THE OFFICIAL® 2000 PRICE GUIDE TO BASEBALL CARDS

BY

DR. JAMES BECKETT

NINETEENTH EDITION

HOUSE OF COLLECTIBLES

The Ballantine Publishing Group • New York

Important Notice: All of the information, including valuations, in this book has been compiled from the most reliable sources, and every effort has been made to eliminate errors and questionable data. Nevertheless, the possibility of error in a work of such scope always exists. The publisher will not be held responsible for losses which may occur in the purchase, sale or other transaction of items because of information contained herein. Readers who feel they have discovered errors are invited to write and inform us, so that they may be corrected in subsequent editions. Those seeking further information on the topics covered in this book are advised to refer to the complete line of Official Price Guides published by the House of Collectibles.

Published by:
House of Collectibles
The Ballantine Publishing Group
201 East 50th Street
New York, New York 10022

Distributed by The Ballantine Publishing Group,
a division of Random House, Inc.,
New York, and simultaneously in Canada by
Random House of Canada Limited, Toronto.

Manufactured in the United States of America

Cover design by Min Choi

Cover photo © Steven Dunn/Allsport

ISSN: 1062-7138

ISBN: 0-676-60156-1

Nineteenth Edition: April 1999

10 9 8 7 6 5 4 3 2 1

Table of Contents

About the Author

Jim Beckett, the leading authority on sport card values in the United States, maintains a wide range of activities in the world of sports. He possesses one of the finest collections of sports cards and autographs in the world, has made numerous appearances on radio and television, and has been frequently cited in many national publications. He was awarded the first "Special Achievement Award" for Contributions to the Hobby by the National Sports Collectors Convention in 1980, the "Jock-Jaspersen Award" for Hobby Dedication in 1983, and the "Buck Barker, Spirit of the Hobby" Award in 1991.

Dr. Beckett is the author of *Beckett Baseball Card Price Guide, The Official Price Guide to Baseball Cards, The Sport Americana Price Guide to Baseball Collectibles, The Sport Americana Baseball Memorabilia and Autograph Price Guide, Beckett Football Card Price Guide, The Official Price Guide to Football Cards, Beckett Hockey Card Price Guide, The Official Price Guide to Hockey Cards, Beckett Basketball Card Price Guide, The Official Price Guide to Basketball Cards,* and *The Sport Americana Baseball Card Alphabetical Checklist.* In addition, he is the founder, publisher, and editor of *Beckett Baseball Card Monthly, Beckett Basketball Monthly, Beckett Football Card Monthly, Beckett Hockey Monthly, Beckett Future Stars, Beckett Racing Monthly,* and *Beckett Tribute* magazines.

Jim Beckett received his Ph.D. in Statistics from Southern Methodist University in 1975. Prior to starting Beckett Publications in 1984, Dr. Beckett served as an Associate Professor of Statistics at Bowling Green State University and as a vice president of a consulting firm in Dallas, Texas. He currently resides in Dallas with his wife, Patti, and their daughters, Christina, Rebecca, and Melissa.

How to Use This Book

Isn't it great? Every year this book gets bigger and bigger with all the new sets coming out. But even more exciting is that every year there are more collectors, more shows, more stores, and more interest in the cards we love so much. This edition has been enhanced and expanded from the previous edition. The cards you collect — who appears on them, what they look like, where they are from, and (most important to most of you) what their current values are — are enumerated within. Many of the features contained in the other *Beckett Price Guides* have been incorporated into this volume since condition grading, terminology, and many other aspects of collecting are common to the card hobby in general. We hope you find the book both interesting and useful in your collecting pursuits.

The *Beckett Guide* has been successful where other attempts have failed because it is complete, current, and valid. This Price Guide contains not just one, but three prices by condition for all the baseball cards listed. The prices were added to the card lists just prior to printing and reflect not the author's opinions or desires but the going retail prices for each card, based on the marketplace (sports memorabilia conventions and shows, sports card shops, hobby papers, current mail-order catalogs, local club meetings, auction results, and other firsthand reportings of actually realized prices).

What is the best price guide available on the market today? Of course, card sellers prefer the price guide with the highest prices, while card buyers naturally prefer the one with the lowest prices. Accuracy, however, is the true test. Use the price guide trusted by more collectors and dealers than all the others combined. Look for the *Beckett®* name. I won't put my name on anything I won't stake my reputation on. Not the lowest and not the highest — but the most accurate, with integrity.

To facilitate your use of this book, read the complete introductory section on the following pages before going to the pricing pages. Every collectible field has its own terminology; we've tried to capture most of these terms and definitions in our glossary. Please read carefully the section on grading and the condition of your cards, as you cannot determine which price column is appropriate for a given card without first knowing its condition.

Welcome to the world of baseball cards.

How to Collect

Each collection is personal and reflects the individuality of its owner. There are no set rules on how to collect cards. Since card collecting is a hobby or leisure pastime, what you collect, how much you collect, and how much time and money you spend collecting are entirely up to you. The funds you have available for collecting and your own personal taste should determine how you collect. Information and ideas presented here are intended to help you get the most enjoyment from this hobby.

It is impossible to collect every card ever produced. Therefore, beginners as well as intermediate and advanced collectors usually specialize in some way. One of the reasons this hobby is popular is that individual collectors can define and tailor their collecting methods to match their own tastes. To give you some ideas of the various approaches to collecting, we will list some of the more popular areas of specialization.

Many collectors select complete sets from particular years. For example, they may concentrate on assembling complete sets from all the years since their birth or since they became avid sports fans. They may try to collect a card for every player during that specified period of time.

Many others wish to acquire only certain players. Usually such players are the superstars of the sport, but occasionally collectors will specialize in all the cards of players who attended a particular college or came from a certain town. Some collectors are only interested in the first cards or Rookie Cards of certain players. A handy guide for collectors interested in pursuing the hobby this way is the *Sport Americana Baseball Card Alphabetical Checklist*.

Another fun way to collect cards is by team. Most fans have a favorite team, and it is natural for that loyalty to be translated into a desire for cards of the players on that favorite team. For most of the recent years, team sets (all the cards from a given team for that year) are readily available at a reasonable price. *The Sport Americana Team Baseball Card Checklist* will open up this field to the collector.

Obtaining Cards

Several avenues are open to card collectors. Cards still can be purchased in the traditional way: by the pack at the local candy, grocery, drug or major discount stores.

But there are also thousands of card shops across the country that specialize in selling cards individually or by the pack, box, or set. Another alternative is the thousands of card shows held each month around the country, which feature anywhere from eight to 800 tables of sports cards and memorabilia for sale.

For many years, it has been possible to purchase complete sets of baseball cards through mail-order advertisers found in traditional sports media publications, such as *The Sporting News, Baseball Digest, Street & Smith* yearbooks, and others. These sets also are advertised in the card collecting periodicals. Many collectors will begin by subscribing to at least one of the hobby periodicals, all with good up-to-date information. In fact, subscription offers can be found in the advertising section of this book.

Most serious card collectors obtain old (and new) cards from one or more of several main sources: (1) trading or buying from other collectors or dealers; (2) responding to sale or auction ads in the hobby publications; (3) buying at a local hobby store; and/or (4) attending sports collectibles shows or conventions.

We advise that you try all four methods since each has its own distinct advantages: (1) trading is a great way to make new friends; (2) hobby periodicals help you keep up with what's going on in the hobby (including when and where the conventions are happening); (3) stores provide the opportunity to enjoy personalized service and consider a great diversity of material in a relaxed sports-oriented atmosphere; and (4) shows allow you to choose from multiple dealers and thousands of cards under one roof in a competitive situation.

Preserving Your Cards

Cards are fragile. They must be handled properly in order to retain their value. Careless handling can easily result in creased or bent cards. It is, however, not recommended that tweezers or tongs be used to pick up your cards since such utensils might mar or indent card surfaces and thus reduce those cards' conditions and values.

In general, your cards should be handled directly as little as possible. This is sometimes easier to say than to do.

Although there are still many who use custom boxes, storage trays, or even shoe boxes, plastic sheets are the preferred method of many collectors for storing cards.

A collection stored in plastic pages in a three-ring album allows you to view your collection at any time without the need to touch the card itself. Cards can also be kept in single holders (of various types and thickness) designed for the enjoyment of each card individually.

For a large collection, some collectors may use a combination of the above methods. When purchasing plastic sheets for your cards, be sure that you find the pocket size that fits the cards snugly. Don't put your 1951 Bowman in a sheet designed to fit 1981 Topps.

Most hobby and collectibles shops and virtually all collectors' conventions will have these plastic pages available in quantity for the various sizes offered, or you can purchase them directly from the advertisers in this book.

Also, remember that pocket size isn't the only factor to consider when looking for plastic sheets. Other factors such as safety, economy, appearance, availability, or personal preference also may indicate which types of sheets a collector may want to buy.

Damp, sunny and/or hot conditions — no, this is not a weather forecast — are three elements to avoid in extremes if you are interested in preserving your collection. Too much (or too little) humidity can cause the gradual deterioration of a card. Direct, bright sun (or fluorescent light) over time will bleach out the color of a card. Extreme heat accelerates the decomposition of the card. On the other hand, many cards have lasted more than 75 years without much scientific intervention. So be cautious, even if the above factors typically present a problem only when present in the extreme. It never hurts to be prudent.

Collecting vs. Investing

Collecting individual players and collecting complete sets are both popular vehicles for investment and speculation.

Most investors and speculators stock up on complete sets or on quantities of players they think have good investment potential.

There is obviously no guarantee in this book, or anywhere else for that matter, that cards will outperform the stock market or other investment alternatives in the future. After all, baseball cards do not pay quarterly dividends and cards cannot be sold at their "current values" as easily as stocks or bonds.

Nevertheless, investors have noticed a favorable long-term trend in the past performance of baseball and other sports collectibles, and certain cards and sets have outperformed just about any other investment in some years.

Many hobbyists maintain that the best investment is and always will be the building of a collection, which traditionally has held up better than outright speculation.

Some of the obvious questions are: Which cards? When to buy? When to sell? The best investment you can make is in your own education.

The more you know about your collection and the hobby, the more informed the decisions you will be able to make. We're not selling investment tips. We're selling information about the current value of baseball cards. It's up to you to use that information to your best advantage.

Terminology

Each hobby has its own language to describe its area of interest. The nomenclature traditionally used for trading cards is derived from the American Card Catalog, published in 1960 by Nostalgia Press. That catalog, written by Jefferson Burdick (who is called the "Father of Card Collecting" for his pioneering work), uses letter and number designations for each separate set of cards. The letter used in the ACC designation refers to the generic type of card. While both sport and non-sport issues are classified in the ACC, we shall confine ourselves to the sport issues. The following list defines the letters and their meanings as used by the American Card Catalog.

(none) or N - 19th Century U.S. Tobacco
B - Blankets
D - Bakery Inserts Including Bread
E - Early Candy and Gum
F - Food Inserts
H - Advertising
M - Periodicals
PC - Postcards
R - Candy and Gum since 1930

Following the letter prefix and an optional hyphen are one-, two-, or three-digit numbers, R(-)999. These typically represent the company or entity issuing the cards. In several cases, the ACC number is extended by an additional hyphen and another one- or two-digit numerical suffix. For example, the 1957 Topps regular-series baseball card issue carries an ACC designation of R414-11. The "R" indicates a Candy or Gum card produced since 1930. The "414" is the ACC designation for Topps Chewing Gum baseball card issues, and the "11" is the ACC designation for the 1957 regular issue (Topps' eleventh baseball set). Like other traditional methods of identification, this system provides order to the process of cataloging cards; however, most serious collectors learn the ACC designation of the popular sets by repetition and familiarity, rather than by attempting to "figure out" what they might or should be. From 1948 forward, collectors and dealers commonly refer to all sets by their year, maker, type of issue, and any other distinguishing characteristic. For example, such a characteristic could be an unusual issue or one of several regular issues put out by a specific maker in a single year. Regional issues are usually referred to by year, maker, and sometimes by title or theme of the set.

Glossary/Legend

Our glossary defines terms used in the card collecting hobby and in this book. Many of these terms are also common to other types of sports memorabilia collecting. Some terms may have several meanings depending on use and context.

ACC - Acronym for American Card Catalog.

ACETATE - A transparent plastic.

ANN- Announcer.

AS - All-Star card. A card portraying an All-Star Player of the previous year that says "All-Star" on its face.

ATG - All-Time Great card.

ATL - All-Time Leaders card.

AU(TO) - Autographed card.

BC - Bonus Card.

BL - Blue letters.

BLANKET - A felt square (normally 5 to 6 inches) portraying a baseball player.

BOX CARD - Card issued on a box (i.e., 1987 Topps Box Bottoms).

BRICK - A group of 50 or more cards having common characteristics that is intended to be bought, sold or traded as a unit.

CABINETS - Popular and highly valuable photographs on thick card stock produced in the 19th and early 20th century.

CHECKLIST - A list of the cards contained in a particular set. The list is always in numerical order if the cards are numbered. Some unnumbered sets are artificially numbered in alphabetical order, by team and alphabetically within the team, or by uniform number for convenience.

CL - Checklist card. A card that lists in order the cards and players in the set or series. Older checklist cards in Mint condition that have not been marked are very desirable and command premiums.

CO - Coach.

COIN - A small disc of metal or plastic portraying a player in its center.

COLLECTOR ISSUE - A set produced for the sake of the card itself with no product or service sponsor. It derives its name from the fact that most of these sets are produced for sale directly to the hobby market.

COM - Card issued by the Post Cereal Company through their mail-in offer.

COMM - Commissioner.

COMMON CARD - The typical card of any set; it has no premium value accruing from subject matter, numerical scarcity, popular demand, or anomaly.

CONVENTION - A gathering of dealers and collectors at a single location for the purpose of buying, selling, and trading sports memorabilia items. Conventions are open to the public and sometimes feature autograph guests, door prizes, contests, seminars, etc. They are frequently referred to simply as "shows."

COOP - Cooperstown.

COR - Corrected card.

COUPON - See Tab.

CY - Cy Young Award.

DEALER - A person who engages in buying, selling, and trading sports collectibles or supplies. A dealer may also be a collector, but as a dealer, his main goal is to earn a profit.

DIE-CUT - A card with part of its stock partially cut, allowing one or more parts to be folded or removed. After removal or appropriate folding, the remaining part of the card can frequently be made to stand up.

DISC - A circular-shaped card.

DISPLAY CARD - A sheet, usually containing three to nine cards, that is printed and used by the manufacturer to advertise and/or display the packages containing his products and cards. The backs of display cards are blank or contain advertisements.

DK - Diamond King.

DL - Division Leaders.

DP - Double Print (a card that was printed in double the quantity compared to the other cards in the same series) or a Draft Pick card.

DUFEX - A method of card manufacturing technology patented by Pinnacle Brands, Inc. It involves a refractive quality to a card with a foil coating.

EMBOSSED - A raised surface; features of a card that are projected from a flat background.

ERA - Earned Run Average.

ERR - Error card. A card with erroneous information, spelling, or depiction on either side of the card. Most errors are not corrected by the producing card company.

ETCHED - Impressions within the surface of a card.

EXHIBIT - The generic name given to thick-stock, postcard-size cards with single color obverse pictures. The name is derived from the Exhibit Supply Co. of Chicago, the principal manufacturer of this type of card. These also are known as Arcade cards since they were found in many arcades.

FDP - First or First Round Draft Pick.

FOIL - Foil embossed stamp on card.

FOLD - Foldout.

FS - Father/son card.

FULL BLEED - A borderless card; a card containing a photo that encompasses the entire card.

FULL SHEET - A complete sheet of cards that has not been cut up into individual cards by the manufacturer. Also called an uncut sheet.

FUN - Fun Cards.

GL - Green letters.

GLOSS - A card with luster; a shiny finish as in a card with UV coating.

HIGH NUMBER - The cards in the last series of numbers in a year in which such higher-numbered cards were printed or distributed in significantly lesser amounts than the lower-numbered cards. The high-number designation refers to a scarcity of the high-numbered cards. Not all years have high numbers in terms of this definition.

HL - Highlight card.

HOF - Hall of Fame, or a card that portrays a Hall of Famer (HOFer).

HOLOGRAM - A three-dimensional photographic image.

HOR - Horizontal pose on card as opposed to the standard vertical orientation found on most cards.

IA - In Action card.

IF - Infielder.

INSERT - A card of a different type or any other sports collectible (typically a poster or sticker) contained and sold in the same package along with a card or cards of a major set. An insert card is either unnumbered or not numbered in the same sequence as the major set. Sometimes the inserts are randomly distributed and are not found in every pack.

INTERACTIVE - A concept that involves collector participation.

ISSUE - Synonymous with set, but usually used in conjunction with a manufacturer, e.g., a Topps issue.

KARAT - A unit of measure for the fineness of gold; i.e. 24K.

LAYERING - The separation or peeling of one or more layers of the card stock, usually at the corner of the card.

LEGITIMATE ISSUE - A set produced to promote or boost sales of a product or service, e.g., bubblegum, cereal, cigarettes, etc. Most collector issues are not legitimate issues in this sense.

LHP - Lefthanded pitcher.

LID - A circular-shaped card (possibly with tab) that forms the top of the container for the product being promoted.

LL - League leaders or large letters on card.

MAJOR SET - A set produced by a national manufacturer of cards containing a large number of cards. Usually 100 or more different cards comprise a major set.

MEM - Memorial card. For example, the 1990 Donruss and Topps Bart Giamatti cards.

METALLIC - A glossy design method that enhances card features.

MG - Manager.

MINI - A small card; for example, a 1975 Topps card of identical design but smaller dimensions than the regular Topps issue of 1975.

ML - Major League.

MULTI-PLAYER CARD - A single card depicting two or more players (but not a team card).

MVP - Most Valuable Player.

NAU - No autograph on card.

NH - No-Hitter.

NNOF - No Name on Front.

NOF - Name on Front.

NON-SPORT CARD - A card from a set whose major theme is a subject other than a sports subject. A card of a sports figure or event that is part of a non-sport set is still a non-sport card, e.g., while the "Look 'N' See" non-sport card set contains a card of Babe Ruth, a sports figure, that card is a non-sport card.

NOTCHING - The grooving of the card, usually caused by fingernails, rubber bands, or bumping card edges against other objects.

OF - Outfield or Outfielder.

OLY - Olympics Card.

ORG - Organist.

P - Pitcher or Pitching pose.

P1 - First Printing.

P2 - Second Printing.

P3 - Third Printing.

PACKS - A means with which cards are issued in terms of pack type (wax, cello, foil, rack, etc.) and channels of distribution (hobby, retail, etc.).

PANEL - An extended card that is composed of two or more individual cards. Often the panel forms the back part of the container for the product being promoted, e.g., a Hostess panel, a Bazooka panel, an Esskay Meat panel.

PARALLEL- A card that is similar in design to its counterpart from a basic set, but offers a distinguishing quality.

PCL - Pacific Coast League.

PF - Profiles.

PLASTIC SHEET - A clear, plastic page that is punched for insertion into a binder (with standard three-ring spacing) containing pockets for displaying cards. Many different styles of sheets exist with pockets of varying sizes to hold the many differing card formats. Also called a display sheet or storage sheet.

PLATINUM - A metallic element used in the process of creating a glossy card.

PR - Printed name on back.

PREMIUM - A card, sometimes on photographic stock, that is purchased or obtained in conjunction with, or redemption for, another card or product. The premium is not packaged in the same unit as the primary item.

PRES - President.

PRISMATIC/PRISM - A glossy or bright design that refracts or disperses light.

PUZZLE CARD - A card whose back contains a part of a picture which, when joined correctly with other puzzle cards, forms the completed picture.

PUZZLE PIECE - A die-cut piece designed to interlock with similar pieces (e.g., early 1980's Donruss).

PVC - Polyvinyl Chloride, a substance used to make many of the popular card display protective sheets. Non-PVC sheets are considered preferable for long-term storage of cards by many.

RARE - A card or series of cards of very limited availability. Unfortunately, "rare" is a subjective term frequently used indiscriminately to hype value. "Rare" cards are harder to obtain than "scarce" cards.

RB - Record Breaker.

REDEMPTION- A program established by multiple card manufacturers that allows collectors to mail in a special card (usually a random insert) in return for special cards, sets or other prizes not available through conventional channels.

REFRACTORS - A card that features a design element which enhances (distorts) its color/appearance through deflecting light.

REGIONAL - A card or set of cards issued and distributed only in a limited geographical area of the country.

REPLICA - An identical copy or reproduction.

REV NEG - Reversed or flopped photo side of the card. This is a major type of error card, but only some are corrected.

RHP - Righthanded pitcher.

ROY - Rookie of the Year.

RP - Relief pitcher.

SA - Super Action card.

SASE - Self-Addressed, Stamped Envelope.

SB - Stolen Bases.

SCARCE - A card or series of cards of limited availability. This subjective term is sometimes used indiscriminately to hype value. "Scarce" cards are not as difficult to obtain as "rare" cards.

SCR - Script name on back.

SD - San Diego Padres.

SEMI-HIGH - A card from the next to last series of a sequentially issued set. It has more value than an average card and generally less value than a high number. A card is not called a semi-high unless the next to last series in which it exists has an additional premium attached to it.

SERIES - The entire set of cards issued by a particular producer in a particular year; e.g., the 1971 Topps series. Also, within a particular set, series can refer to a group of (consecutively numbered) cards printed at the same time; e.g., the first series of the 1957 Topps issue (#1 through #88).

SET - One each of the entire run of cards of the same type produced by a particular manufacturer during a single year. In other words, if you have a complete set of 1976 Topps then you have every card from #1 up to and including #660, i.e., all the different cards that were produced.

SF - Starflics.

SHEEN - Brightness or luster emitted by a card.

SKIP-NUMBERED - A set that has many unissued card numbers between the lowest number in the set and the highest number in the set; e.g., the 1948 Leaf baseball set contains 98 cards skip-numbered from #1 to #168. A major set in which a few numbers were not printed is not considered to be skip-numbered.

SP - Single or Short Print (a card which was printed in lesser quantity compared to the other cards in the same series; see also DP and TP).

SPECIAL CARD - A card that portrays something other than a single player or team; for example, a card that portrays the previous year's statistical leaders or the results from the previous year's World Series.

SS - Shortstop.

STAMP - Adhesive-backed papers depicting a player. The stamp may be individual or in a sheet of many stamps. Moisture must be applied to the adhesive in order for the stamp to be attached to another surface.

STANDARD SIZE - Most modern sports cards measure 2-1/2 by 3-1/2 inches. Exceptions are noted in card descriptions throughout this book.

STAR CARD - A card that portrays a player of some repute, usually determined by his ability, however, sometimes referring to sheer popularity.

STICKER - A card with a removable layer that can be affixed to (stuck onto) another surface.

STOCK - The cardboard or paper on which the card is printed.

STRIP CARDS - A sheet or strip of cards, particularly popular in the 1920s and 1930s, with the individual cards usually separated by broken or dotted lines.

SUPERIMPOSED - To be affixed on top of something, i.e., a player photo over a solid background.

SUPERSTAR CARD - A card that portrays a superstar; e.g., a Hall of Famer or player with strong Hall of Fame potential.

TAB - A card portion set off from the rest of the card, usually with perforations, that may be removed without damaging the central character or event depicted by the card.

TC - Team Checklist.

TEAM CARD - A card that depicts an entire team.

TEST SET - A set, usually containing a small number of cards, issued by a national card producer and distributed in a limited section or sections of the country. Presumably, the purpose of a test set is to test market appeal for a particular type of card.

THREE-DIMENSIONAL (3D) - A visual image that provides an illusion of depth and perspective.

TOPICAL - a subset or group of cards that have a common theme (e.g., MVP award winners).

TP - Triple Print (a card that was printed in triple the quantity compared to the other cards in the same series).

TRANSPARENT - Clear, see through.

TR - Trade reference on card.

TRIMMED - A card cut down from its original size. Trimmed cards are undesirable to most collectors.

UDCA - Upper Deck Classic Alumni.

UER - Uncorrected Error.

UMP - Umpire.

USA - Team USA.

UV - Ultraviolet, a glossy coating used in producing cards.

VAR - Variation card. One of two or more cards from the same series with the same number (or player with identical pose if the series is unnumbered) differing from one another by some aspect, the different feature stemming from the printing or stock of the card. This can be caused when the manufacturer of the cards notices an error in one or more of the cards, makes the changes, and then resumes the print run. In this case there will be two versions or variations of the same card. Sometimes one of the variations is relatively scarce.

VERT - Vertical pose on card.

WAS - Washington National League (1974 Topps).

WC - What's the Call?

WL - White letter on front.

WS - World Series card.

YL - Yellow letters on front

YT - Yellow team name on front.

* - to denote multi-sport sets.

Understanding Card Values

Determining Value

Why are some cards more valuable than others? Obviously, the economic laws of supply and demand are applicable to card collecting just as they are to any other field where a commodity is bought, sold or traded in a free, unregulated market.

Supply (the number of cards available on the market) is less than the total number of cards originally produced since attrition diminishes that original quantity. Each year a percentage of cards is typically thrown away, destroyed or otherwise lost to collectors. This percentage is much, much smaller today than it was in the past because more and more people have become increasingly aware of the value of their cards.

For those who collect only Mint condition cards, the supply of older cards can be quite small indeed. Until recently, collectors were not so conscious of the need to preserve the condition of their cards. For this reason, it is difficult to know exactly how many 1953 Topps are currently available, Mint or otherwise. It is generally accepted that there are fewer 1953 Topps available than 1963, 1973 or 1983 Topps cards. If demand were equal for each of these sets, the law of supply and demand would increase the price for the least available sets. Demand, however, is never equal for all sets, so price correlations can be complicated. The demand for a card is influenced by many factors. These include: (1) the age of the card; (2) the number of cards printed; (3) the player(s) portrayed on the card; (4) the attractiveness and popularity of the set; and (5) the physical condition of the card.

In general, (1) the older the card, (2) the fewer the number of the cards printed, (3) the more famous, popular and talented the player, (4) the more attractive and popular the set, and (5) the better the condition of the card, the higher the value of the card will be. There are exceptions to all but one of these factors: the condition of the card. Given two cards similar in all respects except condition, the one in the best condition will always be valued higher.

While those guidelines help to establish the value of a card, the countless exceptions and peculiarities make any simple, direct mathematical formula to determine card values impossible.

Regional Variation

Since the market varies from region to region, card prices of local players may be higher. This is known as a regional premium. How significant the premium is — and if there is any premium at all — depends on the local popularity of the team and the player.

The largest regional premiums usually do not apply to superstars, who often are so well-known nationwide that the prices of their key cards are too high for local dealers to realize a premium.

Lesser stars often command the strongest premiums. Their popularity is concentrated in their home region, creating local demand that greatly exceeds overall demand.

Regional premiums can apply to popular retired players and sometimes can be found in the areas where the players grew up or starred in college.

A regional discount is the converse of a regional premium. Regional discounts occur when a player has been so popular in his region for so long that local collectors and dealers have accumulated quantities of his key cards. The abundant supply may make the cards available in that area at the lowest prices anywhere.

Set Prices

A somewhat paradoxical situation exists in the price of a complete set vs. the combined cost of the individual cards in the set. In nearly every case, the sum of the prices for the individual cards is higher than the cost for the complete set. This is prevalent especially in the cards of the last few years. The reasons for this apparent anomaly stem from the habits of collectors and from the carrying costs to dealers. Today, each card in a set normally is produced in the same quantity as all other cards in its set.

Many collectors pick up only stars, superstars and particular teams. As a result, the dealer is left with a shortage of certain player cards and an abundance of others. He therefore incurs an expense in simply "carrying" these less desirable cards in stock. On the other hand, if he sells a complete set, he gets rid of large numbers of cards at one time. For this reason, he generally is willing to receive less money for a complete set. By doing this, he recovers all of his costs and also makes a profit.

The disparity between the price of the complete set and the sum of the individual cards also has been influenced by the fact that some of the major manufacturers now are pre-collating card sets. Since "pulling" individual cards from the sets involves a specific type of labor (and cost), the singles or star card market is not affected significantly by pre-collation.

Set prices also do not include rare card varieties, unless specifically stated. Of course, the prices for sets do include one example of each type for the given set, but this is the least expensive variety.

Scarce Series

Scarce series occur because cards issued before 1974 were made available to the public each year in several series of finite numbers of cards, rather than all cards of the set being available for purchase at one time. At some point during the year, usually toward the end of the baseball season, interest in current year baseball cards waned. Consequently, the manufacturers produced smaller numbers of these later-series cards.

Nearly all nationwide issues from post-World War II manufacturers (1948 to 1973) exhibit these series variations. In the past, Topps, for example, may have issued series consisting of many different numbers of cards, including 55, 66, 80, 88 and others. Recently, Topps has settled on what is now its standard sheet size of 132 cards, six of which comprise its 792-card set.

While the number of cards within a given series is usually the same as the number of cards on one printed sheet, this is not always the case. For example, Bowman used 36 cards on its standard printed sheets, but in 1948 substituted 12 cards during later print runs of that year's baseball cards. Twelve of the cards from the initial sheet of 36 cards were removed and replaced by 12 different cards giving, in effect, a first series of 36 cards and a second series of 12 new cards. This replacement produced a scarcity of 24 cards — the 12 cards removed from the original sheet and the 12 new cards added to the sheet. A full sheet of 1948 Bowman cards (second printing) shows that card numbers 37 through 48 have replaced 12 of the cards on the first printing sheet.

The Topps Company also has created scarcities and/or excesses of certain cards in many of its sets. Topps, however, has most frequently gone the other direction by double printing some of the cards. Double printing causes an abundance of cards of the players who are on the same sheet more than one time. During the years from 1978 to 1981, Topps double printed 66 cards out of their large 726-card set. The Topps practice of double printing cards in earlier years is the most logical explanation for the known scarcities of particular cards in some of these Topps sets.

From 1988 through 1990, Donruss short printed and double printed certain cards in its major sets. Ostensibly this was because of its addition of bonus team MVP cards in its regular-issue wax packs. In the last couple of years, card companies have been printing specific subsets (usually young players or rookie cards) in shorter supply than the regular cards.

We are always looking for information or photographs of printing sheets of cards for research. Each year, we try to update the hobby's knowledge of distribution anomalies. Please let us know at the address in this book if you have first-hand knowledge that would be helpful in this pursuit.

Grading Your Cards

Each hobby has its own grading terminology — stamps, coins, comic books, record collecting, etc. Collectors of sports cards are no exception. The one invariable criterion for determining the value of a card is its condition: The better the condition of the card, the more valuable it is. Condition grading, however, is subjective. Individual card dealers and collectors differ in the strictness of their grading, but the stated condition of a card should be determined without regard to whether it is being bought or sold.

No allowance is made for age. A 1952 card is judged by the same standards as a 1992 card. But there are specific sets and cards that are condition sensitive (marked with "!" in the Price Guide) because of their border color, consistently poor centering, etc. Such cards and sets sometimes command premiums above the listed percentages in Mint condition.

Centering

Current centering terminology uses numbers representing the percentage of border on either side of the main design. Obviously, centering is diminished in importance for borderless cards such as Stadium Club.

Slightly Off-Center (60/40): A slightly off-center card is one that, upon close inspection, is found to have one border bigger than the opposite border. This degree once was offensive to only purists, but now some hobbyists try to avoid cards that are anything other than perfectly centered.

Off-Center (70/30): An off-center card has one border that is noticeably more than twice as wide as the opposite border.

Badly Off-Center (80/20 or worse): A badly off-center card has virtually no border on one side of the card.

Miscut: A miscut card actually shows part of the adjacent card in its larger border and consequently a corresponding amount of its card is cut off.

Corner Wear

Corner wear is the most scrutinized grading criteria in the hobby. These are the major categories of corner wear:

Corner with a slight touch of wear: The corner still is sharp, but there is a slight touch of wear showing. On a dark-bordered card, this shows as a dot of white.

Fuzzy corner: The corner still comes to a point, but the point has just begun to fray. A slightly "dinged" corner is considered the same as a fuzzy corner.

Slightly rounded corner: The fraying of the corner has increased to where there is only a hint of a point. Mild layering may be evident. A "dinged" corner is considered the same as a slightly rounded corner.

Rounded corner: The point is completely gone. Some layering is noticeable.

Badly rounded corner: The corner is completely round and rough. Severe layering is evident.

Creases

A third common defect is the crease. The degree of creasing in a card is difficult to show in a drawing or picture. On giving the specific condition of an expensive card for sale, the seller should note any creases additionally. Creases can be categorized as to severity according to the following scale:

Light Crease: A light crease is a crease that is barely noticeable upon close inspection. In fact, when cards are in plastic sheets or holders, a light crease may not be seen (until the card is taken out of the holder). A light crease on the front is much more serious than a light crease on the card back only.

Medium Crease: A medium crease is noticeable when held and studied at arm's length by the naked eye, but does not overly detract from the appearance of the card. It is an obvious crease, but not one that breaks the picture surface of the card.

Heavy Crease: A heavy crease is one that has torn or broken through the card's picture surface, e.g., puts a tear in the photo surface.

Alterations

Deceptive Trimming: This occurs when someone alters the card in order (1) to shave off edge wear, (2) to improve the sharpness of the corners, or (3) to improve centering — obviously their objective is to falsely increase the perceived value of the card to an unsuspecting buyer. The shrinkage usually is evident only if the trimmed card is compared to an adjacent full-sized card or if the trimmed card is itself measured.

Obvious Trimming: Obvious trimming is noticeable and unfortunate. It is usually performed by non-collectors who give no thought to the present or future value of their cards.

Deceptively Retouched Borders: This occurs when the borders (especially on those cards with dark borders) are touched up on the edges and corners with magic marker or crayons of appropriate color in order to make the card appear Mint.

Categorization of Defects—Miscellaneous Flaws

The following are common minor flaws that, depending on severity, lower a card's condition by one to four grades and often render it no better than Excellent-Mint: bubbles (lumps in surface), gum and wax stains, diamond cutting (slanted borders), notching, off-centered backs, paper wrinkles, scratched-off cartoons or puzzles on back, rubber band marks, scratches, surface impressions and warping.

The following are common serious flaws that, depending on severity, lower a card's condition at least four grades and often render it no better than Good: chemical or sun fading, erasure marks, mildew, miscutting (severe off-centering), holes, bleached or re-touched borders, tape marks, tears, trimming, water or coffee stains and writing.

Condition Guide

Grades

Mint (Mt) - A card with no flaws or wear. The card has four perfect corners, 60/40 or better centering from top to bottom and from left to right, original gloss, smooth edges and original color borders. A Mint card does not have print spots, color or focus imperfections.

Near Mint-Mint (NrMt-Mt) - A card with one minor flaw. Any one of the following would lower a Mint card to Near Mint-Mint: one corner with a slight touch of wear, barely noticeable print spots, color or focus imperfections. The card must have 60/40 or better centering in both directions, original gloss, smooth edges and original color borders.

Near Mint (NrMt) - A card with one minor flaw. Any one of the following would lower a Mint card to Near Mint: one fuzzy corner or two to four corners with slight touches of wear, 70/30 to 60/40 centering, slightly rough edges, minor print spots, color or focus imperfections. The card must have original gloss and original color borders.

Excellent-Mint (ExMt) - A card with two or three fuzzy, but not rounded, corners and centering no worse than 80/20. The card may have no more than two of the following: slightly rough edges, very slightly discolored borders, minor print spots, color or focus imperfections. The card must have original gloss.

Excellent (Ex) - A card with four fuzzy but definitely not rounded corners and centering no worse than 80/20. The card may have a small amount of original gloss lost, rough edges, slightly discolored borders and minor print spots, color or focus imperfections.

Very Good (Vg) - A card that has been handled but not abused: slightly rounded corners with slight layering, slight notching on edges, a significant amount of gloss lost from the surface but no scuffing and moderate discoloration of borders. The card may have a few light creases.

Good (G), Fair (F), Poor (P) - A well-worn, mishandled or abused card: badly rounded and layered corners, scuffing, most or all original gloss missing,

Centering

Well-centered

Slightly Off-centered

Off-centered

Badly Off-centered

Miscut

Corner Wear

The partial cards here have been photographed at 300%. This was done in order to magnify each card's corner wear to such a degree that differences could be shown on a printed page.

The 1962 Topps Mickey Mantle card definitely has a rounded corner. Some may say that this card is badly rounded, but that is a judgement call.

The 1962 Topps Hank Aaron card has a slightly rounded corner. Note that there is definite corner wear evident by the fraying and that there is no longer a sharp point to which the corner converges.

The 1962 Topps Gil Hodges card has corner wear; it is slightly better than the Aaron card above. Nevertheless, some collectors might classify this Hodges corner as slightly rounded.

The 1962 Topps Manager's Dream card showing Mantle and Mays has slight corner wear. This is not a fuzzy corner as very slight wear is noticeable on the card's photo surface.

The 1962 Topps Don Mossi card has very slight corner wear such that it might be called a fuzzy corner. A close look at the original card shows that the corner is not perfect, but almost. However, note that coner wear is somewhat academic on this card. As you can plainly see, the heavy crease going across his name breaks through the photo surface.

seriously discolored borders, moderate or heavy creases, and one or more serious flaws. The grade of Good, Fair or Poor depends on the severity of wear and flaws. Good, Fair and Poor cards generally are used only as fillers.

The most widely used grades are defined above. Obviously, many cards will not perfectly fit one of the definitions.

Therefore, categories between the major grades known as in-between grades are used, such as Good to Very Good (G-Vg), Very Good to Excellent (VgEx), and Excellent-Mint to Near Mint (ExMt-NrMt). Such grades indicate a card with all qualities of the lower category but with at least a few qualities of the higher category.

The Official Price Guide to Baseball Cards lists each card and set in three grades, with the middle grade valued at about 40-45% of the top grade, and the bottom grade valued at about 10-15% of the top grade.

The value of cards that fall between the listed columns can also be calculated using a percentage of the top grade. For example, a card that falls between the top and middle grades (Ex, ExMt or NrMt in most cases) will generally be valued at anywhere from 50% to 90% of the top grade.

Similarly, a card that falls between the middle and bottom grades (G-Vg, Vg or VgEx in most cases) will generally be valued at anywhere from 20% to 40% of the top grade.

There are also cases where cards are in better condition than the top grade or worse than the bottom grade. Cards that grade worse than the lowest grade are generally valued at 5-10% of the top grade.

When a card exceeds the top grade by one — such as NrMt-Mt when the top grade is NrMt, or Mint when the top grade is NrMt-Mt — a premium of up to 50% is possible, with 10-20% the usual norm.

When a card exceeds the top grade by two — such as Mint when the top grade is NrMt, or NrMt-Mt when the top grade is ExMt — a premium of 25-50% is the usual norm. But certain condition sensitive cards or sets, particularly those from the pre-war era, can bring premiums of up to 100% or even more.

Unopened packs, boxes and factory-collated sets are considered Mint in their unknown (and presumed perfect) state. Once opened, however, each card can be graded (and valued) in its own right by taking into account any defects that may be present in spite of the fact that the card has never been handled.

Selling Your Cards

Just about every collector sells cards or will sell cards eventually. Someday you may be interested in selling your duplicates or maybe even your whole collection. You may sell to other collectors, friends or dealers. You may even sell cards you purchased from a certain dealer back to that same dealer. In any event, it helps to know some of the mechanics of the typical transaction between buyer and seller.

Dealers will buy cards in order to resell them to other collectors who are interested in the cards. Dealers will always pay a higher percentage for items that (in their opinion) can be resold quickly, and a much lower percentage for those items that are perceived as having low demand and hence are slow moving. In either case, dealers must buy at a price that allows for the expense of doing business and a margin for profit.

If you have cards for sale, the best advice we can give is that you get several offers for your cards — either from card shops or at a card show — and take the best offer, all things considered. Note, the "best" offer may not be the one for the highest amount. And remember, if a dealer really wants your cards, he won't let you get away without making his best competitive offer. Another alternative is to place your cards in an auction as one or several lots.

Many people think nothing of going into a department store and paying $15 for an item of clothing for which the store paid $5. But if you were selling your $15 card to a dealer and he offered you $5 for it, you might consider his mark-up unreasonable. To complete the analogy: Most department stores (and card dealers) that consistently pay $10 for $15 items eventually go out of business. An exception is when the dealer has lined up a willing buyer for the item(s) you are attempting to sell, or if the cards are so Hot that it's likely he'll likely have to hold the cards for just a short period of time.

In those cases, an offer of up to 75 percent of book value still will allow the dealer to make a reasonable profit considering the short time he will need to hold the merchandise. In general, however, most cards and collections will bring offers in the range of 25 to 50 percent of retail price. Also consider that most material from the last five to 10 years is plentiful. If that's what you're selling, don't be surprised if your best offer is well below that range.

Interesting Notes

The first card numerically of an issue is the single card most likely to obtain excessive wear.

Consequently, you typically will find the price on the #1 card (in NrMt or Mint condition) somewhat higher than might otherwise be the case.

Similarly, but to a lesser extent (because normally the less important, reverse side of the card is the one exposed), the last card numerically in an issue also is prone to abnormal wear. This extra wear and tear occurs because the first and last cards are exposed to the elements (human element included) more than any of the other cards. They are generally end cards in any brick formations, rubber bandings, stackings on wet surfaces and like activities.

Sports cards have no intrinsic value. The value of a card, like the value of other collectibles, can be determined only by you and your enjoyment in viewing and possessing these cardboard treasures.

Remember, the buyer ultimately determines the price of each baseball card. You are the determining price factor because you have the ability to say "No" to the price of any card by not exchanging your hard-earned money for a given issue. When the cost of a trading card exceeds the enjoyment you will receive from it, your answer should be "No." We assess and report the prices. You set them!

We are always interested in receiving the price input of collectors and dealers. We happily credit major contributors.

We welcome your opinions, since your contributions assist us in ensuring a better guide each year.

If you would like to join our survey list for the next editions of this book and others authored by Dr. Beckett, please send your name and address to Dr. James Beckett, 15850 Dallas Parkway, Dallas, TX 75248.

History of Baseball Cards

Today's version of the baseball card, with its colorful and oft times high-tech fronts and backs, is a far cry from its earliest predecessors. The issue remains cloudy as to which was the very first baseball card ever produced, but the institution of baseball cards dates from the latter half of the 19th century, more than 100 years ago. Early issues, generally printed on heavy cardboard, were of poor quality, with photographs, drawings, and printing far short of today's standards.

Goodwin & Co., of New York, makers of Gypsy Queen, Old Judge, and other cigarette brands, is considered by many to be the first issuer of baseball and other sports cards. Its issues, predominantly sized 1-1/2 by 2-1/2 inches, generally consisted of photographs of baseball players, boxers, wrestlers, and other subjects mounted on stiff cardboard. More than 2,000 different photos of baseball players alone have been identified. These "Old Judges," a collective name commonly used for the Goodwin & Co. cards, were issued from 1886 to 1890 and are treasured parts of many collections today.

Among the other cigarette companies that issued baseball cards still attracting attention today are Allen & Ginter, D. Buchner & Co. (Gold Coin Chewing Tobacco), and P.H. Mayo & Brother. Cards from the first two companies bear colored line drawings, while the Mayos are sepia photographs on black cardboard. In addition to the small-size cards from this era, several tobacco companies issued cabinet-size baseball cards. These "cabinets" were considerably larger than the small cards, usually about 4-1/4 by 6-1/2 inches, and were printed on heavy stock. Goodwin & Co.'s Old Judge cabinets and the National Tobacco Works' "Newsboy" baseball photos are two that remain popular today.

By 1895, the American Tobacco Company began to dominate its competition. They discontinued baseball card inserts in their cigarette packages (actually slide boxes in those days). The lack of competition in the cigarette market had made these inserts unnecessary. This marked the end of the first era of baseball cards. At the dawn of the 20th century, few baseball cards were being issued. But once again, it was the cigarette companies — particularly, the American Tobacco Company — followed to a lesser extent by the candy and gum makers that revived the practice of including baseball cards with their products. The bulk of these cards, identified in the American Card Catalog (designated hereafter as ACC) as T or E cards for 20th century "Tobacco" or "Early Candy and Gum" issues, respectively, were released from 1909 to 1915.

This romantic and popular era of baseball card collecting produced many desirable items. The most outstanding is the fabled T-206 Honus Wagner card. Other perennial favorites among collectors are the T-206 Eddie Plank card, and the T-206 Magee error card. The former was once the second most valuable card and only recently relinquished that position to a more distinctive and aesthetically pleasing Napoleon Lajoie card from the 1933-34 Goudey Gum series. The latter misspells the player's name as "Magie," the most famous and most valuable blooper card.

The ingenuity and distinctiveness of this era has yet to be surpassed. Highlights include:

• the T-202 Hassan triple-folders, one of the best looking and the most distinctive cards ever issued;

• the durable T-201 Mecca double-folders, one of the first sets with players' records on the reverse;

• the T-3 Turkey Reds, the hobby's most popular cabinet card;

• the E-145 Cracker Jacks, the only major set containing Federal League player cards;

• the T-204 Ramlys, with their distinctive black-and-white oval photos and ornate gold borders.

These are but a few of the varieties issued during this period.

Increasing Popularity

While the American Tobacco Company dominated the field, several other tobacco companies, as well as clothing manufacturers, newspapers and periodicals, game makers, and companies whose identities remain anonymous, also issued cards during this period. In fact, the Collins-McCarthy Candy Company, makers of Zeenuts Pacific Coast League baseball cards, issued cards yearly from 1911 to 1938. Its record for continuous annual card production has been exceeded only by the Topps Chewing Gum Company. The era of the tobacco card issues closed with the onset of World War I, with the exception of the Red Man chewing tobacco sets produced from 1952 to 1955.

The next flurry of card issues broke out in the roaring and prosperous 1920s, the era of the E card. The caramel companies (National Caramel, American Caramel, York Caramel) were the leading distributors of these E cards. In addition, the strip card, a continous strip with several cards divided by dotted lines or other sectioning features, flourished during this time. While the E cards and the strip cards generally are considered less imaginative than the T cards or the recent candy and gum issues, they still are pursued by many advanced collectors.

Another significant event of the 1920s was the introduction of the arcade card. Taking its designation from its issuer, the Exhibit Supply Company of Chicago, it is usually known as the "Exhibit" card. Once a trademark of the penny arcades, amusement parks and county fairs across the country, Exhibit machines dispensed nearly postcard-size photos on thick stock for one penny. These picture cards bore likenesses of a favorite cowboy, actor, actress or baseball player. Exhibit Supply and its associated companies produced baseball cards during a longer time span, although discontinuous, than any other manufacturer. Its first cards appeared in 1921, while its last issue was in 1966. In 1979, the Exhibit Supply Company was bought and somewhat revived by a collector/dealer who has since reprinted Exhibit photos of the past.

If the T card period, from 1909 to 1915, can be designated the "Golden Age" of baseball card collecting, then perhaps the "Silver Age" commenced with the introduction of the Big League Gum series of 239 cards in 1933 (a 240th card was added in 1934). These are the forerunners of today's baseball gum cards, and the Goudey Gum Company of Boston is responsible for their success. This era spanned the period from the Depression days of 1933 to America's formal involvement in World War II in 1941.

Goudey's attractive designs, with full-color line drawings on thick card stock, greatly influenced other cards being issued at that time. As a result, the most attractive and popular vintage cards in history were produced in this "Silver Age." The 1933 Goudey Big League Gum series also owes its popularity to the more than 40 Hall of Fame players in the set. These include four cards of Babe Ruth and two of Lou Gehrig. Goudey's reign continued in 1934, when it issued a 96-card set in color, together with the single remaining card from the 1933 series, #106, the Napoleon Lajoie card.

In addition to Goudey, several other bubblegum manufacturers issued baseball cards during this era. DeLong Gum Company issued an extremely attractive set in 1933. National Chicle Company's 192-card "Batter-Up" series of 1934-1936 became the largest die-cut set in card history. In addition, that company offered the popular "Diamond Stars" series during the same period. Other popular sets included the "Tattoo Orbit" set of 60 color cards issued in 1933 and Gum Products' 75-card "Double Play" set, featuring sepia depictions of two players per card.

In 1939, Gum Inc., which later became Bowman Gum, replaced Goudey Gum as the leading baseball card producer. In 1939 and the following year, it issued two important sets of black-and-white cards. In 1939, its "Play Ball America" set consisted of 162 cards. The larger, 240-card "Play Ball" set of 1940 still is considered by many to be the most attractive black-and-white cards ever produced. That firm introduced its only color set in 1941, consisting of 72 cards titled "Play Ball Sports Hall of Fame." Many of these were colored repeats of poses from the black-and-white 1940 series.

In addition to regular gum cards, many manufacturers distributed premium issues during the 1930s. These premiums were printed on paper or photographic stock, rather than card stock. They were much larger than the regular cards and were sold for a penny across the counter with gum (which was packaged separately from the premium). They often were redeemed at the store or through the mail in exchange for the wrappers of previously purchased gum cards, like proof-of-purchase box-top premiums today. The gum premiums are scarcer than the card issues of the 1930s and in most cases no manufacturer's name is present.

World War II brought an end to this popular era of card collecting when paper and rubber shortages curtailed the production of bubblegum baseball cards. They were resurrected again in 1948 by the Bowman Gum Company (the direct descendent of Gum, Inc.). This marked the beginning of the modern era of card collecting.

In 1948, Bowman Gum issued a 48-card set in black and white consisting of one card and one slab of gum in every 1 cent pack. That same year, the Leaf Gum Company also issued a set of cards. Although rather poor in quality, these cards were issued in color. A squabble over the rights to use players' pictures developed between Bowman and Leaf. Eventually Leaf dropped out of the card market, but not before it had left a lasting heritage to the hobby by issuing some of the rarest cards now in existence. Leaf's baseball card series of 1948-49 contained 98 cards, skip numbered to #168 (not all numbers were printed). Of these 98 cards, 49 are relatively plentiful; the other 49, however, are rare and quite valuable.

Bowman continued its production of cards in 1949 with a color series of 240 cards. Because there are many scarce "high numbers," this series remains the most difficult Bowman regular issue to complete. Although the set was printed in color and commands great interest due to its scarcity, it is considered aesthetically inferior to the Goudey and National Chicle issues of the 1930s. In addition to the regular issue of 1949, Bowman also produced a set of 36 Pacific Coast League players. While this was not a regular issue, it still is prized by collectors. In fact, it has become the most valuable Bowman series.

In 1950 (representing Bowman's one-year monopoly of the baseball card market), the company began a string of top quality cards that continued until its demise in 1955. The 1950 series was itself something of an oddity because the low numbers, rather than the traditional high numbers, were the more difficult cards to obtain.

The year 1951 marked the beginning of the most competitive and perhaps the highest quality period of baseball card production. In that year, Topps Chewing Gum Company of Brooklyn entered the market. Topps' 1951 series consisted of two sets of 52 cards each, one set with red backs and the other with blue backs. In addition, Topps also issued 31 insert cards, three of which remain the rarest Topps cards ("Current All-Stars" Konstanty, Roberts and Stanky). The 1951 Topps cards were unattractive and paled in comparison to the 1951 Bowman issues. They were successful, however, and Topps has continued to produce cards ever since.

Intensified Competition

Topps issued a larger and more attractive card set in 1952. This larger size became standard for the next five years. (Bowman followed with larger-size baseball cards in 1953.) This 1952 Topps set has become, like the 1933

Goudey series and the T-206 white border series, the classic set of its era. The 407-card set is a collector's dream of scarcities, rarities, errors and variations. It also contains the first Topps issues of Mickey Mantle and Willie Mays.

As with Bowman and Leaf in the late 1940s, competition over player rights arose. Ensuing court battles occurred between Topps and Bowman. The market split due to stiff competition, and in January 1956, Topps bought out Bowman. (Topps, using the Bowman name, resurrected Bowman as a later label in 1989.) Topps remained essentially unchallenged as the primary producer of baseball cards through 1980. So, the story of major baseball card sets from 1956 through 1980 is by and large the story of Topps' issues. Notable exceptions include the small sets produced by Fleer Gum in 1959, 1960, 1961 and 1963, and the Kellogg's Cereal and Hostess Cakes baseball cards issued to promote their products.

A court decision in 1980 paved the way for two other large gum companies to enter (or reenter, in Fleer's case) the baseball card arena. Fleer, which had last made photo cards in 1963, and the Donruss Company (then a division of General Mills) secured rights to produce baseball cards of current players, thus breaking Topps' monopoly. Each company issued major card sets in 1981 with bubblegum products.

Then a higher court decision in that year overturned the lower court ruling against Topps. It appeared that Topps had regained its sole position as a producer of baseball cards. Undaunted by the revocation ruling, Fleer and Donruss continued to issue cards in 1982 but without bubblegum or any other edible product. Fleer issued its current player baseball cards with "team logo stickers," while Donruss issued its cards with a piece of a baseball jigsaw puzzle.

Sharing the Pie

From 1981 to 1987, the three major companies solidifed their leadership position. The growth and popularity of these newer cards helped in bringing along two new companies by 1989: Score (debut set in 1988) and Upper Deck (debut set in 1989). These five companies were about to embark on a wild ride through the 1990's.

Upper Deck's successful entry into the market turned out to be very important. The company's card stock, photography, packaging and marketing gave baseball cards a new standard for quality, and began the "premium card" trend that continues today. The second premium baseball card set to be issued was the 1990 Leaf set, named for and issued by the parent company of Donruss. To gauge the significance of the premium card trend, one need only note that two of the most valuable post-1986 regular-issue cards in the hobby are the 1989 Upper Deck Ken Griffey Jr. and 1990 Leaf Frank Thomas Rookie Cards.

The impressive debut of Leaf in 1990 was followed by Studio, Ultra, and Stadium Club in 1991. Of those, Stadium Club with its dramatic borderless photo, Un-coated card fronts made the biggest impact. In 1992, Bowman, and Pinnacle joined the premium fray. In 1992, Donruss and Fleer abandoned the traditional 50-cent pack market and instead produced premium sets comparable to (and presumably designed to compete against) Upper Deck's set. Those moves, combined with the almost instantaneous spread of premium cards to the other major team sports cards, serve as strong indicators that premium cards were here to stay. Bowman had been a lower-level product from 1989 to '91.

In 1993, Fleer, Topps and Upper Deck produced the first "super premium" cards with Flair, Finest and SP, respectively. The success of all three products was an indication the baseball card market was headed toward even higher price levels, and that turned out to be the case in 1994 with the introduction of Bowman's Best (a Topps hybrid of prospect-oriented Bowman and the superpremium Finest) and Leaf Limited. Other 1994 debuts included Upper Deck's entry-level Collector's Choice and Pinnacle's hobby-only Select.

Overall, inserts continued to dominate the hobby scene. Specifically, the parallel chase cards first introduced in 1992 with Topps Gold became the latest major hobby trend. Topps Gold was followed by 1993 Finest Refractors (at the time the scarcest insert ever produced and still a landmark set), and the one-per-box Stadium Club First Day Issue.

Of course, the biggest on-field news of 1994 was the owner-provoked players strike that halted the season prematurely. While the baseball card hobby suffered noticeably from the strike, there was no catastrophic market crash as some had feared. However, the strike pulled the plug on a market that was both strong and growing, and contributed to a serious hobby contraction that continues to this day.

By 1995, parallel insert sets were commonplace and had taken on a new complexion: the most popular ones were those that had announced (or at least suspected) print runs of 500 or less, such as Finest Refractors and Select Artist's Proofs.

This trend continued in 1996, with several parallel inserts that were printed in quantities of 250 or less such as Finest Gold Refractors, Fleer Circa Rave, Studio Silver Press Proofs and three of the six Select Certified parallels. It could be argued that the high price tags on these extremely limited parallel cards (many exceeded the $1000 plateau) were driving many single-player collectors to frustration, and even completely out of the hobby. At the same time, average pack prices soared while average number of cards per pack dropped, making the baseball card hobby increasingly more expensive.

On the positive side, two trends from 1996 clearly brought in new collectors: Topps' Mickey Mantle retrospective inserts in both series of Topps and Stadium Club; and Leaf's Signature Series, which included one certified autograph per pack. While the Mantle craze following his passing seemed to be a short-term phenomenon, the inclusion of autographs in packs seemed to have more long-term significance.

In 1997 the print runs in selected sets got even lower. Both Fleer/SkyBox and Pinnacle brands issued cards of which only one exists.

The growth in popularity of autographs also continued. Many products had autographed cards in their packs. A very positive trend was a return to basics. Many collectors bought Rockie Cards as they understood that concept and worked on finishing sets.

There was also an increase in international players collecting. Hideo Nomo was incredibly popular in Japan while Chan Ho Park was in demand in Korea. This bodes well for an international grouth in the hobby.

Nineteen ninety eight was a year of rebirth and growth for the hobby. Led by the home run chase of Mark McGwire and Sammy Sosa as well as the continued brilliance of stalwarts like Ken Griffey Jr. and Roger Clemens. The baseball card hobby got a considerable boost and positive publicity it had not seen in many years.

The Rookie Cards of these players as well as many others showed significant gains as the hobby started accepting Rookie Cards again as the most popular trend in collecting. Also, cards which were professionally graded by companies such as PSA and SGC were becoming more heavily traded for both older and newer cards.

In addition, the internet and various services (eBay, Beckett Auction Services (part of the burgeoning Beckett on-line service), as well as many others) contributed to the strong growth in collecting interest over the past year.

There were some down sides in 1998, though. Pinnacle brands went out of buisness, leaving a legacy of innovation and promotions not seen by the other companies. In addition, there was still the problems of collectors being frustrated by the extremely short printed cards of their favorite players, making completion almost impossible.

Unfortunately, such positives were clearly overshadowed by the industry's overriding problem: too many products costing too much money, with fewer and fewer buyers willing to ante up. The result? Many dealers going out of business, and a buyer's market in which new products usually were available cheaper to the consumer than original dealer cost from the factory. The hobby still faces this very complex problem with no easy solutions in sight.

Finding Out More

The above has been a thumbnail sketch of card collecting from its inception in the 1880s to the present. It is difficult to tell the whole story in just a few pages — there are several other good sources of information. Serious collectors should subscribe to at least one of the excellent hobby periodicals. We also suggest that collectors visit their local card shop(s) and also attend a sports collectibles show in their area. Card collecting is still a young and informal hobby. You can learn more about it in either place. After all, smart dealers realize that spending a few minutes teaching beginners about the hobby often pays off in the long run.

Additional Reading

Each year Beckett Publications produces comprehensive annual price guides for each of the four major sports: Beckett Baseball Card Price Guide, Beckett Basketball Card Price Guide, Beckett Football Card Price Guide, Beckett Hockey Card Price Guide, Beckett Racing Price Guide and a line of Beckett Alphabetical Checklists Books have been released as well. The aim of these annual guides is to provide information and accurate pricing on a wide array of sports cards, ranging from main issues by the major card manufacturers to various regional, promotional, and food issues. Also alphabetical checklist books are published to assist the collector in identifying all the cards of any particular player. The seasoned collector will find these tools valuable sources of information that will enable him to pursue his hobby interests.

In addition, abridged editions of the Beckett Price Guides have been published for each of these major sports as part of the House of Collectibles series: The Official Price Guide to Baseball Cards, The Official Price Guide to Football Cards, The Official Price Guide to Basketball Cards. Published in a convenient mass-market paperback format, these price guides provide information and accurate pricing on all the main issues by the major card manufacturers.

Advertising

Within this Price Guide you will find advertisements for sports memorabilia material, mail order, and retail sports collectibles establishments. All advertisements were accepted in good faith based on the reputation of the advertiser; however, neither the author, the publisher, the distributors, nor the other advertisers in this Price Guide accept any responsibility for any particular advertiser not complying with the terms of his or her ad.

Readers also should be aware that prices in advertisements are subject to change over the annual period before a new edition of this volume is issued each spring. When replying to an advertisement late in the baseball year, the reader should take this into account, and contact the dealer by phone or in writing for up-to-date price information. Should you come into contact with any of the advertisers in this guide as a result of their advertisement herein, please mention this source as your contact.

Prices in This Guide

Prices found in this guide reflect current retail rates just prior to the printing of this book. They do not reflect the FOR SALE prices of the author, the publisher, the distributors, the advertisers, or any card dealers associated with this guide. No one is obligated in any way to buy, sell or trade his or her cards based on these prices. The price listings were compiled by the author from actual buy/sell transactions at sports conventions, sports card shops, buy/sell advertisements in the hobby papers, for sale prices from dealer catalogs and price lists, and discussions with leading hobbyists in the U.S. and Canada. All prices are in U.S. dollars.

Acknowledgments

A great deal of diligence, hard work, and dedicated effort went into this year's volume. However, the high standards to which we hold ourselves could not have been met without the expert input and generous amount of time contributed by many people. Our sincere thanks are extended to each and every one of you.

A complete list of these invaluable contributors appears after the Price Guide section.

1948 Bowman

	NRMT	VG-E
COMPLETE SET (48)	3400.00	1500.00
COMMON CARD (1-36)	20.00	9.00
COMMON CARD (37-48)	30.00	13.50
WRAPPER (5-CENT)	700.00	325.00

	NRMT	VG-E
❑ 1 Bob Elliott	100.00	15.00
❑ 2 Ewell Blackwell	40.00	18.00
❑ 3 Ralph Kiner	150.00	70.00
❑ 4 Johnny Mize	100.00	45.00
❑ 5 Bob Feller	225.00	100.00
❑ 6 Yogi Berra	450.00	200.00
❑ 7 Pete Reiser SP	120.00	55.00
❑ 8 Phil Rizzuto SP	300.00	135.00
❑ 9 Walker Cooper	20.00	9.00
❑ 10 Buddy Rosar	20.00	9.00
❑ 11 Johnny Lindell	25.00	11.00
❑ 12 Johnny Sain	50.00	22.00
❑ 13 Willard Marshall SP	40.00	18.00
❑ 14 Allie Reynolds	50.00	22.00
❑ 15 Eddie Joost	20.00	9.00
❑ 16 Jack Lohrke SP	40.00	18.00
❑ 17 Enos Slaughter	100.00	45.00
❑ 18 Warren Spahn	350.00	160.00
❑ 19 Tommy Henrich	50.00	22.00
❑ 20 Buddy Kerr SP	40.00	18.00
❑ 21 Ferris Fain	40.00	18.00
❑ 22 Floyd Bevens SP	50.00	22.00
❑ 23 Larry Jansen	25.00	11.00
❑ 24 Dutch Leonard SP	40.00	18.00
❑ 25 Barney McCosky	20.00	9.00
❑ 26 Frank Shea SP	50.00	22.00
❑ 27 Sid Gordon	22.50	10.00
❑ 28 Emil Verban SP	40.00	18.00
❑ 29 Joe Page SP	75.00	34.00
❑ 30 Whitey Lockman SP	50.00	22.00
❑ 31 Bill McCahan	20.00	9.00
❑ 32 Bill Rigney	20.00	9.00
❑ 33 Bill Johnson	25.00	11.00
❑ 34 Sheldon Jones SP	40.00	18.00
❑ 35 Snuffy Stirnweiss	40.00	18.00
❑ 36 Stan Musial	800.00	350.00
❑ 37 Clint Hartung	30.00	13.50
❑ 38 Red Schoendienst	150.00	70.00
❑ 39 Augie Galan	30.00	13.50
❑ 40 Marty Marion	75.00	34.00
❑ 41 Rex Barney	60.00	27.00
❑ 42 Ray Poat	30.00	13.50
❑ 43 Bruce Edwards	30.00	13.50
❑ 44 Johnny Wyrostek	30.00	13.50
❑ 45 Hank Sauer	60.00	27.00
❑ 46 Herman Wehmeier	30.00	13.50
❑ 47 Bobby Thomson	100.00	45.00
❑ 48 Dave Koslo	80.00	19.50

1949 Bowman

	NRMT	VG-E
COMPLETE SET (240)	13000.00	5800.00
COMMON CARD (1-144)	15.00	6.75
COMMON CARD (145-240)	50.00	22.00
WRAPPER (5-CENT,GREEN)	250.00	110.00
WRAPPER (5-CENT,BLUE)	200.00	90.00

JOHNNY VANDER MEER

	NRMT	VG-E
❑ 1 Vern Bickford	100.00	20.00
❑ 2 Whitey Lockman	40.00	18.00
❑ 3 Bob Porterfield	15.00	6.75
❑ 4A Jerry Priddy NNOF	15.00	6.75
❑ 4B Jerry Priddy NOF	40.00	18.00
❑ 5 Hank Sauer	40.00	18.00
❑ 6 Phil Cavarretta	40.00	18.00
❑ 7 Joe Dobson	15.00	6.75
❑ 8 Murry Dickson	15.00	6.75
❑ 9 Ferris Fain	40.00	18.00
❑ 10 Ted Gray	15.00	6.75
❑ 11 Lou Boudreau	60.00	27.00
❑ 12 Cass Michaels	15.00	6.75
❑ 13 Bob Chesnes	15.00	6.75
❑ 14 Curt Simmons	35.00	16.00
❑ 15 Ned Garver	15.00	6.75
❑ 16 Al Kozar	15.00	6.75
❑ 17 Earl Torgeson	15.00	6.75
❑ 18 Bobby Thomson	35.00	16.00
❑ 19 Bobby Brown	35.00	16.00
❑ 20 Gene Hermanski	15.00	6.75
❑ 21 Frank Baumholtz	40.00	18.00
❑ 22 Peanuts Lowrey	15.00	6.75
❑ 23 Bobby Doerr	60.00	27.00
❑ 24 Stan Musial	500.00	220.00
❑ 25 Carl Scheib	15.00	6.75
❑ 26 George Kell	60.00	27.00
❑ 27 Bob Feller	175.00	80.00
❑ 28 Don Kolloway	15.00	6.75
❑ 29 Ralph Kiner	125.00	55.00
❑ 30 Andy Seminick	40.00	18.00
❑ 31 Dick Kokos	15.00	6.75
❑ 32 Eddie Yost	60.00	27.00
❑ 33 Warren Spahn	175.00	80.00
❑ 34 Dave Koslo	15.00	6.75
❑ 35 Vic Raschi	55.00	25.00
❑ 36 Pee Wee Reese	175.00	80.00
❑ 37 Johnny Wyrostek	15.00	6.75
❑ 38 Emil Verban	15.00	6.75
❑ 39 Billy Goodman	15.00	6.75
❑ 40 Red Munger	15.00	6.75
❑ 41 Lou Brissie	15.00	6.75
❑ 42 Hoot Evers	15.00	6.75
❑ 43 Dale Mitchell	40.00	18.00
❑ 44 Dave Philley	15.00	6.75
❑ 45 Wally Westlake	15.00	6.75
❑ 46 Robin Roberts	250.00	110.00
❑ 47 Johnny Sain	25.00	11.00
❑ 48 Willard Marshall	15.00	6.75
❑ 49 Frank Shea	25.00	11.00
❑ 50 Jackie Robinson	1100.00	500.00
❑ 51 Herman Wehmeier	15.00	6.75
❑ 52 Johnny Schmitz	15.00	6.75
❑ 53 Jack Kramer	15.00	6.75
❑ 54 Marty Marion	60.00	27.00
❑ 55 Eddie Joost	15.00	6.75
❑ 56 Pat Mullin	15.00	6.75
❑ 57 Gene Bearden	40.00	18.00
❑ 58 Bob Elliott	40.00	18.00
❑ 59 Jack Lohrke	15.00	6.75
❑ 60 Yogi Berra	275.00	125.00
❑ 61 Rex Barney	40.00	18.00
❑ 62 Grady Hatton	15.00	6.75
❑ 63 Andy Pafko	40.00	18.00
❑ 64 Dom DiMaggio	35.00	16.00
❑ 65 Enos Slaughter	70.00	32.00
❑ 66 Elmer Valo	15.00	6.75
❑ 67 Alvin Dark	35.00	16.00
❑ 68 Sheldon Jones	15.00	6.75
❑ 69 Tommy Henrich	35.00	16.00
❑ 70 Carl Furillo	100.00	45.00
❑ 71 Vern Stephens	15.00	6.75
❑ 72 Tommy Holmes	40.00	18.00
❑ 73 Billy Cox	35.00	16.00
❑ 74 Tom McBride	15.00	6.75
❑ 75 Eddie Mayo	15.00	6.75
❑ 76 Bill Nicholson	25.00	11.00
❑ 77 Ernie Bonham	15.00	6.75
❑ 78A Sam Zoldak NNOF	15.00	6.75
❑ 78B Sam Zoldak NOF	40.00	18.00
❑ 79 Ron Northey	15.00	6.75
❑ 80 Bill McCahan	15.00	6.75
❑ 81 Virgil Stallcup	15.00	6.75
❑ 82 Joe Page	60.00	27.00
❑ 83A Bob Scheffing NNOF	15.00	6.75
❑ 83B Bob Scheffing NOF	40.00	18.00
❑ 84 Roy Campanella	725.00	325.00
❑ 85A Johnny Mize NNOF	80.00	36.00
❑ 85B Johnny Mize NOF	150.00	70.00
❑ 86 Johnny Pesky	60.00	27.00
❑ 87 Randy Gumpert	15.00	6.75
❑ 88A Bill Salkeld NNOF	15.00	6.75
❑ 88B Bill Salkeld NOF	40.00	18.00
❑ 89 Mizell Platt	15.00	6.75
❑ 90 Gil Coan	15.00	6.75
❑ 91 Dick Wakefield	15.00	6.75
❑ 92 Willie Jones	40.00	18.00
❑ 93 Ed Stevens	15.00	6.75
❑ 94 Mickey Vernon	35.00	16.00
❑ 95 Howie Pollet	15.00	6.75
❑ 96 Taft Wright	15.00	6.75
❑ 97 Danny Litwhiler	15.00	6.75
❑ 98A Phil Rizzuto NNOF	125.00	55.00
❑ 98B Phil Rizzuto NOF	200.00	90.00
❑ 99 Frank Gustine	15.00	6.75
❑ 100 Gil Hodges	250.00	110.00
❑ 101 Sid Gordon	15.00	6.75
❑ 102 Stan Spence	15.00	6.75
❑ 103 Joe Tipton	15.00	6.75
❑ 104 Eddie Stanky	35.00	16.00
❑ 105 Bill Kennedy	15.00	6.75
❑ 106 Jake Early	15.00	6.75
❑ 107 Eddie Lake	15.00	6.75
❑ 108 Ken Heintzelman	15.00	6.75
❑ 109A Ed Fitzgerald SCR	15.00	6.75
❑ 109B Ed Fitzgerald PR	40.00	18.00
❑ 110 Early Wynn	125.00	55.00
❑ 111 Red Schoendienst	70.00	32.00
❑ 112 Sam Chapman	60.00	27.00
❑ 113 Ray LaManno	15.00	6.75
❑ 114 Allie Reynolds	40.00	18.00
❑ 115 Dutch Leonard	15.00	6.75
❑ 116 Joe Hatton	15.00	6.75
❑ 117 Walker Cooper	15.00	6.75
❑ 118 Sam Meie	15.00	6.75
❑ 119 Floyd Baker	15.00	6.75
❑ 120 Cliff Fannin	15.00	6.75
❑ 121 Mark Christman	15.00	6.75
❑ 122 George Vico	15.00	6.75
❑ 123 Johnny Blatnick	15.00	6.75
❑ 124A Danny Murtaugh SCR	60.00	27.00
❑ 124B Danny Murtaugh PR	45.00	20.00
❑ 125 Ken Keltner	40.00	18.00
❑ 126A Al Brazle SCR	15.00	6.75
❑ 126B Al Brazle PR	40.00	18.00
❑ 127A Hank Majeski SCR	15.00	6.75
❑ 127B Hank Majeski PR	40.00	18.00
❑ 128 Johnny VanderMeer	60.00	27.00
❑ 129 Bill Johnson	40.00	18.00
❑ 130 Harry Walker	15.00	6.75
❑ 131 Paul Lehner	15.00	6.75
❑ 132A Al Evans SCR	15.00	6.75
❑ 132B Al Evans PR	40.00	18.00
❑ 133 Aaron Robinson	15.00	6.75
❑ 134 Hank Borowy	15.00	6.75
❑ 135 Stan Rojek	15.00	6.75
❑ 136 Hank Edwards	15.00	6.75
❑ 137 Ted Wilks	15.00	6.75
❑ 138 Buddy Rosar	15.00	6.75
❑ 139 Hank Arft	15.00	6.75
❑ 140 Ray Scarborough	15.00	6.75
❑ 141 Tony Lupien	15.00	6.75
❑ 142 Eddie Waitkus	40.00	18.00
❑ 143A Bob Dillinger SCR	25.00	11.00
❑ 143B Bob Dillinger PR	75.00	34.00
❑ 144 Mickey Haefner	15.00	6.75
❑ 145 Sylvester Donnelly	50.00	22.00
❑ 146 Mike McCormick	80.00	36.00
❑ 147 Bert Singleton	50.00	22.00

❑ 148 Bob Swift 50.00 22.00
❑ 149 Roy Partee 50.00 22.00
❑ 150 Allie Clark 50.00 22.00
❑ 151 Mickey Harris 50.00 22.00
❑ 152 Clarence Maddern 50.00 22.00
❑ 153 Phil Masi 50.00 22.00
❑ 154 Clint Hartung 75.00 34.00
❑ 155 Mickey Guerra 50.00 22.00
❑ 156 Al Zarilla 50.00 22.00
❑ 157 Walt Masterson 50.00 22.00
❑ 158 Harry Brecheen 75.00 34.00
❑ 159 Glen Moulder 50.00 22.00
❑ 160 Jim Blackburn 50.00 22.00
❑ 161 Jocko Thompson 50.00 22.00
❑ 162 Preacher Roe 125.00 55.00
❑ 163 Clyde McCullough 50.00 22.00
❑ 164 Vic Wertz 75.00 34.00
❑ 165 Snuffy Stirnweiss 75.00 34.00
❑ 166 Mike Tresh 50.00 22.00
❑ 167 Babe Martin 50.00 22.00
❑ 168 Doyle Lade 50.00 22.00
❑ 169 Jeff Heath 80.00 36.00
❑ 170 Bill Rigney 80.00 36.00
❑ 171 Dick Fowler 50.00 22.00
❑ 172 Eddie Pellagrini 50.00 22.00
❑ 173 Eddie Stewart 50.00 22.00
❑ 174 Terry Moore 100.00 45.00
❑ 175 Luke Appling 125.00 55.00
❑ 176 Ken Raffensberger 50.00 22.00
❑ 177 Stan Lopata 80.00 36.00
❑ 178 Tom Brown 80.00 36.00
❑ 179 Hugh Casey 75.00 34.00
❑ 180 Connie Berry 50.00 22.00
❑ 181 Gus Niarhos 50.00 22.00
❑ 182 Hal Peck 50.00 22.00
❑ 183 Lou Stringer 50.00 22.00
❑ 184 Bob Chipman 50.00 22.00
❑ 185 Pete Reiser 100.00 45.00
❑ 186 Buddy Kerr 50.00 22.00
❑ 187 Phil Marchildon 50.00 22.00
❑ 188 Karl Drews 50.00 22.00
❑ 189 Earl Wooten 50.00 22.00
❑ 190 Jim Hearn 50.00 22.00
❑ 191 Joe Haynes 50.00 22.00
❑ 192 Harry Gumbert 50.00 22.00
❑ 193 Ken Trinkle 50.00 22.00
❑ 194 Ralph Branca 100.00 45.00
❑ 195 Eddie Bockman 50.00 22.00
❑ 196 Fred Hutchinson 75.00 34.00
❑ 197 Johnny Lindell 75.00 34.00
❑ 198 Steve Gromek 50.00 22.00
❑ 199 Tex Hughson 50.00 22.00
❑ 200 Jess Dobernic 50.00 22.00
❑ 201 Sibby Sisti 50.00 22.00
❑ 202 Larry Jansen 75.00 34.00
❑ 203 Barney McCosky 50.00 22.00
❑ 204 Bob Savage 50.00 22.00
❑ 205 Dick Sisler 80.00 36.00
❑ 206 Bruce Edwards 50.00 22.00
❑ 207 Johnny Hopp 50.00 22.00
❑ 208 Dizzy Trout 75.00 34.00
❑ 209 Charlie Keller 100.00 45.00
❑ 210 Joe Gordon 100.00 45.00
❑ 211 Boo Ferriss 50.00 22.00
❑ 212 Ralph Hamner 50.00 22.00
❑ 213 Red Barrett 50.00 22.00
❑ 214 Richie Ashburn 550.00 250.00
❑ 215 Kirby Higbe 50.00 22.00
❑ 216 Schoolboy Rowe 75.00 34.00
❑ 217 Marino Pieretti 50.00 22.00
❑ 218 Dick Kryhoski 50.00 22.00
❑ 219 Virgil Fire Trucks 80.00 36.00
❑ 220 Johnny McCarthy 50.00 22.00
❑ 221 Bob Muncrief 50.00 22.00
❑ 222 Alex Kellner 50.00 22.00
❑ 223 Bobby Hofman 50.00 22.00
❑ 224 Satchell Paige 1000.00 450.00
❑ 225 Jerry Coleman 100.00 45.00
❑ 226 Duke Snider 900.00 400.00
❑ 227 Fritz Ostermueller 50.00 22.00
❑ 228 Jackie Mayo 50.00 22.00
❑ 229 Ed Lopat 125.00 55.00
❑ 230 Augie Galan 80.00 36.00
❑ 231 Earl Johnson 50.00 22.00
❑ 232 George McQuinn 80.00 36.00
❑ 233 Larry Doby 175.00 80.00
❑ 234 Rip Sewell 50.00 22.00
❑ 235 Jim Russell 50.00 22.00
❑ 236 Fred Sanford 50.00 22.00
❑ 237 Monte Kennedy 50.00 22.00
❑ 238 Bob Lemon 200.00 90.00
❑ 239 Frank McCormick 50.00 22.00
❑ 240 Babe Young UER 100.00 25.00
(Photo actually Bobby Young)

1950 Bowman

	NRMT	VG-E
COMPLETE SET (252)	8500.00	3800.00
COMMON CARD (1-72)	50.00	22.00
COMMON CARD (73-252)	15.00	6.75
WRAPPER (1-cent)	250.00	110.00
WRAPPER (5-cent)	250.00	110.00

❑ 1 Mel Parnell 150.00 30.00
❑ 2 Vern Stephens 65.00 29.00
❑ 3 Dom DiMaggio 70.00 32.00
❑ 4 Gus Zernial 65.00 29.00
❑ 5 Bob Kuzava 50.00 22.00
❑ 6 Bob Feller 225.00 100.00
❑ 7 Jim Hegan 60.00 27.00
❑ 8 George Kell 75.00 34.00
❑ 9 Vic Wertz 65.00 29.00
❑ 10 Tommy Henrich 80.00 36.00
❑ 11 Phil Rizzuto 225.00 100.00
❑ 12 Joe Page 75.00 34.00
❑ 13 Ferris Fain 65.00 29.00
❑ 14 Alex Kellner 50.00 22.00
❑ 15 Al Kozar 50.00 22.00
❑ 16 Roy Sievers 80.00 36.00
❑ 17 Sid Hudson 50.00 22.00
❑ 18 Eddie Robinson 50.00 22.00
❑ 19 Warren Spahn 225.00 100.00
❑ 20 Bob Elliott 65.00 29.00
❑ 21 Pee Wee Reese 225.00 100.00
❑ 22 Jackie Robinson 800.00 350.00
❑ 23 Don Newcombe 150.00 70.00
❑ 24 Johnny Schmitz 50.00 22.00
❑ 25 Hank Sauer 65.00 29.00
❑ 26 Grady Hatton 50.00 22.00
❑ 27 Herman Wehmeier 50.00 22.00
❑ 28 Bobby Thomson 70.00 32.00
❑ 29 Eddie Stanky 65.00 29.00
❑ 30 Eddie Waitkus 65.00 29.00
❑ 31 Del Ennis 80.00 36.00
❑ 32 Robin Roberts 150.00 70.00
❑ 33 Ralph Kiner 100.00 45.00
❑ 34 Murry Dickson 50.00 22.00
❑ 35 Enos Slaughter 100.00 45.00
❑ 36 Eddie Kazak 55.00 25.00
❑ 37 Luke Appling 75.00 34.00
❑ 38 Bill Wight 50.00 22.00
❑ 39 Larry Doby 80.00 36.00
❑ 40 Bob Lemon 75.00 34.00
❑ 41 Hoot Evers 50.00 22.00
❑ 42 Art Houtteman 50.00 22.00
❑ 43 Bobby Doerr 75.00 34.00
❑ 44 Joe Dobson 50.00 22.00
❑ 45 Al Zarilla 50.00 22.00
❑ 46 Yogi Berra 325.00 145.00
❑ 47 Jerry Coleman 75.00 34.00
❑ 48 Lou Brissie 50.00 22.00
❑ 49 Elmer Valo 50.00 22.00
❑ 50 Dick Kokos 50.00 22.00
❑ 51 Ned Garver 65.00 29.00
❑ 52 Sam Mele 50.00 22.00
❑ 53 Clyde Vollmer 50.00 22.00
❑ 54 Gil Coan 50.00 22.00
❑ 55 Buddy Kerr 50.00 22.00
❑ 56 Del Crandall 65.00 29.00
❑ 57 Vern Bickford 50.00 22.00
❑ 58 Carl Furillo 80.00 36.00
❑ 59 Ralph Branca 75.00 34.00
❑ 60 Andy Pafko 65.00 29.00
❑ 61 Bob Rush 50.00 22.00
❑ 62 Ted Kluszewski 100.00 45.00
❑ 63 Ewell Blackwell 65.00 29.00
❑ 64 Alvin Dark 65.00 29.00
❑ 65 Dave Koslo 50.00 22.00
❑ 66 Larry Jansen 65.00 29.00
❑ 67 Willie Jones 60.00 27.00
❑ 68 Curt Simmons 65.00 29.00
❑ 69 Wally Westlake 50.00 22.00
❑ 70 Bob Chesnes 50.00 22.00
❑ 71 Red Schoendienst 75.00 34.00
❑ 72 Howie Pollet 50.00 22.00
❑ 73 Willard Marshall 15.00 6.75
❑ 74 Johnny Antonelli 60.00 27.00
❑ 75 Roy Campanella 275.00 125.00
❑ 76 Rex Barney 40.00 18.00
❑ 77 Duke Snider 275.00 125.00
❑ 78 Mickey Owen 25.00 11.00
❑ 79 Johnny VanderMeer 40.00 18.00
❑ 80 Howard Fox 15.00 6.75
❑ 81 Ron Northey 15.00 6.75
❑ 82 Whitey Lockman 25.00 11.00
❑ 83 Sheldon Jones 15.00 6.75
❑ 84 Richie Ashburn 100.00 45.00
❑ 85 Ken Heintzelman 15.00 6.75
❑ 86 Stan Rojek 15.00 6.75
❑ 87 Bill Werle 15.00 6.75
❑ 88 Marty Marion 40.00 18.00
❑ 89 Red Munger 15.00 6.75
❑ 90 Harry Brecheen 40.00 18.00
❑ 91 Cass Michaels 15.00 6.75
❑ 92 Hank Majeski 15.00 6.75
❑ 93 Gene Bearden 40.00 18.00
❑ 94 Lou Boudreau 60.00 27.00
❑ 95 Aaron Robinson 15.00 6.75
❑ 96 Virgil Trucks 25.00 11.00
❑ 97 Maurice McDermott 15.00 6.75
❑ 98 Ted Williams 850.00 375.00
❑ 99 Billy Goodman 25.00 11.00
❑ 100 Vic Raschi 60.00 27.00
❑ 101 Bobby Brown 60.00 27.00
❑ 102 Billy Johnson 25.00 11.00
❑ 103 Eddie Joost 15.00 6.75
❑ 104 Sam Chapman 15.00 6.75
❑ 105 Bob Dillinger 15.00 6.75
❑ 106 Cliff Fannin 15.00 6.75
❑ 107 Sam Dente 15.00 6.75
❑ 108 Ray Scarborough 15.00 6.75
❑ 109 Sid Gordon 15.00 6.75
❑ 110 Tommy Holmes 25.00 11.00
❑ 111 Walker Cooper 15.00 6.75
❑ 112 Gil Hodges 100.00 45.00
❑ 113 Gene Hermanski 15.00 6.75
❑ 114 Wayne Terwilliger 15.00 6.75
❑ 115 Roy Smalley 15.00 6.75
❑ 116 Virgil Stallcup 15.00 6.75
❑ 117 Bill Rigney 15.00 6.75
❑ 118 Clint Hartung 15.00 6.75
❑ 119 Dick Sisler 25.00 11.00
❑ 120 John Thompson 15.00 6.75
❑ 121 Andy Seminick 25.00 11.00
❑ 122 Johnny Hopp 25.00 11.00
❑ 123 Dino Restelli 15.00 6.75
❑ 124 Clyde McCullough 15.00 6.75
❑ 125 Del Rice 15.00 6.75
❑ 126 Al Brazle 15.00 6.75
❑ 127 Dave Philley 15.00 6.75
❑ 128 Phil Masi 15.00 6.75
❑ 129 Joe Gordon 25.00 11.00
❑ 130 Dale Mitchell 25.00 11.00
❑ 131 Steve Gromek 15.00 6.75
❑ 132 Mickey Vernon 25.00 11.00
❑ 133 Don Kolloway 15.00 6.75
❑ 134 Paul Trout 15.00 6.75
❑ 135 Pat Mullin 15.00 6.75

Card	Player	NRMT	VG-E
❑ 136	Warren Rosar	15.00	6.75
❑ 137	Johnny Pesky	25.00	11.00
❑ 138	Allie Reynolds	60.00	27.00
❑ 139	Johnny Mize	75.00	34.00
❑ 140	Pete Suder	15.00	6.75
❑ 141	Joe Coleman	25.00	11.00
❑ 142	Sherman Lollar	40.00	18.00
❑ 143	Eddie Stewart	15.00	6.75
❑ 144	Al Evans	15.00	6.75
❑ 145	Jack Graham	15.00	6.75
❑ 146	Floyd Baker	15.00	6.75
❑ 147	Mike Garcia	40.00	18.00
❑ 148	Early Wynn	75.00	34.00
❑ 149	Bob Swift	15.00	6.75
❑ 150	George Vico	15.00	6.75
❑ 151	Fred Hutchinson	25.00	11.00
❑ 152	Ellis Kinder	15.00	6.75
❑ 153	Walt Masterson	15.00	6.75
❑ 154	Gus Niarhos	15.00	6.75
❑ 155	Frank Shea	25.00	11.00
❑ 156	Fred Sanford	25.00	11.00
❑ 157	Mike Guerra	15.00	6.75
❑ 158	Paul Lehner	15.00	6.75
❑ 159	Joe Tipton	15.00	6.75
❑ 160	Mickey Harris	15.00	6.75
❑ 161	Sherry Robertson	15.00	6.75
❑ 162	Eddie Yost	25.00	11.00
❑ 163	Earl Torgeson	15.00	6.75
❑ 164	Sibby Sisti	15.00	6.75
❑ 165	Bruce Edwards	15.00	6.75
❑ 166	Joe Hatton	15.00	6.75
❑ 167	Preacher Roe	60.00	27.00
❑ 168	Bob Scheffing	15.00	6.75
❑ 169	Hank Edwards	15.00	6.75
❑ 170	Dutch Leonard	15.00	6.75
❑ 171	Harry Gumbert	15.00	6.75
❑ 172	Peanuts Lowrey	15.00	6.75
❑ 173	Lloyd Merriman	15.00	6.75
❑ 174	Hank Thompson	40.00	18.00
❑ 175	Monte Kennedy	15.00	6.75
❑ 176	Sylvester Donnelly	15.00	6.75
❑ 177	Hank Borowy	15.00	6.75
❑ 178	Ed Fitzgerald	15.00	6.75
❑ 179	Chuck Diering	15.00	6.75
❑ 180	Harry Walker	15.00	6.75
❑ 181	Marino Pieretti	15.00	6.75
❑ 182	Sam Zoldak	15.00	6.75
❑ 183	Mickey Haefner	15.00	6.75
❑ 184	Randy Gumpert	15.00	6.75
❑ 185	Howie Judson	15.00	6.75
❑ 186	Ken Keltner	25.00	11.00
❑ 187	Lou Stringer	15.00	6.75
❑ 188	Earl Johnson	15.00	6.75
❑ 189	Owen Friend	15.00	6.75
❑ 190	Ken Wood	15.00	6.75
❑ 191	Dick Starr	15.00	6.75
❑ 192	Bob Chipman	15.00	6.75
❑ 193	Pete Reiser	40.00	18.00
❑ 194	Billy Cox	60.00	27.00
❑ 195	Phil Cavarretta	40.00	18.00
❑ 196	Doyle Lade	15.00	6.75
❑ 197	Johnny Wyrostek	15.00	6.75
❑ 198	Danny Litwhiler	15.00	6.75
❑ 199	Jack Kramer	15.00	6.75
❑ 200	Kirby Higbe	25.00	11.00
❑ 201	Pete Castiglione	15.00	6.75
❑ 202	Cliff Chambers	15.00	6.75
❑ 203	Danny Murtaugh	25.00	11.00
❑ 204	Granny Hamner	40.00	18.00
❑ 205	Mike Goliat	15.00	6.75
❑ 206	Stan Lopata	25.00	11.00
❑ 207	Max Lanier	15.00	6.75
❑ 208	Jim Hearn	15.00	6.75
❑ 209	Johnny Lindell	15.00	6.75
❑ 210	Ted Gray	15.00	6.75
❑ 211	Charlie Keller	25.00	11.00
❑ 212	Jerry Priddy	15.00	6.75
❑ 213	Carl Scheib	15.00	6.75
❑ 214	Dick Fowler	15.00	6.75
❑ 215	Ed Lopat	60.00	27.00
❑ 216	Bob Porterfield	25.00	11.00
❑ 217	Casey Stengel MG	125.00	55.00
❑ 218	Cliff Mapes	25.00	11.00
❑ 219	Hank Bauer	80.00	36.00
❑ 220	Leo Durocher MG	60.00	27.00
❑ 221	Don Mueller	40.00	18.00
❑ 222	Bobby Morgan	15.00	6.75
❑ 223	Jim Russell	15.00	6.75
❑ 224	Jack Banta	15.00	6.75
❑ 225	Eddie Sawyer MG	25.00	11.00
❑ 226	Jim Konstanty	60.00	27.00
❑ 227	Bob Miller	15.00	6.75
❑ 228	Bill Nicholson	25.00	11.00
❑ 229	Frank Frisch MG	60.00	27.00
❑ 230	Bill Serena	15.00	6.75
❑ 231	Preston Ward	15.00	6.75
❑ 232	Al Rosen	60.00	27.00
❑ 233	Allie Clark	15.00	6.75
❑ 234	Bobby Shantz	60.00	27.00
❑ 235	Harold Gilbert	15.00	6.75
❑ 236	Bob Cain	15.00	6.75
❑ 237	Bill Salkeld	15.00	6.75
❑ 238	Nippy Jones	15.00	6.75
❑ 239	Bill Howerton	15.00	6.75
❑ 240	Eddie Lake	15.00	6.75
❑ 241	Neil Berry	15.00	6.75
❑ 242	Dick Kryhoski	15.00	6.75
❑ 243	Johnny Groth	15.00	6.75
❑ 244	Dale Coogan	15.00	6.75
❑ 245	Al Papai	15.00	6.75
❑ 246	Walt Dropo	40.00	18.00
❑ 247	Irv Noren	25.00	11.00
❑ 248	Sam Jethroe	60.00	27.00
❑ 249	Snuffy Stirnweiss	25.00	11.00
❑ 250	Ray Coleman	15.00	6.75
❑ 251	Les Moss	15.00	6.75
❑ 252	Billy DeMars	60.00	16.50

1951 Bowman

	NRMT	VG-E
COMPLETE SET (324)	16000.00	7200.00
COMMON CARD (1-252)	18.00	8.00
COMMON CARD (253-324)	50.00	22.00
WRAPPER (1-cent)	200.00	90.00
WRAPPER (5-cent)	250.00	110.00

Card	Player	NRMT	VG-E
❑ 1	Whitey Ford	800.00	200.00
❑ 2	Yogi Berra	275.00	125.00
❑ 3	Robin Roberts	75.00	34.00
❑ 4	Del Ennis	25.00	11.00
❑ 5	Dale Mitchell	25.00	11.00
❑ 6	Don Newcombe	50.00	22.00
❑ 7	Gil Hodges	90.00	40.00
❑ 8	Paul Lehner	18.00	8.00
❑ 9	Sam Chapman	18.00	8.00
❑ 10	Red Schoendienst	55.00	25.00
❑ 11	Red Munger	18.00	8.00
❑ 12	Hank Majeski	18.00	8.00
❑ 13	Eddie Stanky	25.00	11.00
❑ 14	Alvin Dark	40.00	18.00
❑ 15	Johnny Pesky	25.00	11.00
❑ 16	Maurice McDermott	18.00	8.00
❑ 17	Pete Castiglione	18.00	8.00
❑ 18	Gil Coan	18.00	8.00
❑ 19	Sid Gordon	18.00	8.00
❑ 20	Del Crandall UER (Misspelled Crandell on card)	25.00	11.00
❑ 21	Snuffy Stirnweiss	25.00	11.00
❑ 22	Hank Sauer	25.00	11.00
❑ 23	Hoot Evers	18.00	8.00
❑ 24	Ewell Blackwell	40.00	18.00
❑ 25	Vic Raschi	60.00	27.00
❑ 26	Phil Rizzuto	125.00	55.00
❑ 27	Jim Konstanty	25.00	11.00
❑ 28	Eddie Waitkus	18.00	8.00
❑ 29	Allie Clark	18.00	8.00
❑ 30	Bob Feller	125.00	55.00
❑ 31	Roy Campanella	225.00	100.00
❑ 32	Duke Snider	225.00	100.00
❑ 33	Bob Hooper	18.00	8.00
❑ 34	Marty Marion	40.00	18.00
❑ 35	Al Zarilla	18.00	8.00
❑ 36	Joe Dobson	18.00	8.00
❑ 37	Whitey Lockman	40.00	18.00
❑ 38	Al Evans	18.00	8.00
❑ 39	Ray Scarborough	18.00	8.00
❑ 40	Gus Bell	60.00	27.00
❑ 41	Eddie Yost	25.00	11.00
❑ 42	Vern Bickford	18.00	8.00
❑ 43	Billy DeMars	18.00	8.00
❑ 44	Roy Smalley	18.00	8.00
❑ 45	Art Houtteman	18.00	8.00
❑ 46	George Kell 1941 UER	55.00	25.00
❑ 47	Grady Hatton	18.00	8.00
❑ 48	Ken Raffensberger	18.00	8.00
❑ 49	Jerry Coleman	30.00	13.50
❑ 50	Johnny Mize	55.00	25.00
❑ 51	Andy Seminick	18.00	8.00
❑ 52	Dick Sisler	40.00	18.00
❑ 53	Bob Lemon	55.00	25.00
❑ 54	Ray Boone	35.00	16.00
❑ 55	Gene Hermanski	18.00	8.00
❑ 56	Ralph Branca	60.00	27.00
❑ 57	Alex Kellner	18.00	8.00
❑ 58	Enos Slaughter	55.00	25.00
❑ 59	Randy Gumpert	18.00	8.00
❑ 60	Chico Carrasquel	60.00	27.00
❑ 61	Jim Hearn	22.00	10.00
❑ 62	Lou Boudreau	55.00	25.00
❑ 63	Bob Dillinger	18.00	8.00
❑ 64	Bill Werle	18.00	8.00
❑ 65	Mickey Vernon	40.00	18.00
❑ 66	Bob Elliott	25.00	11.00
❑ 67	Roy Sievers	25.00	11.00
❑ 68	Dick Kokos	18.00	8.00
❑ 69	Johnny Schmitz	18.00	8.00
❑ 70	Ron Northey	18.00	8.00
❑ 71	Jerry Priddy	18.00	8.00
❑ 72	Lloyd Merriman	18.00	8.00
❑ 73	Tommy Byrne	18.00	8.00
❑ 74	Billy Johnson	25.00	11.00
❑ 75	Russ Meyer	25.00	11.00
❑ 76	Stan Lopata	25.00	11.00
❑ 77	Mike Goliat	18.00	8.00
❑ 78	Early Wynn	55.00	25.00
❑ 79	Jim Hegan	25.00	11.00
❑ 80	Pee Wee Reese	125.00	55.00
❑ 81	Carl Furillo	50.00	22.00
❑ 82	Joe Tipton	18.00	8.00
❑ 83	Carl Scheib	18.00	8.00
❑ 84	Barney McCosky	18.00	8.00
❑ 85	Eddie Kazak	18.00	8.00
❑ 86	Harry Brecheen	25.00	11.00
❑ 87	Floyd Baker	18.00	8.00
❑ 88	Eddie Robinson	18.00	8.00
❑ 89	Hank Thompson	25.00	11.00
❑ 90	Dave Koslo	25.00	11.00
❑ 91	Clyde Vollmer	18.00	8.00
❑ 92	Vern Stephens	25.00	11.00
❑ 93	Danny O'Connell	18.00	8.00
❑ 94	Clyde McCullough	18.00	8.00
❑ 95	Sherry Robertson	18.00	8.00
❑ 96	Sandy Consuegra	18.00	8.00
❑ 97	Bob Kuzava	18.00	8.00
❑ 98	Willard Marshall	18.00	8.00
❑ 99	Earl Torgeson	18.00	8.00
❑ 100	Sherm Lollar	25.00	11.00
❑ 101	Owen Friend	18.00	8.00
❑ 102	Dutch Leonard	18.00	8.00
❑ 103	Andy Pafko	40.00	18.00
❑ 104	Virgil Trucks	25.00	11.00
❑ 105	Don Kolloway	18.00	8.00
❑ 106	Pat Mullin	18.00	8.00
❑ 107	Johnny Wyrostek	18.00	8.00
❑ 108	Virgil Stallcup	18.00	8.00
❑ 109	Allie Reynolds	60.00	27.00

❑ 110 Bobby Brown 40.00 18.00
❑ 111 Curt Simmons 18.00 8.00
❑ 112 Willie Jones 18.00 8.00
❑ 113 Bill Nicholson 25.00 11.00
❑ 114 Sam Zoldak 18.00 8.00
❑ 115 Steve Gromek 18.00 8.00
❑ 116 Bruce Edwards 18.00 8.00
❑ 117 Eddie Miksis 18.00 8.00
❑ 118 Preacher Roe 60.00 27.00
❑ 119 Eddie Joost 18.00 8.00
❑ 120 Joe Coleman 25.00 11.00
❑ 121 Jerry Staley 18.00 8.00
❑ 122 Joe Garagiola 80.00 36.00
❑ 123 Howie Judson 18.00 8.00
❑ 124 Gus Niarhos 18.00 8.00
❑ 125 Bill Rigney 25.00 11.00
❑ 126 Bobby Thomson 60.00 27.00
❑ 127 Sal Maglie 55.00 25.00
❑ 128 Ellis Kinder 18.00 8.00
❑ 129 Matt Batts 18.00 8.00
❑ 130 Tom Saffell 18.00 8.00
❑ 131 Cliff Chambers 18.00 8.00
❑ 132 Cass Michaels 18.00 8.00
❑ 133 Sam Dente 18.00 8.00
❑ 134 Warren Spahn 125.00 55.00
❑ 135 Walker Cooper 18.00 8.00
❑ 136 Ray Coleman 18.00 8.00
❑ 137 Dick Starr 18.00 8.00
❑ 138 Phil Cavarretta 25.00 11.00
❑ 139 Doyle Lade 18.00 8.00
❑ 140 Eddie Lake 18.00 8.00
❑ 141 Fred Hutchinson 25.00 11.00
❑ 142 Aaron Robinson 18.00 8.00
❑ 143 Ted Kluszewski 60.00 27.00
❑ 144 Herman Wehmeier 18.00 8.00
❑ 145 Fred Sanford 25.00 11.00
❑ 146 Johnny Hopp 25.00 11.00
❑ 147 Ken Heintzelman 18.00 8.00
❑ 148 Granny Hamner 18.00 8.00
❑ 149 Bubba Church 18.00 8.00
❑ 150 Mike Garcia 25.00 11.00
❑ 151 Larry Doby 60.00 27.00
❑ 152 Cal Abrams 18.00 8.00
❑ 153 Rex Barney 25.00 11.00
❑ 154 Pete Suder 18.00 8.00
❑ 155 Lou Brissie 18.00 8.00
❑ 156 Del Rice 18.00 8.00
❑ 157 Al Brazle 18.00 8.00
❑ 158 Chuck Diering 18.00 8.00
❑ 159 Eddie Stewart 18.00 8.00
❑ 160 Phil Masi 18.00 8.00
❑ 161 Wes Westrum 18.00 8.00
❑ 162 Larry Jansen 25.00 11.00
❑ 163 Monte Kennedy 18.00 8.00
❑ 164 Bill Wight 18.00 8.00
❑ 165 Ted Williams 750.00 350.00
❑ 166 Stan Rojek 18.00 8.00
❑ 167 Murry Dickson 18.00 8.00
❑ 168 Sam Mele 18.00 8.00
❑ 169 Sid Hudson 18.00 8.00
❑ 170 Sibby Sisti 18.00 8.00
❑ 171 Buddy Kerr 18.00 8.00
❑ 172 Ned Garver 18.00 8.00
❑ 173 Hank Arft 18.00 8.00
❑ 174 Mickey Owen 25.00 11.00
❑ 175 Wayne Terwilliger 18.00 8.00
❑ 176 Vic Wertz 40.00 18.00
❑ 177 Charlie Keller 25.00 11.00
❑ 178 Ted Gray 18.00 8.00
❑ 179 Danny Litwhiler 18.00 8.00
❑ 180 Howie Fox 18.00 8.00
❑ 181 Casey Stengel MG 75.00 34.00
❑ 182 Tom Ferrick 18.00 8.00
❑ 183 Hank Bauer 60.00 27.00
❑ 184 Eddie Sawyer MG 40.00 18.00
❑ 185 Jimmy Bloodworth 18.00 8.00
❑ 186 Richie Ashburn 90.00 40.00
❑ 187 Al Rosen 40.00 18.00
❑ 188 Bobby Avila 25.00 11.00
❑ 189 Erv Palica 18.00 8.00
❑ 190 Joe Hatten 18.00 8.00
❑ 191 Billy Hitchcock 18.00 8.00
❑ 192 Hank Wyse 18.00 8.00
❑ 193 Ted Wilks 18.00 8.00
❑ 194 Peanuts Lowrey 18.00 8.00
❑ 195 Paul Richards MG 25.00 11.00
(Caricature)
❑ 196 Billy Pierce 60.00 27.00
❑ 197 Bob Cain 18.00 8.00
❑ 198 Monte Irvin 100.00 45.00
❑ 199 Sheldon Jones 18.00 8.00
❑ 200 Jack Kramer 18.00 8.00
❑ 201 Steve O'Neill MG 18.00 8.00
❑ 202 Mike Guerra 18.00 8.00
❑ 203 Vernon Law 60.00 27.00
❑ 204 Vic Lombardi 18.00 8.00
❑ 205 Mickey Grasso 18.00 8.00
❑ 206 Conrado Marrero 18.00 8.00
❑ 207 Billy Southworth MG 18.00 8.00
❑ 208 Blix Donnelly 18.00 8.00
❑ 209 Ken Wood 18.00 8.00
❑ 210 Les Moss 18.00 8.00
❑ 211 Hal Jeffcoat 18.00 8.00
❑ 212 Bob Rush 18.00 8.00
❑ 213 Neil Berry 18.00 8.00
❑ 214 Bob Swift 18.00 8.00
❑ 215 Ken Peterson 18.00 8.00
❑ 216 Connie Ryan 18.00 8.00
❑ 217 Joe Page 25.00 11.00
❑ 218 Ed Lopat 60.00 27.00
❑ 219 Gene Woodling 60.00 27.00
❑ 220 Bob Miller 18.00 8.00
❑ 221 Dick Whitman 18.00 8.00
❑ 222 Thurman Tucker 18.00 8.00
❑ 223 Johnny VanderMeer 40.00 18.00
❑ 224 Billy Cox 30.00 13.50
❑ 225 Dan Bankhead 40.00 18.00
❑ 226 Jimmy Dykes MG 25.00 11.00
❑ 227 Bobby Schantz UER 25.00 11.00
(Sic, Shantz)
❑ 228 Cloyd Boyer 25.00 11.00
❑ 229 Bill Howerton 18.00 8.00
❑ 230 Max Lanier 18.00 8.00
❑ 231 Luis Aloma 18.00 8.00
❑ 232 Nelson Fox 225.00 100.00
❑ 233 Leo Durocher MG 60.00 27.00
❑ 234 Clint Hartung 25.00 11.00
❑ 235 Jack Lohrke 18.00 8.00
❑ 236 Warren Rosar 18.00 8.00
❑ 237 Billy Goodman 25.00 11.00
❑ 238 Pete Reiser 40.00 18.00
❑ 239 Bill MacDonald 18.00 8.00
❑ 240 Joe Haynes 18.00 8.00
❑ 241 Irv Noren 25.00 11.00
❑ 242 Sam Jethroe 25.00 11.00
❑ 243 Johnny Antonelli 25.00 11.00
❑ 244 Cliff Fannin 18.00 8.00
❑ 245 John Berardino 60.00 27.00
❑ 246 Bill Serena 18.00 8.00
❑ 247 Bob Ramazzotti 18.00 8.00
❑ 248 Johnny Klippstein 18.00 8.00
❑ 249 Johnny Groth 18.00 8.00
❑ 250 Hank Borowy 18.00 8.00
❑ 251 Willard Ramsdell 18.00 8.00
❑ 252 Dixie Howell 18.00 8.00
❑ 253 Mickey Mantle 8000.00 3600.00
❑ 254 Jackie Jensen 100.00 45.00
❑ 255 Milo Candini 50.00 22.00
❑ 256 Ken Sylvestri 50.00 22.00
❑ 257 Birdie Tebbetts 65.00 29.00
❑ 258 Luke Easter 65.00 29.00
❑ 259 Chuck Dressen MG 75.00 34.00
❑ 260 Carl Erskine 100.00 45.00
❑ 261 Wally Moses 60.00 27.00
❑ 262 Gus Zernial 60.00 27.00
❑ 263 Howie Pollet 60.00 27.00
❑ 264 Don Richmond 50.00 22.00
❑ 265 Steve Bilko 60.00 27.00
❑ 266 Harry Dorish 50.00 22.00
❑ 267 Ken Holcombe 50.00 22.00
❑ 268 Don Mueller 60.00 27.00
❑ 269 Ray Noble 50.00 22.00
❑ 270 Willard Nixon 50.00 22.00
❑ 271 Tommy Wright 50.00 22.00
❑ 272 Billy Meyer MG 50.00 22.00
❑ 273 Danny Murtaugh 65.00 29.00
❑ 274 George Metkovich 50.00 22.00
❑ 275 Bucky Harris MG 65.00 29.00
❑ 276 Frank Quinn 50.00 22.00
❑ 277 Roy Hartsfield 50.00 22.00
❑ 278 Norman Roy 50.00 22.00
❑ 279 Jim Delsing 50.00 22.00
❑ 280 Frank Overmire 50.00 22.00
❑ 281 Al Widmar 50.00 22.00
❑ 282 Frank Frisch MG 90.00 40.00
❑ 283 Walt Dubiel 50.00 22.00
❑ 284 Gene Bearden 60.00 27.00
❑ 285 Johnny Lipon 50.00 22.00
❑ 286 Bob Usher 50.00 22.00
❑ 287 Jim Blackburn 50.00 22.00
❑ 288 Bobby Adams 50.00 22.00
❑ 289 Cliff Mapes 60.00 27.00
❑ 290 Bill Dickey CO 100.00 45.00
❑ 291 Tommy Henrich CO 90.00 40.00
❑ 292 Eddie Pellegrini 50.00 22.00
❑ 293 Ken Johnson 50.00 22.00
❑ 294 Jocko Thompson 50.00 22.00
❑ 295 Al Lopez MG 120.00 55.00
❑ 296 Bob Kennedy 60.00 27.00
❑ 297 Dave Philley 50.00 22.00
❑ 298 Joe Astroth 50.00 22.00
❑ 299 Clyde King 50.00 22.00
❑ 300 Hal Rice 50.00 22.00
❑ 301 Tommy Glaviano 50.00 22.00
❑ 302 Jim Busby 50.00 22.00
❑ 303 Marv Rotblatt 50.00 22.00
❑ 304 Al Gettell 50.00 22.00
❑ 305 Willie Mays 3200.00 1450.00
❑ 306 Jim Piersall 100.00 45.00
❑ 307 Walt Masterson 50.00 22.00
❑ 308 Ted Beard 50.00 22.00
❑ 309 Mel Queen 50.00 22.00
❑ 310 Erv Dusak 50.00 22.00
❑ 311 Mickey Harris 50.00 22.00
❑ 312 Gene Mauch 65.00 29.00
❑ 313 Ray Mueller 50.00 22.00
❑ 314 Johnny Sain 65.00 29.00
❑ 315 Zack Taylor MG 50.00 22.00
❑ 316 Duane Pillette 50.00 22.00
❑ 317 Smoky Burgess 75.00 34.00
❑ 318 Warren Hacker 50.00 22.00
❑ 319 Red Rolfe MG 65.00 29.00
❑ 320 Hal White 50.00 22.00
❑ 321 Earl Johnson 50.00 22.00
❑ 322 Luke Sewell MG 65.00 29.00
❑ 323 Joe Adcock 75.00 34.00
❑ 324 Johnny Pramesa 100.00 30.00

1952 Bowman

	NRMT	VG-E
COMPLETE SET (252)	7500.00	3400.00
COMMON CARD (1-216)	15.00	6.75
COMMON CARD (217-252)	60.00	27.00
WRAPPER (1-cent)	200.00	90.00
WRAPPER (5-cent)	100.00	45.00

❑ 1 Yogi Berra 450.00 140.00
❑ 2 Bobby Thomson 40.00 18.00
❑ 3 Fred Hutchinson 25.00 11.00
❑ 4 Robin Roberts 60.00 27.00
❑ 5 Minnie Minoso 135.00 60.00
❑ 6 Virgil Stallcup 15.00 6.75
❑ 7 Mike Garcia 25.00 11.00
❑ 8 Pee Wee Reese 125.00 55.00
❑ 9 Vern Stephens 25.00 11.00
❑ 10 Bob Hooper 15.00 6.75
❑ 11 Ralph Kiner 50.00 22.00

	No.	Player	NRMT	VG-E
❑	12	Max Surkont	15.00	6.75
❑	13	Cliff Mapes	15.00	6.75
❑	14	Cliff Chambers	15.00	6.75
❑	15	Sam Mele	15.00	6.75
❑	16	Turk Lown	15.00	6.75
❑	17	Ed Lopat	40.00	18.00
❑	18	Don Mueller	25.00	11.00
❑	19	Bob Cain	15.00	6.75
❑	20	Willie Jones	15.00	6.75
❑	21	Nellie Fox	90.00	40.00
❑	22	Willard Ramsdell	15.00	6.75
❑	23	Bob Lemon	50.00	22.00
❑	24	Carl Furillo	40.00	18.00
❑	25	Mickey McDermott	15.00	6.75
❑	26	Eddie Joost	15.00	6.75
❑	27	Joe Garagiola	50.00	22.00
❑	28	Roy Hartsfield	15.00	6.75
❑	29	Ned Garver	15.00	6.75
❑	30	Red Schoendienst	50.00	22.00
❑	31	Eddie Yost	25.00	11.00
❑	32	Eddie Miksis	15.00	6.75
❑	33	Gil McDougald	80.00	36.00
❑	34	Alvin Dark	25.00	11.00
❑	35	Granny Hamner	15.00	6.75
❑	36	Cass Michaels	15.00	6.75
❑	37	Vic Raschi	25.00	11.00
❑	38	Whitey Lockman	25.00	11.00
❑	39	Vic Wertz	25.00	11.00
❑	40	Bubba Church	15.00	6.75
❑	41	Chico Carrasquel	25.00	11.00
❑	42	Johnny Wyrostek	15.00	6.75
❑	43	Bob Feller	125.00	55.00
❑	44	Roy Campanella	250.00	110.00
❑	45	Johnny Pesky	25.00	11.00
❑	46	Carl Scheib	15.00	6.75
❑	47	Pete Castiglione	15.00	6.75
❑	48	Vern Bickford	15.00	6.75
❑	49	Jim Hearn	15.00	6.75
❑	50	Jerry Staley	15.00	6.75
❑	51	Gil Coan	15.00	6.75
❑	52	Phil Rizzuto	135.00	60.00
❑	53	Richie Ashburn	90.00	40.00
❑	54	Billy Pierce	25.00	11.00
❑	55	Ken Raffensberger	15.00	6.75
❑	56	Clyde King	25.00	11.00
❑	57	Clyde Vollmer	15.00	6.75
❑	58	Hank Majeski	15.00	6.75
❑	59	Murry Dickson	15.00	6.75
❑	60	Sid Gordon	20.00	9.00
❑	61	Tommy Byrne	15.00	6.75
❑	62	Joe Presko	15.00	6.75
❑	63	Irv Noren	20.00	9.00
❑	64	Roy Smalley	15.00	6.75
❑	65	Hank Bauer	25.00	11.00
❑	66	Sal Maglie	25.00	11.00
❑	67	Johnny Groth	15.00	6.75
❑	68	Jim Busby	15.00	6.75
❑	69	Joe Adcock	25.00	11.00
❑	70	Carl Erskine	35.00	16.00
❑	71	Vernon Law	25.00	11.00
❑	72	Earl Torgeson	15.00	6.75
❑	73	Jerry Coleman	25.00	11.00
❑	74	Wes Westrum	22.00	10.00
❑	75	George Kell	50.00	22.00
❑	76	Del Ennis	25.00	11.00
❑	77	Eddie Robinson	15.00	6.75
❑	78	Lloyd Merriman	15.00	6.75
❑	79	Lou Brissie	15.00	6.75
❑	80	Gil Hodges	90.00	40.00
❑	81	Billy Goodman	20.00	9.00
❑	82	Gus Zernial	20.00	9.00
❑	83	Howie Pollet	15.00	6.75
❑	84	Sam Jethroe	25.00	11.00
❑	85	Marty Marion CO	25.00	11.00
❑	86	Cal Abrams	20.00	9.00
❑	87	Mickey Vernon	25.00	11.00
❑	88	Bruce Edwards	15.00	6.75
❑	89	Billy Hitchcock	15.00	6.75
❑	90	Larry Jansen	25.00	11.00
❑	91	Don Kolloway	15.00	6.75
❑	92	Eddie Waitkus	20.00	9.00
❑	93	Paul Richards MG	20.00	9.00
❑	94	Luke Sewell MG	20.00	9.00
❑	95	Luke Easter	25.00	11.00
❑	96	Ralph Branca	25.00	11.00
❑	97	Willard Marshall	15.00	6.75
❑	98	Jimmy Dykes MG	25.00	11.00
❑	99	Clyde McCullough	15.00	6.75
❑	100	Sibby Sisti	15.00	6.75
❑	101	Mickey Mantle	2500.00	1100.00
❑	102	Peanuts Lowrey	15.00	6.75
❑	103	Joe Haynes	15.00	6.75
❑	104	Hal Jeffcoat	15.00	6.75
❑	105	Bobby Brown	25.00	11.00
❑	106	Randy Gumpert	15.00	6.75
❑	107	Del Rice	15.00	6.75
❑	108	George Metkovich	20.00	9.00
❑	109	Tom Morgan	20.00	9.00
❑	110	Max Lanier	15.00	6.75
❑	111	Hoot Evers	15.00	6.75
❑	112	Smoky Burgess	25.00	11.00
❑	113	Al Zarilla	15.00	6.75
❑	114	Frank Hiller	15.00	6.75
❑	115	Larry Doby	40.00	18.00
❑	116	Duke Snider	200.00	90.00
❑	117	Bill Wight	15.00	6.75
❑	118	Ray Murray	15.00	6.75
❑	119	Bill Howerton	15.00	6.75
❑	120	Chet Nichols	15.00	6.75
❑	121	Al Corwin	15.00	6.75
❑	122	Billy Johnson	15.00	6.75
❑	123	Sid Hudson	15.00	6.75
❑	124	Birdie Tebbetts	25.00	11.00
❑	125	Howie Fox	15.00	6.75
❑	126	Phil Cavarretta	25.00	11.00
❑	127	Dick Sisler	15.00	6.75
❑	128	Don Newcombe	35.00	16.00
❑	129	Gus Niarhos	15.00	6.75
❑	130	Allie Clark	15.00	6.75
❑	131	Bob Swift	15.00	6.75
❑	132	Dave Cole	15.00	6.75
❑	133	Dick Kryhoski	15.00	6.75
❑	134	Al Brazle	15.00	6.75
❑	135	Mickey Harris	15.00	6.75
❑	136	Gene Hermanski	15.00	6.75
❑	137	Stan Rojek	15.00	6.75
❑	138	Ted Wilks	15.00	6.75
❑	139	Jerry Priddy	15.00	6.75
❑	140	Ray Scarborough	15.00	6.75
❑	141	Hank Edwards	15.00	6.75
❑	142	Early Wynn	50.00	22.00
❑	143	Sandy Consuegra	15.00	6.75
❑	144	Joe Hatton	15.00	6.75
❑	145	Johnny Mize	50.00	22.00
❑	146	Leo Durocher MG	50.00	22.00
❑	147	Marlin Stuart	15.00	6.75
❑	148	Ken Heintzelman	15.00	6.75
❑	149	Howie Judson	15.00	6.75
❑	150	Herman Wehmeier	15.00	6.75
❑	151	Al Rosen	25.00	11.00
❑	152	Billy Cox	15.00	6.75
❑	153	Fred Hatfield	15.00	6.75
❑	154	Ferris Fain	20.00	9.00
❑	155	Billy Meyer MG	15.00	6.75
❑	156	Warren Spahn	125.00	55.00
❑	157	Jim Delsing	15.00	6.75
❑	158	Bucky Harris MG	25.00	11.00
❑	159	Dutch Leonard	15.00	6.75
❑	160	Eddie Stanky	25.00	11.00
❑	161	Jackie Jensen	35.00	16.00
❑	162	Monte Irvin	50.00	22.00
❑	163	Johnny Lipon	15.00	6.75
❑	164	Connie Ryan	15.00	6.75
❑	165	Saul Rogovin	15.00	6.75
❑	166	Bobby Adams	15.00	6.75
❑	167	Bobby Avila	25.00	11.00
❑	168	Preacher Roe	25.00	11.00
❑	169	Walt Dropo	20.00	9.00
❑	170	Joe Astroth	15.00	6.75
❑	171	Mel Queen	15.00	6.75
❑	172	Ebba St.Claire	15.00	6.75
❑	173	Gene Bearden	15.00	6.75
❑	174	Mickey Grasso	15.00	6.75
❑	175	Randy Jackson	15.00	6.75
❑	176	Harry Brecheen	20.00	9.00
❑	177	Gene Woodling	25.00	11.00
❑	178	Dave Williams	20.00	9.00
❑	179	Pete Suder	15.00	6.75
❑	180	Ed Fitzgerald	15.00	6.75
❑	181	Joe Collins	25.00	11.00
❑	182	Dave Koslo	15.00	6.75
❑	183	Pat Mullin	15.00	6.75
❑	184	Curt Simmons	25.00	11.00
❑	185	Eddie Stewart	15.00	6.75
❑	186	Frank Smith	15.00	6.75
❑	187	Jim Hegan	20.00	9.00
❑	188	Chuck Dressen MG	25.00	11.00
❑	189	Jimmy Piersall	25.00	11.00
❑	190	Dick Fowler	15.00	6.75
❑	191	Bob Friend	40.00	18.00
❑	192	John Cusick	15.00	6.75
❑	193	Bobby Young	15.00	6.75
❑	194	Bob Porterfield	15.00	6.75
❑	195	Frank Baumholtz	15.00	6.75
❑	196	Stan Musial	600.00	275.00
❑	197	Charlie Silvera	15.00	6.75
❑	198	Chuck Diering	15.00	6.75
❑	199	Ted Gray	15.00	6.75
❑	200	Ken Silvestri	15.00	6.75
❑	201	Ray Coleman	15.00	6.75
❑	202	Harry Perkowski	15.00	6.75
❑	203	Steve Gromek	15.00	6.75
❑	204	Andy Pafko	25.00	11.00
❑	205	Walt Masterson	15.00	6.75
❑	206	Elmer Valo	15.00	6.75
❑	207	George Strickland	15.00	6.75
❑	208	Walker Cooper	15.00	6.75
❑	209	Dick Littlefield	15.00	6.75
❑	210	Archie Wilson	15.00	6.75
❑	211	Paul Minner	15.00	6.75
❑	212	Solly Hemus	15.00	6.75
❑	213	Monte Kennedy	15.00	6.75
❑	214	Ray Boone	25.00	11.00
❑	215	Sheldon Jones	15.00	6.75
❑	216	Matt Batts	15.00	6.75
❑	217	Casey Stengel MG	150.00	70.00
❑	218	Willie Mays	1200.00	550.00
❑	219	Neil Berry	60.00	27.00
❑	220	Russ Meyer	60.00	27.00
❑	221	Lou Kretlow	60.00	27.00
❑	222	Dixie Howell	60.00	27.00
❑	223	Harry Simpson	60.00	27.00
❑	224	Johnny Schmitz	60.00	27.00
❑	225	Del Wilber	60.00	27.00
❑	226	Alex Kellner	60.00	27.00
❑	227	Clyde Sukeforth CO	60.00	27.00
❑	228	Bob Chipman	60.00	27.00
❑	229	Hank Arft	60.00	27.00
❑	230	Frank Shea	60.00	27.00
❑	231	Dee Fondy	60.00	27.00
❑	232	Enos Slaughter	90.00	40.00
❑	233	Bob Kuzava	60.00	27.00
❑	234	Fred Fitzsimmons CO	50.00	22.00
❑	235	Steve Souchock	60.00	27.00
❑	236	Tommy Brown	60.00	27.00
❑	237	Sherm Lollar	50.00	22.00
❑	238	Roy McMillan	50.00	22.00
❑	239	Dale Mitchell	50.00	22.00
❑	240	Billy Loes	50.00	22.00
❑	241	Mel Parnell	50.00	22.00
❑	242	Everett Kell	60.00	27.00
❑	243	Red Munger	60.00	27.00
❑	244	Lew Burdette	50.00	22.00
❑	245	George Schmees	60.00	27.00
❑	246	Jerry Snyder	60.00	27.00
❑	247	Johnny Pramesa	60.00	27.00
❑	248	Bill Werle	60.00	27.00
❑	249	Hank Thompson	50.00	22.00
❑	250	Ike Delock	60.00	27.00
❑	251	Jack Lohrke	60.00	27.00
❑	252	Frank Crosetti CO	110.00	28.00

1953 Bowman B/W

	NRMT	VG-E
COMPLETE SET (64)	2400.00	1100.00
COMMON CARD (1-64)	40.00	18.00
WRAPPER (1-CENT)	350.00	160.00

	No.	Player	NRMT	VG-E
❑	1	Gus Bell	125.00	25.00
❑	2	Willard Nixon	40.00	18.00
❑	3	Bill Rigney	40.00	18.00
❑	4	Pat Mullin	40.00	18.00
❑	5	Dee Fondy	40.00	18.00
❑	6	Ray Murray	40.00	18.00
❑	7	Andy Seminick	40.00	18.00

❑ 8 Pete Suder 40.00 18.00
❑ 9 Walt Masterson 40.00 18.00
❑ 10 Dick Sisler 70.00 32.00
❑ 11 Dick Gernert 40.00 18.00
❑ 12 Randy Jackson 40.00 18.00
❑ 13 Joe Tipton 40.00 18.00
❑ 14 Bill Nicholson 70.00 32.00
❑ 15 Johnny Mize 125.00 55.00
❑ 16 Stu Miller 70.00 32.00
❑ 17 Virgil Trucks 70.00 32.00
❑ 18 Billy Hoeft 40.00 18.00
❑ 19 Paul LaPalme 40.00 18.00
❑ 20 Eddie Robinson 40.00 18.00
❑ 21 Clarence Podbielan 40.00 18.00
❑ 22 Matt Batts 40.00 18.00
❑ 23 Wilmer Mizell 70.00 32.00
❑ 24 Del Wilber 40.00 18.00
❑ 25 Johnny Sain 60.00 27.00
❑ 26 Preacher Roe 60.00 27.00
❑ 27 Bob Lemon 125.00 55.00
❑ 28 Hoyt Wilhelm 125.00 55.00
❑ 29 Sid Hudson 40.00 18.00
❑ 30 Walker Cooper 40.00 18.00
❑ 31 Gene Woodling 60.00 27.00
❑ 32 Rocky Bridges 40.00 18.00
❑ 33 Bob Kuzava 40.00 18.00
❑ 34 Ebba St.Claire 40.00 18.00
❑ 35 Johnny Wyrostek 40.00 18.00
❑ 36 Jimmy Piersall 60.00 27.00
❑ 37 Hal Jeffcoat 40.00 18.00
❑ 38 Dave Cole 40.00 18.00
❑ 39 Casey Stengel MG 325.00 145.00
❑ 40 Larry Jansen 70.00 32.00
❑ 41 Bob Ramazzotti 40.00 18.00
❑ 42 Howie Judson 40.00 18.00
❑ 43 Hal Bevan 40.00 18.00
❑ 44 Jim Delsing 40.00 18.00
❑ 45 Irv Noren 70.00 32.00
❑ 46 Bucky Harris MG 60.00 27.00
❑ 47 Jack Lohrke 40.00 18.00
❑ 48 Steve Ridzik 40.00 18.00
❑ 49 Floyd Baker 40.00 18.00
❑ 50 Dutch Leonard 40.00 18.00
❑ 51 Lou Burdette 60.00 27.00
❑ 52 Ralph Branca 60.00 27.00
❑ 53 Morrie Martin 40.00 18.00
❑ 54 Bill Miller 40.00 18.00
❑ 55 Don Johnson 40.00 18.00
❑ 56 Roy Smalley 40.00 18.00
❑ 57 Andy Pafko 70.00 32.00
❑ 58 Jim Konstanty 70.00 32.00
❑ 59 Duane Pillette 40.00 18.00
❑ 60 Billy Cox 60.00 27.00
❑ 61 Tom Gorman 40.00 18.00
❑ 62 Keith Thomas 40.00 18.00
❑ 63 Steve Gromek 40.00 18.00
❑ 64 Andy Hansen 60.00 19.00

1953 Bowman Color

	NRMT	VG-E
COMPLETE SET (160)	12000.00	5400.00
COMMON CARD (1-112)	40.00	18.00
COMMON CARD (113-128)	80.00	36.00
COMMON CARD (129-160)	60.00	27.00
WRAPPER (1-cent)	400.00	180.00
WRAPPER (5-CENT)	300.00	135.00

❑ 1 Dave Williams 100.00 20.00
❑ 2 Vic Wertz 50.00 22.00
❑ 3 Sam Jethroe 50.00 22.00
❑ 4 Art Houtteman 40.00 18.00
❑ 5 Sid Gordon 40.00 18.00
❑ 6 Joe Ginsberg 40.00 18.00
❑ 7 Harry Chiti 40.00 18.00
❑ 8 Al Rosen 50.00 22.00
❑ 9 Phil Rizzuto 175.00 80.00
❑ 10 Richie Ashburn 150.00 70.00
❑ 11 Bobby Shantz 45.00 20.00
❑ 12 Carl Erskine 50.00 22.00
❑ 13 Gus Zernial 50.00 22.00
❑ 14 Billy Loes 50.00 22.00
❑ 15 Jim Busby 40.00 18.00
❑ 16 Bob Friend 45.00 20.00
❑ 17 Gerry Staley 40.00 18.00
❑ 18 Nellie Fox 150.00 70.00
❑ 19 Alvin Dark 45.00 20.00
❑ 20 Don Lenhardt 40.00 18.00
❑ 21 Joe Garagiola 60.00 27.00
❑ 22 Bob Porterfield 40.00 18.00
❑ 23 Herman Wehmeier 40.00 18.00
❑ 24 Jackie Jensen 50.00 22.00
❑ 25 Hoot Evers 40.00 18.00
❑ 26 Roy McMillan 50.00 22.00
❑ 27 Vic Raschi 50.00 22.00
❑ 28 Smoky Burgess 45.00 20.00
❑ 29 Bobby Avila 45.00 20.00
❑ 30 Phil Cavarretta 45.00 20.00
❑ 31 Jimmy Dykes MG 45.00 20.00
❑ 32 Stan Musial 700.00 325.00
❑ 33 Pee Wee Reese 1000.00 450.00
❑ 34 Gil Coan 40.00 18.00
❑ 35 Maurice McDermott 40.00 18.00
❑ 36 Minnie Minoso 60.00 27.00
❑ 37 Jim Wilson 40.00 18.00
❑ 38 Harry Byrd 40.00 18.00
❑ 39 Paul Richards MG 45.00 20.00
❑ 40 Larry Doby 60.00 27.00
❑ 41 Sammy White 40.00 18.00
❑ 42 Tommy Brown 40.00 18.00
❑ 43 Mike Garcia 50.00 22.00
❑ 44 Yogi Berra 675.00 300.00
Hank Bauer
Mickey Mantle
❑ 45 Walt Dropo 50.00 22.00
❑ 46 Roy Campanella 275.00 125.00
❑ 47 Ned Garver 40.00 18.00
❑ 48 Hank Sauer 45.00 20.00
❑ 49 Eddie Stanky MG 45.00 20.00
❑ 50 Lou Kretlow 40.00 18.00
❑ 51 Monte Irvin 60.00 27.00
❑ 52 Marty Marion MG 50.00 22.00
❑ 53 Del Rice 40.00 18.00
❑ 54 Chico Carrasquel 40.00 18.00
❑ 55 Leo Durocher MG 70.00 32.00
❑ 56 Bob Cain 40.00 18.00
❑ 57 Lou Boudreau MG 60.00 27.00
❑ 58 Willard Marshall 40.00 18.00
❑ 59 Mickey Mantle 3000.00 1350.00
❑ 60 Granny Hamner 40.00 18.00
❑ 61 George Kell 70.00 32.00
❑ 62 Ted Kluszewski 60.00 27.00
❑ 63 Gil McDougald 60.00 27.00
❑ 64 Curt Simmons 45.00 20.00
❑ 65 Robin Roberts 110.00 50.00
❑ 66 Mel Parnell 50.00 22.00
❑ 67 Mel Clark 40.00 18.00
❑ 68 Allie Reynolds 50.00 22.00
❑ 69 Charlie Grimm MG 45.00 20.00
❑ 70 Clint Courtney 40.00 18.00
❑ 71 Paul Minner 40.00 18.00
❑ 72 Ted Gray 40.00 18.00
❑ 73 Billy Pierce 45.00 20.00
❑ 74 Don Mueller 50.00 22.00
❑ 75 Saul Rogovin 40.00 18.00
❑ 76 Jim Hearn 40.00 18.00
❑ 77 Mickey Grasso 40.00 18.00
❑ 78 Carl Furillo 50.00 22.00
❑ 79 Ray Boone 45.00 20.00
❑ 80 Ralph Kiner 70.00 32.00
❑ 81 Enos Slaughter 60.00 27.00
❑ 82 Joe Astroth 40.00 18.00
❑ 83 Jack Daniels 40.00 18.00
❑ 84 Hank Bauer 50.00 22.00
❑ 85 Solly Hemus 40.00 18.00
❑ 86 Harry Simpson 40.00 18.00
❑ 87 Harry Perkowski 40.00 18.00
❑ 88 Joe Dobson 40.00 18.00
❑ 89 Sandy Consuegra 40.00 18.00
❑ 90 Joe Nuxhall 45.00 20.00
❑ 91 Steve Souchock 40.00 18.00
❑ 92 Gil Hodges 175.00 80.00
❑ 93 Phil Rizzuto and 275.00 125.00
Billy Martin
❑ 94 Bob Addis 40.00 18.00
❑ 95 Wally Moses CO 50.00 22.00
❑ 96 Sal Maglie 50.00 22.00
❑ 97 Eddie Mathews 300.00 135.00
❑ 98 Hector Rodriguez 40.00 18.00
❑ 99 Warren Spahn 250.00 110.00
❑ 100 Bill Wight 40.00 18.00
❑ 101 Red Schoendienst 60.00 27.00
❑ 102 Jim Hegan 50.00 22.00
❑ 103 Del Ennis 45.00 20.00
❑ 104 Luke Easter 50.00 22.00
❑ 105 Eddie Joost 40.00 18.00
❑ 106 Ken Raffensberger 40.00 18.00
❑ 107 Alex Kellner 40.00 18.00
❑ 108 Bobby Adams 40.00 18.00
❑ 109 Ken Wood 40.00 18.00
❑ 110 Bob Rush 40.00 18.00
❑ 111 Jim Dyck 40.00 18.00
❑ 112 Toby Atwell 40.00 18.00
❑ 113 Karl Drews 80.00 36.00
❑ 114 Bob Feller 300.00 135.00
❑ 115 Cloyd Boyer 80.00 36.00
❑ 116 Eddie Yost 100.00 45.00
❑ 117 Duke Snider 550.00 250.00
❑ 118 Billy Martin 325.00 145.00
❑ 119 Dale Mitchell 75.00 34.00
❑ 120 Marlin Stuart 80.00 36.00
❑ 121 Yogi Berra 600.00 275.00
❑ 122 Bill Serena 80.00 36.00
❑ 123 Johnny Lipon 80.00 36.00
❑ 124 Charlie Dressen MG 90.00 40.00
❑ 125 Fred Hatfield 80.00 36.00
❑ 126 Al Corwin 80.00 36.00
❑ 127 Dick Kryhoski 80.00 36.00
❑ 128 Whitey Lockman 100.00 45.00
❑ 129 Russ Meyer 60.00 27.00
❑ 130 Cass Michaels 60.00 27.00
❑ 131 Connie Ryan 60.00 27.00
❑ 132 Fred Hutchinson 80.00 36.00
❑ 133 Willie Jones 60.00 27.00
❑ 134 Johnny Pesky 75.00 34.00
❑ 135 Bobby Morgan 60.00 27.00
❑ 136 Jim Brideweser 60.00 27.00
❑ 137 Sam Dente 60.00 27.00
❑ 138 Bubba Church 60.00 27.00
❑ 139 Pete Runnels 75.00 34.00
❑ 140 Al Brazle 60.00 27.00
❑ 141 Frank Shea 60.00 27.00
❑ 142 Larry Miggins 60.00 27.00
❑ 143 Al Lopez MG 75.00 34.00
❑ 144 Warren Hacker 60.00 27.00
❑ 145 George Shuba 80.00 36.00
❑ 146 Early Wynn 125.00 55.00
❑ 147 Clem Koshorek 60.00 27.00
❑ 148 Billy Goodman 80.00 36.00
❑ 149 Al Corwin 60.00 27.00
❑ 150 Carl Scheib 60.00 27.00

No.	Player	NRMT	VG-E
❑ 151	Joe Adcock	75.00	34.00
❑ 152	Clyde Vollmer	60.00	27.00
❑ 153	Whitey Ford	500.00	220.00
❑ 154	Turk Lown	60.00	27.00
❑ 155	Allie Clark	60.00	27.00
❑ 156	Max Surkont	60.00	27.00
❑ 157	Sherm Lollar	80.00	36.00
❑ 158	Howard Fox	60.00	27.00
❑ 159	Mickey Vernon UER (Photo actually Floyd Baker)	75.00	34.00
❑ 160	Cal Abrams	100.00	34.00

1954 Bowman

	NRMT	VG-E
COMPLETE SET (224)	4000.00	1800.00
COMMON CARD (1-224)	12.00	5.50
WRAPPER (1-CENT, DATED)	150.00	70.00
WRAPPER (1-CENT, UNDATED)	200.00	90.00
WRAPPER (5-CENT, DATED)	150.00	70.00
WRAPPER (5-CENT, UNDATED)	60.00	27.00

No.	Player	NRMT	VG-E
❑ 1	Phil Rizzuto	150.00	45.00
❑ 2	Jackie Jensen	20.00	9.00
❑ 3	Marion Fricano	12.00	5.50
❑ 4	Bob Hooper	12.00	5.50
❑ 5	Billy Hunter	12.00	5.50
❑ 6	Nellie Fox	75.00	34.00
❑ 7	Walt Dropo	20.00	9.00
❑ 8	Jim Busby	12.00	5.50
❑ 9	Dave Williams	12.00	5.50
❑ 10	Carl Erskine	20.00	9.00
❑ 11	Sid Gordon	12.00	5.50
❑ 12	Roy McMillan	20.00	9.00
❑ 13	Paul Minner	12.00	5.50
❑ 14	Jerry Staley	12.00	5.50
❑ 15	Richie Ashburn	75.00	34.00
❑ 16	Jim Wilson	12.00	5.50
❑ 17	Tom Gorman	12.00	5.50
❑ 18	Hoot Evers	12.00	5.50
❑ 19	Bobby Shantz	20.00	9.00
❑ 20	Art Houtteman	12.00	5.50
❑ 21	Vic Wertz	20.00	9.00
❑ 22	Sam Mele	12.00	5.50
❑ 23	Harvey Kuenn	35.00	16.00
❑ 24	Bob Porterfield	12.00	5.50
❑ 25	Wes Westrum	20.00	9.00
❑ 26	Billy Cox	20.00	9.00
❑ 27	Dick Cole	12.00	5.50
❑ 28	Jim Greengrass	12.00	5.50
❑ 29	Johnny Klippstein	12.00	5.50
❑ 30	Del Rice	12.00	5.50
❑ 31	Smoky Burgess	20.00	9.00
❑ 32	Del Crandall	20.00	9.00
❑ 33A	Vic Raschi (No mention of trade on back)	20.00	9.00
❑ 33B	Vic Raschi (Traded to St.Louis)	35.00	16.00
❑ 34	Sammy White	12.00	5.50
❑ 35	Eddie Joost	12.00	5.50
❑ 36	George Strickland	12.00	5.50
❑ 37	Dick Kokos	12.00	5.50
❑ 38	Minnie Minoso	25.00	11.00
❑ 39	Ned Garver	12.00	5.50
❑ 40	Gil Coan	12.00	5.50
❑ 41	Alvin Dark	20.00	9.00
❑ 42	Billy Loes	20.00	9.00
❑ 43	Bob Friend	20.00	9.00
❑ 44	Harry Perkowski	12.00	5.50
❑ 45	Ralph Kiner	40.00	18.00
❑ 46	Rip Repulski	12.00	5.50
❑ 47	Granny Hamner	12.00	5.50
❑ 48	Jack Dittmer	12.00	5.50
❑ 49	Harry Byrd	12.00	5.50
❑ 50	George Kell	40.00	18.00
❑ 51	Alex Kellner	12.00	5.50
❑ 52	Joe Ginsberg	12.00	5.50
❑ 53	Don Lenhardt	12.00	5.50
❑ 54	Chico Carrasquel	12.00	5.50
❑ 55	Jim Delsing	12.00	5.50
❑ 56	Maurice McDermott	12.00	5.50
❑ 57	Hoyt Wilhelm	35.00	16.00
❑ 58	Pee Wee Reese	75.00	34.00
❑ 59	Bob Schultz	12.00	5.50
❑ 60	Fred Baczewski	12.00	5.50
❑ 61	Eddie Miksis	12.00	5.50
❑ 62	Enos Slaughter	40.00	18.00
❑ 63	Earl Torgeson	12.00	5.50
❑ 64	Eddie Mathews	75.00	34.00
❑ 65	Mickey Mantle	1400.00	650.00
❑ 66A	Ted Williams	4500.00	2000.00
❑ 66B	Jimmy Piersall	75.00	34.00
❑ 67	Carl Scheib	12.00	5.50
❑ 68	Bobby Avila	20.00	9.00
❑ 69	Clint Courtney	12.00	5.50
❑ 70	Willard Marshall	12.00	5.50
❑ 71	Ted Gray	12.00	5.50
❑ 72	Eddie Yost	20.00	9.00
❑ 73	Don Mueller	20.00	9.00
❑ 74	Jim Gilliam	30.00	13.50
❑ 75	Max Surkont	12.00	5.50
❑ 76	Joe Nuxhall	20.00	9.00
❑ 77	Bob Rush	12.00	5.50
❑ 78	Sal Yvars	12.00	5.50
❑ 79	Curt Simmons	20.00	9.00
❑ 80	Johnny Logan	12.00	5.50
❑ 81	Jerry Coleman	20.00	9.00
❑ 82	Billy Goodman	20.00	9.00
❑ 83	Ray Murray	12.00	5.50
❑ 84	Larry Doby	25.00	11.00
❑ 85	Jim Dyck	12.00	5.50
❑ 86	Harry Dorish	12.00	5.50
❑ 87	Don Lund	12.00	5.50
❑ 88	Tom Umphlett	12.00	5.50
❑ 89	Willie Mays	400.00	180.00
❑ 90	Roy Campanella	175.00	80.00
❑ 91	Cal Abrams	12.00	5.50
❑ 92	Ken Raffensberger	12.00	5.50
❑ 93	Bill Serena	12.00	5.50
❑ 94	Solly Hemus	12.00	5.50
❑ 95	Robin Roberts	50.00	22.00
❑ 96	Joe Adcock	20.00	9.00
❑ 97	Gil McDougald	20.00	9.00
❑ 98	Ellis Kinder	12.00	5.50
❑ 99	Pete Suder	12.00	5.50
❑ 100	Mike Garcia	20.00	9.00
❑ 101	Don Larsen	60.00	27.00
❑ 102	Billy Pierce	20.00	9.00
❑ 103	Steve Souchock	12.00	5.50
❑ 104	Frank Shea	12.00	5.50
❑ 105	Sal Maglie	20.00	9.00
❑ 106	Clem Labine	20.00	9.00
❑ 107	Paul LaPalme	12.00	5.50
❑ 108	Bobby Adams	12.00	5.50
❑ 109	Roy Smalley	12.00	5.50
❑ 110	Red Schoendienst	35.00	16.00
❑ 111	Murry Dickson	12.00	5.50
❑ 112	Andy Pafko	20.00	9.00
❑ 113	Allie Reynolds	20.00	9.00
❑ 114	Willard Nixon	12.00	5.50
❑ 115	Don Bollweg	12.00	5.50
❑ 116	Luke Easter	20.00	9.00
❑ 117	Dick Kryhoski	12.00	5.50
❑ 118	Bob Boyd	12.00	5.50
❑ 119	Fred Hatfield	12.00	5.50
❑ 120	Mel Hoderlein	12.00	5.50
❑ 121	Ray Katt	12.00	5.50
❑ 122	Carl Furillo	25.00	11.00
❑ 123	Toby Atwell	12.00	5.50
❑ 124	Gus Bell	20.00	9.00
❑ 125	Warren Hacker	12.00	5.50
❑ 126	Cliff Chambers	12.00	5.50
❑ 127	Del Ennis	20.00	9.00
❑ 128	Ebba St.Claire	12.00	5.50
❑ 129	Hank Bauer	20.00	9.00
❑ 130	Milt Bolling	12.00	5.50
❑ 131	Joe Astroth	12.00	5.50
❑ 132	Bob Feller	75.00	34.00
❑ 133	Duane Pillette	12.00	5.50
❑ 134	Luis Aloma	12.00	5.50
❑ 135	Johnny Pesky	20.00	9.00
❑ 136	Clyde Vollmer	12.00	5.50
❑ 137	Al Corwin	12.00	5.50
❑ 138	Gil Hodges	75.00	34.00
❑ 139	Preston Ward	12.00	5.50
❑ 140	Saul Rogovin	12.00	5.50
❑ 141	Joe Garagiola	30.00	13.50
❑ 142	Al Brazle	12.00	5.50
❑ 143	Willie Jones	12.00	5.50
❑ 144	Ernie Johnson	25.00	11.00
❑ 145	Billy Martin	75.00	34.00
❑ 146	Dick Gernert	12.00	5.50
❑ 147	Joe DeMaestri	12.00	5.50
❑ 148	Dale Mitchell	20.00	9.00
❑ 149	Bob Young	12.00	5.50
❑ 150	Cass Michaels	12.00	5.50
❑ 151	Pat Mullin	12.00	5.50
❑ 152	Mickey Vernon	20.00	9.00
❑ 153	Whitey Lockman	20.00	9.00
❑ 154	Don Newcombe	30.00	13.50
❑ 155	Frank Thomas	20.00	9.00
❑ 156	Rocky Bridges	12.00	5.50
❑ 157	Turk Lown	12.00	5.50
❑ 158	Stu Miller	20.00	9.00
❑ 159	Johnny Lindell	12.00	5.50
❑ 160	Danny O'Connell	12.00	5.50
❑ 161	Yogi Berra	175.00	80.00
❑ 162	Ted Lepcio	12.00	5.50
❑ 163A	Dave Philley (No mention of trade on back)	20.00	9.00
❑ 163B	Dave Philley (Traded to Cleveland)	36.00	16.00
❑ 164	Early Wynn	50.00	22.00
❑ 165	Johnny Groth	12.00	5.50
❑ 166	Sandy Consuegra	12.00	5.50
❑ 167	Billy Hoeft	12.00	5.50
❑ 168	Ed Fitzgerald	12.00	5.50
❑ 169	Larry Jansen	20.00	9.00
❑ 170	Duke Snider	135.00	60.00
❑ 171	Carlos Bernier	12.00	5.50
❑ 172	Andy Seminick	12.00	5.50
❑ 173	Dee Fondy	12.00	5.50
❑ 174	Pete Castiglione	12.00	5.50
❑ 175	Mel Clark	12.00	5.50
❑ 176	Vern Bickford	12.00	5.50
❑ 177	Whitey Ford	100.00	45.00
❑ 178	Del Wilber	12.00	5.50
❑ 179	Morrie Martin	12.00	5.50
❑ 180	Joe Tipton	12.00	5.50
❑ 181	Les Moss	12.00	5.50
❑ 182	Sherm Lollar	20.00	9.00
❑ 183	Matt Batts	12.00	5.50
❑ 184	Mickey Grasso	12.00	5.50
❑ 185	Daryl Spencer	12.00	5.50
❑ 186	Russ Meyer	12.00	5.50
❑ 187	Vern Law	20.00	9.00
❑ 188	Frank Smith	12.00	5.50
❑ 189	Randy Jackson	12.00	5.50
❑ 190	Joe Presko	12.00	5.50
❑ 191	Karl Drews	12.00	5.50
❑ 192	Lou Burdette	20.00	9.00
❑ 193	Eddie Robinson	12.00	5.50
❑ 194	Sid Hudson	12.00	5.50
❑ 195	Bob Cain	12.00	5.50
❑ 196	Bob Lemon	40.00	18.00
❑ 197	Lou Kretlow	12.00	5.50
❑ 198	Virgil Trucks	12.00	5.50
❑ 199	Steve Gromek	12.00	5.50
❑ 200	Conrado Marrero	12.00	5.50
❑ 201	Bobby Thomson	25.00	11.00
❑ 202	George Shuba	20.00	9.00
❑ 203	Vic Janowicz	20.00	9.00
❑ 204	Jack Collum	12.00	5.50
❑ 205	Hal Jeffcoat	12.00	5.50

		NRMT	VG-E
❑ 206	Steve Bilko	12.00	5.50
❑ 207	Stan Lopata	12.00	5.50
❑ 208	Johnny Antonelli	20.00	9.00
❑ 209	Gene Woodling	12.00	5.50
❑ 210	Jimmy Piersall	20.00	9.00
❑ 211	Al Robertson	12.00	5.50
❑ 212	Owen Friend	12.00	5.50
❑ 213	Dick Littlefield	12.00	5.50
❑ 214	Ferris Fain	20.00	9.00
❑ 215	Johnny Bucha	12.00	5.50
❑ 216	Jerry Snyder	12.00	5.50
❑ 217	Hank Thompson	20.00	9.00
❑ 218	Preacher Roe	25.00	11.00
❑ 219	Hal Rice	12.00	5.50
❑ 220	Hobie Landrith	12.00	5.50
❑ 221	Frank Baumholtz	12.00	5.50
❑ 222	Memo Luna	12.00	5.50
❑ 223	Steve Ridzik	12.00	5.50
❑ 224	Bill Bruton	40.00	10.00

1955 Bowman

	NRMT	VG-E
COMPLETE SET (320)	4600.00	2100.00
COMMON CARD (1-96)	12.00	5.50
COMMON CARD (97-224)	10.00	4.50
COMMON CARD (225-320)	15.00	6.75
COMMON UMPIRE 225-320	30.00	13.50
WRAPPER (1-CENT)	60.00	27.00
WRAPPER (5-CENT)	60.00	27.00

		NRMT	VG-E
❑ 1	Hoyt Wilhelm	100.00	22.00
❑ 2	Alvin Dark	15.00	6.75
❑ 3	Joe Coleman	15.00	6.75
❑ 4	Eddie Waitkus	15.00	6.75
❑ 5	Jim Robertson	12.00	5.50
❑ 6	Pete Suder	12.00	5.50
❑ 7	Gene Baker	12.00	5.50
❑ 8	Warren Hacker	12.00	5.50
❑ 9	Gil McDougald	20.00	9.00
❑ 10	Phil Rizzuto	65.00	29.00
❑ 11	Bill Bruton	15.00	6.75
❑ 12	Andy Pafko	15.00	6.75
❑ 13	Clyde Vollmer	12.00	5.50
❑ 14	Gus Keriazakos	12.00	5.50
❑ 15	Frank Sullivan	12.00	5.50
❑ 16	Jimmy Piersall	15.00	6.75
❑ 17	Del Ennis	15.00	6.75
❑ 18	Stan Lopata	12.00	5.50
❑ 19	Bobby Avila	15.00	6.75
❑ 20	Al Smith	15.00	6.75
❑ 21	Don Hoak	12.00	5.50
❑ 22	Roy Campanella	125.00	55.00
❑ 23	Al Kaline	150.00	70.00
❑ 24	Al Aber	12.00	5.50
❑ 25	Minnie Minoso	25.00	11.00
❑ 26	Virgil Trucks	15.00	6.75
❑ 27	Preston Ward	12.00	5.50
❑ 28	Dick Cole	12.00	5.50
❑ 29	Red Schoendienst	30.00	13.50
❑ 30	Bill Sarni	12.00	5.50
❑ 31	Johnny Temple	15.00	6.75
❑ 32	Wally Post	15.00	6.75
❑ 33	Nellie Fox	45.00	20.00
❑ 34	Clint Courtney	12.00	5.50
❑ 35	Bill Tuttle	12.00	5.50
❑ 36	Wayne Belardi	12.00	5.50
❑ 37	Pee Wee Reese	65.00	29.00
❑ 38	Early Wynn	30.00	13.50
❑ 39	Bob Darnell	15.00	6.75
❑ 40	Vic Wertz	15.00	6.75
❑ 41	Mel Clark	12.00	5.50
❑ 42	Bob Greenwood	12.00	5.50
❑ 43	Bob Buhl	15.00	6.75
❑ 44	Danny O'Connell	12.00	5.50
❑ 45	Tom Umphlett	12.00	5.50
❑ 46	Mickey Vernon	15.00	6.75
❑ 47	Sammy White	12.00	5.50
❑ 48A	Milt Bolling ERR (Name on back is Frank Bolling)	30.00	13.50
❑ 48B	Milt Bolling COR	15.00	6.75
❑ 49	Jim Greengrass	12.00	5.50
❑ 50	Hobie Landrith	12.00	5.50
❑ 51	Elvin Tappe	12.00	5.50
❑ 52	Hal Rice	12.00	5.50
❑ 53	Alex Kellner	12.00	5.50
❑ 54	Don Bollweg	12.00	5.50
❑ 55	Cal Abrams	12.00	5.50
❑ 56	Billy Cox	15.00	6.75
❑ 57	Bob Friend	15.00	6.75
❑ 58	Frank Thomas	15.00	6.75
❑ 59	Whitey Ford	75.00	34.00
❑ 60	Enos Slaughter	30.00	13.50
❑ 61	Paul LaPalme	12.00	5.50
❑ 62	Royce Lint	12.00	5.50
❑ 63	Irv Noren	15.00	6.75
❑ 64	Curt Simmons	15.00	6.75
❑ 65	Don Zimmer	25.00	11.00
❑ 66	George Shuba	20.00	9.00
❑ 67	Don Larsen	20.00	9.00
❑ 68	Elston Howard	75.00	34.00
❑ 69	Billy Hunter	12.00	5.50
❑ 70	Lou Burdette	15.00	6.75
❑ 71	Dave Jolly	12.00	5.50
❑ 72	Chet Nichols	12.00	5.50
❑ 73	Eddie Yost	15.00	6.75
❑ 74	Jerry Snyder	12.00	5.50
❑ 75	Brooks Lawrence	12.00	5.50
❑ 76	Tom Poholsky	12.00	5.50
❑ 77	Jim McDonald	12.00	5.50
❑ 78	Gil Coan	12.00	5.50
❑ 79	Willie Miranda	12.00	5.50
❑ 80	Lou Limmer	12.00	5.50
❑ 81	Bobby Morgan	12.00	5.50
❑ 82	Lee Walls	12.00	5.50
❑ 83	Max Surkont	12.00	5.50
❑ 84	George Freese	12.00	5.50
❑ 85	Cass Michaels	12.00	5.50
❑ 86	Ted Gray	12.00	5.50
❑ 87	Randy Jackson	12.00	5.50
❑ 88	Steve Bilko	12.00	5.50
❑ 89	Lou Boudreau MG	30.00	13.50
❑ 90	Art Ditmar	12.00	5.50
❑ 91	Dick Marlowe	12.00	5.50
❑ 92	George Zuverink	12.00	5.50
❑ 93	Andy Seminick	12.00	5.50
❑ 94	Hank Thompson	15.00	6.75
❑ 95	Sal Maglie	15.00	6.75
❑ 96	Ray Narleski	12.00	5.50
❑ 97	Johnny Podres	25.00	11.00
❑ 98	Jim Gilliam	25.00	11.00
❑ 99	Jerry Coleman	18.00	8.00
❑ 100	Tom Morgan	10.00	4.50
❑ 101A	Don Johnson ERR (Photo actually Ernie Johnson)	15.00	6.75
❑ 101B	Don Johnson COR	30.00	13.50
❑ 102	Bobby Thomson	15.00	6.75
❑ 103	Eddie Mathews	50.00	22.00
❑ 104	Bob Porterfield	10.00	4.50
❑ 105	Johnny Schmitz	10.00	4.50
❑ 106	Del Rice	10.00	4.50
❑ 107	Solly Hemus	10.00	4.50
❑ 108	Lou Kretlow	10.00	4.50
❑ 109	Vern Stephens	15.00	6.75
❑ 110	Bob Miller	10.00	4.50
❑ 111	Steve Ridzik	10.00	4.50
❑ 112	Granny Hamner	10.00	4.50
❑ 113	Bob Hall	10.00	4.50
❑ 114	Vic Janowicz	15.00	6.75
❑ 115	Roger Bowman	10.00	4.50
❑ 116	Sandy Consuegra	10.00	4.50
❑ 117	Johnny Groth	10.00	4.50
❑ 118	Bobby Adams	10.00	4.50
❑ 119	Joe Astroth	10.00	4.50
❑ 120	Ed Burtschy	10.00	4.50
❑ 121	Rufus Crawford	10.00	4.50
❑ 122	Al Corwin	10.00	4.50
❑ 123	Marv Grissom	10.00	4.50
❑ 124	Johnny Antonelli	15.00	6.75
❑ 125	Paul Giel	15.00	6.75
❑ 126	Billy Goodman	15.00	6.75
❑ 127	Hank Majeski	10.00	4.50
❑ 128	Mike Garcia	15.00	6.75
❑ 129	Hal Naragon	10.00	4.50
❑ 130	Richie Ashburn	45.00	20.00
❑ 131	Willard Marshall	10.00	4.50
❑ 132A	Harvey Kueen ERR (Sic, Kuenn)	20.00	9.00
❑ 132B	Harvey Kuenn COR	30.00	13.50
❑ 133	Charles King	10.00	4.50
❑ 134	Bob Feller	70.00	32.00
❑ 135	Lloyd Merriman	10.00	4.50
❑ 136	Rocky Bridges	10.00	4.50
❑ 137	Bob Talbot	10.00	4.50
❑ 138	Davey Williams	20.00	9.00
❑ 139	Shantz Brothers (Wilmer Shantz, Bobby Shantz)	15.00	6.75
❑ 140	Bobby Shantz	20.00	9.00
❑ 141	Wes Westrum	20.00	9.00
❑ 142	Rudy Regalado	10.00	4.50
❑ 143	Don Newcombe	25.00	11.00
❑ 144	Art Houtteman	10.00	4.50
❑ 145	Bob Nieman	10.00	4.50
❑ 146	Don Liddle	10.00	4.50
❑ 147	Sam Mele	10.00	4.50
❑ 148	Bob Chakales	10.00	4.50
❑ 149	Cloyd Boyer	10.00	4.50
❑ 150	Billy Klaus	10.00	4.50
❑ 151	Jim Brideweser	10.00	4.50
❑ 152	Johnny Klippstein	10.00	4.50
❑ 153	Eddie Robinson	10.00	4.50
❑ 154	Frank Lary	15.00	6.75
❑ 155	Gerry Staley	10.00	4.50
❑ 156	Jim Hughes	15.00	6.75
❑ 157A	Ernie Johnson ERR (Photo actually Don Johnson)	20.00	9.00
❑ 157B	Ernie Johnson COR	30.00	13.50
❑ 158	Gil Hodges	45.00	20.00
❑ 159	Harry Byrd	10.00	4.50
❑ 160	Bill Skowron	25.00	11.00
❑ 161	Matt Batts	10.00	4.50
❑ 162	Charlie Maxwell	10.00	4.50
❑ 163	Sid Gordon	15.00	6.75
❑ 164	Toby Atwell	10.00	4.50
❑ 165	Maurice McDermott	10.00	4.50
❑ 166	Jim Busby	10.00	4.50
❑ 167	Bob Grim	25.00	11.00
❑ 168	Yogi Berra	90.00	40.00
❑ 169	Carl Furillo	25.00	11.00
❑ 170	Carl Erskine	25.00	11.00
❑ 171	Robin Roberts	35.00	16.00
❑ 172	Willie Jones	10.00	4.50
❑ 173	Chico Carrasquel	10.00	4.50
❑ 174	Sherm Lollar	15.00	6.75
❑ 175	Wilmer Shantz	10.00	4.50
❑ 176	Joe DeMaestri	10.00	4.50
❑ 177	Willard Nixon	10.00	4.50
❑ 178	Tom Brewer	10.00	4.50
❑ 179	Hank Aaron	200.00	90.00
❑ 180	Johnny Logan	15.00	6.75
❑ 181	Eddie Miksis	10.00	4.50
❑ 182	Bob Rush	10.00	4.50
❑ 183	Ray Katt	10.00	4.50
❑ 184	Willie Mays	225.00	100.00
❑ 185	Vic Raschi	10.00	4.50
❑ 186	Alex Grammas	10.00	4.50
❑ 187	Fred Hatfield	10.00	4.50
❑ 188	Ned Garver	10.00	4.50
❑ 189	Jack Collum	10.00	4.50
❑ 190	Fred Baczewski	10.00	4.50
❑ 191	Bob Lemon	30.00	13.50
❑ 192	George Strickland	10.00	4.50
❑ 193	Howie Judson	10.00	4.50
❑ 194	Joe Nuxhall	15.00	6.75

❑ 195A Erv Palica 15.00 6.75
(Without trade)
❑ 195B Erv Palica 30.00 13.50
(With trade)
❑ 196 Russ Meyer 15.00 6.75
❑ 197 Ralph Kiner 30.00 13.50
❑ 198 Dave Pope 10.00 4.50
❑ 199 Vern Law 15.00 6.75
❑ 200 Dick Littlefield 10.00 4.50
❑ 201 Allie Reynolds 18.00 8.00
❑ 202 Mickey Mantle UER 900.00 400.00
Birthdate listed as 10/30/31
Should be 10/20/31
❑ 203 Steve Gromek 10.00 4.50
❑ 204A Frank Bolling ERR 20.00 9.00
(Name on back is
Milt Bolling)
❑ 204B Frank Bolling COR 20.00 9.00
❑ 205 Rip Repulski 10.00 4.50
❑ 206 Ralph Beard 10.00 4.50
❑ 207 Frank Shea 10.00 4.50
❑ 208 Ed Fitzgerald 10.00 4.50
❑ 209 Smoky Burgess 15.00 6.75
❑ 210 Earl Torgeson 10.00 4.50
❑ 211 Sonny Dixon 10.00 4.50
❑ 212 Jack Dittmer 10.00 4.50
❑ 213 George Kell 30.00 13.50
❑ 214 Billy Pierce 15.00 6.75
❑ 215 Bob Kuzava 10.00 4.50
❑ 216 Preacher Roe 15.00 6.75
❑ 217 Del Crandall 15.00 6.75
❑ 218 Joe Adcock 15.00 6.75
❑ 219 Whitey Lockman 15.00 6.75
❑ 220 Jim Hearn 10.00 4.50
❑ 221 Hector Brown 10.00 4.50
❑ 222 Russ Kemmerer 10.00 4.50
❑ 223 Hal Jeffcoat 10.00 4.50
❑ 224 Dee Fondy 10.00 4.50
❑ 225 Paul Richards MG 15.00 6.75
❑ 226 Bill McKinley UMP 30.00 13.50
❑ 227 Frank Baumholtz 15.00 6.75
❑ 228 John Phillips 15.00 6.75
❑ 229 Jim Brosnan 20.00 9.00
❑ 230 Al Brazle 15.00 6.75
❑ 231 Jim Konstanty 20.00 9.00
❑ 232 Birdie Tebbetts MG 22.00 10.00
❑ 233 Bill Serena 15.00 6.75
❑ 234 Dick Bartell CO 20.00 9.00
❑ 235 Joe Paparella UMP 30.00 13.50
❑ 236 Murry Dickson 15.00 6.75
❑ 237 Johnny Wyrostek 15.00 6.75
❑ 238 Eddie Stanky MG 20.00 9.00
❑ 239 Edwin Rommel UMP 40.00 18.00
❑ 240 Billy Loes 20.00 9.00
❑ 241 Johnny Pesky CO 20.00 9.00
❑ 242 Ernie Banks 350.00 160.00
❑ 243 Gus Bell 20.00 9.00
❑ 244 Duane Pillette 15.00 6.75
❑ 245 Bill Miller 15.00 6.75
❑ 246 Hank Bauer 25.00 11.00
❑ 247 Dutch Leonard CO 15.00 6.75
❑ 248 Harry Dorish 15.00 6.75
❑ 249 Billy Gardner 20.00 9.00
❑ 250 Larry Napp UMP 30.00 13.50
❑ 251 Stan Jok 15.00 6.75
❑ 252 Roy Smalley 15.00 6.75
❑ 253 Jim Wilson 15.00 6.75
❑ 254 Bennett Flowers 15.00 6.75
❑ 255 Pete Runnels 20.00 9.00
❑ 256 Owen Friend 15.00 6.75
❑ 257 Tom Alston 15.00 6.75
❑ 258 John Stevens UMP 30.00 13.50
❑ 259 Don Mossi 25.00 11.00
❑ 260 Edwin Hurley UMP 30.00 13.50
❑ 261 Walt Moryn 20.00 9.00
❑ 262 Jim Lemon 15.00 6.75
❑ 263 Eddie Joost 15.00 6.75
❑ 264 Bill Henry 15.00 6.75
❑ 265 Albert Barlick UMP 75.00 34.00
❑ 266 Mike Fornieles 15.00 6.75
❑ 267 Jim Honochick UMP 75.00 34.00
❑ 268 Roy Lee Hawes 15.00 6.75
❑ 269 Joe Amalfitano 22.00 10.00
❑ 270 Chico Fernandez 20.00 9.00
❑ 271 Bob Hooper 15.00 6.75
❑ 272 John Flaherty UMP 30.00 13.50
❑ 273 Bubba Church 15.00 6.75
❑ 274 Jim Delsing 15.00 6.75
❑ 275 William Grieve UMP 30.00 13.50
❑ 276 Ike Delock 15.00 6.75
❑ 277 Ed Runge UMP 30.00 13.50
❑ 278 Charlie Neal 35.00 16.00
❑ 279 Hank Soar UMP 40.00 18.00
❑ 280 Clyde McCullough 15.00 6.75
❑ 281 Charles Berry UMP 40.00 18.00
❑ 282 Phil Cavarretta 22.00 10.00
❑ 283 Nestor Chylak UMP 30.00 13.50
❑ 284 Bill Jackowski UMP 30.00 13.50
❑ 285 Walt Dropo 20.00 9.00
❑ 286 Frank Secory UMP 30.00 13.50
❑ 287 Ron Mrozinski 15.00 6.75
❑ 288 Dick Smith 15.00 6.75
❑ 289 Arthur Gore UMP 30.00 13.50
❑ 290 Hershell Freeman 15.00 6.75
❑ 291 Frank Dascoli UMP 30.00 13.50
❑ 292 Marv Blaylock 15.00 6.75
❑ 293 Thomas Gorman UMP 40.00 18.00
❑ 294 Wally Moses CO 15.00 6.75
❑ 295 Lee Ballanfant UMP 30.00 13.50
❑ 296 Bill Virdon 35.00 16.00
❑ 297 Dusty Boggess UMP 30.00 13.50
❑ 298 Charlie Grimm MG 22.00 10.00
❑ 299 Lon Warneke UMP 40.00 18.00
❑ 300 Tommy Byrne 20.00 9.00
❑ 301 William Engeln UMP 30.00 13.50
❑ 302 Frank Malzone 30.00 13.50
❑ 303 Jocko Conlan UMP 75.00 34.00
❑ 304 Harry Chiti 15.00 6.75
❑ 305 Frank Umont UMP 30.00 13.50
❑ 306 Bob Cerv 22.00 10.00
❑ 307 Babe Pinelli UMP 40.00 18.00
❑ 308 Al Lopez MG 50.00 22.00
❑ 309 Hal Dixon UMP 30.00 13.50
❑ 310 Ken Lehman 15.00 6.75
❑ 311 Lawrence Goetz UMP 30.00 13.50
❑ 312 Bill Wight 15.00 6.75
❑ 313 Augie Donatelli UMP 50.00 22.00
❑ 314 Dale Mitchell 22.00 10.00
❑ 315 Cal Hubbard UMP 75.00 34.00
❑ 316 Marion Fricano 15.00 6.75
❑ 317 William Summers UMP 20.00 9.00
❑ 318 Sid Hudson 15.00 6.75
❑ 319 Al Schroll 15.00 6.75
❑ 320 George Susce Jr. 50.00 10.00

1989 Bowman

	MINT	NRMT
COMPLETE SET (484)	20.00	9.00
COMP.FACT.SET (484)	20.00	9.00
COMMON CARD (1-484)	.05	.02

❑ 1 Oswald Peraza .05 .02
❑ 2 Brian Holton .05 .02
❑ 3 Jose Bautista .05 .02
❑ 4 Pete Harnisch .10 .05
❑ 5 Dave Schmidt .05 .02
❑ 6 Gregg Olson .20 .09
❑ 7 Jeff Ballard .05 .02
❑ 8 Bob Melvin .05 .02
❑ 9 Cal Ripken .75 .35
❑ 10 Randy Milligan .05 .02
❑ 11 Juan Bell .05 .02
❑ 12 Billy Ripken .05 .02
❑ 13 Jim Traber .05 .02
❑ 14 Pete Stanicek .05 .02
❑ 15 Steve Finley .25 .11
❑ 16 Larry Sheets .05 .02
❑ 17 Phil Bradley .05 .02
❑ 18 Brady Anderson .40 .18
❑ 19 Lee Smith .10 .05
❑ 20 Tom Fischer .05 .02
❑ 21 Mike Boddicker .05 .02
❑ 22 Rob Murphy .05 .02
❑ 23 Wes Gardner .05 .02
❑ 24 John Dopson .05 .02
❑ 25 Bob Stanley .05 .02
❑ 26 Roger Clemens .40 .18
❑ 27 Rich Gedman .05 .02
❑ 28 Marty Barrett .05 .02
❑ 29 Luis Rivera .05 .02
❑ 30 Jody Reed .05 .02
❑ 31 Nick Esasky .05 .02
❑ 32 Wade Boggs .20 .09
❑ 33 Jim Rice .10 .05
❑ 34 Mike Greenwell .05 .02
❑ 35 Dwight Evans .10 .05
❑ 36 Ellis Burks .15 .07
❑ 37 Chuck Finley .10 .05
❑ 38 Kirk McCaskill .05 .02
❑ 39 Jim Abbott .20 .09
❑ 40 Bryan Harvey .05 .02
❑ 41 Bert Blyleven .10 .05
❑ 42 Mike Witt .05 .02
❑ 43 Bob McClure .05 .02
❑ 44 Bill Schroeder .05 .02
❑ 45 Lance Parrish .05 .02
❑ 46 Dick Schofield .05 .02
❑ 47 Wally Joyner .10 .05
❑ 48 Jack Howell .05 .02
❑ 49 Johnny Ray .05 .02
❑ 50 Chili Davis .10 .05
❑ 51 Tony Armas .05 .02
❑ 52 Claudell Washington .05 .02
❑ 53 Brian Downing .05 .02
❑ 54 Devon White .10 .05
❑ 55 Bobby Thigpen .05 .02
❑ 56 Bill Long .05 .02
❑ 57 Jerry Reuss .05 .02
❑ 58 Shawn Hillegas .05 .02
❑ 59 Melido Perez .05 .02
❑ 60 Jeff Bittiger .05 .02
❑ 61 Jack McDowell .10 .05
❑ 62 Carlton Fisk .20 .09
❑ 63 Steve Lyons .05 .02
❑ 64 Ozzie Guillen .05 .02
❑ 65 Robin Ventura .40 .18
❑ 66 Fred Manrique .05 .02
❑ 67 Dan Pasqua .05 .02
❑ 68 Ivan Calderon .05 .02
❑ 69 Ron Kittle .05 .02
❑ 70 Daryl Boston .05 .02
❑ 71 Dave Gallagher .05 .02
❑ 72 Harold Baines .10 .05
❑ 73 Charles Nagy .25 .11
❑ 74 John Farrell .05 .02
❑ 75 Kevin Wickander .05 .02
❑ 76 Greg Swindell .05 .02
❑ 77 Mike Walker .05 .02
❑ 78 Doug Jones .05 .02
❑ 79 Rich Yett .05 .02
❑ 80 Tom Candiotti .05 .02
❑ 81 Jesse Orosco .05 .02
❑ 82 Bud Black .05 .02
❑ 83 Andy Allanson .05 .02
❑ 84 Pete O'Brien .05 .02
❑ 85 Jerry Browne .05 .02
❑ 86 Brook Jacoby .05 .02
❑ 87 Mark Lewis .20 .09
❑ 88 Luis Aguayo .05 .02
❑ 89 Cory Snyder .05 .02
❑ 90 Oddibe McDowell .05 .02
❑ 91 Joe Carter .15 .07
❑ 92 Frank Tanana .05 .02
❑ 93 Jack Morris .10 .05
❑ 94 Doyle Alexander .05 .02
❑ 95 Steve Searcy .05 .02
❑ 96 Randy Bockus .05 .02

❑	97	Jeff M. Robinson	.05	.02
❑	98	Mike Henneman	.05	.02
❑	99	Paul Gibson	.05	.02
❑	100	Frank Williams	.05	.02
❑	101	Matt Nokes	.05	.02
❑	102	Rico Brogna UER (Misspelled Ricco on card back)	.25	.11
❑	103	Lou Whitaker	.10	.05
❑	104	Al Pedrique	.05	.02
❑	105	Alan Trammell	.15	.07
❑	106	Chris Brown	.05	.02
❑	107	Pat Sheridan	.05	.02
❑	108	Chet Lemon	.05	.02
❑	109	Keith Moreland	.05	.02
❑	110	Mel Stottlemyre Jr.	.05	.02
❑	111	Bret Saberhagen	.10	.05
❑	112	Floyd Bannister	.05	.02
❑	113	Jeff Montgomery	.10	.05
❑	114	Steve Farr	.05	.02
❑	115	Tom Gordon UER (Front shows autograph of Don Gordon)	.20	.09
❑	116	Charlie Leibrandt	.05	.02
❑	117	Mark Gubicza	.05	.02
❑	118	Mike Macfarlane	.05	.02
❑	119	Bob Boone	.10	.05
❑	120	Kurt Stillwell	.05	.02
❑	121	George Brett	.40	.18
❑	122	Frank White	.10	.05
❑	123	Kevin Seitzer	.05	.02
❑	124	Willie Wilson	.05	.02
❑	125	Pat Tabler	.05	.02
❑	126	Bo Jackson	.15	.07
❑	127	Hugh Walker	.05	.02
❑	128	Danny Tartabull	.05	.02
❑	129	Teddy Higuera	.05	.02
❑	130	Don August	.05	.02
❑	131	Juan Nieves	.05	.02
❑	132	Mike Birkbeck	.05	.02
❑	133	Dan Plesac	.05	.02
❑	134	Chris Bosio	.05	.02
❑	135	Bill Wegman	.05	.02
❑	136	Chuck Crim	.05	.02
❑	137	B.J. Surhoff	.10	.05
❑	138	Joey Meyer	.05	.02
❑	139	Dale Sveum	.05	.02
❑	140	Paul Molitor	.20	.09
❑	141	Jim Gantner	.05	.02
❑	142	Gary Sheffield	.60	.25
❑	143	Greg Brock	.05	.02
❑	144	Robin Yount	.20	.09
❑	145	Glenn Braggs	.05	.02
❑	146	Rob Deer	.05	.02
❑	147	Fred Toliver	.05	.02
❑	148	Jeff Reardon	.10	.05
❑	149	Allan Anderson	.05	.02
❑	150	Frank Viola	.05	.02
❑	151	Shane Rawley	.05	.02
❑	152	Juan Berenguer	.05	.02
❑	153	Johnny Ard	.05	.02
❑	154	Tim Laudner	.05	.02
❑	155	Brian Harper	.05	.02
❑	156	Al Newman	.05	.02
❑	157	Kent Hrbek	.10	.05
❑	158	Gary Gaetti	.10	.05
❑	159	Wally Backman	.05	.02
❑	160	Gene Larkin	.05	.02
❑	161	Greg Gagne	.05	.02
❑	162	Kirby Puckett	.40	.18
❑	163	Dan Gladden	.05	.02
❑	164	Randy Bush	.05	.02
❑	165	Dave LaPoint	.05	.02
❑	166	Andy Hawkins	.05	.02
❑	167	Dave Righetti	.05	.02
❑	168	Lance McCullers	.05	.02
❑	169	Jimmy Jones	.05	.02
❑	170	Al Leiter	.20	.09
❑	171	John Candelaria	.05	.02
❑	172	Don Slaught	.05	.02
❑	173	Jamie Quirk	.05	.02
❑	174	Rafael Santana	.05	.02
❑	175	Mike Pagliarulo	.05	.02
❑	176	Don Mattingly	.30	.14
❑	177	Ken Phelps	.05	.02
❑	178	Steve Sax	.05	.02
❑	179	Dave Winfield	.20	.09
❑	180	Stan Jefferson	.05	.02
❑	181	Rickey Henderson	.20	.09
❑	182	Bob Brower	.05	.02
❑	183	Roberto Kelly	.10	.05
❑	184	Curt Young	.05	.02
❑	185	Gene Nelson	.05	.02
❑	186	Bob Welch	.05	.02
❑	187	Rick Honeycutt	.05	.02
❑	188	Dave Stewart	.10	.05
❑	189	Mike Moore	.05	.02
❑	190	Dennis Eckersley	.15	.07
❑	191	Eric Plunk	.05	.02
❑	192	Storm Davis	.05	.02
❑	193	Terry Steinbach	.10	.05
❑	194	Ron Hassey	.05	.02
❑	195	Stan Royer	.05	.02
❑	196	Walt Weiss	.05	.02
❑	197	Mark McGwire	1.25	.55
❑	198	Carney Lansford	.10	.05
❑	199	Glenn Hubbard	.05	.02
❑	200	Dave Henderson	.05	.02
❑	201	Jose Canseco	.20	.09
❑	202	Dave Parker	.10	.05
❑	203	Scott Bankhead	.05	.02
❑	204	Tom Niedenfuer	.05	.02
❑	205	Mark Langston	.05	.02
❑	206	Erik Hanson	.10	.05
❑	207	Mike Jackson	.15	.07
❑	208	Dave Valle	.05	.02
❑	209	Scott Bradley	.05	.02
❑	210	Harold Reynolds	.05	.02
❑	211	Tino Martinez	1.00	.45
❑	212	Rich Renteria	.05	.02
❑	213	Rey Quinones	.05	.02
❑	214	Jim Presley	.05	.02
❑	215	Alvin Davis	.05	.02
❑	216	Edgar Martinez	.20	.09
❑	217	Darnell Coles	.05	.02
❑	218	Jeffrey Leonard	.05	.02
❑	219	Jay Buhner	.20	.09
❑	220	Ken Griffey Jr.	15.00	6.75
❑	221	Drew Hall	.05	.02
❑	222	Bobby Witt	.05	.02
❑	223	Jamie Moyer	.05	.02
❑	224	Charlie Hough	.10	.05
❑	225	Nolan Ryan	.75	.35
❑	226	Jeff Russell	.05	.02
❑	227	Jim Sundberg	.05	.02
❑	228	Julio Franco	.05	.02
❑	229	Buddy Bell	.10	.05
❑	230	Scott Fletcher	.05	.02
❑	231	Jeff Kunkel	.05	.02
❑	232	Steve Buechele	.05	.02
❑	233	Monty Fariss	.05	.02
❑	234	Rick Leach	.05	.02
❑	235	Ruben Sierra	.05	.02
❑	236	Cecil Espy	.05	.02
❑	237	Rafael Palmeiro	.20	.09
❑	238	Pete Incaviglia	.05	.02
❑	239	Dave Stieb	.05	.02
❑	240	Jeff Musselman	.05	.02
❑	241	Mike Flanagan	.05	.02
❑	242	Todd Stottlemyre	.15	.07
❑	243	Jimmy Key	.10	.05
❑	244	Tony Castillo	.05	.02
❑	245	Alex Sanchez	.05	.02
❑	246	Tom Henke	.05	.02
❑	247	John Cerutti	.05	.02
❑	248	Ernie Whitt	.05	.02
❑	249	Bob Brenly	.05	.02
❑	250	Rance Mulliniks	.05	.02
❑	251	Kelly Gruber	.05	.02
❑	252	Ed Sprague	.25	.11
❑	253	Fred McGriff	.20	.09
❑	254	Tony Fernandez	.05	.02
❑	255	Tom Lawless	.05	.02
❑	256	George Bell	.05	.02
❑	257	Jesse Barfield	.05	.02
❑	258	Roberto Alomar / Sandy Alomar	.20	.09
❑	259	Ken Griffey Jr. / Ken Griffey Sr.	1.00	.45
❑	260	Cal Ripken Jr. / Cal Ripken Sr.	.30	.14
❑	261	Mel Stottlemyre Jr. / Mel Stottlemyre Sr.	.05	.02
❑	262	Zane Smith	.05	.02
❑	263	Charlie Puleo	.05	.02
❑	264	Derek Lilliquist	.05	.02
❑	265	Paul Assenmacher	.05	.02
❑	266	John Smoltz	.50	.23
❑	267	Tom Glavine	.20	.09
❑	268	Steve Avery	.20	.09
❑	269	Pete Smith	.05	.02
❑	270	Jody Davis	.05	.02
❑	271	Bruce Benedict	.05	.02
❑	272	Andres Thomas	.05	.02
❑	273	Gerald Perry	.05	.02
❑	274	Ron Gant	.10	.05
❑	275	Darrell Evans	.10	.05
❑	276	Dale Murphy	.20	.09
❑	277	Dion James	.05	.02
❑	278	Lonnie Smith	.05	.02
❑	279	Geronimo Berroa	.05	.02
❑	280	Steve Wilson	.05	.02
❑	281	Rick Sutcliffe	.05	.02
❑	282	Kevin Coffman	.05	.02
❑	283	Mitch Williams	.05	.02
❑	284	Greg Maddux	.75	.35
❑	285	Paul Kilgus	.05	.02
❑	286	Mike Harkey	.05	.02
❑	287	Lloyd McClendon	.05	.02
❑	288	Damon Berryhill	.05	.02
❑	289	Ty Griffin	.05	.02
❑	290	Ryne Sandberg	.25	.11
❑	291	Mark Grace	.20	.09
❑	292	Curt Wilkerson	.05	.02
❑	293	Vance Law	.05	.02
❑	294	Shawon Dunston	.05	.02
❑	295	Jerome Walton	.20	.09
❑	296	Mitch Webster	.05	.02
❑	297	Dwight Smith	.10	.05
❑	298	Andre Dawson	.20	.09
❑	299	Jeff Sellers	.05	.02
❑	300	Jose Rijo	.05	.02
❑	301	John Franco	.10	.05
❑	302	Rick Mahler	.05	.02
❑	303	Ron Robinson	.05	.02
❑	304	Danny Jackson	.05	.02
❑	305	Rob Dibble	.10	.05
❑	306	Tom Browning	.05	.02
❑	307	Bo Diaz	.05	.02
❑	308	Manny Trillo	.05	.02
❑	309	Chris Sabo	.05	.02
❑	310	Ron Oester	.05	.02
❑	311	Barry Larkin	.20	.09
❑	312	Todd Benzinger	.05	.02
❑	313	Paul O'Neill	.10	.05
❑	314	Kal Daniels	.05	.02
❑	315	Joel Youngblood	.05	.02
❑	316	Eric Davis	.10	.05
❑	317	Dave Smith	.05	.02
❑	318	Mark Portugal	.05	.02
❑	319	Brian Meyer	.05	.02
❑	320	Jim Deshaies	.05	.02
❑	321	Juan Agosto	.05	.02
❑	322	Mike Scott	.05	.02
❑	323	Rick Rhoden	.05	.02
❑	324	Jim Clancy	.05	.02
❑	325	Larry Andersen	.05	.02
❑	326	Alex Trevino	.05	.02
❑	327	Alan Ashby	.05	.02
❑	328	Craig Reynolds	.05	.02
❑	329	Bill Doran	.05	.02
❑	330	Rafael Ramirez	.05	.02
❑	331	Glenn Davis	.05	.02
❑	332	Willie Ansley	.05	.02
❑	333	Gerald Young	.05	.02
❑	334	Cameron Drew	.05	.02
❑	335	Jay Howell	.05	.02
❑	336	Tim Belcher	.05	.02
❑	337	Fernando Valenzuela	.10	.05
❑	338	Ricky Horton	.05	.02
❑	339	Tim Leary	.05	.02
❑	340	Bill Bene	.05	.02
❑	341	Orel Hershiser	.10	.05
❑	342	Mike Scioscia	.05	.02
❑	343	Rick Dempsey	.05	.02
❑	344	Willie Randolph	.10	.05

	MINT	NRMT
❑ 345 Alfredo Griffin	.05	.02
❑ 346 Eddie Murray	.20	.09
❑ 347 Mickey Hatcher	.05	.02
❑ 348 Mike Sharperson	.05	.02
❑ 349 John Shelby	.05	.02
❑ 350 Mike Marshall	.05	.02
❑ 351 Kirk Gibson	.10	.05
❑ 352 Mike Davis	.05	.02
❑ 353 Bryn Smith	.05	.02
❑ 354 Pascual Perez	.05	.02
❑ 355 Kevin Gross	.05	.02
❑ 356 Andy McGaffigan	.05	.02
❑ 357 Brian Holman	.05	.02
❑ 358 Dave Wainhouse	.05	.02
❑ 359 Dennis Martinez	.10	.05
❑ 360 Tim Burke	.05	.02
❑ 361 Nelson Santovenia	.05	.02
❑ 362 Tim Wallach	.05	.02
❑ 363 Spike Owen	.05	.02
❑ 364 Rex Hudler	.05	.02
❑ 365 Andres Galarraga	.20	.09
❑ 366 Otis Nixon	.10	.05
❑ 367 Hubie Brooks	.05	.02
❑ 368 Mike Aldrete	.05	.02
❑ 369 Tim Raines	.10	.05
❑ 370 Dave Martinez	.05	.02
❑ 371 Bob Ojeda	.05	.02
❑ 372 Ron Darling	.05	.02
❑ 373 Wally Whitehurst	.05	.02
❑ 374 Randy Myers	.10	.05
❑ 375 David Cone	.20	.09
❑ 376 Dwight Gooden	.10	.05
❑ 377 Sid Fernandez	.05	.02
❑ 378 Dave Proctor	.05	.02
❑ 379 Gary Carter	.15	.07
❑ 380 Keith Miller	.05	.02
❑ 381 Gregg Jefferies	.10	.05
❑ 382 Tim Teufel	.05	.02
❑ 383 Kevin Elster	.05	.02
❑ 384 Dave Magadan	.05	.02
❑ 385 Keith Hernandez	.10	.05
❑ 386 Mookie Wilson	.10	.05
❑ 387 Darryl Strawberry	.10	.05
❑ 388 Kevin McReynolds	.05	.02
❑ 389 Mark Carreon	.05	.02
❑ 390 Jeff Parrett	.05	.02
❑ 391 Mike Maddux	.05	.02
❑ 392 Don Carman	.05	.02
❑ 393 Bruce Ruffin	.05	.02
❑ 394 Ken Howell	.05	.02
❑ 395 Steve Bedrosian	.05	.02
❑ 396 Floyd Youmans	.05	.02
❑ 397 Larry McWilliams	.05	.02
❑ 398 Pat Combs	.05	.02
❑ 399 Steve Lake	.05	.02
❑ 400 Dickie Thon	.05	.02
❑ 401 Ricky Jordan	.05	.02
❑ 402 Mike Schmidt	.25	.11
❑ 403 Tom Herr	.05	.02
❑ 404 Chris James	.05	.02
❑ 405 Juan Samuel	.05	.02
❑ 406 Von Hayes	.05	.02
❑ 407 Ron Jones	.05	.02
❑ 408 Curt Ford	.05	.02
❑ 409 Bob Walk	.05	.02
❑ 410 Jeff D. Robinson	.05	.02
❑ 411 Jim Gott	.05	.02
❑ 412 Scott Medvin	.05	.02
❑ 413 John Smiley	.05	.02
❑ 414 Bob Kipper	.05	.02
❑ 415 Brian Fisher	.05	.02
❑ 416 Doug Drabek	.05	.02
❑ 417 Mike LaValliere	.05	.02
❑ 418 Ken Oberkfell	.05	.02
❑ 419 Sid Bream	.05	.02
❑ 420 Austin Manahan	.05	.02
❑ 421 Jose Lind	.05	.02
❑ 422 Bobby Bonilla	.15	.07
❑ 423 Glenn Wilson	.05	.02
❑ 424 Andy Van Slyke	.10	.05
❑ 425 Gary Redus	.05	.02
❑ 426 Barry Bonds	.40	.18
❑ 427 Don Heinkel	.05	.02
❑ 428 Ken Dayley	.05	.02
❑ 429 Todd Worrell	.05	.02
❑ 430 Brad DuVall	.05	.02
❑ 431 Jose DeLeon	.05	.02
❑ 432 Joe Magrane	.05	.02
❑ 433 John Ericks	.05	.02
❑ 434 Frank DiPino	.05	.02
❑ 435 Tony Pena	.05	.02
❑ 436 Ozzie Smith	.25	.11
❑ 437 Terry Pendleton	.10	.05
❑ 438 Jose Oquendo	.05	.02
❑ 439 Tim Jones	.05	.02
❑ 440 Pedro Guerrero	.05	.02
❑ 441 Milt Thompson	.05	.02
❑ 442 Willie McGee	.10	.05
❑ 443 Vince Coleman	.05	.02
❑ 444 Tom Brunansky	.05	.02
❑ 445 Walt Terrell	.05	.02
❑ 446 Eric Show	.05	.02
❑ 447 Mark Davis	.05	.02
❑ 448 Andy Benes	.20	.09
❑ 449 Ed Whitson	.05	.02
❑ 450 Dennis Rasmussen	.05	.02
❑ 451 Bruce Hurst	.05	.02
❑ 452 Pat Clements	.05	.02
❑ 453 Benito Santiago	.05	.02
❑ 454 Sandy Alomar Jr.	.40	.18
❑ 455 Garry Templeton	.05	.02
❑ 456 Jack Clark	.05	.02
❑ 457 Tim Flannery	.05	.02
❑ 458 Roberto Alomar	.30	.14
❑ 459 Carmelo Martinez	.05	.02
❑ 460 John Kruk	.10	.05
❑ 461 Tony Gwynn	.50	.23
❑ 462 Jerald Clark	.05	.02
❑ 463 Don Robinson	.05	.02
❑ 464 Craig Lefferts	.05	.02
❑ 465 Kelly Downs	.05	.02
❑ 466 Rick Reuschel	.05	.02
❑ 467 Scott Garrelts	.05	.02
❑ 468 Wil Tejada	.05	.02
❑ 469 Kirt Manwaring	.05	.02
❑ 470 Terry Kennedy	.05	.02
❑ 471 Jose Uribe	.05	.02
❑ 472 Royce Clayton	.20	.09
❑ 473 Robby Thompson	.05	.02
❑ 474 Kevin Mitchell	.10	.05
❑ 475 Ernie Riles	.05	.02
❑ 476 Will Clark	.20	.09
❑ 477 Donell Nixon	.05	.02
❑ 478 Candy Maldonado	.05	.02
❑ 479 Tracy Jones	.05	.02
❑ 480 Brett Butler	.10	.05
❑ 481 Checklist 1-121	.05	.02
❑ 482 Checklist 122-242	.05	.02
❑ 483 Checklist 243-363	.05	.02
❑ 484 Checklist 364-484	.05	.02

1989 Bowman Tiffany

	MINT	NRMT
COMP.FACT.SET (495)	500.00	220.00
COMMON CARD (1-484)	.25	.11
COMMON REPRINT (R1-R11)	.30	.14

*STARS: 10X TO 20X BASIC CARDS
*ROOKIES: 10X TO 20X BASIC CARDS

1990 Bowman

	MINT	NRMT
COMPLETE SET (528)	18.00	8.00
COMP.FACT.SET (528)	18.00	8.00
COMMON CARD (1-528)	.05	.02

	MINT	NRMT
❑ 1 Tommy Greene	.05	.02
❑ 2 Tom Glavine	.20	.09
❑ 3 Andy Nezelek	.05	.02
❑ 4 Mike Stanton	.05	.02
❑ 5 Rick Luecken	.05	.02
❑ 6 Kent Mercker	.05	.02
❑ 7 Derek Lilliquist	.05	.02
❑ 8 Charlie Leibrandt	.05	.02
❑ 9 Steve Avery	.05	.02
❑ 10 John Smoltz	.20	.09
❑ 11 Mark Lemke	.05	.02
❑ 12 Lonnie Smith	.05	.02
❑ 13 Oddibe McDowell	.05	.02
❑ 14 Tyler Houston	.20	.09
❑ 15 Jeff Blauser	.05	.02
❑ 16 Ernie Whitt	.05	.02
❑ 17 Alexis Infante	.05	.02
❑ 18 Jim Presley	.05	.02
❑ 19 Dale Murphy	.20	.09
❑ 20 Nick Esasky	.05	.02
❑ 21 Rick Sutcliffe	.05	.02
❑ 22 Mike Bielecki	.05	.02
❑ 23 Steve Wilson	.05	.02
❑ 24 Kevin Blankenship	.05	.02
❑ 25 Mitch Williams	.05	.02
❑ 26 Dean Wilkins	.05	.02
❑ 27 Greg Maddux	.60	.25
❑ 28 Mike Harkey	.05	.02
❑ 29 Mark Grace	.20	.09
❑ 30 Ryne Sandberg	.25	.11
❑ 31 Greg Smith	.05	.02
❑ 32 Dwight Smith	.05	.02
❑ 33 Damon Berryhill	.05	.02
❑ 34 Earl Cunningham UER (Errant * by the word "in")	.05	.02
❑ 35 Jerome Walton	.05	.02
❑ 36 Lloyd McClendon	.05	.02
❑ 37 Ty Griffin	.05	.02
❑ 38 Shawon Dunston	.05	.02
❑ 39 Andre Dawson	.20	.09
❑ 40 Luis Salazar	.05	.02
❑ 41 Tim Layana	.05	.02
❑ 42 Rob Dibble	.05	.02
❑ 43 Tom Browning	.05	.02
❑ 44 Danny Jackson	.05	.02
❑ 45 Jose Rijo	.05	.02
❑ 46 Scott Scudder	.05	.02
❑ 47 Randy Myers UER (Career ERA .274, should be 2.74)	.10	.05
❑ 48 Brian Lane	.05	.02
❑ 49 Paul O'Neill	.10	.05
❑ 50 Barry Larkin	.20	.09
❑ 51 Reggie Jefferson	.20	.09
❑ 52 Jeff Branson	.05	.02
❑ 53 Chris Sabo	.05	.02
❑ 54 Joe Oliver	.05	.02
❑ 55 Todd Benzinger	.05	.02
❑ 56 Rolando Roomes	.05	.02
❑ 57 Hal Morris	.05	.02

❑ 58 Eric Davis .10 .05
❑ 59 Scott Bryant .05 .02
❑ 60 Ken Griffey Sr. .05 .02
❑ 61 Darryl Kile .25 .11
❑ 62 Dave Smith .05 .02
❑ 63 Mark Portugal .05 .02
❑ 64 Jeff Juden .05 .02
❑ 65 Bill Gullickson .05 .02
❑ 66 Danny Darwin .05 .02
❑ 67 Larry Andersen .05 .02
❑ 68 Jose Cano .05 .02
❑ 69 Dan Schatzeder .05 .02
❑ 70 Jim Deshaies .05 .02
❑ 71 Mike Scott .05 .02
❑ 72 Gerald Young .05 .02
❑ 73 Ken Caminiti .20 .09
❑ 74 Ken Oberkfell .05 .02
❑ 75 Dave Rohde .05 .02
❑ 76 Bill Doran .05 .02
❑ 77 Andujar Cedeno .05 .02
❑ 78 Craig Biggio .20 .09
❑ 79 Karl Rhodes .05 .02
❑ 80 Glenn Davis .05 .02
❑ 81 Eric Anthony .05 .02
❑ 82 John Wetteland .20 .09
❑ 83 Jay Howell .05 .02
❑ 84 Orel Hershiser .10 .05
❑ 85 Tim Belcher .05 .02
❑ 86 Kiki Jones .05 .02
❑ 87 Mike Hartley .05 .02
❑ 88 Ramon Martinez .15 .07
❑ 89 Mike Scioscia .05 .02
❑ 90 Willie Randolph .10 .05
❑ 91 Juan Samuel .05 .02
❑ 92 Jose Offerman .25 .11
❑ 93 Dave Hansen .05 .02
❑ 94 Jeff Hamilton .05 .02
❑ 95 Alfredo Griffin .05 .02
❑ 96 Tom Goodwin .20 .09
❑ 97 Kirk Gibson .10 .05
❑ 98 Jose Vizcaino .20 .09
❑ 99 Kal Daniels .05 .02
❑ 100 Hubie Brooks .05 .02
❑ 101 Eddie Murray .20 .09
❑ 102 Dennis Boyd .05 .02
❑ 103 Tim Burke .05 .02
❑ 104 Bill Sampen .05 .02
❑ 105 Brett Gideon .05 .02
❑ 106 Mark Gardner .05 .02
❑ 107 Howard Farmer .05 .02
❑ 108 Mel Rojas .20 .09
❑ 109 Kevin Gross .05 .02
❑ 110 Dave Schmidt .05 .02
❑ 111 Denny Martinez .10 .05
❑ 112 Jerry Goff .05 .02
❑ 113 Andres Galarraga .20 .09
❑ 114 Tim Wallach .05 .02
❑ 115 Marquis Grissom .25 .11
❑ 116 Spike Owen .05 .02
❑ 117 Larry Walker 1.00 .45
❑ 118 Tim Raines .10 .05
❑ 119 Delino DeShields .20 .09
❑ 120 Tom Foley .05 .02
❑ 121 Dave Martinez .05 .02
❑ 122 Frank Viola UER .05 .02
(Career ERA .384
should be 3.84)
❑ 123 Julio Valera .05 .02
❑ 124 Alejandro Pena .05 .02
❑ 125 David Cone .20 .09
❑ 126 Dwight Gooden .10 .05
❑ 127 Kevin D. Brown .05 .02
❑ 128 John Franco .10 .05
❑ 129 Terry Bross .05 .02
❑ 130 Blaine Beatty .05 .02
❑ 131 Sid Fernandez .05 .02
❑ 132 Mike Marshall .05 .02
❑ 133 Howard Johnson .05 .02
❑ 134 Jaime Roseboro .05 .02
❑ 135 Alan Zinter .05 .02
❑ 136 Keith Miller .05 .02
❑ 137 Kevin Elster .05 .02
❑ 138 Kevin McReynolds .05 .02
❑ 139 Barry Lyons .05 .02
❑ 140 Gregg Jefferies .10 .05
❑ 141 Darryl Strawberry .10 .05
❑ 142 Todd Hundley .40 .18
❑ 143 Scott Service .05 .02
❑ 144 Chuck Malone .05 .02
❑ 145 Steve Ontiveros .05 .02
❑ 146 Roger McDowell .05 .02
❑ 147 Ken Howell .05 .02
❑ 148 Pat Combs .05 .02
❑ 149 Jeff Parrett .05 .02
❑ 150 Chuck McElroy .05 .02
❑ 151 Jason Grimsley .05 .02
❑ 152 Len Dykstra .10 .05
❑ 153 Mickey Morandini .20 .09
❑ 154 John Kruk .10 .05
❑ 155 Dickie Thon .05 .02
❑ 156 Ricky Jordan .05 .02
❑ 157 Jeff Jackson .05 .02
❑ 158 Darren Daulton .10 .05
❑ 159 Tom Herr .05 .02
❑ 160 Von Hayes .05 .02
❑ 161 Dave Hollins .20 .09
❑ 162 Carmelo Martinez .05 .02
❑ 163 Bob Walk .05 .02
❑ 164 Doug Drabek .05 .02
❑ 165 Walt Terrell .05 .02
❑ 166 Bill Landrum .05 .02
❑ 167 Scott Ruskin .05 .02
❑ 168 Bob Patterson .05 .02
❑ 169 Bobby Bonilla .10 .05
❑ 170 Jose Lind .05 .02
❑ 171 Andy Van Slyke .10 .05
❑ 172 Mike LaValliere .05 .02
❑ 173 Willie Greene .25 .11
❑ 174 Jay Bell .10 .05
❑ 175 Sid Bream .05 .02
❑ 176 Tom Prince .05 .02
❑ 177 Wally Backman .05 .02
❑ 178 Moises Alou .75 .35
❑ 179 Steve Carter .05 .02
❑ 180 Gary Redus .05 .02
❑ 181 Barry Bonds .25 .11
❑ 182 Don Slaught UER .05 .02
(Card back shows
headings for a pitcher)
❑ 183 Joe Magrane .05 .02
❑ 184 Bryn Smith .05 .02
❑ 185 Todd Worrell .05 .02
❑ 186 Jose DeLeon .05 .02
❑ 187 Frank DiPino .05 .02
❑ 188 John Tudor .05 .02
❑ 189 Howard Hilton .05 .02
❑ 190 John Ericks .05 .02
❑ 191 Ken Dayley .05 .02
❑ 192 Ray Lankford .50 .23
❑ 193 Todd Zeile .10 .05
❑ 194 Willie McGee .10 .05
❑ 195 Ozzie Smith .25 .11
❑ 196 Milt Thompson .05 .02
❑ 197 Terry Pendleton .10 .05
❑ 198 Vince Coleman .05 .02
❑ 199 Paul Coleman .05 .02
❑ 200 Jose Oquendo .05 .02
❑ 201 Pedro Guerrero .05 .02
❑ 202 Tom Brunansky .05 .02
❑ 203 Roger Smithberg .05 .02
❑ 204 Eddie Whitson .05 .02
❑ 205 Dennis Rasmussen .05 .02
❑ 206 Craig Lefferts .05 .02
❑ 207 Andy Benes .20 .09
❑ 208 Bruce Hurst .05 .02
❑ 209 Eric Show .05 .02
❑ 210 Rafael Valdez .05 .02
❑ 211 Joey Cora .15 .07
❑ 212 Thomas Howard .05 .02
❑ 213 Rob Nelson .05 .02
❑ 214 Jack Clark .10 .05
❑ 215 Garry Templeton .05 .02
❑ 216 Fred Lynn .05 .02
❑ 217 Tony Gwynn .50 .23
❑ 218 Benito Santiago .05 .02
❑ 219 Mike Pagliarulo .05 .02
❑ 220 Joe Carter .10 .05
❑ 221 Roberto Alomar .25 .11
❑ 222 Bip Roberts .05 .02
❑ 223 Rick Reuschel .05 .02
❑ 224 Russ Swan .05 .02
❑ 225 Eric Gunderson .05 .02
❑ 226 Steve Bedrosian .05 .02
❑ 227 Mike Remlinger .05 .02
❑ 228 Scott Garrelts .05 .02
❑ 229 Ernie Camacho .05 .02
❑ 230 Andres Santana .05 .02
❑ 231 Will Clark .20 .09
❑ 232 Kevin Mitchell .05 .02
❑ 233 Robby Thompson .05 .02
❑ 234 Bill Bathe .05 .02
❑ 235 Tony Perezchica .05 .02
❑ 236 Gary Carter .20 .09
❑ 237 Brett Butler .10 .05
❑ 238 Matt Williams .20 .09
❑ 239 Earnie Riles .05 .02
❑ 240 Kevin Bass .05 .02
❑ 241 Terry Kennedy .05 .02
❑ 242 Steve Hosey .05 .02
❑ 243 Ben McDonald .10 .05
❑ 244 Jeff Ballard .05 .02
❑ 245 Joe Price .05 .02
❑ 246 Curt Schilling .20 .09
❑ 247 Pete Harnisch .05 .02
❑ 248 Mark Williamson .05 .02
❑ 249 Gregg Olson .05 .02
❑ 250 Chris Myers .05 .02
❑ 251 David Segui ERR .25 .11
(Missing vital stats
at top of card back
under name)
❑ 251B David Segui COR .25 .11
❑ 252 Joe Orsulak .05 .02
❑ 253 Craig Worthington .05 .02
❑ 254 Mickey Tettleton .10 .05
❑ 255 Cal Ripken .75 .35
❑ 256 Billy Ripken .05 .02
❑ 257 Randy Milligan .05 .02
❑ 258 Brady Anderson .20 .09
❑ 259 Chris Hoiles UER .20 .09
Baltimore is spelled Balitmore
❑ 260 Mike Devereaux .05 .02
❑ 261 Phil Bradley .05 .02
❑ 262 Leo Gomez .05 .02
❑ 263 Lee Smith .10 .05
❑ 264 Mike Rochford .05 .02
❑ 265 Jeff Reardon .10 .05
❑ 266 Wes Gardner .05 .02
❑ 267 Mike Boddicker .05 .02
❑ 268 Roger Clemens .40 .18
❑ 269 Rob Murphy .05 .02
❑ 270 Mickey Pina .05 .02
❑ 271 Tony Pena .05 .02
❑ 272 Jody Reed .05 .02
❑ 273 Kevin Romine .05 .02
❑ 274 Mike Greenwell .05 .02
❑ 275 Maurice Vaughn 1.50 .70
❑ 276 Danny Heep .05 .02
❑ 277 Scott Cooper .05 .02
❑ 278 Greg Blosser .05 .02
❑ 279 Dwight Evans UER .10 .05
(* by "1990 Team
Breakdown")
❑ 280 Ellis Burks .15 .07
❑ 281 Wade Boggs .20 .09
❑ 282 Marty Barrett .05 .02
❑ 283 Kirk McCaskill .05 .02
❑ 284 Mark Langston .05 .02
❑ 285 Bert Blyleven .10 .05
❑ 286 Mike Fetters .05 .02
❑ 287 Kyle Abbott .05 .02
❑ 288 Jim Abbott .15 .07
❑ 289 Chuck Finley .10 .05
❑ 290 Gary DiSarcina .20 .09
❑ 291 Dick Schofield .05 .02
❑ 292 Devon White .05 .02
❑ 293 Bobby Rose .05 .02
❑ 294 Brian Downing .05 .02
❑ 295 Lance Parrish .05 .02
❑ 296 Jack Howell .05 .02
❑ 297 Claudell Washington .05 .02
❑ 298 John Orton .05 .02
❑ 299 Wally Joyner .10 .05
❑ 300 Lee Stevens .10 .05
❑ 301 Chili Davis .10 .05

❑ 302 Johnny Ray .05 .02
❑ 303 Greg Hibbard .05 .02
❑ 304 Eric King .05 .02
❑ 305 Jack McDowell .05 .02
❑ 306 Bobby Thigpen .05 .02
❑ 307 Adam Peterson .05 .02
❑ 308 Scott Radinsky .05 .02
❑ 309 Wayne Edwards .05 .02
❑ 310 Melido Perez .05 .02
❑ 311 Robin Ventura .20 .09
❑ 312 Sammy Sosa 5.00 2.20
❑ 313 Dan Pasqua .05 .02
❑ 314 Carlton Fisk .20 .09
❑ 315 Ozzie Guillen .05 .02
❑ 316 Ivan Calderon .05 .02
❑ 317 Daryl Boston .05 .02
❑ 318 Craig Grebeck .05 .02
❑ 319 Scott Fletcher .05 .02
❑ 320 Frank Thomas 3.00 1.35
❑ 321 Steve Lyons .05 .02
❑ 322 Carlos Martinez .05 .02
❑ 323 Joe Skalski .05 .02
❑ 324 Tom Candiotti .05 .02
❑ 325 Greg Swindell .05 .02
❑ 326 Steve Olin .10 .05
❑ 327 Kevin Wickander .05 .02
❑ 328 Doug Jones .05 .02
❑ 329 Jeff Shaw .05 .02
❑ 330 Kevin Bearse .05 .02
❑ 331 Dion James .05 .02
❑ 332 Jerry Browne .05 .02
❑ 333 Joey Belle 1.00 .45
❑ 334 Felix Fermin .05 .02
❑ 335 Candy Maldonado .05 .02
❑ 336 Cory Snyder .05 .02
❑ 337 Sandy Alomar Jr. .15 .07
❑ 338 Mark Lewis .05 .02
❑ 339 Carlos Baerga .25 .11
❑ 340 Chris James .05 .02
❑ 341 Brook Jacoby .05 .02
❑ 342 Keith Hernandez .10 .05
❑ 343 Frank Tanana .05 .02
❑ 344 Scott Aldred .05 .02
❑ 345 Mike Henneman .05 .02
❑ 346 Steve Wapnick .05 .02
❑ 347 Greg Gohr .05 .02
❑ 348 Eric Stone .05 .02
❑ 349 Brian DuBois .05 .02
❑ 350 Kevin Ritz .05 .02
❑ 351 Rico Brogna .20 .09
❑ 352 Mike Heath .05 .02
❑ 353 Alan Trammell .15 .07
❑ 354 Chet Lemon .05 .02
❑ 355 Dave Bergman .05 .02
❑ 356 Lou Whitaker .10 .05
❑ 357 Cecil Fielder UER .10 .05
* by 1990 Team Breakdown
❑ 358 Milt Cuyler .05 .02
❑ 359 Tony Phillips .05 .02
❑ 360 Travis Fryman .40 .18
❑ 361 Ed Romero .05 .02
❑ 362 Lloyd Moseby .05 .02
❑ 363 Mark Gubicza .05 .02
❑ 364 Bret Saberhagen .10 .05
❑ 365 Tom Gordon .15 .07
❑ 366 Steve Farr .05 .02
❑ 367 Kevin Appier .15 .07
❑ 368 Storm Davis .05 .02
❑ 369 Mark Davis .05 .02
❑ 370 Jeff Montgomery .10 .05
❑ 371 Frank White .10 .05
❑ 372 Brent Mayne .05 .02
❑ 373 Bob Boone .10 .05
❑ 374 Jim Eisenreich .05 .02
❑ 375 Danny Tartabull .05 .02
❑ 376 Kurt Stillwell .05 .02
❑ 377 Bill Pecota .05 .02
❑ 378 Bo Jackson .10 .05
❑ 379 Bob Hamelin .20 .09
❑ 380 Kevin Seitzer .05 .02
❑ 381 Rey Palacios .05 .02
❑ 382 George Brett .40 .18
❑ 383 Gerald Perry .05 .02
❑ 384 Teddy Higuera .05 .02
❑ 385 Tom Filer .05 .02
❑ 386 Dan Plesac .05 .02
❑ 387 Cal Eldred .10 .05
❑ 388 Jaime Navarro .05 .02
❑ 389 Chris Bosio .05 .02
❑ 390 Randy Veres .05 .02
❑ 391 Gary Sheffield .20 .09
❑ 392 George Canale .05 .02
❑ 393 B.J. Surhoff .10 .05
❑ 394 Tim McIntosh .05 .02
❑ 395 Greg Brock .05 .02
❑ 396 Greg Vaughn .40 .18
❑ 397 Darryl Hamilton .05 .02
❑ 398 Dave Parker .10 .05
❑ 399 Paul Molitor .20 .09
❑ 400 Jim Gantner .05 .02
❑ 401 Rob Deer .05 .02
❑ 402 Billy Spiers .05 .02
❑ 403 Glenn Braggs .05 .02
❑ 404 Robin Yount .20 .09
❑ 405 Rick Aguilera .10 .05
❑ 406 Johnny Ard .05 .02
❑ 407 Kevin Tapani .10 .05
❑ 408 Park Pittman .05 .02
❑ 409 Allan Anderson .05 .02
❑ 410 Juan Berenguer .05 .02
❑ 411 Willie Banks .05 .02
❑ 412 Rich Yett .05 .02
❑ 413 Dave West .05 .02
❑ 414 Greg Gagne .05 .02
❑ 415 Chuck Knoblauch .75 .35
❑ 416 Randy Bush .05 .02
❑ 417 Gary Gaetti .10 .05
❑ 418 Kent Hrbek .10 .05
❑ 419 Al Newman .05 .02
❑ 420 Danny Gladden .05 .02
❑ 421 Paul Sorrento .20 .09
❑ 422 Derek Parks .05 .02
❑ 423 Scott Leius .05 .02
❑ 424 Kirby Puckett .30 .14
❑ 425 Willie Smith .05 .02
❑ 426 Dave Righetti .05 .02
❑ 427 Jeff D. Robinson .05 .02
❑ 428 Alan Mills .05 .02
❑ 429 Tim Leary .05 .02
❑ 430 Pascual Perez .05 .02
❑ 431 Alvaro Espinoza .05 .02
❑ 432 Dave Winfield .20 .09
❑ 433 Jesse Barfield .05 .02
❑ 434 Randy Velarde .05 .02
❑ 435 Rick Cerone .05 .02
❑ 436 Steve Balboni .05 .02
❑ 437 Mel Hall .05 .02
❑ 438 Bob Geren .05 .02
❑ 439 Bernie Williams 1.25 .55
❑ 440 Kevin Maas .10 .05
❑ 441 Mike Blowers .10 .05
❑ 442 Steve Sax .05 .02
❑ 443 Don Mattingly .30 .14
❑ 444 Roberto Kelly .05 .02
❑ 445 Mike Moore .05 .02
❑ 446 Reggie Harris .05 .02
❑ 447 Scott Sanderson .05 .02
❑ 448 Dave Otto .05 .02
❑ 449 Dave Stewart .10 .05
❑ 450 Rick Honeycutt .05 .02
❑ 451 Dennis Eckersley .15 .07
❑ 452 Carney Lansford .10 .05
❑ 453 Scott Hemond .05 .02
❑ 454 Mark McGwire 1.00 .45
❑ 455 Felix Jose .05 .02
❑ 456 Terry Steinbach .10 .05
❑ 457 Rickey Henderson .20 .09
❑ 458 Dave Henderson .05 .02
❑ 459 Mike Gallego .05 .02
❑ 460 Jose Canseco .20 .09
❑ 461 Walt Weiss .05 .02
❑ 462 Ken Phelps .05 .02
❑ 463 Darren Lewis .05 .02
❑ 464 Ron Hassey .05 .02
❑ 465 Roger Salkeld .05 .02
❑ 466 Scott Bankhead .05 .02
❑ 467 Keith Comstock .05 .02
❑ 468 Randy Johnson .30 .14
❑ 469 Erik Hanson .05 .02
❑ 470 Mike Schooler .05 .02
❑ 471 Gary Eave .05 .02
❑ 472 Jeffrey Leonard .05 .02
❑ 473 Dave Valle .05 .02
❑ 474 Omar Vizquel .20 .09
❑ 475 Pete O'Brien .05 .02
❑ 476 Henry Cotto .05 .02
❑ 477 Jay Buhner .20 .09
❑ 478 Harold Reynolds .05 .02
❑ 479 Alvin Davis .05 .02
❑ 480 Darnell Coles .05 .02
❑ 481 Ken Griffey Jr. 2.00 .90
❑ 482 Greg Briley .05 .02
❑ 483 Scott Bradley .05 .02
❑ 484 Tino Martinez .20 .09
❑ 485 Jeff Russell .05 .02
❑ 486 Nolan Ryan .75 .35
❑ 487 Robb Nen .25 .11
❑ 488 Kevin Brown .20 .09
❑ 489 Brian Bohanon .05 .02
❑ 490 Ruben Sierra .05 .02
❑ 491 Pete Incaviglia .05 .02
❑ 492 Juan Gonzalez 3.00 1.35
❑ 493 Steve Buechele .05 .02
❑ 494 Scott Coolbaugh .05 .02
❑ 495 Geno Petralli .05 .02
❑ 496 Rafael Palmeiro .20 .09
❑ 497 Julio Franco .05 .02
❑ 498 Gary Pettis .05 .02
❑ 499 Donald Harris .05 .02
❑ 500 Monty Fariss .05 .02
❑ 501 Harold Baines .10 .05
❑ 502 Cecil Espy .05 .02
❑ 503 Jack Daugherty .05 .02
❑ 504 Willie Blair .05 .02
❑ 505 Dave Stieb .10 .05
❑ 506 Tom Henke .05 .02
❑ 507 John Cerutti .05 .02
❑ 508 Paul Kilgus .05 .02
❑ 509 Jimmy Key .10 .05
❑ 510 John Olerud .50 .23
❑ 511 Ed Sprague .10 .05
❑ 512 Manuel Lee .05 .02
❑ 513 Fred McGriff .20 .09
❑ 514 Glenallen Hill .05 .02
❑ 515 George Bell .05 .02
❑ 516 Mookie Wilson .10 .05
❑ 517 Luis Sojo .05 .02
❑ 518 Nelson Liriano .05 .02
❑ 519 Kelly Gruber .05 .02
❑ 520 Greg Myers .05 .02
❑ 521 Pat Borders .05 .02
❑ 522 Junior Felix .05 .02
❑ 523 Eddie Zosky .05 .02
❑ 524 Tony Fernandez .05 .02
❑ 525 Checklist 1-132 UER .05 .02
(No copyright mark on the back)
❑ 526 Checklist 133-264 .05 .02
❑ 527 Checklist 265-396 .05 .02
❑ 528 Checklist 397-528 .05 .02

1990 Bowman Tiffany

	MINT	NRMT
COMP.FACT.SET (539)	600.00	275.00
COMMON CARD (1-528)	.25	.11
COMMON ART (A1-A11)	.20	.09

*STARS: 10X TO 20X BASIC CARDS
*ROOKIES: 15X TO 30X BASIC CARDS

1991 Bowman

	MINT	NRMT
COMPLETE SET (704)	30.00	13.50
COMP.FACT.SET (704)	30.00	13.50
COMMON CARD (1-704)	.05	.02
❑ 1 Rod Carew I	.20	.09
❑ 2 Rod Carew II	.20	.09
❑ 3 Rod Carew III	.20	.09
❑ 4 Rod Carew IV	.20	.09
❑ 5 Rod Carew V	.20	.09
❑ 6 Willie Fraser	.05	.02
❑ 7 John Olerud	.10	.05
❑ 8 William Suero	.05	.02
❑ 9 Roberto Alomar	.20	.09
❑ 10 Todd Stottlemyre	.10	.05
❑ 11 Joe Carter	.10	.05
❑ 12 Steve Karsay	.10	.05
❑ 13 Mark Whiten	.05	.02
❑ 14 Pat Borders	.05	.02
❑ 15 Mike Timlin	.05	.02
❑ 16 Tom Henke	.05	.02
❑ 17 Eddie Zosky	.05	.02
❑ 18 Kelly Gruber	.05	.02
❑ 19 Jimmy Key	.10	.05
❑ 20 Jerry Schunk	.05	.02
❑ 21 Manuel Lee	.05	.02
❑ 22 Dave Stieb	.10	.05
❑ 23 Pat Hentgen	.40	.18
❑ 24 Glenallen Hill	.05	.02
❑ 25 Rene Gonzales	.05	.02
❑ 26 Ed Sprague	.05	.02
❑ 27 Ken Dayley	.05	.02
❑ 28 Pat Tabler	.05	.02
❑ 29 Denis Boucher	.05	.02
❑ 30 Devon White	.05	.02
❑ 31 Dante Bichette	.20	.09
❑ 32 Paul Molitor	.20	.09
❑ 33 Greg Vaughn	.20	.09
❑ 34 Dan Plesac	.05	.02
❑ 35 Chris George	.05	.02
❑ 36 Tim McIntosh	.05	.02
❑ 37 Franklin Stubbs	.05	.02
❑ 38 Bo Dodson	.05	.02
❑ 39 Ron Robinson	.05	.02
❑ 40 Ed Nunez	.05	.02
❑ 41 Greg Brock	.05	.02
❑ 42 Jaime Navarro	.05	.02
❑ 43 Chris Bosio	.05	.02
❑ 44 B.J. Surhoff	.10	.05
❑ 45 Chris Johnson	.05	.02
❑ 46 Willie Randolph	.10	.05
❑ 47 Narciso Elvira	.05	.02
❑ 48 Jim Gantner	.05	.02
❑ 49 Kevin Brown	.15	.07
❑ 50 Julio Machado	.05	.02
❑ 51 Chuck Crim	.05	.02
❑ 52 Gary Sheffield	.20	.09
❑ 53 Angel Miranda	.05	.02
❑ 54 Teddy Higuera	.05	.02
❑ 55 Robin Yount	.20	.09
❑ 56 Cal Eldred	.05	.02
❑ 57 Sandy Alomar Jr.	.10	.05
❑ 58 Greg Swindell	.05	.02
❑ 59 Brook Jacoby	.05	.02
❑ 60 Efrain Valdez	.05	.02
❑ 61 Ever Magallanes	.05	.02
❑ 62 Tom Candiotti	.05	.02
❑ 63 Eric King	.05	.02
❑ 64 Alex Cole	.05	.02
❑ 65 Charles Nagy	.20	.09
❑ 66 Mitch Webster	.05	.02
❑ 67 Chris James	.05	.02
❑ 68 Jim Thome	1.50	.70
❑ 69 Carlos Baerga	.10	.05
❑ 70 Mark Lewis	.05	.02
❑ 71 Jerry Browne	.05	.02
❑ 72 Jesse Orosco	.05	.02
❑ 73 Mike Huff	.05	.02
❑ 74 Jose Escobar	.05	.02
❑ 75 Jeff Manto	.05	.02
❑ 76 Turner Ward	.05	.02
❑ 77 Doug Jones	.05	.02
❑ 78 Bruce Egloff	.05	.02
❑ 79 Tim Costo	.05	.02
❑ 80 Beau Allred	.05	.02
❑ 81 Albert Belle	.25	.11
❑ 82 John Farrell	.05	.02
❑ 83 Glenn Davis	.05	.02
❑ 84 Joe Orsulak	.05	.02
❑ 85 Mark Williamson	.05	.02
❑ 86 Ben McDonald	.05	.02
❑ 87 Billy Ripken	.05	.02
❑ 88 Leo Gomez UER Baltimore is spelled Balitmore	.05	.02
❑ 89 Bob Melvin	.05	.02
❑ 90 Jeff M. Robinson	.05	.02
❑ 91 Jose Mesa	.05	.02
❑ 92 Gregg Olson	.05	.02
❑ 93 Mike Devereaux	.05	.02
❑ 94 Luis Mercedes	.05	.02
❑ 95 Arthur Rhodes	.10	.05
❑ 96 Juan Bell	.05	.02
❑ 97 Mike Mussina	1.50	.70
❑ 98 Jeff Ballard	.05	.02
❑ 99 Chris Hoiles	.05	.02
❑ 100 Brady Anderson	.20	.09
❑ 101 Bob Milacki	.05	.02
❑ 102 David Segui	.10	.05
❑ 103 Dwight Evans	.10	.05
❑ 104 Cal Ripken	.75	.35
❑ 105 Mike Linskey	.05	.02
❑ 106 Jeff Tackett	.05	.02
❑ 107 Jeff Reardon	.10	.05
❑ 108 Dana Kiecker	.05	.02
❑ 109 Ellis Burks	.10	.05
❑ 110 Dave Owen	.05	.02
❑ 111 Danny Darwin	.05	.02
❑ 112 Mo Vaughn	.40	.18
❑ 113 Jeff McNeely	.05	.02
❑ 114 Tom Bolton	.05	.02
❑ 115 Greg Blosser	.05	.02
❑ 116 Mike Greenwell	.05	.02
❑ 117 Phil Plantier	.05	.02
❑ 118 Roger Clemens	.40	.18
❑ 119 John Marzano	.05	.02
❑ 120 Jody Reed	.05	.02
❑ 121 Scott Taylor	.05	.02
❑ 122 Jack Clark	.10	.05
❑ 123 Derek Livernois	.05	.02
❑ 124 Tony Pena	.05	.02
❑ 125 Tom Brunansky	.05	.02
❑ 126 Carlos Quintana	.05	.02
❑ 127 Tim Naehring	.10	.05
❑ 128 Matt Young	.05	.02
❑ 129 Wade Boggs	.20	.09
❑ 130 Kevin Morton	.05	.02
❑ 131 Pete Incaviglia	.05	.02
❑ 132 Rob Deer	.05	.02
❑ 133 Bill Gullickson	.05	.02
❑ 134 Rico Brogna	.15	.07
❑ 135 Lloyd Moseby	.05	.02
❑ 136 Cecil Fielder	.10	.05
❑ 137 Tony Phillips	.05	.02
❑ 138 Mark Leiter	.05	.02
❑ 139 John Cerutti	.05	.02
❑ 140 Mickey Tettleton	.10	.05
❑ 141 Milt Cuyler	.05	.02
❑ 142 Greg Gohr	.05	.02
❑ 143 Tony Bernazard	.05	.02
❑ 144 Dan Gakeler	.05	.02
❑ 145 Travis Fryman	.20	.09
❑ 146 Dan Petry	.05	.02
❑ 147 Scott Aldred	.05	.02
❑ 148 John DeSilva	.05	.02
❑ 149 Rusty Meacham	.05	.02
❑ 150 Lou Whitaker	.10	.05
❑ 151 Dave Haas	.05	.02
❑ 152 Luis de los Santos	.05	.02
❑ 153 Ivan Cruz	.05	.02
❑ 154 Alan Trammell	.15	.07
❑ 155 Pat Kelly	.05	.02
❑ 156 Carl Everett	.20	.09
❑ 157 Greg Cadaret	.05	.02
❑ 158 Kevin Maas	.05	.02
❑ 159 Jeff Johnson	.05	.02
❑ 160 Willie Smith	.05	.02
❑ 161 Gerald Williams	.05	.02
❑ 162 Mike Humphreys	.05	.02
❑ 163 Alvaro Espinoza	.05	.02
❑ 164 Matt Nokes	.05	.02
❑ 165 Wade Taylor	.05	.02
❑ 166 Roberto Kelly	.05	.02
❑ 167 John Habyan	.05	.02
❑ 168 Steve Farr	.05	.02
❑ 169 Jesse Barfield	.05	.02
❑ 170 Steve Sax	.05	.02
❑ 171 Jim Leyritz	.10	.05
❑ 172 Robert Eenhoorn	.05	.02
❑ 173 Bernie Williams	.30	.14
❑ 174 Scott Lusader	.05	.02
❑ 175 Torey Lovullo	.05	.02
❑ 176 Chuck Cary	.05	.02
❑ 177 Scott Sanderson	.05	.02
❑ 178 Don Mattingly	.30	.14
❑ 179 Mel Hall	.05	.02
❑ 180 Juan Gonzalez	.75	.35
❑ 181 Hensley Meulens	.05	.02
❑ 182 Jose Offerman	.05	.02
❑ 183 Jeff Bagwell	2.50	1.10
❑ 184 Jeff Conine	.25	.11
❑ 185 Henry Rodriguez	.40	.18
❑ 186 Jimmie Reese CO	.10	.05
❑ 187 Kyle Abbott	.05	.02
❑ 188 Lance Parrish	.05	.02
❑ 189 Rafael Montalvo	.05	.02
❑ 190 Floyd Bannister	.05	.02
❑ 191 Dick Schofield	.05	.02
❑ 192 Scott Lewis	.05	.02
❑ 193 Jeff D. Robinson	.05	.02
❑ 194 Kent Anderson	.05	.02
❑ 195 Wally Joyner	.10	.05
❑ 196 Chuck Finley	.10	.05
❑ 197 Luis Sojo	.05	.02
❑ 198 Jeff Richardson	.05	.02
❑ 199 Dave Parker	.10	.05
❑ 200 Jim Abbott	.10	.05
❑ 201 Junior Felix	.05	.02
❑ 202 Mark Langston	.05	.02
❑ 203 Tim Salmon	1.25	.55
❑ 204 Cliff Young	.05	.02
❑ 205 Scott Bailes	.05	.02
❑ 206 Bobby Rose	.05	.02
❑ 207 Gary Gaetti	.10	.05
❑ 208 Ruben Amaro	.05	.02
❑ 209 Luis Polonia	.05	.02
❑ 210 Dave Winfield	.20	.09
❑ 211 Bryan Harvey	.05	.02
❑ 212 Mike Moore	.05	.02
❑ 213 Rickey Henderson	.20	.09
❑ 214 Steve Chitren	.05	.02
❑ 215 Bob Welch	.05	.02
❑ 216 Terry Steinbach	.10	.05
❑ 217 Earnest Riles	.05	.02
❑ 218 Todd Van Poppel	.05	.02
❑ 219 Mike Gallego	.05	.02
❑ 220 Curt Young	.05	.02
❑ 221 Todd Burns	.05	.02
❑ 222 Vance Law	.05	.02
❑ 223 Eric Show	.05	.02
❑ 224 Don Peters	.05	.02
❑ 225 Dave Stewart	.10	.05
❑ 226 Dave Henderson	.05	.02
❑ 227 Jose Canseco	.20	.09
❑ 228 Walt Weiss	.05	.02
❑ 229 Dann Howitt	.05	.02
❑ 230 Willie Wilson	.05	.02

231	Harold Baines	.10	.05
232	Scott Hemond	.05	.02
233	Joe Slusarski	.05	.02
234	Mark McGwire	1.00	.45
235	Kirk Dressendorfer	.05	.02
236	Craig Paquette	.05	.02
237	Dennis Eckersley	.10	.05
238	Dana Allison	.05	.02
239	Scott Bradley	.05	.02
240	Brian Holman	.05	.02
241	Mike Schooler	.05	.02
242	Rich DeLucia	.05	.02
243	Edgar Martinez	.20	.09
244	Henry Cotto	.05	.02
245	Omar Vizquel	.20	.09
246	Ken Griffey Jr. (See also 255)	1.50	.70
247	Jay Buhner	.20	.09
248	Bill Krueger	.05	.02
249	Dave Fleming	.05	.02
250	Patrick Lennon	.05	.02
251	Dave Valle	.05	.02
252	Harold Reynolds	.05	.02
253	Randy Johnson	.25	.11
254	Scott Bankhead	.05	.02
255	Ken Griffey Sr. UER (Card number is 246)	.05	.02
256	Greg Briley	.05	.02
257	Tino Martinez	.20	.09
258	Alvin Davis	.05	.02
259	Pete O'Brien	.05	.02
260	Erik Hanson	.05	.02
261	Bret Boone	.25	.11
262	Roger Salkeld	.05	.02
263	Dave Burba	.05	.02
264	Kerry Woodson	.05	.02
265	Julio Franco	.05	.02
266	Dan Peltier	.05	.02
267	Jeff Russell	.05	.02
268	Steve Buechele	.05	.02
269	Donald Harris	.05	.02
270	Robb Nen	.20	.09
271	Rich Gossage	.10	.05
272	Ivan Rodriguez	2.00	.90
273	Jeff Huson	.05	.02
274	Kevin Brown	.15	.07
275	Dan Smith	.05	.02
276	Gary Pettis	.05	.02
277	Jack Daugherty	.05	.02
278	Mike Jeffcoat	.05	.02
279	Brad Arnsberg	.05	.02
280	Nolan Ryan	.75	.35
281	Eric McCray	.05	.02
282	Scott Chiamparino	.05	.02
283	Ruben Sierra	.05	.02
284	Geno Petralli	.05	.02
285	Monty Fariss	.05	.02
286	Rafael Palmeiro	.20	.09
287	Bobby Witt	.05	.02
288	Dean Palmer UER (Photo is Dan Peltier)	.10	.05
289	Tony Scruggs	.05	.02
290	Kenny Rogers	.05	.02
291	Bret Saberhagen	.10	.05
292	Brian McRae	.20	.09
293	Storm Davis	.05	.02
294	Danny Tartabull	.05	.02
295	David Howard	.05	.02
296	Mike Boddicker	.05	.02
297	Joel Johnston	.05	.02
298	Tim Spehr	.05	.02
299	Hector Wagner	.05	.02
300	George Brett	.40	.18
301	Mike Macfarlane	.05	.02
302	Kirk Gibson	.10	.05
303	Harvey Pulliam	.05	.02
304	Jim Eisenreich	.05	.02
305	Kevin Seitzer	.05	.02
306	Mark Davis	.05	.02
307	Kurt Stillwell	.05	.02
308	Jeff Montgomery	.10	.05
309	Kevin Appier	.10	.05
310	Bob Hamelin	.05	.02
311	Tom Gordon	.10	.05
312	Kerwin Moore	.05	.02
313	Hugh Walker	.05	.02
314	Terry Shumpert	.05	.02
315	Warren Cromartie	.05	.02
316	Gary Thurman	.05	.02
317	Steve Bedrosian	.05	.02
318	Danny Gladden	.05	.02
319	Jack Morris	.10	.05
320	Kirby Puckett	.30	.14
321	Kent Hrbek	.10	.05
322	Kevin Tapani	.05	.02
323	Denny Neagle	.50	.23
324	Rich Garces	.05	.02
325	Larry Casian	.05	.02
326	Shane Mack	.05	.02
327	Allan Anderson	.05	.02
328	Junior Ortiz	.05	.02
329	Paul Abbott	.05	.02
330	Chuck Knoblauch	.25	.11
331	Chili Davis	.10	.05
332	Todd Ritchie	.05	.02
333	Brian Harper	.05	.02
334	Rick Aguilera	.10	.05
335	Scott Erickson	.10	.05
336	Pedro Munoz	.05	.02
337	Scott Leius	.05	.02
338	Greg Gagne	.05	.02
339	Mike Pagliarulo	.05	.02
340	Terry Leach	.05	.02
341	Willie Banks	.05	.02
342	Bobby Thigpen	.05	.02
343	Roberto Hernandez	.20	.09
344	Melido Perez	.05	.02
345	Carlton Fisk	.20	.09
346	Norberto Martin	.05	.02
347	Johnny Ruffin	.05	.02
348	Jeff Carter	.05	.02
349	Lance Johnson	.05	.02
350	Sammy Sosa	1.00	.45
351	Alex Fernandez	.10	.05
352	Jack McDowell	.05	.02
353	Bob Wickman	.05	.02
354	Wilson Alvarez	.20	.09
355	Charlie Hough	.10	.05
356	Ozzie Guillen	.05	.02
357	Cory Snyder	.05	.02
358	Robin Ventura	.20	.09
359	Scott Fletcher	.05	.02
360	Cesar Bernhardt	.05	.02
361	Dan Pasqua	.05	.02
362	Tim Raines	.10	.05
363	Brian Drahman	.05	.02
364	Wayne Edwards	.05	.02
365	Scott Radinsky	.05	.02
366	Frank Thomas	1.00	.45
367	Cecil Fielder SLUG	.05	.02
368	Julio Franco SLUG	.05	.02
369	Kelly Gruber SLUG	.05	.02
370	Alan Trammell SLUG	.10	.05
371	Rickey Henderson SLUG	.10	.05
372	Jose Canseco SLUG	.10	.05
373	Ellis Burks SLUG	.05	.02
374	Lance Parrish SLUG	.05	.02
375	Dave Parker SLUG	.05	.02
376	Eddie Murray SLUG	.10	.05
377	Ryne Sandberg SLUG	.20	.09
378	Matt Williams SLUG	.10	.05
379	Barry Larkin SLUG	.10	.05
380	Barry Bonds SLUG	.20	.09
381	Bobby Bonilla SLUG	.05	.02
382	Darryl Strawberry SLUG	.05	.02
383	Benny Santiago SLUG	.05	.02
384	Don Robinson SLUG	.05	.02
385	Paul Coleman	.05	.02
386	Milt Thompson	.05	.02
387	Lee Smith	.10	.05
388	Ray Lankford	.20	.09
389	Tom Pagnozzi	.05	.02
390	Ken Hill	.10	.05
391	Jamie Moyer	.05	.02
392	Greg Carmona	.05	.02
393	John Ericks	.05	.02
394	Bob Tewksbury	.05	.02
395	Jose Oquendo	.05	.02
396	Rheal Cormier	.05	.02
397	Mike Milchin	.05	.02
398	Ozzie Smith	.25	.11
399	Aaron Holbert	.05	.02
400	Jose DeLeon	.05	.02
401	Felix Jose	.05	.02
402	Juan Agosto	.05	.02
403	Pedro Guerrero	.05	.02
404	Todd Zeile	.10	.05
405	Gerald Perry	.05	.02
406	Donovan Osborne UER (Card number is 410)	.10	.05
407	Bryn Smith	.05	.02
408	Bernard Gilkey	.10	.05
409	Rex Hudler	.05	.02
410	Thomson/Branca Shot (Bobby Thomson, Ralph Branca) (See also 406)	.20	.09
411	Lance Dickson	.05	.02
412	Danny Jackson	.05	.02
413	Jerome Walton	.05	.02
414	Sean Cheetham	.05	.02
415	Joe Girardi	.10	.05
416	Ryne Sandberg	.25	.11
417	Mike Harkey	.05	.02
418	George Bell	.05	.02
419	Rick Wilkins	.05	.02
420	Earl Cunningham	.05	.02
421	Heathcliff Slocumb	.20	.09
422	Mike Bielecki	.05	.02
423	Jessie Hollins	.05	.02
424	Shawon Dunston	.05	.02
425	Dave Smith	.05	.02
426	Greg Maddux	.60	.25
427	Jose Vizcaino	.05	.02
428	Luis Salazar	.05	.02
429	Andre Dawson	.20	.09
430	Rick Sutcliffe	.05	.02
431	Paul Assenmacher	.05	.02
432	Erik Pappas	.05	.02
433	Mark Grace	.20	.09
434	Dennis Martinez	.10	.05
435	Marquis Grissom	.20	.09
436	Wil Cordero	.05	.02
437	Tim Wallach	.05	.02
438	Brian Barnes	.05	.02
439	Barry Jones	.05	.02
440	Ivan Calderon	.05	.02
441	Stan Spencer	.05	.02
442	Larry Walker	.30	.14
443	Chris Haney	.05	.02
444	Hector Rivera	.05	.02
445	Delino DeShields	.10	.05
446	Andres Galarraga	.20	.09
447	Gilberto Reyes	.05	.02
448	Willie Greene	.10	.05
449	Greg Colbrunn	.05	.02
450	Rondell White	.50	.23
451	Steve Frey	.05	.02
452	Shane Andrews	.10	.05
453	Mike Fitzgerald	.05	.02
454	Spike Owen	.05	.02
455	Dave Martinez	.05	.02
456	Dennis Boyd	.05	.02
457	Eric Bullock	.05	.02
458	Reid Cornelius	.05	.02
459	Chris Nabholz	.05	.02
460	David Cone	.10	.05
461	Hubie Brooks	.05	.02
462	Sid Fernandez	.05	.02
463	Doug Simons	.05	.02
464	Howard Johnson	.05	.02
465	Chris Donnels	.05	.02
466	Anthony Young	.05	.02
467	Todd Hundley	.20	.09
468	Rick Cerone	.05	.02
469	Kevin Elster	.05	.02
470	Wally Whitehurst	.05	.02
471	Vince Coleman	.05	.02
472	Dwight Gooden	.10	.05
473	Charlie O'Brien	.05	.02
474	Jeromy Burnitz	.50	.23
475	John Franco	.10	.05
476	Daryl Boston	.05	.02
477	Frank Viola	.05	.02
478	D.J. Dozier	.05	.02

No.	Player	Mint	Nrmt
❑ 479	Kevin McReynolds	.05	.02
❑ 480	Tom Herr	.05	.02
❑ 481	Gregg Jefferies	.05	.02
❑ 482	Pete Schourek	.10	.05
❑ 483	Ron Darling	.05	.02
❑ 484	Dave Magadan	.05	.02
❑ 485	Andy Ashby	.25	.11
❑ 486	Dale Murphy	.20	.09
❑ 487	Von Hayes	.05	.02
❑ 488	Kim Batiste	.05	.02
❑ 489	Tony Longmire	.05	.02
❑ 490	Wally Backman	.05	.02
❑ 491	Jeff Jackson	.05	.02
❑ 492	Mickey Morandini	.05	.02
❑ 493	Darrel Akerfelds	.05	.02
❑ 494	Ricky Jordan	.05	.02
❑ 495	Randy Ready	.05	.02
❑ 496	Darrin Fletcher	.05	.02
❑ 497	Chuck Malone	.05	.02
❑ 498	Pat Combs	.05	.02
❑ 499	Dickie Thon	.05	.02
❑ 500	Roger McDowell	.05	.02
❑ 501	Len Dykstra	.10	.05
❑ 502	Joe Boever	.05	.02
❑ 503	John Kruk	.10	.05
❑ 504	Terry Mulholland	.05	.02
❑ 505	Wes Chamberlain	.05	.02
❑ 506	Mike Lieberthal	.20	.09
❑ 507	Darren Daulton	.10	.05
❑ 508	Charlie Hayes	.05	.02
❑ 509	John Smiley	.05	.02
❑ 510	Gary Varsho	.05	.02
❑ 511	Curt Wilkerson	.05	.02
❑ 512	Orlando Merced	.10	.05
❑ 513	Barry Bonds	.25	.11
❑ 514	Mike LaValliere	.05	.02
❑ 515	Doug Drabek	.05	.02
❑ 516	Gary Redus	.05	.02
❑ 517	William Pennyfeather	.05	.02
❑ 518	Randy Tomlin	.05	.02
❑ 519	Mike Zimmerman	.05	.02
❑ 520	Jeff King	.10	.05
❑ 521	Kurt Miller	.05	.02
❑ 522	Jay Bell	.10	.05
❑ 523	Bill Landrum	.05	.02
❑ 524	Zane Smith	.05	.02
❑ 525	Bobby Bonilla	.10	.05
❑ 526	Bob Walk	.05	.02
❑ 527	Austin Manahan	.05	.02
❑ 528	Joe Ausanio	.05	.02
❑ 529	Andy Van Slyke	.10	.05
❑ 530	Jose Lind	.05	.02
❑ 531	Carlos Garcia	.05	.02
❑ 532	Don Slaught	.05	.02
❑ 533	Gen.Colin Powell	.75	.35
❑ 534	Frank Bolick	.05	.02
❑ 535	Gary Scott	.05	.02
❑ 536	Nikco Riesgo	.05	.02
❑ 537	Reggie Sanders	.25	.11
❑ 538	Tim Howard	.05	.02
❑ 539	Ryan Bowen	.05	.02
❑ 540	Eric Anthony	.05	.02
❑ 541	Jim Deshaies	.05	.02
❑ 542	Tom Nevers	.05	.02
❑ 543	Ken Caminiti	.20	.09
❑ 544	Karl Rhodes	.05	.02
❑ 545	Xavier Hernandez	.05	.02
❑ 546	Mike Scott	.05	.02
❑ 547	Jeff Juden	.05	.02
❑ 548	Darryl Kile	.20	.09
❑ 549	Willie Ansley	.05	.02
❑ 550	Luis Gonzalez	.20	.09
❑ 551	Mike Simms	.05	.02
❑ 552	Mark Portugal	.05	.02
❑ 553	Jimmy Jones	.05	.02
❑ 554	Jim Clancy	.05	.02
❑ 555	Pete Harnisch	.05	.02
❑ 556	Craig Biggio	.20	.09
❑ 557	Eric Yelding	.05	.02
❑ 558	Dave Rohde	.05	.02
❑ 559	Casey Candaele	.05	.02
❑ 560	Curt Schilling	.20	.09
❑ 561	Steve Finley	.20	.09
❑ 562	Javier Ortiz	.05	.02
❑ 563	Andujar Cedeno	.05	.02
❑ 564	Rafael Ramirez	.05	.02
❑ 565	Kenny Lofton	1.25	.55
❑ 566	Steve Avery	.05	.02
❑ 567	Lonnie Smith	.05	.02
❑ 568	Kent Mercker	.05	.02
❑ 569	Chipper Jones	5.00	2.20
❑ 570	Terry Pendleton	.10	.05
❑ 571	Otis Nixon	.10	.05
❑ 572	Juan Berenguer	.05	.02
❑ 573	Charlie Leibrandt	.05	.02
❑ 574	David Justice	.25	.11
❑ 575	Keith Mitchell	.05	.02
❑ 576	Tom Glavine	.20	.09
❑ 577	Greg Olson	.05	.02
❑ 578	Rafael Belliard	.05	.02
❑ 579	Ben Rivera	.05	.02
❑ 580	John Smoltz	.20	.09
❑ 581	Tyler Houston	.05	.02
❑ 582	Mark Wohlers	.10	.05
❑ 583	Ron Gant	.10	.05
❑ 584	Ramon Caraballo	.05	.02
❑ 585	Sid Bream	.05	.02
❑ 586	Jeff Treadway	.05	.02
❑ 587	Javier Lopez	.75	.35
❑ 588	Deion Sanders	.10	.05
❑ 589	Mike Heath	.05	.02
❑ 590	Ryan Klesko	.60	.25
❑ 591	Bob Ojeda	.05	.02
❑ 592	Alfredo Griffin	.05	.02
❑ 593	Raul Mondesi	1.00	.45
❑ 594	Greg Smith	.05	.02
❑ 595	Orel Hershiser	.10	.05
❑ 596	Juan Samuel	.05	.02
❑ 597	Brett Butler	.10	.05
❑ 598	Gary Carter	.20	.09
❑ 599	Stan Javier	.05	.02
❑ 600	Kal Daniels	.05	.02
❑ 601	Jamie McAndrew	.05	.02
❑ 602	Mike Sharperson	.05	.02
❑ 603	Jay Howell	.05	.02
❑ 604	Eric Karros	.50	.23
❑ 605	Tim Belcher	.05	.02
❑ 606	Dan Opperman	.05	.02
❑ 607	Lenny Harris	.05	.02
❑ 608	Tom Goodwin	.10	.05
❑ 609	Darryl Strawberry	.10	.05
❑ 610	Ramon Martinez	.10	.05
❑ 611	Kevin Gross	.05	.02
❑ 612	Zakary Shinall	.05	.02
❑ 613	Mike Scioscia	.05	.02
❑ 614	Eddie Murray	.20	.09
❑ 615	Ronnie Walden	.05	.02
❑ 616	Will Clark	.20	.09
❑ 617	Adam Hyzdu	.05	.02
❑ 618	Matt Williams	.20	.09
❑ 619	Don Robinson	.05	.02
❑ 620	Jeff Brantley	.05	.02
❑ 621	Greg Litton	.05	.02
❑ 622	Steve Decker	.05	.02
❑ 623	Robby Thompson	.05	.02
❑ 624	Mark Leonard	.05	.02
❑ 625	Kevin Bass	.05	.02
❑ 626	Scott Garrelts	.05	.02
❑ 627	Jose Uribe	.05	.02
❑ 628	Eric Gunderson	.05	.02
❑ 629	Steve Hosey	.05	.02
❑ 630	Trevor Wilson	.05	.02
❑ 631	Terry Kennedy	.05	.02
❑ 632	Dave Righetti	.05	.02
❑ 633	Kelly Downs	.05	.02
❑ 634	Johnny Ard	.05	.02
❑ 635	Eric Christopherson	.05	.02
❑ 636	Kevin Mitchell	.05	.02
❑ 637	John Burkett	.05	.02
❑ 638	Kevin Rogers	.05	.02
❑ 639	Bud Black	.05	.02
❑ 640	Willie McGee	.10	.05
❑ 641	Royce Clayton	.15	.07
❑ 642	Tony Fernandez	.05	.02
❑ 643	Ricky Bones	.05	.02
❑ 644	Thomas Howard	.05	.02
❑ 645	Dave Staton	.05	.02
❑ 646	Jim Presley	.05	.02
❑ 647	Tony Gwynn	.50	.23
❑ 648	Marty Barrett	.05	.02
❑ 649	Scott Coolbaugh	.05	.02
❑ 650	Craig Lefferts	.05	.02
❑ 651	Eddie Whitson	.05	.02
❑ 652	Oscar Azocar	.05	.02
❑ 653	Wes Gardner	.05	.02
❑ 654	Bip Roberts	.05	.02
❑ 655	Robbie Beckett	.05	.02
❑ 656	Benito Santiago	.05	.02
❑ 657	Greg W.Harris	.05	.02
❑ 658	Jerald Clark	.05	.02
❑ 659	Fred McGriff	.20	.09
❑ 660	Larry Andersen	.05	.02
❑ 661	Bruce Hurst	.05	.02
❑ 662	Steve Martin UER Card said he pitched at Waterloo He's an outfielder	.05	.02
❑ 663	Rafael Valdez	.05	.02
❑ 664	Paul Faries	.05	.02
❑ 665	Andy Benes	.10	.05
❑ 666	Randy Myers	.10	.05
❑ 667	Rob Dibble	.05	.02
❑ 668	Glenn Sutko	.05	.02
❑ 669	Glenn Braggs	.05	.02
❑ 670	Billy Hatcher	.05	.02
❑ 671	Joe Oliver	.05	.02
❑ 672	Freddy Benavides	.05	.02
❑ 673	Barry Larkin	.20	.09
❑ 674	Chris Sabo	.05	.02
❑ 675	Mariano Duncan	.05	.02
❑ 676	Chris Jones	.05	.02
❑ 677	Gino Minutelli	.05	.02
❑ 678	Reggie Jefferson	.15	.07
❑ 679	Jack Armstrong	.05	.02
❑ 680	Chris Hammond	.05	.02
❑ 681	Jose Rijo	.05	.02
❑ 682	Bill Doran	.05	.02
❑ 683	Terry Lee	.05	.02
❑ 684	Tom Browning	.05	.02
❑ 685	Paul O'Neill	.10	.05
❑ 686	Eric Davis	.10	.05
❑ 687	Dan Wilson	.25	.11
❑ 688	Ted Power	.05	.02
❑ 689	Tim Layana	.05	.02
❑ 690	Norm Charlton	.05	.02
❑ 691	Hal Morris	.05	.02
❑ 692	Rickey Henderson	.20	.09
❑ 693	Sam Militello	.05	.02
❑ 694	Matt Mieske	.05	.02
❑ 695	Paul Russo	.05	.02
❑ 696	Domingo Mota	.05	.02
❑ 697	Todd Guggiana	.05	.02
❑ 698	Marc Newfield	.10	.05
❑ 699	Checklist 1-122	.05	.02
❑ 700	Checklist 123-244	.05	.02
❑ 701	Checklist 245-366	.05	.02
❑ 702	Checklist 367-471	.05	.02
❑ 703	Checklist 472-593	.05	.02
❑ 704	Checklist 594-704	.05	.02

1992 Bowman

	MINT	NRMT
COMPLETE SET (705)	300.00	135.00
COMMON CARD (1-705)	.25	.11

No.	Player	Mint	Nrmt
❑ 1	Ivan Rodriguez	3.00	1.35
❑ 2	Kirk McCaskill	.25	.11
❑ 3	Scott Livingstone	.25	.11

❑	4	Salomon Torres	.25	.11
❑	5	Carlos Hernandez	.25	.11
❑	6	Dave Hollins	.25	.11
❑	7	Scott Fletcher	.25	.11
❑	8	Jorge Fabregas	.25	.11
❑	9	Andujar Cedeno	.25	.11
❑	10	Howard Johnson	.25	.11
❑	11	Trevor Hoffman	3.00	1.35
❑	12	Roberto Kelly	.25	.11
❑	13	Gregg Jefferies	.25	.11
❑	14	Marquis Grissom	.50	.23
❑	15	Mike Ignasiak	.25	.11
❑	16	Jack Morris	.50	.23
❑	17	William Pennyfeather	.25	.11
❑	18	Todd Stottlemyre	.50	.23
❑	19	Chito Martinez	.25	.11
❑	20	Roberto Alomar	1.50	.70
❑	21	Sam Militello	.25	.11
❑	22	Hector Fajardo	.25	.11
❑	23	Paul Quantrill	.25	.11
❑	24	Chuck Knoblauch	1.50	.70
❑	25	Reggie Jefferson	.50	.23
❑	26	Jeremy McGarity	.25	.11
❑	27	Jerome Walton	.25	.11
❑	28	Chipper Jones	40.00	18.00
❑	29	Brian Barber	.25	.11
❑	30	Ron Darling	.25	.11
❑	31	Roberto Petagine	.25	.11
❑	32	Chuck Finley	.50	.23
❑	33	Edgar Martinez	1.00	.45
❑	34	Napoleon Robinson	.25	.11
❑	35	Andy Van Slyke	.50	.23
❑	36	Bobby Thigpen	.25	.11
❑	37	Travis Fryman	.50	.23
❑	38	Eric Christopherson	.25	.11
❑	39	Terry Mulholland	.25	.11
❑	40	Darryl Strawberry	.50	.23
❑	41	Manny Alexander	.50	.23
❑	42	Tracy Sanders	.25	.11
❑	43	Pete Incaviglia	.25	.11
❑	44	Kim Batiste	.25	.11
❑	45	Frank Rodriguez	.50	.23
❑	46	Greg Swindell	.25	.11
❑	47	Delino DeShields	.50	.23
❑	48	John Ericks	.25	.11
❑	49	Franklin Stubbs	.25	.11
❑	50	Tony Gwynn	4.00	1.80
❑	51	Clifton Garrett	.25	.11
❑	52	Mike Gardella	.25	.11
❑	53	Scott Erickson	.50	.23
❑	54	Gary Caraballo	.25	.11
❑	55	Jose Oliva	.25	.11
❑	56	Brook Fordyce	.25	.11
❑	57	Mark Whiten	.25	.11
❑	58	Joe Slusarski	.25	.11
❑	59	J.R. Phillips	.25	.11
❑	60	Barry Bonds	2.00	.90
❑	61	Bob Milacki	.25	.11
❑	62	Keith Mitchell	.25	.11
❑	63	Angel Miranda	.25	.11
❑	64	Raul Mondesi	10.00	4.50
❑	65	Brian Koelling	.25	.11
❑	66	Brian McRae	.50	.23
❑	67	John Patterson	.25	.11
❑	68	John Wetteland	.50	.23
❑	69	Wilson Alvarez	.50	.23
❑	70	Wade Boggs	1.50	.70
❑	71	Darryl Ratliff	.25	.11
❑	72	Jeff Jackson	.25	.11
❑	73	Jeremy Hernandez	.25	.11
❑	74	Darryl Hamilton	.25	.11
❑	75	Rafael Belliard	.25	.11
❑	76	Rick Trlicek	.25	.11
❑	77	Felipe Crespo	.50	.23
❑	78	Carney Lansford	.50	.23
❑	79	Ryan Long	.25	.11
❑	80	Kirby Puckett	2.50	1.10
❑	81	Earl Cunningham	.25	.11
❑	82	Pedro Martinez	15.00	6.75
❑	83	Scott Hatteberg	.25	.11
❑	84	Juan Gonzalez UER (65 doubles vs. Tigers)	5.00	2.20
❑	85	Robert Nutting	.25	.11
❑	86	Calvin Reese	1.00	.45
❑	87	Dave Silvestri	.25	.11
❑	88	Scott Ruffcorn	.25	.11
❑	89	Rick Aguilera	.50	.23
❑	90	Cecil Fielder	.50	.23
❑	91	Kirk Dressendorfer	.25	.11
❑	92	Jerry DiPoto	.25	.11
❑	93	Mike Felder	.25	.11
❑	94	Craig Paquette	.25	.11
❑	95	Elvin Paulino	.25	.11
❑	96	Donovan Osborne	.25	.11
❑	97	Hubie Brooks	.25	.11
❑	98	Derek Lowe	1.00	.45
❑	99	David Zancanaro	.25	.11
❑	100	Ken Griffey Jr.	10.00	4.50
❑	101	Todd Hundley	.50	.23
❑	102	Mike Trombley	.25	.11
❑	103	Ricky Gutierrez	.25	.11
❑	104	Braulio Castillo	.25	.11
❑	105	Craig Lefferts	.25	.11
❑	106	Rick Sutcliffe	.25	.11
❑	107	Dean Palmer	.50	.23
❑	108	Henry Rodriguez	1.50	.70
❑	109	Mark Clark	.25	.11
❑	110	Kenny Lofton	6.00	2.70
❑	111	Mark Carreon	.25	.11
❑	112	J.T. Bruett	.25	.11
❑	113	Gerald Williams	.25	.11
❑	114	Frank Thomas	5.00	2.20
❑	115	Kevin Reimer	.25	.11
❑	116	Sammy Sosa	4.00	1.80
❑	117	Mickey Tettleton	.25	.11
❑	118	Reggie Sanders	.25	.11
❑	119	Trevor Wilson	.25	.11
❑	120	Cliff Brantley	.25	.11
❑	121	Spike Owen	.25	.11
❑	122	Jeff Montgomery	.50	.23
❑	123	Alex Sutherland	.25	.11
❑	124	Brien Taylor	.25	.11
❑	125	Brian Williams	.25	.11
❑	126	Kevin Seitzer	.25	.11
❑	127	Carlos Delgado	12.00	5.50
❑	128	Gary Scott	.25	.11
❑	129	Scott Cooper	.25	.11
❑	130	Domingo Jean	.25	.11
❑	131	Pat Mahomes	.25	.11
❑	132	Mike Boddicker	.25	.11
❑	133	Roberto Hernandez	1.50	.70
❑	134	Dave Valle	.25	.11
❑	135	Kurt Stillwell	.25	.11
❑	136	Brad Pennington	.25	.11
❑	137	Jermaine Swinton	.25	.11
❑	138	Ryan Hawblitzel	.25	.11
❑	139	Tito Navarro	.25	.11
❑	140	Sandy Alomar	.50	.23
❑	141	Todd Benzinger	.25	.11
❑	142	Danny Jackson	.25	.11
❑	143	Melvin Nieves	1.50	.70
❑	144	Jim Campanis	.25	.11
❑	145	Luis Gonzalez	.25	.11
❑	146	Dave Doorneweerd	.25	.11
❑	147	Charlie Hayes	.25	.11
❑	148	Greg Maddux	5.00	2.20
❑	149	Brian Harper	.25	.11
❑	150	Brent Miller	.25	.11
❑	151	Shawn Estes	3.00	1.35
❑	152	Mike Williams	.25	.11
❑	153	Charlie Hough	.50	.23
❑	154	Randy Myers	.50	.23
❑	155	Kevin Young	1.50	.70
❑	156	Rick Wilkins	.25	.11
❑	157	Terry Shumpert	.25	.11
❑	158	Steve Karsay	.25	.11
❑	159	Gary DiSarcina	.25	.11
❑	160	Deion Sanders	.50	.23
❑	161	Tom Browning	.25	.11
❑	162	Dickie Thon	.25	.11
❑	163	Luis Mercedes	.25	.11
❑	164	Riccardo Ingram	.25	.11
❑	165	Tavo Alvarez	.25	.11
❑	166	Rickey Henderson	1.50	.70
❑	167	Jaime Navarro	.25	.11
❑	168	Billy Ashley	.25	.11
❑	169	Phil Dauphin	.25	.11
❑	170	Ivan Cruz	.25	.11
❑	171	Harold Baines	.50	.23
❑	172	Bryan Harvey	.25	.11
❑	173	Alex Cole	.25	.11
❑	174	Curtis Shaw	.25	.11
❑	175	Matt Williams	1.00	.45
❑	176	Felix Jose	.25	.11
❑	177	Sam Horn	.25	.11
❑	178	Randy Johnson	1.50	.70
❑	179	Ivan Calderon	.25	.11
❑	180	Steve Avery	.25	.11
❑	181	William Suero	.25	.11
❑	182	Bill Swift	.25	.11
❑	183	Howard Battle	.25	.11
❑	184	Ruben Amaro	.25	.11
❑	185	Jim Abbott	.50	.23
❑	186	Mike Fitzgerald	.25	.11
❑	187	Bruce Hurst	.25	.11
❑	188	Jeff Juden	.25	.11
❑	189	Jeromy Burnitz	4.00	1.80
❑	190	Dave Burba	.25	.11
❑	191	Kevin Brown	1.00	.45
❑	192	Patrick Lennon	.25	.11
❑	193	Jeff McNeely	.25	.11
❑	194	Wil Cordero	.25	.11
❑	195	Chili Davis	.50	.23
❑	196	Milt Cuyler	.25	.11
❑	197	Von Hayes	.25	.11
❑	198	Todd Revenig	.25	.11
❑	199	Joel Johnston	.25	.11
❑	200	Jeff Bagwell	4.00	1.80
❑	201	Alex Fernandez	.50	.23
❑	202	Todd Jones	1.00	.45
❑	203	Charles Nagy	.50	.23
❑	204	Tim Raines	.50	.23
❑	205	Kevin Maas	.25	.11
❑	206	Julio Franco	.25	.11
❑	207	Randy Velarde	.25	.11
❑	208	Lance Johnson	.25	.11
❑	209	Scott Leius	.25	.11
❑	210	Derek Lee	.25	.11
❑	211	Joe Sondrini	.25	.11
❑	212	Royce Clayton	.25	.11
❑	213	Chris George	.25	.11
❑	214	Gary Sheffield	1.50	.70
❑	215	Mark Gubicza	.25	.11
❑	216	Mike Moore	.25	.11
❑	217	Rick Huisman	.25	.11
❑	218	Jeff Russell	.25	.11
❑	219	D.J. Dozier	.25	.11
❑	220	Dave Martinez	.25	.11
❑	221	Alan Newman	.25	.11
❑	222	Nolan Ryan	6.00	2.70
❑	223	Teddy Higuera	.25	.11
❑	224	Damon Buford	.25	.11
❑	225	Ruben Sierra	.25	.11
❑	226	Tom Nevers	.25	.11
❑	227	Tommy Greene	.25	.11
❑	228	Nigel Wilson	.25	.11
❑	229	John DeSilva	.25	.11
❑	230	Bobby Witt	.25	.11
❑	231	Greg Cadaret	.25	.11
❑	232	John Vander Wal	.25	.11
❑	233	Jack Clark	.50	.23
❑	234	Bill Doran	.25	.11
❑	235	Bobby Bonilla	.50	.23
❑	236	Steve Olin	.25	.11
❑	237	Derek Bell	1.50	.70
❑	238	David Cone	.50	.23
❑	239	Victor Cole	.25	.11
❑	240	Rod Bolton	.25	.11
❑	241	Tom Pagnozzi	.25	.11
❑	242	Rob Dibble	.25	.11
❑	243	Michael Carter	.25	.11
❑	244	Don Peters	.25	.11
❑	245	Mike LaValliere	.25	.11
❑	246	Joe Perona	.25	.11
❑	247	Mitch Williams	.25	.11
❑	248	Jay Buhner	1.00	.45
❑	249	Andy Benes	.50	.23
❑	250	Alex Ochoa	1.00	.45
❑	251	Greg Blosser	.25	.11
❑	252	Jack Armstrong	.25	.11
❑	253	Juan Samuel	.25	.11
❑	254	Terry Pendleton	.25	.11
❑	255	Ramon Martinez	.25	.11
❑	256	Rico Brogna	.50	.23
❑	257	John Smiley	.25	.11

❑ 258 Carl Everett 1.00 .45
❑ 259 Tim Salmon 6.00 2.70
❑ 260 Will Clark 1.50 .70
❑ 261 Ugueth Urbina 1.00 .45
❑ 262 Jason Wood .25 .11
❑ 263 Dave Magadan .25 .11
❑ 264 Dante Bichette 1.00 .45
❑ 265 Jose DeLeon .25 .11
❑ 266 Mike Neill .25 .11
❑ 267 Paul O'Neill .50 .23
❑ 268 Anthony Young .25 .11
❑ 269 Greg W. Harris .25 .11
❑ 270 Todd Van Poppel .25 .11
❑ 271 Pedro Castellano .25 .11
❑ 272 Tony Phillips .25 .11
❑ 273 Mike Gallego .25 .11
❑ 274 Steve Cooke .25 .11
❑ 275 Robin Ventura .50 .23
❑ 276 Kevin Mitchell .50 .23
❑ 277 Doug Linton .25 .11
❑ 278 Robert Eenhoorn .25 .11
❑ 279 Gabe White .25 .11
❑ 280 Dave Stewart .25 .11
❑ 281 Mo Sanford .25 .11
❑ 282 Greg Perschke .25 .11
❑ 283 Kevin Flora .25 .11
❑ 284 Jeff Williams .25 .11
❑ 285 Keith Miller .25 .11
❑ 286 Andy Ashby .50 .23
❑ 287 Doug Dascenzo .25 .11
❑ 288 Eric Karros 2.00 .90
❑ 289 Glenn Murray .25 .11
❑ 290 Troy Percival 2.00 .90
❑ 291 Orlando Merced .25 .11
❑ 292 Peter Hoy .25 .11
❑ 293 Tony Fernandez .25 .11
❑ 294 Juan Guzman .25 .11
❑ 295 Jesse Barfield .25 .11
❑ 296 Sid Fernandez .25 .11
❑ 297 Scott Cepicky .25 .11
❑ 298 Garret Anderson 4.00 1.80
❑ 299 Cal Eldred .25 .11
❑ 300 Ryne Sandberg 2.00 .90
❑ 301 Jim Gantner .25 .11
❑ 302 Mariano Rivera 5.00 2.20
❑ 303 Ron Lockett .25 .11
❑ 304 Jose Offerman .25 .11
❑ 305 Denny Martinez .50 .23
❑ 306 Luis Ortiz .25 .11
❑ 307 David Howard .25 .11
❑ 308 Russ Springer .25 .11
❑ 309 Chris Howard .25 .11
❑ 310 Kyle Abbott .25 .11
❑ 311 Aaron Sele 3.00 1.35
❑ 312 David Justice 1.50 .70
❑ 313 Pete O'Brien .25 .11
❑ 314 Greg Hansell .25 .11
❑ 315 Dave Winfield 1.50 .70
❑ 316 Lance Dickson .25 .11
❑ 317 Eric King .25 .11
❑ 318 Vaughn Eshelman .25 .11
❑ 319 Tim Belcher .25 .11
❑ 320 Andres Galarraga 1.50 .70
❑ 321 Scott Bullett .25 .11
❑ 322 Doug Strange .25 .11
❑ 323 Jerald Clark .25 .11
❑ 324 Dave Righetti .25 .11
❑ 325 Greg Hibbard .25 .11
❑ 326 Eric Hillman .25 .11
❑ 327 Shane Reynolds 3.00 1.35
❑ 328 Chris Hammond .25 .11
❑ 329 Albert Belle 2.00 .90
❑ 330 Rich Becker 1.50 .70
❑ 331 Eddie Williams .25 .11
❑ 332 Donald Harris .25 .11
❑ 333 Dave Smith .25 .11
❑ 334 Steve Fireovid .25 .11
❑ 335 Steve Buechele .25 .11
❑ 336 Mike Schooler .25 .11
❑ 337 Kevin McReynolds .25 .11
❑ 338 Hensley Meulens .25 .11
❑ 339 Benji Gil .25 .11
❑ 340 Don Mattingly 2.50 1.10
❑ 341 Alvin Davis .25 .11
❑ 342 Alan Mills .25 .11
❑ 343 Kelly Downs .25 .11
❑ 344 Leo Gomez .25 .11
❑ 345 Tarrik Brock .25 .11
❑ 346 Ryan Turner .25 .11
❑ 347 John Smoltz 1.00 .45
❑ 348 Bill Sampen .25 .11
❑ 349 Paul Byrd .25 .11
❑ 350 Mike Bordick .25 .11
❑ 351 Jose Lind .25 .11
❑ 352 David Wells .50 .23
❑ 353 Barry Larkin 1.00 .45
❑ 354 Bruce Ruffin .25 .11
❑ 355 Luis Rivera .25 .11
❑ 356 Sid Bream .25 .11
❑ 357 Julian Vasquez .25 .11
❑ 358 Jason Bere .50 .23
❑ 359 Ben McDonald .25 .11
❑ 360 Scott Stahoviak .25 .11
❑ 361 Kirt Manwaring .25 .11
❑ 362 Jeff Johnson .25 .11
❑ 363 Rob Deer .25 .11
❑ 364 Tony Pena .25 .11
❑ 365 Melido Perez .25 .11
❑ 366 Clay Parker .25 .11
❑ 367 Dale Sveum .25 .11
❑ 368 Mike Scioscia .25 .11
❑ 369 Roger Salkeld .25 .11
❑ 370 Mike Stanley .25 .11
❑ 371 Jack McDowell .25 .11
❑ 372 Tim Wallach .25 .11
❑ 373 Billy Ripken .25 .11
❑ 374 Mike Christopher .25 .11
❑ 375 Paul Molitor 1.50 .70
❑ 376 Dave Stieb .25 .11
❑ 377 Pedro Guerrero .25 .11
❑ 378 Russ Swan .25 .11
❑ 379 Bob Ojeda .25 .11
❑ 380 Donn Pall .25 .11
❑ 381 Eddie Zosky .25 .11
❑ 382 Darnell Coles .25 .11
❑ 383 Tom Smith .25 .11
❑ 384 Mark McGwire 8.00 3.60
❑ 385 Gary Carter 1.50 .70
❑ 386 Rich Amaral .25 .11
❑ 387 Alan Embree .25 .11
❑ 388 Jonathan Hurst .25 .11
❑ 389 Bobby Jones 1.00 .45
❑ 390 Rico Rossy .25 .11
❑ 391 Dan Smith .25 .11
❑ 392 Terry Steinbach .50 .23
❑ 393 Jon Farrell .25 .11
❑ 394 Dave Anderson .25 .11
❑ 395 Benny Santiago .25 .11
❑ 396 Mark Wohlers .50 .23
❑ 397 Mo Vaughn 2.50 1.10
❑ 398 Randy Kramer .25 .11
❑ 399 John Jaha .50 .23
❑ 400 Cal Ripken 6.00 2.70
❑ 401 Ryan Bowen .25 .11
❑ 402 Tim McIntosh .25 .11
❑ 403 Bernard Gilkey .50 .23
❑ 404 Junior Felix .25 .11
❑ 405 Cris Colon .25 .11
❑ 406 Marc Newfield .25 .11
❑ 407 Bernie Williams 1.50 .70
❑ 408 Jay Howell .25 .11
❑ 409 Zane Smith .25 .11
❑ 410 Jeff Shaw .25 .11
❑ 411 Kerry Woodson .25 .11
❑ 412 Wes Chamberlain .25 .11
❑ 413 Dave Mlicki .25 .11
❑ 414 Benny Distefano .25 .11
❑ 415 Kevin Rogers .25 .11
❑ 416 Tim Naehring .50 .23
❑ 417 Clemente Nunez .50 .23
❑ 418 Luis Sojo .25 .11
❑ 419 Kevin Ritz .25 .11
❑ 420 Omar Olivares .25 .11
❑ 421 Manuel Lee .25 .11
❑ 422 Julio Valera .25 .11
❑ 423 Omar Vizquel .50 .23
❑ 424 Darren Burton .25 .11
❑ 425 Mel Hall .25 .11
❑ 426 Dennis Powell .25 .11
❑ 427 Lee Stevens .25 .11
❑ 428 Glenn Davis .25 .11
❑ 429 Willie Greene 1.00 .45
❑ 430 Kevin Wickander .25 .11
❑ 431 Dennis Eckersley .50 .23
❑ 432 Joe Orsulak .25 .11
❑ 433 Eddie Murray 1.50 .70
❑ 434 Matt Stairs 2.00 .90
❑ 435 Wally Joyner .50 .23
❑ 436 Rondell White 5.00 2.20
❑ 437 Rob Maurer .25 .11
❑ 438 Joe Redfield .25 .11
❑ 439 Mark Lewis .25 .11
❑ 440 Darren Daulton .50 .23
❑ 441 Mike Henneman .25 .11
❑ 442 John Cangelosi .25 .11
❑ 443 Vince Moore .25 .11
❑ 444 John Wehner .25 .11
❑ 445 Kent Hrbek .50 .23
❑ 446 Mark McLemore .25 .11
❑ 447 Bill Wegman .25 .11
❑ 448 Robby Thompson .25 .11
❑ 449 Mark Anthony .25 .11
❑ 450 Archi Cianfrocco .25 .11
❑ 451 Johnny Ruffin .25 .11
❑ 452 Javier Lopez 8.00 3.60
❑ 453 Greg Gohr .25 .11
❑ 454 Tim Scott .25 .11
❑ 455 Stan Belinda .25 .11
❑ 456 Darrin Jackson .25 .11
❑ 457 Chris Gardner .25 .11
❑ 458 Esteban Beltre .25 .11
❑ 459 Phil Plantier .25 .11
❑ 460 Jim Thome 15.00 6.75
❑ 461 Mike Piazza 60.00 27.00
❑ 462 Matt Sinatro .25 .11
❑ 463 Scott Servais .25 .11
❑ 464 Brian Jordan 5.00 2.20
❑ 465 Doug Drabek .25 .11
❑ 466 Carl Willis .25 .11
❑ 467 Bret Barberie .25 .11
❑ 468 Hal Morris .25 .11
❑ 469 Steve Sax .25 .11
❑ 470 Jerry Willard .25 .11
❑ 471 Dan Wilson .50 .23
❑ 472 Chris Hoiles .25 .11
❑ 473 Rheal Cormier .25 .11
❑ 474 John Morris .25 .11
❑ 475 Jeff Reardon .50 .23
❑ 476 Mark Leiter .25 .11
❑ 477 Tom Gordon .50 .23
❑ 478 Kent Bottenfield .25 .11
❑ 479 Gene Larkin .25 .11
❑ 480 Dwight Gooden .50 .23
❑ 481 B.J. Surhoff .50 .23
❑ 482 Andy Stankiewicz .25 .11
❑ 483 Tino Martinez 1.50 .70
❑ 484 Craig Biggio 1.50 .70
❑ 485 Denny Neagle 2.50 1.10
❑ 486 Rusty Meacham .25 .11
❑ 487 Kal Daniels .25 .11
❑ 488 Dave Henderson .25 .11
❑ 489 Tim Costo .25 .11
❑ 490 Doug Davis .25 .11
❑ 491 Frank Viola .25 .11
❑ 492 Cory Snyder .25 .11
❑ 493 Chris Martin .25 .11
❑ 494 Dion James .25 .11
❑ 495 Randy Tomlin .25 .11
❑ 496 Greg Vaughn 1.00 .45
❑ 497 Dennis Cook .25 .11
❑ 498 Rosario Rodriguez .25 .11
❑ 499 Dave Staton .25 .11
❑ 500 George Brett 3.00 1.35
❑ 501 Brian Barnes .25 .11
❑ 502 Butch Henry .25 .11
❑ 503 Harold Reynolds .25 .11
❑ 504 David Nied .25 .11
❑ 505 Lee Smith .50 .23
❑ 506 Steve Chitren .25 .11
❑ 507 Ken Hill .25 .11
❑ 508 Robbie Beckett .25 .11
❑ 509 Troy Afenir .25 .11
❑ 510 Kelly Gruber .25 .11
❑ 511 Bret Boone .50 .23
❑ 512 Jeff Branson .25 .11

❑ 513	Mike Jackson	.50	.23
❑ 514	Pete Harnisch	.25	.11
❑ 515	Chad Kreuter	.25	.11
❑ 516	Joe Vitko	.25	.11
❑ 517	Orel Hershiser	.50	.23
❑ 518	John Doherty	.25	.11
❑ 519	Jay Bell	.50	.23
❑ 520	Mark Langston	.25	.11
❑ 521	Dann Howitt	.25	.11
❑ 522	Bobby Reed	.25	.11
❑ 523	Roberto Munoz	.25	.11
❑ 524	Todd Ritchie	.25	.11
❑ 525	Bip Roberts	.25	.11
❑ 526	Pat Listach	.25	.11
❑ 527	Scott Brosius	4.00	1.80
❑ 528	John Roper	.25	.11
❑ 529	Phil Hiatt	.25	.11
❑ 530	Denny Walling	.25	.11
❑ 531	Carlos Baerga	.25	.11
❑ 532	Manny Ramirez	35.00	16.00
❑ 533	Pat Clements UER (Mistakenly numbered 553)	.25	.11
❑ 534	Ron Gant	.50	.23
❑ 535	Pat Kelly	.25	.11
❑ 536	Billy Spiers	.25	.11
❑ 537	Darren Reed	.25	.11
❑ 538	Ken Caminiti	1.00	.45
❑ 539	Butch Huskey	2.00	.90
❑ 540	Matt Nokes	.25	.11
❑ 541	John Kruk	.50	.23
❑ 542	John Jaha FOIL	.50	.23
❑ 543	Justin Thompson	3.00	1.35
❑ 544	Steve Hosey	.25	.11
❑ 545	Joe Kmak	.25	.11
❑ 546	John Franco	.50	.23
❑ 547	Devon White	.25	.11
❑ 548	Elston Hansen FOIL	.25	.11
❑ 549	Ryan Klesko	6.00	2.70
❑ 550	Danny Tartabull	.25	.11
❑ 551	Frank Thomas FOIL	5.00	2.20
❑ 552	Kevin Tapani	.25	.11
❑ 553	Willie Banks (See also 533)	.25	.11
❑ 554	B.J. Wallace FOIL	.50	.23
❑ 555	Orlando Miller	.25	.11
❑ 556	Mark Smith	.25	.11
❑ 557	Tim Wallach FOIL	.25	.11
❑ 558	Bill Gullickson	.25	.11
❑ 559	Derek Bell FOIL	.50	.23
❑ 560	Joe Randa FOIL	.50	.23
❑ 561	Frank Seminara	.25	.11
❑ 562	Mark Gardner	.25	.11
❑ 563	Rick Greene FOIL	.25	.11
❑ 564	Gary Gaetti	.25	.11
❑ 565	Ozzie Guillen	.25	.11
❑ 566	Charles Nagy FOIL	.50	.23
❑ 567	Mike Milchin	.25	.11
❑ 568	Ben Shelton	.25	.11
❑ 569	Chris Roberts FOIL	.25	.11
❑ 570	Ellis Burks	.50	.23
❑ 571	Scott Scudder	.25	.11
❑ 572	Jim Abbott FOIL	.25	.11
❑ 573	Joe Carter	.50	.23
❑ 574	Steve Finley	.50	.23
❑ 575	Jim Olander FOIL	.25	.11
❑ 576	Carlos Garcia	.25	.11
❑ 577	Gregg Olson	.25	.11
❑ 578	Greg Swindell FOIL	.25	.11
❑ 579	Matt Williams FOIL	1.00	.45
❑ 580	Mark Grace	1.00	.45
❑ 581	Howard House FOIL	.25	.11
❑ 582	Luis Polonia	.25	.11
❑ 583	Erik Hanson	.25	.11
❑ 584	Salomon Torres FOIL	.25	.11
❑ 585	Carlton Fisk	1.50	.70
❑ 586	Bret Saberhagen	.50	.23
❑ 587	Chad McConnell FOIL	.50	.23
❑ 588	Jimmy Key	.50	.23
❑ 589	Mike Macfarlane	.25	.11
❑ 590	Barry Bonds FOIL	2.00	.90
❑ 591	Jamie McAndrew	.25	.11
❑ 592	Shane Mack	.25	.11
❑ 593	Kerwin Moore	.25	.11
❑ 594	Joe Oliver	.25	.11
❑ 595	Chris Sabo	.25	.11
❑ 596	Alex Gonzalez	1.50	.70
❑ 597	Brett Butler	.50	.23
❑ 598	Mark Hutton	.25	.11
❑ 599	Andy Benes FOIL	.50	.23
❑ 600	Jose Canseco	1.50	.70
❑ 601	Darryl Kile	.50	.23
❑ 602	Matt Stairs FOIL	1.50	.70
❑ 603	Robert Butler FOIL	.25	.11
❑ 604	Willie McGee	.50	.23
❑ 605	Jack McDowell FOIL	.25	.11
❑ 606	Tom Candiotti	.25	.11
❑ 607	Ed Martel	.25	.11
❑ 608	Matt Mieske FOIL	.25	.11
❑ 609	Darrin Fletcher	.25	.11
❑ 610	Rafael Palmeiro	1.00	.45
❑ 611	Bill Swift FOIL	.25	.11
❑ 612	Mike Mussina	2.50	1.10
❑ 613	Vince Coleman	.25	.11
❑ 614	Scott Cepicky FOIL UER (Bats: LEFLT)	.25	.11
❑ 615	Mike Greenwell	.25	.11
❑ 616	Kevin McGehee	.25	.11
❑ 617	Jeffrey Hammonds FOIL	1.00	.45
❑ 618	Scott Taylor	.25	.11
❑ 619	Dave Otto	.25	.11
❑ 620	Mark McGwire FOIL	8.00	3.60
❑ 621	Kevin Tatar	.25	.11
❑ 622	Steve Farr	.25	.11
❑ 623	Ryan Klesko FOIL	1.50	.70
❑ 624	Dave Fleming	.25	.11
❑ 625	Andre Dawson	1.00	.45
❑ 626	Tino Martinez FOIL	1.50	.70
❑ 627	Chad Curtis	1.50	.70
❑ 628	Mickey Morandini	.25	.11
❑ 629	Gregg Olson FOIL	.25	.11
❑ 630	Lou Whitaker	.50	.23
❑ 631	Arthur Rhodes	.25	.11
❑ 632	Brandon Wilson	.25	.11
❑ 633	Lance Jennings	.25	.11
❑ 634	Allen Watson	.25	.11
❑ 635	Len Dykstra	.50	.23
❑ 636	Joe Girardi	.50	.23
❑ 637	Kiki Hernandez FOIL	.25	.11
❑ 638	Mike Hampton	2.00	.90
❑ 639	Al Osuna	.25	.11
❑ 640	Kevin Appier	.50	.23
❑ 641	Rick Helling FOIL	3.00	1.35
❑ 642	Jody Reed	.25	.11
❑ 643	Ray Lankford	1.50	.70
❑ 644	John Olerud	.50	.23
❑ 645	Paul Molitor FOIL	1.50	.70
❑ 646	Pat Borders	.25	.11
❑ 647	Mike Morgan	.25	.11
❑ 648	Larry Walker	1.50	.70
❑ 649	Pedro Castellano FOIL	.25	.11
❑ 650	Fred McGriff	1.00	.45
❑ 651	Walt Weiss	.25	.11
❑ 652	Calvin Murray FOIL	.25	.11
❑ 653	Dave Nilsson	.50	.23
❑ 654	Greg Pirkl	.25	.11
❑ 655	Robin Ventura FOIL	.50	.23
❑ 656	Mark Portugal	.25	.11
❑ 657	Roger McDowell	.25	.11
❑ 658	Rick Hirtensteiner FOIL	.25	.11
❑ 659	Glenallen Hill	.25	.11
❑ 660	Greg Gagne	.25	.11
❑ 661	Charles Johnson FOIL	5.00	2.20
❑ 662	Brian Hunter	.25	.11
❑ 663	Mark Lemke	.25	.11
❑ 664	Tim Belcher FOIL	.25	.11
❑ 665	Rich DeLucia	.25	.11
❑ 666	Bob Walk	.25	.11
❑ 667	Joe Carter FOIL	.50	.23
❑ 668	Jose Guzman	.25	.11
❑ 669	Otis Nixon	.50	.23
❑ 670	Phil Nevin FOIL	.25	.11
❑ 671	Eric Davis	.50	.23
❑ 672	Damion Easley	3.00	1.35
❑ 673	Will Clark FOIL	1.50	.70
❑ 674	Mark Kiefer	.25	.11
❑ 675	Ozzie Smith	2.00	.90
❑ 676	Manny Ramirez FOIL	6.00	2.70
❑ 677	Gregg Olson	.25	.11
❑ 678	Cliff Floyd	4.00	1.80
❑ 679	Duane Singleton	.25	.11
❑ 680	Jose Rijo	.25	.11
❑ 681	Willie Randolph	.50	.23
❑ 682	Michael Tucker FOIL	3.00	1.35
❑ 683	Darren Lewis	.25	.11
❑ 684	Dale Murphy	1.50	.70
❑ 685	Mike Pagliarulo	.25	.11
❑ 686	Paul Miller	.25	.11
❑ 687	Mike Robertson	.25	.11
❑ 688	Mike Devereaux	.25	.11
❑ 689	Pedro Astacio	.25	.11
❑ 690	Alan Trammell	1.00	.45
❑ 691	Roger Clemens	3.00	1.35
❑ 692	Bud Black	.25	.11
❑ 693	Turk Wendell	.50	.23
❑ 694	Barry Larkin FOIL	1.00	.45
❑ 695	Todd Zeile	.25	.11
❑ 696	Pat Hentgen	2.00	.90
❑ 697	Eddie Taubensee	.50	.23
❑ 698	Guillermo Velasquez	.25	.11
❑ 699	Tom Glavine	1.00	.45
❑ 700	Robin Yount	1.50	.70
❑ 701	Checklist 1-141	.25	.11
❑ 702	Checklist 142-282	.25	.11
❑ 703	Checklist 283-423	.25	.11
❑ 704	Checklist 424-564	.25	.11
❑ 705	Checklist 565-705	.25	.11

1993 Bowman

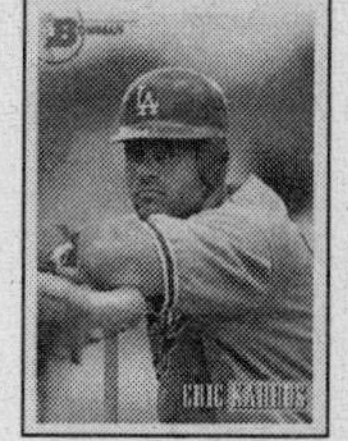

	MINT	NRMT
COMPLETE SET (708)	70.00	32.00
COMMON CARD (1-708)	.15	.07

	Player	MINT	NRMT
❑ 1	Glenn Davis	.15	.07
❑ 2	Hector Roa	.15	.07
❑ 3	Ken Ryan	.15	.07
❑ 4	Derek Wallace	.15	.07
❑ 5	Jorge Fabregas	.15	.07
❑ 6	Joe Oliver	.15	.07
❑ 7	Brandon Wilson	.15	.07
❑ 8	Mark Thompson	.15	.07
❑ 9	Tracy Sanders	.15	.07
❑ 10	Rich Renteria	.15	.07
❑ 11	Lou Whitaker	.30	.14
❑ 12	Brian Hunter	1.00	.45
❑ 13	Joe Vitiello	.15	.07
❑ 14	Eric Karros	.40	.18
❑ 15	Joe Kmak	.15	.07
❑ 16	Tavo Alvarez	.15	.07
❑ 17	Steve Dunn	.15	.07
❑ 18	Tony Fernandez	.15	.07
❑ 19	Melido Perez	.15	.07
❑ 20	Mike Lieberthal	.15	.07
❑ 21	Terry Steinbach	.15	.07
❑ 22	Stan Belinda	.15	.07
❑ 23	Jay Buhner	.40	.18
❑ 24	Allen Watson	.15	.07
❑ 25	Daryl Henderson	.15	.07
❑ 26	Ray McDavid	.15	.07
❑ 27	Shawn Green	1.50	.70
❑ 28	Bud Black	.15	.07
❑ 29	Sherman Obando	.15	.07
❑ 30	Mike Hostetler	.15	.07
❑ 31	Nate Minchey	.15	.07
❑ 32	Randy Myers	.30	.14
❑ 33	Brian Grebeck	.15	.07
❑ 34	John Roper	.15	.07

❑	35	Larry Thomas	.15	.07
❑	36	Alex Cole	.15	.07
❑	37	Tom Kramer	.15	.07
❑	38	Matt Whisenant	.15	.07
❑	39	Chris Gomez	.30	.14
❑	40	Luis Gonzalez	.15	.07
❑	41	Kevin Appier	.30	.14
❑	42	Omar Daal	.30	.14
❑	43	Duane Singleton	.15	.07
❑	44	Bill Risley	.15	.07
❑	45	Pat Meares	.15	.07
❑	46	Butch Huskey	.40	.18
❑	47	Bobby Munoz	.15	.07
❑	48	Juan Bell	.15	.07
❑	49	Scott Lydy	.15	.07
❑	50	Dennis Moeller	.15	.07
❑	51	Marc Newfield	.15	.07
❑	52	Tripp Cromer	.15	.07
❑	53	Kurt Miller	.15	.07
❑	54	Jim Pena	.15	.07
❑	55	Juan Guzman	.15	.07
❑	56	Matt Williams	.40	.18
❑	57	Harold Reynolds	.15	.07
❑	58	Donnie Elliott	.15	.07
❑	59	Jon Shave	.15	.07
❑	60	Kevin Roberson	.15	.07
❑	61	Hilly Hathaway	.15	.07
❑	62	Jose Rijo	.15	.07
❑	63	Kerry Taylor	.15	.07
❑	64	Ryan Hawblitzel	.15	.07
❑	65	Glenallen Hill	.15	.07
❑	66	Ramon Martinez	.30	.14
❑	67	Travis Fryman	.30	.14
❑	68	Tom Nevers	.15	.07
❑	69	Phil Hiatt	.15	.07
❑	70	Tim Wallach	.15	.07
❑	71	B.J. Surhoff	.30	.14
❑	72	Rondell White	.40	.18
❑	73	Denny Hocking	.30	.14
❑	74	Mike Oquist	.15	.07
❑	75	Paul O'Neill	.30	.14
❑	76	Willie Banks	.15	.07
❑	77	Bob Welch	.15	.07
❑	78	Jose Sandoval	.15	.07
❑	79	Bill Haselman	.15	.07
❑	80	Rheal Cormier	.15	.07
❑	81	Dean Palmer	.30	.14
❑	82	Pat Gomez	.15	.07
❑	83	Steve Karsay	.30	.14
❑	84	Carl Hanselman	.15	.07
❑	85	T.R. Lewis	.15	.07
❑	86	Chipper Jones	3.00	1.35
❑	87	Scott Hatteberg	.15	.07
❑	88	Greg Hibbard	.15	.07
❑	89	Lance Painter	.15	.07
❑	90	Chad Mottola	.15	.07
❑	91	Jason Bere	.15	.07
❑	92	Dante Bichette	.30	.14
❑	93	Sandy Alomar Jr.	.30	.14
❑	94	Carl Everett	.30	.14
❑	95	Danny Bautista	.30	.14
❑	96	Steve Finley	.30	.14
❑	97	David Cone	.30	.14
❑	98	Todd Hollandsworth	.75	.35
❑	99	Matt Mieske	.15	.07
❑	100	Larry Walker	.60	.25
❑	101	Shane Mack	.15	.07
❑	102	Aaron Ledesma	.15	.07
❑	103	Andy Pettitte	5.00	2.20
❑	104	Kevin Stocker	.15	.07
❑	105	Mike Mohler	.15	.07
❑	106	Tony Menendez	.15	.07
❑	107	Derek Lowe	.30	.14
❑	108	Basil Shabazz	.15	.07
❑	109	Dan Smith	.15	.07
❑	110	Scott Sanders	.15	.07
❑	111	Todd Stottlemyre	.15	.07
❑	112	Benji Simonton	.15	.07
❑	113	Rick Sutcliffe	.15	.07
❑	114	Lee Heath	.15	.07
❑	115	Jeff Russell	.15	.07
❑	116	Dave Stevens	.15	.07
❑	117	Mark Holzemer	.15	.07
❑	118	Tim Belcher	.15	.07
❑	119	Bobby Thigpen	.15	.07
❑	120	Roger Bailey	.15	.07
❑	121	Tony Mitchell	.15	.07
❑	122	Junior Felix	.15	.07
❑	123	Rich Robertson	.15	.07
❑	124	Andy Cook	.15	.07
❑	125	Brian Bevil	.15	.07
❑	126	Darryl Strawberry	.30	.14
❑	127	Cal Eldred	.15	.07
❑	128	Cliff Floyd	.30	.14
❑	129	Alan Newman	.15	.07
❑	130	Howard Johnson	.15	.07
❑	131	Jim Abbott	.30	.14
❑	132	Chad McConnell	.15	.07
❑	133	Miguel Jimenez	.30	.14
❑	134	Brett Backlund	.15	.07
❑	135	John Cummings	.15	.07
❑	136	Brian Barber	.15	.07
❑	137	Rafael Palmeiro	.40	.18
❑	138	Tim Worrell	.15	.07
❑	139	Jose Pett	.50	.23
❑	140	Barry Bonds	.60	.25
❑	141	Damon Buford	.15	.07
❑	142	Jeff Blauser	.15	.07
❑	143	Frankie Rodriguez	.15	.07
❑	144	Mike Morgan	.15	.07
❑	145	Gary DiSarcina	.15	.07
❑	146	Calvin Reese	.30	.14
❑	147	Johnny Ruffin	.15	.07
❑	148	David Nied	.15	.07
❑	149	Charles Nagy	.30	.14
❑	150	Mike Myers	.15	.07
❑	151	Kenny Carlyle	.15	.07
❑	152	Eric Anthony	.15	.07
❑	153	Jose Lind	.15	.07
❑	154	Pedro Martinez	.75	.35
❑	155	Mark Kiefer	.15	.07
❑	156	Tim Laker	.15	.07
❑	157	Pat Mahomes	.15	.07
❑	158	Bobby Bonilla	.30	.14
❑	159	Domingo Jean	.15	.07
❑	160	Darren Daulton	.30	.14
❑	161	Mark McGwire	3.00	1.35
❑	162	Jason Kendall	4.00	1.80
❑	163	Desi Relaford	.30	.14
❑	164	Ozzie Canseco	.15	.07
❑	165	Rick Helling	.40	.18
❑	166	Steve Pegues	.15	.07
❑	167	Paul Molitor	.60	.25
❑	168	Larry Carter	.15	.07
❑	169	Arthur Rhodes	.15	.07
❑	170	Damon Hollins	.50	.23
❑	171	Frank Viola	.15	.07
❑	172	Steve Trachsel	.30	.14
❑	173	J.T. Snow	1.50	.70
❑	174	Keith Gordon	.15	.07
❑	175	Carlton Fisk	.60	.25
❑	176	Jason Bates	.30	.14
❑	177	Mike Crosby	.15	.07
❑	178	Benny Santiago	.15	.07
❑	179	Mike Moore	.15	.07
❑	180	Jeff Juden	.15	.07
❑	181	Darren Burton	.15	.07
❑	182	Todd Williams	.15	.07
❑	183	John Jaha	.15	.07
❑	184	Mike Lansing	.30	.14
❑	185	Pedro Grifol	.15	.07
❑	186	Vince Coleman	.15	.07
❑	187	Pat Kelly	.15	.07
❑	188	Clemente Alvarez	.15	.07
❑	189	Ron Darling	.15	.07
❑	190	Orlando Merced	.15	.07
❑	191	Chris Bosio	.15	.07
❑	192	Steve Dixon	.15	.07
❑	193	Doug Dascenzo	.15	.07
❑	194	Ray Holbert	.15	.07
❑	195	Howard Battle	.15	.07
❑	196	Willie McGee	.30	.14
❑	197	John O'Donoghue	.15	.07
❑	198	Steve Avery	.15	.07
❑	199	Greg Blosser	.15	.07
❑	200	Ryne Sandberg	.75	.35
❑	201	Joe Grahe	.15	.07
❑	202	Dan Wilson	.30	.14
❑	203	Domingo Martinez	.15	.07
❑	204	Andres Galarraga	.60	.25
❑	205	Jamie Taylor	.15	.07
❑	206	Darrell Whitmore	.15	.07
❑	207	Ben Blomdahl	.15	.07
❑	208	Doug Drabek	.15	.07
❑	209	Keith Miller	.15	.07
❑	210	Billy Ashley	.15	.07
❑	211	Mike Farrell	.15	.07
❑	212	John Wetteland	.30	.14
❑	213	Randy Tomlin	.15	.07
❑	214	Sid Fernandez	.15	.07
❑	215	Quilvio Veras	.75	.35
❑	216	Dave Hollins	.15	.07
❑	217	Mike Neill	.15	.07
❑	218	Andy Van Slyke	.30	.14
❑	219	Bret Boone	.30	.14
❑	220	Tom Pagnozzi	.15	.07
❑	221	Mike Welch	.15	.07
❑	222	Frank Seminara	.15	.07
❑	223	Ron Villone	.15	.07
❑	224	D.J. Thielen	.15	.07
❑	225	Cal Ripken	2.50	1.10
❑	226	Pedro Borbon Jr.	.15	.07
❑	227	Carlos Quintana	.15	.07
❑	228	Tommy Shields	.15	.07
❑	229	Tim Salmon	.60	.25
❑	230	John Smiley	.15	.07
❑	231	Ellis Burks	.30	.14
❑	232	Pedro Castellano	.15	.07
❑	233	Paul Byrd	.15	.07
❑	234	Bryan Harvey	.15	.07
❑	235	Scott Livingstone	.15	.07
❑	236	James Mouton	.30	.14
❑	237	Joe Randa	.15	.07
❑	238	Pedro Astacio	.15	.07
❑	239	Darryl Hamilton	.15	.07
❑	240	Joey Eischen	.30	.14
❑	241	Edgar Herrera	.15	.07
❑	242	Dwight Gooden	.30	.14
❑	243	Sam Militello	.15	.07
❑	244	Ron Blazier	.15	.07
❑	245	Ruben Sierra	.15	.07
❑	246	Al Martin	.15	.07
❑	247	Mike Felder	.15	.07
❑	248	Bob Tewksbury	.15	.07
❑	249	Craig Lefferts	.15	.07
❑	250	Luis Lopez	.15	.07
❑	251	Devon White	.15	.07
❑	252	Will Clark	.60	.25
❑	253	Mark Smith	.15	.07
❑	254	Terry Pendleton	.15	.07
❑	255	Aaron Sele	.60	.25
❑	256	Jose Viera	.15	.07
❑	257	Damion Easley	.30	.14
❑	258	Rod Lofton	.15	.07
❑	259	Chris Snopek	.30	.14
❑	260	Quinton McCracken	1.00	.45
❑	261	Mike Matthews	.15	.07
❑	262	Hector Carrasco	.15	.07
❑	263	Rick Greene	.15	.07
❑	264	Chris Holt	.15	.07
❑	265	George Brett	1.25	.55
❑	266	Rick Gorecki	.15	.07
❑	267	Francisco Gamez	.15	.07
❑	268	Marquis Grissom	.30	.14
❑	269	Kevin Tapani UER (Misspelled Tapan on card front)	.15	.07
❑	270	Ryan Thompson	.15	.07
❑	271	Gerald Williams	.15	.07
❑	272	Paul Fletcher	.15	.07
❑	273	Lance Blankenship	.15	.07
❑	274	Marty Neff	.15	.07
❑	275	Shawn Estes	.60	.25
❑	276	Rene Arocha	.15	.07
❑	277	Scott Eyre	.15	.07
❑	278	Phil Plantier	.15	.07
❑	279	Paul Spoljaric	.15	.07
❑	280	Chris Gambs	.15	.07
❑	281	Harold Baines	.30	.14
❑	282	Jose Oliva	.15	.07
❑	283	Matt Whiteside	.15	.07
❑	284	Brant Brown	2.00	.90
❑	285	Russ Springer	.15	.07
❑	286	Chris Sabo	.15	.07
❑	287	Ozzie Guillen	.15	.07

❑	288	Marcus Moore	.15	.07
❑	289	Chad Ogea	.30	.14
❑	290	Walt Weiss	.15	.07
❑	291	Brian Edmondson	.15	.07
❑	292	Jimmy Gonzalez	.15	.07
❑	293	Danny Miceli	.15	.07
❑	294	Jose Offerman	.15	.07
❑	295	Greg Vaughn	.30	.14
❑	296	Frank Bolick	.15	.07
❑	297	Mike Maksudian	.15	.07
❑	298	John Franco	.30	.14
❑	299	Danny Tartabull	.15	.07
❑	300	Len Dykstra	.30	.14
❑	301	Bobby Witt	.15	.07
❑	302	Trey Beamon	.50	.23
❑	303	Tino Martinez	.60	.25
❑	304	Aaron Holbert	.15	.07
❑	305	Juan Gonzalez	1.50	.70
❑	306	Billy Hall	.15	.07
❑	307	Duane Ward	.15	.07
❑	308	Rod Beck	.30	.14
❑	309	Jose Mercedes	.15	.07
❑	310	Otis Nixon	.15	.07
❑	311	Gettys Glaze	.15	.07
❑	312	Candy Maldonado	.15	.07
❑	313	Chad Curtis	.30	.14
❑	314	Tim Costo	.15	.07
❑	315	Mike Robertson	.15	.07
❑	316	Nigel Wilson	.15	.07
❑	317	Greg McMichael	.15	.07
❑	318	Scott Pose	.15	.07
❑	319	Ivan Cruz	.15	.07
❑	320	Greg Swindell	.15	.07
❑	321	Kevin McReynolds	.15	.07
❑	322	Tom Candiotti	.15	.07
❑	323	Rob Wishnevski	.15	.07
❑	324	Ken Hill	.15	.07
❑	325	Kirby Puckett	1.00	.45
❑	326	Tim Bogar	.15	.07
❑	327	Mariano Rivera	.75	.35
❑	328	Mitch Williams	.15	.07
❑	329	Craig Paquette	.15	.07
❑	330	Jay Bell	.30	.14
❑	331	Jose Martinez	.15	.07
❑	332	Rob Deer	.15	.07
❑	333	Brook Fordyce	.15	.07
❑	334	Matt Nokes	.15	.07
❑	335	Derek Lee	.15	.07
❑	336	Paul Ellis	.15	.07
❑	337	Desi Wilson	.15	.07
❑	338	Roberto Alomar	.60	.25
❑	339	Jim Tatum FOIL	.15	.07
❑	340	J.T. Snow FOIL	.60	.25
❑	341	Tim Salmon FOIL	.60	.25
❑	342	Russ Davis FOIL	1.00	.45
❑	343	Javier Lopez FOIL	.60	.25
❑	344	Troy O'Leary FOIL	1.50	.70
❑	345	Marty Cordova FOIL	1.00	.45
❑	346	Bubba Smith FOIL	.15	.07
❑	347	Chipper Jones FOIL	3.00	1.35
❑	348	Jessie Hollins FOIL	.15	.07
❑	349	Willie Greene FOIL	.15	.07
❑	350	Mark Thompson FOIL	.15	.07
❑	351	Nigel Wilson FOIL	.15	.07
❑	352	Todd Jones FOIL	.30	.14
❑	353	Raul Mondesi FOIL	.75	.35
❑	354	Cliff Floyd FOIL	.30	.14
❑	355	Bobby Jones FOIL	.30	.14
❑	356	Kevin Stocker FOIL	.15	.07
❑	357	Midre Cummings FOIL	.15	.07
❑	358	Allen Watson FOIL	.15	.07
❑	359	Ray McDavid FOIL	.15	.07
❑	360	Steve Hosey FOIL	.15	.07
❑	361	Brad Pennington FOIL	.15	.07
❑	362	Frankie Rodriguez FOIL	.15	.07
❑	363	Troy Percival FOIL	.40	.18
❑	364	Jason Bere FOIL	.15	.07
❑	365	Manny Ramirez FOIL	1.25	.55
❑	366	Justin Thompson FOIL	.40	.18
❑	367	Joe Vitiello FOIL	.15	.07
❑	368	Tyrone Hill FOIL	.15	.07
❑	369	David McCarty FOIL	.15	.07
❑	370	Brien Taylor FOIL	.15	.07
❑	371	Todd Van Poppel FOIL	.15	.07
❑	372	Marc Newfield FOIL	.15	.07
❑	373	Terrell Lowery FOIL	.15	.07
❑	374	Alex Gonzalez FOIL	.40	.18
❑	375	Ken Griffey Jr.	3.00	1.35
❑	376	Donovan Osborne	.15	.07
❑	377	Ritchie Moody	.15	.07
❑	378	Shane Andrews	.15	.07
❑	379	Carlos Delgado	.60	.25
❑	380	Bill Swift	.15	.07
❑	381	Leo Gomez	.15	.07
❑	382	Ron Gant	.30	.14
❑	383	Scott Fletcher	.15	.07
❑	384	Matt Walbeck	.15	.07
❑	385	Chuck Finley	.30	.14
❑	386	Kevin Mitchell	.30	.14
❑	387	Wilson Alvarez UER (Misspelled Alverez on card front)	.30	.14
❑	388	John Burke	.15	.07
❑	389	Alan Embree	.15	.07
❑	390	Trevor Hoffman	.60	.25
❑	391	Alan Trammell	.40	.18
❑	392	Todd Jones	.30	.14
❑	393	Felix Jose	.15	.07
❑	394	Orel Hershiser	.30	.14
❑	395	Pat Listach	.15	.07
❑	396	Gabe White	.15	.07
❑	397	Dan Serafini	.50	.23
❑	398	Todd Hundley	.40	.18
❑	399	Wade Boggs	.60	.25
❑	400	Tyler Green	.15	.07
❑	401	Mike Bordick	.15	.07
❑	402	Scott Bullett	.15	.07
❑	403	LaGrande Russell	.15	.07
❑	404	Ray Lankford	.40	.18
❑	405	Nolan Ryan	2.50	1.10
❑	406	Robbie Beckett	.15	.07
❑	407	Brent Bowers	.30	.14
❑	408	Adell Davenport	.15	.07
❑	409	Brady Anderson	.40	.18
❑	410	Tom Glavine	.40	.18
❑	411	Doug Hecker	.15	.07
❑	412	Jose Guzman	.15	.07
❑	413	Luis Polonia	.15	.07
❑	414	Brian Williams	.15	.07
❑	415	Bo Jackson	.30	.14
❑	416	Eric Young	.60	.25
❑	417	Kenny Lofton	.60	.25
❑	418	Orestes Destrade	.15	.07
❑	419	Tony Phillips	.15	.07
❑	420	Jeff Bagwell	1.00	.45
❑	421	Mark Gardner	.15	.07
❑	422	Brett Butler	.30	.14
❑	423	Graeme Lloyd	.15	.07
❑	424	Delino DeShields	.30	.14
❑	425	Scott Erickson	.15	.07
❑	426	Jeff Kent	.30	.14
❑	427	Jimmy Key	.30	.14
❑	428	Mickey Morandini	.15	.07
❑	429	Marcos Armas	.15	.07
❑	430	Don Slaught	.15	.07
❑	431	Randy Johnson	.60	.25
❑	432	Omar Olivares	.15	.07
❑	433	Charlie Leibrandt	.15	.07
❑	434	Kurt Stillwell	.15	.07
❑	435	Scott Brow	.15	.07
❑	436	Robby Thompson	.15	.07
❑	437	Ben McDonald	.15	.07
❑	438	Deion Sanders	.40	.18
❑	439	Tony Pena	.15	.07
❑	440	Mark Grace	.40	.18
❑	441	Eduardo Perez	.15	.07
❑	442	Tim Pugh	.15	.07
❑	443	Scott Ruffcorn	.15	.07
❑	444	Jay Gainer	.15	.07
❑	445	Albert Belle	.75	.35
❑	446	Bret Barberie	.15	.07
❑	447	Justin Mashore	.15	.07
❑	448	Pete Harnisch	.15	.07
❑	449	Greg Gagne	.15	.07
❑	450	Eric Davis	.30	.14
❑	451	Dave Mlicki	.15	.07
❑	452	Moises Alou	.30	.14
❑	453	Rick Aguilera	.15	.07
❑	454	Eddie Murray	.60	.25
❑	455	Bob Wickman	.15	.07
❑	456	Wes Chamberlain	.15	.07
❑	457	Brent Gates	.15	.07
❑	458	Paul Wagner	.15	.07
❑	459	Mike Hampton	.40	.18
❑	460	Ozzie Smith	.75	.35
❑	461	Tom Henke	.15	.07
❑	462	Ricky Gutierrez	.15	.07
❑	463	Jack Morris	.30	.14
❑	464	Joel Chimelis	.15	.07
❑	465	Gregg Olson	.15	.07
❑	466	Javier Lopez	.60	.25
❑	467	Scott Cooper	.15	.07
❑	468	Willie Wilson	.15	.07
❑	469	Mark Langston	.15	.07
❑	470	Barry Larkin	.40	.18
❑	471	Rod Bolton	.15	.07
❑	472	Freddie Benavides	.15	.07
❑	473	Ken Ramos	.15	.07
❑	474	Chuck Carr	.15	.07
❑	475	Cecil Fielder	.30	.14
❑	476	Eddie Taubensee	.15	.07
❑	477	Chris Eddy	.15	.07
❑	478	Greg Hansell	.15	.07
❑	479	Kevin Reimer	.15	.07
❑	480	Denny Martinez	.30	.14
❑	481	Chuck Knoblauch	.60	.25
❑	482	Mike Draper	.15	.07
❑	483	Spike Owen	.15	.07
❑	484	Terry Mulholland	.15	.07
❑	485	Dennis Eckersley	.30	.14
❑	486	Blas Minor	.15	.07
❑	487	Dave Fleming	.15	.07
❑	488	Dan Cholowsky	.15	.07
❑	489	Ivan Rodriguez	.75	.35
❑	490	Gary Sheffield	.60	.25
❑	491	Ed Sprague	.15	.07
❑	492	Steve Hosey	.15	.07
❑	493	Jimmy Haynes	.75	.35
❑	494	John Smoltz	.30	.14
❑	495	Andre Dawson	.40	.18
❑	496	Rey Sanchez	.15	.07
❑	497	Ty Van Burkleo	.15	.07
❑	498	Bobby Ayala	.15	.07
❑	499	Tim Raines	.30	.14
❑	500	Charlie Hayes	.15	.07
❑	501	Paul Sorrento	.15	.07
❑	502	Richie Lewis	.15	.07
❑	503	Jason Pfaff	.15	.07
❑	504	Ken Caminiti	.40	.18
❑	505	Mike Macfarlane	.15	.07
❑	506	Jody Reed	.15	.07
❑	507	Bobby Hughes	.15	.07
❑	508	Wil Cordero	.15	.07
❑	509	George Tsamis	.15	.07
❑	510	Bret Saberhagen	.30	.14
❑	511	Derek Jeter	10.00	4.50
❑	512	Gene Schall	.15	.07
❑	513	Curtis Shaw	.15	.07
❑	514	Steve Cooke	.15	.07
❑	515	Edgar Martinez	.40	.18
❑	516	Mike Milchin	.15	.07
❑	517	Billy Ripken	.15	.07
❑	518	Andy Benes	.30	.14
❑	519	Juan de la Rosa	.15	.07
❑	520	John Burkett	.15	.07
❑	521	Alex Ochoa	.15	.07
❑	522	Tony Tarasco	.15	.07
❑	523	Luis Ortiz	.15	.07
❑	524	Rick Wilkins	.15	.07
❑	525	Chris Turner	.15	.07
❑	526	Rob Dibble	.15	.07
❑	527	Jack McDowell	.15	.07
❑	528	Daryl Boston	.15	.07
❑	529	Bill Wertz	.15	.07
❑	530	Charlie Hough	.15	.07
❑	531	Sean Bergman	.15	.07
❑	532	Doug Jones	.15	.07
❑	533	Jeff Montgomery	.30	.14
❑	534	Roger Cedeno	.50	.23
❑	535	Robin Yount	.40	.18
❑	536	Mo Vaughn	.75	.35
❑	537	Brian Harper	.15	.07
❑	538	Juan Castillo	.15	.07
❑	539	Steve Farr	.15	.07
❑	540	John Kruk	.30	.14

❑ 541 Troy Neel .15 .07
❑ 542 Danny Clyburn .50 .23
❑ 543 Jim Converse .15 .07
❑ 544 Gregg Jefferies .15 .07
❑ 545 Jose Canseco .60 .25
❑ 546 Julio Bruno .15 .07
❑ 547 Rob Butler .15 .07
❑ 548 Royce Clayton .15 .07
❑ 549 Chris Hoiles .15 .07
❑ 550 Greg Maddux 2.00 .90
❑ 551 Joe Ciccarella .30 .14
❑ 552 Ozzie Timmons .30 .14
❑ 553 Chili Davis .30 .14
❑ 554 Brian Koelling .15 .07
❑ 555 Frank Thomas 2.00 .90
❑ 556 Vinny Castilla 2.00 .90
❑ 557 Reggie Jefferson .30 .14
❑ 558 Rob Natal .15 .07
❑ 559 Mike Henneman .15 .07
❑ 560 Craig Biggio .60 .25
❑ 561 Billy Brewer .15 .07
❑ 562 Dan Melendez .15 .07
❑ 563 Kenny Felder .15 .07
❑ 564 Miguel Batista .30 .14
❑ 565 Dave Winfield .40 .18
❑ 566 Al Shirley .15 .07
❑ 567 Robert Eenhoorn .15 .07
❑ 568 Mike Williams .15 .07
❑ 569 Tanyon Sturtze .15 .07
❑ 570 Tim Wakefield .30 .14
❑ 571 Greg Pirkl .15 .07
❑ 572 Sean Lowe .15 .07
❑ 573 Terry Burrows .15 .07
❑ 574 Kevin Higgins .15 .07
❑ 575 Joe Carter .30 .14
❑ 576 Kevin Rogers .15 .07
❑ 577 Manny Alexander .15 .07
❑ 578 David Justice .60 .25
❑ 579 Brian Conroy .15 .07
❑ 580 Jessie Hollins .15 .07
❑ 581 Ron Watson .15 .07
❑ 582 Bip Roberts .15 .07
❑ 583 Tom Urbani .15 .07
❑ 584 Jason Hutchins .15 .07
❑ 585 Carlos Baerga .15 .07
❑ 586 Jeff Mutis .15 .07
❑ 587 Justin Thompson .40 .18
❑ 588 Orlando Miller .30 .14
❑ 589 Brian McRae .15 .07
❑ 590 Ramon Martinez .30 .14
❑ 591 Dave Nilsson .30 .14
❑ 592 Jose Vidro .75 .35
❑ 593 Rich Becker .30 .14
❑ 594 Preston Wilson 1.00 .45
❑ 595 Don Mattingly 1.00 .45
❑ 596 Tony Longmire .15 .07
❑ 597 Kevin Seitzer .15 .07
❑ 598 Midre Cummings .15 .07
❑ 599 Omar Vizquel .30 .14
❑ 600 Lee Smith .30 .14
❑ 601 David Hulse .15 .07
❑ 602 Darrell Sherman .15 .07
❑ 603 Alex Gonzalez .40 .18
❑ 604 Geronimo Pena .15 .07
❑ 605 Mike Devereaux .15 .07
❑ 606 Sterling Hitchcock 1.00 .45
❑ 607 Mike Greenwell .15 .07
❑ 608 Steve Buechele .15 .07
❑ 609 Troy Percival .40 .18
❑ 610 Roberto Kelly .15 .07
❑ 611 James Baldwin .75 .35
❑ 612 Jerald Clark .15 .07
❑ 613 Albie Lopez .30 .14
❑ 614 Dave Magadan .15 .07
❑ 615 Mickey Tettleton .15 .07
❑ 616 Sean Runyan .15 .07
❑ 617 Bob Hamelin .15 .07
❑ 618 Raul Mondesi .75 .35
❑ 619 Tyrone Hill .15 .07
❑ 620 Darrin Fletcher .15 .07
❑ 621 Mike Trombley .15 .07
❑ 622 Jeromy Burnitz .30 .14
❑ 623 Bernie Williams .60 .25
❑ 624 Mike Farmer .15 .07
❑ 625 Rickey Henderson .60 .25
❑ 626 Carlos Garcia .15 .07
❑ 627 Jeff Darwin .15 .07
❑ 628 Todd Zeile .15 .07
❑ 629 Benji Gil .15 .07
❑ 630 Tony Gwynn 1.50 .70
❑ 631 Aaron Small .15 .07
❑ 632 Joe Rosselli .15 .07
❑ 633 Mike Mussina .60 .25
❑ 634 Ryan Klesko .60 .25
❑ 635 Roger Clemens 1.25 .55
❑ 636 Sammy Sosa 1.50 .70
❑ 637 Orlando Palmeiro .15 .07
❑ 638 Willie Greene .15 .07
❑ 639 George Bell .15 .07
❑ 640 Garvin Alston .15 .07
❑ 641 Pete Janicki .15 .07
❑ 642 Chris Sheff .15 .07
❑ 643 Felipe Lira .30 .14
❑ 644 Roberto Petagine .30 .14
❑ 645 Wally Joyner .30 .14
❑ 646 Mike Piazza 3.00 1.35
❑ 647 Jaime Navarro .15 .07
❑ 648 Jeff Hartsock .15 .07
❑ 649 David McCarty .15 .07
❑ 650 Bobby Jones .40 .18
❑ 651 Mark Hutton .15 .07
❑ 652 Kyle Abbott .15 .07
❑ 653 Steve Cox .50 .23
❑ 654 Jeff King .30 .14
❑ 655 Norm Charlton .15 .07
❑ 656 Mike Gulan .15 .07
❑ 657 Julio Franco .15 .07
❑ 658 Cameron Cairncross .15 .07
❑ 659 John Olerud .40 .18
❑ 660 Salomon Torres .15 .07
❑ 661 Brad Pennington .15 .07
❑ 662 Melvin Nieves .15 .07
❑ 663 Ivan Calderon .15 .07
❑ 664 Turk Wendell .15 .07
❑ 665 Chris Pritchett .15 .07
❑ 666 Reggie Sanders .15 .07
❑ 667 Robin Ventura .30 .14
❑ 668 Joe Girardi .30 .14
❑ 669 Manny Ramirez 1.25 .55
❑ 670 Jeff Conine .15 .07
❑ 671 Greg Gohr .15 .07
❑ 672 Andujar Cedeno .15 .07
❑ 673 Les Norman .15 .07
❑ 674 Mike James .15 .07
❑ 675 Marshall Boze .15 .07
❑ 676 B.J. Wallace .15 .07
❑ 677 Kent Hrbek .30 .14
❑ 678 Jack Voigt .15 .07
❑ 679 Brien Taylor .15 .07
❑ 680 Curt Schilling .15 .07
❑ 681 Todd Van Poppel .15 .07
❑ 682 Kevin Young .15 .07
❑ 683 Tommy Adams .15 .07
❑ 684 Bernard Gilkey .15 .07
❑ 685 Kevin Brown .40 .18
❑ 686 Fred McGriff .40 .18
❑ 687 Pat Borders .15 .07
❑ 688 Kirt Manwaring .15 .07
❑ 689 Sid Bream .15 .07
❑ 690 John Valentin .30 .14
❑ 691 Steve Olsen .15 .07
❑ 692 Roberto Mejia .15 .07
❑ 693 Carlos Delgado FOIL .60 .25
❑ 694 Steve Gibralter FOIL .30 .14
❑ 695 Gary Mota FOIL .15 .07
❑ 696 Jose Malave FOIL .15 .07
❑ 697 Larry Sutton FOIL .15 .07
❑ 698 Dan Frye FOIL .15 .07
❑ 699 Tim Clark FOIL .15 .07
❑ 700 Brian Rupp FOIL .15 .07
❑ 701 Felipe Alou FOIL .30 .14
Moises Alou
❑ 702 Barry Bonds FOIL .60 .25
Bobby Bonds
❑ 703 Ken Griffey Sr. FOIL 1.00 .45
Ken Griffey Jr.
❑ 704 Brian McRae FOIL .15 .07
Hal McRae
❑ 705 Checklist 1 .15 .07
❑ 706 Checklist 2 .15 .07
❑ 707 Checklist 3 .15 .07
❑ 708 Checklist 4 .15 .07

1994 Bowman Previews

	MINT	NRMT
COMPLETE SET (10)	40.00	18.00
COMMON CARD (1-10)	1.00	.45

❑ 1 Frank Thomas 12.00 5.50
❑ 2 Mike Piazza 12.00 5.50
❑ 3 Albert Belle 5.00 2.20
❑ 4 Javier Lopez 2.50 1.10
❑ 5 Cliff Floyd 2.00 .90
❑ 6 Alex Gonzalez 1.00 .45
❑ 7 Ricky Bottalico 2.00 .90
❑ 8 Tony Clark 8.00 3.60
❑ 9 Mac Suzuki 2.00 .90
❑ 10 James Mouton Foil 1.00 .45

1994 Bowman

	MINT	NRMT
COMPLETE SET (682)	125.00	55.00
COMMON CARD (1-682)	.20	.09

❑ 1 Joe Carter .40 .18
❑ 2 Marcus Moore .20 .09
❑ 3 Doug Creek .20 .09
❑ 4 Pedro Martinez .75 .35
❑ 5 Ken Griffey Jr. 4.00 1.80
❑ 6 Greg Swindell .20 .09
❑ 7 J.J. Johnson .40 .18
❑ 8 Homer Bush 1.00 .45
❑ 9 Arquimedez Pozo .40 .18
❑ 10 Bryan Harvey .20 .09
❑ 11 J.T. Snow .40 .18
❑ 12 Alan Benes 3.00 1.35
❑ 13 Chad Kreuter .20 .09
❑ 14 Eric Karros .40 .18
❑ 15 Frank Thomas 2.50 1.10
❑ 16 Bret Saberhagen .40 .18
❑ 17 Terrell Lowery .20 .09
❑ 18 Rod Bolton .20 .09
❑ 19 Harold Baines .40 .18
❑ 20 Matt Walbeck .20 .09
❑ 21 Tom Glavine .75 .35
❑ 22 Todd Jones .20 .09
❑ 23 Alberto Castillo .20 .09
❑ 24 Ruben Sierra .20 .09
❑ 25 Don Mattingly 1.25 .55

❑ 26 Mike Morgan .20 .09
❑ 27 Jim Musselwhite .40 .18
❑ 28 Matt Brunson .20 .09
❑ 29 Adam Meinershagen .20 .09
❑ 30 Joe Girardi .20 .09
❑ 31 Shane Halter .20 .09
❑ 32 Jose Paniagua .40 .18
❑ 33 Paul Perkins .20 .09
❑ 34 John Hudek .20 .09
❑ 35 Frank Viola .20 .09
❑ 36 David Lamb .20 .09
❑ 37 Marshall Boze .20 .09
❑ 38 Jorge Posada 6.00 2.70
❑ 39 Brian Anderson 1.50 .70
❑ 40 Mark Whiten .20 .09
❑ 41 Sean Bergman .40 .18
❑ 42 Jose Parra .40 .18
❑ 43 Mike Robertson .20 .09
❑ 44 Pete Walker .20 .09
❑ 45 Juan Gonzalez 2.00 .90
❑ 46 Cleveland Ladell .40 .18
❑ 47 Mark Smith .20 .09
❑ 48 Kevin Jarvis UER .20 .09
(team listed as Yankees on back)
❑ 49 Amaury Telemaco 1.00 .45
❑ 50 Andy Van Slyke .40 .18
❑ 51 Rikkert Faneyte .20 .09
❑ 52 Curtis Shaw .20 .09
❑ 53 Matt Drews .50 .23
❑ 54 Wilson Alvarez .40 .18
❑ 55 Manny Ramirez 1.00 .45
❑ 56 Bobby Munoz .20 .09
❑ 57 Ed Sprague .20 .09
❑ 58 Jamey Wright .75 .35
❑ 59 Jeff Montgomery .20 .09
❑ 60 Kirk Rueter .20 .09
❑ 61 Edgar Martinez .40 .18
❑ 62 Luis Gonzalez .20 .09
❑ 63 Tim Vanegmond .20 .09
❑ 64 Bip Roberts .20 .09
❑ 65 John Jaha .20 .09
❑ 66 Chuck Carr .20 .09
❑ 67 Chuck Finley .40 .18
❑ 68 Aaron Holbert .20 .09
❑ 69 Cecil Fielder .40 .18
❑ 70 Tom Engle .20 .09
❑ 71 Ron Karkovice .20 .09
❑ 72 Joe Orsulak .20 .09
❑ 73 Duff Brumley .20 .09
❑ 74 Craig Clayton .20 .09
❑ 75 Cal Ripken 3.00 1.35
❑ 76 Brad Fulimer 8.00 3.60
❑ 77 Tony Tarasco .20 .09
❑ 78 Terry Farrar .20 .09
❑ 79 Matt Williams .60 .25
❑ 80 Rickey Henderson .75 .35
❑ 81 Terry Mulholland .20 .09
❑ 82 Sammy Sosa 2.00 .90
❑ 83 Paul Sorrento .20 .09
❑ 84 Pete Incaviglia .20 .09
❑ 85 Darren Hall .20 .09
❑ 86 Scott Klingenbeck .20 .09
❑ 87 Dario Perez .20 .09
❑ 88 Ugueth Urbina .40 .18
❑ 89 Dave Vanhof .20 .09
❑ 90 Domingo Jean .20 .09
❑ 91 Otis Nixon .20 .09
❑ 92 Andres Berumen .20 .09
❑ 93 Jose Valentin .20 .09
❑ 94 Edgar Renteria 4.00 1.80
❑ 95 Chris Turner .20 .09
❑ 96 Ray Lankford .40 .18
❑ 97 Danny Bautista .20 .09
❑ 98 Chan Ho Park 8.00 3.60
❑ 99 Glenn DiSarcina .40 .18
❑ 100 Butch Huskey .40 .18
❑ 101 Ivan Rodriguez 1.00 .45
❑ 102 Johnny Ruffin .20 .09
❑ 103 Alex Ochoa .20 .09
❑ 104 Torii Hunter 1.00 .45
❑ 105 Ryan Klesko .40 .18
❑ 106 Jay Bell .40 .18
❑ 107 Kurt Peltzer .20 .09
❑ 108 Miguel Jimenez .20 .09
❑ 109 Russ Davis .40 .18
❑ 110 Derek Wallace .20 .09
❑ 111 Keith Lockhart .20 .09
❑ 112 Mike Lieberthal .20 .09
❑ 113 Dave Stewart .40 .18
❑ 114 Tom Schmidt .20 .09
❑ 115 Brian McRae .20 .09
❑ 116 Moises Alou .60 .25
❑ 117 Dave Fleming .20 .09
❑ 118 Jeff Bagwell 1.25 .55
❑ 119 Luis Ortiz .20 .09
❑ 120 Tony Gwynn 2.00 .90
❑ 121 Jaime Navarro .20 .09
❑ 122 Benny Santiago .20 .09
❑ 123 Darrell Whitmore .20 .09
❑ 124 John Mabry .50 .23
❑ 125 Mickey Tettleton .20 .09
❑ 126 Tom Candiotti .20 .09
❑ 127 Tim Raines .40 .18
❑ 128 Bobby Bonilla .40 .18
❑ 129 John Dettmer .20 .09
❑ 130 Hector Carrasco .20 .09
❑ 131 Chris Hoiles .20 .09
❑ 132 Rick Aguilera .20 .09
❑ 133 David Justice .75 .35
❑ 134 Esteban Loaiza 1.00 .45
❑ 135 Barry Bonds 1.00 .45
❑ 136 Bob Welch .20 .09
❑ 137 Mike Stanley .20 .09
❑ 138 Roberto Hernandez .20 .09
❑ 139 Sandy Alomar .40 .18
❑ 140 Darren Daulton .40 .18
❑ 141 Angel Martinez .20 .09
❑ 142 Howard Johnson .20 .09
❑ 143 Bob Hamelin UER .20 .09
(name and card number colors don't match)
❑ 144 J.J. Thobe .20 .09
❑ 145 Roger Salkeld .20 .09
❑ 146 Orlando Miller .20 .09
❑ 147 Dmitri Young .40 .18
❑ 148 Tim Hyers .20 .09
❑ 149 Mark Loretta .20 .09
❑ 150 Chris Hammond .20 .09
❑ 151 Joel Moore .20 .09
❑ 152 Todd Zeile .20 .09
❑ 153 Wil Cordero .20 .09
❑ 154 Chris Smith .20 .09
❑ 155 James Baldwin .40 .18
❑ 156 Edgardo Alfonzo 3.00 1.35
❑ 157 Kym Ashworth .40 .18
❑ 158 Paul Bako .20 .09
❑ 159 Rick Krivda .20 .09
❑ 160 Pat Mahomes .20 .09
❑ 161 Damon Hollins .40 .18
❑ 162 Felix Martinez .50 .23
❑ 163 Jason Myers .40 .18
❑ 164 Izzy Molina .40 .18
❑ 165 Brien Taylor .20 .09
❑ 166 Kevin Orie 2.00 .90
❑ 167 Casey Whitten .40 .18
❑ 168 Tony Longmire .20 .09
❑ 169 John Olerud .40 .18
❑ 170 Mark Thompson .20 .09
❑ 171 Jorge Fabregas .20 .09
❑ 172 John Wetteland .40 .18
❑ 173 Dan Wilson .20 .09
❑ 174 Doug Drabek .20 .09
❑ 175 Jeffrey McNeely .20 .09
❑ 176 Melvin Nieves .20 .09
❑ 177 Doug Glanville 2.50 1.10
❑ 178 Javier De La Hoya .20 .09
❑ 179 Chad Curtis .20 .09
❑ 180 Brian Barber .20 .09
❑ 181 Mike Henneman .20 .09
❑ 182 Jose Offerman .20 .09
❑ 183 Robert Ellis .20 .09
❑ 184 John Franco .40 .18
❑ 185 Benji Gil .20 .09
❑ 186 Hal Morris .20 .09
❑ 187 Chris Sabo .20 .09
❑ 188 Blaise Ilsley .20 .09
❑ 189 Steve Avery .20 .09
❑ 190 Rick White .20 .09
❑ 191 Rod Beck .20 .09
❑ 192 Mark McGwire UER 4.00 1.80
(No card number on back)
❑ 193 Jim Abbott .40 .18
❑ 194 Randy Myers .20 .09
❑ 195 Kenny Lofton .75 .35
❑ 196 Mariano Duncan .20 .09
❑ 197 Lee Daniels .20 .09
❑ 198 Armando Reynoso .20 .09
❑ 199 Joe Randa .40 .18
❑ 200 Cliff Floyd .40 .18
❑ 201 Tim Harkrider .20 .09
❑ 202 Kevin Gallaher .20 .09
❑ 203 Scott Cooper .20 .09
❑ 204 Phil Stidham .20 .09
❑ 205 Jeff D'Amico .50 .23
❑ 206 Matt Whisenant .20 .09
❑ 207 De Shawn Warren .40 .18
❑ 208 Rene Arocha .20 .09
❑ 209 Tony Clark 12.00 5.50
❑ 210 Jason Jacome .20 .09
❑ 211 Scott Christman .40 .18
❑ 212 Bill Pulsipher .40 .18
❑ 213 Dean Palmer .40 .18
❑ 214 Chad Mottola .20 .09
❑ 215 Manny Alexander .20 .09
❑ 216 Rich Becker .20 .09
❑ 217 Andre King .20 .09
❑ 218 Carlos Garcia .20 .09
❑ 219 Ron Pezzoni .20 .09
❑ 220 Steve Karsay .20 .09
❑ 221 Jose Musset .20 .09
❑ 222 Karl Rhodes .20 .09
❑ 223 Frank Cimorelli .20 .09
❑ 224 Kevin Jordan .20 .09
❑ 225 Duane Ward .20 .09
❑ 226 John Burke .20 .09
❑ 227 Mike Macfarlane .20 .09
❑ 228 Mike Lansing .40 .18
❑ 229 Chuck Knoblauch .75 .35
❑ 230 Ken Caminiti .60 .25
❑ 231 Gar Finnvold .20 .09
❑ 232 Derrek Lee 8.00 3.60
❑ 233 Brady Anderson .40 .18
❑ 234 Vic Darensbourg .20 .09
❑ 235 Mark Langston .20 .09
❑ 236 T.J. Mathews .40 .18
❑ 237 Lou Whitaker .40 .18
❑ 238 Roger Cedeno .40 .18
❑ 239 Alex Fernandez .20 .09
❑ 240 Ryan Thompson .20 .09
❑ 241 Kerry Lacy .20 .09
❑ 242 Reggie Sanders .40 .18
❑ 243 Brad Pennington .20 .09
❑ 244 Bryan Eversgerd .20 .09
❑ 245 Greg Maddux 2.50 1.10
❑ 246 Jason Kendall .75 .35
❑ 247 J.R. Phillips .20 .09
❑ 248 Bobby Witt .20 .09
❑ 249 Paul O'Neill .40 .18
❑ 250 Ryne Sandberg 1.00 .45
❑ 251 Charles Nagy .40 .18
❑ 252 Kevin Stocker .20 .09
❑ 253 Shawn Green .40 .18
❑ 254 Charlie Hayes .20 .09
❑ 255 Donnie Elliott .20 .09
❑ 256 Rob Fitzpatrick .20 .09
❑ 257 Tim Davis .20 .09
❑ 258 James Mouton .20 .09
❑ 259 Mike Greenwell .20 .09
❑ 260 Ray McDavid .20 .09
❑ 261 Mike Kelly .20 .09
❑ 262 Andy Larkin .40 .18
❑ 263 Marquis Riley UER .20 .09
(No card number on back)
❑ 264 Bob Tewksbury .20 .09
❑ 265 Brian Edmondson .20 .09
❑ 266 Eduardo Lantigua .40 .18
❑ 267 Brandon Wilson .20 .09
❑ 268 Mike Welch .20 .09
❑ 269 Tom Henke .20 .09
❑ 270 Calvin Reese .40 .18
❑ 271 Greg Zaun .20 .09
❑ 272 Todd Ritchie .20 .09
❑ 273 Javier Lopez .60 .25
❑ 274 Kevin Young .20 .09
❑ 275 Kirt Manwaring .20 .09
❑ 276 Bill Taylor .20 .09

❑ 277 Robert Eenhoorn .20 .09
❑ 278 Jessie Hollins .20 .09
❑ 279 Julian Tavarez .40 .18
❑ 280 Gene Schall .20 .09
❑ 281 Paul Molitor .75 .35
❑ 282 Neifi Perez 3.00 1.35
❑ 283 Greg Gagne .20 .09
❑ 284 Marquis Grissom .40 .18
❑ 285 Randy Johnson .75 .35
❑ 286 Pete Harnisch .20 .09
❑ 287 Joel Bennett .20 .09
❑ 288 Derek Bell .40 .18
❑ 289 Darryl Hamilton .20 .09
❑ 290 Gary Sheffield .75 .35
❑ 291 Eduardo Perez .20 .09
❑ 292 Basil Shabazz .20 .09
❑ 293 Eric Davis .40 .18
❑ 294 Pedro Astacio .20 .09
❑ 295 Robin Ventura .40 .18
❑ 296 Jeff Kent .40 .18
❑ 297 Rick Helling .40 .18
❑ 298 Joe Oliver .20 .09
❑ 299 Lee Smith .40 .18
❑ 300 Dave Winfield .75 .35
❑ 301 Deion Sanders .40 .18
❑ 302 Ravelo Manzanillo .20 .09
❑ 303 Mark Portugal .20 .09
❑ 304 Brent Gates .20 .09
❑ 305 Wade Boggs .75 .35
❑ 306 Rick Wilkins .20 .09
❑ 307 Carlos Baerga .40 .18
❑ 308 Curt Schilling .40 .18
❑ 309 Shannon Stewart .40 .18
❑ 310 Darren Holmes .20 .09
❑ 311 Robert Toth .20 .09
❑ 312 Gabe White .20 .09
❑ 313 Mac Suzuki .40 .18
❑ 314 Alvin Morman .20 .09
❑ 315 Mo Vaughn 1.00 .45
❑ 316 Bryce Florie .20 .09
❑ 317 Gabby Martinez .50 .23
❑ 318 Carl Everett .20 .09
❑ 319 Kerwin Moore .20 .09
❑ 320 Tom Pagnozzi .20 .09
❑ 321 Chris Gomez .20 .09
❑ 322 Todd Williams .20 .09
❑ 323 Pat Hentgen .40 .18
❑ 324 Kirk Presley .40 .18
❑ 325 Kevin Brown .40 .18
❑ 326 Jason Isringhausen .50 .23
❑ 327 Rick Forney .20 .09
❑ 328 Carlos Pulido .20 .09
❑ 329 Terrell Wade .20 .09
❑ 330 Al Martin .20 .09
❑ 331 Dan Carlson .20 .09
❑ 332 Mark Acre .20 .09
❑ 333 Sterling Hitchcock .40 .18
❑ 334 Jon Ratliff .40 .18
❑ 335 Alex Ramirez 5.00 2.20
❑ 336 Phil Geisler .20 .09
❑ 337 Eddie Zambrano FOIL .20 .09
❑ 338 Jim Thome FOIL 1.00 .45
❑ 339 James Mouton FOIL .20 .09
❑ 340 Cliff Floyd FOIL .40 .18
❑ 341 Carlos Delgado FOIL .60 .25
❑ 342 Roberto Petagine FOIL .20 .09
❑ 343 Tim Clark FOIL .20 .09
❑ 344 Bubba Smith FOIL .20 .09
❑ 345 Randy Curtis FOIL .20 .09
❑ 346 Joe Biasucci FOIL .20 .09
❑ 347 D.J. Boston FOIL .20 .09
❑ 348 Ruben Rivera FOIL 4.00 1.80
❑ 349 Bryan Link FOIL .20 .09
❑ 350 Mike Bell FOIL .50 .23
❑ 351 Marty Watson FOIL .20 .09
❑ 352 Jason Myers FOIL .40 .18
❑ 353 Chipper Jones FOIL 2.50 1.10
❑ 354 Brooks Kieschnick FOIL .40 .18
❑ 355 Calvin Reese FOIL .40 .18
❑ 356 John Burke FOIL .20 .09
❑ 357 Kurt Miller FOIL .20 .09
❑ 358 Orlando Miller FOIL .20 .09
❑ 359 Todd Hollandsworth FOIL .20 .09
❑ 360 Rondell White FOIL .40 .18
❑ 361 Bill Pulsipher FOIL .40 .18
❑ 362 Tyler Green FOIL .20 .09
❑ 363 Midre Cummings FOIL .20 .09
❑ 364 Brian Barber FOIL .20 .09
❑ 365 Melvin Nieves FOIL .20 .09
❑ 366 Salomon Torres FOIL .20 .09
❑ 367 Alex Ochoa FOIL .20 .09
❑ 368 Frankie Rodriguez FOIL .20 .09
❑ 369 Brian Anderson FOIL 1.50 .70
❑ 370 James Baldwin FOIL .40 .18
❑ 371 Manny Ramirez FOIL 1.00 .45
❑ 372 Justin Thompson FOIL .60 .25
❑ 373 Johnny Damon FOIL .40 .18
❑ 374 Jeff D'Amico FOIL .50 .23
❑ 375 Rich Becker FOIL .20 .09
❑ 376 Derek Jeter FOIL 3.00 1.35
❑ 377 Steve Karsay FOIL .20 .09
❑ 378 Mac Suzuki FOIL .40 .18
❑ 379 Benji Gil FOIL .20 .09
❑ 380 Alex Gonzalez FOIL .20 .09
❑ 381 Jason Bere FOIL .20 .09
❑ 382 Brett Butler FOIL .40 .18
❑ 383 Jeff Conine FOIL .40 .18
❑ 384 Darren Daulton FOIL .40 .18
❑ 385 Jeff Kent FOIL .40 .18
❑ 386 Don Mattingly FOIL 1.25 .55
❑ 387 Mike Piazza FOIL 2.50 1.10
❑ 388 Ryne Sandberg FOIL 1.00 .45
❑ 389 Rich Amaral .20 .09
❑ 390 Craig Biggio .75 .35
❑ 391 Jeff Suppan .50 .23
❑ 392 Andy Benes .40 .18
❑ 393 Cal Eldred .20 .09
❑ 394 Jeff Conine .40 .18
❑ 395 Tim Salmon .75 .35
❑ 396 Ray Suplee .20 .09
❑ 397 Tony Phillips .20 .09
❑ 398 Ramon Martinez .40 .18
❑ 399 Julio Franco .20 .09
❑ 400 Dwight Gooden .40 .18
❑ 401 Kevin Lomon .20 .09
❑ 402 Jose Rijo .20 .09
❑ 403 Mike Devereaux .20 .09
❑ 404 Mike Zolecki .20 .09
❑ 405 Fred McGriff .60 .25
❑ 406 Danny Clyburn .40 .18
❑ 407 Robby Thompson .20 .09
❑ 408 Terry Steinbach .40 .18
❑ 409 Luis Polonia .20 .09
❑ 410 Mark Grace .60 .25
❑ 411 Albert Belle 1.00 .45
❑ 412 John Kruk .40 .18
❑ 413 Scott Spiezio 1.50 .70
❑ 414 Ellis Burks UER .40 .18
(Name spelled Elkis on front)
❑ 415 Joe Vitiello .20 .09
❑ 416 Tim Costo .20 .09
❑ 417 Marc Newfield .20 .09
❑ 418 Oscar Henriquez .75 .35
❑ 419 Matt Perisho .50 .23
❑ 420 Julio Bruno .20 .09
❑ 421 Kenny Felder .20 .09
❑ 422 Tyler Green .20 .09
❑ 423 Jim Edmonds .75 .35
❑ 424 Ozzie Smith 1.00 .45
❑ 425 Rick Greene .20 .09
❑ 426 Todd Hollandsworth .20 .09
❑ 427 Eddie Pearson .40 .18
❑ 428 Quilvio Veras .20 .09
❑ 429 Kenny Rogers .20 .09
❑ 430 Willie Greene .40 .18
❑ 431 Vaughn Eshelman .20 .09
❑ 432 Pat Meares .20 .09
❑ 433 Jermaine Dye 1.00 .45
❑ 434 Steve Cooke .20 .09
❑ 435 Bill Swift .20 .09
❑ 436 Fausto Cruz .20 .09
❑ 437 Mark Hutton .20 .09
❑ 438 Brooks Kieschnick .40 .18
❑ 439 Yorkis Perez .20 .09
❑ 440 Len Dykstra .40 .18
❑ 441 Pat Borders .20 .09
❑ 442 Doug Walls .20 .09
❑ 443 Wally Joyner .40 .18
❑ 444 Ken Hill .20 .09
❑ 445 Eric Anthony .20 .09
❑ 446 Mitch Williams .20 .09
❑ 447 Cory Bailey .20 .09
❑ 448 Dave Staton .20 .09
❑ 449 Greg Vaughn .40 .18
❑ 450 Dave Magadan .20 .09
❑ 451 Chili Davis .40 .18
❑ 452 Gerald Santos .20 .09
❑ 453 Joe Perona .20 .09
❑ 454 Delino DeShields .20 .09
❑ 455 Jack McDowell .20 .09
❑ 456 Todd Hundley .40 .18
❑ 457 Ritchie Moody .20 .09
❑ 458 Bret Boone .40 .18
❑ 459 Ben McDonald .20 .09
❑ 460 Kirby Puckett 1.25 .55
❑ 461 Gregg Olson .20 .09
❑ 462 Rich Aude .20 .09
❑ 463 John Burkett .20 .09
❑ 464 Troy Neel .20 .09
❑ 465 Jimmy Key .40 .18
❑ 466 Ozzie Timmons .20 .09
❑ 467 Eddie Murray .75 .35
❑ 468 Mark Tranberg .20 .09
❑ 469 Alex Gonzalez .20 .09
❑ 470 David Nied .20 .09
❑ 471 Barry Larkin .60 .25
❑ 472 Brian Looney .20 .09
❑ 473 Shawn Estes .40 .18
❑ 474 A.J. Sager .20 .09
❑ 475 Roger Clemens 1.50 .70
❑ 476 Vince Moore .20 .09
❑ 477 Scott Karl .40 .18
❑ 478 Kurt Miller .20 .09
❑ 479 Garret Anderson .75 .35
❑ 480 Allen Watson .20 .09
❑ 481 Jose Lima 1.00 .45
❑ 482 Rick Gorecki .20 .09
❑ 483 Jimmy Hurst .40 .18
❑ 484 Preston Wilson .40 .18
❑ 485 Will Clark .75 .35
❑ 486 Mike Ferry .20 .09
❑ 487 Curtis Goodwin .40 .18
❑ 488 Mike Myers .20 .09
❑ 489 Chipper Jones 2.50 1.10
❑ 490 Jeff King .20 .09
❑ 491 William VanLandingham .20 .09
❑ 492 Carlos Reyes .20 .09
❑ 493 Andy Pettitte 1.50 .70
❑ 494 Brant Brown .40 .18
❑ 495 Daron Kirkreit .20 .09
❑ 496 Ricky Bottalico 1.00 .45
❑ 497 Devon White .40 .18
❑ 498 Jason Johnson .20 .09
❑ 499 Vince Coleman .20 .09
❑ 500 Larry Walker .75 .35
❑ 501 Bobby Ayala .20 .09
❑ 502 Steve Finley .40 .18
❑ 503 Scott Fletcher .20 .09
❑ 504 Brad Ausmus .20 .09
❑ 505 Scott Talanoa .20 .09
❑ 506 Orestes Destrade .20 .09
❑ 507 Gary DiSarcina .20 .09
❑ 508 Willie Smith .20 .09
❑ 509 Alan Trammell .60 .25
❑ 510 Mike Piazza 2.50 1.10
❑ 511 Ozzie Guillen .20 .09
❑ 512 Jeromy Burnitz .40 .18
❑ 513 Darren Oliver 1.00 .45
❑ 514 Kevin Mitchell .20 .09
❑ 515 Rafael Palmeiro .60 .25
❑ 516 David McCarty .20 .09
❑ 517 Jeff Blauser .20 .09
❑ 518 Trey Beamon .20 .09
❑ 519 Royce Clayton .20 .09
❑ 520 Dennis Eckersley .40 .18
❑ 521 Bernie Williams .75 .35
❑ 522 Steve Buechele .20 .09
❑ 523 Denny Martinez .40 .18
❑ 524 Dave Hollins .20 .09
❑ 525 Joey Hamilton .75 .35
❑ 526 Andres Galarraga .75 .35
❑ 527 Jeff Granger .20 .09
❑ 528 Joey Eischen .20 .09
❑ 529 Desi Relaford .40 .18
❑ 530 Roberto Petagine .20 .09

❑ 531 Andre Dawson .60 .25
❑ 532 Ray Holbert .20 .09
❑ 533 Duane Singleton .20 .09
❑ 534 Kurt Abbott .20 .09
❑ 535 Bo Jackson .40 .18
❑ 536 Gregg Jefferies .20 .09
❑ 537 David Mysel .20 .09
❑ 538 Raul Mondesi .75 .35
❑ 539 Chris Snopek .20 .09
❑ 540 Brook Fordyce .20 .09
❑ 541 Ron Frazier .20 .09
❑ 542 Brian Koelling .20 .09
❑ 543 Jimmy Haynes .40 .18
❑ 544 Marty Cordova .40 .18
❑ 545 Jason Green .40 .18
❑ 546 Orlando Merced .20 .09
❑ 547 Lou Pote .20 .09
❑ 548 Todd Van Poppel .20 .09
❑ 549 Pat Kelly .20 .09
❑ 550 Turk Wendell .20 .09
❑ 551 Herbert Perry .20 .09
❑ 552 Ryan Karp .20 .09
❑ 553 Juan Guzman .20 .09
❑ 554 Bryan Rekar .40 .18
❑ 555 Kevin Appier .40 .18
❑ 556 Chris Schwab .40 .18
❑ 557 Jay Buhner .40 .18
❑ 558 Andujar Cedeno .20 .09
❑ 559 Ryan McGuire .40 .18
❑ 560 Ricky Gutierrez .20 .09
❑ 561 Keith Kimsey .20 .09
❑ 562 Tim Clark .20 .09
❑ 563 Damion Easley .40 .18
❑ 564 Clint Davis .20 .09
❑ 565 Mike Moore .20 .09
❑ 566 Orel Hershiser .40 .18
❑ 567 Jason Bere .20 .09
❑ 568 Kevin McReynolds .20 .09
❑ 569 Leland Macon .20 .09
❑ 570 John Courtright .20 .09
❑ 571 Sid Fernandez .20 .09
❑ 572 Chad Roper .20 .09
❑ 573 Terry Pendleton .20 .09
❑ 574 Danny Miceli .20 .09
❑ 575 Joe Rosselli .20 .09
❑ 576 Mike Bordick .20 .09
❑ 577 Danny Tartabull .20 .09
❑ 578 Jose Guzman .20 .09
❑ 579 Omar Vizquel .40 .18
❑ 580 Tommy Greene .20 .09
❑ 581 Paul Spoljaric .20 .09
❑ 582 Walt Weiss .20 .09
❑ 583 Oscar Jimenez .20 .09
❑ 584 Rod Henderson .20 .09
❑ 585 Derek Lowe .20 .09
❑ 586 Richard Hidalgo 5.00 2.20
❑ 587 Shayne Bennett .40 .18
❑ 588 Tim Belk .20 .09
❑ 589 Matt Mieske .20 .09
❑ 590 Nigel Wilson .20 .09
❑ 591 Jeff Knox .20 .09
❑ 592 Bernard Gilkey .20 .09
❑ 593 David Cone .60 .25
❑ 594 Paul LoDuca .40 .18
❑ 595 Scott Ruffcorn .20 .09
❑ 596 Chris Roberts .40 .18
❑ 597 Oscar Munoz .20 .09
❑ 598 Scott Sullivan .40 .18
❑ 599 Matt Jarvis .20 .09
❑ 600 Jose Canseco .75 .35
❑ 601 Tony Graffanino .40 .18
❑ 602 Don Slaught .20 .09
❑ 603 Brett King .40 .18
❑ 604 Jose Herrera .40 .18
❑ 605 Melido Perez .20 .09
❑ 606 Mike Hubbard .20 .09
❑ 607 Chad Ogea .40 .18
❑ 608 Wayne Gomes .20 .09
❑ 609 Roberto Alomar .75 .35
❑ 610 Angel Echevarria .50 .23
❑ 611 Jose Lind .20 .09
❑ 612 Darrin Fletcher .20 .09
❑ 613 Chris Bosio .20 .09
❑ 614 Darryl Kile .40 .18
❑ 615 Frankie Rodriguez .20 .09
❑ 616 Phil Plantier .20 .09
❑ 617 Pat Listach .20 .09
❑ 618 Charlie Hough .20 .09
❑ 619 Ryan Hancock .20 .09
❑ 620 Darrel Deak .20 .09
❑ 621 Travis Fryman .40 .18
❑ 622 Brett Butler .40 .18
❑ 623 Lance Johnson .20 .09
❑ 624 Pete Smith .20 .09
❑ 625 James Hurst .20 .09
❑ 626 Roberto Kelly .20 .09
❑ 627 Mike Mussina .75 .35
❑ 628 Kevin Tapani .20 .09
❑ 629 John Smoltz .40 .18
❑ 630 Midre Cummings .20 .09
❑ 631 Salomon Torres .20 .09
❑ 632 Willie Adams .20 .09
❑ 633 Derek Jeter 3.00 1.35
❑ 634 Steve Trachsel .20 .09
❑ 635 Albie Lopez .20 .09
❑ 636 Jason Moler .20 .09
❑ 637 Carlos Delgado .60 .25
❑ 638 Roberto Mejia .20 .09
❑ 639 Darren Burton .20 .09
❑ 640 B.J. Wallace .20 .09
❑ 641 Brad Clontz .20 .09
❑ 642 Billy Wagner 3.00 1.35
❑ 643 Aaron Sele .40 .18
❑ 644 Cameron Cairncross .20 .09
❑ 645 Brian Harper .20 .09
❑ 646 Marc Valdes UER .20 .09
(No card number on back)
❑ 647 Mark Ratekin .20 .09
❑ 648 Terry Bradshaw .20 .09
❑ 649 Justin Thompson .60 .25
❑ 650 Mike Busch .40 .18
❑ 651 Joe Hall .20 .09
❑ 652 Bobby Jones .20 .09
❑ 653 Kelly Stinnett .20 .09
❑ 654 Rod Steph .20 .09
❑ 655 Jay Powell .40 .18
❑ 656 Keith Garagozzo UER .20 .09
(No card number on back)
❑ 657 Todd Dunn .40 .18
❑ 658 Charles Peterson .50 .23
❑ 659 Darren Lewis .20 .09
❑ 660 John Wasdin .40 .18
❑ 661 Tate Seefried .20 .09
❑ 662 Hector Trinidad .40 .18
❑ 663 John Carter .20 .09
❑ 664 Larry Mitchell .20 .09
❑ 665 David Catlett .20 .09
❑ 666 Dante Bichette .40 .18
❑ 667 Felix Jose .20 .09
❑ 668 Rondell White .40 .18
❑ 669 Tino Martinez .75 .35
❑ 670 Brian L. Hunter .40 .18
❑ 671 Jose Malave .20 .09
❑ 672 Archi Cianfrocco .20 .09
❑ 673 Mike Matheny .20 .09
❑ 674 Bret Barberie .20 .09
❑ 675 Andrew Lorraine .20 .09
❑ 676 Brian Jordan .40 .18
❑ 677 Tim Belcher .20 .09
❑ 678 Antonio Osuna .20 .09
❑ 679 Checklist .20 .09
❑ 680 Checklist .20 .09
❑ 681 Checklist .20 .09
❑ 682 Checklist .20 .09

1995 Bowman

	MINT	NRMT
COMPLETE SET (439)	250.00	110.00
COMMON CARD (1-439)	.25	.11

❑ 1 Billy Wagner .50 .23
❑ 2 Chris Widger .25 .11
❑ 3 Brent Bowers .25 .11
❑ 4 Bob Abreu 5.00 2.20
❑ 5 Lou Collier 1.00 .45
❑ 6 Juan Acevedo .25 .11
❑ 7 Jason Kelley .25 .11
❑ 8 Brian Sackinsky .25 .11
❑ 9 Scott Christman .25 .11
❑ 10 Damon Hollins .25 .11

❑ 11 Willis Otanez .50 .23
❑ 12 Jason Ryan .50 .23
❑ 13 Jason Giambi .50 .23
❑ 14 Andy Taulbee .25 .11
❑ 15 Mark Thompson .25 .11
❑ 16 Hugo Pivaral .50 .23
❑ 17 Brien Taylor .25 .11
❑ 18 Antonio Osuna .25 .11
❑ 19 Edgardo Alfonzo .50 .23
❑ 20 Carl Everett .25 .11
❑ 21 Matt Drews .25 .11
❑ 22 Bartolo Colon 10.00 4.50
❑ 23 Andruw Jones 35.00 16.00
❑ 24 Robert Person .25 .11
❑ 25 Derrek Lee 1.50 .70
❑ 26 John Ambrose .25 .11
❑ 27 Eric Knowles .50 .23
❑ 28 Chris Roberts .25 .11
❑ 29 Don Wengert .25 .11
❑ 30 Marcus Jensen .50 .23
❑ 31 Brian Barber .25 .11
❑ 32 Kevin Brown C .50 .23
❑ 33 Benji Gil .25 .11
❑ 34 Mike Hubbard .25 .11
❑ 35 Bart Evans .25 .11
❑ 36 Enrique Wilson 2.00 .90
❑ 37 Brian Buchanan .50 .23
❑ 38 Ken Ray .25 .11
❑ 39 Micah Franklin .25 .11
❑ 40 Ricky Otero .25 .11
❑ 41 Jason Kendall 1.00 .45
❑ 42 Jimmy Hurst .25 .11
❑ 43 Jerry Wolak .25 .11
❑ 44 Jayson Peterson .25 .11
❑ 45 Allen Battle .25 .11
❑ 46 Scott Stahoviak .25 .11
❑ 47 Steve Schrenk .25 .11
❑ 48 Travis Miller .25 .11
❑ 49 Eddie Rios .25 .11
❑ 50 Mike Hampton .25 .11
❑ 51 Chad Frontera .25 .11
❑ 52 Tom Evans 1.00 .45
❑ 53 C.J. Nitkowski .25 .11
❑ 54 Clay Caruthers .25 .11
❑ 55 Shannon Stewart .50 .23
❑ 56 Jorge Posada .50 .23
❑ 57 Aaron Holbert .25 .11
❑ 58 Harry Berrios .25 .11
❑ 59 Steve Rodriguez .25 .11
❑ 60 Shane Andrews .25 .11
❑ 61 Will Cunnane .50 .23
❑ 62 Richard Hidalgo .75 .35
❑ 63 Bill Selby .25 .11
❑ 64 Jay Cranford .25 .11
❑ 65 Jeff Suppan .50 .23
❑ 66 Curtis Goodwin .25 .11
❑ 67 John Thomson 1.00 .45
❑ 68 Justin Thompson .50 .23
❑ 69 Troy Percival .50 .23
❑ 70 Matt Wagner .50 .23
❑ 71 Terry Bradshaw .25 .11
❑ 72 Greg Hansell .25 .11
❑ 73 John Burke .25 .11
❑ 74 Jeff D'Amico .50 .23
❑ 75 Ernie Young .25 .11
❑ 76 Jason Bates .25 .11
❑ 77 Chris Stynes 1.00 .45
❑ 78 Cade Gaspar .50 .23

❑ 79 Melvin Nieves .25 .11
❑ 80 Rick Gorecki .25 .11
❑ 81 Felix Rodriguez .25 .11
❑ 82 Ryan Hancock .25 .11
❑ 83 Chris Carpenter 2.50 1.10
❑ 84 Ray McDavid .25 .11
❑ 85 Chris Wimmer .25 .11
❑ 86 Doug Glanville .25 .11
❑ 87 DeShawn Warren .25 .11
❑ 88 Damian Moss 1.00 .45
❑ 89 Rafael Orellano .50 .23
❑ 90 Vladimir Guerrero 50.00 22.00
❑ 91 Raul Casanova .75 .35
❑ 92 Karim Garcia 4.00 1.80
❑ 93 Bryce Florie .25 .11
❑ 94 Kevin Orie .50 .23
❑ 95 Ryan Nye .50 .23
❑ 96 Matt Sachse .50 .23
❑ 97 Ivan Arteaga .25 .11
❑ 98 Glenn Murray .25 .11
❑ 99 Stacy Hollins .25 .11
❑ 100 Jim Pittsley .25 .11
❑ 101 Craig Mattson .25 .11
❑ 102 Neifi Perez .50 .23
❑ 103 Keith Williams .25 .11
❑ 104 Roger Cedeno .25 .11
❑ 105 Tony Terry .25 .11
❑ 106 Jose Malave .25 .11
❑ 107 Joe Rosselli .25 .11
❑ 108 Kevin Jordan .25 .11
❑ 109 Sid Roberson .25 .11
❑ 110 Alan Embree .25 .11
❑ 111 Terrell Wade .25 .11
❑ 112 Bob Wolcott .25 .11
❑ 113 Carlos Perez 2.00 .90
❑ 114 Mike Bovee .50 .23
❑ 115 Tommy Davis .50 .23
❑ 116 Jeremey Kendall .25 .11
❑ 117 Rich Aude .25 .11
❑ 118 Rick Huisman .25 .11
❑ 119 Tim Belk .25 .11
❑ 120 Edgar Renteria .50 .23
❑ 121 Calvin Maduro .50 .23
❑ 122 Jerry Martin .25 .11
❑ 123 Ramon Fermin .25 .11
❑ 124 Kimera Bartee .25 .11
❑ 125 Mark Farris .25 .11
❑ 126 Frank Rodriguez .25 .11
❑ 127 Bobby Higginson 6.00 2.70
❑ 128 Bret Wagner .25 .11
❑ 129 Edwin Diaz 1.00 .45
❑ 130 Jimmy Haynes .25 .11
❑ 131 Chris Weinke .50 .23
❑ 132 Damian Jackson 1.00 .45
❑ 133 Felix Martinez .50 .23
❑ 134 Edwin Hurtado .25 .11
❑ 135 Matt Raleigh .25 .11
❑ 136 Paul Wilson .25 .11
❑ 137 Ron Villone .25 .11
❑ 138 Eric Stuckenschneider .25 .11
❑ 139 Tate Seefried .25 .11
❑ 140 Rey Ordonez 2.50 1.10
❑ 141 Eddie Pearson .25 .11
❑ 142 Kevin Gallaher .25 .11
❑ 143 Torii Hunter .50 .23
❑ 144 Daron Kirkreit .25 .11
❑ 145 Craig Wilson .25 .11
❑ 146 Ugueth Urbina .25 .11
❑ 147 Chris Snopek .25 .11
❑ 148 Kym Ashworth .25 .11
❑ 149 Wayne Gomes .25 .11
❑ 150 Mark Loretta .25 .11
❑ 151 Ramon Morel .50 .23
❑ 152 Trot Nixon .50 .23
❑ 153 Desi Relaford .50 .23
❑ 154 Scott Sullivan .25 .11
❑ 155 Marc Barcelo .25 .11
❑ 156 Willie Adams .25 .11
❑ 157 Derrick Gibson 8.00 3.60
❑ 158 Brian Meadows 1.00 .45
❑ 159 Julian Tavarez .25 .11
❑ 160 Bryan Rekar .25 .11
❑ 161 Steve Gibralter .50 .23
❑ 162 Esteban Loaiza .25 .11
❑ 163 John Wasdin .25 .11
❑ 164 Kirk Presley .25 .11
❑ 165 Mariano Rivera 1.00 .45
❑ 166 Andy Larkin .25 .11
❑ 167 Sean Whiteside .25 .11
❑ 168 Matt Apana .25 .11
❑ 169 Shawn Senior .25 .11
❑ 170 Scott Gentile .25 .11
❑ 171 Quilvio Veras .25 .11
❑ 172 Eli Marrero 4.00 1.80
❑ 173 Mendy Lopez .75 .35
❑ 174 Homer Bush .25 .11
❑ 175 Brian Stephenson .50 .23
❑ 176 Jon Nunnally .25 .11
❑ 177 Jose Herrera .25 .11
❑ 178 Corey Avrard .50 .23
❑ 179 David Bell .25 .11
❑ 180 Jason Isringhausen .50 .23
❑ 181 Jamey Wright .50 .23
❑ 182 Lonell Roberts .25 .11
❑ 183 Marty Cordova .25 .11
❑ 184 Amaury Telemaco .25 .11
❑ 185 John Mabry .25 .11
❑ 186 Andrew Vessel .50 .23
❑ 187 Jim Cole .25 .11
❑ 188 Marquis Riley .25 .11
❑ 189 Todd Dunn .50 .23
❑ 190 John Carter .25 .11
❑ 191 Donnie Sadler 2.00 .90
❑ 192 Mike Bell .50 .23
❑ 193 Chris Cumberland .50 .23
❑ 194 Jason Schmidt .50 .23
❑ 195 Matt Brunson .25 .11
❑ 196 James Baldwin .50 .23
❑ 197 Biff Simas .25 .11
❑ 198 Gus Gandarillas .25 .11
❑ 199 Mac Suzuki .50 .23
❑ 200 Rick Holifield .25 .11
❑ 201 Fernando Lunar .50 .23
❑ 202 Kevin Jarvis .25 .11
❑ 203 Everett Stull .25 .11
❑ 204 Steve Wojciechowski .25 .11
❑ 205 Shawn Estes .50 .23
❑ 206 Jermaine Dye .50 .23
❑ 207 Marc Kroon .25 .11
❑ 208 Peter Munro .50 .23
❑ 209 Pat Watkins .50 .23
❑ 210 Matt Smith .25 .11
❑ 211 Joe Vitiello .25 .11
❑ 212 Gerald Witasick Jr. .25 .11
❑ 213 Freddy Garcia 1.00 .45
❑ 214 Glenn Dishman .50 .23
❑ 215 Jay Canizaro .25 .11
❑ 216 Angel Martinez .25 .11
❑ 217 Yamil Benitez 1.00 .45
❑ 218 Fausto Macey .50 .23
❑ 219 Eric Owens .50 .23
❑ 220 Checklist .25 .11
❑ 221 Dwayne Hosey FOIL .25 .11
❑ 222 Brad Woodall FOIL .40 .18
❑ 223 Billy Ashley FOIL .40 .18
❑ 224 Mark Grudzielanek FOIL 2.00 .90
❑ 225 Mark Johnson FOIL .40 .18
❑ 226 Tim Unroe FOIL .40 .18
❑ 227 Todd Greene FOIL 2.50 1.10
❑ 228 Larry Sutton FOIL .40 .18
❑ 229 Derek Jeter FOIL 4.00 1.80
❑ 230 Sal Fasano FOIL .40 .18
❑ 231 Ruben Rivera FOIL .50 .23
❑ 232 Chris Truby FOIL 1.00 .45
❑ 233 John Donati FOIL .40 .18
❑ 234 Decomba Conner FOIL .50 .23
❑ 235 Sergio Nunez FOIL .75 .35
❑ 236 Ray Brown FOIL .40 .18
❑ 237 Juan Melo FOIL 2.00 .90
❑ 238 Hideo Nomo FOIL 10.00 4.50
❑ 239 Jamie Bluma FOIL .40 .18
❑ 240 Jay Payton FOIL .50 .23
❑ 241 Paul Konerko FOIL 10.00 4.50
❑ 242 Scott Elarton FOIL 3.00 1.35
❑ 243 Jeff Abbott FOIL 2.00 .90
❑ 244 Jim Brower FOIL .40 .18
❑ 245 Geoff Blum FOIL .50 .23
❑ 246 Aaron Boone FOIL 1.50 .70
❑ 247 J.R. Phillips FOIL .40 .18
❑ 248 Alex Ochoa FOIL .40 .18
❑ 249 Nomar Garciaparra FOIL 25.00 11.00
❑ 250 Garret Anderson FOIL .50 .23
❑ 251 Ray Durham FOIL .50 .23
❑ 252 Paul Shuey FOIL .40 .18
❑ 253 Tony Clark FOIL 1.50 .70
❑ 254 Johnny Damon FOIL .50 .23
❑ 255 Duane Singleton FOIL .40 .18
❑ 256 LaTroy Hawkins FOIL .40 .18
❑ 257 Andy Pettitte FOIL 1.00 .45
❑ 258 Ben Grieve FOIL 25.00 11.00
❑ 259 Marc Newfield FOIL .40 .18
❑ 260 Terrell Lowery FOIL .40 .18
❑ 261 Shawn Green FOIL .50 .23
❑ 262 Chipper Jones FOIL 2.50 1.10
❑ 263 Brooks Kieschnick FOIL .25 .11
❑ 264 Calvin Reese FOIL .40 .18
❑ 265 Doug Million FOIL .40 .18
❑ 266 Marc Valdes FOIL .40 .18
❑ 267 Brian L.Hunter FOIL .50 .23
❑ 268 Todd Hollandsworth FOIL .25 .11
❑ 269 Rod Henderson FOIL .40 .18
❑ 270 Bill Pulsipher FOIL .40 .18
❑ 271 Scott Rolen FOIL 35.00 16.00
❑ 272 Trey Beamon FOIL .40 .18
❑ 273 Alan Benes FOIL .50 .23
❑ 274 Dustin Hermanson FOIL .50 .23
❑ 275 Ricky Bottalico .50 .23
❑ 276 Albert Belle 1.25 .55
❑ 277 Deion Sanders .50 .23
❑ 278 Matt Williams .50 .23
❑ 279 Jeff Bagwell 1.50 .70
❑ 280 Kirby Puckett 1.50 .70
❑ 281 Dave Hollins .25 .11
❑ 282 Don Mattingly 1.50 .70
❑ 283 Joey Hamilton .50 .23
❑ 284 Bobby Bonilla .50 .23
❑ 285 Moises Alou .75 .35
❑ 286 Tom Glavine 1.00 .45
❑ 287 Brett Butler .50 .23
❑ 288 Chris Hoiles .25 .11
❑ 289 Kenny Rogers .25 .11
❑ 290 Larry Walker 1.00 .45
❑ 291 Tim Raines .50 .23
❑ 292 Kevin Appier .50 .23
❑ 293 Roger Clemens 2.00 .90
❑ 294 Chuck Carr .25 .11
❑ 295 Randy Myers .25 .11
❑ 296 Dave Nilsson .25 .11
❑ 297 Joe Carter .50 .23
❑ 298 Chuck Finley .50 .23
❑ 299 Ray Lankford .50 .23
❑ 300 Roberto Kelly .25 .11
❑ 301 Jon Lieber .25 .11
❑ 302 Travis Fryman .50 .23
❑ 303 Mark McGwire 5.00 2.20
❑ 304 Tony Gwynn 2.50 1.10
❑ 305 Kenny Lofton 1.00 .45
❑ 306 Mark Whiten .25 .11
❑ 307 Doug Drabek .25 .11
❑ 308 Terry Steinbach .50 .23
❑ 309 Ryan Klesko .50 .23
❑ 310 Mike Piazza 3.00 1.35
❑ 311 Ben McDonald .25 .11
❑ 312 Reggie Sanders .50 .23
❑ 313 Alex Fernandez .25 .11
❑ 314 Aaron Sele .50 .23
❑ 315 Gregg Jefferies .25 .11
❑ 316 Rickey Henderson 1.00 .45
❑ 317 Brian Anderson .50 .23
❑ 318 Jose Valentin .25 .11
❑ 319 Rod Beck .25 .11
❑ 320 Marquis Grissom .50 .23
❑ 321 Ken Griffey Jr. 5.00 2.20
❑ 322 Bret Saberhagen .50 .23
❑ 323 Juan Gonzalez 2.50 1.10
❑ 324 Paul Molitor 1.00 .45
❑ 325 Gary Sheffield .75 .35
❑ 326 Darren Daulton .50 .23
❑ 327 Bill Swift .25 .11
❑ 328 Brian McRae .25 .11
❑ 329 Robin Ventura .50 .23
❑ 330 Lee Smith .50 .23
❑ 331 Fred McGriff .75 .35
❑ 332 Delino DeShields .25 .11
❑ 333 Edgar Martinez .50 .23

- ❑ 334 Mike Mussina 1.00 .45
- ❑ 335 Orlando Merced .25 .11
- ❑ 336 Carlos Baerga .50 .23
- ❑ 337 Wil Cordero .25 .11
- ❑ 338 Tom Pagnozzi .25 .11
- ❑ 339 Pat Hentgen .50 .23
- ❑ 340 Chad Curtis .25 .11
- ❑ 341 Darren Lewis .25 .11
- ❑ 342 Jeff Kent .50 .23
- ❑ 343 Bip Roberts .25 .11
- ❑ 344 Ivan Rodriguez 1.25 .55
- ❑ 345 Jeff Montgomery .25 .11
- ❑ 346 Hal Morris .25 .11
- ❑ 347 Danny Tartabull .25 .11
- ❑ 348 Raul Mondesi .75 .35
- ❑ 349 Ken Hill .25 .11
- ❑ 350 Pedro Martinez 1.00 .45
- ❑ 351 Frank Thomas 3.00 1.35
- ❑ 352 Manny Ramirez 1.00 .45
- ❑ 353 Tim Salmon 1.00 .45
- ❑ 354 W. VanLandingham .25 .11
- ❑ 355 Andres Galarraga 1.00 .45
- ❑ 356 Paul O'Neill .50 .23
- ❑ 357 Brady Anderson .50 .23
- ❑ 358 Ramon Martinez .50 .23
- ❑ 359 John Olerud .50 .23
- ❑ 360 Ruben Sierra .25 .11
- ❑ 361 Cal Eldred .25 .11
- ❑ 362 Jay Buhner .50 .23
- ❑ 363 Jay Bell .50 .23
- ❑ 364 Wally Joyner .50 .23
- ❑ 365 Chuck Knoblauch 1.00 .45
- ❑ 366 Len Dykstra .50 .23
- ❑ 367 John Wetteland .50 .23
- ❑ 368 Roberto Alomar 1.00 .45
- ❑ 369 Craig Biggio 1.00 .45
- ❑ 370 Ozzie Smith 1.25 .55
- ❑ 371 Terry Pendleton .25 .11
- ❑ 372 Sammy Sosa 2.50 1.10
- ❑ 373 Carlos Garcia .25 .11
- ❑ 374 Jose Rijo .25 .11
- ❑ 375 Chris Gomez .25 .11
- ❑ 376 Barry Bonds 1.25 .55
- ❑ 377 Steve Avery .25 .11
- ❑ 378 Rick Wilkins .25 .11
- ❑ 379 Pete Harnisch .25 .11
- ❑ 380 Dean Palmer .50 .23
- ❑ 381 Bob Hamelin .25 .11
- ❑ 382 Jason Bere .25 .11
- ❑ 383 Jimmy Key .50 .23
- ❑ 384 Dante Bichette .50 .23
- ❑ 385 Rafael Palmeiro .75 .35
- ❑ 386 David Justice 1.00 .45
- ❑ 387 Chili Davis .50 .23
- ❑ 388 Mike Greenwell .25 .11
- ❑ 389 Todd Zeile .25 .11
- ❑ 390 Jeff Conine .50 .23
- ❑ 391 Rick Aguilera .25 .11
- ❑ 392 Eddie Murray 1.00 .45
- ❑ 393 Mike Stanley .25 .11
- ❑ 394 Cliff Floyd UER .50 .23 (numbered 294)
- ❑ 395 Randy Johnson 1.00 .45
- ❑ 396 David Nied .25 .11
- ❑ 397 Devon White .50 .23
- ❑ 398 Royce Clayton .25 .11
- ❑ 399 Andy Benes .50 .23
- ❑ 400 John Hudek .25 .11
- ❑ 401 Bobby Jones .25 .11
- ❑ 402 Eric Karros .50 .23
- ❑ 403 Will Clark 1.00 .45
- ❑ 404 Mark Langston .25 .11
- ❑ 405 Kevin Brown .75 .35
- ❑ 406 Greg Maddux 3.00 1.35
- ❑ 407 David Cone .75 .35
- ❑ 408 Wade Boggs 1.00 .45
- ❑ 409 Steve Trachsel .25 .11
- ❑ 410 Greg Vaughn .50 .23
- ❑ 411 Mo Vaughn 1.25 .55
- ❑ 412 Wilson Alvarez .50 .23
- ❑ 413 Cal Ripken 4.00 1.80
- ❑ 414 Rico Brogna .25 .11
- ❑ 415 Barry Larkin .75 .35
- ❑ 416 Cecil Fielder .50 .23
- ❑ 417 Jose Canseco 1.00 .45
- ❑ 418 Jack McDowell .25 .11
- ❑ 419 Mike Lieberthal .25 .11
- ❑ 420 Andrew Lorraine .25 .11
- ❑ 421 Rich Becker .25 .11
- ❑ 422 Tony Phillips .25 .11
- ❑ 423 Scott Ruffcorn .25 .11
- ❑ 424 Jeff Granger .25 .11
- ❑ 425 Greg Pirkl .25 .11
- ❑ 426 Dennis Eckersley .50 .23
- ❑ 427 Jose Lima .25 .11
- ❑ 428 Russ Davis .50 .23
- ❑ 429 Armando Benitez .25 .11
- ❑ 430 Alex Gonzalez .25 .11
- ❑ 431 Carlos Delgado .50 .23
- ❑ 432 Chan Ho Park 1.25 .55
- ❑ 433 Mickey Tettleton .25 .11
- ❑ 434 Dave Winfield 1.00 .45
- ❑ 435 John Burkett .25 .11
- ❑ 436 Orlando Miller .25 .11
- ❑ 437 Rondell White .50 .23
- ❑ 438 Jose Oliva .25 .11
- ❑ 439 Checklist .25 .11

1995 Bowman Gold Foil

	MINT	NRMT
COMPLETE SET (54)	150.00	70.00
COMMON CARD (221-274)	1.00	.45

*GOLD: 3X TO 6X BASIC CARDS

1996 Bowman

	MINT	NRMT
COMPLETE SET (385)	125.00	55.00
COMMON CARD (1-385)	.20	.09

- ❑ 1 Cal Ripken 3.00 1.35
- ❑ 2 Ray Durham .40 .18
- ❑ 3 Ivan Rodriguez 1.00 .45
- ❑ 4 Fred McGriff .60 .25
- ❑ 5 Hideo Nomo 1.25 .55
- ❑ 6 Troy Percival .40 .18
- ❑ 7 Moises Alou .60 .25
- ❑ 8 Mike Stanley .20 .09
- ❑ 9 Jay Buhner .40 .18
- ❑ 10 Shawn Green .40 .18
- ❑ 11 Ryan Klesko .40 .18
- ❑ 12 Andres Galarraga .75 .35
- ❑ 13 Dean Palmer .40 .18
- ❑ 14 Jeff Conine .40 .18
- ❑ 15 Brian L.Hunter .40 .18
- ❑ 16 J.T. Snow .40 .18
- ❑ 17 Larry Walker .75 .35
- ❑ 18 Barry Larkin .60 .25
- ❑ 19 Alex Gonzalez .20 .09
- ❑ 20 Edgar Martinez .40 .18
- ❑ 21 Mo Vaughn 1.00 .45
- ❑ 22 Mark McGwire 4.00 1.80
- ❑ 23 Jose Canseco .75 .35
- ❑ 24 Jack McDowell .20 .09
- ❑ 25 Dante Bichette .40 .18
- ❑ 26 Wade Boggs .75 .35
- ❑ 27 Mike Piazza 2.50 1.10
- ❑ 28 Ray Lankford .40 .18
- ❑ 29 Craig Biggio .75 .35
- ❑ 30 Rafael Palmeiro .60 .25
- ❑ 31 Ron Gant .20 .09
- ❑ 32 Javy Lopez .40 .18
- ❑ 33 Brian Jordan .40 .18
- ❑ 34 Paul O'Neill .40 .18
- ❑ 35 Mark Grace .60 .25
- ❑ 36 Matt Williams .40 .18
- ❑ 37 Pedro Martinez .75 .35
- ❑ 38 Rickey Henderson .75 .35
- ❑ 39 Bobby Bonilla .40 .18
- ❑ 40 Todd Hollandsworth .20 .09
- ❑ 41 Jim Thome .75 .35
- ❑ 42 Gary Sheffield .60 .25
- ❑ 43 Tim Salmon .75 .35
- ❑ 44 Gregg Jefferies .20 .09
- ❑ 45 Roberto Alomar .75 .35
- ❑ 46 Carlos Baerga .40 .18
- ❑ 47 Mark Grudzielanek .40 .18
- ❑ 48 Randy Johnson .75 .35
- ❑ 49 Tino Martinez .75 .35
- ❑ 50 Robin Ventura .40 .18
- ❑ 51 Ryne Sandberg 1.00 .45
- ❑ 52 Jay Bell .40 .18
- ❑ 53 Jason Schmidt .20 .09
- ❑ 54 Frank Thomas 2.50 1.10
- ❑ 55 Kenny Lofton .75 .35
- ❑ 56 Ariel Prieto .20 .09
- ❑ 57 David Cone .60 .25
- ❑ 58 Reggie Sanders .40 .18
- ❑ 59 Michael Tucker .40 .18
- ❑ 60 Vinny Castilla .60 .25
- ❑ 61 Len Dykstra .40 .18
- ❑ 62 Todd Hundley .40 .18
- ❑ 63 Brian McRae .20 .09
- ❑ 64 Dennis Eckersley .40 .18
- ❑ 65 Rondell White .40 .18
- ❑ 66 Eric Karros .40 .18
- ❑ 67 Greg Maddux 2.50 1.10
- ❑ 68 Kevin Appier .40 .18
- ❑ 69 Eddie Murray .75 .35
- ❑ 70 John Olerud .40 .18
- ❑ 71 Tony Gwynn 2.00 .90
- ❑ 72 David Justice .75 .35
- ❑ 73 Ken Caminiti .60 .25
- ❑ 74 Terry Steinbach .40 .18
- ❑ 75 Alan Benes .40 .18
- ❑ 76 Chipper Jones 2.00 .90
- ❑ 77 Jeff Bagwell 1.25 .55
- ❑ 78 Barry Bonds 1.00 .45
- ❑ 79 Ken Griffey Jr. 4.00 1.80
- ❑ 80 Roger Cedeno .20 .09
- ❑ 81 Joe Carter .40 .18
- ❑ 82 Henry Rodriguez .40 .18
- ❑ 83 Jason Isringhausen .20 .09
- ❑ 84 Chuck Knoblauch .75 .35
- ❑ 85 Manny Ramirez .75 .35
- ❑ 86 Tom Glavine .75 .35
- ❑ 87 Jeffrey Hammonds .40 .18
- ❑ 88 Paul Molitor .75 .35
- ❑ 89 Roger Clemens 1.50 .70
- ❑ 90 Greg Vaughn .40 .18
- ❑ 91 Marty Cordova .20 .09
- ❑ 92 Albert Belle 1.00 .45
- ❑ 93 Mike Mussina .75 .35
- ❑ 94 Garret Anderson .40 .18
- ❑ 95 Juan Gonzalez 2.00 .90
- ❑ 96 John Valentin .40 .18
- ❑ 97 Jason Giambi .40 .18
- ❑ 98 Kirby Puckett 1.25 .55
- ❑ 99 Jim Edmonds .60 .25
- ❑ 100 Cecil Fielder .40 .18
- ❑ 101 Mike Aldrete .20 .09
- ❑ 102 Marquis Grissom .40 .18
- ❑ 103 Derek Bell .40 .18
- ❑ 104 Raul Mondesi .60 .25
- ❑ 105 Sammy Sosa 2.00 .90
- ❑ 106 Travis Fryman .40 .18
- ❑ 107 Rico Brogna .20 .09
- ❑ 108 Will Clark .75 .35
- ❑ 109 Bernie Williams .75 .35
- ❑ 110 Brady Anderson .40 .18
- ❑ 111 Torii Hunter .40 .18
- ❑ 112 Derek Jeter 2.50 1.10
- ❑ 113 Mike Kusiewicz .50 .23
- ❑ 114 Scott Rolen 4.00 1.80
- ❑ 115 Ramon Castro .40 .18
- ❑ 116 Jose Guillen 6.00 2.70
- ❑ 117 Wade Walker .20 .09

118	Shawn Senior	.20	.09
119	Onan Masaoka	1.00	.45
120	Marlon Anderson	2.50	1.10
121	Katsuhiro Maeda	2.00	.90
122	Garrett Stephenson	.20	.09
123	Butch Huskey	.20	.09
124	D'Angelo Jimenez	2.00	.90
125	Tony Mounce	.50	.23
126	Jay Canizaro	.20	.09
127	Juan Melo	.40	.18
128	Steve Gibralter	.20	.09
129	Freddy Garcia	.20	.09
130	Julio Santana UER Card has him born in 1993	.20	.09
131	Richard Hidalgo	.40	.18
132	Jermaine Dye	.20	.09
133	Willie Adams	.20	.09
134	Everett Stull	.20	.09
135	Ramon Morel	.20	.09
136	Chan Ho Park	.75	.35
137	Jamey Wright	.20	.09
138	Luis Garcia	.20	.09
139	Dan Serafini	.20	.09
140	Ryan Dempster	1.00	.45
141	Tate Seefried	.20	.09
142	Jimmy Hurst	.20	.09
143	Travis Miller	.20	.09
144	Curtis Goodwin	.20	.09
145	Rocky Coppinger	.50	.23
146	Enrique Wilson	.40	.18
147	Jaime Bluma	.20	.09
148	Andrew Vessel	.20	.09
149	Damian Moss	.20	.09
150	Shawn Gallagher	2.50	1.10
151	Pat Watkins	.40	.18
152	Jose Paniagua	.20	.09
153	Danny Graves	.40	.18
154	Bryon Gainey	.50	.23
155	Steve Soderstrom	.20	.09
156	Cliff Brumbaugh	.20	.09
157	Eugene Kingsale	1.00	.45
158	Lou Collier	.40	.18
159	Todd Walker	4.00	1.80
160	Kris Detmers	1.00	.45
161	Josh Booty	1.00	.45
162	Greg Whiteman	.20	.09
163	Damian Jackson	.20	.09
164	Tony Clark	.75	.35
165	Jeff D'Amico	.20	.09
166	Johnny Damon	.40	.18
167	Rafael Orellano	.20	.09
168	Ruben Rivera	.40	.18
169	Alex Ochoa	.20	.09
170	Jay Powell	.20	.09
171	Tom Evans	.40	.18
172	Ron Villone	.20	.09
173	Shawn Estes	.40	.18
174	John Wasdin	.20	.09
175	Bill Simas	.20	.09
176	Kevin Brown	.75	.35
177	Shannon Stewart	.40	.18
178	Todd Greene	.40	.18
179	Bob Wolcott	.20	.09
180	Chris Snopek	.20	.09
181	Nomar Garciaparra	4.00	1.80
182	Cameron Smith	.20	.09
183	Matt Drews	.20	.09
184	Jimmy Haynes	.20	.09
185	Chris Carpenter	.40	.18
186	Desi Relaford	.20	.09
187	Ben Grieve	4.00	1.80
188	Mike Bell	.20	.09
189	Luis Castillo	1.00	.45
190	Ugueth Urbina	.40	.18
191	Paul Wilson	.20	.09
192	Andruw Jones	2.50	1.10
193	Wayne Gomes	.20	.09
194	Craig Counsell	1.00	.45
195	Jim Cole	.20	.09
196	Brooks Kieschnick	.20	.09
197	Trey Beamon	.20	.09
198	Marino Santana	.20	.09
199	Bob Abreu	.40	.18
200	Calvin Reese	.20	.09
201	Dante Powell	1.50	.70
202	George Arias	.20	.09
203	Jorge Velandia	.20	.09
204	George Lombard	8.00	3.60
205	Byron Browne	.20	.09
206	John Frascatore	.20	.09
207	Terry Adams	.20	.09
208	Wilson Delgado	.50	.23
209	Billy McMillon	.20	.09
210	Jeff Abbott	.40	.18
211	Trot Nixon	.20	.09
212	Amaury Telemaco	.20	.09
213	Scott Sullivan	.20	.09
214	Justin Thompson	.40	.18
215	Decomba Conner	.40	.18
216	Ryan McGuire	.20	.09
217	Matt Luke	.20	.09
218	Doug Million	.20	.09
219	Jason Dickson	3.00	1.35
220	Ramon Hernandez	4.00	1.80
221	Mark Bellhorn	2.00	.90
222	Eric Ludwick	.50	.23
223	Luke Wilcox	.20	.09
224	Marty Malloy	.50	.23
225	Gary Coffee	.60	.25
226	Wendell Magee	.40	.18
227	Brett Tomko	2.00	.90
228	Derek Lowe	.20	.09
229	Jose Rosado	1.50	.70
230	Steve Bourgeois	.20	.09
231	Neil Weber	.20	.09
232	Jeff Ware	.20	.09
233	Edwin Diaz	.40	.18
234	Greg Norton	.20	.09
235	Aaron Boone	.20	.09
236	Jeff Suppan	.20	.09
237	Bret Wagner	.20	.09
238	Elieser Marrero	.40	.18
239	Will Cunnane	.40	.18
240	Brian Barkley	.50	.23
241	Jay Payton	.20	.09
242	Marcus Jensen	.20	.09
243	Ryan Nye	.20	.09
244	Chad Mottola	.20	.09
245	Scott McClain	.20	.09
246	Jessie Ibarra	.40	.18
247	Mike Darr	1.50	.70
248	Bobby Estalella	3.00	1.35
249	Michael Barrett	1.25	.55
250	Jamie Lopiccolo	.50	.23
251	Shane Spencer	10.00	4.50
252	Ben Petrick	4.00	1.80
253	Jason Bell	1.00	.45
254	Arnold Gooch	.50	.23
255	T.J. Mathews	.20	.09
256	Jason Ryan	.20	.09
257	Pat Cline	1.50	.70
258	Rafael Carmona	.20	.09
259	Carl Pavano	5.00	2.20
260	Ben Davis	1.00	.45
261	Matt Lawton	2.00	.90
262	Kevin Sefcik	.20	.09
263	Chris Fussell	1.00	.45
264	Mike Cameron	4.00	1.80
265	Marty Janzen	.20	.09
266	Livan Hernandez	4.00	1.80
267	Raul Ibanez	.75	.35
268	Juan Encarnacion	2.00	.90
269	David Yocum	.50	.23
270	Jonathan Johnson	.50	.23
271	Reggie Taylor	.40	.18
272	Danny Buxbaum	1.00	.45
273	Jacob Cruz	.40	.18
274	Bobby Morris	.20	.09
275	Andy Fox	.20	.09
276	Greg Keagle	.20	.09
277	Charles Peterson	.20	.09
278	Derrek Lee	.75	.35
279	Bryant Nelson	.50	.23
280	Antone Williamson	.20	.09
281	Scott Elarton	.40	.18
282	Shad Williams	.20	.09
283	Rich Hunter	.20	.09
284	Chris Sheff	.20	.09
285	Derrick Gibson	.75	.35
286	Felix Rodriguez	.20	.09
287	Brian Banks	.20	.09
288	Jason McDonald	.20	.09
289	Glendon Rusch	1.00	.45
290	Gary Rath	.20	.09
291	Peter Munro	.40	.18
292	Tom Fordham	.20	.09
293	Jason Kendall	.75	.35
294	Russ Johnson	.20	.09
295	Joe Long	.20	.09
296	Robert Smith	2.00	.90
297	Jarrod Washburn	2.00	.90
298	Dave Coggin	.50	.23
299	Jeff Yoder	.50	.23
300	Jed Hansen	.40	.18
301	Matt Morris	3.00	1.35
302	Josh Bishop	.50	.23
303	Dustin Hermanson	.40	.18
304	Mike Gulan	.20	.09
305	Felipe Crespo	.20	.09
306	Quinton McCracken	.40	.18
307	Jim Bonnici	.20	.09
308	Sal Fasano	.20	.09
309	Gabe Alvarez	3.00	1.35
310	Heath Murray	.50	.23
311	Jose Valentin	1.50	.70
312	Bartolo Colon	1.25	.55
313	Olmedo Saenz	.20	.09
314	Norm Hutchins	2.00	.90
315	Chris Holt	.20	.09
316	David Doster	.20	.09
317	Robert Person	.20	.09
318	Donne Wall	.20	.09
319	Adam Riggs	.20	.09
320	Homer Bush	.20	.09
321	Brad Rigby	.20	.09
322	Lou Merloni	1.50	.70
323	Neifi Perez	.20	.09
324	Chris Cumberland	.20	.09
325	Alvie Shepherd	.50	.23
326	Jarrod Patterson	.20	.09
327	Ray Ricken	.40	.18
328	Danny Klassen	1.50	.70
329	David Miller	.50	.23
330	Chad Alexander	.75	.35
331	Matt Beaumont	.20	.09
332	Damon Hollins	.20	.09
333	Todd Dunn	.20	.09
334	Mike Sweeney	1.00	.45
335	Richie Sexson	1.25	.55
336	Billy Wagner	.40	.18
337	Ron Wright	3.00	1.35
338	Paul Konerko	1.50	.70
339	Tommy Phelps	.50	.23
340	Karim Garcia	.40	.18
341	Mike Grace	.20	.09
342	Russell Branyan	6.00	2.70
343	Randy Winn	1.00	.45
344	A.J. Pierzynski	1.00	.45
345	Mike Busby	.20	.09
346	Matt Beech	.50	.23
347	Jose Cepeda	.50	.23
348	Brian Stephenson	.20	.09
349	Rey Ordonez	.40	.18
350	Rich Aurilla	.20	.09
351	Edgard Velazquez	2.00	.90
352	Raul Casanova	.20	.09
353	Carlos Guillen	4.00	1.80
354	Bruce Aven	.20	.09
355	Ryan Jones	1.00	.45
356	Derek Aucoin	.20	.09
357	Brian Rose	4.00	1.80
358	Richard Almanzar	.50	.23
359	Fletcher Bates	.75	.35
360	Russ Ortiz	.20	.09
361	Wilton Guerrero	1.50	.70
362	Geoff Jenkins	3.00	1.35
363	Pete Janicki	.20	.09
364	Yamil Benitez	.20	.09
365	Aaron Holbert	.20	.09
366	Tim Belk	.20	.09
367	Terrell Wade	.20	.09
368	Terrence Long	.40	.18
369	Brad Fullmer	.75	.35
370	Matt Wagner	.20	.09
371	Craig Wilson	.20	.09

❑ 372 Mark Loretta .20 .09
❑ 373 Eric Owens .20 .09
❑ 374 Vladimir Guerrero 3.00 1.35
❑ 375 Tommy Davis .20 .09
❑ 376 Donnie Sadler .40 .18
❑ 377 Edgar Renteria .40 .18
❑ 378 Todd Helton 8.00 3.60
❑ 379 Ralph Milliard .50 .23
❑ 380 Darin Blood 1.50 .70
❑ 381 Shayne Bennett .20 .09
❑ 382 Mark Redman .20 .09
❑ 383 Felix Martinez .20 .09
❑ 384 Sean Watkins .75 .35
❑ 385 Oscar Henriquez .40 .18
❑ M20 1952 Bowman Mantle 10.00 4.50
❑ NNO Unnumbered Checklists .20 .09

1996 Bowman Minor League POY

	MINT	NRMT
COMPLETE SET (15)	40.00	18.00
COMMON CARD (1-15)	1.50	.70

❑ 1 Andruw Jones 8.00 3.60
❑ 2 Derrick Gibson 2.50 1.10
❑ 3 Bob Abreu 1.75 .80
❑ 4 Todd Walker 5.00 2.20
❑ 5 Jamey Wright 1.50 .70
❑ 6 Wes Helms 5.00 2.20
❑ 7 Karim Garcia 1.75 .80
❑ 8 Bartolo Colon 4.00 1.80
❑ 9 Alex Ochoa 1.50 .70
❑ 10 Mike Sweeney 2.00 .90
❑ 11 Ruben Rivera 1.75 .80
❑ 12 Gabe Alvarez 2.50 1.10
❑ 13 Billy Wagner 1.75 .80
❑ 14 Vladimir Guerrero 10.00 4.50
❑ 15 Edgard Velazquez 3.00 1.35

1997 Bowman

	MINT	NRMT
COMPLETE SET (441)	150.00	70.00
COMPLETE SERIES 1 (221)	90.00	40.00
COMPLETE SERIES 2 (220)	60.00	27.00
COMMON CARD (1-441)	.20	.09

❑ 1 Derek Jeter 2.50 1.10
❑ 2 Edgar Renteria .40 .18
❑ 3 Chipper Jones 2.00 .90
❑ 4 Hideo Nomo 1.00 .45
❑ 5 Tim Salmon .75 .35
❑ 6 Jason Giambi .40 .18
❑ 7 Robin Ventura .40 .18
❑ 8 Tony Clark .50 .23
❑ 9 Barry Larkin .50 .23
❑ 10 Paul Molitor .75 .35
❑ 11 Bernard Gilkey .20 .09
❑ 12 Jack McDowell .20 .09
❑ 13 Andy Benes .40 .18
❑ 14 Ryan Klesko .40 .18
❑ 15 Mark McGwire 4.00 1.80
❑ 16 Ken Griffey Jr. 4.00 1.80
❑ 17 Robb Nen .20 .09
❑ 18 Cal Ripken 3.00 1.35
❑ 19 John Valentin .40 .18
❑ 20 Ricky Bottalico .40 .18
❑ 21 Mike Lansing .20 .09
❑ 22 Ryne Sandberg 1.00 .45
❑ 23 Carlos Delgado .40 .18
❑ 24 Craig Biggio .75 .35
❑ 25 Eric Karros .40 .18
❑ 26 Kevin Appier .40 .18
❑ 27 Mariano Rivera .40 .18
❑ 28 Vinny Castilla .50 .23
❑ 29 Juan Gonzalez 2.00 .90
❑ 30 Al Martin .20 .09
❑ 31 Jeff Cirillo .40 .18
❑ 32 Eddie Murray .75 .35
❑ 33 Ray Lankford .40 .18
❑ 34 Manny Ramirez .75 .35
❑ 35 Roberto Alomar .75 .35
❑ 36 Will Clark .75 .35
❑ 37 Chuck Knoblauch .75 .35
❑ 38 Harold Baines .40 .18
❑ 39 Trevor Hoffman .40 .18
❑ 40 Edgar Martinez .40 .18
❑ 41 Geronimo Berroa .20 .09
❑ 42 Rey Ordonez .40 .18
❑ 43 Mike Stanley .20 .09
❑ 44 Mike Mussina .75 .35
❑ 45 Kevin Brown .50 .23
❑ 46 Dennis Eckersley .40 .18
❑ 47 Henry Rodriguez .40 .18
❑ 48 Tino Martinez .75 .35
❑ 49 Eric Young .40 .18
❑ 50 Bret Boone .40 .18
❑ 51 Raul Mondesi .50 .23
❑ 52 Sammy Sosa 2.00 .90
❑ 53 John Smoltz .40 .18
❑ 54 Billy Wagner .40 .18
❑ 55 Jeff D'Amico .20 .09
❑ 56 Ken Caminiti .50 .23
❑ 57 Jason Kendall .50 .23
❑ 58 Wade Boggs .75 .35
❑ 59 Andres Galarraga .75 .35
❑ 60 Jeff Brantley .20 .09
❑ 61 Mel Rojas .20 .09
❑ 62 Brian L. Hunter .40 .18
❑ 63 Bobby Bonilla .40 .18
❑ 64 Roger Clemens 1.50 .70
❑ 65 Jeff Kent .40 .18
❑ 66 Matt Williams .40 .18
❑ 67 Albert Belle 1.00 .45
❑ 68 Jeff King .20 .09
❑ 69 John Wetteland .40 .18
❑ 70 Deion Sanders .40 .18
❑ 71 Bubba Trammell 1.00 .45
❑ 72 Felix Heredia .75 .35
❑ 73 Billy Koch .75 .35
❑ 74 Sidney Ponson 1.00 .45
❑ 75 Ricky Ledee 5.00 2.20
❑ 76 Brett Tomko .40 .18
❑ 77 Braden Looper .50 .23
❑ 78 Damian Jackson .20 .09
❑ 79 Jason Dickson .40 .18
❑ 80 Chad Green .75 .35
❑ 81 R.A. Dickey .50 .23
❑ 82 Jeff Liefer .40 .18
❑ 83 Matt Wagner .20 .09
❑ 84 Richard Hidalgo .40 .18
❑ 85 Adam Riggs .20 .09
❑ 86 Robert Smith .20 .09
❑ 87 Chad Hermansen 4.00 1.80
❑ 88 Felix Martinez .20 .09
❑ 89 J.J. Johnson .20 .09
❑ 90 Todd Dunwoody 1.00 .45
❑ 91 Katsuhiro Maeda .40 .18
❑ 92 Darin Erstad 1.25 .55
❑ 93 Elieser Marrero .40 .18
❑ 94 Bartolo Colon .40 .18
❑ 95 Chris Fussell .20 .09
❑ 96 Ugueth Urbina .40 .18
❑ 97 Josh Paul 1.00 .45
❑ 98 Jaime Bluma .20 .09
❑ 99 Seth Greisinger 1.25 .55
❑ 100 Jose Cruz Jr. 6.00 2.70
❑ 101 Todd Dunn .20 .09
❑ 102 Joe Young .50 .23
❑ 103 Jonathan Johnson .20 .09
❑ 104 Justin Towle 1.00 .45
❑ 105 Brian Rose .75 .35
❑ 106 Jose Guillen .75 .35
❑ 107 Andruw Jones 1.25 .55
❑ 108 Mark Kotsay 3.00 1.35
❑ 109 Wilton Guerrero .20 .09
❑ 110 Jacob Cruz .20 .09
❑ 111 Mike Sweeney .20 .09
❑ 112 Julio Mosquera .20 .09
❑ 113 Matt Morris .40 .18
❑ 114 Wendell Magee .20 .09
❑ 115 John Thomson .20 .09
❑ 116 Javier (Jose) Valentin .40 .18
❑ 117 Tom Fordham .20 .09
❑ 118 Ruben Rivera .40 .18
❑ 119 Mike Drumright .75 .35
❑ 120 Chris Holt .20 .09
❑ 121 Sean Maloney .20 .09
❑ 122 Michael Barrett .40 .18
❑ 123 Tony Saunders .75 .35
❑ 124 Kevin Brown C .20 .09
❑ 125 Richard Almanzar .20 .09
❑ 126 Mark Redman .20 .09
❑ 127 Anthony Sanders 1.25 .55
❑ 128 Jeff Abbott .40 .18
❑ 129 Eugene Kingsale .40 .18
❑ 130 Paul Konerko .75 .35
❑ 131 Randall Simon 2.50 1.10
❑ 132 Andy Larkin .20 .09
❑ 133 Rafael Medina .40 .18
❑ 134 Mendy Lopez .20 .09
❑ 135 Freddy Garcia .20 .09
❑ 136 Karim Garcia .40 .18
❑ 137 Larry Rodriguez .50 .23
❑ 138 Carlos Guillen .40 .18
❑ 139 Aaron Boone .20 .09
❑ 140 Donnie Sadler .40 .18
❑ 141 Brooks Kieschnick .20 .09
❑ 142 Scott Spiezio .20 .09
❑ 143 Everett Stull .20 .09
❑ 144 Enrique Wilson .40 .18
❑ 145 Milton Bradley 4.00 1.80
❑ 146 Kevin Orie .20 .09
❑ 147 Derek Wallace .20 .09
❑ 148 Russ Johnson .20 .09
❑ 149 Joe Lagarde .50 .23
❑ 150 Luis Castillo .40 .18
❑ 151 Jay Payton .20 .09
❑ 152 Joe Long .40 .18
❑ 153 Livan Hernandez .40 .18
❑ 154 Vladimir Nunez 1.00 .45
❑ 155 Calvin Reese UER .20 .09
Card actually numbered 156
❑ 156 George Arias .20 .09
❑ 157 Homer Bush .20 .09
❑ 158 Chris Carpenter UER .40 .18
Card numbered 159
❑ 159 Eric Milton 1.50 .70
❑ 160 Richie Sexson .50 .23
❑ 161 Carl Pavano .75 .35
❑ 162 Chris Gissell .50 .23
❑ 163 Mac Suzuki .20 .09
❑ 164 Pat Cline .40 .18
❑ 165 Ron Wright .40 .18
❑ 166 Dante Powell .40 .18
❑ 167 Mark Bellhorn .40 .18
❑ 168 George Lombard 1.00 .45
❑ 169 Pee Wee Lopez 1.00 .45
❑ 170 Paul Wilder 1.00 .45

❑	171	Brad Fullmer	.50	.23
❑	172	Willie Martinez	1.50	.70
❑	173	Dario Veras	.50	.23
❑	174	Dave Coggin	.20	.09
❑	175	Kris Benson	2.00	.90
❑	176	Torii Hunter	.20	.09
❑	177	D.T. Cromer	.20	.09
❑	178	Nelson Figueroa	.60	.25
❑	179	Hiram Bocachica	1.00	.45
❑	180	Shane Monahan	.40	.18
❑	181	Jimmy Anderson	.75	.35
❑	182	Juan Melo	.40	.18
❑	183	Pablo Ortega	.75	.35
❑	184	Calvin Pickering	5.00	2.20
❑	185	Reggie Taylor	.40	.18
❑	186	Jeff Farnsworth	.50	.23
❑	187	Terrence Long	.40	.18
❑	188	Geoff Jenkins	.40	.18
❑	189	Steve Rain	.50	.23
❑	190	Nerio Rodriguez	.75	.35
❑	191	Derrick Gibson	.50	.23
❑	192	Darin Blood	.20	.09
❑	193	Ben Davis	.75	.35
❑	194	Adrian Beltre	8.00	3.60
❑	195	Damian Sapp UER	2.00	.90
❑	196	Kerry Wood	20.00	9.00
❑	197	Nate Rolison	1.25	.55
❑	198	Fernando Tatis	2.50	1.10
❑	199	Brad Penny	5.00	2.20
❑	200	Jake Westbrook	1.00	.45
❑	201	Edwin Diaz	.20	.09
❑	202	Joe Fontenot	.75	.35
❑	203	Matt Halloran	.60	.25
❑	204	Blake Stein	1.00	.45
❑	205	Onan Masaoka	.40	.18
❑	206	Ben Petrick	.40	.18
❑	207	Matt Clement	3.00	1.35
❑	208	Todd Greene	.40	.18
❑	209	Ray Ricken	.20	.09
❑	210	Eric Chavez	10.00	4.50
❑	211	Edgard Velazquez	.40	.18
❑	212	Bruce Chen	5.00	2.20
❑	213	Danny Patterson	.20	.09
❑	214	Jeff Yoder	.20	.09
❑	215	Luis Ordaz	.75	.35
❑	216	Chris Widger	.20	.09
❑	217	Jason Brester	.40	.18
❑	218	Carlton Loewer	.40	.18
❑	219	Chris Reitsma	.60	.25
❑	220	Neifi Perez	.20	.09
❑	221	Hideki Irabu	4.00	1.80
❑	222	Ellis Burks	.40	.18
❑	223	Pedro Martinez	.75	.35
❑	224	Kenny Lofton	.75	.35
❑	225	Randy Johnson	.75	.35
❑	226	Terry Steinbach	.40	.18
❑	227	Bernie Williams	.75	.35
❑	228	Dean Palmer	.40	.18
❑	229	Alan Benes	.40	.18
❑	230	Marquis Grissom	.40	.18
❑	231	Gary Sheffield	.50	.23
❑	232	Curt Schilling	.40	.18
❑	233	Reggie Sanders	.40	.18
❑	234	Bobby Higginson	.50	.23
❑	235	Moises Alou	.50	.23
❑	236	Tom Glavine	.75	.35
❑	237	Mark Grace	.50	.23
❑	238	Ramon Martinez	.40	.18
❑	239	Rafael Palmeiro	.50	.23
❑	240	John Olerud	.40	.18
❑	241	Dante Bichette	.40	.18
❑	242	Greg Vaughn	.40	.18
❑	243	Jeff Bagwell	1.25	.55
❑	244	Barry Bonds	1.00	.45
❑	245	Pat Hentgen	.40	.18
❑	246	Jim Thome	.75	.35
❑	247	Jermaine Allensworth	.20	.09
❑	248	Andy Pettitte	.50	.23
❑	249	Jay Bell	.40	.18
❑	250	John Jaha	.20	.09
❑	251	Jim Edmonds	.50	.23
❑	252	Ron Gant	.20	.09
❑	253	David Cone	.50	.23
❑	254	Jose Canseco	.75	.35
❑	255	Jay Buhner	.40	.18
❑	256	Greg Maddux	2.50	1.10
❑	257	Brian McRae	.20	.09
❑	258	Lance Johnson	.20	.09
❑	259	Travis Fryman	.40	.18
❑	260	Paul O'Neill	.40	.18
❑	261	Ivan Rodriguez	1.00	.45
❑	262	Gregg Jefferies	.20	.09
❑	263	Fred McGriff	.50	.23
❑	264	Derek Bell	.40	.18
❑	265	Jeff Conine	.40	.18
❑	266	Mike Piazza	2.50	1.10
❑	267	Mark Grudzielanek	.40	.18
❑	268	Brady Anderson	.40	.18
❑	269	Marty Cordova	.20	.09
❑	270	Ray Durham	.40	.18
❑	271	Joe Carter	.40	.18
❑	272	Brian Jordan	.40	.18
❑	273	David Justice	.75	.35
❑	274	Tony Gwynn	2.00	.90
❑	275	Larry Walker	.75	.35
❑	276	Cecil Fielder	.40	.18
❑	277	Mo Vaughn	1.00	.45
❑	278	Alex Fernandez	.20	.09
❑	279	Michael Tucker	.40	.18
❑	280	Jose Valentin	.20	.09
❑	281	Sandy Alomar	.40	.18
❑	282	Todd Hollandsworth	.20	.09
❑	283	Rico Brogna	.20	.09
❑	284	Rusty Greer	.40	.18
❑	285	Roberto Hernandez	.20	.09
❑	286	Hal Morris	.20	.09
❑	287	Johnny Damon	.40	.18
❑	288	Todd Hundley	.40	.18
❑	289	Rondell White	.40	.18
❑	290	Frank Thomas	2.50	1.10
❑	291	Don Denbow	.20	.09
❑	292	Derrek Lee	.50	.23
❑	293	Todd Walker	.75	.35
❑	294	Scott Rolen	2.50	1.10
❑	295	Wes Helms	.40	.18
❑	296	Bob Abreu	.40	.18
❑	297	John Patterson	2.00	.90
❑	298	Alex Gonzalez	1.25	.55
❑	299	Grant Roberts	1.50	.70
❑	300	Jeff Suppan	.20	.09
❑	301	Luke Wilcox	.20	.09
❑	302	Marlon Anderson	.40	.18
❑	303	Ray Brown	.20	.09
❑	304	Mike Caruso	2.50	1.10
❑	305	Sam Marsonek	.50	.23
❑	306	Brady Raggio	.20	.09
❑	307	Kevin McGlinchy	.75	.35
❑	308	Roy Halladay	4.00	1.80
❑	309	Jeremi Gonzalez	1.00	.45
❑	310	Aramis Ramirez	6.00	2.70
❑	311	Dermal Brown	3.00	1.35
❑	312	Justin Thompson	.40	.18
❑	313	Jay Tessmer	.20	.09
❑	314	Mike Johnson	.50	.23
❑	315	Danny Clyburn	.20	.09
❑	316	Bruce Aven	.20	.09
❑	317	Keith Foulke	.20	.09
❑	318	Jimmy Osting	.50	.23
❑	319	Valerio De Los Santos	.75	.35
❑	320	Shannon Stewart	.40	.18
❑	321	Willie Adams	.20	.09
❑	322	Larry Barnes	.40	.18
❑	323	Mark Johnson	.50	.23
❑	324	Chris Stowers	.50	.23
❑	325	Brandon Reed	.50	.23
❑	326	Randy Winn	.20	.09
❑	327	Steve Chavez	.75	.35
❑	328	Nomar Garciaparra	2.50	1.10
❑	329	Jacque Jones	2.50	1.10
❑	330	Chris Clemons	.20	.09
❑	331	Todd Helton	1.50	.70
❑	332	Ryan Brannan	.50	.23
❑	333	Alex Sanchez	1.00	.45
❑	334	Arnold Gooch	.75	.35
❑	335	Russell Branyan	.75	.35
❑	336	Daryle Ward	1.25	.55
❑	337	John LeRoy	.50	.23
❑	338	Steve Cox	.20	.09
❑	339	Kevin Witt	2.00	.90
❑	340	Norm Hutchins	.20	.09
❑	341	Gabby Martinez	.20	.09
❑	342	Kris Detmers	.20	.09
❑	343	Mike Villano	.20	.09
❑	344	Preston Wilson	.40	.18
❑	345	James Manias	.50	.23
❑	346	Deivi Cruz	1.25	.55
❑	347	Donzell McDonald	.60	.25
❑	348	Rod Myers	.75	.35
❑	349	Shawn Chacon	1.00	.45
❑	350	Elvin Hernandez	.50	.23
❑	351	Orlando Cabrera	.75	.35
❑	352	Brian Banks	.20	.09
❑	353	Robbie Bell	.75	.35
❑	354	Brad Rigby	.20	.09
❑	355	Scott Elarton	.40	.18
❑	356	Kevin Sweeney	.50	.23
❑	357	Steve Soderstrom	.20	.09
❑	358	Ryan Nye	.40	.18
❑	359	Marlon Allen	.50	.23
❑	360	Donny Leon	.60	.25
❑	361	Garrett Neubart	.75	.35
❑	362	Abraham Nunez	1.00	.45
❑	363	Adam Eaton	.50	.23
❑	364	Octavio Dotel	1.25	.55
❑	365	Dean Crow	.20	.09
❑	366	Jason Baker	.50	.23
❑	367	Sean Casey	2.50	1.10
❑	368	Joe Lawrence	.75	.35
❑	369	Adam Johnson	1.00	.45
❑	370	Scott Schoeneweis	.75	.35
❑	371	Gerald Witasick Jr.	.20	.09
❑	372	Ronnie Belliard	1.00	.45
❑	373	Russ Ortiz	.20	.09
❑	374	Robert Stratton	.75	.35
❑	375	Bobby Estalella	.40	.18
❑	376	Corey Lee	.60	.25
❑	377	Carlos Beltran	1.25	.55
❑	378	Mike Cameron	.40	.18
❑	379	Scott Randall	.50	.23
❑	380	Corey Erickson	.75	.35
❑	381	Jay Canizaro	.20	.09
❑	382	Kerry Robinson	.50	.23
❑	383	Todd Noel	1.00	.45
❑	384	A.J. Zapp	2.00	.90
❑	385	Jarrod Washburn	.40	.18
❑	386	Ben Grieve	2.00	.90
❑	387	Javier Vazquez	1.00	.45
❑	388	Tony Graffanino	.20	.09
❑	389	Travis Lee	12.00	5.50
❑	390	DaRond Stovall	.20	.09
❑	391	Dennis Reyes	1.00	.45
❑	392	Danny Buxbaum	.20	.09
❑	393	Marc Lewis	1.00	.45
❑	394	Kelvim Escobar	1.25	.55
❑	395	Danny Klassen	.40	.18
❑	396	Ken Cloude	1.00	.45
❑	397	Gabe Alvarez	.40	.18
❑	398	Jaret Wright	8.00	3.60
❑	399	Raul Casanova	.20	.09
❑	400	Clayton Bruner	.75	.35
❑	401	Jason Marquis	1.25	.55
❑	402	Marc Kroon	.20	.09
❑	403	Jamey Wright	.20	.09
❑	404	Matt Snyder	.50	.23
❑	405	Josh Garrett	1.00	.45
❑	406	Juan Encarnacion	.40	.18
❑	407	Heath Murray	.20	.09
❑	408	Brett Herbison	.50	.23
❑	409	Brent Butler	2.50	1.10
❑	410	Danny Peoples	1.25	.55
❑	411	Miguel Tejada	3.00	1.35
❑	412	Damian Moss	.20	.09
❑	413	Jim Pittsley	.20	.09
❑	414	Dmitri Young	.40	.18
❑	415	Glendon Rusch	.20	.09
❑	416	Vladimir Guerrero	1.50	.70
❑	417	Cole Liniak	2.50	1.10
❑	418	Ramon Hernandez UER Card back says 1st Bowman card is 1997, he had a 1996 Bowman	.50	.23
❑	419	Cliff Politte	1.00	.45
❑	420	Mel Rosario	.50	.23
❑	421	Jorge Carrion	.50	.23
❑	422	John Barnes	1.00	.45

Card	MINT	NRMT
❑ 423 Chris Stowe	.50	.23
❑ 424 Vernon Wells	3.00	1.35
❑ 425 Brett Caradonna	2.00	.90
❑ 426 Scott Hodges	.75	.35
❑ 427 Jon Garland	2.00	.90
❑ 428 Nathan Haynes	1.00	.45
❑ 429 Geoff Goetz	.75	.35
❑ 430 Adam Kennedy	1.00	.45
❑ 431 T.J. Tucker	.60	.25
❑ 432 Aaron Akin	.60	.25
❑ 433 Jayson Werth	4.00	1.80
❑ 434 Glenn Davis	1.00	.45
❑ 435 Mark Mangum	.60	.25
❑ 436 Troy Cameron	2.00	.90
❑ 437 J.J. Davis	2.50	1.10
❑ 438 Lance Berkman	6.00	2.70
❑ 439 Jason Standridge	1.00	.45
❑ 440 Jason Dellaero	1.00	.45
❑ 441 Hideki Irabu	2.00	.90

1997 Bowman 1998 ROY Favorites

	MINT	NRMT
COMPLETE SET (15)	40.00	18.00
COMMON CARD (1-15)	1.00	.45

Card	MINT	NRMT
❑ ROY1 Jeff Abbott	1.50	.70
❑ ROY2 Karim Garcia	1.50	.70
❑ ROY3 Todd Helton	4.00	1.80
❑ ROY4 Richard Hidalgo	1.50	.70
❑ ROY5 Geoff Jenkins	1.50	.70
❑ ROY6 Russ Johnson	1.00	.45
❑ ROY7 Paul Konerko	2.00	.90
❑ ROY8 Mark Kotsay	4.00	1.80
❑ ROY9 Ricky Ledee	6.00	2.70
❑ ROY10 Travis Lee	12.00	5.50
❑ ROY11 Derrek Lee	2.00	.90
❑ ROY12 Elieser Marrero	1.50	.70
❑ ROY13 Juan Melo	1.50	.70
❑ ROY14 Brian Rose	1.50	.70
❑ ROY15 Fernando Tatis	3.00	1.35

1997 Bowman Certified Blue Ink Autographs

	MINT	NRMT
COMPLETE SET (90)	1500.00	700.00
COMMON BLUE INK (1-90)	10.00	4.50

Card	MINT	NRMT
❑ CA1 Jeff Abbott	15.00	6.75
❑ CA2 Bob Abreu	15.00	6.75
❑ CA3 Willie Adams	10.00	4.50
❑ CA4 Brian Banks	10.00	4.50
❑ CA5 Kris Benson	20.00	9.00
❑ CA6 Darin Blood	10.00	4.50
❑ CA7 Jaime Bluma	10.00	4.50
❑ CA8 Kevin L. Brown	10.00	4.50
❑ CA9 Ray Brown	10.00	4.50
❑ CA10 Homer Bush	15.00	6.75
❑ CA11 Mike Cameron	15.00	6.75
❑ CA12 Jay Canizaro	10.00	4.50
❑ CA13 Luis Castillo	15.00	6.75
❑ CA14 Dave Coggin	10.00	4.50
❑ CA15 Bartolo Colon	20.00	9.00
❑ CA16 Rocky Coppinger	10.00	4.50
❑ CA17 Jacob Cruz	10.00	4.50
❑ CA18 Jose Cruz Jr.	60.00	27.00
❑ CA19 Jeff D'Amico	10.00	4.50
❑ CA20 Ben Davis	20.00	9.00
❑ CA21 Mike Drumright	15.00	6.75
❑ CA22 Scott Elarton	15.00	6.75
❑ CA23 Darin Erstad	40.00	18.00
❑ CA24 Bobby Estalella	15.00	6.75
❑ CA25 Joe Fontenot	15.00	6.75
❑ CA26 Tom Fordham	10.00	4.50
❑ CA27 Brad Fullmer	25.00	11.00
❑ CA28 Chris Fussell	10.00	4.50
❑ CA29 Karim Garcia	15.00	6.75
❑ CA30 Kris Detmers	10.00	4.50
❑ CA31 Todd Greene	15.00	6.75
❑ CA32 Ben Grieve	60.00	27.00
❑ CA33 Vladimir Guerrero	50.00	22.00
❑ CA34 Jose Guillen	25.00	11.00
❑ CA35 Roy Halladay	40.00	18.00
❑ CA36 Wes Helms	15.00	6.75
❑ CA37 Chad Hermansen	40.00	18.00
❑ CA38 Richard Hidalgo	15.00	6.75
❑ CA39 Todd Hollandsworth	10.00	4.50
❑ CA40 Damian Jackson	10.00	4.50
❑ CA41 Derek Jeter Blue DP	80.00	36.00
❑ CA42 Andruw Jones	40.00	18.00
❑ CA43 Brooks Kieschnick	10.00	4.50
❑ CA44 Eugene Kingsale	15.00	6.75
❑ CA45 Paul Konerko	25.00	11.00
❑ CA46 Marc Kroon	10.00	4.50
❑ CA47 Derrek Lee	20.00	9.00
❑ CA48 Travis Lee	100.00	45.00
❑ CA49 Terrence Long	15.00	6.75
❑ CA50 Curt Lyons	10.00	4.50
❑ CA51 Eli Marrero	15.00	6.75
❑ CA52 Rafael Medina	15.00	6.75
❑ CA53 Juan Melo	15.00	6.75
❑ CA54 Shane Monahan	15.00	6.75
❑ CA55 Julio Mosquera	10.00	4.50
❑ CA56 Heath Murray	10.00	4.50
❑ CA57 Ryan Nye	15.00	6.75
❑ CA58 Kevin Orie	10.00	4.50
❑ CA59 Russ Ortiz	10.00	4.50
❑ CA60 Carl Pavano	20.00	9.00
❑ CA61 Jay Payton	10.00	4.50
❑ CA62 Neifi Perez	10.00	4.50
❑ CA63 Sidney Ponson	20.00	9.00
❑ CA64 Calvin Reese	10.00	4.50
❑ CA65 Ray Ricken	10.00	4.50
❑ CA66 Brad Rigby	10.00	4.50
❑ CA67 Adam Riggs	10.00	4.50
❑ CA68 Ruben Rivera	15.00	6.75
❑ CA69 J.J. Johnson	10.00	4.50
❑ CA70 Scott Rolen	60.00	27.00
❑ CA71 Tony Saunders	15.00	6.75
❑ CA72 Donnie Sadler	15.00	6.75
❑ CA73 Richie Sexson	25.00	11.00
❑ CA74 Scott Spiezio	10.00	4.50
❑ CA75 Everett Stull	10.00	4.50
❑ CA76 Mike Sweeney	10.00	4.50
❑ CA77 Fernando Tatis	25.00	11.00
❑ CA78 Miguel Tejada	30.00	13.50
❑ CA79 Justin Thompson	15.00	6.75
❑ CA80 Justin Towle	20.00	9.00
❑ CA81 Billy Wagner	15.00	6.75
❑ CA82 Todd Walker	25.00	11.00
❑ CA83 Luke Wilcox	10.00	4.50
❑ CA84 Paul Wilder	20.00	9.00
❑ CA85 Enrique Wilson	15.00	6.75
❑ CA86 Kerry Wood	150.00	70.00
❑ CA87 Jamey Wright	10.00	4.50
❑ CA88 Ron Wright	15.00	6.75
❑ CA89 Dmitri Young	15.00	6.75
❑ CA90 Nelson Figueroa	15.00	6.75

1997 Bowman International Best

	MINT	NRMT
COMPLETE SET (20)	80.00	36.00
COMMON CARD (1-20)	1.50	.70

Card	MINT	NRMT
❑ BBI1 Frank Thomas	10.00	4.50
❑ BBI2 Ken Griffey Jr.	15.00	6.75
❑ BBI3 Juan Gonzalez	8.00	3.60
❑ BBI4 Bernie Williams	3.00	1.35
❑ BBI5 Hideo Nomo	4.00	1.80
❑ BBI6 Sammy Sosa	8.00	3.60
❑ BBI7 Larry Walker	3.00	1.35
❑ BBI8 Vinny Castilla	2.00	.90
❑ BBI9 Mariano Rivera	1.50	.70
❑ BBI10 Rafael Palmeiro	2.00	.90
❑ BBI11 Nomar Garciaparra	10.00	4.50
❑ BBI12 Todd Walker	3.00	1.35
❑ BBI13 Andruw Jones	5.00	2.20
❑ BBI14 Vladimir Guerrero	6.00	2.70
❑ BBI15 Ruben Rivera	1.50	.70
❑ BBI16 Bob Abreu	1.50	.70
❑ BBI17 Karim Garcia	1.50	.70
❑ BBI18 Katsuhiro Maeda	1.50	.70
❑ BBI19 Jose Cruz Jr.	8.00	3.60
❑ BBI20 Damian Moss	1.50	.70

1997 Bowman Scout's Honor Roll

	MINT	NRMT
COMPLETE SET (15)	50.00	22.00
COMMON CARD (1-15)	1.00	.45

Card	MINT	NRMT
❑ 1 Dmitri Young	1.25	.55
❑ 2 Bob Abreu	1.25	.55
❑ 3 Vladimir Guerrero	4.00	1.80
❑ 4 Paul Konerko	2.00	.90
❑ 5 Kevin Orie	1.00	.45
❑ 6 Todd Walker	1.50	.70
❑ 7 Ben Grieve	5.00	2.20
❑ 8 Darin Erstad	3.00	1.35

		MINT	NRMT
❑ 9	Derrek Lee	1.50	.70
❑ 10	Jose Cruz Jr.	8.00	3.60
❑ 11	Scott Rolen	5.00	2.20
❑ 12	Travis Lee	12.00	5.50
❑ 13	Andruw Jones	3.00	1.35
❑ 14	Wilton Guerrero	1.00	.45
❑ 15	Nomar Garciaparra	6.00	2.70

1998 Bowman

	MINT	NRMT
COMPLETE SET (441)	140.00	65.00
COMPLETE SERIES 1 (221)	80.00	36.00
COMPLETE SERIES 2 (220)	60.00	27.00
COMMON CARD (1-441)	.20	.09

		MINT	NRMT
❑ 1	Nomar Garciaparra	2.50	1.10
❑ 2	Scott Rolen	2.00	.90
❑ 3	Andy Pettitte	.50	.23
❑ 4	Ivan Rodriguez	1.00	.45
❑ 5	Mark McGwire	5.00	2.20
❑ 6	Jason Dickson	.30	.14
❑ 7	Jose Cruz Jr.	1.00	.45
❑ 8	Jeff Kent	.30	.14
❑ 9	Mike Mussina	.75	.35
❑ 10	Jason Kendall	.30	.14
❑ 11	Brett Tomko	.30	.14
❑ 12	Jeff King	.30	.14
❑ 13	Brad Radke	.30	.14
❑ 14	Robin Ventura	.30	.14
❑ 15	Jeff Bagwell	1.25	.55
❑ 16	Greg Maddux	2.50	1.10
❑ 17	John Jaha	.20	.09
❑ 18	Mike Piazza	2.50	1.10
❑ 19	Edgar Martinez	.30	.14
❑ 20	David Justice	.75	.35
❑ 21	Todd Hundley	.30	.14
❑ 22	Tony Gwynn	2.00	.90
❑ 23	Larry Walker	.75	.35
❑ 24	Bernie Williams	.75	.35
❑ 25	Edgar Renteria	.30	.14
❑ 26	Rafael Palmeiro	.50	.23
❑ 27	Tim Salmon	.75	.35
❑ 28	Matt Morris	.30	.14
❑ 29	Shawn Estes	.30	.14
❑ 30	Vladimir Guerrero	1.25	.55
❑ 31	Fernando Tatis	.30	.14
❑ 32	Justin Thompson	.30	.14
❑ 33	Ken Griffey Jr.	4.00	1.80
❑ 34	Edgardo Alfonzo	.30	.14
❑ 35	Mo Vaughn	1.00	.45
❑ 36	Marty Cordova	.20	.09
❑ 37	Craig Biggio	.75	.35
❑ 38	Roger Clemens	1.50	.70
❑ 39	Mark Grace	.50	.23
❑ 40	Ken Caminiti	.50	.23
❑ 41	Tony Womack	.30	.14
❑ 42	Albert Belle	.75	.35
❑ 43	Tino Martinez	.75	.35
❑ 44	Sandy Alomar	.30	.14
❑ 45	Jeff Cirillo	.30	.14
❑ 46	Jason Giambi	.30	.14
❑ 47	Darin Erstad	1.00	.45
❑ 48	Livan Hernandez	.30	.14
❑ 49	Mark Grudzielanek	.30	.14
❑ 50	Sammy Sosa	2.00	.90
❑ 51	Curt Schilling	.30	.14
❑ 52	Brian Hunter	.30	.14
❑ 53	Neifi Perez	.30	.14
❑ 54	Todd Walker	.50	.23
❑ 55	Jose Guillen	.30	.14
❑ 56	Jim Thome	.75	.35
❑ 57	Tom Glavine	.75	.35
❑ 58	Todd Greene	.30	.14
❑ 59	Rondell White	.30	.14
❑ 60	Roberto Alomar	.75	.35
❑ 61	Tony Clark	.50	.23
❑ 62	Vinny Castilla	.50	.23
❑ 63	Barry Larkin	.50	.23
❑ 64	Hideki Irabu	.50	.23
❑ 65	Johnny Damon	.30	.14
❑ 66	Juan Gonzalez	2.00	.90
❑ 67	John Olerud	.30	.14
❑ 68	Gary Sheffield	.50	.23
❑ 69	Raul Mondesi	.50	.23
❑ 70	Chipper Jones	2.00	.90
❑ 71	David Ortiz	.30	.14
❑ 72	Warren Morris	1.50	.70
❑ 73	Alex Gonzalez	.30	.14
❑ 74	Nick Bierbrodt	1.00	.45
❑ 75	Roy Halladay	.30	.14
❑ 76	Danny Buxbaum	.20	.09
❑ 77	Adam Kennedy	.30	.14
❑ 78	Jared Sandberg	2.50	1.10
❑ 79	Michael Barrett	.30	.14
❑ 80	Gil Meche	1.50	.70
❑ 81	Jayson Werth	.50	.23
❑ 82	Abraham Nunez	.30	.14
❑ 83	Ben Petrick	.30	.14
❑ 84	Brett Caradonna	.30	.14
❑ 85	Mike Lowell	2.00	.90
❑ 86	Clayton Bruner	.30	.14
❑ 87	John Curtice	2.00	.90
❑ 88	Bobby Estalella	.30	.14
❑ 89	Juan Melo	.30	.14
❑ 90	Arnold Gooch	.20	.09
❑ 91	Kevin Millwood	5.00	2.20
❑ 92	Richie Sexson	.50	.23
❑ 93	Orlando Cabrera	.30	.14
❑ 94	Pat Cline	.30	.14
❑ 95	Anthony Sanders	.30	.14
❑ 96	Russ Johnson	.20	.09
❑ 97	Ben Grieve	1.50	.70
❑ 98	Kevin McGlinchy	.30	.14
❑ 99	Paul Wilder	.30	.14
❑ 100	Russ Ortiz	.20	.09
❑ 101	Ryan Jackson	.75	.35
❑ 102	Heath Murray	.20	.09
❑ 103	Brian Rose	.30	.14
❑ 104	Ryan Radmanovich	.75	.35
❑ 105	Ricky Ledee	.30	.14
❑ 106	Jeff Wallace	1.00	.45
❑ 107	Ryan Minor	2.50	1.10
❑ 108	Dennis Reyes	.30	.14
❑ 109	James Manias	.20	.09
❑ 110	Chris Carpenter	.30	.14
❑ 111	Daryle Ward	.30	.14
❑ 112	Vernon Wells	.50	.23
❑ 113	Chad Green	.30	.14
❑ 114	Mike Stoner	2.00	.90
❑ 115	Brad Fullmer	.30	.14
❑ 116	Adam Eaton	.20	.09
❑ 117	Jeff Liefer	.30	.14
❑ 118	Corey Koskie	2.00	.90
❑ 119	Todd Helton	1.00	.45
❑ 120	Jaime Jones	1.00	.45
❑ 121	Mel Rosario	.20	.09
❑ 122	Geoff Goetz	.30	.14
❑ 123	Adrian Beltre	1.00	.45
❑ 124	Jason Dellaero	.30	.14
❑ 125	Gabe Kapler	10.00	4.50
❑ 126	Scott Schoeneweis	.20	.09
❑ 127	Ryan Brannan	.20	.09
❑ 128	Aaron Akin	.20	.09
❑ 129	Ryan Anderson	8.00	3.60
❑ 130	Brad Penny	.50	.23
❑ 131	Bruce Chen	.30	.14
❑ 132	Eli Marrero	.30	.14
❑ 133	Eric Chavez	1.25	.55
❑ 134	Troy Glaus	10.00	4.50
❑ 135	Troy Cameron	.30	.14
❑ 136	Brian Sikorski	.75	.35
❑ 137	Mike Kinkade	1.50	.70
❑ 138	Braden Looper	.30	.14
❑ 139	Mark Mangum	.30	.14
❑ 140	Danny Peoples	.20	.09
❑ 141	J.J. Davis	.30	.14
❑ 142	Ben Davis	.30	.14
❑ 143	Jacque Jones	.30	.14
❑ 144	Derrick Gibson	.30	.14
❑ 145	Bronson Arroyo	1.00	.45
❑ 146	Luis De Los Santos UER Has hitting stat line instead of pitching	1.50	.70
❑ 147	Jeff Abbott	.30	.14
❑ 148	Mike Cuddyer	3.00	1.35
❑ 149	Jason Romano	.30	.14
❑ 150	Shane Monahan	.30	.14
❑ 151	Ntema Ndungidi	1.50	.70
❑ 152	Alex Sanchez	.30	.14
❑ 153	Jack Cust	3.00	1.35
❑ 154	Brent Butler	.30	.14
❑ 155	Ramon Hernandez	.30	.14
❑ 156	Norm Hutchins	.30	.14
❑ 157	Jason Marquis	.30	.14
❑ 158	Jacob Cruz	.20	.09
❑ 159	Rob Burger	1.00	.45
❑ 160	Dave Coggin	.20	.09
❑ 161	Preston Wilson	.30	.14
❑ 162	Jason Fitzgerald	1.00	.45
❑ 163	Dan Serafini	.20	.09
❑ 164	Peter Munro	.20	.09
❑ 165	Trot Nixon	.30	.14
❑ 166	Homer Bush	.20	.09
❑ 167	Dermal Brown	.30	.14
❑ 168	Chad Hermansen	.75	.35
❑ 169	Julio Moreno	1.00	.45
❑ 170	John Roskos	1.50	.70
❑ 171	Grant Roberts	.30	.14
❑ 172	Ken Cloude	.30	.14
❑ 173	Jason Brester	.30	.14
❑ 174	Jason Conti	1.00	.45
❑ 175	Jon Garland	.30	.14
❑ 176	Robbie Bell	.30	.14
❑ 177	Nathan Haynes	.30	.14
❑ 178	Ramon Ortiz	2.50	1.10
❑ 179	Shannon Stewart	.30	.14
❑ 180	Pablo Ortega	.20	.09
❑ 181	Jimmy Rollins	1.50	.70
❑ 182	Sean Casey	.30	.14
❑ 183	Ted Lilly	1.50	.70
❑ 184	Chris Enochs	2.50	1.10
❑ 185	Magglio Ordonez	3.00	1.35
❑ 186	Mike Drumright	.30	.14
❑ 187	Aaron Boone	.20	.09
❑ 188	Matt Clement	.30	.14
❑ 189	Todd Dunwoody	.30	.14
❑ 190	Larry Rodriguez	.20	.09
❑ 191	Todd Noel	.30	.14
❑ 192	Geoff Jenkins	.30	.14
❑ 193	George Lombard	.30	.14
❑ 194	Lance Berkman	.75	.35
❑ 195	Marcus McCain	.30	.14
❑ 196	Ryan McGuire	.20	.09
❑ 197	Jhensy Sandoval	2.50	1.10
❑ 198	Corey Lee	.30	.14
❑ 199	Mario Valdez	1.00	.45
❑ 200	Robert Fick	2.50	1.10
❑ 201	Donnie Sadler	.30	.14
❑ 202	Marc Kroon	.20	.09
❑ 203	David Miller	.20	.09
❑ 204	Jarrod Washburn	.30	.14
❑ 205	Miguel Tejada	.30	.14
❑ 206	Raul Ibanez	.20	.09
❑ 207	John Patterson	.30	.14
❑ 208	Calvin Pickering	.50	.23
❑ 209	Felix Martinez	.20	.09
❑ 210	Mark Redman	.20	.09
❑ 211	Scott Elarton	.30	.14
❑ 212	Jose Amado	.75	.35
❑ 213	Kerry Wood	5.00	2.20
❑ 214	Dante Powell	.30	.14
❑ 215	Aramis Ramirez	.75	.35
❑ 216	A.J. Hinch	.30	.14
❑ 217	Dustin Carr	.75	.35
❑ 218	Mark Kotsay	.50	.23
❑ 219	Jason Standridge	.30	.14
❑ 220	Luis Ordaz	.30	.14

Card	Mint	Nrmt
❑ 221 Orlando Hernandez	10.00	4.50
❑ 222 Cal Ripken	3.00	1.35
❑ 223 Paul Molitor	.75	.35
❑ 224 Derek Jeter	2.00	.90
❑ 225 Barry Bonds	1.00	.45
❑ 226 Jim Edmonds	.50	.23
❑ 227 John Smoltz	.30	.14
❑ 228 Eric Karros	.30	.14
❑ 229 Ray Lankford	.30	.14
❑ 230 Rey Ordonez	.30	.14
❑ 231 Kenny Lofton	.75	.35
❑ 232 Alex Rodriguez	2.50	1.10
❑ 233 Dante Bichette	.30	.14
❑ 234 Pedro Martinez	.75	.35
❑ 235 Carlos Delgado	.30	.14
❑ 236 Rod Beck	.30	.14
❑ 237 Matt Williams	.30	.14
❑ 238 Charles Johnson	.30	.14
❑ 239 Rico Brogna	.30	.14
❑ 240 Frank Thomas	2.50	1.10
❑ 241 Paul O'Neill	.30	.14
❑ 242 Jaret Wright	1.00	.45
❑ 243 Brant Brown	.30	.14
❑ 244 Ryan Klesko	.30	.14
❑ 245 Chuck Finley	.30	.14
❑ 246 Derek Bell	.30	.14
❑ 247 Delino DeShields	.20	.09
❑ 248 Chan Ho Park	.75	.35
❑ 249 Wade Boggs	.75	.35
❑ 250 Jay Buhner	.30	.14
❑ 251 Butch Huskey	.20	.09
❑ 252 Steve Finley	.30	.14
❑ 253 Will Clark	.75	.35
❑ 254 John Valentin	.30	.14
❑ 255 Bobby Higginson	.50	.23
❑ 256 Darryl Strawberry	.30	.14
❑ 257 Randy Johnson	.75	.35
❑ 258 Al Martin	.20	.09
❑ 259 Travis Fryman	.30	.14
❑ 260 Fred McGriff	.50	.23
❑ 261 Jose Valentin	.20	.09
❑ 262 Andruw Jones	1.00	.45
❑ 263 Kenny Rogers	.20	.09
❑ 264 Moises Alou	.50	.23
❑ 265 Denny Neagle	.30	.14
❑ 266 Ugueth Urbina	.30	.14
❑ 267 Derrek Lee	.30	.14
❑ 268 Ellis Burks	.30	.14
❑ 269 Mariano Rivera	.30	.14
❑ 270 Dean Palmer	.30	.14
❑ 271 Eddie Taubensee	.20	.09
❑ 272 Brady Anderson	.30	.14
❑ 273 Brian Giles	.30	.14
❑ 274 Quinton McCracken	.30	.14
❑ 275 Henry Rodriguez	.30	.14
❑ 276 Andres Galarraga	.75	.35
❑ 277 Jose Canseco	.75	.35
❑ 278 David Segui	.30	.14
❑ 279 Bret Saberhagen	.30	.14
❑ 280 Kevin Brown	.50	.23
❑ 281 Chuck Knoblauch	.75	.35
❑ 282 Jeromy Burnitz	.30	.14
❑ 283 Jay Bell	.30	.14
❑ 284 Manny Ramirez	.75	.35
❑ 285 Rick Helling	.30	.14
❑ 286 Francisco Cordova	.20	.09
❑ 287 Bob Abreu	.30	.14
❑ 288 J.T. Snow	.30	.14
❑ 289 Hideo Nomo	1.00	.45
❑ 290 Brian Jordan	.30	.14
❑ 291 Javy Lopez	.30	.14
❑ 292 Travis Lee	1.50	.70
❑ 293 Russell Branyan	.30	.14
❑ 294 Paul Konerko	.75	.35
❑ 295 Masato Yoshii	1.50	.70
❑ 296 Kris Benson	.30	.14
❑ 297 Juan Encarnacion	.30	.14
❑ 298 Eric Milton	.30	.14
❑ 299 Mike Caruso	.30	.14
❑ 300 Ricardo Aramboles	3.00	1.35
❑ 301 Bobby Smith	.30	.14
❑ 302 Billy Koch	.30	.14
❑ 303 Richard Hidalgo	.30	.14
❑ 304 Justin Baughman	1.00	.45
❑ 305 Chris Gissell	.20	.09
❑ 306 Donnie Bridges	1.00	.45
❑ 307 Nelson Lara	1.00	.45
❑ 308 Randy Wolf	1.00	.45
❑ 309 Jason LaRue	1.50	.70
❑ 310 Jason Gooding	.75	.35
❑ 311 Edgard Clemente	.30	.14
❑ 312 Andrew Vessel	.20	.09
❑ 313 Chris Reitsma	.20	.09
❑ 314 Jesus Sanchez	1.25	.55
❑ 315 Buddy Carlyle	1.25	.55
❑ 316 Randy Winn	.20	.09
❑ 317 Luis Rivera	2.50	1.10
❑ 318 Marcus Thames	1.50	.70
❑ 319 A.J. Pierzynski	.30	.14
❑ 320 Scott Randall	.20	.09
❑ 321 Damian Sapp	.30	.14
❑ 322 Eddie Yarnall	3.00	1.35
❑ 323 Luke Allen	1.50	.70
❑ 324 J.D. Smart	.20	.09
❑ 325 Willie Martinez	.30	.14
❑ 326 Alex Ramirez	.30	.14
❑ 327 Eric DuBose	1.25	.55
❑ 328 Kevin Witt	.30	.14
❑ 329 Dan McKinley	.75	.35
❑ 330 Cliff Politte	.30	.14
❑ 331 Vladimir Nunez	.30	.14
❑ 332 John Halama	.20	.09
❑ 333 Nerio Rodriguez	.30	.14
❑ 334 Desi Relaford	.20	.09
❑ 335 Robinson Checo	.30	.14
❑ 336 John Nicholson	1.25	.55
❑ 337 Tom LaRosa	.75	.35
❑ 338 Kevin Nicholson	1.25	.55
❑ 339 Javier Vazquez	.30	.14
❑ 340 A.J. Zapp	.20	.09
❑ 341 Tom Evans	.30	.14
❑ 342 Kerry Robinson	.20	.09
❑ 343 Gabe Gonzalez	.20	.09
❑ 344 Ralph Milliard	.20	.09
❑ 345 Enrique Wilson	.30	.14
❑ 346 Elvin Hernandez	.20	.09
❑ 347 Mike Lincoln	1.50	.70
❑ 348 Cesar King	2.00	.90
❑ 349 Cristian Guzman	1.00	.45
❑ 350 Donzell McDonald	.20	.09
❑ 351 Jim Parque	2.00	.90
❑ 352 Mike Saipe	.20	.09
❑ 353 Carlos Febles	1.50	.70
❑ 354 Dernell Stenson	4.00	1.80
❑ 355 Mark Osborne	1.50	.70
❑ 356 Odalis Perez	2.00	.90
❑ 357 Jason Dewey	1.25	.55
❑ 358 Joe Fontenot	.30	.14
❑ 359 Jason Grilli	1.50	.70
❑ 360 Kevin Haverbusch	1.50	.70
❑ 361 Jay Yennaco	1.00	.45
❑ 362 Brian Buchanan	.20	.09
❑ 363 John Barnes	.30	.14
❑ 364 Chris Fussell	.20	.09
❑ 365 Kevin Gibbs	.75	.35
❑ 366 Joe Lawrence	.30	.14
❑ 367 DaRond Stovall	.20	.09
❑ 368 Brian Fuentes	.75	.35
❑ 369 Jimmy Anderson	.20	.09
❑ 370 Lariel Gonzalez	.75	.35
❑ 371 Scott Williamson	1.00	.45
❑ 372 Milton Bradley	.30	.14
❑ 373 Jason Halper	.75	.35
❑ 374 Brent Billingsley	1.00	.45
❑ 375 Joe DePastino	.75	.35
❑ 376 Jake Westbrook	.30	.14
❑ 377 Octavio Dotel	.30	.14
❑ 378 Jason Williams	.75	.35
❑ 379 Julio Ramirez	2.50	1.10
❑ 380 Seth Greisinger		
❑ 381 Mike Judd	1.25	.55
❑ 382 Ben Ford	.75	.35
❑ 383 Tom Bennett	.75	.35
❑ 384 Adam Butler	.75	.35
❑ 385 Wade Miller	1.00	.45
❑ 386 Kyle Peterson	1.00	.45
❑ 387 Tommy Peterman	1.00	.45
❑ 388 Onan Masaoka	.30	.14
❑ 389 Jason Rakers	.75	.35
❑ 390 Rafael Medina	.30	.14
❑ 391 Luis Lopez	.20	.09
❑ 392 Jeff Yoder	.20	.09
❑ 393 Vance Wilson	.75	.35
❑ 394 Fernando Seguignol	2.50	1.10
❑ 395 Ron Wright	.30	.14
❑ 396 Ruben Mateo	6.00	2.70
❑ 397 Steve Lomasney	1.00	.45
❑ 398 Damian Jackson	.20	.09
❑ 399 Mike Jerzembeck	1.00	.45
❑ 400 Luis Rivas	1.50	.70
❑ 401 Kevin Burford	1.50	.70
❑ 402 Glenn Davis	.30	.14
❑ 403 Robert Luce	.75	.35
❑ 404 Cole Liniak	.30	.14
❑ 405 Matt LeCroy	1.50	.70
❑ 406 Jeremy Giambi	3.00	1.35
❑ 407 Shawn Chacon	.30	.14
❑ 408 Dewayne Wise	2.00	.90
❑ 409 Steve Woodard	.30	.14
❑ 410 Francisco Cordero	.75	.35
❑ 411 Damon Minor	1.00	.45
❑ 412 Lou Collier	.20	.09
❑ 413 Justin Towle	.30	.14
❑ 414 Juan LeBron	.30	.14
❑ 415 Michael Coleman	.30	.14
❑ 416 Felix Rodriguez	.20	.09
❑ 417 Paul Ah Yat	1.00	.45
❑ 418 Kevin Barker	1.00	.45
❑ 419 Brian Meadows	.20	.09
❑ 420 Darnell McDonald	4.00	1.80
❑ 421 Matt Kinney	1.00	.45
❑ 422 Mike Vavrek	1.00	.45
❑ 423 Courtney Duncan	.75	.35
❑ 424 Kevin Millar	2.00	.90
❑ 425 Ruben Rivera	.30	.14
❑ 426 Steve Shoemaker	.20	.09
❑ 427 Dan Reichert	.75	.35
❑ 428 Carlos Lee	3.00	1.35
❑ 429 Rod Barajas	1.00	.45
❑ 430 Pablo Ozuna	4.00	1.80
❑ 431 Todd Belitz	.75	.35
❑ 432 Sidney Ponson	.30	.14
❑ 433 Steve Carver	.20	.09
❑ 434 Esteban Yan	1.50	.70
❑ 435 Cedrick Bowers	1.00	.45
❑ 436 Marlon Anderson	.30	.14
❑ 437 Carl Pavano	.30	.14
❑ 438 Jae Weong Seo	1.50	.70
❑ 439 Jose Taveras	1.50	.70
❑ 440 Matt Anderson	2.00	.90
❑ 441 Darron Ingram	1.50	.70
❑ NNO S.Hasegawa '91 BBM	15.00	6.75
❑ NNO H.Irabu '91 BBM	40.00	18.00
❑ NNO H.Nomo '91 BBM	40.00	18.00

1998 Bowman Golden Anniversary

	MINT	NRMT
COMMON CARD (1-441)	20.00	9.00
MINOR STARS	30.00	13.50
SEMISTARS	50.00	22.00
UNLISTED STARS	80.00	36.00

*STARS: 40X TO 100X BASIC CARDS
*YOUNG STARS: 30X TO 80X BASIC CARDS
*PROSPECTS: 20X TO 50X BASIC CARDS
*ROOKIES: 8X TO 20X BASIC CARDS

1998 Bowman 1999 ROY Favorites

	MINT	NRMT
COMPLETE SET (10)	25.00	11.00
COMMON CARD (ROY1-ROY10)	1.00	.45

	MINT	NRMT
❑ ROY1 Adrian Beltre	4.00	1.80
❑ ROY2 Troy Glaus	10.00	4.50
❑ ROY3 Chad Hermansen		
❑ ROY4 Matt Clement	1.50	.70
❑ ROY5 Eric Chavez	5.00	2.20
❑ ROY6 Kris Benson	1.50	.70
❑ ROY7 Richie Sexson	2.50	1.10
❑ ROY8 Randy Wolf	1.00	.45
❑ ROY9 Ryan Minor	3.00	1.35
❑ ROY10 Alex Gonzalez	1.50	.70

1998 Bowman Certified Blue Autographs

	MINT	NRMT
COMPLETE SET (70)	1500.00	700.00
COMMON CARD (1-70)	15.00	6.75

	MINT	NRMT
❑ 1 Adrian Beltre	40.00	18.00
❑ 2 Brad Fullmer	20.00	9.00
❑ 3 Ricky Ledee	20.00	9.00
❑ 4 David Ortiz	20.00	9.00
❑ 5 Fernando Tatis	15.00	6.75
❑ 6 Kerry Wood	120.00	55.00
❑ 7 Mel Rosario	15.00	6.75
❑ 8 Cole Liniak	15.00	6.75
❑ 9 A.J. Hinch	20.00	9.00
❑ 10 Jhensy Sandoval	25.00	11.00
❑ 11 Jose Cruz Jr.	40.00	18.00
❑ 12 Richard Hidalgo	15.00	6.75
❑ 13 Geoff Jenkins	15.00	6.75
❑ 14 Carl Pavano	20.00	9.00
❑ 15 Richie Sexson	25.00	11.00
❑ 16 Tony Womack	15.00	6.75
❑ 17 Scott Rolen	80.00	36.00
❑ 18 Ryan Minor	25.00	11.00
❑ 19 Eli Marrero	15.00	6.75
❑ 20 Jason Marquis	15.00	6.75
❑ 21 Mike Lowell	20.00	9.00
❑ 22 Todd Helton	40.00	18.00
❑ 23 Chad Green	15.00	6.75
❑ 24 Scott Elarton	15.00	6.75
❑ 25 Russell Branyan	20.00	9.00
❑ 26 Mike Drumright	15.00	6.75
❑ 27 Ben Grieve	60.00	27.00
❑ 28 Jacque Jones	15.00	6.75
❑ 29 Jared Sandberg	25.00	11.00
❑ 30 Grant Roberts	15.00	6.75
❑ 31 Mike Stoner	20.00	9.00
❑ 32 Brian Rose	15.00	6.75
❑ 33 Randy Winn	15.00	6.75
❑ 34 Justin Towle	15.00	6.75
❑ 35 Anthony Sanders	15.00	6.75
❑ 36 Rafael Medina	15.00	6.75
❑ 37 Corey Lee	15.00	6.75
❑ 38 Mike Kinkade	15.00	6.75
❑ 39 Norm Hutchins	15.00	6.75
❑ 40 Jason Brester	15.00	6.75
❑ 41 Ben Davis	20.00	9.00
❑ 42 Nomar Garciaparra	100.00	45.00
❑ 43 Jeff Liefer	15.00	6.75
❑ 44 Eric Milton	15.00	6.75
❑ 45 Preston Wilson	15.00	6.75
❑ 46 Miguel Tejada	15.00	6.75
❑ 47 Luis Ordaz	15.00	6.75
❑ 48 Travis Lee	60.00	27.00
❑ 49 Kris Benson	15.00	6.75
❑ 50 Jacob Cruz	15.00	6.75
❑ 51 Dermal Brown	15.00	6.75
❑ 52 Marc Kroon	15.00	6.75
❑ 53 Chad Hermansen	20.00	9.00
❑ 54 Roy Halladay	20.00	9.00
❑ 55 Eric Chavez	50.00	22.00
❑ 56 Jason Conti	15.00	6.75
❑ 57 Juan Encarnacion	20.00	9.00
❑ 58 Paul Wilder	15.00	6.75
❑ 59 Aramis Ramirez	30.00	13.50
❑ 60 Cliff Politte	15.00	6.75
❑ 61 Todd Dunwoody	15.00	6.75
❑ 62 Paul Konerko	25.00	11.00
❑ 63 Shane Monahan	15.00	6.75
❑ 64 Alex Sanchez	15.00	6.75
❑ 65 Jeff Abbott	15.00	6.75
❑ 66 John Patterson	15.00	6.75
❑ 67 Peter Munro	15.00	6.75
❑ 68 Jarrod Washburn	15.00	6.75
❑ 69 Derrek Lee	20.00	9.00
❑ 70 Ramon Hernandez	20.00	9.00

1998 Bowman Minor League MVP's

	MINT	NRMT
COMPLETE SET (11)	25.00	11.00
COMMON CARD (MVP1-MVP11)	1.25	.55

	MINT	NRMT
❑ MVP1 Jeff Bagwell	3.00	1.35
❑ MVP2 Andres Galarraga	2.00	.90
❑ MVP3 Juan Gonzalez	5.00	2.20
❑ MVP4 Tony Gwynn	5.00	2.20
❑ MVP5 Vladimir Guerrero	3.00	1.35
❑ MVP6 Derek Jeter	5.00	2.20
❑ MVP7 Andruw Jones	2.50	1.10
❑ MVP8 Tino Martinez	2.00	.90
❑ MVP9 Manny Ramirez	2.00	.90
❑ MVP10 Gary Sheffield	1.25	.55
❑ MVP11 Jim Thome	2.00	.90

1998 Bowman Scout's Choice

	MINT	NRMT
COMPLETE SET (21)	50.00	22.00
COMMON CARD (SC1-SC21)	1.50	.70

	MINT	NRMT
❑ SC1 Paul Konerko	2.00	.90
❑ SC2 Richard Hidalgo	2.00	.90
❑ SC3 Mark Kotsay	2.50	1.10
❑ SC4 Ben Grieve	6.00	2.70
❑ SC5 Chad Hermansen		
❑ SC6 Matt Clement	2.00	.90
❑ SC7 Brad Fullmer	2.00	.90
❑ SC8 Eli Marrero	1.50	.70
❑ SC9 Kerry Wood	15.00	6.75
❑ SC10 Adrian Beltre	4.00	1.80
❑ SC11 Ricky Ledee	2.00	.90
❑ SC12 Travis Lee	6.00	2.70
❑ SC13 Abraham Nunez	2.00	.90
❑ SC14 Brian Rose	1.50	.70
❑ SC15 Dermal Brown	2.00	.90
❑ SC16 Juan Encarnacion	2.00	.90
❑ SC17 Aramis Ramirez	3.00	1.35
❑ SC18 Todd Helton	4.00	1.80
❑ SC19 Kris Benson	2.00	.90
❑ SC20 Russell Branyan	2.00	.90
❑ SC21 Mike Stoner	3.00	1.35

1997 Bowman Chrome

	MINT	NRMT
COMPLETE SET (300)	350.00	160.00
COMMON RED (1-100)	.40	.18
COMMON BLUE (101-300)	1.00	.45

	MINT	NRMT
❑ 1 Derek Jeter	5.00	2.20
❑ 2 Chipper Jones	4.00	1.80
❑ 3 Hideo Nomo	2.00	.90
❑ 4 Tim Salmon	1.50	.70
❑ 5 Robin Ventura	.75	.35
❑ 6 Tony Clark	1.00	.45
❑ 7 Barry Larkin	1.00	.45
❑ 8 Paul Molitor	1.50	.70
❑ 9 Andy Benes	.75	.35
❑ 10 Ryan Klesko	.75	.35
❑ 11 Mark McGwire	8.00	3.60
❑ 12 Ken Griffey Jr.	8.00	3.60
❑ 13 Robb Nen	.40	.18
❑ 14 Cal Ripken	6.00	2.70

❑ 15 John Valentin .75 .35
❑ 16 Ricky Bottalico .75 .35
❑ 17 Mike Lansing .40 .18
❑ 18 Ryne Sandberg 2.00 .90
❑ 19 Carlos Delgado .75 .35
❑ 20 Craig Biggio 1.50 .70
❑ 21 Eric Karros .75 .35
❑ 22 Kevin Appier .75 .35
❑ 23 Mariano Rivera .75 .35
❑ 24 Vinny Castilla 1.00 .45
❑ 25 Juan Gonzalez 4.00 1.80
❑ 26 Al Martin .40 .18
❑ 27 Jeff Cirillo .75 .35
❑ 28 Ray Lankford .75 .35
❑ 29 Manny Ramirez 1.50 .70
❑ 30 Roberto Alomar 1.50 .70
❑ 31 Will Clark 1.50 .70
❑ 32 Chuck Knoblauch 1.50 .70
❑ 33 Harold Baines .75 .35
❑ 34 Edgar Martinez .75 .35
❑ 35 Mike Mussina 1.50 .70
❑ 36 Kevin Brown 1.00 .45
❑ 37 Dennis Eckersley .75 .35
❑ 38 Tino Martinez 1.50 .70
❑ 39 Raul Mondesi 1.00 .45
❑ 40 Sammy Sosa 4.00 1.80
❑ 41 John Smoltz .75 .35
❑ 42 Billy Wagner .75 .35
❑ 43 Ken Caminiti 1.00 .45
❑ 44 Wade Boggs 1.50 .70
❑ 45 Andres Galarraga 1.50 .70
❑ 46 Roger Clemens 3.00 1.35
❑ 47 Matt Williams .75 .35
❑ 48 Albert Belle 2.00 .90
❑ 49 Jeff King .40 .18
❑ 50 John Wetteland .75 .35
❑ 51 Deion Sanders .75 .35
❑ 52 Ellis Burks .75 .35
❑ 53 Pedro Martinez 1.50 .70
❑ 54 Kenny Lofton 1.50 .70
❑ 55 Randy Johnson 1.50 .70
❑ 56 Bernie Williams 1.50 .70
❑ 57 Marquis Grissom .75 .35
❑ 58 Gary Sheffield 1.00 .45
❑ 59 Curt Schilling .75 .35
❑ 60 Reggie Sanders .75 .35
❑ 61 Bobby Higginson 1.00 .45
❑ 62 Moises Alou 1.00 .45
❑ 63 Tom Glavine 1.50 .70
❑ 64 Mark Grace 1.00 .45
❑ 65 Rafael Palmeiro 1.00 .45
❑ 66 John Olerud .75 .35
❑ 67 Dante Bichette .75 .35
❑ 68 Jeff Bagwell 2.50 1.10
❑ 69 Barry Bonds 2.00 .90
❑ 70 Pat Hentgen .75 .35
❑ 71 Jim Thome 1.50 .70
❑ 72 Andy Pettitte 1.00 .45
❑ 73 Jay Bell .75 .35
❑ 74 Jim Edmonds 1.00 .45
❑ 75 Ron Gant .40 .18
❑ 76 David Cone 1.00 .45
❑ 77 Jose Canseco 1.50 .70
❑ 78 Jay Buhner .75 .35
❑ 79 Greg Maddux 5.00 2.20
❑ 80 Lance Johnson .40 .18
❑ 81 Travis Fryman .75 .35
❑ 82 Paul O'Neill .75 .35
❑ 83 Ivan Rodriguez 2.00 .90
❑ 84 Fred McGriff 1.00 .45
❑ 85 Mike Piazza 5.00 2.20
❑ 86 Brady Anderson .75 .35
❑ 87 Marty Cordova .40 .18
❑ 88 Joe Carter .75 .35
❑ 89 Brian Jordan .75 .35
❑ 90 David Justice 1.50 .70
❑ 91 Tony Gwynn 2.50 1.10
❑ 92 Larry Walker 1.50 .70
❑ 93 Mo Vaughn 2.00 .90
❑ 94 Sandy Alomar .75 .35
❑ 95 Rusty Greer .75 .35
❑ 96 Roberto Hernandez .40 .18
❑ 97 Hal Morris .40 .18
❑ 98 Todd Hundley .75 .35
❑ 99 Rondell White .75 .35
❑ 100 Frank Thomas 5.00 2.20
❑ 101 Bubba Trammell 3.00 1.35
❑ 102 Sidney Ponson 3.00 1.35
❑ 103 Ricky Ledee 15.00 6.75
❑ 104 Brett Tomko 1.25 .55
❑ 105 Braden Looper 1.50 .70
❑ 106 Jason Dickson 1.25 .55
❑ 107 Chad Green 2.50 1.10
❑ 108 R.A. Dickey 1.50 .70
❑ 109 Jeff Liefer 1.25 .55
❑ 110 Richard Hidalgo 1.25 .55
❑ 111 Chad Hermansen 12.00 5.50
❑ 112 Felix Martinez 1.00 .45
❑ 113 J.J. Johnson 1.00 .45
❑ 114 Todd Dunwoody 1.25 .55
❑ 115 Katsuhiro Maeda 1.25 .55
❑ 116 Darin Erstad 5.00 2.20
❑ 117 Elieser Marrero 1.25 .55
❑ 118 Bartolo Colon 1.25 .55
❑ 119 Ugueth Urbina 1.25 .55
❑ 120 Jaime Bluma 1.00 .45
❑ 121 Seth Greisinger 4.00 1.80
❑ 122 Jose Cruz Jr. 20.00 9.00
❑ 123 Todd Dunn 1.00 .45
❑ 124 Justin Towle 3.00 1.35
❑ 125 Brian Rose 2.00 .90
❑ 126 Jose Guillen 2.00 .90
❑ 127 Andruw Jones 2.50 1.10
❑ 128 Mark Kotsay 10.00 4.50
❑ 129 Wilton Guerrero 1.00 .45
❑ 130 Jacob Cruz 1.00 .45
❑ 131 Mike Sweeney 1.00 .45
❑ 132 Matt Morris 1.25 .55
❑ 133 John Thomson 1.00 .45
❑ 134 Javier Valentin 1.25 .55
❑ 135 Mike Drumright 2.50 1.10
❑ 136 Michael Barrett 1.25 .55
❑ 137 Tony Saunders 2.50 1.10
❑ 138 Kevin Brown 1.50 .70
❑ 139 Anthony Sanders 4.00 1.80
❑ 140 Jeff Abbott 1.25 .55
❑ 141 Eugene Kingsale 1.25 .55
❑ 142 Paul Konerko 1.50 .70
❑ 143 Randall Simon 8.00 3.60
❑ 144 Freddy Garcia 1.00 .45
❑ 145 Karim Garcia 1.25 .55
❑ 146 Carlos Guillen 1.25 .55
❑ 147 Aaron Boone 1.00 .45
❑ 148 Donnie Sadler 1.25 .55
❑ 149 Brooks Kieschnick 1.00 .45
❑ 150 Scott Spiezio 1.00 .45
❑ 151 Kevin Orie 1.00 .45
❑ 152 Russ Johnson 1.00 .45
❑ 153 Livan Hernandez 1.25 .55
❑ 154 Vladimir Nunez 3.00 1.35
❑ 155 Calvin Reese 1.00 .45
❑ 156 Chris Carpenter 1.25 .55
❑ 157 Eric Milton 5.00 2.20
❑ 158 Richie Sexson 1.50 .70
❑ 159 Carl Pavano 2.00 .90
❑ 160 Pat Cline 1.25 .55
❑ 161 Ron Wright 1.25 .55
❑ 162 Dante Powell 1.25 .55
❑ 163 Mark Bellhorn 1.25 .55
❑ 164 George Lombard 2.00 .90
❑ 165 Paul Wilder 3.00 1.35
❑ 166 Brad Fullmer 1.50 .70
❑ 167 Kris Benson 6.00 2.70
❑ 168 Torii Hunter 1.00 .45
❑ 169 D.T. Cromer 1.00 .45
❑ 170 Nelson Figueroa 2.00 .90
❑ 171 Hiram Bocachica 3.00 1.35
❑ 172 Shane Monahan 1.25 .55
❑ 173 Juan Melo 1.25 .55
❑ 174 Calvin Pickering 15.00 6.75
❑ 175 Reggie Taylor 1.25 .55
❑ 176 Geoff Jenkins 1.25 .55
❑ 177 Steve Rain 1.50 .70
❑ 178 Nerio Rodriguez 2.50 1.10
❑ 179 Derrick Gibson 1.50 .70
❑ 180 Darin Blood 1.00 .45
❑ 181 Ben Davis 2.00 .90
❑ 182 Adrian Beltre 25.00 11.00
❑ 183 Kerry Wood 60.00 27.00
❑ 184 Nate Rolison 4.00 1.80
❑ 185 Fernando Tatis 8.00 3.60
❑ 186 Jake Westbrook 3.00 1.35
❑ 187 Edwin Diaz 1.00 .45
❑ 188 Joe Fontenot 2.50 1.10
❑ 189 Matt Halloran 2.00 .90
❑ 190 Matt Clement 10.00 4.50
❑ 191 Todd Greene 1.25 .55
❑ 192 Eric Chavez 30.00 13.50
❑ 193 Edgard Velazquez 1.25 .55
❑ 194 Bruce Chen 15.00 6.75
❑ 195 Jason Brester 1.25 .55
❑ 196 Chris Reitsma 2.00 .90
❑ 197 Neifi Perez 1.00 .45
❑ 198 Hideki Irabu 12.00 5.50
❑ 199 Don Denbow 1.00 .45
❑ 200 Derrek Lee 1.50 .70
❑ 201 Todd Walker 2.00 .90
❑ 202 Scott Rolen 4.00 1.80
❑ 203 Wes Helms 1.25 .55
❑ 204 Bob Abreu 1.25 .55
❑ 205 John Patterson 6.00 2.70
❑ 206 Alex Gonzalez 4.00 1.80
❑ 207 Grant Roberts 5.00 2.20
❑ 208 Jeff Suppan 1.00 .45
❑ 209 Luke Wilcox 1.00 .45
❑ 210 Marlon Anderson 1.25 .55
❑ 211 Mike Caruso 8.00 3.60
❑ 212 Roy Halladay 12.00 5.50
❑ 213 Jeremi Gonzalez 3.00 1.35
❑ 214 Aramis Ramirez 20.00 9.00
❑ 215 Dermal Brown 10.00 4.50
❑ 216 Justin Thompson 1.25 .55
❑ 217 Danny Clyburn 1.00 .45
❑ 218 Bruce Aven 1.00 .45
❑ 219 Keith Foulke 1.00 .45
❑ 220 Shannon Stewart 1.25 .55
❑ 221 Larry Barnes 1.25 .55
❑ 222 Mark Johnson 1.50 .70
❑ 223 Randy Winn 1.00 .45
❑ 224 Nomar Garciaparra 5.00 2.20
❑ 225 Jacque Jones 8.00 3.60
❑ 226 Chris Clemons 1.00 .45
❑ 227 Todd Helton 3.00 1.35
❑ 228 Ryan Brannan 1.50 .70
❑ 229 Alex Sanchez 3.00 1.35
❑ 230 Russell Branyan 2.00 .90
❑ 231 Daryle Ward 4.00 1.80
❑ 232 Kevin Witt 6.00 2.70
❑ 233 Gabby Martinez 1.00 .45
❑ 234 Preston Wilson 1.25 .55
❑ 235 Donzell McDonald 2.00 .90
❑ 236 Orlando Cabrera 2.50 1.10
❑ 237 Brian Banks 1.00 .45
❑ 238 Robbie Bell 2.50 1.10
❑ 239 Brad Rigby 1.00 .45
❑ 240 Scott Elarton 1.25 .55
❑ 241 Donny Leon 2.00 .90
❑ 242 Abraham Nunez 3.00 1.35
❑ 243 Adam Eaton 1.50 .70
❑ 244 Octavio Dotel 4.00 1.80
❑ 245 Sean Casey 8.00 3.60
❑ 246 Joe Lawrence 2.50 1.10
❑ 247 Adam Johnson 3.00 1.35
❑ 248 Ronnie Belliard 3.00 1.35
❑ 249 Bobby Estalella 1.25 .55
❑ 250 Corey Lee 2.00 .90
❑ 251 Mike Cameron 1.25 .55
❑ 252 Kerry Robinson 1.50 .70
❑ 253 A.J. Zapp 6.00 2.70
❑ 254 Jarrod Washburn 1.25 .55
❑ 255 Ben Grieve 4.00 1.80
❑ 256 Javier Vazquez 3.00 1.35
❑ 257 Travis Lee 35.00 16.00
❑ 258 Dennis Reyes 3.00 1.35
❑ 259 Danny Buxbaum 1.00 .45
❑ 260 Kelvim Escobar 4.00 1.80
❑ 261 Danny Klassen 1.25 .55
❑ 262 Ken Cloude 3.00 1.35
❑ 263 Gabe Alvarez 1.25 .55
❑ 264 Clayton Bruner 2.50 1.10
❑ 265 Jason Marquis 4.00 1.80
❑ 266 Jamey Wright 1.00 .45
❑ 267 Matt Snyder 1.50 .70
❑ 268 Josh Garrett 3.00 1.35
❑ 269 Juan Encarnacion 1.25 .55

❑ 270 Heath Murray	1.00	.45
❑ 271 Brent Butler	8.00	3.60
❑ 272 Danny Peoples	4.00	1.80
❑ 273 Miguel Tejada	10.00	4.50
❑ 274 Jim Pittsley	1.00	.45
❑ 275 Dmitri Young	1.25	.55
❑ 276 Vladimir Guerrero	3.00	1.35
❑ 277 Cole Liniak	8.00	3.60
❑ 278 Ramon Hernandez	1.50	.70
❑ 279 Cliff Politte	3.00	1.35
❑ 280 Mel Rosario	1.50	.70
❑ 281 Jorge Carrion	1.50	.70
❑ 282 John Barnes	3.00	1.35
❑ 283 Chris Stowe	1.50	.70
❑ 284 Vernon Wells	10.00	4.50
❑ 285 Brett Caradonna	6.00	2.70
❑ 286 Scott Hodges	2.50	1.10
❑ 287 Jon Garland	6.00	2.70
❑ 288 Nathan Haynes	3.00	1.35
❑ 289 Geoff Goetz	2.50	1.10
❑ 290 Adam Kennedy	3.00	1.35
❑ 291 T.J. Tucker	2.00	.90
❑ 292 Aaron Akin	2.00	.90
❑ 293 Jayson Werth	12.00	5.50
❑ 294 Glenn Davis	3.00	1.35
❑ 295 Mark Mangum	2.00	.90
❑ 296 Troy Cameron	6.00	2.70
❑ 297 J.J. Davis	8.00	3.60
❑ 298 Lance Berkman	20.00	9.00
❑ 299 Jason Standridge	3.00	1.35
❑ 300 Jason Dellaero	3.00	1.35

1997 Bowman Chrome International

	MINT	NRMT
COMPLETE SET (300)	800.00	350.00
COMMON RED (1-100)	1.00	.45
COMMON BLUE (101-300)	1.50	.70

*STARS: 1.25X TO 3X BASIC CARDS
*YOUNG STARS: 1.5X TO 3X BASIC CARDS
*RC'S/PROSPECTS: .5X TO 1.2X BASIC CARDS

1997 Bowman Chrome International Refractors

	MINT	NRMT
COMPLETE SET (300)	4000.00	1800.00
COMMON CARD (1-300)	6.00	2.70

*STARS: 7.5X TO 15X BASIC CARDS
*ROOKIES: 2.5X TO 5X BASIC CARDS

1997 Bowman Chrome Refractors

	MINT	NRMT
COMPLETE SET (300)	3000.00	1350.00
COMMON CARD (1-300)	4.00	1.80

*STARS: 3X TO 8X BASIC CARDS
*YOUNG STARS: 2.5X TO 6X BASIC CARDS
*ROOKIES: 1.5X TO 4X BASIC CARDS

1997 Bowman Chrome 1998 ROY Favorites

	MINT	NRMT
COMPLETE SET (15)	50.00	22.00
COMMON CARD (1-15)	1.50	.70
COMP.REF.SET (15)	100.00	45.00

*REFRACTORS: .75X TO 2X BASIC CARDS
REFRACTOR STATED ODDS 1:72

❑ ROY1 Jeff Abbott	2.00	.90
❑ ROY2 Karim Garcia	2.00	.90
❑ ROY3 Todd Helton	6.00	2.70
❑ ROY4 Richard Hidalgo	2.00	.90
❑ ROY5 Geoff Jenkins	2.00	.90
❑ ROY6 Russ Johnson	1.50	.70
❑ ROY7 Paul Konerko	3.00	1.35
❑ ROY8 Mark Kotsay	6.00	2.70
❑ ROY9 Ricky Ledee	10.00	4.50
❑ ROY10 Travis Lee	20.00	9.00
❑ ROY11 Derrek Lee	3.00	1.35
❑ ROY12 Elieser Marrero	2.00	.90
❑ ROY13 Juan Melo	2.00	.90
❑ ROY14 Brian Rose	2.50	1.10
❑ ROY15 Fernando Tatis	5.00	2.20

1997 Bowman Chrome Scout's Honor Roll

	MINT	NRMT
COMPLETE SET (15)	50.00	22.00
COMMON CARD (1-15)	1.50	.70

❑ SHR1 Dmitri Young	1.50	.70
❑ SHR2 Bob Abreu	1.50	.70
❑ SHR3 Vladimir Guerrero	5.00	2.20
❑ SHR4 Paul Konerko	2.50	1.10
❑ SHR5 Kevin Orie	1.50	.70
❑ SHR6 Todd Walker	3.00	1.35
❑ SHR7 Ben Grieve	6.00	2.70
❑ SHR8 Darin Erstad	4.00	1.80
❑ SHR9 Derrek Lee	2.00	.90
❑ SHR10 Jose Cruz Jr.	10.00	4.50
❑ SHR11 Scott Rolen	6.00	2.70
❑ SHR12 Travis Lee	15.00	6.75
❑ SHR13 Andruw Jones	4.00	1.80
❑ SHR14 Wilton Guerrero	1.50	.70
❑ SHR15 Nomar Garciaparra	8.00	3.60

1998 Bowman Chrome

	MINT	NRMT
COMPLETE SET (441)	350.00	160.00
COMPLETE SERIES 1 (221)	200.00	90.00
COMPLETE SERIES 2 (220)	150.00	70.00
COMMON CARD (1-441)	.40	.18

❑ 1 Nomar Garciaparra	5.00	2.20
❑ 2 Scott Rolen	4.00	1.80
❑ 3 Andy Pettitte	1.00	.45
❑ 4 Ivan Rodriguez	2.00	.90
❑ 5 Mark McGwire	10.00	4.50
❑ 6 Jason Dickson	.60	.25
❑ 7 Jose Cruz Jr.	2.00	.90
❑ 8 Jeff Kent	.60	.25
❑ 9 Mike Mussina	1.50	.70
❑ 10 Jason Kendall	.60	.25
❑ 11 Brett Tomko	.60	.25
❑ 12 Jeff King	.60	.25
❑ 13 Brad Radke	.60	.25
❑ 14 Robin Ventura	.60	.25
❑ 15 Jeff Bagwell	2.50	1.10
❑ 16 Greg Maddux	5.00	2.20
❑ 17 John Jaha	.40	.18
❑ 18 Mike Piazza	5.00	2.20
❑ 19 Edgar Martinez	.60	.25
❑ 20 David Justice	1.50	.70
❑ 21 Todd Hundley	.60	.25
❑ 22 Tony Gwynn	4.00	1.80
❑ 23 Larry Walker	1.50	.70
❑ 24 Bernie Williams	1.50	.70
❑ 25 Edgar Renteria	.60	.25
❑ 26 Rafael Palmeiro	1.00	.45
❑ 27 Tim Salmon	1.50	.70
❑ 28 Matt Morris	.60	.25
❑ 29 Shawn Estes	.60	.25
❑ 30 Vladimir Guerrero	2.50	1.10
❑ 31 Fernando Tatis	.60	.25
❑ 32 Justin Thompson	.60	.25
❑ 33 Ken Griffey Jr.	8.00	3.60
❑ 34 Edgardo Alfonzo	.60	.25
❑ 35 Mo Vaughn	2.00	.90
❑ 36 Marty Cordova	.40	.18
❑ 37 Craig Biggio	1.50	.70
❑ 38 Roger Clemens	3.00	1.35
❑ 39 Mark Grace	1.00	.45
❑ 40 Ken Caminiti	1.00	.45
❑ 41 Tony Womack	.60	.25
❑ 42 Albert Belle	1.50	.70
❑ 43 Tino Martinez	1.50	.70
❑ 44 Sandy Alomar	.60	.25
❑ 45 Jeff Cirillo	.60	.25
❑ 46 Jason Giambi	.60	.25
❑ 47 Darin Erstad	2.00	.90
❑ 48 Livan Hernandez	.60	.25
❑ 49 Mark Grudzielanek	.60	.25
❑ 50 Sammy Sosa	4.00	1.80
❑ 51 Curt Schilling	.60	.25
❑ 52 Brian Hunter	.60	.25
❑ 53 Neifi Perez	.60	.25
❑ 54 Todd Walker	1.00	.45
❑ 55 Jose Guillen	.60	.25
❑ 56 Jim Thome	1.50	.70
❑ 57 Tom Glavine	1.50	.70
❑ 58 Todd Greene	.60	.25
❑ 59 Rondell White	.60	.25
❑ 60 Roberto Alomar	1.50	.70
❑ 61 Tony Clark	1.00	.45
❑ 62 Vinny Castilla	1.00	.45
❑ 63 Barry Larkin	1.00	.45
❑ 64 Hideki Irabu	1.00	.45
❑ 65 Johnny Damon	.60	.25
❑ 66 Juan Gonzalez	4.00	1.80
❑ 67 John Olerud	.60	.25
❑ 68 Gary Sheffield	1.00	.45
❑ 69 Raul Mondesi	1.00	.45
❑ 70 Chipper Jones	4.00	1.80
❑ 71 David Ortiz	.60	.25
❑ 72 Warren Morris	4.00	1.80
❑ 73 Alex Gonzalez	.60	.25
❑ 74 Nick Bierbrodt	2.50	1.10
❑ 75 Roy Halladay	.60	.25
❑ 76 Danny Buxbaum	.40	.18
❑ 77 Adam Kennedy	.60	.25
❑ 78 Jared Sandberg	6.00	2.70
❑ 79 Michael Barrett	.60	.25
❑ 80 Gil Meche	4.00	1.80
❑ 81 Jayson Werth	1.00	.45

❑ 82	Abraham Nunez	.60	.25
❑ 83	Ben Petrick	.60	.25
❑ 84	Brett Caradonna	.60	.25
❑ 85	Mike Lowell	5.00	2.20
❑ 86	Clayton Bruner	.60	.25
❑ 87	John Curtice	5.00	2.20
❑ 88	Bobby Estalella	.60	.25
❑ 89	Juan Melo	.60	.25
❑ 90	Arnold Gooch	.40	.18
❑ 91	Kevin Millwood	12.00	5.50
❑ 92	Richie Sexson	1.00	.45
❑ 93	Orlando Cabrera	.60	.25
❑ 94	Pat Cline	.60	.25
❑ 95	Anthony Sanders	.60	.25
❑ 96	Russ Johnson	.40	.18
❑ 97	Ben Grieve	3.00	1.35
❑ 98	Kevin McGlinchy	.60	.25
❑ 99	Paul Wilder	.60	.25
❑ 100	Russ Ortiz	.40	.18
❑ 101	Ryan Jackson	2.00	.90
❑ 102	Heath Murray	.40	.18
❑ 103	Brian Rose	.60	.25
❑ 104	Ryan Radmanovich	.40	.18
❑ 105	Ricky Ledee	.60	.25
❑ 106	Jeff Wallace	2.50	1.10
❑ 107	Ryan Minor	6.00	2.70
❑ 108	Dennis Reyes	.60	.25
❑ 109	James Manias	.40	.18
❑ 110	Chris Carpenter	.60	.25
❑ 111	Daryle Ward	.60	.25
❑ 112	Vernon Wells	1.00	.45
❑ 113	Chad Green	.60	.25
❑ 114	Mike Stoner	5.00	2.20
❑ 115	Brad Fullmer	.60	.25
❑ 116	Adam Eaton	.40	.18
❑ 117	Jeff Liefer	.60	.25
❑ 118	Corey Koskie	5.00	2.20
❑ 119	Todd Helton	2.00	.90
❑ 120	Jaime Jones	2.50	1.10
❑ 121	Mel Rosario	.40	.18
❑ 122	Geoff Goetz	.60	.25
❑ 123	Adrian Beltre	2.00	.90
❑ 124	Jason Dellaero	.60	.25
❑ 125	Gabe Kapler	25.00	11.00
❑ 126	Scott Schoeneweis	.40	.18
❑ 127	Ryan Brannan	.40	.18
❑ 128	Aaron Akin	.40	.18
❑ 129	Ryan Anderson	20.00	9.00
❑ 130	Brad Penny	1.00	.45
❑ 131	Bruce Chen	.60	.25
❑ 132	Eli Marrero	.60	.25
❑ 133	Eric Chavez	2.50	1.10
❑ 134	Troy Glaus	25.00	11.00
❑ 135	Troy Cameron	.60	.25
❑ 136	Brian Sikorski	2.00	.90
❑ 137	Mike Kinkade	4.00	1.80
❑ 138	Braden Looper	.60	.25
❑ 139	Mark Mangum	.60	.25
❑ 140	Danny Peoples	.40	.18
❑ 141	J.J. Davis	.60	.25
❑ 142	Ben Davis	.60	.25
❑ 143	Jacque Jones	.60	.25
❑ 144	Derrick Gibson	.60	.25
❑ 145	Bronson Arroyo	2.50	1.10
❑ 146	Luis De Los Santos	4.00	1.80
❑ 147	Jeff Abbott	.60	.25
❑ 148	Mike Cuddyer	8.00	3.60
❑ 149	Jason Romano	.60	.25
❑ 150	Shane Monahan	.60	.25
❑ 151	Ntema Ndungidi	4.00	1.80
❑ 152	Alex Sanchez	.60	.25
❑ 153	Jack Cust	8.00	3.60
❑ 154	Brent Butler	.60	.25
❑ 155	Ramon Hernandez	.60	.25
❑ 156	Norm Hutchins	.60	.25
❑ 157	Jason Marquis	.60	.25
❑ 158	Jacob Cruz	.40	.18
❑ 159	Rob Burger	2.50	1.10
❑ 160	Dave Coggin	.40	.18
❑ 161	Preston Wilson	.60	.25
❑ 162	Jason Fitzgerald	2.50	1.10
❑ 163	Dan Serafini	.40	.18
❑ 164	Peter Munro	.40	.18
❑ 165	Trot Nixon	.60	.25
❑ 166	Homer Bush	.40	.18
❑ 167	Dermal Brown	.60	.25
❑ 168	Chad Hermansen	1.50	.70
❑ 169	Julio Moreno	2.50	1.10
❑ 170	John Roskos	4.00	1.80
❑ 171	Grant Roberts	.60	.25
❑ 172	Ken Cloude	.60	.25
❑ 173	Jason Brester	.60	.25
❑ 174	Jason Conti	2.00	.90
❑ 175	Jon Garland	.60	.25
❑ 176	Robbie Bell	.60	.25
❑ 177	Nathan Haynes	.60	.25
❑ 178	Ramon Ortiz	6.00	2.70
❑ 179	Shannon Stewart	.60	.25
❑ 180	Pablo Ortega	.40	.18
❑ 181	Jimmy Rollins	4.00	1.80
❑ 182	Sean Casey	.60	.25
❑ 183	Ted Lilly	4.00	1.80
❑ 184	Chris Enochs	6.00	2.70
❑ 185	Magglio Ordonez	6.00	2.70
❑ 186	Mike Drumright	.60	.25
❑ 187	Aaron Boone	.40	.18
❑ 188	Matt Clement	.60	.25
❑ 189	Todd Dunwoody	.60	.25
❑ 190	Larry Rodriguez	.40	.18
❑ 191	Todd Noel	.60	.25
❑ 192	Geoff Jenkins	.60	.25
❑ 193	George Lombard	.60	.25
❑ 194	Lance Berkman	1.50	.70
❑ 195	Marcus McCain	.60	.25
❑ 196	Ryan McGuire	.40	.18
❑ 197	Jhensy Sandoval	6.00	2.70
❑ 198	Corey Lee	.60	.25
❑ 199	Mario Valdez	2.00	.90
❑ 200	Robert Fick	6.00	2.70
❑ 201	Donnie Sadler	.60	.25
❑ 202	Marc Kroon	.40	.18
❑ 203	David Miller	.40	.18
❑ 204	Jarrod Washburn	.60	.25
❑ 205	Miguel Tejada	.60	.25
❑ 206	Raul Ibanez	.40	.18
❑ 207	John Patterson	.60	.25
❑ 208	Calvin Pickering	1.00	.45
❑ 209	Felix Martinez	.40	.18
❑ 210	Mark Redman	.40	.18
❑ 211	Scott Elarton	.60	.25
❑ 212	Jose Amado	2.00	.90
❑ 213	Kerry Wood	8.00	3.60
❑ 214	Dante Powell	.60	.25
❑ 215	Aramis Ramirez	1.50	.70
❑ 216	A.J. Hinch	.60	.25
❑ 217	Dustin Carr	2.00	.90
❑ 218	Mark Kotsay	1.00	.45
❑ 219	Jason Standridge	.60	.25
❑ 220	Luis Ordaz	.60	.25
❑ 221	Orlando Hernandez	25.00	11.00
❑ 222	Cal Ripken	6.00	2.70
❑ 223	Paul Molitor	.40	.18
❑ 224	Derek Jeter	4.00	1.80
❑ 225	Barry Bonds	2.00	.90
❑ 226	Jim Edmonds	.40	.18
❑ 227	John Smoltz	.40	.18
❑ 228	Eric Karros	.40	.18
❑ 229	Ray Lankford	.40	.18
❑ 230	Rey Ordonez	.40	.18
❑ 231	Kenny Lofton	.40	.18
❑ 232	Alex Rodriguez	5.00	2.20
❑ 233	Dante Bichette	.40	.18
❑ 234	Pedro Martinez	.40	.18
❑ 235	Carlos Delgado	.40	.18
❑ 236	Rod Beck	.40	.18
❑ 237	Matt Williams	.40	.18
❑ 238	Charles Johnson	.40	.18
❑ 239	Rico Brogna	.40	.18
❑ 240	Frank Thomas	5.00	2.20
❑ 241	Paul O'Neill	.40	.18
❑ 242	Jaret Wright	2.00	.90
❑ 243	Brant Brown	.40	.18
❑ 244	Ryan Klesko	.40	.18
❑ 245	Chuck Finley	.40	.18
❑ 246	Derek Bell	.40	.18
❑ 247	Delino DeShields	.40	.18
❑ 248	Chan Ho Park	.40	.18
❑ 249	Wade Boggs	.40	.18
❑ 250	Jay Buhner	.40	.18
❑ 251	Butch Huskey	.40	.18
❑ 252	Steve Finley	.40	.18
❑ 253	Will Clark	.40	.18
❑ 254	John Valentin	.40	.18
❑ 255	Bobby Higginson	.40	.18
❑ 256	Darryl Strawberry	.40	.18
❑ 257	Randy Johnson	.40	.18
❑ 258	Al Martin	.40	.18
❑ 259	Travis Fryman	.40	.18
❑ 260	Fred McGriff	.40	.18
❑ 261	Jose Valentin	.40	.18
❑ 262	Andruw Jones	2.00	.90
❑ 263	Kenny Rogers	.40	.18
❑ 264	Moises Alou	.40	.18
❑ 265	Denny Neagle	.40	.18
❑ 266	Ugueth Urbina	.40	.18
❑ 267	Derrek Lee	.40	.18
❑ 268	Ellis Burks	.40	.18
❑ 269	Mariano Rivera	.40	.18
❑ 270	Dean Palmer	.40	.18
❑ 271	Eddie Taubensee	.40	.18
❑ 272	Brady Anderson	.40	.18
❑ 273	Brian Giles	.40	.18
❑ 274	Quinton McCracken	.40	.18
❑ 275	Henry Rodriguez	.40	.18
❑ 276	Andres Galarraga	.40	.18
❑ 277	Jose Canseco	.40	.18
❑ 278	David Segui	.40	.18
❑ 279	Bret Saberhagen	.40	.18
❑ 280	Kevin Brown	.40	.18
❑ 281	Chuck Knoblauch	.40	.18
❑ 282	Jeromy Burnitz	.40	.18
❑ 283	Jay Bell	.40	.18
❑ 284	Manny Ramirez	.40	.18
❑ 285	Rick Helling	.40	.18
❑ 286	Francisco Cordova	.40	.18
❑ 287	Bob Abreu	.40	.18
❑ 288	J.T. Snow Jr.	.40	.18
❑ 289	Hideo Nomo	2.00	.90
❑ 290	Brian Jordan	.40	.18
❑ 291	Javy Lopez	.40	.18
❑ 292	Travis Lee	3.00	1.35
❑ 293	Russ Branyan	.40	.18
❑ 294	Paul Konerko	.40	.18
❑ 295	Masato Yoshii	4.00	1.80
❑ 296	Kris Benson	.40	.18
❑ 297	Juan Encarnacion	.40	.18
❑ 298	Eric Milton	.40	.18
❑ 299	Mike Caruso	.40	.18
❑ 300	Ricardo Aramboles	8.00	3.60
❑ 301	Bobby Smith	.40	.18
❑ 302	Billy Koch	.40	.18
❑ 303	Richard Hidalgo	.40	.18
❑ 304	Justin Baughman	2.50	1.10
❑ 305	Chris Gissell	.40	.18
❑ 306	Donnie Bridges	2.50	1.10
❑ 307	Nelson Lara	2.50	1.10
❑ 308	Randy Wolf	2.50	1.10
❑ 309	Jason LaRue	4.00	1.80
❑ 310	Jason Gooding	2.00	.90
❑ 311	Edgard Clemente	.40	.18
❑ 312	Andrew Vessel	.40	.18
❑ 313	Chris Reitsma	.40	.18
❑ 314	Jesus Sanchez	3.00	1.35
❑ 315	Buddy Carlyle	3.00	1.35
❑ 316	Randy Winn	.40	.18
❑ 317	Luis Rivera	6.00	2.70
❑ 318	Marcus Thames	4.00	1.80
❑ 319	A.J. Pierzynski	.40	.18
❑ 320	Scott Randall	.40	.18
❑ 321	Damian Sapp	.40	.18
❑ 322	Eddie Yarnall	8.00	3.60
❑ 323	Luke Allen	4.00	1.80
❑ 324	J.D. Smart	.40	.18
❑ 325	Willie Martinez	.40	.18
❑ 326	Alex Ramirez	.40	.18
❑ 327	Eric DuBose	3.00	1.35
❑ 328	Kevin Witt	.40	.18
❑ 329	Dan McKinley	2.00	.90
❑ 330	Cliff Politte	.40	.18
❑ 331	Vladimir Nunez	.40	.18
❑ 332	John Halama	.40	.18
❑ 333	Nerio Rodriguez	.40	.18
❑ 334	Desi Relaford	.40	.18
❑ 335	Robinson Checo	.40	.18
❑ 336	John Nicholson	3.00	1.35

- ❑ 337 Tom LaRosa 2.00 .90
- ❑ 338 Kevin Nicholson 3.00 1.35
- ❑ 339 Javier Vazquez .40 .18
- ❑ 340 A.J. Zapp .40 .18
- ❑ 341 Tom Evans .40 .18
- ❑ 342 Kerry Robinson .40 .18
- ❑ 343 Gabe Gonzalez .40 .18
- ❑ 344 Ralph Milliard .40 .18
- ❑ 345 Enrique Wilson .40 .18
- ❑ 346 Elvin Hernandez .40 .18
- ❑ 347 Mike Lincoln 4.00 1.80
- ❑ 348 Cesar King 5.00 2.20
- ❑ 349 Cristian Guzman 2.50 1.10
- ❑ 350 Donzell McDonald .40 .18
- ❑ 351 Jim Parque 5.00 2.20
- ❑ 352 Mike Saipe .40 .18
- ❑ 353 Carlos Febles 4.00 1.80
- ❑ 354 Dernell Stenson 10.00 4.50
- ❑ 355 Mark Osborne 4.00 1.80
- ❑ 356 Odalis Perez 5.00 2.20
- ❑ 357 Jason Dewey 3.00 1.35
- ❑ 358 Joe Fontenot .40 .18
- ❑ 359 Jason Grilli 4.00 1.80
- ❑ 360 Kevin Haverbusch 4.00 1.80
- ❑ 361 Jay Yennaco 2.50 1.10
- ❑ 362 Brian Buchanan .40 .18
- ❑ 363 John Barnes .40 .18
- ❑ 364 Chris Fussell .40 .18
- ❑ 365 Kevin Gibbs 2.00 .90
- ❑ 366 Joe Lawrence .40 .18
- ❑ 367 DaRond Stovall .40 .18
- ❑ 368 Brian Fuentes 2.00 .90
- ❑ 369 Jimmy Anderson .40 .18
- ❑ 370 Lariel Gonzalez 2.00 .90
- ❑ 371 Scott Williamson 2.50 1.10
- ❑ 372 Milton Bradley .40 .18
- ❑ 373 Jason Halper 2.00 .90
- ❑ 374 Brent Billingsley 2.50 1.10
- ❑ 375 Joe DePastino 2.00 .90
- ❑ 376 Jake Westbrook .40 .18
- ❑ 377 Octavio Dotel .40 .18
- ❑ 378 Jason Williams 2.00 .90
- ❑ 379 Julio Ramirez 6.00 2.70
- ❑ 380 Seth Greisinger .40 .18
- ❑ 381 Mike Judd 3.00 1.35
- ❑ 382 Ben Ford 2.00 .90
- ❑ 383 Tom Bennett 2.00 .90
- ❑ 384 Adam Butler 2.00 .90
- ❑ 385 Wade Miller 2.50 1.10
- ❑ 386 Kyle Peterson 2.50 1.10
- ❑ 387 Tommy Peterman 2.50 1.10
- ❑ 388 Onan Masaoka .40 .18
- ❑ 389 Jason Rakers 2.00 .90
- ❑ 390 Rafael Medina .40 .18
- ❑ 391 Luis Lopez .40 .18
- ❑ 392 Jeff Yoder .40 .18
- ❑ 393 Vance Wilson 2.00 .90
- ❑ 394 Fernando Seguignol 6.00 2.70
- ❑ 395 Ron Wright .40 .18
- ❑ 396 Ruben Mateo 15.00 6.75
- ❑ 397 Steve Lomasney 2.50 1.10
- ❑ 398 Damian Jackson .40 .18
- ❑ 399 Mike Jerzembeck 2.50 1.10
- ❑ 400 Luis Rivas 4.00 1.80
- ❑ 401 Kevin Burford 4.00 1.80
- ❑ 402 Glenn Davis .40 .18
- ❑ 403 Robert Luce 2.00 .90
- ❑ 404 Cole Liniak .40 .18
- ❑ 405 Matt LeCroy 4.00 1.80
- ❑ 406 Jeremy Giambi 8.00 3.60
- ❑ 407 Shawn Chacon .40 .18
- ❑ 408 Dewayne Wise 5.00 2.20
- ❑ 409 Steve Woodard .40 .18
- ❑ 410 Francisco Cordero 2.00 .90
- ❑ 411 Damon Minor 2.50 1.10
- ❑ 412 Lou Collier .40 .18
- ❑ 413 Justin Towle .40 .18
- ❑ 414 Juan LeBron .40 .18
- ❑ 415 Michael Coleman .40 .18
- ❑ 416 Felix Rodriguez .40 .18
- ❑ 417 Paul Ah Yat 2.50 1.10
- ❑ 418 Kevin Barker 2.50 1.10
- ❑ 419 Brian Meadows .40 .18
- ❑ 420 Darnell McDonald 10.00 4.50
- ❑ 421 Matt Kinney 2.50 1.10
- ❑ 422 Mike Vavrek 2.50 1.10
- ❑ 423 Courtney Duncan 2.00 .90
- ❑ 424 Kevin Millar 5.00 2.20
- ❑ 425 Ruben Rivera .40 .18
- ❑ 426 Steve Shoemaker .40 .18
- ❑ 427 Dan Reichert 2.00 .90
- ❑ 428 Carlos Lee 8.00 3.60
- ❑ 429 Rod Barajas 2.50 1.10
- ❑ 430 Pablo Ozuna 10.00 4.50
- ❑ 431 Todd Belitz 2.00 .90
- ❑ 432 Sidney Ponson .40 .18
- ❑ 433 Steve Carver .40 .18
- ❑ 434 Esteban Yan 4.00 1.80
- ❑ 435 Cedrick Bowers 2.50 1.10
- ❑ 436 Marlon Anderson .40 .18
- ❑ 437 Carl Pavano .40 .18
- ❑ 438 Jae Weong Seo 4.00 1.80
- ❑ 439 Jose Taveras 4.00 1.80
- ❑ 440 Matt Anderson 5.00 2.20
- ❑ 441 Darron Ingram 4.00 1.80

1998 Bowman Chrome Golden Anniversary

	MINT	NRMT
COMMON CARD (1-441)	20.00	9.00

*STARS: 25X TO 50X BASIC CARDS
*YOUNG STARS: 20X TO 40X BASIC CARDS
*PROSPECTS:12.5X TO 25X BASIC CARDS
*ROOKIES: 4X TO 8X BASIC CARDS

1998 Bowman Chrome International

	MINT	NRMT
COMPLETE SET (441)	1000.00	450.00
COMPLETE SERIES 1 (221)	600.00	275.00
COMPLETE SERIES 2 (220)	400.00	180.00
COMMON CARD (1-441)	1.00	.45

*STARS: 1X TO 2.5X BASIC CARDS
*YOUNG STARS: 1X TO 2.5X BASIC CARDS
*RC'S/PROSPECTS: .5X TO 1.2X BASIC CARDS

1998 Bowman Chrome International Refractors

	MINT	NRMT
COMPLETE SET (441)	5000.00	2200.00

COMPLETE SERIES 1 (221)	3000.00	1350.00
COMPLETE SERIES 2 (220)	2000.00	900.00
COMMON CARD (1-441)	6.00	2.70

*STARS: 6X TO 15X BASIC CARDS
*YOUNG STARS: 5X TO 12X BASIC CARDS
*PROSPECTS: 4X TO 10X BASIC CARDS
*ROOKIES: 2.5X TO 6X BASIC CARDS

1998 Bowman Chrome Refractors

	MINT	NRMT
COMPLETE SET (441)	3200.00	1450.00
COMPLETE SERIES 1 (221)	2000.00	900.00
COMPLETE SERIES 2 (220)	1200.00	550.00
COMMON CARD (1-441)	3.00	1.35

*STARS: 3X TO 8X BASIC CARDS
*YOUNG STARS: 2.5X TO 6X BASIC CARDS
*PROSPECTS: 2.5X TO 6X BASIC CARDS
*ROOKIES: 1.5X TO 4X BASIC CARDS

1998 Bowman Chrome Reprints

	MINT	NRMT
COMPLETE SET (50)	160.00	70.00
COMPLETE SERIES 1 (25)	80.00	36.00
COMPLETE SERIES 2 (25)	80.00	36.00
COMMON CARD (1-50)	1.50	.70

- ❑ 1 Yogi Berra 8.00 3.60
- ❑ 2 Jackie Robinson 12.00 5.50

		MINT	NRMT
❑ 3	Don Newcombe	1.50	.70
❑ 4	Satchell Paige	8.00	3.60
❑ 5	Willie Mays	12.00	5.50
❑ 6	Gil McDougald	1.50	.70
❑ 7	Don Larsen	1.50	.70
❑ 8	Elston Howard	1.50	.70
❑ 9	Robin Ventura	1.50	.70
❑ 10	Brady Anderson	1.50	.70
❑ 11	Gary Sheffield	2.00	.90
❑ 12	Tino Martinez	3.00	1.35
❑ 13	Ken Griffey Jr.	15.00	6.75
❑ 14	John Smoltz	1.50	.70
❑ 15	Sandy Alomar Jr.	1.50	.70
❑ 16	Larry Walker	3.00	1.35
❑ 17	Todd Hundley	1.50	.70
❑ 18	Mo Vaughn	4.00	1.80
❑ 19	Sammy Sosa	8.00	3.60
❑ 20	Frank Thomas	10.00	4.50
❑ 21	Chuck Knoblauch	3.00	1.35
❑ 22	Bernie Williams	3.00	1.35
❑ 23	Juan Gonzalez	8.00	3.60
❑ 24	Mike Mussina	3.00	1.35
❑ 25	Jeff Bagwell	5.00	2.20
❑ 26	Tim Salmon	3.00	1.35
❑ 27	Ivan Rodriguez	4.00	1.80
❑ 28	Kenny Lofton	3.00	1.35
❑ 29	Chipper Jones	8.00	3.60
❑ 30	Javy Lopez	1.50	.70
❑ 31	Ryan Klesko	1.50	.70
❑ 32	Raul Mondesi	2.00	.90
❑ 33	Jim Thome	3.00	1.35
❑ 34	Carlos Delgado	1.50	.70
❑ 35	Mike Piazza	10.00	4.50
❑ 36	Manny Ramirez	3.00	1.35
❑ 37	Andy Pettitte	2.00	.90
❑ 38	Derek Jeter	8.00	3.60
❑ 39	Brad Fullmer	1.50	.70
❑ 40	Richard Hidalgo	1.50	.70
❑ 41	Tony Clark	2.00	.90
❑ 42	Andruw Jones	4.00	1.80
❑ 43	Vladimir Guerrero	5.00	2.20
❑ 44	Nomar Garciaparra	10.00	4.50
❑ 45	Paul Konerko	3.00	1.35
❑ 46	Ben Grieve	6.00	2.70
❑ 47	Hideo Nomo	4.00	1.80
❑ 48	Scott Rolen	8.00	3.60
❑ 49	Jose Guillen	1.50	.70
❑ 50	Livan Hernandez	1.50	.70

1994 Bowman's Best

		MINT	NRMT
COMPLETE SET (200)		80.00	36.00
COMMON CARD (B1-X110)		.30	.14
❑ B1	Chipper Jones	4.00	1.80
❑ B2	Derek Jeter	5.00	2.20
❑ B3	Bill Pulsipher	.60	.25
❑ B4	James Baldwin	.60	.25
❑ B5	Brooks Kieschnick	.60	.25
❑ B6	Justin Thompson	.75	.35
❑ B7	Midre Cummings	.30	.14
❑ B8	Joey Hamilton	1.25	.55
❑ B9	Calvin Reese	.60	.25
❑ B10	Brian Barber	.30	.14
❑ B11	John Burke	.30	.14
❑ B12	DeShawn Warren	.60	.25
❑ B13	Edgardo Alfonzo	3.00	1.35
❑ B14	Eddie Pearson	.60	.25
❑ B15	Jimmy Haynes	.60	.25
❑ B16	Danny Bautista	.30	.14
❑ B17	Roger Cedeno	.60	.25
❑ B18	Jon Lieber	.30	.14
❑ B19	Billy Wagner	3.00	1.35
❑ B20	Tate Seefried	.30	.14
❑ B21	Chad Mottola	.30	.14
❑ B22	Jose Malave	.30	.14
❑ B23	Terrell Wade	.30	.14
❑ B24	Shane Andrews	.30	.14
❑ B25	Chan Ho Park	8.00	3.60
❑ B26	Kirk Presley	.60	.25
❑ B27	Robbie Beckett	.30	.14
❑ B28	Orlando Miller	.30	.14
❑ B29	Jorge Posada	6.00	2.70
❑ B30	Frankie Rodriguez	.30	.14
❑ B31	Brian L.Hunter	.60	.25
❑ B32	Billy Ashley	.30	.14
❑ B33	Rondell White	.60	.25
❑ B34	John Roper	.30	.14
❑ B35	Marc Valdes	.30	.14
❑ B36	Scott Ruffcorn	.30	.14
❑ B37	Rod Henderson	.30	.14
❑ B38	Curtis Goodwin	.60	.25
❑ B39	Russ Davis	.60	.25
❑ B40	Rick Gorecki	.30	.14
❑ B41	Johnny Damon	.60	.25
❑ B42	Roberto Petagine	.30	.14
❑ B43	Chris Snopek	.30	.14
❑ B44	Mark Acre	.30	.14
❑ B45	Todd Hollandsworth	.30	.14
❑ B46	Shawn Green	.60	.25
❑ B47	John Carter	.30	.14
❑ B48	Jim Pittsley	1.00	.45
❑ B49	John Wasdin	.60	.25
❑ B50	D.J.Boston	.30	.14
❑ B51	Tim Clark	.30	.14
❑ B52	Alex Ochoa	.30	.14
❑ B53	Chad Roper	.30	.14
❑ B54	Mike Kelly	.30	.14
❑ B55	Brad Fullmer	8.00	3.60
❑ B56	Carl Everett	.30	.14
❑ B57	Tim Belk	.30	.14
❑ B58	Jimmy Hurst	.60	.25
❑ B59	Mac Suzuki	.60	.25
❑ B60	Michael Moore	.30	.14
❑ B61	Alan Benes	3.00	1.35
❑ B62	Tony Clark	12.00	5.50
❑ B63	Edgar Renteria	4.00	1.80
❑ B64	Trey Beamon	.30	.14
❑ B65	LaTroy Hawkins	.60	.25
❑ B66	Wayne Gomes	.30	.14
❑ B67	Ray McDavid	.30	.14
❑ B68	John Dettmer	.30	.14
❑ B69	Willie Greene	.60	.25
❑ B70	Dave Stevens	.30	.14
❑ B71	Kevin Orie	2.00	.90
❑ B72	Chad Ogea	.60	.25
❑ B73	Ben Van Ryn	.30	.14
❑ B74	Kym Ashworth	.60	.25
❑ B75	Dmitri Young	.60	.25
❑ B76	Herbert Perry	.30	.14
❑ B77	Joey Eischen	.30	.14
❑ B78	Arquimedez Pozo	.60	.25
❑ B79	Ugueth Urbina	.60	.25
❑ B80	Keith Williams	.60	.25
❑ B81	John Frascatore	.30	.14
❑ B82	Garey Ingram	.30	.14
❑ B83	Aaron Small	.30	.14
❑ B84	Olmedo Saenz	.30	.14
❑ B85	Jesus Tavarez	.30	.14
❑ B86	Jose Silva	.60	.25
❑ B87	Jay Witasick	.60	.25
❑ B88	Jay Maldonado	.30	.14
❑ B89	Keith Heberling	.30	.14
❑ B90	Rusty Greer	8.00	3.60
❑ R1	Paul Molitor	1.25	.55
❑ R2	Eddie Murray	1.25	.55
❑ R3	Ozzie Smith	1.50	.70
❑ R4	Rickey Henderson	1.25	.55
❑ R5	Lee Smith	.60	.25
❑ R6	Dave Winfield	1.25	.55
❑ R7	Roberto Alomar	1.25	.55
❑ R8	Matt Williams	.75	.35
❑ R9	Mark Grace	.75	.35
❑ R10	Lance Johnson	.30	.14
❑ R11	Darren Daulton	.60	.25
❑ R12	Tom Glavine	1.25	.55
❑ R13	Gary Sheffield	1.25	.55
❑ R14	Rod Beck	.30	.14
❑ R15	Fred McGriff	.75	.35
❑ R16	Joe Carter	.60	.25
❑ R17	Dante Bichette	.60	.25
❑ R18	Danny Tartabull	.30	.14
❑ R19	Juan Gonzalez	3.00	1.35
❑ R20	Steve Avery	.30	.14
❑ R21	John Wetteland	.60	.25
❑ R22	Ben McDonald	.30	.14
❑ R23	Jack McDowell	.30	.14
❑ R24	Jose Canseco	1.25	.55
❑ R25	Tim Salmon	1.25	.55
❑ R26	Wilson Alvarez	.60	.25
❑ R27	Gregg Jefferies	.30	.14
❑ R28	John Burkett	.30	.14
❑ R29	Greg Vaughn	.60	.25
❑ R30	Robin Ventura	.60	.25
❑ R31	Paul O'Neill	.60	.25
❑ R32	Cecil Fielder	.60	.25
❑ R33	Kevin Mitchell	.30	.14
❑ R34	Jeff Conine	.60	.25
❑ R35	Carlos Baerga	.60	.25
❑ R36	Greg Maddux	4.00	1.80
❑ R37	Roger Clemens	2.50	1.10
❑ R38	Deion Sanders	.60	.25
❑ R39	Delino DeShields	.30	.14
❑ R40	Ken Griffey Jr.	6.00	2.70
❑ R41	Albert Belle	1.50	.70
❑ R42	Wade Boggs	1.25	.55
❑ R43	Andres Galarraga	1.25	.55
❑ R44	Aaron Sele	.60	.25
❑ R45	Don Mattingly	2.00	.90
❑ R46	David Cone	.75	.35
❑ R47	Len Dykstra	.60	.25
❑ R48	Brett Butler	.60	.25
❑ R49	Bill Swift	.30	.14
❑ R50	Bobby Bonilla	.60	.25
❑ R51	Rafael Palmeiro	.75	.35
❑ R52	Moises Alou	.75	.35
❑ R53	Jeff Bagwell	2.00	.90
❑ R54	Mike Mussina	1.25	.55
❑ R55	Frank Thomas	4.00	1.80
❑ R56	Jose Rijo	.30	.14
❑ R57	Ruben Sierra	.30	.14
❑ R58	Randy Myers	.30	.14
❑ R59	Barry Bonds	1.50	.70
❑ R60	Jimmy Key	.60	.25
❑ R61	Travis Fryman	.60	.25
❑ R62	John Olerud	.60	.25
❑ R63	David Justice	1.25	.55
❑ R64	Ray Lankford	.60	.25
❑ R65	Bob Tewksbury	.30	.14
❑ R66	Chuck Carr	.30	.14
❑ R67	Jay Buhner	.60	.25
❑ R68	Kenny Lofton	1.25	.55
❑ R69	Marquis Grissom	.60	.25
❑ R70	Sammy Sosa	3.00	1.35
❑ R71	Cal Ripken	5.00	2.20
❑ R72	Ellis Burks	.60	.25
❑ R73	Jeff Montgomery	.30	.14
❑ R74	Julio Franco	.30	.14
❑ R75	Kirby Puckett	2.00	.90
❑ R76	Larry Walker	1.25	.55
❑ R77	Andy Van Slyke	.60	.25
❑ R78	Tony Gwynn	3.00	1.35
❑ R79	Will Clark	1.25	.55
❑ R80	Mo Vaughn	1.50	.70
❑ R81	Mike Piazza	4.00	1.80
❑ R82	James Mouton	.30	.14
❑ R83	Carlos Delgado	.75	.35
❑ R84	Ryan Klesko	.60	.25
❑ R85	Javier Lopez	.75	.35
❑ R86	Raul Mondesi	1.25	.55
❑ R87	Cliff Floyd	.60	.25
❑ R88	Manny Ramirez	1.50	.70
❑ R89	Hector Carrasco	.30	.14
❑ R90	Jeff Granger	.30	.14
❑ X91	Frank Thomas Dmitri Young	2.00	.90
❑ X92	Fred McGriff Brooks Kieschnick	1.25	.55

Card	Player	Mint	NrMt
❑ X93	Matt Williams Shane Andrews	.30	.14
❑ X94	Cal Ripken Kevin Orie	2.50	1.10
❑ X95	Barry Larkin Derek Jeter	2.50	1.10
❑ X96	Ken Griffey Jr. Johnny Damon	3.00	1.35
❑ X97	Barry Bonds Rondell White	1.25	.55
❑ X98	Albert Belle Jimmy Hurst	1.25	.55
❑ X99	Raul Mondesi Ruben Rivera	4.00	1.80
❑ X100	Roger Clemens Scott Ruffcorn	.75	.35
❑ X101	Greg Maddux John Wasdin	2.00	.90
❑ X102	Tim Salmon Chad Mottola	.75	.35
❑ X103	Carlos Baerga Arquimedez Pozo	.60	.25
❑ X104	Mike Piazza Bobby Hughes	2.00	.90
❑ X105	Carlos Delgado Melvin Nieves	1.25	.55
❑ X106	Javier Lopez Jorge Posada	1.00	.45
❑ X107	Manny Ramirez Jose Malave	1.25	.55
❑ X108	Travis Fryman Chipper Jones	2.00	.90
❑ X109	Steve Avery Bill Pulsipher	.30	.14
❑ X110	John Olerud Shawn Green	.60	.25

1994 Bowman's Best Refractors

	MINT	NRMT
COMPLETE SET (200)	1200.00	550.00
COMMON CARD	3.00	1.35

*RED STARS: 4X TO 10X BASIC CARDS
*BLUE STARS: 5X TO 12X BASIC CARDS
*BLUE ROOKIES: 2.5X TO 5X BASIC CARDS
*MIRROR IMAGE STARS: 3X TO 6X BASIC CARDS

1995 Bowman's Best

	MINT	NRMT
COMPLETE SET (195)	250.00	110.00
COMMON CARD (B1-R90)	.40	.18
COMMON CARD (X1-X15)	.50	.23

Card	Player	Mint	NrMt
❑ B1	Derek Jeter	5.00	2.20
❑ B2	Vladimir Guerrero	65.00	29.00
❑ B3	Bob Abreu	6.00	2.70
❑ B4	Chan Ho Park	2.00	.90
❑ B5	Paul Wilson	.40	.18
❑ B6	Chad Ogea	.40	.18
❑ B7	Andruw Jones	45.00	20.00
❑ B8	Brian Barber	.40	.18
❑ B9	Andy Larkin	.40	.18
❑ B10	Richie Sexson	20.00	9.00
❑ B11	Everett Stull	.40	.18
❑ B12	Brooks Kieschnick	.40	.18
❑ B13	Matt Murray	.40	.18
❑ B14	John Wasdin	.40	.18
❑ B15	Shannon Stewart	.75	.35
❑ B16	Luis Ortiz	.40	.18
❑ B17	Marc Kroon	.40	.18
❑ B18	Todd Greene	3.00	1.35
❑ B19	Juan Acevedo	.40	.18
❑ B20	Tony Clark	2.00	.90
❑ B21	Jermaine Dye	.75	.35
❑ B22	Derrek Lee	2.00	.90
❑ B23	Pat Watkins	.75	.35
❑ B24	Calvin Reese	.40	.18
❑ B25	Ben Grieve	30.00	13.50
❑ B26	Julio Santana	.40	.18
❑ B27	Felix Rodriguez	.40	.18
❑ B28	Paul Konerko	12.00	5.50
❑ B29	Nomar Garciaparra	30.00	13.50
❑ B30	Pat Ahearne	.40	.18
❑ B31	Jason Schmidt	.75	.35
❑ B32	Billy Wagner	.75	.35
❑ B33	Rey Ordonez	3.00	1.35
❑ B34	Curtis Goodwin	.40	.18
❑ B35	Sergio Nunez	1.00	.45
❑ B36	Tim Belk	.40	.18
❑ B37	Scott Elarton	4.00	1.80
❑ B38	Jason Isringhausen	.75	.35
❑ B39	Trot Nixon	.75	.35
❑ B40	Sid Roberson	.40	.18
❑ B41	Ron Villone	.40	.18
❑ B42	Ruben Rivera	.75	.35
❑ B43	Rick Huisman	.40	.18
❑ B44	Todd Hollandsworth	.40	.18
❑ B45	Johnny Damon	.75	.35
❑ B46	Garret Anderson	.75	.35
❑ B47	Jeff D'Amico	.75	.35
❑ B48	Dustin Hermanson	.75	.35
❑ B49	Juan Encarnacion	25.00	11.00
❑ B50	Andy Pettitte	1.50	.70
❑ B51	Chris Stynes	1.50	.70
❑ B52	Troy Percival	.75	.35
❑ B53	LaTroy Hawkins	.40	.18
❑ B54	Roger Cedeno	.40	.18
❑ B55	Alan Benes	.75	.35
❑ B56	Karim Garcia	5.00	2.20
❑ B57	Andrew Lorraine	.40	.18
❑ B58	Gary Rath	.40	.18
❑ B59	Bret Wagner	.40	.18
❑ B60	Jeff Suppan	.75	.35
❑ B61	Bill Pulsipher	.40	.18
❑ B62	Jay Payton	.75	.35
❑ B63	Alex Ochoa	.40	.18
❑ B64	Ugueth Urbina	.40	.18
❑ B65	Armando Benitez	.40	.18
❑ B66	George Arias	.75	.35
❑ B67	Raul Casanova	1.00	.45
❑ B68	Matt Drews	.40	.18
❑ B69	Jimmy Haynes	.40	.18
❑ B70	Jimmy Hurst	.40	.18
❑ B71	C.J. Nitkowski	.40	.18
❑ B72	Tommy Davis	.75	.35
❑ B73	Bartolo Colon	12.00	5.50
❑ B74	Chris Carpenter	3.00	1.35
❑ B75	Trey Beamon	.40	.18
❑ B76	Bryan Rekar	.40	.18
❑ B77	James Baldwin	.75	.35
❑ B78	Marc Valdes	.40	.18
❑ B79	Tom Fordham	.75	.35
❑ B80	Marc Newfield	.40	.18
❑ B81	Angel Martinez	.40	.18
❑ B82	Brian L. Hunter	.75	.35
❑ B83	Jose Herrera	.40	.18
❑ B84	Glenn Dishman	.75	.35
❑ B85	Jacob Cruz	4.00	1.80
❑ B86	Paul Shuey	.40	.18
❑ B87	Scott Rolen	45.00	20.00
❑ B88	Doug Million	.40	.18
❑ B89	Desi Relaford	.75	.35
❑ B90	Michael Tucker	.75	.35
❑ R1	Randy Johnson	1.50	.70
❑ R2	Joe Carter	.75	.35
❑ R3	Chili Davis	.75	.35
❑ R4	Moises Alou	1.00	.45
❑ R5	Gary Sheffield	1.00	.45
❑ R6	Kevin Appier	.75	.35
❑ R7	Denny Neagle	.75	.35
❑ R8	Ruben Sierra	.40	.18
❑ R9	Darren Daulton	.75	.35
❑ R10	Cal Ripken	6.00	2.70
❑ R11	Bobby Bonilla	.75	.35
❑ R12	Manny Ramirez	1.50	.70
❑ R13	Barry Bonds	2.00	.90
❑ R14	Eric Karros	.75	.35
❑ R15	Greg Maddux	5.00	2.20
❑ R16	Jeff Bagwell	2.50	1.10
❑ R17	Paul Molitor	1.50	.70
❑ R18	Ray Lankford	.75	.35
❑ R19	Mark Grace	1.00	.45
❑ R20	Kenny Lofton	1.50	.70
❑ R21	Tony Gwynn	4.00	1.80
❑ R22	Will Clark	1.50	.70
❑ R23	Roger Clemens	3.00	1.35
❑ R24	Dante Bichette	.75	.35
❑ R25	Barry Larkin	1.00	.45
❑ R26	Wade Boggs	1.50	.70
❑ R27	Kirby Puckett	2.50	1.10
❑ R28	Cecil Fielder	.75	.35
❑ R29	Jose Canseco	1.50	.70
❑ R30	Juan Gonzalez	4.00	1.80
❑ R31	David Cone	1.00	.45
❑ R32	Craig Biggio	1.50	.70
❑ R33	Tim Salmon	1.50	.70
❑ R34	David Justice	1.50	.70
❑ R35	Sammy Sosa	4.00	1.80
❑ R36	Mike Piazza	5.00	2.20
❑ R37	Carlos Baerga	.75	.35
❑ R38	Jeff Conine	.75	.35
❑ R39	Rafael Palmeiro	1.00	.45
❑ R40	Bret Saberhagen	.75	.35
❑ R41	Len Dykstra	.75	.35
❑ R42	Mo Vaughn	2.00	.90
❑ R43	Wally Joyner	.75	.35
❑ R44	Chuck Knoblauch	1.50	.70
❑ R45	Robin Ventura	.75	.35
❑ R46	Don Mattingly	2.50	1.10
❑ R47	Dave Hollins	.40	.18
❑ R48	Andy Benes	.75	.35
❑ R49	Ken Griffey Jr.	8.00	3.60
❑ R50	Albert Belle	2.00	.90
❑ R51	Matt Williams	.75	.35
❑ R52	Rondell White	.75	.35
❑ R53	Raul Mondesi	1.00	.45
❑ R54	Brian Jordan	.75	.35
❑ R55	Greg Vaughn	.75	.35
❑ R56	Fred McGriff	1.00	.45
❑ R57	Roberto Alomar	1.50	.70
❑ R58	Dennis Eckersley	.75	.35
❑ R59	Lee Smith	.75	.35
❑ R60	Eddie Murray	1.50	.70
❑ R61	Kenny Rogers	.40	.18
❑ R62	Ron Gant	.40	.18
❑ R63	Larry Walker	1.50	.70
❑ R64	Chad Curtis	.40	.18
❑ R65	Frank Thomas	5.00	2.20
❑ R66	Paul O'Neill	.75	.35
❑ R67	Kevin Seitzer	.40	.18
❑ R68	Marquis Grissom	.75	.35
❑ R69	Mark McGwire	8.00	3.60
❑ R70	Travis Fryman	.75	.35
❑ R71	Andres Galarraga	1.50	.70
❑ R72	Carlos Perez	2.50	1.10
❑ R73	Tyler Green	.40	.18
❑ R74	Marty Cordova	.40	.18
❑ R75	Shawn Green	.75	.35
❑ R76	Vaughn Eshelman	.40	.18
❑ R77	John Mabry	.40	.18
❑ R78	Jason Bates	.40	.18
❑ R79	Jon Nunnally	.40	.18
❑ R80	Ray Durham	.75	.35
❑ R81	Edgardo Alfonzo	.75	.35
❑ R82	Esteban Loaiza	.40	.18
❑ R83	Hideo Nomo	12.00	5.50
❑ R84	Orlando Miller	.40	.18
❑ R85	Alex Gonzalez	.40	.18
❑ R86	Mark Grudzielanek	2.50	1.10
❑ R87	Julian Tavarez	.40	.18
❑ R88	Benji Gil	.40	.18
❑ R89	Quilvio Veras	.40	.18
❑ R90	Ricky Bottalico	.75	.35
❑ X1	Ben Davis Ivan Rodriguez	6.00	2.70

Card		MINT	NRMT
❑ X2	Mark Redman / Manny Ramirez	1.00	.45
❑ X3	Reggie Taylor / Deion Sanders	2.00	.90
❑ X4	Ryan Jaroncyk / Shawn Green	1.25	.55
❑ X5	Juan LeBron / Juan Gonzalez	2.00	.90
❑ X6	Toby McKnight / Craig Biggio	1.25	.55
❑ X7	Michael Barrett / Travis Fryman	10.00	4.50
❑ X8	Corey Jenkins / Mo Vaughn	2.50	1.10
❑ X9	Ruben Rivera / Frank Thomas	2.50	1.10
❑ X10	Curtis Goodwin / Kenny Lofton	.50	.23
❑ X11	Brian L. Hunter / Tony Gwynn	2.00	.90
❑ X12	Todd Greene / Ken Griffey Jr.	4.00	1.80
❑ X13	Karim Garcia / Matt Williams	2.00	.90
❑ X14	Billy Wagner / Randy Johnson	.50	.23
❑ X15	Pat Watkins / Jeff Bagwell	1.50	.70

1995 Bowman's Best Refractors

	MINT	NRMT
COMPLETE SET (195)	2000.00	900.00
COMMON BLUE (B1-B90)	4.00	1.80
COMMON RED (R1-R90)	3.00	1.35
COMMON MIR.IMAGE (X1-X15)	4.00	1.80

*STARS: 3X TO 8X BASIC CARDS
*YOUNG STARS: 6X TO 12X BASIC CARDS
*RCs: 1.5X TO 3X BASIC CARDS
*MIRROR IMAGE: 2X TO 4X BASIC CARDS

1996 Bowman's Best Previews

	MINT	NRMT
COMPLETE SET (30)	120.00	55.00
COMMON CARD (BBP1-BBP30)	.75	.35

*REFRACTORS: .6X TO 1.5X BASIC PREVIEWS
REFRACTOR STATED ODDS 1:24
*ATOMIC STARS: 1.25X TO 3X BASIC PREVIEWS
ATOMIC STATED ODDS 1:48

Card		MINT	NRMT
❑ BBP1	Chipper Jones	8.00	3.60
❑ BBP2	Alan Benes	1.50	.70
❑ BBP3	Brooks Kieschnick	.75	.35
❑ BBP4	Barry Bonds	4.00	1.80
❑ BBP5	Rey Ordonez	1.50	.70
❑ BBP6	Tim Salmon	3.00	1.35
❑ BBP7	Mike Piazza	10.00	4.50
❑ BBP8	Billy Wagner	1.50	.70
❑ BBP9	Andruw Jones	6.00	2.70
❑ BBP10	Tony Gwynn	8.00	3.60
❑ BBP11	Paul Wilson	.75	.35
❑ BBP12	Calvin Reese	.75	.35
❑ BBP13	Frank Thomas	10.00	4.50
❑ BBP14	Greg Maddux	10.00	4.50
❑ BBP15	Derek Jeter	8.00	3.60
❑ BBP16	Jeff Bagwell	5.00	2.20
❑ BBP17	Barry Larkin	2.00	.90
❑ BBP18	Todd Greene	1.50	.70
❑ BBP19	Ruben Rivera	1.50	.70
❑ BBP20	Richard Hidalgo	1.50	.70
❑ BBP21	Larry Walker	3.00	1.35
❑ BBP22	Carlos Baerga	1.50	.70
❑ BBP23	Derrick Gibson	3.00	1.35
❑ BBP24	Richie Sexson	3.00	1.35
❑ BBP25	Mo Vaughn	4.00	1.80
❑ BBP26	Hideo Nomo	5.00	2.20
❑ BBP27	Nomar Garciaparra	10.00	4.50
❑ BBP28	Cal Ripken	12.00	5.50
❑ BBP29	Karim Garcia	1.50	.70
❑ BBP30	Ken Griffey Jr.	15.00	6.75

1996 Bowman's Best

	MINT	NRMT
COMPLETE SET (180)	100.00	45.00
COMMON GOLD (1-90)	.25	.11
COMMON SILVER (91-180)	.25	.11

Card		MINT	NRMT
❑ 1	Hideo Nomo	2.00	.90
❑ 2	Edgar Martinez	.60	.25
❑ 3	Cal Ripken	5.00	2.20
❑ 4	Wade Boggs	1.25	.55
❑ 5	Cecil Fielder	.60	.25
❑ 6	Albert Belle	1.50	.70
❑ 7	Chipper Jones	3.00	1.35
❑ 8	Ryne Sandberg	1.50	.70
❑ 9	Tim Salmon	1.25	.55
❑ 10	Barry Bonds	1.50	.70
❑ 11	Ken Caminiti	.75	.35
❑ 12	Ron Gant	.25	.11
❑ 13	Frank Thomas	4.00	1.80
❑ 14	Dante Bichette	.60	.25
❑ 15	Jason Kendall	1.25	.55
❑ 16	Mo Vaughn	1.50	.70
❑ 17	Rey Ordonez	.60	.25
❑ 18	Henry Rodriguez	.60	.25
❑ 19	Ryan Klesko	.60	.25
❑ 20	Jeff Bagwell	2.00	.90
❑ 21	Randy Johnson	1.25	.55
❑ 22	Jim Edmonds	.75	.35
❑ 23	Kenny Lofton	1.25	.55
❑ 24	Andy Pettitte	.75	.35
❑ 25	Brady Anderson	.60	.25
❑ 26	Mike Piazza	4.00	1.80
❑ 27	Greg Vaughn	.60	.25
❑ 28	Joe Carter	.60	.25
❑ 29	Jason Giambi	.60	.25
❑ 30	Ivan Rodriguez	1.50	.70
❑ 31	Jeff Conine	.60	.25
❑ 32	Rafael Palmeiro	.75	.35
❑ 33	Roger Clemens	2.50	1.10
❑ 34	Chuck Knoblauch	1.25	.55
❑ 35	Reggie Sanders	.60	.25
❑ 36	Andres Galarraga	1.25	.55
❑ 37	Paul O'Neill	.60	.25
❑ 38	Tony Gwynn	3.00	1.35
❑ 39	Paul Wilson	.25	.11
❑ 40	Garret Anderson	.60	.25
❑ 41	David Justice	1.25	.55
❑ 42	Eddie Murray	1.25	.55
❑ 43	Mike Grace	.25	.11
❑ 44	Marty Cordova	.25	.11
❑ 45	Kevin Appier	.60	.25
❑ 46	Raul Mondesi	.75	.35
❑ 47	Jim Thome	1.25	.55
❑ 48	Sammy Sosa	3.00	1.35
❑ 49	Craig Biggio	1.25	.55
❑ 50	Marquis Grissom	.60	.25
❑ 51	Alan Benes	.60	.25
❑ 52	Manny Ramirez	1.25	.55
❑ 53	Gary Sheffield	.75	.35
❑ 54	Mike Mussina	1.25	.55
❑ 55	Robin Ventura	.60	.25
❑ 56	Johnny Damon	.60	.25
❑ 57	Jose Canseco	1.25	.55
❑ 58	Juan Gonzalez	3.00	1.35
❑ 59	Tino Martinez	1.25	.55
❑ 60	Brian Hunter	.60	.25
❑ 61	Fred McGriff	.75	.35
❑ 62	Jay Buhner	.60	.25
❑ 63	Carlos Delgado	.60	.25
❑ 64	Moises Alou	.75	.35
❑ 65	Roberto Alomar	1.25	.55
❑ 66	Barry Larkin	.75	.35
❑ 67	Vinny Castilla	.75	.35
❑ 68	Ray Durham	.60	.25
❑ 69	Travis Fryman	.60	.25
❑ 70	Jason Isringhausen	.25	.11
❑ 71	Ken Griffey Jr.	6.00	2.70
❑ 72	John Smoltz	.60	.25
❑ 73	Matt Williams	.60	.25
❑ 74	Chan Ho Park	1.25	.55
❑ 75	Mark McGwire	6.00	2.70
❑ 76	Jeffrey Hammonds	.60	.25
❑ 77	Will Clark	1.25	.55
❑ 78	Kirby Puckett	2.00	.90
❑ 79	Derek Jeter	4.00	1.80
❑ 80	Derek Bell	.60	.25
❑ 81	Eric Karros	.60	.25
❑ 82	Len Dykstra	.60	.25
❑ 83	Larry Walker	1.25	.55
❑ 84	Mark Grudzielanek	.60	.25
❑ 85	Greg Maddux	4.00	1.80
❑ 86	Carlos Baerga	.60	.25
❑ 87	Paul Molitor	1.25	.55
❑ 88	John Valentin	.60	.25
❑ 89	Mark Grace	.75	.35
❑ 90	Ray Lankford	.60	.25
❑ 91	Andruw Jones	3.00	1.35
❑ 92	Nomar Garciaparra	5.00	2.20
❑ 93	Alex Ochoa	.25	.11
❑ 94	Derrick Gibson	1.25	.55
❑ 95	Jeff D'Amico	.25	.11
❑ 96	Ruben Rivera	.60	.25
❑ 97	Vladimir Guerrero	4.00	1.80
❑ 98	Calvin Reese	.25	.11
❑ 99	Richard Hidalgo	.60	.25
❑ 100	Bartolo Colon	1.50	.70
❑ 101	Karim Garcia	.60	.25
❑ 102	Ben Davis	1.50	.70
❑ 103	Jay Powell	.25	.11
❑ 104	Chris Snopek	.25	.11
❑ 105	Glendon Rusch	1.25	.55
❑ 106	Enrique Wilson	.60	.25
❑ 107	Antonio Alfonseca	.25	.11
❑ 108	Wilton Guerrero	2.00	.90
❑ 109	Jose Guillen	8.00	3.60
❑ 110	Miguel Mejia	.25	.11
❑ 111	Jay Payton	.25	.11
❑ 112	Scott Elarton	.60	.25
❑ 113	Brooks Kieschnick	.25	.11
❑ 114	Dustin Hermanson	.60	.25
❑ 115	Roger Cedeno	.25	.11
❑ 116	Matt Wagner	.25	.11
❑ 117	Lee Daniels	.25	.11
❑ 118	Ben Grieve	5.00	2.20
❑ 119	Ugueth Urbina	.60	.25
❑ 120	Danny Graves	.60	.25
❑ 121	Dan Donato	.25	.11
❑ 122	Matt Ruebel	.25	.11
❑ 123	Mark Sievert	.25	.11
❑ 124	Chris Stynes	.25	.11
❑ 125	Jeff Abbott	.60	.25
❑ 126	Rocky Coppinger	.75	.35
❑ 127	Jermaine Dye	.25	.11

		MINT	NRMT
❑ 128	Todd Greene	.60	.25
❑ 129	Chris Carpenter	.60	.25
❑ 130	Edgar Renteria	.60	.25
❑ 131	Matt Drews	.25	.11
❑ 132	Edgard Velazquez	2.50	1.10
❑ 133	Casey Whitten	.60	.25
❑ 134	Ryan Jones	1.25	.55
❑ 135	Todd Walker	5.00	2.20
❑ 136	Geoff Jenkins	4.00	1.80
❑ 137	Matt Morris	4.00	1.80
❑ 138	Richie Sexson	2.00	.90
❑ 139	Todd Dunwoody	3.00	1.35
❑ 140	Gabe Alvarez	4.00	1.80
❑ 141	J.J. Johnson	.25	.11
❑ 142	Shannon Stewart	.60	.25
❑ 143	Brad Fullmer	1.25	.55
❑ 144	Julio Santana	.25	.11
❑ 145	Scott Rolen	5.00	2.20
❑ 146	Amaury Telemaco	.25	.11
❑ 147	Trey Beamon	.25	.11
❑ 148	Billy Wagner	.60	.25
❑ 149	Todd Hollandsworth	.25	.11
❑ 150	Doug Million	.25	.11
❑ 151	Jose Valentin	2.00	.90
❑ 152	Wes Helms	4.00	1.80
❑ 153	Jeff Suppan	.25	.11
❑ 154	Luis Castillo	1.25	.55
❑ 155	Bob Abreu	.60	.25
❑ 156	Paul Konerko	2.00	.90
❑ 157	Jamey Wright	.25	.11
❑ 158	Eddie Pearson	.25	.11
❑ 159	Jimmy Haynes	.25	.11
❑ 160	Derrek Lee	1.25	.55
❑ 161	Damian Moss	.25	.11
❑ 162	Carlos Guillen	5.00	2.20
❑ 163	Chris Fussell	1.25	.55
❑ 164	Mike Sweeney	1.25	.55
❑ 165	Donnie Sadler	.60	.25
❑ 166	Desi Relaford	.25	.11
❑ 167	Steve Gibralter	.25	.11
❑ 168	Neifi Perez	.25	.11
❑ 169	Antone Williamson	.25	.11
❑ 170	Marty Janzen	.25	.11
❑ 171	Todd Helton	10.00	4.50
❑ 172	Raul Ibanez	1.00	.45
❑ 173	Bill Selby	.25	.11
❑ 174	Shane Monahan	3.00	1.35
❑ 175	Robin Jennings	.25	.11
❑ 176	Bobby Chouinard	.25	.11
❑ 177	Einar Diaz	.25	.11
❑ 178	Jason Thompson	.25	.11
❑ 179	Rafael Medina	2.00	.90
❑ 180	Kevin Orie	.25	.11
❑ NNO	1952 Mantle Chrome	8.00	3.60
❑ NNO	1952 Mantle Refractor	20.00	9.00
❑ NNO	1952 Mantle Atomic Ref.	40.00	18.00

1996 Bowman's Best Atomic Refractors

	MINT	NRMT
COMMON GOLD (1-90)	5.00	2.20
COMMON SILVER (91-180)	8.00	3.60

*STARS: 7.5X TO 15X BASIC CARDS
*GOLD YNG.STARS: 6X TO 12X BASIC CARDS
*SILVER YNG.STARS: 10X TO 20X BASIC CARDS
*PROSPECTS: 4X TO 8X BASIC CARDS
*ROOKIES: 4X TO 8X BASIC CARDS

1996 Bowman's Best Refractors

	MINT	NRMT
COMPLETE SET (180)	1500.00	700.00
COMMON CARD (1-180)	3.00	1.35

*STARS: 4X TO 10X BASIC CARDS
*GOLD YNG.STARS: 3X TO 8X BASIC CARDS
*SILVER YNG.STARS: 5X TO 10X BASIC CARDS
*PROSPECTS: 2X TO 4X BASIC CARDS
*ROOKIES: 2X TO 4X BASIC CARDS

1996 Bowman's Best Cuts

	MINT	NRMT
COMPLETE SET (15)	200.00	90.00
COMMON CARD (1-15)	1.50	.70

*REFRACTORS: .6X TO 1.5X BASIC CUTS
REF.STATED ODDS 1:48 HOB, 1:80 RET
*ATOMIC REF: 1.25X TO 3X BASIC CUTS
ATOMIC STATED ODDS 1:96 HOB, 1:160 RET

		MINT	NRMT
❑ 1	Ken Griffey Jr.	30.00	13.50
❑ 2	Jason Isringhausen	1.50	.70
❑ 3	Derek Jeter	15.00	6.75
❑ 4	Andruw Jones	12.00	5.50
❑ 5	Chipper Jones	15.00	6.75
❑ 6	Ryan Klesko	2.00	.90
❑ 7	Raul Mondesi	3.00	1.35
❑ 8	Hideo Nomo	10.00	4.50
❑ 9	Mike Piazza	20.00	9.00
❑ 10	Manny Ramirez	6.00	2.70
❑ 11	Cal Ripken	25.00	11.00
❑ 12	Ruben Rivera	2.00	.90
❑ 13	Tim Salmon	6.00	2.70
❑ 14	Frank Thomas	20.00	9.00
❑ 15	Jim Thome	6.00	2.70

1996 Bowman's Best Mirror Image

	MINT	NRMT
COMPLETE SET (10)	120.00	55.00
COMMON CARD (1-10)	2.50	1.10

*REFRACTORS: .6X TO 1.5X BASIC CARDS
REF.STATED ODDS 1:96 HOB, 1:160 RET
*ATOMIC REFRACTORS: 1.25X TO 3X BASIC CARDS
ATOMIC STATED ODDS 1:192 HOB, 1:320 RET

		MINT	NRMT
❑ 1	Jeff Bagwell Todd Helton Frank Thomas Richie Sexson	25.00	11.00
❑ 2	Craig Biggio Luis Castillo Roberto Alomar Desi Relaford	2.50	1.10
❑ 3	Chipper Jones Scott Rolen Wade Boggs George Arias	15.00	6.75
❑ 4	Barry Larkin Neifi Perez Cal Ripken Mark Bellhorn	12.00	5.50
❑ 5	Larry Walker Karim Garcia Albert Belle Ruben Rivera	4.00	1.80
❑ 6	Barry Bonds Andruw Jones Kenny Lofton Donnie Sadler	8.00	3.60
❑ 7	Tony Gwynn Vladimir Guerrero Ken Griffey Ben Grieve	30.00	13.50
❑ 8	Mike Piazza Ben Davis Ivan Rodriguez Jose Valentin	12.00	5.50
❑ 9	Greg Maddux Jamey Wright Mike Mussina Bartolo Colon	10.00	4.50
❑ 10	Tom Glavine Billy Wagner Randy Johnson Jarrod Washburn	2.50	1.10

1997 Bowman's Best Previews

	MINT	NRMT
COMPLETE SET (20)	100.00	45.00
COMMON CARD (1-20)	1.50	.70

*REFRACTORS: .75X TO 2X BASIC PREVIEWS
REFRACTOR STATED ODDS 1:48
*ATOMIC REFRACTORS,1.5X TO 4X BASIC PREVIEWS
ATOMIC STATED ODDS 1:96

		MINT	NRMT
❑ 1	Frank Thomas	10.00	4.50
❑ 2	Ken Griffey Jr.	15.00	6.75
❑ 3	Barry Bonds	4.00	1.80
❑ 4	Derek Jeter	8.00	3.60
❑ 5	Chipper Jones	8.00	3.60
❑ 6	Mark McGwire	15.00	6.75
❑ 7	Cal Ripken	12.00	5.50
❑ 8	Kenny Lofton	2.50	1.10
❑ 9	Gary Sheffield	2.00	.90
❑ 10	Jeff Bagwell	5.00	2.20
❑ 11	Wilton Guerrero	1.50	.70
❑ 12	Scott Rolen	6.00	2.70
❑ 13	Todd Walker	2.50	1.10
❑ 14	Ruben Rivera	1.50	.70
❑ 15	Andruw Jones	4.00	1.80
❑ 16	Nomar Garciaparra	10.00	4.50
❑ 17	Vladimir Guerrero	5.00	2.20
❑ 18	Miguel Tejada	5.00	2.20
❑ 19	Bartolo Colon	1.50	.70
❑ 20	Katsuhiro Maeda	1.50	.70

1997 Bowman's Best

	MINT	NRMT
COMPLETE SET (200)	100.00	45.00
COMMON CARD (1-200)	.25	.11

	Player	MINT	NRMT
❑ 1	Ken Griffey Jr.	5.00	2.20
❑ 2	Cecil Fielder	.50	.23
❑ 3	Albert Belle	1.25	.55
❑ 4	Todd Hundley	.50	.23
❑ 5	Mike Piazza	3.00	1.35
❑ 6	Matt Williams	.50	.23
❑ 7	Mo Vaughn	1.25	.55
❑ 8	Ryne Sandberg	1.25	.55
❑ 9	Chipper Jones	2.50	1.10
❑ 10	Edgar Martinez	.50	.23
❑ 11	Kenny Lofton	1.00	.45
❑ 12	Ron Gant	.25	.11
❑ 13	Moises Alou	.75	.35
❑ 14	Pat Hentgen	.50	.23
❑ 15	Steve Finley	.50	.23
❑ 16	Mark Grace	.75	.35
❑ 17	Jay Buhner	.50	.23
❑ 18	Jeff Conine	.50	.23
❑ 19	Jim Edmonds	.75	.35
❑ 20	Todd Hollandsworth	.25	.11
❑ 21	Andy Pettitte	.75	.35
❑ 22	Jim Thome	1.00	.45
❑ 23	Eric Young	.50	.23
❑ 24	Ray Lankford	.50	.23
❑ 25	Marquis Grissom	.50	.23
❑ 26	Tony Clark	.75	.35
❑ 27	Jermaine Allensworth	.25	.11
❑ 28	Ellis Burks	.50	.23
❑ 29	Tony Gwynn	2.50	1.10
❑ 30	Barry Larkin	.75	.35
❑ 31	John Olerud	.50	.23
❑ 32	Mariano Rivera	.50	.23
❑ 33	Paul Molitor	1.00	.45
❑ 34	Ken Caminiti	.75	.35
❑ 35	Gary Sheffield	.75	.35
❑ 36	Al Martin	.25	.11
❑ 37	John Valentin	.50	.23
❑ 38	Frank Thomas	3.00	1.35
❑ 39	John Jaha	.25	.11
❑ 40	Greg Maddux	3.00	1.35
❑ 41	Alex Fernandez	.25	.11
❑ 42	Dean Palmer	.50	.23
❑ 43	Bernie Williams	1.00	.45
❑ 44	Deion Sanders	.50	.23
❑ 45	Mark McGwire	5.00	2.20
❑ 46	Brian Jordan	.50	.23
❑ 47	Bernard Gilkey	.25	.11
❑ 48	Will Clark	1.00	.45
❑ 49	Kevin Appier	.50	.23
❑ 50	Tom Glavine	1.00	.45
❑ 51	Chuck Knoblauch	1.00	.45
❑ 52	Rondell White	.50	.23
❑ 53	Greg Vaughn	.50	.23
❑ 54	Mike Mussina	1.00	.45
❑ 55	Brian McRae	.25	.11
❑ 56	Chili Davis	.50	.23
❑ 57	Wade Boggs	1.00	.45
❑ 58	Jeff Bagwell	1.50	.70
❑ 59	Roberto Alomar	1.00	.45
❑ 60	Dennis Eckersley	.50	.23
❑ 61	Ryan Klesko	.50	.23
❑ 62	Manny Ramirez	1.00	.45
❑ 63	John Wetteland	.50	.23
❑ 64	Cal Ripken	4.00	1.80
❑ 65	Edgar Renteria	.50	.23
❑ 66	Tino Martinez	1.00	.45
❑ 67	Larry Walker	1.00	.45
❑ 68	Gregg Jefferies	.25	.11
❑ 69	Lance Johnson	.25	.11
❑ 70	Carlos Delgado	.50	.23
❑ 71	Craig Biggio	1.00	.45
❑ 72	Jose Canseco	1.00	.45
❑ 73	Barry Bonds	1.25	.55
❑ 74	Juan Gonzalez	2.50	1.10
❑ 75	Eric Karros	.50	.23
❑ 76	Reggie Sanders	.50	.23
❑ 77	Robin Ventura	.50	.23
❑ 78	Hideo Nomo	1.25	.55
❑ 79	David Justice	1.00	.45
❑ 80	Vinny Castilla	.75	.35
❑ 81	Travis Fryman	.50	.23
❑ 82	Derek Jeter	3.00	1.35
❑ 83	Sammy Sosa	2.50	1.10
❑ 84	Ivan Rodriguez	1.25	.55
❑ 85	Rafael Palmeiro	.75	.35
❑ 86	Roger Clemens	2.00	.90
❑ 87	Jason Giambi	.50	.23
❑ 88	Andres Galarraga	1.00	.45
❑ 89	Jermaine Dye	.25	.11
❑ 90	Joe Carter	.50	.23
❑ 91	Brady Anderson	.50	.23
❑ 92	Derek Bell	.50	.23
❑ 93	Randy Johnson	1.00	.45
❑ 94	Fred McGriff	.75	.35
❑ 95	John Smoltz	.50	.23
❑ 96	Harold Baines	.50	.23
❑ 97	Raul Mondesi	.75	.35
❑ 98	Tim Salmon	1.00	.45
❑ 99	Carlos Baerga	.50	.23
❑ 100	Dante Bichette	.50	.23
❑ 101	Vladimir Guerrero	2.00	.90
❑ 102	Richard Hidalgo	.50	.23
❑ 103	Paul Konerko	1.00	.45
❑ 104	Alex Gonzalez	1.50	.70
❑ 105	Jason Dickson	.50	.23
❑ 106	Jose Rosado	.25	.11
❑ 107	Todd Walker	1.00	.45
❑ 108	Seth Greisinger	1.50	.70
❑ 109	Todd Helton	2.00	.90
❑ 110	Ben Davis	1.00	.45
❑ 111	Bartolo Colon	.50	.23
❑ 112	Elieser Marrero	.50	.23
❑ 113	Jeff D'Amico	.25	.11
❑ 114	Miguel Tejada	4.00	1.80
❑ 115	Darin Erstad	1.50	.70
❑ 116	Kris Benson	2.50	1.10
❑ 117	Adrian Beltre	10.00	4.50
❑ 118	Neifi Perez	.25	.11
❑ 119	Calvin Reese	.25	.11
❑ 120	Carl Pavano	1.00	.45
❑ 121	Juan Melo	.50	.23
❑ 122	Kevin McGlinchy	1.00	.45
❑ 123	Pat Cline	.50	.23
❑ 124	Felix Heredia	1.00	.45
❑ 125	Aaron Boone	.25	.11
❑ 126	Glendon Rusch	.25	.11
❑ 127	Mike Cameron	.50	.23
❑ 128	Justin Thompson	.50	.23
❑ 129	Chad Hermansen	5.00	2.20
❑ 130	Sidney Ponson	1.25	.55
❑ 131	Willie Martinez	2.00	.90
❑ 132	Paul Wilder	1.25	.55
❑ 133	Geoff Jenkins	.50	.23
❑ 134	Roy Halladay	5.00	2.20
❑ 135	Carlos Guillen	.50	.23
❑ 136	Tony Batista	.25	.11
❑ 137	Todd Greene	.50	.23
❑ 138	Luis Castillo	.50	.23
❑ 139	Jimmy Anderson	1.00	.45
❑ 140	Edgard Velazquez	.50	.23
❑ 141	Chris Snopek	.25	.11
❑ 142	Ruben Rivera	.50	.23
❑ 143	Javier Valentin	.50	.23
❑ 144	Brian Rose	1.00	.45
❑ 145	Fernando Tatis	3.00	1.35
❑ 146	Dean Crow	.25	.11
❑ 147	Karim Garcia	.50	.23
❑ 148	Dante Powell	.50	.23
❑ 149	Hideki Irabu	5.00	2.20
❑ 150	Matt Morris	.50	.23
❑ 151	Wes Helms	.50	.23
❑ 152	Russ Johnson	.25	.11
❑ 153	Jarrod Washburn	.50	.23
❑ 154	Kerry Wood	25.00	11.00
❑ 155	Joe Fontenot	1.00	.45
❑ 156	Eugene Kingsale	.50	.23
❑ 157	Terrence Long	.50	.23
❑ 158	Calvin Maduro	.25	.11
❑ 159	Jeff Suppan	.25	.11
❑ 160	DaRond Stovall	.25	.11
❑ 161	Mark Redman	.25	.11
❑ 162	Ken Cloude	1.25	.55
❑ 163	Bobby Estalella	.50	.23
❑ 164	Abraham Nunez	1.25	.55
❑ 165	Derrick Gibson	.75	.35
❑ 166	Mike Drumright	1.00	.45
❑ 167	Katsuhiro Maeda	.50	.23
❑ 168	Jeff Liefer	.50	.23
❑ 169	Ben Grieve	2.50	1.10
❑ 170	Bob Abreu	.50	.23
❑ 171	Shannon Stewart	.50	.23
❑ 172	Braden Looper	.75	.35
❑ 173	Brant Brown	.50	.23
❑ 174	Marlon Anderson	.50	.23
❑ 175	Brad Fullmer	.75	.35
❑ 176	Carlos Beltran	1.50	.70
❑ 177	Nomar Garciaparra	3.00	1.35
❑ 178	Derrek Lee	.75	.35
❑ 179	Valerio De Los Santos	1.00	.45
❑ 180	Dmitri Young	.50	.23
❑ 181	Jamey Wright	.25	.11
❑ 182	Hiram Bocachica	1.25	.55
❑ 183	Wilton Guerrero	.25	.11
❑ 184	Chris Carpenter	.50	.23
❑ 185	Scott Spiezio	.25	.11
❑ 186	Andruw Jones	1.50	.70
❑ 187	Travis Lee	15.00	6.75
❑ 188	Jose Cruz Jr.	8.00	3.60
❑ 189	Jose Guillen	1.00	.45
❑ 190	Jeff Abbott	.50	.23
❑ 191	Ricky Ledee	6.00	2.70
❑ 192	Mike Sweeney	.25	.11
❑ 193	Donnie Sadler	.50	.23
❑ 194	Scott Rolen	2.50	1.10
❑ 195	Kevin Orie	.25	.11
❑ 196	Jason Conti	2.00	.90
❑ 197	Mark Kotsay	4.00	1.80
❑ 198	Eric Milton	2.00	.90
❑ 199	Russell Branyan	1.00	.45
❑ 200	Alex Sanchez	1.25	.55

1997 Bowman's Best Atomic Refractors

	MINT	NRMT
COMPLETE SET (200)	3000.00	1350.00
COMMON CARD (1-200)	5.00	2.20

*STARS: 8X TO 20X BASIC CARDS
*YOUNG STARS: 6X TO 15X BASIC CARDS
*ROOKIES: 3X TO 8X BASIC CARDS

1997 Bowman's Best Autographs

	MINT	NRMT
COMPLETE SET (10)	500.00	220.00
COMMON CARD	12.00	5.50

*REF.STARS: 1X TO 2.5X BASIC CARDS
*REF.YOUNG STARS: .75X TO 2X BASIC CARDS
*REF.CRUZ JR: .6X TO 1.5X BASIC AUTO
*ATOMIC STARS: 2.5X TO 5X BASIC CARDS
*ATOMIC YOUNG STARS: 2X TO 4X BASIC CARDS
*ATOMIC CRUZ JR: 1.5X TO 3X BASIC AUTO

	MINT	NRMT
❑ 29 Tony Gwynn	120.00	55.00
❑ 33 Paul Molitor	50.00	22.00
❑ 82 Derek Jeter	100.00	45.00
❑ 91 Brady Anderson	25.00	11.00
❑ 98 Tim Salmon	40.00	18.00
❑ 107 Todd Walker	25.00	11.00
❑ 183 Wilton Guerrero	12.00	5.50
❑ 185 Scott Spiezio	15.00	6.75
❑ 188 Jose Cruz Jr.	60.00	27.00
❑ 194 Scott Rolen	80.00	36.00

1997 Bowman's Best Best Cuts

	MINT	NRMT
COMPLETE SET (20)	200.00	90.00
COMMON CARD (BC1-BC20)	1.50	.70

*REFRACTORS: .6X TO 1.5X BASIC CARDS
REFRACTOR STATED ODDS 1:48
*ATOMIC REFRACTORS: 1.25X TO 3X BASIC CARDS
ATOMIC STATED ODDS 1:96

	MINT	NRMT
❑ BC1 Derek Jeter	12.00	5.50
❑ BC2 Chipper Jones	12.00	5.50
❑ BC3 Frank Thomas	15.00	6.75
❑ BC4 Cal Ripken	20.00	9.00
❑ BC5 Mark McGwire	25.00	11.00
❑ BC6 Ken Griffey Jr.	25.00	11.00
❑ BC7 Jeff Bagwell	8.00	3.60
❑ BC8 Mike Piazza	15.00	6.75
❑ BC9 Ken Caminiti	3.00	1.35
❑ BC10 Albert Belle	6.00	2.70
❑ BC11 Jose Cruz Jr.	10.00	4.50
❑ BC12 Wilton Guerrero	1.50	.70
❑ BC13 Darin Erstad	8.00	3.60
❑ BC14 Andruw Jones	8.00	3.60
❑ BC15 Scott Rolen	12.00	5.50
❑ BC16 Jose Guillen	5.00	2.20
❑ BC17 Bob Abreu	2.00	.90
❑ BC18 Vladimir Guerrero	10.00	4.50
❑ BC19 Todd Walker	5.00	2.20
❑ BC20 Nomar Garciaparra	15.00	6.75

1997 Bowman's Best Mirror Image

	MINT	NRMT
COMPLETE SET (10)	120.00	55.00
COMMON CARD (MI1-MI10)	5.00	2.20

*REFRACTORS: .6X TO 1.5X BASIC CARDS
REFRACTOR STATED ODDS 1:96
*ATOMIC REFRACTORS: 1.25X TO 3X BASIC CARDS
ATOMIC STATED ODDS 1:192

*INVERTED: 2X VALUE OF NON-INVERTED
INVERTED: RANDOM INSERTS IN PACKS
INVERTED HAVE LARGER ROOKIE PHOTOS

	MINT	NRMT
❑ MI1 Nomar Garciaparra Derek Jeter Hiram Bocachica Barry Larkin	15.00	6.75
❑ MI2 Travis Lee Frank Thomas Derrick Lee Jeff Bagwell	25.00	11.00
❑ MI3 Kerry Wood Greg Maddux Kris Benson John Smoltz	30.00	13.50
❑ MI4 Kevin Brown Ivan Rodriguez Eli Marrero Mike Piazza	12.00	5.50
❑ MI5 Jose Cruz Jr. Ken Griffey Jr. Andruw Jones Barry Bonds	25.00	11.00
❑ MI6 Jose Guillen Juan Gonzalez Richard Hidalgo Gary Sheffield	10.00	4.50
❑ MI7 Paul Konerko Mark McGwire Todd Helton Rafael Palmeiro	25.00	11.00
❑ MI8 Wilton Guerrero Craig Biggio Donnie Sadler Chuck Knoblauch	5.00	2.20
❑ MI9 Russell Branyan Matt Williams Adrian Beltre Chipper Jones	15.00	6.75
❑ MI10 Bob Abreu Kenny Lofton Vladimir Guerrero Albert Belle	8.00	3.60

1998 Bowman's Best

	MINT	NRMT
COMPLETE SET (200)	100.00	45.00
COMMON CARD (1-200)	.25	.11

	MINT	NRMT
❑ 1 Mark McGwire	6.00	2.70
❑ 2 Jeromy Burnitz	.40	.18
❑ 3 Barry Bonds	1.25	.55
❑ 4 Dante Bichette	.40	.18
❑ 5 Chipper Jones	2.50	1.10
❑ 6 Frank Thomas	3.00	1.35
❑ 7 Kevin Brown	.60	.25
❑ 8 Juan Gonzalez	2.50	1.10
❑ 9 Jay Buhner	.40	.18
❑ 10 Chuck Knoblauch	1.00	.45
❑ 11 Cal Ripken	4.00	1.80
❑ 12 Matt Williams	.40	.18
❑ 13 Jim Edmonds	.60	.25
❑ 14 Manny Ramirez	1.00	.45
❑ 15 Tony Clark	.60	.25
❑ 16 Mo Vaughn	1.25	.55
❑ 17 Bernie Williams	1.00	.45
❑ 18 Scott Rolen	2.50	1.10
❑ 19 Gary Sheffield	.60	.25
❑ 20 Albert Belle	1.00	.45
❑ 21 Mike Piazza	3.00	1.35
❑ 22 John Olerud	.40	.18
❑ 23 Tony Gwynn	2.50	1.10
❑ 24 Jay Bell	.40	.18
❑ 25 Jose Cruz Jr.	1.25	.55
❑ 26 Justin Thompson	.40	.18
❑ 27 Ken Griffey Jr.	5.00	2.20
❑ 28 Sandy Alomar	.40	.18
❑ 29 Mark Grudzielanek	.40	.18
❑ 30 Mark Grace	.60	.25
❑ 31 Ron Gant	.25	.11
❑ 32 Javy Lopez	.40	.18
❑ 33 Jeff Bagwell	1.50	.70
❑ 34 Fred McGriff	.60	.25
❑ 35 Rafael Palmeiro	.60	.25
❑ 36 Vinny Castilla	.60	.25
❑ 37 Andy Benes	.40	.18
❑ 38 Pedro Martinez	1.00	.45
❑ 39 Andy Pettitte	.60	.25
❑ 40 Marty Cordova	.25	.11
❑ 41 Rusty Greer	.40	.18
❑ 42 Kevin Orie	.25	.11
❑ 43 Chan Ho Park	1.00	.45
❑ 44 Ryan Klesko	.40	.18
❑ 45 Alex Rodriguez	3.00	1.35
❑ 46 Travis Fryman	.40	.18
❑ 47 Jeff King	.40	.18
❑ 48 Roger Clemens	2.00	.90
❑ 49 Darin Erstad	1.25	.55
❑ 50 Brady Anderson	.40	.18
❑ 51 Jason Kendall	.40	.18
❑ 52 John Valentin	.40	.18
❑ 53 Ellis Burks	.40	.18
❑ 54 Brian Hunter	.40	.18
❑ 55 Paul O'Neill	.40	.18
❑ 56 Ken Caminiti	.60	.25
❑ 57 David Justice	1.00	.45
❑ 58 Eric Karros	.40	.18
❑ 59 Pat Hentgen	.40	.18
❑ 60 Greg Maddux	3.00	1.35
❑ 61 Craig Biggio	1.00	.45
❑ 62 Edgar Martinez	.40	.18
❑ 63 Mike Mussina	1.00	.45
❑ 64 Larry Walker	1.00	.45
❑ 65 Tino Martinez	1.00	.45
❑ 66 Jim Thome	1.00	.45
❑ 67 Tom Glavine	1.00	.45
❑ 68 Raul Mondesi	.60	.25
❑ 69 Marquis Grissom	.40	.18
❑ 70 Randy Johnson	1.00	.45
❑ 71 Steve Finley	.40	.18
❑ 72 Jose Guillen	.40	.18
❑ 73 Nomar Garciaparra	3.00	1.35
❑ 74 Wade Boggs	1.00	.45
❑ 75 Bobby Higginson	.60	.25
❑ 76 Robin Ventura	.40	.18
❑ 77 Derek Jeter	2.50	1.10
❑ 78 Andruw Jones	1.25	.55
❑ 79 Ray Lankford	.40	.18
❑ 80 Vladimir Guerrero	1.50	.70
❑ 81 Kenny Lofton	1.00	.45
❑ 82 Ivan Rodriguez	1.25	.55
❑ 83 Neifi Perez	.40	.18
❑ 84 John Smoltz	.40	.18
❑ 85 Tim Salmon	1.00	.45

		MINT	NRMT
❑ 86	Carlos Delgado	.40	.18
❑ 87	Sammy Sosa	2.50	1.10
❑ 88	Jaret Wright	1.25	.55
❑ 89	Roberto Alomar	1.00	.45
❑ 90	Paul Molitor	1.00	.45
❑ 91	Dean Palmer	.40	.18
❑ 92	Barry Larkin	.60	.25
❑ 93	Jason Giambi	.40	.18
❑ 94	Curt Schilling	.40	.18
❑ 95	Eric Young	.40	.18
❑ 96	Denny Neagle	.40	.18
❑ 97	Moises Alou	.60	.25
❑ 98	Livan Hernandez	.40	.18
❑ 99	Todd Hundley	.40	.18
❑ 100	Andres Galarraga	1.00	.45
❑ 101	Travis Lee	2.00	.90
❑ 102	Lance Berkman	1.00	.45
❑ 103	Orlando Cabrera	.40	.18
❑ 104	Mike Lowell	2.50	1.10
❑ 105	Ben Grieve	2.00	.90
❑ 106	Jae Weong Seo	2.00	.90
❑ 107	Richie Sexson	.60	.25
❑ 108	Eli Marrero	.40	.18
❑ 109	Aramis Ramirez	1.00	.45
❑ 110	Paul Konerko	1.00	.45
❑ 111	Carl Pavano	.40	.18
❑ 112	Brad Fullmer	.40	.18
❑ 113	Matt Clement	.40	.18
❑ 114	Donzell McDonald	.25	.11
❑ 115	Todd Helton	1.25	.55
❑ 116	Mike Caruso	.40	.18
❑ 117	Donnie Sadler	.40	.18
❑ 118	Bruce Chen	.40	.18
❑ 119	Jarrod Washburn	.40	.18
❑ 120	Adrian Beltre	1.25	.55
❑ 121	Ryan Jackson	1.00	.45
❑ 122	Kevin Millar	2.50	1.10
❑ 123	Corey Koskie	2.50	1.10
❑ 124	Dermal Brown	.40	.18
❑ 125	Kerry Wood	5.00	2.20
❑ 126	Juan Melo	.40	.18
❑ 127	Ramon Hernandez	.40	.18
❑ 128	Roy Halladay	.40	.18
❑ 129	Ron Wright	.40	.18
❑ 130	Darnell McDonald	5.00	2.20
❑ 131	Odalis Perez	2.50	1.10
❑ 132	Alex Cora	1.25	.55
❑ 133	Justin Towle	.40	.18
❑ 134	Juan Encarnacion	.40	.18
❑ 135	Brian Rose	.40	.18
❑ 136	Russell Branyan	.40	.18
❑ 137	Cesar King	2.50	1.10
❑ 138	Ruben Rivera	.40	.18
❑ 139	Ricky Ledee	.40	.18
❑ 140	Vernon Wells	.60	.25
❑ 141	Luis Rivas	2.00	.90
❑ 142	Brent Butler	.40	.18
❑ 143	Karim Garcia	.40	.18
❑ 144	George Lombard	.40	.18
❑ 145	Masato Yoshii	2.00	.90
❑ 146	Braden Looper	.40	.18
❑ 147	Alex Sanchez	.40	.18
❑ 148	Kris Benson	.40	.18
❑ 149	Mark Kotsay	.60	.25
❑ 150	Richard Hidalgo	.40	.18
❑ 151	Scott Elarton	.40	.18
❑ 152	Ryan Minor	3.00	1.35
❑ 153	Troy Glaus	12.00	5.50
❑ 154	Carlos Lee	4.00	1.80
❑ 155	Michael Coleman	.40	.18
❑ 156	Jason Grilli	2.00	.90
❑ 157	Julio Ramirez	3.00	1.35
❑ 158	Randy Wolf	1.25	.55
❑ 159	Ryan Brannan	.25	.11
❑ 160	Edgard Clemente	.40	.18
❑ 161	Miguel Tejada	.40	.18
❑ 162	Chad Hermansen	1.00	.45
❑ 163	Ryan Anderson	10.00	4.50
❑ 164	Ben Petrick	.40	.18
❑ 165	Alex Gonzalez	.40	.18
❑ 166	Ben Davis	.40	.18
❑ 167	John Patterson	.40	.18
❑ 168	Cliff Politte	.40	.18
❑ 169	Randall Simon	.40	.18
❑ 170	Javier Vazquez	.40	.18
❑ 171	Kevin Witt	.40	.18
❑ 172	Geoff Jenkins	.40	.18
❑ 173	David Ortiz	.40	.18
❑ 174	Derrick Gibson	.40	.18
❑ 175	Abraham Nunez	.40	.18
❑ 176	A.J. Hinch	.40	.18
❑ 177	Ruben Mateo	8.00	3.60
❑ 178	Magglio Ordonez	3.00	1.35
❑ 179	Todd Dunwoody	.40	.18
❑ 180	Daryle Ward	.40	.18
❑ 181	Mike Kinkade	2.00	.90
❑ 182	Willie Martinez	.40	.18
❑ 183	Orlando Hernandez	12.00	5.50
❑ 184	Eric Milton	.40	.18
❑ 185	Eric Chavez	1.50	.70
❑ 186	Damian Jackson	.25	.11
❑ 187	Jim Parque	2.50	1.10
❑ 188	Dan Reichert	1.00	.45
❑ 189	Mike Drumright	.40	.18
❑ 190	Todd Walker	.60	.25
❑ 191	Shane Monahan	.40	.18
❑ 192	Derrek Lee	.40	.18
❑ 193	Jeremy Giambi	4.00	1.80
❑ 194	Dan McKinley	1.00	.45
❑ 195	Tony Armas Jr.	2.00	.90
❑ 196	Matt Anderson	2.50	1.10
❑ 197	Jim Chamblee	1.00	.45
❑ 198	Francisco Cordero	1.00	.45
❑ 199	Calvin Pickering	.60	.25
❑ 200	Reggie Taylor	.40	.18

1998 Bowman's Best Atomic Refractors

	MINT	NRMT
COMMON CARD (1-200)	15.00	6.75

*STARS: 25X TO 60X BASIC CARDS
*YOUNG STARS: 20X TO 50X BASIC CARDS
*PROSPECTS: 15X TO 40X BASIC CARDS
*ROOKIES: 6X TO 15X BASIC CARDS

1998 Bowman's Best Refractors

	MINT	NRMT
COMPLETE SET (200)	3000.00	1350.00
COMMON CARD (1-200)	5.00	2.20

*STARS: 8X TO 20X BASIC CARDS
*YOUNG STARS: 6X TO 15X BASIC CARDS
*PROSPECTS: 6X TO 15X BASIC CARDS
*ROOKIES: 3X TO 8X BASIC CARDS

1998 Bowman's Best Autographs

	MINT	NRMT
COMPLETE SET (10)	500.00	220.00
COMMON CARD	30.00	13.50

*REFRACTORS: 1.25X TO 2.5X BASIC AU'S
REFRACTOR STATED ODDS 1:2158
*ATOMICS: 2.5X TO 5X BASIC AU'S
ATOMIC STATED ODDS 1:6437

		MINT	NRMT
❑ 5	Chipper Jones	100.00	45.00
❑ 10	Chuck Knoblauch	40.00	18.00
❑ 15	Tony Clark	30.00	13.50
❑ 20	Albert Belle	50.00	22.00
❑ 25	Jose Cruz Jr.	50.00	22.00
❑ 105	Ben Grieve	80.00	36.00
❑ 110	Paul Konerko	30.00	13.50
❑ 115	Todd Helton	50.00	22.00
❑ 120	Adrian Beltre	50.00	22.00
❑ 125	Kerry Wood	120.00	55.00

1998 Bowman's Best Mirror Image Fusion

	MINT	NRMT
COMPLETE SET (20)	200.00	90.00
COMMON CARD (MI1-MI20)	2.00	.90

*REFRACTORS: 5X TO 12X BASIC MIR.IMAGE
REFRACTOR STATED ODDS 1:809
*ATOMIC: 12.5X TO 30X BASIC MIR.IMAGE
ATOMIC STATED ODDS 1:3237
ATOMIC PRINT RUN 25 SERIAL #'d SETS

		MINT	NRMT
❑ MI1	Frank Thomas David Ortiz	15.00	6.75
❑ MI2	Chuck Knoblauch Enrique Wilson	5.00	2.20
❑ MI3	Nomar Garciaparra Miguel Tejada	12.00	5.50
❑ MI4	Alex Rodriguez Mike Caruso	15.00	6.75
❑ MI5	Cal Ripken Ryan Minor	20.00	9.00
❑ MI6	Ken Griffey Jr. Ben Grieve	25.00	11.00
❑ MI7	Juan Gonzalez Juan Encarnacion	12.00	5.50
❑ MI8	Jose Cruz Jr. Ruben Mateo	10.00	4.50

Card	Players	MINT	NRMT
❑ MI9	Randy Johnson / Ryan Anderson	15.00	6.75
❑ MI10	Ivan Rodriguez / A.J. Hinch	6.00	2.70
❑ MI11	Jeff Bagwell / Paul Konerko	8.00	3.60
❑ MI12	Mark McGwire / Travis Lee	30.00	13.50
❑ MI13	Craig Biggio / Chad Hermansen	5.00	2.20
❑ MI14	Mark Grudzielanek / Alex Gonzalez	2.00	.90
❑ MI15	Chipper Jones / Adrian Beltre	12.00	5.50
❑ MI16	Larry Walker / Mark Kotsay	5.00	2.20
❑ MI17	Tony Gwynn / George Lombard	12.00	5.50
❑ MI18	Barry Bonds / Richard Hidalgo	6.00	2.70
❑ MI19	Greg Maddux / Kerry Wood	20.00	9.00
❑ MI20	Mike Piazza / Ben Petrick	15.00	6.75

1998 Bowman's Best Performers

	MINT	NRMT
COMPLETE SET (10)	25.00	11.00
COMMON CARD (BP1-BP10)	1.50	.70

*REFRACTORS: 5X TO 12X BASIC PERF.
REFRACTOR STATED ODDS 1:809
*ATOMIC: 12.5X TO 30X BASIC PERF.
ATOMIC STATED ODDS 1:3237
ATOMIC PRINT RUN 50 SERIAL #'d SETS

Card	Player	MINT	NRMT
❑ BP1	Ben Grieve	5.00	2.20
❑ BP2	Travis Lee	5.00	2.20
❑ BP3	Ryan Minor	3.00	1.35
❑ BP4	Todd Helton	3.00	1.35
❑ BP5	Brad Fullmer	1.50	.70
❑ BP6	Paul Konerko	2.00	.90
❑ BP7	Adrian Beltre	3.00	1.35
❑ BP8	Richie Sexson	2.00	.90
❑ BP9	Aramis Ramirez	2.50	1.10
❑ BP10	Russell Branyan	1.50	.70

1996 Circa

	MINT	NRMT
COMPLETE SET (200)	25.00	11.00
COMMON CARD (1-200)	.15	.07

Card	Player	MINT	NRMT
❑ 1	Roberto Alomar	.60	.25
❑ 2	Brady Anderson	.30	.14
❑ 3	Rocky Coppinger	.60	.25
❑ 4	Eddie Murray	.60	.25
❑ 5	Mike Mussina	.60	.25
❑ 6	Randy Myers	.15	.07
❑ 7	Rafael Palmeiro	.40	.18
❑ 8	Cal Ripken	2.50	1.10
❑ 9	Jose Canseco	.60	.25
❑ 10	Roger Clemens	1.25	.55
❑ 11	Mike Greenwell	.15	.07
❑ 12	Tim Naehring	.15	.07
❑ 13	John Valentin	.30	.14
❑ 14	Mo Vaughn	.75	.35
❑ 15	Tim Wakefield	.30	.14
❑ 16	Jim Abbott	.30	.14
❑ 17	Garret Anderson	.30	.14
❑ 18	Jim Edmonds	.40	.18
❑ 19	Darin Erstad	5.00	2.20
❑ 20	Chuck Finley	.30	.14
❑ 21	Troy Percival	.30	.14
❑ 22	Tim Salmon	.60	.25
❑ 23	J.T. Snow	.30	.14
❑ 24	Wilson Alvarez	.30	.14
❑ 25	Harold Baines	.30	.14
❑ 26	Ray Durham	.30	.14
❑ 27	Alex Fernandez	.15	.07
❑ 28	Tony Phillips	.15	.07
❑ 29	Frank Thomas	2.00	.90
❑ 30	Robin Ventura	.30	.14
❑ 31	Sandy Alomar Jr.	.30	.14
❑ 32	Albert Belle	.75	.35
❑ 33	Kenny Lofton	.60	.25
❑ 34	Dennis Martinez	.30	.14
❑ 35	Jose Mesa	.15	.07
❑ 36	Charles Nagy	.30	.14
❑ 37	Manny Ramirez	.60	.25
❑ 38	Jim Thome	.60	.25
❑ 39	Travis Fryman	.30	.14
❑ 40	Bob Higginson	.60	.25
❑ 41	Melvin Nieves	.15	.07
❑ 42	Alan Trammell	.40	.18
❑ 43	Kevin Appier	.30	.14
❑ 44	Johnny Damon	.30	.14
❑ 45	Keith Lockhart	.15	.07
❑ 46	Jeff Montgomery	.15	.07
❑ 47	Joe Randa	.15	.07
❑ 48	Bip Roberts	.15	.07
❑ 49	Ricky Bones	.15	.07
❑ 50	Jeff Cirillo	.30	.14
❑ 51	Marc Newfield	.15	.07
❑ 52	Dave Nilsson	.15	.07
❑ 53	Kevin Seitzer	.15	.07
❑ 54	Ron Coomer	.15	.07
❑ 55	Marty Cordova	.15	.07
❑ 56	Roberto Kelly	.15	.07
❑ 57	Chuck Knoblauch	.60	.25
❑ 58	Paul Molitor	.60	.25
❑ 59	Kirby Puckett	1.00	.45
❑ 60	Scott Stahoviak	.15	.07
❑ 61	Wade Boggs	.60	.25
❑ 62	David Cone	.40	.18
❑ 63	Cecil Fielder	.30	.14
❑ 64	Dwight Gooden	.30	.14
❑ 65	Derek Jeter	2.00	.90
❑ 66	Tino Martinez	.60	.25
❑ 67	Paul O'Neill	.30	.14
❑ 68	Andy Pettitte	.40	.18
❑ 69	Ruben Rivera	.30	.14
❑ 70	Bernie Williams	.60	.25
❑ 71	Geronimo Berroa	.15	.07
❑ 72	Jason Giambi	.30	.14
❑ 73	Mark McGwire	3.00	1.35
❑ 74	Terry Steinbach	.30	.14
❑ 75	Todd Van Poppel	.15	.07
❑ 76	Jay Buhner	.30	.14
❑ 77	Norm Charlton	.15	.07
❑ 78	Ken Griffey Jr.	3.00	1.35
❑ 79	Randy Johnson	.60	.25
❑ 80	Edgar Martinez	.30	.14
❑ 81	Alex Rodriguez	2.00	.90
❑ 82	Paul Sorrento	.15	.07
❑ 83	Dan Wilson	.15	.07
❑ 84	Will Clark	.60	.25
❑ 85	Kevin Elster	.15	.07
❑ 86	Juan Gonzalez	1.50	.70
❑ 87	Rusty Greer	.40	.18
❑ 88	Ken Hill	.15	.07
❑ 89	Mark McLemore	.15	.07
❑ 90	Dean Palmer	.30	.14
❑ 91	Roger Pavlik	.15	.07
❑ 92	Ivan Rodriguez	.75	.35
❑ 93	Joe Carter	.30	.14
❑ 94	Carlos Delgado	.30	.14
❑ 95	Juan Guzman	.15	.07
❑ 96	John Olerud	.30	.14
❑ 97	Ed Sprague	.15	.07
❑ 98	Jermaine Dye	.15	.07
❑ 99	Tom Glavine	.60	.25
❑ 100	Marquis Grissom	.30	.14
❑ 101	Andruw Jones	1.50	.70
❑ 102	Chipper Jones	1.50	.70
❑ 103	David Justice	.60	.25
❑ 104	Ryan Klesko	.30	.14
❑ 105	Greg Maddux	2.00	.90
❑ 106	Fred McGriff	.40	.18
❑ 107	John Smoltz	.30	.14
❑ 108	Brant Brown	.30	.14
❑ 109	Mark Grace	.40	.18
❑ 110	Brian McRae	.15	.07
❑ 111	Ryne Sandberg	.75	.35
❑ 112	Sammy Sosa	1.50	.70
❑ 113	Steve Trachsel	.15	.07
❑ 114	Bret Boone	.30	.14
❑ 115	Eric Davis	.30	.14
❑ 116	Steve Gibralter	.15	.07
❑ 117	Barry Larkin	.40	.18
❑ 118	Reggie Sanders	.30	.14
❑ 119	John Smiley	.15	.07
❑ 120	Dante Bichette	.30	.14
❑ 121	Ellis Burks	.30	.14
❑ 122	Vinny Castilla	.40	.18
❑ 123	Andres Galarraga	.60	.25
❑ 124	Larry Walker	.60	.25
❑ 125	Eric Young	.15	.07
❑ 126	Kevin Brown	.60	.25
❑ 127	Greg Colbrunn	.15	.07
❑ 128	Jeff Conine	.30	.14
❑ 129	Charles Johnson	.30	.14
❑ 130	Al Leiter	.30	.14
❑ 131	Gary Sheffield	.40	.18
❑ 132	Devon White	.30	.14
❑ 133	Jeff Bagwell	1.00	.45
❑ 134	Derek Bell	.30	.14
❑ 135	Craig Biggio	.60	.25
❑ 136	Doug Drabek	.15	.07
❑ 137	Brian L.Hunter	.30	.14
❑ 138	Darryl Kile	.30	.14
❑ 139	Shane Reynolds	.30	.14
❑ 140	Brett Butler	.30	.14
❑ 141	Eric Karros	.30	.14
❑ 142	Ramon Martinez	.30	.14
❑ 143	Raul Mondesi	.40	.18
❑ 144	Hideo Nomo	1.00	.45
❑ 145	Chan Ho Park	.60	.25
❑ 146	Mike Piazza	2.00	.90
❑ 147	Moises Alou	.40	.18
❑ 148	Yamil Benitez	.15	.07
❑ 149	Mark Grudzielanek	.30	.14
❑ 150	Pedro Martinez	.60	.25
❑ 151	Henry Rodriguez	.30	.14
❑ 152	David Segui	.30	.14
❑ 153	Rondell White	.30	.14
❑ 154	Carlos Baerga	.30	.14
❑ 155	John Franco	.30	.14
❑ 156	Bernard Gilkey	.15	.07
❑ 157	Todd Hundley	.30	.14
❑ 158	Jason Isringhausen	.15	.07
❑ 159	Lance Johnson	.15	.07
❑ 160	Alex Ochoa	.15	.07
❑ 161	Rey Ordonez	.30	.14
❑ 162	Paul Wilson	.15	.07
❑ 163	Ron Blazier	.15	.07
❑ 164	Ricky Bottalico	.30	.14
❑ 165	Jim Eisenreich	.15	.07
❑ 166	Pete Incaviglia	.15	.07

		MINT	NRMT
❑ 167	Mickey Morandini	.15	.07
❑ 168	Ricky Otero	.15	.07
❑ 169	Curt Schilling	.30	.14
❑ 170	Jay Bell	.30	.14
❑ 171	Charlie Hayes	.15	.07
❑ 172	Jason Kendall	.60	.25
❑ 173	Jeff King	.15	.07
❑ 174	Al Martin	.15	.07
❑ 175	Alan Benes	.30	.14
❑ 176	Royce Clayton	.15	.07
❑ 177	Brian Jordan	.30	.14
❑ 178	Ray Lankford	.30	.14
❑ 179	John Mabry	.15	.07
❑ 180	Willie McGee	.30	.14
❑ 181	Ozzie Smith	.75	.35
❑ 182	Todd Stottlemyre	.15	.07
❑ 183	Andy Ashby	.15	.07
❑ 184	Ken Caminiti	.40	.18
❑ 185	Steve Finley	.30	.14
❑ 186	Tony Gwynn	1.50	.70
❑ 187	Rickey Henderson	.60	.25
❑ 188	Wally Joyner	.30	.14
❑ 189	Fernando Valenzuela	.30	.14
❑ 190	Greg Vaughn	.30	.14
❑ 191	Rod Beck	.15	.07
❑ 192	Barry Bonds	.75	.35
❑ 193	Shawon Dunston	.15	.07
❑ 194	Chris Singleton	.15	.07
❑ 195	Robby Thompson	.15	.07
❑ 196	Matt Williams	.30	.14
❑ 197	Barry Bonds CL	.40	.18
❑ 198	Ken Griffey Jr. CL	1.50	.70
❑ 199	Cal Ripken CL	1.25	.55
❑ 200	Frank Thomas CL	1.00	.45

1996 Circa Rave

	MINT	NRMT
COMPLETE SET (200)	5000.00	2200.00
COMMON CARD (1-200)	10.00	4.50

*STARS: 25X TO 60X BASIC CARDS
*YOUNG STARS: 20X TO 50X BASIC CARDS
*ROOKIES: 12.5X TO 30X BASIC CARDS

1996 Circa Access

	MINT	NRMT
COMPLETE SET (30)	120.00	55.00
COMMON CARD (1-30)	2.00	.90

		MINT	NRMT
❑ 1	Cal Ripken	15.00	6.75
❑ 2	Mo Vaughn	5.00	2.20
❑ 3	Tim Salmon	4.00	1.80
❑ 4	Frank Thomas	12.00	5.50
❑ 5	Albert Belle	5.00	2.20
❑ 6	Kenny Lofton	4.00	1.80
❑ 7	Manny Ramirez	4.00	1.80
❑ 8	Paul Molitor	4.00	1.80
❑ 9	Kirby Puckett	6.00	2.70
❑ 10	Paul O'Neill	2.00	.90
❑ 11	Mark McGwire	20.00	9.00
❑ 12	Ken Griffey Jr.	20.00	9.00
❑ 13	Randy Johnson	4.00	1.80
❑ 14	Greg Maddux	12.00	5.50
❑ 15	John Smoltz	2.00	.90
❑ 16	Sammy Sosa	10.00	4.50
❑ 17	Barry Larkin	3.00	1.35
❑ 18	Gary Sheffield	3.00	1.35
❑ 19	Jeff Bagwell	6.00	2.70
❑ 20	Hideo Nomo	6.00	2.70
❑ 21	Mike Piazza	12.00	5.50
❑ 22	Moises Alou	3.00	1.35
❑ 23	Henry Rodriguez	2.00	.90
❑ 24	Rey Ordonez	2.00	.90
❑ 25	Jay Bell	2.00	.90
❑ 26	Ozzie Smith	5.00	2.20
❑ 27	Tony Gwynn	10.00	4.50
❑ 28	Rickey Henderson	4.00	1.80
❑ 29	Barry Bonds	5.00	2.20
❑ 30	Matt Williams	2.00	.90
❑ P30	Matt Williams Promo	1.00	.45

1996 Circa Boss

	MINT	NRMT
COMPLETE SET (50)	100.00	45.00
COMMON CARD (1-50)	1.00	.45

		MINT	NRMT
❑ 1	Roberto Alomar	3.00	1.35
❑ 2	Cal Ripken	12.00	5.50
❑ 3	Jose Canseco	3.00	1.35
❑ 4	Mo Vaughn	3.00	1.35
❑ 5	Tim Salmon	3.00	1.35
❑ 6	Frank Thomas	10.00	4.50
❑ 7	Robin Ventura	1.50	.70
❑ 8	Albert Belle	3.00	1.35
❑ 9	Kenny Lofton	3.00	1.35
❑ 10	Manny Ramirez	3.00	1.35
❑ 11	Dave Nilsson	1.00	.45
❑ 12	Chuck Knoblauch	3.00	1.35
❑ 13	Paul Molitor	3.00	1.35
❑ 14	Kirby Puckett	6.00	2.70
❑ 15	Wade Boggs	3.00	1.35
❑ 16	Dwight Gooden	1.50	.70
❑ 17	Paul O'Neill	1.50	.70
❑ 18	Mark McGwire	15.00	6.75
❑ 19	Jay Buhner	1.50	.70
❑ 20	Ken Griffey Jr.	15.00	6.75
❑ 21	Randy Johnson	3.00	1.35
❑ 22	Will Clark	3.00	1.35
❑ 23	Juan Gonzalez	8.00	3.60
❑ 24	Joe Carter	1.50	.70
❑ 25	Tom Glavine	3.00	1.35
❑ 26	Ryan Klesko	1.50	.70
❑ 27	Greg Maddux	10.00	4.50
❑ 28	John Smoltz	1.50	.70
❑ 29	Ryne Sandberg	3.00	1.35
❑ 30	Sammy Sosa	3.00	1.35
❑ 31	Barry Larkin	2.00	.90
❑ 32	Reggie Sanders	1.50	.70
❑ 33	Dante Bichette	1.50	.70
❑ 34	Andres Galarraga	3.00	1.35
❑ 35	Charles Johnson	1.50	.70
❑ 36	Gary Sheffield	2.00	.90
❑ 37	Jeff Bagwell	5.00	2.20
❑ 38	Hideo Nomo	5.00	2.20
❑ 39	Mike Piazza	10.00	4.50
❑ 40	Moises Alou	2.00	.90
❑ 41	Henry Rodriguez	1.50	.70
❑ 42	Rey Ordonez	1.50	.70
❑ 43	Ricky Otero	1.00	.45
❑ 44	Jay Bell	1.50	.70
❑ 45	Royce Clayton	1.00	.45
❑ 46	Ozzie Smith	3.00	1.35
❑ 47	Tony Gwynn	8.00	3.60
❑ 48	Rickey Henderson	3.00	1.35
❑ 49	Barry Bonds	3.00	1.35
❑ 50	Matt Williams	1.50	.70
❑ P2	Cal Ripken Promo	2.00	.90

1997 Circa

	MINT	NRMT
COMPLETE SET (400)	40.00	18.00
COMMON CARD (1-400)	.15	.07

		MINT	NRMT
❑ 1	Kenny Lofton	.60	.25
❑ 2	Ray Durham	.30	.14
❑ 3	Mariano Rivera	.30	.14
❑ 4	Jon Lieber	.15	.07
❑ 5	Tim Salmon	.60	.25
❑ 6	Mark Grudzielanek	.30	.14
❑ 7	Neifi Perez	.15	.07
❑ 8	Cal Ripken	2.50	1.10
❑ 9	John Olerud	.30	.14
❑ 10	Edgar Renteria	.30	.14
❑ 11	Jose Rosado	.15	.07
❑ 12	Mickey Morandini	.15	.07
❑ 13	Orlando Miller	.15	.07
❑ 14	Ben McDonald	.15	.07
❑ 15	Hideo Nomo	.75	.35
❑ 16	Fred McGriff	.40	.18
❑ 17	Sean Berry	.15	.07
❑ 18	Roger Pavlik	.15	.07
❑ 19	Aaron Sele	.30	.14
❑ 20	Joey Hamilton	.30	.14
❑ 21	Roger Clemens	1.25	.55
❑ 22	Jose Herrera	.15	.07
❑ 23	Ryne Sandberg	.75	.35
❑ 24	Ken Griffey Jr.	3.00	1.35
❑ 25	Barry Bonds	.75	.35
❑ 26	Dan Naulty	.15	.07
❑ 27	Wade Boggs	.60	.25
❑ 28	Ray Lankford	.30	.14
❑ 29	Rico Brogna	.15	.07
❑ 30	Wally Joyner	.30	.14
❑ 31	F.P. Santangelo	.15	.07
❑ 32	Vinny Castilla	.40	.18
❑ 33	Eddie Murray	.60	.25
❑ 34	Kevin Elster	.15	.07
❑ 35	Mike Macfarlane	.15	.07
❑ 36	Jeff Kent	.30	.14
❑ 37	Orlando Merced	.15	.07
❑ 38	Jason Isringhausen	.15	.07
❑ 39	Chad Ogea	.15	.07
❑ 40	Greg Gagne	.15	.07
❑ 41	Curt Lyons	.15	.07
❑ 42	Mo Vaughn	.75	.35
❑ 43	Rusty Greer	.30	.14
❑ 44	Shane Reynolds	.30	.14
❑ 45	Frank Thomas	2.00	.90
❑ 46	Chris Hoiles	.15	.07
❑ 47	Scott Sanders	.15	.07
❑ 48	Mark Lemke	.15	.07
❑ 49	Fernando Vina	.15	.07
❑ 50	Mark McGwire	3.00	1.35
❑ 51	Bernie Williams	.60	.25
❑ 52	Bobby Higginson	.40	.18
❑ 53	Kevin Tapani	.15	.07
❑ 54	Rich Becker	.15	.07
❑ 55	Felix Heredia	.30	.14
❑ 56	Delino DeShields	.15	.07

❑ 57 Rick Wilkins .15 .07
❑ 58 Edgardo Alfonzo .30 .14
❑ 59 Brett Butler .30 .14
❑ 60 Ed Sprague .15 .07
❑ 61 Joe Randa .15 .07
❑ 62 Ugueth Urbina .30 .14
❑ 63 Todd Greene .30 .14
❑ 64 Devon White .30 .14
❑ 65 Bruce Ruffin .15 .07
❑ 66 Mark Gardner .15 .07
❑ 67 Omar Vizquel .30 .14
❑ 68 Luis Gonzalez .15 .07
❑ 69 Tom Glavine .60 .25
❑ 70 Cal Eldred .15 .07
❑ 71 Wm. VanLandingham .15 .07
❑ 72 Jay Buhner .30 .14
❑ 73 James Baldwin .30 .14
❑ 74 Robin Jennings .15 .07
❑ 75 Terry Steinbach .30 .14
❑ 76 Billy Taylor .15 .07
❑ 77 Armando Benitez .15 .07
❑ 78 Joe Girardi .15 .07
❑ 79 Jay Bell .30 .14
❑ 80 Damon Buford .15 .07
❑ 81 Deion Sanders .30 .14
❑ 82 Bill Haselman .15 .07
❑ 83 John Flaherty .15 .07
❑ 84 Todd Stottlemyre .15 .07
❑ 85 J.T. Snow .30 .14
❑ 86 Felipe Lira .15 .07
❑ 87 Steve Avery .15 .07
❑ 88 Trey Beamon .15 .07
❑ 89 Alex Gonzalez .15 .07
❑ 90 Mark Clark .15 .07
❑ 91 Shane Andrews .15 .07
❑ 92 Randy Myers .15 .07
❑ 93 Gary Gaetti .15 .07
❑ 94 Jeff Blauser .15 .07
❑ 95 Tony Batista .15 .07
❑ 96 Todd Worrell .15 .07
❑ 97 Jim Edmonds .40 .18
❑ 98 Eric Young .30 .14
❑ 99 Roberto Kelly .15 .07
❑ 100 Alex Rodriguez 2.00 .90
❑ 101 Julio Franco .30 .14
❑ 102 Jeff Bagwell 1.00 .45
❑ 103 Bobby Witt .15 .07
❑ 104 Tino Martinez .60 .25
❑ 105 Shannon Stewart .30 .14
❑ 106 Brian Banks .15 .07
❑ 107 Eddie Taubensee .15 .07
❑ 108 Terry Mulholland .15 .07
❑ 109 Lyle Mouton .15 .07
❑ 110 Jeff Conine .30 .14
❑ 111 Johnny Damon .30 .14
❑ 112 Quilvio Veras .15 .07
❑ 113 Wilton Guerrero .15 .07
❑ 114 Dmitri Young .30 .14
❑ 115 Garret Anderson .30 .14
❑ 116 Bill Pulsipher .15 .07
❑ 117 Jacob Brumfield .15 .07
❑ 118 Mike Lansing .15 .07
❑ 119 Jose Canseco .60 .25
❑ 120 Mike Bordick .15 .07
❑ 121 Kevin Stocker .15 .07
❑ 122 Frankie Rodriguez .15 .07
❑ 123 Mike Cameron .30 .14
❑ 124 Tony Womack .50 .23
❑ 125 Bret Boone .30 .14
❑ 126 Moises Alou .40 .18
❑ 127 Tim Naehring .15 .07
❑ 128 Brant Brown .30 .14
❑ 129 Todd Zeile .15 .07
❑ 130 Dave Nilsson .15 .07
❑ 131 Donne Wall .15 .07
❑ 132 Jose Mesa .15 .07
❑ 133 Mark McLemore .15 .07
❑ 134 Mike Stanton .15 .07
❑ 135 Dan Wilson .15 .07
❑ 136 Jose Offerman .15 .07
❑ 137 David Justice .60 .25
❑ 138 Kirt Manwaring .15 .07
❑ 139 Raul Casanova .15 .07
❑ 140 Ron Coomer .15 .07
❑ 141 Dave Hollins .15 .07
❑ 142 Shawn Estes .30 .14
❑ 143 Darren Daulton .30 .14
❑ 144 Turk Wendell .15 .07
❑ 145 Darrin Fletcher .15 .07
❑ 146 Marquis Grissom .30 .14
❑ 147 Andy Benes .30 .14
❑ 148 Nomar Garciaparra 2.00 .90
❑ 149 Andy Pettitte .40 .18
❑ 150 Tony Gwynn 1.50 .70
❑ 151 Robb Nen .15 .07
❑ 152 Kevin Seitzer .15 .07
❑ 153 Ariel Prieto .15 .07
❑ 154 Scott Karl .15 .07
❑ 155 Carlos Baerga .30 .14
❑ 156 Wilson Alvarez .30 .14
❑ 157 Thomas Howard .15 .07
❑ 158 Kevin Appier .30 .14
❑ 159 Russ Davis .30 .14
❑ 160 Justin Thompson .30 .14
❑ 161 Pete Schourek .15 .07
❑ 162 John Burkett .15 .07
❑ 163 Roberto Alomar .60 .25
❑ 164 Darren Holmes .15 .07
❑ 165 Travis Miller .15 .07
❑ 166 Mark Langston .30 .14
❑ 167 Juan Guzman .15 .07
❑ 168 Pedro Astacio .15 .07
❑ 169 Mark Johnson .15 .07
❑ 170 Mark Leiter .15 .07
❑ 171 Heathcliff Slocumb .15 .07
❑ 172 Dante Bichette .30 .14
❑ 173 Brian Giles .75 .35
❑ 174 Paul Wilson .15 .07
❑ 175 Eric Davis .30 .14
❑ 176 Charles Johnson .30 .14
❑ 177 Willie Greene .30 .14
❑ 178 Geronimo Berroa .15 .07
❑ 179 Mariano Duncan .15 .07
❑ 180 Robert Person .15 .07
❑ 181 David Segui .30 .14
❑ 182 Ozzie Guillen .15 .07
❑ 183 Osvaldo Fernandez .15 .07
❑ 184 Dean Palmer .30 .14
❑ 185 Bob Wickman .15 .07
❑ 186 Eric Karros .30 .14
❑ 187 Travis Fryman .30 .14
❑ 188 Andy Ashby .15 .07
❑ 189 Scott Stahoviak .15 .07
❑ 190 Norm Charlton .15 .07
❑ 191 Craig Paquette .15 .07
❑ 192 John Smoltz UER .30 .14
Name spelled "Smotlz" on back
❑ 193 Orel Hershiser .30 .14
❑ 194 Glenallen Hill .15 .07
❑ 195 George Arias .15 .07
❑ 196 Brian Jordan .30 .14
❑ 197 Greg Vaughn .30 .14
❑ 198 Rafael Palmeiro .40 .18
❑ 199 Darryl Kile .30 .14
❑ 200 Derek Jeter 2.00 .90
❑ 201 Jose Vizcaino .15 .07
❑ 202 Rick Aguilera .15 .07
❑ 203 Jason Schmidt .15 .07
❑ 204 Trot Nixon .30 .14
❑ 205 Tom Pagnozzi .15 .07
❑ 206 Mark Wohlers .15 .07
❑ 207 Lance Johnson .15 .07
❑ 208 Carlos Delgado .30 .14
❑ 209 Cliff Floyd .30 .14
❑ 210 Kent Mercker .15 .07
❑ 211 Matt Mieske .15 .07
❑ 212 Ismael Valdes .30 .14
❑ 213 Shawon Dunston .15 .07
❑ 214 Melvin Nieves .15 .07
❑ 215 Tony Phillips .15 .07
❑ 216 Scott Spiezio .15 .07
❑ 217 Michael Tucker .30 .14
❑ 218 Matt Williams .30 .14
❑ 219 Ricky Otero .15 .07
❑ 220 Kevin Ritz .15 .07
❑ 221 Darryl Strawberry .30 .14
❑ 222 Troy Percival .30 .14
❑ 223 Eugene Kingsale .30 .14
❑ 224 Julian Tavarez .15 .07
❑ 225 Jermaine Dye .15 .07
❑ 226 Jason Kendall .40 .18
❑ 227 Sterling Hitchcock .30 .14
❑ 228 Jeff Cirillo .30 .14
❑ 229 Roberto Hernandez .15 .07
❑ 230 Ricky Bottalico .30 .14
❑ 231 Bobby Bonilla .30 .14
❑ 232 Edgar Martinez .30 .14
❑ 233 John Valentin .30 .14
❑ 234 Ellis Burks .30 .14
❑ 235 Benito Santiago .15 .07
❑ 236 Terrell Wade .15 .07
❑ 237 Armando Reynoso .15 .07
❑ 238 Danny Graves .15 .07
❑ 239 Ken Hill .15 .07
❑ 240 Dennis Eckersley .30 .14
❑ 241 Darin Erstad 1.00 .45
❑ 242 Lee Smith UER .30 .14
Position 2b
❑ 243 Cecil Fielder .30 .14
❑ 244 Tony Clark .40 .18
❑ 245 Scott Erickson .30 .14
❑ 246 Bob Abreu .30 .14
❑ 247 Ruben Sierra .15 .07
❑ 248 Chili Davis .30 .14
❑ 249 Darryl Hamilton .15 .07
❑ 250 Albert Belle .75 .35
❑ 251 Todd Hollandsworth .15 .07
❑ 252 Terry Adams .15 .07
❑ 253 Rey Ordonez .30 .14
❑ 254 Steve Finley .30 .14
❑ 255 Jose Valentin .15 .07
❑ 256 Royce Clayton .15 .07
❑ 257 Sandy Alomar .30 .14
❑ 258 Mike Lieberthal .15 .07
❑ 259 Ivan Rodriguez .75 .35
❑ 260 Rod Beck .15 .07
❑ 261 Ron Karkovice .15 .07
❑ 262 Mark Gubicza .15 .07
❑ 263 Chris Holt .15 .07
❑ 264 Jaime Bluma UER .15 .07
Name spelled "Jamie" on front and back
❑ 265 Francisco Cordova .15 .07
❑ 266 Javy Lopez .30 .14
❑ 267 Reggie Jefferson .15 .07
❑ 268 Kevin Brown .40 .18
❑ 269 Scott Brosius .30 .14
❑ 270 Dwight Gooden .30 .14
❑ 271 Marty Cordova .15 .07
❑ 272 Jeff Brantley .15 .07
❑ 273 Joe Carter .30 .14
❑ 274 Todd Jones .15 .07
❑ 275 Sammy Sosa 1.50 .70
❑ 276 Randy Johnson .60 .25
❑ 277 B.J. Surhoff .30 .14
❑ 278 Chan Ho Park .60 .25
❑ 279 Jamey Wright .15 .07
❑ 280 Manny Ramirez .60 .25
❑ 281 John Franco .30 .14
❑ 282 Tim Worrell .15 .07
❑ 283 Scott Rolen 1.50 .70
❑ 284 Reggie Sanders .30 .14
❑ 285 Mike Fetters .15 .07
❑ 286 Tim Wakefield .30 .14
❑ 287 Trevor Hoffman .30 .14
❑ 288 Donovan Osborne .15 .07
❑ 289 Phil Nevin .15 .07
❑ 290 Jermaine Allensworth .15 .07
❑ 291 Rocky Coppinger .15 .07
❑ 292 Tim Raines .30 .14
❑ 293 Henry Rodriguez .30 .14
❑ 294 Paul Sorrento .15 .07
❑ 295 Tom Goodwin .15 .07
❑ 296 Raul Mondesi .40 .18
❑ 297 Allen Watson .15 .07
❑ 298 Derek Bell .30 .14
❑ 299 Gary Sheffield .40 .18
❑ 300 Paul Molitor .60 .25
❑ 301 Shawn Green .30 .14
❑ 302 Darren Oliver .15 .07
❑ 303 Jack McDowell .15 .07
❑ 304 Denny Neagle .30 .14
❑ 305 Doug Drabek .15 .07
❑ 306 Mel Rojas .15 .07
❑ 307 Andres Galarraga .60 .25

❑ 308 Alex Ochoa	.15	.07
❑ 309 Gary DiSarcina	.15	.07
❑ 310 Ron Gant	.15	.07
❑ 311 Gregg Jefferies	.15	.07
❑ 312 Ruben Rivera	.30	.14
❑ 313 Vladimir Guerrero	1.25	.55
❑ 314 Willie Adams	.15	.07
❑ 315 Bip Roberts	.15	.07
❑ 316 Mark Grace	.40	.18
❑ 317 Bernard Gilkey	.15	.07
❑ 318 Marc Newfield	.15	.07
❑ 319 Al Leiter	.30	.14
❑ 320 Otis Nixon	.15	.07
❑ 321 Tom Candiotti	.15	.07
❑ 322 Mike Stanley	.15	.07
❑ 323 Jeff Fassero	.15	.07
❑ 324 Billy Wagner	.30	.14
❑ 325 Todd Walker	.60	.25
❑ 326 Chad Curtis	.15	.07
❑ 327 Quinton McCracken	.30	.14
❑ 328 Will Clark	.60	.25
❑ 329 Andruw Jones	1.00	.45
❑ 330 Robin Ventura	.30	.14
❑ 331 Curtis Pride	.15	.07
❑ 332 Barry Larkin	.40	.18
❑ 333 Jimmy Key	.30	.14
❑ 334 David Wells	.40	.18
❑ 335 Mike Holtz	.15	.07
❑ 336 Paul Wagner	.15	.07
❑ 337 Greg Maddux	2.00	.90
❑ 338 Curt Schilling	.30	.14
❑ 339 Steve Trachsel	.15	.07
❑ 340 John Wetteland	.30	.14
❑ 341 Rickey Henderson	.60	.25
❑ 342 Ernie Young	.15	.07
❑ 343 Harold Baines	.30	.14
❑ 344 Bobby Jones	.15	.07
❑ 345 Jeff D'Amico	.15	.07
❑ 346 John Mabry	.15	.07
❑ 347 Pedro Martinez	.60	.25
❑ 348 Mark Lewis	.15	.07
❑ 349 Dan Miceli	.15	.07
❑ 350 Chuck Knoblauch	.60	.25
❑ 351 John Smiley	.15	.07
❑ 352 Brady Anderson	.30	.14
❑ 353 Jim Leyritz	.15	.07
❑ 354 Al Martin	.15	.07
❑ 355 Pat Hentgen	.30	.14
❑ 356 Mike Piazza	2.00	.90
❑ 357 Charles Nagy	.30	.14
❑ 358 Luis Castillo	.30	.14
❑ 359 Paul O'Neill	.30	.14
❑ 360 Steve Reed	.15	.07
❑ 361 Tom Gordon	.15	.07
❑ 362 Craig Biggio	.60	.25
❑ 363 Jeff Montgomery	.15	.07
❑ 364 Jamie Moyer	.15	.07
❑ 365 Ryan Klesko	.30	.14
❑ 366 Todd Hundley	.30	.14
❑ 367 Bobby Estalella	.30	.14
❑ 368 Jason Giambi	.30	.14
❑ 369 Brian Hunter	.30	.14
❑ 370 Ramon Martinez	.30	.14
❑ 371 Carlos Garcia	.15	.07
❑ 372 Hal Morris	.15	.07
❑ 373 Juan Gonzalez	1.50	.70
❑ 374 Brian McRae	.15	.07
❑ 375 Mike Mussina	.60	.25
❑ 376 John Ericks	.15	.07
❑ 377 Larry Walker	.60	.25
❑ 378 Chris Gomez	.15	.07
❑ 379 John Jaha	.15	.07
❑ 380 Rondell White	.30	.14
❑ 381 Chipper Jones	1.50	.70
❑ 382 David Cone	.40	.18
❑ 383 Alan Benes	.30	.14
❑ 384 Troy O'Leary	.30	.14
❑ 385 Ken Caminiti	.40	.18
❑ 386 Jeff King	.15	.07
❑ 387 Mike Hampton	.15	.07
❑ 388 Jaime Navarro	.15	.07
❑ 389 Brad Radke	.30	.14
❑ 390 Joey Cora	.30	.14
❑ 391 Jim Thome	.60	.25
❑ 392 Alex Fernandez	.15	.07
❑ 393 Chuck Finley	.30	.14
❑ 394 Andruw Jones CL	.75	.35
❑ 395 Ken Griffey Jr. CL	1.50	.70
❑ 396 Frank Thomas CL	1.00	.45
❑ 397 Alex Rodriguez CL	1.00	.45
❑ 398 Cal Ripken CL	1.25	.55
❑ 399 Mike Piazza CL	1.00	.45
❑ 400 Greg Maddux CL	1.00	.45
❑ P100 Alex Rodriguez Promo	3.00	1.35

1997 Circa Rave

	MINT	NRMT
COMMON CARD (1-400)	10.00	4.50

*STARS: 25X TO 60X BASIC CARDS
*YOUNG STARS: 20X TO 50X BASIC CARDS
*ROOKIES: 12.5X TO 30X BASIC CARDS

1997 Circa Boss

	MINT	NRMT
COMPLETE SET (20)	40.00	18.00
COMMON CARD (1-20)	.50	.23
COMP.SUPER BOSS SET (20)	150.00	70.00
COMMON CARD (1-20)	2.00	.90
SUPER BOSS STATED ODDS 1:36		
❑ 1 Jeff Bagwell	2.00	.90
❑ 2 Albert Belle	1.25	.55
❑ 3 Barry Bonds	1.50	.70
❑ 4 Ken Caminiti	.75	.35
❑ 5 Juan Gonzalez	3.00	1.35
❑ 6 Ken Griffey Jr.	6.00	2.70
❑ 7 Tony Gwynn	3.00	1.35
❑ 8 Derek Jeter	4.00	1.80
❑ 9 Andruw Jones	2.00	.90
❑ 10 Chipper Jones	3.00	1.35
❑ 11 Greg Maddux	4.00	1.80
❑ 12 Mark McGwire	6.00	2.70
❑ 13 Mike Piazza	4.00	1.80
❑ 14 Manny Ramirez	1.25	.55
❑ 15 Cal Ripken	5.00	2.20
❑ 16 Alex Rodriguez	4.00	1.80
❑ 17 John Smoltz	.50	.23
❑ 18 Frank Thomas	4.00	1.80
❑ 19 Mo Vaughn	1.50	.70
❑ 20 Bernie Williams	1.25	.55

1997 Circa Emerald Autographs

	MINT	NRMT
COMPLETE SET (6)	300.00	135.00
COMMON CARD	12.00	5.50
*EXCH CARDS: .1X TO .25X HI COLUMN		
EXCH CARDS STATED ODDS 1:1000 PACKS		
❑ 100 Alex Rodriguez AU	150.00	70.00
❑ 241 Darin Erstad AU	50.00	22.00
❑ 251 Todd Hollandsworth AU	12.00	5.50
❑ 283 Scott Rolen AU	80.00	36.00
❑ 308 Alex Ochoa AU	12.00	5.50
❑ 325 Todd Walker AU	25.00	11.00

1997 Circa Fast Track

	MINT	NRMT
COMPLETE SET (10)	40.00	18.00
COMMON CARD (1-10)	1.50	.70
❑ 1 Vladimir Guerrero	6.00	2.70
❑ 2 Todd Hollandsworth	1.50	.70
❑ 3 Derek Jeter	8.00	3.60
❑ 4 Andruw Jones	5.00	2.20
❑ 5 Chipper Jones	8.00	3.60
❑ 6 Andy Pettitte	2.00	.90
❑ 7 Mariano Rivera	2.00	.90
❑ 8 Alex Rodriguez	10.00	4.50
❑ 9 Scott Rolen	8.00	3.60
❑ 10 Todd Walker	3.00	1.35

1997 Circa Icons

	MINT	NRMT
COMPLETE SET (12)	100.00	45.00
COMMON CARD (1-12)	2.50	1.10
❑ 1 Juan Gonzalez	10.00	4.50
❑ 2 Ken Griffey Jr.	20.00	9.00
❑ 3 Tony Gwynn	10.00	4.50
❑ 4 Derek Jeter	10.00	4.50
❑ 5 Chipper Jones	10.00	4.50
❑ 6 Greg Maddux	12.00	5.50
❑ 7 Mark McGwire	20.00	9.00
❑ 8 Mike Piazza	12.00	5.50
❑ 9 Cal Ripken	15.00	6.75
❑ 10 Alex Rodriguez	12.00	5.50
❑ 11 Frank Thomas	12.00	5.50
❑ 12 Matt Williams	2.50	1.10

1997 Circa Limited Access

	MINT	NRMT
COMPLETE SET (15)	180.00	80.00
COMMON CARD (1-15)	5.00	2.20
❑ 1 Jeff Bagwell	8.00	3.60
❑ 2 Albert Belle	6.00	2.70
❑ 3 Barry Bonds	6.00	2.70
❑ 4 Juan Gonzalez	12.00	5.50
❑ 5 Ken Griffey Jr.	25.00	11.00
❑ 6 Tony Gwynn	12.00	5.50
❑ 7 Derek Jeter	12.00	5.50
❑ 8 Chipper Jones	12.00	5.50
❑ 9 Greg Maddux	15.00	6.75
❑ 10 Mark McGwire	25.00	11.00
❑ 11 Mike Piazza	15.00	6.75
❑ 12 Cal Ripken	20.00	9.00
❑ 13 Alex Rodriguez	15.00	6.75
❑ 14 Frank Thomas	15.00	6.75
❑ 15 Mo Vaughn	6.00	2.70

1997 Circa Rave Reviews

	MINT	NRMT
COMPLETE SET (12)	400.00	180.00
COMMON CARD (1-12)	12.00	5.50
❑ 1 Albert Belle	20.00	9.00
❑ 2 Barry Bonds	15.00	6.75
❑ 3 Juan Gonzalez	30.00	13.50
❑ 4 Ken Griffey Jr.	60.00	27.00
❑ 5 Tony Gwynn	30.00	13.50
❑ 6 Greg Maddux	40.00	18.00
❑ 7 Mark McGwire	60.00	27.00
❑ 8 Eddie Murray	12.00	5.50
❑ 9 Mike Piazza	40.00	18.00
❑ 10 Cal Ripken	50.00	22.00
❑ 11 Alex Rodriguez	50.00	22.00
❑ 12 Frank Thomas	40.00	18.00

1998 Circa Thunder

	MINT	NRMT
COMPLETE SET (300)	30.00	13.50
COMMON CARD (1-300)	.15	.07
❑ 1 Ben Grieve	1.25	.55
❑ 2 Derek Jeter	1.50	.70
❑ 3 Alex Rodriguez	2.00	.90
❑ 4 Paul Molitor	.60	.25
❑ 5 Nomar Garciaparra	2.00	.90
❑ 6 Fred McGriff	.40	.18
❑ 7 Kenny Lofton	.60	.25
❑ 8 Cal Ripken	2.50	1.10
❑ 9 Matt Williams	.25	.11
❑ 10 Chipper Jones	1.50	.70
❑ 11 Barry Larkin	.40	.18
❑ 12 Steve Finley	.25	.11
❑ 13 Billy Wagner	.25	.11
❑ 14 Rico Brogna	.25	.11
❑ 15 Tim Salmon	.60	.25
❑ 16 Hideo Nomo	.75	.35
❑ 17 Tony Clark	.40	.18
❑ 18 Jason Kendall	.25	.11
❑ 19 Juan Gonzalez	1.50	.70
❑ 20 Jeromy Burnitz	.25	.11
❑ 21 Roger Clemens	1.25	.55
❑ 22 Mark Grace	.40	.18
❑ 23 Robin Ventura	.25	.11
❑ 24 Manny Ramirez	.60	.25
❑ 25 Mark McGwire	4.00	1.80
❑ 26 Gary Sheffield	.40	.18
❑ 27 Vladimir Guerrero	1.00	.45
❑ 28 Butch Huskey	.15	.07
❑ 29 Cecil Fielder	.25	.11
❑ 30 Rod Myers	.15	.07
❑ 31 Greg Maddux	2.00	.90
❑ 32 Bill Mueller	.25	.11
❑ 33 Larry Walker	.60	.25
❑ 34 Henry Rodriguez	.25	.11
❑ 35 Mike Mussina	.60	.25
❑ 36 Ricky Ledee	.25	.11
❑ 37 Bobby Bonilla	.25	.11
❑ 38 Curt Schilling	.25	.11
❑ 39 Luis Gonzalez	.15	.07
❑ 40 Troy Percival	.25	.11
❑ 41 Eric Milton	.25	.11
❑ 42 Mo Vaughn	.75	.35
❑ 43 Raul Mondesi	.40	.18
❑ 44 Kenny Rogers	.15	.07
❑ 45 Frank Thomas	2.00	.90
❑ 46 Jose Canseco	.60	.25
❑ 47 Tom Glavine	.60	.25
❑ 48 Rich Butler	.40	.18
❑ 49 Jay Buhner	.25	.11
❑ 50 Jose Cruz Jr.	.75	.35
❑ 51 Bernie Williams	.60	.25
❑ 52 Doug Glanville	.25	.11
❑ 53 Travis Fryman	.25	.11
❑ 54 Rey Ordonez	.25	.11
❑ 55 Jeff Conine	.25	.11
❑ 56 Trevor Hoffman	.25	.11
❑ 57 Kirk Rueter UER back Reuter	.15	.07
❑ 58 Ron Gant	.15	.07
❑ 59 Carl Everett	.15	.07
❑ 60 Joe Carter	.25	.11
❑ 61 Livan Hernandez	.25	.11
❑ 62 John Jaha	.15	.07
❑ 63 Ivan Rodriguez	.75	.35
❑ 64 Willie Blair	.15	.07
❑ 65 Todd Helton	.75	.35
❑ 66 Kevin Young	.25	.11
❑ 67 Mike Caruso	.25	.11
❑ 68 Steve Trachsel	.15	.07
❑ 69 Marty Cordova	.15	.07
❑ 70 Alex Fernandez	.15	.07
❑ 71 Eric Karros	.25	.11
❑ 72 Reggie Sanders	.25	.11
❑ 73 Russ Davis	.25	.11
❑ 74 Roberto Hernandez	.15	.07
❑ 75 Barry Bonds	.75	.35
❑ 76 Alex Gonzalez	.15	.07
❑ 77 Roberto Alomar	.60	.25
❑ 78 Troy O'Leary	.25	.11
❑ 79 Bernard Gilkey	.15	.07
❑ 80 Ismael Valdes	.25	.11
❑ 81 Travis Lee	1.25	.55
❑ 82 Brant Brown	.25	.11
❑ 83 Gary DiSarcina	.15	.07
❑ 84 Joe Randa	.15	.07
❑ 85 Jaret Wright	.75	.35
❑ 86 Quilvio Veras	.15	.07
❑ 87 Rickey Henderson	.60	.25
❑ 88 Randall Simon	.25	.11
❑ 89 Mariano Rivera	.25	.11
❑ 90 Ugueth Urbina	.25	.11
❑ 91 Fernando Vina	.15	.07
❑ 92 Alan Benes	.25	.11
❑ 93 Dante Bichette	.25	.11
❑ 94 Karim Garcia	.25	.11
❑ 95 A.J. Hinch	.25	.11
❑ 96 Shane Reynolds	.25	.11
❑ 97 Kevin Stocker	.15	.07
❑ 98 John Wetteland	.25	.11
❑ 99 Terry Steinbach	.25	.11
❑ 100 Ken Griffey Jr.	3.00	1.35
❑ 101 Mike Cameron	.25	.11
❑ 102 Damion Easley	.25	.11
❑ 103 Randy Myers	.25	.11
❑ 104 Jason Schmidt	.15	.07
❑ 105 Jeff King	.25	.11
❑ 106 Gregg Jefferies	.15	.07
❑ 107 Sean Casey	.25	.11
❑ 108 Mark Kotsay	.40	.18
❑ 109 Brad Fullmer	.25	.11
❑ 110 Wilson Alvarez	.25	.11
❑ 111 Sandy Alomar Jr.	.25	.11
❑ 112 Walt Weiss	.25	.11
❑ 113 Doug Jones	.15	.07
❑ 114 Andy Benes	.25	.11
❑ 115 Paul O'Neill	.25	.11
❑ 116 Dennis Eckersley	.25	.11
❑ 117 Todd Greene	.25	.11
❑ 118 Bobby Jones	.15	.07
❑ 119 Darrin Fletcher	.15	.07
❑ 120 Eric Young	.25	.11
❑ 121 Jeffrey Hammonds	.25	.11
❑ 122 Mickey Morandini	.15	.07
❑ 123 Chuck Knoblauch	.60	.25
❑ 124 Moises Alou	.40	.18
❑ 125 Miguel Tejada	.25	.11
❑ 126 Brian Anderson	.25	.11
❑ 127 Edgar Renteria	.25	.11
❑ 128 Mike Lansing	.15	.07
❑ 129 Quinton McCracken	.25	.11
❑ 130 Ray Lankford	.25	.11
❑ 131 Andy Ashby	.15	.07
❑ 132 Kelvim Escobar	.25	.11
❑ 133 Mike Lowell	.60	.25
❑ 134 Randy Johnson	.60	.25
❑ 135 Andres Galarraga	.60	.25
❑ 136 Armando Benitez	.15	.07
❑ 137 Rusty Greer	.25	.11
❑ 138 Jose Guillen	.25	.11
❑ 139 Paul Konerko	.60	.25
❑ 140 Edgardo Alfonzo	.25	.11
❑ 141 Jim Leyritz	.15	.07
❑ 142 Mark Clark	.15	.07
❑ 143 Brian Johnson	.15	.07
❑ 144 Scott Rolen	1.50	.70
❑ 145 David Cone	.40	.18
❑ 146 Jeff Shaw	.25	.11
❑ 147 Shannon Stewart	.25	.11
❑ 148 Brian Hunter	.25	.11
❑ 149 Garret Anderson	.25	.11
❑ 150 Jeff Bagwell	1.00	.45
❑ 151 James Baldwin	.25	.11
❑ 152 Devon White	.25	.11
❑ 153 Jim Thome	.60	.25

Card	MINT	NRMT
❑ 154 Wally Joyner	.25	.11
❑ 155 Mark Wohlers	.15	.07
❑ 156 Jeff Cirillo	.25	.11
❑ 157 Jason Giambi	.25	.11
❑ 158 Royce Clayton	.15	.07
❑ 159 Dennis Reyes	.25	.11
❑ 160 Raul Casanova	.15	.07
❑ 161 Pedro Astacio	.15	.07
❑ 162 Todd Dunwoody	.25	.11
❑ 163 Sammy Sosa	1.50	.70
❑ 164 Todd Hundley	.25	.11
❑ 165 Wade Boggs	.60	.25
❑ 166 Robb Nen	.25	.11
❑ 167 Dan Wilson	.15	.07
❑ 168 Hideki Irabu	.40	.18
❑ 169 B.J. Surhoff	.25	.11
❑ 170 Carlos Delgado	.25	.11
❑ 171 Fernando Tatis	.25	.11
❑ 172 Bob Abreu	.25	.11
❑ 173 David Ortiz	.25	.11
❑ 174 Tony Womack	.25	.11
❑ 175 Magglio Ordonez	.75	.35
❑ 176 Aaron Boone	.15	.07
❑ 177 Brian Giles	.25	.11
❑ 178 Kevin Appier	.25	.11
❑ 179 Chuck Finley	.25	.11
❑ 180 Brian Rose	.25	.11
❑ 181 Ryan Klesko	.25	.11
❑ 182 Mike Stanley	.15	.07
❑ 183 Dave Nilsson	.15	.07
❑ 184 Carlos Perez	.25	.11
❑ 185 Jeff Blauser	.15	.07
❑ 186 Richard Hidalgo	.25	.11
❑ 187 Charles Johnson	.25	.11
❑ 188 Vinny Castilla	.40	.18
❑ 189 Joey Hamilton	.25	.11
❑ 190 Bubba Trammell	.25	.11
❑ 191 Eli Marrero	.25	.11
❑ 192 Scott Erickson	.25	.11
❑ 193 Pat Hentgen	.25	.11
❑ 194 Jorge Fabregas	.15	.07
❑ 195 Tino Martinez	.60	.25
❑ 196 Bobby Higginson	.40	.18
❑ 197 Dave Hollins	.15	.07
❑ 198 Rolando Arrojo	1.00	.45
❑ 199 Joey Cora	.25	.11
❑ 200 Mike Piazza	2.00	.90
❑ 201 Reggie Jefferson	.15	.07
❑ 202 John Smoltz	.25	.11
❑ 203 Bobby Smith	.25	.11
❑ 204 Tom Goodwin	.15	.07
❑ 205 Omar Vizquel	.25	.11
❑ 206 John Olerud	.25	.11
❑ 207 Matt Stairs	.25	.11
❑ 208 Bobby Estalella	.25	.11
❑ 209 Miguel Cairo	.25	.11
❑ 210 Shawn Green	.25	.11
❑ 211 Jon Nunnally	.15	.07
❑ 212 Al Leiter	.25	.11
❑ 213 Matt Lawton	.25	.11
❑ 214 Brady Anderson	.25	.11
❑ 215 Jeff Kent	.25	.11
❑ 216 Ray Durham	.25	.11
❑ 217 Al Martin	.15	.07
❑ 218 Jeff D'Amico	.15	.07
❑ 219 Kevin Tapani	.15	.07
❑ 220 Jim Edmonds	.40	.18
❑ 221 Jose Vizcaino	.15	.07
❑ 222 Jay Bell	.25	.11
❑ 223 Ken Caminiti	.40	.18
❑ 224 Craig Biggio	.60	.25
❑ 225 Bartolo Colon	.25	.11
❑ 226 Neifi Perez	.25	.11
❑ 227 Delino DeShields	.15	.07
❑ 228 Javier Lopez	.25	.11
❑ 229 David Wells	.40	.18
❑ 230 Brad Rigby	.15	.07
❑ 231 John Franco	.25	.11
❑ 232 Michael Coleman	.25	.11
❑ 233 Edgar Martinez	.25	.11
❑ 234 Francisco Cordova	.15	.07
❑ 235 Johnny Damon	.25	.11
❑ 236 Deivi Cruz	.15	.07
❑ 237 J.T. Snow	.25	.11
❑ 238 Enrique Wilson	.25	.11
❑ 239 Rondell White	.25	.11
❑ 240 Aaron Sele	.25	.11
❑ 241 Tony Saunders	.15	.07
❑ 242 Ricky Bottalico	.25	.11
❑ 243 Cliff Floyd	.25	.11
❑ 244 Chili Davis	.25	.11
❑ 245 Brian McRae	.15	.07
❑ 246 Brad Radke	.25	.11
❑ 247 Chan Ho Park	.60	.25
❑ 248 Lance Johnson	.15	.07
❑ 249 Rafael Palmeiro	.40	.18
❑ 250 Tony Gwynn	1.50	.70
❑ 251 Denny Neagle	.25	.11
❑ 252 Dean Palmer	.25	.11
❑ 253 Jose Valentin	.15	.07
❑ 254 Matt Morris	.25	.11
❑ 255 Ellis Burks	.25	.11
❑ 256 Jeff Suppan	.15	.07
❑ 257 Jimmy Key	.25	.11
❑ 258 Justin Thompson	.25	.11
❑ 259 Brett Tomko	.25	.11
❑ 260 Mark Grudzielanek	.25	.11
❑ 261 Mike Hampton	.15	.07
❑ 262 Jeff Fassero	.15	.07
❑ 263 Charles Nagy	.25	.11
❑ 264 Pedro Martinez	.60	.25
❑ 265 Todd Zeile	.25	.11
❑ 266 Will Clark	.60	.25
❑ 267 Abraham Nunez	.25	.11
❑ 268 Dave Martinez	.15	.07
❑ 269 Jason Dickson	.25	.11
❑ 270 Eric Davis	.25	.11
❑ 271 Kevin Orie	.15	.07
❑ 272 Derrek Lee	.25	.11
❑ 273 Andruw Jones	.75	.35
❑ 274 Juan Encarnacion	.25	.11
❑ 275 Carlos Baerga	.25	.11
❑ 276 Andy Pettitte	.40	.18
❑ 277 Brent Brede	.15	.07
❑ 278 Paul Sorrento	.15	.07
❑ 279 Mike Lieberthal	.15	.07
❑ 280 Marquis Grissom UER #'d 8 instead of 280	.25	.11
❑ 281 Darin Erstad	.75	.35
❑ 282 Willie Greene	.25	.11
❑ 283 Derek Bell	.25	.11
❑ 284 Scott Spiezio	.15	.07
❑ 285 David Segui	.25	.11
❑ 286 Albert Belle	.60	.25
❑ 287 Ramon Martinez	.25	.11
❑ 288 Jeremi Gonzalez	.25	.11
❑ 289 Shawn Estes	.25	.11
❑ 290 Ron Coomer	.15	.07
❑ 291 John Valentin	.25	.11
❑ 292 Kevin Brown	.40	.18
❑ 293 Michael Tucker	.25	.11
❑ 294 Brian Jordan	.25	.11
❑ 295 Darryl Kile	.25	.11
❑ 296 David Justice	.60	.25
❑ 297 Frank Thomas CL	1.00	.45
❑ 298 Alex Rodriguez CL	1.00	.45
❑ 299 Ken Griffey Jr. CL	1.50	.70
❑ 300 Jose Cruz Jr. CL	.40	.18
❑ P8 Cal Ripken Promo	3.00	1.35

1998 Circa Thunder Rave

	MINT	NRMT
COMMON CARD (1-296)	8.00	3.60

*STARS: 20X TO 50X BASIC CIRCA
*YOUNG STARS: 15X TO 40X BASIC CIRCA
*RC'S/PROSPECTS: 10X TO 25X BASIC CARDS

1998 Circa Thunder Super Rave

	MINT	NRMT
COMMON CARD (1-296)	30.00	13.50

*STARS: 100X TO 200X BASIC CIRCA
*YOUNG STARS: 75X TO 150X BASIC CIRCA
*RC'S/PROSPECTS: 50X TO 100X BASIC CARDS

1998 Circa Thunder Boss

	MINT	NRMT
COMPLETE SET (20)	40.00	18.00
COMMON CARD (1-20)	1.25	.55
❑ 1 Jeff Bagwell	2.00	.90
❑ 2 Barry Bonds	1.50	.70
❑ 3 Roger Clemens	2.50	1.10
❑ 4 Jose Cruz Jr.	1.50	.70
❑ 5 Nomar Garciaparra	4.00	1.80
❑ 6 Juan Gonzalez	3.00	1.35
❑ 7 Ken Griffey Jr.	6.00	2.70
❑ 8 Tony Gwynn	3.00	1.35
❑ 9 Derek Jeter	3.00	1.35
❑ 10 Chipper Jones	3.00	1.35
❑ 11 Travis Lee	2.50	1.10
❑ 12 Greg Maddux	4.00	1.80
❑ 13 Pedro Martinez	1.25	.55
❑ 14 Mark McGwire	8.00	3.60
❑ 15 Mike Piazza	4.00	1.80
❑ 16 Cal Ripken	5.00	2.20
❑ 17 Alex Rodriguez	4.00	1.80
❑ 18 Scott Rolen	3.00	1.35
❑ 19 Frank Thomas	4.00	1.80
❑ 20 Larry Walker	1.25	.55

1998 Circa Thunder Fast Track

	MINT	NRMT
COMPLETE SET (10)	40.00	18.00
COMMON CARD (1-10)	1.00	.45
❑ 1 Jose Cruz Jr.	3.00	1.35
❑ 2 Juan Encarnacion	1.50	.70
❑ 3 Brad Fullmer	1.50	.70
❑ 4 Nomar Garciaparra	8.00	3.60
❑ 5 Todd Helton	3.00	1.35
❑ 6 Livan Hernandez	1.00	.45
❑ 7 Travis Lee	5.00	2.20
❑ 8 Neifi Perez	1.00	.45
❑ 9 Scott Rolen	6.00	2.70
❑ 10 Jaret Wright	3.00	1.35

1998 Circa Thunder Limited Access

	MINT	NRMT
COMPLETE SET (15)	150.00	70.00
COMMON CARD (1-15)	5.00	2.20
❑ 1 Jeff Bagwell	8.00	3.60
❑ 2 Roger Clemens	10.00	4.50
❑ 3 Jose Cruz Jr.	5.00	2.20
❑ 4 Nomar Garciaparra	15.00	6.75
❑ 5 Juan Gonzalez	12.00	5.50
❑ 6 Ken Griffey Jr.	25.00	11.00
❑ 7 Tony Gwynn	12.00	5.50
❑ 8 Derek Jeter	12.00	5.50
❑ 9 Greg Maddux	15.00	6.75
❑ 10 Pedro Martinez	5.00	2.20
❑ 11 Mark McGwire	30.00	13.50
❑ 12 Mike Piazza	15.00	6.75
❑ 13 Alex Rodriguez	15.00	6.75
❑ 14 Frank Thomas	15.00	6.75
❑ 15 Larry Walker	5.00	2.20

1998 Circa Thunder Quick Strike

	MINT	NRMT
COMPLETE SET (12)	100.00	45.00
COMMON CARD (1-12)	4.00	1.80
❑ 1 Jeff Bagwell	6.00	2.70
❑ 2 Roger Clemens	8.00	3.60
❑ 3 Jose Cruz Jr.	10.00	4.50
❑ 4 Nomar Garciaparra	12.00	5.50
❑ 5 Ken Griffey Jr.	20.00	9.00
❑ 6 Greg Maddux	12.00	5.50
❑ 7 Pedro Martinez	4.00	1.80
❑ 8 Mark McGwire	25.00	11.00
❑ 9 Mike Piazza	12.00	5.50
❑ 10 Alex Rodriguez	12.00	5.50
❑ 11 Frank Thomas	12.00	5.50
❑ 12 Larry Walker	4.00	1.80

1998 Circa Thunder Rave Review

	MINT	NRMT
COMPLETE SET (15)	600.00	275.00
COMMON CARD (1-15)	15.00	6.75
❑ 1 Jeff Bagwell	25.00	11.00
❑ 2 Barry Bonds	20.00	9.00
❑ 3 Roger Clemens	30.00	13.50
❑ 4 Jose Cruz Jr.	20.00	9.00
❑ 5 Nomar Garciaparra	50.00	22.00
❑ 6 Juan Gonzalez	40.00	18.00
❑ 7 Ken Griffey Jr.	80.00	36.00
❑ 8 Tony Gwynn	40.00	18.00
❑ 9 Derek Jeter	40.00	18.00
❑ 10 Greg Maddux	50.00	22.00
❑ 11 Mark McGwire	100.00	45.00
❑ 12 Mike Piazza	50.00	22.00
❑ 13 Alex Rodriguez	50.00	22.00
❑ 14 Frank Thomas	50.00	22.00
❑ 15 Larry Walker	15.00	6.75

1998 Circa Thunder Thunder Boomers

	MINT	NRMT
COMPLETE SET (12)	150.00	70.00
COMMON CARD (1-12)	5.00	2.20
❑ 1 Jeff Bagwell	12.00	5.50
❑ 2 Barry Bonds	10.00	4.50
❑ 3 Jay Buhner	5.00	2.20
❑ 4 Andres Galarraga	8.00	3.60
❑ 5 Juan Gonzalez	20.00	9.00
❑ 6 Ken Griffey Jr.	40.00	18.00
❑ 7 Tino Martinez	8.00	3.60
❑ 8 Mark McGwire	50.00	22.00
❑ 9 Mike Piazza	25.00	11.00
❑ 10 Frank Thomas	25.00	11.00
❑ 11 Jim Thome	8.00	3.60
❑ 12 Larry Walker	8.00	3.60

1994 Collector's Choice

	MINT	NRMT
COMPLETE SET (670)	25.00	11.00
COMP.FACT.SET (675)	30.00	13.50
COMPLETE SERIES 1 (320)	10.00	4.50
COMPLETE SERIES 2 (350)	15.00	6.75
COMMON CARD (1-670)	.10	.05
❑ 1 Rich Becker	.10	.05
❑ 2 Greg Blosser	.10	.05
❑ 3 Midre Cummings	.10	.05
❑ 4 Carlos Delgado	.30	.14
❑ 5 Steve Dreyer	.10	.05
❑ 6 Carl Everett	.10	.05
❑ 7 Cliff Floyd	.20	.09
❑ 8 Alex Gonzalez	.10	.05
❑ 9 Shawn Green	.20	.09
❑ 10 Butch Huskey	.20	.09
❑ 11 Mark Hutton	.10	.05
❑ 12 Miguel Jimenez	.10	.05
❑ 13 Steve Karsay	.10	.05
❑ 14 Marc Newfield	.10	.05
❑ 15 Luis Ortiz	.10	.05
❑ 16 Manny Ramirez	.50	.23
❑ 17 Johnny Ruffin	.10	.05
❑ 18 Scott Stahoviak	.10	.05
❑ 19 Salomon Torres	.10	.05
❑ 20 Gabe White	.10	.05
❑ 21 Brian Anderson	.30	.14
❑ 22 Wayne Gomes	.10	.05
❑ 23 Jeff Granger	.10	.05
❑ 24 Steve Soderstrom	.10	.05
❑ 25 Trot Nixon	.50	.23
❑ 26 Kirk Presley	.20	.09
❑ 27 Matt Brunson	.10	.05
❑ 28 Brooks Kieschnick	.20	.09
❑ 29 Billy Wagner	.50	.23
❑ 30 Matt Drews	.20	.09
❑ 31 Kurt Abbott	.10	.05
❑ 32 Luis Alicea	.10	.05
❑ 33 Roberto Alomar	.40	.18
❑ 34 Sandy Alomar Jr.	.20	.09
❑ 35 Moises Alou	.30	.14

	No.	Player	Price	Price
❑	36	Wilson Alvarez	.20	.09
❑	37	Rich Amaral	.10	.05
❑	38	Eric Anthony	.10	.05
❑	39	Luis Aquino	.10	.05
❑	40	Jack Armstrong	.10	.05
❑	41	Rene Arocha	.10	.05
❑	42	Rich Aude	.10	.05
❑	43	Brad Ausmus	.10	.05
❑	44	Steve Avery	.10	.05
❑	45	Bob Ayrault	.10	.05
❑	46	Willie Banks	.10	.05
❑	47	Bret Barberie	.10	.05
❑	48	Kim Batiste	.10	.05
❑	49	Rod Beck	.10	.05
❑	50	Jason Bere	.10	.05
❑	51	Sean Berry	.10	.05
❑	52	Dante Bichette	.20	.09
❑	53	Jeff Blauser	.10	.05
❑	54	Mike Blowers	.10	.05
❑	55	Tim Bogar	.10	.05
❑	56	Tom Bolton	.10	.05
❑	57	Ricky Bones	.10	.05
❑	58	Bobby Bonilla	.20	.09
❑	59	Bret Boone	.20	.09
❑	60	Pat Borders	.10	.05
❑	61	Mike Bordick	.10	.05
❑	62	Daryl Boston	.10	.05
❑	63	Ryan Bowen	.10	.05
❑	64	Jeff Branson	.10	.05
❑	65	George Brett	.75	.35
❑	66	Steve Buechele	.10	.05
❑	67	Dave Burba	.10	.05
❑	68	John Burkett	.10	.05
❑	69	Jeromy Burnitz	.20	.09
❑	70	Brett Bulter	.20	.09
❑	71	Rob Butler	.10	.05
❑	72	Ken Caminiti	.30	.14
❑	73	Cris Carpenter	.10	.05
❑	74	Vinny Castilla	.20	.09
❑	75	Andujar Cedeno	.10	.05
❑	76	Wes Chamberlain	.10	.05
❑	77	Archi Cianfrocco	.10	.05
❑	78	Dave Clark	.10	.05
❑	79	Jerald Clark	.10	.05
❑	80	Royce Clayton	.10	.05
❑	81	David Cone	.30	.14
❑	82	Jeff Conine	.20	.09
❑	83	Steve Cooke	.10	.05
❑	84	Scott Cooper	.10	.05
❑	85	Joey Cora	.20	.09
❑	86	Tim Costo	.10	.05
❑	87	Chad Curtis	.10	.05
❑	88	Ron Darling	.10	.05
❑	89	Danny Darwin	.10	.05
❑	90	Rob Deer	.10	.05
❑	91	Jim Deshaies	.10	.05
❑	92	Delino DeShields	.10	.05
❑	93	Rob Dibble	.10	.05
❑	94	Gary DiSarcina	.10	.05
❑	95	Doug Drabek	.10	.05
❑	96	Scott Erickson	.20	.09
❑	97	Rikkert Faneyte	.10	.05
❑	98	Jeff Fassero	.10	.05
❑	99	Alex Fernandez	.10	.05
❑	100	Cecil Fielder	.20	.09
❑	101	Dave Fleming	.10	.05
❑	102	Darrin Fletcher	.10	.05
❑	103	Scott Fletcher	.10	.05
❑	104	Mike Gallego	.10	.05
❑	105	Carlos Garcia	.10	.05
❑	106	Jeff Gardner	.10	.05
❑	107	Brent Gates	.10	.05
❑	108	Benji Gil	.10	.05
❑	109	Bernard Gilkey	.10	.05
❑	110	Chris Gomez	.10	.05
❑	111	Luis Gonzalez	.10	.05
❑	112	Tom Gordon	.10	.05
❑	113	Jim Gott	.10	.05
❑	114	Mark Grace	.30	.14
❑	115	Tommy Greene	.10	.05
❑	116	Willie Greene	.20	.09
❑	117	Ken Griffey Jr.	2.00	.90
❑	118	Bill Gullickson	.10	.05
❑	119	Ricky Gutierrez	.10	.05
❑	120	Juan Guzman	.10	.05
❑	121	Chris Gwynn	.10	.05
❑	122	Tony Gwynn	1.00	.45
❑	123	Jeffrey Hammonds	.20	.09
❑	124	Erik Hanson	.10	.05
❑	125	Gene Harris	.10	.05
❑	126	Greg W. Harris	.10	.05
❑	127	Bryan Harvey	.10	.05
❑	128	Billy Hatcher	.10	.05
❑	129	Hilly Hathaway	.10	.05
❑	130	Charlie Hayes	.10	.05
❑	131	Rickey Henderson	.40	.18
❑	132	Mike Henneman	.10	.05
❑	133	Pat Hentgen	.20	.09
❑	134	Roberto Hernandez	.10	.05
❑	135	Orel Hershiser	.20	.09
❑	136	Phil Hiatt	.10	.05
❑	137	Glenallen Hill	.10	.05
❑	138	Ken Hill	.10	.05
❑	139	Eric Hillman	.10	.05
❑	140	Chris Hoiles	.10	.05
❑	141	Dave Hollins	.10	.05
❑	142	David Hulse	.10	.05
❑	143	Todd Hundley	.20	.09
❑	144	Pete Incaviglia	.10	.05
❑	145	Danny Jackson	.10	.05
❑	146	John Jaha	.10	.05
❑	147	Domingo Jean	.10	.05
❑	148	Gregg Jefferies	.10	.05
❑	149	Reggie Jefferson	.10	.05
❑	150	Lance Johnson	.10	.05
❑	151	Bobby Jones	.10	.05
❑	152	Chipper Jones	1.25	.55
❑	153	Todd Jones	.10	.05
❑	154	Brian Jordan	.20	.09
❑	155	Wally Joyner	.20	.09
❑	156	David Justice	.40	.18
❑	157	Ron Karkovice	.10	.05
❑	158	Eric Karros	.20	.09
❑	159	Jeff Kent	.20	.09
❑	160	Jimmy Key	.20	.09
❑	161	Mark Kiefer	.10	.05
❑	162	Darryl Kile	.20	.09
❑	163	Jeff King	.10	.05
❑	164	Wayne Kirby	.10	.05
❑	165	Ryan Klesko	.20	.09
❑	166	Chuck Knoblauch	.40	.18
❑	167	Chad Kreuter	.10	.05
❑	168	John Kruk	.20	.09
❑	169	Mark Langston	.10	.05
❑	170	Mike Lansing	.20	.09
❑	171	Barry Larkin	.30	.14
❑	172	Manuel Lee	.10	.05
❑	173	Phil Leftwich	.10	.05
❑	174	Darren Lewis	.10	.05
❑	175	Derek Lilliquist	.10	.05
❑	176	Jose Lind	.10	.05
❑	177	Albie Lopez	.10	.05
❑	178	Javier Lopez	.30	.14
❑	179	Torey Lovullo	.10	.05
❑	180	Scott Lydy	.10	.05
❑	181	Mike Macfarlane	.10	.05
❑	182	Shane Mack	.10	.05
❑	183	Greg Maddux	1.25	.55
❑	184	Dave Magadan	.10	.05
❑	185	Joe Magrane	.10	.05
❑	186	Kirk Manwaring	.10	.05
❑	187	Al Martin	.10	.05
❑	188	Pedro A. Martinez	.10	.05
❑	189	Pedro Martinez	.50	.23
❑	190	Ramon Martinez	.20	.09
❑	191	Tino Martinez	.40	.18
❑	192	Don Mattingly	.60	.25
❑	193	Derrick May	.10	.05
❑	194	David McCarty	.10	.05
❑	195	Ben McDonald	.10	.05
❑	196	Roger McDowell	.10	.05
❑	197	Fred McGriff UER (Stats on back have 73 stolen bases for 1989; should be 7)	.30	.14
❑	198	Mark McLemore	.10	.05
❑	199	Greg McMichael	.10	.05
❑	200	Jeff McNeely	.10	.05
❑	201	Brian McRae	.10	.05
❑	202	Pat Meares	.10	.05
❑	203	Roberto Mejia	.10	.05
❑	204	Orlando Merced	.10	.05
❑	205	Jose Mesa	.10	.05
❑	206	Blas Minor	.10	.05
❑	207	Angel Miranda	.10	.05
❑	208	Paul Molitor	.40	.18
❑	209	Raul Mondesi	.40	.18
❑	210	Jeff Montgomery	.10	.05
❑	211	Mickey Morandini	.10	.05
❑	212	Mike Morgan	.10	.05
❑	213	Jamie Moyer	.10	.05
❑	214	Bobby Munoz	.10	.05
❑	215	Troy Neel	.10	.05
❑	216	Dave Nilsson	.10	.05
❑	217	John O'Donoghue	.10	.05
❑	218	Paul O'Neill	.20	.09
❑	219	Jose Offerman	.10	.05
❑	220	Joe Oliver	.10	.05
❑	221	Greg Olson	.10	.05
❑	222	Donovan Osborne	.10	.05
❑	223	J. Owens	.10	.05
❑	224	Mike Pagliarulo	.10	.05
❑	225	Craig Paquette	.10	.05
❑	226	Roger Pavlik	.10	.05
❑	227	Brad Pennington	.10	.05
❑	228	Eduardo Perez	.10	.05
❑	229	Mike Perez	.10	.05
❑	230	Tony Phillips	.10	.05
❑	231	Hipolito Pichardo	.10	.05
❑	232	Phil Plantier	.10	.05
❑	233	Curtis Pride	.10	.05
❑	234	Tim Pugh	.10	.05
❑	235	Scott Radinsky	.10	.05
❑	236	Pat Rapp	.10	.05
❑	237	Kevin Reimer	.10	.05
❑	238	Armando Reynoso	.10	.05
❑	239	Jose Rijo	.10	.05
❑	240	Cal Ripken	1.50	.70
❑	241	Kevin Roberson	.10	.05
❑	242	Kenny Rogers	.10	.05
❑	243	Kevin Rogers	.10	.05
❑	244	Mel Rojas	.10	.05
❑	245	John Roper	.10	.05
❑	246	Kirk Rueter	.10	.05
❑	247	Scott Ruffcorn	.10	.05
❑	248	Ken Ryan	.10	.05
❑	249	Nolan Ryan	1.50	.70
❑	250	Bret Saberhagen	.20	.09
❑	251	Tim Salmon	.40	.18
❑	252	Reggie Sanders	.20	.09
❑	253	Curt Schilling	.20	.09
❑	254	David Segui	.20	.09
❑	255	Aaron Sele	.20	.09
❑	256	Scott Servais	.10	.05
❑	257	Gary Sheffield	.40	.18
❑	258	Ruben Sierra	.10	.05
❑	259	Don Slaught	.10	.05
❑	260	Lee Smith	.20	.09
❑	261	Cory Snyder	.10	.05
❑	262	Paul Sorrento	.10	.05
❑	263	Sammy Sosa	1.00	.45
❑	264	Bill Spiers	.10	.05
❑	265	Mike Stanley	.10	.05
❑	266	Dave Staton	.10	.05
❑	267	Terry Steinbach	.20	.09
❑	268	Kevin Stocker	.10	.05
❑	269	Todd Stottlemyre	.10	.05
❑	270	Doug Strange	.10	.05
❑	271	Bill Swift	.10	.05
❑	272	Kevin Tapani	.10	.05
❑	273	Tony Tarasco	.10	.05
❑	274	Julian Tavarez	.20	.09
❑	275	Mickey Tettleton	.10	.05
❑	276	Ryan Thompson	.10	.05
❑	277	Chris Turner	.10	.05
❑	278	John Valentin	.20	.09
❑	279	Todd Van Poppel	.10	.05
❑	280	Andy Van Slyke	.20	.09
❑	281	Mo Vaughn	.50	.23
❑	282	Robin Ventura	.20	.09
❑	283	Frank Viola	.10	.05
❑	284	Jose Vizcaino	.10	.05
❑	285	Omar Vizquel	.20	.09
❑	286	Larry Walker	.40	.18
❑	287	Duane Ward	.10	.05

❑	288	Allen Watson	.10	.05
❑	289	Bill Wegman	.10	.05
❑	290	Turk Wendell	.10	.05
❑	291	Lou Whitaker	.20	.09
❑	292	Devon White	.20	.09
❑	293	Rondell White	.20	.09
❑	294	Mark Whiten	.10	.05
❑	295	Darrel Whitmore	.10	.05
❑	296	Bob Wickman	.10	.05
❑	297	Rick Wilkins	.10	.05
❑	298	Bernie Williams	.40	.18
❑	299	Matt Williams	.30	.14
❑	300	Woody Williams	.10	.05
❑	301	Nigel Wilson	.10	.05
❑	302	Dave Winfield	.40	.18
❑	303	Anthony Young	.10	.05
❑	304	Eric Young	.10	.05
❑	305	Todd Zeile	.10	.05
❑	306	Jack McDowell TP John Burkett Tom Glavine	.10	.05
❑	307	Randy Johnson TP	.20	.09
❑	308	Randy Myers TP	.10	.05
❑	309	Jack McDowell TP	.10	.05
❑	310	Mike Piazza TP	.60	.25
❑	311	Barry Bonds TP	.40	.18
❑	312	Andres Galarraga TP	.20	.09
❑	313	Juan Gonzalez TP Barry Bonds	.40	.18
❑	314	Albert Belle TP	.30	.14
❑	315	Kenny Lofton TP	.20	.09
❑	316	Barry Bonds CL	.40	.18
❑	317	Ken Griffey Jr. CL	.50	.23
❑	318	Mike Piazza CL	.60	.25
❑	319	Kirby Puckett CL	.40	.18
❑	320	Nolan Ryan CL	.75	.35
❑	321	Roberto Alomar CL	.20	.09
❑	322	Roger Clemens CL	.40	.18
❑	323	Juan Gonzalez CL	.50	.23
❑	324	Ken Griffey Jr. CL	.50	.23
❑	325	David Justice CL	.20	.09
❑	326	John Kruk CL	.10	.05
❑	327	Frank Thomas CL	.50	.23
❑	328	Tim Salmon TC	.20	.09
❑	329	Jeff Bagwell TC	.40	.18
❑	330	Mark McGwire TC	1.00	.45
❑	331	Roberto Alomar TC	.20	.09
❑	332	David Justice TC	.20	.09
❑	333	Pat Listach TC	.10	.05
❑	334	Ozzie Smith TC	.40	.18
❑	335	Ryne Sandberg TC	.30	.14
❑	336	Mike Piazza TC	.60	.25
❑	337	Cliff Floyd TC	.10	.05
❑	338	Barry Bonds TC	.40	.18
❑	339	Albert Belle TC	.30	.14
❑	340	Ken Griffey Jr. TC	1.00	.45
❑	341	Gary Sheffield TC	.20	.09
❑	342	Dwight Gooden TC	.10	.05
❑	343	Cal Ripken TC	.75	.35
❑	344	Tony Gwynn TC	.50	.23
❑	345	Lenny Dykstra TC	.10	.05
❑	346	Andy Van Slyke TC	.10	.05
❑	347	Juan Gonzalez TC	.50	.23
❑	348	Roger Clemens TC	.40	.18
❑	349	Barry Larkin TC	.10	.05
❑	350	Andres Galarraga TC	.20	.09
❑	351	Kevin Appier TC	.10	.05
❑	352	Cecil Fielder TC	.10	.05
❑	353	Kirby Puckett TC	.40	.18
❑	354	Frank Thomas TC	.60	.25
❑	355	Don Mattingly TC	.30	.14
❑	356	Bo Jackson	.20	.09
❑	357	Randy Johnson	.40	.18
❑	358	Darren Daulton	.20	.09
❑	359	Charlie Hough	.10	.05
❑	360	Andres Galarraga	.40	.18
❑	361	Mike Felder	.10	.05
❑	362	Chris Hammond	.10	.05
❑	363	Shawon Dunston	.10	.05
❑	364	Junior Felix	.10	.05
❑	365	Ray Lankford	.20	.09
❑	366	Darryl Strawberry	.20	.09
❑	367	Dave Magadan	.10	.05
❑	368	Gregg Olson	.10	.05
❑	369	Lenny Dykstra	.20	.09
❑	370	Darrin Jackson	.10	.05
❑	371	Dave Stewart	.20	.09
❑	372	Terry Pendleton	.10	.05
❑	373	Arthur Rhodes	.10	.05
❑	374	Benito Santiago	.10	.05
❑	375	Travis Fryman	.20	.09
❑	376	Scott Brosius	.20	.09
❑	377	Stan Belinda	.10	.05
❑	378	Derek Parks	.10	.05
❑	379	Kevin Seitzer	.10	.05
❑	380	Wade Boggs	.40	.18
❑	381	Wally Whitehurst	.10	.05
❑	382	Scott Leius	.10	.05
❑	383	Danny Tartabull	.10	.05
❑	384	Harold Reynolds	.10	.05
❑	385	Tim Raines	.20	.09
❑	386	Darryl Hamilton	.10	.05
❑	387	Felix Fermin	.10	.05
❑	388	Jim Eisenreich	.10	.05
❑	389	Kurt Abbott	.10	.05
❑	390	Kevin Appier	.20	.09
❑	391	Chris Bosio	.10	.05
❑	392	Randy Tomlin	.10	.05
❑	393	Bob Hamelin	.10	.05
❑	394	Kevin Gross	.10	.05
❑	395	Wil Cordero	.10	.05
❑	396	Joe Girardi	.10	.05
❑	397	Orestes Destrade	.10	.05
❑	398	Chris Haney	.10	.05
❑	399	Xavier Hernandez	.10	.05
❑	400	Mike Piazza	1.25	.55
❑	401	Alex Arias	.10	.05
❑	402	Tom Candiotti	.10	.05
❑	403	Kirk Gibson	.20	.09
❑	404	Chuck Carr	.10	.05
❑	405	Brady Anderson	.20	.09
❑	406	Greg Gagne	.10	.05
❑	407	Bruce Ruffin	.10	.05
❑	408	Scott Hemond	.10	.05
❑	409	Keith Miller	.10	.05
❑	410	John Wetteland	.20	.09
❑	411	Eric Anthony	.10	.05
❑	412	Andre Dawson	.30	.14
❑	413	Doug Henry	.10	.05
❑	414	John Franco	.20	.09
❑	415	Julio Franco	.10	.05
❑	416	Dave Hansen	.10	.05
❑	417	Mike Harkey	.10	.05
❑	418	Jack Armstrong	.10	.05
❑	419	Joe Orsulak	.10	.05
❑	420	John Smoltz	.20	.09
❑	421	Scott Livingstone	.10	.05
❑	422	Darren Holmes	.10	.05
❑	423	Ed Sprague	.10	.05
❑	424	Jay Buhner	.20	.09
❑	425	Kirby Puckett	.60	.25
❑	426	Phil Clark	.10	.05
❑	427	Anthony Young	.10	.05
❑	428	Reggie Jefferson	.10	.05
❑	429	Mariano Duncan	.10	.05
❑	430	Tom Glavine	.40	.18
❑	431	Dave Henderson	.10	.05
❑	432	Melido Perez	.10	.05
❑	433	Paul Wagner	.10	.05
❑	434	Tim Worrell	.10	.05
❑	435	Ozzie Guillen	.10	.05
❑	436	Mike Butcher	.10	.05
❑	437	Jim Deshaies	.10	.05
❑	438	Kevin Young	.10	.05
❑	439	Tom Browning	.10	.05
❑	440	Mike Greenwell	.10	.05
❑	441	Mike Stanton	.10	.05
❑	442	John Doherty	.10	.05
❑	443	John Dopson	.10	.05
❑	444	Carlos Baerga	.20	.09
❑	445	Jack McDowell	.10	.05
❑	446	Kent Mercker	.10	.05
❑	447	Ricky Jordan	.10	.05
❑	448	Jerry Browne	.10	.05
❑	449	Fernando Vina	.10	.05
❑	450	Jim Abbott	.20	.09
❑	451	Teddy Higuera	.10	.05
❑	452	Tim Naehring	.10	.05
❑	453	Jim Leyritz	.20	.09
❑	454	Frank Castillo	.10	.05
❑	455	Joe Carter	.20	.09
❑	456	Craig Biggio	.40	.18
❑	457	Geronimo Pena	.10	.05
❑	458	Alejandro Pena	.10	.05
❑	459	Mike Moore	.10	.05
❑	460	Randy Myers	.10	.05
❑	461	Greg Myers	.10	.05
❑	462	Greg Hibbard	.10	.05
❑	463	Jose Guzman	.10	.05
❑	464	Tom Pagnozzi	.10	.05
❑	465	Marquis Grissom	.20	.09
❑	466	Tim Wallach	.10	.05
❑	467	Joe Grahe	.10	.05
❑	468	Bob Tewksbury	.10	.05
❑	469	B.J. Surhoff	.20	.09
❑	470	Kevin Mitchell	.10	.05
❑	471	Bobby Witt	.10	.05
❑	472	Milt Thompson	.10	.05
❑	473	John Smiley	.10	.05
❑	474	Alan Trammell	.30	.14
❑	475	Mike Mussina	.40	.18
❑	476	Rick Aguilera	.10	.05
❑	477	Jose Valentin	.10	.05
❑	478	Harold Baines	.20	.09
❑	479	Bip Roberts	.10	.05
❑	480	Edgar Martinez	.20	.09
❑	481	Rheal Cormier	.10	.05
❑	482	Hal Morris	.10	.05
❑	483	Pat Kelly	.10	.05
❑	484	Roberto Kelly	.10	.05
❑	485	Chris Sabo	.10	.05
❑	486	Kent Hrbek	.20	.09
❑	487	Scott Kamieniecki	.10	.05
❑	488	Walt Weiss	.10	.05
❑	489	Karl Rhodes	.10	.05
❑	490	Derek Bell	.20	.09
❑	491	Chili Davis	.20	.09
❑	492	Brian Harper	.10	.05
❑	493	Felix Jose	.10	.05
❑	494	Trevor Hoffman	.20	.09
❑	495	Dennis Eckersley	.20	.09
❑	496	Pedro Astacio	.10	.05
❑	497	Jay Bell	.20	.09
❑	498	Randy Velarde	.10	.05
❑	499	David Wells	.30	.14
❑	500	Frank Thomas	1.25	.55
❑	501	Mark Lemke	.10	.05
❑	502	Mike Devereaux	.10	.05
❑	503	Chuck McElroy	.10	.05
❑	504	Luis Polonia	.10	.05
❑	505	Damion Easley	.20	.09
❑	506	Greg A. Harris	.10	.05
❑	507	Chris James	.10	.05
❑	508	Terry Mulholland	.10	.05
❑	509	Pete Smith	.10	.05
❑	510	Rickey Henderson	.40	.18
❑	511	Sid Fernandez	.10	.05
❑	512	Al Leiter	.20	.09
❑	513	Doug Jones	.10	.05
❑	514	Steve Farr	.10	.05
❑	515	Chuck Finley	.20	.09
❑	516	Bobby Thigpen	.10	.05
❑	517	Jim Edmonds	.40	.18
❑	518	Graeme Lloyd	.10	.05
❑	519	Dwight Gooden	.20	.09
❑	520	Pat Listach	.10	.05
❑	521	Kevin Bass	.10	.05
❑	522	Willie Banks	.10	.05
❑	523	Steve Finley	.20	.09
❑	524	Delino DeShields	.10	.05
❑	525	Mark McGwire	2.00	.90
❑	526	Greg Swindell	.10	.05
❑	527	Chris Nabholz	.10	.05
❑	528	Scott Sanders	.10	.05
❑	529	David Segui	.20	.09
❑	530	Howard Johnson	.10	.05
❑	531	Jaime Navarro	.10	.05
❑	532	Jose Vizcaino	.10	.05
❑	533	Mark Lewis	.10	.05
❑	534	Pete Harnisch	.10	.05
❑	535	Robby Thompson	.10	.05
❑	536	Marcus Moore	.10	.05
❑	537	Kevin Brown	.20	.09
❑	538	Mark Clark	.10	.05
❑	539	Sterling Hitchcock	.20	.09

Card	MINT	NRMT
❑ 540 Will Clark	.40	.18
❑ 541 Denis Boucher	.10	.05
❑ 542 Jack Morris	.20	.09
❑ 543 Pedro Munoz	.10	.05
❑ 544 Bret Boone	.20	.09
❑ 545 Ozzie Smith	.50	.23
❑ 546 Dennis Martinez	.20	.09
❑ 547 Dan Wilson	.10	.05
❑ 548 Rick Sutcliffe	.10	.05
❑ 549 Kevin McReynolds	.10	.05
❑ 550 Roger Clemens	.75	.35
❑ 551 Todd Benzinger	,10	.05
❑ 552 Bill Haselman	.10	.05
❑ 553 Bobby Munoz	.10	.05
❑ 554 Ellis Burks	.20	.09
❑ 555 Ryne Sandberg	.50	.23
❑ 556 Lee Smith	.20	.09
❑ 557 Danny Bautista	.10	.05
❑ 558 Rey Sanchez	.10	.05
❑ 559 Norm Charlton	.10	.05
❑ 560 Jose Canseco	.40	.18
❑ 561 Tim Belcher	.10	.05
❑ 562 Denny Neagle	.20	.09
❑ 563 Eric Davis	.20	.09
❑ 564 Jody Reed	.10	.05
❑ 565 Kenny Lofton	.40	.18
❑ 566 Gary Gaetti	.20	.09
❑ 567 Todd Worrell	.10	.05
❑ 568 Mark Portugal	.10	.05
❑ 569 Dick Schofield	.10	.05
❑ 570 Andy Benes	.20	.09
❑ 571 Zane Smith	.10	.05
❑ 572 Bobby Ayala	.10	.05
❑ 573 Chip Hale	.10	.05
❑ 574 Bob Welch	.10	.05
❑ 575 Deion Sanders	.20	.09
❑ 576 Dave Nied	.10	.05
❑ 577 Pat Mahomes	.10	.05
❑ 578 Charles Nagy	.20	.09
❑ 579 Otis Nixon	.10	.05
❑ 580 Dean Palmer	.20	.09
❑ 581 Roberto Petagine	.10	.05
❑ 582 Dwight Smith	.10	.05
❑ 583 Jeff Russell	.10	.05
❑ 584 Mark Dewey	.10	.05
❑ 585 Greg Vaughn	.20	.09
❑ 586 Brian Hunter	.10	.05
❑ 587 Willie McGee	.20	.09
❑ 588 Pedro Martinez	.50	.23
❑ 589 Roger Salkeld	.10	.05
❑ 590 Jeff Bagwell	.60	.25
❑ 591 Spike Owen	.10	.05
❑ 592 Jeff Reardon	.20	.09
❑ 593 Erik Pappas	.10	.05
❑ 594 Brian Williams	.10	.05
❑ 595 Eddie Murray	.40	.18
❑ 596 Henry Rodriguez	.20	.09
❑ 597 Erik Hanson	.10	.05
❑ 598 Stan Javier	.10	.05
❑ 599 Mitch Williams	.10	.05
❑ 600 John Olerud	.20	.09
❑ 601 Vince Coleman	.10	.05
❑ 602 Damon Berryhill	.10	.05
❑ 603 Tom Brunansky	.10	.05
❑ 604 Robb Nen	.10	.05
❑ 605 Rafael Palmeiro	.30	.14
❑ 606 Cal Eldred	.10	.05
❑ 607 Jeff Brantley	.10	.05
❑ 608 Alan Mills	.10	.05
❑ 609 Jeff Nelson	.10	.05
❑ 610 Barry Bonds	.50	.23
❑ 611 Carlos Pulido	.10	.05
❑ 612 Tim Hyers	.10	.05
❑ 613 Steve Howe	.10	.05
❑ 614 Brian Turang	.10	.05
❑ 615 Leo Gomez	.10	.05
❑ 616 Jesse Orosco	.10	.05
❑ 617 Dan Pasqua	.10	.05
❑ 618 Marvin Freeman	.10	.05
❑ 619 Tony Fernandez	.10	.05
❑ 620 Albert Belle	.50	.23
❑ 621 Eddie Taubensee	.10	.05
❑ 622 Mike Jackson	.10	.05
❑ 623 Jose Bautista	.10	.05
❑ 624 Jim Thome	.50	.23
❑ 625 Ivan Rodriguez	.50	.23
❑ 626 Ben Rivera	.10	.05
❑ 627 Dave Valle	.10	.05
❑ 628 Tom Henke	.10	.05
❑ 629 Omar Vizquel	.20	.09
❑ 630 Juan Gonzalez	1.00	.45
❑ 631 Roberto Alomar UP	.20	.09
❑ 632 Barry Bonds UP	.40	.18
❑ 633 Juan Gonzalez UP	.50	.23
❑ 634 Ken Griffey Jr. UP	1.00	.45
❑ 635 Michael Jordan UP	2.50	1.10
❑ 636 David Justice UP	.20	.09
❑ 637 Mike Piazza UP	.60	.25
❑ 638 Kirby Puckett UP	.40	.18
❑ 639 Tim Salmon UP	.20	.09
❑ 640 Frank Thomas UP	.60	.25
❑ 641 Alan Benes FF	.50	.23
❑ 642 Johnny Damon FF	.20	.09
❑ 643 Brad Fullmer FF	1.25	.55
❑ 644 Derek Jeter FF	1.50	.70
❑ 645 Derrek Lee FF	1.25	.55
❑ 646 Alex Ochoa	.10	.05
❑ 647 Alex Rodriguez FF	5.00	2.20
❑ 648 Jose Silva FF	.20	.09
❑ 649 Terrell Wade FF	.10	.05
❑ 650 Preston Wilson FF	.20	.09
❑ 651 Shane Andrews	.10	.05
❑ 652 James Baldwin	.20	.09
❑ 653 Ricky Bottalico	.20	.09
❑ 654 Tavo Alvarez	.10	.05
❑ 655 Donnie Elliott	.10	.05
❑ 656 Joey Eischen	.10	.05
❑ 657 Jason Giambi	.30	.14
❑ 658 Todd Hollandsworth	.10	.05
❑ 659 Brian L. Hunter	.20	.09
❑ 660 Charles Johnson	.20	.09
❑ 661 Michael Jordan	6.00	2.70
❑ 662 Jeff Juden	.10	.05
❑ 663 Mike Kelly	.10	.05
❑ 664 James Mouton	.10	.05
❑ 665 Ray Holbert	.10	.05
❑ 666 Pokey Reese	.20	.09
❑ 667 Ruben Santana	.10	.05
❑ 668 Paul Spoljaric	.10	.05
❑ 669 Luis Lopez	.10	.05
❑ 670 Matt Walbeck	.10	.05
❑ P50 Ken Griffey Jr. Promo	1.00	.45

1994 Collector's Choice Home Run All-Stars

	MINT	NRMT
COMPLETE SET (8)	4.00	1.80
COMMON CARD (HA1-HA8)	.25	.11
❑ HA1 Juan Gonzalez	1.50	.70
❑ HA2 Ken Griffey Jr.	3.00	1.35
❑ HA3 Barry Bonds	.60	.25
❑ HA4 Bobby Bonilla	.25	.11
❑ HA5 Cecil Fielder UER (Card number is HA4)	.25	.11
❑ HA6 Albert Belle	.60	.25
❑ HA7 David Justice	.60	.25
❑ HA8 Mike Piazza	2.00	.90

1995 Collector's Choice

	MINT	NRMT
COMPLETE SET (530)	20.00	9.00
COMP.FACT.SET (545)	25.00	11.00
COMMON CARD (1-530)	.10	.05
COMP.TRADE SET (55)	10.00	4.50
COMMON TRADE (531-585)	.15	.07
COMMON TRADE DP (542-552)	.05	.02
TRADE MINOR STARS	.30	.14
TRADE SEMISTARS	.50	.23
TRADE UNLISTED STARS	.75	.35
COMP.TRADE EXCH.SET (5)	4.00	1.80
COMMON TRD.EXCH. (TC1-TC5)	1.00	.45
❑ 1 Charles Johnson	.20	.09
❑ 2 Scott Ruffcorn	.10	.05
❑ 3 Ray Durham	.20	.09
❑ 4 Armando Benitez	.10	.05
❑ 5 Alex Rodriguez	1.50	.70
❑ 6 Julian Tavarez	.10	.05
❑ 7 Chad Ogea	.10	.05
❑ 8 Quilvio Veras	.10	.05
❑ 9 Phil Nevin	.10	.05
❑ 10 Michael Tucker	.20	.09
❑ 11 Mark Thompson	.10	.05
❑ 12 Rod Henderson	.10	.05
❑ 13 Andrew Lorraine	.10	.05
❑ 14 Joe Randa	.10	.05
❑ 15 Derek Jeter	1.25	.55
❑ 16 Tony Clark	.40	.18
❑ 17 Juan Castillo	.10	.05
❑ 18 Mark Acre	.10	.05
❑ 19 Orlando Miller	.10	.05
❑ 20 Paul Wilson	.10	.05
❑ 21 John Mabry	.10	.05
❑ 22 Garey Ingram	.10	.05
❑ 23 Garret Anderson	.20	.09
❑ 24 Dave Stevens	.10	.05
❑ 25 Dustin Hermanson	.20	.09
❑ 26 Paul Shuey	.10	.05
❑ 27 J.R. Phillips	.10	.05
❑ 28 Ruben Rivera FF	.20	.09
❑ 29 Nomar Garciaparra FF	2.50	1.10
❑ 30 John Wasdin FF	.10	.05
❑ 31 Jim Pittsley FF	.10	.05
❑ 32 Scott Elarton FF	.50	.23
❑ 33 Raul Casanova FF	.10	.05
❑ 34 Todd Greene FF	.20	.09
❑ 35 Bill Pulsipher FF	.10	.05
❑ 36 Trey Beamon FF	.10	.05
❑ 37 Curtis Goodwin FF	.10	.05
❑ 38 Doug Million FF	.10	.05
❑ 39 Karim Garcia FF	.60	.25
❑ 40 Ben Grieve FF	2.50	1.10
❑ 41 Mark Farris FF	.10	.05
❑ 42 Juan Acevedo FF	.10	.05
❑ 43 C.J. Nitkowski FF	.10	.05
❑ 44 Travis Miller FF	.10	.05
❑ 45 Reid Ryan FF	.20	.09
❑ 46 Nolan Ryan	1.50	.70
❑ 47 Robin Yount	.40	.18
❑ 48 Ryne Sandberg	.50	.23
❑ 49 George Brett	.75	.35
❑ 50 Mike Schmidt	.50	.23
❑ 51 Cecil Fielder B90	.10	.05
❑ 52 Nolan Ryan B90	.75	.35

❑ 53 Rickey Henderson B90 .20 .09
❑ 54 George Brett B90 .40 .18
Robin Yount
Dave Winfield
❑ 55 Sid Bream B90 .10 .05
❑ 56 Carlos Baerga B90 .10 .05
❑ 57 Lee Smith B90 .10 .05
❑ 58 Mark Whiten B90 .10 .05
❑ 59 Joe Carter B90 .20 .09
❑ 60 Barry Bonds B90 .30 .14
❑ 61 Tony Gwynn B90 .50 .23
❑ 62 Ken Griffey Jr. B90 1.00 .45
❑ 63 Greg Maddux B90 .60 .25
❑ 64 Frank Thomas B90 .60 .25
❑ 65 Dennis Martinez B90 .10 .05
Kenny Rogers
❑ 66 David Cone .30 .14
❑ 67 Greg Maddux 1.25 .55
❑ 68 Jimmy Key .20 .09
❑ 69 Fred McGriff .30 .14
❑ 70 Ken Griffey Jr. 2.00 .90
❑ 71 Matt Williams .20 .09
❑ 72 Paul O'Neill .20 .09
❑ 73 Tony Gwynn 1.00 .45
❑ 74 Randy Johnson .40 .18
❑ 75 Frank Thomas 1.25 .55
❑ 76 Jeff Bagwell .60 .25
❑ 77 Kirby Puckett .60 .25
❑ 78 Bob Hamelin .10 .05
❑ 79 Raul Mondesi .30 .14
❑ 80 Mike Piazza 1.25 .55
❑ 81 Kenny Lofton .40 .18
❑ 82 Barry Bonds .50 .23
❑ 83 Albert Belle .50 .23
❑ 84 Juan Gonzalez 1.00 .45
❑ 85 Cal Ripken Jr. 1.50 .70
❑ 86 Barry Bonds WC .30 .14
❑ 87 Mike Piazza WC .60 .25
❑ 88 Ken Griffey Jr. WC 1.00 .45
❑ 89 Frank Thomas WC .60 .25
❑ 90 Juan Gonzalez WC .50 .23
❑ 91 Jorge Fabregas .10 .05
❑ 92 J.T. Snow .20 .09
❑ 93 Spike Owen .10 .05
❑ 94 Eduardo Perez .10 .05
❑ 95 Bo Jackson .20 .09
❑ 96 Damion Easley .20 .09
❑ 97 Gary DiSarcina .10 .05
❑ 98 Jim Edmonds .30 .14
❑ 99 Chad Curtis .10 .05
❑ 100 Tim Salmon .40 .18
❑ 101 Chili Davis .20 .09
❑ 102 Chuck Finley .20 .09
❑ 103 Mark Langston .10 .05
❑ 104 Brian Anderson .20 .09
❑ 105 Lee Smith .20 .09
❑ 106 Phil Leftwich .10 .05
❑ 107 Chris Donnels .10 .05
❑ 108 John Hudek .10 .05
❑ 109 Craig Biggio .40 .18
❑ 110 Luis Gonzalez .10 .05
❑ 111 Brian L. Hunter .20 .09
❑ 112 James Mouton .10 .05
❑ 113 Scott Servais .10 .05
❑ 114 Tony Eusebio .10 .05
❑ 115 Derek Bell .20 .09
❑ 116 Doug Drabek .10 .05
❑ 117 Shane Reynolds .20 .09
❑ 118 Darryl Kile .20 .09
❑ 119 Greg Swindell .10 .05
❑ 120 Phil Plantier .10 .05
❑ 121 Todd Jones .10 .05
❑ 122 Steve Ontiveros .10 .05
❑ 123 Bobby Witt .10 .05
❑ 124 Brent Gates .10 .05
❑ 125 Rickey Henderson .40 .18
❑ 126 Scott Brosius .20 .09
❑ 127 Mike Bordick .10 .05
❑ 128 Fausto Cruz .10 .05
❑ 129 Stan Javier .10 .05
❑ 130 Mark McGwire 2.00 .90
❑ 131 Geronimo Berroa .10 .05
❑ 132 Terry Steinbach .20 .09
❑ 133 Steve Karsay .10 .05
❑ 134 Dennis Eckersley .20 .09
❑ 135 Ruben Sierra .10 .05
❑ 136 Ron Darling .10 .05
❑ 137 Todd Van Poppel .10 .05
❑ 138 Alex Gonzalez .10 .05
❑ 139 John Olerud .20 .09
❑ 140 Roberto Alomar .40 .18
❑ 141 Darren Hall .10 .05
❑ 142 Ed Sprague .10 .05
❑ 143 Devon White .20 .09
❑ 144 Shawn Green .20 .09
❑ 145 Paul Molitor .40 .18
❑ 146 Pat Borders .10 .05
❑ 147 Carlos Delgado .20 .09
❑ 148 Juan Guzman .10 .05
❑ 149 Pat Hentgen .20 .09
❑ 150 Joe Carter .20 .09
❑ 151 Dave Stewart .20 .09
❑ 152 Todd Stottlemyre .10 .05
❑ 153 Dick Schofield .10 .05
❑ 154 Chipper Jones 1.00 .45
❑ 155 Ryan Klesko .20 .09
❑ 156 David Justice .40 .18
❑ 157 Mike Kelly .10 .05
❑ 158 Roberto Kelly .10 .05
❑ 159 Tony Tarasco .10 .05
❑ 160 Javier Lopez .20 .09
❑ 161 Steve Avery .10 .05
❑ 162 Greg McMichael .10 .05
❑ 163 Kent Mercker .10 .05
❑ 164 Mark Lemke .10 .05
❑ 165 Tom Glavine .40 .18
❑ 166 Jose Oliva .10 .05
❑ 167 John Smoltz .20 .09
❑ 168 Jeff Blauser .10 .05
❑ 169 Troy O'Leary .20 .09
❑ 170 Greg Vaughn .20 .09
❑ 171 Jody Reed .10 .05
❑ 172 Kevin Seitzer .10 .05
❑ 173 Jeff Cirillo .20 .09
❑ 174 B.J. Surhoff .20 .09
❑ 175 Cal Eldred .10 .05
❑ 176 Jose Valentin .10 .05
❑ 177 Turner Ward .10 .05
❑ 178 Darryl Hamilton .10 .05
❑ 179 Pat Listach .10 .05
❑ 180 Matt Mieske .10 .05
❑ 181 Brian Harper .10 .05
❑ 182 Dave Nilsson .10 .05
❑ 183 Mike Fetters .10 .05
❑ 184 John Jaha .10 .05
❑ 185 Ricky Bones .10 .05
❑ 186 Geronimo Pena .10 .05
❑ 187 Bob Tewksbury .10 .05
❑ 188 Todd Zeile .10 .05
❑ 189 Danny Jackson .10 .05
❑ 190 Ray Lankford .20 .09
❑ 191 Bernard Gilkey .10 .05
❑ 192 Brian Jordan .20 .09
❑ 193 Tom Pagnozzi .10 .05
❑ 194 Rick Sutcliffe .10 .05
❑ 195 Mark Whiten .10 .05
❑ 196 Tom Henke .10 .05
❑ 197 Rene Arocha .10 .05
❑ 198 Allen Watson .10 .05
❑ 199 Mike Perez .10 .05
❑ 200 Ozzie Smith .50 .23
❑ 201 Anthony Young .10 .05
❑ 202 Rey Sanchez .10 .05
❑ 203 Steve Buechele .10 .05
❑ 204 Shawon Dunston .10 .05
❑ 205 Mark Grace .30 .14
❑ 206 Glenallen Hill .10 .05
❑ 207 Eddie Zambrano .10 .05
❑ 208 Rick Wilkins .10 .05
❑ 209 Derrick May .10 .05
❑ 210 Sammy Sosa 1.00 .45
❑ 211 Kevin Roberson .10 .05
❑ 212 Steve Trachsel .10 .05
❑ 213 Willie Banks .10 .05
❑ 214 Kevin Foster .10 .05
❑ 215 Randy Myers .10 .05
❑ 216 Mike Morgan .10 .05
❑ 217 Rafael Bournigal .10 .05
❑ 218 Delino DeShields .10 .05
❑ 219 Tim Wallach .10 .05
❑ 220 Eric Karros .20 .09
❑ 221 Jose Offerman .10 .05
❑ 222 Tom Candiotti .10 .05
❑ 223 Ismael Valdes .20 .09
❑ 224 Henry Rodriguez .20 .09
❑ 225 Billy Ashley .10 .05
❑ 226 Darren Dreifort .20 .09
❑ 227 Ramon Martinez .20 .09
❑ 228 Pedro Astacio .10 .05
❑ 229 Orel Hershiser .20 .09
❑ 230 Brett Butler .20 .09
❑ 231 Todd Hollandsworth .10 .05
❑ 232 Chan Ho Park .50 .23
❑ 233 Mike Lansing .10 .05
❑ 234 Sean Berry .10 .05
❑ 235 Rondell White .20 .09
❑ 236 Ken Hill .10 .05
❑ 237 Marquis Grissom .20 .09
❑ 238 Larry Walker .40 .18
❑ 239 John Wetteland .20 .09
❑ 240 Cliff Floyd .20 .09
❑ 241 Joey Eischen .10 .05
❑ 242 Lou Frazier .10 .05
❑ 243 Darrin Fletcher .10 .05
❑ 244 Pedro J. Martinez .40 .18
❑ 245 Wil Cordero .10 .05
❑ 246 Jeff Fassero .10 .05
❑ 247 Butch Henry .10 .05
❑ 248 Mel Rojas .10 .05
❑ 249 Kirk Rueter .10 .05
❑ 250 Moises Alou .30 .14
❑ 251 Rod Beck .10 .05
❑ 252 John Patterson .10 .05
❑ 253 Robby Thompson .10 .05
❑ 254 Royce Clayton .10 .05
❑ 255 Wm. VanLandingham .10 .05
❑ 256 Darren Lewis .10 .05
❑ 257 Kirt Manwaring .10 .05
❑ 258 Mark Portugal .10 .05
❑ 259 Bill Swift .10 .05
❑ 260 Rikkert Faneyte .10 .05
❑ 261 Mike Jackson .10 .05
❑ 262 Todd Benzinger .10 .05
❑ 263 Bud Black .10 .05
❑ 264 Salomon Torres .10 .05
❑ 265 Eddie Murray .40 .18
❑ 266 Mark Clark .10 .05
❑ 267 Paul Sorrento .10 .05
❑ 268 Jim Thome .40 .18
❑ 269 Omar Vizquel .20 .09
❑ 270 Carlos Baerga .20 .09
❑ 271 Jeff Russell .10 .05
❑ 272 Herbert Perry .10 .05
❑ 273 Sandy Alomar Jr. .20 .09
❑ 274 Dennis Martinez .20 .09
❑ 275 Manny Ramirez .40 .18
❑ 276 Wayne Kirby .10 .05
❑ 277 Charles Nagy .20 .09
❑ 278 Albie Lopez .10 .05
❑ 279 Jeromy Burnitz .20 .09
❑ 280 Dave Winfield .40 .18
❑ 281 Tim Davis .10 .05
❑ 282 Marc Newfield .10 .05
❑ 283 Tino Martinez .40 .18
❑ 284 Mike Blowers .10 .05
❑ 285 Goose Gossage .20 .09
❑ 286 Luis Sojo .10 .05
❑ 287 Edgar Martinez .20 .09
❑ 288 Rich Amaral .10 .05
❑ 289 Felix Fermin .10 .05
❑ 290 Jay Buhner .20 .09
❑ 291 Dan Wilson .10 .05
❑ 292 Bobby Ayala .10 .05
❑ 293 Dave Fleming .10 .05
❑ 294 Greg Pirkl .10 .05
❑ 295 Reggie Jefferson .10 .05
❑ 296 Greg Hibbard .10 .05
❑ 297 Yorkis Perez .10 .05
❑ 298 Kurt Miller .10 .05
❑ 299 Chuck Carr .10 .05
❑ 300 Gary Sheffield .30 .14
❑ 301 Jerry Browne .10 .05
❑ 302 Dave Magadan .10 .05
❑ 303 Kurt Abbott .10 .05
❑ 304 Pat Rapp .10 .05

❑ 305 Jeff Conine .20 .09
❑ 306 Benito Santiago .10 .05
❑ 307 Dave Weathers .10 .05
❑ 308 Robb Nen .10 .05
❑ 309 Chris Hammond .10 .05
❑ 310 Bryan Harvey .10 .05
❑ 311 Charlie Hough .10 .05
❑ 312 Greg Colbrunn .10 .05
❑ 313 David Segui .20 .09
❑ 314 Rico Brogna .10 .05
❑ 315 Jeff Kent .20 .09
❑ 316 Jose Vizcaino .10 .05
❑ 317 Jim Lindeman .10 .05
❑ 318 Carl Everett .10 .05
❑ 319 Ryan Thompson .10 .05
❑ 320 Bobby Bonilla .20 .09
❑ 321 Joe Orsulak .10 .05
❑ 322 Pete Harnisch .10 .05
❑ 323 Doug Linton .10 .05
❑ 324 Todd Hundley .20 .09
❑ 325 Bret Saberhagen .20 .09
❑ 326 Kelly Stinnett .10 .05
❑ 327 Jason Jacome .10 .05
❑ 328 Bobby Jones .10 .05
❑ 329 John Franco .20 .09
❑ 330 Rafael Palmeiro .30 .14
❑ 331 Chris Hoiles .10 .05
❑ 332 Leo Gomez .10 .05
❑ 333 Chris Sabo .10 .05
❑ 334 Brady Anderson .20 .09
❑ 335 Jeffrey Hammonds .20 .09
❑ 336 Dwight Smith .10 .05
❑ 337 Jack Voigt .10 .05
❑ 338 Harold Baines .20 .09
❑ 339 Ben McDonald .10 .05
❑ 340 Mike Mussina .40 .18
❑ 341 Bret Barberie .10 .05
❑ 342 Jamie Moyer .10 .05
❑ 343 Mike Oquist .10 .05
❑ 344 Sid Fernandez .10 .05
❑ 345 Eddie Williams .10 .05
❑ 346 Joey Hamilton .20 .09
❑ 347 Brian Williams .10 .05
❑ 348 Luis Lopez .10 .05
❑ 349 Steve Finley .20 .09
❑ 350 Andy Benes .20 .09
❑ 351 Andujar Cedeno .10 .05
❑ 352 Bip Roberts .10 .05
❑ 353 Ray McDavid .10 .05
❑ 354 Ken Caminiti .30 .14
❑ 355 Trevor Hoffman .20 .09
❑ 356 Mel Nieves .10 .05
❑ 357 Brad Ausmus .10 .05
❑ 358 Andy Ashby .10 .05
❑ 359 Scott Sanders .10 .05
❑ 360 Gregg Jefferies .10 .05
❑ 361 Mariano Duncan .10 .05
❑ 362 Dave Hollins .10 .05
❑ 363 Kevin Stocker .10 .05
❑ 364 Fernando Valenzuela .20 .09
❑ 365 Lenny Dykstra .20 .09
❑ 366 Jim Eisenreich .10 .05
❑ 367 Ricky Bottalico .20 .09
❑ 368 Doug Jones .10 .05
❑ 369 Ricky Jordan .10 .05
❑ 370 Darren Daulton .20 .09
❑ 371 Mike Lieberthal .10 .05
❑ 372 Bobby Munoz .10 .05
❑ 373 John Kruk .20 .09
❑ 374 Curt Schilling .20 .09
❑ 375 Orlando Merced .10 .05
❑ 376 Carlos Garcia .10 .05
❑ 377 Lance Parrish .10 .05
❑ 378 Steve Cooke .10 .05
❑ 379 Jeff King .10 .05
❑ 380 Jay Bell .20 .09
❑ 381 Al Martin .10 .05
❑ 382 Paul Wagner .10 .05
❑ 383 Rick White .10 .05
❑ 384 Midre Cummings .10 .05
❑ 385 Jon Lieber .10 .05
❑ 386 Dave Clark .10 .05
❑ 387 Don Slaught .10 .05
❑ 388 Denny Neagle .20 .09
❑ 389 Zane Smith .10 .05
❑ 390 Andy Van Slyke .20 .09
❑ 391 Ivan Rodriguez .50 .23
❑ 392 David Hulse .10 .05
❑ 393 John Burkett .10 .05
❑ 394 Kevin Brown .30 .14
❑ 395 Dean Palmer .20 .09
❑ 396 Otis Nixon .10 .05
❑ 397 Rick Helling .20 .09
❑ 398 Kenny Rogers .10 .05
❑ 399 Darren Oliver .10 .05
❑ 400 Will Clark .40 .18
❑ 401 Jeff Frye .10 .05
❑ 402 Kevin Gross .10 .05
❑ 403 John Dettmer .10 .05
❑ 404 Manny Lee .10 .05
❑ 405 Rusty Greer .40 .18
❑ 406 Aaron Sele .20 .09
❑ 407 Carlos Rodriguez .10 .05
❑ 408 Scott Cooper .10 .05
❑ 409 John Valentin .20 .09
❑ 410 Roger Clemens .75 .35
❑ 411 Mike Greenwell .10 .05
❑ 412 Tim Vanegmond .10 .05
❑ 413 Tom Brunansky .10 .05
❑ 414 Steve Farr .10 .05
❑ 415 Jose Canseco .40 .18
❑ 416 Joe Hesketh .10 .05
❑ 417 Ken Ryan .10 .05
❑ 418 Tim Naehring .10 .05
❑ 419 Frank Viola .10 .05
❑ 420 Andre Dawson .30 .14
❑ 421 Mo Vaughn .50 .23
❑ 422 Jeff Brantley .10 .05
❑ 423 Pete Schourek .10 .05
❑ 424 Hal Morris .10 .05
❑ 425 Deion Sanders .20 .09
❑ 426 Brian R. Hunter .10 .05
❑ 427 Bret Boone .20 .09
❑ 428 Willie Greene .20 .09
❑ 429 Ron Gant .10 .05
❑ 430 Barry Larkin .30 .14
❑ 431 Reggie Sanders .20 .09
❑ 432 Eddie Taubensee .10 .05
❑ 433 Jack Morris .20 .09
❑ 434 Jose Rijo .10 .05
❑ 435 Johnny Ruffin .10 .05
❑ 436 John Smiley .10 .05
❑ 437 John Roper .10 .05
❑ 438 Dave Nied .10 .05
❑ 439 Roberto Mejia .10 .05
❑ 440 Andres Galarraga .40 .18
❑ 441 Mike Kingery .10 .05
❑ 442 Curt Leskanic .10 .05
❑ 443 Walt Weiss .10 .05
❑ 444 Marvin Freeman .10 .05
❑ 445 Charlie Hayes .10 .05
❑ 446 Eric Young .10 .05
❑ 447 Ellis Burks .20 .09
❑ 448 Joe Girardi .10 .05
❑ 449 Lance Painter .10 .05
❑ 450 Dante Bichette .20 .09
❑ 451 Bruce Ruffin .10 .05
❑ 452 Jeff Granger .10 .05
❑ 453 Wally Joyner .20 .09
❑ 454 Jose Lind .10 .05
❑ 455 Jeff Montgomery .10 .05
❑ 456 Gary Gaetti .20 .09
❑ 457 Greg Gagne .10 .05
❑ 458 Vince Coleman .10 .05
❑ 459 Mike Macfarlane .10 .05
❑ 460 Brian McRae .10 .05
❑ 461 Tom Gordon .10 .05
❑ 462 Kevin Appier .20 .09
❑ 463 Billy Brewer .10 .05
❑ 464 Mark Gubicza .10 .05
❑ 465 Travis Fryman .20 .09
❑ 466 Danny Bautista .10 .05
❑ 467 Sean Bergman .10 .05
❑ 468 Mike Henneman .10 .05
❑ 469 Mike Moore .10 .05
❑ 470 Cecil Fielder .20 .09
❑ 471 Alan Trammell .20 .09
❑ 472 Kirk Gibson .20 .09
❑ 473 Tony Phillips .10 .05
❑ 474 Mickey Tettleton .10 .05
❑ 475 Lou Whitaker .20 .09
❑ 476 Chris Gomez .10 .05
❑ 477 John Doherty .10 .05
❑ 478 Greg Gohr .10 .05
❑ 479 Bill Gullickson .10 .05
❑ 480 Rick Aguilera .10 .05
❑ 481 Matt Walbeck .10 .05
❑ 482 Kevin Tapani .10 .05
❑ 483 Scott Erickson .20 .09
❑ 484 Steve Dunn .10 .05
❑ 485 David McCarty .10 .05
❑ 486 Scott Leius .10 .05
❑ 487 Pat Meares .10 .05
❑ 488 Jeff Reboulet .10 .05
❑ 489 Pedro Munoz .10 .05
❑ 490 Chuck Knoblauch .40 .18
❑ 491 Rich Becker .10 .05
❑ 492 Alex Cole .10 .05
❑ 493 Pat Mahomes .10 .05
❑ 494 Ozzie Guillen .10 .05
❑ 495 Tim Raines .20 .09
❑ 496 Kirk McCaskill .10 .05
❑ 497 Olmedo Saenz .10 .05
❑ 498 Scott Sanderson .10 .05
❑ 499 Lance Johnson .10 .05
❑ 500 Michael Jordan 2.50 1.10
❑ 501 Warren Newson .10 .05
❑ 502 Ron Karkovice .10 .05
❑ 503 Wilson Alvarez .20 .09
❑ 504 Jason Bere .10 .05
❑ 505 Robin Ventura .20 .09
❑ 506 Alex Fernandez .10 .05
❑ 507 Roberto Hernandez .10 .05
❑ 508 Norberto Martin .10 .05
❑ 509 Bob Wickman .10 .05
❑ 510 Don Mattingly .60 .25
❑ 511 Melido Perez .10 .05
❑ 512 Pat Kelly .10 .05
❑ 513 Randy Velarde .10 .05
❑ 514 Tony Fernandez .10 .05
❑ 515 Jack McDowell .10 .05
❑ 516 Luis Polonia .10 .05
❑ 517 Bernie Williams .40 .18
❑ 518 Danny Tartabull .10 .05
❑ 519 Mike Stanley .10 .05
❑ 520 Wade Boggs .40 .18
❑ 521 Jim Leyritz .20 .09
❑ 522 Steve Howe .10 .05
❑ 523 Scott Kamieniecki .10 .05
❑ 524 Russ Davis .20 .09
❑ 525 Jim Abbott .20 .09
❑ 526 Eddie Murray CL .20 .09
❑ 527 Alex Rodriguez CL .75 .35
❑ 528 Jeff Bagwell CL .40 .18
❑ 529 Joe Carter CL .10 .05
❑ 530 Fred McGriff CL .10 .05
❑ 531T Tony Phillips TRADE .15 .07
❑ 532T Dave Magadan TRADE .15 .07
❑ 533T Mike Gallego TRADE .15 .07
❑ 534T Dave Stewart TRADE .30 .14
❑ 535T T. Stottlemyre TRADE .15 .07
❑ 536T David Cone TRADE .50 .23
❑ 537T M. Grissom TRADE .30 .14
❑ 538T Derrick May TRADE .15 .07
❑ 539T Joe Oliver TRADE .15 .07
❑ 540T Scott Cooper TRADE .15 .07
❑ 541T Ken Hill TRADE .15 .07
❑ 542T H. Johnson TRADE DP .15 .07
❑ 543T B. McRae TRADE DP .15 .07
❑ 544T J. Navarro TRADE DP .15 .07
❑ 545T O. Timmons TRADE DP .15 .07
❑ 546T R. Kelly TRADE DP .15 .07
❑ 547T Hideo Nomo TRADE DP 4.00 1.80
❑ 548T S. Andrews TRADE DP .15 .07
❑ 549T M.Grudzi TRADE DP .75 .35
❑ 550T C. Perez TRADE DP .75 .35
❑ 551T H. Rodriguez TRADE DP .30 .14
❑ 552T T. Tarasco TRADE DP .15 .07
❑ 553T Glenallen Hill TRADE .15 .07
❑ 554T T. Mulholland TRADE .15 .07
❑ 555T Orel Hershiser TRADE .30 .14
❑ 556T Darren Bragg TRADE .15 .07
❑ 557T John Burkett TRADE .15 .07
❑ 558T Bobby Witt TRADE .15 .07
❑ 559T Terry Pendleton TRADE .15 .07

❑ 560T Andre Dawson TRADE .50 .23
❑ 561T Brett Butler TRADE...... .30 .14
❑ 562T Kevin Brown TRADE.... .50 .23
❑ 563T Doug Jones TRADE .... .15 .07
❑ 564T Andy Van Slyke TRADE .30 .14
❑ 565T Jody Reed TRADE ...... .15 .07
❑ 566T F. Valenzuela TRADE.. .30 .14
❑ 567T Charlie Hayes TRADE .15 .07
❑ 568T Benji Gil TRADE .... .15 .07
❑ 569T Mark McLemore TRADE.15 .07
❑ 570T Mickey Tettleton TRADE.15 .07
❑ 571T Bob Tewksbury TRADE .15 .07
❑ 572T Rheal Cormier TRADE .15 .07
❑ 573T V. Eshelman TRADE .. .15 .07
❑ 574T M. Macfarlane TRADE .15 .07
❑ 575T Bill Swift TRADE .... .15 .07
❑ 576T Mark Whiten TRADE.... .15 .07
❑ 577T Benito Santiago TRADE .15 .07
❑ 578T Jason Bates TRADE.... .15 .07
❑ 579T Larry Walker TRADE .. .75 .35
❑ 580T Chad Curtis TRADE .... .15 .07
❑ 581T Bob Higginson TRADE 2.50 1.10
❑ 582T Marty Cordova TRADE .15 .07
❑ 583T Mike Devereaux TRADE.15 .07
❑ 584T John Kruk TRADE........ .30 .14
❑ 585T John Wetteland TRADE .30 .14
❑ P172 Ken Griffey Jr. Promo 3.00 1.35
❑ TC1 Larry Walker EXCH .... 2.00 .90
❑ TC2 David Cone EXCH ...... 2.00 .90
❑ TC3 Marquis Grissom EXCH 1.00 .45
❑ TC4 Terry Pendleton EXCH 1.00 .45
❑ TC5 Fernando Valenzuela EXCH1.50 .70

1995 Collector's Choice Crash the Game

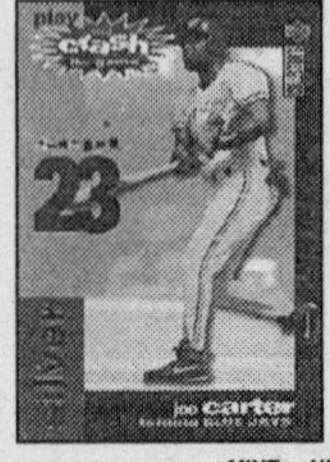

	MINT	NRMT
COMPLETE SET (60)	50.00	22.00
COMMON CARD (CG1-CG20) ..	.10	.05

*GOLD CARDS: 2X TO 5X SILVER CRASH
*GOLD EXCH.CARDS: 1.5X TO 4X SILVER CRASH

❑ CG1 Jeff Bagwell 7/30 .... .75 .35
❑ CG1B Jeff Bagwell 8/13 .... .75 .35
❑ CG1C Jeff Bagwell 9/28......... .75 .35
❑ CG2 Albert Belle 6/18 .... .50 .23
❑ CG2B Albert Belle 8/26 .... .50 .23
❑ CG2C Albert Belle 9/20 .... .50 .23
❑ CG3 Barry Bonds 6/28.......... .50 .23
❑ CG3B Barry Bonds 7/9.......... .50 .23
❑ CG3C Barry Bonds 9/6 .... .50 .23
❑ CG4 Jose Canseco 6/30 W .. .50 .23
❑ CG4B Jose Canseco 7/30 W .50 .23
❑ CG4C Jose Canseco 9/3 ...... .50 .23
❑ CG5 Joe Carter 7/14 .... .20 .09
❑ CG5B Joe Carter 8/9 .... .20 .09
❑ CG5C Joe Carter 9/23 .... .20 .09
❑ CG6 Cecil Fielder 7/4........... .20 .09
❑ CG6B Cecil Fielder 8/2 .... .20 .09
❑ CG6C Cecil Fielder 10/1 ...... .20 .09
❑ CG7 Juan Gonzalez 6/29..... 1.00 .45
❑ CG7B Juan Gonzalez 8/13 1.00 .45
❑ CG7C Juan Gonzalez 9/3 W 1.00 .45
❑ CG8 Ken Griffey Jr. 7/2 ...... 2.00 .90
❑ CG8B Ken Griffey Jr. 8/24 W 2.00 .90
❑ CG8C Ken Griffey Jr. 9/15 .. 2.00 .90
❑ CG9 Bob Hamelin 7/23 .... .10 .05
❑ CG9B Bob Hamelin 8/1 .... .10 .05
❑ CG9C Bob Hamelin 9/29 ...... .10 .05
❑ CG10 David Justice 6/24 ...... .50 .23
❑ CG10B David Justice 7/25.... .50 .23
❑ CG10C David Justice 9/17.... .50 .23
❑ CG11 Ryan Klesko 7/13........ .20 .09
❑ CG11B Ryan Klesko 8/20 .... .20 .09
❑ CG11C Ryan Klesko 9/10 .... .20 .09
❑ CG12 Fred McGriff 8/25........ .30 .14
❑ CG12B Fred McGriff 9/8 ...... .30 .14
❑ CG12C Fred McGriff 9/24 .... .30 .14
❑ CG13 Mark McGwire 7/23 .. 2.00 .90
❑ CG13B Mark McGwire 8/3 W 2.00 .90
❑ CG13C Mark McGwire 9/27 2.00 .90
❑ CG14 Raul Mondesi 7/27 W .30 .14
❑ CG14B Raul Mondesi 8/13 .. .30 .14
❑ CG14C Raul Mondesi 9/15 W .30 .14
❑ CG15 Mike Piazza 7/23 W.. 1.25 .55
❑ CG15B Mike Piazza 8/27 .... 1.25 .55
❑ CG15C Mike Piazza 9/19.... 1.25 .55
❑ CG16 Manny Ramirez 6/21 .. .50 .23
❑ CG16B Manny Ramirez 8/13 .50 .23
❑ CG16C Manny Ramirez 9/26 .50 .23
❑ CG17 Alex Rodriguez 9/10 1.50 .70
❑ CG17B Alex Rodriguez 9/18 1.50 .70
❑ CG17C Alex Rodriguez 9/24 1.50 .70
❑ CG18 Gary Sheffield .... .25 .11
❑ CG18B Gary Sheffield 8/13 .. .25 .11
❑ CG18C Gary Sheffield 9/4 W .25 .11
❑ CG19 Frank Thomas 7/26 .. 1.25 .55
❑ CG19B Frank Thomas 8/17 1.25 .55
❑ CG19C Frank Thomas 9/23 1.25 .55
❑ CG20 Matt Williams 7/29 ...... .20 .09
❑ CG20B Matt Williams 8/12.... .20 .09
❑ CG20C Matt Williams 9/19.... .20 .09

1996 Collector's Choice

	MINT	NRMT
COMPLETE SET (730)	24.00	11.00
COMP.FACT.SET (790)	30.00	13.50
COMPLETE SERIES 1 (365) ..	12.00	5.50
COMPLETE SERIES 2 (365) ..	12.00	5.50
COMMON (1-365/396-760)	.10	.05
COMP.TRADE SET (30)	15.00	6.75
COMMON TRADE (366T-395T)..	.15	.07
COMPLETE UPDATE SET (30)	4.00	1.80
COMMON UPDATE (761-790)....	.25	.11

❑ 1 Cal Ripken........................ 1.50 .70
❑ 2 Edgar Martinez SL .... .40 .18
Tony Gwynn
❑ 3 Albert Belle SL .... .20 .09
Dante Bichette
❑ 4 Albert Belle SL .... .20 .09
Mo Vaughn
Dante Bichette
❑ 5 Kenny Lofton SL .... .20 .09
Quilvio Veras
❑ 6 Mike Mussina SL................ .50 .23
Greg Maddux
❑ 7 Randy Johnson SL .... .40 .18
Hideo Nomo
❑ 8 Randy Johnson SL .... .50 .23
Greg Maddux
❑ 9 Jose Mesa SL .... .10 .05
Randy Myers
❑ 10 Johnny Damon .... .20 .09
❑ 11 Rick Krivda .... .10 .05
❑ 12 Roger Cedeno................. .10 .05
❑ 13 Angel Martinez .... .10 .05
❑ 14 Ariel Prieto....................... .10 .05
❑ 15 John Wasdin .... .10 .05
❑ 16 Edwin Hurtado................. .10 .05
❑ 17 Lyle Mouton..................... .10 .05
❑ 18 Chris Snopek................... .10 .05
❑ 19 Mariano Rivera .... .20 .09
❑ 20 Ruben Rivera .... .20 .09
❑ 21 Juan Castro..................... .10 .05
❑ 22 Jimmy Haynes................. .10 .05
❑ 23 Bob Wolcott..................... .10 .05
❑ 24 Brian Barber .... .10 .05
❑ 25 Frank Rodriguez .... .10 .05
❑ 26 Jesus Tavarez.................. .10 .05
❑ 27 Glenn Dishman .... .10 .05
❑ 28 Jose Herrera .... .10 .05
❑ 29 Chan Ho Park .... .40 .18
❑ 30 Jason Isringhausen.......... .10 .05
❑ 31 Doug Johns...................... .10 .05
❑ 32 Gene Schall..................... .10 .05
❑ 33 Kevin Jordan.................... .10 .05
❑ 34 Matt Lawton...................... .40 .18
❑ 35 Karim Garcia .... .20 .09
❑ 36 George Williams .... .10 .05
❑ 37 Orlando Palmeiro .... .10 .05
❑ 38 Jamie Brewington .... .10 .05
❑ 39 Robert Person.................. .10 .05
❑ 40 Greg Maddux .... 1.25 .55
❑ 41 Marquis Grissom.............. .20 .09
❑ 42 Chipper Jones .... 1.00 .45
❑ 43 David Justice.................... .40 .18
❑ 44 Mark Lemke .... .10 .05
❑ 45 Fred McGriff .... .30 .14
❑ 46 Javier Lopez .... .20 .09
❑ 47 Mark Wohlers .... .10 .05
❑ 48 Jason Schmidt................. .10 .05
❑ 49 John Smoltz .... .20 .09
❑ 50 Curtis Goodwin .... .10 .05
❑ 51 Greg Zaun........................ .10 .05
❑ 52 Armando Benitez.............. .10 .05
❑ 53 Manny Alexander .... .10 .05
❑ 54 Chris Hoiles...................... .10 .05
❑ 55 Harold Baines .... .20 .09
❑ 56 Ben McDonald.................. .10 .05
❑ 57 Scott Erickson .... .20 .09
❑ 58 Jeff Manto .... .10 .05
❑ 59 Luis Alicea........................ .10 .05
❑ 60 Roger Clemens .... .75 .35
❑ 61 Rheal Cormier .... .10 .05
❑ 62 Vaughn Eshelman............ .10 .05
❑ 63 Zane Smith .... .10 .05
❑ 64 Mike Macfarlane .... .10 .05
❑ 65 Erik Hanson...................... .10 .05
❑ 66 Tim Naehring.................... .10 .05
❑ 67 Lee Tinsley .... .10 .05
❑ 68 Troy O'Leary .... .20 .09
❑ 69 Garret Anderson .... .20 .09
❑ 70 Chili Davis........................ .20 .09
❑ 71 Jim Edmonds .... .30 .14
❑ 72 Troy Percival.................... .20 .09
❑ 73 Mark Langston .... .10 .05
❑ 74 Spike Owen...................... .10 .05
❑ 75 Tim Salmon...................... .40 .18
❑ 76 Brian Anderson .... .20 .09
❑ 77 Lee Smith .... .20 .09
❑ 78 Jim Abbott........................ .20 .09
❑ 79 Jim Bullinger .... .10 .05
❑ 80 Mark Grace .... .30 .14
❑ 81 Todd Zeile .... .10 .05
❑ 82 Kevin Foster .... .10 .05
❑ 83 Howard Johnson .... .20 .09
❑ 84 Brian McRae .... .10 .05
❑ 85 Randy Myers.................... .10 .05
❑ 86 Jaime Navarro.................. .10 .05
❑ 87 Luis Gonzalez .... .10 .05
❑ 88 Ozzie Timmons .... .10 .05
❑ 89 Wilson Alvarez .... .20 .09
❑ 90 Frank Thomas .... 1.25 .55
❑ 91 James Baldwin .... .20 .09
❑ 92 Ray Durham .... .20 .09
❑ 93 Alex Fernandez................ .10 .05
❑ 94 Ozzie Guillen.................... .10 .05

❑ 95 Tim Raines .20 .09
❑ 96 Roberto Hernandez .10 .05
❑ 97 Lance Johnson .10 .05
❑ 98 John Kruk .20 .09
❑ 99 Mark Portugal .10 .05
❑ 100 Don Mattingly TT .30 .14
❑ 101 Roger Clemens TT .40 .18
❑ 102 Raul Mondesi TT .10 .05
❑ 103 Cecil Fielder TT .10 .05
❑ 104 Ozzie Smith TT .40 .18
❑ 105 Frank Thomas TT .60 .25
❑ 106 Sammy Sosa TT .50 .23
❑ 107 Fred McGriff TT .10 .05
❑ 108 Barry Bonds TT .30 .14
❑ 109 Thomas Howard .10 .05
❑ 110 Ron Gant .10 .05
❑ 111 Eddie Taubensee .10 .05
❑ 112 Hal Morris .10 .05
❑ 113 Jose Rijo .10 .05
❑ 114 Pete Schourek .10 .05
❑ 115 Reggie Sanders .20 .09
❑ 116 Benito Santiago .10 .05
❑ 117 Jeff Brantley .10 .05
❑ 118 Julian Tavarez .10 .05
❑ 119 Carlos Baerga .20 .09
❑ 120 Jim Thome .40 .18
❑ 121 Jose Mesa .10 .05
❑ 122 Dennis Martinez .20 .09
❑ 123 Dave Winfield .40 .18
❑ 124 Eddie Murray .40 .18
❑ 125 Manny Ramirez .40 .18
❑ 126 Paul Sorrento .10 .05
❑ 127 Kenny Lofton .40 .18
❑ 128 Eric Young .10 .05
❑ 129 Jason Bates .10 .05
❑ 130 Bret Saberhagen .20 .09
❑ 131 Andres Galarraga .40 .18
❑ 132 Joe Girardi .10 .05
❑ 133 John VanderWal .10 .05
❑ 134 David Nied .10 .05
❑ 135 Dante Bichette .20 .09
❑ 136 Vinny Castilla .30 .14
❑ 137 Kevin Ritz .10 .05
❑ 138 Felipe Lira .10 .05
❑ 139 Joe Boever .10 .05
❑ 140 Cecil Fielder .20 .09
❑ 141 John Flaherty .10 .05
❑ 142 Kirk Gibson .20 .09
❑ 143 Brian Maxcy .10 .05
❑ 144 Lou Whitaker .20 .09
❑ 145 Alan Trammell .30 .14
❑ 146 Bobby Higginson .40 .18
❑ 147 Chad Curtis .10 .05
❑ 148 Quilvio Veras .10 .05
❑ 149 Jerry Browne .10 .05
❑ 150 Andre Dawson .30 .14
❑ 151 Robb Nen .10 .05
❑ 152 Greg Colbrunn .10 .05
❑ 153 Chris Hammond .10 .05
❑ 154 Kurt Abbott .10 .05
❑ 155 Charles Johnson .20 .09
❑ 156 Terry Pendleton .10 .05
❑ 157 Dave Weathers .10 .05
❑ 158 Mike Hampton .10 .05
❑ 159 Craig Biggio .40 .18
❑ 160 Jeff Bagwell .60 .25
❑ 161 Brian L.Hunter .20 .09
❑ 162 Mike Henneman .10 .05
❑ 163 Dave Magadan .10 .05
❑ 164 Shane Reynolds .20 .09
❑ 165 Derek Bell .20 .09
❑ 166 Orlando Miller .10 .05
❑ 167 James Mouton .10 .05
❑ 168 Melvin Bunch .10 .05
❑ 169 Tom Gordon .10 .05
❑ 170 Kevin Appier .20 .09
❑ 171 Tom Goodwin .10 .05
❑ 172 Greg Gagne .10 .05
❑ 173 Gary Gaetti .20 .09
❑ 174 Jeff Montgomery .10 .05
❑ 175 Jon Nunnally .10 .05
❑ 176 Michael Tucker .20 .09
❑ 177 Joe Vitiello .10 .05
❑ 178 Billy Ashley .10 .05
❑ 179 Tom Candiotti .10 .05
❑ 180 Hideo Nomo .60 .25
❑ 181 Chad Fonville .10 .05
❑ 182 Todd Hollandsworth .10 .05
❑ 183 Eric Karros .20 .09
❑ 184 Roberto Kelly .10 .05
❑ 185 Mike Piazza 1.25 .55
❑ 186 Ramon Martinez .20 .09
❑ 187 Tim Wallach .10 .05
❑ 188 Jeff Cirillo .20 .09
❑ 189 Sid Roberson .10 .05
❑ 190 Kevin Seitzer .10 .05
❑ 191 Mike Fetters .10 .05
❑ 192 Steve Sparks .10 .05
❑ 193 Matt Mieske .10 .05
❑ 194 Joe Oliver .10 .05
❑ 195 B.J. Surhoff .20 .09
❑ 196 Alberto Reyes .10 .05
❑ 197 Fernando Vina .10 .05
❑ 198 LaTroy Hawkins .10 .05
❑ 199 Marty Cordova .10 .05
❑ 200 Kirby Puckett .60 .25
❑ 201 Brad Radke .20 .09
❑ 202 Pedro Munoz .10 .05
❑ 203 Scott Klingenbeck .10 .05
❑ 204 Pat Meares .10 .05
❑ 205 Chuck Knoblauch .40 .18
❑ 206 Scott Stahoviak .10 .05
❑ 207 Dave Stevens .10 .05
❑ 208 Shane Andrews .10 .05
❑ 209 Moises Alou .30 .14
❑ 210 David Segui .20 .09
❑ 211 Cliff Floyd .20 .09
❑ 212 Carlos Perez .20 .09
❑ 213 Mark Grudzielanek .20 .09
❑ 214 Butch Henry .10 .05
❑ 215 Rondell White .20 .09
❑ 216 Mel Rojas .10 .05
❑ 217 Ugueth Urbina .20 .09
❑ 218 Edgardo Alfonzo .20 .09
❑ 219 Carl Everett .10 .05
❑ 220 John Franco .20 .09
❑ 221 Todd Hundley .20 .09
❑ 222 Bobby Jones .10 .05
❑ 223 Bill Pulsipher .10 .05
❑ 224 Rico Brogna .10 .05
❑ 225 Jeff Kent .20 .09
❑ 226 Chris Jones .10 .05
❑ 227 Butch Huskey .10 .05
❑ 228 Robert Eenhoorn .10 .05
❑ 229 Sterling Hitchcock .20 .09
❑ 230 Wade Boggs .40 .18
❑ 231 Derek Jeter 1.25 .55
❑ 232 Tony Fernandez .10 .05
❑ 233 Jack McDowell .10 .05
❑ 234 Andy Pettitte .30 .14
❑ 235 David Cone .30 .14
❑ 236 Mike Stanley .10 .05
❑ 237 Don Mattingly .60 .25
❑ 238 Geronimo Berroa .10 .05
❑ 239 Scott Brosius .20 .09
❑ 240 Rickey Henderson .40 .18
❑ 241 Terry Steinbach .20 .09
❑ 242 Mike Gallego .10 .05
❑ 243 Jason Giambi .20 .09
❑ 244 Steve Ontiveros .10 .05
❑ 245 Dennis Eckersley .20 .09
❑ 246 Dave Stewart .20 .09
❑ 247 Don Wengert .10 .05
❑ 248 Paul Quantrill .10 .05
❑ 249 Ricky Bottalico .20 .09
❑ 250 Kevin Stocker .10 .05
❑ 251 Lenny Dykstra .20 .09
❑ 252 Tony Longmire .10 .05
❑ 253 Tyler Green .10 .05
❑ 254 Mike Mimbs .10 .05
❑ 255 Charlie Hayes .10 .05
❑ 256 Mickey Morandini .10 .05
❑ 257 Heathcliff Slocumb .10 .05
❑ 258 Jeff King .10 .05
❑ 259 Midre Cummings .10 .05
❑ 260 Mark Johnson .10 .05
❑ 261 Freddy Garcia .10 .05
❑ 262 Jon Lieber .10 .05
❑ 263 Esteban Loaiza .10 .05
❑ 264 Dan Miceli .10 .05
❑ 265 Orlando Merced .10 .05
❑ 266 Denny Neagle .20 .09
❑ 267 Steve Parris .10 .05
❑ 268 Greg Maddux FT .60 .25
❑ 269 Randy Johnson FT .20 .09
❑ 270 Hideo Nomo FT .50 .23
❑ 271 Jose Mesa FT .10 .05
❑ 272 Mike Piazza FT .60 .25
❑ 273 Mo Vaughn FT .30 .14
❑ 274 Craig Biggio FT .20 .09
❑ 275 Edgar Martinez FT .10 .05
❑ 276 Barry Larkin FT .10 .05
❑ 277 Sammy Sosa FT .50 .23
❑ 278 Dante Bichette FT .10 .05
❑ 279 Albert Belle FT .30 .14
❑ 280 Ozzie Smith .50 .23
❑ 281 Mark Sweeney .10 .05
❑ 282 Terry Bradshaw .10 .05
❑ 283 Allen Battle .10 .05
❑ 284 Danny Jackson .10 .05
❑ 285 Tom Henke .10 .05
❑ 286 Scott Cooper .10 .05
❑ 287 Tripp Cromer .10 .05
❑ 288 Bernard Gilkey .10 .05
❑ 289 Brian Jordan .20 .09
❑ 290 Tony Gwynn 1.00 .45
❑ 291 Brad Ausmus .10 .05
❑ 292 Bryce Florie .10 .05
❑ 293 Andres Berumen .10 .05
❑ 294 Ken Caminiti .30 .14
❑ 295 Bip Roberts .10 .05
❑ 296 Trevor Hoffman .20 .09
❑ 297 Roberto Petagine .10 .05
❑ 298 Jody Reed .10 .05
❑ 299 Fernando Valenzuela .20 .09
❑ 300 Barry Bonds .50 .23
❑ 301 Mark Leiter .10 .05
❑ 302 Mark Carreon .10 .05
❑ 303 Royce Clayton .10 .05
❑ 304 Kirt Manwaring .10 .05
❑ 305 Glenallen Hill .10 .05
❑ 306 Deion Sanders .20 .09
❑ 307 Joe Rosselli .10 .05
❑ 308 Robby Thompson .10 .05
❑ 309 W. VanLandingham .10 .05
❑ 310 Ken Griffey Jr. 2.00 .90
❑ 311 Bobby Ayala .10 .05
❑ 312 Joey Cora .20 .09
❑ 313 Mike Blowers .10 .05
❑ 314 Darren Bragg .10 .05
❑ 315 Randy Johnson .40 .18
❑ 316 Alex Rodriguez 1.25 .55
❑ 317 Andy Benes .20 .09
❑ 318 Tino Martinez .40 .18
❑ 319 Dan Wilson .10 .05
❑ 320 Will Clark .40 .18
❑ 321 Jeff Frye .10 .05
❑ 322 Benji Gil .10 .05
❑ 323 Rick Helling .10 .05
❑ 324 Mark McLemore .10 .05
❑ 325 Dave Nilsson IF .10 .05
❑ 326 Larry Walker IF .20 .09
❑ 327 Jose Canseco IF .20 .09
❑ 328 Raul Mondesi IF .10 .05
❑ 329 Manny Ramirez IF .20 .09
❑ 330 Robert Eenhoorn IF .10 .05
❑ 331 Chili Davis IF .10 .05
❑ 332 Hideo Nomo IF .50 .23
❑ 333 Benji Gil IF .10 .05
❑ 334 Fernando Valenzuela IF .10 .05
❑ 335 Dennis Martinez IF .10 .05
❑ 336 Roberto Kelly IF .10 .05
❑ 337 Carlos Baerga IF .10 .05
❑ 338 Juan Gonzalez IF .50 .23
❑ 339 Roberto Alomar IF .20 .09
❑ 340 Chan Ho Park IF .20 .09
❑ 341 Andres Galarraga IF .20 .09
❑ 342 Midre Cummings IF .10 .05
❑ 343 Otis Nixon .10 .05
❑ 344 Jeff Russell .10 .05
❑ 345 Ivan Rodriguez .50 .23
❑ 346 Mickey Tettleton .10 .05
❑ 347 Bob Tewksbury .10 .05
❑ 348 Domingo Cedeno .10 .05
❑ 349 Lance Parrish .10 .05

❑ 350 Joe Carter .20 .09
❑ 351 Devon White .20 .09
❑ 352 Carlos Delgado .20 .09
❑ 353 Alex Gonzalez .10 .05
❑ 354 Darren Hall .10 .05
❑ 355 Paul Molitor .40 .18
❑ 356 Al Leiter .20 .09
❑ 357 Randy Knorr .10 .05
❑ 358 Ken Caminiti CL .20 .09
Steve Finley
Brian Williams
Roberto Petagine
Andujar Cedeno
Phil Plantier
Derek Bell
Pedro A. Martinez
Doug Brocail
Craig Shipley
Ricky Gutierrez
❑ 359 Hideo Nomo CL .50 .23
❑ 360 Ramon A.Martinez CL .20 .09
Ramon J.Martinez
❑ 361 Robin Ventura CL .10 .05
❑ 362 Cal Ripken CL .75 .35
❑ 363 Ken Caminiti CL .10 .05
❑ 364 Albert Belle CL .30 .14
Eddie Murray
❑ 365 Randy Johnson CL .20 .09
❑ 366T Tony Pena TRADE .15 .07
❑ 367T Jim Thome TRADE .75 .35
❑ 368T Don Mattingly TRADE 1.25 .55
❑ 369T Jim Leyritz TRADE .15 .07
❑ 370T Ken Griffey Jr. TRADE 4.00 1.80
❑ 371T Edgar Martinez TRADE .30 .14
❑ 372T Pete Schourek TRADE .15 .07
❑ 373T Mark Lewis TRADE .15 .07
❑ 374T Chipper Jones TRADE 2.00 .90
❑ 375T Fred McGriff TRADE .50 .23
❑ 376T Javy Lopez TRADE .30 .14
❑ 377T Fred McGriff TRADE .50 .23
❑ 378T Charlie O'Brien TRADE .15 .07
❑ 379T Mike Devereaux TRADE .15 .07
❑ 380T Mark Wohlers TRADE .15 .07
❑ 381T Bob Wolcott TRADE .15 .07
❑ 382T Manny Ramirez TRADE .75 .35
❑ 383T Jay Buhner TRADE .30 .14
❑ 384T Orel Hershiser TRADE .30 .14
❑ 385T Kenny Lofton TRADE .40 .18
❑ 386T Greg Maddux TRADE 2.50 1.10
❑ 387T Javier Lopez TRADE .30 .14
❑ 388T Kenny Lofton TRADE .40 .18
❑ 389T Eddie Murray TRADE .75 .35
❑ 390T Luis Polonia TRADE .15 .07
❑ 391T Pedro Borbon TRADE .15 .07
❑ 392T Jim Thome TRADE .75 .35
❑ 393T Orel Hershiser TRADE .30 .14
❑ 394T David Justice TRADE .30 .14
❑ 395T Tom Glavine TRADE .75 .35
❑ 396 Greg Maddux TC .60 .25
❑ 397 Rico Brogna TC .10 .05
❑ 398 Darren Daulton TC .10 .05
❑ 399 Gary Sheffield TC .10 .05
❑ 400 Moises Alou TC .10 .05
❑ 401 Barry Larkin TC .10 .05
❑ 402 Jeff Bagwell TC .40 .18
❑ 403 Sammy Sosa TC .50 .23
❑ 404 Ozzie Smith TC .40 .18
❑ 405 Jay Bell TC .10 .05
❑ 406 Mike Piazza TC .60 .25
❑ 407 Dante Bichette TC .10 .05
❑ 408 Tony Gwynn TC .50 .23
❑ 409 Barry Bonds TC .30 .14
❑ 410 Kenny Lofton TC .20 .09
❑ 411 Johnny Damon TC .10 .05
❑ 412 Frank Thomas TC .60 .25
❑ 413 Greg Vaughn TC .10 .05
❑ 414 Paul Molitor TC .20 .09
❑ 415 Ken Griffey Jr. TC 1.00 .45
❑ 416 Tim Salmon TC .20 .09
❑ 417 Juan Gonzalez TC .50 .23
❑ 418 Mark McGwire TC 1.00 .45
❑ 419 Roger Clemens TC .40 .18
❑ 420 Wade Boggs TC .20 .09
❑ 421 Cal Ripken TC .75 .35
❑ 422 Cecil Fielder TC .10 .05
❑ 423 Joe Carter TC .10 .05
❑ 424 Osvaldo Fernandez .10 .05
❑ 425 Billy Wagner .20 .09
❑ 426 George Arias .10 .05
❑ 427 Mendy Lopez .10 .05
❑ 428 Jeff Suppan .10 .05
❑ 429 Rey Ordonez .20 .09
❑ 430 Brooks Kieschnick .10 .05
❑ 431 Raul Ibanez .10 .05
❑ 432 Livan Hernandez .75 .35
❑ 433 Shannon Stewart .20 .09
❑ 434 Steve Cox .10 .05
❑ 435 Trey Beamon .10 .05
❑ 436 Sergio Nunez .10 .05
❑ 437 Jermaine Dye .10 .05
❑ 438 Mike Sweeney .30 .14
❑ 439 Richard Hidalgo .20 .09
❑ 440 Todd Greene .20 .09
❑ 441 Robert Smith .40 .18
❑ 442 Rafael Orellano .10 .05
❑ 443 Wilton Guerrero .30 .14
❑ 444 David Doster .10 .05
❑ 445 Jason Kendall .40 .18
❑ 446 Edgar Renteria .20 .09
❑ 447 Scott Spiezio .10 .05
❑ 448 Jay Canizaro .10 .05
❑ 449 Enrique Wilson .20 .09
❑ 450 Bob Abreu .20 .09
❑ 451 Dwight Smith .10 .05
❑ 452 Jeff Blauser .10 .05
❑ 453 Steve Avery .10 .05
❑ 454 Brad Clontz .10 .05
❑ 455 Tom Glavine .40 .18
❑ 456 Mike Mordecai .10 .05
❑ 457 Rafael Belliard .10 .05
❑ 458 Greg McMichael .10 .05
❑ 459 Pedro Borbon .10 .05
❑ 460 Ryan Klesko .20 .09
❑ 461 Terrell Wade .10 .05
❑ 462 Brady Anderson .20 .09
❑ 463 Roberto Alomar .40 .18
❑ 464 Bobby Bonilla .20 .09
❑ 465 Mike Mussina .40 .18
❑ 466 Cesar Devarez .10 .05
❑ 467 Jeffrey Hammonds .20 .09
❑ 468 Mike Devereaux .10 .05
❑ 469 B.J. Surhoff .20 .09
❑ 470 Rafael Palmeiro .30 .14
❑ 471 John Valentin .20 .09
❑ 472 Mike Greenwell .10 .05
❑ 473 Dwayne Hosey .10 .05
❑ 474 Tim Wakefield .20 .09
❑ 475 Jose Canseco .40 .18
❑ 476 Aaron Sele .20 .09
❑ 477 Stan Belinda .10 .05
❑ 478 Mike Stanley .10 .05
❑ 479 Jamie Moyer .10 .05
❑ 480 Mo Vaughn .50 .23
❑ 481 Randy Velarde .10 .05
❑ 482 Gary DiSarcina .10 .05
❑ 483 Jorge Fabregas .10 .05
❑ 484 Rex Hudler .10 .05
❑ 485 Chuck Finley .20 .09
❑ 486 Tim Wallach .10 .05
❑ 487 Eduardo Perez .10 .05
❑ 488 Scott Sanderson .10 .05
❑ 489 J.T. Snow .20 .09
❑ 490 Sammy Sosa 1.00 .45
❑ 491 Terry Adams .10 .05
❑ 492 Matt Franco .10 .05
❑ 493 Scott Servais .10 .05
❑ 494 Frank Castillo .10 .05
❑ 495 Ryne Sandberg .50 .23
❑ 496 Rey Sanchez .10 .05
❑ 497 Steve Trachsel .10 .05
❑ 498 Jose Hernandez .10 .05
❑ 499 Dave Martinez .10 .05
❑ 500 Babe Ruth FC 1.00 .45
❑ 501 Ty Cobb FC .40 .18
❑ 502 Walter Johnson FC .30 .14
❑ 503 Christy Mathewson FC .30 .14
❑ 504 Honus Wagner FC .30 .14
❑ 505 Robin Ventura .20 .09
❑ 506 Jason Bere .10 .05
❑ 507 Mike Cameron .75 .35
❑ 508 Ron Karkovice .10 .05
❑ 509 Matt Karchner .10 .05
❑ 510 Harold Baines .20 .09
❑ 511 Kirk McCaskill .10 .05
❑ 512 Larry Thomas .10 .05
❑ 513 Danny Tartabull .10 .05
❑ 514 Steve Gilbralter .10 .05
❑ 515 Bret Boone .20 .09
❑ 516 Jeff Branson .10 .05
❑ 517 Kevin Jarvis .10 .05
❑ 518 Xavier Hernandez .10 .05
❑ 519 Eric Owens .10 .05
❑ 520 Barry Larkin .30 .14
❑ 521 Dave Burba .10 .05
❑ 522 John Smiley .10 .05
❑ 523 Paul Assenmacher .10 .05
❑ 524 Chad Ogea .10 .05
❑ 525 Orel Hershiser .20 .09
❑ 526 Alan Embree .10 .05
❑ 527 Tony Pena .10 .05
❑ 528 Omar Vizquel .20 .09
❑ 529 Mark Clark .10 .05
❑ 530 Albert Belle .50 .23
❑ 531 Charles Nagy .20 .09
❑ 532 Herbert Perry .10 .05
❑ 533 Darren Holmes .10 .05
❑ 534 Ellis Burks .20 .09
❑ 535 Billy Swift .10 .05
❑ 536 Armando Reynoso .10 .05
❑ 537 Curtis Leskanic .10 .05
❑ 538 Quinton McCracken .20 .09
❑ 539 Steve Reed .10 .05
❑ 540 Larry Walker .40 .18
❑ 541 Walt Weiss .10 .05
❑ 542 Bryan Rekar .10 .05
❑ 543 Tony Clark .40 .18
❑ 544 Steve Rodriguez .10 .05
❑ 545 C.J. Nitkowski .10 .05
❑ 546 Todd Steverson .10 .05
❑ 547 Jose Lima .10 .05
❑ 548 Phil Nevin .10 .05
❑ 549 Chris Gomez .10 .05
❑ 550 Travis Fryman .20 .09
❑ 551 Mark Lewis .10 .05
❑ 552 Alex Arias .10 .05
❑ 553 Marc Valdes .10 .05
❑ 554 Kevin Brown .40 .18
❑ 555 Jeff Conine .20 .09
❑ 556 John Burkett .10 .05
❑ 557 Devon White .20 .09
❑ 558 Pat Rapp .10 .05
❑ 559 Jay Powell .10 .05
❑ 560 Gary Sheffield .30 .14
❑ 561 Jim Dougherty .10 .05
❑ 562 Todd Jones .10 .05
❑ 563 Tony Eusebio .10 .05
❑ 564 Darryl Kile .20 .09
❑ 565 Doug Drabek .10 .05
❑ 566 Mike Simms .10 .05
❑ 567 Derrick May .10 .05
❑ 568 Donne Wall .10 .05
❑ 569 Greg Swindell .10 .05
❑ 570 Jim Pittsley .10 .05
❑ 571 Bob Hamelin .10 .05
❑ 572 Mark Gubicza .10 .05
❑ 573 Chris Haney .10 .05
❑ 574 Keith Lockhart .10 .05
❑ 575 Mike Macfarlane .10 .05
❑ 576 Les Norman .10 .05
❑ 577 Joe Randa .10 .05
❑ 578 Chris Stynes .10 .05
❑ 579 Greg Gagne .10 .05
❑ 580 Raul Mondesi .30 .14
❑ 581 Delino DeShields .10 .05
❑ 582 Pedro Astacio .10 .05
❑ 583 Antonio Osuna .10 .05
❑ 584 Brett Butler .20 .09
❑ 585 Todd Worrell .10 .05
❑ 586 Mike Blowers .10 .05
❑ 587 Felix Rodriguez .10 .05
❑ 588 Ismael Valdes .20 .09
❑ 589 Ricky Bones .10 .05
❑ 590 Greg Vaughn .20 .09
❑ 591 Mark Loretta .10 .05
❑ 592 Cal Eldred .10 .05

	Card	Player	Mint	NRMT
❑	593	Chuck Carr	.10	.05
❑	594	Dave Nilsson	.10	.05
❑	595	John Jaha	.10	.05
❑	596	Scott Karl	.10	.05
❑	597	Pat Listach	.10	.05
❑	598	Jose Valentin	.10	.05
❑	599	Mike Trombley	.10	.05
❑	600	Paul Molitor	.40	.18
❑	601	Dave Hollins	.10	.05
❑	602	Ron Coomer	.10	.05
❑	603	Matt Walbeck	.10	.05
❑	604	Roberto Kelly	.10	.05
❑	605	Rick Aguilera	.10	.05
❑	606	Pat Mahomes	.10	.05
❑	607	Jeff Reboulet	.10	.05
❑	608	Rich Becker	.10	.05
❑	609	Tim Scott	.10	.05
❑	610	Pedro J. Martinez	.40	.18
❑	611	Kirk Rueter	.10	.05
❑	612	Tavo Alvarez	.10	.05
❑	613	Yamil Benitez	.10	.05
❑	614	Darrin Fletcher	.10	.05
❑	615	Mike Lansing	.10	.05
❑	616	Henry Rodriguez	.20	.09
❑	617	Tony Tarasco	.10	.05
❑	618	Alex Ochoa	.10	.05
❑	619	Tim Bogar	.10	.05
❑	620	Bernard Gilkey	.10	.05
❑	621	Dave Mlicki	.10	.05
❑	622	Brent Mayne	.10	.05
❑	623	Ryan Thompson	.10	.05
❑	624	Pete Harnisch	.10	.05
❑	625	Lance Johnson	.10	.05
❑	626	Jose Vizcaino	.10	.05
❑	627	Doug Henry	.10	.05
❑	628	Scott Kamieniecki	.10	.05
❑	629	Jim Leyritz	.10	.05
❑	630	Ruben Sierra	.10	.05
❑	631	Pat Kelly	.10	.05
❑	632	Joe Girardi	.10	.05
❑	633	John Wetteland	.20	.09
❑	634	Melido Perez	.10	.05
❑	635	Paul O'Neill	.20	.09
❑	636	Jorge Posada	.20	.09
❑	637	Bernie Williams	.40	.18
❑	638	Mark Acre	.10	.05
❑	639	Mike Bordick	.10	.05
❑	640	Mark McGwire	2.00	.90
❑	641	Fausto Cruz	.10	.05
❑	642	Ernie Young	.10	.05
❑	643	Todd Van Poppel	.10	.05
❑	644	Craig Paquette	.10	.05
❑	645	Brent Gates	.10	.05
❑	646	Pedro Munoz	.10	.05
❑	647	Andrew Lorraine	.10	.05
❑	648	Sid Fernandez	.10	.05
❑	649	Jim Eisenreich	.10	.05
❑	650	Johnny Damon	.20	.09
❑	651	Dustin Hermanson	.20	.09
❑	652	Joe Randa	.10	.05
❑	653	Michael Tucker	.20	.09
❑	654	Alan Benes	.20	.09
❑	655	Chad Fonville	.10	.05
❑	656	David Bell	.10	.05
❑	657	Jon Nunnally	.10	.05
❑	658	Chan Ho Park	.40	.18
❑	659	LaTroy Hawkins	.10	.05
❑	660	Jamie Brewington	.10	.05
❑	661	Quinton McCracken	.20	.09
❑	662	Tim Unroe	.10	.05
❑	663	Jeff Ware	.10	.05
❑	664	Todd Greene	.20	.09
❑	665	Andrew Lorraine	.10	.05
❑	666	Ernie Young	.10	.05
❑	667	Toby Borland	.10	.05
❑	668	Lenny Webster	.10	.05
❑	669	Benito Santiago	.10	.05
❑	670	Gregg Jefferies	.10	.05
❑	671	Darren Daulton	.20	.09
❑	672	Curt Schilling	.20	.09
❑	673	Mark Whiten	.10	.05
❑	674	Todd Zeile	.10	.05
❑	675	Jay Bell	.20	.09
❑	676	Paul Wagner	.10	.05
❑	677	Dave Clark	.10	.05
❑	678	Nelson Liriano	.10	.05
❑	679	Ramon Morel	.10	.05
❑	680	Charlie Hayes	.10	.05
❑	681	Angelo Encarnacion	.10	.05
❑	682	Al Martin	.10	.05
❑	683	Jacob Brumfield	.10	.05
❑	684	Mike Kingery	.10	.05
❑	685	Carlos Garcia	.10	.05
❑	686	Tom Pagnozzi	.10	.05
❑	687	David Bell	.10	.05
❑	688	Todd Stottlemyre	.10	.05
❑	689	Jose Oliva	.10	.05
❑	690	Ray Lankford	.20	.09
❑	691	Mike Morgan	.10	.05
❑	692	John Frascatore	.10	.05
❑	693	John Mabry	.10	.05
❑	694	Mark Petkovsek	.10	.05
❑	695	Alan Benes	.20	.09
❑	696	Steve Finley	.20	.09
❑	697	Marc Newfield	.10	.05
❑	698	Andy Ashby	.10	.05
❑	699	Marc Kroon	.10	.05
❑	700	Wally Joyner	.20	.09
❑	701	Joey Hamilton	.20	.09
❑	702	Dustin Hermanson	.20	.09
❑	703	Scott Sanders	.10	.05
❑	704	Marty Cordova ROY	.10	.05
❑	705	Hideo Nomo ROY	.50	.23
❑	706	Mo Vaughn MVP	.30	.14
❑	707	Barry Larkin MVP	.10	.05
❑	708	Randy Johnson CY	.20	.09
❑	709	Greg Maddux CY	.60	.25
❑	710	Mark McGwire CB	1.00	.45
❑	711	Ron Gant CB	.10	.05
❑	712	Andujar Cedeno	.10	.05
❑	713	Brian Johnson	.10	.05
❑	714	J.R. Phillips	.10	.05
❑	715	Rod Beck	.10	.05
❑	716	Sergio Valdez	.10	.05
❑	717	Marvin Benard	.10	.05
❑	718	Steve Scarsone	.10	.05
❑	719	Rich Aurilia	.10	.05
❑	720	Matt Williams	.20	.09
❑	721	John Patterson	.10	.05
❑	722	Shawn Estes	.20	.09
❑	723	Russ Davis	.20	.09
❑	724	Rich Amaral	.10	.05
❑	725	Edgar Martinez	.20	.09
❑	726	Norm Charlton	.10	.05
❑	727	Paul Sorrento	.10	.05
❑	728	Luis Sojo	.10	.05
❑	729	Arquimedez Pozo	.10	.05
❑	730	Jay Buhner	.20	.09
❑	731	Chris Bosio	.10	.05
❑	732	Chris Widger	.10	.05
❑	733	Kevin Gross	.10	.05
❑	734	Darren Oliver	.10	.05
❑	735	Dean Palmer	.20	.09
❑	736	Matt Whiteside	.10	.05
❑	737	Luis Ortiz	.10	.05
❑	738	Roger Pavlik	.10	.05
❑	739	Damon Buford	.10	.05
❑	740	Juan Gonzalez	1.00	.45
❑	741	Rusty Greer	.30	.14
❑	742	Lou Frazier	.10	.05
❑	743	Pat Hentgen	.20	.09
❑	744	Tomas Perez	.10	.05
❑	745	Juan Guzman	.10	.05
❑	746	Otis Nixon	.10	.05
❑	747	Robert Perez	.10	.05
❑	748	Ed Sprague	.10	.05
❑	749	Tony Castillo	.10	.05
❑	750	John Olerud	.20	.09
❑	751	Shawn Green	.20	.09
❑	752	Jeff Ware	.10	.05
❑	753	Dante Bichette CL Vinny Castilla Andres Galarraga Larry Walker	.20	.09
❑	754	Greg Maddux CL	.60	.25
❑	755	Marty Cordova CL	.10	.05
❑	756	Ozzie Smith CL	.40	.18
❑	757	John Vanderwal CL	.10	.05
❑	758	Andres Galarraga CL	.20	.09
❑	759	Frank Thomas CL	.60	.25
❑	760	Tony Gwynn CL	.50	.23
❑	761	Randy Myers UPD	.25	.11
❑	762	Kent Mercker UPD	.25	.11
❑	763	David Wells UPD	.50	.23
❑	764	Tom Gordon UPD	.25	.11
❑	765	Wil Cordero UPD	.25	.11
❑	766	Dave Magadan UPD	.25	.11
❑	767	Doug Jones UPD	.25	.11
❑	768	Kevin Tapani UPD	.25	.11
❑	769	Curtis Goodwin UPD	.25	.11
❑	770	Julio Franco UPD	.25	.11
❑	771	Jack McDowell UPD	.25	.11
❑	772	Al Leiter UPD	.40	.18
❑	773	Sean Berry UPD	.25	.11
❑	774	Bip Roberts UPD	.25	.11
❑	775	Jose Offerman UPD	.25	.11
❑	776	Ben McDonald UPD	.25	.11
❑	777	Dan Serafini UPD	.25	.11
❑	778	Ryan McGuire UPD	.25	.11
❑	779	Tim Raines UPD	.40	.18
❑	780	Tino Martinez UPD	.75	.35
❑	781	Kenny Rogers UPD	.25	.11
❑	782	Bob Tewksbury UPD	.25	.11
❑	783	Rickey Henderson UPD	.50	.23
❑	784	Ron Gant UPD	.25	.11
❑	785	Gary Gaetti UPD	.40	.18
❑	786	Andy Benes UPD	.40	.18
❑	787	Royce Clayton UPD	.25	.11
❑	788	Darryl Hamilton UPD	.25	.11
❑	789	Ken Hill UPD	.25	.11
❑	790	Erik Hanson UPD	.25	.11
❑	P100	Ken Griffey Jr. Promo	3.00	1.35

1996 Collector's Choice Crash the Game

	MINT	NRMT
COMPLETE SET (90)	50.00	22.00
COMMON CARD (CG1-CG30)	.25	.11
COMP.GOLD SET (90)	250.00	110.00
COMMON CARD (CG1-CG30)	1.25	
GOLD SER.2 STATED ODDS 1:48		
COMP.EXCH.SET (27)	100.00	45.00
COMMON CARD (CG1-CG30)	1.25	
COMP.GOLD EXCH.SET (27)	300.00	135.00
COMMON CARD (CG1-CG30)	5.00	
ONE EXCH.CARD VIA MAIL PER WINNER		

	Card	Player	Mint	NRMT
❑	CG1	Chipper Jones 7/11 W	1.50	.70
❑	CG1B	Chipper Jones 8/27 W	1.50	.70
❑	CG1C	Chipper Jones 9/19	1.50	.70
❑	CG2	Fred McGriff 7/1	.40	.18
❑	CG2B	Fred McGriff 8/30	.40	.18
❑	CG2C	Fred McGriff 9/10 W	.40	.18
❑	CG3	Rafael Palmeiro 7/4 W	.40	.18
❑	CG3B	Rafael Palmeiro 8/29	.40	.18
❑	CG3C	Rafael Palmeiro 9/26	.40	.18
❑	CG4	Cal Ripken 6/27	2.50	1.10
❑	CG4B	Cal Ripken 7/25 W	2.50	1.10
❑	CG4C	Cal Ripken 9/2	2.50	1.10
❑	CG5	Jose Canseco 6/27	.60	.25
❑	CG5B	Jose Canseco 7/11 W	.60	.25
❑	CG5C	Jose Canseco 8/23	.60	.25
❑	CG6	Mo Vaughn 6/21 W	.60	.25
❑	CG6B	Mo Vaughn 7/18 W	.60	.25
❑	CG6C	Mo Vaughn 9/20	.60	.25
❑	CG7	Jim Edmonds 7/18 W	.40	.18

❑ CG7B Jim Edmonds 8/16 W	.40	.18
❑ CG7C Jim Edmonds 9/20	.40	.18
❑ CG8 Tim Salmon 6/20	.60	.25
❑ CG8B Tim Salmon 7/30	.60	.25
❑ CG8C Tim Salmon 9/9	.60	.25
❑ CG9 Sammy Sosa 7/4 W	1.50	.70
❑ CG9B Sammy Sosa 8/1 W	1.50	.70
❑ CG9C Sammy Sosa 9/2	1.50	.70
❑ CG10 Frank Thomas 6/27	2.00	.90
❑ CG10B Frank Thomas 7/4	2.00	.90
❑ CG10C Frank Thomas 9/2 W	2.00	.90
❑ CG11 Albert Belle 6/25	.60	.25
❑ CG11B Albert Belle 8/2 W	.60	.25
❑ CG11C Albert Belle 9/6	.60	.25
❑ CG12 Manny Ramirez 7/18 W	.60	.25
❑ CG12B Manny Ramirez 8/26	.60	.25
❑ CG12C Manny Ramirez 9/9 W	.60	.25
❑ CG13 Jim Thome 6/27	.60	.25
❑ CG13B Jim Thome 7/4 W	.60	.25
❑ CG13C Jim Thome 9/23	.60	.25
❑ CG14 Dante Bichette 7/11 W	.25	.11
❑ CG14B Dante Bichette 8/9	.25	.11
❑ CG14C Dante Bichette 9/9	.25	.11
❑ CG15 Vinny Castilla 7/1	.40	.18
❑ CG15B Vinny Castilla 8/23 W	.40	.18
❑ CG15C Vinny Castilla 9/13 W	.40	.18
❑ CG16 Larry Walker 6/24	.60	.25
❑ CG16B Larry Walker 7/18	.60	.25
❑ CG16C Larry Walker 9/27	.60	.25
❑ CG17 Cecil Fielder 6/27	.25	.11
❑ CG17B Cecil Fielder 7/30 W	.25	.11
❑ CG17C Cecil Fielder 9/17 W	.25	.11
❑ CG18 Gary Sheffield 7/4	.40	.18
❑ CG18B Gary Sheffield 8/2	.40	.18
❑ CG18C Gary Sheffield 9/5 W	.40	.18
❑ CG19 Jeff Bagwell 7/4 W	1.00	.45
❑ CG19B Jeff Bagwell 8/16	1.00	.45
❑ CG19C Jeff Bagwell 9/13	1.00	.45
❑ CG20 Eric Karros 7/4 W	.25	.11
❑ CG20B Eric Karros 8/13 W	.25	.11
❑ CG20C Eric Karros 9/16	.25	.11
❑ CG21 Mike Piazza 6/27 W	2.00	.90
❑ CG21B Mike Piazza 7/26	2.00	.90
❑ CG21C Mike Piazza 9/12 W	2.00	.90
❑ CG22 Ken Caminiti 7/11 W	.40	.18
❑ CG22B Ken Caminiti 8/16 W	.40	.18
❑ CG22C Ken Caminiti 9/19 W	.40	.18
❑ CG23 Barry Bonds 6/27 W	.60	.25
❑ CG23B Barry Bonds 7/22	.60	.25
❑ CG23C Barry Bonds 9/24	.60	.25
❑ CG24 Matt Williams 7/11 W	.25	.11
❑ CG24B Matt Williams 8/19	.25	.11
❑ CG24C Matt Williams 9/27	.25	.11
❑ CG25 Jay Buhner 6/20	.25	.11
❑ CG25B Jay Buhner 7/25	.25	.11
❑ CG25C Jay Buhner 8/29 W	.25	.11
❑ CG26 Ken Griffey Jr. 7/18 W	3.00	1.35
❑ CG26B Ken Griffey Jr. 8/16 W	3.00	1.35
❑ CG26C Ken Griffey Jr. 9/20 W	3.00	1.35
❑ CG27 Ron Gant 6/24 W	.25	.11
❑ CG27B Ron Gant 7/11 W	.25	.11
❑ CG27C Ron Gant 9/27 W	.25	.11
❑ CG28 Juan Gonzalez 6/28 W	1.50	.70
❑ CG28B J. Gonzalez 7/15 W	1.50	.70
❑ CG28C Juan Gonzalez 8/6	1.50	.70
❑ CG29 Mickey Tettleton 7/4 W	.25	.11
❑ CG29B Mickey Tettleton 8/6	.25	.11
❑ CG29C M. Tettleton 9/6 W	.25	.11
❑ CG30 Joe Carter 6/25	.25	.11
❑ CG30B Joe Carter 8/5	.25	.11
❑ CG30C Joe Carter 9/23	.25	.11

1996 Collector's Choice Griffey A Cut Above

	MINT	NRMT
COMPLETE SET (10)	8.00	3.60
COMMON CARD (CA1-CA10)	1.00	.45
❑ CA1 Ken Griffey Jr.	1.00	.45
❑ CA2 Ken Griffey Jr.	1.00	.45
❑ CA3 Ken Griffey Jr.	1.00	.45
❑ CA4 Ken Griffey Jr.	1.00	.45
❑ CA5 Ken Griffey Jr.	1.00	.45
❑ CA6 Ken Griffey Jr.	1.00	.45
❑ CA7 Ken Griffey Jr.	1.00	.45
❑ CA8 Ken Griffey Jr.	1.00	.45
❑ CA9 Ken Griffey Jr.	1.00	.45
❑ CA10 Ken Griffey Jr.	1.00	.45

1996 Collector's Choice Nomo Scrapbook

	MINT	NRMT
COMPLETE SET (5)	5.00	2.20
COMMON CARD (1-5)	1.50	.70
❑ 1 Hideo Nomo Hands at Side	1.50	.70
❑ 2 Hideo Nomo Releasing ball	1.50	.70
❑ 3 Hideo Nomo Back turned to batter	1.50	.70
❑ 4 Hideo Nomo Hands over head	1.50	.70
❑ 5 Hideo Nomo Glove at side	1.50	.70

1996 Collector's Choice You Make the Play

	MINT	NRMT
COMPLETE SET (90)	12.00	5.50
COMMON CARD (1-45)	.10	.05
COMP.GOLD SET (90)	200.00	90.00
COMMON CARD (1-45)	1.50	
GOLD SER.1 STATED ODDS 1:35		
❑ 1 Kevin Appier	.20	.09
❑ 1A Kevin Appier	.20	.09
❑ 2 Carlos Baerga	.20	.09
❑ 2A Carlos Baerga	.20	.09
❑ 3 Jeff Bagwell	.60	.25
❑ 3A Jeff Bagwell	.60	.25
❑ 4 Jay Bell	.20	.09
❑ 4A Jay Bell	.20	.09
❑ 5 Albert Belle	.40	.18
❑ 5A Albert Belle	.40	.18
❑ 6 Craig Biggio	.40	.18
❑ 6A Craig Biggio	.40	.18
❑ 7 Wade Boggs	.40	.18
❑ 7A Wade Boggs	.40	.18
❑ 8 Barry Bonds	.40	.18
❑ 8A Barry Bonds	.50	.23
❑ 9 Bobby Bonilla	.20	.09
❑ 9A Bobby Bonilla	.20	.09
❑ 10 Jose Canseco	.40	.18
❑ 10A Jose Canseco	.40	.18
❑ 11 Joe Carter	.20	.09
❑ 11A Joe Carter	.20	.09
❑ 12 Darren Daulton	.20	.09
❑ 12A Darren Daulton	.20	.09
❑ 13 Cecil Fielder	.20	.09
❑ 13A Cecil Fielder	.20	.09
❑ 14 Ron Gant	.10	.05
❑ 14A Ron Gant	.10	.05
❑ 15 Juan Gonzalez	1.00	.45
❑ 15A Juan Gonzalez	1.00	.45
❑ 16 Ken Griffey Jr.	2.00	.90
❑ 16A Ken Griffey Jr.	2.00	.90
❑ 17 Tony Gwynn	1.00	.45
❑ 17A Tony Gwynn	1.00	.45
❑ 18 Randy Johnson	.50	.23
❑ 18A Randy Johnson	.50	.23
❑ 19 Chipper Jones	1.00	.45
❑ 19A Chipper Jones	1.00	.45
❑ 20 Barry Larkin	.30	.14
❑ 20A Barry Larkin	.30	.14
❑ 21 Kenny Lofton	.40	.18
❑ 21A Kenny Lofton	.40	.18
❑ 22 Greg Maddux	1.25	.55
❑ 22A Greg Maddux	1.25	.55
❑ 23 Don Mattingly	.60	.25
❑ 23A Don Mattingly	.60	.25
❑ 24 Fred McGriff	.30	.14
❑ 24A Fred McGriff	.30	.14
❑ 25 Mark McGwire	2.00	.90
❑ 25A Mark McGwire	2.00	.90
❑ 26 Paul Molitor	.40	.18
❑ 26A Paul Molitor	.40	.18
❑ 27 Raul Mondesi	.30	.14
❑ 27A Raul Mondesi	.30	.14
❑ 28 Eddie Murray	.40	.18
❑ 28A Eddie Murray	.40	.18
❑ 29 Hideo Nomo	.60	.25
❑ 29A Hideo Nomo	.60	.25
❑ 30 Jon Nunnally	.10	.05
❑ 30A Jon Nunnally	.10	.05
❑ 31 Mike Piazza	1.25	.55
❑ 31A Mike Piazza	1.25	.55
❑ 32 Kirby Puckett	.75	.35
❑ 32A Kirby Puckett	.75	.35
❑ 33 Cal Ripken	1.50	.70
❑ 33A Cal Ripken	1.50	.70
❑ 34 Alex Rodriguez	1.25	.55
❑ 34A Alex Rodriguez	1.25	.55
❑ 35 Tim Salmon	.40	.18
❑ 35A Tim Salmon	.40	.18
❑ 36 Gary Sheffield	.30	.14
❑ 36A Gary Sheffield	.30	.14
❑ 37 Lee Smith	.20	.09
❑ 37A Lee Smith	.20	.09
❑ 38 Ozzie Smith	.50	.23
❑ 38A Ozzie Smith	.50	.23
❑ 39 Sammy Sosa	1.00	.45
❑ 39A Sammy Sosa	1.00	.45
❑ 40 Frank Thomas	1.25	.55
❑ 40A Frank Thomas	1.25	.55
❑ 41 Greg Vaughn	.20	.09
❑ 41A Greg Vaughn	.20	.09
❑ 42 Mo Vaughn	.50	.23
❑ 42A Mo Vaughn	.50	.23

Card	MINT	NRMT
❑ 43 Larry Walker	.40	.18
❑ 43A Larry Walker	.40	.18
❑ 44 Rondell White	.20	.09
❑ 44A Rondell White	.20	.09
❑ 45 Matt Williams	.20	.09
❑ 45A Matt Williams	.20	.09

1997 Collector's Choice

	MINT	NRMT
COMPLETE SET (506)	40.00	18.00
COMP.FACT.SET (516)	40.00	18.00
COMPLETE SERIES 1 (246)	20.00	9.00
COMPLETE SERIES 2 (260)	20.00	9.00
COMMON CARD (1-506)	.10	.05

Card	MINT	NRMT
❑ 1 Andruw Jones	.60	.25
❑ 2 Rocky Coppinger	.10	.05
❑ 3 Jeff D'Amico	.10	.05
❑ 4 Dmitri Young	.20	.09
❑ 5 Darin Erstad	.60	.25
❑ 6 Jermaine Allensworth	.10	.05
❑ 7 Damian Jackson	.10	.05
❑ 8 Bill Mueller	.50	.23
❑ 9 Jacob Cruz	.10	.05
❑ 10 Vladimir Guerrero	.75	.35
❑ 11 Marty Janzen	.10	.05
❑ 12 Kevin L. Brown	.10	.05
❑ 13 Willie Adams	.10	.05
❑ 14 Wendell Magee	.10	.05
❑ 15 Scott Rolen	1.00	.45
❑ 16 Matt Beech	.10	.05
❑ 17 Neifi Perez	.10	.05
❑ 18 Jamey Wright	.10	.05
❑ 19 Jose Paniagua	.10	.05
❑ 20 Todd Walker	.40	.18
❑ 21 Justin Thompson	.20	.09
❑ 22 Robin Jennings	.10	.05
❑ 23 Dario Veras	.25	.11
❑ 24 Brian Lesher	.10	.05
❑ 25 Nomar Garciaparra	1.25	.55
❑ 26 Luis Castillo	.20	.09
❑ 27 Brian Giles	.50	.23
❑ 28 Jermaine Dye	.10	.05
❑ 29 Terrell Wade	.10	.05
❑ 30 Fred McGriff	.30	.14
❑ 31 Marquis Grissom	.20	.09
❑ 32 Ryan Klesko	.20	.09
❑ 33 Javier Lopez	.20	.09
❑ 34 Mark Wohlers	.10	.05
❑ 35 Tom Glavine	.40	.18
❑ 36 Denny Neagle	.20	.09
❑ 37 Scott Erickson	.20	.09
❑ 38 Chris Hoiles	.10	.05
❑ 39 Roberto Alomar	.40	.18
❑ 40 Eddie Murray	.40	.18
❑ 41 Cal Ripken	1.50	.70
❑ 42 Randy Myers	.10	.05
❑ 43 B.J. Surhoff	.20	.09
❑ 44 Rick Krivda	.10	.05
❑ 45 Jose Canseco	.40	.18
❑ 46 Heathcliff Slocumb	.10	.05
❑ 47 Jeff Suppan	.10	.05
❑ 48 Tom Gordon	.10	.05
❑ 49 Aaron Sele	.20	.09
❑ 50 Mo Vaughn	.50	.23
❑ 51 Darren Bragg	.10	.05
❑ 52 Wil Cordero	.10	.05
❑ 53 Scott Bullett	.10	.05
❑ 54 Terry Adams	.10	.05
❑ 55 Jackie Robinson	1.00	.45
❑ 56 Tony Gwynn LL	.50	.23
Alex Rodriguez		
❑ 57 Andres Galarraga LL	.25	.11
Mark McGwire		
❑ 58 Andres Galarraga LL	.20	.09
Albert Belle		
❑ 59 Eric Young LL	.20	.09
Kenny Lofton		
❑ 60 John Smoltz LL	.10	.05
Andy Pettitte		
❑ 61 John Smoltz LL	.25	.11
Roger Clemens		
❑ 62 Kevin Brown LL	.10	.05
Juan Guzman		
❑ 63 John Wetteland LL	.10	.05
Todd Worrell		
Jeff Brantley		
❑ 64 Scott Servais	.10	.05
❑ 65 Sammy Sosa	1.00	.45
❑ 66 Ryne Sandberg	.50	.23
❑ 67 Frank Castillo	.10	.05
❑ 68 Rey Sanchez	.10	.05
❑ 69 Steve Trachsel	.10	.05
❑ 70 Robin Ventura	.20	.09
❑ 71 Wilson Alvarez	.20	.09
❑ 72 Tony Phillips	.10	.05
❑ 73 Lyle Mouton	.10	.05
❑ 74 Mike Cameron	.20	.09
❑ 75 Harold Baines	.20	.09
❑ 76 Albert Belle	.50	.23
❑ 77 Chris Snopek	.10	.05
❑ 78 Reggie Sanders	.20	.09
❑ 79 Jeff Brantley	.10	.05
❑ 80 Barry Larkin	.30	.14
❑ 81 Kevin Jarvis	.10	.05
❑ 82 John Smiley	.10	.05
❑ 83 Pete Schourek	.10	.05
❑ 84 Thomas Howard	.10	.05
❑ 85 Lee Smith	.20	.09
❑ 86 Omar Vizquel	.20	.09
❑ 87 Julio Franco	.20	.09
❑ 88 Orel Hershiser	.20	.09
❑ 89 Charles Nagy	.20	.09
❑ 90 Matt Williams	.20	.09
❑ 91 Dennis Martinez	.20	.09
❑ 92 Jose Mesa	.10	.05
❑ 93 Sandy Alomar Jr.	.20	.09
❑ 94 Jim Thome	.40	.18
❑ 95 Vinny Castilla	.30	.14
❑ 96 Armando Reynoso	.10	.05
❑ 97 Kevin Ritz	.10	.05
❑ 98 Larry Walker	.40	.18
❑ 99 Eric Young	.20	.09
❑ 100 Dante Bichette	.20	.09
❑ 101 Quinton McCracken	.20	.09
❑ 102 John Vander Wal	.10	.05
❑ 103 Phil Nevin	.10	.05
❑ 104 Tony Clark	.30	.14
❑ 105 Alan Trammell	.20	.09
❑ 106 Felipe Lira	.10	.05
❑ 107 Curtis Pride	.10	.05
❑ 108 Bobby Higginson	.30	.14
❑ 109 Mark Lewis	.10	.05
❑ 110 Travis Fryman	.20	.09
❑ 111 Al Leiter	.20	.09
❑ 112 Devon White	.20	.09
❑ 113 Jeff Conine	.20	.09
❑ 114 Charles Johnson	.20	.09
❑ 115 Andre Dawson	.30	.14
❑ 116 Edgar Renteria	.20	.09
❑ 117 Robb Nen	.10	.05
❑ 118 Kevin Brown	.30	.14
❑ 119 Derek Bell	.20	.09
❑ 120 Bob Abreu	.20	.09
❑ 121 Mike Hampton	.10	.05
❑ 122 Todd Jones	.10	.05
❑ 123 Billy Wagner	.20	.09
❑ 124 Shane Reynolds	.20	.09
❑ 125 Jeff Bagwell	.60	.25
❑ 126 Brian L. Hunter	.20	.09
❑ 127 Jeff Montgomery	.10	.05
❑ 128 Rod Myers	.20	.09
❑ 129 Tim Belcher	.10	.05
❑ 130 Kevin Appier	.20	.09
❑ 131 Mike Sweeney	.10	.05
❑ 132 Craig Paquette	.10	.05
❑ 133 Joe Randa	.10	.05
❑ 134 Michael Tucker	.20	.09
❑ 135 Raul Mondesi	.30	.14
❑ 136 Tim Wallach	.10	.05
❑ 137 Brett Butler	.20	.09
❑ 138 Karim Garcia	.20	.09
❑ 139 Todd Hollandsworth	.10	.05
❑ 140 Eric Karros	.20	.09
❑ 141 Hideo Nomo	.50	.23
❑ 142 Ismael Valdes	.20	.09
❑ 143 Cal Eldred	.10	.05
❑ 144 Scott Karl	.10	.05
❑ 145 Matt Mieske	.10	.05
❑ 146 Mike Fetters	.10	.05
❑ 147 Mark Loretta	.10	.05
❑ 148 Fernando Vina	.10	.05
❑ 149 Jeff Cirillo	.20	.09
❑ 150 Dave Nilsson	.10	.05
❑ 151 Kirby Puckett	.60	.25
❑ 152 Rich Becker	.10	.05
❑ 153 Chuck Knoblauch	.40	.18
❑ 154 Marty Cordova	.10	.05
❑ 155 Paul Molitor	.40	.18
❑ 156 Rick Aguilera	.10	.05
❑ 157 Pat Meares	.10	.05
❑ 158 Frank Rodriguez	.10	.05
❑ 159 David Segui	.20	.09
❑ 160 Henry Rodriguez	.20	.09
❑ 161 Shane Andrews	.10	.05
❑ 162 Pedro Martinez	.40	.18
❑ 163 Mark Grudzielanek	.20	.09
❑ 164 Mike Lansing	.10	.05
❑ 165 Rondell White	.20	.09
❑ 166 Ugueth Urbina	.20	.09
❑ 167 Rey Ordonez	.20	.09
❑ 168 Robert Person	.10	.05
❑ 169 Carlos Baerga	.20	.09
❑ 170 Bernard Gilkey	.10	.05
❑ 171 John Franco	.20	.09
❑ 172 Pete Harnisch	.10	.05
❑ 173 Butch Huskey	.10	.05
❑ 174 Paul Wilson	.10	.05
❑ 175 Dwight Gooden ERR	.20	.09
incorrectly numbered 175		
❑ 175 Bernie Williams	.40	.18
❑ 177 Wade Boggs	.40	.18
❑ 178 Ruben Rivera	.20	.09
❑ 179 Jim Leyritz	.10	.05
❑ 180 Derek Jeter	1.25	.55
❑ 181 Tino Martinez	.40	.18
❑ 182 Tim Raines	.20	.09
❑ 183 Scott Brosius	.20	.09
❑ 184 Jason Giambi	.20	.09
❑ 185 Geronimo Berroa	.10	.05
❑ 186 Ariel Prieto	.10	.05
❑ 187 Scott Spiezio	.10	.05
❑ 188 John Wasdin	.10	.05
❑ 189 Ernie Young	.10	.05
❑ 190 Mark McGwire	2.00	.90
❑ 191 Jim Eisenreich	.10	.05
❑ 192 Ricky Bottalico	.20	.09
❑ 193 Darren Daulton	.20	.09
❑ 194 David Doster	.10	.05
❑ 195 Gregg Jefferies	.10	.05
❑ 196 Lenny Dykstra	.20	.09
❑ 197 Curt Schilling	.20	.09
❑ 198 Todd Stottlemyre	.10	.05
❑ 199 Willie McGee	.20	.09
❑ 200 Ozzie Smith	.50	.23
❑ 201 Dennis Eckersley	.20	.09
❑ 202 Ray Lankford	.20	.09
❑ 203 John Mabry	.10	.05
❑ 204 Alan Benes	.20	.09
❑ 205 Ron Gant	.10	.05
❑ 206 Archi Cianfrocco	.10	.05
❑ 207 Fernando Valenzuela	.20	.09
❑ 208 Greg Vaughn	.20	.09
❑ 209 Steve Finley	.20	.09
❑ 210 Tony Gwynn	1.00	.45
❑ 211 Rickey Henderson	.40	.18
❑ 212 Trevor Hoffman	.20	.09

❑ 213	Jason Thompson	.10	.05
❑ 214	Osvaldo Fernandez	.10	.05
❑ 215	Glenallen Hill	.10	.05
❑ 216	William VanLandingham	.10	.05
❑ 217	Marvin Benard	.10	.05
❑ 218	Juan Gonzalez POST	.50	.23
❑ 219	Roberto Alomar POST	.20	.09
❑ 220	Brian Jordan POST	.10	.05
❑ 221	John Smoltz POST	.10	.05
❑ 222	Javy Lopez POST	.10	.05
❑ 223	Bernie Williams POST	.20	.09
❑ 224	Jim Leyritz POST John Wetteland	.10	.05
❑ 225	Barry Bonds	.50	.23
❑ 226	Rich Aurilia	.10	.05
❑ 227	Jay Canizaro	.10	.05
❑ 228	Dan Wilson	.10	.05
❑ 229	Bob Wolcott	.10	.05
❑ 230	Ken Griffey Jr.	2.00	.90
❑ 231	Sterling Hitchcock	.20	.09
❑ 232	Edgar Martinez	.20	.09
❑ 233	Joey Cora	.20	.09
❑ 234	Norm Charlton	.10	.05
❑ 235	Alex Rodriguez	1.25	.55
❑ 236	Bobby Witt	.10	.05
❑ 237	Darren Oliver	.10	.05
❑ 238	Kevin Elster	.10	.05
❑ 239	Rusty Greer	.20	.09
❑ 240	Juan Gonzalez	1.00	.45
❑ 241	Will Clark	.40	.18
❑ 242	Dean Palmer	.20	.09
❑ 243	Ivan Rodriguez	.50	.23
❑ 244	Ken Griffey Jr. CL	.25	.11
❑ 245	Ken Griffey Jr. CL	.25	.11
❑ 246	Ken Griffey Jr. CL	.25	.11
❑ 247	Ken Griffey Jr. CL	.25	.11
❑ 248	Ken Griffey Jr. CL	.25	.11
❑ 249	Ken Griffey Jr. CL	.25	.11
❑ 250	Eddie Murray	.40	.18
❑ 251	Troy Percival	.20	.09
❑ 252	Garret Anderson	.20	.09
❑ 253	Allen Watson	.10	.05
❑ 254	Jason Dickson	.20	.09
❑ 255	Jim Edmonds	.30	.14
❑ 256	Chuck Finley	.20	.09
❑ 257	Randy Velarde	.10	.05
❑ 258	Shigetoshi Hasegawa	.25	.11
❑ 259	Todd Greene	.20	.09
❑ 260	Tim Salmon	.40	.18
❑ 261	Mark Langston	.20	.09
❑ 262	Dave Hollins	.10	.05
❑ 263	Gary DiSarcina	.10	.05
❑ 264	Kenny Lofton	.40	.18
❑ 265	John Smoltz	.20	.09
❑ 266	Greg Maddux	1.25	.55
❑ 267	Jeff Blauser	.10	.05
❑ 268	Alan Embree	.10	.05
❑ 269	Mark Lemke	.10	.05
❑ 270	Chipper Jones	1.00	.45
❑ 271	Mike Mussina	.40	.18
❑ 272	Rafael Palmeiro	.30	.14
❑ 273	Jimmy Key	.20	.09
❑ 274	Mike Bordick	.10	.05
❑ 275	Brady Anderson	.20	.09
❑ 276	Eric Davis	.20	.09
❑ 277	Jeffrey Hammonds	.20	.09
❑ 278	Reggie Jefferson	.10	.05
❑ 279	Tim Naehring	.10	.05
❑ 280	John Valentin	.20	.09
❑ 281	Troy O'Leary	.20	.09
❑ 282	Shane Mack	.10	.05
❑ 283	Mike Stanley	.10	.05
❑ 284	Tim Wakefield	.20	.09
❑ 285	Brian McRae	.10	.05
❑ 286	Brooks Kieschnick	.10	.05
❑ 287	Shawon Dunston	.10	.05
❑ 288	Kevin Foster	.10	.05
❑ 289	Mel Rojas	.10	.05
❑ 290	Mark Grace	.30	.14
❑ 291	Brant Brown	.20	.09
❑ 292	Amaury Telemaco	.10	.05
❑ 293	Dave Martinez	.10	.05
❑ 294	Jaime Navarro	.10	.05
❑ 295	Ray Durham	.20	.09
❑ 296	Ozzie Guillen	.10	.05
❑ 297	Roberto Hernandez	.10	.05
❑ 298	Ron Karkovice	.10	.05
❑ 299	James Baldwin	.20	.09
❑ 300	Frank Thomas	1.25	.55
❑ 301	Eddie Taubensee	.10	.05
❑ 302	Bret Boone	.20	.09
❑ 303	Willie Greene	.20	.09
❑ 304	Dave Burba	.10	.05
❑ 305	Deion Sanders	.20	.09
❑ 306	Reggie Sanders	.20	.09
❑ 307	Hal Morris	.10	.05
❑ 308	Pokey Reese	.10	.05
❑ 309	Tony Fernandez	.10	.05
❑ 310	Manny Ramirez	.40	.18
❑ 311	Chad Ogea	.10	.05
❑ 312	Jack McDowell	.10	.05
❑ 313	Kevin Mitchell	.10	.05
❑ 314	Chad Curtis	.10	.05
❑ 315	Steve Kline	.10	.05
❑ 316	Kevin Seitzer	.10	.05
❑ 317	Kirt Manwaring	.10	.05
❑ 318	Billy Swift	.10	.05
❑ 319	Ellis Burks	.20	.09
❑ 320	Andres Galarraga	.40	.18
❑ 321	Bruce Ruffin	.10	.05
❑ 322	Mark Thompson	.10	.05
❑ 323	Walt Weiss	.10	.05
❑ 324	Todd Jones	.10	.05
❑ 325	Andruw Jones GHL	.50	.23
❑ 326	Chipper Jones GHL	.50	.23
❑ 327	Mo Vaughn GHL	.25	.11
❑ 328	Frank Thomas GHL	.60	.25
❑ 329	Albert Belle GHL	.25	.11
❑ 330	Mark McGwire GHL	1.00	.45
❑ 331	Derek Jeter GHL	.60	.25
❑ 332	Alex Rodriguez GHL	.60	.25
❑ 333	Jay Buhner GHL with Ken Griffey Jr.	.10	.05
❑ 334	Ken Griffey Jr. GHL	1.00	.45
❑ 335	Brian L. Hunter	.20	.09
❑ 336	Brian Johnson	.10	.05
❑ 337	Omar Olivares	.10	.05
❑ 338	Deivi Cruz	.30	.14
❑ 339	Damion Easley	.20	.09
❑ 340	Melvin Nieves	.10	.05
❑ 341	Moises Alou	.30	.14
❑ 342	Jim Eisenreich	.10	.05
❑ 343	Mark Hutton	.10	.05
❑ 344	Alex Fernandez	.10	.05
❑ 345	Gary Sheffield	.30	.14
❑ 346	Pat Rapp	.10	.05
❑ 347	Brad Ausmus	.10	.05
❑ 348	Sean Berry	.10	.05
❑ 349	Darryl Kile	.20	.09
❑ 350	Craig Biggio	.40	.18
❑ 351	Chris Holt	.10	.05
❑ 352	Luis Gonzalez	.10	.05
❑ 353	Pat Listach	.10	.05
❑ 354	Jose Rosado	.10	.05
❑ 355	Mike Macfarlane	.10	.05
❑ 356	Tom Goodwin	.10	.05
❑ 357	Chris Haney	.10	.05
❑ 358	Chili Davis	.20	.09
❑ 359	Jose Offerman	.10	.05
❑ 360	Johnny Damon	.20	.09
❑ 361	Bip Roberts	.10	.05
❑ 362	Ramon Martinez	.20	.09
❑ 363	Pedro Astacio	.10	.05
❑ 364	Todd Zeile	.10	.05
❑ 365	Mike Piazza	1.25	.55
❑ 366	Greg Gagne	.10	.05
❑ 367	Chan Ho Park	.40	.18
❑ 368	Wilton Guerrero	.10	.05
❑ 369	Todd Worrell	.10	.05
❑ 370	John Jaha	.10	.05
❑ 371	Steve Sparks	.10	.05
❑ 372	Mike Matheny	.10	.05
❑ 373	Marc Newfield	.10	.05
❑ 374	Jeromy Burnitz	.20	.09
❑ 375	Jose Valentin	.10	.05
❑ 376	Ben McDonald	.10	.05
❑ 377	Roberto Kelly	.10	.05
❑ 378	Bob Tewksbury	.10	.05
❑ 379	Ron Coomer	.10	.05
❑ 380	Brad Radke	.20	.09
❑ 381	Matt Lawton	.20	.09
❑ 382	Dan Naulty	.10	.05
❑ 383	Scott Stahoviak	.10	.05
❑ 384	Matt Wagner	.10	.05
❑ 385	Jim Bullinger	.10	.05
❑ 386	Carlos Perez	.20	.09
❑ 387	Darrin Fletcher	.10	.05
❑ 388	Chris Widger	.10	.05
❑ 389	F.P. Santangelo	.10	.05
❑ 390	Lee Smith	.20	.09
❑ 391	Bobby Jones	.10	.05
❑ 392	John Olerud	.20	.09
❑ 393	Mark Clark	.10	.05
❑ 394	Jason Isringhausen	.10	.05
❑ 395	Todd Hundley	.20	.09
❑ 396	Lance Johnson	.10	.05
❑ 397	Edgardo Alfonzo	.20	.09
❑ 398	Alex Ochoa	.10	.05
❑ 399	Darryl Strawberry	.20	.09
❑ 400	David Cone	.30	.14
❑ 401	Paul O'Neill	.20	.09
❑ 402	Joe Girardi	.10	.05
❑ 403	Charlie Hayes	.10	.05
❑ 404	Andy Pettitte	.30	.14
❑ 405	Mariano Rivera	.20	.09
❑ 406	Mariano Duncan	.10	.05
❑ 407	Kenny Rogers	.10	.05
❑ 408	Cecil Fielder	.20	.09
❑ 409	George Williams	.10	.05
❑ 410	Jose Canseco	.40	.18
❑ 411	Tony Batista	.10	.05
❑ 412	Steve Karsay	.10	.05
❑ 413	Dave Telgheder	.10	.05
❑ 414	Billy Taylor	.10	.05
❑ 415	Mickey Morandini	.10	.05
❑ 416	Calvin Maduro	.10	.05
❑ 417	Mark Leiter	.10	.05
❑ 418	Kevin Stocker	.10	.05
❑ 419	Mike Lieberthal	.10	.05
❑ 420	Rico Brogna	.10	.05
❑ 421	Mark Portugal	.10	.05
❑ 422	Rex Hudler	.10	.05
❑ 423	Mark Johnson	.10	.05
❑ 424	Esteban Loaiza	.10	.05
❑ 425	Lou Collier	.10	.05
❑ 426	Kevin Elster	.10	.05
❑ 427	Francisco Cordova	.10	.05
❑ 428	Marc Wilkins	.10	.05
❑ 429	Joe Randa	.10	.05
❑ 430	Jason Kendall	.30	.14
❑ 431	Jon Lieber	.10	.05
❑ 432	Steve Cooke	.10	.05
❑ 433	Emil Brown	.30	.14
❑ 434	Tony Womack	.30	.14
❑ 435	Al Martin	.10	.05
❑ 436	Jason Schmidt	.10	.05
❑ 437	Andy Benes	.20	.09
❑ 438	Delino DeShields	.10	.05
❑ 439	Royce Clayton	.10	.05
❑ 440	Brian Jordan	.20	.09
❑ 441	Donovan Osborne	.10	.05
❑ 442	Gary Gaetti	.10	.05
❑ 443	Tom Pagnozzi	.10	.05
❑ 444	Joey Hamilton	.20	.09
❑ 445	Wally Joyner	.20	.09
❑ 446	John Flaherty	.10	.05
❑ 447	Chris Gomez	.10	.05
❑ 448	Sterling Hitchcock	.20	.09
❑ 449	Andy Ashby	.10	.05
❑ 450	Ken Caminiti	.30	.14
❑ 451	Tim Worrell	.10	.05
❑ 452	Jose Vizcaino	.10	.05
❑ 453	Rod Beck	.10	.05
❑ 454	Wilson Delgado	.20	.09
❑ 455	Darryl Hamilton	.10	.05
❑ 456	Mark Lewis	.10	.05
❑ 457	Mark Gardner	.10	.05
❑ 458	Rick Wilkins	.10	.05
❑ 459	Scott Sanders	.10	.05
❑ 460	Kevin Orie	.10	.05
❑ 461	Glendon Rusch	.10	.05
❑ 462	Juan Melo	.20	.09
❑ 463	Richie Sexson	.30	.14
❑ 464	Bartolo Colon	.20	.09
❑ 465	Jose Guillen	.40	.18

		MINT	NRMT
❑ 466	Heath Murray	.10	.05
❑ 467	Aaron Boone	.10	.05
❑ 468	Bubba Trammell	.25	.11
❑ 469	Jeff Abbott	.20	.09
❑ 470	Derrick Gibson	.30	.14
❑ 471	Matt Morris	.20	.09
❑ 472	Ryan Jones	.10	.05
❑ 473	Pat Cline	.20	.09
❑ 474	Adam Riggs	.10	.05
❑ 475	Jay Payton	.10	.05
❑ 476	Derrek Lee	.30	.14
❑ 477	Eli Marrero	.20	.09
❑ 478	Lee Tinsley	.10	.05
❑ 479	Jamie Moyer	.10	.05
❑ 480	Jay Buhner	.20	.09
❑ 481	Bob Wells	.10	.05
❑ 482	Jeff Fassero	.10	.05
❑ 483	Paul Sorrento	.10	.05
❑ 484	Russ Davis	.20	.09
❑ 485	Randy Johnson	.40	.18
❑ 486	Roger Pavlik	.10	.05
❑ 487	Damon Buford	.10	.05
❑ 488	Julio Santana	.10	.05
❑ 489	Mark McLemore	.10	.05
❑ 490	Mickey Tettleton	.10	.05
❑ 491	Ken Hill	.10	.05
❑ 492	Benji Gil	.10	.05
❑ 493	Ed Sprague	.10	.05
❑ 494	Mike Timlin	.10	.05
❑ 495	Pat Hentgen	.20	.09
❑ 496	Orlando Merced	.10	.05
❑ 497	Carlos Garcia	.10	.05
❑ 498	Carlos Delgado	.20	.09
❑ 499	Juan Guzman	.10	.05
❑ 500	Roger Clemens	.75	.35
❑ 501	Erik Hanson	.10	.05
❑ 502	Otis Nixon	.10	.05
❑ 503	Shawn Green	.20	.09
❑ 504	Charlie O'Brien	.10	.05
❑ 505	Joe Carter	.20	.09
❑ 506	Alex Gonzalez	.10	.05

1997 Collector's Choice All-Star Connection

	MINT	NRMT
COMPLETE SET (45)	12.00	5.50
COMMON CARD (1-45)	.10	.05

		MINT	NRMT
❑ 1	Mark McGwire	2.00	.90
❑ 2	Chuck Knoblauch	.40	.18
❑ 3	Jim Thome	.40	.18
❑ 4	Alex Rodriguez	1.25	.55
❑ 5	Ken Griffey Jr.	2.00	.90
❑ 6	Brady Anderson	.20	.09
❑ 7	Albert Belle	.50	.23
❑ 8	Ivan Rodriguez	.50	.23
❑ 9	Pat Hentgen	.20	.09
❑ 10	Frank Thomas	1.50	.70
❑ 11	Roberto Alomar	.40	.18
❑ 12	Robin Ventura	.20	.09
❑ 13	Cal Ripken	1.50	.70
❑ 14	Juan Gonzalez	1.00	.45
❑ 15	Manny Ramirez	.40	.18
❑ 16	Bernie Williams	.40	.18
❑ 17	Terry Steinbach	.20	.09
❑ 18	Andy Pettitte	.30	.14
❑ 19	Jeff Bagwell	.75	.35
❑ 20	Craig Biggio	.40	.18
❑ 21	Ken Caminiti	.30	.14
❑ 22	Barry Larkin	.30	.14
❑ 23	Tony Gwynn	1.00	.45
❑ 24	Barry Bonds	.50	.23
❑ 25	Kenny Lofton	.50	.23
❑ 26	Mike Piazza	1.25	.55
❑ 27	John Smoltz	.20	.09
❑ 28	Andres Galarraga	.40	.18
❑ 29	Ryne Sandberg	.50	.23
❑ 30	Chipper Jones	1.25	.55
❑ 31	Mark Grudzielanek	.20	.09
❑ 32	Sammy Sosa	1.00	.45
❑ 33	Steve Finley	.20	.09
❑ 34	Gary Sheffield	.30	.14
❑ 35	Todd Hundley	.20	.09
❑ 36	Greg Maddux	1.25	.55
❑ 37	Mo Vaughn	.40	.18
❑ 38	Eric Young	.20	.09
❑ 39	Vinny Castilla	.30	.14
❑ 40	Derek Jeter	1.25	.55
❑ 41	Lance Johnson	.10	.05
❑ 42	Ellis Burks	.20	.09
❑ 43	Dante Bichette	.20	.09
❑ 44	Javy Lopez	.20	.09
❑ 45	Hideo Nomo	.60	.25

1997 Collector's Choice Big Shots

	MINT	NRMT
COMPLETE SET (19)	60.00	27.00
COMMON CARD (1-19)	1.00	.45
COMP.GOLD SET (20)	250.00	110.00

*GOLD CARDS: 1.5X TO 4X BASIC BIG SHOT
SER.2 STATED ODDS 1:144

		MINT	NRMT
❑ 1	Ken Griffey Jr.	10.00	4.50
❑ 2	Nomar Garciaparra	6.00	2.70
❑ 3	Brian Jordan	1.25	.55
❑ 4	Scott Rolen	5.00	2.20
❑ 5	Alex Rodriguez	6.00	2.70
❑ 6	Larry Walker	2.00	.90
❑ 7	Mariano Rivera	1.25	.55
❑ 8	Cal Ripken	8.00	3.60
❑ 9	Deion Sanders	1.25	.55
❑ 10	Frank Thomas	6.00	2.70
❑ 11	Dean Palmer	1.00	.45
❑ 12	Ken Caminiti	1.50	.70
❑ 13	Derek Jeter	5.00	2.20
❑ 14	Barry Bonds	2.50	1.10
❑ 15	Chipper Jones	5.00	2.20
❑ 16	Mo Vaughn	2.50	1.10
❑ 17	Jay Buhner	1.25	.55
❑ 18	Mike Piazza	6.00	2.70
❑ 19	Tony Gwynn	5.00	2.20

1997 Collector's Choice The Big Show

	MINT	NRMT
COMPLETE SET (45)	10.00	4.50
COMMON CARD (1-45)	.10	.05
COMP.WORLD HQ SET (45)	250.00	110.00

*WHQ STARS: 15X TO 40X BASIC CARDS
WHQ SER.1 STATED ODDS 1:35

		MINT	NRMT
❑ 1	Greg Maddux	1.25	.55
❑ 2	Chipper Jones	1.00	.45
❑ 3	Andruw Jones	.75	.35
❑ 4	John Smoltz	.20	.09
❑ 5	Cal Ripken	1.50	.70
❑ 6	Roberto Alomar	.40	.18
❑ 7	Rafael Palmeiro	.30	.14
❑ 8	Eddie Murray	.40	.18
❑ 9	Jose Canseco	.40	.18
❑ 10	Roger Clemens	.75	.35
❑ 11	Mo Vaughn	.50	.23
❑ 12	Jim Edmonds	.30	.14
❑ 13	Tim Salmon	.40	.18
❑ 14	Sammy Sosa	1.00	.45
❑ 15	Albert Belle	.40	.18
❑ 16	Frank Thomas	1.25	.55
❑ 17	Barry Larkin	.30	.14
❑ 18	Kenny Lofton	.40	.18
❑ 19	Manny Ramirez	.40	.18
❑ 20	Matt Williams	.20	.09
❑ 21	Dante Bichette	.20	.09
❑ 22	Gary Sheffield	.30	.14
❑ 23	Craig Biggio	.40	.18
❑ 24	Jeff Bagwell	.75	.35
❑ 25	Todd Hollandsworth	.10	.05
❑ 26	Raul Mondesi	.30	.14
❑ 27	Hideo Nomo	1.00	.45
❑ 28	Mike Piazza	1.25	.55
❑ 29	Paul Molitor	.40	.18
❑ 30	Kirby Puckett	.40	.18
❑ 31	Rondell White	.20	.09
❑ 32	Rey Ordonez	.20	.09
❑ 33	Paul Wilson	.10	.05
❑ 34	Derek Jeter	1.25	.55
❑ 35	Andy Pettitte	.30	.14
❑ 36	Mark McGwire	2.00	.90
❑ 37	Jason Kendall	.30	.14
❑ 38	Ozzie Smith	.40	.18
❑ 39	Tony Gwynn	1.00	.45
❑ 40	Barry Bonds	.50	.23
❑ 41	Alex Rodriguez	1.25	.55
❑ 42	Jay Buhner	.20	.09
❑ 43	Ken Griffey Jr.	2.00	.90
❑ 44	Randy Johnson	.40	.18
❑ 45	Juan Gonzalez	1.00	.45

1997 Collector's Choice Crash the Game

	MINT	NRMT
COMPLETE SET (90)	60.00	27.00
COMMON CARD (CG1-CG30)	.25	.11

		MINT	NRMT
❑ 1A	R.Klesko July 28-30 L	.50	.23
❑ 1B	R.Klesko Aug 8-11 L	.50	.23
❑ 1C	R.Klesko Sept 19-21 L	.50	.23
❑ 2A	C.Jones Aug 15-17 L	2.50	1.10
❑ 2B	C.Jones Aug 29-31 L	2.50	1.10
❑ 2C	C.Jones Sept 12-14 L	2.50	1.10
❑ 3A	A. Jones Aug 22-24 W	2.00	.90
❑ 3B	A. Jones Sept 1-3	2.00	.90
❑ 3C	A.Jones Sept 19-22 L	2.00	.90
❑ 4A	B. Ander. July 31-Aug 3 W	.25	.11
❑ 4B	B.Anderson Sept 4-7 L	.25	.11
❑ 4C	B.Anderson Sept 19-22 L	.25	.11
❑ 5A	R.Palmeiro July 29-30 L	.50	.23
❑ 5B	R.Palmeiro Aug 29-31 L	.50	.23

Card	MINT	NRMT
❑ 5C R.Palmeiro Sept 26-28 L	.50	.23
❑ 6A Cal Ripken Aug 8-10	3.00	1.35
❑ 6B C.Ripken Sept 1-3 W	3.00	1.35
❑ 6C C.Ripken Sept 11-14 L	3.00	1.35
❑ 7A M.Vaughn Aug 14-17 L	1.00	.45
❑ 7B M.Vaughn Aug 29-31 W	1.00	.45
❑ 7C M.Vaughn Sept 23-25 W	1.00	.45
❑ 8A S.Sosa Aug 1-3 W	2.00	.90
❑ 8B S.Sosa Aug 29-31 L	2.00	.90
❑ 8C S.Sosa Sept 19-21 W	2.00	.90
❑ 9A A.Belle Aug 7-10 L	1.00	.45
❑ 9B A.Belle Sept 11-14 L	1.00	.45
❑ 9C A.Belle Sept 19-21 W	1.00	.45
❑ 10A F.Thomas Aug 29-31 L	2.50	1.10
❑ 10B F.Thomas Sept 1-3 L	2.50	1.10
❑ 10C F.Thomas Sept 23-25 W	2.50	1.10
❑ 11A M.Ramirez Aug 12-14 W	.75	.35
❑ 11B M.Ramirez Aug 29-31 L	.75	.35
❑ 11C M.Ramirez Sept 11-14 W	.75	.35
❑ 12A J.Thome July 28-30 L	.75	.35
❑ 12B J.Thome Aug 15-18 W	.75	.35
❑ 12C J.Thome Sept 19-22 L	.75	.35
❑ 13A M.Williams Aug 4-5 L	.50	.23
❑ 13B M.Williams Sept 1-3 W	.50	.23
❑ 13C M.Williams Sept 23-25 L	.50	.23
❑ 14A D.Bichette July 24-27 W	.25	.11
❑ 14B D.Bichette Aug 28-29 L	.25	.11
❑ 14C D.Bichette Sept 26-28 W	.25	.11
❑ 15A V.Castilla Aug 12-13 L	.25	.11
❑ 15B V.Castilla Sept 4-7 W	.25	.11
❑ 15C V.Castilla Sept 19-21 L	.25	.11
❑ 16A A.Galarraga Aug 8-10 W	.75	.35
❑ 16B A.Galarraga Aug 30-31 L	.75	.35
❑ 16C A.Galarraga Sept 12-14 L	.75	.35
❑ 17A G.Sheffield Aug 1-3 W	.50	.23
❑ 17B G.Sheffield Sept 1-3 W	.50	.23
❑ 17C G.Sheffield Sept 12-14 W	.50	.23
❑ 18A J.Bagwell Sept 9-10 L	1.50	.70
❑ 18B J.Bagwell Sept 19-22 W	1.50	.70
❑ 18C J.Bagwell Sept 23-25 W	1.50	.70
❑ 19A E.Karros Aug 1-3 L	.25	.11
❑ 19B E.Karros Aug 15-17 L	.25	.11
❑ 19C E.Karros Sept 25-28 W	.25	.11
❑ 20A M.Piazza Aug 11-12 L	2.50	1.10
❑ 20B M.Piazza Sept 5-8 W	2.50	1.10
❑ 20C M.Piazza Sept 19-21 W	2.50	1.10
❑ 21A V.Guerrero Aug 22-24 L	1.50	.70
❑ 21B V.Guerrero Aug 29-31 L	1.50	.70
❑ 21C V.Guerrero Sept 19-22 L	1.50	.70
❑ 22A C.Fielder Aug 29-31 L	.25	.11
❑ 22B C.Fielder Sept 4-7 L	.25	.11
❑ 22C C.Fielder Sept 26-28 L	.25	.11
❑ 23A J.Canseco Sept 12-14 L	.75	.35
❑ 23B J.Canseco Sept 22-24 L	.75	.35
❑ 23C J.Canseco Sept 26-28 L	.75	.35
❑ 24A McGwire July 31-Aug 3 L	4.00	1.80
❑ 24B M.McGwire Aug 30-31 L	4.00	1.80
❑ 24C McGwire Sept 19-22 W	4.00	1.80
❑ 25A K.Caminiti Aug 8-10 L	.50	.23
❑ 25B K.Caminiti Sept 4-7 W	.50	.23
❑ 25C K.Caminiti Sept 17-18 W	.50	.23
❑ 26A B.Bonds Aug 5-7 L	1.00	.45
❑ 26B B.Bonds Sept 4-7 L	1.00	.45
❑ 26C B.Bonds Sept 23-24 W	1.00	.45
❑ 27A J.Buhner Aug 7-10 L	.25	.11
❑ 27B J.Buhner Aug 28-29 L	.25	.11
❑ 27C J.Buhner Sept 1-3 L	.25	.11
❑ 28A K.Griffey Aug 22-24 W	4.00	1.80
❑ 28B K.Griffey Aug 28-29 L	4.00	1.80
❑ 28C K.Griffey Sept 19-22 W	4.00	1.80
❑ 29A A.Rodriguez July 29-31 L	2.50	1.10
❑ 29B A.Rodriguez Aug 30-31 L	2.50	1.10
❑ 29C A.Rod. Sept 12-15 L	2.50	1.10
❑ 30A J.Gonzalez Aug 11-13 W	2.00	.90
❑ 30B J.Gonzalez Aug 30-31 L	2.00	.90
❑ 30C J.Gonzalez Sept 19-21 W	2.00	.90

1997 Collector's Choice Crash the Game Exchange

	MINT	NRMT
COMPLETE SET (30)	120.00	55.00
COMMON CARD (CG1-CG30)	1.00	.45
❑ CG1 Ryan Klesko SP	4.00	1.80
❑ CG2 Chipper Jones SP	25.00	11.00
❑ CG3 Andruw Jones	5.00	2.20
❑ CG4 Brady Anderson	1.00	.45
❑ CG5 Rafael Palmeiro SP	6.00	2.70
❑ CG6 Cal Ripken Jr.	10.00	4.50
❑ CG7 Mo Vaughn	3.00	1.35
❑ CG8 Sammy Sosa	6.00	2.70
❑ CG9 Albert Belle	3.00	1.35
❑ CG10 Frank Thomas	10.00	4.50
❑ CG11 Manny Ramirez	2.50	1.10
❑ CG12 Jim Thome	2.50	1.10
❑ CG13 Matt Williams	1.00	.45
❑ CG14 Dante Bichette	1.00	.45
❑ CG15 Vinny Castilla	1.50	.70
❑ CG16 Andres Galarraga	2.00	.90
❑ CG17 Gary Sheffield	1.50	.70
❑ CG18 Jeff Bagwell	5.00	2.20
❑ CG19 Eric Karros	1.00	.45
❑ CG20 Mike Piazza	8.00	3.60
❑ CG21 Vladimir Guerrero SP	15.00	6.75
❑ CG22 Cecil Fielder SP	4.00	1.80
❑ CG23 Jose Canseco SP	10.00	4.50
❑ CG24 Mark McGwire	12.00	5.50
❑ CG25 Ken Caminiti	1.50	.70
❑ CG26 Barry Bonds	3.00	1.35
❑ CG27 Jay Buhner SP	5.00	2.20
❑ CG28 Ken Griffey Jr.	12.00	5.50
❑ CG29 Alex Rodriguez SP	30.00	13.50
❑ CG30 Juan Gonzalez	6.00	2.70

1997 Collector's Choice Griffey Clearly Dominant

	MINT	NRMT
COMPLETE SET (5)	80.00	36.00
COMMON GRIFFEY (CD1-CD5)	20.00	9.00
❑ CD1 Ken Griffey Jr. Cap Worn Backwords	20.00	9.00
❑ CD2 Ken Griffey Jr. With Eye Chalk and Flip Sunglasses	20.00	9.00
❑ CD3 Ken Griffey Jr. Portrait	20.00	9.00
❑ CD4 Ken Griffey Jr. Batting	20.00	9.00
❑ CD5 Ken Griffey Jr.	20.00	9.00

1997 Collector's Choice New Frontier

	MINT	NRMT
COMPLETE SET (40)	450.00	200.00
COMMON CARD (NF1-NF40)	4.00	1.80
❑ NF1 Alex Rodriguez	25.00	11.00
❑ NF2 Tony Gwynn	20.00	9.00
❑ NF3 Jose Canseco	8.00	3.60
❑ NF4 Hideo Nomo	10.00	4.50
❑ NF5 Mark McGwire	40.00	18.00
❑ NF6 Barry Bonds	10.00	4.50
❑ NF7 Juan Gonzalez	20.00	9.00
❑ NF8 Ken Caminiti	5.00	2.20
❑ NF9 Tim Salmon	8.00	3.60
❑ NF10 Mike Piazza	25.00	11.00
❑ NF11 Ken Griffey Jr.	40.00	18.00
❑ NF12 Andres Galarraga	8.00	3.60
❑ NF13 Jay Buhner	4.00	1.80
❑ NF14 Dante Bichette	4.00	1.80
❑ NF15 Frank Thomas	25.00	11.00
❑ NF16 Ryne Sandberg	10.00	4.50
❑ NF17 Roger Clemens	15.00	6.75
❑ NF18 Andruw Jones	10.00	4.50
❑ NF19 Jim Thome	8.00	3.60
❑ NF20 Sammy Sosa	20.00	9.00
❑ NF21 Dave Justice	8.00	3.60
❑ NF22 Deion Sanders	4.00	1.80
❑ NF23 Todd Walker	8.00	3.60
❑ NF24 Kevin Orie	4.00	1.80
❑ NF25 Albert Belle	10.00	4.50
❑ NF26 Jeff Bagwell	12.00	5.50
❑ NF27 Manny Ramirez	8.00	3.60
❑ NF28 Brian Jordan	4.00	1.80
❑ NF29 Derek Jeter	20.00	9.00
❑ NF30 Chipper Jones	20.00	9.00
❑ NF31 Mo Vaughn	10.00	4.50
❑ NF32 Gary Sheffield	5.00	2.20
❑ NF33 Carlos Delgado	4.00	1.80
❑ NF34 Vladimir Guerrero	12.00	5.50
❑ NF35 Cal Ripken	30.00	13.50
❑ NF36 Greg Maddux	25.00	11.00
❑ NF37 Cecil Fielder	4.00	1.80
❑ NF38 Todd Hundley	4.00	1.80
❑ NF39 Mike Mussina	8.00	3.60
❑ NF40 Scott Rolen	20.00	9.00

1997 Collector's Choice Premier Power

	MINT	NRMT
COMPLETE SET (20)	40.00	18.00
COMMON CARD (PP1-PP20)	1.00	.45
❑ PP1 Mark McGwire	10.00	4.50
❑ PP2 Brady Anderson	1.00	.45
❑ PP3 Ken Griffey Jr.	10.00	4.50
❑ PP4 Albert Belle	2.50	1.10
❑ PP5 Juan Gonzalez	5.00	2.20
❑ PP6 Andres Galarraga	2.00	.90
❑ PP7 Jay Buhner	1.00	.45
❑ PP8 Mo Vaughn	2.50	1.10
❑ PP9 Barry Bonds	2.50	1.10
❑ PP10 Gary Sheffield	1.50	.70
❑ PP11 Todd Hundley	1.00	.45
❑ PP12 Frank Thomas	6.00	2.70

❑ PP13 Sammy Sosa	5.00	2.20
❑ PP14 Ken Caminiti	1.50	.70
❑ PP15 Vinny Castilla	1.50	.70
❑ PP16 Ellis Burks	1.00	.45
❑ PP17 Rafael Palmeiro	1.50	.70
❑ PP18 Alex Rodriguez	6.00	2.70
❑ PP19 Mike Piazza	6.00	2.70
❑ PP20 Eddie Murray	2.00	.90

1997 Collector's Choice Stick'Ums

	MINT	NRMT
COMPLETE SET (30)	15.00	6.75
COMMON CARD (1-30)	.25	.11
❑ 1 Ozzie Smith	.60	.25
❑ 2 Andruw Jones	1.25	.55
❑ 3 Alex Rodriguez	2.00	.90
❑ 4 Paul Molitor	.60	.25
❑ 5 Jeff Bagwell	1.25	.55
❑ 6 Manny Ramirez	.60	.25
❑ 7 Kenny Lofton	.75	.35
❑ 8 Albert Belle	.60	.25
❑ 9 Jay Buhner	.25	.11
❑ 10 Chipper Jones	2.00	.90
❑ 11 Barry Larkin	.40	.18
❑ 12 Dante Bichette	.25	.11
❑ 13 Mike Piazza	2.00	.90
❑ 14 Andres Galarraga	.60	.25
❑ 15 Barry Bonds	.75	.35
❑ 16 Brady Anderson	.25	.11
❑ 17 Gary Sheffield	.40	.18
❑ 18 Jim Thome	.60	.25
❑ 19 Tony Gwynn	1.25	.55
❑ 20 Cal Ripken	2.50	1.10
❑ 21 Sammy Sosa	1.50	.70
❑ 22 Juan Gonzalez	1.50	.70
❑ 23 Greg Maddux	2.00	.90
❑ 24 Ken Griffey Jr.	3.00	1.35
❑ 25 Mark McGwire	3.00	1.35
❑ 26 Kirby Puckett	.60	.25
❑ 27 Mo Vaughn	.75	.35
❑ 28 Vladimir Guerrero	1.25	.55
❑ 29 Ken Caminiti	.40	.18
❑ 30 Frank Thomas	2.00	.90

1997 Collector's Choice Toast of the Town

	MINT	NRMT
COMPLETE SET (30)	250.00	110.00
COMMON CARD (T1-T30)	2.50	1.10
❑ T1 Andruw Jones	8.00	3.60
❑ T2 Chipper Jones	12.00	5.50
❑ T3 Greg Maddux	15.00	6.75
❑ T4 John Smoltz	2.50	1.10
❑ T5 Kenny Lofton	5.00	2.20
❑ T6 Brady Anderson	2.50	1.10
❑ T7 Cal Ripken	20.00	9.00
❑ T8 Mo Vaughn	6.00	2.70
❑ T9 Sammy Sosa	12.00	5.50
❑ T10 Albert Belle	6.00	2.70
❑ T11 Frank Thomas	15.00	6.75
❑ T12 Barry Larkin	4.00	1.80
❑ T13 Manny Ramirez	5.00	2.20
❑ T14 Jeff Bagwell	8.00	3.60
❑ T15 Mike Piazza	15.00	6.75
❑ T16 Paul Molitor	5.00	2.20
❑ T17 Vladimir Guerrero	10.00	4.50
❑ T18 Todd Hundley	2.50	1.10
❑ T19 Derek Jeter	12.00	5.50
❑ T20 Andy Pettitte	4.00	1.80
❑ T21 Bernie Williams	5.00	2.20
❑ T22 Mark McGwire	25.00	11.00
❑ T23 Scott Rolen	12.00	5.50
❑ T24 Ken Caminiti	4.00	1.80
❑ T25 Tony Gwynn	12.00	5.50
❑ T26 Barry Bonds	6.00	2.70
❑ T27 Ken Griffey Jr.	25.00	11.00
❑ T28 Alex Rodriguez	15.00	6.75
❑ T29 Juan Gonzalez	12.00	5.50
❑ T30 Roger Clemens	10.00	4.50

1997 Collector's Choice Update

	MINT	NRMT
COMPLETE SET (30)	6.00	2.70
COMMON CARD (U1-U30)	.10	.05
❑ U1 Jim Leyritz	.10	.05
❑ U2 Matt Perisho	.10	.05
❑ U3 Michael Tucker	.20	.09
❑ U4 Mike Johnson	.20	.09
❑ U5 Jaime Navarro	.10	.05
❑ U6 Doug Drabek	.10	.05
❑ U7 Terry Mulholland	.10	.05
❑ U8 Brett Tomko	.20	.09
❑ U9 Marquis Grissom	.20	.09
❑ U10 David Justice	.40	.18
❑ U11 Brian Moehler	.10	.05
❑ U12 Bobby Bonilla	.20	.09
❑ U13 Todd Dunwoody	.20	.09
❑ U14 Tony Saunders	.20	.09
❑ U15 Jay Bell	.20	.09
❑ U16 Jeff King	.10	.05
❑ U17 Terry Steinbach	.20	.09
❑ U18 Steve Bieser	.10	.05
❑ U19 Takashi Kashiwada	.20	.09
❑ U20 Hideki Irabu	1.50	.70
❑ U21 Damon Mashore	.10	.05
❑ U22 Quilvio Veras	.10	.05
❑ U23 Will Cunnane	.10	.05
❑ U24 Jeff Kent	.20	.09
❑ U25 J.T. Snow	.20	.09
❑ U26 Dante Powell	.20	.09
❑ U27 Jose Cruz Jr.	2.50	1.10
❑ U28 John Burkett	.10	.05
❑ U29 John Wetteland	.20	.09
❑ U30 Benito Santiago	.10	.05

1998 Collector's Choice

	MINT	NRMT
COMPLETE SET (530)	36.00	16.00
COMPLETE SERIES 1 (265)	18.00	8.00
COMPLETE SERIES 2 (265)	18.00	8.00
COMP.FACT.SET (530)	40.00	18.00
COMMON CARD (1-530)	.10	.05
❑ 1 Nomar Garciaparra CG	.60	.25
❑ 2 Roger Clemens CG	.40	.18
❑ 3 Larry Walker CG	.15	.07
❑ 4 Mike Piazza CG	.60	.25
❑ 5 Mark McGwire CG	1.25	.55
❑ 6 Tony Gwynn CG	.50	.23
❑ 7 Jose Cruz Jr. CG	.25	.11
❑ 8 Frank Thomas CG	.60	.25
❑ 9 Tino Martinez CG	.15	.07
❑ 10 Ken Griffey Jr. CG	1.00	.45
❑ 11 Barry Bonds CG	.25	.11
❑ 12 Scott Rolen CG	.50	.23
❑ 13 Randy Johnson CG	.15	.07
❑ 14 Ryne Sandberg CG	.25	.11
❑ 15 Eddie Murray CG	.15	.07
❑ 16 Kevin Brown CG	.10	.05
❑ 17 Mike Mussina CG	.15	.07
❑ 18 Sandy Alomar Jr. CG	.10	.05
❑ 19 Ken Griffey Jr. CL Adam Riggs	.15	.07
❑ 20 Nomar Garciaparra CL Charlie O'Brien	.15	.07
❑ 21 Ben Grieve CL Frank Thomas Tony Gwynn	.15	.07
❑ 22 Mark McGwire CL Cal Ripken	.15	.07
❑ 23 Tino Martinez CL	.10	.05
❑ 24 Jason Dickson	.15	.07
❑ 25 Darin Erstad	.50	.23
❑ 26 Todd Greene	.15	.07
❑ 27 Chuck Finley	.15	.07

❑ 28	Garret Anderson	.15	.07
❑ 29	Dave Hollins	.10	.05
❑ 30	Rickey Henderson	.40	.18
❑ 31	John Smoltz	.15	.07
❑ 32	Michael Tucker	.15	.07
❑ 33	Jeff Blauser	.10	.05
❑ 34	Javier Lopez	.15	.07
❑ 35	Andruw Jones	.50	.23
❑ 36	Denny Neagle	.15	.07
❑ 37	Randall Simon	.15	.07
❑ 38	Mark Wohlers	.10	.05
❑ 39	Harold Baines	.15	.07
❑ 40	Cal Ripken	1.50	.70
❑ 41	Mike Bordick	.10	.05
❑ 42	Jimmy Key	.15	.07
❑ 43	Armando Benitez	.10	.05
❑ 44	Scott Erickson	.15	.07
❑ 45	Eric Davis	.15	.07
❑ 46	Bret Saberhagen	.15	.07
❑ 47	Darren Bragg	.10	.05
❑ 48	Steve Avery	.10	.05
❑ 49	Jeff Frye	.10	.05
❑ 50	Aaron Sele	.15	.07
❑ 51	Scott Hatteberg	.10	.05
❑ 52	Tom Gordon	.15	.07
❑ 53	Kevin Orie	.10	.05
❑ 54	Kevin Foster	.10	.05
❑ 55	Ryne Sandberg	.50	.23
❑ 56	Doug Glanville	.15	.07
❑ 57	Tyler Houston	.10	.05
❑ 58	Steve Trachsel	.10	.05
❑ 59	Mark Grace	.25	.11
❑ 60	Frank Thomas	1.25	.55
❑ 61	Scott Eyre	.10	.05
❑ 62	Jeff Abbott	.15	.07
❑ 63	Chris Clemons	.10	.05
❑ 64	Jorge Fabregas	.10	.05
❑ 65	Robin Ventura	.15	.07
❑ 66	Matt Karchner	.10	.05
❑ 67	Jon Nunnally	.10	.05
❑ 68	Aaron Boone	.10	.05
❑ 69	Pokey Reese	.10	.05
❑ 70	Deion Sanders	.15	.07
❑ 71	Jeff Shaw	.15	.07
❑ 72	Eduardo Perez	.10	.05
❑ 73	Brett Tomko	.15	.07
❑ 74	Bartolo Colon	.15	.07
❑ 75	Manny Ramirez	.40	.18
❑ 76	Jose Mesa	.10	.05
❑ 77	Brian Giles	.15	.07
❑ 78	Richie Sexson	.25	.11
❑ 79	Orel Hershiser	.15	.07
❑ 80	Matt Williams	.15	.07
❑ 81	Walt Weiss	.15	.07
❑ 82	Jerry DiPoto	.10	.05
❑ 83	Quinton McCracken	.15	.07
❑ 84	Neifi Perez	.15	.07
❑ 85	Vinny Castilla	.25	.11
❑ 86	Ellis Burks	.15	.07
❑ 87	John Thomson	.10	.05
❑ 88	Willie Blair	.10	.05
❑ 89	Bob Hamelin	.10	.05
❑ 90	Tony Clark	.25	.11
❑ 91	Todd Jones	.10	.05
❑ 92	Deivi Cruz	.10	.05
❑ 93	Frank Catalanotto	.25	.11
❑ 94	Justin Thompson	.15	.07
❑ 95	Gary Sheffield	.25	.11
❑ 96	Kevin Brown	.25	.11
❑ 97	Charles Johnson	.15	.07
❑ 98	Bobby Bonilla	.15	.07
❑ 99	Livan Hernandez	.15	.07
❑ 100	Paul Konerko	.40	.18
❑ 101	Craig Counsell	.10	.05
❑ 102	Magglio Ordonez	.50	.23
❑ 103	Garrett Stephenson	.10	.05
❑ 104	Ken Cloude	.15	.07
❑ 105	Miguel Tejada	.15	.07
❑ 106	Juan Encarnacion	.15	.07
❑ 107	Dennis Reyes	.15	.07
❑ 108	Orlando Cabrera	.15	.07
❑ 109	Kelvim Escobar	.15	.07
❑ 110	Ben Grieve	.75	.35
❑ 111	Brian Rose	.15	.07
❑ 112	Fernando Tatis	.15	.07
❑ 113	Tom Evans	.15	.07
❑ 114	Tom Fordham	.10	.05
❑ 115	Mark Kotsay	.25	.11
❑ 116	Mario Valdez	.15	.07
❑ 117	Jeremi Gonzalez	.15	.07
❑ 118	Todd Dunwoody	.15	.07
❑ 119	Javier Valentin	.15	.07
❑ 120	Todd Helton	.50	.23
❑ 121	Jason Varitek	.10	.05
❑ 122	Chris Carpenter	.15	.07
❑ 123	Kevin Millwood	1.00	.45
❑ 124	Brad Fullmer	.15	.07
❑ 125	Jaret Wright	.50	.23
❑ 126	Brad Rigby	.10	.05
❑ 127	Edgar Renteria	.15	.07
❑ 128	Robb Nen	.15	.07
❑ 129	Tony Pena	.10	.05
❑ 130	Craig Biggio	.40	.18
❑ 131	Brad Ausmus	.10	.05
❑ 132	Shane Reynolds	.15	.07
❑ 133	Mike Hampton	.10	.05
❑ 134	Billy Wagner	.15	.07
❑ 135	Richard Hidalgo	.15	.07
❑ 136	Jose Rosado	.10	.05
❑ 137	Yamil Benitez	.10	.05
❑ 138	Felix Martinez	.10	.05
❑ 139	Jeff King	.15	.07
❑ 140	Jose Offerman	.10	.05
❑ 141	Joe Vitiello	.10	.05
❑ 142	Tim Belcher	.10	.05
❑ 143	Brett Butler	.15	.07
❑ 144	Greg Gagne	.10	.05
❑ 145	Mike Piazza	1.25	.55
❑ 146	Ramon Martinez	.15	.07
❑ 147	Raul Mondesi	.25	.11
❑ 148	Adam Riggs	.10	.05
❑ 149	Eddie Murray	.40	.18
❑ 150	Jeff Cirillo	.15	.07
❑ 151	Scott Karl	.10	.05
❑ 152	Mike Fetters	.10	.05
❑ 153	Dave Nilsson	.10	.05
❑ 154	Antone Williamson	.10	.05
❑ 155	Jeff D'Amico	.10	.05
❑ 156	Jose Valentin	.10	.05
❑ 157	Brad Radke	.15	.07
❑ 158	Torii Hunter	.10	.05
❑ 159	Chuck Knoblauch	.40	.18
❑ 160	Paul Molitor	.40	.18
❑ 161	Travis Miller	.10	.05
❑ 162	Rich Robertson	.10	.05
❑ 163	Ron Coomer	.10	.05
❑ 164	Mark Grudzielanek	.15	.07
❑ 165	Lee Smith	.15	.07
❑ 166	Vladimir Guerrero	.60	.25
❑ 167	Dustin Hermanson	.15	.07
❑ 168	Ugueth Urbina	.15	.07
❑ 169	F.P. Santangelo	.10	.05
❑ 170	Rondell White	.15	.07
❑ 171	Bobby Jones	.10	.05
❑ 172	Edgardo Alfonzo	.15	.07
❑ 173	John Franco	.15	.07
❑ 174	Carlos Baerga	.15	.07
❑ 175	Butch Huskey	.10	.05
❑ 176	Rey Ordonez	.15	.07
❑ 177	Matt Franco	.10	.05
❑ 178	Dwight Gooden	.15	.07
❑ 179	Chad Curtis	.10	.05
❑ 180	Tino Martinez	.40	.18
❑ 181	Charlie O'Brien MM	.10	.05
❑ 182	Sandy Alomar Jr. MM	.10	.05
❑ 183	Raul Casanova MM	.10	.05
❑ 184	Javier Lopez MM	.10	.05
❑ 185	Mike Piazza MM	.60	.25
❑ 186	Ivan Rodriguez MM	.25	.11
❑ 187	Charles Johnson MM	.10	.05
❑ 188	Brad Ausmus MM	.10	.05
❑ 189	Brian Johnson MM	.10	.05
❑ 190	Wade Boggs	.40	.18
❑ 191	David Wells	.25	.11
❑ 192	Tim Raines	.15	.07
❑ 193	Ramiro Mendoza	.15	.07
❑ 194	Willie Adams	.10	.05
❑ 195	Matt Stairs	.15	.07
❑ 196	Jason McDonald	.10	.05
❑ 197	Dave Magadan	.10	.05
❑ 198	Mark Bellhorn	.15	.07
❑ 199	Ariel Prieto	.10	.05
❑ 200	Jose Canseco	.40	.18
❑ 201	Bobby Estalella	.15	.07
❑ 202	Tony Barron	.10	.05
❑ 203	Midre Cummings	.10	.05
❑ 204	Ricky Bottalico	.15	.07
❑ 205	Mike Grace	.10	.05
❑ 206	Rico Brogna	.15	.07
❑ 207	Mickey Morandini	.10	.05
❑ 208	Lou Collier	.10	.05
❑ 209	Kevin Polcovich	.10	.05
❑ 210	Kevin Young	.15	.07
❑ 211	Jose Guillen	.15	.07
❑ 212	Esteban Loaiza	.10	.05
❑ 213	Marc Wilkins	.10	.05
❑ 214	Jason Schmidt	.10	.05
❑ 215	Gary Gaetti	.10	.05
❑ 216	Fernando Valenzuela	.15	.07
❑ 217	Willie McGee	.10	.05
❑ 218	Alan Benes	.15	.07
❑ 219	Eli Marrero	.15	.07
❑ 220	Mark McGwire	2.50	1.10
❑ 221	Matt Morris	.15	.07
❑ 222	Trevor Hoffman	.15	.07
❑ 223	Will Cunnane	.10	.05
❑ 224	Joey Hamilton	.15	.07
❑ 225	Ken Caminiti	.25	.11
❑ 226	Derrek Lee	.15	.07
❑ 227	Mark Sweeney	.10	.05
❑ 228	Carlos Hernandez	.10	.05
❑ 229	Brian Johnson	.10	.05
❑ 230	Jeff Kent	.15	.07
❑ 231	Kirk Rueter	.10	.05
❑ 232	Bill Mueller	.15	.07
❑ 233	Dante Powell	.15	.07
❑ 234	J.T. Snow	.15	.07
❑ 235	Shawn Estes	.15	.07
❑ 236	Dennis Martinez	.15	.07
❑ 237	Jamie Moyer	.10	.05
❑ 238	Dan Wilson	.10	.05
❑ 239	Joey Cora	.15	.07
❑ 240	Ken Griffey Jr.	2.00	.90
❑ 241	Paul Sorrento	.10	.05
❑ 242	Jay Buhner	.15	.07
❑ 243	Hanley Frias	.25	.11
❑ 244	John Burkett	.10	.05
❑ 245	Juan Gonzalez	1.00	.45
❑ 246	Rick Helling	.15	.07
❑ 247	Darren Oliver	.10	.05
❑ 248	Mickey Tettleton	.10	.05
❑ 249	Ivan Rodriguez	.50	.23
❑ 250	Joe Carter	.15	.07
❑ 251	Pat Hentgen	.15	.07
❑ 252	Marty Janzen	.10	.05
❑ 253	Frank Thomas TOP Tony Gwynn	.40	.18
❑ 254	Mark McGwire TOP Ken Griffey Jr. Larry Walker	1.00	.45
❑ 255	Ken Griffey Jr. TOP Andres Galarraga	.50	.23
❑ 256	Brian L.Hunter TOP Tony Womack	.10	.05
❑ 257	Roger Clemens TOP Denny Neagle	.15	.07
❑ 258	Roger Clemens TOP Curt Schilling	.15	.07
❑ 259	Roger Clemens TOP Pedro Martinez	.15	.07
❑ 260	Randy Myers TOP Jeff Shaw	.10	.05
❑ 261	Nomar Garciaparra TOP Scott Rolen	.40	.18
❑ 262	Charlie O'Brien	.10	.05
❑ 263	Shannon Stewart	.15	.07
❑ 264	Robert Person	.10	.05
❑ 265	Carlos Delgado	.15	.07
❑ 266	Matt Williams CL Travis Lee	.15	.07
❑ 267	Nomar Garciaparra CL Cal Ripken	.15	.07
❑ 268	Mark McGwire CL Mike Piazza	.40	.18
❑ 269	Tony Gwynn CL Ken Griffey Jr.	.15	.07

❑	270	Fred McGriff CL Jose Cruz Jr.	.10	.05
❑	271	Andruw Jones GJ	.25	.11
❑	272	Alex Rodriguez GJ	.60	.25
❑	273	Juan Gonzalez GJ	.50	.23
❑	274	Nomar Garciaparra GJ	.60	.25
❑	275	Ken Griffey Jr. GJ	1.00	.45
❑	276	Tino Martinez GJ	.15	.07
❑	277	Roger Clemens GJ	.40	.18
❑	278	Barry Bonds GJ	.25	.11
❑	279	Mike Piazza GJ	.60	.25
❑	280	Tim Salmon	.40	.18
❑	281	Gary DiSarcina	.10	.05
❑	282	Cecil Fielder	.15	.07
❑	283	Ken Hill	.10	.05
❑	284	Troy Percival	.15	.07
❑	285	Jim Edmonds	.25	.11
❑	286	Allen Watson	.10	.05
❑	287	Brian Anderson	.15	.07
❑	288	Jay Bell	.15	.07
❑	289	Jorge Fabregas	.10	.05
❑	290	Devon White	.15	.07
❑	291	Yamil Benitez	.10	.05
❑	292	Jeff Suppan	.10	.05
❑	293	Tony Batista	.10	.05
❑	294	Brent Brede	.10	.05
❑	295	Andy Benes	.15	.07
❑	296	Felix Rodriguez	.10	.05
❑	297	Karim Garcia	.15	.07
❑	298	Omar Daal	.10	.05
❑	299	Andy Stankiewicz	.10	.05
❑	300	Matt Williams	.15	.07
❑	301	Willie Blair	.10	.05
❑	302	Ryan Klesko	.15	.07
❑	303	Tom Glavine	.40	.18
❑	304	Walt Weiss	.15	.07
❑	305	Greg Maddux	1.25	.55
❑	306	Chipper Jones	1.00	.45
❑	307	Keith Lockhart	.10	.05
❑	308	Andres Galarraga	.40	.18
❑	309	Chris Hoiles	.10	.05
❑	310	Roberto Alomar	.40	.18
❑	311	Joe Carter	.15	.07
❑	312	Doug Drabek	.10	.05
❑	313	Jeffrey Hammonds	.15	.07
❑	314	Rafael Palmeiro	.25	.11
❑	315	Mike Mussina	.40	.18
❑	316	Brady Anderson	.15	.07
❑	317	B.J. Surhoff	.15	.07
❑	318	Dennis Eckersley	.15	.07
❑	319	Jim Leyritz	.10	.05
❑	320	Mo Vaughn	.50	.23
❑	321	Nomar Garciaparra	1.25	.55
❑	322	Reggie Jefferson	.10	.05
❑	323	Tim Naehring	.10	.05
❑	324	Troy O'Leary	.15	.07
❑	325	Pedro Martinez	.40	.18
❑	326	John Valentin	.15	.07
❑	327	Mark Clark	.10	.05
❑	328	Rod Beck	.15	.07
❑	329	Mickey Morandini	.10	.05
❑	330	Sammy Sosa	1.00	.45
❑	331	Jeff Blauser	.10	.05
❑	332	Lance Johnson	.10	.05
❑	333	Scott Servais	.10	.05
❑	334	Kevin Tapani	.10	.05
❑	335	Henry Rodriguez	.15	.07
❑	336	Jaime Navarro	.10	.05
❑	337	Benji Gil	.10	.05
❑	338	James Baldwin	.15	.07
❑	339	Mike Cameron	.15	.07
❑	340	Ray Durham	.15	.07
❑	341	Chris Snopek	.10	.05
❑	342	Eddie Taubensee	.10	.05
❑	343	Bret Boone	.15	.07
❑	344	Willie Greene	.15	.07
❑	345	Barry Larkin	.25	.11
❑	346	Chris Stynes	.10	.05
❑	347	Pete Harnisch	.10	.05
❑	348	Dave Burba	.10	.05
❑	349	Sandy Alomar Jr.	.15	.07
❑	350	Kenny Lofton	.40	.18
❑	351	Geronimo Berroa	.10	.05
❑	352	Omar Vizquel	.15	.07
❑	353	Travis Fryman	.15	.07
❑	354	Dwight Gooden	.15	.07
❑	355	Jim Thome	.40	.18
❑	356	David Justice	.40	.18
❑	357	Charles Nagy	.15	.07
❑	358	Chad Ogea	.10	.05
❑	359	Pedro Astacio	.10	.05
❑	360	Larry Walker	.40	.18
❑	361	Mike Lansing	.10	.05
❑	362	Kirt Manwaring	.10	.05
❑	363	Dante Bichette	.15	.07
❑	364	Jamey Wright	.10	.05
❑	365	Darryl Kile	.15	.07
❑	366	Luis Gonzalez	.10	.05
❑	367	Joe Randa	.10	.05
❑	368	Raul Casanova	.10	.05
❑	369	Damion Easley	.15	.07
❑	370	Brian Hunter	.15	.07
❑	371	Bobby Higginson	.25	.11
❑	372	Brian Moehler	.10	.05
❑	373	Scott Sanders	.10	.05
❑	374	Jim Eisenreich	.10	.05
❑	375	Derrek Lee	.15	.07
❑	376	Jay Powell	.10	.05
❑	377	Cliff Floyd	.15	.07
❑	378	Alex Fernandez	.10	.05
❑	379	Felix Heredia	.10	.05
❑	380	Jeff Bagwell	.60	.25
❑	381	Bill Spiers	.10	.05
❑	382	Chris Holt	.10	.05
❑	383	Carl Everett	.10	.05
❑	384	Derek Bell	.15	.07
❑	385	Moises Alou	.25	.11
❑	386	Ramon Garcia	.10	.05
❑	387	Mike Sweeney	.10	.05
❑	388	Glendon Rusch	.10	.05
❑	389	Kevin Appier	.15	.07
❑	390	Dean Palmer	.15	.07
❑	391	Jeff Conine	.15	.07
❑	392	Johnny Damon	.15	.07
❑	393	Jose Vizcaino	.10	.05
❑	394	Todd Hollandsworth	.10	.05
❑	395	Eric Karros	.15	.07
❑	396	Todd Zeile	.15	.07
❑	397	Chan Ho Park	.40	.18
❑	398	Ismael Valdes	.15	.07
❑	399	Eric Young	.15	.07
❑	400	Hideo Nomo	.50	.23
❑	401	Mark Loretta	.10	.05
❑	402	Doug Jones	.10	.05
❑	403	Jeromy Burnitz	.15	.07
❑	404	John Jaha	.10	.05
❑	405	Marquis Grissom	.15	.07
❑	406	Mike Matheny	.10	.05
❑	407	Todd Walker	.25	.11
❑	408	Marty Cordova	.10	.05
❑	409	Matt Lawton	.15	.07
❑	410	Terry Steinbach	.15	.07
❑	411	Pat Meares	.10	.05
❑	412	Rick Aguilera	.10	.05
❑	413	Otis Nixon	.10	.05
❑	414	Derrick May	.10	.05
❑	415	Carl Pavano	.15	.07
❑	416	A.J. Hinch	.15	.07
❑	417	Dave Dellucci	.50	.23
❑	418	Bruce Chen	.15	.07
❑	419	Darron Ingram	.30	.14
❑	420	Sean Casey	.15	.07
❑	421	Mark L. Johnson	.10	.05
❑	422	Gabe Alvarez	.15	.07
❑	423	Alex Gonzalez	.15	.07
❑	424	Daryle Ward	.15	.07
❑	425	Russell Branyan	.15	.07
❑	426	Mike Caruso	.15	.07
❑	427	Mike Kinkade	.30	.14
❑	428	Ramon Hernandez	.15	.07
❑	429	Matt Clement	.15	.07
❑	430	Travis Lee	.75	.35
❑	431	Shane Monahan	.15	.07
❑	432	Rich Butler	.25	.11
❑	433	Chris Widger	.10	.05
❑	434	Jose Vidro	.10	.05
❑	435	Carlos Perez	.15	.07
❑	436	Ryan McGuire	.10	.05
❑	437	Brian McRae	.10	.05
❑	438	Al Leiter	.15	.07
❑	439	Rich Becker	.10	.05
❑	440	Todd Hundley	.15	.07
❑	441	Dave Mlicki	.10	.05
❑	442	Bernard Gilkey	.10	.05
❑	443	John Olerud	.15	.07
❑	444	Paul O'Neill	.15	.07
❑	445	Andy Pettitte	.25	.11
❑	446	David Cone	.25	.11
❑	447	Chili Davis	.15	.07
❑	448	Bernie Williams	.40	.18
❑	449	Joe Girardi	.10	.05
❑	450	Derek Jeter	1.00	.45
❑	451	Mariano Rivera	.15	.07
❑	452	George Williams	.10	.05
❑	453	Kenny Rogers	.10	.05
❑	454	Tom Candiotti	.10	.05
❑	455	Rickey Henderson	.40	.18
❑	456	Jason Giambi	.15	.07
❑	457	Scott Spiezio	.10	.05
❑	458	Doug Glanville	.15	.07
❑	459	Desi Relaford	.10	.05
❑	460	Curt Schilling	.15	.07
❑	461	Bob Abreu	.15	.07
❑	462	Gregg Jefferies	.10	.05
❑	463	Scott Rolen	1.00	.45
❑	464	Mike Lieberthal	.10	.05
❑	465	Tony Womack	.15	.07
❑	466	Jermaine Allensworth	.10	.05
❑	467	Francisco Cordova	.10	.05
❑	468	Jon Lieber	.10	.05
❑	469	Al Martin	.10	.05
❑	470	Jason Kendall	.15	.07
❑	471	Todd Stottlemyre	.15	.07
❑	472	Royce Clayton	.10	.05
❑	473	Brian Jordan	.15	.07
❑	474	John Mabry	.10	.05
❑	475	Ray Lankford	.15	.07
❑	476	Delino DeShields	.10	.05
❑	477	Ron Gant	.10	.05
❑	478	Mark Langston	.10	.05
❑	479	Steve Finley	.15	.07
❑	480	Tony Gwynn	1.00	.45
❑	481	Andy Ashby	.10	.05
❑	482	Wally Joyner	.15	.07
❑	483	Greg Vaughn	.15	.07
❑	484	Sterling Hitchcock	.15	.07
❑	485	Kevin Brown	.25	.11
❑	486	Orel Hershiser	.15	.07
❑	487	Charlie Hayes	.10	.05
❑	488	Darryl Hamilton	.10	.05
❑	489	Mark Gardner	.10	.05
❑	490	Barry Bonds	.50	.23
❑	491	Robb Nen	.15	.07
❑	492	Kirk Rueter	.10	.05
❑	493	Randy Johnson	.40	.18
❑	494	Jeff Fassero	.10	.05
❑	495	Alex Rodriguez	1.25	.55
❑	496	David Segui	.15	.07
❑	497	Rich Amaral	.10	.05
❑	498	Russ Davis	.15	.07
❑	499	Bubba Trammell	.15	.07
❑	500	Wade Boggs	.40	.18
❑	501	Roberto Hernandez	.10	.05
❑	502	Dave Martinez	.10	.05
❑	503	Dennis Springer	.10	.05
❑	504	Paul Sorrento	.10	.05
❑	505	Wilson Alvarez	.15	.07
❑	506	Mike Kelly	.10	.05
❑	507	Albie Lopez	.10	.05
❑	508	Tony Saunders	.10	.05
❑	509	John Flaherty	.10	.05
❑	510	Fred McGriff	.25	.11
❑	511	Quinton McCracken	.15	.07
❑	512	Terrell Wade	.10	.05
❑	513	Kevin Stocker	.10	.05
❑	514	Kevin Elster	.10	.05
❑	515	Will Clark	.40	.18
❑	516	Bobby Witt	.10	.05
❑	517	Tom Goodwin	.10	.05
❑	518	Aaron Sele	.15	.07
❑	519	Lee Stevens	.10	.05
❑	520	Rusty Greer	.15	.07
❑	521	John Wetteland	.15	.07
❑	522	Darrin Fletcher	.10	.05
❑	523	Jose Canseco	.40	.18

❑ 524 Randy Myers .... .15 .07
❑ 525 Jose Cruz Jr. .... .50 .23
❑ 526 Shawn Green .... .15 .07
❑ 527 Tony Fernandez .... .10 .05
❑ 528 Alex Gonzalez .... .10 .05
❑ 529 Ed Sprague .... .10 .05
❑ 530 Roger Clemens .... .75 .35

1998 Collector's Choice Crash the Game

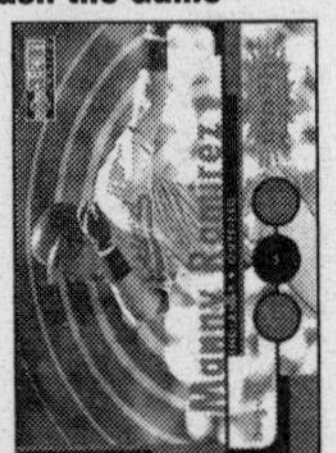

	MINT	NRMT
COMPLETE SET (90)	80.00	36.00
COMMON CARD (CG1-CG30) ..	.40	.18
MINOR STARS	.40	.18
SEMISTARS	.60	.25
UNLISTED STARS	.75	.35

*INSTANT WIN: 10X TO 20X BASIC CRASH
INSTANT WIN SER.2 STATED ODDS 1:721

❑ CG1A K.Griffey June 26-28 W 4.00
1.80
❑ CG1B K.Griffey July 7 L 4.00 1.80
❑ CG1C K.Griffey Sept 21-24 W 4.00 1.80
❑ CG2A T.Lee July 27-30 L .... 1.50 .70
❑ CG2B T.Lee Aug 27-30 L ..... 1.50 .70
❑ CG2C T.Lee Sept 17-20 L .. 1.50 .70
❑ CG3A L.Walker July 17-19 L .75 .35
❑ CG3B L.Walker Aug 27-30 W .75 .35
❑ CG3C L.Walker Sept 25-27 W .75 .35
❑ CG4A T.Clark July 9-12 W .... .60 .25
❑ CG4B T.Clark June 30-July 2 L .60
.25
❑ CG4C T.Clark Sept 4-6 L ...... .60 .25
❑ CG5A C.Ripken June 22-25 W 3.00
1.35
❑ CG5B C.Ripken July 7 L 3.00 1.35
❑ CG5C C.Ripken Sept 4-6 W 3.00 1.35
❑ CG6A T.Salmon June 22-25 L .75 .35
❑ CG6B T.Salmon Aug 28-30 L .75 .35
❑ CG6C T.Salmon Sept 14-15 L .75 .35
❑ CG7A V.Castilla June30-July2 W .60
.25
❑ CG7B V.Castilla Aug 27-30 W .60 .25
❑ CG7C V.Castilla Sept 7-10 W .60 .25
❑ CG8A F.McGriff June 22-25 L .60 .25
❑ CG8B F.McGriff July 3-5 L .... .60 .25
❑ CG8C F.McGriff Sept 18-20 W .60
.25
❑ CG9A M.Williams July 17-19 L .40
.18
❑ CG9B M.Williams Sept 14-16 W .40
.18
❑ CG9C M.Williams Sept 18-20 L .40
.18
❑ CG10A M.McGwire July 7 L 5.00 2.20
❑ CG10B Mark McGwire 5.00 2.20
July24-26 W
❑ CG10C Mark McGwire 5.00 2.20
Aug 18-19 W
❑ CG11A A.Belle July 3-5 L .... .75 .35
❑ CG11B A.Belle Aug 21-23 W .75 .35
❑ CG11C A.Belle Sept 11-13 L .75 .35
❑ CG12A J.Buhner July 9-12 W .40 .18
❑ CG12B J.Buhner Aug 6-9 L .. .40 .18
❑ CG12C J.Buhner Sept 24-27 L .40
.18
❑ CG13A Vladimir Guerrero .. 1.25 .55
June 22-25 L
❑ CG13B Vladimir Guerrero .. 1.25 .55
Aug 10-12 W
❑ CG13C Vladimir Guerrero .. 1.25 .55
Sept 14-16 W
❑ CG14A A.Jones July 16-19 W 1.00 .45
❑ CG14B A.Jones Aug 27-30 W 1.00 .45
❑ CG14C A.Jones Sept 17-20 L 1.00 .45
❑ CG15A Nomar Garciaparra 2.50 1.10
July 9-12 L
❑ CG15B Nomar Garciaparra 2.50 1.10
Aug 13-16 W
❑ CG15C Nomar Garciaparra 2.50 1.10
Sept 24-27
❑ CG16A K.Caminiti June 26-28 W .60
.25
❑ CG16B K.Caminiti July 13-15 W .60
.25
❑ CG16C K.Caminiti Sept 10-13 L .60
.25
❑ CG17A S.Sosa July 9-12 W 2.00 .90
❑ CG17B S.Sosa Aug 27-30 W 2.00 .90
❑ CG17C S.Sosa Sept 18-20 L 2.00 .90
❑ CG18A Ben Grieve .... 1.50 .70
June 30-July 2 W
❑ CG18B B.Grieve Aug 14-16 L 1.50 .70
❑ CG18C B.Grieve Sept 24-27 L 1.50 .70
❑ CG19A M.Vaughn July 7 L .. 1.00 .45
❑ CG19B M.Vaughn Sept 7-9 L 1.00 .45
❑ CG19C Mo Vaughn .... 1.00 .45
Sept 24-27 W
❑ CG20A F.Thomas July 7 L .. 2.50 1.10
❑ CG20B Frank Thomas 2.50 1.10
July 17-19 W
❑ CG20C F.Thomas Sept 4-6 L 2.50 1.10
❑ CG21A Manny Ramirez .... .75 .35
July 9-12 L
❑ CG21B Manny Ramirez .... .75 .35
Aug 13-16 W
❑ CG21C Manny Ramirez .... .75 .35
Sept 18-20 W
❑ CG22A J.Bagwell July 7 L .. 1.25 .55
❑ CG22B Jeff Bagwell .... 1.25 .55
Aug 28-30 W
❑ CG22C J.Bagwell Sept 4-6 W 1.25 .55
❑ CG23A J.Cruz Jr. July 9-12 L 1.00 .45
❑ CG23B Jose Cruz Jr. .... 1.00 .45
Aug 13-16 L
❑ CG23C Jose Cruz Jr. .... 1.00 .45
Sept 18-20 L
❑ CG24A A.Rodriguez July 7 W 2.50 1.10
❑ CG24B Alex Rodriguez 2.50 1.10
Aug 6-9 W
❑ CG24C Alex Rodriguez 2.50 1.10
Sept 21-23 W
❑ CG25A Mike Piazza 2.50 1.10
June 22-25 W
❑ CG25B M.Piazza July 7 L .. 2.50 1.10
❑ CG25C Mike Piazza 2.50 1.10
Sept 10-13 W
❑ CG26A T.Martinez June 26-28 W .75
.35
❑ CG26B T.Martinez July 9-12 L .75 .35
❑ CG26C Tino Martinez .... .75 .35
Aug 13-16 L
❑ CG27A C.Jones July 3-5 L .. 2.00 .90
❑ CG27B C.Jones Aug 23-30 L 2.00 .90
❑ CG27C C.Jones Sept 17-20 L 2.00 .90
❑ CG28A J.Gonzalez July 7 L 2.00 .90
❑ CG28B Juan Gonzalez ...... 2.00 .90
Aug 6-9 W
❑ CG28C Juan Gonzalez ...... 2.00 .90
Sept 11-13 W
❑ CG29A J.Thome June 22-23 L .75
.35
❑ CG29B J.Thome July 23-26 W .75
.35
❑ CG29C J.Thome Sept 24-27 L .75 .35
❑ CG30A B.Bonds July 7 W .. 1.00 .45
❑ CG30B B.Bonds Sept 4-6 L 1.00 .45
❑ CG30C Barry Bonds .... 1.00 .45
Sept 18-20 W

1998 Collector's Choice Evolution Revolution

	MINT	NRMT
COMPLETE SET (28)	60.00	27.00
COMMON CARD (ER1-ER28)	.50	.23

❑ ER1 Tim Salmon .... 2.00 .90
❑ ER2 Greg Maddux 6.00 2.70
❑ ER3 Cal Ripken 8.00 3.60
❑ ER4 Mo Vaughn 2.50 1.10
❑ ER5 Sammy Sosa 5.00 2.20
❑ ER6 Frank Thomas 6.00 2.70
❑ ER7 Barry Larkin .... 1.25 .55
❑ ER8 Jim Thome .... 2.00 .90
❑ ER9 Larry Walker .... 2.00 .90
❑ ER10 Travis Fryman .... 1.00 .45
❑ ER11 Gary Sheffield .... 1.25 .55
❑ ER12 Jeff Bagwell 3.00 1.35
❑ ER13 Johnny Damon .... 1.00 .45
❑ ER14 Mike Piazza 6.00 2.70
❑ ER15 Jeff Cirillo .... 1.00 .45
❑ ER16 Paul Molitor .... 2.00 .90
❑ ER17 Vladimir Guerrero 3.00 1.35
❑ ER18 Todd Hundley .... 1.00 .45
❑ ER19 Tino Martinez .... 2.00 .90
❑ ER20 Jose Canseco .... 2.00 .90
❑ ER21 Scott Rolen 5.00 2.20
❑ ER22 Al Martin .... .50 .23
❑ ER23 Mark McGwire 12.00 5.50
❑ ER24 Tony Gwynn 5.00 2.20
❑ ER25 Barry Bonds 2.50 1.10
❑ ER26 Ken Griffey Jr. 10.00 4.50
❑ ER27 Juan Gonzalez 5.00 2.20
❑ ER28 Roger Clemens 4.00 1.80

1998 Collector's Choice Mini Bobbing Heads

	MINT	NRMT
COMPLETE SET (30)	20.00	9.00
COMMON CARD (1-30)	.25	.11

❑ 1 Tim Salmon .... .60 .25
❑ 2 Travis Lee .... 1.25 .55
❑ 3 Matt Williams .... .25 .11
❑ 4 Chipper Jones .... 1.50 .70
❑ 5 Greg Maddux UER6 .... 2.00 .90
❑ 6 Cal Ripken 2.50 1.10

❑ 7 Nomar Garciaparra .... 2.00 .90
❑ 8 Mo Vaughn .... .75 .35
❑ 9 Sammy Sosa.................... 1.50 .70
❑ 10 Frank Thomas................ 2.00 .90
❑ 11 Kenny Lofton .... .60 .25
❑ 12 Jaret Wright........................ .75 .35
❑ 13 Larry Walker .... .60 .25
❑ 14 Tony Clark........................ .40 .18
❑ 15 Edgar Renteria .... .25 .11
❑ 16 Jeff Bagwell.................. 1.00 .45
❑ 17 Mike Piazza.................. 2.00 .90
❑ 18 Vladimir Guerrero .... 1.00 .45
❑ 19 Derek Jeter .... 1.50 .70
❑ 20 Ben Grieve .... 1.25 .55
❑ 21 Scott Rolen .... 1.50 .70
❑ 22 Mark McGwire................ 4.00 1.80
❑ 23 Tony Gwynn .... 1.50 .70
❑ 24 Barry Bonds .... .75 .35
❑ 25 Ken Griffey Jr. 3.00 1.35
❑ 26 Alex Rodriguez .... 2.00 .90
❑ 27 Fred McGriff .... .40 .18
❑ 28 Juan Gonzalez .... 1.50 .70
❑ 29 Roger Clemens.............. 1.25 .55
❑ 30 Jose Cruz Jr. .... .75 .35

1998 Collector's Choice StarQuest

	MINT	NRMT
COMP.DELIV.SET (45)	20.00	9.00
COMM.DELIVERY (1-45)............	.15	.07
COMP.STUDENT SET (20)	60.00	27.00
COMM.STUDENTS (46-65)	1.50	.70
COMP.POWERS SET (15) ..	100.00	45.00
COMMON POWERS (66-80)	4.00	1.80
COMP.SUPERSTAR SET (10)	300.00	135.00
COM.SUPERSTAR (81-90)	10.00	4.50

❑ SQ1 Nomar Garciaparra SD 1.50 .70
❑ SQ2 Scott Rolen SD .... 1.25 .55
❑ SQ3 Jason Dickson SD .... .25 .11
❑ SQ4 Jaret Wright SD .... .60 .25
❑ SQ5 Kevin Orie SD .... .15 .07
❑ SQ6 Jose Guillen SD............ .25 .11
❑ SQ7 Matt Morris SD.............. .25 .11
❑ SQ8 Mike Cameron SD .... .25 .11
❑ SQ9 Kevin Polcovich SD ...... .15 .07
❑ SQ10 Jose Cruz Jr. SD .... .60 .25
❑ SQ11 Miguel Tejada SD ...... .25 .11
❑ SQ12 Fernando Tatis SD...... .25 .11
❑ SQ13 Todd Helton SD .... .60 .25
❑ SQ14 Ken Cloude SD .... .25 .11
❑ SQ15 Ben Grieve SD.......... 1.00 .45
❑ SQ16 Dante Powell SD .... .25 .11
❑ SQ17 Bubba Trammell SD.... .25 .11
❑ SQ18 Juan Encarnacion SD .25 .11
❑ SQ19 Derrek Lee SD .... .25 .11
❑ SQ20 Paul Konerko SD .... .50 .23
❑ SQ21 Richard Hidalgo SD .... .25 .11
❑ SQ22 Denny Neagle SD ...... .25 .11
❑ SQ23 David Justice SD .... .50 .23
❑ SQ24 Pedro Martinez SD...... .50 .23
❑ SQ25 Greg Maddux SD ...... 1.50 .70
❑ SQ26 Edgar Martinez SD...... .25 .11
❑ SQ27 Cal Ripken SD .... 2.00 .90
❑ SQ28 Tim Salmon SD .... .50 .23
❑ SQ29 Shawn Estes SD .... .25 .11
❑ SQ30 Ken Griffey Jr. SD 2.50 1.10
❑ SQ31 Brad Radke SD .... .25 .11
❑ SQ32 Andy Pettitte SD.......... .30 .14
❑ SQ33 Curt Schilling SD .... .25 .11
❑ SQ34 Raul Mondesi SD........ .30 .14
❑ SQ35 Alex Rodriguez SD.... 1.50 .70
❑ SQ36 Jeff Kent SD................ .25 .11
❑ SQ37 Jeff Bagwell SD .... .75 .35
❑ SQ38 Juan Gonzalez SD .... 1.25 .55
❑ SQ39 Barry Bonds SD .... .60 .25
❑ SQ40 Mark McGwire SD 3.00 1.35
❑ SQ41 Frank Thomas SD .... 1.50 .70
❑ SQ42 Ray Lankford SD .... .25 .11
❑ SQ43 Tony Gwynn SD........ 1.25 .55
❑ SQ44 Mike Piazza SD .... 1.50 .70
❑ SQ45 Tino Martinez SD .... .50 .23
❑ SQ46 Nomar Garciaparra SG 10.00 4.50
❑ SQ47 Paul Molitor SG 3.00 1.35
❑ SQ48 Chuck Knoblauch SG 3.00 1.35
❑ SQ49 Rusty Greer SG .... 1.50 .70
❑ SQ50 Cal Ripken SG 12.00 5.50
❑ SQ51 Roberto Alomar SG .. 3.00 1.35
❑ SQ52 Scott Rolen SG 8.00 3.60
❑ SQ53 Derek Jeter SG 8.00 3.60
❑ SQ54 Mark Grace SG .... 2.00 .90
❑ SQ55 Randy Johnson SG .. 3.00 1.35
❑ SQ56 Craig Biggio SG........ 3.00 1.35
❑ SQ57 Kenny Lofton SG 3.00 1.35
❑ SQ58 Eddie Murray SG 3.00 1.35
❑ SQ59 Ryne Sandberg SG .. 4.00 1.80
❑ SQ60 Rickey Henderson SG 3.00 1.35
❑ SQ61 Darin Erstad SG........ 4.00 1.80
❑ SQ62 Jim Edmonds SG ...... 2.00 .90
❑ SQ63 Ken Caminiti SG ...... 2.00 .90
❑ SQ64 Ivan Rodriguez SG.... 4.00 1.80
❑ SQ65 Tony Gwynn SG........ 8.00 3.60
❑ SQ66 Tony Clark SP 5.00 2.20
❑ SQ67 Andres Galarraga SP 8.00 3.60
❑ SQ68 Rafael Palmeiro SP .. 5.00 2.20
❑ SQ69 Manny Ramirez SP .. 8.00 3.60
❑ SQ70 Albert Belle SP.......... 8.00 3.60
❑ SQ71 Jay Buhner SP 4.00 1.80
❑ SQ72 Mo Vaughn SP........ 10.00 4.50
❑ SQ73 Barry Bonds SP 10.00 4.50
❑ SQ74 Chipper Jones SP .. 20.00 9.00
❑ SQ75 Jeff Bagwell SP 12.00 5.50
❑ SQ76 Jim Thome SP 8.00 3.60
❑ SQ77 Sammy Sosa SP 20.00 9.00
❑ SQ78 Todd Hundley SP...... 4.00 1.80
❑ SQ79 Matt Williams SP 4.00 1.80
❑ SQ80 Vinny Castilla SP 5.00 2.20
❑ SQ81 Jose Cruz Jr. SS 12.00 5.50
❑ SQ82 Frank Thomas SS .. 40.00 18.00
❑ SQ83 Juan Gonzalez SS .. 30.00 13.50
❑ SQ84 Mike Piazza SS 40.00 18.00
❑ SQ85 Alex Rodriguez SS.. 40.00 18.00
❑ SQ86 Larry Walker SS...... 12.00 5.50
❑ SQ87 Tino Martinez SS 12.00 5.50
❑ SQ88 Greg Maddux SS 40.00 18.00
❑ SQ89 Mark McGwire SS .. 80.00 36.00
❑ SQ90 Ken Griffey Jr. SS .. 60.00 27.00

1998 Collector's Choice StarQuest Single

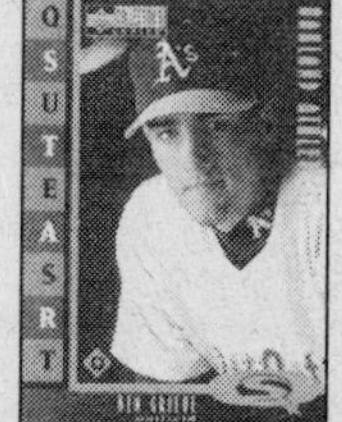

	MINT	NRMT
COMPLETE SET (30)	15.00	6.75
COMMON CARD (1-30)..............	.30	.14

COMP.DOUBLE SET (30) 200.00 90.00
*DOUBLE: 5X TO 10X STARQUEST SINGLE
DOUBLE SER.2 STATED ODDS 1:21
COMP.TRIPLE SET (30) 600.00 275.00
*TRIPLE: 15X TO 30X STARQUEST SINGLE
TRIPLE SER.2 STATED ODDS 1:71
COMP.HOME RUN SET (30) 3000.00 1350.00
*HOME RUN: 60X TO 120X STARQUEST SINGLE
HOME RUN: RANDOM INS.IN SER.2 PACKS
HOME RUN PRINT RUN 100 SERIAL #'d SETS

❑ 1 Ken Griffey Jr. .... 2.00 .90
❑ 2 Jose Cruz Jr. .... .50 .23
❑ 3 Cal Ripken........................ 1.50 .70
❑ 4 Roger Clemens .... .75 .35
❑ 5 Frank Thomas .... 1.25 .55
❑ 6 Derek Jeter .... 1.00 .45
❑ 7 Alex Rodriguez .... 1.25 .55
❑ 8 Andruw Jones .... .50 .23
❑ 9 Vladimir Guerrero .... .60 .25
❑ 10 Mark McGwire................ 2.50 1.10
❑ 11 Kenny Lofton .... .40 .18
❑ 12 Pedro Martinez .... .40 .18
❑ 13 Greg Maddux .... 1.25 .55
❑ 14 Larry Walker .... .40 .18
❑ 15 Barry Bonds .... .50 .23
❑ 16 Chipper Jones.............. 1.00 .45
❑ 17 Jeff Bagwell........................ .60 .25
❑ 18 Juan Gonzalez .... 1.00 .45
❑ 19 Tony Gwynn .... 1.00 .45
❑ 20 Mike Piazza.................... 1.25 .55
❑ 21 Tino Martinez .... .40 .18
❑ 22 Mo Vaughn .... .50 .23
❑ 23 Ben Grieve .... .75 .35
❑ 24 Scott Rolen .... 1.00 .45
❑ 25 Nomar Garciaparra .... 1.25 .55
❑ 26 Paul Konerko...................... .40 .18
❑ 27 Jaret Wright........................ .50 .23
❑ 28 Gary Sheffield .... .30 .14
❑ 29 Todd Helton........................ .50 .23
❑ 30 Travis Lee .... .75 .35

1998 Collector's Choice Stick 'Ums

	MINT	NRMT
COMPLETE SET (30)	20.00	9.00
COMMON CARD (1-30)..............	.25	.11

❑ 1 Andruw Jones .... .75 .35
❑ 2 Chipper Jones.................. 1.50 .70
❑ 3 Cal Ripken........................ 2.50 1.10
❑ 4 Nomar Garciaparra .... 2.00 .90
❑ 5 Mo Vaughn .... .75 .35
❑ 6 Ryne Sandberg.................. .75 .35
❑ 7 Sammy Sosa.................... 1.50 .70
❑ 8 Frank Thomas.................. 2.00 .90
❑ 9 Albert Belle .... .60 .25
❑ 10 Jim Thome .... .60 .25
❑ 11 Manny Ramirez.................. .60 .25
❑ 12 Larry Walker .... .60 .25
❑ 13 Gary Sheffield .... .40 .18
❑ 14 Jeff Bagwell.................... 1.00 .45
❑ 15 Mike Piazza.................... 2.00 .90
❑ 16 Paul Molitor .... .60 .25
❑ 17 Pedro Martinez .... .60 .25

#	Player	MINT	NRMT
18	Todd Hundley	.25	.11
19	Derek Jeter	1.50	.70
20	Tino Martinez	.60	.25
21	Curt Schilling	.25	.11
22	Mark McGwire	4.00	1.80
23	Tony Gwynn	1.50	.70
24	Barry Bonds	.75	.35
25	Ken Griffey Jr.	3.00	1.35
26	Alex Rodriguez	2.00	.90
27	Juan Gonzalez	1.50	.70
28	Ivan Rodriguez	.75	.35
29	Roger Clemens	1.25	.55
30	Jose Cruz Jr.	.75	.35

1995 Collector's Choice SE

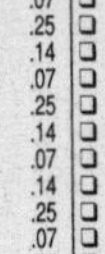

	MINT	NRMT
COMPLETE SET (265)	20.00	9.00
COMMON CARD (1-265)	.15	.07

#	Player	MINT	NRMT
1	Alex Rodriguez	2.50	1.10
2	Derek Jeter	2.00	.90
3	Dustin Hermanson	.30	.14
4	Bill Pulsipher	.15	.07
5	Terrell Wade	.15	.07
6	Darren Dreifort	.30	.14
7	LaTroy Hawkins	.15	.07
8	Alex Ochoa	.15	.07
9	Paul Wilson	.15	.07
10	Rod Henderson	.15	.07
11	Alan Benes	.30	.14
12	Garret Anderson	.30	.14
13	Armando Benitez	.15	.07
14	Mark Thompson	.15	.07
15	Herbert Perry	.15	.07
16	Jose Silva	.15	.07
17	Orlando Miller	.15	.07
18	Russ Davis	.30	.14
19	Jason Isringhausen	.30	.14
20	Ray McDavid	.15	.07
21	Tim VanEgmond	.15	.07
22	Paul Shuey	.15	.07
23	Steve Dunn	.15	.07
24	Mike Lieberthal	.15	.07
25	Chan Ho Park	.75	.35
26	Ken Griffey Jr. RP	1.50	.70
27	Tony Gwynn RP	.75	.35
28	Chuck Knoblauch RP	.60	.25
29	Frank Thomas RP	1.00	.45
30	Matt Williams RP	.15	.07
31	Chili Davis	.30	.14
32	Chad Curtis	.15	.07
33	Brian Anderson	.30	.14
34	Chuck Finley	.30	.14
35	Tim Salmon	.60	.25
36	Bo Jackson	.30	.14
37	Doug Drabek	.15	.07
38	Craig Biggio	.60	.25
39	Ken Caminiti	.40	.18
40	Jeff Bagwell	1.00	.45
41	Darryl Kile	.30	.14
42	John Hudek	.15	.07
43	Brian L. Hunter	.30	.14
44	Dennis Eckersley	.30	.14
45	Mark McGwire	3.00	1.35
46	Brent Gates	.15	.07
47	Steve Karsay	.15	.07
48	Rickey Henderson	.60	.25
49	Terry Steinbach	.30	.14
50	Ruben Sierra	.15	.07
51	Roberto Alomar	.60	.25
52	Carlos Delgado	.30	.14
53	Alex Gonzalez	.15	.07
54	Joe Carter	.30	.14
55	Paul Molitor	.60	.25
56	Juan Guzman	.15	.07
57	John Olerud	.30	.14
58	Shawn Green	.30	.14
59	Tom Glavine	.60	.25
60	Greg Maddux	2.00	.90
61	Roberto Kelly	.15	.07
62	Ryan Klesko	.30	.14
63	Javier Lopez	.30	.14
64	Jose Oliva	.15	.07
65	Fred McGriff	.40	.18
66	Steve Avery	.15	.07
67	David Justice	.60	.25
68	Ricky Bones	.15	.07
69	Cal Eldred	.15	.07
70	Greg Vaughn	.30	.14
71	Dave Nilsson	.15	.07
72	Jose Valentin	.15	.07
73	Matt Mieske	.15	.07
74	Todd Zeile	.15	.07
75	Ozzie Smith	.75	.35
76	Bernard Gilkey	.15	.07
77	Ray Lankford	.30	.14
78	Bob Tewksbury	.15	.07
79	Mark Whiten	.15	.07
80	Gregg Jefferies	.15	.07
81	Randy Myers	.15	.07
82	Shawon Dunston	.15	.07
83	Mark Grace	.40	.18
84	Derrick May	.15	.07
85	Sammy Sosa	1.50	.70
86	Steve Trachsel	.15	.07
87	Brett Butler	.30	.14
88	Delino DeShields	.15	.07
89	Orel Hershiser	.30	.14
90	Mike Piazza	2.00	.90
91	Todd Hollandsworth	.15	.07
92	Eric Karros	.30	.14
93	Ramon Martinez	.30	.14
94	Tim Wallach	.15	.07
95	Raul Mondesi	.40	.18
96	Larry Walker	.60	.25
97	Wil Cordero	.15	.07
98	Marquis Grissom	.30	.14
99	Ken Hill	.15	.07
100	Cliff Floyd	.30	.14
101	Pedro J. Martinez	.60	.25
102	John Wetteland	.30	.14
103	Rondell White	.30	.14
104	Moises Alou	.40	.18
105	Barry Bonds	.75	.35
106	Darren Lewis	.15	.07
107	Mark Portugal	.15	.07
108	Matt Williams	.30	.14
109	William VanLandingham	.15	.07
110	Bill Swift	.15	.07
111	Robby Thompson	.15	.07
112	Rod Beck	.15	.07
113	Darryl Strawberry	.30	.14
114	Jim Thome	.60	.25
115	Dave Winfield	.60	.25
116	Eddie Murray	.60	.25
117	Manny Ramirez	.60	.25
118	Carlos Baerga	.30	.14
119	Kenny Lofton	.60	.25
120	Albert Belle	.75	.35
121	Mark Clark	.15	.07
122	Dennis Martinez	.30	.14
123	Randy Johnson	.60	.25
124	Jay Buhner	.30	.14
125	Ken Griffey Jr.	3.00	1.35
126	Goose Gossage	.30	.14
127	Tino Martinez	.60	.25
128	Reggie Jefferson	.15	.07
129	Edgar Martinez	.30	.14
130	Gary Sheffield	.40	.18
131	Pat Rapp	.15	.07
132	Bret Barberie	.15	.07
133	Chuck Carr	.15	.07
134	Jeff Conine	.30	.14
135	Charles Johnson	.30	.14
136	Benito Santiago	.15	.07
137	Matt Williams STL	.15	.07
138	Jeff Bagwell STL	.60	.25
139	Kenny Lofton STL	.30	.14
140	Tony Gwynn STL	.75	.35
141	Jimmy Key STL	.30	.14
142	Greg Maddux STL	1.00	.45
143	Randy Johnson STL	.30	.14
144	Lee Smith STL	.15	.07
145	Bobby Bonilla	.30	.14
146	Jason Jacome	.15	.07
147	Jeff Kent	.30	.14
148	Ryan Thompson	.15	.07
149	Bobby Jones	.15	.07
150	Bret Saberhagen	.30	.14
151	John Franco	.30	.14
152	Lee Smith	.30	.14
153	Rafael Palmeiro	.40	.18
154	Brady Anderson	.30	.14
155	Cal Ripken Jr.	2.50	1.10
156	Jeffrey Hammonds	.30	.14
157	Mike Mussina	.60	.25
158	Chris Hoiles	.15	.07
159	Ben McDonald	.15	.07
160	Tony Gwynn	1.50	.70
161	Joey Hamilton	.30	.14
162	Andy Benes	.30	.14
163	Trevor Hoffman	.30	.14
164	Phil Plantier	.15	.07
165	Derek Bell	.30	.14
166	Bip Roberts	.15	.07
167	Eddie Williams	.15	.07
168	Fernando Valenzuela	.30	.14
169	Mariano Duncan	.15	.07
170	Lenny Dykstra	.30	.14
171	Darren Daulton	.30	.14
172	Danny Jackson	.15	.07
173	Bobby Munoz	.15	.07
174	Doug Jones	.15	.07
175	Jay Bell	.30	.14
176	Zane Smith	.15	.07
177	Jon Lieber	.15	.07
178	Carlos Garcia	.15	.07
179	Orlando Merced	.15	.07
180	Andy Van Slyke	.30	.14
181	Rick Helling	.30	.14
182	Rusty Greer	.60	.25
183	Kenny Rogers UER (shows 110 wins in 1990)	.15	.07
184	Will Clark	.60	.25
185	Jose Canseco	.60	.25
186	Juan Gonzalez	1.50	.70
187	Dean Palmer	.30	.14
188	Ivan Rodriguez	.75	.35
189	John Valentin	.30	.14
190	Roger Clemens	1.25	.55
191	Aaron Sele	.30	.14
192	Scott Cooper	.15	.07
193	Mike Greenwell	.15	.07
194	Mo Vaughn	.75	.35
195	Andre Dawson	.40	.18
196	Ron Gant	.15	.07
197	Jose Rijo	.15	.07
198	Bret Boone	.30	.14
199	Deion Sanders	.30	.14
200	Barry Larkin	.40	.18
201	Hal Morris	.15	.07
202	Reggie Sanders	.30	.14
203	Kevin Mitchell	.15	.07
204	Marvin Freeman	.15	.07
205	Andres Galarraga	.60	.25
206	Walt Weiss	.15	.07
207	Charlie Hayes	.15	.07
208	Dave Nied	.15	.07
209	Dante Bichette	.30	.14
210	David Cone	.40	.18
211	Jeff Montgomery	.15	.07
212	Felix Jose	.15	.07
213	Mike Macfarlane	.15	.07
214	Wally Joyner	.30	.14
215	Bob Hamelin	.15	.07

❑ 216	Brian McRae	.15	.07
❑ 217	Kirk Gibson	.30	.14
❑ 218	Lou Whitaker	.30	.14
❑ 219	Chris Gomez	.15	.07
❑ 220	Cecil Fielder	.30	.14
❑ 221	Mickey Tettleton	.15	.07
❑ 222	Travis Fryman	.30	.14
❑ 223	Tony Phillips	.15	.07
❑ 224	Rick Aguilera	.15	.07
❑ 225	Scott Erickson	.30	.14
❑ 226	Chuck Knoblauch	.60	.25
❑ 227	Kent Hrbek	.15	.07
❑ 228	Shane Mack	.15	.07
❑ 229	Kevin Tapani	.15	.07
❑ 230	Kirby Puckett	1.00	.45
❑ 231	Julio Franco	.15	.07
❑ 232	Jack McDowell	.15	.07
❑ 233	Jason Bere	.15	.07
❑ 234	Alex Fernandez	.15	.07
❑ 235	Frank Thomas	2.00	.90
❑ 236	Ozzie Guillen	.15	.07
❑ 237	Robin Ventura	.30	.14
❑ 238	Michael Jordan	4.00	1.80
❑ 239	Wilson Alvarez	.30	.14
❑ 240	Don Mattingly	1.00	.45
❑ 241	Jim Abbott	.30	.14
❑ 242	Jim Leyritz	.30	.14
❑ 243	Paul O'Neill	.30	.14
❑ 244	Melido Perez	.15	.07
❑ 245	Wade Boggs	.60	.25
❑ 246	Mike Stanley	.15	.07
❑ 247	Danny Tartabull	.15	.07
❑ 248	Jimmy Key	.30	.14
❑ 249	Greg Maddux FT	1.00	.45
❑ 250	Randy Johnson FT	.30	.14
❑ 251	Bret Saberhagen FT	.30	.14
❑ 252	John Wetteland FT	.30	.14
❑ 253	Mike Piazza FT	1.00	.45
❑ 254	Jeff Bagwell FT	.60	.25
❑ 255	Craig Biggio FT	.30	.14
❑ 256	Matt Williams FT	.15	.07
❑ 257	Wil Cordero FT	.15	.07
❑ 258	Kenny Lofton FT	.30	.14
❑ 259	Barry Bonds FT	.40	.18
❑ 260	Dante Bichette FT	.15	.07
❑ 261	Ken Griffey Jr. CL	1.50	.70
❑ 262	Goose Gossage CL	.15	.07
❑ 263	Cal Ripken CL	1.25	.55
❑ 264	Kenny Rogers CL	.15	.07
❑ 265	John Valentin CL	.15	.07
❑ P125	Ken Griffey Jr. Promo	3.00	1.35

1998 Crown Royale

	MINT	NRMT
COMPLETE SET (144)	150.00	70.00
COMMON CARD (1-144)	.50	.23

❑ 1	Garret Anderson	.75	.35
❑ 2	Jim Edmonds	1.25	.55
❑ 3	Darin Erstad	2.50	1.10
❑ 4	Tim Salmon	2.00	.90
❑ 5	Jarrod Washburn	.75	.35
❑ 6	Dave Dellucci	2.50	1.10
❑ 7	Travis Lee	4.00	1.80
❑ 8	Devon White	.75	.35
❑ 9	Matt Williams	.75	.35
❑ 10	Andres Galarraga	2.00	.90
❑ 11	Tom Glavine	2.00	.90
❑ 12	Andruw Jones	2.50	1.10
❑ 13	Chipper Jones	5.00	2.20
❑ 14	Ryan Klesko	.75	.35
❑ 15	Javy Lopez	.75	.35
❑ 16	Greg Maddux	6.00	2.70
❑ 17	Walt Weiss	.75	.35
❑ 18	Roberto Alomar	2.00	.90
❑ 19	Harold Baines	.75	.35
❑ 20	Eric Davis	.75	.35
❑ 21	Mike Mussina	2.00	.90
❑ 22	Rafael Palmeiro	1.25	.55
❑ 23	Cal Ripken	8.00	3.60
❑ 24	Nomar Garciaparra	6.00	2.70
❑ 25	Pedro Martinez	2.00	.90
❑ 26	Troy O'Leary	.75	.35
❑ 27	Mo Vaughn	2.50	1.10
❑ 28	Tim Wakefield	.50	.23
❑ 29	Mark Grace	1.25	.55
❑ 30	Mickey Morandini	.50	.23
❑ 31	Sammy Sosa	5.00	2.20
❑ 32	Kerry Wood	10.00	4.50
❑ 33	Albert Belle	2.00	.90
❑ 34	Mike Caruso	.75	.35
❑ 35	Ray Durham	.75	.35
❑ 36	Frank Thomas	6.00	2.70
❑ 37	Robin Ventura	.75	.35
❑ 38	Bret Boone	.75	.35
❑ 39	Sean Casey	.75	.35
❑ 40	Barry Larkin	1.25	.55
❑ 41	Reggie Sanders	.75	.35
❑ 42	Sandy Alomar Jr.	.75	.35
❑ 43	David Justice	2.00	.90
❑ 44	Kenny Lofton	2.00	.90
❑ 45	Manny Ramirez	2.00	.90
❑ 46	Jim Thome	2.00	.90
❑ 47	Omar Vizquel	.75	.35
❑ 48	Jaret Wright	2.50	1.10
❑ 49	Dante Bichette	.75	.35
❑ 50	Ellis Burks	.75	.35
❑ 51	Vinny Castilla	1.25	.55
❑ 52	Todd Helton	2.50	1.10
❑ 53	Larry Walker	2.00	.90
❑ 54	Tony Clark	1.25	.55
❑ 55	Damion Easley	.75	.35
❑ 56	Bobby Higginson	1.25	.55
❑ 57	Cliff Floyd	.75	.35
❑ 58	Livan Hernandez	.75	.35
❑ 59	Derrek Lee	.75	.35
❑ 60	Edgar Renteria	.75	.35
❑ 61	Moises Alou	1.25	.55
❑ 62	Jeff Bagwell	3.00	1.35
❑ 63	Derek Bell	.75	.35
❑ 64	Craig Biggio	2.00	.90
❑ 65	Johnny Damon	.75	.35
❑ 66	Jeff King	.75	.35
❑ 67	Hal Morris	.50	.23
❑ 68	Dean Palmer	.75	.35
❑ 69	Bobby Bonilla	.75	.35
❑ 70	Eric Karros	.75	.35
❑ 71	Raul Mondesi	1.25	.55
❑ 72	Gary Sheffield	1.25	.55
❑ 73	Jeromy Burnitz	.75	.35
❑ 74	Jeff Cirillo	.75	.35
❑ 75	Marquis Grissom	.75	.35
❑ 76	Fernando Vina	.50	.23
❑ 77	Marty Cordova	.50	.23
❑ 78	Pat Meares	.50	.23
❑ 79	Paul Molitor	2.00	.90
❑ 80	Terry Steinbach	.75	.35
❑ 81	Todd Walker	1.25	.55
❑ 82	Brad Fullmer	.75	.35
❑ 83	Vladimir Guerrero	3.00	1.35
❑ 84	Carl Pavano	.75	.35
❑ 85	Rondell White	.75	.35
❑ 86	Carlos Baerga	.75	.35
❑ 87	Hideo Nomo	2.50	1.10
❑ 88	John Olerud	.75	.35
❑ 89	Rey Ordonez	.75	.35
❑ 90	Mike Piazza	6.00	2.70
❑ 91	Masato Yoshii	1.50	.70
❑ 92	Orlando Hernandez	10.00	4.50
❑ 93	Hideki Irabu	1.25	.55
❑ 94	Derek Jeter	5.00	2.20
❑ 95	Chuck Knoblauch	2.00	.90
❑ 96	Ricky Ledee	.75	.35
❑ 97	Tino Martinez	2.00	.90
❑ 98	Paul O'Neill	.75	.35
❑ 99	Bernie Williams	2.00	.90
❑ 100	Jason Giambi	.75	.35
❑ 101	Ben Grieve	4.00	1.80
❑ 102	Rickey Henderson	2.00	.90
❑ 103	Matt Stairs	.75	.35
❑ 104	Bob Abreu	.75	.35
❑ 105	Doug Glanville	.75	.35
❑ 106	Scott Rolen	5.00	2.20
❑ 107	Curt Schilling	.75	.35
❑ 108	Jose Guillen	.75	.35
❑ 109	Jason Kendall	.75	.35
❑ 110	Jason Schmidt	.50	.23
❑ 111	Kevin Young	.75	.35
❑ 112	Delino DeShields	.50	.23
❑ 113	Brian Jordan	.75	.35
❑ 114	Ray Lankford	.75	.35
❑ 115	Mark McGwire	12.00	5.50
❑ 116	Tony Gwynn	5.00	2.20
❑ 117	Wally Joyner	.75	.35
❑ 118	Ruben Rivera	.75	.35
❑ 119	Greg Vaughn	.75	.35
❑ 120	Rich Aurilia	.50	.23
❑ 121	Barry Bonds	2.50	1.10
❑ 122	Bill Mueller	.75	.35
❑ 123	Robb Nen	.75	.35
❑ 124	Jay Buhner	.75	.35
❑ 125	Ken Griffey Jr.	10.00	4.50
❑ 126	Edgar Martinez	.75	.35
❑ 127	Shane Monahan	.75	.35
❑ 128	Alex Rodriguez	6.00	2.70
❑ 129	David Segui	.75	.35
❑ 130	Rolando Arrojo	3.00	1.35
❑ 131	Wade Boggs	2.00	.90
❑ 132	Quinton McCracken	.75	.35
❑ 133	Fred McGriff	1.25	.55
❑ 134	Bobby Smith	.75	.35
❑ 135	Will Clark	2.00	.90
❑ 136	Juan Gonzalez	5.00	2.20
❑ 137	Rusty Greer	.75	.35
❑ 138	Ivan Rodriguez	2.50	1.10
❑ 139	Aaron Sele	.75	.35
❑ 140	John Wetteland	.75	.35
❑ 141	Jose Canseco	2.00	.90
❑ 142	Roger Clemens	4.00	1.80
❑ 143	Carlos Delgado	.75	.35
❑ 144	Shawn Green	.75	.35

1998 Crown Royale All-Stars

	MINT	NRMT
COMPLETE SET (20)	400.00	180.00
COMMON CARD (1-20)	4.00	1.80

❑ 1	Roberto Alomar	10.00	4.50
❑ 2	Cal Ripken	40.00	18.00
❑ 3	Kenny Lofton	10.00	4.50
❑ 4	Jim Thome	10.00	4.50
❑ 5	Derek Jeter	25.00	11.00
❑ 6	David Wells	6.00	2.70
❑ 7	Ken Griffey Jr.	50.00	22.00
❑ 8	Alex Rodriguez	30.00	13.50
❑ 9	Juan Gonzalez	25.00	11.00
❑ 10	Ivan Rodriguez	12.00	5.50

		MINT	NRMT
❑ 11	Gary Sheffield	6.00	2.70
❑ 12	Chipper Jones	25.00	11.00
❑ 13	Greg Maddux	30.00	13.50
❑ 14	Walt Weiss	4.00	1.80
❑ 15	Larry Walker	10.00	4.50
❑ 16	Craig Biggio	10.00	4.50
❑ 17	Mike Piazza	30.00	13.50
❑ 18	Mark McGwire	60.00	27.00
❑ 19	Tony Gwynn	25.00	11.00
❑ 20	Barry Bonds	12.00	5.50

1998 Crown Royale Cramer's Choice Premiums

	MINT	NRMT
COMPLETE SET (10)	150.00	70.00
COMMON CARD (1-10)	8.00	3.60
❑ 1 Cal Ripken	20.00	9.00
❑ 2 Ken Griffey Jr.	25.00	11.00
❑ 3 Alex Rodriguez	15.00	6.75
❑ 4 Juan Gonzalez	12.00	5.50
❑ 5 Travis Lee	8.00	3.60
❑ 6 Chipper Jones	12.00	5.50
❑ 7 Greg Maddux	15.00	6.75
❑ 8 Kerry Wood	20.00	9.00
❑ 9 Mark McGwire	30.00	13.50
❑ 10 Tony Gwynn	12.00	5.50

1998 Crown Royale Diamond Knights

	MINT	NRMT
COMPLETE SET (25)	40.00	18.00
COMMON CARD (1-25)	.60	.25
❑ 1 Andres Galarraga	1.00	.45
❑ 2 Chipper Jones	2.50	1.10
❑ 3 Greg Maddux	3.00	1.35
❑ 4 Cal Ripken	4.00	1.80
❑ 5 Nomar Garciaparra	3.00	1.35
❑ 6 Mo Vaughn	1.25	.55
❑ 7 Kerry Wood	5.00	2.20
❑ 8 Frank Thomas	3.00	1.35
❑ 9 Vinny Castilla	.60	.25
❑ 10 Jeff Bagwell	1.50	.70
❑ 11 Craig Biggio	1.00	.45
❑ 12 Paul Molitor	1.00	.45
❑ 13 Mike Piazza	3.00	1.35
❑ 14 Orlando Hernandez	5.00	2.20
❑ 15 Derek Jeter	2.50	1.10
❑ 16 Ricky Ledee	.40	.18
❑ 17 Mark McGwire	6.00	2.70
❑ 18 Tony Gwynn	2.50	1.10
❑ 19 Barry Bonds	1.25	.55
❑ 20 Ken Griffey Jr.	5.00	2.20
❑ 21 Alex Rodriguez	3.00	1.35
❑ 22 Wade Boggs	1.00	.45
❑ 23 Juan Gonzalez	2.50	1.10
❑ 24 Ivan Rodriguez	1.25	.55
❑ 25 Jose Canseco	1.00	.45

1998 Crown Royale Firestone on Baseball

	MINT	NRMT
COMPLETE SET (26)	300.00	135.00
COMMON CARD (1-26)	4.00	1.80
❑ 1 Travis Lee	10.00	4.50
❑ 2 Chipper Jones	15.00	6.75
❑ 3 Greg Maddux	20.00	9.00
❑ 4 Cal Ripken	25.00	11.00
❑ 5 Nomar Garciaparra	20.00	9.00
❑ 6 Mo Vaughn	8.00	3.60
❑ 7 Kerry Wood	25.00	11.00
❑ 8 Frank Thomas	20.00	9.00
❑ 9 Manny Ramirez	6.00	2.70
❑ 10 Larry Walker	6.00	2.70
❑ 11 Gary Sheffield	4.00	1.80
❑ 12 Paul Molitor	6.00	2.70
❑ 13 Hideo Nomo	8.00	3.60
❑ 14 Mike Piazza	20.00	9.00
❑ 15 Ben Grieve	10.00	4.50
❑ 16 Mark McGwire	40.00	18.00
❑ 17 Tony Gwynn	15.00	6.75
❑ 18 Barry Bonds	8.00	3.60
❑ 19 Ken Griffey Jr.	30.00	13.50
❑ 20 Randy Johnson	6.00	2.70
❑ 21 Alex Rodriguez	20.00	9.00
❑ 22 Wade Boggs	6.00	2.70
❑ 23 Juan Gonzalez	15.00	6.75
❑ 24 Ivan Rodriguez	8.00	3.60
❑ 25 Roger Clemens	12.00	5.50
❑ 26 Roy Firestone Tony Gwynn	8.00	3.60

1998 Crown Royale Home Run Fever

	MINT	NRMT
COMPLETE SET (10)	350.00	160.00
COMMON CARD (1-10)	8.00	3.60
❑ 1 Andres Galarraga	15.00	6.75
❑ 2 Sammy Sosa	40.00	18.00
❑ 3 Albert Belle	15.00	6.75
❑ 4 Jim Thome	15.00	6.75
❑ 5 Mark McGwire	100.00	45.00
❑ 6 Greg Vaughn	8.00	3.60
❑ 7 Ken Griffey Jr.	80.00	36.00
❑ 8 Alex Rodriguez	50.00	22.00
❑ 9 Juan Gonzalez	40.00	18.00
❑ 10 Jose Canseco	15.00	6.75

1998 Crown Royale Pillars of the Game

	MINT	NRMT
COMPLETE SET (25)	40.00	18.00
COMMON CARD (1-25)	.60	.25
❑ 1 Jim Edmonds	.60	.25
❑ 2 Travis Lee	2.00	.90
❑ 3 Chipper Jones	2.50	1.10
❑ 4 Tom Glavine John Smoltz Greg Maddux	2.50	1.10
❑ 5 Cal Ripken	4.00	1.80
❑ 6 Nomar Garciaparra	3.00	1.35
❑ 7 Roberto Alomar	1.00	.45
❑ 8 Sammy Sosa	2.50	1.10
❑ 9 Kerry Wood	5.00	2.20
❑ 10 Frank Thomas	3.00	1.35
❑ 11 Jim Thome	1.00	.45
❑ 12 Larry Walker	1.00	.45
❑ 13 Moises Alou	.60	.25
❑ 14 Raul Mondesi	.60	.25
❑ 15 Mike Piazza	3.00	1.35
❑ 16 Hideki Irabu	.60	.25
❑ 17 Bernie Williams	1.00	.45
❑ 18 Ben Grieve	2.00	.90
❑ 19 Scott Rolen	2.50	1.10
❑ 20 Mark McGwire	6.00	2.70
❑ 21 Tony Gwynn	2.50	1.10
❑ 22 Ken Griffey Jr.	5.00	2.20
❑ 23 Alex Rodriguez	3.00	1.35
❑ 24 Juan Gonzalez	2.50	1.10
❑ 25 Roger Clemens	2.00	.90

1981 Donruss

	NRMT	VG-E
COMPLETE SET (605)	25.00	11.00
COMMON CARD (1-605)	.10	.05
❑ 1 Ozzie Smith	4.00	1.80
❑ 2 Rollie Fingers	1.00	.45
❑ 3 Rick Wise	.10	.05
❑ 4 Gene Richards	.10	.05
❑ 5 Alan Trammell	1.00	.45
❑ 6 Tom Brookens	.10	.05
❑ 7A Duffy Dyer P1 1980 batting average	.25	.11

has decimal point
❑ 7B Duffy Dyer P2 .10 .05
1980 batting average
has no decimal point
❑ 8 Mark Fidrych 1.00 .45
❑ 9 Dave Rozema .10 .05
❑ 10 Ricky Peters .10 .05
❑ 11 Mike Schmidt 1.25 .55
❑ 12 Willie Stargell 1.00 .45
❑ 13 Tim Foli .10 .05
❑ 14 Manny Sanguillen .25 .11
❑ 15 Grant Jackson .10 .05
❑ 16 Eddie Solomon .10 .05
❑ 17 Omar Moreno .10 .05
❑ 18 Joe Morgan 1.00 .45
❑ 19 Rafael Landestoy .10 .05
❑ 20 Bruce Bochy .10 .05
❑ 21 Joe Sambito .10 .05
❑ 22 Manny Trillo .10 .05
❑ 23A Dave Smith P1 .25 .11
Line box around stats
is not complete
❑ 23B Dave Smith P2 .25 .11
Box totally encloses
stats at top
❑ 24 Terry Puhl .10 .05
❑ 25 Bump Wills .10 .05
❑ 26A John Ellis P1 ERR .50 .23
Danny Walton photo on front
❑ 26B John Ellis P2 COR .25 .11
❑ 27 Jim Kern .10 .05
❑ 28 Richie Zisk .10 .05
❑ 29 John Mayberry .10 .05
❑ 30 Bob Davis .10 .05
❑ 31 Jackson Todd .10 .05
❑ 32 Alvis Woods .10 .05
❑ 33 Steve Carlton 1.00 .45
❑ 34 Lee Mazzilli .10 .05
❑ 35 John Stearns .10 .05
❑ 36 Roy Lee Jackson .10 .05
❑ 37 Mike Scott .25 .11
❑ 38 Lamar Johnson .10 .05
❑ 39 Kevin Bell .10 .05
❑ 40 Ed Farmer .10 .05
❑ 41 Ross Baumgarten .10 .05
❑ 42 Leo Sutherland .10 .05
❑ 43 Dan Meyer .10 .05
❑ 44 Ron Reed .10 .05
❑ 45 Mario Mendoza .10 .05
❑ 46 Rick Honeycutt .10 .05
❑ 47 Glenn Abbott .10 .05
❑ 48 Leon Roberts .10 .05
❑ 49 Rod Carew 1.00 .45
❑ 50 Bert Campaneris .25 .11
❑ 51A Tom Donahue P1 ERR .25 .11
Name on front
misspelled Donahue
❑ 51B Tom Donohue .10 .05
P2 COR
❑ 52 Dave Frost .10 .05
❑ 53 Ed Halicki .10 .05
❑ 54 Dan Ford .10 .05
❑ 55 Garry Maddox .10 .05
❑ 56A Steve Garvey P1 1.00 .45
Surpassed 25 HR
❑ 56B Steve Garvey P2 1.00 .45
Surpassed 21 HR
❑ 57 Bill Russell .25 .11
❑ 58 Don Sutton 1.00 .45
❑ 59 Reggie Smith .25 .11
❑ 60 Rick Monday .25 .11
❑ 61 Ray Knight .25 .11
❑ 62 Johnny Bench 1.25 .55
❑ 63 Mario Soto .10 .05
❑ 64 Doug Bair .10 .05
❑ 65 George Foster .25 .11
❑ 66 Jeff Burroughs .10 .05
❑ 67 Keith Hernandez .25 .11
❑ 68 Tom Herr .25 .11
❑ 69 Bob Forsch .10 .05
❑ 70 John Fulgham .10 .05
❑ 71A Bobby Bonds P1 ERR 1.00 .45
986 lifetime HR
❑ 71B Bobby Bonds P2 COR .50 .23
326 lifetime HR
❑ 72A Rennie Stennett P1 .25 .11
Breaking broke leg
❑ 72B Rennie Stennett P2 .10 .05
Word "broke" deleted
❑ 73 Joe Strain .10 .05
❑ 74 Ed Whitson .10 .05
❑ 75 Tom Griffin .10 .05
❑ 76 Billy North .10 .05
❑ 77 Gene Garber .10 .05
❑ 78 Mike Hargrove .25 .11
❑ 79 Dave Rosello .10 .05
❑ 80 Ron Hassey .10 .05
❑ 81 Sid Monge .10 .05
❑ 82A Joe Charboneau P1 1.00 .45
'78 highlights
For some reason
❑ 82B Joe Charboneau P2 1.00 .45
Phrase "For some reason" deleted
❑ 83 Cecil Cooper .25 .11
❑ 84 Sal Bando .25 .11
❑ 85 Moose Haas .10 .05
❑ 86 Mike Caldwell .10 .05
❑ 87A Larry Hisle P1 .25 .11
'77 highlights
line ends with "28 RBI"
❑ 87B Larry Hisle P2 .10 .05
Correct line "28 HR"
❑ 88 Luis Gomez .10 .05
❑ 89 Larry Parrish .10 .05
❑ 90 Gary Carter 1.00 .45
❑ 91 Bill Gullickson .50 .23
❑ 92 Fred Norman .10 .05
❑ 93 Tommy Hutton .10 .05
❑ 94 Carl Yastrzemski 1.00 .45
❑ 95 Glenn Hoffman .10 .05
❑ 96 Dennis Eckersley 1.00 .45
❑ 97A Tom Burgmeier P1 .25 .11
ERR Throws: Right
❑ 97B Tom Burgmeier P2 .10 .05
COR Throws: Left
❑ 98 Win Remmerswaal .10 .05
❑ 99 Bob Horner .25 .11
❑ 100 George Brett 2.50 1.10
❑ 101 Dave Chalk .10 .05
❑ 102 Dennis Leonard .10 .05
❑ 103 Renie Martin .10 .05
❑ 104 Amos Otis .25 .11
❑ 105 Graig Nettles .25 .11
❑ 106 Eric Soderholm .10 .05
❑ 107 Tommy John .50 .23
❑ 108 Tom Underwood .10 .05
❑ 109 Lou Piniella .25 .11
❑ 110 Mickey Klutts .10 .05
❑ 111 Bobby Murcer .25 .11
❑ 112 Eddie Murray 2.00 .90
❑ 113 Rick Dempsey .25 .11
❑ 114 Scott McGregor .10 .05
❑ 115 Ken Singleton .25 .11
❑ 116 Gary Roenicke .10 .05
❑ 117 Dave Revering .10 .05
❑ 118 Mike Norris .10 .05
❑ 119 Rickey Henderson 2.50 1.10
❑ 120 Mike Heath .10 .05
❑ 121 Dave Cash .10 .05
❑ 122 Randy Jones .10 .05
❑ 123 Eric Rasmussen .10 .05
❑ 124 Jerry Mumphrey .10 .05
❑ 125 Richie Hebner .10 .05
❑ 126 Mark Wagner .10 .05
❑ 127 Jack Morris 1.00 .45
❑ 128 Dan Petry .10 .05
❑ 129 Bruce Robbins .10 .05
❑ 130 Champ Summers .10 .05
❑ 131 Pete Rose P1 1.25 .55
Last line ends with
see card 251
❑ 131B Pete Rose P2 1.50 .70
Last line corrected
see card 371
❑ 132 Willie Stargell 1.00 .45
❑ 133 Ed Ott .10 .05
❑ 134 Jim Bibby .10 .05
❑ 135 Bert Blyleven .50 .23
❑ 136 Dave Parker .25 .11
❑ 137 Bill Robinson .25 .11
❑ 138 Enos Cabell .10 .05
❑ 139 Dave Bergman .10 .05
❑ 140 J.R. Richard .25 .11
❑ 141 Ken Forsch .10 .05
❑ 142 Larry Bowa UER .25 .11
Shortshop on front
❑ 143 Frank LaCorte UER .10 .05
Photo actually Randy Niemann
❑ 144 Denny Walling .10 .05
❑ 145 Buddy Bell .25 .11
❑ 146 Ferguson Jenkins 1.00 .45
❑ 147 Danny Darwin .25 .11
❑ 148 John Grubb .10 .05
❑ 149 Alfredo Griffin .10 .05
❑ 150 Jerry Garvin .10 .05
❑ 151 Paul Mirabella .10 .05
❑ 152 Rick Bosetti .10 .05
❑ 153 Dick Ruthven .10 .05
❑ 154 Frank Taveras .10 .05
❑ 155 Craig Swan .10 .05
❑ 156 Jeff Reardon 1.00 .45
❑ 157 Steve Henderson .10 .05
❑ 158 Jim Morrison .10 .05
❑ 159 Glenn Borgmann .10 .05
❑ 160 LaMarr Hoyt .25 .11
❑ 161 Rich Wortham .10 .05
❑ 162 Thad Bosley .10 .05
❑ 163 Julio Cruz .10 .05
❑ 164A Del Unser P1 .25 .11
No "3B" heading
❑ 164B Del Unser P2 .10 .05
Batting record on back
corrected "3B"
❑ 165 Jim Anderson .10 .05
❑ 166 Jim Beattie .10 .05
❑ 167 Shane Rawley .10 .05
❑ 168 Joe Simpson .10 .05
❑ 169 Rod Carew 1.00 .45
❑ 170 Fred Patek .10 .05
❑ 171 Frank Tanana .25 .11
❑ 172 Alfredo Martinez .10 .05
❑ 173 Chris Knapp .10 .05
❑ 174 Joe Rudi .25 .11
❑ 175 Greg Luzinski .25 .11
❑ 176 Steve Garvey .50 .23
❑ 177 Joe Ferguson .10 .05
❑ 178 Bob Welch .25 .11
❑ 179 Dusty Baker .50 .23
❑ 180 Rudy Law .10 .05
❑ 181 Dave Concepcion .25 .11
❑ 182 Johnny Bench 1.25 .55
❑ 183 Mike LaCoss .10 .05
❑ 184 Ken Griffey .50 .23
❑ 185 Dave Collins .10 .05
❑ 186 Brian Asselstine .10 .05
❑ 187 Garry Templeton .10 .05
❑ 188 Mike Phillips .10 .05
❑ 189 Pete Vuckovich .25 .11
❑ 190 John Urrea .10 .05
❑ 191 Tony Scott .10 .05
❑ 192 Darrell Evans .25 .11
❑ 193 Milt May .10 .05
❑ 194 Bob Knepper .10 .05
❑ 195 Randy Moffitt .10 .05
❑ 196 Larry Herndon .10 .05
❑ 197 Rick Camp .10 .05
❑ 198 Andre Thornton .25 .11
❑ 199 Tom Veryzer .10 .05

❑ 200 Gary Alexander .10 .05
❑ 201 Rick Waits .10 .05
❑ 202 Rick Manning .10 .05
❑ 203 Paul Molitor 2.00 .90
❑ 204 Jim Gantner .25 .11
❑ 205 Paul Mitchell .10 .05
❑ 206 Reggie Cleveland .10 .05
❑ 207 Sixto Lezcano .10 .05
❑ 208 Bruce Benedict .10 .05
❑ 209 Rodney Scott .10 .05
❑ 210 John Tamargo .10 .05
❑ 211 Bill Lee .25 .11
❑ 212 Andre Dawson UER 1.00 .45
Middle name Fernando
should be Nolan
❑ 213 Rowland Office .10 .05
❑ 214 Carl Yastrzemski 1.00 .45
❑ 215 Jerry Remy .10 .05
❑ 216 Mike Torrez .10 .05
❑ 217 Skip Lockwood .10 .05
❑ 218 Fred Lynn .25 .11
❑ 219 Chris Chambliss .25 .11
❑ 220 Willie Aikens .10 .05
❑ 221 John Wathan .10 .05
❑ 222 Dan Quisenberry .25 .11
❑ 223 Willie Wilson .25 .11
❑ 224 Clint Hurdle .10 .05
❑ 225 Bob Watson .25 .11
❑ 226 Jim Spencer .10 .05
❑ 227 Ron Guidry .25 .11
❑ 228 Reggie Jackson 1.25 .55
❑ 229 Oscar Gamble .10 .05
❑ 230 Jeff Cox .10 .05
❑ 231 Luis Tiant .25 .11
❑ 232 Rich Dauer .10 .05
❑ 233 Dan Graham .10 .05
❑ 234 Mike Flanagan .25 .11
❑ 235 John Lowenstein .10 .05
❑ 236 Benny Ayala .10 .05
❑ 237 Wayne Gross .10 .05
❑ 238 Rick Langford .10 .05
❑ 239 Tony Armas .25 .11
❑ 240A Bob Lacey P1 ERR .50 .23
Name misspelled Lacy
❑ 240B Bob Lacey P2 COR .10 .05
❑ 241 Gene Tenace .25 .11
❑ 242 Bob Shirley .10 .05
❑ 243 Gary Lucas .10 .05
❑ 244 Jerry Turner .10 .05
❑ 245 John Wockenfuss .10 .05
❑ 246 Stan Papi .10 .05
❑ 247 Milt Wilcox .10 .05
❑ 248 Dan Schatzeder .10 .05
❑ 249 Steve Kemp .10 .05
❑ 250 Jim Lentine .10 .05
❑ 251 Pete Rose 1.25 .55
❑ 252 Bill Madlock .25 .11
❑ 253 Dale Berra .10 .05
❑ 254 Kent Tekulve .25 .11
❑ 255 Enrique Romo .10 .05
❑ 256 Mike Easler .10 .05
❑ 257 Chuck Tanner MG .25 .11
❑ 258 Art Howe .10 .05
❑ 259 Alan Ashby .10 .05
❑ 260 Nolan Ryan 5.00 2.20
❑ 261A Vern Ruhle P1 ERR .50 .23
Ken Forsch photo on front
❑ 261B Vern Ruhle P2 COR .25 .11
❑ 262 Bob Boone .25 .11
❑ 263 Cesar Cedeno .25 .11
❑ 264 Jeff Leonard .25 .11
❑ 265 Pat Putnam .10 .05
❑ 266 Jon Matlack .10 .05
❑ 267 Dave Rajsich .10 .05
❑ 268 Billy Sample .10 .05
❑ 269 Damaso Garcia .10 .05
❑ 270 Tom Buskey .10 .05
❑ 271 Joey McLaughlin .10 .05
❑ 272 Barry Bonnell .10 .05
❑ 273 Tug McGraw .25 .11
❑ 274 Mike Jorgensen .10 .05
❑ 275 Pat Zachry .10 .05
❑ 276 Neil Allen .10 .05
❑ 277 Joel Youngblood .10 .05
❑ 278 Greg Pryor .10 .05
❑ 279 Britt Burns .10 .05
❑ 280 Rich Dotson .10 .05
❑ 281 Chet Lemon .10 .05
❑ 282 Rusty Kuntz .10 .05
❑ 283 Ted Cox .10 .05
❑ 284 Sparky Lyle .25 .11
❑ 285 Larry Cox .10 .05
❑ 286 Floyd Bannister .10 .05
❑ 287 Byron McLaughlin .10 .05
❑ 288 Rodney Craig .10 .05
❑ 289 Bobby Grich .25 .11
❑ 290 Dickie Thon .25 .11
❑ 291 Mark Clear .10 .05
❑ 292 Dave Lemanczyk .10 .05
❑ 293 Jason Thompson .10 .05
❑ 294 Rick Miller .10 .05
❑ 295 Lonnie Smith .25 .11
❑ 296 Ron Cey .25 .11
❑ 297 Steve Yeager .10 .05
❑ 298 Bobby Castillo .10 .05
❑ 299 Manny Mota .25 .11
❑ 300 Jay Johnstone .25 .11
❑ 301 Dan Driessen .10 .05
❑ 302 Joe Nolan .10 .05
❑ 303 Paul Householder .10 .05
❑ 304 Harry Spilman .10 .05
❑ 305 Cesar Geronimo .10 .05
❑ 306A Gary Mathews P1 ERR .50 .23
Name misspelled
❑ 306B Gary Matthews P2 .25 .11
COR
❑ 307 Ken Reitz .10 .05
❑ 308 Ted Simmons .25 .11
❑ 309 John Littlefield .10 .05
❑ 310 George Frazier .10 .05
❑ 311 Dane Iorg .10 .05
❑ 312 Mike Ivie .10 .05
❑ 313 Dennis Littlejohn .10 .05
❑ 314 Gary Lavelle .10 .05
❑ 315 Jack Clark .25 .11
❑ 316 Jim Wohlford .10 .05
❑ 317 Rick Matula .10 .05
❑ 318 Toby Harrah .25 .11
❑ 319A Dwane Kuiper P1 ERR .25 .11
Name misspelled
❑ 319B Duane Kuiper P2 COR .10 .05
❑ 320 Len Barker .10 .05
❑ 321 Victor Cruz .10 .05
❑ 322 Dell Alston .10 .05
❑ 323 Robin Yount 1.25 .55
❑ 324 Charlie Moore .10 .05
❑ 325 Lary Sorensen .10 .05
❑ 326A Gorman Thomas P1 .50 .23
2nd line on back:
"30 HR mark 4th"
❑ 326B Gorman Thomas P2 .25 .11
30 HR mark 3rd
❑ 327 Bob Rodgers MG .10 .05
❑ 328 Phil Niekro 1.00 .45
❑ 329 Chris Speier .10 .05
❑ 330A Steve Rodgers P1 .25 .11
ERR Name misspelled
❑ 330B Steve Rogers P2 COR .10 .05
❑ 331 Woodie Fryman .10 .05
❑ 332 Warren Cromartie .10 .05
❑ 333 Jerry White .10 .05
❑ 334 Tony Perez 1.00 .45
❑ 335 Carlton Fisk 1.00 .45
❑ 336 Dick Drago .10 .05
❑ 337 Steve Renko .10 .05
❑ 338 Jim Rice .25 .11
❑ 339 Jerry Royster .10 .05
❑ 340 Frank White .25 .11
❑ 341 Jamie Quirk .10 .05
❑ 342A Paul Spittorff P1 ERR .25 .11
Name misspelled
❑ 342B Paul Splittorff .10 .05
P2 COR
❑ 343 Marty Pattin .10 .05
❑ 344 Pete LaCock .10 .05
❑ 345 Willie Randolph .25 .11
❑ 346 Rick Cerone .10 .05
❑ 347 Rich Gossage .50 .23
❑ 348 Reggie Jackson 1.25 .55
❑ 349 Ruppert Jones .10 .05
❑ 350 Dave McKay .10 .05
❑ 351 Yogi Berra CO .50 .23
❑ 352 Doug DeCinces .25 .11
❑ 353 Jim Palmer 1.00 .45
❑ 354 Tippy Martinez .10 .05
❑ 355 Al Bumbry .25 .11
❑ 356 Earl Weaver MG 1.00 .45
❑ 357A Bob Picciolo P1 ERR .25 .11
Name misspelled
❑ 357B Rob Picciolo P2 COR .10 .05
❑ 358 Matt Keough .10 .05
❑ 359 Dwayne Murphy .10 .05
❑ 360 Brian Kingman .10 .05
❑ 361 Bill Fahey .10 .05
❑ 362 Steve Mura .10 .05
❑ 363 Dennis Kinney .10 .05
❑ 364 Dave Winfield 1.00 .45
❑ 365 Lou Whitaker 1.00 .45
❑ 366 Lance Parrish .25 .11
❑ 367 Tim Corcoran .10 .05
❑ 368 Pat Underwood .10 .05
❑ 369 Al Cowens .10 .05
❑ 370 Sparky Anderson MG .25 .11
❑ 371 Pete Rose 1.25 .55
❑ 372 Phil Garner .25 .11
❑ 373 Steve Nicosia .10 .05
❑ 374 John Candelaria .25 .11
❑ 375 Don Robinson .10 .05
❑ 376 Lee Lacy .10 .05
❑ 377 John Milner .10 .05
❑ 378 Craig Reynolds .10 .05
❑ 379A Luis Pujols P1 ERR .25 .11
Name misspelled Pujois
❑ 379B Luis Pujols P2 COR .10 .05
❑ 380 Joe Niekro .25 .11
❑ 381 Joaquin Andujar .25 .11
❑ 382 Keith Moreland .25 .11
❑ 383 Jose Cruz .25 .11
❑ 384 Bill Virdon MG .10 .05
❑ 385 Jim Sundberg .25 .11
❑ 386 Doc Medich .10 .05
❑ 387 Al Oliver .25 .11
❑ 388 Jim Norris .10 .05
❑ 389 Bob Bailor .10 .05
❑ 390 Ernie Whitt .10 .05
❑ 391 Otto Velez .10 .05
❑ 392 Roy Howell .10 .05
❑ 393 Bob Walk .25 .11
❑ 394 Doug Flynn .10 .05
❑ 395 Pete Falcone .10 .05
❑ 396 Tom Hausman .10 .05
❑ 397 Elliott Maddox .10 .05
❑ 398 Mike Squires .10 .05
❑ 399 Marvis Foley .10 .05
❑ 400 Steve Trout .10 .05
❑ 401 Wayne Nordhagen .10 .05
❑ 402 Tony LaRussa MG .25 .11
❑ 403 Bruce Bochte .10 .05
❑ 404 Bake McBride .10 .05
❑ 405 Jerry Narron .10 .05
❑ 406 Rob Dressler .10 .05
❑ 407 Dave Heaverlo .10 .05
❑ 408 Tom Paciorek .25 .11
❑ 409 Carney Lansford .25 .11
❑ 410 Brian Downing .25 .11
❑ 411 Don Aase .10 .05
❑ 412 Jim Barr .10 .05
❑ 413 Don Baylor .50 .23
❑ 414 Jim Fregosi MG .10 .05
❑ 415 Dallas Green MG .10 .05
❑ 416 Dave Lopes .25 .11
❑ 417 Jerry Reuss .25 .11
❑ 418 Rick Sutcliffe .25 .11
❑ 419 Derrel Thomas .10 .05
❑ 420 Tom Lasorda MG 1.00 .45
❑ 421 Charlie Leibrandt .50 .23
❑ 422 Tom Seaver 1.25 .55
❑ 423 Ron Oester .10 .05
❑ 424 Junior Kennedy .10 .05
❑ 425 Tom Seaver 1.25 .55
❑ 426 Bobby Cox MG .25 .11
❑ 427 Leon Durham .25 .11
❑ 428 Terry Kennedy .10 .05
❑ 429 Silvio Martinez .10 .05
❑ 430 George Hendrick .10 .05

❑ 431 Red Schoendienst MG .. .50 .23
❑ 432 Johnnie LeMaster .... .10 .05
❑ 433 Vida Blue.......................... .25 .11
❑ 434 John Montefusco........... .10 .05
❑ 435 Terry Whitfield................ .10 .05
❑ 436 Dave Bristol MG .... .10 .05
❑ 437 Dale Murphy .... 1.00 .45
❑ 438 Jerry Dybzinski .... .10 .05
❑ 439 Jorge Orta........................ .10 .05
❑ 440 Wayne Garland................ .10 .05
❑ 441 Miguel Dilone .... .10 .05
❑ 442 Dave Garcia MG .... .10 .05
❑ 443 Don Money .... .10 .05
❑ 444A Buck Martinez P1 ERR .25 .11
Reverse negative
❑ 444B Buck Martinez.............. .10 .05
P2 COR
❑ 445 Jerry Augustine.............. .10 .05
❑ 446 Ben Oglivie .... .25 .11
❑ 447 Jim Slaton .... .10 .05
❑ 448 Doyle Alexander .... .10 .05
❑ 449 Tony Bernazard.............. .10 .05
❑ 450 Scott Sanderson .... .10 .05
❑ 451 David Palmer.................. .10 .05
❑ 452 Stan Bahnsen .... .10 .05
❑ 453 Dick Williams MG .... .10 .05
❑ 454 Rick Burleson .... .10 .05
❑ 455 Gary Allenson .... .10 .05
❑ 456 Bob Stanley..................... .10 .05
❑ 457A John Tudor P1 ERR .... .25 .11
Lifetime W-L 9.7
❑ 457B John Tudor P2 COR.... .25 .11
Lifetime W-L 9-7
❑ 458 Dwight Evans .... .50 .23
❑ 459 Glenn Hubbard .... .10 .05
❑ 460 U.L. Washington .... .10 .05
❑ 461 Larry Gura....................... .10 .05
❑ 462 Rich Gale .... .10 .05
❑ 463 Hal McRae .... .25 .11
❑ 464 Jim Frey MG .... .10 .05
❑ 465 Bucky Dent .... .25 .11
❑ 466 Dennis Werth .... .10 .05
❑ 467 Ron Davis .... .10 .05
❑ 468 Reggie Jackson UER .. 1.25 .55
32 HR in 1970
should be 23
❑ 469 Bobby Brown.................. .10 .05
❑ 470 Mike Davis....................... .10 .05
❑ 471 Gaylord Perry .... 1.00 .45
❑ 472 Mark Belanger............... .25 .11
❑ 473 Jim Palmer .... 1.00 .45
❑ 474 Sammy Stewart............. .10 .05
❑ 475 Tim Stoddard.................. .10 .05
❑ 476 Steve Stone.................... .25 .11
❑ 477 Jeff Newman .... .10 .05
❑ 478 Steve McCatty................ .10 .05
❑ 479 Billy Martin MG .... .50 .23
❑ 480 Mitchell Page.................. .10 .05
❑ 481 Steve Carlton CY .... .50 .23
❑ 482 Bill Buckner .... .25 .11
❑ 483A Ivan DeJesus P1 ERR .25 .11
Lifetime hits 702
❑ 483B Ivan DeJesus P2 COR .10 .05
Lifetime hits 642
❑ 484 Cliff Johnson .... .10 .05
❑ 485 Lenny Randle .... .10 .05
❑ 486 Larry Milbourne.............. .10 .05
❑ 487 Roy Smalley .... .10 .05
❑ 488 John Castino.................. .10 .05
❑ 489 Ron Jackson .... .10 .05
❑ 490A Dave Roberts P1 .... .25 .11
Career Highlights
Showed pop in
❑ 490B Dave Roberts P2 .... .10 .05
Declared himself
❑ 491 George Brett MVP........ 1.25 .55
❑ 492 Mike Cubbage .... .10 .05
❑ 493 Rob Wilfong.................... .10 .05
❑ 494 Danny Goodwin.............. .10 .05
❑ 495 Jose Morales.................. .10 .05
❑ 496 Mickey Rivers .... .25 .11
❑ 497 Mike Edwards .... .10 .05
❑ 498 Mike Sadek .... .10 .05
❑ 499 Lenn Sakata .... .10 .05
❑ 500 Gene Michael MG .... .10 .05
❑ 501 Dave Roberts .... .10 .05
❑ 502 Steve Dillard .... .10 .05
❑ 503 Jim Essian....................... .10 .05
❑ 504 Rance Mulliniks.............. .10 .05
❑ 505 Darrell Porter.................. .10 .05
❑ 506 Joe Torre MG .... .25 .11
❑ 507 Terry Crowley .... .10 .05
❑ 508 Bill Travers .... .10 .05
❑ 509 Nelson Norman .... .10 .05
❑ 510 Bob McClure .... .10 .05
❑ 511 Steve Howe..................... .25 .11
❑ 512 Dave Rader..................... .10 .05
❑ 513 Mick Kelleher.................. .10 .05
❑ 514 Kiko Garcia .... .10 .05
❑ 515 Larry Biittner .... .10 .05
❑ 516A Willie Norwood P1 ...... .25 .11
Career Highlights
Spent most of
❑ 516B Willie Norwood P2 ...... .10 .05
Traded to Seattle
❑ 517 Bo Diaz .... .10 .05
❑ 518 Juan Beniquez .... .10 .05
❑ 519 Scot Thompson.............. .10 .05
❑ 520 Jim Tracy........................ .10 .05
❑ 521 Carlos Lezcano .... .10 .05
❑ 522 Joe Amalfitano MG .... .10 .05
❑ 523 Preston Hanna .... .10 .05
❑ 524A Ray Burris P1 .... .25 .11
Career Highlights
Went on O
❑ 524B Ray Burris P2 .... .10 .05
Drafted by O
❑ 525 Broderick Perkins .... .10 .05
❑ 526 Mickey Hatcher .... .25 .11
❑ 527 John Goryl MG .... .10 .05
❑ 528 Dick Davis .... .10 .05
❑ 529 Butch Wynegar .... .10 .05
❑ 530 Sal Butera .... .10 .05
❑ 531 Jerry Koosman .... .25 .11
❑ 532A Geoff Zahn P1 .... .25 .11
(Career Highlights
Was 2nd in
❑ 532B Geoff Zahn P2 .... .10 .05
Signed a 3 year
❑ 533 Dennis Martinez .... .50 .23
❑ 534 Gary Thomasson............ .10 .05
❑ 535 Steve Macko .... .10 .05
❑ 536 Jim Kaat .... .25 .11
❑ 537 Best Hitters .... 1.50 .70
George Brett
Rod Carew
❑ 538 Tim Raines .... 2.00 .90
❑ 539 Keith Smith .... .10 .05
❑ 540 Ken Macha .... .10 .05
❑ 541 Burt Hooton.................... .10 .05
❑ 542 Butch Hobson .... .10 .05
❑ 543 Bill Stein .... .10 .05
❑ 544 Dave Stapleton .... .10 .05
❑ 545 Bob Pate .... .10 .05
❑ 546 Doug Corbett.................. .10 .05
❑ 547 Darrell Jackson .... .10 .05
❑ 548 Pete Redfern .... .10 .05
❑ 549 Roger Erickson .... .10 .05
❑ 550 Al Hrabosky.................... .10 .05
❑ 551 Dick Tidrow .... .10 .05
❑ 552 Dave Ford .... .10 .05
❑ 553 Dave Kingman................ .50 .23
❑ 554A Mike Vail P1 .... .25 .11
Career Highlights
After two
❑ 554B Mike Vail P2 .... .10 .05
Traded to
❑ 555A Jerry Martin P1 .... .25 .11
Career Highlights
Overcame a
❑ 555B Jerry Martin P2............ .10 .05
Traded to
❑ 556A Jesus Figueroa P1 ...... .25 .11
Career Highlights
Had an
❑ 556B Jesus Figueroa P2 ...... .10 .05
Traded to
❑ 557 Don Stanhouse .... .10 .05
❑ 558 Barry Foote .... .10 .05
❑ 559 Tim Blackwell .... .10 .05
❑ 560 Bruce Sutter .... .25 .11
❑ 561 Rick Reuschel................ .25 .11
❑ 562 Lynn McGlothen .... .10 .05
❑ 563A Bob Owchinko P1 .... .25 .11
Career Highlights
Traded to
❑ 563B Bob Owchinko P2........ .10 .05
Involved in a
❑ 564 John Verhoeven .... .10 .05
❑ 565 Ken Landreaux .... .10 .05
❑ 566A Glen Adams P1 ERR .. .25 .11
Name misspelled
❑ 566B Glenn Adams P2 COR .10 .05
❑ 567 Hosken Powell .... .10 .05
❑ 568 Dick Noles...................... .10 .05
❑ 569 Danny Ainge .... 2.00 .90
❑ 570 Bobby Mattick MG.......... .10 .05
❑ 571 Joe Lefebvre .... .10 .05
❑ 572 Bobby Clark.................... .10 .05
❑ 573 Dennis Lamp.................. .10 .05
❑ 574 Randy Lerch .... .10 .05
❑ 575 Mookie Wilson................ .50 .23
❑ 576 Ron LeFlore .... .25 .11
❑ 577 Jim Dwyer .... .10 .05
❑ 578 Bill Castro .... .10 .05
❑ 579 Greg Minton .... .10 .05
❑ 580 Mark Littell...................... .10 .05
❑ 581 Andy Hassler.................. .10 .05
❑ 582 Dave Stieb....................... .25 .11
❑ 583 Ken Oberkfell .... .10 .05
❑ 584 Larry Bradford .... .10 .05
❑ 585 Fred Stanley .... .10 .05
❑ 586 Bill Caudill .... .10 .05
❑ 587 Doug Capilla .... .10 .05
❑ 588 George Riley .... .10 .05
❑ 589 Willie Hernandez............ .25 .11
❑ 590 Mike Schmidt MVP ...... 1.25 .55
❑ 591 Steve Stone CY.............. .10 .05
❑ 592 Rick Sofield.................... .10 .05
❑ 593 Bombo Rivera .... .10 .05
❑ 594 Gary Ward....................... .10 .05
❑ 595A Dave Edwards P1 .... .25 .11
Career Highlights
Sidelined the
❑ 595B Dave Edwards P2........ .10 .05
Traded to
❑ 596 Mike Proly .... .10 .05
❑ 597 Tommy Boggs................ .10 .05
❑ 598 Greg Gross .... .10 .05
❑ 599 Elias Sosa....................... .10 .05
❑ 600 Pat Kelly .... .10 .05
❑ 601A Checklist 1-120 P1 ...... .25 .11
ERR Unnumbered
51 Donahue
❑ 601B Checklist 1-120 P2 ...... .50 .23
COR Unnumbered
51 Donohue
❑ 602 Checklist 121-240 .... .25 .11
Unnumbered
❑ 603A Checklist 241-360 P1 .. .25 .11
ERR Unnumbered
306 Mathews
❑ 603B Checklist 241-360 P2 .. .25 .11
COR Unnumbered
306 Matthews
❑ 604A Checklist 361-480 P1 .. .25 .11
ERR Unnumbered
379 Pujois
❑ 604B Checklist 361-480 P2 .. .25 .11
COR Unnumbered
379 Pujols
❑ 605A Checklist 481-600 P1 .. .25 .11
ERR Unnumbered
566 Glen Adams
❑ 605B Checklist 481-600 P2 .. .25 .11
COR Unnumbered
566 Glenn Adams

1982 Donruss

	NRMT	VG-E
COMPLETE SET (660)	60.00	27.00
COMP.FACT.SET (660)..........	75.00	34.00
COMMON CARD (1-660)...........	.10	.05
COMP.RUTH PUZZLE...........	10.00	4.50

❑ 1 Pete Rose DK 2.00 .90
❑ 2 Gary Carter DK .20 .09
❑ 3 Steve Garvey DK .20 .09
❑ 4 Vida Blue DK .10 .05
❑ 5 Alan Trammell DK COR .40 .18
❑ 5A Alan Trammel DK ERR .75 .35
(Name misspelled)
❑ 6 Len Barker DK .10 .05
❑ 7 Dwight Evans DK .40 .18
❑ 8 Rod Carew DK .75 .35
❑ 9 George Hendrick DK .20 .09
❑ 10 Phil Niekro DK .40 .18
❑ 11 Richie Zisk DK .10 .05
❑ 12 Dave Parker DK .20 .09
❑ 13 Nolan Ryan DK 4.00 1.80
❑ 14 Ivan DeJesus DK .10 .05
❑ 15 George Brett DK .75 .35
❑ 16 Tom Seaver DK 1.00 .45
❑ 17 Dave Kingman DK .20 .09
❑ 18 Dave Winfield DK .40 .18
❑ 19 Mike Norris DK .10 .05
❑ 20 Carlton Fisk DK .40 .18
❑ 21 Ozzie Smith DK 1.25 .55
❑ 22 Roy Smalley DK .20 .09
❑ 23 Buddy Bell DK .20 .09
❑ 24 Ken Singleton DK .10 .05
❑ 25 John Mayberry DK .10 .05
❑ 26 Gorman Thomas DK .20 .09
❑ 27 Earl Weaver MG .40 .18
❑ 28 Rollie Fingers .75 .35
❑ 29 Sparky Anderson MG .20 .09
❑ 30 Dennis Eckersley .75 .35
❑ 31 Dave Winfield .75 .35
❑ 32 Burt Hooton .10 .05
❑ 33 Rick Waits .10 .05
❑ 34 George Brett 1.50 .70
❑ 35 Steve McCatty .10 .05
❑ 36 Steve Rogers .10 .05
❑ 37 Bill Stein .10 .05
❑ 38 Steve Renko .10 .05
❑ 39 Mike Squires .10 .05
❑ 40 George Hendrick .10 .05
❑ 41 Bob Knepper .10 .05
❑ 42 Steve Carlton .75 .35
❑ 43 Larry Biittner .10 .05
❑ 44 Chris Welsh .10 .05
❑ 45 Steve Nicosia .10 .05
❑ 46 Jack Clark .20 .09
❑ 47 Chris Chambliss .20 .09
❑ 48 Ivan DeJesus .10 .05
❑ 49 Lee Mazzilli .10 .05
❑ 50 Julio Cruz .10 .05
❑ 51 Pete Redfern .10 .05
❑ 52 Dave Stieb .20 .09
❑ 53 Doug Corbett .10 .05
❑ 54 Jorge Bell .75 .35
❑ 55 Joe Simpson .10 .05
❑ 56 Rusty Staub .20 .09
❑ 57 Hector Cruz .10 .05
❑ 58 Claudell Washington .10 .05
❑ 59 Enrique Romo .10 .05
❑ 60 Gary Lavelle .10 .05
❑ 61 Tim Flannery .10 .05
❑ 62 Joe Nolan .10 .05
❑ 63 Larry Bowa .20 .09
❑ 64 Sixto Lezcano .10 .05
❑ 65 Joe Sambito .10 .05
❑ 66 Bruce Kison .10 .05
❑ 67 Wayne Nordhagen .10 .05
❑ 68 Woodie Fryman .10 .05
❑ 69 Billy Sample .10 .05
❑ 70 Amos Otis .20 .09
❑ 71 Matt Keough .10 .05
❑ 72 Toby Harrah .20 .09
❑ 73 Dave Righetti .75 .35
❑ 74 Carl Yastrzemski .75 .35
❑ 75 Bob Welch .20 .09
❑ 76 Alan Trammell COR .75 .35
❑ 76A Alan Trammel ERR 1.00 .45
(Name misspelled)
❑ 77 Rick Dempsey .20 .09
❑ 78 Paul Molitor 1.00 .45
❑ 79 Dennis Martinez .40 .18
❑ 80 Jim Slaton .10 .05
❑ 81 Champ Summers .10 .05
❑ 82 Carney Lansford .20 .09
❑ 83 Barry Foote .10 .05
❑ 84 Steve Garvey .40 .18
❑ 85 Rick Manning .10 .05
❑ 86 John Wathan .10 .05
❑ 87 Brian Kingman .10 .05
❑ 88 Andre Dawson UER .75 .35
(Middle name Fernando should be Nolan)
❑ 89 Jim Kern .10 .05
❑ 90 Bobby Grich .20 .09
❑ 91 Bob Forsch .10 .05
❑ 92 Art Howe .20 .09
❑ 93 Marty Bystrom .10 .05
❑ 94 Ozzie Smith 2.00 .90
❑ 95 Dave Parker .20 .09
❑ 96 Doyle Alexander .10 .05
❑ 97 Al Hrabosky .10 .05
❑ 98 Frank Taveras .10 .05
❑ 99 Tim Blackwell .10 .05
❑ 100 Floyd Bannister .10 .05
❑ 101 Alfredo Griffin .10 .05
❑ 102 Dave Engle .10 .05
❑ 103 Mario Soto .10 .05
❑ 104 Ross Baumgarten .10 .05
❑ 105 Ken Singleton .20 .09
❑ 106 Ted Simmons .20 .09
❑ 107 Jack Morris .20 .09
❑ 108 Bob Watson .20 .09
❑ 109 Dwight Evans .40 .18
❑ 110 Tom Lasorda MG .40 .18
❑ 111 Bert Blyleven .40 .18
❑ 112 Dan Quisenberry .20 .09
❑ 113 Rickey Henderson 1.50 .70
❑ 114 Gary Carter .75 .35
❑ 115 Brian Downing .10 .05
❑ 116 Al Oliver .20 .09
❑ 117 LaMarr Hoyt .10 .05
❑ 118 Cesar Cedeno .20 .09
❑ 119 Keith Moreland .10 .05
❑ 120 Bob Shirley .10 .05
❑ 121 Terry Kennedy .10 .05
❑ 122 Frank Pastore .10 .05
❑ 123 Gene Garber .10 .05
❑ 124 Tony Pena .20 .09
❑ 125 Allen Ripley .10 .05
❑ 126 Randy Martz .10 .05
❑ 127 Richie Zisk .10 .05
❑ 128 Mike Scott .20 .09
❑ 129 Lloyd Moseby .10 .05
❑ 130 Rob Wilfong .10 .05
❑ 131 Tim Stoddard .10 .05
❑ 132 Gorman Thomas .20 .09
❑ 133 Dan Petry .10 .05
❑ 134 Bob Stanley .10 .05
❑ 135 Lou Piniella .20 .09
❑ 136 Pedro Guerrero .20 .09
❑ 137 Len Barker .10 .05
❑ 138 Rich Gale .10 .05
❑ 139 Wayne Gross .10 .05
❑ 140 Tim Wallach .40 .18
❑ 141 Gene Mauch MG .10 .05
❑ 142 Doc Medich .10 .05
❑ 143 Tony Bernazard .10 .05
❑ 144 Bill Virdon MG .10 .05
❑ 145 John Littlefield .10 .05
❑ 146 Dave Bergman .10 .05
❑ 147 Dick Davis .10 .05
❑ 148 Tom Seaver 1.00 .45
❑ 149 Matt Sinatro .10 .05
❑ 150 Chuck Tanner MG .10 .05
❑ 151 Leon Durham .10 .05
❑ 152 Gene Tenace .20 .09
❑ 153 Al Bumbry .20 .09
❑ 154 Mark Brouhard .10 .05
❑ 155 Rick Peters .10 .05
❑ 156 Jerry Remy .10 .05
❑ 157 Rick Reuschel .20 .09
❑ 158 Steve Howe .10 .05
❑ 159 Alan Bannister .10 .05
❑ 160 U.L. Washington .10 .05
❑ 161 Rick Langford .10 .05
❑ 162 Bill Gullickson .10 .05
❑ 163 Mark Wagner .10 .05
❑ 164 Geoff Zahn .10 .05
❑ 165 Ron LeFlore .20 .09
❑ 166 Dane Iorg .10 .05
❑ 167 Joe Niekro .20 .09
❑ 168 Pete Rose 1.00 .45
❑ 169 Dave Collins .10 .05
❑ 170 Rick Wise .10 .05
❑ 171 Jim Bibby .10 .05
❑ 172 Larry Herndon .10 .05
❑ 173 Bob Horner .20 .09
❑ 174 Steve Dillard .10 .05
❑ 175 Mookie Wilson .20 .09
❑ 176 Dan Meyer .10 .05
❑ 177 Fernando Arroyo .10 .05
❑ 178 Jackson Todd .10 .05
❑ 179 Darrell Jackson .10 .05
❑ 180 Alvis Woods .10 .05
❑ 181 Jim Anderson .10 .05
❑ 182 Dave Kingman .20 .09
❑ 183 Steve Henderson .10 .05
❑ 184 Brian Asselstine .10 .05
❑ 185 Rod Scurry .10 .05
❑ 186 Fred Breining .10 .05
❑ 187 Danny Boone .10 .05
❑ 188 Junior Kennedy .10 .05
❑ 189 Sparky Lyle .20 .09
❑ 190 Whitey Herzog MG .20 .09
❑ 191 Dave Smith .10 .05
❑ 192 Ed Ott .10 .05
❑ 193 Greg Luzinski .20 .09
❑ 194 Bill Lee .20 .09
❑ 195 Don Zimmer MG .10 .05
❑ 196 Hal McRae .20 .09
❑ 197 Mike Norris .10 .05
❑ 198 Duane Kuiper .10 .05
❑ 199 Rick Cerone .10 .05
❑ 200 Jim Rice .20 .09
❑ 201 Steve Yeager .10 .05
❑ 202 Tom Brookens .10 .05
❑ 203 Jose Morales .10 .05
❑ 204 Roy Howell .10 .05
❑ 205 Tippy Martinez .10 .05
❑ 206 Moose Haas .10 .05
❑ 207 Al Cowens .10 .05
❑ 208 Dave Stapleton .10 .05
❑ 209 Bucky Dent .20 .09
❑ 210 Ron Cey .20 .09
❑ 211 Jorge Orta .10 .05
❑ 212 Jamie Quirk .10 .05
❑ 213 Jeff Jones .10 .05
❑ 214 Tim Raines .75 .35
❑ 215 Jon Matlack .10 .05
❑ 216 Rod Carew .75 .35
❑ 217 Jim Kaat .20 .09
❑ 218 Joe Pittman .10 .05
❑ 219 Larry Christenson .10 .05
❑ 220 Juan Bonilla .10 .05
❑ 221 Mike Easler .10 .05
❑ 222 Vida Blue .20 .09
❑ 223 Rick Camp .10 .05
❑ 224 Mike Jorgensen .10 .05
❑ 225 Jody Davis .10 .05
❑ 226 Mike Parrott .10 .05
❑ 227 Jim Clancy .10 .05
❑ 228 Hosken Powell .10 .05
❑ 229 Tom Hume .10 .05
❑ 230 Britt Burns .10 .05
❑ 231 Jim Palmer .75 .35

❑ 232	Bob Rodgers MG	.10	.05
❑ 233	Milt Wilcox	.10	.05
❑ 234	Dave Revering	.10	.05
❑ 235	Mike Torrez	.10	.05
❑ 236	Robert Castillo	.10	.05
❑ 237	Von Hayes	.20	.09
❑ 238	Renie Martin	.10	.05
❑ 239	Dwayne Murphy	.10	.05
❑ 240	Rodney Scott	.10	.05
❑ 241	Fred Patek	.10	.05
❑ 242	Mickey Rivers	.10	.05
❑ 243	Steve Trout	.10	.05
❑ 244	Jose Cruz	.20	.09
❑ 245	Manny Trillo	.10	.05
❑ 246	Lary Sorensen	.10	.05
❑ 247	Dave Edwards	.10	.05
❑ 248	Dan Driessen	.10	.05
❑ 249	Tommy Boggs	.10	.05
❑ 250	Dale Berra	.10	.05
❑ 251	Ed Whitson	.10	.05
❑ 252	Lee Smith	2.50	1.10
❑ 253	Tom Paciorek	.20	.09
❑ 254	Pat Zachry	.10	.05
❑ 255	Luis Leal	.10	.05
❑ 256	John Castino	.10	.05
❑ 257	Rich Dauer	.10	.05
❑ 258	Cecil Cooper	.20	.09
❑ 259	Dave Rozema	.10	.05
❑ 260	John Tudor	.10	.05
❑ 261	Jerry Mumphrey	.10	.05
❑ 262	Jay Johnstone	.20	.09
❑ 263	Bo Diaz	.10	.05
❑ 264	Dennis Leonard	.10	.05
❑ 265	Jim Spencer	.10	.05
❑ 266	John Milner	.10	.05
❑ 267	Don Aase	.10	.05
❑ 268	Jim Sundberg	.20	.09
❑ 269	Lamar Johnson	.10	.05
❑ 270	Frank LaCorte	.10	.05
❑ 271	Barry Evans	.10	.05
❑ 272	Enos Cabell	.10	.05
❑ 273	Del Unser	.10	.05
❑ 274	George Foster	.20	.09
❑ 275	Brett Butler	1.25	.55
❑ 276	Lee Lacy	.10	.05
❑ 277	Ken Reitz	.10	.05
❑ 278	Keith Hernandez	.20	.09
❑ 279	Doug DeCinces	.20	.09
❑ 280	Charlie Moore	.10	.05
❑ 281	Lance Parrish	.40	.18
❑ 282	Ralph Houk MG	.20	.09
❑ 283	Rich Gossage	.40	.18
❑ 284	Jerry Reuss	.20	.09
❑ 285	Mike Stanton	.10	.05
❑ 286	Frank White	.20	.09
❑ 287	Bob Owchinko	.10	.05
❑ 288	Scott Sanderson	.10	.05
❑ 289	Bump Wills	.10	.05
❑ 290	Dave Frost	.10	.05
❑ 291	Chet Lemon	.10	.05
❑ 292	Tito Landrum	.10	.05
❑ 293	Vern Ruhle	.10	.05
❑ 294	Mike Schmidt	1.00	.45
❑ 295	Sam Mejias	.10	.05
❑ 296	Gary Lucas	.10	.05
❑ 297	John Candelaria	.10	.05
❑ 298	Jerry Martin	.10	.05
❑ 299	Dale Murphy	.75	.35
❑ 300	Mike Lum	.10	.05
❑ 301	Tom Hausman	.10	.05
❑ 302	Glenn Abbott	.10	.05
❑ 303	Roger Erickson	.10	.05
❑ 304	Otto Velez	.10	.05
❑ 305	Danny Goodwin	.10	.05
❑ 306	John Mayberry	.10	.05
❑ 307	Lenny Randle	.10	.05
❑ 308	Bob Bailor	.10	.05
❑ 309	Jerry Morales	.10	.05
❑ 310	Rufino Linares	.10	.05
❑ 311	Kent Tekulve	.20	.09
❑ 312	Joe Morgan	.75	.35
❑ 313	John Urrea	.10	.05
❑ 314	Paul Householder	.10	.05
❑ 315	Garry Maddox	.10	.05
❑ 316	Mike Ramsey	.10	.05
❑ 317	Alan Ashby	.10	.05
❑ 318	Bob Clark	.10	.05
❑ 319	Tony LaRussa MG	.20	.09
❑ 320	Charlie Lea	.10	.05
❑ 321	Danny Darwin	.20	.09
❑ 322	Cesar Geronimo	.10	.05
❑ 323	Tom Underwood	.10	.05
❑ 324	Andre Thornton	.10	.05
❑ 325	Rudy May	.10	.05
❑ 326	Frank Tanana	.20	.09
❑ 327	Dave Lopes	.20	.09
❑ 328	Richie Hebner	.20	.09
❑ 329	Mike Flanagan	.20	.09
❑ 330	Mike Caldwell	.10	.05
❑ 331	Scott McGregor	.10	.05
❑ 332	Jerry Augustine	.10	.05
❑ 333	Stan Papi	.10	.05
❑ 334	Rick Miller	.10	.05
❑ 335	Graig Nettles	.20	.09
❑ 336	Dusty Baker	.40	.18
❑ 337	Dave Garcia MG	.10	.05
❑ 338	Larry Gura	.10	.05
❑ 339	Cliff Johnson	.10	.05
❑ 340	Warren Cromartie	.10	.05
❑ 341	Steve Comer	.10	.05
❑ 342	Rick Burleson	.10	.05
❑ 343	John Martin	.10	.05
❑ 344	Craig Reynolds	.10	.05
❑ 345	Mike Proly	.10	.05
❑ 346	Ruppert Jones	.10	.05
❑ 347	Omar Moreno	.10	.05
❑ 348	Greg Minton	.10	.05
❑ 349	Rick Mahler	.10	.05
❑ 350	Alex Trevino	.10	.05
❑ 351	Mike Krukow	.10	.05
❑ 352A	Shane Rawley ERR (Photo actually Jim Anderson)	.40	.18
❑ 352B	Shane Rawley COR	.10	.05
❑ 353	Garth Iorg	.10	.05
❑ 354	Pete Mackanin	.10	.05
❑ 355	Paul Moskau	.10	.05
❑ 356	Richard Dotson	.10	.05
❑ 357	Steve Stone	.20	.09
❑ 358	Larry Hisle	.10	.05
❑ 359	Aurelio Lopez	.10	.05
❑ 360	Oscar Gamble	.10	.05
❑ 361	Tom Burgmeier	.10	.05
❑ 362	Terry Forster	.10	.05
❑ 363	Joe Charboneau	.20	.09
❑ 364	Ken Brett	.10	.05
❑ 365	Tony Armas	.10	.05
❑ 366	Chris Speier	.10	.05
❑ 367	Fred Lynn	.20	.09
❑ 368	Buddy Bell	.20	.09
❑ 369	Jim Essian	.10	.05
❑ 370	Terry Puhl	.10	.05
❑ 371	Greg Gross	.10	.05
❑ 372	Bruce Sutter	.20	.09
❑ 373	Joe Lefebvre	.10	.05
❑ 374	Ray Knight	.20	.09
❑ 375	Bruce Benedict	.10	.05
❑ 376	Tim Foli	.10	.05
❑ 377	Al Holland	.10	.05
❑ 378	Ken Kravec	.10	.05
❑ 379	Jeff Burroughs	.10	.05
❑ 380	Pete Falcone	.10	.05
❑ 381	Ernie Whitt	.10	.05
❑ 382	Brad Havens	.10	.05
❑ 383	Terry Crowley	.10	.05
❑ 384	Don Money	.10	.05
❑ 385	Dan Schatzeder	.10	.05
❑ 386	Gary Allenson	.10	.05
❑ 387	Yogi Berra CO	.40	.18
❑ 388	Ken Landreaux	.10	.05
❑ 389	Mike Hargrove	.20	.09
❑ 390	Darryl Motley	.10	.05
❑ 391	Dave McKay	.10	.05
❑ 392	Stan Bahnsen	.10	.05
❑ 393	Ken Forsch	.10	.05
❑ 394	Mario Mendoza	.10	.05
❑ 395	Jim Morrison	.10	.05
❑ 396	Mike Ivie	.10	.05
❑ 397	Broderick Perkins	.10	.05
❑ 398	Darrell Evans	.20	.09
❑ 399	Ron Reed	.10	.05
❑ 400	Johnny Bench	1.00	.45
❑ 401	Steve Bedrosian	.20	.09
❑ 402	Bill Robinson	.10	.05
❑ 403	Bill Buckner	.20	.09
❑ 404	Ken Oberkfell	.10	.05
❑ 405	Cal Ripken	40.00	18.00
❑ 406	Jim Gantner	.20	.09
❑ 407	Kirk Gibson	.75	.35
❑ 408	Tony Perez	.75	.35
❑ 409	Tommy John UER (Text says 52-56 as Yankee, should be 52-26)	.40	.18
❑ 410	Dave Stewart	1.00	.45
❑ 411	Dan Spillner	.10	.05
❑ 412	Willie Aikens	.10	.05
❑ 413	Mike Heath	.10	.05
❑ 414	Ray Burris	.10	.05
❑ 415	Leon Roberts	.10	.05
❑ 416	Mike Witt	.20	.09
❑ 417	Bob Molinaro	.10	.05
❑ 418	Steve Braun	.10	.05
❑ 419	Nolan Ryan UER (Nisnumbering of Nolan's no-hitters on card back)	5.00	2.20
❑ 420	Tug McGraw	.20	.09
❑ 421	Dave Concepcion	.20	.09
❑ 422A	Juan Eichelberger ERR (Photo actually Gary Lucas)	.40	.18
❑ 422B	Juan Eichelberger COR	.10	.05
❑ 423	Rick Rhoden	.10	.05
❑ 424	Frank Robinson MG	.40	.18
❑ 425	Eddie Miller	.10	.05
❑ 426	Bill Caudill	.10	.05
❑ 427	Doug Flynn	.10	.05
❑ 428	Larry Andersen UER (Misspelled Anderson on card front)	.10	.05
❑ 429	Al Williams	.10	.05
❑ 430	Jerry Garvin	.10	.05
❑ 431	Glenn Adams	.10	.05
❑ 432	Barry Bonnell	.10	.05
❑ 433	Jerry Narron	.10	.05
❑ 434	John Stearns	.10	.05
❑ 435	Mike Tyson	.10	.05
❑ 436	Glenn Hubbard	.10	.05
❑ 437	Eddie Solomon	.10	.05
❑ 438	Jeff Leonard	.10	.05
❑ 439	Randy Bass	.10	.05
❑ 440	Mike LaCoss	.10	.05
❑ 441	Gary Matthews	.20	.09
❑ 442	Mark Littell	.10	.05
❑ 443	Don Sutton	.75	.35
❑ 444	John Harris	.10	.05
❑ 445	Vada Pinson CO	.20	.09
❑ 446	Elias Sosa	.10	.05
❑ 447	Charlie Hough	.20	.09
❑ 448	Willie Wilson	.20	.09
❑ 449	Fred Stanley	.10	.05
❑ 450	Tom Veryzer	.10	.05
❑ 451	Ron Davis	.10	.05
❑ 452	Mark Clear	.10	.05
❑ 453	Bill Russell	.20	.09
❑ 454	Lou Whitaker	.75	.35
❑ 455	Dan Graham	.10	.05
❑ 456	Reggie Cleveland	.10	.05
❑ 457	Sammy Stewart	.10	.05
❑ 458	Pete Vuckovich	.10	.05
❑ 459	John Wockenfuss	.10	.05
❑ 460	Glenn Hoffman	.10	.05
❑ 461	Willie Randolph	.20	.09
❑ 462	Fernando Valenzuela	.75	.35
❑ 463	Ron Hassey	.10	.05
❑ 464	Paul Splittorff	.10	.05
❑ 465	Rob Picciolo	.10	.05
❑ 466	Larry Parrish	.10	.05
❑ 467	Johnny Grubb	.10	.05
❑ 468	Dan Ford	.10	.05
❑ 469	Silvio Martinez	.10	.05
❑ 470	Kiko Garcia	.10	.05
❑ 471	Bob Boone	.20	.09

❑ 472 Luis Salazar .10 .05
❑ 473 Randy Niemann .10 .05
❑ 474 Tom Griffin .10 .05
❑ 475 Phil Niekro .75 .35
❑ 476 Hubie Brooks .20 .09
❑ 477 Dick Tidrow .10 .05
❑ 478 Jim Beattie .10 .05
❑ 479 Damaso Garcia .10 .05
❑ 480 Mickey Hatcher .10 .05
❑ 481 Joe Price .10 .05
❑ 482 Ed Farmer .10 .05
❑ 483 Eddie Murray 1.00 .45
❑ 484 Ben Oglivie .20 .09
❑ 485 Kevin Saucier .10 .05
❑ 486 Bobby Murcer .20 .09
❑ 487 Bill Campbell .10 .05
❑ 488 Reggie Smith .20 .09
❑ 489 Wayne Garland .10 .05
❑ 490 Jim Wright .10 .05
❑ 491 Billy Martin MG .20 .09
❑ 492 Jim Fanning MG .10 .05
❑ 493 Don Baylor .40 .18
❑ 494 Rick Honeycutt .10 .05
❑ 495 Carlton Fisk .75 .35
❑ 496 Denny Walling .10 .05
❑ 497 Bake McBride .10 .05
❑ 498 Darrell Porter .20 .09
❑ 499 Gene Richards .10 .05
❑ 500 Ron Oester .10 .05
❑ 501 Ken Dayley .10 .05
❑ 502 Jason Thompson .10 .05
❑ 503 Milt May .10 .05
❑ 504 Doug Bird .10 .05
❑ 505 Bruce Bochte .10 .05
❑ 506 Neil Allen .10 .05
❑ 507 Joey McLaughlin .10 .05
❑ 508 Butch Wynegar .10 .05
❑ 509 Gary Roenicke .10 .05
❑ 510 Robin Yount .75 .35
❑ 511 Dave Tobik .10 .05
❑ 512 Rich Gedman .20 .09
❑ 513 Gene Nelson .10 .05
❑ 514 Rick Monday .10 .05
❑ 515 Miguel Dilone .10 .05
❑ 516 Clint Hurdle .10 .05
❑ 517 Jeff Newman .10 .05
❑ 518 Grant Jackson .10 .05
❑ 519 Andy Hassler .10 .05
❑ 520 Pat Putnam .10 .05
❑ 521 Greg Pryor .10 .05
❑ 522 Tony Scott .10 .05
❑ 523 Steve Mura .10 .05
❑ 524 Johnnie LeMaster .10 .05
❑ 525 Dick Ruthven .10 .05
❑ 526 John McNamara MG .10 .05
❑ 527 Larry McWilliams .10 .05
❑ 528 Johnny Ray .20 .09
❑ 529 Pat Tabler .20 .09
❑ 530 Tom Herr .20 .09
❑ 531A San Diego Chicken .75 .35
ERR (Without TM)
❑ 531B San Diego Chicken .75 .35
COR (With TM)
❑ 532 Sal Butera .10 .05
❑ 533 Mike Griffin .10 .05
❑ 534 Kelvin Moore .10 .05
❑ 535 Reggie Jackson 1.00 .45
❑ 536 Ed Romero .10 .05
❑ 537 Derrel Thomas .10 .05
❑ 538 Mike O'Berry .10 .05
❑ 539 Jack O'Connor .10 .05
❑ 540 Bob Ojeda .40 .18
❑ 541 Roy Lee Jackson .10 .05
❑ 542 Lynn Jones .10 .05
❑ 543 Gaylord Perry .75 .35
❑ 544A Phil Garner ERR .40 .18
(Reverse negative)
❑ 544B Phil Garner COR .20 .09
❑ 545 Garry Templeton .10 .05
❑ 546 Rafael Ramirez .10 .05
❑ 547 Jeff Reardon .40 .18
❑ 548 Ron Guidry .20 .09
❑ 549 Tim Laudner .10 .05
❑ 550 John Henry Johnson .10 .05
❑ 551 Chris Bando .10 .05
❑ 552 Bobby Brown .10 .05
❑ 553 Larry Bradford .10 .05
❑ 554 Scott Fletcher .20 .09
❑ 555 Jerry Royster .10 .05
❑ 556 Shooty Babitt UER .10 .05
(Spelled Babbitt
on front)
❑ 557 Kent Hrbek 1.00 .45
❑ 558 Yankee Winners .20 .09
Ron Guidry
Tommy John
❑ 559 Mark Bomback .10 .05
❑ 560 Julio Valdez .10 .05
❑ 561 Buck Martinez .10 .05
❑ 562 Mike A. Marshall .20 .09
❑ 563 Rennie Stennett .10 .05
❑ 564 Steve Crawford .10 .05
❑ 565 Bob Babcock .10 .05
❑ 566 Johnny Podres CO .20 .09
❑ 567 Paul Serna .10 .05
❑ 568 Harold Baines .75 .35
❑ 569 Dave LaRoche .10 .05
❑ 570 Lee May .20 .09
❑ 571 Gary Ward .10 .05
❑ 572 John Denny .10 .05
❑ 573 Roy Smalley .10 .05
❑ 574 Bob Brenly .10 .05
❑ 575 Bronx Bombers 1.50 .70
Reggie Jackson
Dave Winfield
❑ 576 Luis Pujols .10 .05
❑ 577 Butch Hobson .10 .05
❑ 578 Harvey Kuenn MG .20 .09
❑ 579 Cal Ripken Sr. CO .20 .09
❑ 580 Juan Berenguer .10 .05
❑ 581 Benny Ayala .10 .05
❑ 582 Vance Law .10 .05
❑ 583 Rick Leach .10 .05
❑ 584 George Frazier .10 .05
❑ 585 Phillies Finest 1.00 .45
Pete Rose
Mike Schmidt
❑ 586 Joe Rudi .10 .05
❑ 587 Juan Beniquez .10 .05
❑ 588 Luis DeLeon .10 .05
❑ 589 Craig Swan .10 .05
❑ 590 Dave Chalk .10 .05
❑ 591 Billy Gardner MG .10 .05
❑ 592 Sal Bando .20 .09
❑ 593 Bert Campaneris .20 .09
❑ 594 Steve Kemp .10 .05
❑ 595A Randy Lerch ERR .40 .18
(Braves)
❑ 595B Randy Lerch COR .10 .05
(Brewers)
❑ 596 Bryan Clark .10 .05
❑ 597 Dave Ford .10 .05
❑ 598 Mike Scioscia .20 .09
❑ 599 John Lowenstein .10 .05
❑ 600 Rene Lachemann MG .10 .05
❑ 601 Mick Kelleher .10 .05
❑ 602 Ron Jackson .10 .05
❑ 603 Jerry Koosman .20 .09
❑ 604 Dave Goltz .10 .05
❑ 605 Ellis Valentine .10 .05
❑ 606 Lonnie Smith .20 .09
❑ 607 Joaquin Andujar .20 .09
❑ 608 Garry Hancock .10 .05
❑ 609 Jerry Turner .10 .05
❑ 610 Bob Bonner .10 .05
❑ 611 Jim Dwyer .10 .05
❑ 612 Terry Bulling .10 .05
❑ 613 Joel Youngblood .10 .05
❑ 614 Larry Milbourne .10 .05
❑ 615 Gene Roof UER .10 .05
(Name on front
is Phil Roof)
❑ 616 Keith Drumwright .10 .05
❑ 617 Dave Rosello .10 .05
❑ 618 Rickey Keeton .10 .05
❑ 619 Dennis Lamp .10 .05
❑ 620 Sid Monge .10 .05
❑ 621 Jerry White .10 .05
❑ 622 Luis Aguayo .10 .05
❑ 623 Jamie Easterly .10 .05
❑ 624 Steve Sax .75 .35
❑ 625 Dave Roberts .10 .05
❑ 626 Rick Bosetti .10 .05
❑ 627 Terry Francona .10 .05
❑ 628 Pride of Reds 1.00 .45
Tom Seaver
Johnny Bench
❑ 629 Paul Mirabella .10 .05
❑ 630 Rance Mulliniks .10 .05
❑ 631 Kevin Hickey .10 .05
❑ 632 Reid Nichols .10 .05
❑ 633 Dave Geisel .10 .05
❑ 634 Ken Griffey .20 .09
❑ 635 Bob Lemon MG .75 .35
❑ 636 Orlando Sanchez .10 .05
❑ 637 Bill Almon .10 .05
❑ 638 Danny Ainge 1.00 .45
❑ 639 Willie Stargell .75 .35
❑ 640 Bob Sykes .10 .05
❑ 641 Ed Lynch .10 .05
❑ 642 John Ellis .10 .05
❑ 643 Ferguson Jenkins .75 .35
❑ 644 Lenn Sakata .10 .05
❑ 645 Julio Gonzalez .10 .05
❑ 646 Jesse Orosco .10 .05
❑ 647 Jerry Dybzinski .10 .05
❑ 648 Tommy Davis CO .20 .09
❑ 649 Ron Gardenhire .10 .05
❑ 650 Felipe Alou CO .20 .09
❑ 651 Harvey Haddix CO .20 .09
❑ 652 Willie Upshaw .10 .05
❑ 653 Bill Madlock .20 .09
❑ 654A DK Checklist 1-26 .75 .35
ERR (Unnumbered)
(With Trammel)
❑ 654B DK Checklist 1-26 .20 .09
COR (Unnumbered)
(With Trammell)
❑ 655 Checklist 27-130 .20 .09
(Unnumbered)
❑ 656 Checklist 131-234 .20 .09
(Unnumbered)
❑ 657 Checklist 235-338 .20 .09
(Unnumbered)
❑ 658 Checklist 339-442 .20 .09
(Unnumbered)
❑ 659 Checklist 443-544 .20 .09
(Unnumbered)
❑ 660 Checklist 545-653 .20 .09
(Unnumbered)

1983 Donruss

	NRMT	VG-E
COMPLETE SET (660)	80.00	36.00
COMP.FACT.SET (660)	90.00	40.00
COMMON CARD (1-660)	.10	.05
COMP.COBB PUZZLE	5.00	2.20

❑ 1 Fernando Valenzuela DK .40 .18
❑ 2 Rollie Fingers DK .40 .18
❑ 3 Reggie Jackson DK .40 .18
❑ 4 Jim Palmer DK .40 .18
❑ 5 Jack Morris DK .10 .05
❑ 6 George Foster DK .20 .09
❑ 7 Jim Sundberg DK .10 .05
❑ 8 Willie Stargell DK .40 .18
❑ 9 Dave Stieb DK .10 .05

- ❑ 10 Joe Niekro DK .20 .09
- ❑ 11 Rickey Henderson DK .40 .18
- ❑ 12 Dale Murphy DK .40 .18
- ❑ 13 Toby Harrah DK .10 .05
- ❑ 14 Bill Buckner DK .10 .05
- ❑ 15 Willie Wilson DK .10 .05
- ❑ 16 Steve Carlton DK .40 .18
- ❑ 17 Ron Guidry DK .10 .05
- ❑ 18 Steve Rogers DK .10 .05
- ❑ 19 Kent Hrbek DK .10 .05
- ❑ 20 Keith Hernandez DK .20 .09
- ❑ 21 Floyd Bannister DK .10 .05
- ❑ 22 Johnny Bench DK .40 .18
- ❑ 23 Britt Burns DK .10 .05
- ❑ 24 Joe Morgan DK .40 .18
- ❑ 25 Carl Yastrzemski DK .40 .18
- ❑ 26 Terry Kennedy DK .10 .05
- ❑ 27 Gary Roenicke .10 .05
- ❑ 28 Dwight Bernard .10 .05
- ❑ 29 Pat Underwood .10 .05
- ❑ 30 Gary Allenson .10 .05
- ❑ 31 Ron Guidry .20 .09
- ❑ 32 Burt Hooton .10 .05
- ❑ 33 Chris Bando .10 .05
- ❑ 34 Vida Blue .20 .09
- ❑ 35 Rickey Henderson 1.00 .45
- ❑ 36 Ray Burris .10 .05
- ❑ 37 John Butcher .10 .05
- ❑ 38 Don Aase .10 .05
- ❑ 39 Jerry Koosman .20 .09
- ❑ 40 Bruce Sutter .20 .09
- ❑ 41 Jose Cruz .20 .09
- ❑ 42 Pete Rose 1.00 .45
- ❑ 43 Cesar Cedeno .20 .09
- ❑ 44 Floyd Chiffer .10 .05
- ❑ 45 Larry McWilliams .10 .05
- ❑ 46 Alan Fowlkes .10 .05
- ❑ 47 Dale Murphy .75 .35
- ❑ 48 Doug Bird .10 .05
- ❑ 49 Hubie Brooks .20 .09
- ❑ 50 Floyd Bannister .10 .05
- ❑ 51 Jack O'Connor .10 .05
- ❑ 52 Steve Senteney .10 .05
- ❑ 53 Gary Gaetti .75 .35
- ❑ 54 Damaso Garcia .10 .05
- ❑ 55 Gene Nelson .10 .05
- ❑ 56 Mookie Wilson .20 .09
- ❑ 57 Allen Ripley .10 .05
- ❑ 58 Bob Horner .10 .05
- ❑ 59 Tony Pena .10 .05
- ❑ 60 Gary Lavelle .10 .05
- ❑ 61 Tim Lollar .10 .05
- ❑ 62 Frank Pastore .10 .05
- ❑ 63 Garry Maddox .10 .05
- ❑ 64 Bob Forsch .10 .05
- ❑ 65 Harry Spilman .10 .05
- ❑ 66 Geoff Zahn .10 .05
- ❑ 67 Salome Barojas .10 .05
- ❑ 68 David Palmer .10 .05
- ❑ 69 Charlie Hough .20 .09
- ❑ 70 Dan Quisenberry .20 .09
- ❑ 71 Tony Armas .10 .05
- ❑ 72 Rick Sutcliffe .20 .09
- ❑ 73 Steve Balboni .10 .05
- ❑ 74 Jerry Remy .10 .05
- ❑ 75 Mike Scioscia .20 .09
- ❑ 76 John Wockenfuss .10 .05
- ❑ 77 Jim Palmer .75 .35
- ❑ 78 Rollie Fingers .75 .35
- ❑ 79 Joe Nolan .10 .05
- ❑ 80 Pete Vuckovich .10 .05
- ❑ 81 Rick Leach .10 .05
- ❑ 82 Rick Miller .10 .05
- ❑ 83 Graig Nettles .20 .09
- ❑ 84 Ron Cey .20 .09
- ❑ 85 Miguel Dilone .10 .05
- ❑ 86 John Wathan .10 .05
- ❑ 87 Kelvin Moore .10 .05
- ❑ 88A Byrn Smith ERR .20 .09 (Sic, Bryn)
- ❑ 88B Bryn Smith COR .40 .18
- ❑ 89 Dave Hostetler .10 .05
- ❑ 90 Rod Carew .75 .35
- ❑ 91 Lonnie Smith .10 .05
- ❑ 92 Bob Knepper .10 .05
- ❑ 93 Marty Bystrom .10 .05
- ❑ 94 Chris Welsh .10 .05
- ❑ 95 Jason Thompson .10 .05
- ❑ 96 Tom O'Malley .10 .05
- ❑ 97 Phil Niekro .75 .35
- ❑ 98 Neil Allen .10 .05
- ❑ 99 Bill Buckner .20 .09
- ❑ 100 Ed VandeBerg .10 .05
- ❑ 101 Jim Clancy .10 .05
- ❑ 102 Robert Castillo .10 .05
- ❑ 103 Bruce Berenyi .10 .05
- ❑ 104 Carlton Fisk .75 .35
- ❑ 105 Mike Flanagan .20 .09
- ❑ 106 Cecil Cooper .20 .09
- ❑ 107 Jack Morris .20 .09
- ❑ 108 Mike Morgan .10 .05
- ❑ 109 Luis Aponte .10 .05
- ❑ 110 Pedro Guerrero .20 .09
- ❑ 111 Len Barker .10 .05
- ❑ 112 Willie Wilson .20 .09
- ❑ 113 Dave Beard .10 .05
- ❑ 114 Mike Gates .10 .05
- ❑ 115 Reggie Jackson 1.00 .45
- ❑ 116 George Wright .10 .05
- ❑ 117 Vance Law .10 .05
- ❑ 118 Nolan Ryan 4.00 1.80
- ❑ 119 Mike Krukow .10 .05
- ❑ 120 Ozzie Smith 1.50 .70
- ❑ 121 Broderick Perkins .10 .05
- ❑ 122 Tom Seaver 1.00 .45
- ❑ 123 Chris Chambliss .20 .09
- ❑ 124 Chuck Tanner MG .10 .05
- ❑ 125 Johnnie LeMaster .10 .05
- ❑ 126 Mel Hall .20 .09
- ❑ 127 Bruce Bochte .10 .05
- ❑ 128 Charlie Puleo .10 .05
- ❑ 129 Luis Leal .10 .05
- ❑ 130 John Pacella .10 .05
- ❑ 131 Glenn Gulliver .10 .05
- ❑ 132 Don Money .10 .05
- ❑ 133 Dave Rozema .10 .05
- ❑ 134 Bruce Hurst .10 .05
- ❑ 135 Rudy May .10 .05
- ❑ 136 Tom Lasorda MG .40 .18
- ❑ 137 Dan Spillner UER .10 .05 (Photo actually Ed Whitson)
- ❑ 138 Jerry Martin .10 .05
- ❑ 139 Mike Norris .10 .05
- ❑ 140 Al Oliver .20 .09
- ❑ 141 Daryl Sconiers .10 .05
- ❑ 142 Lamar Johnson .10 .05
- ❑ 143 Harold Baines .40 .18
- ❑ 144 Alan Ashby .10 .05
- ❑ 145 Garry Templeton .10 .05
- ❑ 146 Al Holland .10 .05
- ❑ 147 Bo Diaz .10 .05
- ❑ 148 Dave Concepcion .20 .09
- ❑ 149 Rick Camp .10 .05
- ❑ 150 Jim Morrison .10 .05
- ❑ 151 Randy Martz .10 .05
- ❑ 152 Keith Hernandez .20 .09
- ❑ 153 John Lowenstein .10 .05
- ❑ 154 Mike Caldwell .10 .05
- ❑ 155 Milt Wilcox .10 .05
- ❑ 156 Rich Gedman .10 .05
- ❑ 157 Rich Gossage .40 .18
- ❑ 158 Jerry Reuss .20 .09
- ❑ 159 Ron Hassey .10 .05
- ❑ 160 Larry Gura .10 .05
- ❑ 161 Dwayne Murphy .10 .05
- ❑ 162 Woodie Fryman .10 .05
- ❑ 163 Steve Comer .10 .05
- ❑ 164 Ken Forsch .10 .05
- ❑ 165 Dennis Lamp .10 .05
- ❑ 166 David Green .10 .05
- ❑ 167 Terry Puhl .10 .05
- ❑ 168 Mike Schmidt 1.00 .45 (Wearing 37 rather than 20)
- ❑ 169 Eddie Milner .10 .05
- ❑ 170 John Curtis .10 .05
- ❑ 171 Don Robinson .10 .05
- ❑ 172 Rich Gale .10 .05
- ❑ 173 Steve Bedrosian .20 .09
- ❑ 174 Willie Hernandez .20 .09
- ❑ 175 Ron Gardenhire .10 .05
- ❑ 176 Jim Beattie .10 .05
- ❑ 177 Tim Laudner .10 .05
- ❑ 178 Buck Martinez .10 .05
- ❑ 179 Kent Hrbek .20 .09
- ❑ 180 Alfredo Griffin .10 .05
- ❑ 181 Larry Andersen .10 .05
- ❑ 182 Pete Falcone .10 .05
- ❑ 183 Jody Davis .10 .05
- ❑ 184 Glenn Hubbard .10 .05
- ❑ 185 Dale Berra .10 .05
- ❑ 186 Greg Minton .10 .05
- ❑ 187 Gary Lucas .10 .05
- ❑ 188 Dave Van Gorder .10 .05
- ❑ 189 Bob Dernier .10 .05
- ❑ 190 Willie McGee .75 .35
- ❑ 191 Dickie Thon .10 .05
- ❑ 192 Bob Boone .20 .09
- ❑ 193 Britt Burns .10 .05
- ❑ 194 Jeff Reardon .20 .09
- ❑ 195 Jon Matlack .10 .05
- ❑ 196 Don Slaught .40 .18
- ❑ 197 Fred Stanley .10 .05
- ❑ 198 Rick Manning .10 .05
- ❑ 199 Dave Righetti .20 .09
- ❑ 200 Dave Stapleton .10 .05
- ❑ 201 Steve Yeager .10 .05
- ❑ 202 Enos Cabell .10 .05
- ❑ 203 Sammy Stewart .10 .05
- ❑ 204 Moose Haas .10 .05
- ❑ 205 Lenn Sakata .10 .05
- ❑ 206 Charlie Moore .10 .05
- ❑ 207 Alan Trammell .75 .35
- ❑ 208 Jim Rice .20 .09
- ❑ 209 Roy Smalley .10 .05
- ❑ 210 Bill Russell .20 .09
- ❑ 211 Andre Thornton .10 .05
- ❑ 212 Willie Aikens .10 .05
- ❑ 213 Dave McKay .10 .05
- ❑ 214 Tim Blackwell .10 .05
- ❑ 215 Buddy Bell .20 .09
- ❑ 216 Doug DeCinces .20 .09
- ❑ 217 Tom Herr .20 .09
- ❑ 218 Frank LaCorte .10 .05
- ❑ 219 Steve Carlton .75 .35
- ❑ 220 Terry Kennedy .10 .05
- ❑ 221 Mike Easler .10 .05
- ❑ 222 Jack Clark .20 .09
- ❑ 223 Gene Garber .10 .05
- ❑ 224 Scott Holman .10 .05
- ❑ 225 Mike Proly .10 .05
- ❑ 226 Terry Bulling .10 .05
- ❑ 227 Jerry Garvin .10 .05
- ❑ 228 Ron Davis .10 .05
- ❑ 229 Tom Hume .10 .05
- ❑ 230 Marc Hill .10 .05
- ❑ 231 Dennis Martinez .20 .09
- ❑ 232 Jim Gantner .20 .09
- ❑ 233 Larry Pashnick .10 .05
- ❑ 234 Dave Collins .10 .05
- ❑ 235 Tom Burgmeier .10 .05
- ❑ 236 Ken Landreaux .10 .05
- ❑ 237 John Denny .10 .05
- ❑ 238 Hal McRae .20 .09
- ❑ 239 Matt Keough .10 .05
- ❑ 240 Doug Flynn .10 .05
- ❑ 241 Fred Lynn .20 .09
- ❑ 242 Billy Sample .10 .05
- ❑ 243 Tom Paciorek .20 .09
- ❑ 244 Joe Sambito .10 .05
- ❑ 245 Sid Monge .10 .05
- ❑ 246 Ken Oberkfell .10 .05
- ❑ 247 Joe Pittman UER .10 .05 (Photo actually Juan Eichelberger)
- ❑ 248 Mario Soto .10 .05
- ❑ 249 Claudell Washington .10 .05
- ❑ 250 Rick Rhoden .10 .05
- ❑ 251 Darrell Evans .20 .09
- ❑ 252 Steve Henderson .10 .05
- ❑ 253 Manny Castillo .10 .05
- ❑ 254 Craig Swan .10 .05
- ❑ 255 Joey McLaughlin .10 .05
- ❑ 256 Pete Redfern .10 .05

❑ 257 Ken Singleton .10 .05
❑ 258 Robin Yount .75 .35
❑ 259 Elias Sosa .10 .05
❑ 260 Bob Ojeda .10 .05
❑ 261 Bobby Murcer .20 .09
❑ 262 Candy Maldonado .20 .09
❑ 263 Rick Waits .10 .05
❑ 264 Greg Pryor .10 .05
❑ 265 Bob Owchinko .10 .05
❑ 266 Chris Speier .10 .05
❑ 267 Bruce Kison .10 .05
❑ 268 Mark Wagner .10 .05
❑ 269 Steve Kemp .10 .05
❑ 270 Phil Garner .20 .09
❑ 271 Gene Richards .10 .05
❑ 272 Renie Martin .10 .05
❑ 273 Dave Roberts .10 .05
❑ 274 Dan Driessen .10 .05
❑ 275 Rufino Linares .10 .05
❑ 276 Lee Lacy .10 .05
❑ 277 Ryne Sandberg 12.00 5.50
❑ 278 Darrell Porter .10 .05
❑ 279 Cal Ripken 8.00 3.60
❑ 280 Jamie Easterly .10 .05
❑ 281 Bill Fahey .10 .05
❑ 282 Glenn Hoffman .10 .05
❑ 283 Willie Randolph .20 .09
❑ 284 Fernando Valenzuela .40 .18
❑ 285 Alan Bannister .10 .05
❑ 286 Paul Splittorff .10 .05
❑ 287 Joe Rudi .10 .05
❑ 288 Bill Gullickson .20 .09
❑ 289 Danny Darwin .20 .09
❑ 290 Andy Hassler .10 .05
❑ 291 Ernesto Escarrega .10 .05
❑ 292 Steve Mura .10 .05
❑ 293 Tony Scott .10 .05
❑ 294 Manny Trillo .10 .05
❑ 295 Greg Harris .10 .05
❑ 296 Luis DeLeon .10 .05
❑ 297 Kent Tekulve .20 .09
❑ 298 Atlee Hammaker .10 .05
❑ 299 Bruce Benedict .10 .05
❑ 300 Fergie Jenkins .75 .35
❑ 301 Dave Kingman .40 .18
❑ 302 Bill Caudill .10 .05
❑ 303 John Castino .10 .05
❑ 304 Ernie Whitt .10 .05
❑ 305 Randy Johnson .10 .05
❑ 306 Garth Iorg .10 .05
❑ 307 Gaylord Perry .75 .35
❑ 308 Ed Lynch .10 .05
❑ 309 Keith Moreland .10 .05
❑ 310 Rafael Ramirez .10 .05
❑ 311 Bill Madlock .20 .09
❑ 312 Milt May .10 .05
❑ 313 John Montefusco .10 .05
❑ 314 Wayne Krenchicki .10 .05
❑ 315 George Vukovich .10 .05
❑ 316 Joaquin Andujar .10 .05
❑ 317 Craig Reynolds .10 .05
❑ 318 Rick Burleson .10 .05
❑ 319 Richard Dotson .10 .05
❑ 320 Steve Rogers .10 .05
❑ 321 Dave Schmidt .10 .05
❑ 322 Bud Black .20 .09
❑ 323 Jeff Burroughs .10 .05
❑ 324 Von Hayes .20 .09
❑ 325 Butch Wynegar .10 .05
❑ 326 Carl Yastrzemski .75 .35
❑ 327 Ron Roenicke .10 .05
❑ 328 Howard Johnson .75 .35
❑ 329 Rick Dempsey UER .20 .09
(Posing as a left-handed batter)
❑ 330A Jim Slaton .10 .05
(Bio printed black on white)
❑ 330B Jim Slaton .20 .09
(Bio printed black on yellow)
❑ 331 Benny Ayala .10 .05
❑ 332 Ted Simmons .20 .09
❑ 333 Lou Whitaker .40 .18
❑ 334 Chuck Rainey .10 .05
❑ 335 Lou Piniella .20 .09
❑ 336 Steve Sax .20 .09
❑ 337 Toby Harrah .10 .05
❑ 338 George Brett 1.50 .70
❑ 339 Dave Lopes .20 .09
❑ 340 Gary Carter .75 .35
❑ 341 John Grubb .10 .05
❑ 342 Tim Foli .10 .05
❑ 343 Jim Kaat .20 .09
❑ 344 Mike LaCoss .10 .05
❑ 345 Larry Christenson .10 .05
❑ 346 Juan Bonilla .10 .05
❑ 347 Omar Moreno .10 .05
❑ 348 Chili Davis .75 .35
❑ 349 Tommy Boggs .10 .05
❑ 350 Rusty Staub .20 .09
❑ 351 Bump Wills .10 .05
❑ 352 Rick Sweet .10 .05
❑ 353 Jim Gott .10 .05
❑ 354 Terry Felton .10 .05
❑ 355 Jim Kern .10 .05
❑ 356 Bill Almon UER .10 .05
(Expos/Mets in 1983, not Padres/Mets)
❑ 357 Tippy Martinez .10 .05
❑ 358 Roy Howell .10 .05
❑ 359 Dan Petry .10 .05
❑ 360 Jerry Mumphrey .10 .05
❑ 361 Mark Clear .10 .05
❑ 362 Mike Marshall .10 .05
❑ 363 Lary Sorensen .10 .05
❑ 364 Amos Otis .20 .09
❑ 365 Rick Langford .10 .05
❑ 366 Brad Mills .10 .05
❑ 367 Brian Downing .10 .05
❑ 368 Mike Richardt .10 .05
❑ 369 Aurelio Rodriguez .10 .05
❑ 370 Dave Smith .10 .05
❑ 371 Tug McGraw .20 .09
❑ 372 Doug Bair .10 .05
❑ 373 Ruppert Jones .10 .05
❑ 374 Alex Trevino .10 .05
❑ 375 Ken Dayley .10 .05
❑ 376 Rod Scurry .10 .05
❑ 377 Bob Brenly .10 .05
❑ 378 Scot Thompson .10 .05
❑ 379 Julio Cruz .10 .05
❑ 380 John Stearns .10 .05
❑ 381 Dale Murray .10 .05
❑ 382 Frank Viola .75 .35
❑ 383 Al Bumbry .10 .05
❑ 384 Ben Oglivie .10 .05
❑ 385 Dave Tobik .10 .05
❑ 386 Bob Stanley .10 .05
❑ 387 Andre Robertson .10 .05
❑ 388 Jorge Orta .10 .05
❑ 389 Ed Whitson .10 .05
❑ 390 Don Hood .10 .05
❑ 391 Tom Underwood .10 .05
❑ 392 Tim Wallach .20 .09
❑ 393 Steve Renko .10 .05
❑ 394 Mickey Rivers .10 .05
❑ 395 Greg Luzinski .20 .09
❑ 396 Art Howe .20 .09
❑ 397 Alan Wiggins .10 .05
❑ 398 Jim Barr .10 .05
❑ 399 Ivan DeJesus .10 .05
❑ 400 Tom Lawless .10 .05
❑ 401 Bob Walk .10 .05
❑ 402 Jimmy Smith .10 .05
❑ 403 Lee Smith .75 .35
❑ 404 George Hendrick .10 .05
❑ 405 Eddie Murray 1.00 .45
❑ 406 Marshall Edwards .10 .05
❑ 407 Lance Parrish .20 .09
❑ 408 Carney Lansford .20 .09
❑ 409 Dave Winfield .75 .35
❑ 410 Bob Welch .20 .09
❑ 411 Larry Milbourne .10 .05
❑ 412 Dennis Leonard .10 .05
❑ 413 Dan Meyer .10 .05
❑ 414 Charlie Lea .10 .05
❑ 415 Rick Honeycutt .10 .05
❑ 416 Mike Witt .10 .05
❑ 417 Steve Trout .10 .05
❑ 418 Glenn Brummer .10 .05
❑ 419 Denny Walling .10 .05
❑ 420 Gary Matthews .20 .09
❑ 421 Charlie Leibrandt UER .10 .05
(Liebrandt on front of card)
❑ 422 Juan Eichelberger UER .10 .05
(Photo actually Joe Pittman)
❑ 423 Cecilio Guante UER .10 .05
(Listed as Matt on card)
❑ 424 Bill Laskey .10 .05
❑ 425 Jerry Royster .10 .05
❑ 426 Dickie Noles .10 .05
❑ 427 George Foster .20 .09
❑ 428 Mike Moore .20 .09
❑ 429 Gary Ward .10 .05
❑ 430 Barry Bonnell .10 .05
❑ 431 Ron Washington .10 .05
❑ 432 Rance Mulliniks .10 .05
❑ 433 Mike Stanton .10 .05
❑ 434 Jesse Orosco .10 .05
❑ 435 Larry Bowa .20 .09
❑ 436 Biff Pocoroba .10 .05
❑ 437 Johnny Ray .10 .05
❑ 438 Joe Morgan .75 .35
❑ 439 Eric Show .10 .05
❑ 440 Larry Biittner .10 .05
❑ 441 Greg Gross .10 .05
❑ 442 Gene Tenace .20 .09
❑ 443 Danny Heep .10 .05
❑ 444 Bobby Clark .10 .05
❑ 445 Kevin Hickey .10 .05
❑ 446 Scott Sanderson .10 .05
❑ 447 Frank Tanana .20 .09
❑ 448 Cesar Geronimo .10 .05
❑ 449 Jimmy Sexton .10 .05
❑ 450 Mike Hargrove .20 .09
❑ 451 Doyle Alexander .10 .05
❑ 452 Dwight Evans .20 .09
❑ 453 Terry Forster .10 .05
❑ 454 Tom Brookens .10 .05
❑ 455 Rich Dauer .10 .05
❑ 456 Rob Picciolo .10 .05
❑ 457 Terry Crowley .10 .05
❑ 458 Ned Yost .10 .05
❑ 459 Kirk Gibson .75 .35
❑ 460 Reid Nichols .10 .05
❑ 461 Oscar Gamble .10 .05
❑ 462 Dusty Baker .20 .09
❑ 463 Jack Perconte .10 .05
❑ 464 Frank White .20 .09
❑ 465 Mickey Klutts .10 .05
❑ 466 Warren Cromartie .10 .05
❑ 467 Larry Parrish .10 .05
❑ 468 Bobby Grich .20 .09
❑ 469 Dane Iorg .10 .05
❑ 470 Joe Niekro .20 .09
❑ 471 Ed Farmer .10 .05
❑ 472 Tim Flannery .10 .05
❑ 473 Dave Parker .20 .09
❑ 474 Jeff Leonard .10 .05
❑ 475 Al Hrabosky .10 .05
❑ 476 Ron Hodges .10 .05
❑ 477 Leon Durham .10 .05
❑ 478 Jim Essian .10 .05
❑ 479 Roy Lee Jackson .10 .05
❑ 480 Brad Havens .10 .05
❑ 481 Joe Price .10 .05
❑ 482 Tony Bernazard .10 .05
❑ 483 Scott McGregor .10 .05
❑ 484 Paul Molitor 1.00 .45
❑ 485 Mike Ivie .10 .05
❑ 486 Ken Griffey .20 .09
❑ 487 Dennis Eckersley .75 .35
❑ 488 Steve Garvey .40 .18
❑ 489 Mike Fischlin .10 .05
❑ 490 U.L. Washington .10 .05
❑ 491 Steve McCatty .10 .05
❑ 492 Roy Johnson .10 .05
❑ 493 Don Baylor .40 .18
❑ 494 Bobby Johnson .10 .05
❑ 495 Mike Squires .10 .05
❑ 496 Bert Roberge .10 .05

❑ 497 Dick Ruthven .10 .05
❑ 498 Tito Landrum .10 .05
❑ 499 Sixto Lezcano .10 .05
❑ 500 Johnny Bench 1.00 .45
❑ 501 Larry Whisenton .10 .05
❑ 502 Manny Sarmiento .10 .05
❑ 503 Fred Breining .10 .05
❑ 504 Bill Campbell .10 .05
❑ 505 Todd Cruz .10 .05
❑ 506 Bob Bailor .10 .05
❑ 507 Dave Stieb .20 .09
❑ 508 Al Williams .10 .05
❑ 509 Dan Ford .10 .05
❑ 510 Gorman Thomas .10 .05
❑ 511 Chet Lemon .10 .05
❑ 512 Mike Torrez .10 .05
❑ 513 Shane Rawley .10 .05
❑ 514 Mark Belanger .10 .05
❑ 515 Rodney Craig .10 .05
❑ 516 Onix Concepcion .10 .05
❑ 517 Mike Heath .10 .05
❑ 518 Andre Dawson UER .75 .35
(Middle name Fernando, should be Nolan)
❑ 519 Luis Sanchez .10 .05
❑ 520 Terry Bogener .10 .05
❑ 521 Rudy Law .10 .05
❑ 522 Ray Knight .20 .09
❑ 523 Joe Lefebvre .10 .05
❑ 524 Jim Wohlford .10 .05
❑ 525 Julio Franco 1.00 .45
❑ 526 Ron Oester .10 .05
❑ 527 Rick Mahler .10 .05
❑ 528 Steve Nicosia .10 .05
❑ 529 Junior Kennedy .10 .05
❑ 530A Whitey Herzog MG .20 .09
(Bio printed black on white)
❑ 530B Whitey Herzog MG .20 .09
(Bio printed black on yellow)
❑ 531A Don Sutton .75 .35
(Blue border on photo)
❑ 531B Don Sutton .75 .35
(Green border on photo)
❑ 532 Mark Brouhard .10 .05
❑ 533A Sparky Anderson MG .20 .09
(Bio printed black on white)
❑ 533B Sparky Anderson MG .20 .09
(Bio printed black on yellow)
❑ 534 Roger LaFrancois .10 .05
❑ 535 George Frazier .10 .05
❑ 536 Tom Niedenfuer .10 .05
❑ 537 Ed Glynn .10 .05
❑ 538 Lee May .20 .09
❑ 539 Bob Kearney .10 .05
❑ 540 Tim Raines .75 .35
❑ 541 Paul Mirabella .10 .05
❑ 542 Luis Tiant .20 .09
❑ 543 Ron LeFlore .10 .05
❑ 544 Dave LaPoint .10 .05
❑ 545 Randy Moffitt .10 .05
❑ 546 Luis Aguayo .10 .05
❑ 547 Brad Lesley .20 .09
❑ 548 Luis Salazar .10 .05
❑ 549 John Candelaria .10 .05
❑ 550 Dave Bergman .10 .05
❑ 551 Bob Watson .20 .09
❑ 552 Pat Tabler .10 .05
❑ 553 Brent Gaff .10 .05
❑ 554 Al Cowens .10 .05
❑ 555 Tom Brunansky .20 .09
❑ 556 Lloyd Moseby .10 .05
❑ 557A Pascual Perez ERR 2.00 .90
(Twins in glove)
❑ 557B Pascual Perez COR .20 .09
(Braves in glove)
❑ 558 Willie Upshaw .10 .05
❑ 559 Richie Zisk .10 .05
❑ 560 Pat Zachry .10 .05
❑ 561 Jay Johnstone .20 .09
❑ 562 Carlos Diaz .10 .05
❑ 563 John Tudor .10 .05
❑ 564 Frank Robinson MG .40 .18
❑ 565 Dave Edwards .10 .05
❑ 566 Paul Householder .10 .05
❑ 567 Ron Reed .10 .05
❑ 568 Mike Ramsey .10 .05
❑ 569 Kiko Garcia .10 .05
❑ 570 Tommy John .40 .18
❑ 571 Tony LaRussa MG .20 .09
❑ 572 Joel Youngblood .10 .05
❑ 573 Wayne Tolleson .10 .05
❑ 574 Keith Creel .10 .05
❑ 575 Billy Martin MG .20 .09
❑ 576 Jerry Dybzinski .10 .05
❑ 577 Rick Cerone .10 .05
❑ 578 Tony Perez .75 .35
❑ 579 Greg Brock .10 .05
❑ 580 Glenn Wilson .10 .05
❑ 581 Tim Stoddard .10 .05
❑ 582 Bob McClure .10 .05
❑ 583 Jim Dwyer .10 .05
❑ 584 Ed Romero .10 .05
❑ 585 Larry Herndon .10 .05
❑ 586 Wade Boggs 12.00 5.50
❑ 587 Jay Howell .10 .05
❑ 588 Dave Stewart .20 .09
❑ 589 Bert Blyleven .40 .18
❑ 590 Dick Howser MG .10 .05
❑ 591 Wayne Gross .10 .05
❑ 592 Terry Francona .10 .05
❑ 593 Don Werner .10 .05
❑ 594 Bill Stein .10 .05
❑ 595 Jesse Barfield .20 .09
❑ 596 Bob Molinaro .10 .05
❑ 597 Mike Vail .10 .05
❑ 598 Tony Gwynn 30.00 13.50
❑ 599 Gary Rajsich .10 .05
❑ 600 Jerry Ujdur .10 .05
❑ 601 Cliff Johnson .10 .05
❑ 602 Jerry White .10 .05
❑ 603 Bryan Clark .10 .05
❑ 604 Joe Ferguson .10 .05
❑ 605 Guy Sularz .10 .05
❑ 606A Ozzie Virgil .20 .09
(Green border on photo)
❑ 606B Ozzie Virgil .20 .09
(Orange border on photo)
❑ 607 Terry Harper .10 .05
❑ 608 Harvey Kuenn MG .20 .09
❑ 609 Jim Sundberg .20 .09
❑ 610 Willie Stargell .75 .35
❑ 611 Reggie Smith .20 .09
❑ 612 Rob Wilfong .10 .05
❑ 613 The Niekro Brothers .40 .18
Joe Niekro
Phil Niekro
❑ 614 Lee Elia MG .10 .05
❑ 615 Mickey Hatcher .10 .05
❑ 616 Jerry Hairston .10 .05
❑ 617 John Martin .10 .05
❑ 618 Wally Backman .10 .05
❑ 619 Storm Davis .10 .05
❑ 620 Alan Knicely .10 .05
❑ 621 John Stuper .10 .05
❑ 622 Matt Sinatro .10 .05
❑ 623 Geno Petralli .40 .18
❑ 624 Duane Walker .10 .05
❑ 625 Dick Williams MG .10 .05
❑ 626 Pat Corrales MG .10 .05
❑ 627 Vern Ruhle .10 .05
❑ 628 Joe Torre MG .20 .09
❑ 629 Anthony Johnson .10 .05
❑ 630 Steve Howe .10 .05
❑ 631 Gary Woods .10 .05
❑ 632 LaMarr Hoyt .20 .09
❑ 633 Steve Swisher .10 .05
❑ 634 Terry Leach .10 .05
❑ 635 Jeff Newman .10 .05
❑ 636 Brett Butler .75 .35
❑ 637 Gary Gray .10 .05
❑ 638 Lee Mazzilli .10 .05
❑ 639A Ron Jackson ERR 5.00 2.20
(A's in glove)
❑ 639B Ron Jackson COR .10 .05
(Angels in glove, red border on photo)
❑ 639C Ron Jackson COR .75 .35
(Angels in glove, green border on photo)
❑ 640 Juan Beniquez .10 .05
❑ 641 Dave Rucker .10 .05
❑ 642 Luis Pujols .10 .05
❑ 643 Rick Monday .10 .05
❑ 644 Hosken Powell .10 .05
❑ 645 The Chicken .75 .35
❑ 646 Dave Engle .10 .05
❑ 647 Dick Davis .10 .05
❑ 648 Frank Robinson .20 .09
Vida Blue
Joe Morgan
❑ 649 Al Chambers .10 .05
❑ 650 Jesus Vega .10 .05
❑ 651 Jeff Jones .10 .05
❑ 652 Marvis Foley .10 .05
❑ 653 Ty Cobb Puzzle Card .75 .35
❑ 654A Dick Perez/Diamond King Checklist 1-26 .75 .35
(Unnumbered) ERR
(Word "checklist" omitted from back)
❑ 654B Dick Perez/Diamond King Checklist 1-26 .75 .35
(Unnumbered) COR
(Word "checklist" is on back)
❑ 655 Checklist 27-130 .10 .05
(Unnumbered)
❑ 656 Checklist 131-234 .10 .05
(Unnumbered)
❑ 657 Checklist 235-338 .10 .05
(Unnumbered)
❑ 658 Checklist 339-442 .10 .05
(Unnumbered)
❑ 659 Checklist 443-544 .10 .05
(Unnumbered)
❑ 660 Checklist 545-653 .10 .05
(Unnumbered)

1984 Donruss

	NRMT	VG-E
COMPLETE SET (660)	150.00	70.00
COMP.FACT.SET (658)	150.00	70.00
COMMON CARD (1-658)	.25	.11
COMP.SNIDER PUZZLE	5.00	2.20

❑ 1 Robin Yount DK COR 4.00 1.80
❑ 1A Robin Yount DK ERR 3.00 1.35
❑ 2 Dave Concepcion DK COR 1.50 .70
❑ 2A Dave Concepcion DK ERR .75 .35
❑ 3 Dwayne Murphy DK COR .75 .35
❑ 3A Dwayne Murphy DK ERR .25 .11
❑ 4 John Castino DK COR .75 .35
❑ 4A John Castino DK ERR .25 .11
❑ 5 Leon Durham DK COR .75 .35

❑ 5A Leon Durham DK ERR .... .25 .11
❑ 6 Rusty Staub DK COR ...... 1.50 .70
❑ 6A Rusty Staub DK ERR ...... .75 .35
❑ 7 Jack Clark DK COR .... .75 .35
❑ 7A Jack Clark DK ERR .... .75 .35
❑ 8 Dave Dravecky DK .... .75 .35
COR
❑ 8A Dave Dravecky DK .... .75 .35
ERR
❑ 9 Al Oliver DK COR .... 1.50 .70
❑ 9A Al Oliver DK ERR .... .75 .35
❑ 10 Dave Righetti DK............. .75 .35
COR
❑ 10A Dave Righetti DK .... .75 .35
ERR
❑ 11 Hal McRae DK COR ...... 1.50 .70
❑ 11A Hal McRae DK ERR ...... .75 .35
❑ 12 Ray Knight DK COR .... .75 .35
❑ 12A Ray Knight DK ERR .... .75 .35
❑ 13 Bruce Sutter DK COR .... 1.50 .70
❑ 13A Bruce Sutter DK ERR .... .75 .35
❑ 14 Bob Horner DK COR........ .75 .35
❑ 14A Bob Horner DK ERR...... .75 .35
❑ 15 Lance Parrish DK .... 1.50 .70
COR
❑ 15A Lance Parrish DK .... .75 .35
ERR
❑ 16 Matt Young DK COR........ .75 .35
❑ 16A Matt Young DK ERR...... .25 .11
❑ 17 Fred Lynn DK COR.......... .75 .35
❑ 17A Fred Lynn DK ERR........ .25 .11
❑ 18 Ron Kittle DK COR .... .75 .35
❑ 18A Ron Kittle DK ERR .... .25 .11
❑ 19 Jim Clancy DK COR .... .75 .35
❑ 19A Jim Clancy DK ERR ...... .25 .11
❑ 20 Bill Madlock DK COR .... 1.50 .70
❑ 20A Bill Madlock DK ERR .... .75 .35
❑ 21 Larry Parrish DK .... .75 .35
COR
❑ 21A Larry Parrish DK............ .25 .11
ERR
❑ 22 Eddie Murray DK COR .. 3.00 1.35
❑ 22A Eddie Murray DK ERR 1.50 .70
❑ 23 Mike Schmidt DK COR .. 5.00 2.20
❑ 23A Mike Schmidt DK ERR 3.00 1.35
❑ 24 Pedro Guerrero DK.......... .75 .35
COR
❑ 24A Pedro Guerrero DK........ .75 .35
ERR
❑ 25 Andre Thornton DK.......... .75 .35
COR
❑ 25A Andre Thornton DK........ .75 .35
ERR
❑ 26 Wade Boggs DK COR.... 4.00 1.80
❑ 26A Wade Boggs DK ERR.. 2.50 1.10
❑ 27 Joel Skinner RR .... .25 .11
❑ 28 Tommy Dunbar RR............ .25 .11
❑ 29A Mike Stenhouse RR ...... .25 .11
ERR No number on back
❑ 29B Mike Stenhouse RR 3.00 1.35
COR Numbered on back
❑ 30A Ron Darling RR ERR ... .75 .35
(No number on back)
❑ 30B Ron Darling RR COR .. 3.00 1.35
(Numbered on back)
❑ 31 Dion James RR................ .75 .35
❑ 32 Tony Fernandez RR 3.00 1.35
❑ 33 Angel Salazar RR .... .25 .11
❑ 34 Kevin McReynolds RR .. 1.50 .70
❑ 35 Dick Schofield RR............ .75 .35
❑ 36 Brad Komminsk RR.......... .25 .11
❑ 37 Tim Teufel RR.................. .25 .11
❑ 38 Doug Frobel RR .... .25 .11
❑ 39 Greg Gagne RR .... .75 .35
❑ 40 Mike Fuentes RR .... .25 .11
❑ 41 Joe Carter RR.............. 20.00 9.00
❑ 42 Mike Brown RR .... .25 .11
(Angels OF)
❑ 43 Mike Jeffcoat RR.............. .25 .11
❑ 44 Sid Fernandez RR.......... 1.50 .70
❑ 45 Brian Dayett RR .... .25 .11
❑ 46 Chris Smith RR .... .25 .11
❑ 47 Eddie Murray.................. 4.00 1.80
❑ 48 Robin Yount 4.00 1.80
❑ 49 Lance Parrish .... 1.50 .70
❑ 50 Jim Rice .... .75 .35
❑ 51 Dave Winfield 3.00 1.35
❑ 52 Fernando Valenzuela ...... .75 .35
❑ 53 George Brett 8.00 3.60
❑ 54 Rickey Henderson.......... 4.00 1.80
❑ 55 Gary Carter 3.00 1.35
❑ 56 Buddy Bell........................ .75 .35
❑ 57 Reggie Jackson.............. 5.00 2.20
❑ 58 Harold Baines .... 1.50 .70
❑ 59 Ozzie Smith.................... 6.00 2.70
❑ 60 Nolan Ryan UER.......... 20.00 9.00
(Text on back refers to 1972 as the year he struck out 383; the year was 1973)
❑ 61 Pete Rose 5.00 2.20
❑ 62 Ron Oester .... .25 .11
❑ 63 Steve Garvey .... 1.50 .70
❑ 64 Jason Thompson.............. .25 .11
❑ 65 Jack Clark .... .75 .35
❑ 66 Dale Murphy 3.00 1.35
❑ 67 Leon Durham .... .25 .11
❑ 68 Darryl Strawberry 10.00 4.50
❑ 69 Richie Zisk........................ .25 .11
❑ 70 Kent Hrbek .... .75 .35
❑ 71 Dave Stieb.......................... .25 .11
❑ 72 Ken Schrom .... .25 .11
❑ 73 George Bell .... .75 .35
❑ 74 John Moses........................ .25 .11
❑ 75 Ed Lynch .... .25 .11
❑ 76 Chuck Rainey .... .25 .11
❑ 77 Biff Pocoroba...................... .25 .11
❑ 78 Cecilio Guante.................... .25 .11
❑ 79 Jim Barr.............................. .25 .11
❑ 80 Kurt Bevacqua.................... .25 .11
❑ 81 Tom Foley .... .25 .11
❑ 82 Joe Lefebvre .... .25 .11
❑ 83 Andy Van Slyke.............. 3.00 1.35
❑ 84 Bob Lillis MG .... .25 .11
❑ 85 Ricky Adams...................... .25 .11
❑ 86 Jerry Hairston .... .25 .11
❑ 87 Bob James .... .25 .11
❑ 88 Joe Altobelli MG .... .25 .11
❑ 89 Ed Romero .... .25 .11
❑ 90 John Grubb .... .25 .11
❑ 91 John Henry Johnson .... .25 .11
❑ 92 Juan Espino .... .25 .11
❑ 93 Candy Maldonado.............. .25 .11
❑ 94 Andre Thornton .... .25 .11
❑ 95 Onix Concepcion................ .25 .11
❑ 96 Donnie Hill UER .... .25 .11
(Listed as P, should be 2B)
❑ 97 Andre Dawson UER 3.00 1.35
(Wrong middle name, should be Nolan)
❑ 98 Frank Tanana .... .75 .35
❑ 99 Curtis Wilkerson .... .25 .11
❑ 100 Larry Gura.......................... .25 .11
❑ 101 Dwayne Murphy .... .25 .11
❑ 102 Tom Brennan .... .25 .11
❑ 103 Dave Righetti...................... .75 .35
❑ 104 Steve Sax .... .75 .35
❑ 105 Dan Petry .... .75 .35
❑ 106 Cal Ripken.................... 25.00 11.00
❑ 107 Paul Molitor UER.......... 4.00 1.80
('83 stats should say .270 BA, 608 AB, and 164 hits)
❑ 108 Fred Lynn .... .75 .35
❑ 109 Neil Allen............................ .25 .11
❑ 110 Joe Niekro.......................... .75 .35
❑ 111 Steve Carlton 4.00 1.80
❑ 112 Terry Kennedy.................... .25 .11
❑ 113 Bill Madlock........................ .75 .35
❑ 114 Chili Davis .... 1.50 .70
❑ 115 Jim Gantner........................ .75 .35
❑ 116 Tom Seaver.................... 5.00 2.20
❑ 117 Bill Buckner........................ .75 .35
❑ 118 Bill Caudill.......................... .25 .11
❑ 119 Jim Clancy.......................... .25 .11
❑ 120 John Castino...................... .25 .11
❑ 121 Dave Concepcion .... .75 .35
❑ 122 Greg Luzinski .... .75 .35
❑ 123 Mike Boddicker .... .25 .11
❑ 124 Pete Ladd .... .25 .11
❑ 125 Juan Berenguer.............. .25 .11
❑ 126 John Montefusco............ .25 .11
❑ 127 Ed Jurak .... .25 .11
❑ 128 Tom Niedenfuer .... .25 .11
❑ 129 Bert Blyleven.................... .75 .35
❑ 130 Bud Black .... .25 .11
❑ 131 Gorman Heimueller.......... .25 .11
❑ 132 Dan Schatzeder .... .25 .11
❑ 133 Ron Jackson .... .25 .11
❑ 134 Tom Henke .... 1.50 .70
❑ 135 Kevin Hickey .... .25 .11
❑ 136 Mike Scott .... .75 .35
❑ 137 Bo Diaz .... .25 .11
❑ 138 Glenn Brummer................ .25 .11
❑ 139 Sid Monge .... .25 .11
❑ 140 Rich Gale .... .25 .11
❑ 141 Brett Butler .... 1.50 .70
❑ 142 Brian Harper .... .75 .35
❑ 143 John Rabb........................ .25 .11
❑ 144 Gary Woods .... .25 .11
❑ 145 Pat Putnam .... .25 .11
❑ 146 Jim Acker .... .25 .11
❑ 147 Mickey Hatcher .... .25 .11
❑ 148 Todd Cruz .... .25 .11
❑ 149 Tom Tellmann .... .25 .11
❑ 150 John Wockenfuss .... .25 .11
❑ 151 Wade Boggs UER 8.00 3.60
1983 runs 10; should be 100
❑ 152 Don Baylor .... 1.50 .70
❑ 153 Bob Welch........................ .25 .11
❑ 154 Alan Bannister.................. .25 .11
❑ 155 Willie Aikens .... .25 .11
❑ 156 Jeff Burroughs.................. .25 .11
❑ 157 Bryan Little .... .25 .11
❑ 158 Bob Boone .... .75 .35
❑ 159 Dave Hostetler .... .25 .11
❑ 160 Jerry Dybzinski .... .25 .11
❑ 161 Mike Madden.................... .25 .11
❑ 162 Luis DeLeon .... .25 .11
❑ 163 Willie Hernandez.............. .75 .35
❑ 164 Frank Pastore .... .25 .11
❑ 165 Rick Camp........................ .25 .11
❑ 166 Lee Mazzilli .... .25 .11
❑ 167 Scot Thompson................ .25 .11
❑ 168 Bob Forsch .... .25 .11
❑ 169 Mike Flanagan.................. .25 .11
❑ 170 Rick Manning .... .25 .11
❑ 171 Chet Lemon...................... .75 .35
❑ 172 Jerry Remy .... .25 .11
❑ 173 Ron Guidry .... .75 .35
❑ 174 Pedro Guerrero................ .75 .35
❑ 175 Willie Wilson .... .25 .11
❑ 176 Carney Lansford .... .75 .35
❑ 177 Al Oliver............................ .75 .35
❑ 178 Jim Sundberg .... .75 .35
❑ 179 Bobby Grich .... .75 .35
❑ 180 Rich Dotson...................... .25 .11
❑ 181 Joaquin Andujar .... .25 .11
❑ 182 Jose Cruz .... .75 .35
❑ 183 Mike Schmidt.................. 5.00 2.20
❑ 184 Gary Redus...................... .25 .11
❑ 185 Garry Templeton .... .25 .11
❑ 186 Tony Pena........................ .25 .11
❑ 187 Greg Minton .... .25 .11
❑ 188 Phil Niekro.................... 3.00 1.35
❑ 189 Ferguson Jenkins 3.00 1.35
❑ 190 Mookie Wilson.................. .75 .35
❑ 191 Jim Beattie .... .25 .11
❑ 192 Gary Ward........................ .25 .11
❑ 193 Jesse Barfield .... .75 .35
❑ 194 Pete Filson .... .25 .11
❑ 195 Roy Lee Jackson.............. .25 .11
❑ 196 Rick Sweet .... .25 .11
❑ 197 Jesse Orosco .... .25 .11
❑ 198 Steve Lake .... .25 .11
❑ 199 Ken Dayley .... .25 .11
❑ 200 Manny Sarmiento .... .25 .11
❑ 201 Mark Davis .... .25 .11
❑ 202 Tim Flannery .... .25 .11
❑ 203 Bill Scherrer...................... .25 .11
❑ 204 Al Holland .... .25 .11
❑ 205 Dave Von Ohlen .... .25 .11
❑ 206 Mike LaCoss .... .25 .11
❑ 207 Juan Beniquez .... .25 .11
❑ 208 Juan Agosto .... .25 .11

❑ 209 Bobby Ramos .25 .11
❑ 210 Al Bumbry .75 .35
❑ 211 Mark Brouhard .25 .11
❑ 212 Howard Bailey .25 .11
❑ 213 Bruce Hurst .25 .11
❑ 214 Bob Shirley .25 .11
❑ 215 Pat Zachry .25 .11
❑ 216 Julio Franco 1.50 .70
❑ 217 Mike Armstrong .25 .11
❑ 218 Dave Beard .25 .11
❑ 219 Steve Rogers .25 .11
❑ 220 John Butcher .25 .11
❑ 221 Mike Smithson .25 .11
❑ 222 Frank White .75 .35
❑ 223 Mike Heath .25 .11
❑ 224 Chris Bando .25 .11
❑ 225 Roy Smalley .25 .11
❑ 226 Dusty Baker .75 .35
❑ 227 Lou Whitaker 3.00 1.35
❑ 228 John Lowenstein .25 .11
❑ 229 Ben Oglivie .25 .11
❑ 230 Doug DeCinces .25 .11
❑ 231 Lonnie Smith .25 .11
❑ 232 Ray Knight .75 .35
❑ 233 Gary Matthews .75 .35
❑ 234 Juan Bonilla .25 .11
❑ 235 Rod Scurry .25 .11
❑ 236 Atlee Hammaker .25 .11
❑ 237 Mike Caldwell .25 .11
❑ 238 Keith Hernandez .75 .35
❑ 239 Larry Bowa .75 .35
❑ 240 Tony Bernazard .25 .11
❑ 241 Damaso Garcia .25 .11
❑ 242 Tom Brunansky .75 .35
❑ 243 Dan Driessen .25 .11
❑ 244 Ron Kittle .25 .11
❑ 245 Tim Stoddard .25 .11
❑ 246 Bob L. Gibson .25 .11
(Brewers Pitcher)
❑ 247 Marty Castillo .25 .11
❑ 248 Don Mattingly UER 30.00 13.50
("Traiing" on back)
❑ 249 Jeff Newman .25 .11
❑ 250 Alejandro Pena .75 .35
❑ 251 Toby Harrah .75 .35
❑ 252 Cesar Geronimo .25 .11
❑ 253 Tom Underwood .25 .11
❑ 254 Doug Flynn .25 .11
❑ 255 Andy Hassler .25 .11
❑ 256 Odell Jones .25 .11
❑ 257 Rudy Law .25 .11
❑ 258 Harry Spilman .25 .11
❑ 259 Marty Bystrom .25 .11
❑ 260 Dave Rucker .25 .11
❑ 261 Ruppert Jones .25 .11
❑ 262 Jeff R. Jones .25 .11
(Reds OF)
❑ 263 Gerald Perry .75 .35
❑ 264 Gene Tenace .75 .35
❑ 265 Brad Wellman .25 .11
❑ 266 Dickie Noles .25 .11
❑ 267 Jamie Allen .25 .11
❑ 268 Jim Gott .25 .11
❑ 269 Ron Davis .25 .11
❑ 270 Benny Ayala .25 .11
❑ 271 Ned Yost .25 .11
❑ 272 Dave Rozema .25 .11
❑ 273 Dave Stapleton .25 .11
❑ 274 Lou Piniella .75 .35
❑ 275 Jose Morales .25 .11
❑ 276 Broderick Perkins .25 .11
❑ 277 Butch Davis .25 .11
❑ 278 Tony Phillips 3.00 1.35
❑ 279 Jeff Reardon .75 .35
❑ 280 Ken Forsch .25 .11
❑ 281 Pete O'Brien .75 .35
❑ 282 Tom Paciorek .75 .35
❑ 283 Frank LaCorte .25 .11
❑ 284 Tim Lollar .25 .11
❑ 285 Greg Gross .25 .11
❑ 286 Alex Trevino .25 .11
❑ 287 Gene Garber .25 .11
❑ 288 Dave Parker .75 .35
❑ 289 Lee Smith 3.00 1.35
❑ 290 Dave LaPoint .25 .11
❑ 291 John Shelby .25 .11
❑ 292 Charlie Moore .25 .11
❑ 293 Alan Trammell 3.00 1.35
❑ 294 Tony Armas .25 .11
❑ 295 Shane Rawley .25 .11
❑ 296 Greg Brock .25 .11
❑ 297 Hal McRae .75 .35
❑ 298 Mike Davis .25 .11
❑ 299 Tim Raines 1.50 .70
❑ 300 Bucky Dent .75 .35
❑ 301 Tommy John 1.50 .70
❑ 302 Carlton Fisk 3.00 1.35
❑ 303 Darrell Porter .25 .11
❑ 304 Dickie Thon .25 .11
❑ 305 Garry Maddox .25 .11
❑ 306 Cesar Cedeno .75 .35
❑ 307 Gary Lucas .25 .11
❑ 308 Johnny Ray .25 .11
❑ 309 Andy McGaffigan .25 .11
❑ 310 Claudell Washington .25 .11
❑ 311 Ryne Sandberg 12.00 5.50
❑ 312 George Foster .75 .35
❑ 313 Spike Owen .75 .35
❑ 314 Gary Gaetti 1.50 .70
❑ 315 Willie Upshaw .25 .11
❑ 316 Al Williams .25 .11
❑ 317 Jorge Orta .25 .11
❑ 318 Orlando Mercado .25 .11
❑ 319 Junior Ortiz .25 .11
❑ 320 Mike Proly .25 .11
❑ 321 Randy Johnson UER .25 .11
('72-'82 stats are from Twins' Randy Johnson, '83 stats are from Braves' Randy Johnson)
❑ 322 Jim Morrison .25 .11
❑ 323 Max Venable .25 .11
❑ 324 Tony Gwynn 25.00 11.00
❑ 325 Duane Walker .25 .11
❑ 326 Ozzie Virgil .25 .11
❑ 327 Jeff Lahti .25 .11
❑ 328 Bill Dawley .25 .11
❑ 329 Rob Wilfong .25 .11
❑ 330 Marc Hill .25 .11
❑ 331 Ray Burris .25 .11
❑ 332 Allan Ramirez .25 .11
❑ 333 Chuck Porter .25 .11
❑ 334 Wayne Krenchicki .25 .11
❑ 335 Gary Allenson .25 .11
❑ 336 Bobby Meacham .25 .11
❑ 337 Joe Beckwith .25 .11
❑ 338 Rick Sutcliffe .75 .35
❑ 339 Mark Huismann .25 .11
❑ 340 Tim Conroy .25 .11
❑ 341 Scott Sanderson .25 .11
❑ 342 Larry Biittner .25 .11
❑ 343 Dave Stewart .75 .35
❑ 344 Darryl Motley .25 .11
❑ 345 Chris Codiroli .25 .11
❑ 346 Rich Behenna .25 .11
❑ 347 Andre Robertson .25 .11
❑ 348 Mike Marshall .25 .11
❑ 349 Larry Herndon .75 .35
❑ 350 Rich Dauer .25 .11
❑ 351 Cecil Cooper .75 .35
❑ 352 Rod Carew 4.00 1.80
❑ 353 Willie McGee 1.50 .70
❑ 354 Phil Garner .75 .35
❑ 355 Joe Morgan 3.00 1.35
❑ 356 Luis Salazar .25 .11
❑ 357 John Candelaria .25 .11
❑ 358 Bill Laskey .25 .11
❑ 359 Bob McClure .25 .11
❑ 360 Dave Kingman .75 .35
❑ 361 Ron Cey .75 .35
❑ 362 Matt Young .25 .11
❑ 363 Lloyd Moseby .25 .11
❑ 364 Frank Viola 1.50 .70
❑ 365 Eddie Milner .25 .11
❑ 366 Floyd Bannister .25 .11
❑ 367 Dan Ford .25 .11
❑ 368 Moose Haas .25 .11
❑ 369 Doug Bair .25 .11
❑ 370 Ray Fontenot .25 .11
❑ 371 Luis Aponte .25 .11
❑ 372 Jack Fimple .25 .11
❑ 373 Neal Heaton .25 .11
❑ 374 Greg Pryor .25 .11
❑ 375 Wayne Gross .25 .11
❑ 376 Charlie Lea .25 .11
❑ 377 Steve Lubratich .25 .11
❑ 378 Jon Matlack .25 .11
❑ 379 Julio Cruz .25 .11
❑ 380 John Mizerock .25 .11
❑ 381 Kevin Gross .75 .35
❑ 382 Mike Ramsey .25 .11
❑ 383 Doug Gwosdz .25 .11
❑ 384 Kelly Paris .25 .11
❑ 385 Pete Falcone .25 .11
❑ 386 Milt May .25 .11
❑ 387 Fred Breining .25 .11
❑ 388 Craig Lefferts .25 .11
❑ 389 Steve Henderson .25 .11
❑ 390 Randy Moffitt .25 .11
❑ 391 Ron Washington .25 .11
❑ 392 Gary Roenicke .25 .11
❑ 393 Tom Candiotti 3.00 1.35
❑ 394 Larry Pashnick .25 .11
❑ 395 Dwight Evans .75 .35
❑ 396 Goose Gossage 1.50 .70
❑ 397 Derrel Thomas .25 .11
❑ 398 Juan Eichelberger .25 .11
❑ 399 Leon Roberts .25 .11
❑ 400 Dave Lopes .75 .35
❑ 401 Bill Gullickson .25 .11
❑ 402 Geoff Zahn .25 .11
❑ 403 Billy Sample .25 .11
❑ 404 Mike Squires .25 .11
❑ 405 Craig Reynolds .25 .11
❑ 406 Eric Show .25 .11
❑ 407 John Denny .25 .11
❑ 408 Dann Bilardello .25 .11
❑ 409 Bruce Benedict .25 .11
❑ 410 Kent Tekulve .75 .35
❑ 411 Mel Hall .75 .35
❑ 412 John Stuper .25 .11
❑ 413 Rick Dempsey .25 .11
❑ 414 Don Sutton 3.00 1.35
❑ 415 Jack Morris 3.00 1.35
❑ 416 John Tudor .25 .11
❑ 417 Willie Randolph .75 .35
❑ 418 Jerry Reuss .25 .11
❑ 419 Don Slaught .75 .35
❑ 420 Steve McCatty .25 .11
❑ 421 Tim Wallach .75 .35
❑ 422 Larry Parrish .25 .11
❑ 423 Brian Downing .25 .11
❑ 424 Britt Burns .25 .11
❑ 425 David Green .25 .11
❑ 426 Jerry Mumphrey .25 .11
❑ 427 Ivan DeJesus .25 .11
❑ 428 Mario Soto .25 .11
❑ 429 Gene Richards .25 .11
❑ 430 Dale Berra .25 .11
❑ 431 Darrell Evans .75 .35
❑ 432 Glenn Hubbard .25 .11
❑ 433 Jody Davis .25 .11
❑ 434 Danny Heep .25 .11
❑ 435 Ed Nunez .25 .11
❑ 436 Bobby Castillo .25 .11
❑ 437 Ernie Whitt .25 .11
❑ 438 Scott Ullger .25 .11
❑ 439 Doyle Alexander .25 .11
❑ 440 Domingo Ramos .25 .11
❑ 441 Craig Swan .25 .11
❑ 442 Warren Brusstar .25 .11
❑ 443 Len Barker .25 .11
❑ 444 Mike Easler .25 .11
❑ 445 Renie Martin .25 .11
❑ 446 Dennis Rasmussen .25 .11
❑ 447 Ted Power .25 .11
❑ 448 Charles Hudson .25 .11
❑ 449 Danny Cox .25 .11
❑ 450 Kevin Bass .25 .11
❑ 451 Daryl Sconiers .25 .11
❑ 452 Scott Fletcher .25 .11
❑ 453 Bryn Smith .25 .11
❑ 454 Jim Dwyer .25 .11
❑ 455 Rob Picciolo .25 .11
❑ 456 Enos Cabell .25 .11

	No.	Player	NRMT	VG-E
❑	457	Dennis Boyd	.75	.35
❑	458	Butch Wynegar	.25	.11
❑	459	Burt Hooton	.25	.11
❑	460	Ron Hassey	.25	.11
❑	461	Danny Jackson	1.50	.70
❑	462	Bob Kearney	.25	.11
❑	463	Terry Francona	.25	.11
❑	464	Wayne Tolleson	.25	.11
❑	465	Mickey Rivers	.25	.11
❑	466	John Wathan	.25	.11
❑	467	Bill Almon	.25	.11
❑	468	George Vukovich	.25	.11
❑	469	Steve Kemp	.25	.11
❑	470	Ken Landreaux	.25	.11
❑	471	Milt Wilcox	.25	.11
❑	472	Tippy Martinez	.25	.11
❑	473	Ted Simmons	.75	.35
❑	474	Tim Foli	.25	.11
❑	475	George Hendrick	.25	.11
❑	476	Terry Puhl	.25	.11
❑	477	Von Hayes	.25	.11
❑	478	Bobby Brown	.25	.11
❑	479	Lee Lacy	.25	.11
❑	480	Joel Youngblood	.25	.11
❑	481	Jim Slaton	.25	.11
❑	482	Mike Fitzgerald	.25	.11
❑	483	Keith Moreland	.25	.11
❑	484	Ron Roenicke	.25	.11
❑	485	Luis Leal	.25	.11
❑	486	Bryan Oelkers	.25	.11
❑	487	Bruce Berenyi	.25	.11
❑	488	LaMarr Hoyt	.25	.11
❑	489	Joe Nolan	.25	.11
❑	490	Marshall Edwards	.25	.11
❑	491	Mike Laga	.75	.35
❑	492	Rick Cerone	.25	.11
❑	493	Rick Miller UER	.25	.11
		(Listed as Mike on card front)		
❑	494	Rick Honeycutt	.25	.11
❑	495	Mike Hargrove	.75	.35
❑	496	Joe Simpson	.25	.11
❑	497	Keith Atherton	.25	.11
❑	498	Chris Welsh	.25	.11
❑	499	Bruce Kison	.25	.11
❑	500	Bobby Johnson	.25	.11
❑	501	Jerry Koosman	.75	.35
❑	502	Frank DiPino	.25	.11
❑	503	Tony Perez	3.00	1.35
❑	504	Ken Oberkfell	.25	.11
❑	505	Mark Thurmond	.25	.11
❑	506	Joe Price	.25	.11
❑	507	Pascual Perez	.25	.11
❑	508	Marvell Wynne	.25	.11
❑	509	Mike Krukow	.25	.11
❑	510	Dick Ruthven	.25	.11
❑	511	Al Cowens	.25	.11
❑	512	Cliff Johnson	.25	.11
❑	513	Randy Bush	.25	.11
❑	514	Sammy Stewart	.25	.11
❑	515	Bill Schroeder	.25	.11
❑	516	Aurelio Lopez	.75	.35
❑	517	Mike G. Brown	.25	.11
❑	518	Graig Nettles	.75	.35
❑	519	Dave Sax	.25	.11
❑	520	Jerry Willard	.25	.11
❑	521	Paul Splittorff	.25	.11
❑	522	Tom Burgmeier	.25	.11
❑	523	Chris Speier	.25	.11
❑	524	Bobby Clark	.25	.11
❑	525	George Wright	.25	.11
❑	526	Dennis Lamp	.25	.11
❑	527	Tony Scott	.25	.11
❑	528	Ed Whitson	.25	.11
❑	529	Ron Reed	.25	.11
❑	530	Charlie Puleo	.25	.11
❑	531	Jerry Royster	.25	.11
❑	532	Don Robinson	.25	.11
❑	533	Steve Trout	.25	.11
❑	534	Bruce Sutter	.75	.35
❑	535	Bob Horner	.25	.11
❑	536	Pat Tabler	.25	.11
❑	537	Chris Chambliss	.25	.11
❑	538	Bob Ojeda	.25	.11
❑	539	Alan Ashby	.25	.11
❑	540	Jay Johnstone	.75	.35
❑	541	Bob Dernier	.25	.11
❑	542	Brook Jacoby	.75	.35
❑	543	U.L. Washington	.25	.11
❑	544	Danny Darwin	.75	.35
❑	545	Kiko Garcia	.25	.11
❑	546	Vance Law UER	.25	.11
		(Listed as P on card front)		
❑	547	Tug McGraw	.75	.35
❑	548	Dave Smith	.25	.11
❑	549	Len Matuszek	.25	.11
❑	550	Tom Hume	.25	.11
❑	551	Dave Dravecky	.75	.35
❑	552	Rick Rhoden	.25	.11
❑	553	Duane Kuiper	.25	.11
❑	554	Rusty Staub	.75	.35
❑	555	Bill Campbell	.25	.11
❑	556	Mike Torrez	.25	.11
❑	557	Dave Henderson	.75	.35
❑	558	Len Whitehouse	.25	.11
❑	559	Barry Bonnell	.25	.11
❑	560	Rick Lysander	.25	.11
❑	561	Garth Iorg	.25	.11
❑	562	Bryan Clark	.25	.11
❑	563	Brian Giles	.25	.11
❑	564	Vern Ruhle	.25	.11
❑	565	Steve Bedrosian	.25	.11
❑	566	Larry McWilliams	.25	.11
❑	567	Jeff Leonard UER	.25	.11
		(Listed as P on card front)		
❑	568	Alan Wiggins	.25	.11
❑	569	Jeff Russell	.75	.35
❑	570	Salome Barojas	.25	.11
❑	571	Dane Iorg	.25	.11
❑	572	Bob Knepper	.25	.11
❑	573	Gary Lavelle	.25	.11
❑	574	Gorman Thomas	.25	.11
❑	575	Manny Trillo	.25	.11
❑	576	Jim Palmer	4.00	1.80
❑	577	Dale Murray	.25	.11
❑	578	Tom Brookens	.75	.35
❑	579	Rich Gedman	.25	.11
❑	580	Bill Doran	.75	.35
❑	581	Steve Yeager	.25	.11
❑	582	Dan Spillner	.25	.11
❑	583	Dan Quisenberry	.25	.11
❑	584	Rance Mulliniks	.25	.11
❑	585	Storm Davis	.25	.11
❑	586	Dave Schmidt	.25	.11
❑	587	Bill Russell	.75	.35
❑	588	Pat Sheridan	.25	.11
❑	589	Rafael Ramirez	.25	.11
		UER (A's on front)		
❑	590	Bud Anderson	.25	.11
❑	591	George Frazier	.25	.11
❑	592	Lee Tunnell	.25	.11
❑	593	Kirk Gibson	3.00	1.35
❑	594	Scott McGregor	.25	.11
❑	595	Bob Bailor	.25	.11
❑	596	Tommy Herr	.75	.35
❑	597	Luis Sanchez	.25	.11
❑	598	Dave Engle	.25	.11
❑	599	Craig McMurtry	.25	.11
❑	600	Carlos Diaz	.25	.11
❑	601	Tom O'Malley	.25	.11
❑	602	Nick Esasky	.25	.11
❑	603	Ron Hodges	.25	.11
❑	604	Ed VandeBerg	.25	.11
❑	605	Alfredo Griffin	.25	.11
❑	606	Glenn Hoffman	.25	.11
❑	607	Hubie Brooks	.25	.11
❑	608	Richard Barnes UER	.25	.11
		(Photo actually Neal Heaton)		
❑	609	Greg Walker	.75	.35
❑	610	Ken Singleton	.25	.11
❑	611	Mark Clear	.25	.11
❑	612	Buck Martinez	.25	.11
❑	613	Ken Griffey	.75	.35
❑	614	Reid Nichols	.25	.11
❑	615	Doug Sisk	.25	.11
❑	616	Bob Brenly	.25	.11
❑	617	Joey McLaughlin	.25	.11
❑	618	Glenn Wilson	.75	.35
❑	619	Bob Stoddard	.25	.11
❑	620	Lenn Sakata UER	.25	.11
		(Listed as Len on card front)		
❑	621	Mike Young	.25	.11
❑	622	John Stefero	.25	.11
❑	623	Carmelo Martinez	.25	.11
❑	624	Dave Bergman	.25	.11
❑	625	Runnin' Reds UER	3.00	1.35
		(Sic, Redbirds) David Green Willie McGee Lonnie Smith Ozzie Smith		
❑	626	Rudy May	.25	.11
❑	627	Matt Keough	.25	.11
❑	628	Jose DeLeon	.25	.11
❑	629	Jim Essian	.25	.11
❑	630	Darnell Coles	.25	.11
❑	631	Mike Warren	.25	.11
❑	632	Del Crandall MG	.25	.11
❑	633	Dennis Martinez	.75	.35
❑	634	Mike Moore	.75	.35
❑	635	Lary Sorensen	.25	.11
❑	636	Ricky Nelson	.25	.11
❑	637	Omar Moreno	.25	.11
❑	638	Charlie Hough	.75	.35
❑	639	Dennis Eckersley	3.00	1.35
❑	640	Walt Terrell	.25	.11
❑	641	Denny Walling	.25	.11
❑	642	Dave Anderson	.25	.11
❑	643	Jose Oquendo	.75	.35
❑	644	Bob Stanley	.25	.11
❑	645	Dave Geisel	.25	.11
❑	646	Scott Garrelts	.25	.11
❑	647	Gary Pettis	.25	.11
❑	648	Duke Snider	1.50	.70
		Puzzle Card		
❑	649	Johnnie LeMaster	.25	.11
❑	650	Dave Collins	.25	.11
❑	651	The Chicken	1.50	.70
❑	652	DK Checklist 1-26	.75	.35
		(Unnumbered)		
❑	653	Checklist 27-130	.25	.11
		(Unnumbered)		
❑	654	Checklist 131-234	.25	.11
		(Unnumbered)		
❑	655	Checklist 235-338	.25	.11
		(Unnumbered)		
❑	656	Checklist 339-442	.25	.11
		(Unnumbered)		
❑	657	Checklist 443-546	.25	.11
		(Unnumbered)		
❑	658	Checklist 547-651	.25	.11
		(Unnumbered)		
❑	A	Living Legends A	2.50	1.10
		Gaylord Perry Rollie Fingers		
❑	B	Living Legends B	5.00	2.20
		Carl Yastrzemski Johnny Bench		

1985 Donruss

	NRMT	VG-E
COMPLETE SET (660)	100.00	45.00
COMP.FACT.SET (660)	120.00	55.00

COMMON CARD (1-660)	.15	.07
COMP.GEHRIG PUZZLE	4.00	1.80
❑ 1 Ryne Sandberg DK	2.00	.90
❑ 2 Doug DeCinces DK	.15	.07
❑ 3 Richard Dotson DK	.15	.07
❑ 4 Bert Blyleven DK	.15	.07
❑ 5 Lou Whitaker DK	.40	.18
❑ 6 Dan Quisenberry DK	.15	.07
❑ 7 Don Mattingly DK	2.00	.90
❑ 8 Carney Lansford DK	.15	.07
❑ 9 Frank Tanana DK	.15	.07
❑ 10 Willie Upshaw DK	.15	.07
❑ 11 Claudell Washington DK	.15	.07
❑ 12 Mike Marshall DK	.15	.07
❑ 13 Joaquin Andujar DK	.15	.07
❑ 14 Cal Ripken DK	4.00	1.80
❑ 15 Jim Rice DK	.15	.07
❑ 16 Don Sutton DK	.40	.18
❑ 17 Frank Viola DK	.15	.07
❑ 18 Alvin Davis DK	.15	.07
❑ 19 Mario Soto DK	.15	.07
❑ 20 Jose Cruz DK	.15	.07
❑ 21 Charlie Lea DK	.15	.07
❑ 22 Jesse Orosco DK	.15	.07
❑ 23 Juan Samuel DK	.15	.07
❑ 24 Tony Pena DK	.15	.07
❑ 25 Tony Gwynn DK	3.00	1.35
❑ 26 Bob Brenly DK	.15	.07
❑ 27 Danny Tartabull RR	1.50	.70
❑ 28 Mike Bielecki RR	.15	.07
❑ 29 Steve Lyons RR	.40	.18
❑ 30 Jeff Reed RR	.15	.07
❑ 31 Tony Brewer RR	.15	.07
❑ 32 John Morris RR	.15	.07
❑ 33 Daryl Boston RR	.15	.07
❑ 34 Al Pulido RR	.15	.07
❑ 35 Steve Kiefer RR	.15	.07
❑ 36 Larry Sheets RR	.15	.07
❑ 37 Scott Bradley RR	.15	.07
❑ 38 Calvin Schiraldi RR	.15	.07
❑ 39 Shawon Dunston RR	1.50	.70
❑ 40 Charlie Mitchell RR	.15	.07
❑ 41 Billy Hatcher RR	.75	.35
❑ 42 Russ Stephans RR	.15	.07
❑ 43 Alejandro Sanchez RR	.15	.07
❑ 44 Steve Jeltz RR	.15	.07
❑ 45 Jim Traber RR	.15	.07
❑ 46 Doug Loman RR	.15	.07
❑ 47 Eddie Murray	1.50	.70
❑ 48 Robin Yount	1.50	.70
❑ 49 Lance Parrish	.40	.18
❑ 50 Jim Rice	.40	.18
❑ 51 Dave Winfield	1.50	.70
❑ 52 Fernando Valenzuela	.40	.18
❑ 53 George Brett	3.00	1.35
❑ 54 Dave Kingman	.40	.18
❑ 55 Gary Carter	1.50	.70
❑ 56 Buddy Bell	.40	.18
❑ 57 Reggie Jackson	2.00	.90
❑ 58 Harold Baines	.40	.18
❑ 59 Ozzie Smith	2.00	.90
❑ 60 Nolan Ryan UER (Set strikeout record in 1973, not 1972)	8.00	3.60
❑ 61 Mike Schmidt	2.00	.90
❑ 62 Dave Parker	.40	.18
❑ 63 Tony Gwynn	6.00	2.70
❑ 64 Tony Pena	.15	.07
❑ 65 Jack Clark	.40	.18
❑ 66 Dale Murphy	1.50	.70
❑ 67 Ryne Sandberg	3.00	1.35
❑ 68 Keith Hernandez	.40	.18
❑ 69 Alvin Davis	.40	.18
❑ 70 Kent Hrbek	.40	.18
❑ 71 Willie Upshaw	.15	.07
❑ 72 Dave Engle	.15	.07
❑ 73 Alfredo Griffin	.15	.07
❑ 74A Jack Perconte (Career Highlights takes four lines)	.15	.07
❑ 74B Jack Perconte (Career Highlights takes three lines)	.15	.07
❑ 75 Jesse Orosco	.15	.07
❑ 76 Jody Davis	.15	.07
❑ 77 Bob Horner	.15	.07
❑ 78 Larry McWilliams	.15	.07
❑ 79 Joel Youngblood	.15	.07
❑ 80 Alan Wiggins	.15	.07
❑ 81 Ron Oester	.15	.07
❑ 82 Ozzie Virgil	.15	.07
❑ 83 Ricky Horton	.15	.07
❑ 84 Bill Doran	.15	.07
❑ 85 Rod Carew	1.50	.70
❑ 86 LaMarr Hoyt	.15	.07
❑ 87 Tim Wallach	.40	.18
❑ 88 Mike Flanagan	.15	.07
❑ 89 Jim Sundberg	.15	.07
❑ 90 Chet Lemon	.15	.07
❑ 91 Bob Stanley	.15	.07
❑ 92 Willie Randolph	.40	.18
❑ 93 Bill Russell	.40	.18
❑ 94 Julio Franco	.75	.35
❑ 95 Dan Quisenberry	.40	.18
❑ 96 Bill Caudill	.15	.07
❑ 97 Bill Gullickson	.15	.07
❑ 98 Danny Darwin	.40	.18
❑ 99 Curtis Wilkerson	.15	.07
❑ 100 Bud Black	.15	.07
❑ 101 Tony Phillips	.15	.07
❑ 102 Tony Bernazard	.15	.07
❑ 103 Jay Howell	.15	.07
❑ 104 Burt Hooton	.15	.07
❑ 105 Milt Wilcox	.15	.07
❑ 106 Rich Dauer	.15	.07
❑ 107 Don Sutton	1.50	.70
❑ 108 Mike Witt	.15	.07
❑ 109 Bruce Sutter	.40	.18
❑ 110 Enos Cabell	.15	.07
❑ 111 John Denny	.15	.07
❑ 112 Dave Dravecky	.40	.18
❑ 113 Marvell Wynne	.15	.07
❑ 114 Johnnie LeMaster	.15	.07
❑ 115 Chuck Porter	.15	.07
❑ 116 John Gibbons	.15	.07
❑ 117 Keith Moreland	.15	.07
❑ 118 Darnell Coles	.15	.07
❑ 119 Dennis Lamp	.15	.07
❑ 120 Ron Davis	.15	.07
❑ 121 Nick Esasky	.15	.07
❑ 122 Vance Law	.15	.07
❑ 123 Gary Roenicke	.15	.07
❑ 124 Bill Schroeder	.15	.07
❑ 125 Dave Rozema	.15	.07
❑ 126 Bobby Meacham	.15	.07
❑ 127 Marty Barrett	.15	.07
❑ 128 R.J. Reynolds	.15	.07
❑ 129 Ernie Camacho UER (Photo actually Rich Thompson)	.15	.07
❑ 130 Jorge Orta	.15	.07
❑ 131 Lary Sorensen	.15	.07
❑ 132 Terry Francona	.15	.07
❑ 133 Fred Lynn	.40	.18
❑ 134 Bob Jones	.15	.07
❑ 135 Jerry Hairston	.15	.07
❑ 136 Kevin Bass	.15	.07
❑ 137 Garry Maddox	.15	.07
❑ 138 Dave LaPoint	.15	.07
❑ 139 Kevin McReynolds	.40	.18
❑ 140 Wayne Krenchicki	.15	.07
❑ 141 Rafael Ramirez	.15	.07
❑ 142 Rod Scurry	.15	.07
❑ 143 Greg Minton	.15	.07
❑ 144 Tim Stoddard	.15	.07
❑ 145 Steve Henderson	.15	.07
❑ 146 George Bell	.40	.18
❑ 147 Dave Meier	.15	.07
❑ 148 Sammy Stewart	.15	.07
❑ 149 Mark Brouhard	.15	.07
❑ 150 Larry Herndon	.15	.07
❑ 151 Oil Can Boyd	.15	.07
❑ 152 Brian Dayett	.15	.07
❑ 153 Tom Niedenfuer	.15	.07
❑ 154 Brook Jacoby	.15	.07
❑ 155 Onix Concepcion	.15	.07
❑ 156 Tim Conroy	.15	.07
❑ 157 Joe Hesketh	.15	.07
❑ 158 Brian Downing	.15	.07
❑ 159 Tommy Dunbar	.15	.07
❑ 160 Marc Hill	.15	.07
❑ 161 Phil Garner	.40	.18
❑ 162 Jerry Davis	.15	.07
❑ 163 Bill Campbell	.15	.07
❑ 164 John Franco	1.50	.70
❑ 165 Len Barker	.15	.07
❑ 166 Benny Distefano	.15	.07
❑ 167 George Frazier	.15	.07
❑ 168 Tito Landrum	.15	.07
❑ 169 Cal Ripken	8.00	3.60
❑ 170 Cecil Cooper	.40	.18
❑ 171 Alan Trammell	.75	.35
❑ 172 Wade Boggs	2.00	.90
❑ 173 Don Baylor	.40	.18
❑ 174 Pedro Guerrero	.40	.18
❑ 175 Frank White	.40	.18
❑ 176 Rickey Henderson	1.50	.70
❑ 177 Charlie Lea	.15	.07
❑ 178 Pete O'Brien	.15	.07
❑ 179 Doug DeCinces	.15	.07
❑ 180 Ron Kittle	.15	.07
❑ 181 George Hendrick	.15	.07
❑ 182 Joe Niekro	.15	.07
❑ 183 Juan Samuel	.15	.07
❑ 184 Mario Soto	.15	.07
❑ 185 Goose Gossage	.40	.18
❑ 186 Johnny Ray	.15	.07
❑ 187 Bob Brenly	.15	.07
❑ 188 Craig McMurtry	.15	.07
❑ 189 Leon Durham	.15	.07
❑ 190 Dwight Gooden	2.50	1.10
❑ 191 Barry Bonnell	.15	.07
❑ 192 Tim Teufel	.15	.07
❑ 193 Dave Stieb	.40	.18
❑ 194 Mickey Hatcher	.15	.07
❑ 195 Jesse Barfield	.15	.07
❑ 196 Al Cowens	.15	.07
❑ 197 Hubie Brooks	.15	.07
❑ 198 Steve Trout	.15	.07
❑ 199 Glenn Hubbard	.15	.07
❑ 200 Bill Madlock	.40	.18
❑ 201 Jeff D. Robinson	.15	.07
❑ 202 Eric Show	.15	.07
❑ 203 Dave Concepcion	.40	.18
❑ 204 Ivan DeJesus	.15	.07
❑ 205 Neil Allen	.15	.07
❑ 206 Jerry Mumphrey	.15	.07
❑ 207 Mike C. Brown	.15	.07
❑ 208 Carlton Fisk	1.50	.70
❑ 209 Bryn Smith	.15	.07
❑ 210 Tippy Martinez	.15	.07
❑ 211 Dion James	.15	.07
❑ 212 Willie Hernandez	.15	.07
❑ 213 Mike Easler	.15	.07
❑ 214 Ron Guidry	.40	.18
❑ 215 Rick Honeycutt	.15	.07
❑ 216 Brett Butler	.40	.18
❑ 217 Larry Gura	.15	.07
❑ 218 Ray Burris	.15	.07
❑ 219 Steve Rogers	.15	.07
❑ 220 Frank Tanana UER (Bats Left listed twice on card back)	.15	.07
❑ 221 Ned Yost	.15	.07
❑ 222 Bret Saberhagen UER (18 career IP on back)	1.50	.70
❑ 223 Mike Davis	.15	.07
❑ 224 Bert Blyleven	.40	.18
❑ 225 Steve Kemp	.15	.07
❑ 226 Jerry Reuss	.15	.07
❑ 227 Darrell Evans UER (80 homers in 1980)	.40	.18
❑ 228 Wayne Gross	.15	.07
❑ 229 Jim Gantner	.15	.07
❑ 230 Bob Boone	.40	.18
❑ 231 Lonnie Smith	.15	.07
❑ 232 Frank DiPino	.15	.07
❑ 233 Jerry Koosman	.15	.07
❑ 234 Graig Nettles	.40	.18
❑ 235 John Tudor	.15	.07
❑ 236 John Rabb	.15	.07
❑ 237 Rick Manning	.15	.07
❑ 238 Mike Fitzgerald	.15	.07
❑ 239 Gary Matthews	.15	.07

❑ 240 Jim Presley .40 .18
❑ 241 Dave Collins .15 .07
❑ 242 Gary Gaetti .40 .18
❑ 243 Dann Bilardello .15 .07
❑ 244 Rudy Law .15 .07
❑ 245 John Lowenstein .15 .07
❑ 246 Tom Tellmann .15 .07
❑ 247 Howard Johnson .40 .18
❑ 248 Ray Fontenot .15 .07
❑ 249 Tony Armas .15 .07
❑ 250 Candy Maldonado .15 .07
❑ 251 Mike Jeffcoat .15 .07
❑ 252 Dane Iorg .15 .07
❑ 253 Bruce Bochte .15 .07
❑ 254 Pete Rose 2.00 .90
❑ 255 Don Aase .15 .07
❑ 256 George Wright .15 .07
❑ 257 Britt Burns .15 .07
❑ 258 Mike Scott .15 .07
❑ 259 Len Matuszek .15 .07
❑ 260 Dave Rucker .15 .07
❑ 261 Craig Lefferts .15 .07
❑ 262 Jay Tibbs .15 .07
❑ 263 Bruce Benedict .15 .07
❑ 264 Don Robinson .15 .07
❑ 265 Gary Lavelle .15 .07
❑ 266 Scott Sanderson .15 .07
❑ 267 Matt Young .15 .07
❑ 268 Ernie Whitt .15 .07
❑ 269 Houston Jimenez .15 .07
❑ 270 Ken Dixon .15 .07
❑ 271 Pete Ladd .15 .07
❑ 272 Juan Berenguer .15 .07
❑ 273 Roger Clemens 40.00 18.00
❑ 274 Rick Cerone .15 .07
❑ 275 Dave Anderson .15 .07
❑ 276 George Vukovich .15 .07
❑ 277 Greg Pryor .15 .07
❑ 278 Mike Warren .15 .07
❑ 279 Bob James .15 .07
❑ 280 Bobby Grich .40 .18
❑ 281 Mike Mason .15 .07
❑ 282 Ron Reed .15 .07
❑ 283 Alan Ashby .15 .07
❑ 284 Mark Thurmond .15 .07
❑ 285 Joe Lefebvre .15 .07
❑ 286 Ted Power .15 .07
❑ 287 Chris Chambliss .15 .07
❑ 288 Lee Tunnell .15 .07
❑ 289 Rich Bordi .15 .07
❑ 290 Glenn Brummer .15 .07
❑ 291 Mike Boddicker .15 .07
❑ 292 Rollie Fingers 1.50 .70
❑ 293 Lou Whitaker .75 .35
❑ 294 Dwight Evans .40 .18
❑ 295 Don Mattingly 4.00 1.80
❑ 296 Mike Marshall .15 .07
❑ 297 Willie Wilson .15 .07
❑ 298 Mike Heath .15 .07
❑ 299 Tim Raines .40 .18
❑ 300 Larry Parrish .15 .07
❑ 301 Geoff Zahn .15 .07
❑ 302 Rich Dotson .15 .07
❑ 303 David Green .15 .07
❑ 304 Jose Cruz .40 .18
❑ 305 Steve Carlton 1.50 .70
❑ 306 Gary Redus .15 .07
❑ 307 Steve Garvey .75 .35
❑ 308 Jose DeLeon .15 .07
❑ 309 Randy Lerch .15 .07
❑ 310 Claudell Washington .15 .07
❑ 311 Lee Smith .75 .35
❑ 312 Darryl Strawberry 1.50 .70
❑ 313 Jim Beattie .15 .07
❑ 314 John Butcher .15 .07
❑ 315 Damaso Garcia .15 .07
❑ 316 Mike Smithson .15 .07
❑ 317 Luis Leal .15 .07
❑ 318 Ken Phelps .15 .07
❑ 319 Wally Backman .15 .07
❑ 320 Ron Cey .40 .18
❑ 321 Brad Komminsk .15 .07
❑ 322 Jason Thompson .15 .07
❑ 323 Frank Williams .15 .07
❑ 324 Tim Lollar .15 .07
❑ 325 Eric Davis 3.00 1.35
❑ 326 Von Hayes .15 .07
❑ 327 Andy Van Slyke .75 .35
❑ 328 Craig Reynolds .15 .07
❑ 329 Dick Schofield .15 .07
❑ 330 Scott Fletcher .15 .07
❑ 331 Jeff Reardon .40 .18
❑ 332 Rick Dempsey .15 .07
❑ 333 Ben Oglivie .15 .07
❑ 334 Dan Petry .15 .07
❑ 335 Jackie Gutierrez .15 .07
❑ 336 Dave Righetti .40 .18
❑ 337 Alejandro Pena .15 .07
❑ 338 Mel Hall .15 .07
❑ 339 Pat Sheridan .15 .07
❑ 340 Keith Atherton .15 .07
❑ 341 David Palmer .15 .07
❑ 342 Gary Ward .15 .07
❑ 343 Dave Stewart .40 .18
❑ 344 Mark Gubicza .40 .18
❑ 345 Carney Lansford .40 .18
❑ 346 Jerry Willard .15 .07
❑ 347 Ken Griffey .40 .18
❑ 348 Franklin Stubbs .15 .07
❑ 349 Aurelio Lopez .15 .07
❑ 350 Al Bumbry .15 .07
❑ 351 Charlie Moore .15 .07
❑ 352 Luis Sanchez .15 .07
❑ 353 Darrell Porter .15 .07
❑ 354 Bill Dawley .15 .07
❑ 355 Charles Hudson .15 .07
❑ 356 Garry Templeton .15 .07
❑ 357 Cecilio Guante .15 .07
❑ 358 Jeff Leonard .15 .07
❑ 359 Paul Molitor 1.50 .70
❑ 360 Ron Gardenhire .15 .07
❑ 361 Larry Bowa .40 .18
❑ 362 Bob Kearney .15 .07
❑ 363 Garth Iorg .15 .07
❑ 364 Tom Brunansky .40 .18
❑ 365 Brad Gulden .15 .07
❑ 366 Greg Walker .15 .07
❑ 367 Mike Young .15 .07
❑ 368 Rick Waits .15 .07
❑ 369 Doug Bair .15 .07
❑ 370 Bob Shirley .15 .07
❑ 371 Bob Ojeda .15 .07
❑ 372 Bob Welch .15 .07
❑ 373 Neal Heaton .15 .07
❑ 374 Danny Jackson UER .15 .07
(Photo actually
Frank Wills)
❑ 375 Donnie Hill .15 .07
❑ 376 Mike Stenhouse .15 .07
❑ 377 Bruce Kison .15 .07
❑ 378 Wayne Tolleson .15 .07
❑ 379 Floyd Bannister .15 .07
❑ 380 Vern Ruhle .15 .07
❑ 381 Tim Corcoran .15 .07
❑ 382 Kurt Kepshire .15 .07
❑ 383 Bobby Brown .15 .07
❑ 384 Dave Van Gorder .15 .07
❑ 385 Rick Mahler .15 .07
❑ 386 Lee Mazzilli .15 .07
❑ 387 Bill Laskey .15 .07
❑ 388 Thad Bosley .15 .07
❑ 389 Al Chambers .15 .07
❑ 390 Tony Fernandez .40 .18
❑ 391 Ron Washington .15 .07
❑ 392 Bill Swaggerty .15 .07
❑ 393 Bob L. Gibson .15 .07
❑ 394 Marty Castillo .15 .07
❑ 395 Steve Crawford .15 .07
❑ 396 Clay Christiansen .15 .07
❑ 397 Bob Bailor .15 .07
❑ 398 Mike Hargrove .40 .18
❑ 399 Charlie Leibrandt .15 .07
❑ 400 Tom Burgmeier .15 .07
❑ 401 Razor Shines .15 .07
❑ 402 Rob Wilfong .15 .07
❑ 403 Tom Henke .40 .18
❑ 404 Al Jones .15 .07
❑ 405 Mike LaCoss .15 .07
❑ 406 Luis DeLeon .15 .07
❑ 407 Greg Gross .15 .07
❑ 408 Tom Hume .15 .07
❑ 409 Rick Camp .15 .07
❑ 410 Milt May .15 .07
❑ 411 Henry Cotto .15 .07
❑ 412 David Von Ohlen .15 .07
❑ 413 Scott McGregor .15 .07
❑ 414 Ted Simmons .40 .18
❑ 415 Jack Morris .40 .18
❑ 416 Bill Buckner .40 .18
❑ 417 Butch Wynegar .15 .07
❑ 418 Steve Sax .15 .07
❑ 419 Steve Balboni .15 .07
❑ 420 Dwayne Murphy .15 .07
❑ 421 Andre Dawson 1.50 .70
❑ 422 Charlie Hough .40 .18
❑ 423 Tommy John .75 .35
❑ 424A Tom Seaver ERR 2.00 .90
(Photo actually
Floyd Bannister)
❑ 424B Tom Seaver COR 25.00 11.00
❑ 425 Tommy Herr .40 .18
❑ 426 Terry Puhl .15 .07
❑ 427 Al Holland .15 .07
❑ 428 Eddie Milner .15 .07
❑ 429 Terry Kennedy .15 .07
❑ 430 John Candelaria .15 .07
❑ 431 Manny Trillo .15 .07
❑ 432 Ken Oberkfell .15 .07
❑ 433 Rick Sutcliffe .15 .07
❑ 434 Ron Darling .40 .18
❑ 435 Spike Owen .15 .07
❑ 436 Frank Viola .40 .18
❑ 437 Lloyd Moseby .15 .07
❑ 438 Kirby Puckett 20.00 9.00
❑ 439 Jim Clancy .15 .07
❑ 440 Mike Moore .15 .07
❑ 441 Doug Sisk .15 .07
❑ 442 Dennis Eckersley 1.50 .70
❑ 443 Gerald Perry .15 .07
❑ 444 Dale Berra .15 .07
❑ 445 Dusty Baker .40 .18
❑ 446 Ed Whitson .15 .07
❑ 447 Cesar Cedeno .40 .18
❑ 448 Rick Schu .15 .07
❑ 449 Joaquin Andujar .15 .07
❑ 450 Mark Bailey .15 .07
❑ 451 Ron Romanick .15 .07
❑ 452 Julio Cruz .15 .07
❑ 453 Miguel Dilone .15 .07
❑ 454 Storm Davis .15 .07
❑ 455 Jaime Cocanower .15 .07
❑ 456 Barbaro Garbey .15 .07
❑ 457 Rich Gedman .15 .07
❑ 458 Phil Niekro 1.50 .70
❑ 459 Mike Scioscia .15 .07
❑ 460 Pat Tabler .15 .07
❑ 461 Darryl Motley .15 .07
❑ 462 Chris Codiroli .15 .07
❑ 463 Doug Flynn .15 .07
❑ 464 Billy Sample .15 .07
❑ 465 Mickey Rivers .15 .07
❑ 466 John Wathan .15 .07
❑ 467 Bill Krueger .15 .07
❑ 468 Andre Thornton .15 .07
❑ 469 Rex Hudler .15 .07
❑ 470 Sid Bream .40 .18
❑ 471 Kirk Gibson .40 .18
❑ 472 John Shelby .15 .07
❑ 473 Moose Haas .15 .07
❑ 474 Doug Corbett .15 .07
❑ 475 Willie McGee .40 .18
❑ 476 Bob Knepper .15 .07
❑ 477 Kevin Gross .15 .07
❑ 478 Carmelo Martinez .15 .07
❑ 479 Kent Tekulve .15 .07
❑ 480 Chili Davis .40 .18
❑ 481 Bobby Clark .15 .07
❑ 482 Mookie Wilson .40 .18
❑ 483 Dave Owen .15 .07
❑ 484 Ed Nunez .15 .07
❑ 485 Rance Mulliniks .15 .07
❑ 486 Ken Schrom .15 .07
❑ 487 Jeff Russell .15 .07
❑ 488 Tom Paciorek .40 .18
❑ 489 Dan Ford .15 .07

❑ 490 Mike Caldwell .15 .07
❑ 491 Scottie Earl .15 .07
❑ 492 Jose Rijo .75 .35
❑ 493 Bruce Hurst .15 .07
❑ 494 Ken Landreaux .15 .07
❑ 495 Mike Fischlin .15 .07
❑ 496 Don Slaught .15 .07
❑ 497 Steve McCatty .15 .07
❑ 498 Gary Lucas .15 .07
❑ 499 Gary Pettis .15 .07
❑ 500 Marvis Foley .15 .07
❑ 501 Mike Squires .15 .07
❑ 502 Jim Pankovits .15 .07
❑ 503 Luis Aguayo .15 .07
❑ 504 Ralph Citarella .15 .07
❑ 505 Bruce Bochy .15 .07
❑ 506 Bob Owchinko .15 .07
❑ 507 Pascual Perez .15 .07
❑ 508 Lee Lacy .15 .07
❑ 509 Atlee Hammaker .15 .07
❑ 510 Bob Dernier .15 .07
❑ 511 Ed VandeBerg .15 .07
❑ 512 Cliff Johnson .15 .07
❑ 513 Len Whitehouse .15 .07
❑ 514 Dennis Martinez .40 .18
❑ 515 Ed Romero .15 .07
❑ 516 Rusty Kuntz .15 .07
❑ 517 Rick Miller .15 .07
❑ 518 Dennis Rasmussen .15 .07
❑ 519 Steve Yeager .15 .07
❑ 520 Chris Bando .15 .07
❑ 521 U.L. Washington .15 .07
❑ 522 Curt Young .15 .07
❑ 523 Angel Salazar .15 .07
❑ 524 Curt Kaufman .15 .07
❑ 525 Odell Jones .15 .07
❑ 526 Juan Agosto .15 .07
❑ 527 Denny Walling .15 .07
❑ 528 Andy Hawkins .15 .07
❑ 529 Sixto Lezcano .15 .07
❑ 530 Skeeter Barnes .15 .07
❑ 531 Randy Johnson .15 .07
❑ 532 Jim Morrison .15 .07
❑ 533 Warren Brusstar .15 .07
❑ 534A Jeff Pendleton ERR .. 1.50 .70
(Wrong first name)
❑ 534B Terry Pendleton COR 5.00 2.20
❑ 535 Vic Rodriguez .15 .07
❑ 536 Bob McClure .15 .07
❑ 537 Dave Bergman .15 .07
❑ 538 Mark Clear .15 .07
❑ 539 Mike Pagliarulo .15 .07
❑ 540 Terry Whitfield .15 .07
❑ 541 Joe Beckwith .15 .07
❑ 542 Jeff Burroughs .15 .07
❑ 543 Dan Schatzeder .15 .07
❑ 544 Donnie Scott .15 .07
❑ 545 Jim Slaton .15 .07
❑ 546 Greg Luzinski .40 .18
❑ 547 Mark Salas .15 .07
❑ 548 Dave Smith .15 .07
❑ 549 John Wockenfuss .15 .07
❑ 550 Frank Pastore .15 .07
❑ 551 Tim Flannery .15 .07
❑ 552 Rick Rhoden .15 .07
❑ 553 Mark Davis .15 .07
❑ 554 Jeff Dedmon .15 .07
❑ 555 Gary Woods .15 .07
❑ 556 Danny Heep .15 .07
❑ 557 Mark Langston .75 .35
❑ 558 Darrell Brown .15 .07
❑ 559 Jimmy Key 2.00 .90
❑ 560 Rick Lysander .15 .07
❑ 561 Doyle Alexander .15 .07
❑ 562 Mike Stanton .15 .07
❑ 563 Sid Fernandez .40 .18
❑ 564 Richie Hebner .15 .07
❑ 565 Alex Trevino .15 .07
❑ 566 Brian Harper .15 .07
❑ 567 Dan Gladden .40 .18
❑ 568 Luis Salazar .15 .07
❑ 569 Tom Foley .15 .07
❑ 570 Larry Andersen .15 .07
❑ 571 Danny Cox .15 .07
❑ 572 Joe Sambito .15 .07
❑ 573 Juan Beniquez .15 .07
❑ 574 Joel Skinner .15 .07
❑ 575 Randy St.Claire .15 .07
❑ 576 Floyd Rayford .15 .07
❑ 577 Roy Howell .15 .07
❑ 578 John Grubb .15 .07
❑ 579 Ed Jurak .15 .07
❑ 580 John Montefusco .15 .07
❑ 581 Orel Hershiser 2.00 .90
❑ 582 Tom Waddell .15 .07
❑ 583 Mark Huismann .15 .07
❑ 584 Joe Morgan 1.50 .70
❑ 585 Jim Wohlford .15 .07
❑ 586 Dave Schmidt .15 .07
❑ 587 Jeff Kunkel .15 .07
❑ 588 Hal McRae .40 .18
❑ 589 Bill Almon .15 .07
❑ 590 Carmen Castillo .15 .07
❑ 591 Omar Moreno .15 .07
❑ 592 Ken Howell .15 .07
❑ 593 Tom Brookens .15 .07
❑ 594 Joe Nolan .15 .07
❑ 595 Willie Lozado .15 .07
❑ 596 Tom Nieto .15 .07
❑ 597 Walt Terrell .15 .07
❑ 598 Al Oliver .40 .18
❑ 599 Shane Rawley .15 .07
❑ 600 Denny Gonzalez .15 .07
❑ 601 Mark Grant .15 .07
❑ 602 Mike Armstrong .15 .07
❑ 603 George Foster .40 .18
❑ 604 Dave Lopes .40 .18
❑ 605 Salome Barojas .15 .07
❑ 606 Roy Lee Jackson .15 .07
❑ 607 Pete Filson .15 .07
❑ 608 Duane Walker .15 .07
❑ 609 Glenn Wilson .15 .07
❑ 610 Rafael Santana .15 .07
❑ 611 Roy Smith .15 .07
❑ 612 Ruppert Jones .15 .07
❑ 613 Joe Cowley .15 .07
❑ 614 Al Nipper UER .15 .07
(Photo actually
Mike Brown)
❑ 615 Gene Nelson .15 .07
❑ 616 Joe Carter 1.50 .70
❑ 617 Ray Knight .15 .07
❑ 618 Chuck Rainey .15 .07
❑ 619 Dan Driessen .15 .07
❑ 620 Daryl Sconiers .15 .07
❑ 621 Bill Stein .15 .07
❑ 622 Roy Smalley .15 .07
❑ 623 Ed Lynch .15 .07
❑ 624 Jeff Stone .15 .07
❑ 625 Bruce Berenyi .15 .07
❑ 626 Kelvin Chapman .15 .07
❑ 627 Joe Price .15 .07
❑ 628 Steve Bedrosian .15 .07
❑ 629 Vic Mata .15 .07
❑ 630 Mike Krukow .15 .07
❑ 631 Phil Bradley .40 .18
❑ 632 Jim Gott .15 .07
❑ 633 Randy Bush .15 .07
❑ 634 Tom Browning .40 .18
❑ 635 Lou Gehrig 1.50 .70
Puzzle Card
❑ 636 Reid Nichols .15 .07
❑ 637 Dan Pasqua .40 .18
❑ 638 German Rivera .15 .07
❑ 639 Don Schulze .15 .07
❑ 640A Mike Jones .15 .07
(Career Highlights,
takes five lines)
❑ 640B Mike Jones .15 .07
(Career Highlights,
takes four lines)
❑ 641 Pete Rose 2.00 .90
❑ 642 Wade Rowdon .15 .07
❑ 643 Jerry Narron .15 .07
❑ 644 Darrell Miller .15 .07
❑ 645 Tim Hulett .15 .07
❑ 646 Andy McGaffigan .15 .07
❑ 647 Kurt Bevacqua .15 .07
❑ 648 John Russell .15 .07
❑ 649 Ron Robinson .15 .07
❑ 650 Donnie Moore .15 .07
❑ 651A Two for the Title 2.00 .90
Dave Winfield
Don Mattingly
(Yellow letters)
❑ 651B Two for the Title 4.00 1.80
Dave Winfield
Don Mattingly
(White letters)
❑ 652 Tim Laudner .15 .07
❑ 653 Steve Farr .40 .18
❑ 654 DK Checklist 1-26 .15 .07
(Unnumbered)
❑ 655 Checklist 27-130 .15 .07
(Unnumbered)
❑ 656 Checklist 131-234 .15 .07
(Unnumbered)
❑ 657 Checklist 235-338 .15 .07
(Unnumbered)
❑ 658 Checklist 339-442 .15 .07
(Unnumbered)
❑ 659 Checklist 443-546 .15 .07
(Unnumbered)
❑ 660 Checklist 547-653 .15 .07
(Unnumbered)

1986 Donruss

	MINT	NRMT
COMPLETE SET (660)	40.00	18.00
COMP.FACT.SET (660)	60.00	27.00
COMMON CARD (1-660)	.10	.05
COMP.AARON PUZZLE	2.00	.90

❑ 1 Kirk Gibson DK .10 .05
❑ 2 Goose Gossage DK .10 .05
❑ 3 Willie McGee DK .10 .05
❑ 4 George Bell DK .10 .05
❑ 5 Tony Armas DK .10 .05
❑ 6 Chili Davis DK .50 .23
❑ 7 Cecil Cooper DK .10 .05
❑ 8 Mike Boddicker DK .10 .05
❑ 9 Dave Lopes DK .10 .05
❑ 10 Bill Doran DK .10 .05
❑ 11 Bret Saberhagen DK .25 .11
❑ 12 Brett Butler DK .10 .05
❑ 13 Harold Baines DK .50 .23
❑ 14 Mike Davis DK .10 .05
❑ 15 Tony Perez DK .25 .11
❑ 16 Willie Randolph DK .10 .05
❑ 17 Bob Boone DK .10 .05
❑ 18 Orel Hershiser DK .25 .11
❑ 19 Johnny Ray DK .10 .05
❑ 20 Gary Ward DK .10 .05
❑ 21 Rick Mahler DK .10 .05
❑ 22 Phil Bradley DK .10 .05
❑ 23 Jerry Koosman DK .25 .11
❑ 24 Tom Brunansky DK .10 .05
❑ 25 Andre Dawson DK .25 .11
❑ 26 Dwight Gooden DK .25 .11
❑ 27 Kal Daniels RR .25 .11
❑ 28 Fred McGriff RR 6.00 2.70
❑ 29 Cory Snyder RR .10 .05
❑ 30 Jose Guzman RR .10 .05
❑ 31 Ty Gainey RR .10 .05
❑ 32 Johnny Abrego RR .10 .05
❑ 33 Andres Galarraga RR 8.00 3.60
(No accent)

❑ 33B	Andre's Galarraga RR (Accent over e)	6.00	2.70
❑ 34	Dave Shipanoff RR	.10	.05
❑ 35	Mark McLemore RR	.50	.23
❑ 36	Marty Clary RR	.10	.05
❑ 37	Paul O'Neill RR	4.00	1.80
❑ 38	Danny Tartabull RR	.25	.11
❑ 39	Jose Canseco RR	25.00	11.00
❑ 40	Juan Nieves RR	.10	.05
❑ 41	Lance McCullers RR	.10	.05
❑ 42	Rick Surhoff RR	.10	.05
❑ 43	Todd Worrell RR	1.00	.45
❑ 44	Bob Kipper RR	.10	.05
❑ 45	John Habyan RR	.10	.05
❑ 46	Mike Woodard RR	.10	.05
❑ 47	Mike Boddicker	.10	.05
❑ 48	Robin Yount	1.00	.45
❑ 49	Lou Whitaker	.25	.11
❑ 50	Oil Can Boyd	.10	.05
❑ 51	Rickey Henderson	1.00	.45
❑ 52	Mike Marshall	.10	.05
❑ 53	George Brett	2.00	.90
❑ 54	Dave Kingman	.25	.11
❑ 55	Hubie Brooks	.10	.05
❑ 56	Oddibe McDowell	.10	.05
❑ 57	Doug DeCinces	.10	.05
❑ 58	Britt Burns	.10	.05
❑ 59	Ozzie Smith	1.25	.55
❑ 60	Jose Cruz	.25	.11
❑ 61	Mike Schmidt	1.25	.55
❑ 62	Pete Rose	1.25	.55
❑ 63	Steve Garvey	.50	.23
❑ 64	Tony Pena	.10	.05
❑ 65	Chili Davis	.50	.23
❑ 66	Dale Murphy	1.00	.45
❑ 67	Ryne Sandberg	1.25	.55
❑ 68	Gary Carter	1.00	.45
❑ 69	Alvin Davis	.10	.05
❑ 70	Kent Hrbek	.25	.11
❑ 71	George Bell	.25	.11
❑ 72	Kirby Puckett	3.00	1.35
❑ 73	Lloyd Moseby	.10	.05
❑ 74	Bob Kearney	.10	.05
❑ 75	Dwight Gooden	1.00	.45
❑ 76	Gary Matthews	.10	.05
❑ 77	Rick Mahler	.10	.05
❑ 78	Benny Distefano	.10	.05
❑ 79	Jeff Leonard	.10	.05
❑ 80	Kevin McReynolds	.25	.11
❑ 81	Ron Oester	.10	.05
❑ 82	John Russell	.10	.05
❑ 83	Tommy Herr	.10	.05
❑ 84	Jerry Mumphrey	.10	.05
❑ 85	Ron Romanick	.10	.05
❑ 86	Daryl Boston	.10	.05
❑ 87	Andre Dawson	1.00	.45
❑ 88	Eddie Murray	1.00	.45
❑ 89	Dion James	.10	.05
❑ 90	Chet Lemon	.10	.05
❑ 91	Bob Stanley	.10	.05
❑ 92	Willie Randolph	.25	.11
❑ 93	Mike Scioscia	.10	.05
❑ 94	Tom Waddell	.10	.05
❑ 95	Danny Jackson	.10	.05
❑ 96	Mike Davis	.10	.05
❑ 97	Mike Fitzgerald	.10	.05
❑ 98	Gary Ward	.10	.05
❑ 99	Pete O'Brien	.10	.05
❑ 100	Bret Saberhagen	.25	.11
❑ 101	Alfredo Griffin	.10	.05
❑ 102	Brett Butler	.25	.11
❑ 103	Ron Guidry	.25	.11
❑ 104	Jerry Reuss	.10	.05
❑ 105	Jack Morris	.25	.11
❑ 106	Rick Dempsey	.10	.05
❑ 107	Ray Burris	.10	.05
❑ 108	Brian Downing	.10	.05
❑ 109	Willie McGee	.25	.11
❑ 110	Bill Doran	.10	.05
❑ 111	Kent Tekulve	.10	.05
❑ 112	Tony Gwynn	2.50	1.10
❑ 113	Marvell Wynne	.10	.05
❑ 114	David Green	.10	.05
❑ 115	Jim Gantner	.10	.05
❑ 116	George Foster	.25	.11
❑ 117	Steve Trout	.10	.05
❑ 118	Mark Langston	.10	.05
❑ 119	Tony Fernandez	.10	.05
❑ 120	John Butcher	.10	.05
❑ 121	Ron Robinson	.10	.05
❑ 122	Dan Spillner	.10	.05
❑ 123	Mike Young	.10	.05
❑ 124	Paul Molitor	1.00	.45
❑ 125	Kirk Gibson	.25	.11
❑ 126	Ken Griffey	.25	.11
❑ 127	Tony Armas	.10	.05
❑ 128	Mariano Duncan	1.00	.45
❑ 129	Pat Tabler	.10	.05
❑ 130	Frank White	.25	.11
❑ 131	Carney Lansford	.25	.11
❑ 132	Vance Law	.10	.05
❑ 133	Dick Schofield	.10	.05
❑ 134	Wayne Tolleson	.10	.05
❑ 135	Greg Walker	.10	.05
❑ 136	Denny Walling	.10	.05
❑ 137	Ozzie Virgil	.10	.05
❑ 138	Ricky Horton	.10	.05
❑ 139	LaMarr Hoyt	.10	.05
❑ 140	Wayne Krenchicki	.10	.05
❑ 141	Glenn Hubbard	.10	.05
❑ 142	Cecilio Guante	.10	.05
❑ 143	Mike Krukow	.10	.05
❑ 144	Lee Smith	.50	.23
❑ 145	Edwin Nunez	.10	.05
❑ 146	Dave Stieb	.10	.05
❑ 147	Mike Smithson	.10	.05
❑ 148	Ken Dixon	.10	.05
❑ 149	Danny Darwin	.10	.05
❑ 150	Chris Pittaro	.10	.05
❑ 151	Bill Buckner	.25	.11
❑ 152	Mike Pagliarulo	.10	.05
❑ 153	Bill Russell	.10	.05
❑ 154	Brook Jacoby	.10	.05
❑ 155	Pat Sheridan	.10	.05
❑ 156	Mike Gallego	.25	.11
❑ 157	Jim Wohlford	.10	.05
❑ 158	Gary Pettis	.10	.05
❑ 159	Toby Harrah	.10	.05
❑ 160	Richard Dotson	.10	.05
❑ 161	Bob Knepper	.10	.05
❑ 162	Dave Dravecky	.25	.11
❑ 163	Greg Gross	.10	.05
❑ 164	Eric Davis	.50	.23
❑ 165	Gerald Perry	.10	.05
❑ 166	Rick Rhoden	.10	.05
❑ 167	Keith Moreland	.10	.05
❑ 168	Jack Clark	.25	.11
❑ 169	Storm Davis	.10	.05
❑ 170	Cecil Cooper	.25	.11
❑ 171	Alan Trammell	.50	.23
❑ 172	Roger Clemens	4.00	1.80
❑ 173	Don Mattingly	1.50	.70
❑ 174	Pedro Guerrero	.25	.11
❑ 175	Willie Wilson	.10	.05
❑ 176	Dwayne Murphy	.10	.05
❑ 177	Tim Raines	.25	.11
❑ 178	Larry Parrish	.10	.05
❑ 179	Mike Witt	.10	.05
❑ 180	Harold Baines	.50	.23
❑ 181	Vince Coleman UER (BA 2.67 on back)	1.00	.45
❑ 182	Jeff Heathcock	.10	.05
❑ 183	Steve Carlton	1.00	.45
❑ 184	Mario Soto	.10	.05
❑ 185	Goose Gossage	.25	.11
❑ 186	Johnny Ray	.10	.05
❑ 187	Dan Gladden	.10	.05
❑ 188	Bob Horner	.10	.05
❑ 189	Rick Sutcliffe	.10	.05
❑ 190	Keith Hernandez	.25	.11
❑ 191	Phil Bradley	.10	.05
❑ 192	Tom Brunansky	.10	.05
❑ 193	Jesse Barfield	.10	.05
❑ 194	Frank Viola	.25	.11
❑ 195	Willie Upshaw	.10	.05
❑ 196	Jim Beattie	.10	.05
❑ 197	Darryl Strawberry	1.00	.45
❑ 198	Ron Cey	.25	.11
❑ 199	Steve Bedrosian	.10	.05
❑ 200	Steve Kemp	.10	.05
❑ 201	Manny Trillo	.10	.05
❑ 202	Garry Templeton	.10	.05
❑ 203	Dave Parker	.25	.11
❑ 204	John Denny	.10	.05
❑ 205	Terry Pendleton	.50	.23
❑ 206	Terry Puhl	.10	.05
❑ 207	Bobby Grich	.25	.11
❑ 208	Ozzie Guillen	.50	.23
❑ 209	Jeff Reardon	.25	.11
❑ 210	Cal Ripken	4.00	1.80
❑ 211	Bill Schroeder	.10	.05
❑ 212	Dan Petry	.10	.05
❑ 213	Jim Rice	.25	.11
❑ 214	Dave Righetti	.10	.05
❑ 215	Fernando Valenzuela	.25	.11
❑ 216	Julio Franco	.25	.11
❑ 217	Darryl Motley	.10	.05
❑ 218	Dave Collins	.10	.05
❑ 219	Tim Wallach	.10	.05
❑ 220	George Wright	.10	.05
❑ 221	Tommy Dunbar	.10	.05
❑ 222	Steve Balboni	.10	.05
❑ 223	Jay Howell	.10	.05
❑ 224	Joe Carter	1.00	.45
❑ 225	Ed Whitson	.10	.05
❑ 226	Orel Hershiser	.50	.23
❑ 227	Willie Hernandez	.10	.05
❑ 228	Lee Lacy	.10	.05
❑ 229	Rollie Fingers	1.00	.45
❑ 230	Bob Boone	.25	.11
❑ 231	Joaquin Andujar	.10	.05
❑ 232	Craig Reynolds	.10	.05
❑ 233	Shane Rawley	.10	.05
❑ 234	Eric Show	.10	.05
❑ 235	Jose DeLeon	.10	.05
❑ 236	Jose Uribe	.10	.05
❑ 237	Moose Haas	.10	.05
❑ 238	Wally Backman	.10	.05
❑ 239	Dennis Eckersley	1.00	.45
❑ 240	Mike Moore	.10	.05
❑ 241	Damaso Garcia	.10	.05
❑ 242	Tim Teufel	.10	.05
❑ 243	Dave Concepcion	.25	.11
❑ 244	Floyd Bannister	.10	.05
❑ 245	Fred Lynn	.25	.11
❑ 246	Charlie Moore	.10	.05
❑ 247	Walt Terrell	.10	.05
❑ 248	Dave Winfield	1.00	.45
❑ 249	Dwight Evans	.25	.11
❑ 250	Dennis Powell	.10	.05
❑ 251	Andre Thornton	.10	.05
❑ 252	Onix Concepcion	.10	.05
❑ 253	Mike Heath	.10	.05
❑ 254A	David Palmer ERR (Position 2B)	.10	.05
❑ 254B	David Palmer COR (Position P)	1.00	.45
❑ 255	Donnie Moore	.10	.05
❑ 256	Curtis Wilkerson	.10	.05
❑ 257	Julio Cruz	.10	.05
❑ 258	Nolan Ryan	4.00	1.80
❑ 259	Jeff Stone	.10	.05
❑ 260	John Tudor	.10	.05
❑ 261	Mark Thurmond	.10	.05
❑ 262	Jay Tibbs	.10	.05
❑ 263	Rafael Ramirez	.10	.05
❑ 264	Larry McWilliams	.10	.05
❑ 265	Mark Davis	.10	.05
❑ 266	Bob Dernier	.10	.05
❑ 267	Matt Young	.10	.05
❑ 268	Jim Clancy	.10	.05
❑ 269	Mickey Hatcher	.10	.05
❑ 270	Sammy Stewart	.10	.05
❑ 271	Bob L. Gibson	.10	.05
❑ 272	Nelson Simmons	.10	.05
❑ 273	Rich Gedman	.10	.05
❑ 274	Butch Wynegar	.10	.05
❑ 275	Ken Howell	.10	.05
❑ 276	Mel Hall	.10	.05
❑ 277	Jim Sundberg	.10	.05
❑ 278	Chris Codiroli	.10	.05
❑ 279	Herm Winningham	.10	.05
❑ 280	Rod Carew	1.00	.45
❑ 281	Don Slaught	.10	.05
❑ 282	Scott Fletcher	.10	.05

❑ 283 Bill Dawley .10 .05
❑ 284 Andy Hawkins .10 .05
❑ 285 Glenn Wilson .10 .05
❑ 286 Nick Esasky .10 .05
❑ 287 Claudell Washington .10 .05
❑ 288 Lee Mazzilli .10 .05
❑ 289 Jody Davis .10 .05
❑ 290 Darrell Porter .25 .11
❑ 291 Scott McGregor .10 .05
❑ 292 Ted Simmons .25 .11
❑ 293 Aurelio Lopez .10 .05
❑ 294 Marty Barrett .10 .05
❑ 295 Dale Berra .10 .05
❑ 296 Greg Brock .10 .05
❑ 297 Charlie Leibrandt .10 .05
❑ 298 Bill Krueger .10 .05
❑ 299 Bryn Smith .10 .05
❑ 300 Burt Hooton .10 .05
❑ 301 Stu Cliburn .10 .05
❑ 302 Luis Salazar .10 .05
❑ 303 Ken Dayley .10 .05
❑ 304 Frank DiPino .10 .05
❑ 305 Von Hayes .10 .05
❑ 306 Gary Redus .10 .05
❑ 307 Craig Lefferts .10 .05
❑ 308 Sammy Khalifa .10 .05
❑ 309 Scott Garrelts .10 .05
❑ 310 Rick Cerone .10 .05
❑ 311 Shawon Dunston .25 .11
❑ 312 Howard Johnson .25 .11
❑ 313 Jim Presley .10 .05
❑ 314 Gary Gaetti .25 .11
❑ 315 Luis Leal .10 .05
❑ 316 Mark Salas .10 .05
❑ 317 Bill Caudill .10 .05
❑ 318 Dave Henderson .10 .05
❑ 319 Rafael Santana .10 .05
❑ 320 Leon Durham .10 .05
❑ 321 Bruce Sutter .25 .11
❑ 322 Jason Thompson .10 .05
❑ 323 Bob Brenly .10 .05
❑ 324 Carmelo Martinez .10 .05
❑ 325 Eddie Milner .10 .05
❑ 326 Juan Samuel .10 .05
❑ 327 Tom Nieto .10 .05
❑ 328 Dave Smith .10 .05
❑ 329 Urbano Lugo .10 .05
❑ 330 Joel Skinner .10 .05
❑ 331 Bill Gullickson .10 .05
❑ 332 Floyd Rayford .10 .05
❑ 333 Ben Oglivie .10 .05
❑ 334 Lance Parrish .25 .11
❑ 335 Jackie Gutierrez .10 .05
❑ 336 Dennis Rasmussen .10 .05
❑ 337 Terry Whitfield .10 .05
❑ 338 Neal Heaton .10 .05
❑ 339 Jorge Orta .10 .05
❑ 340 Donnie Hill .10 .05
❑ 341 Joe Hesketh .10 .05
❑ 342 Charlie Hough .25 .11
❑ 343 Dave Rozema .10 .05
❑ 344 Greg Pryor .10 .05
❑ 345 Mickey Tettleton 1.00 .45
❑ 346 George Vukovich .10 .05
❑ 347 Don Baylor .50 .23
❑ 348 Carlos Diaz .10 .05
❑ 349 Barbaro Garbey .10 .05
❑ 350 Larry Sheets .10 .05
❑ 351 Ted Higuera .25 .11
❑ 352 Juan Beniquez .10 .05
❑ 353 Bob Forsch .10 .05
❑ 354 Mark Bailey .10 .05
❑ 355 Larry Andersen .10 .05
❑ 356 Terry Kennedy .10 .05
❑ 357 Don Robinson .10 .05
❑ 358 Jim Gott .10 .05
❑ 359 Earnie Riles .10 .05
❑ 360 John Christensen .10 .05
❑ 361 Ray Fontenot .10 .05
❑ 362 Spike Owen .10 .05
❑ 363 Jim Acker .10 .05
❑ 364 Ron Davis .10 .05
❑ 365 Tom Hume .10 .05
❑ 366 Carlton Fisk 1.00 .45
❑ 367 Nate Snell .10 .05
❑ 368 Rick Manning .10 .05
❑ 369 Darrell Evans .25 .11
❑ 370 Ron Hassey .10 .05
❑ 371 Wade Boggs 1.00 .45
❑ 372 Rick Honeycutt .10 .05
❑ 373 Chris Bando .10 .05
❑ 374 Bud Black .10 .05
❑ 375 Steve Henderson .10 .05
❑ 376 Charlie Lea .10 .05
❑ 377 Reggie Jackson 1.25 .55
❑ 378 Dave Schmidt .10 .05
❑ 379 Bob James .10 .05
❑ 380 Glenn Davis .25 .11
❑ 381 Tim Corcoran .10 .05
❑ 382 Danny Cox .10 .05
❑ 383 Tim Flannery .10 .05
❑ 384 Tom Browning .10 .05
❑ 385 Rick Camp .10 .05
❑ 386 Jim Morrison .10 .05
❑ 387 Dave LaPoint .10 .05
❑ 388 Dave Lopes .25 .11
❑ 389 Al Cowens .10 .05
❑ 390 Doyle Alexander .10 .05
❑ 391 Tim Laudner .10 .05
❑ 392 Don Aase .10 .05
❑ 393 Jaime Cocanower .10 .05
❑ 394 Randy O'Neal .10 .05
❑ 395 Mike Easler .10 .05
❑ 396 Scott Bradley .10 .05
❑ 397 Tom Niedenfuer .10 .05
❑ 398 Jerry Willard .10 .05
❑ 399 Lonnie Smith .10 .05
❑ 400 Bruce Bochte .10 .05
❑ 401 Terry Francona .10 .05
❑ 402 Jim Slaton .10 .05
❑ 403 Bill Stein .10 .05
❑ 404 Tim Hulett .10 .05
❑ 405 Alan Ashby .10 .05
❑ 406 Tim Stoddard .10 .05
❑ 407 Garry Maddox .10 .05
❑ 408 Ted Power .10 .05
❑ 409 Len Barker .10 .05
❑ 410 Denny Gonzalez .10 .05
❑ 411 George Frazier .10 .05
❑ 412 Andy Van Slyke .25 .11
❑ 413 Jim Dwyer .10 .05
❑ 414 Paul Householder .10 .05
❑ 415 Alejandro Sanchez .10 .05
❑ 416 Steve Crawford .10 .05
❑ 417 Dan Pasqua .10 .05
❑ 418 Enos Cabell .10 .05
❑ 419 Mike Jones .10 .05
❑ 420 Steve Kiefer .10 .05
❑ 421 Tim Burke .10 .05
❑ 422 Mike Mason .10 .05
❑ 423 Ruppert Jones .10 .05
❑ 424 Jerry Hairston .10 .05
❑ 425 Tito Landrum .10 .05
❑ 426 Jeff Calhoun .10 .05
❑ 427 Don Carman .10 .05
❑ 428 Tony Perez 1.00 .45
❑ 429 Jerry Davis .10 .05
❑ 430 Bob Walk .10 .05
❑ 431 Brad Wellman .10 .05
❑ 432 Terry Forster .10 .05
❑ 433 Billy Hatcher .10 .05
❑ 434 Clint Hurdle .10 .05
❑ 435 Ivan Calderon .25 .11
❑ 436 Pete Filson .10 .05
❑ 437 Tom Henke .25 .11
❑ 438 Dave Engle .10 .05
❑ 439 Tom Filer .10 .05
❑ 440 Gorman Thomas .10 .05
❑ 441 Rick Aguilera 1.00 .45
❑ 442 Scott Sanderson .10 .05
❑ 443 Jeff Dedmon .10 .05
❑ 444 Joe Orsulak .10 .05
❑ 445 Atlee Hammaker .10 .05
❑ 446 Jerry Royster .10 .05
❑ 447 Buddy Bell .25 .11
❑ 448 Dave Rucker .10 .05
❑ 449 Ivan DeJesus .10 .05
❑ 450 Jim Pankovits .10 .05
❑ 451 Jerry Narron .10 .05
❑ 452 Bryan Little .10 .05
❑ 453 Gary Lucas .10 .05
❑ 454 Dennis Martinez .25 .11
❑ 455 Ed Romero .10 .05
❑ 456 Bob Melvin .10 .05
❑ 457 Glenn Hoffman .10 .05
❑ 458 Bob Shirley .10 .05
❑ 459 Bob Welch .10 .05
❑ 460 Carmen Castillo .10 .05
❑ 461 Dave Leeper .10 .05
❑ 462 Tim Birtsas .10 .05
❑ 463 Randy St.Claire .10 .05
❑ 464 Chris Welsh .10 .05
❑ 465 Greg Harris .10 .05
❑ 466 Lynn Jones .10 .05
❑ 467 Dusty Baker .25 .11
❑ 468 Roy Smith .10 .05
❑ 469 Andre Robertson .10 .05
❑ 470 Ken Landreaux .10 .05
❑ 471 Dave Bergman .10 .05
❑ 472 Gary Roenicke .10 .05
❑ 473 Pete Vuckovich .10 .05
❑ 474 Kirk McCaskill .25 .11
❑ 475 Jeff Lahti .10 .05
❑ 476 Mike Scott .10 .05
❑ 477 Darren Daulton 2.00 .90
❑ 478 Graig Nettles .25 .11
❑ 479 Bill Almon .10 .05
❑ 480 Greg Minton .10 .05
❑ 481 Randy Ready .10 .05
❑ 482 Len Dykstra 2.00 .90
❑ 483 Thad Bosley .10 .05
❑ 484 Harold Reynolds 1.00 .45
❑ 485 Al Oliver .25 .11
❑ 486 Roy Smalley .10 .05
❑ 487 John Franco 1.00 .45
❑ 488 Juan Agosto .10 .05
❑ 489 Al Pardo .10 .05
❑ 490 Bill Wegman .10 .05
❑ 491 Frank Tanana .10 .05
❑ 492 Brian Fisher .10 .05
❑ 493 Mark Clear .10 .05
❑ 494 Len Matuszek .10 .05
❑ 495 Ramon Romero .10 .05
❑ 496 John Wathan .10 .05
❑ 497 Rob Picciolo .10 .05
❑ 498 U.L. Washington .10 .05
❑ 499 John Candelaria .10 .05
❑ 500 Duane Walker .10 .05
❑ 501 Gene Nelson .10 .05
❑ 502 John Mizerock .10 .05
❑ 503 Luis Aguayo .10 .05
❑ 504 Kurt Kepshire .10 .05
❑ 505 Ed Wojna .10 .05
❑ 506 Joe Price .10 .05
❑ 507 Milt Thompson .25 .11
❑ 508 Junior Ortiz .10 .05
❑ 509 Vida Blue .25 .11
❑ 510 Steve Engel .10 .05
❑ 511 Karl Best .10 .05
❑ 512 Cecil Fielder 2.50 1.10
❑ 513 Frank Eufemia .10 .05
❑ 514 Tippy Martinez .10 .05
❑ 515 Billy Joe Robidoux .10 .05
❑ 516 Bill Scherrer .10 .05
❑ 517 Bruce Hurst .10 .05
❑ 518 Rich Bordi .10 .05
❑ 519 Steve Yeager .10 .05
❑ 520 Tony Bernazard .10 .05
❑ 521 Hal McRae .25 .11
❑ 522 Jose Rijo .10 .05
❑ 523 Mitch Webster .10 .05
❑ 524 Jack Howell .10 .05
❑ 525 Alan Bannister .10 .05
❑ 526 Ron Kittle .10 .05
❑ 527 Phil Garner .10 .05
❑ 528 Kurt Bevacqua .10 .05
❑ 529 Kevin Gross .10 .05
❑ 530 Bo Diaz .10 .05
❑ 531 Ken Oberkfell .10 .05
❑ 532 Rick Reuschel .10 .05
❑ 533 Ron Meridith .10 .05
❑ 534 Steve Braun .10 .05
❑ 535 Wayne Gross .10 .05
❑ 536 Ray Searage .10 .05
❑ 537 Tom Brookens .10 .05

❑ 538 Al Nipper .10 .05
❑ 539 Billy Sample .10 .05
❑ 540 Steve Sax .10 .05
❑ 541 Dan Quisenberry .10 .05
❑ 542 Tony Phillips .10 .05
❑ 543 Floyd Youmans .10 .05
❑ 544 Steve Buechele .25 .11
❑ 545 Craig Gerber .10 .05
❑ 546 Joe DeSa .10 .05
❑ 547 Brian Harper .10 .05
❑ 548 Kevin Bass .10 .05
❑ 549 Tom Foley .10 .05
❑ 550 Dave Van Gorder .10 .05
❑ 551 Bruce Bochy .10 .05
❑ 552 R.J. Reynolds .10 .05
❑ 553 Chris Brown .10 .05
❑ 554 Bruce Benedict .10 .05
❑ 555 Warren Brusstar .10 .05
❑ 556 Danny Heep .10 .05
❑ 557 Darnell Coles .10 .05
❑ 558 Greg Gagne .10 .05
❑ 559 Ernie Whitt .10 .05
❑ 560 Ron Washington .10 .05
❑ 561 Jimmy Key 1.00 .45
❑ 562 Billy Swift .10 .05
❑ 563 Ron Darling .10 .05
❑ 564 Dick Ruthven .10 .05
❑ 565 Zane Smith .10 .05
❑ 566 Sid Bream .10 .05
❑ 567A Joel Youngblood ERR .10 .05
(Position P)
❑ 567B Joel Youngblood COR 1.00 .45
(Position IF)
❑ 568 Mario Ramirez .10 .05
❑ 569 Tom Runnells .10 .05
❑ 570 Rick Schu .10 .05
❑ 571 Bill Campbell .10 .05
❑ 572 Dickie Thon .10 .05
❑ 573 Al Holland .10 .05
❑ 574 Reid Nichols .10 .05
❑ 575 Bert Roberge .10 .05
❑ 576 Mike Flanagan .10 .05
❑ 577 Tim Leary .10 .05
❑ 578 Mike Laga .10 .05
❑ 579 Steve Lyons .10 .05
❑ 580 Phil Niekro 1.00 .45
❑ 581 Gilberto Reyes .10 .05
❑ 582 Jamie Easterly .10 .05
❑ 583 Mark Gubicza .10 .05
❑ 584 Stan Javier .25 .11
❑ 585 Bill Laskey .10 .05
❑ 586 Jeff Russell .10 .05
❑ 587 Dickie Noles .10 .05
❑ 588 Steve Farr .10 .05
❑ 589 Steve Ontiveros .25 .11
❑ 590 Mike Hargrove .25 .11
❑ 591 Marty Bystrom .10 .05
❑ 592 Franklin Stubbs .10 .05
❑ 593 Larry Herndon .10 .05
❑ 594 Bill Swaggerty .10 .05
❑ 595 Carlos Ponce .10 .05
❑ 596 Pat Perry .10 .05
❑ 597 Ray Knight .25 .11
❑ 598 Steve Lombardozzi .10 .05
❑ 599 Brad Havens .10 .05
❑ 600 Pat Clements .10 .05
❑ 601 Joe Niekro .10 .05
❑ 602 Hank Aaron 1.00 .45
Puzzle Card
❑ 603 Dwayne Henry .10 .05
❑ 604 Mookie Wilson .25 .11
❑ 605 Buddy Biancalana .10 .05
❑ 606 Rance Mulliniks .10 .05
❑ 607 Alan Wiggins .10 .05
❑ 608 Joe Cowley .10 .05
❑ 609 Tom Seaver 1.25 .55
(Green borders
on name)
❑ 609B Tom Seaver 2.00 .90
(Yellow borders
on name)
❑ 610 Neil Allen .10 .05
❑ 611 Don Sutton 1.00 .45
❑ 612 Fred Toliver .10 .05
❑ 613 Jay Baller .10 .05
❑ 614 Marc Sullivan .10 .05
❑ 615 John Grubb .10 .05
❑ 616 Bruce Kison .10 .05
❑ 617 Bill Madlock .10 .05
❑ 618 Chris Chambliss .25 .11
❑ 619 Dave Stewart .25 .11
❑ 620 Tim Lollar .10 .05
❑ 621 Gary Lavelle .10 .05
❑ 622 Charles Hudson .10 .05
❑ 623 Joel Davis .10 .05
❑ 624 Joe Johnson .10 .05
❑ 625 Sid Fernandez .25 .11
❑ 626 Dennis Lamp .10 .05
❑ 627 Terry Harper .10 .05
❑ 628 Jack Lazorko .10 .05
❑ 629 Roger McDowell .25 .11
❑ 630 Mark Funderburk .10 .05
❑ 631 Ed Lynch .10 .05
❑ 632 Rudy Law .10 .05
❑ 633 Roger Mason .10 .05
❑ 634 Mike Felder .10 .05
❑ 635 Ken Schrom .10 .05
❑ 636 Bob Ojeda .10 .05
❑ 637 Ed VandeBerg .10 .05
❑ 638 Bobby Meacham .10 .05
❑ 639 Cliff Johnson .10 .05
❑ 640 Garth Iorg .10 .05
❑ 641 Dan Driessen .10 .05
❑ 642 Mike Brown OF .10 .05
❑ 643 John Shelby .10 .05
❑ 644 Pete Rose .60 .25
(Ty-Breaking)
❑ 645 The Knuckle Brothers .25 .11
Phil Niekro
Joe Niekro
❑ 646 Jesse Orosco .10 .05
❑ 647 Billy Beane .10 .05
❑ 648 Cesar Cedeno .25 .11
❑ 649 Bert Blyleven .25 .11
❑ 650 Max Venable .10 .05
❑ 651 Fleet Feet .10 .05
Vince Coleman
Willie McGee
❑ 652 Calvin Schiraldi .10 .05
❑ 653 King of Kings 1.00 .45
(Pete Rose)
❑ 654 Diamond Kings CL 1-26 .10 .05
(Unnumbered)
❑ 655A CL 1: 27-130 .10 .05
(Unnumbered)
(45 Beane ERR)
❑ 655B CL 1: 27-130 .10 .05
(Unnumbered)
(45 Habyan COR)
❑ 656 CL 2: 131-234 .10 .05
(Unnumbered)
❑ 657 CL 3: 235-338 .10 .05
(Unnumbered)
❑ 658 CL 4: 339-442 .10 .05
(Unnumbered)
❑ 659 CL 5: 443-546 .10 .05
(Unnumbered)
❑ 660 CL 6: 547-653 .10 .05
(Unnumbered)

1986 Donruss Rookies

	MINT	NRMT
COMP.FACT.SET (56)	25.00	11.00
COMMON CARD (1-56)	.10	.05

❑ 1 Wally Joyner 1.00 .45
❑ 2 Tracy Jones .10 .05
❑ 3 Allan Anderson .10 .05
❑ 4 Ed Correa .10 .05
❑ 5 Reggie Williams .10 .05
❑ 6 Charlie Kerfeld .10 .05
❑ 7 Andres Galarraga 3.00 1.35
❑ 8 Bob Tewksbury .25 .11
❑ 9 Al Newman .25 .11
❑ 10 Andres Thomas .10 .05
❑ 11 Barry Bonds 12.00 5.50
❑ 12 Juan Nieves .10 .05
❑ 13 Mark Eichhorn .10 .05
❑ 14 Dan Plesac .10 .05
❑ 15 Cory Snyder .10 .05

❑ 16 Kelly Gruber .10 .05
❑ 17 Kevin Mitchell 1.00 .45
❑ 18 Steve Lombardozzi .10 .05
❑ 19 Mitch Williams .25 .11
❑ 20 John Cerutti .10 .05
❑ 21 Todd Worrell 1.00 .45
❑ 22 Jose Canseco 5.00 2.20
❑ 23 Pete Incaviglia 1.00 .45
❑ 24 Jose Guzman .10 .05
❑ 25 Scott Bailes .10 .05
❑ 26 Greg Mathews .10 .05
❑ 27 Eric King .10 .05
❑ 28 Paul Assenmacher .10 .05
❑ 29 Jeff Sellers .10 .05
❑ 30 Bobby Bonilla 1.50 .70
❑ 31 Doug Drabek 1.00 .45
❑ 32 Will Clark UER 4.00 1.80
(Listed as throwing
right, should be left)
❑ 33 Bip Roberts 1.00 .45
❑ 34 Jim Deshaies .10 .05
❑ 35 Mike LaValliere .10 .05
❑ 36 Scott Bankhead .10 .05
❑ 37 Dale Sveum .10 .05
❑ 38 Bo Jackson 2.00 .90
❑ 39 Robby Thompson .25 .11
❑ 40 Eric Plunk .10 .05
❑ 41 Bill Bathe .10 .05
❑ 42 John Kruk 1.00 .45
❑ 43 Andy Allanson .10 .05
❑ 44 Mark Portugal .25 .11
❑ 45 Danny Tartabull .25 .11
❑ 46 Bob Kipper .10 .05
❑ 47 Gene Walter .10 .05
❑ 48 Rey Quinones UER .10 .05
(Misspelled Quinonez)
❑ 49 Bobby Witt .50 .23
❑ 50 Bill Mooneyham .10 .05
❑ 51 John Cangelosi .10 .05
❑ 52 Ruben Sierra 1.00 .45
❑ 53 Rob Woodward .10 .05
❑ 54 Ed Hearn .10 .05
❑ 55 Joel McKeon .10 .05
❑ 56 Checklist 1-56 .10 .05

1987 Donruss

	MINT	NRMT
COMPLETE SET (660)	70.00	32.00
COMP.FACT.SET (660)	80.00	36.00
COMMON CARD (1-660)	.10	.05

COMP.CLEMENTE PUZZLE .... 1.50 .70

❑ 1 Wally Joyner DK .40 .18
❑ 2 Roger Clemens DK .50 .23
❑ 3 Dale Murphy DK .20 .09
❑ 4 Darryl Strawberry DK .20 .09
❑ 5 Ozzie Smith DK .40 .18
❑ 6 Jose Canseco DK .50 .23
❑ 7 Charlie Hough DK .10 .05
❑ 8 Brook Jacoby DK .10 .05
❑ 9 Fred Lynn DK .20 .09
❑ 10 Rick Rhoden DK .10 .05
❑ 11 Chris Brown DK .10 .05
❑ 12 Von Hayes DK .10 .05
❑ 13 Jack Morris DK .20 .09
❑ 14A Kevin McReynolds DK .. .40 .18
ERR (Yellow strip missing on back)
❑ 14B Kevin McReynolds DK .. .10 .05
COR
❑ 15 George Brett DK .40 .18
❑ 16 Ted Higuera DK .10 .05
❑ 17 Hubie Brooks DK .10 .05
❑ 18 Mike Scott DK .10 .05
❑ 19 Kirby Puckett DK .50 .23
❑ 20 Dave Winfield DK .20 .09
❑ 21 Lloyd Moseby DK .10 .05
❑ 22A Eric Davis DK ERR .40 .18
(Yellow strip missing on back)
❑ 22B Eric Davis DK COR .20 .09
❑ 23 Jim Presley DK .10 .05
❑ 24 Keith Moreland DK .10 .05
❑ 25A Greg Walker DK ERR .40 .18
(Yellow strip missing on back)
❑ 25B Greg Walker DK COR .10 .05
❑ 26 Steve Sax DK .10 .05
❑ 27 DK Checklist 1-26 .10 .05
❑ 28 B.J. Surhoff RR .50 .23
❑ 29 Randy Myers RR .40 .18
❑ 30 Ken Gerhart RR .10 .05
❑ 31 Benito Santiago RR .20 .09
❑ 32 Greg Swindell RR .40 .18
❑ 33 Mike Birkbeck RR .10 .05
❑ 34 Terry Steinbach RR .40 .18
❑ 35 Bo Jackson RR 1.00 .45
❑ 36 Greg Maddux UER 30.00 13.50
(middle name misspelled "Allen")
❑ 37 Jim Lindeman RR .10 .05
❑ 38 Devon White RR .75 .35
❑ 39 Eric Bell RR .10 .05
❑ 40 Willie Fraser RR .10 .05
❑ 41 Jerry Browne RR .10 .05
❑ 42 Chris James RR .10 .05
❑ 43 Rafael Palmeiro RR 4.00 1.80
❑ 44 Pat Dodson RR .10 .05
❑ 45 Duane Ward RR .20 .09
❑ 46 Mark McGwire RR 30.00 13.50
❑ 47 Bruce Fields RR UER .10 .05
(Photo actually Darnell Coles)
❑ 48 Eddie Murray .40 .18
❑ 49 Ted Higuera .10 .05
❑ 50 Kirk Gibson .20 .09
❑ 51 Oil Can Boyd .10 .05
❑ 52 Don Mattingly .60 .25
❑ 53 Pedro Guerrero .10 .05
❑ 54 George Brett .75 .35
❑ 55 Jose Rijo .10 .05
❑ 56 Tim Raines .20 .09
❑ 57 Ed Correa .10 .05
❑ 58 Mike Witt .10 .05
❑ 59 Greg Walker .10 .05
❑ 60 Ozzie Smith .50 .23
❑ 61 Glenn Davis .10 .05
❑ 62 Glenn Wilson .10 .05
❑ 63 Tom Browning .10 .05
❑ 64 Tony Gwynn 1.00 .45
❑ 65 R.J. Reynolds .10 .05
❑ 66 Will Clark 2.00 .90
❑ 67 Ozzie Virgil .10 .05
❑ 68 Rick Sutcliffe .10 .05
❑ 69 Gary Carter .10 .05
❑ 70 Mike Moore .10 .05
❑ 71 Bert Blyleven .20 .09
❑ 72 Tony Fernandez .10 .05
❑ 73 Kent Hrbek .20 .09
❑ 74 Lloyd Moseby .10 .05
❑ 75 Alvin Davis .10 .05
❑ 76 Keith Hernandez .20 .09
❑ 77 Ryne Sandberg .50 .23
❑ 78 Dale Murphy .40 .18
❑ 79 Sid Bream .10 .05
❑ 80 Chris Brown .10 .05
❑ 81 Steve Garvey .10 .05
❑ 82 Mario Soto .10 .05
❑ 83 Shane Rawley .10 .05
❑ 84 Willie McGee .20 .09
❑ 85 Jose Cruz .20 .09
❑ 86 Brian Downing .10 .05
❑ 87 Ozzie Guillen .10 .05
❑ 88 Hubie Brooks .10 .05
❑ 89 Cal Ripken 1.50 .70
❑ 90 Juan Nieves .10 .05
❑ 91 Lance Parrish .20 .09
❑ 92 Jim Rice .20 .09
❑ 93 Ron Guidry .20 .09
❑ 94 Fernando Valenzuela .20 .09
❑ 95 Andy Allanson .10 .05
❑ 96 Willie Wilson .20 .09
❑ 97 Jose Canseco .75 .35
❑ 98 Jeff Reardon .20 .09
❑ 99 Bobby Witt .20 .09
❑ 100 Checklist 28-133 .10 .05
❑ 101 Jose Guzman .10 .05
❑ 102 Steve Balboni .10 .05
❑ 103 Tony Phillips .10 .05
❑ 104 Brook Jacoby .10 .05
❑ 105 Dave Winfield .40 .18
❑ 106 Orel Hershiser .20 .09
❑ 107 Lou Whitaker .20 .09
❑ 108 Fred Lynn .20 .09
❑ 109 Bill Wegman .10 .05
❑ 110 Donnie Moore .10 .05
❑ 111 Jack Clark .20 .09
❑ 112 Bob Knepper .10 .05
❑ 113 Von Hayes .10 .05
❑ 114 Bip Roberts .40 .18
❑ 115 Tony Pena .10 .05
❑ 116 Scott Garrelts .10 .05
❑ 117 Paul Molitor .40 .18
❑ 118 Darryl Strawberry .10 .05
❑ 119 Shawon Dunston .10 .05
❑ 120 Jim Presley .10 .05
❑ 121 Jesse Barfield .10 .05
❑ 122 Gary Gaetti .20 .09
❑ 123 Kurt Stillwell .10 .05
❑ 124 Joel Davis .10 .05
❑ 125 Mike Boddicker .10 .05
❑ 126 Robin Yount .40 .18
❑ 127 Alan Trammell .10 .05
❑ 128 Dave Righetti .10 .05
❑ 129 Dwight Evans .20 .09
❑ 130 Mike Scioscia .10 .05
❑ 131 Julio Franco .10 .05
❑ 132 Bret Saberhagen .20 .09
❑ 133 Mike Davis .10 .05
❑ 134 Joe Hesketh .10 .05
❑ 135 Wally Joyner .40 .18
❑ 136 Don Slaught .10 .05
❑ 137 Daryl Boston .10 .05
❑ 138 Nolan Ryan 1.50 .70
❑ 139 Mike Schmidt .50 .23
❑ 140 Tommy Herr .10 .05
❑ 141 Garry Templeton .10 .05
❑ 142 Kal Daniels .10 .05
❑ 143 Billy Sample .10 .05
❑ 144 Johnny Ray .10 .05
❑ 145 Rob Thompson .20 .09
❑ 146 Bob Dernier .10 .05
❑ 147 Danny Tartabull .10 .05
❑ 148 Ernie Whitt .10 .05
❑ 149 Kirby Puckett .75 .35
❑ 150 Mike Young .10 .05
❑ 151 Ernest Riles .10 .05
❑ 152 Frank Tanana .10 .05
❑ 153 Rich Gedman .10 .05
❑ 154 Willie Randolph .20 .09
❑ 155 Bill Madlock .20 .09
❑ 156 Joe Carter .40 .18
❑ 157 Danny Jackson .10 .05
❑ 158 Carney Lansford .20 .09
❑ 159 Bryn Smith .10 .05
❑ 160 Gary Pettis .10 .05
❑ 161 Oddibe McDowell .10 .05
❑ 162 John Cangelosi .10 .05
❑ 163 Mike Scott .10 .05
❑ 164 Eric Show .10 .05
❑ 165 Juan Samuel .10 .05
❑ 166 Nick Esasky .10 .05
❑ 167 Zane Smith .10 .05
❑ 168 Mike C. Brown OF .10 .05
❑ 169 Keith Moreland .10 .05
❑ 170 John Tudor .10 .05
❑ 171 Ken Dixon .10 .05
❑ 172 Jim Gantner .10 .05
❑ 173 Jack Morris .20 .09
❑ 174 Bruce Hurst .10 .05
❑ 175 Dennis Rasmussen .10 .05
❑ 176 Mike Marshall .10 .05
❑ 177 Dan Quisenberry .10 .05
❑ 178 Eric Plunk .10 .05
❑ 179 Tim Wallach .10 .05
❑ 180 Steve Buechele .10 .05
❑ 181 Don Sutton .40 .18
❑ 182 Dave Schmidt .10 .05
❑ 183 Terry Pendleton .20 .09
❑ 184 Jim Deshaies .10 .05
❑ 185 Steve Bedrosian .10 .05
❑ 186 Pete Rose .50 .23
❑ 187 Dave Dravecky .20 .09
❑ 188 Rick Reuschel .10 .05
❑ 189 Dan Gladden .10 .05
❑ 190 Rick Mahler .10 .05
❑ 191 Thad Bosley .10 .05
❑ 192 Ron Darling .10 .05
❑ 193 Matt Young .10 .05
❑ 194 Tom Brunansky .10 .05
❑ 195 Dave Stieb .10 .05
❑ 196 Frank Viola .10 .05
❑ 197 Tom Henke .10 .05
❑ 198 Karl Best .10 .05
❑ 199 Dwight Gooden .10 .05
❑ 200 Checklist 134-239 .10 .05
❑ 201 Steve Trout .10 .05
❑ 202 Rafael Ramirez .10 .05
❑ 203 Bob Walk .10 .05
❑ 204 Roger Mason .10 .05
❑ 205 Terry Kennedy .10 .05
❑ 206 Ron Oester .10 .05
❑ 207 John Russell .10 .05
❑ 208 Greg Mathews .10 .05
❑ 209 Charlie Kerfeld .10 .05
❑ 210 Reggie Jackson .50 .23
❑ 211 Floyd Bannister .10 .05
❑ 212 Vance Law .10 .05
❑ 213 Rich Bordi .10 .05
❑ 214 Dan Plesac .10 .05
❑ 215 Dave Collins .10 .05
❑ 216 Bob Stanley .10 .05
❑ 217 Joe Niekro .10 .05
❑ 218 Tom Niedenfuer .10 .05
❑ 219 Brett Butler .20 .09
❑ 220 Charlie Leibrandt .10 .05
❑ 221 Steve Ontiveros .10 .05
❑ 222 Tim Burke .10 .05
❑ 223 Curtis Wilkerson .10 .05
❑ 224 Pete Incaviglia .20 .09
❑ 225 Lonnie Smith .10 .05
❑ 226 Chris Codiroli .10 .05
❑ 227 Scott Bailes .10 .05
❑ 228 Rickey Henderson .40 .18
❑ 229 Ken Howell .10 .05
❑ 230 Darnell Coles .10 .05
❑ 231 Don Aase .10 .05
❑ 232 Tim Leary .10 .05
❑ 233 Bob Boone .20 .09
❑ 234 Ricky Horton .10 .05
❑ 235 Mark Bailey .10 .05
❑ 236 Kevin Gross .10 .05
❑ 237 Lance McCullers .10 .05
❑ 238 Cecilio Guante .10 .05
❑ 239 Bob Melvin .10 .05
❑ 240 Billy Joe Robidoux .10 .05

❑ 241 Roger McDowell .10 .05
❑ 242 Leon Durham .10 .05
❑ 243 Ed Nunez .10 .05
❑ 244 Jimmy Key .10 .05
❑ 245 Mike Smithson .10 .05
❑ 246 Bo Diaz .10 .05
❑ 247 Carlton Fisk .40 .18
❑ 248 Larry Sheets .10 .05
❑ 249 Juan Castillo .10 .05
❑ 250 Eric King .10 .05
❑ 251 Doug Drabek .40 .18
❑ 252 Wade Boggs .40 .18
❑ 253 Mariano Duncan .10 .05
❑ 254 Pat Tabler .10 .05
❑ 255 Frank White .20 .09
❑ 256 Alfredo Griffin .10 .05
❑ 257 Floyd Youmans .10 .05
❑ 258 Rob Wilfong .10 .05
❑ 259 Pete O'Brien .10 .05
❑ 260 Tim Hulett .10 .05
❑ 261 Dickie Thon .10 .05
❑ 262 Darren Daulton .10 .05
❑ 263 Vince Coleman .10 .05
❑ 264 Andy Hawkins .10 .05
❑ 265 Eric Davis .10 .05
❑ 266 Andres Thomas .10 .05
❑ 267 Mike Diaz .10 .05
❑ 268 Chili Davis .10 .05
❑ 269 Jody Davis .10 .05
❑ 270 Phil Bradley .10 .05
❑ 271 George Bell .10 .05
❑ 272 Keith Atherton .10 .05
❑ 273 Storm Davis .10 .05
❑ 274 Rob Deer .10 .05
❑ 275 Walt Terrell .10 .05
❑ 276 Roger Clemens 1.00 .45
❑ 277 Mike Easler .10 .05
❑ 278 Steve Sax .10 .05
❑ 279 Andre Thornton .10 .05
❑ 280 Jim Sundberg .10 .05
❑ 281 Bill Bathe .10 .05
❑ 282 Jay Tibbs .10 .05
❑ 283 Dick Schofield .10 .05
❑ 284 Mike Mason .10 .05
❑ 285 Jerry Hairston .10 .05
❑ 286 Bill Doran .10 .05
❑ 287 Tim Flannery .10 .05
❑ 288 Gary Redus .10 .05
❑ 289 John Franco .20 .09
❑ 290 Paul Assenmacher .10 .05
❑ 291 Joe Orsulak .10 .05
❑ 292 Lee Smith .10 .05
❑ 293 Mike Laga .10 .05
❑ 294 Rick Dempsey .20 .09
❑ 295 Mike Felder .10 .05
❑ 296 Tom Brookens .10 .05
❑ 297 Al Nipper .10 .05
❑ 298 Mike Pagliarulo .10 .05
❑ 299 Franklin Stubbs .10 .05
❑ 300 Checklist 240-345 .10 .05
❑ 301 Steve Farr .10 .05
❑ 302 Bill Mooneyham .10 .05
❑ 303 Andres Galarraga .50 .23
❑ 304 Scott Fletcher .10 .05
❑ 305 Jack Howell .10 .05
❑ 306 Russ Morman .10 .05
❑ 307 Todd Worrell .20 .09
❑ 308 Dave Smith .10 .05
❑ 309 Jeff Stone .10 .05
❑ 310 Ron Robinson .10 .05
❑ 311 Bruce Bochy .10 .05
❑ 312 Jim Winn .10 .05
❑ 313 Mark Davis .10 .05
❑ 314 Jeff Dedmon .10 .05
❑ 315 Jamie Moyer .10 .05
❑ 316 Wally Backman .10 .05
❑ 317 Ken Phelps .10 .05
❑ 318 Steve Lombardozzi .10 .05
❑ 319 Rance Mulliniks .10 .05
❑ 320 Tim Laudner .10 .05
❑ 321 Mark Eichhorn .10 .05
❑ 322 Lee Guetterman .10 .05
❑ 323 Sid Fernandez .10 .05
❑ 324 Jerry Mumphrey .10 .05
❑ 325 David Palmer .10 .05
❑ 326 Bill Almon .10 .05
❑ 327 Candy Maldonado .10 .05
❑ 328 John Kruk .40 .18
❑ 329 John Denny .10 .05
❑ 330 Milt Thompson .10 .05
❑ 331 Mike LaValliere .10 .05
❑ 332 Alan Ashby .10 .05
❑ 333 Doug Corbett .10 .05
❑ 334 Ron Karkovice .20 .09
❑ 335 Mitch Webster .10 .05
❑ 336 Lee Lacy .10 .05
❑ 337 Glenn Braggs .10 .05
❑ 338 Dwight Lowry .10 .05
❑ 339 Don Baylor .20 .09
❑ 340 Brian Fisher .10 .05
❑ 341 Reggie Williams .10 .05
❑ 342 Tom Candiotti .10 .05
❑ 343 Rudy Law .10 .05
❑ 344 Curt Young .10 .05
❑ 345 Mike Fitzgerald .10 .05
❑ 346 Ruben Sierra .20 .09
❑ 347 Mitch Williams .20 .09
❑ 348 Jorge Orta .10 .05
❑ 349 Mickey Tettleton .20 .09
❑ 350 Ernie Camacho .10 .05
❑ 351 Ron Kittle .10 .05
❑ 352 Ken Landreaux .10 .05
❑ 353 Chet Lemon .10 .05
❑ 354 John Shelby .10 .05
❑ 355 Mark Clear .10 .05
❑ 356 Doug DeCinces .10 .05
❑ 357 Ken Dayley .10 .05
❑ 358 Phil Garner .10 .05
❑ 359 Steve Jeltz .10 .05
❑ 360 Ed Whitson .10 .05
❑ 361 Barry Bonds 8.00 3.60
❑ 362 Vida Blue .20 .09
❑ 363 Cecil Cooper .20 .09
❑ 364 Bob Ojeda .10 .05
❑ 365 Dennis Eckersley .40 .18
❑ 366 Mike Morgan .10 .05
❑ 367 Willie Upshaw .10 .05
❑ 368 Allan Anderson .10 .05
❑ 369 Bill Gullickson .10 .05
❑ 370 Bobby Thigpen .20 .09
❑ 371 Juan Beniquez .10 .05
❑ 372 Charlie Moore .10 .05
❑ 373 Dan Petry .10 .05
❑ 374 Rod Scurry .10 .05
❑ 375 Tom Seaver .40 .18
❑ 376 Ed VandeBerg .10 .05
❑ 377 Tony Bernazard .10 .05
❑ 378 Greg Pryor .10 .05
❑ 379 Dwayne Murphy .10 .05
❑ 380 Andy McGaffigan .10 .05
❑ 381 Kirk McCaskill .10 .05
❑ 382 Greg Harris .10 .05
❑ 383 Rich Dotson .10 .05
❑ 384 Craig Reynolds .10 .05
❑ 385 Greg Gross .10 .05
❑ 386 Tito Landrum .10 .05
❑ 387 Craig Lefferts .10 .05
❑ 388 Dave Parker .20 .09
❑ 389 Bob Horner .10 .05
❑ 390 Pat Clements .10 .05
❑ 391 Jeff Leonard .10 .05
❑ 392 Chris Speier .10 .05
❑ 393 John Moses .10 .05
❑ 394 Garth Iorg .10 .05
❑ 395 Greg Gagne .10 .05
❑ 396 Nate Snell .10 .05
❑ 397 Bryan Clutterbuck .10 .05
❑ 398 Darrell Evans .20 .09
❑ 399 Steve Crawford .10 .05
❑ 400 Checklist 346-451 .10 .05
❑ 401 Phil Lombardi .10 .05
❑ 402 Rick Honeycutt .10 .05
❑ 403 Ken Schrom .10 .05
❑ 404 Bud Black .10 .05
❑ 405 Donnie Hill .10 .05
❑ 406 Wayne Krenchicki .10 .05
❑ 407 Chuck Finley .40 .18
❑ 408 Toby Harrah .10 .05
❑ 409 Steve Lyons .10 .05
❑ 410 Kevin Bass .10 .05
❑ 411 Marvell Wynne .10 .05
❑ 412 Ron Roenicke .10 .05
❑ 413 Tracy Jones .10 .05
❑ 414 Gene Garber .10 .05
❑ 415 Mike Bielecki .10 .05
❑ 416 Frank DiPino .10 .05
❑ 417 Andy Van Slyke .20 .09
❑ 418 Jim Dwyer .10 .05
❑ 419 Ben Oglivie .10 .05
❑ 420 Dave Bergman .10 .05
❑ 421 Joe Sambito .10 .05
❑ 422 Bob Tewksbury .20 .09
❑ 423 Len Matuszek .10 .05
❑ 424 Mike Kingery .10 .05
❑ 425 Dave Kingman .20 .09
❑ 426 Al Newman .10 .05
❑ 427 Gary Ward .10 .05
❑ 428 Ruppert Jones .10 .05
❑ 429 Harold Baines .20 .09
❑ 430 Pat Perry .10 .05
❑ 431 Terry Puhl .10 .05
❑ 432 Don Carman .10 .05
❑ 433 Eddie Milner .10 .05
❑ 434 LaMarr Hoyt .10 .05
❑ 435 Rick Rhoden .10 .05
❑ 436 Jose Uribe .10 .05
❑ 437 Ken Oberkfell .10 .05
❑ 438 Ron Davis .10 .05
❑ 439 Jesse Orosco .10 .05
❑ 440 Scott Bradley .10 .05
❑ 441 Randy Bush .10 .05
❑ 442 John Cerutti .10 .05
❑ 443 Roy Smalley .10 .05
❑ 444 Kelly Gruber .10 .05
❑ 445 Bob Kearney .10 .05
❑ 446 Ed Hearn .10 .05
❑ 447 Scott Sanderson .10 .05
❑ 448 Bruce Benedict .10 .05
❑ 449 Junior Ortiz .10 .05
❑ 450 Mike Aldrete .20 .09
❑ 451 Kevin McReynolds .10 .05
❑ 452 Rob Murphy .10 .05
❑ 453 Kent Tekulve .10 .05
❑ 454 Curt Ford .10 .05
❑ 455 Dave Lopes .20 .09
❑ 456 Bob Grich .20 .09
❑ 457 Jose DeLeon .10 .05
❑ 458 Andre Dawson .40 .18
❑ 459 Mike Flanagan .10 .05
❑ 460 Joey Meyer .10 .05
❑ 461 Chuck Cary .10 .05
❑ 462 Bill Buckner .20 .09
❑ 463 Bob Shirley .10 .05
❑ 464 Jeff Hamilton .10 .05
❑ 465 Phil Niekro .40 .18
❑ 466 Mark Gubicza .10 .05
❑ 467 Jerry Willard .10 .05
❑ 468 Bob Sebra .10 .05
❑ 469 Larry Parrish .10 .05
❑ 470 Charlie Hough .10 .05
❑ 471 Hal McRae .20 .09
❑ 472 Dave Leiper .10 .05
❑ 473 Mel Hall .10 .05
❑ 474 Dan Pasqua .10 .05
❑ 475 Bob Welch .10 .05
❑ 476 Johnny Grubb .10 .05
❑ 477 Jim Traber .10 .05
❑ 478 Chris Bosio .20 .09
❑ 479 Mark McLemore .20 .09
❑ 480 John Morris .10 .05
❑ 481 Billy Hatcher .10 .05
❑ 482 Dan Schatzeder .10 .05
❑ 483 Rich Gossage .20 .09
❑ 484 Jim Morrison .10 .05
❑ 485 Bob Brenly .10 .05
❑ 486 Bill Schroeder .10 .05
❑ 487 Mookie Wilson .20 .09
❑ 488 Dave Martinez .20 .09
❑ 489 Harold Reynolds .20 .09
❑ 490 Jeff Hearron .10 .05
❑ 491 Mickey Hatcher .10 .05
❑ 492 Barry Larkin 1.50 .70
❑ 493 Bob James .10 .05
❑ 494 John Habyan .10 .05
❑ 495 Jim Adduci .10 .05

❑	496	Mike Heath	.10	.05
❑	497	Tim Stoddard	.10	.05
❑	498	Tony Armas	.10	.05
❑	499	Dennis Powell	.10	.05
❑	500	Checklist 452-557	.10	.05
❑	501	Chris Bando	.10	.05
❑	502	David Cone	4.00	1.80
❑	503	Jay Howell	.10	.05
❑	504	Tom Foley	.10	.05
❑	505	Ray Chadwick	.10	.05
❑	506	Mike Loynd	.10	.05
❑	507	Neil Allen	.10	.05
❑	508	Danny Darwin	.10	.05
❑	509	Rick Schu	.10	.05
❑	510	Jose Oquendo	.10	.05
❑	511	Gene Walter	.10	.05
❑	512	Terry McGriff	.10	.05
❑	513	Ken Griffey	.20	.09
❑	514	Benny Distefano	.10	.05
❑	515	Terry Mulholland	.20	.09
❑	516	Ed Lynch	.10	.05
❑	517	Bill Swift	.10	.05
❑	518	Manny Lee	.10	.05
❑	519	Andre David	.10	.05
❑	520	Scott McGregor	.10	.05
❑	521	Rick Manning	.10	.05
❑	522	Willie Hernandez	.10	.05
❑	523	Marty Barrett	.10	.05
❑	524	Wayne Tolleson	.10	.05
❑	525	Jose Gonzalez	.10	.05
❑	526	Cory Snyder	.10	.05
❑	527	Buddy Biancalana	.10	.05
❑	528	Moose Haas	.10	.05
❑	529	Wilfredo Tejada	.10	.05
❑	530	Stu Cliburn	.10	.05
❑	531	Dale Mohorcic	.10	.05
❑	532	Ron Hassey	.10	.05
❑	533	Ty Gainey	.10	.05
❑	534	Jerry Royster	.10	.05
❑	535	Mike Maddux	.10	.05
❑	536	Ted Power	.10	.05
❑	537	Ted Simmons	.20	.09
❑	538	Rafael Belliard	.10	.05
❑	539	Chico Walker	.10	.05
❑	540	Bob Forsch	.10	.05
❑	541	John Stefero	.10	.05
❑	542	Dale Sveum	.10	.05
❑	543	Mark Thurmond	.10	.05
❑	544	Jeff Sellers	.10	.05
❑	545	Joel Skinner	.10	.05
❑	546	Alex Trevino	.10	.05
❑	547	Randy Kutcher	.10	.05
❑	548	Joaquin Andujar	.10	.05
❑	549	Casey Candaele	.10	.05
❑	550	Jeff Russell	.10	.05
❑	551	John Candelaria	.10	.05
❑	552	Joe Cowley	.10	.05
❑	553	Danny Cox	.10	.05
❑	554	Denny Walling	.10	.05
❑	555	Bruce Ruffin	.10	.05
❑	556	Buddy Bell	.20	.09
❑	557	Jimmy Jones	.10	.05
❑	558	Bobby Bonilla	.75	.35
❑	559	Jeff D. Robinson	.10	.05
❑	560	Ed Olwine	.10	.05
❑	561	Glenallen Hill	.40	.18
❑	562	Lee Mazzilli	.10	.05
❑	563	Mike G. Brown P	.10	.05
❑	564	George Frazier	.10	.05
❑	565	Mike Sharperson	.10	.05
❑	566	Mark Portugal	.20	.09
❑	567	Rick Leach	.10	.05
❑	568	Mark Langston	.10	.05
❑	569	Rafael Santana	.10	.05
❑	570	Manny Trillo	.10	.05
❑	571	Cliff Speck	.10	.05
❑	572	Bob Kipper	.10	.05
❑	573	Kelly Downs	.10	.05
❑	574	Randy Asadoor	.10	.05
❑	575	Dave Magadan	.20	.09
❑	576	Marvin Freeman	.10	.05
❑	577	Jeff Lahti	.10	.05
❑	578	Jeff Calhoun	.10	.05
❑	579	Gus Polidor	.10	.05
❑	580	Gene Nelson	.10	.05
❑	581	Tim Teufel	.10	.05
❑	582	Odell Jones	.10	.05
❑	583	Mark Ryal	.10	.05
❑	584	Randy O'Neal	.10	.05
❑	585	Mike Greenwell	.40	.18
❑	586	Ray Knight	.10	.05
❑	587	Ralph Bryant	.10	.05
❑	588	Carmen Castillo	.10	.05
❑	589	Ed Wojna	.10	.05
❑	590	Stan Javier	.10	.05
❑	591	Jeff Musselman	.10	.05
❑	592	Mike Stanley	.40	.18
❑	593	Darrell Porter	.10	.05
❑	594	Drew Hall	.10	.05
❑	595	Rob Nelson	.10	.05
❑	596	Bryan Oelkers	.10	.05
❑	597	Scott Nielsen	.10	.05
❑	598	Brian Holton	.10	.05
❑	599	Kevin Mitchell	.10	.05
❑	600	Checklist 558-660	.10	.05
❑	601	Jackie Gutierrez	.10	.05
❑	602	Barry Jones	.10	.05
❑	603	Jerry Narron	.10	.05
❑	604	Steve Lake	.10	.05
❑	605	Jim Pankovits	.10	.05
❑	606	Ed Romero	.10	.05
❑	607	Dave LaPoint	.10	.05
❑	608	Don Robinson	.10	.05
❑	609	Mike Krukow	.10	.05
❑	610	Dave Valle	.10	.05
❑	611	Len Dykstra	.10	.05
❑	612	Roberto Clemente PUZ	.50	.23
❑	613	Mike Trujillo	.10	.05
❑	614	Damaso Garcia	.10	.05
❑	615	Neal Heaton	.10	.05
❑	616	Juan Berenguer	.10	.05
❑	617	Steve Carlton	.40	.18
❑	618	Gary Lucas	.10	.05
❑	619	Geno Petralli	.10	.05
❑	620	Rick Aguilera	.20	.09
❑	621	Fred McGriff	.50	.23
❑	622	Dave Henderson	.10	.05
❑	623	Dave Clark	.20	.09
❑	624	Angel Salazar	.10	.05
❑	625	Randy Hunt	.10	.05
❑	626	John Gibbons	.10	.05
❑	627	Kevin Brown	8.00	3.60
❑	628	Bill Dawley	.10	.05
❑	629	Aurelio Lopez	.10	.05
❑	630	Charles Hudson	.10	.05
❑	631	Ray Soff	.10	.05
❑	632	Ray Hayward	.10	.05
❑	633	Spike Owen	.10	.05
❑	634	Glenn Hubbard	.10	.05
❑	635	Kevin Elster	.10	.05
❑	636	Mike LaCoss	.10	.05
❑	637	Dwayne Henry	.10	.05
❑	638	Rey Quinones	.10	.05
❑	639	Jim Clancy	.10	.05
❑	640	Larry Andersen	.10	.05
❑	641	Calvin Schiraldi	.10	.05
❑	642	Stan Jefferson	.10	.05
❑	643	Marc Sullivan	.10	.05
❑	644	Mark Grant	.10	.05
❑	645	Cliff Johnson	.10	.05
❑	646	Howard Johnson	.10	.05
❑	647	Dave Sax	.10	.05
❑	648	Dave Stewart	.20	.09
❑	649	Danny Heep	.10	.05
❑	650	Joe Johnson	.10	.05
❑	651	Bob Brower	.10	.05
❑	652	Rob Woodward	.10	.05
❑	653	John Mizerock	.10	.05
❑	654	Tim Pyznarski	.10	.05
❑	655	Luis Aquino	.10	.05
❑	656	Mickey Brantley	.10	.05
❑	657	Doyle Alexander	.10	.05
❑	658	Sammy Stewart	.10	.05
❑	659	Jim Acker	.10	.05
❑	660	Pete Ladd	.10	.05

1987 Donruss Rookies

	MINT	NRMT
COMP.FACT.SET (56)	40.00	18.00
COMMON CARD (1-56)	.10	.05

❑	1	Mark McGwire	20.00	9.00
❑	2	Eric Bell	.10	.05
❑	3	Mark Williamson	.10	.05
❑	4	Mike Greenwell	.75	.35
❑	5	Ellis Burks	1.50	.70
❑	6	DeWayne Buice	.10	.05
❑	7	Mark McLemore	.25	.11
❑	8	Devon White	.75	.35
❑	9	Willie Fraser	.10	.05
❑	10	Les Lancaster	.10	.05
❑	11	Ken Williams	.10	.05
❑	12	Matt Nokes	.25	.11
❑	13	Jeff M. Robinson	.10	.05
❑	14	Bo Jackson	1.00	.45
❑	15	Kevin Seitzer	.75	.35
❑	16	Billy Ripken	.10	.05
❑	17	B.J. Surhoff	.75	.35
❑	18	Chuck Crim	.10	.05
❑	19	Mike Birkbeck	.10	.05
❑	20	Chris Bosio	.25	.11
❑	21	Les Straker	.10	.05
❑	22	Mark Davidson	.10	.05
❑	23	Gene Larkin	.10	.05
❑	24	Ken Gerhart	.10	.05
❑	25	Luis Polonia	.25	.11
❑	26	Terry Steinbach	.75	.35
❑	27	Mickey Brantley	.10	.05
❑	28	Mike Stanley	.75	.35
❑	29	Jerry Browne	.10	.05
❑	30	Todd Benzinger	.10	.05
❑	31	Fred McGriff	1.00	.45
❑	32	Mike Henneman	.75	.35
❑	33	Casey Candaele	.10	.05
❑	34	Dave Magadan	.25	.11
❑	35	David Cone	2.50	1.10
❑	36	Mike Jackson	.75	.35
❑	37	John Mitchell	.10	.05
❑	38	Mike Dunne	.10	.05
❑	39	John Smiley	.25	.11
❑	40	Joe Magrane	.10	.05
❑	41	Jim Lindeman	.10	.05
❑	42	Shane Mack	.25	.11
❑	43	Stan Jefferson	.10	.05
❑	44	Benito Santiago	.25	.11
❑	45	Matt Williams	2.50	1.10
❑	46	Dave Meads	.10	.05
❑	47	Rafael Palmeiro	2.00	.90
❑	48	Bill Long	.10	.05
❑	49	Bob Brower	.10	.05
❑	50	James Steels	.10	.05
❑	51	Paul Noce	.10	.05
❑	52	Greg Maddux	15.00	6.75
❑	53	Jeff Musselman	.10	.05
❑	54	Brian Holton	.10	.05
❑	55	Chuck Jackson	.10	.05
❑	56	Checklist 1-56	.10	.05

1988 Donruss

	MINT	NRMT
COMPLETE SET (660)	8.00	3.60
COMP.FACT.SET (660)	10.00	4.50
COMMON CARD (1-660)	.05	.02
COMMON SP (648-660)	.07	.03
COMP.MUSIAL PUZZLE	1.00	.45

❑	1	Mark McGwire DK	1.00	.45
❑	2	Tim Raines DK	.07	.03

3	Benito Santiago DK	.05	.02
4	Alan Trammell DK	.10	.05
5	Danny Tartabull DK	.05	.02
6	Ron Darling DK	.05	.02
7	Paul Molitor DK	.20	.09
8	Devon White DK	.05	.02
9	Andre Dawson DK	.20	.09
10	Julio Franco DK	.05	.02
11	Scott Fletcher DK	.05	.02
12	Tony Fernandez DK	.05	.02
13	Shane Rawley DK	.05	.02
14	Kal Daniels DK	.05	.02
15	Jack Clark DK	.10	.05
16	Dwight Evans DK	.05	.02
17	Tommy John DK	.05	.02
18	Andy Van Slyke DK	.05	.02
19	Gary Gaetti DK	.05	.02
20	Mark Langston DK	.05	.02
21	Will Clark DK	.20	.09
22	Glenn Hubbard DK	.05	.02
23	Billy Hatcher DK	.05	.02
24	Bob Welch DK	.05	.02
25	Ivan Calderon DK	.05	.02
26	Cal Ripken DK	.40	.18
27	DK Checklist 1-26	.05	.02
28	Mackey Sasser RR	.05	.02
29	Jeff Treadway RR	.05	.02
30	Mike Campbell RR	.05	.02
31	Lance Johnson RR	.20	.09
32	Nelson Liriano RR	.05	.02
33	Shawn Abner RR	.05	.02
34	Roberto Alomar RR	1.00	.45
35	Shawn Hillegas RR	.05	.02
36	Joey Meyer RR	.05	.02
37	Kevin Elster RR	.05	.02
38	Jose Lind RR	.05	.02
39	Kirt Manwaring RR	.05	.02
40	Mark Grace RR	.60	.25
41	Jody Reed RR	.10	.05
42	John Farrell RR	.05	.02
43	Al Leiter RR	.25	.11
44	Gary Thurman RR	.05	.02
45	Vicente Palacios RR	.05	.02
46	Eddie Williams RR	.05	.02
47	Jack McDowell RR	.20	.09
48	Ken Dixon	.05	.02
49	Mike Birkbeck	.05	.02
50	Eric King	.05	.02
51	Roger Clemens	.40	.18
52	Pat Clements	.05	.02
53	Fernando Valenzuela	.10	.05
54	Mark Gubicza	.05	.02
55	Jay Howell	.05	.02
56	Floyd Youmans	.05	.02
57	Ed Correa	.05	.02
58	DeWayne Buice	.05	.02
59	Jose DeLeon	.05	.02
60	Danny Cox	.05	.02
61	Nolan Ryan	.75	.35
62	Steve Bedrosian	.05	.02
63	Tom Browning	.05	.02
64	Mark Davis	.05	.02
65	R.J. Reynolds	.05	.02
66	Kevin Mitchell	.10	.05
67	Ken Oberkfell	.05	.02
68	Rick Sutcliffe	.05	.02
69	Dwight Gooden	.10	.05
70	Scott Bankhead	.05	.02
71	Bert Blyleven	.10	.05
72	Jimmy Key	.10	.05
73	Les Straker	.05	.02
74	Jim Clancy	.05	.02
75	Mike Moore	.05	.02
76	Ron Darling	.05	.02
77	Ed Lynch	.05	.02
78	Dale Murphy	.20	.09
79	Doug Drabek	.05	.02
80	Scott Garrelts	.05	.02
81	Ed Whitson	.05	.02
82	Rob Murphy	.05	.02
83	Shane Rawley	.05	.02
84	Greg Mathews	.05	.02
85	Jim Deshaies	.05	.02
86	Mike Witt	.05	.02
87	Donnie Hill	.05	.02
88	Jeff Reed	.05	.02
89	Mike Boddicker	.05	.02
90	Ted Higuera	.05	.02
91	Walt Terrell	.05	.02
92	Bob Stanley	.05	.02
93	Dave Righetti	.05	.02
94	Orel Hershiser	.10	.05
95	Chris Bando	.05	.02
96	Bret Saberhagen	.10	.05
97	Curt Young	.05	.02
98	Tim Burke	.05	.02
99	Charlie Hough	.10	.05
100A	Checklist 28-137	.05	.02
100B	Checklist 28-133	.05	.02
101	Bobby Witt	.05	.02
102	George Brett	.40	.18
103	Mickey Tettleton	.10	.05
104	Scott Bailes	.05	.02
105	Mike Pagliarulo	.05	.02
106	Mike Scioscia	.05	.02
107	Tom Brookens	.05	.02
108	Ray Knight	.05	.02
109	Dan Plesac	.05	.02
110	Wally Joyner	.20	.09
111	Bob Forsch	.05	.02
112	Mike Scott	.05	.02
113	Kevin Gross	.05	.02
114	Benito Santiago	.05	.02
115	Bob Kipper	.05	.02
116	Mike Krukow	.05	.02
117	Chris Bosio	.05	.02
118	Sid Fernandez	.05	.02
119	Jody Davis	.05	.02
120	Mike Morgan	.05	.02
121	Mark Eichhorn	.05	.02
122	Jeff Reardon	.10	.05
123	John Franco	.10	.05
124	Richard Dotson	.05	.02
125	Eric Bell	.05	.02
126	Juan Nieves	.05	.02
127	Jack Morris	.10	.05
128	Rick Rhoden	.05	.02
129	Rich Gedman	.05	.02
130	Ken Howell	.05	.02
131	Brook Jacoby	.05	.02
132	Danny Jackson	.05	.02
133	Gene Nelson	.05	.02
134	Neal Heaton	.05	.02
135	Willie Fraser	.05	.02
136	Jose Guzman	.05	.02
137	Ozzie Guillen	.05	.02
138	Bob Knepper	.05	.02
139	Mike Jackson	.20	.09
140	Joe Magrane	.05	.02
141	Jimmy Jones	.05	.02
142	Ted Power	.05	.02
143	Ozzie Virgil	.05	.02
144	Felix Fermin	.05	.02
145	Kelly Downs	.05	.02
146	Shawon Dunston	.05	.02
147	Scott Bradley	.05	.02
148	Dave Stieb	.05	.02
149	Frank Viola	.05	.02
150	Terry Kennedy	.05	.02
151	Bill Wegman	.05	.02
152	Matt Nokes	.05	.02
153	Wade Boggs	.20	.09
154	Wayne Tolleson	.05	.02
155	Mariano Duncan	.05	.02
156	Julio Franco	.05	.02
157	Charlie Leibrandt	.05	.02
158	Terry Steinbach	.10	.05
159	Mike Fitzgerald	.05	.02
160	Jack Lazorko	.05	.02
161	Mitch Williams	.05	.02
162	Greg Walker	.05	.02
163	Alan Ashby	.05	.02
164	Tony Gwynn	.50	.23
165	Bruce Ruffin	.05	.02
166	Ron Robinson	.05	.02
167	Zane Smith	.05	.02
168	Junior Ortiz	.05	.02
169	Jamie Moyer	.05	.02
170	Tony Pena	.05	.02
171	Cal Ripken	.75	.35
172	B.J. Surhoff	.10	.05
173	Lou Whitaker	.10	.05
174	Ellis Burks	.40	.18
175	Ron Guidry	.05	.02
176	Steve Sax	.05	.02
177	Danny Tartabull	.05	.02
178	Carney Lansford	.10	.05
179	Casey Candaele	.05	.02
180	Scott Fletcher	.05	.02
181	Mark McLemore	.05	.02
182	Ivan Calderon	.05	.02
183	Jack Clark	.10	.05
184	Glenn Davis	.05	.02
185	Luis Aguayo	.05	.02
186	Bo Diaz	.05	.02
187	Stan Jefferson	.05	.02
188	Sid Bream	.05	.02
189	Bob Brenly	.05	.02
190	Dion James	.05	.02
191	Leon Durham	.05	.02
192	Jesse Orosco	.05	.02
193	Alvin Davis	.05	.02
194	Gary Gaetti	.10	.05
195	Fred McGriff	.20	.09
196	Steve Lombardozzi	.05	.02
197	Rance Mulliniks	.05	.02
198	Rey Quinones	.05	.02
199	Gary Carter	.15	.07
200A	Checklist 138-247	.05	.02
200B	Checklist 134-239	.05	.02
201	Keith Moreland	.05	.02
202	Ken Griffey	.05	.02
203	Tommy Gregg	.05	.02
204	Will Clark	.25	.11
205	John Kruk	.10	.05
206	Buddy Bell	.10	.05
207	Von Hayes	.05	.02
208	Tommy Herr	.05	.02
209	Craig Reynolds	.05	.02
210	Gary Pettis	.05	.02
211	Harold Baines	.10	.05
212	Vance Law	.05	.02
213	Ken Gerhart	.05	.02
214	Jim Gantner	.05	.02
215	Chet Lemon	.05	.02
216	Dwight Evans	.10	.05
217	Don Mattingly	.30	.14
218	Franklin Stubbs	.05	.02
219	Pat Tabler	.05	.02
220	Bo Jackson	.20	.09
221	Tony Phillips	.05	.02
222	Tim Wallach	.05	.02
223	Ruben Sierra	.05	.02
224	Steve Buechele	.05	.02
225	Frank White	.10	.05
226	Alfredo Griffin	.05	.02
227	Greg Swindell	.05	.02
228	Willie Randolph	.10	.05
229	Mike Marshall	.05	.02
230	Alan Trammell	.15	.07
231	Eddie Murray	.20	.09
232	Dale Sveum	.05	.02
233	Dick Schofield	.05	.02
234	Jose Oquendo	.05	.02
235	Bill Doran	.05	.02
236	Milt Thompson	.05	.02
237	Marvell Wynne	.05	.02
238	Bobby Bonilla	.15	.07

❑ 239	Chris Speier	.05	.02
❑ 240	Glenn Braggs	.05	.02
❑ 241	Wally Backman	.05	.02
❑ 242	Ryne Sandberg	.25	.11
❑ 243	Phil Bradley	.05	.02
❑ 244	Kelly Gruber	.05	.02
❑ 245	Tom Brunansky	.05	.02
❑ 246	Ron Oester	.05	.02
❑ 247	Bobby Thigpen	.05	.02
❑ 248	Fred Lynn	.05	.02
❑ 249	Paul Molitor	.20	.09
❑ 250	Darrell Evans	.10	.05
❑ 251	Gary Ward	.05	.02
❑ 252	Bruce Hurst	.05	.02
❑ 253	Bob Welch	.05	.02
❑ 254	Joe Carter	.20	.09
❑ 255	Willie Wilson	.05	.02
❑ 256	Mark McGwire	2.00	.90
❑ 257	Mitch Webster	.05	.02
❑ 258	Brian Downing	.05	.02
❑ 259	Mike Stanley	.10	.05
❑ 260	Carlton Fisk	.20	.09
❑ 261	Billy Hatcher	.05	.02
❑ 262	Glenn Wilson	.05	.02
❑ 263	Ozzie Smith	.25	.11
❑ 264	Randy Ready	.05	.02
❑ 265	Kurt Stillwell	.05	.02
❑ 266	David Palmer	.05	.02
❑ 267	Mike Diaz	.05	.02
❑ 268	Robby Thompson	.05	.02
❑ 269	Andre Dawson	.20	.09
❑ 270	Lee Guetterman	.05	.02
❑ 271	Willie Upshaw	.05	.02
❑ 272	Randy Bush	.05	.02
❑ 273	Larry Sheets	.05	.02
❑ 274	Rob Deer	.05	.02
❑ 275	Kirk Gibson	.10	.05
❑ 276	Marty Barrett	.05	.02
❑ 277	Rickey Henderson	.20	.09
❑ 278	Pedro Guerrero	.05	.02
❑ 279	Brett Butler	.10	.05
❑ 280	Kevin Seitzer	.10	.05
❑ 281	Mike Davis	.05	.02
❑ 282	Andres Galarraga	.20	.09
❑ 283	Devon White	.10	.05
❑ 284	Pete O'Brien	.05	.02
❑ 285	Jerry Hairston	.05	.02
❑ 286	Kevin Bass	.05	.02
❑ 287	Carmelo Martinez	.05	.02
❑ 288	Juan Samuel	.05	.02
❑ 289	Kal Daniels	.05	.02
❑ 290	Albert Hall	.05	.02
❑ 291	Andy Van Slyke	.10	.05
❑ 292	Lee Smith	.10	.05
❑ 293	Vince Coleman	.05	.02
❑ 294	Tom Niedenfuer	.05	.02
❑ 295	Robin Yount	.20	.09
❑ 296	Jeff M. Robinson	.05	.02
❑ 297	Todd Benzinger	.05	.02
❑ 298	Dave Winfield	.20	.09
❑ 299	Mickey Hatcher	.05	.02
❑ 300A	Checklist 248-357	.05	.02
❑ 300B	Checklist 240-345	.05	.02
❑ 301	Bud Black	.05	.02
❑ 302	Jose Canseco	.20	.09
❑ 303	Tom Foley	.05	.02
❑ 304	Pete Incaviglia	.05	.02
❑ 305	Bob Boone	.10	.05
❑ 306	Bill Long	.05	.02
❑ 307	Willie McGee	.10	.05
❑ 308	Ken Caminiti	.75	.35
❑ 309	Darren Daulton	.10	.05
❑ 310	Tracy Jones	.05	.02
❑ 311	Greg Booker	.05	.02
❑ 312	Mike LaValliere	.05	.02
❑ 313	Chili Davis	.15	.07
❑ 314	Glenn Hubbard	.05	.02
❑ 315	Paul Noce	.05	.02
❑ 316	Keith Hernandez	.10	.05
❑ 317	Mark Langston	.05	.02
❑ 318	Keith Atherton	.05	.02
❑ 319	Tony Fernandez	.05	.02
❑ 320	Kent Hrbek	.10	.05
❑ 321	John Cerutti	.05	.02
❑ 322	Mike Kingery	.05	.02
❑ 323	Dave Magadan	.05	.02
❑ 324	Rafael Palmeiro	.20	.09
❑ 325	Jeff Dedmon	.05	.02
❑ 326	Barry Bonds	.50	.23
❑ 327	Jeffrey Leonard	.05	.02
❑ 328	Tim Flannery	.05	.02
❑ 329	Dave Concepcion	.10	.05
❑ 330	Mike Schmidt	.25	.11
❑ 331	Bill Dawley	.05	.02
❑ 332	Larry Andersen	.05	.02
❑ 333	Jack Howell	.05	.02
❑ 334	Ken Williams	.05	.02
❑ 335	Bryn Smith	.05	.02
❑ 336	Billy Ripken	.05	.02
❑ 337	Greg Brock	.05	.02
❑ 338	Mike Heath	.05	.02
❑ 339	Mike Greenwell	.05	.02
❑ 340	Claudell Washington	.05	.02
❑ 341	Jose Gonzalez	.05	.02
❑ 342	Mel Hall	.05	.02
❑ 343	Jim Eisenreich	.20	.09
❑ 344	Tony Bernazard	.05	.02
❑ 345	Tim Raines	.10	.05
❑ 346	Bob Brower	.05	.02
❑ 347	Larry Parrish	.05	.02
❑ 348	Thad Bosley	.05	.02
❑ 349	Dennis Eckersley	.10	.05
❑ 350	Cory Snyder	.05	.02
❑ 351	Rick Cerone	.05	.02
❑ 352	John Shelby	.05	.02
❑ 353	Larry Herndon	.05	.02
❑ 354	John Habyan	.05	.02
❑ 355	Chuck Crim	.05	.02
❑ 356	Gus Polidor	.05	.02
❑ 357	Ken Dayley	.05	.02
❑ 358	Danny Darwin	.05	.02
❑ 359	Lance Parrish	.05	.02
❑ 360	James Steels	.05	.02
❑ 361	Al Pedrique	.05	.02
❑ 362	Mike Aldrete	.05	.02
❑ 363	Juan Castillo	.05	.02
❑ 364	Len Dykstra	.10	.05
❑ 365	Luis Quinones	.05	.02
❑ 366	Jim Presley	.05	.02
❑ 367	Lloyd Moseby	.05	.02
❑ 368	Kirby Puckett	.30	.14
❑ 369	Eric Davis	.10	.05
❑ 370	Gary Redus	.05	.02
❑ 371	Dave Schmidt	.05	.02
❑ 372	Mark Clear	.05	.02
❑ 373	Dave Bergman	.05	.02
❑ 374	Charles Hudson	.05	.02
❑ 375	Calvin Schiraldi	.05	.02
❑ 376	Alex Trevino	.05	.02
❑ 377	Tom Candiotti	.05	.02
❑ 378	Steve Farr	.05	.02
❑ 379	Mike Gallego	.05	.02
❑ 380	Andy McGaffigan	.05	.02
❑ 381	Kirk McCaskill	.05	.02
❑ 382	Oddibe McDowell	.05	.02
❑ 383	Floyd Bannister	.05	.02
❑ 384	Denny Walling	.05	.02
❑ 385	Don Carman	.05	.02
❑ 386	Todd Worrell	.10	.05
❑ 387	Eric Show	.05	.02
❑ 388	Dave Parker	.10	.05
❑ 389	Rick Mahler	.05	.02
❑ 390	Mike Dunne	.05	.02
❑ 391	Candy Maldonado	.05	.02
❑ 392	Bob Dernier	.05	.02
❑ 393	Dave Valle	.05	.02
❑ 394	Ernie Whitt	.05	.02
❑ 395	Juan Berenguer	.05	.02
❑ 396	Mike Young	.05	.02
❑ 397	Mike Felder	.05	.02
❑ 398	Willie Hernandez	.05	.02
❑ 399	Jim Rice	.10	.05
❑ 400A	Checklist 358-467	.05	.02
❑ 400B	Checklist 346-451	.05	.02
❑ 401	Tommy John	.10	.05
❑ 402	Brian Holton	.05	.02
❑ 403	Carmen Castillo	.05	.02
❑ 404	Jamie Quirk	.05	.02
❑ 405	Dwayne Murphy	.05	.02
❑ 406	Jeff Parrett	.05	.02
❑ 407	Don Sutton	.20	.09
❑ 408	Jerry Browne	.05	.02
❑ 409	Jim Winn	.05	.02
❑ 410	Dave Smith	.05	.02
❑ 411	Shane Mack	.05	.02
❑ 412	Greg Gross	.05	.02
❑ 413	Nick Esasky	.05	.02
❑ 414	Damaso Garcia	.05	.02
❑ 415	Brian Fisher	.05	.02
❑ 416	Brian Dayett	.05	.02
❑ 417	Curt Ford	.05	.02
❑ 418	Mark Williamson	.05	.02
❑ 419	Bill Schroeder	.05	.02
❑ 420	Mike Henneman	.10	.05
❑ 421	John Marzano	.05	.02
❑ 422	Ron Kittle	.05	.02
❑ 423	Matt Young	.05	.02
❑ 424	Steve Balboni	.05	.02
❑ 425	Luis Polonia	.05	.02
❑ 426	Randy St.Claire	.05	.02
❑ 427	Greg Harris	.05	.02
❑ 428	Johnny Ray	.05	.02
❑ 429	Ray Searage	.05	.02
❑ 430	Ricky Horton	.05	.02
❑ 431	Gerald Young	.05	.02
❑ 432	Rick Schu	.05	.02
❑ 433	Paul O'Neill	.15	.07
❑ 434	Rich Gossage	.10	.05
❑ 435	John Cangelosi	.05	.02
❑ 436	Mike LaCoss	.05	.02
❑ 437	Gerald Perry	.05	.02
❑ 438	Dave Martinez	.05	.02
❑ 439	Darryl Strawberry	.10	.05
❑ 440	John Moses	.05	.02
❑ 441	Greg Gagne	.05	.02
❑ 442	Jesse Barfield	.05	.02
❑ 443	George Frazier	.05	.02
❑ 444	Garth Iorg	.05	.02
❑ 445	Ed Nunez	.05	.02
❑ 446	Rick Aguilera	.10	.05
❑ 447	Jerry Mumphrey	.05	.02
❑ 448	Rafael Ramirez	.05	.02
❑ 449	John Smiley	.10	.05
❑ 450	Atlee Hammaker	.05	.02
❑ 451	Lance McCullers	.05	.02
❑ 452	Guy Hoffman	.05	.02
❑ 453	Chris James	.05	.02
❑ 454	Terry Pendleton	.10	.05
❑ 455	Dave Meads	.05	.02
❑ 456	Bill Buckner	.10	.05
❑ 457	John Pawlowski	.05	.02
❑ 458	Bob Sebra	.05	.02
❑ 459	Jim Dwyer	.05	.02
❑ 460	Jay Aldrich	.05	.02
❑ 461	Frank Tanana	.05	.02
❑ 462	Oil Can Boyd	.05	.02
❑ 463	Dan Pasqua	.05	.02
❑ 464	Tim Crews	.05	.02
❑ 465	Andy Allanson	.05	.02
❑ 466	Bill Pecota	.05	.02
❑ 467	Steve Ontiveros	.05	.02
❑ 468	Hubie Brooks	.05	.02
❑ 469	Paul Kilgus	.05	.02
❑ 470	Dale Mohorcic	.05	.02
❑ 471	Dan Quisenberry	.05	.02
❑ 472	Dave Stewart	.10	.05
❑ 473	Dave Clark	.05	.02
❑ 474	Joel Skinner	.05	.02
❑ 475	Dave Anderson	.05	.02
❑ 476	Dan Petry	.05	.02
❑ 477	Carl Nichols	.05	.02
❑ 478	Ernest Riles	.05	.02
❑ 479	George Hendrick	.05	.02
❑ 480	John Morris	.05	.02
❑ 481	Manny Hernandez	.05	.02
❑ 482	Jeff Stone	.05	.02
❑ 483	Chris Brown	.05	.02
❑ 484	Mike Bielecki	.05	.02
❑ 485	Dave Dravecky	.10	.05
❑ 486	Rick Manning	.05	.02
❑ 487	Bill Almon	.05	.02
❑ 488	Jim Sundberg	.05	.02
❑ 489	Ken Phelps	.05	.02
❑ 490	Tom Henke	.05	.02
❑ 491	Dan Gladden	.05	.02

	Card	Mint	NrMt
❑	492 Barry Larkin	.20	.09
❑	493 Fred Manrique	.05	.02
❑	494 Mike Griffin	.05	.02
❑	495 Mark Knudson	.05	.02
❑	496 Bill Madlock	.10	.05
❑	497 Tim Stoddard	.05	.02
❑	498 Sam Horn	.05	.02
❑	499 Tracy Woodson	.05	.02
❑	500A Checklist 468-577	.05	.02
❑	500B Checklist 452-557	.05	.02
❑	501 Ken Schrom	.05	.02
❑	502 Angel Salazar	.05	.02
❑	503 Eric Plunk	.05	.02
❑	504 Joe Hesketh	.05	.02
❑	505 Greg Minton	.05	.02
❑	506 Geno Petralli	.05	.02
❑	507 Bob James	.05	.02
❑	508 Robbie Wine	.05	.02
❑	509 Jeff Calhoun	.05	.02
❑	510 Steve Lake	.05	.02
❑	511 Mark Grant	.05	.02
❑	512 Frank Williams	.05	.02
❑	513 Jeff Blauser	.25	.11
❑	514 Bob Walk	.05	.02
❑	515 Craig Lefferts	.05	.02
❑	516 Manny Trillo	.05	.02
❑	517 Jerry Reed	.05	.02
❑	518 Rick Leach	.05	.02
❑	519 Mark Davidson	.05	.02
❑	520 Jeff Ballard	.05	.02
❑	521 Dave Stapleton	.05	.02
❑	522 Pat Sheridan	.05	.02
❑	523 Al Nipper	.05	.02
❑	524 Steve Trout	.05	.02
❑	525 Jeff Hamilton	.05	.02
❑	526 Tommy Hinzo	.05	.02
❑	527 Lonnie Smith	.05	.02
❑	528 Greg Cadaret	.05	.02
❑	529 Bob McClure UER (Rob on front)	.05	.02
❑	530 Chuck Finley	.15	.07
❑	531 Jeff Russell	.05	.02
❑	532 Steve Lyons	.05	.02
❑	533 Terry Puhl	.05	.02
❑	534 Eric Nolte	.05	.02
❑	535 Kent Tekulve	.05	.02
❑	536 Pat Pacillo	.05	.02
❑	537 Charlie Puleo	.05	.02
❑	538 Tom Prince	.05	.02
❑	539 Greg Maddux	1.25	.55
❑	540 Jim Lindeman	.05	.02
❑	541 Pete Stanicek	.05	.02
❑	542 Steve Kiefer	.05	.02
❑	543A Jim Morrison ERR (No decimal before lifetime average)	.20	.09
❑	543B Jim Morrison COR	.05	.02
❑	544 Spike Owen	.05	.02
❑	545 Jay Buhner	.50	.23
❑	546 Mike Devereaux	.10	.05
❑	547 Jerry Don Gleaton	.05	.02
❑	548 Jose Rijo	.05	.02
❑	549 Dennis Martinez	.10	.05
❑	550 Mike Loynd	.05	.02
❑	551 Darrell Miller	.05	.02
❑	552 Dave LaPoint	.05	.02
❑	553 John Tudor	.05	.02
❑	554 Rocky Childress	.05	.02
❑	555 Wally Ritchie	.05	.02
❑	556 Terry McGriff	.05	.02
❑	557 Dave Leiper	.05	.02
❑	558 Jeff D. Robinson	.05	.02
❑	559 Jose Uribe	.05	.02
❑	560 Ted Simmons	.10	.05
❑	561 Les Lancaster	.05	.02
❑	562 Keith A. Miller	.05	.02
❑	563 Harold Reynolds	.10	.05
❑	564 Gene Larkin	.05	.02
❑	565 Cecil Fielder	.15	.07
❑	566 Roy Smalley	.05	.02
❑	567 Duane Ward	.05	.02
❑	568 Bill Wilkinson	.05	.02
❑	569 Howard Johnson	.05	.02
❑	570 Frank DiPino	.05	.02
❑	571 Pete Smith	.05	.02
❑	572 Darnell Coles	.05	.02
❑	573 Don Robinson	.05	.02
❑	574 Rob Nelson UER (Career 0 RBI, but 1 RBI in '87)	.05	.02
❑	575 Dennis Rasmussen	.05	.02
❑	576 Steve Jeltz UER (Photo actually Juan Samuel; Samuel noted for one batting glove and black bat)	.05	.02
❑	577 Tom Pagnozzi	.10	.05
❑	578 Ty Gainey	.05	.02
❑	579 Gary Lucas	.05	.02
❑	580 Ron Hassey	.05	.02
❑	581 Herm Winningham	.05	.02
❑	582 Rene Gonzales	.05	.02
❑	583 Brad Komminsk	.05	.02
❑	584 Doyle Alexander	.05	.02
❑	585 Jeff Sellers	.05	.02
❑	586 Bill Gullickson	.05	.02
❑	587 Tim Belcher	.10	.05
❑	588 Doug Jones	.20	.09
❑	589 Melido Perez	.05	.02
❑	590 Rick Honeycutt	.05	.02
❑	591 Pascual Perez	.05	.02
❑	592 Curt Wilkerson	.05	.02
❑	593 Steve Howe	.05	.02
❑	594 John Davis	.05	.02
❑	595 Storm Davis	.05	.02
❑	596 Sammy Stewart	.05	.02
❑	597 Neil Allen	.05	.02
❑	598 Alejandro Pena	.05	.02
❑	599 Mark Thurmond	.05	.02
❑	600A Checklist 578-660/BC1-26	.05	.02
❑	600B Checklist 558-660	.05	.02
❑	601 Jose Mesa	.15	.07
❑	602 Don August	.05	.02
❑	603 Terry Leach SP	.07	.03
❑	604 Tom Newell	.05	.02
❑	605 Randall Byers SP	.07	.03
❑	606 Jim Gott	.05	.02
❑	607 Harry Spilman	.05	.02
❑	608 John Candelaria	.05	.02
❑	609 Mike Brumley	.05	.02
❑	610 Mickey Brantley	.05	.02
❑	611 Jose Nunez SP	.07	.03
❑	612 Tom Nieto	.05	.02
❑	613 Rick Reuschel	.05	.02
❑	614 Lee Mazzilli SP	.07	.03
❑	615 Scott Lusader	.05	.02
❑	616 Bobby Meacham	.05	.02
❑	617 Kevin McReynolds SP	.07	.03
❑	618 Gene Garber	.05	.02
❑	619 Barry Lyons SP	.07	.03
❑	620 Randy Myers	.15	.07
❑	621 Donnie Moore	.05	.02
❑	622 Domingo Ramos	.05	.02
❑	623 Ed Romero	.05	.02
❑	624 Greg Myers	.05	.02
❑	625 Ripken Family (Cal Ripken Sr., Cal Ripken Jr., Billy Ripken)	.40	.18
❑	626 Pat Perry	.05	.02
❑	627 Andres Thomas SP	.07	.03
❑	628 Matt Williams SP	.50	.23
❑	629 Dave Hengel	.05	.02
❑	630 Jeff Musselman SP	.07	.03
❑	631 Tim Laudner	.05	.02
❑	632 Bob Ojeda SP	.07	.03
❑	633 Rafael Santana	.05	.02
❑	634 Wes Gardner	.05	.02
❑	635 Roberto Kelly SP	.20	.09
❑	636 Mike Flanagan SP	.07	.03
❑	637 Jay Bell	.25	.11
❑	638 Bob Melvin	.05	.02
❑	639 Damon Berryhill UER (Bats: Swithch)	.05	.02
❑	640 David Wells SP	.75	.35
❑	641 Stan Musial PUZ	.20	.09
❑	642 Doug Sisk	.05	.02
❑	643 Keith Hughes	.05	.02
❑	644 Tom Glavine	1.00	.45
❑	645 Al Newman	.05	.02
❑	646 Scott Sanderson	.05	.02
❑	647 Scott Terry	.05	.02
❑	648 Tim Teufel SP	.07	.03
❑	649 Garry Templeton SP	.07	.03
❑	650 Manny Lee SP	.07	.03
❑	651 Roger McDowell SP	.07	.03
❑	652 Mookie Wilson SP	.20	.09
❑	653 David Cone SP	.25	.11
❑	654 Ron Gant SP	.25	.11
❑	655 Joe Price SP	.07	.03
❑	656 George Bell SP	.10	.05
❑	657 Gregg Jefferies SP	.25	.11
❑	658 Todd Stottlemyre SP	.20	.09
❑	659 Geronimo Berroa SP	.25	.11
❑	660 Jerry Royster SP	.07	.03

1988 Donruss Rookies

		MINT	NRMT
	COMP.FACT.SET (56)	12.00	5.50
	COMMON CARD (1-56)	.15	.07
❑	1 Mark Grace	2.50	1.10
❑	2 Mike Campbell	.15	.07
❑	3 Todd Frohwirth	.15	.07
❑	4 Dave Stapleton	.15	.07
❑	5 Shawn Abner	.15	.07
❑	6 Jose Cecena	.15	.07
❑	7 Dave Gallagher	.15	.07
❑	8 Mark Parent	.15	.07
❑	9 Cecil Espy	.15	.07
❑	10 Pete Smith	.15	.07
❑	11 Jay Buhner	2.00	.90
❑	12 Pat Borders	.30	.14
❑	13 Doug Jennings	.15	.07
❑	14 Brady Anderson	1.50	.70
❑	15 Pete Stanicek	.15	.07
❑	16 Roberto Kelly	.60	.25
❑	17 Jeff Treadway	.15	.07
❑	18 Walt Weiss	.60	.25
❑	19 Paul Gibson	.15	.07
❑	20 Tim Crews	.15	.07
❑	21 Melido Perez	.15	.07
❑	22 Steve Peters	.15	.07
❑	23 Craig Worthington	.15	.07
❑	24 John Trautwein	.15	.07
❑	25 DeWayne Vaughn	.15	.07
❑	26 David Wells	3.00	1.35
❑	27 Al Leiter	1.00	.45
❑	28 Tim Belcher	.30	.14
❑	29 Johnny Paredes	.15	.07
❑	30 Chris Sabo	.30	.14
❑	31 Damon Berryhill	.15	.07
❑	32 Randy Milligan	.15	.07
❑	33 Gary Thurman	.15	.07
❑	34 Kevin Elster	.15	.07
❑	35 Roberto Alomar	4.00	1.80
❑	36 Edgar Martinez UER (Photo actually Edwin Nunez)	2.00	.90
❑	37 Todd Stottlemyre	.60	.25
❑	38 Joey Meyer	.15	.07
❑	39 Carl Nichols	.15	.07
❑	40 Jack McDowell	.60	.25
❑	41 Jose Bautista	.15	.07
❑	42 Sil Campusano	.15	.07
❑	43 John Dopson	.15	.07
❑	44 Jody Reed	.30	.14

❑ 45 Darrin Jackson .15 .07
❑ 46 Mike Capel .15 .07
❑ 47 Ron Gant .60 .25
❑ 48 John Davis .15 .07
❑ 49 Kevin Coffman .15 .07
❑ 50 Cris Carpenter .15 .07
❑ 51 Mackey Sasser .15 .07
❑ 52 Luis Alicea .30 .14
❑ 53 Bryan Harvey .30 .14
❑ 54 Steve Ellsworth .15 .07
❑ 55 Mike Macfarlane .15 .07
❑ 56 Checklist 1-56 .15 .07

1989 Donruss

	MINT	NRMT
COMPLETE SET (660)	20.00	9.00
COMP.FACT.SET (672)	20.00	9.00
COMMON CARD (1-660)	.05	.02
COMP.SPAHN PUZZLE	1.00	.45

❑ 1 Mike Greenwell DK .05 .02
❑ 2 Bobby Bonilla DK DP .10 .05
❑ 3 Pete Incaviglia DK .05 .02
❑ 4 Chris Sabo DK DP .05 .02
❑ 5 Robin Yount DK .10 .05
❑ 6 Tony Gwynn DK DP .20 .09
❑ 7 Carlton Fisk DK UER .10 .05
(OF on back)
❑ 8 Cory Snyder DK .05 .02
❑ 9 David Cone DK UER .10 .05
("hurdlers")
❑ 10 Kevin Seitzer DK .05 .02
❑ 11 Rick Reuschel DK .05 .02
❑ 12 Johnny Ray DK .05 .02
❑ 13 Dave Schmidt DK .05 .02
❑ 14 Andres Galarraga DK .10 .05
❑ 15 Kirk Gibson DK .05 .02
❑ 16 Fred McGriff DK .10 .05
❑ 17 Mark Grace DK .10 .05
❑ 18 Jeff M. Robinson DK .05 .02
❑ 19 Vince Coleman DK DP .05 .02
❑ 20 Dave Henderson DK .05 .02
❑ 21 Harold Reynolds DK .05 .02
❑ 22 Gerald Perry DK .05 .02
❑ 23 Frank Viola DK .05 .02
❑ 24 Steve Bedrosian DK .05 .02
❑ 25 Glenn Davis DK .05 .02
❑ 26 Don Mattingly DK UER .15 .07
(Doesn't mention Don's previous DK in 1985)
❑ 27 DK Checklist 1-26 DP .05 .02
❑ 28 Sandy Alomar Jr. RR .40 .18
❑ 29 Steve Searcy RR .05 .02
❑ 30 Cameron Drew RR .05 .02
❑ 31 Gary Sheffield RR .60 .25
❑ 32 Erik Hanson RR .10 .05
❑ 33 Ken Griffey Jr. RR 15.00 6.75
❑ 34 Greg W. Harris RR .05 .02
❑ 35 Gregg Jefferies RR .10 .05
❑ 36 Luis Medina RR .05 .02
❑ 37 Carlos Quintana RR .05 .02
❑ 38 Felix Jose RR .05 .02
❑ 39 Cris Carpenter RR .05 .02
❑ 40 Ron Jones RR .05 .02
❑ 41 Dave West RR .05 .02
❑ 42 Randy Johnson RR UER 1.25 .55
Card says born in 1964
he was born in 1963
❑ 43 Mike Harkey RR .05 .02
❑ 44 Pete Harnisch RR DP .10 .05
❑ 45 Tom Gordon RR DP .20 .09
❑ 46 Gregg Olson RR DP .20 .09
❑ 47 Alex Sanchez RR DP .05 .02
❑ 48 Ruben Sierra .05 .02
❑ 49 Rafael Palmeiro .20 .09
❑ 50 Ron Gant .10 .05
❑ 51 Cal Ripken .75 .35
❑ 52 Wally Joyner .10 .05
❑ 53 Gary Carter .15 .07
❑ 54 Andy Van Slyke .10 .05
❑ 55 Robin Yount .20 .09
❑ 56 Pete Incaviglia .05 .02
❑ 57 Greg Brock .05 .02
❑ 58 Melido Perez .05 .02
❑ 59 Craig Lefferts .05 .02
❑ 60 Gary Pettis .05 .02
❑ 61 Danny Tartabull .05 .02
❑ 62 Guillermo Hernandez .05 .02
❑ 63 Ozzie Smith .25 .11
❑ 64 Gary Gaetti .10 .05
❑ 65 Mark Davis .05 .02
❑ 66 Lee Smith .10 .05
❑ 67 Dennis Eckersley .15 .07
❑ 68 Wade Boggs .20 .09
❑ 69 Mike Scott .05 .02
❑ 70 Fred McGriff .20 .09
❑ 71 Tom Browning .05 .02
❑ 72 Claudell Washington .05 .02
❑ 73 Mel Hall .05 .02
❑ 74 Don Mattingly .30 .14
❑ 75 Steve Bedrosian .05 .02
❑ 76 Juan Samuel .05 .02
❑ 77 Mike Scioscia .05 .02
❑ 78 Dave Righetti .05 .02
❑ 79 Alfredo Griffin .05 .02
❑ 80 Eric Davis UER .10 .05
(165 games in 1988, should be 135)
❑ 81 Juan Berenguer .05 .02
❑ 82 Todd Worrell .05 .02
❑ 83 Joe Carter .15 .07
❑ 84 Steve Sax .05 .02
❑ 85 Frank White .10 .05
❑ 86 John Kruk .10 .05
❑ 87 Rance Mulliniks .05 .02
❑ 88 Alan Ashby .05 .02
❑ 89 Charlie Leibrandt .05 .02
❑ 90 Frank Tanana .05 .02
❑ 91 Jose Canseco .20 .09
❑ 92 Barry Bonds .40 .18
❑ 93 Harold Reynolds .05 .02
❑ 94 Mark McLemore .05 .02
❑ 95 Mark McGwire 1.25 .55
❑ 96 Eddie Murray .20 .09
❑ 97 Tim Raines .10 .05
❑ 98 Robby Thompson .05 .02
❑ 99 Kevin McReynolds .05 .02
❑ 100 Checklist 28-137 .05 .02
❑ 101 Carlton Fisk .20 .09
❑ 102 Dave Martinez .05 .02
❑ 103 Glenn Braggs .05 .02
❑ 104 Dale Murphy .20 .09
❑ 105 Ryne Sandberg .25 .11
❑ 106 Dennis Martinez .10 .05
❑ 107 Pete O'Brien .05 .02
❑ 108 Dick Schofield .05 .02
❑ 109 Henry Cotto .05 .02
❑ 110 Mike Marshall .05 .02
❑ 111 Keith Moreland .05 .02
❑ 112 Tom Brunansky .05 .02
❑ 113 Kelly Gruber UER .05 .02
(Wrong birthdate)
❑ 114 Brook Jacoby .05 .02
❑ 115 Keith Brown .05 .02
❑ 116 Matt Nokes .05 .02
❑ 117 Keith Hernandez .10 .05
❑ 118 Bob Forsch .05 .02
❑ 119 Bert Blyleven UER .10 .05
(... 3000 strikeouts in 1987, should be 1986)
❑ 120 Willie Wilson .05 .02
❑ 121 Tommy Gregg .05 .02
❑ 122 Jim Rice .10 .05
❑ 123 Bob Knepper .05 .02
❑ 124 Danny Jackson .05 .02
❑ 125 Eric Plunk .05 .02
❑ 126 Brian Fisher .05 .02
❑ 127 Mike Pagliarulo .05 .02
❑ 128 Tony Gwynn .50 .23
❑ 129 Lance McCullers .05 .02
❑ 130 Andres Galarraga .20 .09
❑ 131 Jose Uribe .05 .02
❑ 132 Kirk Gibson UER .10 .05
(Wrong birthdate)
❑ 133 David Palmer .05 .02
❑ 134 R.J. Reynolds .05 .02
❑ 135 Greg Walker .05 .02
❑ 136 Kirk McCaskill UER .05 .02
(Wrong birthdate)
❑ 137 Shawon Dunston .05 .02
❑ 138 Andy Allanson .05 .02
❑ 139 Rob Murphy .05 .02
❑ 140 Mike Aldrete .05 .02
❑ 141 Terry Kennedy .05 .02
❑ 142 Scott Fletcher .05 .02
❑ 143 Steve Balboni .05 .02
❑ 144 Bret Saberhagen .10 .05
❑ 145 Ozzie Virgil .05 .02
❑ 146 Dale Sveum .05 .02
❑ 147 Darryl Strawberry .10 .05
❑ 148 Harold Baines .10 .05
❑ 149 George Bell .05 .02
❑ 150 Dave Parker .10 .05
❑ 151 Bobby Bonilla .15 .07
❑ 152 Mookie Wilson .10 .05
❑ 153 Ted Power .05 .02
❑ 154 Nolan Ryan .75 .35
❑ 155 Jeff Reardon .10 .05
❑ 156 Tim Wallach .05 .02
❑ 157 Jamie Moyer .05 .02
❑ 158 Rich Gossage .10 .05
❑ 159 Dave Winfield .20 .09
❑ 160 Von Hayes .05 .02
❑ 161 Willie McGee .10 .05
❑ 162 Rich Gedman .05 .02
❑ 163 Tony Pena .05 .02
❑ 164 Mike Morgan .05 .02
❑ 165 Charlie Hough .10 .05
❑ 166 Mike Stanley .05 .02
❑ 167 Andre Dawson .20 .09
❑ 168 Joe Boever .05 .02
❑ 169 Pete Stanicek .05 .02
❑ 170 Bob Boone .10 .05
❑ 171 Ron Darling .05 .02
❑ 172 Bob Walk .05 .02
❑ 173 Rob Deer .05 .02
❑ 174 Steve Buechele .05 .02
❑ 175 Ted Higuera .05 .02
❑ 176 Ozzie Guillen .05 .02
❑ 177 Candy Maldonado .05 .02
❑ 178 Doyle Alexander .05 .02
❑ 179 Mark Gubicza .05 .02
❑ 180 Alan Trammell .15 .07
❑ 181 Vince Coleman .05 .02
❑ 182 Kirby Puckett .40 .18
❑ 183 Chris Brown .05 .02
❑ 184 Marty Barrett .05 .02
❑ 185 Stan Javier .05 .02
❑ 186 Mike Greenwell .05 .02
❑ 187 Billy Hatcher .05 .02
❑ 188 Jimmy Key .10 .05
❑ 189 Nick Esasky .05 .02
❑ 190 Don Slaught .05 .02
❑ 191 Cory Snyder .05 .02
❑ 192 John Candelaria .05 .02
❑ 193 Mike Schmidt .25 .11
❑ 194 Kevin Gross .05 .02
❑ 195 John Tudor .05 .02
❑ 196 Neil Allen .05 .02
❑ 197 Orel Hershiser .10 .05
❑ 198 Kal Daniels .05 .02
❑ 199 Kent Hrbek .10 .05
❑ 200 Checklist 138-247 .05 .02
❑ 201 Joe Magrane .05 .02
❑ 202 Scott Bailes .05 .02
❑ 203 Tim Belcher .05 .02
❑ 204 George Brett .40 .18

☐ 205 Benito Santiago .05 .02
☐ 206 Tony Fernandez .05 .02
☐ 207 Gerald Young .05 .02
☐ 208 Bo Jackson .15 .07
☐ 209 Chet Lemon .05 .02
☐ 210 Storm Davis .05 .02
☐ 211 Doug Drabek .05 .02
☐ 212 Mickey Brantley UER .05 .02
(Photo actually
Nelson Simmons)
☐ 213 Devon White .10 .05
☐ 214 Dave Stewart .10 .05
☐ 215 Dave Schmidt .05 .02
☐ 216 Bryn Smith .05 .02
☐ 217 Brett Butler .10 .05
☐ 218 Bob Ojeda .05 .02
☐ 219 Steve Rosenberg .05 .02
☐ 220 Hubie Brooks .05 .02
☐ 221 B.J. Surhoff .10 .05
☐ 222 Rick Mahler .05 .02
☐ 223 Rick Sutcliffe .05 .02
☐ 224 Neal Heaton .05 .02
☐ 225 Mitch Williams .05 .02
☐ 226 Chuck Finley .10 .05
☐ 227 Mark Langston .05 .02
☐ 228 Jesse Orosco .05 .02
☐ 229 Ed Whitson .05 .02
☐ 230 Terry Pendleton .10 .05
☐ 231 Lloyd Moseby .05 .02
☐ 232 Greg Swindell .05 .02
☐ 233 John Franco .10 .05
☐ 234 Jack Morris .10 .05
☐ 235 Howard Johnson .05 .02
☐ 236 Glenn Davis .05 .02
☐ 237 Frank Viola .05 .02
☐ 238 Kevin Seitzer .05 .02
☐ 239 Gerald Perry .05 .02
☐ 240 Dwight Evans .10 .05
☐ 241 Jim Deshaies .05 .02
☐ 242 Bo Diaz .05 .02
☐ 243 Carney Lansford .10 .05
☐ 244 Mike LaValliere .05 .02
☐ 245 Rickey Henderson .20 .09
☐ 246 Roberto Alomar .30 .14
☐ 247 Jimmy Jones .05 .02
☐ 248 Pascual Perez .05 .02
☐ 249 Will Clark .20 .09
☐ 250 Fernando Valenzuela .10 .05
☐ 251 Shane Rawley .05 .02
☐ 252 Sid Bream .05 .02
☐ 253 Steve Lyons .05 .02
☐ 254 Brian Downing .05 .02
☐ 255 Mark Grace .20 .09
☐ 256 Tom Candiotti .05 .02
☐ 257 Barry Larkin .20 .09
☐ 258 Mike Krukow .05 .02
☐ 259 Billy Ripken .05 .02
☐ 260 Cecilio Guante .05 .02
☐ 261 Scott Bradley .05 .02
☐ 262 Floyd Bannister .05 .02
☐ 263 Pete Smith .05 .02
☐ 264 Jim Gantner UER .05 .02
(Wrong birthdate)
☐ 265 Roger McDowell .05 .02
☐ 266 Bobby Thigpen .05 .02
☐ 267 Jim Clancy .05 .02
☐ 268 Terry Steinbach .10 .05
☐ 269 Mike Dunne .05 .02
☐ 270 Dwight Gooden .10 .05
☐ 271 Mike Heath .05 .02
☐ 272 Dave Smith .05 .02
☐ 273 Keith Atherton .05 .02
☐ 274 Tim Burke .05 .02
☐ 275 Damon Berryhill .05 .02
☐ 276 Vance Law .05 .02
☐ 277 Rich Dotson .05 .02
☐ 278 Lance Parrish .05 .02
☐ 279 Denny Walling .05 .02
☐ 280 Roger Clemens .40 .18
☐ 281 Greg Mathews .05 .02
☐ 282 Tom Niedenfuer .05 .02
☐ 283 Paul Kilgus .05 .02
☐ 284 Jose Guzman .05 .02
☐ 285 Calvin Schiraldi .05 .02
☐ 286 Charlie Puleo UER .05 .02
(Career ERA 4.24,
should be 4.23)
☐ 287 Joe Orsulak .05 .02
☐ 288 Jack Howell .05 .02
☐ 289 Kevin Elster .05 .02
☐ 290 Jose Lind .05 .02
☐ 291 Paul Molitor .20 .09
☐ 292 Cecil Espy .05 .02
☐ 293 Bill Wegman .05 .02
☐ 294 Dan Pasqua .05 .02
☐ 295 Scott Garrelts UER .05 .02
(Wrong birthdate)
☐ 296 Walt Terrell .05 .02
☐ 297 Ed Hearn .05 .02
☐ 298 Lou Whitaker .10 .05
☐ 299 Ken Dayley .05 .02
☐ 300 Checklist 248-357 .05 .02
☐ 301 Tommy Herr .05 .02
☐ 302 Mike Brumley .05 .02
☐ 303 Ellis Burks .15 .07
☐ 304 Curt Young UER .05 .02
(Wrong birthdate)
☐ 305 Jody Reed .05 .02
☐ 306 Bill Doran .05 .02
☐ 307 David Wells .05 .02
☐ 308 Ron Robinson .05 .02
☐ 309 Rafael Santana .05 .02
☐ 310 Julio Franco .05 .02
☐ 311 Jack Clark .05 .02
☐ 312 Chris James .05 .02
☐ 313 Milt Thompson .05 .02
☐ 314 John Shelby .05 .02
☐ 315 Al Leiter .20 .09
☐ 316 Mike Davis .05 .02
☐ 317 Chris Sabo .05 .02
☐ 318 Greg Gagne .05 .02
☐ 319 Jose Oquendo .05 .02
☐ 320 John Farrell .05 .02
☐ 321 Franklin Stubbs .05 .02
☐ 322 Kurt Stillwell .05 .02
☐ 323 Shawn Abner .05 .02
☐ 324 Mike Flanagan .05 .02
☐ 325 Kevin Bass .05 .02
☐ 326 Pat Tabler .05 .02
☐ 327 Mike Henneman .05 .02
☐ 328 Rick Honeycutt .05 .02
☐ 329 John Smiley .05 .02
☐ 330 Rey Quinones .05 .02
☐ 331 Johnny Ray .05 .02
☐ 332 Bob Welch .05 .02
☐ 333 Larry Sheets .05 .02
☐ 334 Jeff Parrett .05 .02
☐ 335 Rick Reuschel UER .05 .02
(For Don Robinson,
should be Jeff)
☐ 336 Randy Myers .10 .05
☐ 337 Ken Williams .05 .02
☐ 338 Andy McGaffigan .05 .02
☐ 339 Joey Meyer .05 .02
☐ 340 Dion James .05 .02
☐ 341 Les Lancaster .05 .02
☐ 342 Tom Foley .05 .02
☐ 343 Geno Petralli .05 .02
☐ 344 Dan Petry .05 .02
☐ 345 Alvin Davis .05 .02
☐ 346 Mickey Hatcher .05 .02
☐ 347 Marvell Wynne .05 .02
☐ 348 Danny Cox .05 .02
☐ 349 Dave Stieb .05 .02
☐ 350 Jay Bell .15 .07
☐ 351 Jeff Treadway .05 .02
☐ 352 Luis Salazar .05 .02
☐ 353 Len Dykstra .10 .05
☐ 354 Juan Agosto .05 .02
☐ 355 Gene Larkin .05 .02
☐ 356 Steve Farr .05 .02
☐ 357 Paul Assenmacher .05 .02
☐ 358 Todd Benzinger .05 .02
☐ 359 Larry Andersen .05 .02
☐ 360 Paul O'Neill .10 .05
☐ 361 Ron Hassey .05 .02
☐ 362 Jim Gott .05 .02
☐ 363 Ken Phelps .05 .02
☐ 364 Tim Flannery .05 .02
☐ 365 Randy Ready .05 .02
☐ 366 Nelson Santovenia .05 .02
☐ 367 Kelly Downs .05 .02
☐ 368 Danny Heep .05 .02
☐ 369 Phil Bradley .05 .02
☐ 370 Jeff D. Robinson .05 .02
☐ 371 Ivan Calderon .05 .02
☐ 372 Mike Witt .05 .02
☐ 373 Greg Maddux .75 .35
☐ 374 Carmen Castillo .05 .02
☐ 375 Jose Rijo .05 .02
☐ 376 Joe Price .05 .02
☐ 377 Rene Gonzales .05 .02
☐ 378 Oddibe McDowell .05 .02
☐ 379 Jim Presley .05 .02
☐ 380 Brad Wellman .05 .02
☐ 381 Tom Glavine .20 .09
☐ 382 Dan Plesac .05 .02
☐ 383 Wally Backman .05 .02
☐ 384 Dave Gallagher .05 .02
☐ 385 Tom Henke .05 .02
☐ 386 Luis Polonia .05 .02
☐ 387 Junior Ortiz .05 .02
☐ 388 David Cone .20 .09
☐ 389 Dave Bergman .05 .02
☐ 390 Danny Darwin .05 .02
☐ 391 Dan Gladden .05 .02
☐ 392 John Dopson .05 .02
☐ 393 Frank DiPino .05 .02
☐ 394 Al Nipper .05 .02
☐ 395 Willie Randolph .10 .05
☐ 396 Don Carman .05 .02
☐ 397 Scott Terry .05 .02
☐ 398 Rick Cerone .05 .02
☐ 399 Tom Pagnozzi .05 .02
☐ 400 Checklist 358-467 .05 .02
☐ 401 Mickey Tettleton .10 .05
☐ 402 Curtis Wilkerson .05 .02
☐ 403 Jeff Russell .05 .02
☐ 404 Pat Perry .05 .02
☐ 405 Jose Alvarez .05 .02
☐ 406 Rick Schu .05 .02
☐ 407 Sherman Corbett .05 .02
☐ 408 Dave Magadan .05 .02
☐ 409 Bob Kipper .05 .02
☐ 410 Don August .05 .02
☐ 411 Bob Brower .05 .02
☐ 412 Chris Bosio .05 .02
☐ 413 Jerry Reuss .05 .02
☐ 414 Atlee Hammaker .05 .02
☐ 415 Jim Walewander .05 .02
☐ 416 Mike Macfarlane .05 .02
☐ 417 Pat Sheridan .05 .02
☐ 418 Pedro Guerrero .05 .02
☐ 419 Allan Anderson .05 .02
☐ 420 Mark Parent .05 .02
☐ 421 Bob Stanley .05 .02
☐ 422 Mike Gallego .05 .02
☐ 423 Bruce Hurst .05 .02
☐ 424 Dave Meads .05 .02
☐ 425 Jesse Barfield .05 .02
☐ 426 Rob Dibble .10 .05
☐ 427 Joel Skinner .05 .02
☐ 428 Ron Kittle .05 .02
☐ 429 Rick Rhoden .05 .02
☐ 430 Bob Dernier .05 .02
☐ 431 Steve Jeltz .05 .02
☐ 432 Rick Dempsey .05 .02
☐ 433 Roberto Kelly .10 .05
☐ 434 Dave Anderson .05 .02
☐ 435 Herm Winningham .05 .02
☐ 436 Al Newman .05 .02
☐ 437 Jose DeLeon .05 .02
☐ 438 Doug Jones .05 .02
☐ 439 Brian Holton .05 .02
☐ 440 Jeff Montgomery .10 .05
☐ 441 Dickie Thon .05 .02
☐ 442 Cecil Fielder .10 .05
☐ 443 John Fishel .05 .02
☐ 444 Jerry Don Gleaton .05 .02
☐ 445 Paul Gibson .05 .02
☐ 446 Walt Weiss .05 .02
☐ 447 Glenn Wilson .05 .02
☐ 448 Mike Moore .05 .02
☐ 449 Chili Davis .10 .05
☐ 450 Dave Henderson .05 .02
☐ 451 Jose Bautista .05 .02

❑ 452 Rex Hudler .05 .02
❑ 453 Bob Brenly .05 .02
❑ 454 Mackey Sasser .05 .02
❑ 455 Daryl Boston .05 .02
❑ 456 Mike R. Fitzgerald .05 .02
❑ 457 Jeffrey Leonard .05 .02
❑ 458 Bruce Sutter .05 .02
❑ 459 Mitch Webster .05 .02
❑ 460 Joe Hesketh .05 .02
❑ 461 Bobby Witt .05 .02
❑ 462 Stew Cliburn .05 .02
❑ 463 Scott Bankhead .05 .02
❑ 464 Ramon Martinez .25 .11
❑ 465 Dave Leiper .05 .02
❑ 466 Luis Alicea .05 .02
❑ 467 John Cerutti .05 .02
❑ 468 Ron Washington .05 .02
❑ 469 Jeff Reed .05 .02
❑ 470 Jeff M. Robinson .05 .02
❑ 471 Sid Fernandez .05 .02
❑ 472 Terry Puhl .05 .02
❑ 473 Charlie Lea .05 .02
❑ 474 Israel Sanchez .05 .02
❑ 475 Bruce Benedict .05 .02
❑ 476 Oil Can Boyd .05 .02
❑ 477 Craig Reynolds .05 .02
❑ 478 Frank Williams .05 .02
❑ 479 Greg Cadaret .05 .02
❑ 480 Randy Kramer .05 .02
❑ 481 Dave Eiland .05 .02
❑ 482 Eric Show .05 .02
❑ 483 Garry Templeton .05 .02
❑ 484 Wallace Johnson .05 .02
❑ 485 Kevin Mitchell .10 .05
❑ 486 Tim Crews .05 .02
❑ 487 Mike Maddux .05 .02
❑ 488 Dave LaPoint .05 .02
❑ 489 Fred Manrique .05 .02
❑ 490 Greg Minton .05 .02
❑ 491 Doug Dascenzo UER .05 .02
(Photo actually
Damon Berryhill)
❑ 492 Willie Upshaw .05 .02
❑ 493 Jack Armstrong .05 .02
❑ 494 Kirt Manwaring .05 .02
❑ 495 Jeff Ballard .05 .02
❑ 496 Jeff Kunkel .05 .02
❑ 497 Mike Campbell .05 .02
❑ 498 Gary Thurman .05 .02
❑ 499 Zane Smith .05 .02
❑ 500 Checklist 468-577 DP .05 .02
❑ 501 Mike Birkbeck .05 .02
❑ 502 Terry Leach .05 .02
❑ 503 Shawn Hillegas .05 .02
❑ 504 Manny Lee .05 .02
❑ 505 Doug Jennings .05 .02
❑ 506 Ken Oberkfell .05 .02
❑ 507 Tim Teufel .05 .02
❑ 508 Tom Brookens .05 .02
❑ 509 Rafael Ramirez .05 .02
❑ 510 Fred Toliver .05 .02
❑ 511 Brian Holman .05 .02
❑ 512 Mike Bielecki .05 .02
❑ 513 Jeff Pico .05 .02
❑ 514 Charles Hudson .05 .02
❑ 515 Bruce Ruffin .05 .02
❑ 516 Larry McWilliams UER .05 .02
(New Richland, should
be North Richland)
❑ 517 Jeff Sellers .05 .02
❑ 518 John Costello .05 .02
❑ 519 Brady Anderson .40 .18
❑ 520 Craig McMurtry .05 .02
❑ 521 Ray Hayward DP .05 .02
❑ 522 Drew Hall DP .05 .02
❑ 523 Mark Lemke DP .15 .07
❑ 524 Oswald Peraza DP .05 .02
❑ 525 Bryan Harvey DP .05 .02
❑ 526 Rick Aguilera DP .10 .05
❑ 527 Tom Prince DP .05 .02
❑ 528 Mark Clear DP .05 .02
❑ 529 Jerry Browne DP .05 .02
❑ 530 Juan Castillo DP .05 .02
❑ 531 Jack McDowell DP .10 .05
❑ 532 Chris Speier DP .05 .02
❑ 533 Darrell Evans DP .10 .05
❑ 534 Luis Aquino DP .05 .02
❑ 535 Eric King DP .05 .02
❑ 536 Ken Hill DP .20 .09
❑ 537 Randy Bush DP .05 .02
❑ 538 Shane Mack DP .05 .02
❑ 539 Tom Bolton DP .05 .02
❑ 540 Gene Nelson DP .05 .02
❑ 541 Wes Gardner DP .05 .02
❑ 542 Ken Caminiti DP .20 .09
❑ 543 Duane Ward DP .05 .02
❑ 544 Norm Charlton DP .10 .05
❑ 545 Hal Morris DP .20 .09
❑ 546 Rich Yett DP .05 .02
❑ 547 Hensley Meulens DP .05 .02
❑ 548 Greg A. Harris DP .05 .02
❑ 549 Darren Daulton DP .10 .05
(Posing as right-
handed hitter)
❑ 550 Jeff Hamilton DP .05 .02
❑ 551 Luis Aguayo DP .05 .02
❑ 552 Tim Leary DP .05 .02
(Resembles M.Marshall)
❑ 553 Ron Oester DP .05 .02
❑ 554 Steve Lombardozzi DP .05 .02
❑ 555 Tim Jones DP .05 .02
❑ 556 Bud Black DP .05 .02
❑ 557 Alejandro Pena DP .05 .02
❑ 558 Jose DeJesus DP .05 .02
❑ 559 Dennis Rasmussen DP .05 .02
❑ 560 Pat Borders DP .10 .05
❑ 561 Craig Biggio DP .75 .35
❑ 562 Luis DeLosSantos DP .05 .02
❑ 563 Fred Lynn DP .05 .02
❑ 564 Todd Burns DP .05 .02
❑ 565 Felix Fermin DP .05 .02
❑ 566 Darnell Coles DP .05 .02
❑ 567 Willie Fraser DP .05 .02
❑ 568 Glenn Hubbard DP .05 .02
❑ 569 Craig Worthington DP .05 .02
❑ 570 Johnny Paredes DP .05 .02
❑ 571 Don Robinson DP .05 .02
❑ 572 Barry Lyons DP .05 .02
❑ 573 Bill Long DP .05 .02
❑ 574 Tracy Jones DP .05 .02
❑ 575 Juan Nieves DP .05 .02
❑ 576 Andres Thomas DP .05 .02
❑ 577 Rolando Roomes DP .05 .02
❑ 578 Luis Rivera UER DP .05 .02
(Wrong birthdate)
❑ 579 Chad Kreuter DP .05 .02
❑ 580 Tony Armas DP .05 .02
❑ 581 Jay Buhner .20 .09
❑ 582 Ricky Horton DP .05 .02
❑ 583 Andy Hawkins DP .05 .02
❑ 584 Sil Campusano .05 .02
❑ 585 Dave Clark .05 .02
❑ 586 Van Snider DP .05 .02
❑ 587 Todd Frohwirth DP .05 .02
❑ 588 Warren Spahn DP PUZ .20 .09
❑ 589 William Brennan .05 .02
❑ 590 German Gonzalez .05 .02
❑ 591 Ernie Whitt DP .05 .02
❑ 592 Jeff Blauser .10 .05
❑ 593 Spike Owen DP .05 .02
❑ 594 Matt Williams .20 .09
❑ 595 Lloyd McClendon DP .05 .02
❑ 596 Steve Ontiveros .05 .02
❑ 597 Scott Medvin .05 .02
❑ 598 Hipolito Pena DP .05 .02
❑ 599 Jerald Clark DP .05 .02
❑ 600A Checklist 578-660 DP .05 .02
(635 Kurt Schilling)
❑ 600B Checklist 578-660 DP .05 .02
(635 Curt Schilling;
MVP's not listed
on checklist card)
❑ 600C Checklist 578-660 DP .05 .02
(635 Curt Schilling;
MVP's listed
following 660)
❑ 601 Carmelo Martinez DP .05 .02
❑ 602 Mike LaCoss .05 .02
❑ 603 Mike Devereaux .05 .02
❑ 604 Alex Madrid DP .05 .02
❑ 605 Gary Redus DP .05 .02
❑ 606 Lance Johnson .10 .05
❑ 607 Terry Clark DP .05 .02
❑ 608 Manny Trillo DP .05 .02
❑ 609 Scott Jordan .10 .05
❑ 610 Jay Howell DP .05 .02
❑ 611 Francisco Melendez .05 .02
❑ 612 Mike Boddicker .05 .02
❑ 613 Kevin Brown DP .60 .25
❑ 614 Dave Valle .05 .02
❑ 615 Tim Laudner DP .05 .02
❑ 616 Andy Nezelek UER .05 .02
(Wrong birthdate)
❑ 617 Chuck Crim .05 .02
❑ 618 Jack Savage DP .05 .02
❑ 619 Adam Peterson .05 .02
❑ 620 Todd Stottlemyre .15 .07
❑ 621 Lance Blankenship .05 .02
❑ 622 Miguel Garcia DP .05 .02
❑ 623 Keith A. Miller DP .05 .02
❑ 624 Ricky Jordan DP .10 .05
❑ 625 Ernest Riles DP .05 .02
❑ 626 John Moses DP .05 .02
❑ 627 Nelson Liriano DP .05 .02
❑ 628 Mike Smithson DP .05 .02
❑ 629 Scott Sanderson .05 .02
❑ 630 Dale Mohorcic .05 .02
❑ 631 Marvin Freeman DP .05 .02
❑ 632 Mike Young DP .05 .02
❑ 633 Dennis Lamp .05 .02
❑ 634 Dante Bichette DP .40 .18
❑ 635 Curt Schilling DP .50 .23
❑ 636 Scott May DP .05 .02
❑ 637 Mike Schooler .05 .02
❑ 638 Rick Leach .05 .02
❑ 639 Tom Lampkin UER .05 .02
(Throws Left, should
be Throws Right)
❑ 640 Brian Meyer .05 .02
❑ 641 Brian Harper .05 .02
❑ 642 John Smoltz .50 .23
❑ 643 Jose Canseco .10 .05
(40/40 Club)
❑ 644 Bill Schroeder .05 .02
❑ 645 Edgar Martinez .20 .09
❑ 646 Dennis Cook .05 .02
❑ 647 Barry Jones .05 .02
❑ 648 Orel Hershiser .10 .05
(59 and Counting)
❑ 649 Rod Nichols .05 .02
❑ 650 Jody Davis .05 .02
❑ 651 Bob Milacki .05 .02
❑ 652 Mike Jackson .15 .07
❑ 653 Derek Lilliquist .05 .02
❑ 654 Paul Mirabella .05 .02
❑ 655 Mike Diaz .05 .02
❑ 656 Jeff Musselman .05 .02
❑ 657 Jerry Reed .05 .02
❑ 658 Kevin Blankenship .05 .02
❑ 659 Wayne Tolleson .05 .02
❑ 660 Eric Hetzel .05 .02

1989 Donruss Rookies

	MINT	NRMT
COMP.FACT.SET (56)	20.00	9.00
COMMON CARD (1-56)	.05	.02

❑ 1 Gary Sheffield .60 .25
❑ 2 Gregg Jefferies .10 .05
❑ 3 Ken Griffey Jr. 15.00 6.75
❑ 4 Tom Gordon .20 .09
❑ 5 Billy Spiers .05 .02
❑ 6 Deion Sanders .75 .35
❑ 7 Donn Pall .05 .02
❑ 8 Steve Carter .05 .02
❑ 9 Francisco Oliveras .05 .02
❑ 10 Steve Wilson .05 .02
❑ 11 Bob Geren .05 .02
❑ 12 Tony Castillo .05 .02
❑ 13 Kenny Rogers .20 .09
❑ 14 Carlos Martinez .05 .02
❑ 15 Edgar Martinez .20 .09
❑ 16 Jim Abbott .20 .09
❑ 17 Torey Lovullo .05 .02
❑ 18 Mark Carreon .05 .02
❑ 19 Geronimo Berroa .05 .02
❑ 20 Luis Medina .05 .02
❑ 21 Sandy Alomar Jr. .40 .18
❑ 22 Bob Milacki .05 .02
❑ 23 Joe Girardi .30 .14
❑ 24 German Gonzalez .05 .02
❑ 25 Craig Worthington .05 .02
❑ 26 Jerome Walton .20 .09
❑ 27 Gary Wayne .05 .02
❑ 28 Tim Jones .05 .02
❑ 29 Dante Bichette .40 .18
❑ 30 Alexis Infante .05 .02
❑ 31 Ken Hill .20 .09
❑ 32 Dwight Smith .10 .05
❑ 33 Luis de los Santos .05 .02
❑ 34 Eric Yelding .05 .02
❑ 35 Gregg Olson .20 .09
❑ 36 Phil Stephenson .05 .02
❑ 37 Ken Patterson .05 .02
❑ 38 Rick Wrona .05 .02
❑ 39 Mike Brumley .05 .02
❑ 40 Cris Carpenter .05 .02
❑ 41 Jeff Brantley .20 .09
❑ 42 Ron Jones .05 .02
❑ 43 Randy Johnson 1.25 .55
❑ 44 Kevin Brown .60 .25
❑ 45 Ramon Martinez .15 .07
❑ 46 Greg W.Harris .05 .02
❑ 47 Steve Finley .25 .11
❑ 48 Randy Kramer .05 .02
❑ 49 Erik Hanson .10 .05
❑ 50 Matt Merullo .05 .02
❑ 51 Mike Devereaux .05 .02
❑ 52 Clay Parker .05 .02
❑ 53 Omar Vizquel .40 .18
❑ 54 Derek Lilliquist .05 .02
❑ 55 Junior Felix .05 .02
❑ 56 Checklist 1-56 .05 .02

1989 Donruss Baseball's Best

	MINT	NRMT
COMP.FACT.SET (336)	50.00	22.00
COMMON CARD (1-336)	.10	.05

❑ 1 Don Mattingly .60 .25
❑ 2 Tom Glavine .50 .23
❑ 3 Bert Blyleven .20 .09
❑ 4 Andre Dawson .40 .18
❑ 5 Pete O'Brien .10 .05
❑ 6 Eric Davis .20 .09
❑ 7 George Brett .75 .35
❑ 8 Glenn Davis .10 .05
❑ 9 Ellis Burks .30 .14
❑ 10 Kirk Gibson .20 .09
❑ 11 Carlton Fisk .40 .18
❑ 12 Andres Galarraga .30 .14
❑ 13 Alan Trammell .30 .14
❑ 14 Dwight Gooden .20 .09
❑ 15 Paul Molitor .40 .18
❑ 16 Roger McDowell .10 .05
❑ 17 Doug Drabek .10 .05
❑ 18 Kent Hrbek .20 .09
❑ 19 Vince Coleman .10 .05
❑ 20 Steve Sax .10 .05
❑ 21 Roberto Alomar .60 .25
❑ 22 Carney Lansford .20 .09
❑ 23 Will Clark .40 .18
❑ 24 Alvin Davis .10 .05
❑ 25 Bobby Thigpen .10 .05
❑ 26 Ryne Sandberg .50 .23
❑ 27 Devon White .20 .09
❑ 28 Mike Greenwell .10 .05
❑ 29 Dale Murphy .40 .18
❑ 30 Jeff Ballard .10 .05
❑ 31 Kelly Gruber .10 .05
❑ 32 Julio Franco .10 .05
❑ 33 Bobby Bonilla .30 .14
❑ 34 Tim Wallach .10 .05
❑ 35 Lou Whitaker .20 .09
❑ 36 Jay Howell .10 .05
❑ 37 Greg Maddux 1.50 .70
❑ 38 Bill Doran .10 .05
❑ 39 Danny Tartabull .10 .05
❑ 40 Darryl Strawberry .20 .09
❑ 41 Ron Darling .10 .05
❑ 42 Tony Gwynn 1.00 .45
❑ 43 Mark McGwire 2.50 1.10
❑ 44 Ozzie Smith .50 .23
❑ 45 Andy Van Slyke .20 .09
❑ 46 Juan Berenguer .10 .05
❑ 47 Von Hayes .10 .05
❑ 48 Tony Fernandez .10 .05
❑ 49 Eric Plunk .10 .05
❑ 50 Ernest Riles .10 .05
❑ 51 Harold Reynolds .10 .05
❑ 52 Andy Hawkins .10 .05
❑ 53 Robin Yount .40 .18
❑ 54 Danny Jackson .10 .05
❑ 55 Nolan Ryan 1.50 .70
❑ 56 Joe Carter .25 .11
❑ 57 Jose Canseco .30 .14
❑ 58 Jody Davis .10 .05
❑ 59 Lance Parrish .10 .05
❑ 60 Mitch Williams .10 .05
❑ 61 Brook Jacoby .10 .05
❑ 62 Tom Browning .10 .05
❑ 63 Kurt Stillwell .10 .05
❑ 64 Rafael Ramirez .10 .05
❑ 65 Roger Clemens .75 .35
❑ 66 Mike Scioscia .10 .05
❑ 67 Dave Gallagher .10 .05
❑ 68 Mark Langston .10 .05
❑ 69 Chet Lemon .10 .05
❑ 70 Kevin McReynolds .10 .05
❑ 71 Rob Deer .10 .05
❑ 72 Tommy Herr .10 .05
❑ 73 Barry Bonds .75 .35
❑ 74 Frank Viola .10 .05
❑ 75 Pedro Guerrero .10 .05
❑ 76 Dave Righetti UER .10 .05
(ML total of 7 wins incorrect)
❑ 77 Bruce Hurst .10 .05
❑ 78 Rickey Henderson .25 .11
❑ 79 Robby Thompson .10 .05
❑ 80 Randy Johnson 1.25 .55
❑ 81 Harold Baines .20 .09
❑ 82 Calvin Schiraldi .10 .05
❑ 83 Kirk McCaskill .10 .05
❑ 84 Lee Smith .20 .09
❑ 85 John Smoltz .50 .23
❑ 86 Mickey Tettleton .20 .09
❑ 87 Jimmy Key .20 .09
❑ 88 Rafael Palmeiro .30 .14
❑ 89 Sid Bream .10 .05
❑ 90 Dennis Martinez .20 .09
❑ 91 Frank Tanana .10 .05
❑ 92 Eddie Murray .40 .18
❑ 93 Shawon Dunston .10 .05
❑ 94 Mike Scott .10 .05
❑ 95 Bret Saberhagen .20 .09
❑ 96 David Cone .40 .18
❑ 97 Kevin Elster .10 .05
❑ 98 Jack Clark .10 .05
❑ 99 Dave Stewart .20 .09
❑ 100 Jose Oquendo .10 .05
❑ 101 Jose Lind .10 .05
❑ 102 Gary Gaetti .20 .09
❑ 103 Ricky Jordan .10 .05
❑ 104 Fred McGriff .40 .18
❑ 105 Don Slaught .10 .05
❑ 106 Jose Uribe .10 .05
❑ 107 Jeffrey Leonard .10 .05
❑ 108 Lee Guetterman .10 .05
❑ 109 Chris Bosio .10 .05
❑ 110 Barry Larkin .40 .18
❑ 111 Ruben Sierra .10 .05
❑ 112 Greg Swindell .10 .05
❑ 113 Gary Sheffield .60 .25
❑ 114 Lonnie Smith .10 .05
❑ 115 Chili Davis .20 .09
❑ 116 Damon Berryhill .10 .05
❑ 117 Tom Candiotti .10 .05
❑ 118 Kal Daniels .10 .05
❑ 119 Mark Gubicza .10 .05
❑ 120 Jim Deshaies .10 .05
❑ 121 Dwight Evans .20 .09
❑ 122 Mike Morgan .10 .05
❑ 123 Dan Pasqua .10 .05
❑ 124 Bryn Smith .10 .05
❑ 125 Doyle Alexander .10 .05
❑ 126 Howard Johnson .10 .05
❑ 127 Chuck Crim .10 .05
❑ 128 Darren Daulton .20 .09
❑ 129 Jeff Robinson .10 .05
❑ 130 Kirby Puckett .75 .35
❑ 131 Joe Magrane .10 .05
❑ 132 Jesse Barfield .10 .05
❑ 133 Mark Davis UER .10 .05
(Photo actually Dave Leiper)
❑ 134 Dennis Eckersley .30 .14
❑ 135 Mike Krukow .10 .05
❑ 136 Jay Buhner .40 .18
❑ 137 Ozzie Guillen .10 .05
❑ 138 Rick Sutcliffe .10 .05
❑ 139 Wally Joyner .20 .09
❑ 140 Wade Boggs .25 .11
❑ 141 Jeff Treadway .10 .05
❑ 142 Cal Ripken 1.50 .70
❑ 143 Dave Stieb .10 .05
❑ 144 Pete Incaviglia .10 .05
❑ 145 Bob Walk .10 .05
❑ 146 Nelson Santovenia .10 .05
❑ 147 Mike Heath .10 .05
❑ 148 Willie Randolph .20 .09
❑ 149 Paul Kilgus .10 .05
❑ 150 Billy Hatcher .10 .05
❑ 151 Steve Farr .10 .05
❑ 152 Gregg Jefferies .20 .09
❑ 153 Randy Myers .20 .09
❑ 154 Garry Templeton .10 .05
❑ 155 Walt Weiss .10 .05
❑ 156 Terry Pendleton .20 .09
❑ 157 John Smiley .10 .05
❑ 158 Greg Gagne .10 .05
❑ 159 Len Dykstra .20 .09
❑ 160 Nelson Liriano .10 .05
❑ 161 Alvaro Espinoza .10 .05
❑ 162 Rick Reuschel .10 .05
❑ 163 Omar Vizquel UER .25 .11
(Photo actually Darnell Coles)
❑ 164 Clay Parker .10 .05
❑ 165 Dan Plesac .10 .05
❑ 166 John Franco .20 .09
❑ 167 Scott Fletcher .10 .05

❑ 168 Cory Snyder .10 .05
❑ 169 Bo Jackson .30 .14
❑ 170 Tommy Gregg .10 .05
❑ 171 Jim Abbott .25 .11
❑ 172 Jerome Walton .40 .18
❑ 173 Doug Jones .10 .05
❑ 174 Todd Benzinger .10 .05
❑ 175 Frank White .20 .09
❑ 176 Craig Biggio .75 .35
❑ 177 John Dopson .10 .05
❑ 178 Alfredo Griffin .10 .05
❑ 179 Melido Perez .10 .05
❑ 180 Tim Burke .10 .05
❑ 181 Matt Nokes .10 .05
❑ 182 Gary Carter .30 .14
❑ 183 Ted Higuera .10 .05
❑ 184 Ken Howell .10 .05
❑ 185 Rey Quinones .10 .05
❑ 186 Wally Backman .10 .05
❑ 187 Tom Brunansky .10 .05
❑ 188 Steve Balboni .10 .05
❑ 189 Marvell Wynne .10 .05
❑ 190 Dave Henderson .10 .05
❑ 191 Don Robinson .10 .05
❑ 192 Ken Griffey Jr. 15.00 6.75
❑ 193 Ivan Calderon .10 .05
❑ 194 Mike Bielecki .10 .05
❑ 195 Johnny Ray .10 .05
❑ 196 Rob Murphy .10 .05
❑ 197 Andres Thomas .10 .05
❑ 198 Phil Bradley .10 .05
❑ 199 Junior Felix .10 .05
❑ 200 Jeff Russell .10 .05
❑ 201 Mike LaValliere .10 .05
❑ 202 Kevin Gross .10 .05
❑ 203 Keith Moreland .10 .05
❑ 204 Mike Marshall .10 .05
❑ 205 Dwight Smith .20 .09
❑ 206 Jim Clancy .10 .05
❑ 207 Kevin Seitzer .10 .05
❑ 208 Keith Hernandez .20 .09
❑ 209 Bob Ojeda .10 .05
❑ 210 Ed Whitson .10 .05
❑ 211 Tony Phillips .10 .05
❑ 212 Milt Thompson .10 .05
❑ 213 Randy Kramer .10 .05
❑ 214 Randy Bush .10 .05
❑ 215 Randy Ready .10 .05
❑ 216 Duane Ward .10 .05
❑ 217 Jimmy Jones .10 .05
❑ 218 Scott Garrelts .10 .05
❑ 219 Scott Bankhead .10 .05
❑ 220 Lance McCullers .10 .05
❑ 221 B.J. Surhoff .20 .09
❑ 222 Chris Sabo .10 .05
❑ 223 Steve Buechele .10 .05
❑ 224 Joel Skinner .10 .05
❑ 225 Orel Hershiser .20 .09
❑ 226 Derek Lilliquist .10 .05
❑ 227 Claudell Washington .10 .05
❑ 228 Lloyd McClendon .10 .05
❑ 229 Felix Fermin .10 .05
❑ 230 Paul O'Neill .20 .09
❑ 231 Charlie Leibrandt .10 .05
❑ 232 Dave Smith .10 .05
❑ 233 Bob Stanley .10 .05
❑ 234 Tim Belcher .10 .05
❑ 235 Eric King .10 .05
❑ 236 Spike Owen .10 .05
❑ 237 Mike Henneman .10 .05
❑ 238 Juan Samuel .10 .05
❑ 239 Greg Brock .10 .05
❑ 240 John Kruk .20 .09
❑ 241 Glenn Wilson .10 .05
❑ 242 Jeff Reardon .20 .09
❑ 243 Todd Worrell .10 .05
❑ 244 Dave LaPoint .10 .05
❑ 245 Walt Terrell .10 .05
❑ 246 Mike Moore .10 .05
❑ 247 Kelly Downs .10 .05
❑ 248 Dave Valle .10 .05
❑ 249 Ron Kittle .10 .05
❑ 250 Steve Wilson .10 .05
❑ 251 Dick Schofield .10 .05
❑ 252 Marty Barrett .10 .05
❑ 253 Dion James .10 .05
❑ 254 Bob Milacki .10 .05
❑ 255 Ernie Whitt .10 .05
❑ 256 Kevin Brown .60 .25
❑ 257 R.J. Reynolds .10 .05
❑ 258 Tim Raines .20 .09
❑ 259 Frank Williams .10 .05
❑ 260 Jose Gonzalez .10 .05
❑ 261 Mitch Webster .10 .05
❑ 262 Ken Caminiti .40 .18
❑ 263 Bob Boone .20 .09
❑ 264 Dave Magadan .10 .05
❑ 265 Rick Aguilera .20 .09
❑ 266 Chris James .10 .05
❑ 267 Bob Welch .10 .05
❑ 268 Ken Dayley .10 .05
❑ 269 Junior Ortiz .10 .05
❑ 270 Allan Anderson .10 .05
❑ 271 Steve Jeltz .10 .05
❑ 272 George Bell .10 .05
❑ 273 Roberto Kelly .20 .09
❑ 274 Brett Butler .20 .09
❑ 275 Mike Schooler .10 .05
❑ 276 Ken Phelps .10 .05
❑ 277 Glenn Braggs .10 .05
❑ 278 Jose Rijo .10 .05
❑ 279 Bobby Witt .10 .05
❑ 280 Jerry Browne .10 .05
❑ 281 Kevin Mitchell .20 .09
❑ 282 Craig Worthington .10 .05
❑ 283 Greg Minton .10 .05
❑ 284 Nick Esasky .10 .05
❑ 285 John Farrell .10 .05
❑ 286 Rick Mahler .10 .05
❑ 287 Tom Gordon .40 .18
❑ 288 Gerald Young .10 .05
❑ 289 Jody Reed .10 .05
❑ 290 Jeff Hamilton .10 .05
❑ 291 Gerald Perry .10 .05
❑ 292 Hubie Brooks .10 .05
❑ 293 Bo Diaz .10 .05
❑ 294 Terry Puhl .10 .05
❑ 295 Jim Gantner .10 .05
❑ 296 Jeff Parrett .10 .05
❑ 297 Mike Boddicker .10 .05
❑ 298 Dan Gladden .10 .05
❑ 299 Tony Pena .10 .05
❑ 300 Checklist Card .10 .05
❑ 301 Tom Henke .10 .05
❑ 302 Pascual Perez .10 .05
❑ 303 Steve Bedrosian .10 .05
❑ 304 Ken Hill .25 .11
❑ 305 Jerry Reuss .10 .05
❑ 306 Jim Eisenreich .10 .05
❑ 307 Jack Howell .10 .05
❑ 308 Rick Cerone .10 .05
❑ 309 Tim Leary .10 .05
❑ 310 Joe Orsulak .10 .05
❑ 311 Jim Dwyer .10 .05
❑ 312 Geno Petralli .10 .05
❑ 313 Rick Honeycutt .10 .05
❑ 314 Tom Foley .10 .05
❑ 315 Kenny Rogers .25 .11
❑ 316 Mike Flanagan .10 .05
❑ 317 Bryan Harvey .10 .05
❑ 318 Billy Ripken .10 .05
❑ 319 Jeff Montgomery .20 .09
❑ 320 Erik Hanson .40 .18
❑ 321 Brian Downing .10 .05
❑ 322 Gregg Olson .40 .18
❑ 323 Terry Steinbach .20 .09
❑ 324 Sammy Sosa 40.00 18.00
❑ 325 Gene Harris .10 .05
❑ 326 Mike Devereaux .10 .05
❑ 327 Dennis Cook .10 .05
❑ 328 David Wells .10 .05
❑ 329 Checklist Card .10 .05
❑ 330 Kirt Manwaring .10 .05
❑ 331 Jim Presley .10 .05
❑ 332 Checklist Card .10 .05
❑ 333 Chuck Finley .20 .09
❑ 334 Rob Dibble .20 .09
❑ 335 Cecil Espy .10 .05
❑ 336 Dave Parker .20 .09

1990 Donruss

	MINT	NRMT
COMPLETE SET (716)	10.00	4.50
COMP.FACT.SET (728)	12.00	5.50
COMMON CARD (1-716)	.05	.02
COMP.YAZ PUZZLE	1.00	.45

❑ 1 Bo Jackson DK .10 .05
❑ 2 Steve Sax DK .05 .02
❑ 3A Ruben Sierra DK ERR .05 .02
(No small line on top border on card back)
❑ 3B Ruben Sierra DK COR .05 .02
❑ 4 Ken Griffey Jr. DK .75 .35
❑ 5 Mickey Tettleton DK .05 .02
❑ 6 Dave Stewart DK .05 .02
❑ 7 Jim Deshaies DK DP .05 .02
❑ 8 John Smoltz DK .20 .09
❑ 9 Mike Bielecki DK .05 .02
❑ 10A Brian Downing DK .20 .09
ERR (Reverse negative on card front)
❑ 10B Brian Downing DK .05 .02
COR
❑ 11 Kevin Mitchell DK .05 .02
❑ 12 Kelly Gruber DK .05 .02
❑ 13 Joe Magrane DK .05 .02
❑ 14 John Franco DK .05 .02
❑ 15 Ozzie Guillen DK .05 .02
❑ 16 Lou Whitaker DK .05 .02
❑ 17 John Smiley DK .05 .02
❑ 18 Howard Johnson DK .05 .02
❑ 19 Willie Randolph DK .10 .05
❑ 20 Chris Bosio DK .05 .02
❑ 21 Tommy Herr DK DP .05 .02
❑ 22 Dan Gladden DK .05 .02
❑ 23 Ellis Burks DK .10 .05
❑ 24 Pete O'Brien DK .05 .02
❑ 25 Bryn Smith DK .05 .02
❑ 26 Ed Whitson DK DP .05 .02
❑ 27 DK Checklist 1-27 DP .05 .02
(Comments on Perez-Steele on back)
❑ 28 Robin Ventura RR .20 .09
❑ 29 Todd Zeile RR .10 .05
❑ 30 Sandy Alomar Jr. RR .15 .07
❑ 31 Kent Mercker RR .05 .02
❑ 32 Ben McDonald RR UER .10 .05
(Middle name Benard, not Benjamin)
❑ 33A Juan Gonzalez RR ERR 5.00 2.20
(Reverse negative)
❑ 33B Juan Gonzalez RR COR 3.00 1.35
❑ 34 Eric Anthony RR .05 .02
❑ 35 Mike Fetters RR .05 .02
❑ 36 Marquis Grissom RR .25 .11
❑ 37 Greg Vaughn RR .40 .18
❑ 38 Brian DuBois RR .05 .02
❑ 39 Steve Avery RR UER .05 .02
(Born in MI, not NJ)
❑ 40 Mark Gardner RR .05 .02
❑ 41 Andy Benes RR .20 .09
❑ 42 Delino DeShields RR .20 .09
❑ 43 Scott Coolbaugh RR .05 .02
❑ 44 Pat Combs RR DP .05 .02
❑ 45 Alex Sanchez RR DP .05 .02
❑ 46 Kelly Mann RR DP .05 .02

❑ 47 Julio Machado RR DP ...... .05 .02
❑ 48 Pete Incaviglia .... .05 .02
❑ 49 Shawon Dunston .... .05 .02
❑ 50 Jeff Treadway .... .05 .02
❑ 51 Jeff Ballard .... .05 .02
❑ 52 Claudell Washington .... .05 .02
❑ 53 Juan Samuel .... .05 .02
❑ 54 John Smiley .... .05 .02
❑ 55 Rob Deer .... .05 .02
❑ 56 Geno Petralli .... .05 .02
❑ 57 Chris Bosio .... .05 .02
❑ 58 Carlton Fisk .... .20 .09
❑ 59 Kirt Manwaring .... .05 .02
❑ 60 Chet Lemon .... .05 .02
❑ 61 Bo Jackson .... .10 .05
❑ 62 Doyle Alexander .... .05 .02
❑ 63 Pedro Guerrero .... .05 .02
❑ 64 Allan Anderson .... .05 .02
❑ 65 Greg W. Harris .... .05 .02
❑ 66 Mike Greenwell .... .05 .02
❑ 67 Walt Weiss .... .05 .02
❑ 68 Wade Boggs .... .20 .09
❑ 69 Jim Clancy .... .05 .02
❑ 70 Junior Felix .... .05 .02
❑ 71 Barry Larkin .... .20 .09
❑ 72 Dave LaPoint .... .05 .02
❑ 73 Joel Skinner .... .05 .02
❑ 74 Jesse Barfield .... .05 .02
❑ 75 Tommy Herr .... .05 .02
❑ 76 Ricky Jordan .... .05 .02
❑ 77 Eddie Murray .... .20 .09
❑ 78 Steve Sax .... .05 .02
❑ 79 Tim Belcher .... .05 .02
❑ 80 Danny Jackson .... .05 .02
❑ 81 Kent Hrbek .... .10 .05
❑ 82 Milt Thompson .... .05 .02
❑ 83 Brook Jacoby .... .05 .02
❑ 84 Mike Marshall .... .05 .02
❑ 85 Kevin Seitzer .... .05 .02
❑ 86 Tony Gwynn .... .50 .23
❑ 87 Dave Stieb .... .10 .05
❑ 88 Dave Smith .... .05 .02
❑ 89 Bret Saberhagen .... .10 .05
❑ 90 Alan Trammell .... .15 .07
❑ 91 Tony Phillips .... .05 .02
❑ 92 Doug Drabek .... .05 .02
❑ 93 Jeffrey Leonard .... .05 .02
❑ 94 Wally Joyner .... .10 .05
❑ 95 Carney Lansford .... .10 .05
❑ 96 Cal Ripken .... .75 .35
❑ 97 Andres Galarraga .... .20 .09
❑ 98 Kevin Mitchell .... .05 .02
❑ 99 Howard Johnson .... .05 .02
❑ 100A Checklist 28-129 .... .05 .02
❑ 100B Checklist 28-125 .... .05 .02
❑ 101 Melido Perez .... .05 .02
❑ 102 Spike Owen .... .05 .02
❑ 103 Paul Molitor .... .20 .09
❑ 104 Geronimo Berroa .... .05 .02
❑ 105 Ryne Sandberg .... .25 .11
❑ 106 Bryn Smith .... .05 .02
❑ 107 Steve Buechele .... .05 .02
❑ 108 Jim Abbott .... .15 .07
❑ 109 Alvin Davis .... .05 .02
❑ 110 Lee Smith .... .10 .05
❑ 111 Roberto Alomar .... .25 .11
❑ 112 Rick Reuschel .... .05 .02
❑ 113A Kelly Gruber ERR .... .05 .02
(Born 2/22)
❑ 113B Kelly Gruber COR .... .05 .02
(Born 2/26; corrected in factory sets)
❑ 114 Joe Carter .... .10 .05
❑ 115 Jose Rijo .... .05 .02
❑ 116 Greg Minton .... .05 .02
❑ 117 Bob Ojeda .... .05 .02
❑ 118 Glenn Davis .... .05 .02
❑ 119 Jeff Reardon .... .10 .05
❑ 120 Kurt Stillwell .... .05 .02
❑ 121 John Smoltz .... .20 .09
❑ 122 Dwight Evans .... .10 .05
❑ 123 Eric Yelding .... .05 .02
❑ 124 John Franco .... .10 .05
❑ 125 Jose Canseco .... .20 .09
❑ 126 Barry Bonds .... .25 .11
❑ 127 Lee Guetterman .... .05 .02
❑ 128 Jack Clark .... .10 .05
❑ 129 Dave Valle .... .05 .02
❑ 130 Hubie Brooks .... .05 .02
❑ 131 Ernest Riles .... .05 .02
❑ 132 Mike Morgan .... .05 .02
❑ 133 Steve Jeltz .... .05 .02
❑ 134 Jeff D. Robinson .... .05 .02
❑ 135 Ozzie Guillen .... .05 .02
❑ 136 Chili Davis .... .10 .05
❑ 137 Mitch Webster .... .05 .02
❑ 138 Jerry Browne .... .05 .02
❑ 139 Bo Diaz .... .05 .02
❑ 140 Robby Thompson .... .05 .02
❑ 141 Craig Worthington .... .05 .02
❑ 142 Julio Franco .... .05 .02
❑ 143 Brian Holman .... .05 .02
❑ 144 George Brett .... .40 .18
❑ 145 Tom Glavine .... .20 .09
❑ 146 Robin Yount .... .20 .09
❑ 147 Gary Carter .... .20 .09
❑ 148 Ron Kittle .... .05 .02
❑ 149 Tony Fernandez .... .05 .02
❑ 150 Dave Stewart .... .10 .05
❑ 151 Gary Gaetti .... .10 .05
❑ 152 Kevin Elster .... .05 .02
❑ 153 Gerald Perry .... .05 .02
❑ 154 Jesse Orosco .... .05 .02
❑ 155 Wally Backman .... .05 .02
❑ 156 Dennis Martinez .... .10 .05
❑ 157 Rick Sutcliffe .... .05 .02
❑ 158 Greg Maddux .... .60 .25
❑ 159 Andy Hawkins .... .05 .02
❑ 160 John Kruk .... .10 .05
❑ 161 Jose Oquendo .... .05 .02
❑ 162 John Dopson .... .05 .02
❑ 163 Joe Magrane .... .05 .02
❑ 164 Bill Ripken .... .05 .02
❑ 165 Fred Manrique .... .05 .02
❑ 166 Nolan Ryan UER .... .75 .35
(Did not lead NL in K's in '89 as he was in AL in '89)
❑ 167 Damon Berryhill .... .05 .02
❑ 168 Dale Murphy .... .20 .09
❑ 169 Mickey Tettleton .... .10 .05
❑ 170A Kirk McCaskill ERR ...... .05 .02
(Born 4/19)
❑ 170B Kirk McCaskill COR .... .05 .02
(Born 4/9; corrected in factory sets)
❑ 171 Dwight Gooden .... .10 .05
❑ 172 Jose Lind .... .05 .02
❑ 173 B.J. Surhoff .... .10 .05
❑ 174 Ruben Sierra .... .05 .02
❑ 175 Dan Plesac .... .05 .02
❑ 176 Dan Pasqua .... .05 .02
❑ 177 Kelly Downs .... .05 .02
❑ 178 Matt Nokes .... .05 .02
❑ 179 Luis Aquino .... .05 .02
❑ 180 Frank Tanana .... .05 .02
❑ 181 Tony Pena .... .05 .02
❑ 182 Dan Gladden .... .05 .02
❑ 183 Bruce Hurst .... .05 .02
❑ 184 Roger Clemens .... .40 .18
❑ 185 Mark McGwire .... 1.00 .45
❑ 186 Rob Murphy .... .05 .02
❑ 187 Jim Deshaies .... .05 .02
❑ 188 Fred McGriff .... .20 .09
❑ 189 Rob Dibble .... .05 .02
❑ 190 Don Mattingly .... .30 .14
❑ 191 Felix Fermin .... .05 .02
❑ 192 Roberto Kelly .... .05 .02
❑ 193 Dennis Cook .... .05 .02
❑ 194 Darren Daulton .... .10 .05
❑ 195 Alfredo Griffin .... .05 .02
❑ 196 Eric Plunk .... .05 .02
❑ 197 Orel Hershiser .... .10 .05
❑ 198 Paul O'Neill .... .10 .05
❑ 199 Randy Bush .... .05 .02
❑ 200A Checklist 130-231 .... .05 .02
❑ 200B Checklist 126-223 .... .05 .02
❑ 201 Ozzie Smith .... .25 .11
❑ 202 Pete O'Brien .... .05 .02
❑ 203 Jay Howell .... .05 .02
❑ 204 Mark Gubicza .... .05 .02
❑ 205 Ed Whitson .... .05 .02
❑ 206 George Bell .... .05 .02
❑ 207 Mike Scott .... .05 .02
❑ 208 Charlie Leibrandt .... .05 .02
❑ 209 Mike Heath .... .05 .02
❑ 210 Dennis Eckersley .... .15 .07
❑ 211 Mike LaValliere .... .05 .02
❑ 212 Darnell Coles .... .05 .02
❑ 213 Lance Parrish .... .05 .02
❑ 214 Mike Moore .... .05 .02
❑ 215 Steve Finley .... .20 .09
❑ 216 Tim Raines .... .10 .05
❑ 217A Scott Garrelts ERR ...... .05 .02
(Born 10/20)
❑ 217B Scott Garrelts COR ...... .05 .02
(Born 10/30; corrected in factory sets)
❑ 218 Kevin McReynolds .... .05 .02
❑ 219 Dave Gallagher .... .05 .02
❑ 220 Tim Wallach .... .05 .02
❑ 221 Chuck Crim .... .05 .02
❑ 222 Lonnie Smith .... .05 .02
❑ 223 Andre Dawson .... .20 .09
❑ 224 Nelson Santovenia .... .05 .02
❑ 225 Rafael Palmeiro .... .20 .09
❑ 226 Devon White .... .05 .02
❑ 227 Harold Reynolds .... .05 .02
❑ 228 Ellis Burks .... .15 .07
❑ 229 Mark Parent .... .05 .02
❑ 230 Will Clark .... .20 .09
❑ 231 Jimmy Key .... .10 .05
❑ 232 John Farrell .... .05 .02
❑ 233 Eric Davis .... .10 .05
❑ 234 Johnny Ray .... .05 .02
❑ 235 Darryl Strawberry .... .10 .05
❑ 236 Bill Doran .... .05 .02
❑ 237 Greg Gagne .... .05 .02
❑ 238 Jim Eisenreich .... .05 .02
❑ 239 Tommy Gregg .... .05 .02
❑ 240 Marty Barrett .... .05 .02
❑ 241 Rafael Ramirez .... .05 .02
❑ 242 Chris Sabo .... .05 .02
❑ 243 Dave Henderson .... .05 .02
❑ 244 Andy Van Slyke .... .10 .05
❑ 245 Alvaro Espinoza .... .05 .02
❑ 246 Garry Templeton .... .05 .02
❑ 247 Gene Harris .... .05 .02
❑ 248 Kevin Gross .... .05 .02
❑ 249 Brett Butler .... .10 .05
❑ 250 Willie Randolph .... .10 .05
❑ 251 Roger McDowell .... .05 .02
❑ 252 Rafael Belliard .... .05 .02
❑ 253 Steve Rosenberg .... .05 .02
❑ 254 Jack Howell .... .05 .02
❑ 255 Marvell Wynne .... .05 .02
❑ 256 Tom Candiotti .... .05 .02
❑ 257 Todd Benzinger .... .05 .02
❑ 258 Don Robinson .... .05 .02
❑ 259 Phil Bradley .... .05 .02
❑ 260 Cecil Espy .... .05 .02
❑ 261 Scott Bankhead .... .05 .02
❑ 262 Frank White .... .10 .05
❑ 263 Andres Thomas .... .05 .02
❑ 264 Glenn Braggs .... .05 .02
❑ 265 David Cone .... .20 .09
❑ 266 Bobby Thigpen .... .05 .02
❑ 267 Nelson Liriano .... .05 .02
❑ 268 Terry Steinbach .... .10 .05
❑ 269 Kirby Puckett UER .... .30 .14
(Back doesn't consider Joe Torre's .363 in '71)
❑ 270 Gregg Jefferies .... .10 .05
❑ 271 Jeff Blauser .... .05 .02
❑ 272 Cory Snyder .... .05 .02
❑ 273 Roy Smith .... .05 .02
❑ 274 Tom Foley .... .05 .02
❑ 275 Mitch Williams .... .05 .02
❑ 276 Paul Kilgus .... .05 .02
❑ 277 Don Slaught .... .05 .02
❑ 278 Von Hayes .... .05 .02
❑ 279 Vince Coleman .... .05 .02
❑ 280 Mike Boddicker .... .05 .02
❑ 281 Ken Dayley .... .05 .02
❑ 282 Mike Devereaux .... .05 .02

No.	Player	NRMT	EXC
❑ 283	Kenny Rogers	.10	.05
❑ 284	Jeff Russell	.05	.02
❑ 285	Jerome Walton	.05	.02
❑ 286	Derek Lilliquist	.05	.02
❑ 287	Joe Orsulak	.05	.02
❑ 288	Dick Schofield	.05	.02
❑ 289	Ron Darling	.05	.02
❑ 290	Bobby Bonilla	.10	.05
❑ 291	Jim Gantner	.05	.02
❑ 292	Bobby Witt	.05	.02
❑ 293	Greg Brock	.05	.02
❑ 294	Ivan Calderon	.05	.02
❑ 295	Steve Bedrosian	.05	.02
❑ 296	Mike Henneman	.05	.02
❑ 297	Tom Gordon	.15	.07
❑ 298	Lou Whitaker	.10	.05
❑ 299	Terry Pendleton	.10	.05
❑ 300A	Checklist 232-333	.05	.02
❑ 300B	Checklist 224-321	.05	.02
❑ 301	Juan Berenguer	.05	.02
❑ 302	Mark Davis	.05	.02
❑ 303	Nick Esasky	.05	.02
❑ 304	Rickey Henderson	.20	.09
❑ 305	Rick Cerone	.05	.02
❑ 306	Craig Biggio	.20	.09
❑ 307	Duane Ward	.05	.02
❑ 308	Tom Browning	.05	.02
❑ 309	Walt Terrell	.05	.02
❑ 310	Greg Swindell	.05	.02
❑ 311	Dave Righetti	.05	.02
❑ 312	Mike Maddux	.05	.02
❑ 313	Len Dykstra	.10	.05
❑ 314	Jose Gonzalez	.05	.02
❑ 315	Steve Balboni	.05	.02
❑ 316	Mike Scioscia	.05	.02
❑ 317	Ron Oester	.05	.02
❑ 318	Gary Wayne	.05	.02
❑ 319	Todd Worrell	.05	.02
❑ 320	Doug Jones	.05	.02
❑ 321	Jeff Hamilton	.05	.02
❑ 322	Danny Tartabull	.05	.02
❑ 323	Chris James	.05	.02
❑ 324	Mike Flanagan	.05	.02
❑ 325	Gerald Young	.05	.02
❑ 326	Bob Boone	.10	.05
❑ 327	Frank Williams	.05	.02
❑ 328	Dave Parker	.10	.05
❑ 329	Sid Bream	.05	.02
❑ 330	Mike Schooler	.05	.02
❑ 331	Bert Blyleven	.10	.05
❑ 332	Bob Welch	.05	.02
❑ 333	Bob Milacki	.05	.02
❑ 334	Tim Burke	.05	.02
❑ 335	Jose Uribe	.05	.02
❑ 336	Randy Myers	.10	.05
❑ 337	Eric King	.05	.02
❑ 338	Mark Langston	.05	.02
❑ 339	Teddy Higuera	.05	.02
❑ 340	Oddibe McDowell	.05	.02
❑ 341	Lloyd McClendon	.05	.02
❑ 342	Pascual Perez	.05	.02
❑ 343	Kevin Brown UER (Signed is misspelled as signeed on back)	.20	.09
❑ 344	Chuck Finley	.10	.05
❑ 345	Erik Hanson	.05	.02
❑ 346	Rich Gedman	.05	.02
❑ 347	Bip Roberts	.05	.02
❑ 348	Matt Williams	.20	.09
❑ 349	Tom Henke	.05	.02
❑ 350	Brad Komminsk	.05	.02
❑ 351	Jeff Reed	.05	.02
❑ 352	Brian Downing	.05	.02
❑ 353	Frank Viola	.05	.02
❑ 354	Terry Puhl	.05	.02
❑ 355	Brian Harper	.05	.02
❑ 356	Steve Farr	.05	.02
❑ 357	Joe Boever	.05	.02
❑ 358	Danny Heep	.05	.02
❑ 359	Larry Andersen	.05	.02
❑ 360	Rolando Roomes	.05	.02
❑ 361	Mike Gallego	.05	.02
❑ 362	Bob Kipper	.05	.02
❑ 363	Clay Parker	.05	.02
❑ 364	Mike Pagliarulo	.05	.02
❑ 365	Ken Griffey Jr. UER (Signed through 1990, should be 1991)	2.00	.90
❑ 366	Rex Hudler	.05	.02
❑ 367	Pat Sheridan	.05	.02
❑ 368	Kirk Gibson	.10	.05
❑ 369	Jeff Parrett	.05	.02
❑ 370	Bob Walk	.05	.02
❑ 371	Ken Patterson	.05	.02
❑ 372	Bryan Harvey	.05	.02
❑ 373	Mike Bielecki	.05	.02
❑ 374	Tom Magrann	.05	.02
❑ 375	Rick Mahler	.05	.02
❑ 376	Craig Lefferts	.05	.02
❑ 377	Gregg Olson	.05	.02
❑ 378	Jamie Moyer	.05	.02
❑ 379	Randy Johnson	.30	.14
❑ 380	Jeff Montgomery	.10	.05
❑ 381	Marty Clary	.05	.02
❑ 382	Bill Spiers	.05	.02
❑ 383	Dave Magadan	.05	.02
❑ 384	Greg Hibbard	.05	.02
❑ 385	Ernie Whitt	.05	.02
❑ 386	Rick Honeycutt	.05	.02
❑ 387	Dave West	.05	.02
❑ 388	Keith Hernandez	.10	.05
❑ 389	Jose Alvarez	.05	.02
❑ 390	Joey Belle	1.00	.45
❑ 391	Rick Aguilera	.10	.05
❑ 392	Mike Fitzgerald	.05	.02
❑ 393	Dwight Smith	.05	.02
❑ 394	Steve Wilson	.05	.02
❑ 395	Bob Geren	.05	.02
❑ 396	Randy Ready	.05	.02
❑ 397	Ken Hill	.15	.07
❑ 398	Jody Reed	.05	.02
❑ 399	Tom Brunansky	.05	.02
❑ 400A	Checklist 334-435	.05	.02
❑ 400B	Checklist 322-419	.05	.02
❑ 401	Rene Gonzales	.05	.02
❑ 402	Harold Baines	.10	.05
❑ 403	Cecilio Guante	.05	.02
❑ 404	Joe Girardi	.15	.07
❑ 405A	Sergio Valdez ERR (Card front shows black line crossing S in Sergio)	.05	.02
❑ 405B	Sergio Valdez COR	.05	.02
❑ 406	Mark Williamson	.05	.02
❑ 407	Glenn Hoffman	.05	.02
❑ 408	Jeff Innis	.05	.02
❑ 409	Randy Kramer	.05	.02
❑ 410	Charlie O'Brien	.05	.02
❑ 411	Charlie Hough	.10	.05
❑ 412	Gus Polidor	.05	.02
❑ 413	Ron Karkovice	.05	.02
❑ 414	Trevor Wilson	.05	.02
❑ 415	Kevin Ritz	.05	.02
❑ 416	Gary Thurman	.05	.02
❑ 417	Jeff M. Robinson	.05	.02
❑ 418	Scott Terry	.05	.02
❑ 419	Tim Laudner	.05	.02
❑ 420	Dennis Rasmussen	.05	.02
❑ 421	Luis Rivera	.05	.02
❑ 422	Jim Corsi	.05	.02
❑ 423	Dennis Lamp	.05	.02
❑ 424	Ken Caminiti	.20	.09
❑ 425	David Wells	.15	.07
❑ 426	Norm Charlton	.05	.02
❑ 427	Deion Sanders	.20	.09
❑ 428	Dion James	.05	.02
❑ 429	Chuck Cary	.05	.02
❑ 430	Ken Howell	.05	.02
❑ 431	Steve Lake	.05	.02
❑ 432	Kal Daniels	.05	.02
❑ 433	Lance McCullers	.05	.02
❑ 434	Lenny Harris	.05	.02
❑ 435	Scott Scudder	.05	.02
❑ 436	Gene Larkin	.05	.02
❑ 437	Dan Quisenberry	.05	.02
❑ 438	Steve Olin	.10	.05
❑ 439	Mickey Hatcher	.05	.02
❑ 440	Willie Wilson	.05	.02
❑ 441	Mark Grant	.05	.02
❑ 442	Mookie Wilson	.10	.05
❑ 443	Alex Trevino	.05	.02
❑ 444	Pat Tabler	.05	.02
❑ 445	Dave Bergman	.05	.02
❑ 446	Todd Burns	.05	.02
❑ 447	R.J. Reynolds	.05	.02
❑ 448	Jay Buhner	.20	.09
❑ 449	Lee Stevens	.10	.05
❑ 450	Ron Hassey	.05	.02
❑ 451	Bob Melvin	.05	.02
❑ 452	Dave Martinez	.05	.02
❑ 453	Greg Litton	.05	.02
❑ 454	Mark Carreon	.05	.02
❑ 455	Scott Fletcher	.05	.02
❑ 456	Otis Nixon	.10	.05
❑ 457	Tony Fossas	.05	.02
❑ 458	John Russell	.05	.02
❑ 459	Paul Assenmacher	.05	.02
❑ 460	Zane Smith	.05	.02
❑ 461	Jack Daugherty	.05	.02
❑ 462	Rich Monteleone	.05	.02
❑ 463	Greg Briley	.05	.02
❑ 464	Mike Smithson	.05	.02
❑ 465	Benito Santiago	.05	.02
❑ 466	Jeff Brantley	.05	.02
❑ 467	Jose Nunez	.05	.02
❑ 468	Scott Bailes	.05	.02
❑ 469	Ken Griffey Sr.	.05	.02
❑ 470	Bob McClure	.05	.02
❑ 471	Mackey Sasser	.05	.02
❑ 472	Glenn Wilson	.05	.02
❑ 473	Kevin Tapani	.10	.05
❑ 474	Bill Buckner	.05	.02
❑ 475	Ron Gant	.10	.05
❑ 476	Kevin Romine	.05	.02
❑ 477	Juan Agosto	.05	.02
❑ 478	Herm Winningham	.05	.02
❑ 479	Storm Davis	.05	.02
❑ 480	Jeff King	.10	.05
❑ 481	Kevin Mmahat	.05	.02
❑ 482	Carmelo Martinez	.05	.02
❑ 483	Omar Vizquel	.20	.09
❑ 484	Jim Dwyer	.05	.02
❑ 485	Bob Knepper	.05	.02
❑ 486	Dave Anderson	.05	.02
❑ 487	Ron Jones	.05	.02
❑ 488	Jay Bell	.10	.05
❑ 489	Sammy Sosa	5.00	2.20
❑ 490	Kent Anderson	.05	.02
❑ 491	Domingo Ramos	.05	.02
❑ 492	Dave Clark	.05	.02
❑ 493	Tim Birtsas	.05	.02
❑ 494	Ken Oberkfell	.05	.02
❑ 495	Larry Sheets	.05	.02
❑ 496	Jeff Kunkel	.05	.02
❑ 497	Jim Presley	.05	.02
❑ 498	Mike Macfarlane	.05	.02
❑ 499	Pete Smith	.05	.02
❑ 500A	Checklist 436-537 DP	.05	.02
❑ 500B	Checklist 420-517	.05	.02
❑ 501	Gary Sheffield	.20	.09
❑ 502	Terry Bross	.05	.02
❑ 503	Jerry Kutzler	.05	.02
❑ 504	Lloyd Moseby	.05	.02
❑ 505	Curt Young	.05	.02
❑ 506	Al Newman	.05	.02
❑ 507	Keith Miller	.05	.02
❑ 508	Mike Stanton	.05	.02
❑ 509	Rich Yett	.05	.02
❑ 510	Tim Drummond	.05	.02
❑ 511	Joe Hesketh	.05	.02
❑ 512	Rick Wrona	.05	.02
❑ 513	Luis Salazar	.05	.02
❑ 514	Hal Morris	.05	.02
❑ 515	Terry Mulholland	.05	.02
❑ 516	John Morris	.05	.02
❑ 517	Carlos Quintana	.05	.02
❑ 518	Frank DiPino	.05	.02
❑ 519	Randy Milligan	.05	.02
❑ 520	Chad Kreuter	.05	.02
❑ 521	Mike Jeffcoat	.05	.02
❑ 522	Mike Harkey	.05	.02
❑ 523A	Andy Nezelek ERR (Wrong birth year)	.05	.02
❑ 523B	Andy Nezelek COR (Finally corrected in factory sets)	.20	.09

❑	524	Dave Schmidt	.05	.02
❑	525	Tony Armas	.05	.02
❑	526	Barry Lyons	.05	.02
❑	527	Rick Reed	.05	.02
❑	528	Jerry Reuss	.05	.02
❑	529	Dean Palmer	.25	.11
❑	530	Jeff Peterek	.05	.02
❑	531	Carlos Martinez	.05	.02
❑	532	Atlee Hammaker	.05	.02
❑	533	Mike Brumley	.05	.02
❑	534	Terry Leach	.05	.02
❑	535	Doug Strange	.05	.02
❑	536	Jose DeLeon	.05	.02
❑	537	Shane Rawley	.05	.02
❑	538	Joey Cora	.15	.07
❑	539	Eric Hetzel	.05	.02
❑	540	Gene Nelson	.05	.02
❑	541	Wes Gardner	.05	.02
❑	542	Mark Portugal	.05	.02
❑	543	Al Leiter	.20	.09
❑	544	Jack Armstrong	.05	.02
❑	545	Greg Cadaret	.05	.02
❑	546	Rod Nichols	.05	.02
❑	547	Luis Polonia	.05	.02
❑	548	Charlie Hayes	.05	.02
❑	549	Dickie Thon	.05	.02
❑	550	Tim Crews	.05	.02
❑	551	Dave Winfield	.20	.09
❑	552	Mike Davis	.05	.02
❑	553	Ron Robinson	.05	.02
❑	554	Carmen Castillo	.05	.02
❑	555	John Costello	.05	.02
❑	556	Bud Black	.05	.02
❑	557	Rick Dempsey	.05	.02
❑	558	Jim Acker	.05	.02
❑	559	Eric Show	.05	.02
❑	560	Pat Borders	.05	.02
❑	561	Danny Darwin	.05	.02
❑	562	Rick Luecken	.05	.02
❑	563	Edwin Nunez	.05	.02
❑	564	Felix Jose	.05	.02
❑	565	John Cangelosi	.05	.02
❑	566	Bill Swift	.05	.02
❑	567	Bill Schroeder	.05	.02
❑	568	Stan Javier	.05	.02
❑	569	Jim Traber	.05	.02
❑	570	Wallace Johnson	.05	.02
❑	571	Donell Nixon	.05	.02
❑	572	Sid Fernandez	.05	.02
❑	573	Lance Johnson	.05	.02
❑	574	Andy McGaffigan	.05	.02
❑	575	Mark Knudson	.05	.02
❑	576	Tommy Greene	.05	.02
❑	577	Mark Grace	.20	.09
❑	578	Larry Walker	1.00	.45
❑	579	Mike Stanley	.05	.02
❑	580	Mike Witt DP	.05	.02
❑	581	Scott Bradley	.05	.02
❑	582	Greg A. Harris	.05	.02
❑	583A	Kevin Hickey ERR	.20	.09
❑	583B	Kevin Hickey COR	.05	.02
❑	584	Lee Mazzilli	.05	.02
❑	585	Jeff Pico	.05	.02
❑	586	Joe Oliver	.05	.02
❑	587	Willie Fraser DP	.05	.02
❑	588	Carl Yastrzemski Puzzle Card DP	.20	.09
❑	589	Kevin Bass DP	.05	.02
❑	590	John Moses DP	.05	.02
❑	591	Tom Pagnozzi DP	.05	.02
❑	592	Tony Castillo DP	.05	.02
❑	593	Jerald Clark DP	.05	.02
❑	594	Dan Schatzeder	.05	.02
❑	595	Luis Quinones DP	.05	.02
❑	596	Pete Harnisch DP	.05	.02
❑	597	Gary Redus	.05	.02
❑	598	Mel Hall	.05	.02
❑	599	Rick Schu	.05	.02
❑	600A	Checklist 538-639	.05	.02
❑	600B	Checklist 518-617	.05	.02
❑	601	Mike Kingery DP	.05	.02
❑	602	Terry Kennedy DP	.05	.02
❑	603	Mike Sharperson DP	.05	.02
❑	604	Don Carman DP	.05	.02
❑	605	Jim Gott	.05	.02
❑	606	Donn Pall DP	.05	.02
❑	607	Rance Mulliniks	.05	.02
❑	608	Curt Wilkerson DP	.05	.02
❑	609	Mike Felder DP	.05	.02
❑	610	Guillermo Hernandez DP	.05	.02
❑	611	Candy Maldonado DP	.05	.02
❑	612	Mark Thurmond DP	.05	.02
❑	613	Rick Leach DP	.05	.02
❑	614	Jerry Reed DP	.05	.02
❑	615	Franklin Stubbs	.05	.02
❑	616	Billy Hatcher DP	.05	.02
❑	617	Don August DP	.05	.02
❑	618	Tim Teufel	.05	.02
❑	619	Shawn Hillegas DP	.05	.02
❑	620	Manny Lee	.05	.02
❑	621	Gary Ward DP	.05	.02
❑	622	Mark Guthrie DP	.05	.02
❑	623	Jeff Musselman DP	.05	.02
❑	624	Mark Lemke DP	.05	.02
❑	625	Fernando Valenzuela	.10	.05
❑	626	Paul Sorrento DP	.20	.09
❑	627	Glenallen Hill DP	.05	.02
❑	628	Les Lancaster DP	.05	.02
❑	629	Vance Law DP	.05	.02
❑	630	Randy Velarde DP	.05	.02
❑	631	Todd Frohwirth DP	.05	.02
❑	632	Willie McGee	.10	.05
❑	633	Dennis Boyd DP	.05	.02
❑	634	Cris Carpenter DP	.05	.02
❑	635	Brian Holton	.05	.02
❑	636	Tracy Jones DP	.05	.02
❑	637A	Terry Steinbach AS (Recent Major League Performance)	.05	.02
❑	637B	Terry Steinbach AS (All-Star Game Performance)	.05	.02
❑	638	Brady Anderson	.20	.09
❑	639A	Jack Morris ERR (Card front shows black line crossing J in Jack)	.05	.02
❑	639B	Jack Morris COR	.05	.02
❑	640	Jaime Navarro	.05	.02
❑	641	Darrin Jackson	.05	.02
❑	642	Mike Dyer	.05	.02
❑	643	Mike Schmidt	.25	.11
❑	644	Henry Cotto	.05	.02
❑	645	John Cerutti	.05	.02
❑	646	Francisco Cabrera	.05	.02
❑	647	Scott Sanderson	.05	.02
❑	648	Brian Meyer	.05	.02
❑	649	Ray Searage	.05	.02
❑	650A	Bo Jackson AS (Recent Major League Performance)	.10	.05
❑	650B	Bo Jackson AS (All-Star Game Performance)	.10	.05
❑	651	Steve Lyons	.05	.02
❑	652	Mike LaCoss	.05	.02
❑	653	Ted Power	.05	.02
❑	654A	Howard Johnson AS (Recent Major League Performance)	.05	.02
❑	654B	Howard Johnson AS (All-Star Game Performance)	.05	.02
❑	655	Mauro Gozzo	.05	.02
❑	656	Mike Blowers	.10	.05
❑	657	Paul Gibson	.05	.02
❑	658	Neal Heaton	.05	.02
❑	659	Nolan Ryan 5000K COR (Still an error as Ryan did not lead AL in K's in '75)	.40	.18
❑	659A	Nolan Ryan 5000K (665 King of Kings back) ERR	1.50	.70
❑	660A	Harold Baines AS (Black line through star on front; Recent Major League Performance)	.75	.35
❑	660B	Harold Baines AS (Black line through star on front; All-Star Game Performance)	1.00	.45
❑	660C	Harold Baines AS (Black line behind star on front; Recent Major League Performance)	.20	.09
❑	660D	Harold Baines AS (Black line behind star on front; All-Star Game Performance)	.05	.02
❑	661	Gary Pettis	.05	.02
❑	662	Clint Zavaras	.05	.02
❑	663A	Rick Reuschel AS (Recent Major League Performance)	.05	.02
❑	663B	Rick Reuschel AS (All-Star Game Performance)	.05	.02
❑	664	Alejandro Pena	.05	.02
❑	665	Nolan Ryan KING COR	.40	.18
❑	665A	Nolan Ryan KING (659 5000 K back) ERR	1.50	.70
❑	665C	Nolan Ryan KING ERR (No number on back; in factory sets)	.75	.35
❑	666	Ricky Horton	.05	.02
❑	667	Curt Schilling	.20	.09
❑	668	Bill Landrum	.05	.02
❑	669	Todd Stottlemyre	.10	.05
❑	670	Tim Leary	.05	.02
❑	671	John Wetteland	.20	.09
❑	672	Calvin Schiraldi	.05	.02
❑	673A	Ruben Sierra AS (Recent Major League Performance)	.05	.02
❑	673B	Ruben Sierra AS (All-Star Game Performance)	.05	.02
❑	674A	Pedro Guerrero AS (Recent Major League Performance)	.05	.02
❑	674B	Pedro Guerrero AS (All-Star Game Performance)	.05	.02
❑	675	Ken Phelps	.05	.02
❑	676A	Cal Ripken AS (All-Star Game Performance)	.40	.18
❑	676B	Cal Ripken AS (Recent Major League Performance)	.75	.35
❑	677	Denny Walling	.05	.02
❑	678	Goose Gossage	.10	.05
❑	679	Gary Mielke	.05	.02
❑	680	Bill Bathe	.05	.02
❑	681	Tom Lawless	.05	.02
❑	682	Xavier Hernandez	.05	.02
❑	683A	Kirby Puckett AS (Recent Major League Performance)	.20	.09
❑	683B	Kirby Puckett AS (All-Star Game Performance)	.20	.09
❑	684	Mariano Duncan	.05	.02
❑	685	Ramon Martinez	.15	.07
❑	686	Tim Jones	.05	.02
❑	687	Tom Filer	.05	.02
❑	688	Steve Lombardozzi	.05	.02
❑	689	Bernie Williams	1.25	.55
❑	690	Chip Hale	.05	.02
❑	691	Beau Allred	.05	.02
❑	692A	Ryne Sandberg AS (Recent Major League Performance)	.20	.09
❑	692B	Ryne Sandberg AS (All-Star Game Performance)	.20	.09
❑	693	Jeff Huson	.05	.02
❑	694	Curt Ford	.05	.02
❑	695A	Eric Davis AS (Recent Major League Performance)	.05	.02

Card	MINT	NRMT
❑ 695B Eric Davis AS (All-Star Game Performance)	.05	.02
❑ 696 Scott Lusader	.05	.02
❑ 697A Mark McGwire AS (Recent Major League Performance)	.20	.09
❑ 697B Mark McGwire AS (All-Star Game Performance)	.10	.05
❑ 698 Steve Cummings	.05	.02
❑ 699 George Canale	.05	.02
❑ 700A Checklist 640-715 and BC1-BC26	.20	.09
❑ 700B Checklist 640-716 and BC1-BC26	.10	.05
❑ 700C Checklist 618-716	.05	.02
❑ 701A Julio Franco AS (Recent Major League Performance)	.05	.02
❑ 701B Julio Franco AS (All-Star Game Performance)	.05	.02
❑ 702 Dave Johnson (P)	.05	.02
❑ 703A Dave Stewart AS (Recent Major League Performance)	.05	.02
❑ 703B Dave Stewart AS (All-Star Game Performance)	.05	.02
❑ 704 Dave Justice	.75	.35
❑ 705 Tony Gwynn AS (All-Star Game Performance)	.25	.11
❑ 705A Tony Gwynn AS (Recent Major League Performance)	.20	.09
❑ 706 Greg Myers	.05	.02
❑ 707A Will Clark AS (Recent Major League Performance)	.20	.09
❑ 707B Will Clark AS (All-Star Game Performance)	.20	.09
❑ 708A Benito Santiago AS (Recent Major League Performance)	.05	.02
❑ 708B Benito Santiago AS (All-Star Game Performance)	.05	.02
❑ 709 Larry McWilliams	.05	.02
❑ 710A Ozzie Smith AS (Recent Major League Performance)	.20	.09
❑ 710B Ozzie Smith AS (All-Star Game Performance)	.10	.05
❑ 711 John Olerud	.50	.23
❑ 712A Wade Boggs AS (Recent Major League Performance)	.10	.05
❑ 712B Wade Boggs AS (All-Star Game Performance)	.10	.05
❑ 713 Gary Eave	.05	.02
❑ 714 Bob Tewksbury	.05	.02
❑ 715A Kevin Mitchell AS (Recent Major League Performance)	.05	.02
❑ 715B Kevin Mitchell AS (All-Star Game Performance)	.05	.02
❑ 716 Bart Giamatti COMM (In Memoriam)	.20	.09

1990 Donruss Rookies

	MINT	NRMT
COMP.FACT.SET (56)	2.00	.90
COMMON CARD (1-56)	.05	.02

Card	MINT	NRMT
❑ 1 Sandy Alomar Jr. UER (No stitches on baseball on Donruss logo on card front)	.15	.07
❑ 2 John Olerud	.20	.09
❑ 3 Pat Combs	.05	.02
❑ 4 Brian DuBois	.05	.02
❑ 5 Felix Jose	.05	.02
❑ 6 Delino DeShields	.20	.09
❑ 7 Mike Stanton	.05	.02
❑ 8 Mike Munoz	.05	.02
❑ 9 Craig Grebeck	.05	.02
❑ 10 Joe Kraemer	.05	.02
❑ 11 Jeff Huson	.05	.02
❑ 12 Bill Sampen	.05	.02
❑ 13 Brian Bohanon	.05	.02
❑ 14 Dave Justice	.75	.35
❑ 15 Robin Ventura	.20	.09
❑ 16 Greg Vaughn	.40	.18
❑ 17 Wayne Edwards	.05	.02
❑ 18 Shawn Boskie	.05	.02
❑ 19 Carlos Baerga	.25	.11
❑ 20 Mark Gardner	.05	.02
❑ 21 Kevin Appier	.15	.07
❑ 22 Mike Harkey	.05	.02
❑ 23 Tim Layana	.05	.02
❑ 24 Glenallen Hill	.05	.02
❑ 25 Jerry Kutzler	.05	.02
❑ 26 Mike Blowers	.10	.05
❑ 27 Scott Ruskin	.05	.02
❑ 28 Dana Kiecker	.05	.02
❑ 29 Willie Blair	.05	.02
❑ 30 Ben McDonald	.05	.02
❑ 31 Todd Zeile	.10	.05
❑ 32 Scott Coolbaugh	.05	.02
❑ 33 Xavier Hernandez	.05	.02
❑ 34 Mike Hartley	.05	.02
❑ 35 Kevin Tapani	.10	.05
❑ 36 Kevin Wickander	.05	.02
❑ 37 Carlos Hernandez	.20	.09
❑ 38 Brian Traxler	.05	.02
❑ 39 Marty Brown	.05	.02
❑ 40 Scott Radinsky	.05	.02
❑ 41 Julio Machado	.05	.02
❑ 42 Steve Avery	.05	.02
❑ 43 Mark Lemke	.05	.02
❑ 44 Alan Mills	.05	.02
❑ 45 Marquis Grissom	.20	.09
❑ 46 Greg Olson	.05	.02
❑ 47 Dave Hollins	.20	.09
❑ 48 Jerald Clark	.05	.02
❑ 49 Eric Anthony	.05	.02
❑ 50 Tim Drummond	.05	.02
❑ 51 John Burkett	.10	.05
❑ 52 Brent Knackert	.05	.02
❑ 53 Jeff Shaw	.05	.02
❑ 54 John Orton	.05	.02
❑ 55 Terry Shumpert	.05	.02
❑ 56 Checklist 1-56	.05	.02

1991 Donruss

	MINT	NRMT
COMPLETE SET (770)	8.00	3.60
COMP.FACT.w/LEAF PREV	10.00	4.50
COMP.FACT.w/STUDIO PREV	10.00	4.50
COMMON CARD (1-770)	.05	.02
COMP.STARGELL PUZZLE	1.00	.45

Card	MINT	NRMT
❑ 1 Dave Stieb DK	.05	.02
❑ 2 Craig Biggio DK	.10	.05
❑ 3 Cecil Fielder DK	.05	.02
❑ 4 Barry Bonds DK	.20	.09
❑ 5 Barry Larkin DK	.10	.05
❑ 6 Dave Parker DK	.05	.02
❑ 7 Len Dykstra DK	.05	.02
❑ 8 Bobby Thigpen DK	.05	.02
❑ 9 Roger Clemens DK	.20	.09
❑ 10 Ron Gant DK UER (No trademark on team logo on back)	.10	.05
❑ 11 Delino DeShields DK	.05	.02
❑ 12 Roberto Alomar DK UER (No trademark on team logo on back)	.10	.05
❑ 13 Sandy Alomar Jr. DK	.05	.02
❑ 14 Ryne Sandberg DK UER (Was DK in '85, not '83 as shown)	.20	.09
❑ 15 Ramon Martinez DK	.05	.02
❑ 16 Edgar Martinez DK	.10	.05
❑ 17 Dave Magadan DK	.05	.02
❑ 18 Matt Williams DK	.10	.05
❑ 19 Rafael Palmeiro DK UER (No trademark on team logo on back)	.10	.05
❑ 20 Bob Welch DK	.05	.02
❑ 21 Dave Righetti DK	.05	.02
❑ 22 Brian Harper DK	.05	.02
❑ 23 Gregg Olson DK	.05	.02
❑ 24 Kurt Stillwell DK	.05	.02
❑ 25 Pedro Guerrero DK UER (No trademark on team logo on back)	.05	.02
❑ 26 Chuck Finley DK UER (No trademark on team logo on back)	.05	.02
❑ 27 DK Checklist 1-27	.05	.02
❑ 28 Tino Martinez RR	.20	.09
❑ 29 Mark Lewis RR	.05	.02
❑ 30 Bernard Gilkey RR	.10	.05
❑ 31 Hensley Meulens RR	.05	.02
❑ 32 Derek Bell RR	.20	.09
❑ 33 Jose Offerman RR	.05	.02
❑ 34 Terry Bross RR	.05	.02
❑ 35 Leo Gomez RR	.05	.02
❑ 36 Derrick May RR	.05	.02
❑ 37 Kevin Morton RR	.05	.02
❑ 38 Moises Alou RR	.20	.09
❑ 39 Julio Valera RR	.05	.02
❑ 40 Milt Cuyler RR	.05	.02
❑ 41 Phil Plantier RR	.05	.02
❑ 42 Scott Chiamparino RR	.05	.02
❑ 43 Ray Lankford RR	.20	.09
❑ 44 Mickey Morandini RR	.05	.02
❑ 45 Dave Hansen RR	.05	.02
❑ 46 Kevin Belcher RR	.05	.02
❑ 47 Darrin Fletcher RR	.05	.02
❑ 48 Steve Sax AS	.05	.02
❑ 49 Ken Griffey Jr. AS	.75	.35
❑ 50A Jose Canseco AS ERR (Team in stat box should be AL, not A's)	.10	.05
❑ 50B Jose Canseco AS COR	.75	.35
❑ 51 Sandy Alomar Jr. AS	.05	.02
❑ 52 Cal Ripken AS	.40	.18
❑ 53 Rickey Henderson AS	.10	.05
❑ 54 Bob Welch AS	.05	.02
❑ 55 Wade Boggs AS	.10	.05
❑ 56 Mark McGwire AS	.50	.23
❑ 57A Jack McDowell ERR	.20	.09

(Career stats do not include 1990)
❑ 57B Jack McDowell COR .25 .11
(Career stats do not include 1990)
❑ 58 Jose Lind .05 .02
❑ 59 Alex Fernandez .10 .05
❑ 60 Pat Combs .05 .02
❑ 61 Mike Walker .05 .02
❑ 62 Juan Samuel .05 .02
❑ 63 Mike Blowers UER .05 .02
(Last line has aseball, not baseball)
❑ 64 Mark Guthrie .05 .02
❑ 65 Mark Salas .05 .02
❑ 66 Tim Jones .05 .02
❑ 67 Tim Leary .05 .02
❑ 68 Andres Galarraga .20 .09
❑ 69 Bob Milacki .05 .02
❑ 70 Tim Belcher .05 .02
❑ 71 Todd Zeile .10 .05
❑ 72 Jerome Walton .05 .02
❑ 73 Kevin Seitzer .05 .02
❑ 74 Jerald Clark .05 .02
❑ 75 John Smoltz UER .20 .09
(Born in Detroit, not Warren)
❑ 76 Mike Henneman .05 .02
❑ 77 Ken Griffey Jr. 1.50 .70
❑ 78 Jim Abbott .10 .05
❑ 79 Gregg Jefferies .05 .02
❑ 80 Kevin Reimer .05 .02
❑ 81 Roger Clemens .40 .18
❑ 82 Mike Fitzgerald .05 .02
❑ 83 Bruce Hurst UER .05 .02
(Middle name is Lee, not Vee)
❑ 84 Eric Davis .10 .05
❑ 85 Paul Molitor .20 .09
❑ 86 Will Clark .20 .09
❑ 87 Mike Bielecki .05 .02
❑ 88 Bret Saberhagen .10 .05
❑ 89 Nolan Ryan .75 .35
❑ 90 Bobby Thigpen .05 .02
❑ 91 Dickie Thon .05 .02
❑ 92 Duane Ward .05 .02
❑ 93 Luis Polonia .05 .02
❑ 94 Terry Kennedy .05 .02
❑ 95 Kent Hrbek .10 .05
❑ 96 Danny Jackson .05 .02
❑ 97 Sid Fernandez .05 .02
❑ 98 Jimmy Key .10 .05
❑ 99 Franklin Stubbs .05 .02
❑ 100 Checklist 28-103 .05 .02
❑ 101 R.J. Reynolds .05 .02
❑ 102 Dave Stewart .10 .05
❑ 103 Dan Pasqua .05 .02
❑ 104 Dan Plesac .05 .02
❑ 105 Mark McGwire 1.00 .45
❑ 106 John Farrell .05 .02
❑ 107 Don Mattingly .30 .14
❑ 108 Carlton Fisk .20 .09
❑ 109 Ken Oberkfell .05 .02
❑ 110 Darrel Akerfelds .05 .02
❑ 111 Gregg Olson .05 .02
❑ 112 Mike Scioscia .05 .02
❑ 113 Bryn Smith .05 .02
❑ 114 Bob Geren .05 .02
❑ 115 Tom Candiotti .05 .02
❑ 116 Kevin Tapani .05 .02
❑ 117 Jeff Treadway .05 .02
❑ 118 Alan Trammell .15 .07
❑ 119 Pete O'Brien .05 .02
(Blue shading goes through stats)
❑ 120 Joel Skinner .05 .02
❑ 121 Mike LaValliere .05 .02
❑ 122 Dwight Evans .10 .05
❑ 123 Jody Reed .05 .02
❑ 124 Lee Guetterman .05 .02
❑ 125 Tim Burke .05 .02
❑ 126 Dave Johnson .05 .02
❑ 127 Fernando Valenzuela .10 .05
(Lower large stripe in yellow instead of blue) UER
❑ 128 Jose DeLeon .05 .02
❑ 129 Andre Dawson .20 .09
❑ 130 Gerald Perry .05 .02
❑ 131 Greg W. Harris .05 .02
❑ 132 Tom Glavine .20 .09
❑ 133 Lance McCullers .05 .02
❑ 134 Randy Johnson .25 .11
❑ 135 Lance Parrish UER .05 .02
(Born in McKeesport, not Clairton)
❑ 136 Mackey Sasser .05 .02
❑ 137 Geno Petralli .05 .02
❑ 138 Dennis Lamp .05 .02
❑ 139 Dennis Martinez .10 .05
❑ 140 Mike Pagliarulo .05 .02
❑ 141 Hal Morris .05 .02
❑ 142 Dave Parker .10 .05
❑ 143 Brett Butler .10 .05
❑ 144 Paul Assenmacher .05 .02
❑ 145 Mark Gubicza .05 .02
❑ 146 Charlie Hough .10 .05
❑ 147 Sammy Sosa 1.00 .45
❑ 148 Randy Ready .05 .02
❑ 149 Kelly Gruber .05 .02
❑ 150 Devon White .05 .02
❑ 151 Gary Carter .20 .09
❑ 152 Gene Larkin .05 .02
❑ 153 Chris Sabo .05 .02
❑ 154 David Cone .10 .05
❑ 155 Todd Stottlemyre .10 .05
❑ 156 Glenn Wilson .05 .02
❑ 157 Bob Walk .05 .02
❑ 158 Mike Gallego .05 .02
❑ 159 Greg Hibbard .05 .02
❑ 160 Chris Bosio .05 .02
❑ 161 Mike Moore .05 .02
❑ 162 Jerry Browne UER .05 .02
(Born Christiansted, should be St. Croix)
❑ 163 Steve Sax UER .05 .02
(No asterisk next to his 1989 At Bats)
❑ 164 Melido Perez .05 .02
❑ 165 Danny Darwin .05 .02
❑ 166 Roger McDowell .05 .02
❑ 167 Bill Ripken .05 .02
❑ 168 Mike Sharperson .05 .02
❑ 169 Lee Smith .10 .05
❑ 170 Matt Nokes .05 .02
❑ 171 Jesse Orosco .05 .02
❑ 172 Rick Aguilera .10 .05
❑ 173 Jim Presley .05 .02
❑ 174 Lou Whitaker .10 .05
❑ 175 Harold Reynolds .05 .02
❑ 176 Brook Jacoby .05 .02
❑ 177 Wally Backman .05 .02
❑ 178 Wade Boggs .20 .09
❑ 179 Chuck Cary .05 .02
(Comma after DOB, not on other cards)
❑ 180 Tom Foley .05 .02
❑ 181 Pete Harnisch .05 .02
❑ 182 Mike Morgan .05 .02
❑ 183 Bob Tewksbury .05 .02
❑ 184 Joe Girardi .10 .05
❑ 185 Storm Davis .05 .02
❑ 186 Ed Whitson .05 .02
❑ 187 Steve Avery UER .05 .02
(Born in New Jersey, should be Michigan)
❑ 188 Lloyd Moseby .05 .02
❑ 189 Scott Bankhead .05 .02
❑ 190 Mark Langston .05 .02
❑ 191 Kevin McReynolds .05 .02
❑ 192 Julio Franco .05 .02
❑ 193 John Dopson .05 .02
❑ 194 Dennis Boyd .05 .02
❑ 195 Bip Roberts .05 .02
❑ 196 Billy Hatcher .05 .02
❑ 197 Edgar Diaz .05 .02
❑ 198 Greg Litton .05 .02
❑ 199 Mark Grace .20 .09
❑ 200 Checklist 104-179 .05 .02
❑ 201 George Brett .40 .18
❑ 202 Jeff Russell .05 .02
❑ 203 Ivan Calderon .05 .02
❑ 204 Ken Howell .05 .02
❑ 205 Tom Henke .05 .02
❑ 206 Bryan Harvey .05 .02
❑ 207 Steve Bedrosian .05 .02
❑ 208 Al Newman .05 .02
❑ 209 Randy Myers .10 .05
❑ 210 Daryl Boston .05 .02
❑ 211 Manny Lee .05 .02
❑ 212 Dave Smith .05 .02
❑ 213 Don Slaught .05 .02
❑ 214 Walt Weiss .05 .02
❑ 215 Donn Pall .05 .02
❑ 216 Jaime Navarro .05 .02
❑ 217 Willie Randolph .10 .05
❑ 218 Rudy Seanez .05 .02
❑ 219 Jim Leyritz .10 .05
❑ 220 Ron Karkovice .05 .02
❑ 221 Ken Caminiti .20 .09
❑ 222 Von Hayes .05 .02
❑ 223 Cal Ripken .75 .35
❑ 224 Lenny Harris .05 .02
❑ 225 Milt Thompson .05 .02
❑ 226 Alvaro Espinoza .05 .02
❑ 227 Chris James .05 .02
❑ 228 Dan Gladden .05 .02
❑ 229 Jeff Blauser .05 .02
❑ 230 Mike Heath .05 .02
❑ 231 Omar Vizquel .20 .09
❑ 232 Doug Jones .05 .02
❑ 233 Jeff King .10 .05
❑ 234 Luis Rivera .05 .02
❑ 235 Ellis Burks .10 .05
❑ 236 Greg Cadaret .05 .02
❑ 237 Dave Martinez .05 .02
❑ 238 Mark Williamson .05 .02
❑ 239 Stan Javier .05 .02
❑ 240 Ozzie Smith .25 .11
❑ 241 Shawn Boskie .05 .02
❑ 242 Tom Gordon .10 .05
❑ 243 Tony Gwynn .50 .23
❑ 244 Tommy Gregg .05 .02
❑ 245 Jeff M. Robinson .05 .02
❑ 246 Keith Comstock .05 .02
❑ 247 Jack Howell .05 .02
❑ 248 Keith Miller .05 .02
❑ 249 Bobby Witt .05 .02
❑ 250 Rob Murphy UER .05 .02
(Shown as on Reds in '89 in stats, should be Red Sox)
❑ 251 Spike Owen .05 .02
❑ 252 Garry Templeton .05 .02
❑ 253 Glenn Braggs .05 .02
❑ 254 Ron Robinson .05 .02
❑ 255 Kevin Mitchell .05 .02
❑ 256 Les Lancaster .05 .02
❑ 257 Mel Stottlemyre Jr. .05 .02
❑ 258 Kenny Rogers UER .05 .02
(IP listed as 171, should be 172)
❑ 259 Lance Johnson .05 .02
❑ 260 John Kruk .10 .05
❑ 261 Fred McGriff .20 .09
❑ 262 Dick Schofield .05 .02
❑ 263 Trevor Wilson .05 .02
❑ 264 David West .05 .02
❑ 265 Scott Scudder .05 .02
❑ 266 Dwight Gooden .10 .05
❑ 267 Willie Blair .05 .02
❑ 268 Mark Portugal .05 .02
❑ 269 Doug Drabek .05 .02
❑ 270 Dennis Eckersley .10 .05
❑ 271 Eric King .05 .02
❑ 272 Robin Yount .20 .09
❑ 273 Carney Lansford .10 .05
❑ 274 Carlos Baerga .10 .05
❑ 275 Dave Righetti .05 .02
❑ 276 Scott Fletcher .05 .02
❑ 277 Eric Yelding .05 .02
❑ 278 Charlie Hayes .05 .02
❑ 279 Jeff Ballard .05 .02
❑ 280 Orel Hershiser .10 .05
❑ 281 Jose Oquendo .05 .02
❑ 282 Mike Witt .05 .02

283	Mitch Webster	.05	.02
284	Greg Gagne	.05	.02
285	Greg Olson	.05	.02
286	Tony Phillips UER (Born 4/15 should be 4/25)	.05	.02
287	Scott Bradley	.05	.02
288	Cory Snyder UER (In text, led is repeated and Inglewood is misspelled as Englewood)	.05	.02
289	Jay Bell UER (Born in Pensacola, not Eglin AFB)	.10	.05
290	Kevin Romine	.05	.02
291	Jeff D. Robinson	.05	.02
292	Steve Frey UER (Bats left, should be right)	.05	.02
293	Craig Worthington	.05	.02
294	Tim Crews	.05	.02
295	Joe Magrane	.05	.02
296	Hector Villanueva	.05	.02
297	Terry Shumpert	.05	.02
298	Joe Carter	.10	.05
299	Kent Mercker UER (IP listed as 53, should be 52)	.05	.02
300	Checklist 180-255	.05	.02
301	Chet Lemon	.05	.02
302	Mike Schooler	.05	.02
303	Dante Bichette	.20	.09
304	Kevin Elster	.05	.02
305	Jeff Huson	.05	.02
306	Greg A. Harris	.05	.02
307	Marquis Grissom UER (Middle name Deon, should be Dean)	.20	.09
308	Calvin Schiraldi	.05	.02
309	Mariano Duncan	.05	.02
310	Bill Spiers	.05	.02
311	Scott Garrelts	.05	.02
312	Mitch Williams	.05	.02
313	Mike Macfarlane	.05	.02
314	Kevin Brown	.15	.07
315	Robin Ventura	.20	.09
316	Darren Daulton	.10	.05
317	Pat Borders	.05	.02
318	Mark Eichhorn	.05	.02
319	Jeff Brantley	.05	.02
320	Shane Mack	.05	.02
321	Rob Dibble	.05	.02
322	John Franco	.10	.05
323	Junior Felix	.05	.02
324	Casey Candaele	.05	.02
325	Bobby Bonilla	.10	.05
326	Dave Henderson	.05	.02
327	Wayne Edwards	.05	.02
328	Mark Knudson	.05	.02
329	Terry Steinbach	.10	.05
330	Colby Ward UER (No comma between city and state)	.05	.02
331	Oscar Azocar	.05	.02
332	Scott Radinsky	.05	.02
333	Eric Anthony	.05	.02
334	Steve Lake	.05	.02
335	Bob Melvin	.05	.02
336	Kal Daniels	.05	.02
337	Tom Pagnozzi	.05	.02
338	Alan Mills	.05	.02
339	Steve Olin	.05	.02
340	Juan Berenguer	.05	.02
341	Francisco Cabrera	.05	.02
342	Dave Bergman	.05	.02
343	Henry Cotto	.05	.02
344	Sergio Valdez	.05	.02
345	Bob Patterson	.05	.02
346	John Marzano	.05	.02
347	Dana Kiecker	.05	.02
348	Dion James	.05	.02
349	Hubie Brooks	.05	.02
350	Bill Landrum	.05	.02
351	Bill Sampen	.05	.02
352	Greg Briley	.05	.02
353	Paul Gibson	.05	.02
354	Dave Eiland	.05	.02
355	Steve Finley	.20	.09
356	Bob Boone	.10	.05
357	Steve Buechele	.05	.02
358	Chris Hoiles	.05	.02
359	Larry Walker	.30	.14
360	Frank DiPino	.05	.02
361	Mark Grant	.05	.02
362	Dave Magadan	.05	.02
363	Robby Thompson	.05	.02
364	Lonnie Smith	.05	.02
365	Steve Farr	.05	.02
366	Dave Valle	.05	.02
367	Tim Naehring	.10	.05
368	Jim Acker	.05	.02
369	Jeff Reardon UER (Born in Pittsfield, not Dalton)	.10	.05
370	Tim Teufel	.05	.02
371	Juan Gonzalez	.75	.35
372	Luis Salazar	.05	.02
373	Rick Honeycutt	.05	.02
374	Greg Maddux	.60	.25
375	Jose Uribe UER (Middle name Elta, should be Alta)	.05	.02
376	Donnie Hill	.05	.02
377	Don Carman	.05	.02
378	Craig Grebeck	.05	.02
379	Willie Fraser	.05	.02
380	Glenallen Hill	.05	.02
381	Joe Oliver	.05	.02
382	Randy Bush	.05	.02
383	Alex Cole	.05	.02
384	Norm Charlton	.05	.02
385	Gene Nelson	.05	.02
386	Checklist 256-331	.05	.02
387	Rickey Henderson MVP	.10	.05
388	Lance Parrish MVP	.05	.02
389	Fred McGriff MVP	.10	.05
390	Dave Parker MVP	.05	.02
391	Candy Maldonado MVP	.05	.02
392	Ken Griffey Jr. MVP	.75	.35
393	Gregg Olson MVP	.05	.02
394	Rafael Palmeiro MVP	.10	.05
395	Roger Clemens MVP	.20	.09
396	George Brett MVP	.20	.09
397	Cecil Fielder MVP	.05	.02
398	Brian Harper MVP UER (Major League Performance, should be Career)	.05	.02
399	Bobby Thigpen MVP	.05	.02
400	Roberto Kelly MVP UER (Second Base on front and OF on back)	.05	.02
401	Danny Darwin MVP	.05	.02
402	Dave Justice MVP	.10	.05
403	Lee Smith MVP	.05	.02
404	Ryne Sandberg MVP	.20	.09
405	Eddie Murray MVP	.10	.05
406	Tim Wallach MVP	.05	.02
407	Kevin Mitchell MVP	.05	.02
408	Darryl Strawberry MVP	.05	.02
409	Joe Carter MVP	.05	.02
410	Len Dykstra MVP	.05	.02
411	Doug Drabek MVP	.05	.02
412	Chris Sabo MVP	.05	.02
413	Paul Marak RR	.05	.02
414	Tim McIntosh RR	.05	.02
415	Brian Barnes RR	.05	.02
416	Eric Gunderson RR	.05	.02
417	Mike Gardiner RR	.05	.02
418	Steve Carter RR	.05	.02
419	Gerald Alexander RR	.05	.02
420	Rich Garces RR	.05	.02
421	Chuck Knoblauch RR	.25	.11
422	Scott Aldred RR	.05	.02
423	Wes Chamberlain RR	.05	.02
424	Lance Dickson RR	.05	.02
425	Greg Colbrunn RR	.05	.02
426	Rich DeLucia RR UER (Misspelled Delucia on card)	.05	.02
427	Jeff Conine RR	.25	.11
428	Steve Decker RR	.05	.02
429	Turner Ward RR	.05	.02
430	Mo Vaughn RR	.40	.18
431	Steve Chitren RR	.05	.02
432	Mike Benjamin RR	.05	.02
433	Ryne Sandberg AS	.20	.09
434	Len Dykstra AS	.05	.02
435	Andre Dawson AS	.10	.05
436A	Mike Scioscia AS (White star by name)	.05	.02
436B	Mike Scioscia AS (Yellow star by name)	.05	.02
437	Ozzie Smith AS	.20	.09
438	Kevin Mitchell AS	.05	.02
439	Jack Armstrong AS	.05	.02
440	Chris Sabo AS	.05	.02
441	Will Clark AS	.10	.05
442	Mel Hall	.05	.02
443	Mark Gardner	.05	.02
444	Mike Devereaux	.05	.02
445	Kirk Gibson	.10	.05
446	Terry Pendleton	.10	.05
447	Mike Harkey	.05	.02
448	Jim Eisenreich	.05	.02
449	Benito Santiago	.05	.02
450	Oddibe McDowell	.05	.02
451	Cecil Fielder	.10	.05
452	Ken Griffey Sr.	.05	.02
453	Bert Blyleven	.10	.05
454	Howard Johnson	.05	.02
455	Monty Fariss UER (Misspelled Farris on card)	.05	.02
456	Tony Pena	.05	.02
457	Tim Raines	.10	.05
458	Dennis Rasmussen	.05	.02
459	Luis Quinones	.05	.02
460	B.J. Surhoff	.10	.05
461	Ernest Riles	.05	.02
462	Rick Sutcliffe	.05	.02
463	Danny Tartabull	.05	.02
464	Pete Incaviglia	.05	.02
465	Carlos Martinez	.05	.02
466	Ricky Jordan	.05	.02
467	John Cerutti	.05	.02
468	Dave Winfield	.20	.09
469	Francisco Oliveras	.05	.02
470	Roy Smith	.05	.02
471	Barry Larkin	.20	.09
472	Ron Darling	.05	.02
473	David Wells	.10	.05
474	Glenn Davis	.05	.02
475	Neal Heaton	.05	.02
476	Ron Hassey	.05	.02
477	Frank Thomas	1.00	.45
478	Greg Vaughn	.20	.09
479	Todd Burns	.05	.02
480	Candy Maldonado	.05	.02
481	Dave LaPoint	.05	.02
482	Alvin Davis	.05	.02
483	Mike Scott	.05	.02
484	Dale Murphy	.20	.09
485	Ben McDonald	.05	.02
486	Jay Howell	.05	.02
487	Vince Coleman	.05	.02
488	Alfredo Griffin	.05	.02
489	Sandy Alomar Jr.	.10	.05
490	Kirby Puckett	.30	.14
491	Andres Thomas	.05	.02
492	Jack Morris	.10	.05
493	Matt Young	.05	.02
494	Greg Myers	.05	.02
495	Barry Bonds	.25	.11
496	Scott Cooper UER (No BA for 1990 and career)	.05	.02
497	Dan Schatzeder	.05	.02
498	Jesse Barfield	.05	.02
499	Jerry Goff	.05	.02
500	Checklist 332-408	.05	.02
501	Anthony Telford	.05	.02
502	Eddie Murray	.20	.09
503	Omar Olivares	.05	.02
504	Ryne Sandberg	.25	.11

❑ 505 Jeff Montgomery .10 .05
❑ 506 Mark Parent .05 .02
❑ 507 Ron Gant .10 .05
❑ 508 Frank Tanana .05 .02
❑ 509 Jay Buhner .20 .09
❑ 510 Max Venable .05 .02
❑ 511 Wally Whitehurst .05 .02
❑ 512 Gary Pettis .05 .02
❑ 513 Tom Brunansky .05 .02
❑ 514 Tim Wallach .05 .02
❑ 515 Craig Lefferts .05 .02
❑ 516 Tim Layana .05 .02
❑ 517 Darryl Hamilton .05 .02
❑ 518 Rick Reuschel .05 .02
❑ 519 Steve Wilson .05 .02
❑ 520 Kurt Stillwell .05 .02
❑ 521 Rafael Palmeiro .20 .09
❑ 522 Ken Patterson .05 .02
❑ 523 Len Dykstra .10 .05
❑ 524 Tony Fernandez .05 .02
❑ 525 Kent Anderson .05 .02
❑ 526 Mark Leonard .05 .02
❑ 527 Allan Anderson .05 .02
❑ 528 Tom Browning .05 .02
❑ 529 Frank Viola .05 .02
❑ 530 John Olerud .10 .05
❑ 531 Juan Agosto .05 .02
❑ 532 Zane Smith .05 .02
❑ 533 Scott Sanderson .05 .02
❑ 534 Barry Jones .05 .02
❑ 535 Mike Felder .05 .02
❑ 536 Jose Canseco .20 .09
❑ 537 Felix Fermin .05 .02
❑ 538 Roberto Kelly .05 .02
❑ 539 Brian Holman .05 .02
❑ 540 Mark Davidson .05 .02
❑ 541 Terry Mulholland .05 .02
❑ 542 Randy Milligan .05 .02
❑ 543 Jose Gonzalez .05 .02
❑ 544 Craig Wilson .05 .02
❑ 545 Mike Hartley .05 .02
❑ 546 Greg Swindell .05 .02
❑ 547 Gary Gaetti .10 .05
❑ 548 Dave Justice .25 .11
❑ 549 Steve Searcy .05 .02
❑ 550 Erik Hanson .05 .02
❑ 551 Dave Stieb .10 .05
❑ 552 Andy Van Slyke .10 .05
❑ 553 Mike Greenwell .05 .02
❑ 554 Kevin Maas .05 .02
❑ 555 Delino DeShields .10 .05
❑ 556 Curt Schilling .20 .09
❑ 557 Ramon Martinez .10 .05
❑ 558 Pedro Guerrero .05 .02
❑ 559 Dwight Smith .05 .02
❑ 560 Mark Davis .05 .02
❑ 561 Shawn Abner .05 .02
❑ 562 Charlie Leibrandt .05 .02
❑ 563 John Shelby .05 .02
❑ 564 Bill Swift .05 .02
❑ 565 Mike Fetters .05 .02
❑ 566 Alejandro Pena .05 .02
❑ 567 Ruben Sierra .05 .02
❑ 568 Carlos Quintana .05 .02
❑ 569 Kevin Gross .05 .02
❑ 570 Derek Lilliquist .05 .02
❑ 571 Jack Armstrong .05 .02
❑ 572 Greg Brock .05 .02
❑ 573 Mike Kingery .05 .02
❑ 574 Greg Smith .05 .02
❑ 575 Brian McRae .20 .09
❑ 576 Jack Daugherty .05 .02
❑ 577 Ozzie Guillen .05 .02
❑ 578 Joe Boever .05 .02
❑ 579 Luis Sojo .05 .02
❑ 580 Chili Davis .10 .05
❑ 581 Don Robinson .05 .02
❑ 582 Brian Harper .05 .02
❑ 583 Paul O'Neill .10 .05
❑ 584 Bob Ojeda .05 .02
❑ 585 Mookie Wilson .10 .05
❑ 586 Rafael Ramirez .05 .02
❑ 587 Gary Redus .05 .02
❑ 588 Jamie Quirk .05 .02
❑ 589 Shawn Hillegas .05 .02
❑ 590 Tom Edens .05 .02
❑ 591 Joe Klink .05 .02
❑ 592 Charles Nagy .20 .09
❑ 593 Eric Plunk .05 .02
❑ 594 Tracy Jones .05 .02
❑ 595 Craig Biggio .20 .09
❑ 596 Jose DeJesus .05 .02
❑ 597 Mickey Tettleton .10 .05
❑ 598 Chris Gwynn .05 .02
❑ 599 Rex Hudler .05 .02
❑ 600 Checklist 409-506 .05 .02
❑ 601 Jim Gott .05 .02
❑ 602 Jeff Manto .05 .02
❑ 603 Nelson Liriano .05 .02
❑ 604 Mark Lemke .05 .02
❑ 605 Clay Parker .05 .02
❑ 606 Edgar Martinez .20 .09
❑ 607 Mark Whiten .05 .02
❑ 608 Ted Power .05 .02
❑ 609 Tom Bolton .05 .02
❑ 610 Tom Herr .05 .02
❑ 611 Andy Hawkins UER .05 .02
(Pitched No-Hitter on 7/1, not 7/2)
❑ 612 Scott Ruskin .05 .02
❑ 613 Ron Kittle .05 .02
❑ 614 John Wetteland .20 .09
❑ 615 Mike Perez .05 .02
❑ 616 Dave Clark .05 .02
❑ 617 Brent Mayne .05 .02
❑ 618 Jack Clark .10 .05
❑ 619 Marvin Freeman .05 .02
❑ 620 Edwin Nunez .05 .02
❑ 621 Russ Swan .05 .02
❑ 622 Johnny Ray .05 .02
❑ 623 Charlie O'Brien .05 .02
❑ 624 Joe Bitker .05 .02
❑ 625 Mike Marshall .05 .02
❑ 626 Otis Nixon .10 .05
❑ 627 Andy Benes .10 .05
❑ 628 Ron Oester .05 .02
❑ 629 Ted Higuera .05 .02
❑ 630 Kevin Bass .05 .02
❑ 631 Damon Berryhill .05 .02
❑ 632 Bo Jackson .10 .05
❑ 633 Brad Arnsberg .05 .02
❑ 634 Jerry Willard .05 .02
❑ 635 Tommy Greene .05 .02
❑ 636 Bob MacDonald .05 .02
❑ 637 Kirk McCaskill .05 .02
❑ 638 John Burkett .05 .02
❑ 639 Paul Abbott .05 .02
❑ 640 Todd Benzinger .05 .02
❑ 641 Todd Hundley .20 .09
❑ 642 George Bell .05 .02
❑ 643 Javier Ortiz .05 .02
❑ 644 Sid Bream .05 .02
❑ 645 Bob Welch .05 .02
❑ 646 Phil Bradley .05 .02
❑ 647 Bill Krueger .05 .02
❑ 648 Rickey Henderson .20 .09
❑ 649 Kevin Wickander .05 .02
❑ 650 Steve Balboni .05 .02
❑ 651 Gene Harris .05 .02
❑ 652 Jim Deshaies .05 .02
❑ 653 Jason Grimsley .05 .02
❑ 654 Joe Orsulak .05 .02
❑ 655 Jim Poole .05 .02
❑ 656 Felix Jose .05 .02
❑ 657 Denis Cook .05 .02
❑ 658 Tom Brookens .05 .02
❑ 659 Junior Ortiz .05 .02
❑ 660 Jeff Parrett .05 .02
❑ 661 Jerry Don Gleaton .05 .02
❑ 662 Brent Knackert .05 .02
❑ 663 Rance Mulliniks .05 .02
❑ 664 John Smiley .05 .02
❑ 665 Larry Andersen .05 .02
❑ 666 Willie McGee .10 .05
❑ 667 Chris Nabholz .05 .02
❑ 668 Brady Anderson .20 .09
❑ 669 Darren Holmes UER .05 .02
(19 CG's, should be 0)
❑ 670 Ken Hill .10 .05
❑ 671 Gary Varsho .05 .02
❑ 672 Bill Pecota .05 .02
❑ 673 Fred Lynn .05 .02
❑ 674 Kevin D. Brown .05 .02
❑ 675 Dan Petry .05 .02
❑ 676 Mike Jackson .10 .05
❑ 677 Wally Joyner .10 .05
❑ 678 Danny Jackson .05 .02
❑ 679 Bill Haselman .05 .02
❑ 680 Mike Boddicker .05 .02
❑ 681 Mel Rojas .10 .05
❑ 682 Roberto Alomar .20 .09
❑ 683 Dave Justice ROY .10 .05
❑ 684 Chuck Crim .05 .02
❑ 685 Matt Williams .20 .09
❑ 686 Shawon Dunston .05 .02
❑ 687 Jeff Schulz .05 .02
❑ 688 John Barfield .05 .02
❑ 689 Gerald Young .05 .02
❑ 690 Luis Gonzalez .20 .09
❑ 691 Frank Wills .05 .02
❑ 692 Chuck Finley .10 .05
❑ 693 Sandy Alomar Jr. ROY .05 .02
❑ 694 Tim Drummond .05 .02
❑ 695 Herm Winningham .05 .02
❑ 696 Darryl Strawberry .10 .05
❑ 697 Al Leiter .10 .05
❑ 698 Karl Rhodes .05 .02
❑ 699 Stan Belinda .05 .02
❑ 700 Checklist 507-604 .05 .02
❑ 701 Lance Blankenship .05 .02
❑ 702 Willie Stargell PUZ .20 .09
❑ 703 Jim Gantner .05 .02
❑ 704 Reggie Harris .05 .02
❑ 705 Rob Ducey .05 .02
❑ 706 Tim Hulett .05 .02
❑ 707 Atlee Hammaker .05 .02
❑ 708 Xavier Hernandez .05 .02
❑ 709 Chuck McElroy .05 .02
❑ 710 John Mitchell .05 .02
❑ 711 Carlos Hernandez .10 .05
❑ 712 Geronimo Pena .05 .02
❑ 713 Jim Neidlinger .05 .02
❑ 714 John Orton .05 .02
❑ 715 Terry Leach .05 .02
❑ 716 Mike Stanton .05 .02
❑ 717 Walt Terrell .05 .02
❑ 718 Luis Aquino .05 .02
❑ 719 Bud Black .05 .02
(Blue Jays uniform, but Giants logo)
❑ 720 Bob Kipper .05 .02
❑ 721 Jeff Gray .05 .02
❑ 722 Jose Rijo .05 .02
❑ 723 Curt Young .05 .02
❑ 724 Jose Vizcaino .05 .02
❑ 725 Randy Tomlin .05 .02
❑ 726 Junior Noboa .05 .02
❑ 727 Bob Welch CY .05 .02
❑ 728 Gary Ward .05 .02
❑ 729 Rob Deer .05 .02
(Brewers uniform, but Tigers logo)
❑ 730 David Segui .10 .05
❑ 731 Mark Carreon .05 .02
❑ 732 Vicente Palacios .05 .02
❑ 733 Sam Horn .05 .02
❑ 734 Howard Farmer .05 .02
❑ 735 Ken Dayley .05 .02
(Cardinals uniform, but Blue Jays logo)
❑ 736 Kelly Mann .05 .02
❑ 737 Joe Grahe .05 .02
❑ 738 Kelly Downs .05 .02
❑ 739 Jimmy Kremers .05 .02
❑ 740 Kevin Appier .10 .05
❑ 741 Jeff Reed .05 .02
❑ 742 Jose Rijo WS .05 .02
❑ 743 Dave Rohde .05 .02
❑ 744 Dr.Dirt/Mr.Clean .10 .05
Len Dykstra
Dale Murphy
UER (No '91 Donruss logo on card front)
❑ 745 Paul Sorrento .10 .05
❑ 746 Thomas Howard .05 .02

		MINT	NRMT
❑ 747	Matt Stark	.05	.02
❑ 748	Harold Baines	.10	.05
❑ 749	Doug Dascenzo	.05	.02
❑ 750	Doug Drabek CY	.05	.02
❑ 751	Gary Sheffield	.20	.09
❑ 752	Terry Lee	.05	.02
❑ 753	Jim Vatcher	.05	.02
❑ 754	Lee Stevens	.05	.02
❑ 755	Randy Veres	.05	.02
❑ 756	Bill Doran	.05	.02
❑ 757	Gary Wayne	.05	.02
❑ 758	Pedro Munoz	.05	.02
❑ 759	Chris Hammond	.05	.02
❑ 760	Checklist 605-702	.05	.02
❑ 761	Rickey Henderson MVP	.10	.05
❑ 762	Barry Bonds MVP	.20	.09
❑ 763	Billy Hatcher WS UER (Line 13, on should be one)	.05	.02
❑ 764	Julio Machado	.05	.02
❑ 765	Jose Mesa	.05	.02
❑ 766	Willie Randolph WS	.05	.02
❑ 767	Scott Erickson	.10	.05
❑ 768	Travis Fryman	.20	.09
❑ 769	Rich Rodriguez	.05	.02
❑ 770	Checklist 703-770 and BC1-BC22	.05	.02

1991 Donruss Elite

	MINT	NRMT
COMPLETE SET (10)	500.00	220.00
COMMON CARD (1-8)	12.00	5.50

		MINT	NRMT
❑ 1	Barry Bonds	50.00	22.00
❑ 2	George Brett	80.00	36.00
❑ 3	Jose Canseco	40.00	18.00
❑ 4	Andre Dawson	40.00	18.00
❑ 5	Doug Drabek	12.00	5.50
❑ 6	Cecil Fielder	15.00	6.75
❑ 7	Rickey Henderson	30.00	13.50
❑ 8	Matt Williams	40.00	18.00
❑ L1	Nolan Ryan (Legend)	100.00	45.00
❑ S1	Ryne Sandberg (Signature Series)	250.00	110.00

1991 Donruss Rookies

	MINT	NRMT
COMP.FACT.SET (56)	4.00	1.80
COMMON CARD (1-56)	.05	.02

		MINT	NRMT
❑ 1	Pat Kelly	.05	.02
❑ 2	Rich DeLucia	.05	.02
❑ 3	Wes Chamberlain	.05	.02
❑ 4	Scott Leius	.05	.02
❑ 5	Darryl Kile	.20	.09
❑ 6	Milt Cuyler	.05	.02
❑ 7	Todd Van Poppel	.05	.02
❑ 8	Ray Lankford	.20	.09
❑ 9	Brian R. Hunter	.05	.02
❑ 10	Tony Perezchica	.05	.02
❑ 11	Ced Landrum	.05	.02
❑ 12	Dave Burba	.05	.02
❑ 13	Ramon Garcia	.05	.02
❑ 14	Ed Sprague	.05	.02
❑ 15	Warren Newson	.05	.02
❑ 16	Paul Faries	.05	.02
❑ 17	Luis Gonzalez	.20	.09
❑ 18	Charles Nagy	.20	.09
❑ 19	Chris Hammond	.05	.02
❑ 20	Frank Castillo	.05	.02
❑ 21	Pedro Munoz	.05	.02
❑ 22	Orlando Merced	.10	.05
❑ 23	Jose Melendez	.05	.02
❑ 24	Kirk Dressendorfer	.05	.02
❑ 25	Heathcliff Slocumb	.20	.09
❑ 26	Doug Simons	.05	.02
❑ 27	Mike Timlin	.05	.02
❑ 28	Jeff Fassero	.25	.11
❑ 29	Mark Leiter	.05	.02
❑ 30	Jeff Bagwell	2.00	.90
❑ 31	Brian McRae	.20	.09
❑ 32	Mark Whiten	.05	.02
❑ 33	Ivan Rodriguez	1.50	.70
❑ 34	Wade Taylor	.05	.02
❑ 35	Darren Lewis	.10	.05
❑ 36	Mo Vaughn	.40	.18
❑ 37	Mike Remlinger	.05	.02
❑ 38	Rick Wilkins	.05	.02
❑ 39	Chuck Knoblauch	.25	.11
❑ 40	Kevin Morton	.05	.02
❑ 41	Carlos Rodriguez	.05	.02
❑ 42	Mark Lewis	.05	.02
❑ 43	Brent Mayne	.05	.02
❑ 44	Chris Haney	.05	.02
❑ 45	Denis Boucher	.05	.02
❑ 46	Mike Gardiner	.05	.02
❑ 47	Jeff Johnson	.05	.02
❑ 48	Dean Palmer	.10	.05
❑ 49	Chuck McElroy	.05	.02
❑ 50	Chris Jones	.05	.02
❑ 51	Scott Kamieniecki	.05	.02
❑ 52	Al Osuna	.05	.02
❑ 53	Rusty Meacham	.05	.02
❑ 54	Chito Martinez	.05	.02
❑ 55	Reggie Jefferson	.15	.07
❑ 56	Checklist 1-56	.05	.02

1992 Donruss

	MINT	NRMT
COMPLETE SET (784)	8.00	3.60
COMP.HOBBY SET (788)	15.00	6.75
COMP.RETAIL SET (788)	8.00	3.60
COMPLETE SERIES 1 (396)	4.00	1.80
COMPLETE SERIES 2 (388)	4.00	1.80
COMMON CARD (1-784)	.05	.02
COMP.CAREW PUZZLE	1.00	.45

		MINT	NRMT
❑ 1	Mark Wohlers RR	.10	.05
❑ 2	Wil Cordero RR	.05	.02
❑ 3	Kyle Abbott RR	.05	.02
❑ 4	Dave Nilsson RR	.10	.05
❑ 5	Kenny Lofton RR	.40	.18
❑ 6	Luis Mercedes RR	.05	.02
❑ 7	Roger Salkeld RR	.05	.02
❑ 8	Eddie Zosky RR	.05	.02
❑ 9	Todd Van Poppel RR	.05	.02
❑ 10	Frank Seminara RR	.05	.02
❑ 11	Andy Ashby RR	.10	.05
❑ 12	Reggie Jefferson RR	.10	.05
❑ 13	Ryan Klesko RR	.25	.11
❑ 14	Carlos Garcia RR	.05	.02
❑ 15	John Ramos RR	.05	.02
❑ 16	Eric Karros RR	.20	.09
❑ 17	Patrick Lennon RR	.05	.02
❑ 18	Eddie Taubensee RR	.10	.05
❑ 19	Roberto Hernandez RR	.10	.05
❑ 20	D.J. Dozier RR	.05	.02
❑ 21	Dave Henderson AS	.05	.02
❑ 22	Cal Ripken AS	.20	.09
❑ 23	Wade Boggs AS	.20	.09
❑ 24	Ken Griffey Jr. AS	.60	.25
❑ 25	Jack Morris AS	.05	.02
❑ 26	Danny Tartabull AS	.05	.02
❑ 27	Cecil Fielder AS	.05	.02
❑ 28	Roberto Alomar AS	.10	.05
❑ 29	Sandy Alomar Jr. AS	.10	.05
❑ 30	Rickey Henderson AS	.10	.05
❑ 31	Ken Hill	.05	.02
❑ 32	John Habyan	.05	.02
❑ 33	Otis Nixon HL	.05	.02
❑ 34	Tim Wallach	.05	.02
❑ 35	Cal Ripken	.75	.35
❑ 36	Gary Carter	.20	.09
❑ 37	Juan Agosto	.05	.02
❑ 38	Doug Dascenzo	.05	.02
❑ 39	Kirk Gibson	.10	.05
❑ 40	Benito Santiago	.05	.02
❑ 41	Otis Nixon	.10	.05
❑ 42	Andy Allanson	.05	.02
❑ 43	Brian Holman	.05	.02
❑ 44	Dick Schofield	.05	.02
❑ 45	Dave Magadan	.05	.02
❑ 46	Rafael Palmeiro	.15	.07
❑ 47	Jody Reed	.05	.02
❑ 48	Ivan Calderon	.05	.02
❑ 49	Greg W. Harris	.05	.02
❑ 50	Chris Sabo	.05	.02
❑ 51	Paul Molitor	.20	.09
❑ 52	Robby Thompson	.05	.02
❑ 53	Dave Smith	.05	.02
❑ 54	Mark Davis	.05	.02
❑ 55	Kevin Brown	.15	.07
❑ 56	Donn Pall	.05	.02
❑ 57	Len Dykstra	.10	.05
❑ 58	Roberto Alomar	.20	.09
❑ 59	Jeff D. Robinson	.05	.02
❑ 60	Willie McGee	.10	.05
❑ 61	Jay Buhner	.15	.07
❑ 62	Mike Pagliarulo	.05	.02
❑ 63	Paul O'Neill	.10	.05
❑ 64	Hubie Brooks	.05	.02
❑ 65	Kelly Gruber	.05	.02
❑ 66	Ken Caminiti	.15	.07
❑ 67	Gary Redus	.05	.02
❑ 68	Harold Baines	.10	.05
❑ 69	Charlie Hough	.10	.05
❑ 70	B.J. Surhoff	.10	.05
❑ 71	Walt Weiss	.05	.02
❑ 72	Shawn Hillegas	.05	.02
❑ 73	Roberto Kelly	.05	.02
❑ 74	Jeff Ballard	.05	.02
❑ 75	Craig Biggio	.20	.09
❑ 76	Pat Combs	.05	.02
❑ 77	Jeff M. Robinson	.05	.02
❑ 78	Tim Belcher	.05	.02
❑ 79	Cris Carpenter	.05	.02
❑ 80	Checklist 1-79	.05	.02
❑ 81	Steve Avery	.05	.02
❑ 82	Chris James	.05	.02
❑ 83	Brian Harper	.05	.02
❑ 84	Charlie Leibrandt	.05	.02

❑ 85 Mickey Tettleton .05 .02
❑ 86 Pete O'Brien .05 .02
❑ 87 Danny Darwin .05 .02
❑ 88 Bob Walk .05 .02
❑ 89 Jeff Reardon .10 .05
❑ 90 Bobby Rose .05 .02
❑ 91 Danny Jackson .05 .02
❑ 92 John Morris .05 .02
❑ 93 Bud Black .05 .02
❑ 94 Tommy Greene HL .05 .02
❑ 95 Rick Aguilera .10 .05
❑ 96 Gary Gaetti .05 .02
❑ 97 David Cone .10 .05
❑ 98 John Olerud .10 .05
❑ 99 Joel Skinner .05 .02
❑ 100 Jay Bell .10 .05
❑ 101 Bob Milacki .05 .02
❑ 102 Norm Charlton .05 .02
❑ 103 Chuck Crim .05 .02
❑ 104 Terry Steinbach .10 .05
❑ 105 Juan Samuel .05 .02
❑ 106 Steve Howe .05 .02
❑ 107 Rafael Belliard .05 .02
❑ 108 Joey Cora .10 .05
❑ 109 Tommy Greene .05 .02
❑ 110 Gregg Olson .05 .02
❑ 111 Frank Tanana .05 .02
❑ 112 Lee Smith .10 .05
❑ 113 Greg A. Harris .05 .02
❑ 114 Dwayne Henry .05 .02
❑ 115 Chili Davis .10 .05
❑ 116 Kent Mercker .05 .02
❑ 117 Brian Barnes .05 .02
❑ 118 Rich DeLucia .05 .02
❑ 119 Andre Dawson .15 .07
❑ 120 Carlos Baerga .05 .02
❑ 121 Mike LaValliere .05 .02
❑ 122 Jeff Gray .05 .02
❑ 123 Bruce Hurst .05 .02
❑ 124 Alvin Davis .05 .02
❑ 125 John Candelaria .05 .02
❑ 126 Matt Nokes .05 .02
❑ 127 George Bell .05 .02
❑ 128 Bret Saberhagen .10 .05
❑ 129 Jeff Russell .05 .02
❑ 130 Jim Abbott .10 .05
❑ 131 Bill Gullickson .05 .02
❑ 132 Todd Zeile .05 .02
❑ 133 Dave Winfield .20 .09
❑ 134 Wally Whitehurst .05 .02
❑ 135 Matt Williams .15 .07
❑ 136 Tom Browning .05 .02
❑ 137 Marquis Grissom .10 .05
❑ 138 Erik Hanson .05 .02
❑ 139 Rob Dibble .05 .02
❑ 140 Don August .05 .02
❑ 141 Tom Henke .05 .02
❑ 142 Dan Pasqua .05 .02
❑ 143 George Brett .40 .18
❑ 144 Jerald Clark .05 .02
❑ 145 Robin Ventura .10 .05
❑ 146 Dale Murphy .20 .09
❑ 147 Dennis Eckersley .10 .05
❑ 148 Eric Yelding .05 .02
❑ 149 Mario Diaz .05 .02
❑ 150 Casey Candaele .05 .02
❑ 151 Steve Olin .05 .02
❑ 152 Luis Salazar .05 .02
❑ 153 Kevin Maas .05 .02
❑ 154 Nolan Ryan HL .40 .18
❑ 155 Barry Jones .05 .02
❑ 156 Chris Hoiles .05 .02
❑ 157 Bobby Ojeda .05 .02
❑ 158 Pedro Guerrero .05 .02
❑ 159 Paul Assenmacher .05 .02
❑ 160 Checklist 80-157 .05 .02
❑ 161 Mike Macfarlane .05 .02
❑ 162 Craig Lefferts .05 .02
❑ 163 Brian Hunter .05 .02
❑ 164 Alan Trammell .15 .07
❑ 165 Ken Griffey Jr. 1.25 .55
❑ 166 Lance Parrish .05 .02
❑ 167 Brian Downing .05 .02
❑ 168 John Barfield .05 .02
❑ 169 Jack Clark .10 .05
❑ 170 Chris Nabholz .05 .02
❑ 171 Tim Teufel .05 .02
❑ 172 Chris Hammond .05 .02
❑ 173 Robin Yount .20 .09
❑ 174 Dave Righetti .05 .02
❑ 175 Joe Girardi .10 .05
❑ 176 Mike Boddicker .05 .02
❑ 177 Dean Palmer .10 .05
❑ 178 Greg Hibbard .05 .02
❑ 179 Randy Ready .05 .02
❑ 180 Devon White .05 .02
❑ 181 Mark Eichhorn .05 .02
❑ 182 Mike Felder .05 .02
❑ 183 Joe Klink .05 .02
❑ 184 Steve Bedrosian .05 .02
❑ 185 Barry Larkin .15 .07
❑ 186 John Franco .10 .05
❑ 187 Ed Sprague .05 .02
❑ 188 Mark Portugal .05 .02
❑ 189 Jose Lind .05 .02
❑ 190 Bob Welch .05 .02
❑ 191 Alex Fernandez .10 .05
❑ 192 Gary Sheffield .20 .09
❑ 193 Rickey Henderson .20 .09
❑ 194 Rod Nichols .05 .02
❑ 195 Scott Kamieniecki .05 .02
❑ 196 Mike Flanagan .05 .02
❑ 197 Steve Finley .10 .05
❑ 198 Darren Daulton .10 .05
❑ 199 Leo Gomez .05 .02
❑ 200 Mike Morgan .05 .02
❑ 201 Bob Tewksbury .05 .02
❑ 202 Sid Bream .05 .02
❑ 203 Sandy Alomar Jr. .10 .05
❑ 204 Greg Gagne .05 .02
❑ 205 Juan Berenguer .05 .02
❑ 206 Cecil Fielder .10 .05
❑ 207 Randy Johnson .20 .09
❑ 208 Tony Pena .05 .02
❑ 209 Doug Drabek .05 .02
❑ 210 Wade Boggs .20 .09
❑ 211 Bryan Harvey .05 .02
❑ 212 Jose Vizcaino .05 .02
❑ 213 Alonzo Powell .05 .02
❑ 214 Will Clark .20 .09
❑ 215 Rickey Henderson HL .10 .05
❑ 216 Jack Morris .10 .05
❑ 217 Junior Felix .05 .02
❑ 218 Vince Coleman .05 .02
❑ 219 Jimmy Key .10 .05
❑ 220 Alex Cole .05 .02
❑ 221 Bill Landrum .05 .02
❑ 222 Randy Milligan .05 .02
❑ 223 Jose Rijo .05 .02
❑ 224 Greg Vaughn .10 .05
❑ 225 Dave Stewart .10 .05
❑ 226 Lenny Harris .05 .02
❑ 227 Scott Sanderson .05 .02
❑ 228 Jeff Blauser .05 .02
❑ 229 Ozzie Guillen .05 .02
❑ 230 John Kruk .10 .05
❑ 231 Bob Melvin .05 .02
❑ 232 Milt Cuyler .05 .02
❑ 233 Felix Jose .05 .02
❑ 234 Ellis Burks .10 .05
❑ 235 Pete Harnisch .05 .02
❑ 236 Kevin Tapani .05 .02
❑ 237 Terry Pendleton .05 .02
❑ 238 Mark Gardner .05 .02
❑ 239 Harold Reynolds .05 .02
❑ 240 Checklist 158-237 .05 .02
❑ 241 Mike Harkey .05 .02
❑ 242 Felix Fermin .05 .02
❑ 243 Barry Bonds .25 .11
❑ 244 Roger Clemens .40 .18
❑ 245 Dennis Rasmussen .05 .02
❑ 246 Jose DeLeon .05 .02
❑ 247 Orel Hershiser .10 .05
❑ 248 Mel Hall .05 .02
❑ 249 Rick Wilkins .05 .02
❑ 250 Tom Gordon .10 .05
❑ 251 Kevin Reimer .05 .02
❑ 252 Luis Polonia .05 .02
❑ 253 Mike Henneman .05 .02
❑ 254 Tom Pagnozzi .05 .02
❑ 255 Chuck Finley .10 .05
❑ 256 Mackey Sasser .05 .02
❑ 257 John Burkett .05 .02
❑ 258 Hal Morris .05 .02
❑ 259 Larry Walker .20 .09
❑ 260 Billy Swift .05 .02
❑ 261 Joe Oliver .05 .02
❑ 262 Julio Machado .05 .02
❑ 263 Todd Stottlemyre .10 .05
❑ 264 Matt Merullo .05 .02
❑ 265 Brent Mayne .05 .02
❑ 266 Thomas Howard .05 .02
❑ 267 Lance Johnson .05 .02
❑ 268 Terry Mulholland .05 .02
❑ 269 Rick Honeycutt .05 .02
❑ 270 Luis Gonzalez .05 .02
❑ 271 Jose Guzman .05 .02
❑ 272 Jimmy Jones .05 .02
❑ 273 Mark Lewis .05 .02
❑ 274 Rene Gonzales .05 .02
❑ 275 Jeff Johnson .05 .02
❑ 276 Dennis Martinez HL .05 .02
❑ 277 Delino DeShields .10 .05
❑ 278 Sam Horn .05 .02
❑ 279 Kevin Gross .05 .02
❑ 280 Jose Oquendo .05 .02
❑ 281 Mark Grace .15 .07
❑ 282 Mark Gubicza .05 .02
❑ 283 Fred McGriff .15 .07
❑ 284 Ron Gant .10 .05
❑ 285 Lou Whitaker .10 .05
❑ 286 Edgar Martinez .15 .07
❑ 287 Ron Tingley .05 .02
❑ 288 Kevin McReynolds .05 .02
❑ 289 Ivan Rodriguez .40 .18
❑ 290 Mike Gardiner .05 .02
❑ 291 Chris Haney .05 .02
❑ 292 Darrin Jackson .05 .02
❑ 293 Bill Doran .05 .02
❑ 294 Ted Higuera .05 .02
❑ 295 Jeff Brantley .05 .02
❑ 296 Les Lancaster .05 .02
❑ 297 Jim Eisenreich .05 .02
❑ 298 Ruben Sierra .05 .02
❑ 299 Scott Radinsky .05 .02
❑ 300 Jose DeJesus .05 .02
❑ 301 Mike Timlin .05 .02
❑ 302 Luis Sojo .05 .02
❑ 303 Kelly Downs .05 .02
❑ 304 Scott Bankhead .05 .02
❑ 305 Pedro Munoz .05 .02
❑ 306 Scott Scudder .05 .02
❑ 307 Kevin Elster .05 .02
❑ 308 Duane Ward .05 .02
❑ 309 Darryl Kile .10 .05
❑ 310 Orlando Merced .05 .02
❑ 311 Dave Henderson .05 .02
❑ 312 Tim Raines .10 .05
❑ 313 Mark Lee .05 .02
❑ 314 Mike Gallego .05 .02
❑ 315 Charles Nagy .10 .05
❑ 316 Jesse Barfield .05 .02
❑ 317 Todd Frohwirth .05 .02
❑ 318 Al Osuna .05 .02
❑ 319 Darrin Fletcher .05 .02
❑ 320 Checklist 238-316 .05 .02
❑ 321 David Segui .10 .05
❑ 322 Stan Javier .05 .02
❑ 323 Bryn Smith .05 .02
❑ 324 Jeff Treadway .05 .02
❑ 325 Mark Whiten .05 .02
❑ 326 Kent Hrbek .10 .05
❑ 327 Dave Justice .20 .09
❑ 328 Tony Phillips .05 .02
❑ 329 Rob Murphy .05 .02
❑ 330 Kevin Morton .05 .02
❑ 331 John Smiley .05 .02
❑ 332 Luis Rivera .05 .02
❑ 333 Wally Joyner .10 .05
❑ 334 Heathcliff Slocumb .05 .02
❑ 335 Rick Cerone .05 .02
❑ 336 Mike Remlinger .05 .02
❑ 337 Mike Moore .05 .02
❑ 338 Lloyd McClendon .05 .02
❑ 339 Al Newman .05 .02

❑	340	Kirk McCaskill	.05	.02
❑	341	Howard Johnson	.05	.02
❑	342	Greg Myers	.05	.02
❑	343	Kal Daniels	.05	.02
❑	344	Bernie Williams	.20	.09
❑	345	Shane Mack	.05	.02
❑	346	Gary Thurman	.05	.02
❑	347	Dante Bichette	.15	.07
❑	348	Mark McGwire	1.00	.45
❑	349	Travis Fryman	.10	.05
❑	350	Ray Lankford	.20	.09
❑	351	Mike Jeffcoat	.05	.02
❑	352	Jack McDowell	.05	.02
❑	353	Mitch Williams	.05	.02
❑	354	Mike Devereaux	.05	.02
❑	355	Andres Galarraga	.20	.09
❑	356	Henry Cotto	.05	.02
❑	357	Scott Bailes	.05	.02
❑	358	Jeff Bagwell	.50	.23
❑	359	Scott Leius	.05	.02
❑	360	Zane Smith	.05	.02
❑	361	Bill Pecota	.05	.02
❑	362	Tony Fernandez	.05	.02
❑	363	Glenn Braggs	.05	.02
❑	364	Bill Spiers	.05	.02
❑	365	Vicente Palacios	.05	.02
❑	366	Tim Burke	.05	.02
❑	367	Randy Tomlin	.05	.02
❑	368	Kenny Rogers	.05	.02
❑	369	Brett Butler	.10	.05
❑	370	Pat Kelly	.05	.02
❑	371	Bip Roberts	.05	.02
❑	372	Gregg Jefferies	.05	.02
❑	373	Kevin Bass	.05	.02
❑	374	Ron Karkovice	.05	.02
❑	375	Paul Gibson	.05	.02
❑	376	Bernard Gilkey	.10	.05
❑	377	Dave Gallagher	.05	.02
❑	378	Bill Wegman	.05	.02
❑	379	Pat Borders	.05	.02
❑	380	Ed Whitson	.05	.02
❑	381	Gilberto Reyes	.05	.02
❑	382	Russ Swan	.05	.02
❑	383	Andy Van Slyke	.10	.05
❑	384	Wes Chamberlain	.05	.02
❑	385	Steve Chitren	.05	.02
❑	386	Greg Olson	.05	.02
❑	387	Brian McRae	.10	.05
❑	388	Rich Rodriguez	.05	.02
❑	389	Steve Decker	.05	.02
❑	390	Chuck Knoblauch	.20	.09
❑	391	Bobby Witt	.05	.02
❑	392	Eddie Murray	.20	.09
❑	393	Juan Gonzalez	.60	.25
❑	394	Scott Ruskin	.05	.02
❑	395	Jay Howell	.05	.02
❑	396	Checklist 317-396	.05	.02
❑	397	Royce Clayton RR	.05	.02
❑	398	John Jaha RR	.10	.05
❑	399	Dan Wilson RR	.10	.05
❑	400	Archie Corbin RR	.05	.02
❑	401	Barry Manuel RR	.05	.02
❑	402	Kim Batiste RR	.05	.02
❑	403	Pat Mahomes RR	.05	.02
❑	404	Dave Fleming RR	.05	.02
❑	405	Jeff Juden RR	.05	.02
❑	406	Jim Thome RR	.50	.23
❑	407	Sam Militello RR	.05	.02
❑	408	Jeff Nelson RR	.05	.02
❑	409	Anthony Young RR	.05	.02
❑	410	Tino Martinez RR	.20	.09
❑	411	Jeff Mutis RR	.05	.02
❑	412	Rey Sanchez RR	.05	.02
❑	413	Chris Gardner RR	.05	.02
❑	414	John Vander Wal RR	.05	.02
❑	415	Reggie Sanders RR	.05	.02
❑	416	Brian Williams RR	.05	.02
❑	417	Mo Sanford RR	.05	.02
❑	418	David Weathers RR	.05	.02
❑	419	Hector Fajardo RR	.05	.02
❑	420	Steve Foster RR	.05	.02
❑	421	Lance Dickson RR	.05	.02
❑	422	Andre Dawson AS	.10	.05
❑	423	Ozzie Smith AS	.20	.09
❑	424	Chris Sabo AS	.05	.02
❑	425	Tony Gwynn AS	.25	.11
❑	426	Tom Glavine AS	.15	.07
❑	427	Bobby Bonilla AS	.05	.02
❑	428	Will Clark AS	.10	.05
❑	429	Ryne Sandberg AS	.20	.09
❑	430	Benito Santiago AS	.05	.02
❑	431	Ivan Calderon AS	.05	.02
❑	432	Ozzie Smith	.25	.11
❑	433	Tim Leary	.05	.02
❑	434	Bret Saberhagen HL	.05	.02
❑	435	Mel Rojas	.05	.02
❑	436	Ben McDonald	.05	.02
❑	437	Tim Crews	.05	.02
❑	438	Rex Hudler	.05	.02
❑	439	Chico Walker	.05	.02
❑	440	Kurt Stillwell	.05	.02
❑	441	Tony Gwynn	.50	.23
❑	442	John Smoltz	.15	.07
❑	443	Lloyd Moseby	.05	.02
❑	444	Mike Schooler	.05	.02
❑	445	Joe Grahe	.05	.02
❑	446	Dwight Gooden	.10	.05
❑	447	Oil Can Boyd	.05	.02
❑	448	John Marzano	.05	.02
❑	449	Bret Barberie	.05	.02
❑	450	Mike Maddux	.05	.02
❑	451	Jeff Reed	.05	.02
❑	452	Dale Sveum	.05	.02
❑	453	Jose Uribe	.05	.02
❑	454	Bob Scanlan	.05	.02
❑	455	Kevin Appier	.10	.05
❑	456	Jeff Huson	.05	.02
❑	457	Ken Patterson	.05	.02
❑	458	Ricky Jordan	.05	.02
❑	459	Tom Candiotti	.05	.02
❑	460	Lee Stevens	.05	.02
❑	461	Rod Beck	.20	.09
❑	462	Dave Valle	.05	.02
❑	463	Scott Erickson	.10	.05
❑	464	Chris Jones	.05	.02
❑	465	Mark Carreon	.05	.02
❑	466	Rob Ducey	.05	.02
❑	467	Jim Corsi	.05	.02
❑	468	Jeff King	.10	.05
❑	469	Curt Young	.05	.02
❑	470	Bo Jackson	.10	.05
❑	471	Chris Bosio	.05	.02
❑	472	Jamie Quirk	.05	.02
❑	473	Jesse Orosco	.05	.02
❑	474	Alvaro Espinoza	.05	.02
❑	475	Joe Orsulak	.05	.02
❑	476	Checklist 397-477	.05	.02
❑	477	Gerald Young	.05	.02
❑	478	Wally Backman	.05	.02
❑	479	Juan Bell	.05	.02
❑	480	Mike Scioscia	.05	.02
❑	481	Omar Olivares	.05	.02
❑	482	Francisco Cabrera	.05	.02
❑	483	Greg Swindell UER (Shown on Indians, but listed on Reds)	.05	.02
❑	484	Terry Leach	.05	.02
❑	485	Tommy Gregg	.05	.02
❑	486	Scott Aldred	.05	.02
❑	487	Greg Briley	.05	.02
❑	488	Phil Plantier	.05	.02
❑	489	Curtis Wilkerson	.05	.02
❑	490	Tom Brunansky	.05	.02
❑	491	Mike Fetters	.05	.02
❑	492	Frank Castillo	.05	.02
❑	493	Joe Boever	.05	.02
❑	494	Kirt Manwaring	.05	.02
❑	495	Wilson Alvarez HL	.05	.02
❑	496	Gene Larkin	.05	.02
❑	497	Gary DiSarcina	.05	.02
❑	498	Frank Viola	.05	.02
❑	499	Manuel Lee	.05	.02
❑	500	Albert Belle	.25	.11
❑	501	Stan Belinda	.05	.02
❑	502	Dwight Evans	.10	.05
❑	503	Eric Davis	.10	.05
❑	504	Darren Holmes	.05	.02
❑	505	Mike Bordick	.05	.02
❑	506	Dave Hansen	.05	.02
❑	507	Lee Guetterman	.05	.02
❑	508	Keith Mitchell	.05	.02
❑	509	Melido Perez	.05	.02
❑	510	Dickie Thon	.05	.02
❑	511	Mark Williamson	.05	.02
❑	512	Mark Salas	.05	.02
❑	513	Milt Thompson	.05	.02
❑	514	Mo Vaughn	.30	.14
❑	515	Jim Deshaies	.05	.02
❑	516	Rich Garces	.05	.02
❑	517	Lonnie Smith	.05	.02
❑	518	Spike Owen	.05	.02
❑	519	Tracy Jones	.05	.02
❑	520	Greg Maddux	.60	.25
❑	521	Carlos Martinez	.05	.02
❑	522	Neal Heaton	.05	.02
❑	523	Mike Greenwell	.05	.02
❑	524	Andy Benes	.10	.05
❑	525	Jeff Schaefer UER (Photo actually Tino Martinez)	.05	.02
❑	526	Mike Sharperson	.05	.02
❑	527	Wade Taylor	.05	.02
❑	528	Jerome Walton	.05	.02
❑	529	Storm Davis	.05	.02
❑	530	Jose Hernandez	.05	.02
❑	531	Mark Langston	.05	.02
❑	532	Rob Deer	.05	.02
❑	533	Geronimo Pena	.05	.02
❑	534	Juan Guzman	.05	.02
❑	535	Pete Schourek	.05	.02
❑	536	Todd Benzinger	.05	.02
❑	537	Billy Hatcher	.05	.02
❑	538	Tom Foley	.05	.02
❑	539	Dave Cochrane	.05	.02
❑	540	Mariano Duncan	.05	.02
❑	541	Edwin Nunez	.05	.02
❑	542	Rance Mulliniks	.05	.02
❑	543	Carlton Fisk	.20	.09
❑	544	Luis Aquino	.05	.02
❑	545	Ricky Bones	.05	.02
❑	546	Craig Grebeck	.05	.02
❑	547	Charlie Hayes	.05	.02
❑	548	Jose Canseco	.20	.09
❑	549	Andujar Cedeno	.05	.02
❑	550	Geno Petralli	.05	.02
❑	551	Javier Ortiz	.05	.02
❑	552	Rudy Seanez	.05	.02
❑	553	Rich Gedman	.05	.02
❑	554	Eric Plunk	.05	.02
❑	555	Nolan Ryan HL (With Rich Gossage)	.25	.11
❑	556	Checklist 478-555	.05	.02
❑	557	Greg Colbrunn	.05	.02
❑	558	Chito Martinez	.05	.02
❑	559	Darryl Strawberry	.10	.05
❑	560	Luis Alicea	.05	.02
❑	561	Dwight Smith	.05	.02
❑	562	Terry Shumpert	.05	.02
❑	563	Jim Vatcher	.05	.02
❑	564	Deion Sanders	.20	.09
❑	565	Walt Terrell	.05	.02
❑	566	Dave Burba	.05	.02
❑	567	Dave Howard	.05	.02
❑	568	Todd Hundley	.10	.05
❑	569	Jack Daugherty	.05	.02
❑	570	Scott Cooper	.05	.02
❑	571	Bill Sampen	.05	.02
❑	572	Jose Melendez	.05	.02
❑	573	Freddie Benavides	.05	.02
❑	574	Jim Gantner	.05	.02
❑	575	Trevor Wilson	.05	.02
❑	576	Ryne Sandberg	.25	.11
❑	577	Kevin Seitzer	.05	.02
❑	578	Gerald Alexander	.05	.02
❑	579	Mike Huff	.05	.02
❑	580	Von Hayes	.05	.02
❑	581	Derek Bell	.10	.05
❑	582	Mike Stanley	.05	.02
❑	583	Kevin Mitchell	.10	.05
❑	584	Mike Jackson	.10	.05
❑	585	Dan Gladden	.05	.02
❑	586	Ted Power UER (Wrong year given for signing with Reds)	.05	.02
❑	587	Jeff Innis	.05	.02

- ❑ 588 Bob MacDonald .05 .02
- ❑ 589 Jose Tolentino .05 .02
- ❑ 590 Bob Patterson .05 .02
- ❑ 591 Scott Brosius .25 .11
- ❑ 592 Frank Thomas .60 .25
- ❑ 593 Darryl Hamilton .05 .02
- ❑ 594 Kirk Dressendorfer .05 .02
- ❑ 595 Jeff Shaw .05 .02
- ❑ 596 Don Mattingly .30 .14
- ❑ 597 Glenn Davis .05 .02
- ❑ 598 Andy Mota .05 .02
- ❑ 599 Jason Grimsley .05 .02
- ❑ 600 Jimmy Poole .05 .02
- ❑ 601 Jim Gott .05 .02
- ❑ 602 Stan Royer .05 .02
- ❑ 603 Marvin Freeman .05 .02
- ❑ 604 Denis Boucher .05 .02
- ❑ 605 Denny Neagle .15 .07
- ❑ 606 Mark Lemke .05 .02
- ❑ 607 Jerry Don Gleaton .05 .02
- ❑ 608 Brent Knackert .05 .02
- ❑ 609 Carlos Quintana .05 .02
- ❑ 610 Bobby Bonilla .10 .05
- ❑ 611 Joe Hesketh .05 .02
- ❑ 612 Daryl Boston .05 .02
- ❑ 613 Shawon Dunston .05 .02
- ❑ 614 Danny Cox .05 .02
- ❑ 615 Darren Lewis .05 .02
- ❑ 616 Braves No-Hitter UER .05 .02
  Kent Mercker
  (Misspelled Merker
  on card front)
  Alejandro Pena
  Mark Wohlers
- ❑ 617 Kirby Puckett .30 .14
- ❑ 618 Franklin Stubbs .05 .02
- ❑ 619 Chris Donnels .05 .02
- ❑ 620 David Wells UER .10 .05
  (Career Highlights
  in black not red)
- ❑ 621 Mike Aldrete .05 .02
- ❑ 622 Bob Kipper .05 .02
- ❑ 623 Anthony Telford .05 .02
- ❑ 624 Randy Myers .10 .05
- ❑ 625 Willie Randolph .10 .05
- ❑ 626 Joe Slusarski .05 .02
- ❑ 627 John Wetteland .10 .05
- ❑ 628 Greg Cadaret .05 .02
- ❑ 629 Tom Glavine .15 .07
- ❑ 630 Wilson Alvarez .10 .05
- ❑ 631 Wally Ritchie .05 .02
- ❑ 632 Mike Mussina .30 .14
- ❑ 633 Mark Leiter .05 .02
- ❑ 634 Gerald Perry .05 .02
- ❑ 635 Matt Young .05 .02
- ❑ 636 Checklist 556-635 .05 .02
- ❑ 637 Scott Hemond .05 .02
- ❑ 638 David West .05 .02
- ❑ 639 Jim Clancy .05 .02
- ❑ 640 Doug Piatt UER .05 .02
  (Not born in 1955 as
  on card; incorrect info
  on How Acquired)
- ❑ 641 Omar Vizquel .10 .05
- ❑ 642 Rick Sutcliffe .05 .02
- ❑ 643 Glenallen Hill .05 .02
- ❑ 644 Gary Varsho .05 .02
- ❑ 645 Tony Fossas .05 .02
- ❑ 646 Jack Howell .05 .02
- ❑ 647 Jim Campanis .05 .02
- ❑ 648 Chris Gwynn .05 .02
- ❑ 649 Jim Leyritz .05 .02
- ❑ 650 Chuck McElroy .05 .02
- ❑ 651 Sean Berry .05 .02
- ❑ 652 Donald Harris .05 .02
- ❑ 653 Don Slaught .05 .02
- ❑ 654 Rusty Meacham .05 .02
- ❑ 655 Scott Terry .05 .02
- ❑ 656 Ramon Martinez .10 .05
- ❑ 657 Keith Miller .05 .02
- ❑ 658 Ramon Garcia .05 .02
- ❑ 659 Milt Hill .05 .02
- ❑ 660 Steve Frey .05 .02
- ❑ 661 Bob McClure .05 .02
- ❑ 662 Ced Landrum .05 .02
- ❑ 663 Doug Henry .05 .02
- ❑ 664 Candy Maldonado .05 .02
- ❑ 665 Carl Willis .05 .02
- ❑ 666 Jeff Montgomery .10 .05
- ❑ 667 Craig Shipley .05 .02
- ❑ 668 Warren Newson .05 .02
- ❑ 669 Mickey Morandini .05 .02
- ❑ 670 Brook Jacoby .05 .02
- ❑ 671 Ryan Bowen .05 .02
- ❑ 672 Bill Krueger .05 .02
- ❑ 673 Rob Mallicoat .05 .02
- ❑ 674 Doug Jones .05 .02
- ❑ 675 Scott Livingstone .05 .02
- ❑ 676 Danny Tartabull .05 .02
- ❑ 677 Joe Carter HL .10 .05
- ❑ 678 Cecil Espy .05 .02
- ❑ 679 Randy Velarde .05 .02
- ❑ 680 Bruce Ruffin .05 .02
- ❑ 681 Ted Wood .05 .02
- ❑ 682 Dan Plesac .05 .02
- ❑ 683 Eric Bullock .05 .02
- ❑ 684 Junior Ortiz .05 .02
- ❑ 685 Dave Hollins .05 .02
- ❑ 686 Dennis Martinez .10 .05
- ❑ 687 Larry Andersen .05 .02
- ❑ 688 Doug Simons .05 .02
- ❑ 689 Tim Spehr .05 .02
- ❑ 690 Calvin Jones .05 .02
- ❑ 691 Mark Guthrie .05 .02
- ❑ 692 Alfredo Griffin .05 .02
- ❑ 693 Joe Carter .10 .05
- ❑ 694 Terry Mathews .05 .02
- ❑ 695 Pascual Perez .05 .02
- ❑ 696 Gene Nelson .05 .02
- ❑ 697 Gerald Williams .05 .02
- ❑ 698 Chris Cron .05 .02
- ❑ 699 Steve Buechele .05 .02
- ❑ 700 Paul McClellan .05 .02
- ❑ 701 Jim Lindeman .05 .02
- ❑ 702 Francisco Oliveras .05 .02
- ❑ 703 Rob Maurer .05 .02
- ❑ 704 Pat Hentgen .20 .09
- ❑ 705 Jaime Navarro .05 .02
- ❑ 706 Mike Magnante .05 .02
- ❑ 707 Nolan Ryan .75 .35
- ❑ 708 Bobby Thigpen .05 .02
- ❑ 709 John Cerutti .05 .02
- ❑ 710 Steve Wilson .05 .02
- ❑ 711 Hensley Meulens .05 .02
- ❑ 712 Rheal Cormier .05 .02
- ❑ 713 Scott Bradley .05 .02
- ❑ 714 Mitch Webster .05 .02
- ❑ 715 Roger Mason .05 .02
- ❑ 716 Checklist 636-716 .05 .02
- ❑ 717 Jeff Fassero .10 .05
- ❑ 718 Cal Eldred .05 .02
- ❑ 719 Sid Fernandez .05 .02
- ❑ 720 Bob Zupcic .05 .02
- ❑ 721 Jose Offerman .05 .02
- ❑ 722 Cliff Brantley .05 .02
- ❑ 723 Ron Darling .05 .02
- ❑ 724 Dave Stieb .05 .02
- ❑ 725 Hector Villanueva .05 .02
- ❑ 726 Mike Hartley .05 .02
- ❑ 727 Arthur Rhodes .05 .02
- ❑ 728 Randy Bush .05 .02
- ❑ 729 Steve Sax .05 .02
- ❑ 730 Dave Otto .05 .02
- ❑ 731 John Wehner .05 .02
- ❑ 732 Dave Martinez .05 .02
- ❑ 733 Ruben Amaro .05 .02
- ❑ 734 Billy Ripken .05 .02
- ❑ 735 Steve Farr .05 .02
- ❑ 736 Shawn Abner .05 .02
- ❑ 737 Gil Heredia .05 .02
- ❑ 738 Ron Jones .05 .02
- ❑ 739 Tony Castillo .05 .02
- ❑ 740 Sammy Sosa .50 .23
- ❑ 741 Julio Franco .05 .02
- ❑ 742 Tim Naehring .10 .05
- ❑ 743 Steve Wapnick .05 .02
- ❑ 744 Craig Wilson .05 .02
- ❑ 745 Darrin Chapin .05 .02
- ❑ 746 Chris George .05 .02
- ❑ 747 Mike Simms .05 .02
- ❑ 748 Rosario Rodriguez .05 .02
- ❑ 749 Skeeter Barnes .05 .02
- ❑ 750 Roger McDowell .05 .02
- ❑ 751 Dann Howitt .05 .02
- ❑ 752 Paul Sorrento .05 .02
- ❑ 753 Braulio Castillo .05 .02
- ❑ 754 Yorkis Perez .05 .02
- ❑ 755 Willie Fraser .05 .02
- ❑ 756 Jeremy Hernandez .05 .02
- ❑ 757 Curt Schilling .15 .07
- ❑ 758 Steve Lyons .05 .02
- ❑ 759 Dave Anderson .05 .02
- ❑ 760 Willie Banks .05 .02
- ❑ 761 Mark Leonard .05 .02
- ❑ 762 Jack Armstrong .05 .02
  (Listed on Indians,
  but shown on Reds)
- ❑ 763 Scott Servais .05 .02
- ❑ 764 Ray Stephens .05 .02
- ❑ 765 Junior Noboa .05 .02
- ❑ 766 Jim Olander .05 .02
- ❑ 767 Joe Magrane .05 .02
- ❑ 768 Lance Blankenship .05 .02
- ❑ 769 Mike Humphreys .05 .02
- ❑ 770 Jarvis Brown .05 .02
- ❑ 771 Damon Berryhill .05 .02
- ❑ 772 Alejandro Pena .05 .02
- ❑ 773 Jose Mesa .05 .02
- ❑ 774 Gary Cooper .05 .02
- ❑ 775 Carney Lansford .10 .05
- ❑ 776 Mike Bielecki .05 .02
  (Shown on Cubs,
  but listed on Braves)
- ❑ 777 Charlie O'Brien .05 .02
- ❑ 778 Carlos Hernandez .05 .02
- ❑ 779 Howard Farmer .05 .02
- ❑ 780 Mike Stanton .05 .02
- ❑ 781 Reggie Harris .05 .02
- ❑ 782 Xavier Hernandez .05 .02
- ❑ 783 Bryan Hickerson .05 .02
- ❑ 784 Checklist 717-784 .05 .02
  and BC1-BC8

1992 Donruss Diamond Kings

	MINT	NRMT
COMPLETE SET (27)	20.00	9.00
COMPLETE SERIES 1 (14)	16.00	7.25
COMPLETE SERIES 2 (13)	4.00	1.80
COMMON CARD (DK1-DK27)	.50	.23

- ❑ DK1 Paul Molitor 1.50 .70
- ❑ DK2 Will Clark 1.50 .70
- ❑ DK3 Joe Carter .75 .35
- ❑ DK4 Julio Franco .50 .23
- ❑ DK5 Cal Ripken 6.00 2.70
- ❑ DK6 Dave Justice 1.50 .70
- ❑ DK7 George Bell .50 .23
- ❑ DK8 Frank Thomas 4.00 1.80
- ❑ DK9 Wade Boggs 1.50 .70
- ❑ DK10 Scott Sanderson .50 .23
- ❑ DK11 Jeff Bagwell 3.00 1.35
- ❑ DK12 John Kruk .75 .35
- ❑ DK13 Felix Jose .50 .23
- ❑ DK14 Harold Baines .75 .35
- ❑ DK15 Dwight Gooden .75 .35

Card	Player	MINT	NRMT
❑ DK16	Brian McRae	.75	.35
❑ DK17	Jay Bell	.75	.35
❑ DK18	Brett Butler	.75	.35
❑ DK19	Hal Morris	.50	.23
❑ DK20	Mark Langston	.50	.23
❑ DK21	Scott Erickson	.75	.35
❑ DK22	Randy Johnson	1.50	.70
❑ DK23	Greg Swindell	.50	.23
❑ DK24	Dennis Martinez	.75	.35
❑ DK25	Tony Phillips	.50	.23
❑ DK26	Fred McGriff	1.00	.45
❑ DK27	Checklist 1-26 DP (Dick Perez)	.50	.23

1992 Donruss Elite

	MINT	NRMT
COMPLETE SET (12)	600.00	275.00
COMMON CARD (9-18)	12.00	5.50

Card	Player	MINT	NRMT
❑ 9	Wade Boggs	25.00	11.00
❑ 10	Joe Carter	20.00	9.00
❑ 11	Will Clark	25.00	11.00
❑ 12	Dwight Gooden	20.00	9.00
❑ 13	Ken Griffey Jr.	120.00	55.00
❑ 14	Tony Gwynn	50.00	22.00
❑ 15	Howard Johnson	12.00	5.50
❑ 16	Terry Pendleton	12.00	5.50
❑ 17	Kirby Puckett	40.00	18.00
❑ 18	Frank Thomas	60.00	27.00
❑ L2	Rickey Henderson (Legend Series)	35.00	16.00
❑ S2	Cal Ripken (Signature Series)	300.00	135.00

1992 Donruss Update

	MINT	NRMT
COMPLETE SET (22)	60.00	27.00
COMMON CARD (U1-U22)	1.00	.45

Card	Player	MINT	NRMT
❑ U1	Pat Listach RR	1.00	.45
❑ U2	Andy Stankiewicz RR	1.00	.45
❑ U3	Brian Jordan RR	5.00	2.20
❑ U4	Dan Walters RR	1.50	.70
❑ U5	Chad Curtis RR	5.00	2.20
❑ U6	Kenny Lofton RR	12.00	5.50
❑ U7	Mark McGwire HL	25.00	11.00
❑ U8	Eddie Murray HL	5.00	2.20
❑ U9	Jeff Reardon HL	1.50	.70
❑ U10	Frank Viola	1.00	.45
❑ U11	Gary Sheffield	5.00	2.20
❑ U12	George Bell	1.00	.45
❑ U13	Rick Sutcliffe	1.00	.45
❑ U14	Wally Joyner	1.50	.70
❑ U15	Kevin Seitzer	1.00	.45
❑ U16	Bill Krueger	1.00	.45
❑ U17	Danny Tartabull	1.00	.45
❑ U18	Dave Winfield	5.00	2.20
❑ U19	Gary Carter	5.00	2.20
❑ U20	Bobby Bonilla	1.50	.70
❑ U21	Cory Snyder	1.00	.45
❑ U22	Bill Swift	1.00	.45

1992 Donruss Rookies

	MINT	NRMT
COMPLETE SET (132)	5.00	2.20
COMMON CARD (1-132)	.05	.02

Card	Player	MINT	NRMT
❑ 1	Kyle Abbott	.05	.02
❑ 2	Troy Afenir	.05	.02
❑ 3	Rich Amaral	.05	.02
❑ 4	Ruben Amaro	.05	.02
❑ 5	Billy Ashley	.05	.02
❑ 6	Pedro Astacio	.05	.02
❑ 7	Jim Austin	.05	.02
❑ 8	Robert Ayrault	.05	.02
❑ 9	Kevin Baez	.05	.02
❑ 10	Esteban Beltre	.05	.02
❑ 11	Brian Bohanon	.05	.02
❑ 12	Kent Bottenfield	.05	.02
❑ 13	Jeff Branson	.05	.02
❑ 14	Brad Brink	.05	.02
❑ 15	John Briscoe	.05	.02
❑ 16	Doug Brocail	.05	.02
❑ 17	Rico Brogna	.10	.05
❑ 18	J.T. Bruett	.05	.02
❑ 19	Jacob Brumfield	.05	.02
❑ 20	Jim Bullinger	.05	.02
❑ 21	Kevin Campbell	.05	.02
❑ 22	Pedro Castellano	.05	.02
❑ 23	Mike Christopher	.05	.02
❑ 24	Archi Cianfrocco	.05	.02
❑ 25	Mark Clark	.05	.02
❑ 26	Craig Colbert	.05	.02
❑ 27	Victor Cole	.05	.02
❑ 28	Steve Cooke	.05	.02
❑ 29	Tim Costo	.05	.02
❑ 30	Chad Curtis	.20	.09
❑ 31	Doug Davis	.05	.02
❑ 32	Gary DiSarcina	.05	.02
❑ 33	John Doherty	.05	.02
❑ 34	Mike Draper	.05	.02
❑ 35	Monty Fariss	.05	.02
❑ 36	Bien Figueroa	.05	.02
❑ 37	John Flaherty	.05	.02
❑ 38	Tim Fortugno	.05	.02
❑ 39	Eric Fox	.05	.02
❑ 40	Jeff Frye	.05	.02
❑ 41	Ramon Garcia	.05	.02
❑ 42	Brent Gates	.05	.02
❑ 43	Tom Goodwin	.10	.05
❑ 44	Buddy Groom	.05	.02
❑ 45	Jeff Grotewold	.05	.02
❑ 46	Juan Guerrero	.05	.02
❑ 47	Johnny Guzman	.05	.02
❑ 48	Shawn Hare	.05	.02
❑ 49	Ryan Hawblitzel	.05	.02
❑ 50	Bert Hefferman	.05	.02
❑ 51	Butch Henry	.05	.02
❑ 52	Cesar Hernandez	.05	.02
❑ 53	Vince Horsman	.05	.02
❑ 54	Steve Hosey	.05	.02
❑ 55	Pat Howell	.05	.02
❑ 56	Peter Hoy	.05	.02
❑ 57	Jonathan Hurst	.05	.02
❑ 58	Mark Hutton	.05	.02
❑ 59	Shawn Jeter	.05	.02
❑ 60	Joel Johnston	.05	.02
❑ 61	Jeff Kent	.20	.09
❑ 62	Kurt Knudsen	.05	.02
❑ 63	Kevin Koslofski	.05	.02
❑ 64	Danny Leon	.05	.02
❑ 65	Jesse Levis	.05	.02
❑ 66	Tom Marsh	.05	.02
❑ 67	Ed Martel	.05	.02
❑ 68	Al Martin	.10	.05
❑ 69	Pedro Martinez	.60	.25
❑ 70	Derrick May	.05	.02
❑ 71	Matt Maysey	.05	.02
❑ 72	Russ McGinnis	.05	.02
❑ 73	Tim McIntosh	.05	.02
❑ 74	Jim McNamara	.05	.02
❑ 75	Jeff McNeely	.05	.02
❑ 76	Rusty Meacham	.05	.02
❑ 77	Tony Menendez	.05	.02
❑ 78	Henry Mercedes	.05	.02
❑ 79	Paul Miller	.05	.02
❑ 80	Joe Millette	.05	.02
❑ 81	Blas Minor	.05	.02
❑ 82	Dennis Moeller	.05	.02
❑ 83	Raul Mondesi	.30	.14
❑ 84	Rob Natal	.05	.02
❑ 85	Troy Neel	.05	.02
❑ 86	David Nied	.05	.02
❑ 87	Jerry Nielson	.05	.02
❑ 88	Donovan Osborne	.05	.02
❑ 89	John Patterson	.05	.02
❑ 90	Roger Pavlik	.05	.02
❑ 91	Dan Peltier	.05	.02
❑ 92	Jim Pena	.05	.02
❑ 93	William Pennyfeather	.05	.02
❑ 94	Mike Perez	.05	.02
❑ 95	Hipolito Pichardo	.05	.02
❑ 96	Greg Pirkl	.05	.02
❑ 97	Harvey Pulliam	.05	.02
❑ 98	Manny Ramirez	1.50	.70
❑ 99	Pat Rapp	.05	.02
❑ 100	Jeff Reboulet	.05	.02
❑ 101	Darren Reed	.05	.02
❑ 102	Shane Reynolds	.25	.11
❑ 103	Bill Risley	.05	.02
❑ 104	Ben Rivera	.05	.02
❑ 105	Henry Rodriguez	.20	.09
❑ 106	Rico Rossy	.05	.02
❑ 107	Johnny Ruffin	.05	.02
❑ 108	Steve Scarsone	.05	.02
❑ 109	Tim Scott	.05	.02
❑ 110	Steve Shifflett	.05	.02
❑ 111	Dave Silvestri	.05	.02
❑ 112	Matt Stairs	.20	.09
❑ 113	William Suero	.05	.02
❑ 114	Jeff Tackett	.05	.02
❑ 115	Eddie Taubensee	.10	.05
❑ 116	Rick Trlicek	.05	.02
❑ 117	Scooter Tucker	.05	.02
❑ 118	Shane Turner	.05	.02
❑ 119	Julio Valera	.05	.02
❑ 120	Paul Wagner	.05	.02
❑ 121	Tim Wakefield	.40	.18
❑ 122	Mike Walker	.05	.02
❑ 123	Bruce Walton	.05	.02
❑ 124	Lenny Webster	.05	.02
❑ 125	Bob Wickman	.05	.02
❑ 126	Mike Williams	.05	.02
❑ 127	Kerry Woodson	.05	.02
❑ 128	Eric Young	.20	.09
❑ 129	Kevin Young	.20	.09
❑ 130	Pete Young	.05	.02
❑ 131	Checklist 1-66	.05	.02
❑ 132	Checklist 67-132	.05	.02

1992 Donruss Rookies Phenoms

	MINT	NRMT
COMP.FOIL SET (12)	25.00	11.00
COMMON FOIL (BC1-BC12)	.50	.23
COMP.JUMBO SET (8)	10.00	4.50
COMMON JUMBO (BC13-BC20)	.50	.23

	MINT	NRMT
❑ BC1 Moises Alou	1.50	.70
❑ BC2 Bret Boone	1.00	.45
❑ BC3 Jeff Conine	1.00	.45
❑ BC4 Dave Fleming	.50	.23
❑ BC5 Tyler Green	.50	.23
❑ BC6 Eric Karros	1.50	.70
❑ BC7 Pat Listach	.50	.23
❑ BC8 Kenny Lofton	5.00	2.20
❑ BC9 Mike Piazza	20.00	9.00
❑ BC10 Tim Salmon	5.00	2.20
❑ BC11 Andy Stankiewicz	.50	.23
❑ BC12 Dan Walters	.50	.23
❑ BC13 Ramon Caraballo	.50	.23
❑ BC14 Brian Jordan	1.50	.70
❑ BC15 Ryan Klesko	2.00	.90
❑ BC16 Sam Militello	.50	.23
❑ BC17 Frank Seminara	.50	.23
❑ BC18 Salomon Torres	.50	.23
❑ BC19 John Valentin	1.50	.70
❑ BC20 Wil Cordero	.50	.23

1993 Donruss

	MINT	NRMT
COMPLETE SET (792)	30.00	13.50
COMPLETE SERIES 1 (396)	15.00	6.75
COMPLETE SERIES 2 (396)	15.00	6.75
COMMON CARD (1-792)	.10	.05

	MINT	NRMT
❑ 1 Craig Lefferts	.10	.05
❑ 2 Kent Mercker	.10	.05
❑ 3 Phil Plantier	.10	.05
❑ 4 Alex Arias	.10	.05
❑ 5 Julio Valera	.10	.05
❑ 6 Dan Wilson	.20	.09
❑ 7 Frank Thomas	1.25	.55
❑ 8 Eric Anthony	.10	.05
❑ 9 Derek Lilliquist	.10	.05
❑ 10 Rafael Bournigal	.10	.05
❑ 11 Manny Alexander RR	.10	.05
❑ 12 Bret Barberie	.10	.05
❑ 13 Mickey Tettleton	.10	.05
❑ 14 Anthony Young	.10	.05
❑ 15 Tim Spehr	.10	.05
❑ 16 Bob Ayrault	.10	.05
❑ 17 Bill Wegman	.10	.05
❑ 18 Jay Bell	.20	.09
❑ 19 Rick Aguilera	.10	.05
❑ 20 Todd Zeile	.10	.05
❑ 21 Steve Farr	.10	.05
❑ 22 Andy Benes	.20	.09
❑ 23 Lance Blankenship	.10	.05
❑ 24 Ted Wood	.10	.05
❑ 25 Omar Vizquel	.20	.09
❑ 26 Steve Avery	.10	.05
❑ 27 Brian Bohanon	.10	.05
❑ 28 Rick Wilkins	.10	.05
❑ 29 Devon White	.10	.05
❑ 30 Bobby Ayala	.10	.05
❑ 31 Leo Gomez	.10	.05
❑ 32 Mike Simms	.10	.05
❑ 33 Ellis Burks	.20	.09
❑ 34 Steve Wilson	.10	.05
❑ 35 Jim Abbott	.20	.09
❑ 36 Tim Wallach	.10	.05
❑ 37 Wilson Alvarez	.20	.09
❑ 38 Daryl Boston	.10	.05
❑ 39 Sandy Alomar Jr.	.20	.09
❑ 40 Mitch Williams	.10	.05
❑ 41 Rico Brogna	.20	.09
❑ 42 Gary Varsho	.10	.05
❑ 43 Kevin Appier	.20	.09
❑ 44 Eric Wedge RR	.10	.05
❑ 45 Dante Bichette	.20	.09
❑ 46 Jose Oquendo	.10	.05
❑ 47 Mike Trombley	.10	.05
❑ 48 Dan Walters	.10	.05
❑ 49 Gerald Williams	.10	.05
❑ 50 Bud Black	.10	.05
❑ 51 Bobby Witt	.10	.05
❑ 52 Mark Davis	.10	.05
❑ 53 Shawn Barton	.10	.05
❑ 54 Paul Assenmacher	.10	.05
❑ 55 Kevin Reimer	.10	.05
❑ 56 Billy Ashley RR	.10	.05
❑ 57 Eddie Zosky	.10	.05
❑ 58 Chris Sabo	.10	.05
❑ 59 Billy Ripken	.10	.05
❑ 60 Scooter Tucker	.10	.05
❑ 61 Tim Wakefield RR	.20	.09
❑ 62 Mitch Webster	.10	.05
❑ 63 Jack Clark	.10	.05
❑ 64 Mark Gardner	.10	.05
❑ 65 Lee Stevens	.10	.05
❑ 66 Todd Hundley	.30	.14
❑ 67 Bobby Thigpen	.10	.05
❑ 68 Dave Hollins	.10	.05
❑ 69 Jack Armstrong	.10	.05
❑ 70 Alex Cole	.10	.05
❑ 71 Mark Carreon	.10	.05
❑ 72 Todd Worrell	.10	.05
❑ 73 Steve Shifflett	.10	.05
❑ 74 Jerald Clark	.10	.05
❑ 75 Paul Molitor	.40	.18
❑ 76 Larry Carter	.10	.05
❑ 77 Rich Rowland RR	.10	.05
❑ 78 Damon Berryhill	.10	.05
❑ 79 Willie Banks	.10	.05
❑ 80 Hector Villanueva	.10	.05
❑ 81 Mike Gallego	.10	.05
❑ 82 Tim Belcher	.10	.05
❑ 83 Mike Bordick	.10	.05
❑ 84 Craig Biggio	.40	.18
❑ 85 Lance Parrish	.10	.05
❑ 86 Brett Butler	.20	.09
❑ 87 Mike Timlin	.10	.05
❑ 88 Brian Barnes	.10	.05
❑ 89 Brady Anderson	.30	.14
❑ 90 D.J. Dozier	.10	.05
❑ 91 Frank Viola	.10	.05
❑ 92 Darren Daulton	.20	.09
❑ 93 Chad Curtis	.20	.09
❑ 94 Zane Smith	.10	.05
❑ 95 George Bell	.10	.05
❑ 96 Rex Hudler	.10	.05
❑ 97 Mark Whiten	.10	.05
❑ 98 Tim Teufel	.10	.05
❑ 99 Kevin Ritz	.10	.05
❑ 100 Jeff Brantley	.10	.05
❑ 101 Jeff Conine	.10	.05
❑ 102 Vinny Castilla	.50	.23
❑ 103 Greg Vaughn	.20	.09
❑ 104 Steve Buechele	.10	.05
❑ 105 Darren Reed	.10	.05
❑ 106 Bip Roberts	.10	.05
❑ 107 John Habyan	.10	.05
❑ 108 Scott Servais	.10	.05
❑ 109 Walt Weiss	.10	.05
❑ 110 J.T. Snow RR	.50	.23
❑ 111 Jay Buhner	.30	.14
❑ 112 Darryl Strawberry	.20	.09
❑ 113 Roger Pavlik	.10	.05
❑ 114 Chris Nabholz	.10	.05
❑ 115 Pat Borders	.10	.05
❑ 116 Pat Howell	.10	.05
❑ 117 Gregg Olson	.10	.05
❑ 118 Curt Schilling	.20	.09
❑ 119 Roger Clemens	.75	.35
❑ 120 Victor Cole	.10	.05
❑ 121 Gary DiSarcina	.10	.05
❑ 122 Checklist 1-80 Gary Carter and Kirt Manwaring	.20	.09
❑ 123 Steve Sax	.10	.05
❑ 124 Chuck Carr	.10	.05
❑ 125 Mark Lewis	.10	.05
❑ 126 Tony Gwynn	1.00	.45
❑ 127 Travis Fryman	.20	.09
❑ 128 Dave Burba	.10	.05
❑ 129 Wally Joyner	.20	.09
❑ 130 John Smoltz	.20	.09
❑ 131 Cal Eldred	.10	.05
❑ 132 Checklist 81-159 Roberto Alomar and Devon White	.20	.09
❑ 133 Arthur Rhodes	.10	.05
❑ 134 Jeff Blauser	.10	.05
❑ 135 Scott Cooper	.10	.05
❑ 136 Doug Strange	.10	.05
❑ 137 Luis Sojo	.10	.05
❑ 138 Jeff Branson	.10	.05
❑ 139 Alex Fernandez	.20	.09
❑ 140 Ken Caminiti	.30	.14
❑ 141 Charles Nagy	.20	.09
❑ 142 Tom Candiotti	.10	.05
❑ 143 Willie Greene RR	.10	.05
❑ 144 John Vander Wal	.10	.05
❑ 145 Kurt Knudsen	.10	.05
❑ 146 John Franco	.20	.09
❑ 147 Eddie Pierce	.10	.05
❑ 148 Kim Batiste	.10	.05
❑ 149 Darren Holmes	.10	.05
❑ 150 Steve Cooke	.10	.05
❑ 151 Terry Jorgensen	.10	.05
❑ 152 Mark Clark	.10	.05
❑ 153 Randy Velarde	.10	.05
❑ 154 Greg W. Harris	.10	.05
❑ 155 Kevin Campbell	.10	.05
❑ 156 John Burkett	.10	.05
❑ 157 Kevin Mitchell	.20	.09
❑ 158 Deion Sanders	.30	.14
❑ 159 Jose Canseco	.40	.18
❑ 160 Jeff Hartsock	.10	.05
❑ 161 Tom Quinlan	.10	.05
❑ 162 Tim Pugh	.10	.05
❑ 163 Glenn Davis	.10	.05
❑ 164 Shane Reynolds	.20	.09
❑ 165 Jody Reed	.10	.05
❑ 166 Mike Sharperson	.10	.05
❑ 167 Scott Lewis	.10	.05
❑ 168 Dennis Martinez	.20	.09
❑ 169 Scott Radinsky	.10	.05
❑ 170 Dave Gallagher	.10	.05
❑ 171 Jim Thome	.75	.35
❑ 172 Terry Mulholland	.10	.05
❑ 173 Milt Cuyler	.10	.05
❑ 174 Bob Patterson	.10	.05
❑ 175 Jeff Montgomery	.20	.09
❑ 176 Tim Salmon RR	.40	.18
❑ 177 Franklin Stubbs	.10	.05
❑ 178 Donovan Osborne	.10	.05

❑ 179	Jeff Reboulet	.10	.05
❑ 180	Jeremy Hernandez	.10	.05
❑ 181	Charlie Hayes	.10	.05
❑ 182	Matt Williams	.30	.14
❑ 183	Mike Raczka	.10	.05
❑ 184	Francisco Cabrera	.10	.05
❑ 185	Rich DeLucia	.10	.05
❑ 186	Sammy Sosa	1.00	.45
❑ 187	Ivan Rodriguez	.50	.23
❑ 188	Bret Boone RR	.20	.09
❑ 189	Juan Guzman	.10	.05
❑ 190	Tom Browning	.10	.05
❑ 191	Randy Milligan	.10	.05
❑ 192	Steve Finley	.20	.09
❑ 193	John Patterson RR	.10	.05
❑ 194	Kip Gross	.10	.05
❑ 195	Tony Fossas	.10	.05
❑ 196	Ivan Calderon	.10	.05
❑ 197	Junior Felix	.10	.05
❑ 198	Pete Schourek	.10	.05
❑ 199	Craig Grebeck	.10	.05
❑ 200	Juan Bell	.10	.05
❑ 201	Glenallen Hill	.10	.05
❑ 202	Danny Jackson	.10	.05
❑ 203	John Kiely	.10	.05
❑ 204	Bob Tewksbury	.10	.05
❑ 205	Kevin Koslofski	.10	.05
❑ 206	Craig Shipley	.10	.05
❑ 207	John Jaha	.10	.05
❑ 208	Royce Clayton	.10	.05
❑ 209	Mike Piazza RR	2.00	.90
❑ 210	Ron Gant	.20	.09
❑ 211	Scott Erickson	.10	.05
❑ 212	Doug Dascenzo	.10	.05
❑ 213	Andy Stankiewicz	.10	.05
❑ 214	Geronimo Berroa	.10	.05
❑ 215	Dennis Eckersley	.20	.09
❑ 216	Al Osuna	.10	.05
❑ 217	Tino Martinez	.40	.18
❑ 218	Henry Rodriguez	.20	.09
❑ 219	Ed Sprague	.10	.05
❑ 220	Ken Hill	.10	.05
❑ 221	Chito Martinez	.10	.05
❑ 222	Bret Saberhagen	.20	.09
❑ 223	Mike Greenwell	.10	.05
❑ 224	Mickey Morandini	.10	.05
❑ 225	Chuck Finley	.20	.09
❑ 226	Denny Neagle	.20	.09
❑ 227	Kirk McCaskill	.10	.05
❑ 228	Rheal Cormier	.10	.05
❑ 229	Paul Sorrento	.10	.05
❑ 230	Darrin Jackson	.10	.05
❑ 231	Rob Deer	.10	.05
❑ 232	Bill Swift	.10	.05
❑ 233	Kevin McReynolds	.10	.05
❑ 234	Terry Pendleton	.10	.05
❑ 235	Dave Nilsson	.20	.09
❑ 236	Chuck McElroy	.10	.05
❑ 237	Derek Parks	.10	.05
❑ 238	Norm Charlton	.10	.05
❑ 239	Matt Nokes	.10	.05
❑ 240	Juan Guerrero	.10	.05
❑ 241	Jeff Parrett	.10	.05
❑ 242	Ryan Thompson RR	.10	.05
❑ 243	Dave Fleming	.10	.05
❑ 244	Dave Hansen	.10	.05
❑ 245	Monty Fariss	.10	.05
❑ 246	Archi Cianfrocco	.10	.05
❑ 247	Pat Hentgen	.30	.14
❑ 248	Bill Pecota	.10	.05
❑ 249	Ben McDonald	.10	.05
❑ 250	Cliff Brantley	.10	.05
❑ 251	John Valentin	.20	.09
❑ 252	Jeff King	.20	.09
❑ 253	Reggie Williams	.10	.05
❑ 254	Checklist 160-238 (Damon Berryhill and Alex Arias)	.10	.05
❑ 255	Ozzie Guillen	.10	.05
❑ 256	Mike Perez	.10	.05
❑ 257	Thomas Howard	.10	.05
❑ 258	Kurt Stillwell	.10	.05
❑ 259	Mike Henneman	.10	.05
❑ 260	Steve Decker	.10	.05
❑ 261	Brent Mayne	.10	.05
❑ 262	Otis Nixon	.10	.05
❑ 263	Mark Kiefer	.10	.05
❑ 264	Checklist 239-317 (Don Mattingly and Mike Bordick)	.30	.14
❑ 265	Richie Lewis	.10	.05
❑ 266	Pat Gomez	.10	.05
❑ 267	Scott Taylor	.10	.05
❑ 268	Shawon Dunston	.10	.05
❑ 269	Greg Myers	.10	.05
❑ 270	Tim Costo	.10	.05
❑ 271	Greg Hibbard	.10	.05
❑ 272	Pete Harnisch	.10	.05
❑ 273	Dave Mlicki	.10	.05
❑ 274	Orel Hershiser	.20	.09
❑ 275	Sean Berry RR	.10	.05
❑ 276	Doug Simons	.10	.05
❑ 277	John Doherty	.10	.05
❑ 278	Eddie Murray	.40	.18
❑ 279	Chris Haney	.10	.05
❑ 280	Stan Javier	.10	.05
❑ 281	Jaime Navarro	.10	.05
❑ 282	Orlando Merced	.10	.05
❑ 283	Kent Hrbek	.20	.09
❑ 284	Bernard Gilkey	.10	.05
❑ 285	Russ Springer	.10	.05
❑ 286	Mike Maddux	.10	.05
❑ 287	Eric Fox	.10	.05
❑ 288	Mark Leonard	.10	.05
❑ 289	Tim Leary	.10	.05
❑ 290	Brian Hunter	.10	.05
❑ 291	Donald Harris	.10	.05
❑ 292	Bob Scanlan	.10	.05
❑ 293	Turner Ward	.10	.05
❑ 294	Hal Morris	.10	.05
❑ 295	Jimmy Poole	.10	.05
❑ 296	Doug Jones	.10	.05
❑ 297	Tony Pena	.10	.05
❑ 298	Ramon Martinez	.20	.09
❑ 299	Tim Fortugno	.10	.05
❑ 300	Marquis Grissom	.20	.09
❑ 301	Lance Johnson	.10	.05
❑ 302	Jeff Kent	.20	.09
❑ 303	Reggie Jefferson	.20	.09
❑ 304	Wes Chamberlain	.10	.05
❑ 305	Shawn Hare	.10	.05
❑ 306	Mike LaValliere	.10	.05
❑ 307	Gregg Jefferies	.10	.05
❑ 308	Troy Neel RR	.10	.05
❑ 309	Pat Listach	.10	.05
❑ 310	Geronimo Pena	.10	.05
❑ 311	Pedro Munoz	.10	.05
❑ 312	Guillermo Velasquez	.10	.05
❑ 313	Roberto Kelly	.10	.05
❑ 314	Mike Jackson	.10	.05
❑ 315	Rickey Henderson	.40	.18
❑ 316	Mark Lemke	.10	.05
❑ 317	Erik Hanson	.10	.05
❑ 318	Derrick May	.10	.05
❑ 319	Geno Petralli	.10	.05
❑ 320	Melvin Nieves RR	.10	.05
❑ 321	Doug Linton	.10	.05
❑ 322	Rob Dibble	.10	.05
❑ 323	Chris Hoiles	.10	.05
❑ 324	Jimmy Jones	.10	.05
❑ 325	Dave Staton RR	.10	.05
❑ 326	Pedro Martinez	.50	.23
❑ 327	Paul Quantrill	.10	.05
❑ 328	Greg Colbrunn	.10	.05
❑ 329	Hilly Hathaway	.10	.05
❑ 330	Jeff Innis	.10	.05
❑ 331	Ron Karkovice	.10	.05
❑ 332	Keith Shepherd	.10	.05
❑ 333	Alan Embree	.10	.05
❑ 334	Paul Wagner	.10	.05
❑ 335	Dave Haas	.10	.05
❑ 336	Ozzie Canseco	.10	.05
❑ 337	Bill Sampen	.10	.05
❑ 338	Rich Rodriguez	.10	.05
❑ 339	Dean Palmer	.20	.09
❑ 340	Greg Litton	.10	.05
❑ 341	Jim Tatum RR	.10	.05
❑ 342	Todd Haney	.10	.05
❑ 343	Larry Casian	.10	.05
❑ 344	Ryne Sandberg	.50	.23
❑ 345	Sterling Hitchcock	.40	.18
❑ 346	Chris Hammond	.10	.05
❑ 347	Vince Horsman	.10	.05
❑ 348	Butch Henry	.10	.05
❑ 349	Dann Howitt	.10	.05
❑ 350	Roger McDowell	.10	.05
❑ 351	Jack Morris	.20	.09
❑ 352	Bill Krueger	.10	.05
❑ 353	Cris Colon	.10	.05
❑ 354	Joe Vitko	.10	.05
❑ 355	Willie McGee	.20	.09
❑ 356	Jay Baller	.10	.05
❑ 357	Pat Mahomes	.10	.05
❑ 358	Roger Mason	.10	.05
❑ 359	Jerry Nielsen	.10	.05
❑ 360	Tom Pagnozzi	.10	.05
❑ 361	Kevin Baez	.10	.05
❑ 362	Tim Scott	.10	.05
❑ 363	Domingo Martinez	.10	.05
❑ 364	Kirt Manwaring	.10	.05
❑ 365	Rafael Palmeiro	.30	.14
❑ 366	Ray Lankford	.30	.14
❑ 367	Tim McIntosh	.10	.05
❑ 368	Jessie Hollins	.10	.05
❑ 369	Scott Leius	.10	.05
❑ 370	Bill Doran	.10	.05
❑ 371	Sam Militello	.10	.05
❑ 372	Ryan Bowen	.10	.05
❑ 373	Dave Henderson	.10	.05
❑ 374	Dan Smith RR	.10	.05
❑ 375	Steve Reed RR	.10	.05
❑ 376	Jose Offerman	.10	.05
❑ 377	Kevin Brown	.30	.14
❑ 378	Darrin Fletcher	.10	.05
❑ 379	Duane Ward	.10	.05
❑ 380	Wayne Kirby RR	.10	.05
❑ 381	Steve Scarsone	.10	.05
❑ 382	Mariano Duncan	.10	.05
❑ 383	Ken Ryan	.10	.05
❑ 384	Lloyd McClendon	.10	.05
❑ 385	Brian Holman	.10	.05
❑ 386	Braulio Castillo	.10	.05
❑ 387	Danny Leon	.10	.05
❑ 388	Omar Olivares	.10	.05
❑ 389	Kevin Wickander	.10	.05
❑ 390	Fred McGriff	.30	.14
❑ 391	Phil Clark	.10	.05
❑ 392	Darren Lewis	.10	.05
❑ 393	Phil Hiatt	.10	.05
❑ 394	Mike Morgan	.10	.05
❑ 395	Shane Mack	.10	.05
❑ 396	Checklist 318-396 (Dennis Eckersley and Art Kusnyer CO)	.20	.09
❑ 397	David Segui	.10	.05
❑ 398	Rafael Belliard	.10	.05
❑ 399	Tim Naehring	.10	.05
❑ 400	Frank Castillo	.10	.05
❑ 401	Joe Grahe	.10	.05
❑ 402	Reggie Sanders	.10	.05
❑ 403	Roberto Hernandez	.20	.09
❑ 404	Luis Gonzalez	.10	.05
❑ 405	Carlos Baerga	.10	.05
❑ 406	Carlos Hernandez	.10	.05
❑ 407	Pedro Astacio RR	.10	.05
❑ 408	Mel Rojas	.10	.05
❑ 409	Scott Livingstone	.10	.05
❑ 410	Chico Walker	.10	.05
❑ 411	Brian McRae	.10	.05
❑ 412	Ben Rivera	.10	.05
❑ 413	Ricky Bones	.10	.05
❑ 414	Andy Van Slyke	.20	.09
❑ 415	Chuck Knoblauch	.40	.18
❑ 416	Luis Alicea	.10	.05
❑ 417	Bob Wickman	.10	.05
❑ 418	Doug Brocail	.10	.05
❑ 419	Scott Brosius	.10	.05
❑ 420	Rod Beck	.20	.09
❑ 421	Edgar Martinez	.30	.14
❑ 422	Ryan Klesko	.40	.18
❑ 423	Nolan Ryan	1.50	.70
❑ 424	Rey Sanchez	.10	.05
❑ 425	Roberto Alomar	.40	.18
❑ 426	Barry Larkin	.30	.14
❑ 427	Mike Mussina	.40	.18

❑ 428 Jeff Bagwell .60 .25
❑ 429 Mo Vaughn .50 .23
❑ 430 Eric Karros .30 .14
❑ 431 John Orton .10 .05
❑ 432 Wil Cordero .10 .05
❑ 433 Jack McDowell .10 .05
❑ 434 Howard Johnson .10 .05
❑ 435 Albert Belle .50 .23
❑ 436 John Kruk .20 .09
❑ 437 Skeeter Barnes .10 .05
❑ 438 Don Slaught .10 .05
❑ 439 Rusty Meacham .10 .05
❑ 440 Tim Laker RR .10 .05
❑ 441 Robin Yount .30 .14
❑ 442 Brian Jordan .20 .09
❑ 443 Kevin Tapani .10 .05
❑ 444 Gary Sheffield .40 .18
❑ 445 Rich Monteleone .10 .05
❑ 446 Will Clark .40 .18
❑ 447 Jerry Browne .10 .05
❑ 448 Jeff Treadway .10 .05
❑ 449 Mike Schooler .10 .05
❑ 450 Mike Harkey .10 .05
❑ 451 Julio Franco .10 .05
❑ 452 Kevin Young RR .10 .05
❑ 453 Kelly Gruber .10 .05
❑ 454 Jose Rijo .10 .05
❑ 455 Mike Devereaux .10 .05
❑ 456 Andujar Cedeno .10 .05
❑ 457 Damion Easley RR .20 .09
❑ 458 Kevin Gross .10 .05
❑ 459 Matt Young .10 .05
❑ 460 Matt Stairs .10 .05
❑ 461 Luis Polonia .10 .05
❑ 462 Dwight Gooden .20 .09
❑ 463 Warren Newson .10 .05
❑ 464 Jose DeLeon .10 .05
❑ 465 Jose Mesa .10 .05
❑ 466 Danny Cox .10 .05
❑ 467 Dan Gladden .10 .05
❑ 468 Gerald Perry .10 .05
❑ 469 Mike Boddicker .10 .05
❑ 470 Jeff Gardner .10 .05
❑ 471 Doug Henry .10 .05
❑ 472 Mike Benjamin .10 .05
❑ 473 Dan Peltier RR .10 .05
❑ 474 Mike Stanton .10 .05
❑ 475 John Smiley .10 .05
❑ 476 Dwight Smith .10 .05
❑ 477 Jim Leyritz .10 .05
❑ 478 Dwayne Henry .10 .05
❑ 479 Mark McGwire 2.00 .90
❑ 480 Pete Incaviglia .10 .05
❑ 481 Dave Cochrane .10 .05
❑ 482 Eric Davis .20 .09
❑ 483 John Olerud .30 .14
❑ 484 Kent Bottenfield .10 .05
❑ 485 Mark McLemore .10 .05
❑ 486 Dave Magadan .10 .05
❑ 487 John Marzano .10 .05
❑ 488 Ruben Amaro .10 .05
❑ 489 Rob Ducey .10 .05
❑ 490 Stan Belinda .10 .05
❑ 491 Dan Pasqua .10 .05
❑ 492 Joe Magrane .10 .05
❑ 493 Brook Jacoby .10 .05
❑ 494 Gene Harris .10 .05
❑ 495 Mark Leiter .10 .05
❑ 496 Bryan Hickerson .10 .05
❑ 497 Tom Gordon .20 .09
❑ 498 Pete Smith .10 .05
❑ 499 Chris Bosio .10 .05
❑ 500 Shawn Boskie .10 .05
❑ 501 Dave West .10 .05
❑ 502 Milt Hill .10 .05
❑ 503 Pat Kelly .10 .05
❑ 504 Joe Boever .10 .05
❑ 505 Terry Steinbach .10 .05
❑ 506 Butch Huskey RR .30 .14
❑ 507 David Valle .10 .05
❑ 508 Mike Scioscia .10 .05
❑ 509 Kenny Rogers .10 .05
❑ 510 Moises Alou .20 .09
❑ 511 David Wells .20 .09
❑ 512 Mackey Sasser .10 .05
❑ 513 Todd Frohwirth .10 .05
❑ 514 Ricky Jordan .10 .05
❑ 515 Mike Gardiner .10 .05
❑ 516 Gary Redus .10 .05
❑ 517 Gary Gaetti .10 .05
❑ 518 Checklist .10 .05
❑ 519 Carlton Fisk .40 .18
❑ 520 Ozzie Smith .50 .23
❑ 521 Rod Nichols .10 .05
❑ 522 Benito Santiago .10 .05
❑ 523 Bill Gullickson .10 .05
❑ 524 Robby Thompson .10 .05
❑ 525 Mike Macfarlane .10 .05
❑ 526 Sid Bream .10 .05
❑ 527 Darryl Hamilton .10 .05
❑ 528 Checklist .10 .05
❑ 529 Jeff Tackett .10 .05
❑ 530 Greg Olson .10 .05
❑ 531 Bob Zupcic .10 .05
❑ 532 Mark Grace .30 .14
❑ 533 Steve Frey .10 .05
❑ 534 Dave Martinez .10 .05
❑ 535 Robin Ventura .20 .09
❑ 536 Casey Candaele .10 .05
❑ 537 Kenny Lofton .40 .18
❑ 538 Jay Howell .10 .05
❑ 539 Fernando Ramsey RR .10 .05
❑ 540 Larry Walker .40 .18
❑ 541 Cecil Fielder .20 .09
❑ 542 Lee Guetterman .10 .05
❑ 543 Keith Miller .10 .05
❑ 544 Len Dykstra .20 .09
❑ 545 B.J. Surhoff .20 .09
❑ 546 Bob Walk .10 .05
❑ 547 Brian Harper .10 .05
❑ 548 Lee Smith .20 .09
❑ 549 Danny Tartabull .10 .05
❑ 550 Frank Seminara .10 .05
❑ 551 Henry Mercedes .10 .05
❑ 552 Dave Righetti .10 .05
❑ 553 Ken Griffey Jr. 2.00 .90
❑ 554 Tom Glavine .30 .14
❑ 555 Juan Gonzalez 1.00 .45
❑ 556 Jim Bullinger .10 .05
❑ 557 Derek Bell .20 .09
❑ 558 Cesar Hernandez .10 .05
❑ 559 Cal Ripken 1.50 .70
❑ 560 Eddie Taubensee .10 .05
❑ 561 John Flaherty .10 .05
❑ 562 Todd Benzinger .10 .05
❑ 563 Hubie Brooks .10 .05
❑ 564 Delino DeShields .20 .09
❑ 565 Tim Raines .20 .09
❑ 566 Sid Fernandez .10 .05
❑ 567 Steve Olin .10 .05
❑ 568 Tommy Greene .10 .05
❑ 569 Buddy Groom .10 .05
❑ 570 Randy Tomlin .10 .05
❑ 571 Hipolito Pichardo .10 .05
❑ 572 Rene Arocha RR .10 .05
❑ 573 Mike Fetters .10 .05
❑ 574 Felix Jose .10 .05
❑ 575 Gene Larkin .10 .05
❑ 576 Bruce Hurst .10 .05
❑ 577 Bernie Williams .40 .18
❑ 578 Trevor Wilson .10 .05
❑ 579 Bob Welch .10 .05
❑ 580 David Justice .40 .18
❑ 581 Randy Johnson .40 .18
❑ 582 Jose Vizcaino .10 .05
❑ 583 Jeff Huson .10 .05
❑ 584 Rob Maurer RR .10 .05
❑ 585 Todd Stottlemyre .10 .05
❑ 586 Joe Oliver .10 .05
❑ 587 Bob Milacki .10 .05
❑ 588 Rob Murphy .10 .05
❑ 589 Greg Pirkl RR .10 .05
❑ 590 Lenny Harris .10 .05
❑ 591 Luis Rivera .10 .05
❑ 592 John Wetteland .20 .09
❑ 593 Mark Langston .10 .05
❑ 594 Bobby Bonilla .20 .09
❑ 595 Esteban Beltre .10 .05
❑ 596 Mike Hartley .10 .05
❑ 597 Felix Fermin .10 .05
❑ 598 Carlos Garcia .10 .05
❑ 599 Frank Tanana .10 .05
❑ 600 Pedro Guerrero .10 .05
❑ 601 Terry Shumpert .10 .05
❑ 602 Wally Whitehurst .10 .05
❑ 603 Kevin Seitzer .10 .05
❑ 604 Chris James .10 .05
❑ 605 Greg Gohr RR .10 .05
❑ 606 Mark Wohlers .10 .05
❑ 607 Kirby Puckett .60 .25
❑ 608 Greg Maddux 1.25 .55
❑ 609 Don Mattingly .60 .25
❑ 610 Greg Cadaret .10 .05
❑ 611 Dave Stewart .20 .09
❑ 612 Mark Portugal .10 .05
❑ 613 Pete O'Brien .10 .05
❑ 614 Bobby Ojeda .10 .05
❑ 615 Joe Carter .20 .09
❑ 616 Pete Young .10 .05
❑ 617 Sam Horn .10 .05
❑ 618 Vince Coleman .10 .05
❑ 619 Wade Boggs .40 .18
❑ 620 Todd Pratt .10 .05
❑ 621 Ron Tingley .10 .05
❑ 622 Doug Drabek .10 .05
❑ 623 Scott Hemond .10 .05
❑ 624 Tim Jones .10 .05
❑ 625 Dennis Cook .10 .05
❑ 626 Jose Melendez .10 .05
❑ 627 Mike Munoz .10 .05
❑ 628 Jim Pena .10 .05
❑ 629 Gary Thurman .10 .05
❑ 630 Charlie Leibrandt .10 .05
❑ 631 Scott Fletcher .10 .05
❑ 632 Andre Dawson .30 .14
❑ 633 Greg Gagne .10 .05
❑ 634 Greg Swindell .10 .05
❑ 635 Kevin Maas .10 .05
❑ 636 Xavier Hernandez .10 .05
❑ 637 Ruben Sierra .10 .05
❑ 638 Dmitri Young RR .40 .18
❑ 639 Harold Reynolds .10 .05
❑ 640 Tom Goodwin .10 .05
❑ 641 Todd Burns .10 .05
❑ 642 Jeff Fassero .10 .05
❑ 643 Dave Winfield .30 .14
❑ 644 Willie Randolph .20 .09
❑ 645 Luis Mercedes .10 .05
❑ 646 Dale Murphy .30 .14
❑ 647 Danny Darwin .10 .05
❑ 648 Dennis Moeller .10 .05
❑ 649 Chuck Crim .10 .05
❑ 650 Checklist .10 .05
❑ 651 Shawn Abner .10 .05
❑ 652 Tracy Woodson .10 .05
❑ 653 Scott Scudder .10 .05
❑ 654 Tom Lampkin .10 .05
❑ 655 Alan Trammell .30 .14
❑ 656 Cory Snyder .10 .05
❑ 657 Chris Gwynn .10 .05
❑ 658 Lonnie Smith .10 .05
❑ 659 Jim Austin .10 .05
❑ 660 Checklist .10 .05
❑ 661 Tim Hulett .10 .05
❑ 662 Marvin Freeman .10 .05
❑ 663 Greg A. Harris .10 .05
❑ 664 Heathcliff Slocumb .10 .05
❑ 665 Mike Butcher .10 .05
❑ 666 Steve Foster .10 .05
❑ 667 Donn Pall .10 .05
❑ 668 Darryl Kile .20 .09
❑ 669 Jesse Levis .10 .05
❑ 670 Jim Gott .10 .05
❑ 671 Mark Hutton RR .10 .05
❑ 672 Brian Drahman .10 .05
❑ 673 Chad Kreuter .10 .05
❑ 674 Tony Fernandez .10 .05
❑ 675 Jose Lind .10 .05
❑ 676 Kyle Abbott .10 .05
❑ 677 Dan Plesac .10 .05
❑ 678 Barry Bonds .50 .23
❑ 679 Chili Davis .20 .09
❑ 680 Stan Royer .10 .05
❑ 681 Scott Kamieniecki .10 .05
❑ 682 Carlos Martinez .10 .05

❑ 683 Mike Moore	.10	.05
❑ 684 Candy Maldonado	.10	.05
❑ 685 Jeff Nelson	.10	.05
❑ 686 Lou Whitaker	.20	.09
❑ 687 Jose Guzman	.10	.05
❑ 688 Manuel Lee	.10	.05
❑ 689 Bob MacDonald	.10	.05
❑ 690 Scott Bankhead	.10	.05
❑ 691 Alan Mills	.10	.05
❑ 692 Brian Williams	.10	.05
❑ 693 Tom Brunansky	.10	.05
❑ 694 Lenny Webster	.10	.05
❑ 695 Greg Briley	.10	.05
❑ 696 Paul O'Neill	.20	.09
❑ 697 Joey Cora	.20	.09
❑ 698 Charlie O'Brien	.10	.05
❑ 699 Junior Ortiz	.10	.05
❑ 700 Ron Darling	.10	.05
❑ 701 Tony Phillips	.10	.05
❑ 702 William Pennyfeather	.10	.05
❑ 703 Mark Gubicza	.10	.05
❑ 704 Steve Hosey RR	.10	.05
❑ 705 Henry Cotto	.10	.05
❑ 706 David Hulse	.10	.05
❑ 707 Mike Pagliarulo	.10	.05
❑ 708 Dave Stieb	.20	.09
❑ 709 Melido Perez	.10	.05
❑ 710 Jimmy Key	.20	.09
❑ 711 Jeff Russell	.10	.05
❑ 712 David Cone	.20	.09
❑ 713 Russ Swan	.10	.05
❑ 714 Mark Guthrie	.10	.05
❑ 715 Checklist	.10	.05
❑ 716 Al Martin RR	.10	.05
❑ 717 Randy Knorr	.10	.05
❑ 718 Mike Stanley	.10	.05
❑ 719 Rick Sutcliffe	.10	.05
❑ 720 Terry Leach	.10	.05
❑ 721 Chipper Jones RR	2.00	.90
❑ 722 Jim Eisenreich	.10	.05
❑ 723 Tom Henke	.10	.05
❑ 724 Jeff Frye	.10	.05
❑ 725 Harold Baines	.20	.09
❑ 726 Scott Sanderson	.10	.05
❑ 727 Tom Foley	.10	.05
❑ 728 Bryan Harvey	.10	.05
❑ 729 Tom Edens	.10	.05
❑ 730 Eric Young	.40	.18
❑ 731 Dave Weathers	.10	.05
❑ 732 Spike Owen	.10	.05
❑ 733 Scott Aldred	.10	.05
❑ 734 Cris Carpenter	.10	.05
❑ 735 Dion James	.10	.05
❑ 736 Joe Girardi	.20	.09
❑ 737 Nigel Wilson RR	.10	.05
❑ 738 Scott Chiamparino	.10	.05
❑ 739 Jeff Reardon	.20	.09
❑ 740 Willie Blair	.10	.05
❑ 741 Jim Corsi	.10	.05
❑ 742 Ken Patterson	.10	.05
❑ 743 Andy Ashby	.20	.09
❑ 744 Rob Natal	.10	.05
❑ 745 Kevin Bass	.10	.05
❑ 746 Freddie Benavides	.10	.05
❑ 747 Chris Donnels	.10	.05
❑ 748 Kerry Woodson	.10	.05
❑ 749 Calvin Jones	.10	.05
❑ 750 Gary Scott	.10	.05
❑ 751 Joe Orsulak	.10	.05
❑ 752 Armando Reynoso	.10	.05
❑ 753 Monty Fariss	.10	.05
❑ 754 Billy Hatcher	.10	.05
❑ 755 Denis Boucher	.10	.05
❑ 756 Walt Weiss	.10	.05
❑ 757 Mike Fitzgerald	.10	.05
❑ 758 Rudy Seanez	.10	.05
❑ 759 Bret Barberie	.10	.05
❑ 760 Mo Sanford	.10	.05
❑ 761 Pedro Castellano	.10	.05
❑ 762 Chuck Carr	.10	.05
❑ 763 Steve Howe	.10	.05
❑ 764 Andres Galarraga	.40	.18
❑ 765 Jeff Conine	.10	.05
❑ 766 Ted Power	.10	.05
❑ 767 Butch Henry	.10	.05
❑ 768 Steve Decker	.10	.05
❑ 769 Storm Davis	.10	.05
❑ 770 Vinny Castilla	.50	.23
❑ 771 Junior Felix	.10	.05
❑ 772 Walt Terrell	.10	.05
❑ 773 Brad Ausmus	.10	.05
❑ 774 Jamie McAndrew	.10	.05
❑ 775 Milt Thompson	.10	.05
❑ 776 Charlie Hayes	.10	.05
❑ 777 Jack Armstrong	.10	.05
❑ 778 Dennis Rasmussen	.10	.05
❑ 779 Darren Holmes	.10	.05
❑ 780 Alex Arias	.10	.05
❑ 781 Randy Bush	.10	.05
❑ 782 Javier Lopez RR	.40	.18
❑ 783 Dante Bichette	.20	.09
❑ 784 John Johnstone	.10	.05
❑ 785 Rene Gonzales	.10	.05
❑ 786 Alex Cole	.10	.05
❑ 787 Jeromy Burnitz RR	.20	.09
❑ 788 Michael Huff	.10	.05
❑ 789 Anthony Telford	.10	.05
❑ 790 Jerald Clark	.10	.05
❑ 791 Joel Johnston	.10	.05
❑ 792 David Nied RR	.10	.05

1993 Donruss Diamond Kings

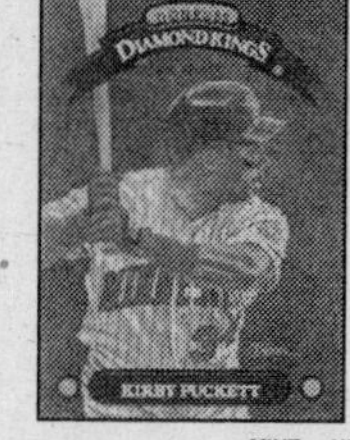

	MINT	NRMT
COMPLETE SET (31)	30.00	13.50
COMPLETE SERIES 1 (15)	20.00	9.00
COMPLETE SERIES 2 (16)	10.00	4.50
COMMON CARD (DK1-DK31)	.75	.35
❑ DK1 Ken Griffey Jr.	12.00	5.50
❑ DK2 Ryne Sandberg	3.00	1.35
❑ DK3 Roger Clemens	5.00	2.20
❑ DK4 Kirby Puckett	3.00	1.35
❑ DK5 Bill Swift	.75	.35
❑ DK6 Larry Walker	2.50	1.10
❑ DK7 Juan Gonzalez	6.00	2.70
❑ DK8 Wally Joyner	1.25	.55
❑ DK9 Andy Van Slyke	.75	.35
❑ DK10 Robin Ventura	1.25	.55
❑ DK11 Bip Roberts	.75	.35
❑ DK12 Roberto Kelly	.75	.35
❑ DK13 Carlos Baerga	.75	.35
❑ DK14 Orel Hershiser	1.25	.55
❑ DK15 Cecil Fielder	1.25	.55
❑ DK16 Robin Yount	2.00	.90
❑ DK17 Darren Daulton	1.25	.55
❑ DK18 Mark McGwire	10.00	4.50
❑ DK19 Tom Glavine	2.00	.90
❑ DK20 Roberto Alomar	2.50	1.10
❑ DK21 Gary Sheffield	2.50	1.10
❑ DK22 Bob Tewksbury	.75	.35
❑ DK23 Brady Anderson	1.25	.55
❑ DK24 Craig Biggio	2.50	1.10
❑ DK25 Eddie Murray	2.50	1.10
❑ DK26 Luis Polonia	.75	.35
❑ DK27 Nigel Wilson	.75	.35
❑ DK28 David Nied	.75	.35
❑ DK29 Pat Listach ROY	.75	.35
❑ DK30 Eric Karros ROY	2.00	.90
❑ DK31 Checklist 1-31	.75	.35

1993 Donruss Elite

	MINT	NRMT
COMPLETE SET (20)	400.00	180.00
COMMON CARD (19-36)	8.00	3.60
❑ 19 Fred McGriff	12.00	5.50
❑ 20 Ryne Sandberg	25.00	11.00
❑ 21 Eddie Murray	20.00	9.00
❑ 22 Paul Molitor	20.00	9.00
❑ 23 Barry Larkin	12.00	5.50
❑ 24 Don Mattingly	30.00	13.50
❑ 25 Dennis Eckersley	12.00	5.50
❑ 26 Roberto Alomar	20.00	9.00
❑ 27 Edgar Martinez	12.00	5.50
❑ 28 Gary Sheffield	20.00	9.00
❑ 29 Darren Daulton	12.00	5.50
❑ 30 Larry Walker	20.00	9.00
❑ 31 Barry Bonds	25.00	11.00
❑ 32 Andy Van Slyke	8.00	3.60
❑ 33 Mark McGwire	100.00	45.00
❑ 34 Cecil Fielder	12.00	5.50
❑ 35 Dave Winfield	12.00	5.50
❑ 36 Juan Gonzalez	50.00	22.00
❑ L3 Robin Yount (Legend Series)	25.00	11.00
❑ S3 Will Clark AU (Signature Series)	100.00	45.00

1993 Donruss Long Ball Leaders

	MINT	NRMT
COMPLETE SET (18)	60.00	27.00
COMPLETE SERIES 1 (9)	30.00	13.50
COMPLETE SERIES 2 (9)	30.00	13.50
COMMON CARD (LL1-LL18)	1.00	.45
❑ LL1 Rob Deer	1.00	.45
❑ LL2 Fred McGriff	2.50	1.10
❑ LL3 Albert Belle	5.00	2.20
❑ LL4 Mark McGwire	20.00	9.00
❑ LL5 David Justice	4.00	1.80
❑ LL6 Jose Canseco	4.00	1.80
❑ LL7 Kent Hrbek	2.00	.90
❑ LL8 Roberto Alomar	4.00	1.80
❑ LL9 Ken Griffey Jr.	20.00	9.00
❑ LL10 Frank Thomas	12.00	5.50
❑ LL11 Darryl Strawberry	2.00	.90
❑ LL12 Felix Jose	1.00	.45

		MINT	NRMT
❑ LL13	Cecil Fielder	2.00	.90
❑ LL14	Juan Gonzalez	10.00	4.50
❑ LL15	Ryne Sandberg	5.00	2.20
❑ LL16	Gary Sheffield	4.00	1.80
❑ LL17	Jeff Bagwell	6.00	2.70
❑ LL18	Larry Walker	4.00	1.80

1993 Donruss MVPs

	MINT	NRMT
COMPLETE SET (26)	30.00	13.50
COMPLETE SERIES 1 (13)	10.00	4.50
COMPLETE SERIES 2 (13)	20.00	9.00
COMMON CARD (1-26)	.50	.23

		MINT	NRMT
❑ 1	Luis Polonia	.50	.23
❑ 2	Frank Thomas	5.00	2.20
❑ 3	George Brett	3.00	1.35
❑ 4	Paul Molitor	1.00	.45
❑ 5	Don Mattingly	3.00	1.35
❑ 6	Roberto Alomar	1.00	.45
❑ 7	Terry Pendleton	.50	.23
❑ 8	Eric Karros	.75	.35
❑ 9	Larry Walker	1.00	.45
❑ 10	Eddie Murray	1.00	.45
❑ 11	Darren Daulton	.60	.25
❑ 12	Ray Lankford	.75	.35
❑ 13	Will Clark	1.00	.45
❑ 14	Cal Ripken	6.00	2.70
❑ 15	Roger Clemens	3.00	1.35
❑ 16	Carlos Baerga	.50	.23
❑ 17	Cecil Fielder	.60	.25
❑ 18	Kirby Puckett	2.50	1.10
❑ 19	Mark McGwire	7.50	3.40
❑ 20	Ken Griffey Jr.	8.00	3.60
❑ 21	Juan Gonzalez	4.00	1.80
❑ 22	Ryne Sandberg	2.00	.90
❑ 23	Bip Roberts	.50	.23
❑ 24	Jeff Bagwell	2.50	1.10
❑ 25	Barry Bonds	2.00	.90
❑ 26	Gary Sheffield	1.00	.45

1993 Donruss Spirit of the Game

	MINT	NRMT
COMPLETE SET (20)	20.00	9.00
COMPLETE SERIES 1 (10)	8.00	3.60
COMPLETE SERIES 2 (10)	12.00	5.50
COMMON CARD (SG1-SG20)	.50	.23

		MINT	NRMT
❑ SG1	Mike Bordick Turning Two	.50	.23
❑ SG2	Dave Justice Play at the Plate	1.50	.70
❑ SG3	Roberto Alomar In There	1.50	.70
❑ SG4	Dennis Eckersley Pumped	.75	.35
❑ SG5	Juan Gonzalez and Jose Canseco Dynamic Duo	4.00	1.80
❑ SG6	George Bell and Frank Thomas ... Gone	1.50	.70
❑ SG7	Wade Boggs and Luis Polonia Safe or Out	1.50	.70
❑ SG8	Will Clark The Thrill	1.50	.70
❑ SG9	Bip Roberts Safe at Home	.50	.23
❑ SG10	Cecil Fielder Rob Deer Mickey Tettleton Thirty 3	.75	.35
❑ SG11	Kenny Lofton Bag Bandit	2.00	.90
❑ SG12	Gary Sheffield Fred McGriff Back to Back	1.50	.70
❑ SG13	Greg Gagne Barry Larkin	.75	.35
❑ SG14	Ryne Sandberg The Ball Stops Here	2.50	1.10
❑ SG15	Carlos Baerga Gary Gaetti Over the Top	.75	.35
❑ SG16	Danny Tartabull At the Wall	.50	.23
❑ SG17	Brady Anderson Head First	.75	.35
❑ SG18	Frank Thomas Big Hurt	8.00	3.60
❑ SG19	Kevin Gross No Hitter	.50	.23
❑ SG20	Robin Yount 3,000 Hits	1.00	.45

1994 Donruss

	MINT	NRMT
COMPLETE SET (660)	40.00	18.00
COMPLETE SERIES 1 (330)	20.00	9.00
COMPLETE SERIES 2 (330)	20.00	9.00
COMMON CARD (1-660)	.15	.07

		MINT	NRMT
❑ 1	Nolan Ryan	3.00	1.35
❑ 2	Mike Piazza	2.00	.90
❑ 3	Moises Alou	.40	.18
❑ 4	Ken Griffey Jr.	3.00	1.35
❑ 5	Gary Sheffield	.60	.25
❑ 6	Roberto Alomar	.60	.25
❑ 7	John Kruk	.30	.14
❑ 8	Gregg Olson	.15	.07
❑ 9	Gregg Jefferies	.15	.07
❑ 10	Tony Gwynn	1.50	.70
❑ 11	Chad Curtis	.15	.07
❑ 12	Craig Biggio	.60	.25
❑ 13	John Burkett	.15	.07
❑ 14	Carlos Baerga	.30	.14
❑ 15	Robin Yount	.60	.25
❑ 16	Dennis Eckersley	.30	.14
❑ 17	Dwight Gooden	.30	.14
❑ 18	Ryne Sandberg	.75	.35
❑ 19	Rickey Henderson	.60	.25
❑ 20	Jack McDowell	.15	.07
❑ 21	Jay Bell	.30	.14
❑ 22	Kevin Brown	.30	.14
❑ 23	Robin Ventura	.30	.14
❑ 24	Paul Molitor	.60	.25
❑ 25	David Justice	.60	.25
❑ 26	Rafael Palmeiro	.40	.18
❑ 27	Cecil Fielder	.30	.14
❑ 28	Chuck Knoblauch	.60	.25
❑ 29	Dave Hollins	.15	.07
❑ 30	Jimmy Key	.30	.14
❑ 31	Mark Langston	.15	.07
❑ 32	Darryl Kile	.30	.14
❑ 33	Ruben Sierra	.15	.07
❑ 34	Ron Gant	.30	.14
❑ 35	Ozzie Smith	.75	.35
❑ 36	Wade Boggs	.60	.25
❑ 37	Marquis Grissom	.30	.14
❑ 38	Will Clark	.60	.25
❑ 39	Kenny Lofton	.60	.25
❑ 40	Cal Ripken	2.50	1.10
❑ 41	Steve Avery	.15	.07
❑ 42	Mo Vaughn	.75	.35
❑ 43	Brian McRae	.15	.07
❑ 44	Mickey Tettleton	.15	.07
❑ 45	Barry Larkin	.40	.18
❑ 46	Charlie Hayes	.15	.07
❑ 47	Kevin Appier	.30	.14
❑ 48	Robby Thompson	.15	.07
❑ 49	Juan Gonzalez	1.50	.70
❑ 50	Paul O'Neill	.30	.14
❑ 51	Marcos Armas	.15	.07
❑ 52	Mike Butcher	.15	.07
❑ 53	Ken Caminiti	.40	.18
❑ 54	Pat Borders	.15	.07
❑ 55	Pedro Munoz	.15	.07
❑ 56	Tim Belcher	.15	.07
❑ 57	Paul Assenmacher	.15	.07
❑ 58	Damon Berryhill	.15	.07
❑ 59	Ricky Bones	.15	.07
❑ 60	Rene Arocha	.15	.07
❑ 61	Shawn Boskie	.15	.07
❑ 62	Pedro Astacio	.15	.07
❑ 63	Frank Bolick	.15	.07
❑ 64	Bud Black	.15	.07
❑ 65	Sandy Alomar Jr.	.30	.14
❑ 66	Rich Amaral	.15	.07
❑ 67	Luis Aquino	.15	.07
❑ 68	Kevin Baez	.15	.07
❑ 69	Mike Devereaux	.15	.07
❑ 70	Andy Ashby	.15	.07
❑ 71	Larry Andersen	.15	.07
❑ 72	Steve Cooke	.15	.07
❑ 73	Mario Diaz	.15	.07
❑ 74	Rob Deer	.15	.07
❑ 75	Bobby Ayala	.15	.07
❑ 76	Freddie Benavides	.15	.07
❑ 77	Stan Belinda	.15	.07
❑ 78	John Doherty	.15	.07
❑ 79	Willie Banks	.15	.07
❑ 80	Spike Owen	.15	.07
❑ 81	Mike Bordick	.15	.07
❑ 82	Chili Davis	.30	.14
❑ 83	Luis Gonzalez	.15	.07
❑ 84	Ed Sprague	.15	.07
❑ 85	Jeff Reboulet	.15	.07
❑ 86	Jason Bere	.15	.07
❑ 87	Mark Hutton	.15	.07
❑ 88	Jeff Blauser	.15	.07
❑ 89	Cal Eldred	.15	.07
❑ 90	Bernard Gilkey	.15	.07
❑ 91	Frank Castillo	.15	.07
❑ 92	Jim Gott	.15	.07
❑ 93	Greg Colbrunn	.15	.07
❑ 94	Jeff Brantley	.15	.07
❑ 95	Jeremy Hernandez	.15	.07
❑ 96	Norm Charlton	.15	.07
❑ 97	Alex Arias	.15	.07

❑ 98 John Franco .30 .14
❑ 99 Chris Hoiles .15 .07
❑ 100 Brad Ausmus .15 .07
❑ 101 Wes Chamberlain .15 .07
❑ 102 Mark Dewey .15 .07
❑ 103 Benji Gil .15 .07
❑ 104 John Dopson .15 .07
❑ 105 John Smiley .15 .07
❑ 106 David Nied .15 .07
❑ 107 George Brett 1.25 .55
❑ 108 Kirk Gibson .30 .14
❑ 109 Larry Casian .15 .07
❑ 110 Ryne Sandberg CL .40 .18
❑ 111 Brent Gates .15 .07
❑ 112 Damion Easley .30 .14
❑ 113 Pete Harnisch .15 .07
❑ 114 Danny Cox .15 .07
❑ 115 Kevin Tapani .15 .07
❑ 116 Roberto Hernandez .15 .07
❑ 117 Domingo Jean .15 .07
❑ 118 Sid Bream .15 .07
❑ 119 Doug Henry .15 .07
❑ 120 Omar Olivares .15 .07
❑ 121 Mike Harkey .15 .07
❑ 122 Carlos Hernandez .15 .07
❑ 123 Jeff Fassero .15 .07
❑ 124 Dave Burba .15 .07
❑ 125 Wayne Kirby .15 .07
❑ 126 John Cummings .15 .07
❑ 127 Bret Barberie .15 .07
❑ 128 Todd Hundley .30 .14
❑ 129 Tim Hulett .15 .07
❑ 130 Phil Clark .15 .07
❑ 131 Danny Jackson .15 .07
❑ 132 Tom Foley .15 .07
❑ 133 Donald Harris .15 .07
❑ 134 Scott Fletcher .15 .07
❑ 135 Johnny Ruffin .15 .07
❑ 136 Jerald Clark .15 .07
❑ 137 Billy Brewer .15 .07
❑ 138 Dan Gladden .15 .07
❑ 139 Eddie Guardado .15 .07
❑ 140 Cal Ripken CL .75 .35
❑ 141 Scott Hemond .15 .07
❑ 142 Steve Frey .15 .07
❑ 143 Xavier Hernandez .15 .07
❑ 144 Mark Eichhorn .15 .07
❑ 145 Ellis Burks .30 .14
❑ 146 Jim Leyritz .30 .14
❑ 147 Mark Lemke .15 .07
❑ 148 Pat Listach .15 .07
❑ 149 Donovan Osborne .15 .07
❑ 150 Glenallen Hill .15 .07
❑ 151 Orel Hershiser .30 .14
❑ 152 Darrin Fletcher .15 .07
❑ 153 Royce Clayton .15 .07
❑ 154 Derek Lilliquist .15 .07
❑ 155 Mike Felder .15 .07
❑ 156 Jeff Conine .30 .14
❑ 157 Ryan Thompson .15 .07
❑ 158 Ben McDonald .15 .07
❑ 159 Ricky Gutierrez .15 .07
❑ 160 Terry Mulholland .15 .07
❑ 161 Carlos Garcia .15 .07
❑ 162 Tom Henke .15 .07
❑ 163 Mike Greenwell .15 .07
❑ 164 Thomas Howard .15 .07
❑ 165 Joe Girardi .15 .07
❑ 166 Hubie Brooks .15 .07
❑ 167 Greg Gohr .15 .07
❑ 168 Chip Hale .15 .07
❑ 169 Rick Honeycutt .15 .07
❑ 170 Hilly Hathaway .15 .07
❑ 171 Todd Jones .15 .07
❑ 172 Tony Fernandez .15 .07
❑ 173 Bo Jackson .30 .14
❑ 174 Bobby Munoz .15 .07
❑ 175 Greg McMichael .15 .07
❑ 176 Graeme Lloyd .15 .07
❑ 177 Tom Pagnozzi .15 .07
❑ 178 Derrick May .15 .07
❑ 179 Pedro Martinez .75 .35
❑ 180 Ken Hill .15 .07
❑ 181 Bryan Hickerson .15 .07
❑ 182 Jose Mesa .15 .07
❑ 183 Dave Fleming .15 .07
❑ 184 Henry Cotto .15 .07
❑ 185 Jeff Kent .30 .14
❑ 186 Mark McLemore .15 .07
❑ 187 Trevor Hoffman .30 .14
❑ 188 Todd Pratt .15 .07
❑ 189 Blas Minor .15 .07
❑ 190 Charlie Leibrandt .15 .07
❑ 191 Tony Pena .15 .07
❑ 192 Larry Luebbers .15 .07
❑ 193 Greg W. Harris .15 .07
❑ 194 David Cone .40 .18
❑ 195 Bill Gullickson .15 .07
❑ 196 Brian Harper .15 .07
❑ 197 Steve Karsay .15 .07
❑ 198 Greg Myers .15 .07
❑ 199 Mark Portugal .15 .07
❑ 200 Pat Hentgen .30 .14
❑ 201 Mike LaValliere .15 .07
❑ 202 Mike Stanley .15 .07
❑ 203 Kent Mercker .15 .07
❑ 204 Dave Nilsson .15 .07
❑ 205 Erik Pappas .15 .07
❑ 206 Mike Morgan .15 .07
❑ 207 Roger McDowell .15 .07
❑ 208 Mike Lansing .30 .14
❑ 209 Kirt Manwaring .15 .07
❑ 210 Randy Milligan .15 .07
❑ 211 Erik Hanson .15 .07
❑ 212 Orestes Destrade .15 .07
❑ 213 Mike Maddux .15 .07
❑ 214 Alan Mills .15 .07
❑ 215 Tim Mauser .15 .07
❑ 216 Ben Rivera .15 .07
❑ 217 Don Slaught .15 .07
❑ 218 Bob Patterson .15 .07
❑ 219 Carlos Quintana .15 .07
❑ 220 Tim Raines CL .15 .07
❑ 221 Hal Morris .15 .07
❑ 222 Darren Holmes .15 .07
❑ 223 Chris Gwynn .15 .07
❑ 224 Chad Kreuter .15 .07
❑ 225 Mike Hartley .15 .07
❑ 226 Scott Lydy .15 .07
❑ 227 Eduardo Perez .15 .07
❑ 228 Greg Swindell .15 .07
❑ 229 Al Leiter .30 .14
❑ 230 Scott Radinsky .15 .07
❑ 231 Bob Wickman .15 .07
❑ 232 Otis Nixon .15 .07
❑ 233 Kevin Reimer .15 .07
❑ 234 Geronimo Pena .15 .07
❑ 235 Kevin Roberson .15 .07
❑ 236 Jody Reed .15 .07
❑ 237 Kirk Rueter .15 .07
❑ 238 Willie McGee .30 .14
❑ 239 Charles Nagy .30 .14
❑ 240 Tim Leary .15 .07
❑ 241 Carl Everett .15 .07
❑ 242 Charlie O'Brien .15 .07
❑ 243 Mike Pagliarulo .15 .07
❑ 244 Kerry Taylor .15 .07
❑ 245 Kevin Stocker .15 .07
❑ 246 Joel Johnston .15 .07
❑ 247 Geno Petralli .15 .07
❑ 248 Jeff Russell .15 .07
❑ 249 Joe Oliver .15 .07
❑ 250 Roberto Mejia .15 .07
❑ 251 Chris Haney .15 .07
❑ 252 Bill Krueger .15 .07
❑ 253 Shane Mack .15 .07
❑ 254 Terry Steinbach .30 .14
❑ 255 Luis Polonia .15 .07
❑ 256 Eddie Taubensee .15 .07
❑ 257 Dave Stewart .30 .14
❑ 258 Tim Raines .30 .14
❑ 259 Bernie Williams .60 .25
❑ 260 John Smoltz .30 .14
❑ 261 Kevin Seitzer .15 .07
❑ 262 Bob Tewksbury .15 .07
❑ 263 Bob Scanlan .15 .07
❑ 264 Henry Rodriguez .30 .14
❑ 265 Tim Scott .15 .07
❑ 266 Scott Sanderson .15 .07
❑ 267 Eric Plunk .15 .07
❑ 268 Edgar Martinez .30 .14
❑ 269 Charlie Hough .15 .07
❑ 270 Joe Orsulak .15 .07
❑ 271 Harold Reynolds .15 .07
❑ 272 Tim Teufel .15 .07
❑ 273 Bobby Thigpen .15 .07
❑ 274 Randy Tomlin .15 .07
❑ 275 Gary Redus .15 .07
❑ 276 Ken Ryan .15 .07
❑ 277 Tim Pugh .15 .07
❑ 278 J. Owens .15 .07
❑ 279 Phil Hiatt .15 .07
❑ 280 Alan Trammell .40 .18
❑ 281 Dave McCarty .15 .07
❑ 282 Bob Welch .15 .07
❑ 283 J.T. Snow .30 .14
❑ 284 Brian Williams .15 .07
❑ 285 Devon White .30 .14
❑ 286 Steve Sax .15 .07
❑ 287 Tony Tarasco .15 .07
❑ 288 Bill Spiers .15 .07
❑ 289 Allen Watson .15 .07
❑ 290 Rickey Henderson CL .30 .14
❑ 291 Jose Vizcaino .15 .07
❑ 292 Darryl Strawberry .30 .14
❑ 293 John Wetteland .30 .14
❑ 294 Bill Swift .15 .07
❑ 295 Jeff Treadway .15 .07
❑ 296 Tino Martinez .60 .25
❑ 297 Richie Lewis .15 .07
❑ 298 Bret Saberhagen .30 .14
❑ 299 Arthur Rhodes .15 .07
❑ 300 Guillermo Velasquez .15 .07
❑ 301 Milt Thompson .15 .07
❑ 302 Doug Strange .15 .07
❑ 303 Aaron Sele .30 .14
❑ 304 Bip Roberts .15 .07
❑ 305 Bruce Ruffin .15 .07
❑ 306 Jose Lind .15 .07
❑ 307 David Wells .40 .18
❑ 308 Bobby Witt .15 .07
❑ 309 Mark Wohlers .15 .07
❑ 310 B.J. Surhoff .30 .14
❑ 311 Mark Whiten .15 .07
❑ 312 Turk Wendell .15 .07
❑ 313 Raul Mondesi .60 .25
❑ 314 Brian Turang .15 .07
❑ 315 Chris Hammond .15 .07
❑ 316 Tim Bogar .15 .07
❑ 317 Brad Pennington .15 .07
❑ 318 Tim Worrell .15 .07
❑ 319 Mitch Williams .15 .07
❑ 320 Rondell White .30 .14
❑ 321 Frank Viola .15 .07
❑ 322 Manny Ramirez .75 .35
❑ 323 Gary Wayne .15 .07
❑ 324 Mike Macfarlane .15 .07
❑ 325 Russ Springer .15 .07
❑ 326 Tim Wallach .15 .07
❑ 327 Salomon Torres .15 .07
❑ 328 Omar Vizquel .30 .14
❑ 329 Andy Tomberlin .15 .07
❑ 330 Chris Sabo .15 .07
❑ 331 Mike Mussina .60 .25
❑ 332 Andy Benes .30 .14
❑ 333 Darren Daulton .30 .14
❑ 334 Orlando Merced .15 .07
❑ 335 Mark McGwire 3.00 1.35
❑ 336 Dave Winfield .60 .25
❑ 337 Sammy Sosa 1.50 .70
❑ 338 Eric Karros .30 .14
❑ 339 Greg Vaughn .30 .14
❑ 340 Don Mattingly 1.00 .45
❑ 341 Frank Thomas 2.00 .90
❑ 342 Fred McGriff .40 .18
❑ 343 Kirby Puckett 1.00 .45
❑ 344 Roberto Kelly .15 .07
❑ 345 Wally Joyner .30 .14
❑ 346 Andres Galarraga .60 .25
❑ 347 Bobby Bonilla .30 .14
❑ 348 Benito Santiago .15 .07
❑ 349 Barry Bonds .75 .35
❑ 350 Delino DeShields .15 .07
❑ 351 Albert Belle .75 .35
❑ 352 Randy Johnson .60 .25

❑ 353 Tim Salmon .60 .25
❑ 354 John Olerud .30 .14
❑ 355 Dean Palmer .30 .14
❑ 356 Roger Clemens 1.25 .55
❑ 357 Jim Abbott .30 .14
❑ 358 Mark Grace .40 .18
❑ 359 Ozzie Guillen .15 .07
❑ 360 Lou Whitaker .30 .14
❑ 361 Jose Rijo .15 .07
❑ 362 Jeff Montgomery .15 .07
❑ 363 Chuck Finley .30 .14
❑ 364 Tom Glavine .60 .25
❑ 365 Jeff Bagwell 1.00 .45
❑ 366 Joe Carter .30 .14
❑ 367 Ray Lankford .30 .14
❑ 368 Ramon Martinez .30 .14
❑ 369 Jay Buhner .30 .14
❑ 370 Matt Williams .40 .18
❑ 371 Larry Walker .60 .25
❑ 372 Jose Canseco .60 .25
❑ 373 Lenny Dykstra .30 .14
❑ 374 Bryan Harvey .15 .07
❑ 375 Andy Van Slyke .30 .14
❑ 376 Ivan Rodriguez .75 .35
❑ 377 Kevin Mitchell .15 .07
❑ 378 Travis Fryman .30 .14
❑ 379 Duane Ward .15 .07
❑ 380 Greg Maddux 2.00 .90
❑ 381 Scott Servais .15 .07
❑ 382 Greg Olson .15 .07
❑ 383 Rey Sanchez .15 .07
❑ 384 Tom Kramer .15 .07
❑ 385 David Valle .15 .07
❑ 386 Eddie Murray .60 .25
❑ 387 Kevin Higgins .15 .07
❑ 388 Dan Wilson .15 .07
❑ 389 Todd Frohwith .15 .07
❑ 390 Gerald Williams .15 .07
❑ 391 Hipolito Pichardo .15 .07
❑ 392 Pat Meares .15 .07
❑ 393 Luis Lopez .15 .07
❑ 394 Ricky Jordan .15 .07
❑ 395 Bob Walk .15 .07
❑ 396 Sid Fernandez .15 .07
❑ 397 Todd Worrell .15 .07
❑ 398 Darryl Hamilton .15 .07
❑ 399 Randy Myers .15 .07
❑ 400 Rod Brewer .15 .07
❑ 401 Lance Blankenship .15 .07
❑ 402 Steve Finley .30 .14
❑ 403 Phil Leftwich .15 .07
❑ 404 Juan Guzman .15 .07
❑ 405 Anthony Young .15 .07
❑ 406 Jeff Gardner .15 .07
❑ 407 Ryan Bowen .15 .07
❑ 408 Fernando Valenzuela .30 .14
❑ 409 David West .40 .18
❑ 410 Kenny Rogers .15 .07
❑ 411 Bob Zupcic .15 .07
❑ 412 Eric Young .15 .07
❑ 413 Bret Boone .30 .14
❑ 414 Danny Tartabull .15 .07
❑ 415 Bob MacDonald .15 .07
❑ 416 Ron Karkovice .15 .07
❑ 417 Scott Cooper .15 .07
❑ 418 Dante Bichette .30 .14
❑ 419 Tripp Cromer .15 .07
❑ 420 Billy Ashley .15 .07
❑ 421 Roger Smithberg .15 .07
❑ 422 Dennis Martinez .30 .14
❑ 423 Mike Blowers .15 .07
❑ 424 Darren Lewis .15 .07
❑ 425 Junior Ortiz .15 .07
❑ 426 Butch Huskey .30 .14
❑ 427 Jimmy Poole .15 .07
❑ 428 Walt Weiss .15 .07
❑ 429 Scott Bankhead .15 .07
❑ 430 Deion Sanders .30 .14
❑ 431 Scott Bullett .15 .07
❑ 432 Jeff Huson .15 .07
❑ 433 Tyler Green .15 .07
❑ 434 Billy Hatcher .15 .07
❑ 435 Bob Hamelin .15 .07
❑ 436 Reggie Sanders .30 .14
❑ 437 Scott Erickson .30 .14
❑ 438 Steve Reed .15 .07
❑ 439 Randy Velarde .15 .07
❑ 440 Tony Gwynn CL .60 .25
❑ 441 Terry Leach .15 .07
❑ 442 Danny Bautista .15 .07
❑ 443 Kent Hrbek .30 .14
❑ 444 Rick Wilkins .15 .07
❑ 445 Tony Phillips .15 .07
❑ 446 Dion James .15 .07
❑ 447 Joey Cora .30 .14
❑ 448 Andre Dawson .40 .18
❑ 449 Pedro Castellano .15 .07
❑ 450 Tom Gordon .15 .07
❑ 451 Rob Dibble .15 .07
❑ 452 Ron Darling .15 .07
❑ 453 Chipper Jones 2.00 .90
❑ 454 Joe Grahe .15 .07
❑ 455 Domingo Cedeno .15 .07
❑ 456 Tom Edens .15 .07
❑ 457 Mitch Webster .15 .07
❑ 458 Jose Bautista .15 .07
❑ 459 Troy O'Leary .30 .14
❑ 460 Todd Zeile .15 .07
❑ 461 Sean Berry .15 .07
❑ 462 Brad Holman .15 .07
❑ 463 Dave Martinez .15 .07
❑ 464 Mark Lewis .15 .07
❑ 465 Paul Carey .15 .07
❑ 466 Jack Armstrong .15 .07
❑ 467 David Telgheder .15 .07
❑ 468 Gene Harris .15 .07
❑ 469 Danny Darwin .15 .07
❑ 470 Kim Batiste .15 .07
❑ 471 Tim Wakefield .30 .14
❑ 472 Craig Lefferts .15 .07
❑ 473 Jacob Brumfield .15 .07
❑ 474 Lance Painter .15 .07
❑ 475 Milt Cuyler .15 .07
❑ 476 Melido Perez .15 .07
❑ 477 Derek Parks .15 .07
❑ 478 Gary DiSarcina .15 .07
❑ 479 Steve Bedrosian .15 .07
❑ 480 Eric Anthony .15 .07
❑ 481 Julio Franco .15 .07
❑ 482 Tommy Greene .15 .07
❑ 483 Pat Kelly .15 .07
❑ 484 Nate Minchey .15 .07
❑ 485 William Pennyfeather .15 .07
❑ 486 Harold Baines .30 .14
❑ 487 Howard Johnson .15 .07
❑ 488 Angel Miranda .15 .07
❑ 489 Scott Sanders .15 .07
❑ 490 Shawon Dunston .15 .07
❑ 491 Mel Rojas .15 .07
❑ 492 Jeff Nelson .15 .07
❑ 493 Archi Cianfrocco .15 .07
❑ 494 Al Martin .15 .07
❑ 495 Mike Gallego .15 .07
❑ 496 Mike Henneman .15 .07
❑ 497 Armando Reynoso .15 .07
❑ 498 Mickey Morandini .15 .07
❑ 499 Rick Renteria .15 .07
❑ 500 Rick Sutcliffe .15 .07
❑ 501 Bobby Jones .15 .07
❑ 502 Gary Gaetti .30 .14
❑ 503 Rick Aguilera .15 .07
❑ 504 Todd Stottlemyre .15 .07
❑ 505 Mike Mohler .15 .07
❑ 506 Mike Stanton .15 .07
❑ 507 Jose Guzman .15 .07
❑ 508 Kevin Rogers .15 .07
❑ 509 Chuck Carr .15 .07
❑ 510 Chris Jones .15 .07
❑ 511 Brent Mayne .15 .07
❑ 512 Greg Harris .15 .07
❑ 513 Dave Henderson .15 .07
❑ 514 Eric Hillman .15 .07
❑ 515 Dan Peltier .15 .07
❑ 516 Craig Shipley .15 .07
❑ 517 John Valentin .30 .14
❑ 518 Wilson Alvarez .30 .14
❑ 519 Andujar Cedeno .15 .07
❑ 520 Troy Neel .15 .07
❑ 521 Tom Candiotti .15 .07
❑ 522 Matt Mieske .15 .07
❑ 523 Jim Thome .75 .35
❑ 524 Lou Frazier .15 .07
❑ 525 Mike Jackson .15 .07
❑ 526 Pedro Martinez .60 .25
❑ 527 Roger Pavlik .15 .07
❑ 528 Kent Bottenfield .15 .07
❑ 529 Felix Jose .15 .07
❑ 530 Mark Guthrie .15 .07
❑ 531 Steve Farr .15 .07
❑ 532 Craig Paquette .15 .07
❑ 533 Doug Jones .15 .07
❑ 534 Luis Alicea .15 .07
❑ 535 Cory Snyder .15 .07
❑ 536 Paul Sorrento .15 .07
❑ 537 Nigel Wilson .15 .07
❑ 538 Jeff King .15 .07
❑ 539 Willie Greene .30 .14
❑ 540 Kirk McCaskill .15 .07
❑ 541 Al Osuna .15 .07
❑ 542 Greg Hibbard .15 .07
❑ 543 Brett Butler .30 .14
❑ 544 Jose Valentin .15 .07
❑ 545 Wil Cordero .15 .07
❑ 546 Chris Bosio .15 .07
❑ 547 Jamie Moyer .15 .07
❑ 548 Jim Eisenreich .15 .07
❑ 549 Vinny Castilla .30 .14
❑ 550 Dave Winfield CL .30 .14
❑ 551 John Roper .15 .07
❑ 552 Lance Johnson .15 .07
❑ 553 Scott Kamieniecki .15 .07
❑ 554 Mike Moore .15 .07
❑ 555 Steve Buechele .15 .07
❑ 556 Terry Pendleton .15 .07
❑ 557 Todd Van Poppel .15 .07
❑ 558 Rob Butler .15 .07
❑ 559 Zane Smith .15 .07
❑ 560 David Hulse .15 .07
❑ 561 Tim Costo .15 .07
❑ 562 John Habyan .15 .07
❑ 563 Terry Jorgensen .15 .07
❑ 564 Matt Nokes .15 .07
❑ 565 Kevin McReynolds .15 .07
❑ 566 Phil Plantier .15 .07
❑ 567 Chris Turner .15 .07
❑ 568 Carlos Delgado .40 .18
❑ 569 John Jaha .15 .07
❑ 570 Dwight Smith .15 .07
❑ 571 John Vander Wal .15 .07
❑ 572 Trevor Wilson .15 .07
❑ 573 Felix Fermin .15 .07
❑ 574 Marc Newfield .15 .07
❑ 575 Jeromy Burnitz .30 .14
❑ 576 Leo Gomez .15 .07
❑ 577 Curt Schilling .30 .14
❑ 578 Kevin Young .15 .07
❑ 579 Jerry Spradlin .15 .07
❑ 580 Curt Leskanic .15 .07
❑ 581 Carl Willis .15 .07
❑ 582 Alex Fernandez .15 .07
❑ 583 Mark Holzemer .15 .07
❑ 584 Domingo Martinez .15 .07
❑ 585 Pete Smith .15 .07
❑ 586 Brian Jordan .30 .14
❑ 587 Kevin Gross .15 .07
❑ 588 J.R. Phillips .15 .07
❑ 589 Chris Nabholz .15 .07
❑ 590 Bill Wertz .15 .07
❑ 591 Derek Bell .30 .14
❑ 592 Brady Anderson .30 .14
❑ 593 Matt Turner .15 .07
❑ 594 Pete Incaviglia .15 .07
❑ 595 Greg Gagne .15 .07
❑ 596 John Flaherty .15 .07
❑ 597 Scott Livingstone .15 .07
❑ 598 Rod Bolton .15 .07
❑ 599 Mike Perez .15 .07
❑ 600 Roger Clemens CL .60 .25
❑ 601 Tony Castillo .15 .07
❑ 602 Henry Mercedes .15 .07
❑ 603 Mike Fetters .15 .07
❑ 604 Rod Beck .15 .07
❑ 605 Damon Buford .15 .07
❑ 606 Matt Whiteside .15 .07
❑ 607 Shawn Green .30 .14

❑ 608 Midre Cummings	.15	.07
❑ 609 Jeff McNeely	.15	.07
❑ 610 Danny Sheaffer	.15	.07
❑ 611 Paul Wagner	.15	.07
❑ 612 Torey Lovullo	.15	.07
❑ 613 Javier Lopez	.40	.18
❑ 614 Mariano Duncan	.15	.07
❑ 615 Doug Brocail	.15	.07
❑ 616 Dave Hansen	.15	.07
❑ 617 Ryan Klesko	.30	.14
❑ 618 Eric Davis	.30	.14
❑ 619 Scott Ruffcorn	.15	.07
❑ 620 Mike Trombley	.15	.07
❑ 621 Jaime Navarro	.15	.07
❑ 622 Rheal Cormier	.15	.07
❑ 623 Jose Offerman	.15	.07
❑ 624 David Segui	.30	.14
❑ 625 Robb Nen	.15	.07
❑ 626 Dave Gallagher	.15	.07
❑ 627 Julian Tavarez	.30	.14
❑ 628 Chris Gomez	.15	.07
❑ 629 Jeffrey Hammonds	.30	.14
❑ 630 Scott Brosius	.30	.14
❑ 631 Willie Blair	.15	.07
❑ 632 Doug Drabek	.15	.07
❑ 633 Bill Wegman	.15	.07
❑ 634 Jeff McKnight	.15	.07
❑ 635 Rich Rodriguez	.15	.07
❑ 636 Steve Trachsel	.15	.07
❑ 637 Buddy Groom	.15	.07
❑ 638 Sterling Hitchcock	.30	.14
❑ 639 Chuck McElroy	.15	.07
❑ 640 Rene Gonzales	.15	.07
❑ 641 Dan Plesac	.15	.07
❑ 642 Jeff Branson	.15	.07
❑ 643 Darrell Whitmore	.15	.07
❑ 644 Paul Quantrill	.15	.07
❑ 645 Rich Rowland	.15	.07
❑ 646 Curtis Pride	.15	.07
❑ 647 Erik Plantenberg	.15	.07
❑ 648 Albie Lopez	.15	.07
❑ 649 Rich Batchelor	.15	.07
❑ 650 Lee Smith	.30	.14
❑ 651 Cliff Floyd	.30	.14
❑ 652 Pete Schourek	.15	.07
❑ 653 Reggie Jefferson	.15	.07
❑ 654 Bill Haselman	.15	.07
❑ 655 Steve Hosey	.15	.07
❑ 656 Mark Clark	.15	.07
❑ 657 Mark Davis	.15	.07
❑ 658 Dave Magadan	.15	.07
❑ 659 Candy Maldonado	.15	.07
❑ 660 Mark Langston CL	.15	.07

1994 Donruss Anniversary '84

	MINT	NRMT
COMPLETE SET (10)	50.00	22.00
COMMON CARD (1-10)	2.00	.90

❑ 1 Joe Carter	2.00	.90
❑ 2 Robin Yount	4.00	1.80
❑ 3 George Brett	6.00	2.70
❑ 4 Rickey Henderson	4.00	1.80
❑ 5 Nolan Ryan	15.00	6.75
❑ 6 Cal Ripken	15.00	6.75
❑ 7 Wade Boggs UER 1983 runs 10, should be 100	4.00	1.80
❑ 8 Don Mattingly	6.00	2.70
❑ 9 Ryne Sandberg	5.00	2.20
❑ 10 Tony Gwynn	10.00	4.50

1994 Donruss Award Winner Jumbos

	MINT	NRMT
COMPLETE SET (10)	90.00	40.00
COMPLETE SERIES 1 (5)	50.00	22.00
COMPLETE SERIES 2 (5)	40.00	18.00
COMMON CARD (1-10)	1.50	.70

❑ 1 Barry Bonds MVP	8.00	3.60
❑ 2 Greg Maddux CY	20.00	9.00
❑ 3 Mike Piazza ROY	20.00	9.00
❑ 4 Barry Bonds HR King	8.00	3.60
❑ 5 Kirby Puckett AS MVP	10.00	4.50
❑ 6 Frank Thomas MVP	20.00	9.00
❑ 7 Jack McDowell CY	1.50	.70
❑ 8 Tim Salmon ROY	6.00	2.70
❑ 9 Juan Gonzalez HR King	15.00	6.75
❑ 10 Paul Molitor WS MVP	6.00	2.70

1994 Donruss Diamond Kings

	MINT	NRMT
COMPLETE SET (30)	50.00	22.00
COMPLETE SERIES 1 (15)	25.00	11.00
COMPLETE SERIES 2 (15)	25.00	11.00
COMMON CARD (1-30)	.50	.23

❑ DK1 Barry Bonds	2.00	.90
❑ DK2 Mo Vaughn	2.00	.90
❑ DK3 Steve Avery	.50	.23
❑ DK4 Tim Salmon	2.00	.90
❑ DK5 Rick Wilkins	.50	.23
❑ DK6 Brian Harper	.50	.23
❑ DK7 Andres Galarraga	2.00	.90
❑ DK8 Albert Belle	2.00	.90
❑ DK9 John Kruk	1.00	.45
❑ DK10 Ivan Rodriguez	2.00	.90
❑ DK11 Tony Gwynn	5.00	2.20
❑ DK12 Brian McRae	.50	.23
❑ DK13 Bobby Bonilla	1.00	.45
❑ DK14 Ken Griffey Jr.	10.00	4.50
❑ DK15 Mike Piazza	6.00	2.70
❑ DK16 Don Mattingly	3.00	1.35
❑ DK17 Barry Larkin	1.25	.55
❑ DK18 Ruben Sierra	.50	.23
❑ DK19 Orlando Merced	.50	.23
❑ DK20 Greg Vaughn	1.00	.45
❑ DK21 Gregg Jefferies	.50	.23
❑ DK22 Cecil Fielder	1.00	.45
❑ DK23 Moises Alou	1.25	.55
❑ DK24 John Olerud	1.00	.45
❑ DK25 Gary Sheffield	2.00	.90
❑ DK26 Mike Mussina	2.00	.90
❑ DK27 Jeff Bagwell	3.00	1.35
❑ DK28 Frank Thomas	6.00	2.70
❑ DK29 Dave Winfield	2.00	.90
❑ DK30 Checklist	.50	.23

1994 Donruss Dominators

	MINT	NRMT
COMPLETE SET (20)	40.00	18.00
COMPLETE SER.1 SET (10)	20.00	9.00
COMPLETE SER.2 SET (10)	20.00	9.00
COMMON SER.1 CARD (A1-A10)	.50	.23

ONE JUMBO DOMINATOR PER HOBBY BOX

❑ A1 Cecil Fielder	1.00	.45
❑ A2 Barry Bonds	2.00	.90
❑ A3 Fred McGriff	1.25	.55
❑ A4 Matt Williams	1.25	.55
❑ A5 Joe Carter	1.00	.45
❑ A6 Juan Gonzalez	5.00	2.20
❑ A7 Jose Canseco	2.00	.90
❑ A8 Ron Gant	1.00	.45
❑ A9 Ken Griffey Jr.	10.00	4.50
❑ A10 Mark McGwire	10.00	4.50
❑ B1 Tony Gwynn	5.00	2.20
❑ B2 Frank Thomas	6.00	2.70
❑ B3 Paul Molitor	2.00	.90
❑ B4 Edgar Martinez	1.00	.45
❑ B5 Kirby Puckett	4.00	1.80
❑ B6 Ken Griffey Jr.	10.00	4.50
❑ B7 Barry Bonds	2.00	.90
❑ B8 Willie McGee	1.00	.45
❑ B9 Lenny Dykstra	.50	.23
❑ B10 John Kruk	1.00	.45

1994 Donruss Elite

	MINT	NRMT
COMPLETE SET (12)	160.00	70.00
COMPLETE SERIES 1 (6)	80.00	36.00
COMPLETE SERIES 2 (6)	80.00	36.00
COMMON CARD (37-48)	8.00	3.60
❑ 37 Frank Thomas	30.00	13.50
❑ 38 Tony Gwynn	25.00	11.00
❑ 39 Tim Salmon	10.00	4.50
❑ 40 Albert Belle	12.00	5.50
❑ 41 John Kruk	10.00	4.50
❑ 42 Juan Gonzalez	25.00	11.00
❑ 43 John Olerud	10.00	4.50
❑ 44 Barry Bonds	12.00	5.50
❑ 45 Ken Griffey Jr.	50.00	22.00
❑ 46 Mike Piazza	30.00	13.50
❑ 47 Jack McDowell	8.00	3.60
❑ 48 Andres Galarraga	10.00	4.50

1994 Donruss Long Ball Leaders

	MINT	NRMT
COMPLETE SET (10)	40.00	18.00
COMMON CARD (1-10)	1.00	.45
❑ 1 Cecil Fielder	1.00	.45
❑ 2 Dean Palmer	1.50	.70
❑ 3 Andres Galarraga	3.00	1.35
❑ 4 Bo Jackson	1.50	.70
❑ 5 Ken Griffey Jr.	15.00	6.75
❑ 6 David Justice	3.00	1.35
❑ 7 Mike Piazza	10.00	4.50
❑ 8 Frank Thomas	10.00	4.50
❑ 9 Barry Bonds	3.00	1.35
❑ 10 Juan Gonzalez	8.00	3.60

1994 Donruss MVPs

	MINT	NRMT
COMPLETE SET (28)	75.00	34.00
COMPLETE SERIES 1 (14)	15.00	6.75
COMPLETE SERIES 2 (14)	60.00	27.00
COMMON CARD (1-28)	.75	.35
❑ 1 David Justice	2.50	1.10
❑ 2 Mark Grace	1.50	.70
❑ 3 Jose Rijo	.75	.35
❑ 4 Andres Galarraga	2.50	1.10
❑ 5 Bryan Harvey	.75	.35
❑ 6 Jeff Bagwell	5.00	2.20
❑ 7 Mike Piazza	10.00	4.50
❑ 8 Moises Alou	1.50	.70
❑ 9 Bobby Bonilla	1.00	.45
❑ 10 Len Dykstra	1.00	.45
❑ 11 Jeff King	.75	.35
❑ 12 Gregg Jefferies	.75	.35
❑ 13 Tony Gwynn	8.00	3.60
❑ 14 Barry Bonds	2.50	1.10
❑ 15 Cal Ripken Jr.	12.00	5.50
❑ 16 Mo Vaughn	2.50	1.10
❑ 17 Tim Salmon	2.50	1.10
❑ 18 Frank Thomas	10.00	4.50
❑ 19 Albert Belle	2.50	1.10
❑ 20 Cecil Fielder	1.00	.45
❑ 21 Wally Joyner	1.00	.45
❑ 22 Greg Vaughn	1.00	.45
❑ 23 Kirby Puckett	6.00	2.70
❑ 24 Don Mattingly	4.00	1.80
❑ 25 Ruben Sierra	.75	.35
❑ 26 Ken Griffey Jr.	15.00	6.75
❑ 27 Juan Gonzalez	8.00	3.60
❑ 28 John Olerud	1.00	.45

1994 Donruss Spirit of the Game

	MINT	NRMT
COMPLETE SET (10)	60.00	27.00
COMPLETE SERIES 1 (5)	30.00	13.50
COMPLETE SERIES 2 (5)	30.00	13.50
COMMON CARD (1-10)	1.00	.45

*JUMBOS: 6X TO 12X BASIC SPIRIT
ONE JUMBO SPIRIT PER MAG.JUMBO BOX

	MINT	NRMT
❑ 1 John Olerud	1.50	.70
❑ 2 Barry Bonds	4.00	1.80
❑ 3 Ken Griffey Jr.	20.00	9.00
❑ 4 Mike Piazza	12.00	5.50
❑ 5 Juan Gonzalez	10.00	4.50
❑ 6 Frank Thomas	12.00	5.50
❑ 7 Tim Salmon	4.00	1.80
❑ 8 David Justice	4.00	1.80
❑ 9 Don Mattingly	5.00	2.20
❑ 10 Lenny Dykstra	1.00	.45

1995 Donruss

	MINT	NRMT
COMPLETE SET (550)	40.00	18.00
COMPLETE SERIES 1 (330)	25.00	11.00
COMPLETE SERIES 2 (220)	15.00	6.75
COMMON CARD (1-550)	.15	.07
❑ 1 David Justice	.60	.25
❑ 2 Rene Arocha	.15	.07
❑ 3 Sandy Alomar Jr.	.30	.14
❑ 4 Luis Lopez	.15	.07
❑ 5 Mike Piazza	2.00	.90
❑ 6 Bobby Jones	.15	.07
❑ 7 Damion Easley	.30	.14
❑ 8 Barry Bonds	.75	.35
❑ 9 Mike Mussina	.60	.25
❑ 10 Kevin Seitzer	.15	.07
❑ 11 John Smiley	.15	.07
❑ 12 Wm.VanLandingham	.15	.07
❑ 13 Ron Darling	.15	.07
❑ 14 Walt Weiss	.15	.07
❑ 15 Mike Lansing	.15	.07
❑ 16 Allen Watson	.15	.07
❑ 17 Aaron Sele	.30	.14
❑ 18 Randy Johnson	.60	.25
❑ 19 Dean Palmer	.30	.14
❑ 20 Jeff Bagwell	1.00	.45
❑ 21 Curt Schilling	.30	.14
❑ 22 Darrell Whitmore	.15	.07
❑ 23 Steve Trachsel	.15	.07
❑ 24 Dan Wilson	.15	.07
❑ 25 Steve Finley	.30	.14
❑ 26 Bret Boone	.30	.14
❑ 27 Charles Johnson	.30	.14
❑ 28 Mike Stanton	.15	.07
❑ 29 Ismael Valdes	.30	.14
❑ 30 Salomon Torres	.15	.07
❑ 31 Eric Anthony	.15	.07
❑ 32 Spike Owen	.15	.07
❑ 33 Joey Cora	.30	.14
❑ 34 Robert Eenhoorn	.15	.07
❑ 35 Rick White	.15	.07
❑ 36 Omar Vizquel	.30	.14
❑ 37 Carlos Delgado	.30	.14
❑ 38 Eddie Williams	.15	.07
❑ 39 Shawon Dunston	.15	.07
❑ 40 Darrin Fletcher	.15	.07
❑ 41 Leo Gomez	.15	.07
❑ 42 Juan Gonzalez	1.50	.70
❑ 43 Luis Alicea	.15	.07
❑ 44 Ken Ryan	.15	.07
❑ 45 Lou Whitaker	.30	.14
❑ 46 Mike Blowers	.15	.07
❑ 47 Willie Blair	.15	.07
❑ 48 Todd Van Poppel	.15	.07
❑ 49 Roberto Alomar	.60	.25
❑ 50 Ozzie Smith	.75	.35
❑ 51 Sterling Hitchcock	.30	.14
❑ 52 Mo Vaughn	.75	.35
❑ 53 Rick Aguilera	.15	.07
❑ 54 Kent Mercker	.15	.07
❑ 55 Don Mattingly	1.00	.45
❑ 56 Bob Scanlan	.15	.07
❑ 57 Wilson Alvarez	.30	.14
❑ 58 Jose Mesa	.15	.07
❑ 59 Scott Kamieniecki	.15	.07
❑ 60 Todd Jones	.15	.07
❑ 61 John Kruk	.30	.14
❑ 62 Mike Stanley	.15	.07
❑ 63 Tino Martinez	.60	.25
❑ 64 Eddie Zambrano	.15	.07
❑ 65 Todd Hundley	.30	.14
❑ 66 Jamie Moyer	.15	.07
❑ 67 Rich Amaral	.15	.07
❑ 68 Jose Valentin	.15	.07
❑ 69 Alex Gonzalez	.15	.07
❑ 70 Kurt Abbott	.15	.07
❑ 71 Delino DeShields	.15	.07
❑ 72 Brian Anderson	.30	.14
❑ 73 John Vander Wal	.15	.07
❑ 74 Turner Ward	.15	.07
❑ 75 Tim Raines	.30	.14
❑ 76 Mark Acre	.15	.07
❑ 77 Jose Offerman	.15	.07
❑ 78 Jimmy Key	.30	.14
❑ 79 Mark Whiten	.15	.07
❑ 80 Mark Gubicza	.15	.07
❑ 81 Darren Hall	.15	.07

❑ 82 Travis Fryman .30 .14
❑ 83 Cal Ripken 2.50 1.10
❑ 84 Geronimo Berroa .15 .07
❑ 85 Bret Barberie .15 .07
❑ 86 Andy Ashby .15 .07
❑ 87 Steve Avery .15 .07
❑ 88 Rich Becker .15 .07
❑ 89 John Valentin .30 .14
❑ 90 Glenallen Hill .15 .07
❑ 91 Carlos Garcia .15 .07
❑ 92 Dennis Martinez .30 .14
❑ 93 Pat Kelly .15 .07
❑ 94 Orlando Miller .15 .07
❑ 95 Felix Jose .15 .07
❑ 96 Mike Kingery .15 .07
❑ 97 Jeff Kent .30 .14
❑ 98 Pete Incaviglia .15 .07
❑ 99 Chad Curtis .15 .07
❑ 100 Thomas Howard .15 .07
❑ 101 Hector Carrasco .15 .07
❑ 102 Tom Pagnozzi .15 .07
❑ 103 Danny Tartabull .15 .07
❑ 104 Donnie Elliott .15 .07
❑ 105 Danny Jackson .15 .07
❑ 106 Steve Dunn .15 .07
❑ 107 Roger Salkeld .15 .07
❑ 108 Jeff King .15 .07
❑ 109 Cecil Fielder .30 .14
❑ 110 Paul Molitor CL .30 .14
❑ 111 Denny Neagle .30 .14
❑ 112 Troy Neel .15 .07
❑ 113 Rod Beck .15 .07
❑ 114 Alex Rodriguez 2.50 1.10
❑ 115 Joey Eischen .15 .07
❑ 116 Tom Candiotti .15 .07
❑ 117 Ray McDavid .15 .07
❑ 118 Vince Coleman .15 .07
❑ 119 Pete Harnisch .15 .07
❑ 120 David Nied .15 .07
❑ 121 Pat Rapp .15 .07
❑ 122 Sammy Sosa 1.50 .70
❑ 123 Steve Reed .15 .07
❑ 124 Jose Oliva .15 .07
❑ 125 Ricky Bottalico .30 .14
❑ 126 Jose DeLeon .15 .07
❑ 127 Pat Hentgen .30 .14
❑ 128 Will Clark .60 .25
❑ 129 Mark Dewey .15 .07
❑ 130 Greg Vaughn .30 .14
❑ 131 Darren Dreifort .30 .14
❑ 132 Ed Sprague .15 .07
❑ 133 Lee Smith .30 .14
❑ 134 Charles Nagy .30 .14
❑ 135 Phil Plantier .15 .07
❑ 136 Jason Jacome .15 .07
❑ 137 Jose Lima .15 .07
❑ 138 J.R. Phillips .15 .07
❑ 139 J.T. Snow .30 .14
❑ 140 Michael Huff .15 .07
❑ 141 Billy Brewer .15 .07
❑ 142 Jeromy Burnitz .30 .14
❑ 143 Ricky Bones .15 .07
❑ 144 Carlos Rodriguez .15 .07
❑ 145 Luis Gonzalez .15 .07
❑ 146 Mark Lemke .15 .07
❑ 147 Al Martin .15 .07
❑ 148 Mike Bordick .15 .07
❑ 149 Robb Nen .15 .07
❑ 150 Wil Cordero .15 .07
❑ 151 Edgar Martinez .30 .14
❑ 152 Gerald Williams .15 .07
❑ 153 Esteban Beltre .15 .07
❑ 154 Mike Moore .15 .07
❑ 155 Mark Langston .15 .07
❑ 156 Mark Clark .15 .07
❑ 157 Bobby Ayala .15 .07
❑ 158 Rick Wilkins .15 .07
❑ 159 Bobby Munoz .15 .07
❑ 160 Brett Butler CL .30 .14
❑ 161 Scott Erickson .30 .14
❑ 162 Paul Molitor .60 .25
❑ 163 Jon Lieber .15 .07
❑ 164 Jason Grimsley .15 .07
❑ 165 Norberto Martin .15 .07
❑ 166 Javier Lopez .30 .14
❑ 167 Brian McRae .15 .07
❑ 168 Gary Sheffield .40 .18
❑ 169 Marcus Moore .15 .07
❑ 170 John Hudek .15 .07
❑ 171 Kelly Stinnett .15 .07
❑ 172 Chris Gomez .15 .07
❑ 173 Rey Sanchez .15 .07
❑ 174 Juan Guzman .15 .07
❑ 175 Chan Ho Park .75 .35
❑ 176 Terry Shumpert .15 .07
❑ 177 Steve Ontiveros .15 .07
❑ 178 Brad Ausmus .15 .07
❑ 179 Tim Davis .15 .07
❑ 180 Billy Ashley .15 .07
❑ 181 Vinny Castilla .40 .18
❑ 182 Bill Spiers .15 .07
❑ 183 Randy Knorr .15 .07
❑ 184 Brian Hunter .30 .14
❑ 185 Pat Meares .15 .07
❑ 186 Steve Buechele .15 .07
❑ 187 Kirt Manwaring .15 .07
❑ 188 Tim Naehring .15 .07
❑ 189 Matt Mieske .15 .07
❑ 190 Josias Manzanillo .15 .07
❑ 191 Greg McMichael .15 .07
❑ 192 Chuck Carr .15 .07
❑ 193 Midre Cummings .15 .07
❑ 194 Darryl Strawberry .30 .14
❑ 195 Greg Gagne .15 .07
❑ 196 Steve Cooke .15 .07
❑ 197 Woody Williams .15 .07
❑ 198 Ron Karkovice .15 .07
❑ 199 Phil Leftwich .15 .07
❑ 200 Jim Thome .60 .25
❑ 201 Brady Anderson .30 .14
❑ 202 Pedro Martinez .60 .25
❑ 203 Steve Karsay .15 .07
❑ 204 Reggie Sanders .30 .14
❑ 205 Bill Risley .15 .07
❑ 206 Jay Bell .30 .14
❑ 207 Kevin Brown .40 .18
❑ 208 Tim Scott .15 .07
❑ 209 Lenny Dykstra .30 .14
❑ 210 Willie Greene .30 .14
❑ 211 Jim Eisenreich .15 .07
❑ 212 Cliff Floyd .30 .14
❑ 213 Otis Nixon .15 .07
❑ 214 Eduardo Perez .15 .07
❑ 215 Manuel Lee .15 .07
❑ 216 Armando Benitez .15 .07
❑ 217 Dave McCarty .15 .07
❑ 218 Scott Livingstone .15 .07
❑ 219 Chad Kreuter .15 .07
❑ 220 Don Mattingly CL .60 .25
❑ 221 Brian Jordan .30 .14
❑ 222 Matt Whiteside .15 .07
❑ 223 Jim Edmonds .40 .18
❑ 224 Tony Gwynn 1.50 .70
❑ 225 Jose Lind .15 .07
❑ 226 Marvin Freeman .15 .07
❑ 227 Ken Hill .15 .07
❑ 228 David Hulse .15 .07
❑ 229 Joe Hesketh .15 .07
❑ 230 Roberto Petagine .15 .07
❑ 231 Jeffrey Hammonds .30 .14
❑ 232 John Jaha .15 .07
❑ 233 John Burkett .15 .07
❑ 234 Hal Morris .15 .07
❑ 235 Tony Castillo .15 .07
❑ 236 Ryan Bowen .15 .07
❑ 237 Wayne Kirby .15 .07
❑ 238 Brent Mayne .15 .07
❑ 239 Jim Bullinger .15 .07
❑ 240 Mike Lieberthal .15 .07
❑ 241 Barry Larkin .40 .18
❑ 242 David Segui .30 .14
❑ 243 Jose Bautista .15 .07
❑ 244 Hector Fajardo .15 .07
❑ 245 Orel Hershiser .30 .14
❑ 246 James Mouton .15 .07
❑ 247 Scott Leius .15 .07
❑ 248 Tom Glavine .60 .25
❑ 249 Danny Bautista .15 .07
❑ 250 Jose Mercedes .15 .07
❑ 251 Marquis Grissom .30 .14
❑ 252 Charlie Hayes .15 .07
❑ 253 Ryan Klesko .30 .14
❑ 254 Vicente Palacios .15 .07
❑ 255 Matias Carrillo .15 .07
❑ 256 Gary DiSarcina .15 .07
❑ 257 Kirk Gibson .30 .14
❑ 258 Garey Ingram .15 .07
❑ 259 Alex Fernandez .15 .07
❑ 260 John Mabry .15 .07
❑ 261 Chris Howard .15 .07
❑ 262 Miguel Jimenez .15 .07
❑ 263 Heath Slocumb .15 .07
❑ 264 Albert Belle .75 .35
❑ 265 Dave Clark .15 .07
❑ 266 Joe Orsulak .15 .07
❑ 267 Joey Hamilton .30 .14
❑ 268 Mark Portugal .15 .07
❑ 269 Kevin Tapani .15 .07
❑ 270 Sid Fernandez .15 .07
❑ 271 Steve Dreyer .15 .07
❑ 272 Denny Hocking .15 .07
❑ 273 Troy O'Leary .30 .14
❑ 274 Milt Cuyler .15 .07
❑ 275 Frank Thomas 2.00 .90
❑ 276 Jorge Fabregas .15 .07
❑ 277 Mike Gallego .15 .07
❑ 278 Mickey Morandini .15 .07
❑ 279 Roberto Hernandez .15 .07
❑ 280 Henry Rodriguez .30 .14
❑ 281 Garret Anderson .30 .14
❑ 282 Bob Wickman .15 .07
❑ 283 Gar Finnvold .15 .07
❑ 284 Paul O'Neill .30 .14
❑ 285 Royce Clayton .15 .07
❑ 286 Chuck Knoblauch .60 .25
❑ 287 Johnny Ruffin .15 .07
❑ 288 Dave Nilsson .15 .07
❑ 289 David Cone .40 .18
❑ 290 Chuck McElroy .15 .07
❑ 291 Kevin Stocker .15 .07
❑ 292 Jose Rijo .15 .07
❑ 293 Sean Berry .15 .07
❑ 294 Ozzie Guillen .15 .07
❑ 295 Chris Hoiles .15 .07
❑ 296 Kevin Foster .15 .07
❑ 297 Jeff Frye .15 .07
❑ 298 Lance Johnson .15 .07
❑ 299 Mike Kelly .15 .07
❑ 300 Ellis Burks .30 .14
❑ 301 Roberto Kelly .15 .07
❑ 302 Dante Bichette .30 .14
❑ 303 Alvaro Ezpinoza .15 .07
❑ 304 Alex Cole .15 .07
❑ 305 Rickey Henderson .60 .25
❑ 306 Dave Weathers .15 .07
❑ 307 Shane Reynolds .30 .14
❑ 308 Bobby Bonilla .30 .14
❑ 309 Junior Felix .15 .07
❑ 310 Jeff Fassero .15 .07
❑ 311 Darren Lewis .15 .07
❑ 312 John Doherty .15 .07
❑ 313 Scott Servais .15 .07
❑ 314 Rick Helling .30 .14
❑ 315 Pedro Martinez .60 .25
❑ 316 Wes Chamberlain .15 .07
❑ 317 Bryan Eversgerd .15 .07
❑ 318 Trevor Hoffman .30 .14
❑ 319 John Patterson .15 .07
❑ 320 Matt Walbeck .15 .07
❑ 321 Jeff Montgomery .15 .07
❑ 322 Mel Rojas .15 .07
❑ 323 Eddie Taubensee .15 .07
❑ 324 Ray Lankford .30 .14
❑ 325 Jose Vizcaino .15 .07
❑ 326 Carlos Baerga .30 .14
❑ 327 Jack Voigt .15 .07
❑ 328 Julio Franco .15 .07
❑ 329 Brent Gates .15 .07
❑ 330 Kirby Puckett CL .60 .25
❑ 331 Greg Maddux 2.00 .90
❑ 332 Jason Bere .15 .07
❑ 333 Bill Wegman .15 .07
❑ 334 Tuffy Rhodes .15 .07
❑ 335 Kevin Young .15 .07
❑ 336 Andy Benes .30 .14

- ❑ 337 Pedro Astacio .15 .07
- ❑ 338 Reggie Jefferson .15 .07
- ❑ 339 Tim Belcher .15 .07
- ❑ 340 Ken Griffey Jr. 3.00 1.35
- ❑ 341 Mariano Duncan .15 .07
- ❑ 342 Andres Galarraga .60 .25
- ❑ 343 Rondell White .30 .14
- ❑ 344 Cory Bailey .15 .07
- ❑ 345 Bryan Harvey .15 .07
- ❑ 346 John Franco .30 .14
- ❑ 347 Greg Swindell .15 .07
- ❑ 348 David West .40 .18
- ❑ 349 Fred McGriff .40 .18
- ❑ 350 Jose Canseco .60 .25
- ❑ 351 Orlando Merced .15 .07
- ❑ 352 Rheal Cormier .15 .07
- ❑ 353 Carlos Pulido .15 .07
- ❑ 354 Terry Steinbach .30 .14
- ❑ 355 Wade Boggs .60 .25
- ❑ 356 B.J. Surhoff .30 .14
- ❑ 357 Rafael Palmeiro .40 .18
- ❑ 358 Anthony Young .15 .07
- ❑ 359 Tom Brunansky .15 .07
- ❑ 360 Todd Stottlemyre .15 .07
- ❑ 361 Chris Turner .15 .07
- ❑ 362 Joe Boever .15 .07
- ❑ 363 Jeff Blauser .15 .07
- ❑ 364 Derek Bell .30 .14
- ❑ 365 Matt Williams .30 .14
- ❑ 366 Jeremy Hernandez .15 .07
- ❑ 367 Joe Girardi .15 .07
- ❑ 368 Mike Devereaux .15 .07
- ❑ 369 Jim Abbott .30 .14
- ❑ 370 Manny Ramirez .60 .25
- ❑ 371 Kenny Lofton .60 .25
- ❑ 372 Mark Smith .15 .07
- ❑ 373 Dave Fleming .15 .07
- ❑ 374 Dave Stewart .30 .14
- ❑ 375 Roger Pavlik .15 .07
- ❑ 376 Hipolito Pichardo .15 .07
- ❑ 377 Bill Taylor .15 .07
- ❑ 378 Robin Ventura .30 .14
- ❑ 379 Bernard Gilkey .15 .07
- ❑ 380 Kirby Puckett 1.00 .45
- ❑ 381 Steve Howe .15 .07
- ❑ 382 Devon White .30 .14
- ❑ 383 Roberto Mejia .15 .07
- ❑ 384 Darrin Jackson .15 .07
- ❑ 385 Mike Morgan .15 .07
- ❑ 386 Rusty Meacham .15 .07
- ❑ 387 Bill Swift .15 .07
- ❑ 388 Lou Frazier .15 .07
- ❑ 389 Andy Van Slyke .30 .14
- ❑ 390 Brett Butler .30 .14
- ❑ 391 Bobby Witt .15 .07
- ❑ 392 Jeff Conine .30 .14
- ❑ 393 Tim Hyers .15 .07
- ❑ 394 Terry Pendleton .15 .07
- ❑ 395 Ricky Jordan .15 .07
- ❑ 396 Eric Plunk .15 .07
- ❑ 397 Melido Perez .15 .07
- ❑ 398 Darryl Kile .30 .14
- ❑ 399 Mark McLemore .15 .07
- ❑ 400 Greg W.Harris .15 .07
- ❑ 401 Jim Leyritz .30 .14
- ❑ 402 Doug Strange .15 .07
- ❑ 403 Tim Salmon .60 .25
- ❑ 404 Terry Mulholland .15 .07
- ❑ 405 Robby Thompson .15 .07
- ❑ 406 Ruben Sierra .15 .07
- ❑ 407 Tony Phillips .15 .07
- ❑ 408 Moises Alou .40 .18
- ❑ 409 Felix Fermin .15 .07
- ❑ 410 Pat Listach .15 .07
- ❑ 411 Kevin Bass .15 .07
- ❑ 412 Ben McDonald .15 .07
- ❑ 413 Scott Cooper .15 .07
- ❑ 414 Jody Reed .15 .07
- ❑ 415 Deion Sanders .30 .14
- ❑ 416 Ricky Gutierrez .15 .07
- ❑ 417 Gregg Jefferies .15 .07
- ❑ 418 Jack McDowell .15 .07
- ❑ 419 Al Leiter .30 .14
- ❑ 420 Tony Longmire .15 .07
- ❑ 421 Paul Wagner .15 .07
- ❑ 422 Geronimo Pena .15 .07
- ❑ 423 Ivan Rodriguez .75 .35
- ❑ 424 Kevin Gross .15 .07
- ❑ 425 Kirk McCaskill .15 .07
- ❑ 426 Greg Myers .15 .07
- ❑ 427 Roger Clemens 1.25 .55
- ❑ 428 Chris Hammond .15 .07
- ❑ 429 Randy Myers .15 .07
- ❑ 430 Roger Mason .15 .07
- ❑ 431 Bret Saberhagen .30 .14
- ❑ 432 Jeff Reboulet .15 .07
- ❑ 433 John Olerud .30 .14
- ❑ 434 Bill Gullickson .15 .07
- ❑ 435 Eddie Murray .60 .25
- ❑ 436 Pedro Munoz .15 .07
- ❑ 437 Charlie O'Brien .15 .07
- ❑ 438 Jeff Nelson .15 .07
- ❑ 439 Mike Macfarlane .15 .07
- ❑ 440 Don Mattingly CL .60 .25
- ❑ 441 Derrick May .15 .07
- ❑ 442 John Roper .15 .07
- ❑ 443 Darryl Hamilton .15 .07
- ❑ 444 Dan Miceli .15 .07
- ❑ 445 Tony Eusebio .15 .07
- ❑ 446 Jerry Browne .15 .07
- ❑ 447 Wally Joyner .30 .14
- ❑ 448 Brian Harper .15 .07
- ❑ 449 Scott Fletcher .15 .07
- ❑ 450 Bip Roberts .15 .07
- ❑ 451 Pete Smith .15 .07
- ❑ 452 Chili Davis .30 .14
- ❑ 453 Dave Hollins .15 .07
- ❑ 454 Tony Pena .15 .07
- ❑ 455 Butch Henry .15 .07
- ❑ 456 Craig Biggio .60 .25
- ❑ 457 Zane Smith .15 .07
- ❑ 458 Ryan Thompson .15 .07
- ❑ 459 Mike Jackson .15 .07
- ❑ 460 Mark McGwire 3.00 1.35
- ❑ 461 John Smoltz .30 .14
- ❑ 462 Steve Scarsone .15 .07
- ❑ 463 Greg Colbrunn .15 .07
- ❑ 464 Shawn Green .30 .14
- ❑ 465 David Wells .40 .18
- ❑ 466 Jose Hernandez .15 .07
- ❑ 467 Chip Hale .15 .07
- ❑ 468 Tony Tarasco .15 .07
- ❑ 469 Kevin Mitchell .15 .07
- ❑ 470 Billy Hatcher .15 .07
- ❑ 471 Jay Buhner .30 .14
- ❑ 472 Ken Caminiti .40 .18
- ❑ 473 Tom Henke .15 .07
- ❑ 474 Todd Worrell .15 .07
- ❑ 475 Mark Eichhorn .15 .07
- ❑ 476 Bruce Ruffin .15 .07
- ❑ 477 Chuck Finley .30 .14
- ❑ 478 Marc Newfield .15 .07
- ❑ 479 Paul Shuey .15 .07
- ❑ 480 Bob Tewksbury .15 .07
- ❑ 481 Ramon J.Martinez .30 .14
- ❑ 482 Melvin Nieves .15 .07
- ❑ 483 Todd Zeile .15 .07
- ❑ 484 Benito Santiago .15 .07
- ❑ 485 Stan Javier .15 .07
- ❑ 486 Kirk Rueter .15 .07
- ❑ 487 Andre Dawson .40 .18
- ❑ 488 Eric Karros .30 .14
- ❑ 489 Dave Magadan .15 .07
- ❑ 490 Joe Carter CL .15 .07
- ❑ 491 Randy Velarde .15 .07
- ❑ 492 Larry Walker .60 .25
- ❑ 493 Cris Carpenter .15 .07
- ❑ 494 Tom Gordon .15 .07
- ❑ 495 Dave Burba .15 .07
- ❑ 496 Darren Bragg .15 .07
- ❑ 497 Darren Daulton .30 .14
- ❑ 498 Don Slaught .15 .07
- ❑ 499 Pat Borders .15 .07
- ❑ 500 Lenny Harris .15 .07
- ❑ 501 Joe Ausanio .15 .07
- ❑ 502 Alan Trammell .30 .14
- ❑ 503 Mike Fetters .15 .07
- ❑ 504 Scott Ruffcorn .15 .07
- ❑ 505 Rich Rowland .15 .07
- ❑ 506 Juan Samuel .15 .07
- ❑ 507 Bo Jackson .30 .14
- ❑ 508 Jeff Branson .15 .07
- ❑ 509 Bernie Williams .60 .25
- ❑ 510 Paul Sorrento .15 .07
- ❑ 511 Dennis Eckersley .30 .14
- ❑ 512 Pat Mahomes .15 .07
- ❑ 513 Rusty Greer .60 .25
- ❑ 514 Luis Polonia .15 .07
- ❑ 515 Willie Banks .15 .07
- ❑ 516 John Wetteland .30 .14
- ❑ 517 Mike LaValliere .15 .07
- ❑ 518 Tommy Greene .15 .07
- ❑ 519 Mark Grace .40 .18
- ❑ 520 Bob Hamelin .15 .07
- ❑ 521 Scott Sanderson .15 .07
- ❑ 522 Joe Carter .30 .14
- ❑ 523 Jeff Brantley .15 .07
- ❑ 524 Andrew Lorraine .15 .07
- ❑ 525 Rico Brogna .15 .07
- ❑ 526 Shane Mack .15 .07
- ❑ 527 Mark Wohlers .15 .07
- ❑ 528 Scott Sanders .15 .07
- ❑ 529 Chris Bosio .15 .07
- ❑ 530 Andujar Cedeno .15 .07
- ❑ 531 Kenny Rogers .15 .07
- ❑ 532 Doug Drabek .15 .07
- ❑ 533 Curt Leskanic .15 .07
- ❑ 534 Craig Shipley .15 .07
- ❑ 535 Craig Grebeck .15 .07
- ❑ 536 Cal Eldred .15 .07
- ❑ 537 Mickey Tettleton .15 .07
- ❑ 538 Harold Baines .30 .14
- ❑ 539 Tim Wallach .15 .07
- ❑ 540 Damon Buford .15 .07
- ❑ 541 Lenny Webster .15 .07
- ❑ 542 Kevin Appier .30 .14
- ❑ 543 Raul Mondesi .40 .18
- ❑ 544 Eric Young .15 .07
- ❑ 545 Russ Davis .30 .14
- ❑ 546 Mike Benjamin .15 .07
- ❑ 547 Mike Greenwell .15 .07
- ❑ 548 Scott Brosius .30 .14
- ❑ 549 Brian Dorsett .15 .07
- ❑ 550 Chili Davis CL .15 .07

1995 Donruss All-Stars

	MINT	NRMT
COMPLETE SET (18)	150.00	70.00
COMPLETE SERIES 1 (9)	90.00	40.00
COMPLETE SERIES 2 (9)	60.00	27.00
COMMON CARD (AL1-NL9)	1.50	.70

- ❑ AL1 Jimmy Key 2.50 1.10
- ❑ AL2 Ivan Rodriguez 8.00 3.60
- ❑ AL3 Frank Thomas 20.00 9.00
- ❑ AL4 Roberto Alomar 6.00 2.70
- ❑ AL5 Wade Boggs 6.00 2.70
- ❑ AL6 Cal Ripken 25.00 11.00
- ❑ AL7 Joe Carter 2.50 1.10
- ❑ AL8 Ken Griffey Jr. 30.00 13.50
- ❑ AL9 Kirby Puckett 10.00 4.50
- ❑ NL1 Greg Maddux 20.00 9.00
- ❑ NL2 Mike Piazza 20.00 9.00
- ❑ NL3 Gregg Jefferies 1.50 .70
- ❑ NL4 Mariano Duncan 1.50 .70
- ❑ NL5 Matt Williams 2.50 1.10
- ❑ NL6 Ozzie Smith 8.00 3.60

		MINT	NRMT
❑ NL7	Barry Bonds	8.00	3.60
❑ NL8	Tony Gwynn	15.00	6.75
❑ NL9	David Justice	6.00	2.70

1995 Donruss Bomb Squad

	MINT	NRMT
COMPLETE SET (6)	15.00	6.75
COMMON CARD (1-6)	1.50	.70
❑ 1 Ken Griffey / Matt Williams	8.00	3.60
❑ 2 Frank Thomas / Jeff Bagwell	6.00	2.70
❑ 3 Albert Belle / Barry Bonds	2.00	.90
❑ 4 Jose Canseco / Fred McGriff	2.50	1.10
❑ 5 Cecil Fielder / Andres Galarraga	1.50	.70
❑ 6 Joe Carter / Kevin Mitchell	2.00	.90

1995 Donruss Diamond Kings

	MINT	NRMT
COMPLETE SET (29)	50.00	22.00
COMPLETE SERIES 1 (14)	20.00	9.00
COMPLETE SERIES 2 (15)	30.00	13.50
COMMON CARD (DK1-DK29)	1.00	.45
❑ DK1 Frank Thomas	8.00	3.60
❑ DK2 Jeff Bagwell	4.00	1.80
❑ DK3 Chili Davis	1.50	.70
❑ DK4 Dante Bichette	1.50	.70
❑ DK5 Ruben Sierra	1.00	.45
❑ DK6 Jeff Conine	1.50	.70
❑ DK7 Paul O'Neill	1.50	.70
❑ DK8 Bobby Bonilla	1.50	.70
❑ DK9 Joe Carter	1.50	.70
❑ DK10 Moises Alou	2.00	.90
❑ DK11 Kenny Lofton	2.50	1.10
❑ DK12 Matt Williams	1.50	.70
❑ DK13 Kevin Seitzer	1.00	.45
❑ DK14 Sammy Sosa	6.00	2.70
❑ DK15 Scott Cooper	1.00	.45
❑ DK16 Raul Mondesi	2.00	.90
❑ DK17 Will Clark	2.50	1.10
❑ DK18 Lenny Dykstra	1.50	.70
❑ DK19 Kirby Puckett	2.50	1.10
❑ DK20 Hal Morris	1.00	.45
❑ DK21 Travis Fryman	1.50	.70
❑ DK22 Greg Maddux	8.00	3.60
❑ DK23 Rafael Palmeiro	2.00	.90
❑ DK24 Tony Gwynn	6.00	2.70
❑ DK25 David Cone	2.00	.90
❑ DK26 Al Martin	1.00	.45
❑ DK27 Ken Griffey Jr.	12.00	5.50
❑ DK28 Gregg Jefferies	1.00	.45
❑ DK29 Checklist	1.00	.45

1995 Donruss Dominators

	MINT	NRMT
COMPLETE SET (9)	25.00	11.00
COMMON CARD (1-9)	1.00	.45
❑ 1 David Cone / Mike Mussina / Greg Maddux	5.00	2.20
❑ 2 Ivan Rodriguez / Mike Piazza / Darren Daulton	5.00	2.20
❑ 3 Fred McGriff / Frank Thomas / Jeff Bagwell	6.00	2.70
❑ 4 Roberto Alomar / Carlos Baerga / Craig Biggio	1.00	.45
❑ 5 Robin Ventura / Travis Fryman / Matt Williams	1.00	.45
❑ 6 Cal Ripken / Barry Larkin / Wil Cordero	6.00	2.70
❑ 7 Albert Belle / Barry Bonds / Moises Alou	2.00	.90
❑ 8 Ken Griffey / Kenny Lofton / Marquis Grissom	8.00	3.60
❑ 9 Kirby Puckett / Paul O'Neill / Tony Gwynn	4.00	1.80

1995 Donruss Elite

	MINT	NRMT
COMPLETE SET (12)	250.00	110.00
COMPLETE SERIES 1 (6)	150.00	70.00
COMPLETE SERIES 2 (6)	100.00	45.00
COMMON CARD (49-60)	6.00	2.70
❑ 49 Jeff Bagwell	20.00	9.00
❑ 50 Paul O'Neill	6.00	2.70
❑ 51 Greg Maddux	40.00	18.00
❑ 52 Mike Piazza	40.00	18.00
❑ 53 Matt Williams	6.00	2.70
❑ 54 Ken Griffey	60.00	27.00
❑ 55 Frank Thomas	40.00	18.00
❑ 56 Barry Bonds	15.00	6.75
❑ 57 Kirby Puckett	20.00	9.00
❑ 58 Fred McGriff	8.00	3.60
❑ 59 Jose Canseco	12.00	5.50
❑ 60 Albert Belle	15.00	6.75

1995 Donruss Long Ball Leaders

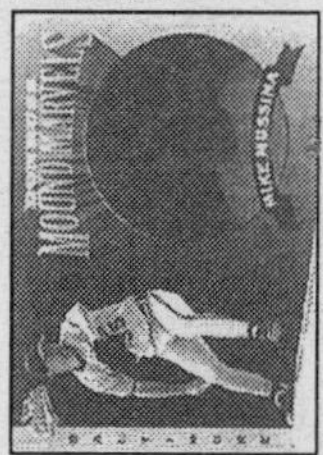

	MINT	NRMT
COMPLETE SET (8)	20.00	9.00
COMMON CARD (1-8)	1.00	.45
❑ 1 Frank Thomas	6.00	2.70
❑ 2 Fred McGriff	1.00	.45
❑ 3 Ken Griffey	8.00	3.60
❑ 4 Matt Williams	1.00	.45
❑ 5 Mike Piazza	6.00	2.70
❑ 6 Jose Canseco	1.50	.70
❑ 7 Barry Bonds	1.50	.70
❑ 8 Jeff Bagwell	3.00	1.35

1995 Donruss Mound Marvels

	MINT	NRMT
COMPLETE SET (8)	20.00	9.00
COMMON CARD (1-8)	1.00	.45
❑ 1 Greg Maddux	10.00	4.50
❑ 2 David Cone	2.00	.90
❑ 3 Mike Mussina	3.00	1.35
❑ 4 Bret Saberhagen	1.50	.70
❑ 5 Jimmy Key	1.50	.70
❑ 6 Doug Drabek	1.00	.45
❑ 7 Randy Johnson	3.00	1.35
❑ 8 Jason Bere	1.00	.45

1996 Donruss

	MINT	NRMT
COMPLETE SET (550)	40.00	18.00
COMPLETE SERIES 1 (330)	25.00	11.00
COMPLETE SERIES 2 (220)	15.00	6.75
COMMON CARD (1-550)	.15	.07
❑ 1 Frank Thomas	2.00	.90
❑ 2 Jason Bates	.15	.07
❑ 3 Steve Sparks	.15	.07
❑ 4 Scott Servais	.15	.07
❑ 5 Angelo Encarnacion	.15	.07
❑ 6 Scott Sanders	.15	.07
❑ 7 Billy Ashley	.15	.07
❑ 8 Alex Rodriguez	2.00	.90
❑ 9 Sean Bergman	.15	.07
❑ 10 Brad Radke	.30	.14
❑ 11 Andy Van Slyke	.15	.07
❑ 12 Joe Girardi	.15	.07
❑ 13 Mark Grudzielanek	.30	.14
❑ 14 Rick Aguilera	.15	.07
❑ 15 Randy Veres	.15	.07
❑ 16 Tim Bogar	.15	.07
❑ 17 Dave Veres	.15	.07
❑ 18 Kevin Stocker	.15	.07
❑ 19 Marquis Grissom	.30	.14
❑ 20 Will Clark	.60	.25
❑ 21 Jay Bell	.30	.14
❑ 22 Allen Battle	.15	.07
❑ 23 Frank Rodriguez	.15	.07
❑ 24 Terry Steinbach	.30	.14
❑ 25 Gerald Williams	.15	.07
❑ 26 Sid Roberson	.15	.07
❑ 27 Greg Zaun	.15	.07
❑ 28 Ozzie Timmons	.15	.07
❑ 29 Vaughn Eshelman	.15	.07
❑ 30 Ed Sprague	.15	.07
❑ 31 Gary DiSarcina	.15	.07
❑ 32 Joe Boever	.15	.07
❑ 33 Steve Avery	.15	.07
❑ 34 Brad Ausmus	.15	.07
❑ 35 Kirt Manwaring	.15	.07
❑ 36 Gary Sheffield	.40	.18
❑ 37 Jason Bere	.15	.07
❑ 38 Jeff Manto	.15	.07
❑ 39 David Cone	.40	.18
❑ 40 Manny Ramirez	.60	.25
❑ 41 Sandy Alomar Jr.	.30	.14
❑ 42 Curtis Goodwin	.15	.07
❑ 43 Tino Martinez	.60	.25
❑ 44 Woody Williams	.15	.07
❑ 45 Dean Palmer	.30	.14
❑ 46 Hipolito Pichardo	.15	.07
❑ 47 Jason Giambi	.30	.14
❑ 48 Lance Johnson	.15	.07
❑ 49 Bernard Gilkey	.15	.07
❑ 50 Kirby Puckett	1.00	.45
❑ 51 Tony Fernandez	.15	.07
❑ 52 Alex Gonzalez	.15	.07
❑ 53 Bret Saberhagen	.30	.14
❑ 54 Lyle Mouton	.15	.07
❑ 55 Brian McRae	.15	.07
❑ 56 Mark Gubicza	.15	.07
❑ 57 Sergio Valdez	.15	.07
❑ 58 Darrin Fletcher	.15	.07
❑ 59 Steve Parris	.15	.07
❑ 60 Johnny Damon	.30	.14
❑ 61 Rickey Henderson	.60	.25
❑ 62 Darrell Whitmore	.15	.07
❑ 63 Roberto Petagine	.15	.07
❑ 64 Trenidad Hubbard	.15	.07
❑ 65 Heathcliff Slocumb	.15	.07
❑ 66 Steve Finley	.30	.14
❑ 67 Mariano Rivera	.30	.14
❑ 68 Brian L.Hunter	.30	.14
❑ 69 Jamie Moyer	.15	.07
❑ 70 Ellis Burks	.30	.14
❑ 71 Pat Kelly	.15	.07
❑ 72 Mickey Tettleton	.15	.07
❑ 73 Garret Anderson	.30	.14
❑ 74 Andy Pettitte	.40	.18
❑ 75 Glenallen Hill	.15	.07
❑ 76 Brent Gates	.15	.07
❑ 77 Lou Whitaker	.30	.14
❑ 78 David Segui	.30	.14
❑ 79 Dan Wilson	.15	.07
❑ 80 Pat Listach	.15	.07
❑ 81 Jeff Bagwell	1.00	.45
❑ 82 Ben McDonald	.15	.07
❑ 83 John Valentin	.30	.14
❑ 84 John Jaha	.15	.07
❑ 85 Pete Schourek	.15	.07
❑ 86 Bryce Florie	.15	.07
❑ 87 Brian Jordan	.30	.14
❑ 88 Ron Karkovice	.15	.07
❑ 89 Al Leiter	.30	.14
❑ 90 Tony Longmire	.15	.07
❑ 91 Nelson Liriano	.15	.07
❑ 92 David Bell	.15	.07
❑ 93 Kevin Gross	.15	.07
❑ 94 Tom Candiotti	.15	.07
❑ 95 Dave Martinez	.15	.07
❑ 96 Greg Myers	.15	.07
❑ 97 Rheal Cormier	.15	.07
❑ 98 Chris Hammond	.15	.07
❑ 99 Randy Myers	.15	.07
❑ 100 Bill Pulsipher	.15	.07
❑ 101 Jason Isringhausen	.15	.07
❑ 102 Dave Stevens	.15	.07
❑ 103 Roberto Alomar	.60	.25
❑ 104 Bob Higginson	.60	.25
❑ 105 Eddie Murray	.60	.25
❑ 106 Matt Walbeck	.15	.07
❑ 107 Mark Wohlers	.15	.07
❑ 108 Jeff Nelson	.15	.07
❑ 109 Tom Goodwin	.15	.07
❑ 110 Cal Ripken CL	1.25	.55
❑ 111 Rey Sanchez	.15	.07
❑ 112 Hector Carrasco	.15	.07
❑ 113 B.J. Surhoff	.30	.14
❑ 114 Dan Miceli	.15	.07
❑ 115 Dean Hartgraves	.15	.07
❑ 116 John Burkett	.15	.07
❑ 117 Gary Gaetti	.30	.14
❑ 118 Ricky Bones	.15	.07
❑ 119 Mike Macfarlane	.15	.07
❑ 120 Bip Roberts	.15	.07
❑ 121 Dave Mlicki	.15	.07
❑ 122 Chili Davis	.30	.14
❑ 123 Mark Whiten	.15	.07
❑ 124 Herbert Perry	.15	.07
❑ 125 Butch Henry	.15	.07
❑ 126 Derek Bell	.30	.14
❑ 127 Al Martin	.15	.07
❑ 128 John Franco	.30	.14
❑ 129 W. VanLandingham	.15	.07
❑ 130 Mike Bordick	.15	.07
❑ 131 Mike Mordecai	.15	.07
❑ 132 Robby Thompson	.15	.07
❑ 133 Greg Colbrunn	.15	.07
❑ 134 Domingo Cedeno	.15	.07
❑ 135 Chad Curtis	.15	.07
❑ 136 Jose Hernandez	.15	.07
❑ 137 Scott Klingenbeck	.15	.07
❑ 138 Ryan Klesko	.30	.14
❑ 139 John Smiley	.15	.07
❑ 140 Charlie Hayes	.15	.07
❑ 141 Jay Buhner	.30	.14
❑ 142 Doug Drabek	.15	.07
❑ 143 Roger Pavlik	.15	.07
❑ 144 Todd Worrell	.15	.07
❑ 145 Cal Ripken	2.50	1.10
❑ 146 Steve Reed	.15	.07
❑ 147 Chuck Finley	.30	.14
❑ 148 Mike Blowers	.15	.07
❑ 149 Orel Hershiser	.30	.14
❑ 150 Allen Watson	.15	.07
❑ 151 Ramon Martinez	.30	.14
❑ 152 Melvin Nieves	.15	.07
❑ 153 Tripp Cromer	.15	.07
❑ 154 Yorkis Perez	.15	.07
❑ 155 Stan Javier	.15	.07
❑ 156 Mel Rojas	.15	.07
❑ 157 Aaron Sele	.30	.14
❑ 158 Eric Karros	.30	.14
❑ 159 Robb Nen	.15	.07
❑ 160 Raul Mondesi	.40	.18
❑ 161 John Wetteland	.30	.14
❑ 162 Tim Scott	.15	.07
❑ 163 Kenny Rogers	.15	.07
❑ 164 Melvin Bunch	.15	.07
❑ 165 Rod Beck	.15	.07
❑ 166 Andy Benes	.30	.14
❑ 167 Lenny Dykstra	.30	.14
❑ 168 Orlando Merced	.15	.07
❑ 169 Tomas Perez	.15	.07
❑ 170 Xavier Hernandez	.15	.07
❑ 171 Ruben Sierra	.15	.07
❑ 172 Alan Trammell	.40	.18
❑ 173 Mike Fetters	.15	.07
❑ 174 Wilson Alvarez	.30	.14
❑ 175 Erik Hanson	.15	.07
❑ 176 Travis Fryman	.30	.14
❑ 177 Jim Abbott	.30	.14
❑ 178 Bret Boone	.30	.14
❑ 179 Sterling Hitchcock	.30	.14
❑ 180 Pat Mahomes	.15	.07
❑ 181 Mark Acre	.15	.07
❑ 182 Charles Nagy	.30	.14
❑ 183 Rusty Greer	.40	.18
❑ 184 Mike Stanley	.15	.07
❑ 185 Jim Bullinger	.15	.07
❑ 186 Shane Andrews	.15	.07
❑ 187 Brian Keyser	.15	.07
❑ 188 Tyler Green	.15	.07
❑ 189 Mark Grace	.40	.18
❑ 190 Bob Hamelin	.15	.07
❑ 191 Luis Ortiz	.15	.07
❑ 192 Joe Carter	.30	.14
❑ 193 Eddie Taubensee	.15	.07
❑ 194 Brian Anderson	.30	.14
❑ 195 Edgardo Alfonzo	.30	.14
❑ 196 Pedro Munoz	.15	.07
❑ 197 David Justice	.60	.25
❑ 198 Trevor Hoffman	.30	.14
❑ 199 Bobby Ayala	.15	.07
❑ 200 Tony Eusebio	.15	.07
❑ 201 Jeff Russell	.15	.07
❑ 202 Mike Hampton	.15	.07
❑ 203 Walt Weiss	.15	.07
❑ 204 Joey Hamilton	.30	.14
❑ 205 Roberto Hernandez	.15	.07
❑ 206 Greg Vaughn	.30	.14
❑ 207 Felipe Lira	.15	.07
❑ 208 Harold Baines	.30	.14
❑ 209 Tim Wallach	.15	.07
❑ 210 Manny Alexander	.15	.07
❑ 211 Tim Laker	.15	.07
❑ 212 Chris Haney	.15	.07
❑ 213 Brian Maxcy	.15	.07
❑ 214 Eric Young	.15	.07
❑ 215 Darryl Strawberry	.30	.14
❑ 216 Barry Bonds	.75	.35
❑ 217 Tim Naehring	.15	.07
❑ 218 Scott Brosius	.30	.14
❑ 219 Reggie Sanders	.30	.14
❑ 220 Eddie Murray CL	.30	.14
❑ 221 Luis Alicea	.15	.07
❑ 222 Albert Belle	.75	.35
❑ 223 Benji Gil	.15	.07
❑ 224 Dante Bichette	.30	.14
❑ 225 Bobby Bonilla	.30	.14
❑ 226 Todd Stottlemyre	.15	.07
❑ 227 Jim Edmonds	.40	.18
❑ 228 Todd Jones	.15	.07
❑ 229 Shawn Green	.30	.14
❑ 230 Javier Lopez	.30	.14

❑	231	Ariel Prieto	.15	.07
❑	232	Tony Phillips	.15	.07
❑	233	James Mouton	.15	.07
❑	234	Jose Oquendo	.15	.07
❑	235	Royce Clayton	.15	.07
❑	236	Chuck Carr	.15	.07
❑	237	Doug Jones	.15	.07
❑	238	Mark McLemore	.15	.07
❑	239	Bill Swift	.15	.07
❑	240	Scott Leius	.15	.07
❑	241	Russ Davis	.30	.14
❑	242	Ray Durham	.30	.14
❑	243	Matt Mieske	.15	.07
❑	244	Brent Mayne	.15	.07
❑	245	Thomas Howard	.15	.07
❑	246	Troy O'Leary	.30	.14
❑	247	Jacob Brumfield	.15	.07
❑	248	Mickey Morandini	.15	.07
❑	249	Todd Hundley	.30	.14
❑	250	Chris Bosio	.15	.07
❑	251	Omar Vizquel	.30	.14
❑	252	Mike Lansing	.15	.07
❑	253	John Mabry	.15	.07
❑	254	Mike Perez	.15	.07
❑	255	Delino DeShields	.15	.07
❑	256	Wil Cordero	.15	.07
❑	257	Mike James	.15	.07
❑	258	Todd Van Poppel	.15	.07
❑	259	Joey Cora	.30	.14
❑	260	Andre Dawson	.40	.18
❑	261	Jerry DiPoto	.15	.07
❑	262	Rick Krivda	.15	.07
❑	263	Glenn Dishman	.15	.07
❑	264	Mike Mimbs	.15	.07
❑	265	John Ericks	.15	.07
❑	266	Jose Canseco	.60	.25
❑	267	Jeff Branson	.15	.07
❑	268	Curt Leskanic	.15	.07
❑	269	Jon Nunnally	.15	.07
❑	270	Scott Stahoviak	.15	.07
❑	271	Jeff Montgomery	.15	.07
❑	272	Hal Morris	.15	.07
❑	273	Esteban Loaiza	.15	.07
❑	274	Rico Brogna	.15	.07
❑	275	Dave Winfield	.60	.25
❑	276	J.R. Phillips	.15	.07
❑	277	Todd Zeile	.15	.07
❑	278	Tom Pagnozzi	.15	.07
❑	279	Mark Lemke	.15	.07
❑	280	Dave Magadan	.15	.07
❑	281	Greg McMichael	.15	.07
❑	282	Mike Morgan	.15	.07
❑	283	Moises Alou	.40	.18
❑	284	Dennis Martinez	.30	.14
❑	285	Jeff Kent	.30	.14
❑	286	Mark Johnson	.15	.07
❑	287	Darren Lewis	.15	.07
❑	288	Brad Clontz	.15	.07
❑	289	Chad Fonville	.15	.07
❑	290	Paul Sorrento	.15	.07
❑	291	Lee Smith	.30	.14
❑	292	Tom Glavine	.60	.25
❑	293	Antonio Osuna	.15	.07
❑	294	Kevin Foster	.15	.07
❑	295	Sandy Martinez	.15	.07
❑	296	Mark Leiter	.15	.07
❑	297	Julian Tavarez	.15	.07
❑	298	Mike Kelly	.15	.07
❑	299	Joe Oliver	.15	.07
❑	300	John Flaherty	.15	.07
❑	301	Don Mattingly	1.00	.45
❑	302	Pat Meares	.15	.07
❑	303	John Doherty	.15	.07
❑	304	Joe Vitiello	.15	.07
❑	305	Vinny Castilla	.40	.18
❑	306	Jeff Brantley	.15	.07
❑	307	Mike Greenwell	.15	.07
❑	308	Midre Cummings	.15	.07
❑	309	Curt Schilling	.30	.14
❑	310	Ken Caminiti	.40	.18
❑	311	Scott Erickson	.30	.14
❑	312	Carl Everett	.15	.07
❑	313	Charles Johnson	.30	.14
❑	314	Alex Diaz	.15	.07
❑	315	Jose Mesa	.15	.07
❑	316	Mark Carreon	.15	.07
❑	317	Carlos Perez	.30	.14
❑	318	Ismael Valdes	.30	.14
❑	319	Frank Castillo	.15	.07
❑	320	Tom Henke	.15	.07
❑	321	Spike Owen	.15	.07
❑	322	Joe Orsulak	.15	.07
❑	323	Paul Menhart	.15	.07
❑	324	Pedro Borbon	.15	.07
❑	325	Paul Molitor CL	.30	.14
❑	326	Jeff Cirillo	.30	.14
❑	327	Edwin Hurtado	.15	.07
❑	328	Orlando Miller	.15	.07
❑	329	Steve Ontiveros	.15	.07
❑	330	Kirby Puckett CL	.60	.25
❑	331	Scott Bullett	.15	.07
❑	332	Andres Galarraga	.60	.25
❑	333	Cal Eldred	.15	.07
❑	334	Sammy Sosa	1.50	.70
❑	335	Don Slaught	.15	.07
❑	336	Jody Reed	.15	.07
❑	337	Roger Cedeno	.15	.07
❑	338	Ken Griffey Jr.	3.00	1.35
❑	339	Todd Hollandsworth	.15	.07
❑	340	Mike Trombley	.15	.07
❑	341	Gregg Jefferies	.15	.07
❑	342	Larry Walker	.60	.25
❑	343	Pedro Martinez	.60	.25
❑	344	Dwayne Hosey	.15	.07
❑	345	Terry Pendleton	.15	.07
❑	346	Pete Harnisch	.15	.07
❑	347	Tony Castillo	.15	.07
❑	348	Paul Quantrill	.15	.07
❑	349	Fred McGriff	.40	.18
❑	350	Ivan Rodriguez	.75	.35
❑	351	Butch Huskey	.15	.07
❑	352	Ozzie Smith	.75	.35
❑	353	Marty Cordova	.15	.07
❑	354	John Wasdin	.15	.07
❑	355	Wade Boggs	.60	.25
❑	356	Dave Nilsson	.15	.07
❑	357	Rafael Palmeiro	.40	.18
❑	358	Luis Gonzalez	.15	.07
❑	359	Reggie Jefferson	.15	.07
❑	360	Carlos Delgado	.30	.14
❑	361	Orlando Palmeiro	.15	.07
❑	362	Chris Gomez	.15	.07
❑	363	John Smoltz	.30	.14
❑	364	Marc Newfield	.15	.07
❑	365	Matt Williams	.30	.14
❑	366	Jesus Tavarez	.15	.07
❑	367	Bruce Ruffin	.15	.07
❑	368	Sean Berry	.15	.07
❑	369	Randy Velarde	.15	.07
❑	370	Tony Pena	.15	.07
❑	371	Jim Thome	.60	.25
❑	372	Jeffrey Hammonds	.30	.14
❑	373	Bob Wolcott	.15	.07
❑	374	Juan Guzman	.15	.07
❑	375	Juan Gonzalez	1.50	.70
❑	376	Michael Tucker	.30	.14
❑	377	Doug Johns	.15	.07
❑	378	Mike Cameron	1.25	.55
❑	379	Ray Lankford	.30	.14
❑	380	Jose Parra	.15	.07
❑	381	Jimmy Key	.30	.14
❑	382	John Olerud	.30	.14
❑	383	Kevin Ritz	.15	.07
❑	384	Tim Raines	.30	.14
❑	385	Rich Amaral	.15	.07
❑	386	Keith Lockhart	.15	.07
❑	387	Steve Scarsone	.15	.07
❑	388	Cliff Floyd	.30	.14
❑	389	Rich Aude	.15	.07
❑	390	Hideo Nomo	1.00	.45
❑	391	Geronimo Berroa	.15	.07
❑	392	Pat Rapp	.15	.07
❑	393	Dustin Hermanson	.30	.14
❑	394	Greg Maddux	2.00	.90
❑	395	Darren Daulton	.30	.14
❑	396	Kenny Lofton	.60	.25
❑	397	Ruben Rivera	.30	.14
❑	398	Billy Wagner	.30	.14
❑	399	Kevin Brown	.60	.25
❑	400	Mike Kingery	.15	.07
❑	401	Bernie Williams	.60	.25
❑	402	Otis Nixon	.15	.07
❑	403	Damion Easley	.30	.14
❑	404	Paul O'Neill	.30	.14
❑	405	Deion Sanders	.30	.14
❑	406	Dennis Eckersley	.30	.14
❑	407	Tony Clark	.60	.25
❑	408	Rondell White	.30	.14
❑	409	Luis Sojo	.15	.07
❑	410	David Hulse	.15	.07
❑	411	Shane Reynolds	.30	.14
❑	412	Chris Hoiles	.15	.07
❑	413	Lee Tinsley	.15	.07
❑	414	Scott Karl	.15	.07
❑	415	Ron Gant	.15	.07
❑	416	Brian Johnson	.15	.07
❑	417	Jose Oliva	.15	.07
❑	418	Jack McDowell	.15	.07
❑	419	Paul Molitor	.60	.25
❑	420	Ricky Bottalico	.30	.14
❑	421	Paul Wagner	.15	.07
❑	422	Terry Bradshaw	.15	.07
❑	423	Bob Tewksbury	.15	.07
❑	424	Mike Piazza	2.00	.90
❑	425	Luis Andujar	.30	.14
❑	426	Mark Langston	.15	.07
❑	427	Stan Belinda	.15	.07
❑	428	Kurt Abbott	.15	.07
❑	429	Shawon Dunston	.15	.07
❑	430	Bobby Jones	.15	.07
❑	431	Jose Vizcaino	.15	.07
❑	432	Matt Lawton	.60	.25
❑	433	Pat Hentgen	.30	.14
❑	434	Cecil Fielder	.30	.14
❑	435	Carlos Baerga	.30	.14
❑	436	Rich Becker	.15	.07
❑	437	Chipper Jones	1.50	.70
❑	438	Bill Risley	.15	.07
❑	439	Kevin Appier	.30	.14
❑	440	Wade Boggs CL	.30	.14
❑	441	Jaime Navarro	.15	.07
❑	442	Barry Larkin	.40	.18
❑	443	Jose Valentin	.15	.07
❑	444	Bryan Rekar	.15	.07
❑	445	Rick Wilkins	.15	.07
❑	446	Quilvio Veras	.15	.07
❑	447	Greg Gagne	.15	.07
❑	448	Mark Kiefer	.15	.07
❑	449	Bobby Witt	.15	.07
❑	450	Andy Ashby	.15	.07
❑	451	Alex Ochoa	.15	.07
❑	452	Jorge Fabregas	.15	.07
❑	453	Gene Schall	.15	.07
❑	454	Ken Hill	.15	.07
❑	455	Tony Tarasco	.15	.07
❑	456	Donnie Wall	.15	.07
❑	457	Carlos Garcia	.15	.07
❑	458	Ryan Thompson	.15	.07
❑	459	Marvin Benard	.15	.07
❑	460	Jose Herrera	.15	.07
❑	461	Jeff Blauser	.15	.07
❑	462	Chris Hook	.15	.07
❑	463	Jeff Conine	.30	.14
❑	464	Devon White	.30	.14
❑	465	Danny Bautista	.15	.07
❑	466	Steve Trachsel	.15	.07
❑	467	C.J. Nitkowski	.15	.07
❑	468	Mike Devereaux	.15	.07
❑	469	David Wells	.40	.18
❑	470	Jim Eisenreich	.15	.07
❑	471	Edgar Martinez	.30	.14
❑	472	Craig Biggio	.60	.25
❑	473	Jeff Frye	.15	.07
❑	474	Karim Garcia	.30	.14
❑	475	Jimmy Haynes	.15	.07
❑	476	Darren Holmes	.15	.07
❑	477	Tim Salmon	.60	.25
❑	478	Randy Johnson	.60	.25
❑	479	Eric Plunk	.15	.07
❑	480	Scott Cooper	.15	.07
❑	481	Chan Ho Park	.60	.25
❑	482	Ray McDavid	.15	.07
❑	483	Mark Petkovsek	.15	.07
❑	484	Greg Swindell	.15	.07
❑	485	George Williams	.15	.07

❑ 486 Yamil Benitez	.15	.07
❑ 487 Tim Wakefield	.30	.14
❑ 488 Kevin Tapani	.15	.07
❑ 489 Derrick May	.15	.07
❑ 490 Ken Griffey Jr. CL	1.50	.70
❑ 491 Derek Jeter	2.00	.90
❑ 492 Jeff Fassero	.15	.07
❑ 493 Benito Santiago	.15	.07
❑ 494 Tom Gordon	.15	.07
❑ 495 Jamie Brewington	.15	.07
❑ 496 Vince Coleman	.15	.07
❑ 497 Kevin Jordan	.15	.07
❑ 498 Jeff King	.15	.07
❑ 499 Mike Simms	.15	.07
❑ 500 Jose Rijo	.15	.07
❑ 501 Denny Neagle	.30	.14
❑ 502 Jose Lima	.15	.07
❑ 503 Kevin Seitzer	.15	.07
❑ 504 Alex Fernandez	.15	.07
❑ 505 Mo Vaughn	.75	.35
❑ 506 Phil Nevin	.15	.07
❑ 507 J.T. Snow	.30	.14
❑ 508 Andujar Cedeno	.15	.07
❑ 509 Ozzie Guillen	.15	.07
❑ 510 Mark Clark	.15	.07
❑ 511 Mark McGwire	3.00	1.35
❑ 512 Jeff Reboulet	.15	.07
❑ 513 Armando Benitez	.15	.07
❑ 514 LaTroy Hawkins	.15	.07
❑ 515 Brett Butler	.30	.14
❑ 516 Tavo Alvarez	.15	.07
❑ 517 Chris Snopek	.15	.07
❑ 518 Mike Mussina	.60	.25
❑ 519 Darryl Kile	.30	.14
❑ 520 Wally Joyner	.30	.14
❑ 521 Willie McGee	.30	.14
❑ 522 Kent Mercker	.15	.07
❑ 523 Mike Jackson	.15	.07
❑ 524 Troy Percival	.30	.14
❑ 525 Tony Gwynn	1.50	.70
❑ 526 Ron Coomer	.15	.07
❑ 527 Darryl Hamilton	.15	.07
❑ 528 Phil Plantier	.15	.07
❑ 529 Norm Charlton	.15	.07
❑ 530 Craig Paquette	.15	.07
❑ 531 Dave Burba	.15	.07
❑ 532 Mike Henneman	.15	.07
❑ 533 Terrell Wade	.15	.07
❑ 534 Eddie Williams	.15	.07
❑ 535 Robin Ventura	.30	.14
❑ 536 Chuck Knoblauch	.60	.25
❑ 537 Les Norman	.15	.07
❑ 538 Brady Anderson	.30	.14
❑ 539 Roger Clemens	1.25	.55
❑ 540 Mark Portugal	.15	.07
❑ 541 Mike Matheny	.15	.07
❑ 542 Jeff Parrett	.15	.07
❑ 543 Roberto Kelly	.15	.07
❑ 544 Damon Buford	.15	.07
❑ 545 Chad Ogea	.15	.07
❑ 546 Jose Offerman	.15	.07
❑ 547 Brian Barber	.15	.07
❑ 548 Danny Tartabull	.15	.07
❑ 549 Duane Singleton	.15	.07
❑ 550 Tony Gwynn CL	.75	.35

1996 Donruss Diamond Kings

	MINT	NRMT
COMPLETE SET (31)	240.00	110.00
COMPLETE SERIES 1 (14)	120.00	55.00
COMPLETE SERIES 2 (17)	120.00	55.00
COMMON CARD (1-31)	3.00	1.35

❑ 1 Frank Thomas	25.00	11.00
❑ 2 Mo Vaughn	10.00	4.50
❑ 3 Manny Ramirez	8.00	3.60
❑ 4 Mark McGwire	40.00	18.00
❑ 5 Juan Gonzalez	20.00	9.00
❑ 6 Roberto Alomar	8.00	3.60
❑ 7 Tim Salmon	8.00	3.60
❑ 8 Barry Bonds	10.00	4.50
❑ 9 Tony Gwynn	20.00	9.00
❑ 10 Reggie Sanders	5.00	2.20

❑ 11 Larry Walker	8.00	3.60
❑ 12 Pedro Martinez	8.00	3.60
❑ 13 Jeff King	3.00	1.35
❑ 14 Mark Grace	5.00	2.20
❑ 15 Greg Maddux	25.00	11.00
❑ 16 Don Mattingly	12.00	5.50
❑ 17 Gregg Jefferies	3.00	1.35
❑ 18 Chad Curtis	3.00	1.35
❑ 19 Jason Isringhausen	3.00	1.35
❑ 20 B.J. Surhoff	5.00	2.20
❑ 21 Jeff Conine	5.00	2.20
❑ 22 Kirby Puckett	12.00	5.50
❑ 23 Derek Bell	5.00	2.20
❑ 24 Wally Joyner	5.00	2.20
❑ 25 Brian Jordan	5.00	2.20
❑ 26 Edgar Martinez	5.00	2.20
❑ 27 Hideo Nomo	12.00	5.50
❑ 28 Mike Mussina	8.00	3.60
❑ 29 Eddie Murray	8.00	3.60
❑ 30 Cal Ripken	30.00	13.50
❑ 31 Checklist	3.00	1.35

1996 Donruss Elite

	MINT	NRMT
COMPLETE SET (12)	200.00	90.00
COMPLETE SERIES 1 (6)	100.00	45.00
COMPLETE SERIES 2 (6)	100.00	45.00
COMMON CARD (61-72)	5.00	2.20

❑ 61 Cal Ripken	40.00	18.00
❑ 62 Hideo Nomo	15.00	6.75
❑ 63 Reggie Sanders	5.00	2.20
❑ 64 Mo Vaughn	12.00	5.50
❑ 65 Tim Salmon	8.00	3.60
❑ 66 Chipper Jones	25.00	11.00
❑ 67 Manny Ramirez	8.00	3.60
❑ 68 Greg Maddux	25.00	11.00
❑ 69 Frank Thomas	25.00	11.00
❑ 70 Ken Griffey Jr.	40.00	18.00
❑ 71 Dante Bichette	6.00	2.70
❑ 72 Tony Gwynn	20.00	9.00

1996 Donruss Freeze Frame

	MINT	NRMT
COMPLETE SET (8)	180.00	80.00
COMMON CARD (1-8)	8.00	3.60

❑ 1 Frank Thomas	25.00	11.00
❑ 2 Ken Griffey Jr.	40.00	18.00
❑ 3 Cal Ripken	30.00	13.50
❑ 4 Hideo Nomo	12.00	5.50
❑ 5 Greg Maddux	25.00	11.00
❑ 6 Albert Belle	10.00	4.50
❑ 7 Chipper Jones	20.00	9.00
❑ 8 Mike Piazza	25.00	11.00

1996 Donruss Hit List

	MINT	NRMT
COMPLETE SET (16)	100.00	45.00
COMPLETE SERIES 1 (8)	60.00	27.00
COMPLETE SERIES 2 (8)	40.00	18.00
COMMON CARD (1-16)	2.50	1.10

❑ 1 Tony Gwynn	12.00	5.50
❑ 2 Ken Griffey Jr.	25.00	11.00
❑ 3 Will Clark	5.00	2.20
❑ 4 Mike Piazza	15.00	6.75
❑ 5 Carlos Baerga	2.50	1.10
❑ 6 Mo Vaughn	6.00	2.70
❑ 7 Mark Grace	3.00	1.35
❑ 8 Kirby Puckett	8.00	3.60
❑ 9 Frank Thomas	15.00	6.75
❑ 10 Barry Bonds	6.00	2.70
❑ 11 Jeff Bagwell	8.00	3.60
❑ 12 Edgar Martinez	2.50	1.10
❑ 13 Tim Salmon	5.00	2.20
❑ 14 Wade Boggs	5.00	2.20
❑ 15 Don Mattingly	8.00	3.60
❑ 16 Eddie Murray	5.00	2.20

1996 Donruss Long Ball Leaders

	MINT	NRMT
COMPLETE SET (8)	120.00	55.00
COMMON CARD (1-8)	4.00	1.80

❑ 1 Barry Bonds	12.00	5.50
❑ 2 Ryan Klesko	6.00	2.70
❑ 3 Mark McGwire	50.00	22.00
❑ 4 Raul Mondesi	6.00	2.70
❑ 5 Cecil Fielder	4.00	1.80
❑ 6 Ken Griffey Jr.	50.00	22.00
❑ 7 Larry Walker	10.00	4.50
❑ 8 Frank Thomas	30.00	13.50

1996 Donruss Power Alley

	MINT	NRMT
COMPLETE SET (10)	120.00	55.00
COMMON CARD (1-10)	4.00	1.80
COMP.DIE CUT SET (10)	400.00	180.00

DIE CUTS: 1.25X TO 3X BASIC CARDS
SER.1 DC STATED ODDS 1:920 HOBBY

	MINT	NRMT
❑ 1 Frank Thomas	30.00	13.50
❑ 2 Barry Bonds	12.00	5.50
❑ 3 Reggie Sanders	4.00	1.80
❑ 4 Albert Belle	12.00	5.50
❑ 5 Tim Salmon	10.00	4.50
❑ 6 Dante Bichette	5.00	2.20
❑ 7 Mo Vaughn	12.00	5.50
❑ 8 Jim Edmonds	6.00	2.70
❑ 9 Manny Ramirez	10.00	4.50
❑ 10 Ken Griffey Jr.	50.00	22.00

1996 Donruss Pure Power

	MINT	NRMT
COMPLETE SET (8)	120.00	55.00
COMMON CARD (1-8)	6.00	2.70

	MINT	NRMT
❑ 1 Raul Mondesi	8.00	3.60
❑ 2 Barry Bonds	12.00	5.50
❑ 3 Albert Belle	15.00	6.75
❑ 4 Frank Thomas	30.00	13.50
❑ 5 Mike Piazza	30.00	13.50
❑ 6 Dante Bichette	6.00	2.70
❑ 7 Manny Ramirez	10.00	4.50
❑ 8 Mo Vaughn	12.00	5.50

1996 Donruss Round Trippers

	MINT	NRMT
COMPLETE SET (10)	150.00	70.00
COMMON CARD (1-10)	5.00	2.20

	MINT	NRMT
❑ 1 Albert Belle	10.00	4.50
❑ 2 Barry Bonds	10.00	4.50
❑ 3 Jeff Bagwell	12.00	5.50
❑ 4 Tim Salmon	8.00	3.60
❑ 5 Mo Vaughn	10.00	4.50
❑ 6 Ken Griffey Jr.	40.00	18.00
❑ 7 Mike Piazza	25.00	11.00
❑ 8 Cal Ripken	30.00	13.50
❑ 9 Frank Thomas	25.00	11.00
❑ 10 Dante Bichette	5.00	2.20

1996 Donruss Showdown

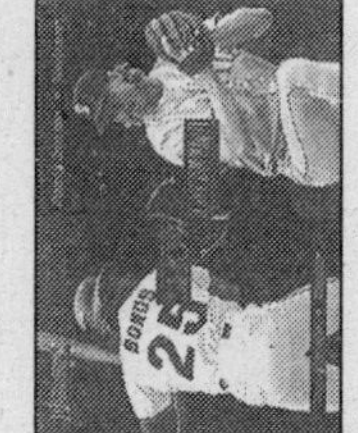

	MINT	NRMT
COMPLETE SET (8)	100.00	45.00
COMMON CARD (1-8)	3.00	1.35

	MINT	NRMT
❑ 1 Frank Thomas Hideo Nomo	20.00	9.00
❑ 2 Barry Bonds Randy Johnson	8.00	3.60
❑ 3 Greg Maddux Ken Griffey Jr.	30.00	13.50
❑ 4 Roger Clemens Tony Gwynn	15.00	6.75
❑ 5 Mike Piazza Mike Mussina	20.00	9.00
❑ 6 Cal Ripken Pedro J.Martinez	25.00	11.00
❑ 7 Tim Wakefield Matt Williams	3.00	1.35
❑ 8 Manny Ramirez Carlos Perez	8.00	3.60

1997 Donruss

	MINT	NRMT
COMPLETE SET (450)	45.00	20.00
COMPLETE SERIES 1 (270)	25.00	11.00
COMPLETE UPDATE (180)	20.00	9.00
COMMON CARD (1-450)	.15	.07

	MINT	NRMT
❑ 1 Juan Gonzalez	1.50	.70
❑ 2 Jim Edmonds	.40	.18
❑ 3 Tony Gwynn	1.50	.70
❑ 4 Andres Galarraga	.60	.25
❑ 5 Joe Carter	.30	.14
❑ 6 Raul Mondesi	.40	.18
❑ 7 Greg Maddux	2.00	.90
❑ 8 Travis Fryman	.30	.14
❑ 9 Brian Jordan	.30	.14
❑ 10 Henry Rodriguez	.30	.14
❑ 11 Manny Ramirez	.60	.25
❑ 12 Mark McGwire	3.00	1.35
❑ 13 Marc Newfield	.15	.07
❑ 14 Craig Biggio	.60	.25
❑ 15 Sammy Sosa	1.50	.70
❑ 16 Brady Anderson	.30	.14
❑ 17 Wade Boggs	.60	.25
❑ 18 Charles Johnson	.30	.14
❑ 19 Matt Williams	.30	.14
❑ 20 Denny Neagle	.30	.14
❑ 21 Ken Griffey Jr.	3.00	1.35
❑ 22 Robin Ventura	.30	.14
❑ 23 Barry Larkin	.40	.18
❑ 24 Todd Zeile	.15	.07
❑ 25 Chuck Knoblauch	.60	.25
❑ 26 Todd Hundley	.30	.14
❑ 27 Roger Clemens	1.25	.55
❑ 28 Michael Tucker	.30	.14
❑ 29 Rondell White	.30	.14
❑ 30 Osvaldo Fernandez	.15	.07
❑ 31 Ivan Rodriguez	.75	.35
❑ 32 Alex Fernandez	.15	.07
❑ 33 Jason Isringhausen	.15	.07
❑ 34 Chipper Jones	1.50	.70
❑ 35 Paul O'Neill	.30	.14
❑ 36 Hideo Nomo	.75	.35
❑ 37 Roberto Alomar	.60	.25
❑ 38 Derek Bell	.30	.14
❑ 39 Paul Molitor	.60	.25
❑ 40 Andy Benes	.30	.14
❑ 41 Steve Trachsel	.15	.07
❑ 42 J.T. Snow	.30	.14
❑ 43 Jason Kendall	.40	.18
❑ 44 Alex Rodriguez	2.00	.90
❑ 45 Joey Hamilton	.30	.14
❑ 46 Carlos Delgado	.30	.14
❑ 47 Jason Giambi	.30	.14
❑ 48 Larry Walker	.60	.25
❑ 49 Derek Jeter	2.00	.90
❑ 50 Kenny Lofton	.60	.25
❑ 51 Devon White	.30	.14
❑ 52 Matt Mieske	.15	.07
❑ 53 Melvin Nieves	.15	.07
❑ 54 Jose Canseco	.60	.25
❑ 55 Tino Martinez	.60	.25
❑ 56 Rafael Palmeiro	.40	.18
❑ 57 Edgardo Alfonzo	.30	.14
❑ 58 Jay Buhner	.30	.14
❑ 59 Shane Reynolds	.30	.14
❑ 60 Steve Finley	.30	.14

❑	61	Bobby Higginson	.40	.18
❑	62	Dean Palmer	.30	.14
❑	63	Terry Pendleton	.15	.07
❑	64	Marquis Grissom	.30	.14
❑	65	Mike Stanley	.15	.07
❑	66	Moises Alou	.40	.18
❑	67	Ray Lankford	.30	.14
❑	68	Marty Cordova	.15	.07
❑	69	John Olerud	.30	.14
❑	70	David Cone	.40	.18
❑	71	Benito Santiago	.15	.07
❑	72	Ryne Sandberg	.75	.35
❑	73	Rickey Henderson	.60	.25
❑	74	Roger Cedeno	.15	.07
❑	75	Wilson Alvarez	.30	.14
❑	76	Tim Salmon	.60	.25
❑	77	Orlando Merced	.15	.07
❑	78	Vinny Castilla	.40	.18
❑	79	Ismael Valdes	.30	.14
❑	80	Dante Bichette	.30	.14
❑	81	Kevin Brown	.40	.18
❑	82	Andy Pettitte	.40	.18
❑	83	Scott Stahoviak	.15	.07
❑	84	Mickey Tettleton	.15	.07
❑	85	Jack McDowell	.15	.07
❑	86	Tom Glavine	.60	.25
❑	87	Gregg Jefferies	.15	.07
❑	88	Chili Davis	.30	.14
❑	89	Randy Johnson	.60	.25
❑	90	John Mabry	.15	.07
❑	91	Billy Wagner	.30	.14
❑	92	Jeff Cirillo	.30	.14
❑	93	Trevor Hoffman	.30	.14
❑	94	Juan Guzman	.15	.07
❑	95	Geronimo Berroa	.15	.07
❑	96	Bernard Gilkey	.15	.07
❑	97	Danny Tartabull	.15	.07
❑	98	Johnny Damon	.30	.14
❑	99	Charlie Hayes	.15	.07
❑	100	Reggie Sanders	.30	.14
❑	101	Robby Thompson	.15	.07
❑	102	Bobby Bonilla	.30	.14
❑	103	Reggie Jefferson	.15	.07
❑	104	John Smoltz	.30	.14
❑	105	Jim Thome	.60	.25
❑	106	Ruben Rivera	.30	.14
❑	107	Darren Oliver	.15	.07
❑	108	Mo Vaughn	.75	.35
❑	109	Roger Pavlik	.15	.07
❑	110	Terry Steinbach	.30	.14
❑	111	Jermaine Dye	.15	.07
❑	112	Mark Grudzielanek	.30	.14
❑	113	Rick Aguilera	.15	.07
❑	114	Jamey Wright	.15	.07
❑	115	Eddie Murray	.60	.25
❑	116	Brian L. Hunter	.30	.14
❑	117	Hal Morris	.15	.07
❑	118	Tom Pagnozzi	.15	.07
❑	119	Mike Mussina	.60	.25
❑	120	Mark Grace	.40	.18
❑	121	Cal Ripken	2.50	1.10
❑	122	Tom Goodwin	.15	.07
❑	123	Paul Sorrento	.15	.07
❑	124	Jay Bell	.30	.14
❑	125	Todd Hollandsworth	.15	.07
❑	126	Edgar Martinez	.30	.14
❑	127	George Arias	.15	.07
❑	128	Greg Vaughn	.30	.14
❑	129	Roberto Hernandez	.15	.07
❑	130	Delino DeShields	.15	.07
❑	131	Bill Pulsipher	.15	.07
❑	132	Joey Cora	.30	.14
❑	133	Mariano Rivera	.30	.14
❑	134	Mike Piazza	2.00	.90
❑	135	Carlos Baerga	.30	.14
❑	136	Jose Mesa	.15	.07
❑	137	Will Clark	.60	.25
❑	138	Frank Thomas	2.00	.90
❑	139	John Wetteland	.30	.14
❑	140	Shawn Estes	.30	.14
❑	141	Garret Anderson	.30	.14
❑	142	Andre Dawson	.40	.18
❑	143	Eddie Taubensee	.15	.07
❑	144	Ryan Klesko	.30	.14
❑	145	Rocky Coppinger	.15	.07
❑	146	Jeff Bagwell	1.00	.45
❑	147	Donovan Osborne	.15	.07
❑	148	Greg Myers	.15	.07
❑	149	Brant Brown	.30	.14
❑	150	Kevin Elster	.15	.07
❑	151	Bob Wells	.15	.07
❑	152	Wally Joyner	.30	.14
❑	153	Rico Brogna	.15	.07
❑	154	Dwight Gooden	.30	.14
❑	155	Jermaine Allensworth	.15	.07
❑	156	Ray Durham	.30	.14
❑	157	Cecil Fielder	.30	.14
❑	158	John Burkett	.15	.07
❑	159	Gary Sheffield	.40	.18
❑	160	Albert Belle	.75	.35
❑	161	Tomas Perez	.15	.07
❑	162	David Doster	.15	.07
❑	163	John Valentin	.30	.14
❑	164	Danny Graves	.15	.07
❑	165	Jose Paniagua	.15	.07
❑	166	Brian Giles	.75	.35
❑	167	Barry Bonds	.75	.35
❑	168	Sterling Hitchcock	.30	.14
❑	169	Bernie Williams	.60	.25
❑	170	Fred McGriff	.40	.18
❑	171	George Williams	.15	.07
❑	172	Amaury Telemaco	.15	.07
❑	173	Ken Caminiti	.40	.18
❑	174	Ron Gant	.15	.07
❑	175	Dave Justice	.60	.25
❑	176	James Baldwin	.30	.14
❑	177	Pat Hentgen	.30	.14
❑	178	Ben McDonald	.15	.07
❑	179	Tim Naehring	.15	.07
❑	180	Jim Eisenreich	.15	.07
❑	181	Ken Hill	.15	.07
❑	182	Paul Wilson	.15	.07
❑	183	Marvin Benard	.15	.07
❑	184	Alan Benes	.30	.14
❑	185	Ellis Burks	.30	.14
❑	186	Scott Servais	.15	.07
❑	187	David Segui	.30	.14
❑	188	Scott Brosius	.30	.14
❑	189	Jose Offerman	.15	.07
❑	190	Eric Davis	.30	.14
❑	191	Brett Butler	.30	.14
❑	192	Curtis Pride	.15	.07
❑	193	Yamil Benitez	.15	.07
❑	194	Chan Ho Park	.60	.25
❑	195	Bret Boone	.30	.14
❑	196	Omar Vizquel	.30	.14
❑	197	Orlando Miller	.15	.07
❑	198	Ramon Martinez	.30	.14
❑	199	Harold Baines	.30	.14
❑	200	Eric Young	.30	.14
❑	201	Fernando Vina	.15	.07
❑	202	Alex Gonzalez	.15	.07
❑	203	Fernando Valenzuela	.30	.14
❑	204	Steve Avery	.15	.07
❑	205	Ernie Young	.15	.07
❑	206	Kevin Appier	.30	.14
❑	207	Randy Myers	.15	.07
❑	208	Jeff Suppan	.15	.07
❑	209	James Mouton	.15	.07
❑	210	Russ Davis	.30	.14
❑	211	Al Martin	.15	.07
❑	212	Troy Percival	.30	.14
❑	213	Al Leiter	.30	.14
❑	214	Dennis Eckersley	.30	.14
❑	215	Mark Johnson	.15	.07
❑	216	Eric Karros	.30	.14
❑	217	Royce Clayton	.15	.07
❑	218	Tony Phillips	.15	.07
❑	219	Tim Wakefield	.30	.14
❑	220	Alan Trammell	.30	.14
❑	221	Eduardo Perez	.15	.07
❑	222	Butch Huskey	.15	.07
❑	223	Tim Belcher	.15	.07
❑	224	Jamie Moyer	.15	.07
❑	225	F.P. Santangelo	.15	.07
❑	226	Rusty Greer	.30	.14
❑	227	Jeff Brantley	.15	.07
❑	228	Mark Langston	.30	.14
❑	229	Ray Montgomery	.15	.07
❑	230	Rich Becker	.15	.07
❑	231	Ozzie Smith	.75	.35
❑	232	Rey Ordonez	.30	.14
❑	233	Ricky Otero	.15	.07
❑	234	Mike Cameron	.30	.14
❑	235	Mike Sweeney	.15	.07
❑	236	Mark Lewis	.15	.07
❑	237	Luis Gonzalez	.15	.07
❑	238	Marcus Jensen	.15	.07
❑	239	Ed Sprague	.15	.07
❑	240	Jose Valentin	.15	.07
❑	241	Jeff Frye	.15	.07
❑	242	Charles Nagy	.30	.14
❑	243	Carlos Garcia	.15	.07
❑	244	Mike Hampton	.15	.07
❑	245	B.J. Surhoff	.30	.14
❑	246	Wilton Guerrero	.15	.07
❑	247	Frank Rodriguez	.15	.07
❑	248	Gary Gaetti	.15	.07
❑	249	Lance Johnson	.15	.07
❑	250	Darren Bragg	.15	.07
❑	251	Darryl Hamilton	.15	.07
❑	252	John Jaha	.15	.07
❑	253	Craig Paquette	.15	.07
❑	254	Jaime Navarro	.15	.07
❑	255	Shawon Dunston	.15	.07
❑	256	Mark Loretta	.15	.07
❑	257	Tim Belk	.15	.07
❑	258	Jeff Darwin	.15	.07
❑	259	Ruben Sierra	.15	.07
❑	260	Chuck Finley	.30	.14
❑	261	Darryl Strawberry	.30	.14
❑	262	Shannon Stewart	.30	.14
❑	263	Pedro Martinez	.60	.25
❑	264	Neifi Perez	.15	.07
❑	265	Jeff Conine	.30	.14
❑	266	Orel Hershiser	.30	.14
❑	267	Eddie Murray CL	.30	.14
❑	268	Paul Molitor CL	.30	.14
❑	269	Barry Bonds CL	.30	.14
❑	270	Mark McGwire CL	1.50	.70
❑	271	Matt Williams	.30	.14
❑	272	Todd Zeile	.15	.07
❑	273	Roger Clemens	1.25	.55
❑	274	Michael Tucker	.30	.14
❑	275	J.T. Snow	.30	.14
❑	276	Kenny Lofton	.60	.25
❑	277	Jose Canseco	.60	.25
❑	278	Marquis Grissom	.30	.14
❑	279	Moises Alou	.40	.18
❑	280	Benito Santiago	.15	.07
❑	281	Willie McGee	.30	.14
❑	282	Chili Davis	.30	.14
❑	283	Ron Coomer	.15	.07
❑	284	Orlando Merced	.15	.07
❑	285	Delino DeShields	.15	.07
❑	286	John Wetteland	.30	.14
❑	287	Darren Daulton	.30	.14
❑	288	Lee Stevens	.15	.07
❑	289	Albert Belle	.75	.35
❑	290	Sterling Hitchcock	.30	.14
❑	291	David Justice	.60	.25
❑	292	Eric Davis	.30	.14
❑	293	Brian Hunter	.30	.14
❑	294	Darryl Hamilton	.15	.07
❑	295	Steve Avery	.15	.07
❑	296	Joe Vitiello	.15	.07
❑	297	Jaime Navarro	.15	.07
❑	298	Eddie Murray	.60	.25
❑	299	Randy Myers	.15	.07
❑	300	Francisco Cordova	.15	.07
❑	301	Javier Lopez	.30	.14
❑	302	Geronimo Berroa	.15	.07
❑	303	Jeffrey Hammonds	.30	.14
❑	304	Deion Sanders	.30	.14
❑	305	Jeff Fassero	.15	.07
❑	306	Curt Schilling	.30	.14
❑	307	Robb Nen	.15	.07
❑	308	Mark McLemore	.15	.07
❑	309	Jimmy Key	.30	.14
❑	310	Quilvio Veras	.15	.07
❑	311	Bip Roberts	.15	.07
❑	312	Esteban Loaiza	.15	.07
❑	313	Andy Ashby	.15	.07
❑	314	Sandy Alomar Jr.	.30	.14
❑	315	Shawn Green	.30	.14

Card	Mint	Nrmt
❑ 316 Luis Castillo	.30	.14
❑ 317 Benji Gil	.15	.07
❑ 318 Otis Nixon	.15	.07
❑ 319 Aaron Sele	.30	.14
❑ 320 Brad Ausmus	.15	.07
❑ 321 Troy O'Leary	.30	.14
❑ 322 Terrell Wade	.15	.07
❑ 323 Jeff King	.15	.07
❑ 324 Kevin Seitzer	.15	.07
❑ 325 Mark Wohlers	.15	.07
❑ 326 Edgar Renteria	.30	.14
❑ 327 Dan Wilson	.15	.07
❑ 328 Brian McRae	.15	.07
❑ 329 Rod Beck	.15	.07
❑ 330 Julio Franco	.30	.14
❑ 331 Dave Nilsson	.15	.07
❑ 332 Glenallen Hill	.15	.07
❑ 333 Kevin Elster	.15	.07
❑ 334 Joe Girardi	.15	.07
❑ 335 David Wells	.40	.18
❑ 336 Jeff Blauser	.15	.07
❑ 337 Darryl Kile	.30	.14
❑ 338 Jeff Kent	.30	.14
❑ 339 Jim Leyritz	.15	.07
❑ 340 Todd Stottlemyre	.15	.07
❑ 341 Tony Clark	.40	.18
❑ 342 Chris Hoiles	.15	.07
❑ 343 Mike Lieberthal	.15	.07
❑ 344 Matt Lawton	.30	.14
❑ 345 Alex Ochoa	.15	.07
❑ 346 Chris Snopek	.15	.07
❑ 347 Rudy Pemberton	.15	.07
❑ 348 Eric Owens	.15	.07
❑ 349 Joe Randa	.15	.07
❑ 350 John Olerud	.30	.14
❑ 351 Steve Karsay	.15	.07
❑ 352 Mark Whiten	.15	.07
❑ 353 Bob Abreu	.30	.14
❑ 354 Bartolo Colon	.30	.14
❑ 355 Vladimir Guerrero	1.25	.55
❑ 356 Darin Erstad	1.00	.45
❑ 357 Scott Rolen	1.50	.70
❑ 358 Andruw Jones	1.00	.45
❑ 359 Scott Spiezio	.15	.07
❑ 360 Karim Garcia	.30	.14
❑ 361 Hideki Irabu	1.50	.70
❑ 362 Nomar Garciaparra	2.00	.90
❑ 363 Dmitri Young	.30	.14
❑ 364 Bubba Trammell	.40	.18
❑ 365 Kevin Orie	.15	.07
❑ 366 Jose Rosado	.15	.07
❑ 367 Jose Guillen	.60	.25
❑ 368 Brooks Kieschnick	.15	.07
❑ 369 Pokey Reese	.15	.07
❑ 370 Glendon Rusch	.15	.07
❑ 371 Jason Dickson	.30	.14
❑ 372 Todd Walker	.60	.25
❑ 373 Justin Thompson	.30	.14
❑ 374 Todd Greene	.30	.14
❑ 375 Jeff Suppan	.15	.07
❑ 376 Trey Beamon	.15	.07
❑ 377 Damon Mashore	.15	.07
❑ 378 Wendell Magee	.15	.07
❑ 379 Shigetoshi Hasegawa	.40	.18
❑ 380 Bill Mueller	.75	.35
❑ 381 Chris Widger	.15	.07
❑ 382 Tony Graffanino	.15	.07
❑ 383 Derrek Lee	.40	.18
❑ 384 Brian Moehler	.15	.07
❑ 385 Quinton McCracken	.30	.14
❑ 386 Matt Morris	.30	.14
❑ 387 Marvin Benard	.15	.07
❑ 388 Deivi Cruz	.50	.23
❑ 389 Javier Valentin	.30	.14
❑ 390 Todd Dunwoody	.30	.14
❑ 391 Derrick Gibson	.40	.18
❑ 392 Raul Casanova	.15	.07
❑ 393 George Arias	.15	.07
❑ 394 Tony Womack	.50	.23
❑ 395 Antone Williamson	.15	.07
❑ 396 Jose Cruz Jr.	2.50	1.10
❑ 397 Desi Relaford	.15	.07
❑ 398 Frank Thomas HIT	1.00	.45
❑ 399 Ken Griffey Jr. HIT	1.50	.70
❑ 400 Cal Ripken HIT	1.25	.55
❑ 401 Chipper Jones HIT	.75	.35
❑ 402 Mike Piazza HIT	1.00	.45
❑ 403 Gary Sheffield HIT	.15	.07
❑ 404 Alex Rodriguez HIT	1.00	.45
❑ 405 Wade Boggs HIT	.30	.14
❑ 406 Juan Gonzalez HIT	.75	.35
❑ 407 Tony Gwynn HIT	.75	.35
❑ 408 Edgar Martinez HIT	.15	.07
❑ 409 Jeff Bagwell HIT	.60	.25
❑ 410 Larry Walker HIT	.30	.14
❑ 411 Kenny Lofton HIT	.30	.14
❑ 412 Manny Ramirez HIT	.30	.14
❑ 413 Mark McGwire HIT	1.50	.70
❑ 414 Roberto Alomar HIT	.30	.14
❑ 415 Derek Jeter HIT	1.00	.45
❑ 416 Brady Anderson HIT	.15	.07
❑ 417 Paul Molitor HIT	.30	.14
❑ 418 Dante Bichette HIT	.15	.07
❑ 419 Jim Edmonds HIT	.15	.07
❑ 420 Mo Vaughn HIT	.40	.18
❑ 421 Barry Bonds HIT	.30	.14
❑ 422 Rusty Greer HIT	.15	.07
❑ 423 Greg Maddux KING	1.00	.45
❑ 424 Andy Pettitte KING	.15	.07
❑ 425 John Smoltz KING	.15	.07
❑ 426 Randy Johnson KING	.30	.14
❑ 427 Hideo Nomo KING	.75	.35
❑ 428 Roger Clemens KING	.60	.25
❑ 429 Tom Glavine KING	.30	.14
❑ 430 Pat Hentgen KING	.15	.07
❑ 431 Kevin Brown KING	.15	.07
❑ 432 Mike Mussina KING	.30	.14
❑ 433 Alex Fernandez KING	.15	.07
❑ 434 Kevin Appier KING	.15	.07
❑ 435 David Cone KING	.15	.07
❑ 436 Jeff Fassero KING	.15	.07
❑ 437 John Wetteland KING	.15	.07
❑ 438 Barry Bonds IS	.25	.11
Ivan Rodriguez		
❑ 439 Ken Griffey Jr. IS	1.00	.45
Andres Galarraga		
❑ 440 Fred McGriff IS	.15	.07
Rafael Palmeiro		
❑ 441 Barry Larkin IS	.15	.07
Jim Thome		
❑ 442 Sammy Sosa IS	.25	.11
Albert Belle		
❑ 443 Bernie Williams IS	.15	.07
Todd Hundley		
❑ 444 Chuck Knoblauch IS	.15	.07
Brian Jordan		
❑ 445 Mo Vaughn IS	.25	.11
Jeff Conine		
❑ 446 Ken Caminiti IS	.15	.07
Jason Giambi		
❑ 447 Raul Mondesi IS	.15	.07
Tim Salmon		
❑ 448 Cal Ripken CL	1.25	.55
❑ 449 Greg Maddux CL	1.00	.45
❑ 450 Ken Griffey Jr. CL	1.50	.70

1997 Donruss Armed and Dangerous

	MINT	NRMT
COMPLETE SET (15)	120.00	55.00
COMMON CARD (1-15)	2.50	1.10
❑ 1 Ken Griffey Jr.	25.00	11.00
❑ 2 Raul Mondesi	4.00	1.80
❑ 3 Chipper Jones	12.00	5.50
❑ 4 Ivan Rodriguez	6.00	2.70
❑ 5 Randy Johnson	5.00	2.20
❑ 6 Alex Rodriguez	15.00	6.75
❑ 7 Larry Walker	5.00	2.20
❑ 8 Cal Ripken	20.00	9.00
❑ 9 Kenny Lofton	5.00	2.20
❑ 10 Barry Bonds	6.00	2.70
❑ 11 Derek Jeter	12.00	5.50
❑ 12 Charles Johnson	2.50	1.10
❑ 13 Greg Maddux	15.00	6.75
❑ 14 Roberto Alomar	5.00	2.20
❑ 15 Barry Larkin	4.00	1.80

1997 Donruss Diamond Kings

	MINT	NRMT
COMPLETE SET (10)	180.00	80.00
COMMON CARD (1-10)	2.00	.90
COMP.CANVAS SET (10)	500.00	220.00
*CANVAS: 1.25X TO 3X BASIC DK'S		
❑ 1 Ken Griffey Jr.	40.00	18.00
❑ 2 Cal Ripken	30.00	13.50
❑ 3 Mo Vaughn	10.00	4.50
❑ 4 Chuck Knoblauch	6.00	2.70
❑ 5 Jeff Bagwell	12.00	5.50
❑ 6 Henry Rodriguez	2.00	.90
❑ 7 Mike Piazza	25.00	11.00
❑ 8 Ivan Rodriguez	10.00	4.50
❑ 9 Frank Thomas	25.00	11.00
❑ 10 Chipper Jones	20.00	9.00

1997 Donruss Dominators

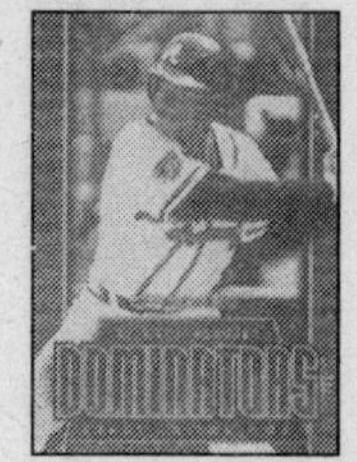

	MINT	NRMT
COMPLETE SET (20)	90.00	40.00
COMMON CARD (1-20)	1.50	.70
❑ 1 Frank Thomas	10.00	4.50
❑ 2 Ken Griffey Jr.	15.00	6.75
❑ 3 Greg Maddux	10.00	4.50
❑ 4 Cal Ripken	12.00	5.50
❑ 5 Alex Rodriguez	10.00	4.50
❑ 6 Albert Belle	4.00	1.80

	MINT	NRMT
❑ 7 Mark McGwire	15.00	6.75
❑ 8 Juan Gonzalez	8.00	3.60
❑ 9 Chipper Jones	8.00	3.60
❑ 10 Hideo Nomo	4.00	1.80
❑ 11 Roger Clemens	6.00	2.70
❑ 12 John Smoltz	1.50	.70
❑ 13 Mike Piazza	10.00	4.50
❑ 14 Sammy Sosa	8.00	3.60
❑ 15 Matt Williams	1.50	.70
❑ 16 Kenny Lofton	4.00	1.80
❑ 17 Barry Larkin	2.00	.90
❑ 18 Rafael Palmeiro	2.00	.90
❑ 19 Ken Caminiti	2.00	.90
❑ 20 Gary Sheffield	2.00	.90

1997 Donruss Elite Inserts

	MINT	NRMT
COMPLETE SET (12)	350.00	160.00
COMMON CARD (1-12)	12.00	5.50
❑ 1 Frank Thomas	40.00	18.00
❑ 2 Paul Molitor	12.00	5.50
❑ 3 Sammy Sosa	30.00	13.50
❑ 4 Barry Bonds	15.00	6.75
❑ 5 Chipper Jones	30.00	13.50
❑ 6 Alex Rodriguez	40.00	18.00
❑ 7 Ken Griffey Jr.	60.00	27.00
❑ 8 Jeff Bagwell	25.00	11.00
❑ 9 Cal Ripken	50.00	22.00
❑ 10 Mo Vaughn	15.00	6.75
❑ 11 Mike Piazza	40.00	18.00
❑ 12 Juan Gonzalez UER name mispelled as Gonzales	30.00	13.50

1997 Donruss Franchise Features

	MINT	NRMT
COMPLETE SET (15)	250.00	110.00
COMMON CARD (1-15)	6.00	2.70
❑ 1 Ken Griffey Jr. Andruw Jones	40.00	18.00
❑ 2 Frank Thomas Darin Erstad	25.00	11.00
❑ 3 Alex Rodriguez Nomar Garciaparra	30.00	13.50
❑ 4 Chuck Knoblauch Wilton Guerrero	6.00	2.70
❑ 5 Juan Gonzalez BubbaTrammell	20.00	9.00
❑ 6 Chipper Jones Todd Walker	20.00	9.00
❑ 7 Barry Bonds Vladimir Guerrero	12.00	5.50
❑ 8 Mark McGwire Dmitri Young	40.00	18.00
❑ 9 Mike Piazza Mike Sweeney	25.00	11.00
❑ 10 Mo Vaughn Tony Clark	10.00	4.50
❑ 11 Gary Sheffield Jose Guillen	6.00	2.70
❑ 12 Kenny Lofton Shannon Stewart	10.00	4.50
❑ 13 Cal Ripken Scott Rolen	30.00	13.50
❑ 14 Derek Jeter Pokey Reese	20.00	9.00
❑ 15 Tony Gwynn Bob Abreu	20.00	9.00

1997 Donruss Longball Leaders

	MINT	NRMT
COMPLETE SET (15)	100.00	45.00
COMMON CARD (1-15)	1.50	.70
❑ 1 Frank Thomas	15.00	6.75
❑ 2 Albert Belle	8.00	3.60
❑ 3 Mo Vaughn	6.00	2.70
❑ 4 Brady Anderson	2.50	1.10
❑ 5 Greg Vaughn	2.50	1.10
❑ 6 Ken Griffey Jr.	25.00	11.00
❑ 7 Jay Buhner	2.50	1.10
❑ 8 Juan Gonzalez	12.00	5.50
❑ 9 Mike Piazza	15.00	6.75
❑ 10 Jeff Bagwell	8.00	3.60
❑ 11 Sammy Sosa	12.00	5.50
❑ 12 Mark McGwire	25.00	11.00
❑ 13 Cecil Fielder	1.50	.70
❑ 14 Ryan Klesko	2.50	1.10
❑ 15 Jose Canseco	5.00	2.20

1997 Donruss Power Alley

	MINT	NRMT
COMPLETE SET (24)	600.00	275.00
COMMON CARD (1-24)	5.00	2.20

*GREEN DIE CUT: 2X TO 5X BASIC GREEN
*BLUE DIE CUT: 1.25X TO 3X BASIC BLUE
*GOLD DIE CUT: .75X TO 2X BASIC GOLD
DIE CUTS: RANDOM INS.IN UPDATE PACKS
DIE CUTS PRINT RUN 250 SERIAL #'d SETS

	MINT	NRMT
❑ 1 Frank Thomas G	60.00	27.00
❑ 2 Ken Griffey Jr. G	100.00	45.00
❑ 3 Cal Ripken G	80.00	36.00
❑ 4 Jeff Bagwell B	20.00	9.00
❑ 5 Mike Piazza B	40.00	18.00
❑ 6 Andruw Jones GR	10.00	4.50
❑ 7 Alex Rodriguez G	60.00	27.00

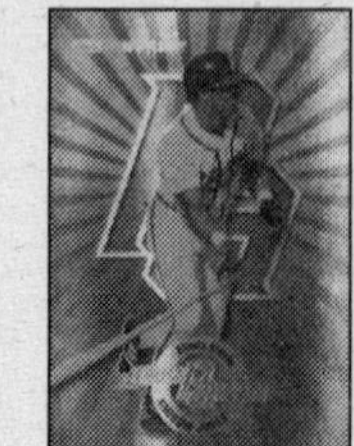

	MINT	NRMT
❑ 8 Albert Belle GR	10.00	4.50
❑ 9 Mo Vaughn GR	10.00	4.50
❑ 10 Chipper Jones B	30.00	13.50
❑ 11 Juan Gonzalez B	30.00	13.50
❑ 12 Ken Caminiti GR	5.00	2.20
❑ 13 Manny Ramirez GR	8.00	3.60
❑ 14 Mark McGwire GR	40.00	18.00
❑ 15 Kenny Lofton B	8.00	3.60
❑ 16 Barry Bonds GR	10.00	4.50
❑ 17 Gary Sheffield GR	5.00	2.20
❑ 18 Tony Gwynn GR	20.00	9.00
❑ 19 Vladimir Guerrero B	20.00	9.00
❑ 20 Ivan Rodriguez B	15.00	6.75
❑ 21 Paul Molitor B	12.00	5.50
❑ 22 Sammy Sosa GR	20.00	9.00
❑ 23 Matt Williams GR	5.00	2.20
❑ 24 Derek Jeter GR	20.00	9.00

1997 Donruss Rated Rookies

	MINT	NRMT
COMPLETE SET (30)	50.00	22.00
COMMON CARD (1-30)	1.00	.45
❑ 1 Jason Thompson	1.00	.45
❑ 2 LaTroy Hawkins	1.00	.45
❑ 3 Scott Rolen	10.00	4.50
❑ 4 Trey Beamon	1.00	.45
❑ 5 Kimera Bartee	1.00	.45
❑ 6 Nerio Rodriguez	1.50	.70
❑ 7 Jeff D'Amico	1.00	.45
❑ 8 Quinton McCracken	1.50	.70
❑ 9 John Wasdin	1.00	.45
❑ 10 Robin Jennings	1.00	.45
❑ 11 Steve Gibralter	1.00	.45
❑ 12 Tyler Houston	1.00	.45
❑ 13 Tony Clark	2.50	1.10
❑ 14 Ugueth Urbina	1.50	.70
❑ 15 Karim Garcia	1.50	.70
❑ 16 Raul Casanova	1.00	.45
❑ 17 Brooks Kieschnick	1.00	.45
❑ 18 Luis Castillo	1.50	.70
❑ 19 Edgar Renteria	1.50	.70
❑ 20 Andruw Jones	6.00	2.70
❑ 21 Chad Mottola	1.00	.45
❑ 22 Mac Suzuki	1.00	.45
❑ 23 Justin Thompson	1.50	.70
❑ 24 Darin Erstad	6.00	2.70
❑ 25 Todd Walker	4.00	1.80

	MINT	NRMT
❑ 26 Todd Greene	1.50	.70
❑ 27 Vladimir Guerrero	8.00	3.60
❑ 28 Darren Dreifort	1.50	.70
❑ 29 John Burke	1.00	.45
❑ 30 Damon Mashore	1.00	.45

1997 Donruss Ripken The Only Way I Know

	MINT	NRMT
COMPLETE SET (9)	100.00	45.00
COMMON CARD (1-9)	12.00	5.50
❑ 1 Cal Ripken	12.00	5.50
❑ 2 Cal Ripken Cal Ripken Sr. Memorial Stadium 1978	12.00	5.50
❑ 3 Cal Ripken Rochester Red Wings	12.00	5.50
❑ 4 Cal Ripken Aberdeen Indians 1970	12.00	5.50
❑ 5 Cal Ripken Eddie Murray	12.00	5.50
❑ 6 Cal Ripken Cal Ripken Sr. Billy Ripken Family Reunion at Camden Yards	12.00	5.50
❑ 7 Cal Ripken Cal Ripken Sr. Billy Ripken Family Day Tri-Cities Atoms	12.00	5.50
❑ 8 Cal Ripken	12.00	5.50
❑ 9 Cal Ripken Victory Lap Game 2131	12.00	5.50
❑ 10 Cal Ripken distributed exclusively with book	6.00	2.70
❑ 10A Cal Ripken AU/2131 distributed exclusively with book	200.00	90.00

1997 Donruss Rocket Launchers

	MINT	NRMT
COMPLETE SET (15)	100.00	45.00
COMMON CARD (1-15)	1.50	.70
❑ 1 Frank Thomas	15.00	6.75
❑ 2 Albert Belle	8.00	3.60
❑ 3 Chipper Jones	12.00	5.50
❑ 4 Mike Piazza	15.00	6.75
❑ 5 Mo Vaughn	6.00	2.70
❑ 6 Juan Gonzalez	12.00	5.50
❑ 7 Fred McGriff	3.00	1.35
❑ 8 Jeff Bagwell	8.00	3.60
❑ 9 Matt Williams	2.00	.90
❑ 10 Gary Sheffield	3.00	1.35
❑ 11 Barry Bonds	6.00	2.70
❑ 12 Manny Ramirez	5.00	2.20
❑ 13 Henry Rodriguez	1.50	.70
❑ 14 Jason Giambi	2.00	.90
❑ 15 Cal Ripken	20.00	9.00

1997 Donruss Rookie Diamond Kings

	MINT	NRMT
COMPLETE SET (10)	110.00	50.00
COMMON CARD (1-10)	4.00	1.80

*CANVAS: 1.25X TO 3X BASIC DK'S
CANVAS PRINT RUN 500 SERIAL #'d SETS

	MINT	NRMT
❑ 1 Andruw Jones	12.00	5.50
❑ 2 Vladimir Guerrero	15.00	6.75
❑ 3 Scott Rolen	20.00	9.00
❑ 4 Todd Walker	6.00	2.70
❑ 5 Bartolo Colon	4.00	1.80
❑ 6 Jose Guillen	6.00	2.70
❑ 7 Nomar Garciaparra	25.00	11.00
❑ 8 Darin Erstad	12.00	5.50
❑ 9 Dmitri Young	4.00	1.80
❑ 10 Wilton Guerrero	4.00	1.80

1998 Donruss

	MINT	NRMT
COMPLETE SET (420)	50.00	22.00
COMPLETE SERIES 1 (170)	20.00	9.00
COMPLETE UPDATE (250)	30.00	13.50
COMMON CARD (1-420)	.10	.05
❑ 1 Paul Molitor	.50	.23
❑ 2 Juan Gonzalez	1.25	.55
❑ 3 Darryl Kile	.20	.09
❑ 4 Randy Johnson	.50	.23
❑ 5 Tom Glavine	.50	.23
❑ 6 Pat Hentgen	.20	.09
❑ 7 David Justice	.50	.23
❑ 8 Kevin Brown	.30	.14
❑ 9 Mike Mussina	.50	.23
❑ 10 Ken Caminiti	.30	.14
❑ 11 Todd Hundley	.20	.09
❑ 12 Frank Thomas	1.50	.70
❑ 13 Ray Lankford	.20	.09
❑ 14 Justin Thompson	.20	.09
❑ 15 Jason Dickson	.20	.09
❑ 16 Kenny Lofton	.50	.23
❑ 17 Ivan Rodriguez	.60	.25
❑ 18 Pedro Martinez	.50	.23
❑ 19 Brady Anderson	.20	.09
❑ 20 Barry Larkin	.30	.14
❑ 21 Chipper Jones	1.25	.55
❑ 22 Tony Gwynn	1.25	.55
❑ 23 Roger Clemens	1.00	.45
❑ 24 Sandy Alomar Jr.	.20	.09
❑ 25 Tino Martinez	.50	.23
❑ 26 Jeff Bagwell	.75	.35
❑ 27 Shawn Estes	.20	.09
❑ 28 Ken Griffey Jr.	2.50	1.10
❑ 29 Javier Lopez	.20	.09
❑ 30 Denny Neagle	.20	.09
❑ 31 Mike Piazza	1.50	.70
❑ 32 Andres Galarraga	.50	.23
❑ 33 Larry Walker	.50	.23
❑ 34 Alex Rodriguez	1.50	.70
❑ 35 Greg Maddux	1.50	.70
❑ 36 Albert Belle	.50	.23
❑ 37 Barry Bonds	.60	.25
❑ 38 Mo Vaughn	.60	.25
❑ 39 Kevin Appier	.20	.09
❑ 40 Wade Boggs	.50	.23
❑ 41 Garret Anderson	.20	.09
❑ 42 Jeffrey Hammonds	.20	.09
❑ 43 Marquis Grissom	.20	.09
❑ 44 Jim Edmonds	.30	.14
❑ 45 Brian Jordan	.20	.09
❑ 46 Raul Mondesi	.30	.14
❑ 47 John Valentin	.20	.09
❑ 48 Brad Radke	.20	.09
❑ 49 Ismael Valdes	.20	.09
❑ 50 Matt Stairs	.20	.09
❑ 51 Matt Williams	.20	.09
❑ 52 Reggie Jefferson	.10	.05
❑ 53 Alan Benes	.20	.09
❑ 54 Charles Johnson	.20	.09
❑ 55 Chuck Knoblauch	.50	.23
❑ 56 Edgar Martinez	.20	.09
❑ 57 Nomar Garciaparra	1.50	.70
❑ 58 Craig Biggio	.50	.23
❑ 59 Bernie Williams	.50	.23
❑ 60 David Cone	.30	.14
❑ 61 Cal Ripken	2.00	.90
❑ 62 Mark McGwire	3.00	1.35
❑ 63 Roberto Alomar	.50	.23
❑ 64 Fred McGriff	.30	.14
❑ 65 Eric Karros	.20	.09
❑ 66 Robin Ventura	.20	.09
❑ 67 Darin Erstad	.60	.25
❑ 68 Michael Tucker	.20	.09
❑ 69 Jim Thome	.50	.23
❑ 70 Mark Grace	.30	.14
❑ 71 Lou Collier	.10	.05
❑ 72 Karim Garcia	.20	.09
❑ 73 Alex Fernandez	.10	.05
❑ 74 J.T. Snow	.20	.09
❑ 75 Reggie Sanders	.20	.09
❑ 76 John Smoltz	.20	.09
❑ 77 Tim Salmon	.50	.23
❑ 78 Paul O'Neill	.20	.09
❑ 79 Vinny Castilla	.30	.14
❑ 80 Rafael Palmeiro	.30	.14
❑ 81 Jaret Wright	.60	.25
❑ 82 Jay Buhner	.20	.09
❑ 83 Brett Butler	.20	.09
❑ 84 Todd Greene	.20	.09
❑ 85 Scott Rolen	1.25	.55
❑ 86 Sammy Sosa	1.25	.55
❑ 87 Jason Giambi	.20	.09
❑ 88 Carlos Delgado	.20	.09
❑ 89 Deion Sanders	.20	.09
❑ 90 Wilton Guerrero	.10	.05
❑ 91 Andy Pettitte	.30	.14
❑ 92 Brian Giles	.20	.09
❑ 93 Dmitri Young	.20	.09
❑ 94 Ron Coomer	.10	.05

❑ 95 Mike Cameron .20 .09
❑ 96 Edgardo Alfonzo .20 .09
❑ 97 Jimmy Key .20 .09
❑ 98 Ryan Klesko .20 .09
❑ 99 Andy Benes .20 .09
❑ 100 Derek Jeter 1.25 .55
❑ 101 Jeff Fassero .10 .05
❑ 102 Neifi Perez .20 .09
❑ 103 Hideo Nomo .60 .25
❑ 104 Andruw Jones .60 .25
❑ 105 Todd Helton .60 .25
❑ 106 Livan Hernandez .20 .09
❑ 107 Brett Tomko .20 .09
❑ 108 Shannon Stewart .20 .09
❑ 109 Bartolo Colon .20 .09
❑ 110 Matt Morris .20 .09
❑ 111 Miguel Tejada .20 .09
❑ 112 Pokey Reese .10 .05
❑ 113 Fernando Tatis .20 .09
❑ 114 Todd Dunwoody .20 .09
❑ 115 Jose Cruz Jr. .60 .25
❑ 116 Chan Ho Park .50 .23
❑ 117 Kevin Young .20 .09
❑ 118 Rickey Henderson .50 .23
❑ 119 Hideki Irabu .30 .14
❑ 120 Francisco Cordova .10 .05
❑ 121 Al Martin .10 .05
❑ 122 Tony Clark .30 .14
❑ 123 Curt Schilling .20 .09
❑ 124 Rusty Greer .20 .09
❑ 125 Jose Canseco .50 .23
❑ 126 Edgar Renteria .20 .09
❑ 127 Todd Walker .30 .14
❑ 128 Wally Joyner .20 .09
❑ 129 Bill Mueller .20 .09
❑ 130 Jose Guillen .20 .09
❑ 131 Manny Ramirez .50 .23
❑ 132 Bobby Higginson .30 .14
❑ 133 Kevin Orie .10 .05
❑ 134 Will Clark .50 .23
❑ 135 Dave Nilsson .10 .05
❑ 136 Jason Kendall .20 .09
❑ 137 Ivan Cruz .10 .05
❑ 138 Gary Sheffield .30 .14
❑ 139 Bubba Trammell .20 .09
❑ 140 Vladimir Guerrero .75 .35
❑ 141 Dennis Reyes .20 .09
❑ 142 Bobby Bonilla .20 .09
❑ 143 Ruben Rivera .20 .09
❑ 144 Ben Grieve 1.00 .45
❑ 145 Moises Alou .30 .14
❑ 146 Tony Womack .20 .09
❑ 147 Eric Young .20 .09
❑ 148 Paul Konerko .50 .23
❑ 149 Dante Bichette .20 .09
❑ 150 Joe Carter .20 .09
❑ 151 Rondell White .20 .09
❑ 152 Chris Holt .10 .05
❑ 153 Shawn Green .20 .09
❑ 154 Mark Grudzielanek .20 .09
UER back rudzielanek
❑ 155 Jermaine Dye .10 .05
❑ 156 Ken Griffey Jr. FC 1.25 .55
❑ 157 Frank Thomas FC .75 .35
❑ 158 Chipper Jones FC .60 .25
❑ 159 Mike Piazza FC .75 .35
❑ 160 Cal Ripken FC 1.00 .45
❑ 161 Greg Maddux FC .75 .35
❑ 162 Juan Gonzalez FC .60 .25
❑ 163 Alex Rodriguez FC .75 .35
❑ 164 Mark McGwire FC 1.50 .70
❑ 165 Derek Jeter FC .60 .25
❑ 166 Larry Walker CL .20 .09
❑ 167 Tony Gwynn CL .60 .25
❑ 168 Tino Martinez CL .20 .09
❑ 169 Scott Rolen CL .60 .25
❑ 170 Nomar Garciaparra CL .75 .35
❑ 171 Mike Sweeney .10 .05
❑ 172 Dustin Hermanson .20 .09
❑ 173 Darren Dreifort .20 .09
❑ 174 Ron Gant .10 .05
❑ 175 Todd Hollandsworth .10 .05
❑ 176 John Jaha .10 .05
❑ 177 Kerry Wood 2.50 1.10
❑ 178 Chris Stynes .10 .05
❑ 179 Kevin Elster .10 .05
❑ 180 Derek Bell .20 .09
❑ 181 Darryl Strawberry .20 .09
❑ 182 Damion Easley .20 .09
❑ 183 Jeff Cirillo .20 .09
❑ 184 John Thomson .10 .05
❑ 185 Dan Wilson .10 .05
❑ 186 Jay Bell .20 .09
❑ 187 Bernard Gilkey .10 .05
❑ 188 Marc Valdes .10 .05
❑ 189 Ramon Martinez .20 .09
❑ 190 Charles Nagy .20 .09
❑ 191 Derek Lowe .10 .05
❑ 192 Andy Benes .20 .09
❑ 193 Delino DeShields .10 .05
❑ 194 Ryan Jackson .25 .11
❑ 195 Kenny Lofton .50 .23
❑ 196 Chuck Knoblauch .50 .23
❑ 197 Andres Galarraga .50 .23
❑ 198 Jose Canseco .50 .23
❑ 199 John Olerud .20 .09
❑ 200 Lance Johnson .10 .05
❑ 201 Darryl Kile .20 .09
❑ 202 Luis Castillo .20 .09
❑ 203 Joe Carter .20 .09
❑ 204 Dennis Eckersley .20 .09
❑ 205 Steve Finley .20 .09
❑ 206 Esteban Loaiza .10 .05
❑ 207 Ryan Christenson UER .25 .11
birthdate says 1988
❑ 208 Deivi Cruz .10 .05
❑ 209 Mariano Rivera .20 .09
❑ 210 Mike Judd .30 .14
❑ 211 Billy Wagner .20 .09
❑ 212 Scott Spiezio .10 .05
❑ 213 Russ Davis .20 .09
❑ 214 Jeff Suppan .10 .05
❑ 215 Doug Glanville .20 .09
❑ 216 Dmitri Young .20 .09
❑ 217 Rey Ordonez .20 .09
❑ 218 Cecil Fielder .20 .09
❑ 219 Masato Yoshii .40 .18
❑ 220 Raul Casanova .10 .05
❑ 221 Rolando Arrojo .75 .35
❑ 222 Ellis Burks .20 .09
❑ 223 Butch Huskey .10 .05
❑ 224 Brian Hunter .20 .09
❑ 225 Marquis Grissom .20 .09
❑ 226 Kevin Brown .30 .14
❑ 227 Joe Randa .10 .05
❑ 228 Henry Rodriguez .20 .09
❑ 229 Omar Vizquel .20 .09
❑ 230 Fred McGriff .30 .14
❑ 231 Matt Williams .20 .09
❑ 232 Moises Alou .30 .14
❑ 233 Travis Fryman .20 .09
❑ 234 Wade Boggs .50 .23
❑ 235 Pedro Martinez .50 .23
❑ 236 Rickey Henderson .50 .23
❑ 237 Bubba Trammell .20 .09
❑ 238 Mike Caruso .20 .09
❑ 239 Wilson Alvarez .20 .09
❑ 240 Geronimo Berroa .10 .05
❑ 241 Eric Milton .20 .09
❑ 242 Scott Erickson .20 .09
❑ 243 Todd Erdos .20 .09
❑ 244 Bobby Hughes .10 .05
❑ 245 Dave Hollins .10 .05
❑ 246 Dean Palmer .20 .09
❑ 247 Carlos Baerga .20 .09
❑ 248 Jose Silva .10 .05
❑ 249 Jose Cabrera .10 .05
❑ 250 Tom Evans .20 .09
❑ 251 Marty Cordova .10 .05
❑ 252 Hanley Frias .25 .11
❑ 253 Javier Valentin .20 .09
❑ 254 Mario Valdez .20 .09
❑ 255 Joey Cora .20 .09
❑ 256 Mike Lansing .10 .05
❑ 257 Jeff Kent .20 .09
❑ 258 Dave Dellucci .60 .25
❑ 259 Curtis King .10 .05
❑ 260 David Segui .20 .09
❑ 261 Royce Clayton .10 .05
❑ 262 Jeff Blauser .10 .05
❑ 263 Manny Aybar .25 .11
❑ 264 Mike Cather .10 .05
❑ 265 Todd Zeile .20 .09
❑ 266 Richard Hidalgo .20 .09
❑ 267 Dante Powell .20 .09
❑ 268 Mike DeJean .10 .05
❑ 269 Ken Cloude .20 .09
❑ 270 Danny Klassen .20 .09
❑ 271 Sean Casey .20 .09
❑ 272 A.J. Hinch .20 .09
❑ 273 Rich Butler .30 .14
❑ 274 Ben Ford .25 .11
❑ 275 Billy McMillon .10 .05
❑ 276 Wilson Delgado .20 .09
❑ 277 Orlando Cabrera .20 .09
❑ 278 Geoff Jenkins .20 .09
❑ 279 Enrique Wilson .20 .09
❑ 280 Derrek Lee .20 .09
❑ 281 Marc Pisciotta .10 .05
❑ 282 Abraham Nunez .20 .09
❑ 283 Aaron Boone .10 .05
❑ 284 Brad Fullmer .20 .09
❑ 285 Rob Stanifer .10 .05
❑ 286 Preston Wilson .20 .09
❑ 287 Greg Norton .10 .05
❑ 288 Bobby Smith .20 .09
❑ 289 Josh Booty .10 .05
❑ 290 Russell Branyan .20 .09
❑ 291 Jeremi Gonzalez .20 .09
❑ 292 Michael Coleman .20 .09
❑ 293 Cliff Politte .20 .09
❑ 294 Eric Ludwick .10 .05
❑ 295 Rafael Medina .20 .09
❑ 296 Jason Varitek .10 .05
❑ 297 Ron Wright .20 .09
❑ 298 Mark Kotsay .30 .14
❑ 299 David Ortiz .20 .09
❑ 300 Frank Catalanotto .25 .11
❑ 301 Robinson Checo .20 .09
❑ 302 Kevin Millwood 1.25 .55
❑ 303 Jacob Cruz .10 .05
❑ 304 Javier Vazquez .20 .09
❑ 305 Magglio Ordonez .60 .25
❑ 306 Kevin Witt .20 .09
❑ 307 Derrick Gibson .20 .09
❑ 308 Shane Monahan .20 .09
❑ 309 Brian Rose .20 .09
❑ 310 Bobby Estalella .20 .09
❑ 311 Felix Heredia .10 .05
❑ 312 Desi Relaford .10 .05
❑ 313 Esteban Yan .40 .18
❑ 314 Ricky Ledee .20 .09
❑ 315 Steve Woodard .20 .09
❑ 316 Pat Watkins .10 .05
❑ 317 Damian Moss .10 .05
❑ 318 Bob Abreu .20 .09
❑ 319 Jeff Abbott .20 .09
❑ 320 Miguel Cairo .20 .09
❑ 321 Rigo Beltran .10 .05
❑ 322 Tony Saunders .10 .05
❑ 323 Randall Simon .20 .09
❑ 324 Hiram Bocachica .20 .09
❑ 325 Richie Sexson .30 .14
❑ 326 Karim Garcia .20 .09
❑ 327 Mike Lowell .50 .23
❑ 328 Pat Cline .20 .09
❑ 329 Matt Clement .20 .09
❑ 330 Scott Elarton .20 .09
❑ 331 Manuel Barrios .25 .11
❑ 332 Bruce Chen .20 .09
❑ 333 Juan Encarnacion .20 .09
❑ 334 Travis Lee 1.00 .45
❑ 335 Wes Helms .20 .09
❑ 336 Chad Fox .10 .05
❑ 337 Donnie Sadler .20 .09
❑ 338 Carlos Mendoza .25 .11
❑ 339 Damian Jackson .10 .05
❑ 340 Julio Ramirez .60 .25
❑ 341 John Halama .10 .05
❑ 342 Edwin Diaz .10 .05
❑ 343 Felix Martinez .10 .05
❑ 344 Eli Marrero .20 .09
❑ 345 Carl Pavano .20 .09
❑ 346 Vladimir Guerrero HL .50 .23
❑ 347 Barry Bonds HL .30 .14

	MINT	NRMT
❑ 348 Darin Erstad HL	.30	.14
❑ 349 Albert Belle HL	.20	.09
❑ 350 Kenny Lofton HL	.20	.09
❑ 351 Mo Vaughn HL	.30	.14
❑ 352 Jose Cruz Jr. HL	.30	.14
❑ 353 Tony Clark HL	.10	.05
❑ 354 Roberto Alomar HL	.20	.09
❑ 355 Manny Ramirez HL	.20	.09
❑ 356 Paul Molitor HL	.20	.09
❑ 357 Jim Thome HL	.20	.09
❑ 358 Tino Martinez HL	.20	.09
❑ 359 Tim Salmon HL	.20	.09
❑ 360 David Justice HL	.20	.09
❑ 361 Raul Mondesi HL	.10	.05
❑ 362 Mark Grace HL	.10	.05
❑ 363 Craig Biggio HL	.20	.09
❑ 364 Larry Walker HL	.20	.09
❑ 365 Mark McGwire HL	1.50	.70
❑ 366 Juan Gonzalez HL	.60	.25
❑ 367 Derek Jeter HL	.60	.25
❑ 368 Chipper Jones HL	.60	.25
❑ 369 Frank Thomas HL	.75	.35
❑ 370 Alex Rodriguez HL	.75	.35
❑ 371 Mike Piazza HL	.75	.35
❑ 372 Tony Gwynn HL	.60	.25
❑ 373 Jeff Bagwell HL	.50	.23
❑ 374 Nomar Garciaparra HL	.75	.35
❑ 375 Ken Griffey Jr. HL	1.25	.55
❑ 376 Livan Hernandez UN	.10	.05
❑ 377 Chan Ho Park UN	.20	.09
❑ 378 Mike Mussina UN	.20	.09
❑ 379 Andy Pettitte UN	.10	.05
❑ 380 Greg Maddux UN	.75	.35
❑ 381 Hideo Nomo UN	.50	.23
❑ 382 Roger Clemens UN	.50	.23
❑ 383 Randy Johnson UN	.20	.09
❑ 384 Pedro Martinez UN	.20	.09
❑ 385 Jaret Wright UN	.30	.14
❑ 386 Ken Griffey Jr. SG	1.25	.55
❑ 387 Todd Helton SG	.30	.14
❑ 388 Paul Konerko SG	.20	.09
❑ 389 Cal Ripken SG	1.00	.45
❑ 390 Larry Walker SG	.20	.09
❑ 391 Ken Caminiti SG	.10	.05
❑ 392 Jose Guillen SG	.10	.05
❑ 393 Jim Edmonds SG	.10	.05
❑ 394 Barry Larkin SG	.10	.05
❑ 395 Bernie Williams SG	.20	.09
❑ 396 Tony Clark SG	.10	.05
❑ 397 Jose Cruz Jr. SG	.30	.14
❑ 398 Ivan Rodriguez SG	.30	.14
❑ 399 Darin Erstad SG	.30	.14
❑ 400 Scott Rolen SG	.50	.23
❑ 401 Mark McGwire SG	1.50	.70
❑ 402 Andruw Jones SG	.30	.14
❑ 403 Juan Gonzalez SG	.60	.25
❑ 404 Derek Jeter SG	.60	.25
❑ 405 Chipper Jones SG	.60	.25
❑ 406 Greg Maddux SG	.75	.35
❑ 407 Frank Thomas SG	.75	.35
❑ 408 Alex Rodriguez SG	.75	.35
❑ 409 Mike Piazza SG	.75	.35
❑ 410 Tony Gwynn SG	.60	.25
❑ 411 Jeff Bagwell SG	.50	.23
❑ 412 Nomar Garciaparra SG	.75	.35
❑ 413 Hideo Nomo SG	.50	.23
❑ 414 Barry Bonds SG	.30	.14
❑ 415 Ben Grieve SG	.50	.23
❑ 416 Barry Bonds CL	.30	.14
❑ 417 Mark McGwire CL	1.50	.70
❑ 418 Roger Clemens CL	.50	.23
❑ 419 Livan Hernandez CL	.10	.05
❑ 420 Ken Griffey Jr. CL	1.25	.55

1998 Donruss Crusade Green

	MINT	NRMT
COMMON CARD (1-100)	8.00	3.60

*PURPLE STARS: .6X TO 1.5X GREEN CRUSADE
*RED STARS: 2X TO 4X GREEN CRUSADE
PURPLE PRINT RUN 100 SERIAL #'d SETS
RED PRINT RUN 25 SERIAL #'d SETS

	MINT	NRMT
❑ 1 Tim Salmon U	25.00	11.00
❑ 2 Garret Anderson U	15.00	6.75
❑ 3 Jim Edmonds CTA L	20.00	9.00
❑ 4 Darin Erstad CTA L	30.00	13.50
❑ 5 Jason Dickson D	15.00	6.75
❑ 6 Todd Greene D	15.00	6.75
❑ 7 Roberto Alomar CTA	30.00	13.50
❑ 8 Cal Ripken D	120.00	55.00
❑ 9 Rafael Palmeiro CTA U	20.00	9.00
❑ 10 Brady Anderson U	15.00	6.75
❑ 11 Mike Mussina L	30.00	13.50
❑ 12 Mo Vaughn CTA	40.00	18.00
❑ 13 Nomar Garciaparra D	100.00	45.00
❑ 14 Frank Thomas CTA U	100.00	45.00
❑ 15 Albert Belle CTA L	30.00	13.50
❑ 16 Mike Cameron D	15.00	6.75
❑ 17 Robin Ventura U	15.00	6.75
❑ 18 Manny Ramirez L	30.00	13.50
❑ 19 Jim Thome CTA L	30.00	13.50
❑ 20 Sandy Alomar Jr. D	15.00	6.75
❑ 21 David Justice D	25.00	11.00
❑ 22 Matt Williams U	15.00	6.75
❑ 23 Tony Clark U	20.00	9.00
❑ 24 Bubba Trammell L	15.00	6.75
❑ 25 Justin Thompson D	15.00	6.75
❑ 26 Bobby Higginson L	20.00	9.00
❑ 27 Kevin Appier D	15.00	6.75
❑ 28 Paul Molitor L	30.00	13.50
❑ 29 Chuck Knoblauch CTA U	25.00	11.00
❑ 30 Todd Walker L	20.00	9.00
❑ 31 Bernie Williams U	30.00	13.50
❑ 32 Derek Jeter CTA U	80.00	36.00
❑ 33 Tino Martinez D	25.00	11.00
❑ 34 Andy Pettitte L	20.00	9.00
❑ 35 Wade Boggs CTA L	30.00	13.50
❑ 36 Hideki Irabu D	20.00	9.00
❑ 37 Jose Canseco D	30.00	13.50
❑ 38 Jason Giambi U	15.00	6.75
❑ 39 Ken Griffey Jr. D	150.00	70.00
❑ 40 Alex Rodriguez CTA L	100.00	45.00
❑ 41 Randy Johnson L	30.00	13.50
❑ 42 Edgar Martinez D	15.00	6.75
❑ 43 Jay Buhner CTA U	15.00	6.75
❑ 44 Juan Gonzalez CTA U	80.00	36.00
❑ 45 Will Clark D	25.00	11.00
❑ 46 Ivan Rodriguez L	40.00	18.00
❑ 47 Rusty Greer D	15.00	6.75
❑ 48 Roger Clemens L	60.00	27.00
❑ 49 Carlos Delgado U	15.00	6.75
❑ 50 Shawn Green D	15.00	6.75
❑ 51 Jose Cruz Jr. D	30.00	13.50
❑ 52 Kenny Lofton D	25.00	11.00
❑ 53 Chipper Jones D	80.00	36.00
❑ 54 Andruw Jones CTA L	30.00	13.50
❑ 55 Greg Maddux U	100.00	45.00
❑ 56 John Smoltz CTA L	15.00	6.75
❑ 57 Tom Glavine U	25.00	11.00
❑ 58 Javier Lopez L	15.00	6.75
❑ 59 Fred McGriff L	20.00	9.00
❑ 60 Mark Grace U	20.00	9.00
❑ 61 Sammy Sosa CTA U	80.00	36.00
❑ 62 Kevin Orie D	8.00	3.60
❑ 63 Barry Larkin CTA U	20.00	9.00
❑ 64 Pokey Reese L	8.00	3.60
❑ 65 Deion Sanders D	15.00	6.75
❑ 66 Andres Galarraga L	25.00	11.00
❑ 67 Larry Walker D	30.00	13.50
❑ 68 Dante Bichette CTA D	15.00	6.75
❑ 69 Neifi Perez U	15.00	6.75
❑ 70 Eric Young L	15.00	6.75
❑ 71 Todd Helton D	30.00	13.50
❑ 72 Gary Sheffield CTA U	20.00	9.00
❑ 73 Moises Alou L	20.00	9.00
❑ 74 Bobby Bonilla D	15.00	6.75
❑ 75 Kevin Brown D	20.00	9.00
❑ 76 Ben Grieve L	50.00	22.00
❑ 77 Jeff Bagwell CTA U	50.00	22.00
❑ 78 Craig Biggio D	25.00	11.00
❑ 79 Mike Piazza L	100.00	45.00
❑ 80 Raul Mondesi U	20.00	9.00
❑ 81 Hideo Nomo CTA U	50.00	22.00
❑ 82 Wilton Guerrero D	8.00	3.60
❑ 83 Rondell White CTA U	15.00	6.75
❑ 84 Vladimir Guerrero CTA U	40.00	18.00
❑ 85 Pedro Martinez D	30.00	13.50
❑ 86 Edgardo Alfonzo D	15.00	6.75
❑ 87 Todd Hundley CTA U	15.00	6.75
❑ 88 Scott Rolen D	60.00	27.00
❑ 89 Francisco Cordova D	8.00	3.60
❑ 90 Jose Guillen D	15.00	6.75
❑ 91 Jason Kendall L	15.00	6.75
❑ 92 Ray Lankford D	15.00	6.75
❑ 93 Mark McGwire CTA D	200.00	90.00
❑ 94 Matt Morris D	15.00	6.75
❑ 95 Alan Benes L	15.00	6.75
❑ 96 Brian Jordan CTA U	15.00	6.75
❑ 97 Tony Gwynn L	80.00	36.00
❑ 98 Ken Caminiti CTA L	20.00	9.00
❑ 99 Barry Bonds CTA U	40.00	18.00
❑ 100 Shawn Estes D	15.00	6.75

1998 Donruss Diamond Kings

	MINT	NRMT
COMPLETE SET (20)	250.00	110.00
COMMON CARD (1-20)	5.00	2.20
COMP.CANVAS SET (20)	800.00	350.00

*CANVAS: 1.25X TO 3X BASIC DIAM.KINGS
CANVAS: RANDOM INSERTS IN PACKS
CANVAS PRINT RUN 500 SERIAL #'d SETS

	MINT	NRMT
❑ 1 Cal Ripken	30.00	13.50
❑ 2 Greg Maddux	25.00	11.00
❑ 3 Ivan Rodriguez	10.00	4.50
❑ 4 Tony Gwynn	20.00	9.00
❑ 5 Paul Molitor	8.00	3.60
❑ 6 Kenny Lofton	8.00	3.60
❑ 7 Andy Pettitte	5.00	2.20
❑ 8 Darin Erstad	8.00	3.60
❑ 9 Randy Johnson	8.00	3.60
❑ 10 Derek Jeter	20.00	9.00
❑ 11 Hideo Nomo	10.00	4.50
❑ 12 David Justice	8.00	3.60
❑ 13 Bernie Williams	8.00	3.60
❑ 14 Roger Clemens	15.00	6.75
❑ 15 Barry Larkin	5.00	2.20
❑ 16 Andruw Jones	8.00	3.60
❑ 17 Mike Piazza	25.00	11.00
❑ 18 Frank Thomas	25.00	11.00
❑ 19 Alex Rodriguez	25.00	11.00
❑ 20 Ken Griffey Jr.	40.00	18.00
❑ S20 Frank Thomas Sample	3.00	1.35

1998 Donruss Dominators

	MINT	NRMT
COMPLETE SET (30)	150.00	70.00
COMMON CARD (1-30)	2.00	.90
❑ 1 Roger Clemens	6.00	2.70
❑ 2 Tony Clark	2.00	.90
❑ 3 Darin Erstad	3.00	1.35
❑ 4 Jeff Bagwell	5.00	2.20
❑ 5 Ken Griffey Jr	15.00	6.75
❑ 6 Andruw Jones	3.00	1.35
❑ 7 Juan Gonzalez	8.00	3.60
❑ 8 Ivan Rodriguez	4.00	1.80
❑ 9 Randy Johnson	3.00	1.35
❑ 10 Tino Martinez	3.00	1.35
❑ 11 Mark McGwire	20.00	9.00
❑ 12 Chuck Knoblauch	3.00	1.35
❑ 13 Jim Thome	3.00	1.35
❑ 14 Alex Rodriguez	10.00	4.50
❑ 15 Hideo Nomo	4.00	1.80
❑ 16 Jose Cruz Jr.	3.00	1.35
❑ 17 Chipper Jones	8.00	3.60
❑ 18 Tony Gwynn	8.00	3.60
❑ 19 Barry Bonds	4.00	1.80
❑ 20 Mo Vaughn	4.00	1.80
❑ 21 Cal Ripken	12.00	5.50
❑ 22 Greg Maddux	10.00	4.50
❑ 23 Manny Ramirez	3.00	1.35
❑ 24 Andres Galarraga	3.00	1.35
❑ 25 Vladimir Guerrero	4.00	1.80
❑ 26 Albert Belle	3.00	1.35
❑ 27 Nomar Garciaparra	10.00	4.50
❑ 28 Kenny Lofton	3.00	1.35
❑ 29 Mike Piazza	10.00	4.50
❑ 30 Frank Thomas	10.00	4.50

1998 Donruss Elite Inserts

	MINT	NRMT
COMPLETE SET (20)	400.00	180.00
COMMON CARD (1-20)	10.00	4.50
❑ 1 Jeff Bagwell	15.00	6.75
❑ 2 Andruw Jones	10.00	4.50
❑ 3 Ken Griffey Jr.	50.00	22.00
❑ 4 Derek Jeter	25.00	11.00
❑ 5 Juan Gonzalez	25.00	11.00
❑ 6 Mark McGwire	60.00	27.00
❑ 7 Ivan Rodriguez	12.00	5.50
❑ 8 Paul Molitor	10.00	4.50
❑ 9 Hideo Nomo	12.00	5.50
❑ 10 Mo Vaughn	12.00	5.50
❑ 11 Chipper Jones	25.00	11.00
❑ 12 Nomar Garciaparra	30.00	13.50
❑ 13 Mike Piazza	30.00	13.50
❑ 14 Frank Thomas	30.00	13.50
❑ 15 Greg Maddux	30.00	13.50
❑ 16 Cal Ripken	40.00	18.00
❑ 17 Alex Rodriguez	30.00	13.50
❑ 18 Jose Cruz Jr.	10.00	4.50
❑ 19 Barry Bonds	12.00	5.50
❑ 20 Tony Gwynn	25.00	11.00

1998 Donruss FANtasy Team

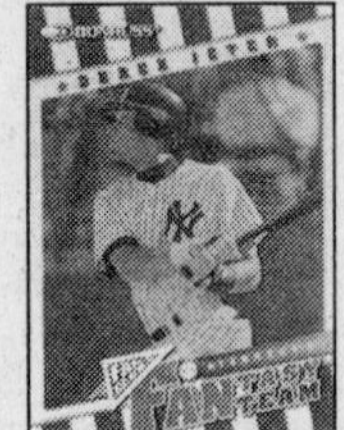

	MINT	NRMT
COMPLETE SET (20)	500.00	220.00
COMMON 1ST TEAM (1-10)	12.00	5.50
COMMON 2ND TEAM (11-20)	3.00	1.35
COMP.DIE CUT SET (20)	1500.00	700.00

*1ST TEAM DIE CUTS: 1.25X TO 3X BASIC FANT.TM
*2ND TEAM DIE CUTS: 2X TO 5X BASIC FANT.TM
DIE CUTS PRINT RUN 250 SERIAL #'d SETS
RANDOM INSERTS IN UPDATE PACKS

	MINT	NRMT
❑ 1 Frank Thomas	40.00	18.00
❑ 2 Ken Griffey Jr.	60.00	27.00
❑ 3 Cal Ripken	50.00	22.00
❑ 4 Jose Cruz Jr.	12.00	5.50
❑ 5 Travis Lee	20.00	9.00
❑ 6 Greg Maddux	40.00	18.00
❑ 7 Alex Rodriguez	40.00	18.00
❑ 8 Mark McGwire	80.00	36.00
❑ 9 Chipper Jones	30.00	13.50
❑ 10 Andruw Jones	12.00	5.50
❑ 11 Mike Piazza	25.00	11.00
❑ 12 Tony Gwynn	20.00	9.00
❑ 13 Larry Walker	8.00	3.60
❑ 14 Nomar Garciaparra	25.00	11.00
❑ 15 Jaret Wright	8.00	3.60
❑ 16 Livan Hernandez	3.00	1.35
❑ 17 Roger Clemens	15.00	6.75
❑ 18 Derek Jeter	20.00	9.00
❑ 19 Scott Rolen	15.00	6.75
❑ 20 Jeff Bagwell	12.00	5.50

1998 Donruss Longball Leaders

	MINT	NRMT
COMPLETE SET (24)	150.00	70.00
COMMON CARD (1-24)	2.50	1.10
❑ 1 Ken Griffey Jr.	25.00	11.00
❑ 2 Mark McGwire	30.00	13.50
❑ 3 Tino Martinez	5.00	2.20
❑ 4 Barry Bonds	6.00	2.70
❑ 5 Frank Thomas	15.00	6.75
❑ 6 Albert Belle	5.00	2.20
❑ 7 Mike Piazza	15.00	6.75

	MINT	NRMT
❑ 8 Chipper Jones	12.00	5.50
❑ 9 Vladimir Guerrero	6.00	2.70
❑ 10 Matt Williams	2.50	1.10
❑ 11 Sammy Sosa	12.00	5.50
❑ 12 Tim Salmon	5.00	2.20
❑ 13 Raul Mondesi	3.00	1.35
❑ 14 Jeff Bagwell	8.00	3.60
❑ 15 Mo Vaughn	6.00	2.70
❑ 16 Manny Ramirez	5.00	2.20
❑ 17 Jim Thome	5.00	2.20
❑ 18 Jim Edmonds	3.00	1.35
❑ 19 Tony Clark	3.00	1.35
❑ 20 Nomar Garciaparra	15.00	6.75
❑ 21 Juan Gonzalez	12.00	5.50
❑ 22 Scott Rolen	10.00	4.50
❑ 23 Larry Walker	5.00	2.20
❑ 24 Andres Galarraga	5.00	2.20

1998 Donruss MLB 99

	MINT	NRMT
COMPLETE SET (20)	10.00	4.50
COMMON CARD (1-20)	.25	.11
❑ 1 Cal Ripken	2.00	.90
❑ 2 Nomar Garciaparra	1.50	.70
❑ 3 Barry Bonds	.60	.25
❑ 4 Mike Mussina	.50	.23
❑ 5 Pedro Martinez	.50	.23
❑ 6 Derek Jeter	1.25	.55
❑ 7 Andruw Jones	.60	.25
❑ 8 Kenny Lofton	.50	.23
❑ 9 Gary Sheffield	.40	.18
❑ 10 Raul Mondesi	.40	.18
❑ 11 Jeff Bagwell	.75	.35
❑ 12 Tim Salmon	.50	.23
❑ 13 Tom Glavine	.50	.23
❑ 14 Ben Grieve	1.00	.45
❑ 15 Matt Williams	.25	.11
❑ 16 Juan Gonzalez	1.25	.55
❑ 17 Mark McGwire	3.00	1.35
❑ 18 Bernie Williams	.50	.23
❑ 19 Andres Galarraga	.50	.23
❑ 20 Jose Cruz Jr.	.60	.25

1998 Donruss Production Line On-Base

	MINT	NRMT
COMPLETE SET (20)	800.00	350.00
COMMON CARD (1-20)	15.00	6.75
❑ 1 Frank Thomas/456	100.00	45.00
❑ 2 Edgar Martinez/456	15.00	6.75
❑ 3 Roberto Alomar/390	30.00	13.50
❑ 4 Chuck Knoblauch/390	30.00	13.50
❑ 5 Mike Piazza/431	100.00	45.00
❑ 6 Barry Larkin/440	20.00	9.00
❑ 7 Kenny Lofton/409	30.00	13.50
❑ 8 Jeff Bagwell/425	50.00	22.00
❑ 9 Barry Bonds/446	40.00	18.00
❑ 10 Rusty Greer/405	15.00	6.75
❑ 11 Gary Sheffield/424	20.00	9.00
❑ 12 Mark McGwire/393	200.00	90.00
❑ 13 Chipper Jones/371	80.00	36.00
❑ 14 Tony Gwynn/409	80.00	36.00
❑ 15 Craig Biggio/415	30.00	13.50
❑ 16 Mo Vaughn/420	40.00	18.00
❑ 17 Bernie Williams/408	30.00	13.50
❑ 18 Ken Griffey Jr./382	150.00	70.00
❑ 19 Brady Anderson/393	15.00	6.75
❑ 20 Derek Jeter/370	80.00	36.00

1998 Donruss Production Line Power Index

	MINT	NRMT
COMPLETE SET (20)	500.00	220.00
COMMON CARD (1-20)	6.00	2.70
❑ 1 Frank Thomas/1067	50.00	22.00
❑ 2 Mark McGwire/1039	100.00	45.00
❑ 3 Barry Bonds/1031	20.00	9.00
❑ 4 Jeff Bagwell/1017	25.00	11.00
❑ 5 Ken Griffey Jr./1028	80.00	36.00
❑ 6 Alex Rodriguez/846	50.00	22.00
❑ 7 Chipper Jones/850	40.00	18.00
❑ 8 Mike Piazza/1070	50.00	22.00
❑ 9 Mo Vaughn/980	20.00	9.00
❑ 10 Brady Anderson/863	6.00	2.70
❑ 11 Manny Ramirez/953	15.00	6.75
❑ 12 Albert Belle/823	15.00	6.75
❑ 13 Jim Thome/1001	15.00	6.75
❑ 14 Bernie Williams/952	15.00	6.75
❑ 15 Scott Rolen/846	30.00	13.50
❑ 16 Vladimir Guerrero/833	20.00	9.00
❑ 17 Larry Walker/1172	15.00	6.75
❑ 18 David Justice/1013	15.00	6.75
❑ 19 Tino Martinez/948	15.00	6.75
❑ 20 Tony Gwynn/957	40.00	18.00

1998 Donruss Production Line Slugging

	MINT	NRMT
COMPLETE SET (20)	800.00	350.00
COMMON CARD (1-20)	15.00	6.75
❑ 1 Mark McGwire/646	150.00	70.00
❑ 2 Ken Griffey Jr./646	120.00	55.00
❑ 3 Andres Galarraga/585	25.00	11.00
❑ 4 Barry Bonds/585	30.00	13.50
❑ 5 Juan Gonzalez/589	60.00	27.00
❑ 6 Mike Piazza/638	80.00	36.00
❑ 7 Jeff Bagwell/592	40.00	18.00
❑ 8 Manny Ramirez/538	25.00	11.00
❑ 9 Jim Thome/579	25.00	11.00
❑ 10 Mo Vaughn/560	30.00	13.50
❑ 11 Larry Walker/720	25.00	11.00
❑ 12 Tino Martinez/577	25.00	11.00
❑ 13 Frank Thomas/611	80.00	36.00
❑ 14 Tim Salmon/517	25.00	11.00
❑ 15 Raul Mondesi/541	15.00	6.75
❑ 16 Alex Rodriguez/496	80.00	36.00
❑ 17 Nomar Garciaparra/534	80.00	36.00
❑ 18 Jose Cruz Jr./499	25.00	11.00
❑ 19 Tony Clark/500	15.00	6.75
❑ 20 Cal Ripken/402	100.00	45.00

1998 Donruss Rated Rookies

	MINT	NRMT
COMPLETE SET (30)	60.00	27.00
COMMON CARD (1-30)	1.00	.45
COMP.MEDALIST SET (30)	600.00	275.00

*MEDALISTS: 4X TO 10X BASIC CARDS
MEDALIST PRINT RUN 250 SETS
RANDOM INSERTS IN PACKS

❑ 1 Mark Kotsay	2.50	1.10
❑ 2 Neifi Perez	1.50	.70
❑ 3 Paul Konerko	4.00	1.80
❑ 4 Jose Cruz Jr.	5.00	2.20
❑ 5 Hideki Irabu	2.50	1.10
❑ 6 Mike Cameron	1.50	.70
❑ 7 Jeff Suppan	1.00	.45
❑ 8 Kevin Orie	1.00	.45
❑ 9 Pokey Reese	1.00	.45
❑ 10 Todd Dunwoody	1.50	.70
❑ 11 Miguel Tejada	1.50	.70
❑ 12 Jose Guillen	1.50	.70
❑ 13 Bartolo Colon	1.50	.70
❑ 14 Derrek Lee	1.50	.70
❑ 15 Antone Williamson	1.00	.45
❑ 16 Wilton Guerrero	1.00	.45
❑ 17 Jaret Wright	5.00	2.20
❑ 18 Todd Helton	5.00	2.20
❑ 19 Shannon Stewart	1.50	.70
❑ 20 Nomar Garciaparra	12.00	5.50
❑ 21 Brett Tomko	1.50	.70
❑ 22 Fernando Tatis	1.50	.70
❑ 23 Raul Ibanez	1.00	.45
❑ 24 Dennis Reyes	1.50	.70
❑ 25 Bobby Estalella	1.50	.70
❑ 26 Lou Collier	1.00	.45
❑ 27 Bubba Trammell	1.50	.70
❑ 28 Ben Grieve	8.00	3.60
❑ 29 Ivan Cruz	1.00	.45
❑ 30 Karim Garcia	1.50	.70

1998 Donruss Rookie Diamond Kings

	MINT	NRMT
COMPLETE SET (12)	80.00	36.00
COMMON CARD (1-12)	1.50	.70

*CANVAS: 1.25X TO 3X BASIC ROOKIE DK'S
CANVAS PRINT RUN 500 SERIAL #'d SETS
RANDOM INSERTS IN UPDATE PACKS

❑ 1 Travis Lee	12.00	5.50
❑ 2 Fernando Tatis	2.50	1.10
❑ 3 Livan Hernandez	2.50	1.10
❑ 4 Todd Helton	8.00	3.60
❑ 5 Derrek Lee	2.50	1.10
❑ 6 Jaret Wright	8.00	3.60
❑ 7 Ben Grieve	12.00	5.50
❑ 8 Paul Konerko	5.00	2.20
❑ 9 Jose Cruz Jr.	8.00	3.60
❑ 10 Mark Kotsay	4.00	1.80
❑ 11 Todd Greene	1.50	.70
❑ 12 Brad Fullmer	2.50	1.10

1998 Donruss Signature Series Previews

	MINT	NRMT
COMMON CARD	30.00	13.50
❑ 1 Sandy Alomar Jr./96	50.00	22.00
❑ 2 Andy Benes/135	40.00	18.00
❑ 3 Russell Branyan/188	40.00	18.00
❑ 4 Tony Clark/188	60.00	27.00

❑ 5	Juan Encarnacion/193	40.00	18.00
❑ 6	Brad Fullmer/396	30.00	13.50
❑ 7	Juan Gonzalez/108	300.00	135.00
❑ 8	Ben Grieve/100	150.00	70.00
❑ 9	Todd Helton/101	100.00	45.00
❑ 10	Richard Hidalgo/380	30.00	13.50
❑ 11	A.J. Hinch/400	30.00	13.50
❑ 12	Damian Jackson/15	120.00	55.00
❑ 13	Chipper Jones/112	300.00	135.00
❑ 14	Chuck Knoblauch/98	100.00	45.00
❑ 15	Travis Lee/101	200.00	90.00
❑ 16	Mike Lowell/450	30.00	13.50
❑ 17	Greg Maddux/92	400.00	180.00
❑ 18	Kevin Millwood/395	80.00	36.00
❑ 19	Maggio Ordonez/420	40.00	18.00
❑ 20	David Ortiz/393	30.00	13.50
❑ 21	Rafael Palmeiro/107	80.00	36.00
❑ 22	Cal Ripken/22	1200.00	550.00
❑ 23	Alex Rodriguez/23	1000.00	450.00
❑ 24	Curt Schilling/100	80.00	36.00
❑ 25	Randall Simon/380	30.00	13.50
❑ 26	Fernando Tatis/400	30.00	13.50
❑ 27	Miguel Tejada/375	30.00	13.50
❑ 28	Robin Ventura/95	60.00	27.00
❑ 29	Kerry Wood/373	150.00	70.00

1998 Donruss Collections Donruss

	MINT	NRMT
COMPLETE SET (200)	120.00	55.00
COMMON (1-170/176-205)	.30	.14

❑ 1	Paul Molitor	1.25	.55
❑ 2	Juan Gonzalez	3.00	1.35
❑ 3	Darryl Kile	.50	.23
❑ 4	Randy Johnson	1.25	.55
❑ 5	Tom Glavine	1.25	.55
❑ 6	Pat Hentgen	.50	.23
❑ 7	David Justice	1.25	.55
❑ 8	Kevin Brown	.75	.35
❑ 9	Mike Mussina	1.25	.55
❑ 10	Ken Caminiti	.75	.35
❑ 11	Todd Hundley	.50	.23
❑ 12	Frank Thomas	4.00	1.80
❑ 13	Ray Lankford	.50	.23
❑ 14	Justin Thompson	.50	.23
❑ 15	Jason Dickson	.50	.23
❑ 16	Kenny Lofton	1.25	.55
❑ 17	Ivan Rodriguez	1.50	.70
❑ 18	Pedro Martinez	1.25	.55
❑ 19	Brady Anderson	.50	.23
❑ 20	Barry Larkin	.75	.35
❑ 21	Chipper Jones	3.00	1.35
❑ 22	Tony Gwynn	3.00	1.35
❑ 23	Roger Clemens	2.50	1.10
❑ 24	Sandy Alomar Jr.	.50	.23
❑ 25	Tino Martinez	1.25	.55
❑ 26	Jeff Bagwell	2.00	.90
❑ 27	Shawn Estes	.50	.23
❑ 28	Ken Griffey Jr.	6.00	2.70
❑ 29	Javier Lopez	.50	.23
❑ 30	Denny Neagle	.50	.23
❑ 31	Mike Piazza	4.00	1.80
❑ 32	Andres Galarraga	1.25	.55
❑ 33	Larry Walker	1.25	.55
❑ 34	Alex Rodriguez	4.00	1.80
❑ 35	Greg Maddux	4.00	1.80
❑ 36	Albert Belle	1.25	.55
❑ 37	Barry Bonds	1.50	.70
❑ 38	Mo Vaughn	1.50	.70
❑ 39	Kevin Appier	.50	.23
❑ 40	Wade Boggs	1.25	.55
❑ 41	Garret Anderson	.50	.23
❑ 42	Jeffrey Hammonds	.50	.23
❑ 43	Marquis Grissom	.50	.23
❑ 44	Jim Edmonds	.75	.35
❑ 45	Brian Jordan	.50	.23
❑ 46	Raul Mondesi	.75	.35
❑ 47	John Valentin	.50	.23
❑ 48	Brad Radke	.50	.23
❑ 49	Ismael Valdes	.50	.23
❑ 50	Matt Stairs	.50	.23
❑ 51	Matt Williams	.50	.23
❑ 52	Reggie Jefferson	.30	.14
❑ 53	Alan Benes	.50	.23
❑ 54	Charles Johnson	.50	.23
❑ 55	Chuck Knoblauch	1.25	.55
❑ 56	Edgar Martinez	.50	.23
❑ 57	Nomar Garciaparra	4.00	1.80
❑ 58	Craig Biggio	1.25	.55
❑ 59	Bernie Williams	1.25	.55
❑ 60	David Cone	.75	.35
❑ 61	Cal Ripken	5.00	2.20
❑ 62	Mark McGwire	8.00	3.60
❑ 63	Roberto Alomar	1.25	.55
❑ 64	Fred McGriff	.75	.35
❑ 65	Eric Karros	.50	.23
❑ 66	Robin Ventura	.50	.23
❑ 67	Darin Erstad	1.50	.70
❑ 68	Michael Tucker	.50	.23
❑ 69	Jim Thome	1.25	.55
❑ 70	Mark Grace	.75	.35
❑ 71	Lou Collier	.30	.14
❑ 72	Karim Garcia	.50	.23
❑ 73	Alex Fernandez	.30	.14
❑ 74	J.T. Snow	.50	.23
❑ 75	Reggie Sanders	.50	.23
❑ 76	John Smoltz	.50	.23
❑ 77	Tim Salmon	1.25	.55
❑ 78	Paul O'Neill	.50	.23
❑ 79	Vinny Castilla	.75	.35
❑ 80	Rafael Palmeiro	.75	.35
❑ 81	Jaret Wright	1.50	.70
❑ 82	Jay Buhner	.50	.23
❑ 83	Brett Butler	.50	.23
❑ 84	Todd Greene	.50	.23
❑ 85	Scott Rolen	3.00	1.35
❑ 86	Sammy Sosa	3.00	1.35
❑ 87	Jason Giambi	.50	.23
❑ 88	Carlos Delgado	.50	.23
❑ 89	Deion Sanders	.50	.23
❑ 90	Wilton Guerrero	.30	.14
❑ 91	Andy Pettitte	.75	.35
❑ 92	Brian Giles	.50	.23
❑ 93	Dmitri Young	.50	.23
❑ 94	Ron Coomer	.30	.14
❑ 95	Mike Cameron	.50	.23
❑ 96	Edgardo Alfonzo	.50	.23
❑ 97	Jimmy Key	.50	.23
❑ 98	Ryan Klesko	.50	.23
❑ 99	Andy Benes	.50	.23
❑ 100	Derek Jeter	3.00	1.35
❑ 101	Jeff Fassero	.30	.14
❑ 102	Neifi Perez	.50	.23
❑ 103	Hideo Nomo	1.50	.70
❑ 104	Andruw Jones	1.50	.70
❑ 105	Todd Helton	1.50	.70
❑ 106	Livan Hernandez	.50	.23
❑ 107	Brett Tomko	.50	.23
❑ 108	Shannon Stewart	.50	.23
❑ 109	Bartolo Colon	.50	.23
❑ 110	Matt Morris	.50	.23
❑ 111	Miguel Tejada	.50	.23
❑ 112	Pokey Reese	.30	.14
❑ 113	Fernando Tatis	.50	.23
❑ 114	Todd Dunwoody	.50	.23
❑ 115	Jose Cruz Jr.	1.50	.70
❑ 116	Chan Ho Park	1.25	.55
❑ 117	Kevin Young	.50	.23
❑ 118	Rickey Henderson	1.25	.55
❑ 119	Hideki Irabu	.75	.35
❑ 120	Francisco Cordova	.30	.14
❑ 121	Al Martin	.30	.14
❑ 122	Tony Clark	.75	.35
❑ 123	Curt Schilling	.50	.23
❑ 124	Rusty Greer	.50	.23
❑ 125	Jose Canseco	1.25	.55
❑ 126	Edgar Renteria	.50	.23
❑ 127	Todd Walker	.75	.35
❑ 128	Wally Joyner	.50	.23
❑ 129	Bill Mueller	.50	.23
❑ 130	Jose Guillen	.50	.23
❑ 131	Manny Ramirez	1.25	.55
❑ 132	Bobby Higginson	.75	.35
❑ 133	Kevin Orie	.30	.14
❑ 134	Will Clark	1.25	.55
❑ 135	Dave Nilsson	.30	.14
❑ 136	Jason Kendall	.50	.23
❑ 137	Ivan Cruz	.30	.14
❑ 138	Gary Sheffield	.75	.35
❑ 139	Bubba Trammell	.50	.23
❑ 140	Vladimir Guerrero	2.00	.90
❑ 141	Dennis Reyes	.50	.23
❑ 142	Bobby Bonilla	.50	.23
❑ 143	Ruben Rivera	.50	.23
❑ 144	Ben Grieve	2.50	1.10
❑ 145	Moises Alou	.75	.35
❑ 146	Tony Womack	.50	.23
❑ 147	Eric Young	.50	.23
❑ 148	Paul Konerko	1.25	.55
❑ 149	Dante Bichette	.50	.23
❑ 150	Joe Carter	.50	.23
❑ 151	Rondell White	.50	.23
❑ 152	Chris Holt	.30	.14
❑ 153	Shawn Green	.50	.23
❑ 154	Mark Grudzielanek	.50	.23
❑ 155	Jermaine Dye	.30	.14
❑ 156	Ken Griffey Jr. FC	3.00	1.35
❑ 157	Frank Thomas FC	2.00	.90
❑ 158	Chipper Jones FC	1.50	.70
❑ 159	Mike Piazza FC	2.00	.90
❑ 160	Cal Ripken FC	2.50	1.10
❑ 161	Greg Maddux FC	2.00	.90
❑ 162	Juan Gonzalez FC	1.50	.70
❑ 163	Alex Rodriguez FC	2.00	.90
❑ 164	Mark McGwire FC	4.00	1.80
❑ 165	Derek Jeter FC	1.50	.70
❑ 166	Larry Walker CL	.50	.23
❑ 167	Tony Gwynn CL	1.50	.70
❑ 168	Tino Martinez CL	.50	.23
❑ 169	Scott Rolen CL	1.50	.70
❑ 170	Nomar Garciaparra CL	2.00	.90
❑ 176	Mark Kotsay RR	.75	.35
❑ 177	Neifi Perez RR	.50	.23
❑ 178	Paul Konerko RR	1.25	.55
❑ 179	Jose Cruz Jr. RR	1.50	.70
❑ 180	Hideki Irabu RR	.75	.35
❑ 181	Mike Cameron RR	.50	.23
❑ 182	Jeff Suppan RR	.30	.14
❑ 183	Kevin Orie RR	.30	.14
❑ 184	Pokey Reese RR	.30	.14
❑ 185	Todd Dunwoody RR	.50	.23
❑ 186	Miguel Tejada RR	.50	.23
❑ 187	Jose Guillen RR	.50	.23
❑ 188	Bartolo Colon RR	.50	.23
❑ 189	Derrek Lee RR	.50	.23
❑ 190	Antone Williamson RR	.30	.14
❑ 191	Wilton Guerrero RR	.30	.14
❑ 192	Jaret Wright RR	1.50	.70

No.	Player	MINT	NRMT
❑ 193	Todd Helton RR	1.50	.70
❑ 194	Shannon Stewart RR	.50	.23
❑ 195	Nomar Garciaparra RR	4.00	1.80
❑ 196	Brett Tomko RR	.50	.23
❑ 197	Fernando Tatis RR	.50	.23
❑ 198	Raul Ibanez RR	.30	.14
❑ 199	Dennis Reyes RR	.50	.23
❑ 200	Bobby Estalella RR	.50	.23
❑ 201	Lou Collier RR	.30	.14
❑ 202	Bubba Trammell RR	.50	.23
❑ 203	Ben Grieve RR	2.50	1.10
❑ 204	Ivan Cruz RR	.30	.14
❑ 205	Karim Garcia RR	.50	.23

1998 Donruss Collections Elite

	MINT	NRMT
COMPLETE SET (150)	200.00	90.00
COMMON CARD (401-550)	.50	.23

No.	Player	MINT	NRMT
❑ 401	Ken Griffey Jr.	10.00	4.50
❑ 402	Frank Thomas	6.00	2.70
❑ 403	Alex Rodriguez	6.00	2.70
❑ 404	Mike Piazza	6.00	2.70
❑ 405	Greg Maddux	6.00	2.70
❑ 406	Cal Ripken	8.00	3.60
❑ 407	Chipper Jones	5.00	2.20
❑ 408	Derek Jeter	5.00	2.20
❑ 409	Tony Gwynn	5.00	2.20
❑ 410	Andruw Jones	2.50	1.10
❑ 411	Juan Gonzalez	5.00	2.20
❑ 412	Jeff Bagwell	3.00	1.35
❑ 413	Mark McGwire	12.00	5.50
❑ 414	Roger Clemens	4.00	1.80
❑ 415	Albert Belle	2.00	.90
❑ 416	Barry Bonds	2.50	1.10
❑ 417	Kenny Lofton	2.00	.90
❑ 418	Ivan Rodriguez	2.50	1.10
❑ 419	Manny Ramirez	2.00	.90
❑ 420	Jim Thome	2.00	.90
❑ 421	Chuck Knoblauch	2.00	.90
❑ 422	Paul Molitor	2.00	.90
❑ 423	Barry Larkin	1.25	.55
❑ 424	Andy Pettitte	1.25	.55
❑ 425	John Smoltz	.75	.35
❑ 426	Randy Johnson	2.00	.90
❑ 427	Bernie Williams	2.00	.90
❑ 428	Larry Walker	2.00	.90
❑ 429	Mo Vaughn	2.50	1.10
❑ 430	Bobby Higginson	1.25	.55
❑ 431	Edgardo Alfonzo	.75	.35
❑ 432	Justin Thompson	.75	.35
❑ 433	Jeff Suppan	.50	.23
❑ 434	Roberto Alomar	2.00	.90
❑ 435	Hideo Nomo	2.50	1.10
❑ 436	Rusty Greer	.75	.35
❑ 437	Tim Salmon	2.00	.90
❑ 438	Jim Edmonds	1.25	.55
❑ 439	Gary Sheffield	1.25	.55
❑ 440	Ken Caminiti	1.25	.55
❑ 441	Sammy Sosa	5.00	2.20
❑ 442	Tony Womack	.75	.35
❑ 443	Matt Williams	.75	.35
❑ 444	Andres Galarraga	2.00	.90
❑ 445	Garret Anderson	.75	.35
❑ 446	Rafael Palmeiro	1.25	.55
❑ 447	Mike Mussina	2.00	.90
❑ 448	Craig Biggio	2.00	.90
❑ 449	Wade Boggs	2.00	.90
❑ 450	Tom Glavine	2.00	.90
❑ 451	Jason Giambi	.75	.35
❑ 452	Will Clark	2.00	.90
❑ 453	David Justice	2.00	.90
❑ 454	Sandy Alomar Jr.	.75	.35
❑ 455	Edgar Martinez	.75	.35
❑ 456	Brady Anderson	.75	.35
❑ 457	Eric Young	.75	.35
❑ 458	Ray Lankford	.75	.35
❑ 459	Kevin Brown	1.25	.55
❑ 460	Raul Mondesi	1.25	.55
❑ 461	Bobby Bonilla	.75	.35
❑ 462	Javier Lopez	.75	.35
❑ 463	Fred McGriff	1.25	.55
❑ 464	Rondell White	.75	.35
❑ 465	Todd Hundley	.75	.35
❑ 466	Mark Grace	1.25	.55
❑ 467	Alan Benes	.75	.35
❑ 468	Jeff Abbott	.75	.35
❑ 469	Bob Abreu	.75	.35
❑ 470	Deion Sanders	.75	.35
❑ 471	Tino Martinez	2.00	.90
❑ 472	Shannon Stewart	.75	.35
❑ 473	Homer Bush	.50	.23
❑ 474	Carlos Delgado	.75	.35
❑ 475	Raul Ibanez	.50	.23
❑ 476	Hideki Irabu	1.25	.55
❑ 477	Jose Cruz Jr.	2.50	1.10
❑ 478	Tony Clark	1.25	.55
❑ 479	Wilton Guerrero	.50	.23
❑ 480	Vladimir Guerrero	3.00	1.35
❑ 481	Scott Rolen	5.00	2.20
❑ 482	Nomar Garciaparra	6.00	2.70
❑ 483	Darin Erstad	2.50	1.10
❑ 484	Chan Ho Park	2.00	.90
❑ 485	Mike Cameron	.75	.35
❑ 486	Todd Walker	1.25	.55
❑ 487	Todd Dunwoody	.75	.35
❑ 488	Neifi Perez	.75	.35
❑ 489	Brett Tomko	.75	.35
❑ 490	Jose Guillen	.75	.35
❑ 491	Matt Morris	.75	.35
❑ 492	Bartolo Colon	.75	.35
❑ 493	Jaret Wright	2.50	1.10
❑ 494	Shawn Estes	.75	.35
❑ 495	Livan Hernandez	.75	.35
❑ 496	Bobby Estalella	.75	.35
❑ 497	Ben Grieve	4.00	1.80
❑ 498	Paul Konerko	2.00	.90
❑ 499	David Ortiz	.75	.35
❑ 500	Todd Helton	2.50	1.10
❑ 501	Juan Encarnacion	.75	.35
❑ 502	Bubba Trammell	.75	.35
❑ 503	Miguel Tejada	.75	.35
❑ 504	Jacob Cruz	.50	.23
❑ 505	Todd Greene	.75	.35
❑ 506	Kevin Orie	.50	.23
❑ 507	Mark Kotsay	1.25	.55
❑ 508	Fernando Tatis	.75	.35
❑ 509	Jay Payton	.50	.23
❑ 510	Pokey Reese	.50	.23
❑ 511	Derrek Lee	.75	.35
❑ 512	Richard Hidalgo	.75	.35
❑ 513	Ricky Ledee	.75	.35
❑ 514	Lou Collier	.50	.23
❑ 515	Ruben Rivera	.75	.35
❑ 516	Shawn Green	.75	.35
❑ 517	Moises Alou	1.25	.55
❑ 518	Ken Griffey Jr. GEN	5.00	2.20
❑ 519	Frank Thomas GEN	3.00	1.35
❑ 520	Alex Rodriguez GEN	3.00	1.35
❑ 521	Mike Piazza GEN	3.00	1.35
❑ 522	Greg Maddux GEN	3.00	1.35
❑ 523	Cal Ripken GEN	4.00	1.80
❑ 524	Chipper Jones GEN	2.50	1.10
❑ 525	Derek Jeter GEN	2.50	1.10
❑ 526	Tony Gwynn GEN	2.50	1.10
❑ 527	Andruw Jones GEN	1.25	.55
❑ 528	Juan Gonzalez GEN	2.50	1.10
❑ 529	Jeff Bagwell GEN	2.00	.90
❑ 530	Mark McGwire GEN	6.00	2.70
❑ 531	Roger Clemens GEN	2.00	.90
❑ 532	Albert Belle GEN	.75	.35
❑ 533	Barry Bonds GEN	1.25	.55
❑ 534	Kenny Lofton GEN	.75	.35
❑ 535	Ivan Rodriguez GEN	1.25	.55
❑ 536	Manny Ramirez GEN	.75	.35
❑ 537	Jim Thome GEN	.75	.35
❑ 538	Chuck Knoblauch GEN	.75	.35
❑ 539	Paul Molitor GEN	.75	.35
❑ 540	Barry Larkin GEN	.50	.23
❑ 541	Mo Vaughn GEN	1.25	.55
❑ 542	Hideki Irabu GEN	.50	.23
❑ 543	Jose Cruz Jr. GEN	1.25	.55
❑ 544	Tony Clark GEN	.50	.23
❑ 545	Vladimir Guerrero GEN	2.00	.90
❑ 546	Scott Rolen GEN	2.50	1.10
❑ 547	Nomar Garciaparra GEN	3.00	1.35
❑ 548	Nomar Garciaparra CL	3.00	1.35
❑ 549	Larry Walker CL	.75	.35
❑ 550	Tino Martinez CL	.75	.35

1998 Donruss Collections Leaf

	MINT	NRMT
COMPLETE SET (200)	100.00	45.00
COMMON CARD (201-400)	.40	.18

No.	Player	MINT	NRMT
❑ 201	Rusty Greer	.60	.25
❑ 202	Tino Martinez	1.50	.70
❑ 203	Bobby Bonilla	.60	.25
❑ 204	Jason Giambi	.60	.25
❑ 205	Matt Morris	.60	.25
❑ 206	Craig Counsell	.40	.18
❑ 207	Reggie Jefferson	.40	.18
❑ 208	Brian Rose	.60	.25
❑ 209	Ruben Rivera	.60	.25
❑ 210	Shawn Estes	.60	.25
❑ 211	Tony Gwynn	4.00	1.80
❑ 212	Jeff Abbott	.60	.25
❑ 213	Jose Cruz Jr.	2.00	.90
❑ 214	Francisco Cordova	.40	.18
❑ 215	Ryan Klesko	.60	.25
❑ 216	Tim Salmon	1.50	.70
❑ 217	Brett Tomko	.60	.25
❑ 218	Matt Williams	.60	.25
❑ 219	Joe Carter	.60	.25
❑ 220	Harold Baines	.60	.25
❑ 221	Gary Sheffield	1.00	.45
❑ 222	Charles Johnson	.60	.25
❑ 223	Aaron Boone	.40	.18
❑ 224	Eddie Murray	1.50	.70
❑ 225	Matt Stairs	.60	.25
❑ 226	David Cone	1.00	.45
❑ 227	Jon Nunnally	.40	.18
❑ 228	Chris Stynes	.40	.18
❑ 229	Enrique Wilson	.60	.25
❑ 230	Randy Johnson	1.50	.70
❑ 231	Garret Anderson	.60	.25
❑ 232	Manny Ramirez	1.50	.70
❑ 233	Jeff Suppan	.40	.18
❑ 234	Rickey Henderson	1.50	.70
❑ 235	Scott Spiezio	.40	.18
❑ 236	Rondell White	.60	.25
❑ 237	Todd Greene	.60	.25
❑ 238	Delino DeShields	.40	.18
❑ 239	Kevin Brown	1.00	.45
❑ 240	Chili Davis	.60	.25

❑ 241 Jimmy Key .60 .25
❑ 242 Mike Mussina 1.50 .70
❑ 243 Joe Randa .40 .18
❑ 244 Chan Ho Park 1.50 .70
❑ 245 Brad Radke .60 .25
❑ 246 Geronimo Berroa .40 .18
❑ 247 Wade Boggs 1.50 .70
❑ 248 Kevin Appier .60 .25
❑ 249 Moises Alou 1.00 .45
❑ 250 David Justice 1.50 .70
❑ 251 Ivan Rodriguez 2.00 .90
❑ 252 J.T. Snow .60 .25
❑ 253 Brian Giles .60 .25
❑ 254 Will Clark 1.50 .70
❑ 255 Justin Thompson .60 .25
❑ 256 Javier Lopez .60 .25
❑ 257 Hideki Irabu 1.00 .45
❑ 258 Mark Grudzielanek .60 .25
❑ 259 Abraham Nunez .60 .25
❑ 260 Todd Hollandsworth .40 .18
❑ 261 Jay Bell .60 .25
❑ 262 Nomar Garciaparra 5.00 2.20
❑ 263 Vinny Castilla 1.00 .45
❑ 264 Lou Collier .40 .18
❑ 265 Kevin Orie .40 .18
❑ 266 John Valentin .60 .25
❑ 267 Robin Ventura .60 .25
❑ 268 Denny Neagle .60 .25
❑ 269 Tony Womack .60 .25
❑ 270 Dennis Reyes .60 .25
❑ 271 Wally Joyner .60 .25
❑ 272 Kevin Brown 1.00 .45
❑ 273 Ray Durham .60 .25
❑ 274 Mike Cameron .60 .25
❑ 275 Dante Bichette .60 .25
❑ 276 Jose Guillen .60 .25
❑ 277 Carlos Delgado .60 .25
❑ 278 Paul Molitor 1.50 .70
❑ 279 Jason Kendall .60 .25
❑ 280 Mark Bellhorn .60 .25
❑ 281 Damian Jackson .40 .18
❑ 282 Bill Mueller .60 .25
❑ 283 Kevin Young .60 .25
❑ 284 Curt Schilling .60 .25
❑ 285 Jeffrey Hammonds .60 .25
❑ 286 Sandy Alomar Jr. .60 .25
❑ 287 Bartolo Colon .60 .25
❑ 288 Wilton Guerrero .40 .18
❑ 289 Bernie Williams 1.50 .70
❑ 290 Deion Sanders .60 .25
❑ 291 Mike Piazza 5.00 2.20
❑ 292 Butch Huskey .40 .18
❑ 293 Edgardo Alfonzo .60 .25
❑ 294 Alan Benes .60 .25
❑ 295 Craig Biggio 1.50 .70
❑ 296 Mark Grace 1.00 .45
❑ 297 Shawn Green .60 .25
❑ 298 Derrek Lee .60 .25
❑ 299 Ken Griffey Jr. 8.00 3.60
❑ 300 Tim Raines .60 .25
❑ 301 Pokey Reese .40 .18
❑ 302 Lee Stevens .40 .18
❑ 303 Shannon Stewart .60 .25
❑ 304 John Smoltz .60 .25
❑ 305 Frank Thomas 5.00 2.20
❑ 306 Jeff Fassero .40 .18
❑ 307 Jay Buhner .60 .25
❑ 308 Jose Canseco 1.50 .70
❑ 309 Omar Vizquel .60 .25
❑ 310 Travis Fryman .60 .25
❑ 311 Dave Nilsson .40 .18
❑ 312 John Olerud .60 .25
❑ 313 Larry Walker 1.50 .70
❑ 314 Jim Edmonds 1.00 .45
❑ 315 Bobby Higginson 1.00 .45
❑ 316 Todd Hundley .60 .25
❑ 317 Paul O'Neill .60 .25
❑ 318 Bip Roberts .40 .18
❑ 319 Ismael Valdes .60 .25
❑ 320 Pedro Martinez 1.50 .70
❑ 321 Jeff Cirillo .60 .25
❑ 322 Andy Benes .60 .25
❑ 323 Bobby Jones .40 .18
❑ 324 Brian Hunter .60 .25
❑ 325 Darryl Kile .60 .25

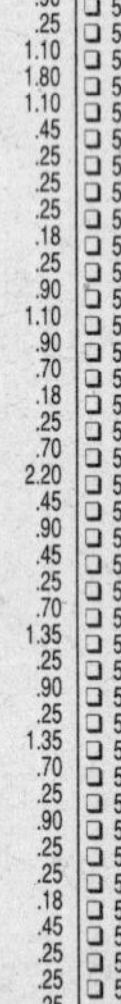

❑ 326 Pat Hentgen .60 .25
❑ 327 Marquis Grissom .60 .25
❑ 328 Eric Davis .60 .25
❑ 329 Chipper Jones 4.00 1.80
❑ 330 Edgar Martinez .60 .25
❑ 331 Andy Pettitte 1.00 .45
❑ 332 Cal Ripken 6.00 2.70
❑ 333 Scott Rolen 4.00 1.80
❑ 334 Ron Coomer .40 .18
❑ 335 Luis Castillo .60 .25
❑ 336 Fred McGriff 1.00 .45
❑ 337 Neifi Perez .60 .25
❑ 338 Eric Karros .60 .25
❑ 339 Alex Fernandez .40 .18
❑ 340 Jason Dickson .60 .25
❑ 341 Lance Johnson .40 .18
❑ 342 Ray Lankford .60 .25
❑ 343 Sammy Sosa 4.00 1.80
❑ 344 Eric Young .60 .25
❑ 345 Bubba Trammell .60 .25
❑ 346 Todd Walker 1.00 .45
❑ 347 Mo Vaughn CC 1.00 .45
❑ 348 Jeff Bagwell CC 1.50 .70
❑ 349 Kenny Lofton CC .60 .25
❑ 350 Raul Mondesi CC .40 .18
❑ 351 Mike Piazza CC 2.50 1.10
❑ 352 Chipper Jones CC 2.00 .90
❑ 353 Larry Walker CC .60 .25
❑ 354 Greg Maddux CC 2.50 1.10
❑ 355 Ken Griffey Jr. CC 4.00 1.80
❑ 356 Frank Thomas CC 2.50 1.10
❑ 357 Darin Erstad GLS 1.00 .45
❑ 358 Roberto Alomar GLS .60 .25
❑ 359 Albert Belle GLS .60 .25
❑ 360 Jim Thome GLS .60 .25
❑ 361 Tony Clark GLS .40 .18
❑ 362 Chuck Knoblauch GLS .60 .25
❑ 363 Derek Jeter GLS 2.00 .90
❑ 364 Alex Rodriguez GLS 2.50 1.10
❑ 365 Tony Gwynn GLS 2.00 .90
❑ 366 Roger Clemens GLS 1.50 .70
❑ 367 Barry Larkin GLS .40 .18
❑ 368 Andres Galarraga GLS .60 .25
❑ 369 Vladimir Guerrero GLS 1.50 .70
❑ 370 Mark McGwire GLS 5.00 2.20
❑ 371 Barry Bonds GLS 1.00 .45
❑ 372 Juan Gonzalez GLS 2.00 .90
❑ 373 Andruw Jones GLS 1.00 .45
❑ 374 Paul Molitor GLS .60 .25
❑ 375 Hideo Nomo GLS 1.50 .70
❑ 376 Cal Ripken GLS 3.00 1.35
❑ 377 Brad Fullmer GLR .60 .25
❑ 378 Jaret Wright GLR 2.00 .90
❑ 379 Bobby Estalella GLR .60 .25
❑ 380 Ben Grieve GLR 3.00 1.35
❑ 381 Paul Konerko GLR 1.50 .70
❑ 382 David Ortiz GLR .60 .25
❑ 383 Todd Helton GLR 2.00 .90
❑ 384 Juan Encarnacion GLR .60 .25
❑ 385 Miguel Tejada GLR .60 .25
❑ 386 Jacob Cruz GLR .40 .18
❑ 387 Mark Kotsay GLR 1.00 .45
❑ 388 Fernando Tatis GLR .60 .25
❑ 389 Ricky Ledee GLR .60 .25
❑ 390 Richard Hidalgo GLR .60 .25
❑ 391 Richie Sexson GLR 1.00 .45
❑ 392 Luis Ordaz GLR .60 .25
❑ 393 Eli Marrero GLR .60 .25
❑ 394 Livan Hernandez GLR .60 .25
❑ 395 Homer Bush GLR .40 .18
❑ 396 Raul Ibanez GLR .40 .18
❑ 397 Nomar Garciaparra CL 2.50 1.10
❑ 398 Scott Rolen CL 2.00 .90
❑ 399 Jose Cruz Jr. CL 1.00 .45
❑ 400 Al Martin .40 .18

1998 Donruss Collections Preferred

	MINT	NRMT
COMPLETE SET (200)	600.00	275.00
COMMON CARD (551-750)	1.50	.70

❑ 551 Ken Griffey Jr. EX 30.00 13.50
❑ 552 Frank Thomas EX 20.00 9.00

❑ 553 Cal Ripken EX 25.00 11.00
❑ 554 Alex Rodriguez EX 20.00 9.00
❑ 555 Greg Maddux EX 20.00 9.00
❑ 556 Mike Piazza EX 20.00 9.00
❑ 557 Chipper Jones EX 15.00 6.75
❑ 558 Tony Gwynn FB 15.00 6.75
❑ 559 Derek Jeter FB 15.00 6.75
❑ 560 Jeff Bagwell EX 10.00 4.50
❑ 561 Juan Gonzalez EX 15.00 6.75
❑ 562 Nomar Garciaparra EX 20.00 9.00
❑ 563 Andruw Jones FB 6.00 2.70
❑ 564 Hideo Nomo FB 8.00 3.60
❑ 565 Roger Clemens FB 12.00 5.50
❑ 566 Mark McGwire FB 40.00 18.00
❑ 567 Scott Rolen FB 15.00 6.75
❑ 568 Vladimir Guerrero FB 10.00 4.50
❑ 569 Barry Bonds FB 8.00 3.60
❑ 570 Darin Erstad FB 8.00 3.60
❑ 571 Albert Belle FB 6.00 2.70
❑ 572 Kenny Lofton FB 6.00 2.70
❑ 573 Mo Vaughn FB 8.00 3.60
❑ 574 Tony Clark FB 4.00 1.80
❑ 575 Ivan Rodriguez FB 8.00 3.60
❑ 576 Larry Walker CB 6.00 2.70
❑ 577 Eddie Murray CB 6.00 2.70
❑ 578 Andy Pettitte CB 4.00 1.80
❑ 579 Roberto Alomar CB 6.00 2.70
❑ 580 Randy Johnson CB 6.00 2.70
❑ 581 Manny Ramirez CB 6.00 2.70
❑ 582 Paul Molitor FB 6.00 2.70
❑ 583 Mike Mussina CB 6.00 2.70
❑ 584 Jim Thome FB 6.00 2.70
❑ 585 Tino Martinez CB 6.00 2.70
❑ 586 Gary Sheffield CB 4.00 1.80
❑ 587 Chuck Knoblauch CB 6.00 2.70
❑ 588 Bernie Williams CB 6.00 2.70
❑ 589 Tim Salmon CB 6.00 2.70
❑ 590 Sammy Sosa CB 15.00 6.75
❑ 591 Wade Boggs GS 6.00 2.70
❑ 592 Will Clark GS 6.00 2.70
❑ 593 Andres Galarraga CB 6.00 2.70
❑ 594 Raul Mondesi CB 4.00 1.80
❑ 595 Rickey Henderson GS 6.00 2.70
❑ 596 Jose Canseco GS 6.00 2.70
❑ 597 Pedro Martinez GS 6.00 2.70
❑ 598 Jay Buhner GS 2.50 1.10
❑ 599 Ryan Klesko GS 2.50 1.10
❑ 600 Barry Larkin CB 4.00 1.80
❑ 601 Charles Johnson GS 2.50 1.10
❑ 602 Tom Glavine GS 6.00 2.70
❑ 603 Edgar Martinez CB 2.50 1.10
❑ 604 Fred McGriff GS 4.00 1.80
❑ 605 Moises Alou ME 4.00 1.80
❑ 606 Dante Bichette GS 2.50 1.10
❑ 607 Jim Edmonds CB 4.00 1.80
❑ 608 Mark Grace ME 4.00 1.80
❑ 609 Chan Ho Park ME 6.00 2.70
❑ 610 Justin Thompson ME 2.50 1.10
❑ 611 John Smoltz ME 2.50 1.10
❑ 612 Craig Biggio CB 6.00 2.70
❑ 613 Ken Caminiti ME 4.00 1.80
❑ 614 Deion Sanders ME 2.50 1.10
❑ 615 Carlos Delgado GS 2.50 1.10
❑ 616 David Justice CB 6.00 2.70
❑ 617 J.T. Snow GS 2.50 1.10
❑ 618 Jason Giambi CB 2.50 1.10
❑ 619 Garret Anderson ME 2.50 1.10
❑ 620 Rondell White ME 2.50 1.10

❑ 621 Matt Williams ME 2.50 1.10
❑ 622 Brady Anderson ME 2.50 1.10
❑ 623 Eric Karros GS 2.50 1.10
❑ 624 Javier Lopez GS 2.50 1.10
❑ 625 Pat Hentgen GS 2.50 1.10
❑ 626 Todd Hundley GS 2.50 1.10
❑ 627 Ray Lankford GS.......... 2.50 1.10
❑ 628 Denny Neagle GS......... 2.50 1.10
❑ 629 Henry Rodriguez GS.... 2.50 1.10
❑ 630 Sandy Alomar Jr. ME .. 2.50 1.10
❑ 631 Rafael Palmeiro ME 4.00 1.80
❑ 632 Robin Ventura GS......... 2.50 1.10
❑ 633 John Olerud GS 2.50 1.10
❑ 634 Omar Vizquel GS 2.50 1.10
❑ 635 Joe Randa GS............. 1.50 .70
❑ 636 Lance Johnson GS ...... 1.50 .70
❑ 637 Kevin Brown GS 4.00 1.80
❑ 638 Curt Schilling GS.......... 2.50 1.10
❑ 639 Ismael Valdes GS 2.50 1.10
❑ 640 Francisco Cordova GS 1.50 .70
❑ 641 David Cone GS 4.00 1.80
❑ 642 Paul O'Neill GS 2.50 1.10
❑ 643 Jimmy Key GS 2.50 1.10
❑ 644 Brad Radke GS........... 2.50 1.10
❑ 645 Kevin Appier GS 2.50 1.10
❑ 646 Al Martin GS .... 1.50 .70
❑ 647 Rusty Greer ME 2.50 1.10
❑ 648 Reggie Jefferson GS.... 1.50 .70
❑ 649 Ron Coomer GS .... 1.50 .70
❑ 650 Vinny Castilla GS 4.00 1.80
❑ 651 Bobby Bonilla ME 2.50 1.10
❑ 652 Eric Young GS 2.50 1.10
❑ 653 Tony Womack GS........ 2.50 1.10
❑ 654 Jason Kendall GS 2.50 1.10
❑ 655 Jeff Suppan GS........... 1.50 .70
❑ 656 Shawn Estes ME.......... 2.50 1.10
❑ 657 Shawn Green GS 2.50 1.10
❑ 658 Edgardo Alfonzo ME 2.50 1.10
❑ 659 Alan Benes ME 2.50 1.10
❑ 660 Bobby Higginson GS.... 4.00 1.80
❑ 661 Mark Grudzielanek GS 2.50 1.10
❑ 662 Wilton Guerrero GS...... 1.50 .70
❑ 663 Todd Greene ME.......... 2.50 1.10
❑ 664 Pokey Reese GS.......... 1.50 .70
❑ 665 Jose Guillen CB 2.50 1.10
❑ 666 Neifi Perez ME 2.50 1.10
❑ 667 Luis Castillo GS........... 2.50 1.10
❑ 668 Edgar Renteria GS 2.50 1.10
❑ 669 Karim Garcia GS.......... 2.50 1.10
❑ 670 Butch Huskey GS .... 1.50 .70
❑ 671 Michael Tucker GS 2.50 1.10
❑ 672 Jason Dickson GS........ 2.50 1.10
❑ 673 Todd Walker ME 4.00 1.80
❑ 674 Brian Jordan GS 2.50 1.10
❑ 675 Joe Carter GS 2.50 1.10
❑ 676 Matt Morris ME 2.50 1.10
❑ 677 Brett Tomko ME 2.50 1.10
❑ 678 Mike Cameron CB......... 2.50 1.10
❑ 679 Russ Davis GS 2.50 1.10
❑ 680 Shannon Stewart ME .. 2.50 1.10
❑ 681 Kevin Orie GS .... 1.50 .70
❑ 682 Scott Spiezio GS.......... 1.50 .70
❑ 683 Brian Giles GS 2.50 1.10
❑ 684 Raul Casanova GS ...... 1.50 .70
❑ 685 Jose Cruz Jr. CB.......... 8.00 3.60
❑ 686 Hideki Irabu GS........... 4.00 1.80
❑ 687 Bubba Trammell GS 2.50 1.10
❑ 688 Richard Hidalgo CB...... 2.50 1.10
❑ 689 Paul Konerko CB.......... 6.00 2.70
❑ 690 Todd Helton FB............ 8.00 3.60
❑ 691 Miguel Tejada CB 2.50 1.10
❑ 692 Fernando Tatis ME 2.50 1.10
❑ 693 Ben Grieve FB........... 12.00 5.50
❑ 694 Travis Lee FB 12.00 5.50
❑ 695 Mark Kotsay CB 4.00 1.80
❑ 696 Eli Marrero ME 2.50 1.10
❑ 697 David Ortiz CB 2.50 1.10
❑ 698 Juan Encarnacion ME .. 2.50 1.10
❑ 699 Jaret Wright ME 8.00 3.60
❑ 700 Livan Hernandez CB.... 2.50 1.10
❑ 701 Ruben Rivera GS 2.50 1.10
❑ 702 Brad Fullmer ME.......... 2.50 1.10
❑ 703 Dennis Reyes GS 2.50 1.10
❑ 704 Enrique Wilson ME 2.50 1.10
❑ 705 Todd Dunwoody ME 2.50 1.10
❑ 706 Derrick Gibson ME 2.50 1.10
❑ 707 Aaron Boone ME......... 1.50 .70
❑ 708 Ron Wright ME 2.50 1.10
❑ 709 Preston Wilson ME 2.50 1.10
❑ 710 Abraham Nunez GS 2.50 1.10
❑ 711 Shane Monahan GS 2.50 1.10
❑ 712 Carl Pavano GS 2.50 1.10
❑ 713 Derrek Lee GS 2.50 1.10
❑ 714 Jeff Abbott GS............. 2.50 1.10
❑ 715 Wes Helms ME 2.50 1.10
❑ 716 Brian Rose GS 2.50 1.10
❑ 717 Bobby Estalella GS...... 2.50 1.10
❑ 718 Ken Griffey Jr. PP GS 15.00 6.75
❑ 719 Frank Thomas PP GS 10.00 4.50
❑ 720 Cal Ripken PP GS...... 12.00 5.50
❑ 721 Alex Rodriguez PP GS 10.00 4.50
❑ 722 Greg Maddux PP GS 10.00 4.50
❑ 723 Mike Piazza PP GS.... 10.00 4.50
❑ 724 Chipper Jones PP GS.. 8.00 3.60
❑ 725 Tony Gwynn PP GS 8.00 3.60
❑ 726 Derek Jeter PP GS 8.00 3.60
❑ 727 Jeff Bagwell PP GS...... 6.00 2.70
❑ 728 Juan Gonzalez PP GS 8.00 3.60
❑ 729 N. Garciaparra PP GS 10.00 4.50
❑ 730 Andruw Jones PP GS .. 4.00 1.80
❑ 731 Hideo Nomo PP GS 6.00 2.70
❑ 732 Roger Clemens PP GS 6.00 2.70
❑ 733 Mark McGwire PP GS 20.00 9.00
❑ 734 Scott Rolen PP GS 8.00 3.60
❑ 735 Barry Bonds PP GS 4.00 1.80
❑ 736 Darin Erstad PP GS 4.00 1.80
❑ 737 Mo Vaughn PP GS 4.00 1.80
❑ 738 Ivan Rodriguez PP GS 4.00 1.80
❑ 739 Larry Walker PP ME 2.50 1.10
❑ 740 Andy Pettitte PP GS .... 1.50 .70
❑ 741 Randy Johnson PP ME 2.50 1.10
❑ 742 Paul Molitor PP GS...... 2.50 1.10
❑ 743 Jim Thome PP GS 2.50 1.10
❑ 744 Tino Martinez PP ME .. 2.50 1.10
❑ 745 Gary Sheffield PP GS .. 1.50 .70
❑ 746 Albert Belle PP GS 2.50 1.10
❑ 747 Jose Cruz Jr. PP GS.... 4.00 1.80
❑ 748 Todd Helton CL GS...... 4.00 1.80
❑ 749 Ben Grieve CL GS 6.00 2.70
❑ 750 Paul Konerko CL GS.... 2.50 1.10

1998 Donruss Prized Collections Donruss

	MINT	NRMT
COMPLETE SET (200)	1200.00	550.00
COMMON (1-170/176-205)	2.50	1.10

*STARS: 3X TO 8X BASIC DONRUSS COLL.
*YOUNG STARS: 2.5X TO 6X BASIC DONRUSS COLL.

1998 Donruss Prized Collections Elite

	MINT	NRMT
COMPLETE SET (150)	2000.00	900.00
COMMON CARD (401-550)......	5.00	2.20

*STARS: 4X TO 10X BASIC ELITE COLL.
*YOUNG STARS: 3X TO 8X BASIC ELITE COLL.

1998 Donruss Prized Collections Leaf

	MINT	NRMT
COMPLETE SET (200)	1000.00	450.00
COMMON CARD (201-400)......	3.00	1.35

*STARS: 3X TO 8X BASIC LEAF COLL.
*YOUNG STARS: 2.5X TO 6X BASIC LEAF COLL.

1998 Donruss Prized Collections Preferred

	MINT	NRMT
COMMON CARD (551-750)....	20.00	9.00

*STARS: 5X TO 12X BASIC PREF.COLL.
*YOUNG STARS: 4X TO 10X BASIC PREF.COLL.

1997 Donruss Elite

	MINT	NRMT
COMPLETE SET (150)	40.00	18.00
COMMON CARD (1-150)...........	.20	.09

❑ 1 Juan Gonzalez .... 2.00 .90
❑ 2 Alex Rodriguez 2.50 1.10
❑ 3 Frank Thomas................. 2.50 1.10
❑ 4 Greg Maddux 2.50 1.10
❑ 5 Ken Griffey Jr. 4.00 1.80
❑ 6 Cal Ripken........................ 3.00 1.35

❑ 7	Mike Piazza	2.50	1.10
❑ 8	Chipper Jones	2.00	.90
❑ 9	Albert Belle	1.00	.45
❑ 10	Andruw Jones	1.25	.55
❑ 11	Vladimir Guerrero	1.50	.70
❑ 12	Mo Vaughn UER front Gonzales	1.00	.45
❑ 13	Ivan Rodriguez	1.00	.45
❑ 14	Andy Pettitte	.50	.23
❑ 15	Tony Gwynn	2.00	.90
❑ 16	Barry Bonds	1.00	.45
❑ 17	Jeff Bagwell	1.25	.55
❑ 18	Manny Ramirez	.75	.35
❑ 19	Kenny Lofton	.75	.35
❑ 20	Roberto Alomar	.75	.35
❑ 21	Mark McGwire	4.00	1.80
❑ 22	Ryan Klesko	.40	.18
❑ 23	Tim Salmon	.75	.35
❑ 24	Derek Jeter	2.50	1.10
❑ 25	Eddie Murray	.75	.35
❑ 26	Jermaine Dye	.20	.09
❑ 27	Ruben Rivera	.40	.18
❑ 28	Jim Edmonds	.50	.23
❑ 29	Mike Mussina	.75	.35
❑ 30	Randy Johnson	.75	.35
❑ 31	Sammy Sosa	2.00	.90
❑ 32	Hideo Nomo	1.00	.45
❑ 33	Chuck Knoblauch	.75	.35
❑ 34	Paul Molitor	.75	.35
❑ 35	Rafael Palmeiro	.50	.23
❑ 36	Brady Anderson	.40	.18
❑ 37	Will Clark	.75	.35
❑ 38	Craig Biggio	.75	.35
❑ 39	Jason Giambi	.40	.18
❑ 40	Roger Clemens	1.50	.70
❑ 41	Jay Buhner	.40	.18
❑ 42	Edgar Martinez	.40	.18
❑ 43	Gary Sheffield	.50	.23
❑ 44	Fred McGriff	.50	.23
❑ 45	Bobby Bonilla	.40	.18
❑ 46	Tom Glavine	.75	.35
❑ 47	Wade Boggs	.75	.35
❑ 48	Jeff Conine	.40	.18
❑ 49	John Smoltz	.40	.18
❑ 50	Jim Thome	.75	.35
❑ 51	Billy Wagner	.40	.18
❑ 52	Jose Canseco	.75	.35
❑ 53	Javy Lopez	.40	.18
❑ 54	Cecil Fielder	.40	.18
❑ 55	Garret Anderson	.40	.18
❑ 56	Alex Ochoa	.20	.09
❑ 57	Scott Rolen	2.00	.90
❑ 58	Darin Erstad	1.25	.55
❑ 59	Rey Ordonez	.40	.18
❑ 60	Dante Bichette	.40	.18
❑ 61	Joe Carter	.40	.18
❑ 62	Moises Alou	.50	.23
❑ 63	Jason Isringhausen	.20	.09
❑ 64	Karim Garcia	.40	.18
❑ 65	Brian Jordan	.40	.18
❑ 66	Ruben Sierra	.20	.09
❑ 67	Todd Hollandsworth	.20	.09
❑ 68	Paul Wilson	.20	.09
❑ 69	Ernie Young	.20	.09
❑ 70	Ryne Sandberg	1.00	.45
❑ 71	Raul Mondesi	.50	.23
❑ 72	George Arias	.20	.09
❑ 73	Ray Durham	.40	.18
❑ 74	Dean Palmer	.40	.18
❑ 75	Shawn Green	.40	.18
❑ 76	Eric Young	.40	.18
❑ 77	Jason Kendall	.50	.23
❑ 78	Greg Vaughn	.40	.18
❑ 79	Terrell Wade	.20	.09
❑ 80	Bill Pulsipher	.20	.09
❑ 81	Bobby Higginson	.50	.23
❑ 82	Mark Grudzielanek	.40	.18
❑ 83	Ken Caminiti	.50	.23
❑ 84	Todd Greene	.40	.18
❑ 85	Carlos Delgado	.40	.18
❑ 86	Mark Grace	.50	.23
❑ 87	Rondell White	.40	.18
❑ 88	Barry Larkin	.50	.23
❑ 89	J.T. Snow	.40	.18
❑ 90	Alex Gonzalez	.20	.09
❑ 91	Raul Casanova	.20	.09
❑ 92	Marc Newfield	.20	.09
❑ 93	Jermaine Allensworth	.20	.09
❑ 94	John Mabry	.20	.09
❑ 95	Kirby Puckett	1.25	.55
❑ 96	Travis Fryman	.40	.18
❑ 97	Kevin Brown	.50	.23
❑ 98	Andres Galarraga	.75	.35
❑ 99	Marty Cordova	.20	.09
❑ 100	Henry Rodriguez	.40	.18
❑ 101	Sterling Hitchcock	.40	.18
❑ 102	Trey Beamon	.20	.09
❑ 103	Brett Butler	.40	.18
❑ 104	Rickey Henderson	.75	.35
❑ 105	Tino Martinez	.75	.35
❑ 106	Kevin Appier	.40	.18
❑ 107	Brian Hunter	.40	.18
❑ 108	Eric Karros	.40	.18
❑ 109	Andre Dawson	.50	.23
❑ 110	Darryl Strawberry	.40	.18
❑ 111	James Baldwin	.40	.18
❑ 112	Chad Mottola	.20	.09
❑ 113	Dave Nilsson	.20	.09
❑ 114	Carlos Baerga	.40	.18
❑ 115	Chan Ho Park	.75	.35
❑ 116	John Jaha	.20	.09
❑ 117	Alan Benes	.40	.18
❑ 118	Mariano Rivera	.40	.18
❑ 119	Ellis Burks	.40	.18
❑ 120	Tony Clark	.50	.23
❑ 121	Todd Walker	.75	.35
❑ 122	Dwight Gooden	.40	.18
❑ 123	Ugueth Urbina	.40	.18
❑ 124	David Cone	.50	.23
❑ 125	Ozzie Smith	1.00	.45
❑ 126	Kimera Bartee	.20	.09
❑ 127	Rusty Greer	.40	.18
❑ 128	Pat Hentgen	.40	.18
❑ 129	Charles Johnson	.40	.18
❑ 130	Quinton McCracken	.40	.18
❑ 131	Troy Percival	.40	.18
❑ 132	Shane Reynolds	.40	.18
❑ 133	Charles Nagy	.40	.18
❑ 134	Tom Goodwin	.20	.09
❑ 135	Ron Gant	.20	.09
❑ 136	Dan Wilson	.20	.09
❑ 137	Matt Williams	.40	.18
❑ 138	LaTroy Hawkins	.20	.09
❑ 139	Kevin Seitzer	.20	.09
❑ 140	Michael Tucker	.40	.18
❑ 141	Todd Hundley	.40	.18
❑ 142	Alex Fernandez	.20	.09
❑ 143	Marquis Grissom	.40	.18
❑ 144	Steve Finley	.40	.18
❑ 145	Curtis Pride	.20	.09
❑ 146	Derek Bell	.40	.18
❑ 147	Butch Huskey	.20	.09
❑ 148	Dwight Gooden CL	.40	.18
❑ 149	Al Leiter CL	.40	.18
❑ 150	Hideo Nomo CL	.75	.35

1997 Donruss Elite Leather and Lumber

	MINT	NRMT
COMPLETE SET (10)	800.00	350.00
COMMON CARD (1-10)	25.00	11.00

❑ 1	Ken Griffey Jr.	150.00	70.00
❑ 2	Alex Rodriguez	100.00	45.00
❑ 3	Frank Thomas	100.00	45.00
❑ 4	Chipper Jones	80.00	36.00
❑ 5	Ivan Rodriguez	40.00	18.00
❑ 6	Cal Ripken	120.00	55.00
❑ 7	Barry Bonds	40.00	18.00
❑ 8	Chuck Knoblauch	25.00	11.00
❑ 9	Manny Ramirez	30.00	13.50
❑ 10	Mark McGwire	150.00	70.00

1997 Donruss Elite Passing the Torch

	MINT	NRMT
COMPLETE SET (12)	500.00	220.00
COMMON CARD (1-12)	6.00	2.70

❑ 1	Cal Ripken	60.00	27.00
❑ 2	Alex Rodriguez	50.00	22.00
❑ 3	Cal Ripken Alex Rodriguez	100.00	45.00
❑ 4	Kirby Puckett	25.00	11.00
❑ 5	Andruw Jones	20.00	9.00
❑ 6	Kirby Puckett Andruw Jones	25.00	11.00
❑ 7	Cecil Fielder	6.00	2.70
❑ 8	Frank Thomas	50.00	22.00
❑ 9	Cecil Fielder Frank Thomas	50.00	22.00
❑ 10	Ozzie Smith	20.00	9.00
❑ 11	Derek Jeter	40.00	18.00
❑ 12	Ozzie Smith Derek Jeter	40.00	18.00

1997 Donruss Elite Passing the Torch Autographs

	MINT	NRMT
COMPLETE SET (12)	5000.00	2200.00
COMMON CARD (1-12)	100.00	45.00

❑ 1	Cal Ripken	600.00	275.00
❑ 2	Alex Rodriguez	500.00	220.00
❑ 3	Cal Ripken Alex Rodriguez	1200.00	550.00
❑ 4	Kirby Puckett	300.00	135.00
❑ 5	Andruw Jones	150.00	70.00

❑ 6 Kirby Puckett Andruw Jones	400.00	180.00
❑ 7 Cecil Fielder	100.00	45.00
❑ 8 Frank Thomas	500.00	220.00
❑ 9 Cecil Fielder Frank Thomas	500.00	220.00
❑ 10 Ozzie Smith	300.00	135.00
❑ 11 Derek Jeter	300.00	135.00
❑ 12 Ozzie Smith Derek Jeter	400.00	180.00

1997 Donruss Elite Turn of the Century

	MINT	NRMT
COMPLETE SET (20)	120.00	55.00
COMMON CARD (1-20)	2.00	.90
COMP.DIE CUT SET (20)	400.00	180.00

*DIE CUTS: 1.25X TO 3X BASIC CARDS
DC STATED PRINT RUN 500 SERIAL #'d SETS
RANDOM INSERTS IN PACKS

❑ 1 Alex Rodriguez	25.00	11.00
❑ 2 Andruw Jones	12.00	5.50
❑ 3 Chipper Jones	20.00	9.00
❑ 4 Todd Walker	8.00	3.60
❑ 5 Scott Rolen	20.00	9.00
❑ 6 Trey Beamon	2.00	.90
❑ 7 Derek Jeter	20.00	9.00
❑ 8 Darin Erstad	12.00	5.50
❑ 9 Tony Clark	6.00	2.70
❑ 10 Todd Greene	4.00	1.80
❑ 11 Jason Giambi	4.00	1.80
❑ 12 Justin Thompson	4.00	1.80
❑ 13 Ernie Young	2.00	.90
❑ 14 Jason Kendall	6.00	2.70
❑ 15 Alex Ochoa	2.00	.90
❑ 16 Brooks Kieschnick	2.00	.90
❑ 17 Bobby Higginson	6.00	2.70
❑ 18 Ruben Rivera	4.00	1.80
❑ 19 Chan Ho Park	8.00	3.60
❑ 20 Chad Mottola	2.00	.90
❑ P5 Scott Rolen Promo	5.00	2.20
❑ P7 Derek Jeter Promo	5.00	2.20

1998 Donruss Elite

	MINT	NRMT
COMPLETE SET (150)	40.00	18.00
COMMON CARD (1-150)	.20	.09

❑ 1 Ken Griffey Jr.	4.00	1.80
❑ 2 Frank Thomas	2.50	1.10
❑ 3 Alex Rodriguez	2.50	1.10
❑ 4 Mike Piazza	2.50	1.10
❑ 5 Greg Maddux	2.50	1.10
❑ 6 Cal Ripken	3.00	1.35
❑ 7 Chipper Jones	2.00	.90
❑ 8 Derek Jeter	2.00	.90
❑ 9 Tony Gwynn	2.00	.90
❑ 10 Andruw Jones	1.00	.45
❑ 11 Juan Gonzalez	2.00	.90
❑ 12 Jeff Bagwell	1.25	.55
❑ 13 Mark McGwire	5.00	2.20
❑ 14 Roger Clemens	1.50	.70
❑ 15 Albert Belle	.75	.35
❑ 16 Barry Bonds	1.00	.45
❑ 17 Kenny Lofton	.75	.35
❑ 18 Ivan Rodriguez	1.00	.45
❑ 19 Manny Ramirez	.75	.35
❑ 20 Jim Thome	.75	.35
❑ 21 Chuck Knoblauch	.75	.35
❑ 22 Paul Molitor	.75	.35
❑ 23 Barry Larkin	.50	.23
❑ 24 Andy Pettitte	.50	.23
❑ 25 John Smoltz	.30	.14
❑ 26 Randy Johnson	.75	.35
❑ 27 Bernie Williams	.75	.35
❑ 28 Larry Walker	.75	.35
❑ 29 Mo Vaughn	1.00	.45
❑ 30 Bobby Higginson	.50	.23
❑ 31 Edgardo Alfonzo	.30	.14
❑ 32 Justin Thompson	.30	.14
❑ 33 Jeff Suppan	.20	.09
❑ 34 Roberto Alomar	.75	.35
❑ 35 Hideo Nomo	1.00	.45
❑ 36 Rusty Greer	.30	.14
❑ 37 Tim Salmon	.75	.35
❑ 38 Jim Edmonds	.50	.23
❑ 39 Gary Sheffield	.50	.23
❑ 40 Ken Caminiti	.50	.23
❑ 41 Sammy Sosa	2.00	.90
❑ 42 Tony Womack	.30	.14
❑ 43 Matt Williams	.30	.14
❑ 44 Andres Galarraga	.75	.35
❑ 45 Garret Anderson	.30	.14
❑ 46 Rafael Palmeiro	.50	.23
❑ 47 Mike Mussina	.75	.35
❑ 48 Craig Biggio	.75	.35
❑ 49 Wade Boggs	.75	.35
❑ 50 Tom Glavine	.75	.35
❑ 51 Jason Giambi	.30	.14
❑ 52 Will Clark	.75	.35
❑ 53 David Justice	.75	.35
❑ 54 Sandy Alomar Jr.	.30	.14
❑ 55 Edgar Martinez	.30	.14
❑ 56 Brady Anderson	.30	.14
❑ 57 Eric Young	.30	.14
❑ 58 Ray Lankford	.30	.14
❑ 59 Kevin Brown	.50	.23
❑ 60 Raul Mondesi	.50	.23
❑ 61 Bobby Bonilla	.30	.14
❑ 62 Javier Lopez	.30	.14
❑ 63 Fred McGriff	.50	.23
❑ 64 Rondell White	.30	.14
❑ 65 Todd Hundley	.30	.14
❑ 66 Mark Grace	.50	.23
❑ 67 Alan Benes	.30	.14
❑ 68 Jeff Abbott	.30	.14
❑ 69 Bob Abreu	.30	.14
❑ 70 Deion Sanders	.30	.14
❑ 71 Tino Martinez	.75	.35
❑ 72 Shannon Stewart	.30	.14
❑ 73 Homer Bush	.20	.09
❑ 74 Carlos Delgado	.30	.14
❑ 75 Raul Ibanez	.20	.09
❑ 76 Hideki Irabu	.50	.23
❑ 77 Jose Cruz Jr.	1.00	.45
❑ 78 Tony Clark	.50	.23
❑ 79 Wilton Guerrero	.20	.09
❑ 80 Vladimir Guerrero	1.25	.55
❑ 81 Scott Rolen	2.00	.90
❑ 82 Nomar Garciaparra	2.50	1.10
❑ 83 Darin Erstad	1.00	.45
❑ 84 Chan Ho Park	.75	.35
❑ 85 Mike Cameron	.30	.14
❑ 86 Todd Walker	.50	.23
❑ 87 Todd Dunwoody	.30	.14
❑ 88 Neifi Perez	.30	.14
❑ 89 Brett Tomko	.30	.14
❑ 90 Jose Guillen	.30	.14
❑ 91 Matt Morris	.30	.14
❑ 92 Bartolo Colon	.30	.14
❑ 93 Jaret Wright	1.00	.45
❑ 94 Shawn Estes	.30	.14
❑ 95 Livan Hernandez	.30	.14
❑ 96 Bobby Estalella	.30	.14
❑ 97 Ben Grieve	1.50	.70
❑ 98 Paul Konerko	.75	.35
❑ 99 David Ortiz	.30	.14
❑ 100 Todd Helton	1.00	.45
❑ 101 Juan Encarnacion	.30	.14
❑ 102 Bubba Trammell	.30	.14
❑ 103 Miguel Tejada	.30	.14
❑ 104 Jacob Cruz	.20	.09
❑ 105 Todd Greene	.30	.14
❑ 106 Kevin Orie	.20	.09
❑ 107 Mark Kotsay	.50	.23
❑ 108 Fernando Tatis	.30	.14
❑ 109 Jay Payton	.20	.09
❑ 110 Pokey Reese	.20	.09
❑ 111 Derrek Lee	.30	.14
❑ 112 Richard Hidalgo	.30	.14
❑ 113 Ricky Ledee UER front Rickey	.30	.14
❑ 114 Lou Collier	.20	.09
❑ 115 Ruben Rivera	.30	.14
❑ 116 Shawn Green	.30	.14
❑ 117 Moises Alou	.50	.23
❑ 118 Ken Griffey Jr. GEN	2.00	.90
❑ 119 Frank Thomas GEN	1.25	.55
❑ 120 Alex Rodriguez GEN	1.25	.55
❑ 121 Mike Piazza GEN	1.25	.55
❑ 122 Greg Maddux GEN	1.25	.55
❑ 123 Cal Ripken GEN	1.50	.70
❑ 124 Chipper Jones GEN	1.00	.45
❑ 125 Derek Jeter GEN	1.00	.45
❑ 126 Tony Gwynn GEN	1.00	.45
❑ 127 Andruw Jones GEN	.50	.23
❑ 128 Juan Gonzalez GEN	1.00	.45
❑ 129 Jeff Bagwell GEN	.75	.35
❑ 130 Mark McGwire GEN	2.50	1.10
❑ 131 Roger Clemens GEN	.75	.35
❑ 132 Albert Belle GEN	.30	.14
❑ 133 Barry Bonds GEN	.50	.23
❑ 134 Kenny Lofton GEN	.30	.14
❑ 135 Ivan Rodriguez GEN	.50	.23
❑ 136 Manny Ramirez GEN	.30	.14
❑ 137 Jim Thome GEN	.30	.14
❑ 138 Chuck Knoblauch GEN	.30	.14
❑ 139 Paul Molitor GEN	.30	.14
❑ 140 Barry Larkin GEN	.20	.09
❑ 141 Mo Vaughn GEN	.50	.23
❑ 142 Hideki Irabu GEN	.20	.09
❑ 143 Jose Cruz Jr. GEN	.50	.23
❑ 144 Tony Clark GEN	.20	.09
❑ 145 Vladimir Guerrero GEN	.75	.35
❑ 146 Scott Rolen GEN	1.00	.45
❑ 147 Nomar Garciaparra GEN	1.25	.55
❑ 148 Nomar Garciaparra CL	1.25	.55
❑ 149 Larry Walker CL	.30	.14
❑ 150 Tino Martinez CL	.30	.14
❑ AU2 F.Thomas AUTO/100	400.00	180.00

1998 Donruss Elite Status

	MINT	NRMT
COMPLETE SET (150)	8000.00	3600.00
COMMON CARD (1-150)	15.00	6.75

*STARS: 30X TO 80X BASIC CARDS
*YOUNG STARS: 25X TO 60X BASIC CARDS

1998 Donruss Elite Back to the Future

	MINT	NRMT
COMPLETE SET (8)	300.00	135.00
COMMON CARD (1-8)	20.00	9.00
❑ 1 Cal Ripken .... Paul Konerko	50.00	22.00
❑ 2 Jeff Bagwell .... Todd Helton	20.00	9.00
❑ 3 Eddie Matthews .... Chipper Jones	30.00	13.50
❑ 4 Juan Gonzalez .... Ben Grieve	40.00	18.00
❑ 5 Hank Aaron .... Jose Cruz Jr.	30.00	13.50
❑ 6 Frank Thomas .... David Ortiz 1-100	40.00	18.00
❑ 7 Nolan Ryan .... Greg Maddux	60.00	27.00
❑ 8 Alex Rodriguez .... Nomar Garciaparra	50.00	22.00

1998 Donruss Elite Back to the Future Autographs

	MINT	NRMT
COMPLETE SET (8)	3500.00	1600.00
COMMON CARD (1A-5/7-8) ..	60.00	27.00
❑ 1A Cal Ripken .... Paul Konerko Redeemed/100 Redeemed card signed only by Konerko	60.00	27.00
❑ 1B C. Ripken AU/200 ...... Redeemed card signed only by Ripken	500.00	220.00
❑ 2 Jeff Bagwell .... Todd Helton	250.00	110.00
❑ 3 Eddie Matthews .... Chipper Jones	400.00	180.00
❑ 4 Juan Gonzalez .... Ben Grieve	400.00	180.00
❑ 5 Hank Aaron .... Jose Cruz Jr.	400.00	180.00
❑ 7 Nolan Ryan .... Greg Maddux	1200.00	550.00
❑ 8 Alex Rodriguez .... Nomar Garciaparra	600.00	275.00
❑ NNO C. Ripken AU EXCH100	500.00	220.00

1998 Donruss Elite Craftsmen

	MINT	NRMT
COMPLETE SET (30)	250.00	110.00
COMMON CARD (1-30)	4.00	1.80
COMP.MASTER SET (30) ..	2500.00	1100.00

*MASTERS: 4X TO 8X BASIC CRAFTSMEN
MASTER PRINT RUN 100 SERIAL #'d SETS

	MINT	NRMT
❑ 1 Ken Griffey Jr.	30.00	13.50
❑ 2 Frank Thomas	20.00	9.00
❑ 3 Alex Rodriguez	20.00	9.00
❑ 4 Cal Ripken	25.00	11.00
❑ 5 Greg Maddux	20.00	9.00
❑ 6 Mike Piazza	20.00	9.00
❑ 7 Chipper Jones	15.00	6.75
❑ 8 Derek Jeter	15.00	6.75
❑ 9 Tony Gwynn	15.00	6.75
❑ 10 Nomar Garciaparra	20.00	9.00
❑ 11 Scott Rolen	12.00	5.50
❑ 12 Jose Cruz Jr.	6.00	2.70
❑ 13 Tony Clark	4.00	1.80
❑ 14 Vladimir Guerrero	8.00	3.60
❑ 15 Todd Helton	6.00	2.70
❑ 16 Ben Grieve	10.00	4.50
❑ 17 Andruw Jones	6.00	2.70
❑ 18 Jeff Bagwell	10.00	4.50
❑ 19 Mark McGwire	40.00	18.00
❑ 20 Juan Gonzalez	15.00	6.75
❑ 21 Roger Clemens	12.00	5.50
❑ 22 Albert Belle	6.00	2.70
❑ 23 Barry Bonds	8.00	3.60
❑ 24 Kenny Lofton	6.00	2.70
❑ 25 Ivan Rodriguez	8.00	3.60
❑ 26 Paul Molitor	6.00	2.70
❑ 27 Barry Larkin	4.00	1.80
❑ 28 Mo Vaughn	8.00	3.60
❑ 29 Larry Walker	6.00	2.70
❑ 30 Tino Martinez	6.00	2.70

1998 Donruss Elite Prime Numbers

	MINT	NRMT
COMPLETE SET (36)	4000.00	1800.00
COMMON CARD (1-36)	20.00	9.00
❑ 1A Ken Griffey Jr. 2 (94)	300.00	135.00
❑ 1B Ken Griffey Jr. 9 (204)	150.00	70.00
❑ 1C Ken Griffey Jr. 4 (290)	120.00	55.00
❑ 2A Frank Thomas 4 (56)	250.00	110.00
❑ 2B Frank Thomas 5 (406)	60.00	27.00

	MINT	NRMT
❑ 2C Frank Thomas 6 (450)	60.00	27.00
❑ 3A Mark McGwire 3 (87)	400.00	180.00
❑ 3B Mark McGwire 8 (307)	150.00	70.00
❑ 3C Mark McGwire 7 (380)	150.00	70.00
❑ 4A Cal Ripken 5 (17)	1000.00	450.00
❑ 4B Cal Ripken 1 (507)	80.00	36.00
❑ 4C Cal Ripken 7 (510)	80.00	36.00
❑ 5A Mike Piazza 5 (76)	200.00	90.00
❑ 5B Mike Piazza 7 (506)	60.00	27.00
❑ 5C Mike Piazza 6 (570)	60.00	27.00
❑ 6A Chipper Jones 4 (89)	150.00	70.00
❑ 6B Chipper Jones 8 (409)	50.00	22.00
❑ 6C Chipper Jones 9 (480)	50.00	22.00
❑ 7A Tony Gwynn 3 (72)	150.00	70.00
❑ 7B Tony Gwynn 7 (302)	60.00	27.00
❑ 7C Tony Gwynn 2 (370)	60.00	27.00
❑ 8A Barry Bonds 3 (74)	80.00	36.00
❑ 8B Barry Bonds 7 (304)	30.00	13.50
❑ 8C Barry Bonds 4 (370)	30.00	13.50
❑ 9A Jeff Bagwell 4 (25)	250.00	110.00
❑ 9B Jeff Bagwell 2 (405)	30.00	13.50
❑ 9C Jeff Bagwell 5 (420)	30.00	13.50
❑ 10A Juan Gonzalez 5 (89)	150.00	70.00
❑ 10B Juan Gonzalez 8 (509)	50.00	22.00
❑ 10C Juan Gonzalez 9 (580)	50.00	22.00
❑ 11A Alex Rodriguez 5 (34)	300.00	135.00
❑ 11B Alex Rodriguez 3 (504)	60.00	27.00
❑ 11C Alex Rodriguez 4 (530)	60.00	27.00
❑ 12A Kenny Lofton 3 (54) ..	60.00	27.00
❑ 12B Kenny Lofton 5 (304)	20.00	9.00
❑ 12C Kenny Lofton 4 (350)	20.00	9.00

1998 Donruss Elite Prime Numbers Die Cuts

	MINT	NRMT
COMMON CARD (1-36)	20.00	9.00
❑ 1A Ken Griffey Jr. 2 (200)	150.00	70.00
❑ 1B Ken Griffey Jr. 9 (90)	300.00	135.00
❑ 1C Ken Griffey Jr. 4 (4)		
❑ 2A Frank Thomas 4 (400)	60.00	27.00
❑ 2B Frank Thomas 5 (50)	250.00	110.00
❑ 2C Frank Thomas 6 (6)		
❑ 3A Mark McGwire 3 (300)	150.00	70.00
❑ 3B Mark McGwire 8 (80)	400.00	180.00
❑ 3C Mark McGwire 7 (7)		
❑ 4A Cal Ripken 5 (500)	80.00	36.00
❑ 4B Cal Ripken 1 (10)		
❑ 4C Cal Ripken 7 (7)		

❑ 5A Mike Piazza 5 (500) 60.00 27.00
❑ 5B Mike Piazza 7 (70) 200.00 90.00
❑ 5C Mike Piazza 6 (6)
❑ 6A Chipper Jones 4 (400) 50.00 22.00
❑ 6B Chipper Jones 8 (80) 150.00 70.00
❑ 6C Chipper Jones 9 (9) 40.00 18.00
❑ 7A Tony Gwynn 3 (300) 60.00 27.00
❑ 7B Tony Gwynn 7 (70) 150.00 70.00
❑ 7C Tony Gwynn 2 (2)
❑ 8A Barry Bonds 3 (300) 30.00 13.50
❑ 8B Barry Bonds 7 (70) 80.00 36.00
❑ 8C Barry Bonds 4 (4)
❑ 9A Jeff Bagwell 4 (400) 30.00 13.50
❑ 9B Jeff Bagwell 2 (20) 300.00 135.00
❑ 9C Jeff Bagwell 5 (5)
❑ 10A Juan Gonzalez 5 (500) 50.00 22.00
❑ 10B Juan Gonzalez 8 (80) 150.00 70.00
❑ 10C Juan Gonzalez 9 (9)
❑ 11A Alex Rodriguez 5 (500) 60.00 27.00
❑ 11B Alex Rodriguez 3 (30) 400.00 180.00
❑ 11C Alex Rodriguez 4 (4)
❑ 12A Kenny Lofton 3 (300) 20.00 9.00
❑ 12B Kenny Lofton 5 (50) .. 60.00 27.00
❑ 12C Kenny Lofton 4 (4)

1997 Donruss Limited

	MINT	NRMT
COMPLETE SET (200)	1500.00	700.00
COMP.COUNTER SET (100)..	30.00	13.50
COMMON COUNTERPART	.20	.09
COUNTERPART UNLISTED	.75	.35
COMP.DOUBLE SET (40)	100.00	45.00
COMMON DOUBLE TEAM	1.25	.55
COMP.STAR FACT.SET (40)	800.00	350.00
COMMON STAR FACTOR	4.00	1.80
COMP.UNLIMITED SET (20)	600.00	275.00
COMMON UNLIMITED	3.00	1.35

❑ 1 Ken Griffey Jr. C 4.00 1.80
Rondell White
❑ 2 Greg Maddux C................ 2.50 1.10
David Cone
❑ 3 Gary Sheffield D 5.00 2.20
Moises Alou
❑ 4 Frank Thomas S 50.00 22.00
❑ 5 Cal Ripken C..................... 3.00 1.35
Kevin Orie
❑ 6 Vladimir Guerrero U 20.00 9.00
Barry Bonds
❑ 7 Eddie Murray C.................. .75 .35
Reggie Jefferson
❑ 8 Manny Ramirez D 5.00 2.20
Marquis Grissom
❑ 9 Mike Piazza S 50.00 22.00
❑ 10 Barry Larkin C.................. .75 .35
Rey Ordonez
❑ 11 Jeff Bagwell C................ 1.25 .55
Eric Karros
❑ 12 Chuck Knoblauch C .... .75 .35
Ray Durham
❑ 13 Alex Rodriguez C 2.50 1.10
Edgar Renteria
❑ 14 Matt Williams C................ .75 .35
Vinny Castilla
❑ 15 Todd Hollandsworth C...... .40 .18
Bob Abreu
❑ 16 John Smoltz C.................. .75 .35
Pedro Martinez
❑ 17 Jose Canseco C .... .75 .35
Chili Davis
❑ 18 Jose Cruz Jr. U 80.00 36.00
Ken Griffey Jr.
❑ 19 Ken Griffey Jr. S 80.00 36.00
❑ 20 Paul Molitor C .... .75 .35
John Olerud
❑ 21 Roberto Alomar C .... .75 .35
Luis Castillo
❑ 22 Derek Jeter C .... 2.00 .90
Lou Collier
❑ 23 Chipper Jones C .... 2.00 .90
Robin Ventura
❑ 24 Gary Sheffield C .... .75 .35
Ron Gant
❑ 25 Ramon Martinez C .... .40 .18
Bobby Jones
❑ 26 Mike Piazza D.............. 15.00 6.75
Raul Mondesi
❑ 27 Darin Erstad U............... 30.00 13.50
Jeff Bagwell
❑ 28 Ivan Rodriguez S.......... 20.00 9.00
❑ 29 J.T.Snow C .... .40 .18
Kevin Young
❑ 30 Ryne Sandberg C .... 1.00 .45
Julio Franco
❑ 31 Travis Fryman C.............. .40 .18
Chris Snopek
❑ 32 Wade Boggs C .... .75 .35
Russ Davis
❑ 33 Brooks Kieschnick C .... .40 .18
Marty Cordova
❑ 34 Andy Pettitte C .... .75 .35
Denny Neagle
❑ 35 Paul Molitor D 5.00 2.20
Matt Lawton
❑ 36 Scott Rolen U 60.00 27.00
Cal Ripken
❑ 37 Cal Ripken S................ 60.00 27.00
❑ 38 Jim Thome C..................... .75 .35
Dave Nilsson
❑ 39 Tony Womack C .... .75 .35
Carlos Baerga
❑ 40 Nomar Garciaparra C 2.50 1.10
Mark Grudzielanek
❑ 41 Todd Greene C .... .40 .18
Chris Widger
❑ 42 Deion Sanders C.............. .40 .18
Bernard Gilkey
❑ 43 Hideo Nomo C................ 1.00 .45
Charles Nagy
❑ 44 Ivan Rodriguez D 6.00 2.70
Rusty Greer
❑ 45 Todd Walker U 30.00 13.50
Chipper Jones
❑ 46 Greg Maddux S............ 50.00 22.00
❑ 47 Mo Vaughn C .... 1.00 .45
Cecil Fielder
❑ 48 Craig Biggio C.................. .75 .35
Scott Spiezio
❑ 49 Pokey Reese C .... .40 .18
Jeff Blauser
❑ 50 Ken Caminiti C .... .75 .35
Joe Randa
❑ 51 Albert Belle C .... 1.25 .55
Shawn Green
❑ 52 Randy Johnson C .... .75 .35
Jason Dickson
❑ 53 Hideo Nomo D............... 6.00 2.70
Chan Ho Park
❑ 54 Scott Spiezio U 12.00 5.50
Chuck Knoblauch
❑ 55 Chipper Jones S 40.00 18.00
❑ 56 Tino Martinez C................ .75 .35
Ryan McGuire
❑ 57 Eric Young C .... .20 .09
Wilton Guerrero
❑ 58 Ron Coomer C .... .20 .09
Dave Hollins
❑ 59 Sammy Sosa C .... 2.00 .90
Angel Echevarria
❑ 60 Dennis Reyes C .... .60 .25
Jimmy Key
❑ 61 Barry Larkin D............... 4.00 1.80
Deion Sanders
❑ 62 Wilton Guerrero U 12.00 5.50
Roberto Alomar
❑ 63 Albert Belle S 25.00 11.00
❑ 64 Mark McGwire C 4.00 1.80
Andre Galarraga
❑ 65 Edgar Martinez C .... .75 .35
Todd Walker
❑ 66 Steve Finley C.................. .40 .18
Rich Becker
❑ 67 Tom Glavine C .... .40 .18
Andy Ashby
❑ 68 Sammy Sosa D 12.00 5.50
Ryne Sandberg
❑ 69 Nomar Garciaparra U .. 50.00 22.00
Alex Rodriguez
❑ 70 Jeff Bagwell S 30.00 13.50
❑ 71 Darin Erstad C............... 1.25 .55
Mark Grace
❑ 72 Scott Rolen C .... 2.00 .90
Edgardo Alfonzo
❑ 73 Kenny Lofton C .... .75 .35
Lance Johnson
❑ 74 Joey Hamilton C .... .40 .18
Brett Tomko
❑ 75 Eddie Murray D 5.00 2.20
Tim Salmon
❑ 76 Dmitri Young U 15.00 6.75
Mo Vaughn
❑ 77 Juan Gonzalez S......... 40.00 18.00
❑ 78 Frank Thomas C 2.50 1.10
Tony Clark
❑ 79 Shannon Stewart C.......... .40 .18
Bip Roberts
❑ 80 Shawn Estes C .... .40 .18
Alex Fernandez
❑ 81 John Smoltz D............... 2.50 1.10
Javier Lopez
❑ 82 Todd Greene U 40.00 18.00
Mike Piazza
❑ 83 Derek Jeter S 40.00 18.00
❑ 84 Dmitri Young C .... .40 .18
Antone Williamson
❑ 85 Rickey Henderson C .... .75 .35
Darryl Hamilton
❑ 86 Billy Wagner C .... .40 .18
Dennis Eckersley
❑ 87 Larry Walker D 5.00 2.20
Eric Young
❑ 88 Mark Kotsay U............. 40.00 18.00
Juan Gonzalez
❑ 89 Barry Bonds S............. 20.00 9.00
❑ 90 Will Clark C .... .75 .35
Jeff Conine
❑ 91 Tony Gwynn C .... 2.00 .90
Brett Butler
❑ 92 John Wetteland C .... .20 .09
Rod Beck
❑ 93 Bernie Williams D 5.00 2.20
Tony Martinez
❑ 94 Andruw Jones U 15.00 6.75
Kenny Lofton
❑ 95 Mo Vaughn S 20.00 9.00
❑ 96 Joe Carter C .... .75 .35
Derrek Lee
❑ 97 John Mabry C .... .20 .09
F.P. Santangelo
❑ 98 Esteban Loaiza C .... .20 .09
Wilson Alvarez
❑ 99 Matt Williams D 5.00 2.20
David Justice
❑ 100 Derrek Lee U.............. 40.00 18.00
Frank Thomas
❑ 101 Mark McGwire S 80.00 36.00
❑ 102 Fred McGriff C................ .75 .35
Paul Sorrento
❑ 103 Jermaine Allensworth C .75 .35
Bernie Williams
❑ 104 Ismael Valdes C .... .40 .18
Chris Holt
❑ 105 Fred McGriff D.............. 4.00 1.80
Ryan Klesko
❑ 106 Tony Clark U 60.00 27.00
Mark McGwire
❑ 107 Tony Gwynn S........... 40.00 18.00
❑ 108 Jeffrey Hammonds C .... .40 .18
Ellis Burks

❑ 109 Shane Reynolds C .... .40 .18
Andy Benes
❑ 110 Roger Clemens D 10.00 4.50
Carlos Delgado
❑ 111 Karim Garcia U 25.00 11.00
Albert Belle
❑ 112 Paul Molitor S 15.00 6.75
❑ 113 Trey Beamon C .... .20 .09
Eric Owens
❑ 114 Curt Schilling C .... .40 .18
Darryl Kile
❑ 115 Tom Glavine D 2.50 1.10
Michael Tucker
❑ 116 Pokey Reese U 30.00 13.50
Derek Jeter
❑ 117 Manny Ramirez S 15.00 6.75
❑ 118 Juan Gonzalez C.......... 2.00 .90
Brant Brown
❑ 119 Juan Guzman C .... .20 .09
Francisco Cordova
❑ 120 Randy Johnson D 5.00 2.20
Edgar Martinez
❑ 121 Hideki Irabu U 40.00 18.00
Greg Maddux
❑ 122 Alex Rodriguez S 50.00 22.00
❑ 123 Barry Bonds C............. 1.00 .45
Quinton McCracken
❑ 124 Roger Clemens C .... 1.50 .70
Andy Benes
❑ 125 Wade Boggs D 5.00 2.20
Paul O'Neill
❑ 126 Mike Cameron U 12.00 5.50
Larry Walker
❑ 127 Gary Sheffield S 15.00 6.75
❑ 128 Andruw Jones C .... 1.25 .55
Raul Mondesi
❑ 129 Brady Anderson C.......... .40 .18
Terrell Wade
❑ 130 Brady Anderson D........ 4.00 1.80
Rafael Palmeiro
❑ 131 Neifi Perez U............. 10.00 4.50
Barry Larkin
❑ 132 Ken Caminiti S 12.00 5.50
❑ 133 Larry Walker C .... .75 .35
Rusty Greer
❑ 134 Mariano Rivera C .... .40 .18
Mark Wohlers
❑ 135 Hideki Irabu D 8.00 3.60
Andy Pettitte
❑ 136 Jose Guillen U............ 30.00 13.50
Tony Gwynn
❑ 137 Hideo Nomo S............ 20.00 9.00
❑ 138 Vladimir Guerrero C .... 1.50 .70
Jim Edmonds
❑ 139 Justin Thompson C .... .40 .18
Dwight Gooden
❑ 140 Andres Galarraga D 5.00 2.20
Dante Bichette
❑ 141 Kenny Lofton S 15.00 6.75
❑ 142 Tim Salmon C .... .75 .35
Manny Ramirez
❑ 143 Kevin Brown C .... .40 .18
Matt Morris
❑ 144 Craig Biggio D............. 4.00 1.80
Bob Abreu
❑ 145 Roberto Alomar S 15.00 6.75
❑ 146 Jose Guillen C................ .75 .35
Brian Jordan
❑ 147 Bartolo Colon C.............. .40 .18
Kevin Appier
❑ 148 Ray Lankford D............ 2.50 1.10
Brian Jordan
❑ 149 Chuck Knoblauch S.... 15.00 6.75
❑ 150 Henry Rodriguez C .... .40 .18
Ray Lankford
❑ 151 Jaret Wright C 4.00 1.80
Ben McDonald
❑ 152 Bobby Bonilla D............ 2.50 1.10
Kevin Brown
❑ 153 Barry Larkin S 12.00 5.50
❑ 154 David Justice C................ .75 .35
Reggie Sanders
❑ 155 Mike Mussina C.............. .75 .35
Ken Hill
❑ 156 Mark Grace D 4.00 1.80
Brooks Kieschnick
❑ 157 Jim Thome S.............. 15.00 6.75
❑ 158 Michael Tucker C .... .40 .18
Curtis Goodwin
❑ 159 Jeff Suppan C .... .40 .18
Jeff Fassero
❑ 160 Mike Mussina D............. 5.00 2.20
Jeffrey Hammonds
❑ 161 John Smoltz S........... 10.00 4.50
❑ 162 Moises Alou C .... .40 .18
Eric Davis
❑ 163 Sandy Alomar Jr. C........ .40 .18
Dan Wilson
❑ 164 Rondell White D 2.50 1.10
Henry Rodriguez
❑ 165 Roger Clemens S 30.00 13.50
❑ 166 Brady Anderson C.......... .40 .18
Al Martin
❑ 167 Jason Kendall C .... .40 .18
Charles Johnson
❑ 168 Jason Giambi D............ 4.00 1.80
Jose Canseco
❑ 169 Larry Walker S 15.00 6.75
❑ 170 Jay Buhner C .... .40 .18
Geronimo Berroa
❑ 171 Ivan Rodriguez C .... 1.00 .45
Mike Sweeney
❑ 172 Kevin Appier D 2.50 1.10
Jose Rosado
❑ 173 Bernie Williams S 15.00 6.75
❑ 174 Todd Dunwoody C ...... 1.00 .45
Brian Giles
❑ 175 Javier Lopez C .... .40 .18
Scott Hatteberg
❑ 176 John Jaha D 2.50 1.10
Jeff Cirillo
❑ 177 Andy Pettitte S 15.00 6.75
❑ 178 Dante Bichette C........... .40 .18
Butch Huskey
❑ 179 Raul Casanova C .... .40 .18
Todd Hundley
❑ 180 Jim Edmonds D........... 4.00 1.80
Garrett Anderson
❑ 181 Deion Sanders S....... 10.00 4.50
❑ 182 Ryan Klesko C .... .75 .35
Paul O'Neill
❑ 183 Joe Carter D 2.50 1.10
Pat Hentgen
❑ 184 Brady Anderson S...... 12.00 5.50
❑ 185 Carlos Delgado C .... .40 .18
Wally Joyner
❑ 186 Jermaine Dye D .... 1.25 .55
Johnny Damon
❑ 187 Randy Johnson S 15.00 6.75
❑ 188 Todd Hundley D 2.50 1.10
Carlos Baerga
❑ 189 Tom Glavine S 10.00 4.50
❑ 190 Damon Mashore D ...... 1.25 .55
Jason McDonald
❑ 191 Wade Boggs S 15.00 6.75
❑ 192 Al Martin D 2.50 1.10
Jason Kendall
❑ 193 Matt Williams S 8.00 3.60
❑ 194 Will Clark D 4.00 1.80
Dean Palmer
❑ 195 Sammy Sosa S 40.00 18.00
❑ 196 Jose Cruz Jr. D 15.00 6.75
Jay Buhner
❑ 197 Eddie Murray S 15.00 6.75
❑ 198 Darin Erstad D............. 8.00 3.60
Jason Dickson
❑ 199 Fred McGriff S............ 10.00 4.50
❑ 200 Bubba Trammell D 3.00 1.35
Bobby Higginson

1997 Donruss Limited Exposure

	MINT	NRMT
COMPLETE SET (200)	10000.00	4500.00
COMP.COUNTER SET (100)	600.00	275.00
COMMON COUNTERPART	2.50	1.10
*COUNTER.STARS: 5X TO 12X BASIC CARDS		
*COUNTER.ROOKIES: 2X TO 5X BASIC CARDS		
COMP.DOUBLE SET (40)	800.00	350.00
COMMON DOUBLE TEAM	10.00	4.50
*DOUBLE TEAM: 3X TO 8X BASIC CARDS		
COMP.STAR FACT.SET (40)	5000.00	2200.00
COMMON STAR FACTOR	25.00	11.00
*STAR FACTOR: 2.5X TO 6X BASIC CARDS		
COMP.UNLIMITED SET (20)	4000.00	1800.00
COMMON UNLIMITED	20.00	9.00
*UNLIMITED: 2.5X TO 6X BASIC CARDS		
*NON-GLOSS: .1X TO .25X BASIC EXPOSURE		

1997 Donruss Limited Fabric of the Game

	MINT	NRMT
COMPLETE SET (69)	2000.00	900.00
COMMON MAJOR LG MAT.	3.00	1.35
COMMON STAR MAT.............	5.00	2.20
COMMON SUPERSTAR MAT.	12.00	5.50
COMMON HOF MAT..............	20.00	9.00
COMMON LEGEND...............	50.00	22.00

❑ 1 Cal Ripken HF............. 150.00 70.00
❑ 2 Tony Gwynn SS 60.00 27.00
❑ 3 Ivan Rodriguez S........... 25.00 11.00
❑ 4 Rickey Henderson L 60.00 27.00
❑ 5 Ken Griffey Jr. SS 120.00 55.00
❑ 6 Chipper Jones ML.......... 40.00 18.00
❑ 7 Sammy Sosa S 50.00 22.00
❑ 8 Wade Boggs HF 40.00 18.00
❑ 9 Manny Ramirez ML 12.00 5.50
❑ 10 Barry Bonds HF........... 50.00 22.00
❑ 11 Mike Piazza S 60.00 27.00
❑ 12 Rondell White ML 5.00 2.20
❑ 13 Albert Belle S 25.00 11.00
❑ 14 Tony Clark ML................ 8.00 3.60
❑ 15 Edgar Martinez SS 15.00 6.75
❑ 16 Deion Sanders S............ 8.00 3.60
❑ 17 Juan Gonzalez SS 60.00 27.00
❑ 18 Nomar Garciaparra ML 50.00 22.00
❑ 19 Rafael Palmeiro SS...... 15.00 6.75
❑ 20 Dave Justice S 20.00 9.00
❑ 21 Bob Abreu ML 5.00 2.20
❑ 22 Paul Molitor L 80.00 36.00
❑ 23 Vladimir Guerrero ML .. 25.00 11.00
❑ 24 Chuck Knoblauch SS .. 25.00 11.00
❑ 25 Tony Gwynn HF 100.00 45.00
❑ 26 Darin Erstad ML 20.00 9.00
❑ 27 Mark McGwire HF...... 200.00 90.00
❑ 28 Larry Walker S 20.00 9.00
❑ 29 Gary Sheffield S 12.00 5.50
❑ 30 Jose Cruz Jr. ML......... 30.00 13.50
❑ 31 Kenny Lofton HF 40.00 18.00
❑ 32 Andres Galarraga SS .. 25.00 11.00
❑ 33 Raul Mondesi ML 8.00 3.60
❑ 34 Eddie Murray L 80.00 36.00
❑ 35 Tino Martinez ML 12.00 5.50
❑ 36 Todd Walker ML 12.00 5.50
❑ 37 Frank Thomas SS........ 80.00 36.00
❑ 38 Ken Caminiti S 12.00 5.50
❑ 39 Pokey Reese ML............ 3.00 1.35
❑ 40 Barry Bonds HF........... 50.00 22.00
❑ 41 Barry Larkin SS........... 15.00 6.75
❑ 42 Bernie Williams S 20.00 9.00
❑ 43 Cal Ripken HF............ 150.00 70.00
❑ 44 Bobby Bonilla SS 15.00 6.75
❑ 45 Ken Griffey Jr. S 100.00 45.00
❑ 46 Tim Salmon S 20.00 9.00

❑ 47	Ryne Sandberg HF	50.00	22.00
❑ 48	Rusty Greer ML	5.00	2.20
❑ 49	Matt Williams SS	15.00	6.75
❑ 50	Eric Young S	8.00	3.60
❑ 51	Andruw Jones ML	20.00	9.00
❑ 52	Jeff Bagwell S	30.00	13.50
❑ 53	Wilton Guerrero ML	3.00	1.35
❑ 54	Fred McGriff HF	25.00	11.00
❑ 55	Jose Guillen ML	12.00	5.50
❑ 56	Brady Anderson SS	15.00	6.75
❑ 57	Mo Vaughn S	25.00	11.00
❑ 58	Craig Biggio SS	25.00	11.00
❑ 59	Dmitri Young ML	5.00	2.20
❑ 60	Frank Thomas S	60.00	27.00
❑ 61	Derek Jeter ML	40.00	18.00
❑ 62	Albert Belle SS	30.00	13.50
❑ 63	Scott Rolen ML	30.00	13.50
❑ 64	Roberto Alomar HF	40.00	18.00
❑ 65	Jeff Bagwell S	30.00	13.50
❑ 66	Mark Grace SS	15.00	6.75
❑ 67	Gary Sheffield S	12.00	5.50
❑ 68	Joe Carter HF	20.00	9.00
❑ 69	Jim Thome ML	12.00	5.50

1997 Donruss Preferred

	MINT	NRMT
COMPLETE SET (200)	800.00	350.00
COMP.BRONZE SET (100)	30.00	13.50
COMMON BRONZE	.20	.09
COMP.SILVER SET (60)	120.00	55.00
COMMON SILVER	1.25	.55
COMP.GOLD SET (30)	250.00	110.00
COMMON GOLD	2.50	1.10
COMP.PLAT.SET (10)	400.00	180.00
COMMON PLATINUM	25.00	11.00

❑ 1	Frank Thomas P	40.00	18.00
❑ 2	Ken Griffey Jr. P	60.00	27.00
❑ 3	Cecil Fielder B	.40	.18
❑ 4	Chuck Knoblauch G	10.00	4.50
❑ 5	Garret Anderson B	.40	.18
❑ 6	Greg Maddux P	40.00	18.00
❑ 7	Matt Williams S	2.00	.90
❑ 8	Marquis Grissom S	2.00	.90
❑ 9	Jason Isringhausen B	.20	.09
❑ 10	Larry Walker S	5.00	2.20
❑ 11	Charles Nagy B	.40	.18
❑ 12	Dan Wilson B	.20	.09
❑ 13	Albert Belle G	15.00	6.75
❑ 14	Javier Lopez B	.40	.18
❑ 15	David Cone B	.60	.25
❑ 16	Bernard Gilkey B	.20	.09
❑ 17	Andres Galarraga S	5.00	2.20
❑ 18	Bill Pulsipher B	.20	.09
❑ 19	Alex Fernandez B	.20	.09
❑ 20	Andy Pettitte S	3.00	1.35
❑ 21	Mark Grudzielanek B	.40	.18
❑ 22	Juan Gonzalez P	30.00	13.50
❑ 23	Reggie Sanders B	.40	.18
❑ 24	Kenny Lofton G	10.00	4.50
❑ 25	Andy Ashby B	.20	.09
❑ 26	John Wetteland B	.40	.18
❑ 27	Bobby Bonilla B	.40	.18
❑ 28	Hideo Nomo G	12.00	5.50
❑ 29	Joe Carter B	.40	.18
❑ 30	Jose Canseco B	.75	.35
❑ 31	Ellis Burks B	.40	.18
❑ 32	Edgar Martinez S	2.00	.90
❑ 33	Chan Ho Park B	.75	.35
❑ 34	Dave Justice B	.75	.35
❑ 35	Carlos Delgado B	.40	.18
❑ 36	Jeff Cirillo S	2.00	.90
❑ 37	Charles Johnson B	.40	.18
❑ 38	Manny Ramirez G	10.00	4.50
❑ 39	Greg Vaughn B	.40	.18
❑ 40	Henry Rodriguez B	.40	.18
❑ 41	Darryl Strawberry B	.40	.18
❑ 42	Jim Thome G	10.00	4.50
❑ 43	Ryan Klesko S	2.00	.90
❑ 44	Ruben Sierra B	.20	.09
❑ 45	Brian Jordan G	4.00	1.80
❑ 46	Tony Gwynn P	30.00	13.50
❑ 47	Rafael Palmeiro G	6.00	2.70
❑ 48	Dante Bichette S	2.00	.90
❑ 49	Ivan Rodriguez G	12.00	5.50
❑ 50	Mark McGwire G	50.00	22.00
❑ 51	Tim Salmon S	5.00	2.20
❑ 52	Roger Clemens B	1.50	.70
❑ 53	Matt Lawton B	.40	.18
❑ 54	Wade Boggs S	5.00	2.20
❑ 55	Travis Fryman B	.40	.18
❑ 56	Bobby Higginson S	3.00	1.35
❑ 57	John Jaha S	1.25	.55
❑ 58	Rondell White S	2.00	.90
❑ 59	Tom Glavine S	5.00	2.20
❑ 60	Eddie Murray S	5.00	2.20
❑ 61	Vinny Castilla B	.60	.25
❑ 62	Todd Hundley B	.40	.18
❑ 63	Jay Buhner S	2.00	.90
❑ 64	Paul O'Neill B	.40	.18
❑ 65	Steve Finley B	.40	.18
❑ 66	Kevin Appier B	.40	.18
❑ 67	Ray Durham B	.40	.18
❑ 68	Dave Nilsson B	.20	.09
❑ 69	Jeff Bagwell G	15.00	6.75
❑ 70	Al Martin S	1.25	.55
❑ 71	Paul Molitor G	10.00	4.50
❑ 72	Kevin Brown S	3.00	1.35
❑ 73	Ron Gant B	.20	.09
❑ 74	Dwight Gooden B	.40	.18
❑ 75	Quinton McCracken B	.40	.18
❑ 76	Rusty Greer S	2.00	.90
❑ 77	Juan Guzman B	.20	.09
❑ 78	Fred McGriff S	3.00	1.35
❑ 79	Tino Martinez B	.75	.35
❑ 80	Ray Lankford B	.40	.18
❑ 81	Ken Caminiti G	6.00	2.70
❑ 82	James Baldwin B	.40	.18
❑ 83	Jermaine Dye G	2.50	1.10
❑ 84	Mark Grace S	3.00	1.35
❑ 85	Pat Hentgen S	2.00	.90
❑ 86	Jason Giambi S	2.00	.90
❑ 87	Brian Hunter B	.40	.18
❑ 88	Andy Benes B	.40	.18
❑ 89	Jose Rosado B	.20	.09
❑ 90	Shawn Green B	.40	.18
❑ 91	Jason Kendall B	.60	.25
❑ 92	Alex Rodriguez P	40.00	18.00
❑ 93	Chipper Jones P	30.00	13.50
❑ 94	Barry Bonds G	12.00	5.50
❑ 95	Brady Anderson G	4.00	1.80
❑ 96	Ryne Sandberg S	6.00	2.70
❑ 97	Lance Johnson B	.20	.09
❑ 98	Cal Ripken P	50.00	22.00
❑ 99	Craig Biggio S	10.00	4.50
❑ 100	Dean Palmer B	.40	.18
❑ 101	Gary Sheffield G	6.00	2.70
❑ 102	Johnny Damon B	.40	.18
❑ 103	Mo Vaughn G	12.00	5.50
❑ 104	Randy Johnson S	5.00	2.20
❑ 105	Raul Mondesi S	3.00	1.35
❑ 106	Roberto Alomar G	10.00	4.50
❑ 107	Mike Piazza P	40.00	18.00
❑ 108	Rey Ordonez B	.40	.18
❑ 109	Barry Larkin G	6.00	2.70
❑ 110	Tony Clark S	3.00	1.35
❑ 111	Bernie Williams S	5.00	2.20
❑ 112	John Smoltz G	4.00	1.80
❑ 113	Moises Alou B	.60	.25
❑ 114	Will Clark B	.75	.35
❑ 115	Sammy Sosa G	25.00	11.00
❑ 116	Jim Edmonds S	3.00	1.35
❑ 117	Jeff Conine B	.40	.18
❑ 118	Joey Hamilton B	.40	.18
❑ 119	Todd Hollandsworth B	.20	.09
❑ 120	Troy Percival B	.40	.18
❑ 121	Paul Wilson B	.20	.09
❑ 122	Ken Hill B	.20	.09
❑ 123	Mariano Rivera S	2.00	.90
❑ 124	Eric Karros B	.40	.18
❑ 125	Derek Jeter G	25.00	11.00
❑ 126	Eric Young S	.40	.18
❑ 127	John Mabry B	.20	.09
❑ 128	Gregg Jefferies B	.20	.09
❑ 129	Ismael Valdes S	2.00	.90
❑ 130	Marty Cordova B	.20	.09
❑ 131	Omar Vizquel B	.40	.18
❑ 132	Mike Mussina S	5.00	2.20
❑ 133	Darin Erstad B	1.25	.55
❑ 134	Edgar Renteria S	2.00	.90
❑ 135	Billy Wagner B	.40	.18
❑ 136	Alex Ochoa B	.20	.09
❑ 137	Luis Castillo B	.40	.18
❑ 138	Rocky Coppinger B	.20	.09
❑ 139	Mike Sweeney B	.20	.09
❑ 140	Michael Tucker B	.40	.18
❑ 141	Chris Snopek B	.20	.09
❑ 142	Dmitri Young S	2.00	.90
❑ 143	Andruw Jones P	15.00	6.75
❑ 144	Mike Cameron S	2.00	.90
❑ 145	Brant Brown B	.40	.18
❑ 146	Todd Walker G	10.00	4.50
❑ 147	Nomar Garciaparra G	30.00	13.50
❑ 148	Glendon Rusch B	.20	.09
❑ 149	Karim Garcia S	2.00	.90
❑ 150	Bubba Trammell S	3.00	1.35
❑ 151	Todd Greene B	.40	.18
❑ 152	Wilton Guerrero G	2.50	1.10
❑ 153	Scott Spiezio B	.20	.09
❑ 154	Brooks Kieschnick B	.20	.09
❑ 155	Vladimir Guerrero G	15.00	6.75
❑ 156	Brian Giles S	6.00	2.70
❑ 157	Pokey Reese B	.20	.09
❑ 158	Jason Dickson G	4.00	1.80
❑ 159	Kevin Orie S	2.50	1.10
❑ 160	Scott Rolen G	20.00	9.00
❑ 161	Bartolo Colon S	2.00	.90
❑ 162	Shannon Stewart G	4.00	1.80
❑ 163	Wendell Magee B	.20	.09
❑ 164	Jose Guillen S	5.00	2.20
❑ 165	Bob Abreu S	2.00	.90
❑ 166	Deivi Cruz B	1.00	.45
❑ 167	Alex Rodriguez NT B	2.50	1.10
❑ 168	Frank Thomas NT B	2.50	1.10
❑ 169	Cal Ripken NT B	3.00	1.35
❑ 170	Chipper Jones NT B	2.00	.90
❑ 171	Mike Piazza NT B	2.50	1.10
❑ 172	Tony Gwynn NT S	12.00	5.50
❑ 173	Juan Gonzalez NT B	2.00	.90
❑ 174	Kenny Lofton NT S	5.00	2.20
❑ 175	Ken Griffey Jr. NT B	4.00	1.80
❑ 176	Mark McGwire NT B	4.00	1.80
❑ 177	Jeff Bagwell NT B	1.25	.55
❑ 178	Paul Molitor NT S	5.00	2.20
❑ 179	Andruw Jones NT B	1.25	.55
❑ 180	Manny Ramirez NT S	5.00	2.20
❑ 181	Ken Caminiti NT S	3.00	1.35
❑ 182	Barry Bonds NT B	1.00	.45
❑ 183	Mo Vaughn NT B	1.00	.45
❑ 184	Derek Jeter NT B	2.50	1.10
❑ 185	Barry Larkin NT S	3.00	1.35
❑ 186	Ivan Rodriguez NT B	1.00	.45
❑ 187	Albert Belle NT S	8.00	3.60
❑ 188	John Smoltz NT S	2.00	.90
❑ 189	Chuck Knoblauch NT S	5.00	2.20
❑ 190	Brian Jordan NT S	2.00	.90
❑ 191	Gary Sheffield NT S	3.00	1.35
❑ 192	Jim Thome NT S	5.00	2.20
❑ 193	Brady Anderson NT S	2.00	.90
❑ 194	Hideo Nomo NT S	6.00	2.70
❑ 195	Sammy Sosa NT S	12.00	5.50
❑ 196	Greg Maddux NT B	2.50	1.10
❑ 197	Vladimir Guerrero CL B	1.25	.55
❑ 198	Scott Rolen CL B	1.50	.70
❑ 199	Todd Walker CL B	.40	.18
❑ 200	Nomar Garciaparra CL B	2.00	.90

1997 Donruss Preferred Cut to the Chase

	MINT	NRMT
COMP.BRONZE SET (100) ..	300.00	135.00
COMMON BRONZE	1.50	.70
*BRONZE STARS: 3X TO 8X BASIC CARDS		
*BRONZE YNG.STARS: 2.5X TO 6X BASIC CARDS		
COMP.SILVER SET (60)	500.00	220.00
COMMON SILVER	6.00	2.70
*SILVER STARS: 1.5X TO 4X BASIC CARDS		
*SILVER YNG.STARS: 1.25X TO 3X BASIC CARDS		
COMP.GOLD SET (30)	600.00	275.00
COMMON GOLD	12.00	5.50
*GOLD STARS: 1X TO 2.5X BASIC CARDS		
*GOLD YOUNG STARS: .75X TO 2X BASIC CARDS		
COMP.PLAT.SET (10)	1200.00	550.00
COMMON PLATINUM	100.00	45.00
*PLAT.STARS: 1.25X TO 3X BASIC CARDS		
*PLAT.YNG.STARS: 1X TO 2.5X BASIC CARDS		

1997 Donruss Preferred Precious Metals

	MINT	NRMT
COMPLETE SET (25)	5000.00	2200.00
COMMON CARD (1-25)	50.00	22.00
❑ 1 Frank Thomas P	300.00	135.00
❑ 2 Ken Griffey Jr. P	500.00	220.00
❑ 3 Greg Maddux P	300.00	135.00
❑ 4 Albert Belle G	100.00	45.00
❑ 5 Juan Gonzalez P	250.00	110.00
❑ 6 Kenny Lofton G	80.00	36.00
❑ 7 Tony Gwynn P	250.00	110.00
❑ 8 Ivan Rodriguez G	120.00	55.00
❑ 9 Mark McGwire G	500.00	220.00
❑ 10 Matt Williams S	50.00	22.00
❑ 11 Wade Boggs S	100.00	45.00
❑ 12 Eddie Murray S	100.00	45.00
❑ 13 Jeff Bagwell G	150.00	70.00
❑ 14 Ken Caminiti G	60.00	27.00
❑ 15 Alex Rodriguez P	300.00	135.00
❑ 16 Chipper Jones P	250.00	110.00
❑ 17 Barry Bonds G	120.00	55.00
❑ 18 Cal Ripken P	400.00	180.00
❑ 19 Mo Vaughn G	120.00	55.00
❑ 20 Mike Piazza P	300.00	135.00
❑ 21 Derek Jeter G	250.00	110.00
❑ 22 Bernie Williams S	100.00	45.00
❑ 23 Andruw Jones P	120.00	55.00
❑ 24 Vladimir Guerrero G ..	150.00	70.00
❑ 25 Jose Guillen S	50.00	22.00

1997 Donruss Preferred Staremasters

	MINT	NRMT
COMPLETE SET (20)	500.00	220.00
COMMON CARD (1-20)	8.00	3.60
❑ 1 Alex Rodriguez	40.00	18.00
❑ 2 Frank Thomas	40.00	18.00
❑ 3 Chipper Jones	30.00	13.50
❑ 4 Cal Ripken	50.00	22.00
❑ 5 Mike Piazza	40.00	18.00
❑ 6 Juan Gonzalez	30.00	13.50
❑ 7 Derek Jeter	30.00	13.50
❑ 8 Jeff Bagwell	20.00	9.00
❑ 9 Ken Griffey Jr.	60.00	27.00
❑ 10 Tony Gwynn	30.00	13.50
❑ 11 Barry Bonds	15.00	6.75
❑ 12 Albert Belle	20.00	9.00
❑ 13 Greg Maddux	40.00	18.00
❑ 14 Mark McGwire	60.00	27.00
❑ 15 Ken Caminiti	8.00	3.60
❑ 16 Hideo Nomo	15.00	6.75
❑ 17 Gary Sheffield	8.00	3.60
❑ 18 Andruw Jones	15.00	6.75
❑ 19 Mo Vaughn	15.00	6.75
❑ 20 Ivan Rodriguez	15.00	6.75

1997 Donruss Preferred Tin Packs

	MINT	NRMT
COMPLETE SET (25)	20.00	9.00
COMMON PACK (1-25)	.25	.11
COMP.GOLD PACK SET (25)	250.00	110.00
*GOLD PACKS: 4X TO 10X HI COLUMN		
*GOLD SEALED PACKS: 7.5X TO 15X HI		
ONE GOLD PACK PER BOX	.25	.11
GOLD PACKS: 1200 SERIAL #'d SETS		
COMP.BLUE BOX SET (25)	150.00	70.00
*BLUE BOXES: 3X TO 8X HI COLUMN		
BLUE BOXES: 1200 SERIAL #'d SETS		
COMP.GOLD BOX SET (25)	500.00	220.00
*GOLD BOXES: 8X TO 20X HI COLUMN		
GOLD BOXES: 299 SERIAL #'d SETS		
PRICES BELOW REFER TO OPENED PACKS		
.25	.11	
❑ 1 Jeff Bagwell	.75	.35
❑ 2 Albert Belle	.60	.25
❑ 3 Barry Bonds	.60	.25
❑ 4 Roger Clemens	1.00	.45
❑ 5 Juan Gonzalez	1.25	.55
❑ 6 Ken Griffey Jr.	2.50	1.10
❑ 7 Tony Gwynn	1.25	.55
❑ 8 Derek Jeter	1.50	.70
❑ 9 Andruw Jones	.75	.35
❑ 10 Chipper Jones	1.25	.55
❑ 11 Kenny Lofton	.50	.23
❑ 12 Greg Maddux	1.50	.70
❑ 13 Mark McGwire	2.50	1.10
❑ 14 Hideo Nomo	.60	.25
❑ 15 Mike Piazza	1.50	.70
❑ 16 Manny Ramirez	.50	.23
❑ 17 Cal Ripken	2.00	.90
❑ 18 Alex Rodriguez	1.50	.70
❑ 19 Ivan Rodriguez	.60	.25
❑ 20 Ryne Sandberg	.60	.25
❑ 21 Gary Sheffield	.40	.18
❑ 22 John Smoltz	.25	.11
❑ 23 Sammy Sosa	1.25	.55
❑ 24 Frank Thomas	1.50	.70
❑ 25 Mo Vaughn	.60	.25

1997 Donruss Preferred X-Ponential Power

	MINT	NRMT
COMPLETE SET (10)	250.00	110.00
COMMON CARD (1A-10B)	5.00	2.20
❑ 1A Manny Ramirez	8.00	3.60
❑ 1B Jim Thome	8.00	3.60
❑ 2A Paul Molitor	8.00	3.60
❑ 2B Chuck Knoblauch	8.00	3.60
❑ 3A Ivan Rodriguez	10.00	4.50
❑ 3B Juan Gonzalez	20.00	9.00
❑ 4A Albert Belle	12.00	5.50
❑ 4B Frank Thomas	25.00	11.00
❑ 5A Roberto Alomar	8.00	3.60
❑ 5B Cal Ripken	30.00	13.50
❑ 6A Tim Salmon	8.00	3.60
❑ 6B Jim Edmonds	6.00	2.70
❑ 7A Ken Griffey Jr.	40.00	18.00
❑ 7B Alex Rodriguez	25.00	11.00
❑ 8A Chipper Jones	20.00	9.00
❑ 8B Andruw Jones	10.00	4.50
❑ 9A Mike Piazza	25.00	11.00
❑ 9B Raul Mondesi	6.00	2.70
❑ 10A Tony Gwynn	20.00	9.00
❑ 10B Ken Caminiti	5.00	2.20

1998 Donruss Preferred

	MINT	NRMT
COMPLETE SET (200)	1100.00	500.00
COMP.GRAND STAND (100)	30.00	13.50
COMMON GRAND STAND	.20	.09
COMP.MEZZANINE (40)	100.00	45.00
COMMON MEZZANINE	2.50	1.10
COMP.CLUB LEVEL (30)	200.00	90.00
COMMON CLUB LEVEL	4.00	1.80
COMP.FIELD BOX (20)	300.00	135.00
COMMON FIELD BOX	8.00	3.60
COMP.EXEC.SUITE (10)	500.00	220.00
COMMON EXEC.SUITE	30.00	13.50
❑ 1 Ken Griffey Jr. EX	100.00	45.00
❑ 2 Frank Thomas EX	60.00	27.00
❑ 3 Cal Ripken EX	80.00	36.00
❑ 4 Alex Rodriguez EX	60.00	27.00
❑ 5 Greg Maddux EX	60.00	27.00
❑ 6 Mike Piazza EX	60.00	27.00
❑ 7 Chipper Jones EX	50.00	22.00
❑ 8 Tony Gwynn FB	30.00	13.50
❑ 9 Derek Jeter FB	30.00	13.50

❑ 10 Jeff Bagwell EX 30.00 13.50
❑ 11 Juan Gonzalez EX 50.00 22.00
❑ 12 Nomar Garciaparra EX 60.00 27.00
❑ 13 Andruw Jones FB 12.00 5.50
❑ 14 Hideo Nomo FB 15.00 6.75
❑ 15 Roger Clemens FB 25.00 11.00
❑ 16 Mark McGwire FB 80.00 36.00
❑ 17 Scott Rolen FB 25.00 11.00
❑ 18 Vladimir Guerrero FB 15.00 6.75
❑ 19 Barry Bonds FB 15.00 6.75
❑ 20 Darin Erstad FB 12.00 5.50
❑ 21 Albert Belle FB 12.00 5.50
❑ 22 Kenny Lofton FB 12.00 5.50
❑ 23 Mo Vaughn FB 15.00 6.75
❑ 24 Tony Clark FB 10.00 4.50
❑ 25 Ivan Rodriguez FB 15.00 6.75
❑ 26 Larry Walker CB 10.00 4.50
❑ 27 Eddie Murray CB 10.00 4.50
❑ 28 Andy Pettitte CB 6.00 2.70
❑ 29 Roberto Alomar CB 10.00 4.50
❑ 30 Randy Johnson CB 10.00 4.50
❑ 31 Manny Ramirez CB 10.00 4.50
❑ 32 Paul Molitor FB 12.00 5.50
❑ 33 Mike Mussina CB 10.00 4.50
❑ 34 Jim Thome FB 12.00 5.50
❑ 35 Tino Martinez CB 10.00 4.50
❑ 36 Gary Sheffield CB 6.00 2.70
❑ 37 Chuck Knoblauch CB 10.00 4.50
❑ 38 Bernie Williams CB 10.00 4.50
❑ 39 Tim Salmon CB 10.00 4.50
❑ 40 Sammy Sosa CB 25.00 11.00
❑ 41 Wade Boggs ME .75 .35
❑ 42 Will Clark GS .75 .35
❑ 43 Andres Galarraga CB 10.00 4.50
❑ 44 Raul Mondesi CB 6.00 2.70
❑ 45 Rickey Henderson GS .75 .35
❑ 46 Jose Canseco GS .75 .35
❑ 47 Pedro Martinez GS .75 .35
❑ 48 Jay Buhner GS .30 .14
❑ 49 Ryan Klesko GS .30 .14
❑ 50 Barry Larkin CB 6.00 2.70
❑ 51 Charles Johnson GS .30 .14
❑ 52 Tom Glavine GS .75 .35
❑ 53 Edgar Martinez CB 4.00 1.80
❑ 54 Fred McGriff GS .50 .23
❑ 55 Moises Alou ME 4.00 1.80
❑ 56 Dante Bichette GS .30 .14
❑ 57 Jim Edmonds CB 6.00 2.70
❑ 58 Mark Grace ME 4.00 1.80
❑ 59 Chan Ho Park ME 6.00 2.70
❑ 60 Justin Thompson ME 2.50 1.10
❑ 61 John Smoltz ME 2.50 1.10
❑ 62 Craig Biggio CB 10.00 4.50
❑ 63 Ken Caminiti ME 4.00 1.80
❑ 64 Deion Sanders ME 2.50 1.10
❑ 65 Carlos Delgado GS .30 .14
❑ 66 David Justice CB 10.00 4.50
❑ 67 J.T. Snow GS .30 .14
❑ 68 Jason Giambi CB 4.00 1.80
❑ 69 Garret Anderson ME 2.50 1.10
❑ 70 Rondell White ME 2.50 1.10
❑ 71 Matt Williams ME 2.50 1.10
❑ 72 Brady Anderson ME 2.50 1.10
❑ 73 Eric Karros GS .30 .14
❑ 74 Javier Lopez GS .30 .14
❑ 75 Pat Hentgen GS .30 .14
❑ 76 Todd Hundley GS .30 .14
❑ 77 Ray Lankford GS .30 .14
❑ 78 Denny Neagle GS .30 .14
❑ 79 Henry Rodriguez GS .30 .14
❑ 80 Sandy Alomar Jr. ME 2.50 1.10
❑ 81 Rafael Palmeiro ME 4.00 1.80
❑ 82 Robin Ventura GS .30 .14
❑ 83 John Olerud GS .30 .14
❑ 84 Omar Vizquel GS .30 .14
❑ 85 Joe Randa GS .20 .09
❑ 86 Lance Johnson GS .20 .09
❑ 87 Kevin Brown GS .50 .23
❑ 88 Curt Schilling GS .30 .14
❑ 89 Ismael Valdes GS .30 .14
❑ 90 Francisco Cordova GS .20 .09
❑ 91 David Cone GS .50 .23
❑ 92 Paul O'Neill GS .30 .14
❑ 93 Jimmy Key GS .30 .14
❑ 94 Brad Radke GS .30 .14
❑ 95 Kevin Appier GS .30 .14
❑ 96 Al Martin GS .20 .09
❑ 97 Rusty Greer ME 2.50 1.10
❑ 98 Reggie Jefferson GS .20 .09
❑ 99 Ron Coomer GS .20 .09
❑ 100 Vinny Castilla GS .50 .23
❑ 101 Bobby Bonilla ME 2.50 1.10
❑ 102 Eric Young GS .30 .14
❑ 103 Tony Womack GS .30 .14
❑ 104 Jason Kendall GS .30 .14
❑ 105 Jeff Suppan GS .20 .09
❑ 106 Shawn Estes ME 2.50 1.10
❑ 107 Shawn Green GS .30 .14
❑ 108 Edgardo Alfonzo ME 2.50 1.10
❑ 109 Alan Benes ME 2.50 1.10
❑ 110 Bobby Higginson GS .50 .23
❑ 111 Mark Grudzielanek GS .30 .14
❑ 112 Wilton Guerrero GS .20 .09
❑ 113 Todd Greene ME 2.50 1.10
❑ 114 Pokey Reese GS .20 .09
❑ 115 Jose Guillen CB 4.00 1.80
❑ 116 Neifi Perez ME 2.50 1.10
❑ 117 Luis Castillo GS .30 .14
❑ 118 Edgar Renteria GS .30 .14
❑ 119 Karim Garcia GS .30 .14
❑ 120 Butch Huskey GS .20 .09
❑ 121 Michael Tucker GS .30 .14
❑ 122 Jason Dickson GS .30 .14
❑ 123 Todd Walker ME 4.00 1.80
❑ 124 Brian Jordan GS .30 .14
❑ 125 Joe Carter GS .30 .14
❑ 126 Matt Morris ME 2.50 1.10
❑ 127 Brett Tomko ME 2.50 1.10
❑ 128 Mike Cameron CB 4.00 1.80
❑ 129 Russ Davis GS .30 .14
❑ 130 Shannon Stewart ME 2.50 1.10
❑ 131 Kevin Orie GS .20 .09
❑ 132 Scott Spiezio GS .20 .09
❑ 133 Brian Giles GS .30 .14
❑ 134 Raul Casanova GS .20 .09
❑ 135 Jose Cruz Jr. CB 10.00 4.50
❑ 136 Hideki Irabu GS .50 .23
❑ 137 Bubba Trammell GS .30 .14
❑ 138 Richard Hidalgo CB 4.00 1.80
❑ 139 Paul Konerko CB 10.00 4.50
❑ 140 Todd Helton FB 12.00 5.50
❑ 141 Miguel Tejada CB 4.00 1.80
❑ 142 Fernando Tatis ME 2.50 1.10
❑ 143 Ben Grieve FB 20.00 9.00
❑ 144 Travis Lee FB 20.00 9.00
❑ 145 Mark Kotsay CB 6.00 2.70
❑ 146 Eli Marrero ME 2.50 1.10
❑ 147 David Ortiz CB 4.00 1.80
❑ 148 Juan Encarnacion ME 2.50 1.10
❑ 149 Jaret Wright ME 6.00 2.70
❑ 150 Livan Hernandez CB 4.00 1.80
❑ 151 Ruben Rivera GS .30 .14
❑ 152 Brad Fullmer ME 2.50 1.10
❑ 153 Dennis Reyes GS .30 .14
❑ 154 Enrique Wilson ME 2.50 1.10
❑ 155 Todd Dunwoody ME 2.50 1.10
❑ 156 Derrick Gibson ME 2.50 1.10
❑ 157 Aaron Boone ME 2.50 1.10
❑ 158 Ron Wright ME 2.50 1.10
❑ 159 Preston Wilson ME 2.50 1.10
❑ 160 Abraham Nunez GS .30 .14
❑ 161 Shane Monahan GS .30 .14
❑ 162 Carl Pavano GS .30 .14
❑ 163 Derrek Lee GS .30 .14
❑ 164 Jeff Abbott GS .30 .14
❑ 165 Wes Helms ME 2.50 1.10
❑ 166 Brian Rose GS .30 .14
❑ 167 Bobby Estalella GS .30 .14
❑ 168 Ken Griffey Jr. PP GS 4.00 1.80
❑ 169 Frank Thomas PP GS 2.50 1.10
❑ 170 Cal Ripken PP GS 3.00 1.35
❑ 171 Alex Rodriguez PP GS 2.50 1.10
❑ 172 Greg Maddux PP GS 2.50 1.10
❑ 173 Mike Piazza PP GS 2.50 1.10
❑ 174 Chipper Jones PP GS 2.00 .90
❑ 175 Tony Gwynn PP GS 2.00 .90
❑ 176 Derek Jeter PP GS 2.00 .90
❑ 177 Jeff Bagwell PP GS 1.25 .55
❑ 178 Juan Gonzalez PP GS 2.00 .90
❑ 179 N. Garciaparra PP GS 2.50 1.10
❑ 180 Andruw Jones PP GS 1.00 .45
❑ 181 Hideo Nomo PP GS 1.00 .45
❑ 182 Roger Clemens PP GS 1.50 .70
❑ 183 Mark McGwire PP GS 5.00 2.20
❑ 184 Scott Rolen PP GS 2.00 .90
❑ 185 Barry Bonds PP GS 1.00 .45
❑ 186 Darin Erstad PP GS 1.00 .45
❑ 187 Mo Vaughn PP GS 1.00 .45
❑ 188 Ivan Rodriguez PP GS 1.00 .45
❑ 189 Larry Walker PP ME 6.00 2.70
❑ 190 Andy Pettitte PP GS .50 .23
❑ 191 Randy Johnson PP ME 6.00 2.70
❑ 192 Paul Molitor PP GS .75 .35
❑ 193 Jim Thome PP GS .75 .35
❑ 194 Tino Martinez PP ME 6.00 2.70
❑ 195 Gary Sheffield PP GS .50 .23
❑ 196 Albert Belle PP GS .75 .35
❑ 197 Jose Cruz Jr. PP GS 1.00 .45
❑ 198 Todd Helton CL GS 1.00 .45
❑ 199 Ben Grieve CL GS 1.50 .70
❑ 200 Paul Konerko CL GS .75 .35

1998 Donruss Preferred Seating

	MINT	NRMT
COMPLETE SET (200)	4500.00	2000.00
COMP.GRAND STAND (100)	400.00	180.00
COMMON GRAND STAND	2.00	.90
*GRAND STAND STARS: 4X TO 10X BASIC CARDS		
*GRAND STAND YOUNG STARS: 3X TO 8X BASIC CARDS		
COMP.MEZZANINE (40)	300.00	135.00
COMMON MEZZANINE	8.00	3.60
*MEZZANINE STARS: .75X TO 2X BASIC CARDS		
COMP.CLUB LEVEL (30)	600.00	275.00
COMMON CLUB LEVEL	12.00	5.50
*CLUB LEVEL STARS: .75X TO 2X BASIC CARDS		
COMP.FIELD BOX (20)	1200.00	550.00
COMMON FIELD BOX	30.00	13.50
*FIELD X STARS: .75X TO 2X BASIC CARDS		
COMP.EXEC.SUITE (10)	2000.00	900.00
COMMON EXEC.SUITE	60.00	27.00
*EXEC.SUITE STARS: .75X TO 2X BASIC CARDS		

1998 Donruss Preferred Great X-Pectations

	MINT	NRMT
COMPLETE SET (26)	400.00	180.00
COMMON CARD (1-26)	5.00	2.20
COMP.DIE CUT SET (26)	1200.00	550.00
*DIE CUT SINGLES: 1.25X TO 3X HI COLUMN		
DIE CUT PRINT RUN 300 SERIAL #'d SETS		

❑ 1 Jeff Bagwell 12.00 5.50
Travis Lee
❑ 2 Jose Cruz Jr. 40.00 18.00
Ken Griffey Jr.
❑ 3 Larry Walker 12.00 5.50
Ben Grieve
❑ 4 Frank Thomas 25.00 11.00
Todd Helton

❑ 5 Jim Thome Paul Konerko	8.00	3.60
❑ 6 Alex Rodriguez Miguel Tejada	25.00	11.00
❑ 7 Greg Maddux Livan Hernandez	25.00	11.00
❑ 8 Roger Clemens Jaret Wright	15.00	6.75
❑ 9 Albert Belle Juan Encarnacion	8.00	3.60
❑ 10 Mo Vaughn David Ortiz	10.00	4.50
❑ 11 Manny Ramirez Mark Kotsay	8.00	3.60
❑ 12 Tim Salmon Brad Fullmer UER misspelled Fulmer	8.00	3.60
❑ 13 Cal Ripken Fernando Tatis	30.00	13.50
❑ 14 Hideo Nomo Hideki Irabu	10.00	4.50
❑ 15 Mike Piazza Todd Greene	25.00	11.00
❑ 16 Gary Sheffield Richard Hidalgo	5.00	2.20
❑ 17 Paul Molitor Darin Erstad	8.00	3.60
❑ 18 Ivan Rodriguez Eli Marrero	10.00	4.50
❑ 19 Ken Caminiti Todd Walker	5.00	2.20
❑ 20 Tony Gwynn Jose Guillen	20.00	9.00
❑ 21 Deter Jeter Nomar Garciaparra	25.00	11.00
❑ 22 Chipper Jones Scott Rolen	20.00	9.00
❑ 23 Juan Gonzalez Andruw Jones	20.00	9.00
❑ 24 Barry Bonds Vladimir Guerrero	10.00	4.50
❑ 25 Mark McGwire Tony Clark	50.00	22.00
❑ 26 Bernie Williams Mike Cameron	8.00	3.60

1998 Donruss Preferred Precious Metals

	MINT	NRMT
COMPLETE SET (30)	7500.00	3400.00
COMMON CARD (1-30)	60.00	27.00
❑ 1 Ken Griffey Jr.	600.00	275.00
❑ 2 Frank Thomas	400.00	180.00
❑ 3 Cal Ripken	500.00	220.00
❑ 4 Alex Rodriguez	400.00	180.00
❑ 5 Greg Maddux	400.00	180.00
❑ 6 Mike Piazza	400.00	180.00
❑ 7 Chipper Jones	300.00	135.00
❑ 8 Tony Gwynn	300.00	135.00
❑ 9 Derek Jeter	300.00	135.00
❑ 10 Jeff Bagwell	200.00	90.00
❑ 11 Juan Gonzalez	300.00	135.00
❑ 12 Nomar Garciaparra	400.00	180.00
❑ 13 Andruw Jones	120.00	55.00
❑ 14 Hideo Nomo	200.00	90.00
❑ 15 Roger Clemens	250.00	110.00
❑ 16 Mark McGwire	800.00	350.00
❑ 17 Scott Rolen	250.00	110.00
❑ 18 Barry Bonds	150.00	70.00
❑ 19 Darin Erstad	120.00	55.00
❑ 20 Kenny Lofton	100.00	45.00
❑ 21 Mo Vaughn	150.00	70.00
❑ 22 Ivan Rodriguez	150.00	70.00
❑ 23 Randy Johnson	120.00	55.00
❑ 24 Paul Molitor	120.00	55.00
❑ 25 Jose Cruz Jr.	120.00	55.00
❑ 26 Paul Konerko	80.00	36.00
❑ 27 Todd Helton	120.00	55.00
❑ 28 Ben Grieve	200.00	90.00
❑ 29 Travis Lee	200.00	90.00
❑ 30 Mark Kotsay	60.00	27.00

1998 Donruss Preferred Tin Packs

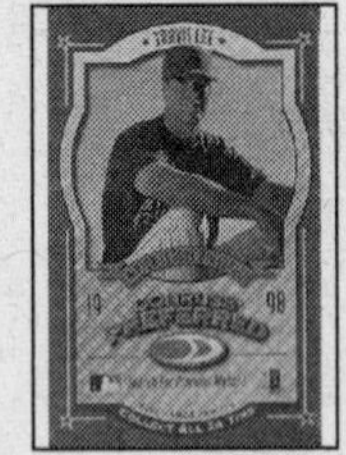

	MINT	NRMT
COMPLETE SET (24)	20.00	9.00
COMMON PACK (1-24)	.50	.23
COMMON SEALED PACK	5.00	2.20

*SEALED: 1.25X TO 3X BASIC PACKS ON 2.00+ PACKS
COMP.GOLD PACK SET (24) 600.00 275.00
*GOLD PACKS: 10X TO 25X BASIC PACKS
*GOLD SEALED PACKS: 12.5X TO 30X BASIC PACKS
GOLD PACKS: RANDOM INSERTS IN BOXES
GOLD PACKS PRINT RUN 199 SERIAL #'d SETS
COMP.SILVER PACK SET (24) 250.00 110.00
*SILVER PACK: 4X TO 10X BASIC PACKS
*SILVER SEALED PACKS: 5X TO 12X BASIC PACKS
SILVER PACKS: RANDOM INSERTS IN BOXES
SILVER PACK PRINT RUN 999 SERIAL #'d SETS
COMP.GREEN BOX SET (24) 250.00 110.00
*GREEN BOXES: 4X TO 10X BASIC PACKS
GREEN BOX PRINT RUN 999 SERIAL #'d SETS
COMP.GOLD BOX SET (24) 600.00 275.00
*GOLD BOXES: 10X TO 25X BASIC PACKS
GOLD BOXES PRINT RUN 199 SERIAL #'d SETS
PRICES BELOW REFER TO OPENED PACKS

❑ 1 Todd Helton	.60	.25
❑ 2 Ben Grieve	1.00	.45
❑ 3 Cal Ripken	2.00	.90
❑ 4 Alex Rodriguez	1.50	.70
❑ 5 Greg Maddux	1.50	.70
❑ 6 Mike Piazza	1.50	.70
❑ 7 Chipper Jones	1.25	.55
❑ 8 Travis Lee	1.00	.45
❑ 9 Derek Jeter	1.25	.55
❑ 10 Jeff Bagwell	.75	.35
❑ 11 Juan Gonzalez	1.25	.55
❑ 12 Mark McGwire	3.00	1.35
❑ 13 Hideo Nomo	.60	.25
❑ 14 Roger Clemens	1.00	.45
❑ 15 Andruw Jones	.60	.25
❑ 16 Paul Molitor	.50	.23
❑ 17 Vladimir Guerrero	.75	.35
❑ 18 Jose Cruz Jr.	.60	.25
❑ 19 Nomar Garciaparra PH	1.50	.70
❑ 20 Scott Rolen PH	1.25	.55
❑ 21 Ken Griffey Jr. PH	2.50	1.10
❑ 22 Larry Walker PH	.50	.23
❑ 23 Frank Thomas PH	1.50	.70
❑ 24 Tony Gwynn PH	1.25	.55

1998 Donruss Preferred Tin Packs Double-Wide

	MINT	NRMT
COMPLETE SET (12)	25.00	11.00
COMMON PACK (1-12)	1.00	.45
❑ 1 Todd Helton Ben Grieve	1.50	.70
❑ 2 Cal Ripken Alex Rodriguez	3.00	1.35
❑ 3 Greg Maddux Mike Piazza	2.50	1.10
❑ 4 Chipper Jones Travis Lee	2.00	.90
❑ 5 Derek Jeter Jeff Bagwell	2.00	.90
❑ 6 Juan Gonzalez Mark McGwire	5.00	2.20
❑ 7 Hideo Nomo Roger Clemens	1.50	.70
❑ 8 Andruw Jones Paul Molitor	1.00	.45
❑ 9 Vladimir Guerrero Jose Cruz Jr.	1.25	.55
❑ 10 Nomar Garciaparra Scott Rolen PH	2.50	1.10
❑ 11 Ken Griffey Jr. Larry Walker PH	4.00	1.80
❑ 12 Frank Thomas Tony Gwynn PH	2.50	1.10

1998 Donruss Preferred Title Waves

	MINT	NRMT
COMPLETE SET (30)	600.00	275.00
COMMON CARD (1-30)	10.00	4.50
❑ 1 Nomar Garciaparra 97 AL ROY	40.00	18.00

- ❑ 2 Scott Rolen 25.00 11.00
  97 NL ROY
- ❑ 3 Roger Clemens 25.00 11.00
  97 AL Cy Young
- ❑ 4 Gary Sheffield 10.00 4.50
  97 World Series
- ❑ 5 Jeff Bagwell 20.00 9.00
  97 Wildcard
- ❑ 6 Cal Ripken 50.00 22.00
  97 AL East Penn.
- ❑ 7 Frank Thomas 40.00 18.00
  97 AL Batting
- ❑ 8 Ken Griffey Jr. 60.00 27.00
  97 AL HR
- ❑ 9 Larry Walker 12.00 5.50
  97 NL HR
- ❑ 10 Derek Jeter 30.00 13.50
  96 AL ROY
- ❑ 11 Juan Gonzalez 30.00 13.50
  96 AL MVP
- ❑ 12 Bernie Williams 12.00 5.50
  96 ALCS MVP
- ❑ 13 Andruw Jones 12.00 5.50
  96 NLCS
- ❑ 14 Andy Pettitte 10.00 4.50
  96 World Series
- ❑ 15 Ivan Rodriguez 15.00 6.75
  96 AL West Penn.
- ❑ 16 Alex Rodriguez 40.00 18.00
  96 AL Batting
- ❑ 17 Mark McGwire 80.00 36.00
  96 AL HR
- ❑ 18 Andres Galarraga 12.00 5.50
  96 NL HR
- ❑ 19 Hideo Nomo 15.00 6.75
  95 ROY
- ❑ 20 Mo Vaughn 15.00 6.75
  95 AL MVP
- ❑ 21 Randy Johnson 12.00 5.50
  95 AL Cy Young
- ❑ 22 Chipper Jones 30.00 13.50
  95 World Series
- ❑ 23 Greg Maddux 40.00 18.00
  95 World Series
- ❑ 24 Manny Ramirez 12.00 5.50
  95 ALCS
- ❑ 25 Tony Gwynn 30.00 13.50
  95 NL Batting
- ❑ 26 Albert Belle 12.00 5.50
  95 AL HR
- ❑ 27 Kenny Lofton 12.00 5.50
  95 AL SB
- ❑ 28 Mike Piazza 40.00 18.00
  93 NL ROY
- ❑ 29 Paul Molitor 12.00 5.50
  93 World Series
- ❑ 30 Barry Bonds 15.00 6.75
  93 NL HR

1997 Donruss Signature

	MINT	NRMT
COMPLETE SET (100)	50.00	22.00
COMMON CARD (1-100)	.25	.11

❑ 1 Mark McGwire	6.00	2.70
❑ 2 Kenny Lofton	1.00	.45
❑ 3 Tony Gwynn	2.50	1.10
❑ 4 Tony Clark	.75	.35
❑ 5 Tim Salmon	1.00	.45
❑ 6 Ken Griffey Jr.	5.00	2.20
❑ 7 Mike Piazza	3.00	1.35
❑ 8 Greg Maddux	3.00	1.35
❑ 9 Roberto Alomar	1.00	.45
❑ 10 Andres Galarraga	1.00	.45
❑ 11 Roger Clemens	2.00	.90
❑ 12 Bernie Williams	1.00	.45
❑ 13 Rondell White	.50	.23
❑ 14 Kevin Appier	.50	.23
❑ 15 Ray Lankford	.50	.23
❑ 16 Frank Thomas	3.00	1.35
❑ 17 Will Clark	1.00	.45
❑ 18 Chipper Jones	2.50	1.10
❑ 19 Jeff Bagwell	1.50	.70
❑ 20 Manny Ramirez	1.00	.45
❑ 21 Ryne Sandberg	1.25	.55
❑ 22 Paul Molitor	1.00	.45
❑ 23 Gary Sheffield	.75	.35
❑ 24 Jim Edmonds	.75	.35
❑ 25 Barry Larkin	.75	.35
❑ 26 Rafael Palmeiro	.75	.35
❑ 27 Alan Benes	.50	.23
❑ 28 Dave Justice	1.00	.45
❑ 29 Randy Johnson	1.00	.45
❑ 30 Barry Bonds	1.25	.55
❑ 31 Mo Vaughn	1.25	.55
❑ 32 Michael Tucker	.50	.23
❑ 33 Larry Walker	1.00	.45
❑ 34 Tino Martinez	1.00	.45
❑ 35 Jose Guillen	1.00	.45
❑ 36 Carlos Delgado	.50	.23
❑ 37 Jason Dickson	.50	.23
❑ 38 Tom Glavine	1.00	.45
❑ 39 Raul Mondesi	.75	.35
❑ 40 Jose Cruz Jr.	4.00	1.80
❑ 41 Johnny Damon	.50	.23
❑ 42 Mark Grace	.75	.35
❑ 43 Juan Gonzalez	2.50	1.10
❑ 44 Vladimir Guerrero	2.00	.90
❑ 45 Kevin Brown	.75	.35
❑ 46 Justin Thompson	.50	.23
❑ 47 Eric Young	.50	.23
❑ 48 Ron Coomer	.25	.11
❑ 49 Mark Kotsay	2.00	.90
❑ 50 Scott Rolen	2.50	1.10
❑ 51 Derek Jeter	3.00	1.35
❑ 52 Jim Thome	1.00	.45
❑ 53 Fred McGriff	.75	.35
❑ 54 Albert Belle	1.25	.55
❑ 55 Garret Anderson	.50	.23
❑ 56 Wilton Guerrero	.25	.11
❑ 57 Jose Canseco	1.00	.45
❑ 58 Cal Ripken	4.00	1.80
❑ 59 Sammy Sosa	2.50	1.10
❑ 60 Dmitri Young	.50	.23
❑ 61 Alex Rodriguez	3.00	1.35
❑ 62 Javier Lopez	.50	.23
❑ 63 Sandy Alomar Jr.	.50	.23
❑ 64 Joe Carter	.50	.23
❑ 65 Dante Bichette	.50	.23
❑ 66 Al Martin	.25	.11
❑ 67 Darin Erstad	1.50	.70
❑ 68 Pokey Reese	.25	.11
❑ 69 Brady Anderson	.50	.23
❑ 70 Andruw Jones	1.50	.70
❑ 71 Ivan Rodriguez	1.25	.55
❑ 72 Nomar Garciaparra	3.00	1.35
❑ 73 Moises Alou	.75	.35
❑ 74 Andy Pettitte	.75	.35
❑ 75 Jay Buhner	.50	.23
❑ 76 Craig Biggio	1.00	.45
❑ 77 Wade Boggs	1.00	.45
❑ 78 Shawn Estes	.50	.23
❑ 79 Neifi Perez	.25	.11
❑ 80 Rusty Greer	.50	.23
❑ 81 Pedro Martinez	1.00	.45
❑ 82 Mike Mussina	1.00	.45
❑ 83 Jason Giambi	.50	.23
❑ 84 Hideo Nomo	1.25	.55
❑ 85 Todd Hundley	.50	.23
❑ 86 Deion Sanders	.50	.23
❑ 87 Mike Cameron	.50	.23
❑ 88 Bobby Bonilla	.50	.23
❑ 89 Todd Greene	.50	.23
❑ 90 Kevin Orie	.25	.11
❑ 91 Ken Caminiti	.75	.35
❑ 92 Chuck Knoblauch	1.00	.45
❑ 93 Matt Morris	.50	.23
❑ 94 Matt Williams	.50	.23
❑ 95 Pat Hentgen	.50	.23
❑ 96 John Smoltz	.50	.23
❑ 97 Edgar Martinez	.50	.23
❑ 98 Jason Kendall	.75	.35
❑ 99 Ken Griffey Jr. CL	2.50	1.10
❑ 100 Frank Thomas CL	1.50	.70

1997 Donruss Signature Autographs

	MINT	NRMT
COMPLETE SET (117)	2000.00	900.00
COMMON CARD	5.00	2.20

❑ 1 Jeff Abbott/3900	8.00	3.60
❑ 2 Bob Abreu/3900	8.00	3.60
❑ 3 Edgardo Alfonzo/3900	8.00	3.60
❑ 4 Roberto Alomar/150 *	120.00	55.00
❑ 5 Sandy Alomar Jr./1400	15.00	6.75
❑ 6 Moises Alou/900	30.00	13.50
❑ 7 Garret Anderson/3900	10.00	4.50
❑ 8 Andy Ashby/3900	5.00	2.20
❑ 9 Trey Beamon/3900	5.00	2.20
❑ 10 Alan Benes/3900	8.00	3.60
❑ 11 Geronimo Berroa/3900	5.00	2.20
❑ 12 Wade Boggs/150 *	120.00	55.00
❑ 13 Kevin Brown C/3900	5.00	2.20
❑ 14 Brett Butler/1400	20.00	9.00
❑ 15 Mike Cameron/3900	8.00	3.60
❑ 16 Giovanni Carrara/2900	5.00	2.20
❑ 17 Luis Castillo/3900	8.00	3.60
❑ 18 Tony Clark/3900	15.00	6.75
❑ 19 Will Clark/1400	30.00	13.50
❑ 20 Lou Collier/3900	5.00	2.20
❑ 21 Bartolo Colon/3900	12.00	5.50
❑ 22 Ron Coomer/3900	5.00	2.20
❑ 23 Marty Cordova/3900	5.00	2.20
❑ 24 Jacob Cruz/3900 *	5.00	2.20
❑ 25 Jose Cruz Jr./900 *	80.00	36.00
❑ 26 Russ Davis/3900	8.00	3.60
❑ 27 Jason Dickson/3900	8.00	3.60
❑ 28 Todd Dunwoody/3900	8.00	3.60
❑ 29 Jermaine Dye/3900	5.00	2.20
❑ 30 Jim Edmonds/3900	15.00	6.75
❑ 31 Darin Erstad/900 *	50.00	22.00
❑ 32 Bobby Estalella/3900	8.00	3.60
❑ 33 Shawn Estes/3900	8.00	3.60
❑ 34 Jeff Fassero/3900	5.00	2.20
❑ 35 Andres Galarraga/900	40.00	18.00
❑ 36 Karim Garcia/3900	8.00	3.60
❑ 37 Derrick Gibson/3900	10.00	4.50
❑ 38 Brian Giles/3900	8.00	3.60
❑ 39 Tom Glavine/150	100.00	45.00
❑ 40 Rick Gorecki/900	10.00	4.50
❑ 41 Shawn Green/1900	15.00	6.75
❑ 42 Todd Greene/3900	8.00	3.60
❑ 43 Rusty Greer/3900	10.00	4.50
❑ 44 Ben Grieve/3900	30.00	13.50
❑ 45 Mark Grudzielanek/3900	8.00	3.60
❑ 46 Vladimir Guerrero/1900 *	40.00	18.00
❑ 47 Wilton Guerrero/2150	10.00	4.50

Card	Mint	NrMt
❑ 48 Jose Guillen/2900	12.00	5.50
❑ 49 Jeffrey Hammonds/2150	10.00	4.50
❑ 50 Todd Helton/1400	30.00	13.50
❑ 51 Todd Hollandsworth/2900	10.00	4.50
❑ 52 Trenidad Hubbard/900	10.00	4.50
❑ 53 Todd Hundley/1400	15.00	6.75
❑ 54 Bobby Jones/3900	5.00	2.20
❑ 55 Brian Jordan/1400	15.00	6.75
❑ 56 David Justice/900	30.00	13.50
❑ 57 Eric Karros/650	25.00	11.00
❑ 58 Jason Kendall/3900	10.00	4.50
❑ 59 Jimmy Key/3900	8.00	3.60
❑ 60 Brooks Kieschnick/3900	5.00	2.20
❑ 61 Ryan Klesko/225	40.00	18.00
❑ 62 Paul Konerko/3900	12.00	5.50
❑ 63 Mark Kotsay/2400	15.00	6.75
❑ 64 Ray Lankford/3900	10.00	4.50
❑ 65 Barry Larkin/150 *	80.00	36.00
❑ 66 Derrek Lee/3900	12.00	5.50
❑ 67 Esteban Loaiza/3900	5.00	2.20
❑ 68 Javier Lopez/1400	20.00	9.00
❑ 69 Edgar Martinez/150 *	60.00	27.00
❑ 70 Pedro Martinez/900	50.00	22.00
❑ 71 Rafael Medina/3900	8.00	3.60
❑ 72 Raul Mondesi EXCH/650	40.00	18.00
❑ 73 Matt Morris/3900	8.00	3.60
❑ 74 Paul O'Neill/900	25.00	11.00
❑ 75 Kevin Orie/3900	5.00	2.20
❑ 76 David Ortiz/3900	12.00	5.50
❑ 77 Rafael Palmeiro/900	30.00	13.50
❑ 78 Jay Payton/3900	5.00	2.20
❑ 79 Neifi Perez/3900	5.00	2.20
❑ 80 Manny Ramirez/900	50.00	22.00
❑ 81 Joe Randa/3900	5.00	2.20
❑ 82 Calvin Reese/3900	5.00	2.20
❑ 83 Edgar Renteria EXCH SP	25.00	11.00
❑ 84 Dennis Reyes/3900	10.00	4.50
❑ 85 Henry Rodriguez/3900	8.00	3.60
❑ 86 Scott Rolen/1900 *	50.00	22.00
❑ 87 Kirk Rueter/2900	8.00	3.60
❑ 88 Ryne Sandberg/400	120.00	55.00
❑ 89 Dwight Smith/2900	8.00	3.60
❑ 90 J.T. Snow/900	15.00	6.75
❑ 91 Scott Spiezio/3900	5.00	2.20
❑ 92 Shannon Stewart/2900	10.00	4.50
❑ 93 Jeff Suppan/1900	10.00	4.50
❑ 94 Mike Sweeney/3900	5.00	2.20
❑ 95 Miguel Tejada/3900	15.00	6.75
❑ 96 Justin Thompson/2400	12.00	5.50
❑ 97 Brett Tomko/3900	8.00	3.60
❑ 98 Bubba Trammell/3900	12.00	5.50
❑ 99 Michael Tucker/3900	8.00	3.60
❑ 100 Javier Valentin/3900	8.00	3.60
❑ 101 Mo Vaughn/150 *	120.00	55.00
❑ 102 Robin Ventura/1400	20.00	9.00
❑ 103 Terrell Wade/3900	5.00	2.20
❑ 104 Billy Wagner/3900	8.00	3.60
❑ 105 Larry Walker/900	40.00	18.00
❑ 106 Todd Walker/2400	15.00	6.75
❑ 107 Rondell White/3900	8.00	3.60
❑ 108 Kevin Wickander/900	10.00	4.50
❑ 109 Chris Widger/3900	5.00	2.20
❑ 110 Matt Williams/150 *	60.00	27.00
❑ 111 Antone Williamson/3900	5.00	2.20
❑ 112 Dan Wilson/3900	5.00	2.20
❑ 113 Tony Womack/3900	12.00	5.50
❑ 114 Jaret Wright/3900	25.00	11.00
❑ 115 Dmitri Young/3900	8.00	3.60
❑ 116 Eric Young/3900	8.00	3.60
❑ 117 Kevin Young/3900	8.00	3.60

1997 Donruss Signature Autographs Century

	MINT	NRMT
COMMON CARD	40.00	18.00
MINOR STARS	80.00	36.00
❑ 4 Roberto Alomar *	150.00	70.00
❑ 9 Jeff Bagwell	250.00	110.00
❑ 11 Albert Belle	150.00	70.00
❑ 14 Wade Boggs *	150.00	70.00
❑ 15 Barry Bonds	200.00	90.00
❑ 19 Jay Buhner	80.00	36.00
❑ 24 Tony Clark	100.00	45.00

Card	Mint	NrMt
❑ 25 Will Clark	120.00	55.00
❑ 26 Roger Clemens *	300.00	135.00
❑ 32 Jose Cruz Jr. *	200.00	90.00
❑ 37 Jim Edmonds	100.00	45.00
❑ 38 Darin Erstad *	120.00	55.00
❑ 42 Andres Galarraga	120.00	55.00
❑ 44 N. Garciaparra SP62 *	500.00	220.00
❑ 48 Juan Gonzalez	400.00	180.00
❑ 53 Ben Grieve	150.00	70.00
❑ 55 Vladimir Guerrero *	150.00	70.00
❑ 57 Jose Guillen	150.00	70.00
❑ 58 Tony Gwynn *	400.00	180.00
❑ 60 Todd Helton	100.00	45.00
❑ 64 Derek Jeter *	400.00	180.00
❑ 65 Andruw Jones *	150.00	70.00
❑ 67 Chipper Jones *	400.00	180.00
❑ 69 David Justice	100.00	45.00
❑ 74 Ryan Klesko	80.00	36.00
❑ 75 Chuck Knoblauch *	100.00	45.00
❑ 76 Paul Konerko	150.00	70.00
❑ 77 Mark Kotsay	100.00	45.00
❑ 79 Barry Larkin *	100.00	45.00
❑ 83 Greg Maddux *	500.00	220.00
❑ 84 Edgar Martinez *	80.00	36.00
❑ 85 Pedro Martinez	150.00	70.00
❑ 86 Tino Martinez *	120.00	55.00
❑ 88 Raul Mondesi EXCH	100.00	45.00
❑ 90 Eddie Murray EXCH*	150.00	70.00
❑ 91 Mike Mussina	150.00	70.00
❑ 95 Rafael Palmeiro	100.00	45.00
❑ 98 Andy Pettitte *	100.00	45.00
❑ 99 Manny Ramirez	150.00	70.00
❑ 104 Cal Ripken	600.00	275.00
❑ 105 Alex Rodriguez	500.00	220.00
❑ 107 Ivan Rodriguez	200.00	90.00
❑ 108 Scott Rolen *	200.00	90.00
❑ 110 Ryne Sandberg	250.00	110.00
❑ 111 Gary Sheffield *	100.00	45.00
❑ 118 Miguel Tejada	100.00	45.00
❑ 119 Frank Thomas	500.00	220.00
❑ 120 Jim Thome EXCH	150.00	70.00
❑ 126 Mo Vaughn *	150.00	70.00
❑ 130 Larry Walker	120.00	55.00
❑ 135 Bernie Williams	150.00	70.00
❑ 136 Matt Williams *	80.00	36.00
❑ 140 Jaret Wright	150.00	70.00

1997 Donruss Signature Autographs Millenium

	MINT	NRMT
COMPLETE SET (143)	6500.00	2900.00
COMMON CARD	15.00	6.75
❑ 1 Jeff Abbott	30.00	13.50
❑ 2 Bob Abreu	20.00	9.00
❑ 3 Edgardo Alfonzo	20.00	9.00
❑ 4 Roberto Alomar *	60.00	27.00
❑ 5 Sandy Alomar Jr.	30.00	13.50
❑ 6 Moises Alou	40.00	18.00
❑ 7 Garret Anderson	30.00	13.50
❑ 8 Andy Ashby	15.00	6.75
❑ 9 Jeff Bagwell/400	150.00	70.00
❑ 10 Trey Beamon	15.00	6.75
❑ 11 Albert Belle/400	100.00	45.00
❑ 12 Alan Benes	30.00	13.50
❑ 13 Geronimo Berroa	15.00	6.75
❑ 14 Wade Boggs *	60.00	27.00
❑ 15 Barry Bonds/400	150.00	70.00
❑ 16 Bobby Bonilla/900 *	30.00	13.50
❑ 17 Kevin Brown/900	50.00	22.00
❑ 18 Kevin Brown C	15.00	6.75
❑ 19 Jay Buhner/900	30.00	13.50
❑ 20 Brett Butler	30.00	13.50
❑ 21 Mike Cameron	30.00	13.50
❑ 22 Giovanni Carrara	15.00	6.75
❑ 23 Luis Castillo	20.00	9.00
❑ 24 Tony Clark	40.00	18.00
❑ 25 Will Clark	50.00	22.00
❑ 26 Roger Clemens/400 *	200.00	90.00
❑ 27 Lou Collier	15.00	6.75
❑ 28 Bartolo Colon	20.00	9.00
❑ 29 Ron Coomer	15.00	6.75
❑ 30 Marty Cordova	15.00	6.75
❑ 31 Jacob Cruz	20.00	9.00
❑ 32 Jose Cruz Jr. *	80.00	36.00
❑ 33 Russ Davis	30.00	13.50
❑ 34 Jason Dickson	20.00	9.00
❑ 35 Todd Dunwoody	30.00	13.50
❑ 36 Jermaine Dye	15.00	6.75
❑ 37 Jim Edmonds	40.00	18.00
❑ 38 Darin Erstad *	60.00	27.00
❑ 39 Bobby Estalella	20.00	9.00
❑ 40 Shawn Estes	30.00	13.50
❑ 41 Jeff Fassero	15.00	6.75
❑ 42 Andres Galarraga	50.00	22.00
❑ 43 Karim Garcia	20.00	9.00
❑ 44 Nomar Garciaparra/650 *	200.00	90.00
❑ 45 Derrick Gibson	30.00	13.50
❑ 46 Brian Giles	30.00	13.50
❑ 47 Tom Glavine	60.00	27.00
❑ 48 Juan Gonzalez/900	150.00	70.00
❑ 49 Rick Gorecki	15.00	6.75
❑ 50 Shawn Green	30.00	13.50
❑ 51 Todd Greene	20.00	9.00
❑ 52 Rusty Greer	30.00	13.50
❑ 53 Ben Grieve	60.00	27.00
❑ 54 Mark Grudzielanek	30.00	13.50
❑ 55 Vladimir Guerrero *	80.00	36.00
❑ 56 Wilton Guerrero	15.00	6.75
❑ 57 Jose Guillen	40.00	18.00
❑ 58 Tony Gwynn/900 *	150.00	70.00
❑ 59 Jeffrey Hammonds	30.00	13.50
❑ 60 Todd Helton	50.00	22.00
❑ 61 Todd Hundley	30.00	13.50
❑ 62 Todd Hollandsworth	15.00	6.75
❑ 63 Trenidad Hubbard	15.00	6.75
❑ 64 Derek Jeter/400 *	200.00	90.00
❑ 65 Andruw Jones/900 *	60.00	27.00
❑ 66 Bobby Jones	15.00	6.75
❑ 67 Chipper Jones/900 *	150.00	70.00
❑ 68 Brian Jordan	30.00	13.50
❑ 69 David Justice	40.00	18.00
❑ 70 Eric Karros	30.00	13.50
❑ 71 Jason Kendall	40.00	18.00
❑ 72 Jimmy Key	30.00	13.50
❑ 73 Brooks Kieschnick	15.00	6.75
❑ 74 Ryan Klesko	30.00	13.50
❑ 75 Chuck Knoblauch/900 *	40.00	18.00
❑ 76 Paul Konerko	60.00	27.00
❑ 77 Mark Kotsay	40.00	18.00
❑ 78 Ray Lankford	30.00	13.50
❑ 79 Barry Larkin *	40.00	18.00
❑ 80 Derrek Lee	30.00	13.50
❑ 81 Esteban Loaiza	15.00	6.75

Card	Mint	NrMt
❑ 82 Javier Lopez	30.00	13.50
❑ 83 Greg Maddux/400 *	300.00	135.00
❑ 84 Edgar Martinez *	30.00	13.50
❑ 85 Pedro Martinez	60.00	27.00
❑ 86 Tino Martinez/900 *	50.00	22.00
❑ 87 Rafael Medina	20.00	9.00
❑ 88 Raul Mondesi EXCH	40.00	18.00
❑ 89 Matt Morris	20.00	9.00
❑ 90 Eddie Murray/900 *	60.00	27.00
❑ 91 Mike Mussina/900	60.00	27.00
❑ 92 Paul O'Neill	30.00	13.50
❑ 93 Kevin Orie	20.00	9.00
❑ 94 David Ortiz	20.00	9.00
❑ 95 Rafael Palmeiro	40.00	18.00
❑ 96 Jay Payton	15.00	6.75
❑ 97 Neifi Perez	20.00	9.00
❑ 98 Andy Pettitte/900 *	40.00	18.00
❑ 99 Manny Ramirez	60.00	27.00
❑ 100 Joe Randa	15.00	6.75
❑ 101 Calvin Reese	15.00	6.75
❑ 102 Edgar Renteria EXCH SP	40.00	18.00
❑ 103 Dennis Reyes	20.00	9.00
❑ 104 Cal Ripken/400	400.00	180.00
❑ 105 Alex Rodriguez/400	300.00	135.00
❑ 106 Henry Rodriguez	30.00	13.50
❑ 107 Ivan Rodriguez/900	80.00	36.00
❑ 108 Scott Rolen *	80.00	36.00
❑ 109 Kirk Rueter	15.00	6.75
❑ 110 Ryne Sandberg	100.00	45.00
❑ 111 Gary Sheffield/400 *	60.00	27.00
❑ 112 Dwight Smith	15.00	6.75
❑ 113 J.T. Snow	30.00	13.50
❑ 114 Scott Spiezio	20.00	9.00
❑ 115 Shannon Stewart	20.00	9.00
❑ 116 Jeff Suppan	20.00	9.00
❑ 117 Mike Sweeney	20.00	9.00
❑ 118 Miguel Tejada	40.00	18.00
❑ 119 Frank Thomas/400	300.00	135.00
❑ 120 Jim Thome EXCH/900	60.00	27.00
❑ 121 Justin Thompson	30.00	13.50
❑ 122 Brett Tomko	20.00	9.00
❑ 123 Bubba Trammell	30.00	13.50
❑ 124 Michael Tucker	20.00	9.00
❑ 125 Javier Valentin	20.00	9.00
❑ 126 Mo Vaughn *	60.00	27.00
❑ 127 Robin Ventura	30.00	13.50
❑ 128 Terrell Wade	15.00	6.75
❑ 129 Billy Wagner	30.00	13.50
❑ 130 Larry Walker	50.00	22.00
❑ 131 Todd Walker	20.00	9.00
❑ 132 Rondell White	30.00	13.50
❑ 133 Kevin Wickander	15.00	6.75
❑ 134 Chris Widger	15.00	6.75
❑ 135 Bernie Williams/400	100.00	45.00
❑ 136 Matt Williams *	30.00	13.50
❑ 137 Antone Williamson	15.00	6.75
❑ 138 Dan Wilson	15.00	6.75
❑ 139 Tony Womack	20.00	9.00
❑ 140 Jaret Wright	60.00	27.00
❑ 141 Dmitri Young	30.00	13.50
❑ 142 Eric Young	30.00	13.50
❑ 143 Kevin Young	30.00	13.50

1997 Donruss Signature Notable Nicknames

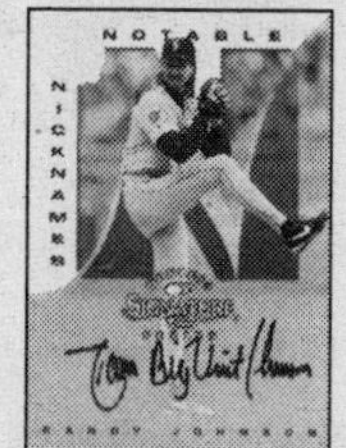

	MINT	NRMT
COMPLETE SET (10)	1800.00	800.00
COMMON CARD	60.00	27.00
❑ 1 Ernie Banks Mr. Cub	250.00	110.00
❑ 2 Tony Clark The Tiger	100.00	45.00
❑ 3 Roger Clemens The Rocket	300.00	135.00
❑ 4 Reggie Jackson Mr. October	250.00	110.00
❑ 5 Randy Johnson The Big Unit	120.00	55.00
❑ 6 Stan Musial The Man	300.00	135.00
❑ 7 Ivan Rodriguez Pudge	150.00	70.00
❑ 8 Frank Thomas The Big Hurt	400.00	180.00
❑ 9 Mo Vaughn The Hit Dog	120.00	55.00
❑ 10 Billy Wagner The Kid	60.00	27.00

1997 Donruss Signature Significant Signatures

	MINT	NRMT
COMPLETE SET (22)	1000.00	450.00
COMMON CARD	30.00	13.50
❑ 1 Ernie Banks	50.00	22.00
❑ 2 Johnny Bench	60.00	27.00
❑ 3 Yogi Berra	60.00	27.00
❑ 4 George Brett	60.00	27.00
❑ 5 Lou Brock	40.00	18.00
❑ 6 Rod Carew	40.00	18.00
❑ 7 Steve Carlton	40.00	18.00
❑ 8 Larry Doby	30.00	13.50
❑ 9 Carlton Fisk	40.00	18.00
❑ 10 Bob Gibson	40.00	18.00
❑ 11A Reggie Jackson	60.00	27.00
❑ 11B R.Jackson Silver Ink	150.00	70.00
❑ 12 Al Kaline	50.00	22.00
❑ 13 Harmon Killebrew	40.00	18.00
❑ 14 Don Mattingly	100.00	45.00
❑ 15 Stan Musial	80.00	36.00
❑ 16 Jim Palmer	40.00	18.00
❑ 17 Brooks Robinson	40.00	18.00
❑ 18 Frank Robinson	50.00	22.00
❑ 19 Mike Schmidt	80.00	36.00
❑ 20 Tom Seaver	60.00	27.00
❑ 21 Duke Snider	60.00	27.00
❑ 22 Carl Yastrzemski	60.00	27.00

1995 Emotion

	MINT	NRMT
COMPLETE SET (200)	40.00	18.00
COMMON CARD (1-200)	.25	.11
❑ 1 Brady Anderson	.50	.23
❑ 2 Kevin Brown	.75	.35
❑ 3 Curtis Goodwin	.25	.11
❑ 4 Jeffrey Hammonds	.50	.23
❑ 5 Ben McDonald	.25	.11
❑ 6 Mike Mussina	1.00	.45
❑ 7 Rafael Palmeiro	.75	.35
❑ 8 Cal Ripken Jr.	4.00	1.80

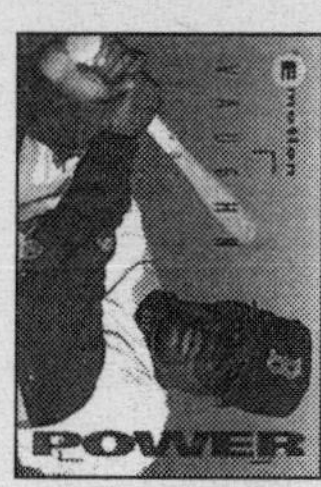

Card	Mint	NrMt
❑ 9 Jose Canseco	1.00	.45
❑ 10 Roger Clemens	2.00	.90
❑ 11 Vaughn Eshelman	.25	.11
❑ 12 Mike Greenwell	.25	.11
❑ 13 Erik Hanson	.25	.11
❑ 14 Tim Naehring	.25	.11
❑ 15 Aaron Sele	.50	.23
❑ 16 John Valentin	.50	.23
❑ 17 Mo Vaughn	1.25	.55
❑ 18 Chili Davis	.50	.23
❑ 19 Gary DiSarcina	.25	.11
❑ 20 Chuck Finley	.50	.23
❑ 21 Tim Salmon	1.00	.45
❑ 22 Lee Smith	.50	.23
❑ 23 J.T. Snow	.50	.23
❑ 24 Jim Abbott	.50	.23
❑ 25 Jason Bere	.25	.11
❑ 26 Ray Durham	.50	.23
❑ 27 Ozzie Guillen	.25	.11
❑ 28 Tim Raines	.50	.23
❑ 29 Frank Thomas	3.00	1.35
❑ 30 Robin Ventura	.50	.23
❑ 31 Carlos Baerga	.50	.23
❑ 32 Albert Belle	1.25	.55
❑ 33 Orel Hershiser	.50	.23
❑ 34 Kenny Lofton	1.00	.45
❑ 35 Dennis Martinez	.50	.23
❑ 36 Eddie Murray	1.00	.45
❑ 37 Manny Ramirez	1.00	.45
❑ 38 Julian Tavarez	.25	.11
❑ 39 Jim Thome	1.00	.45
❑ 40 Dave Winfield	1.00	.45
❑ 41 Chad Curtis	.25	.11
❑ 42 Cecil Fielder	.50	.23
❑ 43 Travis Fryman	.50	.23
❑ 44 Kirk Gibson	.50	.23
❑ 45 Bob Higginson	2.50	1.10
❑ 46 Alan Trammell	.50	.23
❑ 47 Lou Whitaker	.50	.23
❑ 48 Kevin Appier	.50	.23
❑ 49 Gary Gaetti	.50	.23
❑ 50 Jeff Montgomery	.25	.11
❑ 51 Jon Nunnally	.25	.11
❑ 52 Ricky Bones	.25	.11
❑ 53 Cal Eldred	.25	.11
❑ 54 Joe Oliver	.25	.11
❑ 55 Kevin Seitzer	.25	.11
❑ 56 Marty Cordova	.25	.11
❑ 57 Chuck Knoblauch	1.00	.45
❑ 58 Kirby Puckett	1.50	.70
❑ 59 Wade Boggs	1.00	.45
❑ 60 Derek Jeter	3.00	1.35
❑ 61 Jimmy Key	.50	.23
❑ 62 Don Mattingly	1.50	.70
❑ 63 Jack McDowell	.25	.11
❑ 64 Paul O'Neill	.50	.23
❑ 65 Andy Pettitte	1.00	.45
❑ 66 Ruben Rivera	.50	.23
❑ 67 Mike Stanley	.25	.11
❑ 68 John Wetteland	.50	.23
❑ 69 Geronimo Berroa	.25	.11
❑ 70 Dennis Eckersley	.50	.23
❑ 71 Rickey Henderson	1.00	.45
❑ 72 Mark McGwire	5.00	2.20
❑ 73 Steve Ontiveros	.25	.11
❑ 74 Ruben Sierra	.25	.11
❑ 75 Terry Steinbach	.50	.23
❑ 76 Jay Buhner	.50	.23

❑ 77 Ken Griffey Jr. 5.00 2.20
❑ 78 Randy Johnson 1.00 .45
❑ 79 Edgar Martinez .50 .23
❑ 80 Tino Martinez 1.00 .45
❑ 81 Marc Newfield .25 .11
❑ 82 Alex Rodriguez 4.00 1.80
❑ 83 Will Clark 1.00 .45
❑ 84 Benji Gil .25 .11
❑ 85 Juan Gonzalez 2.50 1.10
❑ 86 Rusty Greer 1.00 .45
❑ 87 Dean Palmer .50 .23
❑ 88 Ivan Rodriguez 1.25 .55
❑ 89 Kenny Rogers .25 .11
❑ 90 Roberto Alomar 1.00 .45
❑ 91 Joe Carter .50 .23
❑ 92 David Cone .75 .35
❑ 93 Alex Gonzalez .25 .11
❑ 94 Shawn Green .50 .23
❑ 95 Pat Hentgen .50 .23
❑ 96 Paul Molitor 1.00 .45
❑ 97 John Olerud .50 .23
❑ 98 Devon White .50 .23
❑ 99 Steve Avery .25 .11
❑ 100 Tom Glavine 1.00 .45
❑ 101 Marquis Grissom .50 .23
❑ 102 Chipper Jones 2.50 1.10
❑ 103 David Justice 1.00 .45
❑ 104 Ryan Klesko .50 .23
❑ 105 Javier Lopez .50 .23
❑ 106 Greg Maddux 3.00 1.35
❑ 107 Fred McGriff .75 .35
❑ 108 John Smoltz .50 .23
❑ 109 Shawon Dunston .25 .11
❑ 110 Mark Grace .75 .35
❑ 111 Brian McRae .25 .11
❑ 112 Randy Myers .25 .11
❑ 113 Sammy Sosa 2.50 1.10
❑ 114 Steve Trachsel .25 .11
❑ 115 Bret Boone .50 .23
❑ 116 Ron Gant .25 .11
❑ 117 Barry Larkin .75 .35
❑ 118 Deion Sanders .50 .23
❑ 119 Reggie Sanders .50 .23
❑ 120 Pete Schourek .25 .11
❑ 121 John Smiley .25 .11
❑ 122 Jason Bates .25 .11
❑ 123 Dante Bichette .50 .23
❑ 124 Vinny Castilla .75 .35
❑ 125 Andres Galarraga 1.00 .45
❑ 126 Larry Walker 1.00 .45
❑ 127 Greg Colbrunn .25 .11
❑ 128 Jeff Conine .50 .23
❑ 129 Andre Dawson .75 .35
❑ 130 Chris Hammond .25 .11
❑ 131 Charles Johnson .50 .23
❑ 132 Gary Sheffield .75 .35
❑ 133 Quilvio Veras .25 .11
❑ 134 Jeff Bagwell 1.50 .70
❑ 135 Derek Bell .50 .23
❑ 136 Craig Biggio 1.00 .45
❑ 137 Jim Dougherty .25 .11
❑ 138 John Hudek .25 .11
❑ 139 Orlando Miller .25 .11
❑ 140 Phil Plantier .25 .11
❑ 141 Eric Karros .50 .23
❑ 142 Ramon Martinez .50 .23
❑ 143 Raul Mondesi .75 .35
❑ 144 Hideo Nomo 4.00 1.80
❑ 145 Mike Piazza 3.00 1.35
❑ 146 Ismael Valdes .50 .23
❑ 147 Todd Worrell .25 .11
❑ 148 Moises Alou .75 .35
❑ 149 Yamil Benitez .75 .35
❑ 150 Wil Cordero .25 .11
❑ 151 Jeff Fassero .25 .11
❑ 152 Cliff Floyd .50 .23
❑ 153 Pedro Martinez 1.00 .45
❑ 154 Carlos Perez .75 .35
❑ 155 Tony Tarasco .25 .11
❑ 156 Rondell White .50 .23
❑ 157 Edgardo Alfonzo .50 .23
❑ 158 Bobby Bonilla .50 .23
❑ 159 Rico Brogna .25 .11
❑ 160 Bobby Jones .25 .11
❑ 161 Bill Pulsipher .25 .11
❑ 162 Bret Saberhagen .50 .23
❑ 163 Ricky Bottalico .50 .23
❑ 164 Darren Daulton .50 .23
❑ 165 Lenny Dykstra .50 .23
❑ 166 Charlie Hayes .25 .11
❑ 167 Dave Hollins .25 .11
❑ 168 Gregg Jefferies .25 .11
❑ 169 Michael Mimbs .25 .11
❑ 170 Curt Schilling .50 .23
❑ 171 Heathcliff Slocumb .25 .11
❑ 172 Jay Bell .50 .23
❑ 173 Micah Franklin .25 .11
❑ 174 Mark Johnson .25 .11
❑ 175 Jeff King .25 .11
❑ 176 Al Martin .25 .11
❑ 177 Dan Miceli .25 .11
❑ 178 Denny Neagle .50 .23
❑ 179 Bernard Gilkey .25 .11
❑ 180 Ken Hill .25 .11
❑ 181 Brian Jordan .50 .23
❑ 182 Ray Lankford .50 .23
❑ 183 Ozzie Smith 1.25 .55
❑ 184 Andy Benes .50 .23
❑ 185 Ken Caminiti .75 .35
❑ 186 Steve Finley .50 .23
❑ 187 Tony Gwynn 2.50 1.10
❑ 188 Joey Hamilton .50 .23
❑ 189 Melvin Nieves .25 .11
❑ 190 Scott Sanders .25 .11
❑ 191 Rod Beck .25 .11
❑ 192 Barry Bonds 1.25 .55
❑ 193 Royce Clayton .25 .11
❑ 194 Glenallen Hill .25 .11
❑ 195 Darren Lewis .25 .11
❑ 196 Mark Portugal .25 .11
❑ 197 Matt Williams .50 .23
❑ 198 Checklist 1-82 .25 .11
❑ 199 Checklist 83-162 .25 .11
❑ 200 Checklist 163-200/Inserts .25 .11
❑ P8 Cal Ripken Promo 3.00 1.35

1995 Emotion Masters

	MINT	NRMT
COMPLETE SET (10)	60.00	27.00
COMMON CARD (1-10)	2.00	.90

❑ 1 Barry Bonds 3.00 1.35
❑ 2 Juan Gonzalez 8.00 3.60
❑ 3 Ken Griffey Jr. 15.00 6.75
❑ 4 Tony Gwynn 8.00 3.60
❑ 5 Kenny Lofton 3.00 1.35
❑ 6 Greg Maddux 10.00 4.50
❑ 7 Raul Mondesi 2.00 .90
❑ 8 Cal Ripken 12.00 5.50
❑ 9 Frank Thomas 10.00 4.50
❑ 10 Matt Williams 2.00 .90

1995 Emotion N-Tense

	MINT	NRMT
COMPLETE SET (12)	150.00	70.00
COMMON CARD (1-12)	3.00	1.35

❑ 1 Jeff Bagwell 12.00 5.50
❑ 2 Albert Belle 10.00 4.50
❑ 3 Barry Bonds 10.00 4.50
❑ 4 Cecil Fielder 4.00 1.80
❑ 5 Ron Gant 3.00 1.35
❑ 6 Ken Griffey Jr. 40.00 18.00
❑ 7 Mark McGwire 40.00 18.00
❑ 8 Mike Piazza 25.00 11.00
❑ 9 Manny Ramirez 8.00 3.60
❑ 10 Frank Thomas 25.00 11.00
❑ 11 Mo Vaughn 10.00 4.50
❑ 12 Matt Williams 4.00 1.80

1995 Emotion Ripken

	MINT	NRMT
COMPLETE SET (10)	50.00	22.00
COMMON CARD (1-10)	6.00	2.70
COMMON MAIL-IN (11-15)	6.00	2.70

❑ 1 Cal Ripken 6.00 2.70
High School Pitcher
❑ 2 Cal Ripken 6.00 2.70
Role Model
❑ 3 Cal Ripken 6.00 2.70
Rookie of the Year
❑ 4 Cal Ripken 6.00 2.70
1st MVP Season
❑ 5 Cal Ripken 6.00 2.70
95 Consecutived Errorless Games
❑ 6 Cal Ripken 6.00 2.70
All-Star MVP
❑ 7 Cal Ripken 6.00 2.70
Conditioning
❑ 8 Cal Ripken 6.00 2.70
Shortstop HR Record
❑ 9 Cal Ripken 6.00 2.70
Literacy Work
❑ 10 Cal Ripken 6.00 2.70
2000th Consecutive Game
❑ 11 Cal Ripken 6.00 2.70
1995 All-Star Selection
❑ 12 Cal Ripken 6.00 2.70
35th Birthday
❑ 13 Cal Ripken 6.00 2.70
Game 2,130
❑ 14 Cal Ripken 6.00 2.70
Game 2,131
❑ 15 Cal Ripken 6.00 2.70
2,153 and Counting

1995 Emotion Rookies

	MINT	NRMT
COMPLETE SET (10)	25.00	11.00

COMMON CARD (1-10)	1.00	.45
❑ 1 Edgardo Alfonzo	2.00	.90
❑ 2 Jason Bates	1.00	.45
❑ 3 Marty Cordova	1.00	.45
❑ 4 Ray Durham	2.00	.90
❑ 5 Alex Gonzalez	1.00	.45
❑ 6 Shawn Green	2.00	.90
❑ 7 Charles Johnson	2.00	.90
❑ 8 Chipper Jones	8.00	3.60
❑ 9 Hideo Nomo	6.00	2.70
❑ 10 Alex Rodriguez	10.00	4.50

1996 Emotion-XL

	MINT	NRMT
COMPLETE SET (300)	80.00	36.00
COMMON CARD (1-300)	.40	.18
❑ 1 Roberto Alomar	1.50	.70
❑ 2 Brady Anderson	.75	.35
❑ 3 Bobby Bonilla	.75	.35
❑ 4 Jeffrey Hammonds	.75	.35
❑ 5 Chris Hoiles	.40	.18
❑ 6 Mike Mussina	1.50	.70
❑ 7 Randy Myers	.40	.18
❑ 8 Rafael Palmeiro	1.00	.45
❑ 9 Cal Ripken	6.00	2.70
❑ 10 B.J. Surhoff	.75	.35
❑ 11 Jose Canseco	1.50	.70
❑ 12 Roger Clemens	3.00	1.35
❑ 13 Wil Cordero	.40	.18
❑ 14 Mike Greenwell	.40	.18
❑ 15 Dwayne Hosey	.40	.18
❑ 16 Tim Naehring	.40	.18
❑ 17 Troy O'Leary	.75	.35
❑ 18 Mike Stanley	.40	.18
❑ 19 John Valentin	.75	.35
❑ 20 Mo Vaughn	2.00	.90
❑ 21 Jim Abbott	.75	.35
❑ 22 Garret Anderson	.75	.35
❑ 23 George Arias	.40	.18
❑ 24 Chili Davis	.75	.35
❑ 25 Jim Edmonds	1.00	.45
❑ 26 Chuck Finley	.75	.35
❑ 27 Todd Greene	.75	.35
❑ 28 Mark Langston	.40	.18
❑ 29 Troy Percival	.75	.35
❑ 30 Tim Salmon	1.50	.70
❑ 31 Lee Smith	.75	.35
❑ 32 J.T. Snow	.75	.35
❑ 33 Harold Baines	.75	.35
❑ 34 Jason Bere	.40	.18
❑ 35 Ray Durham	.75	.35
❑ 36 Alex Fernandez	.40	.18
❑ 37 Ozzie Guillen	.40	.18
❑ 38 Darren Lewis	.40	.18
❑ 39 Lyle Mouton	.40	.18
❑ 40 Tony Phillips	.40	.18
❑ 41 Danny Tartabull	.40	.18
❑ 42 Frank Thomas	5.00	2.20
❑ 43 Robin Ventura	.75	.35
❑ 44 Sandy Alomar Jr.	.75	.35
❑ 45 Carlos Baerga	.75	.35
❑ 46 Albert Belle	2.00	.90
❑ 47 Julio Franco	.40	.18
❑ 48 Orel Hershiser	.75	.35
❑ 49 Kenny Lofton	1.50	.70
❑ 50 Dennis Martinez	.75	.35
❑ 51 Jack McDowell	.40	.18
❑ 52 Jose Mesa	.40	.18
❑ 53 Eddie Murray	1.50	.70
❑ 54 Charles Nagy	.75	.35
❑ 55 Manny Ramirez	1.50	.70
❑ 56 Jim Thome	1.50	.70
❑ 57 Omar Vizquel	.75	.35
❑ 58 Chad Curtis	.40	.18
❑ 59 Cecil Fielder	.75	.35
❑ 60 Travis Fryman	.75	.35
❑ 61 Chris Gomez	.40	.18
❑ 62 Felipe Lira	.40	.18
❑ 63 Alan Trammell	1.00	.45
❑ 64 Kevin Appier	.75	.35
❑ 65 Johnny Damon	.75	.35
❑ 66 Tom Goodwin	.40	.18
❑ 67 Mark Gubicza	.40	.18
❑ 68 Jeff Montgomery	.40	.18
❑ 69 Jon Nunnally	.40	.18
❑ 70 Bip Roberts	.40	.18
❑ 71 Ricky Bones	.40	.18
❑ 72 Chuck Carr	.40	.18
❑ 73 John Jaha	.40	.18
❑ 74 Ben McDonald	.40	.18
❑ 75 Matt Mieske	.40	.18
❑ 76 Dave Nilsson	.40	.18
❑ 77 Kevin Seitzer	.40	.18
❑ 78 Greg Vaughn	.75	.35
❑ 79 Rick Aguilera	.40	.18
❑ 80 Marty Cordova	.40	.18
❑ 81 Roberto Kelly	.40	.18
❑ 82 Chuck Knoblauch	1.50	.70
❑ 83 Pat Meares	.40	.18
❑ 84 Paul Molitor	1.50	.70
❑ 85 Kirby Puckett	2.50	1.10
❑ 86 Brad Radke	.75	.35
❑ 87 Wade Boggs	1.50	.70
❑ 88 David Cone	1.00	.45
❑ 89 Dwight Gooden	.75	.35
❑ 90 Derek Jeter	5.00	2.20
❑ 91 Tino Martinez	1.50	.70
❑ 92 Paul O'Neill	.75	.35
❑ 93 Andy Pettitte	1.00	.45
❑ 94 Tim Raines	.75	.35
❑ 95 Ruben Rivera	.75	.35
❑ 96 Kenny Rogers	.40	.18
❑ 97 Ruben Sierra	.40	.18
❑ 98 John Wetteland	.75	.35
❑ 99 Bernie Williams	1.50	.70
❑ 100 Allen Battle	.40	.18
❑ 101 Geronimo Berroa	.40	.18
❑ 102 Brent Gates	.40	.18
❑ 103 Doug Johns	.40	.18
❑ 104 Mark McGwire	8.00	3.60
❑ 105 Pedro Munoz	.40	.18
❑ 106 Ariel Prieto	.40	.18
❑ 107 Terry Steinbach	.75	.35
❑ 108 Todd Van Poppel	.40	.18
❑ 109 Chris Bosio	.40	.18
❑ 110 Jay Buhner	.75	.35
❑ 111 Joey Cora	.75	.35
❑ 112 Russ Davis	.75	.35
❑ 113 Ken Griffey Jr.	8.00	3.60
❑ 114 Sterling Hitchcock	.75	.35
❑ 115 Randy Johnson	1.50	.70
❑ 116 Edgar Martinez	.75	.35
❑ 117 Alex Rodriguez	5.00	2.20
❑ 118 Paul Sorrento	.40	.18
❑ 119 Dan Wilson	.40	.18
❑ 120 Will Clark	1.50	.70
❑ 121 Juan Gonzalez	4.00	1.80
❑ 122 Rusty Greer	1.00	.45
❑ 123 Kevin Gross	.40	.18
❑ 124 Ken Hill	.40	.18
❑ 125 Dean Palmer	.75	.35
❑ 126 Roger Pavlik	.40	.18
❑ 127 Ivan Rodriguez	2.00	.90
❑ 128 Mickey Tettleton	.40	.18
❑ 129 Joe Carter	.75	.35
❑ 130 Carlos Delgado	.75	.35
❑ 131 Alex Gonzalez	.40	.18
❑ 132 Shawn Green	.75	.35
❑ 133 Erik Hanson	.40	.18
❑ 134 Pat Hentgen	.75	.35
❑ 135 Otis Nixon	.40	.18
❑ 136 John Olerud	.75	.35
❑ 137 Ed Sprague	.40	.18
❑ 138 Steve Avery	.40	.18
❑ 139 Jermaine Dye	.40	.18
❑ 140 Tom Glavine	1.50	.70
❑ 141 Marquis Grissom	.75	.35
❑ 142 Chipper Jones	4.00	1.80
❑ 143 David Justice	1.50	.70
❑ 144 Ryan Klesko	.75	.35
❑ 145 Javier Lopez	.75	.35
❑ 146 Greg Maddux	5.00	2.20
❑ 147 Fred McGriff	1.00	.45
❑ 148 Jason Schmidt	.40	.18
❑ 149 John Smoltz	.75	.35
❑ 150 Mark Wohlers	.40	.18
❑ 151 Jim Bullinger	.40	.18
❑ 152 Frank Castillo	.40	.18
❑ 153 Kevin Foster	.40	.18
❑ 154 Luis Gonzalez	.40	.18
❑ 155 Mark Grace	1.00	.45
❑ 156 Brian McRae	.40	.18
❑ 157 Jaime Navarro	.40	.18
❑ 158 Rey Sanchez	.40	.18
❑ 159 Ryne Sandberg	2.00	.90
❑ 160 Sammy Sosa	4.00	1.80
❑ 161 Bret Boone	.75	.35
❑ 162 Jeff Brantley	.40	.18
❑ 163 Vince Coleman	.40	.18
❑ 164 Steve Gibralter	.40	.18
❑ 165 Barry Larkin	1.00	.45
❑ 166 Hal Morris	.40	.18
❑ 167 Mark Portugal	.40	.18
❑ 168 Reggie Sanders	.75	.35
❑ 169 Pete Schourek	.40	.18
❑ 170 John Smiley	.40	.18
❑ 171 Jason Bates	.40	.18
❑ 172 Dante Bichette	.75	.35
❑ 173 Ellis Burks	.75	.35
❑ 174 Vinny Castilla	1.00	.45
❑ 175 Andres Galarraga	1.50	.70
❑ 176 Kevin Ritz	.40	.18
❑ 177 Bill Swift	.40	.18
❑ 178 Larry Walker	1.50	.70
❑ 179 Walt Weiss	.40	.18
❑ 180 Eric Young	.40	.18
❑ 181 Kurt Abbott	.40	.18
❑ 182 Kevin Brown	1.50	.70
❑ 183 John Burkett	.40	.18
❑ 184 Greg Colbrunn	.40	.18
❑ 185 Jeff Conine	.75	.35
❑ 186 Chris Hammond	.40	.18
❑ 187 Charles Johnson	.75	.35
❑ 188 Terry Pendleton	.40	.18
❑ 189 Pat Rapp	.40	.18
❑ 190 Gary Sheffield	1.00	.45
❑ 191 Quilvio Veras	.40	.18
❑ 192 Devon White	.75	.35
❑ 193 Jeff Bagwell	2.50	1.10
❑ 194 Derek Bell	.75	.35
❑ 195 Sean Berry	.40	.18
❑ 196 Craig Biggio	1.50	.70
❑ 197 Doug Drabek	.40	.18
❑ 198 Tony Eusebio	.40	.18
❑ 199 Mike Hampton	.40	.18
❑ 200 Brian L.Hunter	.75	.35
❑ 201 Derrick May	.40	.18
❑ 202 Orlando Miller	.40	.18

❑ 203 Shane Reynolds .75 .35
❑ 204 Mike Blowers .40 .18
❑ 205 Tom Candiotti .40 .18
❑ 206 Delino DeShields .40 .18
❑ 207 Greg Gagne .40 .18
❑ 208 Karim Garcia .75 .35
❑ 209 Todd Hollandsworth .40 .18
❑ 210 Eric Karros .75 .35
❑ 211 Ramon Martinez .75 .35
❑ 212 Raul Mondesi 1.00 .45
❑ 213 Hideo Nomo 2.50 1.10
❑ 214 Chan Ho Park 1.50 .70
❑ 215 Mike Piazza 5.00 2.20
❑ 216 Ismael Valdes .75 .35
❑ 217 Todd Worrell .40 .18
❑ 218 Moises Alou 1.00 .45
❑ 219 Yamil Benitez .40 .18
❑ 220 Jeff Fassero .40 .18
❑ 221 Darrin Fletcher .40 .18
❑ 222 Cliff Floyd .75 .35
❑ 223 Pedro Martinez 1.50 .70
❑ 224 Carlos Perez .75 .35
❑ 225 Mel Rojas .40 .18
❑ 226 David Segui .75 .35
❑ 227 Rondell White .75 .35
❑ 228 Rico Brogna .40 .18
❑ 229 Carl Everett .40 .18
❑ 230 John Franco .75 .35
❑ 231 Bernard Gilkey .40 .18
❑ 232 Todd Hundley .75 .35
❑ 233 Jason Isringhausen .40 .18
❑ 234 Lance Johnson .40 .18
❑ 235 Bobby Jones .40 .18
❑ 236 Jeff Kent .75 .35
❑ 237 Rey Ordonez .75 .35
❑ 238 Bill Pulsipher .40 .18
❑ 239 Jose Vizcaino .40 .18
❑ 240 Paul Wilson .40 .18
❑ 241 Ricky Bottalico .75 .35
❑ 242 Darren Daulton .75 .35
❑ 243 Lenny Dykstra .75 .35
❑ 244 Jim Eisenreich .40 .18
❑ 245 Sid Fernandez .40 .18
❑ 246 Gregg Jefferies .40 .18
❑ 247 Mickey Morandini .40 .18
❑ 248 Benito Santiago .40 .18
❑ 249 Curt Schilling .75 .35
❑ 250 Mark Whiten .40 .18
❑ 251 Todd Zeile .40 .18
❑ 252 Jay Bell .75 .35
❑ 253 Carlos Garcia .40 .18
❑ 254 Charlie Hayes .40 .18
❑ 255 Jason Kendall 1.50 .70
❑ 256 Jeff King .40 .18
❑ 257 Al Martin .40 .18
❑ 258 Orlando Merced .40 .18
❑ 259 Dan Miceli .40 .18
❑ 260 Denny Neagle .75 .35
❑ 261 Alan Benes .75 .35
❑ 262 Andy Benes .75 .35
❑ 263 Royce Clayton .40 .18
❑ 264 Dennis Eckersley .75 .35
❑ 265 Gary Gaetti .75 .35
❑ 266 Ron Gant .40 .18
❑ 267 Brian Jordan .75 .35
❑ 268 Ray Lankford .75 .35
❑ 269 John Mabry .40 .18
❑ 270 Tom Pagnozzi .40 .18
❑ 271 Ozzie Smith 2.00 .90
❑ 272 Todd Stottlemyre .40 .18
❑ 273 Andy Ashby .40 .18
❑ 274 Brad Ausmus .40 .18
❑ 275 Ken Caminiti 1.00 .45
❑ 276 Steve Finley .75 .35
❑ 277 Tony Gwynn 4.00 1.80
❑ 278 Joey Hamilton .75 .35
❑ 279 Rickey Henderson 1.50 .70
❑ 280 Trevor Hoffman .75 .35
❑ 281 Wally Joyner .75 .35
❑ 282 Jody Reed .40 .18
❑ 283 Bob Tewksbury .40 .18
❑ 284 Fernando Valenzuela .75 .35
❑ 285 Rod Beck .40 .18
❑ 286 Barry Bonds 2.00 .90
❑ 287 Mark Carreon .40 .18
❑ 288 Shawon Dunston .40 .18
❑ 289 Osvaldo Fernandez .40 .18
❑ 290 Glenallen Hill .40 .18
❑ 291 Stan Javier .40 .18
❑ 292 Mark Leiter .40 .18
❑ 293 Kirt Manwaring .40 .18
❑ 294 Robby Thompson .40 .18
❑ 295 William VanLandingham .40 .18
❑ 296 Allen Watson .40 .18
❑ 297 Matt Williams .75 .35
❑ 298 Checklist .40 .18
❑ 299 Checklist .40 .18
❑ 300 Checklist .40 .18
❑ P55 Manny Ramirez 2.00 .90
Promo

1996 Emotion-XL D-Fense

	MINT	NRMT
COMPLETE SET (10)	25.00	11.00
COMMON CARD (1-10)	1.00	.45

❑ 1 Roberto Alomar 1.50 .70
❑ 2 Barry Bonds 1.50 .70
❑ 3 Mark Grace 1.00 .45
❑ 4 Ken Griffey Jr. 10.00 4.50
❑ 5 Kenny Lofton 1.50 .70
❑ 6 Greg Maddux 6.00 2.70
❑ 7 Raul Mondesi 1.00 .45
❑ 8 Cal Ripken 8.00 3.60
❑ 9 Ivan Rodriguez 1.50 .70
❑ 10 Matt Williams 1.00 .45

1996 Emotion-XL Legion of Boom

	MINT	NRMT
COMPLETE SET (12)	200.00	90.00
COMMON CARD (1-12)	6.00	2.70

❑ 1 Albert Belle 12.00 5.50
❑ 2 Barry Bonds 12.00 5.50
❑ 3 Juan Gonzalez 25.00 11.00
❑ 4 Ken Griffey Jr. 50.00 22.00
❑ 5 Mark McGwire 50.00 22.00
❑ 6 Mike Piazza 30.00 13.50
❑ 7 Manny Ramirez 10.00 4.50
❑ 8 Tim Salmon 10.00 4.50
❑ 9 Sammy Sosa 25.00 11.00
❑ 10 Frank Thomas 30.00 13.50
❑ 11 Mo Vaughn 12.00 5.50
❑ 12 Matt Williams 6.00 2.70

1996 Emotion-XL N-Tense

	MINT	NRMT
COMPLETE SET (10)	100.00	45.00
COMMON CARD (1-10)	3.00	1.35

❑ 1 Albert Belle 5.00 2.20
❑ 2 Barry Bonds 6.00 2.70
❑ 3 Jose Canseco 5.00 2.20
❑ 4 Ken Griffey Jr. 25.00 11.00
❑ 5 Tony Gwynn 12.00 5.50
❑ 6 Randy Johnson 5.00 2.20
❑ 7 Greg Maddux 15.00 6.75
❑ 8 Cal Ripken 20.00 9.00
❑ 9 Frank Thomas 15.00 6.75
❑ 10 Matt Williams 3.00 1.35

1997 E-X2000

	MINT	NRMT
COMPLETE SET (100)	100.00	45.00
COMMON CARD (1-100)	.50	.23

❑ 1 Jim Edmonds 1.50 .70
❑ 2 Darin Erstad 3.00 1.35
❑ 3 Eddie Murray 2.00 .90
❑ 4 Roberto Alomar 2.00 .90
❑ 5 Brady Anderson 1.00 .45
❑ 6 Mike Mussina 2.00 .90
❑ 7 Rafael Palmeiro 1.50 .70
❑ 8 Cal Ripken 8.00 3.60
❑ 9 Steve Avery .50 .23
❑ 10 Nomar Garciaparra 6.00 2.70
❑ 11 Mo Vaughn 2.50 1.10
❑ 12 Albert Belle 2.50 1.10
❑ 13 Mike Cameron 1.00 .45
❑ 14 Ray Durham 1.00 .45
❑ 15 Frank Thomas 6.00 2.70
❑ 16 Robin Ventura 1.00 .45
❑ 17 Manny Ramirez 2.00 .90
❑ 18 Jim Thome 2.00 .90
❑ 19 Matt Williams 1.00 .45
❑ 20 Tony Clark 1.50 .70
❑ 21 Travis Fryman 1.00 .45

		MINT	NRMT
❑ 22	Bob Higginson	1.50	.70
❑ 23	Kevin Appier	1.00	.45
❑ 24	Johnny Damon	1.00	.45
❑ 25	Jermaine Dye	.50	.23
❑ 26	Jeff Cirillo	1.00	.45
❑ 27	Ben McDonald	.50	.23
❑ 28	Chuck Knoblauch	2.00	.90
❑ 29	Paul Molitor	2.00	.90
❑ 30	Todd Walker	2.00	.90
❑ 31	Wade Boggs	2.00	.90
❑ 32	Cecil Fielder	1.00	.45
❑ 33	Derek Jeter	6.00	2.70
❑ 34	Andy Pettitte	1.50	.70
❑ 35	Ruben Rivera	1.00	.45
❑ 36	Bernie Williams	2.00	.90
❑ 37	Jose Canseco	2.00	.90
❑ 38	Mark McGwire	10.00	4.50
❑ 39	Jay Buhner	1.00	.45
❑ 40	Ken Griffey Jr.	10.00	4.50
❑ 41	Randy Johnson	2.00	.90
❑ 42	Edgar Martinez	1.00	.45
❑ 43	Alex Rodriguez	6.00	2.70
❑ 44	Dan Wilson	.50	.23
❑ 45	Will Clark	2.00	.90
❑ 46	Juan Gonzalez	5.00	2.20
❑ 47	Ivan Rodriguez	2.50	1.10
❑ 48	Joe Carter	1.00	.45
❑ 49	Roger Clemens	4.00	1.80
❑ 50	Juan Guzman	.50	.23
❑ 51	Pat Hentgen	1.00	.45
❑ 52	Tom Glavine	2.00	.90
❑ 53	Andruw Jones	3.00	1.35
❑ 54	Chipper Jones	5.00	2.20
❑ 55	Ryan Klesko	1.00	.45
❑ 56	Kenny Lofton	2.00	.90
❑ 57	Greg Maddux	6.00	2.70
❑ 58	Fred McGriff	1.50	.70
❑ 59	John Smoltz	1.00	.45
❑ 60	Mark Wohlers	.50	.23
❑ 61	Mark Grace	1.50	.70
❑ 62	Ryne Sandberg	2.50	1.10
❑ 63	Sammy Sosa	5.00	2.20
❑ 64	Barry Larkin	1.50	.70
❑ 65	Deion Sanders	1.00	.45
❑ 66	Reggie Sanders	1.00	.45
❑ 67	Dante Bichette	1.00	.45
❑ 68	Ellis Burks	1.00	.45
❑ 69	Andres Galarraga	2.00	.90
❑ 70	Moises Alou	1.50	.70
❑ 71	Kevin Brown	1.50	.70
❑ 72	Cliff Floyd	1.00	.45
❑ 73	Edgar Renteria	1.00	.45
❑ 74	Gary Sheffield	1.50	.70
❑ 75	Bob Abreu	1.00	.45
❑ 76	Jeff Bagwell	3.00	1.35
❑ 77	Craig Biggio	2.00	.90
❑ 78	Todd Hollandsworth	.50	.23
❑ 79	Eric Karros	1.00	.45
❑ 80	Raul Mondesi	1.50	.70
❑ 81	Hideo Nomo	2.50	1.10
❑ 82	Mike Piazza	6.00	2.70
❑ 83	Vladimir Guerrero	4.00	1.80
❑ 84	Henry Rodriguez	1.00	.45
❑ 85	Todd Hundley	1.00	.45
❑ 86	Alex Ochoa	.50	.23
❑ 87	Rey Ordonez	1.00	.45
❑ 88	Gregg Jefferies	.50	.23
❑ 89	Scott Rolen	5.00	2.20
❑ 90	Jermaine Allensworth	.50	.23
❑ 91	Jason Kendall	1.50	.70
❑ 92	Ken Caminiti	1.50	.70
❑ 93	Tony Gwynn	5.00	2.20
❑ 94	Rickey Henderson	2.00	.90
❑ 95	Barry Bonds	2.50	1.10
❑ 96	J.T. Snow	1.00	.45
❑ 97	Dennis Eckersley	1.00	.45
❑ 98	Ron Gant	.50	.23
❑ 99	Brian Jordan	1.00	.45
❑ 100	Ray Lankford	1.00	.45
❑ 101	Checklist	.50	.23
❑ 102	Checklist	.50	.23
❑ P43	Alex Rodriguez Three card promo strip	3.00	1.35
❑ S43	Alex Rodriguez Mailed to Dealers who ordered Cases Card is numbered out of 3,000	20.00	9.00
❑ NNO	Alex Rodriguez Ball Exch 100 produced	150.00	70.00

1997 E-X2000 Essential Credentials

	MINT	NRMT
COMMON CARD (1-100)	20.00	9.00

*STARS: 15X TO 40X BASIC CARDS
*YOUNG STARS: 12.5X TO 30X BASIC CARDS

1997 E-X2000 A Cut Above

		MINT	NRMT
COMPLETE SET (10)		400.00	180.00
COMMON CARD (1-10)		12.00	5.50
❑ 1	Frank Thomas	60.00	27.00
❑ 2	Ken Griffey Jr.	100.00	45.00
❑ 3	Alex Rodriguez	60.00	27.00
❑ 4	Albert Belle	30.00	13.50
❑ 5	Juan Gonzalez	50.00	22.00
❑ 6	Mark McGwire	100.00	45.00
❑ 7	Mo Vaughn	25.00	11.00
❑ 8	Manny Ramirez	20.00	9.00
❑ 9	Barry Bonds	25.00	11.00
❑ 10	Fred McGriff	12.00	5.50

1997 E-X2000 Emerald Autographs

		MINT	NRMT
COMPLETE SET (6)		400.00	180.00
COMMON CARD		15.00	6.75
❑ 2	Darin Erstad	80.00	36.00
❑ 30	Todd Walker	30.00	13.50
❑ 43	Alex Rodriguez	200.00	90.00
❑ 78	Todd Hollandsworth	15.00	6.75
❑ 86	Alex Ochoa	15.00	6.75
❑ 89	Scott Rolen	100.00	45.00

1997 E-X2000 Hall or Nothing

		MINT	NRMT
COMPLETE SET (20)		300.00	135.00
COMMON CARD (1-20)		3.00	1.35
❑ 1	Frank Thomas	25.00	11.00
❑ 2	Ken Griffey Jr.	40.00	18.00
❑ 3	Eddie Murray	8.00	3.60
❑ 4	Cal Ripken	30.00	13.50
❑ 5	Ryne Sandberg	10.00	4.50
❑ 6	Wade Boggs	8.00	3.60
❑ 7	Roger Clemens	15.00	6.75
❑ 8	Tony Gwynn	20.00	9.00
❑ 9	Alex Rodriguez	25.00	11.00
❑ 10	Mark McGwire	40.00	18.00
❑ 11	Barry Bonds	10.00	4.50
❑ 12	Greg Maddux	25.00	11.00
❑ 13	Juan Gonzalez	20.00	9.00
❑ 14	Albert Belle	12.00	5.50
❑ 15	Mike Piazza	25.00	11.00
❑ 16	Jeff Bagwell	12.00	5.50
❑ 17	Dennis Eckersley	3.00	1.35
❑ 18	Mo Vaughn	10.00	4.50
❑ 19	Roberto Alomar	8.00	3.60
❑ 20	Kenny Lofton	8.00	3.60

1997 E-X2000 Star Date 2000

		MINT	NRMT
COMPLETE SET (15)		50.00	22.00
COMMON CARD (1-15)		1.50	.70
❑ 1	Alex Rodriguez	10.00	4.50
❑ 2	Andruw Jones	5.00	2.20
❑ 3	Andy Pettitte	2.00	.90
❑ 4	Brooks Kieschnick	1.50	.70
❑ 5	Chipper Jones	8.00	3.60
❑ 6	Darin Erstad	5.00	2.20
❑ 7	Derek Jeter	8.00	3.60
❑ 8	Jason Kendall	2.00	.90
❑ 9	Jermaine Dye	1.50	.70
❑ 10	Neifi Perez	1.50	.70
❑ 11	Scott Rolen	8.00	3.60
❑ 12	Todd Hollandsworth	1.50	.70
❑ 13	Todd Walker	3.00	1.35
❑ 14	Tony Clark	2.00	.90
❑ 15	Vladimir Guerrero	6.00	2.70

1998 E-X2001

	MINT	NRMT
COMPLETE SET (100)	120.00	55.00

COMMON CARD (1-100) .50 .23

❑ 1 Alex Rodriguez 6.00 2.70
❑ 2 Barry Bonds 2.50 1.10
❑ 3 Greg Maddux 6.00 2.70
❑ 4 Roger Clemens 4.00 1.80
❑ 5 Juan Gonzalez 5.00 2.20
❑ 6 Chipper Jones 5.00 2.20
❑ 7 Derek Jeter 5.00 2.20
❑ 8 Frank Thomas 6.00 2.70
❑ 9 Cal Ripken 8.00 3.60
❑ 10 Ken Griffey Jr. 10.00 4.50
❑ 11 Mark McGwire 12.00 5.50
❑ 12 Hideo Nomo 2.50 1.10
❑ 13 Tony Gwynn 5.00 2.20
❑ 14 Ivan Rodriguez 2.50 1.10
❑ 15 Mike Piazza 6.00 2.70
❑ 16 Roberto Alomar 2.00 .90
❑ 17 Jeff Bagwell 3.00 1.35
❑ 18 Andruw Jones 2.50 1.10
❑ 19 Albert Belle 2.00 .90
❑ 20 Mo Vaughn 2.50 1.10
❑ 21 Kenny Lofton 2.00 .90
❑ 22 Gary Sheffield 1.25 .55
❑ 23 Tony Clark 1.25 .55
❑ 24 Mike Mussina 2.00 .90
❑ 25 Barry Larkin 1.25 .55
❑ 26 Moises Alou 1.25 .55
❑ 27 Brady Anderson .75 .35
❑ 28 Andy Pettitte 1.25 .55
❑ 29 Sammy Sosa 5.00 2.20
❑ 30 Raul Mondesi 1.25 .55
❑ 31 Andres Galarraga 2.00 .90
❑ 32 Chuck Knoblauch 2.00 .90
❑ 33 Jim Thome 2.00 .90
❑ 34 Craig Biggio 2.00 .90
❑ 35 Jay Buhner .75 .35
❑ 36 Rafael Palmeiro 1.25 .55
❑ 37 Curt Schilling .75 .35
❑ 38 Tino Martinez 2.00 .90
❑ 39 Pedro Martinez 2.00 .90
❑ 40 Jose Canseco 2.00 .90
❑ 41 Jeff Cirillo .75 .35
❑ 42 Dean Palmer .75 .35
❑ 43 Tim Salmon 2.00 .90
❑ 44 Jason Giambi .75 .35
❑ 45 Bobby Higginson 1.25 .55
❑ 46 Jim Edmonds 1.25 .55
❑ 47 David Justice 2.00 .90
❑ 48 John Olerud .75 .35
❑ 49 Ray Lankford .75 .35
❑ 50 Al Martin .50 .23
❑ 51 Mike Lieberthal .50 .23
❑ 52 Henry Rodriguez .75 .35
❑ 53 Edgar Renteria .75 .35
❑ 54 Eric Karros .75 .35
❑ 55 Marquis Grissom .75 .35
❑ 56 Wilson Alvarez .75 .35
❑ 57 Darryl Kile .75 .35
❑ 58 Jeff King .75 .35
❑ 59 Shawn Estes .75 .35
❑ 60 Tony Womack .75 .35
❑ 61 Willie Greene .75 .35
❑ 62 Ken Caminiti 1.25 .55
❑ 63 Vinny Castilla 1.25 .55
❑ 64 Mark Grace 1.25 .55
❑ 65 Ryan Klesko .75 .35
❑ 66 Robin Ventura .75 .35
❑ 67 Todd Hundley .75 .35
❑ 68 Travis Fryman .75 .35
❑ 69 Edgar Martinez .75 .35
❑ 70 Matt Williams .75 .35
❑ 71 Paul Molitor 2.00 .90
❑ 72 Kevin Brown 1.25 .55
❑ 73 Randy Johnson 2.00 .90
❑ 74 Bernie Williams 2.00 .90
❑ 75 Manny Ramirez 2.00 .90
❑ 76 Fred McGriff 1.25 .55
❑ 77 Tom Glavine 2.00 .90
❑ 78 Carlos Delgado .75 .35
❑ 79 Larry Walker 2.00 .90
❑ 80 Hideki Irabu 1.25 .55
❑ 81 Ryan McGuire .50 .23
❑ 82 Justin Thompson .75 .35
❑ 83 Kevin Orie .50 .23
❑ 84 Jon Nunnally .50 .23
❑ 85 Mark Kotsay 1.25 .55
❑ 86 Todd Walker 1.25 .55
❑ 87 Jason Dickson .75 .35
❑ 88 Fernando Tatis .75 .35
❑ 89 Karim Garcia .75 .35
❑ 90 Ricky Ledee .75 .35
❑ 91 Paul Konerko 2.00 .90
❑ 92 Jaret Wright 2.50 1.10
❑ 93 Darin Erstad 2.50 1.10
❑ 94 Livan Hernandez .75 .35
❑ 95 Nomar Garciaparra 6.00 2.70
❑ 96 Jose Cruz Jr. 2.50 1.10
❑ 97 Scott Rolen 5.00 2.20
❑ 98 Ben Grieve 4.00 1.80
❑ 99 Vladimir Guerrero 3.00 1.35
❑ 100 Travis Lee 4.00 1.80
❑ 101 Kerry Wood Redemption 20.00 9.00
❑ NNO Kerry Wood EXCH 15.00 6.75
❑ NNO Alex Rodriguez Sample 3.00 1.35

1998 E-X2001 Essential Credentials Future

MINT NRMT

COMMON CARD (1-100) 25.00 11.00

❑ 1 Alex Rodriguez (100) 250.00 110.00
❑ 2 Barry Bonds (99) 100.00 45.00
❑ 3 Greg Maddux (98) 250.00 110.00
❑ 4 Roger Clemens (97) 150.00 70.00
❑ 5 Juan Gonzalez (96) 200.00 90.00
❑ 6 Chipper Jones (95) 200.00 90.00
❑ 7 Derek Jeter (94) 200.00 90.00
❑ 8 Frank Thomas (93) 250.00 110.00
❑ 9 Cal Ripken (92) 300.00 135.00
❑ 10 Ken Griffey Jr. (91) 400.00 180.00
❑ 11 Mark McGwire (90) 500.00 220.00
❑ 12 Hideo Nomo (89) 100.00 45.00
❑ 13 Tony Gwynn (88) 200.00 90.00
❑ 14 Ivan Rodriguez (87) 100.00 45.00
❑ 15 Mike Piazza (86) 250.00 110.00
❑ 16 Roberto Alomar (85) 80.00 36.00
❑ 17 Jeff Bagwell (84) 120.00 55.00
❑ 18 Andruw Jones (83) 80.00 36.00
❑ 19 Albert Belle (82) 80.00 36.00
❑ 20 Mo Vaughn (81) 100.00 45.00
❑ 21 Kenny Lofton (80) 60.00 27.00
❑ 22 Gary Sheffield (79) 50.00 22.00
❑ 23 Tony Clark (78) 50.00 22.00
❑ 24 Mike Mussina (77) 80.00 36.00
❑ 25 Barry Larkin (76) 50.00 22.00
❑ 26 Moises Alou (75) 50.00 22.00
❑ 27 Brady Anderson (74) 40.00 18.00
❑ 28 Andy Pettitte (73) 50.00 22.00
❑ 29 Sammy Sosa (72) 200.00 90.00
❑ 30 Raul Mondesi (71) 50.00 22.00
❑ 31 Andres Galarraga (70) 80.00 36.00
❑ 32 Chuck Knoblauch (69) 80.00 36.00
❑ 33 Jim Thome (68) 100.00 45.00
❑ 34 Craig Biggio (67) 80.00 36.00
❑ 35 Jay Buhner (66) 40.00 18.00
❑ 36 Rafael Palmeiro (65) 60.00 27.00
❑ 37 Curt Schilling (64) 40.00 18.00
❑ 38 Tino Martinez (63) 80.00 36.00
❑ 39 Pedro Martinez (62) 100.00 45.00
❑ 40 Jose Canseco (61) 100.00 45.00
❑ 41 Jeff Cirillo (60) 40.00 18.00
❑ 42 Dean Palmer (59) 40.00 18.00
❑ 43 Tim Salmon (58) 80.00 36.00
❑ 44 Jason Giambi (57) 40.00 18.00
❑ 45 Bobby Higginson (56) 60.00 27.00
❑ 46 Jim Edmonds (55) 60.00 27.00
❑ 47 David Justice (54) 80.00 36.00
❑ 48 John Olerud (53) 40.00 18.00
❑ 49 Ray Lankford (52) 40.00 18.00
❑ 50 Al Martin (51) 25.00 11.00
❑ 51 Mike Lieberthal (50) 25.00 11.00
❑ 52 Henry Rodriguez (49) 40.00 18.00
❑ 53 Edgar Renteria (48) 40.00 18.00
❑ 54 Eric Karros (47) 40.00 18.00
❑ 55 Marquis Grissom (46) 40.00 18.00
❑ 56 Wilson Alvarez (45) 40.00 18.00
❑ 57 Darryl Kile (44) 40.00 18.00
❑ 58 Jeff King (43) 40.00 18.00
❑ 59 Shawn Estes (42) 40.00 18.00
❑ 60 Tony Womack (41) 40.00 18.00
❑ 61 Willie Greene (40) 40.00 18.00
❑ 62 Ken Caminiti (39) 80.00 36.00
❑ 63 Vinny Castilla (38) 60.00 27.00
❑ 64 Mark Grace (37) 80.00 36.00
❑ 65 Ryan Klesko (36) 40.00 18.00
❑ 66 Robin Ventura (35) 80.00 36.00
❑ 67 Todd Hundley (34) 40.00 18.00
❑ 68 Travis Fryman (33) 40.00 18.00
❑ 69 Edgar Martinez (32) 80.00 36.00
❑ 70 Matt Williams (31) 80.00 36.00
❑ 71 Paul Molitor (30) 200.00 90.00
❑ 72 Kevin Brown (29) 80.00 36.00
❑ 73 Randy Johnson (28) 200.00 90.00
❑ 74 Bernie Williams (27) 200.00 90.00
❑ 75 Manny Ramirez (26) 200.00 90.00
❑ 76 Fred McGriff (25) 120.00 55.00
❑ 77 Tom Glavine (24) 150.00 70.00
❑ 78 Carlos Delgado (23) 100.00 45.00
❑ 79 Larry Walker (22) 250.00 110.00
❑ 80 Hideki Irabu (21) 150.00 70.00
❑ 81 Ryan McGuire (20) 60.00 27.00
❑ 82 Justin Thompson (19) 80.00 36.00
❑ 83 Kevin Orie (18) 60.00 27.00
❑ 84 Jon Nunnally (17) 60.00 27.00
❑ 85 Mark Kotsay (16) 120.00 55.00
❑ 86 Todd Walker (15)
❑ 87 Jason Dickson (14)
❑ 88 Fernando Tatis (13)
❑ 89 Karim Garcia (12)
❑ 90 Ricky Ledee (11)
❑ 91 Paul Konerko (10)
❑ 92 Jaret Wright (9)
❑ 93 Darin Erstad (8)
❑ 94 Livan Hernandez (7)
❑ 95 Nomar Garciaparra (6)
❑ 96 Jose Cruz Jr. (5)
❑ 97 Scott Rolen (4)
❑ 98 Ben Grieve (3)
❑ 99 Vladimir Guerrero (2)
❑ 100 Travis Lee (1)

1998 E-X2001 Essential Credentials Now

	MINT	NRMT
COMMON CARD (1-100)	20.00	9.00
❑ 1 Alex Rodriguez (1)		
❑ 2 Barry Bonds (2)		
❑ 3 Greg Maddux (3)		
❑ 4 Roger Clemens (4)		
❑ 5 Juan Gonzalez (5)		
❑ 6 Chipper Jones (6)		
❑ 7 Derek Jeter (7)		
❑ 8 Frank Thomas (8)		
❑ 9 Cal Ripken (9)		
❑ 10 Ken Griffey Jr. (10)		
❑ 11 Mark McGwire (11)		
❑ 12 Hideo Nomo (12)		
❑ 13 Tony Gwynn (13)		
❑ 14 Ivan Rodriguez (14)		
❑ 15 Mike Piazza (15)		
❑ 16 Roberto Alomar (16)	250.00	110.00
❑ 17 Jeff Bagwell (17)	400.00	180.00
❑ 18 Andruw Jones (18)	250.00	110.00
❑ 19 Albert Belle (19)	250.00	110.00
❑ 20 Mo Vaughn (20)	300.00	135.00
❑ 21 Kenny Lofton (21)	200.00	90.00
❑ 22 Gary Sheffield (22)	150.00	70.00
❑ 23 Tony Clark (23)	120.00	55.00
❑ 24 Mike Mussina (24)	250.00	110.00
❑ 25 Barry Larkin (25)	120.00	55.00
❑ 26 Moises Alou (26)	100.00	45.00
❑ 27 Brady Anderson (27)	80.00	36.00
❑ 28 Andy Pettitte (28)	120.00	55.00
❑ 29 Sammy Sosa (29)	500.00	220.00
❑ 30 Raul Mondesi (30)	120.00	55.00
❑ 31 Andres Galarraga (31)	120.00	55.00
❑ 32 Chuck Knoblauch (32)	120.00	55.00
❑ 33 Jim Thome (33)	150.00	70.00
❑ 34 Craig Biggio (34)	120.00	55.00
❑ 35 Jay Buhner (35)	80.00	36.00
❑ 36 Rafael Palmeiro (36)	80.00	36.00
❑ 37 Curt Schilling (37)	60.00	27.00
❑ 38 Tino Martinez (38)	100.00	45.00
❑ 39 Pedro Martinez (39)	120.00	55.00
❑ 40 Jose Canseco (40)	120.00	55.00
❑ 41 Jeff Cirillo (41)	40.00	18.00
❑ 42 Dean Palmer (42)	40.00	18.00
❑ 43 Tim Salmon (43)	80.00	36.00
❑ 44 Jason Giambi (44)	40.00	18.00
❑ 45 Bobby Higginson (45)	60.00	27.00
❑ 46 Jim Edmonds (46)	60.00	27.00
❑ 47 David Justice (47)	80.00	36.00
❑ 48 John Olerud (48)	40.00	18.00
❑ 49 Ray Lankford (49)	40.00	18.00
❑ 50 Al Martin (50)	20.00	9.00
❑ 51 Mike Lieberthal (51)	20.00	9.00
❑ 52 Henry Rodriguez (52)	40.00	18.00
❑ 53 Edgar Renteria (53)	40.00	18.00
❑ 54 Eric Karros (54)	40.00	18.00
❑ 55 Marquis Grissom (55)	40.00	18.00
❑ 56 Wilson Alvarez (56)	40.00	18.00
❑ 57 Darryl Kile (57)	40.00	18.00
❑ 58 Jeff King (58)	40.00	18.00
❑ 59 Shawn Estes (59)	40.00	18.00
❑ 60 Tony Womack (60)	40.00	18.00
❑ 61 Willie Greene (61)	40.00	18.00
❑ 62 Ken Caminiti (62)	60.00	27.00
❑ 63 Vinny Castilla (63)	50.00	22.00
❑ 64 Mark Grace (64)	60.00	27.00
❑ 65 Ryan Klesko (65)	40.00	18.00
❑ 66 Robin Ventura (66)	40.00	18.00
❑ 67 Todd Hundley (67)	40.00	18.00
❑ 68 Travis Fryman (68)	40.00	18.00
❑ 69 Edgar Martinez (69)	40.00	18.00
❑ 70 Matt Williams (70)	40.00	18.00
❑ 71 Paul Molitor (71)	80.00	36.00
❑ 72 Kevin Brown (72)	50.00	22.00
❑ 73 Randy Johnson (73)	80.00	36.00
❑ 74 Bernie Williams (74)	80.00	36.00
❑ 75 Manny Ramirez (75)	80.00	36.00
❑ 76 Fred McGriff (76)	50.00	22.00
❑ 77 Tom Glavine (77)	60.00	27.00
❑ 78 Carlos Delgado (78)	40.00	18.00
❑ 79 Larry Walker (79)	80.00	36.00
❑ 80 Hideki Irabu (80)	50.00	22.00
❑ 81 Ryan McGuire (81)	20.00	9.00
❑ 82 Justin Thompson (82)	40.00	18.00
❑ 83 Kevin Orie (83)	20.00	9.00
❑ 84 Jon Nunnally (84)	20.00	9.00
❑ 85 Mark Kotsay (85)	50.00	22.00
❑ 86 Todd Walker (86)	50.00	22.00
❑ 87 Jason Dickson (87)	40.00	18.00
❑ 88 Fernando Tatis (88)	40.00	18.00
❑ 89 Karim Garcia (89)	40.00	18.00
❑ 90 Ricky Ledee (90)	40.00	18.00
❑ 91 Paul Konerko (91)	60.00	27.00
❑ 92 Jaret Wright (92)	80.00	36.00
❑ 93 Darin Erstad (93)	80.00	36.00
❑ 94 Livan Hernandez (94)	40.00	18.00
❑ 95 Nomar Garciaparra (95)	250.00	110.00
❑ 96 Jose Cruz Jr. (96)	80.00	36.00
❑ 97 Scott Rolen (97)	150.00	70.00
❑ 98 Ben Grieve (98)	120.00	55.00
❑ 99 Vladimir Guerrero (99)	100.00	45.00
❑ 100 Travis Lee (100)	120.00	55.00

1998 E-X2001 Cheap Seat Treats

	MINT	NRMT
COMPLETE SET (20)	200.00	90.00
COMMON CARD (1-20)	4.00	1.80
❑ 1 Frank Thomas	20.00	9.00
❑ 2 Ken Griffey Jr.	30.00	13.50
❑ 3 Mark McGwire	40.00	18.00
❑ 4 Tino Martinez	6.00	2.70
❑ 5 Larry Walker	6.00	2.70
❑ 6 Juan Gonzalez	15.00	6.75
❑ 7 Mike Piazza	20.00	9.00
❑ 8 Jeff Bagwell	10.00	4.50
❑ 9 Tony Clark	4.00	1.80
❑ 10 Albert Belle	6.00	2.70
❑ 11 Andres Galarraga	6.00	2.70
❑ 12 Jim Thome	6.00	2.70
❑ 13 Mo Vaughn	8.00	3.60
❑ 14 Barry Bonds	8.00	3.60
❑ 15 Vladimir Guerrero	8.00	3.60
❑ 16 Scott Rolen	12.00	5.50
❑ 17 Travis Lee	10.00	4.50
❑ 18 David Justice	6.00	2.70
❑ 19 Jose Cruz Jr.	6.00	2.70
❑ 20 Andruw Jones	6.00	2.70

1998 E-X2001 Destination Cooperstown

	MINT	NRMT
COMPLETE SET (15)	1800.00	800.00
COMMON CARD (1-15)	50.00	22.00
❑ 1 Alex Rodriguez	150.00	70.00
❑ 2 Frank Thomas	150.00	70.00
❑ 3 Cal Ripken	200.00	90.00
❑ 4 Roger Clemens	100.00	45.00
❑ 5 Greg Maddux	150.00	70.00
❑ 6 Chipper Jones	120.00	55.00
❑ 7 Ken Griffey Jr.	250.00	110.00
❑ 8 Mark McGwire	300.00	135.00
❑ 9 Tony Gwynn	120.00	55.00
❑ 10 Mike Piazza	150.00	70.00
❑ 11 Jeff Bagwell	80.00	36.00
❑ 12 Jose Cruz Jr.	50.00	22.00
❑ 13 Derek Jeter	120.00	55.00
❑ 14 Hideo Nomo	80.00	36.00
❑ 15 Ivan Rodriguez	60.00	27.00

1998 E-X2001 Signature 2001

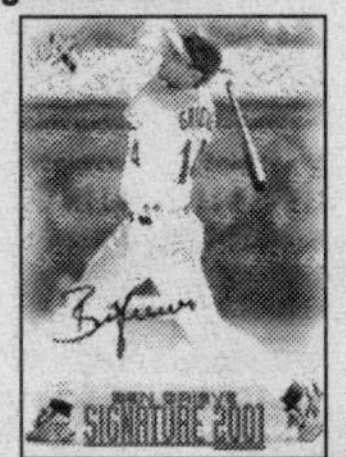

	MINT	NRMT
COMPLETE SET (17)	500.00	220.00
COMMON CARD (1-17)	20.00	9.00
❑ 1 Ricky Ledee	25.00	11.00
❑ 2 Derrick Gibson	20.00	9.00
❑ 3 Mark Kotsay	20.00	9.00
❑ 4 Kevin Millwood	50.00	22.00
❑ 5 Brad Fullmer	25.00	11.00
❑ 6 Todd Walker	25.00	11.00
❑ 7 Ben Grieve	50.00	22.00
❑ 8 Tony Clark	25.00	11.00
❑ 9 Jaret Wright	30.00	13.50
❑ 10 Randall Simon	20.00	9.00
❑ 11 Paul Konerko	25.00	11.00
❑ 12 Todd Helton	30.00	13.50
❑ 13 David Ortiz	20.00	9.00
❑ 14 Alex Gonzalez	20.00	9.00
❑ 15 Bobby Estalella	20.00	9.00
❑ 16 Alex Rodriguez SP	150.00	70.00
❑ 17 Mike Lowell	20.00	9.00

1998 E-X2001 Star Date 2001

	MINT	NRMT
COMPLETE SET (15)	40.00	18.00
COMMON CARD (1-15)	1.50	.70
❑ 1 Travis Lee	8.00	3.60
❑ 2 Jose Cruz Jr.	5.00	2.20
❑ 3 Paul Konerko	4.00	1.80
❑ 4 Bobby Estalella	1.50	.70
❑ 5 Magglio Ordonez	5.00	2.20
❑ 6 Juan Encarnacion	1.50	.70
❑ 7 Richard Hidalgo	1.50	.70
❑ 8 Abraham Nunez	1.50	.70
❑ 9 Sean Casey	1.50	.70
❑ 10 Todd Helton	5.00	2.20
❑ 11 Brad Fullmer	1.50	.70
❑ 12 Ben Grieve	8.00	3.60
❑ 13 Livan Hernandez	1.50	.70
❑ 14 Jaret Wright	5.00	2.20
❑ 15 Todd Dunwoody	1.50	.70

1993 Finest

	MINT	NRMT
COMPLETE SET (199)	250.00	110.00
COMMON CARD (1-199)	1.00	.45
❑ 1 David Justice	5.00	2.20
❑ 2 Lou Whitaker	1.50	.70
❑ 3 Bryan Harvey	1.00	.45
❑ 4 Carlos Garcia	1.00	.45
❑ 5 Sid Fernandez	1.00	.45
❑ 6 Brett Butler	1.50	.70
❑ 7 Scott Cooper	1.00	.45
❑ 8 B.J. Surhoff	1.50	.70
❑ 9 Steve Finley	1.50	.70
❑ 10 Curt Schilling	1.50	.70
❑ 11 Jeff Bagwell	8.00	3.60
❑ 12 Alex Cole	1.00	.45
❑ 13 John Olerud	3.00	1.35
❑ 14 John Smiley	1.00	.45
❑ 15 Bip Roberts	1.00	.45
❑ 16 Albert Belle	6.00	2.70
❑ 17 Duane Ward	1.00	.45
❑ 18 Alan Trammell	3.00	1.35
❑ 19 Andy Benes	1.50	.70
❑ 20 Reggie Sanders	1.00	.45
❑ 21 Todd Zeile	1.00	.45
❑ 22 Rick Aguilera	1.00	.45
❑ 23 Dave Hollins	1.00	.45
❑ 24 Jose Rijo	1.00	.45
❑ 25 Matt Williams	3.00	1.35
❑ 26 Sandy Alomar	1.50	.70
❑ 27 Alex Fernandez	1.50	.70
❑ 28 Ozzie Smith	6.00	2.70
❑ 29 Ramon Martinez	1.50	.70
❑ 30 Bernie Williams	5.00	2.20
❑ 31 Gary Sheffield	5.00	2.20
❑ 32 Eric Karros	3.00	1.35
❑ 33 Frank Viola	1.00	.45
❑ 34 Kevin Young	1.00	.45
❑ 35 Ken Hill	1.00	.45
❑ 36 Tony Fernandez	1.00	.45
❑ 37 Tim Wakefield	1.50	.70
❑ 38 John Kruk	1.50	.70
❑ 39 Chris Sabo	1.00	.45
❑ 40 Marquis Grissom	1.50	.70
❑ 41 Glenn Davis	1.00	.45
❑ 42 Jeff Montgomery	1.50	.70
❑ 43 Kenny Lofton	5.00	2.20
❑ 44 John Burkett	1.00	.45
❑ 45 Darryl Hamilton	1.00	.45
❑ 46 Jim Abbott	1.50	.70
❑ 47 Ivan Rodriguez	6.00	2.70
❑ 48 Eric Young	5.00	2.20
❑ 49 Mitch Williams	1.00	.45
❑ 50 Harold Reynolds	1.00	.45
❑ 51 Brian Harper	1.00	.45
❑ 52 Rafael Palmeiro	3.00	1.35
❑ 53 Bret Saberhagen	1.50	.70
❑ 54 Jeff Conine	1.00	.45
❑ 55 Ivan Calderon	1.00	.45
❑ 56 Juan Guzman	1.00	.45
❑ 57 Carlos Baerga	1.00	.45
❑ 58 Charles Nagy	1.50	.70
❑ 59 Wally Joyner	1.50	.70
❑ 60 Charlie Hayes	1.00	.45
❑ 61 Shane Mack	1.00	.45
❑ 62 Pete Harnisch	1.00	.45
❑ 63 George Brett	10.00	4.50
❑ 64 Lance Johnson	1.00	.45
❑ 65 Ben McDonald	1.00	.45
❑ 66 Bobby Bonilla	1.50	.70
❑ 67 Terry Steinbach	1.00	.45
❑ 68 Ron Gant	1.50	.70
❑ 69 Doug Jones	1.00	.45
❑ 70 Paul Molitor	5.00	2.20
❑ 71 Brady Anderson	3.00	1.35
❑ 72 Chuck Finley	1.50	.70
❑ 73 Mark Grace	3.00	1.35
❑ 74 Mike Devereaux	1.00	.45
❑ 75 Tony Phillips	1.00	.45
❑ 76 Chuck Knoblauch	5.00	2.20
❑ 77 Tony Gwynn	12.00	5.50
❑ 78 Kevin Appier	1.50	.70
❑ 79 Sammy Sosa	12.00	5.50
❑ 80 Mickey Tettleton	1.00	.45
❑ 81 Felix Jose	1.00	.45
❑ 82 Mark Langston	1.00	.45
❑ 83 Gregg Jefferies	1.00	.45
❑ 84 Andre Dawson AS	3.00	1.35
❑ 85 Greg Maddux AS	15.00	6.75
❑ 86 Rickey Henderson AS	5.00	2.20
❑ 87 Tom Glavine AS	3.00	1.35
❑ 88 Roberto Alomar AS	5.00	2.20
❑ 89 Darryl Strawberry AS	1.50	.70
❑ 90 Wade Boggs AS	5.00	2.20
❑ 91 Bo Jackson AS	1.50	.70
❑ 92 Mark McGwire AS	25.00	11.00
❑ 93 Robin Ventura AS	1.50	.70
❑ 94 Joe Carter AS	1.50	.70
❑ 95 Lee Smith AS	1.50	.70
❑ 96 Cal Ripken AS	20.00	9.00
❑ 97 Larry Walker AS	5.00	2.20
❑ 98 Don Mattingly AS	8.00	3.60
❑ 99 Jose Canseco AS	5.00	2.20
❑ 100 Dennis Eckersley AS	1.00	.45
❑ 101 Terry Pendleton AS	1.00	.45
❑ 102 Frank Thomas AS	15.00	6.75
❑ 103 Barry Bonds AS	6.00	2.70
❑ 104 Roger Clemens AS	10.00	4.50
❑ 105 Ryne Sandberg AS	6.00	2.70
❑ 106 Fred McGriff AS	3.00	1.35
❑ 107 Nolan Ryan AS	20.00	9.00
❑ 108 Will Clark AS	5.00	2.20
❑ 109 Pat Listach AS	1.00	.45
❑ 110 Ken Griffey Jr. AS	25.00	11.00
❑ 111 Cecil Fielder AS	1.50	.70
❑ 112 Kirby Puckett AS	8.00	3.60
❑ 113 Dwight Gooden AS	1.50	.70
❑ 114 Barry Larkin AS	3.00	1.35
❑ 115 David Cone AS	1.50	.70
❑ 116 Juan Gonzalez AS	12.00	5.50
❑ 117 Kent Hrbek	1.50	.70
❑ 118 Tim Wallach	1.00	.45
❑ 119 Craig Biggio	5.00	2.20
❑ 120 Roberto Kelly	1.00	.45
❑ 121 Gregg Olson	1.00	.45
❑ 122 Eddie Murray UER 122 career strikeouts should be 1224	5.00	2.20
❑ 123 Wil Cordero	1.00	.45
❑ 124 Jay Buhner	3.00	1.35
❑ 125 Carlton Fisk	5.00	2.20
❑ 126 Eric Davis	1.50	.70
❑ 127 Doug Drabek	1.00	.45
❑ 128 Ozzie Guillen	1.00	.45
❑ 129 John Wetteland	1.50	.70
❑ 130 Andres Galarraga	5.00	2.20
❑ 131 Ken Caminiti	3.00	1.35
❑ 132 Tom Candiotti	1.00	.45
❑ 133 Pat Borders	1.00	.45
❑ 134 Kevin Brown	3.00	1.35
❑ 135 Travis Fryman	1.50	.70
❑ 136 Kevin Mitchell	1.50	.70
❑ 137 Greg Swindell	1.00	.45
❑ 138 Benito Santiago	1.00	.45
❑ 139 Reggie Jefferson	1.50	.70
❑ 140 Chris Bosio	1.00	.45
❑ 141 Deion Sanders	3.00	1.35
❑ 142 Scott Erickson	1.00	.45
❑ 143 Howard Johnson	1.00	.45
❑ 144 Orestes Destrade	1.00	.45
❑ 145 Jose Guzman	1.00	.45
❑ 146 Chad Curtis	1.50	.70
❑ 147 Cal Eldred	1.00	.45
❑ 148 Willie Greene	1.00	.45
❑ 149 Tommy Greene	1.00	.45
❑ 150 Erik Hanson	1.00	.45
❑ 151 Bob Welch	1.00	.45
❑ 152 John Jaha	1.00	.45
❑ 153 Harold Baines	1.50	.70
❑ 154 Randy Johnson	5.00	2.20
❑ 155 Al Martin	1.00	.45
❑ 156 J.T. Snow	6.00	2.70
❑ 157 Mike Mussina	6.00	2.70
❑ 158 Ruben Sierra	1.00	.45
❑ 159 Dean Palmer	1.50	.70
❑ 160 Steve Avery	1.00	.45
❑ 161 Julio Franco	1.00	.45
❑ 162 Dave Winfield	3.00	1.35
❑ 163 Tim Salmon	5.00	2.20
❑ 164 Tom Henke	1.00	.45
❑ 165 Mo Vaughn	6.00	2.70
❑ 166 John Smoltz	1.50	.70
❑ 167 Danny Tartabull	1.00	.45
❑ 168 Delino DeShields	1.50	.70
❑ 169 Charlie Hough	1.50	.70
❑ 170 Paul O'Neill	1.50	.70
❑ 171 Darren Daulton	1.50	.70
❑ 172 Jack McDowell	1.00	.45
❑ 173 Junior Felix	1.00	.45
❑ 174 Jimmy Key	1.50	.70
❑ 175 George Bell	1.00	.45
❑ 176 Mike Stanton	1.00	.45
❑ 177 Len Dykstra	1.50	.70
❑ 178 Norm Charlton	1.00	.45
❑ 179 Eric Anthony	1.00	.45
❑ 180 Rob Dibble	1.00	.45
❑ 181 Otis Nixon	1.00	.45
❑ 182 Randy Myers	1.50	.70
❑ 183 Tim Raines	1.50	.70
❑ 184 Orel Hershiser	1.50	.70
❑ 185 Andy Van Slyke	1.50	.70
❑ 186 Mike Lansing	1.50	.70
❑ 187 Ray Lankford	3.00	1.35
❑ 188 Mike Morgan	1.00	.45
❑ 189 Moises Alou	1.50	.70

	MINT	NRMT
❑ 190 Edgar Martinez	3.00	1.35
❑ 191 John Franco	1.50	.70
❑ 192 Robin Yount	3.00	1.35
❑ 193 Bob Tewksbury	1.00	.45
❑ 194 Jay Bell	1.50	.70
❑ 195 Luis Gonzalez	1.00	.45
❑ 196 Dave Fleming	1.00	.45
❑ 197 Mike Greenwell	1.00	.45
❑ 198 David Nied	1.00	.45
❑ 199 Mike Piazza	25.00	11.00

1993 Finest Refractors

	MINT	NRMT
COMPLETE SET (199)	15000.00	6800.00
COMMON CARD (1-199)	30.00	13.50
MINOR STARS	60.00	27.00

1993 Finest Jumbos

	MINT	NRMT
COMPLETE SET (33)	500.00	220.00
COMMON CARD (84-116)	5.00	2.20
❑ 84 Andre Dawson	8.00	3.60
❑ 85 Greg Maddux	40.00	18.00
❑ 86 Rickey Henderson	12.00	5.50
❑ 87 Tom Glavine	8.00	3.60
❑ 88 Roberto Alomar	12.00	5.50
❑ 89 Darryl Strawberry	6.00	2.70
❑ 90 Wade Boggs	12.00	5.50
❑ 91 Bo Jackson	6.00	2.70
❑ 92 Mark McGwire	60.00	27.00
❑ 93 Robin Ventura	6.00	2.70
❑ 94 Joe Carter	6.00	2.70
❑ 95 Lee Smith	6.00	2.70
❑ 96 Cal Ripken	50.00	22.00
❑ 97 Larry Walker	12.00	5.50
❑ 98 Don Mattingly	20.00	9.00
❑ 99 Jose Canseco	12.00	5.50
❑ 100 Dennis Eckersley	6.00	2.70
❑ 101 Terry Pendleton	5.00	2.20
❑ 102 Frank Thomas	40.00	18.00
❑ 103 Barry Bonds	15.00	6.75
❑ 104 Roger Clemens	25.00	11.00
❑ 105 Ryne Sandberg	15.00	6.75
❑ 106 Fred McGriff	8.00	3.60
❑ 107 Nolan Ryan	50.00	22.00
❑ 108 Will Clark	12.00	5.50
❑ 109 Pat Listach	5.00	2.20
❑ 110 Ken Griffey Jr.	60.00	27.00
❑ 111 Cecil Fielder	6.00	2.70
❑ 112 Kirby Puckett	20.00	9.00
❑ 113 Dwight Gooden	6.00	2.70
❑ 114 Barry Larkin	8.00	3.60
❑ 115 David Cone	6.00	2.70
❑ 116 Juan Gonzalez	30.00	13.50

1994 Finest Pre-Production

	MINT	NRMT
COMPLETE SET (40)	200.00	90.00
COMMON CARD	3.00	1.35
❑ 22P Deion Sanders	6.00	2.70
❑ 23P Jose Offerman	3.00	1.35
❑ 26P Alex Fernandez	3.00	1.35
❑ 31P Steve Finley	6.00	2.70
❑ 35P Andres Galarraga	15.00	6.75
❑ 43P Reggie Sanders	6.00	2.70
❑ 47P Dave Hollins	3.00	1.35
❑ 52P David Cone	12.00	5.50
❑ 59P Dante Bichette	6.00	2.70
❑ 61P Orlando Merced	3.00	1.35
❑ 62P Brian McRae	3.00	1.35
❑ 66P Mike Mussina	20.00	9.00
❑ 76P Mike Stanley	3.00	1.35
❑ 78P Mark McGwire	100.00	45.00
❑ 79P Pat Listach	3.00	1.35
❑ 82P Dwight Gooden	6.00	2.70
❑ 84P Phil Plantier	3.00	1.35
❑ 90P Jeff Russell	3.00	1.35
❑ 92P Gregg Jefferies	3.00	1.35
❑ 93P Jose Guzman	3.00	1.35
❑ 100P John Smoltz	6.00	2.70
❑ 102P Jim Thome	25.00	11.00
❑ 121P Moises Alou	12.00	5.50
❑ 125P Devon White	6.00	2.70
❑ 126P Ivan Rodriguez	25.00	11.00
❑ 130P Dave Magadan	3.00	1.35
❑ 136P Ozzie Smith	25.00	11.00
❑ 141P Chris Hoiles	3.00	1.35
❑ 149P Jim Abbott	6.00	2.70
❑ 151P Bill Swift	3.00	1.35
❑ 154P Edgar Martinez	6.00	2.70
❑ 157P J.T. Snow	6.00	2.70
❑ 159P Alan Trammell	12.00	5.50
❑ 163P Roberto Kelly	3.00	1.35
❑ 166P Scott Erickson	6.00	2.70
❑ 168P Scott Cooper	3.00	1.35
❑ 169P Rod Beck	3.00	1.35
❑ 177P Dean Palmer	6.00	2.70
❑ 182P Todd Van Poppel	3.00	1.35
❑ 185P Paul Sorrento	3.00	1.35

1994 Finest

	MINT	NRMT
COMPLETE SET (440)	150.00	70.00
COMPLETE SERIES 1 (220)	80.00	36.00
COMPLETE SERIES 2 (220)	80.00	36.00
COMMON CARD (1-440)	.50	.23
❑ 1 Mike Piazza FIN	8.00	3.60
❑ 2 Kevin Stocker FIN	.50	.23
❑ 3 Greg McMichael FIN	.50	.23
❑ 4 Jeff Conine FIN	1.00	.45
❑ 5 Rene Arocha FIN	.50	.23
❑ 6 Aaron Sele FIN	1.00	.45
❑ 7 Brent Gates FIN	.50	.23
❑ 8 Chuck Carr FIN	.50	.23
❑ 9 Kirk Rueter FIN	.50	.23
❑ 10 Mike Lansing FIN	1.00	.45
❑ 11 Al Martin FIN	.50	.23
❑ 12 Jason Bere FIN	.50	.23
❑ 13 Troy Neel FIN	.50	.23
❑ 14 Armando Reynoso FIN	.50	.23
❑ 15 Jeromy Burnitz FIN	1.00	.45
❑ 16 Rich Amaral FIN	.50	.23
❑ 17 David McCarty FIN	.50	.23
❑ 18 Tim Salmon FIN	2.50	1.10
❑ 19 Steve Cooke FIN	.50	.23
❑ 20 Wil Cordero FIN	.50	.23
❑ 21 Kevin Tapani	.50	.23
❑ 22 Deion Sanders	1.00	.45
❑ 23 Jose Offerman	.50	.23
❑ 24 Mark Langston	.50	.23
❑ 25 Ken Hill	.50	.23
❑ 26 Alex Fernandez	.50	.23
❑ 27 Jeff Blauser	.50	.23
❑ 28 Royce Clayton	.50	.23
❑ 29 Brad Ausmus	.50	.23
❑ 30 Ryan Bowen	.50	.23
❑ 31 Steve Finley	1.00	.45
❑ 32 Charlie Hayes	.50	.23
❑ 33 Jeff Kent	1.00	.45
❑ 34 Mike Henneman	.50	.23
❑ 35 Andres Galarraga	2.50	1.10
❑ 36 Wayne Kirby	.50	.23
❑ 37 Joe Oliver	.50	.23
❑ 38 Terry Steinbach	1.00	.45
❑ 39 Ryan Thompson	.50	.23
❑ 40 Luis Alicea	.50	.23
❑ 41 Randy Velarde	.50	.23
❑ 42 Bob Tewksbury	.50	.23
❑ 43 Reggie Sanders	1.00	.45
❑ 44 Brian Williams	.50	.23
❑ 45 Joe Orsulak	.50	.23
❑ 46 Jose Lind	.50	.23
❑ 47 Dave Hollins	.50	.23
❑ 48 Graeme Lloyd	.50	.23
❑ 49 Jim Gott	.50	.23
❑ 50 Andre Dawson	1.50	.70
❑ 51 Steve Buechele	.50	.23
❑ 52 David Cone	1.50	.70
❑ 53 Ricky Gutierrez	.50	.23
❑ 54 Lance Johnson	.50	.23
❑ 55 Tino Martinez	2.50	1.10
❑ 56 Phil Hiatt	.50	.23
❑ 57 Carlos Garcia	.50	.23
❑ 58 Danny Darwin	.50	.23
❑ 59 Dante Bichette	1.00	.45
❑ 60 Scott Kamieniecki	.50	.23
❑ 61 Orlando Merced	.50	.23
❑ 62 Brian McRae	.50	.23
❑ 63 Pat Kelly	.50	.23
❑ 64 Tom Henke	.50	.23
❑ 65 Jeff King	.50	.23
❑ 66 Mike Mussina	2.50	1.10
❑ 67 Tim Pugh	.50	.23
❑ 68 Robby Thompson	.50	.23
❑ 69 Paul O'Neill	1.00	.45
❑ 70 Hal Morris	.50	.23
❑ 71 Ron Karkovice	.50	.23
❑ 72 Joe Girardi	.50	.23
❑ 73 Eduardo Perez	.50	.23
❑ 74 Raul Mondesi	2.50	1.10
❑ 75 Mike Gallego	.50	.23
❑ 76 Mike Stanley	.50	.23
❑ 77 Kevin Roberson	.50	.23
❑ 78 Mark McGwire	12.00	5.50
❑ 79 Pat Listach	.50	.23
❑ 80 Eric Davis	1.00	.45
❑ 81 Mike Bordick	.50	.23
❑ 82 Doc Gooden	1.00	.45
❑ 83 Mike Moore	.50	.23
❑ 84 Phil Plantier	.50	.23
❑ 85 Darren Lewis	.50	.23
❑ 86 Rick Wilkins	.50	.23
❑ 87 Darryl Strawberry	1.00	.45
❑ 88 Rob Dibble	.50	.23
❑ 89 Greg Vaughn	1.00	.45
❑ 90 Jeff Russell	.50	.23
❑ 91 Mark Lewis	.50	.23
❑ 92 Gregg Jefferies	.50	.23
❑ 93 Jose Guzman	.50	.23
❑ 94 Kenny Rogers	.50	.23
❑ 95 Mark Lemke	.50	.23
❑ 96 Mike Morgan	.50	.23
❑ 97 Andujar Cedeno	.50	.23
❑ 98 Orel Hershiser	1.00	.45
❑ 99 Greg Swindell	.50	.23
❑ 100 John Smoltz	1.00	.45
❑ 101 Pedro Martinez	2.50	1.10
❑ 102 Jim Thome	3.00	1.35
❑ 103 David Segui	1.00	.45
❑ 104 Charles Nagy	1.00	.45
❑ 105 Shane Mack	.50	.23
❑ 106 John Jaha	.50	.23
❑ 107 Tom Candiotti	.50	.23

❑ 108 David Wells 1.50 .70
❑ 109 Bobby Jones .50 .23
❑ 110 Bob Hamelin .50 .23
❑ 111 Bernard Gilkey .50 .23
❑ 112 Chili Davis 1.00 .45
❑ 113 Todd Stottlemyre .50 .23
❑ 114 Derek Bell 1.00 .45
❑ 115 Mark McLemore .50 .23
❑ 116 Mark Whiten .50 .23
❑ 117 Mike Devereaux .50 .23
❑ 118 Terry Pendleton .50 .23
❑ 119 Pat Meares .50 .23
❑ 120 Pete Harnisch .50 .23
❑ 121 Moises Alou 1.50 .70
❑ 122 Jay Buhner 1.00 .45
❑ 123 Wes Chamberlain .50 .23
❑ 124 Mike Perez .50 .23
❑ 125 Devon White 1.00 .45
❑ 126 Ivan Rodriguez 3.00 1.35
❑ 127 Don Slaught .50 .23
❑ 128 John Valentin 1.00 .45
❑ 129 Jaime Navarro .50 .23
❑ 130 Dave Magadan .50 .23
❑ 131 Brady Anderson 1.00 .45
❑ 132 Juan Guzman .50 .23
❑ 133 John Wetteland 1.00 .45
❑ 134 Dave Stewart 1.00 .45
❑ 135 Scott Servais .50 .23
❑ 136 Ozzie Smith 3.00 1.35
❑ 137 Darrin Fletcher .50 .23
❑ 138 Jose Mesa .50 .23
❑ 139 Wilson Alvarez 1.00 .45
❑ 140 Pete Incaviglia .50 .23
❑ 141 Chris Hoiles .50 .23
❑ 142 Darryl Hamilton .50 .23
❑ 143 Chuck Finley 1.00 .45
❑ 144 Archi Cianfrocco .50 .23
❑ 145 Bill Wegman .50 .23
❑ 146 Joey Cora 1.00 .45
❑ 147 Darrell Whitmore .50 .23
❑ 148 David Hulse .50 .23
❑ 149 Jim Abbott 1.00 .45
❑ 150 Curt Schilling 1.00 .45
❑ 151 Bill Swift .50 .23
❑ 152 Tommy Greene .50 .23
❑ 153 Roberto Mejia .50 .23
❑ 154 Edgar Martinez 1.00 .45
❑ 155 Roger Pavlik .50 .23
❑ 156 Randy Tomlin .50 .23
❑ 157 J.T. Snow 1.00 .45
❑ 158 Bob Welch .50 .23
❑ 159 Alan Trammell 1.50 .70
❑ 160 Ed Sprague .50 .23
❑ 161 Ben McDonald .50 .23
❑ 162 Derrick May .50 .23
❑ 163 Roberto Kelly .50 .23
❑ 164 Bryan Harvey .50 .23
❑ 165 Ron Gant 1.00 .45
❑ 166 Scott Erickson 1.00 .45
❑ 167 Anthony Young .50 .23
❑ 168 Scott Cooper .50 .23
❑ 169 Rod Beck .50 .23
❑ 170 John Franco 1.00 .45
❑ 171 Gary DiSarcina .50 .23
❑ 172 Dave Fleming .50 .23
❑ 173 Wade Boggs 2.50 1.10
❑ 174 Kevin Appier 1.00 .45
❑ 175 Jose Bautista .50 .23
❑ 176 Wally Joyner 1.00 .45
❑ 177 Dean Palmer 1.00 .45
❑ 178 Tony Phillips .50 .23
❑ 179 John Smiley .50 .23
❑ 180 Charlie Hough .50 .23
❑ 181 Scott Fletcher .50 .23
❑ 182 Todd Van Poppel .50 .23
❑ 183 Mike Blowers .50 .23
❑ 184 Willie McGee 1.00 .45
❑ 185 Paul Sorrento .50 .23
❑ 186 Eric Young .50 .23
❑ 187 Bret Barberie .50 .23
❑ 188 Manuel Lee .50 .23
❑ 189 Jeff Branson .50 .23
❑ 190 Jim Deshaies .50 .23
❑ 191 Ken Caminiti 1.50 .70
❑ 192 Tim Raines 1.00 .45
❑ 193 Joe Grahe .50 .23
❑ 194 Hipolito Pichardo .50 .23
❑ 195 Denny Neagle 1.00 .45
❑ 196 Jeff Gardner .50 .23
❑ 197 Mike Benjamin .50 .23
❑ 198 Milt Thompson .50 .23
❑ 199 Bruce Ruffin .50 .23
❑ 200 Chris Hammond UER .50 .23
(Back of card has Mariners; should be Marlins)
❑ 201 Tony Gwynn FIN 6.00 2.70
❑ 202 Robin Ventura FIN 1.00 .45
❑ 203 Frank Thomas FIN 8.00 3.60
❑ 204 Kirby Puckett FIN 4.00 1.80
❑ 205 Roberto Alomar FIN 2.50 1.10
❑ 206 Dennis Eckersley FIN 1.00 .45
❑ 207 Joe Carter FIN 1.00 .45
❑ 208 Albert Belle FIN 3.00 1.35
❑ 209 Greg Maddux FIN 8.00 3.60
❑ 210 Ryne Sandberg FIN 3.00 1.35
❑ 211 Juan Gonzalez FIN 6.00 2.70
❑ 212 Jeff Bagwell FIN 4.00 1.80
❑ 213 Randy Johnson FIN 2.50 1.10
❑ 214 Matt Williams FIN 1.50 .70
❑ 215 Dave Winfield FIN 2.50 1.10
❑ 216 Larry Walker FIN 2.50 1.10
❑ 217 Roger Clemens FIN 5.00 2.20
❑ 218 Kenny Lofton FIN 2.50 1.10
❑ 219 Cecil Fielder FIN 1.00 .45
❑ 220 Darren Daulton FIN 1.00 .45
❑ 221 John Olerud FIN 1.00 .45
❑ 222 Jose Canseco FIN 2.50 1.10
❑ 223 Rickey Henderson FIN 2.50 1.10
❑ 224 Fred McGriff FIN 1.50 .70
❑ 225 Gary Sheffield FIN 2.50 1.10
❑ 226 Jack McDowell FIN .50 .23
❑ 227 Rafael Palmeiro FIN 1.50 .70
❑ 228 Travis Fryman FIN 1.00 .45
❑ 229 Marquis Grissom FIN 1.00 .45
❑ 230 Barry Bonds FIN 3.00 1.35
❑ 231 Carlos Baerga FIN 1.00 .45
❑ 232 Ken Griffey Jr. FIN 12.00 5.50
❑ 233 David Justice FIN 2.50 1.10
❑ 234 Bobby Bonilla FIN 1.00 .45
❑ 235 Cal Ripken FIN 10.00 4.50
❑ 236 Sammy Sosa FIN 6.00 2.70
❑ 237 Len Dykstra FIN 1.00 .45
❑ 238 Will Clark FIN 2.50 1.10
❑ 239 Paul Molitor FIN 2.50 1.10
❑ 240 Barry Larkin FIN 1.50 .70
❑ 241 Bo Jackson 1.00 .45
❑ 242 Mitch Williams .50 .23
❑ 243 Ron Darling .50 .23
❑ 244 Darryl Kile 1.00 .45
❑ 245 Geronimo Berroa .50 .23
❑ 246 Gregg Olson .50 .23
❑ 247 Brian Harper .50 .23
❑ 248 Rheal Cormier .50 .23
❑ 249 Rey Sanchez .50 .23
❑ 250 Jeff Fassero .50 .23
❑ 251 Sandy Alomar 1.00 .45
❑ 252 Chris Bosio .50 .23
❑ 253 Andy Stankiewicz .50 .23
❑ 254 Harold Baines 1.00 .45
❑ 255 Andy Ashby .50 .23
❑ 256 Tyler Green .50 .23
❑ 257 Kevin Brown 1.00 .45
❑ 258 Mo Vaughn 3.00 1.35
❑ 259 Mike Harkey .50 .23
❑ 260 Dave Henderson .50 .23
❑ 261 Kent Hrbek 1.00 .45
❑ 262 Darrin Jackson .50 .23
❑ 263 Bob Wickman .50 .23
❑ 264 Spike Owen .50 .23
❑ 265 Todd Jones .50 .23
❑ 266 Pat Borders .50 .23
❑ 267 Tom Glavine 2.50 1.10
❑ 268 Dave Nilsson .50 .23
❑ 269 Rich Batchelor .50 .23
❑ 270 Delino DeShields .50 .23
❑ 271 Felix Fermin .50 .23
❑ 272 Orestes Destrade .50 .23
❑ 273 Mickey Morandini .50 .23
❑ 274 Otis Nixon .50 .23
❑ 275 Ellis Burks 1.00 .45
❑ 276 Greg Gagne .50 .23
❑ 277 John Doherty .50 .23
❑ 278 Julio Franco .50 .23
❑ 279 Bernie Williams 2.50 1.10
❑ 280 Rick Aguilera .50 .23
❑ 281 Mickey Tettleton .50 .23
❑ 282 David Nied .50 .23
❑ 283 Johnny Ruffin .50 .23
❑ 284 Dan Wilson .50 .23
❑ 285 Omar Vizquel 1.00 .45
❑ 286 Willie Banks .50 .23
❑ 287 Erik Pappas .50 .23
❑ 288 Cal Eldred .50 .23
❑ 289 Bobby Witt .50 .23
❑ 290 Luis Gonzalez .50 .23
❑ 291 Greg Pirkl .50 .23
❑ 292 Alex Cole .50 .23
❑ 293 Ricky Bones .50 .23
❑ 294 Denis Boucher .50 .23
❑ 295 John Burkett .50 .23
❑ 296 Steve Trachsel .50 .23
❑ 297 Ricky Jordan .50 .23
❑ 298 Mark Dewey .50 .23
❑ 299 Jimmy Key 1.00 .45
❑ 300 Mike Macfarlane .50 .23
❑ 301 Tim Belcher .50 .23
❑ 302 Carlos Reyes .50 .23
❑ 303 Greg A. Harris .50 .23
❑ 304 Brian Anderson 1.50 .70
❑ 305 Terry Mulholland .50 .23
❑ 306 Felix Jose .50 .23
❑ 307 Darren Holmes .50 .23
❑ 308 Jose Rijo .50 .23
❑ 309 Paul Wagner .50 .23
❑ 310 Bob Scanlan .50 .23
❑ 311 Mike Jackson .50 .23
❑ 312 Jose Vizcaino .50 .23
❑ 313 Rob Butler .50 .23
❑ 314 Kevin Seitzer .50 .23
❑ 315 Geronimo Pena .50 .23
❑ 316 Hector Carrasco .50 .23
❑ 317 Eddie Murray 2.50 1.10
❑ 318 Roger Salkeld .50 .23
❑ 319 Todd Hundley 1.00 .45
❑ 320 Danny Jackson .50 .23
❑ 321 Kevin Young .50 .23
❑ 322 Mike Greenwell .50 .23
❑ 323 Kevin Mitchell .50 .23
❑ 324 Chuck Knoblauch 2.50 1.10
❑ 325 Danny Tartabull .50 .23
❑ 326 Vince Coleman .50 .23
❑ 327 Marvin Freeman .50 .23
❑ 328 Andy Benes 1.00 .45
❑ 329 Mike Kelly .50 .23
❑ 330 Karl Rhodes .50 .23
❑ 331 Allen Watson .50 .23
❑ 332 Damion Easley 1.00 .45
❑ 333 Reggie Jefferson .50 .23
❑ 334 Kevin McReynolds .50 .23
❑ 335 Arthur Rhodes .50 .23
❑ 336 Brian R. Hunter .50 .23
❑ 337 Tom Browning .50 .23
❑ 338 Pedro Munoz .50 .23
❑ 339 Billy Ripken .50 .23
❑ 340 Gene Harris .50 .23
❑ 341 Fernando Vina .50 .23
❑ 342 Sean Berry .50 .23
❑ 343 Pedro Astacio .50 .23
❑ 344 B.J. Surhoff 1.00 .45
❑ 345 Doug Drabek .50 .23
❑ 346 Jody Reed .50 .23
❑ 347 Ray Lankford 1.00 .45
❑ 348 Steve Farr .50 .23
❑ 349 Eric Anthony .50 .23
❑ 350 Pete Smith .50 .23
❑ 351 Lee Smith 1.00 .45
❑ 352 Mariano Duncan .50 .23
❑ 353 Doug Strange .50 .23
❑ 354 Tim Bogar .50 .23
❑ 355 Dave Weathers .50 .23
❑ 356 Eric Karros 1.00 .45
❑ 357 Randy Myers .50 .23
❑ 358 Chad Curtis .50 .23
❑ 359 Steve Avery .50 .23
❑ 360 Brian Jordan 1.00 .45

No.	Player	Mint	NrMt
361	Tim Wallach	.50	.23
362	Pedro Martinez	3.00	1.35
363	Bip Roberts	.50	.23
364	Lou Whitaker	1.00	.45
365	Luis Polonia	.50	.23
366	Benny Santiago	.50	.23
367	Brett Butler	1.00	.45
368	Shawon Dunston	.50	.23
369	Kelly Stinnett	.50	.23
370	Chris Turner	.50	.23
371	Ruben Sierra	.50	.23
372	Greg A. Harris	.50	.23
373	Xavier Hernandez	.50	.23
374	Howard Johnson	.50	.23
375	Duane Ward	.50	.23
376	Roberto Hernandez	.50	.23
377	Scott Leius	.50	.23
378	Dave Valle	.50	.23
379	Sid Fernandez	.50	.23
380	Doug Jones	.50	.23
381	Zane Smith	.50	.23
382	Craig Biggio	2.50	1.10
383	Rick White	.50	.23
384	Tom Pagnozzi	.50	.23
385	Chris James	.50	.23
386	Bret Boone	1.00	.45
387	Jeff Montgomery	.50	.23
388	Chad Kreuter	.50	.23
389	Greg Hibbard	.50	.23
390	Mark Grace	1.50	.70
391	Phil Leftwich	.50	.23
392	Don Mattingly	4.00	1.80
393	Ozzie Guillen	.50	.23
394	Gary Gaetti	1.00	.45
395	Erik Hanson	.50	.23
396	Scott Brosius	1.00	.45
397	Tom Gordon	.50	.23
398	Bill Gullickson	.50	.23
399	Matt Mieske	.50	.23
400	Pat Hentgen	1.00	.45
401	Walt Weiss	.50	.23
402	Greg Blosser	.50	.23
403	Stan Javier	.50	.23
404	Doug Henry	.50	.23
405	Ramon Martinez	1.00	.45
406	Frank Viola	.50	.23
407	Mike Hampton	.50	.23
408	Andy Van Slyke	1.00	.45
409	Bobby Ayala	.50	.23
410	Todd Zeile	.50	.23
411	Jay Bell	1.00	.45
412	Denny Martinez	1.00	.45
413	Mark Portugal	.50	.23
414	Bobby Munoz	.50	.23
415	Kirt Manwaring	.50	.23
416	John Kruk	1.00	.45
417	Trevor Hoffman	1.00	.45
418	Chris Sabo	.50	.23
419	Bret Saberhagen	1.00	.45
420	Chris Nabholz	.50	.23
421	James Mouton FIN	.50	.23
422	Tony Tarasco FIN	.50	.23
423	Carlos Delgado FIN	1.50	.70
424	Rondell White FIN	1.00	.45
425	Javier Lopez FIN	1.50	.70
426	Chan Ho Park FIN	12.00	5.50
427	Cliff Floyd FIN	1.00	.45
428	Dave Staton FIN	.50	.23
429	J.R. Phillips FIN	.50	.23
430	Manny Ramirez FIN	3.00	1.35
431	Kurt Abbott FIN	.50	.23
432	Melvin Nieves FIN	.50	.23
433	Alex Gonzalez FIN	.50	.23
434	Rick Helling FIN	1.00	.45
435	Danny Bautista FIN	.50	.23
436	Matt Walbeck FIN	.50	.23
437	Ryan Klesko FIN	1.00	.45
438	Steve Karsay FIN	.50	.23
439	Salomon Torres FIN	.50	.23
440	Scott Ruffcorn FIN	.50	.23

1995 Finest

	MINT	NRMT
COMPLETE SET (330)	100.00	45.00
COMPLETE SERIES 1 (220)	70.00	32.00
COMPLETE SERIES 2 (110)	30.00	13.50
COMMON CARD (1-330)	.40	.18

No.	Player	Mint	NrMt
1	Raul Mondesi	1.25	.55
2	Kurt Abbott	.40	.18
3	Chris Gomez	.40	.18
4	Manny Ramirez	2.00	.90
5	Rondell White	.75	.35
6	William VanLandingham	.40	.18
7	Jon Lieber	.40	.18
8	Ryan Klesko	.75	.35
9	John Hudek	.40	.18
10	Joey Hamilton	.75	.35
11	Bob Hamelin	.40	.18
12	Brian Anderson	.75	.35
13	Mike Lieberthal	.40	.18
14	Rico Brogna	.40	.18
15	Rusty Greer	2.00	.90
16	Carlos Delgado	.75	.35
17	Jim Edmonds	1.25	.55
18	Steve Trachsel	.40	.18
19	Matt Walbeck	.40	.18
20	Armando Benitez	.40	.18
21	Steve Karsay	.40	.18
22	Jose Oliva	.40	.18
23	Cliff Floyd	.75	.35
24	Kevin Foster	.40	.18
25	Javier Lopez	.75	.35
26	Jose Valentin	.40	.18
27	James Mouton	.40	.18
28	Hector Carrasco	.40	.18
29	Orlando Miller	.40	.18
30	Garret Anderson	.75	.35
31	Marvin Freeman	.40	.18
32	Brett Butler	.75	.35
33	Roberto Kelly	.40	.18
34	Rod Beck	.40	.18
35	Jose Rijo	.40	.18
36	Edgar Martinez	.75	.35
37	Jim Thome	2.00	.90
38	Rick Wilkins	.40	.18
39	Wally Joyner	.75	.35
40	Wil Cordero	.40	.18
41	Tommy Greene	.40	.18
42	Travis Fryman	.75	.35
43	Don Slaught	.40	.18
44	Brady Anderson	.75	.35
45	Matt Williams	.75	.35
46	Rene Arocha	.40	.18
47	Rickey Henderson	2.00	.90
48	Mike Mussina	2.00	.90
49	Greg McMichael	.40	.18
50	Jody Reed	.40	.18
51	Tino Martinez	2.00	.90
52	Dave Clark	.40	.18
53	John Valentin	.75	.35
54	Bret Boone	.75	.35
55	Walt Weiss	.40	.18
56	Kenny Lofton	2.00	.90
57	Scott Leius	.40	.18
58	Eric Karros	.75	.35
59	John Olerud	.75	.35
60	Chris Hoiles	.40	.18
61	Sandy Alomar Jr.	.75	.35
62	Tim Wallach	.40	.18
63	Cal Eldred	.40	.18
64	Tom Glavine	2.00	.90
65	Mark Grace	1.25	.55
66	Rey Sanchez	.40	.18
67	Bobby Ayala	.40	.18
68	Dante Bichette	.75	.35
69	Andres Galarraga	2.00	.90
70	Chuck Carr	.40	.18
71	Bobby Witt	.40	.18
72	Steve Avery	.40	.18
73	Bobby Jones	.40	.18
74	Delino DeShields	.40	.18
75	Kevin Tapani	.40	.18
76	Randy Johnson	2.00	.90
77	David Nied	.40	.18
78	Pat Hentgen	.75	.35
79	Tim Salmon	2.00	.90
80	Todd Zeile	.40	.18
81	John Wetteland	.75	.35
82	Albert Belle	2.50	1.10
83	Ben McDonald	.40	.18
84	Bobby Munoz	.40	.18
85	Bip Roberts	.40	.18
86	Mo Vaughn	2.50	1.10
87	Chuck Finley	.75	.35
88	Chuck Knoblauch	2.00	.90
89	Frank Thomas	6.00	2.70
90	Danny Tartabull	.40	.18
91	Dean Palmer	.75	.35
92	Len Dykstra	.75	.35
93	J.R. Phillips	.40	.18
94	Tom Candiotti	.40	.18
95	Marquis Grissom	.75	.35
96	Barry Larkin	1.25	.55
97	Bryan Harvey	.40	.18
98	David Justice	2.00	.90
99	David Cone	1.25	.55
100	Wade Boggs	2.00	.90
101	Jason Bere	.40	.18
102	Hal Morris	.40	.18
103	Fred McGriff	1.25	.55
104	Bobby Bonilla	.75	.35
105	Jay Buhner	.75	.35
106	Allen Watson	.40	.18
107	Mickey Tettleton	.40	.18
108	Kevin Appier	.75	.35
109	Ivan Rodriguez	2.50	1.10
110	Carlos Garcia	.40	.18
111	Andy Benes	.75	.35
112	Eddie Murray	2.00	.90
113	Mike Piazza	6.00	2.70
114	Greg Vaughn	.75	.35
115	Paul Molitor	2.00	.90
116	Terry Steinbach	.75	.35
117	Jeff Bagwell	3.00	1.35
118	Ken Griffey Jr.	10.00	4.50
119	Gary Sheffield	1.25	.55
120	Cal Ripken	8.00	3.60
121	Jeff Kent	.75	.35
122	Jay Bell	.75	.35
123	Will Clark	2.00	.90
124	Cecil Fielder	.75	.35
125	Alex Fernandez	.40	.18
126	Don Mattingly	3.00	1.35
127	Reggie Sanders	.75	.35
128	Moises Alou	1.25	.55
129	Craig Biggio	2.00	.90
130	Eddie Williams	.40	.18
131	John Franco	.75	.35
132	John Kruk	.75	.35
133	Jeff King	.40	.18
134	Royce Clayton	.40	.18
135	Doug Drabek	.40	.18
136	Ray Lankford	.75	.35
137	Roberto Alomar	2.00	.90
138	Todd Hundley	.75	.35
139	Alex Cole	.40	.18
140	Shawon Dunston	.40	.18
141	John Roper	.40	.18
142	Mark Langston	.40	.18
143	Tom Pagnozzi	.40	.18
144	Wilson Alvarez	.75	.35
145	Scott Cooper	.40	.18
146	Kevin Mitchell	.40	.18
147	Mark Whiten	.40	.18
148	Jeff Conine	.75	.35
149	Chili Davis	.75	.35
150	Luis Gonzalez	.40	.18

❑ 151 Juan Guzman .40 .18
❑ 152 Mike Greenwell .40 .18
❑ 153 Mike Henneman .40 .18
❑ 154 Rick Aguilera .40 .18
❑ 155 Dennis Eckersley .75 .35
❑ 156 Darrin Fletcher .40 .18
❑ 157 Darren Lewis .40 .18
❑ 158 Juan Gonzalez 5.00 2.20
❑ 159 Dave Hollins .40 .18
❑ 160 Jimmy Key .75 .35
❑ 161 Roberto Hernandez .40 .18
❑ 162 Randy Myers .40 .18
❑ 163 Joe Carter .75 .35
❑ 164 Darren Daulton .75 .35
❑ 165 Mike Macfarlane .40 .18
❑ 166 Bret Saberhagen .75 .35
❑ 167 Kirby Puckett 3.00 1.35
❑ 168 Lance Johnson .40 .18
❑ 169 Mark McGwire 10.00 4.50
❑ 170 Jose Canseco 2.00 .90
❑ 171 Mike Stanley .40 .18
❑ 172 Lee Smith .75 .35
❑ 173 Robin Ventura .75 .35
❑ 174 Greg Gagne .40 .18
❑ 175 Brian McRae .40 .18
❑ 176 Mike Bordick .40 .18
❑ 177 Rafael Palmeiro 1.25 .55
❑ 178 Kenny Rogers .40 .18
❑ 179 Chad Curtis .40 .18
❑ 180 Devon White .75 .35
❑ 181 Paul O'Neill .75 .35
❑ 182 Ken Caminiti 1.25 .55
❑ 183 Dave Nilsson .40 .18
❑ 184 Tim Naehring .40 .18
❑ 185 Roger Clemens 4.00 1.80
❑ 186 Otis Nixon .40 .18
❑ 187 Tim Raines .75 .35
❑ 188 Denny Martinez .75 .35
❑ 189 Pedro Martinez 2.00 .90
❑ 190 Jim Abbott .75 .35
❑ 191 Ryan Thompson .40 .18
❑ 192 Barry Bonds 2.50 1.10
❑ 193 Joe Girardi .40 .18
❑ 194 Steve Finley .75 .35
❑ 195 John Jaha .40 .18
❑ 196 Tony Gwynn 5.00 2.20
❑ 197 Sammy Sosa 5.00 2.20
❑ 198 John Burkett .40 .18
❑ 199 Carlos Baerga .75 .35
❑ 200 Ramon Martinez .75 .35
❑ 201 Aaron Sele .75 .35
❑ 202 Eduardo Perez .40 .18
❑ 203 Alan Trammell .75 .35
❑ 204 Orlando Merced .40 .18
❑ 205 Deion Sanders .75 .35
❑ 206 Robb Nen .40 .18
❑ 207 Jack McDowell .40 .18
❑ 208 Ruben Sierra .40 .18
❑ 209 Bernie Williams 2.00 .90
❑ 210 Kevin Seitzer .40 .18
❑ 211 Charles Nagy .75 .35
❑ 212 Tony Phillips .40 .18
❑ 213 Greg Maddux 6.00 2.70
❑ 214 Jeff Montgomery .40 .18
❑ 215 Larry Walker 2.00 .90
❑ 216 Andy Van Slyke .75 .35
❑ 217 Ozzie Smith 2.50 1.10
❑ 218 Geronimo Pena .40 .18
❑ 219 Gregg Jefferies .40 .18
❑ 220 Lou Whitaker .75 .35
❑ 221 Chipper Jones 5.00 2.20
❑ 222 Benji Gil .40 .18
❑ 223 Tony Phillips .40 .18
❑ 224 Trevor Wilson .40 .18
❑ 225 Tony Tarasco .40 .18
❑ 226 Roberto Petagine .40 .18
❑ 227 Mike Macfarlane .40 .18
❑ 228 Hideo Nomo UER 12.00 5.50
(In 3rd line agianst)
❑ 229 Mark McLemore .40 .18
❑ 230 Ron Gant .40 .18
❑ 231 Andujar Cedeno .40 .18
❑ 232 Mike Mimbs .40 .18
❑ 233 Jim Abbott .75 .35
❑ 234 Ricky Bones .40 .18
❑ 235 Marty Cordova .40 .18
❑ 236 Mark Johnson .40 .18
❑ 237 Marquis Grissom .75 .35
❑ 238 Tom Henke .40 .18
❑ 239 Terry Pendleton .40 .18
❑ 240 John Wetteland .75 .35
❑ 241 Lee Smith .75 .35
❑ 242 Jaime Navarro .40 .18
❑ 243 Luis Alicea .40 .18
❑ 244 Scott Cooper .40 .18
❑ 245 Gary Gaetti .75 .35
❑ 246 Edgardo Alfonzo UER .75 .35
(Incomplete career BA)
❑ 247 Brad Clontz .40 .18
❑ 248 Dave Mlicki .40 .18
❑ 249 Dave Winfield 2.00 .90
❑ 250 Mark Grudzielanek 2.50 1.10
❑ 251 Alex Gonzalez .40 .18
❑ 252 Kevin Brown 1.25 .55
❑ 253 Esteban Loaiza .40 .18
❑ 254 Vaughn Eshelman .40 .18
❑ 255 Bill Swift .40 .18
❑ 256 Brian McRae .40 .18
❑ 257 Bobby Higginson 8.00 3.60
❑ 258 Jack McDowell .40 .18
❑ 259 Scott Stahoviak .40 .18
❑ 260 Jon Nunnally .40 .18
❑ 261 Charlie Hayes .40 .18
❑ 262 Jacob Brumfield .40 .18
❑ 263 Chad Curtis .40 .18
❑ 264 Heathcliff Slocumb .40 .18
❑ 265 Mark Whiten .40 .18
❑ 266 Mickey Tettleton .40 .18
❑ 267 Jose Mesa .40 .18
❑ 268 Doug Jones .40 .18
❑ 269 Trevor Hoffman .75 .35
❑ 270 Paul Sorrento .40 .18
❑ 271 Shane Andrews .40 .18
❑ 272 Brett Butler .75 .35
❑ 273 Curtis Goodwin .40 .18
❑ 274 Larry Walker 2.00 .90
❑ 275 Phil Plantier .40 .18
❑ 276 Ken Hill .40 .18
❑ 277 Vinny Castilla UER 1.25 .55
Rockies spelled Rockie
❑ 278 Billy Ashley .40 .18
❑ 279 Derek Jeter 6.00 2.70
❑ 280 Bob Tewksbury .40 .18
❑ 281 Jose Offerman .40 .18
❑ 282 Glenallen Hill .40 .18
❑ 283 Tony Fernandez .40 .18
❑ 284 Mike Devereaux .40 .18
❑ 285 John Burkett .40 .18
❑ 286 Geronimo Berroa .40 .18
❑ 287 Quilvio Veras .40 .18
❑ 288 Jason Bates .40 .18
❑ 289 Lee Tinsley .40 .18
❑ 290 Derek Bell .75 .35
❑ 291 Jeff Fassero .40 .18
❑ 292 Ray Durham .75 .35
❑ 293 Chad Ogea .40 .18
❑ 294 Bill Pulsipher .40 .18
❑ 295 Phil Nevin .40 .18
❑ 296 Carlos Perez 2.50 1.10
❑ 297 Roberto Kelly .40 .18
❑ 298 Tim Wakefield .75 .35
❑ 299 Jeff Manto .40 .18
❑ 300 Brian Hunter .75 .35
❑ 301 C.J. Nitkowski .40 .18
❑ 302 Dustin Hermanson .75 .35
❑ 303 John Mabry .40 .18
❑ 304 Orel Hershiser .75 .35
❑ 305 Ron Villone .40 .18
❑ 306 Sean Bergman .40 .18
❑ 307 Tom Goodwin .40 .18
❑ 308 Al Reyes .40 .18
❑ 309 Todd Stottlemyre .40 .18
❑ 310 Rich Becker .40 .18
❑ 311 Joey Cora .75 .35
❑ 312 Ed Sprague .40 .18
❑ 313 John Smoltz UER .75 .35
(3rd line; from spelled as form)
❑ 314 Frank Castillo .40 .18
❑ 315 Chris Hammond .40 .18
❑ 316 Ismael Valdes .75 .35
❑ 317 Pete Harnisch .40 .18
❑ 318 Bernard Gilkey .40 .18
❑ 319 John Kruk .75 .35
❑ 320 Marc Newfield .40 .18
❑ 321 Brian Johnson .40 .18
❑ 322 Mark Portugal .40 .18
❑ 323 David Hulse .40 .18
❑ 324 Luis Ortiz UER .40 .18
(Below spelled beloe)
❑ 325 Mike Benjamin .40 .18
❑ 326 Brian Jordan .75 .35
❑ 327 Shawn Green .75 .35
❑ 328 Joe Oliver .40 .18
❑ 329 Felipe Lira .40 .18
❑ 330 Andre Dawson 1.25 .55

1995 Finest Flame Throwers

	MINT	NRMT
COMPLETE SET (9)	40.00	18.00
COMMON CARD (1-9)	3.00	1.35

❑ FT1 Jason Bere 3.00 1.35
❑ FT2 Roger Clemens 25.00 11.00
❑ FT3 Juan Guzman 3.00 1.35
❑ FT4 John Hudek 3.00 1.35
❑ FT5 Randy Johnson 12.00 5.50
❑ FT6 Pedro Martinez 12.00 5.50
❑ FT7 Jose Rijo 3.00 1.35
❑ FT8 Bret Saberhagen 4.00 1.80
❑ FT9 John Wetteland 4.00 1.80

1995 Finest Power Kings

	MINT	NRMT
COMPLETE SET (18)	200.00	90.00
COMMON CARD (1-18)	4.00	1.80

❑ PK1 Bob Hamelin 4.00 1.80
❑ PK2 Raul Mondesi 6.00 2.70
❑ PK3 Ryan Klesko 5.00 2.20
❑ PK4 Carlos Delgado 5.00 2.20
❑ PK5 Manny Ramirez 10.00 4.50
❑ PK6 Mike Piazza 30.00 13.50
❑ PK7 Jeff Bagwell 15.00 6.75
❑ PK8 Mo Vaughn 12.00 5.50
❑ PK9 Frank Thomas 30.00 13.50

Card	Player	Mint	NrMt
❑ PK10	Ken Griffey Jr.	50.00	22.00
❑ PK11	Albert Belle	12.00	5.50
❑ PK12	Sammy Sosa	25.00	11.00
❑ PK13	Dante Bichette	5.00	2.20
❑ PK14	Gary Sheffield	6.00	2.70
❑ PK15	Matt Williams	5.00	2.20
❑ PK16	Fred McGriff	6.00	2.70
❑ PK17	Barry Bonds	12.00	5.50
❑ PK18	Cecil Fielder	5.00	2.20

1996 Finest

	MINT	NRMT
COMPLETE SET (359)	1000.00	450.00
COMPLETE SERIES 1 (191)	650.00	300.00
COMPLETE SERIES 2 (168)	350.00	160.00
COMP.BRONZE SET (220)	50.00	22.00
COMP.BRONZE SER.1 (110)	25.00	11.00
COMP.BRONZE SER.2 (110)	30.00	13.50
COMMON BRONZE	.25	.11
COMP.GOLD SET (48)	750.00	350.00
COMP.GOLD SER.1 (26)	500.00	220.00
COMP.GOLD SER.2 (22)	250.00	110.00
COMMON GOLD	6.00	2.70
COMP.SILVER SET (91)	230.00	105.00
COMP.SILVER SER.1 (55)	150.00	70.00
COMP.SILVER SER.2 (36)	80.00	36.00
COMMON SILVER	1.50	.70

Card	Player	Mint	NrMt
❑ B5	Roberto Hernandez B	.25	.11
❑ B8	Terry Pendleton B	.25	.11
❑ B12	Ken Caminiti B	.75	.35
❑ B15	Dan Miceli B	.25	.11
❑ B16	Chipper Jones B	2.50	1.10
❑ B17	John Wetteland B	.50	.23
❑ B19	Tim Naehring B	.25	.11
❑ B21	Eddie Murray B	1.00	.45
❑ B23	Kevin Appier B	.50	.23
❑ B24	Ken Griffey Jr. B	5.00	2.20
❑ B26	Brian McRae B	.25	.11
❑ B27	Pedro Martinez B	1.00	.45
❑ B28	Brian Jordan B	.50	.23
❑ B29	Mike Fetters B	.25	.11
❑ B30	Carlos Delgado B	.50	.23
❑ B31	Shane Reynolds B	.50	.23
❑ B32	Terry Steinbach B	.50	.23
❑ B34	Mark Leiter B	.25	.11
❑ B36	David Segui B	.50	.23
❑ B40	Fred McGriff B	.75	.35
❑ B44	Glenallen Hill B	.25	.11
❑ B45	Brady Anderson B	.50	.23
❑ B47	Jim Thome B	1.00	.45
❑ B48	Frank Thomas B	3.00	1.35
❑ B49	Chuck Knoblauch B	1.00	.45
❑ B50	Len Dykstra B	.50	.23
❑ B53	Tom Pagnozzi B	.25	.11
❑ B55	Ricky Bones B	.25	.11
❑ B56	David Justice B	1.00	.45
❑ B57	Steve Avery B	.25	.11
❑ B58	Robby Thompson B	.25	.11
❑ B61	Tony Gwynn B	2.50	1.10
❑ B63	Denny Neagle B	.50	.23
❑ B67	Robin Ventura B	.50	.23
❑ B70	Kevin Seitzer B	.25	.11
❑ B71	Ramon Martinez B	.50	.23
❑ B75	Brian L.Hunter B	.50	.23
❑ B76	Alan Benes B	.50	.23
❑ B80	Ozzie Guillen B	.25	.11
❑ B82	Benji Gil B	.25	.11
❑ B85	Todd Hundley B	.50	.23
❑ B87	Pat Hentgen B	.50	.23
❑ B89	Chuck Finley B	.50	.23
❑ B92	Derek Jeter B	3.00	1.35
❑ B93	Paul O'Neill B	.50	.23
❑ B94	Darrin Fletcher B	.25	.11
❑ B96	Delino DeShields B	.25	.11
❑ B97	Tim Salmon B	1.00	.45
❑ B98	John Olerud B	.50	.23
❑ B101	Tim Wakefield B	.50	.23
❑ B103	Dave Stevens B	.25	.11
❑ B104	Orlando Merced B	.25	.11
❑ B106	Jay Bell B	.50	.23
❑ B107	John Burkett B	.25	.11
❑ B108	Chris Hoiles B	.25	.11
❑ B110	Dave Nilsson B	.25	.11
❑ B111	Rod Beck B	.25	.11
❑ B113	Mike Piazza B	3.00	1.35
❑ B114	Mark Langston B	.25	.11
❑ B116	Rico Brogna B	.25	.11
❑ B118	Tom Goodwin B	.25	.11
❑ B119	Bryan Rekar B	.25	.11
❑ B120	David Cone B	.75	.35
❑ B122	Andy Pettitte B	.75	.35
❑ B123	Chili Davis B	.50	.23
❑ B124	John Smoltz B	.50	.23
❑ B125	Heathcliff Slocumb B	.25	.11
❑ B126	Dante Bichette B	.50	.23
❑ B128	Alex Gonzalez B	.25	.11
❑ B129	Jeff Montgomery B	.25	.11
❑ B131	Denny Martinez B	.50	.23
❑ B132	Mel Rojas B	.25	.11
❑ B133	Derek Bell B	.50	.23
❑ B134	Trevor Hoffman B	.50	.23
❑ B136	Darren Daulton B	.50	.23
❑ B137	Pete Schourek B	.25	.11
❑ B138	Phil Nevin B	.25	.11
❑ B139	Andres Galarraga B	1.00	.45
❑ B140	Chad Fonville B	.25	.11
❑ B144	J.T. Snow B	.50	.23
❑ B146	Barry Bonds B	1.25	.55
❑ B147	Orel Hershiser B	.50	.23
❑ B148	Quilvio Veras B	.25	.11
❑ B149	Will Clark B	1.00	.45
❑ B150	Jose Rijo B	.25	.11
❑ B152	Travis Fryman B	.50	.23
❑ B154	Alex Fernandez B	.25	.11
❑ B155	Wade Boggs B	1.00	.45
❑ B156	Troy Percival B	.50	.23
❑ B157	Moises Alou B	.75	.35
❑ B158	Javy Lopez B	.50	.23
❑ B159	Jason Giambi B	.50	.23
❑ B162	Mark McGwire B	5.00	2.20
❑ B163	Eric Karros B	.50	.23
❑ B166	Mickey Tettleton B	.25	.11
❑ B167	Barry Larkin B	.75	.35
❑ B169	Ruben Sierra B	.25	.11
❑ B170	Bill Swift B	.25	.11
❑ B172	Chad Curtis B	.25	.11
❑ B173	Dean Palmer B	.50	.23
❑ B175	Bobby Bonilla B	.50	.23
❑ B176	Greg Colbrunn B	.25	.11
❑ B177	Jose Mesa B	.25	.11
❑ B178	Mike Greenwell B	.25	.11
❑ B181	Doug Drabek B	.25	.11
❑ B183	Wilson Alvarez B	.50	.23
❑ B184	Marty Cordova B	.25	.11
❑ B185	Hal Morris B	.25	.11
❑ B187	Carlos Garcia B	.25	.11
❑ B190	Marquis Grissom B	.50	.23
❑ B193	Will Clark B	1.00	.45
❑ B194	Paul Molitor B	1.00	.45
❑ B195	Kenny Rogers B	.25	.11
❑ B196	Reggie Sanders B	.50	.23
❑ B199	Raul Mondesi B	.75	.35
❑ B200	Lance Johnson B	.25	.11
❑ B201	Alvin Morman B	.25	.11
❑ B203	Jack McDowell B	.25	.11
❑ B204	Randy Myers B	.25	.11
❑ B205	Harold Baines B	.50	.23
❑ B206	Marty Cordova B	.25	.11
❑ B207	Rich Hunter B	.25	.11
❑ B208	Al Leiter B	.50	.23
❑ B209	Greg Gagne B	.25	.11
❑ B210	Ben McDonald B	.25	.11
❑ B212	Terry Adams B	.25	.11
❑ B213	Paul Sorrento B	.25	.11
❑ B214	Albert Belle B	1.25	.55
❑ B215	Mike Blowers B	.25	.11
❑ B216	Jim Edmonds B	.75	.35
❑ B217	Felipe Crespo B	.25	.11
❑ B219	Shawon Dunston B	.25	.11
❑ B220	Jimmy Haynes B	.25	.11
❑ B221	Jose Canseco B	1.00	.45
❑ B222	Eric Davis B	.50	.23
❑ B224	Tim Raines B	.50	.23
❑ B225	Tony Phillips B	.25	.11
❑ B226	Charlie Hayes B	.25	.11
❑ B227	Eric Owens B	.25	.11
❑ B228	Roberto Alomar B	1.00	.45
❑ B233	Kenny Lofton B	1.00	.45
❑ B236	Mark McGwire B	5.00	2.20
❑ B237	Jay Buhner B	.50	.23
❑ B238	Craig Biggio B	1.00	.45
❑ B240	Barry Bonds B	1.25	.55
❑ B244	Ron Gant B	.25	.11
❑ B245	Paul Wilson B	.25	.11
❑ B246	Todd Hollandsworth B	.25	.11
❑ B247	Todd Zeile B	.25	.11
❑ B248	David Justice B	1.00	.45
❑ B250	Moises Alou B	.75	.35
❑ B251	Bob Wolcott B	.25	.11
❑ B252	David Wells B	.75	.35
❑ B253	Juan Gonzalez B	2.50	1.10
❑ B254	Andres Galarraga B	1.00	.45
❑ B255	Dave Hollins B	.25	.11
❑ B257	Sammy Sosa B	2.50	1.10
❑ B258	Ivan Rodriguez B	1.00	.45
❑ B259	Bip Roberts B	.25	.11
❑ B260	Tino Martinez B	1.00	.45
❑ B262	Mike Stanley B	.25	.11
❑ B264	Butch Huskey B	.25	.11
❑ B265	Jeff Conine B	.50	.23
❑ B267	Mark Grace B	.75	.35
❑ B268	Jason Schmidt B	.25	.11
❑ B269	Otis Nixon B	.25	.11
❑ B271	Kirby Puckett B	1.50	.70
❑ B273	Andy Benes B	.50	.23
❑ B275	Mike Piazza B	3.00	1.35
❑ B276	Rey Ordonez B	.50	.23
❑ B278	Gary Gaetti B	.50	.23
❑ B280	Robin Ventura B	.50	.23
❑ B281	Cal Ripken B	4.00	1.80
❑ B282	Carlos Baerga B	.50	.23
❑ B283	Roger Cedeno B	.25	.11
❑ B285	Terrell Wade B	.25	.11
❑ B286	Kevin Brown B	1.00	.45
❑ B287	Rafael Palmeiro B	.75	.35
❑ B288	Mo Vaughn B	1.25	.55
❑ B292	Bob Tewksbury B	.25	.11
❑ B297	T.J. Mathews B	.25	.11
❑ B298	Manny Ramirez B	1.00	.45
❑ B299	Jeff Bagwell B	1.50	.70
❑ B301	Wade Boggs B	1.00	.45
❑ B303	Steve Gibralter B	.25	.11
❑ B304	B.J. Surhoff B	.50	.23
❑ B306	Royce Clayton B	.25	.11
❑ B307	Sal Fasano B	.25	.11
❑ B309	Gary Sheffield B	.75	.35
❑ B310	Ken Hill B	.25	.11
❑ B311	Joe Girardi B	.25	.11
❑ B312	Matt Lawton B	1.00	.45
❑ B314	Julio Franco B	.25	.11
❑ B315	Joe Carter B	.50	.23
❑ B316	Brooks Kieschnick B	.25	.11
❑ B318	Heathcliff Slocumb B	.25	.11
❑ B319	Barry Larkin B	.75	.35
❑ B320	Tony Gwynn B	2.50	1.10
❑ B322	Frank Thomas B	3.00	1.35
❑ B323	Edgar Martinez B	.50	.23
❑ B325	Henry Rodriguez B	.50	.23
❑ B326	Marvin Benard B	.25	.11
❑ B329	Ugueth Urbina B	.50	.23
❑ B331	Roger Salkeld B	.25	.11
❑ B332	Edgar Renteria B	.50	.23
❑ B333	Ryan Klesko B	.50	.23
❑ B334	Ray Lankford B	.50	.23
❑ B336	Justin Thompson B	.50	.23
❑ B339	Mark Clark B	.25	.11

Card	Mint	NRMT
❑ B340 Ruben Rivera B	.50	.23
❑ B342 Matt Williams B	.50	.23
❑ B343 Francisco Cordova B	.25	.11
❑ B344 Cecil Fielder B	.50	.23
❑ B348 Mark Grudzielanek B	.50	.23
❑ B349 Ron Coomer B	.25	.11
❑ B351 Rich Aurilia B	.25	.11
❑ B352 Jose Herrera B	.25	.11
❑ B356 Tony Clark B	1.00	.45
❑ B358 Dan Naulty B	.25	.11
❑ B359 Checklist B	.25	.11
❑ G4 Marty Cordova G	6.00	2.70
❑ G6 Tony Gwynn G	30.00	13.50
❑ G9 Albert Belle G	20.00	9.00
❑ G18 Kirby Puckett G	20.00	9.00
❑ G20 Karim Garcia G	8.00	3.60
❑ G25 Cal Ripken G	50.00	22.00
❑ G33 Hideo Nomo G	20.00	9.00
❑ G39 Ryne Sandberg G	15.00	6.75
❑ G42 Jeff Bagwell G	20.00	9.00
❑ G51 Jason Isringhausen G	6.00	2.70
❑ G64 Mo Vaughn G	15.00	6.75
❑ G66 Dante Bichette G	8.00	3.60
❑ G74 Mark McGwire G	60.00	27.00
❑ G81 Kenny Lofton G	12.00	5.50
❑ G83 Jim Edmonds G	8.00	3.60
❑ G90 Mike Mussina G	12.00	5.50
❑ G100 Jeff Conine G	8.00	3.60
❑ G102 Johnny Damon G	8.00	3.60
❑ G105 Barry Bonds G	15.00	6.75
❑ G117 Jose Canseco G	12.00	5.50
❑ G135 Ken Griffey Jr. G	60.00	27.00
❑ G141 Chipper Jones G	30.00	13.50
❑ G145 Greg Maddux G	40.00	18.00
❑ G164 Jay Buhner G	8.00	3.60
❑ G186 Frank Thomas G	40.00	18.00
❑ G191 Checklist G	6.00	2.70
❑ G192 Chipper Jones G	30.00	13.50
❑ G197 Roberto Alomar G	12.00	5.50
❑ G198 Dennis Eckersley G	8.00	3.60
❑ G202 George Arias G	6.00	2.70
❑ G232 Hideo Nomo G	20.00	9.00
❑ G243 Chris Snopek G	6.00	2.70
❑ G249 Tim Salmon G	12.00	5.50
❑ G266 Matt Williams G	8.00	3.60
❑ G270 Randy Johnson G	12.00	5.50
❑ G279 Paul Molitor G	12.00	5.50
❑ G290 Cecil Fielder G	8.00	3.60
❑ G294 Livan Hernandez G	20.00	9.00
❑ G300 Marty Janzen G	6.00	2.70
❑ G308 Ron Gant G	6.00	2.70
❑ G321 Ryan Klesko G	8.00	3.60
❑ G324 Jermaine Dye G	6.00	2.70
❑ G330 Jason Giambi G	8.00	3.60
❑ G335 Edgar Martinez G	8.00	3.60
❑ G338 Rey Ordonez G	8.00	3.60
❑ G347 Sammy Sosa G	30.00	13.50
❑ G354 Juan Gonzalez G	30.00	13.50
❑ G355 Craig Biggio G	12.00	5.50
❑ S1 Greg Maddux S UER	15.00	6.75
95 stats listed as Mariners		
❑ S2 Bernie Williams S	5.00	2.20
❑ S3 Ivan Rodriguez S	6.00	2.70
❑ S7 Barry Larkin S	3.00	1.35
❑ S10 Ray Lankford S	2.50	1.10
❑ S11 Mike Piazza S	15.00	6.75
❑ S13 Larry Walker S	5.00	2.20
❑ S14 Matt Williams S	2.50	1.10
❑ S22 Tim Salmon S	5.00	2.20
❑ S35 Edgar Martinez S	2.50	1.10
❑ S37 Gregg Jefferies S	1.50	.70
❑ S38 Bill Pulsipher S	1.50	.70
❑ S41 Shawn Green S	2.50	1.10
❑ S43 Jim Abbott S	2.50	1.10
❑ S46 Roger Clemens S	10.00	4.50
❑ S52 Rondell White S	2.50	1.10
❑ S54 Dennis Eckersley S	2.50	1.10
❑ S59 Hideo Nomo S	8.00	3.60
❑ S60 Gary Sheffield S	3.00	1.35
❑ S62 Will Clark S	5.00	2.20
❑ S65 Bret Boone S	2.50	1.10
❑ S68 Rafael Palmeiro S	3.00	1.35
❑ S69 Carlos Baerga S	2.50	1.10
❑ S72 Tom Glavine S	5.00	2.20
❑ S73 Garret Anderson S	2.50	1.10
❑ S77 Randy Johnson S	5.00	2.20
❑ S78 Jeff King S	2.50	1.10
❑ S79 Kirby Puckett S	8.00	3.60
❑ S84 Cecil Fielder S	2.50	1.10
❑ S86 Reggie Sanders S	1.50	.70
❑ S88 Ryan Klesko S	2.50	1.10
❑ S91 John Valentin S	2.50	1.10
❑ S95 Manny Ramirez S	5.00	2.20
❑ S99 Vinny Castilla S	3.00	1.35
❑ S109 Carlos Perez S	2.50	1.10
❑ S112 Craig Biggio S	5.00	2.20
❑ S115 Juan Gonzalez S	12.00	5.50
❑ S121 Ray Durham S	2.50	1.10
❑ S127 C.J. Nitkowski S	1.50	.70
❑ S130 Raul Mondesi S	3.00	1.35
❑ S142 Lee Smith S	2.50	1.10
❑ S143 Joe Carter S	2.50	1.10
❑ S151 Mo Vaughn S	6.00	2.70
❑ S153 Frank Rodriguez S	1.50	.70
❑ S160 Steve Finley S	2.50	1.10
❑ S161 Jeff Bagwell S	8.00	3.60
❑ S165 Cal Ripken S	20.00	9.00
❑ S168 Lyle Mouton S	1.50	.70
❑ S171 Sammy Sosa S	12.00	5.50
❑ S174 John Franco S	2.50	1.10
❑ S179 Greg Vaughn S	2.50	1.10
❑ S180 Mark Wohlers S	1.50	.70
❑ S182 Paul O'Neill S	2.50	1.10
❑ S188 Albert Belle S	6.00	2.70
❑ S189 Mark Grace S	3.00	1.35
❑ S211 Ernie Young S	1.50	.70
❑ S218 Fred McGriff S	3.00	1.35
❑ S223 Kimera Bartee S	1.50	.70
❑ S229 Rickey Henderson S	5.00	2.20
❑ S230 Sterling Hitchcock S	2.50	1.10
❑ S231 Bernard Gilkey S	1.50	.70
❑ S234 Ryne Sandberg S	6.00	2.70
❑ S235 Greg Maddux S	15.00	6.75
❑ S239 Todd Stottlemyre S	1.50	.70
❑ S241 Jason Kendall S	5.00	2.20
❑ S242 Paul O'Neill S	2.50	1.10
❑ S256 Devon White S	2.50	1.10
❑ S261 Chuck Knoblauch S	5.00	2.20
❑ S263 Wally Joyner S	2.50	1.10
❑ S272 Andy Fox S	1.50	.70
❑ S274 Sean Berry S	1.50	.70
❑ S277 Benito Santiago S	1.50	.70
❑ S284 Chad Mottola S	1.50	.70
❑ S289 Dante Bichette S	2.50	1.10
❑ S291 Doc Gooden S	2.50	1.10
❑ S293 Kevin Mitchell S	1.50	.70
❑ S295 Russ Davis S	2.50	1.10
❑ S296 Chan Ho Park S	5.00	2.20
❑ S302 Larry Walker S	5.00	2.20
❑ S305 Ken Griffey Jr. S	25.00	11.00
❑ S313 Billy Wagner S	2.50	1.10
❑ S317 Mike Grace S	1.50	.70
❑ S327 Kenny Lofton S	5.00	2.20
❑ S328 Derek Bell S	2.50	1.10
❑ S337 Gary Sheffield S	5.00	2.20
❑ S341 Mark Grace S	3.00	1.35
❑ S345 Andres Galarraga S	5.00	2.20
❑ S346 Brady Anderson S	2.50	1.10
❑ S350 Derek Jeter S	12.00	5.50
❑ S353 Jay Buhner S	2.50	1.10
❑ S357 Tino Martinez S	5.00	2.20

1996 Finest Refractors

	MINT	NRMT
COMPLETE SET (359)	4500.00	2000.00
COMPLETE SERIES 1 (191)	2600.00	1150.00
COMPLETE SERIES 2 (168)	1900.00	850.00
COMP.BRONZE SET (220)	1100.00	500.00
COMP.BRONZE SER.1 (110)	500.00	220.00
COMP.BRONZE SER.2 (110)	600.00	275.00
COMMON BRONZE	3.00	1.35
*BRONZE STARS: 5X to 12X BASIC CARDS		
COMP.GOLD SET (48)	2300.00	1050.00
COMP.GOLD SER.1 (26)	1500.00	700.00
COMP.GOLD SER.2 (22)	800.00	350.00
COMMON GOLD	20.00	9.00
*GOLD STARS: 1.25X TO 3X BASIC CARDS		
COMP.SILVER SET (91)	1100.00	500.00
COMP.SILVER SER.1 (55)	600.00	275.00
COMP.SILVER SER.2 (36)	500.00	220.00
COMMON SILVER	5.00	2.20
*SILVER STARS: 1.5X TO 4X BASIC CARDS		

1997 Finest

	MINT	NRMT
COMPLETE SET (350)	1050.00	475.00
COMPLETE SERIES 1 (175)	550.00	250.00
COMPLETE SERIES 2 (175)	500.00	220.00
COMP.BRONZE SET (200)	60.00	27.00
COMP.BRONZE SER.1 (100)	30.00	13.50
COMP.BRONZE SER.2 (100)	30.00	13.50
COM.BRON.(1-100/176-275)	.25	.11
COMP.SILVER SET (100)	350.00	160.00
COMP.SILVER SER.1 (50)	150.00	70.00
COMP.SILVER SER.2 (50)	200.00	90.00
COM.SILV.(101-150/276-325)	1.50	.70
COMP.GOLD SET (50)	700.00	325.00
COMP.GOLD SER.1 (25)	400.00	180.00
COMP.GOLD SER.2 (25)	300.00	135.00
COM.GOLD (151-175/326-350)	6.00	2.70

Card	Mint	NRMT
❑ 1 Barry Bonds B	1.25	.55
❑ 2 Ryne Sandberg B	1.25	.55
❑ 3 Brian Jordan B	.50	.23
❑ 4 Rocky Coppinger B	.25	.11
❑ 5 Dante Bichette B UER	.50	.23
Card is erroneously numbered 155		
❑ 6 Al Martin B	.25	.11
❑ 7 Charles Nagy B	.50	.23
❑ 8 Otis Nixon B	.25	.11
❑ 9 Mark Johnson B	.25	.11
❑ 10 Jeff Bagwell B	1.50	.70
❑ 11 Ken Hill B	.25	.11
❑ 12 Willie Adams B	.25	.11
❑ 13 Raul Mondesi B	.75	.35
❑ 14 Reggie Sanders B	.50	.23
❑ 15 Derek Jeter B	3.00	1.35
❑ 16 Jermaine Dye B	.25	.11
❑ 17 Edgar Renteria B	.50	.23
❑ 18 Travis Fryman B	.50	.23
❑ 19 Roberto Hernandez B	.25	.11
❑ 20 Sammy Sosa B	2.50	1.10
❑ 21 Garret Anderson B	.50	.23
❑ 22 Rey Ordonez B	.50	.23
❑ 23 Glenallen Hill B	.25	.11
❑ 24 Dave Nilsson B	.25	.11
❑ 25 Kevin Brown B	.75	.35
❑ 26 Brian McRae B	.25	.11
❑ 27 Joey Hamilton B	.50	.23
❑ 28 Jamey Wright B	.25	.11
❑ 29 Frank Thomas B	3.00	1.35
❑ 30 Mark McGwire B	5.00	2.20
❑ 31 Ramon Martinez B	.50	.23
❑ 32 Jaime Bluma B	.25	.11
❑ 33 Frank Rodriguez B	.25	.11
❑ 34 Andy Benes B	.50	.23
❑ 35 Jay Buhner B	.50	.23
❑ 36 Justin Thompson B	.50	.23
❑ 37 Darin Erstad B	1.50	.70
❑ 38 Gregg Jefferies B	.25	.11
❑ 39 Jeff D'Amico B	.25	.11
❑ 40 Pedro Martinez B	1.00	.45
❑ 41 Nomar Garciaparra B	3.00	1.35
❑ 42 Jose Valentin B	.25	.11
❑ 43 Pat Hentgen B	.50	.23
❑ 44 Will Clark B	1.00	.45
❑ 45 Bernie Williams B	1.00	.45

❑ 46 Luis Castillo B .50 .23
❑ 47 B.J. Surhoff B .50 .23
❑ 48 Greg Gagne B .25 .11
❑ 49 Pete Schourek B .25 .11
❑ 50 Mike Piazza B 3.00 1.35
❑ 51 Dwight Gooden B .50 .23
❑ 52 Javy Lopez B .50 .23
❑ 53 Chuck Finley B .50 .23
❑ 54 James Baldwin B .50 .23
❑ 55 Jack McDowell B .25 .11
❑ 56 Royce Clayton B .25 .11
❑ 57 Carlos Delgado B .50 .23
❑ 58 Neifi Perez B .25 .11
❑ 59 Eddie Taubensee B .25 .11
❑ 60 Rafael Palmeiro B .75 .35
❑ 61 Marty Cordova B .25 .11
❑ 62 Wade Boggs B 1.00 .45
❑ 63 Rickey Henderson B 1.00 .45
❑ 64 Mike Hampton B .25 .11
❑ 65 Troy Percival B .50 .23
❑ 66 Barry Larkin B .75 .35
❑ 67 Jermaine Allensworth B .25 .11
❑ 68 Mark Clark B .25 .11
❑ 69 Mike Lansing B .25 .11
❑ 70 Mark Grudzielanek B .50 .23
❑ 71 Todd Stottlemyre B .25 .11
❑ 72 Juan Guzman B .25 .11
❑ 73 John Burkett B .25 .11
❑ 74 Wilson Alvarez B .50 .23
❑ 75 Ellis Burks B .50 .23
❑ 76 Bobby Higginson B .75 .35
❑ 77 Ricky Bottalico B .50 .23
❑ 78 Omar Vizquel B .50 .23
❑ 79 Paul Sorrento B .25 .11
❑ 80 Denny Neagle B .50 .23
❑ 81 Roger Pavlik B .25 .11
❑ 82 Mike Lieberthal B .25 .11
❑ 83 Devon White B .50 .23
❑ 84 John Olerud B .50 .23
❑ 85 Kevin Appier B .50 .23
❑ 86 Joe Girardi B .25 .11
❑ 87 Paul O'Neill B .50 .23
❑ 88 Mike Sweeney B .25 .11
❑ 89 John Smiley B .25 .11
❑ 90 Ivan Rodriguez B 1.25 .55
❑ 91 Randy Myers B .25 .11
❑ 92 Bip Roberts B .25 .11
❑ 93 Jose Mesa B .25 .11
❑ 94 Paul Wilson B .25 .11
❑ 95 Mike Mussina B 1.00 .45
❑ 96 Ben McDonald B .25 .11
❑ 97 John Mabry B .25 .11
❑ 98 Tom Goodwin B .25 .11
❑ 99 Edgar Martinez B .50 .23
❑ 100 Andruw Jones B 1.50 .70
❑ 101 Jose Canseco S 5.00 2.20
❑ 102 Billy Wagner S 2.50 1.10
❑ 103 Dante Bichette S 2.50 1.10
❑ 104 Curt Schilling S 2.50 1.10
❑ 105 Dean Palmer S 2.50 1.10
❑ 106 Larry Walker S 5.00 2.20
❑ 107 Bernie Williams S 5.00 2.20
❑ 108 Chipper Jones S 12.00 5.50
❑ 109 Gary Sheffield S 3.00 1.35
❑ 110 Randy Johnson S 5.00 2.20
❑ 111 Roberto Alomar S 5.00 2.20
❑ 112 Todd Walker S 5.00 2.20
❑ 113 Sandy Alomar Jr. S 2.50 1.10
❑ 114 John Jaha S 1.50 .70
❑ 115 Ken Caminiti S UER 3.00 1.35
Card is numbered 135
❑ 116 Ryan Klesko S 2.50 1.10
❑ 117 Mariano Rivera S 2.50 1.10
❑ 118 Jason Giambi S 2.50 1.10
❑ 119 Lance Johnson S 1.50 .70
❑ 120 Robin Ventura S 2.50 1.10
❑ 121 Todd Hollandsworth S 1.50 .70
❑ 122 Johnny Damon S 2.50 1.10
❑ 123 W. VanLandingham S 1.50 .70
❑ 124 Jason Kendall S 3.00 1.35
❑ 125 Vinny Castilla S 3.00 1.35
❑ 126 Harold Baines S 2.50 1.10
❑ 127 Joe Carter S 2.50 1.10
❑ 128 Craig Biggio S 5.00 2.20
❑ 129 Tony Clark S 3.00 1.35
❑ 130 Ron Gant S 1.50 .70
❑ 131 David Segui S 2.50 1.10
❑ 132 Steve Trachsel S 1.50 .70
❑ 133 Scott Rolen S 12.00 5.50
❑ 134 Mike Stanley S 1.50 .70
❑ 135 Cal Ripken S 20.00 9.00
❑ 136 John Smoltz S 2.50 1.10
❑ 137 Bobby Jones S 1.50 .70
❑ 138 Manny Ramirez S 12.00 5.50
❑ 139 Ken Griffey Jr. S 25.00 11.00
❑ 140 Chuck Knoblauch S 5.00 2.20
❑ 141 Mark Grace S 3.00 1.35
❑ 142 Chris Snopek S 1.50 .70
❑ 143 Hideo Nomo S 6.00 2.70
❑ 144 Tim Salmon S 5.00 2.20
❑ 145 David Cone S 3.00 1.35
❑ 146 Eric Young S 2.50 1.10
❑ 147 Jeff Brantley S 1.50 .70
❑ 148 Jim Thome S 5.00 2.20
❑ 149 Trevor Hoffman S 2.50 1.10
❑ 150 Juan Gonzalez S 12.00 5.50
❑ 151 Mike Piazza G 40.00 18.00
❑ 152 Ivan Rodriguez G 15.00 6.75
❑ 153 Mo Vaughn G 15.00 6.75
❑ 154 Brady Anderson G 8.00 3.60
❑ 155 Mark McGwire G 60.00 27.00
❑ 156 Rafael Palmeiro G 10.00 4.50
❑ 157 Barry Larkin G 10.00 4.50
❑ 158 Greg Maddux G 40.00 18.00
❑ 159 Jeff Bagwell G 20.00 9.00
❑ 160 Frank Thomas G 40.00 18.00
❑ 161 Ken Caminiti G 10.00 4.50
❑ 162 Andruw Jones G 20.00 9.00
❑ 163 Dennis Eckersley G 8.00 3.60
❑ 164 Jeff Conine G 8.00 3.60
❑ 165 Jim Edmonds G 10.00 4.50
❑ 166 Derek Jeter G 30.00 13.50
❑ 167 Vladimir Guerrero G 25.00 11.00
❑ 168 Sammy Sosa G 30.00 13.50
❑ 169 Tony Gwynn G 30.00 13.50
❑ 170 Andres Galarraga G 12.00 5.50
❑ 171 Todd Hundley G 8.00 3.60
❑ 172 Jay Buhner G UER 8.00 3.60
Card is numbered 164
❑ 173 Paul Molitor G 12.00 5.50
❑ 174 Kenny Lofton G 12.00 5.50
❑ 175 Barry Bonds G 15.00 6.75
❑ 176 Gary Sheffield B .75 .35
❑ 177 Dmitri Young B .50 .23
❑ 178 Jay Bell B .50 .23
❑ 179 David Wells B .75 .35
❑ 180 Walt Weiss B .25 .11
❑ 181 Paul Molitor B 1.00 .45
❑ 182 Jose Guillen B 1.00 .45
❑ 183 Al Leiter B .50 .23
❑ 184 Mike Fetters B .25 .11
❑ 185 Mark Langston B .50 .23
❑ 186 Fred McGriff B .75 .35
❑ 187 Darrin Fletcher B .25 .11
❑ 188 Brant Brown B .50 .23
❑ 189 Geronimo Berroa B .25 .11
❑ 190 Jim Thome B 1.00 .45
❑ 191 Jose Vizcaino B .25 .11
❑ 192 Andy Ashby B .25 .11
❑ 193 Rusty Greer B .50 .23
❑ 194 Brian Hunter B .50 .23
❑ 195 Chris Hoiles B .25 .11
❑ 196 Orlando Merced B .25 .11
❑ 197 Brett Butler B .50 .23
❑ 198 Derek Bell B .50 .23
❑ 199 Bobby Bonilla B .50 .23
❑ 200 Alex Ochoa B .25 .11
❑ 201 Wally Joyner B .50 .23
❑ 202 Mo Vaughn B 1.25 .55
❑ 203 Doug Drabek B .25 .11
❑ 204 Tino Martinez B 1.00 .45
❑ 205 Roberto Alomar B 1.00 .45
❑ 206 Brian Giles B 1.25 .55
❑ 207 Todd Worrell B .25 .11
❑ 208 Alan Benes B .50 .23
❑ 209 Jim Leyritz B .25 .11
❑ 210 Darryl Hamilton B .25 .11
❑ 211 Jimmy Key B .50 .23
❑ 212 Juan Gonzalez B 2.50 1.10
❑ 213 Vinny Castilla B .75 .35
❑ 214 Chuck Knoblauch B 1.00 .45
❑ 215 Tony Phillips B .25 .11
❑ 216 Jeff Cirillo B .50 .23
❑ 217 Carlos Garcia B .25 .11
❑ 218 Brooks Kieschnick B .25 .11
❑ 219 Marquis Grissom B .50 .23
❑ 220 Dan Wilson B .25 .11
❑ 221 Greg Vaughn B .50 .23
❑ 222 John Wetteland B .50 .23
❑ 223 Andres Galarraga B 1.00 .45
❑ 224 Ozzie Guillen B .25 .11
❑ 225 Kevin Elster B .25 .11
❑ 226 Bernard Gilkey B .25 .11
❑ 227 Mike Macfarlane B .25 .11
❑ 228 Heathcliff Slocumb B .25 .11
❑ 229 Wendell Magee Jr. B .25 .11
❑ 230 Carlos Baerga B .50 .23
❑ 231 Kevin Seitzer B .25 .11
❑ 232 Henry Rodriguez B .50 .23
❑ 233 Roger Clemens B 2.00 .90
❑ 234 Mark Wohlers B .25 .11
❑ 235 Eddie Murray B 1.00 .45
❑ 236 Todd Zeile B .25 .11
❑ 237 J.T. Snow B .50 .23
❑ 238 Ken Griffey Jr. B 5.00 2.20
❑ 239 Sterling Hitchcock B .50 .23
❑ 240 Albert Belle B 1.25 .55
❑ 241 Terry Steinbach B .50 .23
❑ 242 Robb Nen B .25 .11
❑ 243 Mark McLemore B .25 .11
❑ 244 Jeff King B .25 .11
❑ 245 Tony Clark B .75 .35
❑ 246 Tim Salmon B 1.00 .45
❑ 247 Benito Santiago B .25 .11
❑ 248 Robin Ventura B .50 .23
❑ 249 Bubba Trammell B .75 .35
❑ 250 Chili Davis B .50 .23
❑ 251 John Valentin B .50 .23
❑ 252 Cal Ripken B 4.00 1.80
❑ 253 Matt Williams B .50 .23
❑ 254 Jeff Kent B .50 .23
❑ 255 Eric Karros B .50 .23
❑ 256 Ray Lankford B .50 .23
❑ 257 Ed Sprague B .25 .11
❑ 258 Shane Reynolds B .50 .23
❑ 259 Jaime Navarro B .25 .11
❑ 260 Eric Davis B .50 .23
❑ 261 Orel Hershiser B .50 .23
❑ 262 Mark Grace B .75 .35
❑ 263 Rod Beck B .25 .11
❑ 264 Ismael Valdes B .50 .23
❑ 265 Manny Ramirez B 1.00 .45
❑ 266 Ken Caminiti B .75 .35
❑ 267 Tim Naehring B .25 .11
❑ 268 Jose Rosado B .25 .11
❑ 269 Greg Colbrunn B .25 .11
❑ 270 Dean Palmer B .50 .23
❑ 271 David Justice B 1.00 .45
❑ 272 Scott Spiezio B .25 .11
❑ 273 Chipper Jones B 2.50 1.10
❑ 274 Mel Rojas B .25 .11
❑ 275 Bartolo Colon B .50 .23
❑ 276 Darin Erstad S 8.00 3.60
❑ 277 Sammy Sosa S 12.00 5.50
❑ 278 Rafael Palmeiro S 3.00 1.35
❑ 279 Frank Thomas S 15.00 6.75
❑ 280 Ruben Rivera S 2.50 1.10
❑ 281 Hal Morris S 1.50 .70
❑ 282 Jay Buhner S 2.50 1.10
❑ 283 Kenny Lofton S 5.00 2.20
❑ 284 Jose Canseco S 5.00 2.20
❑ 285 Alex Fernandez S 1.50 .70
❑ 286 Todd Helton S 10.00 4.50
❑ 287 Andy Pettitte S 3.00 1.35
❑ 288 John Franco S 2.50 1.10
❑ 289 Ivan Rodriguez S 6.00 2.70
❑ 290 Ellis Burks S 2.50 1.10
❑ 291 Julio Franco S 2.50 1.10
❑ 292 Mike Piazza S 15.00 6.75
❑ 293 Brian Jordan S 2.50 1.10
❑ 294 Greg Maddux S 15.00 6.75
❑ 295 Bob Abreu S 2.50 1.10
❑ 296 Rondell White S 2.50 1.10
❑ 297 Moises Alou S 3.00 1.35
❑ 298 Tony Gwynn S 12.00 5.50

❑ 299 Deion Sanders S 2.50 1.10
❑ 300 Jeff Montgomery S ...... 1.50 .70
❑ 301 Ray Durham S 2.50 1.10
❑ 302 John Wasdin S .... 1.50 .70
❑ 303 Ryne Sandberg S 6.00 2.70
❑ 304 Delino DeShields S ...... 1.50 .70
❑ 305 Mark McGwire S 25.00 11.00
❑ 306 Andruw Jones S 8.00 3.60
❑ 307 Kevin Orie S .... 1.50 .70
❑ 308 Matt Williams S 2.50 1.10
❑ 309 Karim Garcia S 2.50 1.10
❑ 310 Derek Jeter S 12.00 5.50
❑ 311 Mo Vaughn S 6.00 2.70
❑ 312 Brady Anderson S 2.50 1.10
❑ 313 Barry Bonds S 6.00 2.70
❑ 314 Steve Finley S 2.50 1.10
❑ 315 Vladimir Guerrero S .. 10.00 4.50
❑ 316 Matt Morris S 2.50 1.10
❑ 317 Tom Glavine S 5.00 2.20
❑ 318 Jeff Bagwell S 8.00 3.60
❑ 319 Albert Belle S 6.00 2.70
❑ 320 Hideki Irabu S 12.00 5.50
❑ 321 Andres Galarraga S 5.00 2.20
❑ 322 Cecil Fielder S 2.50 1.10
❑ 323 Barry Larkin S 3.00 1.35
❑ 324 Todd Hundley S 2.50 1.10
❑ 325 Fred McGriff S 3.00 1.35
❑ 326 Gary Sheffield G 10.00 4.50
❑ 327 Craig Biggio G 12.00 5.50
❑ 328 Raul Mondesi G 10.00 4.50
❑ 329 Edgar Martinez G 8.00 3.60
❑ 330 Chipper Jones G 30.00 13.50
❑ 331 Bernie Williams G 12.00 5.50
❑ 332 Juan Gonzalez G 30.00 13.50
❑ 333 Ron Gant G 6.00 2.70
❑ 334 Cal Ripken G 50.00 22.00
❑ 335 Larry Walker G 12.00 5.50
❑ 336 Matt Williams G 8.00 3.60
❑ 337 Jose Cruz Jr. G 50.00 22.00
❑ 338 Joe Carter G 8.00 3.60
❑ 339 Wilton Guerrero G 6.00 2.70
❑ 340 Cecil Fielder G 8.00 3.60
❑ 341 Todd Walker G 12.00 5.50
❑ 342 Ken Griffey Jr. G 60.00 27.00
❑ 343 Ryan Klesko G 8.00 3.60
❑ 344 Roger Clemens G 25.00 11.00
❑ 345 Hideo Nomo G 15.00 6.75
❑ 346 Dante Bichette G 8.00 3.60
❑ 347 Albert Belle G 20.00 9.00
❑ 348 Randy Johnson G 12.00 5.50
❑ 349 Manny Ramirez G 12.00 5.50
❑ 350 John Smoltz G 8.00 3.60

1997 Finest Embossed

	MINT	NRMT
COMPLETE SET (150)	2600.00	1150.00
COMPLETE SERIES 1 (75)	1300.00	575.00
COMPLETE SERIES 2 (75)	1300.00	575.00
COMP.SILVER SER.1 (50) ..	300.00	135.00
COMP.SILVER SER.2 (50) ..	500.00	220.00
COM.SILV.(101-150/276-325) ..	2.50	1.10

*SILV.STARS: .75X TO 2X BASIC CARD
*SILVER YOUNG STARS: .6X TO 1.5X BASIC CARD

	MINT	NRMT
COMP.GOLD SER.1 (25)	800.00	350.00
COMP.GOLD SER.2 (25)	600.00	275.00
COM.GOLD (151-175/326-350)	12.00	5.50

*GOLD STARS: .75X TO 2X BASIC CARD
*GOLD YNG.STARS: .6X TO 1.5X BASIC CARD

1997 Finest Embossed Refractors

	MINT	NRMT
COM.SILV.(101-150/276-325)	15.00	6.75

*SILVER STARS: 5X TO 10X BASIC CARDS
*SILVER YNG.STARS: 4X TO 8X BASIC CARDS

	MINT	NRMT
COM.SER.1 GOLD (151-175)	30.00	13.50

*SER.1 GOLD STARS: 2.5X TO 6X BASIC CARDS
*SER.1 GOLD YNG.STARS: 2X TO 5X BASIC

	MINT	NRMT
COM.SER.2 GOLD (326-350)	60.00	27.00

*SER.2 GOLD STARS: 6X TO 12X BASIC CARDS
*SER.2 GOLD YNG.STARS: 5X TO 10X BASIC

1997 Finest Refractors

	MINT	NRMT
COMPLETE SET (350)	6200.00	2800.00
COMPLETE SERIES 1 (175)	3200.00	1450.00
COMPLETE SERIES 2 (175)	3000.00	1350.00
COMP.BRONZE SER.1 (100)	500.00	220.00
COMP.BRONZE SER.2 (100)	400.00	180.00
COM.BRON.(1-100/176-275)	3.00	1.35

*BRONZE STARS: 5X TO 12X BASIC CARD
*BRONZE YOUNG STARS: 4X TO 10X BASIC CARD

	MINT	NRMT
COMP.SILVER SER.1 (50) ..	600.00	275.00
COMP.SILVER SER.2 (50)	1000.00	450.00
COM.SILV.(101-150/276-325) ..	5.00	2.20

*SILVER STARS: 1.5X TO 4X BASIC CARD
*SILVER YNG.STARS: 1.25X TO 3X BASIC CARD

	MINT	NRMT
COMP.GOLD SER.1 (25)	1000.00	450.00
COMP.GOLD SER.2 (25)	800.00	350.00
COM.GOLD (151-175/326-350)	15.00	6.75

*GOLD STARS: 1.25X TO 3X BASIC CARD
*GOLD YNG.STARS: 1X TO 2.5X BASIC CARD

1998 Finest

	MINT	NRMT
COMPLETE SET (275)	90.00	40.00
COMPLETE SERIES 1 (150) ..	50.00	22.00
COMPLETE SERIES 2 (125) ..	40.00	18.00
COMMON CARD (1-275)	.25	.11

❑ 1 Larry Walker .... 1.00 .45
❑ 2 Andruw Jones .... 1.25 .55
❑ 3 Ramon Martinez .... .40 .18
❑ 4 Geronimo Berroa .... .25 .11
❑ 5 David Justice .... 1.00 .45
❑ 6 Rusty Greer .... .40 .18
❑ 7 Chad Ogea .... .25 .11
❑ 8 Tom Goodwin .... .25 .11
❑ 9 Tino Martinez .... 1.00 .45
❑ 10 Jose Guillen .... .40 .18
❑ 11 Jeffrey Hammonds .... .40 .18
❑ 12 Brian McRae .... .25 .11
❑ 13 Jeremi Gonzalez .... .40 .18
❑ 14 Craig Counsell .... .25 .11
❑ 15 Mike Piazza 3.00 1.35
❑ 16 Greg Maddux 3.00 1.35
❑ 17 Todd Greene .... .40 .18
❑ 18 Rondell White .... .40 .18
❑ 19 Kirk Rueter .... .25 .11
❑ 20 Tony Clark .... .60 .25
❑ 21 Brad Radke .... .40 .18
❑ 22 Jaret Wright .... 1.25 .55
❑ 23 Carlos Delgado .... .40 .18
❑ 24 Dustin Hermanson .... .40 .18
❑ 25 Gary Sheffield .... .60 .25
❑ 26 Jose Canseco .... 1.00 .45
❑ 27 Kevin Young .... .40 .18
❑ 28 David Wells .... .60 .25
❑ 29 Mariano Rivera .... .40 .18
❑ 30 Reggie Sanders .... .40 .18
❑ 31 Mike Cameron .... .40 .18
❑ 32 Bobby Witt .... .25 .11
❑ 33 Kevin Orie .... .25 .11
❑ 34 Royce Clayton .... .25 .11
❑ 35 Edgar Martinez .... .40 .18
❑ 36 Neifi Perez .... .40 .18
❑ 37 Kevin Appier .... .40 .18
❑ 38 Darryl Hamilton .... .25 .11
❑ 39 Michael Tucker .... .40 .18
❑ 40 Roger Clemens .... 2.00 .90
❑ 41 Carl Everett .... .25 .11
❑ 42 Mike Sweeney .... .25 .11
❑ 43 Pat Meares .... .25 .11
❑ 44 Brian Giles .... .40 .18
❑ 45 Matt Morris .... .40 .18
❑ 46 Jason Dickson .... .40 .18
❑ 47 Rich Loiselle .... .40 .18
❑ 48 Joe Girardi .... .25 .11
❑ 49 Steve Trachsel .... .25 .11
❑ 50 Ben Grieve .... 2.00 .90
❑ 51 Brian Johnson .... .25 .11
❑ 52 Hideki Irabu .... .60 .25
❑ 53 J.T. Snow .... .40 .18
❑ 54 Mike Hampton .... .25 .11
❑ 55 Dave Nilsson .... .25 .11
❑ 56 Alex Fernandez .... .25 .11
❑ 57 Brett Tomko .... .40 .18
❑ 58 Wally Joyner .... .40 .18
❑ 59 Kelvim Escobar .... .40 .18
❑ 60 Roberto Alomar .... 1.00 .45
❑ 61 Todd Jones .... .25 .11
❑ 62 Paul O'Neill .... .40 .18
❑ 63 Jamie Moyer .... .25 .11
❑ 64 Mark Wohlers .... .25 .11
❑ 65 Jose Cruz Jr. .... 1.25 .55
❑ 66 Troy Percival .... .40 .18
❑ 67 Rick Reed .... .25 .11
❑ 68 Will Clark .... 1.00 .45
❑ 69 Jamey Wright .... .25 .11
❑ 70 Mike Mussina .... 1.00 .45
❑ 71 David Cone .... .60 .25
❑ 72 Ryan Klesko .... .40 .18
❑ 73 Scott Hatteberg .... .25 .11
❑ 74 James Baldwin .... .40 .18
❑ 75 Tony Womack .... .40 .18
❑ 76 Carlos Perez .... .40 .18
❑ 77 Charles Nagy .... .40 .18
❑ 78 Jeromy Burnitz .... .40 .18
❑ 79 Shane Reynolds .... .40 .18
❑ 80 Cliff Floyd .... .40 .18
❑ 81 Jason Kendall .... .40 .18
❑ 82 Chad Curtis .... .25 .11
❑ 83 Matt Karchner .... .25 .11
❑ 84 Ricky Bottalico .... .40 .18
❑ 85 Sammy Sosa 2.50 1.10
❑ 86 Javy Lopez .... .40 .18
❑ 87 Jeff Kent .... .40 .18
❑ 88 Shawn Green .... .40 .18
❑ 89 Joey Cora .... .40 .18
❑ 90 Tony Gwynn 2.50 1.10
❑ 91 Bob Tewksbury .... .25 .11
❑ 92 Derek Jeter 2.50 1.10
❑ 93 Eric Davis .... .40 .18
❑ 94 Jeff Fassero .... .25 .11
❑ 95 Denny Neagle .... .40 .18
❑ 96 Ismael Valdes .... .40 .18
❑ 97 Tim Salmon .... 1.00 .45
❑ 98 Mark Grudzielanek .... .40 .18
❑ 99 Curt Schilling .... .40 .18
❑ 100 Ken Griffey Jr. 5.00 2.20
❑ 101 Edgardo Alfonzo .... .40 .18
❑ 102 Vinny Castilla .... .60 .25
❑ 103 Jose Rosado .... .25 .11
❑ 104 Scott Erickson .... .40 .18
❑ 105 Alan Benes .... .40 .18
❑ 106 Shannon Stewart .... .40 .18
❑ 107 Delino DeShields .... .25 .11
❑ 108 Mark Loretta .... .25 .11
❑ 109 Todd Hundley .... .40 .18
❑ 110 Chuck Knoblauch .... 1.00 .45
❑ 111 Todd Helton .... 1.25 .55
❑ 112 F.P. Santangelo .... .25 .11
❑ 113 Jeff Cirillo .... .40 .18
❑ 114 Omar Vizquel .... .40 .18
❑ 115 John Valentin .... .40 .18
❑ 116 Damion Easley .... .40 .18
❑ 117 Matt Lawton .... .40 .18
❑ 118 Jim Thome .... 1.00 .45

❑ 119 Sandy Alomar .40 .18
❑ 120 Albert Belle 1.25 .55
❑ 121 Chris Stynes .25 .11
❑ 122 Butch Huskey .25 .11
❑ 123 Shawn Estes .40 .18
❑ 124 Terry Adams .25 .11
❑ 125 Ivan Rodriguez 1.25 .55
❑ 126 Ron Gant .25 .11
❑ 127 John Mabry .25 .11
❑ 128 Jeff Shaw .40 .18
❑ 129 Jeff Montgomery .25 .11
❑ 130 Justin Thompson .40 .18
❑ 131 Livan Hernandez .40 .18
❑ 132 Ugueth Urbina .40 .18
❑ 133 Scott Servais .25 .11
❑ 134 Troy O'Leary .40 .18
❑ 135 Cal Ripken 4.00 1.80
❑ 136 Quilvio Veras .25 .11
❑ 137 Pedro Astacio .25 .11
❑ 138 Willie Greene .40 .18
❑ 139 Lance Johnson .25 .11
❑ 140 Nomar Garciaparra 3.00 1.35
❑ 141 Jose Offerman .25 .11
❑ 142 Scott Rolen 2.50 1.10
❑ 143 Derek Bell .40 .18
❑ 144 Johnny Damon .40 .18
❑ 145 Mark McGwire 6.00 2.70
❑ 146 Chan Ho Park 1.00 .45
❑ 147 Edgar Renteria .40 .18
❑ 148 Eric Young .40 .18
❑ 149 Craig Biggio 1.00 .45
❑ 150 Checklist (1-150) .25 .11
❑ 151 Frank Thomas 3.00 1.35
❑ 152 John Wetteland .40 .18
❑ 153 Mike Lansing .25 .11
❑ 154 Pedro Martinez 1.00 .45
❑ 155 Rico Brogna .40 .18
❑ 156 Kevin Brown .60 .25
❑ 157 Alex Rodriguez 3.00 1.35
❑ 158 Wade Boggs 1.00 .45
❑ 159 Richard Hidalgo .40 .18
❑ 160 Mark Grace .60 .25
❑ 161 Jose Mesa .25 .11
❑ 162 John Olerud .40 .18
❑ 163 Tim Belcher .25 .11
❑ 164 Chuck Finley .40 .18
❑ 165 Brian Hunter .40 .18
❑ 166 Joe Carter .40 .18
❑ 167 Stan Javier .25 .11
❑ 168 Jay Bell .40 .18
❑ 169 Ray Lankford .40 .18
❑ 170 John Smoltz .40 .18
❑ 171 Ed Sprague .25 .11
❑ 172 Jason Giambi .40 .18
❑ 173 Todd Walker .60 .25
❑ 174 Paul Konerko 1.00 .45
❑ 175 Rey Ordonez .40 .18
❑ 176 Dante Bichette .40 .18
❑ 177 Bernie Williams 1.00 .45
❑ 178 Jon Nunnally .25 .11
❑ 179 Rafael Palmeiro .60 .25
❑ 180 Jay Buhner .40 .18
❑ 181 Devon White .40 .18
❑ 182 Jeff D'Amico .25 .11
❑ 183 Walt Weiss .40 .18
❑ 184 Scott Spiezio .25 .11
❑ 185 Moises Alou .60 .25
❑ 186 Carlos Baerga .40 .18
❑ 187 Todd Zeile .40 .18
❑ 188 Gregg Jefferies .25 .11
❑ 189 Mo Vaughn 1.25 .55
❑ 190 Terry Steinbach .40 .18
❑ 191 Ray Durham .40 .18
❑ 192 Robin Ventura .40 .18
❑ 193 Jeff Reed .25 .11
❑ 194 Ken Caminiti .60 .25
❑ 195 Eric Karros .40 .18
❑ 196 Wilson Alvarez .40 .18
❑ 197 Gary Gaetti .25 .11
❑ 198 Andres Galarraga 1.00 .45
❑ 199 Alex Gonzalez .25 .11
❑ 200 Garret Anderson .40 .18
❑ 201 Andy Benes .40 .18
❑ 202 Harold Baines .40 .18
❑ 203 Ron Coomer .25 .11
❑ 204 Dean Palmer .40 .18
❑ 205 Reggie Jefferson .25 .11
❑ 206 John Burkett .25 .11
❑ 207 Jermaine Allensworth .25 .11
❑ 208 Bernard Gilkey .25 .11
❑ 209 Jeff Bagwell 1.50 .70
❑ 210 Kenny Lofton 1.00 .45
❑ 211 Bobby Jones .25 .11
❑ 212 Bartolo Colon .40 .18
❑ 213 Jim Edmonds .60 .25
❑ 214 Pat Hentgen .40 .18
❑ 215 Matt Williams .40 .18
❑ 216 Bob Abreu .40 .18
❑ 217 Jorge Posada .40 .18
❑ 218 Marty Cordova .25 .11
❑ 219 Ken Hill .25 .11
❑ 220 Steve Finley .40 .18
❑ 221 Jeff King .40 .18
❑ 222 Quinton McCracken .40 .18
❑ 223 Matt Stairs .40 .18
❑ 224 Darin Erstad 1.25 .55
❑ 225 Fred McGriff .60 .25
❑ 226 Marquis Grissom .40 .18
❑ 227 Doug Glanville .40 .18
❑ 228 Tom Glavine 1.00 .45
❑ 229 John Franco .40 .18
❑ 230 Darren Bragg .25 .11
❑ 231 Barry Larkin .60 .25
❑ 232 Trevor Hoffman .40 .18
❑ 233 Brady Anderson .40 .18
❑ 234 Al Martin .25 .11
❑ 235 B.J. Surhoff .40 .18
❑ 236 Ellis Burks .40 .18
❑ 237 Randy Johnson 1.00 .45
❑ 238 Mark Clark .25 .11
❑ 239 Tony Saunders .25 .11
❑ 240 Hideo Nomo 1.25 .55
❑ 241 Brad Fullmer .40 .18
❑ 242 Chipper Jones 2.50 1.10
❑ 243 Jose Valentin .25 .11
❑ 244 Manny Ramirez 1.00 .45
❑ 245 Derrek Lee .40 .18
❑ 246 Jimmy Key .40 .18
❑ 247 Tim Naehring .25 .11
❑ 248 Bobby Higginson .60 .25
❑ 249 Charles Johnson .40 .18
❑ 250 Chili Davis .40 .18
❑ 251 Tom Gordon .40 .18
❑ 252 Mike Lieberthal .25 .11
❑ 253 Billy Wagner .40 .18
❑ 254 Juan Guzman .25 .11
❑ 255 Todd Stottlemyre .40 .18
❑ 256 Brian Jordan .40 .18
❑ 257 Barry Bonds 1.25 .55
❑ 258 Dan Wilson .25 .11
❑ 259 Paul Molitor 1.00 .45
❑ 260 Juan Gonzalez 2.50 1.10
❑ 261 Francisco Cordova .25 .11
❑ 262 Cecil Fielder .40 .18
❑ 263 Travis Lee 2.00 .90
❑ 264 Kevin Tapani .25 .11
❑ 265 Raul Mondesi .60 .25
❑ 266 Travis Fryman .40 .18
❑ 267 Armando Benitez .25 .11
❑ 268 Pokey Reese .25 .11
❑ 269 Rick Aguilera .25 .11
❑ 270 Andy Pettitte .60 .25
❑ 271 Jose Vizcaino .25 .11
❑ 272 Kerry Wood 5.00 2.20
❑ 273 Vladimir Guerrero 1.50 .70
❑ 274 John Smiley .25 .11
❑ 275 Checklist (151-275) .25 .11

1998 Finest No-Protectors Refractors

	MINT	NRMT
COMPLETE SET (275)	2200.00	1000.00
COMPLETE SERIES 1 (150)	1200.00	550.00
COMPLETE SERIES 2 (125)	1000.00	450.00
COMMON CARD (1-275)	6.00	2.70

*STARS: 10X TO 25X BASIC CARDS
*YOUNG STARS: 8X TO 20X BASIC CARDS

1998 Finest Oversize

	MINT	NRMT
COMPLETE SERIES 1 (8)	120.00	55.00
COMPLETE SERIES 2 (8)	80.00	36.00
COMMON CARD (A1-B8)	6.00	2.70
COMP.REF.SER.1 (8)	250.00	110.00
COMP.REF.SER.2 (8)	150.00	70.00

*REFRACTORS: 1X TO 2X BASIC OVERSIZE

❑ A1 Mark McGwire 40.00 18.00
❑ A2 Cal Ripken 25.00 11.00
❑ A3 Nomar Garciaparra 20.00 9.00
❑ A4 Mike Piazza 20.00 9.00
❑ A5 Greg Maddux 20.00 9.00
❑ A6 Jose Cruz Jr. 6.00 2.70
❑ A7 Roger Clemens 12.00 5.50
❑ A8 Ken Griffey Jr. 30.00 13.50
❑ B1 Frank Thomas 20.00 9.00
❑ B2 Bernie Williams 6.00 2.70
❑ B3 Randy Johnson 6.00 2.70
❑ B4 Chipper Jones 15.00 6.75
❑ B5 Manny Ramirez 6.00 2.70
❑ B6 Barry Bonds 8.00 3.60
❑ B7 Juan Gonzalez 15.00 6.75
❑ B8 Jeff Bagwell 10.00 4.50

1998 Finest Refractors

	MINT	NRMT
COMPLETE SET (275)	1100.00	500.00
COMPLETE SERIES 1 (150)	600.00	275.00
COMPLETE SERIES 2 (125)	500.00	220.00
COMMON CARD (1-275)	3.00	1.35

*STARS: 5X TO 12X BASIC CARDS
*YOUNG STARS: 4X TO 10X BASIC CARDS

1998 Finest Centurions

	MINT	NRMT
COMPLETE SET (20)	1000.00	450.00
COMMON CARD (C1-C20)	10.00	4.50
COMP.REF.SET (20)	3000.00	1350.00

*REFRACTORS: 1.5X TO 3X BASIC CENTURIONS

❑ C1 Andruw Jones 25.00 11.00
❑ C2 Vladimir Guerrero 30.00 13.50
❑ C3 Nomar Garciaparra 80.00 36.00
❑ C4 Scott Rolen 50.00 22.00

❑ C5 Ken Griffey Jr. 120.00 55.00
❑ C6 Jose Cruz Jr. 25.00 11.00
❑ C7 Barry Bonds 30.00 13.50
❑ C8 Mark McGwire 150.00 70.00
❑ C9 Juan Gonzalez 60.00 27.00
❑ C10 Jeff Bagwell 40.00 18.00
❑ C11 Frank Thomas 80.00 36.00
❑ C12 Paul Konerko 25.00 11.00
❑ C13 Alex Rodriguez 80.00 36.00
❑ C14 Mike Piazza 80.00 36.00
❑ C15 Travis Lee 40.00 18.00
❑ C16 Chipper Jones 60.00 27.00
❑ C17 Larry Walker 25.00 11.00
❑ C18 Mo Vaughn 30.00 13.50
❑ C19 Livan Hernandez 10.00 4.50
❑ C20 Jaret Wright 25.00 11.00

1998 Finest The Man

	MINT	NRMT
COMPLETE SET (20)	1000.00	450.00
COMMON CARD (TM1-TM20)	25.00	11.00
COMP.REF.SET (20)	3000.00	1350.00

*REFRACTORS: 1.5X TO 3X BASIC THE MAN

❑ TM1 Ken Griffey Jr. 120.00 55.00
❑ TM2 Barry Bonds 30.00 13.50
❑ TM3 Frank Thomas 80.00 36.00
❑ TM4 Chipper Jones 60.00 27.00
❑ TM5 Cal Ripken 100.00 45.00
❑ TM6 Nomar Garciaparra 80.00 36.00
❑ TM7 Mark McGwire 150.00 70.00
❑ TM8 Mike Piazza 80.00 36.00
❑ TM9 Derek Jeter 60.00 27.00
❑ TM10 Alex Rodriguez 80.00 36.00
❑ TM11 Jose Cruz Jr. 25.00 11.00
❑ TM12 Larry Walker 25.00 11.00
❑ TM13 Jeff Bagwell 40.00 18.00
❑ TM14 Tony Gwynn 60.00 27.00
❑ TM15 Travis Lee 40.00 18.00
❑ TM16 Juan Gonzalez 60.00 27.00
❑ TM17 Scott Rolen 50.00 22.00
❑ TM18 Randy Johnson 25.00 11.00
❑ TM19 Roger Clemens 50.00 22.00
❑ TM20 Greg Maddux 80.00 36.00

1998 Finest Mystery Finest 1

	MINT	NRMT
COMPLETE SET (50)	1000.00	450.00
COMMON CARD (M1-M50)	8.00	3.60
COMP.REF.SET (50)	2500.00	1100.00

*REFRACTORS: 1X TO 2.5X BASIC MYSTERY FINEST

❑ M1 Frank Thomas 40.00 18.00
Ken Griffey Jr.
❑ M2 Frank Thomas 25.00 11.00
Mike Piazza
❑ M3 Frank Thomas 50.00 22.00
Mark McGwire
❑ M4 Frank Thomas 30.00 13.50
Frank Thomas
❑ M5 Ken Griffey Jr. 40.00 18.00
Mike Piazza
❑ M6 Ken Griffey Jr. 60.00 27.00
Mark McGwire
❑ M7 Ken Griffey Jr. 50.00 22.00
Ken Griffey Jr.
❑ M8 Mike Piazza 50.00 22.00
Mark McGwire
❑ M9 Mike Piazza 30.00 13.50
Mike Piazza
❑ M10 Mark McGwire 60.00 27.00
Mark McGwire
❑ M11 Nomar Garciaparra 25.00 11.00
Jose Cruz Jr.
❑ M12 Nomar Garciaparra 30.00 13.50
Derek Jeter
❑ M13 Nomar Garciaparra 25.00 11.00
Andruw Jones
❑ M14 Nomar Garciaparra 30.00 13.50
Nomar Garciaparra
❑ M15 Jose Cruz Jr. 20.00 9.00
Derek Jeter
❑ M16 Jose Cruz Jr. 8.00 3.60
Andruw Jones
❑ M17 Jose Cruz Jr. 8.00 3.60
Jose Cruz Jr.
❑ M18 Derek Jeter 15.00 6.75
Andruw Jones
❑ M19 Derek Jeter 25.00 11.00
Derek Jeter
❑ M20 Andruw Jones 10.00 4.50
Andruw Jones
❑ M21 Cal Ripken 30.00 13.50
Tony Gwynn
❑ M22 Cal Ripken 30.00 13.50
Barry Bonds
❑ M23 Cal Ripken 30.00 13.50
Greg Maddux
❑ M24 Cal Ripken 40.00 18.00
Cal Ripken
❑ M25 Tony Gwynn 20.00 9.00
Barry Bonds
❑ M26 Tony Gwynn 25.00 11.00
Greg Maddux
❑ M27 Tony Gwynn 25.00 11.00
Tony Gwynn
❑ M28 Barry Bonds 25.00 11.00
Greg Maddux
❑ M29 Barry Bonds 12.00 5.50
Barry Bonds
❑ M30 Greg Maddux 30.00 13.50
Greg Maddux
❑ M31 Juan Gonzalez 20.00 9.00
Larry Walker
❑ M32 Juan Gonzalez 20.00 9.00
Andres Galarraga
❑ M33 Juan Gonzalez 25.00 11.00
Chipper Jones
❑ M34 Juan Gonzalez 25.00 11.00
Juan Gonzalez
❑ M35 Larry Walker 10.00 4.50
Andres Galarraga
❑ M36 Larry Walker 20.00 9.00
Chipper Jones
❑ M37 Larry Walker 10.00 4.50
Larry Walker
❑ M38 Andres Galarraga 20.00 9.00
Chipper Jones
❑ M39 Andres Galarraga 10.00 4.50
Andres Galarraga
❑ M40 Chipper Jones 25.00 11.00
Chipper Jones
❑ M41 Gary Sheffield 20.00 9.00
Sammy Sosa
❑ M42 Gary Sheffield 15.00 6.75
Jeff Bagwell
❑ M43 Gary Sheffield 8.00 3.60
Tino Martinez
❑ M44 Gary Sheffield 8.00 3.60
Gary Sheffield
❑ M45 Sammy Sosa 20.00 9.00
Jeff Bagwell
❑ M46 Sammy Sosa 20.00 9.00
Tino Martinez
❑ M47 Sammy Sosa 25.00 11.00
Sammy Sosa
❑ M48 Jeff Bagwell 12.00 5.50
Tino Martinez
❑ M49 Jeff Bagwell 15.00 6.75
Jeff Bagwell
❑ M50 Tino Martinez 8.00 3.60
Tino Martinez

1998 Finest Mystery Finest 2

	MINT	NRMT
COMPLETE SET (40)	800.00	350.00
COMMON CARD (M1-M40)	6.00	2.70
COMP.REF.SET (40)	2000.00	900.00

*REFRACTORS: 1X TO 2.5X BASIC MYS.FINEST 2
REF.SER.2 ODDS 1:144

❑ M1 Nomar Garciaparra 30.00 13.50
Frank Thomas
❑ M2 Nomar Garciaparra 25.00 11.00
Albert Belle
❑ M3 Nomar Garciaparra 25.00 11.00
Scott Rolen
❑ M4 Frank Thomas 25.00 11.00
Albert Belle
❑ M5 Frank Thomas 25.00 11.00
Scott Rolen
❑ M6 Albert Belle 15.00 6.75
Scott Rolen
❑ M7 Ken Griffey Jr. 40.00 18.00
Jose Cruz Jr.

		MINT	NRMT
❑ M8	Ken Griffey Jr. / Alex Rodriguez	40.00	18.00
❑ M9	Ken Griffey Jr. / Roger Clemens	40.00	18.00
❑ M10	Jose Cruz Jr. / Alex Rodriguez	25.00	11.00
❑ M11	Jose Cruz Jr. / Roger Clemens	15.00	6.75
❑ M12	Alex Rodriguez / Roger Clemens	25.00	11.00
❑ M13	Mike Piazza / Barry Bonds	25.00	11.00
❑ M14	Mike Piazza / Derek Jeter	25.00	11.00
❑ M15	Mike Piazza / Bernie Williams	25.00	11.00
❑ M16	Barry Bonds / Derek Jeter	20.00	9.00
❑ M17	Barry Bonds / Bernie Williams	10.00	4.50
❑ M18	Deter Jeter / Bernie Williams	20.00	9.00
❑ M19	Mark McGwire / Jeff Bagwell	50.00	22.00
❑ M20	Mark McGwire / Mo Vaughn	50.00	22.00
❑ M21	Mark McGwire / Jim Thome	50.00	22.00
❑ M22	Jeff Bagwell / Mo Vaughn	12.00	5.50
❑ M23	Jeff Bagwell / Jim Thome	12.00	5.50
❑ M24	Mo Vaughn / Jim Thome	10.00	4.50
❑ M25	Juan Gonzalez / Travis Lee	20.00	9.00
❑ M26	Juan Gonzalez / Ben Grieve	20.00	9.00
❑ M27	Juan Gonzalez / Fred McGriff	20.00	9.00
❑ M28	Travis Lee / Ben Grieve	15.00	6.75
❑ M29	Travis Lee / Fred McGriff	12.00	5.50
❑ M30	Ben Grieve / Fred McGriff	12.00	5.50
❑ M31	Albert Belle / Albert Belle	10.00	4.50
❑ M32	Scott Rolen / Scott Rolen	20.00	9.00
❑ M33	Alex Rodriguez / Alex Rodriguez	30.00	13.50
❑ M34	Roger Clemens / Roger Clemens	20.00	9.00
❑ M35	Bernie Williams / Bernie Williams	10.00	4.50
❑ M36	Mo Vaughn / Mo Vaughn	12.00	5.50
❑ M37	Jim Thome / Jim Thome	10.00	4.50
❑ M38	Travis Lee / Travis Lee	15.00	6.75
❑ M39	Fred McGriff / Fred McGriff	6.00	2.70
❑ M40	Ben Grieve / Ben Grieve	15.00	6.75

1998 Finest Power Zone

	MINT	NRMT
COMPLETE SET (20)	400.00	180.00
COMMON CARD (P1-P20)	6.00	2.70
❑ P1 Ken Griffey Jr.	60.00	27.00
❑ P2 Jeff Bagwell	20.00	9.00
❑ P3 Jose Cruz Jr.	12.00	5.50
❑ P4 Barry Bonds	15.00	6.75
❑ P5 Mark McGwire	80.00	36.00
❑ P6 Jim Thome	12.00	5.50
❑ P7 Mo Vaughn	15.00	6.75
❑ P8 Gary Sheffield	8.00	3.60
❑ P9 Andres Galarraga	12.00	5.50
❑ P10 Nomar Garciaparra	40.00	18.00
❑ P11 Rafael Palmeiro	8.00	3.60
❑ P12 Sammy Sosa	30.00	13.50
❑ P13 Jay Buhner	6.00	2.70
❑ P14 Tony Clark	8.00	3.60
❑ P15 Mike Piazza	40.00	18.00
❑ P16 Larry Walker	12.00	5.50
❑ P17 Albert Belle	15.00	6.75
❑ P18 Tino Martinez	12.00	5.50
❑ P19 Juan Gonzalez	30.00	13.50
❑ P20 Frank Thomas	40.00	18.00

1998 Finest Stadium Stars

	MINT	NRMT
COMPLETE SET (24)	600.00	275.00
COMMON CARD (SS1-SS24)	10.00	4.50
❑ SS1 Ken Griffey Jr.	80.00	36.00
❑ SS2 Alex Rodriguez	50.00	22.00
❑ SS3 Mo Vaughn	20.00	9.00
❑ SS4 Nomar Garciaparra	50.00	22.00
❑ SS5 Frank Thomas	50.00	22.00
❑ SS6 Albert Belle	15.00	6.75
❑ SS7 Derek Jeter	40.00	18.00
❑ SS8 Chipper Jones	40.00	18.00
❑ SS9 Cal Ripken	60.00	27.00
❑ SS10 Jim Thome	15.00	6.75
❑ SS11 Mike Piazza	50.00	22.00
❑ SS12 Juan Gonzalez	40.00	18.00
❑ SS13 Jeff Bagwell	25.00	11.00
❑ SS14 Sammy Sosa	40.00	18.00
❑ SS15 Jose Cruz Jr.	15.00	6.75
❑ SS16 Gary Sheffield	10.00	4.50
❑ SS17 Larry Walker	15.00	6.75
❑ SS18 Tony Gwynn	40.00	18.00
❑ SS19 Mark McGwire	100.00	45.00
❑ SS20 Barry Bonds	20.00	9.00
❑ SS21 Tino Martinez	15.00	6.75
❑ SS22 Manny Ramirez	15.00	6.75
❑ SS23 Ken Caminiti	10.00	4.50
❑ SS24 Andres Galarraga	15.00	6.75

1993 Flair

	MINT	NRMT
COMPLETE SET (300)	60.00	27.00
COMMON CARD (1-300)	.40	.18
❑ 1 Steve Avery	.40	.18
❑ 2 Jeff Blauser	.40	.18
❑ 3 Ron Gant	.60	.25
❑ 4 Tom Glavine	1.00	.45
❑ 5 David Justice	1.50	.70
❑ 6 Mark Lemke	.40	.18
❑ 7 Greg Maddux	5.00	2.20
❑ 8 Fred McGriff	1.00	.45
❑ 9 Terry Pendleton	.40	.18
❑ 10 Deion Sanders	1.00	.45
❑ 11 John Smoltz	.60	.25
❑ 12 Mike Stanton	.40	.18
❑ 13 Steve Buechele	.40	.18
❑ 14 Mark Grace	1.00	.45
❑ 15 Greg Hibbard	.40	.18
❑ 16 Derrick May	.40	.18
❑ 17 Chuck McElroy	.40	.18
❑ 18 Mike Morgan	.40	.18
❑ 19 Randy Myers	.60	.25
❑ 20 Ryne Sandberg	2.00	.90
❑ 21 Dwight Smith	.40	.18
❑ 22 Sammy Sosa	4.00	1.80
❑ 23 Jose Vizcaino	.40	.18
❑ 24 Tim Belcher	.40	.18
❑ 25 Rob Dibble	.40	.18
❑ 26 Roberto Kelly	.40	.18
❑ 27 Barry Larkin	1.00	.45
❑ 28 Kevin Mitchell	.60	.25
❑ 29 Hal Morris	.40	.18
❑ 30 Joe Oliver	.40	.18
❑ 31 Jose Rijo	.40	.18
❑ 32 Bip Roberts	.40	.18
❑ 33 Chris Sabo	.40	.18
❑ 34 Reggie Sanders	.40	.18
❑ 35 Dante Bichette	.60	.25
❑ 36 Willie Blair	.40	.18
❑ 37 Jerald Clark	.40	.18
❑ 38 Alex Cole	.40	.18
❑ 39 Andres Galarraga	1.50	.70
❑ 40 Joe Girardi	.60	.25
❑ 41 Charlie Hayes	.40	.18
❑ 42 Chris Jones	.40	.18
❑ 43 David Nied	.40	.18
❑ 44 Eric Young	1.50	.70
❑ 45 Alex Arias	.40	.18
❑ 46 Jack Armstrong	.40	.18
❑ 47 Bret Barberie	.40	.18
❑ 48 Chuck Carr	.40	.18
❑ 49 Jeff Conine	.40	.18
❑ 50 Orestes Destrade	.40	.18
❑ 51 Chris Hammond	.40	.18
❑ 52 Bryan Harvey	.40	.18
❑ 53 Benito Santiago	.40	.18
❑ 54 Gary Sheffield	1.50	.70
❑ 55 Walt Weiss	.40	.18
❑ 56 Eric Anthony	.40	.18
❑ 57 Jeff Bagwell	2.50	1.10
❑ 58 Craig Biggio	1.50	.70
❑ 59 Ken Caminiti	1.00	.45
❑ 60 Andujar Cedeno	.40	.18
❑ 61 Doug Drabek	.40	.18
❑ 62 Steve Finley	.60	.25
❑ 63 Luis Gonzalez	.40	.18
❑ 64 Pete Harnisch	.40	.18
❑ 65 Doug Jones	.40	.18
❑ 66 Darryl Kile	.60	.25
❑ 67 Greg Swindell	.40	.18
❑ 68 Brett Butler	.60	.25
❑ 69 Jim Gott	.40	.18
❑ 70 Orel Hershiser	.60	.25
❑ 71 Eric Karros	1.00	.45
❑ 72 Pedro Martinez	2.00	.90

❑ 73 Ramon Martinez .60 .25
❑ 74 Roger McDowell .40 .18
❑ 75 Mike Piazza 8.00 3.60
❑ 76 Jody Reed .40 .18
❑ 77 Tim Wallach .40 .18
❑ 78 Moises Alou .60 .25
❑ 79 Greg Colbrunn .40 .18
❑ 80 Wil Cordero .40 .18
❑ 81 Delino DeShields .60 .25
❑ 82 Jeff Fassero .40 .18
❑ 83 Marquis Grissom .60 .25
❑ 84 Ken Hill .40 .18
❑ 85 Mike Lansing .60 .25
❑ 86 Dennis Martinez .60 .25
❑ 87 Larry Walker 1.50 .70
❑ 88 John Wetteland .60 .25
❑ 89 Bobby Bonilla .60 .25
❑ 90 Vince Coleman .40 .18
❑ 91 Dwight Gooden .60 .25
❑ 92 Todd Hundley 1.00 .45
❑ 93 Howard Johnson .40 .18
❑ 94 Eddie Murray 1.50 .70
❑ 95 Joe Orsulak .40 .18
❑ 96 Bret Saberhagen .60 .25
❑ 97 Darren Daulton .60 .25
❑ 98 Mariano Duncan .40 .18
❑ 99 Len Dykstra .60 .25
❑ 100 Jim Eisenreich .40 .18
❑ 101 Tommy Greene .40 .18
❑ 102 Dave Hollins .40 .18
❑ 103 Pete Incaviglia .40 .18
❑ 104 Danny Jackson .40 .18
❑ 105 John Kruk .60 .25
❑ 106 Terry Mulholland .40 .18
❑ 107 Curt Schilling .60 .25
❑ 108 Mitch Williams .40 .18
❑ 109 Stan Belinda .40 .18
❑ 110 Jay Bell .60 .25
❑ 111 Steve Cooke .40 .18
❑ 112 Carlos Garcia .40 .18
❑ 113 Jeff King .60 .25
❑ 114 Al Martin .40 .18
❑ 115 Orlando Merced .40 .18
❑ 116 Don Slaught .40 .18
❑ 117 Andy Van Slyke .60 .25
❑ 118 Tim Wakefield .60 .25
❑ 119 Rene Arocha .40 .18
❑ 120 Bernard Gilkey .40 .18
❑ 121 Gregg Jefferies .40 .18
❑ 122 Ray Lankford 1.00 .45
❑ 123 Donovan Osborne .40 .18
❑ 124 Tom Pagnozzi .40 .18
❑ 125 Erik Pappas .40 .18
❑ 126 Geronimo Pena .40 .18
❑ 127 Lee Smith .60 .25
❑ 128 Ozzie Smith 2.00 .90
❑ 129 Bob Tewksbury .40 .18
❑ 130 Mark Whiten .40 .18
❑ 131 Derek Bell .60 .25
❑ 132 Andy Benes .60 .25
❑ 133 Tony Gwynn 4.00 1.80
❑ 134 Gene Harris .40 .18
❑ 135 Trevor Hoffman 1.50 .70
❑ 136 Phil Plantier .40 .18
❑ 137 Rod Beck .60 .25
❑ 138 Barry Bonds 2.00 .90
❑ 139 John Burkett .40 .18
❑ 140 Will Clark 1.50 .70
❑ 141 Royce Clayton .40 .18
❑ 142 Mike Jackson .40 .18
❑ 143 Darren Lewis .40 .18
❑ 144 Kirt Manwaring .40 .18
❑ 145 Willie McGee .60 .25
❑ 146 Bill Swift .40 .18
❑ 147 Robby Thompson .40 .18
❑ 148 Matt Williams 1.00 .45
❑ 149 Brady Anderson 1.00 .45
❑ 150 Mike Devereaux .40 .18
❑ 151 Chris Hoiles .40 .18
❑ 152 Ben McDonald .40 .18
❑ 153 Mark McLemore .40 .18
❑ 154 Mike Mussina 1.50 .70
❑ 155 Gregg Olson .40 .18
❑ 156 Harold Reynolds .40 .18
❑ 157 Cal Ripken UER 6.00 2.70
(Back refers to his games streak going into 1992; should be 1993)
Also streak is spelled steak
❑ 158 Rick Sutcliffe .40 .18
❑ 159 Fernando Valenzuela .60 .25
❑ 160 Roger Clemens 3.00 1.35
❑ 161 Scott Cooper .40 .18
❑ 162 Andre Dawson 1.00 .45
❑ 163 Scott Fletcher .40 .18
❑ 164 Mike Greenwell .40 .18
❑ 165 Greg A. Harris .40 .18
❑ 166 Billy Hatcher .40 .18
❑ 167 Jeff Russell .40 .18
❑ 168 Mo Vaughn 2.00 .90
❑ 169 Frank Viola .40 .18
❑ 170 Chad Curtis .60 .25
❑ 171 Chili Davis .60 .25
❑ 172 Gary DiSarcina .40 .18
❑ 173 Damion Easley .60 .25
❑ 174 Chuck Finley .60 .25
❑ 175 Mark Langston .40 .18
❑ 176 Luis Polonia .40 .18
❑ 177 Tim Salmon 1.50 .70
❑ 178 Scott Sanderson .40 .18
❑ 179 J.T.Snow 2.00 .90
❑ 180 Wilson Alvarez .60 .25
❑ 181 Ellis Burks .60 .25
❑ 182 Joey Cora .60 .25
❑ 183 Alex Fernandez .60 .25
❑ 184 Ozzie Guillen .40 .18
❑ 185 Roberto Hernandez .60 .25
❑ 186 Bo Jackson .60 .25
❑ 187 Lance Johnson .40 .18
❑ 188 Jack McDowell .40 .18
❑ 189 Frank Thomas 5.00 2.20
❑ 190 Robin Ventura .60 .25
❑ 191 Carlos Baerga .40 .18
❑ 192 Albert Belle 2.00 .90
❑ 193 Wayne Kirby .40 .18
❑ 194 Derek Lilliquist .40 .18
❑ 195 Kenny Lofton 1.50 .70
❑ 196 Carlos Martinez .40 .18
❑ 197 Jose Mesa .40 .18
❑ 198 Eric Plunk .40 .18
❑ 199 Paul Sorrento .40 .18
❑ 200 John Doherty .40 .18
❑ 201 Cecil Fielder .60 .25
❑ 202 Travis Fryman .60 .25
❑ 203 Kirk Gibson .60 .25
❑ 204 Mike Henneman .40 .18
❑ 205 Chad Kreuter .40 .18
❑ 206 Scott Livingstone .40 .18
❑ 207 Tony Phillips .40 .18
❑ 208 Mickey Tettleton .40 .18
❑ 209 Alan Trammell 1.00 .45
❑ 210 David Wells .60 .25
❑ 211 Lou Whitaker .60 .25
❑ 212 Kevin Appier .60 .25
❑ 213 George Brett 3.00 1.35
❑ 214 David Cone .60 .25
❑ 215 Tom Gordon .60 .25
❑ 216 Phil Hiatt .40 .18
❑ 217 Felix Jose .40 .18
❑ 218 Wally Joyner .60 .25
❑ 219 Jose Lind .40 .18
❑ 220 Mike Macfarlane .40 .18
❑ 221 Brian McRae .40 .18
❑ 222 Jeff Montgomery .60 .25
❑ 223 Cal Eldred .40 .18
❑ 224 Darryl Hamilton .40 .18
❑ 225 John Jaha .40 .18
❑ 226 Pat Listach .40 .18
❑ 227 Graeme Lloyd .40 .18
❑ 228 Kevin Reimer .40 .18
❑ 229 Bill Spiers .40 .18
❑ 230 B.J.Surhoff .60 .25
❑ 231 Greg Vaughn .60 .25
❑ 232 Robin Yount 1.00 .45
❑ 233 Rick Aguilera .40 .18
❑ 234 Jim Deshaies .40 .18
❑ 235 Brian Harper .40 .18
❑ 236 Kent Hrbek .60 .25
❑ 237 Chuck Knoblauch 1.50 .70
❑ 238 Shane Mack .40 .18
❑ 239 David McCarty .40 .18
❑ 240 Pedro Munoz .40 .18
❑ 241 Mike Pagliarulo .40 .18
❑ 242 Kirby Puckett 2.50 1.10
❑ 243 Dave Winfield 1.00 .45
❑ 244 Jim Abbott .60 .25
❑ 245 Wade Boggs 1.50 .70
❑ 246 Pat Kelly .40 .18
❑ 247 Jimmy Key .60 .25
❑ 248 Jim Leyritz .40 .18
❑ 249 Don Mattingly 2.50 1.10
❑ 250 Matt Nokes .40 .18
❑ 251 Paul O'Neill .60 .25
❑ 252 Mike Stanley .40 .18
❑ 253 Danny Tartabull .40 .18
❑ 254 Bob Wickman .40 .18
❑ 255 Bernie Williams 1.50 .70
❑ 256 Mike Bordick .40 .18
❑ 257 Dennis Eckersley .60 .25
❑ 258 Brent Gates .40 .18
❑ 259 Goose Gossage .60 .25
❑ 260 Rickey Henderson 1.50 .70
❑ 261 Mark McGwire 8.00 3.60
❑ 262 Ruben Sierra .40 .18
❑ 263 Terry Steinbach .40 .18
❑ 264 Bob Welch .40 .18
❑ 265 Bobby Witt .40 .18
❑ 266 Rich Amaral .40 .18
❑ 267 Chris Bosio .40 .18
❑ 268 Jay Buhner 1.00 .45
❑ 269 Norm Charlton .40 .18
❑ 270 Ken Griffey Jr. 8.00 3.60
❑ 271 Erik Hanson .40 .18
❑ 272 Randy Johnson 1.50 .70
❑ 273 Edgar Martinez 1.00 .45
❑ 274 Tino Martinez 1.50 .70
❑ 275 Dave Valle .40 .18
❑ 276 Omar Vizquel .60 .25
❑ 277 Kevin Brown 1.00 .45
❑ 278 Jose Canseco 1.50 .70
❑ 279 Julio Franco .40 .18
❑ 280 Juan Gonzalez 4.00 1.80
❑ 281 Tom Henke .40 .18
❑ 282 David Hulse .40 .18
❑ 283 Rafael Palmeiro 1.00 .45
❑ 284 Dean Palmer .60 .25
❑ 285 Ivan Rodriguez 2.00 .90
❑ 286 Nolan Ryan 6.00 2.70
❑ 287 Roberto Alomar 1.50 .70
❑ 288 Pat Borders .40 .18
❑ 289 Joe Carter .60 .25
❑ 290 Juan Guzman .40 .18
❑ 291 Pat Hentgen 1.00 .45
❑ 292 Paul Molitor 1.50 .70
❑ 293 John Olerud 1.00 .45
❑ 294 Ed Sprague .40 .18
❑ 295 Dave Stewart .60 .25
❑ 296 Duane Ward .40 .18
❑ 297 Devon White .40 .18
❑ 298 Checklist 1-100 .40 .18
❑ 299 Checklist 101-200 .40 .18
❑ 300 Checklist 201-300 .40 .18

1993 Flair Wave of the Future

	MINT	NRMT
COMPLETE SET (20)	40.00	18.00
COMMON CARD (1-20)	1.00	.45

❑ 1 Jason Bere	1.00	.45
❑ 2 Jeromy Burnitz	1.50	.70
❑ 3 Russ Davis	1.50	.70
❑ 4 Jim Edmonds	10.00	4.50
❑ 5 Cliff Floyd	3.00	1.35
❑ 6 Jeffrey Hammonds	1.50	.70
❑ 7 Trevor Hoffman	3.00	1.35
❑ 8 Domingo Jean	1.00	.45
❑ 9 David McCarty	1.00	.45
❑ 10 Bobby Munoz	1.00	.45
❑ 11 Brad Pennington	1.00	.45
❑ 12 Mike Piazza	15.00	6.75
❑ 13 Manny Ramirez	8.00	3.60
❑ 14 John Roper	1.00	.45
❑ 15 Tim Salmon	4.00	1.80
❑ 16 Aaron Sele	3.00	1.35
❑ 17 Allen Watson	1.00	.45
❑ 18 Rondell White	2.00	.90
❑ 19 Darrell Whitmore UER (Nigel Wilson back)	1.00	.45
❑ 20 Nigel Wilson UER (Darrell Whitmore back)	1.00	.45

1994 Flair

	MINT	NRMT
COMPLETE SET (450)	100.00	45.00
COMPLETE SERIES 1 (250)	25.00	11.00
COMPLETE SERIES 2 (200)	75.00	34.00
COMMON CARD (1-450)	.25	.11

❑ 1 Harold Baines	.50	.23
❑ 2 Jeffrey Hammonds	.50	.23
❑ 3 Chris Hoiles	.25	.11
❑ 4 Ben McDonald	.25	.11
❑ 5 Mark McLemore	.25	.11
❑ 6 Jamie Moyer	.25	.11
❑ 7 Jim Poole	.25	.11
❑ 8 Cal Ripken Jr.	4.00	1.80
❑ 9 Chris Sabo	.25	.11
❑ 10 Scott Bankhead	.25	.11
❑ 11 Scott Cooper	.25	.11
❑ 12 Danny Darwin	.25	.11
❑ 13 Andre Dawson	.75	.35
❑ 14 Billy Hatcher	.25	.11
❑ 15 Aaron Sele	.50	.23
❑ 16 John Valentin	.50	.23
❑ 17 Dave Valle	.25	.11
❑ 18 Mo Vaughn	1.25	.55
❑ 19 Brian Anderson	.75	.35
❑ 20 Gary DiSarcina	.25	.11
❑ 21 Jim Edmonds	1.00	.45
❑ 22 Chuck Finley	.50	.23
❑ 23 Bo Jackson	.50	.23
❑ 24 Mark Leiter	.25	.11
❑ 25 Greg Myers	.25	.11
❑ 26 Eduardo Perez	.25	.11
❑ 27 Tim Salmon	1.00	.45
❑ 28 Wilson Alvarez	.50	.23
❑ 29 Jason Bere	.25	.11
❑ 30 Alex Fernandez	.25	.11
❑ 31 Ozzie Guillen	.25	.11
❑ 32 Joe Hall	.25	.11
❑ 33 Darrin Jackson	.25	.11
❑ 34 Kirk McCaskill	.25	.11
❑ 35 Tim Raines	.50	.23
❑ 36 Frank Thomas	3.00	1.35
❑ 37 Carlos Baerga	.50	.23
❑ 38 Albert Belle	1.25	.55
❑ 39 Mark Clark	.25	.11
❑ 40 Wayne Kirby	.25	.11
❑ 41 Dennis Martinez	.50	.23
❑ 42 Charles Nagy	.50	.23
❑ 43 Manny Ramirez	1.25	.55
❑ 44 Paul Sorrento	.25	.11
❑ 45 Jim Thome	1.25	.55
❑ 46 Eric Davis	.50	.23
❑ 47 John Doherty	.25	.11
❑ 48 Junior Felix	.25	.11
❑ 49 Cecil Fielder	.50	.23
❑ 50 Kirk Gibson	.50	.23
❑ 51 Mike Moore	.25	.11
❑ 52 Tony Phillips	.25	.11
❑ 53 Alan Trammell	.75	.35
❑ 54 Kevin Appier	.50	.23
❑ 55 Stan Belinda	.25	.11
❑ 56 Vince Coleman	.25	.11
❑ 57 Greg Gagne	.25	.11
❑ 58 Bob Hamelin	.25	.11
❑ 59 Dave Henderson	.25	.11
❑ 60 Wally Joyner	.50	.23
❑ 61 Mike Macfarlane	.25	.11
❑ 62 Jeff Montgomery	.25	.11
❑ 63 Ricky Bones	.25	.11
❑ 64 Jeff Bronkey	.25	.11
❑ 65 Alex Diaz	.25	.11
❑ 66 Cal Eldred	.25	.11
❑ 67 Darryl Hamilton	.25	.11
❑ 68 John Jaha	.25	.11
❑ 69 Mark Kiefer	.25	.11
❑ 70 Kevin Seitzer	.25	.11
❑ 71 Turner Ward	.25	.11
❑ 72 Rich Becker	.25	.11
❑ 73 Scott Erickson	.50	.23
❑ 74 Keith Garagozzo	.25	.11
❑ 75 Kent Hrbek	.50	.23
❑ 76 Scott Leius	.25	.11
❑ 77 Kirby Puckett	1.50	.70
❑ 78 Matt Walbeck	.25	.11
❑ 79 Dave Winfield	1.00	.45
❑ 80 Mike Gallego	.25	.11
❑ 81 Xavier Hernandez	.25	.11
❑ 82 Jimmy Key	.50	.23
❑ 83 Jim Leyritz	.50	.23
❑ 84 Don Mattingly	1.50	.70
❑ 85 Matt Nokes	.25	.11
❑ 86 Paul O'Neill	.50	.23
❑ 87 Melido Perez	.25	.11
❑ 88 Danny Tartabull	.25	.11
❑ 89 Mike Bordick	.25	.11
❑ 90 Ron Darling	.25	.11
❑ 91 Dennis Eckersley	.50	.23
❑ 92 Stan Javier	.25	.11
❑ 93 Steve Karsay	.25	.11
❑ 94 Mark McGwire	5.00	2.20
❑ 95 Troy Neel	.25	.11
❑ 96 Terry Steinbach	.50	.23
❑ 97 Bill Taylor	.25	.11
❑ 98 Eric Anthony	.25	.11
❑ 99 Chris Bosio	.25	.11
❑ 100 Tim Davis	.25	.11
❑ 101 Felix Fermin	.25	.11
❑ 102 Dave Fleming	.25	.11
❑ 103 Ken Griffey Jr.	5.00	2.20
❑ 104 Greg Hibbard	.25	.11
❑ 105 Reggie Jefferson	.25	.11
❑ 106 Tino Martinez	1.00	.45
❑ 107 Jack Armstrong	.25	.11
❑ 108 Will Clark	1.00	.45
❑ 109 Juan Gonzalez	2.50	1.10
❑ 110 Rick Helling	.50	.23
❑ 111 Tom Henke	.25	.11
❑ 112 David Hulse	.25	.11
❑ 113 Manuel Lee	.25	.11
❑ 114 Doug Strange	.25	.11
❑ 115 Roberto Alomar	1.00	.45
❑ 116 Joe Carter	.50	.23
❑ 117 Carlos Delgado	.75	.35
❑ 118 Pat Hentgen	.50	.23
❑ 119 Paul Molitor	1.00	.45
❑ 120 John Olerud	.50	.23
❑ 121 Dave Stewart	.50	.23
❑ 122 Todd Stottlemyre	.25	.11
❑ 123 Mike Timlin	.25	.11
❑ 124 Jeff Blauser	.25	.11
❑ 125 Tom Glavine	1.00	.45
❑ 126 David Justice	1.00	.45
❑ 127 Mike Kelly	.25	.11
❑ 128 Ryan Klesko	.50	.23
❑ 129 Javier Lopez	.75	.35
❑ 130 Greg Maddux	3.00	1.35
❑ 131 Fred McGriff	.75	.35
❑ 132 Kent Mercker	.25	.11
❑ 133 Mark Wohlers	.25	.11
❑ 134 Willie Banks	.25	.11
❑ 135 Steve Buechele	.25	.11
❑ 136 Shawon Dunston	.25	.11
❑ 137 Jose Guzman	.25	.11
❑ 138 Glenallen Hill	.25	.11
❑ 139 Randy Myers	.25	.11
❑ 140 Karl Rhodes	.25	.11
❑ 141 Ryne Sandberg	1.25	.55
❑ 142 Steve Trachsel	.25	.11
❑ 143 Bret Boone	.50	.23
❑ 144 Tom Browning	.25	.11
❑ 145 Hector Carrasco	.25	.11
❑ 146 Barry Larkin	.75	.35
❑ 147 Hal Morris	.25	.11
❑ 148 Jose Rijo	.25	.11
❑ 149 Reggie Sanders	.50	.23
❑ 150 John Smiley	.25	.11
❑ 151 Dante Bichette	.50	.23
❑ 152 Ellis Burks	.50	.23
❑ 153 Joe Girardi	.25	.11
❑ 154 Mike Harkey	.25	.11
❑ 155 Roberto Mejia	.25	.11
❑ 156 Marcus Moore	.25	.11
❑ 157 Armando Reynoso	.25	.11
❑ 158 Bruce Ruffin	.25	.11
❑ 159 Eric Young	.25	.11
❑ 160 Kurt Abbott	.25	.11
❑ 161 Jeff Conine	.50	.23
❑ 162 Orestes Destrade	.25	.11
❑ 163 Chris Hammond	.25	.11
❑ 164 Bryan Harvey	.25	.11
❑ 165 Dave Magadan	.25	.11
❑ 166 Gary Sheffield	1.00	.45
❑ 167 David Weathers	.25	.11
❑ 168 Andujar Cedeno	.25	.11
❑ 169 Tom Edens	.25	.11
❑ 170 Luis Gonzalez	.25	.11
❑ 171 Pete Harnisch	.25	.11
❑ 172 Todd Jones	.25	.11
❑ 173 Darryl Kile	.50	.23
❑ 174 James Mouton	.25	.11
❑ 175 Scott Servais	.25	.11
❑ 176 Mitch Williams	.25	.11
❑ 177 Pedro Astacio	.25	.11
❑ 178 Orel Hershiser	.50	.23
❑ 179 Raul Mondesi	1.00	.45
❑ 180 Jose Offerman	.25	.11
❑ 181 Chan Ho Park	5.00	2.20
❑ 182 Mike Piazza	3.00	1.35
❑ 183 Cory Snyder	.25	.11
❑ 184 Tim Wallach	.25	.11
❑ 185 Todd Worrell	.25	.11
❑ 186 Sean Berry	.25	.11
❑ 187 Wil Cordero	.25	.11
❑ 188 Darrin Fletcher	.25	.11
❑ 189 Cliff Floyd	.50	.23
❑ 190 Marquis Grissom	.50	.23
❑ 191 Rod Henderson	.25	.11
❑ 192 Ken Hill	.25	.11
❑ 193 Pedro Martinez	1.25	.55
❑ 194 Kirk Rueter	.25	.11
❑ 195 Jeromy Burnitz	.50	.23
❑ 196 John Franco	.50	.23
❑ 197 Dwight Gooden	.50	.23
❑ 198 Todd Hundley	.50	.23
❑ 199 Bobby Jones	.25	.11
❑ 200 Jeff Kent	.50	.23
❑ 201 Mike Maddux	.25	.11
❑ 202 Ryan Thompson	.25	.11
❑ 203 Jose Vizcaino	.25	.11
❑ 204 Darren Daulton	.50	.23
❑ 205 Lenny Dykstra	.50	.23
❑ 206 Jim Eisenreich	.25	.11
❑ 207 Dave Hollins	.25	.11

❑ 208 Danny Jackson .25 .11
❑ 209 Doug Jones .25 .11
❑ 210 Jeff Juden .25 .11
❑ 211 Ben Rivera .25 .11
❑ 212 Kevin Stocker .25 .11
❑ 213 Milt Thompson .25 .11
❑ 214 Jay Bell .50 .23
❑ 215 Steve Cooke .25 .11
❑ 216 Mark Dewey .25 .11
❑ 217 Al Martin .25 .11
❑ 218 Orlando Merced .25 .11
❑ 219 Don Slaught .25 .11
❑ 220 Zane Smith .25 .11
❑ 221 Rick White .25 .11
❑ 222 Kevin Young .25 .11
❑ 223 Rene Arocha .25 .11
❑ 224 Rheal Cormier .25 .11
❑ 225 Brian Jordan .50 .23
❑ 226 Ray Lankford .50 .23
❑ 227 Mike Perez .25 .11
❑ 228 Ozzie Smith 1.25 .55
❑ 229 Mark Whiten .25 .11
❑ 230 Todd Zeile .25 .11
❑ 231 Derek Bell .50 .23
❑ 232 Archi Cianfrocco .25 .11
❑ 233 Ricky Gutierrez .25 .11
❑ 234 Trevor Hoffman .50 .23
❑ 235 Phil Plantier .25 .11
❑ 236 Dave Staton .25 .11
❑ 237 Wally Whitehurst .25 .11
❑ 238 Todd Benzinger .25 .11
❑ 239 Barry Bonds 1.25 .55
❑ 240 John Burkett .25 .11
❑ 241 Royce Clayton .25 .11
❑ 242 Bryan Hickerson .25 .11
❑ 243 Mike Jackson .25 .11
❑ 244 Darren Lewis .25 .11
❑ 245 Kirt Manwaring .25 .11
❑ 246 Mark Portugal .25 .11
❑ 247 Salomon Torres .25 .11
❑ 248 Checklist .25 .11
❑ 249 Checklist .25 .11
❑ 250 Checklist .25 .11
❑ 251 Brady Anderson .50 .23
❑ 252 Mike Devereaux .25 .11
❑ 253 Sid Fernandez .25 .11
❑ 254 Leo Gomez .25 .11
❑ 255 Mike Mussina 1.00 .45
❑ 256 Mike Oquist .25 .11
❑ 257 Rafael Palmeiro .75 .35
❑ 258 Lee Smith .50 .23
❑ 259 Damon Berryhill .25 .11
❑ 260 Wes Chamberlain .25 .11
❑ 261 Roger Clemens 2.00 .90
❑ 262 Gar Finnvold .25 .11
❑ 263 Mike Greenwell .25 .11
❑ 264 Tim Naehring .25 .11
❑ 265 Otis Nixon .25 .11
❑ 266 Ken Ryan .25 .11
❑ 267 Chad Curtis .25 .11
❑ 268 Chili Davis .50 .23
❑ 269 Damion Easley .50 .23
❑ 270 Jorge Fabregas .25 .11
❑ 271 Mark Langston .25 .11
❑ 272 Phil Leftwich .25 .11
❑ 273 Harold Reynolds .25 .11
❑ 274 J.T. Snow .50 .23
❑ 275 Joey Cora .50 .23
❑ 276 Julio Franco .25 .11
❑ 277 Roberto Hernandez .25 .11
❑ 278 Lance Johnson .25 .11
❑ 279 Ron Karkovice .25 .11
❑ 280 Jack McDowell .25 .11
❑ 281 Robin Ventura .50 .23
❑ 282 Sandy Alomar Jr. .50 .23
❑ 283 Kenny Lofton 1.00 .45
❑ 284 Jose Mesa .25 .11
❑ 285 Jack Morris .50 .23
❑ 286 Eddie Murray 1.00 .45
❑ 287 Chad Ogea .50 .23
❑ 288 Eric Plunk .25 .11
❑ 289 Paul Shuey .25 .11
❑ 290 Omar Vizquel .50 .23
❑ 291 Danny Bautista .25 .11
❑ 292 Travis Fryman .50 .23
❑ 293 Greg Gohr .25 .11
❑ 294 Chris Gomez .25 .11
❑ 295 Mickey Tettleton .25 .11
❑ 296 Lou Whitaker .50 .23
❑ 297 David Cone .75 .35
❑ 298 Gary Gaetti .50 .23
❑ 299 Tom Gordon .25 .11
❑ 300 Felix Jose .25 .11
❑ 301 Jose Lind .25 .11
❑ 302 Brian McRae .25 .11
❑ 303 Mike Fetters .25 .11
❑ 304 Brian Harper .25 .11
❑ 305 Pat Listach .25 .11
❑ 306 Matt Mieske .25 .11
❑ 307 Dave Nilsson .25 .11
❑ 308 Jody Reed .25 .11
❑ 309 Greg Vaughn .50 .23
❑ 310 Bill Wegman .25 .11
❑ 311 Rick Aguilera .25 .11
❑ 312 Alex Cole .25 .11
❑ 313 Denny Hocking .25 .11
❑ 314 Chuck Knoblauch 1.00 .45
❑ 315 Shane Mack .25 .11
❑ 316 Pat Meares .25 .11
❑ 317 Kevin Tapani .25 .11
❑ 318 Jim Abbott .50 .23
❑ 319 Wade Boggs 1.00 .45
❑ 320 Sterling Hitchcock .50 .23
❑ 321 Pat Kelly .25 .11
❑ 322 Terry Mulholland .25 .11
❑ 323 Luis Polonia .25 .11
❑ 324 Mike Stanley .25 .11
❑ 325 Bob Wickman .25 .11
❑ 326 Bernie Williams 1.00 .45
❑ 327 Mark Acre .25 .11
❑ 328 Geronimo Berroa .25 .11
❑ 329 Scott Brosius .50 .23
❑ 330 Brent Gates .25 .11
❑ 331 Rickey Henderson 1.00 .45
❑ 332 Carlos Reyes .25 .11
❑ 333 Ruben Sierra .25 .11
❑ 334 Bobby Witt .25 .11
❑ 335 Bobby Ayala .25 .11
❑ 336 Jay Buhner .50 .23
❑ 337 Randy Johnson 1.00 .45
❑ 338 Edgar Martinez .50 .23
❑ 339 Bill Risley .25 .11
❑ 340 Alex Rodriguez 60.00 27.00
❑ 341 Roger Salkeld .25 .11
❑ 342 Dan Wilson .25 .11
❑ 343 Kevin Brown .50 .23
❑ 344 Jose Canseco 1.00 .45
❑ 345 Dean Palmer .50 .23
❑ 346 Ivan Rodriguez 1.25 .55
❑ 347 Kenny Rogers .25 .11
❑ 348 Pat Borders .25 .11
❑ 349 Juan Guzman .25 .11
❑ 350 Ed Sprague .25 .11
❑ 351 Devon White .50 .23
❑ 352 Steve Avery .25 .11
❑ 353 Roberto Kelly .25 .11
❑ 354 Mark Lemke .25 .11
❑ 355 Greg McMichael .25 .11
❑ 356 Terry Pendleton .25 .11
❑ 357 John Smoltz .50 .23
❑ 358 Mike Stanton .25 .11
❑ 359 Tony Tarasco .25 .11
❑ 360 Mark Grace .75 .35
❑ 361 Derrick May .25 .11
❑ 362 Rey Sanchez .25 .11
❑ 363 Sammy Sosa 2.50 1.10
❑ 364 Rick Wilkins .25 .11
❑ 365 Jeff Brantley .25 .11
❑ 366 Tony Fernandez .25 .11
❑ 367 Chuck McElroy .25 .11
❑ 368 Kevin Mitchell .25 .11
❑ 369 John Roper .25 .11
❑ 370 Johnny Ruffin .25 .11
❑ 371 Deion Sanders .50 .23
❑ 372 Marvin Freeman .25 .11
❑ 373 Andres Galarraga 1.00 .45
❑ 374 Charlie Hayes .25 .11
❑ 375 Nelson Liriano .25 .11
❑ 376 David Nied .25 .11
❑ 377 Walt Weiss .25 .11
❑ 378 Bret Barberie .25 .11
❑ 379 Jerry Browne .25 .11
❑ 380 Chuck Carr .25 .11
❑ 381 Greg Colbrunn .25 .11
❑ 382 Charlie Hough .25 .11
❑ 383 Kurt Miller .25 .11
❑ 384 Benito Santiago .25 .11
❑ 385 Jeff Bagwell 1.50 .70
❑ 386 Craig Biggio 1.00 .45
❑ 387 Ken Caminiti .75 .35
❑ 388 Doug Drabek .25 .11
❑ 389 Steve Finley .50 .23
❑ 390 John Hudek .25 .11
❑ 391 Orlando Miller .25 .11
❑ 392 Shane Reynolds .50 .23
❑ 393 Brett Butler .50 .23
❑ 394 Tom Candiotti .25 .11
❑ 395 Delino DeShields .25 .11
❑ 396 Kevin Gross .25 .11
❑ 397 Eric Karros .50 .23
❑ 398 Ramon Martinez .50 .23
❑ 399 Henry Rodriguez .50 .23
❑ 400 Moises Alou .75 .35
❑ 401 Jeff Fassero .25 .11
❑ 402 Mike Lansing .50 .23
❑ 403 Mel Rojas .25 .11
❑ 404 Larry Walker 1.00 .45
❑ 405 John Wetteland .50 .23
❑ 406 Gabe White .25 .11
❑ 407 Bobby Bonilla .50 .23
❑ 408 Josias Manzanillo .25 .11
❑ 409 Bret Saberhagen .50 .23
❑ 410 David Segui .50 .23
❑ 411 Mariano Duncan .25 .11
❑ 412 Tommy Greene .25 .11
❑ 413 Billy Hatcher .25 .11
❑ 414 Ricky Jordan .25 .11
❑ 415 John Kruk .50 .23
❑ 416 Bobby Munoz .25 .11
❑ 417 Curt Schilling .50 .23
❑ 418 Fernando Valenzuela .50 .23
❑ 419 David West .75 .35
❑ 420 Carlos Garcia .25 .11
❑ 421 Brian Hunter .25 .11
❑ 422 Jeff King .25 .11
❑ 423 Jon Lieber .25 .11
❑ 424 Ravelo Manzanillo .25 .11
❑ 425 Denny Neagle .50 .23
❑ 426 Andy Van Slyke .50 .23
❑ 427 Bryan Eversgerd .25 .11
❑ 428 Bernard Gilkey .25 .11
❑ 429 Gregg Jefferies .25 .11
❑ 430 Tom Pagnozzi .25 .11
❑ 431 Bob Tewksbury .25 .11
❑ 432 Allen Watson .25 .11
❑ 433 Andy Ashby .25 .11
❑ 434 Andy Benes .50 .23
❑ 435 Donnie Elliott .25 .11
❑ 436 Tony Gwynn 2.50 1.10
❑ 437 Joey Hamilton 1.00 .45
❑ 438 Tim Hyers .25 .11
❑ 439 Luis Lopez .25 .11
❑ 440 Bip Roberts .25 .11
❑ 441 Scott Sanders .25 .11
❑ 442 Rod Beck .25 .11
❑ 443 Dave Burba .25 .11
❑ 444 Darryl Strawberry .50 .23
❑ 445 Bill Swift .25 .11
❑ 446 Robby Thompson .25 .11
❑ 447 Bill VanLandingham .25 .11
❑ 448 Matt Williams .75 .35
❑ 449 Checklist .25 .11
❑ 450 Checklist .25 .11
❑ P15 Aaron Sele Promo 1.50 .70

1994 Flair Hot Gloves

	MINT	NRMT
COMPLETE SET (10)	180.00	80.00
COMMON CARD (1-10)	8.00	3.60

❑ 1 Barry Bonds 15.00 6.75
❑ 2 Will Clark 12.00 5.50
❑ 3 Ken Griffey Jr. 60.00 27.00
❑ 4 Kenny Lofton 12.00 5.50
❑ 5 Greg Maddux 40.00 18.00

	MINT	NRMT
❑ 6 Don Mattingly	20.00	9.00
❑ 7 Kirby Puckett	20.00	9.00
❑ 8 Cal Ripken Jr.	50.00	22.00
❑ 9 Tim Salmon	12.00	5.50
❑ 10 Matt Williams	8.00	3.60

1994 Flair Hot Numbers

	MINT	NRMT
COMPLETE SET (10)	80.00	36.00
COMMON CARD (1-10)	1.50	.70
❑ 1 Roberto Alomar	6.00	2.70
❑ 2 Carlos Baerga	1.50	.70
❑ 3 Will Clark	6.00	2.70
❑ 4 Fred McGriff	4.00	1.80
❑ 5 Paul Molitor	6.00	2.70
❑ 6 John Olerud	3.00	1.35
❑ 7 Mike Piazza	20.00	9.00
❑ 8 Cal Ripken Jr.	25.00	11.00
❑ 9 Ryne Sandberg	8.00	3.60
❑ 10 Frank Thomas	20.00	9.00

1994 Flair Infield Power

	MINT	NRMT
COMPLETE SET (10)	18.00	8.00
COMMON CARD (1-10)	.50	.23
❑ 1 Jeff Bagwell	2.50	1.10
❑ 2 Will Clark	1.50	.70
❑ 3 Darren Daulton	.50	.23
❑ 4 Don Mattingly	1.50	.70
❑ 5 Fred McGriff	1.00	.45
❑ 6 Rafael Palmeiro	1.00	.45
❑ 7 Mike Piazza	5.00	2.20
❑ 8 Cal Ripken Jr.	6.00	2.70
❑ 9 Frank Thomas	5.00	2.20
❑ 10 Matt Williams	1.00	.45

1994 Flair Outfield Power

	MINT	NRMT
COMPLETE SET (10)	25.00	11.00
COMMON CARD (1-10)	.50	.23
❑ 1 Albert Belle	2.00	.90
❑ 2 Barry Bonds	2.00	.90
❑ 3 Joe Carter	1.00	.45
❑ 4 Lenny Dykstra	.50	.23
❑ 5 Juan Gonzalez	5.00	2.20
❑ 6 Ken Griffey Jr.	10.00	4.50
❑ 7 David Justice	2.00	.90
❑ 8 Kirby Puckett	4.00	1.80
❑ 9 Tim Salmon	2.00	.90
❑ 10 Dave Winfield	2.00	.90

1994 Flair Wave of the Future

	MINT	NRMT
COMPLETE SER.1 SET (10)	15.00	6.75
COMPLETE SER.2 SET (10)	60.00	27.00
COMMON CARD (A1-B10)	1.00	.45
❑ A1 Kurt Abbott	1.00	.45
❑ A2 Carlos Delgado	2.50	1.10
❑ A3 Steve Karsay	1.00	.45
❑ A4 Ryan Klesko	2.00	.90
❑ A5 Javier Lopez	2.50	1.10
❑ A6 Raul Mondesi	3.00	1.35
❑ A7 James Mouton	1.00	.45
❑ A8 Chan Ho Park	10.00	4.50
❑ A9 Dave Staton	1.00	.45
❑ A10 Rick White	1.00	.45
❑ B1 Mark Acre	1.00	.45
❑ B2 Chris Gomez	1.00	.45
❑ B3 Joey Hamilton	2.50	1.10
❑ B4 John Hudek	1.00	.45
❑ B5 Jon Lieber	1.00	.45
❑ B6 Matt Mieske	1.00	.45
❑ B7 Orlando Miller	1.00	.45
❑ B8 Alex Rodriguez	50.00	22.00
❑ B9 Tony Tarasco	1.00	.45
❑ B10 William VanLandingham	1.00	.45

1995 Flair

	MINT	NRMT
COMPLETE SET (432)	80.00	36.00
COMPLETE SERIES 1 (216)	50.00	22.00
COMPLETE SERIES (216)	30.00	13.50
COMMON CARD (1-432)	.25	.11
❑ 1 Brady Anderson	.50	.23
❑ 2 Harold Baines	.50	.23
❑ 3 Leo Gomez	.25	.11
❑ 4 Alan Mills	.25	.11
❑ 5 Jamie Moyer	.25	.11
❑ 6 Mike Mussina	1.00	.45
❑ 7 Mike Oquist	.25	.11
❑ 8 Arthur Rhodes	.25	.11
❑ 9 Cal Ripken Jr.	4.00	1.80
❑ 10 Roger Clemens	2.00	.90
❑ 11 Scott Cooper	.25	.11
❑ 12 Mike Greenwell	.25	.11
❑ 13 Aaron Sele	.50	.23
❑ 14 John Valentin	.50	.23
❑ 15 Mo Vaughn	1.25	.55
❑ 16 Chad Curtis	.25	.11
❑ 17 Gary DiSarcina	.25	.11
❑ 18 Chuck Finley	.50	.23
❑ 19 Andrew Lorraine	.25	.11
❑ 20 Spike Owen	.25	.11
❑ 21 Tim Salmon	1.00	.45
❑ 22 J.T. Snow	.50	.23
❑ 23 Wilson Alvarez	.50	.23
❑ 24 Jason Bere	.25	.11
❑ 25 Ozzie Guillen	.25	.11
❑ 26 Mike LaValliere	.25	.11
❑ 27 Frank Thomas	3.00	1.35
❑ 28 Robin Ventura	.50	.23
❑ 29 Carlos Baerga	.50	.23
❑ 30 Albert Belle	1.25	.55
❑ 31 Jason Grimsley	.25	.11
❑ 32 Dennis Martinez	.50	.23
❑ 33 Eddie Murray	1.00	.45
❑ 34 Charles Nagy	.50	.23
❑ 35 Manny Ramirez	1.00	.45
❑ 36 Paul Sorrento	.25	.11
❑ 37 John Doherty	.25	.11
❑ 38 Cecil Fielder	.50	.23
❑ 39 Travis Fryman	.50	.23
❑ 40 Chris Gomez	.25	.11
❑ 41 Tony Phillips	.25	.11
❑ 42 Lou Whitaker	.50	.23
❑ 43 David Cone	.75	.35
❑ 44 Gary Gaetti	.50	.23
❑ 45 Mark Gubicza	.25	.11
❑ 46 Bob Hamelin	.25	.11
❑ 47 Wally Joyner	.50	.23
❑ 48 Rusty Meacham	.25	.11
❑ 49 Jeff Montgomery	.25	.11
❑ 50 Ricky Bones	.25	.11
❑ 51 Cal Eldred	.25	.11
❑ 52 Pat Listach	.25	.11
❑ 53 Matt Mieske	.25	.11
❑ 54 Dave Nilsson	.25	.11
❑ 55 Greg Vaughn	.50	.23

❑ 56 Bill Wegman .25 .11
❑ 57 Chuck Knoblauch 1.00 .45
❑ 58 Scott Leius .25 .11
❑ 59 Pat Mahomes .25 .11
❑ 60 Pat Meares .25 .11
❑ 61 Pedro Munoz .25 .11
❑ 62 Kirby Puckett 1.50 .70
❑ 63 Wade Boggs 1.00 .45
❑ 64 Jimmy Key .50 .23
❑ 65 Jim Leyritz .50 .23
❑ 66 Don Mattingly 1.50 .70
❑ 67 Paul O'Neill .50 .23
❑ 68 Melido Perez .25 .11
❑ 69 Danny Tartabull .25 .11
❑ 70 John Briscoe .25 .11
❑ 71 Scott Brosius .50 .23
❑ 72 Ron Darling .25 .11
❑ 73 Brent Gates .25 .11
❑ 74 Rickey Henderson 1.00 .45
❑ 75 Stan Javier .25 .11
❑ 76 Mark McGwire 5.00 2.20
❑ 77 Todd Van Poppel .25 .11
❑ 78 Bobby Ayala .25 .11
❑ 79 Mike Blowers .25 .11
❑ 80 Jay Buhner .50 .23
❑ 81 Ken Griffey Jr. 5.00 2.20
❑ 82 Randy Johnson 1.00 .45
❑ 83 Tino Martinez 1.00 .45
❑ 84 Jeff Nelson .25 .11
❑ 85 Alex Rodriguez 4.00 1.80
❑ 86 Will Clark 1.00 .45
❑ 87 Jeff Frye .25 .11
❑ 88 Juan Gonzalez 2.50 1.10
❑ 89 Rusty Greer 1.00 .45
❑ 90 Darren Oliver .25 .11
❑ 91 Dean Palmer .50 .23
❑ 92 Ivan Rodriguez 1.25 .55
❑ 93 Matt Whiteside .25 .11
❑ 94 Roberto Alomar 1.00 .45
❑ 95 Joe Carter .50 .23
❑ 96 Tony Castillo .25 .11
❑ 97 Juan Guzman .25 .11
❑ 98 Pat Hentgen .50 .23
❑ 99 Mike Huff .25 .11
❑ 100 John Olerud .50 .23
❑ 101 Woody Williams .25 .11
❑ 102 Roberto Kelly .25 .11
❑ 103 Ryan Klesko .50 .23
❑ 104 Javier Lopez .50 .23
❑ 105 Greg Maddux 3.00 1.35
❑ 106 Fred McGriff .75 .35
❑ 107 Jose Oliva .25 .11
❑ 108 John Smoltz .50 .23
❑ 109 Tony Tarasco .25 .11
❑ 110 Mark Wohlers .25 .11
❑ 111 Jim Bullinger .25 .11
❑ 112 Shawon Dunston .25 .11
❑ 113 Derrick May .25 .11
❑ 114 Randy Myers .25 .11
❑ 115 Karl Rhodes .25 .11
❑ 116 Rey Sanchez .25 .11
❑ 117 Steve Trachsel .25 .11
❑ 118 Eddie Zambrano .25 .11
❑ 119 Bret Boone .50 .23
❑ 120 Brian Dorsett .25 .11
❑ 121 Hal Morris .25 .11
❑ 122 Jose Rijo .25 .11
❑ 123 John Roper .25 .11
❑ 124 Reggie Sanders .50 .23
❑ 125 Pete Schourek .25 .11
❑ 126 John Smiley .25 .11
❑ 127 Ellis Burks .50 .23
❑ 128 Vinny Castilla .75 .35
❑ 129 Marvin Freeman .25 .11
❑ 130 Andres Galarraga 1.00 .45
❑ 131 Mike Munoz .25 .11
❑ 132 David Nied .25 .11
❑ 133 Bruce Ruffin .25 .11
❑ 134 Walt Weiss .25 .11
❑ 135 Eric Young .25 .11
❑ 136 Greg Colbrunn .25 .11
❑ 137 Jeff Conine .50 .23
❑ 138 Jeremy Hernandez .25 .11
❑ 139 Charles Johnson .50 .23
❑ 140 Robb Nen .25 .11
❑ 141 Gary Sheffield .75 .35
❑ 142 Dave Weathers .25 .11
❑ 143 Jeff Bagwell 1.50 .70
❑ 144 Craig Biggio 1.00 .45
❑ 145 Tony Eusebio .25 .11
❑ 146 Luis Gonzalez .25 .11
❑ 147 John Hudek .25 .11
❑ 148 Darryl Kile .50 .23
❑ 149 Dave Veres .25 .11
❑ 150 Billy Ashley .25 .11
❑ 151 Pedro Astacio .25 .11
❑ 152 Rafael Bournigal .25 .11
❑ 153 Delino DeShields .25 .11
❑ 154 Raul Mondesi .75 .35
❑ 155 Mike Piazza 3.00 1.35
❑ 156 Rudy Seanez .25 .11
❑ 157 Ismael Valdes .50 .23
❑ 158 Tim Wallach .25 .11
❑ 159 Todd Worrell .25 .11
❑ 160 Moises Alou .75 .35
❑ 161 Cliff Floyd .50 .23
❑ 162 Gil Heredia .25 .11
❑ 163 Mike Lansing .25 .11
❑ 164 Pedro Martinez 1.00 .45
❑ 165 Kirk Rueter .25 .11
❑ 166 Tim Scott .25 .11
❑ 167 Jeff Shaw .25 .11
❑ 168 Rondell White .50 .23
❑ 169 Bobby Bonilla .50 .23
❑ 170 Rico Brogna .25 .11
❑ 171 Todd Hundley .50 .23
❑ 172 Jeff Kent .50 .23
❑ 173 Jim Lindeman .25 .11
❑ 174 Joe Orsulak .25 .11
❑ 175 Bret Saberhagen .50 .23
❑ 176 Toby Borland .25 .11
❑ 177 Darren Daulton .50 .23
❑ 178 Lenny Dykstra .50 .23
❑ 179 Jim Eisenreich .25 .11
❑ 180 Tommy Greene .25 .11
❑ 181 Tony Longmire .25 .11
❑ 182 Bobby Munoz .25 .11
❑ 183 Kevin Stocker .25 .11
❑ 184 Jay Bell .50 .23
❑ 185 Steve Cooke .25 .11
❑ 186 Ravelo Manzanillo .25 .11
❑ 187 Al Martin .25 .11
❑ 188 Denny Neagle .50 .23
❑ 189 Don Slaught .25 .11
❑ 190 Paul Wagner .25 .11
❑ 191 Rene Arocha .25 .11
❑ 192 Bernard Gilkey .25 .11
❑ 193 Jose Oquendo .25 .11
❑ 194 Tom Pagnozzi .25 .11
❑ 195 Ozzie Smith 1.25 .55
❑ 196 Allen Watson .25 .11
❑ 197 Mark Whiten .25 .11
❑ 198 Andy Ashby .25 .11
❑ 199 Donnie Elliott .25 .11
❑ 200 Bryce Florie .25 .11
❑ 201 Tony Gwynn 2.50 1.10
❑ 202 Trevor Hoffman .50 .23
❑ 203 Brian Johnson .25 .11
❑ 204 Tim Mauser .25 .11
❑ 205 Bip Roberts .25 .11
❑ 206 Rod Beck .25 .11
❑ 207 Barry Bonds 1.25 .55
❑ 208 Royce Clayton .25 .11
❑ 209 Darren Lewis .25 .11
❑ 210 Mark Portugal .25 .11
❑ 211 Kevin Rogers .25 .11
❑ 212 Wm. VanLandingham .25 .11
❑ 213 Matt Williams .50 .23
❑ 214 Checklist .25 .11
❑ 215 Checklist .25 .11
❑ 216 Checklist .25 .11
❑ 217 Bret Barberie .25 .11
❑ 218 Armando Benitez .25 .11
❑ 219 Kevin Brown .75 .35
❑ 220 Sid Fernandez .25 .11
❑ 221 Chris Hoiles .25 .11
❑ 222 Doug Jones .25 .11
❑ 223 Ben McDonald .25 .11
❑ 224 Rafael Palmeiro .75 .35
❑ 225 Andy Van Slyke .50 .23
❑ 226 Jose Canseco 1.00 .45
❑ 227 Vaughn Eshelman .25 .11
❑ 228 Mike Macfarlane .25 .11
❑ 229 Tim Naehring .25 .11
❑ 230 Frank Rodriguez .25 .11
❑ 231 Lee Tinsley .25 .11
❑ 232 Mark Whiten .25 .11
❑ 233 Garret Anderson .50 .23
❑ 234 Chili Davis .50 .23
❑ 235 Jim Edmonds .75 .35
❑ 236 Mark Langston .25 .11
❑ 237 Troy Percival .50 .23
❑ 238 Tony Phillips .25 .11
❑ 239 Lee Smith .50 .23
❑ 240 Jim Abbott .50 .23
❑ 241 James Baldwin .50 .23
❑ 242 Mike Devereaux .25 .11
❑ 243 Ray Durham .50 .23
❑ 244 Alex Fernandez .25 .11
❑ 245 Roberto Hernandez .25 .11
❑ 246 Lance Johnson .25 .11
❑ 247 Ron Karkovice .25 .11
❑ 248 Tim Raines .50 .23
❑ 249 Sandy Alomar Jr. .50 .23
❑ 250 Orel Hershiser .50 .23
❑ 251 Julian Tavarez .25 .11
❑ 252 Jim Thome 1.00 .45
❑ 253 Omar Vizquel .50 .23
❑ 254 Dave Winfield 1.00 .45
❑ 255 Chad Curtis .25 .11
❑ 256 Kirk Gibson .50 .23
❑ 257 Mike Henneman .25 .11
❑ 258 Bob Higginson 2.50 1.10
❑ 259 Felipe Lira .25 .11
❑ 260 Rudy Pemberton .25 .11
❑ 261 Alan Trammell .50 .23
❑ 262 Kevin Appier .50 .23
❑ 263 Pat Borders .25 .11
❑ 264 Tom Gordon .25 .11
❑ 265 Jose Lind .25 .11
❑ 266 Jon Nunnally .25 .11
❑ 267 Dilson Torres .25 .11
❑ 268 Michael Tucker .50 .23
❑ 269 Jeff Cirillo .50 .23
❑ 270 Darryl Hamilton .25 .11
❑ 271 David Hulse .25 .11
❑ 272 Mark Kiefer .25 .11
❑ 273 Graeme Lloyd .25 .11
❑ 274 Joe Oliver .25 .11
❑ 275 Al Reyes .25 .11
❑ 276 Kevin Seitzer .25 .11
❑ 277 Rick Aguilera .25 .11
❑ 278 Marty Cordova .25 .11
❑ 279 Scott Erickson .50 .23
❑ 280 LaTroy Hawkins .25 .11
❑ 281 Brad Radke 1.25 .55
❑ 282 Kevin Tapani .25 .11
❑ 283 Tony Fernandez .25 .11
❑ 284 Sterling Hitchcock .50 .23
❑ 285 Pat Kelly .25 .11
❑ 286 Jack McDowell .25 .11
❑ 287 Andy Pettitte 1.00 .45
❑ 288 Mike Stanley .25 .11
❑ 289 John Wetteland .50 .23
❑ 290 Bernie Williams 1.00 .45
❑ 291 Mark Acre .25 .11
❑ 292 Geronimo Berroa .25 .11
❑ 293 Dennis Eckersley .50 .23
❑ 294 Steve Ontiveros .25 .11
❑ 295 Ruben Sierra .25 .11
❑ 296 Terry Steinbach .50 .23
❑ 297 Dave Stewart .50 .23
❑ 298 Todd Stottlemyre .25 .11
❑ 299 Darren Bragg .25 .11
❑ 300 Joey Cora .50 .23
❑ 301 Edgar Martinez .50 .23
❑ 302 Bill Risley .25 .11
❑ 303 Ron Villone .25 .11
❑ 304 Dan Wilson .25 .11
❑ 305 Benji Gil .25 .11
❑ 306 Wilson Heredia .25 .11
❑ 307 Mark McLemore .25 .11
❑ 308 Otis Nixon .25 .11
❑ 309 Kenny Rogers .25 .11
❑ 310 Jeff Russell .25 .11

❑ 311	Mickey Tettleton	.25	.11
❑ 312	Bob Tewksbury	.25	.11
❑ 313	David Cone	.75	.35
❑ 314	Carlos Delgado	.50	.23
❑ 315	Alex Gonzalez	.25	.11
❑ 316	Shawn Green	.50	.23
❑ 317	Paul Molitor	1.00	.45
❑ 318	Ed Sprague	.25	.11
❑ 319	Devon White	.50	.23
❑ 320	Steve Avery	.25	.11
❑ 321	Jeff Blauser	.25	.11
❑ 322	Brad Clontz	.25	.11
❑ 323	Tom Glavine	1.00	.45
❑ 324	Marquis Grissom	.50	.23
❑ 325	Chipper Jones	2.50	1.10
❑ 326	David Justice	1.00	.45
❑ 327	Mark Lemke	.25	.11
❑ 328	Kent Mercker	.25	.11
❑ 329	Jason Schmidt	.50	.23
❑ 330	Steve Buechele	.25	.11
❑ 331	Kevin Foster	.25	.11
❑ 332	Mark Grace	.75	.35
❑ 333	Brian McRae	.25	.11
❑ 334	Sammy Sosa	2.50	1.10
❑ 335	Ozzie Timmons	.25	.11
❑ 336	Rick Wilkins	.25	.11
❑ 337	Hector Carrasco	.25	.11
❑ 338	Ron Gant	.25	.11
❑ 339	Barry Larkin	.75	.35
❑ 340	Deion Sanders	.50	.23
❑ 341	Benito Santiago	.25	.11
❑ 342	Roger Bailey	.25	.11
❑ 343	Jason Bates	.25	.11
❑ 344	Dante Bichette	.50	.23
❑ 345	Joe Girardi	.25	.11
❑ 346	Bill Swift	.25	.11
❑ 347	Mark Thompson	.25	.11
❑ 348	Larry Walker	1.00	.45
❑ 349	Kurt Abbott	.25	.11
❑ 350	John Burkett	.25	.11
❑ 351	Chuck Carr	.25	.11
❑ 352	Andre Dawson	.75	.35
❑ 353	Chris Hammond	.25	.11
❑ 354	Charles Johnson	.50	.23
❑ 355	Terry Pendleton	.25	.11
❑ 356	Quilvio Veras	.25	.11
❑ 357	Derek Bell	.50	.23
❑ 358	Jim Dougherty	.25	.11
❑ 359	Doug Drabek	.25	.11
❑ 360	Todd Jones	.25	.11
❑ 361	Orlando Miller	.25	.11
❑ 362	James Mouton	.25	.11
❑ 363	Phil Plantier	.25	.11
❑ 364	Shane Reynolds	.50	.23
❑ 365	Todd Hollandsworth	.25	.11
❑ 366	Eric Karros	.50	.23
❑ 367	Ramon Martinez	.50	.23
❑ 368	Hideo Nomo	4.00	1.80
❑ 369	Jose Offerman	.25	.11
❑ 370	Antonio Osuna	.25	.11
❑ 371	Todd Williams	.25	.11
❑ 372	Shane Andrews	.25	.11
❑ 373	Wil Cordero	.25	.11
❑ 374	Jeff Fassero	.25	.11
❑ 375	Darrin Fletcher	.25	.11
❑ 376	Mark Grudzielanek	.75	.35
❑ 377	Carlos Perez	.75	.35
❑ 378	Mel Rojas	.25	.11
❑ 379	Tony Tarasco	.25	.11
❑ 380	Edgardo Alfonzo	.50	.23
❑ 381	Brett Butler	.50	.23
❑ 382	Carl Everett	.25	.11
❑ 383	John Franco	.50	.23
❑ 384	Pete Harnisch	.25	.11
❑ 385	Bobby Jones	.25	.11
❑ 386	Dave Mlicki	.25	.11
❑ 387	Jose Vizcaino	.25	.11
❑ 388	Ricky Bottalico	.50	.23
❑ 389	Tyler Green	.25	.11
❑ 390	Charlie Hayes	.25	.11
❑ 391	Dave Hollins	.25	.11
❑ 392	Gregg Jefferies	.25	.11
❑ 393	Michael Mimbs	.25	.11
❑ 394	Mickey Morandini	.25	.11
❑ 395	Curt Schilling	.50	.23
❑ 396	Heathcliff Slocumb	.25	.11
❑ 397	Jason Christiansen	.25	.11
❑ 398	Midre Cummings	.25	.11
❑ 399	Carlos Garcia	.25	.11
❑ 400	Mark Johnson	.25	.11
❑ 401	Jeff King	.25	.11
❑ 402	Jon Lieber	.25	.11
❑ 403	Esteban Loaiza	.25	.11
❑ 404	Orlando Merced	.25	.11
❑ 405	Gary Wilson	.25	.11
❑ 406	Scott Cooper	.25	.11
❑ 407	Tom Henke	.25	.11
❑ 408	Ken Hill	.25	.11
❑ 409	Danny Jackson	.25	.11
❑ 410	Brian Jordan	.50	.23
❑ 411	Ray Lankford	.50	.23
❑ 412	John Mabry	.25	.11
❑ 413	Todd Zeile	.25	.11
❑ 414	Andy Benes	.50	.23
❑ 415	Andres Berumen	.25	.11
❑ 416	Ken Caminiti	.75	.35
❑ 417	Andujar Cedeno	.25	.11
❑ 418	Steve Finley	.50	.23
❑ 419	Joey Hamilton	.50	.23
❑ 420	Dustin Hermanson	.50	.23
❑ 421	Melvin Nieves	.25	.11
❑ 422	Roberto Petagine	.25	.11
❑ 423	Eddie Williams	.25	.11
❑ 424	Glenallen Hill	.25	.11
❑ 425	Kirt Manwaring	.25	.11
❑ 426	Terry Mulholland	.25	.11
❑ 427	J.R. Phillips	.25	.11
❑ 428	Joe Rosselli	.25	.11
❑ 429	Robby Thompson	.25	.11
❑ 430	Checklist	.25	.11
❑ 431	Checklist	.25	.11
❑ 432	Checklist	.25	.11

1995 Flair Hot Gloves

	MINT	NRMT
COMPLETE SET (12)	150.00	70.00
COMMON CARD (1-12)	5.00	2.20
❑ 1 Roberto Alomar	12.00	5.50
❑ 2 Barry Bonds	15.00	6.75
❑ 3 Ken Griffey Jr.	60.00	27.00
❑ 4 Marquis Grissom	6.00	2.70
❑ 5 Barry Larkin	8.00	3.60
❑ 6 Darren Lewis	5.00	2.20
❑ 7 Kenny Lofton	12.00	5.50
❑ 8 Don Mattingly	20.00	9.00
❑ 9 Cal Ripken	50.00	22.00
❑ 10 Ivan Rodriguez	15.00	6.75
❑ 11 Devon White	6.00	2.70
❑ 12 Matt Williams	6.00	2.70

1995 Flair Hot Numbers

	MINT	NRMT
COMPLETE SET (10)	60.00	27.00
COMMON CARD (1-10)	2.00	.90
❑ 1 Jeff Bagwell	5.00	2.20
❑ 2 Albert Belle	3.00	1.35
❑ 3 Barry Bonds	3.00	1.35
❑ 4 Ken Griffey Jr.	15.00	6.75
❑ 5 Kenny Lofton	3.00	1.35

❑ 6 Greg Maddux	10.00	4.50
❑ 7 Mike Piazza	10.00	4.50
❑ 8 Cal Ripken	8.00	3.60
❑ 9 Frank Thomas	10.00	4.50
❑ 10 Matt Williams	2.00	.90

1995 Flair Infield Power

	MINT	NRMT
COMPLETE SET (10)	15.00	6.75
COMMON CARD (1-10)	.75	.35
❑ 1 Jeff Bagwell	2.50	1.10
❑ 2 Darren Daulton	.75	.35
❑ 3 Cecil Fielder	.75	.35
❑ 4 Andres Galarraga	1.50	.70
❑ 5 Fred McGriff	1.00	.45
❑ 6 Rafael Palmeiro	1.00	.45
❑ 7 Mike Piazza	5.00	2.20
❑ 8 Frank Thomas	4.00	1.80
❑ 9 Mo Vaughn	1.50	.70
❑ 10 Matt Williams	.75	.35

1995 Flair Outfield Power

	MINT	NRMT
COMPLETE SET (10)	15.00	6.75
COMMON CARD (1-10)	.50	.23
❑ 1 Albert Belle	1.50	.70
❑ 2 Dante Bichette	.75	.35
❑ 3 Barry Bonds	1.50	.70

	MINT	NRMT
❑ 4 Jose Canseco	1.50	.70
❑ 5 Joe Carter	.75	.35
❑ 6 Juan Gonzalez	4.00	1.80
❑ 7 Ken Griffey Jr.	8.00	3.60
❑ 8 Kirby Puckett	1.50	.70
❑ 9 Gary Sheffield	1.00	.45
❑ 10 Ruben Sierra	.50	.23

1995 Flair Ripken

	MINT	NRMT
COMPLETE SET (10)	80.00	36.00
COMMON CARD (1-10)	10.00	4.50
COMMON MAIL-IN (11-15)	6.00	2.70
❑ 1 Cal Ripken Rookie of the Year	10.00	4.50
❑ 2 Cal Ripken 1st MVP Season	10.00	4.50
❑ 3 Cal Ripken World Series Highlight	10.00	4.50
❑ 4 Cal Ripken Family Tradition	10.00	4.50
❑ 5 Cal Ripken 8,243 Consecutive Innings	10.00	4.50
❑ 6 Cal Ripken 95 Consecutive Errorless Games	10.00	4.50
❑ 7 Cal Ripken All-Star MVP	10.00	4.50
❑ 8 Cal Ripken 1,000th RBI	10.00	4.50
❑ 9 Cal Ripken 287th Home Run	10.00	4.50
❑ 10 Cal Ripken 2,000th Consecutive Game	10.00	4.50
❑ 11 Cal Ripken Literacy	6.00	2.70
❑ 12 Cal Ripken Game 2,130	6.00	2.70
❑ 13 Cal Ripken Game 2,131	6.00	2.70
❑ 14 Cal Ripken Defensive Prowess	6.00	2.70
❑ 15 Cal Ripken 2,153 and Counting	6.00	2.70

1995 Flair Today's Spotlight

	MINT	NRMT
COMPLETE SET (12)	100.00	45.00
COMMON CARD (1-12)	4.00	1.80
❑ 1 Jeff Bagwell	15.00	6.75
❑ 2 Jason Bere	4.00	1.80
❑ 3 Cliff Floyd	5.00	2.20
❑ 4 Chuck Knoblauch	10.00	4.50
❑ 5 Kenny Lofton	10.00	4.50
❑ 6 Javier Lopez	5.00	2.20
❑ 7 Raul Mondesi	6.00	2.70
❑ 8 Mike Mussina	10.00	4.50
❑ 9 Mike Piazza	30.00	13.50
❑ 10 Manny Ramirez	10.00	4.50
❑ 11 Tim Salmon	10.00	4.50
❑ 12 Frank Thomas	30.00	13.50

1995 Flair Wave of the Future

	MINT	NRMT
COMPLETE SET (10)	25.00	11.00
COMMON CARD (1-10)	1.00	.45
❑ 1 Jason Bates	1.00	.45
❑ 2 Armando Benitez	1.00	.45
❑ 3 Marty Cordova	1.00	.45
❑ 4 Ray Durham	2.00	.90
❑ 5 Vaughn Eshelman	1.00	.45
❑ 6 Carl Everett	1.00	.45
❑ 7 Shawn Green	2.00	.90
❑ 8 Dustin Hermanson	2.00	.90
❑ 9 Chipper Jones	10.00	4.50
❑ 10 Hideo Nomo	8.00	3.60

1996 Flair

	MINT	NRMT
COMPLETE SET (400)	200.00	90.00
COMMON CARD (1-400)	.50	.23
❑ 1 Roberto Alomar	2.00	.90
❑ 2 Brady Anderson	.75	.35
❑ 3 Bobby Bonilla	.75	.35
❑ 4 Scott Erickson	.75	.35
❑ 5 Jeffrey Hammonds	.75	.35
❑ 6 Jimmy Haynes	.50	.23
❑ 7 Chris Hoiles	.50	.23
❑ 8 Kent Mercker	.50	.23
❑ 9 Mike Mussina	2.00	.90
❑ 10 Randy Myers	.50	.23
❑ 11 Rafael Palmeiro	1.25	.55
❑ 12 Cal Ripken	8.00	3.60
❑ 13 B.J. Surhoff	.75	.35
❑ 14 David Wells	1.25	.55
❑ 15 Jose Canseco	2.00	.90
❑ 16 Roger Clemens	4.00	1.80
❑ 17 Wil Cordero	.50	.23
❑ 18 Tom Gordon	.50	.23
❑ 19 Mike Greenwell	.50	.23
❑ 20 Dwayne Hosey	.50	.23
❑ 21 Jose Malave	.50	.23
❑ 22 Tim Naehring	.50	.23
❑ 23 Troy O'Leary	.75	.35
❑ 24 Aaron Sele	.75	.35
❑ 25 Heathcliff Slocumb	.50	.23
❑ 26 Mike Stanley	.50	.23
❑ 27 Jeff Suppan	.50	.23
❑ 28 John Valentin	.75	.35
❑ 29 Mo Vaughn	2.50	1.10
❑ 30 Tim Wakefield	.75	.35
❑ 31 Jim Abbott	.75	.35
❑ 32 Garret Anderson	.75	.35
❑ 33 George Arias	.50	.23
❑ 34 Chili Davis	.75	.35
❑ 35 Gary DiSarcina	.50	.23
❑ 36 Jim Edmonds	1.25	.55
❑ 37 Chuck Finley	.75	.35
❑ 38 Todd Greene	.75	.35
❑ 39 Mark Langston	.50	.23
❑ 40 Troy Percival	.75	.35
❑ 41 Tim Salmon	2.00	.90
❑ 42 Lee Smith	.75	.35
❑ 43 J.T. Snow	.75	.35
❑ 44 Randy Velarde	.50	.23
❑ 45 Tim Wallach	.50	.23
❑ 46 Wilson Alvarez	.75	.35
❑ 47 Harold Baines	.75	.35
❑ 48 Jason Bere	.50	.23
❑ 49 Ray Durham	.75	.35
❑ 50 Alex Fernandez	.50	.23
❑ 51 Ozzie Guillen	.50	.23
❑ 52 Roberto Hernandez	.50	.23
❑ 53 Ron Karkovice	.50	.23
❑ 54 Darren Lewis	.50	.23
❑ 55 Lyle Mouton	.50	.23
❑ 56 Tony Phillips	.50	.23
❑ 57 Chris Snopek	.50	.23
❑ 58 Kevin Tapani	.50	.23
❑ 59 Danny Tartabull	.50	.23
❑ 60 Frank Thomas	6.00	2.70
❑ 61 Robin Ventura	.75	.35
❑ 62 Sandy Alomar Jr.	.75	.35
❑ 63 Carlos Baerga	.75	.35
❑ 64 Albert Belle	2.50	1.10
❑ 65 Julio Franco	.50	.23
❑ 66 Orel Hershiser	.75	.35
❑ 67 Kenny Lofton	2.00	.90
❑ 68 Dennis Martinez	.75	.35
❑ 69 Jack McDowell	.50	.23
❑ 70 Jose Mesa	.50	.23
❑ 71 Eddie Murray	2.00	.90
❑ 72 Charles Nagy	.75	.35
❑ 73 Tony Pena	.50	.23
❑ 74 Manny Ramirez	2.00	.90
❑ 75 Julian Tavarez	.50	.23
❑ 76 Jim Thome	2.00	.90
❑ 77 Omar Vizquel	.75	.35
❑ 78 Chad Curtis	.50	.23
❑ 79 Cecil Fielder	.75	.35
❑ 80 Travis Fryman	.75	.35
❑ 81 Chris Gomez	.50	.23
❑ 82 Bob Higginson	2.00	.90
❑ 83 Mark Lewis	.50	.23
❑ 84 Felipe Lira	.50	.23
❑ 85 Alan Trammell	1.25	.55
❑ 86 Kevin Appier	.75	.35
❑ 87 Johnny Damon	.75	.35
❑ 88 Tom Goodwin	.50	.23
❑ 89 Mark Gubicza	.50	.23
❑ 90 Bob Hamelin	.50	.23
❑ 91 Keith Lockhart	.50	.23
❑ 92 Jeff Montgomery	.50	.23
❑ 93 Jon Nunnally	.50	.23
❑ 94 Bip Roberts	.50	.23
❑ 95 Michael Tucker	.75	.35

❑ 96 Joe Vitiello .50 .23
❑ 97 Ricky Bones .50 .23
❑ 98 Chuck Carr .50 .23
❑ 99 Jeff Cirillo .75 .35
❑ 100 Mike Fetters .50 .23
❑ 101 John Jaha .50 .23
❑ 102 Mike Matheny .50 .23
❑ 103 Ben McDonald .50 .23
❑ 104 Matt Mieske .50 .23
❑ 105 Dave Nilsson .50 .23
❑ 106 Kevin Seitzer .50 .23
❑ 107 Steve Sparks .50 .23
❑ 108 Jose Valentin .50 .23
❑ 109 Greg Vaughn .75 .35
❑ 110 Rick Aguilera .50 .23
❑ 111 Rich Becker .50 .23
❑ 112 Marty Cordova .50 .23
❑ 113 LaTroy Hawkins .50 .23
❑ 114 Dave Hollins .50 .23
❑ 115 Roberto Kelly .50 .23
❑ 116 Chuck Knoblauch 2.00 .90
❑ 117 Matt Lawton 2.00 .90
❑ 118 Pat Meares .50 .23
❑ 119 Paul Molitor 2.00 .90
❑ 120 Kirby Puckett 3.00 1.35
❑ 121 Brad Radke .75 .35
❑ 122 Frank Rodriguez .50 .23
❑ 123 Scott Stahoviak .50 .23
❑ 124 Matt Walbeck .50 .23
❑ 125 Wade Boggs 2.00 .90
❑ 126 David Cone 1.25 .55
❑ 127 Joe Girardi .50 .23
❑ 128 Dwight Gooden .75 .35
❑ 129 Derek Jeter 6.00 2.70
❑ 130 Jimmy Key .75 .35
❑ 131 Jim Leyritz .50 .23
❑ 132 Tino Martinez 2.00 .90
❑ 133 Paul O'Neill .75 .35
❑ 134 Andy Pettitte 1.25 .55
❑ 135 Tim Raines .75 .35
❑ 136 Ruben Rivera .75 .35
❑ 137 Kenny Rogers .50 .23
❑ 138 Ruben Sierra .50 .23
❑ 139 John Wetteland .75 .35
❑ 140 Bernie Williams 2.00 .90
❑ 141 Tony Batista .50 .23
❑ 142 Allen Battle .50 .23
❑ 143 Geronimo Berroa .50 .23
❑ 144 Mike Bordick .50 .23
❑ 145 Scott Brosius .75 .35
❑ 146 Steve Cox .50 .23
❑ 147 Brent Gates .50 .23
❑ 148 Jason Giambi .75 .35
❑ 149 Doug Johns .50 .23
❑ 150 Mark McGwire 10.00 4.50
❑ 151 Pedro Munoz .50 .23
❑ 152 Ariel Prieto .50 .23
❑ 153 Terry Steinbach .75 .35
❑ 154 Todd Van Poppel .50 .23
❑ 155 Bobby Ayala .50 .23
❑ 156 Chris Bosio .50 .23
❑ 157 Jay Buhner .75 .35
❑ 158 Joey Cora .75 .35
❑ 159 Russ Davis .75 .35
❑ 160 Ken Griffey Jr. 10.00 4.50
❑ 161 Sterling Hitchcock .75 .35
❑ 162 Randy Johnson 2.00 .90
❑ 163 Edgar Martinez .75 .35
❑ 164 Alex Rodriguez 6.00 2.70
❑ 165 Paul Sorrento .50 .23
❑ 166 Dan Wilson .50 .23
❑ 167 Will Clark 2.00 .90
❑ 168 Benji Gil .50 .23
❑ 169 Juan Gonzalez 5.00 2.20
❑ 170 Rusty Greer 1.25 .55
❑ 171 Kevin Gross .50 .23
❑ 172 Darryl Hamilton .50 .23
❑ 173 Mike Henneman .50 .23
❑ 174 Ken Hill .50 .23
❑ 175 Mark McLemore .50 .23
❑ 176 Dean Palmer .75 .35
❑ 177 Roger Pavlik .50 .23
❑ 178 Ivan Rodriguez 2.50 1.10
❑ 179 Mickey Tettleton .50 .23
❑ 180 Bobby Witt .50 .23
❑ 181 Joe Carter .75 .35
❑ 182 Felipe Crespo .50 .23
❑ 183 Alex Gonzalez .50 .23
❑ 184 Shawn Green .75 .35
❑ 185 Juan Guzman .50 .23
❑ 186 Erik Hanson .50 .23
❑ 187 Pat Hentgen .75 .35
❑ 188 Sandy Martinez .50 .23
❑ 189 Otis Nixon .50 .23
❑ 190 John Olerud .75 .35
❑ 191 Paul Quantrill .50 .23
❑ 192 Bill Risley .50 .23
❑ 193 Ed Sprague .50 .23
❑ 194 Steve Avery .50 .23
❑ 195 Jeff Blauser .50 .23
❑ 196 Brad Clontz .50 .23
❑ 197 Jermaine Dye .50 .23
❑ 198 Tom Glavine 2.00 .90
❑ 199 Marquis Grissom .75 .35
❑ 200 Chipper Jones 5.00 2.20
❑ 201 David Justice 2.00 .90
❑ 202 Ryan Klesko .75 .35
❑ 203 Mark Lemke .50 .23
❑ 204 Javier Lopez .75 .35
❑ 205 Greg Maddux 6.00 2.70
❑ 206 Fred McGriff 1.25 .55
❑ 207 Greg McMichael .50 .23
❑ 208 Wonderful Monds .50 .23
❑ 209 Jason Schmidt .50 .23
❑ 210 John Smoltz .75 .35
❑ 211 Mark Wohlers .50 .23
❑ 212 Jim Bullinger .50 .23
❑ 213 Frank Castillo .50 .23
❑ 214 Kevin Foster .50 .23
❑ 215 Luis Gonzalez .50 .23
❑ 216 Mark Grace 1.25 .55
❑ 217 Robin Jennings .50 .23
❑ 218 Doug Jones .50 .23
❑ 219 Dave Magadan .50 .23
❑ 220 Brian McRae .50 .23
❑ 221 Jaime Navarro .50 .23
❑ 222 Rey Sanchez .50 .23
❑ 223 Ryne Sandberg 2.50 1.10
❑ 224 Scott Servais .50 .23
❑ 225 Sammy Sosa 5.00 2.20
❑ 226 Ozzie Timmons .50 .23
❑ 227 Bret Boone .75 .35
❑ 228 Jeff Branson .50 .23
❑ 229 Jeff Brantley .50 .23
❑ 230 Dave Burba .50 .23
❑ 231 Vince Coleman .50 .23
❑ 232 Steve Gibralter .50 .23
❑ 233 Mike Kelly .50 .23
❑ 234 Barry Larkin 1.25 .55
❑ 235 Hal Morris .50 .23
❑ 236 Mark Portugal .50 .23
❑ 237 Jose Rijo .50 .23
❑ 238 Reggie Sanders .75 .35
❑ 239 Pete Schourek .50 .23
❑ 240 John Smiley .50 .23
❑ 241 Eddie Taubensee .50 .23
❑ 242 Jason Bates .50 .23
❑ 243 Dante Bichette .75 .35
❑ 244 Ellis Burks .75 .35
❑ 245 Vinny Castilla 1.25 .55
❑ 246 Andres Galarraga 2.00 .90
❑ 247 Darren Holmes .50 .23
❑ 248 Curt Leskanic .50 .23
❑ 249 Steve Reed .50 .23
❑ 250 Kevin Rtiz .50 .23
❑ 251 Bret Saberhagen .75 .35
❑ 252 Bill Swift .50 .23
❑ 253 Larry Walker 2.00 .90
❑ 254 Walt Weiss .50 .23
❑ 255 Eric Young .50 .23
❑ 256 Kurt Abbott .50 .23
❑ 257 Kevin Brown 2.00 .90
❑ 258 John Burkett .50 .23
❑ 259 Greg Colbrunn .50 .23
❑ 260 Jeff Conine .75 .35
❑ 261 Andre Dawson 1.25 .55
❑ 262 Chris Hammond .50 .23
❑ 263 Charles Johnson .75 .35
❑ 264 Al Leiter .75 .35
❑ 265 Robb Nen .50 .23
❑ 266 Terry Pendleton .50 .23
❑ 267 Pat Rapp .50 .23
❑ 268 Gary Sheffield 1.25 .55
❑ 269 Quilvio Veras .50 .23
❑ 270 Devon White .75 .35
❑ 271 Bob Abreu .75 .35
❑ 272 Jeff Bagwell 3.00 1.35
❑ 273 Derek Bell .75 .35
❑ 274 Sean Berry .50 .23
❑ 275 Craig Biggio 2.00 .90
❑ 276 Doug Drabek .50 .23
❑ 277 Tony Eusebio .50 .23
❑ 278 Richard Hidalgo .75 .35
❑ 279 Brian L.Hunter .75 .35
❑ 280 Todd Jones .50 .23
❑ 281 Derrick May .50 .23
❑ 282 Orlando Miller .50 .23
❑ 283 James Mouton .50 .23
❑ 284 Shane Reynolds .75 .35
❑ 285 Greg Swindell .50 .23
❑ 286 Mike Blowers .50 .23
❑ 287 Brett Butler .75 .35
❑ 288 Tom Candiotti .50 .23
❑ 289 Roger Cedeno .50 .23
❑ 290 Delino DeShields .50 .23
❑ 291 Greg Gagne .50 .23
❑ 292 Karim Garcia .75 .35
❑ 293 Todd Hollandsworth .50 .23
❑ 294 Eric Karros .75 .35
❑ 295 Ramon Martinez .75 .35
❑ 296 Raul Mondesi 1.25 .55
❑ 297 Hideo Nomo 3.00 1.35
❑ 298 Mike Piazza 6.00 2.70
❑ 299 Ismael Valdes .75 .35
❑ 300 Todd Worrell .50 .23
❑ 301 Moises Alou 1.25 .55
❑ 302 Shane Andrews .50 .23
❑ 303 Yamil Benitez .50 .23
❑ 304 Jeff Fassero .50 .23
❑ 305 Darrin Fletcher .50 .23
❑ 306 Cliff Floyd .75 .35
❑ 307 Mark Grudzielanek .75 .35
❑ 308 Mike Lansing .50 .23
❑ 309 Pedro Martinez 2.00 .90
❑ 310 Ryan McGuire .50 .23
❑ 311 Carlos Perez .75 .35
❑ 312 Mel Rojas .50 .23
❑ 313 David Segui .75 .35
❑ 314 Rondell White .75 .35
❑ 315 Edgardo Alfonzo .75 .35
❑ 316 Rico Brogna .50 .23
❑ 317 Carl Everett .50 .23
❑ 318 John Franco .75 .35
❑ 319 Bernard Gilkey .50 .23
❑ 320 Todd Hundley .75 .35
❑ 321 Jason Isringhausen .50 .23
❑ 322 Lance Johnson .50 .23
❑ 323 Bobby Jones .50 .23
❑ 324 Jeff Kent .75 .35
❑ 325 Rey Ordonez .75 .35
❑ 326 Bill Pulsipher .50 .23
❑ 327 Jose Vizcaino .50 .23
❑ 328 Paul Wilson .50 .23
❑ 329 Ricky Bottalico .75 .35
❑ 330 Darren Daulton .75 .35
❑ 331 David Doster .50 .23
❑ 332 Lenny Dykstra .75 .35
❑ 333 Jim Eisenreich .50 .23
❑ 334 Sid Fernandez .50 .23
❑ 335 Gregg Jefferies .50 .23
❑ 336 Mickey Morandini .50 .23
❑ 337 Benito Santiago .50 .23
❑ 338 Curt Schilling .75 .35
❑ 339 Kevin Stocker .50 .23
❑ 340 David West .50 .23
❑ 341 Mark Whiten .50 .23
❑ 342 Todd Zeile .50 .23
❑ 343 Jay Bell .75 .35
❑ 344 John Ericks .50 .23
❑ 345 Carlos Garcia .50 .23
❑ 346 Charlie Hayes .50 .23
❑ 347 Jason Kendall 2.00 .90
❑ 348 Jeff King .50 .23
❑ 349 Mike Kingery .50 .23
❑ 350 Al Martin .50 .23

		MINT	NRMT
❑ 351	Orlando Merced	.50	.23
❑ 352	Dan Miceli	.50	.23
❑ 353	Denny Neagle	.75	.35
❑ 354	Alan Benes	.75	.35
❑ 355	Andy Benes	.75	.35
❑ 356	Royce Clayton	.50	.23
❑ 357	Dennis Eckersley	.75	.35
❑ 358	Gary Gaetti	.75	.35
❑ 359	Ron Gant	.50	.23
❑ 360	Brian Jordan	.75	.35
❑ 361	Ray Lankford	.75	.35
❑ 362	John Mabry	.50	.23
❑ 363	T.J. Mathews	.50	.23
❑ 364	Mike Morgan	.50	.23
❑ 365	Donovan Osborne	.50	.23
❑ 366	Tom Pagnozzi	.50	.23
❑ 367	Ozzie Smith	2.50	1.10
❑ 368	Todd Stottlemyre	.50	.23
❑ 369	Andy Ashby	.50	.23
❑ 370	Brad Ausmus	.50	.23
❑ 371	Ken Caminiti	1.25	.55
❑ 372	Andujar Cedeno	.50	.23
❑ 373	Steve Finley	.75	.35
❑ 374	Tony Gwynn	5.00	2.20
❑ 375	Joey Hamilton	.75	.35
❑ 376	Rickey Henderson	2.00	.90
❑ 377	Trevor Hoffman	.75	.35
❑ 378	Wally Joyner	.75	.35
❑ 379	Marc Newfield	.50	.23
❑ 380	Jody Reed	.50	.23
❑ 381	Bob Tewksbury	.50	.23
❑ 382	Fernando Valenzuela	.75	.35
❑ 383	Rod Beck	.50	.23
❑ 384	Barry Bonds	2.50	1.10
❑ 385	Mark Carreon	.50	.23
❑ 386	Shawon Dunston	.50	.23
❑ 387	Osvaldo Fernandez	.50	.23
❑ 388	Glenallen Hill	.50	.23
❑ 389	Stan Javier	.50	.23
❑ 390	Mark Leiter	.50	.23
❑ 391	Kirt Manwaring	.50	.23
❑ 392	Robby Thompson	.50	.23
❑ 393	William VanLandingham	.50	.23
❑ 394	Allen Watson	.50	.23
❑ 395	Matt Williams	.75	.35
❑ 396	Checklist 1-92	.50	.23
❑ 397	Checklist 93-180	.50	.23
❑ 398	Checklist 181-272	.50	.23
❑ 399	Checklist 273-365	.50	.23
❑ 400	Checklist 366-400/Inserts	.50	.23

1996 Flair Diamond Cuts

		MINT	NRMT
COMPLETE SET (12)		120.00	55.00
COMMON CARD (1-12)		3.00	1.35
❑ 1	Jeff Bagwell	8.00	3.60
❑ 2	Albert Belle	6.00	2.70
❑ 3	Barry Bonds	6.00	2.70
❑ 4	Juan Gonzalez	12.00	5.50
❑ 5	Ken Griffey Jr.	25.00	11.00
❑ 6	Greg Maddux	15.00	6.75
❑ 7	Eddie Murray	5.00	2.20
❑ 8	Mike Piazza	15.00	6.75
❑ 9	Cal Ripken	20.00	9.00
❑ 10	Frank Thomas	15.00	6.75
❑ 11	Mo Vaughn	6.00	2.70
❑ 12	Matt Williams	3.00	1.35

1996 Flair Hot Gloves

		MINT	NRMT
COMPLETE SET (10)		400.00	180.00
COMMON CARD (1-10)		15.00	6.75
❑ 1	Roberto Alomar	25.00	11.00
❑ 2	Barry Bonds	30.00	13.50
❑ 3	Will Clark	25.00	11.00
❑ 4	Ken Griffey Jr.	120.00	55.00
❑ 5	Kenny Lofton	25.00	11.00
❑ 6	Greg Maddux	80.00	36.00
❑ 7	Mike Piazza	80.00	36.00
❑ 8	Cal Ripken	100.00	45.00
❑ 9	Ivan Rodriguez	30.00	13.50
❑ 10	Matt Williams	15.00	6.75

1996 Flair Powerline

		MINT	NRMT
COMPLETE SET (10)		30.00	13.50
COMMON CARD (1-10)		1.50	.70
❑ 1	Albert Belle	2.00	.90
❑ 2	Barry Bonds	2.00	.90
❑ 3	Juan Gonzalez	5.00	2.20
❑ 4	Ken Griffey Jr.	10.00	4.50
❑ 5	Mark McGwire	10.00	4.50
❑ 6	Mike Piazza	6.00	2.70
❑ 7	Manny Ramirez	2.00	.90
❑ 8	Sammy Sosa	5.00	2.20
❑ 9	Frank Thomas	6.00	2.70
❑ 10	Matt Williams	1.50	.70

1996 Flair Wave of the Future

		MINT	NRMT
COMPLETE SET (20)		200.00	90.00
COMMON CARD (1-20)		10.00	4.50
❑ 1	Bob Abreu	15.00	6.75
❑ 2	George Arias	10.00	4.50
❑ 3	Tony Batista	10.00	4.50
❑ 4	Alan Benes	12.00	5.50
❑ 5	Yamil Benitez	10.00	4.50

		MINT	NRMT
❑ 6	Steve Cox	10.00	4.50
❑ 7	David Doster	10.00	4.50
❑ 8	Jermaine Dye	10.00	4.50
❑ 9	Osvaldo Fernandez	10.00	4.50
❑ 10	Karim Garcia	15.00	6.75
❑ 11	Steve Gibralter	10.00	4.50
❑ 12	Todd Greene	12.00	5.50
❑ 13	Richard Hidalgo	15.00	6.75
❑ 14	Robin Jennings	10.00	4.50
❑ 15	Jason Kendall	30.00	13.50
❑ 16	Jose Malave	10.00	4.50
❑ 17	Wonderful Monds	10.00	4.50
❑ 18	Rey Ordonez	12.00	5.50
❑ 19	Ruben Rivera	12.00	5.50
❑ 20	Paul Wilson	10.00	4.50

1997 Flair Showcase Row 2

		MINT	NRMT
COMPLETE SET (180)		80.00	36.00
COMMON CARD (1-60)		.25	.11
COMMON CARD (61-120)		.40	.18
COMMON CARD (121-180)		.30	.14
❑ 1	Andruw Jones	1.50	.70
❑ 2	Derek Jeter	3.00	1.35
❑ 3	Alex Rodriguez	3.00	1.35
❑ 4	Paul Molitor	1.00	.45
❑ 5	Jeff Bagwell	1.50	.70
❑ 6	Scott Rolen	2.50	1.10
❑ 7	Kenny Lofton	1.00	.45
❑ 8	Cal Ripken	4.00	1.80
❑ 9	Brady Anderson	.40	.18
❑ 10	Chipper Jones	2.50	1.10
❑ 11	Todd Greene	.40	.18
❑ 12	Todd Walker	1.00	.45
❑ 13	Billy Wagner	.40	.18
❑ 14	Craig Biggio	1.00	.45
❑ 15	Kevin Orie	.25	.11
❑ 16	Hideo Nomo	1.25	.55
❑ 17	Kevin Appier	.40	.18
❑ 18	Bubba Trammell STY	.60	.25
❑ 19	Juan Gonzalez	2.50	1.10
❑ 20	Randy Johnson	1.00	.45
❑ 21	Roger Clemens	2.00	.90
❑ 22	Johnny Damon	.40	.18
❑ 23	Ryne Sandberg	1.25	.55
❑ 24	Ken Griffey Jr.	5.00	2.20
❑ 25	Barry Bonds	1.25	.55

Card	MINT	NRMT
❑ 26 Nomar Garciaparra	3.00	1.35
❑ 27 Vladimir Guerrero	2.00	.90
❑ 28 Ron Gant	.25	.11
❑ 29 Joe Carter	.40	.18
❑ 30 Tim Salmon	1.00	.45
❑ 31 Mike Piazza	3.00	1.35
❑ 32 Barry Larkin	.60	.25
❑ 33 Manny Ramirez	1.00	.45
❑ 34 Sammy Sosa	2.50	1.10
❑ 35 Frank Thomas	3.00	1.35
❑ 36 Melvin Nieves	.25	.11
❑ 37 Tony Gwynn	2.50	1.10
❑ 38 Gary Sheffield	.60	.25
❑ 39 Darin Erstad	1.50	.70
❑ 40 Ken Caminiti	.60	.25
❑ 41 Jermaine Dye	.25	.11
❑ 42 Mo Vaughn	1.25	.55
❑ 43 Raul Mondesi	.60	.25
❑ 44 Greg Maddux	3.00	1.35
❑ 45 Chuck Knoblauch	1.00	.45
❑ 46 Andy Pettitte	.60	.25
❑ 47 Deion Sanders	.40	.18
❑ 48 Albert Belle	1.25	.55
❑ 49 Jamey Wright	.25	.11
❑ 50 Rey Ordonez	.40	.18
❑ 51 Bernie Williams	1.00	.45
❑ 52 Mark McGwire	5.00	2.20
❑ 53 Mike Mussina	1.00	.45
❑ 54 Bob Abreu	.40	.18
❑ 55 Reggie Sanders	.40	.18
❑ 56 Brian Jordan	.40	.18
❑ 57 Ivan Rodriguez	1.25	.55
❑ 58 Roberto Alomar	1.00	.45
❑ 59 Tim Naehring	.25	.11
❑ 60 Edgar Renteria	.40	.18
❑ 61 Dean Palmer	.60	.25
❑ 62 Benito Santiago	.40	.18
❑ 63 David Cone	1.00	.45
❑ 64 Carlos Delgado	.60	.25
❑ 65 Brian Giles	1.25	.55
❑ 66 Alex Ochoa	.40	.18
❑ 67 Rondell White	.60	.25
❑ 68 Robin Ventura	.60	.25
❑ 69 Eric Karros	.60	.25
❑ 70 Jose Valentin	.40	.18
❑ 71 Rafael Palmeiro	1.00	.45
❑ 72 Chris Snopek	.40	.18
❑ 73 David Justice	1.25	.55
❑ 74 Tom Glavine	1.25	.55
❑ 75 Rudy Pemberton	.40	.18
❑ 76 Larry Walker	1.50	.70
❑ 77 Jim Thome	1.50	.70
❑ 78 Charles Johnson	.60	.25
❑ 79 Dante Powell	.60	.25
❑ 80 Derrek Lee	1.00	.45
❑ 81 Jason Kendall	1.00	.45
❑ 82 Todd Hollandsworth	.40	.18
❑ 83 Bernard Gilkey	.40	.18
❑ 84 Mel Rojas	.40	.18
❑ 85 Dmitri Young	.60	.25
❑ 86 Bret Boone	.60	.25
❑ 87 Pat Hentgen	.60	.25
❑ 88 Bobby Bonilla	.60	.25
❑ 89 John Wetteland	.60	.25
❑ 90 Todd Hundley	.60	.25
❑ 91 Wilton Guerrero	.40	.18
❑ 92 Geronimo Berroa	.40	.18
❑ 93 Al Martin	.40	.18
❑ 94 Danny Tartabull	.40	.18
❑ 95 Brian McRae	.40	.18
❑ 96 Steve Finley	.60	.25
❑ 97 Todd Stottlemyre	.40	.18
❑ 98 John Smoltz	.60	.25
❑ 99 Matt Williams	.60	.25
❑ 100 Eddie Murray	1.50	.70
❑ 101 Henry Rodriguez	.60	.25
❑ 102 Marty Cordova	.40	.18
❑ 103 Juan Guzman	.40	.18
❑ 104 Chili Davis	.60	.25
❑ 105 Eric Young	.60	.25
❑ 106 Jeff Abbott	.60	.25
❑ 107 Shannon Stewart	.60	.25
❑ 108 Rocky Coppinger	.40	.18
❑ 109 Jose Canseco	1.25	.55
❑ 110 Dante Bichette	.60	.25
❑ 111 Dwight Gooden	.60	.25
❑ 112 Scott Brosius	.60	.25
❑ 113 Steve Avery	.40	.18
❑ 114 Andres Galarraga	1.25	.55
❑ 115 Sandy Alomar Jr.	.60	.25
❑ 116 Ray Lankford	.60	.25
❑ 117 Jorge Posada	.60	.25
❑ 118 Ryan Klesko	.60	.25
❑ 119 Jay Buhner	.60	.25
❑ 120 Jose Guillen	1.25	.55
❑ 121 Paul O'Neill	.50	.23
❑ 122 Jimmy Key	.50	.23
❑ 123 Hal Morris	.30	.14
❑ 124 Travis Fryman	.50	.23
❑ 125 Jim Edmonds	.75	.35
❑ 126 Jeff Cirillo	.50	.23
❑ 127 Fred McGriff	.75	.35
❑ 128 Alan Benes	.50	.23
❑ 129 Derek Bell	.50	.23
❑ 130 Tony Graffanino	.30	.14
❑ 131 Shawn Green	.50	.23
❑ 132 Denny Neagle	.50	.23
❑ 133 Alex Fernandez	.30	.14
❑ 134 Mickey Morandini	.30	.14
❑ 135 Royce Clayton	.30	.14
❑ 136 Jose Mesa	.30	.14
❑ 137 Edgar Martinez	.50	.23
❑ 138 Curt Schilling	.50	.23
❑ 139 Lance Johnson	.30	.14
❑ 140 Andy Benes	.50	.23
❑ 141 Charles Nagy	.50	.23
❑ 142 Mariano Rivera	.50	.23
❑ 143 Mark Wohlers	.30	.14
❑ 144 Ken Hill	.30	.14
❑ 145 Jay Bell	.50	.23
❑ 146 Bob Higginson	.75	.35
❑ 147 Mark Grudzielanek	.50	.23
❑ 148 Ray Durham	.50	.23
❑ 149 John Olerud	.50	.23
❑ 150 Joey Hamilton	.50	.23
❑ 151 Trevor Hoffman	.50	.23
❑ 152 Dan Wilson	.30	.14
❑ 153 J.T. Snow	.50	.23
❑ 154 Marquis Grissom	.50	.23
❑ 155 Yamil Benitez	.30	.14
❑ 156 Rusty Greer	.50	.23
❑ 157 Darryl Kile	.50	.23
❑ 158 Ismael Valdes	.50	.23
❑ 159 Jeff Conine	.50	.23
❑ 160 Darren Daulton	.50	.23
❑ 161 Chan Ho Park	1.00	.45
❑ 162 Troy Percival	.50	.23
❑ 163 Wade Boggs	1.00	.45
❑ 164 Dave Nilsson	.30	.14
❑ 165 Vinny Castilla	.75	.35
❑ 166 Kevin Brown	.75	.35
❑ 167 Dennis Eckersley	.50	.23
❑ 168 Wendell Magee Jr.	.30	.14
❑ 169 John Jaha	.30	.14
❑ 170 Garret Anderson	.50	.23
❑ 171 Jason Giambi	.50	.23
❑ 172 Mark Grace	.75	.35
❑ 173 Tony Clark	.75	.35
❑ 174 Moises Alou	.75	.35
❑ 175 Brett Butler	.50	.23
❑ 176 Cecil Fielder	.50	.23
❑ 177 Chris Widger	.30	.14
❑ 178 Doug Drabek	.30	.14
❑ 179 Ellis Burks	.50	.23
❑ 180 Shigetoshi Hasegawa	.75	.35
❑ NNO A. Rod. Glove EXCH	800.00	350.00

1997 Flair Showcase Row 1

	MINT	NRMT
COMPLETE SET (180)	200.00	90.00
COMMON CARD (1-60)	.60	.25
*STARS 1-60: 1X TO 2.5X ROW2		
COMMON CARD (61-120)	.50	.23
*STARS 61-120: .5X TO 1.2X ROW 2		
COMMON CARD (121-180)	1.00	.45
*STARS 121-180: 1.25X TO 3X ROW 2		

1997 Flair Showcase Row 0

	MINT	NRMT
COMPLETE SET (180)	1500.00	700.00
COMMON CARD (1-60)	6.00	2.70
*STARS 1-60: 8X TO 20X ROW 2		
*YOUNG STARS 1-60: 6X TO 15X ROW 2		
COMMON CARD (61-120)	2.50	1.10
*STARS 61-120: 2.5X TO 6X ROW 2		
*YOUNG STARS 61-120: 2X TO 5X ROW 2		
COMMON CARD (121-180)	1.00	.45
*STARS 121-180: 1.5X TO 4X ROW 2		
*YOUNG STARS 121-180: 1.25X TO 3X ROW 2		

1997 Flair Showcase Legacy Collection

	MINT	NRMT
COMMON CARD (1-180)	15.00	6.75
*STARS 1-60: 30X TO 60X BASIC CARDS		
*STARS 61-120: 20X TO 40X BASIC CARDS		
*STARS 121-180: 25X TO 50X BASIC CARDS		

1997 Flair Showcase Diamond Cuts

	MINT	NRMT
COMPLETE SET (20)	250.00	110.00
COMMON CARD (1-20)	3.00	1.35
❑ 1 Jeff Bagwell	10.00	4.50
❑ 2 Albert Belle	8.00	3.60
❑ 3 Ken Caminiti	4.00	1.80
❑ 4 Juan Gonzalez	15.00	6.75
❑ 5 Ken Griffey Jr.	30.00	13.50
❑ 6 Tony Gwynn	15.00	6.75
❑ 7 Todd Hundley	3.00	1.35
❑ 8 Andruw Jones	8.00	3.60
❑ 9 Chipper Jones	15.00	6.75
❑ 10 Greg Maddux	20.00	9.00
❑ 11 Mark McGwire	30.00	13.50
❑ 12 Mike Piazza	20.00	9.00
❑ 13 Derek Jeter	15.00	6.75
❑ 14 Manny Ramirez	6.00	2.70
❑ 15 Cal Ripken	25.00	11.00
❑ 16 Alex Rodriguez	20.00	9.00
❑ 17 Frank Thomas	20.00	9.00
❑ 18 Mo Vaughn	8.00	3.60
❑ 19 Bernie Williams	6.00	2.70
❑ 20 Matt Williams	3.00	1.35

1997 Flair Showcase Hot Gloves

	MINT	NRMT
COMPLETE SET (15)	600.00	275.00
COMMON CARD (1-15)	10.00	4.50
❑ 1 Roberto Alomar	20.00	9.00
❑ 2 Barry Bonds	25.00	11.00
❑ 3 Juan Gonzalez	50.00	22.00
❑ 4 Ken Griffey Jr.	100.00	45.00
❑ 5 Marquis Grissom	10.00	4.50
❑ 6 Derek Jeter	50.00	22.00
❑ 7 Chipper Jones	50.00	22.00

❑ 8 Barry Larkin	12.00	5.50
❑ 9 Kenny Lofton	20.00	9.00
❑ 10 Greg Maddux	60.00	27.00
❑ 11 Mike Piazza	60.00	27.00
❑ 12 Cal Ripken	80.00	36.00
❑ 13 Alex Rodriguez	60.00	27.00
❑ 14 Ivan Rodriguez	25.00	11.00
❑ 15 Frank Thomas	60.00	27.00

1997 Flair Showcase Wave of the Future

	MINT	NRMT
COMPLETE SET (27)	60.00	27.00
COMMON (1-25/WF1-WF2)	1.00	.45
❑ 1 Todd Greene	1.50	.70
❑ 2 Andruw Jones	4.00	1.80
❑ 3 Randall Simon	4.00	1.80
❑ 4 Wady Almonte	1.50	.70
❑ 5 Pat Cline	1.50	.70
❑ 6 Jeff Abbott	1.50	.70
❑ 7 Justin Towle	2.00	.90
❑ 8 Richie Sexson	3.00	1.35
❑ 9 Bubba Trammell	2.50	1.10
❑ 10 Bob Abreu	1.50	.70
❑ 11 David Arias-Ortiz	5.00	2.20
❑ 12 Todd Walker	2.50	1.10
❑ 13 Orlando Cabrera	1.50	.70
❑ 14 Vladimir Guerrero	5.00	2.20
❑ 15 Ricky Ledee	8.00	3.60
❑ 16 Jorge Posada	1.50	.70
❑ 17 Ruben Rivera	1.50	.70
❑ 18 Scott Spiezio	1.00	.45
❑ 19 Scott Rolen	6.00	2.70
❑ 20 Emil Brown	2.00	.90
❑ 21 Jose Guillen	2.50	1.10
❑ 22 T.J. Staton	1.50	.70
❑ 23 Eli Marrero	1.50	.70
❑ 24 Fernando Tatis	4.00	1.80
❑ 25 Ryan Jones	1.00	.45
❑ WF1 Hideki Irabu	6.00	2.70
❑ WF2 Jose Cruz Jr.	10.00	4.50

1998 Flair Showcase Row 3

	MINT	NRMT
COMPLETE SET (120)	80.00	36.00
COMMON CARD (1-30)	.40	.18
COMMON CARD (31-60)	.40	.18
COMMON CARD (61-90)	.50	.23
COMMON CARD (91-120)	.60	.25
❑ 1 Ken Griffey Jr.	5.00	2.20
❑ 2 Travis Lee	2.00	.90
❑ 3 Frank Thomas	3.00	1.35
❑ 4 Ben Grieve	2.00	.90
❑ 5 Nomar Garciaparra	3.00	1.35
❑ 6 Jose Cruz Jr.	1.25	.55
❑ 7 Alex Rodriguez	3.00	1.35
❑ 8 Cal Ripken	4.00	1.80
❑ 9 Mark McGwire	6.00	2.70
❑ 10 Chipper Jones	2.50	1.10
❑ 11 Paul Konerko	1.00	.45
❑ 12 Todd Helton	1.25	.55
❑ 13 Greg Maddux	3.00	1.35
❑ 14 Derek Jeter	2.50	1.10
❑ 15 Jaret Wright	1.25	.55
❑ 16 Livan Hernandez	.50	.23
❑ 17 Mike Piazza	3.00	1.35
❑ 18 Juan Encarnacion	.50	.23
❑ 19 Tony Gwynn	2.50	1.10
❑ 20 Scott Rolen	2.50	1.10
❑ 21 Roger Clemens	2.00	.90
❑ 22 Tony Clark	.60	.25
❑ 23 Albert Belle	1.00	.45
❑ 24 Mo Vaughn	1.25	.55
❑ 25 Andruw Jones	1.25	.55
❑ 26 Jason Dickson	.50	.23
❑ 27 Fernando Tatis	.50	.23
❑ 28 Ivan Rodriguez	1.25	.55
❑ 29 Ricky Ledee	.50	.23
❑ 30 Darin Erstad	1.25	.55
❑ 31 Brian Rose	.50	.23
❑ 32 Maggio Ordonez	1.25	.55
❑ 33 Larry Walker	1.00	.45
❑ 34 Bobby Higginson	.60	.25
❑ 35 Chili Davis	.50	.23
❑ 36 Barry Bonds	1.25	.55
❑ 37 Vladimir Guerrero	1.50	.70
❑ 38 Jeff Bagwell	1.50	.70
❑ 39 Kenny Lofton	1.00	.45
❑ 40 Ryan Klesko	.50	.23
❑ 41 Mike Cameron	.50	.23
❑ 42 Charles Johnson	.50	.23
❑ 43 Andy Pettitte	.60	.25
❑ 44 Juan Gonzalez	2.50	1.10
❑ 45 Tim Salmon	1.00	.45
❑ 46 Hideki Irabu	.60	.25
❑ 47 Paul Molitor	1.00	.45
❑ 48 Edgar Renteria	.50	.23
❑ 49 Manny Ramirez	1.00	.45
❑ 50 Jim Edmonds	.60	.25
❑ 51 Bernie Williams	1.00	.45
❑ 52 Roberto Alomar	1.00	.45
❑ 53 David Justice	1.00	.45
❑ 54 Rey Ordonez	.50	.23
❑ 55 Ken Caminiti	.60	.25
❑ 56 Jose Guillen	.50	.23
❑ 57 Randy Johnson	1.00	.45
❑ 58 Brady Anderson	.50	.23
❑ 59 Hideo Nomo	1.25	.55
❑ 60 Tino Martinez	1.00	.45
❑ 61 John Smoltz	.60	.25
❑ 62 Joe Carter	.60	.25
❑ 63 Matt Williams	.60	.25
❑ 64 Robin Ventura	.60	.25
❑ 65 Barry Larkin	.75	.35
❑ 66 Dante Bichette	.60	.25
❑ 67 Travis Fryman	.60	.25
❑ 68 Gary Sheffield	.75	.35
❑ 69 Eric Karros	.60	.25
❑ 70 Matt Stairs	.60	.25
❑ 71 Al Martin	.50	.23
❑ 72 Jay Buhner	.60	.25
❑ 73 Ray Lankford	.60	.25
❑ 74 Carlos Delgado	.60	.25
❑ 75 Edgardo Alfonzo	.60	.25
❑ 76 Rondell White	.60	.25
❑ 77 Chuck Knoblauch	1.25	.55
❑ 78 Raul Mondesi	.75	.35
❑ 79 Johnny Damon	.60	.25
❑ 80 Matt Morris	.60	.25
❑ 81 Tom Glavine	1.25	.55
❑ 82 Kevin Brown	.75	.35
❑ 83 Garret Anderson	.60	.25
❑ 84 Mike Mussina	1.25	.55
❑ 85 Pedro Martinez	1.25	.55
❑ 86 Craig Biggio	1.25	.55
❑ 87 Darryl Kile	.60	.25
❑ 88 Rafael Palmeiro	.75	.35
❑ 89 Jim Thome	1.25	.55
❑ 90 Andres Galarraga	1.25	.55
❑ 91 Sammy Sosa	4.00	1.80
❑ 92 Willie Greene	.75	.35
❑ 93 Vinny Castilla	1.00	.45
❑ 94 Justin Thompson	.75	.35
❑ 95 Jeff King	.75	.35
❑ 96 Jeff Cirillo	.75	.35
❑ 97 Mark Grudzielanek	.75	.35
❑ 98 Brad Radke	.75	.35
❑ 99 John Olerud	.75	.35
❑ 100 Curt Schilling	.75	.35
❑ 101 Steve Finley	.75	.35
❑ 102 J.T. Snow	.75	.35
❑ 103 Edgar Martinez	.75	.35
❑ 104 Wilson Alvarez	.75	.35
❑ 105 Rusty Greer	.75	.35
❑ 106 Pat Hentgen	.75	.35
❑ 107 David Cone	1.00	.45
❑ 108 Fred McGriff	1.00	.45
❑ 109 Jason Giambi	.75	.35
❑ 110 Tony Womack	.75	.35
❑ 111 Bernard Gilkey	.60	.25
❑ 112 Alan Benes	.75	.35
❑ 113 Mark Grace	1.00	.45
❑ 114 Reggie Sanders	.75	.35
❑ 115 Moises Alou	1.00	.45
❑ 116 John Jaha	.60	.25
❑ 117 Henry Rodriguez	.75	.35
❑ 118 Dean Palmer	.75	.35
❑ 119 Mike Lieberthal	.60	.25
❑ 120 Shawn Estes	.75	.35

1998 Flair Showcase Row 2

	MINT	NRMT
COMPLETE SET (120)	150.00	70.00
COMMON CARD (1-30)	1.00	.45
*STARS 1-30: 1X TO 2.5X ROW 3		
COMMON CARD (31-60)	.75	.35
*STARS 31-60: .75X TO 2X ROW 3		
COMMON CARD (61-90)	1.25	.55
*STARS 61-90: 1X TO 2.5X ROW 3		

COMMON CARD (91-120)	1.25	.55
*STARS 91-120: .75X TO 2X ROW 3		

1998 Flair Showcase Row 1

	MINT	NRMT
COMPLETE SET (120)	600.00	275.00
COMMON CARD (1-30)	3.00	1.35
*STARS 1-30: 3X TO 8X ROW 3		
COMMON CARD (31-60)	4.00	1.80
*STARS 31-60: 4X TO 10X ROW 3		
COMMON CARD (61-90)	1.50	.70
*STARS 61-90: 1.25X TO 3X ROW 3		
COMMON CARD (91-120)	2.50	1.10
*STARS 91-120: 1.5X TO 4X ROW 3		

1998 Flair Showcase Row 0

	MINT	NRMT
COMPLETE SET (120)	2500.00	1100.00
COMMON CARD (1-30)	12.00	5.50
*STARS 1-30: 15X TO 30X ROW 3		
COMMON CARD (31-60)	8.00	3.60
*STARS 31-60: 10X TO 20X ROW 3		
COMMON CARD (61-90)	6.00	2.70
*STARS 61-90: 6X TO 12X ROW 3		
COMMON CARD (91-120)	4.00	1.80
*STARS 91-120: 3X TO 6X ROW 3		

1998 Flair Showcase Perfect 10

	MINT	NRMT
COMMON CARD (1-10)		
NO PRICING AVAILABLE DUE TO SCARCITY		

- ❑ 1 Ken Griffey Jr.
- ❑ 2 Cal Ripken
- ❑ 3 Frank Thomas
- ❑ 4 Mike Piazza
- ❑ 5 Greg Maddux
- ❑ 6 Nomar Garciaparra
- ❑ 7 Mark McGwire
- ❑ 8 Scott Rolen
- ❑ 9 Alex Rodriguez
- ❑ 10 Roger Clemens

1998 Flair Showcase Legacy Collection

	MINT	NRMT
COMMON CARD (1-120)	25.00	11.00

1998 Flair Showcase Wave of the Future

	MINT	NRMT
COMPLETE SET (12)	60.00	27.00
COMMON CARD (1-12)	3.00	1.35
❑ 1 Travis Lee	12.00	5.50
❑ 2 Todd Helton	8.00	3.60
❑ 3 Ben Grieve	12.00	5.50
❑ 4 Juan Encarnacion	3.00	1.35
❑ 5 Brad Fullmer	3.00	1.35
❑ 6 Ruben Rivera	3.00	1.35
❑ 7 Paul Konerko	5.00	2.20
❑ 8 Derrek Lee	3.00	1.35
❑ 9 Mike Lowell	5.00	2.20
❑ 10 Magglio Ordonez	6.00	2.70
❑ 11 Rich Butler	4.00	1.80
❑ 12 Eli Marrero	3.00	1.35

1963 Fleer

	NRMT	VG-E
COMPLETE SET (67)	2000.00	900.00
COMMON CARD (1-66)	15.00	6.75
WRAPPER (5-CENT)	100.00	45.00
❑ 1 Steve Barber	30.00	9.00
❑ 2 Ron Hansen	15.00	6.75
❑ 3 Milt Pappas	20.00	9.00
❑ 4 Brooks Robinson	100.00	45.00
❑ 5 Willie Mays	200.00	90.00
❑ 6 Lou Clinton	15.00	6.75
❑ 7 Bill Monbouquette	15.00	6.75
❑ 8 Carl Yastrzemski	120.00	55.00
❑ 9 Ray Herbert	15.00	6.75
❑ 10 Jim Landis	15.00	6.75
❑ 11 Dick Donovan	15.00	6.75
❑ 12 Tito Francona	15.00	6.75
❑ 13 Jerry Kindall	15.00	6.75
❑ 14 Frank Lary	20.00	9.00
❑ 15 Dick Howser	20.00	9.00
❑ 16 Jerry Lumpe	15.00	6.75
❑ 17 Norm Siebern	15.00	6.75
❑ 18 Don Lee	15.00	6.75
❑ 19 Albie Pearson	20.00	9.00
❑ 20 Bob Rodgers	20.00	9.00
❑ 21 Leon Wagner	15.00	6.75
❑ 22 Jim Kaat	20.00	9.00
❑ 23 Vic Power	20.00	9.00
❑ 24 Rich Rollins	20.00	9.00
❑ 25 Bobby Richardson	30.00	13.50
❑ 26 Ralph Terry	20.00	9.00
❑ 27 Tom Cheney	15.00	6.75
❑ 28 Chuck Cottier	15.00	6.75
❑ 29 Jimmy Piersall	20.00	9.00
❑ 30 Dave Stenhouse	15.00	6.75
❑ 31 Glen Hobbie	15.00	6.75
❑ 32 Ron Santo	20.00	9.00
❑ 33 Gene Freese	15.00	6.75
❑ 34 Vada Pinson	20.00	9.00
❑ 35 Bob Purkey	15.00	6.75
❑ 36 Joe Amalfitano	15.00	6.75
❑ 37 Bob Aspromonte	15.00	6.75
❑ 38 Dick Farrell	15.00	6.75
❑ 39 Al Spangler	15.00	6.75
❑ 40 Tommy Davis	20.00	9.00
❑ 41 Don Drysdale	70.00	32.00
❑ 42 Sandy Koufax	200.00	90.00
❑ 43 Maury Wills	100.00	45.00
❑ 44 Frank Bolling	15.00	6.75
❑ 45 Warren Spahn	70.00	32.00
❑ 46 Joe Adcock SP	200.00	90.00
❑ 47 Roger Craig	20.00	9.00
❑ 48 Al Jackson	20.00	9.00
❑ 49 Rod Kanehl	20.00	9.00
❑ 50 Ruben Amaro	15.00	6.75
❑ 51 Johnny Callison	20.00	9.00
❑ 52 Clay Dalrymple	15.00	6.75
❑ 53 Don Demeter	15.00	6.75
❑ 54 Art Mahaffey	15.00	6.75
❑ 55 Smoky Burgess	20.00	9.00
❑ 56 Roberto Clemente	250.00	110.00
❑ 57 Roy Face	20.00	9.00
❑ 58 Vern Law	20.00	9.00
❑ 59 Bill Mazeroski	30.00	13.50
❑ 60 Ken Boyer	20.00	9.00
❑ 61 Bob Gibson	70.00	32.00
❑ 62 Gene Oliver	15.00	6.75
❑ 63 Bill White	20.00	9.00
❑ 64 Orlando Cepeda	30.00	13.50
❑ 65 Jim Davenport	15.00	6.75
❑ 66 Billy O'Dell	30.00	9.00
❑ NNO Checklist card	700.00	230.00

1981 Fleer

	NRMT	VG-E
COMPLETE SET (660)	25.00	11.00
COMMON CARD (1-660)	.10	.05
❑ 1 Pete Rose UER (270 hits in '63, should be 170)	1.25	.55
❑ 2 Larry Bowa	.25	.11
❑ 3 Manny Trillo	.10	.05
❑ 4 Bob Boone	.25	.11
❑ 5 Mike Schmidt (See also 640A)	1.25	.55
❑ 6 Steve Carlton P1 Golden Arm (Back "1066 Cardinals"; Number on back 6)	1.00	.45

❑ 6B Steve Carlton P2 1.50 .70
Pitcher of Year
(Back "1066 Cardinals")
❑ 6C Steve Carlton P3 2.00 .90
(1966 Cardinals)
❑ 7 Tug McGraw .25 .11
(See 657A)
❑ 8 Larry Christenson .10 .05
❑ 9 Bake McBride .10 .05
❑ 10 Greg Luzinski .25 .11
❑ 11 Ron Reed .10 .05
❑ 12 Dickie Noles .10 .05
❑ 13 Keith Moreland .25 .11
❑ 14 Bob Walk .25 .11
❑ 15 Lonnie Smith .25 .11
❑ 16 Dick Ruthven .10 .05
❑ 17 Sparky Lyle .25 .11
❑ 18 Greg Gross .10 .05
❑ 19 Garry Maddox .10 .05
❑ 20 Nino Espinosa .10 .05
❑ 21 George Vukovich .10 .05
❑ 22 John Vukovich .10 .05
❑ 23 Ramon Aviles .10 .05
❑ 24A Kevin Saucier P1 .10 .05
(Name on back "Ken")
❑ 24B Kevin Saucier P2 .10 .05
(Name on back "Ken")
❑ 24C Kevin Saucier P3 1.00 .45
(Name on back "Kevin")
❑ 25 Randy Lerch .10 .05
❑ 26 Del Unser .10 .05
❑ 27 Tim McCarver .50 .23
❑ 28 George Brett 2.50 1.10
(See also 655A)
❑ 29 Willie Wilson .25 .11
(See also 653A)
❑ 30 Paul Splittorff .10 .05
❑ 31 Dan Quisenberry .25 .11
❑ 32A Amos Otis P1 .25 .11
(Batting Pose;
"Outfield";
32 on back)
❑ 32B Amos Otis P2 .25 .11
Series Starter
483 on back
❑ 33 Steve Busby .10 .05
❑ 34 U.L. Washington .10 .05
❑ 35 Dave Chalk .10 .05
❑ 36 Darrell Porter .10 .05
❑ 37 Marty Pattin .10 .05
❑ 38 Larry Gura .10 .05
❑ 39 Renie Martin .10 .05
❑ 40 Rich Gale .10 .05
❑ 41A Hal McRae P1 .50 .23
("Royals" on front
in black letters)
❑ 41B Hal McRae P2 .25 .11
("Royals" on front
in blue letters)
❑ 42 Dennis Leonard .10 .05
❑ 43 Willie Aikens .10 .05
❑ 44 Frank White .25 .11
❑ 45 Clint Hurdle .10 .05
❑ 46 John Wathan .10 .05
❑ 47 Pete LaCock .10 .05
❑ 48 Rance Mulliniks .10 .05
❑ 49 Jeff Twitty .10 .05
❑ 50 Jamie Quirk .10 .05
❑ 51 Art Howe .10 .05
❑ 52 Ken Forsch .10 .05
❑ 53 Vern Ruhle .10 .05
❑ 54 Joe Niekro .25 .11
❑ 55 Frank LaCorte .10 .05
❑ 56 J.R. Richard .25 .11
❑ 57 Nolan Ryan 5.00 2.20
❑ 58 Enos Cabell .10 .05
❑ 59 Cesar Cedeno .25 .11
❑ 60 Jose Cruz .25 .11
❑ 61 Bill Virdon MG .10 .05
❑ 62 Terry Puhl .10 .05
❑ 63 Joaquin Andujar .25 .11
❑ 64 Alan Ashby .10 .05
❑ 65 Joe Sambito .10 .05
❑ 66 Denny Walling .10 .05
❑ 67 Jeff Leonard .25 .11
❑ 68 Luis Pujols .10 .05
❑ 69 Bruce Bochy .10 .05
❑ 70 Rafael Landestoy .10 .05
❑ 71 Dave Smith .25 .11
❑ 72 Danny Heep .10 .05
❑ 73 Julio Gonzalez .10 .05
❑ 74 Craig Reynolds .10 .05
❑ 75 Gary Woods .10 .05
❑ 76 Dave Bergman .10 .05
❑ 77 Randy Niemann .10 .05
❑ 78 Joe Morgan 1.00 .45
❑ 79 Reggie Jackson 1.25 .55
(See also 650A)
❑ 80 Bucky Dent .25 .11
❑ 81 Tommy John .50 .23
❑ 82 Luis Tiant .25 .11
❑ 83 Rick Cerone .10 .05
❑ 84 Dick Howser MG .25 .11
❑ 85 Lou Piniella .25 .11
❑ 86 Ron Davis .10 .05
❑ 87A Graig Nettles P1 5.00 2.20
ERR (Name on back
misspelled "Craig")
❑ 87B Graig Nettles P2 COR .25 .11
("Graig")
❑ 88 Ron Guidry .25 .11
❑ 89 Rich Gossage .50 .23
❑ 90 Rudy May .10 .05
❑ 91 Gaylord Perry 1.00 .45
❑ 92 Eric Soderholm .10 .05
❑ 93 Bob Watson .25 .11
❑ 94 Bobby Murcer .25 .11
❑ 95 Bobby Brown .10 .05
❑ 96 Jim Spencer .10 .05
❑ 97 Tom Underwood .10 .05
❑ 98 Oscar Gamble .10 .05
❑ 99 Johnny Oates .25 .11
❑ 100 Fred Stanley .10 .05
❑ 101 Ruppert Jones .10 .05
❑ 102 Dennis Werth .10 .05
❑ 103 Joe Lefebvre .10 .05
❑ 104 Brian Doyle .10 .05
❑ 105 Aurelio Rodriguez .10 .05
❑ 106 Doug Bird .10 .05
❑ 107 Mike Griffin .10 .05
❑ 108 Tim Lollar .10 .05
❑ 109 Willie Randolph .25 .11
❑ 110 Steve Garvey .50 .23
❑ 111 Reggie Smith .25 .11
❑ 112 Don Sutton 1.00 .45
❑ 113 Burt Hooton .10 .05
❑ 114A Dave Lopes P1 .50 .23
(Small hand on back)
❑ 114B Dave Lopes P2 .25 .11
(No hand)
❑ 115 Dusty Baker .50 .23
❑ 116 Tom Lasorda MG .25 .11
❑ 117 Bill Russell .25 .11
❑ 118 Jerry Reuss UER .25 .11
("Home:" omitted)
❑ 119 Terry Forster .10 .05
❑ 120A Bob Welch P1 .25 .11
(Name on back
is "Bob")
❑ 120B Bob Welch P2 .50 .23
(Name on back
is "Robert")
❑ 121 Don Stanhouse .10 .05
❑ 122 Rick Monday .25 .11
❑ 123 Derrel Thomas .10 .05
❑ 124 Joe Ferguson .10 .05
❑ 125 Rick Sutcliffe .25 .11
❑ 126A Ron Cey P1 .50 .23
(Small hand on back)
❑ 126B Ron Cey P2 .25 .11
(No hand)
❑ 127 Dave Goltz .10 .05
❑ 128 Jay Johnstone .25 .11
❑ 129 Steve Yeager .10 .05
❑ 130 Gary Weiss .10 .05
❑ 131 Mike Scioscia 1.00 .45
❑ 132 Vic Davalillo .10 .05
❑ 133 Doug Rau .10 .05
❑ 134 Pepe Frias .10 .05
❑ 135 Mickey Hatcher .25 .11
❑ 136 Steve Howe .25 .11
❑ 137 Robert Castillo .10 .05
❑ 138 Gary Thomasson .10 .05
❑ 139 Rudy Law .10 .05
❑ 140 Fernando Valenzuela 2.00 .90
UER (Misspelled
Fernand on card)
❑ 141 Manny Mota .25 .11
❑ 142 Gary Carter 1.00 .45
❑ 143 Steve Rogers .10 .05
❑ 144 Warren Cromartie .10 .05
❑ 145 Andre Dawson 1.00 .45
❑ 146 Larry Parrish .10 .05
❑ 147 Rowland Office .10 .05
❑ 148 Ellis Valentine .10 .05
❑ 149 Dick Williams MG .10 .05
❑ 150 Bill Gullickson .50 .23
❑ 151 Elias Sosa .10 .05
❑ 152 John Tamargo .10 .05
❑ 153 Chris Speier .10 .05
❑ 154 Ron LeFlore .25 .11
❑ 155 Rodney Scott .10 .05
❑ 156 Stan Bahnsen .10 .05
❑ 157 Bill Lee .25 .11
❑ 158 Fred Norman .10 .05
❑ 159 Woodie Fryman .10 .05
❑ 160 David Palmer .10 .05
❑ 161 Jerry White .10 .05
❑ 162 Roberto Ramos .10 .05
❑ 163 John D'Acquisto .10 .05
❑ 164 Tommy Hutton .10 .05
❑ 165 Charlie Lea .10 .05
❑ 166 Scott Sanderson .10 .05
❑ 167 Ken Macha .10 .05
❑ 168 Tony Bernazard .10 .05
❑ 169 Jim Palmer 1.00 .45
❑ 170 Steve Stone .25 .11
❑ 171 Mike Flanagan .25 .11
❑ 172 Al Bumbry .25 .11
❑ 173 Doug DeCinces .25 .11
❑ 174 Scott McGregor .10 .05
❑ 175 Mark Belanger .25 .11
❑ 176 Tim Stoddard .10 .05
❑ 177A Rick Dempsey P1 .50 .23
(Small hand on front)
❑ 177B Rick Dempsey P2 .25 .11
(No hand)
❑ 178 Earl Weaver MG 1.00 .45
❑ 179 Tippy Martinez .10 .05
❑ 180 Dennis Martinez .50 .23
❑ 181 Sammy Stewart .10 .05
❑ 182 Rich Dauer .10 .05
❑ 183 Lee May .25 .11
❑ 184 Eddie Murray 2.00 .90
❑ 185 Benny Ayala .10 .05
❑ 186 John Lowenstein .10 .05
❑ 187 Gary Roenicke .10 .05
❑ 188 Ken Singleton .25 .11
❑ 189 Dan Graham .10 .05
❑ 190 Terry Crowley .10 .05
❑ 191 Kiko Garcia .10 .05
❑ 192 Dave Ford .10 .05
❑ 193 Mark Corey .10 .05
❑ 194 Lenn Sakata .10 .05
❑ 195 Doug DeCinces .25 .11
❑ 196 Johnny Bench 1.25 .55
❑ 197 Dave Concepcion .25 .11
❑ 198 Ray Knight .25 .11

No.	Player		
❑ 199	Ken Griffey	.50	.23
❑ 200	Tom Seaver	1.25	.55
❑ 201	Dave Collins	.10	.05
❑ 202A	George Foster P1 Slugger (Number on back 216)	.50	.23
❑ 202B	George Foster P2 Slugger (Number on back 202)	.50	.23
❑ 203	Junior Kennedy	.10	.05
❑ 204	Frank Pastore	.10	.05
❑ 205	Dan Driessen	.10	.05
❑ 206	Hector Cruz	.10	.05
❑ 207	Paul Moskau	.10	.05
❑ 208	Charlie Leibrandt	.50	.23
❑ 209	Harry Spilman	.10	.05
❑ 210	Joe Price	.10	.05
❑ 211	Tom Hume	.10	.05
❑ 212	Joe Nolan	.10	.05
❑ 213	Doug Bair	.10	.05
❑ 214	Mario Soto	.10	.05
❑ 215A	Bill Bonham P1 (Small hand on back)	.50	.23
❑ 215B	Bill Bonham P2 (No hand)	.10	.05
❑ 216	George Foster (See 202)	.25	.11
❑ 217	Paul Householder	.10	.05
❑ 218	Ron Oester	.10	.05
❑ 219	Sam Mejias	.10	.05
❑ 220	Sheldon Burnside	.10	.05
❑ 221	Carl Yastrzemski	1.00	.45
❑ 222	Jim Rice	.25	.11
❑ 223	Fred Lynn	.25	.11
❑ 224	Carlton Fisk	1.00	.45
❑ 225	Rick Burleson	.10	.05
❑ 226	Dennis Eckersley	1.00	.45
❑ 227	Butch Hobson	.10	.05
❑ 228	Tom Burgmeier	.10	.05
❑ 229	Garry Hancock	.10	.05
❑ 230	Don Zimmer MG	.10	.05
❑ 231	Steve Renko	.10	.05
❑ 232	Dwight Evans	.50	.23
❑ 233	Mike Torrez	.10	.05
❑ 234	Bob Stanley	.10	.05
❑ 235	Jim Dwyer	.10	.05
❑ 236	Dave Stapleton	.10	.05
❑ 237	Glenn Hoffman	.10	.05
❑ 238	Jerry Remy	.10	.05
❑ 239	Dick Drago	.10	.05
❑ 240	Bill Campbell	.10	.05
❑ 241	Tony Perez	1.00	.45
❑ 242	Phil Niekro	1.00	.45
❑ 243	Dale Murphy	1.00	.45
❑ 244	Bob Horner	.25	.11
❑ 245	Jeff Burroughs	.10	.05
❑ 246	Rick Camp	.10	.05
❑ 247	Bobby Cox MG	.25	.11
❑ 248	Bruce Benedict	.10	.05
❑ 249	Gene Garber	.10	.05
❑ 250	Jerry Royster	.10	.05
❑ 251A	Gary Matthews P1 (Small hand on back)	.50	.23
❑ 251B	Gary Matthews P2 (No hand)	.25	.11
❑ 252	Chris Chambliss	.25	.11
❑ 253	Luis Gomez	.10	.05
❑ 254	Bill Nahorodny	.10	.05
❑ 255	Doyle Alexander	.10	.05
❑ 256	Brian Asselstine	.10	.05
❑ 257	Biff Pocoroba	.10	.05
❑ 258	Mike Lum	.10	.05
❑ 259	Charlie Spikes	.10	.05
❑ 260	Glenn Hubbard	.10	.05
❑ 261	Tommy Boggs	.10	.05
❑ 262	Al Hrabosky	.10	.05
❑ 263	Rick Matula	.10	.05
❑ 264	Preston Hanna	.10	.05
❑ 265	Larry Bradford	.10	.05
❑ 266	Rafael Ramirez	.10	.05
❑ 267	Larry McWilliams	.10	.05
❑ 268	Rod Carew	1.00	.45
❑ 269	Bobby Grich	.25	.11
❑ 270	Carney Lansford	.25	.11
❑ 271	Don Baylor	.50	.23
❑ 272	Joe Rudi	.25	.11
❑ 273	Dan Ford	.10	.05
❑ 274	Jim Fregosi MG	.10	.05
❑ 275	Dave Frost	.10	.05
❑ 276	Frank Tanana	.25	.11
❑ 277	Dickie Thon	.25	.11
❑ 278	Jason Thompson	.10	.05
❑ 279	Rick Miller	.10	.05
❑ 280	Bert Campaneris	.25	.11
❑ 281	Tom Donohue	.10	.05
❑ 282	Brian Downing	.25	.11
❑ 283	Fred Patek	.10	.05
❑ 284	Bruce Kison	.10	.05
❑ 285	Dave LaRoche	.10	.05
❑ 286	Don Aase	.10	.05
❑ 287	Jim Barr	.10	.05
❑ 288	Alfredo Martinez	.10	.05
❑ 289	Larry Harlow	.10	.05
❑ 290	Andy Hassler	.10	.05
❑ 291	Dave Kingman	.50	.23
❑ 292	Bill Buckner	.25	.11
❑ 293	Rick Reuschel	.25	.11
❑ 294	Bruce Sutter	.25	.11
❑ 295	Jerry Martin	.10	.05
❑ 296	Scot Thompson	.10	.05
❑ 297	Ivan DeJesus	.10	.05
❑ 298	Steve Dillard	.10	.05
❑ 299	Dick Tidrow	.10	.05
❑ 300	Randy Martz	.10	.05
❑ 301	Lenny Randle	.10	.05
❑ 302	Lynn McGlothen	.10	.05
❑ 303	Cliff Johnson	.10	.05
❑ 304	Tim Blackwell	.10	.05
❑ 305	Dennis Lamp	.10	.05
❑ 306	Bill Caudill	.10	.05
❑ 307	Carlos Lezcano	.10	.05
❑ 308	Jim Tracy	.10	.05
❑ 309	Doug Capilla UER (Cubs on front but Braves on back)	.10	.05
❑ 310	Willie Hernandez	.25	.11
❑ 311	Mike Vail	.10	.05
❑ 312	Mike Krukow	.10	.05
❑ 313	Barry Foote	.10	.05
❑ 314	Larry Biittner	.10	.05
❑ 315	Mike Tyson	.10	.05
❑ 316	Lee Mazzilli	.10	.05
❑ 317	John Stearns	.10	.05
❑ 318	Alex Trevino	.10	.05
❑ 319	Craig Swan	.10	.05
❑ 320	Frank Taveras	.10	.05
❑ 321	Steve Henderson	.10	.05
❑ 322	Neil Allen	.10	.05
❑ 323	Mark Bomback	.10	.05
❑ 324	Mike Jorgensen	.10	.05
❑ 325	Joe Torre MG	.25	.11
❑ 326	Elliott Maddox	.10	.05
❑ 327	Pete Falcone	.10	.05
❑ 328	Ray Burris	.10	.05
❑ 329	Claudell Washington	.10	.05
❑ 330	Doug Flynn	.10	.05
❑ 331	Joel Youngblood	.10	.05
❑ 332	Bill Almon	.10	.05
❑ 333	Tom Hausman	.10	.05
❑ 334	Pat Zachry	.10	.05
❑ 335	Jeff Reardon	1.00	.45
❑ 336	Wally Backman	.25	.11
❑ 337	Dan Norman	.10	.05
❑ 338	Jerry Morales	.10	.05
❑ 339	Ed Farmer	.10	.05
❑ 340	Bob Molinaro	.10	.05
❑ 341	Todd Cruz	.10	.05
❑ 342A	Britt Burns P1 (Small hand on front)	.50	.23
❑ 342B	Britt Burns P2 (No hand)	.25	.11
❑ 343	Kevin Bell	.10	.05
❑ 344	Tony LaRussa MG	.25	.11
❑ 345	Steve Trout	.10	.05
❑ 346	Harold Baines	1.50	.70
❑ 347	Richard Wortham	.10	.05
❑ 348	Wayne Nordhagen	.10	.05
❑ 349	Mike Squires	.10	.05
❑ 350	Lamar Johnson	.10	.05
❑ 351	Rickey Henderson (Most Stolen Bases AL)	1.00	.45
❑ 352	Francisco Barrios	.10	.05
❑ 353	Thad Bosley	.10	.05
❑ 354	Chet Lemon	.10	.05
❑ 355	Bruce Kimm	.10	.05
❑ 356	Richard Dotson	.10	.05
❑ 357	Jim Morrison	.10	.05
❑ 358	Mike Proly	.10	.05
❑ 359	Greg Pryor	.10	.05
❑ 360	Dave Parker	.25	.11
❑ 361	Omar Moreno	.10	.05
❑ 362A	Kent Tekulve P1 (Back "1071 Waterbury" and "1078 Pirates")	.25	.11
❑ 362B	Kent Tekulve P2 ("1971 Waterbury" and "1978 Pirates")	.25	.11
❑ 363	Willie Stargell	1.00	.45
❑ 364	Phil Garner	.25	.11
❑ 365	Ed Ott	.10	.05
❑ 366	Don Robinson	.10	.05
❑ 367	Chuck Tanner MG	.25	.11
❑ 368	Jim Rooker	.10	.05
❑ 369	Dale Berra	.10	.05
❑ 370	Jim Bibby	.10	.05
❑ 371	Steve Nicosia	.10	.05
❑ 372	Mike Easler	.10	.05
❑ 373	Bill Robinson	.25	.11
❑ 374	Lee Lacy	.10	.05
❑ 375	John Candelaria	.25	.11
❑ 376	Manny Sanguillen	.25	.11
❑ 377	Rick Rhoden	.10	.05
❑ 378	Grant Jackson	.10	.05
❑ 379	Tim Foli	.10	.05
❑ 380	Rod Scurry	.10	.05
❑ 381	Bill Madlock	.25	.11
❑ 382A	Kurt Bevacqua P1 ERR (P on cap backwards)	.25	.11
❑ 382B	Kurt Bevacqua P2 COR	.10	.05
❑ 383	Bert Blyleven	.50	.23
❑ 384	Eddie Solomon	.10	.05
❑ 385	Enrique Romo	.10	.05
❑ 386	John Milner	.10	.05
❑ 387	Mike Hargrove	.25	.11
❑ 388	Jorge Orta	.10	.05
❑ 389	Toby Harrah	.25	.11
❑ 390	Tom Veryzer	.10	.05
❑ 391	Miguel Dilone	.10	.05
❑ 392	Dan Spillner	.10	.05
❑ 393	Jack Brohamer	.10	.05
❑ 394	Wayne Garland	.10	.05
❑ 395	Sid Monge	.10	.05
❑ 396	Rick Waits	.10	.05
❑ 397	Joe Charboneau	1.00	.45
❑ 398	Gary Alexander	.10	.05
❑ 399	Jerry Dybzinski	.10	.05
❑ 400	Mike Stanton	.10	.05
❑ 401	Mike Paxton	.10	.05
❑ 402	Gary Gray	.10	.05
❑ 403	Rick Manning	.10	.05
❑ 404	Bo Diaz	.10	.05
❑ 405	Ron Hassey	.10	.05
❑ 406	Ross Grimsley	.10	.05
❑ 407	Victor Cruz	.10	.05
❑ 408	Len Barker	.10	.05
❑ 409	Bob Bailor	.10	.05
❑ 410	Otto Velez	.10	.05
❑ 411	Ernie Whitt	.10	.05
❑ 412	Jim Clancy	.10	.05
❑ 413	Barry Bonnell	.10	.05
❑ 414	Dave Stieb	.25	.11
❑ 415	Damaso Garcia	.10	.05
❑ 416	John Mayberry	.10	.05
❑ 417	Roy Howell	.10	.05
❑ 418	Danny Ainge	2.00	.90
❑ 419A	Jesse Jefferson P1 (Back says Pirates)	.10	.05
❑ 419B	Jesse Jefferson P2 (Back says Pirates)	.10	.05
❑ 419C	Jesse Jefferson P3 (Back says Blue Jays)	1.00	.45
❑ 420	Joey McLaughlin	.10	.05
❑ 421	Lloyd Moseby	.25	.11
❑ 422	Alvis Woods	.10	.05

❑ 423 Garth Iorg .10 .05
❑ 424 Doug Ault .10 .05
❑ 425 Ken Schrom .10 .05
❑ 426 Mike Willis .10 .05
❑ 427 Steve Braun .10 .05
❑ 428 Bob Davis .10 .05
❑ 429 Jerry Garvin .10 .05
❑ 430 Alfredo Griffin .10 .05
❑ 431 Bob Mattick MG .10 .05
❑ 432 Vida Blue .25 .11
❑ 433 Jack Clark .25 .11
❑ 434 Willie McCovey 1.00 .45
❑ 435 Mike Ivie .10 .05
❑ 436A Darrel Evans P1 ERR .50 .23
(Name on front "Darrel")
❑ 436B Darrell Evans P2 COR .50 .23
(Name on front "Darrell")
❑ 437 Terry Whitfield .10 .05
❑ 438 Rennie Stennett .10 .05
❑ 439 John Montefusco .10 .05
❑ 440 Jim Wohlford .10 .05
❑ 441 Bill North .10 .05
❑ 442 Milt May .10 .05
❑ 443 Max Venable .10 .05
❑ 444 Ed Whitson .10 .05
❑ 445 Al Holland .10 .05
❑ 446 Randy Moffitt .10 .05
❑ 447 Bob Knepper .10 .05
❑ 448 Gary Lavelle .10 .05
❑ 449 Greg Minton .10 .05
❑ 450 Johnnie LeMaster .10 .05
❑ 451 Larry Herndon .10 .05
❑ 452 Rich Murray .10 .05
❑ 453 Joe Pettini .10 .05
❑ 454 Allen Ripley .10 .05
❑ 455 Dennis Littlejohn .10 .05
❑ 456 Tom Griffin .10 .05
❑ 457 Alan Hargesheimer .10 .05
❑ 458 Joe Strain .10 .05
❑ 459 Steve Kemp .10 .05
❑ 460 Sparky Anderson MG .25 .11
❑ 461 Alan Trammell 1.00 .45
❑ 462 Mark Fidrych 1.00 .45
❑ 463 Lou Whitaker 1.00 .45
❑ 464 Dave Rozema .10 .05
❑ 465 Milt Wilcox .10 .05
❑ 466 Champ Summers .10 .05
❑ 467 Lance Parrish .25 .11
❑ 468 Dan Petry .10 .05
❑ 469 Pat Underwood .10 .05
❑ 470 Rick Peters .10 .05
❑ 471 Al Cowens .10 .05
❑ 472 John Wockenfuss .10 .05
❑ 473 Tom Brookens .10 .05
❑ 474 Richie Hebner .10 .05
❑ 475 Jack Morris 1.00 .45
❑ 476 Jim Lentine .10 .05
❑ 477 Bruce Robbins .10 .05
❑ 478 Mark Wagner .10 .05
❑ 479 Tim Corcoran .10 .05
❑ 480A Stan Papi P1 .25 .11
(Front as Pitcher)
❑ 480B Stan Papi P2 .10 .05
(Front as Shortstop)
❑ 481 Kirk Gibson 2.00 .90
❑ 482 Dan Schatzeder .10 .05
❑ 483A Amos Otis P1 .25 .11
(See card 32)
❑ 483B Amos Otis P2 .25 .11
(See card 32)
❑ 484 Dave Winfield 1.00 .45
❑ 485 Rollie Fingers 1.00 .45
❑ 486 Gene Richards .10 .05
❑ 487 Randy Jones .10 .05
❑ 488 Ozzie Smith 4.00 1.80
❑ 489 Gene Tenace .25 .11
❑ 490 Bill Fahey .10 .05
❑ 491 John Curtis .10 .05
❑ 492 Dave Cash .10 .05
❑ 493A Tim Flannery P1 .25 .11
(Batting right)
❑ 493B Tim Flannery P2 .10 .05
(Batting left)
❑ 494 Jerry Mumphrey .10 .05
❑ 495 Bob Shirley .10 .05
❑ 496 Steve Mura .10 .05
❑ 497 Eric Rasmussen .10 .05
❑ 498 Broderick Perkins .10 .05
❑ 499 Barry Evans .10 .05
❑ 500 Chuck Baker .10 .05
❑ 501 Luis Salazar .10 .05
❑ 502 Gary Lucas .10 .05
❑ 503 Mike Armstrong .10 .05
❑ 504 Jerry Turner .10 .05
❑ 505 Dennis Kinney .10 .05
❑ 506 Willie Montanez UER .10 .05
(Misspelled Willy on card front)
❑ 507 Gorman Thomas .25 .11
❑ 508 Ben Oglivie .25 .11
❑ 509 Larry Hisle .10 .05
❑ 510 Sal Bando .25 .11
❑ 511 Robin Yount 1.25 .55
❑ 512 Mike Caldwell .10 .05
❑ 513 Sixto Lezcano .10 .05
❑ 514A Bill Travers P1 ERR .25 .11
("Jerry Augustine" with Augustine back)
❑ 514B Bill Travers P2 COR .10 .05
❑ 515 Paul Molitor 2.00 .90
❑ 516 Moose Haas .10 .05
❑ 517 Bill Castro .10 .05
❑ 518 Jim Slaton .10 .05
❑ 519 Lary Sorensen .10 .05
❑ 520 Bob McClure .10 .05
❑ 521 Charlie Moore .10 .05
❑ 522 Jim Gantner .25 .11
❑ 523 Reggie Cleveland .10 .05
❑ 524 Don Money .10 .05
❑ 525 Bill Travers .10 .05
❑ 526 Buck Martinez .10 .05
❑ 527 Dick Davis .10 .05
❑ 528 Ted Simmons .25 .11
❑ 529 Garry Templeton .10 .05
❑ 530 Ken Reitz .10 .05
❑ 531 Tony Scott .10 .05
❑ 532 Ken Oberkfell .10 .05
❑ 533 Bob Sykes .10 .05
❑ 534 Keith Smith .10 .05
❑ 535 John Littlefield .10 .05
❑ 536 Jim Kaat .25 .11
❑ 537 Bob Forsch .10 .05
❑ 538 Mike Phillips .10 .05
❑ 539 Terry Landrum .10 .05
❑ 540 Leon Durham .25 .11
❑ 541 Terry Kennedy .10 .05
❑ 542 George Hendrick .10 .05
❑ 543 Dane Iorg .10 .05
❑ 544 Mark Littell .10 .05
❑ 545 Keith Hernandez .25 .11
❑ 546 Silvio Martinez .10 .05
❑ 547A Don Hood P1 ERR .25 .11
("Pete Vuckovich" with Vuckovich back)
❑ 547B Don Hood P2 COR .10 .05
❑ 548 Bobby Bonds .25 .11
❑ 549 Mike Ramsey .10 .05
❑ 550 Tom Herr .25 .11
❑ 551 Roy Smalley .10 .05
❑ 552 Jerry Koosman .25 .11
❑ 553 Ken Landreaux .10 .05
❑ 554 John Castino .10 .05
❑ 555 Doug Corbett .10 .05
❑ 556 Bombo Rivera .10 .05
❑ 557 Ron Jackson .10 .05
❑ 558 Butch Wynegar .10 .05
❑ 559 Hosken Powell .10 .05
❑ 560 Pete Redfern .10 .05
❑ 561 Roger Erickson .10 .05
❑ 562 Glenn Adams .10 .05
❑ 563 Rick Sofield .10 .05
❑ 564 Geoff Zahn .10 .05
❑ 565 Pete Mackanin .10 .05
❑ 566 Mike Cubbage .10 .05
❑ 567 Darrell Jackson .10 .05
❑ 568 Dave Edwards .10 .05
❑ 569 Rob Wilfong .10 .05
❑ 570 Sal Butera .10 .05
❑ 571 Jose Morales .10 .05
❑ 572 Rick Langford .10 .05
❑ 573 Mike Norris .10 .05
❑ 574 Rickey Henderson 2.50 1.10
❑ 575 Tony Armas .25 .11
❑ 576 Dave Revering .10 .05
❑ 577 Jeff Newman .10 .05
❑ 578 Bob Lacey .10 .05
❑ 579 Brian Kingman .10 .05
❑ 580 Mitchell Page .10 .05
❑ 581 Billy Martin MG .50 .23
❑ 582 Rob Picciolo .10 .05
❑ 583 Mike Heath .10 .05
❑ 584 Mickey Klutts .10 .05
❑ 585 Orlando Gonzalez .10 .05
❑ 586 Mike Davis .10 .05
❑ 587 Wayne Gross .10 .05
❑ 588 Matt Keough .10 .05
❑ 589 Steve McCatty .10 .05
❑ 590 Dwayne Murphy .10 .05
❑ 591 Mario Guerrero .10 .05
❑ 592 Dave McKay .10 .05
❑ 593 Jim Essian .10 .05
❑ 594 Dave Heaverlo .10 .05
❑ 595 Maury Wills MG .25 .11
❑ 596 Juan Beniquez .10 .05
❑ 597 Rodney Craig .10 .05
❑ 598 Jim Anderson .10 .05
❑ 599 Floyd Bannister .10 .05
❑ 600 Bruce Bochte .10 .05
❑ 601 Julio Cruz .10 .05
❑ 602 Ted Cox .10 .05
❑ 603 Dan Meyer .10 .05
❑ 604 Larry Cox .10 .05
❑ 605 Bill Stein .10 .05
❑ 606 Steve Garvey .50 .23
(Most Hits NL)
❑ 607 Dave Roberts .10 .05
❑ 608 Leon Roberts .10 .05
❑ 609 Reggie Walton .10 .05
❑ 610 Dave Edler .10 .05
❑ 611 Larry Milbourne .10 .05
❑ 612 Kim Allen .10 .05
❑ 613 Mario Mendoza .10 .05
❑ 614 Tom Paciorek .25 .11
❑ 615 Glenn Abbott .10 .05
❑ 616 Joe Simpson .10 .05
❑ 617 Mickey Rivers .25 .11
❑ 618 Jim Kern .10 .05
❑ 619 Jim Sundberg .25 .11
❑ 620 Richie Zisk .10 .05
❑ 621 Jon Matlack .10 .05
❑ 622 Ferguson Jenkins 1.00 .45
❑ 623 Pat Corrales MG .10 .05
❑ 624 Ed Figueroa .10 .05
❑ 625 Buddy Bell .25 .11
❑ 626 Al Oliver .25 .11
❑ 627 Doc Medich .10 .05
❑ 628 Bump Wills .10 .05
❑ 629 Rusty Staub .25 .11
❑ 630 Pat Putnam .10 .05
❑ 631 John Grubb .10 .05
❑ 632 Danny Darwin .25 .11
❑ 633 Ken Clay .10 .05
❑ 634 Jim Norris .10 .05
❑ 635 John Butcher .10 .05
❑ 636 Dave Roberts .10 .05
❑ 637 Billy Sample .10 .05
❑ 638 Carl Yastrzemski 1.00 .45
❑ 639 Cecil Cooper .25 .11
❑ 640 Mike Schmidt P1 1.25 .55
(Portrait; "Third Base"; number on back 5)
❑ 640B Mike Schmidt P2 2.00 .90
("1980 Home Run King"; 640 on back)
❑ 641A CL: Phils/Royals P1 .25 .11
41 is Hal McRae
❑ 641B CL: Phils/Royals P2 .25 .11
(41 is Hal McRae, Double Threat)
❑ 642 CL: Astros/Yankees .10 .05
❑ 643 CL: Expos/Dodgers .10 .05
❑ 644A CL: Reds/Orioles P1 .25 .11
(202 is George Foster;

Joe Nolan pitcher, should be catcher)		
❑ 644B CL: Reds/Orioles P2 (202 is Foster Slugger; Joe Nolan pitcher, should be catcher)	.25	.11
❑ 645 Pete Rose Larry Bowa Mike Schmidt Triple Threat P1 (No number on back)	1.25	.55
❑ 645B Pete Rose Larry Bowa Mike Schmidt Triple Threat P2 (Back numbered 645)	2.50	1.10
❑ 646 CL: Braves/Red Sox	.10	.05
❑ 647 CL: Cubs/Angels	.10	.05
❑ 648 CL: Mets/White Sox	.10	.05
❑ 649 CL: Indians/Pirates	.10	.05
❑ 650 Reggie Jackson Mr. Baseball P1 (Number on back 79)	1.25	.55
❑ 650B Reggie Jackson Mr. Baseball P2 (Number on back 650)	1.25	.55
❑ 651 CL: Giants/Blue Jays	.10	.05
❑ 652A CL: Tigers/Padres P1 (483 is listed)	.25	.11
❑ 652B CL: Tigers/Padres P2 (483 is deleted)	.25	.11
❑ 653A Willie Wilson P1 Most Hits Most Runs (Number on back 29)	.25	.11
❑ 653B Willie Wilson P2 Most Hits Most Runs (Number on back 653)	.25	.11
❑ 654A CL:Brewers/Cards P1 (514 Jerry Augustine; 547 Pete Vuckovich)	.25	.11
❑ 654B CL:Brewers/Cards P2 (514 Billy Travers; 547 Don Hood)	.25	.11
❑ 655 George Brett P1 .390 Average (Number on back 28)	2.50	1.10
❑ 655B George Brett P2 .390 Average (Number on back 655)	4.00	1.80
❑ 656 CL: Twins/Oakland A's	.25	.11
❑ 657A Tug McGraw P1 Game Saver (Number on back 7)	.25	.11
❑ 657B Tug McGraw P2 Game Saver (Number on back 657)	.25	.11
❑ 658 CL: Rangers/Mariners	.10	.05
❑ 659A Checklist P1 of Special Cards (Last lines on front, Wilson Most Hits)	.10	.05
❑ 659B Checklist P2 of Special Cards (Last lines on front, Otis Series Starter)	.10	.05
❑ 660 Steve Carlton P1 Golden Arm (Number on back 660 Back 1066 Cardinals)	1.00	.45
❑ 660B Steve Carlton P2 Golden Arm (1966 Cardinals)	1.50	.70

1982 Fleer

	NRMT	VG-E
COMPLETE SET (660)	60.00	27.00
COMMON CARD (1-660)	.10	.05
❑ 1 Dusty Baker	.40	.18
❑ 2 Robert Castillo	.10	.05
❑ 3 Ron Cey	.20	.09
❑ 4 Terry Forster	.10	.05
❑ 5 Steve Garvey	.40	.18
❑ 6 Dave Goltz	.10	.05
❑ 7 Pedro Guerrero	.20	.09

❑ 8 Burt Hooton	.10	.05
❑ 9 Steve Howe	.10	.05
❑ 10 Jay Johnstone	.20	.09
❑ 11 Ken Landreaux	.10	.05
❑ 12 Dave Lopes	.20	.09
❑ 13 Mike A. Marshall	.20	.09
❑ 14 Bobby Mitchell	.10	.05
❑ 15 Rick Monday	.10	.05
❑ 16 Tom Niedenfuer	.10	.05
❑ 17 Ted Power	.10	.05
❑ 18 Jerry Reuss UER ("Home:" omitted)	.20	.09
❑ 19 Ron Roenicke	.10	.05
❑ 20 Bill Russell	.20	.09
❑ 21 Steve Sax	.75	.35
❑ 22 Mike Scioscia	.20	.09
❑ 23 Reggie Smith	.20	.09
❑ 24 Dave Stewart	1.00	.45
❑ 25 Rick Sutcliffe	.20	.09
❑ 26 Derrel Thomas	.10	.05
❑ 27 Fernando Valenzuela	.75	.35
❑ 28 Bob Welch	.20	.09
❑ 29 Steve Yeager	.10	.05
❑ 30 Bobby Brown	.10	.05
❑ 31 Rick Cerone	.10	.05
❑ 32 Ron Davis	.10	.05
❑ 33 Bucky Dent	.20	.09
❑ 34 Barry Foote	.10	.05
❑ 35 George Frazier	.10	.05
❑ 36 Oscar Gamble	.10	.05
❑ 37 Rich Gossage	.40	.18
❑ 38 Ron Guidry	.20	.09
❑ 39 Reggie Jackson	1.00	.45
❑ 40 Tommy John	.40	.18
❑ 41 Rudy May	.10	.05
❑ 42 Larry Milbourne	.10	.05
❑ 43 Jerry Mumphrey	.10	.05
❑ 44 Bobby Murcer	.20	.09
❑ 45 Gene Nelson	.10	.05
❑ 46 Graig Nettles	.20	.09
❑ 47 Johnny Oates	.20	.09
❑ 48 Lou Piniella	.20	.09
❑ 49 Willie Randolph	.20	.09
❑ 50 Rick Reuschel	.20	.09
❑ 51 Dave Revering	.10	.05
❑ 52 Dave Righetti	.75	.35
❑ 53 Aurelio Rodriguez	.10	.05
❑ 54 Bob Watson	.20	.09
❑ 55 Dennis Werth	.10	.05
❑ 56 Dave Winfield	.75	.35
❑ 57 Johnny Bench	1.00	.45
❑ 58 Bruce Berenyi	.10	.05
❑ 59 Larry Biittner	.10	.05
❑ 60 Scott Brown	.10	.05
❑ 61 Dave Collins	.10	.05
❑ 62 Geoff Combe	.10	.05
❑ 63 Dave Concepcion	.20	.09
❑ 64 Dan Driessen	.10	.05
❑ 65 Joe Edelen	.10	.05
❑ 66 George Foster	.20	.09
❑ 67 Ken Griffey	.20	.09
❑ 68 Paul Householder	.10	.05
❑ 69 Tom Hume	.10	.05
❑ 70 Junior Kennedy	.10	.05
❑ 71 Ray Knight	.20	.09
❑ 72 Mike LaCoss	.10	.05
❑ 73 Rafael Landestoy	.10	.05
❑ 74 Charlie Leibrandt	.10	.05
❑ 75 Sam Mejias	.10	.05
❑ 76 Paul Moskau	.10	.05
❑ 77 Joe Nolan	.10	.05
❑ 78 Mike O'Berry	.10	.05
❑ 79 Ron Oester	.10	.05
❑ 80 Frank Pastore	.10	.05
❑ 81 Joe Price	.10	.05
❑ 82 Tom Seaver	1.00	.45
❑ 83 Mario Soto	.10	.05
❑ 84 Mike Vail	.10	.05
❑ 85 Tony Armas	.10	.05
❑ 86 Shooty Babitt	.10	.05
❑ 87 Dave Beard	.10	.05
❑ 88 Rick Bosetti	.10	.05
❑ 89 Keith Drumwright	.10	.05
❑ 90 Wayne Gross	.10	.05
❑ 91 Mike Heath	.10	.05
❑ 92 Rickey Henderson	1.50	.70
❑ 93 Cliff Johnson	.10	.05
❑ 94 Jeff Jones	.10	.05
❑ 95 Matt Keough	.10	.05
❑ 96 Brian Kingman	.10	.05
❑ 97 Mickey Klutts	.10	.05
❑ 98 Rick Langford	.10	.05
❑ 99 Steve McCatty	.10	.05
❑ 100 Dave McKay	.10	.05
❑ 101 Dwayne Murphy	.10	.05
❑ 102 Jeff Newman	.10	.05
❑ 103 Mike Norris	.10	.05
❑ 104 Bob Owchinko	.10	.05
❑ 105 Mitchell Page	.10	.05
❑ 106 Rob Picciolo	.10	.05
❑ 107 Jim Spencer	.10	.05
❑ 108 Fred Stanley	.10	.05
❑ 109 Tom Underwood	.10	.05
❑ 110 Joaquin Andujar	.20	.09
❑ 111 Steve Braun	.10	.05
❑ 112 Bob Forsch	.10	.05
❑ 113 George Hendrick	.10	.05
❑ 114 Keith Hernandez	.20	.09
❑ 115 Tom Herr	.20	.09
❑ 116 Dane Iorg	.10	.05
❑ 117 Jim Kaat	.20	.09
❑ 118 Tito Landrum	.10	.05
❑ 119 Sixto Lezcano	.10	.05
❑ 120 Mark Littell	.10	.05
❑ 121 John Martin	.10	.05
❑ 122 Silvio Martinez	.10	.05
❑ 123 Ken Oberkfell	.10	.05
❑ 124 Darrell Porter	.20	.09
❑ 125 Mike Ramsey	.10	.05
❑ 126 Orlando Sanchez	.10	.05
❑ 127 Bob Shirley	.10	.05
❑ 128 Lary Sorensen	.10	.05
❑ 129 Bruce Sutter	.20	.09
❑ 130 Bob Sykes	.10	.05
❑ 131 Garry Templeton	.10	.05
❑ 132 Gene Tenace	.20	.09
❑ 133 Jerry Augustine	.10	.05
❑ 134 Sal Bando	.20	.09
❑ 135 Mark Brouhard	.10	.05
❑ 136 Mike Caldwell	.10	.05
❑ 137 Reggie Cleveland	.10	.05
❑ 138 Cecil Cooper	.20	.09
❑ 139 Jamie Easterly	.10	.05
❑ 140 Marshall Edwards	.10	.05
❑ 141 Rollie Fingers	.75	.35
❑ 142 Jim Gantner	.20	.09
❑ 143 Moose Haas	.10	.05
❑ 144 Larry Hisle	.10	.05
❑ 145 Roy Howell	.10	.05
❑ 146 Rickey Keeton	.10	.05
❑ 147 Randy Lerch	.10	.05
❑ 148 Paul Molitor	1.00	.45
❑ 149 Don Money	.10	.05
❑ 150 Charlie Moore	.10	.05
❑ 151 Ben Oglivie	.20	.09
❑ 152 Ted Simmons	.20	.09
❑ 153 Jim Slaton	.10	.05
❑ 154 Gorman Thomas	.20	.09
❑ 155 Robin Yount	.75	.35
❑ 156 Pete Vuckovich (Should precede Yount in the team order)	.10	.05
❑ 157 Benny Ayala	.10	.05

	No.	Player		
❑	158	Mark Belanger	.20	.09
❑	159	Al Bumbry	.20	.09
❑	160	Terry Crowley	.10	.05
❑	161	Rich Dauer	.10	.05
❑	162	Doug DeCinces	.20	.09
❑	163	Rick Dempsey	.20	.09
❑	164	Jim Dwyer	.10	.05
❑	165	Mike Flanagan	.20	.09
❑	166	Dave Ford	.10	.05
❑	167	Dan Graham	.10	.05
❑	168	Wayne Krenchicki	.10	.05
❑	169	John Lowenstein	.10	.05
❑	170	Dennis Martinez	.40	.18
❑	171	Tippy Martinez	.10	.05
❑	172	Scott McGregor	.10	.05
❑	173	Jose Morales	.10	.05
❑	174	Eddie Murray	1.00	.45
❑	175	Jim Palmer	.75	.35
❑	176	Cal Ripken (Fleer Ripken cards from 1982 through 1993 erroneously have 22 games played in 1981;not 23.)	40.00	18.00
❑	177	Gary Roenicke	.10	.05
❑	178	Lenn Sakata	.10	.05
❑	179	Ken Singleton	.20	.09
❑	180	Sammy Stewart	.10	.05
❑	181	Tim Stoddard	.10	.05
❑	182	Steve Stone	.20	.09
❑	183	Stan Bahnsen	.10	.05
❑	184	Ray Burris	.10	.05
❑	185	Gary Carter	.75	.35
❑	186	Warren Cromartie	.10	.05
❑	187	Andre Dawson	.75	.35
❑	188	Terry Francona	.10	.05
❑	189	Woodie Fryman	.10	.05
❑	190	Bill Gullickson	.10	.05
❑	191	Grant Jackson	.10	.05
❑	192	Wallace Johnson	.10	.05
❑	193	Charlie Lea	.10	.05
❑	194	Bill Lee	.20	.09
❑	195	Jerry Manuel	.10	.05
❑	196	Brad Mills	.10	.05
❑	197	John Milner	.10	.05
❑	198	Rowland Office	.10	.05
❑	199	David Palmer	.10	.05
❑	200	Larry Parrish	.10	.05
❑	201	Mike Phillips	.10	.05
❑	202	Tim Raines	.75	.35
❑	203	Bobby Ramos	.10	.05
❑	204	Jeff Reardon	.40	.18
❑	205	Steve Rogers	.10	.05
❑	206	Scott Sanderson	.10	.05
❑	207	Rodney Scott UER (Photo actually Tim Raines)	.40	.18
❑	208	Elias Sosa	.10	.05
❑	209	Chris Speier	.10	.05
❑	210	Tim Wallach	.40	.18
❑	211	Jerry White	.10	.05
❑	212	Alan Ashby	.10	.05
❑	213	Cesar Cedeno	.20	.09
❑	214	Jose Cruz	.20	.09
❑	215	Kiko Garcia	.10	.05
❑	216	Phil Garner	.20	.09
❑	217	Danny Heep	.10	.05
❑	218	Art Howe	.20	.09
❑	219	Bob Knepper	.10	.05
❑	220	Frank LaCorte	.10	.05
❑	221	Joe Niekro	.20	.09
❑	222	Joe Pittman	.10	.05
❑	223	Terry Puhl	.10	.05
❑	224	Luis Pujols	.10	.05
❑	225	Craig Reynolds	.10	.05
❑	226	J.R. Richard	.20	.09
❑	227	Dave Roberts	.10	.05
❑	228	Vern Ruhle	.10	.05
❑	229	Nolan Ryan	5.00	2.20
❑	230	Joe Sambito	.10	.05
❑	231	Tony Scott	.10	.05
❑	232	Dave Smith	.10	.05
❑	233	Harry Spilman	.10	.05
❑	234	Don Sutton	.75	.35
❑	235	Dickie Thon	.10	.05
❑	236	Denny Walling	.10	.05
❑	237	Gary Woods	.10	.05
❑	238	Luis Aguayo	.10	.05
❑	239	Ramon Aviles	.10	.05
❑	240	Bob Boone	.20	.09
❑	241	Larry Bowa	.20	.09
❑	242	Warren Brusstar	.10	.05
❑	243	Steve Carlton	.75	.35
❑	244	Larry Christenson	.10	.05
❑	245	Dick Davis	.10	.05
❑	246	Greg Gross	.10	.05
❑	247	Sparky Lyle	.20	.09
❑	248	Garry Maddox	.10	.05
❑	249	Gary Matthews	.20	.09
❑	250	Bake McBride	.10	.05
❑	251	Tug McGraw	.20	.09
❑	252	Keith Moreland	.10	.05
❑	253	Dickie Noles	.10	.05
❑	254	Mike Proly	.10	.05
❑	255	Ron Reed	.10	.05
❑	256	Pete Rose	1.00	.45
❑	257	Dick Ruthven	.10	.05
❑	258	Mike Schmidt	1.00	.45
❑	259	Lonnie Smith	.20	.09
❑	260	Manny Trillo	.10	.05
❑	261	Del Unser	.10	.05
❑	262	George Vukovich	.10	.05
❑	263	Tom Brookens	.10	.05
❑	264	George Cappuzzello	.10	.05
❑	265	Marty Castillo	.10	.05
❑	266	Al Cowens	.10	.05
❑	267	Kirk Gibson	.75	.35
❑	268	Richie Hebner	.20	.09
❑	269	Ron Jackson	.10	.05
❑	270	Lynn Jones	.10	.05
❑	271	Steve Kemp	.10	.05
❑	272	Rick Leach	.10	.05
❑	273	Aurelio Lopez	.10	.05
❑	274	Jack Morris	.20	.09
❑	275	Kevin Saucier	.10	.05
❑	276	Lance Parrish	.40	.18
❑	277	Rick Peters	.10	.05
❑	278	Dan Petry	.10	.05
❑	279	Dave Rozema	.10	.05
❑	280	Stan Papi	.10	.05
❑	281	Dan Schatzeder	.10	.05
❑	282	Champ Summers	.10	.05
❑	283	Alan Trammell	.75	.35
❑	284	Lou Whitaker	.75	.35
❑	285	Milt Wilcox	.10	.05
❑	286	John Wockenfuss	.10	.05
❑	287	Gary Allenson	.10	.05
❑	288	Tom Burgmeier	.10	.05
❑	289	Bill Campbell	.10	.05
❑	290	Mark Clear	.10	.05
❑	291	Steve Crawford	.10	.05
❑	292	Dennis Eckersley	.75	.35
❑	293	Dwight Evans	.40	.18
❑	294	Rich Gedman	.20	.09
❑	295	Garry Hancock	.10	.05
❑	296	Glenn Hoffman	.10	.05
❑	297	Bruce Hurst	.10	.05
❑	298	Carney Lansford	.20	.09
❑	299	Rick Miller	.10	.05
❑	300	Reid Nichols	.10	.05
❑	301	Bob Ojeda	.40	.18
❑	302	Tony Perez	.75	.35
❑	303	Chuck Rainey	.10	.05
❑	304	Jerry Remy	.10	.05
❑	305	Jim Rice	.20	.09
❑	306	Joe Rudi	.10	.05
❑	307	Bob Stanley	.10	.05
❑	308	Dave Stapleton	.10	.05
❑	309	Frank Tanana	.20	.09
❑	310	Mike Torrez	.10	.05
❑	311	John Tudor	.10	.05
❑	312	Carl Yastrzemski	.75	.35
❑	313	Buddy Bell	.20	.09
❑	314	Steve Comer	.10	.05
❑	315	Danny Darwin	.20	.09
❑	316	John Ellis	.10	.05
❑	317	John Grubb	.10	.05
❑	318	Rick Honeycutt	.10	.05
❑	319	Charlie Hough	.20	.09
❑	320	Ferguson Jenkins	.75	.35
❑	321	John Henry Johnson	.10	.05
❑	322	Jim Kern	.10	.05
❑	323	Jon Matlack	.10	.05
❑	324	Doc Medich	.10	.05
❑	325	Mario Mendoza	.10	.05
❑	326	Al Oliver	.20	.09
❑	327	Pat Putnam	.10	.05
❑	328	Mickey Rivers	.10	.05
❑	329	Leon Roberts	.10	.05
❑	330	Billy Sample	.10	.05
❑	331	Bill Stein	.10	.05
❑	332	Jim Sundberg	.20	.09
❑	333	Mark Wagner	.10	.05
❑	334	Bump Wills	.10	.05
❑	335	Bill Almon	.10	.05
❑	336	Harold Baines	.75	.35
❑	337	Ross Baumgarten	.10	.05
❑	338	Tony Bernazard	.10	.05
❑	339	Britt Burns	.10	.05
❑	340	Richard Dotson	.10	.05
❑	341	Jim Essian	.10	.05
❑	342	Ed Farmer	.10	.05
❑	343	Carlton Fisk	.75	.35
❑	344	Kevin Hickey	.10	.05
❑	345	LaMarr Hoyt	.10	.05
❑	346	Lamar Johnson	.10	.05
❑	347	Jerry Koosman	.20	.09
❑	348	Rusty Kuntz	.10	.05
❑	349	Dennis Lamp	.10	.05
❑	350	Ron LeFlore	.20	.09
❑	351	Chet Lemon	.10	.05
❑	352	Greg Luzinski	.20	.09
❑	353	Bob Molinaro	.10	.05
❑	354	Jim Morrison	.10	.05
❑	355	Wayne Nordhagen	.10	.05
❑	356	Greg Pryor	.10	.05
❑	357	Mike Squires	.10	.05
❑	358	Steve Trout	.10	.05
❑	359	Alan Bannister	.10	.05
❑	360	Len Barker	.10	.05
❑	361	Bert Blyleven	.40	.18
❑	362	Joe Charboneau	.20	.09
❑	363	John Denny	.10	.05
❑	364	Bo Diaz	.10	.05
❑	365	Miguel Dilone	.10	.05
❑	366	Jerry Dybzinski	.10	.05
❑	367	Wayne Garland	.10	.05
❑	368	Mike Hargrove	.20	.09
❑	369	Toby Harrah	.20	.09
❑	370	Ron Hassey	.10	.05
❑	371	Von Hayes	.20	.09
❑	372	Pat Kelly	.10	.05
❑	373	Duane Kuiper	.10	.05
❑	374	Rick Manning	.10	.05
❑	375	Sid Monge	.10	.05
❑	376	Jorge Orta	.10	.05
❑	377	Dave Rosello	.10	.05
❑	378	Dan Spillner	.10	.05
❑	379	Mike Stanton	.10	.05
❑	380	Andre Thornton	.10	.05
❑	381	Tom Veryzer	.10	.05
❑	382	Rick Waits	.10	.05
❑	383	Doyle Alexander	.10	.05
❑	384	Vida Blue	.20	.09
❑	385	Fred Breining	.10	.05
❑	386	Enos Cabell	.10	.05
❑	387	Jack Clark	.20	.09
❑	388	Darrell Evans	.20	.09
❑	389	Tom Griffin	.10	.05
❑	390	Larry Herndon	.10	.05
❑	391	Al Holland	.10	.05
❑	392	Gary Lavelle	.10	.05
❑	393	Johnnie LeMaster	.10	.05
❑	394	Jerry Martin	.10	.05
❑	395	Milt May	.10	.05
❑	396	Greg Minton	.10	.05
❑	397	Joe Morgan	.75	.35
❑	398	Joe Pettini	.10	.05
❑	399	Allen Ripley	.10	.05
❑	400	Billy Smith	.10	.05
❑	401	Rennie Stennett	.10	.05
❑	402	Ed Whitson	.10	.05
❑	403	Jim Wohlford	.10	.05
❑	404	Willie Aikens	.10	.05
❑	405	George Brett	1.50	.70
❑	406	Ken Brett	.10	.05
❑	407	Dave Chalk	.10	.05

❑ 408 Rich Gale .10 .05
❑ 409 Cesar Geronimo .10 .05
❑ 410 Larry Gura .10 .05
❑ 411 Clint Hurdle .10 .05
❑ 412 Mike Jones .10 .05
❑ 413 Dennis Leonard .10 .05
❑ 414 Renie Martin .10 .05
❑ 415 Lee May .20 .09
❑ 416 Hal McRae .20 .09
❑ 417 Darryl Motley .10 .05
❑ 418 Rance Mulliniks .10 .05
❑ 419 Amos Otis .20 .09
❑ 420 Ken Phelps .10 .05
❑ 421 Jamie Quirk .10 .05
❑ 422 Dan Quisenberry .20 .09
❑ 423 Paul Splittorff .10 .05
❑ 424 U.L. Washington .10 .05
❑ 425 John Wathan .10 .05
❑ 426 Frank White .20 .09
❑ 427 Willie Wilson .20 .09
❑ 428 Brian Asselstine .10 .05
❑ 429 Bruce Benedict .10 .05
❑ 430 Tommy Boggs .10 .05
❑ 431 Larry Bradford .10 .05
❑ 432 Rick Camp .10 .05
❑ 433 Chris Chambliss .20 .09
❑ 434 Gene Garber .10 .05
❑ 435 Preston Hanna .10 .05
❑ 436 Bob Horner .20 .09
❑ 437 Glenn Hubbard .10 .05
❑ 438A All Hrabosky ERR 10.00 4.50
(Height 5'1"
All on reverse)
❑ 438B Al Hrabosky ERR .40 .18
(Height 5'1")
❑ 438C Al Hrabosky .20 .09
(Height 5'10")
❑ 439 Rufino Linares .10 .05
❑ 440 Rick Mahler .10 .05
❑ 441 Ed Miller .10 .05
❑ 442 John Montefusco .10 .05
❑ 443 Dale Murphy .75 .35
❑ 444 Phil Niekro .75 .35
❑ 445 Gaylord Perry .75 .35
❑ 446 Biff Pocoroba .10 .05
❑ 447 Rafael Ramirez .10 .05
❑ 448 Jerry Royster .10 .05
❑ 449 Claudell Washington .10 .05
❑ 450 Don Aase .10 .05
❑ 451 Don Baylor .40 .18
❑ 452 Juan Beniquez .10 .05
❑ 453 Rick Burleson .10 .05
❑ 454 Bert Campaneris .20 .09
❑ 455 Rod Carew .75 .35
❑ 456 Bob Clark .10 .05
❑ 457 Brian Downing .10 .05
❑ 458 Dan Ford .10 .05
❑ 459 Ken Forsch .10 .05
❑ 460A Dave Frost (5 mm .10 .05
space before ERA)
❑ 460B Dave Frost .10 .05
(1 mm space)
❑ 461 Bobby Grich .20 .09
❑ 462 Larry Harlow .10 .05
❑ 463 John Harris .10 .05
❑ 464 Andy Hassler .10 .05
❑ 465 Butch Hobson .10 .05
❑ 466 Jesse Jefferson .10 .05
❑ 467 Bruce Kison .10 .05
❑ 468 Fred Lynn .20 .09
❑ 469 Angel Moreno .10 .05
❑ 470 Ed Ott .10 .05
❑ 471 Fred Patek .10 .05
❑ 472 Steve Renko .10 .05
❑ 473 Mike Witt .20 .09
❑ 474 Geoff Zahn .10 .05
❑ 475 Gary Alexander .10 .05
❑ 476 Dale Berra .10 .05
❑ 477 Kurt Bevacqua .10 .05
❑ 478 Jim Bibby .10 .05
❑ 479 John Candelaria .10 .05
❑ 480 Victor Cruz .10 .05
❑ 481 Mike Easler .10 .05
❑ 482 Tim Foli .10 .05
❑ 483 Lee Lacy .10 .05
❑ 484 Vance Law .10 .05
❑ 485 Bill Madlock .20 .09
❑ 486 Willie Montanez .10 .05
❑ 487 Omar Moreno .10 .05
❑ 488 Steve Nicosia .10 .05
❑ 489 Dave Parker .20 .09
❑ 490 Tony Pena .20 .09
❑ 491 Pascual Perez .10 .05
❑ 492 Johnny Ray .20 .09
❑ 493 Rick Rhoden .10 .05
❑ 494 Bill Robinson .10 .05
❑ 495 Don Robinson .10 .05
❑ 496 Enrique Romo .10 .05
❑ 497 Rod Scurry .10 .05
❑ 498 Eddie Solomon .10 .05
❑ 499 Willie Stargell .75 .35
❑ 500 Kent Tekulve .20 .09
❑ 501 Jason Thompson .10 .05
❑ 502 Glenn Abbott .10 .05
❑ 503 Jim Anderson .10 .05
❑ 504 Floyd Bannister .10 .05
❑ 505 Bruce Bochte .10 .05
❑ 506 Jeff Burroughs .10 .05
❑ 507 Bryan Clark .10 .05
❑ 508 Ken Clay .10 .05
❑ 509 Julio Cruz .10 .05
❑ 510 Dick Drago .10 .05
❑ 511 Gary Gray .10 .05
❑ 512 Dan Meyer .10 .05
❑ 513 Jerry Narron .10 .05
❑ 514 Tom Paciorek .20 .09
❑ 515 Casey Parsons .10 .05
❑ 516 Lenny Randle .10 .05
❑ 517 Shane Rawley .10 .05
❑ 518 Joe Simpson .10 .05
❑ 519 Richie Zisk .10 .05
❑ 520 Neil Allen .10 .05
❑ 521 Bob Bailor .10 .05
❑ 522 Hubie Brooks .20 .09
❑ 523 Mike Cubbage .10 .05
❑ 524 Pete Falcone .10 .05
❑ 525 Doug Flynn .10 .05
❑ 526 Tom Hausman .10 .05
❑ 527 Ron Hodges .10 .05
❑ 528 Randy Jones .10 .05
❑ 529 Mike Jorgensen .10 .05
❑ 530 Dave Kingman .20 .09
❑ 531 Ed Lynch .10 .05
❑ 532 Mike G. Marshall .10 .05
❑ 533 Lee Mazzilli .10 .05
❑ 534 Dyar Miller .10 .05
❑ 535 Mike Scott .20 .09
❑ 536 Rusty Staub .20 .09
❑ 537 John Stearns .10 .05
❑ 538 Craig Swan .10 .05
❑ 539 Frank Taveras .10 .05
❑ 540 Alex Trevino .10 .05
❑ 541 Ellis Valentine .10 .05
❑ 542 Mookie Wilson .20 .09
❑ 543 Joel Youngblood .10 .05
❑ 544 Pat Zachry .10 .05
❑ 545 Glenn Adams .10 .05
❑ 546 Fernando Arroyo .10 .05
❑ 547 John Verhoeven .10 .05
❑ 548 Sal Butera .10 .05
❑ 549 John Castino .10 .05
❑ 550 Don Cooper .10 .05
❑ 551 Doug Corbett .10 .05
❑ 552 Dave Engle .10 .05
❑ 553 Roger Erickson .10 .05
❑ 554 Danny Goodwin .10 .05
❑ 555A Darrell Jackson .40 .18
(Black cap)
❑ 555B Darrell Jackson .20 .09
(Red cap with T)
❑ 555C Darrell Jackson 3.00 1.35
(Red cap, no emblem)
❑ 556 Pete Mackanin .10 .05
❑ 557 Jack O'Connor .10 .05
❑ 558 Hosken Powell .10 .05
❑ 559 Pete Redfern .10 .05
❑ 560 Roy Smalley .10 .05
❑ 561 Chuck Baker UER .10 .05
(Shortshop on front)
❑ 562 Gary Ward .10 .05
❑ 563 Rob Wilfong .10 .05
❑ 564 Al Williams .10 .05
❑ 565 Butch Wynegar .10 .05
❑ 566 Randy Bass .10 .05
❑ 567 Juan Bonilla .10 .05
❑ 568 Danny Boone .10 .05
❑ 569 John Curtis .10 .05
❑ 570 Juan Eichelberger .10 .05
❑ 571 Barry Evans .10 .05
❑ 572 Tim Flannery .10 .05
❑ 573 Ruppert Jones .10 .05
❑ 574 Terry Kennedy .10 .05
❑ 575 Joe Lefebvre .10 .05
❑ 576A John Littlefield ERR 200.00 90.00
(Left handed;
reverse negative)
❑ 576B John Littlefield COR .20 .09
(Right handed)
❑ 577 Gary Lucas .10 .05
❑ 578 Steve Mura .10 .05
❑ 579 Broderick Perkins .10 .05
❑ 580 Gene Richards .10 .05
❑ 581 Luis Salazar .10 .05
❑ 582 Ozzie Smith 2.00 .90
❑ 583 John Urrea .10 .05
❑ 584 Chris Welsh .10 .05
❑ 585 Rick Wise .10 .05
❑ 586 Doug Bird .10 .05
❑ 587 Tim Blackwell .10 .05
❑ 588 Bobby Bonds .20 .09
❑ 589 Bill Buckner .20 .09
❑ 590 Bill Caudill .10 .05
❑ 591 Hector Cruz .10 .05
❑ 592 Jody Davis .10 .05
❑ 593 Ivan DeJesus .10 .05
❑ 594 Steve Dillard .10 .05
❑ 595 Leon Durham .10 .05
❑ 596 Rawly Eastwick .10 .05
❑ 597 Steve Henderson .10 .05
❑ 598 Mike Krukow .10 .05
❑ 599 Mike Lum .10 .05
❑ 600 Randy Martz .10 .05
❑ 601 Jerry Morales .10 .05
❑ 602 Ken Reitz .10 .05
❑ 603 Lee Smith ERR 2.50 1.10
(Cubs logo reversed)
❑ 603B Lee Smith COR 2.50 1.10
❑ 604 Dick Tidrow .10 .05
❑ 605 Jim Tracy .10 .05
❑ 606 Mike Tyson .10 .05
❑ 607 Ty Waller .10 .05
❑ 608 Danny Ainge 1.00 .45
❑ 609 Jorge Bell .75 .35
❑ 610 Mark Bomback .10 .05
❑ 611 Barry Bonnell .10 .05
❑ 612 Jim Clancy .10 .05
❑ 613 Damaso Garcia .10 .05
❑ 614 Jerry Garvin .10 .05
❑ 615 Alfredo Griffin .10 .05
❑ 616 Garth Iorg .10 .05
❑ 617 Luis Leal .10 .05
❑ 618 Ken Macha .10 .05
❑ 619 John Mayberry .10 .05
❑ 620 Joey McLaughlin .10 .05
❑ 621 Lloyd Moseby .10 .05
❑ 622 Dave Stieb .20 .09
❑ 623 Jackson Todd .10 .05
❑ 624 Willie Upshaw .10 .05
❑ 625 Otto Velez .10 .05
❑ 626 Ernie Whitt .10 .05
❑ 627 Alvis Woods .10 .05
❑ 628 All Star Game .20 .09
Cleveland, Ohio
❑ 629 All Star Infielders .20 .09
Frank White
Bucky Dent
❑ 630 Big Red Machine .20 .09
Dan Driessen
Dave Concepcion
George Foster
❑ 631 Bruce Sutter .10 .05
Top NL Relief Pitcher
❑ 632 Steve and Carlton .40 .18
Steve Carlton
Carlton Fisk

Card	NRMT	VG-E
❑ 633 Carl Yastrzemski	.75	.35
3000th Game		
❑ 634 Dynamic Duo	1.00	.45
Johnny Bench		
Tom Seaver		
❑ 635 West Meets East	.20	.09
Fernando Valenzuela		
Gary Carter		
❑ 636A Fernando Valenzuela:	.75	.35
NL SO King ("he" NL)		
❑ 636B Fernando Valenzuela:	.75	.35
NL SO King ("the" NL)		
❑ 637 Mike Schmidt	.40	.18
Home Run King		
❑ 638 NL All Stars	.20	.09
Gary Carter		
Dave Parker		
❑ 639 Perfect Game UER	.20	.09
Len Barker		
Bo Diaz		
(Catcher actually		
Ron Hassey)		
❑ 640 Pete and Re-Pete	.75	.35
Pete Rose		
Pete Rose Jr.		
❑ 641 Phillies Finest	.75	.35
Lonnie Smith		
Mike Schmidt		
Steve Carlton		
❑ 642 Red Sox Reunion	.20	.09
Fred Lynn		
Dwight Evans		
❑ 643 Rickey Henderson	.75	.35
Most Hits and Runs		
❑ 644 Rollie Fingers	.20	.09
Most Saves AL		
❑ 645 Tom Seaver	.40	.18
Most 1981 Wins		
❑ 646 Yankee Powerhouse	2.00	.90
Reggie Jackson		
Dave Winfield		
(Comma on back		
after outfielder)		
❑ 646B Yankee Powerhouse	2.00	.90
Reggie Jackson		
Dave Winfield		
(No comma)		
❑ 647 CL: Yankees/Dodgers	.10	.05
❑ 648 CL: A's/Reds	.10	.05
❑ 649 CL: Cards/Brewers	.10	.05
❑ 650 CL: Expos/Orioles	.10	.05
❑ 651 CL: Astros/Phillies	.10	.05
❑ 652 CL: Tigers/Red Sox	.10	.05
❑ 653 CL: Rangers/White Sox	.10	.05
❑ 654 CL: Giants/Indians	.10	.05
❑ 655 CL: Royals/Braves	.10	.05
❑ 656 CL: Angels/Pirates	.10	.05
❑ 657 CL: Mariners/Mets	.10	.05
❑ 658 CL: Padres/Twins	.10	.05
❑ 659 CL: Blue Jays/Cubs	.10	.05
❑ 660 Specials Checklist	.10	.05

1983 Fleer

	NRMT	VG-E
COMPLETE SET (660)	80.00	36.00
COMMON CARD (1-660)	.10	.05

Card	NRMT	VG-E
❑ 1 Joaquin Andujar	.10	.05
❑ 2 Doug Bair	.10	.05
❑ 3 Steve Braun	.10	.05
❑ 4 Glenn Brummer	.10	.05
❑ 5 Bob Forsch	.10	.05
❑ 6 David Green	.10	.05
❑ 7 George Hendrick	.10	.05
❑ 8 Keith Hernandez	.20	.09
❑ 9 Tom Herr	.20	.09
❑ 10 Dane Iorg	.10	.05
❑ 11 Jim Kaat	.20	.09
❑ 12 Jeff Lahti	.10	.05
❑ 13 Tito Landrum	.10	.05
❑ 14 Dave LaPoint	.10	.05
❑ 15 Willie McGee	.75	.35
❑ 16 Steve Mura	.10	.05
❑ 17 Ken Oberkfell	.10	.05
❑ 18 Darrell Porter	.10	.05
❑ 19 Mike Ramsey	.10	.05
❑ 20 Gene Roof	.10	.05
❑ 21 Lonnie Smith	.10	.05
❑ 22 Ozzie Smith	1.50	.70
❑ 23 John Stuper	.10	.05
❑ 24 Bruce Sutter	.20	.09
❑ 25 Gene Tenace	.20	.09
❑ 26 Jerry Augustine	.10	.05
❑ 27 Dwight Bernard	.10	.05
❑ 28 Mark Brouhard	.10	.05
❑ 29 Mike Caldwell	.10	.05
❑ 30 Cecil Cooper	.20	.09
❑ 31 Jamie Easterly	.10	.05
❑ 32 Marshall Edwards	.10	.05
❑ 33 Rollie Fingers	.75	.35
❑ 34 Jim Gantner	.20	.09
❑ 35 Moose Haas	.10	.05
❑ 36 Roy Howell	.10	.05
❑ 37 Pete Ladd	.10	.05
❑ 38 Bob McClure	.10	.05
❑ 39 Doc Medich	.10	.05
❑ 40 Paul Molitor	1.00	.45
❑ 41 Don Money	.10	.05
❑ 42 Charlie Moore	.10	.05
❑ 43 Ben Oglivie	.10	.05
❑ 44 Ed Romero	.10	.05
❑ 45 Ted Simmons	.20	.09
❑ 46 Jim Slaton	.10	.05
❑ 47 Don Sutton	.75	.35
❑ 48 Gorman Thomas	.10	.05
❑ 49 Pete Vuckovich	.10	.05
❑ 50 Ned Yost	.10	.05
❑ 51 Robin Yount	.75	.35
❑ 52 Benny Ayala	.10	.05
❑ 53 Bob Bonner	.10	.05
❑ 54 Al Bumbry	.10	.05
❑ 55 Terry Crowley	.10	.05
❑ 56 Storm Davis	.10	.05
❑ 57 Rich Dauer	.10	.05
❑ 58 Rick Dempsey UER	.20	.09
(Posing batting lefty)		
❑ 59 Jim Dwyer	.10	.05
❑ 60 Mike Flanagan	.20	.09
❑ 61 Dan Ford	.10	.05
❑ 62 Glenn Gulliver	.10	.05
❑ 63 John Lowenstein	.10	.05
❑ 64 Dennis Martinez	.20	.09
❑ 65 Tippy Martinez	.10	.05
❑ 66 Scott McGregor	.10	.05
❑ 67 Eddie Murray	1.00	.45
❑ 68 Joe Nolan	.10	.05
❑ 69 Jim Palmer	.75	.35
❑ 70 Cal Ripken	8.00	3.60
❑ 71 Gary Roenicke	.10	.05
❑ 72 Lenn Sakata	.10	.05
❑ 73 Ken Singleton	.10	.05
❑ 74 Sammy Stewart	.10	.05
❑ 75 Tim Stoddard	.10	.05
❑ 76 Don Aase	.10	.05
❑ 77 Don Baylor	.40	.18
❑ 78 Juan Beniquez	.10	.05
❑ 79 Bob Boone	.20	.09
❑ 80 Rick Burleson	.10	.05
❑ 81 Rod Carew	.75	.35
❑ 82 Bobby Clark	.10	.05
❑ 83 Doug Corbett	.10	.05
❑ 84 John Curtis	.10	.05
❑ 85 Doug DeCinces	.20	.09
❑ 86 Brian Downing	.10	.05
❑ 87 Joe Ferguson	.10	.05
❑ 88 Tim Foli	.10	.05
❑ 89 Ken Forsch	.10	.05
❑ 90 Dave Goltz	.10	.05
❑ 91 Bobby Grich	.20	.09
❑ 92 Andy Hassler	.10	.05
❑ 93 Reggie Jackson	1.00	.45
❑ 94 Ron Jackson	.10	.05
❑ 95 Tommy John	.40	.18
❑ 96 Bruce Kison	.10	.05
❑ 97 Fred Lynn	.20	.09
❑ 98 Ed Ott	.10	.05
❑ 99 Steve Renko	.10	.05
❑ 100 Luis Sanchez	.10	.05
❑ 101 Rob Wilfong	.10	.05
❑ 102 Mike Witt	.10	.05
❑ 103 Geoff Zahn	.10	.05
❑ 104 Willie Aikens	.10	.05
❑ 105 Mike Armstrong	.10	.05
❑ 106 Vida Blue	.20	.09
❑ 107 Bud Black	.20	.09
❑ 108 George Brett	1.50	.70
❑ 109 Bill Castro	.10	.05
❑ 110 Onix Concepcion	.10	.05
❑ 111 Dave Frost	.10	.05
❑ 112 Cesar Geronimo	.10	.05
❑ 113 Larry Gura	.10	.05
❑ 114 Steve Hammond	.10	.05
❑ 115 Don Hood	.10	.05
❑ 116 Dennis Leonard	.10	.05
❑ 117 Jerry Martin	.10	.05
❑ 118 Lee May	.20	.09
❑ 119 Hal McRae	.20	.09
❑ 120 Amos Otis	.20	.09
❑ 121 Greg Pryor	.10	.05
❑ 122 Dan Quisenberry	.20	.09
❑ 123 Don Slaught	.40	.18
❑ 124 Paul Splittorff	.10	.05
❑ 125 U.L. Washington	.10	.05
❑ 126 John Wathan	.10	.05
❑ 127 Frank White	.20	.09
❑ 128 Willie Wilson	.20	.09
❑ 129 Steve Bedrosian UER	.20	.09
(Height 6'33")		
❑ 130 Bruce Benedict	.10	.05
❑ 131 Tommy Boggs	.10	.05
❑ 132 Brett Butler	.75	.35
❑ 133 Rick Camp	.10	.05
❑ 134 Chris Chambliss	.20	.09
❑ 135 Ken Dayley	.10	.05
❑ 136 Gene Garber	.10	.05
❑ 137 Terry Harper	.10	.05
❑ 138 Bob Horner	.10	.05
❑ 139 Glenn Hubbard	.10	.05
❑ 140 Rufino Linares	.10	.05
❑ 141 Rick Mahler	.10	.05
❑ 142 Dale Murphy	.75	.35
❑ 143 Phil Niekro	.75	.35
❑ 144 Pascual Perez	.10	.05
❑ 145 Biff Pocoroba	.10	.05
❑ 146 Rafael Ramirez	.10	.05
❑ 147 Jerry Royster	.10	.05
❑ 148 Ken Smith	.10	.05
❑ 149 Bob Walk	.10	.05
❑ 150 Claudell Washington	.10	.05
❑ 151 Bob Watson	.20	.09
❑ 152 Larry Whisenton	.10	.05
❑ 153 Porfirio Altamirano	.10	.05
❑ 154 Marty Bystrom	.10	.05
❑ 155 Steve Carlton	.75	.35
❑ 156 Larry Christenson	.10	.05
❑ 157 Ivan DeJesus	.10	.05
❑ 158 John Denny	.10	.05
❑ 159 Bob Dernier	.10	.05
❑ 160 Bo Diaz	.10	.05
❑ 161 Ed Farmer	.10	.05
❑ 162 Greg Gross	.10	.05
❑ 163 Mike Krukow	.10	.05
❑ 164 Garry Maddox	.10	.05
❑ 165 Gary Matthews	.20	.09
❑ 166 Tug McGraw	.20	.09
❑ 167 Bob Molinaro	.10	.05
❑ 168 Sid Monge	.10	.05

- ❑ 169 Ron Reed .10 .05
- ❑ 170 Bill Robinson .10 .05
- ❑ 171 Pete Rose 1.00 .45
- ❑ 172 Dick Ruthven .10 .05
- ❑ 173 Mike Schmidt 1.00 .45
- ❑ 174 Manny Trillo .10 .05
- ❑ 175 Ozzie Virgil .10 .05
- ❑ 176 George Vukovich .10 .05
- ❑ 177 Gary Allenson .10 .05
- ❑ 178 Luis Aponte .10 .05
- ❑ 179 Wade Boggs 12.00 5.50
- ❑ 180 Tom Burgmeier .10 .05
- ❑ 181 Mark Clear .10 .05
- ❑ 182 Dennis Eckersley .75 .35
- ❑ 183 Dwight Evans .20 .09
- ❑ 184 Rich Gedman .10 .05
- ❑ 185 Glenn Hoffman .10 .05
- ❑ 186 Bruce Hurst .10 .05
- ❑ 187 Carney Lansford .20 .09
- ❑ 188 Rick Miller .10 .05
- ❑ 189 Reid Nichols .10 .05
- ❑ 190 Bob Ojeda .10 .05
- ❑ 191 Tony Perez .75 .35
- ❑ 192 Chuck Rainey .10 .05
- ❑ 193 Jerry Remy .10 .05
- ❑ 194 Jim Rice .20 .09
- ❑ 195 Bob Stanley .10 .05
- ❑ 196 Dave Stapleton .10 .05
- ❑ 197 Mike Torrez .10 .05
- ❑ 198 John Tudor .10 .05
- ❑ 199 Julio Valdez .10 .05
- ❑ 200 Carl Yastrzemski .75 .35
- ❑ 201 Dusty Baker .20 .09
- ❑ 202 Joe Beckwith .10 .05
- ❑ 203 Greg Brock .10 .05
- ❑ 204 Ron Cey .20 .09
- ❑ 205 Terry Forster .10 .05
- ❑ 206 Steve Garvey .40 .18
- ❑ 207 Pedro Guerrero .20 .09
- ❑ 208 Burt Hooton .10 .05
- ❑ 209 Steve Howe .10 .05
- ❑ 210 Ken Landreaux .10 .05
- ❑ 211 Mike Marshall .10 .05
- ❑ 212 Candy Maldonado .20 .09
- ❑ 213 Rick Monday .10 .05
- ❑ 214 Tom Niedenfuer .10 .05
- ❑ 215 Jorge Orta .10 .05
- ❑ 216 Jerry Reuss UER .20 .09
  ("Home:" omitted)
- ❑ 217 Ron Roenicke .10 .05
- ❑ 218 Vicente Romo .10 .05
- ❑ 219 Bill Russell .20 .09
- ❑ 220 Steve Sax .20 .09
- ❑ 221 Mike Scioscia .20 .09
- ❑ 222 Dave Stewart .20 .09
- ❑ 223 Derrel Thomas .10 .05
- ❑ 224 Fernando Valenzuela .40 .18
- ❑ 225 Bob Welch .20 .09
- ❑ 226 Ricky Wright .10 .05
- ❑ 227 Steve Yeager .10 .05
- ❑ 228 Bill Almon .10 .05
- ❑ 229 Harold Baines .40 .18
- ❑ 230 Salome Barojas .10 .05
- ❑ 231 Tony Bernazard .10 .05
- ❑ 232 Britt Burns .10 .05
- ❑ 233 Richard Dotson .10 .05
- ❑ 234 Ernesto Escarrega .10 .05
- ❑ 235 Carlton Fisk .75 .35
- ❑ 236 Jerry Hairston .10 .05
- ❑ 237 Kevin Hickey .10 .05
- ❑ 238 LaMarr Hoyt .20 .09
- ❑ 239 Steve Kemp .10 .05
- ❑ 240 Jim Kern .10 .05
- ❑ 241 Ron Kittle .40 .18
- ❑ 242 Jerry Koosman .20 .09
- ❑ 243 Dennis Lamp .10 .05
- ❑ 244 Rudy Law .10 .05
- ❑ 245 Vance Law .10 .05
- ❑ 246 Ron LeFlore .10 .05
- ❑ 247 Greg Luzinski .20 .09
- ❑ 248 Tom Paciorek .20 .09
- ❑ 249 Aurelio Rodriguez .10 .05
- ❑ 250 Mike Squires .10 .05
- ❑ 251 Steve Trout .10 .05
- ❑ 252 Jim Barr .10 .05
- ❑ 253 Dave Bergman .10 .05
- ❑ 254 Fred Breining .10 .05
- ❑ 255 Bob Brenly .10 .05
- ❑ 256 Jack Clark .20 .09
- ❑ 257 Chili Davis .75 .35
- ❑ 258 Darrell Evans .20 .09
- ❑ 259 Alan Fowlkes .10 .05
- ❑ 260 Rich Gale .10 .05
- ❑ 261 Atlee Hammaker .10 .05
- ❑ 262 Al Holland .10 .05
- ❑ 263 Duane Kuiper .10 .05
- ❑ 264 Bill Laskey .10 .05
- ❑ 265 Gary Lavelle .10 .05
- ❑ 266 Johnnie LeMaster .10 .05
- ❑ 267 Renie Martin .10 .05
- ❑ 268 Milt May .10 .05
- ❑ 269 Greg Minton .10 .05
- ❑ 270 Joe Morgan .75 .35
- ❑ 271 Tom O'Malley .10 .05
- ❑ 272 Reggie Smith .20 .09
- ❑ 273 Guy Sularz .10 .05
- ❑ 274 Champ Summers .10 .05
- ❑ 275 Max Venable .10 .05
- ❑ 276 Jim Wohlford .10 .05
- ❑ 277 Ray Burris .10 .05
- ❑ 278 Gary Carter .75 .35
- ❑ 279 Warren Cromartie .10 .05
- ❑ 280 Andre Dawson .75 .35
- ❑ 281 Terry Francona .10 .05
- ❑ 282 Doug Flynn .10 .05
- ❑ 283 Woodie Fryman .10 .05
- ❑ 284 Bill Gullickson .20 .09
- ❑ 285 Wallace Johnson .10 .05
- ❑ 286 Charlie Lea .10 .05
- ❑ 287 Randy Lerch .10 .05
- ❑ 288 Brad Mills .10 .05
- ❑ 289 Dan Norman .10 .05
- ❑ 290 Al Oliver .20 .09
- ❑ 291 David Palmer .10 .05
- ❑ 292 Tim Raines .75 .35
- ❑ 293 Jeff Reardon .20 .09
- ❑ 294 Steve Rogers .10 .05
- ❑ 295 Scott Sanderson .10 .05
- ❑ 296 Dan Schatzeder .10 .05
- ❑ 297 Bryn Smith .10 .05
- ❑ 298 Chris Speier .10 .05
- ❑ 299 Tim Wallach .20 .09
- ❑ 300 Jerry White .10 .05
- ❑ 301 Joel Youngblood .10 .05
- ❑ 302 Ross Baumgarten .10 .05
- ❑ 303 Dale Berra .10 .05
- ❑ 304 John Candelaria .10 .05
- ❑ 305 Dick Davis .10 .05
- ❑ 306 Mike Easler .10 .05
- ❑ 307 Richie Hebner .20 .09
- ❑ 308 Lee Lacy .10 .05
- ❑ 309 Bill Madlock .20 .09
- ❑ 310 Larry McWilliams .10 .05
- ❑ 311 John Milner .10 .05
- ❑ 312 Omar Moreno .10 .05
- ❑ 313 Jim Morrison .10 .05
- ❑ 314 Steve Nicosia .10 .05
- ❑ 315 Dave Parker .20 .09
- ❑ 316 Tony Pena .10 .05
- ❑ 317 Johnny Ray .10 .05
- ❑ 318 Rick Rhoden .10 .05
- ❑ 319 Don Robinson .10 .05
- ❑ 320 Enrique Romo .10 .05
- ❑ 321 Manny Sarmiento .10 .05
- ❑ 322 Rod Scurry .10 .05
- ❑ 323 Jimmy Smith .10 .05
- ❑ 324 Willie Stargell .75 .35
- ❑ 325 Jason Thompson .10 .05
- ❑ 326 Kent Tekulve .20 .09
- ❑ 327A Tom Brookens .10 .05
  (Short .375" brown box shaded in on card back)
- ❑ 327B Tom Brookens .10 .05
  (Longer 1.25" brown box shaded in on card back)
- ❑ 328 Enos Cabell .10 .05
- ❑ 329 Kirk Gibson .75 .35
- ❑ 330 Larry Herndon .10 .05
- ❑ 331 Mike Ivie .10 .05
- ❑ 332 Howard Johnson .75 .35
- ❑ 333 Lynn Jones .10 .05
- ❑ 334 Rick Leach .10 .05
- ❑ 335 Chet Lemon .10 .05
- ❑ 336 Jack Morris .20 .09
- ❑ 337 Lance Parrish .20 .09
- ❑ 338 Larry Pashnick .10 .05
- ❑ 339 Dan Petry .10 .05
- ❑ 340 Dave Rozema .10 .05
- ❑ 341 Dave Rucker .10 .05
- ❑ 342 Elias Sosa .10 .05
- ❑ 343 Dave Tobik .10 .05
- ❑ 344 Alan Trammell .75 .35
- ❑ 345 Jerry Turner .10 .05
- ❑ 346 Jerry Ujdur .10 .05
- ❑ 347 Pat Underwood .10 .05
- ❑ 348 Lou Whitaker .40 .18
- ❑ 349 Milt Wilcox .10 .05
- ❑ 350 Glenn Wilson .20 .09
- ❑ 351 John Wockenfuss .10 .05
- ❑ 352 Kurt Bevacqua .10 .05
- ❑ 353 Juan Bonilla .10 .05
- ❑ 354 Floyd Chiffer .10 .05
- ❑ 355 Luis DeLeon .10 .05
- ❑ 356 Dave Dravecky .75 .35
- ❑ 357 Dave Edwards .10 .05
- ❑ 358 Juan Eichelberger .10 .05
- ❑ 359 Tim Flannery .10 .05
- ❑ 360 Tony Gwynn 30.00 13.50
- ❑ 361 Ruppert Jones .10 .05
- ❑ 362 Terry Kennedy .10 .05
- ❑ 363 Joe Lefebvre .10 .05
- ❑ 364 Sixto Lezcano .10 .05
- ❑ 365 Tim Lollar .10 .05
- ❑ 366 Gary Lucas .10 .05
- ❑ 367 John Montefusco .10 .05
- ❑ 368 Broderick Perkins .10 .05
- ❑ 369 Joe Pittman .10 .05
- ❑ 370 Gene Richards .10 .05
- ❑ 371 Luis Salazar .10 .05
- ❑ 372 Eric Show .10 .05
- ❑ 373 Garry Templeton .10 .05
- ❑ 374 Chris Welsh .10 .05
- ❑ 375 Alan Wiggins .10 .05
- ❑ 376 Rick Cerone .10 .05
- ❑ 377 Dave Collins .10 .05
- ❑ 378 Roger Erickson .10 .05
- ❑ 379 George Frazier .10 .05
- ❑ 380 Oscar Gamble .10 .05
- ❑ 381 Rich Gossage .40 .18
- ❑ 382 Ken Griffey .20 .09
- ❑ 383 Ron Guidry .20 .09
- ❑ 384 Dave LaRoche .10 .05
- ❑ 385 Rudy May .10 .05
- ❑ 386 John Mayberry .10 .05
- ❑ 387 Lee Mazzilli .10 .05
- ❑ 388 Mike Morgan .10 .05
- ❑ 389 Jerry Mumphrey .10 .05
- ❑ 390 Bobby Murcer .20 .09
- ❑ 391 Graig Nettles .20 .09
- ❑ 392 Lou Piniella .20 .09
- ❑ 393 Willie Randolph .20 .09
- ❑ 394 Shane Rawley .10 .05
- ❑ 395 Dave Righetti .20 .09
- ❑ 396 Andre Robertson .10 .05
- ❑ 397 Roy Smalley .10 .05
- ❑ 398 Dave Winfield .75 .35
- ❑ 399 Butch Wynegar .10 .05
- ❑ 400 Chris Bando .10 .05
- ❑ 401 Alan Bannister .10 .05
- ❑ 402 Len Barker .10 .05
- ❑ 403 Tom Brennan .10 .05
- ❑ 404 Carmelo Castillo .10 .05
- ❑ 405 Miguel Dilone .10 .05
- ❑ 406 Jerry Dybzinski .10 .05
- ❑ 407 Mike Fischlin .10 .05
- ❑ 408 Ed Glynn UER .10 .05
  (Photo actually Bud Anderson)
- ❑ 409 Mike Hargrove .20 .09
- ❑ 410 Toby Harrah .10 .05
- ❑ 411 Ron Hassey .10 .05
- ❑ 412 Von Hayes .20 .09
- ❑ 413 Rick Manning .10 .05
- ❑ 414 Bake McBride .10 .05
- ❑ 415 Larry Milbourne .10 .05

No.	Player		
❑ 416	Bill Nahorodny	.10	.05
❑ 417	Jack Perconte	.10	.05
❑ 418	Lary Sorensen	.10	.05
❑ 419	Dan Spillner	.10	.05
❑ 420	Rick Sutcliffe	.20	.09
❑ 421	Andre Thornton	.10	.05
❑ 422	Rick Waits	.10	.05
❑ 423	Eddie Whitson	.10	.05
❑ 424	Jesse Barfield	.20	.09
❑ 425	Barry Bonnell	.10	.05
❑ 426	Jim Clancy	.10	.05
❑ 427	Damaso Garcia	.10	.05
❑ 428	Jerry Garvin	.10	.05
❑ 429	Alfredo Griffin	.10	.05
❑ 430	Garth Iorg	.10	.05
❑ 431	Roy Lee Jackson	.10	.05
❑ 432	Luis Leal	.10	.05
❑ 433	Buck Martinez	.10	.05
❑ 434	Joey McLaughlin	.10	.05
❑ 435	Lloyd Moseby	.10	.05
❑ 436	Rance Mulliniks	.10	.05
❑ 437	Dale Murray	.10	.05
❑ 438	Wayne Nordhagen	.10	.05
❑ 439	Geno Petralli	.20	.09
❑ 440	Hosken Powell	.10	.05
❑ 441	Dave Stieb	.20	.09
❑ 442	Willie Upshaw	.10	.05
❑ 443	Ernie Whitt	.10	.05
❑ 444	Alvis Woods	.10	.05
❑ 445	Alan Ashby	.10	.05
❑ 446	Jose Cruz	.20	.09
❑ 447	Kiko Garcia	.10	.05
❑ 448	Phil Garner	.20	.09
❑ 449	Danny Heep	.10	.05
❑ 450	Art Howe	.20	.09
❑ 451	Bob Knepper	.10	.05
❑ 452	Alan Knicely	.10	.05
❑ 453	Ray Knight	.20	.09
❑ 454	Frank LaCorte	.10	.05
❑ 455	Mike LaCoss	.10	.05
❑ 456	Randy Moffitt	.10	.05
❑ 457	Joe Niekro	.20	.09
❑ 458	Terry Puhl	.10	.05
❑ 459	Luis Pujols	.10	.05
❑ 460	Craig Reynolds	.10	.05
❑ 461	Bert Roberge	.10	.05
❑ 462	Vern Ruhle	.10	.05
❑ 463	Nolan Ryan	4.00	1.80
❑ 464	Joe Sambito	.10	.05
❑ 465	Tony Scott	.10	.05
❑ 466	Dave Smith	.10	.05
❑ 467	Harry Spilman	.10	.05
❑ 468	Dickie Thon	.10	.05
❑ 469	Denny Walling	.10	.05
❑ 470	Larry Andersen	.10	.05
❑ 471	Floyd Bannister	.10	.05
❑ 472	Jim Beattie	.10	.05
❑ 473	Bruce Bochte	.10	.05
❑ 474	Manny Castillo	.10	.05
❑ 475	Bill Caudill	.10	.05
❑ 476	Bryan Clark	.10	.05
❑ 477	Al Cowens	.10	.05
❑ 478	Julio Cruz	.10	.05
❑ 479	Todd Cruz	.10	.05
❑ 480	Gary Gray	.10	.05
❑ 481	Dave Henderson	.10	.05
❑ 482	Mike Moore	.20	.09
❑ 483	Gaylord Perry	.75	.35
❑ 484	Dave Revering	.10	.05
❑ 485	Joe Simpson	.10	.05
❑ 486	Mike Stanton	.10	.05
❑ 487	Rick Sweet	.10	.05
❑ 488	Ed VandeBerg	.10	.05
❑ 489	Richie Zisk	.10	.05
❑ 490	Doug Bird	.10	.05
❑ 491	Larry Bowa	.20	.09
❑ 492	Bill Buckner	.20	.09
❑ 493	Bill Campbell	.10	.05
❑ 494	Jody Davis	.10	.05
❑ 495	Leon Durham	.10	.05
❑ 496	Steve Henderson	.10	.05
❑ 497	Willie Hernandez	.20	.09
❑ 498	Ferguson Jenkins	.75	.35
❑ 499	Jay Johnstone	.20	.09
❑ 500	Junior Kennedy	.10	.05
❑ 501	Randy Martz	.10	.05
❑ 502	Jerry Morales	.10	.05
❑ 503	Keith Moreland	.10	.05
❑ 504	Dickie Noles	.10	.05
❑ 505	Mike Proly	.10	.05
❑ 506	Allen Ripley	.10	.05
❑ 507	Ryne Sandberg UER.. (Should say High School in Spokane, Washington)	12.00	5.50
❑ 508	Lee Smith	.75	.35
❑ 509	Pat Tabler	.10	.05
❑ 510	Dick Tidrow	.10	.05
❑ 511	Bump Wills	.10	.05
❑ 512	Gary Woods	.10	.05
❑ 513	Tony Armas	.10	.05
❑ 514	Dave Beard	.10	.05
❑ 515	Jeff Burroughs	.10	.05
❑ 516	John D'Acquisto	.10	.05
❑ 517	Wayne Gross	.10	.05
❑ 518	Mike Heath	.10	.05
❑ 519	Rickey Henderson UER (Brock record listed as 120 steals)	1.00	.45
❑ 520	Cliff Johnson	.10	.05
❑ 521	Matt Keough	.10	.05
❑ 522	Brian Kingman	.10	.05
❑ 523	Rick Langford	.10	.05
❑ 524	Dave Lopes	.20	.09
❑ 525	Steve McCatty	.10	.05
❑ 526	Dave McKay	.10	.05
❑ 527	Dan Meyer	.10	.05
❑ 528	Dwayne Murphy	.10	.05
❑ 529	Jeff Newman	.10	.05
❑ 530	Mike Norris	.10	.05
❑ 531	Bob Owchinko	.10	.05
❑ 532	Joe Rudi	.10	.05
❑ 533	Jimmy Sexton	.10	.05
❑ 534	Fred Stanley	.10	.05
❑ 535	Tom Underwood	.10	.05
❑ 536	Neil Allen	.10	.05
❑ 537	Wally Backman	.10	.05
❑ 538	Bob Bailor	.10	.05
❑ 539	Hubie Brooks	.20	.09
❑ 540	Carlos Diaz	.10	.05
❑ 541	Pete Falcone	.10	.05
❑ 542	George Foster	.20	.09
❑ 543	Ron Gardenhire	.10	.05
❑ 544	Brian Giles	.10	.05
❑ 545	Ron Hodges	.10	.05
❑ 546	Randy Jones	.10	.05
❑ 547	Mike Jorgensen	.10	.05
❑ 548	Dave Kingman	.40	.18
❑ 549	Ed Lynch	.10	.05
❑ 550	Jesse Orosco	.10	.05
❑ 551	Rick Ownbey	.10	.05
❑ 552	Charlie Puleo	.10	.05
❑ 553	Gary Rajsich	.10	.05
❑ 554	Mike Scott	.20	.09
❑ 555	Rusty Staub	.20	.09
❑ 556	John Stearns	.10	.05
❑ 557	Craig Swan	.10	.05
❑ 558	Ellis Valentine	.10	.05
❑ 559	Tom Veryzer	.10	.05
❑ 560	Mookie Wilson	.20	.09
❑ 561	Pat Zachry	.10	.05
❑ 562	Buddy Bell	.20	.09
❑ 563	John Butcher	.10	.05
❑ 564	Steve Comer	.10	.05
❑ 565	Danny Darwin	.20	.09
❑ 566	Bucky Dent	.20	.09
❑ 567	John Grubb	.10	.05
❑ 568	Rick Honeycutt	.10	.05
❑ 569	Dave Hostetler	.10	.05
❑ 570	Charlie Hough	.20	.09
❑ 571	Lamar Johnson	.10	.05
❑ 572	Jon Matlack	.10	.05
❑ 573	Paul Mirabella	.10	.05
❑ 574	Larry Parrish	.10	.05
❑ 575	Mike Richardt	.10	.05
❑ 576	Mickey Rivers	.10	.05
❑ 577	Billy Sample	.10	.05
❑ 578	Dave Schmidt	.10	.05
❑ 579	Bill Stein	.10	.05
❑ 580	Jim Sundberg	.20	.09
❑ 581	Frank Tanana	.20	.09
❑ 582	Mark Wagner	.10	.05
❑ 583	George Wright	.10	.05
❑ 584	Johnny Bench	1.00	.45
❑ 585	Bruce Berenyi	.10	.05
❑ 586	Larry Biittner	.10	.05
❑ 587	Cesar Cedeno	.20	.09
❑ 588	Dave Concepcion	.20	.09
❑ 589	Dan Driessen	.10	.05
❑ 590	Greg Harris	.10	.05
❑ 591	Ben Hayes	.10	.05
❑ 592	Paul Householder	.10	.05
❑ 593	Tom Hume	.10	.05
❑ 594	Wayne Krenchicki	.10	.05
❑ 595	Rafael Landestoy	.10	.05
❑ 596	Charlie Leibrandt	.10	.05
❑ 597	Eddie Milner	.10	.05
❑ 598	Ron Oester	.10	.05
❑ 599	Frank Pastore	.10	.05
❑ 600	Joe Price	.10	.05
❑ 601	Tom Seaver	1.00	.45
❑ 602	Bob Shirley	.10	.05
❑ 603	Mario Soto	.10	.05
❑ 604	Alex Trevino	.10	.05
❑ 605	Mike Vail	.10	.05
❑ 606	Duane Walker	.10	.05
❑ 607	Tom Brunansky	.20	.09
❑ 608	Bobby Castillo	.10	.05
❑ 609	John Castino	.10	.05
❑ 610	Ron Davis	.10	.05
❑ 611	Lenny Faedo	.10	.05
❑ 612	Terry Felton	.10	.05
❑ 613	Gary Gaetti	.75	.35
❑ 614	Mickey Hatcher	.10	.05
❑ 615	Brad Havens	.10	.05
❑ 616	Kent Hrbek	.20	.09
❑ 617	Randy Johnson	.10	.05
❑ 618	Tim Laudner	.10	.05
❑ 619	Jeff Little	.10	.05
❑ 620	Bobby Mitchell	.10	.05
❑ 621	Jack O'Connor	.10	.05
❑ 622	John Pacella	.10	.05
❑ 623	Pete Redfern	.10	.05
❑ 624	Jesus Vega	.10	.05
❑ 625	Frank Viola	.75	.35
❑ 626	Ron Washington	.10	.05
❑ 627	Gary Ward	.10	.05
❑ 628	Al Williams	.10	.05
❑ 629	Red Sox All-Stars Carl Yastrzemski Dennis Eckersley Mark Clear	.75	.35
❑ 630	300 Career Wins Gaylord Perry Terry Bulling 5/6/82	.20	.09
❑ 631	Pride of Venezuela Dave Concepcion and Manny Trillo	.20	.09
❑ 632	All-Star Infielders Robin Yount and Buddy Bell	.75	.35
❑ 633	Mr.Vet and Mr.Rookie Dave Winfield and Kent Hrbek	.40	.18
❑ 634	Fountain of Youth Willie Stargell and Pete Rose	.75	.35
❑ 635	Big Chiefs Toby Harrah and Andre Thornton	.20	.09
❑ 636	Smith Brothers Ozzie Smith Lonnie Smith	.75	.35
❑ 637	Base Stealers' Threat Bo Diaz and Gary Carter	.20	.09
❑ 638	All-Star Catchers Carlton Fisk and Gary Carter	.75	.35
❑ 639	The Silver Shoe Rickey Henderson	.40	.18
❑ 640	Home Run Threats Ben Oglivie and Reggie Jackson	.75	.35
❑ 641	Two Teams Same Day .. Joel Youngblood August 4, 1982	.10	.05

❑ 642 Last Perfect Game .20 .09
Ron Hassey and
Len Barker
❑ 643 Black and Blue .20 .09
Vida Blue
❑ 644 Black and Blue .10 .05
Bud Black
❑ 645 Speed and Power .40 .18
Reggie Jackson
❑ 646 Speed and Power .40 .18
Rickey Henderson
❑ 647 CL: Cards/Brewers .10 .05
❑ 648 CL: Orioles/Angels .10 .05
❑ 649 CL: Royals/Braves .10 .05
❑ 650 CL: Phillies/Red Sox .10 .05
❑ 651 CL: Dodgers/White Sox .10 .05
❑ 652 CL: Giants/Expos .10 .05
❑ 653 CL: Pirates/Tigers .10 .05
❑ 654 CL: Padres/Yankees .10 .05
❑ 655 CL: Indians/Blue Jays .10 .05
❑ 656 CL: Astros/Mariners .10 .05
❑ 657 CL: Cubs/A's .10 .05
❑ 658 CL: Mets/Rangers .10 .05
❑ 659 CL: Reds/Twins .10 .05
❑ 660 CL: Specials/Teams .10 .05

1984 Fleer

	NRMT	VG-E
COMPLETE SET (660)	80.00	36.00
COMMON CARD (1-660)	.15	.07

❑ 1 Mike Boddicker .15 .07
❑ 2 Al Bumbry .40 .18
❑ 3 Todd Cruz .15 .07
❑ 4 Rich Dauer .15 .07
❑ 5 Storm Davis .15 .07
❑ 6 Rick Dempsey .15 .07
❑ 7 Jim Dwyer .15 .07
❑ 8 Mike Flanagan .15 .07
❑ 9 Dan Ford .15 .07
❑ 10 John Lowenstein .15 .07
❑ 11 Dennis Martinez .40 .18
❑ 12 Tippy Martinez .15 .07
❑ 13 Scott McGregor .15 .07
❑ 14 Eddie Murray 1.50 .70
❑ 15 Joe Nolan .15 .07
❑ 16 Jim Palmer 1.50 .70
❑ 17 Cal Ripken 10.00 4.50
❑ 18 Gary Roenicke .15 .07
❑ 19 Lenn Sakata .15 .07
❑ 20 John Shelby .15 .07
❑ 21 Ken Singleton .15 .07
❑ 22 Sammy Stewart .15 .07
❑ 23 Tim Stoddard .15 .07
❑ 24 Marty Bystrom .15 .07
❑ 25 Steve Carlton 1.50 .70
❑ 26 Ivan DeJesus .15 .07
❑ 27 John Denny .15 .07
❑ 28 Bob Dernier .15 .07
❑ 29 Bo Diaz .15 .07
❑ 30 Kiko Garcia .15 .07
❑ 31 Greg Gross .15 .07
❑ 32 Kevin Gross .40 .18
❑ 33 Von Hayes .15 .07
❑ 34 Willie Hernandez .40 .18
❑ 35 Al Holland .15 .07
❑ 36 Charles Hudson .15 .07
❑ 37 Joe Lefebvre .15 .07
❑ 38 Sixto Lezcano .15 .07
❑ 39 Garry Maddox .15 .07
❑ 40 Gary Matthews .40 .18
❑ 41 Len Matuszek .15 .07
❑ 42 Tug McGraw .40 .18
❑ 43 Joe Morgan 1.50 .70
❑ 44 Tony Perez 1.50 .70
❑ 45 Ron Reed .15 .07
❑ 46 Pete Rose 2.00 .90
❑ 47 Juan Samuel .75 .35
❑ 48 Mike Schmidt 2.00 .90
❑ 49 Ozzie Virgil .15 .07
❑ 50 Juan Agosto .15 .07
❑ 51 Harold Baines .75 .35
❑ 52 Floyd Bannister .15 .07
❑ 53 Salome Barojas .15 .07
❑ 54 Britt Burns .15 .07
❑ 55 Julio Cruz .15 .07
❑ 56 Richard Dotson .15 .07
❑ 57 Jerry Dybzinski .15 .07
❑ 58 Carlton Fisk 1.50 .70
❑ 59 Scott Fletcher .15 .07
❑ 60 Jerry Hairston .15 .07
❑ 61 Kevin Hickey .15 .07
❑ 62 Marc Hill .15 .07
❑ 63 LaMarr Hoyt .15 .07
❑ 64 Ron Kittle .15 .07
❑ 65 Jerry Koosman .40 .18
❑ 66 Dennis Lamp .15 .07
❑ 67 Rudy Law .15 .07
❑ 68 Vance Law .15 .07
❑ 69 Greg Luzinski .40 .18
❑ 70 Tom Paciorek .40 .18
❑ 71 Mike Squires .15 .07
❑ 72 Dick Tidrow .15 .07
❑ 73 Greg Walker .40 .18
❑ 74 Glenn Abbott .15 .07
❑ 75 Howard Bailey .15 .07
❑ 76 Doug Bair .15 .07
❑ 77 Juan Berenguer .15 .07
❑ 78 Tom Brookens .40 .18
❑ 79 Enos Cabell .15 .07
❑ 80 Kirk Gibson 1.50 .70
❑ 81 John Grubb .15 .07
❑ 82 Larry Herndon .40 .18
❑ 83 Wayne Krenchicki .15 .07
❑ 84 Rick Leach .15 .07
❑ 85 Chet Lemon .40 .18
❑ 86 Aurelio Lopez .40 .18
❑ 87 Jack Morris 1.50 .70
❑ 88 Lance Parrish .75 .35
❑ 89 Dan Petry .40 .18
❑ 90 Dave Rozema .15 .07
❑ 91 Alan Trammell 1.50 .70
❑ 92 Lou Whitaker 1.50 .70
❑ 93 Milt Wilcox .15 .07
❑ 94 Glenn Wilson .40 .18
❑ 95 John Wockenfuss .15 .07
❑ 96 Dusty Baker .40 .18
❑ 97 Joe Beckwith .15 .07
❑ 98 Greg Brock .15 .07
❑ 99 Jack Fimple .15 .07
❑ 100 Pedro Guerrero .40 .18
❑ 101 Rick Honeycutt .15 .07
❑ 102 Burt Hooton .15 .07
❑ 103 Steve Howe .15 .07
❑ 104 Ken Landreaux .15 .07
❑ 105 Mike Marshall .15 .07
❑ 106 Rick Monday .15 .07
❑ 107 Jose Morales .15 .07
❑ 108 Tom Niedenfuer .15 .07
❑ 109 Alejandro Pena .40 .18
❑ 110 Jerry Reuss UER .15 .07
("Home:" omitted)
❑ 111 Bill Russell .40 .18
❑ 112 Steve Sax .40 .18
❑ 113 Mike Scioscia .15 .07
❑ 114 Derrel Thomas .15 .07
❑ 115 Fernando Valenzuela .40 .18
❑ 116 Bob Welch .15 .07
❑ 117 Steve Yeager .15 .07
❑ 118 Pat Zachry .15 .07
❑ 119 Don Baylor .75 .35
❑ 120 Bert Campaneris .40 .18
❑ 121 Rick Cerone .15 .07
❑ 122 Ray Fontenot .15 .07
❑ 123 George Frazier .15 .07
❑ 124 Oscar Gamble .15 .07
❑ 125 Rich Gossage .75 .35
❑ 126 Ken Griffey .40 .18
❑ 127 Ron Guidry .40 .18
❑ 128 Jay Howell .15 .07
❑ 129 Steve Kemp .15 .07
❑ 130 Matt Keough .15 .07
❑ 131 Don Mattingly 20.00 9.00
❑ 132 John Montefusco .15 .07
❑ 133 Omar Moreno .15 .07
❑ 134 Dale Murray .15 .07
❑ 135 Graig Nettles .40 .18
❑ 136 Lou Piniella .40 .18
❑ 137 Willie Randolph .40 .18
❑ 138 Shane Rawley .15 .07
❑ 139 Dave Righetti .40 .18
❑ 140 Andre Robertson .15 .07
❑ 141 Bob Shirley .15 .07
❑ 142 Roy Smalley .15 .07
❑ 143 Dave Winfield 1.50 .70
❑ 144 Butch Wynegar .15 .07
❑ 145 Jim Acker .15 .07
❑ 146 Doyle Alexander .15 .07
❑ 147 Jesse Barfield .40 .18
❑ 148 Jorge Bell .40 .18
❑ 149 Barry Bonnell .15 .07
❑ 150 Jim Clancy .15 .07
❑ 151 Dave Collins .15 .07
❑ 152 Tony Fernandez 1.50 .70
❑ 153 Damaso Garcia .15 .07
❑ 154 Dave Geisel .15 .07
❑ 155 Jim Gott .15 .07
❑ 156 Alfredo Griffin .15 .07
❑ 157 Garth Iorg .15 .07
❑ 158 Roy Lee Jackson .15 .07
❑ 159 Cliff Johnson .15 .07
❑ 160 Luis Leal .15 .07
❑ 161 Buck Martinez .15 .07
❑ 162 Joey McLaughlin .15 .07
❑ 163 Randy Moffitt .15 .07
❑ 164 Lloyd Moseby .15 .07
❑ 165 Rance Mulliniks .15 .07
❑ 166 Jorge Orta .15 .07
❑ 167 Dave Stieb .15 .07
❑ 168 Willie Upshaw .15 .07
❑ 169 Ernie Whitt .15 .07
❑ 170 Len Barker .15 .07
❑ 171 Steve Bedrosian .15 .07
❑ 172 Bruce Benedict .15 .07
❑ 173 Brett Butler .75 .35
❑ 174 Rick Camp .15 .07
❑ 175 Chris Chambliss .15 .07
❑ 176 Ken Dayley .15 .07
❑ 177 Pete Falcone .15 .07
❑ 178 Terry Forster .15 .07
❑ 179 Gene Garber .15 .07
❑ 180 Terry Harper .15 .07
❑ 181 Bob Horner .15 .07
❑ 182 Glenn Hubbard .15 .07
❑ 183 Randy Johnson .15 .07
❑ 184 Craig McMurtry .15 .07
❑ 185 Donnie Moore .15 .07
❑ 186 Dale Murphy 1.50 .70
❑ 187 Phil Niekro 1.50 .70
❑ 188 Pascual Perez .15 .07
❑ 189 Biff Pocoroba .15 .07
❑ 190 Rafael Ramirez .15 .07
❑ 191 Jerry Royster .15 .07
❑ 192 Claudell Washington .15 .07
❑ 193 Bob Watson .40 .18
❑ 194 Jerry Augustine .15 .07
❑ 195 Mark Brouhard .15 .07
❑ 196 Mike Caldwell .15 .07
❑ 197 Tom Candiotti 1.50 .70
❑ 198 Cecil Cooper .40 .18
❑ 199 Rollie Fingers 1.50 .70
❑ 200 Jim Gantner .40 .18
❑ 201 Bob L. Gibson .15 .07
❑ 202 Moose Haas .15 .07
❑ 203 Roy Howell .15 .07
❑ 204 Pete Ladd .15 .07
❑ 205 Rick Manning .15 .07

❑ 206 Bob McClure .15 .07
❑ 207 Paul Molitor UER 3.00 1.35
('83 stats should say .270 BA and 608 AB)
❑ 208 Don Money .15 .07
❑ 209 Charlie Moore .15 .07
❑ 210 Ben Oglivie .15 .07
❑ 211 Chuck Porter .15 .07
❑ 212 Ed Romero .15 .07
❑ 213 Ted Simmons .40 .18
❑ 214 Jim Slaton .15 .07
❑ 215 Don Sutton 1.50 .70
❑ 216 Tom Tellmann .15 .07
❑ 217 Pete Vuckovich .15 .07
❑ 218 Ned Yost .15 .07
❑ 219 Robin Yount 1.50 .70
❑ 220 Alan Ashby .15 .07
❑ 221 Kevin Bass .15 .07
❑ 222 Jose Cruz .40 .18
❑ 223 Bill Dawley .15 .07
❑ 224 Frank DiPino .15 .07
❑ 225 Bill Doran .40 .18
❑ 226 Phil Garner .40 .18
❑ 227 Art Howe .40 .18
❑ 228 Bob Knepper .15 .07
❑ 229 Ray Knight .40 .18
❑ 230 Frank LaCorte .15 .07
❑ 231 Mike LaCoss .15 .07
❑ 232 Mike Madden .15 .07
❑ 233 Jerry Mumphrey .15 .07
❑ 234 Joe Niekro .40 .18
❑ 235 Terry Puhl .15 .07
❑ 236 Luis Pujols .15 .07
❑ 237 Craig Reynolds .15 .07
❑ 238 Vern Ruhle .15 .07
❑ 239 Nolan Ryan 10.00 4.50
❑ 240 Mike Scott .40 .18
❑ 241 Tony Scott .15 .07
❑ 242 Dave Smith .15 .07
❑ 243 Dickie Thon .15 .07
❑ 244 Denny Walling .15 .07
❑ 245 Dale Berra .15 .07
❑ 246 Jim Bibby .15 .07
❑ 247 John Candelaria .15 .07
❑ 248 Jose DeLeon .15 .07
❑ 249 Mike Easler .15 .07
❑ 250 Cecilio Guante .15 .07
❑ 251 Richie Hebner .15 .07
❑ 252 Lee Lacy .15 .07
❑ 253 Bill Madlock .40 .18
❑ 254 Milt May .15 .07
❑ 255 Lee Mazzilli .15 .07
❑ 256 Larry McWilliams .15 .07
❑ 257 Jim Morrison .15 .07
❑ 258 Dave Parker .40 .18
❑ 259 Tony Pena .15 .07
❑ 260 Johnny Ray .15 .07
❑ 261 Rick Rhoden .15 .07
❑ 262 Don Robinson .15 .07
❑ 263 Manny Sarmiento .15 .07
❑ 264 Rod Scurry .15 .07
❑ 265 Kent Tekulve .40 .18
❑ 266 Gene Tenace .40 .18
❑ 267 Jason Thompson .15 .07
❑ 268 Lee Tunnell .15 .07
❑ 269 Marvell Wynne .15 .07
❑ 270 Ray Burris .15 .07
❑ 271 Gary Carter 1.50 .70
❑ 272 Warren Cromartie .15 .07
❑ 273 Andre Dawson 1.50 .70
❑ 274 Doug Flynn .15 .07
❑ 275 Terry Francona .15 .07
❑ 276 Bill Gullickson .15 .07
❑ 277 Bob James .15 .07
❑ 278 Charlie Lea .15 .07
❑ 279 Bryan Little .15 .07
❑ 280 Al Oliver .40 .18
❑ 281 Tim Raines .75 .35
❑ 282 Bobby Ramos .15 .07
❑ 283 Jeff Reardon .40 .18
❑ 284 Steve Rogers .15 .07
❑ 285 Scott Sanderson .15 .07
❑ 286 Dan Schatzeder .15 .07
❑ 287 Bryn Smith .15 .07
❑ 288 Chris Speier .15 .07
❑ 289 Manny Trillo .15 .07
❑ 290 Mike Vail .15 .07
❑ 291 Tim Wallach .40 .18
❑ 292 Chris Welsh .15 .07
❑ 293 Jim Wohlford .15 .07
❑ 294 Kurt Bevacqua .15 .07
❑ 295 Juan Bonilla .15 .07
❑ 296 Bobby Brown .15 .07
❑ 297 Luis DeLeon .15 .07
❑ 298 Dave Dravecky .40 .18
❑ 299 Tim Flannery .15 .07
❑ 300 Steve Garvey .75 .35
❑ 301 Tony Gwynn 10.00 4.50
❑ 302 Andy Hawkins .15 .07
❑ 303 Ruppert Jones .15 .07
❑ 304 Terry Kennedy .15 .07
❑ 305 Tim Lollar .15 .07
❑ 306 Gary Lucas .15 .07
❑ 307 Kevin McReynolds .75 .35
❑ 308 Sid Monge .15 .07
❑ 309 Mario Ramirez .15 .07
❑ 310 Gene Richards .15 .07
❑ 311 Luis Salazar .15 .07
❑ 312 Eric Show .15 .07
❑ 313 Elias Sosa .15 .07
❑ 314 Garry Templeton .15 .07
❑ 315 Mark Thurmond .15 .07
❑ 316 Ed Whitson .15 .07
❑ 317 Alan Wiggins .15 .07
❑ 318 Neil Allen .15 .07
❑ 319 Joaquin Andujar .15 .07
❑ 320 Steve Braun .15 .07
❑ 321 Glenn Brummer .15 .07
❑ 322 Bob Forsch .15 .07
❑ 323 David Green .15 .07
❑ 324 George Hendrick .15 .07
❑ 325 Tom Herr .40 .18
❑ 326 Dane Iorg .15 .07
❑ 327 Jeff Lahti .15 .07
❑ 328 Dave LaPoint .15 .07
❑ 329 Willie McGee .75 .35
❑ 330 Ken Oberkfell .15 .07
❑ 331 Darrell Porter .15 .07
❑ 332 Jamie Quirk .15 .07
❑ 333 Mike Ramsey .15 .07
❑ 334 Floyd Rayford .15 .07
❑ 335 Lonnie Smith .15 .07
❑ 336 Ozzie Smith 2.50 1.10
❑ 337 John Stuper .15 .07
❑ 338 Bruce Sutter .40 .18
❑ 339 Andy Van Slyke UER 1.50 .70
(Batting and throwing both wrong on card back)
❑ 340 Dave Von Ohlen .15 .07
❑ 341 Willie Aikens .15 .07
❑ 342 Mike Armstrong .15 .07
❑ 343 Bud Black .15 .07
❑ 344 George Brett 3.00 1.35
❑ 345 Onix Concepcion .15 .07
❑ 346 Keith Creel .15 .07
❑ 347 Larry Gura .15 .07
❑ 348 Don Hood .15 .07
❑ 349 Dennis Leonard .15 .07
❑ 350 Hal McRae .40 .18
❑ 351 Amos Otis .40 .18
❑ 352 Gaylord Perry 1.50 .70
❑ 353 Greg Pryor .15 .07
❑ 354 Dan Quisenberry .15 .07
❑ 355 Steve Renko .15 .07
❑ 356 Leon Roberts .15 .07
❑ 357 Pat Sheridan .15 .07
❑ 358 Joe Simpson .15 .07
❑ 359 Don Slaught .40 .18
❑ 360 Paul Splittorff .15 .07
❑ 361 U.L. Washington .15 .07
❑ 362 John Wathan .15 .07
❑ 363 Frank White .40 .18
❑ 364 Willie Wilson .15 .07
❑ 365 Jim Barr .15 .07
❑ 366 Dave Bergman .15 .07
❑ 367 Fred Breining .15 .07
❑ 368 Bob Brenly .15 .07
❑ 369 Jack Clark .40 .18
❑ 370 Chili Davis .75 .35
❑ 371 Mark Davis .15 .07
❑ 372 Darrell Evans .40 .18
❑ 373 Atlee Hammaker .15 .07
❑ 374 Mike Krukow .15 .07
❑ 375 Duane Kuiper .15 .07
❑ 376 Bill Laskey .15 .07
❑ 377 Gary Lavelle .15 .07
❑ 378 Johnnie LeMaster .15 .07
❑ 379 Jeff Leonard .15 .07
❑ 380 Randy Lerch .15 .07
❑ 381 Renie Martin .15 .07
❑ 382 Andy McGaffigan .15 .07
❑ 383 Greg Minton .15 .07
❑ 384 Tom O'Malley .15 .07
❑ 385 Max Venable .15 .07
❑ 386 Brad Wellman .15 .07
❑ 387 Joel Youngblood .15 .07
❑ 388 Gary Allenson .15 .07
❑ 389 Luis Aponte .15 .07
❑ 390 Tony Armas .15 .07
❑ 391 Doug Bird .15 .07
❑ 392 Wade Boggs 3.00 1.35
❑ 393 Dennis Boyd .40 .18
❑ 394 Mike Brown UER P .15 .07
(shown with record of 31-104)
❑ 395 Mark Clear .15 .07
❑ 396 Dennis Eckersley 1.50 .70
❑ 397 Dwight Evans .40 .18
❑ 398 Rich Gedman .15 .07
❑ 399 Glenn Hoffman .15 .07
❑ 400 Bruce Hurst .15 .07
❑ 401 John Henry Johnson .15 .07
❑ 402 Ed Jurak .15 .07
❑ 403 Rick Miller .15 .07
❑ 404 Jeff Newman .15 .07
❑ 405 Reid Nichols .15 .07
❑ 406 Bob Ojeda .15 .07
❑ 407 Jerry Remy .15 .07
❑ 408 Jim Rice .40 .18
❑ 409 Bob Stanley .15 .07
❑ 410 Dave Stapleton .15 .07
❑ 411 John Tudor .15 .07
❑ 412 Carl Yastrzemski 1.50 .70
❑ 413 Buddy Bell .40 .18
❑ 414 Larry Biittner .15 .07
❑ 415 John Butcher .15 .07
❑ 416 Danny Darwin .40 .18
❑ 417 Bucky Dent .40 .18
❑ 418 Dave Hostetler .15 .07
❑ 419 Charlie Hough .40 .18
❑ 420 Bobby Johnson .15 .07
❑ 421 Odell Jones .15 .07
❑ 422 Jon Matlack .15 .07
❑ 423 Pete O'Brien .40 .18
❑ 424 Larry Parrish .15 .07
❑ 425 Mickey Rivers .15 .07
❑ 426 Billy Sample .15 .07
❑ 427 Dave Schmidt .15 .07
❑ 428 Mike Smithson .15 .07
❑ 429 Bill Stein .15 .07
❑ 430 Dave Stewart .40 .18
❑ 431 Jim Sundberg .40 .18
❑ 432 Frank Tanana .40 .18
❑ 433 Dave Tobik .15 .07
❑ 434 Wayne Tolleson .15 .07
❑ 435 George Wright .15 .07
❑ 436 Bill Almon .15 .07
❑ 437 Keith Atherton .15 .07
❑ 438 Dave Beard .15 .07
❑ 439 Tom Burgmeier .15 .07
❑ 440 Jeff Burroughs .15 .07
❑ 441 Chris Codiroli .15 .07
❑ 442 Tim Conroy .15 .07
❑ 443 Mike Davis .15 .07
❑ 444 Wayne Gross .15 .07
❑ 445 Garry Hancock .15 .07
❑ 446 Mike Heath .15 .07
❑ 447 Rickey Henderson 1.50 .70
❑ 448 Donnie Hill .15 .07
❑ 449 Bob Kearney .15 .07
❑ 450 Bill Krueger .15 .07
❑ 451 Rick Langford .15 .07
❑ 452 Carney Lansford .40 .18
❑ 453 Dave Lopes .40 .18
❑ 454 Steve McCatty .15 .07

❑ 455 Dan Meyer .15 .07
❑ 456 Dwayne Murphy .15 .07
❑ 457 Mike Norris .15 .07
❑ 458 Ricky Peters .15 .07
❑ 459 Tony Phillips 1.50 .70
❑ 460 Tom Underwood .15 .07
❑ 461 Mike Warren .15 .07
❑ 462 Johnny Bench 2.00 .90
❑ 463 Bruce Berenyi .15 .07
❑ 464 Dann Bilardello .15 .07
❑ 465 Cesar Cedeno .40 .18
❑ 466 Dave Concepcion .40 .18
❑ 467 Dan Driessen .15 .07
❑ 468 Nick Esasky .15 .07
❑ 469 Rich Gale .15 .07
❑ 470 Ben Hayes .15 .07
❑ 471 Paul Householder .15 .07
❑ 472 Tom Hume .15 .07
❑ 473 Alan Knicely .15 .07
❑ 474 Eddie Milner .15 .07
❑ 475 Ron Oester .15 .07
❑ 476 Kelly Paris .15 .07
❑ 477 Frank Pastore .15 .07
❑ 478 Ted Power .15 .07
❑ 479 Joe Price .15 .07
❑ 480 Charlie Puleo .15 .07
❑ 481 Gary Redus .15 .07
❑ 482 Bill Scherrer .15 .07
❑ 483 Mario Soto .15 .07
❑ 484 Alex Trevino .15 .07
❑ 485 Duane Walker .15 .07
❑ 486 Larry Bowa .40 .18
❑ 487 Warren Brusstar .15 .07
❑ 488 Bill Buckner .40 .18
❑ 489 Bill Campbell .15 .07
❑ 490 Ron Cey .40 .18
❑ 491 Jody Davis .15 .07
❑ 492 Leon Durham .15 .07
❑ 493 Mel Hall .40 .18
❑ 494 Ferguson Jenkins 1.50 .70
❑ 495 Jay Johnstone .40 .18
❑ 496 Craig Lefferts .15 .07
❑ 497 Carmelo Martinez .15 .07
❑ 498 Jerry Morales .15 .07
❑ 499 Keith Moreland .15 .07
❑ 500 Dickie Noles .15 .07
❑ 501 Mike Proly .15 .07
❑ 502 Chuck Rainey .15 .07
❑ 503 Dick Ruthven .15 .07
❑ 504 Ryne Sandberg 5.00 2.20
❑ 505 Lee Smith 1.50 .70
❑ 506 Steve Trout .15 .07
❑ 507 Gary Woods .15 .07
❑ 508 Juan Beniquez .15 .07
❑ 509 Bob Boone .40 .18
❑ 510 Rick Burleson .15 .07
❑ 511 Rod Carew 1.50 .70
❑ 512 Bobby Clark .15 .07
❑ 513 John Curtis .15 .07
❑ 514 Doug DeCinces .15 .07
❑ 515 Brian Downing .15 .07
❑ 516 Tim Foli .15 .07
❑ 517 Ken Forsch .15 .07
❑ 518 Bobby Grich .40 .18
❑ 519 Andy Hassler .15 .07
❑ 520 Reggie Jackson 2.00 .90
❑ 521 Ron Jackson .15 .07
❑ 522 Tommy John .75 .35
❑ 523 Bruce Kison .15 .07
❑ 524 Steve Lubratich .15 .07
❑ 525 Fred Lynn .40 .18
❑ 526 Gary Pettis .15 .07
❑ 527 Luis Sanchez .15 .07
❑ 528 Daryl Sconiers .15 .07
❑ 529 Ellis Valentine .15 .07
❑ 530 Rob Wilfong .15 .07
❑ 531 Mike Witt .15 .07
❑ 532 Geoff Zahn .15 .07
❑ 533 Bud Anderson .15 .07
❑ 534 Chris Bando .15 .07
❑ 535 Alan Bannister .15 .07
❑ 536 Bert Blyleven .40 .18
❑ 537 Tom Brennan .15 .07
❑ 538 Jamie Easterly .15 .07
❑ 539 Juan Eichelberger .15 .07
❑ 540 Jim Essian .15 .07
❑ 541 Mike Fischlin .15 .07
❑ 542 Julio Franco .75 .35
❑ 543 Mike Hargrove .40 .18
❑ 544 Toby Harrah .40 .18
❑ 545 Ron Hassey .15 .07
❑ 546 Neal Heaton .15 .07
❑ 547 Bake McBride .15 .07
❑ 548 Broderick Perkins .15 .07
❑ 549 Lary Sorensen .15 .07
❑ 550 Dan Spillner .15 .07
❑ 551 Rick Sutcliffe .40 .18
❑ 552 Pat Tabler .15 .07
❑ 553 Gorman Thomas .15 .07
❑ 554 Andre Thornton .15 .07
❑ 555 George Vukovich .15 .07
❑ 556 Darrell Brown .15 .07
❑ 557 Tom Brunansky .40 .18
❑ 558 Randy Bush .15 .07
❑ 559 Bobby Castillo .15 .07
❑ 560 John Castino .15 .07
❑ 561 Ron Davis .15 .07
❑ 562 Dave Engle .15 .07
❑ 563 Lenny Faedo .15 .07
❑ 564 Pete Filson .15 .07
❑ 565 Gary Gaetti .75 .35
❑ 566 Mickey Hatcher .15 .07
❑ 567 Kent Hrbek .40 .18
❑ 568 Rusty Kuntz .15 .07
❑ 569 Tim Laudner .15 .07
❑ 570 Rick Lysander .15 .07
❑ 571 Bobby Mitchell .15 .07
❑ 572 Ken Schrom .15 .07
❑ 573 Ray Smith .15 .07
❑ 574 Tim Teufel .15 .07
❑ 575 Frank Viola .75 .35
❑ 576 Gary Ward .15 .07
❑ 577 Ron Washington .15 .07
❑ 578 Len Whitehouse .15 .07
❑ 579 Al Williams .15 .07
❑ 580 Bob Bailor .15 .07
❑ 581 Mark Bradley .15 .07
❑ 582 Hubie Brooks .15 .07
❑ 583 Carlos Diaz .15 .07
❑ 584 George Foster .40 .18
❑ 585 Brian Giles .15 .07
❑ 586 Danny Heep .15 .07
❑ 587 Keith Hernandez .40 .18
❑ 588 Ron Hodges .15 .07
❑ 589 Scott Holman .15 .07
❑ 590 Dave Kingman .75 .35
❑ 591 Ed Lynch .15 .07
❑ 592 Jose Oquendo .40 .18
❑ 593 Jesse Orosco .15 .07
❑ 594 Junior Ortiz .15 .07
❑ 595 Tom Seaver 2.00 .90
❑ 596 Doug Sisk .15 .07
❑ 597 Rusty Staub .40 .18
❑ 598 John Stearns .15 .07
❑ 599 Darryl Strawberry 5.00 2.20
❑ 600 Craig Swan .15 .07
❑ 601 Walt Terrell .15 .07
❑ 602 Mike Torrez .15 .07
❑ 603 Mookie Wilson .40 .18
❑ 604 Jamie Allen .15 .07
❑ 605 Jim Beattie .15 .07
❑ 606 Tony Bernazard .15 .07
❑ 607 Manny Castillo .15 .07
❑ 608 Bill Caudill .15 .07
❑ 609 Bryan Clark .15 .07
❑ 610 Al Cowens .15 .07
❑ 611 Dave Henderson .40 .18
❑ 612 Steve Henderson .15 .07
❑ 613 Orlando Mercado .15 .07
❑ 614 Mike Moore .15 .07
❑ 615 Ricky Nelson UER .15 .07
(Jamie Nelson's
stats on back)
❑ 616 Spike Owen .40 .18
❑ 617 Pat Putnam .15 .07
❑ 618 Ron Roenicke .15 .07
❑ 619 Mike Stanton .15 .07
❑ 620 Bob Stoddard .15 .07
❑ 621 Rick Sweet .15 .07
❑ 622 Roy Thomas .15 .07
❑ 623 Ed VandeBerg .15 .07
❑ 624 Matt Young .15 .07
❑ 625 Richie Zisk .15 .07
❑ 626 Fred Lynn .40 .18
1982 AS Game RB
❑ 627 Manny Trillo .15 .07
1983 AS Game RB
❑ 628 Steve Garvey .40 .18
NL Iron Man
❑ 629 Rod Carew .75 .35
AL Batting Runner-Up
❑ 630 Wade Boggs 1.50 .70
AL Batting Champion
❑ 631 Tim Raines: Letting .40 .18
Go of the Raines
❑ 632 Al Oliver .40 .18
Double Trouble
❑ 633 Steve Sax .15 .07
AS Second Base
❑ 634 Dickie Thon .15 .07
AS Shortstop
❑ 635 Ace Firemen .15 .07
Dan Quisenberry
and Tippy Martinez
❑ 636 Reds Reunited 1.50 .70
Joe Morgan
Pete Rose
Tony Perez
❑ 637 Backstop Stars .75 .35
Lance Parrish
Bob Boone
❑ 638 George Brett and 2.00 .90
Gaylord Perry
Pine Tar 7/24/83
❑ 639 1983 No Hitters .75 .35
Dave Righetti
Mike Warren
Bob Forsch
❑ 640 Johnny Bench and 2.00 .90
Carl Yastrzemski
Retiring Superstars
❑ 641 Gaylord Perry 1.50 .70
Going Out In Style
❑ 642 Steve Carlton .75 .35
300 Club and
Strikeout Record
❑ 643 Joe Altobelli and .15 .07
Paul Owens
World Series Managers
❑ 644 Rick Dempsey .40 .18
World Series MVP
❑ 645 Mike Boddicker .15 .07
WS Rookie Winner
❑ 646 Scott McGregor .15 .07
WS Clincher
❑ 647 CL: Orioles/Royals .15 .07
Joe Altobelli MG
❑ 648 CL: Phillies/Giants .15 .07
Paul Owens MG
❑ 649 CL: White Sox/Red Sox .75 .35
Tony LaRussa MG
❑ 650 CL: Tigers/Rangers .75 .35
Sparky Anderson MG
❑ 651 CL: Dodgers/A's .75 .35
Tommy Lasorda MG
❑ 652 CL: Yankees/Reds .75 .35
Billy Martin MG
❑ 653 CL: Blue Jays/Cubs .40 .18
Bobby Cox MG
❑ 654 CL: Braves/Angels .75 .35
Joe Torre MG
❑ 655 CL: Brewers/Indians .15 .07
Rene Lachemann MG
❑ 656 CL: Astros/Twins .15 .07
Bob Lillis MG
❑ 657 CL: Pirates/Mets .15 .07
Chuck Tanner MG
❑ 658 CL: Expos/Mariners .15 .07
Bill Virdon MG
❑ 659 CL: Padres/Specials .40 .18
Dick Williams MG
❑ 660 CL: Cardinals/Teams .75 .35
Whitey Herzog MG

1984 Fleer Update

	NRMT	VG-E
COMP.FACT.SET (132)	400.00	180.00
COMMON CARD (1-132)	1.00	.45
❑ 1 Willie Aikens	1.00	.45
❑ 2 Luis Aponte	1.00	.45
❑ 3 Mark Bailey	1.00	.45
❑ 4 Bob Bailor	1.00	.45
❑ 5 Dusty Baker	3.00	1.35
❑ 6 Steve Balboni	1.00	.45
❑ 7 Alan Bannister	1.00	.45
❑ 8 Marty Barrett	3.00	1.35
❑ 9 Dave Beard	1.00	.45
❑ 10 Joe Beckwith	1.00	.45
❑ 11 Dave Bergman	1.00	.45
❑ 12 Tony Bernazard	1.00	.45
❑ 13 Bruce Bochte	1.00	.45
❑ 14 Barry Bonnell	1.00	.45
❑ 15 Phil Bradley	3.00	1.35
❑ 16 Fred Breining	1.00	.45
❑ 17 Mike C. Brown	1.00	.45
❑ 18 Bill Buckner	3.00	1.35
❑ 19 Ray Burris	1.00	.45
❑ 20 John Butcher	1.00	.45
❑ 21 Brett Butler	5.00	2.20
❑ 22 Enos Cabell	1.00	.45
❑ 23 Bill Campbell	1.00	.45
❑ 24 Bill Caudill	1.00	.45
❑ 25 Bobby Clark	1.00	.45
❑ 26 Bryan Clark	1.00	.45
❑ 27 Roger Clemens	250.00	110.00
❑ 28 Jaime Cocanower	1.00	.45
❑ 29 Ron Darling	5.00	2.20
❑ 30 Alvin Davis	3.00	1.35
❑ 31 Bob Dernier	1.00	.45
❑ 32 Carlos Diaz	1.00	.45
❑ 33 Mike Easler	1.00	.45
❑ 34 Dennis Eckersley	5.00	2.20
❑ 35 Jim Essian	1.00	.45
❑ 36 Darrell Evans	3.00	1.35
❑ 37 Mike Fitzgerald	1.00	.45
❑ 38 Tim Foli	1.00	.45
❑ 39 John Franco	6.00	2.70
❑ 40 George Frazier	1.00	.45
❑ 41 Rich Gale	1.00	.45
❑ 42 Barbaro Garbey	1.00	.45
❑ 43 Dwight Gooden	20.00	9.00
❑ 44 Rich Gossage	5.00	2.20
❑ 45 Wayne Gross	1.00	.45
❑ 46 Mark Gubicza	3.00	1.35
❑ 47 Jackie Gutierrez	1.00	.45
❑ 48 Toby Harrah	3.00	1.35
❑ 49 Ron Hassey	1.00	.45
❑ 50 Richie Hebner	1.00	.45
❑ 51 Willie Hernandez	3.00	1.35
❑ 52 Ed Hodge	1.00	.45
❑ 53 Ricky Horton	1.00	.45
❑ 54 Art Howe	3.00	1.35
❑ 55 Dane Iorg	1.00	.45
❑ 56 Brook Jacoby	3.00	1.35
❑ 57 Dion James	3.00	1.35
❑ 58 Mike Jeffcoat	1.00	.45
❑ 59 Ruppert Jones	1.00	.45
❑ 60 Bob Kearney	1.00	.45
❑ 61 Jimmy Key	15.00	6.75
❑ 62 Dave Kingman	5.00	2.20
❑ 63 Brad Komminsk	1.00	.45
❑ 64 Jerry Koosman	3.00	1.35
❑ 65 Wayne Krenchicki	1.00	.45
❑ 66 Rusty Kuntz	1.00	.45
❑ 67 Frank LaCorte	1.00	.45
❑ 68 Dennis Lamp	1.00	.45
❑ 69 Tito Landrum	1.00	.45
❑ 70 Mark Langston	6.00	2.70
❑ 71 Rick Leach	1.00	.45
❑ 72 Craig Lefferts	3.00	1.35
❑ 73 Gary Lucas	1.00	.45
❑ 74 Jerry Martin	1.00	.45
❑ 75 Carmelo Martinez	1.00	.45
❑ 76 Mike Mason	1.00	.45
❑ 77 Gary Matthews	3.00	1.35
❑ 78 Andy McGaffigan	1.00	.45
❑ 79 Joey McLaughlin	1.00	.45
❑ 80 Joe Morgan	6.00	2.70
❑ 81 Darryl Motley	1.00	.45
❑ 82 Graig Nettles	3.00	1.35
❑ 83 Phil Niekro	6.00	2.70
❑ 84 Ken Oberkfell	1.00	.45
❑ 85 Al Oliver	3.00	1.35
❑ 86 Jorge Orta	1.00	.45
❑ 87 Amos Otis	3.00	1.35
❑ 88 Bob Owchinko	1.00	.45
❑ 89 Dave Parker	3.00	1.35
❑ 90 Jack Perconte	1.00	.45
❑ 91 Tony Perez	6.00	2.70
❑ 92 Gerald Perry	3.00	1.35
❑ 93 Kirby Puckett	125.00	55.00
❑ 94 Shane Rawley	1.00	.45
❑ 95 Floyd Rayford	1.00	.45
❑ 96 Ron Reed	1.00	.45
❑ 97 R.J. Reynolds	1.00	.45
❑ 98 Gene Richards	1.00	.45
❑ 99 Jose Rijo	6.00	2.70
❑ 100 Jeff D. Robinson	1.00	.45
❑ 101 Ron Romanick	1.00	.45
❑ 102 Pete Rose	12.00	5.50
❑ 103 Bret Saberhagen	12.00	5.50
❑ 104 Scott Sanderson	1.00	.45
❑ 105 Dick Schofield	3.00	1.35
❑ 106 Tom Seaver	12.00	5.50
❑ 107 Jim Slaton	1.00	.45
❑ 108 Mike Smithson	1.00	.45
❑ 109 Lary Sorensen	1.00	.45
❑ 110 Tim Stoddard	1.00	.45
❑ 111 Jeff Stone	1.00	.45
❑ 112 Champ Summers	1.00	.45
❑ 113 Jim Sundberg	3.00	1.35
❑ 114 Rick Sutcliffe	5.00	2.20
❑ 115 Craig Swan	1.00	.45
❑ 116 Derrel Thomas	1.00	.45
❑ 117 Gorman Thomas	1.00	.45
❑ 118 Alex Trevino	1.00	.45
❑ 119 Manny Trillo	1.00	.45
❑ 120 John Tudor	1.00	.45
❑ 121 Tom Underwood	1.00	.45
❑ 122 Mike Vail	1.00	.45
❑ 123 Tom Waddell	1.00	.45
❑ 124 Gary Ward	1.00	.45
❑ 125 Terry Whitfield	1.00	.45
❑ 126 Curtis Wilkerson	1.00	.45
❑ 127 Frank Williams	1.00	.45
❑ 128 Glenn Wilson	1.00	.45
❑ 129 John Wockenfuss	1.00	.45
❑ 130 Ned Yost	1.00	.45
❑ 131 Mike Young	1.00	.45
❑ 132 Checklist 1-132	1.00	.45

1985 Fleer

	NRMT	VG-E
COMPLETE SET (660)	100.00	45.00
COMMON CARD (1-660)	.15	.07
❑ 1 Doug Bair	.15	.07
❑ 2 Juan Berenguer	.15	.07
❑ 3 Dave Bergman	.15	.07
❑ 4 Tom Brookens	.15	.07
❑ 5 Marty Castillo	.15	.07
❑ 6 Darrell Evans	.40	.18
❑ 7 Barbaro Garbey	.15	.07
❑ 8 Kirk Gibson	.40	.18
❑ 9 John Grubb	.15	.07
❑ 10 Willie Hernandez	.15	.07
❑ 11 Larry Herndon	.15	.07
❑ 12 Howard Johnson	.40	.18
❑ 13 Ruppert Jones	.15	.07
❑ 14 Rusty Kuntz	.15	.07
❑ 15 Chet Lemon	.15	.07
❑ 16 Aurelio Lopez	.15	.07
❑ 17 Sid Monge	.15	.07
❑ 18 Jack Morris	.40	.18
❑ 19 Lance Parrish	.40	.18
❑ 20 Dan Petry	.15	.07
❑ 21 Dave Rozema	.15	.07
❑ 22 Bill Scherrer	.15	.07
❑ 23 Alan Trammell	.75	.35
❑ 24 Lou Whitaker	.75	.35
❑ 25 Milt Wilcox	.15	.07
❑ 26 Kurt Bevacqua	.15	.07
❑ 27 Greg Booker	.15	.07
❑ 28 Bobby Brown	.15	.07
❑ 29 Luis DeLeon	.15	.07
❑ 30 Dave Dravecky	.40	.18
❑ 31 Tim Flannery	.15	.07
❑ 32 Steve Garvey	.75	.35
❑ 33 Rich Gossage	.40	.18
❑ 34 Tony Gwynn	6.00	2.70
❑ 35 Greg Harris	.15	.07
❑ 36 Andy Hawkins	.15	.07
❑ 37 Terry Kennedy	.15	.07
❑ 38 Craig Lefferts	.15	.07
❑ 39 Tim Lollar	.15	.07
❑ 40 Carmelo Martinez	.15	.07
❑ 41 Kevin McReynolds	.40	.18
❑ 42 Graig Nettles	.40	.18
❑ 43 Luis Salazar	.15	.07
❑ 44 Eric Show	.15	.07
❑ 45 Garry Templeton	.15	.07
❑ 46 Mark Thurmond	.15	.07
❑ 47 Ed Whitson	.15	.07
❑ 48 Alan Wiggins	.15	.07
❑ 49 Rich Bordi	.15	.07
❑ 50 Larry Bowa	.40	.18
❑ 51 Warren Brusstar	.15	.07
❑ 52 Ron Cey	.40	.18
❑ 53 Henry Cotto	.15	.07
❑ 54 Jody Davis	.15	.07
❑ 55 Bob Dernier	.15	.07
❑ 56 Leon Durham	.15	.07
❑ 57 Dennis Eckersley	1.50	.70
❑ 58 George Frazier	.15	.07
❑ 59 Richie Hebner	.15	.07
❑ 60 Dave Lopes	.40	.18
❑ 61 Gary Matthews	.15	.07
❑ 62 Keith Moreland	.15	.07
❑ 63 Rick Reuschel	.15	.07
❑ 64 Dick Ruthven	.15	.07
❑ 65 Ryne Sandberg	3.00	1.35
❑ 66 Scott Sanderson	.15	.07
❑ 67 Lee Smith	.75	.35
❑ 68 Tim Stoddard	.15	.07
❑ 69 Rick Sutcliffe	.15	.07
❑ 70 Steve Trout	.15	.07
❑ 71 Gary Woods	.15	.07
❑ 72 Wally Backman	.15	.07
❑ 73 Bruce Berenyi	.15	.07
❑ 74 Hubie Brooks UER (Kelvin Chapman's stats on card back)	.15	.07
❑ 75 Kelvin Chapman	.15	.07

	No.	Player		
❑	76	Ron Darling	.40	.18
❑	77	Sid Fernandez	.40	.18
❑	78	Mike Fitzgerald	.15	.07
❑	79	George Foster	.40	.18
❑	80	Brent Gaff	.15	.07
❑	81	Ron Gardenhire	.15	.07
❑	82	Dwight Gooden	2.50	1.10
❑	83	Tom Gorman	.15	.07
❑	84	Danny Heep	.15	.07
❑	85	Keith Hernandez	.40	.18
❑	86	Ray Knight	.15	.07
❑	87	Ed Lynch	.15	.07
❑	88	Jose Oquendo	.15	.07
❑	89	Jesse Orosco	.15	.07
❑	90	Rafael Santana	.15	.07
❑	91	Doug Sisk	.15	.07
❑	92	Rusty Staub	.40	.18
❑	93	Darryl Strawberry	1.50	.70
❑	94	Walt Terrell	.15	.07
❑	95	Mookie Wilson	.40	.18
❑	96	Jim Acker	.15	.07
❑	97	Willie Aikens	.15	.07
❑	98	Doyle Alexander	.15	.07
❑	99	Jesse Barfield	.15	.07
❑	100	George Bell	.40	.18
❑	101	Jim Clancy	.15	.07
❑	102	Dave Collins	.15	.07
❑	103	Tony Fernandez	.40	.18
❑	104	Damaso Garcia	.15	.07
❑	105	Jim Gott	.15	.07
❑	106	Alfredo Griffin	.15	.07
❑	107	Garth Iorg	.15	.07
❑	108	Roy Lee Jackson	.15	.07
❑	109	Cliff Johnson	.15	.07
❑	110	Jimmy Key	2.00	.90
❑	111	Dennis Lamp	.15	.07
❑	112	Rick Leach	.15	.07
❑	113	Luis Leal	.15	.07
❑	114	Buck Martinez	.15	.07
❑	115	Lloyd Moseby	.15	.07
❑	116	Rance Mulliniks	.15	.07
❑	117	Dave Stieb	.40	.18
❑	118	Willie Upshaw	.15	.07
❑	119	Ernie Whitt	.15	.07
❑	120	Mike Armstrong	.15	.07
❑	121	Don Baylor	.40	.18
❑	122	Marty Bystrom	.15	.07
❑	123	Rick Cerone	.15	.07
❑	124	Joe Cowley	.15	.07
❑	125	Brian Dayett	.15	.07
❑	126	Tim Foli	.15	.07
❑	127	Ray Fontenot	.15	.07
❑	128	Ken Griffey	.40	.18
❑	129	Ron Guidry	.40	.18
❑	130	Toby Harrah	.15	.07
❑	131	Jay Howell	.15	.07
❑	132	Steve Kemp	.15	.07
❑	133	Don Mattingly	4.00	1.80
❑	134	Bobby Meacham	.15	.07
❑	135	John Montefusco	.15	.07
❑	136	Omar Moreno	.15	.07
❑	137	Dale Murray	.15	.07
❑	138	Phil Niekro	1.50	.70
❑	139	Mike Pagliarulo	.15	.07
❑	140	Willie Randolph	.40	.18
❑	141	Dennis Rasmussen	.15	.07
❑	142	Dave Righetti	.40	.18
❑	143	Jose Rijo	.75	.35
❑	144	Andre Robertson	.15	.07
❑	145	Bob Shirley	.15	.07
❑	146	Dave Winfield	1.50	.70
❑	147	Butch Wynegar	.15	.07
❑	148	Gary Allenson	.15	.07
❑	149	Tony Armas	.15	.07
❑	150	Marty Barrett	.15	.07
❑	151	Wade Boggs	2.00	.90
❑	152	Dennis Boyd	.15	.07
❑	153	Bill Buckner	.40	.18
❑	154	Mark Clear	.15	.07
❑	155	Roger Clemens	40.00	18.00
❑	156	Steve Crawford	.15	.07
❑	157	Mike Easler	.15	.07
❑	158	Dwight Evans	.40	.18
❑	159	Rich Gedman	.15	.07
❑	160	Jackie Gutierrez (Wade Boggs shown on deck)	.40	.18
❑	161	Bruce Hurst	.15	.07
❑	162	John Henry Johnson	.15	.07
❑	163	Rick Miller	.15	.07
❑	164	Reid Nichols	.15	.07
❑	165	Al Nipper	.15	.07
❑	166	Bob Ojeda	.15	.07
❑	167	Jerry Remy	.15	.07
❑	168	Jim Rice	.40	.18
❑	169	Bob Stanley	.15	.07
❑	170	Mike Boddicker	.15	.07
❑	171	Al Bumbry	.15	.07
❑	172	Todd Cruz	.15	.07
❑	173	Rich Dauer	.15	.07
❑	174	Storm Davis	.15	.07
❑	175	Rick Dempsey	.15	.07
❑	176	Jim Dwyer	.15	.07
❑	177	Mike Flanagan	.15	.07
❑	178	Dan Ford	.15	.07
❑	179	Wayne Gross	.15	.07
❑	180	John Lowenstein	.15	.07
❑	181	Dennis Martinez	.40	.18
❑	182	Tippy Martinez	.15	.07
❑	183	Scott McGregor	.15	.07
❑	184	Eddie Murray	1.50	.70
❑	185	Joe Nolan	.15	.07
❑	186	Floyd Rayford	.15	.07
❑	187	Cal Ripken	8.00	3.60
❑	188	Gary Roenicke	.15	.07
❑	189	Lenn Sakata	.15	.07
❑	190	John Shelby	.15	.07
❑	191	Ken Singleton	.15	.07
❑	192	Sammy Stewart	.15	.07
❑	193	Bill Swaggerty	.15	.07
❑	194	Tom Underwood	.15	.07
❑	195	Mike Young	.15	.07
❑	196	Steve Balboni	.15	.07
❑	197	Joe Beckwith	.15	.07
❑	198	Bud Black	.15	.07
❑	199	George Brett	3.00	1.35
❑	200	Onix Concepcion	.15	.07
❑	201	Mark Gubicza	.40	.18
❑	202	Larry Gura	.15	.07
❑	203	Mark Huismann	.15	.07
❑	204	Dane Iorg	.15	.07
❑	205	Danny Jackson	.15	.07
❑	206	Charlie Leibrandt	.15	.07
❑	207	Hal McRae	.40	.18
❑	208	Darryl Motley	.15	.07
❑	209	Jorge Orta	.15	.07
❑	210	Greg Pryor	.15	.07
❑	211	Dan Quisenberry	.40	.18
❑	212	Bret Saberhagen	1.50	.70
❑	213	Pat Sheridan	.15	.07
❑	214	Don Slaught	.15	.07
❑	215	U.L. Washington	.15	.07
❑	216	John Wathan	.15	.07
❑	217	Frank White	.40	.18
❑	218	Willie Wilson	.15	.07
❑	219	Neil Allen	.15	.07
❑	220	Joaquin Andujar	.15	.07
❑	221	Steve Braun	.15	.07
❑	222	Danny Cox	.15	.07
❑	223	Bob Forsch	.15	.07
❑	224	David Green	.15	.07
❑	225	George Hendrick	.15	.07
❑	226	Tom Herr	.15	.07
❑	227	Ricky Horton	.15	.07
❑	228	Art Howe	.15	.07
❑	229	Mike Jorgensen	.15	.07
❑	230	Kurt Kepshire	.15	.07
❑	231	Jeff Lahti	.15	.07
❑	232	Tito Landrum	.15	.07
❑	233	Dave LaPoint	.15	.07
❑	234	Willie McGee	.40	.18
❑	235	Tom Nieto	.15	.07
❑	236	Terry Pendleton	1.50	.70
❑	237	Darrell Porter	.15	.07
❑	238	Dave Rucker	.15	.07
❑	239	Lonnie Smith	.15	.07
❑	240	Ozzie Smith	2.00	.90
❑	241	Bruce Sutter	.40	.18
❑	242	Andy Van Slyke UER (Bats Right, Throws Left)	.75	.35
❑	243	Dave Von Ohlen	.15	.07
❑	244	Larry Andersen	.15	.07
❑	245	Bill Campbell	.15	.07
❑	246	Steve Carlton	1.50	.70
❑	247	Tim Corcoran	.15	.07
❑	248	Ivan DeJesus	.15	.07
❑	249	John Denny	.15	.07
❑	250	Bo Diaz	.15	.07
❑	251	Greg Gross	.15	.07
❑	252	Kevin Gross	.15	.07
❑	253	Von Hayes	.15	.07
❑	254	Al Holland	.15	.07
❑	255	Charles Hudson	.15	.07
❑	256	Jerry Koosman	.15	.07
❑	257	Joe Lefebvre	.15	.07
❑	258	Sixto Lezcano	.15	.07
❑	259	Garry Maddox	.15	.07
❑	260	Len Matuszek	.15	.07
❑	261	Tug McGraw	.40	.18
❑	262	Al Oliver	.40	.18
❑	263	Shane Rawley	.15	.07
❑	264	Juan Samuel	.15	.07
❑	265	Mike Schmidt	2.00	.90
❑	266	Jeff Stone	.15	.07
❑	267	Ozzie Virgil	.15	.07
❑	268	Glenn Wilson	.15	.07
❑	269	John Wockenfuss	.15	.07
❑	270	Darrell Brown	.15	.07
❑	271	Tom Brunansky	.40	.18
❑	272	Randy Bush	.15	.07
❑	273	John Butcher	.15	.07
❑	274	Bobby Castillo	.15	.07
❑	275	Ron Davis	.15	.07
❑	276	Dave Engle	.15	.07
❑	277	Pete Filson	.15	.07
❑	278	Gary Gaetti	.40	.18
❑	279	Mickey Hatcher	.15	.07
❑	280	Ed Hodge	.15	.07
❑	281	Kent Hrbek	.40	.18
❑	282	Houston Jimenez	.15	.07
❑	283	Tim Laudner	.15	.07
❑	284	Rick Lysander	.15	.07
❑	285	Dave Meier	.15	.07
❑	286	Kirby Puckett	20.00	9.00
❑	287	Pat Putnam	.15	.07
❑	288	Ken Schrom	.15	.07
❑	289	Mike Smithson	.15	.07
❑	290	Tim Teufel	.15	.07
❑	291	Frank Viola	.40	.18
❑	292	Ron Washington	.15	.07
❑	293	Don Aase	.15	.07
❑	294	Juan Beniquez	.15	.07
❑	295	Bob Boone	.40	.18
❑	296	Mike C. Brown	.15	.07
❑	297	Rod Carew	1.50	.70
❑	298	Doug Corbett	.15	.07
❑	299	Doug DeCinces	.15	.07
❑	300	Brian Downing	.15	.07
❑	301	Ken Forsch	.15	.07
❑	302	Bobby Grich	.40	.18
❑	303	Reggie Jackson	2.00	.90
❑	304	Tommy John	.75	.35
❑	305	Curt Kaufman	.15	.07
❑	306	Bruce Kison	.15	.07
❑	307	Fred Lynn	.40	.18
❑	308	Gary Pettis	.15	.07
❑	309	Ron Romanick	.15	.07
❑	310	Luis Sanchez	.15	.07
❑	311	Dick Schofield	.15	.07
❑	312	Daryl Sconiers	.15	.07
❑	313	Jim Slaton	.15	.07
❑	314	Derrel Thomas	.15	.07
❑	315	Rob Wilfong	.15	.07
❑	316	Mike Witt	.15	.07
❑	317	Geoff Zahn	.15	.07
❑	318	Len Barker	.15	.07
❑	319	Steve Bedrosian	.15	.07
❑	320	Bruce Benedict	.15	.07
❑	321	Rick Camp	.15	.07
❑	322	Chris Chambliss	.15	.07
❑	323	Jeff Dedmon	.15	.07
❑	324	Terry Forster	.15	.07
❑	325	Gene Garber	.15	.07
❑	326	Albert Hall	.15	.07
❑	327	Terry Harper	.15	.07

	No.	Player		
❑	328	Bob Horner	.15	.07
❑	329	Glenn Hubbard	.15	.07
❑	330	Randy Johnson	.15	.07
❑	331	Brad Komminsk	.15	.07
❑	332	Rick Mahler	.15	.07
❑	333	Craig McMurtry	.15	.07
❑	334	Donnie Moore	.15	.07
❑	335	Dale Murphy	1.50	.70
❑	336	Ken Oberkfell	.15	.07
❑	337	Pascual Perez	.15	.07
❑	338	Gerald Perry	.15	.07
❑	339	Rafael Ramirez	.15	.07
❑	340	Jerry Royster	.15	.07
❑	341	Alex Trevino	.15	.07
❑	342	Claudell Washington	.15	.07
❑	343	Alan Ashby	.15	.07
❑	344	Mark Bailey	.15	.07
❑	345	Kevin Bass	.15	.07
❑	346	Enos Cabell	.15	.07
❑	347	Jose Cruz	.40	.18
❑	348	Bill Dawley	.15	.07
❑	349	Frank DiPino	.15	.07
❑	350	Bill Doran	.15	.07
❑	351	Phil Garner	.40	.18
❑	352	Bob Knepper	.15	.07
❑	353	Mike LaCoss	.15	.07
❑	354	Jerry Mumphrey	.15	.07
❑	355	Joe Niekro	.15	.07
❑	356	Terry Puhl	.15	.07
❑	357	Craig Reynolds	.15	.07
❑	358	Vern Ruhle	.15	.07
❑	359	Nolan Ryan	8.00	3.60
❑	360	Joe Sambito	.15	.07
❑	361	Mike Scott	.15	.07
❑	362	Dave Smith	.15	.07
❑	363	Julio Solano	.15	.07
❑	364	Dickie Thon	.15	.07
❑	365	Denny Walling	.15	.07
❑	366	Dave Anderson	.15	.07
❑	367	Bob Bailor	.15	.07
❑	368	Greg Brock	.15	.07
❑	369	Carlos Diaz	.15	.07
❑	370	Pedro Guerrero	.40	.18
❑	371	Orel Hershiser	2.00	.90
❑	372	Rick Honeycutt	.15	.07
❑	373	Burt Hooton	.15	.07
❑	374	Ken Howell	.15	.07
❑	375	Ken Landreaux	.15	.07
❑	376	Candy Maldonado	.15	.07
❑	377	Mike Marshall	.15	.07
❑	378	Tom Niedenfuer	.15	.07
❑	379	Alejandro Pena	.15	.07
❑	380	Jerry Reuss UER ("Home:" omitted)	.15	.07
❑	381	R.J. Reynolds	.15	.07
❑	382	German Rivera	.15	.07
❑	383	Bill Russell	.40	.18
❑	384	Steve Sax	.15	.07
❑	385	Mike Scioscia	.15	.07
❑	386	Franklin Stubbs	.15	.07
❑	387	Fernando Valenzuela	.40	.18
❑	388	Bob Welch	.15	.07
❑	389	Terry Whitfield	.15	.07
❑	390	Steve Yeager	.15	.07
❑	391	Pat Zachry	.15	.07
❑	392	Fred Breining	.15	.07
❑	393	Gary Carter	1.50	.70
❑	394	Andre Dawson	1.50	.70
❑	395	Miguel Dilone	.15	.07
❑	396	Dan Driessen	.15	.07
❑	397	Doug Flynn	.15	.07
❑	398	Terry Francona	.15	.07
❑	399	Bill Gullickson	.15	.07
❑	400	Bob James	.15	.07
❑	401	Charlie Lea	.15	.07
❑	402	Bryan Little	.15	.07
❑	403	Gary Lucas	.15	.07
❑	404	David Palmer	.15	.07
❑	405	Tim Raines	.40	.18
❑	406	Mike Ramsey	.15	.07
❑	407	Jeff Reardon	.40	.18
❑	408	Steve Rogers	.15	.07
❑	409	Dan Schatzeder	.15	.07
❑	410	Bryn Smith	.15	.07
❑	411	Mike Stenhouse	.15	.07
❑	412	Tim Wallach	.40	.18
❑	413	Jim Wohlford	.15	.07
❑	414	Bill Almon	.15	.07
❑	415	Keith Atherton	.15	.07
❑	416	Bruce Bochte	.15	.07
❑	417	Tom Burgmeier	.15	.07
❑	418	Ray Burris	.15	.07
❑	419	Bill Caudill	.15	.07
❑	420	Chris Codiroli	.15	.07
❑	421	Tim Conroy	.15	.07
❑	422	Mike Davis	.15	.07
❑	423	Jim Essian	.15	.07
❑	424	Mike Heath	.15	.07
❑	425	Rickey Henderson	1.50	.70
❑	426	Donnie Hill	.15	.07
❑	427	Dave Kingman	.40	.18
❑	428	Bill Krueger	.15	.07
❑	429	Carney Lansford	.40	.18
❑	430	Steve McCatty	.15	.07
❑	431	Joe Morgan	1.50	.70
❑	432	Dwayne Murphy	.15	.07
❑	433	Tony Phillips	.15	.07
❑	434	Lary Sorensen	.15	.07
❑	435	Mike Warren	.15	.07
❑	436	Curt Young	.15	.07
❑	437	Luis Aponte	.15	.07
❑	438	Chris Bando	.15	.07
❑	439	Tony Bernazard	.15	.07
❑	440	Bert Blyleven	.40	.18
❑	441	Brett Butler	.40	.18
❑	442	Ernie Camacho	.15	.07
❑	443	Joe Carter	1.50	.70
❑	444	Carmelo Castillo	.15	.07
❑	445	Jamie Easterly	.15	.07
❑	446	Steve Farr	.40	.18
❑	447	Mike Fischlin	.15	.07
❑	448	Julio Franco	.75	.35
❑	449	Mel Hall	.15	.07
❑	450	Mike Hargrove	.40	.18
❑	451	Neal Heaton	.15	.07
❑	452	Brook Jacoby	.15	.07
❑	453	Mike Jeffcoat	.15	.07
❑	454	Don Schulze	.15	.07
❑	455	Roy Smith	.15	.07
❑	456	Pat Tabler	.15	.07
❑	457	Andre Thornton	.15	.07
❑	458	George Vukovich	.15	.07
❑	459	Tom Waddell	.15	.07
❑	460	Jerry Willard	.15	.07
❑	461	Dale Berra	.15	.07
❑	462	John Candelaria	.15	.07
❑	463	Jose DeLeon	.15	.07
❑	464	Doug Frobel	.15	.07
❑	465	Cecilio Guante	.15	.07
❑	466	Brian Harper	.15	.07
❑	467	Lee Lacy	.15	.07
❑	468	Bill Madlock	.40	.18
❑	469	Lee Mazzilli	.15	.07
❑	470	Larry McWilliams	.15	.07
❑	471	Jim Morrison	.15	.07
❑	472	Tony Pena	.15	.07
❑	473	Johnny Ray	.15	.07
❑	474	Rick Rhoden	.15	.07
❑	475	Don Robinson	.15	.07
❑	476	Rod Scurry	.15	.07
❑	477	Kent Tekulve	.15	.07
❑	478	Jason Thompson	.15	.07
❑	479	John Tudor	.15	.07
❑	480	Lee Tunnell	.15	.07
❑	481	Marvell Wynne	.15	.07
❑	482	Salome Barojas	.15	.07
❑	483	Dave Beard	.15	.07
❑	484	Jim Beattie	.15	.07
❑	485	Barry Bonnell	.15	.07
❑	486	Phil Bradley	.40	.18
❑	487	Al Cowens	.15	.07
❑	488	Alvin Davis	.40	.18
❑	489	Dave Henderson	.15	.07
❑	490	Steve Henderson	.15	.07
❑	491	Bob Kearney	.15	.07
❑	492	Mark Langston	.75	.35
❑	493	Larry Milbourne	.15	.07
❑	494	Paul Mirabella	.15	.07
❑	495	Mike Moore	.15	.07
❑	496	Edwin Nunez	.15	.07
❑	497	Spike Owen	.15	.07
❑	498	Jack Perconte	.15	.07
❑	499	Ken Phelps	.15	.07
❑	500	Jim Presley	.40	.18
❑	501	Mike Stanton	.15	.07
❑	502	Bob Stoddard	.15	.07
❑	503	Gorman Thomas	.15	.07
❑	504	Ed VandeBerg	.15	.07
❑	505	Matt Young	.15	.07
❑	506	Juan Agosto	.15	.07
❑	507	Harold Baines	.40	.18
❑	508	Floyd Bannister	.15	.07
❑	509	Britt Burns	.15	.07
❑	510	Julio Cruz	.15	.07
❑	511	Richard Dotson	.15	.07
❑	512	Jerry Dybzinski	.15	.07
❑	513	Carlton Fisk	1.50	.70
❑	514	Scott Fletcher	.15	.07
❑	515	Jerry Hairston	.15	.07
❑	516	Marc Hill	.15	.07
❑	517	LaMarr Hoyt	.15	.07
❑	518	Ron Kittle	.15	.07
❑	519	Rudy Law	.15	.07
❑	520	Vance Law	.15	.07
❑	521	Greg Luzinski	.40	.18
❑	522	Gene Nelson	.15	.07
❑	523	Tom Paciorek	.40	.18
❑	524	Ron Reed	.15	.07
❑	525	Bert Roberge	.15	.07
❑	526	Tom Seaver	2.00	.90
❑	527	Roy Smalley	.15	.07
❑	528	Dan Spillner	.15	.07
❑	529	Mike Squires	.15	.07
❑	530	Greg Walker	.15	.07
❑	531	Cesar Cedeno	.40	.18
❑	532	Dave Concepcion	.40	.18
❑	533	Eric Davis	3.00	1.35
❑	534	Nick Esasky	.15	.07
❑	535	Tom Foley	.15	.07
❑	536	John Franco UER (Koufax misspelled as Kofax on back)	1.50	.70
❑	537	Brad Gulden	.15	.07
❑	538	Tom Hume	.15	.07
❑	539	Wayne Krenchicki	.15	.07
❑	540	Andy McGaffigan	.15	.07
❑	541	Eddie Milner	.15	.07
❑	542	Ron Oester	.15	.07
❑	543	Bob Owchinko	.15	.07
❑	544	Dave Parker	.40	.18
❑	545	Frank Pastore	.15	.07
❑	546	Tony Perez	1.50	.70
❑	547	Ted Power	.15	.07
❑	548	Joe Price	.15	.07
❑	549	Gary Redus	.15	.07
❑	550	Pete Rose	2.00	.90
❑	551	Jeff Russell	.15	.07
❑	552	Mario Soto	.15	.07
❑	553	Jay Tibbs	.15	.07
❑	554	Duane Walker	.15	.07
❑	555	Alan Bannister	.15	.07
❑	556	Buddy Bell	.40	.18
❑	557	Danny Darwin	.40	.18
❑	558	Charlie Hough	.40	.18
❑	559	Bobby Jones	.15	.07
❑	560	Odell Jones	.15	.07
❑	561	Jeff Kunkel	.15	.07
❑	562	Mike Mason	.15	.07
❑	563	Pete O'Brien	.15	.07
❑	564	Larry Parrish	.15	.07
❑	565	Mickey Rivers	.15	.07
❑	566	Billy Sample	.15	.07
❑	567	Dave Schmidt	.15	.07
❑	568	Donnie Scott	.15	.07
❑	569	Dave Stewart	.40	.18
❑	570	Frank Tanana	.15	.07
❑	571	Wayne Tolleson	.15	.07
❑	572	Gary Ward	.15	.07
❑	573	Curtis Wilkerson	.15	.07
❑	574	George Wright	.15	.07
❑	575	Ned Yost	.15	.07
❑	576	Mark Brouhard	.15	.07
❑	577	Mike Caldwell	.15	.07
❑	578	Bobby Clark	.15	.07
❑	579	Jaime Cocanower	.15	.07

❑ 580 Cecil Cooper .40 .18
❑ 581 Rollie Fingers 1.50 .70
❑ 582 Jim Gantner .15 .07
❑ 583 Moose Haas .15 .07
❑ 584 Dion James .15 .07
❑ 585 Pete Ladd .15 .07
❑ 586 Rick Manning .15 .07
❑ 587 Bob McClure .15 .07
❑ 588 Paul Molitor 1.50 .70
❑ 589 Charlie Moore .15 .07
❑ 590 Ben Oglivie .15 .07
❑ 591 Chuck Porter .15 .07
❑ 592 Randy Ready .15 .07
❑ 593 Ed Romero .15 .07
❑ 594 Bill Schroeder .15 .07
❑ 595 Ray Searage .15 .07
❑ 596 Ted Simmons .40 .18
❑ 597 Jim Sundberg .15 .07
❑ 598 Don Sutton 1.50 .70
❑ 599 Tom Tellmann .15 .07
❑ 600 Rick Waits .15 .07
❑ 601 Robin Yount 1.50 .70
❑ 602 Dusty Baker .40 .18
❑ 603 Bob Brenly .15 .07
❑ 604 Jack Clark .40 .18
❑ 605 Chili Davis .40 .18
❑ 606 Mark Davis .15 .07
❑ 607 Dan Gladden .40 .18
❑ 608 Atlee Hammaker .15 .07
❑ 609 Mike Krukow .15 .07
❑ 610 Duane Kuiper .15 .07
❑ 611 Bob Lacey .15 .07
❑ 612 Bill Laskey .15 .07
❑ 613 Gary Lavelle .15 .07
❑ 614 Johnnie LeMaster .15 .07
❑ 615 Jeff Leonard .15 .07
❑ 616 Randy Lerch .15 .07
❑ 617 Greg Minton .15 .07
❑ 618 Steve Nicosia .15 .07
❑ 619 Gene Richards .15 .07
❑ 620 Jeff D. Robinson .15 .07
❑ 621 Scot Thompson .15 .07
❑ 622 Manny Trillo .15 .07
❑ 623 Brad Wellman .15 .07
❑ 624 Frank Williams .15 .07
❑ 625 Joel Youngblood .15 .07
❑ 626 Cal Ripken IA 4.00 1.80
❑ 627 Mike Schmidt IA .75 .35
❑ 628 Giving The Signs .40 .18
Sparky Anderson
❑ 629 AL Pitcher's Nightmare 1.50 .70
Dave Winfield
Rickey Henderson
❑ 630 NL Pitcher's Nightmare 1.50 .70
Mike Schmidt
Ryne Sandberg
❑ 631 NL All-Stars 1.50 .70
Darryl Strawberry
Gary Carter
Steve Garvey
Ozzie Smith
❑ 632 A-S Winning Battery .75 .35
Gary Carter
Charlie Lea
❑ 633 NL Pennant Clinchers .75 .35
Steve Garvey
Rich Gossage
❑ 634 NL Rookie Phenoms 1.50 .70
Dwight Gooden
Juan Samuel
❑ 635 Toronto's Big Guns .15 .07
Willie Upshaw
❑ 636 Toronto's Big Guns .15 .07
Lloyd Moseby
❑ 637 HOLLAND: Al Holland .15 .07
❑ 638 TUNNELL: Lee Tunnell .15 .07
❑ 639 Reggie Jackson 1.50 .70
500th Homer
❑ 640 4000th Hit 1.50 .70
Pete Rose
❑ 641 Father and Son 4.00 1.80
Cal Ripken Jr.
Cal Ripken Sr.
❑ 642 Cubs: Division Champs .40 .18
❑ 643 Two Perfect Games .40 .18
and One No-Hitter:
Mike Witt
David Palmer
Jack Morris
❑ 644 Willie Lozado and .15 .07
Vic Mata
❑ 645 Kelly Gruber and .40 .18
Randy O'Neal
❑ 646 Jose Roman and .15 .07
Joel Skinner
❑ 647 Steve Kiefer and 1.50 .70
Danny Tartabull
❑ 648 Rob Deer and .40 .18
Alejandro Sanchez
❑ 649 Billy Hatcher and 1.50 .70
Shawon Dunston
❑ 650 Ron Robinson and .15 .07
Mike Bielecki
❑ 651 Zane Smith and .40 .18
Paul Zuvella
❑ 652 Joe Hesketh and .40 .18
Glenn Davis
❑ 653 John Russell and .15 .07
Steve Jeltz
❑ 654 CL: Tigers/Padres .15 .07
and Cubs/Mets
❑ 655 CL: Blue Jays/Yankees .15 .07
and Red Sox/Orioles
❑ 656 CL: Royals/Cardinals .15 .07
and Phillies/Twins
❑ 657 CL: Angels/Braves .15 .07
and Astros/Dodgers
❑ 658 CL: Expos/A's .15 .07
and Indians/Pirates
❑ 659 CL: Mariners/White Sox .15 .07
and Reds/Rangers
❑ 660 CL: Brewers/Giants .15 .07
and Special Cards

1985 Fleer Update

	NRMT	VG-E
COMP.FACT.SET (132)	12.00	5.50
COMMON CARD (1-132)	.15	.07

❑ 1 Don Aase .15 .07
❑ 2 Bill Almon .15 .07
❑ 3 Dusty Baker .40 .18
❑ 4 Dale Berra .15 .07
❑ 5 Karl Best .15 .07
❑ 6 Tim Birtsas .15 .07
❑ 7 Vida Blue .40 .18
❑ 8 Rich Bordi .15 .07
❑ 9 Daryl Boston .15 .07
❑ 10 Hubie Brooks .15 .07
❑ 11 Chris Brown .15 .07
❑ 12 Tom Browning .40 .18
❑ 13 Al Bumbry .15 .07
❑ 14 Tim Burke .15 .07
❑ 15 Ray Burris .15 .07
❑ 16 Jeff Burroughs .15 .07
❑ 17 Ivan Calderon .15 .07
❑ 18 Jeff Calhoun .15 .07
❑ 19 Bill Campbell .15 .07
❑ 20 Don Carman .15 .07
❑ 21 Gary Carter 1.00 .45
❑ 22 Bobby Castillo .15 .07
❑ 23 Bill Caudill .15 .07
❑ 24 Rick Cerone .15 .07
❑ 25 Jack Clark .40 .18
❑ 26 Pat Clements .15 .07
❑ 27 Stewart Cliburn .15 .07
❑ 28 Vince Coleman 1.00 .45
❑ 29 Dave Collins .15 .07
❑ 30 Fritz Connally .15 .07
❑ 31 Henry Cotto .15 .07
❑ 32 Danny Darwin .40 .18
❑ 33 Darren Daulton 5.00 2.20
❑ 34 Jerry Davis .15 .07
❑ 35 Brian Dayett .15 .07
❑ 36 Ken Dixon .15 .07
❑ 37 Tommy Dunbar .15 .07
❑ 38 Mariano Duncan 1.00 .45
❑ 39 Bob Fallon .15 .07
❑ 40 Brian Fisher .15 .07
❑ 41 Mike Fitzgerald .15 .07
❑ 42 Ray Fontenot .15 .07
❑ 43 Greg Gagne .40 .18
❑ 44 Oscar Gamble .15 .07
❑ 45 Jim Gott .15 .07
❑ 46 David Green .15 .07
❑ 47 Alfredo Griffin .15 .07
❑ 48 Ozzie Guillen 1.50 .70
❑ 49 Toby Harrah .15 .07
❑ 50 Ron Hassey .15 .07
❑ 51 Rickey Henderson 1.00 .45
❑ 52 Steve Henderson .15 .07
❑ 53 George Hendrick .15 .07
❑ 54 Teddy Higuera .40 .18
❑ 55 Al Holland .15 .07
❑ 56 Burt Hooton .15 .07
❑ 57 Jay Howell .15 .07
❑ 58 LaMarr Hoyt .15 .07
❑ 59 Tim Hulett .15 .07
❑ 60 Bob James .15 .07
❑ 61 Cliff Johnson .15 .07
❑ 62 Howard Johnson .40 .18
❑ 63 Ruppert Jones .15 .07
❑ 64 Steve Kemp .15 .07
❑ 65 Bruce Kison .15 .07
❑ 66 Mike LaCoss .15 .07
❑ 67 Lee Lacy .15 .07
❑ 68 Dave LaPoint .15 .07
❑ 69 Gary Lavelle .15 .07
❑ 70 Vance Law .15 .07
❑ 71 Manny Lee .15 .07
❑ 72 Sixto Lezcano .15 .07
❑ 73 Tim Lollar .15 .07
❑ 74 Urbano Lugo .15 .07
❑ 75 Fred Lynn .40 .18
❑ 76 Steve Lyons .40 .18
❑ 77 Mickey Mahler .15 .07
❑ 78 Ron Mathis .15 .07
❑ 79 Len Matuszek .15 .07
❑ 80 Oddibe McDowell UER .40 .18
(Part of bio
actually Roger's)
❑ 81 Roger McDowell UER .40 .18
(Part of bio
actually Oddibe's)
❑ 82 Donnie Moore .15 .07
❑ 83 Ron Musselman .15 .07
❑ 84 Al Oliver .40 .18
❑ 85 Joe Orsulak .40 .18
❑ 86 Dan Pasqua .40 .18
❑ 87 Chris Pittaro .15 .07
❑ 88 Rick Reuschel .15 .07
❑ 89 Earnie Riles .15 .07
❑ 90 Jerry Royster .15 .07
❑ 91 Dave Rozema .15 .07
❑ 92 Dave Rucker .15 .07
❑ 93 Vern Ruhle .15 .07
❑ 94 Mark Salas .15 .07
❑ 95 Luis Salazar .15 .07
❑ 96 Joe Sambito .15 .07
❑ 97 Billy Sample .15 .07
❑ 98 Alejandro Sanchez .15 .07
❑ 99 Calvin Schiraldi .15 .07
❑ 100 Rick Schu .15 .07
❑ 101 Larry Sheets .15 .07
❑ 102 Ron Shephard .15 .07
❑ 103 Nelson Simmons .15 .07
❑ 104 Don Slaught .15 .07
❑ 105 Roy Smalley .15 .07

❑ 106 Lonnie Smith .15 .07
❑ 107 Nate Snell .15 .07
❑ 108 Lary Sorensen .15 .07
❑ 109 Chris Speier .15 .07
❑ 110 Mike Stenhouse .15 .07
❑ 111 Tim Stoddard .15 .07
❑ 112 John Stuper .15 .07
❑ 113 Jim Sundberg .15 .07
❑ 114 Bruce Sutter .40 .18
❑ 115 Don Sutton 1.00 .45
❑ 116 Bruce Tanner .15 .07
❑ 117 Kent Tekulve .15 .07
❑ 118 Walt Terrell .15 .07
❑ 119 Mickey Tettleton 1.50 .70
❑ 120 Rich Thompson .15 .07
❑ 121 Louis Thornton .15 .07
❑ 122 Alex Trevino .15 .07
❑ 123 John Tudor .15 .07
❑ 124 Jose Uribe .15 .07
❑ 125 Dave Valle .15 .07
❑ 126 Dave Von Ohlen .15 .07
❑ 127 Curt Wardle .15 .07
❑ 128 U.L. Washington .15 .07
❑ 129 Ed Whitson .15 .07
❑ 130 Herm Winningham .15 .07
❑ 131 Rich Yett .15 .07
❑ 132 Checklist U1-U132 .15 .07

1986 Fleer

	MINT	NRMT
COMPLETE SET (660)	40.00	18.00
COMP.FACT.SET (660)	70.00	32.00
COMMON CARD (1-660)	.10	.05

❑ 1 Steve Balboni .10 .05
❑ 2 Joe Beckwith .10 .05
❑ 3 Buddy Biancalana .10 .05
❑ 4 Bud Black .10 .05
❑ 5 George Brett 2.00 .90
❑ 6 Onix Concepcion .10 .05
❑ 7 Steve Farr .10 .05
❑ 8 Mark Gubicza .10 .05
❑ 9 Dane Iorg .10 .05
❑ 10 Danny Jackson .10 .05
❑ 11 Lynn Jones .10 .05
❑ 12 Mike Jones .10 .05
❑ 13 Charlie Leibrandt .10 .05
❑ 14 Hal McRae .25 .11
❑ 15 Omar Moreno .10 .05
❑ 16 Darryl Motley .10 .05
❑ 17 Jorge Orta .10 .05
❑ 18 Dan Quisenberry .10 .05
❑ 19 Bret Saberhagen .25 .11
❑ 20 Pat Sheridan .10 .05
❑ 21 Lonnie Smith .10 .05
❑ 22 Jim Sundberg .10 .05
❑ 23 John Wathan .10 .05
❑ 24 Frank White .25 .11
❑ 25 Willie Wilson .10 .05
❑ 26 Joaquin Andujar .10 .05
❑ 27 Steve Braun .10 .05
❑ 28 Bill Campbell .10 .05
❑ 29 Cesar Cedeno .25 .11
❑ 30 Jack Clark .25 .11
❑ 31 Vince Coleman 1.00 .45
❑ 32 Danny Cox .10 .05
❑ 33 Ken Dayley .10 .05
❑ 34 Ivan DeJesus .10 .05
❑ 35 Bob Forsch .10 .05
❑ 36 Brian Harper .10 .05
❑ 37 Tom Herr .10 .05
❑ 38 Ricky Horton .10 .05
❑ 39 Kurt Kepshire .10 .05
❑ 40 Jeff Lahti .10 .05
❑ 41 Tito Landrum .10 .05
❑ 42 Willie McGee .25 .11
❑ 43 Tom Nieto .10 .05
❑ 44 Terry Pendleton .50 .23
❑ 45 Darrell Porter .25 .11
❑ 46 Ozzie Smith 1.25 .55
❑ 47 John Tudor .10 .05
❑ 48 Andy Van Slyke .25 .11
❑ 49 Todd Worrell 1.00 .45
❑ 50 Jim Acker .10 .05
❑ 51 Doyle Alexander .10 .05
❑ 52 Jesse Barfield .10 .05
❑ 53 George Bell .25 .11
❑ 54 Jeff Burroughs .10 .05
❑ 55 Bill Caudill .10 .05
❑ 56 Jim Clancy .10 .05
❑ 57 Tony Fernandez .10 .05
❑ 58 Tom Filer .10 .05
❑ 59 Damaso Garcia .10 .05
❑ 60 Tom Henke .25 .11
❑ 61 Garth Iorg .10 .05
❑ 62 Cliff Johnson .10 .05
❑ 63 Jimmy Key 1.00 .45
❑ 64 Dennis Lamp .10 .05
❑ 65 Gary Lavelle .10 .05
❑ 66 Buck Martinez .10 .05
❑ 67 Lloyd Moseby .10 .05
❑ 68 Rance Mulliniks .10 .05
❑ 69 Al Oliver .25 .11
❑ 70 Dave Stieb .10 .05
❑ 71 Louis Thornton .10 .05
❑ 72 Willie Upshaw .10 .05
❑ 73 Ernie Whitt .10 .05
❑ 74 Rick Aguilera 1.00 .45
❑ 75 Wally Backman .10 .05
❑ 76 Gary Carter 1.00 .45
❑ 77 Ron Darling .10 .05
❑ 78 Len Dykstra 2.00 .90
❑ 79 Sid Fernandez .25 .11
❑ 80 George Foster .25 .11
❑ 81 Dwight Gooden 1.00 .45
❑ 82 Tom Gorman .10 .05
❑ 83 Danny Heep .10 .05
❑ 84 Keith Hernandez .25 .11
❑ 85 Howard Johnson .25 .11
❑ 86 Ray Knight .25 .11
❑ 87 Terry Leach .10 .05
❑ 88 Ed Lynch .10 .05
❑ 89 Roger McDowell .25 .11
❑ 90 Jesse Orosco .10 .05
❑ 91 Tom Paciorek .25 .11
❑ 92 Ronn Reynolds .10 .05
❑ 93 Rafael Santana .10 .05
❑ 94 Doug Sisk .10 .05
❑ 95 Rusty Staub .25 .11
❑ 96 Darryl Strawberry 1.00 .45
❑ 97 Mookie Wilson .25 .11
❑ 98 Neil Allen .10 .05
❑ 99 Don Baylor .50 .23
❑ 100 Dale Berra .10 .05
❑ 101 Rich Bordi .10 .05
❑ 102 Marty Bystrom .10 .05
❑ 103 Joe Cowley .10 .05
❑ 104 Brian Fisher .10 .05
❑ 105 Ken Griffey .25 .11
❑ 106 Ron Guidry .25 .11
❑ 107 Ron Hassey .10 .05
❑ 108 Rickey Henderson UER 1.00 .45
(SB Record of 120, sic)
❑ 109 Don Mattingly 1.50 .70
❑ 110 Bobby Meacham .10 .05
❑ 111 John Montefusco .10 .05
❑ 112 Phil Niekro 1.00 .45
❑ 113 Mike Pagliarulo .10 .05
❑ 114 Dan Pasqua .10 .05
❑ 115 Willie Randolph .25 .11
❑ 116 Dave Righetti .10 .05
❑ 117 Andre Robertson .10 .05
❑ 118 Billy Sample .10 .05
❑ 119 Bob Shirley .10 .05
❑ 120 Ed Whitson .10 .05
❑ 121 Dave Winfield 1.00 .45
❑ 122 Butch Wynegar .10 .05
❑ 123 Dave Anderson .10 .05
❑ 124 Bob Bailor .10 .05
❑ 125 Greg Brock .10 .05
❑ 126 Enos Cabell .10 .05
❑ 127 Bobby Castillo .10 .05
❑ 128 Carlos Diaz .10 .05
❑ 129 Mariano Duncan 1.00 .45
❑ 130 Pedro Guerrero .25 .11
❑ 131 Orel Hershiser .50 .23
❑ 132 Rick Honeycutt .10 .05
❑ 133 Ken Howell .10 .05
❑ 134 Ken Landreaux .10 .05
❑ 135 Bill Madlock .10 .05
❑ 136 Candy Maldonado .10 .05
❑ 137 Mike Marshall .10 .05
❑ 138 Len Matuszek .10 .05
❑ 139 Tom Niedenfuer .10 .05
❑ 140 Alejandro Pena .10 .05
❑ 141 Jerry Reuss .10 .05
❑ 142 Bill Russell .25 .11
❑ 143 Steve Sax .10 .05
❑ 144 Mike Scioscia .10 .05
❑ 145 Fernando Valenzuela .25 .11
❑ 146 Bob Welch .10 .05
❑ 147 Terry Whitfield .10 .05
❑ 148 Juan Beniquez .10 .05
❑ 149 Bob Boone .25 .11
❑ 150 John Candelaria .10 .05
❑ 151 Rod Carew 1.00 .45
❑ 152 Stewart Cliburn .10 .05
❑ 153 Doug DeCinces .10 .05
❑ 154 Brian Downing .10 .05
❑ 155 Ken Forsch .10 .05
❑ 156 Craig Gerber .10 .05
❑ 157 Bobby Grich .25 .11
❑ 158 George Hendrick .10 .05
❑ 159 Al Holland .10 .05
❑ 160 Reggie Jackson 1.25 .55
❑ 161 Ruppert Jones .10 .05
❑ 162 Urbano Lugo .10 .05
❑ 163 Kirk McCaskill .25 .11
❑ 164 Donnie Moore .10 .05
❑ 165 Gary Pettis .10 .05
❑ 166 Ron Romanick .10 .05
❑ 167 Dick Schofield .10 .05
❑ 168 Daryl Sconiers .10 .05
❑ 169 Jim Slaton .10 .05
❑ 170 Don Sutton 1.00 .45
❑ 171 Mike Witt .10 .05
❑ 172 Buddy Bell .25 .11
❑ 173 Tom Browning .10 .05
❑ 174 Dave Concepcion .25 .11
❑ 175 Eric Davis .50 .23
❑ 176 Bo Diaz .10 .05
❑ 177 Nick Esasky .10 .05
❑ 178 John Franco 1.00 .45
❑ 179 Tom Hume .10 .05
❑ 180 Wayne Krenchicki .10 .05
❑ 181 Andy McGaffigan .10 .05
❑ 182 Eddie Milner .10 .05
❑ 183 Ron Oester .10 .05
❑ 184 Dave Parker .25 .11
❑ 185 Frank Pastore .10 .05
❑ 186 Tony Perez 1.00 .45
❑ 187 Ted Power .10 .05
❑ 188 Joe Price .10 .05
❑ 189 Gary Redus .10 .05
❑ 190 Ron Robinson .10 .05
❑ 191 Pete Rose 1.25 .55
❑ 192 Mario Soto .10 .05
❑ 193 John Stuper .10 .05
❑ 194 Jay Tibbs .10 .05
❑ 195 Dave Van Gorder .10 .05
❑ 196 Max Venable .10 .05
❑ 197 Juan Agosto .10 .05
❑ 198 Harold Baines .50 .23
❑ 199 Floyd Bannister .10 .05
❑ 200 Britt Burns .10 .05
❑ 201 Julio Cruz .10 .05
❑ 202 Joel Davis .10 .05

❑ 203 Richard Dotson .10 .05
❑ 204 Carlton Fisk 1.00 .45
❑ 205 Scott Fletcher .10 .05
❑ 206 Ozzie Guillen .50 .23
❑ 207 Jerry Hairston .10 .05
❑ 208 Tim Hulett .10 .05
❑ 209 Bob James .10 .05
❑ 210 Ron Kittle .10 .05
❑ 211 Rudy Law .10 .05
❑ 212 Bryan Little .10 .05
❑ 213 Gene Nelson .10 .05
❑ 214 Reid Nichols .10 .05
❑ 215 Luis Salazar .10 .05
❑ 216 Tom Seaver 1.25 .55
❑ 217 Dan Spillner .10 .05
❑ 218 Bruce Tanner .10 .05
❑ 219 Greg Walker .10 .05
❑ 220 Dave Wehrmeister .10 .05
❑ 221 Juan Berenguer .10 .05
❑ 222 Dave Bergman .10 .05
❑ 223 Tom Brookens .10 .05
❑ 224 Darrell Evans .25 .11
❑ 225 Barbaro Garbey .10 .05
❑ 226 Kirk Gibson .25 .11
❑ 227 John Grubb .10 .05
❑ 228 Willie Hernandez .10 .05
❑ 229 Larry Herndon .10 .05
❑ 230 Chet Lemon .10 .05
❑ 231 Aurelio Lopez .10 .05
❑ 232 Jack Morris .25 .11
❑ 233 Randy O'Neal .10 .05
❑ 234 Lance Parrish .25 .11
❑ 235 Dan Petry .10 .05
❑ 236 Alejandro Sanchez .10 .05
❑ 237 Bill Scherrer .10 .05
❑ 238 Nelson Simmons .10 .05
❑ 239 Frank Tanana .10 .05
❑ 240 Walt Terrell .10 .05
❑ 241 Alan Trammell .50 .23
❑ 242 Lou Whitaker .25 .11
❑ 243 Milt Wilcox .10 .05
❑ 244 Hubie Brooks .10 .05
❑ 245 Tim Burke .10 .05
❑ 246 Andre Dawson 1.00 .45
❑ 247 Mike Fitzgerald .10 .05
❑ 248 Terry Francona .10 .05
❑ 249 Bill Gullickson .10 .05
❑ 250 Joe Hesketh .10 .05
❑ 251 Bill Laskey .10 .05
❑ 252 Vance Law .10 .05
❑ 253 Charlie Lea .10 .05
❑ 254 Gary Lucas .10 .05
❑ 255 David Palmer .10 .05
❑ 256 Tim Raines .25 .11
❑ 257 Jeff Reardon .25 .11
❑ 258 Bert Roberge .10 .05
❑ 259 Dan Schatzeder .10 .05
❑ 260 Bryn Smith .10 .05
❑ 261 Randy St.Claire .10 .05
❑ 262 Scot Thompson .10 .05
❑ 263 Tim Wallach .10 .05
❑ 264 U.L. Washington .10 .05
❑ 265 Mitch Webster .10 .05
❑ 266 Herm Winningham .10 .05
❑ 267 Floyd Youmans .10 .05
❑ 268 Don Aase .10 .05
❑ 269 Mike Boddicker .10 .05
❑ 270 Rich Dauer .10 .05
❑ 271 Storm Davis .10 .05
❑ 272 Rick Dempsey .10 .05
❑ 273 Ken Dixon .10 .05
❑ 274 Jim Dwyer .10 .05
❑ 275 Mike Flanagan .10 .05
❑ 276 Wayne Gross .10 .05
❑ 277 Lee Lacy .10 .05
❑ 278 Fred Lynn .25 .11
❑ 279 Tippy Martinez .10 .05
❑ 280 Dennis Martinez .25 .11
❑ 281 Scott McGregor .10 .05
❑ 282 Eddie Murray 1.00 .45
❑ 283 Floyd Rayford .10 .05
❑ 284 Cal Ripken 4.00 1.80
❑ 285 Gary Roenicke .10 .05
❑ 286 Larry Sheets .10 .05
❑ 287 John Shelby .10 .05
❑ 288 Nate Snell .10 .05
❑ 289 Sammy Stewart .10 .05
❑ 290 Alan Wiggins .10 .05
❑ 291 Mike Young .10 .05
❑ 292 Alan Ashby .10 .05
❑ 293 Mark Bailey .10 .05
❑ 294 Kevin Bass .10 .05
❑ 295 Jeff Calhoun .10 .05
❑ 296 Jose Cruz .25 .11
❑ 297 Glenn Davis .25 .11
❑ 298 Bill Dawley .10 .05
❑ 299 Frank DiPino .10 .05
❑ 300 Bill Doran .10 .05
❑ 301 Phil Garner .10 .05
❑ 302 Jeff Heathcock .10 .05
❑ 303 Charlie Kerfeld .10 .05
❑ 304 Bob Knepper .10 .05
❑ 305 Ron Mathis .10 .05
❑ 306 Jerry Mumphrey .10 .05
❑ 307 Jim Pankovits .10 .05
❑ 308 Terry Puhl .10 .05
❑ 309 Craig Reynolds .10 .05
❑ 310 Nolan Ryan 4.00 1.80
❑ 311 Mike Scott .10 .05
❑ 312 Dave Smith .10 .05
❑ 313 Dickie Thon .10 .05
❑ 314 Denny Walling .10 .05
❑ 315 Kurt Bevacqua .10 .05
❑ 316 Al Bumbry .10 .05
❑ 317 Jerry Davis .10 .05
❑ 318 Luis DeLeon .10 .05
❑ 319 Dave Dravecky .25 .11
❑ 320 Tim Flannery .10 .05
❑ 321 Steve Garvey .50 .23
❑ 322 Rich Gossage .25 .11
❑ 323 Tony Gwynn 2.50 1.10
❑ 324 Andy Hawkins .10 .05
❑ 325 LaMarr Hoyt .10 .05
❑ 326 Roy Lee Jackson .10 .05
❑ 327 Terry Kennedy .10 .05
❑ 328 Craig Lefferts .10 .05
❑ 329 Carmelo Martinez .10 .05
❑ 330 Lance McCullers .10 .05
❑ 331 Kevin McReynolds .10 .05
❑ 332 Graig Nettles .25 .11
❑ 333 Jerry Royster .10 .05
❑ 334 Eric Show .10 .05
❑ 335 Tim Stoddard .10 .05
❑ 336 Garry Templeton .10 .05
❑ 337 Mark Thurmond .10 .05
❑ 338 Ed Wojna .10 .05
❑ 339 Tony Armas .10 .05
❑ 340 Marty Barrett .10 .05
❑ 341 Wade Boggs 1.00 .45
❑ 342 Dennis Boyd .10 .05
❑ 343 Bill Buckner .25 .11
❑ 344 Mark Clear .10 .05
❑ 345 Roger Clemens 4.00 1.80
❑ 346 Steve Crawford .10 .05
❑ 347 Mike Easler .10 .05
❑ 348 Dwight Evans .25 .11
❑ 349 Rich Gedman .10 .05
❑ 350 Jackie Gutierrez .10 .05
❑ 351 Glenn Hoffman .10 .05
❑ 352 Bruce Hurst .10 .05
❑ 353 Bruce Kison .10 .05
❑ 354 Tim Lollar .10 .05
❑ 355 Steve Lyons .10 .05
❑ 356 Al Nipper .10 .05
❑ 357 Bob Ojeda .10 .05
❑ 358 Jim Rice .25 .11
❑ 359 Bob Stanley .10 .05
❑ 360 Mike Trujillo .10 .05
❑ 361 Thad Bosley .10 .05
❑ 362 Warren Brusstar .10 .05
❑ 363 Ron Cey .25 .11
❑ 364 Jody Davis .10 .05
❑ 365 Bob Dernier .10 .05
❑ 366 Shawon Dunston .25 .11
❑ 367 Leon Durham .10 .05
❑ 368 Dennis Eckersley 1.00 .45
❑ 369 Ray Fontenot .10 .05
❑ 370 George Frazier .10 .05
❑ 371 Billy Hatcher .10 .05
❑ 372 Dave Lopes .25 .11
❑ 373 Gary Matthews .10 .05
❑ 374 Ron Meridith .10 .05
❑ 375 Keith Moreland .10 .05
❑ 376 Reggie Patterson .10 .05
❑ 377 Dick Ruthven .10 .05
❑ 378 Ryne Sandberg 1.25 .55
❑ 379 Scott Sanderson .10 .05
❑ 380 Lee Smith .50 .23
❑ 381 Lary Sorensen .10 .05
❑ 382 Chris Speier .10 .05
❑ 383 Rick Sutcliffe .10 .05
❑ 384 Steve Trout .10 .05
❑ 385 Gary Woods .10 .05
❑ 386 Bert Blyleven .25 .11
❑ 387 Tom Brunansky .10 .05
❑ 388 Randy Bush .10 .05
❑ 389 John Butcher .10 .05
❑ 390 Ron Davis .10 .05
❑ 391 Dave Engle .10 .05
❑ 392 Frank Eufemia .10 .05
❑ 393 Pete Filson .10 .05
❑ 394 Gary Gaetti .25 .11
❑ 395 Greg Gagne .10 .05
❑ 396 Mickey Hatcher .10 .05
❑ 397 Kent Hrbek .25 .11
❑ 398 Tim Laudner .10 .05
❑ 399 Rick Lysander .10 .05
❑ 400 Dave Meier .10 .05
❑ 401 Kirby Puckett UER 3.00 1.35
(Card has him in NL, should be AL)
❑ 402 Mark Salas .10 .05
❑ 403 Ken Schrom .10 .05
❑ 404 Roy Smalley .10 .05
❑ 405 Mike Smithson .10 .05
❑ 406 Mike Stenhouse .10 .05
❑ 407 Tim Teufel .10 .05
❑ 408 Frank Viola .25 .11
❑ 409 Ron Washington .10 .05
❑ 410 Keith Atherton .10 .05
❑ 411 Dusty Baker .25 .11
❑ 412 Tim Birtsas .10 .05
❑ 413 Bruce Bochte .10 .05
❑ 414 Chris Codiroli .10 .05
❑ 415 Dave Collins .10 .05
❑ 416 Mike Davis .10 .05
❑ 417 Alfredo Griffin .10 .05
❑ 418 Mike Heath .10 .05
❑ 419 Steve Henderson .10 .05
❑ 420 Donnie Hill .10 .05
❑ 421 Jay Howell .10 .05
❑ 422 Tommy John 1.00 .45
❑ 423 Dave Kingman .25 .11
❑ 424 Bill Krueger .10 .05
❑ 425 Rick Langford .10 .05
❑ 426 Carney Lansford .25 .11
❑ 427 Steve McCatty .10 .05
❑ 428 Dwayne Murphy .10 .05
❑ 429 Steve Ontiveros .25 .11
❑ 430 Tony Phillips .10 .05
❑ 431 Jose Rijo .10 .05
❑ 432 Mickey Tettleton 1.00 .45
❑ 433 Luis Aguayo .10 .05
❑ 434 Larry Andersen .10 .05
❑ 435 Steve Carlton 1.00 .45
❑ 436 Don Carman .10 .05
❑ 437 Tim Corcoran .10 .05
❑ 438 Darren Daulton 2.00 .90
❑ 439 John Denny .10 .05
❑ 440 Tom Foley .10 .05
❑ 441 Greg Gross .10 .05
❑ 442 Kevin Gross .10 .05
❑ 443 Von Hayes .10 .05
❑ 444 Charles Hudson .10 .05
❑ 445 Garry Maddox .10 .05
❑ 446 Shane Rawley .10 .05
❑ 447 Dave Rucker .10 .05
❑ 448 John Russell .10 .05
❑ 449 Juan Samuel .10 .05
❑ 450 Mike Schmidt 1.25 .55
❑ 451 Rick Schu .10 .05
❑ 452 Dave Shipanoff .10 .05
❑ 453 Dave Stewart .25 .11
❑ 454 Jeff Stone .10 .05
❑ 455 Kent Tekulve .10 .05

❑	456	Ozzie Virgil	.10	.05
❑	457	Glenn Wilson	.10	.05
❑	458	Jim Beattie	.10	.05
❑	459	Karl Best	.10	.05
❑	460	Barry Bonnell	.10	.05
❑	461	Phil Bradley	.10	.05
❑	462	Ivan Calderon	.25	.11
❑	463	Al Cowens	.10	.05
❑	464	Alvin Davis	.10	.05
❑	465	Dave Henderson	.10	.05
❑	466	Bob Kearney	.10	.05
❑	467	Mark Langston	.10	.05
❑	468	Bob Long	.10	.05
❑	469	Mike Moore	.10	.05
❑	470	Edwin Nunez	.10	.05
❑	471	Spike Owen	.10	.05
❑	472	Jack Perconte	.10	.05
❑	473	Jim Presley	.10	.05
❑	474	Donnie Scott	.10	.05
❑	475	Bill Swift	.10	.05
❑	476	Danny Tartabull	.25	.11
❑	477	Gorman Thomas	.10	.05
❑	478	Roy Thomas	.10	.05
❑	479	Ed VandeBerg	.10	.05
❑	480	Frank Wills	.10	.05
❑	481	Matt Young	.10	.05
❑	482	Ray Burris	.10	.05
❑	483	Jaime Cocanower	.10	.05
❑	484	Cecil Cooper	.25	.11
❑	485	Danny Darwin	.10	.05
❑	486	Rollie Fingers	1.00	.45
❑	487	Jim Gantner	.10	.05
❑	488	Bob L. Gibson	.10	.05
❑	489	Moose Haas	.10	.05
❑	490	Teddy Higuera	.25	.11
❑	491	Paul Householder	.10	.05
❑	492	Pete Ladd	.10	.05
❑	493	Rick Manning	.10	.05
❑	494	Bob McClure	.10	.05
❑	495	Paul Molitor	1.00	.45
❑	496	Charlie Moore	.10	.05
❑	497	Ben Oglivie	.10	.05
❑	498	Randy Ready	.10	.05
❑	499	Earnie Riles	.10	.05
❑	500	Ed Romero	.10	.05
❑	501	Bill Schroeder	.10	.05
❑	502	Ray Searage	.10	.05
❑	503	Ted Simmons	.25	.11
❑	504	Pete Vuckovich	.10	.05
❑	505	Rick Waits	.10	.05
❑	506	Robin Yount	1.00	.45
❑	507	Len Barker	.10	.05
❑	508	Steve Bedrosian	.10	.05
❑	509	Bruce Benedict	.10	.05
❑	510	Rick Camp	.10	.05
❑	511	Rick Cerone	.10	.05
❑	512	Chris Chambliss	.25	.11
❑	513	Jeff Dedmon	.10	.05
❑	514	Terry Forster	.10	.05
❑	515	Gene Garber	.10	.05
❑	516	Terry Harper	.10	.05
❑	517	Bob Horner	.10	.05
❑	518	Glenn Hubbard	.10	.05
❑	519	Joe Johnson	.10	.05
❑	520	Brad Komminsk	.10	.05
❑	521	Rick Mahler	.10	.05
❑	522	Dale Murphy	1.00	.45
❑	523	Ken Oberkfell	.10	.05
❑	524	Pascual Perez	.10	.05
❑	525	Gerald Perry	.10	.05
❑	526	Rafael Ramirez	.10	.05
❑	527	Steve Shields	.10	.05
❑	528	Zane Smith	.10	.05
❑	529	Bruce Sutter	.25	.11
❑	530	Milt Thompson	.25	.11
❑	531	Claudell Washington	.10	.05
❑	532	Paul Zuvella	.10	.05
❑	533	Vida Blue	.25	.11
❑	534	Bob Brenly	.10	.05
❑	535	Chris Brown	.10	.05
❑	536	Chili Davis	.50	.23
❑	537	Mark Davis	.10	.05
❑	538	Rob Deer	.10	.05
❑	539	Dan Driessen	.10	.05
❑	540	Scott Garrelts	.10	.05
❑	541	Dan Gladden	.10	.05
❑	542	Jim Gott	.10	.05
❑	543	David Green	.10	.05
❑	544	Atlee Hammaker	.10	.05
❑	545	Mike Jeffcoat	.10	.05
❑	546	Mike Krukow	.10	.05
❑	547	Dave LaPoint	.10	.05
❑	548	Jeff Leonard	.10	.05
❑	549	Greg Minton	.10	.05
❑	550	Alex Trevino	.10	.05
❑	551	Manny Trillo	.10	.05
❑	552	Jose Uribe	.10	.05
❑	553	Brad Wellman	.10	.05
❑	554	Frank Williams	.10	.05
❑	555	Joel Youngblood	.10	.05
❑	556	Alan Bannister	.10	.05
❑	557	Glenn Brummer	.10	.05
❑	558	Steve Buechele	.25	.11
❑	559	Jose Guzman	.10	.05
❑	560	Toby Harrah	.10	.05
❑	561	Greg Harris	.10	.05
❑	562	Dwayne Henry	.10	.05
❑	563	Burt Hooton	.10	.05
❑	564	Charlie Hough	.25	.11
❑	565	Mike Mason	.10	.05
❑	566	Oddibe McDowell	.10	.05
❑	567	Dickie Noles	.10	.05
❑	568	Pete O'Brien	.10	.05
❑	569	Larry Parrish	.10	.05
❑	570	Dave Rozema	.10	.05
❑	571	Dave Schmidt	.10	.05
❑	572	Don Slaught	.10	.05
❑	573	Wayne Tolleson	.10	.05
❑	574	Duane Walker	.10	.05
❑	575	Gary Ward	.10	.05
❑	576	Chris Welsh	.10	.05
❑	577	Curtis Wilkerson	.10	.05
❑	578	George Wright	.10	.05
❑	579	Chris Bando	.10	.05
❑	580	Tony Bernazard	.10	.05
❑	581	Brett Butler	.25	.11
❑	582	Ernie Camacho	.10	.05
❑	583	Joe Carter	1.00	.45
❑	584	Carmen Castillo	.10	.05
❑	585	Jamie Easterly	.10	.05
❑	586	Julio Franco	.25	.11
❑	587	Mel Hall	.10	.05
❑	588	Mike Hargrove	.25	.11
❑	589	Neal Heaton	.10	.05
❑	590	Brook Jacoby	.10	.05
❑	591	Otis Nixon	1.00	.45
❑	592	Jerry Reed	.10	.05
❑	593	Vern Ruhle	.10	.05
❑	594	Pat Tabler	.10	.05
❑	595	Rich Thompson	.10	.05
❑	596	Andre Thornton	.10	.05
❑	597	Dave Von Ohlen	.10	.05
❑	598	George Vukovich	.10	.05
❑	599	Tom Waddell	.10	.05
❑	600	Curt Wardle	.10	.05
❑	601	Jerry Willard	.10	.05
❑	602	Bill Almon	.10	.05
❑	603	Mike Bielecki	.10	.05
❑	604	Sid Bream	.10	.05
❑	605	Mike C. Brown	.10	.05
❑	606	Pat Clements	.10	.05
❑	607	Jose DeLeon	.10	.05
❑	608	Denny Gonzalez	.10	.05
❑	609	Cecilio Guante	.10	.05
❑	610	Steve Kemp	.10	.05
❑	611	Sammy Khalifa	.10	.05
❑	612	Lee Mazzilli	.10	.05
❑	613	Larry McWilliams	.10	.05
❑	614	Jim Morrison	.10	.05
❑	615	Joe Orsulak	.10	.05
❑	616	Tony Pena	.10	.05
❑	617	Johnny Ray	.10	.05
❑	618	Rick Reuschel	.10	.05
❑	619	R.J. Reynolds	.10	.05
❑	620	Rick Rhoden	.10	.05
❑	621	Don Robinson	.10	.05
❑	622	Jason Thompson	.10	.05
❑	623	Lee Tunnell	.10	.05
❑	624	Jim Winn	.10	.05
❑	625	Marvell Wynne	.10	.05
❑	626	Dwight Gooden IA	.25	.11
❑	627	Don Mattingly IA	1.25	.55
❑	628	4192 (Pete Rose)	.60	.25
❑	629	3000 Career Hits Rod Carew	1.00	.45
❑	630	300 Career Wins Tom Seaver Phil Niekro	1.00	.45
❑	631	Ouch (Don Baylor)	.25	.11
❑	632	Instant Offense Darryl Strawberry Tim Raines	.50	.23
❑	633	Shortstops Supreme Cal Ripken Alan Trammell	2.00	.90
❑	634	Boggs and "Hero" Wade Boggs George Brett	1.00	.45
❑	635	Braves Dynamic Duo Bob Horner Dale Murphy	.25	.11
❑	636	Cardinal Ignitors Willie McGee Vince Coleman	.25	.11
❑	637	Terror on Basepaths Vince Coleman	.25	.11
❑	638	Charlie Hustle / Dr.K Pete Rose Dwight Gooden	1.00	.45
❑	639	1984 and 1985 AL Batting Champs Wade Boggs Don Mattingly	1.00	.45
❑	640	NL West Sluggers Dale Murphy Steve Garvey Dave Parker	.25	.11
❑	641	Staff Aces Fernando Valenzuela Dwight Gooden	.25	.11
❑	642	Blue Jay Stoppers Jimmy Key Dave Stieb	.25	.11
❑	643	AL All-Star Backstops Carlton Fisk Rich Gedman	.25	.11
❑	644	Gene Walter and Benito Santiago	1.00	.45
❑	645	Mike Woodard and Colin Ward	.10	.05
❑	646	Kal Daniels and Paul O'Neill	3.00	1.35
❑	647	Andres Galarraga and Fred Toliver	6.00	2.70
❑	648	Bob Kipper and Curt Ford	.10	.05
❑	649	Jose Canseco and Eric Plunk	12.00	5.50
❑	650	Mark McLemore and Gus Polidor	1.00	.45
❑	651	Rob Woodward and Mickey Brantley	.10	.05
❑	652	Billy Joe Robidoux and Mark Funderburk	.10	.05
❑	653	Cecil Fielder and Cory Snyder	2.00	.90
❑	654	CL: Royals/Cardinals Blue Jays/Mets	.10	.05
❑	655	CL: Yankees/Dodgers Angels/Reds UER (168 Darly Sconiers)	.10	.05
❑	656	CL: White Sox/Tigers Expos/Orioles (279 Dennis, 280 Tippy)	.10	.05
❑	657	CL: Astros/Padres Red Sox/Cubs	.10	.05
❑	658	CL: Twins/A's Phillies/Mariners	.10	.05
❑	659	CL: Brewers/Braves Giants/Rangers	.10	.05
❑	660	CL: Indians/Pirates Special Cards	.10	.05

1986 Fleer All-Stars

	MINT	NRMT
COMPLETE SET (12)	30.00	13.50
COMMON CARD (1-12)	.25	.11

	MINT	NRMT
❑ 1 Don Mattingly	6.00	2.70
❑ 2 Tom Herr	.25	.11
❑ 3 George Brett	6.00	2.70
❑ 4 Gary Carter	.75	.35
❑ 5 Cal Ripken	15.00	6.75
❑ 6 Dave Parker	.35	.16
❑ 7 Rickey Henderson UER (Misspelled Ricky on card back)	2.50	1.10
❑ 8 Pedro Guerrero	.35	.16
❑ 9 Dan Quisenberry	.25	.11
❑ 10 Dwight Gooden	.75	.35
❑ 11 Gorman Thomas	.25	.11
❑ 12 John Tudor	.25	.11

1986 Fleer Future Hall of Famers

	MINT	NRMT
COMPLETE SET (6)	15.00	6.75
COMMON CARD (1-6)	2.00	.90

	MINT	NRMT
❑ 1 Pete Rose	3.00	1.35
❑ 2 Steve Carlton	2.00	.90
❑ 3 Tom Seaver	2.00	.90
❑ 4 Rod Carew	2.00	.90
❑ 5 Nolan Ryan	10.00	4.50
❑ 6 Reggie Jackson	2.50	1.10

1986 Fleer Update

	MINT	NRMT
COMP.FACT.SET (132)	15.00	6.75
COMMON CARD (1-132)	.10	.05

	MINT	NRMT
❑ 1 Mike Aldrete	.10	.05
❑ 2 Andy Allanson	.10	.05
❑ 3 Neil Allen	.10	.05
❑ 4 Joaquin Andujar	.10	.05
❑ 5 Paul Assenmacher	.10	.05
❑ 6 Scott Bailes	.10	.05
❑ 7 Jay Baller	.10	.05
❑ 8 Scott Bankhead	.10	.05
❑ 9 Bill Bathe	.10	.05
❑ 10 Don Baylor	.40	.18
❑ 11 Billy Beane	.10	.05
❑ 12 Steve Bedrosian	.10	.05
❑ 13 Juan Beniquez	.10	.05
❑ 14 Barry Bonds	10.00	4.50
❑ 15 Bobby Bonilla UER (Wrong birthday)	1.25	.55
❑ 16 Rich Bordi	.10	.05
❑ 17 Bill Campbell	.10	.05
❑ 18 Tom Candiotti	.10	.05
❑ 19 John Cangelosi	.10	.05
❑ 20 Jose Canseco UER (Headings on back for a pitcher)	3.00	1.35
❑ 21 Chuck Cary	.10	.05
❑ 22 Juan Castillo	.10	.05
❑ 23 Rick Cerone	.10	.05
❑ 24 John Cerutti	.10	.05
❑ 25 Will Clark	3.00	1.35
❑ 26 Mark Clear	.10	.05
❑ 27 Darnell Coles	.10	.05
❑ 28 Dave Collins	.10	.05
❑ 29 Tim Conroy	.10	.05
❑ 30 Ed Correa	.10	.05
❑ 31 Joe Cowley	.10	.05
❑ 32 Bill Dawley	.10	.05
❑ 33 Rob Deer	.20	.09
❑ 34 John Denny	.10	.05
❑ 35 Jim Deshaies	.10	.05
❑ 36 Doug Drabek	.75	.35
❑ 37 Mike Easler	.10	.05
❑ 38 Mark Eichhorn	.10	.05
❑ 39 Dave Engle	.10	.05
❑ 40 Mike Fischlin	.10	.05
❑ 41 Scott Fletcher	.10	.05
❑ 42 Terry Forster	.10	.05
❑ 43 Terry Francona	.10	.05
❑ 44 Andres Galarraga	2.50	1.10
❑ 45 Lee Guetterman	.10	.05
❑ 46 Bill Gullickson	.10	.05
❑ 47 Jackie Gutierrez	.10	.05
❑ 48 Moose Haas	.10	.05
❑ 49 Billy Hatcher	.10	.05
❑ 50 Mike Heath	.10	.05
❑ 51 Guy Hoffman	.10	.05
❑ 52 Tom Hume	.10	.05
❑ 53 Pete Incaviglia	.75	.35
❑ 54 Dane Iorg	.10	.05
❑ 55 Chris James	.10	.05
❑ 56 Stan Javier	.20	.09
❑ 57 Tommy John	.75	.35
❑ 58 Tracy Jones	.10	.05
❑ 59 Wally Joyner	.75	.35
❑ 60 Wayne Krenchicki	.10	.05
❑ 61 John Kruk	.75	.35
❑ 62 Mike LaCoss	.10	.05
❑ 63 Pete Ladd	.10	.05
❑ 64 Dave LaPoint	.10	.05
❑ 65 Mike LaValliere	.10	.05
❑ 66 Rudy Law	.10	.05
❑ 67 Dennis Leonard	.10	.05
❑ 68 Steve Lombardozzi	.10	.05
❑ 69 Aurelio Lopez	.10	.05
❑ 70 Mickey Mahler	.10	.05
❑ 71 Candy Maldonado	.10	.05
❑ 72 Roger Mason	.10	.05
❑ 73 Greg Mathews	.10	.05
❑ 74 Andy McGaffigan	.10	.05
❑ 75 Joel McKeon	.10	.05
❑ 76 Kevin Mitchell	.75	.35
❑ 77 Bill Mooneyham	.10	.05
❑ 78 Omar Moreno	.10	.05
❑ 79 Jerry Mumphrey	.10	.05
❑ 80 Al Newman	.20	.09
❑ 81 Phil Niekro	.75	.35
❑ 82 Randy Niemann	.10	.05
❑ 83 Juan Nieves	.10	.05
❑ 84 Bob Ojeda	.10	.05
❑ 85 Rick Ownbey	.10	.05
❑ 86 Tom Paciorek	.20	.09
❑ 87 David Palmer	.10	.05
❑ 88 Jeff Parrett	.10	.05
❑ 89 Pat Perry	.10	.05
❑ 90 Dan Plesac	.10	.05
❑ 91 Darrell Porter	.20	.09
❑ 92 Luis Quinones	.10	.05
❑ 93 Rey Quinones UER (Misspelled Quinonez)	.10	.05
❑ 94 Gary Redus	.10	.05
❑ 95 Jeff Reed	.10	.05
❑ 96 Bip Roberts	.75	.35
❑ 97 Billy Joe Robidoux	.10	.05
❑ 98 Gary Roenicke	.10	.05
❑ 99 Ron Roenicke	.10	.05
❑ 100 Angel Salazar	.10	.05
❑ 101 Joe Sambito	.10	.05
❑ 102 Billy Sample	.10	.05
❑ 103 Dave Schmidt	.10	.05
❑ 104 Ken Schrom	.10	.05
❑ 105 Ruben Sierra	.75	.35
❑ 106 Ted Simmons	.20	.09
❑ 107 Sammy Stewart	.10	.05
❑ 108 Kurt Stillwell	.10	.05
❑ 109 Dale Sveum	.10	.05
❑ 110 Tim Teufel	.10	.05
❑ 111 Bob Tewksbury	.20	.09
❑ 112 Andres Thomas	.10	.05
❑ 113 Jason Thompson	.10	.05
❑ 114 Milt Thompson	.20	.09
❑ 115 Robby Thompson	.20	.09
❑ 116 Jay Tibbs	.10	.05
❑ 117 Fred Toliver	.10	.05
❑ 118 Wayne Tolleson	.10	.05
❑ 119 Alex Trevino	.10	.05
❑ 120 Manny Trillo	.10	.05
❑ 121 Ed VandeBerg	.10	.05
❑ 122 Ozzie Virgil	.10	.05
❑ 123 Tony Walker	.10	.05
❑ 124 Gene Walter	.10	.05
❑ 125 Duane Ward	.20	.09
❑ 126 Jerry Willard	.10	.05
❑ 127 Mitch Williams	.20	.09
❑ 128 Reggie Williams	.10	.05
❑ 129 Bobby Witt	.40	.18
❑ 130 Marvell Wynne	.10	.05
❑ 131 Steve Yeager	.10	.05
❑ 132 Checklist 1-132	.10	.05

1987 Fleer

	MINT	NRMT
COMPLETE SET (660)	40.00	18.00
COMP.FACT.SET (672)	50.00	22.00
COMMON CARD (1-660)	.20	.09

	MINT	NRMT
❑ 1 Rick Aguilera	.40	.18

❑ 2 Richard Anderson .20 .09
❑ 3 Wally Backman .20 .09
❑ 4 Gary Carter .60 .25
❑ 5 Ron Darling .20 .09
❑ 6 Len Dykstra .60 .25
❑ 7 Kevin Elster .60 .25
❑ 8 Sid Fernandez .20 .09
❑ 9 Dwight Gooden .60 .25
❑ 10 Ed Hearn .20 .09
❑ 11 Danny Heep .20 .09
❑ 12 Keith Hernandez .40 .18
❑ 13 Howard Johnson .20 .09
❑ 14 Ray Knight .20 .09
❑ 15 Lee Mazzilli .20 .09
❑ 16 Roger McDowell .20 .09
❑ 17 Kevin Mitchell .60 .25
❑ 18 Randy Niemann .20 .09
❑ 19 Bob Ojeda .20 .09
❑ 20 Jesse Orosco .20 .09
❑ 21 Rafael Santana .20 .09
❑ 22 Doug Sisk .20 .09
❑ 23 Darryl Strawberry .60 .25
❑ 24 Tim Teufel .20 .09
❑ 25 Mookie Wilson .40 .18
❑ 26 Tony Armas .20 .09
❑ 27 Marty Barrett .20 .09
❑ 28 Don Baylor .40 .18
❑ 29 Wade Boggs .75 .35
❑ 30 Oil Can Boyd .20 .09
❑ 31 Bill Buckner .40 .18
❑ 32 Roger Clemens 2.00 .90
❑ 33 Steve Crawford .20 .09
❑ 34 Dwight Evans .40 .18
❑ 35 Rich Gedman .20 .09
❑ 36 Dave Henderson .20 .09
❑ 37 Bruce Hurst .20 .09
❑ 38 Tim Lollar .20 .09
❑ 39 Al Nipper .20 .09
❑ 40 Spike Owen .20 .09
❑ 41 Jim Rice .40 .18
❑ 42 Ed Romero .20 .09
❑ 43 Joe Sambito .20 .09
❑ 44 Calvin Schiraldi .20 .09
❑ 45 Tom Seaver UER .75 .35
Lifetime saves total 0, should be 1
❑ 46 Jeff Sellers .20 .09
❑ 47 Bob Stanley .20 .09
❑ 48 Sammy Stewart .20 .09
❑ 49 Larry Andersen .20 .09
❑ 50 Alan Ashby .20 .09
❑ 51 Kevin Bass .20 .09
❑ 52 Jeff Calhoun .20 .09
❑ 53 Jose Cruz .40 .18
❑ 54 Danny Darwin .20 .09
❑ 55 Glenn Davis .20 .09
❑ 56 Jim Deshaies .20 .09
❑ 57 Bill Doran .20 .09
❑ 58 Phil Garner .20 .09
❑ 59 Billy Hatcher .20 .09
❑ 60 Charlie Kerfeld .20 .09
❑ 61 Bob Knepper .20 .09
❑ 62 Dave Lopes .40 .18
❑ 63 Aurelio Lopez .20 .09
❑ 64 Jim Pankovits .20 .09
❑ 65 Terry Puhl .20 .09
❑ 66 Craig Reynolds .20 .09
❑ 67 Nolan Ryan 3.00 1.35
❑ 68 Mike Scott .20 .09
❑ 69 Dave Smith .20 .09
❑ 70 Dickie Thon .20 .09
❑ 71 Tony Walker .20 .09
❑ 72 Denny Walling .20 .09
❑ 73 Bob Boone .40 .18
❑ 74 Rick Burleson .20 .09
❑ 75 John Candelaria .20 .09
❑ 76 Doug Corbett .20 .09
❑ 77 Doug DeCinces .20 .09
❑ 78 Brian Downing .20 .09
❑ 79 Chuck Finley .75 .35
❑ 80 Terry Forster .20 .09
❑ 81 Bob Grich .40 .18
❑ 82 George Hendrick .20 .09
❑ 83 Jack Howell .20 .09
❑ 84 Reggie Jackson 1.00 .45
❑ 85 Ruppert Jones .20 .09
❑ 86 Wally Joyner 1.00 .45
❑ 87 Gary Lucas .20 .09
❑ 88 Kirk McCaskill .20 .09
❑ 89 Donnie Moore .20 .09
❑ 90 Gary Pettis .20 .09
❑ 91 Vern Ruhle .20 .09
❑ 92 Dick Schofield .20 .09
❑ 93 Don Sutton .75 .35
❑ 94 Rob Wilfong .20 .09
❑ 95 Mike Witt .20 .09
❑ 96 Doug Drabek .75 .35
❑ 97 Mike Easler .20 .09
❑ 98 Mike Fischlin .20 .09
❑ 99 Brian Fisher .20 .09
❑ 100 Ron Guidry .40 .18
❑ 101 Rickey Henderson .75 .35
❑ 102 Tommy John .40 .18
❑ 103 Ron Kittle .20 .09
❑ 104 Don Mattingly 1.25 .55
❑ 105 Bobby Meacham .20 .09
❑ 106 Joe Niekro .20 .09
❑ 107 Mike Pagliarulo .20 .09
❑ 108 Dan Pasqua .20 .09
❑ 109 Willie Randolph .40 .18
❑ 110 Dennis Rasmussen .20 .09
❑ 111 Dave Righetti .20 .09
❑ 112 Gary Roenicke .20 .09
❑ 113 Rod Scurry .20 .09
❑ 114 Bob Shirley .20 .09
❑ 115 Joel Skinner .20 .09
❑ 116 Tim Stoddard .20 .09
❑ 117 Bob Tewksbury .40 .18
❑ 118 Wayne Tolleson .20 .09
❑ 119 Claudell Washington .20 .09
❑ 120 Dave Winfield .75 .35
❑ 121 Steve Buechele .20 .09
❑ 122 Ed Correa .20 .09
❑ 123 Scott Fletcher .20 .09
❑ 124 Jose Guzman .20 .09
❑ 125 Toby Harrah .20 .09
❑ 126 Greg Harris .20 .09
❑ 127 Charlie Hough .20 .09
❑ 128 Pete Incaviglia .40 .18
❑ 129 Mike Mason .20 .09
❑ 130 Oddibe McDowell .20 .09
❑ 131 Dale Mohorcic .20 .09
❑ 132 Pete O'Brien .20 .09
❑ 133 Tom Paciorek .40 .18
❑ 134 Larry Parrish .20 .09
❑ 135 Geno Petralli .20 .09
❑ 136 Darrell Porter .20 .09
❑ 137 Jeff Russell .20 .09
❑ 138 Ruben Sierra 1.00 .45
❑ 139 Don Slaught .20 .09
❑ 140 Gary Ward .20 .09
❑ 141 Curtis Wilkerson .20 .09
❑ 142 Mitch Williams .40 .18
❑ 143 Bobby Witt UER .40 .18
(Tulsa misspelled as Tusla; ERA should be 6.43, not .643)
❑ 144 Dave Bergman .20 .09
❑ 145 Tom Brookens .20 .09
❑ 146 Bill Campbell .20 .09
❑ 147 Chuck Cary .20 .09
❑ 148 Darnell Coles .20 .09
❑ 149 Dave Collins .20 .09
❑ 150 Darrell Evans .40 .18
❑ 151 Kirk Gibson .40 .18
❑ 152 John Grubb .20 .09
❑ 153 Willie Hernandez .20 .09
❑ 154 Larry Herndon .20 .09
❑ 155 Eric King .20 .09
❑ 156 Chet Lemon .20 .09
❑ 157 Dwight Lowry .20 .09
❑ 158 Jack Morris .40 .18
❑ 159 Randy O'Neal .20 .09
❑ 160 Lance Parrish .40 .18
❑ 161 Dan Petry .20 .09
❑ 162 Pat Sheridan .20 .09
❑ 163 Jim Slaton .20 .09
❑ 164 Frank Tanana .20 .09
❑ 165 Walt Terrell .20 .09
❑ 166 Mark Thurmond .20 .09
❑ 167 Alan Trammell .60 .25
❑ 168 Lou Whitaker .40 .18
❑ 169 Luis Aguayo .20 .09
❑ 170 Steve Bedrosian .20 .09
❑ 171 Don Carman .20 .09
❑ 172 Darren Daulton .60 .25
❑ 173 Greg Gross .20 .09
❑ 174 Kevin Gross .20 .09
❑ 175 Von Hayes .20 .09
❑ 176 Charles Hudson .20 .09
❑ 177 Tom Hume .20 .09
❑ 178 Steve Jeltz .20 .09
❑ 179 Mike Maddux .20 .09
❑ 180 Shane Rawley .20 .09
❑ 181 Gary Redus .20 .09
❑ 182 Ron Roenicke .20 .09
❑ 183 Bruce Ruffin .20 .09
❑ 184 John Russell .20 .09
❑ 185 Juan Samuel .20 .09
❑ 186 Dan Schatzeder .20 .09
❑ 187 Mike Schmidt 1.00 .45
❑ 188 Rick Schu .20 .09
❑ 189 Jeff Stone .20 .09
❑ 190 Kent Tekulve .20 .09
❑ 191 Milt Thompson .20 .09
❑ 192 Glenn Wilson .20 .09
❑ 193 Buddy Bell .40 .18
❑ 194 Tom Browning .20 .09
❑ 195 Sal Butera .20 .09
❑ 196 Dave Concepcion .40 .18
❑ 197 Kal Daniels .20 .09
❑ 198 Eric Davis .60 .25
❑ 199 John Denny .20 .09
❑ 200 Bo Diaz .20 .09
❑ 201 Nick Esasky .20 .09
❑ 202 John Franco .40 .18
❑ 203 Bill Gullickson .20 .09
❑ 204 Barry Larkin 4.00 1.80
❑ 205 Eddie Milner .20 .09
❑ 206 Rob Murphy .20 .09
❑ 207 Ron Oester .20 .09
❑ 208 Dave Parker .40 .18
❑ 209 Tony Perez .75 .35
❑ 210 Ted Power .20 .09
❑ 211 Joe Price .20 .09
❑ 212 Ron Robinson .20 .09
❑ 213 Pete Rose 1.00 .45
❑ 214 Mario Soto .20 .09
❑ 215 Kurt Stillwell .20 .09
❑ 216 Max Venable .20 .09
❑ 217 Chris Welsh .20 .09
❑ 218 Carl Willis .20 .09
❑ 219 Jesse Barfield .20 .09
❑ 220 George Bell .20 .09
❑ 221 Bill Caudill .20 .09
❑ 222 John Cerutti .20 .09
❑ 223 Jim Clancy .20 .09
❑ 224 Mark Eichhorn .20 .09
❑ 225 Tony Fernandez .20 .09
❑ 226 Damaso Garcia .20 .09
❑ 227 Kelly Gruber ERR .20 .09
(Wrong birth year)
❑ 228 Tom Henke .20 .09
❑ 229 Garth Iorg .20 .09
❑ 230 Joe Johnson .20 .09
❑ 231 Cliff Johnson .20 .09
❑ 232 Jimmy Key .60 .25
❑ 233 Dennis Lamp .20 .09
❑ 234 Rick Leach .20 .09
❑ 235 Buck Martinez .20 .09
❑ 236 Lloyd Moseby .20 .09
❑ 237 Rance Mulliniks .20 .09
❑ 238 Dave Stieb .20 .09
❑ 239 Willie Upshaw .20 .09
❑ 240 Ernie Whitt .20 .09
❑ 241 Andy Allanson .20 .09
❑ 242 Scott Bailes .20 .09
❑ 243 Chris Bando .20 .09
❑ 244 Tony Bernazard .20 .09
❑ 245 John Butcher .20 .09
❑ 246 Brett Butler .40 .18
❑ 247 Ernie Camacho .20 .09
❑ 248 Tom Candiotti .20 .09
❑ 249 Joe Carter .75 .35
❑ 250 Carmen Castillo .20 .09
❑ 251 Julio Franco .40 .18

❑	252	Mel Hall	.20	.09
❑	253	Brook Jacoby	.20	.09
❑	254	Phil Niekro	.75	.35
❑	255	Otis Nixon	.60	.25
❑	256	Dickie Noles	.20	.09
❑	257	Bryan Oelkers	.20	.09
❑	258	Ken Schrom	.20	.09
❑	259	Don Schulze	.20	.09
❑	260	Cory Snyder	.20	.09
❑	261	Pat Tabler	.20	.09
❑	262	Andre Thornton	.20	.09
❑	263	Rich Yett	.20	.09
❑	264	Mike Aldrete	.40	.18
❑	265	Juan Berenguer	.20	.09
❑	266	Vida Blue	.40	.18
❑	267	Bob Brenly	.20	.09
❑	268	Chris Brown	.20	.09
❑	269	Will Clark	5.00	2.20
❑	270	Chili Davis	.60	.25
❑	271	Mark Davis	.20	.09
❑	272	Kelly Downs	.20	.09
❑	273	Scott Garrelts	.20	.09
❑	274	Dan Gladden	.20	.09
❑	275	Mike Krukow	.20	.09
❑	276	Randy Kutcher	.20	.09
❑	277	Mike LaCoss	.20	.09
❑	278	Jeff Leonard	.20	.09
❑	279	Candy Maldonado	.20	.09
❑	280	Roger Mason	.20	.09
❑	281	Bob Melvin	.20	.09
❑	282	Greg Minton	.20	.09
❑	283	Jeff D. Robinson	.20	.09
❑	284	Harry Spilman	.20	.09
❑	285	Robby Thompson	.40	.18
❑	286	Jose Uribe	.20	.09
❑	287	Frank Williams	.20	.09
❑	288	Joel Youngblood	.20	.09
❑	289	Jack Clark	.40	.18
❑	290	Vince Coleman	.20	.09
❑	291	Tim Conroy	.20	.09
❑	292	Danny Cox	.20	.09
❑	293	Ken Dayley	.20	.09
❑	294	Curt Ford	.20	.09
❑	295	Bob Forsch	.20	.09
❑	296	Tom Herr	.20	.09
❑	297	Ricky Horton	.20	.09
❑	298	Clint Hurdle	.20	.09
❑	299	Jeff Lahti	.20	.09
❑	300	Steve Lake	.20	.09
❑	301	Tito Landrum	.20	.09
❑	302	Mike LaValliere	.20	.09
❑	303	Greg Mathews	.20	.09
❑	304	Willie McGee	.40	.18
❑	305	Jose Oquendo	.20	.09
❑	306	Terry Pendleton	.40	.18
❑	307	Pat Perry	.20	.09
❑	308	Ozzie Smith	1.00	.45
❑	309	Ray Soff	.20	.09
❑	310	John Tudor	.20	.09
❑	311	Andy Van Slyke UER (Bats R, Throws L)	.40	.18
❑	312	Todd Worrell	.40	.18
❑	313	Dann Bilardello	.20	.09
❑	314	Hubie Brooks	.20	.09
❑	315	Tim Burke	.20	.09
❑	316	Andre Dawson	.75	.35
❑	317	Mike Fitzgerald	.20	.09
❑	318	Tom Foley	.20	.09
❑	319	Andres Galarraga	1.00	.45
❑	320	Joe Hesketh	.20	.09
❑	321	Wallace Johnson	.20	.09
❑	322	Wayne Krenchicki	.20	.09
❑	323	Vance Law	.20	.09
❑	324	Dennis Martinez	.40	.18
❑	325	Bob McClure	.20	.09
❑	326	Andy McGaffigan	.20	.09
❑	327	Al Newman	.20	.09
❑	328	Tim Raines	.40	.18
❑	329	Jeff Reardon	.40	.18
❑	330	Luis Rivera	.20	.09
❑	331	Bob Sebra	.20	.09
❑	332	Bryn Smith	.20	.09
❑	333	Jay Tibbs	.20	.09
❑	334	Tim Wallach	.20	.09
❑	335	Mitch Webster	.20	.09
❑	336	Jim Wohlford	.20	.09
❑	337	Floyd Youmans	.20	.09
❑	338	Chris Bosio	.40	.18
❑	339	Glenn Braggs	.20	.09
❑	340	Rick Cerone	.20	.09
❑	341	Mark Clear	.20	.09
❑	342	Bryan Clutterbuck	.20	.09
❑	343	Cecil Cooper	.40	.18
❑	344	Rob Deer	.20	.09
❑	345	Jim Gantner	.20	.09
❑	346	Ted Higuera	.20	.09
❑	347	John Henry Johnson	.20	.09
❑	348	Tim Leary	.20	.09
❑	349	Rick Manning	.20	.09
❑	350	Paul Molitor	.75	.35
❑	351	Charlie Moore	.20	.09
❑	352	Juan Nieves	.20	.09
❑	353	Ben Oglivie	.20	.09
❑	354	Dan Plesac	.20	.09
❑	355	Ernest Riles	.20	.09
❑	356	Billy Joe Robidoux	.20	.09
❑	357	Bill Schroeder	.20	.09
❑	358	Dale Sveum	.20	.09
❑	359	Gorman Thomas	.20	.09
❑	360	Bill Wegman	.20	.09
❑	361	Robin Yount	.75	.35
❑	362	Steve Balboni	.20	.09
❑	363	Scott Bankhead	.20	.09
❑	364	Buddy Biancalana	.20	.09
❑	365	Bud Black	.20	.09
❑	366	George Brett	1.50	.70
❑	367	Steve Farr	.20	.09
❑	368	Mark Gubicza	.20	.09
❑	369	Bo Jackson	2.50	1.10
❑	370	Danny Jackson	.20	.09
❑	371	Mike Kingery	.20	.09
❑	372	Rudy Law	.20	.09
❑	373	Charlie Leibrandt	.20	.09
❑	374	Dennis Leonard	.20	.09
❑	375	Hal McRae	.40	.18
❑	376	Jorge Orta	.20	.09
❑	377	Jamie Quirk	.20	.09
❑	378	Dan Quisenberry	.20	.09
❑	379	Bret Saberhagen	.40	.18
❑	380	Angel Salazar	.20	.09
❑	381	Lonnie Smith	.20	.09
❑	382	Jim Sundberg	.20	.09
❑	383	Frank White	.40	.18
❑	384	Willie Wilson	.40	.18
❑	385	Joaquin Andujar	.20	.09
❑	386	Doug Bair	.20	.09
❑	387	Dusty Baker	.40	.18
❑	388	Bruce Bochte	.20	.09
❑	389	Jose Canseco	1.50	.70
❑	390	Chris Codiroli	.20	.09
❑	391	Mike Davis	.20	.09
❑	392	Alfredo Griffin	.20	.09
❑	393	Moose Haas	.20	.09
❑	394	Donnie Hill	.20	.09
❑	395	Jay Howell	.20	.09
❑	396	Dave Kingman	.40	.18
❑	397	Carney Lansford	.40	.18
❑	398	Dave Leiper	.20	.09
❑	399	Bill Mooneyham	.20	.09
❑	400	Dwayne Murphy	.20	.09
❑	401	Steve Ontiveros	.20	.09
❑	402	Tony Phillips	.20	.09
❑	403	Eric Plunk	.20	.09
❑	404	Jose Rijo	.20	.09
❑	405	Terry Steinbach	1.00	.45
❑	406	Dave Stewart	.40	.18
❑	407	Mickey Tettleton	.40	.18
❑	408	Dave Von Ohlen	.20	.09
❑	409	Jerry Willard	.20	.09
❑	410	Curt Young	.20	.09
❑	411	Bruce Bochy	.20	.09
❑	412	Dave Dravecky	.40	.18
❑	413	Tim Flannery	.20	.09
❑	414	Steve Garvey	.60	.25
❑	415	Rich Gossage	.40	.18
❑	416	Tony Gwynn	2.00	.90
❑	417	Andy Hawkins	.20	.09
❑	418	LaMarr Hoyt	.20	.09
❑	419	Terry Kennedy	.20	.09
❑	420	John Kruk	1.00	.45
❑	421	Dave LaPoint	.20	.09
❑	422	Craig Lefferts	.20	.09
❑	423	Carmelo Martinez	.20	.09
❑	424	Lance McCullers	.20	.09
❑	425	Kevin McReynolds	.20	.09
❑	426	Graig Nettles	.40	.18
❑	427	Bip Roberts	1.00	.45
❑	428	Jerry Royster	.20	.09
❑	429	Benito Santiago	.40	.18
❑	430	Eric Show	.20	.09
❑	431	Bob Stoddard	.20	.09
❑	432	Garry Templeton	.20	.09
❑	433	Gene Walter	.20	.09
❑	434	Ed Whitson	.20	.09
❑	435	Marvell Wynne	.20	.09
❑	436	Dave Anderson	.20	.09
❑	437	Greg Brock	.20	.09
❑	438	Enos Cabell	.20	.09
❑	439	Mariano Duncan	.20	.09
❑	440	Pedro Guerrero	.20	.09
❑	441	Orel Hershiser	.40	.18
❑	442	Rick Honeycutt	.20	.09
❑	443	Ken Howell	.20	.09
❑	444	Ken Landreaux	.20	.09
❑	445	Bill Madlock	.40	.18
❑	446	Mike Marshall	.20	.09
❑	447	Len Matuszek	.20	.09
❑	448	Tom Niedenfuer	.20	.09
❑	449	Alejandro Pena	.20	.09
❑	450	Dennis Powell	.20	.09
❑	451	Jerry Reuss	.20	.09
❑	452	Bill Russell	.20	.09
❑	453	Steve Sax	.20	.09
❑	454	Mike Scioscia	.20	.09
❑	455	Franklin Stubbs	.20	.09
❑	456	Alex Trevino	.20	.09
❑	457	Fernando Valenzuela	.40	.18
❑	458	Ed VandeBerg	.20	.09
❑	459	Bob Welch	.20	.09
❑	460	Reggie Williams	.20	.09
❑	461	Don Aase	.20	.09
❑	462	Juan Beniquez	.20	.09
❑	463	Mike Boddicker	.20	.09
❑	464	Juan Bonilla	.20	.09
❑	465	Rich Bordi	.20	.09
❑	466	Storm Davis	.20	.09
❑	467	Rick Dempsey	.40	.18
❑	468	Ken Dixon	.20	.09
❑	469	Jim Dwyer	.20	.09
❑	470	Mike Flanagan	.20	.09
❑	471	Jackie Gutierrez	.20	.09
❑	472	Brad Havens	.20	.09
❑	473	Lee Lacy	.20	.09
❑	474	Fred Lynn	.40	.18
❑	475	Scott McGregor	.20	.09
❑	476	Eddie Murray	.75	.35
❑	477	Tom O'Malley	.20	.09
❑	478	Cal Ripken Jr.	3.00	1.35
❑	479	Larry Sheets	.20	.09
❑	480	John Shelby	.20	.09
❑	481	Nate Snell	.20	.09
❑	482	Jim Traber	.20	.09
❑	483	Mike Young	.20	.09
❑	484	Neil Allen	.20	.09
❑	485	Harold Baines	.40	.18
❑	486	Floyd Bannister	.20	.09
❑	487	Daryl Boston	.20	.09
❑	488	Ivan Calderon	.20	.09
❑	489	John Cangelosi	.20	.09
❑	490	Steve Carlton	.75	.35
❑	491	Joe Cowley	.20	.09
❑	492	Julio Cruz	.20	.09
❑	493	Bill Dawley	.20	.09
❑	494	Jose DeLeon	.20	.09
❑	495	Richard Dotson	.20	.09
❑	496	Carlton Fisk	.75	.35
❑	497	Ozzie Guillen	.20	.09
❑	498	Jerry Hairston	.20	.09
❑	499	Ron Hassey	.20	.09
❑	500	Tim Hulett	.20	.09
❑	501	Bob James	.20	.09
❑	502	Steve Lyons	.20	.09
❑	503	Joel McKeon	.20	.09
❑	504	Gene Nelson	.20	.09
❑	505	Dave Schmidt	.20	.09

	Card	Mint	NrMt
❑ 506	Ray Searage	.20	.09
❑ 507	Bobby Thigpen	.40	.18
❑ 508	Greg Walker	.20	.09
❑ 509	Jim Acker	.20	.09
❑ 510	Doyle Alexander	.20	.09
❑ 511	Paul Assenmacher	.60	.25
❑ 512	Bruce Benedict	.20	.09
❑ 513	Chris Chambliss	.20	.09
❑ 514	Jeff Dedmon	.20	.09
❑ 515	Gene Garber	.20	.09
❑ 516	Ken Griffey	.40	.18
❑ 517	Terry Harper	.20	.09
❑ 518	Bob Horner	.20	.09
❑ 519	Glenn Hubbard	.20	.09
❑ 520	Rick Mahler	.20	.09
❑ 521	Omar Moreno	.20	.09
❑ 522	Dale Murphy	.75	.35
❑ 523	Ken Oberkfell	.20	.09
❑ 524	Ed Olwine	.20	.09
❑ 525	David Palmer	.20	.09
❑ 526	Rafael Ramirez	.20	.09
❑ 527	Billy Sample	.20	.09
❑ 528	Ted Simmons	.40	.18
❑ 529	Zane Smith	.20	.09
❑ 530	Bruce Sutter	.20	.09
❑ 531	Andres Thomas	.20	.09
❑ 532	Ozzie Virgil	.20	.09
❑ 533	Allan Anderson	.20	.09
❑ 534	Keith Atherton	.20	.09
❑ 535	Billy Beane	.20	.09
❑ 536	Bert Blyleven	.40	.18
❑ 537	Tom Brunansky	.20	.09
❑ 538	Randy Bush	.20	.09
❑ 539	George Frazier	.20	.09
❑ 540	Gary Gaetti	.40	.18
❑ 541	Greg Gagne	.20	.09
❑ 542	Mickey Hatcher	.20	.09
❑ 543	Neal Heaton	.20	.09
❑ 544	Kent Hrbek	.40	.18
❑ 545	Roy Lee Jackson	.20	.09
❑ 546	Tim Laudner	.20	.09
❑ 547	Steve Lombardozzi	.20	.09
❑ 548	Mark Portugal	.40	.18
❑ 549	Kirby Puckett	1.50	.70
❑ 550	Jeff Reed	.20	.09
❑ 551	Mark Salas	.20	.09
❑ 552	Roy Smalley	.20	.09
❑ 553	Mike Smithson	.20	.09
❑ 554	Frank Viola	.20	.09
❑ 555	Thad Bosley	.20	.09
❑ 556	Ron Cey	.40	.18
❑ 557	Jody Davis	.20	.09
❑ 558	Ron Davis	.20	.09
❑ 559	Bob Dernier	.20	.09
❑ 560	Frank DiPino	.20	.09
❑ 561	Shawon Dunston UER	.20	.09
	(Wrong birth year listed on card back)		
❑ 562	Leon Durham	.20	.09
❑ 563	Dennis Eckersley	.75	.35
❑ 564	Terry Francona	.40	.18
❑ 565	Dave Gumpert	.20	.09
❑ 566	Guy Hoffman	.20	.09
❑ 567	Ed Lynch	.20	.09
❑ 568	Gary Matthews	.20	.09
❑ 569	Keith Moreland	.20	.09
❑ 570	Jamie Moyer	.60	.25
❑ 571	Jerry Mumphrey	.20	.09
❑ 572	Ryne Sandberg	1.00	.45
❑ 573	Scott Sanderson	.20	.09
❑ 574	Lee Smith	.60	.25
❑ 575	Chris Speier	.20	.09
❑ 576	Rick Sutcliffe	.20	.09
❑ 577	Manny Trillo	.20	.09
❑ 578	Steve Trout	.20	.09
❑ 579	Karl Best	.20	.09
❑ 580	Scott Bradley	.20	.09
❑ 581	Phil Bradley	.20	.09
❑ 582	Mickey Brantley	.20	.09
❑ 583	Mike G. Brown P	.20	.09
❑ 584	Alvin Davis	.20	.09
❑ 585	Lee Guetterman	.20	.09
❑ 586	Mark Huismann	.20	.09
❑ 587	Bob Kearney	.20	.09
❑ 588	Pete Ladd	.20	.09
❑ 589	Mark Langston	.20	.09
❑ 590	Mike Moore	.20	.09
❑ 591	Mike Morgan	.20	.09
❑ 592	John Moses	.20	.09
❑ 593	Ken Phelps	.20	.09
❑ 594	Jim Presley	.20	.09
❑ 595	Rey Quinones UER	.20	.09
	(Quinonez on front)		
❑ 596	Harold Reynolds	.40	.18
❑ 597	Billy Swift	.20	.09
❑ 598	Danny Tartabull	.20	.09
❑ 599	Steve Yeager	.20	.09
❑ 600	Matt Young	.20	.09
❑ 601	Bill Almon	.20	.09
❑ 602	Rafael Belliard	.20	.09
❑ 603	Mike Bielecki	.20	.09
❑ 604	Barry Bonds	35.00	16.00
❑ 605	Bobby Bonilla	2.00	.90
❑ 606	Sid Bream	.20	.09
❑ 607	Mike C. Brown	.20	.09
❑ 608	Pat Clements	.20	.09
❑ 609	Mike Diaz	.20	.09
❑ 610	Cecilio Guante	.20	.09
❑ 611	Barry Jones	.20	.09
❑ 612	Bob Kipper	.20	.09
❑ 613	Larry McWilliams	.20	.09
❑ 614	Jim Morrison	.20	.09
❑ 615	Joe Orsulak	.20	.09
❑ 616	Junior Ortiz	.20	.09
❑ 617	Tony Pena	.20	.09
❑ 618	Johnny Ray	.20	.09
❑ 619	Rick Reuschel	.20	.09
❑ 620	R.J. Reynolds	.20	.09
❑ 621	Rick Rhoden	.20	.09
❑ 622	Don Robinson	.20	.09
❑ 623	Bob Walk	.20	.09
❑ 624	Jim Winn	.20	.09
❑ 625	Youthful Power	.75	.35
	Pete Incaviglia		
	Jose Canseco		
❑ 626	300 Game Winners	.60	.25
	Don Sutton		
	Phil Niekro		
❑ 627	AL Firemen	.20	.09
	Dave Righetti		
	Don Aase		
❑ 628	Rookie All-Stars	.75	.35
	Wally Joyner		
	Jose Canseco		
❑ 629	Magic Mets	.60	.25
	Gary Carter		
	Sid Fernandez		
	Dwight Gooden		
	Keith Hernandez		
	Darryl Strawberry		
❑ 630	NL Best Righties	.20	.09
	Mike Scott		
	Mike Krukow		
❑ 631	Sensational Southpaws	.20	.09
	Fernando Valenzuela		
	John Franco		
❑ 632	Count'Em	.20	.09
	Bob Horner		
❑ 633	AL Pitcher's Nightmare	1.00	.45
	Jose Canseco		
	Jim Rice		
	Kirby Puckett		
❑ 634	All-Star Battery	.40	.18
	Gary Carter		
	Roger Clemens		
❑ 635	4000 Strikeouts	.40	.18
	Steve Carlton		
❑ 636	Big Bats at First	.75	.35
	Glenn Davis		
	Eddie Murray		
❑ 637	On Base	.40	.18
	Wade Boggs		
	Keith Hernandez		
❑ 638	Sluggers Left Side	.75	.35
	Don Mattingly		
	Darryl Strawberry		
❑ 639	Former MVP's	.40	.18
	Dave Parker		
	Ryne Sandberg		
❑ 640	Dr. K and Super K	.60	.25
	Dwight Gooden		
	Roger Clemens		
❑ 641	AL West Stoppers	.20	.09
	Mike Witt		
	Charlie Hough		
❑ 642	Doubles and Triples	.40	.18
	Juan Samuel		
	Tim Raines		
❑ 643	Outfielders with Punch	.40	.18
	Harold Baines		
	Jesse Barfield		
❑ 644	Dave Clark and	.75	.35
	Greg Swindell		
❑ 645	Ron Karkovice and	.40	.18
	Russ Morman		
❑ 646	Devon White and	2.00	.90
	Willie Fraser		
❑ 647	Mike Stanley and	.75	.35
	Jerry Browne		
❑ 648	Dave Magadan and	.40	.18
	Phil Lombardi		
❑ 649	Jose Gonzalez and	.20	.09
	Ralph Bryant		
❑ 650	Jimmy Jones and	.20	.09
	Randy Asadoor		
❑ 651	Tracy Jones and	.20	.09
	Marvin Freeman		
❑ 652	John Stefero and	.75	.35
	Kevin Seitzer		
❑ 653	Rob Nelson and	.20	.09
	Steve Fireovid		
❑ 654	CL: Mets/Red Sox	.20	.09
	Astros/Angels		
❑ 655	CL: Yankees/Rangers	.20	.09
	Tigers/Phillies		
❑ 656	CL: Reds/Blue Jays	.20	.09
	Indians/Giants		
	ERR (230/231 wrong)		
❑ 657	CL: Cardinals/Expos	.20	.09
	Brewers/Royals		
❑ 658	CL: A's/Padres	.20	.09
	Dodgers/Orioles		
❑ 659	CL: White Sox/Braves	.20	.09
	Twins/Cubs		
❑ 660	CL: Mariners/Pirates	.20	.09
	Special Cards		
	ER (580/581 wrong)		

1987 Fleer Glossy

	MINT	NRMT
COMP.FACT.SET (672)	60.00	27.00
COMMON CARD (1-660)	.20	.09
COMMON WS (1-12)	.10	.05

*STARS: .6X TO 1.2X BASIC CARDS
*ROOKIES: .6X TO 1.2X BASIC CARDS

1987 Fleer All-Stars

	MINT	NRMT
COMPLETE SET (12)	20.00	9.00
COMMON CARD (1-12)	.30	.14
❑ 1 Don Mattingly	6.00	2.70
❑ 2 Gary Carter	1.50	.70
❑ 3 Tony Fernandez	.30	.14
❑ 4 Steve Sax	.30	.14
❑ 5 Kirby Puckett	8.00	3.60
❑ 6 Mike Schmidt	2.50	1.10

	MINT	NRMT
❑ 7 Mike Easler	.30	.14
❑ 8 Todd Worrell	.75	.35
❑ 9 George Bell	.30	.14
❑ 10 Fernando Valenzuela	.75	.35
❑ 11 Roger Clemens	5.00	2.20
❑ 12 Tim Raines	.75	.35

1987 Fleer Headliners

	MINT	NRMT
COMPLETE SET (6)	6.00	2.70
COMMON CARD (1-6)	.50	.23
❑ 1 Wade Boggs	1.50	.70
❑ 2 Jose Canseco	4.00	1.80
❑ 3 Dwight Gooden	.75	.35
❑ 4 Rickey Henderson	1.50	.70
❑ 5 Keith Hernandez	.50	.23
❑ 6 Jim Rice	.50	.23

1987 Fleer Update

	MINT	NRMT
COMP.FACT.SET (132)	30.00	13.50
COMMON CARD (1-132)	.10	.05
❑ 1 Scott Bankhead	.10	.05
❑ 2 Eric Bell	.10	.05
❑ 3 Juan Beniquez	.10	.05
❑ 4 Juan Berenguer	.10	.05
❑ 5 Mike Birkbeck	.10	.05
❑ 6 Randy Bockus	.10	.05
❑ 7 Rod Booker	.10	.05
❑ 8 Thad Bosley	.10	.05
❑ 9 Greg Brock	.10	.05
❑ 10 Bob Brower	.10	.05
❑ 11 Chris Brown	.10	.05
❑ 12 Jerry Browne	.10	.05
❑ 13 Ralph Bryant	.10	.05
❑ 14 DeWayne Buice	.10	.05
❑ 15 Ellis Burks	1.00	.45
❑ 16 Casey Candaele	.10	.05
❑ 17 Steve Carlton	.50	.23
❑ 18 Juan Castillo	.10	.05
❑ 19 Chuck Crim	.10	.05
❑ 20 Mark Davidson	.10	.05
❑ 21 Mark Davis	.10	.05
❑ 22 Storm Davis	.10	.05
❑ 23 Bill Dawley	.10	.05
❑ 24 Andre Dawson	.50	.23
❑ 25 Brian Dayett	.10	.05
❑ 26 Rick Dempsey	.25	.11
❑ 27 Ken Dowell	.10	.05
❑ 28 Dave Dravecky	.25	.11
❑ 29 Mike Dunne	.10	.05
❑ 30 Dennis Eckersley	.50	.23
❑ 31 Cecil Fielder	.10	.05
❑ 32 Brian Fisher	.10	.05
❑ 33 Willie Fraser	.10	.05
❑ 34 Ken Gerhart	.10	.05
❑ 35 Jim Gott	.10	.05
❑ 36 Dan Gladden	.10	.05
❑ 37 Mike Greenwell	.50	.23
❑ 38 Cecilio Guante	.10	.05
❑ 39 Albert Hall	.10	.05
❑ 40 Atlee Hammaker	.10	.05
❑ 41 Mickey Hatcher	.10	.05
❑ 42 Mike Heath	.10	.05
❑ 43 Neal Heaton	.10	.05
❑ 44 Mike Henneman	.50	.23
❑ 45 Guy Hoffman	.10	.05
❑ 46 Charles Hudson	.10	.05
❑ 47 Chuck Jackson	.10	.05
❑ 48 Mike Jackson	.50	.23
❑ 49 Reggie Jackson	.60	.25
❑ 50 Chris James	.10	.05
❑ 51 Dion James	.10	.05
❑ 52 Stan Javier	.10	.05
❑ 53 Stan Jefferson	.10	.05
❑ 54 Jimmy Jones	.10	.05
❑ 55 Tracy Jones	.10	.05
❑ 56 Terry Kennedy	.10	.05
❑ 57 Mike Kingery	.10	.05
❑ 58 Ray Knight	.10	.05
❑ 59 Gene Larkin	.10	.05
❑ 60 Mike LaValliere	.10	.05
❑ 61 Jack Lazorko	.10	.05
❑ 62 Terry Leach	.10	.05
❑ 63 Rick Leach	.10	.05
❑ 64 Craig Lefferts	.10	.05
❑ 65 Jim Lindeman	.10	.05
❑ 66 Bill Long	.10	.05
❑ 67 Mike Loynd	.10	.05
❑ 68 Greg Maddux	12.00	5.50
❑ 69 Bill Madlock	.25	.11
❑ 70 Dave Magadan	.25	.11
❑ 71 Joe Magrane	.10	.05
❑ 72 Fred Manrique	.10	.05
❑ 73 Mike Mason	.10	.05
❑ 74 Lloyd McClendon	.10	.05
❑ 75 Fred McGriff	.60	.25
❑ 76 Mark McGwire	20.00	9.00
❑ 77 Mark McLemore	.25	.11
❑ 78 Kevin McReynolds	.10	.05
❑ 79 Dave Meads	.10	.05
❑ 80 Greg Minton	.10	.05
❑ 81 John Mitchell	.10	.05
❑ 82 Kevin Mitchell	.10	.05
❑ 83 John Morris	.10	.05
❑ 84 Jeff Musselman	.10	.05
❑ 85 Randy Myers	.50	.23
❑ 86 Gene Nelson	.10	.05
❑ 87 Joe Niekro	.10	.05
❑ 88 Tom Nieto	.10	.05
❑ 89 Reid Nichols	.10	.05
❑ 90 Matt Nokes	.25	.11
❑ 91 Dickie Noles	.10	.05
❑ 92 Edwin Nunez	.10	.05
❑ 93 Jose Nunez	.10	.05
❑ 94 Paul O'Neill	.50	.23
❑ 95 Jim Paciorek	.10	.05
❑ 96 Lance Parrish	.25	.11
❑ 97 Bill Pecota	.10	.05
❑ 98 Tony Pena	.10	.05
❑ 99 Luis Polonia	.25	.11
❑ 100 Randy Ready	.10	.05
❑ 101 Jeff Reardon	.25	.11
❑ 102 Gary Redus	.10	.05
❑ 103 Rick Rhoden	.10	.05
❑ 104 Wally Ritchie	.10	.05
❑ 105 Jeff M. Robinson UER (Wrong Jeff's stats on back)	.10	.05
❑ 106 Mark Salas	.10	.05
❑ 107 Dave Schmidt	.10	.05
❑ 108 Kevin Seitzer UER (Wrong birth year)	.25	.11
❑ 109 John Shelby	.10	.05
❑ 110 John Smiley	.25	.11
❑ 111 Lary Sorensen	.10	.05
❑ 112 Chris Speier	.10	.05
❑ 113 Randy St.Claire	.10	.05
❑ 114 Jim Sundberg	.10	.05
❑ 115 B.J. Surhoff	.50	.23
❑ 116 Greg Swindell	.50	.23
❑ 117 Danny Tartabull	.10	.05
❑ 118 Dorn Taylor	.10	.05
❑ 119 Lee Tunnell	.10	.05
❑ 120 Ed VandeBerg	.10	.05
❑ 121 Andy Van Slyke	.25	.11
❑ 122 Gary Ward	.10	.05
❑ 123 Devon White	.50	.23
❑ 124 Alan Wiggins	.10	.05
❑ 125 Bill Wilkinson	.10	.05
❑ 126 Jim Winn	.10	.05
❑ 127 Frank Williams	.10	.05
❑ 128 Ken Williams	.10	.05
❑ 129 Matt Williams	1.50	.70
❑ 130 Herm Willingham	.10	.05
❑ 131 Matt Young	.10	.05
❑ 132 Checklist 1-132	.10	.05

1987 Fleer Update Glossy

	MINT	NRMT
COMP.FACT.SET (132)	40.00	18.00
COMMON CARD (1-132)	.15	.07

*STARS: .6X TO 1.2X BASIC CARDS
*ROOKIES: .6X TO 1.2X BASIC CARDS

1988 Fleer

	MINT	NRMT
COMPLETE SET (660)	20.00	9.00
COMP.RETAIL SET (660)	20.00	9.00
COMP.HOBBY SET (672)	25.00	11.00
COMMON CARD (1-660)	.10	.05
❑ 1 Keith Atherton	.10	.05
❑ 2 Don Baylor	.20	.09
❑ 3 Juan Berenguer	.10	.05
❑ 4 Bert Blyleven	.20	.09
❑ 5 Tom Brunansky	.10	.05
❑ 6 Randy Bush	.10	.05
❑ 7 Steve Carlton	.40	.18
❑ 8 Mark Davidson	.10	.05
❑ 9 George Frazier	.10	.05
❑ 10 Gary Gaetti	.20	.09
❑ 11 Greg Gagne	.10	.05
❑ 12 Dan Gladden	.10	.05
❑ 13 Kent Hrbek	.20	.09
❑ 14 Gene Larkin	.10	.05
❑ 15 Tim Laudner	.10	.05
❑ 16 Steve Lombardozzi	.10	.05
❑ 17 Al Newman	.10	.05
❑ 18 Joe Niekro	.10	.05
❑ 19 Kirby Puckett	.60	.25
❑ 20 Jeff Reardon	.20	.09
❑ 21A Dan Schatzeder ERR (Misspelled Schatzader on card front)	.20	.09
❑ 21B Dan Schatzeder COR	.10	.05
❑ 22 Roy Smalley	.10	.05
❑ 23 Mike Smithson	.10	.05

❑ 24 Les Straker .10 .05
❑ 25 Frank Viola .10 .05
❑ 26 Jack Clark .20 .09
❑ 27 Vince Coleman .10 .05
❑ 28 Danny Cox .10 .05
❑ 29 Bill Dawley .10 .05
❑ 30 Ken Dayley .10 .05
❑ 31 Doug DeCinces .10 .05
❑ 32 Curt Ford .10 .05
❑ 33 Bob Forsch .10 .05
❑ 34 David Green .10 .05
❑ 35 Tom Herr .10 .05
❑ 36 Ricky Horton .10 .05
❑ 37 Lance Johnson .40 .18
❑ 38 Steve Lake .10 .05
❑ 39 Jim Lindeman .10 .05
❑ 40 Joe Magrane .10 .05
❑ 41 Greg Mathews .10 .05
❑ 42 Willie McGee .20 .09
❑ 43 John Morris .10 .05
❑ 44 Jose Oquendo .10 .05
❑ 45 Tony Pena .10 .05
❑ 46 Terry Pendleton .20 .09
❑ 47 Ozzie Smith .50 .23
❑ 48 John Tudor .10 .05
❑ 49 Lee Tunnell .10 .05
❑ 50 Todd Worrell .20 .09
❑ 51 Doyle Alexander .10 .05
❑ 52 Dave Bergman .10 .05
❑ 53 Tom Brookens .10 .05
❑ 54 Darrell Evans .20 .09
❑ 55 Kirk Gibson .20 .09
❑ 56 Mike Heath .10 .05
❑ 57 Mike Henneman .20 .09
❑ 58 Willie Hernandez .10 .05
❑ 59 Larry Herndon .10 .05
❑ 60 Eric King .10 .05
❑ 61 Chet Lemon .10 .05
❑ 62 Scott Lusader .10 .05
❑ 63 Bill Madlock .20 .09
❑ 64 Jack Morris .20 .09
❑ 65 Jim Morrison .10 .05
❑ 66 Matt Nokes .10 .05
❑ 67 Dan Petry .10 .05
❑ 68A Jeff M. Robinson ERR .. .40 .18
(Stats for Jeff D. Robinson on card back, Born 12-13-60)
❑ 68B Jeff M. Robinson COR .. .10 .05
(Born 12-14-61)
❑ 69 Pat Sheridan .10 .05
❑ 70 Nate Snell .10 .05
❑ 71 Frank Tanana .10 .05
❑ 72 Walt Terrell .10 .05
❑ 73 Mark Thurmond .10 .05
❑ 74 Alan Trammell .10 .05
❑ 75 Lou Whitaker .20 .09
❑ 76 Mike Aldrete .10 .05
❑ 77 Bob Brenly .10 .05
❑ 78 Will Clark .50 .23
❑ 79 Chili Davis .10 .05
❑ 80 Kelly Downs .10 .05
❑ 81 Dave Dravecky .20 .09
❑ 82 Scott Garrelts .10 .05
❑ 83 Atlee Hammaker .10 .05
❑ 84 Dave Henderson .10 .05
❑ 85 Mike Krukow .10 .05
❑ 86 Mike LaCoss .10 .05
❑ 87 Craig Lefferts .10 .05
❑ 88 Jeff Leonard .10 .05
❑ 89 Candy Maldonado .10 .05
❑ 90 Eddie Milner .10 .05
❑ 91 Bob Melvin .10 .05
❑ 92 Kevin Mitchell .20 .09
❑ 93 Jon Perlman .10 .05
❑ 94 Rick Reuschel .10 .05
❑ 95 Don Robinson .10 .05
❑ 96 Chris Speier .10 .05
❑ 97 Harry Spilman .10 .05
❑ 98 Robby Thompson .10 .05
❑ 99 Jose Uribe .10 .05
❑ 100 Mark Wasinger .10 .05
❑ 101 Matt Williams 1.50 .70
❑ 102 Jesse Barfield .10 .05
❑ 103 George Bell .10 .05
❑ 104 Juan Beniquez .10 .05
❑ 105 John Cerutti .10 .05
❑ 106 Jim Clancy .10 .05
❑ 107 Rob Ducey .10 .05
❑ 108 Mark Eichhorn .10 .05
❑ 109 Tony Fernandez .10 .05
❑ 110 Cecil Fielder .10 .05
❑ 111 Kelly Gruber .10 .05
❑ 112 Tom Henke .10 .05
❑ 113A Garth Iorg ERR .40 .18
(Misspelled lorq on card front)
❑ 113B Garth Iorg COR .10 .05
❑ 114 Jimmy Key .20 .09
❑ 115 Rick Leach .10 .05
❑ 116 Manny Lee .10 .05
❑ 117 Nelson Liriano .10 .05
❑ 118 Fred McGriff .40 .18
❑ 119 Lloyd Moseby .10 .05
❑ 120 Rance Mulliniks .10 .05
❑ 121 Jeff Musselman .10 .05
❑ 122 Jose Nunez .10 .05
❑ 123 Dave Stieb .10 .05
❑ 124 Willie Upshaw .10 .05
❑ 125 Duane Ward .10 .05
❑ 126 Ernie Whitt .10 .05
❑ 127 Rick Aguilera .20 .09
❑ 128 Wally Backman .10 .05
❑ 129 Mark Carreon .20 .09
❑ 130 Gary Carter .10 .05
❑ 131 David Cone .50 .23
❑ 132 Ron Darling .10 .05
❑ 133 Len Dykstra .20 .09
❑ 134 Sid Fernandez .10 .05
❑ 135 Dwight Gooden .20 .09
❑ 136 Keith Hernandez .20 .09
❑ 137 Gregg Jefferies .50 .23
❑ 138 Howard Johnson .10 .05
❑ 139 Terry Leach .10 .05
❑ 140 Barry Lyons .10 .05
❑ 141 Dave Magadan .10 .05
❑ 142 Roger McDowell .10 .05
❑ 143 Kevin McReynolds .10 .05
❑ 144 Keith A. Miller .10 .05
❑ 145 John Mitchell .10 .05
❑ 146 Randy Myers .10 .05
❑ 147 Bob Ojeda .10 .05
❑ 148 Jesse Orosco .10 .05
❑ 149 Rafael Santana .10 .05
❑ 150 Doug Sisk .10 .05
❑ 151 Darryl Strawberry .20 .09
❑ 152 Tim Teufel .10 .05
❑ 153 Gene Walter .10 .05
❑ 154 Mookie Wilson .20 .09
❑ 155 Jay Aldrich .10 .05
❑ 156 Chris Bosio .10 .05
❑ 157 Glenn Braggs .10 .05
❑ 158 Greg Brock .10 .05
❑ 159 Juan Castillo .10 .05
❑ 160 Mark Clear .10 .05
❑ 161 Cecil Cooper .20 .09
❑ 162 Chuck Crim .10 .05
❑ 163 Rob Deer .10 .05
❑ 164 Mike Felder .10 .05
❑ 165 Jim Gantner .10 .05
❑ 166 Ted Higuera .10 .05
❑ 167 Steve Kiefer .10 .05
❑ 168 Rick Manning .10 .05
❑ 169 Paul Molitor .40 .18
❑ 170 Juan Nieves .10 .05
❑ 171 Dan Plesac .10 .05
❑ 172 Earnest Riles .10 .05
❑ 173 Bill Schroeder .10 .05
❑ 174 Steve Stanicek .10 .05
❑ 175 B.J. Surhoff .20 .09
❑ 176 Dale Sveum .10 .05
❑ 177 Bill Wegman .10 .05
❑ 178 Robin Yount .40 .18
❑ 179 Hubie Brooks .10 .05
❑ 180 Tim Burke .10 .05
❑ 181 Casey Candaele .10 .05
❑ 182 Mike Fitzgerald .10 .05
❑ 183 Tom Foley .10 .05
❑ 184 Andres Galarraga .40 .18
❑ 185 Neal Heaton .10 .05
❑ 186 Wallace Johnson .10 .05
❑ 187 Vance Law .10 .05
❑ 188 Dennis Martinez .20 .09
❑ 189 Bob McClure .10 .05
❑ 190 Andy McGaffigan .10 .05
❑ 191 Reid Nichols .10 .05
❑ 192 Pascual Perez .10 .05
❑ 193 Tim Raines .20 .09
❑ 194 Jeff Reed .10 .05
❑ 195 Bob Sebra .10 .05
❑ 196 Bryn Smith .10 .05
❑ 197 Randy St.Claire .10 .05
❑ 198 Tim Wallach .10 .05
❑ 199 Mitch Webster .10 .05
❑ 200 Herm Winningham .10 .05
❑ 201 Floyd Youmans .10 .05
❑ 202 Brad Arnsberg .10 .05
❑ 203 Rick Cerone .10 .05
❑ 204 Pat Clements .10 .05
❑ 205 Henry Cotto .10 .05
❑ 206 Mike Easler .10 .05
❑ 207 Ron Guidry .10 .05
❑ 208 Bill Gullickson .10 .05
❑ 209 Rickey Henderson .40 .18
❑ 210 Charles Hudson .10 .05
❑ 211 Tommy John .20 .09
❑ 212 Roberto Kelly .40 .18
❑ 213 Ron Kittle .10 .05
❑ 214 Don Mattingly .60 .25
❑ 215 Bobby Meacham .10 .05
❑ 216 Mike Pagliarulo .10 .05
❑ 217 Dan Pasqua .10 .05
❑ 218 Willie Randolph .20 .09
❑ 219 Rick Rhoden .10 .05
❑ 220 Dave Righetti .10 .05
❑ 221 Jerry Royster .10 .05
❑ 222 Tim Stoddard .10 .05
❑ 223 Wayne Tolleson .10 .05
❑ 224 Gary Ward .10 .05
❑ 225 Claudell Washington .10 .05
❑ 226 Dave Winfield .40 .18
❑ 227 Buddy Bell .20 .09
❑ 228 Tom Browning .10 .05
❑ 229 Dave Concepcion .20 .09
❑ 230 Kal Daniels .10 .05
❑ 231 Eric Davis .20 .09
❑ 232 Bo Diaz .10 .05
❑ 233 Nick Esasky .10 .05
(Has a dollar sign before '87 SB totals)
❑ 234 John Franco .20 .09
❑ 235 Guy Hoffman .10 .05
❑ 236 Tom Hume .10 .05
❑ 237 Tracy Jones .10 .05
❑ 238 Bill Landrum .10 .05
❑ 239 Barry Larkin .40 .18
❑ 240 Terry McGriff .10 .05
❑ 241 Rob Murphy .10 .05
❑ 242 Ron Oester .10 .05
❑ 243 Dave Parker .20 .09
❑ 244 Pat Perry .10 .05
❑ 245 Ted Power .10 .05
❑ 246 Dennis Rasmussen .10 .05
❑ 247 Ron Robinson .10 .05
❑ 248 Kurt Stillwell .10 .05
❑ 249 Jeff Treadway .10 .05
❑ 250 Frank Williams .10 .05
❑ 251 Steve Balboni .10 .05
❑ 252 Bud Black .10 .05
❑ 253 Thad Bosley .10 .05
❑ 254 George Brett .75 .35
❑ 255 John Davis .10 .05
❑ 256 Steve Farr .10 .05
❑ 257 Gene Garber .10 .05
❑ 258 Jerry Don Gleaton .10 .05
❑ 259 Mark Gubicza .10 .05
❑ 260 Bo Jackson .40 .18
❑ 261 Danny Jackson .10 .05
❑ 262 Ross Jones .10 .05
❑ 263 Charlie Leibrandt .10 .05
❑ 264 Bill Pecota .10 .05
❑ 265 Melido Perez .10 .05
❑ 266 Jamie Quirk .10 .05
❑ 267 Dan Quisenberry .10 .05
❑ 268 Bret Saberhagen .20 .09

❑ 269	Angel Salazar	.10	.05
❑ 270	Kevin Seitzer UER (Wrong birth year)	.20	.09
❑ 271	Danny Tartabull	.10	.05
❑ 272	Gary Thurman	.10	.05
❑ 273	Frank White	.20	.09
❑ 274	Willie Wilson	.10	.05
❑ 275	Tony Bernazard	.10	.05
❑ 276	Jose Canseco	.40	.18
❑ 277	Mike Davis	.10	.05
❑ 278	Storm Davis	.10	.05
❑ 279	Dennis Eckersley	.20	.09
❑ 280	Alfredo Griffin	.10	.05
❑ 281	Rick Honeycutt	.10	.05
❑ 282	Jay Howell	.10	.05
❑ 283	Reggie Jackson	.50	.23
❑ 284	Dennis Lamp	.10	.05
❑ 285	Carney Lansford	.20	.09
❑ 286	Mark McGwire	4.00	1.80
❑ 287	Dwayne Murphy	.10	.05
❑ 288	Gene Nelson	.10	.05
❑ 289	Steve Ontiveros	.10	.05
❑ 290	Tony Phillips	.10	.05
❑ 291	Eric Plunk	.10	.05
❑ 292	Luis Polonia	.10	.05
❑ 293	Rick Rodriguez	.10	.05
❑ 294	Terry Steinbach	.20	.09
❑ 295	Dave Stewart	.20	.09
❑ 296	Curt Young	.10	.05
❑ 297	Luis Aguayo	.10	.05
❑ 298	Steve Bedrosian	.10	.05
❑ 299	Jeff Calhoun	.10	.05
❑ 300	Don Carman	.10	.05
❑ 301	Todd Frohwirth	.10	.05
❑ 302	Greg Gross	.10	.05
❑ 303	Kevin Gross	.10	.05
❑ 304	Von Hayes	.10	.05
❑ 305	Keith Hughes	.10	.05
❑ 306	Mike Jackson	.40	.18
❑ 307	Chris James	.10	.05
❑ 308	Steve Jeltz	.10	.05
❑ 309	Mike Maddux	.10	.05
❑ 310	Lance Parrish	.10	.05
❑ 311	Shane Rawley	.10	.05
❑ 312	Wally Ritchie	.10	.05
❑ 313	Bruce Ruffin	.10	.05
❑ 314	Juan Samuel	.10	.05
❑ 315	Mike Schmidt	.50	.23
❑ 316	Rick Schu	.10	.05
❑ 317	Jeff Stone	.10	.05
❑ 318	Kent Tekulve	.10	.05
❑ 319	Milt Thompson	.10	.05
❑ 320	Glenn Wilson	.10	.05
❑ 321	Rafael Belliard	.10	.05
❑ 322	Barry Bonds	1.00	.45
❑ 323	Bobby Bonilla UER (Wrong birth year)	.10	.05
❑ 324	Sid Bream	.10	.05
❑ 325	John Cangelosi	.10	.05
❑ 326	Mike Diaz	.10	.05
❑ 327	Doug Drabek	.10	.05
❑ 328	Mike Dunne	.10	.05
❑ 329	Brian Fisher	.10	.05
❑ 330	Brett Gideon	.10	.05
❑ 331	Terry Harper	.10	.05
❑ 332	Bob Kipper	.10	.05
❑ 333	Mike LaValliere	.10	.05
❑ 334	Jose Lind	.10	.05
❑ 335	Junior Ortiz	.10	.05
❑ 336	Vicente Palacios	.10	.05
❑ 337	Bob Patterson	.10	.05
❑ 338	Al Pedrique	.10	.05
❑ 339	R.J. Reynolds	.10	.05
❑ 340	John Smiley	.20	.09
❑ 341	Andy Van Slyke UER (Wrong batting and throwing listed)	.20	.09
❑ 342	Bob Walk	.10	.05
❑ 343	Marty Barrett	.10	.05
❑ 344	Todd Benzinger	.10	.05
❑ 345	Wade Boggs	.40	.18
❑ 346	Tom Bolton	.10	.05
❑ 347	Oil Can Boyd	.10	.05
❑ 348	Ellis Burks	1.25	.55
❑ 349	Roger Clemens	.75	.35
❑ 350	Steve Crawford	.10	.05
❑ 351	Dwight Evans	.20	.09
❑ 352	Wes Gardner	.10	.05
❑ 353	Rich Gedman	.10	.05
❑ 354	Mike Greenwell	.10	.05
❑ 355	Sam Horn	.10	.05
❑ 356	Bruce Hurst	.10	.05
❑ 357	John Marzano	.10	.05
❑ 358	Al Nipper	.10	.05
❑ 359	Spike Owen	.10	.05
❑ 360	Jody Reed	.20	.09
❑ 361	Jim Rice	.20	.09
❑ 362	Ed Romero	.10	.05
❑ 363	Kevin Romine	.10	.05
❑ 364	Joe Sambito	.10	.05
❑ 365	Calvin Schiraldi	.10	.05
❑ 366	Jeff Sellers	.10	.05
❑ 367	Bob Stanley	.10	.05
❑ 368	Scott Bankhead	.10	.05
❑ 369	Phil Bradley	.10	.05
❑ 370	Scott Bradley	.10	.05
❑ 371	Mickey Brantley	.10	.05
❑ 372	Mike Campbell	.10	.05
❑ 373	Alvin Davis	.10	.05
❑ 374	Lee Guetterman	.10	.05
❑ 375	Dave Hengel	.10	.05
❑ 376	Mike Kingery	.10	.05
❑ 377	Mark Langston	.10	.05
❑ 378	Edgar Martinez	1.50	.70
❑ 379	Mike Moore	.10	.05
❑ 380	Mike Morgan	.10	.05
❑ 381	John Moses	.10	.05
❑ 382	Donell Nixon	.10	.05
❑ 383	Edwin Nunez	.10	.05
❑ 384	Ken Phelps	.10	.05
❑ 385	Jim Presley	.10	.05
❑ 386	Rey Quinones	.10	.05
❑ 387	Jerry Reed	.10	.05
❑ 388	Harold Reynolds	.20	.09
❑ 389	Dave Valle	.10	.05
❑ 390	Bill Wilkinson	.10	.05
❑ 391	Harold Baines	.20	.09
❑ 392	Floyd Bannister	.10	.05
❑ 393	Daryl Boston	.10	.05
❑ 394	Ivan Calderon	.10	.05
❑ 395	Jose DeLeon	.10	.05
❑ 396	Richard Dotson	.10	.05
❑ 397	Carlton Fisk	.40	.18
❑ 398	Ozzie Guillen	.10	.05
❑ 399	Ron Hassey	.10	.05
❑ 400	Donnie Hill	.10	.05
❑ 401	Bob James	.10	.05
❑ 402	Dave LaPoint	.10	.05
❑ 403	Bill Lindsey	.10	.05
❑ 404	Bill Long	.10	.05
❑ 405	Steve Lyons	.10	.05
❑ 406	Fred Manrique	.10	.05
❑ 407	Jack McDowell	.40	.18
❑ 408	Gary Redus	.10	.05
❑ 409	Ray Searage	.10	.05
❑ 410	Bobby Thigpen	.10	.05
❑ 411	Greg Walker	.10	.05
❑ 412	Ken Williams	.10	.05
❑ 413	Jim Winn	.10	.05
❑ 414	Jody Davis	.10	.05
❑ 415	Andre Dawson	.40	.18
❑ 416	Brian Dayett	.10	.05
❑ 417	Bob Dernier	.10	.05
❑ 418	Frank DiPino	.10	.05
❑ 419	Shawon Dunston	.10	.05
❑ 420	Leon Durham	.10	.05
❑ 421	Les Lancaster	.10	.05
❑ 422	Ed Lynch	.10	.05
❑ 423	Greg Maddux	2.50	1.10
❑ 424	Dave Martinez	.10	.05
❑ 425A	Keith Moreland ERR (Photo actually Jody Davis)	1.50	.70
❑ 425B	Keith Moreland COR (Bat on shoulder)	.20	.09
❑ 426	Jamie Moyer	.10	.05
❑ 427	Jerry Mumphrey	.10	.05
❑ 428	Paul Noce	.10	.05
❑ 429	Rafael Palmeiro	.40	.18
❑ 430	Wade Rowdon	.10	.05
❑ 431	Ryne Sandberg	.50	.23
❑ 432	Scott Sanderson	.10	.05
❑ 433	Lee Smith	.20	.09
❑ 434	Jim Sundberg	.10	.05
❑ 435	Rick Sutcliffe	.10	.05
❑ 436	Manny Trillo	.10	.05
❑ 437	Juan Agosto	.10	.05
❑ 438	Larry Andersen	.10	.05
❑ 439	Alan Ashby	.10	.05
❑ 440	Kevin Bass	.10	.05
❑ 441	Ken Caminiti	2.50	1.10
❑ 442	Rocky Childress	.10	.05
❑ 443	Jose Cruz	.10	.05
❑ 444	Danny Darwin	.10	.05
❑ 445	Glenn Davis	.10	.05
❑ 446	Jim Deshaies	.10	.05
❑ 447	Bill Doran	.10	.05
❑ 448	Ty Gainey	.10	.05
❑ 449	Billy Hatcher	.10	.05
❑ 450	Jeff Heathcock	.10	.05
❑ 451	Bob Knepper	.10	.05
❑ 452	Rob Mallicoat	.10	.05
❑ 453	Dave Meads	.10	.05
❑ 454	Craig Reynolds	.10	.05
❑ 455	Nolan Ryan	1.50	.70
❑ 456	Mike Scott	.10	.05
❑ 457	Dave Smith	.10	.05
❑ 458	Denny Walling	.10	.05
❑ 459	Robbie Wine	.10	.05
❑ 460	Gerald Young	.10	.05
❑ 461	Bob Brower	.10	.05
❑ 462A	Jerry Browne ERR (Photo actually Bob Brower, white player)	1.50	.70
❑ 462B	Jerry Browne COR (Black player)	.20	.09
❑ 463	Steve Buechele	.10	.05
❑ 464	Edwin Correa	.10	.05
❑ 465	Cecil Espy	.10	.05
❑ 466	Scott Fletcher	.10	.05
❑ 467	Jose Guzman	.10	.05
❑ 468	Greg Harris	.10	.05
❑ 469	Charlie Hough	.20	.09
❑ 470	Pete Incaviglia	.10	.05
❑ 471	Paul Kilgus	.10	.05
❑ 472	Mike Loynd	.10	.05
❑ 473	Oddibe McDowell	.10	.05
❑ 474	Dale Mohorcic	.10	.05
❑ 475	Pete O'Brien	.10	.05
❑ 476	Larry Parrish	.10	.05
❑ 477	Geno Petralli	.10	.05
❑ 478	Jeff Russell	.10	.05
❑ 479	Ruben Sierra	.10	.05
❑ 480	Mike Stanley	.20	.09
❑ 481	Curtis Wilkerson	.10	.05
❑ 482	Mitch Williams	.10	.05
❑ 483	Bobby Witt	.10	.05
❑ 484	Tony Armas	.10	.05
❑ 485	Bob Boone	.20	.09
❑ 486	Bill Buckner	.20	.09
❑ 487	DeWayne Buice	.10	.05
❑ 488	Brian Downing	.10	.05
❑ 489	Chuck Finley	.10	.05
❑ 490	Willie Fraser UER (Wrong bio stats, for George Hendrick)	.10	.05
❑ 491	Jack Howell	.10	.05
❑ 492	Ruppert Jones	.10	.05
❑ 493	Wally Joyner	.10	.05
❑ 494	Jack Lazorko	.10	.05
❑ 495	Gary Lucas	.10	.05
❑ 496	Kirk McCaskill	.10	.05
❑ 497	Mark McLemore	.10	.05
❑ 498	Darrell Miller	.10	.05
❑ 499	Greg Minton	.10	.05
❑ 500	Donnie Moore	.10	.05
❑ 501	Gus Polidor	.10	.05
❑ 502	Johnny Ray	.10	.05
❑ 503	Mark Ryal	.10	.05
❑ 504	Dick Schofield	.10	.05
❑ 505	Don Sutton	.40	.18
❑ 506	Devon White	.20	.09
❑ 507	Mike Witt	.10	.05
❑ 508	Dave Anderson	.10	.05

❑ 509 Tim Belcher .20 .09
❑ 510 Ralph Bryant .10 .05
❑ 511 Tim Crews .10 .05
❑ 512 Mike Devereaux .20 .09
❑ 513 Mariano Duncan .10 .05
❑ 514 Pedro Guerrero .10 .05
❑ 515 Jeff Hamilton .10 .05
❑ 516 Mickey Hatcher .10 .05
❑ 517 Brad Havens .10 .05
❑ 518 Orel Hershiser .20 .09
❑ 519 Shawn Hillegas .10 .05
❑ 520 Ken Howell .10 .05
❑ 521 Tim Leary .10 .05
❑ 522 Mike Marshall .10 .05
❑ 523 Steve Sax .10 .05
❑ 524 Mike Scioscia .10 .05
❑ 525 Mike Sharperson .10 .05
❑ 526 John Shelby .10 .05
❑ 527 Franklin Stubbs .10 .05
❑ 528 Fernando Valenzuela .20 .09
❑ 529 Bob Welch .10 .05
❑ 530 Matt Young .10 .05
❑ 531 Jim Acker .10 .05
❑ 532 Paul Assenmacher .10 .05
❑ 533 Jeff Blauser .50 .23
❑ 534 Joe Boever .10 .05
❑ 535 Martin Clary .10 .05
❑ 536 Kevin Coffman .10 .05
❑ 537 Jeff Dedmon .10 .05
❑ 538 Ron Gant .50 .23
❑ 539 Tom Glavine 3.00 1.35
❑ 540 Ken Griffey .10 .05
❑ 541 Albert Hall .10 .05
❑ 542 Glenn Hubbard .10 .05
❑ 543 Dion James .10 .05
❑ 544 Dale Murphy .40 .18
❑ 545 Ken Oberkfell .10 .05
❑ 546 David Palmer .10 .05
❑ 547 Gerald Perry .10 .05
❑ 548 Charlie Puleo .10 .05
❑ 549 Ted Simmons .20 .09
❑ 550 Zane Smith .10 .05
❑ 551 Andres Thomas .10 .05
❑ 552 Ozzie Virgil .10 .05
❑ 553 Don Aase .10 .05
❑ 554 Jeff Ballard .10 .05
❑ 555 Eric Bell .10 .05
❑ 556 Mike Boddicker .10 .05
❑ 557 Ken Dixon .10 .05
❑ 558 Jim Dwyer .10 .05
❑ 559 Ken Gerhart .10 .05
❑ 560 Rene Gonzales .10 .05
❑ 561 Mike Griffin .10 .05
❑ 562 John Habyan UER .10 .05
(Misspelled Hayban on both sides of card)
❑ 563 Terry Kennedy .10 .05
❑ 564 Ray Knight .10 .05
❑ 565 Lee Lacy .10 .05
❑ 566 Fred Lynn .10 .05
❑ 567 Eddie Murray .40 .18
❑ 568 Tom Niedenfuer .10 .05
❑ 569 Bill Ripken .10 .05
❑ 570 Cal Ripken 1.50 .70
❑ 571 Dave Schmidt .10 .05
❑ 572 Larry Sheets .10 .05
❑ 573 Pete Stanicek .10 .05
❑ 574 Mark Williamson .10 .05
❑ 575 Mike Young .10 .05
❑ 576 Shawn Abner .10 .05
❑ 577 Greg Booker .10 .05
❑ 578 Chris Brown .10 .05
❑ 579 Keith Comstock .10 .05
❑ 580 Joey Cora .75 .35
❑ 581 Mark Davis .10 .05
❑ 582 Tim Flannery .40 .18
(With surfboard)
❑ 583 Goose Gossage .10 .05
❑ 584 Mark Grant .10 .05
❑ 585 Tony Gwynn 1.00 .45
❑ 586 Andy Hawkins .10 .05
❑ 587 Stan Jefferson .10 .05
❑ 588 Jimmy Jones .10 .05
❑ 589 John Kruk .20 .09
❑ 590 Shane Mack .10 .05
❑ 591 Carmelo Martinez .10 .05
❑ 592 Lance McCullers UER .10 .05
(6'11" tall)
❑ 593 Eric Nolte .10 .05
❑ 594 Randy Ready .10 .05
❑ 595 Luis Salazar .10 .05
❑ 596 Benito Santiago .10 .05
❑ 597 Eric Show .10 .05
❑ 598 Garry Templeton .10 .05
❑ 599 Ed Whitson .10 .05
❑ 600 Scott Bailes .10 .05
❑ 601 Chris Bando .10 .05
❑ 602 Jay Bell .75 .35
❑ 603 Brett Butler .20 .09
❑ 604 Tom Candiotti .10 .05
❑ 605 Joe Carter .40 .18
❑ 606 Carmen Castillo .10 .05
❑ 607 Brian Dorsett .10 .05
❑ 608 John Farrell .10 .05
❑ 609 Julio Franco .10 .05
❑ 610 Mel Hall .10 .05
❑ 611 Tommy Hinzo .10 .05
❑ 612 Brook Jacoby .10 .05
❑ 613 Doug Jones .40 .18
❑ 614 Ken Schrom .10 .05
❑ 615 Cory Snyder .10 .05
❑ 616 Sammy Stewart .10 .05
❑ 617 Greg Swindell .10 .05
❑ 618 Pat Tabler .10 .05
❑ 619 Ed VandeBerg .10 .05
❑ 620 Eddie Williams .20 .09
❑ 621 Rich Yett .10 .05
❑ 622 Slugging Sophomores .20 .09
Wally Joyner
Cory Snyder
❑ 623 Dominican Dynamite .10 .05
George Bell
Pedro Guerrero
❑ 624 Oakland's Power Team 1.50 .70
Mark McGwire
Jose Canseco
❑ 625 Classic Relief .10 .05
Dave Righetti
Dan Plesac
❑ 626 All Star Righties .20 .09
Bret Saberhagen
Mike Witt
Jack Morris
❑ 627 Game Closers .10 .05
John Franco
Steve Bedrosian
❑ 628 Masters/Double Play .50 .23
Ozzie Smith
Ryne Sandberg
❑ 629 Rookie Record Setter 2.00 .90
Mark McGwire
❑ 630 Changing the Guard .40 .18
Mike Greenwell
Ellis Burks
Todd Benzinger
❑ 631 NL Batting Champs .40 .18
Tony Gwynn
Tim Raines
❑ 632 Pitching Magic .20 .09
Mike Scott
Orel Hershiser
❑ 633 Big Bats at First 1.50 .70
Pat Tabler
Mark McGwire
❑ 634 Hitting King/Thief .40 .18
Tony Gwynn
Vince Coleman
❑ 635 Slugging Shortstops .50 .23
Tony Fernandez
Cal Ripken
Alan Trammell
❑ 636 Tried/True Sluggers .10 .05
Mike Schmidt
Gary Carter
❑ 637 Crunch Time .20 .09
Darryl Strawberry
Eric Davis
❑ 638 AL All-Stars .10 .05
Matt Nokes
Kirby Puckett
❑ 639 NL All-Stars .20 .09
Keith Hernandez
Dale Murphy
❑ 640 The O's Brothers .75 .35
Billy Ripken
Cal Ripken
❑ 641 Mark Grace and 2.00 .90
Darrin Jackson
❑ 642 Damon Berryhill and .40 .18
Jeff Montgomery
❑ 643 Felix Fermin and .10 .05
Jesse Reid
❑ 644 Greg Myers and .10 .05
Greg Tabor
❑ 645 Joey Meyer and .10 .05
Jim Eppard
❑ 646 Adam Peterson and .20 .09
Randy Velarde
❑ 647 Pete Smith and .20 .09
Chris Gwynn
❑ 648 Tom Newell and .10 .05
Greg Jelks
❑ 649 Mario Diaz and .10 .05
Clay Parker
❑ 650 Jack Savage and .10 .05
Todd Simmons
❑ 651 John Burkett and .40 .18
Kirt Manwaring
❑ 652 Dave Otto and .50 .23
Walt Weiss
❑ 653 Jeff King and .50 .23
Randell Byers
❑ 654 CL: Twins/Cards .10 .05
Tigers/Giants UER
(90 Bob Melvin, 91 Eddie Milner)
❑ 655 CL: Blue Jays/Mets .10 .05
Brewers/Expos UER
(Mets listed before Blue Jays on card)
❑ 656 CL: Yankees/Reds .10 .05
Royals/A's
❑ 657 CL: Phillies/Pirates .10 .05
Red Sox/Mariners
❑ 658 CL: White Sox/Cubs .10 .05
Astros/Rangers
❑ 659 CL: Angels/Dodgers .10 .05
Braves/Orioles
❑ 660 CL: Padres/Indians .10 .05
Rookies/Specials

1988 Fleer Glossy

	MINT	NRMT
COMPLETE FACT.SET (672)	60.00	27.00
COMMON CARD (1-660)	.20	.09
COMMON WS (1-12)	.05	.02

*STARS: 1.25X TO 2.5X BASIC CARDS
*ROOKIES: 2.5X TO 5X BASIC CARDS

1988 Fleer All-Stars

	MINT	NRMT
COMPLETE SET (12)	6.00	2.70
COMMON CARD (1-12)	.30	.14

❑ 1 Matt Nokes .30 .14
❑ 2 Tom Henke .30 .14

		MINT	NRMT
❑ 3	Ted Higuera	.30	.14
❑ 4	Roger Clemens	3.00	1.35
❑ 5	George Bell	.30	.14
❑ 6	Andre Dawson	1.00	.45
❑ 7	Eric Davis	.75	.35
❑ 8	Wade Boggs	1.00	.45
❑ 9	Alan Trammell	.40	.18
❑ 10	Juan Samuel	.30	.14
❑ 11	Jack Clark	.75	.35
❑ 12	Paul Molitor	1.50	.70

1988 Fleer Headliners

	MINT	NRMT
COMPLETE SET (6)	6.00	2.70
COMMON CARD (1-6)	.75	.35

		MINT	NRMT
❑ 1	Don Mattingly	1.00	.45
❑ 2	Mark McGwire	5.00	2.20
❑ 3	Jack Morris	1.00	.45
❑ 4	Darryl Strawberry	1.00	.45
❑ 5	Dwight Gooden	1.00	.45
❑ 6	Tim Raines	.75	.35

1988 Fleer Update

	MINT	NRMT
COMP.FACT.SET (132)	8.00	3.60
COMMON CARD (1-132)	.10	.05

		MINT	NRMT
❑ 1	Jose Bautista	.10	.05
❑ 2	Joe Orsulak	.10	.05
❑ 3	Doug Sisk	.10	.05
❑ 4	Craig Worthington	.10	.05
❑ 5	Mike Boddicker	.10	.05
❑ 6	Rick Cerone	.10	.05
❑ 7	Larry Parrish	.10	.05
❑ 8	Lee Smith	.20	.09
❑ 9	Mike Smithson	.10	.05
❑ 10	John Trautwein	.10	.05
❑ 11	Sherman Corbett	.10	.05
❑ 12	Chili Davis	.30	.14
❑ 13	Jim Eppard	.10	.05
❑ 14	Bryan Harvey	.20	.09
❑ 15	John Davis	.10	.05
❑ 16	Dave Gallagher	.10	.05
❑ 17	Ricky Horton	.10	.05
❑ 18	Dan Pasqua	.10	.05
❑ 19	Melido Perez	.10	.05
❑ 20	Jose Segura	.10	.05
❑ 21	Andy Allanson	.10	.05
❑ 22	Jon Perlman	.10	.05
❑ 23	Domingo Ramos	.10	.05
❑ 24	Rick Rodriguez	.10	.05
❑ 25	Willie Upshaw	.10	.05
❑ 26	Paul Gibson	.10	.05
❑ 27	Don Heinkel	.10	.05
❑ 28	Ray Knight	.10	.05
❑ 29	Gary Pettis	.10	.05
❑ 30	Luis Salazar	.10	.05
❑ 31	Mike Macfarlane	.10	.05
❑ 32	Jeff Montgomery	.50	.23
❑ 33	Ted Power	.10	.05
❑ 34	Israel Sanchez	.10	.05
❑ 35	Kurt Stillwell	.10	.05
❑ 36	Pat Tabler	.10	.05
❑ 37	Don August	.10	.05
❑ 38	Darryl Hamilton	.20	.09
❑ 39	Jeff Leonard	.10	.05
❑ 40	Joey Meyer	.10	.05
❑ 41	Allan Anderson	.10	.05
❑ 42	Brian Harper	.10	.05
❑ 43	Tom Herr	.10	.05
❑ 44	Charlie Lea	.10	.05
❑ 45	John Moses (Listed as Hohn on checklist card)	.10	.05
❑ 46	John Candelaria	.10	.05
❑ 47	Jack Clark	.20	.09
❑ 48	Richard Dotson	.10	.05
❑ 49	Al Leiter	.60	.25
❑ 50	Rafael Santana	.10	.05
❑ 51	Don Slaught	.10	.05
❑ 52	Todd Burns	.10	.05
❑ 53	Dave Henderson	.10	.05
❑ 54	Doug Jennings	.10	.05
❑ 55	Dave Parker	.20	.09
❑ 56	Walt Weiss	.50	.23
❑ 57	Bob Welch	.10	.05
❑ 58	Henry Cotto	.10	.05
❑ 59	Mario Diaz UER (Listed as Marion on card front)	.10	.05
❑ 60	Mike Jackson	.50	.23
❑ 61	Bill Swift	.10	.05
❑ 62	Jose Cecena	.10	.05
❑ 63	Ray Hayward	.10	.05
❑ 64	Jim Steels UER (Listed as Jim Steele on card back)	.10	.05
❑ 65	Pat Borders	.20	.09
❑ 66	Sil Campusano	.10	.05
❑ 67	Mike Flanagan	.10	.05
❑ 68	Todd Stottlemyre	.50	.23
❑ 69	David Wells	3.00	1.35
❑ 70	Jose Alvarez	.10	.05
❑ 71	Paul Runge	.10	.05
❑ 72	Cesar Jimenez (Card was intended for German Jiminez, it's his photo)	.10	.05
❑ 73	Pete Smith	.10	.05
❑ 74	John Smoltz	2.00	.90
❑ 75	Damon Berryhill	.10	.05
❑ 76	Goose Gossage	.30	.14
❑ 77	Mark Grace	1.50	.70
❑ 78	Darrin Jackson	.10	.05
❑ 79	Vance Law	.10	.05
❑ 80	Jeff Pico	.10	.05
❑ 81	Gary Varsho	.10	.05
❑ 82	Tim Birtsas	.10	.05
❑ 83	Rob Dibble	.20	.09
❑ 84	Danny Jackson	.10	.05
❑ 85	Paul O'Neill	.30	.14
❑ 86	Jose Rijo	.10	.05
❑ 87	Chris Sabo	.20	.09
❑ 88	John Fishel	.10	.05
❑ 89	Craig Biggio	3.00	1.35
❑ 90	Terry Puhl	.10	.05
❑ 91	Rafael Ramirez	.10	.05
❑ 92	Louie Meadows	.10	.05
❑ 93	Kirk Gibson	.50	.23
❑ 94	Alfredo Griffin	.10	.05
❑ 95	Jay Howell	.10	.05
❑ 96	Jesse Orosco	.10	.05
❑ 97	Alejandro Pena	.10	.05
❑ 98	Tracy Woodson	.10	.05
❑ 99	John Dopson	.10	.05
❑ 100	Brian Holman	.10	.05
❑ 101	Rex Hudler	.10	.05
❑ 102	Jeff Parrett	.10	.05
❑ 103	Nelson Santovenia	.10	.05
❑ 104	Kevin Elster	.10	.05
❑ 105	Jeff Innis	.10	.05
❑ 106	Mackey Sasser	.10	.05
❑ 107	Phil Bradley	.10	.05
❑ 108	Danny Clay	.10	.05
❑ 109	Greg A.Harris	.10	.05
❑ 110	Ricky Jordan	.20	.09
❑ 111	David Palmer	.10	.05
❑ 112	Jim Gott	.10	.05
❑ 113	Tommy Gregg UER (Photo actually Randy Milligan)	.10	.05
❑ 114	Barry Jones	.10	.05
❑ 115	Randy Milligan	.10	.05
❑ 116	Luis Alicea	.20	.09
❑ 117	Tom Brunansky	.10	.05
❑ 118	John Costello	.10	.05
❑ 119	Jose DeLeon	.10	.05
❑ 120	Bob Horner	.10	.05
❑ 121	Scott Terry	.10	.05
❑ 122	Roberto Alomar	4.00	1.80
❑ 123	Dave Leiper	.10	.05
❑ 124	Keith Moreland	.10	.05
❑ 125	Mark Parent	.10	.05
❑ 126	Dennis Rasmussen	.10	.05
❑ 127	Randy Bockus	.10	.05
❑ 128	Brett Butler	.20	.09
❑ 129	Donell Nixon	.10	.05
❑ 130	Earnest Riles	.10	.05
❑ 131	Roger Samuels	.10	.05
❑ 132	Checklist U1-U132	.10	.05

1988 Fleer Update Glossy

	MINT	NRMT
COMP.FACT.SET (132)	60.00	27.00
COMMON CARD (1-132)	.25	.11

*STARS: $1.5X TO 3X BASIC CARDS
*ROOKIES: 2.5X TO 5X BASIC CARDS

1989 Fleer

	MINT	NRMT
COMPLETE SET (660)	20.00	9.00
COMP.RETAIL SET (660)	10.00	4.50
COMP.HOBBY SET (672)	20.00	9.00
COMMON CARD (1-660)	.05	.02

		MINT	NRMT
❑ 1	Don Baylor	.10	.05
❑ 2	Lance Blankenship	.05	.02
❑ 3	Todd Burns UER (Wrong birthdate; before/after All-Star stats missing)	.05	.02
❑ 4	Greg Cadaret UER (All-Star Break stats show 3 losses, should be 2)	.05	.02
❑ 5	Jose Canseco	.20	.09
❑ 6	Storm Davis	.05	.02
❑ 7	Dennis Eckersley	.05	.02

- ❑ 8 Mike Gallego .05 .02
- ❑ 9 Ron Hassey .05 .02
- ❑ 10 Dave Henderson .05 .02
- ❑ 11 Rick Honeycutt .05 .02
- ❑ 12 Glenn Hubbard .05 .02
- ❑ 13 Stan Javier .05 .02
- ❑ 14 Doug Jennings .05 .02
- ❑ 15 Felix Jose .05 .02
- ❑ 16 Carney Lansford .10 .05
- ❑ 17 Mark McGwire 1.25 .55
- ❑ 18 Gene Nelson .05 .02
- ❑ 19 Dave Parker .10 .05
- ❑ 20 Eric Plunk .05 .02
- ❑ 21 Luis Polonia .05 .02
- ❑ 22 Terry Steinbach .10 .05
- ❑ 23 Dave Stewart .10 .05
- ❑ 24 Walt Weiss .05 .02
- ❑ 25 Bob Welch .05 .02
- ❑ 26 Curt Young .05 .02
- ❑ 27 Rick Aguilera .10 .05
- ❑ 28 Wally Backman .05 .02
- ❑ 29 Mark Carreon UER .05 .02 (After All-Star Break batting 7.14)
- ❑ 30 Gary Carter .05 .02
- ❑ 31 David Cone .20 .09
- ❑ 32 Ron Darling .05 .02
- ❑ 33 Len Dykstra .10 .05
- ❑ 34 Kevin Elster .05 .02
- ❑ 35 Sid Fernandez .05 .02
- ❑ 36 Dwight Gooden .10 .05
- ❑ 37 Keith Hernandez .10 .05
- ❑ 38 Gregg Jefferies .10 .05
- ❑ 39 Howard Johnson .05 .02
- ❑ 40 Terry Leach .05 .02
- ❑ 41 Dave Magadan UER .05 .02 (Bio says 15 doubles, should be 13)
- ❑ 42 Bob McClure .05 .02
- ❑ 43 Roger McDowell UER .05 .02 (Led Mets with 58, should be 62)
- ❑ 44 Kevin McReynolds .05 .02
- ❑ 45 Keith A. Miller .05 .02
- ❑ 46 Randy Myers .10 .05
- ❑ 47 Bob Ojeda .05 .02
- ❑ 48 Mackey Sasser .05 .02
- ❑ 49 Darryl Strawberry .10 .05
- ❑ 50 Tim Teufel .05 .02
- ❑ 51 Dave West .05 .02
- ❑ 52 Mookie Wilson .10 .05
- ❑ 53 Dave Anderson .05 .02
- ❑ 54 Tim Belcher .05 .02
- ❑ 55 Mike Davis .05 .02
- ❑ 56 Mike Devereaux .05 .02
- ❑ 57 Kirk Gibson .10 .05
- ❑ 58 Alfredo Griffin .05 .02
- ❑ 59 Chris Gwynn .05 .02
- ❑ 60 Jeff Hamilton .05 .02
- ❑ 61A Danny Heep .20 .09 (Home: Lake Hills)
- ❑ 61B Danny Heep .05 .02 (Home: San Antonio)
- ❑ 62 Orel Hershiser .10 .05
- ❑ 63 Brian Holton .05 .02
- ❑ 64 Jay Howell .05 .02
- ❑ 65 Tim Leary .05 .02
- ❑ 66 Mike Marshall .05 .02
- ❑ 67 Ramon Martinez .25 .11
- ❑ 68 Jesse Orosco .05 .02
- ❑ 69 Alejandro Pena .05 .02
- ❑ 70 Steve Sax .05 .02
- ❑ 71 Mike Scioscia .05 .02
- ❑ 72 Mike Sharperson .05 .02
- ❑ 73 John Shelby .05 .02
- ❑ 74 Franklin Stubbs .05 .02
- ❑ 75 John Tudor .05 .02
- ❑ 76 Fernando Valenzuela .10 .05
- ❑ 77 Tracy Woodson .05 .02
- ❑ 78 Marty Barrett .05 .02
- ❑ 79 Todd Benzinger .05 .02
- ❑ 80 Mike Boddicker UER .05 .02 (Rochester in '76, should be '78)
- ❑ 81 Wade Boggs .20 .09
- ❑ 82 Oil Can Boyd .05 .02
- ❑ 83 Ellis Burks .05 .02
- ❑ 84 Rick Cerone .05 .02
- ❑ 85 Roger Clemens .40 .18
- ❑ 86 Steve Curry .05 .02
- ❑ 87 Dwight Evans .10 .05
- ❑ 88 Wes Gardner .05 .02
- ❑ 89 Rich Gedman .05 .02
- ❑ 90 Mike Greenwell .05 .02
- ❑ 91 Bruce Hurst .05 .02
- ❑ 92 Dennis Lamp .05 .02
- ❑ 93 Spike Owen .05 .02
- ❑ 94 Larry Parrish UER .05 .02 (Before All-Star Break batting 1.90)
- ❑ 95 Carlos Quintana .05 .02
- ❑ 96 Jody Reed .05 .02
- ❑ 97 Jim Rice .10 .05
- ❑ 98A Kevin Romine ERR .20 .09 (Photo actually Randy Kutcher batting)
- ❑ 98B Kevin Romine COR .05 .02 (Arms folded)
- ❑ 99 Lee Smith .10 .05
- ❑ 100 Mike Smithson .05 .02
- ❑ 101 Bob Stanley .05 .02
- ❑ 102 Allan Anderson .05 .02
- ❑ 103 Keith Atherton .05 .02
- ❑ 104 Juan Berenguer .05 .02
- ❑ 105 Bert Blyleven .10 .05
- ❑ 106 Eric Bullock UER .05 .02 (Bats/Throws Right, should be Left)
- ❑ 107 Randy Bush .05 .02
- ❑ 108 John Christensen .05 .02
- ❑ 109 Mark Davidson .05 .02
- ❑ 110 Gary Gaetti .10 .05
- ❑ 111 Greg Gagne .05 .02
- ❑ 112 Dan Gladden .05 .02
- ❑ 113 German Gonzalez .05 .02
- ❑ 114 Brian Harper .05 .02
- ❑ 115 Tom Herr .05 .02
- ❑ 116 Kent Hrbek .10 .05
- ❑ 117 Gene Larkin .05 .02
- ❑ 118 Tim Laudner .05 .02
- ❑ 119 Charlie Lea .05 .02
- ❑ 120 Steve Lombardozzi .05 .02
- ❑ 121A John Moses .20 .09 (Home: Tempe)
- ❑ 121B John Moses .05 .02 (Home: Phoenix)
- ❑ 122 Al Newman .05 .02
- ❑ 123 Mark Portugal .05 .02
- ❑ 124 Kirby Puckett .40 .18
- ❑ 125 Jeff Reardon .10 .05
- ❑ 126 Fred Toliver .05 .02
- ❑ 127 Frank Viola .05 .02
- ❑ 128 Doyle Alexander .05 .02
- ❑ 129 Dave Bergman .05 .02
- ❑ 130A Tom Brookens ERR .75 .35 (Mike Heath back)
- ❑ 130B Tom Brookens COR .05 .02
- ❑ 131 Paul Gibson .05 .02
- ❑ 132A Mike Heath ERR .75 .35 (Tom Brookens back)
- ❑ 132B Mike Heath COR .05 .02
- ❑ 133 Don Heinkel .05 .02
- ❑ 134 Mike Henneman .05 .02
- ❑ 135 Guillermo Hernandez .05 .02
- ❑ 136 Eric King .05 .02
- ❑ 137 Chet Lemon .05 .02
- ❑ 138 Fred Lynn UER .05 .02 ('74, '75 stats missing)
- ❑ 139 Jack Morris .10 .05
- ❑ 140 Matt Nokes .05 .02
- ❑ 141 Gary Pettis .05 .02
- ❑ 142 Ted Power .05 .02
- ❑ 143 Jeff M. Robinson .05 .02
- ❑ 144 Luis Salazar .05 .02
- ❑ 145 Steve Searcy .05 .02
- ❑ 146 Pat Sheridan .05 .02
- ❑ 147 Frank Tanana .05 .02
- ❑ 148 Alan Trammell .05 .02
- ❑ 149 Walt Terrell .05 .02
- ❑ 150 Jim Walewander .05 .02
- ❑ 151 Lou Whitaker .10 .05
- ❑ 152 Tim Birtsas .05 .02
- ❑ 153 Tom Browning .05 .02
- ❑ 154 Keith Brown .05 .02
- ❑ 155 Norm Charlton .10 .05
- ❑ 156 Dave Concepcion .10 .05
- ❑ 157 Kal Daniels .05 .02
- ❑ 158 Eric Davis .10 .05
- ❑ 159 Bo Diaz .05 .02
- ❑ 160 Rob Dibble .10 .05
- ❑ 161 Nick Esasky .05 .02
- ❑ 162 John Franco .10 .05
- ❑ 163 Danny Jackson .05 .02
- ❑ 164 Barry Larkin .20 .09
- ❑ 165 Rob Murphy .05 .02
- ❑ 166 Paul O'Neill .10 .05
- ❑ 167 Jeff Reed .05 .02
- ❑ 168 Jose Rijo .05 .02
- ❑ 169 Ron Robinson .05 .02
- ❑ 170 Chris Sabo .05 .02
- ❑ 171 Candy Sierra .05 .02
- ❑ 172 Van Snider .05 .02
- ❑ 173A Jeff Treadway 5.00 2.20 (Target registration mark above head on front in light blue)
- ❑ 173B Jeff Treadway .05 .02 (No target on front)
- ❑ 174 Frank Williams .05 .02 (After All-Star Break stats are jumbled)
- ❑ 175 Herm Winningham .05 .02
- ❑ 176 Jim Adduci .05 .02
- ❑ 177 Don August .05 .02
- ❑ 178 Mike Birkbeck .05 .02
- ❑ 179 Chris Bosio .05 .02
- ❑ 180 Glenn Braggs .05 .02
- ❑ 181 Greg Brock .05 .02
- ❑ 182 Mark Clear .05 .02
- ❑ 183 Chuck Crim .05 .02
- ❑ 184 Rob Deer .05 .02
- ❑ 185 Tom Filer .05 .02
- ❑ 186 Jim Gantner .05 .02
- ❑ 187 Darryl Hamilton .10 .05
- ❑ 188 Ted Higuera .05 .02
- ❑ 189 Odell Jones .05 .02
- ❑ 190 Jeffrey Leonard .05 .02
- ❑ 191 Joey Meyer .05 .02
- ❑ 192 Paul Mirabella .05 .02
- ❑ 193 Paul Molitor .20 .09
- ❑ 194 Charlie O'Brien .05 .02
- ❑ 195 Dan Plesac .05 .02
- ❑ 196 Gary Sheffield .60 .25
- ❑ 197 B.J. Surhoff .10 .05
- ❑ 198 Dale Sveum .05 .02
- ❑ 199 Bill Wegman .05 .02
- ❑ 200 Robin Yount .20 .09
- ❑ 201 Rafael Belliard .05 .02
- ❑ 202 Barry Bonds .40 .18
- ❑ 203 Bobby Bonilla .05 .02
- ❑ 204 Sid Bream .05 .02
- ❑ 205 Benny Distefano .05 .02
- ❑ 206 Doug Drabek .05 .02
- ❑ 207 Mike Dunne .05 .02
- ❑ 208 Felix Fermin .05 .02
- ❑ 209 Brian Fisher .05 .02
- ❑ 210 Jim Gott .05 .02
- ❑ 211 Bob Kipper .05 .02
- ❑ 212 Dave LaPoint .05 .02
- ❑ 213 Mike LaValliere .05 .02
- ❑ 214 Jose Lind .05 .02
- ❑ 215 Junior Ortiz .05 .02
- ❑ 216 Vicente Palacios .05 .02
- ❑ 217 Tom Prince .05 .02
- ❑ 218 Gary Redus .05 .02
- ❑ 219 R.J. Reynolds .05 .02
- ❑ 220 Jeff D. Robinson .05 .02
- ❑ 221 John Smiley .05 .02
- ❑ 222 Andy Van Slyke .10 .05
- ❑ 223 Bob Walk .05 .02
- ❑ 224 Glenn Wilson .05 .02
- ❑ 225 Jesse Barfield .05 .02
- ❑ 226 George Bell .05 .02

❑ 227 Pat Borders .10 .05
❑ 228 John Cerutti .05 .02
❑ 229 Jim Clancy .05 .02
❑ 230 Mark Eichhorn .05 .02
❑ 231 Tony Fernandez .05 .02
❑ 232 Cecil Fielder .10 .05
❑ 233 Mike Flanagan .05 .02
❑ 234 Kelly Gruber .05 .02
❑ 235 Tom Henke .05 .02
❑ 236 Jimmy Key .10 .05
❑ 237 Rick Leach .05 .02
❑ 238 Manny Lee UER .05 .02
(Bio says regular shortstop, sic, Tony Fernandez)
❑ 239 Nelson Liriano .05 .02
❑ 240 Fred McGriff .20 .09
❑ 241 Lloyd Moseby .05 .02
❑ 242 Rance Mulliniks .05 .02
❑ 243 Jeff Musselman .05 .02
❑ 244 Dave Stieb .05 .02
❑ 245 Todd Stottlemyre .05 .02
❑ 246 Duane Ward .05 .02
❑ 247 David Wells .20 .09
❑ 248 Ernie Whitt UER .05 .02
(HR total 21, should be 121)
❑ 249 Luis Aguayo .05 .02
❑ 250A Neil Allen .75 .35
(Home: Sarasota, FL)
❑ 250B Neil Allen .05 .02
(Home: Syosset, NY)
❑ 251 John Candelaria .05 .02
❑ 252 Jack Clark .05 .02
❑ 253 Richard Dotson .05 .02
❑ 254 Rickey Henderson .20 .09
❑ 255 Tommy John .10 .05
❑ 256 Roberto Kelly .10 .05
❑ 257 Al Leiter .20 .09
❑ 258 Don Mattingly .30 .14
❑ 259 Dale Mohorcic .05 .02
❑ 260 Hal Morris .20 .09
❑ 261 Scott Nielsen .05 .02
❑ 262 Mike Pagliarulo UER .05 .02
(Wrong birthdate)
❑ 263 Hipolito Pena .05 .02
❑ 264 Ken Phelps .05 .02
❑ 265 Willie Randolph .10 .05
❑ 266 Rick Rhoden .05 .02
❑ 267 Dave Righetti .05 .02
❑ 268 Rafael Santana .05 .02
❑ 269 Steve Shields .05 .02
❑ 270 Joel Skinner .05 .02
❑ 271 Don Slaught .05 .02
❑ 272 Claudell Washington .05 .02
❑ 273 Gary Ward .05 .02
❑ 274 Dave Winfield .20 .09
❑ 275 Luis Aquino .05 .02
❑ 276 Floyd Bannister .05 .02
❑ 277 George Brett .40 .18
❑ 278 Bill Buckner .10 .05
❑ 279 Nick Capra .05 .02
❑ 280 Jose DeJesus .05 .02
❑ 281 Steve Farr .05 .02
❑ 282 Jerry Don Gleaton .05 .02
❑ 283 Mark Gubicza .05 .02
❑ 284 Tom Gordon UER .20 .09
(16.2 innings in '88, should be 15.2)
❑ 285 Bo Jackson .05 .02
❑ 286 Charlie Leibrandt .05 .02
❑ 287 Mike Macfarlane .05 .02
❑ 288 Jeff Montgomery .10 .05
❑ 289 Bill Pecota UER .05 .02
(Photo actually Brad Wellman)
❑ 290 Jamie Quirk .05 .02
❑ 291 Bret Saberhagen .10 .05
❑ 292 Kevin Seitzer .05 .02
❑ 293 Kurt Stillwell .05 .02
❑ 294 Pat Tabler .05 .02
❑ 295 Danny Tartabull .05 .02
❑ 296 Gary Thurman .05 .02
❑ 297 Frank White .10 .05
❑ 298 Willie Wilson .05 .02
❑ 299 Roberto Alomar .30 .14
❑ 300 Sandy Alomar Jr. UER .. .40 .18
(Wrong birthdate, says 6/16/66, should say 6/18/66)
❑ 301 Chris Brown .05 .02
❑ 302 Mike Brumley UER .05 .02
(133 hits in '88, should be 134)
❑ 303 Mark Davis .05 .02
❑ 304 Mark Grant .05 .02
❑ 305 Tony Gwynn .50 .23
❑ 306 Greg W. Harris .05 .02
❑ 307 Andy Hawkins .05 .02
❑ 308 Jimmy Jones .05 .02
❑ 309 John Kruk .10 .05
❑ 310 Dave Leiper .05 .02
❑ 311 Carmelo Martinez .05 .02
❑ 312 Lance McCullers .05 .02
❑ 313 Keith Moreland .05 .02
❑ 314 Dennis Rasmussen .05 .02
❑ 315 Randy Ready UER .05 .02
(1214 games in '88, should be 114)
❑ 316 Benito Santiago .05 .02
❑ 317 Eric Show .05 .02
❑ 318 Todd Simmons .05 .02
❑ 319 Garry Templeton .05 .02
❑ 320 Dickie Thon .05 .02
❑ 321 Ed Whitson .05 .02
❑ 322 Marvell Wynne .05 .02
❑ 323 Mike Aldrete .05 .02
❑ 324 Brett Butler .10 .05
❑ 325 Will Clark UER .20 .09
(Three consecutive 100 RBI seasons)
❑ 326 Kelly Downs UER .05 .02
('88 stats missing)
❑ 327 Dave Dravecky .10 .05
❑ 328 Scott Garrelts .05 .02
❑ 329 Atlee Hammaker .05 .02
❑ 330 Charlie Hayes .20 .09
❑ 331 Mike Krukow .05 .02
❑ 332 Craig Lefferts .05 .02
❑ 333 Candy Maldonado .05 .02
❑ 334 Kirt Manwaring UER .05 .02
(Bats Rights)
❑ 335 Bob Melvin .05 .02
❑ 336 Kevin Mitchell .10 .05
❑ 337 Donell Nixon .05 .02
❑ 338 Tony Perezchica .05 .02
❑ 339 Joe Price .05 .02
❑ 340 Rick Reuschel .05 .02
❑ 341 Earnest Riles .05 .02
❑ 342 Don Robinson .05 .02
❑ 343 Chris Speier .05 .02
❑ 344 Robby Thompson UER .. .05 .02
(West Plam Beach)
❑ 345 Jose Uribe .05 .02
❑ 346 Matt Williams .20 .09
❑ 347 Trevor Wilson .05 .02
❑ 348 Juan Agosto .05 .02
❑ 349 Larry Andersen .05 .02
❑ 350A Alan Ashby ERR 2.00 .90
(Throws Rig)
❑ 350B Alan Ashby COR .05 .02
❑ 351 Kevin Bass .05 .02
❑ 352 Buddy Bell .10 .05
❑ 353 Craig Biggio .75 .35
❑ 354 Danny Darwin .05 .02
❑ 355 Glenn Davis .05 .02
❑ 356 Jim Deshaies .05 .02
❑ 357 Bill Doran .05 .02
❑ 358 John Fishel .05 .02
❑ 359 Billy Hatcher .05 .02
❑ 360 Bob Knepper .05 .02
❑ 361 Louie Meadows UER .05 .02
(Bio says 10 EBH's and 6 SB's in '88, should be 3 and 4)
❑ 362 Dave Meads .05 .02
❑ 363 Jim Pankovits .05 .02
❑ 364 Terry Puhl .05 .02
❑ 365 Rafael Ramirez .05 .02
❑ 366 Craig Reynolds .05 .02
❑ 367 Mike Scott .05 .02
(Card number listed as 368 on Astros CL)
❑ 368 Nolan Ryan .75 .35
(Card number listed as 367 on Astros CL)
❑ 369 Dave Smith .05 .02
❑ 370 Gerald Young .05 .02
❑ 371 Hubie Brooks .05 .02
❑ 372 Tim Burke .05 .02
❑ 373 John Dopson .05 .02
❑ 374 Mike R. Fitzgerald .05 .02
❑ 375 Tom Foley .05 .02
❑ 376 Andres Galarraga UER .. .20 .09
(Home: Caracus)
❑ 377 Neal Heaton .05 .02
❑ 378 Joe Hesketh .05 .02
❑ 379 Brian Holman .05 .02
❑ 380 Rex Hudler .05 .02
❑ 381 Randy Johnson UER 1.25 .55
(Innings for '85 and '86 shown as 27 and 120, should be 27.1 and 119.2)
❑ 382 Wallace Johnson .05 .02
❑ 383 Tracy Jones .05 .02
❑ 384 Dave Martinez .05 .02
❑ 385 Dennis Martinez .10 .05
❑ 386 Andy McGaffigan .05 .02
❑ 387 Otis Nixon .10 .05
❑ 388 Johnny Paredes .05 .02
❑ 389 Jeff Parrett .05 .02
❑ 390 Pascual Perez .05 .02
❑ 391 Tim Raines .10 .05
❑ 392 Luis Rivera .05 .02
❑ 393 Nelson Santovenia .05 .02
❑ 394 Bryn Smith .05 .02
❑ 395 Tim Wallach .05 .02
❑ 396 Andy Allanson UER .05 .02
(1214 hits in '88, should be 114)
❑ 397 Rod Allen .05 .02
❑ 398 Scott Bailes .05 .02
❑ 399 Tom Candiotti .05 .02
❑ 400 Joe Carter .05 .02
❑ 401 Carmen Castillo UER .05 .02
(After All-Star Break batting 2.50)
❑ 402 Dave Clark UER .05 .02
(Card front shows position as Rookie; after All-Star Break batting 3.14)
❑ 403 John Farrell UER .05 .02
(Typo in runs allowed in '88)
❑ 404 Julio Franco .05 .02
❑ 405 Don Gordon .05 .02
❑ 406 Mel Hall .05 .02
❑ 407 Brad Havens .05 .02
❑ 408 Brook Jacoby .05 .02
❑ 409 Doug Jones .05 .02
❑ 410 Jeff Kaiser .05 .02
❑ 411 Luis Medina .05 .02
❑ 412 Cory Snyder .05 .02
❑ 413 Greg Swindell .05 .02
❑ 414 Ron Tingley UER .05 .02
(Hit HR in first ML at-bat, should be first AL at-bat)
❑ 415 Willie Upshaw .05 .02
❑ 416 Ron Washington .05 .02
❑ 417 Rich Yett .05 .02
❑ 418 Damon Berryhill .05 .02
❑ 419 Mike Bielecki .05 .02
❑ 420 Doug Dascenzo .05 .02
❑ 421 Jody Davis UER .05 .02
(Braves stats for '88 missing)
❑ 422 Andre Dawson .20 .09
❑ 423 Frank DiPino .05 .02
❑ 424 Shawon Dunston .05 .02
❑ 425 Rich Gossage .10 .05
❑ 426 Mark Grace UER .20 .09
(Minor League stats for '88 missing)

❑ 427 Mike Harkey .05 .02
❑ 428 Darrin Jackson .05 .02
❑ 429 Les Lancaster .05 .02
❑ 430 Vance Law .05 .02
❑ 431 Greg Maddux .75 .35
❑ 432 Jamie Moyer .05 .02
❑ 433 Al Nipper .05 .02
❑ 434 Rafael Palmeiro UER .20 .09
(170 hits in '88, should be 178)
❑ 435 Pat Perry .05 .02
❑ 436 Jeff Pico .05 .02
❑ 437 Ryne Sandberg .25 .11
❑ 438 Calvin Schiraldi .05 .02
❑ 439 Rick Sutcliffe .05 .02
❑ 440A Manny Trillo ERR 2.00 .90
(Throws Rig)
❑ 440B Manny Trillo COR .05 .02
❑ 441 Gary Varsho UER .05 .02
(Wrong birthdate; .303 should be .302; 11/28 should be 9/19)
❑ 442 Mitch Webster .05 .02
❑ 443 Luis Alicea .05 .02
❑ 444 Tom Brunansky .05 .02
❑ 445 Vince Coleman UER .05 .02
(Third straight with 83, should be fourth straight with 81)
❑ 446 John Costello UER .05 .02
(Home California, should be New York)
❑ 447 Danny Cox .05 .02
❑ 448 Ken Dayley .05 .02
❑ 449 Jose DeLeon .05 .02
❑ 450 Curt Ford .05 .02
❑ 451 Pedro Guerrero .05 .02
❑ 452 Bob Horner .05 .02
❑ 453 Tim Jones .05 .02
❑ 454 Steve Lake .05 .02
❑ 455 Joe Magrane UER .05 .02
(Des Moines, IO)
❑ 456 Greg Mathews .05 .02
❑ 457 Willie McGee .10 .05
❑ 458 Larry McWilliams .05 .02
❑ 459 Jose Oquendo .05 .02
❑ 460 Tony Pena .05 .02
❑ 461 Terry Pendleton .10 .05
❑ 462 Steve Peters UER .05 .02
(Lives in Harrah, not Harah)
❑ 463 Ozzie Smith .25 .11
❑ 464 Scott Terry .05 .02
❑ 465 Denny Walling .05 .02
❑ 466 Todd Worrell .05 .02
❑ 467 Tony Armas UER .05 .02
(Before All-Star Break batting 2.39)
❑ 468 Dante Bichette .40 .18
❑ 469 Bob Boone .10 .05
❑ 470 Terry Clark .05 .02
❑ 471 Stew Cliburn .05 .02
❑ 472 Mike Cook UER .05 .02
(TM near Angels logo missing from front)
❑ 473 Sherman Corbett .05 .02
❑ 474 Chili Davis .10 .05
❑ 475 Brian Downing .05 .02
❑ 476 Jim Eppard .05 .02
❑ 477 Chuck Finley .10 .05
❑ 478 Willie Fraser .05 .02
❑ 479 Bryan Harvey UER .05 .02
(ML record shows 0-0, should be 7-5)
❑ 480 Jack Howell .05 .02
❑ 481 Wally Joyner UER .10 .05
(Yorba Linda, GA)
❑ 482 Jack Lazorko .05 .02
❑ 483 Kirk McCaskill .05 .02
❑ 484 Mark McLemore .05 .02
❑ 485 Greg Minton .05 .02
❑ 486 Dan Petry .05 .02
❑ 487 Johnny Ray .05 .02
❑ 488 Dick Schofield .05 .02
❑ 489 Devon White .10 .05
❑ 490 Mike Witt .05 .02
❑ 491 Harold Baines .10 .05
❑ 492 Daryl Boston .05 .02
❑ 493 Ivan Calderon UER .05 .02
('80 stats shifted)
❑ 494 Mike Diaz .05 .02
❑ 495 Carlton Fisk .20 .09
❑ 496 Dave Gallagher .05 .02
❑ 497 Ozzie Guillen .05 .02
❑ 498 Shawn Hillegas .05 .02
❑ 499 Lance Johnson .10 .05
❑ 500 Barry Jones .05 .02
❑ 501 Bill Long .05 .02
❑ 502 Steve Lyons .05 .02
❑ 503 Fred Manrique .05 .02
❑ 504 Jack McDowell .10 .05
❑ 505 Donn Pall .05 .02
❑ 506 Kelly Paris .05 .02
❑ 507 Dan Pasqua .05 .02
❑ 508 Ken Patterson .05 .02
❑ 509 Melido Perez .05 .02
❑ 510 Jerry Reuss .05 .02
❑ 511 Mark Salas .05 .02
❑ 512 Bobby Thigpen UER .05 .02
('86 ERA 4.69, should be 4.68)
❑ 513 Mike Woodard .05 .02
❑ 514 Bob Brower .05 .02
❑ 515 Steve Buechele .05 .02
❑ 516 Jose Cecena .05 .02
❑ 517 Cecil Espy .05 .02
❑ 518 Scott Fletcher .05 .02
❑ 519 Cecilio Guante .05 .02
('87 Yankee stats are off-centered)
❑ 520 Jose Guzman .05 .02
❑ 521 Ray Hayward .05 .02
❑ 522 Charlie Hough .10 .05
❑ 523 Pete Incaviglia .05 .02
❑ 524 Mike Jeffcoat .05 .02
❑ 525 Paul Kilgus .05 .02
❑ 526 Chad Kreuter .05 .02
❑ 527 Jeff Kunkel .05 .02
❑ 528 Oddibe McDowell .05 .02
❑ 529 Pete O'Brien .05 .02
❑ 530 Geno Petralli .05 .02
❑ 531 Jeff Russell .05 .02
❑ 532 Ruben Sierra .05 .02
❑ 533 Mike Stanley .05 .02
❑ 534A Ed VandeBerg ERR .. 2.00 .90
(Throws Lef)
❑ 534B Ed VandeBerg COR .05 .02
❑ 535 Curtis Wilkerson ERR .05 .02
(Pitcher headings at bottom)
❑ 536 Mitch Williams .05 .02
❑ 537 Bobby Witt UER .05 .02
('85 ERA .643, should be 6.43)
❑ 538 Steve Balboni .05 .02
❑ 539 Scott Bankhead .05 .02
❑ 540 Scott Bradley .05 .02
❑ 541 Mickey Brantley .05 .02
❑ 542 Jay Buhner .20 .09
❑ 543 Mike Campbell .05 .02
❑ 544 Darnell Coles .05 .02
❑ 545 Henry Cotto .05 .02
❑ 546 Alvin Davis .05 .02
❑ 547 Mario Diaz .05 .02
❑ 548 Ken Griffey Jr. 15.00 6.75
❑ 549 Erik Hanson .10 .05
❑ 550 Mike Jackson UER .05 .02
(Lifetime ERA 3.345, should be 3.45)
❑ 551 Mark Langston .05 .02
❑ 552 Edgar Martinez .20 .09
❑ 553 Bill McGuire .05 .02
❑ 554 Mike Moore .05 .02
❑ 555 Jim Presley .05 .02
❑ 556 Rey Quinones .05 .02
❑ 557 Jerry Reed .05 .02
❑ 558 Harold Reynolds .05 .02
❑ 559 Mike Schooler .05 .02
❑ 560 Bill Swift .05 .02
❑ 561 Dave Valle .05 .02
❑ 562 Steve Bedrosian .05 .02
❑ 563 Phil Bradley .05 .02
❑ 564 Don Carman .05 .02
❑ 565 Bob Dernier .05 .02
❑ 566 Marvin Freeman .05 .02
❑ 567 Todd Frohwirth .05 .02
❑ 568 Greg Gross .05 .02
❑ 569 Kevin Gross .05 .02
❑ 570 Greg A. Harris .05 .02
❑ 571 Von Hayes .05 .02
❑ 572 Chris James .05 .02
❑ 573 Steve Jeltz .05 .02
❑ 574 Ron Jones UER .05 .02
(Led IL in '88 with 85, should be 75)
❑ 575 Ricky Jordan .10 .05
❑ 576 Mike Maddux .05 .02
❑ 577 David Palmer .05 .02
❑ 578 Lance Parrish .05 .02
❑ 579 Shane Rawley .05 .02
❑ 580 Bruce Ruffin .05 .02
❑ 581 Juan Samuel .05 .02
❑ 582 Mike Schmidt .25 .11
❑ 583 Kent Tekulve .05 .02
❑ 584 Milt Thompson UER .05 .02
(19 hits in '88, should be 109)
❑ 585 Jose Alvarez .05 .02
❑ 586 Paul Assenmacher .05 .02
❑ 587 Bruce Benedict .05 .02
❑ 588 Jeff Blauser .10 .05
❑ 589 Terry Blocker .05 .02
❑ 590 Ron Gant .10 .05
❑ 591 Tom Glavine .20 .09
❑ 592 Tommy Gregg .05 .02
❑ 593 Albert Hall .05 .02
❑ 594 Dion James .05 .02
❑ 595 Rick Mahler .05 .02
❑ 596 Dale Murphy .20 .09
❑ 597 Gerald Perry .05 .02
❑ 598 Charlie Puleo .05 .02
❑ 599 Ted Simmons .10 .05
❑ 600 Pete Smith .05 .02
❑ 601 Zane Smith .05 .02
❑ 602 John Smoltz .50 .23
❑ 603 Bruce Sutter .05 .02
❑ 604 Andres Thomas .05 .02
❑ 605 Ozzie Virgil .05 .02
❑ 606 Brady Anderson .40 .18
❑ 607 Jeff Ballard .05 .02
❑ 608 Jose Bautista .05 .02
❑ 609 Ken Gerhart .05 .02
❑ 610 Terry Kennedy .05 .02
❑ 611 Eddie Murray .20 .09
❑ 612 Carl Nichols UER .05 .02
(Before All-Star Break batting 1.88)
❑ 613 Tom Niedenfuer .05 .02
❑ 614 Joe Orsulak .05 .02
❑ 615 Oswald Peraza UER .05 .02
(Shown as Oswaldo)
❑ 616A Bill Ripken ERR 5.00 2.20
(Rick Face written on knob of bat)
❑ 616B Bill Ripken 25.00 11.00
(Bat knob whited out)
❑ 616C Bill Ripken 5.00 2.20
(Words on bat knob scribbled out)
❑ 616D Bill Ripken DP .10 .05
(Black box covering bat knob)
❑ 617 Cal Ripken .75 .35
❑ 618 Dave Schmidt .05 .02
❑ 619 Rick Schu .05 .02
❑ 620 Larry Sheets .05 .02
❑ 621 Doug Sisk .05 .02
❑ 622 Pete Stanicek .05 .02
❑ 623 Mickey Tettleton .10 .05
❑ 624 Jay Tibbs .05 .02
❑ 625 Jim Traber .05 .02
❑ 626 Mark Williamson .05 .02
❑ 627 Craig Worthington .05 .02
❑ 628 Speed/Power .10 .05
Jose Canseco

❑ 629	Pitcher Perfect Tom Browning	.05	.02
❑ 630	Like Father/Like Sons Roberto Alomar Sandy Alomar Jr. (Names on card listed in wrong order) UER	.20	.09
❑ 631	NL All Stars UER Will Clark Rafael Palmeiro (Gallaraga, sic; Clark 3 consecutive 100 RBI seasons; third with 102 RBI's)	.20	.09
❑ 632	Homeruns - Coast to Coast UER Darryl Strawberry Will Clark (Homeruns should be two words)	.10	.05
❑ 633	Hot Corners - Hot Hitters UER Wade Boggs Carney Lansford (Boggs hit .366 in '86, should be '88)	.10	.05
❑ 634	Triple A's Jose Canseco Terry Steinbach Mark McGwire	.50	.23
❑ 635	Dual Heat Mark Davis Dwight Gooden	.10	.05
❑ 636	NL Pitching Power UER Danny Jackson David Cone (Hersheiser, sic)	.10	.05
❑ 637	Cannon Arms UER Chris Sabo Bobby Bonilla (Bobby Bonds, sic)	.10	.05
❑ 638	Double Trouble UER Andres Galarraga (Misspelled Gallaraga on card back) Gerald Perry	.10	.05
❑ 639	Power Center Kirby Puckett Eric Davis	.20	.09
❑ 640	Steve Wilson and Cameron Drew	.05	.02
❑ 641	Kevin Brown and Kevin Reimer	.60	.25
❑ 642	Brad Pounders and Jerald Clark	.05	.02
❑ 643	Mike Capel and Drew Hall	.05	.02
❑ 644	Joe Girardi and Rolando Roomes	.30	.14
❑ 645	Lenny Harris and Marty Brown	.10	.05
❑ 646	Luis DeLosSantos and Jim Campbell	.05	.02
❑ 647	Randy Kramer and Miguel Garcia	.05	.02
❑ 648	Torey Lovullo and Robert Palacios	.05	.02
❑ 649	Jim Corsi and Bob Milacki	.05	.02
❑ 650	Grady Hall and Mike Rochford	.05	.02
❑ 651	Terry Taylor and Vance Lovelace	.05	.02
❑ 652	Ken Hill and Dennis Cook	.20	.09
❑ 653	Scott Service and Shane Turner	.05	.02
❑ 654	CL: Oakland/Mets Dodgers/Red Sox (10 Hendersor; 68 Jess Orosco)	.05	.02
❑ 655A	CL: Twins/Tigers ERR Reds/Brewers (179 Boslo and Twins/Tigers positions listed)	.05	.02
❑ 655B	CL: Twins/Tigers COR Reds/Brewers (179 Boslo but Twins/Tigers positions not listed)	.05	.02
❑ 656	CL: Pirates/Blue Jays Yankees/Royals (225 Jess Barfield)	.05	.02
❑ 657	CL: Padres/Giants Astros/Expos (367/368 wrong)	.05	.02
❑ 658	CL: Indians/Cubs Cardinals/Angels (449 Deleon)	.05	.02
❑ 659	CL: White Sox/Rangers Mariners/Phillies	.05	.02
❑ 660	CL: Braves/Orioles Specials/Checklists (632 hyphenated differently and 650 Hali; 595 Rich Mahler; 619 Rich Schu)	.05	.02

1989 Fleer Glossy

	MINT	NRMT
COMP.FACT.SET (672)	150.00	70.00
COMMON CARD (1-660)	.15	.07
COMMON WS (1-12)	.10	.05

*STARS: 4X TO 8X BASIC CARDS
*ROOKIES: 5X TO 10X BASIC CARDS

1989 Fleer All-Stars

	MINT	NRMT
COMPLETE SET (12)	5.00	2.20
COMMON CARD (1-12)	.25	.11

		MINT	NRMT
❑ 1	Bobby Bonilla	.40	.18
❑ 2	Jose Canseco	.50	.23
❑ 3	Will Clark	.50	.23
❑ 4	Dennis Eckersley	.40	.18
❑ 5	Julio Franco	.25	.11
❑ 6	Mike Greenwell	.25	.11
❑ 7	Orel Hershiser	.40	.18
❑ 8	Paul Molitor	.50	.23
❑ 9	Mike Scioscia	.25	.11
❑ 10	Darryl Strawberry	.35	.16
❑ 11	Alan Trammell	.40	.18
❑ 12	Frank Viola	.25	.11

1989 Fleer For The Record

	MINT	NRMT
COMPLETE SET (6)	8.00	3.60
COMMON CARD (1-6)	.30	.14

		MINT	NRMT
❑ 1	Wade Boggs	.75	.35
❑ 2	Roger Clemens	2.50	1.10
❑ 3	Andres Galarraga	.75	.35
❑ 4	Kirk Gibson	.30	.14
❑ 5	Greg Maddux	5.00	2.20
❑ 6	Don Mattingly UER (Won batting title '83, should say '84)	2.00	.90

1989 Fleer Update

	MINT	NRMT
COMP.FACT.SET (132)	5.00	2.20
COMMON CARD (1-132)	.05	.02

		MINT	NRMT
❑ 1	Phil Bradley	.05	.02
❑ 2	Mike Devereaux	.05	.02
❑ 3	Steve Finley	.25	.11
❑ 4	Kevin Hickey	.05	.02
❑ 5	Brian Holton	.05	.02
❑ 6	Bob Milacki	.05	.02
❑ 7	Randy Milligan	.05	.02
❑ 8	John Dopson	.05	.02
❑ 9	Nick Esasky	.05	.02
❑ 10	Rob Murphy	.05	.02
❑ 11	Jim Abbott	.20	.09
❑ 12	Bert Blyleven	.10	.05
❑ 13	Jeff Manto	.05	.02
❑ 14	Bob McClure	.05	.02
❑ 15	Lance Parrish	.05	.02
❑ 16	Lee Stevens	.25	.11
❑ 17	Claudell Washington	.05	.02
❑ 18	Mark Davis	.05	.02
❑ 19	Eric King	.05	.02
❑ 20	Ron Kittle	.05	.02
❑ 21	Matt Merullo	.05	.02
❑ 22	Steve Rosenberg	.05	.02
❑ 23	Robin Ventura	.40	.18
❑ 24	Keith Atherton	.05	.02
❑ 25	Joey Belle	3.00	1.35
❑ 26	Jerry Browne	.05	.02
❑ 27	Felix Fermin	.05	.02
❑ 28	Brad Komminsk	.05	.02
❑ 29	Pete O'Brien	.05	.02
❑ 30	Mike Brumley	.05	.02
❑ 31	Tracy Jones	.05	.02
❑ 32	Mike Schwabe	.05	.02
❑ 33	Gary Ward	.05	.02
❑ 34	Frank Williams	.05	.02
❑ 35	Kevin Appier	.25	.11
❑ 36	Bob Boone	.10	.05
❑ 37	Luis DeLosSantos	.05	.02
❑ 38	Jim Eisenreich	.05	.02
❑ 39	Jaime Navarro	.10	.05
❑ 40	Bill Spiers	.05	.02
❑ 41	Greg Vaughn	1.25	.55
❑ 42	Randy Veres	.05	.02
❑ 43	Wally Backman	.05	.02
❑ 44	Shane Rawley	.05	.02

❑ 45 Steve Balboni .05 .02
❑ 46 Jesse Barfield .05 .02
❑ 47 Alvaro Espinoza .05 .02
❑ 48 Bob Geren .05 .02
❑ 49 Mel Hall .05 .02
❑ 50 Andy Hawkins .05 .02
❑ 51 Hensley Meulens .05 .02
❑ 52 Steve Sax .05 .02
❑ 53 Deion Sanders .75 .35
❑ 54 Rickey Henderson .20 .09
❑ 55 Mike Moore .05 .02
❑ 56 Tony Phillips .05 .02
❑ 57 Greg Briley .05 .02
❑ 58 Gene Harris .05 .02
❑ 59 Randy Johnson 1.25 .55
❑ 60 Jeffrey Leonard .05 .02
❑ 61 Dennis Powell .05 .02
❑ 62 Omar Vizquel .40 .18
❑ 63 Kevin Brown .60 .25
❑ 64 Julio Franco .05 .02
❑ 65 Jamie Moyer .05 .02
❑ 66 Rafael Palmeiro .20 .09
❑ 67 Nolan Ryan 1.50 .70
❑ 68 Francisco Cabrera .10 .05
❑ 69 Junior Felix .05 .02
❑ 70 Al Leiter .20 .09
❑ 71 Alex Sanchez .05 .02
❑ 72 Geronimo Berroa .05 .02
❑ 73 Derek Lilliquist .05 .02
❑ 74 Lonnie Smith .05 .02
❑ 75 Jeff Treadway .05 .02
❑ 76 Paul Kilgus .05 .02
❑ 77 Lloyd McClendon .05 .02
❑ 78 Scott Sanderson .05 .02
❑ 79 Dwight Smith .10 .05
❑ 80 Jerome Walton .20 .09
❑ 81 Mitch Williams .05 .02
❑ 82 Steve Wilson .05 .02
❑ 83 Todd Benzinger .05 .02
❑ 84 Ken Griffey Sr. .05 .02
❑ 85 Rick Mahler .05 .02
❑ 86 Rolando Roomes .05 .02
❑ 87 Scott Scudder .05 .02
❑ 88 Jim Clancy .05 .02
❑ 89 Rick Rhoden .05 .02
❑ 90 Dan Schatzeder .05 .02
❑ 91 Mike Morgan .05 .02
❑ 92 Eddie Murray .20 .09
❑ 93 Willie Randolph .10 .05
❑ 94 Ray Searage .05 .02
❑ 95 Mike Aldrete .05 .02
❑ 96 Kevin Gross .05 .02
❑ 97 Mark Langston .05 .02
❑ 98 Spike Owen .05 .02
❑ 99 Zane Smith .05 .02
❑ 100 Don Aase .05 .02
❑ 101 Barry Lyons .05 .02
❑ 102 Juan Samuel .05 .02
❑ 103 Wally Whitehurst .05 .02
❑ 104 Dennis Cook .05 .02
❑ 105 Len Dykstra .10 .05
❑ 106 Charlie Hayes .20 .09
❑ 107 Tommy Herr .05 .02
❑ 108 Ken Howell .05 .02
❑ 109 John Kruk .10 .05
❑ 110 Roger McDowell .05 .02
❑ 111 Terry Mulholland .05 .02
❑ 112 Jeff Parrett .05 .02
❑ 113 Neal Heaton .05 .02
❑ 114 Jeff King .10 .05
❑ 115 Randy Kramer .05 .02
❑ 116 Bill Landrum .05 .02
❑ 117 Cris Carpenter .05 .02
❑ 118 Frank DiPino .05 .02
❑ 119 Ken Hill .20 .09
❑ 120 Dan Quisenberry .05 .02
❑ 121 Milt Thompson .05 .02
❑ 122 Todd Zeile .20 .09
❑ 123 Jack Clark .05 .02
❑ 124 Bruce Hurst .05 .02
❑ 125 Mark Parent .05 .02
❑ 126 Bip Roberts .10 .05
❑ 127 Jeff Brantley UER .10 .05
(Photo actually Joe Kmak)
❑ 128 Terry Kennedy .05 .02
❑ 129 Mike LaCoss .05 .02
❑ 130 Greg Litton .05 .02
❑ 131 Mike Schmidt .50 .23
❑ 132 Checklist 1-132 .05 .02

1990 Fleer

	MINT	NRMT
COMPLETE SET (660)	10.00	4.50
COMP.RETAIL SET (660)	8.00	3.60
COMP.HOBBY SET (672)	12.00	5.50
COMMON CARD (1-660)	.05	.02

❑ 1 Lance Blankenship .05 .02
❑ 2 Todd Burns .05 .02
❑ 3 Jose Canseco .20 .09
❑ 4 Jim Corsi .05 .02
❑ 5 Storm Davis .05 .02
❑ 6 Dennis Eckersley .15 .07
❑ 7 Mike Gallego .05 .02
❑ 8 Ron Hassey .05 .02
❑ 9 Dave Henderson .05 .02
❑ 10 Rickey Henderson .20 .09
❑ 11 Rick Honeycutt .05 .02
❑ 12 Stan Javier .05 .02
❑ 13 Felix Jose .05 .02
❑ 14 Carney Lansford .10 .05
❑ 15 Mark McGwire UER 1.00 .45
(1989 runs listed as 4, should be 74)
❑ 16 Mike Moore .05 .02
❑ 17 Gene Nelson .05 .02
❑ 18 Dave Parker .10 .05
❑ 19 Tony Phillips .05 .02
❑ 20 Terry Steinbach .10 .05
❑ 21 Dave Stewart .10 .05
❑ 22 Walt Weiss .05 .02
❑ 23 Bob Welch .05 .02
❑ 24 Curt Young .05 .02
❑ 25 Paul Assenmacher .05 .02
❑ 26 Damon Berryhill .05 .02
❑ 27 Mike Bielecki .05 .02
❑ 28 Kevin Blankenship .05 .02
❑ 29 Andre Dawson .20 .09
❑ 30 Shawon Dunston .05 .02
❑ 31 Joe Girardi .15 .07
❑ 32 Mark Grace .20 .09
❑ 33 Mike Harkey .05 .02
❑ 34 Paul Kilgus .05 .02
❑ 35 Les Lancaster .05 .02
❑ 36 Vance Law .05 .02
❑ 37 Greg Maddux .60 .25
❑ 38 Lloyd McClendon .05 .02
❑ 39 Jeff Pico .05 .02
❑ 40 Ryne Sandberg .25 .11
❑ 41 Scott Sanderson .05 .02
❑ 42 Dwight Smith .05 .02
❑ 43 Rick Sutcliffe .05 .02
❑ 44 Jerome Walton .05 .02
❑ 45 Mitch Webster .05 .02
❑ 46 Curt Wilkerson .05 .02
❑ 47 Dean Wilkins .05 .02
❑ 48 Mitch Williams .05 .02
❑ 49 Steve Wilson .05 .02
❑ 50 Steve Bedrosian .05 .02
❑ 51 Mike Benjamin .05 .02
❑ 52 Jeff Brantley .05 .02
❑ 53 Brett Butler .10 .05
❑ 54 Will Clark UER .20 .09
(Did You Know says first in runs, should say tied for first)
❑ 55 Kelly Downs .05 .02
❑ 56 Scott Garrelts .05 .02
❑ 57 Atlee Hammaker .05 .02
❑ 58 Terry Kennedy .05 .02
❑ 59 Mike LaCoss .05 .02
❑ 60 Craig Lefferts .05 .02
❑ 61 Greg Litton .05 .02
❑ 62 Candy Maldonado .05 .02
❑ 63 Kirt Manwaring UER .05 .02
(No '88 Phoenix stats as noted in box)
❑ 64 Randy McCament .05 .02
❑ 65 Kevin Mitchell .05 .02
❑ 66 Donell Nixon .05 .02
❑ 67 Ken Oberkfell .05 .02
❑ 68 Rick Reuschel .05 .02
❑ 69 Ernest Riles .05 .02
❑ 70 Don Robinson .05 .02
❑ 71 Pat Sheridan .05 .02
❑ 72 Chris Speier .05 .02
❑ 73 Robby Thompson .05 .02
❑ 74 Jose Uribe .05 .02
❑ 75 Matt Williams .20 .09
❑ 76 George Bell .05 .02
❑ 77 Pat Borders .05 .02
❑ 78 John Cerutti .05 .02
❑ 79 Junior Felix .05 .02
❑ 80 Tony Fernandez .05 .02
❑ 81 Mike Flanagan .05 .02
❑ 82 Mauro Gozzo .05 .02
❑ 83 Kelly Gruber .05 .02
❑ 84 Tom Henke .05 .02
❑ 85 Jimmy Key .10 .05
❑ 86 Manny Lee .05 .02
❑ 87 Nelson Liriano UER .05 .02
(Should say "led the IL" instead of "led the TL")
❑ 88 Lee Mazzilli .05 .02
❑ 89 Fred McGriff .20 .09
❑ 90 Lloyd Moseby .05 .02
❑ 91 Rance Mulliniks .05 .02
❑ 92 Alex Sanchez .05 .02
❑ 93 Dave Stieb .10 .05
❑ 94 Todd Stottlemyre .10 .05
❑ 95 Duane Ward UER .05 .02
(Double line of '87 Syracuse stats)
❑ 96 David Wells .15 .07
❑ 97 Ernie Whitt .05 .02
❑ 98 Frank Wills .05 .02
❑ 99 Mookie Wilson .10 .05
❑ 100 Kevin Appier .15 .07
❑ 101 Luis Aquino .05 .02
❑ 102 Bob Boone .10 .05
❑ 103 George Brett .40 .18
❑ 104 Jose DeJesus .05 .02
❑ 105 Luis De Los Santos .05 .02
❑ 106 Jim Eisenreich .05 .02
❑ 107 Steve Farr .05 .02
❑ 108 Tom Gordon .15 .07
❑ 109 Mark Gubicza .05 .02
❑ 110 Bo Jackson .10 .05
❑ 111 Terry Leach .05 .02
❑ 112 Charlie Leibrandt .05 .02
❑ 113 Rick Luecken .05 .02
❑ 114 Mike Macfarlane .05 .02
❑ 115 Jeff Montgomery .10 .05
❑ 116 Bret Saberhagen .10 .05
❑ 117 Kevin Seitzer .05 .02
❑ 118 Kurt Stillwell .05 .02
❑ 119 Pat Tabler .05 .02
❑ 120 Danny Tartabull .05 .02
❑ 121 Gary Thurman .05 .02
❑ 122 Frank White .10 .05
❑ 123 Willie Wilson .05 .02
❑ 124 Matt Winters .05 .02
❑ 125 Jim Abbott .15 .07
❑ 126 Tony Armas .05 .02
❑ 127 Dante Bichette .20 .09

❑ 128 Bert Blyleven .10 .05
❑ 129 Chili Davis .10 .05
❑ 130 Brian Downing .05 .02
❑ 131 Mike Fetters .05 .02
❑ 132 Chuck Finley .10 .05
❑ 133 Willie Fraser .05 .02
❑ 134 Bryan Harvey .05 .02
❑ 135 Jack Howell .05 .02
❑ 136 Wally Joyner .10 .05
❑ 137 Jeff Manto .05 .02
❑ 138 Kirk McCaskill .05 .02
❑ 139 Bob McClure .05 .02
❑ 140 Greg Minton .05 .02
❑ 141 Lance Parrish .05 .02
❑ 142 Dan Petry .05 .02
❑ 143 Johnny Ray .05 .02
❑ 144 Dick Schofield .05 .02
❑ 145 Lee Stevens .10 .05
❑ 146 Claudell Washington .05 .02
❑ 147 Devon White .05 .02
❑ 148 Mike Witt .05 .02
❑ 149 Roberto Alomar .25 .11
❑ 150 Sandy Alomar Jr. .15 .07
❑ 151 Andy Benes .20 .09
❑ 152 Jack Clark .10 .05
❑ 153 Pat Clements .05 .02
❑ 154 Joey Cora .15 .07
❑ 155 Mark Davis .05 .02
❑ 156 Mark Grant .05 .02
❑ 157 Tony Gwynn .50 .23
❑ 158 Greg W. Harris .05 .02
❑ 159 Bruce Hurst .05 .02
❑ 160 Darrin Jackson .05 .02
❑ 161 Chris James .05 .02
❑ 162 Carmelo Martinez .05 .02
❑ 163 Mike Pagliarulo .05 .02
❑ 164 Mark Parent .05 .02
❑ 165 Dennis Rasmussen .05 .02
❑ 166 Bip Roberts .05 .02
❑ 167 Benito Santiago .05 .02
❑ 168 Calvin Schiraldi .05 .02
❑ 169 Eric Show .05 .02
❑ 170 Garry Templeton .05 .02
❑ 171 Ed Whitson .05 .02
❑ 172 Brady Anderson .20 .09
❑ 173 Jeff Ballard .05 .02
❑ 174 Phil Bradley .05 .02
❑ 175 Mike Devereaux .05 .02
❑ 176 Steve Finley .20 .09
❑ 177 Pete Harnisch .05 .02
❑ 178 Kevin Hickey .05 .02
❑ 179 Brian Holton .05 .02
❑ 180 Ben McDonald .10 .05
❑ 181 Bob Melvin .05 .02
❑ 182 Bob Milacki .05 .02
❑ 183 Randy Milligan UER .05 .02
(Double line of
'87 stats)
❑ 184 Gregg Olson .05 .02
❑ 185 Joe Orsulak .05 .02
❑ 186 Bill Ripken .05 .02
❑ 187 Cal Ripken .75 .35
❑ 188 Dave Schmidt .05 .02
❑ 189 Larry Sheets .05 .02
❑ 190 Mickey Tettleton .10 .05
❑ 191 Mark Thurmond .05 .02
❑ 192 Jay Tibbs .05 .02
❑ 193 Jim Traber .05 .02
❑ 194 Mark Williamson .05 .02
❑ 195 Craig Worthington .05 .02
❑ 196 Don Aase .05 .02
❑ 197 Blaine Beatty .05 .02
❑ 198 Mark Carreon .05 .02
❑ 199 Gary Carter .20 .09
❑ 200 David Cone .20 .09
❑ 201 Ron Darling .05 .02
❑ 202 Kevin Elster .05 .02
❑ 203 Sid Fernandez .05 .02
❑ 204 Dwight Gooden .10 .05
❑ 205 Keith Hernandez .10 .05
❑ 206 Jeff Innis .05 .02
❑ 207 Gregg Jefferies .10 .05
❑ 208 Howard Johnson .05 .02
❑ 209 Barry Lyons UER .05 .02
(Double line of
'87 stats)

❑ 210 Dave Magadan .05 .02
❑ 211 Kevin McReynolds .05 .02
❑ 212 Jeff Musselman .05 .02
❑ 213 Randy Myers .10 .05
❑ 214 Bob Ojeda .05 .02
❑ 215 Juan Samuel .05 .02
❑ 216 Mackey Sasser .05 .02
❑ 217 Darryl Strawberry .10 .05
❑ 218 Tim Teufel .05 .02
❑ 219 Frank Viola .05 .02
❑ 220 Juan Agosto .05 .02
❑ 221 Larry Andersen .05 .02
❑ 222 Eric Anthony .05 .02
❑ 223 Kevin Bass .05 .02
❑ 224 Craig Biggio .20 .09
❑ 225 Ken Caminiti .20 .09
❑ 226 Jim Clancy .05 .02
❑ 227 Danny Darwin .05 .02
❑ 228 Glenn Davis .05 .02
❑ 229 Jim Deshaies .05 .02
❑ 230 Bill Doran .05 .02
❑ 231 Bob Forsch .05 .02
❑ 232 Brian Meyer .05 .02
❑ 233 Terry Puhl .05 .02
❑ 234 Rafael Ramirez .05 .02
❑ 235 Rick Rhoden .05 .02
❑ 236 Dan Schatzeder .05 .02
❑ 237 Mike Scott .05 .02
❑ 238 Dave Smith .05 .02
❑ 239 Alex Trevino .05 .02
❑ 240 Glenn Wilson .05 .02
❑ 241 Gerald Young .05 .02
❑ 242 Tom Brunansky .05 .02
❑ 243 Cris Carpenter .05 .02
❑ 244 Alex Cole .05 .02
❑ 245 Vince Coleman .05 .02
❑ 246 John Costello .05 .02
❑ 247 Ken Dayley .05 .02
❑ 248 Jose DeLeon .05 .02
❑ 249 Frank DiPino .05 .02
❑ 250 Pedro Guerrero .05 .02
❑ 251 Ken Hill .15 .07
❑ 252 Joe Magrane .05 .02
❑ 253 Willie McGee UER .10 .05
(No decimal point
before 353)
❑ 254 John Morris .05 .02
❑ 255 Jose Oquendo .05 .02
❑ 256 Tony Pena .05 .02
❑ 257 Terry Pendleton .10 .05
❑ 258 Ted Power .05 .02
❑ 259 Dan Quisenberry .05 .02
❑ 260 Ozzie Smith .25 .11
❑ 261 Scott Terry .05 .02
❑ 262 Milt Thompson .05 .02
❑ 263 Denny Walling .05 .02
❑ 264 Todd Worrell .05 .02
❑ 265 Todd Zeile .10 .05
❑ 266 Marty Barrett .05 .02
❑ 267 Mike Boddicker .05 .02
❑ 268 Wade Boggs .20 .09
❑ 269 Ellis Burks .15 .07
❑ 270 Rick Cerone .05 .02
❑ 271 Roger Clemens .40 .18
❑ 272 John Dopson .05 .02
❑ 273 Nick Esasky .05 .02
❑ 274 Dwight Evans .10 .05
❑ 275 Wes Gardner .05 .02
❑ 276 Rich Gedman .05 .02
❑ 277 Mike Greenwell .05 .02
❑ 278 Danny Heep .05 .02
❑ 279 Eric Hetzel .05 .02
❑ 280 Dennis Lamp .05 .02
❑ 281 Rob Murphy UER .05 .02
('89 stats say Reds,
should say Red Sox)
❑ 282 Joe Price .05 .02
❑ 283 Carlos Quintana .05 .02
❑ 284 Jody Reed .05 .02
❑ 285 Luis Rivera .05 .02
❑ 286 Kevin Romine .05 .02
❑ 287 Lee Smith .10 .05
❑ 288 Mike Smithson .05 .02
❑ 289 Bob Stanley .05 .02
❑ 290 Harold Baines .10 .05

❑ 291 Kevin Brown .20 .09
❑ 292 Steve Buechele .05 .02
❑ 293 Scott Coolbaugh .05 .02
❑ 294 Jack Daugherty .05 .02
❑ 295 Cecil Espy .05 .02
❑ 296 Julio Franco .05 .02
❑ 297 Juan Gonzalez 3.00 1.35
❑ 298 Cecilio Guante .05 .02
❑ 299 Drew Hall .05 .02
❑ 300 Charlie Hough .10 .05
❑ 301 Pete Incaviglia .05 .02
❑ 302 Mike Jeffcoat .05 .02
❑ 303 Chad Kreuter .05 .02
❑ 304 Jeff Kunkel .05 .02
❑ 305 Rick Leach .05 .02
❑ 306 Fred Manrique .05 .02
❑ 307 Jamie Moyer .05 .02
❑ 308 Rafael Palmeiro .20 .09
❑ 309 Geno Petralli .05 .02
❑ 310 Kevin Reimer .05 .02
❑ 311 Kenny Rogers .10 .05
❑ 312 Jeff Russell .05 .02
❑ 313 Nolan Ryan .75 .35
❑ 314 Ruben Sierra .05 .02
❑ 315 Bobby Witt .05 .02
❑ 316 Chris Bosio .05 .02
❑ 317 Glenn Braggs UER .05 .02
(Stats say 111 K's,
but bio says 117 K's)
❑ 318 Greg Brock .05 .02
❑ 319 Chuck Crim .05 .02
❑ 320 Rob Deer .05 .02
❑ 321 Mike Felder .05 .02
❑ 322 Tom Filer .05 .02
❑ 323 Tony Fossas .05 .02
❑ 324 Jim Gantner .05 .02
❑ 325 Darryl Hamilton .05 .02
❑ 326 Teddy Higuera .05 .02
❑ 327 Mark Knudson .05 .02
❑ 328 Bill Krueger UER .05 .02
('86 stats missing)
❑ 329 Tim McIntosh .05 .02
❑ 330 Paul Molitor .20 .09
❑ 331 Jaime Navarro .05 .02
❑ 332 Charlie O'Brien .05 .02
❑ 333 Jeff Peterek .05 .02
❑ 334 Dan Plesac .05 .02
❑ 335 Jerry Reuss .05 .02
❑ 336 Gary Sheffield UER .20 .09
(Bio says played for
3 teams in '87, but
stats say in '88)
❑ 337 Bill Spiers .05 .02
❑ 338 B.J. Surhoff .10 .05
❑ 339 Greg Vaughn .40 .18
❑ 340 Robin Yount .20 .09
❑ 341 Hubie Brooks .05 .02
❑ 342 Tim Burke .05 .02
❑ 343 Mike Fitzgerald .05 .02
❑ 344 Tom Foley .05 .02
❑ 345 Andres Galarraga .20 .09
❑ 346 Damaso Garcia .05 .02
❑ 347 Marquis Grissom .25 .11
❑ 348 Kevin Gross .05 .02
❑ 349 Joe Hesketh .05 .02
❑ 350 Jeff Huson .05 .02
❑ 351 Wallace Johnson .05 .02
❑ 352 Mark Langston .05 .02
❑ 353A Dave Martinez 2.00 .90
(Yellow on front)
❑ 353B Dave Martinez .05 .02
(Red on front)
❑ 354 Dennis Martinez UER .10 .05
('87 ERA is 616,
should be 6.16)
❑ 355 Andy McGaffigan .05 .02
❑ 356 Otis Nixon .10 .05
❑ 357 Spike Owen .05 .02
❑ 358 Pascual Perez .05 .02
❑ 359 Tim Raines .10 .05
❑ 360 Nelson Santovenia .05 .02
❑ 361 Bryn Smith .05 .02
❑ 362 Zane Smith .05 .02
❑ 363 Larry Walker 1.00 .45
❑ 364 Tim Wallach .05 .02

❑ 365 Rick Aguilera .10 .05
❑ 366 Allan Anderson .05 .02
❑ 367 Wally Backman .05 .02
❑ 368 Doug Baker .05 .02
❑ 369 Juan Berenguer .05 .02
❑ 370 Randy Bush .05 .02
❑ 371 Carmen Castillo .05 .02
❑ 372 Mike Dyer .05 .02
❑ 373 Gary Gaetti .10 .05
❑ 374 Greg Gagne .05 .02
❑ 375 Dan Gladden .05 .02
❑ 376 German Gonzalez UER .05 .02
(Bio says 31 saves in '88, but stats say 30)
❑ 377 Brian Harper .05 .02
❑ 378 Kent Hrbek .10 .05
❑ 379 Gene Larkin .05 .02
❑ 380 Tim Laudner UER .05 .02
(No decimal point before '85 BA of 238)
❑ 381 John Moses .05 .02
❑ 382 Al Newman .05 .02
❑ 383 Kirby Puckett .30 .14
❑ 384 Shane Rawley .05 .02
❑ 385 Jeff Reardon .10 .05
❑ 386 Roy Smith .05 .02
❑ 387 Gary Wayne .05 .02
❑ 388 Dave West .05 .02
❑ 389 Tim Belcher .05 .02
❑ 390 Tim Crews UER .05 .02
(Stats say 163 IP for '83, but bio says 136)
❑ 391 Mike Davis .05 .02
❑ 392 Rick Dempsey .05 .02
❑ 393 Kirk Gibson .10 .05
❑ 394 Jose Gonzalez .05 .02
❑ 395 Alfredo Griffin .05 .02
❑ 396 Jeff Hamilton .05 .02
❑ 397 Lenny Harris .05 .02
❑ 398 Mickey Hatcher .05 .02
❑ 399 Orel Hershiser .10 .05
❑ 400 Jay Howell .05 .02
❑ 401 Mike Marshall .05 .02
❑ 402 Ramon Martinez .15 .07
❑ 403 Mike Morgan .05 .02
❑ 404 Eddie Murray .20 .09
❑ 405 Alejandro Pena .05 .02
❑ 406 Willie Randolph .10 .05
❑ 407 Mike Scioscia .05 .02
❑ 408 Ray Searage .05 .02
❑ 409 Fernando Valenzuela .10 .05
❑ 410 Jose Vizcaino .20 .09
❑ 411 John Wetteland .20 .09
❑ 412 Jack Armstrong .05 .02
❑ 413 Todd Benzinger UER .05 .02
(Bio says .323 at Pawtucket, but stats say .321)
❑ 414 Tim Birtsas .05 .02
❑ 415 Tom Browning .05 .02
❑ 416 Norm Charlton .05 .02
❑ 417 Eric Davis .10 .05
❑ 418 Rob Dibble .05 .02
❑ 419 John Franco .10 .05
❑ 420 Ken Griffey Sr. .05 .02
❑ 421 Chris Hammond .05 .02
(No 1989 used for "Did Not Play" stat, actually did play for Nashville in 1989)
❑ 422 Danny Jackson .05 .02
❑ 423 Barry Larkin .20 .09
❑ 424 Tim Leary .05 .02
❑ 425 Rick Mahler .05 .02
❑ 426 Joe Oliver .05 .02
❑ 427 Paul O'Neill .10 .05
❑ 428 Luis Quinones UER .05 .02
('86-'88 stats are omitted from card but included in totals)
❑ 429 Jeff Reed .05 .02
❑ 430 Jose Rijo .05 .02
❑ 431 Ron Robinson .05 .02
❑ 432 Rolando Roomes .05 .02
❑ 433 Chris Sabo .05 .02
❑ 434 Scott Scudder .05 .02
❑ 435 Herm Winningham .05 .02
❑ 436 Steve Balboni .05 .02
❑ 437 Jesse Barfield .05 .02
❑ 438 Mike Blowers .10 .05
❑ 439 Tom Brookens .05 .02
❑ 440 Greg Cadaret .05 .02
❑ 441 Alvaro Espinoza UER .05 .02
(Career games say 218, should be 219)
❑ 442 Bob Geren .05 .02
❑ 443 Lee Guetterman .05 .02
❑ 444 Mel Hall .05 .02
❑ 445 Andy Hawkins .05 .02
❑ 446 Roberto Kelly .05 .02
❑ 447 Don Mattingly .30 .14
❑ 448 Lance McCullers .05 .02
❑ 449 Hensley Meulens .05 .02
❑ 450 Dale Mohorcic .05 .02
❑ 451 Clay Parker .05 .02
❑ 452 Eric Plunk .05 .02
❑ 453 Dave Righetti .05 .02
❑ 454 Deion Sanders .20 .09
❑ 455 Steve Sax .05 .02
❑ 456 Don Slaught .05 .02
❑ 457 Walt Terrell .05 .02
❑ 458 Dave Winfield .20 .09
❑ 459 Jay Bell .10 .05
❑ 460 Rafael Belliard .05 .02
❑ 461 Barry Bonds .25 .11
❑ 462 Bobby Bonilla .10 .05
❑ 463 Sid Bream .05 .02
❑ 464 Benny Distefano .05 .02
❑ 465 Doug Drabek .05 .02
❑ 466 Jim Gott .05 .02
❑ 467 Billy Hatcher UER .05 .02
(.1 hits for Cubs in 1984)
❑ 468 Neal Heaton .05 .02
❑ 469 Jeff King .10 .05
❑ 470 Bob Kipper .05 .02
❑ 471 Randy Kramer .05 .02
❑ 472 Bill Landrum .05 .02
❑ 473 Mike LaValliere .05 .02
❑ 474 Jose Lind .05 .02
❑ 475 Junior Ortiz .05 .02
❑ 476 Gary Redus .05 .02
❑ 477 Rick Reed .05 .02
❑ 478 R.J. Reynolds .05 .02
❑ 479 Jeff D. Robinson .05 .02
❑ 480 John Smiley .05 .02
❑ 481 Andy Van Slyke .10 .05
❑ 482 Bob Walk .05 .02
❑ 483 Andy Allanson .05 .02
❑ 484 Scott Bailes .05 .02
❑ 485 Joey Belle UER 1.00 .45
(Has Jay Bell "Did You Know")
❑ 486 Bud Black .05 .02
❑ 487 Jerry Browne .05 .02
❑ 488 Tom Candiotti .05 .02
❑ 489 Joe Carter .10 .05
❑ 490 Dave Clark .05 .02
(No '84 stats)
❑ 491 John Farrell .05 .02
❑ 492 Felix Fermin .05 .02
❑ 493 Brook Jacoby .05 .02
❑ 494 Dion James .05 .02
❑ 495 Doug Jones .05 .02
❑ 496 Brad Komminsk .05 .02
❑ 497 Rod Nichols .05 .02
❑ 498 Pete O'Brien .05 .02
❑ 499 Steve Olin .10 .05
❑ 500 Jesse Orosco .05 .02
❑ 501 Joel Skinner .05 .02
❑ 502 Cory Snyder .05 .02
❑ 503 Greg Swindell .05 .02
❑ 504 Rich Yett .05 .02
❑ 505 Scott Bankhead .05 .02
❑ 506 Scott Bradley .05 .02
❑ 507 Greg Briley UER .05 .02
(28 SB's in bio, but 27 in stats)
❑ 508 Jay Buhner .20 .09
❑ 509 Darnell Coles .05 .02
❑ 510 Keith Comstock .05 .02
❑ 511 Henry Cotto .05 .02
❑ 512 Alvin Davis .05 .02
❑ 513 Ken Griffey Jr. 2.00 .90
❑ 514 Erik Hanson .05 .02
❑ 515 Gene Harris .05 .02
❑ 516 Brian Holman .05 .02
❑ 517 Mike Jackson .10 .05
❑ 518 Randy Johnson .30 .14
❑ 519 Jeffrey Leonard .05 .02
❑ 520 Edgar Martinez .20 .09
❑ 521 Dennis Powell .05 .02
❑ 522 Jim Presley .05 .02
❑ 523 Jerry Reed .05 .02
❑ 524 Harold Reynolds .05 .02
❑ 525 Mike Schooler .05 .02
❑ 526 Bill Swift .05 .02
❑ 527 Dave Valle .05 .02
❑ 528 Omar Vizquel .20 .09
❑ 529 Ivan Calderon .05 .02
❑ 530 Carlton Fisk UER .20 .09
(Bellow Falls, should be Bellows Falls)
❑ 531 Scott Fletcher .05 .02
❑ 532 Dave Gallagher .05 .02
❑ 533 Ozzie Guillen .05 .02
❑ 534 Greg Hibbard .05 .02
❑ 535 Shawn Hillegas .05 .02
❑ 536 Lance Johnson .05 .02
❑ 537 Eric King .05 .02
❑ 538 Ron Kittle .05 .02
❑ 539 Steve Lyons .05 .02
❑ 540 Carlos Martinez .05 .02
❑ 541 Tom McCarthy .05 .02
❑ 542 Matt Merullo .05 .02
(Had 5 ML runs scored entering '90, not 6)
❑ 543 Donn Pall UER .05 .02
(Stats say pro career began in '85, bio says '88)
❑ 544 Dan Pasqua .05 .02
❑ 545 Ken Patterson .05 .02
❑ 546 Melido Perez .05 .02
❑ 547 Steve Rosenberg .05 .02
❑ 548 Sammy Sosa 5.00 2.20
❑ 549 Bobby Thigpen .05 .02
❑ 550 Robin Ventura .20 .09
❑ 551 Greg Walker .05 .02
❑ 552 Don Carman .05 .02
❑ 553 Pat Combs .05 .02
(6 walks for Phillies in '89 in stats, brief bio says 4)
❑ 554 Dennis Cook .05 .02
❑ 555 Darren Daulton .10 .05
❑ 556 Len Dykstra .10 .05
❑ 557 Curt Ford .05 .02
❑ 558 Charlie Hayes .05 .02
❑ 559 Von Hayes .05 .02
❑ 560 Tommy Herr .05 .02
❑ 561 Ken Howell .05 .02
❑ 562 Steve Jeltz .05 .02
❑ 563 Ron Jones .05 .02
❑ 564 Ricky Jordan UER .05 .02
(Duplicate line of statistics on back)
❑ 565 John Kruk .10 .05
❑ 566 Steve Lake .05 .02
❑ 567 Roger McDowell .05 .02
❑ 568 Terry Mulholland UER .05 .02
(Did You Know refers to Dave Magadan)
❑ 569 Dwayne Murphy .05 .02
❑ 570 Jeff Parrett .05 .02
❑ 571 Randy Ready .05 .02
❑ 572 Bruce Ruffin .05 .02
❑ 573 Dickie Thon .05 .02
❑ 574 Jose Alvarez UER .05 .02
('78 and '79 stats are reversed)
❑ 575 Geronimo Berroa .05 .02
❑ 576 Jeff Blauser .05 .02
❑ 577 Joe Boever .05 .02
❑ 578 Marty Clary UER .05 .02
(No comma between

city and state)
❑ 579 Jody Davis .05 .02
❑ 580 Mark Eichhorn .05 .02
❑ 581 Darrell Evans .10 .05
❑ 582 Ron Gant .10 .05
❑ 583 Tom Glavine .20 .09
❑ 584 Tommy Greene .05 .02
❑ 585 Tommy Gregg .05 .02
❑ 586 Dave Justice UER .75 .35
(Actually had 16 2B
in Sumter in '86)
❑ 587 Mark Lemke .05 .02
❑ 588 Derek Lilliquist .05 .02
❑ 589 Oddibe McDowell .05 .02
❑ 590 Kent Mercker ERA .05 .02
(Bio says 2.75 ERA,
stats say 2.68 ERA)
❑ 591 Dale Murphy .20 .09
❑ 592 Gerald Perry .05 .02
❑ 593 Lonnie Smith .05 .02
❑ 594 Pete Smith .05 .02
❑ 595 John Smoltz .20 .09
❑ 596 Mike Stanton UER .05 .02
(No comma between
city and state)
❑ 597 Andres Thomas .05 .02
❑ 598 Jeff Treadway .05 .02
❑ 599 Doyle Alexander .05 .02
❑ 600 Dave Bergman .05 .02
❑ 601 Brian DuBois .05 .02
❑ 602 Paul Gibson .05 .02
❑ 603 Mike Heath .05 .02
❑ 604 Mike Henneman .05 .02
❑ 605 Guillermo Hernandez .05 .02
❑ 606 Shawn Holman .05 .02
❑ 607 Tracy Jones .05 .02
❑ 608 Chet Lemon .05 .02
❑ 609 Fred Lynn .05 .02
❑ 610 Jack Morris .10 .05
❑ 611 Matt Nokes .05 .02
❑ 612 Gary Pettis .05 .02
❑ 613 Kevin Ritz .05 .02
❑ 614 Jeff M. Robinson .05 .02
('88 stats are
not in line)
❑ 615 Steve Searcy .05 .02
❑ 616 Frank Tanana .05 .02
❑ 617 Alan Trammell .15 .07
❑ 618 Gary Ward .05 .02
❑ 619 Lou Whitaker .10 .05
❑ 620 Frank Williams .05 .02
❑ 621A George Brett '80 1.50 .70
ERR (Had 10 .390
hitting seasons)
❑ 621B George Brett '80 .20 .09
COR
❑ 622 Fern.Valenzuela '81 .05 .02
❑ 623 Dale Murphy '82 .10 .05
❑ 624A Cal Ripken '83 ERR .. 5.00 2.20
(Misspelled Ripkin
on card back)
❑ 624B Cal Ripken '83 COR .40 .18
❑ 625 Ryne Sandberg '84 .20 .09
❑ 626 Don Mattingly '85 .20 .09
❑ 627 Roger Clemens '86 .20 .09
❑ 628 George Bell '87 .05 .02
❑ 629 Jose Canseco '88 UER .. .10 .05
(Reggie won MVP in
'83, should say '73)
❑ 630A Will Clark '89 ERR 1.00 .45
(32 total bases
on card back)
❑ 630B Will Clark '89 COR .20 .09
(321 total bases;
technically still
an error, listing
only 24 runs)
❑ 631 Game Savers .05 .02
Mark Davis
Mitch Williams
❑ 632 Boston Igniters .20 .09
Wade Boggs
Mike Greenwell
❑ 633 Starter and Stopper .05 .02
Mark Gubicza
Jeff Russell
❑ 634 League's Best .25 .11
Shortstops
Tony Fernandez
Cal Ripken
❑ 635 Human Dynamos .20 .09
Kirby Puckett
Bo Jackson
❑ 636 300 Strikeout Club .25 .11
Nolan Ryan
Mike Scott
❑ 637 The Dynamic Duo .10 .05
Will Clark
Kevin Mitchell
❑ 638 AL All-Stars .50 .23
Don Mattingly
Mark McGwire
❑ 639 NL East Rivals .20 .09
Howard Johnson
Ryne Sandberg
❑ 640 Rudy Seanez .05 .02
Colin Charland
❑ 641 George Canale .10 .05
Kevin Maas UER
(Canale listed as INF
on front, 1B on back)
❑ 642 Kelly Mann .05 .02
and Dave Hansen
❑ 643 Greg Smith .05 .02
and Stu Tate
❑ 644 Tom Drees .05 .02
and Dann Howitt
❑ 645 Mike Roesler .20 .09
and Derrick May
❑ 646 Scott Hemond .05 .02
and Mark Gardner
❑ 647 John Orton .05 .02
and Scott Leius
❑ 648 Rich Monteleone .05 .02
and Dana Williams
❑ 649 Mike Huff .05 .02
and Steve Frey
❑ 650 Chuck McElroy .75 .35
and Moises Alou
❑ 651 Bobby Rose .05 .02
and Mike Hartley
❑ 652 Matt Kinzer .05 .02
and Wayne Edwards
❑ 653 Delino DeShields .20 .09
and Jason Grimsley
❑ 654 CL: A's/Cubs .05 .02
Giants/Blue Jays
❑ 655 CL: Royals/Angels .05 .02
Padres/Orioles
❑ 656 CL: Mets/Astros .05 .02
Cards/Red Sox
❑ 657 CL: Rangers/Brewers .05 .02
Expos/Twins
❑ 658 CL: Dodgers/Reds .05 .02
Yankees/Pirates
❑ 659 CL: Indians/Mariners .05 .02
White Sox/Phillies
❑ 660A CL: Braves/Tigers .05 .02
Specials/Checklists
(Checklist-660 in small-
er print on card front)
❑ 660B CL: Braves/Tigers .05 .02
Specials/Checklists
(Checklist-660 in nor-
mal print on card front)

1990 Fleer All-Stars

	MINT	NRMT
COMPLETE SET (12)	3.00	1.35
COMMON CARD (1-12)	.15	.07

❑ 1 Harold Baines .35 .16
❑ 2 Will Clark .75 .35
❑ 3 Mark Davis .15 .07
❑ 4 Howard Johnson UER .15 .07
(In middle of 5th
line, the is
misspelled th)
❑ 5 Joe Magrane .15 .07
❑ 6 Kevin Mitchell .15 .07
❑ 7 Kirby Puckett .75 .35
❑ 8 Cal Ripken 2.00 .90
❑ 9 Ryne Sandberg .75 .35
❑ 10 Mike Scott UER .15 .07
Astros spelled Asatros on back
❑ 11 Ruben Sierra .15 .07
❑ 12 Mickey Tettleton .35 .16

1990 Fleer League Standouts

	MINT	NRMT
COMPLETE SET (6)	6.00	2.70
COMMON CARD (1-6)	.50	.23

❑ 1 Barry Larkin 1.50 .70
❑ 2 Don Mattingly 2.50 1.10
❑ 3 Darryl Strawberry .50 .23
❑ 4 Jose Canseco 1.50 .70
❑ 5 Wade Boggs 1.50 .70
❑ 6 Mark Grace UER .75 .35
(Chris Sabo misspelled
as Cris)

1990 Fleer Soaring Stars

	MINT	NRMT
COMPLETE SET (12)	25.00	11.00
COMMON CARD (1-12)	.50	.23

❑ 1 Todd Zeile 1.00 .45
❑ 2 Mike Stanton .50 .23

	Card	MINT	NRMT
❑ 3	Larry Walker	6.00	2.70
❑ 4	Robin Ventura	2.00	.90
❑ 5	Scott Coolbaugh	.50	.23
❑ 6	Ken Griffey Jr.	15.00	6.75
❑ 7	Tom Gordon	1.50	.70
❑ 8	Jerome Walton	.50	.23
❑ 9	Junior Felix	.50	.23
❑ 10	Jim Abbott	1.50	.70
❑ 11	Ricky Jordan	.50	.23
❑ 12	Dwight Smith	.50	.23

1990 Fleer Update

	MINT	NRMT
COMP.FACT.SET (132)	5.00	2.20
COMMON CARD (1-132)	.05	.02

	Card	MINT	NRMT
❑ 1	Steve Avery	.05	.02
❑ 2	Francisco Cabrera	.05	.02
❑ 3	Nick Esasky	.05	.02
❑ 4	Jim Kremers	.05	.02
❑ 5	Greg Olson	.05	.02
❑ 6	Jim Presley	.05	.02
❑ 7	Shawn Boskie	.05	.02
❑ 8	Joe Kraemer	.05	.02
❑ 9	Luis Salazar	.05	.02
❑ 10	Hector Villanueva	.05	.02
❑ 11	Glenn Braggs	.05	.02
❑ 12	Mariano Duncan	.05	.02
❑ 13	Billy Hatcher	.05	.02
❑ 14	Tim Layana	.05	.02
❑ 15	Hal Morris	.05	.02
❑ 16	Javier Ortiz	.05	.02
❑ 17	Dave Rohde	.05	.02
❑ 18	Eric Yelding	.05	.02
❑ 19	Hubie Brooks	.05	.02
❑ 20	Kal Daniels	.05	.02
❑ 21	Dave Hansen	.05	.02
❑ 22	Mike Hartley	.05	.02
❑ 23	Stan Javier	.05	.02
❑ 24	Jose Offerman	.25	.11
❑ 25	Juan Samuel	.05	.02
❑ 26	Dennis Boyd	.05	.02
❑ 27	Delino DeShields	.20	.09
❑ 28	Steve Frey	.05	.02
❑ 29	Mark Gardner	.05	.02
❑ 30	Chris Nabholz	.05	.02
❑ 31	Bill Sampen	.05	.02
❑ 32	Dave Schmidt	.05	.02
❑ 33	Daryl Boston	.05	.02
❑ 34	Chuck Carr	.20	.09
❑ 35	John Franco	.10	.05
❑ 36	Todd Hundley	.40	.18
❑ 37	Julio Machado	.05	.02
❑ 38	Alejandro Pena	.05	.02
❑ 39	Darren Reed	.05	.02
❑ 40	Kelvin Torve	.05	.02
❑ 41	Darrel Akerfelds	.05	.02
❑ 42	Jose DeJesus	.05	.02
❑ 43	Dave Hollins UER (Misspelled Dane on card back)	.20	.09
❑ 44	Carmelo Martinez	.05	.02
❑ 45	Brad Moore	.05	.02
❑ 46	Dale Murphy	.20	.09
❑ 47	Wally Backman	.05	.02
❑ 48	Stan Belinda	.05	.02
❑ 49	Bob Patterson	.05	.02
❑ 50	Ted Power	.05	.02
❑ 51	Don Slaught	.05	.02
❑ 52	Geronimo Pena	.05	.02
❑ 53	Lee Smith	.10	.05
❑ 54	John Tudor	.05	.02
❑ 55	Joe Carter	.10	.05
❑ 56	Thomas Howard	.05	.02
❑ 57	Craig Lefferts	.05	.02
❑ 58	Rafael Valdez	.05	.02
❑ 59	Dave Anderson	.05	.02
❑ 60	Kevin Bass	.05	.02
❑ 61	John Burkett	.10	.05
❑ 62	Gary Carter	.20	.09
❑ 63	Rick Parker	.05	.02
❑ 64	Trevor Wilson	.05	.02
❑ 65	Chris Hoiles	.20	.09
❑ 66	Tim Hulett	.05	.02
❑ 67	Dave Johnson	.05	.02
❑ 68	Curt Schilling	.20	.09
❑ 69	David Segui	.25	.11
❑ 70	Tom Brunansky	.05	.02
❑ 71	Greg A. Harris	.05	.02
❑ 72	Dana Kiecker	.05	.02
❑ 73	Tim Naehring	.20	.09
❑ 74	Tony Pena	.05	.02
❑ 75	Jeff Reardon	.10	.05
❑ 76	Jerry Reed	.05	.02
❑ 77	Mark Eichhorn	.05	.02
❑ 78	Mark Langston	.05	.02
❑ 79	John Orton	.05	.02
❑ 80	Luis Polonia	.05	.02
❑ 81	Dave Winfield	.20	.09
❑ 82	Cliff Young	.05	.02
❑ 83	Wayne Edwards	.05	.02
❑ 84	Alex Fernandez	.25	.11
❑ 85	Craig Grebeck	.05	.02
❑ 86	Scott Radinsky	.05	.02
❑ 87	Frank Thomas	3.00	1.35
❑ 88	Beau Allred	.05	.02
❑ 89	Sandy Alomar Jr.	.15	.07
❑ 90	Carlos Baerga	.25	.11
❑ 91	Kevin Bearse	.05	.02
❑ 92	Chris James	.05	.02
❑ 93	Candy Maldonado	.05	.02
❑ 94	Jeff Manto	.05	.02
❑ 95	Cecil Fielder	.10	.05
❑ 96	Travis Fryman	.40	.18
❑ 97	Lloyd Moseby	.05	.02
❑ 98	Edwin Nunez	.05	.02
❑ 99	Tony Phillips	.05	.02
❑ 100	Larry Sheets	.05	.02
❑ 101	Mark Davis	.05	.02
❑ 102	Storm Davis	.05	.02
❑ 103	Gerald Perry	.05	.02
❑ 104	Terry Shumpert	.05	.02
❑ 105	Edgar Diaz	.05	.02
❑ 106	Dave Parker	.10	.05
❑ 107	Tim Drummond	.05	.02
❑ 108	Junior Ortiz	.05	.02
❑ 109	Park Pittman	.05	.02
❑ 110	Kevin Tapani	.10	.05
❑ 111	Oscar Azocar	.05	.02
❑ 112	Jim Leyritz	.20	.09
❑ 113	Kevin Maas	.10	.05
❑ 114	Alan Mills	.05	.02
❑ 115	Matt Nokes	.05	.02
❑ 116	Pascual Perez	.05	.02
❑ 117	Ozzie Canseco	.05	.02
❑ 118	Scott Sanderson	.05	.02
❑ 119	Tino Martinez	.40	.18
❑ 120	Jeff Schaefer	.05	.02
❑ 121	Matt Young	.05	.02
❑ 122	Brian Bohanon	.05	.02
❑ 123	Jeff Huson	.05	.02
❑ 124	Ramon Manon	.05	.02
❑ 125	Gary Mielke UER (Shown as Blue Jay on front)	.05	.02
❑ 126	Willie Blair	.05	.02
❑ 127	Glenallen Hill	.05	.02
❑ 128	John Olerud UER (Listed as throwing right, should be left)	.50	.23
❑ 129	Luis Sojo	.05	.02
❑ 130	Mark Whiten	.05	.02
❑ 131	Nolan Ryan	.75	.35
❑ 132	Checklist U1-U132	.05	.02

1991 Fleer

	MINT	NRMT
COMPLETE SET (720)	8.00	3.60
COMP.RETAIL SET (732)	10.00	4.50
COMP.HOBBY SET (732)	10.00	4.50
COMMON CARD (1-720)	.05	.02

	Card	MINT	NRMT
❑ 1	Troy Afenir	.05	.02
❑ 2	Harold Baines	.10	.05
❑ 3	Lance Blankenship	.05	.02
❑ 4	Todd Burns	.05	.02
❑ 5	Jose Canseco	.20	.09
❑ 6	Dennis Eckersley	.10	.05
❑ 7	Mike Gallego	.05	.02
❑ 8	Ron Hassey	.05	.02
❑ 9	Dave Henderson	.05	.02
❑ 10	Rickey Henderson	.20	.09
❑ 11	Rick Honeycutt	.05	.02
❑ 12	Doug Jennings	.05	.02
❑ 13	Joe Klink	.05	.02
❑ 14	Carney Lansford	.10	.05
❑ 15	Darren Lewis	.10	.05
❑ 16	Willie McGee UER (Height 6'11")	.10	.05
❑ 17	Mark McGwire UER (183 extra base hits in 1987)	1.00	.45
❑ 18	Mike Moore	.05	.02
❑ 19	Gene Nelson	.05	.02
❑ 20	Dave Otto	.05	.02
❑ 21	Jamie Quirk	.05	.02
❑ 22	Willie Randolph	.10	.05
❑ 23	Scott Sanderson	.05	.02
❑ 24	Terry Steinbach	.10	.05
❑ 25	Dave Stewart	.10	.05
❑ 26	Walt Weiss	.05	.02
❑ 27	Bob Welch	.05	.02
❑ 28	Curt Young	.05	.02
❑ 29	Wally Backman	.05	.02
❑ 30	Stan Belinda UER (Born in Huntington, should be State College)	.05	.02
❑ 31	Jay Bell	.10	.05
❑ 32	Rafael Belliard	.05	.02
❑ 33	Barry Bonds	.25	.11
❑ 34	Bobby Bonilla	.10	.05
❑ 35	Sid Bream	.05	.02
❑ 36	Doug Drabek	.05	.02
❑ 37	Carlos Garcia	.05	.02
❑ 38	Neal Heaton	.05	.02
❑ 39	Jeff King	.10	.05
❑ 40	Bob Kipper	.05	.02
❑ 41	Bill Landrum	.05	.02
❑ 42	Mike LaValliere	.05	.02
❑ 43	Jose Lind	.05	.02
❑ 44	Carmelo Martinez	.05	.02
❑ 45	Bob Patterson	.05	.02
❑ 46	Ted Power	.05	.02
❑ 47	Gary Redus	.05	.02
❑ 48	R.J. Reynolds	.05	.02
❑ 49	Don Slaught	.05	.02
❑ 50	John Smiley	.05	.02
❑ 51	Zane Smith	.05	.02
❑ 52	Randy Tomlin	.05	.02

❑ 53 Andy Van Slyke .10 .05
❑ 54 Bob Walk .05 .02
❑ 55 Jack Armstrong .05 .02
❑ 56 Todd Benzinger .05 .02
❑ 57 Glenn Braggs .05 .02
❑ 58 Keith Brown .05 .02
❑ 59 Tom Browning .05 .02
❑ 60 Norm Charlton .05 .02
❑ 61 Eric Davis .10 .05
❑ 62 Rob Dibble .05 .02
❑ 63 Bill Doran .05 .02
❑ 64 Mariano Duncan .05 .02
❑ 65 Chris Hammond .05 .02
❑ 66 Billy Hatcher .05 .02
❑ 67 Danny Jackson .05 .02
❑ 68 Barry Larkin .20 .09
❑ 69 Tim Layana .05 .02
(Black line over made in first text line)
❑ 70 Terry Lee .05 .02
❑ 71 Rick Mahler .05 .02
❑ 72 Hal Morris .05 .02
❑ 73 Randy Myers .10 .05
❑ 74 Ron Oester .05 .02
❑ 75 Joe Oliver .05 .02
❑ 76 Paul O'Neill .10 .05
❑ 77 Luis Quinones .05 .02
❑ 78 Jeff Reed .05 .02
❑ 79 Jose Rijo .05 .02
❑ 80 Chris Sabo .05 .02
❑ 81 Scott Scudder .05 .02
❑ 82 Herm Winningham .05 .02
❑ 83 Larry Andersen .05 .02
❑ 84 Marty Barrett .05 .02
❑ 85 Mike Boddicker .05 .02
❑ 86 Wade Boggs .20 .09
❑ 87 Tom Bolton .05 .02
❑ 88 Tom Brunansky .05 .02
❑ 89 Ellis Burks .10 .05
❑ 90 Roger Clemens .40 .18
❑ 91 Scott Cooper .05 .02
❑ 92 John Dopson .05 .02
❑ 93 Dwight Evans .10 .05
❑ 94 Wes Gardner .05 .02
❑ 95 Jeff Gray .05 .02
❑ 96 Mike Greenwell .05 .02
❑ 97 Greg A. Harris .05 .02
❑ 98 Daryl Irvine .05 .02
❑ 99 Dana Kiecker .05 .02
❑ 100 Randy Kutcher .05 .02
❑ 101 Dennis Lamp .05 .02
❑ 102 Mike Marshall .05 .02
❑ 103 John Marzano .05 .02
❑ 104 Rob Murphy .05 .02
❑ 105 Tim Naehring .10 .05
❑ 106 Tony Pena .05 .02
❑ 107 Phil Plantier .05 .02
❑ 108 Carlos Quintana .05 .02
❑ 109 Jeff Reardon .10 .05
❑ 110 Jerry Reed .05 .02
❑ 111 Jody Reed .05 .02
❑ 112 Luis Rivera UER .05 .02
(Born 1/3/84)
❑ 113 Kevin Romine .05 .02
❑ 114 Phil Bradley .05 .02
❑ 115 Ivan Calderon .05 .02
❑ 116 Wayne Edwards .05 .02
❑ 117 Alex Fernandez .10 .05
❑ 118 Carlton Fisk .20 .09
❑ 119 Scott Fletcher .05 .02
❑ 120 Craig Grebeck .05 .02
❑ 121 Ozzie Guillen .05 .02
❑ 122 Greg Hibbard .05 .02
❑ 123 Lance Johnson UER .05 .02
(Born Cincinnati, should be Lincoln Heights)
❑ 124 Barry Jones .05 .02
❑ 125 Ron Karkovice .05 .02
❑ 126 Eric King .05 .02
❑ 127 Steve Lyons .05 .02
❑ 128 Carlos Martinez .05 .02
❑ 129 Jack McDowell UER .05 .02
(Stanford misspelled as Standford on back)
❑ 130 Donn Pall .05 .02
(No dots over any i's in text)
❑ 131 Dan Pasqua .05 .02
❑ 132 Ken Patterson .05 .02
❑ 133 Melido Perez .05 .02
❑ 134 Adam Peterson .05 .02
❑ 135 Scott Radinsky .05 .02
❑ 136 Sammy Sosa 1.00 .45
❑ 137 Bobby Thigpen .05 .02
❑ 138 Frank Thomas 1.00 .45
❑ 139 Robin Ventura .20 .09
❑ 140 Daryl Boston .05 .02
❑ 141 Chuck Carr .05 .02
❑ 142 Mark Carreon .05 .02
❑ 143 David Cone .10 .05
❑ 144 Ron Darling .05 .02
❑ 145 Kevin Elster .05 .02
❑ 146 Sid Fernandez .05 .02
❑ 147 John Franco .10 .05
❑ 148 Dwight Gooden .10 .05
❑ 149 Tom Herr .05 .02
❑ 150 Todd Hundley .20 .09
❑ 151 Gregg Jefferies .05 .02
❑ 152 Howard Johnson .05 .02
❑ 153 Dave Magadan .05 .02
❑ 154 Kevin McReynolds .05 .02
❑ 155 Keith Miller UER .05 .02
(Text says Rochester in '87, stats say Tidewater, mixed up with other Keith Miller)
❑ 156 Bob Ojeda .05 .02
❑ 157 Tom O'Malley .05 .02
❑ 158 Alejandro Pena .05 .02
❑ 159 Darren Reed .05 .02
❑ 160 Mackey Sasser .05 .02
❑ 161 Darryl Strawberry .10 .05
❑ 162 Tim Teufel .05 .02
❑ 163 Kelvin Torve .05 .02
❑ 164 Julio Valera .05 .02
❑ 165 Frank Viola .05 .02
❑ 166 Wally Whitehurst .05 .02
❑ 167 Jim Acker .05 .02
❑ 168 Derek Bell .20 .09
❑ 169 George Bell .05 .02
❑ 170 Willie Blair .05 .02
❑ 171 Pat Borders .05 .02
❑ 172 John Cerutti .05 .02
❑ 173 Junior Felix .05 .02
❑ 174 Tony Fernandez .05 .02
❑ 175 Kelly Gruber UER .05 .02
(Born in Houston, should be Bellaire)
❑ 176 Tom Henke .05 .02
❑ 177 Glenallen Hill .05 .02
❑ 178 Jimmy Key .10 .05
❑ 179 Manny Lee .05 .02
❑ 180 Fred McGriff .20 .09
❑ 181 Rance Mulliniks .05 .02
❑ 182 Greg Myers .05 .02
❑ 183 John Olerud UER .10 .05
(Listed as throwing right, should be left)
❑ 184 Luis Sojo .05 .02
❑ 185 Dave Stieb .10 .05
❑ 186 Todd Stottlemyre .10 .05
❑ 187 Duane Ward .05 .02
❑ 188 David Wells .10 .05
❑ 189 Mark Whiten .05 .02
❑ 190 Ken Williams .05 .02
❑ 191 Frank Wills .05 .02
❑ 192 Mookie Wilson .10 .05
❑ 193 Don Aase .05 .02
❑ 194 Tim Belcher UER .05 .02
(Born Sparta, Ohio, should say Mt. Gilead)
❑ 195 Hubie Brooks .05 .02
❑ 196 Dennis Cook .05 .02
❑ 197 Tim Crews .05 .02
❑ 198 Kal Daniels .05 .02
❑ 199 Kirk Gibson .10 .05
❑ 200 Jim Gott .05 .02
❑ 201 Alfredo Griffin .05 .02
❑ 202 Chris Gwynn .05 .02
❑ 203 Dave Hansen .05 .02
❑ 204 Lenny Harris .05 .02
❑ 205 Mike Hartley .05 .02
❑ 206 Mickey Hatcher .05 .02
❑ 207 Carlos Hernandez .10 .05
❑ 208 Orel Hershiser .10 .05
❑ 209 Jay Howell UER .05 .02
(No 1982 Yankee stats)
❑ 210 Mike Huff .05 .02
❑ 211 Stan Javier .05 .02
❑ 212 Ramon Martinez .10 .05
❑ 213 Mike Morgan .05 .02
❑ 214 Eddie Murray .20 .09
❑ 215 Jim Neidlinger .05 .02
❑ 216 Jose Offerman .05 .02
❑ 217 Jim Poole .05 .02
❑ 218 Juan Samuel .05 .02
❑ 219 Mike Scioscia .05 .02
❑ 220 Ray Searage .05 .02
❑ 221 Mike Sharperson .05 .02
❑ 222 Fernando Valenzuela .10 .05
❑ 223 Jose Vizcaino .05 .02
❑ 224 Mike Aldrete .05 .02
❑ 225 Scott Anderson .05 .02
❑ 226 Dennis Boyd .05 .02
❑ 227 Tim Burke .05 .02
❑ 228 Delino DeShields .10 .05
❑ 229 Mike Fitzgerald .05 .02
❑ 230 Tom Foley .05 .02
❑ 231 Steve Frey .05 .02
❑ 232 Andres Galarraga .20 .09
❑ 233 Mark Gardner .05 .02
❑ 234 Marquis Grissom .20 .09
❑ 235 Kevin Gross .05 .02
(No date given for first Expos win)
❑ 236 Drew Hall .05 .02
❑ 237 Dave Martinez .05 .02
❑ 238 Dennis Martinez .10 .05
❑ 239 Dale Mohorcic .05 .02
❑ 240 Chris Nabholz .05 .02
❑ 241 Otis Nixon .10 .05
❑ 242 Junior Noboa .05 .02
❑ 243 Spike Owen .05 .02
❑ 244 Tim Raines .10 .05
❑ 245 Mel Rojas UER .10 .05
(Stats show 3.60 ERA, bio says 3.19 ERA)
❑ 246 Scott Ruskin .05 .02
❑ 247 Bill Sampen .05 .02
❑ 248 Nelson Santovenia .05 .02
❑ 249 Dave Schmidt .05 .02
❑ 250 Larry Walker .30 .14
❑ 251 Tim Wallach .05 .02
❑ 252 Dave Anderson .05 .02
❑ 253 Kevin Bass .05 .02
❑ 254 Steve Bedrosian .05 .02
❑ 255 Jeff Brantley .05 .02
❑ 256 John Burkett .05 .02
❑ 257 Brett Butler .10 .05
❑ 258 Gary Carter .20 .09
❑ 259 Will Clark .20 .09
❑ 260 Steve Decker .05 .02
❑ 261 Kelly Downs .05 .02
❑ 262 Scott Garrelts .05 .02
❑ 263 Terry Kennedy .05 .02
❑ 264 Mike LaCoss .05 .02
❑ 265 Mark Leonard .05 .02
❑ 266 Greg Litton .05 .02
❑ 267 Kevin Mitchell .05 .02
❑ 268 Randy O'Neal .05 .02
❑ 269 Rick Parker .05 .02
❑ 270 Rick Reuschel .05 .02
❑ 271 Ernest Riles .05 .02
❑ 272 Don Robinson .05 .02
❑ 273 Robby Thompson .05 .02
❑ 274 Mark Thurmond .05 .02
❑ 275 Jose Uribe .05 .02
❑ 276 Matt Williams .20 .09
❑ 277 Trevor Wilson .05 .02
❑ 278 Gerald Alexander .05 .02
❑ 279 Brad Arnsberg .05 .02
❑ 280 Kevin Belcher .05 .02
❑ 281 Joe Bitker .05 .02
❑ 282 Kevin Brown .15 .07
❑ 283 Steve Buechele .05 .02
❑ 284 Jack Daugherty .05 .02

❑ 285 Julio Franco .05 .02
❑ 286 Juan Gonzalez .75 .35
❑ 287 Bill Haselman .05 .02
❑ 288 Charlie Hough .10 .05
❑ 289 Jeff Huson .05 .02
❑ 290 Pete Incaviglia .05 .02
❑ 291 Mike Jeffcoat .05 .02
❑ 292 Jeff Kunkel .05 .02
❑ 293 Gary Mielke .05 .02
❑ 294 Jamie Moyer .05 .02
❑ 295 Rafael Palmeiro .20 .09
❑ 296 Geno Petralli .05 .02
❑ 297 Gary Pettis .05 .02
❑ 298 Kevin Reimer .05 .02
❑ 299 Kenny Rogers .05 .02
❑ 300 Jeff Russell .05 .02
❑ 301 John Russell .05 .02
❑ 302 Nolan Ryan .75 .35
❑ 303 Ruben Sierra .05 .02
❑ 304 Bobby Witt .05 .02
❑ 305 Jim Abbott UER .10 .05
(Text on back states he won Sullivan Award (outstanding amateur athlete) in 1989;should be '88)
❑ 306 Kent Anderson .05 .02
❑ 307 Dante Bichette .20 .09
❑ 308 Bert Blyleven .10 .05
❑ 309 Chili Davis .10 .05
❑ 310 Brian Downing .05 .02
❑ 311 Mark Eichhorn .05 .02
❑ 312 Mike Fetters .05 .02
❑ 313 Chuck Finley .10 .05
❑ 314 Willie Fraser .05 .02
❑ 315 Bryan Harvey .05 .02
❑ 316 Donnie Hill .05 .02
❑ 317 Wally Joyner .10 .05
❑ 318 Mark Langston .05 .02
❑ 319 Kirk McCaskill .05 .02
❑ 320 John Orton .05 .02
❑ 321 Lance Parrish .05 .02
❑ 322 Luis Polonia UER .05 .02
(1984 Madfison, should be Madison)
❑ 323 Johnny Ray .05 .02
❑ 324 Bobby Rose .05 .02
❑ 325 Dick Schofield .05 .02
❑ 326 Rick Schu .05 .02
❑ 327 Lee Stevens .05 .02
❑ 328 Devon White .05 .02
❑ 329 Dave Winfield .20 .09
❑ 330 Cliff Young .05 .02
❑ 331 Dave Bergman .05 .02
❑ 332 Phil Clark .05 .02
❑ 333 Darnell Coles .05 .02
❑ 334 Milt Cuyler .05 .02
❑ 335 Cecil Fielder .10 .05
❑ 336 Travis Fryman .20 .09
❑ 337 Paul Gibson .05 .02
❑ 338 Jerry Don Gleaton .05 .02
❑ 339 Mike Heath .05 .02
❑ 340 Mike Henneman .05 .02
❑ 341 Chet Lemon .05 .02
❑ 342 Lance McCullers .05 .02
❑ 343 Jack Morris .10 .05
❑ 344 Lloyd Moseby .05 .02
❑ 345 Edwin Nunez .05 .02
❑ 346 Clay Parker .05 .02
❑ 347 Dan Petry .05 .02
❑ 348 Tony Phillips .05 .02
❑ 349 Jeff M. Robinson .05 .02
❑ 350 Mark Salas .05 .02
❑ 351 Mike Schwabe .05 .02
❑ 352 Larry Sheets .05 .02
❑ 353 John Shelby .05 .02
❑ 354 Frank Tanana .05 .02
❑ 355 Alan Trammell .15 .07
❑ 356 Gary Ward .05 .02
❑ 357 Lou Whitaker .10 .05
❑ 358 Beau Allred .05 .02
❑ 359 Sandy Alomar Jr. .10 .05
❑ 360 Carlos Baerga .10 .05
❑ 361 Kevin Bearse .05 .02
❑ 362 Tom Brookens .05 .02
❑ 363 Jerry Browne UER .05 .02
(No dot over i in first text line)
❑ 364 Tom Candiotti .05 .02
❑ 365 Alex Cole .05 .02
❑ 366 John Farrell UER .05 .02
(Born in Neptune, should be Monmouth)
❑ 367 Felix Fermin .05 .02
❑ 368 Keith Hernandez .10 .05
❑ 369 Brook Jacoby .05 .02
❑ 370 Chris James .05 .02
❑ 371 Dion James .05 .02
❑ 372 Doug Jones .05 .02
❑ 373 Candy Maldonado .05 .02
❑ 374 Steve Olin .05 .02
❑ 375 Jesse Orosco .05 .02
❑ 376 Rudy Seanez .05 .02
❑ 377 Joel Skinner .05 .02
❑ 378 Cory Snyder .05 .02
❑ 379 Greg Swindell .05 .02
❑ 380 Sergio Valdez .05 .02
❑ 381 Mike Walker .05 .02
❑ 382 Colby Ward .05 .02
❑ 383 Turner Ward .05 .02
❑ 384 Mitch Webster .05 .02
❑ 385 Kevin Wickander .05 .02
❑ 386 Darrel Akerfelds .05 .02
❑ 387 Joe Boever .05 .02
❑ 388 Rod Booker .05 .02
❑ 389 Sil Campusano .05 .02
❑ 390 Don Carman .05 .02
❑ 391 Wes Chamberlain .05 .02
❑ 392 Pat Combs .05 .02
❑ 393 Darren Daulton .10 .05
❑ 394 Jose DeJesus .05 .02
❑ 395A Len Dykstra .10 .05
Name spelled Lenny on back
❑ 395B Len Dykstra .10 .05
Name spelled Len on back
❑ 396 Jason Grimsley .05 .02
❑ 397 Charlie Hayes .05 .02
❑ 398 Von Hayes .05 .02
❑ 399 David Hollins UER .05 .02
(Atl-bats, should say at-bats)
❑ 400 Ken Howell .05 .02
❑ 401 Ricky Jordan .05 .02
❑ 402 John Kruk .10 .05
❑ 403 Steve Lake .05 .02
❑ 404 Chuck Malone .05 .02
❑ 405 Roger McDowell UER .05 .02
(Says Phillies is saves, should say in)
❑ 406 Chuck McElroy .05 .02
❑ 407 Mickey Morandini .05 .02
❑ 408 Terry Mulholland .05 .02
❑ 409 Dale Murphy .20 .09
❑ 410A Randy Ready ERR .05 .02
(No Brewers stats listed for 1983)
❑ 410B Randy Ready COR .05 .02
❑ 411 Bruce Ruffin .05 .02
❑ 412 Dickie Thon .05 .02
❑ 413 Paul Assenmacher .05 .02
❑ 414 Damon Berryhill .05 .02
❑ 415 Mike Bielecki .05 .02
❑ 416 Shawn Boskie .05 .02
❑ 417 Dave Clark .05 .02
❑ 418 Doug Dascenzo .05 .02
❑ 419A Andre Dawson ERR .20 .09
(No stats for 1976)
❑ 419B Andre Dawson COR .20 .09
❑ 420 Shawon Dunston .05 .02
❑ 421 Joe Girardi .10 .05
❑ 422 Mark Grace .20 .09
❑ 423 Mike Harkey .05 .02
❑ 424 Les Lancaster .05 .02
❑ 425 Bill Long .05 .02
❑ 426 Greg Maddux .60 .25
❑ 427 Derrick May .05 .02
❑ 428 Jeff Pico .05 .02
❑ 429 Domingo Ramos .05 .02
❑ 430 Luis Salazar .05 .02
❑ 431 Ryne Sandberg .25 .11
❑ 432 Dwight Smith .05 .02
❑ 433 Greg Smith .05 .02
❑ 434 Rick Sutcliffe .05 .02
❑ 435 Gary Varsho .05 .02
❑ 436 Hector Villanueva .05 .02
❑ 437 Jerome Walton .05 .02
❑ 438 Curtis Wilkerson .05 .02
❑ 439 Mitch Williams .05 .02
❑ 440 Steve Wilson .05 .02
❑ 441 Marvell Wynne .05 .02
❑ 442 Scott Bankhead .05 .02
❑ 443 Scott Bradley .05 .02
❑ 444 Greg Briley .05 .02
❑ 445 Mike Brumley UER .05 .02
(Text 40 SB's in 1988, stats say 41)
❑ 446 Jay Buhner .20 .09
❑ 447 Dave Burba .05 .02
❑ 448 Henry Cotto .05 .02
❑ 449 Alvin Davis .05 .02
❑ 450 Ken Griffey Jr. 1.50 .70
(Bat around .300)
❑ 450A Ken Griffey Jr. 1.50 .70
(Bat .300)
❑ 451 Erik Hanson .05 .02
❑ 452 Gene Harris UER .05 .02
(63 career runs, should be 73)
❑ 453 Brian Holman .05 .02
❑ 454 Mike Jackson .10 .05
❑ 455 Randy Johnson .25 .11
❑ 456 Jeffrey Leonard .05 .02
❑ 457 Edgar Martinez .20 .09
❑ 458 Tino Martinez .20 .09
❑ 459 Pete O'Brien UER .05 .02
(1987 BA .266, should be .286)
❑ 460 Harold Reynolds .05 .02
❑ 461 Mike Schooler .05 .02
❑ 462 Bill Swift .05 .02
❑ 463 David Valle .05 .02
❑ 464 Omar Vizquel .20 .09
❑ 465 Matt Young .05 .02
❑ 466 Brady Anderson .20 .09
❑ 467 Jeff Ballard UER .05 .02
(Missing top of right parenthesis after Saberhagen in last text line)
❑ 468 Juan Bell .05 .02
❑ 469A Mike Devereaux .10 .05
(First line of text ends with six)
❑ 469B Mike Devereaux .10 .05
(First line of text ends with runs)
❑ 470 Steve Finley .20 .09
❑ 471 Dave Gallagher .05 .02
❑ 472 Leo Gomez .05 .02
❑ 473 Rene Gonzales .05 .02
❑ 474 Pete Harnisch .05 .02
❑ 475 Kevin Hickey .05 .02
❑ 476 Chris Hoiles .05 .02
❑ 477 Sam Horn .05 .02
❑ 478 Tim Hulett .05 .02
(Photo shows National Leaguer sliding into second base)
❑ 479 Dave Johnson .05 .02
❑ 480 Ron Kittle UER .05 .02
(Edmonton misspelled as Edmundton)
❑ 481 Ben McDonald .05 .02
❑ 482 Bob Melvin .05 .02
❑ 483 Bob Milacki .05 .02
❑ 484 Randy Milligan .05 .02
❑ 485 John Mitchell .05 .02
❑ 486 Gregg Olson .05 .02
❑ 487 Joe Orsulak .05 .02
❑ 488 Joe Price .05 .02
❑ 489 Bill Ripken .05 .02
❑ 490 Cal Ripken .75 .35
❑ 491 Curt Schilling .20 .09
❑ 492 David Segui .10 .05
❑ 493 Anthony Telford .05 .02
❑ 494 Mickey Tettleton .10 .05
❑ 495 Mark Williamson .05 .02
❑ 496 Craig Worthington .05 .02

- ❑ 497 Juan Agosto .05 .02
- ❑ 498 Eric Anthony .05 .02
- ❑ 499 Craig Biggio .20 .09
- ❑ 500 Ken Caminiti UER .20 .09
  (Born 4/4, should be 4/21)
- ❑ 501 Casey Candaele .05 .02
- ❑ 502 Andujar Cedeno .05 .02
- ❑ 503 Danny Darwin .05 .02
- ❑ 504 Mark Davidson .05 .02
- ❑ 505 Glenn Davis .05 .02
- ❑ 506 Jim Deshaies .05 .02
- ❑ 507 Luis Gonzalez .20 .09
- ❑ 508 Bill Gullickson .05 .02
- ❑ 509 Xavier Hernandez .05 .02
- ❑ 510 Brian Meyer .05 .02
- ❑ 511 Ken Oberkfell .05 .02
- ❑ 512 Mark Portugal .05 .02
- ❑ 513 Rafael Ramirez .05 .02
- ❑ 514 Karl Rhodes .05 .02
- ❑ 515 Mike Scott .05 .02
- ❑ 516 Mike Simms .05 .02
- ❑ 517 Dave Smith .05 .02
- ❑ 518 Franklin Stubbs .05 .02
- ❑ 519 Glenn Wilson .05 .02
- ❑ 520 Eric Yelding UER .05 .02
  (Text has 63 steals, stats have 64, which is correct)
- ❑ 521 Gerald Young .05 .02
- ❑ 522 Shawn Abner .05 .02
- ❑ 523 Roberto Alomar .20 .09
- ❑ 524 Andy Benes .10 .05
- ❑ 525 Joe Carter .10 .05
- ❑ 526 Jack Clark .10 .05
- ❑ 527 Joey Cora .10 .05
- ❑ 528 Paul Faries .05 .02
- ❑ 529 Tony Gwynn .50 .23
- ❑ 530 Atlee Hammaker .05 .02
- ❑ 531 Greg W. Harris .05 .02
- ❑ 532 Thomas Howard .05 .02
- ❑ 533 Bruce Hurst .05 .02
- ❑ 534 Craig Lefferts .05 .02
- ❑ 535 Derek Lilliquist .05 .02
- ❑ 536 Fred Lynn .05 .02
- ❑ 537 Mike Pagliarulo .05 .02
- ❑ 538 Mark Parent .05 .02
- ❑ 539 Dennis Rasmussen .05 .02
- ❑ 540 Bip Roberts .05 .02
- ❑ 541 Richard Rodriguez .05 .02
- ❑ 542 Benito Santiago .05 .02
- ❑ 543 Calvin Schiraldi .05 .02
- ❑ 544 Eric Show .05 .02
- ❑ 545 Phil Stephenson .05 .02
- ❑ 546 Garry Templeton UER .05 .02
  (Born 3/24/57, should be 3/24/56)
- ❑ 547 Ed Whitson .05 .02
- ❑ 548 Eddie Williams .05 .02
- ❑ 549 Kevin Appier .10 .05
- ❑ 550 Luis Aquino .05 .02
- ❑ 551 Bob Boone .10 .05
- ❑ 552 George Brett .40 .18
- ❑ 553 Jeff Conine .25 .11
- ❑ 554 Steve Crawford .05 .02
- ❑ 555 Mark Davis .05 .02
- ❑ 556 Storm Davis .05 .02
- ❑ 557 Jim Eisenreich .05 .02
- ❑ 558 Steve Farr .05 .02
- ❑ 559 Tom Gordon .10 .05
- ❑ 560 Mark Gubicza .05 .02
- ❑ 561 Bo Jackson .10 .05
- ❑ 562 Mike Macfarlane .05 .02
- ❑ 563 Brian McRae .20 .09
- ❑ 564 Jeff Montgomery .10 .05
- ❑ 565 Bill Pecota .05 .02
- ❑ 566 Gerald Perry .05 .02
- ❑ 567 Bret Saberhagen .10 .05
- ❑ 568 Jeff Schulz .05 .02
- ❑ 569 Kevin Seitzer .05 .02
- ❑ 570 Terry Shumpert .05 .02
- ❑ 571 Kurt Stillwell .05 .02
- ❑ 572 Danny Tartabull .05 .02
- ❑ 573 Gary Thurman .05 .02
- ❑ 574 Frank White .10 .05
- ❑ 575 Willie Wilson .05 .02
- ❑ 576 Chris Bosio .05 .02
- ❑ 577 Greg Brock .05 .02
- ❑ 578 George Canale .05 .02
- ❑ 579 Chuck Crim .05 .02
- ❑ 580 Rob Deer .05 .02
- ❑ 581 Edgar Diaz .05 .02
- ❑ 582 Tom Edens .05 .02
- ❑ 583 Mike Felder .05 .02
- ❑ 584 Jim Gantner .05 .02
- ❑ 585 Darryl Hamilton .05 .02
- ❑ 586 Ted Higuera .05 .02
- ❑ 587 Mark Knudson .05 .02
- ❑ 588 Bill Krueger .05 .02
- ❑ 589 Tim McIntosh .05 .02
- ❑ 590 Paul Mirabella .05 .02
- ❑ 591 Paul Molitor .20 .09
- ❑ 592 Jaime Navarro .05 .02
- ❑ 593 Dave Parker .10 .05
- ❑ 594 Dan Plesac .05 .02
- ❑ 595 Ron Robinson .05 .02
- ❑ 596 Gary Sheffield .20 .09
- ❑ 597 Bill Spiers .05 .02
- ❑ 598 B.J. Surhoff .10 .05
- ❑ 599 Greg Vaughn .20 .09
- ❑ 600 Randy Veres .05 .02
- ❑ 601 Robin Yount .20 .09
- ❑ 602 Rick Aguilera .10 .05
- ❑ 603 Allan Anderson .05 .02
- ❑ 604 Juan Berenguer .05 .02
- ❑ 605 Randy Bush .05 .02
- ❑ 606 Carmen Castillo .05 .02
- ❑ 607 Tim Drummond .05 .02
- ❑ 608 Scott Erickson .10 .05
- ❑ 609 Gary Gaetti .10 .05
- ❑ 610 Greg Gagne .05 .02
- ❑ 611 Dan Gladden .05 .02
- ❑ 612 Mark Guthrie .05 .02
- ❑ 613 Brian Harper .05 .02
- ❑ 614 Kent Hrbek .10 .05
- ❑ 615 Gene Larkin .05 .02
- ❑ 616 Terry Leach .05 .02
- ❑ 617 Nelson Liriano .05 .02
- ❑ 618 Shane Mack .05 .02
- ❑ 619 John Moses .05 .02
- ❑ 620 Pedro Munoz .05 .02
- ❑ 621 Al Newman .05 .02
- ❑ 622 Junior Ortiz .05 .02
- ❑ 623 Kirby Puckett .30 .14
- ❑ 624 Roy Smith .05 .02
- ❑ 625 Kevin Tapani .05 .02
- ❑ 626 Gary Wayne .05 .02
- ❑ 627 David West .05 .02
- ❑ 628 Cris Carpenter .05 .02
- ❑ 629 Vince Coleman .05 .02
- ❑ 630 Ken Dayley .05 .02
- ❑ 631A Jose DeLeon ERR .05 .02
  (missing '79 Bradenton stats)
- ❑ 631B Jose DeLeon COR .05 .02
  (with '79 Bradenton stats)
- ❑ 632 Frank DiPino .05 .02
- ❑ 633 Bernard Gilkey .10 .05
- ❑ 634A Pedro Guerrero ERR .15 .07
  (career SB shown as "$91")
- ❑ 634B Pedro Guerrero COR .10 .05
- ❑ 635 Ken Hill .10 .05
- ❑ 636 Felix Jose .05 .02
- ❑ 637 Ray Lankford .20 .09
- ❑ 638 Joe Magrane .05 .02
- ❑ 639 Tom Niedenfuer .05 .02
- ❑ 640 Jose Oquendo .05 .02
- ❑ 641 Tom Pagnozzi .05 .02
- ❑ 642 Terry Pendleton .10 .05
- ❑ 643 Mike Perez .05 .02
- ❑ 644 Bryn Smith .05 .02
- ❑ 645 Lee Smith .10 .05
- ❑ 646 Ozzie Smith .25 .11
- ❑ 647 Scott Terry .05 .02
- ❑ 648 Bob Tewksbury .05 .02
- ❑ 649 Milt Thompson .05 .02
- ❑ 650 John Tudor .05 .02
- ❑ 651 Denny Walling .05 .02
- ❑ 652 Craig Wilson .05 .02
- ❑ 653 Todd Worrell .05 .02
- ❑ 654 Todd Zeile .10 .05
- ❑ 655 Oscar Azocar .05 .02
- ❑ 656 Steve Balboni UER .05 .02
  (Born 1/5/57, should be 1/16)
- ❑ 657 Jesse Barfield .05 .02
- ❑ 658 Greg Cadaret .05 .02
- ❑ 659 Chuck Cary .05 .02
- ❑ 660 Rick Cerone .05 .02
- ❑ 661 Dave Eiland .05 .02
- ❑ 662 Alvaro Espinoza .05 .02
- ❑ 663 Bob Geren .05 .02
- ❑ 664 Lee Guetterman .05 .02
- ❑ 665 Mel Hall .05 .02
- ❑ 666 Andy Hawkins .05 .02
- ❑ 667 Jimmy Jones .05 .02
- ❑ 668 Roberto Kelly .05 .02
- ❑ 669 Dave LaPoint UER .05 .02
  (No '81 Brewers stats, totals also are wrong)
- ❑ 670 Tim Leary .05 .02
- ❑ 671 Jim Leyritz .10 .05
- ❑ 672 Kevin Maas .05 .02
- ❑ 673 Don Mattingly .30 .14
- ❑ 674 Matt Nokes .05 .02
- ❑ 675 Pascual Perez .05 .02
- ❑ 676 Eric Plunk .05 .02
- ❑ 677 Dave Righetti .05 .02
- ❑ 678 Jeff D. Robinson .05 .02
- ❑ 679 Steve Sax .05 .02
- ❑ 680 Mike Witt .05 .02
- ❑ 681 Steve Avery UER .05 .02
  (Born in New Jersey, should say Michigan)
- ❑ 682 Mike Bell .05 .02
- ❑ 683 Jeff Blauser .05 .02
- ❑ 684 Francisco Cabrera UER .05 .02
  (Born 10/16, should say 10/10)
- ❑ 685 Tony Castillo .05 .02
- ❑ 686 Marty Clary UER .05 .02
  (Shown pitching righty, but bio has left)
- ❑ 687 Nick Esasky .05 .02
- ❑ 688 Ron Gant .10 .05
- ❑ 689 Tom Glavine .20 .09
- ❑ 690 Mark Grant .05 .02
- ❑ 691 Tommy Gregg .05 .02
- ❑ 692 Dwayne Henry .05 .02
- ❑ 693 Dave Justice .25 .11
- ❑ 694 Jimmy Kremers .05 .02
- ❑ 695 Charlie Leibrandt .05 .02
- ❑ 696 Mark Lemke .05 .02
- ❑ 697 Oddibe McDowell .05 .02
- ❑ 698 Greg Olson .05 .02
- ❑ 699 Jeff Parrett .05 .02
- ❑ 700 Jim Presley .05 .02
- ❑ 701 Victor Rosario .05 .02
- ❑ 702 Lonnie Smith .05 .02
- ❑ 703 Pete Smith .05 .02
- ❑ 704 John Smoltz .20 .09
- ❑ 705 Mike Stanton .05 .02
- ❑ 706 Andres Thomas .05 .02
- ❑ 707 Jeff Treadway .05 .02
- ❑ 708 Jim Vatcher .05 .02
- ❑ 709 Ryne Sandberg .20 .09
  Cecil Fielder
  Home Run Kings
- ❑ 710 Barry Bonds .50 .23
  Ken Griffey Jr.
  2nd Generation Stars
- ❑ 711 Bobby Bonilla .20 .09
  Barry Larkin
  NLCS Team Leaders
- ❑ 712 Bobby Thigpen .05 .02
  John Franco
  Top Game Savers
- ❑ 713 Chicago's 100 Club .10 .05
  Andre Dawson
  Ryne Sandberg UER
  (Ryno misspelled Rhino)
- ❑ 714 CL:A's/Pirates .05 .02
  Reds/Red Sox
- ❑ 715 CL:White Sox/Mets .05 .02
  Blue Jays/Dodgers
- ❑ 716 CL:Expos/Giants .05 .02
  Rangers/Angels

		MINT	NRMT
❑ 717	CL:Tigers/Indians Phillies/Cubs	.05	.02
❑ 718	CL:Mariners/Orioles Astros/Padres	.05	.02
❑ 719	CL:Royals/Brewers Twins/Cardinals	.05	.02
❑ 720	CL:Yankees/Braves Superstars/Specials	.05	.02

1991 Fleer All-Stars

	MINT	NRMT
COMPLETE SET (10)	15.00	6.75
COMMON CARD (1-10)	.50	.23

		MINT	NRMT
❑ 1	Ryne Sandberg	2.00	.90
❑ 2	Barry Larkin	2.50	1.10
❑ 3	Matt Williams	2.50	1.10
❑ 4	Cecil Fielder	1.00	.45
❑ 5	Barry Bonds	2.00	.90
❑ 6	Rickey Henderson	2.50	1.10
❑ 7	Ken Griffey Jr.	12.00	5.50
❑ 8	Jose Canseco	2.50	1.10
❑ 9	Benito Santiago	.50	.23
❑ 10	Roger Clemens	3.00	1.35

1991 Fleer Pro-Visions

	MINT	NRMT
COMPLETE REG.SET (12)	4.00	1.80
COMP.FACT.SET (4)	2.00	.90
COMMON REG.CARD (R1-R12)	.20	.09
COMMON FACT.CARD (F1-F4)	.25	.11

		MINT	NRMT
❑ 1	Kirby Puckett UER (.326 average, should be .328)	1.00	.45
❑ 2	Will Clark UER (On tenth line, pennant misspelled pennent)	.50	.23
❑ 3	Ruben Sierra UER (No apostrophe in hasn't)	.20	.09
❑ 4	Mark McGwire UER (Fisk won ROY in '72, not '82)	3.00	1.35
❑ 5	Bo Jackson (Bio says 6', others have him at 6'1")	.30	.14
❑ 6	Jose Canseco UER (Bio 6'3", 230, text has 6'4", 240)	.50	.23
❑ 7	Dwight Gooden UER (2.80 ERA in Lynchburg, should be 2.50)	.30	.14
❑ 8	Mike Greenwell UER (.328 BA and 87 RBI, should be .325 and 95)	.20	.09
❑ 9	Roger Clemens	1.25	.55
❑ 10	Eric Davis	.30	.14
❑ 11	Don Mattingly	1.00	.45
❑ 12	Darryl Strawberry	.30	.14
❑ F1	Barry Bonds	.75	.35
❑ F2	Rickey Henderson	.50	.23
❑ F3	Ryne Sandberg	.75	.35
❑ F4	Dave Stewart	.25	.11

1991 Fleer Update

	MINT	NRMT
COMP.FACT.SET (132)	4.00	1.80
COMMON CARD (1-132)	.05	.02

		MINT	NRMT
❑ 1	Glenn Davis	.05	.02
❑ 2	Dwight Evans	.10	.05
❑ 3	Jose Mesa	.05	.02
❑ 4	Jack Clark	.10	.05
❑ 5	Danny Darwin	.05	.02
❑ 6	Steve Lyons	.05	.02
❑ 7	Mo Vaughn	.40	.18
❑ 8	Floyd Bannister	.05	.02
❑ 9	Gary Gaetti	.10	.05
❑ 10	Dave Parker	.10	.05
❑ 11	Joey Cora	.10	.05
❑ 12	Charlie Hough	.10	.05
❑ 13	Matt Merullo	.05	.02
❑ 14	Warren Newson	.05	.02
❑ 15	Tim Raines	.10	.05
❑ 16	Albert Belle	.25	.11
❑ 17	Glenallen Hill	.05	.02
❑ 18	Shawn Hillegas	.05	.02
❑ 19	Mark Lewis	.05	.02
❑ 20	Charles Nagy	.20	.09
❑ 21	Mark Whiten	.05	.02
❑ 22	John Cerutti	.05	.02
❑ 23	Rob Deer	.05	.02
❑ 24	Mickey Tettleton	.10	.05
❑ 25	Warren Cromartie	.05	.02
❑ 26	Kirk Gibson	.10	.05
❑ 27	David Howard	.05	.02
❑ 28	Brent Mayne	.05	.02
❑ 29	Dante Bichette	.20	.09
❑ 30	Mark Lee	.05	.02
❑ 31	Julio Machado	.05	.02
❑ 32	Edwin Nunez	.05	.02
❑ 33	Willie Randolph	.10	.05
❑ 34	Franklin Stubbs	.05	.02
❑ 35	Bill Wegman	.05	.02
❑ 36	Chili Davis	.10	.05
❑ 37	Chuck Knoblauch	.25	.11
❑ 38	Scott Leius	.05	.02
❑ 39	Jack Morris	.10	.05
❑ 40	Mike Pagliarulo	.05	.02
❑ 41	Lenny Webster	.05	.02
❑ 42	John Habyan	.05	.02
❑ 43	Steve Howe	.05	.02
❑ 44	Jeff Johnson	.05	.02
❑ 45	Scott Kamieniecki	.05	.02
❑ 46	Pat Kelly	.05	.02
❑ 47	Hensley Meulens	.05	.02
❑ 48	Wade Taylor	.05	.02
❑ 49	Bernie Williams	.30	.14
❑ 50	Kirk Dressendorfer	.05	.02
❑ 51	Ernest Riles	.05	.02
❑ 52	Rich DeLucia	.05	.02
❑ 53	Tracy Jones	.05	.02
❑ 54	Bill Krueger	.05	.02
❑ 55	Alonzo Powell	.05	.02
❑ 56	Jeff Schaefer	.05	.02
❑ 57	Russ Swan	.05	.02
❑ 58	John Barfield	.05	.02
❑ 59	Rich Gossage	.10	.05
❑ 60	Jose Guzman	.05	.02
❑ 61	Dean Palmer	.10	.05
❑ 62	Ivan Rodriguez	1.50	.70
❑ 63	Roberto Alomar	.20	.09
❑ 64	Tom Candiotti	.05	.02
❑ 65	Joe Carter	.10	.05
❑ 66	Ed Sprague	.05	.02
❑ 67	Pat Tabler	.05	.02
❑ 68	Mike Timlin	.05	.02
❑ 69	Devon White	.05	.02
❑ 70	Rafael Belliard	.05	.02
❑ 71	Juan Berenguer	.05	.02
❑ 72	Sid Bream	.05	.02
❑ 73	Marvin Freeman	.05	.02
❑ 74	Kent Mercker	.05	.02
❑ 75	Otis Nixon	.10	.05
❑ 76	Terry Pendleton	.10	.05
❑ 77	George Bell	.05	.02
❑ 78	Danny Jackson	.05	.02
❑ 79	Chuck McElroy	.05	.02
❑ 80	Gary Scott	.05	.02
❑ 81	Heathcliff Slocumb	.20	.09
❑ 82	Dave Smith	.05	.02
❑ 83	Rick Wilkins	.05	.02
❑ 84	Freddie Benavides	.05	.02
❑ 85	Ted Power	.05	.02
❑ 86	Mo Sanford	.05	.02
❑ 87	Jeff Bagwell	2.00	.90
❑ 88	Steve Finley	.20	.09
❑ 89	Pete Harnisch	.05	.02
❑ 90	Darryl Kile	.20	.09
❑ 91	Brett Butler	.10	.05
❑ 92	John Candelaria	.05	.02
❑ 93	Gary Carter	.20	.09
❑ 94	Kevin Gross	.05	.02
❑ 95	Bob Ojeda	.05	.02
❑ 96	Darryl Strawberry	.10	.05
❑ 97	Ivan Calderon	.05	.02
❑ 98	Ron Hassey	.05	.02
❑ 99	Gilberto Reyes	.05	.02
❑ 100	Hubie Brooks	.05	.02
❑ 101	Rick Cerone	.05	.02
❑ 102	Vince Coleman	.05	.02
❑ 103	Jeff Innis	.05	.02
❑ 104	Pete Schourek	.10	.05
❑ 105	Andy Ashby	.25	.11
❑ 106	Wally Backman	.05	.02
❑ 107	Darrin Fletcher	.05	.02
❑ 108	Tommy Greene	.05	.02
❑ 109	John Morris	.05	.02
❑ 110	Mitch Williams	.05	.02
❑ 111	Lloyd McClendon	.05	.02
❑ 112	Orlando Merced	.10	.05
❑ 113	Vicente Palacios	.05	.02
❑ 114	Gary Varsho	.05	.02
❑ 115	John Wehner	.05	.02
❑ 116	Rex Hudler	.05	.02
❑ 117	Tim Jones	.05	.02
❑ 118	Geronimo Pena	.05	.02
❑ 119	Gerald Perry	.05	.02
❑ 120	Larry Andersen	.05	.02
❑ 121	Jerald Clark	.05	.02
❑ 122	Scott Coolbaugh	.05	.02
❑ 123	Tony Fernandez	.05	.02
❑ 124	Darrin Jackson	.05	.02
❑ 125	Fred McGriff	.20	.09
❑ 126	Jose Mota	.05	.02
❑ 127	Tim Teufel	.05	.02
❑ 128	Bud Black	.05	.02
❑ 129	Mike Felder	.05	.02
❑ 130	Willie McGee	.10	.05
❑ 131	Dave Righetti	.05	.02
❑ 132	Checklist U1-U132	.05	.02

1992 Fleer

	MINT	NRMT
COMPLETE SET (720)	10.00	4.50
COMP.HOBBY SET (732)	20.00	9.00
COMP.RETAIL SET (732)	20.00	9.00
COMMON CARD (1-720)	.05	.02
❑ 1 Brady Anderson	.15	.07
❑ 2 Jose Bautista	.05	.02
❑ 3 Juan Bell	.05	.02
❑ 4 Glenn Davis	.05	.02
❑ 5 Mike Devereaux	.05	.02
❑ 6 Dwight Evans	.10	.05
❑ 7 Mike Flanagan	.05	.02
❑ 8 Leo Gomez	.05	.02
❑ 9 Chris Hoiles	.05	.02
❑ 10 Sam Horn	.05	.02
❑ 11 Tim Hulett	.05	.02
❑ 12 Dave Johnson	.05	.02
❑ 13 Chito Martinez	.05	.02
❑ 14 Ben McDonald	.05	.02
❑ 15 Bob Melvin	.05	.02
❑ 16 Luis Mercedes	.05	.02
❑ 17 Jose Mesa	.05	.02
❑ 18 Bob Milacki	.05	.02
❑ 19 Randy Milligan	.05	.02
❑ 20 Mike Mussina UER (Card back refers to him as Jeff)	.30	.14
❑ 21 Gregg Olson	.05	.02
❑ 22 Joe Orsulak	.05	.02
❑ 23 Jim Poole	.05	.02
❑ 24 Arthur Rhodes	.05	.02
❑ 25 Billy Ripken	.05	.02
❑ 26 Cal Ripken	.75	.35
❑ 27 David Segui	.10	.05
❑ 28 Roy Smith	.05	.02
❑ 29 Anthony Telford	.05	.02
❑ 30 Mark Williamson	.05	.02
❑ 31 Craig Worthington	.05	.02
❑ 32 Wade Boggs	.20	.09
❑ 33 Tom Bolton	.05	.02
❑ 34 Tom Brunansky	.05	.02
❑ 35 Ellis Burks	.10	.05
❑ 36 Jack Clark	.10	.05
❑ 37 Roger Clemens	.40	.18
❑ 38 Danny Darwin	.05	.02
❑ 39 Mike Greenwell	.05	.02
❑ 40 Joe Hesketh	.05	.02
❑ 41 Daryl Irvine	.05	.02
❑ 42 Dennis Lamp	.05	.02
❑ 43 Tony Pena	.05	.02
❑ 44 Phil Plantier	.05	.02
❑ 45 Carlos Quintana	.05	.02
❑ 46 Jeff Reardon	.10	.05
❑ 47 Jody Reed	.05	.02
❑ 48 Luis Rivera	.05	.02
❑ 49 Mo Vaughn	.30	.14
❑ 50 Jim Abbott	.10	.05
❑ 51 Kyle Abbott	.05	.02
❑ 52 Ruben Amaro Jr.	.05	.02
❑ 53 Scott Bailes	.05	.02
❑ 54 Chris Beasley	.05	.02
❑ 55 Mark Eichhorn	.05	.02
❑ 56 Mike Fetters	.05	.02
❑ 57 Chuck Finley	.10	.05
❑ 58 Gary Gaetti	.05	.02
❑ 59 Dave Gallagher	.05	.02
❑ 60 Donnie Hill	.05	.02
❑ 61 Bryan Harvey UER (Lee Smith led the Majors with 47 saves)	.05	.02
❑ 62 Wally Joyner	.10	.05
❑ 63 Mark Langston	.05	.02
❑ 64 Kirk McCaskill	.05	.02
❑ 65 John Orton	.05	.02
❑ 66 Lance Parrish	.05	.02
❑ 67 Luis Polonia	.05	.02
❑ 68 Bobby Rose	.05	.02
❑ 69 Dick Schofield	.05	.02
❑ 70 Luis Sojo	.05	.02
❑ 71 Lee Stevens	.05	.02
❑ 72 Dave Winfield	.20	.09
❑ 73 Cliff Young	.05	.02
❑ 74 Wilson Alvarez	.10	.05
❑ 75 Esteban Beltre	.05	.02
❑ 76 Joey Cora	.10	.05
❑ 77 Brian Drahman	.05	.02
❑ 78 Alex Fernandez	.10	.05
❑ 79 Carlton Fisk	.20	.09
❑ 80 Scott Fletcher	.05	.02
❑ 81 Craig Grebeck	.05	.02
❑ 82 Ozzie Guillen	.05	.02
❑ 83 Greg Hibbard	.05	.02
❑ 84 Charlie Hough	.10	.05
❑ 85 Mike Huff	.05	.02
❑ 86 Bo Jackson	.10	.05
❑ 87 Lance Johnson	.05	.02
❑ 88 Ron Karkovice	.05	.02
❑ 89 Jack McDowell	.05	.02
❑ 90 Matt Merullo	.05	.02
❑ 91 Warren Newson	.05	.02
❑ 92 Donn Pall UER (Called Dunn on card back)	.05	.02
❑ 93 Dan Pasqua	.05	.02
❑ 94 Ken Patterson	.05	.02
❑ 95 Melido Perez	.05	.02
❑ 96 Scott Radinsky	.05	.02
❑ 97 Tim Raines	.10	.05
❑ 98 Sammy Sosa	.50	.23
❑ 99 Bobby Thigpen	.05	.02
❑ 100 Frank Thomas	.60	.25
❑ 101 Robin Ventura	.10	.05
❑ 102 Mike Aldrete	.05	.02
❑ 103 Sandy Alomar Jr.	.10	.05
❑ 104 Carlos Baerga	.05	.02
❑ 105 Albert Belle	.25	.11
❑ 106 Willie Blair	.05	.02
❑ 107 Jerry Browne	.05	.02
❑ 108 Alex Cole	.05	.02
❑ 109 Felix Fermin	.05	.02
❑ 110 Glenallen Hill	.05	.02
❑ 111 Shawn Hillegas	.05	.02
❑ 112 Chris James	.05	.02
❑ 113 Reggie Jefferson	.10	.05
❑ 114 Doug Jones	.05	.02
❑ 115 Eric King	.05	.02
❑ 116 Mark Lewis	.05	.02
❑ 117 Carlos Martinez	.05	.02
❑ 118 Charles Nagy UER (Throws right, but card says left)	.10	.05
❑ 119 Rod Nichols	.05	.02
❑ 120 Steve Olin	.05	.02
❑ 121 Jesse Orosco	.05	.02
❑ 122 Rudy Seanez	.05	.02
❑ 123 Joel Skinner	.05	.02
❑ 124 Greg Swindell	.05	.02
❑ 125 Jim Thome	.50	.23
❑ 126 Mark Whiten	.05	.02
❑ 127 Scott Aldred	.05	.02
❑ 128 Andy Allanson	.05	.02
❑ 129 John Cerutti	.05	.02
❑ 130 Milt Cuyler	.05	.02
❑ 131 Mike Dalton	.05	.02
❑ 132 Rob Deer	.05	.02
❑ 133 Cecil Fielder	.10	.05
❑ 134 Travis Fryman	.10	.05
❑ 135 Dan Gakeler	.05	.02
❑ 136 Paul Gibson	.05	.02
❑ 137 Bill Gullickson	.05	.02
❑ 138 Mike Henneman	.05	.02
❑ 139 Pete Incaviglia	.05	.02
❑ 140 Mark Leiter	.05	.02
❑ 141 Scott Livingstone	.05	.02
❑ 142 Lloyd Moseby	.05	.02
❑ 143 Tony Phillips	.05	.02
❑ 144 Mark Salas	.05	.02
❑ 145 Frank Tanana	.05	.02
❑ 146 Walt Terrell	.05	.02
❑ 147 Mickey Tettleton	.05	.02
❑ 148 Alan Trammell	.15	.07
❑ 149 Lou Whitaker	.10	.05
❑ 150 Kevin Appier	.10	.05
❑ 151 Luis Aquino	.05	.02
❑ 152 Todd Benzinger	.05	.02
❑ 153 Mike Boddicker	.05	.02
❑ 154 George Brett	.40	.18
❑ 155 Storm Davis	.05	.02
❑ 156 Jim Eisenreich	.05	.02
❑ 157 Kirk Gibson	.10	.05
❑ 158 Tom Gordon	.10	.05
❑ 159 Mark Gubicza	.05	.02
❑ 160 David Howard	.05	.02
❑ 161 Mike Macfarlane	.05	.02
❑ 162 Brent Mayne	.05	.02
❑ 163 Brian McRae	.10	.05
❑ 164 Jeff Montgomery	.10	.05
❑ 165 Bill Pecota	.05	.02
❑ 166 Harvey Pulliam	.05	.02
❑ 167 Bret Saberhagen	.10	.05
❑ 168 Kevin Seitzer	.05	.02
❑ 169 Terry Shumpert	.05	.02
❑ 170 Kurt Stillwell	.05	.02
❑ 171 Danny Tartabull	.05	.02
❑ 172 Gary Thurman	.05	.02
❑ 173 Dante Bichette	.15	.07
❑ 174 Kevin D. Brown	.05	.02
❑ 175 Chuck Crim	.05	.02
❑ 176 Jim Gantner	.05	.02
❑ 177 Darryl Hamilton	.05	.02
❑ 178 Ted Higuera	.05	.02
❑ 179 Darren Holmes	.05	.02
❑ 180 Mark Lee	.05	.02
❑ 181 Julio Machado	.05	.02
❑ 182 Paul Molitor	.20	.09
❑ 183 Jaime Navarro	.05	.02
❑ 184 Edwin Nunez	.05	.02
❑ 185 Dan Plesac	.05	.02
❑ 186 Willie Randolph	.10	.05
❑ 187 Ron Robinson	.05	.02
❑ 188 Gary Sheffield	.20	.09
❑ 189 Bill Spiers	.05	.02
❑ 190 B.J. Surhoff	.10	.05
❑ 191 Dale Sveum	.05	.02
❑ 192 Greg Vaughn	.10	.05
❑ 193 Bill Wegman	.05	.02
❑ 194 Robin Yount	.20	.09
❑ 195 Rick Aguilera	.10	.05
❑ 196 Allan Anderson	.05	.02
❑ 197 Steve Bedrosian	.05	.02
❑ 198 Randy Bush	.05	.02
❑ 199 Larry Casian	.05	.02
❑ 200 Chili Davis	.10	.05
❑ 201 Scott Erickson	.10	.05
❑ 202 Greg Gagne	.05	.02
❑ 203 Dan Gladden	.05	.02
❑ 204 Brian Harper	.05	.02
❑ 205 Kent Hrbek	.10	.05
❑ 206 Chuck Knoblauch UER (Career hit total of 59 is wrong)	.20	.09
❑ 207 Gene Larkin	.05	.02
❑ 208 Terry Leach	.05	.02
❑ 209 Scott Leius	.05	.02
❑ 210 Shane Mack	.05	.02
❑ 211 Jack Morris	.10	.05
❑ 212 Pedro Munoz	.05	.02
❑ 213 Denny Neagle	.15	.07
❑ 214 Al Newman	.05	.02
❑ 215 Junior Ortiz	.05	.02
❑ 216 Mike Pagliarulo	.05	.02
❑ 217 Kirby Puckett	.30	.14
❑ 218 Paul Sorrento	.05	.02
❑ 219 Kevin Tapani	.05	.02
❑ 220 Lenny Webster	.05	.02

❑ 221 Jesse Barfield	.05	.02
❑ 222 Greg Cadaret	.05	.02
❑ 223 Dave Eiland	.05	.02
❑ 224 Alvaro Espinoza	.05	.02
❑ 225 Steve Farr	.05	.02
❑ 226 Bob Geren	.05	.02
❑ 227 Lee Guetterman	.05	.02
❑ 228 John Habyan	.05	.02
❑ 229 Mel Hall	.05	.02
❑ 230 Steve Howe	.05	.02
❑ 231 Mike Humphreys	.05	.02
❑ 232 Scott Kamieniecki	.05	.02
❑ 233 Pat Kelly	.05	.02
❑ 234 Roberto Kelly	.05	.02
❑ 235 Tim Leary	.05	.02
❑ 236 Kevin Maas	.05	.02
❑ 237 Don Mattingly	.30	.14
❑ 238 Hensley Meulens	.05	.02
❑ 239 Matt Nokes	.05	.02
❑ 240 Pascual Perez	.05	.02
❑ 241 Eric Plunk	.05	.02
❑ 242 John Ramos	.05	.02
❑ 243 Scott Sanderson	.05	.02
❑ 244 Steve Sax	.05	.02
❑ 245 Wade Taylor	.05	.02
❑ 246 Randy Velarde	.05	.02
❑ 247 Bernie Williams	.20	.09
❑ 248 Troy Afenir	.05	.02
❑ 249 Harold Baines	.10	.05
❑ 250 Lance Blankenship	.05	.02
❑ 251 Mike Bordick	.05	.02
❑ 252 Jose Canseco	.20	.09
❑ 253 Steve Chitren	.05	.02
❑ 254 Ron Darling	.05	.02
❑ 255 Dennis Eckersley	.10	.05
❑ 256 Mike Gallego	.05	.02
❑ 257 Dave Henderson	.05	.02
❑ 258 Rickey Henderson UER (Wearing 24 on front and 22 on back)	.20	.09
❑ 259 Rick Honeycutt	.05	.02
❑ 260 Brook Jacoby	.05	.02
❑ 261 Carney Lansford	.10	.05
❑ 262 Mark McGwire	1.00	.45
❑ 263 Mike Moore	.05	.02
❑ 264 Gene Nelson	.05	.02
❑ 265 Jamie Quirk	.05	.02
❑ 266 Joe Slusarski	.05	.02
❑ 267 Terry Steinbach	.10	.05
❑ 268 Dave Stewart	.10	.05
❑ 269 Todd Van Poppel	.05	.02
❑ 270 Walt Weiss	.05	.02
❑ 271 Bob Welch	.05	.02
❑ 272 Curt Young	.05	.02
❑ 273 Scott Bradley	.05	.02
❑ 274 Greg Briley	.05	.02
❑ 275 Jay Buhner	.15	.07
❑ 276 Henry Cotto	.05	.02
❑ 277 Alvin Davis	.05	.02
❑ 278 Rich DeLucia	.05	.02
❑ 279 Ken Griffey Jr.	1.25	.55
❑ 280 Erik Hanson	.05	.02
❑ 281 Brian Holman	.05	.02
❑ 282 Mike Jackson	.10	.05
❑ 283 Randy Johnson	.20	.09
❑ 284 Tracy Jones	.05	.02
❑ 285 Bill Krueger	.05	.02
❑ 286 Edgar Martinez	.15	.07
❑ 287 Tino Martinez	.20	.09
❑ 288 Rob Murphy	.05	.02
❑ 289 Pete O'Brien	.05	.02
❑ 290 Alonzo Powell	.05	.02
❑ 291 Harold Reynolds	.05	.02
❑ 292 Mike Schooler	.05	.02
❑ 293 Russ Swan	.05	.02
❑ 294 Bill Swift	.05	.02
❑ 295 Dave Valle	.05	.02
❑ 296 Omar Vizquel	.10	.05
❑ 297 Gerald Alexander	.05	.02
❑ 298 Brad Arnsberg	.05	.02
❑ 299 Kevin Brown	.15	.07
❑ 300 Jack Daugherty	.05	.02
❑ 301 Mario Diaz	.05	.02
❑ 302 Brian Downing	.05	.02
❑ 303 Julio Franco	.05	.02
❑ 304 Juan Gonzalez	.60	.25
❑ 305 Rich Gossage	.10	.05
❑ 306 Jose Guzman	.05	.02
❑ 307 Jose Hernandez	.05	.02
❑ 308 Jeff Huson	.05	.02
❑ 309 Mike Jeffcoat	.05	.02
❑ 310 Terry Mathews	.05	.02
❑ 311 Rafael Palmeiro	.15	.07
❑ 312 Dean Palmer	.10	.05
❑ 313 Geno Petralli	.05	.02
❑ 314 Gary Pettis	.05	.02
❑ 315 Kevin Reimer	.05	.02
❑ 316 Ivan Rodriguez	.40	.18
❑ 317 Kenny Rogers	.05	.02
❑ 318 Wayne Rosenthal	.05	.02
❑ 319 Jeff Russell	.05	.02
❑ 320 Nolan Ryan	.75	.35
❑ 321 Ruben Sierra	.05	.02
❑ 322 Jim Acker	.05	.02
❑ 323 Roberto Alomar	.20	.09
❑ 324 Derek Bell	.10	.05
❑ 325 Pat Borders	.05	.02
❑ 326 Tom Candiotti	.05	.02
❑ 327 Joe Carter	.10	.05
❑ 328 Rob Ducey	.05	.02
❑ 329 Kelly Gruber	.05	.02
❑ 330 Juan Guzman	.05	.02
❑ 331 Tom Henke	.05	.02
❑ 332 Jimmy Key	.10	.05
❑ 333 Manny Lee	.05	.02
❑ 334 Al Leiter	.10	.05
❑ 335 Bob MacDonald	.05	.02
❑ 336 Candy Maldonado	.05	.02
❑ 337 Rance Mulliniks	.05	.02
❑ 338 Greg Myers	.05	.02
❑ 339 John Olerud UER (1991 BA has .256, but text says .258)	.10	.05
❑ 340 Ed Sprague	.05	.02
❑ 341 Dave Stieb	.05	.02
❑ 342 Todd Stottlemyre	.10	.05
❑ 343 Mike Timlin	.05	.02
❑ 344 Duane Ward	.05	.02
❑ 345 David Wells	.10	.05
❑ 346 Devon White	.05	.02
❑ 347 Mookie Wilson	.10	.05
❑ 348 Eddie Zosky	.05	.02
❑ 349 Steve Avery	.05	.02
❑ 350 Mike Bell	.05	.02
❑ 351 Rafael Belliard	.05	.02
❑ 352 Juan Berenguer	.05	.02
❑ 353 Jeff Blauser	.05	.02
❑ 354 Sid Bream	.05	.02
❑ 355 Francisco Cabrera	.05	.02
❑ 356 Marvin Freeman	.05	.02
❑ 357 Ron Gant	.10	.05
❑ 358 Tom Glavine	.15	.07
❑ 359 Brian Hunter	.05	.02
❑ 360 Dave Justice	.20	.09
❑ 361 Charlie Leibrandt	.05	.02
❑ 362 Mark Lemke	.05	.02
❑ 363 Kent Mercker	.05	.02
❑ 364 Keith Mitchell	.05	.02
❑ 365 Greg Olson	.05	.02
❑ 366 Terry Pendleton	.05	.02
❑ 367 Armando Reynoso	.05	.02
❑ 368 Deion Sanders	.20	.09
❑ 369 Lonnie Smith	.05	.02
❑ 370 Pete Smith	.05	.02
❑ 371 John Smoltz	.15	.07
❑ 372 Mike Stanton	.05	.02
❑ 373 Jeff Treadway	.05	.02
❑ 374 Mark Wohlers	.10	.05
❑ 375 Paul Assenmacher	.05	.02
❑ 376 George Bell	.05	.02
❑ 377 Shawn Boskie	.05	.02
❑ 378 Frank Castillo	.05	.02
❑ 379 Andre Dawson	.15	.07
❑ 380 Shawon Dunston	.05	.02
❑ 381 Mark Grace	.15	.07
❑ 382 Mike Harkey	.05	.02
❑ 383 Danny Jackson	.05	.02
❑ 384 Les Lancaster	.05	.02
❑ 385 Ced Landrum	.05	.02
❑ 386 Greg Maddux	.60	.25
❑ 387 Derrick May	.05	.02
❑ 388 Chuck McElroy	.05	.02
❑ 389 Ryne Sandberg	.25	.11
❑ 390 Heathcliff Slocumb	.05	.02
❑ 391 Dave Smith	.05	.02
❑ 392 Dwight Smith	.05	.02
❑ 393 Rick Sutcliffe	.05	.02
❑ 394 Hector Villanueva	.05	.02
❑ 395 Chico Walker	.05	.02
❑ 396 Jerome Walton	.05	.02
❑ 397 Rick Wilkins	.05	.02
❑ 398 Jack Armstrong	.05	.02
❑ 399 Freddie Benavides	.05	.02
❑ 400 Glenn Braggs	.05	.02
❑ 401 Tom Browning	.05	.02
❑ 402 Norm Charlton	.05	.02
❑ 403 Eric Davis	.10	.05
❑ 404 Rob Dibble	.05	.02
❑ 405 Bill Doran	.05	.02
❑ 406 Mariano Duncan	.05	.02
❑ 407 Kip Gross	.05	.02
❑ 408 Chris Hammond	.05	.02
❑ 409 Billy Hatcher	.05	.02
❑ 410 Chris Jones	.05	.02
❑ 411 Barry Larkin	.15	.07
❑ 412 Hal Morris	.05	.02
❑ 413 Randy Myers	.10	.05
❑ 414 Joe Oliver	.05	.02
❑ 415 Paul O'Neill	.10	.05
❑ 416 Ted Power	.05	.02
❑ 417 Luis Quinones	.05	.02
❑ 418 Jeff Reed	.05	.02
❑ 419 Jose Rijo	.05	.02
❑ 420 Chris Sabo	.05	.02
❑ 421 Reggie Sanders	.05	.02
❑ 422 Scott Scudder	.05	.02
❑ 423 Glenn Sutko	.05	.02
❑ 424 Eric Anthony	.05	.02
❑ 425 Jeff Bagwell	.50	.23
❑ 426 Craig Biggio	.20	.09
❑ 427 Ken Caminiti	.15	.07
❑ 428 Casey Candaele	.05	.02
❑ 429 Mike Capel	.05	.02
❑ 430 Andujar Cedeno	.05	.02
❑ 431 Jim Corsi	.05	.02
❑ 432 Mark Davidson	.05	.02
❑ 433 Steve Finley	.10	.05
❑ 434 Luis Gonzalez	.05	.02
❑ 435 Pete Harnisch	.05	.02
❑ 436 Dwayne Henry	.05	.02
❑ 437 Xavier Hernandez	.05	.02
❑ 438 Jimmy Jones	.05	.02
❑ 439 Darryl Kile	.10	.05
❑ 440 Rob Mallicoat	.05	.02
❑ 441 Andy Mota	.05	.02
❑ 442 Al Osuna	.05	.02
❑ 443 Mark Portugal	.05	.02
❑ 444 Scott Servais	.05	.02
❑ 445 Mike Simms	.05	.02
❑ 446 Gerald Young	.05	.02
❑ 447 Tim Belcher	.05	.02
❑ 448 Brett Butler	.10	.05
❑ 449 John Candelaria	.05	.02
❑ 450 Gary Carter	.20	.09
❑ 451 Dennis Cook	.05	.02
❑ 452 Tim Crews	.05	.02
❑ 453 Kal Daniels	.05	.02
❑ 454 Jim Gott	.05	.02
❑ 455 Alfredo Griffin	.05	.02
❑ 456 Kevin Gross	.05	.02
❑ 457 Chris Gwynn	.05	.02
❑ 458 Lenny Harris	.05	.02
❑ 459 Orel Hershiser	.10	.05
❑ 460 Jay Howell	.05	.02
❑ 461 Stan Javier	.05	.02
❑ 462 Eric Karros	.20	.09
❑ 463 Ramon Martinez UER (Card says bats right, should be left)	.10	.05
❑ 464 Roger McDowell UER (Wins add up to 54, totals have 51)	.05	.02
❑ 465 Mike Morgan	.05	.02
❑ 466 Eddie Murray	.20	.09
❑ 467 Jose Offerman	.05	.02

❑ 468	Bob Ojeda	.05	.02
❑ 469	Juan Samuel	.05	.02
❑ 470	Mike Scioscia	.05	.02
❑ 471	Darryl Strawberry	.10	.05
❑ 472	Bret Barberie	.05	.02
❑ 473	Brian Barnes	.05	.02
❑ 474	Eric Bullock	.05	.02
❑ 475	Ivan Calderon	.05	.02
❑ 476	Delino DeShields	.10	.05
❑ 477	Jeff Fassero	.10	.05
❑ 478	Mike Fitzgerald	.05	.02
❑ 479	Steve Frey	.05	.02
❑ 480	Andres Galarraga	.20	.09
❑ 481	Mark Gardner	.05	.02
❑ 482	Marquis Grissom	.10	.05
❑ 483	Chris Haney	.05	.02
❑ 484	Barry Jones	.05	.02
❑ 485	Dave Martinez	.05	.02
❑ 486	Dennis Martinez	.10	.05
❑ 487	Chris Nabholz	.05	.02
❑ 488	Spike Owen	.05	.02
❑ 489	Gilberto Reyes	.05	.02
❑ 490	Mel Rojas	.05	.02
❑ 491	Scott Ruskin	.05	.02
❑ 492	Bill Sampen	.05	.02
❑ 493	Larry Walker	.20	.09
❑ 494	Tim Wallach	.05	.02
❑ 495	Daryl Boston	.05	.02
❑ 496	Hubie Brooks	.05	.02
❑ 497	Tim Burke	.05	.02
❑ 498	Mark Carreon	.05	.02
❑ 499	Tony Castillo	.05	.02
❑ 500	Vince Coleman	.05	.02
❑ 501	David Cone	.10	.05
❑ 502	Kevin Elster	.05	.02
❑ 503	Sid Fernandez	.05	.02
❑ 504	John Franco	.10	.05
❑ 505	Dwight Gooden	.10	.05
❑ 506	Todd Hundley	.10	.05
❑ 507	Jeff Innis	.05	.02
❑ 508	Gregg Jefferies	.05	.02
❑ 509	Howard Johnson	.05	.02
❑ 510	Dave Magadan	.05	.02
❑ 511	Terry McDaniel	.05	.02
❑ 512	Kevin McReynolds	.05	.02
❑ 513	Keith Miller	.05	.02
❑ 514	Charlie O'Brien	.05	.02
❑ 515	Mackey Sasser	.05	.02
❑ 516	Pete Schourek	.05	.02
❑ 517	Julio Valera	.05	.02
❑ 518	Frank Viola	.05	.02
❑ 519	Wally Whitehurst	.05	.02
❑ 520	Anthony Young	.05	.02
❑ 521	Andy Ashby	.10	.05
❑ 522	Kim Batiste	.05	.02
❑ 523	Joe Boever	.05	.02
❑ 524	Wes Chamberlain	.05	.02
❑ 525	Pat Combs	.05	.02
❑ 526	Danny Cox	.05	.02
❑ 527	Darren Daulton	.10	.05
❑ 528	Jose DeJesus	.05	.02
❑ 529	Len Dykstra	.10	.05
❑ 530	Darrin Fletcher	.05	.02
❑ 531	Tommy Greene	.05	.02
❑ 532	Jason Grimsley	.05	.02
❑ 533	Charlie Hayes	.05	.02
❑ 534	Von Hayes	.05	.02
❑ 535	Dave Hollins	.05	.02
❑ 536	Ricky Jordan	.05	.02
❑ 537	John Kruk	.10	.05
❑ 538	Jim Lindeman	.05	.02
❑ 539	Mickey Morandini	.05	.02
❑ 540	Terry Mulholland	.05	.02
❑ 541	Dale Murphy	.20	.09
❑ 542	Randy Ready	.05	.02
❑ 543	Wally Ritchie UER (Letters in data are cut off on card)	.05	.02
❑ 544	Bruce Ruffin	.05	.02
❑ 545	Steve Searcy	.05	.02
❑ 546	Dickie Thon	.05	.02
❑ 547	Mitch Williams	.05	.02
❑ 548	Stan Belinda	.05	.02
❑ 549	Jay Bell	.10	.05
❑ 550	Barry Bonds	.25	.11
❑ 551	Bobby Bonilla	.10	.05
❑ 552	Steve Buechele	.05	.02
❑ 553	Doug Drabek	.05	.02
❑ 554	Neal Heaton	.05	.02
❑ 555	Jeff King	.10	.05
❑ 556	Bob Kipper	.05	.02
❑ 557	Bill Landrum	.05	.02
❑ 558	Mike LaValliere	.05	.02
❑ 559	Jose Lind	.05	.02
❑ 560	Lloyd McClendon	.05	.02
❑ 561	Orlando Merced	.05	.02
❑ 562	Bob Patterson	.05	.02
❑ 563	Joe Redfield	.05	.02
❑ 564	Gary Redus	.05	.02
❑ 565	Rosario Rodriguez	.05	.02
❑ 566	Don Slaught	.05	.02
❑ 567	John Smiley	.05	.02
❑ 568	Zane Smith	.05	.02
❑ 569	Randy Tomlin	.05	.02
❑ 570	Andy Van Slyke	.10	.05
❑ 571	Gary Varsho	.05	.02
❑ 572	Bob Walk	.05	.02
❑ 573	John Wehner UER (Actually played for Carolina in 1991, not Cards)	.05	.02
❑ 574	Juan Agosto	.05	.02
❑ 575	Cris Carpenter	.05	.02
❑ 576	Jose DeLeon	.05	.02
❑ 577	Rich Gedman	.05	.02
❑ 578	Bernard Gilkey	.10	.05
❑ 579	Pedro Guerrero	.05	.02
❑ 580	Ken Hill	.05	.02
❑ 581	Rex Hudler	.05	.02
❑ 582	Felix Jose	.05	.02
❑ 583	Ray Lankford	.20	.09
❑ 584	Omar Olivares	.05	.02
❑ 585	Jose Oquendo	.05	.02
❑ 586	Tom Pagnozzi	.05	.02
❑ 587	Geronimo Pena	.05	.02
❑ 588	Mike Perez	.05	.02
❑ 589	Gerald Perry	.05	.02
❑ 590	Bryn Smith	.05	.02
❑ 591	Lee Smith	.10	.05
❑ 592	Ozzie Smith	.25	.11
❑ 593	Scott Terry	.05	.02
❑ 594	Bob Tewksbury	.05	.02
❑ 595	Milt Thompson	.05	.02
❑ 596	Todd Zeile	.05	.02
❑ 597	Larry Andersen	.05	.02
❑ 598	Oscar Azocar	.05	.02
❑ 599	Andy Benes	.10	.05
❑ 600	Ricky Bones	.05	.02
❑ 601	Jerald Clark	.05	.02
❑ 602	Pat Clements	.05	.02
❑ 603	Paul Faries	.05	.02
❑ 604	Tony Fernandez	.05	.02
❑ 605	Tony Gwynn	.50	.23
❑ 606	Greg W. Harris	.05	.02
❑ 607	Thomas Howard	.05	.02
❑ 608	Bruce Hurst	.05	.02
❑ 609	Darrin Jackson	.05	.02
❑ 610	Tom Lampkin	.05	.02
❑ 611	Craig Lefferts	.05	.02
❑ 612	Jim Lewis	.05	.02
❑ 613	Mike Maddux	.05	.02
❑ 614	Fred McGriff	.15	.07
❑ 615	Jose Melendez	.05	.02
❑ 616	Jose Mota	.05	.02
❑ 617	Dennis Rasmussen	.05	.02
❑ 618	Bip Roberts	.05	.02
❑ 619	Rich Rodriguez	.05	.02
❑ 620	Benito Santiago	.05	.02
❑ 621	Craig Shipley	.05	.02
❑ 622	Tim Teufel	.05	.02
❑ 623	Kevin Ward	.05	.02
❑ 624	Ed Whitson	.05	.02
❑ 625	Dave Anderson	.05	.02
❑ 626	Kevin Bass	.05	.02
❑ 627	Rod Beck	.20	.09
❑ 628	Bud Black	.05	.02
❑ 629	Jeff Brantley	.05	.02
❑ 630	John Burkett	.05	.02
❑ 631	Will Clark	.20	.09
❑ 632	Royce Clayton	.05	.02
❑ 633	Steve Decker	.05	.02
❑ 634	Kelly Downs	.05	.02
❑ 635	Mike Felder	.05	.02
❑ 636	Scott Garrelts	.05	.02
❑ 637	Eric Gunderson	.05	.02
❑ 638	Bryan Hickerson	.05	.02
❑ 639	Darren Lewis	.05	.02
❑ 640	Greg Litton	.05	.02
❑ 641	Kirt Manwaring	.05	.02
❑ 642	Paul McClellan	.05	.02
❑ 643	Willie McGee	.10	.05
❑ 644	Kevin Mitchell	.10	.05
❑ 645	Francisco Oliveras	.05	.02
❑ 646	Mike Remlinger	.05	.02
❑ 647	Dave Righetti	.05	.02
❑ 648	Robby Thompson	.05	.02
❑ 649	Jose Uribe	.05	.02
❑ 650	Matt Williams	.15	.07
❑ 651	Trevor Wilson	.05	.02
❑ 652	Tom Goodwin MLP UER (Timed in 3.5, should be be timed)	.10	.05
❑ 653	Terry Bross MLP	.05	.02
❑ 654	Mike Christopher MLP	.05	.02
❑ 655	Kenny Lofton MLP	.40	.18
❑ 656	Chris Cron MLP	.05	.02
❑ 657	Willie Banks MLP	.05	.02
❑ 658	Pat Rice MLP	.05	.02
❑ 659A	Rob Maurer MLP ERR (Name misspelled as Mauer on card front)	.75	.35
❑ 659B	Rob Maurer MLP COR	.10	.05
❑ 660	Don Harris MLP	.05	.02
❑ 661	Henry Rodriguez MLP	.20	.09
❑ 662	Cliff Brantley MLP	.05	.02
❑ 663	Mike Linskey MLP UER (220 pounds in data, 200 in text)	.05	.02
❑ 664	Gary DiSarcina MLP	.05	.02
❑ 665	Gil Heredia MLP	.05	.02
❑ 666	Vinny Castilla MLP	2.00	.90
❑ 667	Paul Abbott MLP	.05	.02
❑ 668	Monty Fariss MLP UER (Called Paul on back)	.05	.02
❑ 669	Jarvis Brown MLP	.05	.02
❑ 670	Wayne Kirby MLP	.05	.02
❑ 671	Scott Brosius MLP	.25	.11
❑ 672	Bob Hamelin MLP	.05	.02
❑ 673	Joel Johnston MLP	.05	.02
❑ 674	Tim Spehr MLP	.05	.02
❑ 675A	Jeff Gardner MLP ERR (P on front, should be SS)	.75	.35
❑ 675B	Jeff Gardner MLP COR	.25	.11
❑ 676	Rico Rossy MLP	.05	.02
❑ 677	Roberto Hernandez MLP	.10	.05
❑ 678	Ted Wood MLP	.05	.02
❑ 679	Cal Eldred MLP	.05	.02
❑ 680	Sean Berry MLP	.05	.02
❑ 681	Rickey Henderson RS	.10	.05
❑ 682	Nolan Ryan RS	.40	.18
❑ 683	Dennis Martinez RS	.05	.02
❑ 684	Wilson Alvarez RS	.05	.02
❑ 685	Joe Carter RS	.05	.02
❑ 686	Dave Winfield RS	.10	.05
❑ 687	David Cone RS	.05	.02
❑ 688	Jose Canseco LL UER (Text on back has 42 stolen bases in '88; should be 40)	.10	.05
❑ 689	Howard Johnson LL	.05	.02
❑ 690	Julio Franco LL	.05	.02
❑ 691	Terry Pendleton LL	.05	.02
❑ 692	Cecil Fielder LL	.05	.02
❑ 693	Scott Erickson LL	.05	.02
❑ 694	Tom Glavine LL	.10	.05
❑ 695	Dennis Martinez LL	.05	.02
❑ 696	Bryan Harvey LL	.05	.02
❑ 697	Lee Smith LL	.05	.02
❑ 698	Super Siblings: Roberto Alomar, Sandy Alomar Jr.	.10	.05
❑ 699	The Indispensables: Bobby Bonilla, Will Clark	.10	.05
❑ 700	Teamwork: Mark Wohlers	.05	.02

		MINT	NRMT
	Kent Mercker Alejandro Pena		
❑ 701	Tiger Tandems Stacy Jones Bo Jackson Gregg Olson Frank Thomas	.40	.18
❑ 702	The Ignitors Paul Molitor Brett Butler	.20	.09
❑ 703	Indispensables II Cal Ripken Joe Carter	.40	.18
❑ 704	Power Packs Barry Larkin Kirby Puckett	.20	.09
❑ 705	Today and Tomorrow Mo Vaughn Cecil Fielder	.20	.09
❑ 706	Teenage Sensations Ramon Martinez Ozzie Guillen	.10	.05
❑ 707	Designated Hitters Harold Baines Wade Boggs	.15	.07
❑ 708	Robin Yount PV	.10	.05
❑ 709	Ken Griffey Jr. PV UER (Missing quotations on back; BA has .322, but was actually .327)	.60	.25
❑ 710	Nolan Ryan PV	.40	.18
❑ 711	Cal Ripken PV	.20	.09
❑ 712	Frank Thomas PV	.40	.18
❑ 713	Dave Justice PV	.10	.05
❑ 714	Checklist 1-101	.05	.02
❑ 715	Checklist 102-194	.05	.02
❑ 716	Checklist 195-296	.05	.02
❑ 717	Checklist 297-397	.05	.02
❑ 718	Checklist 398-494	.05	.02
❑ 719	Checklist 495-596	.05	.02
❑ 720A	Checklist 597-720 ERR (659 Rob Mauer)	.05	.02
❑ 720B	Checklist 597-720 COR (659 Rob Maurer)	.05	.02

1992 Fleer All-Stars

	MINT	NRMT
COMPLETE SET (24)	35.00	16.00
COMMON CARD (1-24)	.50	.23
❑ 1 Felix Jose	.50	.23
❑ 2 Tony Gwynn	4.00	1.80
❑ 3 Barry Bonds	2.00	.90
❑ 4 Bobby Bonilla	1.00	.45
❑ 5 Mike LaValliere	.50	.23
❑ 6 Tom Glavine	1.50	.70
❑ 7 Ramon Martinez	1.00	.45
❑ 8 Lee Smith	1.00	.45
❑ 9 Mickey Tettleton	.50	.23
❑ 10 Scott Erickson	1.00	.45
❑ 11 Frank Thomas	5.00	2.20
❑ 12 Danny Tartabull	.50	.23
❑ 13 Will Clark	2.00	.90
❑ 14 Ryne Sandberg	1.50	.70
❑ 15 Terry Pendleton	.50	.23
❑ 16 Barry Larkin	1.50	.70
❑ 17 Rafael Palmeiro	1.50	.70
❑ 18 Julio Franco	.50	.23
❑ 19 Robin Ventura	1.00	.45
❑ 20 Cal Ripken UER (Candidte; total bases misspelled as based)	6.00	2.70
❑ 21 Joe Carter	1.00	.45
❑ 22 Kirby Puckett	2.50	1.10
❑ 23 Ken Griffey Jr.	10.00	4.50
❑ 24 Jose Canseco	2.00	.90

1992 Fleer Clemens

	MINT	NRMT
COMPLETE SET (12)	10.00	4.50
COMMON CLEMENS (1-12)	1.00	.45
COMMON MAIL-IN (13-15)	1.00	.45
❑ 1 Roger Clemens Quiet Storm	1.00	.45
❑ 2 Roger Clemens Courted By Mets and Twins	1.00	.45
❑ 3 Roger Clemens The Show	1.00	.45
❑ 4 Roger Clemens Rocket Launched	1.00	.45
❑ 5 Roger Clemens Time Of Trial	1.00	.45
❑ 6 Roger Clemens Break Through	1.00	.45
❑ 7 Roger Clemens Play It Again Roger	1.00	.45
❑ 8 Roger Clemens Business As Usual	1.00	.45
❑ 9 Roger Clemens Heeee's Back	1.00	.45
❑ 10 Roger Clemens Blood, Sweat and Tears	1.00	.45
❑ 11 Roger Clemens Prime Of Life	1.00	.45
❑ 12 Roger Clemens Man For Every Season	1.00	.45
❑ 13 Roger Clemens Cooperstown Bound	1.00	.45
❑ 14 Roger Clemens The Heat of the Moment	1.00	.45
❑ 15 Roger Clemens Final Words Q and A with "The Rocket"	1.00	.45
❑ AU0 Roger Clemens AU	80.00	36.00
❑ NNO Roger Clemens Promo with Paul Mullan	6.00	2.70

1992 Fleer Lumber Company

	MINT	NRMT
COMPLETE SET (9)	10.00	4.50
COMMON CARD (L1-L9)	.50	.23
❑ L1 Cecil Fielder	.75	.35
❑ L2 Mickey Tettleton	.50	.23
❑ L3 Darryl Strawberry	.75	.35
❑ L4 Ryne Sandberg	1.50	.70
❑ L5 Jose Canseco	1.50	.70
❑ L6 Matt Williams UER In 17th line, cycle is spelled cyle	1.00	.45
❑ L7 Cal Ripken	6.00	2.70

	MINT	NRMT
❑ L8 Barry Bonds	1.50	.70
❑ L9 Ron Gant	.75	.35

1992 Fleer Rookie Sensations

	MINT	NRMT
COMPLETE SET (20)	50.00	22.00
COMMON CARD (1-20)	1.00	.45
❑ 1 Frank Thomas	20.00	9.00
❑ 2 Todd Van Poppel	1.00	.45
❑ 3 Orlando Merced	1.00	.45
❑ 4 Jeff Bagwell	10.00	4.50
❑ 5 Jeff Fassero	2.00	.90
❑ 6 Darren Lewis	1.00	.45
❑ 7 Milt Cuyler	1.00	.45
❑ 8 Mike Timlin	1.00	.45
❑ 9 Brian McRae	2.00	.90
❑ 10 Chuck Knoblauch	4.00	1.80
❑ 11 Rich DeLucia	1.00	.45
❑ 12 Ivan Rodriguez	8.00	3.60
❑ 13 Juan Guzman	1.00	.45
❑ 14 Steve Chitren	1.00	.45
❑ 15 Mark Wohlers	2.00	.90
❑ 16 Wes Chamberlain	1.00	.45
❑ 17 Ray Lankford	4.00	1.80
❑ 18 Chito Martinez	1.00	.45
❑ 19 Phil Plantier	1.00	.45
❑ 20 Scott Leius UER (Misspelled Lieus on card front)	1.00	.45

1992 Fleer Smoke 'n Heat

	MINT	NRMT
COMPLETE SET (12)	10.00	4.50
COMMON CARD (S1-S12)	.50	.23
❑ S1 Lee Smith	.75	.35
❑ S2 Jack McDowell	.50	.23
❑ S3 David Cone	.75	.35
❑ S4 Roger Clemens	3.00	1.35
❑ S5 Nolan Ryan	6.00	2.70
❑ S6 Scott Erickson	.75	.35
❑ S7 Tom Glavine	1.00	.45
❑ S8 Dwight Gooden	.75	.35
❑ S9 Andy Benes	.75	.35

	MINT	NRMT
❑ S10 Steve Avery	.50	.23
❑ S11 Randy Johnson	1.50	.70
❑ S12 Jim Abbott	.75	.35

1992 Fleer Team Leaders

	MINT	NRMT
COMPLETE SET (20)	40.00	18.00
COMMON CARD (1-20)	1.00	.45
❑ 1 Don Mattingly	5.00	2.20
❑ 2 Howard Johnson	1.00	.45
❑ 3 Chris Sabo UER (Where he it, should be Where he hit)	1.00	.45
❑ 4 Carlton Fisk	4.00	1.80
❑ 5 Kirby Puckett	5.00	2.20
❑ 6 Cecil Fielder	2.00	.90
❑ 7 Tony Gwynn	8.00	3.60
❑ 8 Will Clark	4.00	1.80
❑ 9 Bobby Bonilla	2.00	.90
❑ 10 Len Dykstra	2.00	.90
❑ 11 Tom Glavine	2.50	1.10
❑ 12 Rafael Palmeiro	2.50	1.10
❑ 13 Wade Boggs	4.00	1.80
❑ 14 Joe Carter	2.00	.90
❑ 15 Ken Griffey Jr.	20.00	9.00
❑ 16 Darryl Strawberry	2.00	.90
❑ 17 Cal Ripken	12.00	5.50
❑ 18 Danny Tartabull	1.00	.45
❑ 19 Jose Canseco	4.00	1.80
❑ 20 Andre Dawson	2.50	1.10

1992 Fleer Update

	MINT	NRMT
COMP.FACT.SET (136)	160.00	70.00
COMPLETE SET (132)	150.00	70.00
COMMON CARD (U1-U132)	.25	.11
❑ 1 Todd Frohwirth	.25	.11
❑ 2 Alan Mills	.25	.11
❑ 3 Rick Sutcliffe	.25	.11
❑ 4 John Valentin	2.00	.90
❑ 5 Frank Viola	.25	.11
❑ 6 Bob Zupcic	.25	.11
❑ 7 Mike Butcher	.25	.11
❑ 8 Chad Curtis	2.00	.90
❑ 9 Damion Easley	4.00	1.80
❑ 10 Tim Salmon	15.00	6.75
❑ 11 Julio Valera	.25	.11
❑ 12 George Bell	.25	.11
❑ 13 Roberto Hernandez	.75	.35
❑ 14 Shawn Jeter	.25	.11
❑ 15 Thomas Howard	.25	.11
❑ 16 Jesse Levis	.25	.11
❑ 17 Kenny Lofton	15.00	6.75
❑ 18 Paul Sorrento	.25	.11
❑ 19 Rico Brogna	.75	.35
❑ 20 John Doherty	.25	.11
❑ 21 Dan Gladden	.25	.11
❑ 22 Buddy Groom	.25	.11
❑ 23 Shawn Hare	.25	.11
❑ 24 John Kiely	.25	.11
❑ 25 Kurt Knudsen	.25	.11
❑ 26 Gregg Jefferies	.25	.11
❑ 27 Wally Joyner	.75	.35
❑ 28 Kevin Koslofski	.25	.11
❑ 29 Kevin McReynolds	.25	.11
❑ 30 Rusty Meacham	.25	.11
❑ 31 Keith Miller	.25	.11
❑ 32 Hipolito Pichardo	.25	.11
❑ 33 James Austin	.25	.11
❑ 34 Scott Fletcher	.25	.11
❑ 35 John Jaha	.75	.35
❑ 36 Pat Listach	.25	.11
❑ 37 Dave Nilsson	2.00	.90
❑ 38 Kevin Seitzer	.25	.11
❑ 39 Tom Edens	.25	.11
❑ 40 Pat Mahomes	.25	.11
❑ 41 John Smiley	.25	.11
❑ 42 Charlie Hayes	.25	.11
❑ 43 Sam Militello	.25	.11
❑ 44 Andy Stankiewicz	.25	.11
❑ 45 Danny Tartabull	.25	.11
❑ 46 Bob Wickman	.25	.11
❑ 47 Jerry Browne	.25	.11
❑ 48 Kevin Campbell	.25	.11
❑ 49 Vince Horsman	.25	.11
❑ 50 Troy Neel	.25	.11
❑ 51 Ruben Sierra	.25	.11
❑ 52 Bruce Walton	.25	.11
❑ 53 Willie Wilson	.25	.11
❑ 54 Bret Boone	.75	.35
❑ 55 Dave Fleming	.25	.11
❑ 56 Kevin Mitchell	.75	.35
❑ 57 Jeff Nelson	.25	.11
❑ 58 Shane Turner	.25	.11
❑ 59 Jose Canseco	2.50	1.10
❑ 60 Jeff Frye	.25	.11
❑ 61 Danny Leon	.25	.11
❑ 62 Roger Pavlik	.25	.11
❑ 63 David Cone	.75	.35
❑ 64 Pat Hentgen	4.00	1.80
❑ 65 Randy Knorr	.25	.11
❑ 66 Jack Morris	.75	.35
❑ 67 Dave Winfield	2.00	.90
❑ 68 David Nied	.25	.11
❑ 69 Otis Nixon	.75	.35
❑ 70 Alejandro Pena	.25	.11
❑ 71 Jeff Reardon	.75	.35
❑ 72 Alex Arias	.25	.11
❑ 73 Jim Bullinger	.25	.11
❑ 74 Mike Morgan	.25	.11
❑ 75 Rey Sanchez	.25	.11
❑ 76 Bob Scanlan	.25	.11
❑ 77 Sammy Sosa	15.00	6.75
❑ 78 Scott Bankhead	.25	.11
❑ 79 Tim Belcher	.25	.11
❑ 80 Steve Foster	.25	.11
❑ 81 Willie Greene	2.00	.90
❑ 82 Bip Roberts	.25	.11
❑ 83 Scott Ruskin	.25	.11
❑ 84 Greg Swindell	.25	.11
❑ 85 Juan Guerrero	.25	.11
❑ 86 Butch Henry	.25	.11
❑ 87 Doug Jones	.25	.11
❑ 88 Brian Williams	.25	.11
❑ 89 Tom Candiotti	.25	.11
❑ 90 Eric Davis	.75	.35
❑ 91 Carlos Hernandez	.25	.11
❑ 92 Mike Piazza	100.00	45.00
❑ 93 Mike Sharperson	.25	.11
❑ 94 Eric Young	2.00	.90
❑ 95 Moises Alou	6.00	2.70
❑ 96 Greg Colbrunn	.25	.11
❑ 97 Wil Cordero	.25	.11
❑ 98 Ken Hill	.75	.35
❑ 99 John Vander Wal	.25	.11
❑ 100 John Wetteland	.75	.35
❑ 101 Bobby Bonilla	.75	.35
❑ 102 Eric Hillman	.25	.11
❑ 103 Pat Howell	.25	.11
❑ 104 Jeff Kent	4.00	1.80
❑ 105 Dick Schofield	.25	.11
❑ 106 Ryan Thompson	.25	.11
❑ 107 Chico Walker	.25	.11
❑ 108 Juan Bell	.25	.11
❑ 109 Mariano Duncan	.25	.11
❑ 110 Jeff Grotewold	.25	.11
❑ 111 Ben Rivera	.25	.11
❑ 112 Curt Schilling	4.00	1.80
❑ 113 Victor Cole	.25	.11
❑ 114 Al Martin	.75	.35
❑ 115 Roger Mason	.25	.11
❑ 116 Blas Minor	.25	.11
❑ 117 Tim Wakefield	2.00	.90
❑ 118 Mark Clark	.25	.11
❑ 119 Rheal Cormier	.25	.11
❑ 120 Donovan Osborne	.25	.11
❑ 121 Todd Worrell	.25	.11
❑ 122 Jeremy Hernandez	.25	.11
❑ 123 Randy Myers	.75	.35
❑ 124 Frank Seminara	.25	.11
❑ 125 Gary Sheffield	2.00	.90
❑ 126 Dan Walters	.25	.11
❑ 127 Steve Hosey	.25	.11
❑ 128 Mike Jackson	.75	.35
❑ 129 Jim Pena	.25	.11
❑ 130 Cory Snyder	.25	.11
❑ 131 Bill Swift	.25	.11
❑ 132 Checklist U1-U132	.25	.11

1992 Fleer Update Headliners

	MINT	NRMT
COMPLETE SET (4)	15.00	6.75
COMMON CARD (1-4)	.50	.23
❑ 1 Ken Griffey Jr.	12.00	5.50
❑ 2 Robin Yount	2.00	.90
❑ 3 Jeff Reardon	.50	.23
❑ 4 Cecil Fielder	1.00	.45

1993 Fleer

	MINT	NRMT
COMPLETE SET (720)	40.00	18.00
COMPLETE SERIES 1 (360)	20.00	9.00
COMPLETE SERIES 2 (360)	20.00	9.00
COMMON CARD (1-720)	.10	.05

	No.	Player	MINT	NRMT
❑	1	Steve Avery	.10	.05
❑	2	Sid Bream	.10	.05
❑	3	Ron Gant	.20	.09
❑	4	Tom Glavine	.30	.14
❑	5	Brian Hunter	.10	.05
❑	6	Ryan Klesko	.40	.18
❑	7	Charlie Leibrandt	.10	.05
❑	8	Kent Mercker	.10	.05
❑	9	David Nied	.10	.05
❑	10	Otis Nixon	.10	.05
❑	11	Greg Olson	.10	.05
❑	12	Terry Pendleton	.10	.05
❑	13	Deion Sanders	.30	.14
❑	14	John Smoltz	.20	.09
❑	15	Mike Stanton	.10	.05
❑	16	Mark Wohlers	.10	.05
❑	17	Paul Assenmacher	.10	.05
❑	18	Steve Buechele	.10	.05
❑	19	Shawon Dunston	.10	.05
❑	20	Mark Grace	.30	.14
❑	21	Derrick May	.10	.05
❑	22	Chuck McElroy	.10	.05
❑	23	Mike Morgan	.10	.05
❑	24	Rey Sanchez	.10	.05
❑	25	Ryne Sandberg	.50	.23
❑	26	Bob Scanlan	.10	.05
❑	27	Sammy Sosa	1.00	.45
❑	28	Rick Wilkins	.10	.05
❑	29	Bobby Ayala	.10	.05
❑	30	Tim Belcher	.10	.05
❑	31	Jeff Branson	.10	.05
❑	32	Norm Charlton	.10	.05
❑	33	Steve Foster	.10	.05
❑	34	Willie Greene	.10	.05
❑	35	Chris Hammond	.10	.05
❑	36	Milt Hill	.10	.05
❑	37	Hal Morris	.10	.05
❑	38	Joe Oliver	.10	.05
❑	39	Paul O'Neill	.20	.09
❑	40	Tim Pugh	.10	.05
❑	41	Jose Rijo	.10	.05
❑	42	Bip Roberts	.10	.05
❑	43	Chris Sabo	.10	.05
❑	44	Reggie Sanders	.10	.05
❑	45	Eric Anthony	.10	.05
❑	46	Jeff Bagwell	.60	.25
❑	47	Craig Biggio	.40	.18
❑	48	Joe Boever	.10	.05
❑	49	Casey Candaele	.10	.05
❑	50	Steve Finley	.20	.09
❑	51	Luis Gonzalez	.10	.05
❑	52	Pete Harnisch	.10	.05
❑	53	Xavier Hernandez	.10	.05
❑	54	Doug Jones	.10	.05
❑	55	Eddie Taubensee	.10	.05
❑	56	Brian Williams	.10	.05
❑	57	Pedro Astacio	.10	.05
❑	58	Todd Benzinger	.10	.05
❑	59	Brett Butler	.20	.09
❑	60	Tom Candiotti	.10	.05
❑	61	Lenny Harris	.10	.05
❑	62	Carlos Hernandez	.10	.05
❑	63	Orel Hershiser	.20	.09
❑	64	Eric Karros	.30	.14
❑	65	Ramon Martinez	.20	.09
❑	66	Jose Offerman	.10	.05
❑	67	Mike Scioscia	.10	.05
❑	68	Mike Sharperson	.10	.05
❑	69	Eric Young	.40	.18
❑	70	Moises Alou	.20	.09
❑	71	Ivan Calderon	.10	.05
❑	72	Archi Cianfrocco	.10	.05
❑	73	Wil Cordero	.10	.05
❑	74	Delino DeShields	.20	.09
❑	75	Mark Gardner	.10	.05
❑	76	Ken Hill	.10	.05
❑	77	Tim Laker	.10	.05
❑	78	Chris Nabholz	.10	.05
❑	79	Mel Rojas	.10	.05
❑	80	John Vander Wal UER (Misspelled Vander Wall in letters on back)	.10	.05
❑	81	Larry Walker	.40	.18
❑	82	Tim Wallach	.10	.05
❑	83	John Wetteland	.20	.09
❑	84	Bobby Bonilla	.20	.09
❑	85	Daryl Boston	.10	.05
❑	86	Sid Fernandez	.10	.05
❑	87	Eric Hillman	.10	.05
❑	88	Todd Hundley	.30	.14
❑	89	Howard Johnson	.10	.05
❑	90	Jeff Kent	.20	.09
❑	91	Eddie Murray	.40	.18
❑	92	Bill Pecota	.10	.05
❑	93	Bret Saberhagen	.20	.09
❑	94	Dick Schofield	.10	.05
❑	95	Pete Schourek	.10	.05
❑	96	Anthony Young	.10	.05
❑	97	Ruben Amaro Jr.	.10	.05
❑	98	Juan Bell	.10	.05
❑	99	Wes Chamberlain	.10	.05
❑	100	Darren Daulton	.20	.09
❑	101	Mariano Duncan	.10	.05
❑	102	Mike Hartley	.10	.05
❑	103	Ricky Jordan	.10	.05
❑	104	John Kruk	.20	.09
❑	105	Mickey Morandini	.10	.05
❑	106	Terry Mulholland	.10	.05
❑	107	Ben Rivera	.10	.05
❑	108	Curt Schilling	.20	.09
❑	109	Keith Shepherd	.10	.05
❑	110	Stan Belinda	.10	.05
❑	111	Jay Bell	.20	.09
❑	112	Barry Bonds	.50	.23
❑	113	Jeff King	.20	.09
❑	114	Mike LaValliere	.10	.05
❑	115	Jose Lind	.10	.05
❑	116	Roger Mason	.10	.05
❑	117	Orlando Merced	.10	.05
❑	118	Bob Patterson	.10	.05
❑	119	Don Slaught	.10	.05
❑	120	Zane Smith	.10	.05
❑	121	Randy Tomlin	.10	.05
❑	122	Andy Van Slyke	.20	.09
❑	123	Tim Wakefield	.20	.09
❑	124	Rheal Cormier	.10	.05
❑	125	Bernard Gilkey	.10	.05
❑	126	Felix Jose	.10	.05
❑	127	Ray Lankford	.30	.14
❑	128	Bob McClure	.10	.05
❑	129	Donovan Osborne	.10	.05
❑	130	Tom Pagnozzi	.10	.05
❑	131	Geronimo Pena	.10	.05
❑	132	Mike Perez	.10	.05
❑	133	Lee Smith	.20	.09
❑	134	Bob Tewksbury	.10	.05
❑	135	Todd Worrell	.10	.05
❑	136	Todd Zeile	.10	.05
❑	137	Jerald Clark	.10	.05
❑	138	Tony Gwynn	1.00	.45
❑	139	Greg W. Harris	.10	.05
❑	140	Jeremy Hernandez	.10	.05
❑	141	Darrin Jackson	.10	.05
❑	142	Mike Maddux	.10	.05
❑	143	Fred McGriff	.30	.14
❑	144	Jose Melendez	.10	.05
❑	145	Rich Rodriguez	.10	.05
❑	146	Frank Seminara	.10	.05
❑	147	Gary Sheffield	.40	.18
❑	148	Kurt Stillwell	.10	.05
❑	149	Dan Walters	.10	.05
❑	150	Rod Beck	.20	.09
❑	151	Bud Black	.10	.05
❑	152	Jeff Brantley	.10	.05
❑	153	John Burkett	.10	.05
❑	154	Will Clark	.40	.18
❑	155	Royce Clayton	.10	.05
❑	156	Mike Jackson	.10	.05
❑	157	Darren Lewis	.10	.05
❑	158	Kirt Manwaring	.10	.05
❑	159	Willie McGee	.20	.09
❑	160	Cory Snyder	.10	.05
❑	161	Bill Swift	.10	.05
❑	162	Trevor Wilson	.10	.05
❑	163	Brady Anderson	.30	.14
❑	164	Glenn Davis	.10	.05
❑	165	Mike Devereaux	.10	.05
❑	166	Todd Frohwirth	.10	.05
❑	167	Leo Gomez	.10	.05
❑	168	Chris Hoiles	.10	.05
❑	169	Ben McDonald	.10	.05
❑	170	Randy Milligan	.10	.05
❑	171	Alan Mills	.10	.05
❑	172	Mike Mussina	.40	.18
❑	173	Gregg Olson	.10	.05
❑	174	Arthur Rhodes	.10	.05
❑	175	David Segui	.10	.05
❑	176	Ellis Burks	.20	.09
❑	177	Roger Clemens	.75	.35
❑	178	Scott Cooper	.10	.05
❑	179	Danny Darwin	.10	.05
❑	180	Tony Fossas	.10	.05
❑	181	Paul Quantrill	.10	.05
❑	182	Jody Reed	.10	.05
❑	183	John Valentin	.20	.09
❑	184	Mo Vaughn	.50	.23
❑	185	Frank Viola	.10	.05
❑	186	Bob Zupcic	.10	.05
❑	187	Jim Abbott	.20	.09
❑	188	Gary DiSarcina	.10	.05
❑	189	Damion Easley	.20	.09
❑	190	Junior Felix	.10	.05
❑	191	Chuck Finley	.20	.09
❑	192	Joe Grahe	.10	.05
❑	193	Bryan Harvey	.10	.05
❑	194	Mark Langston	.10	.05
❑	195	John Orton	.10	.05
❑	196	Luis Polonia	.10	.05
❑	197	Tim Salmon	.40	.18
❑	198	Luis Sojo	.10	.05
❑	199	Wilson Alvarez	.20	.09
❑	200	George Bell	.10	.05
❑	201	Alex Fernandez	.20	.09
❑	202	Craig Grebeck	.10	.05
❑	203	Ozzie Guillen	.10	.05
❑	204	Lance Johnson	.10	.05
❑	205	Ron Karkovice	.10	.05
❑	206	Kirk McCaskill	.10	.05
❑	207	Jack McDowell	.10	.05
❑	208	Scott Radinsky	.10	.05
❑	209	Tim Raines	.20	.09
❑	210	Frank Thomas	1.25	.55
❑	211	Robin Ventura	.20	.09
❑	212	Sandy Alomar Jr.	.20	.09
❑	213	Carlos Baerga	.10	.05
❑	214	Dennis Cook	.10	.05
❑	215	Thomas Howard	.10	.05
❑	216	Mark Lewis	.10	.05
❑	217	Derek Lilliquist	.10	.05
❑	218	Kenny Lofton	.40	.18
❑	219	Charles Nagy	.20	.09
❑	220	Steve Olin	.10	.05
❑	221	Paul Sorrento	.10	.05
❑	222	Jim Thome	.75	.35
❑	223	Mark Whiten	.10	.05
❑	224	Milt Cuyler	.10	.05
❑	225	Rob Deer	.10	.05
❑	226	John Doherty	.10	.05
❑	227	Cecil Fielder	.20	.09
❑	228	Travis Fryman	.20	.09
❑	229	Mike Henneman	.10	.05

❑ 230	John Kiely UER	.10	.05
	(Card has batting stats of Pat Kelly)		
❑ 231	Kurt Knudsen	.10	.05
❑ 232	Scott Livingstone	.10	.05
❑ 233	Tony Phillips	.10	.05
❑ 234	Mickey Tettleton	.10	.05
❑ 235	Kevin Appier	.20	.09
❑ 236	George Brett	.75	.35
❑ 237	Tom Gordon	.20	.09
❑ 238	Gregg Jefferies	.10	.05
❑ 239	Wally Joyner	.20	.09
❑ 240	Kevin Koslofski	.10	.05
❑ 241	Mike Macfarlane	.10	.05
❑ 242	Brian McRae	.10	.05
❑ 243	Rusty Meacham	.10	.05
❑ 244	Keith Miller	.10	.05
❑ 245	Jeff Montgomery	.20	.09
❑ 246	Hipolito Pichardo	.10	.05
❑ 247	Ricky Bones	.10	.05
❑ 248	Cal Eldred	.10	.05
❑ 249	Mike Fetters	.10	.05
❑ 250	Darryl Hamilton	.10	.05
❑ 251	Doug Henry	.10	.05
❑ 252	John Jaha	.10	.05
❑ 253	Pat Listach	.10	.05
❑ 254	Paul Molitor	.40	.18
❑ 255	Jaime Navarro	.10	.05
❑ 256	Kevin Seitzer	.10	.05
❑ 257	B.J. Surhoff	.20	.09
❑ 258	Greg Vaughn	.20	.09
❑ 259	Bill Wegman	.10	.05
❑ 260	Robin Yount	.30	.14
❑ 261	Rick Aguilera	.10	.05
❑ 262	Chili Davis	.20	.09
❑ 263	Scott Erickson	.10	.05
❑ 264	Greg Gagne	.10	.05
❑ 265	Mark Guthrie	.10	.05
❑ 266	Brian Harper	.10	.05
❑ 267	Kent Hrbek	.20	.09
❑ 268	Terry Jorgensen	.10	.05
❑ 269	Gene Larkin	.10	.05
❑ 270	Scott Leius	.10	.05
❑ 271	Pat Mahomes	.10	.05
❑ 272	Pedro Munoz	.10	.05
❑ 273	Kirby Puckett	.60	.25
❑ 274	Kevin Tapani	.10	.05
❑ 275	Carl Willis	.10	.05
❑ 276	Steve Farr	.10	.05
❑ 277	John Habyan	.10	.05
❑ 278	Mel Hall	.10	.05
❑ 279	Charlie Hayes	.10	.05
❑ 280	Pat Kelly	.10	.05
❑ 281	Don Mattingly	.60	.25
❑ 282	Sam Militello	.10	.05
❑ 283	Matt Nokes	.10	.05
❑ 284	Melido Perez	.10	.05
❑ 285	Andy Stankiewicz	.10	.05
❑ 286	Danny Tartabull	.10	.05
❑ 287	Randy Velarde	.10	.05
❑ 288	Bob Wickman	.10	.05
❑ 289	Bernie Williams	.40	.18
❑ 290	Lance Blankenship	.10	.05
❑ 291	Mike Bordick	.10	.05
❑ 292	Jerry Browne	.10	.05
❑ 293	Dennis Eckersley	.20	.09
❑ 294	Rickey Henderson	.40	.18
❑ 295	Vince Horsman	.10	.05
❑ 296	Mark McGwire	2.00	.90
❑ 297	Jeff Parrett	.10	.05
❑ 298	Ruben Sierra	.10	.05
❑ 299	Terry Steinbach	.10	.05
❑ 300	Walt Weiss	.10	.05
❑ 301	Bob Welch	.10	.05
❑ 302	Willie Wilson	.10	.05
❑ 303	Bobby Witt	.10	.05
❑ 304	Bret Boone	.20	.09
❑ 305	Jay Buhner	.30	.14
❑ 306	Dave Fleming	.10	.05
❑ 307	Ken Griffey Jr.	2.00	.90
❑ 308	Erik Hanson	.10	.05
❑ 309	Edgar Martinez	.30	.14
❑ 310	Tino Martinez	.40	.18
❑ 311	Jeff Nelson	.10	.05
❑ 312	Dennis Powell	.10	.05

❑ 313	Mike Schooler	.10	.05
❑ 314	Russ Swan	.10	.05
❑ 315	Dave Valle	.10	.05
❑ 316	Omar Vizquel	.20	.09
❑ 317	Kevin Brown	.30	.14
❑ 318	Todd Burns	.10	.05
❑ 319	Jose Canseco	.40	.18
❑ 320	Julio Franco	.10	.05
❑ 321	Jeff Frye	.10	.05
❑ 322	Juan Gonzalez	1.00	.45
❑ 323	Jose Guzman	.10	.05
❑ 324	Jeff Huson	.10	.05
❑ 325	Dean Palmer	.20	.09
❑ 326	Kevin Reimer	.10	.05
❑ 327	Ivan Rodriguez	.50	.23
❑ 328	Kenny Rogers	.10	.05
❑ 329	Dan Smith	.10	.05
❑ 330	Roberto Alomar	.40	.18
❑ 331	Derek Bell	.20	.09
❑ 332	Pat Borders	.10	.05
❑ 333	Joe Carter	.20	.09
❑ 334	Kelly Gruber	.10	.05
❑ 335	Tom Henke	.10	.05
❑ 336	Jimmy Key	.20	.09
❑ 337	Manuel Lee	.10	.05
❑ 338	Candy Maldonado	.10	.05
❑ 339	John Olerud	.30	.14
❑ 340	Todd Stottlemyre	.10	.05
❑ 341	Duane Ward	.10	.05
❑ 342	Devon White	.10	.05
❑ 343	Dave Winfield	.30	.14
❑ 344	Edgar Martinez LL	.20	.09
❑ 345	Cecil Fielder LL	.10	.05
❑ 346	Kenny Lofton LL	.40	.18
❑ 347	Jack Morris LL	.10	.05
❑ 348	Roger Clemens LL	.40	.18
❑ 349	Fred McGriff RT	.20	.09
❑ 350	Barry Bonds RT	.30	.14
❑ 351	Gary Sheffield RT	.20	.09
❑ 352	Darren Daulton RT	.10	.05
❑ 353	Dave Hollins RT	.10	.05
❑ 354	Brothers in Blue	.10	.05
	Pedro Martinez		
	Ramon Martinez		
❑ 355	Power Packs	.50	.23
	Ivan Rodriguez		
	Kirby Puckett		
❑ 356	Triple Threats	1.00	.45
	Ryne Sandberg		
	Gary Sheffield		
❑ 357	Infield Trifecta	.40	.18
	Roberto Alomar		
	Chuck Knoblauch		
	Carlos Baerga		
❑ 358	Checklist 1-120	.10	.05
❑ 359	Checklist 121-240	.10	.05
❑ 360	Checklist 241-360	.10	.05
❑ 361	Rafael Belliard	.10	.05
❑ 362	Damon Berryhill	.10	.05
❑ 363	Mike Bielecki	.10	.05
❑ 364	Jeff Blauser	.10	.05
❑ 365	Francisco Cabrera	.10	.05
❑ 366	Marvin Freeman	.10	.05
❑ 367	David Justice	.40	.18
❑ 368	Mark Lemke	.10	.05
❑ 369	Alejandro Pena	.10	.05
❑ 370	Jeff Reardon	.20	.09
❑ 371	Lonnie Smith	.10	.05
❑ 372	Pete Smith	.10	.05
❑ 373	Shawn Boskie	.10	.05
❑ 374	Jim Bullinger	.10	.05
❑ 375	Frank Castillo	.10	.05
❑ 376	Doug Dascenzo	.10	.05
❑ 377	Andre Dawson	.30	.14
❑ 378	Mike Harkey	.10	.05
❑ 379	Greg Hibbard	.10	.05
❑ 380	Greg Maddux	1.25	.55
❑ 381	Ken Patterson	.10	.05
❑ 382	Jeff D. Robinson	.10	.05
❑ 383	Luis Salazar	.10	.05
❑ 384	Dwight Smith	.10	.05
❑ 385	Jose Vizcaino	.10	.05
❑ 386	Scott Bankhead	.10	.05
❑ 387	Tom Browning	.10	.05
❑ 388	Darnell Coles	.10	.05

❑ 389	Rob Dibble	.10	.05
❑ 390	Bill Doran	.10	.05
❑ 391	Dwayne Henry	.10	.05
❑ 392	Cesar Hernandez	.10	.05
❑ 393	Roberto Kelly	.10	.05
❑ 394	Barry Larkin	.30	.14
❑ 395	Dave Martinez	.10	.05
❑ 396	Kevin Mitchell	.20	.09
❑ 397	Jeff Reed	.10	.05
❑ 398	Scott Ruskin	.10	.05
❑ 399	Greg Swindell	.10	.05
❑ 400	Dan Wilson	.20	.09
❑ 401	Andy Ashby	.20	.09
❑ 402	Freddie Benavides	.10	.05
❑ 403	Dante Bichette	.20	.09
❑ 404	Willie Blair	.10	.05
❑ 405	Denis Boucher	.10	.05
❑ 406	Vinny Castilla	.50	.23
❑ 407	Braulio Castillo	.10	.05
❑ 408	Alex Cole	.10	.05
❑ 409	Andres Galarraga	.40	.18
❑ 410	Joe Girardi	.20	.09
❑ 411	Butch Henry	.10	.05
❑ 412	Darren Holmes	.10	.05
❑ 413	Calvin Jones	.10	.05
❑ 414	Steve Reed	.10	.05
❑ 415	Kevin Ritz	.10	.05
❑ 416	Jim Tatum	.10	.05
❑ 417	Jack Armstrong	.10	.05
❑ 418	Bret Barberie	.10	.05
❑ 419	Ryan Bowen	.10	.05
❑ 420	Cris Carpenter	.10	.05
❑ 421	Chuck Carr	.10	.05
❑ 422	Scott Chiamparino	.10	.05
❑ 423	Jeff Conine	.10	.05
❑ 424	Jim Corsi	.10	.05
❑ 425	Steve Decker	.10	.05
❑ 426	Chris Donnels	.10	.05
❑ 427	Monty Fariss	.10	.05
❑ 428	Bob Natal	.10	.05
❑ 429	Pat Rapp	.10	.05
❑ 430	Dave Weathers	.10	.05
❑ 431	Nigel Wilson	.10	.05
❑ 432	Ken Caminiti	.30	.14
❑ 433	Andujar Cedeno	.10	.05
❑ 434	Tom Edens	.10	.05
❑ 435	Juan Guerrero	.10	.05
❑ 436	Pete Incaviglia	.10	.05
❑ 437	Jimmy Jones	.10	.05
❑ 438	Darryl Kile	.20	.09
❑ 439	Rob Murphy	.10	.05
❑ 440	Al Osuna	.10	.05
❑ 441	Mark Portugal	.10	.05
❑ 442	Scott Servais	.10	.05
❑ 443	John Candelaria	.10	.05
❑ 444	Tim Crews	.10	.05
❑ 445	Eric Davis	.20	.09
❑ 446	Tom Goodwin	.10	.05
❑ 447	Jim Gott	.10	.05
❑ 448	Kevin Gross	.10	.05
❑ 449	Dave Hansen	.10	.05
❑ 450	Jay Howell	.10	.05
❑ 451	Roger McDowell	.10	.05
❑ 452	Bob Ojeda	.10	.05
❑ 453	Henry Rodriguez	.20	.09
❑ 454	Darryl Strawberry	.20	.09
❑ 455	Mitch Webster	.10	.05
❑ 456	Steve Wilson	.10	.05
❑ 457	Brian Barnes	.10	.05
❑ 458	Sean Berry	.10	.05
❑ 459	Jeff Fassero	.10	.05
❑ 460	Darrin Fletcher	.10	.05
❑ 461	Marquis Grissom	.20	.09
❑ 462	Dennis Martinez	.20	.09
❑ 463	Spike Owen	.10	.05
❑ 464	Matt Stairs	.10	.05
❑ 465	Sergio Valdez	.10	.05
❑ 466	Kevin Bass	.10	.05
❑ 467	Vince Coleman	.10	.05
❑ 468	Mark Dewey	.10	.05
❑ 469	Kevin Elster	.10	.05
❑ 470	Tony Fernandez	.10	.05
❑ 471	John Franco	.20	.09
❑ 472	Dave Gallagher	.10	.05
❑ 473	Paul Gibson	.10	.05

❑	474	Dwight Gooden	.20	.09
❑	475	Lee Guetterman	.10	.05
❑	476	Jeff Innis	.10	.05
❑	477	Dave Magadan	.10	.05
❑	478	Charlie O'Brien	.10	.05
❑	479	Willie Randolph	.20	.09
❑	480	Mackey Sasser	.10	.05
❑	481	Ryan Thompson	.10	.05
❑	482	Chico Walker	.10	.05
❑	483	Kyle Abbott	.10	.05
❑	484	Bob Ayrault	.10	.05
❑	485	Kim Batiste	.10	.05
❑	486	Cliff Brantley	.10	.05
❑	487	Jose DeLeon	.10	.05
❑	488	Len Dykstra	.20	.09
❑	489	Tommy Greene	.10	.05
❑	490	Jeff Grotewold	.10	.05
❑	491	Dave Hollins	.10	.05
❑	492	Danny Jackson	.10	.05
❑	493	Stan Javier	.10	.05
❑	494	Tom Marsh	.10	.05
❑	495	Greg Mathews	.10	.05
❑	496	Dale Murphy	.30	.14
❑	497	Todd Pratt	.10	.05
❑	498	Mitch Williams	.10	.05
❑	499	Danny Cox	.10	.05
❑	500	Doug Drabek	.10	.05
❑	501	Carlos Garcia	.10	.05
❑	502	Lloyd McClendon	.10	.05
❑	503	Denny Neagle	.20	.09
❑	504	Gary Redus	.10	.05
❑	505	Bob Walk	.10	.05
❑	506	John Wehner	.10	.05
❑	507	Luis Alicea	.10	.05
❑	508	Mark Clark	.10	.05
❑	509	Pedro Guerrero	.10	.05
❑	510	Rex Hudler	.10	.05
❑	511	Brian Jordan	.20	.09
❑	512	Omar Olivares	.10	.05
❑	513	Jose Oquendo	.10	.05
❑	514	Gerald Perry	.10	.05
❑	515	Bryn Smith	.10	.05
❑	516	Craig Wilson	.10	.05
❑	517	Tracy Woodson	.10	.05
❑	518	Larry Andersen	.10	.05
❑	519	Andy Benes	.20	.09
❑	520	Jim Deshaies	.10	.05
❑	521	Bruce Hurst	.10	.05
❑	522	Randy Myers	.20	.09
❑	523	Benito Santiago	.10	.05
❑	524	Tim Scott	.10	.05
❑	525	Tim Teufel	.10	.05
❑	526	Mike Benjamin	.10	.05
❑	527	Dave Burba	.10	.05
❑	528	Craig Colbert	.10	.05
❑	529	Mike Felder	.10	.05
❑	530	Bryan Hickerson	.10	.05
❑	531	Chris James	.10	.05
❑	532	Mark Leonard	.10	.05
❑	533	Greg Litton	.10	.05
❑	534	Francisco Oliveras	.10	.05
❑	535	John Patterson	.10	.05
❑	536	Jim Pena	.10	.05
❑	537	Dave Righetti	.10	.05
❑	538	Robby Thompson	.10	.05
❑	539	Jose Uribe	.10	.05
❑	540	Matt Williams	.30	.14
❑	541	Storm Davis	.10	.05
❑	542	Sam Horn	.10	.05
❑	543	Tim Hulett	.10	.05
❑	544	Craig Lefferts	.10	.05
❑	545	Chito Martinez	.10	.05
❑	546	Mark McLemore	.10	.05
❑	547	Luis Mercedes	.10	.05
❑	548	Bob Milacki	.10	.05
❑	549	Joe Orsulak	.10	.05
❑	550	Billy Ripken	.10	.05
❑	551	Cal Ripken Jr.	1.50	.70
❑	552	Rick Sutcliffe	.10	.05
❑	553	Jeff Tackett	.10	.05
❑	554	Wade Boggs	.40	.18
❑	555	Tom Brunansky	.10	.05
❑	556	Jack Clark	.10	.05
❑	557	John Dopson	.10	.05
❑	558	Mike Gardiner	.10	.05
❑	559	Mike Greenwell	.10	.05
❑	560	Greg A. Harris	.10	.05
❑	561	Billy Hatcher	.10	.05
❑	562	Joe Hesketh	.10	.05
❑	563	Tony Pena	.10	.05
❑	564	Phil Plantier	.10	.05
❑	565	Luis Rivera	.10	.05
❑	566	Herm Winningham	.10	.05
❑	567	Matt Young	.10	.05
❑	568	Bert Blyleven	.20	.09
❑	569	Mike Butcher	.10	.05
❑	570	Chuck Crim	.10	.05
❑	571	Chad Curtis	.20	.09
❑	572	Tim Fortugno	.10	.05
❑	573	Steve Frey	.10	.05
❑	574	Gary Gaetti	.10	.05
❑	575	Scott Lewis	.10	.05
❑	576	Lee Stevens	.10	.05
❑	577	Ron Tingley	.10	.05
❑	578	Julio Valera	.10	.05
❑	579	Shawn Abner	.10	.05
❑	580	Joey Cora	.20	.09
❑	581	Chris Cron	.10	.05
❑	582	Carlton Fisk	.40	.18
❑	583	Roberto Hernandez	.20	.09
❑	584	Charlie Hough	.20	.09
❑	585	Terry Leach	.10	.05
❑	586	Donn Pall	.10	.05
❑	587	Dan Pasqua	.10	.05
❑	588	Steve Sax	.10	.05
❑	589	Bobby Thigpen	.10	.05
❑	590	Albert Belle	.50	.23
❑	591	Felix Fermin	.10	.05
❑	592	Glenallen Hill	.10	.05
❑	593	Brook Jacoby	.10	.05
❑	594	Reggie Jefferson	.20	.09
❑	595	Carlos Martinez	.10	.05
❑	596	Jose Mesa	.10	.05
❑	597	Rod Nichols	.10	.05
❑	598	Junior Ortiz	.10	.05
❑	599	Eric Plunk	.10	.05
❑	600	Ted Power	.10	.05
❑	601	Scott Scudder	.10	.05
❑	602	Kevin Wickander	.10	.05
❑	603	Skeeter Barnes	.10	.05
❑	604	Mark Carreon	.10	.05
❑	605	Dan Gladden	.10	.05
❑	606	Bill Gullickson	.10	.05
❑	607	Chad Kreuter	.10	.05
❑	608	Mark Leiter	.10	.05
❑	609	Mike Munoz	.10	.05
❑	610	Rich Rowland	.10	.05
❑	611	Frank Tanana	.10	.05
❑	612	Walt Terrell	.10	.05
❑	613	Alan Trammell	.30	.14
❑	614	Lou Whitaker	.20	.09
❑	615	Luis Aquino	.10	.05
❑	616	Mike Boddicker	.10	.05
❑	617	Jim Eisenreich	.10	.05
❑	618	Mark Gubicza	.10	.05
❑	619	David Howard	.10	.05
❑	620	Mike Magnante	.10	.05
❑	621	Brent Mayne	.10	.05
❑	622	Kevin McReynolds	.10	.05
❑	623	Ed Pierce	.10	.05
❑	624	Bill Sampen	.10	.05
❑	625	Steve Shifflett	.10	.05
❑	626	Gary Thurman	.10	.05
❑	627	Curtis Wilkerson	.10	.05
❑	628	Chris Bosio	.10	.05
❑	629	Scott Fletcher	.10	.05
❑	630	Jim Gantner	.10	.05
❑	631	Dave Nilsson	.20	.09
❑	632	Jesse Orosco	.10	.05
❑	633	Dan Plesac	.10	.05
❑	634	Ron Robinson	.10	.05
❑	635	Bill Spiers	.10	.05
❑	636	Franklin Stubbs	.10	.05
❑	637	Willie Banks	.10	.05
❑	638	Randy Bush	.10	.05
❑	639	Chuck Knoblauch	.40	.18
❑	640	Shane Mack	.10	.05
❑	641	Mike Pagliarulo	.10	.05
❑	642	Jeff Reboulet	.10	.05
❑	643	John Smiley	.10	.05
❑	644	Mike Trombley	.10	.05
❑	645	Gary Wayne	.10	.05
❑	646	Lenny Webster	.10	.05
❑	647	Tim Burke	.10	.05
❑	648	Mike Gallego	.10	.05
❑	649	Dion James	.10	.05
❑	650	Jeff Johnson	.10	.05
❑	651	Scott Kamieniecki	.10	.05
❑	652	Kevin Maas	.10	.05
❑	653	Rich Monteleone	.10	.05
❑	654	Jerry Nielsen	.10	.05
❑	655	Scott Sanderson	.10	.05
❑	656	Mike Stanley	.10	.05
❑	657	Gerald Williams	.10	.05
❑	658	Curt Young	.10	.05
❑	659	Harold Baines	.20	.09
❑	660	Kevin Campbell	.10	.05
❑	661	Ron Darling	.10	.05
❑	662	Kelly Downs	.10	.05
❑	663	Eric Fox	.10	.05
❑	664	Dave Henderson	.10	.05
❑	665	Rick Honeycutt	.10	.05
❑	666	Mike Moore	.10	.05
❑	667	Jamie Quirk	.10	.05
❑	668	Jeff Russell	.10	.05
❑	669	Dave Stewart	.20	.09
❑	670	Greg Briley	.10	.05
❑	671	Dave Cochrane	.10	.05
❑	672	Henry Cotto	.10	.05
❑	673	Rich DeLucia	.10	.05
❑	674	Brian Fisher	.10	.05
❑	675	Mark Grant	.10	.05
❑	676	Randy Johnson	.40	.18
❑	677	Tim Leary	.10	.05
❑	678	Pete O'Brien	.10	.05
❑	679	Lance Parrish	.10	.05
❑	680	Harold Reynolds	.10	.05
❑	681	Shane Turner	.10	.05
❑	682	Jack Daugherty	.10	.05
❑	683	David Hulse	.10	.05
❑	684	Terry Mathews	.10	.05
❑	685	Al Newman	.10	.05
❑	686	Edwin Nunez	.10	.05
❑	687	Rafael Palmeiro	.30	.14
❑	688	Roger Pavlik	.10	.05
❑	689	Geno Petralli	.10	.05
❑	690	Nolan Ryan	1.50	.70
❑	691	David Cone	.20	.09
❑	692	Alfredo Griffin	.10	.05
❑	693	Juan Guzman	.10	.05
❑	694	Pat Hentgen	.30	.14
❑	695	Randy Knorr	.10	.05
❑	696	Bob MacDonald	.10	.05
❑	697	Jack Morris	.20	.09
❑	698	Ed Sprague	.10	.05
❑	699	Dave Stieb	.20	.09
❑	700	Pat Tabler	.10	.05
❑	701	Mike Timlin	.10	.05
❑	702	David Wells	.20	.09
❑	703	Eddie Zosky	.10	.05
❑	704	Gary Sheffield LL	.20	.09
❑	705	Darren Daulton LL	.10	.05
❑	706	Marquis Grissom LL	.10	.05
❑	707	Greg Maddux LL	.60	.25
❑	708	Bill Swift LL	.10	.05
❑	709	Juan Gonzalez RT	.50	.23
❑	710	Mark McGwire RT	1.00	.45
❑	711	Cecil Fielder RT	.10	.05
❑	712	Albert Belle RT	.20	.09
❑	713	Joe Carter RT	.10	.05
❑	714	Cecil Fielder SS Frank Thomas Power Brokers	.50	.23
❑	715	Larry Walker SS Darren Daulton Unsung Heroes	.40	.18
❑	716	Edgar Martinez SS Robin Ventura Hot Corner Hammers	.20	.09
❑	717	Roger Clemens SS Dennis Eckersley Start to Finish	.40	.18
❑	718	Checklist 361-480	.10	.05
❑	719	Checklist 481-600	.10	.05
❑	720	Checklist 601-720	.10	.05

1993 Fleer All-Stars

	MINT	NRMT
COMPLETE SET (24)	40.00	18.00
COMPLETE SER.1 (12)	25.00	11.00
COMPLETE SER.2 (12)	15.00	6.75
COMMON CARD (AL1-NL12)	.50	.23
❑ AL1 Frank Thomas	8.00	3.60
❑ AL2 Roberto Alomar	2.50	1.10
❑ AL3 Edgar Martinez	1.50	.70
❑ AL4 Pat Listach	.50	.23
❑ AL5 Cecil Fielder	1.00	.45
❑ AL6 Juan Gonzalez	6.00	2.70
❑ AL7 Ken Griffey Jr.	12.00	5.50
❑ AL8 Joe Carter	1.00	.45
❑ AL9 Kirby Puckett	4.00	1.80
❑ AL10 Brian Harper	.50	.23
❑ AL11 Dave Fleming	.50	.23
❑ AL12 Jack McDowell	.50	.23
❑ NL1 Fred McGriff	1.50	.70
❑ NL2 Delino DeShields	.50	.23
❑ NL3 Gary Sheffield	2.50	1.10
❑ NL4 Barry Larkin	1.50	.70
❑ NL5 Felix Jose	.50	.23
❑ NL6 Larry Walker	2.50	1.10
❑ NL7 Barry Bonds	3.00	1.35
❑ NL8 Andy Van Slyke	1.00	.45
❑ NL9 Darren Daulton	1.00	.45
❑ NL10 Greg Maddux	8.00	3.60
❑ NL11 Tom Glavine	1.50	.70
❑ NL12 Lee Smith	1.00	.45

1993 Fleer Glavine

	MINT	NRMT
COMPLETE SET (12)	4.00	1.80
COMMON GLAVINE (1-12)	.50	.23
COMMON MAIL-IN (13-15)	2.00	.90
❑ 1 Tom Glavine The Glavine family ... (Throwing to first)	.50	.23
❑ 2 Tom Glavine High School baseball ... (Pitching, with arm behind head, shot from left side)	.50	.23
❑ 3 Tom Glavine Despite being drafted ... (Pitching, close-up shot from left side)	.50	.23
❑ 4 Tom Glavine Unflappable is ... (Pitching, shot from almost directly in front)	.50	.23
❑ 5 Tom Glavine In 1989 Tom ... (Pitching, shot from right angle)	.50	.23
❑ 6 Tom Glavine Tom Glavine had ... (Pitching, with ball below waist)	.50	.23
❑ 7 Tom Glavine Tom Glavine's dream ... (Pitching, close-up shot with ball behind head)	.50	.23
❑ 8 Tom Glavine After Winning ... (Pitching, shot from directly in front)	.50	.23
❑ 9 Tom Glavine Little Leaguers ... (Pitching, just after release with left leg in air)	.50	.23
❑ 10 Tom Glavine Will success spoil ... (Pitching, ball below waist and right leg slightly raised)	.50	.23
❑ 11 Tom Glavine What makes Tom ... (Batting)	.50	.23
❑ 12 Tom Glavine It was a day ... (Pitching, close-up shot wearing dark blue top)	.50	.23
❑ 13 Tom Glavine Send-Off 1	2.00	.90
❑ 14 Tom Glavine Send-Off 2	2.00	.90
❑ 15 Tom Glavine Send-Off 3	2.00	.90
❑ AU0 Tom Glavine AU (Certified signature)	80.00	36.00

1993 Fleer Golden Moments

	MINT	NRMT
COMPLETE SET (6)	12.00	5.50
COMPLETE SER.1 (3)	4.00	1.80
COMPLETE SER.2 (3)	8.00	3.60
COMMON SERIES 1 (A1-B3)	.50	.23
❑ A1 George Brett	4.00	1.80
❑ A2 Mickey Morandini	.50	.23
❑ A3 Dave Winfield	1.50	.70
❑ B1 Dennis Eckersley	1.00	.45
❑ B2 Bip Roberts	.50	.23
❑ B3 Frank Thomas and Juan Gonzalez	8.00	3.60

1993 Fleer Major League Prospects

	MINT	NRMT
COMPLETE SET (36)	30.00	13.50
COMPLETE SERIES 1 (18)	20.00	9.00
COMPLETE SERIES 2 (18)	10.00	4.50
COMMON SERIES 1 (A1-A18)	.50	.23
COMMON SERIES 2 (B1-B18)	.50	.23
❑ A1 Melvin Nieves	.50	.23
❑ A2 Sterling Hitchcock	.50	.23
❑ A3 Tim Costo	.50	.23
❑ A4 Manny Alexander	.50	.23
❑ A5 Alan Embree	.50	.23
❑ A6 Kevin Young	.50	.23
❑ A7 J.T. Snow	1.50	.70
❑ A8 Russ Springer	.50	.23
❑ A9 Billy Ashley	.50	.23
❑ A10 Kevin Rogers	.50	.23
❑ A11 Steve Hosey	.50	.23
❑ A12 Eric Wedge	.50	.23
❑ A13 Mike Piazza	15.00	6.75
❑ A14 Jesse Levis	.50	.23
❑ A15 Rico Brogna	.75	.35
❑ A16 Alex Arias	.50	.23
❑ A17 Rod Brewer	.50	.23
❑ A18 Troy Neel	.50	.23
❑ B1 Scooter Tucker	.50	.23
❑ B2 Kerry Woodson	.50	.23
❑ B3 Greg Colbrunn	.50	.23
❑ B4 Pedro Martinez	5.00	2.20
❑ B5 Dave Silvestri	.50	.23
❑ B6 Kent Bottenfield	.50	.23
❑ B7 Rafael Bournigal	.50	.23
❑ B8 J.T. Bruett	.50	.23
❑ B9 Dave Mlicki	.50	.23
❑ B10 Paul Wagner	.50	.23
❑ B11 Mike Williams	.50	.23
❑ B12 Henry Mercedes	.50	.23
❑ B13 Scott Taylor	.50	.23
❑ B14 Dennis Moeller	.50	.23
❑ B15 Javier Lopez	2.50	1.10
❑ B16 Steve Cooke	.50	.23
❑ B17 Pete Young	.50	.23
❑ B18 Ken Ryan	.50	.23

1993 Fleer Pro-Visions

	MINT	NRMT
COMPLETE SET (6)	5.00	2.20
COMPLETE SERIES 1 (3)	3.00	1.35
COMPLETE SERIES 2 (3)	2.00	.90
COMMON CARD (A1-B3)	.75	.35

	MINT	NRMT
❑ A1 Roberto Alomar	2.00	.90
❑ A2 Dennis Eckersley	1.00	.45
❑ A3 Gary Sheffield	2.00	.90
❑ B1 Andy Van Slyke	.75	.35
❑ B2 Tom Glavine	1.50	.70
❑ B3 Cecil Fielder	1.00	.45

1993 Fleer Rookie Sensations

	MINT	NRMT
COMPLETE SET (20)	25.00	11.00
COMPLETE SERIES 1 (10)	15.00	6.75
COMPLETE SERIES 2 (10)	10.00	4.50
COMMON CARD (RSA1-RSB10)	1.00	.45

	MINT	NRMT
❑ RSA1 Kenny Lofton	5.00	2.20
❑ RSA2 Cal Eldred	1.00	.45
❑ RSA3 Pat Listach	1.00	.45
❑ RSA4 Roberto Hernandez	2.50	1.10
❑ RSA5 Dave Fleming	1.00	.45
❑ RSA6 Eric Karros	3.00	1.35
❑ RSA7 Reggie Sanders	1.00	.45
❑ RSA8 Derrick May	1.00	.45
❑ RSA9 Mike Perez	1.00	.45
❑ RSA10 Donovan Osborne	1.00	.45
❑ RSB1 Moises Alou	5.00	2.20
❑ RSB2 Pedro Astacio	1.00	.45
❑ RSB3 Jim Austin	1.00	.45
❑ RSB4 Chad Curtis	2.50	1.10
❑ RSB5 Gary DiSarcina	1.00	.45
❑ RSB6 Scott Livingstone	1.00	.45
❑ RSB7 Sam Militello	1.00	.45
❑ RSB8 Arthur Rhodes	1.00	.45
❑ RSB9 Tim Wakefield	2.50	1.10
❑ RSB10 Bob Zupcic	1.00	.45

1993 Fleer Team Leaders

	MINT	NRMT
COMPLETE SET (20)	70.00	32.00
COMPLETE SERIES 1 (10)	50.00	22.00
COMPLETE SERIES 2 (10)	20.00	9.00
COMMON CARD (AL1-NL10)	1.00	.45

	MINT	NRMT
❑ AL1 Kirby Puckett	6.00	2.70
❑ AL2 Mark McGwire	20.00	9.00
❑ AL3 Pat Listach	1.00	.45
❑ AL4 Roger Clemens	8.00	3.60
❑ AL5 Frank Thomas	12.00	5.50
❑ AL6 Carlos Baerga	1.00	.45
❑ AL7 Brady Anderson	2.00	.90
❑ AL8 Juan Gonzalez	10.00	4.50
❑ AL9 Roberto Alomar	4.00	1.80
❑ AL10 Ken Griffey Jr.	20.00	9.00
❑ NL1 Will Clark	4.00	1.80
❑ NL2 Terry Pendleton	1.00	.45
❑ NL3 Ray Lankford	2.00	.90
❑ NL4 Eric Karros	2.50	1.10
❑ NL5 Gary Sheffield	4.00	1.80
❑ NL6 Ryne Sandberg	5.00	2.20
❑ NL7 Marquis Grissom	2.00	.90
❑ NL8 John Kruk	2.00	.90
❑ NL9 Jeff Bagwell	6.00	2.70
❑ NL10 Andy Van Slyke	2.00	.90

1993 Fleer Final Edition

	MINT	NRMT
COMP.FACT.SET (310)	10.00	4.50
COMPLETE SET (300)	6.00	2.70
COMMON CARD (F1-F300)	.10	.05

	MINT	NRMT
❑ 1 Steve Bedrosian	.10	.05
❑ 2 Jay Howell	.10	.05
❑ 3 Greg Maddux	1.25	.55
❑ 4 Greg McMichael	.10	.05
❑ 5 Tony Tarasco	.10	.05
❑ 6 Jose Bautista	.10	.05
❑ 7 Jose Guzman	.10	.05
❑ 8 Greg Hibbard	.10	.05
❑ 9 Candy Maldonado	.10	.05
❑ 10 Randy Myers	.20	.09
❑ 11 Matt Walbeck	.10	.05
❑ 12 Turk Wendell	.10	.05
❑ 13 Willie Wilson	.10	.05
❑ 14 Greg Cadaret	.10	.05
❑ 15 Roberto Kelly	.10	.05
❑ 16 Randy Milligan	.10	.05
❑ 17 Kevin Mitchell	.20	.09
❑ 18 Jeff Reardon	.20	.09
❑ 19 John Roper	.10	.05
❑ 20 John Smiley	.10	.05
❑ 21 Andy Ashby	.20	.09
❑ 22 Dante Bichette	.20	.09
❑ 23 Willie Blair	.10	.05
❑ 24 Pedro Castellano	.10	.05
❑ 25 Vinny Castilla	.50	.23
❑ 26 Jerald Clark	.10	.05
❑ 27 Alex Cole	.10	.05
❑ 28 Scott Fredrickson	.10	.05
❑ 29 Jay Gainer	.10	.05
❑ 30 Andres Galarraga	.40	.18
❑ 31 Joe Girardi	.20	.09
❑ 32 Ryan Hawblitzel	.10	.05
❑ 33 Charlie Hayes	.10	.05
❑ 34 Darren Holmes	.10	.05
❑ 35 Chris Jones	.10	.05
❑ 36 David Nied	.10	.05
❑ 37 J.Owens	.10	.05
❑ 38 Lance Painter	.10	.05
❑ 39 Jeff Parrett	.10	.05
❑ 40 Steve Reed	.10	.05
❑ 41 Armando Reynoso	.10	.05
❑ 42 Bruce Ruffin	.10	.05
❑ 43 Danny Sheaffer	.10	.05
❑ 44 Keith Shepherd	.10	.05
❑ 45 Jim Tatum	.10	.05
❑ 46 Gary Wayne	.10	.05
❑ 47 Eric Young	.40	.18
❑ 48 Luis Aquino	.10	.05
❑ 49 Alex Arias	.10	.05
❑ 50 Jack Armstrong	.10	.05
❑ 51 Bret Barberie	.10	.05
❑ 52 Geronimo Berroa	.10	.05
❑ 53 Ryan Bowen	.10	.05
❑ 54 Greg Briley	.10	.05
❑ 55 Cris Carpenter	.10	.05
❑ 56 Chuck Carr	.10	.05
❑ 57 Jeff Conine	.10	.05
❑ 58 Jim Corsi	.10	.05
❑ 59 Orestes Destrade	.10	.05
❑ 60 Junior Felix	.10	.05
❑ 61 Chris Hammond	.10	.05
❑ 62 Bryan Harvey	.10	.05
❑ 63 Charlie Hough	.20	.09
❑ 64 Joe Klink	.10	.05
❑ 65 Richie Lewis UER (Refers to place of birth and residence as Illinois instead of Indiana)	.10	.05
❑ 66 Mitch Lyden	.10	.05
❑ 67 Bob Natal	.10	.05
❑ 68 Scott Pose	.10	.05
❑ 69 Rich Renteria	.10	.05
❑ 70 Benito Santiago	.10	.05
❑ 71 Gary Sheffield	.40	.18
❑ 72 Matt Turner	.10	.05
❑ 73 Walt Weiss	.10	.05
❑ 74 Darrell Whitmore	.10	.05
❑ 75 Nigel Wilson	.10	.05
❑ 76 Kevin Bass	.10	.05
❑ 77 Doug Drabek	.10	.05
❑ 78 Tom Edens	.10	.05
❑ 79 Chris James	.10	.05
❑ 80 Greg Swindell	.10	.05
❑ 81 Omar Daal	.20	.09
❑ 82 Raul Mondesi	.50	.23
❑ 83 Jody Reed	.10	.05
❑ 84 Cory Snyder	.10	.05
❑ 85 Rick Trlicek	.10	.05
❑ 86 Tim Wallach	.10	.05
❑ 87 Todd Worrell	.10	.05
❑ 88 Tavo Alvarez	.10	.05
❑ 89 Frank Bolick	.10	.05
❑ 90 Kent Bottenfield	.10	.05
❑ 91 Greg Colbrunn	.10	.05
❑ 92 Cliff Floyd	.40	.18
❑ 93 Lou Frazier	.10	.05
❑ 94 Mike Gardiner	.10	.05
❑ 95 Mike Lansing	.20	.09
❑ 96 Bill Risley	.10	.05
❑ 97 Jeff Shaw	.10	.05
❑ 98 Kevin Baez	.10	.05
❑ 99 Tim Bogar	.10	.05
❑ 100 Jeromy Burnitz	.20	.09
❑ 101 Mike Draper	.10	.05
❑ 102 Darrin Jackson	.10	.05
❑ 103 Mike Maddux	.10	.05
❑ 104 Joe Orsulak	.10	.05
❑ 105 Doug Saunders	.10	.05
❑ 106 Frank Tanana	.10	.05
❑ 107 Dave Telgheder	.10	.05
❑ 108 Larry Andersen	.10	.05
❑ 109 Jim Eisenreich	.10	.05
❑ 110 Pete Incaviglia	.10	.05
❑ 111 Danny Jackson	.10	.05
❑ 112 David West	.10	.05
❑ 113 Al Martin	.10	.05
❑ 114 Blas Minor	.10	.05
❑ 115 Dennis Moeller	.10	.05
❑ 116 William Pennyfeather	.10	.05
❑ 117 Rich Robertson	.10	.05
❑ 118 Ben Shelton	.10	.05
❑ 119 Lonnie Smith	.10	.05
❑ 120 Freddie Toliver	.10	.05

❑ 121 Paul Wagner .10 .05
❑ 122 Kevin Young .10 .05
❑ 123 Rene Arocha .10 .05
❑ 124 Gregg Jefferies .10 .05
❑ 125 Paul Kilgus .10 .05
❑ 126 Les Lancaster .10 .05
❑ 127 Joe Magrane .10 .05
❑ 128 Rob Murphy .10 .05
❑ 129 Erik Pappas .10 .05
❑ 130 Stan Royer .10 .05
❑ 131 Ozzie Smith .50 .23
❑ 132 Tom Urbani .10 .05
❑ 133 Mark Whiten .10 .05
❑ 134 Derek Bell .20 .09
❑ 135 Doug Brocail .10 .05
❑ 136 Phil Clark .10 .05
❑ 137 Mark Ettles .10 .05
❑ 138 Jeff Gardner .10 .05
❑ 139 Pat Gomez .10 .05
❑ 140 Ricky Gutierrez .10 .05
❑ 141 Gene Harris .10 .05
❑ 142 Kevin Higgins .10 .05
❑ 143 Trevor Hoffman .40 .18
❑ 144 Phil Plantier .10 .05
❑ 145 Kerry Taylor .10 .05
❑ 146 Guillermo Velasquez .10 .05
❑ 147 Wally Whitehurst .10 .05
❑ 148 Tim Worrell .10 .05
❑ 149 Todd Benzinger .10 .05
❑ 150 Barry Bonds .50 .23
❑ 151 Greg Brummett .10 .05
❑ 152 Mark Carreon .10 .05
❑ 153 Dave Martinez .10 .05
❑ 154 Jeff Reed .10 .05
❑ 155 Kevin Rogers .10 .05
❑ 156 Harold Baines .20 .09
❑ 157 Damon Buford .10 .05
❑ 158 Paul Carey .10 .05
❑ 159 Jeffrey Hammonds .20 .09
❑ 160 Jamie Moyer .10 .05
❑ 161 Sherman Obando .10 .05
❑ 162 John O'Donoghue .10 .05
❑ 163 Brad Pennington .10 .05
❑ 164 Jim Poole .10 .05
❑ 165 Harold Reynolds .10 .05
❑ 166 Fernando Valenzuela .20 .09
❑ 167 Jack Voigt .10 .05
❑ 168 Mark Williamson .10 .05
❑ 169 Scott Bankhead .10 .05
❑ 170 Greg Blosser .10 .05
❑ 171 Jim Byrd .10 .05
❑ 172 Ivan Calderon .10 .05
❑ 173 Andre Dawson .30 .14
❑ 174 Scott Fletcher .10 .05
❑ 175 Jose Melendez .10 .05
❑ 176 Carlos Quintana .10 .05
❑ 177 Jeff Russell .10 .05
❑ 178 Aaron Sele .40 .18
❑ 179 Rod Correia .10 .05
❑ 180 Chili Davis .20 .09
❑ 181 Jim Edmonds 1.00 .45
❑ 182 Rene Gonzales .10 .05
❑ 183 Hilly Hathaway .10 .05
❑ 184 Torey Lovullo .10 .05
❑ 185 Greg Myers .10 .05
❑ 186 Gene Nelson .10 .05
❑ 187 Troy Percival .30 .14
❑ 188 Scott Sanderson .10 .05
❑ 189 Darryl Scott .10 .05
❑ 190 J.T. Snow .50 .23
❑ 191 Russ Springer .10 .05
❑ 192 Jason Bere .10 .05
❑ 193 Rodney Bolton .10 .05
❑ 194 Ellis Burks .20 .09
❑ 195 Bo Jackson .20 .09
❑ 196 Mike LaValliere .10 .05
❑ 197 Scott Ruffcorn .10 .05
❑ 198 Jeff Schwartz .10 .05
❑ 199 Jerry DiPoto .10 .05
❑ 200 Alvaro Espinoza .10 .05
❑ 201 Wayne Kirby .10 .05
❑ 202 Tom Kramer .10 .05
❑ 203 Jesse Levis .10 .05
❑ 204 Manny Ramirez .75 .35
❑ 205 Jeff Treadway .10 .05
❑ 206 Bill Wertz .10 .05
❑ 207 Cliff Young .10 .05
❑ 208 Matt Young .10 .05
❑ 209 Kirk Gibson .20 .09
❑ 210 Greg Gohr .10 .05
❑ 211 Bill Krueger .10 .05
❑ 212 Bob MacDonald .10 .05
❑ 213 Mike Moore .10 .05
❑ 214 David Wells .20 .09
❑ 215 Billy Brewer .10 .05
❑ 216 David Cone .20 .09
❑ 217 Greg Gagne .10 .05
❑ 218 Mark Gardner .10 .05
❑ 219 Chris Haney .10 .05
❑ 220 Phil Hiatt .10 .05
❑ 221 Jose Lind .10 .05
❑ 222 Juan Bell .10 .05
❑ 223 Tom Brunansky .10 .05
❑ 224 Mike Ignasiak .10 .05
❑ 225 Joe Kmak .10 .05
❑ 226 Tom Lampkin .10 .05
❑ 227 Graeme Lloyd .10 .05
❑ 228 Carlos Maldonado .10 .05
❑ 229 Matt Mieske .10 .05
❑ 230 Angel Miranda .10 .05
❑ 231 Troy O'Leary .40 .18
❑ 232 Kevin Reimer .10 .05
❑ 233 Larry Casian .10 .05
❑ 234 Jim Deshaies .10 .05
❑ 235 Eddie Guardado .10 .05
❑ 236 Chip Hale .10 .05
❑ 237 Mike Maksudian .10 .05
❑ 238 David McCarty .10 .05
❑ 239 Pat Meares .10 .05
❑ 240 George Tsamis .10 .05
❑ 241 Dave Winfield .30 .14
❑ 242 Jim Abbott .20 .09
❑ 243 Wade Boggs .40 .18
❑ 244 Andy Cook .10 .05
❑ 245 Russ Davis .40 .18
❑ 246 Mike Humphreys .10 .05
❑ 247 Jimmy Key .20 .09
❑ 248 Jim Leyritz .10 .05
❑ 249 Bobby Munoz .10 .05
❑ 250 Paul O'Neill .20 .09
❑ 251 Spike Owen .10 .05
❑ 252 Dave Silvestri .10 .05
❑ 253 Marcos Armas .10 .05
❑ 254 Brent Gates .10 .05
❑ 255 Goose Gossage .20 .09
❑ 256 Scott Lydy .10 .05
❑ 257 Henry Mercedes .10 .05
❑ 258 Mike Mohler .10 .05
❑ 259 Troy Neel .10 .05
❑ 260 Edwin Nunez .10 .05
❑ 261 Craig Paquette .10 .05
❑ 262 Kevin Seitzer .10 .05
❑ 263 Rich Amaral .10 .05
❑ 264 Mike Blowers .10 .05
❑ 265 Chris Bosio .10 .05
❑ 266 Norm Charlton .10 .05
❑ 267 Jim Converse .10 .05
❑ 268 John Cummings .10 .05
❑ 269 Mike Felder .10 .05
❑ 270 Mike Hampton .30 .14
❑ 271 Bill Haselman .10 .05
❑ 272 Dwayne Henry .10 .05
❑ 273 Greg Litton .10 .05
❑ 274 Mackey Sasser .10 .05
❑ 275 Lee Tinsley .20 .09
❑ 276 David Wainhouse .10 .05
❑ 277 Jeff Bronkey .10 .05
❑ 278 Benji Gil .10 .05
❑ 279 Tom Henke .10 .05
❑ 280 Charlie Leibrandt .10 .05
❑ 281 Robb Nen .30 .14
❑ 282 Bill Ripken .10 .05
❑ 283 Jon Shave .10 .05
❑ 284 Doug Strange .10 .05
❑ 285 Matt Whiteside .10 .05
❑ 286 Scott Brow .10 .05
❑ 287 Willie Canate .10 .05
❑ 288 Tony Castillo .10 .05
❑ 289 Domingo Cedeno .10 .05
❑ 290 Darnell Coles .10 .05
❑ 291 Danny Cox .10 .05
❑ 292 Mark Eichhorn .10 .05
❑ 293 Tony Fernandez .10 .05
❑ 294 Al Leiter .20 .09
❑ 295 Paul Molitor .40 .18
❑ 296 Dave Stewart .20 .09
❑ 297 Woody Williams .25 .11
❑ 298 Checklist F1-F100 .10 .05
❑ 299 Checklist F101-F200 .10 .05
❑ 300 Checklist F201-F300 .10 .05

1993 Fleer Final Edition Diamond Tribute

	MINT	NRMT
COMPLETE SET (10)	4.00	1.80
COMMON CARD (1-10)	.20	.09

❑ 1 Wade Boggs .50 .23
❑ 2 George Brett 1.25 .55
❑ 3 Andre Dawson .30 .14
❑ 4 Carlton Fisk .50 .23
❑ 5 Paul Molitor .50 .23
❑ 6 Nolan Ryan 2.00 .90
❑ 7 Lee Smith .20 .09
❑ 8 Ozzie Smith .75 .35
❑ 9 Dave Winfield .30 .14
❑ 10 Robin Yount .30 .14

1994 Fleer

	MINT	NRMT
COMPLETE SET (720)	50.00	22.00
COMMON CARD (1-720)	.15	.07

❑ 1 Brady Anderson .30 .14
❑ 2 Harold Baines .30 .14
❑ 3 Mike Devereaux .15 .07
❑ 4 Todd Frohwirth .15 .07
❑ 5 Jeffrey Hammonds .30 .14
❑ 6 Chris Hoiles .15 .07
❑ 7 Tim Hulett .15 .07
❑ 8 Ben McDonald .15 .07
❑ 9 Mark McLemore .15 .07
❑ 10 Alan Mills .15 .07
❑ 11 Jamie Moyer .15 .07
❑ 12 Mike Mussina .60 .25
❑ 13 Gregg Olson .15 .07
❑ 14 Mike Pagliarulo .15 .07
❑ 15 Brad Pennington .15 .07

❑ 16 Jim Poole .15 .07
❑ 17 Harold Reynolds .15 .07
❑ 18 Arthur Rhodes .15 .07
❑ 19 Cal Ripken Jr. 2.50 1.10
❑ 20 David Segui .30 .14
❑ 21 Rick Sutcliffe .15 .07
❑ 22 Fernando Valenzuela .30 .14
❑ 23 Jack Voigt .15 .07
❑ 24 Mark Williamson .15 .07
❑ 25 Scott Bankhead .15 .07
❑ 26 Roger Clemens 1.25 .55
❑ 27 Scott Cooper .15 .07
❑ 28 Danny Darwin .15 .07
❑ 29 Andre Dawson .40 .18
❑ 30 Rob Deer .15 .07
❑ 31 John Dopson .15 .07
❑ 32 Scott Fletcher .15 .07
❑ 33 Mike Greenwell .15 .07
❑ 34 Greg A. Harris .15 .07
❑ 35 Billy Hatcher .15 .07
❑ 36 Bob Melvin .15 .07
❑ 37 Tony Pena .15 .07
❑ 38 Paul Quantrill .15 .07
❑ 39 Carlos Quintana .15 .07
❑ 40 Ernest Riles .15 .07
❑ 41 Jeff Russell .15 .07
❑ 42 Ken Ryan .15 .07
❑ 43 Aaron Sele .30 .14
❑ 44 John Valentin .30 .14
❑ 45 Mo Vaughn .75 .35
❑ 46 Frank Viola .15 .07
❑ 47 Bob Zupcic .15 .07
❑ 48 Mike Butcher .15 .07
❑ 49 Rod Correia .15 .07
❑ 50 Chad Curtis .15 .07
❑ 51 Chili Davis .30 .14
❑ 52 Gary DiSarcina .15 .07
❑ 53 Damion Easley .30 .14
❑ 54 Jim Edmonds .60 .25
❑ 55 Chuck Finley .30 .14
❑ 56 Steve Frey .15 .07
❑ 57 Rene Gonzales .15 .07
❑ 58 Joe Grahe .15 .07
❑ 59 Hilly Hathaway .15 .07
❑ 60 Stan Javier .15 .07
❑ 61 Mark Langston .15 .07
❑ 62 Phil Leftwich .15 .07
❑ 63 Torey Lovullo .15 .07
❑ 64 Joe Magrane .15 .07
❑ 65 Greg Myers .15 .07
❑ 66 Ken Patterson .15 .07
❑ 67 Eduardo Perez .15 .07
❑ 68 Luis Polonia .15 .07
❑ 69 Tim Salmon .60 .25
❑ 70 J.T. Snow .30 .14
❑ 71 Ron Tingley .15 .07
❑ 72 Julio Valera .15 .07
❑ 73 Wilson Alvarez .30 .14
❑ 74 Tim Belcher .15 .07
❑ 75 George Bell .15 .07
❑ 76 Jason Bere .15 .07
❑ 77 Rod Bolton .15 .07
❑ 78 Ellis Burks .30 .14
❑ 79 Joey Cora .30 .14
❑ 80 Alex Fernandez .15 .07
❑ 81 Craig Grebeck .15 .07
❑ 82 Ozzie Guillen .15 .07
❑ 83 Roberto Hernandez .15 .07
❑ 84 Bo Jackson .30 .14
❑ 85 Lance Johnson .15 .07
❑ 86 Ron Karkovice .15 .07
❑ 87 Mike LaValliere .15 .07
❑ 88 Kirk McCaskill .15 .07
❑ 89 Jack McDowell .15 .07
❑ 90 Warren Newson .15 .07
❑ 91 Dan Pasqua .15 .07
❑ 92 Scott Radinsky .15 .07
❑ 93 Tim Raines .30 .14
❑ 94 Steve Sax .15 .07
❑ 95 Jeff Schwarz .15 .07
❑ 96 Frank Thomas 2.00 .90
❑ 97 Robin Ventura .30 .14
❑ 98 Sandy Alomar Jr. .30 .14
❑ 99 Carlos Baerga .30 .14
❑ 100 Albert Belle .75 .35

❑ 101 Mark Clark .15 .07
❑ 102 Jerry DiPoto .15 .07
❑ 103 Alvaro Espinoza .15 .07
❑ 104 Felix Fermin .15 .07
❑ 105 Jeremy Hernandez .15 .07
❑ 106 Reggie Jefferson .15 .07
❑ 107 Wayne Kirby .15 .07
❑ 108 Tom Kramer .15 .07
❑ 109 Mark Lewis .15 .07
❑ 110 Derek Lilliquist .15 .07
❑ 111 Kenny Lofton .60 .25
❑ 112 Candy Maldonado .15 .07
❑ 113 Jose Mesa .15 .07
❑ 114 Jeff Mutis .15 .07
❑ 115 Charles Nagy .30 .14
❑ 116 Bob Ojeda .15 .07
❑ 117 Junior Ortiz .15 .07
❑ 118 Eric Plunk .15 .07
❑ 119 Manny Ramirez .75 .35
❑ 120 Paul Sorrento .15 .07
❑ 121 Jim Thome .75 .35
❑ 122 Jeff Treadway .15 .07
❑ 123 Bill Wertz .15 .07
❑ 124 Skeeter Barnes .15 .07
❑ 125 Milt Cuyler .15 .07
❑ 126 Eric Davis .30 .14
❑ 127 John Doherty .15 .07
❑ 128 Cecil Fielder .30 .14
❑ 129 Travis Fryman .30 .14
❑ 130 Kirk Gibson .30 .14
❑ 131 Dan Gladden .15 .07
❑ 132 Greg Gohr .15 .07
❑ 133 Chris Gomez .15 .07
❑ 134 Bill Gullickson .15 .07
❑ 135 Mike Henneman .15 .07
❑ 136 Kurt Knudsen .15 .07
❑ 137 Chad Kreuter .15 .07
❑ 138 Bill Krueger .15 .07
❑ 139 Scott Livingstone .15 .07
❑ 140 Bob MacDonald .15 .07
❑ 141 Mike Moore .15 .07
❑ 142 Tony Phillips .15 .07
❑ 143 Mickey Tettleton .15 .07
❑ 144 Alan Trammell .40 .18
❑ 145 David Wells .40 .18
❑ 146 Lou Whitaker .30 .14
❑ 147 Kevin Appier .30 .14
❑ 148 Stan Belinda .15 .07
❑ 149 George Brett 1.25 .55
❑ 150 Billy Brewer .15 .07
❑ 151 Hubie Brooks .15 .07
❑ 152 David Cone .40 .18
❑ 153 Gary Gaetti .30 .14
❑ 154 Greg Gagne .15 .07
❑ 155 Tom Gordon .15 .07
❑ 156 Mark Gubicza .15 .07
❑ 157 Chris Gwynn .15 .07
❑ 158 John Habyan .15 .07
❑ 159 Chris Haney .15 .07
❑ 160 Phil Hiatt .15 .07
❑ 161 Felix Jose .15 .07
❑ 162 Wally Joyner .30 .14
❑ 163 Jose Lind .15 .07
❑ 164 Mike Macfarlane .15 .07
❑ 165 Mike Magnante .15 .07
❑ 166 Brent Mayne .15 .07
❑ 167 Brian McRae .15 .07
❑ 168 Kevin McReynolds .15 .07
❑ 169 Keith Miller .15 .07
❑ 170 Jeff Montgomery .15 .07
❑ 171 Hipolito Pichardo .15 .07
❑ 172 Rico Rossy .15 .07
❑ 173 Juan Bell .15 .07
❑ 174 Ricky Bones .15 .07
❑ 175 Cal Eldred .15 .07
❑ 176 Mike Fetters .15 .07
❑ 177 Darryl Hamilton .15 .07
❑ 178 Doug Henry .15 .07
❑ 179 Mike Ignasiak .15 .07
❑ 180 John Jaha .15 .07
❑ 181 Pat Listach .15 .07
❑ 182 Graeme Lloyd .15 .07
❑ 183 Matt Mieske .15 .07
❑ 184 Angel Miranda .15 .07
❑ 185 Jaime Navarro .15 .07

❑ 186 Dave Nilsson .15 .07
❑ 187 Troy O'Leary .30 .14
❑ 188 Jesse Orosco .15 .07
❑ 189 Kevin Reimer .15 .07
❑ 190 Kevin Seitzer .15 .07
❑ 191 Bill Spiers .15 .07
❑ 192 B.J. Surhoff .30 .14
❑ 193 Dickie Thon .15 .07
❑ 194 Jose Valentin .15 .07
❑ 195 Greg Vaughn .30 .14
❑ 196 Bill Wegman .15 .07
❑ 197 Robin Yount .60 .25
❑ 198 Rick Aguilera .15 .07
❑ 199 Willie Banks .15 .07
❑ 200 Bernardo Brito .15 .07
❑ 201 Larry Casian .15 .07
❑ 202 Scott Erickson .30 .14
❑ 203 Eddie Guardado .15 .07
❑ 204 Mark Guthrie .15 .07
❑ 205 Chip Hale .15 .07
❑ 206 Brian Harper .15 .07
❑ 207 Mike Hartley .15 .07
❑ 208 Kent Hrbek .30 .14
❑ 209 Terry Jorgensen .15 .07
❑ 210 Chuck Knoblauch .60 .25
❑ 211 Gene Larkin .15 .07
❑ 212 Shane Mack .15 .07
❑ 213 David McCarty .15 .07
❑ 214 Pat Meares .15 .07
❑ 215 Pedro Munoz .15 .07
❑ 216 Derek Parks .15 .07
❑ 217 Kirby Puckett 1.00 .45
❑ 218 Jeff Reboulet .15 .07
❑ 219 Kevin Tapani .15 .07
❑ 220 Mike Trombley .15 .07
❑ 221 George Tsamis .15 .07
❑ 222 Carl Willis .15 .07
❑ 223 Dave Winfield .60 .25
❑ 224 Jim Abbott .30 .14
❑ 225 Paul Assenmacher .15 .07
❑ 226 Wade Boggs .60 .25
❑ 227 Russ Davis .30 .14
❑ 228 Steve Farr .15 .07
❑ 229 Mike Gallego .15 .07
❑ 230 Paul Gibson .15 .07
❑ 231 Steve Howe .15 .07
❑ 232 Dion James .15 .07
❑ 233 Domingo Jean .15 .07
❑ 234 Scott Kamieniecki .15 .07
❑ 235 Pat Kelly .15 .07
❑ 236 Jimmy Key .30 .14
❑ 237 Jim Leyritz .30 .14
❑ 238 Kevin Maas .15 .07
❑ 239 Don Mattingly 1.00 .45
❑ 240 Rich Monteleone .15 .07
❑ 241 Bobby Munoz .15 .07
❑ 242 Matt Nokes .15 .07
❑ 243 Paul O'Neill .30 .14
❑ 244 Spike Owen .15 .07
❑ 245 Melido Perez .15 .07
❑ 246 Lee Smith .30 .14
❑ 247 Mike Stanley .15 .07
❑ 248 Danny Tartabull .15 .07
❑ 249 Randy Velarde .15 .07
❑ 250 Bob Wickman .15 .07
❑ 251 Bernie Williams .60 .25
❑ 252 Mike Aldrete .15 .07
❑ 253 Marcos Armas .15 .07
❑ 254 Lance Blankenship .15 .07
❑ 255 Mike Bordick .15 .07
❑ 256 Scott Brosius .30 .14
❑ 257 Jerry Browne .15 .07
❑ 258 Ron Darling .15 .07
❑ 259 Kelly Downs .15 .07
❑ 260 Dennis Eckersley .30 .14
❑ 261 Brent Gates .15 .07
❑ 262 Goose Gossage .30 .14
❑ 263 Scott Hemond .15 .07
❑ 264 Dave Henderson .15 .07
❑ 265 Rick Honeycutt .15 .07
❑ 266 Vince Horsman .15 .07
❑ 267 Scott Lydy .15 .07
❑ 268 Mark McGwire 3.00 1.35
❑ 269 Mike Mohler .15 .07
❑ 270 Troy Neel .15 .07

❑	271	Edwin Nunez	.15	.07
❑	272	Craig Paquette	.15	.07
❑	273	Ruben Sierra	.15	.07
❑	274	Terry Steinbach	.30	.14
❑	275	Todd Van Poppel	.15	.07
❑	276	Bob Welch	.15	.07
❑	277	Bobby Witt	.15	.07
❑	278	Rich Amaral	.15	.07
❑	279	Mike Blowers	.15	.07
❑	280	Bret Boone UER (Name spelled Brett on front)	.30	.14
❑	281	Chris Bosio	.15	.07
❑	282	Jay Buhner	.30	.14
❑	283	Norm Charlton	.15	.07
❑	284	Mike Felder	.15	.07
❑	285	Dave Fleming	.15	.07
❑	286	Ken Griffey Jr.	3.00	1.35
❑	287	Erik Hanson	.15	.07
❑	288	Bill Haselman	.15	.07
❑	289	Brad Holman	.15	.07
❑	290	Randy Johnson	.60	.25
❑	291	Tim Leary	.15	.07
❑	292	Greg Litton	.15	.07
❑	293	Dave Magadan	.15	.07
❑	294	Edgar Martinez	.30	.14
❑	295	Tino Martinez	.60	.25
❑	296	Jeff Nelson	.15	.07
❑	297	Erik Plantenberg	.15	.07
❑	298	Mackey Sasser	.15	.07
❑	299	Brian Turang	.15	.07
❑	300	Dave Valle	.15	.07
❑	301	Omar Vizquel	.30	.14
❑	302	Brian Bohanon	.15	.07
❑	303	Kevin Brown	.30	.14
❑	304	Jose Canseco UER (Back mentions 1991 as his 40/40 MVP season; should be '88)	.60	.25
❑	305	Mario Diaz	.15	.07
❑	306	Julio Franco	.15	.07
❑	307	Juan Gonzalez	1.50	.70
❑	308	Tom Henke	.15	.07
❑	309	David Hulse	.15	.07
❑	310	Manuel Lee	.15	.07
❑	311	Craig Lefferts	.15	.07
❑	312	Charlie Leibrandt	.15	.07
❑	313	Rafael Palmeiro	.40	.18
❑	314	Dean Palmer	.30	.14
❑	315	Roger Pavlik	.15	.07
❑	316	Dan Peltier	.15	.07
❑	317	Gene Petralli	.15	.07
❑	318	Gary Redus	.15	.07
❑	319	Ivan Rodriguez	.75	.35
❑	320	Kenny Rogers	.15	.07
❑	321	Nolan Ryan	2.50	1.10
❑	322	Doug Strange	.15	.07
❑	323	Matt Whiteside	.15	.07
❑	324	Roberto Alomar	.60	.25
❑	325	Pat Borders	.15	.07
❑	326	Joe Carter	.30	.14
❑	327	Tony Castillo	.15	.07
❑	328	Darnell Coles	.15	.07
❑	329	Danny Cox	.15	.07
❑	330	Mark Eichhorn	.15	.07
❑	331	Tony Fernandez	.15	.07
❑	332	Alfredo Griffin	.15	.07
❑	333	Juan Guzman	.15	.07
❑	334	Rickey Henderson	.60	.25
❑	335	Pat Hentgen	.30	.14
❑	336	Randy Knorr	.15	.07
❑	337	Al Leiter	.30	.14
❑	338	Paul Molitor	.60	.25
❑	339	Jack Morris	.30	.14
❑	340	John Olerud	.30	.14
❑	341	Dick Schofield	.15	.07
❑	342	Ed Sprague	.15	.07
❑	343	Dave Stewart	.30	.14
❑	344	Todd Stottlemyre	.15	.07
❑	345	Mike Timlin	.15	.07
❑	346	Duane Ward	.15	.07
❑	347	Turner Ward	.15	.07
❑	348	Devon White	.30	.14
❑	349	Woody Williams	.15	.07
❑	350	Steve Avery	.15	.07
❑	351	Steve Bedrosian	.15	.07
❑	352	Rafael Belliard	.15	.07
❑	353	Damon Berryhill	.15	.07
❑	354	Jeff Blauser	.15	.07
❑	355	Sid Bream	.15	.07
❑	356	Francisco Cabrera	.15	.07
❑	357	Marvin Freeman	.15	.07
❑	358	Ron Gant	.30	.14
❑	359	Tom Glavine	.60	.25
❑	360	Jay Howell	.15	.07
❑	361	David Justice	.60	.25
❑	362	Ryan Klesko	.30	.14
❑	363	Mark Lemke	.15	.07
❑	364	Javier Lopez	.40	.18
❑	365	Greg Maddux	2.00	.90
❑	366	Fred McGriff	.40	.18
❑	367	Greg McMichael	.15	.07
❑	368	Kent Mercker	.15	.07
❑	369	Otis Nixon	.15	.07
❑	370	Greg Olson	.15	.07
❑	371	Bill Pecota	.15	.07
❑	372	Terry Pendleton	.15	.07
❑	373	Deion Sanders	.30	.14
❑	374	Pete Smith	.15	.07
❑	375	John Smoltz	.30	.14
❑	376	Mike Stanton	.15	.07
❑	377	Tony Tarasco	.15	.07
❑	378	Mark Wohlers	.15	.07
❑	379	Jose Bautista	.15	.07
❑	380	Shawn Boskie	.15	.07
❑	381	Steve Buechele	.15	.07
❑	382	Frank Castillo	.15	.07
❑	383	Mark Grace	.40	.18
❑	384	Jose Guzman	.15	.07
❑	385	Mike Harkey	.15	.07
❑	386	Greg Hibbard	.15	.07
❑	387	Glenallen Hill	.15	.07
❑	388	Steve Lake	.15	.07
❑	389	Derrick May	.15	.07
❑	390	Chuck McElroy	.15	.07
❑	391	Mike Morgan	.15	.07
❑	392	Randy Myers	.15	.07
❑	393	Dan Plesac	.15	.07
❑	394	Kevin Roberson	.15	.07
❑	395	Rey Sanchez	.15	.07
❑	396	Ryne Sandberg	.75	.35
❑	397	Bob Scanlan	.15	.07
❑	398	Dwight Smith	.15	.07
❑	399	Sammy Sosa	2.00	.90
❑	400	Jose Vizcaino	.15	.07
❑	401	Rick Wilkins	.15	.07
❑	402	Willie Wilson	.15	.07
❑	403	Eric Yelding	.15	.07
❑	404	Bobby Ayala	.15	.07
❑	405	Jeff Branson	.15	.07
❑	406	Tom Browning	.15	.07
❑	407	Jacob Brumfield	.15	.07
❑	408	Tim Costo	.15	.07
❑	409	Rob Dibble	.15	.07
❑	410	Willie Greene	.30	.14
❑	411	Thomas Howard	.15	.07
❑	412	Roberto Kelly	.15	.07
❑	413	Bill Landrum	.15	.07
❑	414	Barry Larkin	.40	.18
❑	415	Larry Luebbers	.15	.07
❑	416	Kevin Mitchell	.15	.07
❑	417	Hal Morris	.15	.07
❑	418	Joe Oliver	.15	.07
❑	419	Tim Pugh	.15	.07
❑	420	Jeff Reardon	.30	.14
❑	421	Jose Rijo	.15	.07
❑	422	Bip Roberts	.15	.07
❑	423	John Roper	.15	.07
❑	424	Johnny Ruffin	.15	.07
❑	425	Chris Sabo	.15	.07
❑	426	Juan Samuel	.15	.07
❑	427	Reggie Sanders	.30	.14
❑	428	Scott Service	.15	.07
❑	429	John Smiley	.15	.07
❑	430	Jerry Spradlin	.15	.07
❑	431	Kevin Wickander	.15	.07
❑	432	Freddie Benavides	.15	.07
❑	433	Dante Bichette	.30	.14
❑	434	Willie Blair	.15	.07
❑	435	Daryl Boston	.15	.07
❑	436	Kent Bottenfield	.15	.07
❑	437	Vinny Castilla	.30	.14
❑	438	Jerald Clark	.15	.07
❑	439	Alex Cole	.15	.07
❑	440	Andres Galarraga	.60	.25
❑	441	Joe Girardi	.15	.07
❑	442	Greg W. Harris	.15	.07
❑	443	Charlie Hayes	.15	.07
❑	444	Darren Holmes	.15	.07
❑	445	Chris Jones	.15	.07
❑	446	Roberto Mejia	.15	.07
❑	447	David Nied	.15	.07
❑	448	J. Owens	.15	.07
❑	449	Jeff Parrett	.15	.07
❑	450	Steve Reed	.15	.07
❑	451	Armando Reynoso	.15	.07
❑	452	Bruce Ruffin	.15	.07
❑	453	Mo Sanford	.15	.07
❑	454	Danny Sheaffer	.15	.07
❑	455	Jim Tatum	.15	.07
❑	456	Gary Wayne	.15	.07
❑	457	Eric Young	.15	.07
❑	458	Luis Aquino	.15	.07
❑	459	Alex Arias	.15	.07
❑	460	Jack Armstrong	.15	.07
❑	461	Bret Barberie	.15	.07
❑	462	Ryan Bowen	.15	.07
❑	463	Chuck Carr	.15	.07
❑	464	Jeff Conine	.30	.14
❑	465	Henry Cotto	.15	.07
❑	466	Orestes Destrade	.15	.07
❑	467	Chris Hammond	.15	.07
❑	468	Bryan Harvey	.15	.07
❑	469	Charlie Hough	.15	.07
❑	470	Joe Klink	.15	.07
❑	471	Richie Lewis	.15	.07
❑	472	Bob Natal	.15	.07
❑	473	Pat Rapp	.15	.07
❑	474	Rich Renteria	.15	.07
❑	475	Rich Rodriguez	.15	.07
❑	476	Benito Santiago	.15	.07
❑	477	Gary Sheffield	.60	.25
❑	478	Matt Turner	.15	.07
❑	479	David Weathers	.15	.07
❑	480	Walt Weiss	.15	.07
❑	481	Darrell Whitmore	.15	.07
❑	482	Eric Anthony	.15	.07
❑	483	Jeff Bagwell	1.00	.45
❑	484	Kevin Bass	.15	.07
❑	485	Craig Biggio	.60	.25
❑	486	Ken Caminiti	.40	.18
❑	487	Andujar Cedeno	.15	.07
❑	488	Chris Donnels	.15	.07
❑	489	Doug Drabek	.15	.07
❑	490	Steve Finley	.30	.14
❑	491	Luis Gonzalez	.15	.07
❑	492	Pete Harnisch	.15	.07
❑	493	Xavier Hernandez	.15	.07
❑	494	Doug Jones	.15	.07
❑	495	Todd Jones	.15	.07
❑	496	Darryl Kile	.30	.14
❑	497	Al Osuna	.15	.07
❑	498	Mark Portugal	.15	.07
❑	499	Scott Servais	.15	.07
❑	500	Greg Swindell	.15	.07
❑	501	Eddie Taubensee	.15	.07
❑	502	Jose Uribe	.15	.07
❑	503	Brian Williams	.15	.07
❑	504	Billy Ashley	.15	.07
❑	505	Pedro Astacio	.15	.07
❑	506	Brett Butler	.30	.14
❑	507	Tom Candiotti	.15	.07
❑	508	Omar Daal	.15	.07
❑	509	Jim Gott	.15	.07
❑	510	Kevin Gross	.15	.07
❑	511	Dave Hansen	.15	.07
❑	512	Carlos Hernandez	.15	.07
❑	513	Orel Hershiser	.30	.14
❑	514	Eric Karros	.30	.14
❑	515	Pedro Martinez	.75	.35
❑	516	Ramon Martinez	.30	.14
❑	517	Roger McDowell	.15	.07
❑	518	Raul Mondesi	.60	.25
❑	519	Jose Offerman	.15	.07
❑	520	Mike Piazza	2.00	.90
❑	521	Jody Reed	.15	.07
❑	522	Henry Rodriguez	.30	.14

❑ 523 Mike Sharperson .15 .07
❑ 524 Cory Snyder .15 .07
❑ 525 Darryl Strawberry .30 .14
❑ 526 Rick Trlicek .15 .07
❑ 527 Tim Wallach .15 .07
❑ 528 Mitch Webster .15 .07
❑ 529 Steve Wilson .15 .07
❑ 530 Todd Worrell .15 .07
❑ 531 Moises Alou .40 .18
❑ 532 Brian Barnes .15 .07
❑ 533 Sean Berry .15 .07
❑ 534 Greg Colbrunn .15 .07
❑ 535 Delino DeShields .15 .07
❑ 536 Jeff Fassero .15 .07
❑ 537 Darrin Fletcher .15 .07
❑ 538 Cliff Floyd .30 .14
❑ 539 Lou Frazier .15 .07
❑ 540 Marquis Grissom .30 .14
❑ 541 Butch Henry .15 .07
❑ 542 Ken Hill .15 .07
❑ 543 Mike Lansing .30 .14
❑ 544 Brian Looney .15 .07
❑ 545 Dennis Martinez .30 .14
❑ 546 Chris Nabholz .15 .07
❑ 547 Randy Ready .15 .07
❑ 548 Mel Rojas .15 .07
❑ 549 Kirk Rueter .15 .07
❑ 550 Tim Scott .15 .07
❑ 551 Jeff Shaw .15 .07
❑ 552 Tim Spehr .15 .07
❑ 553 John VanderWal .15 .07
❑ 554 Larry Walker .60 .25
❑ 555 John Wetteland .30 .14
❑ 556 Rondell White .30 .14
❑ 557 Tim Bogar .15 .07
❑ 558 Bobby Bonilla .30 .14
❑ 559 Jeromy Burnitz .30 .14
❑ 560 Sid Fernandez .15 .07
❑ 561 John Franco .30 .14
❑ 562 Dave Gallagher .15 .07
❑ 563 Dwight Gooden .30 .14
❑ 564 Eric Hillman .15 .07
❑ 565 Todd Hundley .30 .14
❑ 566 Jeff Innis .15 .07
❑ 567 Darrin Jackson .15 .07
❑ 568 Howard Johnson .15 .07
❑ 569 Bobby Jones .15 .07
❑ 570 Jeff Kent .30 .14
❑ 571 Mike Maddux .15 .07
❑ 572 Jeff McKnight .15 .07
❑ 573 Eddie Murray .60 .25
❑ 574 Charlie O'Brien .15 .07
❑ 575 Joe Orsulak .15 .07
❑ 576 Bret Saberhagen .30 .14
❑ 577 Pete Schourek .15 .07
❑ 578 Dave Telgheder .15 .07
❑ 579 Ryan Thompson .15 .07
❑ 580 Anthony Young .15 .07
❑ 581 Ruben Amaro .15 .07
❑ 582 Larry Andersen .15 .07
❑ 583 Kim Batiste .15 .07
❑ 584 Wes Chamberlain .15 .07
❑ 585 Darren Daulton .30 .14
❑ 586 Mariano Duncan .15 .07
❑ 587 Lenny Dykstra .30 .14
❑ 588 Jim Eisenreich .15 .07
❑ 589 Tommy Greene .15 .07
❑ 590 Dave Hollins .15 .07
❑ 591 Pete Incaviglia .15 .07
❑ 592 Danny Jackson .15 .07
❑ 593 Ricky Jordan .15 .07
❑ 594 John Kruk .30 .14
❑ 595 Roger Mason .15 .07
❑ 596 Mickey Morandini .15 .07
❑ 597 Terry Mulholland .15 .07
❑ 598 Todd Pratt .15 .07
❑ 599 Ben Rivera .15 .07
❑ 600 Curt Schilling .30 .14
❑ 601 Kevin Stocker .15 .07
❑ 602 Milt Thompson .15 .07
❑ 603 David West .40 .18
❑ 604 Mitch Williams .15 .07
❑ 605 Jay Bell .30 .14
❑ 606 Dave Clark .15 .07
❑ 607 Steve Cooke .15 .07
❑ 608 Tom Foley .15 .07
❑ 609 Carlos Garcia .15 .07
❑ 610 Joel Johnston .15 .07
❑ 611 Jeff King .15 .07
❑ 612 Al Martin .15 .07
❑ 613 Lloyd McClendon .15 .07
❑ 614 Orlando Merced .15 .07
❑ 615 Blas Minor .15 .07
❑ 616 Denny Neagle .30 .14
❑ 617 Mark Petkovsek .15 .07
❑ 618 Tom Prince .15 .07
❑ 619 Don Slaught .15 .07
❑ 620 Zane Smith .15 .07
❑ 621 Randy Tomlin .15 .07
❑ 622 Andy Van Slyke .30 .14
❑ 623 Paul Wagner .15 .07
❑ 624 Tim Wakefield .30 .14
❑ 625 Bob Walk .15 .07
❑ 626 Kevin Young .15 .07
❑ 627 Luis Alicea .15 .07
❑ 628 Rene Arocha .15 .07
❑ 629 Rod Brewer .15 .07
❑ 630 Rheal Cormier .15 .07
❑ 631 Bernard Gilkey .15 .07
❑ 632 Lee Guetterman .15 .07
❑ 633 Gregg Jefferies .15 .07
❑ 634 Brian Jordan .30 .14
❑ 635 Les Lancaster .15 .07
❑ 636 Ray Lankford .30 .14
❑ 637 Rob Murphy .15 .07
❑ 638 Omar Olivares .15 .07
❑ 639 Jose Oquendo .15 .07
❑ 640 Donovan Osborne .15 .07
❑ 641 Tom Pagnozzi .15 .07
❑ 642 Erik Pappas .15 .07
❑ 643 Geronimo Pena .15 .07
❑ 644 Mike Perez .15 .07
❑ 645 Gerald Perry .15 .07
❑ 646 Ozzie Smith .75 .35
❑ 647 Bob Tewksbury .15 .07
❑ 648 Allen Watson .15 .07
❑ 649 Mark Whiten .15 .07
❑ 650 Tracy Woodson .15 .07
❑ 651 Todd Zeile .15 .07
❑ 652 Andy Ashby .15 .07
❑ 653 Brad Ausmus .15 .07
❑ 654 Billy Bean .15 .07
❑ 655 Derek Bell .30 .14
❑ 656 Andy Benes .30 .14
❑ 657 Doug Brocail .15 .07
❑ 658 Jarvis Brown .15 .07
❑ 659 Archi Cianfrocco .15 .07
❑ 660 Phil Clark .15 .07
❑ 661 Mark Davis .15 .07
❑ 662 Jeff Gardner .15 .07
❑ 663 Pat Gomez .15 .07
❑ 664 Ricky Gutierrez .15 .07
❑ 665 Tony Gwynn 1.50 .70
❑ 666 Gene Harris .15 .07
❑ 667 Kevin Higgins .15 .07
❑ 668 Trevor Hoffman .30 .14
❑ 669 Pedro Martinez .15 .07
❑ 670 Tim Mauser .15 .07
❑ 671 Melvin Nieves .15 .07
❑ 672 Phil Plantier .15 .07
❑ 673 Frank Seminara .15 .07
❑ 674 Craig Shipley .15 .07
❑ 675 Kerry Taylor .15 .07
❑ 676 Tim Teufel .15 .07
❑ 677 Guillermo Velasquez .15 .07
❑ 678 Wally Whitehurst .15 .07
❑ 679 Tim Worrell .15 .07
❑ 680 Rod Beck .15 .07
❑ 681 Mike Benjamin .15 .07
❑ 682 Todd Benzinger .15 .07
❑ 683 Bud Black .15 .07
❑ 684 Barry Bonds .75 .35
❑ 685 Jeff Brantley .15 .07
❑ 686 Dave Burba .15 .07
❑ 687 John Burkett .15 .07
❑ 688 Mark Carreon .15 .07
❑ 689 Will Clark .60 .25
❑ 690 Royce Clayton .15 .07
❑ 691 Bryan Hickerson .15 .07
❑ 692 Mike Jackson .15 .07
❑ 693 Darren Lewis .15 .07
❑ 694 Kirt Manwaring .15 .07
❑ 695 Dave Martinez .15 .07
❑ 696 Willie McGee .30 .14
❑ 697 John Patterson .15 .07
❑ 698 Jeff Reed .15 .07
❑ 699 Kevin Rogers .15 .07
❑ 700 Scott Sanderson .15 .07
❑ 701 Steve Scarsone .15 .07
❑ 702 Billy Swift .15 .07
❑ 703 Robby Thompson .15 .07
❑ 704 Matt Williams .40 .18
❑ 705 Trevor Wilson .15 .07
❑ 706 Brave New World .60 .25
Fred McGriff
Ron Gant
David Justice
❑ 707 1-2 Punch .30 .14
John Olerud
Paul Molitor
❑ 708 American Heat .30 .14
Mike Mussina
Jack McDowell
❑ 709 Together Again .40 .18
Lou Whitaker
Alan Trammell
❑ 710 Lone Star Lumber .40 .18
Rafael Palmeiro
Juan Gonzalez
❑ 711 Batmen .40 .18
Brett Butler
Tony Gwynn
❑ 712 Twin Peaks .60 .25
Kirby Puckett
Chuck Knoblauch
❑ 713 Back to Back .75 .35
Mike Piazza
Eric Karros
❑ 714 Checklist 1 .15 .07
❑ 715 Checklist 2 .15 .07
❑ 716 Checklist 3 .15 .07
❑ 717 Checklist 4 .15 .07
❑ 718 Checklist 5 .15 .07
❑ 719 Checklist 6 .15 .07
❑ 720 Checklist 7 .15 .07
❑ P69 Tim Salmon Promo 1.00 .45

1994 Fleer All-Stars

	MINT	NRMT
COMPLETE SET (50)	25.00	11.00
COMMON CARD (1-50)	.25	.11

❑ 1 Roberto Alomar .75 .35
❑ 2 Carlos Baerga .40 .18
❑ 3 Albert Belle .75 .35
❑ 4 Wade Boggs .75 .35
❑ 5 Joe Carter .40 .18
❑ 6 Scott Cooper .25 .11
❑ 7 Cecil Fielder .40 .18
❑ 8 Travis Fryman .40 .18
❑ 9 Juan Gonzalez 2.00 .90
❑ 10 Ken Griffey Jr. 4.00 1.80
❑ 11 Pat Hentgen .40 .18
❑ 12 Randy Johnson .75 .35
❑ 13 Jimmy Key .40 .18
❑ 14 Mark Langston .25 .11
❑ 15 Jack McDowell .25 .11

	MINT	NRMT
❑ 16 Paul Molitor	.75	.35
❑ 17 Jeff Montgomery	.25	.11
❑ 18 Mike Mussina	.75	.35
❑ 19 John Olerud	.40	.18
❑ 20 Kirby Puckett	1.50	.70
❑ 21 Cal Ripken	3.00	1.35
❑ 22 Ivan Rodriguez	.75	.35
❑ 23 Frank Thomas	2.50	1.10
❑ 24 Greg Vaughn	.40	.18
❑ 25 Duane Ward	.25	.11
❑ 26 Steve Avery	.25	.11
❑ 27 Rod Beck	.25	.11
❑ 28 Jay Bell	.40	.18
❑ 29 Andy Benes	.40	.18
❑ 30 Jeff Blauser	.25	.11
❑ 31 Barry Bonds	.75	.35
❑ 32 Bobby Bonilla	.40	.18
❑ 33 John Burkett	.25	.11
❑ 34 Darren Daulton	.40	.18
❑ 35 Andres Galarraga	.75	.35
❑ 36 Tom Glavine	.75	.35
❑ 37 Mark Grace	.50	.23
❑ 38 Marquis Grissom	.40	.18
❑ 39 Tony Gwynn	2.00	.90
❑ 40 Bryan Harvey	.25	.11
❑ 41 Dave Hollins	.25	.11
❑ 42 David Justice	.75	.35
❑ 43 Darryl Kile	.40	.18
❑ 44 John Kruk	.40	.18
❑ 45 Barry Larkin	.50	.23
❑ 46 Terry Mulholland	.25	.11
❑ 47 Mike Piazza	2.50	1.10
❑ 48 Ryne Sandberg	1.00	.45
❑ 49 Gary Sheffield	.75	.35
❑ 50 John Smoltz	.40	.18

1994 Fleer Award Winners

	MINT	NRMT
COMPLETE SET (6)	12.00	5.50
COMMON CARD (1-6)	.25	.11
❑ 1 Frank Thomas	3.00	1.35
❑ 2 Barry Bonds	1.00	.45
❑ 3 Jack McDowell	.25	.11
❑ 4 Greg Maddux	3.00	1.35
❑ 5 Tim Salmon	1.00	.45
❑ 6 Mike Piazza	3.00	1.35

1994 Fleer Golden Moments

	MINT	NRMT
COMPLETE SET (10)	40.00	18.00
COMMON CARD (1-10)	.75	.35

*JUMBOS: 1.5X TO 4X BASIC CARDS
ONE JUMBO SET PER HOBBY CASE

	MINT	NRMT
❑ 1 Mark Whiten	.75	.35
❑ 2 Carlos Baerga	1.00	.45
❑ 3 Dave Winfield	2.50	1.10
❑ 4 Ken Griffey Jr.	15.00	6.75
❑ 5 Bo Jackson	1.00	.45
❑ 6 George Brett	5.00	2.20
❑ 7 Nolan Ryan	12.00	5.50
❑ 8 Fred McGriff	1.50	.70

	MINT	NRMT
❑ 9 Frank Thomas	10.00	4.50
❑ 10 Chris Bosio Jim Abbott Darryl Kile	.75	.35

1994 Fleer League Leaders

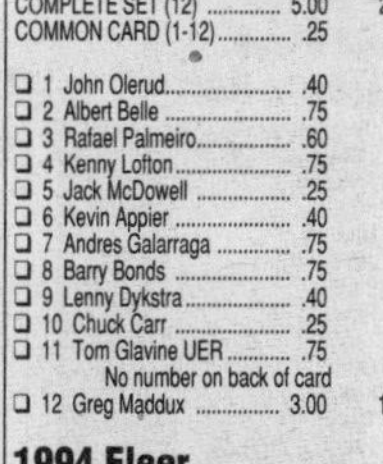

	MINT	NRMT
COMPLETE SET (12)	5.00	2.20
COMMON CARD (1-12)	.25	.11
❑ 1 John Olerud	.40	.18
❑ 2 Albert Belle	.75	.35
❑ 3 Rafael Palmeiro	.60	.25
❑ 4 Kenny Lofton	.75	.35
❑ 5 Jack McDowell	.25	.11
❑ 6 Kevin Appier	.40	.18
❑ 7 Andres Galarraga	.75	.35
❑ 8 Barry Bonds	.75	.35
❑ 9 Lenny Dykstra	.40	.18
❑ 10 Chuck Carr	.25	.11
❑ 11 Tom Glavine UER No number on back of card	.75	.35
❑ 12 Greg Maddux	3.00	1.35

1994 Fleer Lumber Company

	MINT	NRMT
COMPLETE SET (10)	12.00	5.50
COMMON CARD (1-10)	.40	.18
❑ 1 Albert Belle	1.00	.45
❑ 2 Barry Bonds	1.00	.45
❑ 3 Ron Gant	.40	.18
❑ 4 Juan Gonzalez	2.50	1.10
❑ 5 Ken Griffey Jr.	5.00	2.20
❑ 6 David Justice	1.00	.45
❑ 7 Fred McGriff	.75	.35
❑ 8 Rafael Palmeiro	.75	.35
❑ 9 Frank Thomas	3.00	1.35
❑ 10 Matt Williams	.75	.35

1994 Fleer Major League Prospects

	MINT	NRMT
COMPLETE SET (35)	15.00	6.75
COMMON CARD (1-35)	.25	.11
❑ 1 Kurt Abbott	.25	.11
❑ 2 Brian Anderson	1.00	.45
❑ 3 Rich Aude	.25	.11
❑ 4 Cory Bailey	.25	.11
❑ 5 Danny Bautista	.25	.11
❑ 6 Marty Cordova	.50	.23
❑ 7 Tripp Cromer	.25	.11
❑ 8 Midre Cummings	.25	.11
❑ 9 Carlos Delgado	2.00	.90
❑ 10 Steve Dreyer	.25	.11
❑ 11 Steve Dunn	.25	.11
❑ 12 Jeff Granger	.25	.11
❑ 13 Tyrone Hill	.25	.11
❑ 14 Denny Hocking	.25	.11
❑ 15 John Hope	.25	.11
❑ 16 Butch Huskey	.50	.23
❑ 17 Miguel Jimenez	.25	.11
❑ 18 Chipper Jones	6.00	2.70
❑ 19 Steve Karsay	.25	.11
❑ 20 Mike Kelly	.25	.11
❑ 21 Mike Lieberthal	.25	.11
❑ 22 Albie Lopez	.25	.11
❑ 23 Jeff McNeely	.25	.11
❑ 24 Dan Miceli	.25	.11
❑ 25 Nate Minchey	.25	.11
❑ 26 Marc Newfield	.25	.11
❑ 27 Darren Oliver	.50	.23
❑ 28 Luis Ortiz	.25	.11
❑ 29 Curtis Pride	.25	.11
❑ 30 Roger Salkeld	.25	.11
❑ 31 Scott Sanders	.25	.11
❑ 32 Dave Staton	.25	.11
❑ 33 Salomon Torres	.25	.11
❑ 34 Steve Trachsel	.25	.11
❑ 35 Chris Turner	.25	.11

1994 Fleer Pro-Visions

	MINT	NRMT
COMPLETE SET (9)	4.00	1.80
COMMON CARD (1-9)	.25	.11
❑ 1 Darren Daulton	.40	.18
❑ 2 John Olerud	.40	.18
❑ 3 Matt Williams	.60	.25
❑ 4 Carlos Baerga	.40	.18
❑ 5 Ozzie Smith	1.00	.45
❑ 6 Juan Gonzalez	2.00	.90
❑ 7 Jack McDowell	.25	.11

	MINT	NRMT
❑ 8 Mike Piazza	2.50	1.10
❑ 9 Tony Gwynn	2.00	.90

1994 Fleer Rookie Sensations

	MINT	NRMT
COMPLETE SET (20)	18.00	8.00
COMMON CARD (1-20)	.75	.35
❑ 1 Rene Arocha	.75	.35
❑ 2 Jason Bere	.75	.35
❑ 3 Jeromy Burnitz	1.50	.70
❑ 4 Chuck Carr	.75	.35
❑ 5 Jeff Conine	1.50	.70
❑ 6 Steve Cooke	.75	.35
❑ 7 Cliff Floyd	1.50	.70
❑ 8 Jeffrey Hammonds	1.50	.70
❑ 9 Wayne Kirby	.75	.35
❑ 10 Mike Lansing	1.50	.70
❑ 11 Al Martin	.75	.35
❑ 12 Greg McMichael	.75	.35
❑ 13 Troy Neel	.75	.35
❑ 14 Mike Piazza	12.00	5.50
❑ 15 Armando Reynoso	.75	.35
❑ 16 Kirk Rueter	.75	.35
❑ 17 Tim Salmon	2.50	1.10
❑ 18 Aaron Sele	1.50	.70
❑ 19 J.T. Snow	1.50	.70
❑ 20 Kevin Stocker	.75	.35

1994 Fleer Salmon

	MINT	NRMT
COMPLETE SET (12)	25.00	11.00
COMMON CARD (1-12)	2.50	1.10
COMMON MAIL-IN (13-15)	2.50	1.10
❑ 1 Tim Salmon Watching flight of ball after hit	2.50	1.10
❑ 2 Tim Salmon Trotting in to catch ball	2.50	1.10
❑ 3 Tim Salmon Follow through weight on front leg	2.50	1.10
❑ 4 Tim Salmon Middle of swing horizontal pose	2.50	1.10
❑ 5 Tim Salmon Sliding into base	2.50	1.10
❑ 6 Tim Salmon Pose swing end of bat in camera angle	2.50	1.10
❑ 7 Tim Salmon Running with shades on	2.50	1.10
❑ 8 Tim Salmon Bat cocked awaiting pitch	2.50	1.10
❑ 9 Tim Salmon Adjusting batting gloves bat under arm	2.50	1.10
❑ 10 Tim Salmon Running to base	2.50	1.10
❑ 11 Tim Salmon Awaiting pitch shot from left side with catcher in view	2.50	1.10
❑ 12 Tim Salmon Ready to play	2.50	1.10
❑ 13 Tim Salmon Awaiting a pitch	2.50	1.10
❑ 14 Tim Salmon Fielding	2.50	1.10
❑ 15 Tim Salmon Running the bases	2.50	1.10
❑ AU0 Tim Salmon AU (Certified autograph)	80.00	36.00

1994 Fleer Smoke 'n Heat

	MINT	NRMT
COMPLETE SET (12)	60.00	27.00
COMMON CARD (1-12)	1.50	.70
❑ 1 Roger Clemens	12.00	5.50
❑ 2 David Cone	4.00	1.80
❑ 3 Juan Guzman	1.50	.70
❑ 4 Pete Harnisch	1.50	.70
❑ 5 Randy Johnson	6.00	2.70
❑ 6 Mark Langston	1.50	.70
❑ 7 Greg Maddux	20.00	9.00
❑ 8 Mike Mussina	6.00	2.70
❑ 9 Jose Rijo	1.50	.70
❑ 10 Nolan Ryan	25.00	11.00
❑ 11 Curt Schilling	2.50	1.10
❑ 12 John Smoltz	2.50	1.10

1994 Fleer Team Leaders

	MINT	NRMT
COMPLETE SET (28)	25.00	11.00
COMMON CARD (1-28)	.25	.11
❑ 1 Cal Ripken	4.00	1.80
❑ 2 Mo Vaughn	1.00	.45
❑ 3 Tim Salmon	1.00	.45
❑ 4 Frank Thomas	3.00	1.35
❑ 5 Carlos Baerga	.50	.23
❑ 6 Cecil Fielder	.50	.23
❑ 7 Brian McRae	.25	.11
❑ 8 Greg Vaughn	.50	.23
❑ 9 Kirby Puckett	1.50	.70
❑ 10 Don Mattingly	1.25	.55
❑ 11 Mark McGwire	5.00	2.20
❑ 12 Ken Griffey Jr.	5.00	2.20
❑ 13 Juan Gonzalez	2.50	1.10
❑ 14 Paul Molitor	1.00	.45
❑ 15 David Justice	1.00	.45
❑ 16 Ryne Sandberg	1.25	.55
❑ 17 Barry Larkin	.75	.35
❑ 18 Andres Galarraga	1.00	.45
❑ 19 Gary Sheffield	1.00	.45
❑ 20 Jeff Bagwell	2.00	.90
❑ 21 Mike Piazza	3.00	1.35
❑ 22 Marquis Grissom	.50	.23
❑ 23 Bobby Bonilla	.50	.23
❑ 24 Lenny Dykstra	.50	.23
❑ 25 Jay Bell	.50	.23
❑ 26 Gregg Jefferies	.25	.11
❑ 27 Tony Gwynn	2.50	1.10
❑ 28 Will Clark	1.00	.45

1994 Fleer Update

	MINT	NRMT
COMP.FACT.SET (210)	60.00	27.00
COMPLETE SET (200)	15.00	6.75
COMMON CARD (U1-U200)	.15	.07
❑ 1 Mark Eichhorn	.15	.07
❑ 2 Sid Fernandez	.15	.07
❑ 3 Leo Gomez	.15	.07
❑ 4 Mike Oquist	.15	.07
❑ 5 Rafael Palmeiro	.50	.23
❑ 6 Chris Sabo	.15	.07
❑ 7 Dwight Smith	.15	.07

❑ 8 Lee Smith .25 .11
❑ 9 Damon Berryhill .15 .07
❑ 10 Wes Chamberlain .15 .07
❑ 11 Gar Finnvold .15 .07
❑ 12 Chris Howard .15 .07
❑ 13 Tim Naehring .15 .07
❑ 14 Otis Nixon .15 .07
❑ 15 Brian Anderson .50 .23
❑ 16 Jorge Fabregas .15 .07
❑ 17 Rex Hudler .15 .07
❑ 18 Bo Jackson .25 .11
❑ 19 Mark Leiter .15 .07
❑ 20 Spike Owen .15 .07
❑ 21 Harold Reynolds .15 .07
❑ 22 Chris Turner .15 .07
❑ 23 Dennis Cook .15 .07
❑ 24 Jose DeLeon .15 .07
❑ 25 Julio Franco .15 .07
❑ 26 Joe Hall .15 .07
❑ 27 Darrin Jackson .15 .07
❑ 28 Dane Johnson .15 .07
❑ 29 Norberto Martin .15 .07
❑ 30 Scott Sanderson .15 .07
❑ 31 Jason Grimsley .15 .07
❑ 32 Dennis Martinez .25 .11
❑ 33 Jack Morris .25 .11
❑ 34 Eddie Murray 1.00 .45
❑ 35 Chad Ogea .25 .11
❑ 36 Tony Pena .15 .07
❑ 37 Paul Shuey .15 .07
❑ 38 Omar Vizquel .25 .11
❑ 39 Danny Bautista .15 .07
❑ 40 Tim Belcher .15 .07
❑ 41 Joe Boever .15 .07
❑ 42 Storm Davis .15 .07
❑ 43 Junior Felix .15 .07
❑ 44 Mike Gardiner .15 .07
❑ 45 Buddy Groom .15 .07
❑ 46 Juan Samuel .15 .07
❑ 47 Vince Coleman .15 .07
❑ 48 Bob Hamelin .15 .07
❑ 49 Dave Henderson .15 .07
❑ 50 Rusty Meacham .15 .07
❑ 51 Terry Shumpert .15 .07
❑ 52 Jeff Bronkey .15 .07
❑ 53 Alex Diaz .15 .07
❑ 54 Brian Harper .15 .07
❑ 55 Jose Mercedes .15 .07
❑ 56 Jody Reed .15 .07
❑ 57 Bob Scanlan .15 .07
❑ 58 Turner Ward .15 .07
❑ 59 Rich Becker .15 .07
❑ 60 Alex Cole .15 .07
❑ 61 Denny Hocking .15 .07
❑ 62 Scott Leius .15 .07
❑ 63 Pat Mahomes .15 .07
❑ 64 Carlos Pulido .15 .07
❑ 65 Dave Stevens .15 .07
❑ 66 Matt Walbeck .15 .07
❑ 67 Xavier Hernandez .15 .07
❑ 68 Sterling Hitchcock .25 .11
❑ 69 Terry Mulholland .15 .07
❑ 70 Luis Polonia .15 .07
❑ 71 Gerald Williams .15 .07
❑ 72 Mark Acre .15 .07
❑ 73 Geronimo Berroa .15 .07
❑ 74 Rickey Henderson 1.00 .45
❑ 75 Stan Javier .15 .07
❑ 76 Steve Karsay .15 .07
❑ 77 Carlos Reyes .15 .07
❑ 78 Bill Taylor .15 .07
❑ 79 Eric Anthony .15 .07
❑ 80 Bobby Ayala .15 .07
❑ 81 Tim Davis .15 .07
❑ 82 Felix Fermin .15 .07
❑ 83 Reggie Jefferson .15 .07
❑ 84 Keith Mitchell .15 .07
❑ 85 Bill Risley .15 .07
❑ 86 Alex Rodriguez 50.00 22.00
❑ 87 Roger Salkeld .15 .07
❑ 88 Dan Wilson .15 .07
❑ 89 Cris Carpenter .15 .07
❑ 90 Will Clark 1.00 .45
❑ 91 Jeff Frye .15 .07
❑ 92 Rick Helling .25 .11
❑ 93 Chris James .15 .07
❑ 94 Oddibe McDowell .15 .07
❑ 95 Billy Ripken .15 .07
❑ 96 Carlos Delgado .50 .23
❑ 97 Alex Gonzalez .15 .07
❑ 98 Shawn Green .25 .11
❑ 99 Darren Hall .15 .07
❑ 100 Mike Huff .15 .07
❑ 101 Mike Kelly .15 .07
❑ 102 Roberto Kelly .15 .07
❑ 103 Charlie O'Brien .15 .07
❑ 104 Jose Oliva .15 .07
❑ 105 Gregg Olson .15 .07
❑ 106 Willie Banks .15 .07
❑ 107 Jim Bullinger .15 .07
❑ 108 Chuck Crim .15 .07
❑ 109 Shawon Dunston .15 .07
❑ 110 Karl Rhodes .15 .07
❑ 111 Steve Trachsel .15 .07
❑ 112 Anthony Young .15 .07
❑ 113 Eddie Zambrano .15 .07
❑ 114 Bret Boone .25 .11
❑ 115 Jeff Brantley .15 .07
❑ 116 Hector Carrasco .15 .07
❑ 117 Tony Fernandez .15 .07
❑ 118 Tim Fortugno .15 .07
❑ 119 Erik Hanson .15 .07
❑ 120 Chuck McElroy .15 .07
❑ 121 Deion Sanders .25 .11
❑ 122 Ellis Burks .25 .11
❑ 123 Marvin Freeman .15 .07
❑ 124 Mike Harkey .15 .07
❑ 125 Howard Johnson .15 .07
❑ 126 Mike Kingery .15 .07
❑ 127 Nelson Liriano .15 .07
❑ 128 Marcus Moore .15 .07
❑ 129 Mike Munoz .15 .07
❑ 130 Kevin Ritz .15 .07
❑ 131 Walt Weiss .15 .07
❑ 132 Kurt Abbott .15 .07
❑ 133 Jerry Browne .15 .07
❑ 134 Greg Colbrunn .15 .07
❑ 135 Jeremy Hernandez .15 .07
❑ 136 Dave Magadan .15 .07
❑ 137 Kurt Miller .15 .07
❑ 138 Robb Nen .15 .07
❑ 139 Jesus Tavarez .15 .07
❑ 140 Sid Bream .15 .07
❑ 141 Tom Edens .15 .07
❑ 142 Tony Eusebio .15 .07
❑ 143 John Hudek .15 .07
❑ 144 Brian L. Hunter .25 .11
❑ 145 Orlando Miller .15 .07
❑ 146 James Mouton .15 .07
❑ 147 Shane Reynolds .25 .11
❑ 148 Rafael Bournigal .15 .07
❑ 149 Delino DeShields .15 .07
❑ 150 Garey Ingram .15 .07
❑ 151 Chan Ho Park 3.00 1.35
❑ 152 Wil Cordero .15 .07
❑ 153 Pedro Martinez 1.25 .55
❑ 154 Randy Milligan .15 .07
❑ 155 Lenny Webster .15 .07
❑ 156 Rico Brogna .15 .07
❑ 157 Josias Manzanillo .15 .07
❑ 158 Kevin McReynolds .15 .07
❑ 159 Mike Remlinger .15 .07
❑ 160 David Segui .25 .11
❑ 161 Pete Smith .15 .07
❑ 162 Kelly Stinnett .15 .07
❑ 163 Jose Vizcaino .15 .07
❑ 164 Billy Hatcher .15 .07
❑ 165 Doug Jones .15 .07
❑ 166 Mike Lieberthal .15 .07
❑ 167 Tony Longmire .15 .07
❑ 168 Bobby Munoz .15 .07
❑ 169 Paul Quantrill .15 .07
❑ 170 Heathcliff Slocumb .15 .07
❑ 171 Fernando Valenzuela .25 .11
❑ 172 Mark Dewey .15 .07
❑ 173 Brian R. Hunter .15 .07
❑ 174 Jon Lieber .15 .07
❑ 175 Ravelo Manzanillo .15 .07
❑ 176 Dan Miceli .15 .07
❑ 177 Rick White .15 .07
❑ 178 Bryan Eversgerd .15 .07
❑ 179 John Habyan .15 .07
❑ 180 Terry McGriff .15 .07
❑ 181 Vicente Palacios .15 .07
❑ 182 Rich Rodriguez .15 .07
❑ 183 Rick Sutcliffe .15 .07
❑ 184 Donnie Elliott .15 .07
❑ 185 Joey Hamilton 1.00 .45
❑ 186 Tim Hyers .15 .07
❑ 187 Luis Lopez .15 .07
❑ 188 Ray McDavid .15 .07
❑ 189 Bip Roberts .15 .07
❑ 190 Scott Sanders .15 .07
❑ 191 Eddie Williams .15 .07
❑ 192 Steve Frey .15 .07
❑ 193 Pat Gomez .15 .07
❑ 194 Rich Monteleone .15 .07
❑ 195 Mark Portugal .15 .07
❑ 196 Darryl Strawberry .25 .11
❑ 197 Salomon Torres .15 .07
❑ 198 W.VanLandingham .15 .07
❑ 199 Checklist .15 .07
❑ 200 Checklist .15 .07

1994 Fleer Update Diamond Tribute

	MINT	NRMT
COMPLETE SET (10)	2.00	.90
COMMON CARD (1-10)	.15	.07

❑ 1 Barry Bonds .30 .14
❑ 2 Joe Carter .15 .07
❑ 3 Will Clark .30 .14
❑ 4 Roger Clemens .60 .25
❑ 5 Tony Gwynn .75 .35
❑ 6 Don Mattingly .40 .18
❑ 7 Fred McGriff .25 .11
❑ 8 Eddie Murray .30 .14
❑ 9 Kirby Puckett .50 .23
❑ 10 Cal Ripken 1.25 .55

1995 Fleer

	MINT	NRMT
COMPLETE SET (600)	50.00	22.00
COMMON CARD (1-600)	.15	.07

❑ 1 Brady Anderson .30 .14
❑ 2 Harold Baines .30 .14

3	Damon Buford	.15	.07
4	Mike Devereaux	.15	.07
5	Mark Eichhorn	.15	.07
6	Sid Fernandez	.15	.07
7	Leo Gomez	.15	.07
8	Jeffrey Hammonds	.30	.14
9	Chris Hoiles	.15	.07
10	Rick Krivda	.15	.07
11	Ben McDonald	.15	.07
12	Mark McLemore	.15	.07
13	Alan Mills	.15	.07
14	Jamie Moyer	.15	.07
15	Mike Mussina	.60	.25
16	Mike Oquist	.15	.07
17	Rafael Palmeiro	.40	.18
18	Arthur Rhodes	.15	.07
19	Cal Ripken Jr.	2.50	1.10
20	Chris Sabo	.15	.07
21	Lee Smith	.30	.14
22	Jack Voigt	.15	.07
23	Damon Berryhill	.15	.07
24	Tom Brunansky	.15	.07
25	Wes Chamberlain	.15	.07
26	Roger Clemens	1.25	.55
27	Scott Cooper	.15	.07
28	Andre Dawson	.40	.18
29	Gar Finnvold	.15	.07
30	Tony Fossas	.15	.07
31	Mike Greenwell	.15	.07
32	Joe Hesketh	.15	.07
33	Chris Howard	.15	.07
34	Chris Nabholz	.15	.07
35	Tim Naehring	.15	.07
36	Otis Nixon	.15	.07
37	Carlos Rodriguez	.15	.07
38	Rich Rowland	.15	.07
39	Ken Ryan	.15	.07
40	Aaron Sele	.30	.14
41	John Valentin	.30	.14
42	Mo Vaughn	.75	.35
43	Frank Viola	.15	.07
44	Danny Bautista	.15	.07
45	Joe Boever	.15	.07
46	Milt Cuyler	.15	.07
47	Storm Davis	.15	.07
48	John Doherty	.15	.07
49	Junior Felix	.15	.07
50	Cecil Fielder	.30	.14
51	Travis Fryman	.30	.14
52	Mike Gardiner	.15	.07
53	Kirk Gibson	.30	.14
54	Chris Gomez	.15	.07
55	Buddy Groom	.15	.07
56	Mike Henneman	.15	.07
57	Chad Kreuter	.15	.07
58	Mike Moore	.15	.07
59	Tony Phillips	.15	.07
60	Juan Samuel	.15	.07
61	Mickey Tettleton	.15	.07
62	Alan Trammell	.30	.14
63	David Wells	.40	.18
64	Lou Whitaker	.30	.14
65	Jim Abbott	.30	.14
66	Joe Ausanio	.15	.07
67	Wade Boggs	.60	.25
68	Mike Gallego	.15	.07
69	Xavier Hernandez	.15	.07
70	Sterling Hitchcock	.30	.14
71	Steve Howe	.15	.07
72	Scott Kamieniecki	.15	.07
73	Pat Kelly	.15	.07
74	Jimmy Key	.30	.14
75	Jim Leyritz	.30	.14
76	Don Mattingly UER Photo is a reversed negative	1.00	.45
77	Terry Mulholland	.15	.07
78	Paul O'Neill	.30	.14
79	Melido Perez	.15	.07
80	Luis Polonia	.15	.07
81	Mike Stanley	.15	.07
82	Danny Tartabull	.15	.07
83	Randy Velarde	.15	.07
84	Bob Wickman	.15	.07
85	Bernie Williams	.60	.25
86	Gerald Williams	.15	.07
87	Roberto Alomar	.60	.25
88	Pat Borders	.15	.07
89	Joe Carter	.30	.14
90	Tony Castillo	.15	.07
91	Brad Cornett	.15	.07
92	Carlos Delgado	.30	.14
93	Alex Gonzalez	.15	.07
94	Shawn Green	.30	.14
95	Juan Guzman	.15	.07
96	Darren Hall	.15	.07
97	Pat Hentgen	.30	.14
98	Mike Huff	.15	.07
99	Randy Knorr	.15	.07
100	Al Leiter	.30	.14
101	Paul Molitor	.60	.25
102	John Olerud	.30	.14
103	Dick Schofield	.15	.07
104	Ed Sprague	.15	.07
105	Dave Stewart	.30	.14
106	Todd Stottlemyre	.15	.07
107	Devon White	.30	.14
108	Woody Williams	.15	.07
109	Wilson Alvarez	.30	.14
110	Paul Assenmacher	.15	.07
111	Jason Bere	.15	.07
112	Dennis Cook	.15	.07
113	Joey Cora	.30	.14
114	Jose DeLeon	.15	.07
115	Alex Fernandez	.15	.07
116	Julio Franco	.15	.07
117	Craig Grebeck	.15	.07
118	Ozzie Guillen	.15	.07
119	Roberto Hernandez	.15	.07
120	Darrin Jackson	.15	.07
121	Lance Johnson	.15	.07
122	Ron Karkovice	.15	.07
123	Mike LaValliere	.15	.07
124	Norberto Martin	.15	.07
125	Kirk McCaskill	.15	.07
126	Jack McDowell	.15	.07
127	Tim Raines	.30	.14
128	Frank Thomas	2.00	.90
129	Robin Ventura	.30	.14
130	Sandy Alomar Jr.	.30	.14
131	Carlos Baerga	.30	.14
132	Albert Belle	.75	.35
133	Mark Clark	.15	.07
134	Alvaro Espinoza	.15	.07
135	Jason Grimsley	.15	.07
136	Wayne Kirby	.15	.07
137	Kenny Lofton	.60	.25
138	Albie Lopez	.15	.07
139	Dennis Martinez	.30	.14
140	Jose Mesa	.15	.07
141	Eddie Murray	.60	.25
142	Charles Nagy	.30	.14
143	Tony Pena	.15	.07
144	Eric Plunk	.15	.07
145	Manny Ramirez	.60	.25
146	Jeff Russell	.15	.07
147	Paul Shuey	.15	.07
148	Paul Sorrento	.15	.07
149	Jim Thome	.60	.25
150	Omar Vizquel	.30	.14
151	Dave Winfield	.60	.25
152	Kevin Appier	.30	.14
153	Billy Brewer	.15	.07
154	Vince Coleman	.15	.07
155	David Cone	.40	.18
156	Gary Gaetti	.30	.14
157	Greg Gagne	.15	.07
158	Tom Gordon	.15	.07
159	Mark Gubicza	.15	.07
160	Bob Hamelin	.15	.07
161	Dave Henderson	.15	.07
162	Felix Jose	.15	.07
163	Wally Joyner	.30	.14
164	Jose Lind	.15	.07
165	Mike Macfarlane	.15	.07
166	Mike Magnante	.15	.07
167	Brent Mayne	.15	.07
168	Brian McRae	.15	.07
169	Rusty Meacham	.15	.07
170	Jeff Montgomery	.15	.07
171	Hipolito Pichardo	.15	.07
172	Terry Shumpert	.15	.07
173	Michael Tucker	.30	.14
174	Ricky Bones	.15	.07
175	Jeff Cirillo	.30	.14
176	Alex Diaz	.15	.07
177	Cal Eldred	.15	.07
178	Mike Fetters	.15	.07
179	Darryl Hamilton	.15	.07
180	Brian Harper	.15	.07
181	John Jaha	.15	.07
182	Pat Listach	.15	.07
183	Graeme Lloyd	.15	.07
184	Jose Mercedes	.15	.07
185	Matt Mieske	.15	.07
186	Dave Nilsson	.15	.07
187	Jody Reed	.15	.07
188	Bob Scanlan	.15	.07
189	Kevin Seitzer	.15	.07
190	Bill Spiers	.15	.07
191	B.J. Surhoff	.30	.14
192	Jose Valentin	.15	.07
193	Greg Vaughn	.30	.14
194	Turner Ward	.15	.07
195	Bill Wegman	.15	.07
196	Rick Aguilera	.15	.07
197	Rich Becker	.15	.07
198	Alex Cole	.15	.07
199	Marty Cordova	.15	.07
200	Steve Dunn	.15	.07
201	Scott Erickson	.30	.14
202	Mark Guthrie	.15	.07
203	Chip Hale	.15	.07
204	LaTroy Hawkins	.15	.07
205	Denny Hocking	.15	.07
206	Chuck Knoblauch	.60	.25
207	Scott Leius	.15	.07
208	Shane Mack	.15	.07
209	Pat Mahomes	.15	.07
210	Pat Meares	.15	.07
211	Pedro Munoz	.15	.07
212	Kirby Puckett	1.00	.45
213	Jeff Reboulet	.15	.07
214	Dave Stevens	.15	.07
215	Kevin Tapani	.15	.07
216	Matt Walbeck	.15	.07
217	Carl Willis	.15	.07
218	Brian Anderson	.30	.14
219	Chad Curtis	.15	.07
220	Chili Davis	.30	.14
221	Gary DiSarcina	.15	.07
222	Damion Easley	.30	.14
223	Jim Edmonds	.40	.18
224	Chuck Finley	.30	.14
225	Joe Grahe	.15	.07
226	Rex Hudler	.15	.07
227	Bo Jackson	.30	.14
228	Mark Langston	.15	.07
229	Phil Leftwich	.15	.07
230	Mark Leiter	.15	.07
231	Spike Owen	.15	.07
232	Bob Patterson	.15	.07
233	Troy Percival	.30	.14
234	Eduardo Perez	.15	.07
235	Tim Salmon	.60	.25
236	J.T. Snow	.30	.14
237	Chris Turner	.15	.07
238	Mark Acre	.15	.07
239	Geronimo Berroa	.15	.07
240	Mike Bordick	.15	.07
241	John Briscoe	.15	.07
242	Scott Brosius	.30	.14
243	Ron Darling	.15	.07
244	Dennis Eckersley	.30	.14
245	Brent Gates	.15	.07
246	Rickey Henderson	.60	.25
247	Stan Javier	.15	.07
248	Steve Karsay	.15	.07
249	Mark McGwire	3.00	1.35
250	Troy Neel	.15	.07
251	Steve Ontiveros	.15	.07
252	Carlos Reyes	.15	.07
253	Ruben Sierra	.15	.07
254	Terry Steinbach	.30	.14
255	Bill Taylor	.15	.07
256	Todd Van Poppel	.15	.07

❑ 257 Bobby Witt .15 .07
❑ 258 Rich Amaral .15 .07
❑ 259 Eric Anthony .15 .07
❑ 260 Bobby Ayala .15 .07
❑ 261 Mike Blowers .15 .07
❑ 262 Chris Bosio .15 .07
❑ 263 Jay Buhner .30 .14
❑ 264 John Cummings .15 .07
❑ 265 Tim Davis .15 .07
❑ 266 Felix Fermin .15 .07
❑ 267 Dave Fleming .15 .07
❑ 268 Goose Gossage .30 .14
❑ 269 Ken Griffey Jr. 3.00 1.35
❑ 270 Reggie Jefferson .15 .07
❑ 271 Randy Johnson .60 .25
❑ 272 Edgar Martinez .30 .14
❑ 273 Tino Martinez .60 .25
❑ 274 Greg Pirkl .15 .07
❑ 275 Bill Risley .15 .07
❑ 276 Roger Salkeld .15 .07
❑ 277 Luis Sojo .15 .07
❑ 278 Mac Suzuki .30 .14
❑ 279 Dan Wilson .15 .07
❑ 280 Kevin Brown .40 .18
❑ 281 Jose Canseco .60 .25
❑ 282 Cris Carpenter .15 .07
❑ 283 Will Clark .60 .25
❑ 284 Jeff Frye .15 .07
❑ 285 Juan Gonzalez 1.50 .70
❑ 286 Rick Helling .30 .14
❑ 287 Tom Henke .15 .07
❑ 288 David Hulse .15 .07
❑ 289 Chris James .15 .07
❑ 290 Manuel Lee .15 .07
❑ 291 Oddibe McDowell .15 .07
❑ 292 Dean Palmer .30 .14
❑ 293 Roger Pavlik .15 .07
❑ 294 Bill Ripken .15 .07
❑ 295 Ivan Rodriguez .75 .35
❑ 296 Kenny Rogers .15 .07
❑ 297 Doug Strange .15 .07
❑ 298 Matt Whiteside .15 .07
❑ 299 Steve Avery .15 .07
❑ 300 Steve Bedrosian .15 .07
❑ 301 Rafael Belliard .15 .07
❑ 302 Jeff Blauser .15 .07
❑ 303 Dave Gallagher .15 .07
❑ 304 Tom Glavine .60 .25
❑ 305 David Justice .60 .25
❑ 306 Mike Kelly .15 .07
❑ 307 Roberto Kelly .15 .07
❑ 308 Ryan Klesko .30 .14
❑ 309 Mark Lemke .15 .07
❑ 310 Javier Lopez .30 .14
❑ 311 Greg Maddux 2.00 .90
❑ 312 Fred McGriff .40 .18
❑ 313 Greg McMichael .15 .07
❑ 314 Kent Mercker .15 .07
❑ 315 Charlie O'Brien .15 .07
❑ 316 Jose Oliva .15 .07
❑ 317 Terry Pendleton .15 .07
❑ 318 John Smoltz .30 .14
❑ 319 Mike Stanton .15 .07
❑ 320 Tony Tarasco .15 .07
❑ 321 Terrell Wade .15 .07
❑ 322 Mark Wohlers .15 .07
❑ 323 Kurt Abbott .15 .07
❑ 324 Luis Aquino .15 .07
❑ 325 Bret Barberie .15 .07
❑ 326 Ryan Bowen .15 .07
❑ 327 Jerry Browne .15 .07
❑ 328 Chuck Carr .15 .07
❑ 329 Matias Carrillo .15 .07
❑ 330 Greg Colbrunn .15 .07
❑ 331 Jeff Conine .30 .14
❑ 332 Mark Gardner .15 .07
❑ 333 Chris Hammond .15 .07
❑ 334 Bryan Harvey .15 .07
❑ 335 Richie Lewis .15 .07
❑ 336 Dave Magadan .15 .07
❑ 337 Terry Mathews .15 .07
❑ 338 Robb Nen .15 .07
❑ 339 Yorkis Perez .15 .07
❑ 340 Pat Rapp .15 .07
❑ 341 Benito Santiago .15 .07
❑ 342 Gary Sheffield .40 .18
❑ 343 Dave Weathers .15 .07
❑ 344 Moises Alou .40 .18
❑ 345 Sean Berry .15 .07
❑ 346 Wil Cordero .15 .07
❑ 347 Joey Eischen .15 .07
❑ 348 Jeff Fassero .15 .07
❑ 349 Darrin Fletcher .15 .07
❑ 350 Cliff Floyd .30 .14
❑ 351 Marquis Grissom .30 .14
❑ 352 Butch Henry .15 .07
❑ 353 Gil Heredia .15 .07
❑ 354 Ken Hill .15 .07
❑ 355 Mike Lansing .15 .07
❑ 356 Pedro Martinez .60 .25
❑ 357 Mel Rojas .15 .07
❑ 358 Kirk Rueter .15 .07
❑ 359 Tim Scott .15 .07
❑ 360 Jeff Shaw .15 .07
❑ 361 Larry Walker .60 .25
❑ 362 Lenny Webster .15 .07
❑ 363 John Wetteland .30 .14
❑ 364 Rondell White .30 .14
❑ 365 Bobby Bonilla .30 .14
❑ 366 Rico Brogna .15 .07
❑ 367 Jeromy Burnitz .30 .14
❑ 368 John Franco .30 .14
❑ 369 Dwight Gooden .30 .14
❑ 370 Todd Hundley .30 .14
❑ 371 Jason Jacome .15 .07
❑ 372 Bobby Jones .15 .07
❑ 373 Jeff Kent .30 .14
❑ 374 Jim Lindeman .15 .07
❑ 375 Josias Manzanillo .15 .07
❑ 376 Roger Mason .15 .07
❑ 377 Kevin McReynolds .15 .07
❑ 378 Joe Orsulak .15 .07
❑ 379 Bill Pulsipher .15 .07
❑ 380 Bret Saberhagen .30 .14
❑ 381 David Segui .30 .14
❑ 382 Pete Smith .15 .07
❑ 383 Kelly Stinnett .15 .07
❑ 384 Ryan Thompson .15 .07
❑ 385 Jose Vizcaino .15 .07
❑ 386 Toby Borland .15 .07
❑ 387 Ricky Bottalico .30 .14
❑ 388 Darren Daulton .30 .14
❑ 389 Mariano Duncan .15 .07
❑ 390 Lenny Dykstra .30 .14
❑ 391 Jim Eisenreich .15 .07
❑ 392 Tommy Greene .15 .07
❑ 393 Dave Hollins .15 .07
❑ 394 Pete Incaviglia .15 .07
❑ 395 Danny Jackson .15 .07
❑ 396 Doug Jones .15 .07
❑ 397 Ricky Jordan .15 .07
❑ 398 John Kruk .30 .14
❑ 399 Mike Lieberthal .15 .07
❑ 400 Tony Longmire .15 .07
❑ 401 Mickey Morandini .15 .07
❑ 402 Bobby Munoz .15 .07
❑ 403 Curt Schilling .30 .14
❑ 404 Heathcliff Slocumb .15 .07
❑ 405 Kevin Stocker .15 .07
❑ 406 Fernando Valenzuela .30 .14
❑ 407 David West .40 .18
❑ 408 Willie Banks .15 .07
❑ 409 Jose Bautista .15 .07
❑ 410 Steve Buechele .15 .07
❑ 411 Jim Bullinger .15 .07
❑ 412 Chuck Crim .15 .07
❑ 413 Shawon Dunston .15 .07
❑ 414 Kevin Foster .15 .07
❑ 415 Mark Grace .40 .18
❑ 416 Jose Hernandez .15 .07
❑ 417 Glenallen Hill .15 .07
❑ 418 Brooks Kieschnick .15 .07
❑ 419 Derrick May .15 .07
❑ 420 Randy Myers .15 .07
❑ 421 Dan Plesac .15 .07
❑ 422 Karl Rhodes .15 .07
❑ 423 Rey Sanchez .15 .07
❑ 424 Sammy Sosa 1.50 .70
❑ 425 Steve Trachsel .15 .07
❑ 426 Rick Wilkins .15 .07
❑ 427 Anthony Young .15 .07
❑ 428 Eddie Zambrano .15 .07
❑ 429 Bret Boone .30 .14
❑ 430 Jeff Branson .15 .07
❑ 431 Jeff Brantley .15 .07
❑ 432 Hector Carrasco .15 .07
❑ 433 Brian Dorsett .15 .07
❑ 434 Tony Fernandez .15 .07
❑ 435 Tim Fortugno .15 .07
❑ 436 Erik Hanson .15 .07
❑ 437 Thomas Howard .15 .07
❑ 438 Kevin Jarvis .15 .07
❑ 439 Barry Larkin .40 .18
❑ 440 Chuck McElroy .15 .07
❑ 441 Kevin Mitchell .15 .07
❑ 442 Hal Morris .15 .07
❑ 443 Jose Rijo .15 .07
❑ 444 John Roper .15 .07
❑ 445 Johnny Ruffin .15 .07
❑ 446 Deion Sanders .30 .14
❑ 447 Reggie Sanders .30 .14
❑ 448 Pete Schourek .15 .07
❑ 449 John Smiley .15 .07
❑ 450 Eddie Taubensee .15 .07
❑ 451 Jeff Bagwell 1.00 .45
❑ 452 Kevin Bass .15 .07
❑ 453 Craig Biggio .60 .25
❑ 454 Ken Caminiti .40 .18
❑ 455 Andujar Cedeno .15 .07
❑ 456 Doug Drabek .15 .07
❑ 457 Tony Eusebio .15 .07
❑ 458 Mike Felder .15 .07
❑ 459 Steve Finley .30 .14
❑ 460 Luis Gonzalez .15 .07
❑ 461 Mike Hampton .15 .07
❑ 462 Pete Harnisch .15 .07
❑ 463 John Hudek .15 .07
❑ 464 Todd Jones .15 .07
❑ 465 Darryl Kile .30 .14
❑ 466 James Mouton .15 .07
❑ 467 Shane Reynolds .30 .14
❑ 468 Scott Servais .15 .07
❑ 469 Greg Swindell .15 .07
❑ 470 Dave Veres .15 .07
❑ 471 Brian Williams .15 .07
❑ 472 Jay Bell .30 .14
❑ 473 Jacob Brumfield .15 .07
❑ 474 Dave Clark .15 .07
❑ 475 Steve Cooke .15 .07
❑ 476 Midre Cummings .15 .07
❑ 477 Mark Dewey .15 .07
❑ 478 Tom Foley .15 .07
❑ 479 Carlos Garcia .15 .07
❑ 480 Jeff King .15 .07
❑ 481 Jon Lieber .15 .07
❑ 482 Ravelo Manzanillo .15 .07
❑ 483 Al Martin .15 .07
❑ 484 Orlando Merced .15 .07
❑ 485 Danny Miceli .15 .07
❑ 486 Denny Neagle .30 .14
❑ 487 Lance Parrish .15 .07
❑ 488 Don Slaught .15 .07
❑ 489 Zane Smith .15 .07
❑ 490 Andy Van Slyke .30 .14
❑ 491 Paul Wagner .15 .07
❑ 492 Rick White .15 .07
❑ 493 Luis Alicea .15 .07
❑ 494 Rene Arocha .15 .07
❑ 495 Rheal Cormier .15 .07
❑ 496 Bryan Eversgerd .15 .07
❑ 497 Bernard Gilkey .15 .07
❑ 498 John Habyan .15 .07
❑ 499 Gregg Jefferies .15 .07
❑ 500 Brian Jordan .30 .14
❑ 501 Ray Lankford .30 .14
❑ 502 John Mabry .15 .07
❑ 503 Terry McGriff .15 .07
❑ 504 Tom Pagnozzi .15 .07
❑ 505 Vicente Palacios .15 .07
❑ 506 Geronimo Pena .15 .07
❑ 507 Gerald Perry .15 .07
❑ 508 Rich Rodriguez .15 .07
❑ 509 Ozzie Smith .75 .35
❑ 510 Bob Tewksbury .15 .07
❑ 511 Allen Watson .15 .07

❑	512 Mark Whiten	.15	.07
❑	513 Todd Zeile	.15	.07
❑	514 Dante Bichette	.30	.14
❑	515 Willie Blair	.15	.07
❑	516 Ellis Burks	.30	.14
❑	517 Marvin Freeman	.15	.07
❑	518 Andres Galarraga	.60	.25
❑	519 Joe Girardi	.15	.07
❑	520 Greg W. Harris	.15	.07
❑	521 Charlie Hayes	.15	.07
❑	522 Mike Kingery	.15	.07
❑	523 Nelson Liriano	.15	.07
❑	524 Mike Munoz	.15	.07
❑	525 David Nied	.15	.07
❑	526 Steve Reed	.15	.07
❑	527 Kevin Ritz	.15	.07
❑	528 Bruce Ruffin	.15	.07
❑	529 John Vander Wal	.15	.07
❑	530 Walt Weiss	.15	.07
❑	531 Eric Young	.15	.07
❑	532 Billy Ashley	.15	.07
❑	533 Pedro Astacio	.15	.07
❑	534 Rafael Bournigal	.15	.07
❑	535 Brett Butler	.30	.14
❑	536 Tom Candiotti	.15	.07
❑	537 Omar Daal	.15	.07
❑	538 Delino DeShields	.15	.07
❑	539 Darren Dreifort	.30	.14
❑	540 Kevin Gross	.15	.07
❑	541 Orel Hershiser	.30	.14
❑	542 Garey Ingram	.15	.07
❑	543 Eric Karros	.30	.14
❑	544 Ramon Martinez	.30	.14
❑	545 Raul Mondesi	.40	.18
❑	546 Chan Ho Park	.75	.35
❑	547 Mike Piazza	2.00	.90
❑	548 Henry Rodriguez	.30	.14
❑	549 Rudy Seanez	.15	.07
❑	550 Ismael Valdes	.30	.14
❑	551 Tim Wallach	.15	.07
❑	552 Todd Worrell	.15	.07
❑	553 Andy Ashby	.15	.07
❑	554 Brad Ausmus	.15	.07
❑	555 Derek Bell	.30	.14
❑	556 Andy Benes	.30	.14
❑	557 Phil Clark	.15	.07
❑	558 Donnie Elliott	.15	.07
❑	559 Ricky Gutierrez	.15	.07
❑	560 Tony Gwynn	1.50	.70
❑	561 Joey Hamilton	.30	.14
❑	562 Trevor Hoffman	.30	.14
❑	563 Luis Lopez	.15	.07
❑	564 Pedro A. Martinez	.15	.07
❑	565 Tim Mauser	.15	.07
❑	566 Phil Plantier	.15	.07
❑	567 Bip Roberts	.15	.07
❑	568 Scott Sanders	.15	.07
❑	569 Craig Shipley	.15	.07
❑	570 Jeff Tabaka	.15	.07
❑	571 Eddie Williams	.15	.07
❑	572 Rod Beck	.15	.07
❑	573 Mike Benjamin	.15	.07
❑	574 Barry Bonds	.75	.35
❑	575 Dave Burba	.15	.07
❑	576 John Burkett	.15	.07
❑	577 Mark Carreon	.15	.07
❑	578 Royce Clayton	.15	.07
❑	579 Steve Frey	.15	.07
❑	580 Bryan Hickerson	.15	.07
❑	581 Mike Jackson	.15	.07
❑	582 Darren Lewis	.15	.07
❑	583 Kirt Manwaring	.15	.07
❑	584 Rich Monteleone	.15	.07
❑	585 John Patterson	.15	.07
❑	586 J.R. Phillips	.15	.07
❑	587 Mark Portugal	.15	.07
❑	588 Joe Rosselli	.15	.07
❑	589 Darryl Strawberry	.30	.14
❑	590 Bill Swift	.15	.07
❑	591 Robby Thompson	.15	.07
❑	592 William VanLandingham	.15	.07
❑	593 Matt Williams	.30	.14
❑	594 Checklist	.15	.07
❑	595 Checklist	.15	.07
❑	596 Checklist	.15	.07
❑	597 Checklist	.15	.07
❑	598 Checklist	.15	.07
❑	599 Checklist	.15	.07
❑	600 Checklist	.15	.07

1995 Fleer All-Fleer

		MINT	NRMT
	COMPLETE SET (9)	10.00	4.50
	COMMON CARD (1-9)	.40	.18
❑	1 Mike Piazza	2.00	.90
❑	2 Frank Thomas	2.00	.90
❑	3 Roberto Alomar	.60	.25
❑	4 Cal Ripken	2.50	1.10
❑	5 Matt Williams	.40	.18
❑	6 Barry Bonds	.60	.25
❑	7 Ken Griffey Jr.	3.00	1.35
❑	8 Tony Gwynn	1.00	.45
❑	9 Greg Maddux	2.00	.90

1995 Fleer All-Rookies

		MINT	NRMT
	COMPLETE SET (9)	3.00	1.35
	COMMON CARD (M1-M9)	.25	.11
❑	M1 Edgardo Alfonzo	1.00	.45
❑	M2 Jason Bates	.25	.11
❑	M3 Brian Boehringer	.25	.11
❑	M4 Darren Bragg	.25	.11
❑	M5 Brad Clontz	.25	.11
❑	M6 Jim Dougherty	.25	.11
❑	M7 Todd Hollandsworth	.25	.11
❑	M8 Rudy Pemberton	.25	.11
❑	M9 Frank Rodriguez	.25	.11
❑	NNO Expired All-Rookie Exch.	1.00	.45

1995 Fleer All-Stars

		MINT	NRMT
	COMPLETE SET (25)	12.00	5.50
	COMMON CARD (1-25)	.25	.11
❑	1 Ivan Rodriguez	2.00	.90
	Mike Piazza		
❑	2 Frank Thomas	2.00	.90
	Gregg Jefferies		
❑	3 Robert Alomar	.60	.25
	Mariano Duncan		
❑	4 Wade Boggs	.60	.25
	Matt Williams		
❑	5 Cal Ripken Jr.	2.50	1.10
	Ozzie Smith		
❑	6 Joe Carter	.75	.35
	Barry Bonds		
❑	7 Ken Griffey Jr.	4.00	1.80
	Tony Gwynn		
❑	8 Kirby Puckett	1.00	.45
	David Justice		
❑	9 Jimmy Key	2.00	.90
	Greg Maddux		
❑	10 Chuck Knoblauch	.60	.25
	Wil Cordero		
❑	11 Scott Cooper	.40	.18
	Ken Caminiti		
❑	12 Will Clark	.50	.23
	Carlos Garcia		
❑	13 Paul Molitor	1.00	.45
	Jeff Bagwell		
❑	14 Travis Fryman	.50	.23
	Craig Biggio		
❑	15 Mickey Tettleton	.50	.23
	Fred McGriff		
❑	16 Kenny Lofton	.75	.35
	Moises Alou		
❑	17 Albert Belle	.75	.35
	Marquis Grissom		
❑	18 Paul O'Neill	.40	.18
	Dante Bichette		
❑	19 David Cone	.50	.23
	Ken Hill		
❑	20 Mike Mussina	.60	.25
	Doug Drabek		
❑	21 Randy Johnson	.60	.25
	John Hudek		
❑	22 Pat Hentgen	.25	.11
	Danny Jackson		
❑	23 Wilson Alvarez	.25	.11
	Rod Beck		
❑	24 Lee Smith	.25	.11
	Randy Myers		
❑	25 Jason Bere	.25	.11
	Doug Jones		

1995 Fleer Award Winners

		MINT	NRMT
	COMPLETE SET (6)	8.00	3.60
	COMMON CARD (1-6)	.50	.23

❑ 1 Frank Thomas	3.00	1.35
❑ 2 Jeff Bagwell	1.50	.70
❑ 3 David Cone	1.00	.45
❑ 4 Greg Maddux	3.00	1.35
❑ 5 Bob Hamelin	.50	.23
❑ 6 Raul Mondesi	1.00	.45

1995 Fleer League Leaders

	MINT	NRMT
COMPLETE SET (10)	8.00	3.60
COMMON CARD (1-10)	.50	.23

❑ 1 Paul O'Neill	.50	.23
❑ 2 Ken Griffey Jr.	5.00	2.20
❑ 3 Kirby Puckett	1.00	.45
❑ 4 Jimmy Key	.50	.23
❑ 5 Randy Johnson	1.00	.45
❑ 6 Tony Gwynn	2.50	1.10
❑ 7 Matt Williams	.50	.23
❑ 8 Jeff Bagwell	1.50	.70
❑ 9 Greg Maddux Ken Hill	1.50	.70
❑ 10 Andy Benes	.50	.23

1995 Fleer Lumber Company

	MINT	NRMT
COMPLETE SET (10)	40.00	18.00
COMMON CARD (1-10)	1.00	.45

❑ 1 Jeff Bagwell	5.00	2.20
❑ 2 Albert Belle	2.50	1.10
❑ 3 Barry Bonds	2.50	1.10
❑ 4 Jose Canseco	2.50	1.10
❑ 5 Joe Carter	1.50	.70
❑ 6 Ken Griffey Jr.	15.00	6.75
❑ 7 Fred McGriff	2.00	.90
❑ 8 Kevin Mitchell	1.00	.45
❑ 9 Frank Thomas	10.00	4.50
❑ 10 Matt Williams	1.50	.70

1995 Fleer Major League Prospects

	MINT	NRMT
COMPLETE SET (10)	10.00	4.50
COMMON CARD (1-10)	.50	.23

❑ 1 Garret Anderson	.75	.35
❑ 2 James Baldwin	.75	.35
❑ 3 Alan Benes	.75	.35
❑ 4 Armando Benitez	.50	.23
❑ 5 Ray Durham	.75	.35
❑ 6 Brian L. Hunter	.75	.35
❑ 7 Derek Jeter	4.00	1.80
❑ 8 Charles Johnson	.75	.35
❑ 9 Orlando Miller	.50	.23
❑ 10 Alex Rodriguez	5.00	2.20

1995 Fleer Pro-Visions

	MINT	NRMT
COMPLETE SET (6)	3.00	1.35
COMMON CARD (1-6)	.50	.23

❑ 1 Mike Mussina	.60	.25
❑ 2 Raul Mondesi	.50	.23
❑ 3 Jeff Bagwell	1.00	.45
❑ 4 Greg Maddux	2.00	.90
❑ 5 Tim Salmon	.60	.25
❑ 6 Manny Ramirez	.60	.25

1995 Fleer Rookie Sensations

	MINT	NRMT
COMPLETE SET (20)	40.00	18.00
COMMON CARD (1-20)	2.00	.90

❑ 1 Kurt Abbott	2.00	.90
❑ 2 Rico Brogna	2.00	.90
❑ 3 Hector Carrasco	2.00	.90
❑ 4 Kevin Foster	2.00	.90
❑ 5 Chris Gomez	2.00	.90
❑ 6 Darren Hall	2.00	.90
❑ 7 Bob Hamelin	2.00	.90
❑ 8 Joey Hamilton	3.00	1.35
❑ 9 John Hudek	2.00	.90
❑ 10 Ryan Klesko	3.00	1.35
❑ 11 Javier Lopez	3.00	1.35
❑ 12 Matt Mieske	2.00	.90

❑ 13 Raul Mondesi	6.00	2.70
❑ 14 Manny Ramirez	10.00	4.50
❑ 15 Shane Reynolds	3.00	1.35
❑ 16 Bill Risley	2.00	.90
❑ 17 Johnny Ruffin	2.00	.90
❑ 18 Steve Trachsel	2.00	.90
❑ 19 William VanLandingham	2.00	.90
❑ 20 Rondell White	3.00	1.35

1995 Fleer Team Leaders

	MINT	NRMT
COMPLETE SET (28)	200.00	90.00
COMMON CARD (1-28)	2.50	1.10

❑ 1 Cal Ripken Jr. Mike Mussina	30.00	13.50
❑ 2 Mo Vaughn Roger Clemens	15.00	6.75
❑ 3 Tim Salmon Chuck Finley	2.50	1.10
❑ 4 Frank Thomas Jack McDowell	25.00	11.00
❑ 5 Albert Belle Dennis Martinez	10.00	4.50
❑ 6 Cecil Fielder Mike Moore	4.00	1.80
❑ 7 Bob Hamelin David Cone	2.50	1.10
❑ 8 Greg Vaughn Ricky Bones	2.50	1.10
❑ 9 Kirby Puckett Rick Aguilera	12.00	5.50
❑ 10 Don Mattingly Jimmy Key	12.00	5.50
❑ 11 Ruben Sierra Dennis Eckersley	2.50	1.10
❑ 12 Ken Griffey Jr. Randy Johnson	40.00	18.00
❑ 13 Jose Canseco Kenny Rogers	5.00	2.20
❑ 14 Joe Carter Pat Hentgen	4.00	1.80
❑ 15 David Justice Greg Maddux	25.00	11.00
❑ 16 Sammy Sosa Steve Trachsel	20.00	9.00
❑ 17 Kevin Mitchell Jose Rijo	2.50	1.10

	MINT	NRMT
❑ 18 Dante Bichette / Bruce Ruffin	2.50	1.10
❑ 19 Jeff Conine / Robb Nen	2.50	1.10
❑ 20 Jeff Bagwell / Doug Drabek	12.00	5.50
❑ 21 Mike Piazza / Ramon Martinez	20.00	9.00
❑ 22 Moises Alou / Ken Hill	4.00	1.80
❑ 23 Bobby Bonilla / Bret Saberhagen	2.50	1.10
❑ 24 Darren Daulton / Danny Jackson	4.00	1.80
❑ 25 Jay Bell / Zane Smith	4.00	1.80
❑ 26 Gregg Jefferies / Bob Tewksbury	2.50	1.10
❑ 27 Tony Gwynn / Andy Benes	20.00	9.00
❑ 28 Matt Williams / Rod Beck	2.50	1.10

1995 Fleer Update

	MINT	NRMT
COMPLETE SET (200)	15.00	6.75
COMMON CARD (1-200)	.10	.05

	MINT	NRMT
❑ 1 Manny Alexander	.10	.05
❑ 2 Bret Barberie	.10	.05
❑ 3 Armando Benitez	.10	.05
❑ 4 Kevin Brown	.30	.14
❑ 5 Doug Jones	.10	.05
❑ 6 Sherman Obando	.10	.05
❑ 7 Andy Van Slyke	.20	.09
❑ 8 Stan Belinda	.10	.05
❑ 9 Jose Canseco	.40	.18
❑ 10 Vaughn Eshelman	.10	.05
❑ 11 Mike Macfarlane	.10	.05
❑ 12 Troy O'Leary	.20	.09
❑ 13 Steve Rodriguez	.10	.05
❑ 14 Lee Tinsley	.10	.05
❑ 15 Tim Vanegmond	.10	.05
❑ 16 Mark Whiten	.10	.05
❑ 17 Sean Bergman	.10	.05
❑ 18 Chad Curtis	.10	.05
❑ 19 John Flaherty	.10	.05
❑ 20 Bob Higginson	1.00	.45
❑ 21 Felipe Lira	.10	.05
❑ 22 Shannon Penn	.10	.05
❑ 23 Todd Steverson	.10	.05
❑ 24 Sean Whiteside	.10	.05
❑ 25 Tony Fernandez	.10	.05
❑ 26 Jack McDowell	.10	.05
❑ 27 Andy Pettitte	.40	.18
❑ 28 John Wetteland	.20	.09
❑ 29 David Cone	.30	.14
❑ 30 Mike Timlin	.10	.05
❑ 31 Duane Ward	.10	.05
❑ 32 Jim Abbott	.20	.09
❑ 33 James Baldwin	.20	.09
❑ 34 Mike Devereaux	.10	.05
❑ 35 Ray Durham	.20	.09
❑ 36 Tim Fortugno	.10	.05
❑ 37 Scott Ruffcorn	.10	.05
❑ 38 Chris Sabo	.10	.05
❑ 39 Paul Assenmacher	.10	.05
❑ 40 Bud Black	.10	.05
❑ 41 Orel Hershiser	.20	.09
❑ 42 Julian Tavarez	.10	.05
❑ 43 Dave Winfield	.40	.18
❑ 44 Pat Borders	.10	.05
❑ 45 Melvin Bunch	.10	.05
❑ 46 Tom Goodwin	.10	.05
❑ 47 Jon Nunnally	.10	.05
❑ 48 Joe Randa	.10	.05
❑ 49 Dilson Torres	.10	.05
❑ 50 Joe Vitiello	.10	.05
❑ 51 David Hulse	.10	.05
❑ 52 Scott Karl	.10	.05
❑ 53 Mark Kiefer	.10	.05
❑ 54 Derrick May	.10	.05
❑ 55 Joe Oliver	.10	.05
❑ 56 Al Reyes	.10	.05
❑ 57 Steve Sparks	.10	.05
❑ 58 Jerald Clark	.10	.05
❑ 59 Eddie Guardado	.10	.05
❑ 60 Kevin Maas	.10	.05
❑ 61 David McCarty	.10	.05
❑ 62 Brad Radke	.50	.23
❑ 63 Scott Stahoviak	.10	.05
❑ 64 Garret Anderson	.20	.09
❑ 65 Shawn Boskie	.10	.05
❑ 66 Mike James	.10	.05
❑ 67 Tony Phillips	.10	.05
❑ 68 Lee Smith	.20	.09
❑ 69 Mitch Williams	.10	.05
❑ 70 Jim Corsi	.10	.05
❑ 71 Mark Harkey	.10	.05
❑ 72 Dave Stewart	.20	.09
❑ 73 Todd Stottlemyre	.10	.05
❑ 74 Joey Cora	.20	.09
❑ 75 Chad Kreuter	.10	.05
❑ 76 Jeff Nelson	.10	.05
❑ 77 Alex Rodriguez	1.50	.70
❑ 78 Ron Villone	.10	.05
❑ 79 Bob Wells	.10	.05
❑ 80 Jose Alberro	.10	.05
❑ 81 Terry Burrows	.10	.05
❑ 82 Kevin Gross	.10	.05
❑ 83 Wilson Heredia	.10	.05
❑ 84 Mark McLemore	.10	.05
❑ 85 Otis Nixon	.10	.05
❑ 86 Jeff Russell	.10	.05
❑ 87 Mickey Tettleton	.10	.05
❑ 88 Bob Tewksbury	.10	.05
❑ 89 Pedro Borbon	.10	.05
❑ 90 Marquis Grissom	.20	.09
❑ 91 Chipper Jones	1.00	.45
❑ 92 Mike Mordecai	.10	.05
❑ 93 Jason Schmidt	.20	.09
❑ 94 John Burkett	.10	.05
❑ 95 Andre Dawson	.30	.14
❑ 96 Matt Dunbar	.10	.05
❑ 97 Charles Johnson	.20	.09
❑ 98 Terry Pendleton	.10	.05
❑ 99 Rich Scheid	.10	.05
❑ 100 Quilvio Veras	.10	.05
❑ 101 Bobby Witt	.10	.05
❑ 102 Eddie Zosky	.10	.05
❑ 103 Shane Andrews	.10	.05
❑ 104 Reid Cornelius	.10	.05
❑ 105 Chad Fonville	.10	.05
❑ 106 Mark Grudzielanek	.30	.14
❑ 107 Roberto Kelly	.10	.05
❑ 108 Carlos Perez	.30	.14
❑ 109 Tony Tarasco	.10	.05
❑ 110 Brett Butler	.20	.09
❑ 111 Carl Everett	.10	.05
❑ 112 Pete Harnisch	.10	.05
❑ 113 Doug Henry	.10	.05
❑ 114 Kevin Lomon	.10	.05
❑ 115 Blas Minor	.10	.05
❑ 116 Dave Mlicki	.10	.05
❑ 117 Ricky Otero	.10	.05
❑ 118 Norm Charlton	.10	.05
❑ 119 Tyler Green	.10	.05
❑ 120 Gene Harris	.10	.05
❑ 121 Charlie Hayes	.10	.05
❑ 122 Gregg Jefferies	.10	.05
❑ 123 Michael Mimbs	.10	.05
❑ 124 Paul Quantrill	.10	.05
❑ 125 Frank Castillo	.10	.05
❑ 126 Brian McRae	.10	.05
❑ 127 Jaime Navarro	.10	.05
❑ 128 Mike Perez	.10	.05
❑ 129 Tanyon Sturtze	.10	.05
❑ 130 Ozzie Timmons	.10	.05
❑ 131 John Courtright	.10	.05
❑ 132 Ron Gant	.10	.05
❑ 133 Xavier Hernandez	.10	.05
❑ 134 Brian Hunter	.10	.05
❑ 135 Benito Santiago	.10	.05
❑ 136 Pete Smith	.10	.05
❑ 137 Scott Sullivan	.10	.05
❑ 138 Derek Bell	.20	.09
❑ 139 Doug Brocail	.10	.05
❑ 140 Ricky Gutierrez	.10	.05
❑ 141 Pedro Martinez	.40	.18
❑ 142 Orlando Miller	.10	.05
❑ 143 Phil Plantier	.10	.05
❑ 144 Craig Shipley	.10	.05
❑ 145 Rich Aude	.10	.05
❑ 146 Jason Christiansen	.10	.05
❑ 147 Freddy Garcia	.10	.05
❑ 148 Jim Gott	.10	.05
❑ 149 Mark Johnson	.10	.05
❑ 150 Esteban Loaiza	.10	.05
❑ 151 Dan Plesac	.10	.05
❑ 152 Gary Wilson	.10	.05
❑ 153 Allen Battle	.10	.05
❑ 154 Terry Bradshaw	.10	.05
❑ 155 Scott Cooper	.10	.05
❑ 156 Tripp Cromer	.10	.05
❑ 157 John Frascatore	.10	.05
❑ 158 John Habyan	.10	.05
❑ 159 Tom Henke	.10	.05
❑ 160 Ken Hill	.10	.05
❑ 161 Danny Jackson	.10	.05
❑ 162 Donovan Osborne	.10	.05
❑ 163 Tom Urbani	.10	.05
❑ 164 Roger Bailey	.10	.05
❑ 165 Jorge Brito	.10	.05
❑ 166 Vinny Castilla	.30	.14
❑ 167 Darren Holmes	.10	.05
❑ 168 Roberto Mejia	.10	.05
❑ 169 Bill Swift	.10	.05
❑ 170 Mark Thompson	.10	.05
❑ 171 Larry Walker	.40	.18
❑ 172 Greg Hansell	.10	.05
❑ 173 Dave Hansen	.10	.05
❑ 174 Carlos Hernandez	.10	.05
❑ 175 Hideo Nomo	1.50	.70
❑ 176 Jose Offerman	.10	.05
❑ 177 Antonio Osuna	.10	.05
❑ 178 Reggie Williams	.10	.05
❑ 179 Todd Williams	.10	.05
❑ 180 Andres Berumen	.10	.05
❑ 181 Ken Caminiti	.30	.14
❑ 182 Andujar Cedeno	.10	.05
❑ 183 Steve Finley	.20	.09
❑ 184 Bryce Florie	.10	.05
❑ 185 Dustin Hermanson	.20	.09
❑ 186 Ray Holbert	.10	.05
❑ 187 Melvin Nieves	.10	.05
❑ 188 Roberto Petagine	.10	.05
❑ 189 Jody Reed	.10	.05
❑ 190 Fernando Valenzuela	.20	.09
❑ 191 Brian Williams	.10	.05
❑ 192 Mark Dewey	.10	.05
❑ 193 Glenallen Hill	.10	.05
❑ 194 Chris Hook	.10	.05
❑ 195 Terry Mulholland	.10	.05
❑ 196 Steve Scarsone	.10	.05
❑ 197 Trevor Wilson	.10	.05
❑ 198 Checklist	.10	.05
❑ 199 Checklist	.10	.05
❑ 200 Checklist	.10	.05

1995 Fleer Update Diamond Tribute

	MINT	NRMT
COMPLETE SET (10)	8.00	3.60
COMMON CARD (1-10)	.30	.14

	MINT	NRMT
❑ 1 Jeff Bagwell	1.00	.45

Card	MINT	NRMT
❑ 2 Albert Belle	.60	.25
❑ 3 Barry Bonds	.60	.25
❑ 4 David Cone	.50	.23
❑ 5 Dennis Eckersley	.30	.14
❑ 6 Ken Griffey Jr.	3.00	1.35
❑ 7 Rickey Henderson	.60	.25
❑ 8 Greg Maddux	2.00	.90
❑ 9 Frank Thomas	2.00	.90
❑ 10 Matt Williams	.30	.14

1995 Fleer Update Headliners

	MINT	NRMT
COMPLETE SET (20)	12.00	5.50
COMMON CARD (1-20)	.25	.11
❑ 1 Jeff Bagwell	1.00	.45
❑ 2 Albert Belle	.60	.25
❑ 3 Barry Bonds	.60	.25
❑ 4 Jose Canseco	.60	.25
❑ 5 Joe Carter	.25	.11
❑ 6 Will Clark	.60	.25
❑ 7 Roger Clemens	1.25	.55
❑ 8 Lenny Dykstra	.25	.11
❑ 9 Cecil Fielder	.25	.11
❑ 10 Juan Gonzalez	1.50	.70
❑ 11 Ken Griffey Jr.	3.00	1.35
❑ 12 Kenny Lofton	.60	.25
❑ 13 Greg Maddux	2.00	.90
❑ 14 Fred McGriff	.50	.23
❑ 15 Mike Piazza	2.00	.90
❑ 16 Kirby Puckett	.60	.25
❑ 17 Tim Salmon	.60	.25
❑ 18 Frank Thomas	2.00	.90
❑ 19 Mo Vaughn	.60	.25
❑ 20 Matt Williams	.25	.11

1995 Fleer Update Rookie Update

	MINT	NRMT
COMPLETE SET (10)	15.00	6.75
COMMON CARD (1-10)	.25	.11
❑ 1 Shane Andrews	.25	.11
❑ 2 Ray Durham	.50	.23
❑ 3 Shawn Green	.50	.23
❑ 4 Charles Johnson	.50	.23

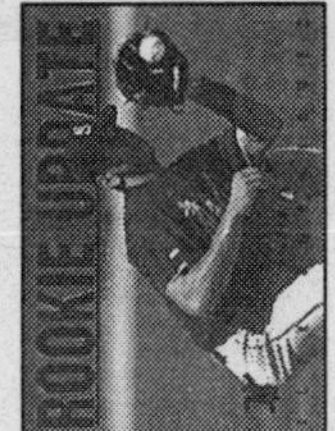

Card	MINT	NRMT
❑ 5 Chipper Jones	4.00	1.80
❑ 6 Esteban Loaiza	.25	.11
❑ 7 Hideo Nomo	3.00	1.35
❑ 8 Jon Nunnally	.25	.11
❑ 9 Alex Rodriguez	5.00	2.20
❑ 10 Julian Tavarez	.25	.11

1995 Fleer Update Smooth Leather

	MINT	NRMT
COMPLETE SET (10)	25.00	11.00
COMMON CARD (1-10)	.75	.35
❑ 1 Roberto Alomar	2.00	.90
❑ 2 Barry Bonds	2.00	.90
❑ 3 Ken Griffey Jr.	10.00	4.50
❑ 4 Marquis Grissom	.75	.35
❑ 5 Darren Lewis	.75	.35
❑ 6 Kenny Lofton	2.00	.90
❑ 7 Don Mattingly	3.00	1.35
❑ 8 Cal Ripken	8.00	3.60
❑ 9 Ivan Rodriguez	2.00	.90
❑ 10 Matt Williams	.75	.35

1995 Fleer Update Soaring Stars

	MINT	NRMT
COMPLETE SET (9)	50.00	22.00
COMMON CARD (1-9)	2.50	1.10
❑ 1 Moises Alou UER (says .399 BA in 1994)	5.00	2.20
❑ 2 Jason Bere	2.50	1.10
❑ 3 Jeff Conine	3.00	1.35
❑ 4 Cliff Floyd	3.00	1.35
❑ 5 Pat Hentgen	3.00	1.35
❑ 6 Kenny Lofton	10.00	4.50
❑ 7 Raul Mondesi	5.00	2.20
❑ 8 Mike Piazza	30.00	13.50
❑ 9 Tim Salmon	10.00	4.50

1996 Fleer

	MINT	NRMT
COMPLETE SET (600)	80.00	36.00
COMMON CARD (1-600)	.15	.07
❑ 1 Manny Alexander	.15	.07
❑ 2 Brady Anderson	.30	.14
❑ 3 Harold Baines	.30	.14
❑ 4 Armando Benitez	.15	.07
❑ 5 Bobby Bonilla	.30	.14
❑ 6 Kevin Brown	.60	.25
❑ 7 Scott Erickson	.30	.14
❑ 8 Curtis Goodwin	.15	.07
❑ 9 Jeffrey Hammonds	.30	.14
❑ 10 Jimmy Haynes	.15	.07
❑ 11 Chris Hoiles	.15	.07
❑ 12 Doug Jones	.15	.07
❑ 13 Rick Krivda	.15	.07
❑ 14 Jeff Manto	.15	.07
❑ 15 Ben McDonald	.15	.07
❑ 16 Jamie Moyer	.15	.07
❑ 17 Mike Mussina	.60	.25
❑ 18 Jesse Orosco	.15	.07
❑ 19 Rafael Palmeiro	.40	.18
❑ 20 Cal Ripken	2.50	1.10
❑ 21 Rick Aguilera	.15	.07
❑ 22 Luis Alicea	.15	.07
❑ 23 Stan Belinda	.15	.07
❑ 24 Jose Canseco	.60	.25
❑ 25 Roger Clemens	1.25	.55
❑ 26 Vaughn Eshelman	.15	.07
❑ 27 Mike Greenwell	.15	.07
❑ 28 Erik Hanson	.15	.07
❑ 29 Dwayne Hosey	.15	.07
❑ 30 Mike Macfarlane UER	.15	.07
❑ 31 Tim Naehring	.15	.07
❑ 32 Troy O'Leary	.30	.14
❑ 33 Aaron Sele	.30	.14
❑ 34 Zane Smith	.15	.07
❑ 35 Jeff Suppan	.15	.07
❑ 36 Lee Tinsley	.15	.07
❑ 37 John Valentin	.30	.14
❑ 38 Mo Vaughn	.75	.35
❑ 39 Tim Wakefield	.30	.14
❑ 40 Jim Abbott	.30	.14
❑ 41 Brian Anderson	.30	.14
❑ 42 Garret Anderson	.30	.14
❑ 43 Chili Davis	.30	.14
❑ 44 Gary DiSarcina	.15	.07
❑ 45 Damion Easley	.30	.14
❑ 46 Jim Edmonds	.40	.18
❑ 47 Chuck Finley	.30	.14
❑ 48 Todd Greene	.30	.14
❑ 49 Mike Harkey	.15	.07
❑ 50 Mike James	.15	.07
❑ 51 Mark Langston	.15	.07

❑	52	Greg Myers	.15	.07
❑	53	Orlando Palmeiro	.15	.07
❑	54	Bob Patterson	.15	.07
❑	55	Troy Percival	.30	.14
❑	56	Tony Phillips	.15	.07
❑	57	Tim Salmon	.60	.25
❑	58	Lee Smith	.30	.14
❑	59	J.T. Snow	.30	.14
❑	60	Randy Velarde	.15	.07
❑	61	Wilson Alvarez	.30	.14
❑	62	Luis Andujar	.15	.07
❑	63	Jason Bere	.15	.07
❑	64	Ray Durham	.30	.14
❑	65	Alex Fernandez	.15	.07
❑	66	Ozzie Guillen	.15	.07
❑	67	Roberto Hernandez	.15	.07
❑	68	Lance Johnson	.15	.07
❑	69	Matt Karchner	.15	.07
❑	70	Ron Karkovice	.15	.07
❑	71	Norberto Martin	.15	.07
❑	72	Dave Martinez	.15	.07
❑	73	Kirk McCaskill	.15	.07
❑	74	Lyle Mouton	.15	.07
❑	75	Tim Raines	.30	.14
❑	76	Mike Sirotka	.15	.07
❑	77	Frank Thomas	2.00	.90
❑	78	Larry Thomas	.15	.07
❑	79	Robin Ventura	.30	.14
❑	80	Sandy Alomar Jr.	.30	.14
❑	81	Paul Assenmacher	.15	.07
❑	82	Carlos Baerga	.30	.14
❑	83	Albert Belle	.75	.35
❑	84	Mark Clark	.15	.07
❑	85	Alan Embree	.15	.07
❑	86	Alvaro Espinoza	.15	.07
❑	87	Orel Hershiser	.30	.14
❑	88	Ken Hill	.15	.07
❑	89	Kenny Lofton	.60	.25
❑	90	Dennis Martinez	.30	.14
❑	91	Jose Mesa	.15	.07
❑	92	Eddie Murray	.60	.25
❑	93	Charles Nagy	.30	.14
❑	94	Chad Ogea	.15	.07
❑	95	Tony Pena	.15	.07
❑	96	Herb Perry	.15	.07
❑	97	Eric Plunk	.15	.07
❑	98	Jim Poole	.15	.07
❑	99	Manny Ramirez	.60	.25
❑	100	Paul Sorrento	.15	.07
❑	101	Julian Tavarez	.15	.07
❑	102	Jim Thome	.60	.25
❑	103	Omar Vizquel	.30	.14
❑	104	Dave Winfield	.60	.25
❑	105	Danny Bautista	.15	.07
❑	106	Joe Boever	.15	.07
❑	107	Chad Curtis	.15	.07
❑	108	John Doherty	.15	.07
❑	109	Cecil Fielder	.30	.14
❑	110	John Flaherty	.15	.07
❑	111	Travis Fryman	.30	.14
❑	112	Chris Gomez	.15	.07
❑	113	Bob Higginson	.60	.25
❑	114	Mark Lewis	.15	.07
❑	115	Jose Lima	.15	.07
❑	116	Felipe Lira	.15	.07
❑	117	Brian Maxcy	.15	.07
❑	118	C.J. Nitkowski	.15	.07
❑	119	Phil Plantier	.15	.07
❑	120	Clint Sodowsky	.15	.07
❑	121	Alan Trammell	.40	.18
❑	122	Lou Whitaker	.30	.14
❑	123	Kevin Appier	.30	.14
❑	124	Johnny Damon	.30	.14
❑	125	Gary Gaetti	.30	.14
❑	126	Tom Goodwin	.15	.07
❑	127	Tom Gordon	.15	.07
❑	128	Mark Gubicza	.15	.07
❑	129	Bob Hamelin	.15	.07
❑	130	David Howard	.15	.07
❑	131	Jason Jacome	.15	.07
❑	132	Wally Joyner	.30	.14
❑	133	Keith Lockhart	.15	.07
❑	134	Brent Mayne	.15	.07
❑	135	Jeff Montgomery	.15	.07
❑	136	Jon Nunnally	.15	.07
❑	137	Juan Samuel	.15	.07
❑	138	Mike Sweeney	.40	.18
❑	139	Michael Tucker	.30	.14
❑	140	Joe Vitiello	.15	.07
❑	141	Ricky Bones	.15	.07
❑	142	Chuck Carr	.15	.07
❑	143	Jeff Cirillo	.30	.14
❑	144	Mike Fetters	.15	.07
❑	145	Darryl Hamilton	.15	.07
❑	146	David Hulse	.15	.07
❑	147	John Jaha	.15	.07
❑	148	Scott Karl	.15	.07
❑	149	Mark Kiefer	.15	.07
❑	150	Pat Listach	.15	.07
❑	151	Mark Loretta	.15	.07
❑	152	Mike Matheny	.15	.07
❑	153	Matt Mieske	.15	.07
❑	154	Dave Nilsson	.15	.07
❑	155	Joe Oliver	.15	.07
❑	156	Al Reyes	.15	.07
❑	157	Kevin Seitzer	.15	.07
❑	158	Steve Sparks	.15	.07
❑	159	B.J. Surhoff	.30	.14
❑	160	Jose Valentin	.15	.07
❑	161	Greg Vaughn	.30	.14
❑	162	Fernando Vina	.15	.07
❑	163	Rich Becker	.15	.07
❑	164	Ron Coomer	.15	.07
❑	165	Marty Cordova	.15	.07
❑	166	Chuck Knoblauch	.60	.25
❑	167	Matt Lawton	.60	.25
❑	168	Pat Meares	.15	.07
❑	169	Paul Molitor	.60	.25
❑	170	Pedro Munoz	.15	.07
❑	171	Jose Parra	.15	.07
❑	172	Kirby Puckett	1.00	.45
❑	173	Brad Radke	.30	.14
❑	174	Jeff Reboulet	.15	.07
❑	175	Rich Robertson	.15	.07
❑	176	Frank Rodriguez	.15	.07
❑	177	Scott Stahoviak	.15	.07
❑	178	Dave Stevens	.15	.07
❑	179	Matt Walbeck	.15	.07
❑	180	Wade Boggs	.60	.25
❑	181	David Cone	.40	.18
❑	182	Tony Fernandez	.15	.07
❑	183	Joe Girardi	.15	.07
❑	184	Derek Jeter	2.00	.90
❑	185	Scott Kamieniecki	.15	.07
❑	186	Pat Kelly	.15	.07
❑	187	Jim Leyritz	.15	.07
❑	188	Tino Martinez	.60	.25
❑	189	Don Mattingly	1.00	.45
❑	190	Jack McDowell	.15	.07
❑	191	Jeff Nelson	.15	.07
❑	192	Paul O'Neill	.30	.14
❑	193	Melido Perez	.15	.07
❑	194	Andy Pettitte	.40	.18
❑	195	Mariano Rivera	.30	.14
❑	196	Ruben Sierra	.15	.07
❑	197	Mike Stanley	.15	.07
❑	198	Darryl Strawberry	.30	.14
❑	199	John Wetteland	.30	.14
❑	200	Bob Wickman	.15	.07
❑	201	Bernie Williams	.60	.25
❑	202	Mark Acre	.15	.07
❑	203	Geronimo Berroa	.15	.07
❑	204	Mike Bordick	.15	.07
❑	205	Scott Brosius	.30	.14
❑	206	Dennis Eckersley	.30	.14
❑	207	Brent Gates	.15	.07
❑	208	Jason Giambi	.30	.14
❑	209	Rickey Henderson	.60	.25
❑	210	Jose Herrera	.15	.07
❑	211	Stan Javier	.15	.07
❑	212	Doug Johns	.15	.07
❑	213	Mark McGwire	3.00	1.35
❑	214	Steve Ontiveros	.15	.07
❑	215	Craig Paquette	.15	.07
❑	216	Ariel Prieto	.15	.07
❑	217	Carlos Reyes	.15	.07
❑	218	Terry Steinbach	.30	.14
❑	219	Todd Stottlemyre	.15	.07
❑	220	Danny Tartabull	.15	.07
❑	221	Todd Van Poppel	.15	.07
❑	222	John Wasdin	.15	.07
❑	223	George Williams	.15	.07
❑	224	Steve Wojciechowski	.15	.07
❑	225	Rich Amaral	.15	.07
❑	226	Bobby Ayala	.15	.07
❑	227	Tim Belcher	.15	.07
❑	228	Andy Benes	.30	.14
❑	229	Chris Bosio	.15	.07
❑	230	Darren Bragg	.15	.07
❑	231	Jay Buhner	.30	.14
❑	232	Norm Charlton	.15	.07
❑	233	Vince Coleman	.15	.07
❑	234	Joey Cora	.30	.14
❑	235	Russ Davis	.30	.14
❑	236	Alex Diaz	.15	.07
❑	237	Felix Fermin	.15	.07
❑	238	Ken Griffey Jr.	3.00	1.35
❑	239	Sterling Hitchcock	.30	.14
❑	240	Randy Johnson	.60	.25
❑	241	Edgar Martinez	.30	.14
❑	242	Bill Risley	.15	.07
❑	243	Alex Rodriguez	2.00	.90
❑	244	Luis Sojo	.15	.07
❑	245	Dan Wilson	.15	.07
❑	246	Bob Wolcott	.15	.07
❑	247	Will Clark	.60	.25
❑	248	Jeff Frye	.15	.07
❑	249	Benji Gil	.15	.07
❑	250	Juan Gonzalez	1.50	.70
❑	251	Rusty Greer	.40	.18
❑	252	Kevin Gross	.15	.07
❑	253	Roger McDowell	.15	.07
❑	254	Mark McLemore	.15	.07
❑	255	Otis Nixon	.15	.07
❑	256	Luis Ortiz	.15	.07
❑	257	Mike Pagliarulo	.15	.07
❑	258	Dean Palmer	.30	.14
❑	259	Roger Pavlik	.15	.07
❑	260	Ivan Rodriguez	.75	.35
❑	261	Kenny Rogers	.15	.07
❑	262	Jeff Russell	.15	.07
❑	263	Mickey Tettleton	.15	.07
❑	264	Bob Tewksbury	.15	.07
❑	265	Dave Valle	.15	.07
❑	266	Matt Whiteside	.15	.07
❑	267	Roberto Alomar	.60	.25
❑	268	Joe Carter	.30	.14
❑	269	Tony Castillo	.15	.07
❑	270	Domingo Cedeno	.15	.07
❑	271	Tim Crabtree UER	.15	.07
❑	272	Carlos Delgado	.30	.14
❑	273	Alex Gonzalez	.15	.07
❑	274	Shawn Green	.30	.14
❑	275	Juan Guzman	.15	.07
❑	276	Pat Hentgen	.30	.14
❑	277	Al Leiter	.30	.14
❑	278	Sandy Martinez	.15	.07
❑	279	Paul Menhart	.15	.07
❑	280	John Olerud	.30	.14
❑	281	Paul Quantrill	.15	.07
❑	282	Ken Robinson	.15	.07
❑	283	Ed Sprague	.15	.07
❑	284	Mike Timlin	.15	.07
❑	285	Steve Avery	.15	.07
❑	286	Rafael Belliard	.15	.07
❑	287	Jeff Blauser	.15	.07
❑	288	Pedro Borbon	.15	.07
❑	289	Brad Clontz	.15	.07
❑	290	Mike Devereaux	.15	.07
❑	291	Tom Glavine	.60	.25
❑	292	Marquis Grissom	.30	.14
❑	293	Chipper Jones	1.50	.70
❑	294	David Justice	.60	.25
❑	295	Mike Kelly	.15	.07
❑	296	Ryan Klesko	.30	.14
❑	297	Mark Lemke	.15	.07
❑	298	Javier Lopez	.30	.14
❑	299	Greg Maddux	2.00	.90
❑	300	Fred McGriff	.40	.18
❑	301	Greg McMichael	.15	.07
❑	302	Kent Mercker	.15	.07
❑	303	Mike Mordecai	.15	.07
❑	304	Charlie O'Brien	.15	.07
❑	305	Eduardo Perez	.15	.07
❑	306	Luis Polonia	.15	.07

❑ 307 Jason Schmidt .15 .07
❑ 308 John Smoltz .30 .14
❑ 309 Terrell Wade .15 .07
❑ 310 Mark Wohlers .15 .07
❑ 311 Scott Bullett .15 .07
❑ 312 Jim Bullinger .15 .07
❑ 313 Larry Casian .15 .07
❑ 314 Frank Castillo .15 .07
❑ 315 Shawon Dunston .15 .07
❑ 316 Kevin Foster .15 .07
❑ 317 Matt Franco .15 .07
❑ 318 Luis Gonzalez .15 .07
❑ 319 Mark Grace .40 .18
❑ 320 Jose Hernandez .15 .07
❑ 321 Mike Hubbard .15 .07
❑ 322 Brian McRae .15 .07
❑ 323 Randy Myers .15 .07
❑ 324 Jaime Navarro .15 .07
❑ 325 Mark Parent .15 .07
❑ 326 Mike Perez .15 .07
❑ 327 Rey Sanchez .15 .07
❑ 328 Ryne Sandberg .75 .35
❑ 329 Scott Servais .15 .07
❑ 330 Sammy Sosa 1.50 .70
❑ 331 Ozzie Timmons .15 .07
❑ 332 Steve Trachsel .15 .07
❑ 333 Todd Zeile .15 .07
❑ 334 Bret Boone .30 .14
❑ 335 Jeff Branson .15 .07
❑ 336 Jeff Brantley .15 .07
❑ 337 Dave Burba .15 .07
❑ 338 Hector Carrasco .15 .07
❑ 339 Mariano Duncan .15 .07
❑ 340 Ron Gant .15 .07
❑ 341 Lenny Harris .15 .07
❑ 342 Xavier Hernandez .15 .07
❑ 343 Thomas Howard .15 .07
❑ 344 Mike Jackson .15 .07
❑ 345 Barry Larkin .40 .18
❑ 346 Darren Lewis .15 .07
❑ 347 Hal Morris .15 .07
❑ 348 Eric Owens .15 .07
❑ 349 Mark Portugal .15 .07
❑ 350 Jose Rijo .15 .07
❑ 351 Reggie Sanders .30 .14
❑ 352 Benito Santiago .15 .07
❑ 353 Pete Schourek .15 .07
❑ 354 John Smiley .15 .07
❑ 355 Eddie Taubensee .15 .07
❑ 356 Jerome Walton .15 .07
❑ 357 David Wells .40 .18
❑ 358 Roger Bailey .15 .07
❑ 359 Jason Bates .15 .07
❑ 360 Dante Bichette .30 .14
❑ 361 Ellis Burks .30 .14
❑ 362 Vinny Castilla .40 .18
❑ 363 Andres Galarraga .60 .25
❑ 364 Darren Holmes .15 .07
❑ 365 Mike Kingery .15 .07
❑ 366 Curt Leskanic .15 .07
❑ 367 Quinton McCracken .30 .14
❑ 368 Mike Munoz .15 .07
❑ 369 David Nied .15 .07
❑ 370 Steve Reed .15 .07
❑ 371 Bryan Rekar .15 .07
❑ 372 Kevin Ritz .15 .07
❑ 373 Bruce Ruffin .15 .07
❑ 374 Bret Saberhagen .30 .14
❑ 375 Bill Swift .15 .07
❑ 376 John Vander Wal .15 .07
❑ 377 Larry Walker .60 .25
❑ 378 Walt Weiss .15 .07
❑ 379 Eric Young .15 .07
❑ 380 Kurt Abbott .15 .07
❑ 381 Alex Arias .15 .07
❑ 382 Jerry Browne .15 .07
❑ 383 John Burkett .15 .07
❑ 384 Greg Colbrunn .15 .07
❑ 385 Jeff Conine .30 .14
❑ 386 Andre Dawson .40 .18
❑ 387 Chris Hammond .15 .07
❑ 388 Charles Johnson .30 .14
❑ 389 Terry Mathews .15 .07
❑ 390 Robb Nen .15 .07
❑ 391 Joe Orsulak .15 .07
❑ 392 Terry Pendleton .15 .07
❑ 393 Pat Rapp .15 .07
❑ 394 Gary Sheffield .40 .18
❑ 395 Jesus Tavarez .15 .07
❑ 396 Marc Valdes .15 .07
❑ 397 Quilvio Veras .15 .07
❑ 398 Randy Veres .15 .07
❑ 399 Devon White .30 .14
❑ 400 Jeff Bagwell 1.00 .45
❑ 401 Derek Bell .30 .14
❑ 402 Craig Biggio .60 .25
❑ 403 John Cangelosi .15 .07
❑ 404 Jim Dougherty .15 .07
❑ 405 Doug Drabek .15 .07
❑ 406 Tony Eusebio .15 .07
❑ 407 Ricky Gutierrez .15 .07
❑ 408 Mike Hampton .15 .07
❑ 409 Dean Hartgraves .15 .07
❑ 410 John Hudek .15 .07
❑ 411 Brian L. Hunter .30 .14
❑ 412 Todd Jones .15 .07
❑ 413 Darryl Kile .30 .14
❑ 414 Dave Magadan .15 .07
❑ 415 Derrick May .15 .07
❑ 416 Orlando Miller .15 .07
❑ 417 James Mouton .15 .07
❑ 418 Shane Reynolds .30 .14
❑ 419 Greg Swindell .15 .07
❑ 420 Jeff Tabaka .15 .07
❑ 421 Dave Veres .15 .07
❑ 422 Billy Wagner .30 .14
❑ 423 Donne Wall .15 .07
❑ 424 Rick Wilkins .15 .07
❑ 425 Billy Ashley .15 .07
❑ 426 Mike Blowers .15 .07
❑ 427 Brett Butler .30 .14
❑ 428 Tom Candiotti .15 .07
❑ 429 Juan Castro .15 .07
❑ 430 John Cummings .15 .07
❑ 431 Delino DeShields .15 .07
❑ 432 Joey Eischen .15 .07
❑ 433 Chad Fonville .15 .07
❑ 434 Greg Gagne .15 .07
❑ 435 Dave Hansen .15 .07
❑ 436 Carlos Hernandez .15 .07
❑ 437 Todd Hollandsworth .15 .07
❑ 438 Eric Karros .30 .14
❑ 439 Roberto Kelly .15 .07
❑ 440 Ramon Martinez .30 .14
❑ 441 Raul Mondesi .40 .18
❑ 442 Hideo Nomo 1.00 .45
❑ 443 Antonio Osuna .15 .07
❑ 444 Chan Ho Park .60 .25
❑ 445 Mike Piazza 2.00 .90
❑ 446 Felix Rodriguez .15 .07
❑ 447 Kevin Tapani .15 .07
❑ 448 Ismael Valdes .30 .14
❑ 449 Todd Worrell .15 .07
❑ 450 Moises Alou .40 .18
❑ 451 Shane Andrews .15 .07
❑ 452 Yamil Benitez .15 .07
❑ 453 Sean Berry .15 .07
❑ 454 Wil Cordero .15 .07
❑ 455 Jeff Fassero .15 .07
❑ 456 Darrin Fletcher .15 .07
❑ 457 Cliff Floyd .30 .14
❑ 458 Mark Grudzielanek .30 .14
❑ 459 Gil Heredia .15 .07
❑ 460 Tim Laker .15 .07
❑ 461 Mike Lansing .15 .07
❑ 462 Pedro J.Martinez .60 .25
❑ 463 Carlos Perez .30 .14
❑ 464 Curtis Pride .15 .07
❑ 465 Mel Rojas .15 .07
❑ 466 Kirk Rueter .15 .07
❑ 467 F.P. Santangelo .15 .07
❑ 468 Tim Scott .15 .07
❑ 469 David Segui .30 .14
❑ 470 Tony Tarasco .15 .07
❑ 471 Rondell White .30 .14
❑ 472 Edgardo Alfonzo .30 .14
❑ 473 Tim Bogar .15 .07
❑ 474 Rico Brogna .15 .07
❑ 475 Damon Buford .15 .07
❑ 476 Paul Byrd .15 .07
❑ 477 Carl Everett .15 .07
❑ 478 John Franco .30 .14
❑ 479 Todd Hundley .30 .14
❑ 480 Butch Huskey .15 .07
❑ 481 Jason Isringhausen .15 .07
❑ 482 Bobby Jones .15 .07
❑ 483 Chris Jones .15 .07
❑ 484 Jeff Kent .30 .14
❑ 485 Dave Mlicki .15 .07
❑ 486 Robert Person .15 .07
❑ 487 Bill Pulsipher .15 .07
❑ 488 Kelly Stinnett .15 .07
❑ 489 Ryan Thompson .15 .07
❑ 490 Jose Vizcaino .15 .07
❑ 491 Howard Battle .15 .07
❑ 492 Toby Borland .15 .07
❑ 493 Ricky Bottalico .30 .14
❑ 494 Darren Daulton .30 .14
❑ 495 Lenny Dykstra .30 .14
❑ 496 Jim Eisenreich .15 .07
❑ 497 Sid Fernandez .15 .07
❑ 498 Tyler Green .15 .07
❑ 499 Charlie Hayes .15 .07
❑ 500 Gregg Jefferies .15 .07
❑ 501 Kevin Jordan .15 .07
❑ 502 Tony Longmire .15 .07
❑ 503 Tom Marsh .15 .07
❑ 504 Michael Mimbs .15 .07
❑ 505 Mickey Morandini .15 .07
❑ 506 Gene Schall .15 .07
❑ 507 Curt Schilling .30 .14
❑ 508 Heathcliff Slocumb .15 .07
❑ 509 Kevin Stocker .15 .07
❑ 510 Andy Van Slyke .15 .07
❑ 511 Lenny Webster .15 .07
❑ 512 Mark Whiten .15 .07
❑ 513 Mike Williams .15 .07
❑ 514 Jay Bell .30 .14
❑ 515 Jacob Brumfield .15 .07
❑ 516 Jason Christiansen .15 .07
❑ 517 Dave Clark .15 .07
❑ 518 Midre Cummings .15 .07
❑ 519 Angelo Encarnacion .15 .07
❑ 520 John Ericks .15 .07
❑ 521 Carlos Garcia .15 .07
❑ 522 Mark Johnson .15 .07
❑ 523 Jeff King .15 .07
❑ 524 Nelson Liriano .15 .07
❑ 525 Esteban Loaiza .15 .07
❑ 526 Al Martin .15 .07
❑ 527 Orlando Merced .15 .07
❑ 528 Dan Miceli .15 .07
❑ 529 Ramon Morel .15 .07
❑ 530 Denny Neagle .30 .14
❑ 531 Steve Parris .15 .07
❑ 532 Dan Plesac .15 .07
❑ 533 Don Slaught .15 .07
❑ 534 Paul Wagner .15 .07
❑ 535 John Wehner .15 .07
❑ 536 Kevin Young .15 .07
❑ 537 Allen Battle .15 .07
❑ 538 David Bell .15 .07
❑ 539 Alan Benes .30 .14
❑ 540 Scott Cooper .15 .07
❑ 541 Tripp Cromer .15 .07
❑ 542 Tony Fossas .15 .07
❑ 543 Bernard Gilkey .15 .07
❑ 544 Tom Henke .15 .07
❑ 545 Brian Jordan .30 .14
❑ 546 Ray Lankford .30 .14
❑ 547 John Mabry .15 .07
❑ 548 T.J. Mathews .15 .07
❑ 549 Mike Morgan .15 .07
❑ 550 Jose Oliva .15 .07
❑ 551 Jose Oquendo .15 .07
❑ 552 Donovan Osborne .15 .07
❑ 553 Tom Pagnozzi .15 .07
❑ 554 Mark Petkovsek .15 .07
❑ 555 Danny Sheaffer .15 .07
❑ 556 Ozzie Smith .75 .35
❑ 557 Mark Sweeney .15 .07
❑ 558 Allen Watson .15 .07
❑ 559 Andy Ashby .15 .07
❑ 560 Brad Ausmus .15 .07
❑ 561 Willie Blair .15 .07

		MINT	NRMT
❑ 562	Ken Caminiti	.40	.18
❑ 563	Andujar Cedeno	.15	.07
❑ 564	Glenn Dishman	.15	.07
❑ 565	Steve Finley	.30	.14
❑ 566	Bryce Florie	.15	.07
❑ 567	Tony Gwynn	1.50	.70
❑ 568	Joey Hamilton	.30	.14
❑ 569	Dustin Hermanson UER	.30	.14
❑ 570	Trevor Hoffman	.30	.14
❑ 571	Brian Johnson	.15	.07
❑ 572	Marc Kroon	.15	.07
❑ 573	Scott Livingstone	.15	.07
❑ 574	Marc Newfield	.15	.07
❑ 575	Melvin Nieves	.15	.07
❑ 576	Jody Reed	.15	.07
❑ 577	Bip Roberts	.15	.07
❑ 578	Scott Sanders	.15	.07
❑ 579	Fernando Valenzuela	.30	.14
❑ 580	Eddie Williams	.15	.07
❑ 581	Rod Beck	.15	.07
❑ 582	Marvin Benard	.15	.07
❑ 583	Barry Bonds	.75	.35
❑ 584	Jamie Brewington	.15	.07
❑ 585	Mark Carreon	.15	.07
❑ 586	Royce Clayton	.15	.07
❑ 587	Shawn Estes	.30	.14
❑ 588	Glenallen Hill	.15	.07
❑ 589	Mark Leiter	.15	.07
❑ 590	Kirt Manwaring	.15	.07
❑ 591	David McCarty	.15	.07
❑ 592	Terry Mulholland	.15	.07
❑ 593	John Patterson	.15	.07
❑ 594	J.R. Phillips	.15	.07
❑ 595	Deion Sanders	.30	.14
❑ 596	Steve Scarsone	.15	.07
❑ 597	Robby Thompson	.15	.07
❑ 598	Sergio Valdez	.15	.07
❑ 599	William Van Landingham	.15	.07
❑ 600	Matt Williams	.30	.14
❑ P20	Cal Ripken Promo	2.00	.90

1996 Fleer Checklists

	MINT	NRMT
COMPLETE SET (10)	4.00	1.80
COMMON CARD (1-10)	.20	.09
❑ 1 Barry Bonds	.40	.18
❑ 2 Ken Griffey Jr.	1.50	.70
❑ 3 Chipper Jones	.75	.35
❑ 4 Greg Maddux	1.00	.45
❑ 5 Mike Piazza	1.00	.45
❑ 6 Manny Ramirez	.40	.18
❑ 7 Cal Ripken	1.25	.55
❑ 8 Frank Thomas	1.00	.45
❑ 9 Mo Vaughn	.40	.18
❑ 10 Matt Williams	.20	.09

1996 Fleer Golden Memories

	MINT	NRMT
COMPLETE SET (10)	8.00	3.60
COMMON CARD (1-10)	.30	.14
❑ 1 Albert Belle	.75	.35
❑ 2 Barry Bonds Sammy Sosa	1.50	.70
❑ 3 Greg Maddux	2.50	1.10
❑ 4 Edgar Martinez	.30	.14
❑ 5 Ramon Martinez	.30	.14
❑ 6 Mark McGwire	4.00	1.80
❑ 7 Eddie Murray	.75	.35
❑ 8 Cal Ripken	3.00	1.35
❑ 9 Frank Thomas	2.50	1.10
❑ 10 Alan Trammell Lou Whitaker	.50	.23

1996 Fleer Lumber Company

	MINT	NRMT
COMPLETE SET (12)	25.00	11.00
COMMON CARD (1-12)	1.00	.45
❑ 1 Albert Belle	2.50	1.10
❑ 2 Dante Bichette	1.00	.45
❑ 3 Barry Bonds	2.50	1.10
❑ 4 Ken Griffey Jr.	10.00	4.50
❑ 5 Mark McGwire	4.00	1.80
❑ 6 Mike Piazza	6.00	2.70
❑ 7 Manny Ramirez	2.00	.90
❑ 8 Tim Salmon	2.00	.90
❑ 9 Sammy Sosa	5.00	2.20
❑ 10 Frank Thomas	6.00	2.70
❑ 11 Mo Vaughn	2.50	1.10
❑ 12 Matt Williams	1.50	.70

1996 Fleer Postseason Glory

	MINT	NRMT
COMPLETE SET (5)	2.00	.90
COMMON CARD (1-5)	.10	.05
❑ 1 Tom Glavine	.30	.14
❑ 2 Ken Griffey Jr.	1.50	.70
❑ 3 Orel Hershiser	.10	.05
❑ 4 Randy Johnson	.30	.14
❑ 5 Jim Thome	.30	.14

1996 Fleer Prospects

	MINT	NRMT
COMPLETE SET (10)	5.00	2.20
COMMON CARD (1-10)	.25	.11
❑ 1 Yamil Benitez	.25	.11
❑ 2 Roger Cedeno	.25	.11
❑ 3 Tony Clark	1.50	.70
❑ 4 Micah Franklin	.25	.11
❑ 5 Karim Garcia	1.25	.55
❑ 6 Todd Greene	.50	.23
❑ 7 Alex Ochoa	.25	.11
❑ 8 Ruben Rivera	.50	.23
❑ 9 Chris Snopek	.25	.11
❑ 10 Shannon Stewart	.50	.23

1996 Fleer Road Warriors

	MINT	NRMT
COMPLETE SET (10)	12.00	5.50
COMMON CARD (1-10)	.40	.18
❑ 1 Derek Bell	.60	.25
❑ 2 Tony Gwynn	2.50	1.10
❑ 3 Greg Maddux	3.00	1.35
❑ 4 Mark McGwire	5.00	2.20
❑ 5 Mike Piazza	3.00	1.35
❑ 6 Manny Ramirez	.75	.35
❑ 7 Tim Salmon	.75	.35
❑ 8 Frank Thomas	3.00	1.35

	MINT	NRMT
❑ 9 Mo Vaughn	.75	.35
❑ 10 Matt Williams	.60	.25

1996 Fleer Rookie Sensations

	MINT	NRMT
COMPLETE SET (15)	15.00	6.75
COMMON CARD (1-15)	1.00	.45
❑ 1 Garret Anderson	1.50	.70
❑ 2 Marty Cordova	1.00	.45
❑ 3 Johnny Damon	1.50	.70
❑ 4 Ray Durham	1.50	.70
❑ 5 Carl Everett	1.00	.45
❑ 6 Shawn Green	1.50	.70
❑ 7 Brian L.Hunter	1.50	.70
❑ 8 Jason Isringhausen	1.00	.45
❑ 9 Charles Johnson	1.50	.70
❑ 10 Chipper Jones	8.00	3.60
❑ 11 John Mabry	1.00	.45
❑ 12 Hideo Nomo	5.00	2.20
❑ 13 Troy Percival	1.50	.70
❑ 14 Andy Pettitte	2.00	.90
❑ 15 Quilvio Veras	1.00	.45

1996 Fleer Smoke 'n Heat

	MINT	NRMT
COMPLETE SET (10)	6.00	2.70
COMMON CARD (1-10)	.25	.11
❑ 1 Kevin Appier	.40	.18
❑ 2 Roger Clemens	2.00	.90
❑ 3 David Cone	.75	.35
❑ 4 Chuck Finley	.40	.18
❑ 5 Randy Johnson	1.00	.45
❑ 6 Greg Maddux	3.00	1.35
❑ 7 Pedro Martinez	1.00	.45
❑ 8 Hideo Nomo	1.50	.70
❑ 9 John Smoltz	.40	.18
❑ 10 Todd Stottlemyre	.25	.11

1996 Fleer Team Leaders

	MINT	NRMT
COMPLETE SET (28)	80.00	36.00

	MINT	NRMT
COMMON CARD (1-28)	.75	.35
❑ 1 Cal Ripken	12.00	5.50
❑ 2 Mo Vaughn	3.00	1.35
❑ 3 Jim Edmonds	2.00	.90
❑ 4 Frank Thomas	10.00	4.50
❑ 5 Kenny Lofton	3.00	1.35
❑ 6 Travis Fryman	1.50	.70
❑ 7 Gary Gaetti	1.50	.70
❑ 8 B.J. Surhoff	1.50	.70
❑ 9 Kirby Puckett	6.00	2.70
❑ 10 Don Mattingly	5.00	2.20
❑ 11 Mark McGwire	15.00	6.75
❑ 12 Ken Griffey Jr.	15.00	6.75
❑ 13 Juan Gonzalez	8.00	3.60
❑ 14 Joe Carter	1.50	.70
❑ 15 Greg Maddux	10.00	4.50
❑ 16 Sammy Sosa	8.00	3.60
❑ 17 Barry Larkin	2.00	.90
❑ 18 Dante Bichette	1.50	.70
❑ 19 Jeff Conine	1.50	.70
❑ 20 Jeff Bagwell	5.00	2.20
❑ 21 Mike Piazza	10.00	4.50
❑ 22 Rondell White	1.50	.70
❑ 23 Rico Brogna	.75	.35
❑ 24 Darren Daulton	1.50	.70
❑ 25 Jeff King	.75	.35
❑ 26 Ray Lankford	1.50	.70
❑ 27 Tony Gwynn	8.00	3.60
❑ 28 Barry Bonds	3.00	1.35

1996 Fleer Tomorrow's Legends

	MINT	NRMT
COMPLETE SET (10)	10.00	4.50
COMMON CARD (1-10)	1.00	.45
❑ 1 Garret Anderson	1.25	.55
❑ 2 Jim Edmonds	1.50	.70
❑ 3 Brian L.Hunter	1.25	.55
❑ 4 Jason Isringhausen	1.00	.45
❑ 5 Charles Johnson	1.25	.55
❑ 6 Chipper Jones	5.00	2.20
❑ 7 Ryan Klesko	1.25	.55
❑ 8 Hideo Nomo	3.00	1.35
❑ 9 Manny Ramirez	2.00	.90
❑ 10 Rondell White	1.25	.55

1996 Fleer Zone

	MINT	NRMT
COMPLETE SET (12)	150.00	70.00
COMMON CARD (1-12)	5.00	2.20
❑ 1 Albert Belle	10.00	4.50
❑ 2 Barry Bonds	10.00	4.50
❑ 3 Ken Griffey Jr.	40.00	18.00
❑ 4 Tony Gwynn	20.00	9.00
❑ 5 Randy Johnson	8.00	3.60
❑ 6 Kenny Lofton	8.00	3.60
❑ 7 Greg Maddux	25.00	11.00
❑ 8 Edgar Martinez	5.00	2.20
❑ 9 Mike Piazza	25.00	11.00
❑ 10 Frank Thomas	25.00	11.00
❑ 11 Mo Vaughn	10.00	4.50
❑ 12 Matt Williams	5.00	2.20

1996 Fleer Update

	MINT	NRMT
COMPLETE SET (250)	30.00	13.50
COMMON CARD (U1-U250)	.15	.07
❑ U1 Roberto Alomar	.60	.25
❑ U2 Mike Devereaux	.15	.07
❑ U3 Scott McClain	.15	.07
❑ U4 Roger McDowell	.15	.07
❑ U5 Kent Mercker	.15	.07
❑ U6 Jimmy Myers	.15	.07
❑ U7 Randy Myers	.15	.07
❑ U8 B.J. Surhoff	.30	.14
❑ U9 Tony Tarasco	.15	.07
❑ U10 David Wells	.40	.18
❑ U11 Wil Cordero	.15	.07
❑ U12 Tom Gordon	.15	.07
❑ U13 Reggie Jefferson	.15	.07
❑ U14 Jose Malave	.15	.07
❑ U15 Kevin Mitchell	.15	.07
❑ U16 Jamie Moyer	.15	.07
❑ U17 Heathcliff Slocumb	.15	.07
❑ U18 Mike Stanley	.15	.07
❑ U19 George Arias	.15	.07
❑ U20 Jorge Fabregas	.15	.07
❑ U21 Don Slaught	.15	.07
❑ U22 Randy Velarde	.15	.07
❑ U23 Harold Baines	.30	.14
❑ U24 Mike Cameron	1.25	.55
❑ U25 Darren Lewis	.15	.07
❑ U26 Tony Phillips	.15	.07

❑ U27 Bill Simas .15 .07
❑ U28 Chris Snopek .15 .07
❑ U29 Kevin Tapani .15 .07
❑ U30 Danny Tartabull .15 .07
❑ U31 Julio Franco .15 .07
❑ U32 Jack McDowell .15 .07
❑ U33 Kimera Bartee .15 .07
❑ U34 Mark Lewis .15 .07
❑ U35 Melvin Nieves .15 .07
❑ U36 Mark Parent .15 .07
❑ U37 Eddie Williams .15 .07
❑ U38 Tim Belcher .15 .07
❑ U39 Sal Fasano .15 .07
❑ U40 Chris Haney .15 .07
❑ U41 Mike Macfarlane .15 .07
❑ U42 Jose Offerman .15 .07
❑ U43 Joe Randa .15 .07
❑ U44 Bip Roberts .15 .07
❑ U45 Chuck Carr .15 .07
❑ U46 Bobby Hughes .15 .07
❑ U47 Graeme Lloyd .15 .07
❑ U48 Ben McDonald .15 .07
❑ U49 Kevin Wickander .15 .07
❑ U50 Rick Aguilera .15 .07
❑ U51 Mike Durant .15 .07
❑ U52 Chip Hale .15 .07
❑ U53 LaTroy Hawkins .15 .07
❑ U54 Dave Hollins .15 .07
❑ U55 Roberto Kelly .15 .07
❑ U56 Paul Molitor .60 .25
❑ U57 Dan Naulty .15 .07
❑ U58 Mariano Duncan .15 .07
❑ U59 Andy Fox .15 .07
❑ U60 Joe Girardi .15 .07
❑ U61 Dwight Gooden .30 .14
❑ U62 Jimmy Key .30 .14
❑ U63 Matt Luke .15 .07
❑ U64 Tino Martinez .60 .25
❑ U65 Jeff Nelson .15 .07
❑ U66 Tim Raines .30 .14
❑ U67 Ruben Rivera .30 .14
❑ U68 Kenny Rogers .15 .07
❑ U69 Gerald Williams .15 .07
❑ U70 Tony Batista .15 .07
❑ U71 Allen Battle .15 .07
❑ U72 Jim Corsi .15 .07
❑ U73 Steve Cox .15 .07
❑ U74 Pedro Munoz .15 .07
❑ U75 Phil Plantier .15 .07
❑ U76 Scott Spiezio .15 .07
❑ U77 Ernie Young .15 .07
❑ U78 Russ Davis .30 .14
❑ U79 Sterling Hitchcock .30 .14
❑ U80 Edwin Hurtado .15 .07
❑ U81 Raul Ibanez .15 .07
❑ U82 Mike Jackson .15 .07
❑ U83 Ricky Jordan .15 .07
❑ U84 Paul Sorrento .15 .07
❑ U85 Doug Strange .15 .07
❑ U86 Mark Brandenburg .15 .07
❑ U87 Damon Buford .15 .07
❑ U88 Kevin Elster .15 .07
❑ U89 Darryl Hamilton .15 .07
❑ U90 Ken Hill .15 .07
❑ U91 Ed Vosberg .15 .07
❑ U92 Craig Worthington .15 .07
❑ U93 Tilson Brito .15 .07
❑ U94 Giovanni Carrara .15 .07
❑ U95 Felipe Crespo .15 .07
❑ U96 Erik Hanson .15 .07
❑ U97 Marty Janzen .15 .07
❑ U98 Otis Nixon .15 .07
❑ U99 Charlie O'Brien .15 .07
❑ U100 Robert Perez .15 .07
❑ U101 Paul Quantrill .15 .07
❑ U102 Bill Risley .15 .07
❑ U103 Juan Samuel .15 .07
❑ U104 Jermaine Dye .15 .07
❑ U105 Wonderful Monds .15 .07
❑ U106 Dwight Smith .15 .07
❑ U107 Jerome Walton .15 .07
❑ U108 Terry Adams .15 .07
❑ U109 Leo Gomez .15 .07
❑ U110 Robin Jennings .15 .07
❑ U111 Doug Jones .15 .07
❑ U112 Brooks Kieschnick .15 .07
❑ U113 Dave Magadan .15 .07
❑ U114 Jason Maxwell .15 .07
❑ U115 Rodney Myers .15 .07
❑ U116 Eric Anthony .15 .07
❑ U117 Vince Coleman .15 .07
❑ U118 Eric Davis .30 .14
❑ U119 Steve Gibralter .15 .07
❑ U120 Curtis Goodwin .15 .07
❑ U121 Willie Greene .30 .14
❑ U122 Mike Kelly .15 .07
❑ U123 Marcus Moore .15 .07
❑ U124 Chad Mottola .15 .07
❑ U125 Chris Sabo .15 .07
❑ U126 Roger Salkeld .15 .07
❑ U127 Pedro Castellano .15 .07
❑ U128 Trenidad Hubbard .15 .07
❑ U129 Jayhawk Owens .15 .07
❑ U130 Jeff Reed .15 .07
❑ U131 Kevin Brown .60 .25
❑ U132 Al Leiter .30 .14
❑ U133 Matt Mantei .15 .07
❑ U134 Dave Weathers .15 .07
❑ U135 Devon White .30 .14
❑ U136 Bob Abreu .30 .14
❑ U137 Sean Berry .15 .07
❑ U138 Doug Brocail .15 .07
❑ U139 Richard Hidalgo .30 .14
❑ U140 Alvin Morman .15 .07
❑ U141 Mike Blowers .15 .07
❑ U142 Roger Cedeno .15 .07
❑ U143 Greg Gagne .15 .07
❑ U144 Karim Garcia .30 .14
❑ U145 Wilton Guerrero .50 .23
❑ U146 Israel Alcantara .15 .07
❑ U147 Omar Daal .15 .07
❑ U148 Ryan McGuire .15 .07
❑ U149 Sherman Obando .15 .07
❑ U150 Jose Paniagua .15 .07
❑ U151 Henry Rodriguez .30 .14
❑ U152 Andy Stankiewicz .15 .07
❑ U153 Dave Veres .15 .07
❑ U154 Juan Acevedo .15 .07
❑ U155 Mark Clark .15 .07
❑ U156 Bernard Gilkey .15 .07
❑ U157 Pete Harnisch .15 .07
❑ U158 Lance Johnson .15 .07
❑ U159 Brent Mayne .15 .07
❑ U160 Rey Ordonez .30 .14
❑ U161 Kevin Roberson .15 .07
❑ U162 Paul Wilson .15 .07
❑ U163 David Doster .15 .07
❑ U164 Mike Grace .15 .07
❑ U165 Rich Hunter .15 .07
❑ U166 Pete Incaviglia .15 .07
❑ U167 Mike Lieberthal .15 .07
❑ U168 Terry Mulholland .15 .07
❑ U169 Ken Ryan .15 .07
❑ U170 Benito Santiago .15 .07
❑ U171 Kevin Sefcik .15 .07
❑ U172 Lee Tinsley .15 .07
❑ U173 Todd Zeile .15 .07
❑ U174 Francisco Cordova .15 .07
❑ U175 Danny Darwin .15 .07
❑ U176 Charlie Hayes .15 .07
❑ U177 Jason Kendall .60 .25
❑ U178 Mike Kingery .15 .07
❑ U179 Jon Lieber .15 .07
❑ U180 Zane Smith .15 .07
❑ U181 Luis Alicea .15 .07
❑ U182 Cory Bailey .15 .07
❑ U183 Andy Benes .30 .14
❑ U184 Pat Borders .15 .07
❑ U185 Mike Busby .15 .07
❑ U186 Royce Clayton .15 .07
❑ U187 Dennis Eckersley .30 .14
❑ U188 Gary Gaetti .30 .14
❑ U189 Ron Gant .15 .07
❑ U190 Aaron Holbert .15 .07
❑ U191 Willie McGee .30 .14
❑ U192 Miguel Mejia .15 .07
❑ U193 Jeff Parrett .15 .07
❑ U194 Todd Stottlemyre .15 .07
❑ U195 Sean Bergman .15 .07
❑ U196 Archi Cianfrocco .15 .07
❑ U197 Rickey Henderson .60 .25
❑ U198 Wally Joyner .30 .14
❑ U199 Craig Shipley .15 .07
❑ U200 Bob Tewksbury .15 .07
❑ U201 Tim Worrell .15 .07
❑ U202 Rich Aurilia .15 .07
❑ U203 Doug Creek .15 .07
❑ U204 Shawon Dunston .15 .07
❑ U205 Osvaldo Fernandez .15 .07
❑ U206 Mark Gardner .15 .07
❑ U207 Stan Javier .15 .07
❑ U208 Marcus Jensen .15 .07
❑ U209 Chris Singleton .15 .07
❑ U210 Allen Watson .15 .07
❑ U211 Jeff Bagwell ENC 1.00 .45
❑ U212 Derek Bell ENC .15 .07
❑ U213 Albert Belle ENC .75 .35
❑ U214 Wade Boggs ENC .30 .14
❑ U215 Barry Bonds ENC .75 .35
❑ U216 Jose Canseco ENC .30 .14
❑ U217 Marty Cordova ENC .15 .07
❑ U218 Jim Edmonds ENC .15 .07
❑ U219 Cecil Fielder ENC .15 .07
❑ U220 Andres Galarraga ENC .30 .14
❑ U221 Juan Gonzalez ENC 1.50 .70
❑ U222 Mark Grace ENC .15 .07
❑ U223 Ken Griffey Jr. ENC 3.00 1.35
❑ U224 Tony Gwynn ENC 1.50 .70
❑ U225 J. Isringhausen ENC .15 .07
❑ U226 Derek Jeter ENC 2.00 .90
❑ U227 Randy Johnson ENC .30 .14
❑ U228 Chipper Jones ENC 1.50 .70
❑ U229 Ryan Klesko ENC .15 .07
❑ U230 Barry Larkin ENC .15 .07
❑ U231 Kenny Lofton ENC .30 .14
❑ U232 Greg Maddux ENC 2.00 .90
❑ U233 Raul Mondesi ENC .15 .07
❑ U234 Hideo Nomo ENC 1.00 .45
❑ U235 Mike Piazza ENC 2.00 .90
❑ U236 Manny Ramirez ENC .30 .14
❑ U237 Cal Ripken ENC 1.50 .70
❑ U238 Tim Salmon ENC .30 .14
❑ U239 Ryne Sandberg ENC .75 .35
❑ U240 Reggie Sanders ENC .15 .07
❑ U241 Gary Sheffield ENC .15 .07
❑ U242 Sammy Sosa ENC 1.50 .70
❑ U243 Frank Thomas ENC 2.00 .90
❑ U244 Mo Vaughn ENC .75 .35
❑ U245 Matt Williams ENC .30 .14
❑ U246 Barry Bonds CL .40 .18
❑ U247 Ken Griffey Jr. CL 1.50 .70
❑ U248 Rey Ordonez CL .15 .07
❑ U249 Ryne Sandberg CL .60 .25
❑ U250 Frank Thomas CL 1.00 .45

1996 Fleer Update Diamond Tribute

	MINT	NRMT
COMPLETE SET (10)	150.00	70.00
COMMON CARD (1-10)	5.00	2.20

❑ 1 Wade Boggs 8.00 3.60
❑ 2 Barry Bonds 10.00 4.50
❑ 3 Ken Griffey Jr. 40.00 18.00
❑ 4 Tony Gwynn 15.00 6.75
❑ 5 Rickey Henderson 8.00 3.60

	MINT	NRMT
❑ 6 Greg Maddux	25.00	11.00
❑ 7 Eddie Murray	5.00	2.20
❑ 8 Cal Ripken	30.00	13.50
❑ 9 Ozzie Smith	10.00	4.50
❑ 10 Frank Thomas	25.00	11.00

1996 Fleer Update Headliners

	MINT	NRMT
COMPLETE SET (20)	40.00	18.00
COMMON CARD (1-20)	.75	.35
❑ 1 Roberto Alomar	1.50	.70
❑ 2 Jeff Bagwell	2.50	1.10
❑ 3 Albert Belle	1.50	.70
❑ 4 Barry Bonds	1.50	.70
❑ 5 Cecil Fielder	.75	.35
❑ 6 Juan Gonzalez	4.00	1.80
❑ 7 Ken Griffey Jr.	8.00	3.60
❑ 8 Tony Gwynn	4.00	1.80
❑ 9 Randy Johnson	1.50	.70
❑ 10 Chipper Jones	4.00	1.80
❑ 11 Ryan Klesko	.75	.35
❑ 12 Kenny Lofton	1.50	.70
❑ 13 Greg Maddux	5.00	2.20
❑ 14 Hideo Nomo	2.50	1.10
❑ 15 Mike Piazza	5.00	2.20
❑ 16 Manny Ramirez	1.50	.70
❑ 17 Cal Ripken	6.00	2.70
❑ 18 Tim Salmon	1.50	.70
❑ 19 Frank Thomas	5.00	2.20
❑ 20 Matt Williams	.75	.35

1996 Fleer Update New Horizons

	MINT	NRMT
COMPLETE SET (20)	15.00	6.75
COMMON CARD (1-20)	.25	.11
❑ 1 Bob Abreu	.50	.23
❑ 2 George Arias	.25	.11
❑ 3 Tony Batista	.25	.11
❑ 4 Steve Cox	.25	.11
❑ 5 Jermaine Dye	.25	.11
❑ 6 Andy Fox	.25	.11
❑ 7 Mike Grace	.25	.11
❑ 8 Todd Greene	.50	.23
❑ 9 Wilton Guerrero	2.00	.90
❑ 10 Richard Hidalgo	2.00	.90
❑ 11 Raul Ibanez	.25	.11
❑ 12 Robin Jennings	.25	.11
❑ 13 Marcus Jensen	.25	.11
❑ 14 Jason Kendall	2.00	.90
❑ 15 Jason Maxwell	.25	.11
❑ 16 Ryan McGuire	.25	.11
❑ 17 Miguel Mejia	.25	.11
❑ 18 Wonderful Monds	.25	.11
❑ 19 Rey Ordonez	.50	.23
❑ 20 Paul Wilson	.25	.11

1996 Fleer Update Smooth Leather

	MINT	NRMT
COMPLETE SET (10)	10.00	4.50
COMMON CARD (1-10)	.25	.11
❑ 1 Roberto Alomar	.75	.35
❑ 2 Barry Bonds	.75	.35
❑ 3 Will Clark	.75	.35
❑ 4 Ken Griffey Jr.	4.00	1.80
❑ 5 Kenny Lofton	.75	.35
❑ 6 Greg Maddux	2.50	1.10
❑ 7 Raul Mondesi	.50	.23
❑ 8 Rey Ordonez	.25	.11
❑ 9 Cal Ripken	3.00	1.35
❑ 10 Matt Williams	.25	.11

1996 Fleer Update Soaring Stars

	MINT	NRMT
COMPLETE SET (10)	25.00	11.00
COMMON CARD (1-10)	1.00	.45
❑ 1 Jeff Bagwell	2.50	1.10
❑ 2 Barry Bonds	1.50	.70
❑ 3 Juan Gonzalez	4.00	1.80
❑ 4 Ken Griffey Jr.	8.00	3.60
❑ 5 Chipper Jones	4.00	1.80
❑ 6 Greg Maddux	5.00	2.20
❑ 7 Mike Piazza	5.00	2.20
❑ 8 Manny Ramirez	1.50	.70
❑ 9 Frank Thomas	5.00	2.20
❑ 10 Matt Williams	1.00	.45

1997 Fleer

	MINT	NRMT
COMPLETE SET (761)	90.00	40.00
COMPLETE SERIES 1 (500)	50.00	22.00
COMPLETE SERIES 2 (261)	40.00	18.00
COMMON CARD (1-750)	.15	.07
COMMON CARD (751-761)	.25	.11
❑ 1 Roberto Alomar	.60	.25
❑ 2 Brady Anderson	.30	.14
❑ 3 Bobby Bonilla	.30	.14
❑ 4 Rocky Coppinger	.15	.07
❑ 5 Cesar Devarez	.15	.07
❑ 6 Scott Erickson	.30	.14
❑ 7 Jeffrey Hammonds	.30	.14
❑ 8 Chris Hoiles	.15	.07
❑ 9 Eddie Murray	.60	.25
❑ 10 Mike Mussina	.60	.25
❑ 11 Randy Myers	.15	.07
❑ 12 Rafael Palmeiro	.40	.18
❑ 13 Cal Ripken	2.50	1.10
❑ 14 B.J. Surhoff	.30	.14
❑ 15 David Wells	.40	.18
❑ 16 Todd Zeile	.15	.07
❑ 17 Darren Bragg	.15	.07
❑ 18 Jose Canseco	.60	.25
❑ 19 Roger Clemens	1.25	.55
❑ 20 Wil Cordero	.15	.07
❑ 21 Jeff Frye	.15	.07
❑ 22 Nomar Garciaparra	2.00	.90
❑ 23 Tom Gordon	.15	.07
❑ 24 Mike Greenwell	.15	.07
❑ 25 Reggie Jefferson	.15	.07
❑ 26 Jose Malave	.15	.07
❑ 27 Tim Naehring	.15	.07
❑ 28 Troy O'Leary	.30	.14
❑ 29 Heathcliff Slocumb	.15	.07
❑ 30 Mike Stanley	.15	.07
❑ 31 John Valentin	.30	.14
❑ 32 Mo Vaughn	.75	.35
❑ 33 Tim Wakefield	.30	.14
❑ 34 Garret Anderson	.30	.14
❑ 35 George Arias	.15	.07
❑ 36 Shawn Boskie	.15	.07
❑ 37 Chili Davis	.30	.14
❑ 38 Jason Dickson	.30	.14
❑ 39 Gary DiSarcina	.15	.07
❑ 40 Jim Edmonds	.40	.18
❑ 41 Darin Erstad	1.00	.45
❑ 42 Jorge Fabregas	.15	.07
❑ 43 Chuck Finley	.30	.14
❑ 44 Todd Greene	.30	.14
❑ 45 Mike Holtz	.15	.07
❑ 46 Rex Hudler	.15	.07
❑ 47 Mike James	.15	.07
❑ 48 Mark Langston	.30	.14
❑ 49 Troy Percival	.30	.14
❑ 50 Tim Salmon	.60	.25
❑ 51 Jeff Schmidt	.15	.07
❑ 52 J.T. Snow	.30	.14
❑ 53 Randy Velarde	.15	.07
❑ 54 Wilson Alvarez	.30	.14
❑ 55 Harold Baines	.30	.14
❑ 56 James Baldwin	.30	.14
❑ 57 Jason Bere	.15	.07
❑ 58 Mike Cameron	.30	.14
❑ 59 Ray Durham	.30	.14

❑	60	Alex Fernandez	.15	.07
❑	61	Ozzie Guillen	.15	.07
❑	62	Roberto Hernandez	.15	.07
❑	63	Ron Karkovice	.15	.07
❑	64	Darren Lewis	.15	.07
❑	65	Dave Martinez	.15	.07
❑	66	Lyle Mouton	.15	.07
❑	67	Greg Norton	.15	.07
❑	68	Tony Phillips	.15	.07
❑	69	Chris Snopek	.15	.07
❑	70	Kevin Tapani	.15	.07
❑	71	Danny Tartabull	.15	.07
❑	72	Frank Thomas	2.00	.90
❑	73	Robin Ventura	.30	.14
❑	74	Sandy Alomar Jr.	.30	.14
❑	75	Albert Belle	.75	.35
❑	76	Mark Carreon	.15	.07
❑	77	Julio Franco	.30	.14
❑	78	Brian Giles	.75	.35
❑	79	Orel Hershiser	.30	.14
❑	80	Kenny Lofton	.60	.25
❑	81	Dennis Martinez	.30	.14
❑	82	Jack McDowell	.15	.07
❑	83	Jose Mesa	.15	.07
❑	84	Charles Nagy	.30	.14
❑	85	Chad Ogea	.15	.07
❑	86	Eric Plunk	.15	.07
❑	87	Manny Ramirez	.60	.25
❑	88	Kevin Seitzer	.15	.07
❑	89	Julian Tavarez	.15	.07
❑	90	Jim Thome	.60	.25
❑	91	Jose Vizcaino	.15	.07
❑	92	Omar Vizquel	.30	.14
❑	93	Brad Ausmus	.15	.07
❑	94	Kimera Bartee	.15	.07
❑	95	Raul Casanova	.15	.07
❑	96	Tony Clark	.40	.18
❑	97	John Cummings	.15	.07
❑	98	Travis Fryman	.30	.14
❑	99	Bob Higginson	.40	.18
❑	100	Mark Lewis	.15	.07
❑	101	Felipe Lira	.15	.07
❑	102	Phil Nevin	.15	.07
❑	103	Melvin Nieves	.15	.07
❑	104	Curtis Pride	.15	.07
❑	105	A.J. Sager	.15	.07
❑	106	Ruben Sierra	.15	.07
❑	107	Justin Thompson	.30	.14
❑	108	Alan Trammell	.30	.14
❑	109	Kevin Appier	.30	.14
❑	110	Tim Belcher	.15	.07
❑	111	Jaime Bluma	.15	.07
❑	112	Johnny Damon	.30	.14
❑	113	Tom Goodwin	.15	.07
❑	114	Chris Haney	.15	.07
❑	115	Keith Lockhart	.15	.07
❑	116	Mike Macfarlane	.15	.07
❑	117	Jeff Montgomery	.15	.07
❑	118	Jose Offerman	.15	.07
❑	119	Craig Paquette	.15	.07
❑	120	Joe Randa	.15	.07
❑	121	Bip Roberts	.15	.07
❑	122	Jose Rosado	.15	.07
❑	123	Mike Sweeney	.15	.07
❑	124	Michael Tucker	.30	.14
❑	125	Jeromy Burnitz	.30	.14
❑	126	Jeff Cirillo	.30	.14
❑	127	Jeff D'Amico	.15	.07
❑	128	Mike Fetters	.15	.07
❑	129	John Jaha	.15	.07
❑	130	Scott Karl	.15	.07
❑	131	Jesse Levis	.15	.07
❑	132	Mark Loretta	.15	.07
❑	133	Mike Matheny	.15	.07
❑	134	Ben McDonald	.15	.07
❑	135	Matt Mieske	.15	.07
❑	136	Marc Newfield	.15	.07
❑	137	Dave Nilsson	.15	.07
❑	138	Jose Valentin	.15	.07
❑	139	Fernando Vina	.15	.07
❑	140	Bob Wickman	.15	.07
❑	141	Gerald Williams	.15	.07
❑	142	Rick Aguilera	.15	.07
❑	143	Rich Becker	.15	.07
❑	144	Ron Coomer	.15	.07
❑	145	Marty Cordova	.15	.07
❑	146	Roberto Kelly	.15	.07
❑	147	Chuck Knoblauch	.60	.25
❑	148	Matt Lawton	.30	.14
❑	149	Pat Meares	.15	.07
❑	150	Travis Miller	.15	.07
❑	151	Paul Molitor	.60	.25
❑	152	Greg Myers	.15	.07
❑	153	Dan Naulty	.15	.07
❑	154	Kirby Puckett	1.00	.45
❑	155	Brad Radke	.30	.14
❑	156	Frank Rodriguez	.15	.07
❑	157	Scott Stahoviak	.15	.07
❑	158	Dave Stevens	.15	.07
❑	159	Matt Walbeck	.15	.07
❑	160	Todd Walker	.60	.25
❑	161	Wade Boggs	.60	.25
❑	162	David Cone	.40	.18
❑	163	Mariano Duncan	.15	.07
❑	164	Cecil Fielder	.30	.14
❑	165	Joe Girardi	.15	.07
❑	166	Dwight Gooden	.30	.14
❑	167	Charlie Hayes	.15	.07
❑	168	Derek Jeter	2.00	.90
❑	169	Jimmy Key	.30	.14
❑	170	Jim Leyritz	.15	.07
❑	171	Tino Martinez	.60	.25
❑	172	Ramiro Mendoza	.50	.23
❑	173	Jeff Nelson	.15	.07
❑	174	Paul O'Neill	.30	.14
❑	175	Andy Pettitte	.40	.18
❑	176	Mariano Rivera	.30	.14
❑	177	Ruben Rivera	.30	.14
❑	178	Kenny Rogers	.15	.07
❑	179	Darryl Strawberry	.30	.14
❑	180	John Wetteland	.30	.14
❑	181	Bernie Williams	.60	.25
❑	182	Willie Adams	.15	.07
❑	183	Tony Batista	.15	.07
❑	184	Geronimo Berroa	.15	.07
❑	185	Mike Bordick	.15	.07
❑	186	Scott Brosius	.30	.14
❑	187	Bobby Chouinard	.15	.07
❑	188	Jim Corsi	.15	.07
❑	189	Brent Gates	.15	.07
❑	190	Jason Giambi	.30	.14
❑	191	Jose Herrera	.15	.07
❑	192	Damon Mashore	.15	.07
❑	193	Mark McGwire	3.00	1.35
❑	194	Mike Mohler	.15	.07
❑	195	Scott Spiezio	.15	.07
❑	196	Terry Steinbach	.30	.14
❑	197	Bill Taylor	.15	.07
❑	198	John Wasdin	.15	.07
❑	199	Steve Wojciechowski	.15	.07
❑	200	Ernie Young	.15	.07
❑	201	Rich Amaral	.15	.07
❑	202	Jay Buhner	.30	.14
❑	203	Norm Charlton	.15	.07
❑	204	Joey Cora	.30	.14
❑	205	Russ Davis	.30	.14
❑	206	Ken Griffey Jr.	3.00	1.35
❑	207	Sterling Hitchcock	.30	.14
❑	208	Brian Hunter	.30	.14
❑	209	Raul Ibanez	.15	.07
❑	210	Randy Johnson	.60	.25
❑	211	Edgar Martinez	.30	.14
❑	212	Jamie Moyer	.15	.07
❑	213	Alex Rodriguez	2.00	.90
❑	214	Paul Sorrento	.15	.07
❑	215	Matt Wagner	.15	.07
❑	216	Bob Wells	.15	.07
❑	217	Dan Wilson	.15	.07
❑	218	Damon Buford	.15	.07
❑	219	Will Clark	.60	.25
❑	220	Kevin Elster	.15	.07
❑	221	Juan Gonzalez	1.50	.70
❑	222	Rusty Greer	.30	.14
❑	223	Kevin Gross	.15	.07
❑	224	Darryl Hamilton	.15	.07
❑	225	Mike Henneman	.15	.07
❑	226	Ken Hill	.15	.07
❑	227	Mark McLemore	.15	.07
❑	228	Darren Oliver	.15	.07
❑	229	Dean Palmer	.30	.14
❑	230	Roger Pavlik	.15	.07
❑	231	Ivan Rodriguez	.75	.35
❑	232	Mickey Tettleton	.15	.07
❑	233	Bobby Witt	.15	.07
❑	234	Jacob Brumfield	.15	.07
❑	235	Joe Carter	.30	.14
❑	236	Tim Crabtree	.15	.07
❑	237	Carlos Delgado	.30	.14
❑	238	Huck Flener	.15	.07
❑	239	Alex Gonzalez	.15	.07
❑	240	Shawn Green	.30	.14
❑	241	Juan Guzman	.15	.07
❑	242	Pat Hentgen	.30	.14
❑	243	Marty Janzen	.15	.07
❑	244	Sandy Martinez	.15	.07
❑	245	Otis Nixon	.15	.07
❑	246	Charlie O'Brien	.15	.07
❑	247	John Olerud	.30	.14
❑	248	Robert Perez	.15	.07
❑	249	Ed Sprague	.15	.07
❑	250	Mike Timlin	.15	.07
❑	251	Steve Avery	.15	.07
❑	252	Jeff Blauser	.15	.07
❑	253	Brad Clontz	.15	.07
❑	254	Jermaine Dye	.15	.07
❑	255	Tom Glavine	.60	.25
❑	256	Marquis Grissom	.30	.14
❑	257	Andruw Jones	1.00	.45
❑	258	Chipper Jones	1.50	.70
❑	259	David Justice	.60	.25
❑	260	Ryan Klesko	.30	.14
❑	261	Mark Lemke	.15	.07
❑	262	Javier Lopez	.30	.14
❑	263	Greg Maddux	2.00	.90
❑	264	Fred McGriff	.40	.18
❑	265	Greg McMichael	.15	.07
❑	266	Denny Neagle	.30	.14
❑	267	Terry Pendleton	.15	.07
❑	268	Eddie Perez	.15	.07
❑	269	John Smoltz	.30	.14
❑	270	Terrell Wade	.15	.07
❑	271	Mark Wohlers	.15	.07
❑	272	Terry Adams	.15	.07
❑	273	Brant Brown	.30	.14
❑	274	Leo Gomez	.15	.07
❑	275	Luis Gonzalez	.15	.07
❑	276	Mark Grace	.40	.18
❑	277	Tyler Houston	.15	.07
❑	278	Robin Jennings	.15	.07
❑	279	Brooks Kieschnick	.15	.07
❑	280	Brian McRae	.15	.07
❑	281	Jaime Navarro	.15	.07
❑	282	Ryne Sandberg	.75	.35
❑	283	Scott Servais	.15	.07
❑	284	Sammy Sosa	1.50	.70
❑	285	Dave Swartzbaugh	.15	.07
❑	286	Amaury Telemaco	.15	.07
❑	287	Steve Trachsel	.15	.07
❑	288	Pedro Valdes	.15	.07
❑	289	Turk Wendell	.15	.07
❑	290	Bret Boone	.30	.14
❑	291	Jeff Branson	.15	.07
❑	292	Jeff Brantley	.15	.07
❑	293	Eric Davis	.30	.14
❑	294	Willie Greene	.30	.14
❑	295	Thomas Howard	.15	.07
❑	296	Barry Larkin	.40	.18
❑	297	Kevin Mitchell	.15	.07
❑	298	Hal Morris	.15	.07
❑	299	Chad Mottola	.15	.07
❑	300	Joe Oliver	.15	.07
❑	301	Mark Portugal	.15	.07
❑	302	Roger Salkeld	.15	.07
❑	303	Reggie Sanders	.30	.14
❑	304	Pete Schourek	.15	.07
❑	305	John Smiley	.15	.07
❑	306	Eddie Taubensee	.15	.07
❑	307	Dante Bichette	.30	.14
❑	308	Ellis Burks	.30	.14
❑	309	Vinny Castilla	.40	.18
❑	310	Andres Galarraga	.60	.25
❑	311	Curt Leskanic	.15	.07
❑	312	Quinton McCracken	.30	.14
❑	313	Neifi Perez	.15	.07
❑	314	Jeff Reed	.15	.07

❑ 315	Steve Reed	.15	.07
❑ 316	Armando Reynoso	.15	.07
❑ 317	Kevin Ritz	.15	.07
❑ 318	Bruce Ruffin	.15	.07
❑ 319	Larry Walker	.60	.25
❑ 320	Walt Weiss	.15	.07
❑ 321	Jamey Wright	.15	.07
❑ 322	Eric Young	.30	.14
❑ 323	Kurt Abbott	.15	.07
❑ 324	Alex Arias	.15	.07
❑ 325	Kevin Brown	.40	.18
❑ 326	Luis Castillo	.30	.14
❑ 327	Greg Colbrunn	.15	.07
❑ 328	Jeff Conine	.30	.14
❑ 329	Andre Dawson	.40	.18
❑ 330	Charles Johnson	.30	.14
❑ 331	Al Leiter	.30	.14
❑ 332	Ralph Milliard	.15	.07
❑ 333	Robb Nen	.15	.07
❑ 334	Pat Rapp	.15	.07
❑ 335	Edgar Renteria	.30	.14
❑ 336	Gary Sheffield	.40	.18
❑ 337	Devon White	.30	.14
❑ 338	Bob Abreu	.30	.14
❑ 339	Jeff Bagwell	1.00	.45
❑ 340	Derek Bell	.30	.14
❑ 341	Sean Berry	.15	.07
❑ 342	Craig Biggio	.60	.25
❑ 343	Doug Drabek	.15	.07
❑ 344	Tony Eusebio	.15	.07
❑ 345	Ricky Gutierrez	.15	.07
❑ 346	Mike Hampton	.15	.07
❑ 347	Brian Hunter	.30	.14
❑ 348	Todd Jones	.15	.07
❑ 349	Darryl Kile	.30	.14
❑ 350	Derrick May	.15	.07
❑ 351	Orlando Miller	.15	.07
❑ 352	James Mouton	.15	.07
❑ 353	Shane Reynolds	.30	.14
❑ 354	Billy Wagner	.30	.14
❑ 355	Donne Wall	.15	.07
❑ 356	Mike Blowers	.15	.07
❑ 357	Brett Butler	.30	.14
❑ 358	Roger Cedeno	.15	.07
❑ 359	Chad Curtis	.15	.07
❑ 360	Delino DeShields	.15	.07
❑ 361	Greg Gagne	.15	.07
❑ 362	Karim Garcia	.30	.14
❑ 363	Wilton Guerrero	.15	.07
❑ 364	Todd Hollandsworth	.15	.07
❑ 365	Eric Karros	.30	.14
❑ 366	Ramon Martinez	.30	.14
❑ 367	Raul Mondesi	.40	.18
❑ 368	Hideo Nomo	.75	.35
❑ 369	Antonio Osuna	.15	.07
❑ 370	Chan Ho Park	.60	.25
❑ 371	Mike Piazza	2.00	.90
❑ 372	Ismael Valdes	.30	.14
❑ 373	Todd Worrell	.15	.07
❑ 374	Moises Alou	.40	.18
❑ 375	Shane Andrews	.15	.07
❑ 376	Yamil Benitez	.15	.07
❑ 377	Jeff Fassero	.15	.07
❑ 378	Darrin Fletcher	.15	.07
❑ 379	Cliff Floyd	.30	.14
❑ 380	Mark Grudzielanek	.30	.14
❑ 381	Mike Lansing	.15	.07
❑ 382	Barry Manuel	.15	.07
❑ 383	Pedro Martinez	.60	.25
❑ 384	Henry Rodriguez	.30	.14
❑ 385	Mel Rojas	.15	.07
❑ 386	F.P. Santangelo	.15	.07
❑ 387	David Segui	.30	.14
❑ 388	Ugueth Urbina	.30	.14
❑ 389	Rondell White	.30	.14
❑ 390	Edgardo Alfonzo	.30	.14
❑ 391	Carlos Baerga	.30	.14
❑ 392	Mark Clark	.15	.07
❑ 393	Alvaro Espinoza	.15	.07
❑ 394	John Franco	.30	.14
❑ 395	Bernard Gilkey	.15	.07
❑ 396	Pete Harnisch	.15	.07
❑ 397	Todd Hundley	.30	.14
❑ 398	Butch Huskey	.15	.07
❑ 399	Jason Isringhausen	.15	.07
❑ 400	Lance Johnson	.15	.07
❑ 401	Bobby Jones	.15	.07
❑ 402	Alex Ochoa	.15	.07
❑ 403	Rey Ordonez	.30	.14
❑ 404	Robert Person	.15	.07
❑ 405	Paul Wilson	.15	.07
❑ 406	Matt Beech	.15	.07
❑ 407	Ron Blazier	.15	.07
❑ 408	Ricky Bottalico	.30	.14
❑ 409	Lenny Dykstra	.30	.14
❑ 410	Jim Eisenreich	.15	.07
❑ 411	Bobby Estalella	.30	.14
❑ 412	Mike Grace	.15	.07
❑ 413	Gregg Jefferies	.15	.07
❑ 414	Mike Lieberthal	.15	.07
❑ 415	Wendell Magee	.15	.07
❑ 416	Mickey Morandini	.15	.07
❑ 417	Ricky Otero	.15	.07
❑ 418	Scott Rolen	1.50	.70
❑ 419	Ken Ryan	.15	.07
❑ 420	Benito Santiago	.15	.07
❑ 421	Curt Schilling	.30	.14
❑ 422	Kevin Sefcik	.15	.07
❑ 423	Jermaine Allensworth	.15	.07
❑ 424	Trey Beamon	.15	.07
❑ 425	Jay Bell	.30	.14
❑ 426	Francisco Cordova	.15	.07
❑ 427	Carlos Garcia	.15	.07
❑ 428	Mark Johnson	.15	.07
❑ 429	Jason Kendall	.40	.18
❑ 430	Jeff King	.15	.07
❑ 431	Jon Lieber	.15	.07
❑ 432	Al Martin	.15	.07
❑ 433	Orlando Merced	.15	.07
❑ 434	Ramon Morel	.15	.07
❑ 435	Matt Ruebel	.15	.07
❑ 436	Jason Schmidt	.15	.07
❑ 437	Marc Wilkins	.15	.07
❑ 438	Alan Benes	.30	.14
❑ 439	Andy Benes	.30	.14
❑ 440	Royce Clayton	.15	.07
❑ 441	Dennis Eckersley	.30	.14
❑ 442	Gary Gaetti	.15	.07
❑ 443	Ron Gant	.15	.07
❑ 444	Aaron Holbert	.15	.07
❑ 445	Brian Jordan	.30	.14
❑ 446	Ray Lankford	.30	.14
❑ 447	John Mabry	.15	.07
❑ 448	T.J. Mathews	.15	.07
❑ 449	Willie McGee	.30	.14
❑ 450	Donovan Osborne	.15	.07
❑ 451	Tom Pagnozzi	.15	.07
❑ 452	Ozzie Smith	.75	.35
❑ 453	Todd Stottlemyre	.15	.07
❑ 454	Mark Sweeney	.15	.07
❑ 455	Dmitri Young	.30	.14
❑ 456	Andy Ashby	.15	.07
❑ 457	Ken Caminiti	.40	.18
❑ 458	Archi Cianfrocco	.15	.07
❑ 459	Steve Finley	.30	.14
❑ 460	John Flaherty	.15	.07
❑ 461	Chris Gomez	.15	.07
❑ 462	Tony Gwynn	1.50	.70
❑ 463	Joey Hamilton	.30	.14
❑ 464	Rickey Henderson	.60	.25
❑ 465	Trevor Hoffman	.30	.14
❑ 466	Brian Johnson	.15	.07
❑ 467	Wally Joyner	.30	.14
❑ 468	Jody Reed	.15	.07
❑ 469	Scott Sanders	.15	.07
❑ 470	Bob Tewksbury	.15	.07
❑ 471	Fernando Valenzuela	.30	.14
❑ 472	Greg Vaughn	.30	.14
❑ 473	Tim Worrell	.15	.07
❑ 474	Rich Aurilia	.15	.07
❑ 475	Rod Beck	.15	.07
❑ 476	Marvin Benard	.15	.07
❑ 477	Barry Bonds	.75	.35
❑ 478	Jay Canizaro	.15	.07
❑ 479	Shawon Dunston	.15	.07
❑ 480	Shawn Estes	.30	.14
❑ 481	Mark Gardner	.15	.07
❑ 482	Glenallen Hill	.15	.07
❑ 483	Stan Javier	.15	.07
❑ 484	Marcus Jensen	.15	.07
❑ 485	Bill Mueller	.75	.35
❑ 486	Wm. VanLandingham	.15	.07
❑ 487	Allen Watson	.15	.07
❑ 488	Rick Wilkins	.15	.07
❑ 489	Matt Williams	.30	.14
❑ 490	Desi Wilson	.15	.07
❑ 491	Albert Belle CL	.30	.14
❑ 492	Ken Griffey Jr. CL	1.50	.70
❑ 493	Andruw Jones CL	.75	.35
❑ 494	Chipper Jones CL	.75	.35
❑ 495	Mark McGwire CL	1.50	.70
❑ 496	Paul Molitor CL	.30	.14
❑ 497	Mike Piazza CL	1.00	.45
❑ 498	Cal Ripken CL	1.25	.55
❑ 499	Alex Rodriguez CL	1.00	.45
❑ 500	Frank Thomas CL	1.00	.45
❑ 501	Kenny Lofton	.60	.25
❑ 502	Carlos Perez	.30	.14
❑ 503	Tim Raines	.30	.14
❑ 504	Danny Patterson	.15	.07
❑ 505	Derrick May	.15	.07
❑ 506	Dave Hollins	.15	.07
❑ 507	Felipe Crespo	.15	.07
❑ 508	Brian Banks	.15	.07
❑ 509	Jeff Kent	.30	.14
❑ 510	Bubba Trammell	.40	.18
❑ 511	Robert Person	.15	.07
❑ 512	David Arias-Ortiz	1.25	.55
❑ 513	Ryan Jones	.15	.07
❑ 514	David Justice	.60	.25
❑ 515	Will Cunnane	.15	.07
❑ 516	Russ Johnson	.15	.07
❑ 517	John Burkett	.15	.07
❑ 518	Robinson Checo	.15	.07
❑ 519	Ricardo Rincon	.15	.07
❑ 520	Woody Williams	.15	.07
❑ 521	Rick Helling	.30	.14
❑ 522	Jorge Posada	.30	.14
❑ 523	Kevin Orie	.15	.07
❑ 524	Fernando Tatis	1.00	.45
❑ 525	Jermaine Dye	.15	.07
❑ 526	Brian Hunter	.30	.14
❑ 527	Greg McMichael	.15	.07
❑ 528	Matt Wagner	.15	.07
❑ 529	Richie Sexson	.40	.18
❑ 530	Scott Ruffcorn	.15	.07
❑ 531	Luis Gonzalez	.15	.07
❑ 532	Mike Johnson	.40	.18
❑ 533	Mark Petkovsek	.15	.07
❑ 534	Doug Drabek	.15	.07
❑ 535	Jose Canseco	.60	.25
❑ 536	Bobby Bonilla	.30	.14
❑ 537	J.T. Snow	.30	.14
❑ 538	Shawon Dunston	.15	.07
❑ 539	John Ericks	.15	.07
❑ 540	Terry Steinbach	.30	.14
❑ 541	Jay Bell	.30	.14
❑ 542	Joe Borowski	.15	.07
❑ 543	David Wells	.40	.18
❑ 544	Justin Towle	.40	.18
❑ 545	Mike Blowers	.15	.07
❑ 546	Shannon Stewart	.30	.14
❑ 547	Rudy Pemberton	.15	.07
❑ 548	Bill Swift	.15	.07
❑ 549	Osvaldo Fernandez	.15	.07
❑ 550	Eddie Murray	.60	.25
❑ 551	Don Wengert	.15	.07
❑ 552	Brad Ausmus	.15	.07
❑ 553	Carlos Garcia	.15	.07
❑ 554	Jose Guillen	.60	.25
❑ 555	Rheal Cormier	.15	.07
❑ 556	Doug Brocail	.15	.07
❑ 557	Rex Hudler	.15	.07
❑ 558	Armando Benitez	.15	.07
❑ 559	Eli Marrero	.30	.14
❑ 560	Ricky Ledee	2.00	.90
❑ 561	Bartolo Colon	.30	.14
❑ 562	Quilvio Veras	.15	.07
❑ 563	Alex Fernandez	.15	.07
❑ 564	Darren Dreifort	.30	.14
❑ 565	Benji Gil	.15	.07
❑ 566	Kent Mercker	.15	.07
❑ 567	Glendon Rusch	.15	.07
❑ 568	Ramon Tatis	.15	.07
❑ 569	Roger Clemens	1.25	.55

❑ 570 Mark Lewis .15 .07
❑ 571 Emil Brown .40 .18
❑ 572 Jaime Navarro .15 .07
❑ 573 Sherman Obando .15 .07
❑ 574 John Wasdin .15 .07
❑ 575 Calvin Maduro .15 .07
❑ 576 Todd Jones .15 .07
❑ 577 Orlando Merced .15 .07
❑ 578 Cal Eldred .15 .07
❑ 579 Mark Gubicza .15 .07
❑ 580 Michael Tucker .30 .14
❑ 581 Tony Saunders .30 .14
❑ 582 Garvin Alston .15 .07
❑ 583 Joe Roa .15 .07
❑ 584 Brady Raggio .15 .07
❑ 585 Jimmy Key .30 .14
❑ 586 Marc Sagmoen .15 .07
❑ 587 Jim Bullinger .15 .07
❑ 588 Yorkis Perez .15 .07
❑ 589 Jose Cruz Jr. 2.50 1.10
❑ 590 Mike Stanton .15 .07
❑ 591 Deivi Cruz .50 .23
❑ 592 Steve Karsay .15 .07
❑ 593 Mike Trombley .15 .07
❑ 594 Doug Glanville .30 .14
❑ 595 Scott Sanders .15 .07
❑ 596 Thomas Howard .15 .07
❑ 597 T.J. Staton .40 .18
❑ 598 Garrett Stephenson .15 .07
❑ 599 Rico Brogna .15 .07
❑ 600 Albert Belle .75 .35
❑ 601 Jose Vizcaino .15 .07
❑ 602 Chili Davis .30 .14
❑ 603 Shane Mack .15 .07
❑ 604 Jim Eisenreich .15 .07
❑ 605 Todd Zeile .15 .07
❑ 606 Brian Boehringer .15 .07
❑ 607 Paul Shuey .15 .07
❑ 608 Kevin Tapani .15 .07
❑ 609 John Wetteland .30 .14
❑ 610 Jim Leyritz .15 .07
❑ 611 Ray Montgomery .15 .07
❑ 612 Doug Bochtler .15 .07
❑ 613 Wady Almonte .40 .18
❑ 614 Danny Tartabull .15 .07
❑ 615 Orlando Miller .15 .07
❑ 616 Bobby Ayala .15 .07
❑ 617 Tony Graffanino .15 .07
❑ 618 Marc Valdes .15 .07
❑ 619 Ron Villone .15 .07
❑ 620 Derrek Lee .40 .18
❑ 621 Greg Colbrunn .15 .07
❑ 622 Felix Heredia .30 .14
❑ 623 Carl Everett .15 .07
❑ 624 Mark Thompson .15 .07
❑ 625 Jeff Granger .15 .07
❑ 626 Damian Jackson .15 .07
❑ 627 Mark Leiter .15 .07
❑ 628 Chris Holt .15 .07
❑ 629 Dario Veras .40 .18
❑ 630 Dave Burba .15 .07
❑ 631 Darryl Hamilton .15 .07
❑ 632 Mark Acre .15 .07
❑ 633 Fernando Hernandez .15 .07
❑ 634 Terry Mulholland .15 .07
❑ 635 Dustin Hermanson .30 .14
❑ 636 Delino DeShields .15 .07
❑ 637 Steve Avery .15 .07
❑ 638 Tony Womack .50 .23
❑ 639 Mark Whiten .15 .07
❑ 640 Marquis Grissom .30 .14
❑ 641 Xavier Hernandez .15 .07
❑ 642 Eric Davis .30 .14
❑ 643 Bob Tewksbury .15 .07
❑ 644 Dante Powell .30 .14
❑ 645 Carlos Castillo .40 .18
❑ 646 Chris Widger .15 .07
❑ 647 Moises Alou .40 .18
❑ 648 Pat Listach .15 .07
❑ 649 Edgar Ramos .40 .18
❑ 650 Deion Sanders .30 .14
❑ 651 John Olerud .30 .14
❑ 652 Todd Dunwoody .30 .14
❑ 653 Randall Simon 1.00 .45
❑ 654 Dan Carlson .15 .07
❑ 655 Matt Williams .30 .14
❑ 656 Jeff King .15 .07
❑ 657 Luis Alicea .15 .07
❑ 658 Brian Moehler .15 .07
❑ 659 Ariel Prieto .15 .07
❑ 660 Kevin Elster .15 .07
❑ 661 Mark Hutton .15 .07
❑ 662 Aaron Sele .30 .14
❑ 663 Graeme Lloyd .15 .07
❑ 664 John Burke .15 .07
❑ 665 Mel Rojas .15 .07
❑ 666 Sid Fernandez .15 .07
❑ 667 Pedro Astacio .15 .07
❑ 668 Jeff Abbott .30 .14
❑ 669 Darren Daulton .30 .14
❑ 670 Mike Bordick .15 .07
❑ 671 Sterling Hitchcock .30 .14
❑ 672 Damion Easley .30 .14
❑ 673 Armando Reynoso .15 .07
❑ 674 Pat Cline .30 .14
❑ 675 Orlando Cabrera .30 .14
❑ 676 Alan Embree .15 .07
❑ 677 Brian Bevil .15 .07
❑ 678 David Weathers .15 .07
❑ 679 Cliff Floyd .30 .14
❑ 680 Joe Randa .15 .07
❑ 681 Bill Haselman .15 .07
❑ 682 Jeff Fassero .15 .07
❑ 683 Matt Morris .30 .14
❑ 684 Mark Portugal .15 .07
❑ 685 Lee Smith .30 .14
❑ 686 Pokey Reese .15 .07
❑ 687 Benito Santiago .15 .07
❑ 688 Brian Johnson .15 .07
❑ 689 Brent Brede .15 .07
❑ 690 Shigetoshi Hasegawa .40 .18
❑ 691 Julio Santana .15 .07
❑ 692 Steve Kline .15 .07
❑ 693 Julian Tavarez .15 .07
❑ 694 John Hudek .15 .07
❑ 695 Manny Alexander .15 .07
❑ 696 Roberto Alomar ENC .30 .14
❑ 697 Jeff Bagwell ENC .60 .25
❑ 698 Barry Bonds ENC .30 .14
❑ 699 Ken Caminiti ENC .15 .07
❑ 700 Juan Gonzalez ENC .75 .35
❑ 701 Ken Griffey Jr. ENC 1.50 .70
❑ 702 Tony Gwynn ENC .75 .35
❑ 703 Derek Jeter ENC 1.00 .45
❑ 704 Andruw Jones ENC .75 .35
❑ 705 Chipper Jones ENC .75 .35
❑ 706 Barry Larkin ENC .15 .07
❑ 707 Greg Maddux ENC 1.00 .45
❑ 708 Mark McGwire ENC 1.50 .70
❑ 709 Paul Molitor ENC .30 .14
❑ 710 Hideo Nomo ENC .60 .25
❑ 711 Andy Pettitte ENC .15 .07
❑ 712 Mike Piazza ENC 1.00 .45
❑ 713 Manny Ramirez ENC .30 .14
❑ 714 Cal Ripken ENC 1.25 .55
❑ 715 Alex Rodriguez ENC 1.00 .45
❑ 716 Ryne Sandberg ENC .60 .25
❑ 717 John Smoltz ENC .15 .07
❑ 718 Frank Thomas ENC 1.00 .45
❑ 719 Mo Vaughn ENC .40 .18
❑ 720 Bernie Williams ENC .30 .14
❑ 721 Tim Salmon CL .30 .14
❑ 722 Greg Maddux CL 1.00 .45
❑ 723 Cal Ripken CL 1.25 .55
❑ 724 Mo Vaughn CL .40 .18
❑ 725 Ryne Sandberg CL .60 .25
❑ 726 Frank Thomas CL 1.00 .45
❑ 727 Barry Larkin CL .15 .07
❑ 728 Manny Ramirez CL .30 .14
❑ 729 Andres Galarraga CL .30 .14
❑ 730 Tony Clark CL .15 .07
❑ 731 Gary Sheffield CL .15 .07
❑ 732 Jeff Bagwell CL .60 .25
❑ 733 Kevin Appier CL .15 .07
❑ 734 Mike Piazza CL 1.00 .45
❑ 735 Jeff Cirillo CL .15 .07
❑ 736 Paul Molitor CL .30 .14
❑ 737 Henry Rodriguez CL .15 .07
❑ 738 Todd Hundley CL .15 .07
❑ 739 Derek Jeter CL 1.00 .45
❑ 740 Mark McGwire CL 1.50 .70
❑ 741 Curt Schilling CL .15 .07
❑ 742 Jason Kendall CL .15 .07
❑ 743 Tony Gwynn CL .75 .35
❑ 744 Barry Bonds CL .30 .14
❑ 745 Ken Griffey Jr. CL 1.50 .70
❑ 746 Brian Jordan CL .15 .07
❑ 747 Juan Gonzalez CL .75 .35
❑ 748 Joe Carter CL .15 .07
❑ 749 Arizona Diamondbacks CL .30 .14
❑ 750 Tampa Bay Devil Rays CL .30 .14
❑ 751 Hideki Irabu 3.00 1.35
❑ 752 Jeremi Gonzalez .75 .35
❑ 753 Mario Valdez .75 .35
❑ 754 Aaron Boone .25 .11
❑ 755 Brett Tomko .25 .11
❑ 756 Jaret Wright 8.00 3.60
❑ 757 Ryan McGuire .25 .11
❑ 758 Jason McDonald .25 .11
❑ 759 Adrian Brown .25 .11
❑ 760 Keith Foulke .25 .11
❑ 761 Bonus Checklist .25 .11
❑ P489 Matt Williams Promo 1.00 .45
❑ NNO Andruw Jones 100.00 45.00
Circa AU/200

1997 Fleer Bleacher Blasters

	MINT	NRMT
COMPLETE SET (10)	100.00	45.00
COMMON CARD (1-10)	3.00	1.35

❑ 1 Albert Belle 6.00 2.70
❑ 2 Barry Bonds 6.00 2.70
❑ 3 Juan Gonzalez 12.00 5.50
❑ 4 Ken Griffey Jr. 25.00 11.00
❑ 5 Mark McGwire 25.00 11.00
❑ 6 Mike Piazza 15.00 6.75
❑ 7 Alex Rodriguez 15.00 6.75
❑ 8 Frank Thomas 15.00 6.75
❑ 9 Mo Vaughn 6.00 2.70
❑ 10 Matt Williams 3.00 1.35

1997 Fleer Decade of Excellence

	MINT	NRMT
COMPLETE SET (12)	60.00	27.00
COMMON CARD (1-12)	2.50	1.10
*RARE TRADITION: 2.5X TO 5X BASIC DECADE		
RARE TRAD.STATED ODDS 1:360 HOBBY		

	MINT	NRMT
❑ 1 Wade Boggs	4.00	1.80
❑ 2 Barry Bonds	5.00	2.20
❑ 3 Roger Clemens	8.00	3.60
❑ 4 Tony Gwynn	10.00	4.50
❑ 5 Rickey Henderson	4.00	1.80
❑ 6 Greg Maddux	12.00	5.50
❑ 7 Mark McGwire	20.00	9.00
❑ 8 Paul Molitor	4.00	1.80
❑ 9 Eddie Murray	4.00	1.80
❑ 10 Cal Ripken	15.00	6.75
❑ 11 Ryne Sandberg	5.00	2.20
❑ 12 Matt Williams	2.50	1.10

1997 Fleer Diamond Tribute

	MINT	NRMT
COMPLETE SET (12)	600.00	275.00
COMMON CARD (1-12)	20.00	9.00

	MINT	NRMT
❑ 1 Albert Belle	25.00	11.00
❑ 2 Barry Bonds	25.00	11.00
❑ 3 Juan Gonzalez	50.00	22.00
❑ 4 Ken Griffey Jr.	100.00	45.00
❑ 5 Tony Gwynn	50.00	22.00
❑ 6 Greg Maddux	60.00	27.00
❑ 7 Mark McGwire	100.00	45.00
❑ 8 Eddie Murray	20.00	9.00
❑ 9 Mike Piazza	60.00	27.00
❑ 10 Cal Ripken	80.00	36.00
❑ 11 Alex Rodriguez	60.00	27.00
❑ 12 Frank Thomas	60.00	27.00

1997 Fleer Golden Memories

	MINT	NRMT
COMPLETE SET (10)	10.00	4.50
COMMON CARD (1-10)	.50	.23

	MINT	NRMT
❑ 1 Barry Bonds	1.25	.55
❑ 2 Dwight Gooden	.50	.23
❑ 3 Todd Hundley	.50	.23
❑ 4 Mark McGwire	5.00	2.20
❑ 5 Paul Molitor	1.00	.45
❑ 6 Eddie Murray	1.00	.45
❑ 7 Hideo Nomo	1.50	.70
❑ 8 Mike Piazza	4.00	1.80
❑ 9 Cal Ripken	4.00	1.80
❑ 10 Ozzie Smith	1.50	.70

1997 Fleer Goudey Greats

	MINT	NRMT
COMPLETE SET (15)	30.00	13.50
COMMON CARD (1-15)	1.00	.45
*FOIL CARDS: 25X TO 60X BASIC GOUDEY		

	MINT	NRMT
❑ 1 Barry Bonds	1.25	.55
❑ 2 Ken Griffey Jr.	5.00	2.20
❑ 3 Tony Gwynn	2.50	1.10
❑ 4 Derek Jeter	3.00	1.35
❑ 5 Chipper Jones	2.50	1.10
❑ 6 Kenny Lofton	1.00	.45
❑ 7 Greg Maddux	3.00	1.35
❑ 8 Mark McGwire	5.00	2.20
❑ 9 Eddie Murray	1.00	.45
❑ 10 Mike Piazza	3.00	1.35
❑ 11 Cal Ripken	4.00	1.80
❑ 12 Alex Rodriguez	3.00	1.35
❑ 13 Ryne Sandberg	1.25	.55
❑ 14 Frank Thomas	3.00	1.35
❑ 15 Mo Vaughn	1.25	.55

1997 Fleer Headliners

	MINT	NRMT
COMPLETE SET (20)	12.00	5.50
COMMON CARD (1-20)	.20	.09

	MINT	NRMT
❑ 1 Jeff Bagwell	.60	.25
❑ 2 Albert Belle	.40	.18
❑ 3 Barry Bonds	.50	.23
❑ 4 Ken Caminiti	.30	.14
❑ 5 Juan Gonzalez	1.00	.45
❑ 6 Ken Griffey Jr.	2.00	.90
❑ 7 Tony Gwynn	1.00	.45
❑ 8 Derek Jeter	1.25	.55
❑ 9 Andruw Jones	.75	.35
❑ 10 Chipper Jones	1.00	.45
❑ 11 Greg Maddux	1.25	.55
❑ 12 Mark McGwire	2.00	.90
❑ 13 Paul Molitor	.40	.18
❑ 14 Eddie Murray	.40	.18
❑ 15 Mike Piazza	1.25	.55
❑ 16 Cal Ripken	1.50	.70
❑ 17 Alex Rodriguez	1.25	.55
❑ 18 Ryne Sandberg	.50	.23
❑ 19 John Smoltz	.20	.09
❑ 20 Frank Thomas	1.50	.70

1997 Fleer Lumber Company

	MINT	NRMT
COMPLETE SET (18)	180.00	80.00
COMMON CARD (1-18)	3.00	1.35

	MINT	NRMT
❑ 1 Brady Anderson	3.00	1.35
❑ 2 Jeff Bagwell	10.00	4.50
❑ 3 Albert Belle	8.00	3.60
❑ 4 Barry Bonds	8.00	3.60
❑ 5 Jay Buhner	3.00	1.35
❑ 6 Ellis Burks	3.00	1.35
❑ 7 Andres Galarraga	6.00	2.70
❑ 8 Juan Gonzalez	15.00	6.75
❑ 9 Ken Griffey Jr.	30.00	13.50
❑ 10 Todd Hundley	3.00	1.35
❑ 11 Ryan Klesko	3.00	1.35
❑ 12 Mark McGwire	30.00	13.50
❑ 13 Mike Piazza	20.00	9.00
❑ 14 Alex Rodriguez	20.00	9.00
❑ 15 Gary Sheffield	4.00	1.80
❑ 16 Sammy Sosa	15.00	6.75
❑ 17 Frank Thomas	20.00	9.00
❑ 18 Mo Vaughn	8.00	3.60

1997-98 Fleer Million Dollar Moments

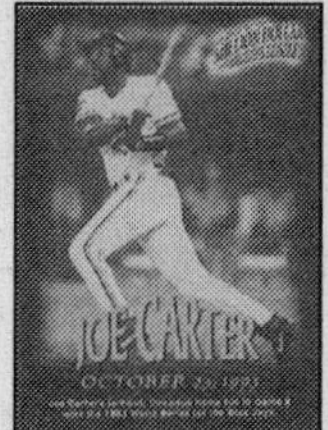

	MINT	NRMT
COMPLETE SET (45)	8.00	3.60
COMMON CARD (1-45)	.10	.05

	MINT	NRMT
❑ 1 Checklist	.10	.05
❑ 2 Derek Jeter	.60	.25
❑ 3 Babe Ruth	1.50	.70
❑ 4 Barry Bonds	.25	.11
❑ 5 Brooks Robinson	.25	.11
❑ 6 Todd Hundley	.10	.05

❑ 7 Johnny Vander Meer	.10	.05
❑ 8 Cal Ripken	.75	.35
❑ 9 Bill Mazeroski	.10	.05
❑ 10 Chipper Jones	.50	.23
❑ 11 Frank Robinson	.25	.11
❑ 12 Roger Clemens	.40	.18
❑ 13 Bob Feller	.10	.05
❑ 14 Mike Piazza	.60	.25
❑ 15 Joe Nuxhall	.10	.05
❑ 16 Hideo Nomo	.25	.11
❑ 17 Jackie Robinson	1.00	.45
❑ 18 Orel Hershiser	.10	.05
❑ 19 Bobby Thomson	.10	.05
❑ 20 Joe Carter	.10	.05
❑ 21 Al Kaline	.25	.11
❑ 22 Bernie Williams	.25	.11
❑ 23 Don Larsen	.10	.05
❑ 24 Rickey Henderson	.25	.11
❑ 25 Maury Wills	.10	.05
❑ 26 Andruw Jones	.30	.14
❑ 27 Bobby Richardson	.10	.05
❑ 28 Alex Rodriguez	.60	.25
❑ 29 Jim Bunning	.10	.05
❑ 30 Ken Caminiti	.15	.07
❑ 31 Bob Gibson	.25	.11
❑ 32 Frank Thomas	.60	.25
❑ 33 Mickey Lolich	.10	.05
❑ 34 John Smoltz	.10	.05
❑ 35 Ron Swoboda	.10	.05
❑ 36 Albert Belle	.25	.11
❑ 37 Chris Chambliss	.10	.05
❑ 38 Juan Gonzalez	.50	.23
❑ 39 Ron Blomberg	.10	.05
❑ 40 John Wetteland	.10	.05
❑ 41 Carlton Fisk	.25	.11
❑ 42 Mo Vaughn	.25	.11
❑ 43 Bucky Dent	.10	.05
❑ 44 Greg Maddux	.60	.25
❑ 45 Willie Stargell	.25	.11
❑ 46 Tony Gwynn SP		
❑ 47 Joel Youngblood SP		
❑ 48 Andy Pettitte SP		
❑ 49 Mookie Wilson SP		
❑ 50 Jeff Bagwell SP		

1997 Fleer New Horizons

	MINT	NRMT
COMPLETE SET (15)	10.00	4.50
COMMON CARD (1-15)	.25	.11
❑ 1 Bob Abreu	.25	.11
❑ 2 Jose Cruz Jr.	2.50	1.10
❑ 3 Darin Erstad	1.25	.55
❑ 4 Nomar Garciaparra	2.50	1.10
❑ 5 Vladimir Guerrero	1.50	.70
❑ 6 Wilton Guerrero	.25	.11
❑ 7 Jose Guillen	1.00	.45
❑ 8 Hideki Irabu	1.50	.70
❑ 9 Andruw Jones	2.00	.90
❑ 10 Kevin Orie	.25	.11
❑ 11 Scott Rolen	2.00	.90
❑ 12 Scott Spiezio	.25	.11
❑ 13 Bubba Trammell	.75	.35
❑ 14 Todd Walker	.75	.35
❑ 15 Dmitri Young	.25	.11

1997 Fleer Night and Day

	MINT	NRMT
COMPLETE SET (10)	300.00	135.00
COMMON CARD (1-10)	8.00	3.60
❑ 1 Barry Bonds	20.00	9.00
❑ 2 Ellis Burks	8.00	3.60
❑ 3 Juan Gonzalez	40.00	18.00
❑ 4 Ken Griffey Jr.	80.00	36.00
❑ 5 Mark McGwire	80.00	36.00
❑ 6 Mike Piazza	50.00	22.00
❑ 7 Manny Ramirez	15.00	6.75
❑ 8 Alex Rodriguez	50.00	22.00
❑ 9 John Smoltz	8.00	3.60
❑ 10 Frank Thomas	50.00	22.00

1997 Fleer Rookie Sensations

	MINT	NRMT
COMPLETE SET (20)	25.00	11.00
COMMON CARD (1-20)	.40	.18
❑ 1 Jermaine Allensworth	.40	.18
❑ 2 James Baldwin	.60	.25
❑ 3 Alan Benes	.60	.25
❑ 4 Jermaine Dye	.40	.18
❑ 5 Darin Erstad	2.50	1.10
❑ 6 Todd Hollandsworth	.40	.18
❑ 7 Derek Jeter	6.00	2.70
❑ 8 Jason Kendall	1.00	.45
❑ 9 Alex Ochoa	.40	.18
❑ 10 Rey Ordonez	.60	.25
❑ 11 Edgar Renteria	.60	.25
❑ 12 Bob Abreu	.60	.25
❑ 13 Nomar Garciaparra	5.00	2.20
❑ 14 Wilton Guerrero	.40	.18
❑ 15 Andruw Jones	4.00	1.80
❑ 16 Wendell Magee	.40	.18
❑ 17 Neifi Perez	.40	.18
❑ 18 Scott Rolen	4.00	1.80
❑ 19 Scott Spiezio	.40	.18
❑ 20 Todd Walker	1.50	.70

1997 Fleer Soaring Stars

	MINT	NRMT
COMPLETE SET (12)	40.00	18.00
COMMON CARD (1-12)	1.50	.70

*GLOWING: 8X TO 20X BASIC CARDS
GLOWING: RANDOM INSERTS IN SER.2 PACKS

❑ 1 Albert Belle	1.50	.70
❑ 2 Barry Bonds	1.50	.70
❑ 3 Juan Gonzalez	3.00	1.35
❑ 4 Ken Griffey Jr.	6.00	2.70
❑ 5 Derek Jeter	4.00	1.80
❑ 6 Andruw Jones	2.50	1.10
❑ 7 Chipper Jones	3.00	1.35
❑ 8 Greg Maddux	4.00	1.80
❑ 9 Mark McGwire	6.00	2.70
❑ 10 Mike Piazza	4.00	1.80
❑ 11 Alex Rodriguez	4.00	1.80
❑ 12 Frank Thomas	4.00	1.80

1997 Fleer Team Leaders

	MINT	NRMT
COMPLETE SET (28)	100.00	45.00
COMMON CARD (1-28)	1.00	.45
❑ 1 Cal Ripken	15.00	6.75
❑ 2 Mo Vaughn	5.00	2.20
❑ 3 Jim Edmonds	2.50	1.10
❑ 4 Frank Thomas	12.00	5.50
❑ 5 Albert Belle	5.00	2.20
❑ 6 Bob Higginson	2.50	1.10
❑ 7 Kevin Appier	2.00	.90
❑ 8 John Jaha	1.00	.45
❑ 9 Paul Molitor	4.00	1.80
❑ 10 Andy Pettitte	2.50	1.10
❑ 11 Mark McGwire	20.00	9.00
❑ 12 Ken Griffey Jr.	20.00	9.00
❑ 13 Juan Gonzalez	10.00	4.50
❑ 14 Pat Hentgen	2.00	.90
❑ 15 Chipper Jones	10.00	4.50
❑ 16 Mark Grace	2.50	1.10
❑ 17 Barry Larkin	2.50	1.10
❑ 18 Ellis Burks	2.00	.90
❑ 19 Gary Sheffield	2.50	1.10

❑ 20 Jeff Bagwell	6.00	2.70
❑ 21 Mike Piazza	12.00	5.50
❑ 22 Henry Rodriguez	2.00	.90
❑ 23 Todd Hundley	2.00	.90
❑ 24 Curt Schilling	2.00	.90
❑ 25 Jeff King	1.00	.45
❑ 26 Brian Jordan	2.00	.90
❑ 27 Tony Gwynn	10.00	4.50
❑ 28 Barry Bonds	5.00	2.20

1997 Fleer Zone

	MINT	NRMT
COMPLETE SET (20)	250.00	110.00
COMMON CARD (1-20)	2.00	.90
❑ 1 Jeff Bagwell	12.00	5.50
❑ 2 Albert Belle	10.00	4.50
❑ 3 Barry Bonds	10.00	4.50
❑ 4 Ken Caminiti	5.00	2.20
❑ 5 Andres Galarraga	8.00	3.60
❑ 6 Juan Gonzalez	20.00	9.00
❑ 7 Ken Griffey Jr.	40.00	18.00
❑ 8 Tony Gwynn	20.00	9.00
❑ 9 Chipper Jones	20.00	9.00
❑ 10 Greg Maddux	25.00	11.00
❑ 11 Mark McGwire	40.00	18.00
❑ 12 Dean Palmer	2.00	.90
❑ 13 Andy Pettitte	5.00	2.20
❑ 14 Mike Piazza	25.00	11.00
❑ 15 Alex Rodriguez	25.00	11.00
❑ 16 Gary Sheffield	5.00	2.20
❑ 17 John Smoltz	4.00	1.80
❑ 18 Frank Thomas	25.00	11.00
❑ 19 Jim Thome	8.00	3.60
❑ 20 Matt Williams	4.00	1.80

1998 Fleer

	MINT	NRMT
COMPLETE SET (600)	170.00	75.00
COMPLETE SERIES 1 (350)	100.00	45.00
COMPLETE SERIES 2 (250)	70.00	32.00
COMMON CARD (1-600)	.15	.07
COMMON GM (311-320)	.40	.18
GM MINOR STARS	.40	.18
COMMON TT (321-340)	.50	.23
COMMON UM (576-600)	.60	.25
❑ 1 Ken Griffey Jr.	3.00	1.35
❑ 2 Derek Jeter	1.50	.70
❑ 3 Gerald Williams	.15	.07
❑ 4 Carlos Delgado	.25	.11
❑ 5 Nomar Garciaparra	2.00	.90
❑ 6 Gary Sheffield	.40	.18
❑ 7 Jeff King	.25	.11
❑ 8 Cal Ripken	2.50	1.10
❑ 9 Matt Williams	.25	.11
❑ 10 Chipper Jones	1.50	.70
❑ 11 Chuck Knoblauch	.60	.25
❑ 12 Mark Grudzielanek	.25	.11
❑ 13 Edgardo Alfonzo	.25	.11
❑ 14 Andres Galarraga	.60	.25
❑ 15 Tim Salmon	.60	.25
❑ 16 Reggie Sanders	.25	.11
❑ 17 Tony Clark	.40	.18
❑ 18 Jason Kendall	.25	.11
❑ 19 Juan Gonzalez	1.50	.70
❑ 20 Ben Grieve	1.25	.55
❑ 21 Roger Clemens	1.25	.55
❑ 22 Raul Mondesi	.40	.18
❑ 23 Robin Ventura	.25	.11
❑ 24 Derrek Lee	.25	.11
❑ 25 Mark McGwire	4.00	1.80
❑ 26 Luis Gonzalez	.15	.07
❑ 27 Kevin Brown	.40	.18
❑ 28 Kirk Rueter	.15	.07
❑ 29 Bobby Estalella	.25	.11
❑ 30 Shawn Green	.25	.11
❑ 31 Greg Maddux	2.00	.90
❑ 32 Jorge Velandia	.15	.07
❑ 33 Larry Walker	.60	.25
❑ 34 Joey Cora	.25	.11
❑ 35 Frank Thomas	2.00	.90
❑ 36 Curtis King	.15	.07
❑ 37 Aaron Boone	.15	.07
❑ 38 Curt Schilling	.25	.11
❑ 39 Bruce Aven	.15	.07
❑ 40 Ben McDonald	.15	.07
❑ 41 Andy Ashby	.15	.07
❑ 42 Jason McDonald	.15	.07
❑ 43 Eric Davis	.25	.11
❑ 44 Mark Grace	.40	.18
❑ 45 Pedro Martinez	.60	.25
❑ 46 Lou Collier	.15	.07
❑ 47 Chan Ho Park	.60	.25
❑ 48 Shane Halter	.15	.07
❑ 49 Brian Hunter	.25	.11
❑ 50 Jeff Bagwell	1.00	.45
❑ 51 Bernie Williams	.60	.25
❑ 52 J.T. Snow	.25	.11
❑ 53 Todd Greene	.25	.11
❑ 54 Shannon Stewart	.25	.11
❑ 55 Darren Bragg	.15	.07
❑ 56 Fernando Tatis	.25	.11
❑ 57 Darryl Kile	.25	.11
❑ 58 Chris Stynes	.15	.07
❑ 59 Javier Valentin	.25	.11
❑ 60 Brian McRae	.15	.07
❑ 61 Tom Evans	.25	.11
❑ 62 Randall Simon	.25	.11
❑ 63 Darrin Fletcher	.15	.07
❑ 64 Jaret Wright	.75	.35
❑ 65 Luis Ordaz	.25	.11
❑ 66 Jose Canseco	.60	.25
❑ 67 Edgar Renteria	.25	.11
❑ 68 Jay Buhner	.25	.11
❑ 69 Paul Konerko	.60	.25
❑ 70 Adrian Brown	.25	.11
❑ 71 Chris Carpenter	.25	.11
❑ 72 Mike Lieberthal	.15	.07
❑ 73 Dean Palmer	.25	.11
❑ 74 Jorge Fabregas	.15	.07
❑ 75 Stan Javier	.15	.07
❑ 76 Damion Easley	.25	.11
❑ 77 David Cone	.40	.18
❑ 78 Aaron Sele	.25	.11
❑ 79 Antonio Alfonseca	.15	.07
❑ 80 Bobby Jones	.15	.07
❑ 81 David Justice	.60	.25
❑ 82 Jeffrey Hammonds	.25	.11
❑ 83 Doug Glanville	.25	.11
❑ 84 Jason Dickson	.25	.11
❑ 85 Brad Radke	.25	.11
❑ 86 David Segui	.25	.11
❑ 87 Greg Vaughn	.25	.11
❑ 88 Mike Cather	.15	.07
❑ 89 Alex Fernandez	.15	.07
❑ 90 Billy Taylor	.15	.07
❑ 91 Jason Schmidt	.15	.07
❑ 92 Mike DeJean	.15	.07
❑ 93 Domingo Cedeno	.15	.07
❑ 94 Jeff Cirillo	.25	.11
❑ 95 Manny Aybar	.25	.11
❑ 96 Jaime Navarro	.15	.07
❑ 97 Dennis Reyes	.25	.11
❑ 98 Barry Larkin	.40	.18
❑ 99 Troy O'Leary	.25	.11
❑ 100 Alex Rodriguez	2.00	.90
❑ 101 Pat Hentgen	.25	.11
❑ 102 Bubba Trammell	.25	.11
❑ 103 Glendon Rusch	.15	.07
❑ 104 Kenny Lofton	.60	.25
❑ 105 Craig Biggio	.60	.25
❑ 106 Kelvim Escobar	.25	.11
❑ 107 Mark Kotsay	.40	.18
❑ 108 Rondell White	.25	.11
❑ 109 Darren Oliver	.15	.07
❑ 110 Jim Thome	.60	.25
❑ 111 Rich Becker	.15	.07
❑ 112 Chad Curtis	.15	.07
❑ 113 Dave Hollins	.15	.07
❑ 114 Bill Mueller	.25	.11
❑ 115 Antone Williamson	.15	.07
❑ 116 Tony Womack	.25	.11
❑ 117 Randy Myers	.25	.11
❑ 118 Rico Brogna	.25	.11
❑ 119 Pat Watkins	.15	.07
❑ 120 Eli Marrero	.25	.11
❑ 121 Jay Bell	.25	.11
❑ 122 Kevin Tapani	.15	.07
❑ 123 Todd Erdos	.25	.11
❑ 124 Neifi Perez	.25	.11
❑ 125 Todd Hundley	.25	.11
❑ 126 Jeff Abbott	.25	.11
❑ 127 Todd Zeile	.25	.11
❑ 128 Travis Fryman	.25	.11
❑ 129 Sandy Alomar	.25	.11
❑ 130 Fred McGriff	.40	.18
❑ 131 Richard Hidalgo	.25	.11
❑ 132 Scott Spiezio	.15	.07
❑ 133 John Valentin	.25	.11
❑ 134 Quilvio Veras	.15	.07
❑ 135 Mike Lansing	.15	.07
❑ 136 Paul Molitor	.60	.25
❑ 137 Randy Johnson	.60	.25
❑ 138 Harold Baines	.25	.11
❑ 139 Doug Jones	.15	.07
❑ 140 Abraham Nunez	.25	.11
❑ 141 Alan Benes	.25	.11
❑ 142 Matt Perisho	.15	.07
❑ 143 Chris Clemons	.15	.07
❑ 144 Andy Pettitte	.40	.18
❑ 145 Jason Giambi	.25	.11
❑ 146 Moises Alou	.40	.18
❑ 147 Chad Fox	.15	.07
❑ 148 Felix Martinez	.15	.07
❑ 149 Carlos Mendoza	.25	.11
❑ 150 Scott Rolen	1.50	.70
❑ 151 Jose Cabrera	.15	.07
❑ 152 Justin Thompson	.25	.11
❑ 153 Ellis Burks	.25	.11
❑ 154 Pokey Reese	.15	.07
❑ 155 Bartolo Colon	.25	.11
❑ 156 Ray Durham	.25	.11
❑ 157 Ugueth Urbina	.25	.11
❑ 158 Tom Goodwin	.15	.07
❑ 159 Dave Dellucci	.75	.35
❑ 160 Rod Beck	.25	.11
❑ 161 Ramon Martinez	.25	.11
❑ 162 Joe Carter	.25	.11
❑ 163 Kevin Orie	.15	.07
❑ 164 Trevor Hoffman	.25	.11
❑ 165 Emil Brown	.25	.11
❑ 166 Robb Nen	.25	.11
❑ 167 Paul O'Neill	.25	.11
❑ 168 Ryan Long	.15	.07
❑ 169 Ray Lankford	.25	.11
❑ 170 Ivan Rodriguez	.75	.35
❑ 171 Rick Aguilera	.15	.07
❑ 172 Deivi Cruz	.15	.07

No.	Player	Price 1	Price 2
❑ 173	Ricky Bottalico	.25	.11
❑ 174	Garret Anderson	.25	.11
❑ 175	Jose Vizcaino	.15	.07
❑ 176	Omar Vizquel	.25	.11
❑ 177	Jeff Blauser	.15	.07
❑ 178	Orlando Cabrera	.25	.11
❑ 179	Russ Johnson	.15	.07
❑ 180	Matt Stairs	.25	.11
❑ 181	Will Cunnane	.15	.07
❑ 182	Adam Riggs	.15	.07
❑ 183	Matt Morris	.25	.11
❑ 184	Mario Valdez	.25	.11
❑ 185	Larry Sutton	.15	.07
❑ 186	Marc Pisciotta	.15	.07
❑ 187	Dan Wilson	.15	.07
❑ 188	John Franco	.25	.11
❑ 189	Darren Daulton	.25	.11
❑ 190	Todd Helton	.75	.35
❑ 191	Brady Anderson	.25	.11
❑ 192	Ricardo Rincon	.15	.07
❑ 193	Kevin Stocker	.15	.07
❑ 194	Jose Valentin	.15	.07
❑ 195	Ed Sprague	.15	.07
❑ 196	Ryan McGuire	.15	.07
❑ 197	Scott Eyre	.15	.07
❑ 198	Steve Finley	.25	.11
❑ 199	T.J. Mathews	.15	.07
❑ 200	Mike Piazza	2.00	.90
❑ 201	Mark Wohlers	.15	.07
❑ 202	Brian Giles	.25	.11
❑ 203	Eduardo Perez	.15	.07
❑ 204	Shigetoshi Hasegawa	.25	.11
❑ 205	Mariano Rivera	.25	.11
❑ 206	Jose Rosado	.15	.07
❑ 207	Michael Coleman	.25	.11
❑ 208	James Baldwin	.25	.11
❑ 209	Russ Davis	.25	.11
❑ 210	Billy Wagner	.25	.11
❑ 211	Sammy Sosa	1.50	.70
❑ 212	Frank Catalanotto	.25	.11
❑ 213	Delino DeShields	.15	.07
❑ 214	John Olerud	.25	.11
❑ 215	Heath Murray	.15	.07
❑ 216	Jose Vidro	.15	.07
❑ 217	Jim Edmonds	.40	.18
❑ 218	Shawon Dunston	.15	.07
❑ 219	Homer Bush	.15	.07
❑ 220	Midre Cummings	.15	.07
❑ 221	Tony Saunders	.15	.07
❑ 222	Jeromy Burnitz	.25	.11
❑ 223	Enrique Wilson	.25	.11
❑ 224	Chili Davis	.25	.11
❑ 225	Jerry DiPoto	.15	.07
❑ 226	Dante Powell	.25	.11
❑ 227	Javier Lopez	.25	.11
❑ 228	Kevin Polcovich	.15	.07
❑ 229	Deion Sanders	.25	.11
❑ 230	Jimmy Key	.25	.11
❑ 231	Rusty Greer	.25	.11
❑ 232	Reggie Jefferson	.15	.07
❑ 233	Ron Coomer	.15	.07
❑ 234	Bobby Higginson	.40	.18
❑ 235	Magglio Ordonez	.75	.35
❑ 236	Miguel Tejada	.25	.11
❑ 237	Rick Gorecki	.15	.07
❑ 238	Charles Johnson	.25	.11
❑ 239	Lance Johnson	.15	.07
❑ 240	Derek Bell	.25	.11
❑ 241	Will Clark	.60	.25
❑ 242	Brady Raggio	.15	.07
❑ 243	Orel Hershiser	.25	.11
❑ 244	Vladimir Guerrero	1.00	.45
❑ 245	John LeRoy	.15	.07
❑ 246	Shawn Estes	.25	.11
❑ 247	Brett Tomko	.25	.11
❑ 248	Dave Nilsson	.15	.07
❑ 249	Edgar Martinez	.25	.11
❑ 250	Tony Gwynn	1.50	.70
❑ 251	Mark Bellhorn	.25	.11
❑ 252	Jed Hansen	.15	.07
❑ 253	Butch Huskey	.15	.07
❑ 254	Eric Young	.25	.11
❑ 255	Vinny Castilla	.40	.18
❑ 256	Hideki Irabu	.40	.18
❑ 257	Mike Cameron	.25	.11
❑ 258	Juan Encarnacion	.25	.11
❑ 259	Brian Rose	.25	.11
❑ 260	Brad Ausmus	.15	.07
❑ 261	Dan Serafini	.15	.07
❑ 262	Willie Greene	.25	.11
❑ 263	Troy Percival	.25	.11
❑ 264	Jeff Wallace	.25	.11
❑ 265	Richie Sexson	.40	.18
❑ 266	Rafael Palmeiro	.40	.18
❑ 267	Brad Fullmer	.25	.11
❑ 268	Jeremi Gonzalez	.25	.11
❑ 269	Rob Stanifer	.15	.07
❑ 270	Mickey Morandini	.15	.07
❑ 271	Andruw Jones	.75	.35
❑ 272	Royce Clayton	.15	.07
❑ 273	Takashi Kashiwada	.40	.18
❑ 274	Steve Woodard	.25	.11
❑ 275	Jose Cruz Jr.	.75	.35
❑ 276	Keith Foulke	.15	.07
❑ 277	Brad Rigby	.15	.07
❑ 278	Tino Martinez	.60	.25
❑ 279	Todd Jones	.15	.07
❑ 280	John Wetteland	.25	.11
❑ 281	Alex Gonzalez	.15	.07
❑ 282	Ken Cloude	.25	.11
❑ 283	Jose Guillen	.25	.11
❑ 284	Danny Clyburn	.15	.07
❑ 285	David Ortiz	.25	.11
❑ 286	John Thomson	.15	.07
❑ 287	Kevin Appier	.25	.11
❑ 288	Ismael Valdes	.25	.11
❑ 289	Gary DiSarcina	.15	.07
❑ 290	Todd Dunwoody	.25	.11
❑ 291	Wally Joyner	.25	.11
❑ 292	Charles Nagy	.25	.11
❑ 293	Jeff Shaw	.25	.11
❑ 294	Kevin Millwood	1.50	.70
❑ 295	Rigo Beltran	.15	.07
❑ 296	Jeff Frye	.15	.07
❑ 297	Oscar Henriquez	.25	.11
❑ 298	Mike Thurman	.15	.07
❑ 299	Garrett Stephenson	.15	.07
❑ 300	Barry Bonds	.75	.35
❑ 301	Roger Clemens SH	.60	.25
❑ 302	David Cone SH	.40	.18
❑ 303	Hideki Irabu SH	.25	.11
❑ 304	Randy Johnson SH	.40	.18
❑ 305	Greg Maddux SH	1.00	.45
❑ 306	Pedro Martinez SH	.40	.18
❑ 307	Mike Mussina SH	.40	.18
❑ 308	Andy Pettitte SH	.25	.11
❑ 309	Curt Schilling SH	.25	.11
❑ 310	John Smoltz SH	.25	.11
❑ 311	Roger Clemens GM	2.00	.90
❑ 312	Jose Cruz JR. GM	1.25	.55
❑ 313	Nomar Garciaparra GM	3.00	1.35
❑ 314	Ken Griffey Jr. GM	5.00	2.20
❑ 315	Tony Gwynn GM	2.50	1.10
❑ 316	Hideki Irabu GM	.60	.25
❑ 317	Randy Johnson GM	1.00	.45
❑ 318	Mark McGwire GM	6.00	2.70
❑ 319	Curt Schilling GM	.40	.18
❑ 320	Larry Walker GM	1.00	.45
❑ 321	Jeff Bagwell TT	2.00	.90
❑ 322	Albert Belle TT	1.50	.70
❑ 323	Barry Bonds TT	1.50	.70
❑ 324	Jay Buhner TT	.50	.23
❑ 325	Tony Clark TT	.75	.35
❑ 326	Jose Cruz Jr. TT	1.50	.70
❑ 327	Andres Galarraga TT	1.25	.55
❑ 328	Juan Gonzalez TT	3.00	1.35
❑ 329	Ken Griffey Jr. TT	6.00	2.70
❑ 330	Andruw Jones TT	1.50	.70
❑ 331	Tino Martinez TT	1.25	.55
❑ 332	Mark McGwire TT	8.00	3.60
❑ 333	Rafael Palmeiro TT	.75	.35
❑ 334	Mike Piazza TT	4.00	1.80
❑ 335	Manny Ramirez TT	1.25	.55
❑ 336	Alex Rodriguez TT	4.00	1.80
❑ 337	Frank Thomas TT	4.00	1.80
❑ 338	Jim Thome TT	1.25	.55
❑ 339	Mo Vaughn TT	1.50	.70
❑ 340	Larry Walker TT	1.25	.55
❑ 341	Jose Cruz Jr. CL	.40	.18
❑ 342	Ken Griffey Jr. CL	1.50	.70
❑ 343	Derek Jeter CL	.75	.35
❑ 344	Andruw Jones CL	.40	.18
❑ 345	Chipper Jones CL	.75	.35
❑ 346	Greg Maddux CL	1.00	.45
❑ 347	Mike Piazza CL	1.00	.45
❑ 348	Cal Ripken CL	1.25	.55
❑ 349	Alex Rodriguez CL	1.00	.45
❑ 350	Frank Thomas CL	1.00	.45
❑ 351	Mo Vaughn	.75	.35
❑ 352	Andres Galarraga	.60	.25
❑ 353	Roberto Alomar	.60	.25
❑ 354	Darin Erstad	.75	.35
❑ 355	Albert Belle	.60	.25
❑ 356	Matt Williams	.25	.11
❑ 357	Darryl Kile	.25	.11
❑ 358	Kenny Lofton	.60	.25
❑ 359	Orel Hershiser	.25	.11
❑ 360	Bob Abreu	.25	.11
❑ 361	Chris Widger	.15	.07
❑ 362	Glenallen Hill	.15	.07
❑ 363	Chili Davis	.25	.11
❑ 364	Kevin Brown	.40	.18
❑ 365	Marquis Grissom	.25	.11
❑ 366	Livan Hernandez	.25	.11
❑ 367	Moises Alou	.40	.18
❑ 368	Matt Lawton	.25	.11
❑ 369	Rey Ordonez	.25	.11
❑ 370	Kenny Rogers	.15	.07
❑ 371	Lee Stevens	.15	.07
❑ 372	Wade Boggs	.60	.25
❑ 373	Luis Gonzalez	.15	.07
❑ 374	Jeff Conine	.25	.11
❑ 375	Esteban Loaiza	.15	.07
❑ 376	Jose Canseco	.60	.25
❑ 377	Henry Rodriguez	.25	.11
❑ 378	Dave Burba	.15	.07
❑ 379	Todd Hollandsworth	.15	.07
❑ 380	Ron Gant	.15	.07
❑ 381	Pedro Martinez	.60	.25
❑ 382	Ryan Klesko	.25	.11
❑ 383	Derrek Lee	.25	.11
❑ 384	Doug Glanville	.25	.11
❑ 385	David Wells	.40	.18
❑ 386	Ken Caminiti	.40	.18
❑ 387	Damon Hollins	.15	.07
❑ 388	Manny Ramirez	.60	.25
❑ 389	Mike Mussina	.60	.25
❑ 390	Jay Bell	.25	.11
❑ 391	Mike Piazza	2.00	.90
❑ 392	Mike Lansing	.15	.07
❑ 393	Mike Hampton	.15	.07
❑ 394	Geoff Jenkins	.25	.11
❑ 395	Jimmy Haynes	.15	.07
❑ 396	Scott Servais	.15	.07
❑ 397	Kent Mercker	.15	.07
❑ 398	Jeff Kent	.25	.11
❑ 399	Kevin Elster	.15	.07
❑ 400	Masato Yoshii	.50	.23
❑ 401	Jose Vizcaino	.15	.07
❑ 402	Javier Martinez	.40	.18
❑ 403	David Segui	.25	.11
❑ 404	Tony Saunders	.15	.07
❑ 405	Karim Garcia	.25	.11
❑ 406	Armando Benitez	.15	.07
❑ 407	Joe Randa	.15	.07
❑ 408	Vic Darensbourg	.15	.07
❑ 409	Sean Casey	.25	.11
❑ 410	Eric Milton	.25	.11
❑ 411	Trey Moore	.15	.07
❑ 412	Mike Stanley	.15	.07
❑ 413	Tom Gordon	.25	.11
❑ 414	Hal Morris	.15	.07
❑ 415	Braden Looper	.25	.11
❑ 416	Mike Kelly	.15	.07
❑ 417	John Smoltz	.25	.11
❑ 418	Roger Cedeno	.15	.07
❑ 419	Al Leiter	.25	.11
❑ 420	Chuck Knoblauch	.60	.25
❑ 421	Felix Rodriguez	.15	.07
❑ 422	Bip Roberts	.15	.07
❑ 423	Ken Hill	.15	.07
❑ 424	Jermaine Allensworth	.15	.07
❑ 425	Esteban Yan	.50	.23
❑ 426	Scott Karl	.15	.07
❑ 427	Sean Berry	.15	.07

❑ 428 Rafael Medina .25 .11
❑ 429 Javier Vazquez .25 .11
❑ 430 Rickey Henderson .60 .25
❑ 431 Adam Butler .25 .11
❑ 432 Todd Stottlemyre .25 .11
❑ 433 Yamil Benitez .15 .07
❑ 434 Sterling Hitchcock .25 .11
❑ 435 Paul Sorrento .15 .07
❑ 436 Bobby Ayala .15 .07
❑ 437 Tim Raines .25 .11
❑ 438 Chris Hoiles .15 .07
❑ 439 Rod Beck .25 .11
❑ 440 Donnie Sadler .25 .11
❑ 441 Charles Johnson .25 .11
❑ 442 Russ Ortiz .15 .07
❑ 443 Pedro Astacio .15 .07
❑ 444 Wilson Alvarez .25 .11
❑ 445 Mike Blowers .15 .07
❑ 446 Todd Zeile .25 .11
❑ 447 Mel Rojas .15 .07
❑ 448 F.P. Santangelo .15 .07
❑ 449 Dmitri Young .25 .11
❑ 450 Brian Anderson .25 .11
❑ 451 Cecil Fielder .25 .11
❑ 452 Roberto Hernandez .15 .07
❑ 453 Todd Walker .40 .18
❑ 454 Tyler Green .15 .07
❑ 455 Jorge Posada .25 .11
❑ 456 Geronimo Berroa .15 .07
❑ 457 Jose Silva .15 .07
❑ 458 Bobby Bonilla .25 .11
❑ 459 Walt Weiss .25 .11
❑ 460 Darren Dreifort .25 .11
❑ 461 B.J. Surhoff .25 .11
❑ 462 Quinton McCracken .25 .11
❑ 463 Derek Lowe .15 .07
❑ 464 Jorge Fabregas .15 .07
❑ 465 Joey Hamilton .25 .11
❑ 466 Brian Jordan .25 .11
❑ 467 Allen Watson .15 .07
❑ 468 John Jaha .15 .07
❑ 469 Heathcliff Slocumb .15 .07
❑ 470 Gregg Jefferies .15 .07
❑ 471 Scott Brosius .25 .11
❑ 472 Chad Ogea .15 .07
❑ 473 A.J. Hinch .25 .11
❑ 474 Bobby Smith .25 .11
❑ 475 Brian Moehler .15 .07
❑ 476 DaRond Stovall .15 .07
❑ 477 Kevin Young .25 .11
❑ 478 Jeff Suppan .15 .07
❑ 479 Marty Cordova .15 .07
❑ 480 John Halama .15 .07
❑ 481 Bubba Trammell .25 .11
❑ 482 Mike Caruso .25 .11
❑ 483 Eric Karros .25 .11
❑ 484 Jamey Wright .15 .07
❑ 485 Mike Sweeney .15 .07
❑ 486 Aaron Sele .25 .11
❑ 487 Cliff Floyd .25 .11
❑ 488 Jeff Brantley .15 .07
❑ 489 Jim Leyritz .15 .07
❑ 490 Denny Neagle .25 .11
❑ 491 Travis Fryman .25 .11
❑ 492 Carlos Baerga .25 .11
❑ 493 Eddie Taubensee .15 .07
❑ 494 Darryl Strawberry .25 .11
❑ 495 Brian Johnson .15 .07
❑ 496 Randy Myers .25 .11
❑ 497 Jeff Blauser .15 .07
❑ 498 Jason Wood .15 .07
❑ 499 Rolando Arrojo 1.00 .45
❑ 500 Johnny Damon .25 .11
❑ 501 Jose Mercedes .15 .07
❑ 502 Tony Batista .15 .07
❑ 503 Mike Piazza Mets 2.00 .90
❑ 504 Hideo Nomo .75 .35
❑ 505 Chris Gomez .15 .07
❑ 506 Jesus Sanchez .40 .18
❑ 507 Al Martin .15 .07
❑ 508 Brian Edmondson .15 .07
❑ 509 Joe Girardi .15 .07
❑ 510 Shayne Bennett .15 .07
❑ 511 Joe Carter .25 .11
❑ 512 Dave Mlicki .15 .07
❑ 513 Rich Butler .40 .18
❑ 514 Dennis Eckersley .25 .11
❑ 515 Travis Lee 1.25 .55
❑ 516 John Mabry .15 .07
❑ 517 Jose Mesa .15 .07
❑ 518 Phil Nevin .15 .07
❑ 519 Raul Casanova .15 .07
❑ 520 Mike Fetters .15 .07
❑ 521 Gary Sheffield .40 .18
❑ 522 Terry Steinbach .25 .11
❑ 523 Steve Trachsel .15 .07
❑ 524 Josh Booty .15 .07
❑ 525 Darryl Hamilton .15 .07
❑ 526 Mark McLemore .15 .07
❑ 527 Kevin Stocker .15 .07
❑ 528 Bret Boone .25 .11
❑ 529 Shane Andrews .15 .07
❑ 530 Robb Nen .25 .11
❑ 531 Carl Everett .15 .07
❑ 532 LaTroy Hawkins .15 .07
❑ 533 Fernando Vina .15 .07
❑ 534 Michael Tucker .25 .11
❑ 535 Mark Langston .15 .07
❑ 536 Mickey Mantle 5.00 2.20
❑ 537 Bernard Gilkey .15 .07
❑ 538 Francisco Cordova .15 .07
❑ 539 Mike Bordick .15 .07
❑ 540 Fred McGriff .40 .18
❑ 541 Cliff Politte .25 .11
❑ 542 Jason Varitek .15 .07
❑ 543 Shawon Dunston .15 .07
❑ 544 Brian Meadows .15 .07
❑ 545 Pat Meares .15 .07
❑ 546 Carlos Perez .25 .11
❑ 547 Desi Relaford .15 .07
❑ 548 Antonio Osuna .15 .07
❑ 549 Devon White .25 .11
❑ 550 Sean Runyan .15 .07
❑ 551 Mickey Morandini .15 .07
❑ 552 Dave Martinez .15 .07
❑ 553 Jeff Fassero .15 .07
❑ 554 Ryan Jackson .25 .11
❑ 555 Stan Javier .15 .07
❑ 556 Jaime Navarro .15 .07
❑ 557 Jose Offerman .15 .07
❑ 558 Mike Lowell .60 .25
❑ 559 Darrin Fletcher .15 .07
❑ 560 Mark Lewis .15 .07
❑ 561 Dante Bichette .25 .11
❑ 562 Chuck Finley .25 .11
❑ 563 Kerry Wood 3.00 1.35
❑ 564 Andy Benes .25 .11
❑ 565 Freddy Garcia .15 .07
❑ 566 Tom Glavine .60 .25
❑ 567 Jon Nunnally .15 .07
❑ 568 Miguel Cairo .25 .11
❑ 569 Shane Reynolds .25 .11
❑ 570 Roberto Kelly .15 .07
❑ 571 Jose Cruz Jr. CL .40 .18
❑ 572 Ken Griffey Jr. CL 1.50 .70
❑ 573 Mark McGwire CL 2.00 .90
❑ 574 Cal Ripken CL 1.25 .55
❑ 575 Frank Thomas CL 1.00 .45
❑ 576 Jeff Bagwell UM 2.50 1.10
❑ 577 Barry Bonds UM 2.00 .90
❑ 578 Tony Clark UM 1.00 .45
❑ 579 Roger Clemens UM 3.00 1.35
❑ 580 Jose Cruz Jr. UM 2.00 .90
❑ 581 Nomar Garciaparra UM 5.00 2.20
❑ 582 Juan Gonzalez UM 4.00 1.80
❑ 583 Ben Grieve UM 3.00 1.35
❑ 584 Ken Griffey Jr. UM 8.00 3.60
❑ 585 Tony Gwynn UM 4.00 1.80
❑ 586 Derek Jeter UM 4.00 1.80
❑ 587 Randy Johnson UM 1.50 .70
❑ 588 Chipper Jones UM 4.00 1.80
❑ 589 Greg Maddux UM 5.00 2.20
❑ 590 Mark McGwire UM 10.00 4.50
❑ 591 Paul Molitor UM 1.50 .70
❑ 592 Andy Pettitte UM 1.00 .45
❑ 593 Cal Ripken UM 6.00 2.70
❑ 594 Alex Rodriguez UM 5.00 2.20
❑ 595 Scott Rolen UM 4.00 1.80
❑ 596 Curt Schilling UM .60 .25
❑ 597 Frank Thomas UM 5.00 2.20
❑ 598 Jim Thome UM 1.50 .70
❑ 599 Larry Walker UM 1.50 .70
❑ 600 Bernie Williams UM 1.50 .70
❑ P100 Alex Rodriguez Promo 3.00 1.35

1998 Fleer Vintage '63

	MINT	NRMT
COMPLETE SET (128)	50.00	22.00
COMPLETE SERIES 1 (64)	25.00	11.00
COMPLETE SERIES 2 (64)	25.00	11.00
COMMON CARD (1-126/CL'S)	.20	.09

❑ 1 Jason Dickson .30 .14
❑ 2 Tim Salmon .75 .35
❑ 3 Andruw Jones 1.00 .45
❑ 4 Chipper Jones 2.00 .90
❑ 5 Kenny Lofton .75 .35
❑ 6 Greg Maddux 2.50 1.10
❑ 7 Rafael Palmeiro .50 .23
❑ 8 Cal Ripken 3.00 1.35
❑ 9 Nomar Garciaparra 2.50 1.10
❑ 10 Mark Grace .50 .23
❑ 11 Sammy Sosa 2.00 .90
❑ 12 Frank Thomas 2.50 1.10
❑ 13 Deion Sanders .30 .14
❑ 14 Sandy Alomar .30 .14
❑ 15 David Justice .75 .35
❑ 16 Jim Thome .75 .35
❑ 17 Matt Williams .30 .14
❑ 18 Jaret Wright 1.00 .45
❑ 19 Vinny Castilla .50 .23
❑ 20 Andres Galarraga .75 .35
❑ 21 Todd Helton 1.00 .45
❑ 22 Larry Walker .75 .35
❑ 23 Tony Clark .50 .23
❑ 24 Moises Alou .50 .23
❑ 25 Kevin Brown .50 .23
❑ 26 Charles Johnson .30 .14
❑ 27 Edgar Renteria .30 .14
❑ 28 Gary Sheffield .50 .23
❑ 29 Jeff Bagwell 1.25 .55
❑ 30 Craig Biggio .75 .35
❑ 31 Raul Mondesi .50 .23
❑ 32 Mike Piazza 2.50 1.10
❑ 33 Chuck Knoblauch .75 .35
❑ 34 Paul Molitor .75 .35
❑ 35 Vladimir Guerrero 1.25 .55
❑ 36 Pedro Martinez .75 .35
❑ 37 Todd Hundley .30 .14
❑ 38 Derek Jeter 2.00 .90
❑ 39 Tino Martinez .75 .35
❑ 40 Paul O'Neill .30 .14
❑ 41 Andy Pettitte .50 .23
❑ 42 Mariano Rivera .30 .14
❑ 43 Bernie Williams .75 .35
❑ 44 Ben Grieve 1.50 .70
❑ 45 Scott Rolen 2.00 .90
❑ 46 Curt Schilling .30 .14
❑ 47 Jason Kendall .30 .14
❑ 48 Tony Womack .30 .14
❑ 49 Ray Lankford .30 .14
❑ 50 Mark McGwire 5.00 2.20
❑ 51 Matt Morris .30 .14
❑ 52 Tony Gwynn 2.00 .90
❑ 53 Barry Bonds 1.00 .45
❑ 54 Jay Buhner .30 .14
❑ 55 Ken Griffey Jr. 4.00 1.80

❑ 56 Randy Johnson	.75	.35
❑ 57 Edgar Martinez	.30	.14
❑ 58 Alex Rodriguez	2.50	1.10
❑ 59 Juan Gonzalez	2.00	.90
❑ 60 Rusty Greer	.30	.14
❑ 61 Ivan Rodriguez	1.00	.45
❑ 62 Roger Clemens	1.50	.70
❑ 63 Jose Cruz Jr.	1.00	.45
❑ 64 Darin Erstad	1.00	.45
❑ 65 Jay Bell	.30	.14
❑ 66 Andy Benes	.30	.14
❑ 67 Mickey Mantle	5.00	2.20
❑ 68 Karim Garcia	.30	.14
❑ 69 Travis Lee	1.50	.70
❑ 70 Matt Williams	.30	.14
❑ 71 Andres Galarraga	.75	.35
❑ 72 Tom Glavine	.75	.35
❑ 73 Ryan Klesko	.30	.14
❑ 74 Denny Neagle	.30	.14
❑ 75 John Smoltz	.30	.14
❑ 76 Roberto Alomar	.75	.35
❑ 77 Joe Carter	.30	.14
❑ 78 Mike Mussina	.75	.35
❑ 79 B.J. Surhoff	.30	.14
❑ 80 Dennis Eckersley	.30	.14
❑ 81 Pedro Martinez	.75	.35
❑ 82 Mo Vaughn	1.00	.45
❑ 83 Henry Rodriguez	.30	.14
❑ 84 Kerry Wood	4.00	1.80
❑ 85 Albert Belle	.75	.35
❑ 86 Sean Casey	.30	.14
❑ 87 Travis Fryman	.30	.14
❑ 88 Kenny Lofton	.75	.35
❑ 89 Darryl Kile	.30	.14
❑ 90 Mike Lansing	.20	.09
❑ 91 Bobby Bonilla	.30	.14
❑ 92 Cliff Floyd	.30	.14
❑ 93 Livan Hernandez	.30	.14
❑ 94 Derrek Lee	.30	.14
❑ 95 Moises Alou	.50	.23
❑ 96 Shane Reynolds	.30	.14
❑ 97 Mike Piazza	2.50	1.10
❑ 98 Johnny Damon	.30	.14
❑ 99 Eric Karros	.30	.14
❑ 100 Hideo Nomo	1.00	.45
❑ 101 Marquis Grissom	.30	.14
❑ 102 Matt Lawton	.30	.14
❑ 103 Todd Walker	.50	.23
❑ 104 Gary Sheffield	.50	.23
❑ 105 Bernard Gilkey	.20	.09
❑ 106 Rey Ordonez	.30	.14
❑ 107 Chili Davis	.30	.14
❑ 108 Chuck Knoblauch	.75	.35
❑ 109 Charles Johnson	.30	.14
❑ 110 Rickey Henderson	.75	.35
❑ 111 Bob Abreu	.30	.14
❑ 112 Doug Glanville	.30	.14
❑ 113 Gregg Jefferies	.20	.09
❑ 114 Al Martin	.20	.09
❑ 115 Kevin Young	.30	.14
❑ 116 Ron Gant	.20	.09
❑ 117 Kevin Brown	.50	.23
❑ 118 Ken Caminiti	.50	.23
❑ 119 Joey Hamilton	.30	.14
❑ 120 Jeff Kent	.30	.14
❑ 121 Wade Boggs	.75	.35
❑ 122 Quinton McCracken	.30	.14
❑ 123 Fred McGriff	.50	.23
❑ 124 Paul Sorrento	.20	.09
❑ 125 Jose Canseco	.75	.35
❑ 126 Randy Myers	.30	.14
❑ NNO Checklist 1	.20	.09
❑ NNO Checklist 2	.20	.09

1998 Fleer Vintage '63 Classic

	MINT	NRMT
COMMON CARD (1-126/CL'S)	20.00	9.00

*STARS: 50X TO 100X '63 VINTAGE
*YOUNG STARS: 40X TO 80X '63 VINTAGE

1998 Fleer Decade of Excellence

	MINT	NRMT
COMPLETE SET (12)	120.00	55.00
COMMON CARD (1-12)	4.00	1.80

*RARE TRADITIONS: 2.5X TO 5X BASIC DECADES
RARE TRAD. STATED ODDS 1:720 HOBBY

❑ 1 Roberto Alomar	8.00	3.60
❑ 2 Barry Bonds	10.00	4.50
❑ 3 Roger Clemens	15.00	6.75
❑ 4 David Cone	5.00	2.20
❑ 5 Andres Galarraga	8.00	3.60
❑ 6 Mark Grace	5.00	2.20
❑ 7 Tony Gwynn	20.00	9.00
❑ 8 Randy Johnson	8.00	3.60
❑ 9 Greg Maddux	25.00	11.00
❑ 10 Mark McGwire	50.00	22.00
❑ 11 Paul O'Neill	4.00	1.80
❑ 12 Cal Ripken	30.00	13.50

1998 Fleer Diamond Ink

	MINT	NRMT
J.BUHNER POINT	.10	.05
R.CLEMENS POINT	.30	.14
J.CRUZ JR. POINT	.25	.11
N.GARCIAPARRA POINT	.20	.09
T.GWYNN POINT	.30	.14
R.HERNANDEZ POINT	.05	.02
G.MADDUX POINT	.40	.18
A.RODRIGUEZ POINT	.30	.14
S.ROLEN POINT	.20	.09
T.WOMACK POINT	.05	.02

1998 Fleer Diamond Standouts

	MINT	NRMT
COMPLETE SET (20)	50.00	22.00
COMMON CARD (1-20)	.75	.35

❑ 1 Jeff Bagwell	2.50	1.10
❑ 2 Barry Bonds	2.00	.90
❑ 3 Roger Clemens	3.00	1.35
❑ 4 Jose Cruz Jr.	1.50	.70
❑ 5 Andres Galarraga	1.50	.70
❑ 6 Nomar Garciaparra	5.00	2.20

❑ 7 Juan Gonzalez	4.00	1.80
❑ 8 Ken Griffey Jr.	8.00	3.60
❑ 9 Derek Jeter	4.00	1.80
❑ 10 Randy Johnson	1.50	.70
❑ 11 Chipper Jones	4.00	1.80
❑ 12 Kenny Lofton	1.50	.70
❑ 13 Greg Maddux	5.00	2.20
❑ 14 Pedro Martinez	1.50	.70
❑ 15 Mark McGwire	10.00	4.50
❑ 16 Mike Piazza	5.00	2.20
❑ 17 Alex Rodriguez	5.00	2.20
❑ 18 Curt Schilling	.75	.35
❑ 19 Frank Thomas	5.00	2.20
❑ 20 Larry Walker	1.50	.70

1998 Fleer Diamond Tribute

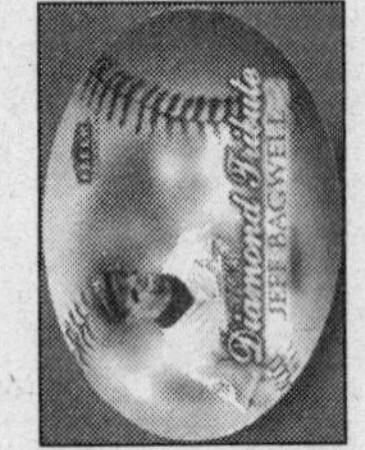

	MINT	NRMT
COMPLETE SET (10)	600.00	275.00
COMMON CARD (DT1-DT10)	30.00	13.50

❑ DT1 Jeff Bagwell	30.00	13.50
❑ DT2 Roger Clemens	40.00	18.00
❑ DT3 Nomar Garciaparra	60.00	27.00
❑ DT4 Juan Gonzalez	50.00	22.00
❑ DT5 Ken Griffey Jr.	100.00	45.00
❑ DT6 Mark McGwire	120.00	55.00
❑ DT7 Mike Piazza	60.00	27.00
❑ DT8 Cal Ripken	80.00	36.00
❑ DT9 Alex Rodriguez	60.00	27.00
❑ DT10 Frank Thomas	60.00	27.00

1998 Fleer In The Clutch

	MINT	NRMT
COMPLETE SET (15)	100.00	45.00
COMMON CARD (IC1-IC15)	3.00	1.35
MINOR STARS	3.00	1.35
SEMISTARS	3.00	1.35
UNLISTED STARS	3.00	1.35

❑ IC1 Jeff Bagwell	5.00	2.20
❑ IC2 Barry Bonds	4.00	1.80
❑ IC3 Roger Clemens	6.00	2.70
❑ IC4 Jose Cruz Jr.	3.00	1.35
❑ IC5 Nomar Garciaparra	10.00	4.50
❑ IC6 Juan Gonzalez	8.00	3.60

		MINT	NRMT
❑ IC7	Ken Griffey Jr.	15.00	6.75
❑ IC8	Tony Gwynn	8.00	3.60
❑ IC9	Derek Jeter	8.00	3.60
❑ IC10	Chipper Jones	8.00	3.60
❑ IC11	Greg Maddux	10.00	4.50
❑ IC12	Mark McGwire	20.00	9.00
❑ IC13	Mike Piazza	10.00	4.50
❑ IC14	Frank Thomas	10.00	4.50
❑ IC15	Larry Walker	3.00	1.35

1998 Fleer Lumber Company

	MINT	NRMT
COMPLETE SET (15)	150.00	70.00
COMMON CARD (1-15)	5.00	2.20

		MINT	NRMT
❑ 1	Jeff Bagwell	8.00	3.60
❑ 2	Barry Bonds	6.00	2.70
❑ 3	Jose Cruz Jr.	5.00	2.20
❑ 4	Nomar Garciaparra	15.00	6.75
❑ 5	Juan Gonzalez	12.00	5.50
❑ 6	Ken Griffey Jr.	25.00	11.00
❑ 7	Tony Gwynn	12.00	5.50
❑ 8	Chipper Jones	12.00	5.50
❑ 9	Tino Martinez	5.00	2.20
❑ 10	Mark McGwire	30.00	13.50
❑ 11	Mike Piazza	15.00	6.75
❑ 12	Cal Ripken	20.00	9.00
❑ 13	Alex Rodriguez	15.00	6.75
❑ 14	Frank Thomas	15.00	6.75
❑ 15	Larry Walker	5.00	2.20

1998 Fleer Mickey Mantle Monumental Moments

	MINT	NRMT
COMPLETE SET (10)	225.00	100.00
COMMON CARD (1-10)	25.00	11.00
COMP.GOLD SET (10)	3000.00	1350.00
COMMON GOLD (1-10)	300.00	135.00

GOLD: RANDOM INSERTS IN SER.2 PACKS
GOLD PRINT RUN 51 SERIAL #'d SETS

❑ 1 Mickey Mantle 25.00 11.00
Armed and Dangerous
❑ 2 Mickey Mantle 25.00 11.00
Getting Ready in Spring Training

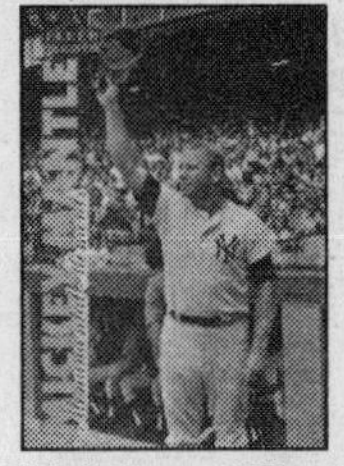

❑ 3 Mickey Mantle 25.00 11.00
Phil Rizzuto
Mantle and Rizzuto Celebrate
❑ 4 Mickey Mantle 25.00 11.00
Posed for Action
❑ 5 Mickey Mantle 25.00 11.00
Signed, Sealed and Ready to Deliver
❑ 6 Mickey Mantle 25.00 11.00
Triple Crown 1956 Season
❑ 7 Mickey Mantle 25.00 11.00
Number 7 on Yankee Pinstripes
Never to be Worn Again
❑ 8 Mickey Mantle 25.00 11.00
Mantle's Powerful Swing Produces
Another Homer
❑ 9 Mickey Mantle 25.00 11.00
Old-Timer's Day Introduction
❑ 10 Mickey Mantle 25.00 11.00
Portrait of Determination

1998 Fleer Power Game

	MINT	NRMT
COMPLETE SET (20)	120.00	55.00
COMMON CARD (1-20)	2.50	1.10

		MINT	NRMT
❑ 1	Jeff Bagwell	8.00	3.60
❑ 2	Albert Belle	6.00	2.70
❑ 3	Barry Bonds	6.00	2.70
❑ 4	Tony Clark	3.00	1.35
❑ 5	Roger Clemens	10.00	4.50
❑ 6	Jose Cruz Jr.	5.00	2.20
❑ 7	Andres Galarraga	5.00	2.20
❑ 8	Nomar Garciaparra	15.00	6.75
❑ 9	Juan Gonzalez	12.00	5.50
❑ 10	Ken Griffey Jr.	25.00	11.00
❑ 11	Randy Johnson	5.00	2.20
❑ 12	Greg Maddux	15.00	6.75
❑ 13	Pedro Martinez	5.00	2.20
❑ 14	Tino Martinez	5.00	2.20
❑ 15	Mark McGwire	30.00	13.50
❑ 16	Mike Piazza	15.00	6.75
❑ 17	Curt Schilling	2.50	1.10
❑ 18	Frank Thomas	15.00	6.75
❑ 19	Jim Thome	5.00	2.20
❑ 20	Larry Walker	5.00	2.20

1998 Fleer Promising Forecast

	MINT	NRMT
COMPLETE SET (20)	25.00	11.00
COMMON CARD (PF1-PF20)	.50	.23

		MINT	NRMT
❑ PF1	Rolando Arrojo	2.50	1.10
❑ PF2	Sean Casey	.75	.35
❑ PF3	Brad Fullmer	.75	.35
❑ PF4	Karim Garcia	.75	.35
❑ PF5	Ben Grieve	3.00	1.35
❑ PF6	Todd Helton	2.00	.90
❑ PF7	Richard Hidalgo	.75	.35
❑ PF8	A.J. Hinch	.75	.35
❑ PF9	Paul Konerko	1.50	.70
❑ PF10	Mark Kotsay	1.00	.45
❑ PF11	Derrek Lee	.75	.35
❑ PF12	Travis Lee	3.00	1.35
❑ PF13	Eric Milton	.75	.35
❑ PF14	Magglio Ordonez	2.00	.90
❑ PF15	David Ortiz	.75	.35
❑ PF16	Brian Rose	.75	.35
❑ PF17	Miguel Tejada	.75	.35
❑ PF18	Jason Varitek	.50	.23
❑ PF19	Enrique Wilson	.75	.35
❑ PF20	Kerry Wood	8.00	3.60

1998 Fleer Rookie Sensations

	MINT	NRMT
COMPLETE SET (20)	60.00	27.00
COMMON CARD (1-20)	1.00	.45

		MINT	NRMT
❑ 1	Mike Cameron	1.50	.70
❑ 2	Jose Cruz Jr.	4.00	1.80
❑ 3	Jason Dickson	1.50	.70
❑ 4	Kelvim Escobar	1.50	.70
❑ 5	Nomar Garciaparra	10.00	4.50
❑ 6	Ben Grieve	6.00	2.70
❑ 7	Vladimir Guerrero	5.00	2.20
❑ 8	Wilton Guerrero	1.00	.45
❑ 9	Jose Guillen	1.50	.70
❑ 10	Todd Helton	4.00	1.80
❑ 11	Livan Hernandez	1.50	.70
❑ 12	Hideki Irabu	2.00	.90
❑ 13	Andruw Jones	4.00	1.80
❑ 14	Matt Morris	1.50	.70

❑ 15 Magglio Ordonez	3.00	1.35
❑ 16 Neifi Perez	1.50	.70
❑ 17 Scott Rolen	8.00	3.60
❑ 18 Fernando Tatis	1.50	.70
❑ 19 Brett Tomko	1.50	.70
❑ 20 Jaret Wright	4.00	1.80

1998 Fleer Zone

	MINT	NRMT
COMPLETE SET (15)	600.00	275.00
COMMON CARD (1-15)	20.00	9.00
❑ 1 Jeff Bagwell	30.00	13.50
❑ 2 Barry Bonds	25.00	11.00
❑ 3 Roger Clemens	40.00	18.00
❑ 4 Jose Cruz Jr.	20.00	9.00
❑ 5 Nomar Garciaparra	60.00	27.00
❑ 6 Juan Gonzalez	50.00	22.00
❑ 7 Ken Griffey Jr.	100.00	45.00
❑ 8 Tony Gwynn	50.00	22.00
❑ 9 Chipper Jones	50.00	22.00
❑ 10 Greg Maddux	60.00	27.00
❑ 11 Mark McGwire	120.00	55.00
❑ 12 Mike Piazza	60.00	27.00
❑ 13 Alex Rodriguez	60.00	27.00
❑ 14 Frank Thomas	60.00	27.00
❑ 15 Larry Walker	20.00	9.00

1998 Fleer Update

	MINT	NRMT
COMP.FACT.SET (100)	60.00	27.00
COMMON CARD (1-100)	.15	.07
❑ U1 Mark McGwire HL	4.00	1.80
❑ U2 Sammy Sosa HL	1.50	.70
❑ U3 Roger Clemens HL	1.25	.55
❑ U4 Barry Bonds HL	.75	.35
❑ U5 Kerry Wood HL	3.00	1.35
❑ U6 Paul Molitor HL	.25	.11
❑ U7 Ken Griffey Jr. HL	3.00	1.35
❑ U8 Cal Ripken HL	2.50	1.10
❑ U9 David Wells HL	.25	.11
❑ U10 Alex Rodriguez HL	2.00	.90
❑ U11 Angel Pena	1.50	.70
❑ U12 Bruce Chen	.40	.18
❑ U13 Craig Wilson	.15	.07
❑ U14 Orlando Hernandez	8.00	3.60
❑ U15 Aramis Ramirez	.75	.35
❑ U16 Aaron Boone	.25	.11
❑ U17 Bob Henley	.15	.07
❑ U18 Juan Guzman	.15	.07
❑ U19 Darryl Hamilton	.15	.07
❑ U20 Jay Payton	.15	.07
❑ U21 Jeremy Powell	.15	.07
❑ U22 Ben Davis	.25	.11
❑ U23 Preston Wilson	.15	.07
❑ U24 Jim Parque	1.50	.70
❑ U25 Odalis Perez	1.50	.70
❑ U26 Ronnie Belliard	.25	.11
❑ U27 Royce Clayton	.15	.07
❑ U28 George Lombard	.40	.18
❑ U29 Tony Phillips	.15	.07
❑ U30 Fernando Seguignol	2.00	.90
❑ U31 Armando Rios	.60	.25
❑ U32 Jerry Hairston Jr.	2.00	.90
❑ U33 Justin Baughman	.75	.35
❑ U34 Seth Greisinger	.15	.07
❑ U35 Alex Gonzalez	.25	.11
❑ U36 Michael Barrett	.40	.18
❑ U37 Carlos Beltran	.40	.18
❑ U38 Ellis Burks	.15	.07
❑ U39 Jose Jimenez	.75	.35
❑ U40 Carlos Guillen	.25	.11
❑ U41 Marlon Anderson	.25	.11
❑ U42 Scott Elarton	.15	.07
❑ U43 Glenallen Hill	.15	.07
❑ U44 Shane Monahan	.25	.11
❑ U45 Dennis Martinez	.25	.11
❑ U46 Carlos Febles	1.25	.55
❑ U47 Carlos Perez	.15	.07
❑ U48 Wilton Guerrero	.15	.07
❑ U49 Randy Johnson	.60	.25
❑ U50 Brian Simmons	.50	.23
❑ U51 Carlton Loewer	.15	.07
❑ U52 Mark DeRosa	.75	.35
❑ U53 Tim Young	.50	.23
❑ U54 Gary Gaetti	.25	.11
❑ U55 Eric Chavez	1.00	.45
❑ U56 Carl Pavano	.15	.07
❑ U57 Mike Stanley	.15	.07
❑ U58 Todd Stottlemyre	.15	.07
❑ U59 Gabe Kapler	8.00	3.60
❑ U60 Mike Jerzembeck	.75	.35
❑ U61 Mitch Meluskey	1.00	.45
❑ U62 Bill Pulsipher	.15	.07
❑ U63 Derrick Gibson	.25	.11
❑ U64 John Rocker	1.50	.70
❑ U65 Calvin Pickering	.60	.25
❑ U66 Blake Stein	.15	.07
❑ U67 Fernando Tatis	.25	.11
❑ U68 Gabe Alvarez	.15	.07
❑ U69 Jeffrey Hammonds	.15	.07
❑ U70 Adrian Beltre	.75	.35
❑ U71 Ryan Bradley	2.00	.90
❑ U72 Edgard Clemente	.25	.11
❑ U73 Rick Croushore	.15	.07
❑ U74 Matt Clement	.25	.11
❑ U75 Dermal Brown	.25	.11
❑ U76 Paul Bako	.15	.07
❑ U77 Placido Polanco	.75	.35
❑ U78 Jay Tessmer	.15	.07
❑ U79 Jarrod Washburn	.15	.07
❑ U80 Kevin Witt	.15	.07
❑ U81 Mike Metcalfe	.15	.07
❑ U82 Daryle Ward	.25	.11
❑ U83 Benj Sampson	1.00	.45
❑ U84 Mike Kinkade	1.25	.55
❑ U85 Randy Winn	.15	.07
❑ U86 Jeff Shaw	.15	.07
❑ U87 Troy Glaus	8.00	3.60
❑ U88 Hideo Nomo	.75	.35
❑ U89 Mark Grudzielanek	.15	.07
❑ U90 Mike Frank	1.50	.70
❑ U91 Bobby Howry	.60	.25
❑ U92 Ryan Minor	2.00	.90
❑ U93 Corey Koskie	1.50	.70
❑ U94 Matt Anderson	1.50	.70
❑ U95 Joe Carter	.25	.11
❑ U96 Paul Konerko	.60	.25
❑ U97 Sidney Ponson	.15	.07
❑ U98 Jeremy Giambi	2.50	1.10
❑ U99 Jeff Kubenka	.50	.23
❑ U100 J.D. Drew RC	45.00	20.00

1949 Leaf

	NRMT	VG-E
COMPLETE SET (98)	25000.00	11200.00
COMMON CARD (1-168)	25.00	11.00
COMMON SP's	300.00	135.00
WRAPPER (1-CENT)	160.00	70.00
❑ 1 Joe DiMaggio	2200.00	900.00
❑ 3 Babe Ruth	2500.00	1100.00
❑ 4 Stan Musial	850.00	375.00
❑ 5 Virgil Trucks SP	350.00	160.00
❑ 8 Satchel Paige SP	2500.00	1100.00
❑ 10 Dizzy Trout	35.00	16.00
❑ 11 Phil Rizzuto	250.00	110.00
❑ 13 Cass Michaels SP	300.00	135.00
❑ 14 Billy Johnson	40.00	18.00
❑ 17 Frank Overmire	25.00	11.00
❑ 19 Johnny Wyrostek SP	300.00	135.00
❑ 20 Hank Sauer SP	350.00	160.00
❑ 22 Al Evans	25.00	11.00
❑ 26 Sam Chapman	35.00	16.00
❑ 27 Mickey Harris	25.00	11.00
❑ 28 Jim Hegan	35.00	16.00
❑ 29 Elmer Valo	35.00	16.00
❑ 30 Billy Goodman SP	300.00	135.00
❑ 31 Lou Brissie	25.00	11.00
❑ 32 Warren Spahn	275.00	125.00
❑ 33 Peanuts Lowrey SP	300.00	135.00
❑ 36 Al Zarilla SP	300.00	135.00
❑ 38 Ted Kluszewski	150.00	70.00
❑ 39 Ewell Blackwell	55.00	25.00
❑ 42 Kent Peterson	25.00	11.00
❑ 43 Ed Stevens SP	300.00	135.00
❑ 45 Ken Keltner SP	300.00	135.00
❑ 46 Johnny Mize	100.00	45.00
❑ 47 George Vico	25.00	11.00
❑ 48 Johnny Schmitz SP	300.00	135.00
❑ 49 Del Ennis	55.00	25.00
❑ 50 Dick Wakefield	25.00	11.00
❑ 51 Al Dark SP	450.00	200.00
❑ 53 Johnny VanderMeer	100.00	45.00
❑ 54 Bobby Adams SP	300.00	135.00
❑ 55 Tommy Henrich SP	450.00	200.00
❑ 56 Larry Jansen UER (Misspelled Jensen)	35.00	16.00
❑ 57 Bob McCall	25.00	11.00
❑ 59 Luke Appling	100.00	45.00
❑ 61 Jake Early	25.00	11.00
❑ 62 Eddie Joost SP	300.00	135.00
❑ 63 Barney McCosky SP	300.00	135.00
❑ 65 Robert Elliott UER (Misspelled Elliot on card front)	100.00	45.00
❑ 66 Orval Grove SP	300.00	135.00
❑ 68 Eddie Miller SP	300.00	135.00
❑ 70 Honus Wagner CO	300.00	135.00
❑ 72 Hank Edwards	25.00	11.00
❑ 73 Pat Seerey	25.00	11.00
❑ 75 Dom DiMaggio SP	550.00	250.00
❑ 76 Ted Williams	900.00	400.00
❑ 77 Roy Smalley	25.00	11.00
❑ 78 Hoot Evers SP	300.00	135.00
❑ 79 Jackie Robinson	1100.00	500.00
❑ 81 Whitey Kurowski SP	300.00	135.00
❑ 82 Johnny Lindell	35.00	16.00
❑ 83 Bobby Doerr	100.00	45.00
❑ 84 Sid Hudson	25.00	11.00
❑ 85 Dave Philley SP	300.00	135.00
❑ 86 Ralph Weigel	25.00	11.00

❑ 88 Frank Gustine SP 300.00 135.00
❑ 91 Ralph Kiner 200.00 90.00
❑ 93 Bob Feller SP 1300.00 575.00
❑ 95 George Stirnweiss........ 35.00 16.00
❑ 97 Marty Marion 55.00 25.00
❑ 98 Hal Newhouser SP 550.00 250.00
❑ 102A Gene Hermansk ERR 250.00 110.00
❑ 102B Gene Hermanski COR 40.00 18.00
❑ 104 Eddie Stewart SP 300.00 135.00
❑ 106 Lou Boudreau 100.00 45.00
❑ 108 Matt Batts SP 300.00 135.00
❑ 111 Jerry Priddy............... 25.00 11.00
❑ 113 Dutch Leonard SP.... 300.00 135.00
❑ 117 Joe Gordon 35.00 16.00
❑ 120 George Kell SP 550.00 250.00
❑ 121 Johnny Pesky SP 350.00 160.00
❑ 123 Cliff Fannin SP 300.00 135.00
❑ 125 Andy Pafko 25.00 11.00
❑ 127 Enos Slaughter SP .. 650.00 300.00
❑ 128 Buddy Rosar 25.00 11.00
❑ 129 Kirby Higbe SP 400.00 180.00
❑ 131 Sid Gordon SP 400.00 180.00
❑ 133 Tommy Holmes SP .. 450.00 200.00
❑ 136A Cliff Aberson 25.00 11.00
(Full sleeve)
❑ 136B Cliff Aberson 250.00 110.00
(Short sleeve)
❑ 137 Harry Walker SP 275.00 125.00
❑ 138 Larry Doby SP.......... 650.00 300.00
❑ 139 Johnny Hopp.............. 25.00 11.00
❑ 142 Danny Murtaugh SP 350.00 160.00
❑ 143 Dick Sisler SP 300.00 135.00
❑ 144 Bob Dillinger SP 400.00 180.00
❑ 146 Pete Reiser SP 450.00 200.00
❑ 149 Hank Majeski SP...... 300.00 135.00
❑ 153 Floyd Baker SP 300.00 135.00
❑ 158 Harry Brecheen SP .. 350.00 160.00
❑ 159 Mizell Platt................. 25.00 11.00
❑ 160 Bob Scheffing SP 225.00 100.00
❑ 161 Vern Stephens SP.... 350.00 160.00
❑ 163 Fred Hutchinson SP 350.00 160.00
❑ 165 Dale Mitchell SP 350.00 160.00
❑ 168 Phil Cavarretta SP UER 450.00 180.00
Name spelled Cavaretta

1990 Leaf

	MINT	NRMT
COMPLETE SET (528)	275.00	125.00
COMPLETE SERIES 1 (264)	175.00	80.00
COMPLETE SERIES 2 (264)	100.00	45.00
COMMON CARD (1-528)...........	.25	.11
COMP. BERRA PUZZLE	1.00	.45

❑ 1 Introductory Card .... .25 .11
❑ 2 Mike Henneman .... .25 .11
❑ 3 Steve Bedrosian .... .25 .11
❑ 4 Mike Scott .... .25 .11
❑ 5 Allan Anderson .... .25 .11
❑ 6 Rick Sutcliffe .... .25 .11
❑ 7 Gregg Olson .... .25 .11
❑ 8 Kevin Elster........................ .25 .11
❑ 9 Pete O'Brien .... .25 .11
❑ 10 Carlton Fisk..................... 1.50 .70
❑ 11 Joe Magrane .... .25 .11
❑ 12 Roger Clemens 3.00 1.35
❑ 13 Tom Glavine 3.00 1.35
❑ 14 Tom Gordon .... 1.00 .45
❑ 15 Todd Benzinger............... .25 .11
❑ 16 Hubie Brooks.................... .25 .11
❑ 17 Roberto Kelly.................... .25 .11
❑ 18 Barry Larkin.................. 1.50 .70
❑ 19 Mike Boddicker .... .25 .11
❑ 20 Roger McDowell .... .25 .11
❑ 21 Nolan Ryan 6.00 2.70
❑ 22 John Farrell .... .25 .11
❑ 23 Bruce Hurst .... .25 .11
❑ 24 Wally Joyner .... .50 .23
❑ 25 Greg Maddux 15.00 6.75
❑ 26 Chris Bosio .... .25 .11
❑ 27 John Cerutti........................ .25 .11
❑ 28 Tim Burke .... .25 .11
❑ 29 Dennis Eckersley .... 1.00 .45
❑ 30 Glenn Davis......................... .25 .11
❑ 31 Jim Abbott .... 1.00 .45
❑ 32 Mike LaValliere .... .25 .11
❑ 33 Andres Thomas.................. .25 .11
❑ 34 Lou Whitaker...................... .50 .23
❑ 35 Alvin Davis .... .25 .11
❑ 36 Melido Perez .... .25 .11
❑ 37 Craig Biggio.................... 1.50 .70
❑ 38 Rick Aguilera .... .50 .23
❑ 39 Pete Harnisch .... .25 .11
❑ 40 David Cone .... 1.50 .70
❑ 41 Scott Garrelts .... .25 .11
❑ 42 Jay Howell.......................... .25 .11
❑ 43 Eric King .... .25 .11
❑ 44 Pedro Guerrero .... .25 .11
❑ 45 Mike Bielecki .... .25 .11
❑ 46 Bob Boone .... .50 .23
❑ 47 Kevin Brown 2.50 1.10
❑ 48 Jerry Browne .... .25 .11
❑ 49 Mike Scioscia .... .25 .11
❑ 50 Chuck Cary .... .25 .11
❑ 51 Wade Boggs .... 1.50 .70
❑ 52 Von Hayes........................... .25 .11
❑ 53 Tony Fernandez .... .25 .11
❑ 54 Dennis Martinez .... .50 .23
❑ 55 Tom Candiotti .... .25 .11
❑ 56 Andy Benes.................... 1.50 .70
❑ 57 Rob Dibble .... .25 .11
❑ 58 Chuck Crim .... .25 .11
❑ 59 John Smoltz 2.50 1.10
❑ 60 Mike Heath .... .25 .11
❑ 61 Kevin Gross.......................... .25 .11
❑ 62 Mark McGwire 8.00 3.60
❑ 63 Bert Blyleven .... .50 .23
❑ 64 Bob Walk.............................. .25 .11
❑ 65 Mickey Tettleton .... .50 .23
❑ 66 Sid Fernandez....................... .25 .11
❑ 67 Terry Kennedy...................... .25 .11
❑ 68 Fernando Valenzuela .... .50 .23
❑ 69 Don Mattingly 2.50 1.10
❑ 70 Paul O'Neill .... .50 .23
❑ 71 Robin Yount .... 1.50 .70
❑ 72 Bret Saberhagen.................. .50 .23
❑ 73 Geno Petralli .... .25 .11
❑ 74 Brook Jacoby .... .25 .11
❑ 75 Roberto Alomar .... 2.00 .90
❑ 76 Devon White .... .25 .11
❑ 77 Jose Lind.............................. .25 .11
❑ 78 Pat Combs .... .25 .11
❑ 79 Dave Stieb............................ .50 .23
❑ 80 Tim Wallach .... .25 .11
❑ 81 Dave Stewart........................ .50 .23
❑ 82 Eric Anthony .... .25 .11
❑ 83 Randy Bush........................... .25 .11
❑ 84 Rickey Henderson CL .... .50 .23
❑ 85 Jaime Navarro....................... .25 .11
❑ 86 Tommy Gregg .... .25 .11
❑ 87 Frank Tanana .... .25 .11
❑ 88 Omar Vizquel .... 2.00 .90
❑ 89 Ivan Calderon .... .25 .11
❑ 90 Vince Coleman .... .25 .11
❑ 91 Barry Bonds .... 2.00 .90
❑ 92 Randy Milligan...................... .25 .11
❑ 93 Frank Viola .... .25 .11
❑ 94 Matt Williams.................... 2.00 .90
❑ 95 Alfredo Griffin .... .25 .11
❑ 96 Steve Sax .... .25 .11
❑ 97 Gary Gaetti .... .50 .23
❑ 98 Ryne Sandberg .... 2.00 .90
❑ 99 Danny Tartabull..................... .25 .11
❑ 100 Rafael Palmeiro............ 1.50 .70
❑ 101 Jesse Orosco .... .25 .11
❑ 102 Garry Templeton .... .25 .11
❑ 103 Frank DiPino .... .25 .11
❑ 104 Tony Pena......................... .25 .11
❑ 105 Dickie Thon .... .25 .11
❑ 106 Kelly Gruber .... .25 .11
❑ 107 Marquis Grissom .... 2.00 .90
❑ 108 Jose Canseco .... 1.50 .70
❑ 109 Mike Blowers..................... .50 .23
❑ 110 Tom Browning .... .25 .11
❑ 111 Greg Vaughn................. 6.00 2.70
❑ 112 Oddibe McDowell .... .25 .11
❑ 113 Gary Ward......................... .25 .11
❑ 114 Jay Buhner .... 1.50 .70
❑ 115 Eric Show .... .25 .11
❑ 116 Bryan Harvey .... .25 .11
❑ 117 Andy Van Slyke................. .50 .23
❑ 118 Jeff Ballard .... .25 .11
❑ 119 Barry Lyons .... .25 .11
❑ 120 Kevin Mitchell .... .25 .11
❑ 121 Mike Gallego .... .25 .11
❑ 122 Dave Smith .... .25 .11
❑ 123 Kirby Puckett................. 2.50 1.10
❑ 124 Jerome Walton .... .25 .11
❑ 125 Bo Jackson .... .50 .23
❑ 126 Harold Baines .... .50 .23
❑ 127 Scott Bankhead.................. .25 .11
❑ 128 Ozzie Guillen...................... .25 .11
❑ 129 Jose Oquendo UER .... .25 .11
(League misspelled
as Legue)
❑ 130 John Dopson...................... .25 .11
❑ 131 Charlie Hayes .... .25 .11
❑ 132 Fred McGriff .... 1.50 .70
❑ 133 Chet Lemon......................... .25 .11
❑ 134 Gary Carter .... 1.50 .70
❑ 135 Rafael Ramirez .... .25 .11
❑ 136 Shane Mack .... .25 .11
❑ 137 Mark Grace UER.......... 1.50 .70
(Card back has OB:L,
should be B:L)
❑ 138 Phil Bradley........................ .25 .11
❑ 139 Dwight Gooden .... .50 .23
❑ 140 Harold Reynolds .... .25 .11
❑ 141 Scott Fletcher .... .25 .11
❑ 142 Ozzie Smith.................... 2.00 .90
❑ 143 Mike Greenwell .... .25 .11
❑ 144 Pete Smith.......................... .25 .11
❑ 145 Mark Gubicza .... .25 .11
❑ 146 Chris Sabo .... .25 .11
❑ 147 Ramon Martinez .... 1.00 .45
❑ 148 Tim Leary .... .25 .11
❑ 149 Randy Myers...................... .50 .23
❑ 150 Jody Reed........................... .25 .11
❑ 151 Bruce Ruffin .... .25 .11
❑ 152 Jeff Russell .... .25 .11
❑ 153 Doug Jones......................... .25 .11
❑ 154 Tony Gwynn 4.00 1.80
❑ 155 Mark Langston .... .25 .11
❑ 156 Mitch Williams.................... .25 .11
❑ 157 Gary Sheffield 3.00 1.35
❑ 158 Tom Henke .... .25 .11
❑ 159 Oil Can Boyd...................... .25 .11
❑ 160 Rickey Henderson........ 1.50 .70
❑ 161 Bill Doran............................. .25 .11
❑ 162 Chuck Finley .... .50 .23
❑ 163 Jeff King .... .50 .23
❑ 164 Nick Esasky......................... .25 .11
❑ 165 Cecil Fielder .... .50 .23
❑ 166 Dave Valle........................... .25 .11
❑ 167 Robin Ventura .... 2.00 .90
❑ 168 Jim Deshaies....................... .25 .11
❑ 169 Juan Berenguer.................. .25 .11
❑ 170 Craig Worthington .... .25 .11
❑ 171 Gregg Jefferies .... .50 .23
❑ 172 Will Clark .... 1.50 .70
❑ 173 Kirk Gibson .... .50 .23
❑ 174 Carlton Fisk CL .... 1.00 .45
❑ 175 Bobby Thigpen .... .25 .11
❑ 176 John Tudor .... .25 .11
❑ 177 Andre Dawson............... 1.50 .70
❑ 178 George Brett 3.00 1.35
❑ 179 Steve Buechele .... .25 .11
❑ 180 Joey Belle 25.00 11.00

No.	Player	Price	Price
❑ 181	Eddie Murray	1.50	.70
❑ 182	Bob Geren	.25	.11
❑ 183	Rob Murphy	.25	.11
❑ 184	Tom Herr	.25	.11
❑ 185	George Bell	.25	.11
❑ 186	Spike Owen	.25	.11
❑ 187	Cory Snyder	.25	.11
❑ 188	Fred Lynn	.25	.11
❑ 189	Eric Davis	.50	.23
❑ 190	Dave Parker	.50	.23
❑ 191	Jeff Blauser	.25	.11
❑ 192	Matt Nokes	.25	.11
❑ 193	Delino DeShields	1.50	.70
❑ 194	Scott Sanderson	.25	.11
❑ 195	Lance Parrish	.25	.11
❑ 196	Bobby Bonilla	.50	.23
❑ 197	Cal Ripken UER (Reistertown, should be Reisterstown)	6.00	2.70
❑ 198	Kevin McReynolds	.25	.11
❑ 199	Robby Thompson	.25	.11
❑ 200	Tim Belcher	.25	.11
❑ 201	Jesse Barfield	.25	.11
❑ 202	Mariano Duncan	.25	.11
❑ 203	Bill Spiers	.25	.11
❑ 204	Frank White	.50	.23
❑ 205	Julio Franco	.25	.11
❑ 206	Greg Swindell	.25	.11
❑ 207	Benito Santiago	.25	.11
❑ 208	Johnny Ray	.25	.11
❑ 209	Gary Redus	.25	.11
❑ 210	Jeff Parrett	.25	.11
❑ 211	Jimmy Key	.50	.23
❑ 212	Tim Raines	.50	.23
❑ 213	Carney Lansford	.50	.23
❑ 214	Gerald Young	.25	.11
❑ 215	Gene Larkin	.25	.11
❑ 216	Dan Plesac	.25	.11
❑ 217	Lonnie Smith	.25	.11
❑ 218	Alan Trammell	1.00	.45
❑ 219	Jeffrey Leonard	.25	.11
❑ 220	Sammy Sosa	80.00	36.00
❑ 221	Todd Zeile	.50	.23
❑ 222	Bill Landrum	.25	.11
❑ 223	Mike Devereaux	.25	.11
❑ 224	Mike Marshall	.25	.11
❑ 225	Jose Uribe	.25	.11
❑ 226	Juan Samuel	.25	.11
❑ 227	Mel Hall	.25	.11
❑ 228	Kent Hrbek	.50	.23
❑ 229	Shawon Dunston	.25	.11
❑ 230	Kevin Seitzer	.25	.11
❑ 231	Pete Incaviglia	.25	.11
❑ 232	Sandy Alomar Jr.	2.00	.90
❑ 233	Bip Roberts	.25	.11
❑ 234	Scott Terry	.25	.11
❑ 235	Dwight Evans	.50	.23
❑ 236	Ricky Jordan	.25	.11
❑ 237	John Olerud	5.00	2.20
❑ 238	Zane Smith	.25	.11
❑ 239	Walt Weiss	.25	.11
❑ 240	Alvaro Espinoza	.25	.11
❑ 241	Billy Hatcher	.25	.11
❑ 242	Paul Molitor	1.50	.70
❑ 243	Dale Murphy	1.50	.70
❑ 244	Dave Bergman	.25	.11
❑ 245	Ken Griffey Jr.	25.00	11.00
❑ 246	Ed Whitson	.25	.11
❑ 247	Kirk McCaskill	.25	.11
❑ 248	Jay Bell	.50	.23
❑ 249	Ben McDonald	.50	.23
❑ 250	Darryl Strawberry	.50	.23
❑ 251	Brett Butler	.50	.23
❑ 252	Terry Steinbach	.50	.23
❑ 253	Ken Caminiti	2.50	1.10
❑ 254	Dan Gladden	.25	.11
❑ 255	Dwight Smith	.25	.11
❑ 256	Kurt Stillwell	.25	.11
❑ 257	Ruben Sierra	.25	.11
❑ 258	Mike Schooler	.25	.11
❑ 259	Lance Johnson	.25	.11
❑ 260	Terry Pendleton	.50	.23
❑ 261	Ellis Burks	1.00	.45
❑ 262	Len Dykstra	.50	.23
❑ 263	Mookie Wilson	.50	.23
❑ 264	Nolan Ryan CL UER (No TM after Ranger logo)	1.50	.70
❑ 265	Nolan Ryan (No Hit King)	3.00	1.35
❑ 266	Brian DuBois	.25	.11
❑ 267	Don Robinson	.25	.11
❑ 268	Glenn Wilson	.25	.11
❑ 269	Kevin Tapani	.50	.23
❑ 270	Marvell Wynne	.25	.11
❑ 271	Billy Ripken	.25	.11
❑ 272	Howard Johnson	.25	.11
❑ 273	Brian Holman	.25	.11
❑ 274	Dan Pasqua	.25	.11
❑ 275	Ken Dayley	.25	.11
❑ 276	Jeff Reardon	.50	.23
❑ 277	Jim Presley	.25	.11
❑ 278	Jim Eisenreich	.25	.11
❑ 279	Danny Jackson	.25	.11
❑ 280	Orel Hershiser	.50	.23
❑ 281	Andy Hawkins	.25	.11
❑ 282	Jose Rijo	.25	.11
❑ 283	Luis Rivera	.25	.11
❑ 284	John Kruk	.50	.23
❑ 285	Jeff Huson	.25	.11
❑ 286	Joel Skinner	.25	.11
❑ 287	Jack Clark	.50	.23
❑ 288	Chili Davis	.50	.23
❑ 289	Joe Girardi	1.00	.45
❑ 290	B.J. Surhoff	.50	.23
❑ 291	Luis Sojo	.25	.11
❑ 292	Tom Foley	.25	.11
❑ 293	Mike Moore	.25	.11
❑ 294	Ken Oberkfell	.25	.11
❑ 295	Luis Polonia	.25	.11
❑ 296	Doug Drabek	.25	.11
❑ 297	Dave Justice	8.00	3.60
❑ 298	Paul Gibson	.25	.11
❑ 299	Edgar Martinez	1.50	.70
❑ 300	Frank Thomas UER (No B in front of birthdate)	60.00	27.00
❑ 301	Eric Yelding	.25	.11
❑ 302	Greg Gagne	.25	.11
❑ 303	Brad Komminsk	.25	.11
❑ 304	Ron Darling	.25	.11
❑ 305	Kevin Bass	.25	.11
❑ 306	Jeff Hamilton	.25	.11
❑ 307	Ron Karkovice	.25	.11
❑ 308	Milt Thompson UER (Ray Lankford pictured on card back)	1.50	.70
❑ 309	Mike Harkey	.25	.11
❑ 310	Mel Stottlemyre Jr.	.25	.11
❑ 311	Kenny Rogers	.50	.23
❑ 312	Mitch Webster	.25	.11
❑ 313	Kal Daniels	.25	.11
❑ 314	Matt Nokes	.25	.11
❑ 315	Dennis Lamp	.25	.11
❑ 316	Ken Howell	.25	.11
❑ 317	Glenallen Hill	.25	.11
❑ 318	Dave Martinez	.25	.11
❑ 319	Chris James	.25	.11
❑ 320	Mike Pagliarulo	.25	.11
❑ 321	Hal Morris	.25	.11
❑ 322	Rob Deer	.25	.11
❑ 323	Greg Olson	.25	.11
❑ 324	Tony Phillips	.25	.11
❑ 325	Larry Walker	12.00	5.50
❑ 326	Ron Hassey	.25	.11
❑ 327	Jack Howell	.25	.11
❑ 328	John Smiley	.25	.11
❑ 329	Steve Finley	1.50	.70
❑ 330	Dave Magadan	.25	.11
❑ 331	Greg Litton	.25	.11
❑ 332	Mickey Hatcher	.25	.11
❑ 333	Lee Guetterman	.25	.11
❑ 334	Norm Charlton	.25	.11
❑ 335	Edgar Diaz	.25	.11
❑ 336	Willie Wilson	.25	.11
❑ 337	Bobby Witt	.25	.11
❑ 338	Candy Maldonado	.25	.11
❑ 339	Craig Lefferts	.25	.11
❑ 340	Dante Bichette	2.00	.90
❑ 341	Wally Backman	.25	.11
❑ 342	Dennis Cook	.25	.11
❑ 343	Pat Borders	.25	.11
❑ 344	Wallace Johnson	.25	.11
❑ 345	Willie Randolph	.50	.23
❑ 346	Danny Darwin	.25	.11
❑ 347	Al Newman	.25	.11
❑ 348	Mark Knudson	.25	.11
❑ 349	Joe Boever	.25	.11
❑ 350	Larry Sheets	.25	.11
❑ 351	Mike Jackson	.50	.23
❑ 352	Wayne Edwards	.25	.11
❑ 353	Bernard Gilkey	2.00	.90
❑ 354	Don Slaught	.25	.11
❑ 355	Joe Orsulak	.25	.11
❑ 356	John Franco	.50	.23
❑ 357	Jeff Brantley	.25	.11
❑ 358	Mike Morgan	.25	.11
❑ 359	Deion Sanders	3.00	1.35
❑ 360	Terry Leach	.25	.11
❑ 361	Les Lancaster	.25	.11
❑ 362	Storm Davis	.25	.11
❑ 363	Scott Coolbaugh	.25	.11
❑ 364	Ozzie Smith CL	1.00	.45
❑ 365	Cecilio Guante	.25	.11
❑ 366	Joey Cora	1.00	.45
❑ 367	Willie McGee	.50	.23
❑ 368	Jerry Reed	.25	.11
❑ 369	Darren Daulton	.50	.23
❑ 370	Manny Lee	.25	.11
❑ 371	Mark Gardner	.25	.11
❑ 372	Rick Honeycutt	.25	.11
❑ 373	Steve Balboni	.25	.11
❑ 374	Jack Armstrong	.25	.11
❑ 375	Charlie O'Brien	.25	.11
❑ 376	Ron Gant	.50	.23
❑ 377	Lloyd Moseby	.25	.11
❑ 378	Gene Harris	.25	.11
❑ 379	Joe Carter	.50	.23
❑ 380	Scott Bailes	.25	.11
❑ 381	R.J. Reynolds	.25	.11
❑ 382	Bob Melvin	.25	.11
❑ 383	Tim Teufel	.25	.11
❑ 384	John Burkett	.50	.23
❑ 385	Felix Jose	.25	.11
❑ 386	Larry Andersen	.25	.11
❑ 387	David West	.25	.11
❑ 388	Luis Salazar	.25	.11
❑ 389	Mike Macfarlane	.25	.11
❑ 390	Charlie Hough	.50	.23
❑ 391	Greg Briley	.25	.11
❑ 392	Donn Pall	.25	.11
❑ 393	Bryn Smith	.25	.11
❑ 394	Carlos Quintana	.25	.11
❑ 395	Steve Lake	.25	.11
❑ 396	Mark Whiten	.25	.11
❑ 397	Edwin Nunez	.25	.11
❑ 398	Rick Parker	.25	.11
❑ 399	Mark Portugal	.25	.11
❑ 400	Roy Smith	.25	.11
❑ 401	Hector Villanueva	.25	.11
❑ 402	Bob Milacki	.25	.11
❑ 403	Alejandro Pena	.25	.11
❑ 404	Scott Bradley	.25	.11
❑ 405	Ron Kittle	.25	.11
❑ 406	Bob Tewksbury	.25	.11
❑ 407	Wes Gardner	.25	.11
❑ 408	Ernie Whitt	.25	.11
❑ 409	Terry Shumpert	.25	.11
❑ 410	Tim Layana	.25	.11
❑ 411	Chris Gwynn	.25	.11
❑ 412	Jeff D. Robinson	.25	.11
❑ 413	Scott Scudder	.25	.11
❑ 414	Kevin Romine	.25	.11
❑ 415	Jose DeJesus	.25	.11
❑ 416	Mike Jeffcoat	.25	.11
❑ 417	Rudy Seanez	.25	.11
❑ 418	Mike Dunne	.25	.11
❑ 419	Dick Schofield	.25	.11
❑ 420	Steve Wilson	.25	.11
❑ 421	Bill Krueger	.25	.11
❑ 422	Junior Felix	.25	.11
❑ 423	Drew Hall	.25	.11
❑ 424	Curt Young	.25	.11
❑ 425	Franklin Stubbs	.25	.11
❑ 426	Dave Winfield	1.50	.70
❑ 427	Rick Reed	.25	.11

❑ 428	Charlie Leibrandt	.25	.11
❑ 429	Jeff M. Robinson	.25	.11
❑ 430	Erik Hanson	.25	.11
❑ 431	Barry Jones	.25	.11
❑ 432	Alex Trevino	.25	.11
❑ 433	John Moses	.25	.11
❑ 434	Dave Johnson	.25	.11
❑ 435	Mackey Sasser	.25	.11
❑ 436	Rick Leach	.25	.11
❑ 437	Lenny Harris	.25	.11
❑ 438	Carlos Martinez	.25	.11
❑ 439	Rex Hudler	.25	.11
❑ 440	Domingo Ramos	.25	.11
❑ 441	Gerald Perry	.25	.11
❑ 442	Jeff Russell	.25	.11
❑ 443	Carlos Baerga	2.00	.90
❑ 444	Will Clark CL	.50	.23
❑ 445	Stan Javier	.25	.11
❑ 446	Kevin Maas	.50	.23
❑ 447	Tom Brunansky	.25	.11
❑ 448	Carmelo Martinez	.25	.11
❑ 449	Willie Blair	.25	.11
❑ 450	Andres Galarraga	1.50	.70
❑ 451	Bud Black	.25	.11
❑ 452	Greg W. Harris	.25	.11
❑ 453	Joe Oliver	.25	.11
❑ 454	Greg Brock	.25	.11
❑ 455	Jeff Treadway	.25	.11
❑ 456	Lance McCullers	.25	.11
❑ 457	Dave Schmidt	.25	.11
❑ 458	Todd Burns	.25	.11
❑ 459	Max Venable	.25	.11
❑ 460	Neal Heaton	.25	.11
❑ 461	Mark Williamson	.25	.11
❑ 462	Keith Miller	.25	.11
❑ 463	Mike LaCoss	.25	.11
❑ 464	Jose Offerman	2.00	.90
❑ 465	Jim Leyritz	2.00	.90
❑ 466	Glenn Braggs	.25	.11
❑ 467	Ron Robinson	.25	.11
❑ 468	Mark Davis	.25	.11
❑ 469	Gary Pettis	.25	.11
❑ 470	Keith Hernandez	.50	.23
❑ 471	Dennis Rasmussen	.25	.11
❑ 472	Mark Eichhorn	.25	.11
❑ 473	Ted Power	.25	.11
❑ 474	Terry Mulholland	.25	.11
❑ 475	Todd Stottlemyre	.50	.23
❑ 476	Jerry Goff	.25	.11
❑ 477	Gene Nelson	.25	.11
❑ 478	Rich Gedman	.25	.11
❑ 479	Brian Harper	.25	.11
❑ 480	Mike Felder	.25	.11
❑ 481	Steve Avery	1.50	.70
❑ 482	Jack Morris	.50	.23
❑ 483	Randy Johnson	5.00	2.20
❑ 484	Scott Radinsky	.25	.11
❑ 485	Jose DeLeon	.25	.11
❑ 486	Stan Belinda	.25	.11
❑ 487	Brian Holton	.25	.11
❑ 488	Mark Carreon	.25	.11
❑ 489	Trevor Wilson	.25	.11
❑ 490	Mike Sharperson	.25	.11
❑ 491	Alan Mills	.25	.11
❑ 492	John Candelaria	.25	.11
❑ 493	Paul Assenmacher	.25	.11
❑ 494	Steve Crawford	.25	.11
❑ 495	Brad Arnsberg	.25	.11
❑ 496	Sergio Valdez	.25	.11
❑ 497	Mark Parent	.25	.11
❑ 498	Tom Pagnozzi	.25	.11
❑ 499	Greg A. Harris	.25	.11
❑ 500	Randy Ready	.25	.11
❑ 501	Duane Ward	.25	.11
❑ 502	Nelson Santovenia	.25	.11
❑ 503	Joe Klink	.25	.11
❑ 504	Eric Plunk	.25	.11
❑ 505	Jeff Reed	.25	.11
❑ 506	Ted Higuera	.25	.11
❑ 507	Joe Hesketh	.25	.11
❑ 508	Dan Petry	.25	.11
❑ 509	Matt Young	.25	.11
❑ 510	Jerald Clark	.25	.11
❑ 511	John Orton	.25	.11
❑ 512	Scott Ruskin	.25	.11
❑ 513	Chris Hoiles	1.50	.70
❑ 514	Daryl Boston	.25	.11
❑ 515	Francisco Oliveras	.25	.11
❑ 516	Ozzie Canseco	.25	.11
❑ 517	Xavier Hernandez	.25	.11
❑ 518	Fred Manrique	.25	.11
❑ 519	Shawn Boskie	.25	.11
❑ 520	Jeff Montgomery	.50	.23
❑ 521	Jack Daugherty	.25	.11
❑ 522	Keith Comstock	.25	.11
❑ 523	Greg Hibbard	.25	.11
❑ 524	Lee Smith	.50	.23
❑ 525	Dana Kiecker	.25	.11
❑ 526	Darrel Akerfelds	.25	.11
❑ 527	Greg Myers	.25	.11
❑ 528	Ryne Sandberg CL	1.50	.70

1991 Leaf Previews

		MINT	NRMT
COMPLETE SET (26)		30.00	13.50
COMMON CARD (1-26)		1.00	.45
❑ 1	Dave Justice	3.00	1.35
❑ 2	Ryne Sandberg	4.00	1.80
❑ 3	Barry Larkin	3.00	1.35
❑ 4	Craig Biggio	3.00	1.35
❑ 5	Ramon Martinez	1.50	.70
❑ 6	Tim Wallach	1.00	.45
❑ 7	Dwight Gooden	1.50	.70
❑ 8	Len Dykstra	1.50	.70
❑ 9	Barry Bonds	4.00	1.80
❑ 10	Ray Lankford	3.00	1.35
❑ 11	Tony Gwynn	8.00	3.60
❑ 12	Will Clark	3.00	1.35
❑ 13	Leo Gomez	1.00	.45
❑ 14	Wade Boggs	3.00	1.35
❑ 15	Chuck Finley UER (Position on card back is First Base)	1.00	.45
❑ 16	Carlton Fisk	3.00	1.35
❑ 17	Sandy Alomar Jr.	1.50	.70
❑ 18	Cecil Fielder	1.50	.70
❑ 19	Bo Jackson	1.50	.70
❑ 20	Paul Molitor	3.00	1.35
❑ 21	Kirby Puckett	5.00	2.20
❑ 22	Don Mattingly	5.00	2.20
❑ 23	Rickey Henderson	3.00	1.35
❑ 24	Tino Martinez	3.00	1.35
❑ 25	Nolan Ryan	12.00	5.50
❑ 26	Dave Stieb	1.50	.70

1991 Leaf

		MINT	NRMT
COMPLETE SET (528)		15.00	6.75
COMPLETE SERIES 1 (264)		5.00	2.20
COMPLETE SERIES 2 (264)		10.00	4.50
COMMON CARD (1-528)		.10	.05
COMP. KILLEBREW PUZZLE		1.00	.45
❑ 1	The Leaf Card	.10	.05
❑ 2	Kurt Stillwell	.10	.05
❑ 3	Bobby Witt	.10	.05
❑ 4	Tony Phillips	.10	.05
❑ 5	Scott Garrelts	.10	.05
❑ 6	Greg Swindell	.10	.05
❑ 7	Billy Ripken	.10	.05

❑ 8	Dave Martinez	.10	.05
❑ 9	Kelly Gruber	.10	.05
❑ 10	Juan Samuel	.10	.05
❑ 11	Brian Holman	.10	.05
❑ 12	Craig Biggio	.40	.18
❑ 13	Lonnie Smith	.10	.05
❑ 14	Ron Robinson	.10	.05
❑ 15	Mike LaValliere	.10	.05
❑ 16	Mark Davis	.10	.05
❑ 17	Jack Daugherty	.10	.05
❑ 18	Mike Henneman	.10	.05
❑ 19	Mike Greenwell	.10	.05
❑ 20	Dave Magadan	.10	.05
❑ 21	Mark Williamson	.10	.05
❑ 22	Marquis Grissom	.40	.18
❑ 23	Pat Borders	.10	.05
❑ 24	Mike Scioscia	.10	.05
❑ 25	Shawon Dunston	.10	.05
❑ 26	Randy Bush	.10	.05
❑ 27	John Smoltz	.40	.18
❑ 28	Chuck Crim	.10	.05
❑ 29	Don Slaught	.10	.05
❑ 30	Mike Macfarlane	.10	.05
❑ 31	Wally Joyner	.30	.14
❑ 32	Pat Combs	.10	.05
❑ 33	Tony Pena	.10	.05
❑ 34	Howard Johnson	.10	.05
❑ 35	Leo Gomez	.10	.05
❑ 36	Spike Owen	.10	.05
❑ 37	Eric Davis	.30	.14
❑ 38	Roberto Kelly	.10	.05
❑ 39	Jerome Walton	.10	.05
❑ 40	Shane Mack	.10	.05
❑ 41	Kent Mercker	.10	.05
❑ 42	B.J. Surhoff	.30	.14
❑ 43	Jerry Browne	.10	.05
❑ 44	Lee Smith	.20	.09
❑ 45	Chuck Finley	.30	.14
❑ 46	Terry Mulholland	.10	.05
❑ 47	Tom Bolton	.10	.05
❑ 48	Tom Herr	.10	.05
❑ 49	Jim Deshaies	.10	.05
❑ 50	Walt Weiss	.10	.05
❑ 51	Hal Morris	.10	.05
❑ 52	Lee Guetterman	.10	.05
❑ 53	Paul Assenmacher	.10	.05
❑ 54	Brian Harper	.10	.05
❑ 55	Paul Gibson	.10	.05
❑ 56	John Burkett	.10	.05
❑ 57	Doug Jones	.10	.05
❑ 58	Jose Oquendo	.10	.05
❑ 59	Dick Schofield	.10	.05
❑ 60	Dickie Thon	.10	.05
❑ 61	Ramon Martinez	.30	.14
❑ 62	Jay Buhner	.40	.18
❑ 63	Mark Portugal	.10	.05
❑ 64	Bob Welch	.10	.05
❑ 65	Chris Sabo	.10	.05
❑ 66	Chuck Cary	.10	.05
❑ 67	Mark Langston	.10	.05
❑ 68	Joe Boever	.10	.05
❑ 69	Jody Reed	.10	.05
❑ 70	Alejandro Pena	.10	.05
❑ 71	Jeff King	.30	.14
❑ 72	Tom Pagnozzi	.10	.05
❑ 73	Joe Oliver	.10	.05
❑ 74	Mike Witt	.10	.05
❑ 75	Hector Villanueva	.10	.05

- ❑ 76 Dan Gladden .10 .05
- ❑ 77 Dave Justice .50 .23
- ❑ 78 Mike Gallego .10 .05
- ❑ 79 Tom Candiotti .10 .05
- ❑ 80 Ozzie Smith .50 .23
- ❑ 81 Luis Polonia .10 .05
- ❑ 82 Randy Ready .10 .05
- ❑ 83 Greg A. Harris .10 .05
- ❑ 84 David Justice CL .20 .09
- ❑ 85 Kevin Mitchell .10 .05
- ❑ 86 Mark McLemore .10 .05
- ❑ 87 Terry Steinbach .30 .14
- ❑ 88 Tom Browning .10 .05
- ❑ 89 Matt Nokes .10 .05
- ❑ 90 Mike Harkey .10 .05
- ❑ 91 Omar Vizquel .40 .18
- ❑ 92 Dave Bergman .10 .05
- ❑ 93 Matt Williams .40 .18
- ❑ 94 Steve Olin .10 .05
- ❑ 95 Craig Wilson .10 .05
- ❑ 96 Dave Stieb .20 .09
- ❑ 97 Ruben Sierra .10 .05
- ❑ 98 Jay Howell .10 .05
- ❑ 99 Scott Bradley .10 .05
- ❑ 100 Eric Yelding .10 .05
- ❑ 101 Rickey Henderson .40 .18
- ❑ 102 Jeff Reed .10 .05
- ❑ 103 Jimmy Key .30 .14
- ❑ 104 Terry Shumpert .10 .05
- ❑ 105 Kenny Rogers .10 .05
- ❑ 106 Cecil Fielder .30 .14
- ❑ 107 Robby Thompson .10 .05
- ❑ 108 Alex Cole .10 .05
- ❑ 109 Randy Milligan .10 .05
- ❑ 110 Andres Galarraga .40 .18
- ❑ 111 Bill Spiers .10 .05
- ❑ 112 Kal Daniels .10 .05
- ❑ 113 Henry Cotto .10 .05
- ❑ 114 Casey Candaele .10 .05
- ❑ 115 Jeff Blauser .10 .05
- ❑ 116 Robin Yount .40 .18
- ❑ 117 Ben McDonald .10 .05
- ❑ 118 Bret Saberhagen .20 .09
- ❑ 119 Juan Gonzalez 1.50 .70
- ❑ 120 Lou Whitaker .30 .14
- ❑ 121 Ellis Burks .20 .09
- ❑ 122 Charlie O'Brien .10 .05
- ❑ 123 John Smiley .10 .05
- ❑ 124 Tim Burke .10 .05
- ❑ 125 John Olerud .30 .14
- ❑ 126 Eddie Murray .40 .18
- ❑ 127 Greg Maddux 1.25 .55
- ❑ 128 Kevin Tapani .10 .05
- ❑ 129 Ron Gant .30 .14
- ❑ 130 Jay Bell .30 .14
- ❑ 131 Chris Hoiles .10 .05
- ❑ 132 Tom Gordon .20 .09
- ❑ 133 Kevin Seitzer .10 .05
- ❑ 134 Jeff Huson .10 .05
- ❑ 135 Jerry Don Gleaton .10 .05
- ❑ 136 Jeff Brantley UER .10 .05 (Photo actually Rick Leach on back)
- ❑ 137 Felix Fermin .10 .05
- ❑ 138 Mike Devereaux .10 .05
- ❑ 139 Delino DeShields .20 .09
- ❑ 140 David Wells .20 .09
- ❑ 141 Tim Crews .10 .05
- ❑ 142 Erik Hanson .10 .05
- ❑ 143 Mark Davidson .10 .05
- ❑ 144 Tommy Gregg .10 .05
- ❑ 145 Jim Gantner .10 .05
- ❑ 146 Jose Lind .10 .05
- ❑ 147 Danny Tartabull .10 .05
- ❑ 148 Geno Petralli .10 .05
- ❑ 149 Travis Fryman .40 .18
- ❑ 150 Tim Naehring .30 .14
- ❑ 151 Kevin McReynolds .10 .05
- ❑ 152 Joe Orsulak .10 .05
- ❑ 153 Steve Frey .10 .05
- ❑ 154 Duane Ward .10 .05
- ❑ 155 Stan Javier .10 .05
- ❑ 156 Damon Berryhill .10 .05
- ❑ 157 Gene Larkin .10 .05
- ❑ 158 Greg Olson .10 .05
- ❑ 159 Mark Knudson .10 .05
- ❑ 160 Carmelo Martinez .10 .05
- ❑ 161 Storm Davis .10 .05
- ❑ 162 Jim Abbott .20 .09
- ❑ 163 Len Dykstra .30 .14
- ❑ 164 Tom Brunansky .10 .05
- ❑ 165 Dwight Gooden .30 .14
- ❑ 166 Jose Mesa .10 .05
- ❑ 167 Oil Can Boyd .10 .05
- ❑ 168 Barry Larkin .40 .18
- ❑ 169 Scott Sanderson .10 .05
- ❑ 170 Mark Grace .40 .18
- ❑ 171 Mark Guthrie .10 .05
- ❑ 172 Tom Glavine .40 .18
- ❑ 173 Gary Sheffield .40 .18
- ❑ 174 Roger Clemens CL .40 .18
- ❑ 175 Chris James .10 .05
- ❑ 176 Milt Thompson .10 .05
- ❑ 177 Donnie Hill .10 .05
- ❑ 178 Wes Chamberlain .10 .05
- ❑ 179 John Marzano .10 .05
- ❑ 180 Frank Viola .10 .05
- ❑ 181 Eric Anthony .10 .05
- ❑ 182 Jose Canseco .40 .18
- ❑ 183 Scott Scudder .10 .05
- ❑ 184 Dave Eiland .10 .05
- ❑ 185 Luis Salazar .10 .05
- ❑ 186 Pedro Munoz .10 .05
- ❑ 187 Steve Searcy .10 .05
- ❑ 188 Don Robinson .10 .05
- ❑ 189 Sandy Alomar Jr. .20 .09
- ❑ 190 Jose DeLeon .10 .05
- ❑ 191 John Orton .10 .05
- ❑ 192 Darren Daulton .30 .14
- ❑ 193 Mike Morgan .10 .05
- ❑ 194 Greg Briley .10 .05
- ❑ 195 Karl Rhodes .10 .05
- ❑ 196 Harold Baines .20 .09
- ❑ 197 Bill Doran .10 .05
- ❑ 198 Alvaro Espinoza .10 .05
- ❑ 199 Kirk McCaskill .10 .05
- ❑ 200 Jose DeJesus .10 .05
- ❑ 201 Jack Clark .20 .09
- ❑ 202 Daryl Boston .10 .05
- ❑ 203 Randy Tomlin .10 .05
- ❑ 204 Pedro Guerrero .10 .05
- ❑ 205 Billy Hatcher .10 .05
- ❑ 206 Tim Leary .10 .05
- ❑ 207 Ryne Sandberg .50 .23
- ❑ 208 Kirby Puckett .60 .25
- ❑ 209 Charlie Leibrandt .10 .05
- ❑ 210 Rick Honeycutt .10 .05
- ❑ 211 Joel Skinner .10 .05
- ❑ 212 Rex Hudler .10 .05
- ❑ 213 Bryan Harvey .10 .05
- ❑ 214 Charlie Hayes .10 .05
- ❑ 215 Matt Young .10 .05
- ❑ 216 Terry Kennedy .10 .05
- ❑ 217 Carl Nichols .10 .05
- ❑ 218 Mike Moore .10 .05
- ❑ 219 Paul O'Neill .30 .14
- ❑ 220 Steve Sax .10 .05
- ❑ 221 Shawn Boskie .10 .05
- ❑ 222 Rich DeLucia .10 .05
- ❑ 223 Lloyd Moseby .10 .05
- ❑ 224 Mike Kingery .10 .05
- ❑ 225 Carlos Baerga .30 .14
- ❑ 226 Bryn Smith .10 .05
- ❑ 227 Todd Stottlemyre .20 .09
- ❑ 228 Julio Franco .10 .05
- ❑ 229 Jim Gott .10 .05
- ❑ 230 Mike Schooler .10 .05
- ❑ 231 Steve Finley .40 .18
- ❑ 232 Dave Henderson .10 .05
- ❑ 233 Luis Quinones .10 .05
- ❑ 234 Mark Whiten .10 .05
- ❑ 235 Brian McRae .40 .18
- ❑ 236 Rich Gossage .30 .14
- ❑ 237 Rob Deer .10 .05
- ❑ 238 Will Clark .40 .18
- ❑ 239 Albert Belle .50 .23
- ❑ 240 Bob Melvin .10 .05
- ❑ 241 Larry Walker .60 .25
- ❑ 242 Dante Bichette .40 .18
- ❑ 243 Orel Hershiser .30 .14
- ❑ 244 Pete O'Brien .10 .05
- ❑ 245 Pete Harnisch .10 .05
- ❑ 246 Jeff Treadway .10 .05
- ❑ 247 Julio Machado .10 .05
- ❑ 248 Dave Johnson .10 .05
- ❑ 249 Kirk Gibson .30 .14
- ❑ 250 Kevin Brown .30 .14
- ❑ 251 Milt Cuyler .10 .05
- ❑ 252 Jeff Reardon .20 .09
- ❑ 253 David Cone .30 .14
- ❑ 254 Gary Redus .10 .05
- ❑ 255 Junior Noboa .10 .05
- ❑ 256 Greg Myers .10 .05
- ❑ 257 Dennis Cook .10 .05
- ❑ 258 Joe Girardi .30 .14
- ❑ 259 Allan Anderson .10 .05
- ❑ 260 Paul Marak .10 .05
- ❑ 261 Barry Bonds .50 .23
- ❑ 262 Juan Bell .10 .05
- ❑ 263 Russ Morman .10 .05
- ❑ 264 George Brett CL .40 .18
- ❑ 265 Jerald Clark .10 .05
- ❑ 266 Dwight Evans .30 .14
- ❑ 267 Roberto Alomar .40 .18
- ❑ 268 Danny Jackson .10 .05
- ❑ 269 Brian Downing .10 .05
- ❑ 270 John Cerutti .10 .05
- ❑ 271 Robin Ventura .40 .18
- ❑ 272 Gerald Perry .10 .05
- ❑ 273 Wade Boggs .40 .18
- ❑ 274 Dennis Martinez .30 .14
- ❑ 275 Andy Benes .20 .09
- ❑ 276 Tony Fossas .10 .05
- ❑ 277 Franklin Stubbs .10 .05
- ❑ 278 John Kruk .30 .14
- ❑ 279 Kevin Gross .10 .05
- ❑ 280 Von Hayes .10 .05
- ❑ 281 Frank Thomas 2.00 .90
- ❑ 282 Rob Dibble .10 .05
- ❑ 283 Mel Hall .10 .05
- ❑ 284 Rick Mahler .10 .05
- ❑ 285 Dennis Eckersley .20 .09
- ❑ 286 Bernard Gilkey .30 .14
- ❑ 287 Dan Plesac .10 .05
- ❑ 288 Jason Grimsley .10 .05
- ❑ 289 Mark Lewis .10 .05
- ❑ 290 Tony Gwynn 1.00 .45
- ❑ 291 Jeff Russell .10 .05
- ❑ 292 Curt Schilling .40 .18
- ❑ 293 Pascual Perez .10 .05
- ❑ 294 Jack Morris .30 .14
- ❑ 295 Hubie Brooks .10 .05
- ❑ 296 Alex Fernandez .20 .09
- ❑ 297 Harold Reynolds .10 .05
- ❑ 298 Craig Worthington .10 .05
- ❑ 299 Willie Wilson .10 .05
- ❑ 300 Mike Maddux .10 .05
- ❑ 301 Dave Righetti .10 .05
- ❑ 302 Paul Molitor .40 .18
- ❑ 303 Gary Gaetti .20 .09
- ❑ 304 Terry Pendleton .30 .14
- ❑ 305 Kevin Elster .10 .05
- ❑ 306 Scott Fletcher .10 .05
- ❑ 307 Jeff Robinson .10 .05
- ❑ 308 Jesse Barfield .10 .05
- ❑ 309 Mike LaCoss .10 .05
- ❑ 310 Andy Van Slyke .30 .14
- ❑ 311 Glenallen Hill .10 .05
- ❑ 312 Bud Black .10 .05
- ❑ 313 Kent Hrbek .30 .14
- ❑ 314 Tim Teufel .10 .05
- ❑ 315 Tony Fernandez .10 .05
- ❑ 316 Beau Allred .10 .05
- ❑ 317 Curtis Wilkerson .10 .05
- ❑ 318 Bill Sampen .10 .05
- ❑ 319 Randy Johnson .50 .23
- ❑ 320 Mike Heath .10 .05
- ❑ 321 Sammy Sosa 2.00 .90
- ❑ 322 Mickey Tettleton .30 .14
- ❑ 323 Jose Vizcaino .10 .05
- ❑ 324 John Candelaria .10 .05
- ❑ 325 Dave Howard .10 .05
- ❑ 326 Jose Rijo .10 .05
- ❑ 327 Todd Zeile .30 .14
- ❑ 328 Gene Nelson .10 .05

❑ 329 Dwayne Henry .10 .05
❑ 330 Mike Boddicker .10 .05
❑ 331 Ozzie Guillen .10 .05
❑ 332 Sam Horn .10 .05
❑ 333 Wally Whitehurst .10 .05
❑ 334 Dave Parker .30 .14
❑ 335 George Brett .75 .35
❑ 336 Bobby Thigpen .10 .05
❑ 337 Ed Whitson .10 .05
❑ 338 Ivan Calderon .10 .05
❑ 339 Mike Pagliarulo .10 .05
❑ 340 Jack McDowell .10 .05
❑ 341 Dana Kiecker .10 .05
❑ 342 Fred McGriff .40 .18
❑ 343 Mark Lee .10 .05
❑ 344 Alfredo Griffin .10 .05
❑ 345 Scott Bankhead .10 .05
❑ 346 Darrin Jackson .10 .05
❑ 347 Rafael Palmeiro .40 .18
❑ 348 Steve Farr .10 .05
❑ 349 Hensley Meulens .10 .05
❑ 350 Danny Cox .10 .05
❑ 351 Alan Trammell .20 .09
❑ 352 Edwin Nunez .10 .05
❑ 353 Joe Carter .20 .09
❑ 354 Eric Show .10 .05
❑ 355 Vance Law .10 .05
❑ 356 Jeff Gray .10 .05
❑ 357 Bobby Bonilla .20 .09
❑ 358 Ernest Riles .10 .05
❑ 359 Ron Hassey .10 .05
❑ 360 Willie McGee .20 .09
❑ 361 Mackey Sasser .10 .05
❑ 362 Glenn Braggs .10 .05
❑ 363 Mario Diaz .10 .05
❑ 364 Barry Bonds CL .40 .18
❑ 365 Kevin Bass .10 .05
❑ 366 Pete Incaviglia .10 .05
❑ 367 Luis Sojo UER .10 .05
(1989 stats interspersed with 1990's)
❑ 368 Lance Parrish .10 .05
❑ 369 Mark Leonard .10 .05
❑ 370 Heathcliff Slocumb .40 .18
❑ 371 Jimmy Jones .10 .05
❑ 372 Ken Griffey Jr. 3.00 1.35
❑ 373 Chris Hammond .10 .05
❑ 374 Chili Davis .30 .14
❑ 375 Joey Cora .20 .09
❑ 376 Ken Hill .30 .14
❑ 377 Darryl Strawberry .30 .14
❑ 378 Ron Darling .10 .05
❑ 379 Sid Bream .10 .05
❑ 380 Bill Swift .10 .05
❑ 381 Shawn Abner .10 .05
❑ 382 Eric King .10 .05
❑ 383 Mickey Morandini .10 .05
❑ 384 Carlton Fisk .40 .18
❑ 385 Steve Lake .10 .05
❑ 386 Mike Jeffcoat .10 .05
❑ 387 Darren Holmes .10 .05
❑ 388 Tim Wallach .10 .05
❑ 389 George Bell .10 .05
❑ 390 Craig Lefferts .10 .05
❑ 391 Ernie Whitt .10 .05
❑ 392 Felix Jose .10 .05
❑ 393 Kevin Maas .10 .05
❑ 394 Devon White .10 .05
❑ 395 Otis Nixon .30 .14
❑ 396 Chuck Knoblauch .50 .23
❑ 397 Scott Coolbaugh .10 .05
❑ 398 Glenn Davis .10 .05
❑ 399 Manny Lee .10 .05
❑ 400 Andre Dawson .40 .18
❑ 401 Scott Chiamparino .10 .05
❑ 402 Bill Gullickson .10 .05
❑ 403 Lance Johnson .10 .05
❑ 404 Juan Agosto .10 .05
❑ 405 Danny Darwin .10 .05
❑ 406 Barry Jones .10 .05
❑ 407 Larry Andersen .10 .05
❑ 408 Luis Rivera .10 .05
❑ 409 Jaime Navarro .10 .05
❑ 410 Roger McDowell .10 .05
❑ 411 Brett Butler .30 .14
❑ 412 Dale Murphy .40 .18
❑ 413 Tim Raines UER .20 .09
(Listed as hitting .500 in 1980, should be .050)
❑ 414 Norm Charlton .10 .05
❑ 415 Greg Cadaret .10 .05
❑ 416 Chris Nabholz .10 .05
❑ 417 Dave Stewart .30 .14
❑ 418 Rich Gedman .10 .05
❑ 419 Willie Randolph .30 .14
❑ 420 Mitch Williams .10 .05
❑ 421 Brook Jacoby .10 .05
❑ 422 Greg W. Harris .10 .05
❑ 423 Nolan Ryan 1.50 .70
❑ 424 Dave Rohde .10 .05
❑ 425 Don Mattingly .60 .25
❑ 426 Greg Gagne .10 .05
❑ 427 Vince Coleman .10 .05
❑ 428 Dan Pasqua .10 .05
❑ 429 Alvin Davis .10 .05
❑ 430 Cal Ripken 1.50 .70
❑ 431 Jamie Quirk .10 .05
❑ 432 Benito Santiago .10 .05
❑ 433 Jose Uribe .10 .05
❑ 434 Candy Maldonado .10 .05
❑ 435 Junior Felix .10 .05
❑ 436 Deion Sanders .20 .09
❑ 437 John Franco .20 .09
❑ 438 Greg Hibbard .10 .05
❑ 439 Floyd Bannister .10 .05
❑ 440 Steve Howe .10 .05
❑ 441 Steve Decker .10 .05
❑ 442 Vicente Palacios .10 .05
❑ 443 Pat Tabler .10 .05
❑ 444 Darryl Strawberry CL .30 .14
❑ 445 Mike Felder .10 .05
❑ 446 Al Newman .10 .05
❑ 447 Chris Donnels .10 .05
❑ 448 Rich Rodriguez .10 .05
❑ 449 Turner Ward .10 .05
❑ 450 Bob Walk .10 .05
❑ 451 Gilberto Reyes .10 .05
❑ 452 Mike Jackson .20 .09
❑ 453 Rafael Belliard .10 .05
❑ 454 Wayne Edwards .10 .05
❑ 455 Andy Allanson .10 .05
❑ 456 Dave Smith .10 .05
❑ 457 Gary Carter .40 .18
❑ 458 Warren Cromartie .10 .05
❑ 459 Jack Armstrong .10 .05
❑ 460 Bob Tewksbury .10 .05
❑ 461 Joe Klink .10 .05
❑ 462 Xavier Hernandez .10 .05
❑ 463 Scott Radinsky .10 .05
❑ 464 Jeff Robinson .10 .05
❑ 465 Gregg Jefferies .10 .05
❑ 466 Denny Neagle 1.00 .45
❑ 467 Carmelo Martinez .10 .05
❑ 468 Donn Pall .10 .05
❑ 469 Bruce Hurst .10 .05
❑ 470 Eric Bullock .10 .05
❑ 471 Rick Aguilera .30 .14
❑ 472 Charlie Hough .20 .09
❑ 473 Carlos Quintana .10 .05
❑ 474 Marty Barrett .10 .05
❑ 475 Kevin D. Brown .10 .05
❑ 476 Bobby Ojeda .10 .05
❑ 477 Edgar Martinez .40 .18
❑ 478 Bip Roberts .10 .05
❑ 479 Mike Flanagan .10 .05
❑ 480 John Habyan .10 .05
❑ 481 Larry Casian .10 .05
❑ 482 Wally Backman .10 .05
❑ 483 Doug Dascenzo .10 .05
❑ 484 Rick Dempsey .10 .05
❑ 485 Ed Sprague .10 .05
❑ 486 Steve Chitren .10 .05
❑ 487 Mark McGwire 2.00 .90
❑ 488 Roger Clemens .75 .35
❑ 489 Orlando Merced .20 .09
❑ 490 Rene Gonzales .10 .05
❑ 491 Mike Stanton .10 .05
❑ 492 Al Osuna .10 .05
❑ 493 Rick Cerone .10 .05
❑ 494 Mariano Duncan .10 .05
❑ 495 Zane Smith .10 .05
❑ 496 John Morris .10 .05
❑ 497 Frank Tanana .10 .05
❑ 498 Junior Ortiz .10 .05
❑ 499 Dave Winfield .40 .18
❑ 500 Gary Varsho .10 .05
❑ 501 Chico Walker .10 .05
❑ 502 Ken Caminiti .40 .18
❑ 503 Ken Griffey Sr. .10 .05
❑ 504 Randy Myers .20 .09
❑ 505 Steve Bedrosian .10 .05
❑ 506 Cory Snyder .10 .05
❑ 507 Cris Carpenter .10 .05
❑ 508 Tim Belcher .10 .05
❑ 509 Jeff Hamilton .10 .05
❑ 510 Steve Avery .10 .05
❑ 511 Dave Valle .10 .05
❑ 512 Tom Lampkin .10 .05
❑ 513 Shawn Hillegas .10 .05
❑ 514 Reggie Jefferson .30 .14
❑ 515 Ron Karkovice .10 .05
❑ 516 Doug Drabek .10 .05
❑ 517 Tom Henke .10 .05
❑ 518 Chris Bosio .10 .05
❑ 519 Gregg Olson .10 .05
❑ 520 Bob Scanlan .10 .05
❑ 521 Alonzo Powell .10 .05
❑ 522 Jeff Ballard .10 .05
❑ 523 Ray Lankford .40 .18
❑ 524 Tommy Greene .10 .05
❑ 525 Mike Timlin .10 .05
❑ 526 Juan Berenguer .10 .05
❑ 527 Scott Erickson .30 .14
❑ 528 Sandy Alomar Jr. CL .10 .05

1991 Leaf Gold Rookies

	MINT	NRMT
COMPLETE SET (26)	20.00	9.00
COMMON CARD (BC1-BC26)	.50	.23

❑ BC1 Scott Leius .50 .23
❑ BC2 Luis Gonzalez 1.25 .55
❑ BC3 Wil Cordero .50 .23
❑ BC4 Gary Scott .50 .23
❑ BC5 Willie Banks .50 .23
❑ BC6 Arthur Rhodes .75 .35
❑ BC7 Mo Vaughn 5.00 2.20
❑ BC8 Henry Rodriguez 1.50 .70
❑ BC9 Todd Van Poppel .50 .23
❑ BC10 Reggie Sanders 1.00 .45
❑ BC11 Rico Brogna 1.00 .45
❑ BC12 Mike Mussina 3.00 1.35
❑ BC13 Kirk Dressendorfer .50 .23
❑ BC14 Jeff Bagwell 5.00 2.20
❑ BC15 Pete Schourek .75 .35
❑ BC16 Wade Taylor .50 .23
❑ BC17 Pat Kelly .50 .23
❑ BC18 Tim Costo .50 .23
❑ BC19 Roger Salkeld .50 .23
❑ BC20 Andujar Cedeno .50 .23
❑ BC21 Ryan Klesko UER 2.50 1.10
(1990 Sumter BA .289; should be .368)
❑ BC22 Mike Huff .50 .23
❑ BC23 Anthony Young .50 .23
❑ BC24 Eddie Zosky .50 .23
❑ BC25 Nolan Ryan DP UER 1.50 .70

		MINT	NRMT
	No Hitter 7 (Word other repeated in 7th line)		
❑	BC26 Rickey Henderson DP Record Steal	.75	.35

1992 Leaf Previews

	MINT	NRMT
COMPLETE SET (26)	50.00	22.00
COMMON CARD (1-26)	.50	.23
❑ 1 Steve Avery	.50	.23
❑ 2 Ryne Sandberg	2.50	1.10
❑ 3 Chris Sabo	.50	.23
❑ 4 Jeff Bagwell	5.00	2.20
❑ 5 Darryl Strawberry	1.00	.45
❑ 6 Bret Barberie	.50	.23
❑ 7 Howard Johnson	.50	.23
❑ 8 John Kruk	1.00	.45
❑ 9 Andy Van Slyke	1.00	.45
❑ 10 Felix Jose	.50	.23
❑ 11 Fred McGriff	1.50	.70
❑ 12 Will Clark	2.00	.90
❑ 13 Cal Ripken	8.00	3.60
❑ 14 Phil Plantier	.50	.23
❑ 15 Lee Stevens	.50	.23
❑ 16 Frank Thomas	6.00	2.70
❑ 17 Mark Whiten	.50	.23
❑ 18 Cecil Fielder	1.00	.45
❑ 19 George Brett	4.00	1.80
❑ 20 Robin Yount	2.00	.90
❑ 21 Scott Erickson	1.00	.45
❑ 22 Don Mattingly	3.00	1.35
❑ 23 Jose Canseco	2.00	.90
❑ 24 Ken Griffey Jr.	12.00	5.50
❑ 25 Nolan Ryan	8.00	3.60
❑ 26 Joe Carter	1.00	.45

1992 Leaf

	MINT	NRMT
COMPLETE SET (528)	15.00	6.75
COMPLETE SERIES 1 (264)	5.00	2.20
COMPLETE SERIES 2 (264)	10.00	4.50
COMMON CARD (1-528)	.05	.02
❑ 1 Jim Abbott	.15	.07
❑ 2 Cal Eldred	.05	.02
❑ 3 Bud Black	.05	.02
❑ 4 Dave Howard	.05	.02
❑ 5 Luis Sojo	.05	.02
❑ 6 Gary Scott	.05	.02
❑ 7 Joe Oliver	.05	.02
❑ 8 Chris Gardner	.05	.02
❑ 9 Sandy Alomar Jr.	.15	.07
❑ 10 Greg W. Harris	.05	.02
❑ 11 Doug Drabek	.05	.02
❑ 12 Darryl Hamilton	.05	.02
❑ 13 Mike Mussina	.50	.23
❑ 14 Kevin Tapani	.05	.02
❑ 15 Ron Gant	.15	.07
❑ 16 Mark McGwire	1.50	.70
❑ 17 Robin Ventura	.15	.07
❑ 18 Pedro Guerrero	.05	.02
❑ 19 Roger Clemens	.60	.25
❑ 20 Steve Farr	.05	.02
❑ 21 Frank Tanana	.05	.02
❑ 22 Joe Hesketh	.05	.02
❑ 23 Erik Hanson	.05	.02
❑ 24 Greg Cadaret	.05	.02
❑ 25 Rex Hudler	.05	.02
❑ 26 Mark Grace	.20	.09
❑ 27 Kelly Gruber	.05	.02
❑ 28 Jeff Bagwell	.75	.35
❑ 29 Darryl Strawberry	.15	.07
❑ 30 Dave Smith	.05	.02
❑ 31 Kevin Appier	.15	.07
❑ 32 Steve Chitren	.05	.02
❑ 33 Kevin Gross	.05	.02
❑ 34 Rick Aguilera	.15	.07
❑ 35 Juan Guzman	.05	.02
❑ 36 Joe Orsulak	.05	.02
❑ 37 Tim Raines	.15	.07
❑ 38 Harold Reynolds	.05	.02
❑ 39 Charlie Hough	.15	.07
❑ 40 Tony Phillips	.05	.02
❑ 41 Nolan Ryan	1.25	.55
❑ 42 Vince Coleman	.05	.02
❑ 43 Andy Van Slyke	.15	.07
❑ 44 Tim Burke	.05	.02
❑ 45 Luis Polonia	.05	.02
❑ 46 Tom Browning	.05	.02
❑ 47 Willie McGee	.15	.07
❑ 48 Gary DiSarcina	.05	.02
❑ 49 Mark Lewis	.05	.02
❑ 50 Phil Plantier	.05	.02
❑ 51 Doug Dascenzo	.05	.02
❑ 52 Cal Ripken	1.25	.55
❑ 53 Pedro Munoz	.05	.02
❑ 54 Carlos Hernandez	.05	.02
❑ 55 Jerald Clark	.05	.02
❑ 56 Jeff Brantley	.05	.02
❑ 57 Don Mattingly	.50	.23
❑ 58 Roger McDowell	.05	.02
❑ 59 Steve Avery	.05	.02
❑ 60 John Olerud	.15	.07
❑ 61 Bill Gullickson	.05	.02
❑ 62 Juan Gonzalez	1.00	.45
❑ 63 Felix Jose	.05	.02
❑ 64 Robin Yount	.30	.14
❑ 65 Greg Briley	.05	.02
❑ 66 Steve Finley	.15	.07
❑ 67 Frank Thomas CL	.30	.14
❑ 68 Tom Gordon	.15	.07
❑ 69 Rob Dibble	.05	.02
❑ 70 Glenallen Hill	.05	.02
❑ 71 Calvin Jones	.05	.02
❑ 72 Joe Girardi	.15	.07
❑ 73 Barry Larkin	.20	.09
❑ 74 Andy Benes	.15	.07
❑ 75 Milt Cuyler	.05	.02
❑ 76 Kevin Bass	.05	.02
❑ 77 Pete Harnisch	.05	.02
❑ 78 Wilson Alvarez	.15	.07
❑ 79 Mike Devereaux	.05	.02
❑ 80 Doug Henry	.05	.02
❑ 81 Orel Hershiser	.15	.07
❑ 82 Shane Mack	.05	.02
❑ 83 Mike Macfarlane	.05	.02
❑ 84 Thomas Howard	.05	.02
❑ 85 Alex Fernandez	.15	.07
❑ 86 Reggie Jefferson	.15	.07
❑ 87 Leo Gomez	.05	.02
❑ 88 Mel Hall	.05	.02
❑ 89 Mike Greenwell	.05	.02
❑ 90 Jeff Russell	.05	.02
❑ 91 Steve Buechele	.05	.02
❑ 92 David Cone	.15	.07
❑ 93 Kevin Reimer	.05	.02
❑ 94 Mark Lemke	.05	.02
❑ 95 Bob Tewksbury	.05	.02
❑ 96 Zane Smith	.05	.02
❑ 97 Mark Eichhorn	.05	.02
❑ 98 Kirby Puckett	.50	.23
❑ 99 Paul O'Neill	.15	.07
❑ 100 Dennis Eckersley	.15	.07
❑ 101 Duane Ward	.05	.02
❑ 102 Matt Nokes	.05	.02
❑ 103 Mo Vaughn	.50	.23
❑ 104 Pat Kelly	.05	.02
❑ 105 Ron Karkovice	.05	.02
❑ 106 Bill Spiers	.05	.02
❑ 107 Gary Gaetti	.05	.02
❑ 108 Mackey Sasser	.05	.02
❑ 109 Robby Thompson	.05	.02
❑ 110 Marvin Freeman	.05	.02
❑ 111 Jimmy Key	.15	.07
❑ 112 Dwight Gooden	.15	.07
❑ 113 Charlie Leibrandt	.05	.02
❑ 114 Devon White	.05	.02
❑ 115 Charles Nagy	.15	.07
❑ 116 Rickey Henderson	.30	.14
❑ 117 Paul Assenmacher	.05	.02
❑ 118 Junior Felix	.05	.02
❑ 119 Julio Franco	.05	.02
❑ 120 Norm Charlton	.05	.02
❑ 121 Scott Servais	.05	.02
❑ 122 Gerald Perry	.05	.02
❑ 123 Brian McRae	.15	.07
❑ 124 Don Slaught	.05	.02
❑ 125 Juan Samuel	.05	.02
❑ 126 Harold Baines	.15	.07
❑ 127 Scott Livingstone	.05	.02
❑ 128 Jay Buhner	.20	.09
❑ 129 Darrin Jackson	.05	.02
❑ 130 Luis Mercedes	.05	.02
❑ 131 Brian Harper	.05	.02
❑ 132 Howard Johnson	.05	.02
❑ 133 Nolan Ryan CL	.30	.14
❑ 134 Dante Bichette	.20	.09
❑ 135 Dave Righetti	.05	.02
❑ 136 Jeff Montgomery	.15	.07
❑ 137 Joe Grahe	.05	.02
❑ 138 Delino DeShields	.15	.07
❑ 139 Jose Rijo	.05	.02
❑ 140 Ken Caminiti	.20	.09
❑ 141 Steve Olin	.05	.02
❑ 142 Kurt Stillwell	.05	.02
❑ 143 Jay Bell	.15	.07
❑ 144 Jaime Navarro	.05	.02
❑ 145 Ben McDonald	.05	.02
❑ 146 Greg Gagne	.05	.02
❑ 147 Jeff Blauser	.05	.02
❑ 148 Carney Lansford	.15	.07
❑ 149 Ozzie Guillen	.05	.02
❑ 150 Milt Thompson	.05	.02
❑ 151 Jeff Reardon	.15	.07
❑ 152 Scott Sanderson	.05	.02
❑ 153 Cecil Fielder	.15	.07
❑ 154 Greg A. Harris	.05	.02
❑ 155 Rich DeLucia	.05	.02
❑ 156 Roberto Kelly	.05	.02
❑ 157 Bryn Smith	.05	.02
❑ 158 Chuck McElroy	.05	.02
❑ 159 Tom Henke	.05	.02
❑ 160 Luis Gonzalez	.05	.02
❑ 161 Steve Wilson	.05	.02
❑ 162 Shawn Boskie	.05	.02
❑ 163 Mark Davis	.05	.02
❑ 164 Mike Moore	.05	.02
❑ 165 Mike Scioscia	.05	.02
❑ 166 Scott Erickson	.15	.07
❑ 167 Todd Stottlemyre	.15	.07
❑ 168 Alvin Davis	.05	.02
❑ 169 Greg Hibbard	.05	.02
❑ 170 David Valle	.05	.02
❑ 171 Dave Winfield	.30	.14
❑ 172 Alan Trammell	.20	.09
❑ 173 Kenny Rogers	.05	.02
❑ 174 John Franco	.15	.07

❑ 175 Jose Lind .05 .02
❑ 176 Pete Schourek .05 .02
❑ 177 Von Hayes .05 .02
❑ 178 Chris Hammond .05 .02
❑ 179 John Burkett .05 .02
❑ 180 Dickie Thon .05 .02
❑ 181 Joel Skinner .05 .02
❑ 182 Scott Cooper .05 .02
❑ 183 Andre Dawson .20 .09
❑ 184 Billy Ripken .05 .02
❑ 185 Kevin Mitchell .15 .07
❑ 186 Brett Butler .15 .07
❑ 187 Tony Fernandez .05 .02
❑ 188 Cory Snyder .05 .02
❑ 189 John Habyan .05 .02
❑ 190 Dennis Martinez .15 .07
❑ 191 John Smoltz .20 .09
❑ 192 Greg Myers .05 .02
❑ 193 Rob Deer .05 .02
❑ 194 Ivan Rodriguez .60 .25
❑ 195 Ray Lankford .30 .14
❑ 196 Bill Wegman .05 .02
❑ 197 Edgar Martinez .20 .09
❑ 198 Darryl Kile .15 .07
❑ 199 Cal Ripken CL .30 .14
❑ 200 Brent Mayne .05 .02
❑ 201 Larry Walker .30 .14
❑ 202 Carlos Baerga .05 .02
❑ 203 Russ Swan .05 .02
❑ 204 Mike Morgan .05 .02
❑ 205 Hal Morris .05 .02
❑ 206 Tony Gwynn .75 .35
❑ 207 Mark Leiter .05 .02
❑ 208 Kirt Manwaring .05 .02
❑ 209 Al Osuna .05 .02
❑ 210 Bobby Thigpen .05 .02
❑ 211 Chris Hoiles .05 .02
❑ 212 B.J. Surhoff .15 .07
❑ 213 Lenny Harris .05 .02
❑ 214 Scott Leius .05 .02
❑ 215 Gregg Jefferies .05 .02
❑ 216 Bruce Hurst .05 .02
❑ 217 Steve Sax .05 .02
❑ 218 Dave Otto .05 .02
❑ 219 Sam Horn .05 .02
❑ 220 Charlie Hayes .05 .02
❑ 221 Frank Viola .05 .02
❑ 222 Jose Guzman .05 .02
❑ 223 Gary Redus .05 .02
❑ 224 Dave Gallagher .05 .02
❑ 225 Dean Palmer .15 .07
❑ 226 Greg Olson .05 .02
❑ 227 Jose DeLeon .05 .02
❑ 228 Mike LaValliere .05 .02
❑ 229 Mark Langston .05 .02
❑ 230 Chuck Knoblauch .30 .14
❑ 231 Bill Doran .05 .02
❑ 232 Dave Henderson .05 .02
❑ 233 Roberto Alomar .30 .14
❑ 234 Scott Fletcher .05 .02
❑ 235 Tim Naehring .15 .07
❑ 236 Mike Gallego .05 .02
❑ 237 Lance Johnson .05 .02
❑ 238 Paul Molitor .30 .14
❑ 239 Dan Gladden .05 .02
❑ 240 Willie Randolph .15 .07
❑ 241 Will Clark .30 .14
❑ 242 Sid Bream .05 .02
❑ 243 Derek Bell .15 .07
❑ 244 Bill Pecota .05 .02
❑ 245 Terry Pendleton .05 .02
❑ 246 Randy Ready .05 .02
❑ 247 Jack Armstrong .05 .02
❑ 248 Todd Van Poppel .05 .02
❑ 249 Shawon Dunston .05 .02
❑ 250 Bobby Rose .05 .02
❑ 251 Jeff Huson .05 .02
❑ 252 Bip Roberts .05 .02
❑ 253 Doug Jones .05 .02
❑ 254 Lee Smith .15 .07
❑ 255 George Brett .60 .25
❑ 256 Randy Tomlin .05 .02
❑ 257 Todd Benzinger .05 .02
❑ 258 Dave Stewart .15 .07
❑ 259 Mark Carreon .05 .02
❑ 260 Pete O'Brien .05 .02
❑ 261 Tim Teufel .05 .02
❑ 262 Bob Milacki .05 .02
❑ 263 Mark Guthrie .05 .02
❑ 264 Darrin Fletcher .05 .02
❑ 265 Omar Vizquel .15 .07
❑ 266 Chris Bosio .05 .02
❑ 267 Jose Canseco .30 .14
❑ 268 Mike Boddicker .05 .02
❑ 269 Lance Parrish .05 .02
❑ 270 Jose Vizcaino .05 .02
❑ 271 Chris Sabo .05 .02
❑ 272 Royce Clayton .05 .02
❑ 273 Marquis Grissom .15 .07
❑ 274 Fred McGriff .20 .09
❑ 275 Barry Bonds .40 .18
❑ 276 Greg Vaughn .15 .07
❑ 277 Gregg Olson .05 .02
❑ 278 Dave Hollins .05 .02
❑ 279 Tom Glavine .20 .09
❑ 280 Bryan Hickerson UER .05 .02
Name spelled Brian on front
❑ 281 Scott Radinsky .05 .02
❑ 282 Omar Olivares .05 .02
❑ 283 Ivan Calderon .05 .02
❑ 284 Kevin Maas .05 .02
❑ 285 Mickey Tettleton .05 .02
❑ 286 Wade Boggs .30 .14
❑ 287 Stan Belinda .05 .02
❑ 288 Bret Barberie .05 .02
❑ 289 Jose Oquendo .05 .02
❑ 290 Frank Castillo .05 .02
❑ 291 Dave Stieb .05 .02
❑ 292 Tommy Greene .05 .02
❑ 293 Eric Karros .30 .14
❑ 294 Greg Maddux 1.00 .45
❑ 295 Jim Eisenreich .05 .02
❑ 296 Rafael Palmeiro .20 .09
❑ 297 Ramon Martinez .15 .07
❑ 298 Tim Wallach .05 .02
❑ 299 Jim Thome .75 .35
❑ 300 Chito Martinez .05 .02
❑ 301 Mitch Williams .05 .02
❑ 302 Randy Johnson .30 .14
❑ 303 Carlton Fisk .30 .14
❑ 304 Travis Fryman .15 .07
❑ 305 Bobby Witt .05 .02
❑ 306 Dave Magadan .05 .02
❑ 307 Alex Cole .05 .02
❑ 308 Bobby Bonilla .15 .07
❑ 309 Bryan Harvey .05 .02
❑ 310 Rafael Belliard .05 .02
❑ 311 Mariano Duncan .05 .02
❑ 312 Chuck Crim .05 .02
❑ 313 John Kruk .15 .07
❑ 314 Ellis Burks .15 .07
❑ 315 Craig Biggio .30 .14
❑ 316 Glenn Davis .05 .02
❑ 317 Ryne Sandberg .40 .18
❑ 318 Mike Sharperson .05 .02
❑ 319 Rich Rodriguez .05 .02
❑ 320 Lee Guetterman .05 .02
❑ 321 Benito Santiago .05 .02
❑ 322 Jose Offerman .05 .02
❑ 323 Tony Pena .05 .02
❑ 324 Pat Borders .05 .02
❑ 325 Mike Henneman .05 .02
❑ 326 Kevin Brown .20 .09
❑ 327 Chris Nabholz .05 .02
❑ 328 Franklin Stubbs .05 .02
❑ 329 Tino Martinez .30 .14
❑ 330 Mickey Morandini .05 .02
❑ 331 Ryne Sandberg CL .30 .14
❑ 332 Mark Gubicza .05 .02
❑ 333 Bill Landrum .05 .02
❑ 334 Mark Whiten .05 .02
❑ 335 Darren Daulton .15 .07
❑ 336 Rick Wilkins .05 .02
❑ 337 Brian Jordan .60 .25
❑ 338 Kevin Ward .05 .02
❑ 339 Ruben Amaro .05 .02
❑ 340 Trevor Wilson .05 .02
❑ 341 Andujar Cedeno .05 .02
❑ 342 Michael Huff .05 .02
❑ 343 Brady Anderson .20 .09
❑ 344 Craig Grebeck .05 .02
❑ 345 Bobby Ojeda .05 .02
❑ 346 Mike Pagliarulo .05 .02
❑ 347 Terry Shumpert .05 .02
❑ 348 Dann Bilardello .05 .02
❑ 349 Frank Thomas 1.00 .45
❑ 350 Albert Belle .40 .18
❑ 351 Jose Mesa .05 .02
❑ 352 Rich Monteleone .05 .02
❑ 353 Bob Walk .05 .02
❑ 354 Monty Fariss .05 .02
❑ 355 Luis Rivera .05 .02
❑ 356 Anthony Young .05 .02
❑ 357 Geno Petralli .05 .02
❑ 358 Otis Nixon .15 .07
❑ 359 Tom Pagnozzi .05 .02
❑ 360 Reggie Sanders .05 .02
❑ 361 Lee Stevens .05 .02
❑ 362 Kent Hrbek .15 .07
❑ 363 Orlando Merced .05 .02
❑ 364 Mike Bordick .05 .02
❑ 365 Dion James UER .05 .02
(Blue Jays logo on card back)
❑ 366 Jack Clark .15 .07
❑ 367 Mike Stanley .05 .02
❑ 368 Randy Velarde .05 .02
❑ 369 Dan Pasqua .05 .02
❑ 370 Pat Listach .05 .02
❑ 371 Mike Fitzgerald .05 .02
❑ 372 Tom Foley .05 .02
❑ 373 Matt Williams .20 .09
❑ 374 Brian Hunter .05 .02
❑ 375 Joe Carter .15 .07
❑ 376 Bret Saberhagen .15 .07
❑ 377 Mike Stanton .05 .02
❑ 378 Hubie Brooks .05 .02
❑ 379 Eric Bell .05 .02
❑ 380 Walt Weiss .05 .02
❑ 381 Danny Jackson .05 .02
❑ 382 Manuel Lee .05 .02
❑ 383 Ruben Sierra .05 .02
❑ 384 Greg Swindell .05 .02
❑ 385 Ryan Bowen .05 .02
❑ 386 Kevin Ritz .05 .02
❑ 387 Curtis Wilkerson .05 .02
❑ 388 Gary Varsho .05 .02
❑ 389 Dave Hansen .05 .02
❑ 390 Bob Welch .05 .02
❑ 391 Lou Whitaker .15 .07
❑ 392 Ken Griffey Jr. 2.00 .90
❑ 393 Mike Maddux .05 .02
❑ 394 Arthur Rhodes .05 .02
❑ 395 Chili Davis .15 .07
❑ 396 Eddie Murray .30 .14
❑ 397 Robin Yount CL .20 .09
❑ 398 Dave Cochrane .05 .02
❑ 399 Kevin Seitzer .05 .02
❑ 400 Ozzie Smith .40 .18
❑ 401 Paul Sorrento .05 .02
❑ 402 Les Lancaster .05 .02
❑ 403 Junior Noboa .05 .02
❑ 404 David Justice .30 .14
❑ 405 Andy Ashby .15 .07
❑ 406 Danny Tartabull .05 .02
❑ 407 Bill Swift .05 .02
❑ 408 Craig Lefferts .05 .02
❑ 409 Tom Candiotti .05 .02
❑ 410 Lance Blankenship .05 .02
❑ 411 Jeff Tackett .05 .02
❑ 412 Sammy Sosa .75 .35
❑ 413 Jody Reed .05 .02
❑ 414 Bruce Ruffin .05 .02
❑ 415 Gene Larkin .05 .02
❑ 416 John Vander Wal .05 .02
❑ 417 Tim Belcher .05 .02
❑ 418 Steve Frey .05 .02
❑ 419 Dick Schofield .05 .02
❑ 420 Jeff King .15 .07
❑ 421 Kim Batiste .05 .02
❑ 422 Jack McDowell .05 .02
❑ 423 Damon Berryhill .05 .02
❑ 424 Gary Wayne .05 .02
❑ 425 Jack Morris .15 .07
❑ 426 Moises Alou .30 .14

#	Player	MINT	NRMT
❑ 427	Mark McLemore	.05	.02
❑ 428	Juan Guerrero	.05	.02
❑ 429	Scott Scudder	.05	.02
❑ 430	Eric Davis	.15	.07
❑ 431	Joe Slusarski	.05	.02
❑ 432	Todd Zeile	.05	.02
❑ 433	Dwayne Henry	.05	.02
❑ 434	Cliff Brantley	.05	.02
❑ 435	Butch Henry	.05	.02
❑ 436	Todd Worrell	.05	.02
❑ 437	Bob Scanlan	.05	.02
❑ 438	Wally Joyner	.15	.07
❑ 439	John Flaherty	.05	.02
❑ 440	Brian Downing	.05	.02
❑ 441	Darren Lewis	.05	.02
❑ 442	Gary Carter	.30	.14
❑ 443	Wally Ritchie	.05	.02
❑ 444	Chris Jones	.05	.02
❑ 445	Jeff Kent	.30	.14
❑ 446	Gary Sheffield	.30	.14
❑ 447	Ron Darling	.05	.02
❑ 448	Deion Sanders	.30	.14
❑ 449	Andres Galarraga	.30	.14
❑ 450	Chuck Finley	.15	.07
❑ 451	Derek Lilliquist	.05	.02
❑ 452	Carl Willis	.05	.02
❑ 453	Wes Chamberlain	.05	.02
❑ 454	Roger Mason	.05	.02
❑ 455	Spike Owen	.05	.02
❑ 456	Thomas Howard	.05	.02
❑ 457	Dave Martinez	.05	.02
❑ 458	Pete Incaviglia	.05	.02
❑ 459	Keith A. Miller	.05	.02
❑ 460	Mike Fetters	.05	.02
❑ 461	Paul Gibson	.05	.02
❑ 462	George Bell	.05	.02
❑ 463	Bobby Bonilla CL	.15	.07
❑ 464	Terry Mulholland	.05	.02
❑ 465	Storm Davis	.05	.02
❑ 466	Gary Pettis	.05	.02
❑ 467	Randy Bush	.05	.02
❑ 468	Ken Hill	.05	.02
❑ 469	Rheal Cormier	.05	.02
❑ 470	Andy Stankiewicz	.05	.02
❑ 471	Dave Burba	.05	.02
❑ 472	Henry Cotto	.05	.02
❑ 473	Dale Sveum	.05	.02
❑ 474	Rich Gossage	.15	.07
❑ 475	William Suero	.05	.02
❑ 476	Doug Strange	.05	.02
❑ 477	Bill Krueger	.05	.02
❑ 478	John Wetteland	.15	.07
❑ 479	Melido Perez	.05	.02
❑ 480	Lonnie Smith	.05	.02
❑ 481	Mike Jackson	.15	.07
❑ 482	Mike Gardiner	.05	.02
❑ 483	David Wells	.15	.07
❑ 484	Barry Jones	.05	.02
❑ 485	Scott Bankhead	.05	.02
❑ 486	Terry Leach	.05	.02
❑ 487	Vince Horsman	.05	.02
❑ 488	Dave Eiland	.05	.02
❑ 489	Alejandro Pena	.05	.02
❑ 490	Julio Valera	.05	.02
❑ 491	Joe Boever	.05	.02
❑ 492	Paul Miller	.05	.02
❑ 493	Archi Cianfrocco	.05	.02
❑ 494	Dave Fleming	.05	.02
❑ 495	Kyle Abbott	.05	.02
❑ 496	Chad Kreuter	.05	.02
❑ 497	Chris James	.05	.02
❑ 498	Donnie Hill	.05	.02
❑ 499	Jacob Brumfield	.05	.02
❑ 500	Ricky Bones	.05	.02
❑ 501	Terry Steinbach	.15	.07
❑ 502	Bernard Gilkey	.15	.07
❑ 503	Dennis Cook	.05	.02
❑ 504	Len Dykstra	.15	.07
❑ 505	Mike Bielecki	.05	.02
❑ 506	Bob Kipper	.05	.02
❑ 507	Jose Melendez	.05	.02
❑ 508	Rick Sutcliffe	.05	.02
❑ 509	Ken Patterson	.05	.02
❑ 510	Andy Allanson	.05	.02
❑ 511	Al Newman	.05	.02
❑ 512	Mark Gardner	.05	.02
❑ 513	Jeff Schaefer	.05	.02
❑ 514	Jim McNamara	.05	.02
❑ 515	Peter Hoy	.05	.02
❑ 516	Curt Schilling	.20	.09
❑ 517	Kirk McCaskill	.05	.02
❑ 518	Chris Gwynn	.05	.02
❑ 519	Sid Fernandez	.05	.02
❑ 520	Jeff Parrett	.05	.02
❑ 521	Scott Ruskin	.05	.02
❑ 522	Kevin McReynolds	.05	.02
❑ 523	Rick Cerone	.05	.02
❑ 524	Jesse Orosco	.05	.02
❑ 525	Troy Afenir	.05	.02
❑ 526	John Smiley	.05	.02
❑ 527	Dale Murphy	.30	.14
❑ 528	Leaf Set Card	.05	.02

1992 Leaf Gold Rookies

	MINT	NRMT
COMPLETE SET (24)	18.00	8.00
COMPLETE SERIES 1 (12)	12.00	5.50
COMPLETE SERIES 2 (12)	6.00	2.70
COMMON CARD (BC1-BC24)	.50	.23

#	Player	MINT	NRMT
❑ BC1	Chad Curtis	1.50	.70
❑ BC2	Brent Gates	.50	.23
❑ BC3	Pedro Martinez	6.00	2.70
❑ BC4	Kenny Lofton	5.00	2.20
❑ BC5	Turk Wendell	1.00	.45
❑ BC6	Mark Hutton	.50	.23
❑ BC7	Todd Hundley	1.00	.45
❑ BC8	Matt Stairs	1.50	.70
❑ BC9	Eddie Taubensee	1.00	.45
❑ BC10	David Nied	.50	.23
❑ BC11	Salomon Torres	.50	.23
❑ BC12	Bret Boone	1.00	.45
❑ BC13	Johnny Ruffin	.50	.23
❑ BC14	Ed Martel	.50	.23
❑ BC15	Rick Trlicek	.50	.23
❑ BC16	Raul Mondesi	4.00	1.80
❑ BC17	Pat Mahomes	.50	.23
❑ BC18	Dan Wilson	1.00	.45
❑ BC19	Donovan Osborne	.50	.23
❑ BC20	Dave Silvestri	.50	.23
❑ BC21	Gary DiSarcina	.50	.23
❑ BC22	Denny Neagle	1.25	.55
❑ BC23	Steve Hosey	.50	.23
❑ BC24	John Doherty	.50	.23

1993 Leaf

	MINT	NRMT
COMPLETE SET (550)	35.00	16.00
COMPLETE SERIES 1 (220)	15.00	6.75
COMPLETE SERIES 2 (220)	15.00	6.75
COMPLETE UPDATE (110)	5.00	2.20
COMMON CARD (1-550)	.15	.07

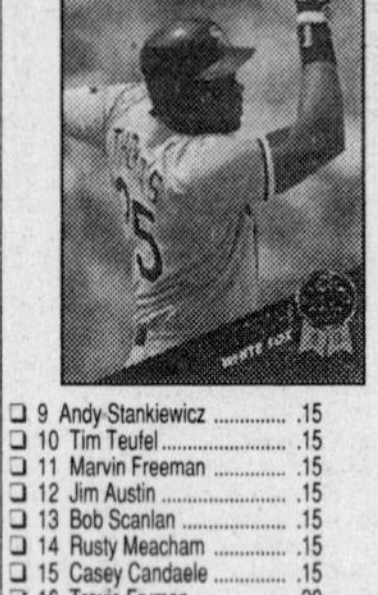

#	Player	MINT	NRMT
❑ 1	Ben McDonald	.15	.07
❑ 2	Sid Fernandez	.15	.07
❑ 3	Juan Guzman	.15	.07
❑ 4	Curt Schilling	.30	.14
❑ 5	Ivan Rodriguez	.75	.35
❑ 6	Don Slaught	.15	.07
❑ 7	Terry Steinbach	.15	.07
❑ 8	Todd Zeile	.15	.07
❑ 9	Andy Stankiewicz	.15	.07
❑ 10	Tim Teufel	.15	.07
❑ 11	Marvin Freeman	.15	.07
❑ 12	Jim Austin	.15	.07
❑ 13	Bob Scanlan	.15	.07
❑ 14	Rusty Meacham	.15	.07
❑ 15	Casey Candaele	.15	.07
❑ 16	Travis Fryman	.30	.14
❑ 17	Jose Offerman	.15	.07
❑ 18	Albert Belle	.75	.35
❑ 19	John Vander Wal	.15	.07
❑ 20	Dan Pasqua	.15	.07
❑ 21	Frank Viola	.15	.07
❑ 22	Terry Mulholland	.15	.07
❑ 23	Gregg Olson	.15	.07
❑ 24	Randy Tomlin	.15	.07
❑ 25	Todd Stottlemyre	.15	.07
❑ 26	Jose Oquendo	.15	.07
❑ 27	Julio Franco	.15	.07
❑ 28	Tony Gwynn	1.50	.70
❑ 29	Ruben Sierra	.15	.07
❑ 30	Robby Thompson	.15	.07
❑ 31	Jim Bullinger	.15	.07
❑ 32	Rick Aguilera	.15	.07
❑ 33	Scott Servais	.15	.07
❑ 34	Cal Eldred	.15	.07
❑ 35	Mike Piazza	3.00	1.35
❑ 36	Brent Mayne	.15	.07
❑ 37	Wil Cordero	.15	.07
❑ 38	Milt Cuyler	.15	.07
❑ 39	Howard Johnson	.15	.07
❑ 40	Kenny Lofton	.60	.25
❑ 41	Alex Fernandez	.30	.14
❑ 42	Denny Neagle	.30	.14
❑ 43	Tony Pena	.15	.07
❑ 44	Bob Tewksbury	.15	.07
❑ 45	Glenn Davis	.15	.07
❑ 46	Fred McGriff	.40	.18
❑ 47	John Olerud	.40	.18
❑ 48	Steve Hosey	.15	.07
❑ 49	Rafael Palmeiro	.40	.18
❑ 50	David Justice	.60	.25
❑ 51	Pete Harnisch	.15	.07
❑ 52	Sam Militello	.15	.07
❑ 53	Orel Hershiser	.30	.14
❑ 54	Pat Mahomes	.15	.07
❑ 55	Greg Colbrunn	.15	.07
❑ 56	Greg Vaughn	.30	.14
❑ 57	Vince Coleman	.15	.07
❑ 58	Brian McRae	.15	.07
❑ 59	Len Dykstra	.30	.14
❑ 60	Dan Gladden	.15	.07
❑ 61	Ted Power	.15	.07
❑ 62	Donovan Osborne	.15	.07
❑ 63	Ron Karkovice	.15	.07
❑ 64	Frank Seminara	.15	.07
❑ 65	Bob Zupcic	.15	.07
❑ 66	Kirt Manwaring	.15	.07
❑ 67	Mike Devereaux	.15	.07
❑ 68	Mark Lemke	.15	.07
❑ 69	Devon White	.15	.07
❑ 70	Sammy Sosa	1.50	.70
❑ 71	Pedro Astacio	.15	.07
❑ 72	Dennis Eckersley	.30	.14
❑ 73	Chris Nabholz	.15	.07
❑ 74	Melido Perez	.15	.07
❑ 75	Todd Hundley	.40	.18
❑ 76	Kent Hrbek	.30	.14

❑ 77 Mickey Morandini .15 .07
❑ 78 Tim McIntosh .15 .07
❑ 79 Andy Van Slyke .30 .14
❑ 80 Kevin McReynolds .15 .07
❑ 81 Mike Henneman .15 .07
❑ 82 Greg W. Harris .15 .07
❑ 83 Sandy Alomar Jr. .30 .14
❑ 84 Mike Jackson .15 .07
❑ 85 Ozzie Guillen .15 .07
❑ 86 Jeff Blauser .15 .07
❑ 87 John Valentin .30 .14
❑ 88 Rey Sanchez .15 .07
❑ 89 Rick Sutcliffe .15 .07
❑ 90 Luis Gonzalez .15 .07
❑ 91 Jeff Fassero .15 .07
❑ 92 Kenny Rogers .15 .07
❑ 93 Bret Saberhagen .30 .14
❑ 94 Bob Welch .15 .07
❑ 95 Darren Daulton .30 .14
❑ 96 Mike Gallego .15 .07
❑ 97 Orlando Merced .15 .07
❑ 98 Chuck Knoblauch .60 .25
❑ 99 Bernard Gilkey .15 .07
❑ 100 Billy Ashley .15 .07
❑ 101 Kevin Appier .30 .14
❑ 102 Jeff Brantley .15 .07
❑ 103 Bill Gullickson .15 .07
❑ 104 John Smoltz .30 .14
❑ 105 Paul Sorrento .15 .07
❑ 106 Steve Buechele .15 .07
❑ 107 Steve Sax .15 .07
❑ 108 Andujar Cedeno .15 .07
❑ 109 Billy Hatcher .15 .07
❑ 110 Checklist .15 .07
❑ 111 Alan Mills .15 .07
❑ 112 John Franco .30 .14
❑ 113 Jack Morris .30 .14
❑ 114 Mitch Williams .15 .07
❑ 115 Nolan Ryan 2.50 1.10
❑ 116 Jay Bell .30 .14
❑ 117 Mike Bordick .15 .07
❑ 118 Geronimo Pena .15 .07
❑ 119 Danny Tartabull .15 .07
❑ 120 Checklist .15 .07
❑ 121 Steve Avery .15 .07
❑ 122 Ricky Bones .15 .07
❑ 123 Mike Morgan .15 .07
❑ 124 Jeff Montgomery .30 .14
❑ 125 Jeff Bagwell 1.00 .45
❑ 126 Tony Phillips .15 .07
❑ 127 Lenny Harris .15 .07
❑ 128 Glenallen Hill .15 .07
❑ 129 Marquis Grissom .30 .14
❑ 130 Gerald Williams UER .15 .07
(Bernie Williams
picture and stats)
❑ 131 Greg A. Harris .15 .07
❑ 132 Tommy Greene .15 .07
❑ 133 Chris Hoiles .15 .07
❑ 134 Bob Walk .15 .07
❑ 135 Duane Ward .15 .07
❑ 136 Tom Pagnozzi .15 .07
❑ 137 Jeff Huson .15 .07
❑ 138 Kurt Stillwell .15 .07
❑ 139 Dave Henderson .15 .07
❑ 140 Darrin Jackson .15 .07
❑ 141 Frank Castillo .15 .07
❑ 142 Scott Erickson .15 .07
❑ 143 Darryl Kile .30 .14
❑ 144 Bill Wegman .15 .07
❑ 145 Steve Wilson .15 .07
❑ 146 George Brett 1.25 .55
❑ 147 Moises Alou .30 .14
❑ 148 Lou Whitaker .30 .14
❑ 149 Chico Walker .15 .07
❑ 150 Jerry Browne .15 .07
❑ 151 Kirk McCaskill .15 .07
❑ 152 Zane Smith .15 .07
❑ 153 Matt Young .15 .07
❑ 154 Lee Smith .30 .14
❑ 155 Leo Gomez .15 .07
❑ 156 Dan Walters .15 .07
❑ 157 Pat Borders .15 .07
❑ 158 Matt Williams .40 .18
❑ 159 Dean Palmer .30 .14
❑ 160 John Patterson .15 .07
❑ 161 Doug Jones .15 .07
❑ 162 John Habyan .15 .07
❑ 163 Pedro Martinez .75 .35
❑ 164 Carl Willis .15 .07
❑ 165 Darrin Fletcher .15 .07
❑ 166 B.J. Surhoff .30 .14
❑ 167 Eddie Murray .60 .25
❑ 168 Keith Miller .15 .07
❑ 169 Ricky Jordan .15 .07
❑ 170 Juan Gonzalez 1.50 .70
❑ 171 Charles Nagy .30 .14
❑ 172 Mark Clark .15 .07
❑ 173 Bobby Thigpen .15 .07
❑ 174 Tim Scott .15 .07
❑ 175 Scott Cooper .15 .07
❑ 176 Royce Clayton .15 .07
❑ 177 Brady Anderson .40 .18
❑ 178 Sid Bream .15 .07
❑ 179 Derek Bell .30 .14
❑ 180 Otis Nixon .15 .07
❑ 181 Kevin Gross .15 .07
❑ 182 Ron Darling .15 .07
❑ 183 John Wetteland .30 .14
❑ 184 Mike Stanley .15 .07
❑ 185 Jeff Kent .30 .14
❑ 186 Brian Harper .15 .07
❑ 187 Mariano Duncan .15 .07
❑ 188 Robin Yount .40 .18
❑ 189 Al Martin .15 .07
❑ 190 Eddie Zosky .15 .07
❑ 191 Mike Munoz .15 .07
❑ 192 Andy Benes .30 .14
❑ 193 Dennis Cook .15 .07
❑ 194 Bill Swift .15 .07
❑ 195 Frank Thomas 2.00 .90
❑ 196 Damon Berryhill .15 .07
❑ 197 Mike Greenwell .15 .07
❑ 198 Mark Grace .40 .18
❑ 199 Darryl Hamilton .15 .07
❑ 200 Derrick May .15 .07
❑ 201 Ken Hill .15 .07
❑ 202 Kevin Brown .40 .18
❑ 203 Dwight Gooden .30 .14
❑ 204 Bobby Witt .15 .07
❑ 205 Juan Bell .15 .07
❑ 206 Kevin Maas .15 .07
❑ 207 Jeff King .30 .14
❑ 208 Scott Leius .15 .07
❑ 209 Rheal Cormier .15 .07
❑ 210 Darryl Strawberry .30 .14
❑ 211 Tom Gordon .30 .14
❑ 212 Bud Black .15 .07
❑ 213 Mickey Tettleton .15 .07
❑ 214 Pete Smith .15 .07
❑ 215 Felix Fermin .15 .07
❑ 216 Rick Wilkins .15 .07
❑ 217 George Bell .15 .07
❑ 218 Eric Anthony .15 .07
❑ 219 Pedro Munoz .15 .07
❑ 220 Checklist .15 .07
❑ 221 Lance Blankenship .15 .07
❑ 222 Deion Sanders .40 .18
❑ 223 Craig Biggio .60 .25
❑ 224 Ryne Sandberg .75 .35
❑ 225 Ron Gant .30 .14
❑ 226 Tom Brunansky .15 .07
❑ 227 Chad Curtis .30 .14
❑ 228 Joe Carter .30 .14
❑ 229 Brian Jordan .30 .14
❑ 230 Brett Butler .30 .14
❑ 231 Frank Bolick .15 .07
❑ 232 Rod Beck .30 .14
❑ 233 Carlos Baerga .15 .07
❑ 234 Eric Karros .40 .18
❑ 235 Jack Armstrong .15 .07
❑ 236 Bobby Bonilla .30 .14
❑ 237 Don Mattingly 1.00 .45
❑ 238 Jeff Gardner .15 .07
❑ 239 Dave Hollins .15 .07
❑ 240 Steve Cooke .15 .07
❑ 241 Jose Canseco .60 .25
❑ 242 Ivan Calderon .15 .07
❑ 243 Tim Belcher .15 .07
❑ 244 Freddie Benavides .15 .07
❑ 245 Roberto Alomar .60 .25
❑ 246 Rob Deer .15 .07
❑ 247 Will Clark .60 .25
❑ 248 Mike Felder .15 .07
❑ 249 Harold Baines .30 .14
❑ 250 David Cone .30 .14
❑ 251 Mark Guthrie .15 .07
❑ 252 Ellis Burks .30 .14
❑ 253 Jim Abbott .30 .14
❑ 254 Chili Davis .30 .14
❑ 255 Chris Bosio .15 .07
❑ 256 Bret Barberie .15 .07
❑ 257 Hal Morris .15 .07
❑ 258 Dante Bichette .30 .14
❑ 259 Storm Davis .15 .07
❑ 260 Gary DiSarcina .15 .07
❑ 261 Ken Caminiti .40 .18
❑ 262 Paul Molitor .60 .25
❑ 263 Joe Oliver .15 .07
❑ 264 Pat Listach .15 .07
❑ 265 Gregg Jefferies .15 .07
❑ 266 Jose Guzman .15 .07
❑ 267 Eric Davis .30 .14
❑ 268 Delino DeShields .30 .14
❑ 269 Barry Bonds .75 .35
❑ 270 Mike Bielecki .15 .07
❑ 271 Jay Buhner .40 .18
❑ 272 Scott Pose .15 .07
❑ 273 Tony Fernandez .15 .07
❑ 274 Chito Martinez .15 .07
❑ 275 Phil Plantier .15 .07
❑ 276 Pete Incaviglia .15 .07
❑ 277 Carlos Garcia .15 .07
❑ 278 Tom Henke .15 .07
❑ 279 Roger Clemens 1.25 .55
❑ 280 Rob Dibble .15 .07
❑ 281 Daryl Boston .15 .07
❑ 282 Greg Gagne .15 .07
❑ 283 Cecil Fielder .30 .14
❑ 284 Carlton Fisk .60 .25
❑ 285 Wade Boggs .60 .25
❑ 286 Damion Easley .30 .14
❑ 287 Norm Charlton .15 .07
❑ 288 Jeff Conine .15 .07
❑ 289 Roberto Kelly .15 .07
❑ 290 Jerald Clark .15 .07
❑ 291 Rickey Henderson .60 .25
❑ 292 Chuck Finley .30 .14
❑ 293 Doug Drabek .15 .07
❑ 294 Dave Stewart .30 .14
❑ 295 Tom Glavine .40 .18
❑ 296 Jaime Navarro .15 .07
❑ 297 Ray Lankford .40 .18
❑ 298 Greg Hibbard .15 .07
❑ 299 Jody Reed .15 .07
❑ 300 Dennis Martinez .30 .14
❑ 301 Dave Martinez .15 .07
❑ 302 Reggie Jefferson .30 .14
❑ 303 John Cummings .15 .07
❑ 304 Orestes Destrade .15 .07
❑ 305 Mike Maddux .15 .07
❑ 306 David Segui .15 .07
❑ 307 Gary Sheffield .60 .25
❑ 308 Danny Jackson .15 .07
❑ 309 Craig Lefferts .15 .07
❑ 310 Andre Dawson .40 .18
❑ 311 Barry Larkin .40 .18
❑ 312 Alex Cole .15 .07
❑ 313 Mark Gardner .15 .07
❑ 314 Kirk Gibson .30 .14
❑ 315 Shane Mack .15 .07
❑ 316 Bo Jackson .30 .14
❑ 317 Jimmy Key .30 .14
❑ 318 Greg Myers .15 .07
❑ 319 Ken Griffey Jr. 3.00 1.35
❑ 320 Monty Fariss .15 .07
❑ 321 Kevin Mitchell .30 .14
❑ 322 Andres Galarraga .60 .25
❑ 323 Mark McGwire 3.00 1.35
❑ 324 Mark Langston .15 .07
❑ 325 Steve Finley .30 .14
❑ 326 Greg Maddux 2.00 .90
❑ 327 Dave Nilsson .30 .14
❑ 328 Ozzie Smith .75 .35
❑ 329 Candy Maldonado .15 .07

	No.	Player	Mint	NRMT
❑	330	Checklist	.15	.07
❑	331	Tim Pugh	.15	.07
❑	332	Joe Girardi	.30	.14
❑	333	Junior Felix	.15	.07
❑	334	Greg Swindell	.15	.07
❑	335	Ramon Martinez	.30	.14
❑	336	Sean Berry	.15	.07
❑	337	Joe Orsulak	.15	.07
❑	338	Wes Chamberlain	.15	.07
❑	339	Stan Belinda	.15	.07
❑	340	Checklist UER (306 Luis Mercedes)	.15	.07
❑	341	Bruce Hurst	.15	.07
❑	342	John Burkett	.15	.07
❑	343	Mike Mussina	.60	.25
❑	344	Scott Fletcher	.15	.07
❑	345	Rene Gonzales	.15	.07
❑	346	Roberto Hernandez	.30	.14
❑	347	Carlos Martinez	.15	.07
❑	348	Bill Krueger	.15	.07
❑	349	Felix Jose	.15	.07
❑	350	John Jaha	.15	.07
❑	351	Willie Banks	.15	.07
❑	352	Matt Nokes	.15	.07
❑	353	Kevin Seitzer	.15	.07
❑	354	Erik Hanson	.15	.07
❑	355	David Hulse	.15	.07
❑	356	Domingo Martinez	.15	.07
❑	357	Greg Olson	.15	.07
❑	358	Randy Myers	.30	.14
❑	359	Tom Browning	.15	.07
❑	360	Charlie Hayes	.15	.07
❑	361	Bryan Harvey	.15	.07
❑	362	Eddie Taubensee	.15	.07
❑	363	Tim Wallach	.15	.07
❑	364	Mel Rojas	.15	.07
❑	365	Frank Tanana	.15	.07
❑	366	John Kruk	.30	.14
❑	367	Tim Laker	.15	.07
❑	368	Rich Rodriguez	.15	.07
❑	369	Darren Lewis	.15	.07
❑	370	Harold Reynolds	.15	.07
❑	371	Jose Melendez	.15	.07
❑	372	Joe Grahe	.15	.07
❑	373	Lance Johnson	.15	.07
❑	374	Jose Mesa	.15	.07
❑	375	Scott Livingstone	.15	.07
❑	376	Wally Joyner	.30	.14
❑	377	Kevin Reimer	.15	.07
❑	378	Kirby Puckett	1.00	.45
❑	379	Paul O'Neill	.30	.14
❑	380	Randy Johnson	.60	.25
❑	381	Manuel Lee	.15	.07
❑	382	Dick Schofield	.15	.07
❑	383	Darren Holmes	.15	.07
❑	384	Charlie Hough	.30	.14
❑	385	John Orton	.15	.07
❑	386	Edgar Martinez	.40	.18
❑	387	Terry Pendleton	.15	.07
❑	388	Dan Plesac	.15	.07
❑	389	Jeff Reardon	.30	.14
❑	390	David Nied	.15	.07
❑	391	Dave Magadan	.15	.07
❑	392	Larry Walker	.60	.25
❑	393	Ben Rivera	.15	.07
❑	394	Lonnie Smith	.15	.07
❑	395	Craig Shipley	.15	.07
❑	396	Willie McGee	.30	.14
❑	397	Arthur Rhodes	.15	.07
❑	398	Mike Stanton	.15	.07
❑	399	Luis Polonia	.15	.07
❑	400	Jack McDowell	.15	.07
❑	401	Mike Moore	.15	.07
❑	402	Jose Lind	.15	.07
❑	403	Bill Spiers	.15	.07
❑	404	Kevin Tapani	.15	.07
❑	405	Spike Owen	.15	.07
❑	406	Tino Martinez	.60	.25
❑	407	Charlie Leibrandt	.15	.07
❑	408	Ed Sprague	.15	.07
❑	409	Bryn Smith	.15	.07
❑	410	Benito Santiago	.15	.07
❑	411	Jose Rijo	.15	.07
❑	412	Pete O'Brien	.15	.07
❑	413	Willie Wilson	.15	.07
❑	414	Bip Roberts	.15	.07
❑	415	Eric Young	.60	.25
❑	416	Walt Weiss	.15	.07
❑	417	Milt Thompson	.15	.07
❑	418	Chris Sabo	.15	.07
❑	419	Scott Sanderson	.15	.07
❑	420	Tim Raines	.30	.14
❑	421	Alan Trammell	.40	.18
❑	422	Mike Macfarlane	.15	.07
❑	423	Dave Winfield	.40	.18
❑	424	Bob Wickman	.15	.07
❑	425	David Valle	.15	.07
❑	426	Gary Redus	.15	.07
❑	427	Turner Ward	.15	.07
❑	428	Reggie Sanders	.15	.07
❑	429	Todd Worrell	.15	.07
❑	430	Julio Valera	.15	.07
❑	431	Cal Ripken Jr.	2.50	1.10
❑	432	Mo Vaughn	.75	.35
❑	433	John Smiley	.15	.07
❑	434	Omar Vizquel	.30	.14
❑	435	Billy Ripken	.15	.07
❑	436	Cory Snyder	.15	.07
❑	437	Carlos Quintana	.15	.07
❑	438	Omar Olivares	.15	.07
❑	439	Robin Ventura	.30	.14
❑	440	Checklist	.15	.07
❑	441	Kevin Higgins	.15	.07
❑	442	Carlos Hernandez	.15	.07
❑	443	Dan Peltier	.15	.07
❑	444	Derek Lilliquist	.15	.07
❑	445	Tim Salmon	.60	.25
❑	446	Sherman Obando	.15	.07
❑	447	Pat Kelly	.15	.07
❑	448	Todd Van Poppel	.15	.07
❑	449	Mark Whiten	.15	.07
❑	450	Checklist	.15	.07
❑	451	Pat Meares	.15	.07
❑	452	Tony Tarasco	.15	.07
❑	453	Chris Gwynn	.15	.07
❑	454	Armando Reynoso	.15	.07
❑	455	Danny Darwin	.15	.07
❑	456	Willie Greene	.15	.07
❑	457	Mike Blowers	.15	.07
❑	458	Kevin Roberson	.15	.07
❑	459	Graeme Lloyd	.15	.07
❑	460	David West	.15	.07
❑	461	Joey Cora	.30	.14
❑	462	Alex Arias	.15	.07
❑	463	Chad Kreuter	.15	.07
❑	464	Mike Lansing	.30	.14
❑	465	Mike Timlin	.15	.07
❑	466	Paul Wagner	.15	.07
❑	467	Mark Portugal	.15	.07
❑	468	Jim Leyritz	.15	.07
❑	469	Ryan Klesko	.60	.25
❑	470	Mario Diaz	.15	.07
❑	471	Guillermo Velasquez	.15	.07
❑	472	Fernando Valenzuela	.30	.14
❑	473	Raul Mondesi	.75	.35
❑	474	Mike Pagliarulo	.15	.07
❑	475	Chris Hammond	.15	.07
❑	476	Torey Lovullo	.15	.07
❑	477	Trevor Wilson	.15	.07
❑	478	Marcos Armas	.15	.07
❑	479	Dave Gallagher	.15	.07
❑	480	Jeff Treadway	.15	.07
❑	481	Jeff Branson	.15	.07
❑	482	Dickie Thon	.15	.07
❑	483	Eduardo Perez	.15	.07
❑	484	David Wells	.30	.14
❑	485	Brian Williams	.15	.07
❑	486	Domingo Cedeno	.15	.07
❑	487	Tom Candiotti	.15	.07
❑	488	Steve Frey	.15	.07
❑	489	Greg McMichael	.15	.07
❑	490	Marc Newfield	.15	.07
❑	491	Larry Andersen	.15	.07
❑	492	Damon Buford	.15	.07
❑	493	Ricky Gutierrez	.15	.07
❑	494	Jeff Russell	.15	.07
❑	495	Vinny Castilla	.75	.35
❑	496	Wilson Alvarez	.30	.14
❑	497	Scott Bullett	.15	.07
❑	498	Larry Casian	.15	.07
❑	499	Jose Vizcaino	.15	.07
❑	500	J.T. Snow	.75	.35
❑	501	Bryan Hickerson	.15	.07
❑	502	Jeremy Hernandez	.15	.07
❑	503	Jeromy Burnitz	.30	.14
❑	504	Steve Farr	.15	.07
❑	505	J. Owens	.15	.07
❑	506	Craig Paquette	.15	.07
❑	507	Jim Eisenreich	.15	.07
❑	508	Matt Whiteside	.15	.07
❑	509	Luis Aquino	.15	.07
❑	510	Mike LaValliere	.15	.07
❑	511	Jim Gott	.15	.07
❑	512	Mark McLemore	.15	.07
❑	513	Randy Milligan	.15	.07
❑	514	Gary Gaetti	.15	.07
❑	515	Lou Frazier	.15	.07
❑	516	Rich Amaral	.15	.07
❑	517	Gene Harris	.15	.07
❑	518	Aaron Sele	.60	.25
❑	519	Mark Wohlers	.15	.07
❑	520	Scott Kamieniecki	.15	.07
❑	521	Kent Mercker	.15	.07
❑	522	Jim Deshaies	.15	.07
❑	523	Kevin Stocker	.15	.07
❑	524	Jason Bere	.15	.07
❑	525	Tim Bogar	.15	.07
❑	526	Brad Pennington	.15	.07
❑	527	Curt Leskanic	.15	.07
❑	528	Wayne Kirby	.15	.07
❑	529	Tim Costo	.15	.07
❑	530	Doug Henry	.15	.07
❑	531	Trevor Hoffman	.60	.25
❑	532	Kelly Gruber	.15	.07
❑	533	Mike Harkey	.15	.07
❑	534	John Doherty	.15	.07
❑	535	Erik Pappas	.15	.07
❑	536	Brent Gates	.15	.07
❑	537	Roger McDowell	.15	.07
❑	538	Chris Haney	.15	.07
❑	539	Blas Minor	.15	.07
❑	540	Pat Hentgen	.40	.18
❑	541	Chuck Carr	.15	.07
❑	542	Doug Strange	.15	.07
❑	543	Xavier Hernandez	.15	.07
❑	544	Paul Quantrill	.15	.07
❑	545	Anthony Young	.15	.07
❑	546	Bret Boone	.30	.14
❑	547	Dwight Smith	.15	.07
❑	548	Bobby Munoz	.15	.07
❑	549	Russ Springer	.15	.07
❑	550	Roger Pavlik	.15	.07
❑	DW	Dave Winfield 3000 Hits	1.00	.45
❑	FT	Frank Thomas AU/3500 (Certified autograph)	150.00	70.00

1993 Leaf Fasttrack

	MINT	NRMT
COMPLETE SET (20)	100.00	45.00
COMPLETE SERIES 1 (10)	60.00	27.00
COMPLETE SERIES 2 (10)	40.00	18.00
COMMON CARD (1-20)	2.00	.90

	No.	Player	MINT	NRMT
❑	1	Frank Thomas	25.00	11.00
❑	2	Tim Wakefield	3.00	1.35
❑	3	Kenny Lofton	7.50	3.40

❑ 4 Mike Mussina	8.00	3.60
❑ 5 Juan Gonzalez	20.00	9.00
❑ 6 Chuck Knoblauch	8.00	3.60
❑ 7 Eric Karros	5.00	2.20
❑ 8 Ray Lankford	5.00	2.20
❑ 9 Juan Guzman	2.00	.90
❑ 10 Pat Listach	2.00	.90
❑ 11 Carlos Baerga	2.00	.90
❑ 12 Felix Jose	2.00	.90
❑ 13 Steve Avery	2.00	.90
❑ 14 Robin Ventura	3.00	1.35
❑ 15 Ivan Rodriguez	10.00	4.50
❑ 16 Cal Eldred	2.00	.90
❑ 17 Jeff Bagwell	12.00	5.50
❑ 18 David Justice	8.00	3.60
❑ 19 Travis Fryman	3.00	1.35
❑ 20 Marquis Grissom	3.00	1.35

1993 Leaf Gold All-Stars

	MINT	NRMT
COMPLETE REG.SET (20)	40.00	18.00
COMPLETE UPDATE SET (10)	12.00	5.50
COMMON CARD (R1-U10)	.50	.23
❑ R1 Ivan Rodriguez	.75	.35
Darren Daulton		
❑ R2 Don Mattingly	1.50	.70
Fred McGriff		
❑ R3 Cecil Fielder	1.50	.70
Jeff Bagwell		
❑ R4 Carlos Baerga	1.50	.70
Ryne Sandberg		
❑ R5 Chuck Knoblauch	1.00	.45
Delino DeShields		
❑ R6 Robin Ventura	.50	.23
Terry Pendleton		
❑ R7 Ken Griffey Jr.	5.00	2.20
Andy Van Slyke		
❑ R8 Joe Carter	.75	.35
Dave Justice		
❑ R9 Jose Canseco	2.50	1.10
Tony Gwynn		
❑ R10 Dennis Eckersley	.50	.23
Rob Dibble		
❑ R11 Mark McGwire	5.00	2.20
Will Clark		
❑ R12 Frank Thomas	3.00	1.35
Mark Grace		
❑ R13 Roberto Alomar	1.50	.70
Craig Biggio		
❑ R14 Cal Ripken	4.00	1.80
Barry Larkin		
❑ R15 Edgar Martinez	1.00	.45
Gary Sheffield		
❑ R16 Juan Gonzalez	2.50	1.10
Barry Bonds		
❑ R17 Kirby Puckett	1.50	.70
Marquis Grissom		
❑ R18 Jim Abbott	.75	.35
Tom Glavine		
❑ R19 Nolan Ryan	8.00	3.60
Greg Maddux		
❑ R20 Roger Clemens	1.00	.45
Doug Drabek		
❑ U1 Mark Langston	.50	.23
Terry Mulholland		
❑ U2 Ivan Rodriguez	.75	.35
Darren Daulton		
❑ U3 John Olerud	.50	.23
John Kruk		
❑ U4 Roberto Alomar	1.50	.70
Ryne Sandberg		
❑ U5 Wade Boggs	1.50	.70
Gary Sheffield		
❑ U6 Cal Ripken	4.00	1.80
Barry Larkin		
❑ U7 Kirby Puckett	2.00	.90
Barry Bonds		
❑ U8 Ken Griffey Jr.	5.00	2.20
Marquis Grissom		
❑ U9 Joe Carter	1.00	.45
David Justice		
❑ U10 Paul Molitor	1.00	.45
Mark Grace		

1993 Leaf Gold Rookies

	MINT	NRMT
COMPLETE REG.SET (20)	40.00	18.00
COMPLETE UPDATE SET (5)	20.00	9.00
COMMON CARD (R1-U5)	1.00	.45
*JUMBOS:2X BASIC GOLD ROOKIES		
❑ R1 Kevin Young	1.25	.55
❑ R2 Wil Cordero	1.00	.45
❑ R3 Mark Kiefer	1.00	.45
❑ R4 Gerald Williams	1.00	.45
❑ R5 Brandon Wilson	1.00	.45
❑ R6 Greg Gohr	1.00	.45
❑ R7 Ryan Thompson	1.00	.45
❑ R8 Tim Wakefield	1.25	.55
❑ R9 Troy Neel	1.00	.45
❑ R10 Tim Salmon	6.00	2.70
❑ R11 Kevin Rogers	1.00	.45
❑ R12 Rod Bolton	1.00	.45
❑ R13 Ken Ryan	1.00	.45
❑ R14 Phil Hiatt	1.00	.45
❑ R15 Rene Arocha	1.00	.45
❑ R16 Nigel Wilson	1.00	.45
❑ R17 J.T. Snow	3.00	1.35
❑ R18 Benji Gil	1.00	.45
❑ R19 Chipper Jones	20.00	9.00
❑ R20 Darrell Sherman	1.00	.45
❑ U1 Allen Watson	1.00	.45
❑ U2 Jeffrey Hammonds	1.25	.55
❑ U3 Dave McCarty	1.00	.45
❑ U4 Mike Piazza	15.00	6.75
❑ U5 Roberto Mejia	1.00	.45

1993 Leaf Heading for the Hall

	MINT	NRMT
COMPLETE SET (10)	30.00	13.50
COMPLETE SERIES 1 (5)	20.00	9.00
COMPLETE SERIES 2 (5)	10.00	4.50
COMMON CARD (1-10)	2.00	.90
❑ 1 Nolan Ryan	10.00	4.50
❑ 2 Tony Gwynn	6.00	2.70
❑ 3 Robin Yount	2.00	.90
❑ 4 Eddie Murray	2.50	1.10
❑ 5 Cal Ripken	10.00	4.50
❑ 6 Roger Clemens	5.00	2.20
❑ 7 George Brett	5.00	2.20
❑ 8 Ryne Sandberg	3.00	1.35
❑ 9 Kirby Puckett	4.00	1.80
❑ 10 Ozzie Smith	3.00	1.35

1993 Leaf Thomas

	MINT	NRMT
COMPLETE SET (10)	40.00	18.00
COMMON THOMAS (1-10)	5.00	2.20
❑ 1 Frank Thomas	5.00	2.20
Aggressive		
❑ 2 Frank Thomas	5.00	2.20
Serious		
❑ 3 Frank Thomas	5.00	2.20
Intense		
❑ 4 Frank Thomas	5.00	2.20
Confident		
❑ 5 Frank Thomas	5.00	2.20
Assertive		
❑ 6 Frank Thomas	5.00	2.20
Power		
❑ 7 Frank Thomas	5.00	2.20
Control		
❑ 8 Frank Thomas	5.00	2.20
Strength		
❑ 9 Frank Thomas	5.00	2.20
Concentration		
❑ 10 Frank Thomas	5.00	2.20
Preparation		

1994 Leaf

	MINT	NRMT
COMPLETE SET (440)	24.00	11.00
COMPLETE SERIES 1 (220)	12.00	5.50
COMPLETE SERIES 2 (220)	12.00	5.50
COMMON CARD (1-440)	.15	.07
❑ 1 Cal Ripken Jr.	2.50	1.10
❑ 2 Tony Tarasco	.15	.07
❑ 3 Joe Girardi	.15	.07
❑ 4 Bernie Williams	.60	.25
❑ 5 Chad Kreuter	.15	.07
❑ 6 Troy Neel	.15	.07
❑ 7 Tom Pagnozzi	.15	.07
❑ 8 Kirk Rueter	.15	.07
❑ 9 Chris Bosio	.15	.07
❑ 10 Dwight Gooden	.30	.14
❑ 11 Mariano Duncan	.15	.07
❑ 12 Jay Bell	.30	.14

❑ 13 Lance Johnson .15 .07
❑ 14 Richie Lewis .15 .07
❑ 15 Dave Martinez .15 .07
❑ 16 Orel Hershiser .30 .14
❑ 17 Rob Butler .15 .07
❑ 18 Glenallen Hill .15 .07
❑ 19 Chad Curtis .15 .07
❑ 20 Mike Stanton .15 .07
❑ 21 Tim Wallach .15 .07
❑ 22 Milt Thompson .15 .07
❑ 23 Kevin Young .15 .07
❑ 24 John Smiley .15 .07
❑ 25 Jeff Montgomery .15 .07
❑ 26 Robin Ventura .30 .14
❑ 27 Scott Lydy .15 .07
❑ 28 Todd Stottlemyre .15 .07
❑ 29 Mark Whiten .15 .07
❑ 30 Robby Thompson .15 .07
❑ 31 Bobby Bonilla .30 .14
❑ 32 Andy Ashby .15 .07
❑ 33 Greg Myers .15 .07
❑ 34 Billy Hatcher .15 .07
❑ 35 Brad Holman .15 .07
❑ 36 Mark McLemore .15 .07
❑ 37 Scott Sanders .15 .07
❑ 38 Jim Abbott .30 .14
❑ 39 David Wells .40 .18
❑ 40 Roberto Kelly .15 .07
❑ 41 Jeff Conine .30 .14
❑ 42 Sean Berry .15 .07
❑ 43 Mark Grace .40 .18
❑ 44 Eric Young .15 .07
❑ 45 Rick Aguilera .15 .07
❑ 46 Chipper Jones 2.00 .90
❑ 47 Mel Rojas .15 .07
❑ 48 Ryan Thompson .15 .07
❑ 49 Al Martin .15 .07
❑ 50 Cecil Fielder .30 .14
❑ 51 Pat Kelly .15 .07
❑ 52 Kevin Tapani .15 .07
❑ 53 Tim Costo .15 .07
❑ 54 Dave Hollins .15 .07
❑ 55 Kirt Manwaring .15 .07
❑ 56 Gregg Jefferies .15 .07
❑ 57 Ron Darling .15 .07
❑ 58 Bill Haselman .15 .07
❑ 59 Phil Plantier .15 .07
❑ 60 Frank Viola .15 .07
❑ 61 Todd Zeile .15 .07
❑ 62 Bret Barberie .15 .07
❑ 63 Roberto Mejia .15 .07
❑ 64 Chuck Knoblauch .60 .25
❑ 65 Jose Lind .15 .07
❑ 66 Brady Anderson .30 .14
❑ 67 Ruben Sierra .15 .07
❑ 68 Jose Vizcaino .15 .07
❑ 69 Joe Grahe .15 .07
❑ 70 Kevin Appier .30 .14
❑ 71 Wilson Alvarez .30 .14
❑ 72 Tom Candiotti .15 .07
❑ 73 John Burkett .15 .07
❑ 74 Anthony Young .15 .07
❑ 75 Scott Cooper .15 .07
❑ 76 Nigel Wilson .15 .07
❑ 77 John Valentin .30 .14
❑ 78 Dave McCarty .15 .07
❑ 79 Archi Cianfrocco .15 .07
❑ 80 Lou Whitaker .30 .14
❑ 81 Dante Bichette .30 .14
❑ 82 Mark Dewey .15 .07
❑ 83 Danny Jackson .15 .07
❑ 84 Harold Baines .30 .14
❑ 85 Todd Benzinger .15 .07
❑ 86 Damion Easley .30 .14
❑ 87 Danny Cox .15 .07
❑ 88 Jose Bautista .15 .07
❑ 89 Mike Lansing .30 .14
❑ 90 Phil Hiatt .15 .07
❑ 91 Tim Pugh .15 .07
❑ 92 Tino Martinez .60 .25
❑ 93 Raul Mondesi .60 .25
❑ 94 Greg Maddux 2.00 .90
❑ 95 Al Leiter .30 .14
❑ 96 Benito Santiago .15 .07
❑ 97 Lenny Dykstra .30 .14
❑ 98 Sammy Sosa 2.00 .90
❑ 99 Tim Bogar .15 .07
❑ 100 Checklist .15 .07
❑ 101 Deion Sanders .30 .14
❑ 102 Bobby Witt .15 .07
❑ 103 Wil Cordero .15 .07
❑ 104 Rich Amaral .15 .07
❑ 105 Mike Mussina .60 .25
❑ 106 Reggie Sanders .30 .14
❑ 107 Ozzie Guillen .15 .07
❑ 108 Paul O'Neill .30 .14
❑ 109 Tim Salmon .60 .25
❑ 110 Rheal Cormier .15 .07
❑ 111 Billy Ashley .15 .07
❑ 112 Jeff Kent .30 .14
❑ 113 Derek Bell .30 .14
❑ 114 Danny Darwin .15 .07
❑ 115 Chip Hale .15 .07
❑ 116 Tim Raines .30 .14
❑ 117 Ed Sprague .15 .07
❑ 118 Darrin Fletcher .15 .07
❑ 119 Darren Holmes .15 .07
❑ 120 Alan Trammell .40 .18
❑ 121 Don Mattingly 1.00 .45
❑ 122 Greg Gagne .15 .07
❑ 123 Jose Offerman .15 .07
❑ 124 Joe Orsulak .15 .07
❑ 125 Jack McDowell .15 .07
❑ 126 Barry Larkin .40 .18
❑ 127 Ben McDonald .15 .07
❑ 128 Mike Bordick .15 .07
❑ 129 Devon White .30 .14
❑ 130 Mike Perez .15 .07
❑ 131 Jay Buhner .30 .14
❑ 132 Phil Leftwich .15 .07
❑ 133 Tommy Greene .15 .07
❑ 134 Charlie Hayes .15 .07
❑ 135 Don Slaught .15 .07
❑ 136 Mike Gallego .15 .07
❑ 137 Dave Winfield .60 .25
❑ 138 Steve Avery .15 .07
❑ 139 Derrick May .15 .07
❑ 140 Bryan Harvey .15 .07
❑ 141 Wally Joyner .30 .14
❑ 142 Andre Dawson .40 .18
❑ 143 Andy Benes .30 .14
❑ 144 John Franco .30 .14
❑ 145 Jeff King .15 .07
❑ 146 Joe Oliver .15 .07
❑ 147 Bill Gullickson .15 .07
❑ 148 Armando Reynoso .15 .07
❑ 149 Dave Fleming .15 .07
❑ 150 Checklist .15 .07
❑ 151 Todd Van Poppel .15 .07
❑ 152 Bernard Gilkey .15 .07
❑ 153 Kevin Gross .15 .07
❑ 154 Mike Devereaux .15 .07
❑ 155 Tim Wakefield .30 .14
❑ 156 Andres Galarraga .60 .25
❑ 157 Pat Meares .15 .07
❑ 158 Jim Leyritz .30 .14
❑ 159 Mike Macfarlane .15 .07
❑ 160 Tony Phillips .15 .07
❑ 161 Brent Gates .15 .07
❑ 162 Mark Langston .15 .07
❑ 163 Allen Watson .15 .07
❑ 164 Randy Johnson .60 .25
❑ 165 Doug Brocail .15 .07
❑ 166 Rob Dibble .15 .07
❑ 167 Roberto Hernandez .15 .07
❑ 168 Felix Jose .15 .07
❑ 169 Steve Cooke .15 .07
❑ 170 Darren Daulton .30 .14
❑ 171 Eric Karros .30 .14
❑ 172 Geronimo Pena .15 .07
❑ 173 Gary DiSarcina .15 .07
❑ 174 Marquis Grissom .30 .14
❑ 175 Joey Cora .30 .14
❑ 176 Jim Eisenreich .15 .07
❑ 177 Brad Pennington .15 .07
❑ 178 Terry Steinbach .30 .14
❑ 179 Pat Borders .15 .07
❑ 180 Steve Buechele .15 .07
❑ 181 Jeff Fassero .15 .07
❑ 182 Mike Greenwell .15 .07
❑ 183 Mike Henneman .15 .07
❑ 184 Ron Karkovice .15 .07
❑ 185 Pat Hentgen .30 .14
❑ 186 Jose Guzman .15 .07
❑ 187 Brett Butler .30 .14
❑ 188 Charlie Hough .15 .07
❑ 189 Terry Pendleton .15 .07
❑ 190 Melido Perez .15 .07
❑ 191 Orestes Destrade .15 .07
❑ 192 Mike Morgan .15 .07
❑ 193 Joe Carter .30 .14
❑ 194 Jeff Blauser .15 .07
❑ 195 Chris Hoiles .15 .07
❑ 196 Ricky Gutierrez .15 .07
❑ 197 Mike Moore .15 .07
❑ 198 Carl Willis .15 .07
❑ 199 Aaron Sele .30 .14
❑ 200 Checklist .15 .07
❑ 201 Tim Naehring .15 .07
❑ 202 Scott Livingstone .15 .07
❑ 203 Luis Alicea .15 .07
❑ 204 Torey Lovullo .15 .07
❑ 205 Jim Gott .15 .07
❑ 206 Bob Wickman .15 .07
❑ 207 Greg McMichael .15 .07
❑ 208 Scott Brosius .30 .14
❑ 209 Chris Gwynn .15 .07
❑ 210 Steve Sax .15 .07
❑ 211 Dick Schofield .15 .07
❑ 212 Robb Nen .15 .07
❑ 213 Ben Rivera .15 .07
❑ 214 Vinny Castilla .30 .14
❑ 215 Jamie Moyer .15 .07
❑ 216 Wally Whitehurst .15 .07
❑ 217 Frank Castillo .15 .07
❑ 218 Mike Blowers .15 .07
❑ 219 Tim Scott .15 .07
❑ 220 Paul Wagner .15 .07
❑ 221 Jeff Bagwell 1.00 .45
❑ 222 Ricky Bones .15 .07
❑ 223 Sandy Alomar Jr. .30 .14
❑ 224 Rod Beck .15 .07
❑ 225 Roberto Alomar .60 .25
❑ 226 Jack Armstrong .15 .07
❑ 227 Scott Erickson .30 .14
❑ 228 Rene Arocha .15 .07
❑ 229 Eric Anthony .15 .07
❑ 230 Jeromy Burnitz .30 .14
❑ 231 Kevin Brown .30 .14
❑ 232 Tim Belcher .15 .07
❑ 233 Bret Boone .30 .14
❑ 234 Dennis Eckersley .30 .14
❑ 235 Tom Glavine .60 .25
❑ 236 Craig Biggio .60 .25
❑ 237 Pedro Astacio .15 .07
❑ 238 Ryan Bowen .15 .07
❑ 239 Brad Ausmus .15 .07
❑ 240 Vince Coleman .15 .07
❑ 241 Jason Bere .15 .07
❑ 242 Ellis Burks .30 .14
❑ 243 Wes Chamberlain .15 .07
❑ 244 Ken Caminiti .40 .18
❑ 245 Willie Banks .15 .07
❑ 246 Sid Fernandez .15 .07
❑ 247 Carlos Baerga .30 .14
❑ 248 Carlos Garcia .15 .07
❑ 249 Jose Canseco .60 .25
❑ 250 Alex Diaz .15 .07

❑ 251 Albert Belle .75 .35
❑ 252 Moises Alou .40 .18
❑ 253 Bobby Ayala .15 .07
❑ 254 Tony Gwynn 1.50 .70
❑ 255 Roger Clemens 1.25 .55
❑ 256 Eric Davis .30 .14
❑ 257 Wade Boggs .60 .25
❑ 258 Chili Davis .30 .14
❑ 259 Rickey Henderson .60 .25
❑ 260 Andujar Cedeno .15 .07
❑ 261 Cris Carpenter .15 .07
❑ 262 Juan Guzman .15 .07
❑ 263 David Justice .60 .25
❑ 264 Barry Bonds .75 .35
❑ 265 Pete Incaviglia .15 .07
❑ 266 Tony Fernandez .15 .07
❑ 267 Cal Eldred .15 .07
❑ 268 Alex Fernandez .15 .07
❑ 269 Kent Hrbek .30 .14
❑ 270 Steve Farr .15 .07
❑ 271 Doug Drabek .15 .07
❑ 272 Brian Jordan .30 .14
❑ 273 Xavier Hernandez .15 .07
❑ 274 David Cone .40 .18
❑ 275 Brian Hunter .15 .07
❑ 276 Mike Harkey .15 .07
❑ 277 Delino DeShields .15 .07
❑ 278 David Hulse .15 .07
❑ 279 Mickey Tettleton .15 .07
❑ 280 Kevin McReynolds .15 .07
❑ 281 Darryl Hamilton .15 .07
❑ 282 Ken Hill .15 .07
❑ 283 Wayne Kirby .15 .07
❑ 284 Chris Hammond .15 .07
❑ 285 Mo Vaughn .75 .35
❑ 286 Ryan Klesko .30 .14
❑ 287 Rick Wilkins .15 .07
❑ 288 Bill Swift .15 .07
❑ 289 Rafael Palmeiro .40 .18
❑ 290 Brian Harper .15 .07
❑ 291 Chris Turner .15 .07
❑ 292 Luis Gonzalez .15 .07
❑ 293 Kenny Rogers .15 .07
❑ 294 Kirby Puckett 1.00 .45
❑ 295 Mike Stanley .15 .07
❑ 296 Carlos Reyes .15 .07
❑ 297 Charles Nagy .30 .14
❑ 298 Reggie Jefferson .15 .07
❑ 299 Bip Roberts .15 .07
❑ 300 Darrin Jackson .15 .07
❑ 301 Mike Jackson .15 .07
❑ 302 Dave Nilsson .15 .07
❑ 303 Ramon Martinez .30 .14
❑ 304 Bobby Jones .15 .07
❑ 305 Johnny Ruffin .15 .07
❑ 306 Brian McRae .15 .07
❑ 307 Bo Jackson .30 .14
❑ 308 Dave Stewart .30 .14
❑ 309 John Smoltz .30 .14
❑ 310 Dennis Martinez .30 .14
❑ 311 Dean Palmer .30 .14
❑ 312 David Nied .15 .07
❑ 313 Eddie Murray .60 .25
❑ 314 Darryl Kile .30 .14
❑ 315 Rick Sutcliffe .15 .07
❑ 316 Shawon Dunston .15 .07
❑ 317 John Jaha .15 .07
❑ 318 Salomon Torres .15 .07
❑ 319 Gary Sheffield .60 .25
❑ 320 Curt Schilling .30 .14
❑ 321 Greg Vaughn .30 .14
❑ 322 Jay Howell .15 .07
❑ 323 Todd Hundley .30 .14
❑ 324 Chris Sabo .15 .07
❑ 325 Stan Javier .15 .07
❑ 326 Willie Greene .30 .14
❑ 327 Hipolito Pichardo .15 .07
❑ 328 Doug Strange .15 .07
❑ 329 Dan Wilson .15 .07
❑ 330 Checklist .15 .07
❑ 331 Omar Vizquel .30 .14
❑ 332 Scott Servais .15 .07
❑ 333 Bob Tewksbury .15 .07
❑ 334 Matt Williams .40 .18
❑ 335 Tom Foley .15 .07
❑ 336 Jeff Russell .15 .07
❑ 337 Scott Leius .15 .07
❑ 338 Ivan Rodriguez .75 .35
❑ 339 Kevin Seitzer .15 .07
❑ 340 Jose Rijo .15 .07
❑ 341 Eduardo Perez .15 .07
❑ 342 Kirk Gibson .30 .14
❑ 343 Randy Milligan .15 .07
❑ 344 Edgar Martinez .30 .14
❑ 345 Fred McGriff .40 .18
❑ 346 Kurt Abbott .15 .07
❑ 347 John Kruk .30 .14
❑ 348 Mike Felder .15 .07
❑ 349 Dave Staton .15 .07
❑ 350 Kenny Lofton .60 .25
❑ 351 Graeme Lloyd .15 .07
❑ 352 David Segui .30 .14
❑ 353 Danny Tartabull .15 .07
❑ 354 Bob Welch .15 .07
❑ 355 Duane Ward .15 .07
❑ 356 Karl Rhodes .15 .07
❑ 357 Lee Smith .30 .14
❑ 358 Chris James .15 .07
❑ 359 Walt Weiss .15 .07
❑ 360 Pedro Munoz .15 .07
❑ 361 Paul Sorrento .15 .07
❑ 362 Todd Worrell .15 .07
❑ 363 Bob Hamelin .15 .07
❑ 364 Julio Franco .15 .07
❑ 365 Roberto Petagine .15 .07
❑ 366 Willie McGee .30 .14
❑ 367 Pedro Martinez .75 .35
❑ 368 Ken Griffey Jr. 3.00 1.35
❑ 369 B.J. Surhoff .30 .14
❑ 370 Kevin Mitchell .15 .07
❑ 371 John Doherty .15 .07
❑ 372 Manuel Lee .15 .07
❑ 373 Terry Mulholland .15 .07
❑ 374 Zane Smith .15 .07
❑ 375 Otis Nixon .15 .07
❑ 376 Jody Reed .15 .07
❑ 377 Doug Jones .15 .07
❑ 378 John Olerud .30 .14
❑ 379 Greg Swindell .15 .07
❑ 380 Checklist .15 .07
❑ 381 Royce Clayton .15 .07
❑ 382 Jim Thome .75 .35
❑ 383 Steve Finley .30 .14
❑ 384 Ray Lankford .30 .14
❑ 385 Henry Rodriguez .30 .14
❑ 386 Dave Magadan .15 .07
❑ 387 Gary Redus .15 .07
❑ 388 Orlando Merced .15 .07
❑ 389 Tom Gordon .15 .07
❑ 390 Luis Polonia .15 .07
❑ 391 Mark McGwire 3.00 1.35
❑ 392 Mark Lemke .15 .07
❑ 393 Doug Henry .15 .07
❑ 394 Chuck Finley .30 .14
❑ 395 Paul Molitor .60 .25
❑ 396 Randy Myers .15 .07
❑ 397 Larry Walker .60 .25
❑ 398 Pete Harnisch .15 .07
❑ 399 Darren Lewis .15 .07
❑ 400 Frank Thomas 2.00 .90
❑ 401 Jack Morris .30 .14
❑ 402 Greg Hibbard .15 .07
❑ 403 Jeffrey Hammonds .30 .14
❑ 404 Will Clark .60 .25
❑ 405 Travis Fryman .30 .14
❑ 406 Scott Sanderson .15 .07
❑ 407 Gene Harris .15 .07
❑ 408 Chuck Carr .15 .07
❑ 409 Ozzie Smith .75 .35
❑ 410 Kent Mercker .15 .07
❑ 411 Andy Van Slyke .30 .14
❑ 412 Jimmy Key .30 .14
❑ 413 Pat Mahomes .15 .07
❑ 414 John Wetteland .30 .14
❑ 415 Todd Jones .15 .07
❑ 416 Greg Harris .15 .07
❑ 417 Kevin Stocker .15 .07
❑ 418 Juan Gonzalez 1.50 .70
❑ 419 Pete Smith .15 .07
❑ 420 Pat Listach .15 .07
❑ 421 Trevor Hoffman .30 .14
❑ 422 Scott Fletcher .15 .07
❑ 423 Mark Lewis .15 .07
❑ 424 Mickey Morandini .15 .07
❑ 425 Ryne Sandberg .75 .35
❑ 426 Erik Hanson .15 .07
❑ 427 Gary Gaetti .30 .14
❑ 428 Harold Reynolds .15 .07
❑ 429 Mark Portugal .15 .07
❑ 430 David Valle .15 .07
❑ 431 Mitch Williams .15 .07
❑ 432 Howard Johnson .15 .07
❑ 433 Hal Morris .15 .07
❑ 434 Tom Henke .15 .07
❑ 435 Shane Mack .15 .07
❑ 436 Mike Piazza 2.00 .90
❑ 437 Bret Saberhagen .30 .14
❑ 438 Jose Mesa .15 .07
❑ 439 Jaime Navarro .15 .07
❑ 440 Checklist .15 .07
❑ A300 Frank Thomas 2.00 .90
Leaf 5th Anniversary

1994 Leaf Clean-Up Crew

	MINT	NRMT
COMPLETE SET (12)	50.00	22.00
COMPLETE SERIES 1 (6)	10.00	4.50
COMPLETE SERIES 2 (6)	40.00	18.00
COMMON CARD (1-12)	3.00	1.35

❑ 1 Larry Walker 10.00 4.50
❑ 2 Andres Galarraga 10.00 4.50
❑ 3 Dave Hollins 3.00 1.35
❑ 4 Bobby Bonilla 4.00 1.80
❑ 5 Cecil Fielder 4.00 1.80
❑ 6 Danny Tartabull 3.00 1.35
❑ 7 Juan Gonzalez 25.00 11.00
❑ 8 Joe Carter 4.00 1.80
❑ 9 Fred McGriff 6.00 2.70
❑ 10 Matt Williams 6.00 2.70
❑ 11 Albert Belle 12.00 5.50
❑ 12 Harold Baines 4.00 1.80

1994 Leaf Gamers

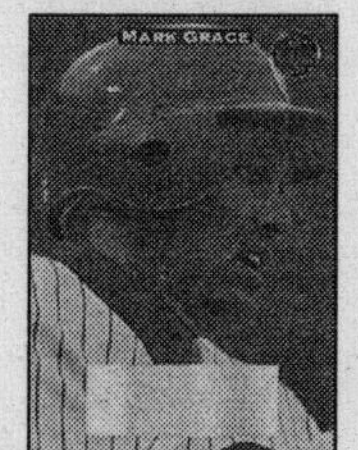

	MINT	NRMT
COMPLETE SET (12)	150.00	70.00
COMPLETE SERIES 1 (6)	70.00	32.00

	MINT	NRMT
COMPLETE SERIES 2 (6)	80.00	36.00
COMMON CARD (1-12)	2.50	1.10
❑ 1 Ken Griffey Jr.	40.00	18.00
❑ 2 Lenny Dykstra	2.50	1.10
❑ 3 Juan Gonzalez	20.00	9.00
❑ 4 Don Mattingly	12.00	5.50
❑ 5 David Justice	8.00	3.60
❑ 6 Mark Grace	5.00	2.20
❑ 7 Frank Thomas	25.00	11.00
❑ 8 Barry Bonds	10.00	4.50
❑ 9 Kirby Puckett	12.00	5.50
❑ 10 Will Clark	8.00	3.60
❑ 11 John Kruk	4.00	1.80
❑ 12 Mike Piazza	25.00	11.00

1994 Leaf Gold Rookies

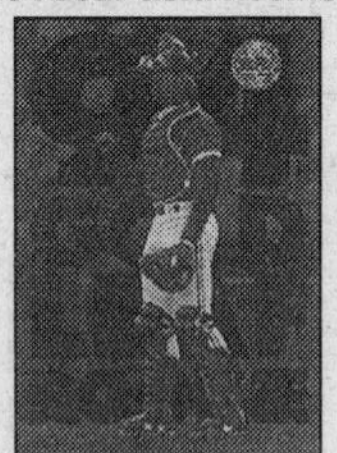

	MINT	NRMT
COMPLETE SET (20)	16.00	7.25
COMPLETE SERIES 1 (10)	12.00	5.50
COMPLETE SERIES 2 (10)	4.00	1.80
COMMON CARD (1-20)	.50	.23
❑ 1 Javier Lopez	1.50	.70
❑ 2 Rondell White	1.00	.45
❑ 3 Butch Huskey	1.00	.45
❑ 4 Midre Cummings	.50	.23
❑ 5 Scott Ruffcorn	.50	.23
❑ 6 Manny Ramirez	4.00	1.80
❑ 7 Danny Bautista	.50	.23
❑ 8 Russ Davis	1.00	.45
❑ 9 Steve Karsay	.50	.23
❑ 10 Carlos Delgado	2.00	.90
❑ 11 Bob Hamelin	.50	.23
❑ 12 Marcus Moore	.50	.23
❑ 13 Miguel Jimenez	.50	.23
❑ 14 Matt Walbeck	.50	.23
❑ 15 James Mouton	.50	.23
❑ 16 Rich Becker	.50	.23
❑ 17 Brian Anderson	1.50	.70
❑ 18 Cliff Floyd	1.00	.45
❑ 19 Steve Trachsel	.50	.23
❑ 20 Hector Carrasco	.50	.23

1994 Leaf Gold Stars

	MINT	NRMT
COMPLETE SET (15)	200.00	90.00
COMPLETE SERIES 1 (8)	120.00	55.00
COMPLETE SERIES 2 (7)	80.00	36.00
COMMON CARD (1-15)	5.00	2.20
❑ 1 Roberto Alomar	10.00	4.50
❑ 2 Barry Bonds	12.00	5.50
❑ 3 David Justice	10.00	4.50
❑ 4 Ken Griffey Jr.	50.00	22.00
❑ 5 Lenny Dykstra	6.00	2.70
❑ 6 Don Mattingly	15.00	6.75
❑ 7 Andres Galarraga	10.00	4.50
❑ 8 Greg Maddux	30.00	13.50
❑ 9 Carlos Baerga	6.00	2.70
❑ 10 Paul Molitor	10.00	4.50
❑ 11 Frank Thomas	30.00	13.50
❑ 12 John Olerud	6.00	2.70
❑ 13 Juan Gonzalez	25.00	11.00
❑ 14 Fred McGriff	8.00	3.60
❑ 15 Jack McDowell	5.00	2.20

1994 Leaf MVP Contenders

	MINT	NRMT
COMPLETE SET (30)	150.00	70.00
COMMON CARD	1.50	.70
COMP.GOLD SET (30)	150.00	70.00

*GOLD: SAME PRICE AS BASIC MVPS
ONE GOLD SET PER A13 OR N1 VIA MAIL
ONE THOMAS J400 PER A13 OR N1 VIA MAIL
THOMAS JUMBO PRINT RUN 20,000 #'d CARDS

	MINT	NRMT
❑ A1 Carlos Baerga	2.50	1.10
❑ A2 Albert Belle	8.00	3.60
❑ A3 Jose Canseco	6.00	2.70
❑ A4 Joe Carter	2.50	1.10
❑ A5 Will Clark	6.00	2.70
❑ A6 Cecil Fielder	2.50	1.10
❑ A7 Juan Gonzalez	15.00	6.75
❑ A8 Ken Griffey Jr.	30.00	13.50
❑ A9 Paul Molitor	6.00	2.70
❑ A10 Rafael Palmeiro	4.00	1.80
❑ A11 Kirby Puckett	10.00	4.50
❑ A12 Cal Ripken Jr.	25.00	11.00
❑ A13 Frank Thomas W	20.00	9.00
❑ A14 Mo Vaughn	8.00	3.60
❑ A15 AL Bonus Card	1.50	.70
❑ N1 Jeff Bagwell W	10.00	4.50
❑ N2 Dante Bichette	2.50	1.10
❑ N3 Barry Bonds	8.00	3.60
❑ N4 Darren Daulton	2.50	1.10
❑ N5 Andres Galarraga	6.00	2.70
❑ N6 Gregg Jefferies	1.50	.70
❑ N7 David Justice	6.00	2.70
❑ N8 Ray Lankford	2.50	1.10
❑ N9 Barry Larkin	4.00	1.80
❑ N10 Fred McGriff	4.00	1.80
❑ N11 Mike Piazza	20.00	9.00
❑ N12 Deion Sanders	2.50	1.10
❑ N13 Gary Sheffield	6.00	2.70
❑ N14 Matt Williams	4.00	1.80
❑ N15 NL Bonus Card	1.50	.70
❑ J400 Frank Thomas Jumbo	10.00	4.50

1994 Leaf Power Brokers

	MINT	NRMT
COMPLETE SET (10)	20.00	9.00
COMMON CARD (1-10)	.75	.35
❑ 1 Frank Thomas	5.00	2.20
❑ 2 David Justice	1.50	.70
❑ 3 Barry Bonds	1.50	.70
❑ 4 Juan Gonzalez	4.00	1.80
❑ 5 Ken Griffey Jr.	8.00	3.60
❑ 6 Mike Piazza	5.00	2.20
❑ 7 Cecil Fielder	.75	.35
❑ 8 Fred McGriff	1.00	.45
❑ 9 Joe Carter	.75	.35
❑ 10 Albert Belle	1.50	.70

1994 Leaf Slideshow

	MINT	NRMT
COMPLETE SET (10)	60.00	27.00
COMPLETE SERIES 1 (5)	30.00	13.50
COMPLETE SERIES 2 (5)	30.00	13.50
COMMON CARD (1-10)	2.00	.90
❑ 1 Frank Thomas	12.00	5.50
❑ 2 Mike Piazza	12.00	5.50
❑ 3 Darren Daulton	2.00	.90
❑ 4 Ryne Sandberg	5.00	2.20
❑ 5 Roberto Alomar	4.00	1.80
❑ 6 Barry Bonds	4.00	1.80
❑ 7 Juan Gonzalez	10.00	4.50
❑ 8 Tim Salmon	4.00	1.80
❑ 9 Ken Griffey Jr.	20.00	9.00
❑ 10 David Justice	4.00	1.80

1994 Leaf Statistical Standouts

	MINT	NRMT
COMPLETE SET (10)	20.00	9.00
COMMON CARD (1-10)	.50	.23
❑ 1 Frank Thomas	3.00	1.35
❑ 2 Barry Bonds	1.00	.45
❑ 3 Juan Gonzalez	2.50	1.10
❑ 4 Mike Piazza	3.00	1.35
❑ 5 Greg Maddux	3.00	1.35
❑ 6 Ken Griffey Jr.	5.00	2.20

❑ 7 Joe Carter	.50	.23
❑ 8 Dave Winfield	1.00	.45
❑ 9 Tony Gwynn	2.50	1.10
❑ 10 Cal Ripken	4.00	1.80

1995 Leaf

	MINT	NRMT
COMPLETE SET (400)	40.00	18.00
COMPLETE SERIES 1 (200)	15.00	6.75
COMPLETE SERIES 2 (200)	25.00	11.00
COMMON CARD (1-400)	.15	.07

❑ 1 Frank Thomas	2.00	.90
❑ 2 Carlos Garcia	.15	.07
❑ 3 Todd Hundley	.30	.14
❑ 4 Damion Easley	.30	.14
❑ 5 Roberto Mejia	.15	.07
❑ 6 John Mabry	.15	.07
❑ 7 Aaron Sele	.30	.14
❑ 8 Kenny Lofton	.60	.25
❑ 9 John Doherty	.15	.07
❑ 10 Joe Carter	.30	.14
❑ 11 Mike Lansing	.15	.07
❑ 12 John Valentin	.30	.14
❑ 13 Ismael Valdes	.30	.14
❑ 14 Dave McCarty	.15	.07
❑ 15 Melvin Nieves	.15	.07
❑ 16 Bobby Jones	.15	.07
❑ 17 Trevor Hoffman	.30	.14
❑ 18 John Smoltz	.30	.14
❑ 19 Leo Gomez	.15	.07
❑ 20 Roger Pavlik	.15	.07
❑ 21 Dean Palmer	.30	.14
❑ 22 Rickey Henderson	.60	.25
❑ 23 Eddie Taubensee	.15	.07
❑ 24 Damon Buford	.15	.07
❑ 25 Mark Wohlers	.15	.07
❑ 26 Jim Edmonds	.40	.18
❑ 27 Wilson Alvarez	.30	.14
❑ 28 Matt Williams	.30	.14
❑ 29 Jeff Montgomery	.15	.07
❑ 30 Shawon Dunston	.15	.07
❑ 31 Tom Pagnozzi	.15	.07
❑ 32 Jose Lind	.15	.07
❑ 33 Royce Clayton	.15	.07
❑ 34 Cal Eldred	.15	.07
❑ 35 Chris Gomez	.15	.07
❑ 36 Henry Rodriguez	.30	.14
❑ 37 Dave Fleming	.15	.07
❑ 38 Jon Lieber	.15	.07
❑ 39 Scott Servais	.15	.07
❑ 40 Wade Boggs	.60	.25
❑ 41 John Olerud	.30	.14
❑ 42 Eddie Williams	.15	.07
❑ 43 Paul Sorrento	.15	.07
❑ 44 Ron Karkovice	.15	.07
❑ 45 Kevin Foster	.15	.07
❑ 46 Miguel Jimenez	.15	.07
❑ 47 Reggie Sanders	.30	.14
❑ 48 Rondell White	.30	.14
❑ 49 Scott Leius	.15	.07
❑ 50 Jose Valentin	.15	.07
❑ 51 Wm. VanLandingham	.15	.07
❑ 52 Denny Hocking	.15	.07
❑ 53 Jeff Fassero	.15	.07
❑ 54 Chris Hoiles	.15	.07
❑ 55 Walt Weiss	.15	.07
❑ 56 Geronimo Berroa	.15	.07
❑ 57 Rich Rowland	.15	.07
❑ 58 Dave Weathers	.15	.07
❑ 59 Sterling Hitchcock	.30	.14
❑ 60 Raul Mondesi	.40	.18
❑ 61 Rusty Greer	.60	.25
❑ 62 David Justice	.60	.25
❑ 63 Cecil Fielder	.30	.14
❑ 64 Brian Jordan	.30	.14
❑ 65 Mike Lieberthal	.15	.07
❑ 66 Rick Aguilera	.15	.07
❑ 67 Chuck Finley	.30	.14
❑ 68 Andy Ashby	.15	.07
❑ 69 Alex Fernandez	.15	.07
❑ 70 Ed Sprague	.15	.07
❑ 71 Steve Buechele	.15	.07
❑ 72 Willie Greene	.30	.14
❑ 73 Dave Nilsson	.15	.07
❑ 74 Bret Saberhagen	.30	.14
❑ 75 Jimmy Key	.30	.14
❑ 76 Darren Lewis	.15	.07
❑ 77 Steve Cooke	.15	.07
❑ 78 Kirk Gibson	.30	.14
❑ 79 Ray Lankford	.30	.14
❑ 80 Paul O'Neill	.30	.14
❑ 81 Mike Bordick	.15	.07
❑ 82 Wes Chamberlain	.15	.07
❑ 83 Rico Brogna	.15	.07
❑ 84 Kevin Appier	.30	.14
❑ 85 Juan Guzman	.15	.07
❑ 86 Kevin Seitzer	.15	.07
❑ 87 Mickey Morandini	.15	.07
❑ 88 Pedro Martinez	.60	.25
❑ 89 Matt Mieske	.15	.07
❑ 90 Tino Martinez	.60	.25
❑ 91 Paul Shuey	.15	.07
❑ 92 Bip Roberts	.15	.07
❑ 93 Chili Davis	.30	.14
❑ 94 Deion Sanders	.30	.14
❑ 95 Darrell Whitmore	.15	.07
❑ 96 Joe Orsulak	.15	.07
❑ 97 Bret Boone	.30	.14
❑ 98 Kent Mercker	.15	.07
❑ 99 Scott Livingstone	.15	.07
❑ 100 Brady Anderson	.30	.14
❑ 101 James Mouton	.15	.07
❑ 102 Jose Rijo	.15	.07
❑ 103 Bobby Munoz	.15	.07
❑ 104 Ramon Martinez	.30	.14
❑ 105 Bernie Williams	.60	.25
❑ 106 Troy Neel	.15	.07
❑ 107 Ivan Rodriguez	.75	.35
❑ 108 Salomon Torres	.15	.07
❑ 109 Johnny Ruffin	.15	.07
❑ 110 Darryl Kile	.30	.14
❑ 111 Bobby Ayala	.15	.07
❑ 112 Ron Darling	.15	.07
❑ 113 Jose Lima	.15	.07
❑ 114 Joey Hamilton	.30	.14
❑ 115 Greg Maddux	2.00	.90
❑ 116 Greg Colbrunn	.15	.07
❑ 117 Ozzie Guillen	.15	.07
❑ 118 Brian Anderson	.30	.14
❑ 119 Jeff Bagwell	1.00	.45
❑ 120 Pat Listach	.15	.07
❑ 121 Sandy Alomar Jr.	.30	.14
❑ 122 Jose Vizcaino	.15	.07
❑ 123 Rick Helling	.30	.14
❑ 124 Allen Watson	.15	.07
❑ 125 Pedro Munoz	.15	.07
❑ 126 Craig Biggio	.60	.25
❑ 127 Kevin Stocker	.15	.07
❑ 128 Wil Cordero	.15	.07
❑ 129 Rafael Palmeiro	.40	.18
❑ 130 Gar Finnvold	.15	.07
❑ 131 Darren Hall	.15	.07
❑ 132 Heath Slocumb	.15	.07
❑ 133 Darrin Fletcher	.15	.07
❑ 134 Cal Ripken	2.50	1.10
❑ 135 Dante Bichette	.30	.14
❑ 136 Don Slaught	.15	.07
❑ 137 Pedro Astacio	.15	.07
❑ 138 Ryan Thompson	.15	.07
❑ 139 Greg Gohr	.15	.07
❑ 140 Javier Lopez	.30	.14
❑ 141 Lenny Dykstra	.30	.14
❑ 142 Pat Rapp	.15	.07
❑ 143 Mark Kiefer	.15	.07
❑ 144 Greg Gagne	.15	.07
❑ 145 Eduardo Perez	.15	.07
❑ 146 Felix Fermin	.15	.07
❑ 147 Jeff Frye	.15	.07
❑ 148 Terry Steinbach	.30	.14
❑ 149 Jim Eisenreich	.15	.07
❑ 150 Brad Ausmus	.15	.07
❑ 151 Randy Myers	.15	.07
❑ 152 Rick White	.15	.07
❑ 153 Mark Portugal	.15	.07
❑ 154 Delino DeShields	.15	.07
❑ 155 Scott Cooper	.15	.07
❑ 156 Pat Hentgen	.30	.14
❑ 157 Mark Gubicza	.15	.07
❑ 158 Carlos Baerga	.30	.14
❑ 159 Joe Girardi	.15	.07
❑ 160 Rey Sanchez	.15	.07
❑ 161 Todd Jones	.15	.07
❑ 162 Luis Polonia	.15	.07
❑ 163 Steve Trachsel	.15	.07
❑ 164 Roberto Hernandez	.15	.07
❑ 165 John Patterson	.15	.07
❑ 166 Rene Arocha	.15	.07
❑ 167 Will Clark	.60	.25
❑ 168 Jim Leyritz	.30	.14
❑ 169 Todd Van Poppel	.15	.07
❑ 170 Robb Nen	.15	.07
❑ 171 Midre Cummings	.15	.07
❑ 172 Jay Buhner	.30	.14
❑ 173 Kevin Tapani	.15	.07
❑ 174 Mark Lemke	.15	.07
❑ 175 Marcus Moore	.15	.07
❑ 176 Wayne Kirby	.15	.07
❑ 177 Rich Amaral	.15	.07
❑ 178 Lou Whitaker	.30	.14
❑ 179 Jay Bell	.30	.14
❑ 180 Rick Wilkins	.15	.07
❑ 181 Paul Molitor	.60	.25
❑ 182 Gary Sheffield	.40	.18
❑ 183 Kirby Puckett	1.00	.45
❑ 184 Cliff Floyd	.30	.14
❑ 185 Darren Oliver	.15	.07
❑ 186 Tim Naehring	.15	.07
❑ 187 John Hudek	.15	.07
❑ 188 Eric Young	.15	.07
❑ 189 Roger Salkeld	.15	.07
❑ 190 Kirt Manwaring	.15	.07
❑ 191 Kurt Abbott	.15	.07
❑ 192 David Nied	.15	.07
❑ 193 Todd Zeile	.15	.07
❑ 194 Wally Joyner	.30	.14
❑ 195 Dennis Martinez	.30	.14
❑ 196 Billy Ashley	.15	.07
❑ 197 Ben McDonald	.15	.07
❑ 198 Bob Hamelin	.15	.07
❑ 199 Chris Turner	.15	.07
❑ 200 Lance Johnson	.15	.07
❑ 201 Willie Banks	.15	.07
❑ 202 Juan Gonzalez	1.50	.70
❑ 203 Scott Sanders	.15	.07
❑ 204 Scott Brosius	.30	.14
❑ 205 Curt Schilling	.30	.14
❑ 206 Alex Gonzalez	.15	.07
❑ 207 Travis Fryman	.30	.14
❑ 208 Tim Raines	.30	.14

		MINT	NRMT
❑ 209	Steve Avery	.15	.07
❑ 210	Hal Morris	.15	.07
❑ 211	Ken Griffey Jr.	3.00	1.35
❑ 212	Ozzie Smith	.75	.35
❑ 213	Chuck Carr	.15	.07
❑ 214	Ryan Klesko	.30	.14
❑ 215	Robin Ventura	.30	.14
❑ 216	Luis Gonzalez	.15	.07
❑ 217	Ken Ryan	.15	.07
❑ 218	Mike Piazza	2.00	.90
❑ 219	Matt Walbeck	.15	.07
❑ 220	Jeff Kent	.30	.14
❑ 221	Orlando Miller	.15	.07
❑ 222	Kenny Rogers	.15	.07
❑ 223	J.T. Snow	.30	.14
❑ 224	Alan Trammell	.30	.14
❑ 225	John Franco	.30	.14
❑ 226	Gerald Williams	.15	.07
❑ 227	Andy Benes	.30	.14
❑ 228	Dan Wilson	.15	.07
❑ 229	Dave Hollins	.15	.07
❑ 230	Vinny Castilla	.40	.18
❑ 231	Devon White	.30	.14
❑ 232	Fred McGriff	.40	.18
❑ 233	Quilvio Veras	.15	.07
❑ 234	Tom Candiotti	.15	.07
❑ 235	Jason Bere	.15	.07
❑ 236	Mark Langston	.15	.07
❑ 237	Mel Rojas	.15	.07
❑ 238	Chuck Knoblauch	.60	.25
❑ 239	Bernard Gilkey	.15	.07
❑ 240	Mark McGwire	3.00	1.35
❑ 241	Kirk Rueter	.15	.07
❑ 242	Pat Kelly	.15	.07
❑ 243	Ruben Sierra	.15	.07
❑ 244	Randy Johnson	.60	.25
❑ 245	Shane Reynolds	.30	.14
❑ 246	Danny Tartabull	.15	.07
❑ 247	Darryl Hamilton	.15	.07
❑ 248	Danny Bautista	.15	.07
❑ 249	Tom Gordon	.15	.07
❑ 250	Tom Glavine	.60	.25
❑ 251	Orlando Merced	.15	.07
❑ 252	Eric Karros	.30	.14
❑ 253	Benji Gil	.15	.07
❑ 254	Sean Bergman	.15	.07
❑ 255	Roger Clemens	1.25	.55
❑ 256	Roberto Alomar	.60	.25
❑ 257	Benito Santiago	.15	.07
❑ 258	Robby Thompson	.15	.07
❑ 259	Marvin Freeman	.15	.07
❑ 260	Jose Offerman	.15	.07
❑ 261	Greg Vaughn	.30	.14
❑ 262	David Segui	.30	.14
❑ 263	Geronimo Pena	.15	.07
❑ 264	Tim Salmon	.60	.25
❑ 265	Eddie Murray	.60	.25
❑ 266	Mariano Duncan	.15	.07
❑ 267	Hideo Nomo	2.50	1.10
❑ 268	Derek Bell	.30	.14
❑ 269	Mo Vaughn	.75	.35
❑ 270	Jeff King	.15	.07
❑ 271	Edgar Martinez	.30	.14
❑ 272	Sammy Sosa	1.50	.70
❑ 273	Scott Ruffcorn	.15	.07
❑ 274	Darren Daulton	.30	.14
❑ 275	John Jaha	.15	.07
❑ 276	Andres Galarraga	.60	.25
❑ 277	Mark Grace	.40	.18
❑ 278	Mike Moore	.15	.07
❑ 279	Barry Bonds	.75	.35
❑ 280	Manny Ramirez	.60	.25
❑ 281	Ellis Burks	.30	.14
❑ 282	Greg Swindell	.15	.07
❑ 283	Barry Larkin	.40	.18
❑ 284	Albert Belle	.75	.35
❑ 285	Shawn Green	.30	.14
❑ 286	John Roper	.15	.07
❑ 287	Scott Erickson	.30	.14
❑ 288	Moises Alou	.40	.18
❑ 289	Mike Blowers	.15	.07
❑ 290	Brent Gates	.15	.07
❑ 291	Sean Berry	.15	.07
❑ 292	Mike Stanley	.15	.07
❑ 293	Jeff Conine	.30	.14
❑ 294	Tim Wallach	.15	.07
❑ 295	Bobby Bonilla	.30	.14
❑ 296	Bruce Ruffin	.15	.07
❑ 297	Chad Curtis	.15	.07
❑ 298	Mike Greenwell	.15	.07
❑ 299	Tony Gwynn	1.50	.70
❑ 300	Russ Davis	.30	.14
❑ 301	Danny Jackson	.15	.07
❑ 302	Pete Harnisch	.15	.07
❑ 303	Don Mattingly	1.00	.45
❑ 304	Rheal Cormier	.15	.07
❑ 305	Larry Walker	.60	.25
❑ 306	Hector Carrasco	.15	.07
❑ 307	Jason Jacome	.15	.07
❑ 308	Phil Plantier	.15	.07
❑ 309	Harold Baines	.30	.14
❑ 310	Mitch Williams	.15	.07
❑ 311	Charles Nagy	.30	.14
❑ 312	Ken Caminiti	.40	.18
❑ 313	Alex Rodriguez	2.50	1.10
❑ 314	Chris Sabo	.15	.07
❑ 315	Gary Gaetti	.30	.14
❑ 316	Andre Dawson	.40	.18
❑ 317	Mark Clark	.15	.07
❑ 318	Vince Coleman	.15	.07
❑ 319	Brad Clontz	.15	.07
❑ 320	Steve Finley	.30	.14
❑ 321	Doug Drabek	.15	.07
❑ 322	Mark McLemore	.15	.07
❑ 323	Stan Javier	.15	.07
❑ 324	Ron Gant	.15	.07
❑ 325	Charlie Hayes	.15	.07
❑ 326	Carlos Delgado	.30	.14
❑ 327	Ricky Bottalico	.30	.14
❑ 328	Rod Beck	.15	.07
❑ 329	Mark Acre	.15	.07
❑ 330	Chris Bosio	.15	.07
❑ 331	Tony Phillips	.15	.07
❑ 332	Garret Anderson	.30	.14
❑ 333	Pat Meares	.15	.07
❑ 334	Todd Worrell	.15	.07
❑ 335	Marquis Grissom	.30	.14
❑ 336	Brent Mayne	.15	.07
❑ 337	Lee Tinsley	.15	.07
❑ 338	Terry Pendleton	.15	.07
❑ 339	David Cone	.40	.18
❑ 340	Tony Fernandez	.15	.07
❑ 341	Jim Bullinger	.15	.07
❑ 342	Armando Benitez	.15	.07
❑ 343	John Smiley	.15	.07
❑ 344	Dan Miceli	.15	.07
❑ 345	Charles Johnson	.30	.14
❑ 346	Lee Smith	.30	.14
❑ 347	Brian McRae	.15	.07
❑ 348	Jim Thome	.60	.25
❑ 349	Jose Oliva	.15	.07
❑ 350	Terry Mulholland	.15	.07
❑ 351	Tom Henke	.15	.07
❑ 352	Dennis Eckersley	.30	.14
❑ 353	Sid Fernandez	.15	.07
❑ 354	Paul Wagner	.15	.07
❑ 355	John Dettmer	.15	.07
❑ 356	John Wetteland	.30	.14
❑ 357	John Burkett	.15	.07
❑ 358	Marty Cordova	.15	.07
❑ 359	Norm Charlton	.15	.07
❑ 360	Mike Devereaux	.15	.07
❑ 361	Alex Cole	.15	.07
❑ 362	Brett Butler	.30	.14
❑ 363	Mickey Tettleton	.15	.07
❑ 364	Al Martin	.15	.07
❑ 365	Tony Tarasco	.15	.07
❑ 366	Pat Mahomes	.15	.07
❑ 367	Gary DiSarcina	.15	.07
❑ 368	Bill Swift	.15	.07
❑ 369	Chipper Jones	1.50	.70
❑ 370	Orel Hershiser	.30	.14
❑ 371	Kevin Gross	.15	.07
❑ 372	Dave Winfield	.60	.25
❑ 373	Andujar Cedeno	.15	.07
❑ 374	Jim Abbott	.30	.14
❑ 375	Glenallen Hill	.15	.07
❑ 376	Otis Nixon	.15	.07
❑ 377	Roberto Kelly	.15	.07
❑ 378	Chris Hammond	.15	.07
❑ 379	Mike Macfarlane	.15	.07
❑ 380	J.R. Phillips	.15	.07
❑ 381	Luis Alicea	.15	.07
❑ 382	Bret Barberie	.15	.07
❑ 383	Tom Goodwin	.15	.07
❑ 384	Mark Whiten	.15	.07
❑ 385	Jeffrey Hammonds	.30	.14
❑ 386	Omar Vizquel	.30	.14
❑ 387	Mike Mussina	.60	.25
❑ 388	Ricky Bones	.15	.07
❑ 389	Steve Ontiveros	.15	.07
❑ 390	Jeff Blauser	.15	.07
❑ 391	Jose Canseco	.60	.25
❑ 392	Bob Tewksbury	.15	.07
❑ 393	Jacob Brumfield	.15	.07
❑ 394	Doug Jones	.15	.07
❑ 395	Ken Hill	.15	.07
❑ 396	Pat Borders	.15	.07
❑ 397	Carl Everett	.15	.07
❑ 398	Gregg Jefferies	.15	.07
❑ 399	Jack McDowell	.15	.07
❑ 400	Denny Neagle	.30	.14

1995 Leaf Checklists

	MINT	NRMT
COMPLETE SET (8)	8.00	3.60
COMMON CARD (1-8)	.15	.07
❑ 1 Bob Hamelin UER (Name spelled Hamlin)	.15	.07
❑ 2 David Cone	.40	.18
❑ 3 Frank Thomas	2.00	.90
❑ 4 Paul O'Neill	.25	.11
❑ 5 Raul Mondesi	.40	.18
❑ 6 Greg Maddux	2.00	.90
❑ 7 Tony Gwynn	1.50	.70
❑ 8 Jeff Bagwell	1.00	.45

1995 Leaf Cornerstones

	MINT	NRMT
COMPLETE SET (6)	10.00	4.50
COMMON CARD (1-6)	1.00	.45
❑ 1 Frank Thomas Robin Ventura	4.00	1.80
❑ 2 Cecil Fielder Travis Fryman	1.00	.45
❑ 3 Don Mattingly Wade Boggs	2.00	.90

		MINT	NRMT
❑ 4	Jeff Bagwell / Ken Caminiti	2.00	.90
❑ 5	Will Clark / Dean Palmer	1.50	.70
❑ 6	J.R. Phillips / Matt Williams	1.00	.45

1995 Leaf Gold Rookies

	MINT	NRMT
COMPLETE SET (16)	6.00	2.70
COMMON CARD (1-16)	.25	.11
❑ 1 Alex Rodriguez	4.00	1.80
❑ 2 Garret Anderson	.50	.23
❑ 3 Shawn Green	.50	.23
❑ 4 Armando Benitez	.25	.11
❑ 5 Darren Dreifort	.50	.23
❑ 6 Orlando Miller	.25	.11
❑ 7 Jose Oliva	.25	.11
❑ 8 Ricky Bottalico	.50	.23
❑ 9 Charles Johnson	.50	.23
❑ 10 Brian L.Hunter	.50	.23
❑ 11 Ray McDavid	.25	.11
❑ 12 Chan Ho Park	1.50	.70
❑ 13 Mike Kelly	.25	.11
❑ 14 Cory Bailey	.25	.11
❑ 15 Alex Gonzalez	.25	.11
❑ 16 Andrew Lorraine	.25	.11

1995 Leaf Gold Stars

	MINT	NRMT
COMPLETE SET (14)	240.00	110.00
COMPLETE SERIES 1 (8)	120.00	55.00
COMPLETE SERIES 2 (6)	120.00	55.00
COMMON CARD (1-14)	8.00	3.60
❑ 1 Jeff Bagwell	15.00	6.75
❑ 2 Albert Belle	12.00	5.50
❑ 3 Tony Gwynn	25.00	11.00
❑ 4 Ken Griffey Jr.	50.00	22.00
❑ 5 Barry Bonds	12.00	5.50
❑ 6 Don Mattingly	15.00	6.75
❑ 7 Raul Mondesi	8.00	3.60
❑ 8 Joe Carter	8.00	3.60
❑ 9 Greg Maddux	30.00	13.50
❑ 10 Frank Thomas	30.00	13.50
❑ 11 Mike Piazza	30.00	13.50
❑ 12 Jose Canseco	10.00	4.50
❑ 13 Kirby Puckett	20.00	9.00
❑ 14 Matt Williams	8.00	3.60

1995 Leaf Great Gloves

	MINT	NRMT
COMPLETE SET (16)	10.00	4.50
COMMON CARD (1-16)	.25	.11
❑ 1 Jeff Bagwell	1.00	.45
❑ 2 Roberto Alomar	.60	.25
❑ 3 Barry Bonds	.60	.25
❑ 4 Wade Boggs	.60	.25
❑ 5 Andres Galarraga	.60	.25
❑ 6 Ken Griffey Jr.	3.00	1.35
❑ 7 Marquis Grissom	.25	.11
❑ 8 Kenny Lofton	.60	.25
❑ 9 Barry Larkin	.40	.18
❑ 10 Don Mattingly	.75	.35
❑ 11 Greg Maddux	2.00	.90
❑ 12 Kirby Puckett	.60	.25
❑ 13 Ozzie Smith	.60	.25
❑ 14 Cal Ripken Jr.	2.50	1.10
❑ 15 Matt Williams	.25	.11
❑ 16 Ivan Rodriguez	.60	.25

1995 Leaf Heading for the Hall

	MINT	NRMT
COMPLETE SET (8)	250.00	110.00
COMMON CARD (1-8)	12.00	5.50
❑ 1 Frank Thomas	40.00	18.00
❑ 2 Ken Griffey Jr.	60.00	27.00
❑ 3 Jeff Bagwell	20.00	9.00
❑ 4 Barry Bonds	15.00	6.75
❑ 5 Kirby Puckett	20.00	9.00
❑ 6 Cal Ripken	50.00	22.00
❑ 7 Tony Gwynn	30.00	13.50
❑ 8 Paul Molitor	12.00	5.50

1995 Leaf Slideshow

	MINT	NRMT
COMPLETE SET (16)	80.00	36.00
COMPLETE SERIES 1 (8)	40.00	18.00
COMPLETE SERIES 2 (8)	40.00	18.00
COMMON CARD (1-8)	2.00	.90
❑ 1A Raul Mondesi	2.00	.90
❑ 1B Raul Mondesi	2.00	.90
❑ 2A Frank Thomas	10.00	4.50

	MINT	NRMT
❑ 2B Frank Thomas	10.00	4.50
❑ 3A Fred McGriff	2.00	.90
❑ 3B Fred McGriff	2.00	.90
❑ 4A Cal Ripken	12.00	5.50
❑ 4B Cal Ripken	12.00	5.50
❑ 5A Jeff Bagwell	5.00	2.20
❑ 5B Jeff Bagwell	5.00	2.20
❑ 6A Will Clark	2.50	1.10
❑ 6B Will Clark	2.50	1.10
❑ 7A Matt Williams	2.00	.90
❑ 7B Matt Williams	2.00	.90
❑ 8A Ken Griffey Jr.	15.00	6.75
❑ 8B Ken Griffey Jr.	15.00	6.75

1995 Leaf Statistical Standouts

	MINT	NRMT
COMPLETE SET (9)	400.00	180.00
COMMON CARD (1-9)	15.00	6.75
❑ 1 Joe Carter	15.00	6.75
❑ 2 Ken Griffey Jr.	120.00	55.00
❑ 3 Don Mattingly	40.00	18.00
❑ 4 Fred McGriff	20.00	9.00
❑ 5 Paul Molitor	25.00	11.00
❑ 6 Kirby Puckett	40.00	18.00
❑ 7 Cal Ripken	100.00	45.00
❑ 8 Frank Thomas	80.00	36.00
❑ 9 Matt Williams	15.00	6.75

1995 Leaf Thomas

	MINT	NRMT
COMPLETE SET (6)	25.00	11.00
COMMON CARD (1-6)	5.00	2.20
1 Frank Thomas The Rookie	5.00	2.20
2 Frank Thomas Sophomore Stardom	5.00	2.20
3 Frank Thomas Superstar	5.00	2.20
4 Frank Thomas AL MVP	5.00	2.20
5 Frank Thomas Back-To-Back	5.00	2.20
6 Frank Thomas The Big Hurt	5.00	2.20

1995 Leaf 300 Club

	MINT	NRMT
COMPLETE SET (18)	120.00	55.00
COMPLETE SERIES 1 (9)	50.00	22.00
COMPLETE SERIES 2 (9)	70.00	32.00
COMMON CARD (1-18)	1.50	.70
1 Frank Thomas	15.00	6.75
2 Paul Molitor	5.00	2.20
3 Mike Piazza	15.00	6.75
4 Moises Alou	4.00	1.80
5 Mike Greenwell	1.50	.70
6 Will Clark	5.00	2.20
7 Hal Morris	1.50	.70
8 Edgar Martinez	3.00	1.35
9 Carlos Baerga	3.00	1.35
10 Ken Griffey Jr.	25.00	11.00
11 Wade Boggs	5.00	2.20
12 Jeff Bagwell	8.00	3.60
13 Tony Gwynn	12.00	5.50
14 John Kruk	3.00	1.35
15 Don Mattingly	8.00	3.60
16 Mark Grace	4.00	1.80
17 Kirby Puckett	5.00	2.20
18 Kenny Lofton	5.00	2.20

1996 Leaf

	MINT	NRMT
COMPLETE SET (220)	20.00	9.00
COMMON CARD (1-220)	.15	.07
1 John Smoltz	.30	.14
2 Dennis Eckersley	.30	.14
3 Delino DeShields	.15	.07
4 Cliff Floyd	.30	.14
5 Chuck Finley	.30	.14
6 Cecil Fielder	.30	.14
7 Tim Naehring	.15	.07
8 Carlos Perez	.30	.14
9 Brad Ausmus	.15	.07
10 Matt Lawton	.60	.25
11 Alan Trammell	.40	.18
12 Steve Finley	.30	.14
13 Paul O'Neill	.30	.14
14 Gary Sheffield	.40	.18
15 Mark McGwire	3.00	1.35
16 Bernie Williams	.60	.25
17 Jeff Montgomery	.15	.07
18 Chan Ho Park	.60	.25
19 Greg Vaughn	.30	.14
20 Jeff Kent	.30	.14
21 Cal Ripken	2.50	1.10
22 Charles Johnson	.30	.14
23 Eric Karros	.30	.14
24 Alex Rodriguez	2.00	.90
25 Chris Snopek	.15	.07
26 Jason Isringhausen	.15	.07
27 Chili Davis	.30	.14
28 Chipper Jones	1.50	.70
29 Bret Saberhagen	.30	.14
30 Tony Clark	.60	.25
31 Marty Cordova	.15	.07
32 Dwayne Hosey	.15	.07
33 Fred McGriff	.40	.18
34 Deion Sanders	.30	.14
35 Orlando Merced	.15	.07
36 Brady Anderson	.30	.14
37 Ray Lankford	.30	.14
38 Manny Ramirez	.60	.25
39 Alex Fernandez	.15	.07
40 Greg Colbrunn	.15	.07
41 Ken Griffey, Jr.	3.00	1.35
42 Mickey Morandini	.15	.07
43 Chuck Knoblauch	.60	.25
44 Quinton McCracken	.30	.14
45 Tim Salmon	.60	.25
46 Jose Mesa	.15	.07
47 Marquis Grissom	.30	.14
48 Checklist	.15	.07
49 Raul Mondesi	.40	.18
50 Mark Grudzielanek	.30	.14
51 Ray Durham	.30	.14
52 Matt Williams	.30	.14
53 Bob Hamelin	.15	.07
54 Lenny Dykstra	.30	.14
55 Jeff King	.15	.07
56 LaTroy Hawkins	.15	.07
57 Terry Pendleton	.15	.07
58 Kevin Stocker	.15	.07
59 Ozzie Timmons	.15	.07
60 David Justice	.60	.25
61 Ricky Bottalico	.30	.14
62 Andy Ashby	.15	.07
63 Larry Walker	.60	.25
64 Jose Canseco	.60	.25
65 Bret Boone	.30	.14
66 Shawn Green	.30	.14
67 Chad Curtis	.15	.07
68 Travis Fryman	.30	.14
69 Roger Clemens	1.25	.55
70 David Bell	.15	.07
71 Rusty Greer	.40	.18
72 Bob Higginson	.60	.25
73 Joey Hamilton	.30	.14
74 Kevin Seitzer	.15	.07
75 Julian Tavarez	.15	.07
76 Troy Percival	.30	.14
77 Kirby Puckett	1.00	.45
78 Barry Bonds	.75	.35
79 Michael Tucker	.30	.14
80 Paul Molitor	.60	.25
81 Carlos Garcia	.15	.07
82 Johnny Damon	.30	.14
83 Mike Hampton	.15	.07
84 Ariel Prieto	.15	.07
85 Tony Tarasco	.15	.07
86 Pete Schourek	.15	.07
87 Tom Glavine	.60	.25
88 Rondell White	.30	.14
89 Jim Edmonds	.40	.18
90 Robby Thompson	.15	.07
91 Wade Boggs	.60	.25
92 Pedro Martinez	.60	.25
93 Gregg Jefferies	.15	.07
94 Albert Belle	.75	.35
95 Benji Gil	.15	.07
96 Denny Neagle	.30	.14
97 Mark Langston	.15	.07
98 Sandy Alomar Jr.	.30	.14
99 Tony Gwynn	1.50	.70
100 Todd Hundley	.30	.14
101 Dante Bichette	.30	.14
102 Eddie Murray	.60	.25
103 Lyle Mouton	.15	.07
104 John Jaha	.15	.07
105 Checklist	.15	.07
106 Jon Nunnally	.15	.07
107 Juan Gonzalez	1.50	.70
108 Kevin Appier	.30	.14
109 Brian McRae	.15	.07
110 Lee Smith	.30	.14
111 Tim Wakefield	.30	.14
112 Sammy Sosa	1.50	.70
113 Jay Buhner	.30	.14
114 Garret Anderson	.30	.14
115 Edgar Martinez	.30	.14
116 Edgardo Alfonzo	.30	.14
117 Billy Ashley	.15	.07
118 Joe Carter	.30	.14
119 Javy Lopez	.30	.14
120 Bobby Bonilla	.30	.14
121 Ken Caminiti	.40	.18
122 Barry Larkin	.40	.18
123 Shannon Stewart	.30	.14
124 Orel Hershiser	.30	.14
125 Jeff Conine	.30	.14
126 Mark Grace	.40	.18
127 Kenny Lofton	.60	.25
128 Luis Gonzalez	.15	.07
129 Rico Brogna	.15	.07
130 Mo Vaughn	.75	.35
131 Brad Radke	.30	.14
132 Jose Herrera	.15	.07
133 Rick Aguilera	.15	.07
134 Gary DiSarcina	.15	.07
135 Andres Galarraga	.60	.25
136 Carl Everett	.15	.07
137 Steve Avery	.15	.07
138 Vinny Castilla	.40	.18
139 Dennis Martinez	.30	.14
140 John Wetteland	.30	.14
141 Alex Gonzalez	.15	.07
142 Brian Jordan	.30	.14
143 Todd Hollandsworth	.15	.07
144 Terrell Wade	.15	.07
145 Wilson Alvarez	.30	.14
146 Reggie Sanders	.30	.14
147 Will Clark	.60	.25
148 Hideo Nomo	1.00	.45
149 J.T.Snow	.30	.14
150 Frank Thomas	2.00	.90
151 Ivan Rodriguez	.75	.35
152 Jay Bell	.30	.14
153 Checklist	.15	.07
154 David Cone	.40	.18
155 Roberto Alomar	.60	.25
156 Carlos Delgado	.30	.14
157 Carlos Baerga	.30	.14
158 Geronimo Berroa	.15	.07
159 Joe Vitiello	.15	.07
160 Terry Steinbach	.30	.14
161 Doug Drabek	.15	.07
162 David Segui	.30	.14
163 Ozzie Smith	.75	.35
164 Kurt Abbott	.15	.07
165 Randy Johnson	.60	.25
166 John Valentin	.30	.14
167 Mickey Tettleton	.15	.07
168 Ruben Sierra	.15	.07
169 Jim Thome	.60	.25
170 Mike Greenwell	.15	.07
171 Quilvio Veras	.15	.07

❑ 172 Robin Ventura	.30	.14
❑ 173 Bill Pulsipher	.15	.07
❑ 174 Rafael Palmeiro	.40	.18
❑ 175 Hal Morris	.15	.07
❑ 176 Ryan Klesko	.30	.14
❑ 177 Eric Young	.15	.07
❑ 178 Shane Andrews	.15	.07
❑ 179 Brian L.Hunter	.30	.14
❑ 180 Brett Butler	.30	.14
❑ 181 John Olerud	.30	.14
❑ 182 Moises Alou	.40	.18
❑ 183 Glenallen Hill	.15	.07
❑ 184 Ismael Valdes	.30	.14
❑ 185 Andy Pettitte	.40	.18
❑ 186 Yamil Benitez	.15	.07
❑ 187 Jason Bere	.15	.07
❑ 188 Dean Palmer	.30	.14
❑ 189 Jimmy Haynes	.15	.07
❑ 190 Trevor Hoffman	.30	.14
❑ 191 Mike Mussina	.60	.25
❑ 192 Greg Maddux	2.00	.90
❑ 193 Ozzie Guillen	.15	.07
❑ 194 Pat Listach	.15	.07
❑ 195 Derek Bell	.30	.14
❑ 196 Darren Daulton	.30	.14
❑ 197 John Mabry	.15	.07
❑ 198 Ramon Martinez	.30	.14
❑ 199 Jeff Bagwell	1.00	.45
❑ 200 Mike Piazza	2.00	.90
❑ 201 Al Martin	.15	.07
❑ 202 Aaron Sele	.30	.14
❑ 203 Ed Sprague	.15	.07
❑ 204 Rod Beck	.15	.07
❑ 205 Checklist	.15	.07
❑ 206 Mike Lansing	.15	.07
❑ 207 Craig Biggio	.60	.25
❑ 208 Jeffrey Hammonds	.30	.14
❑ 209 Dave Nilsson	.15	.07
❑ 210 Checklist	.15	.07
❑ 211 Derek Jeter	2.00	.90
❑ 212 Alan Benes	.30	.14
❑ 213 Jason Schmidt	.15	.07
❑ 214 Alex Ochoa	.15	.07
❑ 215 Ruben Rivera	.30	.14
❑ 216 Roger Cedeno	.15	.07
❑ 217 Jeff Suppan	.15	.07
❑ 218 Billy Wagner	.30	.14
❑ 219 Mark Loretta	.15	.07
❑ 220 Karim Garcia	.30	.14

1996 Leaf All-Star Game MVP Contenders

	MINT	NRMT
COMPLETE SET (20	40.00	18.00
COMMON CARD (1-20)	.25	.11
COMP.GOLD SET (20)	40.00	18.00

*GOLD CARDS: SAME PRICE AS BASIC MVPS
ONE GOLD SET PER PIAZZA VIA MAIL

❑ 1 Frank Thomas	4.00	1.80
❑ 2 Mike Piazza W	6.00	2.70
❑ 3 Sammy Sosa	3.00	1.35
❑ 4 Cal Ripken	5.00	2.20
❑ 5 Jeff Bagwell	2.00	.90
❑ 6 Reggie Sanders	.50	.23
❑ 7 Mo Vaughn	1.25	.55
❑ 8 Tony Gwynn	3.00	1.35
❑ 9 Dante Bichette	.50	.23
❑ 10 Tim Salmon	1.25	.55
❑ 11 Chipper Jones	3.00	1.35
❑ 12 Kenny Lofton	1.25	.55
❑ 13 Manny Ramirez	1.25	.55
❑ 14 Barry Bonds	1.25	.55
❑ 15 Raul Mondesi	.75	.35
❑ 16 Kirby Puckett	2.50	1.10
❑ 17 Albert Belle	1.25	.55
❑ 18 Ken Griffey Jr.	6.00	2.70
❑ 19 Greg Maddux	4.00	1.80
❑ 20 Bonus Card	.25	.11

1996 Leaf Gold Stars

	MINT	NRMT
COMPLETE SET (15)	450.00	200.00
COMMON CARD (1-15)	10.00	4.50
❑ 1 Frank Thomas	50.00	22.00
❑ 2 Dante Bichette	10.00	4.50
❑ 3 Sammy Sosa	40.00	18.00
❑ 4 Ken Griffey Jr.	80.00	36.00
❑ 5 Mike Piazza	50.00	22.00
❑ 6 Tim Salmon	15.00	6.75
❑ 7 Hideo Nomo	25.00	11.00
❑ 8 Cal Ripken	60.00	27.00
❑ 9 Chipper Jones	40.00	18.00
❑ 10 Albert Belle	20.00	9.00
❑ 11 Tony Gwynn	40.00	18.00
❑ 12 Mo Vaughn	20.00	9.00
❑ 13 Barry Larkin	12.00	5.50
❑ 14 Manny Ramirez	15.00	6.75
❑ 15 Greg Maddux	50.00	22.00

1996 Leaf Hats Off

	MINT	NRMT
COMPLETE SET (8)	200.00	90.00
COMMON CARD (1-8)	5.00	2.20
❑ 1 Cal Ripken	30.00	13.50
❑ 2 Barry Larkin	5.00	2.20
❑ 3 Frank Thomas	25.00	11.00
❑ 4 Mo Vaughn	10.00	4.50
❑ 5 Ken Griffey Jr.	40.00	18.00
❑ 6 Hideo Nomo	12.00	5.50
❑ 7 Albert Belle	10.00	4.50
❑ 8 Greg Maddux	25.00	11.00

1996 Leaf Picture Perfect

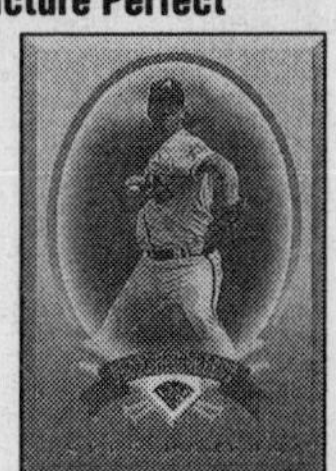

	MINT	NRMT
COMPLETE SET (12)	250.00	110.00
COMMON CARD (1-12)	8.00	3.60
❑ 1 Frank Thomas	25.00	11.00
❑ 2 Cal Ripken	30.00	13.50
❑ 3 Greg Maddux	25.00	11.00
❑ 4 Manny Ramirez	8.00	3.60
❑ 5 Chipper Jones	20.00	9.00
❑ 6 Tony Gwynn	20.00	9.00
❑ 7 Ken Griffey Jr.	40.00	18.00
❑ 8 Albert Belle	10.00	4.50
❑ 9 Jeff Bagwell	12.00	5.50
❑ 10 Mike Piazza	25.00	11.00
❑ 11 Mo Vaughn	8.00	3.60
❑ 12 Barry Bonds	8.00	3.60
❑ P10 Mike Piazza Promo	3.00	1.35

1996 Leaf Statistical Standouts

	MINT	NRMT
COMPLETE SET (8)	350.00	160.00
COMMON CARD (1-8)	15.00	6.75
❑ 1 Cal Ripken	60.00	27.00
❑ 2 Tony Gwynn	40.00	18.00
❑ 3 Frank Thomas	50.00	22.00
❑ 4 Ken Griffey Jr.	80.00	36.00
❑ 5 Hideo Nomo	25.00	11.00
❑ 6 Greg Maddux	50.00	22.00
❑ 7 Albert Belle	25.00	11.00
❑ 8 Chipper Jones	40.00	18.00

1996 Leaf Thomas Greatest Hits

	MINT	NRMT
COMPLETE SET (8)	150.00	70.00
COMMON CARD (1-7)	25.00	11.00
COMMON EXCHANGE (8)	30.00	13.50
❑ 1 Frank Thomas 1990	25.00	11.00
❑ 2 Frank Thomas 1991	25.00	11.00
❑ 3 Frank Thomas 1992	25.00	11.00
❑ 4 Frank Thomas 1993	25.00	11.00

Card	MINT	NRMT
❑ 5 Frank Thomas 1994	25.00	11.00
❑ 6 Frank Thomas 1995	25.00	11.00
❑ 7 Frank Thomas Career	25.00	11.00
❑ 8 Frank Thomas MVP	30.00	13.50

1996 Leaf Total Bases

	MINT	NRMT
COMPLETE SET (12)	120.00	55.00
COMMON CARD (1-12)	3.00	1.35
❑ 1 Frank Thomas	20.00	9.00
❑ 2 Albert Belle	8.00	3.60
❑ 3 Rafael Palmeiro	5.00	2.20
❑ 4 Barry Bonds	8.00	3.60
❑ 5 Kirby Puckett	10.00	4.50
❑ 6 Joe Carter	4.00	1.80
❑ 7 Paul Molitor	6.00	2.70
❑ 8 Fred McGriff	5.00	2.20
❑ 9 Ken Griffey Jr.	30.00	13.50
❑ 10 Carlos Baerga	3.00	1.35
❑ 11 Juan Gonzalez	15.00	6.75
❑ 12 Cal Ripken	25.00	11.00

1997 Leaf

	MINT	NRMT
COMPLETE SET (400)	40.00	18.00
COMPLETE SERIES 1 (200)	20.00	9.00
COMPLETE SERIES 2 (200)	20.00	9.00
COMMON CARD (1-400)	.15	.07
❑ 1 Wade Boggs	.60	.25
❑ 2 Brian McRae	.15	.07
❑ 3 Jeff D'Amico	.15	.07
❑ 4 George Arias	.15	.07
❑ 5 Billy Wagner	.30	.14
❑ 6 Ray Lankford	.30	.14
❑ 7 Will Clark	.60	.25
❑ 8 Edgar Renteria	.30	.14
❑ 9 Alex Ochoa	.15	.07
❑ 10 Roberto Hernandez	.15	.07
❑ 11 Joe Carter	.30	.14
❑ 12 Gregg Jefferies	.15	.07
❑ 13 Mark Grace	.40	.18
❑ 14 Roberto Alomar	.60	.25
❑ 15 Joe Randa	.15	.07
❑ 16 Alex Rodriguez	2.00	.90
❑ 17 Tony Gwynn	1.50	.70
❑ 18 Steve Gibralter	.15	.07
❑ 19 Scott Stahoviak	.15	.07
❑ 20 Matt Williams	.30	.14
❑ 21 Quinton McCracken	.30	.14
❑ 22 Ugueth Urbina	.30	.14
❑ 23 Jermaine Allensworth	.15	.07
❑ 24 Paul Molitor	.60	.25
❑ 25 Carlos Delgado	.30	.14
❑ 26 Bob Abreu	.30	.14
❑ 27 John Jaha	.15	.07
❑ 28 Rusty Greer	.30	.14
❑ 29 Kimera Bartee	.15	.07
❑ 30 Ruben Rivera	.30	.14
❑ 31 Jason Kendall	.40	.18
❑ 32 Lance Johnson	.15	.07
❑ 33 Robin Ventura	.30	.14
❑ 34 Kevin Appier	.30	.14
❑ 35 John Mabry	.15	.07
❑ 36 Ricky Otero	.15	.07
❑ 37 Mike Lansing	.15	.07
❑ 38 Mark McGwire	3.00	1.35
❑ 39 Tim Naehring	.15	.07
❑ 40 Tom Glavine	.60	.25
❑ 41 Rey Ordonez	.30	.14
❑ 42 Tony Clark	.40	.18
❑ 43 Rafael Palmeiro	.40	.18
❑ 44 Pedro Martinez	.60	.25
❑ 45 Keith Lockhart	.15	.07
❑ 46 Dan Wilson	.15	.07
❑ 47 John Wetteland	.30	.14
❑ 48 Chan Ho Park	.60	.25
❑ 49 Gary Sheffield	.40	.18
❑ 50 Shawn Estes	.30	.14
❑ 51 Royce Clayton	.15	.07
❑ 52 Jaime Navarro	.15	.07
❑ 53 Raul Casanova	.15	.07
❑ 54 Jeff Bagwell	1.00	.45
❑ 55 Barry Larkin	.40	.18
❑ 56 Charles Nagy	.30	.14
❑ 57 Ken Caminiti	.40	.18
❑ 58 Todd Hollandsworth	.15	.07
❑ 59 Pat Hentgen	.30	.14
❑ 60 Jose Valentin	.15	.07
❑ 61 Frank Rodriguez	.15	.07
❑ 62 Mickey Tettleton	.15	.07
❑ 63 Marty Cordova	.15	.07
❑ 64 Cecil Fielder	.30	.14
❑ 65 Barry Bonds	.75	.35
❑ 66 Scott Servais	.15	.07
❑ 67 Ernie Young	.15	.07
❑ 68 Wilson Alvarez	.30	.14
❑ 69 Mike Grace	.15	.07
❑ 70 Shane Reynolds	.30	.14
❑ 71 Henry Rodriguez	.30	.14
❑ 72 Eric Karros	.30	.14
❑ 73 Mark Langston	.30	.14
❑ 74 Scott Karl	.15	.07
❑ 75 Trevor Hoffman	.30	.14
❑ 76 Orel Hershiser	.30	.14
❑ 77 John Smoltz	.30	.14
❑ 78 Raul Mondesi	.40	.18
❑ 79 Jeff Brantley	.15	.07
❑ 80 Donne Wall	.15	.07
❑ 81 Joey Cora	.30	.14
❑ 82 Mel Rojas	.15	.07
❑ 83 Chad Mottola	.15	.07
❑ 84 Omar Vizquel	.30	.14
❑ 85 Greg Maddux	2.00	.90
❑ 86 Jamey Wright	.15	.07
❑ 87 Chuck Finley	.30	.14
❑ 88 Brady Anderson	.30	.14
❑ 89 Alex Gonzalez	.15	.07
❑ 90 Andy Benes	.30	.14
❑ 91 Reggie Jefferson	.15	.07
❑ 92 Paul O'Neill	.30	.14
❑ 93 Javier Lopez	.30	.14
❑ 94 Mark Grudzielanek	.30	.14
❑ 95 Marc Newfield	.15	.07
❑ 96 Kevin Ritz	.15	.07
❑ 97 Fred McGriff	.40	.18
❑ 98 Dwight Gooden	.30	.14
❑ 99 Hideo Nomo	.75	.35
❑ 100 Steve Finley	.30	.14
❑ 101 Juan Gonzalez	1.50	.70
❑ 102 Jay Buhner	.30	.14
❑ 103 Paul Wilson	.15	.07
❑ 104 Alan Benes	.30	.14
❑ 105 Manny Ramirez	.60	.25
❑ 106 Kevin Elster	.15	.07
❑ 107 Frank Thomas	2.00	.90
❑ 108 Orlando Miller	.15	.07
❑ 109 Ramon Martinez	.30	.14
❑ 110 Kenny Lofton	.60	.25
❑ 111 Bernie Williams	.60	.25
❑ 112 Robby Thompson	.15	.07
❑ 113 Bernard Gilkey	.15	.07
❑ 114 Ray Durham	.30	.14
❑ 115 Jeff Cirillo	.30	.14
❑ 116 Brian Jordan	.30	.14
❑ 117 Rich Becker	.15	.07
❑ 118 Al Leiter	.30	.14
❑ 119 Mark Johnson	.15	.07
❑ 120 Ellis Burks	.30	.14
❑ 121 Sammy Sosa	1.50	.70
❑ 122 Willie Greene	.30	.14
❑ 123 Michael Tucker	.30	.14
❑ 124 Eddie Murray	.60	.25
❑ 125 Joey Hamilton	.30	.14
❑ 126 Antonio Osuna	.15	.07
❑ 127 Bobby Higginson	.40	.18
❑ 128 Tomas Perez	.15	.07
❑ 129 Tim Salmon	.60	.25
❑ 130 Mark Wohlers	.15	.07
❑ 131 Charles Johnson	.30	.14
❑ 132 Randy Johnson	.60	.25
❑ 133 Brooks Kieschnick	.15	.07
❑ 134 Al Martin	.15	.07
❑ 135 Dante Bichette	.30	.14
❑ 136 Andy Pettitte	.40	.18
❑ 137 Jason Giambi	.30	.14
❑ 138 James Baldwin	.30	.14
❑ 139 Ben McDonald	.15	.07
❑ 140 Shawn Green	.30	.14
❑ 141 Geronimo Berroa	.15	.07
❑ 142 Jose Offerman	.15	.07
❑ 143 Curtis Pride	.15	.07
❑ 144 Terrell Wade	.15	.07
❑ 145 Ismael Valdes	.30	.14
❑ 146 Mike Mussina	.60	.25
❑ 147 Mariano Rivera	.30	.14
❑ 148 Ken Hill	.15	.07
❑ 149 Darin Erstad	1.00	.45
❑ 150 Jay Bell	.30	.14
❑ 151 Mo Vaughn	.75	.35
❑ 152 Ozzie Smith	.75	.35
❑ 153 Jose Mesa	.15	.07
❑ 154 Osvaldo Fernandez	.15	.07
❑ 155 Vinny Castilla	.40	.18
❑ 156 Jason Isringhausen	.15	.07
❑ 157 B.J. Surhoff	.30	.14
❑ 158 Robert Perez	.15	.07
❑ 159 Ron Coomer	.15	.07
❑ 160 Darren Oliver	.15	.07
❑ 161 Mike Mohler	.15	.07
❑ 162 Russ Davis	.30	.14
❑ 163 Bret Boone	.30	.14
❑ 164 Ricky Bottalico	.30	.14
❑ 165 Derek Jeter	2.00	.90
❑ 166 Orlando Merced	.15	.07
❑ 167 John Valentin	.30	.14
❑ 168 Andruw Jones	1.00	.45
❑ 169 Angel Echevarria	.15	.07
❑ 170 Todd Walker	.60	.25
❑ 171 Desi Relaford	.15	.07

No.	Player	Mint	Nrmt
❑ 172	Trey Beamon	.15	.07
❑ 173	Brian Giles	.75	.35
❑ 174	Scott Rolen	1.50	.70
❑ 175	Shannon Stewart	.30	.14
❑ 176	Dmitri Young	.30	.14
❑ 177	Justin Thompson	.30	.14
❑ 178	Trot Nixon	.30	.14
❑ 179	Josh Booty	.15	.07
❑ 180	Robin Jennings	.15	.07
❑ 181	Marvin Benard	.15	.07
❑ 182	Luis Castillo	.30	.14
❑ 183	Wendell Magee	.15	.07
❑ 184	Vladimir Guerrero	1.25	.55
❑ 185	Nomar Garciaparra	2.00	.90
❑ 186	Ryan Hancock	.15	.07
❑ 187	Mike Cameron	.30	.14
❑ 188	Cal Ripken LG	1.25	.55
❑ 189	Chipper Jones LG	.75	.35
❑ 190	Albert Belle LG	.30	.14
❑ 191	Mike Piazza LG	1.00	.45
❑ 192	Chuck Knoblauch LG	.30	.14
❑ 193	Ken Griffey Jr. LG	1.50	.70
❑ 194	Ivan Rodriguez LG	.40	.18
❑ 195	Jose Canseco LG	.60	.25
❑ 196	Ryne Sandberg LG	.60	.25
❑ 197	Jim Thome LG	.30	.14
❑ 198	Andy Pettitte CL	.15	.07
❑ 199	Andruw Jones CL	.75	.35
❑ 200	Derek Jeter CL	1.00	.45
❑ 201	Chipper Jones	1.50	.70
❑ 202	Albert Belle	.75	.35
❑ 203	Mike Piazza	2.00	.90
❑ 204	Ken Griffey Jr.	3.00	1.35
❑ 205	Ryne Sandberg	.75	.35
❑ 206	Jose Canseco	.60	.25
❑ 207	Chili Davis	.30	.14
❑ 208	Roger Clemens	1.25	.55
❑ 209	Deion Sanders	.30	.14
❑ 210	Darryl Hamilton	.15	.07
❑ 211	Jermaine Dye	.15	.07
❑ 212	Matt Williams	.30	.14
❑ 213	Kevin Elster	.15	.07
❑ 214	John Wetteland	.30	.14
❑ 215	Garret Anderson	.30	.14
❑ 216	Kevin Brown	.40	.18
❑ 217	Matt Lawton	.30	.14
❑ 218	Cal Ripken	2.50	1.10
❑ 219	Moises Alou	.40	.18
❑ 220	Chuck Knoblauch	.60	.25
❑ 221	Ivan Rodriguez	.75	.35
❑ 222	Travis Fryman	.30	.14
❑ 223	Jim Thome	.60	.25
❑ 224	Eddie Murray	.60	.25
❑ 225	Eric Young	.30	.14
❑ 226	Ron Gant	.15	.07
❑ 227	Tony Phillips	.15	.07
❑ 228	Reggie Sanders	.30	.14
❑ 229	Johnny Damon	.30	.14
❑ 230	Bill Pulsipher	.15	.07
❑ 231	Jim Edmonds	.40	.18
❑ 232	Melvin Nieves	.15	.07
❑ 233	Ryan Klesko	.30	.14
❑ 234	David Cone	.40	.18
❑ 235	Derek Bell	.30	.14
❑ 236	Julio Franco	.30	.14
❑ 237	Juan Guzman	.15	.07
❑ 238	Larry Walker	.60	.25
❑ 239	Delino DeShields	.15	.07
❑ 240	Troy Percival	.30	.14
❑ 241	Andres Galarraga	.60	.25
❑ 242	Rondell White	.30	.14
❑ 243	John Burkett	.15	.07
❑ 244	J.T. Snow	.30	.14
❑ 245	Alex Fernandez	.15	.07
❑ 246	Edgar Martinez	.30	.14
❑ 247	Craig Biggio	.60	.25
❑ 248	Todd Hundley	.30	.14
❑ 249	Jimmy Key	.30	.14
❑ 250	Cliff Floyd	.30	.14
❑ 251	Jeff Conine	.30	.14
❑ 252	Curt Schilling	.30	.14
❑ 253	Jeff King	.15	.07
❑ 254	Tino Martinez	.60	.25
❑ 255	Carlos Baerga	.30	.14
❑ 256	Jeff Fassero	.15	.07
❑ 257	Dean Palmer	.30	.14
❑ 258	Robb Nen	.15	.07
❑ 259	Sandy Alomar Jr.	.30	.14
❑ 260	Carlos Perez	.30	.14
❑ 261	Rickey Henderson	.60	.25
❑ 262	Bobby Bonilla	.30	.14
❑ 263	Darren Daulton	.30	.14
❑ 264	Jim Leyritz	.15	.07
❑ 265	Dennis Martinez	.30	.14
❑ 266	Butch Huskey	.15	.07
❑ 267	Joe Vitiello	.15	.07
❑ 268	Steve Trachsel	.15	.07
❑ 269	Glenallen Hill	.15	.07
❑ 270	Terry Steinbach	.30	.14
❑ 271	Mark McLemore	.15	.07
❑ 272	Devon White	.30	.14
❑ 273	Jeff Kent	.30	.14
❑ 274	Tim Raines	.30	.14
❑ 275	Carlos Garcia	.15	.07
❑ 276	Hal Morris	.15	.07
❑ 277	Gary Gaetti	.15	.07
❑ 278	John Olerud	.30	.14
❑ 279	Wally Joyner	.30	.14
❑ 280	Brian Hunter	.30	.14
❑ 281	Steve Karsay	.15	.07
❑ 282	Denny Neagle	.30	.14
❑ 283	Jose Herrera	.15	.07
❑ 284	Todd Stottlemyre	.15	.07
❑ 285	Bip Roberts	.15	.07
❑ 286	Kevin Seitzer	.15	.07
❑ 287	Benji Gil	.15	.07
❑ 288	Dennis Eckersley	.30	.14
❑ 289	Brad Ausmus	.15	.07
❑ 290	Otis Nixon	.15	.07
❑ 291	Darryl Strawberry	.30	.14
❑ 292	Marquis Grissom	.30	.14
❑ 293	Darryl Kile	.30	.14
❑ 294	Quilvio Veras	.15	.07
❑ 295	Tom Goodwin	.15	.07
❑ 296	Benito Santiago	.15	.07
❑ 297	Mike Bordick	.15	.07
❑ 298	Roberto Kelly	.15	.07
❑ 299	David Justice	.60	.25
❑ 300	Carl Everett	.15	.07
❑ 301	Mark Whiten	.15	.07
❑ 302	Aaron Sele	.30	.14
❑ 303	Darren Dreifort	.30	.14
❑ 304	Bobby Jones	.15	.07
❑ 305	Fernando Vina	.15	.07
❑ 306	Ed Sprague	.15	.07
❑ 307	Andy Ashby	.15	.07
❑ 308	Tony Fernandez	.15	.07
❑ 309	Roger Pavlik	.15	.07
❑ 310	Mark Clark	.15	.07
❑ 311	Mariano Duncan	.15	.07
❑ 312	Tyler Houston	.15	.07
❑ 313	Eric Davis	.30	.14
❑ 314	Greg Vaughn	.30	.14
❑ 315	David Segui	.30	.14
❑ 316	Dave Nilsson	.15	.07
❑ 317	F.P. Santangelo	.15	.07
❑ 318	Wilton Guerrero	.15	.07
❑ 319	Jose Guillen	.60	.25
❑ 320	Kevin Orie	.15	.07
❑ 321	Derrek Lee	.40	.18
❑ 322	Bubba Trammell	.40	.18
❑ 323	Pokey Reese	.15	.07
❑ 324	Hideki Irabu	1.50	.70
❑ 325	Scott Spiezio	.15	.07
❑ 326	Bartolo Colon	.30	.14
❑ 327	Damon Mashore	.15	.07
❑ 329	Chris Carpenter	.30	.14
❑ 330	Jose Cruz Jr.	2.50	1.10
❑ 331	Todd Greene	.30	.14
❑ 332	Brian Moehler	.15	.07
❑ 333	Mike Sweeney	.15	.07
❑ 334	Neifi Perez	.15	.07
❑ 335	Matt Morris	.30	.14
❑ 336	Marvin Benard	.15	.07
❑ 337	Karim Garcia	.30	.14
❑ 338	Jason Dickson	.30	.14
❑ 339	Brant Brown	.30	.14
❑ 340	Jeff Suppan	.15	.07
❑ 341	Deivi Cruz	.50	.23
❑ 342	Antone Williamson	.15	.07
❑ 343	Curtis Goodwin	.15	.07
❑ 344	Brooks Kieschnick	.15	.07
❑ 345	Tony Womack	.50	.23
❑ 346	Rudy Pemberton	.15	.07
❑ 347	Todd Dunwoody	.30	.14
❑ 348	Frank Thomas LG	1.00	.45
❑ 349	Andruw Jones LG	.75	.35
❑ 350	Alex Rodriguez LG	1.00	.45
❑ 351	Greg Maddux LG	1.00	.45
❑ 352	Jeff Bagwell LG	.60	.25
❑ 353	Juan Gonzalez LG	.75	.35
❑ 354	Barry Bonds LG	.30	.14
❑ 355	Mark McGwire LG	1.50	.70
❑ 356	Tony Gwynn LG	.75	.35
❑ 357	Gary Sheffield LG	.15	.07
❑ 358	Derek Jeter LG	1.00	.45
❑ 359	Manny Ramirez LG	.30	.14
❑ 360	Hideo Nomo LG	1.00	.45
❑ 361	Sammy Sosa LG	.75	.35
❑ 362	Paul Molitor LG	.30	.14
❑ 363	Kenny Lofton LG	.30	.14
❑ 364	Eddie Murray LG	.30	.14
❑ 365	Barry Larkin LG	.15	.07
❑ 366	Roger Clemens LG	.60	.25
❑ 367	John Smoltz LG	.15	.07
❑ 368	Alex Rodriguez GM	1.00	.45
❑ 369	Frank Thomas GM	1.00	.45
❑ 370	Cal Ripken GM	1.25	.55
❑ 371	Ken Griffey Jr. GM	1.50	.70
❑ 372	Greg Maddux GM	1.00	.45
❑ 373	Mike Piazza GM	1.00	.45
❑ 374	Chipper Jones GM	.75	.35
❑ 375	Albert Belle GM	.60	.25
❑ 376	Chuck Knoblauch GM	.30	.14
❑ 377	Brady Anderson GM	.15	.07
❑ 378	David Justice GM	.30	.14
❑ 379	Randy Johnson GM	.30	.14
❑ 380	Wade Boggs GM	.30	.14
❑ 381	Kevin Brown GM	.15	.07
❑ 382	Tom Glavine GM	.30	.14
❑ 383	Raul Mondesi GM	.15	.07
❑ 384	Ivan Rodriguez GM	.40	.18
❑ 385	Larry Walker GM	.30	.14
❑ 386	Bernie Williams GM	.30	.14
❑ 387	Rusty Greer GM	.30	.14
❑ 388	Rafael Palmeiro GM	.15	.07
❑ 389	Matt Williams GM	.15	.07
❑ 390	Eric Young GM	.15	.07
❑ 391	Fred McGriff GM	.15	.07
❑ 392	Ken Caminiti GM	.15	.07
❑ 393	Roberto Alomar GM	.30	.14
❑ 394	Brian Jordan GM	.15	.07
❑ 395	Mark Grace GM	.15	.07
❑ 396	Jim Edmonds GM	.15	.07
❑ 397	Deion Sanders GM	.30	.14
❑ 398	Vladimir Guerrero CL	.75	.35
❑ 399	Darin Erstad CL	.60	.25
❑ 400	N. Garciaparra CL	1.00	.45
❑ NNO	J.Robinson Reprint	30.00	13.50

1997 Leaf Fractal Matrix

	MINT	NRMT
COMPLETE SET(400)	5000.00	2200.00
COMPLETE SERIES 1 (200)	2500.00	1100.00
COMPLETE SERIES 2 (200)	2500.00	1100.00
COMMON BRONZE	1.25	.55
COMMON SILVER	3.00	1.35
COMMON GOLD	5.00	2.20

No.	Player	Mint	Nrmt
❑ 1	Wade Boggs GY	40.00	18.00
❑ 2	Brian McRae BY	1.25	.55
❑ 3	Jeff D'Amico BY	1.25	.55
❑ 4	George Arias SY	3.00	1.35
❑ 5	Billy Wagner SY	5.00	2.20
❑ 6	Ray Lankford BZ	2.00	.90
❑ 7	Will Clark SY	12.00	5.50
❑ 8	Edgar Renteria SY	5.00	2.20
❑ 9	Alex Ochoa SY	3.00	1.35
❑ 10	Roberto Hernandez BX	1.25	.55
❑ 11	Joe Carter SY	5.00	2.20
❑ 12	Gregg Jefferies BY	1.25	.55
❑ 13	Mark Grace SY	8.00	3.60
❑ 14	Roberto Alomar GY	25.00	11.00

❑ 15 Joe Randa BX 1.25 .55
❑ 16 Alex Rodriguez GZ 60.00 27.00
❑ 17 Tony Gwynn GZ 50.00 22.00
❑ 18 Steve Gibralter BY 1.25 .55
❑ 19 Scott Stahoviak BX 1.25 .55
❑ 20 Matt Williams SZ 5.00 2.20
❑ 21 Quinton McCracken BY 2.00 .90
❑ 22 Ugueth Urbina BX 2.00 .90
❑ 23 Jermaine Allensworth SX 3.00 1.35
❑ 24 Paul Molitor GX 50.00 22.00
❑ 25 Carlos Delgado SY 5.00 2.20
❑ 26 Bob Abreu SY 5.00 2.20
❑ 27 John Jaha SY 3.00 1.35
❑ 28 Rusty Greer SZ 5.00 2.20
❑ 29 Kimera Bartee BX 1.25 .55
❑ 30 Ruben Rivera SY 5.00 2.20
❑ 31 Jason Kendall SY 8.00 3.60
❑ 32 Lance Johnson BX 1.25 .55
❑ 33 Robin Ventura BY 2.00 .90
❑ 34 Kevin Appier SX 5.00 2.20
❑ 35 John Mabry SY 3.00 1.35
❑ 36 Ricky Otero BX 1.25 .55
❑ 37 Mike Lansing BX 1.25 .55
❑ 38 Mark McGwire GZ 100.00 45.00
❑ 39 Tim Naehring BX 1.25 .55
❑ 40 Tom Glavine SZ 12.00 5.50
❑ 41 Rey Ordonez SY 5.00 2.20
❑ 42 Tony Clark SY 8.00 3.60
❑ 43 Rafael Palmeiro SZ 8.00 3.60
❑ 44 Pedro Martinez BX 5.00 2.20
❑ 45 Keith Lockhart BX 1.25 .55
❑ 46 Dan Wilson BY 1.25 .55
❑ 47 John Wetteland BY 2.00 .90
❑ 48 Chan Ho Park BX 5.00 2.20
❑ 49 Gary Sheffield GZ 12.00 5.50
❑ 50 Shawn Estes BX 2.00 .90
❑ 51 Royce Clayton BX 1.25 .55
❑ 52 Jaime Navarro BX 1.25 .55
❑ 53 Raul Casanova BX 1.25 .55
❑ 54 Jeff Bagwell GZ 30.00 13.50
❑ 55 Barry Larkin GX 30.00 13.50
❑ 56 Charles Nagy BY 2.00 .90
❑ 57 Ken Caminiti GY 12.00 5.50
❑ 58 Todd Hollandsworth SZ 3.00 1.35
❑ 59 Pat Hentgen SX 5.00 2.20
❑ 60 Jose Valentin BX 1.25 .55
❑ 61 Frank Rodriguez BX 1.25 .55
❑ 62 Mickey Tettleton BX 1.25 .55
❑ 63 Marty Cordova GX 5.00 2.20
❑ 64 Cecil Fielder SX 5.00 2.20
❑ 65 Barry Bonds GZ 25.00 11.00
❑ 66 Scott Servais BX 1.25 .55
❑ 67 Ernie Young BX 1.25 .55
❑ 68 Wilson Alvarez BX 2.00 .90
❑ 69 Mike Grace BX 1.25 .55
❑ 70 Shane Reynolds SX 5.00 2.20
❑ 71 Henry Rodriguez SY 5.00 2.20
❑ 72 Eric Karros BX 2.00 .90
❑ 73 Mark Langston BX 2.00 .90
❑ 74 Scott Karl BX 1.25 .55
❑ 75 Trevor Hoffman BX 2.00 .90
❑ 76 Orel Hershiser SX 5.00 2.20
❑ 77 John Smoltz GY 8.00 3.60
❑ 78 Raul Mondesi GZ 12.00 5.50
❑ 79 Jeff Brantley BX 1.25 .55
❑ 80 Donne Wall BX 1.25 .55
❑ 81 Joey Cora BX 2.00 .90
❑ 82 Mel Rojas BX 1.25 .55
❑ 83 Chad Mottola BX 1.25 .55
❑ 84 Omar Vizquel BX 2.00 .90
❑ 85 Greg Maddux GZ 60.00 27.00
❑ 86 Jamey Wright SY 3.00 1.35
❑ 87 Chuck Finley BX 2.00 .90
❑ 88 Brady Anderson GY 8.00 3.60
❑ 89 Alex Gonzalez SX 3.00 1.35
❑ 90 Andy Benes BX 2.00 .90
❑ 91 Reggie Jefferson BX 1.25 .55
❑ 92 Paul O'Neill BY 2.00 .90
❑ 93 Javier Lopez SX 5.00 2.20
❑ 94 Mark Grudzielanek SX 5.00 2.20
❑ 95 Marc Newfield BX 1.25 .55
❑ 96 Kevin Ritz BX 1.25 .55
❑ 97 Fred McGriff GY 12.00 5.50
❑ 98 Dwight Gooden SX 5.00 2.20
❑ 99 Hideo Nomo SY 25.00 11.00
❑ 100 Steve Finley BX 2.00 .90
❑ 101 Juan Gonzalez GZ 50.00 22.00
❑ 102 Jay Buhner SZ 5.00 2.20
❑ 103 Paul Wilson SY 3.00 1.35
❑ 104 Alan Benes BY 2.00 .90
❑ 105 Manny Ramirez GZ 20.00 9.00
❑ 106 Kevin Elster BX 1.25 .55
❑ 107 Frank Thomas GZ 60.00 27.00
❑ 108 Orlando Miller BX 1.25 .55
❑ 109 Ramon Martinez BX 2.00 .90
❑ 110 Kenny Lofton GZ 20.00 9.00
❑ 111 Bernie Williams GY 20.00 9.00
❑ 112 Robby Thompson BX 1.25 .55
❑ 113 Bernard Gilkey BZ 1.25 .55
❑ 114 Ray Durham BX 2.00 .90
❑ 115 Jeff Cirillo SZ 5.00 2.20
❑ 116 Brian Jordan GZ 8.00 3.60
❑ 117 Rich Becker SY 3.00 1.35
❑ 118 Al Leiter BX 2.00 .90
❑ 119 Mark Johnson BX 1.25 .55
❑ 120 Ellis Burks BY 2.00 .90
❑ 121 Sammy Sosa GZ 50.00 22.00
❑ 122 Willie Greene BX 2.00 .90
❑ 123 Michael Tucker BX 2.00 .90
❑ 124 Eddie Murray GY 25.00 11.00
❑ 125 Joey Hamilton SY 5.00 2.20
❑ 126 Antonio Osuna BX 1.25 .55
❑ 127 Bobby Higginson SY 8.00 3.60
❑ 128 Tomas Perez BX 1.25 .55
❑ 129 Tim Salmon GZ 20.00 9.00
❑ 130 Mark Wohlers BX 1.25 .55
❑ 131 Charles Johnson SX 5.00 2.20
❑ 132 Randy Johnson SY 12.00 5.50
❑ 133 Brooks Kieschnick SX 3.00 1.35
❑ 134 Al Martin SY 5.00 2.20
❑ 135 Dante Bichette BX 2.00 .90
❑ 136 Andy Pettitte GZ 12.00 5.50
❑ 137 Jason Giambi GY 8.00 3.60
❑ 138 James Baldwin SX 5.00 2.20
❑ 139 Ben McDonald BX 1.25 .55
❑ 140 Shawn Green SX 5.00 2.20
❑ 141 Geronimo Berroa BY 1.25 .55
❑ 142 Jose Offerman BX 1.25 .55
❑ 143 Curtis Pride BX 1.25 .55
❑ 144 Terrell Wade BX 1.25 .55
❑ 145 Ismael Valdes SX 5.00 2.20
❑ 146 Mike Mussina SY 12.00 5.50
❑ 147 Mariano Rivera SX 5.00 2.20
❑ 148 Ken Hill BY 1.25 .55
❑ 149 Darin Erstad GZ 25.00 11.00
❑ 150 Jay Bell BX 2.00 .90
❑ 151 Mo Vaughn GZ 25.00 11.00
❑ 152 Ozzie Smith GY 30.00 13.50
❑ 153 Jose Mesa BX 1.25 .55
❑ 154 Osvaldo Fernandez BX 1.25 .55
❑ 155 Vinny Castilla BY 3.00 1.35
❑ 156 Jason Isringhausen SY 3.00 1.35
❑ 157 B.J. Surhoff BX 2.00 .90
❑ 158 Robert Perez BX 1.25 .55
❑ 159 Ron Coomer BX 1.25 .55
❑ 160 Darren Oliver BX 1.25 .55
❑ 161 Mike Mohler BX 1.25 .55
❑ 162 Russ Davis BX 2.00 .90
❑ 163 Bret Boone BX 2.00 .90
❑ 164 Ricky Bottalico BX 2.00 .90
❑ 165 Derek Jeter GZ 50.00 22.00
❑ 166 Orlando Merced BX 1.25 .55
❑ 167 John Valentin BX 2.00 .90
❑ 168 Andruw Jones GZ 25.00 11.00
❑ 169 Angel Echevarria BX 1.25 .55
❑ 170 Todd Walker GZ 20.00 9.00
❑ 171 Desi Relaford BY 1.25 .55
❑ 172 Trey Beamon SX 3.00 1.35
❑ 173 Brian Giles SY 5.00 2.20
❑ 174 Scott Rolen GZ 40.00 18.00
❑ 175 Shannon Stewart SZ 5.00 2.20
❑ 176 Dmitri Young GZ 8.00 3.60
❑ 177 Justin Thompson BX 2.00 .90
❑ 178 Trot Nixon SY 5.00 2.20
❑ 179 Josh Booty SY 3.00 1.35
❑ 180 Robin Jennings BX 1.25 .55
❑ 181 Marvin Benard BX 1.25 .55
❑ 182 Luis Castillo BY 2.00 .90
❑ 183 Wendell Magee BX 1.25 .55
❑ 184 Vladimir Guerrero GX 60.00 27.00
❑ 185 Nomar Garciaparra GX 150.00 70.00
❑ 186 Ryan Hancock BX 1.25 .55
❑ 187 Mike Cameron SX 5.00 2.20
❑ 188 Cal Ripken LG BZ 20.00 9.00
❑ 189 Chipper Jones LG SZ 30.00 13.50
❑ 190 Albert Belle LG SZ 20.00 9.00
❑ 191 Mike Piazza LG BZ 15.00 6.75
❑ 192 Chuck Knoblauch LG SY 12.00 5.50
❑ 193 Ken Griffey Jr. LG BZ 25.00 11.00
❑ 194 Ivan Rodriguez LG GZ 25.00 11.00
❑ 195 Jose Canseco LG SX 12.00 5.50
❑ 196 Ryne Sandberg LG SX 15.00 6.75
❑ 197 Jim Thome LG GY 25.00 11.00
❑ 198 Andy Pettitte CL BY 3.00 1.35
❑ 199 Andruw Jones CL BY 6.00 2.70
❑ 200 Derek Jeter CL SY 30.00 13.50
❑ 201 Chipper Jones GX 150.00 70.00
❑ 202 Albert Belle GY 25.00 11.00
❑ 203 Mike Piazza GY 80.00 36.00
❑ 204 Ken Griffey Jr. GX 300.00 135.00
❑ 205 Ryne Sandberg GZ 25.00 11.00
❑ 206 Jose Canseco SY 12.00 5.50
❑ 207 Chili Davis BX 2.00 .90
❑ 208 Roger Clemens GZ 40.00 18.00
❑ 209 Deion Sanders GZ 8.00 3.60
❑ 210 Darryl Hamilton BX 1.25 .55
❑ 211 Jermaine Dye SX 3.00 1.35
❑ 212 Matt Williams GY 8.00 3.60
❑ 213 Kevin Elster BX 1.25 .55
❑ 214 John Wetteland SX 5.00 2.20
❑ 215 Garret Anderson GZ 8.00 3.60
❑ 216 Kevin Brown GY 12.00 5.50
❑ 217 Matt Lawton SY 5.00 2.20
❑ 218 Cal Ripken GX 250.00 110.00
❑ 219 Moises Alou GY 12.00 5.50
❑ 220 Chuck Knoblauch GZ 20.00 9.00
❑ 221 Ivan Rodriguez GY 30.00 13.50
❑ 222 Travis Fryman BY 2.00 .90
❑ 223 Jim Thome GZ 20.00 9.00
❑ 224 Eddie Murray SZ 12.00 5.50
❑ 225 Eric Young GZ 8.00 3.60
❑ 226 Ron Gant SX 3.00 1.35
❑ 227 Tony Phillips BX 1.25 .55
❑ 228 Reggie Sanders BY 2.00 .90
❑ 229 Johnny Damon SZ 5.00 2.20
❑ 230 Bill Pulsipher BX 1.25 .55
❑ 231 Jim Edmonds GZ 12.00 5.50
❑ 232 Melvin Nieves BX 1.25 .55
❑ 233 Ryan Klesko GZ 8.00 3.60
❑ 234 David Cone SX 8.00 3.60
❑ 235 Derek Bell BY 2.00 .90
❑ 236 Julio Franco SX 5.00 2.20
❑ 237 Juan Guzman BX 1.25 .55
❑ 238 Larry Walker GZ 20.00 9.00
❑ 239 Delino DeShields BX 1.25 .55
❑ 240 Troy Percival BY 2.00 .90
❑ 241 Andres Galarraga GZ 20.00 9.00
❑ 242 Rondell White GZ 8.00 3.60
❑ 243 John Burkett BX 1.25 .55
❑ 244 J.T. Snow BY 2.00 .90
❑ 245 Alex Fernandez SY 3.00 1.35
❑ 246 Edgar Martinez GZ 8.00 3.60
❑ 247 Craig Biggio GZ 20.00 9.00
❑ 248 Todd Hundley GY 8.00 3.60
❑ 249 Jimmy Key SX 5.00 2.20
❑ 250 Cliff Floyd BY 2.00 .90
❑ 251 Jeff Conine BY 2.00 .90
❑ 252 Curt Schilling BX 2.00 .90
❑ 253 Jeff King BX 1.25 .55
❑ 254 Tino Martinez GZ 20.00 9.00
❑ 255 Carlos Baerga SY 5.00 2.20
❑ 256 Jeff Fassero BY 1.25 .55
❑ 257 Dean Palmer SY 5.00 2.20
❑ 258 Robb Nen BX 1.25 .55
❑ 259 Sandy Alomar Jr. SY 5.00 2.20
❑ 260 Carlos Perez BX 2.00 .90
❑ 261 Rickey Henderson SY 12.00 5.50
❑ 262 Bobby Bonilla SY 5.00 2.20
❑ 263 Darren Daulton BX 2.00 .90
❑ 264 Jim Leyritz BX 1.25 .55
❑ 265 Dennis Martinez BX 2.00 .90
❑ 266 Butch Huskey BX 1.25 .55
❑ 267 Joe Vitiello SY 3.00 1.35
❑ 268 Steve Trachsel BX 1.25 .55
❑ 269 Glenallen Hill BX 1.25 .55

❑ 270 Terry Steinbach BX 2.00 .90
❑ 271 Mark McLemore BX 1.25 .55
❑ 272 Devon White BX 2.00 .90
❑ 273 Jeff Kent BX 2.00 .90
❑ 274 Tim Raines BX 2.00 .90
❑ 275 Carlos Garcia BX 1.25 .55
❑ 276 Hal Morris BX 1.25 .55
❑ 277 Gary Gaetti BX 1.25 .55
❑ 278 John Olerud SY 5.00 2.20
❑ 279 Wally Joyner BX 2.00 .90
❑ 280 Brian Hunter SX 5.00 2.20
❑ 281 Steve Karsay BX 1.25 .55
❑ 282 Denny Neagle SX 5.00 2.20
❑ 283 Jose Herrera BX 1.25 .55
❑ 284 Todd Stottlemyre BX 1.25 .55
❑ 285 Bip Roberts SX 3.00 1.35
❑ 286 Kevin Seitzer BX 1.25 .55
❑ 287 Benji Gil BX 1.25 .55
❑ 288 Dennis Eckersley SX 5.00 2.20
❑ 289 Brad Ausmus BX 1.25 .55
❑ 290 Otis Nixon BX 1.25 .55
❑ 291 Darryl Strawberry BX 2.00 .90
❑ 292 Marquis Grissom SY 5.00 2.20
❑ 293 Darryl Kile BX 2.00 .90
❑ 294 Quilvio Veras BX 1.25 .55
❑ 295 Tom Goodwin BX 1.25 .55
❑ 296 Benito Santiago BX 1.25 .55
❑ 297 Mike Bordick BX 1.25 .55
❑ 298 Roberto Kelly BX 1.25 .55
❑ 299 David Justice GZ 20.00 9.00
❑ 300 Carl Everett BX 1.25 .55
❑ 301 Mark Whiten BX 1.25 .55
❑ 302 Aaron Sele BX 2.00 .90
❑ 303 Darren Dreifort BX 2.00 .90
❑ 304 Bobby Jones BX 1.25 .55
❑ 305 Fernando Vina BX 1.25 .55
❑ 306 Ed Sprague BX 1.25 .55
❑ 307 Andy Ashby SX 3.00 1.35
❑ 308 Tony Fernandez BX 1.25 .55
❑ 309 Roger Pavlik BX 1.25 .55
❑ 310 Mark Clark BX 1.25 .55
❑ 311 Mariano Duncan BX 1.25 .55
❑ 312 Tyler Houston BX 1.25 .55
❑ 313 Eric Davis SY 5.00 2.20
❑ 314 Greg Vaughn BY 2.00 .90
❑ 315 David Segui SY 5.00 2.20
❑ 316 Dave Nilsson SX 3.00 1.35
❑ 317 F.P. Santangelo SX 3.00 1.35
❑ 318 Wilton Guerrero GZ 5.00 2.20
❑ 319 Jose Guillen GZ 20.00 9.00
❑ 320 Kevin Orie SY 3.00 1.35
❑ 321 Derrek Lee GZ 12.00 5.50
❑ 322 Bubba Trammell SY 12.00 5.50
❑ 323 Pokey Reese GZ 5.00 2.20
❑ 324 Hideki Irabu GX 50.00 22.00
❑ 325 Scott Spiezio SZ 3.00 1.35
❑ 326 Bartolo Colon GZ 8.00 3.60
❑ 327 Damon Mashore SY 3.00 1.35
❑ 328 Ryan McGuire SY 3.00 1.35
❑ 329 Chris Carpenter BX 2.00 .90
❑ 330 Jose Cruz Jr. GX 80.00 36.00
❑ 331 Todd Greene SZ 5.00 2.20
❑ 332 Brian Moehler BX 1.25 .55
❑ 333 Mike Sweeney BY 1.25 .55
❑ 334 Neifi Perez GZ 5.00 2.20
❑ 335 Matt Morris SY 5.00 2.20
❑ 336 Marvin Benard BY 1.25 .55
❑ 337 Karim Garcia SZ 5.00 2.20
❑ 338 Jason Dickson SY 5.00 2.20
❑ 339 Brant Brown SY 5.00 2.20
❑ 340 Jeff Suppan SZ 3.00 1.35
❑ 341 Deivi Cruz BX 5.00 2.20
❑ 342 Antone Williamson GZ 5.00 2.20
❑ 343 Curtis Goodwin BX 1.25 .55
❑ 344 Brooks Kieschnick SY 3.00 1.35
❑ 345 Tony Womack BX 5.00 2.20
❑ 346 Rudy Pemberton BX 1.25 .55
❑ 347 Todd Dunwoody BX 2.00 .90
❑ 348 Frank Thomas LG SY 40.00 18.00
❑ 349 Andruw Jones LG SX 15.00 6.75
❑ 350 Alex Rodriguez LG BY 15.00 6.75
❑ 351 Greg Maddux LG SY 40.00 18.00
❑ 352 Jeff Bagwell LG BY 8.00 3.60
❑ 353 Juan Gonzalez LG SY 30.00 13.50
❑ 354 Barry Bonds LG BY 6.00 2.70
❑ 355 Mark McGwire LG BY 25.00 11.00
❑ 356 Tony Gwynn LG BY 12.00 5.50
❑ 357 Gary Sheffield LG BX 3.00 1.35
❑ 358 Derek Jeter LG SX 30.00 13.50
❑ 359 Manny Ramirez LG SY 12.00 5.50
❑ 360 Hideo Nomo LG GZ 40.00 18.00
❑ 361 Sammy Sosa LG BX 12.00 5.50
❑ 362 Paul Molitor LG SZ 12.00 5.50
❑ 363 Kenny Lofton LG BY 5.00 2.20
❑ 364 Eddie Murray LG BX 5.00 2.20
❑ 365 Barry Larkin LG SZ 8.00 3.60
❑ 366 Roger Clemens LG SY 25.00 11.00
❑ 367 John Smoltz LG BZ 2.00 .90
❑ 368 Alex Rodriguez GM SX 40.00 18.00
❑ 369 Frank Thomas GM BX 15.00 6.75
❑ 370 Cal Ripken GM SY 50.00 22.00
❑ 371 Ken Griffey Jr. GM SY 60.00 27.00
❑ 372 Greg Maddux GM BX 15.00 6.75
❑ 373 Mike Piazza GM SX 40.00 18.00
❑ 374 Chipper Jones GM BY 12.00 5.50
❑ 375 Albert Belle GM BX 8.00 3.60
❑ 376 Chuck Knoblauch GM BX 5.00 2.20
❑ 377 Brady Anderson GM BZ 2.00 .90
❑ 378 David Justice GM SX 12.00 5.50
❑ 379 Randy Johnson GM BZ 5.00 2.20
❑ 380 Wade Boggs GM BX 5.00 2.20
❑ 381 Kevin Brown GM BX 1.25 .55
❑ 382 Tom Glavine GM GY 20.00 9.00
❑ 383 Raul Mondesi GM SX 8.00 3.60
❑ 384 Ivan Rodriguez GM SX 15.00 6.75
❑ 385 Larry Walker GM BY 5.00 2.20
❑ 386 Bernie Williams GM BZ 5.00 2.20
❑ 387 Rusty Greer GM GY 8.00 3.60
❑ 388 Rafael Palmeiro GM GY 8.00 3.60
❑ 389 Matt Williams GM BX 2.00 .90
❑ 390 Eric Young GM BX 2.00 .90
❑ 391 Fred McGriff GM BX 3.00 1.35
❑ 392 Ken Caminiti GM BX 3.00 1.35
❑ 393 Roberto Alomar GM BZ 5.00 2.20
❑ 394 Brian Jordan GM BX 2.00 .90
❑ 395 Mark Grace GM GZ 3.00 1.35
❑ 396 Jim Edmonds GM BY 3.00 1.35
❑ 397 Deion Sanders GM SY 5.00 2.20
❑ 398 Vladimir Guerrero CL SZ 20.00 9.00
❑ 399 Darin Erstad CL SY 15.00 6.75
❑ 400 N. Garciaparra CL SZ 40.00 18.00

1997 Leaf Fractal Matrix Die Cuts

	MINT	NRMT
COMPLETE SET (400)	10000.00	4500.00
COMPLETE SERIES 1 (200)	5000.00	2200.00
COMPLETE SERIES 2 (200)	5000.00	2200.00
COMMON X-AXIS	5.00	2.20
COMMON Y-AXIS	8.00	3.60
COMMON Z-AXIS	12.00	5.50

❑ 1 Wade Boggs GY 50.00 22.00
❑ 2 Brian McRae BY 5.00 2.20
❑ 3 Jeff D'Amico BY 5.00 2.20
❑ 4 George Arias SY 8.00 3.60
❑ 5 Billy Wagner SY 12.00 5.50
❑ 6 Ray Lankford BZ 8.00 3.60
❑ 7 Will Clark SY 30.00 13.50
❑ 8 Edgar Renteria SY 12.00 5.50
❑ 9 Alex Ochoa SY 8.00 3.60
❑ 10 Roberto Hernandez BX 5.00 2.20
❑ 11 Joe Carter SY 12.00 5.50
❑ 12 Gregg Jefferies BY 5.00 2.20
❑ 13 Mark Grace SY 20.00 9.00
❑ 14 Roberto Alomar GY 50.00 22.00
❑ 15 Joe Randa BX 5.00 2.20
❑ 16 Alex Rodriguez GZ 150.00 70.00
❑ 17 Tony Gwynn GZ 120.00 55.00
❑ 18 Steve Gibralter BY 5.00 2.20
❑ 19 Scott Stahoviak BX 5.00 2.20
❑ 20 Matt Williams SZ 12.00 5.50
❑ 21 Quinton McCracken BY 8.00 3.60
❑ 22 Ugueth Urbina BX 8.00 3.60
❑ 23 Jermaine Allensworth SX 8.00 3.60
❑ 24 Paul Molitor GX 50.00 22.00
❑ 25 Carlos Delgado SY 12.00 5.50
❑ 26 Bob Abreu SY 12.00 5.50
❑ 27 John Jaha SY 8.00 3.60
❑ 28 Rusty Greer SZ 12.00 5.50
❑ 29 Kimera Bartee BX 5.00 2.20
❑ 30 Ruben Rivera SY 12.00 5.50
❑ 31 Jason Kendall SY 20.00 9.00
❑ 32 Lance Johnson BX 5.00 2.20
❑ 33 Robin Ventura BY 8.00 3.60
❑ 34 Kevin Appier SX 12.00 5.50
❑ 35 John Mabry SY 8.00 3.60
❑ 36 Ricky Otero BX 5.00 2.20
❑ 37 Mike Lansing BX 5.00 2.20
❑ 38 Mark McGwire GZ 250.00 110.00
❑ 39 Tim Naehring BX 5.00 2.20
❑ 40 Tom Glavine SZ 30.00 13.50
❑ 41 Rey Ordonez SY 12.00 5.50
❑ 42 Tony Clark SY 20.00 9.00
❑ 43 Rafael Palmeiro SZ 20.00 9.00
❑ 44 Pedro Martinez BX 20.00 9.00
❑ 45 Keith Lockhart BX 5.00 2.20
❑ 46 Dan Wilson BY 5.00 2.20
❑ 47 John Wetteland BY 8.00 3.60
❑ 48 Chan Ho Park BX 20.00 9.00
❑ 49 Gary Sheffield GZ 30.00 13.50
❑ 50 Shawn Estes BX 8.00 3.60
❑ 51 Royce Clayton BX 5.00 2.20
❑ 52 Jaime Navarro BX 5.00 2.20
❑ 53 Raul Casanova BX 5.00 2.20
❑ 54 Jeff Bagwell GZ 80.00 36.00
❑ 55 Barry Larkin GX 30.00 13.50
❑ 56 Charles Nagy BY 8.00 3.60
❑ 57 Ken Caminiti GY 30.00 13.50
❑ 58 Todd Hollandsworth SZ 8.00 3.60
❑ 59 Pat Hentgen SX 12.00 5.50
❑ 60 Jose Valentin BX 5.00 2.20
❑ 61 Frank Rodriguez BX 5.00 2.20
❑ 62 Mickey Tettleton BX 5.00 2.20
❑ 63 Marty Cordova GX 12.00 5.50
❑ 64 Cecil Fielder SX 12.00 5.50
❑ 65 Barry Bonds GZ 60.00 27.00
❑ 66 Scott Servais BX 5.00 2.20
❑ 67 Ernie Young BX 5.00 2.20
❑ 68 Wilson Alvarez BX 8.00 3.60
❑ 69 Mike Grace BX 5.00 2.20
❑ 70 Shane Reynolds SX 12.00 5.50
❑ 71 Henry Rodriguez SY 12.00 5.50
❑ 72 Eric Karros BX 8.00 3.60
❑ 73 Mark Langston BX 8.00 3.60
❑ 74 Scott Karl BX 5.00 2.20
❑ 75 Trevor Hoffman BX 8.00 3.60
❑ 76 Orel Hershiser SX 12.00 5.50
❑ 77 John Smoltz GY 20.00 9.00
❑ 78 Raul Mondesi GZ 30.00 13.50
❑ 79 Jeff Brantley BX 5.00 2.20
❑ 80 Donne Wall BX 5.00 2.20
❑ 81 Joey Cora BX 8.00 3.60
❑ 82 Mel Rojas BX 5.00 2.20
❑ 83 Chad Mottola BX 5.00 2.20
❑ 84 Omar Vizquel BX 8.00 3.60
❑ 85 Greg Maddux GZ 150.00 70.00
❑ 86 Jamey Wright SY 8.00 3.60
❑ 87 Chuck Finley BX 8.00 3.60
❑ 88 Brady Anderson GY 20.00 9.00
❑ 89 Alex Gonzalez SX 8.00 3.60
❑ 90 Andy Benes BX 8.00 3.60
❑ 91 Reggie Jefferson BX 5.00 2.20
❑ 92 Paul O'Neill BY 8.00 3.60
❑ 93 Javier Lopez SX 12.00 5.50
❑ 94 Mark Grudzielanek SX 12.00 5.50
❑ 95 Marc Newfield BX 5.00 2.20
❑ 96 Kevin Ritz BX 5.00 2.20
❑ 97 Fred McGriff GY 30.00 13.50
❑ 98 Dwight Gooden SX 12.00 5.50
❑ 99 Hideo Nomo SY 60.00 27.00
❑ 100 Steve Finley BX 8.00 3.60
❑ 101 Juan Gonzalez GZ 120.00 55.00
❑ 102 Jay Buhner SZ 12.00 5.50
❑ 103 Paul Wilson SY 8.00 3.60
❑ 104 Alan Benes BY 8.00 3.60
❑ 105 Manny Ramirez GZ 50.00 22.00
❑ 106 Kevin Elster BX 5.00 2.20
❑ 107 Frank Thomas GZ 150.00 70.00
❑ 108 Orlando Miller BX 5.00 2.20
❑ 109 Ramon Martinez BX 8.00 3.60
❑ 110 Kenny Lofton GZ 50.00 22.00
❑ 111 Bernie Williams GY 50.00 22.00
❑ 112 Robby Thompson BX 5.00 2.20

❑ 113 Bernard Gilkey BZ 5.00 2.20
❑ 114 Ray Durham BX 8.00 3.60
❑ 115 Jeff Cirillo SZ 12.00 5.50
❑ 116 Brian Jordan GZ 20.00 9.00
❑ 117 Rich Becker SY 8.00 3.60
❑ 118 Al Leiter BX 8.00 3.60
❑ 119 Mark Johnson BX 5.00 2.20
❑ 120 Ellis Burks BY 8.00 3.60
❑ 121 Sammy Sosa GZ 120.00 55.00
❑ 122 Willie Greene BX 8.00 3.60
❑ 123 Michael Tucker BX 8.00 3.60
❑ 124 Eddie Murray GY 50.00 22.00
❑ 125 Joey Hamilton SY 12.00 5.50
❑ 126 Antonio Osuna BX 5.00 2.20
❑ 127 Bobby Higginson SY 20.00 9.00
❑ 128 Tomas Perez BX 5.00 2.20
❑ 129 Tim Salmon GZ 50.00 22.00
❑ 130 Mark Wohlers BX 5.00 2.20
❑ 131 Charles Johnson SX 12.00 5.50
❑ 132 Randy Johnson SY 30.00 13.50
❑ 133 Brooks Kieschnick SX 8.00 3.60
❑ 134 Al Martin SY 12.00 5.50
❑ 135 Dante Bichette BX 8.00 3.60
❑ 136 Andy Pettitte GZ 30.00 13.50
❑ 137 Jason Giambi GY 20.00 9.00
❑ 138 James Baldwin SX 12.00 5.50
❑ 139 Ben McDonald BX 5.00 2.20
❑ 140 Shawn Green SX 12.00 5.50
❑ 141 Geronimo Berroa BY 5.00 2.20
❑ 142 Jose Offerman BX 5.00 2.20
❑ 143 Curtis Pride BX 5.00 2.20
❑ 144 Terrell Wade BX 5.00 2.20
❑ 145 Ismael Valdes SX 12.00 5.50
❑ 146 Mike Mussina SY 30.00 13.50
❑ 147 Mariano Rivera SX 12.00 5.50
❑ 148 Ken Hill BY 5.00 2.20
❑ 149 Darin Erstad GZ 60.00 27.00
❑ 150 Jay Bell BX 8.00 3.60
❑ 151 Mo Vaughn GZ 60.00 27.00
❑ 152 Ozzie Smith GY 40.00 18.00
❑ 153 Jose Mesa BX 5.00 2.20
❑ 154 Osvaldo Fernandez BX 5.00 2.20
❑ 155 Vinny Castilla BY 12.00 5.50
❑ 156 Jason Isringhausen SY 8.00 3.60
❑ 157 B.J. Surhoff BX 8.00 3.60
❑ 158 Robert Perez BX 5.00 2.20
❑ 159 Ron Coomer BX 5.00 2.20
❑ 160 Darren Oliver BX 5.00 2.20
❑ 161 Mike Mohler BX 5.00 2.20
❑ 162 Russ Davis BX 8.00 3.60
❑ 163 Bret Boone BX 8.00 3.60
❑ 164 Ricky Bottalico BX 8.00 3.60
❑ 165 Derek Jeter GZ 120.00 55.00
❑ 166 Orlando Merced BX 5.00 2.20
❑ 167 John Valentin BX 8.00 3.60
❑ 168 Andruw Jones GZ 60.00 27.00
❑ 169 Angel Echevarria BX 5.00 2.20
❑ 170 Todd Walker GZ 50.00 22.00
❑ 171 Desi Relaford BY 5.00 2.20
❑ 172 Trey Beamon SX 8.00 3.60
❑ 173 Brian Giles SY 12.00 5.50
❑ 174 Scott Rolen GZ 100.00 45.00
❑ 175 Shannon Stewart SZ 12.00 5.50
❑ 176 Dmitri Young GZ 20.00 9.00
❑ 177 Justin Thompson BX 8.00 3.60
❑ 178 Trot Nixon SY 12.00 5.50
❑ 179 Josh Booty SY 8.00 3.60
❑ 180 Robin Jennings BX 5.00 2.20
❑ 181 Marvin Benard BX 5.00 2.20
❑ 182 Luis Castillo BY 8.00 3.60
❑ 183 Wendell Magee BX 5.00 2.20
❑ 184 Vladimir Guerrero GX 30.00 13.50
❑ 185 Nomar Garciaparra GX 60.00 27.00
❑ 186 Ryan Hancock BX 5.00 2.20
❑ 187 Mike Cameron SX 12.00 5.50
❑ 188 Cal Ripken LGD BZ 200.00 90.00
❑ 189 Chipper Jones LGD SZ 120.00 55.00
❑ 190 Albert Belle LGD SZ 80.00 36.00
❑ 191 Mike Piazza LGD BZ 150.00 70.00
❑ 192 Chuck Knoblauch LGD SY 30.00
13.50
❑ 193 Ken Griffey Jr. LGD BZ 250.00 110.00
❑ 194 Ivan Rodriguez LGD GZ 60.00 27.00
❑ 195 Jose Canseco LGD SX 30.00 13.50
❑ 196 Ryne Sandberg LGD SX 25.00 11.00
❑ 197 Jim Thome LGD GY 50.00 22.00
❑ 198 Andy Pettitte CL BY 12.00 5.50
❑ 199 Andruw Jones CL BY 40.00 18.00
❑ 200 Derek Jeter CL SY 80.00 36.00
❑ 201 Chipper Jones GX 50.00 22.00
❑ 202 Albert Belle GY 50.00 22.00
❑ 203 Mike Piazza GY 100.00 45.00
❑ 204 Ken Griffey Jr. GX 100.00 45.00
❑ 205 Ryne Sandberg GZ 60.00 27.00
❑ 206 Jose Canseco SY 30.00 13.50
❑ 207 Chili Davis BX 8.00 3.60
❑ 208 Roger Clemens GZ 100.00 45.00
❑ 209 Deion Sanders GZ 20.00 9.00
❑ 210 Darryl Hamilton BX 5.00 2.20
❑ 211 Jermaine Dye SX 8.00 3.60
❑ 212 Matt Williams GY 20.00 9.00
❑ 213 Kevin Elster BX 5.00 2.20
❑ 214 John Wetteland SX 12.00 5.50
❑ 215 Garret Anderson GZ 20.00 9.00
❑ 216 Kevin Brown GY 30.00 13.50
❑ 217 Matt Lawton SY 12.00 5.50
❑ 218 Cal Ripken GX 80.00 36.00
❑ 219 Moises Alou GY 30.00 13.50
❑ 220 Chuck Knoblauch GZ 50.00 22.00
❑ 221 Ivan Rodriguez GY 40.00 18.00
❑ 222 Travis Fryman BY 8.00 3.60
❑ 223 Jim Thome GZ 50.00 22.00
❑ 224 Eddie Murray SZ 30.00 13.50
❑ 225 Eric Young GZ 20.00 9.00
❑ 226 Ron Gant SX 8.00 3.60
❑ 227 Tony Phillips BX 5.00 2.20
❑ 228 Reggie Sanders BY 8.00 3.60
❑ 229 Johnny Damon SZ 12.00 5.50
❑ 230 Bill Pulsipher BX 5.00 2.20
❑ 231 Jim Edmonds GZ 30.00 13.50
❑ 232 Melvin Nieves BX 5.00 2.20
❑ 233 Ryan Klesko GZ 20.00 9.00
❑ 234 David Cone SX 20.00 9.00
❑ 235 Derek Bell BY 8.00 3.60
❑ 236 Julio Franco SX 12.00 5.50
❑ 237 Juan Guzman BX 5.00 2.20
❑ 238 Larry Walker GZ 50.00 22.00
❑ 239 Delino DeShields BX 5.00 2.20
❑ 240 Troy Percival BY 8.00 3.60
❑ 241 Andres Galarraga GZ 50.00 22.00
❑ 242 Rondell White GZ 20.00 9.00
❑ 243 John Burkett BX 5.00 2.20
❑ 244 J.T. Snow BY 8.00 3.60
❑ 245 Alex Fernandez SY 8.00 3.60
❑ 246 Edgar Martinez GZ 20.00 9.00
❑ 247 Craig Biggio GZ 50.00 22.00
❑ 248 Todd Hundley GY 20.00 9.00
❑ 249 Jimmy Key SX 12.00 5.50
❑ 250 Cliff Floyd BY 8.00 3.60
❑ 251 Jeff Conine BY 8.00 3.60
❑ 252 Curt Schilling BX 8.00 3.60
❑ 253 Jeff King BX 5.00 2.20
❑ 254 Tino Martinez GZ 50.00 22.00
❑ 255 Carlos Baerga SY 12.00 5.50
❑ 256 Jeff Fassero BY 5.00 2.20
❑ 257 Dean Palmer SY 12.00 5.50
❑ 258 Robb Nen BX 5.00 2.20
❑ 259 Sandy Alomar Jr. SY 12.00 5.50
❑ 260 Carlos Perez BX 8.00 3.60
❑ 261 Rickey Henderson SY 30.00 13.50
❑ 262 Bobby Bonilla SY 12.00 5.50
❑ 263 Darren Daulton BX 8.00 3.60
❑ 264 Jim Leyritz BX 5.00 2.20
❑ 265 Dennis Martinez BX 8.00 3.60
❑ 266 Butch Huskey BX 5.00 2.20
❑ 267 Joe Vitiello SY 8.00 3.60
❑ 268 Steve Trachsel BX 5.00 2.20
❑ 269 Glenallen Hill BX 5.00 2.20
❑ 270 Terry Steinbach BX 8.00 3.60
❑ 271 Mark McLemore BX 5.00 2.20
❑ 272 Devon White BX 8.00 3.60
❑ 273 Jeff Kent BX 8.00 3.60
❑ 274 Tim Raines BX 8.00 3.60
❑ 275 Carlos Garcia BX 5.00 2.20
❑ 276 Hal Morris BX 5.00 2.20
❑ 277 Gary Gaetti BX 5.00 2.20
❑ 278 John Olerud SY 12.00 5.50
❑ 279 Wally Joyner BX 8.00 3.60
❑ 280 Brian Hunter SX 12.00 5.50
❑ 281 Steve Karsay BX 5.00 2.20
❑ 282 Denny Neagle SX 12.00 5.50
❑ 283 Jose Herrera BX 5.00 2.20
❑ 284 Todd Stottlemyre BX 5.00 2.20
❑ 285 Bip Roberts SX 8.00 3.60
❑ 286 Kevin Seitzer BX 5.00 2.20
❑ 287 Benji Gil BX 5.00 2.20
❑ 288 Dennis Eckersley SX 12.00 5.50
❑ 289 Brad Ausmus BX 5.00 2.20
❑ 290 Otis Nixon BX 5.00 2.20
❑ 291 Darryl Strawberry BX 8.00 3.60
❑ 292 Marquis Grissom SY 12.00 5.50
❑ 293 Darryl Kile BX 8.00 3.60
❑ 294 Quilvio Veras BX 5.00 2.20
❑ 295 Tom Goodwin BX 5.00 2.20
❑ 296 Benito Santiago BX 5.00 2.20
❑ 297 Mike Bordick BX 5.00 2.20
❑ 298 Roberto Kelly BX 5.00 2.20
❑ 299 David Justice GZ 50.00 22.00
❑ 300 Carl Everett BX 5.00 2.20
❑ 301 Mark Whiten BX 5.00 2.20
❑ 302 Aaron Sele BX 8.00 3.60
❑ 303 Darren Dreifort BX 8.00 3.60
❑ 304 Bobby Jones BX 5.00 2.20
❑ 305 Fernando Vina BX 5.00 2.20
❑ 306 Ed Sprague BX 5.00 2.20
❑ 307 Andy Ashby SX 8.00 3.60
❑ 308 Tony Fernandez BX 5.00 2.20
❑ 309 Roger Pavlik BX 5.00 2.20
❑ 310 Mark Clark BX 5.00 2.20
❑ 311 Mariano Duncan BX 5.00 2.20
❑ 312 Tyler Houston BX 5.00 2.20
❑ 313 Eric Davis SY 12.00 5.50
❑ 314 Greg Vaughn BY 8.00 3.60
❑ 315 David Segui SY 12.00 5.50
❑ 316 Dave Nilsson SX 8.00 3.60
❑ 317 F.P. Santangelo SX 8.00 3.60
❑ 318 Wilton Guerrero GZ 12.00 5.50
❑ 319 Jose Guillen GZ 50.00 22.00
❑ 320 Kevin Orie SY 8.00 3.60
❑ 321 Derrek Lee GZ 30.00 13.50
❑ 322 Bubba Trammell SY 30.00 13.50
❑ 323 Pokey Reese GZ 12.00 5.50
❑ 324 Hideki Irabu GX 20.00 9.00
❑ 325 Scott Spiezio SZ 8.00 3.60
❑ 326 Bartolo Colon GZ 20.00 9.00
❑ 327 Damon Mashore SY 8.00 3.60
❑ 328 Ryan McGuire SY 8.00 3.60
❑ 329 Chris Carpenter BX 8.00 3.60
❑ 330 Jose Cruz Jr. GX 30.00 13.50
❑ 331 Todd Greene SZ 12.00 5.50
❑ 332 Brian Moehler BX 5.00 2.20
❑ 333 Mike Sweeney BY 5.00 2.20
❑ 334 Neifi Perez GZ 12.00 5.50
❑ 335 Matt Morris SY 12.00 5.50
❑ 336 Marvin Benard BY 5.00 2.20
❑ 337 Karim Garcia SZ 12.00 5.50
❑ 338 Jason Dickson SY 12.00 5.50
❑ 339 Brant Brown SY 12.00 5.50
❑ 340 Jeff Suppan SZ 8.00 3.60
❑ 341 Deivi Cruz BX 20.00 9.00
❑ 342 Antone Williamson GZ 12.00 5.50
❑ 343 Curtis Goodwin BX 5.00 2.20
❑ 344 Brooks Kieschnick SY 8.00 3.60
❑ 345 Tony Womack BX 20.00 9.00
❑ 346 Rudy Pemberton BX 5.00 2.20
❑ 347 Todd Dunwoody BX 8.00 3.60
❑ 348 Frank Thomas LG SY 100.00 45.00
❑ 349 Andruw Jones LG SX 25.00 11.00
❑ 350 Alex Rodriguez LG BY 100.00 45.00
❑ 351 Greg Maddux LG SY 100.00 45.00
❑ 352 Jeff Bagwell LG BY 50.00 22.00
❑ 353 Juan Gonzalez LG SY 80.00 36.00
❑ 354 Barry Bonds LG BY 40.00 18.00
❑ 355 Mark McGwire LG BY 150.00 70.00
❑ 356 Tony Gwynn LG BY 80.00 36.00
❑ 357 Gary Sheffield LG BX 12.00 5.50
❑ 358 Derek Jeter LG SX 50.00 22.00
❑ 359 Manny Ramirez LG SY 30.00 13.50
❑ 360 Hideo Nomo LG GZ 100.00 45.00
❑ 361 Sammy Sosa LG BX 50.00 22.00
❑ 362 Paul Molitor LG SZ 30.00 13.50
❑ 363 Kenny Lofton LG BY 20.00 9.00
❑ 364 Eddie Murray LG BX 20.00 9.00
❑ 365 Barry Larkin LG SZ 20.00 9.00
❑ 366 Roger Clemens LG SY 60.00 27.00

❑ 367 John Smoltz LG BZ	8.00	3.60
❑ 368 Alex Rodriguez GM SX	60.00	27.00
❑ 369 Frank Thomas GM BX	60.00	27.00
❑ 370 Cal Ripken GM SY	120.00	55.00
❑ 371 Ken Griffey Jr. GM SY	150.00	70.00
❑ 372 Greg Maddux GM BX	60.00	27.00
❑ 373 Mike Piazza GM SX	60.00	27.00
❑ 374 Chipper Jones GM BY	80.00	36.00
❑ 375 Albert Belle GM BX	30.00	13.50
❑ 376 Chuck Knoblauch GM BX	20.00	9.00
❑ 377 Brady Anderson GM BZ	8.00	3.60
❑ 378 David Justice GM SX	30.00	13.50
❑ 379 Randy Johnson GM BZ	20.00	9.00
❑ 380 Wade Boggs GM BX	20.00	9.00
❑ 381 Kevin Brown GM BX	5.00	2.20
❑ 382 Tom Glavine GM GY	50.00	22.00
❑ 383 Raul Mondesi GM SX	20.00	9.00
❑ 384 Ivan Rodriguez GM SX	25.00	11.00
❑ 385 Larry Walker GM BY	20.00	9.00
❑ 386 Bernie Williams GM BZ	20.00	9.00
❑ 387 Rusty Greer GM GY	20.00	9.00
❑ 388 Rafael Palmeiro GM GY	20.00	9.00
❑ 389 Matt Williams GM BX	8.00	3.60
❑ 390 Eric Young GM BX	8.00	3.60
❑ 391 Fred McGriff GM BX	12.00	5.50
❑ 392 Ken Caminiti GM BX	12.00	5.50
❑ 393 Roberto Alomar GM BZ	20.00	9.00
❑ 394 Brian Jordan GM BX	8.00	3.60
❑ 395 Mark Grace GM GZ	12.00	5.50
❑ 396 Jim Edmonds GM BY	12.00	5.50
❑ 397 Deion Sanders GM SY	12.00	5.50
❑ 398 Vladimir Guerrero CL SZ	80.00	36.00
❑ 399 Darin Erstad CL SY	40.00	18.00
❑ 400 N. Garciaparra CL SZ	150.00	70.00

1997 Leaf Banner Season

	MINT	NRMT
COMPLETE SET (15)	250.00	110.00
COMMON CARD (1-15)	2.50	1.10
❑ 1 Jeff Bagwell	15.00	6.75
❑ 2 Ken Griffey Jr.	50.00	22.00
❑ 3 Juan Gonzalez	25.00	11.00
❑ 4 Frank Thomas	30.00	13.50
❑ 5 Alex Rodriguez	30.00	13.50
❑ 6 Kenny Lofton	10.00	4.50
❑ 7 Chuck Knoblauch	10.00	4.50
❑ 8 Mo Vaughn	12.00	5.50
❑ 9 Chipper Jones	25.00	11.00
❑ 10 Ken Caminiti	6.00	2.70
❑ 11 Craig Biggio	10.00	4.50
❑ 12 John Smoltz	5.00	2.20
❑ 13 Pat Hentgen	5.00	2.20
❑ 14 Derek Jeter	25.00	11.00
❑ 15 Todd Hollandsworth	2.50	1.10

1997 Leaf Dress for Success

	MINT	NRMT
COMPLETE SET (18)	250.00	110.00
COMMON CARD (1-18)	3.00	1.35
❑ 1 Greg Maddux	20.00	9.00
❑ 2 Cal Ripken	25.00	11.00
❑ 3 Albert Belle	10.00	4.50
❑ 4 Frank Thomas	20.00	9.00
❑ 5 Dante Bichette	3.00	1.35
❑ 6 Gary Sheffield	4.00	1.80
❑ 7 Jeff Bagwell	10.00	4.50
❑ 8 Mike Piazza	20.00	9.00
❑ 9 Mark McGwire	30.00	13.50
❑ 10 Ken Caminiti	4.00	1.80
❑ 11 Alex Rodriguez	20.00	9.00
❑ 12 Ken Griffey Jr.	30.00	13.50
❑ 13 Juan Gonzalez	15.00	6.75
❑ 14 Brian Jordan	3.00	1.35
❑ 15 Mo Vaughn	8.00	3.60
❑ 16 Ivan Rodriguez	8.00	3.60
❑ 17 Andruw Jones	8.00	3.60
❑ 18 Chipper Jones	15.00	6.75

1997 Leaf Get-A-Grip

	MINT	NRMT
COMPLETE SET (16)	250.00	110.00
COMMON CARD (1-16)	6.00	2.70
❑ 1 Ken Griffey Jr. / Greg Maddux	40.00	18.00
❑ 2 John Smoltz / Frank Thomas	20.00	9.00
❑ 3 Mike Piazza / Andy Pettitte	20.00	9.00
❑ 4 Randy Johnson / Chipper Jones	15.00	6.75
❑ 5 Tom Glavine / Alex Rodriguez	20.00	9.00
❑ 6 Pat Hentgen / Jeff Bagwell	10.00	4.50
❑ 7 Kevin Brown / Juan Gonzalez	15.00	6.75
❑ 8 Barry Bonds / Mike Mussina	8.00	3.60
❑ 9 Hideo Nomo / Albert Belle	8.00	3.60
❑ 10 Troy Percival / Andruw Jones	8.00	3.60
❑ 11 Roger Clemens / Brian Jordan	12.00	5.50
❑ 12 Paul Wilson / Ivan Rodriguez	8.00	3.60
❑ 13 Alan Benes / Mo Vaughn	8.00	3.60
❑ 14 Al Leiter / Derek Jeter	15.00	6.75
❑ 15 Bill Pulsipher / Cal Ripken	25.00	11.00
❑ 16 Mariano Rivera / Ken Caminiti	6.00	2.70

1997 Leaf Gold Stars

	MINT	NRMT
COMPLETE SET (36)	500.00	220.00
COMMON CARD (1-36)	2.50	1.10
❑ 1 Frank Thomas	30.00	13.50
❑ 2 Alex Rodriguez	30.00	13.50
❑ 3 Ken Griffey Jr.	50.00	22.00
❑ 4 Andruw Jones	12.00	5.50
❑ 5 Chipper Jones	25.00	11.00
❑ 6 Jeff Bagwell	15.00	6.75
❑ 7 Derek Jeter	25.00	11.00
❑ 8 Deion Sanders	4.00	1.80
❑ 9 Ivan Rodriguez	12.00	5.50
❑ 10 Juan Gonzalez	25.00	11.00
❑ 11 Greg Maddux	30.00	13.50
❑ 12 Andy Pettitte	6.00	2.70
❑ 13 Roger Clemens	20.00	9.00
❑ 14 Hideo Nomo	12.00	5.50
❑ 15 Tony Gwynn	25.00	11.00
❑ 16 Barry Bonds	12.00	5.50
❑ 17 Kenny Lofton	10.00	4.50
❑ 18 Paul Molitor	10.00	4.50
❑ 19 Jim Thome	10.00	4.50
❑ 20 Albert Belle	15.00	6.75
❑ 21 Cal Ripken	40.00	18.00
❑ 22 Mark McGwire	50.00	22.00
❑ 23 Barry Larkin	6.00	2.70
❑ 24 Mike Piazza	30.00	13.50
❑ 25 Darin Erstad	12.00	5.50
❑ 26 Chuck Knoblauch	10.00	4.50
❑ 27 Vladimir Guerrero	15.00	6.75
❑ 28 Tony Clark	6.00	2.70
❑ 29 Scott Rolen	20.00	9.00
❑ 30 Nomar Garciaparra	30.00	13.50
❑ 31 Eric Young	2.50	1.10
❑ 32 Ryne Sandberg	12.00	5.50
❑ 33 Roberto Alomar	10.00	4.50
❑ 34 Eddie Murray	10.00	4.50
❑ 35 Rafael Palmeiro	6.00	2.70
❑ 36 Jose Guillen	10.00	4.50

1997 Leaf Knot-Hole Gang

	MINT	NRMT
COMPLETE SET (12)	120.00	55.00
COMMON CARD (1-12)	2.50	1.10
❑ 1 Chuck Knoblauch	5.00	2.20
❑ 2 Ken Griffey Jr.	25.00	11.00
❑ 3 Frank Thomas	15.00	6.75
❑ 4 Tony Gwynn	12.00	5.50
❑ 5 Mike Piazza	15.00	6.75
❑ 6 Jeff Bagwell	8.00	3.60
❑ 7 Rusty Greer	2.50	1.10
❑ 8 Cal Ripken	20.00	9.00
❑ 9 Chipper Jones	12.00	5.50
❑ 10 Ryan Klesko	2.50	1.10
❑ 11 Barry Larkin	4.00	1.80
❑ 12 Paul Molitor	5.00	2.20
❑ P10 Ryan Klesko Promo	2.00	.90

1997 Leaf Leagues of the Nation

	MINT	NRMT
COMPLETE SET (15)	300.00	135.00
COMMON CARD (1-15)	10.00	4.50
❑ 1 Juan Gonzalez / Barry Bonds	25.00	11.00
❑ 2 Cal Ripken / Chipper Jones	40.00	18.00
❑ 3 Mark McGwire / Ken Caminiti	50.00	22.00
❑ 4 Derek Jeter / Kenny Lofton	25.00	11.00
❑ 5 Ivan Rodriguez / Mike Piazza	30.00	13.50
❑ 6 Ken Griffey Jr. / Larry Walker	50.00	22.00
❑ 7 Frank Thomas / Sammy Sosa	40.00	18.00
❑ 8 Paul Molitor / Barry Larkin	10.00	4.50
❑ 9 Albert Belle / Deion Sanders	12.00	5.50
❑ 10 Matt Williams / Jeff Bagwell	15.00	6.75
❑ 11 Mo Vaughn / Gary Sheffield	12.00	5.50
❑ 12 Alex Rodriguez / Tony Gwynn	40.00	18.00
❑ 13 Tino Martinez / Scott Rolen	20.00	9.00
❑ 14 Darin Erstad / Wilton Guerrero	12.00	5.50
❑ 15 Tony Clark / Vladimir Guerrero	15.00	6.75

1997 Leaf Statistical Standouts

	MINT	NRMT
COMPLETE SET (15)	750.00	350.00
COMMON CARD (1-15)	10.00	4.50
❑ 1 Albert Belle	40.00	18.00
❑ 2 Juan Gonzalez	50.00	22.00
❑ 3 Ken Griffey Jr.	100.00	45.00
❑ 4 Alex Rodriguez	60.00	27.00
❑ 5 Frank Thomas	60.00	27.00
❑ 6 Chipper Jones	50.00	22.00
❑ 7 Greg Maddux	60.00	27.00
❑ 8 Mike Piazza	60.00	27.00
❑ 9 Cal Ripken	80.00	36.00
❑ 10 Mark McGwire	100.00	45.00
❑ 11 Barry Bonds	25.00	11.00
❑ 12 Derek Jeter	50.00	22.00
❑ 13 Ken Caminiti	12.00	5.50
❑ 14 John Smoltz	10.00	4.50
❑ 15 Paul Molitor	20.00	9.00

1997 Leaf Thomas Collection

	MINT	NRMT
COMPLETE SET (6)	2500.00	1100.00
COMMON CARD (1-6)	400.00	180.00
❑ 1 Frank Thomas / Game Hat/Blue Text	400.00	180.00
❑ 2 Frank Thomas / Home Jersey/Orange Text	500.00	220.00
❑ 3 Frank Thomas / Batting Glove/Yellow Text	400.00	180.00
❑ 4 Frank Thomas / Bat/Green Text	400.00	180.00
❑ 5 Frank Thomas / Sweatband/Purple Text	400.00	180.00
❑ 6 Frank Thomas / Away Jersey/Red Text	500.00	220.00

1997 Leaf Warning Track

	MINT	NRMT
COMPLETE SET (18)	100.00	45.00
COMMON CARD (1-18)	3.00	1.35
❑ 1 Ken Griffey Jr.	30.00	13.50
❑ 2 Albert Belle	8.00	3.60
❑ 3 Barry Bonds	8.00	3.60
❑ 4 Andruw Jones	8.00	3.60
❑ 5 Kenny Lofton	6.00	2.70
❑ 6 Tony Gwynn	15.00	6.75
❑ 7 Manny Ramirez	6.00	2.70
❑ 8 Rusty Greer	3.00	1.35
❑ 9 Bernie Williams	6.00	2.70
❑ 10 Gary Sheffield	4.00	1.80
❑ 11 Juan Gonzalez	15.00	6.75
❑ 12 Raul Mondesi	4.00	1.80
❑ 13 Brady Anderson	3.00	1.35
❑ 14 Rondell White	3.00	1.35
❑ 15 Sammy Sosa	15.00	6.75
❑ 16 Deion Sanders	3.00	1.35
❑ 17 Dave Justice	6.00	2.70
❑ 18 Jim Edmonds	4.00	1.80

1998 Leaf

	MINT	NRMT
COMPLETE SET (200)	200.00	90.00
COMP.SET w/o SP's (147)	15.00	6.75
COMMON CARD (1-201)	.15	.07
COMMON SP (148-197)	1.00	.45
❑ 1 Rusty Greer	.25	.11
❑ 2 Tino Martinez	.60	.25
❑ 3 Bobby Bonilla	.25	.11
❑ 4 Jason Giambi	.25	.11
❑ 5 Matt Morris	.25	.11
❑ 6 Craig Counsell	.15	.07
❑ 7 Reggie Jefferson	.15	.07
❑ 8 Brian Rose	.25	.11
❑ 9 Ruben Rivera	.25	.11
❑ 10 Shawn Estes	.25	.11
❑ 11 Tony Gwynn	1.50	.70
❑ 12 Jeff Abbott	.25	.11
❑ 13 Jose Cruz Jr.	.75	.35
❑ 14 Francisco Cordova	.15	.07
❑ 15 Ryan Klesko	.25	.11
❑ 16 Tim Salmon	.60	.25
❑ 17 Brett Tomko	.25	.11
❑ 18 Matt Williams	.25	.11
❑ 19 Joe Carter	.25	.11
❑ 20 Harold Baines	.25	.11
❑ 21 Gary Sheffield	.40	.18
❑ 22 Charles Johnson	.25	.11
❑ 23 Aaron Boone	.15	.07
❑ 24 Eddie Murray	.60	.25
❑ 25 Matt Stairs	.25	.11
❑ 26 David Cone	.40	.18
❑ 27 Jon Nunnally	.15	.07
❑ 28 Chris Stynes	.15	.07
❑ 29 Enrique Wilson	.25	.11
❑ 30 Randy Johnson	.60	.25
❑ 31 Garret Anderson	.25	.11
❑ 32 Manny Ramirez	.60	.25
❑ 33 Jeff Suppan	.15	.07
❑ 34 Rickey Henderson	.60	.25

❑ 35 Scott Spiezio	.15	.07
❑ 36 Rondell White	.25	.11
❑ 37 Todd Greene	.25	.11
❑ 38 Delino DeShields	.15	.07
❑ 39 Kevin Brown	.40	.18
❑ 40 Chili Davis	.25	.11
❑ 41 Jimmy Key	.25	.11
❑ 43 Mike Mussina	.60	.25
❑ 44 Joe Randa	.15	.07
❑ 45 Chan Ho Park	.60	.25
❑ 46 Brad Radke	.25	.11
❑ 47 Geronimo Berroa	.15	.07
❑ 48 Wade Boggs	.60	.25
❑ 49 Kevin Appier	.25	.11
❑ 50 Moises Alou	.40	.18
❑ 51 David Justice	.60	.25
❑ 52 Ivan Rodriguez	.75	.35
❑ 53 J.T. Snow	.25	.11
❑ 54 Brian Giles	.25	.11
❑ 55 Will Clark	.60	.25
❑ 56 Justin Thompson	.25	.11
❑ 57 Javier Lopez	.25	.11
❑ 58 Hideki Irabu	.40	.18
❑ 59 Mark Grudzielanek	.25	.11
❑ 60 Abraham Nunez	.25	.11
❑ 61 Todd Hollandsworth	.15	.07
❑ 62 Jay Bell	.25	.11
❑ 63 Nomar Garciaparra	2.00	.90
❑ 64 Vinny Castilla	.40	.18
❑ 65 Lou Collier	.15	.07
❑ 66 Kevin Orie	.15	.07
❑ 67 John Valentin	.25	.11
❑ 68 Robin Ventura	.25	.11
❑ 69 Denny Neagle	.25	.11
❑ 70 Tony Womack	.25	.11
❑ 71 Dennis Reyes	.25	.11
❑ 72 Wally Joyner	.25	.11
❑ 73 Kevin Brown	.40	.18
❑ 74 Ray Durham	.25	.11
❑ 75 Mike Cameron	.25	.11
❑ 76 Dante Bichette	.25	.11
❑ 77 Jose Guillen	.25	.11
❑ 78 Carlos Delgado	.25	.11
❑ 79 Paul Molitor	.60	.25
❑ 80 Jason Kendall	.25	.11
❑ 81 Mark Bellhorn	.25	.11
❑ 82 Damian Jackson	.15	.07
❑ 83 Bill Mueller	.25	.11
❑ 84 Kevin Young	.25	.11
❑ 85 Curt Schilling	.25	.11
❑ 86 Jeffrey Hammonds	.25	.11
❑ 87 Sandy Alomar Jr.	.25	.11
❑ 88 Bartolo Colon	.25	.11
❑ 89 Wilton Guerrero	.15	.07
❑ 90 Bernie Williams	.60	.25
❑ 91 Deion Sanders	.25	.11
❑ 92 Mike Piazza	2.00	.90
❑ 93 Butch Huskey	.15	.07
❑ 94 Edgardo Alfonzo	.25	.11
❑ 95 Alan Benes	.25	.11
❑ 96 Craig Biggio	.60	.25
❑ 97 Mark Grace	.40	.18
❑ 98 Shawn Green	.25	.11
❑ 99 Derrek Lee	.25	.11
❑ 100 Ken Griffey Jr.	3.00	1.35
❑ 101 Tim Raines	.25	.11
❑ 102 Pokey Reese	.15	.07
❑ 103 Lee Stevens	.15	.07
❑ 104 Shannon Stewart	.25	.11
❑ 105 John Smoltz	.25	.11
❑ 106 Frank Thomas	2.00	.90
❑ 107 Jeff Fassero	.15	.07
❑ 108 Jay Buhner	.25	.11
❑ 109 Jose Canseco	.60	.25
❑ 110 Omar Vizquel	.25	.11
❑ 111 Travis Fryman	.25	.11
❑ 112 Dave Nilsson	.15	.07
❑ 113 John Olerud	.25	.11
❑ 114 Larry Walker	.60	.25
❑ 115 Jim Edmonds	.40	.18
❑ 116 Bobby Higginson	.40	.18
❑ 117 Todd Hundley	.25	.11
❑ 118 Paul O'Neill	.25	.11
❑ 119 Bip Roberts	.15	.07
❑ 120 Ismael Valdes	.25	.11
❑ 121 Pedro Martinez	.60	.25
❑ 122 Jeff Cirillo	.25	.11
❑ 123 Andy Benes	.25	.11
❑ 124 Bobby Jones	.15	.07
❑ 125 Brian Hunter	.25	.11
❑ 126 Darryl Kile	.25	.11
❑ 127 Pat Hentgen	.25	.11
❑ 128 Marquis Grissom	.25	.11
❑ 129 Eric Davis	.25	.11
❑ 130 Chipper Jones	1.50	.70
❑ 131 Edgar Martinez	.25	.11
❑ 132 Andy Pettitte	.40	.18
❑ 133 Cal Ripken	2.50	1.10
❑ 134 Scott Rolen	1.50	.70
❑ 135 Ron Coomer	.15	.07
❑ 136 Luis Castillo	.25	.11
❑ 137 Fred McGriff	.40	.18
❑ 138 Neifi Perez	.25	.11
❑ 139 Eric Karros	.25	.11
❑ 140 Alex Fernandez	.15	.07
❑ 141 Jason Dickson	.25	.11
❑ 142 Lance Johnson	.15	.07
❑ 143 Ray Lankford	.25	.11
❑ 144 Sammy Sosa	1.50	.70
❑ 145 Eric Young	.25	.11
❑ 146 Bubba Trammell	.25	.11
❑ 147 Todd Walker	.40	.18
❑ 148 Mo Vaughn CC	4.00	1.80
❑ 149 Jeff Bagwell CC	5.00	2.20
❑ 150 Kenny Lofton CC	3.00	1.35
❑ 151 Raul Mondesi CC	2.00	.90
❑ 152 Mike Piazza CC	10.00	4.50
❑ 153 Chipper Jones CC	8.00	3.60
❑ 154 Larry Walker CC	3.00	1.35
❑ 155 Greg Maddux CC	10.00	4.50
❑ 156 Ken Griffey Jr. CC	15.00	6.75
❑ 157 Frank Thomas CC	10.00	4.50
❑ 158 Darin Erstad GLS	3.00	1.35
❑ 159 Roberto Alomar GLS	3.00	1.35
❑ 160 Albert Belle GLS	4.00	1.80
❑ 161 Jim Thome GLS	3.00	1.35
❑ 162 Tony Clark GLS	2.00	.90
❑ 163 Chuck Knoblauch GLS	3.00	1.35
❑ 164 Derek Jeter GLS	8.00	3.60
❑ 165 Alex Rodriguez GLS	10.00	4.50
❑ 166 Tony Gwynn GLS	8.00	3.60
❑ 167 Roger Clemens GLS	6.00	2.70
❑ 168 Barry Larkin GLS	2.00	.90
❑ 169 Andres Galarraga GLS	3.00	1.35
❑ 170 Vladimir Guerrero GLS	4.00	1.80
❑ 171 Mark McGwire GLS	20.00	9.00
❑ 172 Barry Bonds GLS	4.00	1.80
❑ 173 Juan Gonzalez GLS	8.00	3.60
❑ 174 Andruw Jones GLS	3.00	1.35
❑ 175 Paul Molitor GLS	3.00	1.35
❑ 176 Hideo Nomo GLS	4.00	1.80
❑ 177 Cal Ripken GLS	12.00	5.50
❑ 178 Brad Fullmer GLR	1.50	.70
❑ 179 Jaret Wright GLR	4.00	1.80
❑ 180 Bobby Estalella GLR	1.50	.70
❑ 181 Ben Grieve GLR	6.00	2.70
❑ 182 Paul Konerko GLR	3.00	1.35
❑ 183 David Ortiz GLR	1.50	.70
❑ 184 Todd Helton GLR	4.00	1.80
❑ 185 Juan Encarnacion GLR	1.50	.70
❑ 186 Miguel Tejada GLR	1.50	.70
❑ 187 Jacob Cruz GLR	1.00	.45
❑ 188 Mark Kotsay GLR	2.00	.90
❑ 189 Fernando Tatis GLR	1.50	.70
❑ 190 Ricky Ledee GLR	1.50	.70
❑ 191 Richard Hidalgo GLR	1.50	.70
❑ 192 Richie Sexson GLR	2.00	.90
❑ 193 Luis Ordaz GLR	1.50	.70
❑ 194 Eli Marrero GLR	1.50	.70
❑ 195 Livan Hernandez GLR	1.50	.70
❑ 196 Homer Bush GLR	1.00	.45
❑ 197 Raul Ibanez GLR	1.00	.45
❑ 198 Nomar Garciaparra CL	1.00	.45
❑ 199 Scott Rolen CL	.75	.35
❑ 200 Jose Cruz Jr. CL	.40	.18
❑ 201 Al Martin	.15	.07

1998 Leaf Fractal Diamond Axis

	MINT	NRMT
COMMON (1-41/43-201)	20.00	9.00

*STARS 1-147/198-201: 50X TO 120X BASIC CARDS
*YOUNG STARS 1-147/198-201: 40X TO 100X BASIC CARDS
*SP STARS 148-177: 10X TO 25X BASIC SP'S
*SP YG.STARS 148-177: 8X TO 20X BASE SP'S

1998 Leaf Fractal Matrix

	MINT	NRMT
COMPLETE SET (200)	3000.00	1350.00
COMMON BRONZE	1.25	.55
COMMON SILVER	3.00	1.35
COMMON GOLD	8.00	3.60

❑ 1 Rusty Greer GZ	10.00	4.50
❑ 2 Tino Martinez GZ	20.00	9.00
❑ 3 Bobby Bonilla SY	5.00	2.20
❑ 4 Jason Giambi SY	5.00	2.20
❑ 5 Matt Morris SY	5.00	2.20
❑ 6 Craig Counsell BX	1.25	.55
❑ 7 Reggie Jefferson BX	1.25	.55
❑ 8 Brian Rose SY	5.00	2.20
❑ 9 Ruben Rivera BX	2.00	.90
❑ 10 Shawn Estes SY	5.00	2.20
❑ 11 Tony Gwynn GZ	50.00	22.00
❑ 12 Jeff Abbott BY	2.00	.90
❑ 13 Jose Cruz Jr. GZ	20.00	9.00
❑ 14 Francisco Cordova BX	1.25	.55
❑ 15 Ryan Klesko BX	2.00	.90
❑ 16 Tim Salmon GY	20.00	9.00
❑ 17 Brett Tomko BX	2.00	.90
❑ 18 Matt Williams SY	5.00	2.20
❑ 19 Joe Carter BX	2.00	.90
❑ 20 Harold Baines BX	2.00	.90
❑ 21 Gary Sheffield SZ	8.00	3.60
❑ 22 Charles Johnson SX	5.00	2.20
❑ 23 Aaron Boone BX	1.25	.55
❑ 24 Eddie Murray GY	25.00	11.00
❑ 25 Matt Stairs BX	2.00	.90
❑ 26 David Cone BX	3.00	1.35
❑ 27 Jon Nunnally BX	1.25	.55
❑ 28 Chris Stynes BX	1.25	.55
❑ 29 Enrique Wilson BY	2.00	.90
❑ 30 Randy Johnson SZ	12.00	5.50
❑ 31 Garret Anderson SY	5.00	2.20
❑ 32 Manny Ramirez GZ	20.00	9.00
❑ 33 Jeff Suppan SX	3.00	1.35
❑ 34 Rickey Henderson BX	5.00	2.20
❑ 35 Scott Spiezio BX	1.25	.55
❑ 36 Rondell White SY	5.00	2.20
❑ 37 Todd Greene SZ	5.00	2.20
❑ 38 Delino DeShields BX	1.25	.55
❑ 39 Kevin Brown P SX	8.00	3.60
❑ 40 Chili Davis BX	2.00	.90
❑ 41 Jimmy Key BX	2.00	.90
❑ 43 Mike Mussina GY	25.00	11.00
❑ 44 Joe Randa BX	1.25	.55
❑ 45 Chan Ho Park SZ	12.00	5.50
❑ 46 Brad Radke BX	2.00	.90
❑ 47 Geronimo Berroa BX	1.25	.55
❑ 48 Wade Boggs SY	12.00	5.50
❑ 49 Kevin Appier BX	2.00	.90
❑ 50 Moises Alou SY	8.00	3.60
❑ 51 David Justice GY	20.00	9.00
❑ 52 Ivan Rodriguez GZ	25.00	11.00
❑ 53 J.T. Snow BX	2.00	.90
❑ 54 Brian Giles BX	2.00	.90
❑ 55 Will Clark BY	5.00	2.20
❑ 56 Justin Thompson SY	5.00	2.20
❑ 57 Javier Lopez SX	5.00	2.20
❑ 58 Hideki Irabu BZ	3.00	1.35
❑ 59 Mark Grudzielanek BX	2.00	.90
❑ 60 Abraham Nunez SX	5.00	2.20
❑ 61 Todd Hollandsworth BX	1.25	.55
❑ 62 Jay Bell BX	2.00	.90
❑ 63 Nomar Garciaparra GZ	60.00	27.00

	No.	Player	Mint	NRMT
❑	64	Vinny Castilla BY	3.00	1.35
❑	65	Lou Collier BY	1.25	.55
❑	66	Kevin Orie SX	3.00	1.35
❑	67	John Valentin BX	2.00	.90
❑	68	Robin Ventura BX	2.00	.90
❑	69	Denny Neagle BX	2.00	.90
❑	70	Tony Womack SY	5.00	2.20
❑	71	Dennis Reyes SY	5.00	2.20
❑	72	Wally Joyner BX	2.00	.90
❑	73	Kevin Brown C BY	1.25	.55
❑	74	Ray Durham BX	2.00	.90
❑	75	Mike Cameron SZ	5.00	2.20
❑	76	Dante Bichette BX	2.00	.90
❑	77	Jose Guillen GY	10.00	4.50
❑	78	Carlos Delgado BY	2.00	.90
❑	79	Paul Molitor GZ	20.00	9.00
❑	80	Jason Kendall BX	2.00	.90
❑	81	Mark Bellhorn BX	2.00	.90
❑	82	Damian Jackson BX	1.25	.55
❑	83	Bill Mueller BX	2.00	.90
❑	84	Kevin Young BX	2.00	.90
❑	85	Curt Schilling BX	2.00	.90
❑	86	Jeffrey Hammonds BX	2.00	.90
❑	87	Sandy Alomar Jr. SY	5.00	2.20
❑	88	Bartolo Colon BY	2.00	.90
❑	89	Wilton Guerrero BY	1.25	.55
❑	90	Bernie Williams GY	25.00	11.00
❑	91	Deion Sanders SY	5.00	2.20
❑	92	Mike Piazza GX	150.00	70.00
❑	93	Butch Huskey BX	1.25	.55
❑	94	Edgardo Alfonzo SX	5.00	2.20
❑	95	Alan Benes SY	5.00	2.20
❑	96	Craig Biggio SY	12.00	5.50
❑	97	Mark Grace SY	8.00	3.60
❑	98	Shawn Green SY	5.00	2.20
❑	99	Derrek Lee SY	5.00	2.20
❑	100	Ken Griffey Jr. GZ	100.00	45.00
❑	101	Tim Raines BX	2.00	.90
❑	102	Pokey Reese SX	3.00	1.35
❑	103	Lee Stevens BX	1.25	.55
❑	104	Shannon Stewart SY	5.00	2.20
❑	105	John Smoltz SY	5.00	2.20
❑	106	Frank Thomas GX	150.00	70.00
❑	107	Jeff Fassero BX	1.25	.55
❑	108	Jay Buhner BY	2.00	.90
❑	109	Jose Canseco BX	5.00	2.20
❑	110	Omar Vizquel BX	2.00	.90
❑	111	Travis Fryman BX	2.00	.90
❑	112	Dave Nilsson BX	1.25	.55
❑	113	John Olerud BX	2.00	.90
❑	114	Larry Walker GZ	20.00	9.00
❑	115	Jim Edmonds SY	8.00	3.60
❑	116	Bobby Higginson SX	8.00	3.60
❑	117	Todd Hundley SX	5.00	2.20
❑	118	Paul O'Neill BX	2.00	.90
❑	119	Bip Roberts BX	1.25	.55
❑	120	Ismael Valdes BX	2.00	.90
❑	121	Pedro Martinez SY	12.00	5.50
❑	122	Jeff Cirillo BX	2.00	.90
❑	123	Andy Benes BX	2.00	.90
❑	124	Bobby Jones BX	1.25	.55
❑	125	Brian Hunter BX	2.00	.90
❑	126	Darryl Kile BX	2.00	.90
❑	127	Pat Hentgen BX	2.00	.90
❑	128	Marquis Grissom BX	2.00	.90
❑	129	Eric Davis BX	2.00	.90
❑	130	Chipper Jones GZ	50.00	22.00
❑	131	Edgar Martinez SZ	5.00	2.20
❑	132	Andy Pettitte GZ	12.00	5.50
❑	133	Cal Ripken GX	200.00	90.00
❑	134	Scott Rolen GZ	40.00	18.00
❑	135	Ron Coomer BX	1.25	.55
❑	136	Luis Castillo BY	2.00	.90
❑	137	Fred McGriff BY	3.00	1.35
❑	138	Neifi Perez SY	5.00	2.20
❑	139	Eric Karros BX	2.00	.90
❑	140	Alex Fernandez BX	1.25	.55
❑	141	Jason Dickson BX	2.00	.90
❑	142	Lance Johnson BX	1.25	.55
❑	143	Ray Lankford BY	2.00	.90
❑	144	Sammy Sosa GY	60.00	27.00
❑	145	Eric Young BY	2.00	.90
❑	146	Bubba Trammell SY	5.00	2.20
❑	147	Todd Walker SY	8.00	3.60
❑	148	Mo Vaughn CC SX	15.00	6.75
❑	149	Jeff Bagwell CC SX	20.00	9.00
❑	150	Kenny Lofton CC SX	12.00	5.50
❑	151	Raul Mondesi CC SX	8.00	3.60
❑	152	Mike Piazza CC SX	40.00	18.00
❑	153	Chipper Jones CC SX	30.00	13.50
❑	154	Larry Walker CC SX	12.00	5.50
❑	155	Greg Maddux CC SX	40.00	18.00
❑	156	Ken Griffey Jr. CC SX	60.00	27.00
❑	157	Frank Thomas CC SX	40.00	18.00
❑	158	Darin Erstad GLS BZ	5.00	2.20
❑	159	Roberto Alomar GLS BY	5.00	2.20
❑	160	Albert Belle GLS GY	25.00	11.00
❑	161	Jim Thome GLS GY	25.00	11.00
❑	162	Tony Clark GLS GY	12.00	5.50
❑	163	C. Knoblauch GLS BY	5.00	2.20
❑	164	Derek Jeter GLS GZ	50.00	22.00
❑	165	Alex Rodriguez GLS GZ	60.00	27.00
❑	166	Tony Gwynn GLS BX	12.00	5.50
❑	167	Roger Clemens GLS GZ	40.00	18.00
❑	168	Barry Larkin GLS BY	3.00	1.35
❑	169	A. Galarraga GLS BY	5.00	2.20
❑	170	V. Guerrero GLS GZ	25.00	11.00
❑	171	Mark McGwire GLS BZ	30.00	13.50
❑	172	Barry Bonds GLS BZ	6.00	2.70
❑	173	Juan Gonzalez GLS GZ	50.00	22.00
❑	174	Andruw Jones GLS GZ	20.00	9.00
❑	175	Paul Molitor GLS BX	5.00	2.20
❑	176	Hideo Nomo GLS BZ	6.00	2.70
❑	177	Cal Ripken GLS BX	20.00	9.00
❑	178	Brad Fullmer GLR SZ	5.00	2.20
❑	179	Jaret Wright GLR GZ	20.00	9.00
❑	180	Bobby Estalella GLR BY	2.00	.90
❑	181	Ben Grieve GLR GX	80.00	36.00
❑	182	Paul Konerko GLR GZ	20.00	9.00
❑	183	David Ortiz GLR GZ	10.00	4.50
❑	184	Todd Helton GLR GX	50.00	22.00
❑	185	J. Encarnacion GLR GZ	10.00	4.50
❑	186	Miguel Tejada GLR GZ	10.00	4.50
❑	187	Jacob Cruz GLR BY	1.25	.55
❑	188	Mark Kotsay GLR GZ	12.00	5.50
❑	189	Fernando Tatis GLR SZ	5.00	2.20
❑	190	Ricky Ledee GLR SY	5.00	2.20
❑	191	Richard Hidalgo GLR SY	5.00	2.20
❑	192	Richie Sexson GLR SY	8.00	3.60
❑	193	Luis Ordaz GLR BX	2.00	.90
❑	194	Eli Marrero GLR SZ	5.00	2.20
❑	195	Livan Hernandez GLR SZ	5.00	2.20
❑	196	Homer Bush GLR BX	1.25	.55
❑	197	Raul Ibanez GLR BX	1.25	.55
❑	198	N. Garciaparra CL BX	15.00	6.75
❑	199	Scott Rolen CL BX	10.00	4.50
❑	200	Jose Cruz Jr. CL BX	3.00	1.35
❑	201	Al Martin BX	1.25	.55

1998 Leaf Fractal Matrix Die Cuts

	MINT	NRMT
COMPLETE SET (200)	6000.00	2700.00
COMMON X-AXIS	5.00	2.20
COMMON Y-AXIS	8.00	3.60
COMMON Z-AXIS	20.00	9.00

	No.	Player	Mint	NRMT
❑	1	Rusty Greer GZ	20.00	9.00
❑	2	Tino Martinez GZ	50.00	22.00
❑	3	Bobby Bonilla SY	12.00	5.50
❑	4	Jason Giambi SY	12.00	5.50
❑	5	Matt Morris SY	12.00	5.50
❑	6	Craig Counsell BX	5.00	2.20
❑	7	Reggie Jefferson BX	5.00	2.20
❑	8	Brian Rose SY	12.00	5.50
❑	9	Ruben Rivera BX	8.00	3.60
❑	10	Shawn Estes SY	12.00	5.50
❑	11	Tony Gwynn GZ	120.00	55.00
❑	12	Jeff Abbott BY	12.00	5.50
❑	13	Jose Cruz Jr. GZ	50.00	22.00
❑	14	Francisco Cordova BX	5.00	2.20
❑	15	Ryan Klesko BX	8.00	3.60
❑	16	Tim Salmon GY	30.00	13.50
❑	17	Brett Tomko BX	8.00	3.60
❑	18	Matt Williams SY	12.00	5.50
❑	19	Joe Carter BX	8.00	3.60
❑	20	Harold Baines BX	8.00	3.60
❑	21	Gary Sheffield SZ	30.00	13.50
❑	22	Charles Johnson SX	8.00	3.60
❑	23	Aaron Boone BX	5.00	2.20
❑	24	Eddie Murray GY	30.00	13.50
❑	25	Matt Stairs BX	8.00	3.60
❑	26	David Cone BX	12.00	5.50
❑	27	Jon Nunnally BX	5.00	2.20
❑	28	Chris Stynes BX	5.00	2.20
❑	29	Enrique Wilson BY	12.00	5.50
❑	30	Randy Johnson SZ	50.00	22.00
❑	31	Garret Anderson SY	12.00	5.50
❑	32	Manny Ramirez GZ	50.00	22.00
❑	33	Jeff Suppan SX	5.00	2.20
❑	34	Rickey Henderson BX	20.00	9.00
❑	35	Scott Spiezio BX	5.00	2.20
❑	36	Rondell White SY	12.00	5.50
❑	37	Todd Greene SZ	20.00	9.00
❑	38	Delino DeShields BX	5.00	2.20
❑	39	Kevin Brown P SX	12.00	5.50
❑	40	Chili Davis BX	8.00	3.60
❑	41	Jimmy Key BX	8.00	3.60
❑	43	Mike Mussina GY	30.00	13.50
❑	44	Joe Randa BX	5.00	2.20
❑	45	Chan Ho Park SZ	50.00	22.00
❑	46	Brad Radke BX	8.00	3.60
❑	47	Geronimo Berroa BX	5.00	2.20
❑	48	Wade Boggs SY	30.00	13.50
❑	49	Kevin Appier BX	8.00	3.60
❑	50	Moises Alou SY	20.00	9.00
❑	51	David Justice GY	30.00	13.50
❑	52	Ivan Rodriguez GZ	60.00	27.00
❑	53	J.T. Snow BX	8.00	3.60
❑	54	Brian Giles BX	8.00	3.60
❑	55	Will Clark BY	30.00	13.50
❑	56	Justin Thompson SY	12.00	5.50
❑	57	Javier Lopez SX	8.00	3.60
❑	58	Hideki Irabu BZ	30.00	13.50
❑	59	Mark Grudzielanek BX	8.00	3.60
❑	60	Abraham Nunez SX	8.00	3.60
❑	61	Todd Hollandsworth BX	5.00	2.20
❑	62	Jay Bell BX	8.00	3.60
❑	63	Nomar Garciaparra GZ	150.00	70.00
❑	64	Vinny Castilla BY	20.00	9.00
❑	65	Lou Collier BY	8.00	3.60
❑	66	Kevin Orie SX	5.00	2.20
❑	67	John Valentin BX	8.00	3.60
❑	68	Robin Ventura BX	8.00	3.60
❑	69	Denny Neagle BX	8.00	3.60
❑	70	Tony Womack SY	12.00	5.50
❑	71	Dennis Reyes SY	12.00	5.50
❑	72	Wally Joyner BX	8.00	3.60
❑	73	Kevin Brown C BY	8.00	3.60
❑	74	Ray Durham BX	8.00	3.60
❑	75	Mike Cameron SZ	20.00	9.00
❑	76	Dante Bichette BX	8.00	3.60
❑	77	Jose Guillen GY	12.00	5.50
❑	78	Carlos Delgado BY	12.00	5.50
❑	79	Paul Molitor GZ	50.00	22.00
❑	80	Jason Kendall BX	8.00	3.60
❑	81	Mark Bellhorn BX	8.00	3.60
❑	82	Damian Jackson BX	5.00	2.20
❑	83	Bill Mueller BX	8.00	3.60
❑	84	Kevin Young BX	8.00	3.60
❑	85	Curt Schilling BX	8.00	3.60
❑	86	Jeffrey Hammonds BX	8.00	3.60
❑	87	Sandy Alomar Jr. SY	12.00	5.50
❑	88	Bartolo Colon BY	12.00	5.50
❑	89	Wilton Guerrero BY	8.00	3.60
❑	90	Bernie Williams GY	30.00	13.50
❑	91	Deion Sanders SY	12.00	5.50
❑	92	Mike Piazza GX	60.00	27.00
❑	93	Butch Huskey BX	5.00	2.20
❑	94	Edgardo Alfonzo SX	8.00	3.60
❑	95	Alan Benes SY	12.00	5.50
❑	96	Craig Biggio SY	30.00	13.50
❑	97	Mark Grace SY	20.00	9.00
❑	98	Shawn Green SY	12.00	5.50
❑	99	Derrek Lee SY	12.00	5.50
❑	100	Ken Griffey Jr. GZ	250.00	110.00
❑	101	Tim Raines BX	8.00	3.60
❑	102	Pokey Reese SX	5.00	2.20
❑	103	Lee Stevens BX	5.00	2.20
❑	104	Shannon Stewart SY	12.00	5.50
❑	105	John Smoltz SY	12.00	5.50
❑	106	Frank Thomas GX	60.00	27.00
❑	107	Jeff Fassero BX	5.00	2.20
❑	108	Jay Buhner BY	12.00	5.50

❑ 109 Jose Canseco BX 20.00 9.00
❑ 110 Omar Vizquel BX.......... 8.00 3.60
❑ 111 Travis Fryman BX 8.00 3.60
❑ 112 Dave Nilsson BX 5.00 2.20
❑ 113 John Olerud BX............ 8.00 3.60
❑ 114 Larry Walker GZ 50.00 22.00
❑ 115 Jim Edmonds SY.......... 20.00 9.00
❑ 116 Bobby Higginson SX.. 12.00 5.50
❑ 117 Todd Hundley SX 8.00 3.60
❑ 118 Paul O'Neill BX 8.00 3.60
❑ 119 Bip Roberts BX 5.00 2.20
❑ 120 Ismael Valdes BX 8.00 3.60
❑ 121 Pedro Martinez SY 30.00 13.50
❑ 122 Jeff Cirillo BX................ 8.00 3.60
❑ 123 Andy Benes BX............ 8.00 3.60
❑ 124 Bobby Jones BX 5.00 2.20
❑ 125 Brian Hunter BX 8.00 3.60
❑ 126 Darryl Kile BX 8.00 3.60
❑ 127 Pat Hentgen BX 8.00 3.60
❑ 128 Marquis Grissom BX.... 8.00 3.60
❑ 129 Eric Davis BX 8.00 3.60
❑ 130 Chipper Jones GZ..... 120.00 55.00
❑ 131 Edgar Martinez SZ 20.00 9.00
❑ 132 Andy Pettitte GZ 30.00 13.50
❑ 133 Cal Ripken GX 80.00 36.00
❑ 134 Scott Rolen GZ 100.00 45.00
❑ 135 Ron Coomer BX 5.00 2.20
❑ 136 Luis Castillo BY.......... 12.00 5.50
❑ 137 Fred McGriff BY 20.00 9.00
❑ 138 Neifi Perez SY............ 12.00 5.50
❑ 139 Eric Karros BX.............. 8.00 3.60
❑ 140 Alex Fernandez BX...... 5.00 2.20
❑ 141 Jason Dickson BX........ 8.00 3.60
❑ 142 Lance Johnson BX 5.00 2.20
❑ 143 Ray Lankford BY........ 12.00 5.50
❑ 144 Sammy Sosa GY........ 80.00 36.00
❑ 145 Eric Young BY............ 12.00 5.50
❑ 146 Bubba Trammell SY .. 12.00 5.50
❑ 147 Todd Walker SY 20.00 9.00
❑ 148 Mo Vaughn CC SX 25.00 11.00
❑ 149 Jeff Bagwell CC SX.... 30.00 13.50
❑ 150 Kenny Lofton CC SX.. 20.00 9.00
❑ 151 Raul Mondesi CC SX 12.00 5.50
❑ 152 Mike Piazza CC SX.... 60.00 27.00
❑ 153 Chipper Jones CC SX 50.00 22.00
❑ 154 Larry Walker CC SX .. 20.00 9.00
❑ 155 Greg Maddux CC SX 60.00 27.00
❑ 156 Ken Griffey Jr. CC SX 100.00 45.00
❑ 157 Frank Thomas CC SX 60.00 27.00
❑ 158 Darin Erstad GLS BZ 50.00 22.00
❑ 159 Roberto Alomar GLS BY 30.00 13.50
❑ 160 Albert Belle GLS GY .. 50.00 22.00
❑ 161 Jim Thome GLS GY .. 30.00 13.50
❑ 162 Tony Clark GLS GY .. 20.00 9.00
❑ 163 C. Knoblauch GLS BY 30.00 13.50
❑ 164 Derek Jeter GLS GZ 120.00 55.00
❑ 165 Alex Rodriguez GLS GZ 150.00 70.00
❑ 166 Tony Gwynn GLS BX 50.00 22.00
❑ 167 Roger Clemens GLS GZ 100.00 45.00
❑ 168 Barry Larkin GLS BY.. 20.00 9.00
❑ 169 A. Galarraga GLS BY 30.00 13.50
❑ 170 V. Guerrero GLS GZ.. 60.00 27.00
❑ 171 Mark McGwire GLS BZ 300.00 135.00
❑ 172 Barry Bonds GLS BZ.. 60.00 27.00
❑ 173 Juan Gonzalez GLS GZ 120.00 55.00
❑ 174 Andruw Jones GLS GZ 50.00 22.00
❑ 175 Paul Molitor GLS BX .. 20.00 9.00
❑ 176 Hideo Nomo GLS BZ 60.00 27.00
❑ 177 Cal Ripken GLS BX.... 80.00 36.00
❑ 178 Brad Fullmer GLR SZ 20.00 9.00
❑ 179 Jaret Wright GLR GZ 50.00 22.00
❑ 180 Bobby Estalella GLR BY 12.00 5.50
❑ 181 Ben Grieve GLR GX .. 30.00 13.50
❑ 182 Paul Konerko GLR GZ 50.00 22.00
❑ 183 David Ortiz GLR GZ .. 20.00 9.00
❑ 184 Todd Helton GLR GX 20.00 9.00
❑ 185 J. Encarnacion GLR GZ 20.00 9.00
❑ 186 Miguel Tejada GLR GZ 20.00 9.00
❑ 187 Jacob Cruz GLR BY 8.00 3.60
❑ 188 Mark Kotsay GLR GZ 30.00 13.50
❑ 189 Fernando Tatis GLR SZ 20.00 9.00
❑ 190 Ricky Ledee GLR SY 12.00 5.50
❑ 191 Richard Hidalgo GLR SY 12.00 5.50
❑ 192 Richie Sexson GLR SY 20.00 9.00
❑ 193 Luis Ordaz GLR BX...... 8.00 3.60
❑ 194 Eli Marrero GLR SZ.... 20.00 9.00
❑ 195 Livan Hernandez GLR SZ 20.00 9.00
❑ 196 Homer Bush GLR BX .. 5.00 2.20
❑ 197 Raul Ibanez GLR BX.... 5.00 2.20
❑ 198 N. Garciaparra CL BX 30.00 13.50
❑ 199 Scott Rolen CL BX 20.00 9.00
❑ 200 Jose Cruz Jr. CL BX .. 12.00 5.50
❑ 201 Al Martin BX 5.00 2.20

1998 Leaf Crusade Green

MINT NRMT

PLEASE SEE 1998 DONRUSS CRUSADE

1998 Leaf Heading for the Hall

	MINT	NRMT
COMPLETE SET (20)	250.00	110.00
COMMON CARD (1-20)...........	5.00	2.20

❑ 1 Roberto Alomar............... 8.00 3.60
❑ 2 Jeff Bagwell.................... 12.00 5.50
❑ 3 Albert Belle 10.00 4.50
❑ 4 Wade Boggs 8.00 3.60
❑ 5 Barry Bonds 10.00 4.50
❑ 6 Roger Clemens 15.00 6.75
❑ 7 Juan Gonzalez 20.00 9.00
❑ 8 Ken Griffey Jr. 40.00 18.00
❑ 9 Tony Gwynn 20.00 9.00
❑ 10 Barry Larkin................. 5.00 2.20
❑ 11 Kenny Lofton.............. 8.00 3.60
❑ 12 Greg Maddux 25.00 11.00
❑ 13 Mark McGwire............. 50.00 22.00
❑ 14 Paul Molitor 8.00 3.60
❑ 15 Eddie Murray................ 8.00 3.60
❑ 16 Mike Piazza................ 25.00 11.00
❑ 17 Cal Ripken.................. 30.00 13.50
❑ 18 Ivan Rodriguez 10.00 4.50
❑ 19 Ryne Sandberg 10.00 4.50
❑ 20 Frank Thomas 25.00 11.00

1998 Leaf State Representatives

	MINT	NRMT
COMPLETE SET (30)	250.00	110.00
COMMON CARD (1-30)...........	2.50	1.10

❑ 1 Ken Griffey Jr. 25.00 11.00
❑ 2 Frank Thomas 15.00 6.75
❑ 3 Alex Rodriguez 15.00 6.75
❑ 4 Cal Ripken...................... 20.00 9.00
❑ 5 Chipper Jones 12.00 5.50
❑ 6 Andruw Jones 5.00 2.20
❑ 7 Scott Rolen 10.00 4.50
❑ 8 Nomar Garciaparra 15.00 6.75
❑ 9 Tim Salmon.................... 5.00 2.20
❑ 10 Manny Ramirez 5.00 2.20
❑ 11 Jose Cruz Jr. 5.00 2.20
❑ 12 Vladimir Guerrero 6.00 2.70
❑ 13 Tino Martinez 5.00 2.20
❑ 14 Larry Walker 5.00 2.20
❑ 15 Mo Vaughn 6.00 2.70
❑ 16 Jim Thome 5.00 2.20
❑ 17 Tony Clark.................... 3.00 1.35
❑ 18 Derek Jeter 12.00 5.50
❑ 19 Juan Gonzalez 12.00 5.50
❑ 20 Jeff Bagwell.................. 8.00 3.60
❑ 21 Ivan Rodriguez 6.00 2.70
❑ 22 Mark McGwire............. 30.00 13.50
❑ 23 David Justice................ 5.00 2.20
❑ 24 Chuck Knoblauch 5.00 2.20
❑ 25 Andy Pettitte 3.00 1.35
❑ 26 Raul Mondesi 3.00 1.35
❑ 27 Randy Johnson 5.00 2.20
❑ 28 Greg Maddux 15.00 6.75
❑ 29 Bernie Williams 5.00 2.20
❑ 30 Rusty Greer.................. 2.50 1.10

1998 Leaf Statistical Standouts

	MINT	NRMT
COMPLETE SET (24)	600.00	275.00
COMMON CARD (1-24)...........	8.00	3.60

❑ 1 Frank Thomas 40.00 18.00
❑ 2 Ken Griffey Jr. 60.00 27.00
❑ 3 Alex Rodriguez 40.00 18.00
❑ 4 Mike Piazza................... 40.00 18.00
❑ 5 Greg Maddux 40.00 18.00
❑ 6 Cal Ripken..................... 50.00 22.00
❑ 7 Chipper Jones 30.00 13.50
❑ 8 Juan Gonzalez 30.00 13.50
❑ 9 Jeff Bagwell.................. 20.00 9.00
❑ 10 Mark McGwire............. 80.00 36.00
❑ 11 Tony Gwynn 30.00 13.50
❑ 12 Mo Vaughn 15.00 6.75
❑ 13 Nomar Garciaparra 40.00 18.00
❑ 14 Jose Cruz Jr. 12.00 5.50
❑ 15 Vladimir Guerrero 15.00 6.75
❑ 16 Scott Rolen 25.00 11.00
❑ 17 Andy Pettitte 10.00 4.50
❑ 18 Randy Johnson 12.00 5.50
❑ 19 Larry Walker 12.00 5.50
❑ 20 Kenny Lofton............... 12.00 5.50
❑ 21 Tony Clark.................... 8.00 3.60
❑ 22 David Justice............... 10.00 4.50
❑ 23 Derek Jeter 30.00 13.50
❑ 24 Barry Bonds 15.00 6.75

1998 Leaf Fractal Foundations

	MINT	NRMT
COMPLETE SET (200)	400.00	180.00
COMMON (1-41/43-201)	1.50	.70

	MINT	NRMT
❑ 1 Rusty Greer	2.00	.90
❑ 2 Tino Martinez	5.00	2.20
❑ 3 Bobby Bonilla	2.00	.90
❑ 4 Jason Giambi	2.00	.90
❑ 5 Matt Morris	2.00	.90
❑ 6 Craig Counsell	1.50	.70
❑ 7 Reggie Jefferson	1.50	.70
❑ 8 Brian Rose	2.00	.90
❑ 9 Ruben Rivera	2.00	.90
❑ 10 Shawn Estes	2.00	.90
❑ 11 Tony Gwynn	12.00	5.50
❑ 12 Jeff Abbott	2.00	.90
❑ 13 Jose Cruz Jr.	5.00	2.20
❑ 14 Francisco Cordova	1.50	.70
❑ 15 Ryan Klesko	2.00	.90
❑ 16 Tim Salmon	5.00	2.20
❑ 17 Brett Tomko	2.00	.90
❑ 18 Matt Williams	2.00	.90
❑ 19 Joe Carter	2.00	.90
❑ 20 Harold Baines	2.00	.90
❑ 21 Gary Sheffield	3.00	1.35
❑ 22 Charles Johnson	2.00	.90
❑ 23 Aaron Boone	1.50	.70
❑ 24 Eddie Murray	5.00	2.20
❑ 25 Matt Stairs	2.00	.90
❑ 26 David Cone	3.00	1.35
❑ 27 Jon Nunnally	1.50	.70
❑ 28 Chris Stynes	1.50	.70
❑ 29 Enrique Wilson	2.00	.90
❑ 30 Randy Johnson	5.00	2.20
❑ 31 Garret Anderson	2.00	.90
❑ 32 Manny Ramirez	5.00	2.20
❑ 33 Jeff Suppan	1.50	.70
❑ 34 Rickey Henderson	5.00	2.20
❑ 35 Scott Spiezio	1.50	.70
❑ 36 Rondell White	2.00	.90
❑ 37 Todd Greene	2.00	.90
❑ 38 Delino DeShields	1.50	.70
❑ 39 Kevin Brown	3.00	1.35
❑ 40 Chili Davis	2.00	.90
❑ 41 Jimmy Key	2.00	.90
❑ 43 Mike Mussina	5.00	2.20
❑ 44 Joe Randa	1.50	.70
❑ 45 Chan Ho Park	5.00	2.20
❑ 46 Brad Radke	2.00	.90
❑ 47 Geronimo Berroa	1.50	.70
❑ 48 Wade Boggs	5.00	2.20
❑ 49 Kevin Appier	2.00	.90
❑ 50 Moises Alou	3.00	1.35
❑ 51 David Justice	5.00	2.20
❑ 52 Ivan Rodriguez	6.00	2.70
❑ 53 J.T. Snow	2.00	.90
❑ 54 Brian Giles	2.00	.90
❑ 55 Will Clark	5.00	2.20
❑ 56 Justin Thompson	2.00	.90
❑ 57 Javier Lopez	2.00	.90
❑ 58 Hideki Irabu	3.00	1.35
❑ 59 Mark Grudzielanek	2.00	.90
❑ 60 Abraham Nunez	2.00	.90
❑ 61 Todd Hollandsworth	1.50	.70
❑ 62 Jay Bell	2.00	.90
❑ 63 Nomar Garciaparra	15.00	6.75
❑ 64 Vinny Castilla	3.00	1.35
❑ 65 Lou Collier	1.50	.70
❑ 66 Kevin Orie	1.50	.70
❑ 67 John Valentin	2.00	.90
❑ 68 Robin Ventura	2.00	.90
❑ 69 Denny Neagle	2.00	.90
❑ 70 Tony Womack	2.00	.90
❑ 71 Dennis Reyes	2.00	.90
❑ 72 Wally Joyner	2.00	.90
❑ 73 Kevin Brown	3.00	1.35
❑ 74 Ray Durham	2.00	.90
❑ 75 Mike Cameron	2.00	.90
❑ 76 Dante Bichette	2.00	.90
❑ 77 Jose Guillen	2.00	.90
❑ 78 Carlos Delgado	2.00	.90
❑ 79 Paul Molitor	5.00	2.20
❑ 80 Jason Kendall	2.00	.90
❑ 81 Mark Bellhorn	2.00	.90
❑ 82 Damian Jackson	1.50	.70
❑ 83 Bill Mueller	2.00	.90
❑ 84 Kevin Young	2.00	.90
❑ 85 Curt Schilling	2.00	.90
❑ 86 Jeffrey Hammonds	2.00	.90
❑ 87 Sandy Alomar Jr.	2.00	.90
❑ 88 Bartolo Colon	2.00	.90
❑ 89 Wilton Guerrero	1.50	.70
❑ 90 Bernie Williams	5.00	2.20
❑ 91 Deion Sanders	2.00	.90
❑ 92 Mike Piazza	15.00	6.75
❑ 93 Butch Huskey	1.50	.70
❑ 94 Edgardo Alfonzo	2.00	.90
❑ 95 Alan Benes	2.00	.90
❑ 96 Craig Biggio	5.00	2.20
❑ 97 Mark Grace	3.00	1.35
❑ 98 Shawn Green	2.00	.90
❑ 99 Derrek Lee	2.00	.90
❑ 100 Ken Griffey Jr.	25.00	11.00
❑ 101 Tim Raines	2.00	.90
❑ 102 Pokey Reese	1.50	.70
❑ 103 Lee Stevens	1.50	.70
❑ 104 Shannon Stewart	2.00	.90
❑ 105 John Smoltz	2.00	.90
❑ 106 Frank Thomas	15.00	6.75
❑ 107 Jeff Fassero	1.50	.70
❑ 108 Jay Buhner	2.00	.90
❑ 109 Jose Canseco	5.00	2.20
❑ 110 Omar Vizquel	2.00	.90
❑ 111 Travis Fryman	2.00	.90
❑ 112 Dave Nilsson	1.50	.70
❑ 113 John Olerud	2.00	.90
❑ 114 Larry Walker	5.00	2.20
❑ 115 Jim Edmonds	3.00	1.35
❑ 116 Bobby Higginson	3.00	1.35
❑ 117 Todd Hundley	2.00	.90
❑ 118 Paul O'Neill	2.00	.90
❑ 119 Bip Roberts	1.50	.70
❑ 120 Ismael Valdes	2.00	.90
❑ 121 Pedro Martinez	5.00	2.20
❑ 122 Jeff Cirillo	2.00	.90
❑ 123 Andy Benes	2.00	.90
❑ 124 Bobby Jones	1.50	.70
❑ 125 Brian Hunter	2.00	.90
❑ 126 Darryl Kile	2.00	.90
❑ 127 Pat Hentgen	2.00	.90
❑ 128 Marquis Grissom	2.00	.90
❑ 129 Eric Davis	2.00	.90
❑ 130 Chipper Jones	12.00	5.50
❑ 131 Edgar Martinez	2.00	.90
❑ 132 Andy Pettitte	3.00	1.35
❑ 133 Cal Ripken	20.00	9.00
❑ 134 Scott Rolen	10.00	4.50
❑ 135 Ron Coomer	1.50	.70
❑ 136 Luis Castillo	2.00	.90
❑ 137 Fred McGriff	3.00	1.35
❑ 138 Neifi Perez	2.00	.90
❑ 139 Eric Karros	2.00	.90
❑ 140 Alex Fernandez	1.50	.70
❑ 141 Jason Dickson	2.00	.90
❑ 142 Lance Johnson	1.50	.70
❑ 143 Ray Lankford	2.00	.90
❑ 144 Sammy Sosa	12.00	5.50
❑ 145 Eric Young	2.00	.90
❑ 146 Bubba Trammell	2.00	.90
❑ 147 Todd Walker	3.00	1.35
❑ 148 Mo Vaughn CC	6.00	2.70
❑ 149 Jeff Bagwell CC	8.00	3.60
❑ 150 Kenny Lofton CC	5.00	2.20
❑ 151 Raul Mondesi CC	3.00	1.35
❑ 152 Mike Piazza CC	15.00	6.75
❑ 153 Chipper Jones CC	12.00	5.50
❑ 154 Larry Walker CC	5.00	2.20
❑ 155 Greg Maddux CC	15.00	6.75
❑ 156 Ken Griffey Jr. CC	25.00	11.00
❑ 157 Frank Thomas CC	15.00	6.75
❑ 158 Darin Erstad GLS	5.00	2.20
❑ 159 Roberto Alomar GLS	5.00	2.20
❑ 160 Albert Belle GLS	6.00	2.70
❑ 161 Jim Thome GLS	5.00	2.20
❑ 162 Tony Clark GLS	3.00	1.35
❑ 163 Chuck Knoblauch GLS	5.00	2.20
❑ 164 Derek Jeter GLS	12.00	5.50
❑ 165 Alex Rodriguez GLS	15.00	6.75
❑ 166 Tony Gwynn GLS	12.00	5.50
❑ 167 Roger Clemens GLS	10.00	4.50
❑ 168 Barry Larkin GLS	3.00	1.35
❑ 169 A. Galarraga GLS	5.00	2.20
❑ 170 V. Guerrero GLS	6.00	2.70
❑ 171 Mark McGwire GLS	30.00	13.50
❑ 172 Barry Bonds GLS	6.00	2.70
❑ 173 Juan Gonzalez GLS	12.00	5.50
❑ 174 Andruw Jones GLS	5.00	2.20
❑ 175 Paul Molitor GLS	5.00	2.20
❑ 176 Hideo Nomo GLS	6.00	2.70
❑ 177 Cal Ripken GLS	20.00	9.00
❑ 178 Brad Fullmer GLR	2.00	.90
❑ 179 Jaret Wright GLR	5.00	2.20
❑ 180 Bobby Estalella GLR	2.00	.90
❑ 181 Ben Grieve GLR	8.00	3.60
❑ 182 Paul Konerko GLR	5.00	2.20
❑ 183 David Ortiz GLR	2.00	.90
❑ 184 Todd Helton GLR	5.00	2.20
❑ 185 J. Encarnacion GLR	2.00	.90
❑ 186 Miguel Tejada GLR	2.00	.90
❑ 187 Jacob Cruz GLR	1.50	.70
❑ 188 Mark Kotsay GLR	3.00	1.35
❑ 189 Fernando Tatis GLR	2.00	.90
❑ 190 Ricky Ledee GLR	2.00	.90
❑ 191 Richard Hidalgo GLR	2.00	.90
❑ 192 Richie Sexson GLR	3.00	1.35
❑ 193 Luis Ordaz GLR	2.00	.90
❑ 194 Eli Marrero GLR	2.00	.90
❑ 195 Livan Hernandez GLR	2.00	.90
❑ 196 Homer Bush GLR	1.50	.70
❑ 197 Raul Ibanez GLR	1.50	.70
❑ 198 N. Garciaparra CL	8.00	3.60
❑ 199 Scott Rolen CL	6.00	2.70
❑ 200 Jose Cruz Jr. CL	3.00	1.35
❑ 201 Al Martin CL	1.50	.70

1998 Leaf Fractal Materials

	MINT	NRMT
COMPLETE SET (200)	3000.00	1350.00
COMMON PLASTIC	2.00	.90
COMMON LEATHER	3.00	1.35
COMMON NYLON	8.00	3.60
COMMON WOOD	25.00	11.00

	MINT	NRMT
❑ 1 Rusty Greer NZ	10.00	4.50

❑ 2 Tino Martinez WY 30.00 13.50
❑ 3 Bobby Bonilla NY 10.00 4.50
❑ 4 Jason Giambi NZ 10.00 4.50
❑ 5 Matt Morris LY 5.00 2.20
❑ 6 Craig Counsell PX .... 2.00 .90
❑ 7 Reggie Jefferson PX .... 2.00 .90
❑ 8 Brian Rose PX 2.50 1.10
❑ 9 Ruben Rivera LY 5.00 2.20
❑ 10 Shawn Estes LY 5.00 2.20
❑ 11 Tony Gwynn WX 250.00 110.00
❑ 12 Jeff Abbott PY 2.50 1.10
❑ 13 Jose Cruz Jr. WZ 30.00 13.50
❑ 14 Francisco Cordova PY .. 2.00 .90
❑ 15 Ryan Klesko LX 5.00 2.20
❑ 16 Tim Salmon WY 30.00 13.50
❑ 17 Brett Tomko LY 5.00 2.20
❑ 18 Matt Williams NY 10.00 4.50
❑ 19 Joe Carter PX 2.50 1.10
❑ 20 Harold Baines PX .... 2.00 .90
❑ 21 Gary Sheffield NZ 12.00 5.50
❑ 22 Charles Johnson LY 5.00 2.20
❑ 23 Aaron Boone PY .... 2.00 .90
❑ 24 Eddie Murray NY 20.00 9.00
❑ 25 Matt Stairs PX 2.50 1.10
❑ 26 David Cone PX 4.00 1.80
❑ 27 Jon Nunnally PX .... 2.00 .90
❑ 28 Chris Stynes PX .... 2.00 .90
❑ 29 Enrique Wilson PY 2.50 1.10
❑ 30 Randy Johnson WY 40.00 18.00
❑ 31 Garret Anderson NY 10.00 4.50
❑ 32 Manny Ramirez WY 40.00 18.00
❑ 33 Jeff Suppan LY 3.00 1.35
❑ 34 Rickey Henderson NX.. 20.00 9.00
❑ 35 Scott Spiezio PY .... 2.00 .90
❑ 36 Rondell White LY 5.00 2.20
❑ 37 Todd Greene NZ 10.00 4.50
❑ 38 Delino DeShields PY .... 2.00 .90
❑ 39 Kevin Brown LX 8.00 3.60
❑ 40 Chili Davis PX 2.50 1.10
❑ 41 Jimmy Key PX 2.50 1.10
❑ 43 Mike Mussina NZ 20.00 9.00
❑ 44 Joe Randa PX .... 2.00 .90
❑ 45 Chan Ho Park NY 20.00 9.00
❑ 46 Brad Radke PX 2.50 1.10
❑ 47 Geronimo Berroa PX .... 2.00 .90
❑ 48 Wade Boggs NY 20.00 9.00
❑ 49 Kevin Appier PX 2.50 1.10
❑ 50 Moises Alou NX 12.00 5.50
❑ 51 David Justice NZ 20.00 9.00
❑ 52 Ivan Rodriguez WX 120.00 55.00
❑ 53 J.T. Snow LX 5.00 2.20
❑ 54 Brian Giles PY 2.50 1.10
❑ 55 Will Clark LX 12.00 5.50
❑ 56 Justin Thompson NY 10.00 4.50
❑ 57 Javier Lopez PY 2.50 1.10
❑ 58 Hideki Irabu LX 8.00 3.60
❑ 59 Mark Grudzielanek PX .. 2.50 1.10
❑ 60 Abraham Nunez PZ 2.50 1.10
❑ 61 Todd Hollandsworth PX 2.00 .90
❑ 62 Jay Bell PX 2.50 1.10
❑ 63 Nomar Garciaparra WZ 100.00 45.00
❑ 64 Vinny Castilla PY 4.00 1.80
❑ 65 Lou Collier PY .... 2.00 .90
❑ 66 Kevin Orie LX 3.00 1.35
❑ 67 John Valentin PX 2.50 1.10
❑ 68 Robin Ventura PX 2.50 1.10
❑ 69 Denny Neagle PX 2.50 1.10
❑ 70 Tony Womack LX 5.00 2.20
❑ 71 Dennis Reyes LY 5.00 2.20
❑ 72 Wally Joyner PX 2.50 1.10
❑ 73 Kevin Brown PX 4.00 1.80
❑ 74 Ray Durham PX 2.50 1.10
❑ 75 Mike Cameron NY 10.00 4.50
❑ 76 Dante Bichette LX 5.00 2.20
❑ 77 Jose Guillen NZ 10.00 4.50
❑ 78 Carlos Delgado LY 5.00 2.20
❑ 79 Paul Molitor WX 100.00 45.00
❑ 80 Jason Kendall PX 2.50 1.10
❑ 81 Mark Bellhorn LX 5.00 2.20
❑ 82 Damian Jackson PY .... 2.00 .90
❑ 83 Bill Mueller PX 2.50 1.10
❑ 84 Kevin Young PX 2.50 1.10
❑ 85 Curt Schilling PX 2.50 1.10
❑ 86 Jeffrey Hammonds PX .. 2.50 1.10
❑ 87 Sandy Alomar Jr. LY 5.00 2.20
❑ 88 Bartolo Colon PY 2.50 1.10
❑ 89 Wilton Guerrero LY 3.00 1.35
❑ 90 Bernie Williams NZ 20.00 9.00
❑ 91 Deion Sanders NY 10.00 4.50
❑ 92 Mike Piazza WZ 100.00 45.00
❑ 93 Butch Huskey LX 3.00 1.35
❑ 94 Edgardo Alfonzo LY 5.00 2.20
❑ 95 Alan Benes LZ 5.00 2.20
❑ 96 Craig Biggio NX 20.00 9.00
❑ 97 Mark Grace LY 8.00 3.60
❑ 98 Shawn Green LY 5.00 2.20
❑ 99 Derrek Lee LY 5.00 2.20
❑ 100 Ken Griffey Jr. WZ.... 150.00 70.00
❑ 101 Tim Raines PX 2.50 1.10
❑ 102 Pokey Reese PY .... 2.00 .90
❑ 103 Lee Stevens PX .... 2.00 .90
❑ 104 Shannon Stewart NX.. 10.00 4.50
❑ 105 John Smoltz LY 5.00 2.20
❑ 106 Frank Thomas WZ .. 100.00 45.00
❑ 107 Jeff Fassero PX .... 2.00 .90
❑ 108 Jay Buhner LY 5.00 2.20
❑ 109 Jose Canseco LX 12.00 5.50
❑ 110 Omar Vizquel PX 2.50 1.10
❑ 111 Travis Fryman PX 2.50 1.10
❑ 112 Dave Nilsson PX .... 2.00 .90
❑ 113 John Olerud PX 2.50 1.10
❑ 114 Larry Walker WX 100.00 45.00
❑ 115 Jim Edmonds NZ 12.00 5.50
❑ 116 Bobby Higginson LY 8.00 3.60
❑ 117 Todd Hundley LZ 5.00 2.20
❑ 118 Paul O'Neill PX 2.50 1.10
❑ 119 Bip Roberts PX .... 2.00 .90
❑ 120 Ismael Valdes PX 2.50 1.10
❑ 121 Pedro Martinez NX 25.00 11.00
❑ 122 Jeff Cirillo PX 2.50 1.10
❑ 123 Andy Benes PX 2.50 1.10
❑ 124 Bobby Jones PX .... 2.00 .90
❑ 125 Brian Hunter PX 2.50 1.10
❑ 126 Darryl Kile PX 2.50 1.10
❑ 127 Pat Hentgen PX 2.50 1.10
❑ 128 Marquis Grissom PX 2.50 1.10
❑ 129 Eric Davis PX 2.50 1.10
❑ 130 Chipper Jones WZ 80.00 36.00
❑ 131 Edgar Martinez NZ 10.00 4.50
❑ 132 Andy Pettitte WY 25.00 11.00
❑ 133 Cal Ripken WZ 120.00 55.00
❑ 134 Scott Rolen WX 200.00 90.00
❑ 135 Ron Coomer PX .... 2.00 .90
❑ 136 Luis Castillo LX 5.00 2.20
❑ 137 Fred McGriff LX 8.00 3.60
❑ 138 Neifi Perez LY 5.00 2.20
❑ 139 Eric Karros PX 2.50 1.10
❑ 140 Alex Fernandez PX .... 2.00 .90
❑ 141 Jason Dickson PX 2.50 1.10
❑ 142 Lance Johnson PX .... 2.00 .90
❑ 143 Ray Lankford PY 2.50 1.10
❑ 144 Sammy Sosa NY 50.00 22.00
❑ 145 Eric Young PY 2.50 1.10
❑ 146 Bubba Trammell LZ 5.00 2.20
❑ 147 Todd Walker LZ 8.00 3.60
❑ 148 Mo Vaughn CC PX 8.00 3.60
❑ 149 Jeff Bagwell CC PX.... 10.00 4.50
❑ 150 Kenny Lofton CC PX.... 6.00 2.70
❑ 151 Raul Mondesi CC PX .. 4.00 1.80
❑ 152 Mike Piazza CC PX.... 20.00 9.00
❑ 153 Chipper Jones CC PX 15.00 6.75
❑ 154 Larry Walker CC PX 6.00 2.70
❑ 155 Greg Maddux CC PX 20.00 9.00
❑ 156 Ken Griffey Jr. CC PX 30.00 13.50
❑ 157 Frank Thomas CC PX 20.00 9.00
❑ 158 Darin Erstad GLS LY.. 12.00 5.50
❑ 159 Roberto Alomar GLS PX 6.00 2.70
❑ 160 Albert Belle GLS LX .. 15.00 6.75
❑ 161 Jim Thome GLS LX.... 12.00 5.50
❑ 162 Tony Clark GLS LZ 8.00 3.60
❑ 163 Chuck Knoblauch GLS LZ 12.00 5.50
❑ 164 Derek Jeter GLS PX .. 15.00 6.75
❑ 165 Alex Rodriguez GLS PY 20.00 9.00
❑ 166 Tony Gwynn GLS PX 15.00 6.75
❑ 167 Roger Clemens GLS LY 25.00 11.00
❑ 168 Barry Larkin GLS PY.... 4.00 1.80
❑ 169 A. Galarraga GLS PY .. 6.00 2.70
❑ 170 V. Guerrero GLS LY .. 15.00 6.75
❑ 171 Mark McGwire GLS LZ 80.00 36.00
❑ 172 Barry Bonds GLS LY.. 15.00 6.75
❑ 173 Juan Gonzalez GLS PY 15.00 6.75
❑ 174 Andruw Jones GLS PX 6.00 2.70
❑ 175 Paul Molitor GLS PX 6.00 2.70
❑ 176 Hideo Nomo GLS LZ.. 15.00 6.75
❑ 177 Cal Ripken GLS PX.... 25.00 11.00
❑ 178 Brad Fullmer GLR PZ .. 2.50 1.10
❑ 179 Jaret Wright GLR NZ.. 20.00 9.00
❑ 180 Bobby Estalella GLR PY 2.50 1.10
❑ 181 Ben Grieve GLR WZ .. 50.00 22.00
❑ 182 Paul Konerko GLR WZ 30.00 13.50
❑ 183 David Ortiz GLR NZ .. 10.00 4.50
❑ 184 Todd Helton GLR WZ 30.00 13.50
❑ 185 J. Encarnacion GLR NZ 10.00 4.50
❑ 186 Miguel Tejada GLR NZ 10.00 4.50
❑ 187 Jacob Cruz GLR PX .... 2.00 .90
❑ 188 Mark Kotsay GLR NZ 12.00 5.50
❑ 189 Fernando Tatis GLR LY 5.00 2.20
❑ 190 Ricky Ledee GLR PX .. 2.50 1.10
❑ 191 Richard Hidalgo GLR PZ 2.50 1.10
❑ 192 Richie Sexson GLR PZ 4.00 1.80
❑ 193 Luis Ordaz GLR PX 2.50 1.10
❑ 194 Eli Marrero GLR LZ 5.00 2.20
❑ 195 Livan Hernandez GLR LZ 5.00 2.20
❑ 196 Homer Bush GLR PX .. 2.00 .90
❑ 197 Raul Ibanez GLR PX.... 2.00 .90
❑ 198 N. Garciaparra CL PX 20.00 9.00
❑ 199 Scott Rolen CL PZ 12.00 5.50
❑ 200 Jose Cruz Jr. CL PX 6.00 2.70
❑ 201 Al Martin LY 3.00 1.35

1998 Leaf Fractal Materials Die Cuts

	MINT	NRMT
COMMON X-AXIS	8.00	3.60
COMMON Y-AXIS	15.00	6.75
COMMON Z-AXIS	30.00	13.50

❑ 1 Rusty Greer NZ 30.00 13.50
❑ 2 Tino Martinez WY 60.00 27.00
❑ 3 Bobby Bonilla NY 25.00 11.00
❑ 4 Jason Giambi NZ 30.00 13.50
❑ 5 Matt Morris LY 25.00 11.00
❑ 6 Craig Counsell PX 8.00 3.60
❑ 7 Reggie Jefferson PX 8.00 3.60
❑ 8 Brian Rose PX 12.00 5.50
❑ 9 Ruben Rivera LY 25.00 11.00
❑ 10 Shawn Estes LY 25.00 11.00
❑ 11 Tony Gwynn WX 80.00 36.00
❑ 12 Jeff Abbott PY 25.00 11.00
❑ 13 Jose Cruz Jr. WZ 80.00 36.00
❑ 14 Francisco Cordova PY 15.00 6.75
❑ 15 Ryan Klesko LX 12.00 5.50
❑ 16 Tim Salmon WY 60.00 27.00
❑ 17 Brett Tomko LY 25.00 11.00
❑ 18 Matt Williams NY 25.00 11.00
❑ 19 Joe Carter PX 12.00 5.50
❑ 20 Harold Baines PX 12.00 5.50
❑ 21 Gary Sheffield NZ 50.00 22.00
❑ 22 Charles Johnson LY 25.00 11.00
❑ 23 Aaron Boone PY 15.00 6.75
❑ 24 Eddie Murray NY 60.00 27.00
❑ 25 Matt Stairs PX 12.00 5.50
❑ 26 David Cone PX 20.00 9.00
❑ 27 Jon Nunnally PX 8.00 3.60
❑ 28 Chris Stynes PX 8.00 3.60

❑ 29 Enrique Wilson PY 25.00 11.00
❑ 30 Randy Johnson WY 60.00 27.00
❑ 31 Garret Anderson NY 25.00 11.00
❑ 32 Manny Ramirez WY 60.00 27.00
❑ 33 Jeff Suppan LY 15.00 6.75
❑ 34 Rickey Henderson NX.. 30.00 13.50
❑ 35 Scott Spiezio PY 15.00 6.75
❑ 36 Rondell White LY 25.00 11.00
❑ 37 Todd Greene NZ 30.00 13.50
❑ 38 Delino DeShields PY.... 15.00 6.75
❑ 39 Kevin Brown P LX 20.00 9.00
❑ 40 Chili Davis PX 12.00 5.50
❑ 41 Jimmy Key PX.............. 12.00 5.50
❑ 43 Mike Mussina NZ 80.00 36.00
❑ 44 Joe Randa PX............... 8.00 3.60
❑ 45 Chan Ho Park NY 60.00 27.00
❑ 46 Brad Radke PX 12.00 5.50
❑ 47 Geronimo Berroa PX...... 8.00 3.60
❑ 48 Wade Boggs NY 60.00 27.00
❑ 49 Kevin Appier PX 12.00 5.50
❑ 50 Moises Alou NX............ 20.00 9.00
❑ 51 David Justice NZ.......... 80.00 36.00
❑ 52 Ivan Rodriguez WX 40.00 18.00
❑ 53 J.T. Snow LX................ 12.00 5.50
❑ 54 Brian Giles PY.............. 25.00 11.00
❑ 55 Will Clark LX 30.00 13.50
❑ 56 Justin Thompson NY.... 25.00 11.00
❑ 57 Javier Lopez PY 25.00 11.00
❑ 58 Hideki Irabu LX 20.00 9.00
❑ 59 Mark Grudzielanek PX 12.00 5.50
❑ 60 Abraham Nunez PZ...... 30.00 13.50
❑ 61 Todd Hollandsworth PX 8.00 3.60
❑ 62 Jay Bell PX 12.00 5.50
❑ 63 Nomar Garciaparra WZ 250.00 110.00
❑ 64 Vinny Castilla PY.......... 40.00 18.00
❑ 65 Lou Collier PY 15.00 6.75
❑ 66 Kevin Orie LX 8.00 3.60
❑ 67 John Valentin PX.......... 12.00 5.50
❑ 68 Robin Ventura PX 12.00 5.50
❑ 69 Denny Neagle PX 12.00 5.50
❑ 70 Tony Womack LX 12.00 5.50
❑ 71 Dennis Reyes LY 25.00 11.00
❑ 72 Wally Joyner PX 12.00 5.50
❑ 73 Kevin Brown C PX.......... 8.00 3.60
❑ 74 Ray Durham PX 12.00 5.50
❑ 75 Mike Cameron NY........ 25.00 11.00
❑ 76 Dante Bichette LX........ 12.00 5.50
❑ 77 Jose Guillen NZ............ 30.00 13.50
❑ 78 Carlos Delgado LY 25.00 11.00
❑ 79 Paul Molitor WX 30.00 13.50
❑ 80 Jason Kendall PX 12.00 5.50
❑ 81 Mark Bellhorn LX.......... 12.00 5.50
❑ 82 Damian Jackson PY 15.00 6.75
❑ 83 Bill Mueller PX.............. 12.00 5.50
❑ 84 Kevin Young PX 12.00 5.50
❑ 85 Curt Schilling PX.......... 12.00 5.50
❑ 86 Jeffrey Hammonds PX 12.00 5.50
❑ 87 Sandy Alomar Jr. LY 25.00 11.00
❑ 88 Bartolo Colon PY.......... 25.00 11.00
❑ 89 Wilton Guerrero LY 15.00 6.75
❑ 90 Bernie Williams NZ 80.00 36.00
❑ 91 Deion Sanders NY 25.00 11.00
❑ 92 Mike Piazza WZ 250.00 110.00
❑ 93 Butch Huskey LX............ 8.00 3.60
❑ 94 Edgardo Alfonzo LY 25.00 11.00
❑ 95 Alan Benes LZ.............. 30.00 13.50
❑ 96 Craig Biggio NX............ 30.00 13.50
❑ 97 Mark Grace LY 40.00 18.00
❑ 98 Shawn Green LY.......... 25.00 11.00
❑ 99 Derrek Lee LY.............. 25.00 11.00
❑ 100 Ken Griffey Jr. WZ.... 400.00 180.00
❑ 101 Tim Raines PX 12.00 5.50
❑ 102 Pokey Reese PY........ 15.00 6.75
❑ 103 Lee Stevens PX 8.00 3.60
❑ 104 Shannon Stewart NX.. 12.00 5.50
❑ 105 John Smoltz LY.......... 25.00 11.00
❑ 106 Frank Thomas WZ .. 250.00 110.00
❑ 107 Jeff Fassero PX............ 8.00 3.60
❑ 108 Jay Buhner LY............ 25.00 11.00
❑ 109 Jose Canseco LX 30.00 13.50
❑ 110 Omar Vizquel PX........ 12.00 5.50
❑ 111 Travis Fryman PX 12.00 5.50
❑ 112 Dave Nilsson PX 8.00 3.60
❑ 113 John Olerud PX.......... 12.00 5.50
❑ 114 Larry Walker WX 30.00 13.50
❑ 115 Jim Edmonds NZ........ 50.00 22.00
❑ 116 Bobby Higginson LY .. 40.00 18.00
❑ 117 Todd Hundley LZ........ 30.00 13.50
❑ 118 Paul O'Neill PX 12.00 5.50
❑ 119 Bip Roberts PX 8.00 3.60
❑ 120 Ismael Valdes PX 12.00 5.50
❑ 121 Pedro Martinez NX 30.00 13.50
❑ 122 Jeff Cirillo PX.............. 12.00 5.50
❑ 123 Andy Benes PX.......... 12.00 5.50
❑ 124 Bobby Jones PX 8.00 3.60
❑ 125 Brian Hunter PX 12.00 5.50
❑ 126 Darryl Kile PX 12.00 5.50
❑ 127 Pat Hentgen PX 12.00 5.50
❑ 128 Marquis Grissom PX .. 12.00 5.50
❑ 129 Eric Davis PX 12.00 5.50
❑ 130 Chipper Jones WZ .. 200.00 90.00
❑ 131 Edgar Martinez NZ 30.00 13.50
❑ 132 Andy Pettitte WY........ 40.00 18.00
❑ 133 Cal Ripken WZ 300.00 135.00
❑ 134 Scott Rolen WX.......... 60.00 27.00
❑ 135 Ron Coomer PX 8.00 3.60
❑ 136 Luis Castillo LX 12.00 5.50
❑ 137 Fred McGriff LX.......... 20.00 9.00
❑ 138 Neifi Perez LY 25.00 11.00
❑ 139 Eric Karros PX............ 12.00 5.50
❑ 140 Alex Fernandez PX 8.00 3.60
❑ 141 Jason Dickson PX...... 12.00 5.50
❑ 142 Lance Johnson PX 8.00 3.60
❑ 143 Ray Lankford PY........ 25.00 11.00
❑ 144 Sammy Sosa NY...... 150.00 70.00
❑ 145 Eric Young PY............ 25.00 11.00
❑ 146 Bubba Trammell LZ.... 30.00 13.50
❑ 147 Todd Walker LZ.......... 50.00 22.00
❑ 148 Mo Vaughn CC PX 40.00 18.00
❑ 149 Jeff Bagwell CC PX.... 50.00 22.00
❑ 150 Kenny Lofton CC PX.. 30.00 13.50
❑ 151 Raul Mondesi CC PX 20.00 9.00
❑ 152 Mike Piazza CC PX.. 100.00 45.00
❑ 153 Chipper Jones CC PX 80.00 36.00
❑ 154 Larry Walker CC PX .. 30.00 13.50
❑ 155 Greg Maddux CC PX 100.00 45.00
❑ 156 Ken Griffey Jr. CC PX 150.00 70.00
❑ 157 Frank Thomas CC PX 100.00 45.00
❑ 158 Darin Erstad GLS LY.. 60.00 27.00
❑ 159 Roberto Alomar GLS PX 30.00 13.50
❑ 160 Albert Belle GLS LX .. 50.00 22.00
❑ 161 Jim Thome GLS LX ... 30.00 13.50
❑ 162 Tony Clark GLS LZ 50.00 22.00
❑ 163 Chuck Knoblauch GLS LZ 80.00 36.00
❑ 164 Derek Jeter GLS PX .. 80.00 36.00
❑ 165 Alex Rodriguez GLS PY 200.00 90.00
❑ 166 Tony Gwynn GLS PX 80.00 36.00
❑ 167 Roger Clemens GLS LY 120.00 55.00
❑ 168 Barry Larkin GLS PY.. 40.00 18.00
❑ 169 A. Galarraga GLS PY 60.00 27.00
❑ 170 V. Guerrero GLS LY .. 80.00 36.00
❑ 171 Mark McGwire GLS LZ 500.00 220.00
❑ 172 Barry Bonds GLS LY.. 80.00 36.00
❑ 173 Juan Gonzalez GLS PY 150.00 70.00
❑ 174 Andruw Jones GLS PX 30.00 13.50
❑ 175 Paul Molitor GLS PX .. 30.00 13.50
❑ 176 Hideo Nomo GLS LZ 100.00 45.00
❑ 177 Cal Ripken GLS PX.. 120.00 55.00
❑ 178 Brad Fullmer GLR PZ 30.00 13.50
❑ 179 Jaret Wright GLR NZ.. 80.00 36.00
❑ 180 Bobby Estalella GLR PY 25.00 11.00
❑ 181 Ben Grieve GLR WZ 120.00 55.00
❑ 182 Paul Konerko GLR WZ 80.00 36.00
❑ 183 David Ortiz GLR NZ .. 30.00 13.50
❑ 184 Todd Helton GLR WZ 80.00 36.00
❑ 185 J. Encarnacion GLR NZ 30.00 13.50
❑ 186 Miguel Tejada GLR NZ 30.00 13.50
❑ 187 Jacob Cruz GLR PX ... 8.00 3.60
❑ 188 Mark Kotsay GLR NZ 50.00 22.00
❑ 189 Fernando Tatis GLR LY 25.00 11.00
❑ 190 Ricky Ledee GLR PX 12.00 5.50
❑ 191 Richard Hidalgo GLR PZ 30.00 13.50
❑ 192 Richie Sexson GLR PZ 50.00 22.00
❑ 193 Luis Ordaz GLR PX.... 12.00 5.50
❑ 194 Eli Marrero GLR LZ 30.00 13.50
❑ 195 Livan Hernandez GLR LZ 30.00 13.50
❑ 196 Homer Bush GLR PX .. 8.00 3.60
❑ 197 Raul Ibanez GLR PX.... 8.00 3.60
❑ 198 N. Garciaparra CL PX 60.00 27.00
❑ 199 Scott Rolen CL PZ .. 100.00 45.00
❑ 200 Jose Cruz Jr. CL PX .. 20.00 9.00
❑ 201 Al Martin LY................ 15.00 6.75

1998 Leaf Fractal Materials Z2 Axis

	MINT	NRMT
COMMON (1-41/43-201)	50.00	22.00

*STARS: 20X TO 40X BASIC FOUNDATION
*YOUNG STARS: 20X TO 40X BASIC FOUNDATION

1994 Leaf Limited

	MINT	NRMT
COMPLETE SET (160)	80.00	36.00
COMMON CARD (1-160)............	.50	.23

❑ 1 Jeffrey Hammonds .... .75 .35
❑ 2 Ben McDonald.................. .50 .23
❑ 3 Mike Mussina .... 2.00 .90
❑ 4 Rafael Palmeiro................ 1.25 .55
❑ 5 Cal Ripken Jr. 8.00 3.60
❑ 6 Lee Smith .... .75 .35
❑ 7 Roger Clemens 4.00 1.80
❑ 8 Scott Cooper .... .50 .23
❑ 9 Andre Dawson.................. 1.25 .55
❑ 10 Mike Greenwell .... .50 .23
❑ 11 Aaron Sele .... .75 .35
❑ 12 Mo Vaughn 2.50 1.10
❑ 13 Brian Anderson .... 1.25 .55
❑ 14 Chad Curtis .... .50 .23
❑ 15 Chili Davis .... .75 .35
❑ 16 Gary DiSarcina .... .50 .23
❑ 17 Mark Langston .... .50 .23
❑ 18 Tim Salmon .... 2.00 .90
❑ 19 Wilson Alvarez .... .75 .35
❑ 20 Jason Bere .... .50 .23
❑ 21 Julio Franco.................... .50 .23
❑ 22 Jack McDowell .... .50 .23
❑ 23 Tim Raines .... .75 .35
❑ 24 Frank Thomas................ 6.00 2.70
❑ 25 Robin Ventura .... .75 .35
❑ 26 Carlos Baerga .... .75 .35
❑ 27 Albert Belle 2.50 1.10
❑ 28 Kenny Lofton.................. 2.00 .90
❑ 29 Eddie Murray.................. 2.00 .90
❑ 30 Manny Ramirez 2.50 1.10

		MINT	NRMT
❑ 31	Cecil Fielder	.75	.35
❑ 32	Travis Fryman	.75	.35
❑ 33	Mickey Tettleton	.50	.23
❑ 34	Alan Trammell	1.25	.55
❑ 35	Lou Whitaker	.75	.35
❑ 36	David Cone	1.25	.55
❑ 37	Gary Gaetti	.75	.35
❑ 38	Greg Gagne	.50	.23
❑ 39	Bob Hamelin	.50	.23
❑ 40	Wally Joyner	.75	.35
❑ 41	Brian McRae	.50	.23
❑ 42	Ricky Bones	.50	.23
❑ 43	Brian Harper	.50	.23
❑ 44	John Jaha	.50	.23
❑ 45	Pat Listach	.50	.23
❑ 46	Dave Nilsson	.50	.23
❑ 47	Greg Vaughn	.75	.35
❑ 48	Kent Hrbek	.75	.35
❑ 49	Chuck Knoblauch	2.00	.90
❑ 50	Shane Mack	.50	.23
❑ 51	Kirby Puckett	3.00	1.35
❑ 52	Dave Winfield	2.00	.90
❑ 53	Jim Abbott	.75	.35
❑ 54	Wade Boggs	2.00	.90
❑ 55	Jimmy Key	.75	.35
❑ 56	Don Mattingly	3.00	1.35
❑ 57	Paul O'Neill	.75	.35
❑ 58	Danny Tartabull	.50	.23
❑ 59	Dennis Eckersley	.75	.35
❑ 60	Rickey Henderson	2.00	.90
❑ 61	Mark McGwire	10.00	4.50
❑ 62	Troy Neel	.50	.23
❑ 63	Ruben Sierra	.50	.23
❑ 64	Eric Anthony	.50	.23
❑ 65	Jay Buhner	.75	.35
❑ 66	Ken Griffey Jr.	10.00	4.50
❑ 67	Randy Johnson	2.00	.90
❑ 68	Edgar Martinez	.75	.35
❑ 69	Tino Martinez	2.00	.90
❑ 70	Jose Canseco	2.00	.90
❑ 71	Will Clark	2.00	.90
❑ 72	Juan Gonzalez	5.00	2.20
❑ 73	Dean Palmer	.75	.35
❑ 74	Ivan Rodriguez	2.50	1.10
❑ 75	Roberto Alomar	2.00	.90
❑ 76	Joe Carter	.75	.35
❑ 77	Carlos Delgado	1.25	.55
❑ 78	Paul Molitor	2.00	.90
❑ 79	John Olerud	.75	.35
❑ 80	Devon White	.75	.35
❑ 81	Steve Avery	.50	.23
❑ 82	Tom Glavine	2.00	.90
❑ 83	David Justice	2.00	.90
❑ 84	Roberto Kelly	.50	.23
❑ 85	Ryan Klesko	.75	.35
❑ 86	Javier Lopez	1.25	.55
❑ 87	Greg Maddux	6.00	2.70
❑ 88	Fred McGriff	1.25	.55
❑ 89	Shawon Dunston	.50	.23
❑ 90	Mark Grace	1.25	.55
❑ 91	Derrick May	.50	.23
❑ 92	Sammy Sosa	6.00	2.70
❑ 93	Rick Wilkins	.50	.23
❑ 94	Bret Boone	.75	.35
❑ 95	Barry Larkin	1.25	.55
❑ 96	Kevin Mitchell	.50	.23
❑ 97	Hal Morris	.50	.23
❑ 98	Deion Sanders	.75	.35
❑ 99	Reggie Sanders	.75	.35
❑ 100	Dante Bichette	.75	.35
❑ 101	Ellis Burks	.75	.35
❑ 102	Andres Galarraga	2.00	.90
❑ 103	Joe Girardi	.50	.23
❑ 104	Charlie Hayes	.50	.23
❑ 105	Chuck Carr	.50	.23
❑ 106	Jeff Conine	.75	.35
❑ 107	Bryan Harvey	.50	.23
❑ 108	Benito Santiago	.50	.23
❑ 109	Gary Sheffield	2.00	.90
❑ 110	Jeff Bagwell	3.00	1.35
❑ 111	Craig Biggio	2.00	.90
❑ 112	Ken Caminiti	1.25	.55
❑ 113	Andujar Cedeno	.50	.23
❑ 114	Doug Drabek	.50	.23
❑ 115	Luis Gonzalez	.50	.23
❑ 116	Brett Butler	.75	.35
❑ 117	Delino DeShields	.50	.23
❑ 118	Eric Karros	.75	.35
❑ 119	Raul Mondesi	2.00	.90
❑ 120	Mike Piazza	6.00	2.70
❑ 121	Henry Rodriguez	.75	.35
❑ 122	Tim Wallach	.50	.23
❑ 123	Moises Alou	1.25	.55
❑ 124	Cliff Floyd	.75	.35
❑ 125	Marquis Grissom	.75	.35
❑ 126	Ken Hill	.50	.23
❑ 127	Larry Walker	2.00	.90
❑ 128	John Wetteland	.75	.35
❑ 129	Bobby Bonilla	.75	.35
❑ 130	John Franco	.75	.35
❑ 131	Jeff Kent	.75	.35
❑ 132	Bret Saberhagen	.75	.35
❑ 133	Ryan Thompson	.50	.23
❑ 134	Darren Daulton	.75	.35
❑ 135	Mariano Duncan	.50	.23
❑ 136	Lenny Dykstra	.75	.35
❑ 137	Danny Jackson	.50	.23
❑ 138	John Kruk	.75	.35
❑ 139	Jay Bell	.75	.35
❑ 140	Jeff King	.50	.23
❑ 141	Al Martin	.50	.23
❑ 142	Orlando Merced	.50	.23
❑ 143	Andy Van Slyke	.75	.35
❑ 144	Bernard Gilkey	.50	.23
❑ 145	Gregg Jefferies	.50	.23
❑ 146	Ray Lankford	.75	.35
❑ 147	Ozzie Smith	2.50	1.10
❑ 148	Mark Whiten	.50	.23
❑ 149	Todd Zeile	.50	.23
❑ 150	Derek Bell	.75	.35
❑ 151	Andy Benes	.75	.35
❑ 152	Tony Gwynn	5.00	2.20
❑ 153	Phil Plantier	.50	.23
❑ 154	Bip Roberts	.50	.23
❑ 155	Rod Beck	.50	.23
❑ 156	Barry Bonds	2.50	1.10
❑ 157	John Burkett	.50	.23
❑ 158	Royce Clayton	.50	.23
❑ 159	Bill Swift	.50	.23
❑ 160	Matt Williams	1.25	.55

1994 Leaf Limited Gold All-Stars

	MINT	NRMT
COMPLETE SET (18)	150.00	70.00
COMMON CARD (1-18)	1.50	.70

		MINT	NRMT
❑ 1	Frank Thomas	20.00	9.00
❑ 2	Gregg Jefferies	1.50	.70
❑ 3	Roberto Alomar	6.00	2.70
❑ 4	Mariano Duncan	1.50	.70
❑ 5	Wade Boggs	6.00	2.70
❑ 6	Matt Williams	4.00	1.80
❑ 7	Cal Ripken Jr.	25.00	11.00
❑ 8	Ozzie Smith	8.00	3.60
❑ 9	Kirby Puckett	10.00	4.50
❑ 10	Barry Bonds	8.00	3.60
❑ 11	Ken Griffey Jr.	30.00	13.50
❑ 12	Tony Gwynn	15.00	6.75
❑ 13	Joe Carter	2.50	1.10
❑ 14	David Justice	6.00	2.70
❑ 15	Ivan Rodriguez	8.00	3.60
❑ 16	Mike Piazza	20.00	9.00
❑ 17	Jimmy Key	2.50	1.10
❑ 18	Greg Maddux	20.00	9.00

1994 Leaf Limited Rookies

	MINT	NRMT
COMPLETE SET (80)	25.00	11.00
COMMON CARD (1-80)	.40	.18

		MINT	NRMT
❑ 1	Charles Johnson	.75	.35
❑ 2	Rico Brogna	.40	.18
❑ 3	Melvin Nieves	.40	.18
❑ 4	Rich Becker	.40	.18
❑ 5	Russ Davis	.75	.35
❑ 6	Matt Mieske	.40	.18
❑ 7	Paul Shuey	.40	.18
❑ 8	Hector Carrasco	.40	.18
❑ 9	J.R. Phillips	.40	.18
❑ 10	Scott Ruffcorn	.40	.18
❑ 11	Kurt Abbott	.40	.18
❑ 12	Danny Bautista	.40	.18
❑ 13	Rick White	.40	.18
❑ 14	Steve Dunn	.40	.18
❑ 15	Joe Ausanio	.40	.18
❑ 16	Salomon Torres	.40	.18
❑ 17	Ricky Bottalico	1.00	.45
❑ 18	Johnny Ruffin	.40	.18
❑ 19	Kevin Foster	.40	.18
❑ 20	W.VanLandingham	.40	.18
❑ 21	Troy O'Leary	.75	.35
❑ 22	Mark Acre	.40	.18
❑ 23	Norberto Martin	.40	.18
❑ 24	Jason Jacome	.40	.18
❑ 25	Steve Trachsel	.40	.18
❑ 26	Denny Hocking	.40	.18
❑ 27	Mike Lieberthal	.40	.18
❑ 28	Gerald Williams	.40	.18
❑ 29	John Mabry	.40	.18
❑ 30	Greg Blosser	.40	.18
❑ 31	Carl Everett	.40	.18
❑ 32	Steve Karsay	.40	.18
❑ 33	Jose Valentin	.40	.18
❑ 34	Jon Lieber	.40	.18
❑ 35	Chris Gomez	.40	.18
❑ 36	Jesus Tavarez	.40	.18
❑ 37	Tony Longmire	.40	.18
❑ 38	Luis Lopez	.40	.18
❑ 39	Matt Walbeck	.40	.18
❑ 40	Rikkert Faneyte	.40	.18
❑ 41	Shane Reynolds	.75	.35
❑ 42	Joey Hamilton	1.50	.70
❑ 43	Ismael Valdes	2.00	.90
❑ 44	Danny Miceli	.40	.18
❑ 45	Darren Bragg	.40	.18
❑ 46	Alex Gonzalez	.40	.18
❑ 47	Rick Helling	.75	.35
❑ 48	Jose Oliva	.40	.18
❑ 49	Jim Edmonds	1.50	.70
❑ 50	Miguel Jimenez	.40	.18
❑ 51	Tony Eusebio	.40	.18
❑ 52	Shawn Green	.75	.35
❑ 53	Billy Ashley	.40	.18
❑ 54	Rondell White	.75	.35
❑ 55	Cory Bailey	.40	.18

Card	MINT	NRMT
❑ 56 Tim Davis	.40	.18
❑ 57 John Hudek	.40	.18
❑ 58 Darren Hall	.40	.18
❑ 59 Darren Dreifort	.75	.35
❑ 60 Mike Kelly	.40	.18
❑ 61 Marcus Moore	.40	.18
❑ 62 Garret Anderson	1.50	.70
❑ 63 Brian L.Hunter	.75	.35
❑ 64 Mark Smith	.40	.18
❑ 65 Garey Ingram	.40	.18
❑ 66 Rusty Greer	8.00	3.60
❑ 67 Marc Newfield	.40	.18
❑ 68 Gar Finnvold	.40	.18
❑ 69 Paul Spoljaric	.40	.18
❑ 70 Ray McDavid	.40	.18
❑ 71 Orlando Miller	.40	.18
❑ 72 Jorge Fabregas	.40	.18
❑ 73 Ray Holbert	.40	.18
❑ 74 Armando Benitez	.40	.18
❑ 75 Ernie Young	.40	.18
❑ 76 James Mouton	.40	.18
❑ 77 Robert Perez	.40	.18
❑ 78 Chan Ho Park	8.00	3.60
❑ 79 Roger Salkeld	.40	.18
❑ 80 Tony Tarasco	.40	.18

1994 Leaf Limited Rookies Phenoms

	MINT	NRMT
COMPLETE SET (10)	150.00	70.00
COMMON CARD (1-10)	8.00	3.60
❑ 1 Raul Mondesi	15.00	6.75
❑ 2 Bob Hamelin	8.00	3.60
❑ 3 Midre Cummings	8.00	3.60
❑ 4 Carlos Delgado	12.00	5.50
❑ 5 Cliff Floyd	10.00	4.50
❑ 6 Jeffrey Hammonds	10.00	4.50
❑ 7 Ryan Klesko	10.00	4.50
❑ 8 Javier Lopez	12.00	5.50
❑ 9 Manny Ramirez	25.00	11.00
❑ 10 Alex Rodriguez	80.00	36.00

1995 Leaf Limited

	MINT	NRMT
COMPLETE SET (192)	50.00	22.00
COMPLETE SERIES 1 (96)	25.00	11.00
COMPLETE SERIES 2 (96)	25.00	11.00
COMMON CARD (1-192)	.25	.11
❑ 1 Frank Thomas	4.00	1.80
❑ 2 Geronimo Berroa	.25	.11
❑ 3 Tony Phillips	.25	.11
❑ 4 Roberto Alomar	1.25	.55
❑ 5 Steve Avery	.25	.11
❑ 6 Darryl Hamilton	.25	.11
❑ 7 Scott Cooper	.25	.11
❑ 8 Mark Grace	.75	.35
❑ 9 Billy Ashley	.25	.11
❑ 10 Wil Cordero	.25	.11
❑ 11 Barry Bonds	1.50	.70
❑ 12 Kenny Lofton	1.25	.55
❑ 13 Jay Buhner	.50	.23
❑ 14 Alex Rodriguez	5.00	2.20
❑ 15 Bobby Bonilla	.50	.23
❑ 16 Brady Anderson	.50	.23
❑ 17 Ken Caminiti	.75	.35
❑ 18 Charlie Hayes	.25	.11
❑ 19 Jay Bell	.50	.23
❑ 20 Will Clark	1.25	.55
❑ 21 Jose Canseco	1.25	.55
❑ 22 Bret Boone	.50	.23
❑ 23 Dante Bichette	.50	.23
❑ 24 Kevin Appier	.50	.23
❑ 25 Chad Curtis	.25	.11
❑ 26 Marty Cordova	.25	.11
❑ 27 Jason Bere	.25	.11
❑ 28 Jimmy Key	.50	.23
❑ 29 Rickey Henderson	1.25	.55
❑ 30 Tim Salmon	1.25	.55
❑ 31 Joe Carter	.50	.23
❑ 32 Tom Glavine	1.25	.55
❑ 33 Pat Listach	.25	.11
❑ 34 Brian Jordan	.50	.23
❑ 35 Brian McRae	.25	.11
❑ 36 Eric Karros	.50	.23
❑ 37 Pedro Martinez	1.25	.55
❑ 38 Royce Clayton	.25	.11
❑ 39 Eddie Murray	1.25	.55
❑ 40 Randy Johnson	1.25	.55
❑ 41 Jeff Conine	.50	.23
❑ 42 Brett Butler	.50	.23
❑ 43 Jeffrey Hammonds	.50	.23
❑ 44 Andujar Cedeno	.25	.11
❑ 45 Dave Hollins	.25	.11
❑ 46 Jeff King	.25	.11
❑ 47 Benji Gil	.25	.11
❑ 48 Roger Clemens	2.50	1.10
❑ 49 Barry Larkin	.75	.35
❑ 50 Joe Girardi	.25	.11
❑ 51 Bob Hamelin	.25	.11
❑ 52 Travis Fryman	.50	.23
❑ 53 Chuck Knoblauch	1.25	.55
❑ 54 Ray Durham	.50	.23
❑ 55 Don Mattingly	2.00	.90
❑ 56 Ruben Sierra	.25	.11
❑ 57 J.T. Snow	.50	.23
❑ 58 Derek Bell	.50	.23
❑ 59 David Cone	.75	.35
❑ 60 Marquis Grissom	.50	.23
❑ 61 Kevin Seitzer	.25	.11
❑ 62 Ozzie Smith	1.50	.70
❑ 63 Rick Wilkins	.25	.11
❑ 64 Hideo Nomo	5.00	2.20
❑ 65 Tony Tarasco	.25	.11
❑ 66 Manny Ramirez	1.25	.55
❑ 67 Charles Johnson	.50	.23
❑ 68 Craig Biggio	1.25	.55
❑ 69 Bobby Jones	.25	.11
❑ 70 Mike Mussina	1.25	.55
❑ 71 Alex Gonzalez	.25	.11
❑ 72 Gregg Jefferies	.25	.11
❑ 73 Rusty Greer	1.25	.55
❑ 74 Mike Greenwell	.25	.11
❑ 75 Hal Morris	.25	.11
❑ 76 Paul O'Neill	.50	.23
❑ 77 Luis Gonzalez	.25	.11
❑ 78 Chipper Jones	3.00	1.35
❑ 79 Mike Piazza	4.00	1.80
❑ 80 Rondell White	.50	.23
❑ 81 Glenallen Hill	.25	.11
❑ 82 Shawn Green	.50	.23
❑ 83 Bernie Williams	1.25	.55
❑ 84 Jim Thome	1.25	.55
❑ 85 Terry Pendleton	.25	.11
❑ 86 Rafael Palmeiro	.75	.35
❑ 87 Tony Gwynn	3.00	1.35
❑ 88 Mickey Tettleton	.25	.11
❑ 89 John Valentin	.50	.23
❑ 90 Deion Sanders	.50	.23
❑ 91 Larry Walker	1.25	.55
❑ 92 Michael Tucker	.50	.23
❑ 93 Alan Trammell	.50	.23
❑ 94 Tim Raines	.50	.23
❑ 95 David Justice	1.25	.55
❑ 96 Tino Martinez	1.25	.55
❑ 97 Cal Ripken Jr.	5.00	2.20
❑ 98 Deion Sanders	.50	.23
❑ 99 Darren Daulton	.50	.23
❑ 100 Paul Molitor	1.25	.55
❑ 101 Randy Myers	.25	.11
❑ 102 Wally Joyner	.50	.23
❑ 103 Carlos Perez	1.00	.45
❑ 104 Brian Hunter	.50	.23
❑ 105 Wade Boggs	1.25	.55
❑ 106 Bob Higginson	3.00	1.35
❑ 107 Jeff Kent	.50	.23
❑ 108 Jose Offerman	.25	.11
❑ 109 Dennis Eckersley	.50	.23
❑ 110 Dave Nilsson	.25	.11
❑ 111 Chuck Finley	.50	.23
❑ 112 Devon White	.50	.23
❑ 113 Bip Roberts	.25	.11
❑ 114 Ramon Martinez	.50	.23
❑ 115 Greg Maddux	4.00	1.80
❑ 116 Curtis Goodwin	.25	.11
❑ 117 John Jaha	.25	.11
❑ 118 Ken Griffey Jr.	6.00	2.70
❑ 119 Geronimo Pena	.25	.11
❑ 120 Shawon Dunston	.25	.11
❑ 121 Ariel Prieto	.25	.11
❑ 122 Kirby Puckett	2.00	.90
❑ 123 Carlos Baerga	.50	.23
❑ 124 Todd Hundley	.50	.23
❑ 125 Tim Naehring	.25	.11
❑ 126 Gary Sheffield	.75	.35
❑ 127 Dean Palmer	.50	.23
❑ 128 Rondell White	.50	.23
❑ 129 Greg Gagne	.25	.11
❑ 130 Jose Rijo	.25	.11
❑ 131 Ivan Rodriguez	1.50	.70
❑ 132 Jeff Bagwell	2.00	.90
❑ 133 Greg Vaughn	.50	.23
❑ 134 Chili Davis	.50	.23
❑ 135 Al Martin	.25	.11
❑ 136 Kenny Rogers	.25	.11
❑ 137 Aaron Sele	.50	.23
❑ 138 Raul Mondesi	.75	.35
❑ 139 Cecil Fielder	.50	.23
❑ 140 Tim Wallach	.25	.11
❑ 141 Andres Galarraga	1.25	.55
❑ 142 Lou Whitaker	.50	.23
❑ 143 Jack McDowell	.25	.11
❑ 144 Matt Williams	.50	.23
❑ 145 Ryan Klesko	.50	.23
❑ 146 Carlos Garcia	.25	.11
❑ 147 Albert Belle	2.00	.90
❑ 148 Ryan Thompson	.25	.11
❑ 149 Roberto Kelly	.25	.11
❑ 150 Edgar Martinez	.50	.23
❑ 151 Robby Thompson	.25	.11
❑ 152 Mo Vaughn	1.50	.70
❑ 153 Todd Zeile	.25	.11
❑ 154 Harold Baines	.50	.23
❑ 155 Phil Plantier	.25	.11
❑ 156 Mike Stanley	.25	.11
❑ 157 Ed Sprague	.25	.11
❑ 158 Moises Alou	.75	.35
❑ 159 Quilvio Veras	.25	.11
❑ 160 Reggie Sanders	.50	.23
❑ 161 Delino DeShields	.25	.11
❑ 162 Rico Brogna	.25	.11
❑ 163 Greg Colbrunn	.25	.11
❑ 164 Steve Finley	.50	.23
❑ 165 Orlando Merced	.25	.11
❑ 166 Mark McGwire	6.00	2.70
❑ 167 Garret Anderson	.50	.23
❑ 168 Paul Sorrento	.25	.11

❑ 169 Mark Langston .25 .11
❑ 170 Danny Tartabull .25 .11
❑ 171 Vinny Castilia .75 .35
❑ 172 Javier Lopez .50 .23
❑ 173 Bret Saberhagen .50 .23
❑ 174 Eddie Williams .25 .11
❑ 175 Scott Leius .25 .11
❑ 176 Juan Gonzalez 3.00 1.35
❑ 177 Gary Gaetti .50 .23
❑ 178 Jim Edmonds .75 .35
❑ 179 John Olerud .50 .23
❑ 180 Lenny Dykstra .50 .23
❑ 181 Ray Lankford .50 .23
❑ 182 Ron Gant .25 .11
❑ 183 Doug Drabek .25 .11
❑ 184 Fred McGriff .75 .35
❑ 185 Andy Benes .50 .23
❑ 186 Kurt Abbott .25 .11
❑ 187 Bernard Gilkey .25 .11
❑ 188 Sammy Sosa 3.00 1.35
❑ 189 Lee Smith .50 .23
❑ 190 Dennis Martinez .50 .23
❑ 191 Ozzie Guillen .25 .11
❑ 192 Robin Ventura .50 .23

1995 Leaf Limited Bat Patrol

	MINT	NRMT
COMPLETE SET (24)	25.00	11.00
COMMON CARD (1-24)	.50	.23

❑ 1 Frank Thomas 5.00 2.20
❑ 2 Tony Gwynn 4.00 1.80
❑ 3 Wade Boggs 1.50 .70
❑ 4 Larry Walker 1.50 .70
❑ 5 Ken Griffey, Jr. 8.00 3.60
❑ 6 Jeff Bagwell 2.50 1.10
❑ 7 Manny Ramirez 1.50 .70
❑ 8 Mark Grace 1.25 .55
❑ 9 Kenny Lofton 1.50 .70
❑ 10 Mike Piazza 5.00 2.20
❑ 11 Will Clark 1.50 .70
❑ 12 Mo Vaughn 1.50 .70
❑ 13 Carlos Baerga .50 .23
❑ 14 Rafael Palmeiro 1.25 .55
❑ 15 Barry Bonds 1.50 .70
❑ 16 Kirby Puckett 1.50 .70
❑ 17 Roberto Alomar 1.50 .70
❑ 18 Barry Larkin 1.25 .55
❑ 19 Eddie Murray 1.50 .70
❑ 20 Tim Salmon 1.50 .70
❑ 21 Don Mattingly 2.50 1.10
❑ 22 Fred McGriff 1.25 .55
❑ 23 Albert Belle 1.50 .70
❑ 24 Dante Bichette .75 .35

1995 Leaf Limited Lumberjacks

	MINT	NRMT
COMPLETE SET (16)	300.00	135.00
COMPLETE SERIES 1 (8)	180.00	80.00
COMPLETE SERIES 2 (8)	120.00	55.00
COMMON CARD (1-16)	6.00	2.70

❑ 1 Albert Belle 20.00 9.00

❑ 2 Barry Bonds 15.00 6.75
❑ 3 Juan Gonzalez 30.00 13.50
❑ 4 Ken Griffey Jr. 60.00 27.00
❑ 5 Fred McGriff 8.00 3.60
❑ 6 Mike Piazza 30.00 13.50
❑ 7 Kirby Puckett 20.00 9.00
❑ 8 Mo Vaughn 15.00 6.75
❑ 9 Frank Thomas 40.00 18.00
❑ 10 Jeff Bagwell 20.00 9.00
❑ 11 Matt Williams 6.00 2.70
❑ 12 Jose Canseco 12.00 5.50
❑ 13 Raul Mondesi 8.00 3.60
❑ 14 Manny Ramirez 12.00 5.50
❑ 15 Cecil Fielder 6.00 2.70
❑ 16 Cal Ripken Jr. 50.00 22.00

1996 Leaf Limited

	MINT	NRMT
COMPLETE SET (90)	50.00	22.00
COMMON CARD (1-90)	.30	.14

❑ 1 Ivan Rodriguez 1.50 .70
❑ 2 Roger Clemens 2.50 1.10
❑ 3 Gary Sheffield .75 .35
❑ 4 Tino Martinez 1.25 .55
❑ 5 Sammy Sosa 3.00 1.35
❑ 6 Reggie Sanders .50 .23
❑ 7 Ray Lankford .50 .23
❑ 8 Manny Ramirez 1.25 .55
❑ 9 Jeff Bagwell 2.00 .90
❑ 10 Greg Maddux 4.00 1.80
❑ 11 Ken Griffey Jr. 6.00 2.70
❑ 12 Rondell White .50 .23
❑ 13 Mike Piazza 4.00 1.80
❑ 14 Marc Newfield .30 .14
❑ 15 Cal Ripken 5.00 2.20
❑ 16 Carlos Delgado .50 .23
❑ 17 Tim Salmon 1.25 .55
❑ 18 Andres Galarraga 1.25 .55
❑ 19 Chuck Knoblauch 1.25 .55
❑ 20 Matt Williams .50 .23
❑ 21 Mark McGwire 6.00 2.70
❑ 22 Ben McDonald .30 .14
❑ 23 Frank Thomas 4.00 1.80
❑ 24 Johnny Damon .50 .23
❑ 25 Gregg Jefferies .30 .14
❑ 26 Travis Fryman .50 .23
❑ 27 Chipper Jones 3.00 1.35
❑ 28 David Cone .75 .35
❑ 29 Kenny Lofton 1.25 .55
❑ 30 Mike Mussina 1.25 .55
❑ 31 Alex Rodriguez 4.00 1.80
❑ 32 Carlos Baerga .50 .23
❑ 33 Brian Hunter .50 .23
❑ 34 Juan Gonzalez 3.00 1.35
❑ 35 Bernie Williams 1.25 .55
❑ 36 Wally Joyner .50 .23
❑ 37 Fred McGriff .75 .35
❑ 38 Randy Johnson 1.25 .55
❑ 39 Marty Cordova .30 .14
❑ 40 Garret Anderson .50 .23
❑ 41 Albert Belle 2.00 .90
❑ 42 Edgar Martinez .50 .23
❑ 43 Barry Larkin .75 .35
❑ 44 Paul O'Neill .50 .23
❑ 45 Cecil Fielder .50 .23
❑ 46 Rusty Greer .75 .35
❑ 47 Mo Vaughn 1.50 .70
❑ 48 Dante Bichette .50 .23
❑ 49 Ryan Klesko .50 .23
❑ 50 Roberto Alomar 1.25 .55
❑ 51 Raul Mondesi .75 .35
❑ 52 Robin Ventura .50 .23
❑ 53 Tony Gwynn 3.00 1.35
❑ 54 Mark Grace .75 .35
❑ 55 Jim Thome 1.25 .55
❑ 56 Jason Giambi .50 .23
❑ 57 Tom Glavine 1.25 .55
❑ 58 Jim Edmonds .75 .35
❑ 59 Pedro Martinez 1.25 .55
❑ 60 Charles Johnson .50 .23
❑ 61 Wade Boggs 1.25 .55
❑ 62 Orlando Merced .30 .14
❑ 63 Craig Biggio 1.25 .55
❑ 64 Brady Anderson .50 .23
❑ 65 Hideo Nomo 2.00 .90
❑ 66 Ozzie Smith 1.50 .70
❑ 67 Eddie Murray 1.25 .55
❑ 68 Will Clark 1.25 .55
❑ 69 Jay Buhner .50 .23
❑ 70 Kirby Puckett 2.00 .90
❑ 71 Barry Bonds 1.50 .70
❑ 72 Ray Durham .50 .23
❑ 73 Sterling Hitchcock .50 .23
❑ 74 John Smoltz .50 .23
❑ 75 Andre Dawson .75 .35
❑ 76 Joe Carter .50 .23
❑ 77 Ryne Sandberg 1.50 .70
❑ 78 Rickey Henderson 1.25 .55
❑ 79 Brian Jordan .50 .23
❑ 80 Greg Vaughn .50 .23
❑ 81 Andy Pettitte .75 .35
❑ 82 Dean Palmer .50 .23
❑ 83 Paul Molitor 1.25 .55
❑ 84 Rafael Palmeiro .75 .35
❑ 85 Henry Rodriguez .50 .23
❑ 86 Larry Walker 1.25 .55
❑ 87 Ismael Valdes .50 .23
❑ 88 Derek Bell .50 .23
❑ 89 J.T. Snow .50 .23
❑ 90 Jack McDowell .30 .14

1996 Leaf Limited Lumberjacks

	MINT	NRMT
COMPLETE SET (10)	200.00	90.00
COMMON CARD (1-10)	10.00	4.50

*BLACK: 1.5X TO 4X BASIC CARDS
BLACK PRINT RUN 500 SERIAL #'d SETS

Card	MINT	NRMT
❑ 1 Ken Griffey Jr.	40.00	18.00
❑ 2 Sammy Sosa	20.00	9.00
❑ 3 Cal Ripken	30.00	13.50
❑ 4 Frank Thomas	25.00	11.00
❑ 5 Alex Rodriguez	25.00	11.00
❑ 6 Mo Vaughn	10.00	4.50
❑ 7 Chipper Jones	20.00	9.00
❑ 8 Mike Piazza	25.00	11.00
❑ 9 Jeff Bagwell	12.00	5.50
❑ 10 Mark McGwire	40.00	18.00
❑ P8 Mike Piazza Promo	5.00	2.20

1996 Leaf Limited Pennant Craze

	MINT	NRMT
COMPLETE SET (10)	400.00	180.00
COMMON CARD (1-10)	15.00	6.75

Card	MINT	NRMT
❑ 1 Juan Gonzalez	40.00	18.00
❑ 2 Cal Ripken	60.00	27.00
❑ 3 Frank Thomas	50.00	22.00
❑ 4 Ken Griffey Jr.	80.00	36.00
❑ 5 Albert Belle	20.00	9.00
❑ 6 Greg Maddux	50.00	22.00
❑ 7 Paul Molitor	15.00	6.75
❑ 8 Alex Rodriguez	50.00	22.00
❑ 9 Barry Bonds	20.00	9.00
❑ 10 Chipper Jones	40.00	18.00

1996 Leaf Limited Rookies

	MINT	NRMT
COMPLETE SET (10)	50.00	22.00
COMMON CARD (1-10)	2.50	1.10
COMP.GOLD SET (10)	120.00	55.00

*GOLD: 1X TO 2.5X BASIC CARDS
GOLD: RANDOM INSERTS IN PACKS

Card	MINT	NRMT
❑ 1 Alex Ochoa	2.50	1.10
❑ 2 Darin Erstad	15.00	6.75
❑ 3 Ruben Rivera	3.00	1.35
❑ 4 Derek Jeter	12.00	5.50
❑ 5 Jermaine Dye	2.50	1.10
❑ 6 Jason Kendall	5.00	2.20
❑ 7 Mike Grace	2.50	1.10
❑ 8 Andruw Jones	8.00	3.60
❑ 9 Rey Ordonez	3.00	1.35
❑ 10 George Arias	2.50	1.10

1996 Leaf Preferred

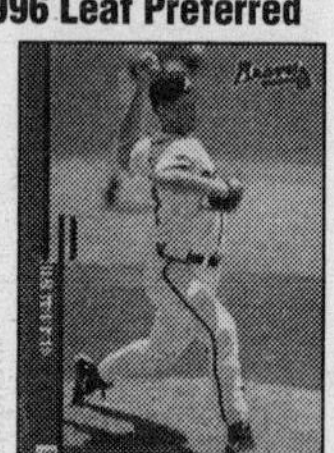

	MINT	NRMT
COMPLETE SET (150)	25.00	11.00
COMMON CARD (1-150)	.15	.07

Card	MINT	NRMT
❑ 1 Ken Griffey Jr.	3.00	1.35
❑ 2 Rico Brogna	.15	.07
❑ 3 Gregg Jefferies	.15	.07
❑ 4 Reggie Sanders	.30	.14
❑ 5 Manny Ramirez	.60	.25
❑ 6 Shawn Green	.30	.14
❑ 7 Tino Martinez	.60	.25
❑ 8 Jeff Bagwell	1.00	.45
❑ 9 Marc Newfield	.15	.07
❑ 10 Ray Lankford	.30	.14
❑ 11 Jay Bell	.30	.14
❑ 12 Greg Maddux	2.00	.90
❑ 13 Frank Thomas	2.00	.90
❑ 14 Travis Fryman	.30	.14
❑ 15 Mark McGwire	3.00	1.35
❑ 16 Chuck Knoblauch	.60	.25
❑ 17 Sammy Sosa	1.50	.70
❑ 18 Matt Williams	.30	.14
❑ 19 Roger Clemens	1.25	.55
❑ 20 Rondell White	.30	.14
❑ 21 Ivan Rodriguez	.75	.35
❑ 22 Cal Ripken	2.50	1.10
❑ 23 Ben McDonald	.15	.07
❑ 24 Kenny Lofton	.60	.25
❑ 25 Mike Piazza	2.00	.90
❑ 26 David Cone	.40	.18
❑ 27 Gary Sheffield	.40	.18
❑ 28 Tim Salmon	.60	.25
❑ 29 Andres Galarraga	.60	.25
❑ 30 Johnny Damon	.30	.14
❑ 31 Ozzie Smith	.75	.35
❑ 32 Carlos Baerga	.30	.14
❑ 33 Raul Mondesi	.40	.18
❑ 34 Moises Alou	.40	.18
❑ 35 Alex Rodriguez	2.00	.90
❑ 36 Mike Mussina	.60	.25
❑ 37 Jason Isringhausen	.15	.07
❑ 38 Barry Larkin	.40	.18
❑ 39 Bernie Williams	.60	.25
❑ 40 Chipper Jones	1.50	.70
❑ 41 Joey Hamilton	.30	.14
❑ 42 Charles Johnson	.30	.14
❑ 43 Juan Gonzalez	1.50	.70
❑ 44 Greg Vaughn	.30	.14
❑ 45 Robin Ventura	.30	.14
❑ 46 Albert Belle	.75	.35
❑ 47 Rafael Palmeiro	.40	.18
❑ 48 Brian L.Hunter	.30	.14
❑ 49 Mo Vaughn	.75	.35
❑ 50 Paul O'Neill	.30	.14
❑ 51 Mark Grace	.40	.18
❑ 52 Randy Johnson	.60	.25
❑ 53 Pedro Martinez	.60	.25
❑ 54 Marty Cordova	.15	.07
❑ 55 Garret Anderson	.30	.14
❑ 56 Joe Carter	.30	.14
❑ 57 Jim Thome	.60	.25
❑ 58 Edgardo Alfonzo	.30	.14
❑ 59 Dante Bichette	.30	.14
❑ 60 Darryl Hamilton	.15	.07
❑ 61 Roberto Alomar	.60	.25
❑ 62 Fred McGriff	.40	.18
❑ 63 Kirby Puckett	1.00	.45
❑ 64 Hideo Nomo	1.00	.45
❑ 65 Alex Fernandez	.15	.07
❑ 66 Ryan Klesko	.30	.14
❑ 67 Wade Boggs	.60	.25
❑ 68 Eddie Murray	.60	.25
❑ 69 Eric Karros	.30	.14
❑ 70 Jim Edmonds	.40	.18
❑ 71 Edgar Martinez	.30	.14
❑ 72 Andy Pettitte	.40	.18
❑ 73 Mark Grudzielanek	.30	.14
❑ 74 Tom Glavine	.60	.25
❑ 75 Ken Caminiti	.40	.18
❑ 76 Will Clark	.60	.25
❑ 77 Craig Biggio	.60	.25
❑ 78 Brady Anderson	.30	.14
❑ 79 Tony Gwynn	1.50	.70
❑ 80 Larry Walker	.60	.25
❑ 81 Brian Jordan	.30	.14
❑ 82 Lenny Dykstra	.30	.14
❑ 83 Butch Huskey	.15	.07
❑ 84 Jack McDowell	.15	.07
❑ 85 Cecil Fielder	.30	.14
❑ 86 Jose Canseco	.60	.25
❑ 87 Jason Giambi	.30	.14
❑ 88 Rickey Henderson	.60	.25
❑ 89 Kevin Seitzer	.15	.07
❑ 90 Carlos Delgado	.30	.14
❑ 91 Ryne Sandberg	.75	.35
❑ 92 Dwight Gooden	.30	.14
❑ 93 Michael Tucker	.30	.14
❑ 94 Barry Bonds	.75	.35
❑ 95 Eric Young	.15	.07
❑ 96 Dean Palmer	.30	.14
❑ 97 Henry Rodriguez	.30	.14
❑ 98 John Mabry	.15	.07
❑ 99 J.T. Snow	.30	.14
❑ 100 Andre Dawson	.40	.18
❑ 101 Ismael Valdes	.30	.14
❑ 102 Charles Nagy	.30	.14
❑ 103 Jay Buhner	.30	.14
❑ 104 Derek Bell	.30	.14
❑ 105 Paul Molitor	.60	.25
❑ 106 Hal Morris	.15	.07
❑ 107 Ray Durham	.30	.14
❑ 108 Bernard Gilkey	.15	.07
❑ 109 John Valentin	.30	.14
❑ 110 Melvin Nieves	.15	.07
❑ 111 John Smoltz	.30	.14
❑ 112 Terrell Wade	.15	.07
❑ 113 Chad Mottola	.15	.07
❑ 114 Tony Clark	.60	.25
❑ 115 John Wasdin	.15	.07
❑ 116 Derek Jeter	2.00	.90
❑ 117 Rey Ordonez	.30	.14
❑ 118 Jason Thompson	.15	.07
❑ 119 Robin Jennings	.15	.07
❑ 120 Rocky Coppinger	.60	.25
❑ 121 Billy Wagner	.30	.14
❑ 122 Steve Gibralter	.15	.07
❑ 123 Jermaine Dye	.15	.07
❑ 124 Jason Kendall	.60	.25
❑ 125 Mike Grace	.15	.07
❑ 126 Jason Schmidt	.15	.07
❑ 127 Paul Wilson	.15	.07
❑ 128 Alan Benes	.30	.14
❑ 129 Justin Thompson	.30	.14
❑ 130 Brooks Kieschnick	.15	.07
❑ 131 George Arias	.15	.07
❑ 132 Osvaldo Fernandez	.15	.07
❑ 133 Todd Hollandsworth	.15	.07
❑ 134 Eric Owens	.15	.07
❑ 135 Chan Ho Park	.60	.25
❑ 136 Mark Loretta	.15	.07
❑ 137 Ruben Rivera	.30	.14
❑ 138 Jeff Suppan	.15	.07
❑ 139 Ugueth Urbina	.30	.14
❑ 140 LaTroy Hawkins	.15	.07
❑ 141 Chris Snopek	.15	.07
❑ 142 Edgar Renteria	.30	.14

		MINT	NRMT
❑ 143	Raul Casanova	.15	.07
❑ 144	Jose Herrera	.15	.07
❑ 145	Matt Lawton	.60	.25
❑ 146	Ralph Milliard	.15	.07
❑ 147	Frank Thomas CL	1.00	.45
❑ 148	Jeff Bagwell CL	.60	.25
❑ 149	Ken Griffey Jr. CL	1.50	.70
❑ 150	Mike Piazza CL	1.00	.45

1996 Leaf Preferred Staremaster

	MINT	NRMT
COMPLETE SET (12)	400.00	180.00
COMMON CARD (1-12)	12.00	5.50

		MINT	NRMT
❑ 1	Chipper Jones	30.00	13.50
❑ 2	Alex Rodriguez	40.00	18.00
❑ 3	Derek Jeter	30.00	13.50
❑ 4	Tony Gwynn	30.00	13.50
❑ 5	Frank Thomas	40.00	18.00
❑ 6	Ken Griffey Jr.	60.00	27.00
❑ 7	Cal Ripken	50.00	22.00
❑ 8	Greg Maddux	40.00	18.00
❑ 9	Albert Belle	15.00	6.75
❑ 10	Barry Bonds	15.00	6.75
❑ 11	Jeff Bagwell	20.00	9.00
❑ 12	Mike Piazza	40.00	18.00

1996 Leaf Preferred Steel

	MINT	NRMT
COMPLETE SET (77)	120.00	55.00
COMMON CARD (1-77)	.50	.23
COMP.GOLD SET (77)	1200.00	550.00

*GOLD STARS: 4X TO 10X BASIC CARDS
*GOLD YOUNG STARS: 3X TO 8X BASIC CARDS
GOLD: RANDOM INSERTS IN PACKS

		MINT	NRMT
❑ 1	Frank Thomas	6.00	2.70
❑ 2	Paul Molitor	2.00	.90
❑ 3	Kenny Lofton	2.00	.90
❑ 4	Travis Fryman	.75	.35
❑ 5	Jeff Conine	.75	.35
❑ 6	Barry Bonds	2.50	1.10
❑ 7	Gregg Jefferies	.50	.23
❑ 8	Alex Rodriguez	6.00	2.70
❑ 9	Wade Boggs	2.00	.90
❑ 10	David Justice	2.00	.90
❑ 11	Hideo Nomo	3.00	1.35
❑ 12	Roberto Alomar	2.00	.90
❑ 13	Todd Hollandsworth	.50	.23
❑ 14	Mark McGwire	10.00	4.50
❑ 15	Rafael Palmeiro	1.25	.55
❑ 16	Will Clark	2.00	.90
❑ 17	Cal Ripken	8.00	3.60
❑ 18	Derek Bell	.75	.35
❑ 19	Gary Sheffield	1.25	.55
❑ 20	Juan Gonzalez	5.00	2.20
❑ 21	Garret Anderson	.75	.35
❑ 22	Mo Vaughn	2.50	1.10
❑ 23	Robin Ventura	.75	.35
❑ 24	Carlos Baerga	.75	.35
❑ 25	Tim Salmon	2.00	.90
❑ 26	Matt Williams	.75	.35
❑ 27	Fred McGriff	1.25	.55
❑ 28	Rondell White	.75	.35
❑ 29	Ray Lankford	.75	.35
❑ 30	Lenny Dykstra	.75	.35
❑ 31	J.T. Snow	.75	.35
❑ 32	Sammy Sosa	5.00	2.20
❑ 33	Chipper Jones	5.00	2.20
❑ 34	Bobby Bonilla	.75	.35
❑ 35	Paul Wilson	.50	.23
❑ 36	Darren Daulton	.75	.35
❑ 37	Larry Walker	2.00	.90
❑ 38	Raul Mondesi	1.25	.55
❑ 39	Jeff Bagwell	3.00	1.35
❑ 40	Derek Jeter	5.00	2.20
❑ 41	Kirby Puckett	3.00	1.35
❑ 42	Jason Isringhausen	.50	.23
❑ 43	Vinny Castilla	1.25	.55
❑ 44	Jim Edmonds	1.25	.55
❑ 45	Ron Gant	.50	.23
❑ 46	Carlos Delgado	.75	.35
❑ 47	Jose Canseco	2.00	.90
❑ 48	Tony Gwynn	5.00	2.20
❑ 49	Mike Mussina	2.00	.90
❑ 50	Charles Johnson	.75	.35
❑ 51	Mike Piazza	6.00	2.70
❑ 52	Ken Griffey Jr.	10.00	4.50
❑ 53	Greg Maddux	6.00	2.70
❑ 54	Mark Grace	1.25	.55
❑ 55	Ryan Klesko	.75	.35
❑ 56	Dennis Eckersley	.75	.35
❑ 57	Rickey Henderson	2.00	.90
❑ 58	Michael Tucker	.75	.35
❑ 59	Joe Carter	.75	.35
❑ 60	Randy Johnson	2.00	.90
❑ 61	Brian Jordan	.75	.35
❑ 62	Shawn Green	.75	.35
❑ 63	Roger Clemens	4.00	1.80
❑ 64	Andres Galarraga	2.00	.90
❑ 65	Johnny Damon	.75	.35
❑ 66	Ryne Sandberg	2.50	1.10
❑ 67	Alan Benes	.75	.35
❑ 68	Albert Belle	2.50	1.10
❑ 69	Barry Larkin	1.25	.55
❑ 70	Marty Cordova	.50	.23
❑ 71	Dante Bichette	.75	.35
❑ 72	Craig Biggio	2.00	.90
❑ 73	Reggie Sanders	.75	.35
❑ 74	Moises Alou	1.25	.55
❑ 75	Chuck Knoblauch	2.00	.90
❑ 76	Cecil Fielder	.75	.35
❑ 77	Manny Ramirez	2.00	.90

1996 Leaf Preferred Steel Power

	MINT	NRMT
COMPLETE SET (8)	150.00	70.00
COMMON CARD (1-8)	8.00	3.60

		MINT	NRMT
❑ 1	Albert Belle	10.00	4.50
❑ 2	Mo Vaughn	10.00	4.50
❑ 3	Ken Griffey Jr.	40.00	18.00
❑ 4	Cal Ripken	30.00	13.50
❑ 5	Mike Piazza	25.00	11.00
❑ 6	Barry Bonds	10.00	4.50
❑ 7	Jeff Bagwell	12.00	5.50
❑ 8	Frank Thomas	25.00	11.00

1996 Leaf Signature

	MINT	NRMT
COMPLETE SET (150)	100.00	45.00
COMPLETE SERIES 1 (100)	60.00	27.00
COMMON CARD (1-100)	.25	.11
COMPLETE SERIES 2 (50)	40.00	18.00
COMMON CARD (101-150)	.50	.23

		MINT	NRMT
❑ 1	Mike Piazza	3.00	1.35
❑ 2	Juan Gonzalez	2.50	1.10
❑ 3	Greg Maddux	3.00	1.35
❑ 4	Marc Newfield	.25	.11
❑ 5	Wade Boggs	1.00	.45
❑ 6	Ray Lankford	.50	.23
❑ 7	Frank Thomas	3.00	1.35
❑ 8	Rico Brogna	.25	.11
❑ 9	Tim Salmon	1.00	.45
❑ 10	Ken Griffey Jr.	5.00	2.20
❑ 11	Manny Ramirez	1.00	.45
❑ 12	Cecil Fielder	.50	.23
❑ 13	Gregg Jefferies	.25	.11
❑ 14	Rondell White	.50	.23
❑ 15	Cal Ripken	4.00	1.80
❑ 16	Alex Rodriguez	3.00	1.35
❑ 17	Bernie Williams	1.00	.45
❑ 18	Andres Galarraga	1.00	.45
❑ 19	Mike Mussina	1.00	.45
❑ 20	Chuck Knoblauch	1.00	.45
❑ 21	Joe Carter	.50	.23
❑ 22	Jeff Bagwell	1.50	.70
❑ 23	Mark McGwire	5.00	2.20
❑ 24	Sammy Sosa	2.50	1.10
❑ 25	Reggie Sanders	.50	.23
❑ 26	Chipper Jones	2.50	1.10
❑ 27	Jeff Cirillo	.50	.23
❑ 28	Roger Clemens	2.00	.90
❑ 29	Craig Biggio	1.00	.45
❑ 30	Gary Sheffield	.75	.35
❑ 31	Paul O'Neill	.50	.23
❑ 32	Johnny Damon	.50	.23
❑ 33	Jason Isringhausen	.25	.11
❑ 34	Jay Bell	.50	.23
❑ 35	Henry Rodriguez	.50	.23
❑ 36	Matt Williams	.50	.23
❑ 37	Randy Johnson	1.00	.45
❑ 38	Fred McGriff	.75	.35
❑ 39	Jason Giambi	.50	.23
❑ 40	Ivan Rodriguez	1.25	.55
❑ 41	Raul Mondesi	.75	.35
❑ 42	Barry Larkin	.75	.35
❑ 43	Ryan Klesko	.50	.23
❑ 44	Joey Hamilton	.50	.23
❑ 45	Todd Hundley	.50	.23
❑ 46	Jim Edmonds	.75	.35
❑ 47	Dante Bichette	.50	.23
❑ 48	Roberto Alomar	1.00	.45
❑ 49	Mark Grace	.75	.35
❑ 50	Brady Anderson	.50	.23
❑ 51	Hideo Nomo	1.50	.70
❑ 52	Ozzie Smith	1.25	.55
❑ 53	Robin Ventura	.50	.23
❑ 54	Andy Pettitte	.75	.35
❑ 55	Kenny Lofton	1.00	.45
❑ 56	John Mabry	.25	.11
❑ 57	Paul Molitor	1.00	.45
❑ 58	Rey Ordonez	.50	.23
❑ 59	Albert Belle	1.25	.55

- ❑ 60 Charles Johnson .50 .23
- ❑ 61 Edgar Martinez .50 .23
- ❑ 62 Derek Bell .50 .23
- ❑ 63 Carlos Delgado .50 .23
- ❑ 64 Raul Casanova .25 .11
- ❑ 65 Ismael Valdes .50 .23
- ❑ 66 J.T. Snow .50 .23
- ❑ 67 Derek Jeter 3.00 1.35
- ❑ 68 Jason Kendall 1.00 .45
- ❑ 69 John Smoltz .50 .23
- ❑ 70 Chad Mottola .25 .11
- ❑ 71 Jim Thome 1.00 .45
- ❑ 72 Will Clark 1.00 .45
- ❑ 73 Mo Vaughn 1.25 .55
- ❑ 74 John Wasdin .25 .11
- ❑ 75 Rafael Palmeiro .75 .35
- ❑ 76 Mark Grudzielanek .50 .23
- ❑ 77 Larry Walker 1.00 .45
- ❑ 78 Alan Benes .50 .23
- ❑ 79 Michael Tucker .50 .23
- ❑ 80 Billy Wagner .50 .23
- ❑ 81 Paul Wilson .25 .11
- ❑ 82 Greg Vaughn .50 .23
- ❑ 83 Dean Palmer .50 .23
- ❑ 84 Ryne Sandberg 1.25 .55
- ❑ 85 Eric Young .25 .11
- ❑ 86 Jay Buhner .50 .23
- ❑ 87 Tony Clark 1.00 .45
- ❑ 88 Jermaine Dye .25 .11
- ❑ 89 Barry Bonds 1.25 .55
- ❑ 90 Ugueth Urbina .50 .23
- ❑ 91 Charles Nagy .50 .23
- ❑ 92 Ruben Rivera .50 .23
- ❑ 93 Todd Hollandsworth .25 .11
- ❑ 94 Darin Erstad 10.00 4.50
- ❑ 95 Brooks Kieschnick .25 .11
- ❑ 96 Edgar Renteria .50 .23
- ❑ 97 Lenny Dykstra .50 .23
- ❑ 98 Tony Gwynn 2.50 1.10
- ❑ 99 Kirby Puckett 1.50 .70
- ❑ 100 Checklist .25 .11
- ❑ 101 Andruw Jones 3.00 1.35
- ❑ 102 Alex Ochoa .50 .23
- ❑ 103 David Cone 1.50 .70
- ❑ 104 Rusty Greer 1.50 .70
- ❑ 105 Jose Canseco 2.00 .90
- ❑ 106 Ken Caminiti 1.50 .70
- ❑ 107 Mariano Rivera 1.00 .45
- ❑ 108 Ron Gant .50 .23
- ❑ 109 Darryl Strawberry 1.00 .45
- ❑ 110 Vladimir Guerrero 4.00 1.80
- ❑ 111 George Arias .50 .23
- ❑ 112 Jeff Conine 1.00 .45
- ❑ 113 Bobby Higginson 2.00 .90
- ❑ 114 Eric Karros 1.00 .45
- ❑ 115 Brian Hunter 1.00 .45
- ❑ 116 Eddie Murray 2.00 .90
- ❑ 117 Todd Walker 4.00 1.80
- ❑ 118 Chan Ho Park 2.00 .90
- ❑ 119 John Jaha .50 .23
- ❑ 120 Dave Justice 2.00 .90
- ❑ 121 Makoto Suzuki 1.00 .45
- ❑ 122 Scott Rolen 5.00 2.20
- ❑ 123 Tino Martinez 2.00 .90
- ❑ 124 Kimera Bartee .50 .23
- ❑ 125 Garret Anderson 1.00 .45
- ❑ 126 Brian Jordan 1.00 .45
- ❑ 127 Andre Dawson 1.50 .70
- ❑ 128 Javier Lopez 1.00 .45
- ❑ 129 Bill Pulsipher .50 .23
- ❑ 130 Dwight Gooden 1.00 .45
- ❑ 131 Al Martin .50 .23
- ❑ 132 Terrell Wade .50 .23
- ❑ 133 Steve Gibralter .50 .23
- ❑ 134 Tom Glavine 2.00 .90
- ❑ 135 Kevin Appier 1.00 .45
- ❑ 136 Tim Raines 1.00 .45
- ❑ 137 Curtis Pride .50 .23
- ❑ 138 Todd Greene 1.00 .45
- ❑ 139 Bobby Bonilla 1.00 .45
- ❑ 140 Trey Beamon .50 .23
- ❑ 141 Marty Cordova .50 .23
- ❑ 142 Rickey Henderson 2.00 .90
- ❑ 143 Ellis Burks 1.00 .45
- ❑ 144 Dennis Eckersley 1.00 .45
- ❑ 145 Kevin Brown 2.00 .90
- ❑ 146 Carlos Baerga 1.00 .45
- ❑ 147 Brett Butler 1.00 .45
- ❑ 148 Marquis Grissom 1.00 .45
- ❑ 149 Karim Garcia 1.00 .45
- ❑ 150 Frank Thomas CL 3.00 1.35

1996 Leaf Signature Autographs

	MINT	NRMT
COMPLETE SET (251)	2200.00	1000.00
COMMON CARD (1-251)	3.00	1.35
COMMON SILVER (1-251)	4.00	1.80
COMMON GOLD (1-251)	5.00	2.20

- ❑ 1 Kurt Abbott 3.00 1.35
- ❑ 2 Juan Acevedo 3.00 1.35
- ❑ 3 Terry Adams 3.00 1.35
- ❑ 4 Manny Alexander 3.00 1.35
- ❑ 5 Roberto Alomar SP 120.00 55.00
- ❑ 6 Moises Alou 12.00 5.50
- ❑ 7 Wilson Alvarez 8.00 3.60
- ❑ 8 Garret Anderson 8.00 3.60
- ❑ 9 Shane Andrews 3.00 1.35
- ❑ 10 Andy Ashby 3.00 1.35
- ❑ 11 Pedro Astacio 3.00 1.35
- ❑ 12 Brad Ausmus 3.00 1.35
- ❑ 13 Bobby Ayala 3.00 1.35
- ❑ 14 Carlos Baerga 8.00 3.60
- ❑ 15 Harold Baines 8.00 3.60
- ❑ 16 Jason Bates 3.00 1.35
- ❑ 17 Allen Battle 3.00 1.35
- ❑ 18 Rich Becker 3.00 1.35
- ❑ 19 David Bell 3.00 1.35
- ❑ 20 Rafael Belliard 3.00 1.35
- ❑ 21 Andy Benes 8.00 3.60
- ❑ 22 Armando Benitez 3.00 1.35
- ❑ 23 Jason Bere 3.00 1.35
- ❑ 24 Geronimo Berroa 3.00 1.35
- ❑ 25 Willie Blair 3.00 1.35
- ❑ 26 Mike Blowers 3.00 1.35
- ❑ 27 Wade Boggs SP 200.00 90.00
- ❑ 28 Ricky Bones 3.00 1.35
- ❑ 29 Mike Bordick 3.00 1.35
- ❑ 30 Toby Borland 3.00 1.35
- ❑ 31 Ricky Bottalico 8.00 3.60
- ❑ 32 Darren Bragg 3.00 1.35
- ❑ 33 Jeff Branson 3.00 1.35
- ❑ 34 Tilson Brito 3.00 1.35
- ❑ 35 Rico Brogna 3.00 1.35
- ❑ 36 Scott Brosius 8.00 3.60
- ❑ 37 Damon Buford 3.00 1.35
- ❑ 38 Mike Busby 3.00 1.35
- ❑ 39 Tom Candiotti 3.00 1.35
- ❑ 40 Frank Castillo 3.00 1.35
- ❑ 41 Andujar Cedeno 3.00 1.35
- ❑ 42 Domingo Cedeno 3.00 1.35
- ❑ 43 Roger Cedeno 3.00 1.35
- ❑ 44 Norm Charlton 3.00 1.35
- ❑ 45 Jeff Cirillo 8.00 3.60
- ❑ 46 Will Clark 20.00 9.00
- ❑ 47 Jeff Conine 8.00 3.60
- ❑ 48 Steve Cooke 3.00 1.35
- ❑ 49 Joey Cora 8.00 3.60
- ❑ 50 Marty Cordova 3.00 1.35
- ❑ 51 Rheal Cormier 3.00 1.35
- ❑ 52 Felipe Crespo 3.00 1.35
- ❑ 53 Chad Curtis 3.00 1.35
- ❑ 54 Johnny Damon 8.00 3.60
- ❑ 55 Russ Davis 8.00 3.60
- ❑ 56 Andre Dawson 15.00 6.75
- ❑ 57 Carlos Delgado 8.00 3.60
- ❑ 58 Doug Drabek 3.00 1.35
- ❑ 59 Darren Dreifort 8.00 3.60
- ❑ 60 Shawon Dunston 3.00 1.35
- ❑ 61 Ray Durham 8.00 3.60
- ❑ 62 Jim Edmonds 15.00 6.75
- ❑ 63 Joey Eischen 3.00 1.35
- ❑ 64 Jim Eisenreich 3.00 1.35
- ❑ 65 Sal Fasano 3.00 1.35
- ❑ 66 Jeff Fassero 3.00 1.35
- ❑ 67 Alex Fernandez 3.00 1.35
- ❑ 68 Darrin Fletcher 3.00 1.35
- ❑ 69 Chad Fonville 3.00 1.35
- ❑ 70 Kevin Foster 3.00 1.35
- ❑ 71 John Franco 8.00 3.60
- ❑ 72 Julio Franco 3.00 1.35
- ❑ 73 Marvin Freeman 3.00 1.35
- ❑ 74 Travis Fryman 8.00 3.60
- ❑ 75 Gary Gaetti 8.00 3.60
- ❑ 76 Carlos Garcia 3.00 1.35
- ❑ 77 Jason Giambi 8.00 3.60
- ❑ 78 Benji Gil 3.00 1.35
- ❑ 79 Greg Gohr 3.00 1.35
- ❑ 80 Chris Gomez 3.00 1.35
- ❑ 81 Leo Gomez 3.00 1.35
- ❑ 82 Tom Goodwin 3.00 1.35
- ❑ 83 Mike Grace 3.00 1.35
- ❑ 84 Mike Greenwell 3.00 1.35
- ❑ 85 Rusty Greer 12.00 5.50
- ❑ 86 Mark Grudzielanek 8.00 3.60
- ❑ 87 Mark Gubicza 3.00 1.35
- ❑ 88 Juan Guzman 3.00 1.35
- ❑ 89 Darryl Hamilton 3.00 1.35
- ❑ 90 Joey Hamilton 8.00 3.60
- ❑ 91 Chris Hammond 3.00 1.35
- ❑ 92 Mike Hampton 3.00 1.35
- ❑ 93 Chris Haney 3.00 1.35
- ❑ 94 Todd Haney 3.00 1.35
- ❑ 95 Erik Hanson 3.00 1.35
- ❑ 96 Pete Harnisch 3.00 1.35
- ❑ 97 LaTroy Hawkins 3.00 1.35
- ❑ 98 Charlie Hayes 3.00 1.35
- ❑ 99 Jimmy Haynes 3.00 1.35
- ❑ 100 Roberto Hernandez 3.00 1.35
- ❑ 101 Bobby Higginson 20.00 9.00
- ❑ 102 Glenallen Hill 3.00 1.35
- ❑ 103 Ken Hill 3.00 1.35
- ❑ 104 Sterling Hitchcock 8.00 3.60
- ❑ 105 Trevor Hoffman 8.00 3.60
- ❑ 106 Dave Hollins 3.00 1.35
- ❑ 107 Dwayne Hosey 3.00 1.35
- ❑ 108 Thomas Howard 3.00 1.35
- ❑ 109 Steve Howe 3.00 1.35
- ❑ 110 John Hudek 3.00 1.35
- ❑ 111 Rex Hudler 3.00 1.35
- ❑ 112 Brian L. Hunter 8.00 3.60
- ❑ 113 Butch Huskey 3.00 1.35
- ❑ 114 Mark Hutton 3.00 1.35
- ❑ 115 Jason Jacome 3.00 1.35
- ❑ 116 John Jaha 3.00 1.35
- ❑ 117 Reggie Jefferson 3.00 1.35
- ❑ 118 Derek Jeter SP 175.00 80.00
- ❑ 119 Bobby Jones 3.00 1.35
- ❑ 120 Todd Jones 3.00 1.35
- ❑ 121 Brian Jordan 8.00 3.60
- ❑ 122 Kevin Jordan 3.00 1.35
- ❑ 123 Jeff Juden 3.00 1.35
- ❑ 124 Ron Karkovice 3.00 1.35
- ❑ 125 Roberto Kelly 3.00 1.35
- ❑ 126 Mark Kiefer 3.00 1.35
- ❑ 127 Brooks Kieschnick 3.00 1.35
- ❑ 128 Jeff King 3.00 1.35
- ❑ 129 Mike Lansing 3.00 1.35
- ❑ 130 Matt Lawton 20.00 9.00
- ❑ 131 Al Leiter 8.00 3.60
- ❑ 132 Mark Leiter 3.00 1.35
- ❑ 133 Curtis Leskanic 3.00 1.35
- ❑ 134 Darren Lewis 3.00 1.35
- ❑ 135 Mark Lewis 3.00 1.35
- ❑ 136 Felipe Lira 3.00 1.35

❑ 137 Pat Listach 3.00 1.35
❑ 138 Keith Lockhart 3.00 1.35
❑ 139 Kenny Lofton SP 80.00 36.00
❑ 140 John Mabry 3.00 1.35
❑ 141 Mike Macfarlane 3.00 1.35
❑ 142 Kirt Manwaring 3.00 1.35
❑ 143 Al Martin 3.00 1.35
❑ 144 Norberto Martin 3.00 1.35
❑ 145 Dennis Martinez 8.00 3.60
❑ 146 Pedro Martinez 25.00 11.00
❑ 147 Sandy Martinez 3.00 1.35
❑ 148 Mike Matheny 3.00 1.35
❑ 149 T.J. Mathews 3.00 1.35
❑ 150 David McCarty 3.00 1.35
❑ 151 Ben McDonald 3.00 1.35
❑ 152 Pat Meares 3.00 1.35
❑ 153 Orlando Merced 3.00 1.35
❑ 154 Jose Mesa 3.00 1.35
❑ 155 Matt Mieske 3.00 1.35
❑ 156 Orlando Miller 3.00 1.35
❑ 157 Mike Mimbs 3.00 1.35
❑ 158 Paul Molitor SP 100.00 45.00
❑ 159 Raul Mondesi SP 60.00 27.00
❑ 160 Jeff Montgomery 3.00 1.35
❑ 161 Mickey Morandini 3.00 1.35
❑ 162 Lyle Mouton 3.00 1.35
❑ 163 James Mouton 3.00 1.35
❑ 164 Jamie Moyer 3.00 1.35
❑ 165 Rodney Myers 3.00 1.35
❑ 166 Denny Neagle 12.00 5.50
❑ 167 Robb Nen 3.00 1.35
❑ 168 Marc Newfield 3.00 1.35
❑ 169 Dave Nilsson 3.00 1.35
❑ 170 Jon Nunnally 3.00 1.35
❑ 171 Chad Ogea 3.00 1.35
❑ 172 Troy O'Leary 8.00 3.60
❑ 173 Rey Ordonez 8.00 3.60
❑ 174 Jayhawk Owens 3.00 1.35
❑ 175 Tom Pagnozzi 3.00 1.35
❑ 176 Dean Palmer 8.00 3.60
❑ 177 Roger Pavlik 3.00 1.35
❑ 178 Troy Percival 8.00 3.60
❑ 179 Carlos Perez 8.00 3.60
❑ 180 Robert Perez 3.00 1.35
❑ 181 Andy Pettitte 20.00 9.00
❑ 182 Phil Plantier 3.00 1.35
❑ 183 Mike Potts 3.00 1.35
❑ 184 Curtis Pride 3.00 1.35
❑ 185 Ariel Prieto 3.00 1.35
❑ 186 Bill Pulsipher 3.00 1.35
❑ 187 Brad Radke 8.00 3.60
❑ 188 Manny Ramirez SP 60.00 27.00
❑ 189 Joe Randa 3.00 1.35
❑ 190 Pat Rapp 3.00 1.35
❑ 191 Bryan Rekar 3.00 1.35
❑ 192 Shane Reynolds 8.00 3.60
❑ 193 Arthur Rhodes 3.00 1.35
❑ 194 Mariano Rivera 12.00 5.50
❑ 195 Alex Rodriguez SP 200.00 90.00
❑ 196 Frank Rodriguez 3.00 1.35
❑ 197 Mel Rojas 3.00 1.35
❑ 198 Ken Ryan 3.00 1.35
❑ 199 Bret Saberhagen 8.00 3.60
❑ 200 Tim Salmon 20.00 9.00
❑ 201 Rey Sanchez 3.00 1.35
❑ 202 Scott Sanders 3.00 1.35
❑ 203 Steve Scarsone 3.00 1.35
❑ 204 Curt Schilling 8.00 3.60
❑ 205 Jason Schmidt 3.00 1.35
❑ 206 David Segui 8.00 3.60
❑ 207 Kevin Seitzer 3.00 1.35
❑ 208 Scott Servais 3.00 1.35
❑ 209 Don Slaught 3.00 1.35
❑ 210 Zane Smith 3.00 1.35
❑ 211 Paul Sorrento 3.00 1.35
❑ 212 Scott Stahoviak 3.00 1.35
❑ 213 Mike Stanley 3.00 1.35
❑ 214 Terry Steinbach 8.00 3.60
❑ 215 Kevin Stocker 3.00 1.35
❑ 216 Jeff Suppan 3.00 1.35
❑ 217 Bill Swift 3.00 1.35
❑ 218 Greg Swindell 3.00 1.35
❑ 219 Kevin Tapani 3.00 1.35
❑ 220 Danny Tartabull 3.00 1.35
❑ 221 Julian Tavarez 3.00 1.35
❑ 222 Frank Thomas SP 150.00 70.00
❑ 223 Ozzie Timmons 3.00 1.35
❑ 224 Michael Tucker 8.00 3.60
❑ 225 Ismael Valdes 8.00 3.60
❑ 226 Jose Valentin 3.00 1.35
❑ 227 Todd Van Poppel 3.00 1.35
❑ 228 Mo Vaughn SP 100.00 45.00
❑ 229 Quilvio Veras 3.00 1.35
❑ 230 Fernando Vina 3.00 1.35
❑ 231 Joe Vitiello 3.00 1.35
❑ 232 Jose Vizcaino 3.00 1.35
❑ 233 Omar Vizquel 8.00 3.60
❑ 234 Terrell Wade 3.00 1.35
❑ 235 Paul Wagner 3.00 1.35
❑ 236 Matt Walbeck 3.00 1.35
❑ 237 Jerome Walton 3.00 1.35
❑ 238 Turner Ward 3.00 1.35
❑ 239 Allen Watson 3.00 1.35
❑ 240 David Weathers 3.00 1.35
❑ 241 Walt Weiss 3.00 1.35
❑ 242 Turk Wendell 3.00 1.35
❑ 243 Rondell White 8.00 3.60
❑ 244 Brian Williams 3.00 1.35
❑ 245 George Williams 3.00 1.35
❑ 246 Paul Wilson 3.00 1.35
❑ 247 Bobby Witt 3.00 1.35
❑ 248 Bob Wolcott 3.00 1.35
❑ 249 Eric Young 3.00 1.35
❑ 250 Ernie Young 3.00 1.35
❑ 251 Greg Zaun 3.00 1.35
❑ NNO F.Thomas Jumbo AU 80.00 36.00

1996 Leaf Signature Extended Autographs

	MINT	NRMT
COMPLETE SET (217)	2500.00	1100.00
COMMON CARD (1-217)	4.00	1.80

❑ 1 Scott Aldred 4.00 1.80
❑ 2 Mike Aldrete 4.00 1.80
❑ 3 Rich Amaral 4.00 1.80
❑ 4 Alex Arias 4.00 1.80
❑ 5 Paul Assenmacher 4.00 1.80
❑ 6 Roger Bailey 4.00 1.80
❑ 7 Erik Bennett 4.00 1.80
❑ 8 Sean Bergman 4.00 1.80
❑ 9 Doug Bochtler 4.00 1.80
❑ 10 Tim Bogar 4.00 1.80
❑ 11 Pat Borders 4.00 1.80
❑ 12 Pedro Borbon 4.00 1.80
❑ 13 Shawn Boskie 4.00 1.80
❑ 14 Rafael Bournigal 4.00 1.80
❑ 15 Mark Brandenburg 4.00 1.80
❑ 16 John Briscoe 4.00 1.80
❑ 17 Jorge Brito 4.00 1.80
❑ 18 Doug Brocail 4.00 1.80
❑ 19 Jay Buhner SP1000 30.00 13.50
❑ 20 Scott Bullett 4.00 1.80
❑ 21 Dave Burba 4.00 1.80
❑ 22 Ken Caminiti SP1000 40.00 18.00
❑ 23 John Cangelosi 4.00 1.80
❑ 24 Cris Carpenter 4.00 1.80
❑ 25 Chuck Carr 4.00 1.80
❑ 26 Larry Casian 4.00 1.80
❑ 27 Tony Castillo 4.00 1.80
❑ 28 Jason Christiansen 4.00 1.80
❑ 29 Archi Cianfrocco 4.00 1.80
❑ 30 Mark Clark 4.00 1.80
❑ 31 Terry Clark 4.00 1.80
❑ 32 Roger Clemens SP1000 150.00 70.00
❑ 33 Jim Converse 4.00 1.80
❑ 34 Dennis Cook 4.00 1.80
❑ 35 Francisco Cordova 4.00 1.80
❑ 36 Jim Corsi 4.00 1.80
❑ 37 Tim Crabtree 4.00 1.80
❑ 38 Doug Creek SP1950 10.00 4.50
❑ 39 John Cummings 4.00 1.80
❑ 40 Omar Daal 4.00 1.80
❑ 41 Rich DeLucia 4.00 1.80
❑ 42 Mark Dewey 4.00 1.80
❑ 43 Alex Diaz 4.00 1.80
❑ 44 Jermaine Dye SP2500 8.00 3.60
❑ 45 Ken Edenfield 4.00 1.80
❑ 46 Mark Eichhorn 4.00 1.80
❑ 47 John Ericks 4.00 1.80
❑ 48 Darin Erstad 40.00 18.00
❑ 49 Alvaro Espinoza 4.00 1.80
❑ 50 Jorge Fabregas 4.00 1.80
❑ 51 Mike Fetters 4.00 1.80
❑ 52 John Flaherty 4.00 1.80
❑ 53 Bryce Florie 4.00 1.80
❑ 54 Tony Fossas 4.00 1.80
❑ 55 Lou Frazier 4.00 1.80
❑ 56 Mike Gallego 4.00 1.80
❑ 57 Karim Garcia SP2500 10.00 4.50
❑ 58 Jason Giambi 6.00 2.70
❑ 59 Ed Giovanola 4.00 1.80
❑ 60 Tom Glavine SP1250 40.00 18.00
❑ 61 Juan Gonzalez SP1000 150.00 70.00
❑ 62 Craig Grebeck 4.00 1.80
❑ 63 Buddy Groom 4.00 1.80
❑ 64 Kevin Gross 4.00 1.80
❑ 65 Eddie Guardado 4.00 1.80
❑ 66 Mark Guthrie 4.00 1.80
❑ 67 Tony Gwynn SP1000 150.00 70.00
❑ 68 Chip Hale 4.00 1.80
❑ 69 Darren Hall 4.00 1.80
❑ 70 Lee Hancock 4.00 1.80
❑ 71 Dave Hansen 4.00 1.80
❑ 72 Bryan Harvey 4.00 1.80
❑ 73 Bill Haselman 4.00 1.80
❑ 74 Mike Henneman 4.00 1.80
❑ 75 Doug Henry 4.00 1.80
❑ 76 Gil Heredia 4.00 1.80
❑ 77 Carlos Hernandez 4.00 1.80
❑ 78 Jose Hernandez 4.00 1.80
❑ 79 Darren Holmes 4.00 1.80
❑ 80 Mark Holzemer 4.00 1.80
❑ 81 Rick Honeycutt 4.00 1.80
❑ 82 Chris Hook 4.00 1.80
❑ 83 Chris Howard 4.00 1.80
❑ 84 Jack Howell 4.00 1.80
❑ 85 David Hulse 4.00 1.80
❑ 86 Edwin Hurtado 4.00 1.80
❑ 87 Jeff Huson 4.00 1.80
❑ 88 Mike James 4.00 1.80
❑ 89 Derek Jeter SP1000 150.00 70.00
❑ 90 Brian Johnson 4.00 1.80
❑ 91 Randy Johnson SP1000 60.00 27.00
❑ 92 Mark Johnson 4.00 1.80
❑ 93 Andruw Jones SP2000 60.00 27.00
❑ 94 Chris Jones 4.00 1.80
❑ 95 Ricky Jordan 4.00 1.80
❑ 96 Matt Karchner 4.00 1.80
❑ 97 Scott Karl 4.00 1.80
❑ 98 Jason Kendall SP2500 25.00 11.00
❑ 99 Brian Keyser 4.00 1.80
❑ 100 Mike Kingery 4.00 1.80
❑ 101 Wayne Kirby 4.00 1.80
❑ 102 Ryan Klesko SP1000 25.00 11.00
❑ 103 Chuck Knoblauch SP1000 50.00
22.00
❑ 104 Chad Kreuter 4.00 1.80
❑ 105 Tom Lampkin 4.00 1.80
❑ 106 Scott Leius 4.00 1.80
❑ 107 Jon Lieber 4.00 1.80
❑ 108 Nelson Liriano 4.00 1.80
❑ 109 Scott Livingstone 4.00 1.80
❑ 110 Graeme Lloyd 4.00 1.80
❑ 111 Kenny Lofton SP1000 50.00 22.00
❑ 112 Luis Lopez 4.00 1.80

❑ 113 Torey Lovullo	4.00	1.80
❑ 114 Greg Maddux SP500	400.00	180.00
❑ 115 Mike Maddux	4.00	1.80
❑ 116 Dave Magadan	4.00	1.80
❑ 117 Mike Magnante	4.00	1.80
❑ 118 Joe Magrane	4.00	1.80
❑ 119 Pat Mahomes	4.00	1.80
❑ 120 Matt Mantei	4.00	1.80
❑ 121 John Marzano	4.00	1.80
❑ 122 Terry Mathews	4.00	1.80
❑ 123 Chuck McElroy	4.00	1.80
❑ 124 Fred McGriff SP1000	40.00	18.00
❑ 125 Mark McLemore	4.00	1.80
❑ 126 Greg McMichael	4.00	1.80
❑ 127 Blas Minor	4.00	1.80
❑ 128 Dave Mlicki	4.00	1.80
❑ 129 Mike Mohler	4.00	1.80
❑ 130 Paul Molitor SP1000	80.00	36.00
❑ 131 Steve Montgomery	4.00	1.80
❑ 132 Mike Mordecai	4.00	1.80
❑ 133 Mike Morgan	4.00	1.80
❑ 134 Mike Munoz	4.00	1.80
❑ 135 Greg Myers	4.00	1.80
❑ 136 Jimmy Myers	4.00	1.80
❑ 137 Mike Myers	4.00	1.80
❑ 138 Bob Natal	4.00	1.80
❑ 139 Dan Naulty	4.00	1.80
❑ 140 Jeff Nelson	4.00	1.80
❑ 141 Warren Newson	4.00	1.80
❑ 142 Chris Nichting	4.00	1.80
❑ 143 Melvin Nieves	4.00	1.80
❑ 144 Charlie O'Brien	4.00	1.80
❑ 145 Alex Ochoa	4.00	1.80
❑ 146 Omar Olivares	4.00	1.80
❑ 147 Joe Oliver	4.00	1.80
❑ 148 Lance Painter	4.00	1.80
❑ 149 Rafael Palmeiro SP2000	25.00	11.00
❑ 150 Mark Parent	4.00	1.80
❑ 151 Steve Parris SP1800	10.00	4.50
❑ 152 Bob Patterson	4.00	1.80
❑ 153 Tony Pena	4.00	1.80
❑ 154 Eddie Perez	4.00	1.80
❑ 155 Yorkis Perez	4.00	1.80
❑ 156 Robert Person	4.00	1.80
❑ 157 Mark Petkovsek	4.00	1.80
❑ 158 Andy Pettitte SP1000	50.00	22.00
❑ 159 J.R. Phillips	4.00	1.80
❑ 160 Hipolito Pichardo	4.00	1.80
❑ 161 Eric Plunk	4.00	1.80
❑ 162 Jimmy Poole	4.00	1.80
❑ 163 Kirby Puckett SP1000	120.00	55.00
❑ 164 Paul Quantrill	4.00	1.80
❑ 165 Tom Quinlan	4.00	1.80
❑ 166 Jeff Reboulet	4.00	1.80
❑ 167 Jeff Reed	4.00	1.80
❑ 168 Steve Reed	4.00	1.80
❑ 169 Carlos Reyes	4.00	1.80
❑ 170 Bill Risley	4.00	1.80
❑ 171 Kevin Ritz	4.00	1.80
❑ 172 Kevin Roberson	4.00	1.80
❑ 173 Rich Robertson	4.00	1.80
❑ 174 Alex Rodriguez SP500	300.00	135.00
❑ 175 Ivan Rodriguez SP1250	80.00	36.00
❑ 176 Bruce Ruffin	4.00	1.80
❑ 177 Juan Samuel	4.00	1.80
❑ 178 Tim Scott	4.00	1.80
❑ 179 Kevin Sefcik	4.00	1.80
❑ 180 Jeff Shaw	4.00	1.80
❑ 181 Danny Sheaffer	4.00	1.80
❑ 182 Craig Shipley	4.00	1.80
❑ 183 Dave Silvestri	4.00	1.80
❑ 184 Aaron Small	4.00	1.80
❑ 185 John Smoltz SP1000	30.00	13.50
❑ 186 Luis Sojo	4.00	1.80
❑ 187 Sammy Sosa SP1000	150.00	70.00
❑ 188 Steve Sparks	4.00	1.80
❑ 189 Tim Spehr	4.00	1.80
❑ 190 Russ Springer	4.00	1.80
❑ 191 Matt Stairs	6.00	2.70
❑ 192 Andy Stankiewicz	4.00	1.80
❑ 193 Mike Stanton	4.00	1.80
❑ 194 Kelly Stinnett	4.00	1.80
❑ 195 Doug Strange	4.00	1.80
❑ 196 Mark Sweeney	4.00	1.80
❑ 197 Jeff Tabaka	4.00	1.80
❑ 198 Jesus Tavarez	4.00	1.80
❑ 199 Frank Thomas SP1000	120.00	55.00
❑ 200 Larry Thomas	4.00	1.80
❑ 201 Mark Thompson	4.00	1.80
❑ 202 Mike Timlin	4.00	1.80
❑ 203 Steve Trachsel	4.00	1.80
❑ 204 Tom Urbani	4.00	1.80
❑ 205 Julio Valera	4.00	1.80
❑ 206 Dave Valle	4.00	1.80
❑ 207 William VanLandingham	4.00	1.80
❑ 208 Mo Vaughn SP1000	80.00	36.00
❑ 209 Dave Veres	4.00	1.80
❑ 210 Ed Vosberg	4.00	1.80
❑ 211 Don Wengert	4.00	1.80
❑ 212 Matt Whiteside	4.00	1.80
❑ 213 Bob Wickman	4.00	1.80
❑ 214 Matt Williams SP1250	30.00	13.50
❑ 215 Mike Williams	4.00	1.80
❑ 216 Woody Williams	4.00	1.80
❑ 217 Craig Worthington	4.00	1.80
❑ NNO F.Thomas Jumbo AU	80.00	36.00

1996 Leaf Signature Extended Autographs Century Marks

	MINT	NRMT
COMPLETE SET (31)	3500.00	1600.00
COMMON CARD (1-31)	40.00	18.00
❑ 1 Jay Buhner	80.00	36.00
❑ 2 Ken Caminiti	100.00	45.00
❑ 3 Roger Clemens	400.00	180.00
❑ 4 Jermaine Dye	40.00	18.00
❑ 5 Darin Erstad	200.00	90.00
❑ 6 Karim Garcia	50.00	22.00
❑ 7 Jason Giambi	60.00	27.00
❑ 8 Tom Glavine	120.00	55.00
❑ 9 Juan Gonzalez	400.00	180.00
❑ 10 Tony Gwynn	400.00	180.00
❑ 11 Derek Jeter	300.00	135.00
❑ 12 Randy Johnson	150.00	70.00
❑ 13 Andruw Jones	250.00	110.00
❑ 14 Jason Kendall	100.00	45.00
❑ 15 Ryan Klesko	60.00	27.00
❑ 16 Chuck Knoblauch	120.00	55.00
❑ 17 Kenny Lofton	120.00	55.00
❑ 18 Greg Maddux	600.00	275.00
❑ 19 Fred McGriff	100.00	45.00
❑ 20 Paul Molitor	150.00	70.00
❑ 21 Alex Ochoa	40.00	18.00
❑ 22 Rafael Palmeiro	100.00	45.00
❑ 23 Andy Pettitte	120.00	55.00
❑ 24 Kirby Puckett	250.00	110.00
❑ 25 Alex Rodriguez	400.00	180.00
❑ 26 Ivan Rodriguez	200.00	90.00
❑ 27 John Smoltz	80.00	36.00
❑ 28 Sammy Sosa	400.00	180.00
❑ 29 Frank Thomas	400.00	180.00
❑ 30 Mo Vaughn	200.00	90.00
❑ 31 Matt Williams	80.00	36.00

1996 Metal Universe

	MINT	NRMT
COMPLETE SET (250)	40.00	18.00
COMMON CARD (1-250)	.15	.07
❑ 1 Roberto Alomar	.60	.25
❑ 2 Brady Anderson	.30	.14
❑ 3 Bobby Bonilla	.30	.14
❑ 4 Chris Hoiles	.15	.07
❑ 5 Ben McDonald	.15	.07
❑ 6 Mike Mussina	.60	.25
❑ 7 Randy Myers	.15	.07
❑ 8 Rafael Palmeiro	.40	.18
❑ 9 Cal Ripken	2.50	1.10
❑ 10 B.J. Surhoff	.30	.14
❑ 11 Luis Alicea	.15	.07
❑ 12 Jose Canseco	.60	.25
❑ 13 Roger Clemens	1.25	.55
❑ 14 Wil Cordero	.15	.07
❑ 15 Tom Gordon	.15	.07
❑ 16 Mike Greenwall	.15	.07
❑ 17 Tim Naehring	.15	.07
❑ 18 Troy O'Leary	.30	.14
❑ 19 Mike Stanley	.15	.07
❑ 20 John Valentin	.30	.14
❑ 21 Mo Vaughn	.75	.35
❑ 22 Tim Wakefield	.30	.14
❑ 23 Garret Anderson	.30	.14
❑ 24 Chili Davis	.30	.14
❑ 25 Gary DiSarcina	.15	.07
❑ 26 Jim Edmonds	.40	.18
❑ 27 Chuck Finley	.30	.14
❑ 28 Todd Greene	.30	.14
❑ 29 Mark Langston	.15	.07
❑ 30 Troy Percival	.30	.14
❑ 31 Tony Phillips	.15	.07
❑ 32 Tim Salmon	.60	.25
❑ 33 Lee Smith	.30	.14
❑ 34 J.T. Snow	.30	.14
❑ 35 Ray Durham	.30	.14
❑ 36 Alex Fernandez	.15	.07
❑ 37 Ozzie Guillen	.15	.07
❑ 38 Roberto Hernandez	.15	.07
❑ 39 Lyle Mouton	.15	.07
❑ 40 Frank Thomas	2.00	.90
❑ 41 Robin Ventura	.30	.14
❑ 42 Sandy Alomar Jr.	.30	.14
❑ 43 Carlos Baerga	.30	.14
❑ 44 Albert Belle	.75	.35
❑ 45 Orel Hershiser	.30	.14
❑ 46 Kenny Lofton	.60	.25
❑ 47 Dennis Martinez	.30	.14
❑ 48 Jack McDowell	.15	.07
❑ 49 Jose Mesa	.15	.07
❑ 50 Eddie Murray	.60	.25
❑ 51 Charles Nagy	.30	.14
❑ 52 Manny Ramirez	.60	.25
❑ 53 Julian Tavarez	.15	.07
❑ 54 Jim Thome	.60	.25
❑ 55 Omar Vizquel	.30	.14
❑ 56 Chad Curtis	.15	.07
❑ 57 Cecil Fielder	.30	.14
❑ 58 John Flaherty	.15	.07
❑ 59 Travis Fryman	.30	.14
❑ 60 Chris Gomez	.15	.07
❑ 61 Felipe Lira	.15	.07
❑ 62 Kevin Appier	.30	.14
❑ 63 Johnny Damon	.30	.14
❑ 64 Tom Goodwin	.15	.07
❑ 65 Mark Gubicza	.15	.07
❑ 66 Jeff Montgomery	.15	.07
❑ 67 Jon Nunnally	.15	.07
❑ 68 Ricky Bones	.15	.07
❑ 69 Jeff Cirillo	.30	.14
❑ 70 John Jaha	.15	.07
❑ 71 Dave Nilsson	.15	.07
❑ 72 Joe Oliver	.15	.07
❑ 73 Kevin Seitzer	.15	.07
❑ 74 Greg Vaughn	.30	.14
❑ 75 Marty Cordova	.15	.07
❑ 76 Chuck Knoblauch	.60	.25
❑ 77 Pat Meares	.15	.07
❑ 78 Paul Molitor	.60	.25
❑ 79 Pedro Munoz	.15	.07
❑ 80 Kirby Puckett	1.00	.45
❑ 81 Brad Radke	.30	.14
❑ 82 Scott Stahoviak	.15	.07
❑ 83 Matt Walbeck	.15	.07
❑ 84 Wade Boggs	.60	.25
❑ 85 David Cone	.40	.18

❑ 86 Joe Girardi .15 .07
❑ 87 Derek Jeter 2.00 .90
❑ 88 Jim Leyritz .15 .07
❑ 89 Tino Martinez .60 .25
❑ 90 Don Mattingly 1.00 .45
❑ 91 Paul O'Neill .30 .14
❑ 92 Andy Pettitte .40 .18
❑ 93 Tim Raines .30 .14
❑ 94 Kenny Rogers .15 .07
❑ 95 Ruben Sierra .15 .07
❑ 96 John Wetteland .30 .14
❑ 97 Bernie Williams .60 .25
❑ 98 Geronimo Berroa .15 .07
❑ 99 Dennis Eckersley .30 .14
❑ 100 Brent Gates .15 .07
❑ 101 Mark McGwire 3.00 1.35
❑ 102 Steve Ontiveros .15 .07
❑ 103 Terry Steinbach .30 .14
❑ 104 Jay Buhner .30 .14
❑ 105 Vince Coleman .15 .07
❑ 106 Joey Cora .30 .14
❑ 107 Ken Griffey, Jr. 3.00 1.35
❑ 108 Randy Johnson .60 .25
❑ 109 Edgar Martinez .30 .14
❑ 110 Alex Rodriguez 2.00 .90
❑ 111 Paul Sorrento .15 .07
❑ 112 Will Clark .60 .25
❑ 113 Juan Gonzalez 1.50 .70
❑ 114 Rusty Greer .40 .18
❑ 115 Dean Palmer .30 .14
❑ 116 Ivan Rodriguez .75 .35
❑ 117 Mickey Tettleton .15 .07
❑ 118 Joe Carter .30 .14
❑ 119 Alex Gonzalez .15 .07
❑ 120 Shawn Green .30 .14
❑ 121 Erik Hanson .15 .07
❑ 122 Pat Hentgen .30 .14
❑ 123 Sandy Martinez .15 .07
❑ 124 Otis Nixon .15 .07
❑ 125 John Olerud .30 .14
❑ 126 Steve Avery .15 .07
❑ 127 Tom Glavine .60 .25
❑ 128 Marquis Grissom .30 .14
❑ 129 Chipper Jones 1.50 .70
❑ 130 David Justice .60 .25
❑ 131 Ryan Klesko .30 .14
❑ 132 Mark Lemke .15 .07
❑ 133 Javier Lopez .30 .14
❑ 134 Greg Maddux 2.00 .90
❑ 135 Fred McGriff .40 .18
❑ 136 John Smoltz .30 .14
❑ 137 Mark Wohlers .15 .07
❑ 138 Frank Castillo .15 .07
❑ 139 Shawon Dunston .15 .07
❑ 140 Luis Gonzalez .15 .07
❑ 141 Mark Grace .40 .18
❑ 142 Brian McRae .15 .07
❑ 143 Jaime Navarro .15 .07
❑ 144 Rey Sanchez .15 .07
❑ 145 Ryne Sandberg .75 .35
❑ 146 Sammy Sosa 1.50 .70
❑ 147 Bret Boone .30 .14
❑ 148 Curtis Goodwin .15 .07
❑ 149 Barry Larkin .40 .18
❑ 150 Hal Morris .15 .07
❑ 151 Reggie Sanders .30 .14
❑ 152 Pete Schourek .15 .07
❑ 153 John Smiley .15 .07
❑ 154 Dante Bichette .30 .14
❑ 155 Vinny Castilla .40 .18
❑ 156 Andres Galarraga .60 .25
❑ 157 Bret Saberhagen .30 .14
❑ 158 Bill Swift .15 .07
❑ 159 Larry Walker .60 .25
❑ 160 Walt Weiss .15 .07
❑ 161 Kurt Abbott .15 .07
❑ 162 John Burkett .15 .07
❑ 163 Greg Colbrunn .15 .07
❑ 164 Jeff Conine .30 .14
❑ 165 Chris Hammond .15 .07
❑ 166 Charles Johnson .30 .14
❑ 167 Al Leiter .30 .14
❑ 168 Pat Rapp .15 .07
❑ 169 Gary Sheffield .40 .18
❑ 170 Quilvio Veras .15 .07
❑ 171 Devon White .30 .14
❑ 172 Jeff Bagwell 1.00 .45
❑ 173 Derek Bell .30 .14
❑ 174 Sean Berry .15 .07
❑ 175 Craig Biggio .60 .25
❑ 176 Doug Drabek .15 .07
❑ 177 Tony Eusebio .15 .07
❑ 178 Brian L.Hunter .30 .14
❑ 179 Orlando Miller .15 .07
❑ 180 Shane Reynolds .30 .14
❑ 181 Mike Blowers .15 .07
❑ 182 Roger Cedeno .15 .07
❑ 183 Eric Karros .30 .14
❑ 184 Ramon Martinez .30 .14
❑ 185 Raul Mondesi .40 .18
❑ 186 Hideo Nomo 1.00 .45
❑ 187 Mike Piazza 2.00 .90
❑ 188 Moises Alou .40 .18
❑ 189 Yamil Benitez .15 .07
❑ 190 Darrin Fletcher .15 .07
❑ 191 Cliff Floyd .30 .14
❑ 192 Pedro Martinez .60 .25
❑ 193 Carlos Perez .30 .14
❑ 194 David Segui .30 .14
❑ 195 Tony Tarasco .15 .07
❑ 196 Rondell White .30 .14
❑ 197 Edgardo Alfonzo .30 .14
❑ 198 Rico Brogna .15 .07
❑ 199 Carl Everett .15 .07
❑ 200 Todd Hundley .30 .14
❑ 201 Jason Isringhausen .15 .07
❑ 202 Lance Johnson .15 .07
❑ 203 Bobby Jones .15 .07
❑ 204 Jeff Kent .30 .14
❑ 205 Bill Pulsipher .15 .07
❑ 206 Jose Vizcaino .15 .07
❑ 207 Ricky Bottalico .30 .14
❑ 208 Darren Daulton .30 .14
❑ 209 Lenny Dykstra .30 .14
❑ 210 Jim Eisenreich .15 .07
❑ 211 Gregg Jefferies .15 .07
❑ 212 Mickey Morandini .15 .07
❑ 213 Heathcliff Slocumb .15 .07
❑ 214 Jay Bell .30 .14
❑ 215 Carlos Garcia .15 .07
❑ 216 Jeff King .15 .07
❑ 217 Al Martin .15 .07
❑ 218 Orlando Merced .15 .07
❑ 219 Dan Miceli .15 .07
❑ 220 Denny Neagle .30 .14
❑ 221 Andy Benes .30 .14
❑ 222 Royce Clayton .15 .07
❑ 223 Gary Gaetti .30 .14
❑ 224 Ron Gant .15 .07
❑ 225 Bernard Gilkey .15 .07
❑ 226 Brian Jordan .30 .14
❑ 227 Ray Lankford .30 .14
❑ 228 John Mabry .15 .07
❑ 229 Ozzie Smith .75 .35
❑ 230 Todd Stottlemyre .15 .07
❑ 231 Andy Ashby .15 .07
❑ 232 Brad Ausmus .15 .07
❑ 233 Ken Caminiti .40 .18
❑ 234 Steve Finley .30 .14
❑ 235 Tony Gwynn 1.50 .70
❑ 236 Joey Hamilton .30 .14
❑ 237 Rickey Henderson .60 .25
❑ 238 Trevor Hoffman .30 .14
❑ 239 Wally Joyner .30 .14
❑ 240 Rod Beck .15 .07
❑ 241 Barry Bonds .75 .35
❑ 242 Glenallen Hill .15 .07
❑ 243 Stan Javier .15 .07
❑ 244 Mark Leiter .15 .07
❑ 245 Deion Sanders .30 .14
❑ 246 William Van Landingham .15 .07
❑ 247 Matt Williams .30 .14
❑ 248 Checklist .15 .07
❑ 249 Checklist .15 .07
❑ 250 Checklist .15 .07

1996 Metal Universe Heavy Metal

	MINT	NRMT
COMPLETE SET (10)	25.00	11.00
COMMON CARD (1-10)	1.25	.55
❑ 1 Albert Belle	1.50	.70
❑ 2 Barry Bonds	1.50	.70
❑ 3 Juan Gonzalez	5.00	2.20
❑ 4 Ken Griffey Jr.	10.00	4.50
❑ 5 Mark McGwire	10.00	4.50
❑ 6 Mike Piazza	6.00	2.70
❑ 7 Sammy Sosa	5.00	2.20
❑ 8 Frank Thomas	6.00	2.70
❑ 9 Mo Vaughn	1.50	.70
❑ 10 Matt Williams	1.25	.55

1996 Metal Universe Mining For Gold

	MINT	NRMT
COMPLETE SET (12)	60.00	27.00
COMMON CARD (1-12)	1.50	.70
❑ 1 Yamil Benitez	1.50	.70
❑ 2 Marty Cordova	1.50	.70
❑ 3 Shawn Green	2.50	1.10
❑ 4 Todd Greene	2.50	1.10
❑ 5 Brian Hunter	2.50	1.10
❑ 6 Derek Jeter	15.00	6.75
❑ 7 Charles Johnson	2.50	1.10
❑ 8 Chipper Jones	15.00	6.75
❑ 9 Hideo Nomo	10.00	4.50
❑ 10 Alex Ochoa	1.50	.70
❑ 11 Andy Pettitte	4.00	1.80
❑ 12 Quilvio Veras	1.50	.70

1996 Metal Universe Mother Lode

	MINT	NRMT
COMPLETE SET (12)	60.00	27.00
COMMON CARD (1-12)	2.00	.90
❑ 1 Barry Bonds	3.00	1.35
❑ 2 Jim Edmonds	2.00	.90
❑ 3 Ken Griffey Jr.	15.00	6.75
❑ 4 Kenny Lofton	3.00	1.35

		MINT	NRMT
❑ 5	Raul Mondesi	2.00	.90
❑ 6	Rafael Palmeiro	2.00	.90
❑ 7	Manny Ramirez	3.00	1.35
❑ 8	Cal Ripken	12.00	5.50
❑ 9	Tim Salmon	3.00	1.35
❑ 10	Ryne Sandberg	3.00	1.35
❑ 11	Frank Thomas	10.00	4.50
❑ 12	Matt Williams	2.00	.90

1996 Metal Universe Platinum Portraits

	MINT	NRMT
COMPLETE SET (10)	12.00	5.50
COMMON CARD (1-10)	.50	.23

		MINT	NRMT
❑ 1	Garret Anderson	.75	.35
❑ 2	Marty Cordova	.50	.23
❑ 3	Jim Edmonds	1.00	.45
❑ 4	Jason Isringhausen	.50	.23
❑ 5	Chipper Jones	5.00	2.20
❑ 6	Ryan Klesko	.75	.35
❑ 7	Hideo Nomo	2.50	1.10
❑ 8	Carlos Perez	.75	.35
❑ 9	Manny Ramirez	1.50	.70
❑ 10	Rondell White	.75	.35

1996 Metal Universe Titanium

	MINT	NRMT
COMPLETE SET (10)	120.00	55.00
COMMON CARD (1-10)	3.00	1.35

		MINT	NRMT
❑ 1	Albert Belle	6.00	2.70
❑ 2	Barry Bonds	6.00	2.70
❑ 3	Ken Griffey Jr.	25.00	11.00
❑ 4	Tony Gwynn	12.00	5.50
❑ 5	Greg Maddux	15.00	6.75
❑ 6	Mike Piazza	15.00	6.75
❑ 7	Cal Ripken	20.00	9.00
❑ 8	Frank Thomas	15.00	6.75
❑ 9	Mo Vaughn	6.00	2.70
❑ 10	Matt Williams	3.00	1.35

1997 Metal Universe

	MINT	NRMT
COMPLETE SET (250)	40.00	18.00
COMMON CARD (1-250)	.15	.07

		MINT	NRMT
❑ 1	Roberto Alomar	.60	.25
❑ 2	Brady Anderson	.30	.14
❑ 3	Rocky Coppinger	.15	.07
❑ 4	Chris Hoiles	.15	.07
❑ 5	Eddie Murray	.60	.25
❑ 6	Mike Mussina	.60	.25
❑ 7	Rafael Palmeiro	.40	.18
❑ 8	Cal Ripken	2.50	1.10
❑ 9	B.J. Surhoff	.30	.14
❑ 10	Brant Brown	.30	.14
❑ 11	Mark Grace	.40	.18
❑ 12	Brian McRae	.15	.07
❑ 13	Jaime Navarro	.15	.07
❑ 14	Ryne Sandberg	.75	.35
❑ 15	Sammy Sosa	1.50	.70
❑ 16	Amaury Telemaco	.15	.07
❑ 17	Steve Trachsel	.15	.07
❑ 18	Darren Bragg	.15	.07
❑ 19	Jose Canseco	.60	.25
❑ 20	Roger Clemens	1.25	.55
❑ 21	Nomar Garciaparra	2.00	.90
❑ 22	Tom Gordon	.15	.07
❑ 23	Tim Naehring	.15	.07
❑ 24	Mike Stanley	.15	.07
❑ 25	John Valentin	.30	.14
❑ 26	Mo Vaughn	.75	.35
❑ 27	Jermaine Dye	.15	.07
❑ 28	Tom Glavine	.60	.25
❑ 29	Marquis Grissom	.30	.14
❑ 30	Andruw Jones	1.00	.45
❑ 31	Chipper Jones	1.50	.70
❑ 32	Ryan Klesko	.30	.14
❑ 33	Greg Maddux	2.00	.90
❑ 34	Fred McGriff	.40	.18
❑ 35	John Smoltz	.30	.14
❑ 36	Garret Anderson	.30	.14
❑ 37	George Arias	.15	.07
❑ 38	Gary DiSarcina	.15	.07
❑ 39	Jim Edmonds	.40	.18
❑ 40	Darin Erstad	1.00	.45
❑ 41	Chuck Finley	.30	.14
❑ 42	Troy Percival	.30	.14
❑ 43	Tim Salmon	.60	.25
❑ 44	Bret Boone	.30	.14
❑ 45	Jeff Brantley	.15	.07
❑ 46	Eric Davis	.30	.14
❑ 47	Barry Larkin	.40	.18
❑ 48	Hal Morris	.15	.07
❑ 49	Mark Portugal	.15	.07
❑ 50	Reggie Sanders	.30	.14
❑ 51	John Smiley	.15	.07
❑ 52	Wilson Alvarez	.30	.14
❑ 53	Harold Baines	.30	.14
❑ 54	James Baldwin	.30	.14
❑ 55	Albert Belle	1.00	.45
❑ 56	Mike Cameron	.30	.14
❑ 57	Ray Durham	.30	.14
❑ 58	Alex Fernandez	.15	.07
❑ 59	Roberto Hernandez	.15	.07
❑ 60	Tony Phillips	.15	.07
❑ 61	Frank Thomas	2.00	.90
❑ 62	Robin Ventura	.30	.14
❑ 63	Jeff Cirillo	.30	.14
❑ 64	Jeff D'Amico	.15	.07
❑ 65	John Jaha	.15	.07
❑ 66	Scott Karl	.15	.07
❑ 67	Ben McDonald	.15	.07
❑ 68	Marc Newfield	.15	.07
❑ 69	Dave Nilsson	.15	.07
❑ 70	Jose Valentin	.15	.07
❑ 71	Dante Bichette	.30	.14
❑ 72	Ellis Burks	.30	.14
❑ 73	Vinny Castilla	.40	.18
❑ 74	Andres Galarraga	.60	.25
❑ 75	Kevin Ritz	.15	.07
❑ 76	Larry Walker	.60	.25
❑ 77	Walt Weiss	.15	.07
❑ 78	Jamey Wright	.15	.07
❑ 79	Eric Young	.30	.14
❑ 80	Julio Franco	.30	.14
❑ 81	Orel Hershiser	.30	.14
❑ 82	Kenny Lofton	.60	.25
❑ 83	Jack McDowell	.15	.07
❑ 84	Jose Mesa	.15	.07
❑ 85	Charles Nagy	.30	.14
❑ 86	Manny Ramirez	.60	.25
❑ 87	Jim Thome	.60	.25
❑ 88	Omar Vizquel	.30	.14
❑ 89	Matt Williams	.30	.14
❑ 90	Kevin Appier	.30	.14
❑ 91	Johnny Damon	.30	.14
❑ 92	Chili Davis	.30	.14
❑ 93	Tom Goodwin	.15	.07
❑ 94	Keith Lockhart	.15	.07
❑ 95	Jeff Montgomery	.15	.07
❑ 96	Craig Paquette	.15	.07
❑ 97	Jose Rosado	.15	.07
❑ 98	Michael Tucker	.30	.14
❑ 99	Wilton Guerrero	.15	.07
❑ 100	Todd Hollandsworth	.15	.07
❑ 101	Eric Karros	.30	.14
❑ 102	Ramon Martinez	.30	.14
❑ 103	Raul Mondesi	.40	.18
❑ 104	Hideo Nomo	.60	.25
❑ 105	Mike Piazza	2.00	.90
❑ 106	Ismael Valdes	.30	.14
❑ 107	Todd Worrell	.15	.07
❑ 108	Tony Clark	.40	.18
❑ 109	Travis Fryman	.30	.14
❑ 110	Bob Higginson	.40	.18
❑ 111	Mark Lewis	.15	.07
❑ 112	Melvin Nieves	.15	.07
❑ 113	Justin Thompson	.30	.14
❑ 114	Wade Boggs	.60	.25
❑ 115	David Cone	.40	.18
❑ 116	Cecil Fielder	.30	.14
❑ 117	Dwight Gooden	.30	.14
❑ 118	Derek Jeter	2.00	.90
❑ 119	Tino Martinez	.60	.25
❑ 120	Paul O'Neill	.30	.14
❑ 121	Andy Pettitte	.40	.18
❑ 122	Mariano Rivera	.30	.14
❑ 123	Darryl Strawberry	.30	.14
❑ 124	John Wetteland	.30	.14
❑ 125	Bernie Williams	.60	.25
❑ 126	Tony Batista	.15	.07
❑ 127	Geronimo Berroa	.15	.07
❑ 128	Scott Brosius	.30	.14
❑ 129	Jason Giambi	.30	.14
❑ 130	Jose Herrera	.15	.07
❑ 131	Mark McGwire	3.00	1.35
❑ 132	John Wasdin	.15	.07
❑ 133	Bob Abreu	.30	.14
❑ 134	Jeff Bagwell	1.00	.45

❑ 135	Derek Bell	.30	.14
❑ 136	Craig Biggio	.60	.25
❑ 137	Brian Hunter	.30	.14
❑ 138	Darryl Kile	.30	.14
❑ 139	Orlando Miller	.15	.07
❑ 140	Shane Reynolds	.30	.14
❑ 141	Billy Wagner	.30	.14
❑ 142	Donne Wall	.15	.07
❑ 143	Jay Buhner	.30	.14
❑ 144	Jeff Fassero	.15	.07
❑ 145	Ken Griffey Jr.	3.00	1.35
❑ 146	Sterling Hitchcock	.30	.14
❑ 147	Randy Johnson	.60	.25
❑ 148	Edgar Martinez	.30	.14
❑ 149	Alex Rodriguez	2.00	.90
❑ 150	Paul Sorrento	.15	.07
❑ 151	Dan Wilson	.15	.07
❑ 152	Moises Alou	.40	.18
❑ 153	Darrin Fletcher	.15	.07
❑ 154	Cliff Floyd	.30	.14
❑ 155	Mark Grudzielanek	.30	.14
❑ 156	Vladimir Guerrero	1.25	.55
❑ 157	Mike Lansing	.15	.07
❑ 158	Pedro Martinez	.60	.25
❑ 159	Henry Rodriguez	.30	.14
❑ 160	Rondell White	.30	.14
❑ 161	Will Clark	.60	.25
❑ 162	Juan Gonzalez	1.50	.70
❑ 163	Rusty Greer	.30	.14
❑ 164	Ken Hill	.15	.07
❑ 165	Mark McLemore	.15	.07
❑ 166	Dean Palmer	.30	.14
❑ 167	Roger Pavlik	.15	.07
❑ 168	Ivan Rodriguez	.75	.35
❑ 169	Mickey Tettleton	.15	.07
❑ 170	Bobby Bonilla	.30	.14
❑ 171	Kevin Brown	.40	.18
❑ 172	Greg Colbrunn	.15	.07
❑ 173	Jeff Conine	.30	.14
❑ 174	Jim Eisenreich	.15	.07
❑ 175	Charles Johnson	.30	.14
❑ 176	Al Leiter	.30	.14
❑ 177	Robb Nen	.15	.07
❑ 178	Edgar Renteria	.30	.14
❑ 179	Gary Sheffield	.40	.18
❑ 180	Devon White	.30	.14
❑ 181	Joe Carter	.30	.14
❑ 182	Carlos Delgado	.30	.14
❑ 183	Alex Gonzalez	.15	.07
❑ 184	Shawn Green	.30	.14
❑ 185	Juan Guzman	.15	.07
❑ 186	Pat Hentgen	.30	.14
❑ 187	Orlando Merced	.15	.07
❑ 188	John Olerud	.30	.14
❑ 189	Robert Perez	.15	.07
❑ 190	Ed Sprague	.15	.07
❑ 191	Mark Clark	.15	.07
❑ 192	John Franco	.30	.14
❑ 193	Bernard Gilkey	.15	.07
❑ 194	Todd Hundley	.30	.14
❑ 195	Lance Johnson	.15	.07
❑ 196	Bobby Jones	.15	.07
❑ 197	Alex Ochoa	.15	.07
❑ 198	Rey Ordonez	.30	.14
❑ 199	Paul Wilson	.15	.07
❑ 200	Ricky Bottalico	.30	.14
❑ 201	Gregg Jefferies	.15	.07
❑ 202	Wendell Magee	.15	.07
❑ 203	Mickey Morandini	.15	.07
❑ 204	Ricky Otero	.15	.07
❑ 205	Scott Rolen	1.50	.70
❑ 206	Benito Santiago	.15	.07
❑ 207	Curt Schilling	.30	.14
❑ 208	Rich Becker	.15	.07
❑ 209	Marty Cordova	.15	.07
❑ 210	Chuck Knoblauch	.60	.25
❑ 211	Pat Meares	.15	.07
❑ 212	Paul Molitor	.60	.25
❑ 213	Frank Rodriguez	.15	.07
❑ 214	Terry Steinbach	.30	.14
❑ 215	Todd Walker	.60	.25
❑ 216	Andy Ashby	.15	.07
❑ 217	Ken Caminiti	.40	.18
❑ 218	Steve Finley	.30	.14
❑ 219	Tony Gwynn	1.50	.70
❑ 220	Joey Hamilton	.30	.14
❑ 221	Rickey Henderson	.60	.25
❑ 222	Trevor Hoffman	.30	.14
❑ 223	Wally Joyner	.30	.14
❑ 224	Scott Sanders	.15	.07
❑ 225	Fernando Valenzuela	.30	.14
❑ 226	Greg Vaughn	.30	.14
❑ 227	Alan Benes	.30	.14
❑ 228	Andy Benes	.30	.14
❑ 229	Dennis Eckersley	.30	.14
❑ 230	Ron Gant	.15	.07
❑ 231	Brian Jordan	.30	.14
❑ 232	Ray Lankford	.30	.14
❑ 233	John Mabry	.15	.07
❑ 234	Tom Pagnozzi	.15	.07
❑ 235	Todd Stottlemyre	.15	.07
❑ 236	Jermaine Allensworth	.15	.07
❑ 237	Francisco Cordova	.15	.07
❑ 238	Jason Kendall	.40	.18
❑ 239	Jeff King	.15	.07
❑ 240	Al Martin	.15	.07
❑ 241	Rod Beck	.15	.07
❑ 242	Barry Bonds	.75	.35
❑ 243	Shawn Estes	.30	.14
❑ 244	Mark Gardner	.15	.07
❑ 245	Glenallen Hill	.15	.07
❑ 246	Bill Mueller	.75	.35
❑ 247	J.T. Snow	.30	.14
❑ 248	Checklist 1-107	.15	.07
❑ 249	Checklist 108-207	.15	.07
❑ 250	Checklist 208-250/inserts	.15	.07
❑ P149	Alex Rodriguez Promo	2.00	.90

1997 Metal Universe Blast Furnace

		MINT	NRMT
COMPLETE SET (12)		200.00	90.00
COMMON CARD (1-12)		4.00	1.80
❑ 1	Jeff Bagwell	12.00	5.50
❑ 2	Albert Belle	10.00	4.50
❑ 3	Barry Bonds	10.00	4.50
❑ 4	Andres Galarraga	8.00	3.60
❑ 5	Juan Gonzalez	20.00	9.00
❑ 6	Ken Griffey Jr.	40.00	18.00
❑ 7	Todd Hundley	4.00	1.80
❑ 8	Mark McGwire	40.00	18.00
❑ 9	Mike Piazza	25.00	11.00
❑ 10	Alex Rodriguez	25.00	11.00
❑ 11	Frank Thomas	25.00	11.00
❑ 12	Mo Vaughn	10.00	4.50

1997 Metal Universe Emerald Autographs

		MINT	NRMT
COMPLETE SET (6)		300.00	135.00
COMMON CARD		12.00	5.50
❑ AU1	Darin Erstad	50.00	22.00
❑ AU2	Todd Hollandsworth	12.00	5.50
❑ AU3	Alex Ochoa	12.00	5.50
❑ AU4	Alex Rodriguez	150.00	70.00
❑ AU5	Scott Rolen	80.00	36.00
❑ AU6	Todd Walker	25.00	11.00

1997 Metal Universe Magnetic Field

		MINT	NRMT
COMPLETE SET (10)		40.00	18.00
COMMON CARD (1-10)		1.00	.45
❑ 1	Roberto Alomar	2.50	1.10
❑ 2	Jeff Bagwell	4.00	1.80
❑ 3	Barry Bonds	3.00	1.35
❑ 4	Ken Griffey Jr.	12.00	5.50
❑ 5	Derek Jeter	6.00	2.70
❑ 6	Kenny Lofton	3.00	1.35
❑ 7	Edgar Renteria	1.00	.45
❑ 8	Cal Ripken	10.00	4.50
❑ 9	Alex Rodriguez	8.00	3.60
❑ 10	Matt Williams	1.00	.45

1997 Metal Universe Mining for Gold

		MINT	NRMT
COMPLETE SET (10)		20.00	9.00
COMMON CARD (1-10)		1.00	.45
❑ 1	Bob Abreu	1.00	.45
❑ 2	Kevin Brown C	1.00	.45
❑ 3	Nomar Garciaparra	6.00	2.70
❑ 4	Vladimir Guerrero	4.00	1.80
❑ 5	Wilton Guerrero	1.00	.45
❑ 6	Andruw Jones	3.00	1.35

		MINT	NRMT
❑ 7	Curt Lyons	1.00	.45
❑ 8	Neifi Perez	1.00	.45
❑ 9	Scott Rolen	5.00	2.20
❑ 10	Todd Walker	1.50	.70

1997 Metal Universe Mother Lode

	MINT	NRMT
COMPLETE SET (12)	600.00	275.00
COMMON CARD (1-12)	15.00	6.75
❑ 1 Roberto Alomar	20.00	9.00
❑ 2 Jeff Bagwell	30.00	13.50
❑ 3 Barry Bonds	25.00	11.00
❑ 4 Ken Griffey Jr.	100.00	45.00
❑ 5 Andruw Jones	25.00	11.00
❑ 6 Chipper Jones	50.00	22.00
❑ 7 Kenny Lofton	20.00	9.00
❑ 8 Mike Piazza	60.00	27.00
❑ 9 Cal Ripken	80.00	36.00
❑ 10 Alex Rodriguez	60.00	27.00
❑ 11 Frank Thomas	60.00	27.00
❑ 12 Matt Williams	15.00	6.75

1997 Metal Universe Platinum Portraits

	MINT	NRMT
COMPLETE SET (10)	50.00	22.00
COMMON CARD (1-10)	1.50	.70
❑ 1 James Baldwin	3.00	1.35
❑ 2 Jermaine Dye	1.50	.70
❑ 3 Todd Hollandsworth	1.50	.70
❑ 4 Derek Jeter	15.00	6.75
❑ 5 Chipper Jones	15.00	6.75
❑ 6 Jason Kendall	4.00	1.80
❑ 7 Rey Ordonez	3.00	1.35
❑ 8 Andy Pettitte	4.00	1.80
❑ 9 Edgar Renteria	3.00	1.35
❑ 10 Alex Rodriguez	20.00	9.00

1997 Metal Universe Titanium

	MINT	NRMT
COMPLETE SET (10)	100.00	45.00
COMMON CARD (1-10)	4.00	1.80
❑ 1 Jeff Bagwell	6.00	2.70
❑ 2 Albert Belle	5.00	2.20
❑ 3 Ken Griffey Jr.	20.00	9.00
❑ 4 Chipper Jones	10.00	4.50
❑ 5 Greg Maddux	12.00	5.50
❑ 6 Mark McGwire	20.00	9.00
❑ 7 Mike Piazza	12.00	5.50
❑ 8 Cal Ripken	15.00	6.75
❑ 9 Alex Rodriguez	12.00	5.50
❑ 10 Frank Thomas	12.00	5.50

1998 Metal Universe

	MINT	NRMT
COMPLETE SET (220)	40.00	18.00
COMMON CARD (1-220)	.15	.07
❑ 1 Jose Cruz Jr.	.75	.35
❑ 2 Jeff Abbott	.25	.11
❑ 3 Rafael Palmeiro	.40	.18
❑ 4 Ivan Rodriguez	.75	.35
❑ 5 Jaret Wright	.75	.35
❑ 6 Derek Bell	.25	.11
❑ 7 Chuck Finley	.25	.11
❑ 8 Travis Fryman	.25	.11
❑ 9 Randy Johnson	.60	.25
❑ 10 Derrek Lee	.25	.11
❑ 11 Bernie Williams	.60	.25
❑ 12 Carlos Baerga	.25	.11
❑ 13 Ricky Bottalico	.25	.11
❑ 14 Ellis Burks	.25	.11
❑ 15 Russ Davis	.25	.11
❑ 16 Nomar Garciaparra	2.00	.90
❑ 17 Joey Hamilton	.25	.11
❑ 18 Jason Kendall	.25	.11
❑ 19 Darryl Kile	.25	.11
❑ 20 Edgardo Alfonzo	.25	.11
❑ 21 Moises Alou	.40	.18
❑ 22 Bobby Bonilla	.25	.11
❑ 23 Jim Edmonds	.40	.18
❑ 24 Jose Guillen	.25	.11
❑ 25 Chuck Knoblauch	.60	.25
❑ 26 Javy Lopez	.25	.11
❑ 27 Billy Wagner	.25	.11
❑ 28 Kevin Appier	.25	.11
❑ 29 Joe Carter	.25	.11
❑ 30 Todd Dunwoody	.25	.11
❑ 31 Gary Gaetti	.15	.07
❑ 32 Juan Gonzalez	1.50	.70
❑ 33 Jeffrey Hammonds	.25	.11
❑ 34 Roberto Hernandez	.15	.07
❑ 35 Dave Nilsson	.15	.07
❑ 36 Manny Ramirez	.60	.25
❑ 37 Robin Ventura	.25	.11
❑ 38 Rondell White	.25	.11
❑ 39 Vinny Castilla	.40	.18
❑ 40 Will Clark	.60	.25
❑ 41 Scott Hatteberg	.15	.07
❑ 42 Russ Johnson	.15	.07
❑ 43 Ricky Ledee	.25	.11
❑ 44 Kenny Lofton	.60	.25
❑ 45 Paul Molitor	.60	.25
❑ 46 Justin Thompson	.25	.11
❑ 47 Craig Biggio	.60	.25
❑ 48 Damion Easley	.25	.11
❑ 49 Brad Radke	.25	.11
❑ 50 Ben Grieve	1.25	.55
❑ 51 Mark Bellhorn	.25	.11
❑ 52 Henry Blanco	.15	.07
❑ 53 Mariano Rivera	.25	.11
❑ 54 Reggie Sanders	.25	.11
❑ 55 Paul Sorrento	.15	.07
❑ 56 Terry Steinbach	.25	.11
❑ 57 Mo Vaughn	.75	.35
❑ 58 Brady Anderson	.25	.11
❑ 59 Tom Glavine	.60	.25
❑ 60 Sammy Sosa	1.50	.70
❑ 61 Larry Walker	.60	.25
❑ 62 Rod Beck	.25	.11
❑ 63 Jose Canseco	.60	.25
❑ 64 Steve Finley	.25	.11
❑ 65 Pedro Martinez	.60	.25
❑ 66 John Olerud	.25	.11
❑ 67 Scott Rolen	1.50	.70
❑ 68 Ismael Valdes	.25	.11
❑ 69 Andrew Vessel	.15	.07
❑ 70 Mark Grudzielanek	.25	.11
❑ 71 Eric Karros	.25	.11
❑ 72 Jeff Shaw	.25	.11
❑ 73 Lou Collier	.15	.07
❑ 74 Edgar Martinez	.25	.11
❑ 75 Vladimir Guerrero	1.00	.45
❑ 76 Paul Konerko	.60	.25
❑ 77 Kevin Orie	.15	.07
❑ 78 Kevin Polcovich	.15	.07
❑ 79 Brett Tomko	.25	.11
❑ 80 Jeff Bagwell	1.00	.45
❑ 81 Barry Bonds	.75	.35
❑ 82 David Justice	.60	.25
❑ 83 Hideo Nomo	.75	.35
❑ 84 Ryne Sandberg	.75	.35
❑ 85 Shannon Stewart	.25	.11
❑ 86 Derek Wallace	.15	.07
❑ 87 Tony Womack	.25	.11
❑ 88 Jason Giambi	.25	.11
❑ 89 Mark Grace	.40	.18
❑ 90 Pat Hentgen	.25	.11
❑ 91 Raul Mondesi	.40	.18
❑ 92 Matt Morris	.25	.11
❑ 93 Matt Perisho	.15	.07
❑ 94 Tim Salmon	.60	.25
❑ 95 Jeremi Gonzalez	.25	.11
❑ 96 Shawn Green	.25	.11
❑ 97 Todd Greene	.25	.11
❑ 98 Ruben Rivera	.25	.11
❑ 99 Deion Sanders	.25	.11
❑ 100 Alex Rodriguez	2.00	.90
❑ 101 Will Cunnane	.15	.07
❑ 102 Ray Lankford	.25	.11
❑ 103 Ryan McGuire	.15	.07
❑ 104 Charles Nagy	.25	.11
❑ 105 Rey Ordonez	.25	.11
❑ 106 Mike Piazza	2.00	.90
❑ 107 Tony Saunders	.15	.07
❑ 108 Curt Schilling	.25	.11
❑ 109 Fernando Tatis	.25	.11
❑ 110 Mark McGwire	4.00	1.80
❑ 111 Dave Dellucci	.75	.35
❑ 112 Garret Anderson	.25	.11
❑ 113 Shane Bowers	.15	.07
❑ 114 David Cone	.40	.18
❑ 115 Jeff King	.25	.11
❑ 116 Matt Williams	.25	.11
❑ 117 Aaron Boone	.15	.07
❑ 118 Dennis Eckersley	.25	.11
❑ 119 Livan Hernandez	.25	.11

❑ 120 Richard Hidalgo	.25	.11
❑ 121 Bobby Higginson	.40	.18
❑ 122 Tino Martinez	.60	.25
❑ 123 Tim Naehring	.15	.07
❑ 124 Jose Vidro	.15	.07
❑ 125 John Wetteland	.25	.11
❑ 126 Jay Bell	.25	.11
❑ 127 Albert Belle	.75	.35
❑ 128 Marty Cordova	.15	.07
❑ 129 Chili Davis	.25	.11
❑ 130 Jason Dickson	.25	.11
❑ 131 Rusty Greer	.25	.11
❑ 132 Hideki Irabu	.40	.18
❑ 133 Greg Maddux	2.00	.90
❑ 134 Billy Taylor	.15	.07
❑ 135 Jim Thome	.60	.25
❑ 136 Gerald Williams	.15	.07
❑ 137 Jeff Cirillo	.25	.11
❑ 138 Delino DeShields	.15	.07
❑ 139 Andres Galarraga	.60	.25
❑ 140 Willie Greene	.25	.11
❑ 141 John Jaha	.15	.07
❑ 142 Charles Johnson	.25	.11
❑ 143 Ryan Klesko	.25	.11
❑ 144 Paul O'Neill	.25	.11
❑ 146 Roberto Alomar	.60	.25
❑ 147 Wilson Alvarez	.25	.11
❑ 148 Bobby Jones	.15	.07
❑ 149 Raul Casanova	.15	.07
❑ 150 Andruw Jones	.75	.35
❑ 151 Mike Lansing	.15	.07
❑ 152 Mickey Morandini	.15	.07
❑ 153 Neifi Perez	.25	.11
❑ 154 Pokey Reese	.15	.07
❑ 155 Edgar Renteria	.25	.11
❑ 156 Eric Young	.25	.11
❑ 157 Darin Erstad	.75	.35
❑ 158 Kelvim Escobar	.25	.11
❑ 159 Carl Everett	.15	.07
❑ 160 Tom Gordon	.25	.11
❑ 161 Ken Griffey Jr.	3.00	1.35
❑ 162 Al Martin	.15	.07
❑ 163 Bubba Trammell	.25	.11
❑ 164 Carlos Delgado	.25	.11
❑ 165 Kevin Brown	.40	.18
❑ 166 Ken Caminiti	.40	.18
❑ 167 Roger Clemens	1.25	.55
❑ 168 Ron Gant	.15	.07
❑ 169 Jeff Kent	.25	.11
❑ 170 Mike Mussina	.60	.25
❑ 171 Dean Palmer	.25	.11
❑ 172 Henry Rodriguez	.25	.11
❑ 173 Matt Stairs	.25	.11
❑ 174 Jay Buhner	.25	.11
❑ 175 Frank Thomas	2.00	.90
❑ 176 Mike Cameron	.25	.11
❑ 177 Johnny Damon	.25	.11
❑ 178 Tony Gwynn	1.50	.70
❑ 179 John Smoltz	.25	.11
❑ 180 B.J. Surhoff	.25	.11
❑ 181 Antone Williamson	.15	.07
❑ 182 Alan Benes	.25	.11
❑ 183 Jeromy Burnitz	.25	.11
❑ 184 Tony Clark	.40	.18
❑ 185 Shawn Estes	.25	.11
❑ 186 Todd Helton	.75	.35
❑ 187 Todd Hundley	.25	.11
❑ 188 Chipper Jones	1.50	.70
❑ 189 Mark Kotsay	.40	.18
❑ 190 Barry Larkin	.40	.18
❑ 191 Mike Lieberthal	.15	.07
❑ 192 Andy Pettitte	.40	.18
❑ 193 Gary Sheffield	.40	.18
❑ 194 Jeff Suppan	.15	.07
❑ 195 Mark Wohlers	.15	.07
❑ 196 Dante Bichette	.25	.11
❑ 197 Trevor Hoffman	.25	.11
❑ 198 J.T. Snow	.25	.11
❑ 199 Derek Jeter	1.50	.70
❑ 200 Cal Ripken	2.50	1.10
❑ 201 Steve Woodard	.25	.11
❑ 202 Ray Durham	.25	.11
❑ 203 Barry Bonds HG	.40	.18
❑ 204 Tony Clark HG	.15	.07
❑ 205 Roger Clemens HG	.60	.25
❑ 206 Ken Griffey Jr. HG	1.50	.70
❑ 207 Deion Sanders HG	.15	.07
❑ 208 Derek Jeter HG	.75	.35
❑ 209 Randy Johnson HG	.25	.11
❑ 210 Brady Anderson HG	.15	.07
❑ 211 Hideo Nomo HG	.60	.25
❑ 212 Mike Piazza HG	1.00	.45
❑ 213 Cal Ripken HG	1.25	.55
❑ 214 Alex Rodriguez HG	1.00	.45
❑ 215 Frank Thomas HG	1.00	.45
❑ 216 Mo Vaughn HG	.40	.18
❑ 217 Larry Walker HG	.25	.11
❑ 218 Ken Griffey JR. CL	1.50	.70
❑ 219 Alex Rodriguez CL	1.00	.45
❑ 220 Frank Thomas CL	.75	.35
❑ NNO Alex Rodriguez Promo	3.00	1.35

1998 Metal Universe Precious Metal Gems

	MINT	NRMT
COMMON CARD (1-217)	20.00	9.00

*STARS: 60X TO 120X BASIC CARDS
*YOUNG STARS: 50X TO 100X BASIC CARDS
*ROOKIES: 40X TO 80X BASIC CARDS

1998 Metal Universe All-Galactic Team

	MINT	NRMT
COMPLETE SET (18)	800.00	350.00
COMMON CARD (1-18)	20.00	9.00
❑ 1 Ken Griffey Jr.	100.00	45.00
❑ 2 Frank Thomas	60.00	27.00
❑ 3 Chipper Jones	50.00	22.00
❑ 4 Albert Belle	20.00	9.00
❑ 5 Juan Gonzalez	50.00	22.00
❑ 6 Jeff Bagwell	30.00	13.50
❑ 7 Andruw Jones	20.00	9.00
❑ 8 Cal Ripken	80.00	36.00
❑ 9 Derek Jeter	50.00	22.00
❑ 10 Nomar Garciaparra	60.00	27.00
❑ 11 Darin Erstad	20.00	9.00
❑ 12 Greg Maddux	60.00	27.00
❑ 13 Alex Rodriguez	60.00	27.00
❑ 14 Mike Piazza	60.00	27.00
❑ 15 Vladimir Guerrero	25.00	11.00
❑ 16 Jose Cruz Jr.	20.00	9.00
❑ 17 Mark McGwire	120.00	55.00
❑ 18 Scott Rolen	40.00	18.00

1998 Metal Universe Diamond Heroes

	MINT	NRMT
COMPLETE SET (6)	30.00	13.50
COMMON CARD (1-6)	2.50	1.10
❑ 1 Ken Griffey Jr.	10.00	4.50
❑ 2 Frank Thomas	6.00	2.70
❑ 3 Andruw Jones	2.50	1.10
❑ 4 Alex Rodriguez	6.00	2.70
❑ 5 Jose Cruz Jr.	2.50	1.10
❑ 6 Cal Ripken	8.00	3.60

1998 Metal Universe Platinum Portraits

	MINT	NRMT
COMPLETE SET (12)	800.00	350.00
COMMON CARD (1-12)	25.00	11.00
❑ 1 Ken Griffey Jr.	120.00	55.00
❑ 2 Frank Thomas	80.00	36.00
❑ 3 Chipper Jones	60.00	27.00
❑ 4 Jose Cruz Jr.	25.00	11.00
❑ 5 Andruw Jones	25.00	11.00
❑ 6 Cal Ripken	100.00	45.00
❑ 7 Derek Jeter	60.00	27.00
❑ 8 Darin Erstad	25.00	11.00
❑ 9 Greg Maddux	80.00	36.00
❑ 10 Alex Rodriguez	80.00	36.00
❑ 11 Mike Piazza	80.00	36.00
❑ 12 Vladimir Guerrero	30.00	13.50

1998 Metal Universe Titanium

	MINT	NRMT
COMPLETE SET (15)	300.00	135.00
COMMON CARD (1-15)	10.00	4.50
❑ 1 Ken Griffey Jr.	50.00	22.00
❑ 2 Frank Thomas	30.00	13.50
❑ 3 Chipper Jones	25.00	11.00
❑ 4 Jose Cruz Jr.	10.00	4.50
❑ 5 Juan Gonzalez	25.00	11.00

❑ 6	Scott Rolen	20.00	9.00
❑ 7	Andruw Jones	10.00	4.50
❑ 8	Cal Ripken	40.00	18.00
❑ 9	Derek Jeter	25.00	11.00
❑ 10	Nomar Garciaparra	30.00	13.50
❑ 11	Darin Erstad	10.00	4.50
❑ 12	Greg Maddux	30.00	13.50
❑ 13	Alex Rodriguez	30.00	13.50
❑ 14	Mike Piazza	30.00	13.50
❑ 15	Vladimir Guerrero	12.00	5.50

1998 Metal Universe Universal Language

		MINT	NRMT
COMPLETE SET (20)		80.00	36.00
COMMON CARD (1-20)		2.00	.90
❑ 1	Ken Griffey Jr.	10.00	4.50
❑ 2	Frank Thomas	6.00	2.70
❑ 3	Chipper Jones	5.00	2.20
❑ 4	Albert Belle	2.50	1.10
❑ 5	Juan Gonzalez	5.00	2.20
❑ 6	Jeff Bagwell	3.00	1.35
❑ 7	Andruw Jones	2.50	1.10
❑ 8	Cal Ripken	8.00	3.60
❑ 9	Derek Jeter	5.00	2.20
❑ 10	Nomar Garciaparra	6.00	2.70
❑ 11	Darin Erstad	2.50	1.10
❑ 12	Greg Maddux	6.00	2.70
❑ 13	Alex Rodriguez	6.00	2.70
❑ 14	Mike Piazza	6.00	2.70
❑ 15	Vladimir Guerrero	3.00	1.35
❑ 16	Jose Cruz Jr.	2.50	1.10
❑ 17	Hideo Nomo	2.50	1.10
❑ 18	Kenny Lofton	2.00	.90
❑ 19	Tony Gwynn	5.00	2.20
❑ 20	Scott Rolen	5.00	2.20

1997 New Pinnacle

		MINT	NRMT
COMPLETE SET (200)		25.00	11.00
COMMON CARD (1-200)		.15	.07
❑ 1	Ken Griffey Jr.	3.00	1.35
❑ 2	Sammy Sosa	1.50	.70
❑ 3	Greg Maddux	2.00	.90
❑ 4	Matt Williams	.30	.14
❑ 5	Jason Isringhausen	.15	.07
❑ 6	Gregg Jefferies	.15	.07
❑ 7	Chili Davis	.30	.14
❑ 8	Paul O'Neill	.30	.14
❑ 9	Larry Walker	.60	.25
❑ 10	Ellis Burks	.30	.14
❑ 11	Cliff Floyd	.30	.14
❑ 12	Albert Belle	.75	.35
❑ 13	Javier Lopez	.30	.14
❑ 14	David Cone	.40	.18
❑ 15	Jose Canseco	.60	.25
❑ 16	Todd Zeile	.15	.07
❑ 17	Bernard Gilkey	.15	.07
❑ 18	Andres Galarraga	.60	.25
❑ 19	Chris Snopek	.15	.07
❑ 20	Tim Salmon	.60	.25
❑ 21	Roger Clemens	1.25	.55
❑ 22	Reggie Sanders	.30	.14
❑ 23	John Jaha	.15	.07
❑ 24	Andy Pettitte	.40	.18
❑ 25	Kenny Lofton	.60	.25
❑ 26	Robb Nen	.15	.07
❑ 27	John Wetteland	.30	.14
❑ 28	Bobby Bonilla	.30	.14
❑ 29	Hideo Nomo	.75	.35
❑ 30	Cecil Fielder	.30	.14
❑ 31	Garret Anderson	.30	.14
❑ 32	Pat Hentgen	.30	.14
❑ 33	Dave Justice	.60	.25
❑ 34	Billy Wagner	.30	.14
❑ 35	Al Leiter	.30	.14
❑ 36	Mark Wohlers	.15	.07
❑ 37	Rondell White	.30	.14
❑ 38	Charles Johnson	.30	.14
❑ 39	Mark Grace	.40	.18
❑ 40	Pedro Martinez	.60	.25
❑ 41	Tom Goodwin	.15	.07
❑ 42	Manny Ramirez	.60	.25
❑ 43	Greg Vaughn	.30	.14
❑ 44	Brian Jordan	.30	.14
❑ 45	Mike Piazza	2.00	.90
❑ 46	Roberto Hernandez	.15	.07
❑ 47	Wade Boggs	.60	.25
❑ 48	Scott Sanders	.15	.07
❑ 49	Alex Gonzalez	.15	.07
❑ 50	Kevin Brown	.40	.18
❑ 51	Bob Higginson	.40	.18
❑ 52	Ken Caminiti	.40	.18
❑ 53	Derek Jeter	2.00	.90
❑ 54	Carlos Baerga	.30	.14
❑ 55	Jay Buhner	.30	.14
❑ 56	Tim Naehring	.15	.07
❑ 57	Jeff Bagwell	1.00	.45
❑ 58	Steve Finley	.30	.14
❑ 59	Kevin Appier	.30	.14
❑ 60	Jay Bell	.30	.14
❑ 61	Ivan Rodriguez	.75	.35
❑ 62	Terrell Wade	.15	.07
❑ 63	Rusty Greer	.30	.14
❑ 64	Juan Guzman	.15	.07
❑ 65	Fred McGriff	.40	.18
❑ 66	Tino Martinez	.60	.25
❑ 67	Ray Lankford	.30	.14
❑ 68	Juan Gonzalez	1.50	.70
❑ 69	Ron Gant	.15	.07
❑ 70	Jack McDowell	.15	.07
❑ 71	Tony Gwynn	1.50	.70
❑ 72	Joe Carter	.30	.14
❑ 73	Wilson Alvarez	.30	.14
❑ 74	Jason Giambi	.30	.14
❑ 75	Brian Hunter	.30	.14
❑ 76	Michael Tucker	.30	.14
❑ 77	Andy Benes	.30	.14
❑ 78	Brady Anderson	.30	.14
❑ 79	Ramon Martinez	.30	.14
❑ 80	Troy Percival	.30	.14
❑ 81	Alex Rodriguez	2.00	.90
❑ 82	Jim Thome	.60	.25
❑ 83	Denny Neagle	.30	.14
❑ 84	Rafael Palmeiro	.40	.18
❑ 85	Jose Valentin	.15	.07
❑ 86	Marc Newfield	.15	.07
❑ 87	Mariano Rivera	.30	.14
❑ 88	Alan Benes	.30	.14
❑ 89	Jimmy Key	.30	.14
❑ 90	Joe Randa	.15	.07
❑ 91	Cal Ripken	2.50	1.10
❑ 92	Craig Biggio	.60	.25
❑ 93	Dean Palmer	.30	.14
❑ 94	Gary Sheffield	.40	.18
❑ 95	Ismael Valdes	.30	.14
❑ 96	John Valentin	.30	.14
❑ 97	Johnny Damon	.30	.14
❑ 98	Mo Vaughn	.75	.35
❑ 99	Paul Sorrento	.15	.07
❑ 100	Randy Johnson	.60	.25
❑ 101	Raul Mondesi	.40	.18
❑ 102	Roberto Alomar	.60	.25
❑ 103	Royce Clayton	.15	.07
❑ 104	Mark Grudzielanek	.30	.14
❑ 105	Wally Joyner	.30	.14
❑ 106	Wil Cordero	.15	.07
❑ 107	Will Clark	.60	.25
❑ 108	Chuck Knoblauch	.60	.25
❑ 109	Derek Bell	.30	.14
❑ 110	Henry Rodriguez	.30	.14
❑ 111	Edgar Renteria	.30	.14
❑ 112	Travis Fryman	.30	.14
❑ 113	Eric Young	.30	.14
❑ 114	Sandy Alomar Jr.	.30	.14
❑ 115	Darin Erstad	1.00	.45
❑ 116	Barry Larkin	.40	.18
❑ 117	Barry Bonds	.75	.35
❑ 118	Frank Thomas	2.00	.90
❑ 119	Carlos Delgado	.30	.14
❑ 120	Jason Kendall	.40	.18
❑ 121	Todd Hollandsworth	.15	.07
❑ 122	Jim Edmonds	.40	.18
❑ 123	Chipper Jones	1.50	.70
❑ 124	Jeff Fassero	.15	.07
❑ 125	Deion Sanders	.30	.14
❑ 126	Matt Lawton	.30	.14
❑ 127	Ryan Klesko	.30	.14
❑ 128	Mike Mussina	.60	.25
❑ 129	Paul Molitor	.60	.25
❑ 130	Dante Bichette	.30	.14
❑ 131	Bill Pulsipher	.15	.07
❑ 132	Todd Hundley	.30	.14
❑ 133	J.T. Snow	.30	.14
❑ 134	Chuck Finley	.30	.14
❑ 135	Shawn Green	.30	.14
❑ 136	Charles Nagy	.30	.14
❑ 137	Willie Greene	.30	.14
❑ 138	Marty Cordova	.15	.07
❑ 139	Eddie Murray	.60	.25
❑ 140	Ryne Sandberg	.75	.35
❑ 141	Alex Fernandez	.15	.07
❑ 142	Mark McGwire	3.00	1.35
❑ 143	Eric Davis	.30	.14
❑ 144	Jermaine Dye	.15	.07
❑ 145	Ruben Sierra	.15	.07
❑ 146	Damon Buford	.15	.07
❑ 147	John Smoltz	.30	.14
❑ 148	Alex Ochoa	.15	.07
❑ 149	Moises Alou	.40	.18
❑ 150	Rico Brogna	.15	.07
❑ 151	Terry Steinbach	.30	.14
❑ 152	Jeff King	.15	.07
❑ 153	Carlos Garcia	.15	.07
❑ 154	Tom Glavine	.60	.25
❑ 155	Edgar Martinez	.30	.14
❑ 156	Kevin Elster	.15	.07
❑ 157	Darryl Hamilton	.15	.07
❑ 158	Jason Dickson	.30	.14

❑ 159 Kevin Orie .15 .07
❑ 160 Bubba Trammell .40 .18
❑ 161 Jose Guillen .60 .25
❑ 162 Brant Brown .30 .14
❑ 163 Wendell Magee .15 .07
❑ 164 Scott Spiezio .15 .07
❑ 165 Todd Walker .60 .25
❑ 166 Rod Myers .30 .14
❑ 167 Damon Mashore .15 .07
❑ 168 Wilton Guerrero .15 .07
❑ 169 Vladimir Guerrero 1.25 .55
❑ 170 Nomar Garciaparra 2.00 .90
❑ 171 Shannon Stewart .30 .14
❑ 172 Scott Rolen 1.50 .70
❑ 173 Bob Abreu .30 .14
❑ 174 Danny Patterson .15 .07
❑ 175 Andruw Jones 1.00 .45
❑ 176 Brian Giles .75 .35
❑ 177 Dmitri Young .30 .14
❑ 178 Cal Ripken EMW 1.25 .55
❑ 179 Chuck Knoblauch EMW .30 .14
❑ 180 Alex Rodriguez EMW.. 1.00 .45
❑ 181 Andres Galarraga EMW .30 .14
❑ 182 Pedro Martinez EMW .30 .14
❑ 183 Brady Anderson EMW .. .15 .07
❑ 184 Barry Bonds EMW .30 .14
❑ 185 Ivan Rodriguez EMW .40 .18
❑ 186 Gary Sheffield EMW .15 .07
❑ 187 Denny Neagle EMW .15 .07
❑ 188 Mark McGwire AURA .. 1.50 .70
❑ 189 Ellis Burks AURA .15 .07
❑ 190 Alex Rodriguez AURA.. 1.00 .45
❑ 191 Mike Piazza AURA 1.00 .45
❑ 192 Barry Bonds AURA .30 .14
❑ 193 Albert Belle AURA .30 .14
❑ 194 Chipper Jones AURA .75 .35
❑ 195 Juan Gonzalez AURA .75 .35
❑ 196 Brady Anderson AURA .. .15 .07
❑ 197 Frank Thomas AURA .. 1.00 .45
❑ 198 Vladimir Guerrero CL .60 .25
❑ 199 Todd Walker CL .30 .14
❑ 200 Scott Rolen CL .75 .35

1997 New Pinnacle Artist's Proof

	MINT	NRMT
COMPLETE SET (200)	4300.00	1900.00
COMP.RED SET (125)	500.00	220.00
COMMON RED	4.00	1.80
COMP.BLUE SET (50)	1000.00	450.00
COMMON BLUE	8.00	3.60
COMP.GREEN SET (25)	2000.00	900.00
COMMON GREEN	20.00	9.00

❑ 1 Ken Griffey Jr. G 200.00 90.00
❑ 2 Sammy Sosa B 80.00 36.00
❑ 3 Greg Maddux G 120.00 55.00
❑ 4 Matt Williams B 15.00 6.75
❑ 5 Jason Isringhausen R 4.00 1.80
❑ 6 Gregg Jefferies R 4.00 1.80
❑ 7 Chili Davis R 6.00 2.70
❑ 8 Paul O'Neill R 6.00 2.70
❑ 9 Larry Walker R 12.00 5.50
❑ 10 Ellis Burks B 15.00 6.75
❑ 11 Cliff Floyd R 6.00 2.70
❑ 12 Albert Belle G 40.00 18.00
❑ 13 Javier Lopez R 6.00 2.70
❑ 14 David Cone R 10.00 4.50
❑ 15 Jose Canseco B 30.00 13.50
❑ 16 Todd Zeile R 4.00 1.80
❑ 17 Bernard Gilkey B 8.00 3.60
❑ 18 Andres Galarraga B 30.00 13.50
❑ 19 Chris Snopek R 4.00 1.80
❑ 20 Tim Salmon B 30.00 13.50
❑ 21 Roger Clemens B 60.00 27.00
❑ 22 Reggie Sanders R 6.00 2.70
❑ 23 John Jaha R 4.00 1.80
❑ 24 Andy Pettitte B 25.00 11.00
❑ 25 Kenny Lofton G 30.00 13.50
❑ 26 Robb Nen R 4.00 1.80
❑ 27 John Wetteland B 15.00 6.75
❑ 28 Bobby Bonilla R 6.00 2.70
❑ 29 Hideo Nomo G 80.00 36.00
❑ 30 Cecil Fielder R 6.00 2.70
❑ 31 Garret Anderson R 6.00 2.70
❑ 32 Pat Hentgen R 6.00 2.70
❑ 33 Dave Justice R 12.00 5.50
❑ 34 Billy Wagner R 6.00 2.70
❑ 35 Al Leiter R 6.00 2.70
❑ 36 Mark Wohlers R 4.00 1.80
❑ 37 Rondell White R 6.00 2.70
❑ 38 Charles Johnson R 6.00 2.70
❑ 39 Mark Grace R 10.00 4.50
❑ 40 Pedro Martinez R 12.00 5.50
❑ 41 Tom Goodwin R 4.00 1.80
❑ 42 Manny Ramirez B 30.00 13.50
❑ 43 Greg Vaughn R 6.00 2.70
❑ 44 Brian Jordan B 15.00 6.75
❑ 45 Mike Piazza G 120.00 55.00
❑ 46 Roberto Hernandez R 4.00 1.80
❑ 47 Wade Boggs B 30.00 13.50
❑ 48 Scott Sanders R 4.00 1.80
❑ 49 Alex Gonzalez R 4.00 1.80
❑ 50 Kevin Brown R 10.00 4.50
❑ 51 Bob Higginson B 25.00 11.00
❑ 52 Ken Caminiti B 25.00 11.00
❑ 53 Derek Jeter G 100.00 45.00
❑ 54 Carlos Baerga R 6.00 2.70
❑ 55 Jay Buhner B 15.00 6.75
❑ 56 Tim Naehring R 4.00 1.80
❑ 57 Jeff Bagwell G 60.00 27.00
❑ 58 Steve Finley R 6.00 2.70
❑ 59 Kevin Appier R 6.00 2.70
❑ 60 Jay Bell R 6.00 2.70
❑ 61 Ivan Rodriguez B 40.00 18.00
❑ 62 Terrell Wade R 4.00 1.80
❑ 63 Rusty Greer R 6.00 2.70
❑ 64 Juan Guzman R 4.00 1.80
❑ 65 Fred McGriff R 10.00 4.50
❑ 66 Tino Martinez R 12.00 5.50
❑ 67 Ray Lankford R 6.00 2.70
❑ 68 Juan Gonzalez G 100.00 45.00
❑ 69 Ron Gant R 4.00 1.80
❑ 70 Jack McDowell R 4.00 1.80
❑ 71 Tony Gwynn B 80.00 36.00
❑ 72 Joe Carter B 15.00 6.75
❑ 73 Wilson Alvarez R 6.00 2.70
❑ 74 Jason Giambi R 6.00 2.70
❑ 75 Brian Hunter R 6.00 2.70
❑ 76 Michael Tucker R 6.00 2.70
❑ 77 Andy Benes R 6.00 2.70
❑ 78 Brady Anderson B 15.00 6.75
❑ 79 Ramon Martinez R 6.00 2.70
❑ 80 Troy Percival B 15.00 6.75
❑ 81 Alex Rodriguez G 120.00 55.00
❑ 82 Jim Thome B 30.00 13.50
❑ 83 Denny Neagle R 6.00 2.70
❑ 84 Rafael Palmeiro B 25.00 11.00
❑ 85 Jose Valentin R 4.00 1.80
❑ 86 Marc Newfield R 4.00 1.80
❑ 87 Mariano Rivera B 15.00 6.75
❑ 88 Alan Benes R 6.00 2.70
❑ 89 Jimmy Key R 6.00 2.70
❑ 90 Joe Randa R 4.00 1.80
❑ 91 Cal Ripken G 150.00 70.00
❑ 92 Craig Biggio R 12.00 5.50
❑ 93 Dean Palmer R 6.00 2.70
❑ 94 Gary Sheffield B 25.00 11.00
❑ 95 Ismael Valdes R 6.00 2.70
❑ 96 John Valentin R 6.00 2.70
❑ 97 Johnny Damon R 6.00 2.70
❑ 98 Mo Vaughn G 50.00 22.00
❑ 99 Paul Sorrento R 4.00 1.80
❑ 100 Randy Johnson B 30.00 13.50
❑ 101 Raul Mondesi B 25.00 11.00
❑ 102 Roberto Alomar B 30.00 13.50
❑ 103 Royce Clayton R 4.00 1.80
❑ 104 Mark Grudzielanek R .. 6.00 2.70
❑ 105 Wally Joyner R 6.00 2.70
❑ 106 Wil Cordero R 4.00 1.80
❑ 107 Will Clark B 30.00 13.50
❑ 108 Chuck Knoblauch B 30.00 13.50
❑ 109 Derek Bell R 6.00 2.70
❑ 110 Henry Rodriguez R 6.00 2.70
❑ 111 Edgar Renteria R 6.00 2.70
❑ 112 Travis Fryman R 6.00 2.70
❑ 113 Eric Young R 6.00 2.70
❑ 114 Sandy Alomar Jr. R 6.00 2.70
❑ 115 Darin Erstad B 40.00 18.00
❑ 116 Barry Larkin B 25.00 11.00
❑ 117 Barry Bonds B 40.00 18.00
❑ 118 Frank Thomas G 120.00 55.00
❑ 119 Carlos Delgado R 6.00 2.70
❑ 120 Jason Kendall R 10.00 4.50
❑ 121 Todd Hollandsworth R.. 4.00 1.80
❑ 122 Jim Edmonds R 10.00 4.50
❑ 123 Chipper Jones G 100.00 45.00
❑ 124 Jeff Fassero R 4.00 1.80
❑ 125 Deion Sanders B 15.00 6.75
❑ 126 Matt Lawton R 6.00 2.70
❑ 127 Ryan Klesko R 6.00 2.70
❑ 128 Mike Mussina R 12.00 5.50
❑ 129 Paul Molitor B 30.00 13.50
❑ 130 Dante Bichette R 6.00 2.70
❑ 131 Bill Pulsipher R 4.00 1.80
❑ 132 Todd Hundley B 15.00 6.75
❑ 133 J.T. Snow R 6.00 2.70
❑ 134 Chuck Finley R 6.00 2.70
❑ 135 Shawn Green R 6.00 2.70
❑ 136 Charles Nagy R 6.00 2.70
❑ 137 Willie Greene R 6.00 2.70
❑ 138 Marty Cordova R 4.00 1.80
❑ 139 Eddie Murray R 12.00 5.50
❑ 140 Ryne Sandberg R 15.00 6.75
❑ 141 Alex Fernandez R 4.00 1.80
❑ 142 Mark McGwire G 200.00 90.00
❑ 143 Eric Davis R 6.00 2.70
❑ 144 Jermaine Dye R 4.00 1.80
❑ 145 Ruben Sierra R 4.00 1.80
❑ 146 Damon Buford R 4.00 1.80
❑ 147 John Smoltz B 15.00 6.75
❑ 148 Alex Ochoa R 4.00 1.80
❑ 149 Moises Alou R 10.00 4.50
❑ 150 Rico Brogna R 4.00 1.80
❑ 151 Terry Steinbach R 6.00 2.70
❑ 152 Jeff King R 4.00 1.80
❑ 153 Carlos Garcia R 4.00 1.80
❑ 154 Tom Glavine R 12.00 5.50
❑ 155 Edgar Martinez B 15.00 6.75
❑ 156 Kevin Elster R 4.00 1.80
❑ 157 Darryl Hamilton R 4.00 1.80
❑ 158 Jason Dickson R 6.00 2.70
❑ 159 Kevin Orie R 4.00 1.80
❑ 160 Bubba Trammell R 12.00 5.50
❑ 161 Jose Guillen B 30.00 13.50
❑ 162 Brant Brown R 6.00 2.70
❑ 163 Wendell Magee R 4.00 1.80
❑ 164 Scott Spiezio R 4.00 1.80
❑ 165 Todd Walker B 30.00 13.50
❑ 166 Rod Myers R 6.00 2.70
❑ 167 Damon Mashore R 4.00 1.80
❑ 168 Wilton Guerrero B 8.00 3.60
❑ 169 Vladimir Guerrero G .. 60.00 27.00
❑ 170 Nomar Garciaparra B 100.00 45.00
❑ 171 Shannon Stewart R 6.00 2.70
❑ 172 Scott Rolen R 25.00 11.00
❑ 173 Bob Abreu R 6.00 2.70
❑ 174 Danny Patterson R 4.00 1.80
❑ 175 Andruw Jones G 50.00 22.00
❑ 176 Brian Giles R 6.00 2.70
❑ 177 Dmitri Young R 6.00 2.70
❑ 178 Cal Ripken EMW G 80.00 36.00
❑ 179 Chuck Knoblauch EMW B 15.00 6.75
❑ 180 Alex Rodriguez EMW G 60.00 27.00
❑ 181 A. Galarraga EMW R .. 6.00 2.70
❑ 182 Pedro Martinez EMW R 6.00 2.70
❑ 183 Brady Anderson EMW R 6.00 2.70
❑ 184 Barry Bonds EMW B .. 15.00 6.75
❑ 185 Ivan Rodriguez EMW B 25.00 11.00
❑ 186 Gary Sheffield EMW B 8.00 3.60
❑ 187 Denny Neagle EMW B 15.00 6.75
❑ 188 Mark McGwire AURA B 100.00 45.00
❑ 189 Ellis Burks AURA R 6.00 2.70
❑ 190 Alex Rodriguez AURA G 60.00 27.00
❑ 191 Mike Piazza AURA G 60.00 27.00
❑ 192 Barry Bonds AURA B 15.00 6.75
❑ 193 Albert Belle AURA G .. 20.00 9.00
❑ 194 Chipper Jones AURA G 50.00 22.00
❑ 195 Juan Gonzalez AURA G 50.00 22.00
❑ 196 Brady Anderson AURA B 15.00 6.75
❑ 197 Frank Thomas AURA G 60.00 27.00
❑ 198 Vladimir Guerrero CL R 12.00 5.50
❑ 199 Todd Walker CL R 6.00 2.70
❑ 200 Scott Rolen CL R 12.00 5.50

1997 New Pinnacle Interleague Encounter

	MINT	NRMT
COMPLETE SET (10)	600.00	275.00
COMMON CARD (1-10)	25.00	11.00
❑ 1 Albert Belle / Brian Jordan	25.00	11.00
❑ 2 Andruw Jones / Brady Anderson	30.00	13.50
❑ 3 Ken Griffey Jr. / Tony Gwynn	120.00	55.00
❑ 4 Cal Ripken / Chipper Jones	100.00	45.00
❑ 5 Mike Piazza / Ivan Rodriguez	80.00	36.00
❑ 6 Derek Jeter / Vladimir Guerrero	60.00	27.00
❑ 7 Greg Maddux / Mo Vaughn	80.00	36.00
❑ 8 Alex Rodriguez / Hideo Nomo	80.00	36.00
❑ 9 Juan Gonzalez / Barry Bonds	60.00	27.00
❑ 10 Frank Thomas / Jeff Bagwell	80.00	36.00

1997 New Pinnacle Keeping the Pace

	MINT	NRMT
COMPLETE SET (18)	600.00	275.00
COMMON CARD (1-18)	4.00	1.80
❑ 1 Juan Gonzalez	40.00	18.00
❑ 2 Greg Maddux	50.00	22.00
❑ 3 Ivan Rodriguez	20.00	9.00
❑ 4 Ken Griffey Jr.	80.00	36.00
❑ 5 Alex Rodriguez	50.00	22.00
❑ 6 Barry Bonds	20.00	9.00
❑ 7 Frank Thomas	50.00	22.00
❑ 8 Chuck Knoblauch	15.00	6.75
❑ 9 Derek Jeter	40.00	18.00
❑ 10 Roger Clemens	30.00	13.50
❑ 11 Kenny Lofton	15.00	6.75
❑ 12 Tony Gwynn	40.00	18.00
❑ 13 Troy Percival	4.00	1.80
❑ 14 Cal Ripken	60.00	27.00
❑ 15 Andy Pettitte	10.00	4.50
❑ 16 Hideo Nomo	20.00	9.00
❑ 17 Randy Johnson	15.00	6.75
❑ 18 Mike Piazza	50.00	22.00

1997 New Pinnacle Spellbound

	MINT	NRMT
COMMON A.BELLE CARD	5.00	2.20
COMMON A.JONES CARD	6.00	2.70
COMMON A.RODRIGUEZ CARD	15.00	6.75
COMMON C.JONES CARD	12.00	5.50
COMMON C.RIPKEN CARD	20.00	9.00
COMMON F.THOMAS CARD	15.00	6.75
COMMON I.RODRIGUEZ CARD	6.00	2.70
COMMON K.GRIFFEY JR. CARD	25.00	11.00
COMMON M.PIAZZA CARD	15.00	6.75
❑ AB1 Albert Belle B	15.00	6.75
❑ AB2 Albert Belle E	15.00	6.75
❑ AB3 Albert Belle L	15.00	6.75
❑ AB4 Albert Belle L	15.00	6.75
❑ AB5 Albert Belle E	15.00	6.75
❑ AJ1 Andruw Jones A	6.00	2.70
❑ AJ2 Andruw Jones N	6.00	2.70
❑ AJ3 Andruw Jones D	6.00	2.70
❑ AJ4 Andruw Jones R	6.00	2.70
❑ AJ5 Andruw Jones U	6.00	2.70
❑ AJ6 Andruw Jones W	6.00	2.70
❑ AR1 Alex Rodriguez A	15.00	6.75
❑ AR2 Alex Rodriguez L	15.00	6.75
❑ AR3 Alex Rodriguez E	15.00	6.75
❑ AR4 Alex Rodriguez X	15.00	6.75
❑ CJ1 Chipper Jones C	12.00	5.50
❑ CJ2 Chipper Jones H	12.00	5.50
❑ CJ3 Chipper Jones I	12.00	5.50
❑ CJ4 Chipper Jones P	12.00	5.50
❑ CJ5 Chipper Jones P	12.00	5.50
❑ CJ6 Chipper Jones E	12.00	5.50
❑ CJ7 Chipper Jones P	12.00	5.50
❑ CR1 Cal Ripken R	20.00	9.00
❑ CR2 Cal Ripken I	20.00	9.00
❑ CR3 Cal Ripken P	20.00	9.00
❑ CR4 Cal Ripken K	20.00	9.00
❑ CR5 Cal Ripken E	20.00	9.00
❑ CR6 Cal Ripken N	20.00	9.00
❑ FT1 Frank Thomas F	15.00	6.75
❑ FT2 Frank Thomas R	15.00	6.75
❑ FT3 Frank Thomas A	15.00	6.75
❑ FT4 Frank Thomas N	15.00	6.75
❑ FT5 Frank Thomas K	15.00	6.75
❑ IR1 Ivan Rodriguez P	6.00	2.70
❑ IR2 Ivan Rodriguez U	6.00	2.70
❑ IR3 Ivan Rodriguez D	6.00	2.70
❑ IR4 Ivan Rodriguez G	6.00	2.70
❑ IR5 Ivan Rodriguez E	6.00	2.70
❑ KG1 Ken Griffey Jr. J	25.00	11.00
❑ KG2 Ken Griffey Jr. U	25.00	11.00
❑ KG3 Ken Griffey Jr. N	25.00	11.00
❑ KG4 Ken Griffey Jr. I	25.00	11.00
❑ KG5 Ken Griffey Jr. O	25.00	11.00
❑ KG6 Ken Griffey Jr. R	25.00	11.00
❑ MP1 Mike Piazza P	15.00	6.75
❑ MP2 Mike Piazza I	15.00	6.75
❑ MP3 Mike Piazza A	15.00	6.75
❑ MP4 Mike Piazza Z	15.00	6.75
❑ MP5 Mike Piazza Z	15.00	6.75
❑ MP6 Mike Piazza A	15.00	6.75

1994 Pacific

	MINT	NRMT
COMPLETE SET (660)	35.00	16.00
COMMON CARD (1-660)	.10	.05
COMP.CHECKLIST SET (6)	2.00	.90
COMMON CHECKLIST	.35	.16
❑ 1 Steve Avery	.10	.05
❑ 2 Steve Bedrosian	.10	.05
❑ 3 Damon Berryhill	.10	.05
❑ 4 Jeff Blauser	.10	.05
❑ 5 Sid Bream	.10	.05
❑ 6 Francisco Cabrera	.10	.05
❑ 7 Ramon Caraballo	.10	.05
❑ 8 Ron Gant	.20	.09
❑ 9 Tom Glavine	.40	.18
❑ 10 Chipper Jones	1.25	.55
❑ 11 Dave Justice	.40	.18
❑ 12 Ryan Klesko	.20	.09
❑ 13 Mark Lemke	.10	.05
❑ 14 Javier Lopez	.30	.14
❑ 15 Greg Maddux	1.25	.55
❑ 16 Fred McGriff	.30	.14
❑ 17 Greg McMichael	.10	.05
❑ 18 Kent Mercker	.10	.05
❑ 19 Otis Nixon	.10	.05
❑ 20 Terry Pendleton	.10	.05
❑ 21 Deion Sanders	.20	.09
❑ 22 John Smoltz	.20	.09
❑ 23 Tony Tarasco	.10	.05
❑ 24 Manny Alexander	.10	.05
❑ 25 Brady Anderson	.20	.09
❑ 26 Harold Baines	.20	.09
❑ 27 Damon Buford	.10	.05
❑ 28 Paul Carey	.10	.05
❑ 29 Mike Devereaux	.10	.05
❑ 30 Todd Frohwirth	.10	.05
❑ 31 Leo Gomez	.10	.05
❑ 32 Jeffrey Hammonds	.20	.09
❑ 33 Chris Hoiles	.10	.05
❑ 34 Tim Hulett	.10	.05
❑ 35 Ben McDonald	.10	.05
❑ 36 Mark McLemore	.10	.05
❑ 37 Alan Mills	.10	.05
❑ 38 Mike Mussina	.40	.18
❑ 39 Sherman Obando	.10	.05
❑ 40 Gregg Olson	.10	.05
❑ 41 Mike Pagliarulo	.10	.05
❑ 42 Jim Poole	.10	.05
❑ 43 Harold Reynolds	.10	.05
❑ 44 Cal Ripken	1.50	.70
❑ 45 David Segui	.20	.09
❑ 46 Fernando Valenzuela	.20	.09
❑ 47 Jack Voigt	.10	.05
❑ 48 Scott Bankhead	.10	.05
❑ 49 Roger Clemens	.75	.35
❑ 50 Scott Cooper	.10	.05
❑ 51 Danny Darwin	.10	.05
❑ 52 Andre Dawson	.30	.14
❑ 53 John Dopson	.10	.05
❑ 54 Scott Fletcher	.10	.05
❑ 55 Tony Fossas	.10	.05
❑ 56 Mike Greenwell	.10	.05
❑ 57 Billy Hatcher	.10	.05

❑ 58	Jeff McNeely	.10	.05
❑ 59	Jose Melendez	.10	.05
❑ 60	Tim Naehring	.10	.05
❑ 61	Tony Pena	.10	.05
❑ 62	Carlos Quintana	.10	.05
❑ 63	Paul Quantrill	.10	.05
❑ 64	Luis Rivera	.10	.05
❑ 65	Jeff Russell	.10	.05
❑ 66	Aaron Sele	.20	.09
❑ 67	John Valentin	.20	.09
❑ 68	Mo Vaughn	.50	.23
❑ 69	Frank Viola	.10	.05
❑ 70	Bob Zupcic	.10	.05
❑ 71	Mike Butcher	.10	.05
❑ 72	Rod Correia	.10	.05
❑ 73	Chad Curtis	.10	.05
❑ 74	Chili Davis	.20	.09
❑ 75	Gary DiSarcina	.10	.05
❑ 76	Damion Easley	.20	.09
❑ 77	John Farrell	.10	.05
❑ 78	Chuck Finley	.20	.09
❑ 79	Joe Grahe	.10	.05
❑ 80	Stan Javier	.10	.05
❑ 81	Mark Langston	.10	.05
❑ 82	Phil Leftwich	.10	.05
❑ 83	Torey Lovullo	.10	.05
❑ 84	Joe Magrane	.10	.05
❑ 85	Greg Myers	.10	.05
❑ 86	Eduardo Perez	.10	.05
❑ 87	Luis Polonia	.10	.05
❑ 88	Tim Salmon	.40	.18
❑ 89	J.T. Snow	.20	.09
❑ 90	Kurt Stillwell	.10	.05
❑ 91	Ron Tingley	.10	.05
❑ 92	Chris Turner	.10	.05
❑ 93	Julio Valera	.10	.05
❑ 94	Jose Bautista	.10	.05
❑ 95	Shawn Boskie	.10	.05
❑ 96	Steve Buechele	.10	.05
❑ 97	Frank Castillo	.10	.05
❑ 98	Mark Grace UER (stats have 98 home runs in 1993; should be 14)	.30	.14
❑ 99	Jose Guzman	.10	.05
❑ 100	Mike Harkey	.10	.05
❑ 101	Greg Hibbard	.10	.05
❑ 102	Doug Jennings	.10	.05
❑ 103	Derrick May	.10	.05
❑ 104	Mike Morgan	.10	.05
❑ 105	Randy Myers	.10	.05
❑ 106	Karl Rhodes	.10	.05
❑ 107	Kevin Roberson	.10	.05
❑ 108	Rey Sanchez	.10	.05
❑ 109	Ryne Sandberg	.50	.23
❑ 110	Tommy Shields	.10	.05
❑ 111	Dwight Smith	.10	.05
❑ 112	Sammy Sosa	1.00	.45
❑ 113	Jose Vizcaino	.10	.05
❑ 114	Turk Wendell	.10	.05
❑ 115	Rick Wilkins	.10	.05
❑ 116	Willie Wilson	.10	.05
❑ 117	Eduardo Zambrano	.10	.05
❑ 118	Wilson Alvarez	.20	.09
❑ 119	Tim Belcher	.10	.05
❑ 120	Jason Bere	.10	.05
❑ 121	Rodney Bolton	.10	.05
❑ 122	Ellis Burks	.20	.09
❑ 123	Joey Cora	.20	.09
❑ 124	Alex Fernandez	.10	.05
❑ 125	Ozzie Guillen	.10	.05
❑ 126	Craig Grebeck	.10	.05
❑ 127	Roberto Hernandez	.10	.05
❑ 128	Bo Jackson	.20	.09
❑ 129	Lance Johnson	.10	.05
❑ 130	Ron Karkovice	.10	.05
❑ 131	Mike LaValliere	.10	.05
❑ 132	Norberto Martin	.10	.05
❑ 133	Kirk McCaskill	.10	.05
❑ 134	Jack McDowell	.10	.05
❑ 135	Scott Radinsky	.10	.05
❑ 136	Tim Raines	.20	.09
❑ 137	Steve Sax	.10	.05
❑ 138	Frank Thomas	1.25	.55
❑ 139	Dan Pasqua	.10	.05
❑ 140	Robin Ventura	.20	.09
❑ 141	Jeff Branson	.10	.05
❑ 142	Tom Browning	.10	.05
❑ 143	Jacob Brumfield	.10	.05
❑ 144	Tim Costo	.10	.05
❑ 145	Rob Dibble	.10	.05
❑ 146	Brian Dorsett	.10	.05
❑ 147	Steve Foster	.10	.05
❑ 148	Cesar Hernandez	.10	.05
❑ 149	Roberto Kelly	.10	.05
❑ 150	Barry Larkin	.30	.14
❑ 151	Larry Luebbers	.10	.05
❑ 152	Kevin Mitchell	.10	.05
❑ 153	Joe Oliver	.10	.05
❑ 154	Tim Pugh	.10	.05
❑ 155	Jeff Reardon	.20	.09
❑ 156	Jose Rijo	.10	.05
❑ 157	Bip Roberts	.10	.05
❑ 158	Chris Sabo	.10	.05
❑ 159	Juan Samuel	.10	.05
❑ 160	Reggie Sanders	.20	.09
❑ 161	John Smiley	.10	.05
❑ 162	Jerry Spradlin	.10	.05
❑ 163	Gary Varsho	.10	.05
❑ 164	Sandy Alomar Jr.	.20	.09
❑ 165	Albert Belle	.50	.23
❑ 166	Carlos Baerga	.20	.09
❑ 167	Mark Clark	.10	.05
❑ 168	Alvaro Espinoza	.10	.05
❑ 169	Felix Fermin	.10	.05
❑ 170	Reggie Jefferson	.10	.05
❑ 171	Wayne Kirby	.10	.05
❑ 172	Tom Kramer	.10	.05
❑ 173	Kenny Lofton	.40	.18
❑ 174	Jesse Levis	.10	.05
❑ 175	Candy Maldonado	.10	.05
❑ 176	Carlos Martinez	.10	.05
❑ 177	Jose Mesa	.10	.05
❑ 178	Jeff Mutis	.10	.05
❑ 179	Charles Nagy	.20	.09
❑ 180	Bob Ojeda	.10	.05
❑ 181	Junior Ortiz	.10	.05
❑ 182	Eric Plunk	.10	.05
❑ 183	Manny Ramirez	.50	.23
❑ 184	Paul Sorrento	.10	.05
❑ 185	Jeff Treadway	.10	.05
❑ 186	Bill Wertz	.10	.05
❑ 187	Freddie Benavides	.10	.05
❑ 188	Dante Bichette	.20	.09
❑ 189	Willie Blair	.10	.05
❑ 190	Daryl Boston	.10	.05
❑ 191	Pedro Castellano	.10	.05
❑ 192	Vinny Castilla	.20	.09
❑ 193	Jerald Clark	.10	.05
❑ 194	Alex Cole	.10	.05
❑ 195	Andres Galarraga	.40	.18
❑ 196	Joe Girardi	.10	.05
❑ 197	Charlie Hayes	.10	.05
❑ 198	Darren Holmes	.10	.05
❑ 199	Chris Jones	.10	.05
❑ 200	Curt Leskanic	.10	.05
❑ 201	Roberto Mejia	.10	.05
❑ 202	David Nied	.10	.05
❑ 203	J. Owens	.10	.05
❑ 204	Steve Reed	.10	.05
❑ 205	Armando Reynoso	.10	.05
❑ 206	Bruce Ruffin	.10	.05
❑ 207	Keith Shepherd	.10	.05
❑ 208	Jim Tatum	.10	.05
❑ 209	Eric Young	.10	.05
❑ 210	Skeeter Barnes	.10	.05
❑ 211	Danny Bautista	.10	.05
❑ 212	Tom Bolton	.10	.05
❑ 213	Eric Davis	.20	.09
❑ 214	Storm Davis	.10	.05
❑ 215	Cecil Fielder	.20	.09
❑ 216	Travis Fryman	.20	.09
❑ 217	Kirk Gibson	.20	.09
❑ 218	Dan Gladden	.10	.05
❑ 219	John Doherty	.10	.05
❑ 220	Chris Gomez	.10	.05
❑ 221	David Haas	.10	.05
❑ 222	Bill Krueger	.10	.05
❑ 223	Chad Kreuter	.10	.05
❑ 224	Mark Leiter	.10	.05
❑ 225	Bob MacDonald	.10	.05
❑ 226	Mike Moore	.10	.05
❑ 227	Tony Phillips	.10	.05
❑ 228	Rich Rowland	.10	.05
❑ 229	Mickey Tettleton	.10	.05
❑ 230	Alan Trammell	.30	.14
❑ 231	David Wells	.30	.14
❑ 232	Lou Whitaker	.20	.09
❑ 233	Luis Aquino	.10	.05
❑ 234	Alex Arias	.10	.05
❑ 235	Jack Armstrong	.10	.05
❑ 236	Ryan Bowen	.10	.05
❑ 237	Chuck Carr	.10	.05
❑ 238	Matias Carrillo	.10	.05
❑ 239	Jeff Conine	.20	.09
❑ 240	Henry Cotto	.10	.05
❑ 241	Orestes Destrade	.10	.05
❑ 242	Chris Hammond	.10	.05
❑ 243	Bryan Harvey	.10	.05
❑ 244	Charlie Hough	.10	.05
❑ 245	Richie Lewis	.10	.05
❑ 246	Mitch Lyden	.10	.05
❑ 247	Dave Magadan	.10	.05
❑ 248	Bob Natal	.10	.05
❑ 249	Benito Santiago	.10	.05
❑ 250	Gary Sheffield	.40	.18
❑ 251	Matt Turner	.10	.05
❑ 252	David Weathers	.10	.05
❑ 253	Walt Weiss	.10	.05
❑ 254	Darrell Whitmore	.10	.05
❑ 255	Nigel Wilson	.10	.05
❑ 256	Eric Anthony	.10	.05
❑ 257	Jeff Bagwell	.60	.25
❑ 258	Kevin Bass	.10	.05
❑ 259	Craig Biggio	.40	.18
❑ 260	Ken Caminiti	.30	.14
❑ 261	Andujar Cedeno	.10	.05
❑ 262	Chris Donnels	.10	.05
❑ 263	Doug Drabek	.10	.05
❑ 264	Tom Edens	.10	.05
❑ 265	Steve Finley	.20	.09
❑ 266	Luis Gonzalez	.10	.05
❑ 267	Pete Harnisch	.10	.05
❑ 268	Xavier Hernandez	.10	.05
❑ 269	Todd Jones	.10	.05
❑ 270	Darryl Kile	.20	.09
❑ 271	Al Osuna	.10	.05
❑ 272	Rick Parker	.10	.05
❑ 273	Mark Portugal	.10	.05
❑ 274	Scott Servais	.10	.05
❑ 275	Greg Swindell	.10	.05
❑ 276	Eddie Taubensee	.10	.05
❑ 277	Jose Uribe	.10	.05
❑ 278	Brian Williams	.10	.05
❑ 279	Kevin Appier	.20	.09
❑ 280	Billy Brewer	.10	.05
❑ 281	David Cone	.30	.14
❑ 282	Greg Gagne	.10	.05
❑ 283	Tom Gordon	.10	.05
❑ 284	Chris Gwynn	.10	.05
❑ 285	John Habyan	.10	.05
❑ 286	Chris Haney	.10	.05
❑ 287	Phil Hiatt	.10	.05
❑ 288	David Howard	.10	.05
❑ 289	Felix Jose	.10	.05
❑ 290	Wally Joyner	.20	.09
❑ 291	Kevin Koslofski	.10	.05
❑ 292	Jose Lind	.10	.05
❑ 293	Brent Mayne	.10	.05
❑ 294	Mike Macfarlane	.10	.05
❑ 295	Brian McRae	.10	.05
❑ 296	Kevin McReynolds	.10	.05
❑ 297	Keith Miller	.10	.05
❑ 298	Jeff Montgomery	.10	.05
❑ 299	Hipolito Pichardo	.10	.05
❑ 300	Rico Rossy	.10	.05
❑ 301	Curtis Wilkerson	.10	.05
❑ 302	Pedro Astacio	.10	.05
❑ 303	Rafael Bournigal	.10	.05
❑ 304	Brett Butler	.20	.09
❑ 305	Tom Candiotti	.10	.05
❑ 306	Omar Daal	.10	.05
❑ 307	Jim Gott	.10	.05
❑ 308	Kevin Gross	.10	.05
❑ 309	Dave Hansen	.10	.05
❑ 310	Carlos Hernandez	.10	.05

❑	311	Orel Hershiser	.20	.09
❑	312	Eric Karros	.20	.09
❑	313	Pedro Martinez	.50	.23
❑	314	Ramon Martinez	.20	.09
❑	315	Roger McDowell	.10	.05
❑	316	Raul Mondesi	.40	.18
❑	317	Jose Offerman	.10	.05
❑	318	Mike Piazza	1.25	.55
❑	319	Jody Reed	.10	.05
❑	320	Henry Rodriguez	.20	.09
❑	321	Cory Snyder	.10	.05
❑	322	Darryl Strawberry	.20	.09
❑	323	Tim Wallach	.10	.05
❑	324	Steve Wilson	.10	.05
❑	325	Juan Bell	.10	.05
❑	326	Ricky Bones	.10	.05
❑	327	Alex Diaz	.10	.05
❑	328	Cal Eldred	.10	.05
❑	329	Darryl Hamilton	.10	.05
❑	330	Doug Henry	.10	.05
❑	331	John Jaha	.10	.05
❑	332	Pat Listach	.10	.05
❑	333	Graeme Lloyd	.10	.05
❑	334	Carlos Maldonado	.10	.05
❑	335	Angel Miranda	.10	.05
❑	336	Jaime Navarro	.10	.05
❑	337	Dave Nilsson	.10	.05
❑	338	Rafael Novoa	.10	.05
❑	339	Troy O'Leary	.20	.09
❑	340	Jesse Orosco	.10	.05
❑	341	Kevin Seitzer	.10	.05
❑	342	Bill Spiers	.10	.05
❑	343	William Suero	.10	.05
❑	344	B.J. Surhoff	.20	.09
❑	345	Dickie Thon	.10	.05
❑	346	Jose Valentin	.10	.05
❑	347	Greg Vaughn	.20	.09
❑	348	Robin Yount	.40	.18
❑	349	Willie Banks	.10	.05
❑	350	Bernardo Brito	.10	.05
❑	351	Scott Erickson	.20	.09
❑	352	Mark Guthrie	.10	.05
❑	353	Chip Hale	.10	.05
❑	354	Brian Harper	.10	.05
❑	355	Kent Hrbek	.20	.09
❑	356	Terry Jorgensen	.10	.05
❑	357	Chuck Knoblauch	.40	.18
❑	358	Gene Larkin	.10	.05
❑	359	Scott Leius	.10	.05
❑	360	Shane Mack	.10	.05
❑	361	David McCarty	.10	.05
❑	362	Pat Meares	.10	.05
❑	363	Pedro Munoz	.10	.05
❑	364	Derek Parks	.10	.05
❑	365	Kirby Puckett	.60	.25
❑	366	Jeff Reboulet	.10	.05
❑	367	Kevin Tapani	.10	.05
❑	368	Mike Trombley	.10	.05
❑	369	George Tsamis	.10	.05
❑	370	Carl Willis	.10	.05
❑	371	Dave Winfield	.40	.18
❑	372	Moises Alou	.30	.14
❑	373	Brian Barnes	.10	.05
❑	374	Sean Berry	.10	.05
❑	375	Frank Bolick	.10	.05
❑	376	Wil Cordero	.10	.05
❑	377	Delino DeShields	.10	.05
❑	378	Jeff Fassero	.10	.05
❑	379	Darrin Fletcher	.10	.05
❑	380	Cliff Floyd	.20	.09
❑	381	Lou Frazier	.10	.05
❑	382	Marquis Grissom	.20	.09
❑	383	Gil Heredia	.10	.05
❑	384	Mike Lansing	.20	.09
❑	385	Oreste Marrero	.10	.05
❑	386	Dennis Martinez	.20	.09
❑	387	Curtis Pride	.10	.05
❑	388	Mel Rojas	.10	.05
❑	389	Kirk Rueter	.10	.05
❑	390	Joe Siddall	.10	.05
❑	391	John Vander Wal	.10	.05
❑	392	Larry Walker	.40	.18
❑	393	John Wetteland	.20	.09
❑	394	Rondell White	.20	.09
❑	395	Tim Bogar	.10	.05
❑	396	Bobby Bonilla	.20	.09
❑	397	Jeromy Burnitz	.20	.09
❑	398	Mike Draper	.10	.05
❑	399	Sid Fernandez	.10	.05
❑	400	John Franco	.20	.09
❑	401	Dave Gallagher	.10	.05
❑	402	Dwight Gooden	.20	.09
❑	403	Eric Hillman	.10	.05
❑	404	Todd Hundley	.20	.09
❑	405	Butch Huskey	.20	.09
❑	406	Jeff Innis	.10	.05
❑	407	Howard Johnson	.10	.05
❑	408	Jeff Kent	.20	.09
❑	409	Ced Landrum	.10	.05
❑	410	Mike Maddux	.10	.05
❑	411	Josias Manzanillo	.10	.05
❑	412	Jeff McKnight	.10	.05
❑	413	Eddie Murray	.40	.18
❑	414	Tito Navarro	.10	.05
❑	415	Joe Orsulak	.10	.05
❑	416	Bret Saberhagen	.20	.09
❑	417	Dave Telgheder	.10	.05
❑	418	Ryan Thompson	.10	.05
❑	419	Chico Walker	.10	.05
❑	420	Jim Abbott	.20	.09
❑	421	Wade Boggs	.40	.18
❑	422	Mike Gallego	.10	.05
❑	423	Mark Hutton	.10	.05
❑	424	Dion James	.10	.05
❑	425	Domingo Jean	.10	.05
❑	426	Pat Kelly	.10	.05
❑	427	Jimmy Key	.20	.09
❑	428	Jim Leyritz	.20	.09
❑	429	Kevin Maas	.10	.05
❑	430	Don Mattingly	.60	.25
❑	431	Bobby Munoz	.10	.05
❑	432	Matt Nokes	.10	.05
❑	433	Paul O'Neill	.20	.09
❑	434	Spike Owen	.10	.05
❑	435	Melido Perez	.10	.05
❑	436	Lee Smith	.20	.09
❑	437	Andy Stankiewicz	.10	.05
❑	438	Mike Stanley	.10	.05
❑	439	Danny Tartabull	.10	.05
❑	440	Randy Velarde	.10	.05
❑	441	Bernie Williams	.40	.18
❑	442	Gerald Williams	.10	.05
❑	443	Mike Witt	.10	.05
❑	444	Marcos Armas	.10	.05
❑	445	Lance Blankenship	.10	.05
❑	446	Mike Bordick	.10	.05
❑	447	Ron Darling UER Reversed negative on front	.10	.05
❑	448	Dennis Eckersley	.20	.09
❑	449	Brent Gates	.10	.05
❑	450	Goose Gossage	.20	.09
❑	451	Scott Hemond	.10	.05
❑	452	Dave Henderson	.10	.05
❑	453	Shawn Hillegas	.10	.05
❑	454	Rick Honeycutt	.10	.05
❑	455	Scott Lydy	.10	.05
❑	456	Mark McGwire	2.00	.90
❑	457	Henry Mercedes	.10	.05
❑	458	Mike Mohler	.10	.05
❑	459	Troy Neel	.10	.05
❑	460	Edwin Nunez	.10	.05
❑	461	Craig Paquette	.10	.05
❑	462	Ruben Sierra	.10	.05
❑	463	Terry Steinbach	.20	.09
❑	464	Todd Van Poppel	.10	.05
❑	465	Bob Welch	.10	.05
❑	466	Bobby Witt	.10	.05
❑	467	Ruben Amaro	.10	.05
❑	468	Larry Andersen	.10	.05
❑	469	Kim Batiste	.10	.05
❑	470	Wes Chamberlain	.10	.05
❑	471	Darren Daulton	.20	.09
❑	472	Mariano Duncan	.10	.05
❑	473	Len Dykstra	.20	.09
❑	474	Jim Eisenreich	.10	.05
❑	475	Tommy Greene	.10	.05
❑	476	Dave Hollins	.10	.05
❑	477	Pete Incaviglia	.10	.05
❑	478	Danny Jackson	.10	.05
❑	479	John Kruk	.20	.09
❑	480	Tony Longmire	.10	.05
❑	481	Jeff Manto	.10	.05
❑	482	Mickey Morandini	.10	.05
❑	483	Terry Mulholland	.10	.05
❑	484	Todd Pratt	.10	.05
❑	485	Ben Rivera	.10	.05
❑	486	Curt Schilling	.20	.09
❑	487	Kevin Stocker	.10	.05
❑	488	Milt Thompson	.10	.05
❑	489	David West	.30	.14
❑	490	Mitch Williams	.10	.05
❑	491	Jeff Ballard	.10	.05
❑	492	Jay Bell	.20	.09
❑	493	Scott Bullett	.10	.05
❑	494	Dave Clark	.10	.05
❑	495	Steve Cooke	.10	.05
❑	496	Midre Cummings	.10	.05
❑	497	Mark Dewey	.10	.05
❑	498	Carlos Garcia	.10	.05
❑	499	Jeff King	.10	.05
❑	500	Al Martin	.10	.05
❑	501	Lloyd McClendon	.10	.05
❑	502	Orlando Merced	.10	.05
❑	503	Blas Minor	.10	.05
❑	504	Denny Neagle	.20	.09
❑	505	Tom Prince	.10	.05
❑	506	Don Slaught	.10	.05
❑	507	Zane Smith	.10	.05
❑	508	Randy Tomlin	.10	.05
❑	509	Andy Van Slyke	.20	.09
❑	510	Paul Wagner	.10	.05
❑	511	Tim Wakefield	.20	.09
❑	512	Bob Walk	.10	.05
❑	513	John Wehner	.10	.05
❑	514	Kevin Young	.10	.05
❑	515	Billy Bean	.10	.05
❑	516	Andy Benes	.20	.09
❑	517	Derek Bell	.20	.09
❑	518	Doug Brocail	.10	.05
❑	519	Jarvis Brown	.10	.05
❑	520	Phil Clark	.10	.05
❑	521	Mark Davis	.10	.05
❑	522	Jeff Gardner	.10	.05
❑	523	Pat Gomez	.10	.05
❑	524	Ricky Gutierrez	.10	.05
❑	525	Tony Gwynn	1.00	.45
❑	526	Gene Harris	.10	.05
❑	527	Kevin Higgins	.10	.05
❑	528	Trevor Hoffman	.20	.09
❑	529	Luis Lopez	.10	.05
❑	530	Pedro A.Martinez	.10	.05
❑	531	Melvin Nieves	.10	.05
❑	532	Phil Plantier	.10	.05
❑	533	Frank Seminara	.10	.05
❑	534	Craig Shipley	.10	.05
❑	535	Tim Teufel	.10	.05
❑	536	Guillermo Velasquez	.10	.05
❑	537	Wally Whitehurst	.10	.05
❑	538	Rod Beck	.10	.05
❑	539	Todd Benzinger	.10	.05
❑	540	Barry Bonds	.50	.23
❑	541	Jeff Brantley	.10	.05
❑	542	Dave Burba	.10	.05
❑	543	John Burkett	.10	.05
❑	544	Will Clark	.40	.18
❑	545	Royce Clayton	.10	.05
❑	546	Bryan Hickerson	.10	.05
❑	547	Mike Jackson	.10	.05
❑	548	Darren Lewis	.10	.05
❑	549	Kirt Manwaring	.10	.05
❑	550	Dave Martinez	.10	.05
❑	551	Willie McGee	.20	.09
❑	552	Jeff Reed	.10	.05
❑	553	Dave Righetti	.10	.05
❑	554	Kevin Rogers	.10	.05
❑	555	Steve Scarsone	.10	.05
❑	556	Bill Swift	.10	.05
❑	557	Robby Thompson	.10	.05
❑	558	Salomon Torres	.10	.05
❑	559	Matt Williams	.30	.14
❑	560	Trevor Wilson	.10	.05
❑	561	Rich Amaral	.10	.05
❑	562	Mike Blowers	.10	.05
❑	563	Chris Bosio	.10	.05
❑	564	Jay Buhner	.20	.09

	MINT	NRMT
❑ 565 Norm Charlton	.10	.05
❑ 566 Jim Converse	.10	.05
❑ 567 Rich DeLucia	.10	.05
❑ 568 Mike Felder	.10	.05
❑ 569 Dave Fleming	.10	.05
❑ 570 Ken Griffey Jr.	2.00	.90
❑ 571 Bill Haselman	.10	.05
❑ 572 Dwayne Henry	.10	.05
❑ 573 Brad Holman	.10	.05
❑ 574 Randy Johnson	.40	.18
❑ 575 Greg Litton	.10	.05
❑ 576 Edgar Martinez	.20	.09
❑ 577 Tino Martinez	.40	.18
❑ 578 Jeff Nelson	.10	.05
❑ 579 Marc Newfield	.10	.05
❑ 580 Roger Salkeld	.10	.05
❑ 581 Mackey Sasser	.10	.05
❑ 582 Brian Turang	.10	.05
❑ 583 Omar Vizquel	.20	.09
❑ 584 Dave Valle	.10	.05
❑ 585 Luis Alicea	.10	.05
❑ 586 Rene Arocha	.10	.05
❑ 587 Rheal Cormier	.10	.05
❑ 588 Tripp Cromer	.10	.05
❑ 589 Bernard Gilkey	.10	.05
❑ 590 Lee Guetterman	.10	.05
❑ 591 Gregg Jefferies	.10	.05
❑ 592 Tim Jones	.10	.05
❑ 593 Paul Kilgus	.10	.05
❑ 594 Les Lancaster	.10	.05
❑ 595 Omar Olivares	.10	.05
❑ 596 Jose Oquendo	.10	.05
❑ 597 Donovan Osborne	.10	.05
❑ 598 Tom Pagnozzi	.10	.05
❑ 599 Erik Pappas	.10	.05
❑ 600 Geronimo Pena	.10	.05
❑ 601 Mike Perez	.10	.05
❑ 602 Gerald Perry	.10	.05
❑ 603 Stan Royer	.10	.05
❑ 604 Ozzie Smith	.50	.23
❑ 605 Bob Tewksbury	.10	.05
❑ 606 Allen Watson	.10	.05
❑ 607 Mark Whiten	.10	.05
❑ 608 Todd Zeile	.10	.05
❑ 609 Jeff Bronkey	.10	.05
❑ 610 Kevin Brown	.20	.09
❑ 611 Jose Canseco	.40	.18
❑ 612 Doug Dascenzo	.10	.05
❑ 613 Butch Davis	.10	.05
❑ 614 Mario Diaz	.10	.05
❑ 615 Julio Franco	.10	.05
❑ 616 Benji Gil	.10	.05
❑ 617 Juan Gonzalez	1.00	.45
❑ 618 Tom Henke	.10	.05
❑ 619 Jeff Huson	.10	.05
❑ 620 David Hulse	.10	.05
❑ 621 Craig Lefferts	.10	.05
❑ 622 Rafael Palmeiro	.30	.14
❑ 623 Dean Palmer	.20	.09
❑ 624 Bob Patterson	.10	.05
❑ 625 Roger Pavlik	.10	.05
❑ 626 Gary Redus	.10	.05
❑ 627 Ivan Rodriguez	.50	.23
❑ 628 Kenny Rogers	.10	.05
❑ 629 Jon Shave	.10	.05
❑ 630 Doug Strange	.10	.05
❑ 631 Matt Whiteside	.10	.05
❑ 632 Roberto Alomar	.40	.18
❑ 633 Pat Borders	.10	.05
❑ 634 Scott Brow	.10	.05
❑ 635 Rob Butler	.10	.05
❑ 636 Joe Carter	.20	.09
❑ 637 Tony Castillo	.10	.05
❑ 638 Mark Eichhorn	.10	.05
❑ 639 Tony Fernandez	.10	.05
❑ 640 Huck Flener	.10	.05
❑ 641 Alfredo Griffin	.10	.05
❑ 642 Juan Guzman	.10	.05
❑ 643 Rickey Henderson	.40	.18
❑ 644 Pat Hentgen	.20	.09
❑ 645 Randy Knorr	.10	.05
❑ 646 Al Leiter	.20	.09
❑ 647 Domingo Martinez	.10	.05
❑ 648 Paul Molitor	.40	.18
❑ 649 Jack Morris	.20	.09
❑ 650 John Olerud	.20	.09
❑ 651 Ed Sprague	.10	.05
❑ 652 Dave Stewart	.20	.09
❑ 653 Devon White	.20	.09
❑ 654 Woody Williams	.10	.05
❑ 655 Barry Bonds MVP	.40	.18
❑ 656 Greg Maddux CY	.60	.25
❑ 657 Jack McDowell CY	.10	.05
❑ 658 Mike Piazza ROY	.60	.25
❑ 659 Tim Salmon ROY	.20	.09
❑ 660 Frank Thomas MVP	.60	.25

1994 Pacific All-Latino

	MINT	NRMT
COMPLETE SET (20)	25.00	11.00
COMMON CARD (1-20)	1.00	.45
❑ 1 Benito Santiago	1.00	.45
❑ 2 Dave Magadan	1.00	.45
❑ 3 Andres Galarraga	4.00	1.80
❑ 4 Luis Gonzalez	1.00	.45
❑ 5 Jose Offerman	1.00	.45
❑ 6 Bobby Bonilla	2.00	.90
❑ 7 Dennis Martinez	2.00	.90
❑ 8 Mariano Duncan	1.00	.45
❑ 9 Orlando Merced	1.00	.45
❑ 10 Jose Rijo	1.00	.45
❑ 11 Danny Tartabull	1.00	.45
❑ 12 Ruben Sierra	1.00	.45
❑ 13 Ivan Rodriguez	4.00	1.80
❑ 14 Juan Gonzalez	12.00	5.50
❑ 15 Jose Canseco	4.00	1.80
❑ 16 Rafael Palmeiro	3.00	1.35
❑ 17 Roberto Alomar	4.00	1.80
❑ 18 Eduardo Perez	1.00	.45
❑ 19 Alex Fernandez	1.00	.45
❑ 20 Omar Vizquel	2.00	.90

1994 Pacific Gold Prisms

	MINT	NRMT
COMPLETE SET (20)	90.00	40.00
COMMON CARD (1-20)	1.00	.45
❑ 1 Juan Gonzalez	12.00	5.50
❑ 2 Ken Griffey Jr.	25.00	11.00
❑ 3 Frank Thomas	15.00	6.75
❑ 4 Albert Belle	4.00	1.80
❑ 5 Rafael Palmeiro	3.00	1.35
❑ 6 Joe Carter	2.00	.90
❑ 7 Dean Palmer	2.00	.90
❑ 8 Mickey Tettleton	1.00	.45
❑ 9 Tim Salmon	4.00	1.80
❑ 10 Danny Tartabull	1.00	.45
❑ 11 Barry Bonds	4.00	1.80
❑ 12 Dave Justice	4.00	1.80
❑ 13 Matt Williams	3.00	1.35
❑ 14 Fred McGriff	3.00	1.35
❑ 15 Ron Gant	2.00	.90
❑ 16 Mike Piazza	15.00	6.75
❑ 17 Bobby Bonilla	2.00	.90
❑ 18 Phil Plantier	1.00	.45
❑ 19 Sammy Sosa	12.00	5.50
❑ 20 Rick Wilkins	1.00	.45

1994 Pacific Silver Prisms

	MINT	NRMT
COMPLETE SET (36)	125.00	55.00
COMMON CARD (1-36)	1.00	.45
COMP.CIRCULAR SET (36)	60.00	27.00

*CIRCULAR STARS: 2X TO 5X BASIC CARDS
ONE CIRCULAR PER BLACK RETAIL PACK

	MINT	NRMT
❑ 1 Robin Yount	3.00	1.35
❑ 2 Juan Gonzalez	10.00	4.50
❑ 3 Rafael Palmeiro	2.50	1.10
❑ 4 Paul Molitor	3.00	1.35
❑ 5 Roberto Alomar	3.00	1.35
❑ 6 John Olerud	2.00	.90
❑ 7 Randy Johnson	3.00	1.35
❑ 8 Ken Griffey Jr.	20.00	9.00
❑ 9 Wade Boggs	3.00	1.35
❑ 10 Don Mattingly	6.00	2.70
❑ 11 Kirby Puckett	8.00	3.60
❑ 12 Tim Salmon	3.00	1.35
❑ 13 Frank Thomas	12.00	5.50
❑ 14 Fernando Valenzuela	2.00	.90
❑ 15 Cal Ripken	15.00	6.75
❑ 16 Carlos Baerga	2.00	.90
❑ 17 Kenny Lofton	3.00	1.35
❑ 18 Cecil Fielder	2.00	.90
❑ 19 John Burkett	1.00	.45
❑ 20 Andres Galarraga	3.00	1.35
❑ 21 Charlie Hayes	1.00	.45
❑ 22 Orestes Destrade	1.00	.45
❑ 23 Jeff Conine	2.00	.90
❑ 24 Jeff Bagwell	6.00	2.70
❑ 25 Mark Grace	2.50	1.10
❑ 26 Ryne Sandberg	5.00	2.20
❑ 27 Gregg Jefferies	1.00	.45
❑ 28 Barry Bonds	3.00	1.35
❑ 29 Mike Piazza	12.00	5.50
❑ 30 Greg Maddux	12.00	5.50
❑ 31 Darren Daulton	2.00	.90
❑ 32 John Kruk	2.00	.90
❑ 33 Lenny Dykstra	2.00	.90
❑ 34 Orlando Merced	1.00	.45
❑ 35 Tony Gwynn	10.00	4.50
❑ 36 Robby Thompson	1.00	.45

1995 Pacific

	MINT	NRMT
COMPLETE SET (450)	30.00	13.50
COMMON CARD (1-450)	.10	.05
❑ 1 Steve Avery	.10	.05
❑ 2 Rafael Belliard	.10	.05
❑ 3 Jeff Blauser	.10	.05
❑ 4 Tom Glavine	.40	.18
❑ 5 David Justice	.40	.18
❑ 6 Mike Kelly	.10	.05
❑ 7 Roberto Kelly	.10	.05
❑ 8 Ryan Klesko	.20	.09
❑ 9 Mark Lemke	.10	.05
❑ 10 Javier Lopez	.20	.09
❑ 11 Greg Maddux	1.25	.55
❑ 12 Fred McGriff	.30	.14
❑ 13 Greg McMichael	.10	.05
❑ 14 Jose Oliva	.10	.05
❑ 15 John Smoltz	.20	.09
❑ 16 Tony Tarasco	.10	.05
❑ 17 Brady Anderson	.20	.09
❑ 18 Harold Baines	.20	.09
❑ 19 Armando Benitez	.10	.05
❑ 20 Mike Devereaux	.10	.05
❑ 21 Leo Gomez	.10	.05
❑ 22 Jeffrey Hammonds	.20	.09
❑ 23 Chris Hoiles	.10	.05
❑ 24 Ben McDonald	.10	.05
❑ 25 Mark McLemore	.10	.05
❑ 26 Jamie Moyer	.10	.05
❑ 27 Mike Mussina	.40	.18
❑ 28 Rafael Palmeiro	.30	.14
❑ 29 Jim Poole	.10	.05
❑ 30 Cal Ripken Jr.	1.50	.70
❑ 31 Lee Smith	.20	.09
❑ 32 Mark Smith	.10	.05
❑ 33 Jose Canseco	.40	.18
❑ 34 Roger Clemens	.75	.35
❑ 35 Scott Cooper	.10	.05
❑ 36 Andre Dawson	.30	.14
❑ 37 Tony Fossas	.10	.05
❑ 38 Mike Greenwell	.10	.05
❑ 39 Chris Howard	.10	.05
❑ 40 Jose Melendez	.10	.05
❑ 41 Nate Minchey	.10	.05
❑ 42 Tim Naehring	.10	.05
❑ 43 Otis Nixon	.10	.05
❑ 44 Carlos Rodriguez	.10	.05
❑ 45 Aaron Sele	.20	.09
❑ 46 Lee Tinsley	.10	.05
❑ 47 Sergio Valdez	.10	.05
❑ 48 John Valentin	.20	.09
❑ 49 Mo Vaughn	.50	.23
❑ 50 Brian Anderson	.20	.09
❑ 51 Garret Anderson	.20	.09
❑ 52 Rod Correia	.10	.05
❑ 53 Chad Curtis	.10	.05
❑ 54 Mark Dalesandro	.10	.05
❑ 55 Chili Davis	.20	.09
❑ 56 Gary DiSarcina	.10	.05
❑ 57 Damion Easley	.20	.09
❑ 58 Jim Edmonds	.30	.14
❑ 59 Jorge Fabregas	.10	.05
❑ 60 Chuck Finley	.20	.09
❑ 61 Bo Jackson	.20	.09
❑ 62 Mark Langston	.10	.05
❑ 63 Eduardo Perez	.10	.05
❑ 64 Tim Salmon	.40	.18
❑ 65 J.T. Snow	.20	.09
❑ 66 Willie Banks	.10	.05
❑ 67 Jose Bautista	.10	.05
❑ 68 Shawon Dunston	.10	.05
❑ 69 Kevin Foster	.10	.05
❑ 70 Mark Grace	.30	.14
❑ 71 Jose Guzman	.10	.05
❑ 72 Jose Hernandez	.10	.05
❑ 73 Blaise Ilsley	.10	.05
❑ 74 Derrick May	.10	.05
❑ 75 Randy Myers	.10	.05
❑ 76 Karl Rhodes	.10	.05
❑ 77 Kevin Roberson	.10	.05
❑ 78 Rey Sanchez	.10	.05
❑ 79 Sammy Sosa	1.00	.45
❑ 80 Steve Trachsel	.10	.05
❑ 81 Eddie Zambrano	.10	.05
❑ 82 Wilson Alvarez	.20	.09
❑ 83 Jason Bere	.10	.05
❑ 84 Joey Cora	.20	.09
❑ 85 Jose DeLeon	.10	.05
❑ 86 Alex Fernandez	.10	.05
❑ 87 Julio Franco	.10	.05
❑ 88 Ozzie Guillen	.10	.05
❑ 89 Joe Hall	.10	.05
❑ 90 Roberto Hernandez	.10	.05
❑ 91 Darrin Jackson	.10	.05
❑ 92 Lance Johnson	.10	.05
❑ 93 Norberto Martin	.10	.05
❑ 94 Jack McDowell	.10	.05
❑ 95 Tim Raines	.20	.09
❑ 96 Olmedo Saenz	.10	.05
❑ 97 Frank Thomas	1.25	.55
❑ 98 Robin Ventura	.20	.09
❑ 99 Bret Boone	.20	.09
❑ 100 Jeff Brantley	.10	.05
❑ 101 Jacob Brumfield	.10	.05
❑ 102 Hector Carrasco	.10	.05
❑ 103 Brian Dorsett	.10	.05
❑ 104 Tony Fernandez	.10	.05
❑ 105 Willie Greene	.20	.09
❑ 106 Erik Hanson	.10	.05
❑ 107 Kevin Jarvis	.10	.05
❑ 108 Barry Larkin	.30	.14
❑ 109 Kevin Mitchell	.10	.05
❑ 110 Hal Morris	.10	.05
❑ 111 Jose Rijo	.10	.05
❑ 112 Johnny Ruffin	.10	.05
❑ 113 Deion Sanders	.20	.09
❑ 114 Reggie Sanders	.20	.09
❑ 115 Sandy Alomar Jr.	.20	.09
❑ 116 Ruben Amaro	.10	.05
❑ 117 Carlos Baerga	.20	.09
❑ 118 Albert Belle	.50	.23
❑ 119 Alvaro Espinoza	.10	.05
❑ 120 Rene Gonzales	.10	.05
❑ 121 Wayne Kirby	.10	.05
❑ 122 Kenny Lofton	.40	.18
❑ 123 Candy Maldonado	.10	.05
❑ 124 Dennis Martinez	.20	.09
❑ 125 Eddie Murray	.40	.18
❑ 126 Charles Nagy	.20	.09
❑ 127 Tony Pena	.10	.05
❑ 128 Manny Ramirez	.40	.18
❑ 129 Paul Sorrento	.10	.05
❑ 130 Jim Thome	.40	.18
❑ 131 Omar Vizquel	.20	.09
❑ 132 Dante Bichette	.20	.09
❑ 133 Ellis Burks	.20	.09
❑ 134 Vinny Castilla	.30	.14
❑ 135 Marvin Freeman	.10	.05
❑ 136 Andres Galarraga	.40	.18
❑ 137 Joe Girardi	.10	.05
❑ 138 Charlie Hayes	.10	.05
❑ 139 Mike Kingery	.10	.05
❑ 140 Nelson Liriano	.10	.05
❑ 141 Roberto Mejia	.10	.05
❑ 142 David Nied	.10	.05
❑ 143 Steve Reed	.10	.05
❑ 144 Armando Reynoso	.10	.05
❑ 145 Bruce Ruffin	.10	.05
❑ 146 John VanderWal	.10	.05
❑ 147 Walt Weiss	.10	.05
❑ 148 Skeeter Barnes	.10	.05
❑ 149 Tim Belcher	.10	.05
❑ 150 Junior Felix	.10	.05
❑ 151 Cecil Fielder	.20	.09
❑ 152 Travis Fryman	.20	.09
❑ 153 Kirk Gibson	.20	.09
❑ 154 Chris Gomez	.10	.05
❑ 155 Buddy Groom	.10	.05
❑ 156 Chad Kreuter	.10	.05
❑ 157 Mike Moore	.10	.05
❑ 158 Tony Phillips	.10	.05
❑ 159 Juan Samuel	.10	.05
❑ 160 Mickey Tettleton	.10	.05
❑ 161 Alan Trammell	.20	.09
❑ 162 David Wells	.30	.14
❑ 163 Lou Whitaker	.20	.09
❑ 164 Kurt Abbott	.10	.05
❑ 165 Luis Aquino	.10	.05
❑ 166 Alex Arias	.10	.05
❑ 167 Bret Barberie	.10	.05
❑ 168 Jerry Browne	.10	.05
❑ 169 Chuck Carr	.10	.05
❑ 170 Matias Carrillo	.10	.05
❑ 171 Greg Colbrunn	.10	.05
❑ 172 Jeff Conine	.20	.09
❑ 173 Carl Everett	.10	.05
❑ 174 Robb Nen	.10	.05
❑ 175 Yorkis Perez	.10	.05
❑ 176 Pat Rapp	.10	.05
❑ 177 Benito Santiago	.10	.05
❑ 178 Gary Sheffield	.30	.14
❑ 179 Darrell Whitmore	.10	.05
❑ 180 Jeff Bagwell	.60	.25
❑ 181 Kevin Bass	.10	.05
❑ 182 Craig Biggio	.40	.18
❑ 183 Andujar Cedeno	.10	.05
❑ 184 Doug Drabek	.10	.05
❑ 185 Tony Eusebio	.10	.05
❑ 186 Steve Finley	.20	.09
❑ 187 Luis Gonzalez	.10	.05
❑ 188 Pete Harnisch	.10	.05
❑ 189 John Hudek	.10	.05
❑ 190 Orlando Miller	.10	.05
❑ 191 James Mouton	.10	.05
❑ 192 Roberto Petagine	.10	.05
❑ 193 Shane Reynolds	.20	.09
❑ 194 Greg Swindell	.10	.05
❑ 195 Dave Veres	.10	.05
❑ 196 Kevin Appier	.20	.09
❑ 197 Stan Belinda	.10	.05
❑ 198 Vince Coleman	.10	.05
❑ 199 David Cone	.30	.14
❑ 200 Gary Gaetti	.20	.09
❑ 201 Greg Gagne	.10	.05
❑ 202 Mark Gubicza	.10	.05
❑ 203 Bob Hamelin	.10	.05
❑ 204 Dave Henderson	.10	.05
❑ 205 Felix Jose	.10	.05
❑ 206 Wally Joyner	.20	.09
❑ 207 Jose Lind	.10	.05
❑ 208 Mike Macfarlane	.10	.05
❑ 209 Brian McRae	.10	.05
❑ 210 Jeff Montgomery	.10	.05
❑ 211 Hipolito Pichardo	.10	.05
❑ 212 Pedro Astacio	.10	.05
❑ 213 Brett Butler	.20	.09
❑ 214 Omar Daal	.10	.05
❑ 215 Delino DeShields	.10	.05
❑ 216 Darren Dreifort	.20	.09
❑ 217 Carlos Hernandez	.10	.05
❑ 218 Orel Hershiser	.20	.09
❑ 219 Garey Ingram	.10	.05
❑ 220 Eric Karros	.20	.09
❑ 221 Ramon Martinez	.20	.09
❑ 222 Raul Mondesi	.30	.14
❑ 223 Jose Offerman	.10	.05
❑ 224 Mike Piazza	1.25	.55
❑ 225 Henry Rodriguez	.20	.09
❑ 226 Ismael Valdes	.20	.09
❑ 227 Tim Wallach	.10	.05
❑ 228 Jeff Cirillo	.20	.09
❑ 229 Alex Diaz	.10	.05
❑ 230 Cal Eldred	.10	.05
❑ 231 Mike Fetters	.10	.05
❑ 232 Brian Harper	.10	.05

Card	Mint	NrMt
❑ 233 Ted Higuera	.10	.05
❑ 234 John Jaha	.10	.05
❑ 235 Graeme Lloyd	.10	.05
❑ 236 Jose Mercedes	.10	.05
❑ 237 Jaime Navarro	.10	.05
❑ 238 Dave Nilsson	.10	.05
❑ 239 Jesse Orosco	.10	.05
❑ 240 Jody Reed	.10	.05
❑ 241 Jose Valentin	.10	.05
❑ 242 Greg Vaughn	.20	.09
❑ 243 Turner Ward	.10	.05
❑ 244 Rick Aguilera	.10	.05
❑ 245 Rich Becker	.10	.05
❑ 246 Jim Deshaies	.10	.05
❑ 247 Steve Dunn	.10	.05
❑ 248 Scott Erickson	.20	.09
❑ 249 Kent Hrbek	.10	.05
❑ 250 Chuck Knoblauch	.40	.18
❑ 251 Scott Leius	.10	.05
❑ 252 David McCarty	.10	.05
❑ 253 Pat Meares	.10	.05
❑ 254 Pedro Munoz	.10	.05
❑ 255 Kirby Puckett	.60	.25
❑ 256 Carlos Pulido	.10	.05
❑ 257 Kevin Tapani	.10	.05
❑ 258 Matt Walbeck	.10	.05
❑ 259 Dave Winfield	.40	.18
❑ 260 Moises Alou	.30	.14
❑ 261 Juan Bell	.10	.05
❑ 262 Freddie Benavides	.10	.05
❑ 263 Sean Berry	.10	.05
❑ 264 Wil Cordero	.10	.05
❑ 265 Jeff Fassero	.10	.05
❑ 266 Darrin Fletcher	.10	.05
❑ 267 Cliff Floyd	.20	.09
❑ 268 Marquis Grissom	.20	.09
❑ 269 Gil Heredia	.10	.05
❑ 270 Ken Hill	.10	.05
❑ 271 Pedro J. Martinez	.40	.18
❑ 272 Mel Rojas	.10	.05
❑ 273 Larry Walker	.40	.18
❑ 274 John Wetteland	.20	.09
❑ 275 Rondell White	.20	.09
❑ 276 Tim Bogar	.10	.05
❑ 277 Bobby Bonilla	.20	.09
❑ 278 Rico Brogna	.10	.05
❑ 279 Jeromy Burnitz	.20	.09
❑ 280 John Franco	.20	.09
❑ 281 Eric Hillman	.10	.05
❑ 282 Todd Hundley	.20	.09
❑ 283 Jeff Kent	.20	.09
❑ 284 Mike Maddux	.10	.05
❑ 285 Joe Orsulak	.10	.05
❑ 286 Luis Rivera	.10	.05
❑ 287 Bret Saberhagen	.20	.09
❑ 288 David Segui	.20	.09
❑ 289 Ryan Thompson	.10	.05
❑ 290 Fernando Vina	.10	.05
❑ 291 Jose Vizcaino	.10	.05
❑ 292 Jim Abbott	.20	.09
❑ 293 Wade Boggs	.40	.18
❑ 294 Russ Davis	.20	.09
❑ 295 Mike Gallego	.10	.05
❑ 296 Xavier Hernandez	.10	.05
❑ 297 Steve Howe	.10	.05
❑ 298 Jimmy Key	.20	.09
❑ 299 Don Mattingly	.60	.25
❑ 300 Terry Mulholland	.10	.05
❑ 301 Paul O'Neill	.20	.09
❑ 302 Luis Polonia	.10	.05
❑ 303 Mike Stanley	.10	.05
❑ 304 Danny Tartabull	.10	.05
❑ 305 Randy Velarde	.10	.05
❑ 306 Bob Wickman	.10	.05
❑ 307 Bernie Williams	.40	.18
❑ 308 Mark Acre	.10	.05
❑ 309 Geronimo Berroa	.10	.05
❑ 310 Mike Bordick	.10	.05
❑ 311 Dennis Eckersley	.20	.09
❑ 312 Rickey Henderson	.40	.18
❑ 313 Stan Javier	.10	.05
❑ 314 Miguel Jimenez	.10	.05
❑ 315 Francisco Matos	.10	.05
❑ 316 Mark McGwire	2.00	.90
❑ 317 Troy Neel	.10	.05
❑ 318 Steve Ontiveros	.10	.05
❑ 319 Carlos Reyes	.10	.05
❑ 320 Ruben Sierra	.10	.05
❑ 321 Terry Steinbach	.20	.09
❑ 322 Bob Welch	.10	.05
❑ 323 Bobby Witt	.10	.05
❑ 324 Larry Andersen	.10	.05
❑ 325 Kim Batiste	.10	.05
❑ 326 Darren Daulton	.20	.09
❑ 327 Mariano Duncan	.10	.05
❑ 328 Lenny Dykstra	.20	.09
❑ 329 Jim Eisenreich	.10	.05
❑ 330 Danny Jackson	.10	.05
❑ 331 John Kruk	.20	.09
❑ 332 Tony Longmire	.10	.05
❑ 333 Tom Marsh	.10	.05
❑ 334 Mickey Morandini	.10	.05
❑ 335 Bobby Munoz	.10	.05
❑ 336 Todd Pratt	.10	.05
❑ 337 Tom Quinlan	.10	.05
❑ 338 Kevin Stocker	.10	.05
❑ 339 Fernando Valenzuela	.20	.09
❑ 340 Jay Bell	.20	.09
❑ 341 Dave Clark	.10	.05
❑ 342 Steve Cooke	.10	.05
❑ 343 Carlos Garcia	.10	.05
❑ 344 Jeff King	.10	.05
❑ 345 Jon Lieber	.10	.05
❑ 346 Ravelo Manzanillo	.10	.05
❑ 347 Al Martin	.10	.05
❑ 348 Orlando Merced	.10	.05
❑ 349 Denny Neagle	.20	.09
❑ 350 Alejandro Pena	.10	.05
❑ 351 Don Slaught	.10	.05
❑ 352 Zane Smith	.10	.05
❑ 353 Andy Van Slyke	.20	.09
❑ 354 Rick White	.10	.05
❑ 355 Kevin Young	.10	.05
❑ 356 Andy Ashby	.10	.05
❑ 357 Derek Bell	.20	.09
❑ 358 Andy Benes	.20	.09
❑ 359 Phil Clark	.10	.05
❑ 360 Donnie Elliott	.10	.05
❑ 361 Ricky Gutierrez	.10	.05
❑ 362 Tony Gwynn	1.00	.45
❑ 363 Trevor Hoffman	.20	.09
❑ 364 Tim Hyers	.10	.05
❑ 365 Luis Lopez	.10	.05
❑ 366 Jose Martinez	.10	.05
❑ 367 Pedro A. Martinez	.10	.05
❑ 368 Phil Plantier	.10	.05
❑ 369 Bip Roberts	.10	.05
❑ 370 A.J. Sager	.10	.05
❑ 371 Jeff Tabaka	.10	.05
❑ 372 Todd Benzinger	.10	.05
❑ 373 Barry Bonds	.50	.23
❑ 374 John Burkett	.10	.05
❑ 375 Mark Carreon	.10	.05
❑ 376 Royce Clayton	.10	.05
❑ 377 Pat Gomez	.10	.05
❑ 378 Erik Johnson	.10	.05
❑ 379 Darren Lewis	.10	.05
❑ 380 Kirt Manwaring	.10	.05
❑ 381 Dave Martinez	.10	.05
❑ 382 John Patterson	.10	.05
❑ 383 Mark Portugal	.10	.05
❑ 384 Darryl Strawberry	.20	.09
❑ 385 Salomon Torres	.10	.05
❑ 386 Wm. VanLandingham	.10	.05
❑ 387 Matt Williams	.20	.09
❑ 388 Rich Amaral	.10	.05
❑ 389 Bobby Ayala	.10	.05
❑ 390 Mike Blowers	.10	.05
❑ 391 Chris Bosio	.10	.05
❑ 392 Jay Buhner	.20	.09
❑ 393 Jim Converse	.10	.05
❑ 394 Tim Davis	.10	.05
❑ 395 Felix Fermin	.10	.05
❑ 396 Dave Fleming	.10	.05
❑ 397 Goose Gossage	.20	.09
❑ 398 Ken Griffey Jr.	2.00	.90
❑ 399 Randy Johnson	.40	.18
❑ 400 Edgar Martinez	.20	.09
❑ 401 Tino Martinez	.40	.18
❑ 402 Alex Rodriguez	1.50	.70
❑ 403 Dan Wilson	.10	.05
❑ 404 Luis Alicea	.10	.05
❑ 405 Rene Arocha	.10	.05
❑ 406 Bernard Gilkey	.10	.05
❑ 407 Gregg Jefferies	.10	.05
❑ 408 Ray Lankford	.20	.09
❑ 409 Terry McGriff	.10	.05
❑ 410 Omar Olivares	.10	.05
❑ 411 Jose Oquendo	.10	.05
❑ 412 Vicente Palacios	.10	.05
❑ 413 Geronimo Pena	.10	.05
❑ 414 Mike Perez	.10	.05
❑ 415 Gerald Perry	.10	.05
❑ 416 Ozzie Smith	.50	.23
❑ 417 Bob Tewksbury	.10	.05
❑ 418 Mark Whiten	.10	.05
❑ 419 Todd Zeile	.10	.05
❑ 420 Esteban Beltre	.10	.05
❑ 421 Kevin Brown	.30	.14
❑ 422 Cris Carpenter	.10	.05
❑ 423 Will Clark	.40	.18
❑ 424 Hector Fajardo	.10	.05
❑ 425 Jeff Frye	.10	.05
❑ 426 Juan Gonzalez	1.00	.45
❑ 427 Rusty Greer	.40	.18
❑ 428 Rick Honeycutt	.10	.05
❑ 429 David Hulse	.10	.05
❑ 430 Manny Lee	.10	.05
❑ 431 Junior Ortiz	.10	.05
❑ 432 Dean Palmer	.20	.09
❑ 433 Ivan Rodriguez	.50	.23
❑ 434 Dan Smith	.10	.05
❑ 435 Roberto Alomar	.40	.18
❑ 436 Pat Borders	.10	.05
❑ 437 Scott Brow	.10	.05
❑ 438 Rob Butler	.10	.05
❑ 439 Joe Carter	.20	.09
❑ 440 Tony Castillo	.10	.05
❑ 441 Domingo Cedeno	.10	.05
❑ 442 Brad Cornett	.10	.05
❑ 443 Carlos Delgado	.20	.09
❑ 444 Alex Gonzalez	.10	.05
❑ 445 Juan Guzman	.10	.05
❑ 446 Darren Hall	.10	.05
❑ 447 Paul Molitor	.40	.18
❑ 448 John Olerud	.20	.09
❑ 449 Robert Perez	.10	.05
❑ 450 Devon White	.20	.09

1995 Pacific Gold Crown Die Cuts

	MINT	NRMT
COMPLETE SET (20)	150.00	70.00
COMMON CARD (1-20)	2.50	1.10
❑ 1 Greg Maddux	20.00	9.00
❑ 2 Fred McGriff	4.00	1.80
❑ 3 Rafael Palmeiro	4.00	1.80
❑ 4 Cal Ripken Jr.	25.00	11.00
❑ 5 Jose Canseco	6.00	2.70
❑ 6 Frank Thomas	20.00	9.00
❑ 7 Albert Belle	8.00	3.60
❑ 8 Manny Ramirez	6.00	2.70
❑ 9 Andres Galarraga	6.00	2.70
❑ 10 Jeff Bagwell	10.00	4.50
❑ 11 Chan Ho Park	6.00	2.70

Card	MINT	NRMT
❑ 12 Raul Mondesi	4.00	1.80
❑ 13 Mike Piazza	20.00	9.00
❑ 14 Kirby Puckett	10.00	4.50
❑ 15 Barry Bonds	8.00	3.60
❑ 16 Ken Griffey Jr.	30.00	13.50
❑ 17 Alex Rodriguez	25.00	11.00
❑ 18 Juan Gonzalez	15.00	6.75
❑ 19 Roberto Alomar	6.00	2.70
❑ 20 Carlos Delgado	2.50	1.10

1995 Pacific Gold Prisms

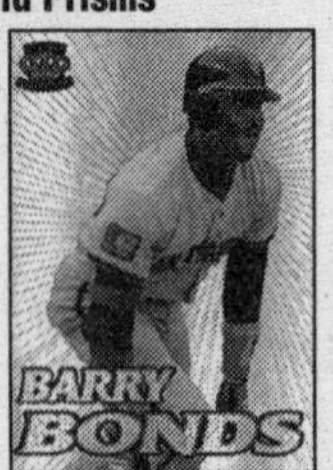

	MINT	NRMT
COMPLETE SET (36)	120.00	55.00
COMMON CARD (1-36)	1.25	.55

Card	MINT	NRMT
❑ 1 Jose Canseco	4.00	1.80
❑ 2 Gregg Jefferies	1.25	.55
❑ 3 Fred McGriff	3.00	1.35
❑ 4 Joe Carter	2.00	.90
❑ 5 Tim Salmon	4.00	1.80
❑ 6 Wade Boggs	4.00	1.80
❑ 7 Dave Winfield	4.00	1.80
❑ 8 Bob Hamelin	1.25	.55
❑ 9 Cal Ripken Jr.	20.00	9.00
❑ 10 Don Mattingly	10.00	4.50
❑ 11 Juan Gonzalez	12.00	5.50
❑ 12 Carlos Delgado	2.00	.90
❑ 13 Barry Bonds	4.00	1.80
❑ 14 Albert Belle	4.00	1.80
❑ 15 Raul Mondesi	3.00	1.35
❑ 16 Jeff Bagwell	8.00	3.60
❑ 17 Mike Piazza	15.00	6.75
❑ 18 Rafael Palmeiro	3.00	1.35
❑ 19 Frank Thomas	15.00	6.75
❑ 20 Matt Williams	2.00	.90
❑ 21 Ken Griffey Jr.	25.00	11.00
❑ 22 Will Clark	4.00	1.80
❑ 23 Bobby Bonilla	2.00	.90
❑ 24 Kenny Lofton	4.00	1.80
❑ 25 Paul Molitor	4.00	1.80
❑ 26 Kirby Puckett	4.00	1.80
❑ 27 David Justice	4.00	1.80
❑ 28 Jeff Conine	2.00	.90
❑ 29 Bret Boone	2.00	.90
❑ 30 Larry Walker	4.00	1.80
❑ 31 Cecil Fielder	2.00	.90
❑ 32 Manny Ramirez	4.00	1.80
❑ 33 Javier Lopez	2.00	.90
❑ 34 Jimmy Key	2.00	.90
❑ 35 Andres Galarraga	4.00	1.80
❑ 36 Tony Gwynn	12.00	5.50

1995 Pacific Latinos Destacados

	MINT	NRMT
COMPLETE SET (36)	50.00	22.00
COMMON CARD (1-36)	1.00	.45

Card	MINT	NRMT
❑ 1 Roberto Alomar	3.00	1.35
❑ 2 Moises Alou	2.50	1.10
❑ 3 Wilson Alvarez	1.50	.70
❑ 4 Carlos Baerga	1.50	.70
❑ 5 Geronimo Berroa	1.00	.45
❑ 6 Jose Canseco	3.00	1.35
❑ 7 Hector Carrasco	1.00	.45
❑ 8 Wil Cordero	1.00	.45
❑ 9 Carlos Delgado	1.50	.70
❑ 10 Damion Easley	1.50	.70
❑ 11 Tony Eusebio	1.00	.45
❑ 12 Hector Fajardo	1.00	.45
❑ 13 Andres Galarraga	3.00	1.35
❑ 14 Carlos Garcia	1.00	.45
❑ 15 Chris Gomez	1.00	.45
❑ 16 Alex Gonzalez	1.00	.45
❑ 17 Juan Gonzalez	10.00	4.50
❑ 18 Luis Gonzalez	1.00	.45
❑ 19 Felix Jose	1.00	.45
❑ 20 Javier Lopez	1.50	.70
❑ 21 Luis Lopez	1.00	.45
❑ 22 Dennis Martinez	1.50	.70
❑ 23 Orlando Miller	1.00	.45
❑ 24 Raul Mondesi	2.50	1.10
❑ 25 Jose Oliva	1.00	.45
❑ 26 Rafael Palmeiro	2.50	1.10
❑ 27 Yorkis Perez	1.00	.45
❑ 28 Manny Ramirez	3.00	1.35
❑ 29 Jose Rijo	1.00	.45
❑ 30 Alex Rodriguez	15.00	6.75
❑ 31 Ivan Rodriguez	3.00	1.35
❑ 32 Carlos Rodriguez	1.00	.45
❑ 33 Sammy Sosa	10.00	4.50
❑ 34 Tony Tarasco	1.00	.45
❑ 35 Ismael Valdes	1.50	.70
❑ 36 Bernie Williams	3.00	1.35

1996 Pacific

	MINT	NRMT
COMPLETE SET (450)	35.00	16.00
COMMON CARD (1-450)	.10	.05

Card	MINT	NRMT
❑ 1 Steve Avery	.10	.05
❑ 2 Ryan Klesko	.20	.09
❑ 3 Pedro Borbon	.10	.05
❑ 4 Chipper Jones	1.00	.45
❑ 5 Kent Mercker	.10	.05
❑ 6 Greg Maddux	1.25	.55
❑ 7 Greg McMichael	.10	.05
❑ 8 Mark Wohlers	.10	.05
❑ 9 Fred McGriff	.30	.14
❑ 10 John Smoltz	.20	.09
❑ 11 Rafael Belliard	.10	.05
❑ 12 Mark Lemke	.10	.05
❑ 13 Tom Glavine	.40	.18
❑ 14 Javier Lopez	.20	.09
❑ 15 Jeff Blauser	.10	.05
❑ 16 David Justice	.40	.18
❑ 17 Marquis Grissom	.20	.09
❑ 18 Greg Maddux CY	.60	.25
❑ 19 Randy Myers	.10	.05
❑ 20 Scott Servais	.10	.05
❑ 21 Sammy Sosa	1.00	.45
❑ 22 Kevin Foster	.10	.05
❑ 23 Jose Hernandez	.10	.05
❑ 24 Jim Bullinger	.10	.05
❑ 25 Mike Perez	.10	.05
❑ 26 Shawon Dunston	.10	.05
❑ 27 Rey Sanchez	.10	.05
❑ 28 Frank Castillo	.10	.05
❑ 29 Jaime Navarro	.10	.05
❑ 30 Brian McRae	.10	.05
❑ 31 Mark Grace	.30	.14
❑ 32 Roberto Rivera	.10	.05
❑ 33 Luis Gonzalez	.10	.05
❑ 34 Hector Carrasco	.10	.05
❑ 35 Bret Boone	.20	.09
❑ 36 Thomas Howard	.10	.05
❑ 37 Hal Morris	.10	.05
❑ 38 John Smiley	.10	.05
❑ 39 Jeff Brantley	.10	.05
❑ 40 Barry Larkin	.30	.14
❑ 41 Mariano Duncan	.10	.05
❑ 42 Xavier Hernandez	.10	.05
❑ 43 Pete Schourek	.10	.05
❑ 44 Reggie Sanders	.20	.09
❑ 45 Dave Burba	.10	.05
❑ 46 Jeff Branson	.10	.05
❑ 47 Mark Portugal	.10	.05
❑ 48 Ron Gant	.10	.05
❑ 49 Benito Santiago	.10	.05
❑ 50 Barry Larkin MVP	.10	.05
❑ 51 Steve Reed	.10	.05
❑ 52 Kevin Ritz	.10	.05
❑ 53 Dante Bichette	.20	.09
❑ 54 Darren Holmes	.10	.05
❑ 55 Ellis Burks	.20	.09
❑ 56 Walt Weiss	.10	.05
❑ 57 Armando Reynoso	.10	.05
❑ 58 Vinny Castilla	.30	.14
❑ 59 Jason Bates	.10	.05
❑ 60 Mike Kingery	.10	.05
❑ 61 Bryan Rekar	.10	.05
❑ 62 Curtis Leskanic	.10	.05
❑ 63 Bret Saberhagen	.20	.09
❑ 64 Andres Galarraga	.40	.18
❑ 65 Larry Walker	.40	.18
❑ 66 Joe Girardi	.10	.05
❑ 67 Quilvio Veras	.10	.05
❑ 68 Robb Nen	.10	.05
❑ 69 Mario Diaz	.10	.05
❑ 70 Chuck Carr	.10	.05
❑ 71 Alex Arias	.10	.05
❑ 72 Pat Rapp	.10	.05
❑ 73 Rich Garces	.10	.05
❑ 74 Kurt Abbott	.10	.05
❑ 75 Andre Dawson	.30	.14
❑ 76 Greg Colbrunn	.10	.05
❑ 77 John Burkett	.10	.05
❑ 78 Terry Pendleton	.10	.05
❑ 79 Jesus Tavarez	.10	.05
❑ 80 Charles Johnson	.20	.09
❑ 81 Yorkis Perez	.10	.05
❑ 82 Jeff Conine	.20	.09
❑ 83 Gary Sheffield	.30	.14
❑ 84 Brian L. Hunter	.20	.09
❑ 85 Derrick May	.10	.05
❑ 86 Greg Swindell	.10	.05
❑ 87 Derek Bell	.20	.09
❑ 88 Dave Veres	.10	.05
❑ 89 Jeff Bagwell	.60	.25
❑ 90 Todd Jones	.10	.05
❑ 91 Orlando Miller	.10	.05
❑ 92 Pedro A. Martinez	.10	.05
❑ 93 Tony Eusebio	.10	.05
❑ 94 Craig Biggio	.40	.18
❑ 95 Shane Reynolds	.20	.09
❑ 96 James Mouton	.10	.05
❑ 97 Doug Drabek	.10	.05
❑ 98 Dave Magadan	.10	.05
❑ 99 Ricky Gutierrez	.10	.05

❑ 100 Hideo Nomo .60 .25
❑ 101 Delino DeShields .10 .05
❑ 102 Tom Candiotti .10 .05
❑ 103 Mike Piazza 1.25 .55
❑ 104 Ramon Martinez .20 .09
❑ 105 Pedro Astacio .10 .05
❑ 106 Chad Fonville .10 .05
❑ 107 Raul Mondesi .30 .14
❑ 108 Ismael Valdes .20 .09
❑ 109 Jose Offerman .10 .05
❑ 110 Todd Worrell .10 .05
❑ 111 Eric Karros .20 .09
❑ 112 Brett Butler .20 .09
❑ 113 Juan Castro .10 .05
❑ 114 Roberto Kelly .10 .05
❑ 115 Omar Daal .10 .05
❑ 116 Antonio Osuna .10 .05
❑ 117 Hideo Nomo ROY .50 .23
❑ 118 Mike Lansing .10 .05
❑ 119 Mel Rojas .10 .05
❑ 120 Sean Berry .10 .05
❑ 121 David Segui .20 .09
❑ 122 Tavo Alvarez .10 .05
❑ 123 Pedro J.Martinez .40 .18
❑ 124 F.P. Santangelo .10 .05
❑ 125 Rondell White .20 .09
❑ 126 Cliff Floyd .20 .09
❑ 127 Henry Rodriguez .20 .09
❑ 128 Tony Tarasco .10 .05
❑ 129 Yamil Benitez .10 .05
❑ 130 Carlos Perez .20 .09
❑ 131 Wil Cordero .10 .05
❑ 132 Jeff Fassero .10 .05
❑ 133 Moises Alou .30 .14
❑ 134 John Franco .20 .09
❑ 135 Rico Brogna .10 .05
❑ 136 Dave Mlicki .10 .05
❑ 137 Bill Pulsipher .10 .05
❑ 138 Jose Vizcaino .10 .05
❑ 139 Carl Everett .10 .05
❑ 140 Edgardo Alfonzo .20 .09
❑ 141 Bobby Jones .10 .05
❑ 142 Alberto Castillo .10 .05
❑ 143 Joe Orsulak .10 .05
❑ 144 Jeff Kent .20 .09
❑ 145 Ryan Thompson .10 .05
❑ 146 Jason Isringhausen .10 .05
❑ 147 Todd Hundley .20 .09
❑ 148 Alex Ochoa .10 .05
❑ 149 Charlie Hayes .10 .05
❑ 150 Michael Mimbs .10 .05
❑ 151 Darren Daulton .20 .09
❑ 152 Toby Borland .10 .05
❑ 153 Andy Van Slyke .10 .05
❑ 154 Mickey Morandini .10 .05
❑ 155 Sid Fernandez .10 .05
❑ 156 Tom Marsh .10 .05
❑ 157 Kevin Stocker .10 .05
❑ 158 Paul Quantrill .10 .05
❑ 159 Gregg Jefferies .10 .05
❑ 160 Ricky Bottalico .20 .09
❑ 161 Lenny Dykstra .20 .09
❑ 162 Mark Whiten .10 .05
❑ 163 Tyler Green .10 .05
❑ 164 Jim Eisenreich .10 .05
❑ 165 Heathcliff Slocumb .10 .05
❑ 166 Esteban Loaiza .10 .05
❑ 167 Rich Aude .10 .05
❑ 168 Jason Christiansen .10 .05
❑ 169 Ramon Morel .10 .05
❑ 170 Orlando Merced .10 .05
❑ 171 Paul Wagner .10 .05
❑ 172 Jeff King .10 .05
❑ 173 Jay Bell .20 .09
❑ 174 Jacob Brumfield .10 .05
❑ 175 Nelson Liriano .10 .05
❑ 176 Dan Miceli .10 .05
❑ 177 Carlos Garcia .10 .05
❑ 178 Denny Neagle .20 .09
❑ 179 Angelo Encarnacion .10 .05
❑ 180 Al Martin .10 .05
❑ 181 Midre Cummings .10 .05
❑ 182 Eddie Williams .10 .05
❑ 183 Roberto Petagine .10 .05
❑ 184 Tony Gwynn 1.00 .45
❑ 185 Andy Ashby .10 .05
❑ 186 Melvin Nieves .10 .05
❑ 187 Phil Clark .10 .05
❑ 188 Brad Ausmus .10 .05
❑ 189 Bip Roberts .10 .05
❑ 190 Fernando Valenzuela .20 .09
❑ 191 Marc Newfield .10 .05
❑ 192 Steve Finley .20 .09
❑ 193 Trevor Hoffman .20 .09
❑ 194 Andujar Cedeno .10 .05
❑ 195 Jody Reed .10 .05
❑ 196 Ken Caminiti .30 .14
❑ 197 Joey Hamilton .20 .09
❑ 198 Tony Gwynn BAC .50 .23
❑ 199 Shawn Barton .10 .05
❑ 200 Deion Sanders .20 .09
❑ 201 Rikkert Faneyte .10 .05
❑ 202 Barry Bonds .50 .23
❑ 203 Matt Williams .20 .09
❑ 204 Jose Bautista .10 .05
❑ 205 Mark Leiter .10 .05
❑ 206 Mark Carreon .10 .05
❑ 207 Robby Thompson .10 .05
❑ 208 Terry Mulholland .10 .05
❑ 209 Rod Beck .10 .05
❑ 210 Royce Clayton .10 .05
❑ 211 J.R. Phillips .10 .05
❑ 212 Kirt Manwaring .10 .05
❑ 213 Glenallen Hill .10 .05
❑ 214 William VanLandingham .10 .05
❑ 215 Scott Cooper .10 .05
❑ 216 Bernard Gilkey .10 .05
❑ 217 Allen Watson .10 .05
❑ 218 Donovan Osborne .10 .05
❑ 219 Ray Lankford .20 .09
❑ 220 Tony Fossas .10 .05
❑ 221 Tom Pagnozzi .10 .05
❑ 222 John Mabry .10 .05
❑ 223 Tripp Cromer .10 .05
❑ 224 Mark Petkovsek .10 .05
❑ 225 Mike Morgan .10 .05
❑ 226 Ozzie Smith .50 .23
❑ 227 Tom Henke .10 .05
❑ 228 Jose Oquendo .10 .05
❑ 229 Brian Jordan .20 .09
❑ 230 Cal Ripken 1.50 .70
❑ 231 Scott Erickson .20 .09
❑ 232 Harold Baines .20 .09
❑ 233 Jeff Manto .10 .05
❑ 234 Jesse Orosco .10 .05
❑ 235 Jeffrey Hammonds .20 .09
❑ 236 Brady Anderson .20 .09
❑ 237 Manny Alexander .10 .05
❑ 238 Chris Hoiles .10 .05
❑ 239 Rafael Palmeiro .30 .14
❑ 240 Ben McDonald .10 .05
❑ 241 Curtis Goodwin .10 .05
❑ 242 Bobby Bonilla .20 .09
❑ 243 Mike Mussina .40 .18
❑ 244 Kevin Brown .40 .18
❑ 245 Armando Benitez .10 .05
❑ 246 Jose Canseco .40 .18
❑ 247 Erik Hanson .10 .05
❑ 248 Mo Vaughn .50 .23
❑ 249 Tim Naehring .10 .05
❑ 250 Vaughn Eshelman .10 .05
❑ 251 Mike Greenwell .10 .05
❑ 252 Troy O'Leary .20 .09
❑ 253 Tim Wakefield .20 .09
❑ 254 Dwayne Hosey .10 .05
❑ 255 John Valentin .20 .09
❑ 256 Rick Aguilera .10 .05
❑ 257 Mike Macfarlane .10 .05
❑ 258 Roger Clemens .75 .35
❑ 259 Luis Alicea .10 .05
❑ 260 Mo Vaughn MVP .30 .14
❑ 261 Mark Langston .10 .05
❑ 262 Jim Edmonds .30 .14
❑ 263 Rod Correia .10 .05
❑ 264 Tim Salmon .40 .18
❑ 265 J.T. Snow .20 .09
❑ 266 Orlando Palmeiro .10 .05
❑ 267 Jorge Fabregas .10 .05
❑ 268 Jim Abbott .20 .09
❑ 269 Eduardo Perez .10 .05
❑ 270 Lee Smith .20 .09
❑ 271 Gary DiSarcina .10 .05
❑ 272 Damion Easley .20 .09
❑ 273 Tony Phillips .10 .05
❑ 274 Garret Anderson .20 .09
❑ 275 Chuck Finley .20 .09
❑ 276 Chili Davis .20 .09
❑ 277 Lance Johnson .10 .05
❑ 278 Alex Fernandez .10 .05
❑ 279 Robin Ventura .20 .09
❑ 280 Chris Snopek .10 .05
❑ 281 Brian Keyser .10 .05
❑ 282 Lyle Mouton .10 .05
❑ 283 Luis Andujar .10 .05
❑ 284 Tim Raines .20 .09
❑ 285 Larry Thomas .10 .05
❑ 286 Ozzie Guillen .10 .05
❑ 287 Frank Thomas 1.25 .55
❑ 288 Roberto Hernandez .10 .05
❑ 289 Dave Martinez .10 .05
❑ 290 Ray Durham .20 .09
❑ 291 Ron Karkovice .10 .05
❑ 292 Wilson Alvarez .20 .09
❑ 293 Omar Vizquel .20 .09
❑ 294 Eddie Murray .40 .18
❑ 295 Sandy Alomar Jr. .20 .09
❑ 296 Orel Hershiser .20 .09
❑ 297 Jose Mesa .10 .05
❑ 298 Julian Tavarez .10 .05
❑ 299 Dennis Martinez .20 .09
❑ 300 Carlos Baerga .20 .09
❑ 301 Manny Ramirez .40 .18
❑ 302 Jim Thome .40 .18
❑ 303 Kenny Lofton .40 .18
❑ 304 Tony Pena .10 .05
❑ 305 Alvaro Espinoza .10 .05
❑ 306 Paul Sorrento .10 .05
❑ 307 Albert Belle .50 .23
❑ 308 Danny Bautista .10 .05
❑ 309 Chris Gomez .10 .05
❑ 310 Jose Lima .10 .05
❑ 311 Phil Nevin .10 .05
❑ 312 Alan Trammell .30 .14
❑ 313 Chad Curtis .10 .05
❑ 314 John Flaherty .10 .05
❑ 315 Travis Fryman .20 .09
❑ 316 Todd Steverson .10 .05
❑ 317 Brian Bohanon .10 .05
❑ 318 Lou Whitaker .20 .09
❑ 319 Bobby Higginson .40 .18
❑ 320 Steve Rodriguez .10 .05
❑ 321 Cecil Fielder .20 .09
❑ 322 Felipe Lira .10 .05
❑ 323 Juan Samuel .10 .05
❑ 324 Bob Hamelin .10 .05
❑ 325 Tom Goodwin .10 .05
❑ 326 Johnny Damon .20 .09
❑ 327 Hipolito Pichardo .10 .05
❑ 328 Dilson Torres .10 .05
❑ 329 Kevin Appier .20 .09
❑ 330 Mark Gubicza .10 .05
❑ 331 Jon Nunnally .10 .05
❑ 332 Gary Gaetti .20 .09
❑ 333 Brent Mayne .10 .05
❑ 334 Brent Cookson .10 .05
❑ 335 Tom Gordon .10 .05
❑ 336 Wally Joyner .20 .09
❑ 337 Greg Gagne .10 .05
❑ 338 Fernando Vina .10 .05
❑ 339 Joe Oliver .10 .05
❑ 340 John Jaha .10 .05
❑ 341 Jeff Cirillo .20 .09
❑ 342 Pat Listach .10 .05
❑ 343 Dave Nilsson .10 .05
❑ 344 Steve Sparks .10 .05
❑ 345 Ricky Bones .10 .05
❑ 346 David Hulse .10 .05
❑ 347 Scott Karl .10 .05
❑ 348 Darryl Hamilton .10 .05
❑ 349 B.J. Surhoff .20 .09
❑ 350 Angel Miranda .10 .05
❑ 351 Sid Roberson .10 .05
❑ 352 Matt Mieske .10 .05
❑ 353 Jose Valentin .10 .05
❑ 354 Matt Lawton .40 .18

Card	Player	Mint	NrMt
❑ 355	Eddie Guardado	.10	.05
❑ 356	Brad Radke	.20	.09
❑ 357	Pedro Munoz	.10	.05
❑ 358	Scott Stahoviak	.10	.05
❑ 359	Erik Schullstrom	.10	.05
❑ 360	Pat Meares	.10	.05
❑ 361	Marty Cordova	.10	.05
❑ 362	Scott Leius	.10	.05
❑ 363	Matt Walbeck	.10	.05
❑ 364	Rich Becker	.10	.05
❑ 365	Kirby Puckett	.60	.25
❑ 366	Oscar Munoz	.10	.05
❑ 367	Chuck Knoblauch	.40	.18
❑ 368	Marty Cordova ROY	.10	.05
❑ 369	Bernie Williams	.40	.18
❑ 370	Mike Stanley	.10	.05
❑ 371	Andy Pettitte	.30	.14
❑ 372	Jack McDowell	.10	.05
❑ 373	Sterling Hitchcock	.20	.09
❑ 374	David Cone	.30	.14
❑ 375	Randy Velarde	.10	.05
❑ 376	Don Mattingly	.60	.25
❑ 377	Melido Perez	.10	.05
❑ 378	Wade Boggs	.40	.18
❑ 379	Ruben Sierra	.10	.05
❑ 380	Tony Fernandez	.10	.05
❑ 381	John Wetteland	.20	.09
❑ 382	Mariano Rivera	.20	.09
❑ 383	Derek Jeter	1.25	.55
❑ 384	Paul O'Neill	.20	.09
❑ 385	Mark McGwire	2.00	.90
❑ 386	Scott Brosius	.20	.09
❑ 387	Don Wengert	.10	.05
❑ 388	Terry Steinbach	.20	.09
❑ 389	Brent Gates	.10	.05
❑ 390	Craig Paquette	.10	.05
❑ 391	Mike Bordick	.10	.05
❑ 392	Ariel Prieto	.10	.05
❑ 393	Dennis Eckersley	.20	.09
❑ 394	Carlos Reyes	.10	.05
❑ 395	Todd Stottlemyre	.10	.05
❑ 396	Rickey Henderson	.40	.18
❑ 397	Geronimo Berroa	.10	.05
❑ 398	Steve Ontiveros	.10	.05
❑ 399	Mike Gallego	.10	.05
❑ 400	Stan Javier	.10	.05
❑ 401	Randy Johnson	.40	.18
❑ 402	Norm Charlton	.10	.05
❑ 403	Mike Blowers	.10	.05
❑ 404	Tino Martinez	.40	.18
❑ 405	Dan Wilson	.10	.05
❑ 406	Andy Benes	.20	.09
❑ 407	Alex Diaz	.10	.05
❑ 408	Edgar Martinez	.20	.09
❑ 409	Chris Bosio	.10	.05
❑ 410	Ken Griffey, Jr.	2.00	.90
❑ 411	Luis Sojo	.10	.05
❑ 412	Bob Wolcott	.10	.05
❑ 413	Vince Coleman	.10	.05
❑ 414	Rich Amaral	.10	.05
❑ 415	Jay Buhner	.20	.09
❑ 416	Alex Rodriguez	1.25	.55
❑ 417	Joey Cora	.20	.09
❑ 418	Randy Johnson CY	.20	.09
❑ 419	Edgar Martinez BAC	.10	.05
❑ 420	Ivan Rodriguez	.50	.23
❑ 421	Mark McLemore	.10	.05
❑ 422	Mickey Tettleton	.10	.05
❑ 423	Juan Gonzalez	1.00	.45
❑ 424	Will Clark	.40	.18
❑ 425	Kevin Gross	.10	.05
❑ 426	Dean Palmer	.20	.09
❑ 427	Kenny Rogers	.10	.05
❑ 428	Bob Tewksbury	.10	.05
❑ 429	Benji Gil	.10	.05
❑ 430	Jeff Russell	.10	.05
❑ 431	Rusty Greer	.30	.14
❑ 432	Roger Pavlik	.10	.05
❑ 433	Esteban Beltre	.10	.05
❑ 434	Otis Nixon	.10	.05
❑ 435	Paul Molitor	.40	.18
❑ 436	Carlos Delgado	.20	.09
❑ 437	Ed Sprague	.10	.05
❑ 438	Juan Guzman	.10	.05
❑ 439	Domingo Cedeno	.10	.05
❑ 440	Pat Hentgen	.20	.09
❑ 441	Tomas Perez	.10	.05
❑ 442	John Olerud	.20	.09
❑ 443	Shawn Green	.20	.09
❑ 444	Al Leiter	.20	.09
❑ 445	Joe Carter	.20	.09
❑ 446	Robert Perez	.10	.05
❑ 447	Devon White	.20	.09
❑ 448	Tony Castillo	.10	.05
❑ 449	Alex Gonzalez	.10	.05
❑ 450	Roberto Alomar	.40	.18

1996 Pacific Cramer's Choice

	MINT	NRMT
COMPLETE SET (10)	1200.00	550.00
COMMON CARD (CC1-CC10)	25.00	11.00

Card	Player	Mint	NrMt
❑ CC1	Roberto Alomar	50.00	22.00
❑ CC2	Wade Boggs	50.00	22.00
❑ CC3	Cal Ripken	200.00	90.00
❑ CC4	Greg Maddux	150.00	70.00
❑ CC5	Frank Thomas	150.00	70.00
❑ CC6	Tony Gwynn	120.00	55.00
❑ CC7	Mike Piazza	150.00	70.00
❑ CC8	Ken Griffey Jr.	250.00	110.00
❑ CC9	Manny Ramirez	50.00	22.00
❑ CC10	Edgar Martinez	25.00	11.00

1996 Pacific Estrellas Latinas

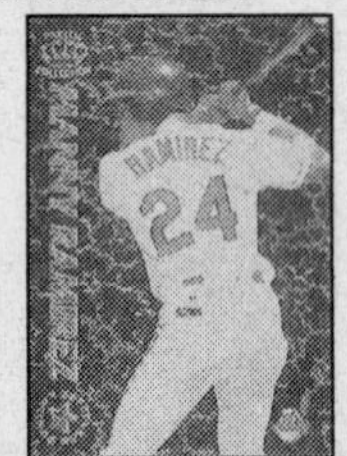

	MINT	NRMT
COMPLETE SET (36)	50.00	22.00
COMMON CARD (EL1-EL36)	.75	.35

Card	Player	Mint	NrMt
❑ EL1	Roberto Alomar	2.50	1.10
❑ EL2	Moises Alou	2.00	.90
❑ EL3	Carlos Baerga	1.25	.55
❑ EL4	Geronimo Berroa	.75	.35
❑ EL5	Ricky Bones	.75	.35
❑ EL6	Bobby Bonilla	1.25	.55
❑ EL7	Jose Canseco	2.50	1.10
❑ EL8	Vinny Castilla	2.00	.90
❑ EL9	Pedro Martinez	2.50	1.10
❑ EL10	John Valentin	1.25	.55
❑ EL11	Andres Galarraga	2.50	1.10
❑ EL12	Juan Gonzalez	8.00	3.60
❑ EL13	Ozzie Guillen	.75	.35
❑ EL14	Esteban Loaiza	.75	.35
❑ EL15	Javier Lopez	1.25	.55
❑ EL16	Dennis Martinez	1.25	.55
❑ EL17	Edgar Martinez	1.25	.55
❑ EL18	Tino Martinez	2.50	1.10
❑ EL19	Orlando Merced	.75	.35
❑ EL20	Jose Mesa	.75	.35
❑ EL21	Raul Mondesi	2.00	.90
❑ EL22	Jaime Navarro	.75	.35
❑ EL23	Rafael Palmeiro	2.00	.90
❑ EL24	Carlos Perez	1.25	.55
❑ EL25	Manny Ramirez	2.50	1.10
❑ EL26	Alex Rodriguez	10.00	4.50
❑ EL27	Ivan Rodriguez	2.50	1.10
❑ EL28	David Segui	1.25	.55
❑ EL29	Ruben Sierra	.75	.35
❑ EL30	Sammy Sosa	8.00	3.60
❑ EL31	Julian Tavarez	.75	.35
❑ EL32	Ismael Valdes	1.25	.55
❑ EL33	Fernando Valenzuela	1.25	.55
❑ EL34	Quilvio Veras	.75	.35
❑ EL35	Omar Vizquel	1.25	.55
❑ EL36	Bernie Williams	2.50	1.10

1996 Pacific Gold Crown Die Cuts

	MINT	NRMT
COMPLETE SET (36)	400.00	180.00
COMMON CARD (DC1-DC36)	3.00	1.35

Card	Player	Mint	NrMt
❑ DC1	Roberto Alomar	8.00	3.60
❑ DC2	Will Clark	8.00	3.60
❑ DC3	Johnny Damon	4.00	1.80
❑ DC4	Don Mattingly	12.00	5.50
❑ DC5	Edgar Martinez	4.00	1.80
❑ DC6	Manny Ramirez	8.00	3.60
❑ DC7	Mike Piazza	25.00	11.00
❑ DC8	Quilvio Veras	3.00	1.35
❑ DC9	Rickey Henderson	8.00	3.60
❑ DC10	Jeff Bagwell	12.00	5.50
❑ DC11	Andres Galarraga	8.00	3.60
❑ DC12	Tim Salmon	8.00	3.60
❑ DC13	Ken Griffey Jr.	40.00	18.00
❑ DC14	Sammy Sosa	20.00	9.00
❑ DC15	Cal Ripken	30.00	13.50
❑ DC16	Raul Mondesi	5.00	2.20
❑ DC17	Jose Canseco	8.00	3.60
❑ DC18	Frank Thomas	25.00	11.00
❑ DC19	Hideo Nomo	12.00	5.50
❑ DC20	Wade Boggs	8.00	3.60
❑ DC21	Reggie Sanders	4.00	1.80
❑ DC22	Carlos Baerga	4.00	1.80
❑ DC23	Mo Vaughn	10.00	4.50
❑ DC24	Ivan Rodriguez	10.00	4.50
❑ DC25	Kirby Puckett	12.00	5.50
❑ DC26	Albert Belle	10.00	4.50
❑ DC27	Vinny Castilla	5.00	2.20
❑ DC28	Greg Maddux	25.00	11.00
❑ DC29	Dante Bichette	4.00	1.80
❑ DC30	Deion Sanders	4.00	1.80
❑ DC31	Chipper Jones	20.00	9.00
❑ DC32	Cecil Fielder	4.00	1.80
❑ DC33	Randy Johnson	8.00	3.60
❑ DC34	Mark McGwire	40.00	18.00
❑ DC35	Tony Gwynn	20.00	9.00
❑ DC36	Barry Bonds	10.00	4.50

1996 Pacific Hometowns

	MINT	NRMT
COMPLETE SET (20)	100.00	45.00
COMMON CARD (HP1-HP20)	1.50	.70

	MINT	NRMT
❑ HP1 Mike Piazza	12.00	5.50
❑ HP2 Greg Maddux	12.00	5.50
❑ HP3 Tony Gwynn	10.00	4.50
❑ HP4 Carlos Baerga	2.00	.90
❑ HP5 Don Mattingly	6.00	2.70
❑ HP6 Cal Ripken	15.00	6.75
❑ HP7 Chipper Jones	10.00	4.50
❑ HP8 Andres Galarraga	4.00	1.80
❑ HP9 Manny Ramirez	4.00	1.80
❑ HP10 Roberto Alomar	4.00	1.80
❑ HP11 Ken Griffey Jr.	20.00	9.00
❑ HP12 Jose Canseco	4.00	1.80
❑ HP13 Frank Thomas	12.00	5.50
❑ HP14 Vinny Castilla	2.50	1.10
❑ HP15 Roberto Kelly	1.50	.70
❑ HP16 Dennis Martinez	2.00	.90
❑ HP17 Kirby Puckett	6.00	2.70
❑ HP18 Raul Mondesi	2.50	1.10
❑ HP19 Hideo Nomo	6.00	2.70
❑ HP20 Edgar Martinez	2.00	.90

1996 Pacific Milestones

	MINT	NRMT
COMPLETE SET (10)	60.00	27.00
COMMON CARD (M1-M10)	2.50	1.10

	MINT	NRMT
❑ M1 Albert Belle	5.00	2.20
❑ M2 Don Mattingly	6.00	2.70
❑ M3 Tony Gwynn	10.00	4.50
❑ M4 Jose Canseco	4.00	1.80
❑ M5 Marty Cordova	2.50	1.10
❑ M6 Wade Boggs	4.00	1.80
❑ M7 Greg Maddux	12.00	5.50
❑ M8 Eddie Murray	4.00	1.80
❑ M9 Ken Griffey Jr.	20.00	9.00
❑ M10 Cal Ripken	15.00	6.75

1996 Pacific October Moments

	MINT	NRMT
COMPLETE SET (20)	150.00	70.00
COMMON CARD (OM1-OM20)	2.00	.90

	MINT	NRMT
❑ OM1 Carlos Baerga	2.00	.90
❑ OM2 Albert Belle	8.00	3.60
❑ OM3 Dante Bichette	3.00	1.35
❑ OM4 Jose Canseco	6.00	2.70
❑ OM5 Tom Glavine	6.00	2.70
❑ OM6 Ken Griffey Jr.	30.00	13.50
❑ OM7 Randy Johnson	6.00	2.70
❑ OM8 Chipper Jones	15.00	6.75
❑ OM9 David Justice	6.00	2.70
❑ OM10 Ryan Klesko	3.00	1.35
❑ OM11 Kenny Lofton	6.00	2.70
❑ OM12 Javier Lopez	3.00	1.35
❑ OM13 Greg Maddux	20.00	9.00
❑ OM14 Edgar Martinez	3.00	1.35
❑ OM15 Don Mattingly	10.00	4.50
❑ OM16 Hideo Nomo	10.00	4.50
❑ OM17 Mike Piazza	20.00	9.00
❑ OM18 Manny Ramirez	6.00	2.70
❑ OM19 Reggie Sanders	2.00	.90
❑ OM20 Jim Thome	6.00	2.70

1997 Pacific

	MINT	NRMT
COMPLETE SET (450)	40.00	18.00
COMMON CARD (1-450)	.15	.07

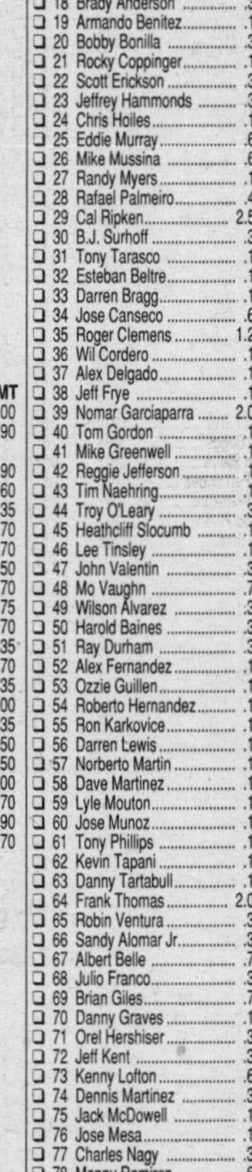

	MINT	NRMT
❑ 1 Garret Anderson	.30	.14
❑ 2 George Arias	.15	.07
❑ 3 Chili Davis	.30	.14
❑ 4 Gary DiSarcina	.15	.07
❑ 5 Jim Edmonds	.40	.18
❑ 6 Darin Erstad	1.00	.45
❑ 7 Jorge Fabregas	.15	.07
❑ 8 Chuck Finley	.30	.14
❑ 9 Rex Hudler	.15	.07
❑ 10 Mark Langston	.30	.14
❑ 11 Orlando Palmeiro	.15	.07
❑ 12 Troy Percival	.30	.14
❑ 13 Tim Salmon	.60	.25
❑ 14 J.T. Snow	.30	.14
❑ 15 Randy Velarde	.15	.07
❑ 16 Manny Alexander	.15	.07
❑ 17 Roberto Alomar	.60	.25
❑ 18 Brady Anderson	.30	.14
❑ 19 Armando Benitez	.15	.07
❑ 20 Bobby Bonilla	.30	.14
❑ 21 Rocky Coppinger	.15	.07
❑ 22 Scott Erickson	.30	.14
❑ 23 Jeffrey Hammonds	.30	.14
❑ 24 Chris Hoiles	.15	.07
❑ 25 Eddie Murray	.60	.25
❑ 26 Mike Mussina	.60	.25
❑ 27 Randy Myers	.15	.07
❑ 28 Rafael Palmeiro	.40	.18
❑ 29 Cal Ripken	2.50	1.10
❑ 30 B.J. Surhoff	.30	.14
❑ 31 Tony Tarasco	.15	.07
❑ 32 Esteban Beltre	.15	.07
❑ 33 Darren Bragg	.15	.07
❑ 34 Jose Canseco	.60	.25
❑ 35 Roger Clemens	1.25	.55
❑ 36 Wil Cordero	.15	.07
❑ 37 Alex Delgado	.15	.07
❑ 38 Jeff Frye	.15	.07
❑ 39 Nomar Garciaparra	2.00	.90
❑ 40 Tom Gordon	.15	.07
❑ 41 Mike Greenwell	.15	.07
❑ 42 Reggie Jefferson	.15	.07
❑ 43 Tim Naehring	.15	.07
❑ 44 Troy O'Leary	.30	.14
❑ 45 Heathcliff Slocumb	.15	.07
❑ 46 Lee Tinsley	.15	.07
❑ 47 John Valentin	.30	.14
❑ 48 Mo Vaughn	.75	.35
❑ 49 Wilson Alvarez	.30	.14
❑ 50 Harold Baines	.30	.14
❑ 51 Ray Durham	.30	.14
❑ 52 Alex Fernandez	.15	.07
❑ 53 Ozzie Guillen	.15	.07
❑ 54 Roberto Hernandez	.15	.07
❑ 55 Ron Karkovice	.15	.07
❑ 56 Darren Lewis	.15	.07
❑ 57 Norberto Martin	.15	.07
❑ 58 Dave Martinez	.15	.07
❑ 59 Lyle Mouton	.15	.07
❑ 60 Jose Munoz	.15	.07
❑ 61 Tony Phillips	.15	.07
❑ 62 Kevin Tapani	.15	.07
❑ 63 Danny Tartabull	.15	.07
❑ 64 Frank Thomas	2.00	.90
❑ 65 Robin Ventura	.30	.14
❑ 66 Sandy Alomar Jr.	.30	.14
❑ 67 Albert Belle	.75	.35
❑ 68 Julio Franco	.30	.14
❑ 69 Brian Giles	.75	.35
❑ 70 Danny Graves	.15	.07
❑ 71 Orel Hershiser	.30	.14
❑ 72 Jeff Kent	.30	.14
❑ 73 Kenny Lofton	.60	.25
❑ 74 Dennis Martinez	.30	.14
❑ 75 Jack McDowell	.15	.07
❑ 76 Jose Mesa	.15	.07
❑ 77 Charles Nagy	.30	.14
❑ 78 Manny Ramirez	.60	.25
❑ 79 Julian Tavarez	.15	.07
❑ 80 Jim Thome	.60	.25
❑ 81 Jose Vizcaino	.15	.07
❑ 82 Omar Vizquel	.30	.14
❑ 83 Brad Ausmus	.15	.07
❑ 84 Kimera Bartee	.15	.07
❑ 85 Raul Casanova	.15	.07
❑ 86 Tony Clark	.40	.18
❑ 87 Travis Fryman	.30	.14
❑ 88 Bobby Higginson	.40	.18
❑ 89 Mark Lewis	.15	.07
❑ 90 Jose Lima	.15	.07
❑ 91 Felipe Lira	.15	.07
❑ 92 Phil Nevin	.15	.07
❑ 93 Melvin Nieves	.15	.07
❑ 94 Curtis Pride	.15	.07
❑ 95 Ruben Sierra	.15	.07
❑ 96 Alan Trammell	.30	.14
❑ 97 Kevin Appier	.30	.14
❑ 98 Tim Belcher	.15	.07
❑ 99 Johnny Damon	.30	.14
❑ 100 Tom Goodwin	.15	.07
❑ 101 Bob Hamelin	.15	.07

❑	102	David Howard	.15	.07
❑	103	Jason Jacome	.15	.07
❑	104	Keith Lockhart	.15	.07
❑	105	Mike Macfarlane	.15	.07
❑	106	Jeff Montgomery	.15	.07
❑	107	Jose Offerman	.15	.07
❑	108	Hipolito Pichardo	.15	.07
❑	109	Joe Randa	.15	.07
❑	110	Bip Roberts	.15	.07
❑	111	Chris Stynes	.15	.07
❑	112	Mike Sweeney	.15	.07
❑	113	Joe Vitiello	.15	.07
❑	114	Jeromy Burnitz	.30	.14
❑	115	Chuck Carr	.15	.07
❑	116	Jeff Cirillo	.30	.14
❑	117	Mike Fetters	.15	.07
❑	118	David Hulse	.15	.07
❑	119	John Jaha	.15	.07
❑	120	Scott Karl	.15	.07
❑	121	Jesse Levis	.15	.07
❑	122	Mark Loretta	.15	.07
❑	123	Mike Matheny	.15	.07
❑	124	Ben McDonald	.15	.07
❑	125	Matt Mieske	.15	.07
❑	126	Angel Miranda	.15	.07
❑	127	Dave Nilsson	.15	.07
❑	128	Jose Valentin	.15	.07
❑	129	Fernando Vina	.15	.07
❑	130	Ron Villone	.15	.07
❑	131	Gerald Williams	.15	.07
❑	132	Rick Aguilera	.15	.07
❑	133	Rich Becker	.15	.07
❑	134	Ron Coomer	.15	.07
❑	135	Marty Cordova	.15	.07
❑	136	Eddie Guardado	.15	.07
❑	137	Denny Hocking	.15	.07
❑	138	Roberto Kelly	.15	.07
❑	139	Chuck Knoblauch	.60	.25
❑	140	Matt Lawton	.30	.14
❑	141	Pat Meares	.15	.07
❑	142	Paul Molitor	.60	.25
❑	143	Greg Myers	.15	.07
❑	144	Jeff Reboulet	.15	.07
❑	145	Scott Stahoviak	.15	.07
❑	146	Todd Walker	.60	.25
❑	147	Wade Boggs	.60	.25
❑	148	David Cone	.40	.18
❑	149	Mariano Duncan	.15	.07
❑	150	Cecil Fielder	.30	.14
❑	151	Dwight Gooden	.30	.14
❑	152	Derek Jeter	2.00	.90
❑	153	Jim Leyritz	.15	.07
❑	154	Tino Martinez	.60	.25
❑	155	Paul O'Neill	.30	.14
❑	156	Andy Pettitte	.40	.18
❑	157	Tim Raines	.30	.14
❑	158	Mariano Rivera	.30	.14
❑	159	Ruben Rivera	.30	.14
❑	160	Kenny Rogers	.15	.07
❑	161	Darryl Strawberry	.30	.14
❑	162	John Wetteland	.30	.14
❑	163	Bernie Williams	.60	.25
❑	164	Tony Batista	.15	.07
❑	165	Geronimo Berroa	.15	.07
❑	166	Mike Bordick	.15	.07
❑	167	Scott Brosius	.30	.14
❑	168	Brent Gates	.15	.07
❑	169	Jason Giambi	.30	.14
❑	170	Jose Herrera	.15	.07
❑	171	Brian Lesher	.15	.07
❑	172	Damon Mashore	.15	.07
❑	173	Mark McGwire	3.00	1.35
❑	174	Ariel Prieto	.15	.07
❑	175	Carlos Reyes	.15	.07
❑	176	Matt Stairs	.30	.14
❑	177	Terry Steinbach	.30	.14
❑	178	John Wasdin	.15	.07
❑	179	Ernie Young	.15	.07
❑	180	Rich Amaral	.15	.07
❑	181	Bobby Ayala	.15	.07
❑	182	Jay Buhner	.30	.14
❑	183	Rafael Carmona	.15	.07
❑	184	Norm Charlton	.15	.07
❑	185	Joey Cora	.30	.14
❑	186	Ken Griffey Jr.	3.00	1.35
❑	187	Sterling Hitchcock	.30	.14
❑	188	Dave Hollins	.15	.07
❑	189	Randy Johnson	.60	.25
❑	190	Edgar Martinez	.30	.14
❑	191	Jamie Moyer	.15	.07
❑	192	Alex Rodriguez	2.00	.90
❑	193	Paul Sorrento	.15	.07
❑	194	Salomon Torres	.15	.07
❑	195	Bob Wells	.15	.07
❑	196	Dan Wilson	.15	.07
❑	197	Will Clark	.60	.25
❑	198	Kevin Elster	.15	.07
❑	199	Rene Gonzales	.15	.07
❑	200	Juan Gonzalez	1.50	.70
❑	201	Rusty Greer	.30	.14
❑	202	Darryl Hamilton	.15	.07
❑	203	Mike Henneman	.15	.07
❑	204	Ken Hill	.15	.07
❑	205	Mark McLemore	.15	.07
❑	206	Darren Oliver	.15	.07
❑	207	Dean Palmer	.30	.14
❑	208	Roger Pavlik	.15	.07
❑	209	Ivan Rodriguez	.75	.35
❑	210	Kurt Stillwell	.15	.07
❑	211	Mickey Tettleton	.15	.07
❑	212	Bobby Witt	.15	.07
❑	213	Tilson Brito	.15	.07
❑	214	Jacob Brumfield	.15	.07
❑	215	Miguel Cairo	.30	.14
❑	216	Joe Carter	.30	.14
❑	217	Felipe Crespo	.15	.07
❑	218	Carlos Delgado	.30	.14
❑	219	Alex Gonzalez	.15	.07
❑	220	Shawn Green	.30	.14
❑	221	Juan Guzman	.15	.07
❑	222	Pat Hentgen	.30	.14
❑	223	Charlie O'Brien	.15	.07
❑	224	John Olerud	.30	.14
❑	225	Robert Perez	.15	.07
❑	226	Tomas Perez	.15	.07
❑	227	Juan Samuel	.15	.07
❑	228	Ed Sprague	.15	.07
❑	229	Mike Timlin	.15	.07
❑	230	Rafael Belliard	.15	.07
❑	231	Jermaine Dye	.15	.07
❑	232	Tom Glavine	.60	.25
❑	233	Marquis Grissom	.30	.14
❑	234	Andruw Jones	1.00	.45
❑	235	Chipper Jones	1.50	.70
❑	236	David Justice	.60	.25
❑	237	Ryan Klesko	.30	.14
❑	238	Mark Lemke	.15	.07
❑	239	Javier Lopez	.30	.14
❑	240	Greg Maddux	2.00	.90
❑	241	Fred McGriff	.40	.18
❑	242	Denny Neagle	.30	.14
❑	243	Eddie Perez	.15	.07
❑	244	John Smoltz	.30	.14
❑	245	Mark Wohlers	.15	.07
❑	246	Brant Brown	.30	.14
❑	247	Scott Bullett	.15	.07
❑	248	Leo Gomez	.15	.07
❑	249	Luis Gonzalez	.15	.07
❑	250	Mark Grace	.40	.18
❑	251	Jose Hernandez	.15	.07
❑	252	Brooks Kieschnick	.15	.07
❑	253	Brian McRae	.15	.07
❑	254	Jaime Navarro	.15	.07
❑	255	Mike Perez	.15	.07
❑	256	Rey Sanchez	.15	.07
❑	257	Ryne Sandberg	.75	.35
❑	258	Scott Servais	.15	.07
❑	259	Sammy Sosa	1.50	.70
❑	260	Pedro Valdes	.15	.07
❑	261	Turk Wendell	.15	.07
❑	262	Bret Boone	.30	.14
❑	263	Jeff Branson	.15	.07
❑	264	Jeff Brantley	.15	.07
❑	265	Dave Burba	.15	.07
❑	266	Hector Carrasco	.15	.07
❑	267	Eric Davis	.30	.14
❑	268	Willie Greene	.30	.14
❑	269	Lenny Harris	.15	.07
❑	270	Thomas Howard	.15	.07
❑	271	Barry Larkin	.40	.18
❑	272	Hal Morris	.15	.07
❑	273	Joe Oliver	.15	.07
❑	274	Eric Owens	.15	.07
❑	275	Jose Rijo	.15	.07
❑	276	Reggie Sanders	.30	.14
❑	277	Eddie Taubensee	.15	.07
❑	278	Jason Bates	.15	.07
❑	279	Dante Bichette	.30	.14
❑	280	Ellis Burks	.30	.14
❑	281	Vinny Castilla	.40	.18
❑	282	Andres Galarraga	.60	.25
❑	283	Quinton McCracken	.30	.14
❑	284	Jayhawk Owens	.15	.07
❑	285	Jeff Reed	.15	.07
❑	286	Bryan Rekar	.15	.07
❑	287	Armando Reynoso	.15	.07
❑	288	Kevin Ritz	.15	.07
❑	289	Bruce Ruffin	.15	.07
❑	290	John Vander Wal	.15	.07
❑	291	Larry Walker	.60	.25
❑	292	Walt Weiss	.15	.07
❑	293	Eric Young	.30	.14
❑	294	Kurt Abbott	.15	.07
❑	295	Alex Arias	.15	.07
❑	296	Miguel Batista	.15	.07
❑	297	Kevin Brown	.40	.18
❑	298	Luis Castillo	.30	.14
❑	299	Greg Colbrunn	.15	.07
❑	300	Jeff Conine	.30	.14
❑	301	Charles Johnson	.30	.14
❑	302	Al Leiter	.30	.14
❑	303	Robb Nen	.15	.07
❑	304	Joe Orsulak	.15	.07
❑	305	Yorkis Perez	.15	.07
❑	306	Edgar Renteria	.30	.14
❑	307	Gary Sheffield	.40	.18
❑	308	Jesus Tavarez	.15	.07
❑	309	Quilvio Veras	.15	.07
❑	310	Devon White	.30	.14
❑	311	Jeff Bagwell	1.00	.45
❑	312	Derek Bell	.30	.14
❑	313	Sean Berry	.15	.07
❑	314	Craig Biggio	.60	.25
❑	315	Doug Drabek	.15	.07
❑	316	Tony Eusebio	.15	.07
❑	317	Ricky Gutierrez	.15	.07
❑	318	Xavier Hernandez	.15	.07
❑	319	Brian L. Hunter	.30	.14
❑	320	Darryl Kile	.30	.14
❑	321	Derrick May	.15	.07
❑	322	Orlando Miller	.15	.07
❑	323	James Mouton	.15	.07
❑	324	Bill Spiers	.15	.07
❑	325	Pedro Astacio	.15	.07
❑	326	Brett Butler	.30	.14
❑	327	Juan Castro	.15	.07
❑	328	Roger Cedeno	.15	.07
❑	329	Delino DeShields	.15	.07
❑	330	Karim Garcia	.30	.14
❑	331	Todd Hollandsworth	.15	.07
❑	332	Eric Karros	.30	.14
❑	333	Oreste Marrero	.15	.07
❑	334	Ramon Martinez	.30	.14
❑	335	Raul Mondesi	.40	.18
❑	336	Hideo Nomo	.75	.35
❑	337	Antonio Osuna	.15	.07
❑	338	Chan Ho Park	.60	.25
❑	339	Mike Piazza	2.00	.90
❑	340	Ismael Valdes	.30	.14
❑	341	Moises Alou	.40	.18
❑	342	Omar Daal	.15	.07
❑	343	Jeff Fassero	.15	.07
❑	344	Cliff Floyd	.30	.14
❑	345	Mark Grudzielanek	.30	.14
❑	346	Mike Lansing	.15	.07
❑	347	Pedro Martinez	.60	.25
❑	348	Sherman Obando	.15	.07
❑	349	Jose Paniagua	.15	.07
❑	350	Henry Rodriguez	.30	.14
❑	351	Mel Rojas	.15	.07
❑	352	F.P. Santangelo	.15	.07
❑	353	David Segui	.30	.14
❑	354	Dave Silvestri	.15	.07
❑	355	Ugueth Urbina	.30	.14
❑	356	Rondell White	.30	.14

❑ 357 Edgardo Alfonzo	.30	.14
❑ 358 Carlos Baerga	.30	.14
❑ 359 Tim Bogar	.15	.07
❑ 360 Rico Brogna	.15	.07
❑ 361 Alvaro Espinoza	.15	.07
❑ 362 Carl Everett	.15	.07
❑ 363 John Franco	.30	.14
❑ 364 Bernard Gilkey	.15	.07
❑ 365 Todd Hundley	.30	.14
❑ 366 Butch Huskey	.15	.07
❑ 367 Jason Isringhausen	.15	.07
❑ 368 Bobby Jones	.15	.07
❑ 369 Lance Johnson	.15	.07
❑ 370 Brent Mayne	.15	.07
❑ 371 Alex Ochoa	.15	.07
❑ 372 Rey Ordonez	.30	.14
❑ 373 Ron Blazier	.15	.07
❑ 374 Ricky Bottalico	.30	.14
❑ 375 David Doster	.15	.07
❑ 376 Lenny Dykstra	.30	.14
❑ 377 Jim Eisenreich	.15	.07
❑ 378 Bobby Estalella	.30	.14
❑ 379 Gregg Jefferies	.15	.07
❑ 380 Kevin Jordan	.15	.07
❑ 381 Ricardo Jordan	.15	.07
❑ 382 Mickey Morandini	.15	.07
❑ 383 Ricky Otero	.15	.07
❑ 384 Benito Santiago	.15	.07
❑ 385 Gene Schall	.15	.07
❑ 386 Curt Schilling	.30	.14
❑ 387 Kevin Sefcik	.15	.07
❑ 388 Kevin Stocker	.15	.07
❑ 389 Jermaine Allensworth	.15	.07
❑ 390 Jay Bell	.30	.14
❑ 391 Jason Christiansen	.15	.07
❑ 392 Francisco Cordova	.15	.07
❑ 393 Mark Johnson	.15	.07
❑ 394 Jason Kendall	.40	.18
❑ 395 Jeff King	.15	.07
❑ 396 Jon Lieber	.15	.07
❑ 397 Nelson Liriano	.15	.07
❑ 398 Esteban Loaiza	.15	.07
❑ 399 Al Martin	.15	.07
❑ 400 Orlando Merced	.15	.07
❑ 401 Ramon Morel	.15	.07
❑ 402 Luis Alicea	.15	.07
❑ 403 Alan Benes	.30	.14
❑ 404 Andy Benes	.30	.14
❑ 405 Terry Bradshaw	.15	.07
❑ 406 Royce Clayton	.15	.07
❑ 407 Dennis Eckersley	.30	.14
❑ 408 Gary Gaetti	.15	.07
❑ 409 Mike Gallego	.15	.07
❑ 410 Ron Gant	.15	.07
❑ 411 Brian Jordan	.30	.14
❑ 412 Ray Lankford	.30	.14
❑ 413 John Mabry	.15	.07
❑ 414 Willie McGee	.30	.14
❑ 415 Tom Pagnozzi	.15	.07
❑ 416 Ozzie Smith	.75	.35
❑ 417 Todd Stottlemyre	.15	.07
❑ 418 Mark Sweeney	.15	.07
❑ 419 Andy Ashby	.15	.07
❑ 420 Ken Caminiti	.40	.18
❑ 421 Archi Cianfrocco	.15	.07
❑ 422 Steve Finley	.30	.14
❑ 423 Chris Gomez	.15	.07
❑ 424 Tony Gwynn	1.50	.70
❑ 425 Joey Hamilton	.30	.14
❑ 426 Rickey Henderson	.60	.25
❑ 427 Trevor Hoffman	.30	.14
❑ 428 Brian Johnson	.15	.07
❑ 429 Wally Joyner	.30	.14
❑ 430 Scott Livingstone	.15	.07
❑ 431 Jody Reed	.15	.07
❑ 432 Craig Shipley	.15	.07
❑ 433 Fernando Valenzuela	.30	.14
❑ 434 Greg Vaughn	.30	.14
❑ 435 Rich Aurilia	.15	.07
❑ 436 Kim Batiste	.15	.07
❑ 437 Jose Bautista	.15	.07
❑ 438 Rod Beck	.15	.07
❑ 439 Marvin Benard	.15	.07
❑ 440 Barry Bonds	.75	.35
❑ 441 Shawon Dunston	.15	.07
❑ 442 Shawn Estes	.30	.14
❑ 443 Osvaldo Fernandez	.15	.07
❑ 444 Stan Javier	.15	.07
❑ 445 David McCarty	.15	.07
❑ 446 Bill Mueller	.75	.35
❑ 447 Steve Scarsone	.15	.07
❑ 448 Robby Thompson	.15	.07
❑ 449 Rick Wilkins	.15	.07
❑ 450 Matt Williams	.30	.14

1997 Pacific Card-Supials

	MINT	NRMT
COMP.LARGE SET (36)	300.00	135.00
COMMON LARGE (1-36)	1.50	.70
COMP.MINI SET (36)	200.00	90.00

*MINIS: .25X TO .6X BASIC CARDS
STATED ODDS 1:37
LARGE CARDS LISTED BELOW

❑ 1 Roberto Alomar	6.00	2.70
❑ 2 Brady Anderson	3.00	1.35
❑ 3 Eddie Murray	6.00	2.70
❑ 4 Cal Ripken	25.00	11.00
❑ 5 Jose Canseco	6.00	2.70
❑ 6 Mo Vaughn	8.00	3.60
❑ 7 Frank Thomas	20.00	9.00
❑ 8 Albert Belle	8.00	3.60
❑ 9 Omar Vizquel	3.00	1.35
❑ 10 Chuck Knoblauch	6.00	2.70
❑ 11 Paul Molitor	6.00	2.70
❑ 12 Wade Boggs	6.00	2.70
❑ 13 Derek Jeter	15.00	6.75
❑ 14 Andy Pettitte	4.00	1.80
❑ 15 Mark McGwire	30.00	13.50
❑ 16 Jay Buhner	3.00	1.35
❑ 17 Ken Griffey Jr.	30.00	13.50
❑ 18 Alex Rodriguez	20.00	9.00
❑ 19 Juan Gonzalez	15.00	6.75
❑ 20 Ivan Rodriguez	8.00	3.60
❑ 21 Andruw Jones	10.00	4.50
❑ 22 Chipper Jones	15.00	6.75
❑ 23 Ryan Klesko	3.00	1.35
❑ 24 Greg Maddux	20.00	9.00
❑ 25 Ryne Sandberg	8.00	3.60
❑ 26 Andres Galarraga	6.00	2.70
❑ 27 Gary Sheffield	4.00	1.80
❑ 28 Jeff Bagwell	10.00	4.50
❑ 29 Todd Hollandsworth	1.50	.70
❑ 30 Hideo Nomo	8.00	3.60
❑ 31 Mike Piazza	20.00	9.00
❑ 32 Todd Hundley	3.00	1.35
❑ 33 Dennis Eckersley	3.00	1.35
❑ 34 Ken Caminiti	4.00	1.80
❑ 35 Tony Gwynn	15.00	6.75
❑ 36 Barry Bonds	8.00	3.60

1997 Pacific Cramer's Choice

	MINT	NRMT
COMPLETE SET (10)	800.00	350.00
COMMON CARD (1-10)	20.00	9.00

❑ 1 Roberto Alomar	40.00	18.00
❑ 2 Frank Thomas	120.00	55.00
❑ 3 Albert Belle	40.00	18.00
❑ 4 Andy Pettitte	25.00	11.00
❑ 5 Ken Griffey Jr.	200.00	90.00
❑ 6 Alex Rodriguez	120.00	55.00
❑ 7 Chipper Jones	100.00	45.00
❑ 8 John Smoltz	20.00	9.00
❑ 9 Mike Piazza	120.00	55.00
❑ 10 Tony Gwynn	100.00	45.00

1997 Pacific Fireworks Die Cuts

	MINT	NRMT
COMPLETE SET (20)	400.00	180.00
COMMON CARD (1-20)	2.50	1.10

❑ 1 Roberto Alomar	10.00	4.50
❑ 2 Brady Anderson	5.00	2.20
❑ 3 Eddie Murray	10.00	4.50
❑ 4 Cal Ripken	40.00	18.00
❑ 5 Frank Thomas	30.00	13.50
❑ 6 Albert Belle	12.00	5.50
❑ 7 Derek Jeter	25.00	11.00
❑ 8 Andy Pettitte	6.00	2.70
❑ 9 Bernie Williams	10.00	4.50
❑ 10 Mark McGwire	50.00	22.00
❑ 11 Ken Griffey Jr.	50.00	22.00
❑ 12 Alex Rodriguez	30.00	13.50
❑ 13 Juan Gonzalez	25.00	11.00
❑ 14 Andruw Jones	12.00	5.50
❑ 15 Chipper Jones	25.00	11.00
❑ 16 Hideo Nomo	12.00	5.50
❑ 17 Mike Piazza	30.00	13.50
❑ 18 Henry Rodriguez	2.50	1.10
❑ 19 Tony Gwynn	25.00	11.00
❑ 20 Barry Bonds	12.00	5.50

1997 Pacific Gold Crown Die Cuts

	MINT	NRMT
COMPLETE SET (36)	400.00	180.00
COMMON CARD (1-36)	2.00	.90

❑ 1 Roberto Alomar	8.00	3.60
❑ 2 Brady Anderson	4.00	1.80
❑ 3 Mike Mussina	8.00	3.60
❑ 4 Eddie Murray	8.00	3.60
❑ 5 Cal Ripken	30.00	13.50

❑ 6 Jose Canseco	8.00	3.60
❑ 7 Frank Thomas	25.00	11.00
❑ 8 Albert Belle	8.00	3.60
❑ 9 Omar Vizquel	4.00	1.80
❑ 10 Wade Boggs	8.00	3.60
❑ 11 Derek Jeter	20.00	9.00
❑ 12 Andy Pettitte	5.00	2.20
❑ 13 Mariano Rivera	4.00	1.80
❑ 14 Bernie Williams	8.00	3.60
❑ 15 Mark McGwire	40.00	18.00
❑ 16 Ken Griffey Jr.	40.00	18.00
❑ 17 Edgar Martinez	4.00	1.80
❑ 18 Alex Rodriguez	25.00	11.00
❑ 19 Juan Gonzalez	20.00	9.00
❑ 20 Ivan Rodriguez	10.00	4.50
❑ 21 Andruw Jones	10.00	4.50
❑ 22 Chipper Jones	20.00	9.00
❑ 23 Ryan Klesko	4.00	1.80
❑ 24 John Smoltz	4.00	1.80
❑ 25 Ryne Sandberg	10.00	4.50
❑ 26 Andres Galarraga	8.00	3.60
❑ 27 Edgar Renteria	4.00	1.80
❑ 28 Jeff Bagwell	12.00	5.50
❑ 29 Todd Hollandsworth	2.00	.90
❑ 30 Hideo Nomo	10.00	4.50
❑ 31 Mike Piazza	25.00	11.00
❑ 32 Todd Hundley	4.00	1.80
❑ 33 Brian Jordan	4.00	1.80
❑ 34 Ken Caminiti	5.00	2.20
❑ 35 Tony Gwynn	20.00	9.00
❑ 36 Barry Bonds	10.00	4.50

1997 Pacific Latinos of the Major Leagues

	MINT	NRMT
COMPLETE SET (36)	80.00	36.00
COMMON CARD (1-36)	1.00	.45
❑ 1 George Arias	1.00	.45
❑ 2 Roberto Alomar	4.00	1.80
❑ 3 Rafael Palmeiro	2.50	1.10
❑ 4 Bobby Bonilla	2.00	.90
❑ 5 Jose Canseco	4.00	1.80
❑ 6 Wilson Alvarez	2.00	.90
❑ 7 Dave Martinez	1.00	.45
❑ 8 Julio Franco	2.00	.90
❑ 9 Manny Ramirez	4.00	1.80
❑ 10 Omar Vizquel	2.00	.90
❑ 11 Marty Cordova	1.00	.45
❑ 12 Roberto Kelly	1.00	.45
❑ 13 Tino Martinez	4.00	1.80
❑ 14 Mariano Rivera	2.00	.90
❑ 15 Ruben Rivera	2.00	.90
❑ 16 Bernie Williams	4.00	1.80
❑ 17 Geronimo Berroa	1.00	.45
❑ 18 Joey Cora	2.00	.90
❑ 19 Edgar Martinez	2.00	.90
❑ 20 Alex Rodriguez	12.00	5.50
❑ 21 Juan Gonzalez	10.00	4.50
❑ 22 Ivan Rodriguez	5.00	2.20
❑ 23 Andruw Jones	6.00	2.70
❑ 24 Javier Lopez	2.00	.90
❑ 25 Sammy Sosa	10.00	4.50
❑ 26 Vinny Castilla	2.50	1.10
❑ 27 Andres Galarraga	4.00	1.80
❑ 28 Ramon Martinez	2.00	.90
❑ 29 Raul Mondesi	2.50	1.10
❑ 30 Ismael Valdes	2.00	.90
❑ 31 Pedro Martinez	4.00	1.80
❑ 32 Henry Rodriguez	2.00	.90
❑ 33 Carlos Baerga	2.00	.90
❑ 34 Rey Ordonez	2.00	.90
❑ 35 Fernando Valenzuela	2.00	.90
❑ 36 Osvaldo Fernandez	1.00	.45

1997 Pacific Triple Crown Die Cuts

	MINT	NRMT
COMPLETE SET (20)	600.00	275.00
COMMON CARD (1-20)	8.00	3.60
❑ 1 Brady Anderson	8.00	3.60
❑ 2 Rafael Palmeiro	10.00	4.50
❑ 3 Mo Vaughn	20.00	9.00
❑ 4 Frank Thomas	50.00	22.00
❑ 5 Albert Belle	20.00	9.00
❑ 6 Jim Thome	15.00	6.75
❑ 7 Cecil Fielder	8.00	3.60
❑ 8 Mark McGwire	80.00	36.00
❑ 9 Ken Griffey Jr.	80.00	36.00
❑ 10 Alex Rodriguez	50.00	22.00
❑ 11 Juan Gonzalez	40.00	18.00
❑ 12 Andruw Jones	20.00	9.00
❑ 13 Chipper Jones	40.00	18.00
❑ 14 Dante Bichette	8.00	3.60
❑ 15 Ellis Burks	8.00	3.60
❑ 16 Andres Galarraga	15.00	6.75
❑ 17 Jeff Bagwell	25.00	11.00
❑ 18 Mike Piazza	50.00	22.00
❑ 19 Ken Caminiti	10.00	4.50
❑ 20 Barry Bonds	20.00	9.00

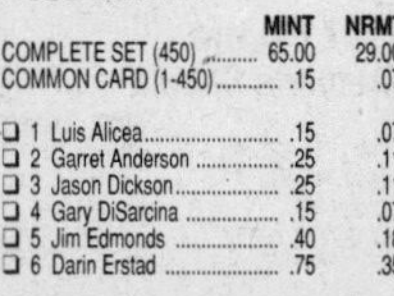

1998 Pacific

	MINT	NRMT
COMPLETE SET (450)	65.00	29.00
COMMON CARD (1-450)	.15	.07
❑ 1 Luis Alicea	.15	.07
❑ 2 Garret Anderson	.25	.11
❑ 3 Jason Dickson	.25	.11
❑ 4 Gary DiSarcina	.15	.07
❑ 5 Jim Edmonds	.40	.18
❑ 6 Darin Erstad	.75	.35

❑ 7 Chuck Finley	.25	.11
❑ 8 Shigetoshi Hasegawa	.25	.11
❑ 9 Rickey Henderson	.60	.25
❑ 10 Dave Hollins	.15	.07
❑ 11 Mark Langston	.15	.07
❑ 12 Orlando Palmeiro	.15	.07
❑ 13 Troy Percival	.25	.11
❑ 14 Tony Phillips	.15	.07
❑ 15 Tim Salmon	.60	.25
❑ 16 Allen Watson	.15	.07
❑ 17 Roberto Alomar	.60	.25
❑ 18 Brady Anderson	.25	.11
❑ 19 Harold Baines	.25	.11
❑ 20 Armando Benitez	.15	.07
❑ 21 Geronimo Berroa	.15	.07
❑ 22 Mike Bordick	.15	.07
❑ 23 Eric Davis	.25	.11
❑ 24 Scott Erickson	.25	.11
❑ 25 Chris Hoiles	.15	.07
❑ 26 Jimmy Key	.25	.11
❑ 27 Aaron Ledesma	.15	.07
❑ 28 Mike Mussina	.60	.25
❑ 29 Randy Myers	.25	.11
❑ 30 Jesse Orosco	.15	.07
❑ 31 Rafael Palmeiro	.40	.18
❑ 32 Jeff Reboulet	.15	.07
❑ 33 Cal Ripken	2.50	1.10
❑ 34 B.J. Surhoff	.25	.11
❑ 35 Steve Avery	.15	.07
❑ 36 Darren Bragg	.15	.07
❑ 37 Wil Cordero	.15	.07
❑ 38 Jeff Frye	.15	.07
❑ 39 Nomar Garciaparra	2.00	.90
❑ 40 Tom Gordon	.25	.11
❑ 41 Bill Haselman	.15	.07
❑ 42 Scott Hatteberg	.15	.07
❑ 43 Butch Henry	.15	.07
❑ 44 Reggie Jefferson	.15	.07
❑ 45 Tim Naehring	.15	.07
❑ 46 Troy O'Leary	.25	.11
❑ 47 Jeff Suppan	.15	.07
❑ 48 John Valentin	.25	.11
❑ 49 Mo Vaughn	.75	.35
❑ 50 Tim Wakefield	.15	.07
❑ 51 James Baldwin	.25	.11
❑ 52 Albert Belle	.75	.35
❑ 53 Tony Castillo	.15	.07
❑ 54 Doug Drabek	.15	.07
❑ 55 Ray Durham	.25	.11
❑ 56 Jorge Fabregas	.15	.07
❑ 57 Ozzie Guillen	.15	.07
❑ 58 Matt Karchner	.15	.07
❑ 59 Norberto Martin	.15	.07
❑ 60 Dave Martinez	.15	.07
❑ 61 Lyle Mouton	.15	.07
❑ 62 Jaime Navarro	.15	.07
❑ 63 Frank Thomas	2.00	.90
❑ 64 Mario Valdez	.25	.11
❑ 65 Robin Ventura	.25	.11
❑ 66 Sandy Alomar Jr.	.25	.11
❑ 67 Paul Assenmacher	.15	.07
❑ 68 Tony Fernandez	.15	.07
❑ 69 Brian Giles	.25	.11
❑ 70 Marquis Grissom	.25	.11
❑ 71 Orel Hershiser	.25	.11
❑ 72 Mike Jackson	.15	.07
❑ 73 David Justice	.60	.25
❑ 74 Albie Lopez	.15	.07

- ❑ 75 Jose Mesa .15 .07
- ❑ 76 Charles Nagy .25 .11
- ❑ 77 Chad Ogea .15 .07
- ❑ 78 Manny Ramirez .60 .25
- ❑ 79 Jim Thome .60 .25
- ❑ 80 Omar Vizquel .25 .11
- ❑ 81 Matt Williams .25 .11
- ❑ 82 Jaret Wright .75 .35
- ❑ 83 Willie Blair .15 .07
- ❑ 84 Raul Casanova .15 .07
- ❑ 85 Tony Clark .40 .18
- ❑ 86 Deivi Cruz .15 .07
- ❑ 87 Damion Easley .25 .11
- ❑ 88 Travis Fryman .25 .11
- ❑ 89 Bobby Higginson .40 .18
- ❑ 90 Brian L. Hunter .25 .11
- ❑ 91 Todd Jones .15 .07
- ❑ 92 Dan Miceli .15 .07
- ❑ 93 Brian Moehler .15 .07
- ❑ 94 Mel Nieves .15 .07
- ❑ 95 Jody Reed .15 .07
- ❑ 96 Justin Thompson .25 .11
- ❑ 97 Bubba Trammell .25 .11
- ❑ 98 Kevin Appier .25 .11
- ❑ 99 Jay Bell .25 .11
- ❑ 100 Yamil Benitez .15 .07
- ❑ 101 Johnny Damon .25 .11
- ❑ 102 Chili Davis .25 .11
- ❑ 103 Jermaine Dye .15 .07
- ❑ 104 Jed Hansen .15 .07
- ❑ 105 Jeff King .25 .11
- ❑ 106 Mike Macfarlane .15 .07
- ❑ 107 Felix Martinez .15 .07
- ❑ 108 Jeff Montgomery .15 .07
- ❑ 109 Jose Offerman .15 .07
- ❑ 110 Dean Palmer .25 .11
- ❑ 111 Hipolito Pichardo .15 .07
- ❑ 112 Jose Rosado .15 .07
- ❑ 113 Jeromy Burnitz .25 .11
- ❑ 114 Jeff Cirillo .25 .11
- ❑ 115 Cal Eldred .15 .07
- ❑ 116 John Jaha .15 .07
- ❑ 117 Doug Jones .15 .07
- ❑ 118 Scott Karl .15 .07
- ❑ 119 Jesse Levis .15 .07
- ❑ 120 Mark Loretta .15 .07
- ❑ 121 Ben McDonald .15 .07
- ❑ 122 Jose Mercedes .15 .07
- ❑ 123 Matt Mieske .15 .07
- ❑ 124 Dave Nilsson .15 .07
- ❑ 125 Jose Valentin .15 .07
- ❑ 126 Fernando Vina .15 .07
- ❑ 127 Gerald Williams .15 .07
- ❑ 128 Rick Aguilera .15 .07
- ❑ 129 Rich Becker .15 .07
- ❑ 130 Ron Coomer .15 .07
- ❑ 131 Marty Cordova .15 .07
- ❑ 132 Eddie Guardado .15 .07
- ❑ 133 LaTroy Hawkins .15 .07
- ❑ 134 Denny Hocking .15 .07
- ❑ 135 Chuck Knoblauch .60 .25
- ❑ 136 Matt Lawton .25 .11
- ❑ 137 Pat Meares .15 .07
- ❑ 138 Paul Molitor .60 .25
- ❑ 139 David Ortiz .25 .11
- ❑ 140 Brad Radke .25 .11
- ❑ 141 Terry Steinbach .25 .11
- ❑ 142 Bob Tewksbury .15 .07
- ❑ 143 Javier Valentin .25 .11
- ❑ 144 Wade Boggs .60 .25
- ❑ 145 David Cone .40 .18
- ❑ 146 Chad Curtis .15 .07
- ❑ 147 Cecil Fielder .25 .11
- ❑ 148 Joe Girardi .15 .07
- ❑ 149 Dwight Gooden .25 .11
- ❑ 150 Hideki Irabu .40 .18
- ❑ 151 Derek Jeter 1.50 .70
- ❑ 152 Tino Martinez .60 .25
- ❑ 153 Ramiro Mendoza .25 .11
- ❑ 154 Paul O'Neill .25 .11
- ❑ 155 Andy Pettitte .40 .18
- ❑ 156 Jorge Posada .25 .11
- ❑ 157 Mariano Rivera .25 .11
- ❑ 158 Rey Sanchez .15 .07
- ❑ 159 Luis Sojo .15 .07
- ❑ 160 David Wells .40 .18
- ❑ 161 Bernie Williams .60 .25
- ❑ 162 Rafael Bournigal .15 .07
- ❑ 163 Scott Brosius .25 .11
- ❑ 164 Jose Canseco .60 .25
- ❑ 165 Jason Giambi .25 .11
- ❑ 166 Ben Grieve 1.25 .55
- ❑ 167 Dave Magadan .15 .07
- ❑ 168 Brent Mayne .15 .07
- ❑ 169 Jason McDonald .15 .07
- ❑ 170 Izzy Molina .15 .07
- ❑ 171 Ariel Prieto .15 .07
- ❑ 172 Carlos Reyes .15 .07
- ❑ 173 Scott Spiezio .15 .07
- ❑ 174 Matt Stairs .25 .11
- ❑ 175 Bill Taylor .15 .07
- ❑ 176 Dave Telgheder .15 .07
- ❑ 177 Steve Wojciechowski .15 .07
- ❑ 178 Rich Amaral .15 .07
- ❑ 179 Bobby Ayala .15 .07
- ❑ 180 Jay Buhner .25 .11
- ❑ 181 Rafael Carmona .15 .07
- ❑ 182 Ken Cloude .25 .11
- ❑ 183 Joey Cora .25 .11
- ❑ 184 Russ Davis .25 .11
- ❑ 185 Jeff Fassero .15 .07
- ❑ 186 Ken Griffey Jr. 3.00 1.35
- ❑ 187 Raul Ibanez .15 .07
- ❑ 188 Randy Johnson .60 .25
- ❑ 189 Roberto Kelly .15 .07
- ❑ 190 Edgar Martinez .25 .11
- ❑ 191 Jamie Moyer .15 .07
- ❑ 192 Omar Olivares .15 .07
- ❑ 193 Alex Rodriguez 2.00 .90
- ❑ 194 Heathcliff Slocumb .15 .07
- ❑ 195 Paul Sorrento .15 .07
- ❑ 196 Dan Wilson .15 .07
- ❑ 197 Scott Bailes .15 .07
- ❑ 198 John Burkett .15 .07
- ❑ 199 Domingo Cedeno .15 .07
- ❑ 200 Will Clark .60 .25
- ❑ 201 Hanley Frias .25 .11
- ❑ 202 Juan Gonzalez 1.50 .70
- ❑ 203 Tom Goodwin .15 .07
- ❑ 204 Rusty Greer .25 .11
- ❑ 205 Wilson Heredia .15 .07
- ❑ 206 Darren Oliver .15 .07
- ❑ 207 Bill Ripken .15 .07
- ❑ 208 Ivan Rodriguez .60 .25
- ❑ 209 Lee Stevens .15 .07
- ❑ 210 Fernando Tatis .25 .11
- ❑ 211 John Wetteland .25 .11
- ❑ 212 Bobby Witt .15 .07
- ❑ 213 Jacob Brumfield .15 .07
- ❑ 214 Joe Carter .25 .11
- ❑ 215 Roger Clemens 1.25 .55
- ❑ 216 Felipe Crespo .15 .07
- ❑ 217 Jose Cruz Jr. .75 .35
- ❑ 218 Carlos Delgado .25 .11
- ❑ 219 Mariano Duncan .15 .07
- ❑ 220 Carlos Garcia .15 .07
- ❑ 221 Alex Gonzalez .15 .07
- ❑ 222 Juan Guzman .15 .07
- ❑ 223 Pat Hentgen .25 .11
- ❑ 224 Orlando Merced .15 .07
- ❑ 225 Tomas Perez .15 .07
- ❑ 226 Paul Quantrill .15 .07
- ❑ 227 Benito Santiago .15 .07
- ❑ 228 Woody Williams .15 .07
- ❑ 229 Rafael Belliard .15 .07
- ❑ 230 Jeff Blauser .15 .07
- ❑ 231 Pedro Borbon .15 .07
- ❑ 232 Tom Glavine .60 .25
- ❑ 233 Tony Graffanino .15 .07
- ❑ 234 Andruw Jones .75 .35
- ❑ 235 Chipper Jones 1.50 .70
- ❑ 236 Ryan Klesko .25 .11
- ❑ 237 Mark Lemke .15 .07
- ❑ 238 Kenny Lofton .60 .25
- ❑ 239 Javier Lopez .25 .11
- ❑ 240 Fred McGriff .40 .18
- ❑ 241 Greg Maddux 2.00 .90
- ❑ 242 Denny Neagle .25 .11
- ❑ 243 John Smoltz .25 .11
- ❑ 244 Michael Tucker .25 .11
- ❑ 245 Mark Wohlers .15 .07
- ❑ 246 Manny Alexander .15 .07
- ❑ 247 Miguel Batista .15 .07
- ❑ 248 Mark Clark .15 .07
- ❑ 249 Doug Glanville .25 .11
- ❑ 250 Jeremi Gonzalez .25 .11
- ❑ 251 Mark Grace .40 .18
- ❑ 252 Jose Hernandez .15 .07
- ❑ 253 Lance Johnson .15 .07
- ❑ 254 Brooks Kieschnick .15 .07
- ❑ 255 Kevin Orie .15 .07
- ❑ 256 Ryne Sandberg .75 .35
- ❑ 257 Scott Servais .15 .07
- ❑ 258 Sammy Sosa 1.50 .70
- ❑ 259 Kevin Tapani .15 .07
- ❑ 260 Ramon Tatis .15 .07
- ❑ 261 Bret Boone .25 .11
- ❑ 262 Dave Burba .15 .07
- ❑ 263 Brook Fordyce .15 .07
- ❑ 264 Willie Greene .25 .11
- ❑ 265 Barry Larkin .40 .18
- ❑ 266 Pedro A. Martinez .15 .07
- ❑ 267 Hal Morris .15 .07
- ❑ 268 Joe Oliver .15 .07
- ❑ 269 Eduardo Perez .15 .07
- ❑ 270 Pokey Reese .15 .07
- ❑ 271 Felix Rodriguez .15 .07
- ❑ 272 Deion Sanders .25 .11
- ❑ 273 Reggie Sanders .25 .11
- ❑ 274 Jeff Shaw .25 .11
- ❑ 275 Scott Sullivan .15 .07
- ❑ 276 Brett Tomko .25 .11
- ❑ 277 Roger Bailey .15 .07
- ❑ 278 Dante Bichette .25 .11
- ❑ 279 Ellis Burks .25 .11
- ❑ 280 Vinny Castilla .40 .18
- ❑ 281 Frank Castillo .15 .07
- ❑ 282 Mike DeJean .15 .07
- ❑ 283 Andres Galarraga .60 .25
- ❑ 284 Darren Holmes .15 .07
- ❑ 285 Kirt Manwaring .15 .07
- ❑ 286 Quinton McCracken .25 .11
- ❑ 287 Neifi Perez .25 .11
- ❑ 288 Steve Reed .15 .07
- ❑ 289 John Thomson .15 .07
- ❑ 290 Larry Walker .60 .25
- ❑ 291 Walt Weiss .25 .11
- ❑ 292 Kurt Abbott .15 .07
- ❑ 293 Antonio Alfonseca .15 .07
- ❑ 294 Moises Alou .40 .18
- ❑ 295 Alex Arias .15 .07
- ❑ 296 Bobby Bonilla .25 .11
- ❑ 297 Kevin Brown .40 .18
- ❑ 298 Craig Counsell .15 .07
- ❑ 299 Darren Daulton .25 .11
- ❑ 300 Jim Eisenreich .15 .07
- ❑ 301 Alex Fernandez .15 .07
- ❑ 302 Felix Heredia .15 .07
- ❑ 303 Livan Hernandez .25 .11
- ❑ 304 Charles Johnson .25 .11
- ❑ 305 Al Leiter .25 .11
- ❑ 306 Robb Nen .25 .11
- ❑ 307 Edgar Renteria .25 .11
- ❑ 308 Gary Sheffield .40 .18
- ❑ 309 Devon White .25 .11
- ❑ 310 Bob Abreu .25 .11
- ❑ 311 Brad Ausmus .15 .07
- ❑ 312 Jeff Bagwell 1.00 .45
- ❑ 313 Derek Bell .25 .11
- ❑ 314 Sean Berry .15 .07
- ❑ 315 Craig Biggio .60 .25
- ❑ 316 Ramon Garcia .15 .07
- ❑ 317 Luis Gonzalez .15 .07
- ❑ 318 Ricky Gutierrez .15 .07
- ❑ 319 Mike Hampton .15 .07
- ❑ 320 Richard Hidalgo .25 .11
- ❑ 321 Thomas Howard .15 .07
- ❑ 322 Darryl Kile .25 .11
- ❑ 323 Jose Lima .15 .07
- ❑ 324 Shane Reynolds .25 .11
- ❑ 325 Bill Spiers .15 .07
- ❑ 326 Tom Candiotti .15 .07
- ❑ 327 Roger Cedeno .15 .07
- ❑ 328 Greg Gagne .15 .07
- ❑ 329 Karim Garcia .25 .11

❑ 330 Wilton Guerrero .... .15 .07
❑ 331 Todd Hollandsworth .... .15 .07
❑ 332 Eric Karros .... .25 .11
❑ 333 Ramon Martinez .... .25 .11
❑ 334 Raul Mondesi .... .40 .18
❑ 335 Otis Nixon .... .15 .07
❑ 336 Hideo Nomo .... .75 .35
❑ 337 Antonio Osuna .... .15 .07
❑ 338 Chan Ho Park .... .60 .25
❑ 339 Mike Piazza .... 2.00 .90
❑ 340 Dennis Reyes .... .25 .11
❑ 341 Ismael Valdes .... .25 .11
❑ 342 Todd Worrell .... .15 .07
❑ 343 Todd Zeile .... .25 .11
❑ 344 Darrin Fletcher .... .15 .07
❑ 345 Mark Grudzielanek .... .25 .11
❑ 346 Vladimir Guerrero .... 1.00 .45
❑ 347 Dustin Hermanson .... .25 .11
❑ 348 Mike Lansing .... .15 .07
❑ 349 Pedro Martinez .... .60 .25
❑ 350 Ryan McGuire .... .15 .07
❑ 351 Jose Paniagua .... .15 .07
❑ 352 Carlos Perez .... .25 .11
❑ 353 Henry Rodriguez .... .25 .11
❑ 354 F.P. Santangelo .... .15 .07
❑ 355 David Segui .... .25 .11
❑ 356 Ugueth Urbina .... .25 .11
❑ 357 Marc Valdes .... .15 .07
❑ 358 Jose Vidro .... .15 .07
❑ 359 Rondell White .... .25 .11
❑ 360 Juan Acevedo .... .15 .07
❑ 361 Edgardo Alfonzo .... .25 .11
❑ 362 Carlos Baerga .... .25 .11
❑ 363 Carl Everett .... .15 .07
❑ 364 John Franco .... .25 .11
❑ 365 Bernard Gilkey .... .15 .07
❑ 366 Todd Hundley .... .25 .11
❑ 367 Butch Huskey .... .15 .07
❑ 368 Bobby Jones .... .15 .07
❑ 369 Takashi Kashiwada .... .40 .18
❑ 370 Greg McMichael .... .15 .07
❑ 371 Brian McRae .... .15 .07
❑ 372 Alex Ochoa .... .15 .07
❑ 373 John Olerud .... .25 .11
❑ 374 Rey Ordonez .... .25 .11
❑ 375 Turk Wendell .... .15 .07
❑ 376 Ricky Bottalico .... .25 .11
❑ 377 Rico Brogna .... .25 .11
❑ 378 Len Dykstra .... .25 .11
❑ 379 Bobby Estalella .... .25 .11
❑ 380 Wayne Gomes .... .15 .07
❑ 381 Tyler Green .... .15 .07
❑ 382 Gregg Jefferies .... .15 .07
❑ 383 Mark Leiter .... .15 .07
❑ 384 Mike Lieberthal .... .15 .07
❑ 385 Mickey Morandini .... .15 .07
❑ 386 Scott Rolen .... 1.50 .70
❑ 387 Curt Schilling .... .25 .11
❑ 388 Kevin Stocker .... .15 .07
❑ 389 Danny Tartabull .... .15 .07
❑ 390 Jermaine Allensworth .... .15 .07
❑ 391 Adrian Brown .... .25 .11
❑ 392 Jason Christiansen .... .15 .07
❑ 393 Steve Cooke .... .15 .07
❑ 394 Francisco Cordova .... .15 .07
❑ 395 Jose Guillen .... .25 .11
❑ 396 Jason Kendall .... .25 .11
❑ 397 Jon Lieber .... .15 .07
❑ 398 Esteban Loaiza .... .15 .07
❑ 399 Al Martin .... .15 .07
❑ 400 Kevin Polcovich .... .15 .07
❑ 401 Joe Randa .... .15 .07
❑ 402 Ricardo Rincon .... .15 .07
❑ 403 Tony Womack .... .25 .11
❑ 404 Kevin Young .... .25 .11
❑ 405 Andy Benes .... .25 .11
❑ 406 Royce Clayton .... .15 .07
❑ 407 Delino DeShields .... .15 .07
❑ 408 Mike Difelice .... .15 .07
❑ 409 Dennis Eckersley .... .25 .11
❑ 410 John Frascatore .... .15 .07
❑ 411 Gary Gaetti .... .15 .07
❑ 412 Ron Gant .... .15 .07
❑ 413 Brian Jordan .... .25 .11
❑ 414 Ray Lankford .... .25 .11
❑ 415 Willie McGee .... .15 .07
❑ 416 Mark McGwire 4.00 1.80
❑ 417 Matt Morris .... .25 .11
❑ 418 Luis Ordaz .... .25 .11
❑ 419 Todd Stottlemyre .... .25 .11
❑ 420 Andy Ashby .... .15 .07
❑ 421 Jim Bruske .... .15 .07
❑ 422 Ken Caminiti .... .40 .18
❑ 423 Will Cunnane .... .15 .07
❑ 424 Steve Finley .... .25 .11
❑ 425 John Flaherty .... .15 .07
❑ 426 Chris Gomez .... .15 .07
❑ 427 Tony Gwynn .... 1.50 .70
❑ 428 Joey Hamilton .... .25 .11
❑ 429 Carlos Hernandez .... .15 .07
❑ 430 Sterling Hitchcock .... .25 .11
❑ 431 Trevor Hoffman .... .25 .11
❑ 432 Wally Joyner .... .25 .11
❑ 433 Greg Vaughn .... .25 .11
❑ 434 Quilvio Veras .... .15 .07
❑ 435 Wilson Alvarez .... .25 .11
❑ 436 Rod Beck .... .25 .11
❑ 437 Barry Bonds .... .75 .35
❑ 438 Jacob Cruz .... .15 .07
❑ 439 Shawn Estes .... .25 .11
❑ 440 Darryl Hamilton .... .15 .07
❑ 441 Roberto Hernandez .... .15 .07
❑ 442 Glenallen Hill .... .15 .07
❑ 443 Stan Javier .... .15 .07
❑ 444 Brian Johnson .... .15 .07
❑ 445 Jeff Kent .... .25 .11
❑ 446 Bill Mueller .... .25 .11
❑ 447 Kirk Rueter .... .15 .07
❑ 448 J.T. Snow .... .25 .11
❑ 449 Julian Tavarez .... .15 .07
❑ 450 Jose Vizcaino .... .15 .07

1998 Pacific Platinum Blue

	MINT	NRMT
COMPLETE SET (450)	8000.00	3600.00
COMMON CARD (1-450)	15.00	6.75

*STARS: 40X TO 100X BASIC CARDS
*YOUNG STARS: 30X TO 80X BASIC CARDS

1998 Pacific Cramer's Choice

	MINT	NRMT
COMPLETE SET (10)	1000.00	450.00
COMMON CARD (1-10)	40.00	18.00

❑ 1 Greg Maddux 120.00 55.00
❑ 2 Roberto Alomar 40.00 18.00
❑ 3 Cal Ripken 150.00 70.00
❑ 4 Nomar Garciaparra 120.00 55.00
❑ 5 Larry Walker 40.00 18.00
❑ 6 Mike Piazza 120.00 55.00
❑ 7 Mark McGwire 250.00 110.00
❑ 8 Tony Gwynn 100.00 45.00
❑ 9 Ken Griffey Jr. 200.00 90.00
❑ 10 Roger Clemens 80.00 36.00

1998 Pacific Gold Crown Die Cuts

	MINT	NRMT
COMPLETE SET (36)	450.00	200.00
COMMON CARD (1-36)	3.00	1.35

❑ 1 Chipper Jones 20.00 9.00
❑ 2 Greg Maddux 25.00 11.00
❑ 3 Denny Neagle 3.00 1.35
❑ 4 Roberto Alomar 8.00 3.60
❑ 5 Rafael Palmeiro 5.00 2.20
❑ 6 Cal Ripken 30.00 13.50
❑ 7 Nomar Garciaparra 25.00 11.00
❑ 8 Mo Vaughn 10.00 4.50
❑ 9 Frank Thomas 25.00 11.00
❑ 10 Sandy Alomar Jr. 3.00 1.35
❑ 11 David Justice 8.00 3.60
❑ 12 Manny Ramirez 8.00 3.60
❑ 13 Andres Galarraga 8.00 3.60
❑ 14 Larry Walker 8.00 3.60
❑ 15 Moises Alou 5.00 2.20
❑ 16 Livan Hernandez 3.00 1.35
❑ 17 Gary Sheffield 5.00 2.20
❑ 18 Jeff Bagwell 12.00 5.50
❑ 19 Raul Mondesi 5.00 2.20
❑ 20 Hideo Nomo 10.00 4.50
❑ 21 Mike Piazza 25.00 11.00
❑ 22 Derek Jeter 20.00 9.00
❑ 23 Tino Martinez 8.00 3.60
❑ 24 Bernie Williams 8.00 3.60
❑ 25 Ben Grieve 12.00 5.50
❑ 26 Mark McGwire 50.00 22.00
❑ 27 Tony Gwynn 20.00 9.00
❑ 28 Barry Bonds 10.00 4.50
❑ 29 Ken Griffey Jr. 40.00 18.00
❑ 30 Randy Johnson 8.00 3.60
❑ 31 Edgar Martinez 3.00 1.35
❑ 32 Alex Rodriguez 25.00 11.00
❑ 33 Juan Gonzalez 20.00 9.00
❑ 34 Ivan Rodriguez 10.00 4.50
❑ 35 Roger Clemens 15.00 6.75
❑ 36 Jose Cruz Jr. 8.00 3.60

1998 Pacific Home Run Hitters

	MINT	NRMT
COMPLETE SET (20)	300.00	135.00
COMMON CARD (1-20)	5.00	2.20

❑ 1	Rafael Palmeiro	6.00	2.70
❑ 2	Mo Vaughn	12.00	5.50
❑ 3	Sammy Sosa	25.00	11.00
❑ 4	Albert Belle	12.00	5.50
❑ 5	Frank Thomas	30.00	13.50
❑ 6	David Justice	10.00	4.50
❑ 7	Jim Thome	10.00	4.50
❑ 8	Matt Williams	5.00	2.20
❑ 9	Vinny Castilla	6.00	2.70
❑ 10	Andres Galarraga	10.00	4.50
❑ 11	Larry Walker	10.00	4.50
❑ 12	Jeff Bagwell	15.00	6.75
❑ 13	Mike Piazza	30.00	13.50
❑ 14	Tino Martinez	10.00	4.50
❑ 15	Mark McGwire	60.00	27.00
❑ 16	Barry Bonds	12.00	5.50
❑ 17	Jay Buhner	5.00	2.20
❑ 18	Ken Griffey Jr.	50.00	22.00
❑ 19	Alex Rodriguez	30.00	13.50
❑ 20	Juan Gonzalez	25.00	11.00

1998 Pacific In The Cage

	MINT	NRMT
COMPLETE SET (20)	600.00	275.00
COMMON CARD (1-20)	6.00	2.70

❑ 1	Chipper Jones	40.00	18.00
❑ 2	Roberto Alomar	15.00	6.75
❑ 3	Cal Ripken	60.00	27.00
❑ 4	Nomar Garciaparra	50.00	22.00
❑ 5	Frank Thomas	50.00	22.00
❑ 6	Sandy Alomar Jr.	6.00	2.70
❑ 7	David Justice	15.00	6.75
❑ 8	Larry Walker	15.00	6.75
❑ 9	Bobby Bonilla	6.00	2.70
❑ 10	Mike Piazza	50.00	22.00
❑ 11	Tino Martinez	15.00	6.75
❑ 12	Bernie Williams	15.00	6.75
❑ 13	Mark McGwire	100.00	45.00
❑ 14	Tony Gwynn	40.00	18.00
❑ 15	Barry Bonds	20.00	9.00
❑ 16	Ken Griffey Jr.	80.00	36.00
❑ 17	Edgar Martinez	6.00	2.70
❑ 18	Alex Rodriguez	50.00	22.00
❑ 19	Juan Gonzalez	40.00	18.00
❑ 20	Ivan Rodriguez	20.00	9.00

1998 Pacific Latinos of the Major Leagues

	MINT	NRMT
COMPLETE SET (36)	80.00	36.00
COMMON CARD (1-36)	1.00	.45

❑ 1	Andruw Jones	4.00	1.80
❑ 2	Javier Lopez	1.50	.70
❑ 3	Roberto Alomar	4.00	1.80
❑ 4	Geronimo Berroa	1.00	.45
❑ 5	Rafael Palmeiro	2.50	1.10
❑ 6	Nomar Garciaparra	12.00	5.50
❑ 7	Sammy Sosa	10.00	4.50
❑ 8	Ozzie Guillen	1.00	.45
❑ 9	Sandy Alomar Jr.	1.50	.70
❑ 10	Manny Ramirez	4.00	1.80
❑ 11	Omar Vizquel	1.50	.70
❑ 12	Vinny Castilla	2.50	1.10
❑ 13	Andres Galarraga	4.00	1.80
❑ 14	Moises Alou	2.50	1.10
❑ 15	Bobby Bonilla	1.50	.70
❑ 16	Livan Hernandez	1.50	.70
❑ 17	Edgar Renteria	1.50	.70
❑ 18	Wilton Guerrero	1.00	.45
❑ 19	Raul Mondesi	2.50	1.10
❑ 20	Ismael Valdes	1.50	.70
❑ 21	Fernando Vina	1.00	.45
❑ 22	Pedro Martinez	4.00	1.80
❑ 23	Edgardo Alfonzo	1.50	.70
❑ 24	Carlos Baerga	1.50	.70
❑ 25	Rey Ordonez	1.50	.70
❑ 26	Tino Martinez	4.00	1.80
❑ 27	Mariano Rivera	1.50	.70
❑ 28	Bernie Williams	4.00	1.80
❑ 29	Jose Canseco	4.00	1.80
❑ 30	Joey Cora	1.50	.70
❑ 31	Roberto Kelly	1.00	.45
❑ 32	Edgar Martinez	1.50	.70
❑ 33	Alex Rodriguez	12.00	5.50
❑ 34	Juan Gonzalez	10.00	4.50
❑ 35	Ivan Rodriguez	5.00	2.20
❑ 36	Jose Cruz Jr.	4.00	1.80

1998 Pacific Team Checklists

	MINT	NRMT
COMPLETE SET (30)	300.00	135.00
COMMON CARD (1-30)	2.00	.90

❑ 1	Tim Salmon Jim Edmonds	6.00	2.70
❑ 2	Cal Ripken Roberto Alomar	25.00	11.00
❑ 3	Nomar Garciaparra Mo Vaughn	20.00	9.00
❑ 4	Frank Thomas Albert Belle	20.00	9.00
❑ 5	Sandy Alomar Jr. Manny Ramirez	6.00	2.70
❑ 6	Justin Thompson Tony Clark	4.00	1.80
❑ 7	Johnny Damon Jermaine Dye	2.00	.90
❑ 8	Dave Nilsson Jeff Cirillo	2.00	.90
❑ 9	Paul Molitor Chuck Knoblauch	6.00	2.70
❑ 10	Tino Martinez Derek Jeter	15.00	6.75
❑ 11	Ben Grieve Jose Canseco	10.00	4.50
❑ 12	Ken Griffey Jr. Alex Rodriguez	40.00	18.00
❑ 13	Juan Gonzalez Ivan Rodriguez	15.00	6.75
❑ 14	Jose Cruz Jr. Roger Clemens	12.00	5.50
❑ 15	Greg Maddux Chipper Jones	25.00	11.00
❑ 16	Sammy Sosa Mark Grace	15.00	6.75
❑ 17	Barry Larkin Deion Sanders	4.00	1.80
❑ 18	Larry Walker Andres Galarraga	6.00	2.70
❑ 19	Moises Alou Bobby Bonilla	4.00	1.80
❑ 20	Jeff Bagwell Craig Biggio	10.00	4.50
❑ 21	Mike Piazza Hideo Nomo	20.00	9.00
❑ 22	Pedro Martinez Henry Rodriguez	6.00	2.70
❑ 23	Rey Ordonez Carlos Baerga	2.00	.90
❑ 24	Curt Schilling Scott Rolen	12.00	5.50
❑ 25	Al Martin Tony Womack	2.00	.90
❑ 26	Mark McGwire Dennis Eckersley	40.00	18.00
❑ 27	Tony Gwynn Wally Joyner	15.00	6.75
❑ 28	Barry Bonds J.T.Snow	8.00	3.60
❑ 29	Matt Williams Jay Bell	2.50	1.10
❑ 30	Fred McGriff Roberto Hernandez	4.00	1.80

1999 Pacific

	MINT	NRMT
COMPLETE SET (500)	80.00	36.00
COMMON CARD (1-450)	.15	.07

❑ 1	Garret Anderson	.25	.11
❑ 2	Jason Dickson	.25	.11
❑ 3	Gary DiSarcina	.15	.07
❑ 4	Jim Edmonds	.40	.18
❑ 5	Darin Erstad	.75	.35
❑ 6	Chuck Finley	.15	.07
❑ 7	Shigetoshi Hasegawa	.25	.11
❑ 8	Ken Hill	.15	.07
❑ 9	Dave Hollins	.15	.07
❑ 10	Phil Nevin	.15	.07
❑ 11	Troy Percival	.25	.11
❑ 12	Tim Salmon *	.60	.25
❑ 12A	Tim Salmon Headshot	.60	.25
❑ 13	Brian Anderson	.25	.11
❑ 14	Tony Batista	.15	.07

- ❑ 15 Jay Bell .25 .11
- ❑ 16 Andy Benes .25 .11
- ❑ 17 Yamil Benitez .15 .07
- ❑ 18 Omar Daal .15 .07
- ❑ 19 David Dellucci .25 .11
- ❑ 20 Karim Garcia .25 .11
- ❑ 21 Bernard Gilkey .15 .07
- ❑ 22 Travis Lee * 1.00 .45
- ❑ 22A Travis Lee Headshot 1.00 .45
- ❑ 23 Aaron Small .15 .07
- ❑ 24 Kelly Stinnett .15 .07
- ❑ 25 Devon White .25 .11
- ❑ 26 Matt Williams .25 .11
- ❑ 27 Bruce Chen * .25 .11
- ❑ 27A Bruce Chen Headshot .15 .07
- ❑ 28 Andres Galarraga * .60 .25
- ❑ 28A A. Galarraga Headshot .60 .25
- ❑ 29 Tom Glavine .60 .25
- ❑ 30 Ozzie Guillen .15 .07
- ❑ 31 Andruw Jones .75 .35
- ❑ 32 Chipper Jones * 1.50 .70
- ❑ 32A Chipper Jones Headshot 1.50 .70
- ❑ 33 Ryan Klesko .25 .11
- ❑ 34 George Lombard .25 .11
- ❑ 35 Javy Lopez .25 .11
- ❑ 36 Greg Maddux * 2.00 .90
- ❑ 36A Greg Maddux Headshot 2.00 .90
- ❑ 37 Marty Malloy * .15 .07
- ❑ 37A Marty Malloy Headshot .15 .07
- ❑ 38 Dennis Martinez .25 .11
- ❑ 39 Kevin Millwood .25 .11
- ❑ 40 Alex Rodriguez * 2.00 .90
- ❑ 40A A. Rodriguez Headshot 2.00 .90
- ❑ 41 Denny Neagle .25 .11
- ❑ 42 John Smoltz .25 .11
- ❑ 43 Michael Tucker .15 .07
- ❑ 44 Walt Weiss .25 .11
- ❑ 45 Roberto Alomar * .60 .25
- ❑ 45A R. Alomar Headshot .60 .25
- ❑ 46 Brady Anderson .25 .11
- ❑ 47 Harold Baines .25 .11
- ❑ 48 Mike Bordick .15 .07
- ❑ 49 Danny Clyburn * .15 .07
- ❑ 49A Danny Clyburn Headshot .15 .07
- ❑ 50 Eric Davis .25 .11
- ❑ 51 Scott Erickson .25 .11
- ❑ 52 Chris Hoiles .15 .07
- ❑ 53 Jimmy Key .25 .11
- ❑ 54 Ryan Minor * .25 .11
- ❑ 54A Ryan Minor Headshot .50 .23
- ❑ 55 Mike Mussina .60 .25
- ❑ 56 Jesse Orosco .15 .07
- ❑ 57 Rafael Palmeiro * .40 .18
- ❑ 57A R. Palmeiro Headshot .40 .18
- ❑ 58 Sidney Ponson .25 .11
- ❑ 59 Arthur Rhodes .15 .07
- ❑ 60 Cal Ripken * 2.50 1.10
- ❑ 60A Cal Ripken Headshot .15 .07
- ❑ 61 B.J. Surhoff .25 .11
- ❑ 62 Steve Avery .15 .07
- ❑ 63 Darren Bragg .15 .07
- ❑ 64 Dennis Eckersley .25 .11
- ❑ 65 Nomar Garciaparra * 2.00 .90
- ❑ 65A Nomar Garciaparra Headshot 2.00 .90
- ❑ 66 Sammy Sosa * 1.50 .70
- ❑ 66A Sammy Sosa Headshot 1.50 .70
- ❑ 67 Tom Gordon .25 .11
- ❑ 68 Reggie Jefferson .15 .07
- ❑ 69 Darren Lewis .15 .07
- ❑ 70 Mark McGwire * 4.00 1.80
- ❑ 70A Mark McGwire Headshot 4.00 1.80
- ❑ 71 Pedro Martinez .60 .25
- ❑ 72 Troy O'Leary .25 .11
- ❑ 73 Bret Saberhagen .25 .11
- ❑ 74 Mike Stanley .15 .07
- ❑ 75 John Valentin .25 .11
- ❑ 76 Jason Varitek .15 .07
- ❑ 77 Mo Vaughn .75 .35
- ❑ 78 Tim Wakefield .25 .11
- ❑ 79 Manny Alexander .15 .07
- ❑ 80 Rod Beck .25 .11
- ❑ 81 Brant Brown .25 .11
- ❑ 82 Mark Clark .15 .07
- ❑ 83 Gary Gaetti .15 .07
- ❑ 84 Mark Grace .40 .18
- ❑ 85 Jose Hernandez .15 .07
- ❑ 86 Lance Johnson .15 .07
- ❑ 87 Jason Maxwell * .15 .07
- ❑ 87A Jason Maxwell Headshot .15 .07
- ❑ 88 Mickey Morandini .15 .07
- ❑ 89 Terry Mulholland .15 .07
- ❑ 90 Henry Rodriguez .25 .11
- ❑ 91 Scott Servais .15 .07
- ❑ 92 Kevin Tapani .15 .07
- ❑ 93 Pedro Valdes .15 .07
- ❑ 94 Kerry Wood 2.00 .90
- ❑ 95 Jeff Abbott .15 .07
- ❑ 96 James Baldwin .25 .11
- ❑ 97 Albert Belle .60 .25
- ❑ 98 Mike Cameron .25 .11
- ❑ 99 Mike Caruso .25 .11
- ❑ 100 Wil Cordero .15 .07
- ❑ 101 Ray Durham .25 .11
- ❑ 102 Jaime Navarro .15 .07
- ❑ 103 Greg Norton .15 .07
- ❑ 104 Magglio Ordonez .25 .11
- ❑ 105 Mike Sirotka .15 .07
- ❑ 106 Frank Thomas * 2.00 .90
- ❑ 106A F. Thomas Headshot 2.00 .90
- ❑ 107 Robin Ventura .25 .11
- ❑ 108 Craig Wilson .15 .07
- ❑ 109 Aaron Boone .15 .07
- ❑ 110 Bret Boone .25 .11
- ❑ 111 Sean Casey .25 .11
- ❑ 112 Pete Harnisch .15 .07
- ❑ 113 John Hudek .15 .07
- ❑ 114 Barry Larkin .40 .18
- ❑ 115 Eduardo Perez .15 .07
- ❑ 116 Mike Remlinger .15 .07
- ❑ 117 Reggie Sanders .15 .07
- ❑ 118 Chris Stynes .15 .07
- ❑ 119 Eddie Taubensee .15 .07
- ❑ 120 Brett Tomko .25 .11
- ❑ 121 Pat Watkins .15 .07
- ❑ 122 Dmitri Young .25 .11
- ❑ 123 Sandy Alomar Jr. .25 .11
- ❑ 124 Dave Burba .15 .07
- ❑ 125 Bartolo Colon .25 .11
- ❑ 126 Joey Cora .25 .11
- ❑ 127 Brian Giles .25 .11
- ❑ 128 Dwight Gooden .25 .11
- ❑ 129 Mike Jackson .15 .07
- ❑ 130 David Justice .60 .25
- ❑ 131 Kenny Lofton .60 .25
- ❑ 132 Charles Nagy .25 .11
- ❑ 133 Chad Ogea .15 .07
- ❑ 134 Manny Ramirez * .60 .25
- ❑ 134A M. Ramirez Headshot .60 .25
- ❑ 135 Richie Sexson .40 .18
- ❑ 136 Jim Thome * .60 .25
- ❑ 136A Jim Thome Headshot .60 .25
- ❑ 137 Omar Vizquel .25 .11
- ❑ 138 Jaret Wright .60 .25
- ❑ 139 Pedro Astacio .15 .07
- ❑ 140 Jason Bates .15 .07
- ❑ 141 Dante Bichette * .25 .11
- ❑ 141A Dante Bichette Headshot .25
  .11
- ❑ 142 Vinny Castilla * .40 .18
- ❑ 142A Vinny Castilla Headshot .40 .18
- ❑ 143 Edgard Clemente * .25 .11
- ❑ 143A E. Clemente Headshot .25 .11
- ❑ 144 Derrick Gibson * .25 .11
- ❑ 144A D. Gibson Headshot .25 .11
- ❑ 145 Curtis Goodwin .15 .07
- ❑ 146 Todd Helton * .75 .35
- ❑ 146A Todd Helton Headshot .75 .35
- ❑ 147 Bobby Jones .15 .07
- ❑ 148 Darryl Kile .25 .11
- ❑ 149 Mike Lansing .15 .07
- ❑ 150 Chuck McElroy .15 .07
- ❑ 151 Neifi Perez .25 .11
- ❑ 152 Jeff Reed .15 .07
- ❑ 153 John Thomson .15 .07
- ❑ 154 Larry Walker * .60 .25
- ❑ 154A Larry Walker Headshot .60 .25
- ❑ 155 Jamey Wright .15 .07
- ❑ 156 Kimera Bartee .15 .07
- ❑ 157 Geronimo Berroa .15 .07
- ❑ 158 Raul Casanova .15 .07
- ❑ 159 Frank Catalanotto .15 .07
- ❑ 160 Tony Clark .40 .18
- ❑ 161 Deivi Cruz .15 .07
- ❑ 162 Damion Easley .25 .11
- ❑ 163 Juan Encarnacion .25 .11
- ❑ 164 Luis Gonzalez .15 .07
- ❑ 165 Seth Greisinger .25 .11
- ❑ 166 Bob Higginson .40 .18
- ❑ 167 Brian L.Hunter .25 .11
- ❑ 168 Todd Jones .15 .07
- ❑ 169 Justin Thompson .25 .11
- ❑ 170 Antonio Alfonseca .15 .07
- ❑ 171 Dave Berg .15 .07
- ❑ 172 John Cangelosi .15 .07
- ❑ 173 Craig Counsell .15 .07
- ❑ 174 Todd Dunwoody .25 .11
- ❑ 175 Cliff Floyd .25 .11
- ❑ 176 Alex Gonzalez .25 .11
- ❑ 177 Livan Hernandez .25 .11
- ❑ 178 Ryan Jackson .15 .07
- ❑ 179 Mark Kotsay .25 .11
- ❑ 180 Derrek Lee .25 .11
- ❑ 181 Matt Mantei .15 .07
- ❑ 182 Brian Meadows .15 .07
- ❑ 183 Edgar Renteria .25 .11
- ❑ 184 Moises Alou * .40 .18
- ❑ 184A Moises Alou Headshot .40 .18
- ❑ 185 Brad Ausmus .15 .07
- ❑ 186 Jeff Bagwell * 1.00 .45
- ❑ 186A Jeff Bagwell Headshot .15 .07
- ❑ 187 Derek Bell .25 .11
- ❑ 188 Sean Berry .15 .07
- ❑ 189 Craig Biggio .60 .25
- ❑ 190 Carl Everett .15 .07
- ❑ 191 Ricky Gutierrez .15 .07
- ❑ 192 Mike Hampton .15 .07
- ❑ 193 Doug Henry .15 .07
- ❑ 194 Richard Hidalgo .25 .11
- ❑ 195 Randy Johnson .60 .25
- ❑ 196 Russ Johnson * .15 .07
- ❑ 196A Russ Johnson Headshot .15 .07
- ❑ 197 Shane Reynolds .25 .11
- ❑ 198 Bill Spiers .15 .07
- ❑ 199 Kevin Appier .25 .11
- ❑ 200 Tim Belcher .15 .07
- ❑ 201 Jeff Conine .25 .11
- ❑ 202 Johnny Damon .25 .11
- ❑ 203 Jermaine Dye .15 .07
- ❑ 204 Jeremy Giambi * .60 .25
- ❑ 204A J. Giambi Headshot .60 .25
- ❑ 205 Jeff King .25 .11
- ❑ 206 Shane Mack .15 .07
- ❑ 207 Jeff Montgomery .25 .11
- ❑ 208 Hal Morris .15 .07
- ❑ 209 Jose Offerman .15 .07
- ❑ 210 Dean Palmer .25 .11
- ❑ 211 Jose Rosado .15 .07
- ❑ 212 Glendon Rusch .15 .07
- ❑ 213 Larry Sutton .15 .07
- ❑ 214 Mike Sweeney .15 .07
- ❑ 215 Bobby Bonilla .25 .11
- ❑ 216 Alex Cora .25 .11
- ❑ 217 Darren Dreifort .15 .07
- ❑ 218 Mark Grudzielanek .25 .11
- ❑ 219 Todd Hollandsworth .15 .07
- ❑ 220 Trenidad Hubbard .15 .07
- ❑ 221 Charles Johnson .25 .11
- ❑ 222 Eric Karros .25 .11
- ❑ 223 Matt Luke .15 .07
- ❑ 224 Ramon Martinez .25 .11
- ❑ 225 Raul Mondesi .40 .18
- ❑ 226 Chan Ho Park .60 .25
- ❑ 227 Jeff Shaw .25 .11
- ❑ 228 Gary Sheffield .40 .18
- ❑ 229 Eric Young .15 .07
- ❑ 230 Jeromy Burnitz .25 .11
- ❑ 231 Jeff Cirillo .25 .11
- ❑ 232 Marquis Grissom .25 .11
- ❑ 233 Bobby Hughes .15 .07
- ❑ 234 John Jaha .15 .07
- ❑ 235 Geoff Jenkins .25 .11
- ❑ 236 Scott Karl .15 .07
- ❑ 237 Mark Loretta .15 .07

❑ 238 Mike Matheny .15 .07
❑ 239 Mike Myers .15 .07
❑ 240 Dave Nilsson .15 .07
❑ 241 Bob Wickman .15 .07
❑ 242 Jose Valentin .15 .07
❑ 243 Fernando Vina .15 .07
❑ 244 Rick Aguilera .15 .07
❑ 245 Ron Coomer .15 .07
❑ 246 Marty Cordova .15 .07
❑ 247 Denny Hocking .15 .07
❑ 248 Matt Lawton .25 .11
❑ 249 Pat Meares .15 .07
❑ 250 Paul Molitor * .60 .25
❑ 250A Paul Molitor Headshot .60 .25
❑ 251 Otis Nixon .15 .07
❑ 252 Alex Ochoa .15 .07
❑ 253 David Ortiz .25 .11
❑ 254 A.J. Pierzynski .25 .11
❑ 255 Brad Radke .25 .11
❑ 256 Terry Steinbach .25 .11
❑ 257 Bob Tewksbury .15 .07
❑ 258 Todd Walker .40 .18
❑ 259 Shane Andrews .15 .07
❑ 260 Shayne Bennett .15 .07
❑ 261 Orlando Cabrera .25 .11
❑ 262 Brad Fullmer .25 .11
❑ 263 Vladimir Guerrero 1.00 .45
❑ 264 Wilton Guerrero .15 .07
❑ 265 Dustin Hermanson .25 .11
❑ 266 Terry Jones .15 .07
❑ 267 Steve Kline .15 .07
❑ 268 Carl Pavano .25 .11
❑ 269 F.P. Santangelo .15 .07
❑ 270 Fernando Seguignol * .40 .18
❑ 270A F. Seguignol Headshot .40 .18
❑ 271 Ugueth Urbina .25 .11
❑ 272 Jose Vidro .15 .07
❑ 273 Chris Widger .15 .07
❑ 274 Edgardo Alfonzo .25 .11
❑ 275 Carlos Baerga .25 .11
❑ 276 John Franco .25 .11
❑ 277 Todd Hundley .25 .11
❑ 278 Butch Huskey .15 .07
❑ 279 Bobby Jones .15 .07
❑ 280 Al Leiter .15 .07
❑ 281 Greg McMichael .15 .07
❑ 282 Brian McRae .15 .07
❑ 283 Hideo Nomo .75 .35
❑ 284 John Olerud .25 .11
❑ 285 Rey Ordonez .25 .11
❑ 286 Mike Piazza * 2.00 .90
❑ 286A Mike Piazza Headshot 2.00 .90
❑ 287 Turk Wendell .15 .07
❑ 288 Masato Yoshii .25 .11
❑ 289 David Cone .40 .18
❑ 290 Chad Curtis .15 .07
❑ 291 Joe Girardi .15 .07
❑ 292 Orlando Hernandez 1.00 .45
❑ 293 Hideki Irabu * .40 .18
❑ 293A Hideki Irabu Headshot .40 .18
❑ 294 Derek Jeter * 1.50 .70
❑ 294A Derek Jeter Headshot 1.50 .70
❑ 295 Chuck Knoblauch .40 .18
❑ 296 Mike Lowell * .25 .11
❑ 296A Mike Lowell Headshot .25 .11
❑ 297 Tino Martinez .60 .25
❑ 298 Ramiro Mendoza .25 .11
❑ 299 Paul O'Neill .25 .11
❑ 300 Andy Pettitte .40 .18
❑ 301 Jorge Posada .25 .11
❑ 302 Tim Raines .25 .11
❑ 303 Mariano Rivera .25 .11
❑ 304 David Wells .40 .18
❑ 305 Bernie Williams * .60 .25
❑ 305A B. Williams Headshot .60 .25
❑ 306 Mike Blowers .15 .07
❑ 307 Tom Candiotti .15 .07
❑ 308 Eric Chavez * .75 .35
❑ 308A Eric Chavez Headshot .75 .35
❑ 309 Ryan Christenson .15 .07
❑ 310 Jason Giambi .25 .11
❑ 311 Ben Grieve * 1.25 .55
❑ 311A Ben Grieve Headshot 1.25 .55
❑ 312 Rickey Henderson .60 .25
❑ 313 A.J. Hinch .25 .11
❑ 314 Jason McDonald .15 .07
❑ 315 Bip Roberts .15 .07
❑ 316 Kenny Rogers .15 .07
❑ 317 Scott Spiezio .15 .07
❑ 318 Matt Stairs .25 .11
❑ 319 Miguel Tejada .25 .11
❑ 320 Bob Abreu .25 .11
❑ 321 Alex Arias .15 .07
❑ 322 Gary Bennett .15 .07
❑ 322A Gary Bennett Headshot .15 .07
❑ 323 Ricky Bottalico .25 .11
❑ 324 Rico Brogna .25 .11
❑ 325 Bobby Estalella .25 .11
❑ 326 Doug Glanville .25 .11
❑ 327 Kevin Jordan .15 .07
❑ 328 Mark Leiter .15 .07
❑ 329 Wendell Magee .15 .07
❑ 330 Mark Portugal .15 .07
❑ 331 Desi Relaford .15 .07
❑ 332 Scott Rolen 1.50 .70
❑ 333 Curt Schilling .25 .11
❑ 334 Kevin Sefcik .15 .07
❑ 335 Adrian Brown .15 .07
❑ 336 Emil Brown .15 .07
❑ 337 Lou Collier .15 .07
❑ 338 Francisco Cordova .15 .07
❑ 339 Freddy Garcia .15 .07
❑ 340 Jose Guillen .25 .11
❑ 341 Jason Kendall .25 .11
❑ 342 Al Martin .15 .07
❑ 343 Abraham Nunez .25 .11
❑ 344 Aramis Ramirez .60 .25
❑ 345 Ricardo Rincon .15 .07
❑ 346 Jason Schmidt .25 .11
❑ 347 Turner Ward .15 .07
❑ 348 Tony Womack .15 .07
❑ 349 Kevin Young .25 .11
❑ 350 Juan Acevedo .15 .07
❑ 351 Delino DeShields .15 .07
❑ 352 J.D. Drew * 12.00 5.50
❑ 352A J.D. Drew Headshot 12.00 5.50
❑ 353 Ron Gant .15 .07
❑ 354 Brian Jordan .25 .11
❑ 355 Ray Lankford .25 .11
❑ 356 Eli Marrero .25 .11
❑ 357 Kent Mercker .15 .07
❑ 358 Matt Morris .25 .11
❑ 359 Luis Ordaz .15 .07
❑ 360 Donovan Osborne .15 .07
❑ 361 Placido Polanco .25 .11
❑ 362 Fernando Tatis .25 .11
❑ 363 Andy Ashby .15 .07
❑ 364 Kevin Brown .40 .18
❑ 365 Ken Caminiti .40 .18
❑ 366 Steve Finley .25 .11
❑ 367 Chris Gomez .15 .07
❑ 368 Tony Gwynn * 1.50 .70
❑ 368A T. Gwynn Headshot 1.50 .70
❑ 369 Joey Hamilton .25 .11
❑ 370 Carlos Hernandez .15 .07
❑ 371 Trevor Hoffman .25 .11
❑ 372 Wally Joyner .25 .11
❑ 373 Jim Leyritz .15 .07
❑ 374 Ruben Rivera .25 .11
❑ 375 Greg Vaughn .25 .11
❑ 376 Quilvio Veras .15 .07
❑ 377 Rich Aurilia .15 .07
❑ 378 Barry Bonds * .75 .35
❑ 378A Barry Bonds Headshot .75 .35
❑ 379 Ellis Burks .25 .11
❑ 380 Joe Carter .25 .11
❑ 381 Stan Javier .15 .07
❑ 382 Brian Johnson .15 .07
❑ 383 Jeff Kent .25 .11
❑ 384 Jose Mesa .15 .07
❑ 385 Bill Mueller .25 .11
❑ 386 Robb Nen .25 .11
❑ 387 Armando Rios * .25 .11
❑ 387A Armando Rios Headshot .25 .11
❑ 388 Kirk Rueter .15 .07
❑ 389 Rey Sanchez .15 .07
❑ 390 J.T. Snow .25 .11
❑ 391 David Bell .15 .07
❑ 392 Jay Buhner .25 .11
❑ 393 Ken Cloude .25 .11
❑ 394 Russ Davis .15 .07
❑ 395 Jeff Fassero .15 .07
❑ 396 Ken Griffey Jr. * 3.00 1.35
❑ 396A K. Griffey Jr. Headshot 3.00 1.35
❑ 397 Giomar Guevara .25 .11
❑ 398 Carlos Guillen .25 .11
❑ 399 Edgar Martinez .25 .11
❑ 400 Shane Monahan .25 .11
❑ 401 Jamie Moyer .15 .07
❑ 402 David Segui .25 .11
❑ 403 Makoto Suzuki .15 .07
❑ 404 Mike Timlin .15 .07
❑ 405 Dan Wilson .15 .07
❑ 406 Wilson Alvarez .15 .07
❑ 407 Rolando Arrojo .60 .25
❑ 408 Wade Boggs .60 .25
❑ 409 Miguel Cairo .25 .11
❑ 410 Roberto Hernandez .15 .07
❑ 411 Mike Kelly .15 .07
❑ 412 Aaron Ledesma .15 .07
❑ 413 Albie Lopez .15 .07
❑ 414 Dave Martinez .15 .07
❑ 415 Quinton McCracken .25 .11
❑ 416 Fred McGriff .40 .18
❑ 417 Bryan Rekar .15 .07
❑ 418 Paul Sorrento .15 .07
❑ 419 Randy Winn .15 .07
❑ 420 John Burkett .15 .07
❑ 421 Will Clark .60 .25
❑ 422 Royce Clayton .15 .07
❑ 423 Juan Gonzalez * 1.50 .70
❑ 423A J. Gonzalez Headshot 1.50 .70
❑ 424 Tom Goodwin .15 .07
❑ 425 Rusty Greer .25 .11
❑ 426 Rick Helling .25 .11
❑ 427 Roberto Kelly .15 .07
❑ 428 Mark McLemore .15 .07
❑ 429 Ivan Rodriguez * .75 .35
❑ 429A I. Rodriguez Headshot .75 .35
❑ 430 Aaron Sele .25 .11
❑ 431 Lee Stevens .15 .07
❑ 432 Todd Stottlemyre .25 .11
❑ 433 John Wetteland .25 .11
❑ 434 Todd Zeile .25 .11
❑ 435 Jose Canseco * .60 .25
❑ 435A Jose Canseco Headshot .60 .25
❑ 436 Roger Clemens * 1.25 .55
❑ 436A R. Clemens Headshot 1.25 .55
❑ 437 Felipe Crespo .15 .07
❑ 438 Jose Cruz Jr. .60 .25
❑ 439 Carlos Delgado .25 .11
❑ 440 Tom Evans * .25 .11
❑ 440A Tom Evans Headshot .25 .11
❑ 441 Tony Fernandez .15 .07
❑ 442 Darrin Fletcher .15 .07
❑ 443 Alex Gonzalez .15 .07
❑ 444 Shawn Green .25 .11
❑ 445 Roy Halladay .25 .11
❑ 446 Pat Hentgen .25 .11
❑ 447 Juan Samuel .15 .07
❑ 448 Benito Santiago .15 .07
❑ 449 Shannon Stewart .25 .11
❑ 450 Woody Williams .15 .07
❑ NNO Tony Gwynn Sample 3.00 1.35

1999 Pacific Platinum Blue

	MINT	NRMT
COMMON CARD (1-450)	8.00	3.60

*STARS: 20X TO 50X BASIC CARDS
*YOUNG STARS: 15X TO 40X BASIC CARDS

1999 Pacific Cramer's Choice

	MINT	NRMT
COMPLETE SET (10)	1000.00	450.00
COMMON CARD (1-10)	80.00	36.00
❑ 1 Cal Ripken	120.00	55.00
❑ 2 Nomar Garciaparra	100.00	45.00
❑ 3 Frank Thomas	100.00	45.00

Card	MINT	NRMT
❑ 4 Ken Griffey Jr.	150.00	70.00
❑ 5 Alex Rodriguez	100.00	45.00
❑ 6 Greg Maddux	100.00	45.00
❑ 7 Sammy Sosa	80.00	36.00
❑ 8 Kerry Wood	80.00	36.00
❑ 9 Mark McGwire	200.00	90.00
❑ 10 Tony Gwynn	80.00	36.00

1999 Pacific Dynagon Diamond

	MINT	NRMT
COMPLETE SET (20)	120.00	55.00
COMMON CARD (1-20)	3.00	1.35

Card	MINT	NRMT
❑ 1 Cal Ripken	10.00	4.50
❑ 2 Nomar Garciaparra	8.00	3.60
❑ 3 Frank Thomas	8.00	3.60
❑ 4 Derek Jeter	6.00	2.70
❑ 5 Ben Grieve	4.00	1.80
❑ 6 Ken Griffey Jr.	12.00	5.50
❑ 7 Alex Rodriguez	8.00	3.60
❑ 8 Juan Gonzalez	6.00	2.70
❑ 9 Travis Lee	3.00	1.35
❑ 10 Chipper Jones	6.00	2.70
❑ 11 Greg Maddux	8.00	3.60
❑ 12 Sammy Sosa	6.00	2.70
❑ 13 Kerry Wood	6.00	2.70
❑ 14 Jeff Bagwell	4.00	1.80
❑ 15 Hideo Nomo	3.00	1.35
❑ 16 Mike Piazza	8.00	3.60
❑ 17 J.D. Drew	25.00	11.00
❑ 18 Mark McGwire	15.00	6.75
❑ 19 Tony Gwynn	6.00	2.70
❑ 20 Barry Bonds	3.00	1.35

1999 Pacific Gold Crown Die Cuts

	MINT	NRMT
COMPLETE SET (36)	500.00	220.00
COMMON CARD (1-36)	5.00	2.20

Card	MINT	NRMT
❑ 1 Darin Erstad	8.00	3.60
❑ 2 Cal Ripken	30.00	13.50
❑ 3 Nomar Garciaparra	25.00	11.00
❑ 4 Pedro Martinez	8.00	3.60
❑ 5 Mo Vaughn	10.00	4.50
❑ 6 Frank Thomas	25.00	11.00
❑ 7 Kenny Lofton	8.00	3.60
❑ 8 Manny Ramirez	8.00	3.60
❑ 9 Paul Molitor	8.00	3.60
❑ 10 Derek Jeter	20.00	9.00
❑ 11 Bernie Williams	8.00	3.60
❑ 12 Ben Grieve	12.00	5.50
❑ 13 Ken Griffey Jr.	40.00	18.00
❑ 14 Alex Rodriguez	25.00	11.00
❑ 15 Wade Boggs	8.00	3.60
❑ 16 Juan Gonzalez	20.00	9.00
❑ 17 Ivan Rodriguez	10.00	4.50
❑ 18 Jose Canseco	8.00	3.60
❑ 19 Roger Clemens	15.00	6.75
❑ 20 Travis Lee	10.00	4.50
❑ 21 Chipper Jones	20.00	9.00
❑ 22 Greg Maddux	25.00	11.00
❑ 23 Sammy Sosa	20.00	9.00
❑ 24 Kerry Wood	20.00	9.00
❑ 25 Todd Helton	8.00	3.60
❑ 26 Larry Walker	8.00	3.60
❑ 27 Jeff Bagwell	12.00	5.50
❑ 28 Craig Biggio	8.00	3.60
❑ 29 Raul Mondesi	5.00	2.20
❑ 30 Vladimir Guerrero	10.00	4.50
❑ 31 Mike Piazza	25.00	11.00
❑ 32 Scott Rolen	15.00	6.75
❑ 33 J.D. Drew	60.00	27.00
❑ 34 Mark McGwire	50.00	22.00
❑ 35 Tony Gwynn	20.00	9.00
❑ 36 Barry Bonds	10.00	4.50

1999 Pacific Team Checklists

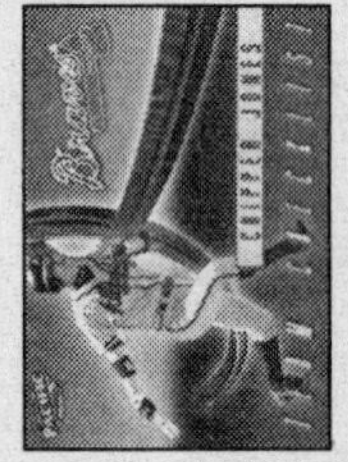

	MINT	NRMT
COMPLETE SET (30)	150.00	70.00
COMMON CARD (1-30)	1.50	.70

Card	MINT	NRMT
❑ 1 Darin Erstad	4.00	1.80
❑ 2 Cal Ripken	15.00	6.75
❑ 3 Nomar Garciaparra	12.00	5.50
❑ 4 Frank Thomas	12.00	5.50
❑ 5 Manny Ramirez	4.00	1.80
❑ 6 Damion Easley	1.50	.70
❑ 7 Jeff King	1.50	.70
❑ 8 Paul Molitor	4.00	1.80
❑ 9 Derek Jeter	10.00	4.50
❑ 10 Ben Grieve	6.00	2.70
❑ 11 Ken Griffey Jr.	20.00	9.00
❑ 12 Wade Boggs	4.00	1.80
❑ 13 Juan Gonzalez	10.00	4.50
❑ 14 Roger Clemens	8.00	3.60
❑ 15 Travis Lee	5.00	2.20
❑ 16 Chipper Jones	10.00	4.50
❑ 17 Sammy Sosa	10.00	4.50
❑ 18 Barry Larkin	2.50	1.10
❑ 19 Todd Helton	4.00	1.80
❑ 20 Mark Kotsay	1.50	.70
❑ 21 Jeff Bagwell	6.00	2.70
❑ 22 Raul Mondesi	2.50	1.10
❑ 23 Jeff Cirillo	1.50	.70
❑ 24 Vladimir Guerrero	5.00	2.20
❑ 25 Mike Piazza	12.00	5.50
❑ 26 Scott Rolen	8.00	3.60
❑ 27 Jason Kendall	1.50	.70
❑ 28 Mark McGwire	25.00	11.00
❑ 29 Tony Gwynn	10.00	4.50
❑ 30 Barry Bonds	5.00	2.20

1999 Pacific Timelines

	MINT	NRMT
COMPLETE SET (20)	1200.00	550.00
COMMON CARD (1-20)	30.00	13.50

Card	MINT	NRMT
❑ 1 Cal Ripken	120.00	55.00
❑ 2 Frank Thomas	100.00	45.00
❑ 3 Jim Thome	25.00	11.00
❑ 4 Paul Molitor	25.00	11.00
❑ 5 Bernie Williams	25.00	11.00
❑ 6 Derek Jeter	80.00	36.00
❑ 7 Ken Griffey Jr.	150.00	70.00
❑ 8 Alex Rodriguez	100.00	45.00
❑ 9 Wade Boggs	25.00	11.00
❑ 10 Jose Canseco	25.00	11.00
❑ 11 Roger Clemens	60.00	27.00
❑ 12 Andres Galarraga	25.00	11.00
❑ 13 Chipper Jones	80.00	36.00
❑ 14 Greg Maddux	100.00	45.00
❑ 15 Sammy Sosa	80.00	36.00
❑ 16 Larry Walker	25.00	11.00
❑ 17 Randy Johnson	25.00	11.00
❑ 18 Mike Piazza	100.00	45.00
❑ 19 Mark McGwire	200.00	90.00
❑ 20 Tony Gwynn	80.00	36.00

1998 Pacific Aurora

	MINT	NRMT
COMPLETE SET (200)	55.00	25.00
COMMON CARD (1-200)	.20	.09

❑ 1 Garret Anderson .30 .14
❑ 2 Jim Edmonds .50 .23
❑ 3 Darin Erstad 1.00 .45
❑ 4 Cecil Fielder .30 .14
❑ 5 Chuck Finley .30 .14
❑ 6 Todd Greene .30 .14
❑ 7 Ken Hill .20 .09
❑ 8 Tim Salmon .75 .35
❑ 9 Roberto Alomar .75 .35
❑ 10 Brady Anderson .30 .14
❑ 11 Joe Carter .30 .14
❑ 12 Mike Mussina .75 .35
❑ 13 Rafael Palmeiro .50 .23
❑ 14 Cal Ripken 3.00 1.35
❑ 15 B.J. Surhoff .30 .14
❑ 16 Steve Avery .20 .09
❑ 17 Nomar Garciaparra 2.50 1.10
❑ 18 Pedro Martinez .75 .35
❑ 19 John Valentin .30 .14
❑ 20 Jason Varitek .20 .09
❑ 21 Mo Vaughn 1.00 .45
❑ 22 Albert Belle .60 .25
❑ 23 Ray Durham .30 .14
❑ 24 Maggio Ordonez 1.00 .45
❑ 25 Frank Thomas 2.50 1.10
❑ 26 Robin Ventura .30 .14
❑ 27 Sandy Alomar Jr. .30 .14
❑ 28 Travis Fryman .30 .14
❑ 29 Dwight Gooden .30 .14
❑ 30 David Justice .75 .35
❑ 31 Kenny Lofton .75 .35
❑ 32 Manny Ramirez .75 .35
❑ 33 Jim Thome .75 .35
❑ 34 Omar Vizquel .30 .14
❑ 35 Enrique Wilson .30 .14
❑ 36 Jaret Wright 1.00 .45
❑ 37 Tony Clark .50 .23
❑ 38 Bobby Higginson .50 .23
❑ 39 Brian Hunter .30 .14
❑ 40 Bip Roberts .20 .09
❑ 41 Justin Thompson .30 .14
❑ 42 Jeff Conine .30 .14
❑ 43 Johnny Damon .30 .14
❑ 44 Jermaine Dye .20 .09
❑ 45 Jeff King .30 .14
❑ 46 Jeff Montgomery .20 .09
❑ 47 Hal Morris .20 .09
❑ 48 Dean Palmer .30 .14
❑ 49 Terry Pendleton .30 .14
❑ 50 Rick Aguilera .20 .09
❑ 51 Marty Cordova .20 .09
❑ 52 Paul Molitor .75 .35
❑ 53 Otis Nixon .20 .09
❑ 54 Brad Radke .30 .14
❑ 55 Terry Steinbach .30 .14
❑ 56 Todd Walker .50 .23
❑ 57 Chili Davis .30 .14
❑ 58 Derek Jeter 2.00 .90
❑ 59 Chuck Knoblauch .75 .35
❑ 60 Tino Martinez .75 .35
❑ 61 Paul O'Neill .30 .14
❑ 62 Andy Pettitte .50 .23
❑ 63 Mariano Rivera .30 .14
❑ 64 Bernie Williams .75 .35
❑ 65 Jason Giambi .30 .14
❑ 66 Ben Grieve 1.50 .70
❑ 67 Rickey Henderson .75 .35
❑ 68 A.J. Hinch .30 .14
❑ 69 Kenny Rogers .20 .09
❑ 70 Jay Buhner .30 .14
❑ 71 Joey Cora .30 .14
❑ 72 Ken Griffey Jr. 4.00 1.80
❑ 73 Randy Johnson .75 .35
❑ 74 Edgar Martinez .30 .14
❑ 75 Jamie Moyer .20 .09
❑ 76 Alex Rodriguez 2.50 1.10
❑ 77 David Segui .30 .14
❑ 78 Rolando Arrojo 1.25 .55
❑ 79 Wade Boggs .75 .35
❑ 80 Roberto Hernandez .20 .09
❑ 81 Dave Martinez .20 .09
❑ 82 Fred McGriff .50 .23
❑ 83 Paul Sorrento .20 .09
❑ 84 Kevin Stocker .20 .09
❑ 85 Will Clark .75 .35
❑ 86 Juan Gonzalez 2.00 .90
❑ 87 Tom Goodwin .20 .09
❑ 88 Rusty Greer .30 .14
❑ 89 Ivan Rodriguez 1.00 .45
❑ 90 John Wetteland .30 .14
❑ 91 Jose Canseco .75 .35
❑ 92 Roger Clemens 1.50 .70
❑ 93 Jose Cruz Jr. 1.00 .45
❑ 94 Carlos Delgado .30 .14
❑ 95 Pat Hentgen .30 .14
❑ 96 Jay Bell .30 .14
❑ 97 Andy Benes .30 .14
❑ 98 Karim Garcia .30 .14
❑ 99 Travis Lee 1.50 .70
❑ 100 Devon White .30 .14
❑ 101 Matt Williams .30 .14
❑ 102 Andres Galarraga .75 .35
❑ 103 Tom Glavine .75 .35
❑ 104 Andruw Jones 1.00 .45
❑ 105 Chipper Jones 2.00 .90
❑ 106 Ryan Klesko .30 .14
❑ 107 Javy Lopez .30 .14
❑ 108 Greg Maddux 2.50 1.10
❑ 109 Walt Weiss .30 .14
❑ 110 Rod Beck .30 .14
❑ 111 Jeff Blauser .20 .09
❑ 112 Mark Grace .50 .23
❑ 113 Lance Johnson .20 .09
❑ 114 Mickey Morandini .20 .09
❑ 115 Henry Rodriguez .30 .14
❑ 116 Sammy Sosa 2.00 .90
❑ 117 Kerry Wood 4.00 1.80
❑ 118 Lenny Harris .20 .09
❑ 119 Damian Jackson .20 .09
❑ 120 Barry Larkin .50 .23
❑ 121 Reggie Sanders .30 .14
❑ 122 Brett Tomko .30 .14
❑ 123 Dante Bichette .30 .14
❑ 124 Ellis Burks .30 .14
❑ 125 Vinny Castilla .50 .23
❑ 126 Todd Helton 1.00 .45
❑ 127 Darryl Kile .30 .14
❑ 128 Larry Walker .75 .35
❑ 129 Bobby Bonilla .30 .14
❑ 130 Livan Hernandez .30 .14
❑ 131 Charles Johnson .30 .14
❑ 132 Derrek Lee .30 .14
❑ 133 Edgar Renteria .30 .14
❑ 134 Gary Sheffield .50 .23
❑ 135 Moises Alou .50 .23
❑ 136 Jeff Bagwell 1.25 .55
❑ 137 Derek Bell .30 .14
❑ 138 Craig Biggio .75 .35
❑ 139 John Halama .20 .09
❑ 140 Mike Hampton .20 .09
❑ 141 Richard Hidalgo .30 .14
❑ 142 Wilton Guerrero .20 .09
❑ 143 Todd Hollandsworth .20 .09
❑ 144 Eric Karros .30 .14
❑ 145 Paul Konerko .75 .35
❑ 146 Raul Mondesi .50 .23
❑ 147 Hideo Nomo 1.00 .45
❑ 148 Chan Ho Park .75 .35
❑ 149 Mike Piazza 2.50 1.10
❑ 150 Jeromy Burnitz .30 .14
❑ 151 Todd Dunn .20 .09
❑ 152 Marquis Grissom .30 .14
❑ 153 John Jaha .20 .09
❑ 154 Dave Nilsson .20 .09
❑ 155 Fernando Vina .20 .09
❑ 156 Mark Grudzielanek .30 .14
❑ 157 Vladimir Guerrero 1.25 .55
❑ 158 F.P. Santangelo .20 .09
❑ 159 Jose Vidro .20 .09
❑ 160 Rondell White .30 .14
❑ 161 Edgardo Alfonzo .30 .14
❑ 162 Carlos Baerga .30 .14
❑ 163 John Franco .30 .14
❑ 164 Todd Hundley .30 .14
❑ 165 Brian McRae .20 .09
❑ 166 John Olerud .30 .14
❑ 167 Rey Ordonez .30 .14
❑ 168 Masato Yoshii .60 .25
❑ 169 Ricky Bottalico .30 .14
❑ 170 Doug Glanville .30 .14
❑ 171 Gregg Jefferies .20 .09
❑ 172 Desi Relaford .20 .09
❑ 173 Scott Rolen 2.00 .90
❑ 174 Curt Schilling .30 .14
❑ 175 Jose Guillen .30 .14
❑ 176 Jason Kendall .30 .14
❑ 177 Al Martin .20 .09
❑ 178 Doug Strange .20 .09
❑ 179 Kevin Young .30 .14
❑ 180 Royce Clayton .20 .09
❑ 181 Delino DeShields .20 .09
❑ 182 Gary Gaetti .20 .09
❑ 183 Ron Gant .20 .09
❑ 184 Brian Jordan .30 .14
❑ 185 Ray Lankford .30 .14
❑ 186 Willie McGee .20 .09
❑ 187 Mark McGwire 5.00 2.20
❑ 188 Kevin Brown .50 .23
❑ 189 Ken Caminiti .50 .23
❑ 190 Steve Finley .30 .14
❑ 191 Tony Gwynn 2.00 .90
❑ 192 Wally Joyner .30 .14
❑ 193 Ruben Rivera .30 .14
❑ 194 Quilvio Veras .20 .09
❑ 195 Barry Bonds 1.00 .45
❑ 196 Shawn Estes .30 .14
❑ 197 Orel Hershiser .30 .14
❑ 198 Jeff Kent .30 .14
❑ 199 Robb Nen .30 .14
❑ 200 J.T. Snow .30 .14
❑ NNO Tony Gwynn Sample 3.00 1.35

1998 Pacific Aurora Cubes

	MINT	NRMT
COMPLETE SET (20)	200.00	90.00
COMMON CARD (1-20)	5.00	2.20

❑ 1 Travis Lee 8.00 3.60
❑ 2 Chipper Jones 12.00 5.50
❑ 3 Greg Maddux 15.00 6.75
❑ 4 Cal Ripken 20.00 9.00
❑ 5 Nomar Garciaparra 15.00 6.75
❑ 6 Frank Thomas 15.00 6.75
❑ 7 Manny Ramirez 5.00 2.20
❑ 8 Larry Walker 5.00 2.20
❑ 9 Hideo Nomo 6.00 2.70
❑ 10 Mike Piazza 15.00 6.75
❑ 11 Derek Jeter 12.00 5.50
❑ 12 Ben Grieve 8.00 3.60
❑ 13 Mark McGwire 30.00 13.50
❑ 14 Tony Gwynn 12.00 5.50
❑ 15 Barry Bonds 6.00 2.70
❑ 16 Ken Griffey Jr. 25.00 11.00
❑ 17 Alex Rodriguez 15.00 6.75
❑ 18 Wade Boggs 5.00 2.20
❑ 19 Juan Gonzalez 12.00 5.50
❑ 20 Jose Cruz Jr. 5.00 2.20

1998 Pacific Aurora Hardball Cel-Fusions

	MINT	NRMT
COMPLETE SET (20)	600.00	275.00
COMMON CARD (1-20)	10.00	4.50

❑ 1 Travis Lee	20.00	9.00
❑ 2 Chipper Jones	30.00	13.50
❑ 3 Greg Maddux	40.00	18.00
❑ 4 Cal Ripken	50.00	22.00
❑ 5 Nomar Garciaparra	40.00	18.00
❑ 6 Frank Thomas	40.00	18.00
❑ 7 David Justice	10.00	4.50
❑ 8 Jeff Bagwell	20.00	9.00
❑ 9 Hideo Nomo	15.00	6.75
❑ 10 Mike Piazza	40.00	18.00
❑ 11 Derek Jeter	30.00	13.50
❑ 12 Ben Grieve	20.00	9.00
❑ 13 Scott Rolen	25.00	11.00
❑ 14 Mark McGwire	80.00	36.00
❑ 15 Tony Gwynn	30.00	13.50
❑ 16 Ken Griffey Jr.	60.00	27.00
❑ 17 Alex Rodriguez	40.00	18.00
❑ 18 Ivan Rodriguez	15.00	6.75
❑ 19 Roger Clemens	25.00	11.00
❑ 20 Jose Cruz Jr.	10.00	4.50

1998 Pacific Aurora Kings of the Major Leagues

	MINT	NRMT
COMPLETE SET (10)	900.00	400.00
COMMON CARD (1-10)	80.00	36.00
❑ 1 Chipper Jones	80.00	36.00
❑ 2 Greg Maddux	100.00	45.00
❑ 3 Cal Ripken	120.00	55.00
❑ 4 Nomar Garciaparra	100.00	45.00
❑ 5 Frank Thomas	100.00	45.00
❑ 6 Mike Piazza	100.00	45.00
❑ 7 Mark McGwire	200.00	90.00
❑ 8 Tony Gwynn	80.00	36.00
❑ 9 Ken Griffey Jr.	150.00	70.00
❑ 10 Alex Rodriguez	100.00	45.00

1998 Pacific Aurora On Deck Laser Cuts

	MINT	NRMT
COMPLETE SET (20)	120.00	55.00
COMMON CARD (1-20)	3.00	1.35
❑ 1 Travis Lee	5.00	2.20
❑ 2 Chipper Jones	8.00	3.60

❑ 3 Greg Maddux	10.00	4.50
❑ 4 Cal Ripken	12.00	5.50
❑ 5 Nomar Garciaparra	10.00	4.50
❑ 6 Frank Thomas	10.00	4.50
❑ 7 Manny Ramirez	3.00	1.35
❑ 8 Larry Walker	3.00	1.35
❑ 9 Hideo Nomo	4.00	1.80
❑ 10 Mike Piazza	10.00	4.50
❑ 11 Derek Jeter	8.00	3.60
❑ 12 Ben Grieve	5.00	2.20
❑ 13 Mark McGwire	20.00	9.00
❑ 14 Tony Gwynn	8.00	3.60
❑ 15 Barry Bonds	4.00	1.80
❑ 16 Ken Griffey Jr.	15.00	6.75
❑ 17 Alex Rodriguez	10.00	4.50
❑ 18 Wade Boggs	3.00	1.35
❑ 19 Juan Gonzalez	8.00	3.60
❑ 20 Jose Cruz Jr.	3.00	1.35

1998 Pacific Aurora Pennant Fever

	MINT	NRMT
COMPLETE SET (50)	30.00	13.50
COMMON CARD (1-50)	.30	.14
COMP.RED SET (50)	150.00	70.00
COMMON RED (1-50)	1.25	.55

*RED STARS: 1.5X TO 4X BASIC PEN.FEVER
*RED YOUNG STARS: 1.25X TO 3X BASIC PEN.FEVER
RED STATED ODDS 1:4 RETAIL
*SILVER STARS: 12.5X TO 30X BASIC PENNANTS
*SILVER YOUNG STARS: 10X TO 25X BASIC PENNANTS
SILVER: RANDOM INSERTS IN RETAIL PACKS
SILVER PRINT RUN 250 SERIAL #'d SETS
*PLAT.BLUE STARS: 25X TO 60X BASIC PENNANTS
*PLAT.BLUE YOUNG STARS: 20X TO 50X BASIC PENNANTS
PLAT.BLUE: RANDOM INSERTS IN ALL PACKS
PLAT.BLUE PRINT RUN 100 SERIAL #'d SETS
*COPPER STARS: 100X TO 200X BASIC PENNANT
*COPPER YOUNG STARS: 75X TO 150X BASIC PENNANT
COPPER: RANDOM INSERTS IN HOBBY PACKS
COPPER PRINT RUN 20 SERIAL #'d SETS

❑ 1 Tony Gwynn	2.00	.90
❑ 2 Derek Jeter	2.00	.90
❑ 3 Alex Rodriguez	2.50	1.10
❑ 4 Paul Molitor	.75	.35
❑ 5 Nomar Garciaparra	2.50	1.10
❑ 6 Jeff Bagwell	1.25	.55
❑ 7 Ivan Rodriguez	1.00	.45
❑ 8 Cal Ripken	3.00	1.35
❑ 9 Matt Williams	.40	.18
❑ 10 Chipper Jones	2.00	.90
❑ 11 Edgar Martinez	.40	.18
❑ 12 Wade Boggs	.75	.35
❑ 13 Paul Konerko	.75	.35
❑ 14 Ben Grieve	1.50	.70
❑ 15 Sandy Alomar Jr.	.40	.18
❑ 16 Travis Lee	1.50	.70
❑ 17 Scott Rolen	2.00	.90
❑ 18 Ryan Klesko	.40	.18
❑ 19 Juan Gonzalez	2.00	.90
❑ 20 Albert Belle	1.50	.70
❑ 21 Roger Clemens	1.50	.70
❑ 22 Javy Lopez	.40	.18
❑ 23 Jose Cruz Jr.	1.00	.45
❑ 24 Ken Griffey Jr.	4.00	1.80
❑ 25 Mark McGwire	5.00	2.20
❑ 26 Brady Anderson	.40	.18
❑ 27 Jaret Wright	1.00	.45
❑ 28 Roberto Alomar	.75	.35
❑ 29 Joe Carter	.40	.18
❑ 30 Hideo Nomo	1.00	.45
❑ 31 Mike Piazza	2.50	1.10
❑ 32 Andres Galarraga	.75	.35
❑ 33 Larry Walker	.75	.35
❑ 34 Tim Salmon	.75	.35
❑ 35 Frank Thomas	2.50	1.10
❑ 36 Moises Alou	.50	.23
❑ 37 David Justice	.75	.35
❑ 38 Manny Ramirez	.75	.35
❑ 39 Jim Edmonds	.50	.23
❑ 40 Barry Bonds	1.00	.45
❑ 41 Jim Thome	.75	.35
❑ 42 Mo Vaughn	1.00	.45
❑ 43 Rafael Palmeiro	.50	.23
❑ 44 Darin Erstad	1.00	.45
❑ 45 Pedro Martinez	.75	.35
❑ 46 Greg Maddux	2.50	1.10
❑ 47 Jose Canseco	.75	.35
❑ 48 Vladimir Guerrero	1.25	.55
❑ 49 Bernie Williams	.75	.35
❑ 50 Randy Johnson	.75	.35

1998 Pacific Invincible

	MINT	NRMT
COMPLETE SET (150)	180.00	80.00
COMMON CARD (1-150)	.75	.35
❑ 1 Garret Anderson	1.25	.55
❑ 2 Jim Edmonds	2.00	.90
❑ 3 Darin Erstad	3.00	1.35
❑ 4 Chuck Finley	1.25	.55
❑ 5 Tim Salmon	3.00	1.35
❑ 6 Roberto Alomar	3.00	1.35
❑ 7 Brady Anderson	1.25	.55
❑ 8 Geronimo Berroa	.75	.35

	Player	MINT	NRMT
❑ 9	Eric Davis	1.25	.55
❑ 10	Mike Mussina	3.00	1.35
❑ 11	Rafael Palmeiro	2.00	.90
❑ 12	Cal Ripken	12.00	5.50
❑ 13	Steve Avery	.75	.35
❑ 14	Nomar Garciaparra	10.00	4.50
❑ 15	John Valentin	1.25	.55
❑ 16	Mo Vaughn	4.00	1.80
❑ 17	Albert Belle	4.00	1.80
❑ 18	Ozzie Guillen	.75	.35
❑ 19	Norberto Martin	.75	.35
❑ 20	Frank Thomas	10.00	4.50
❑ 21	Robin Ventura	1.25	.55
❑ 22	Sandy Alomar Jr.	1.25	.55
❑ 23	David Justice	3.00	1.35
❑ 24	Kenny Lofton	3.00	1.35
❑ 25	Manny Ramirez	3.00	1.35
❑ 26	Jim Thome	3.00	1.35
❑ 27	Omar Vizquel	1.25	.55
❑ 28	Matt Williams	1.25	.55
❑ 29	Jaret Wright	3.00	1.35
❑ 30	Raul Casanova	.75	.35
❑ 31	Tony Clark	2.00	.90
❑ 32	Deivi Cruz	.75	.35
❑ 33	Bobby Higginson	2.00	.90
❑ 34	Justin Thompson	1.25	.55
❑ 35	Yamil Benitez	.75	.35
❑ 36	Johnny Damon	1.25	.55
❑ 37	Jermaine Dye	.75	.35
❑ 38	Jed Hansen	.75	.35
❑ 39	Larry Sutton	.75	.35
❑ 40	Jeromy Burnitz	1.25	.55
❑ 41	Jeff Cirillo	1.25	.55
❑ 42	Dave Nilsson	.75	.35
❑ 43	Jose Valentin	.75	.35
❑ 44	Fernando Vina	.75	.35
❑ 45	Marty Cordova	.75	.35
❑ 46	Chuck Knoblauch	3.00	1.35
❑ 47	Paul Molitor	3.00	1.35
❑ 48	Brad Radke	1.25	.55
❑ 49	Terry Steinbach	1.25	.55
❑ 50	Wade Boggs	3.00	1.35
❑ 51	Hideki Irabu	2.00	.90
❑ 52	Derek Jeter	8.00	3.60
❑ 53	Tino Martinez	3.00	1.35
❑ 54	Andy Pettitte	2.00	.90
❑ 55	Mariano Rivera	1.25	.55
❑ 56	Bernie Williams	3.00	1.35
❑ 57	Jose Canseco	3.00	1.35
❑ 58	Jason Giambi	1.25	.55
❑ 59	Ben Grieve	5.00	2.20
❑ 60	Aaron Small	.75	.35
❑ 61	Jay Buhner	1.25	.55
❑ 62	Ken Cloude	1.25	.55
❑ 63	Joey Cora	1.25	.55
❑ 64	Ken Griffey Jr.	15.00	6.75
❑ 65	Randy Johnson	3.00	1.35
❑ 66	Edgar Martinez	1.25	.55
❑ 67	Alex Rodriguez	10.00	4.50
❑ 68	Will Clark	3.00	1.35
❑ 69	Juan Gonzalez	8.00	3.60
❑ 70	Rusty Greer	1.25	.55
❑ 71	Ivan Rodriguez	4.00	1.80
❑ 72	Joe Carter	1.25	.55
❑ 73	Roger Clemens	6.00	2.70
❑ 74	Jose Cruz Jr.	3.00	1.35
❑ 75	Carlos Delgado	1.25	.55
❑ 76	Andruw Jones	3.00	1.35
❑ 77	Chipper Jones	8.00	3.60
❑ 78	Ryan Klesko	1.25	.55
❑ 79	Javier Lopez	1.25	.55
❑ 80	Greg Maddux	10.00	4.50
❑ 81	Miguel Batista	.75	.35
❑ 82	Jeremi Gonzalez	1.25	.55
❑ 83	Mark Grace	2.00	.90
❑ 84	Kevin Orie	.75	.35
❑ 85	Sammy Sosa	8.00	3.60
❑ 86	Barry Larkin	2.00	.90
❑ 87	Deion Sanders	1.25	.55
❑ 88	Reggie Sanders	1.25	.55
❑ 89	Chris Stynes	.75	.35
❑ 90	Dante Bichette	1.25	.55
❑ 91	Vinny Castilla	2.00	.90
❑ 92	Andres Galarraga	3.00	1.35
❑ 93	Neifi Perez	1.25	.55
❑ 94	Larry Walker	3.00	1.35
❑ 95	Moises Alou	2.00	.90
❑ 96	Bobby Bonilla	1.25	.55
❑ 97	Kevin Brown	2.00	.90
❑ 98	Craig Counsell	.75	.35
❑ 99	Livan Hernandez	1.25	.55
❑ 100	Edgar Renteria	1.25	.55
❑ 101	Gary Sheffield	2.00	.90
❑ 102	Jeff Bagwell	5.00	2.20
❑ 103	Craig Biggio	3.00	1.35
❑ 104	Luis Gonzalez	.75	.35
❑ 105	Darryl Kile	1.25	.55
❑ 106	Wilton Guerrero	.75	.35
❑ 107	Eric Karros	1.25	.55
❑ 108	Ramon Martinez	1.25	.55
❑ 109	Raul Mondesi	2.00	.90
❑ 110	Hideo Nomo	4.00	1.80
❑ 111	Chan Ho Park	3.00	1.35
❑ 112	Mike Piazza	10.00	4.50
❑ 113	Mark Grudzielanek	1.25	.55
❑ 114	Vladimir Guerrero	4.00	1.80
❑ 115	Pedro Martinez	3.00	1.35
❑ 116	Henry Rodriguez	1.25	.55
❑ 117	David Segui	1.25	.55
❑ 118	Edgardo Alfonzo	1.25	.55
❑ 119	Carlos Baerga	1.25	.55
❑ 120	John Franco	1.25	.55
❑ 121	John Olerud	1.25	.55
❑ 122	Rey Ordonez	1.25	.55
❑ 123	Ricky Bottalico	1.25	.55
❑ 124	Gregg Jefferies	.75	.35
❑ 125	Mickey Morandini	.75	.35
❑ 126	Scott Rolen	6.00	2.70
❑ 127	Curt Schilling	1.25	.55
❑ 128	Jose Guillen	1.25	.55
❑ 129	Esteban Loaiza	.75	.35
❑ 130	Al Martin	.75	.35
❑ 131	Tony Womack	1.25	.55
❑ 132	Dennis Eckersley	1.25	.55
❑ 133	Gary Gaetti	.75	.35
❑ 134	Curtis King	.75	.35
❑ 135	Ray Lankford	1.25	.55
❑ 136	Mark McGwire	20.00	9.00
❑ 137	Ken Caminiti	2.00	.90
❑ 138	Steve Finley	1.25	.55
❑ 139	Tony Gwynn	8.00	3.60
❑ 140	Carlos Hernandez	.75	.35
❑ 141	Wally Joyner	1.25	.55
❑ 142	Barry Bonds	4.00	1.80
❑ 143	Jacob Cruz	.75	.35
❑ 144	Shawn Estes	1.25	.55
❑ 145	Stan Javier	.75	.35
❑ 146	J.T. Snow	1.25	.55
❑ 147	Nomar Garciaparra ROY	5.00	2.20
❑ 148	Scott Rolen ROY	3.00	1.35
❑ 149	Ken Griffey Jr. MVP	8.00	3.60
❑ 150	Larry Walker MVP	1.25	.55

1998 Pacific Invincible Platinum Blue

	MINT	NRMT
COMMON CARD (1-150)	12.00	5.50
*STARS: 6X TO 15X BASIC CARDS		

1998 Pacific Invincible

Cramer's Choice Green

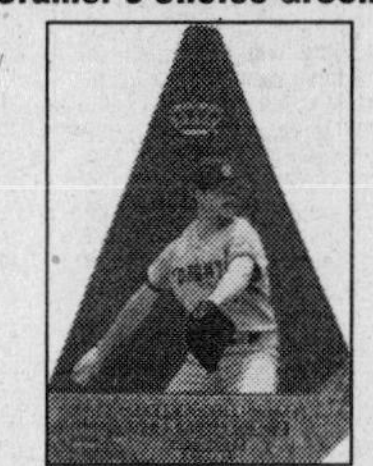

	MINT	NRMT
COMP.GREEN SET (10)	1500.00	700.00
COMMON GREEN (1-10)	60.00	27.00

*DARK BLUE: .6X TO 1.2X GREEN
*LIGHT BLUE: .75X TO 1.5X GREEN
*RED: 1.25X TO 2.5X GREEN
*GOLD: 2X TO 4X GREEN
*PURPLE: 3X TO 6X GREEN
GREEN PRINT RUN 99 SERIAL #'d SETS
DARK BLUE PRINT RUN 80 SERIAL #'d SETS
LIGHT BLUE PRINT RUN 50 SERIAL #'d SETS
RED PRINT RUN 25 SERIAL#'d SETS
GOLD PRINT RUN 15 SERIAL #'d SETS
PURPLE PRINT RUN 10 SERIAL #'d SETS
RANDOM INSERTS IN PACKS
GREEN CARDS LISTED BELOW!

	Player	MINT	NRMT
❑ 1	Greg Maddux	200.00	90.00
❑ 2	Roberto Alomar	60.00	27.00
❑ 3	Cal Ripken	250.00	110.00
❑ 4	Nomar Garciaparra	200.00	90.00
❑ 5	Larry Walker	60.00	27.00
❑ 6	Mike Piazza	200.00	90.00
❑ 7	Mark McGwire	400.00	180.00
❑ 8	Tony Gwynn	150.00	70.00
❑ 9	Ken Griffey Jr.	300.00	135.00
❑ 10	Roger Clemens	120.00	55.00

1998 Pacific Invincible Gems of the Diamond

	MINT	NRMT
COMPLETE SET (220)	40.00	18.00
COMMON CARD (1-220)	.15	.07

	Player	MINT	NRMT
❑ 1	Jim Edmonds	.40	.18
❑ 2	Todd Greene	.25	.11
❑ 3	Ken Hill	.15	.07
❑ 4	Mike Holtz	.15	.07
❑ 5	Mike James	.15	.07
❑ 6	Chad Kreuter	.15	.07
❑ 7	Tim Salmon	.60	.25
❑ 8	Roberto Alomar	.60	.25
❑ 9	Brady Anderson	.25	.11
❑ 10	Dave Dellucci	.60	.25
❑ 11	Jeffrey Hammonds	.25	.11
❑ 12	Mike Mussina	.60	.25
❑ 13	Rafael Palmeiro	.40	.18

❑ 14 Arthur Rhodes .15 .07
❑ 15 Cal Ripken 2.50 1.10
❑ 16 Nerio Rodriguez .25 .11
❑ 17 Tony Tarasco .15 .07
❑ 18 Lenny Webster .15 .07
❑ 19 Mike Benjamin .15 .07
❑ 20 Rich Garces .15 .07
❑ 21 Nomar Garciaparra 2.00 .90
❑ 22 Shane Mack .15 .07
❑ 23 Jose Malave .15 .07
❑ 24 Jesus Tavarez .15 .07
❑ 25 Mo Vaughn .75 .35
❑ 26 John Wasdin .15 .07
❑ 27 Jeff Abbott .25 .11
❑ 28 Albert Belle .75 .35
❑ 29 Mike Cameron .25 .11
❑ 30 Al Levine .15 .07
❑ 31 Robert Machado .15 .07
❑ 32 Greg Norton .15 .07
❑ 33 Magglio Ordonez .75 .35
❑ 34 Mike Sirotka .15 .07
❑ 35 Frank Thomas 2.00 .90
❑ 36 Mario Valdez .25 .11
❑ 37 Sandy Alomar Jr. .25 .11
❑ 38 David Justice .60 .25
❑ 39 Jack McDowell .15 .07
❑ 40 Eric Plunk .15 .07
❑ 41 Manny Ramirez .60 .25
❑ 42 Kevin Seitzer .15 .07
❑ 43 Paul Shuey .15 .07
❑ 44 Omar Vizquel .25 .11
❑ 45 Kimera Bartee .15 .07
❑ 46 Glenn Dishman .15 .07
❑ 47 Orlando Miller .15 .07
❑ 48 Mike Myers .15 .07
❑ 49 Phil Nevin .15 .07
❑ 50 A.J. Sager .15 .07
❑ 51 Ricky Bones .15 .07
❑ 52 Scott Cooper .15 .07
❑ 53 Shane Halter .15 .07
❑ 54 David Howard .15 .07
❑ 55 Glendon Rusch .15 .07
❑ 56 Joe Vitiello .15 .07
❑ 57 Jeff D'Amico .15 .07
❑ 58 Mike Fetters .15 .07
❑ 59 Mike Matheny .15 .07
❑ 60 Jose Mercedes .15 .07
❑ 61 Ron Villone .15 .07
❑ 62 Jack Voigt .15 .07
❑ 63 Brent Brede .15 .07
❑ 64 Chuck Knoblauch .60 .25
❑ 65 Paul Molitor .60 .25
❑ 66 Todd Ritchie .15 .07
❑ 67 Frankie Rodriguez .15 .07
❑ 68 Scott Stahoviak .15 .07
❑ 69 Greg Swindell .15 .07
❑ 70 Todd Walker .40 .18
❑ 71 Wade Boggs .60 .25
❑ 72 Hideki Irabu .40 .18
❑ 73 Derek Jeter 1.50 .70
❑ 74 Pat Kelly .15 .07
❑ 75 Graeme Lloyd .15 .07
❑ 76 Tino Martinez .60 .25
❑ 77 Jeff Nelson .15 .07
❑ 78 Scott Pose .15 .07
❑ 79 Mike Stanton .15 .07
❑ 80 Darryl Strawberry .25 .11
❑ 81 Bernie Williams .60 .25
❑ 82 Tony Batista .15 .07
❑ 83 Mark Bellhorn .25 .11
❑ 84 Ben Grieve 1.25 .55
❑ 85 Pat Lennon .15 .07
❑ 86 Brian Lesher .15 .07
❑ 87 Miguel Tejada .25 .11
❑ 88 George Williams .15 .07
❑ 89 Joey Cora .25 .11
❑ 90 Rob Ducey .15 .07
❑ 91 Ken Griffey Jr. 3.00 1.35
❑ 92 Randy Johnson .60 .25
❑ 93 Edgar Martinez .25 .11
❑ 94 John Marzano .15 .07
❑ 95 Greg McCarthy .15 .07
❑ 96 Alex Rodriguez 2.00 .90
❑ 97 Andy Sheets .15 .07
❑ 98 Mike Timlin .15 .07
❑ 99 Lee Tinsley .15 .07
❑ 100 Damon Buford .15 .07
❑ 101 Alex Diaz .15 .07
❑ 102 Benji Gil .15 .07
❑ 103 Juan Gonzalez 1.50 .70
❑ 104 Eric Gunderson .15 .07
❑ 105 Danny Patterson .15 .07
❑ 106 Ivan Rodriguez .75 .35
❑ 107 Mike Simms .15 .07
❑ 108 Luis Andujar .15 .07
❑ 109 Joe Carter .25 .11
❑ 110 Roger Clemens 1.25 .55
❑ 111 Jose Cruz Jr. .75 .35
❑ 112 Shawn Green .25 .11
❑ 113 Robert Perez .15 .07
❑ 114 Juan Samuel .15 .07
❑ 115 Ed Sprague Jr. .15 .07
❑ 116 Shannon Stewart .25 .11
❑ 117 Danny Bautista .15 .07
❑ 118 Chipper Jones 1.50 .70
❑ 119 Ryan Klesko .25 .11
❑ 120 Keith Lockhart .15 .07
❑ 121 Javier Lopez .25 .11
❑ 122 Greg Maddux 2.00 .90
❑ 123 Kevin Millwood .60 .25
❑ 124 Mike Mordecai .15 .07
❑ 125 Eddie Perez .15 .07
❑ 126 Randall Simon .25 .11
❑ 127 Miguel Cairo .25 .11
❑ 128 Dave Clark .15 .07
❑ 129 Kevin Foster .15 .07
❑ 130 Mark Grace .40 .18
❑ 131 Tyler Houston .15 .07
❑ 132 Mike Hubbard .15 .07
❑ 133 Kevin Orie .15 .07
❑ 134 Ryne Sandberg .75 .35
❑ 135 Sammy Sosa 1.50 .70
❑ 136 Lenny Harris .15 .07
❑ 137 Kent Mercker .15 .07
❑ 138 Mike Morgan .15 .07
❑ 139 Deion Sanders .25 .11
❑ 140 Chris Stynes .15 .07
❑ 141 Gabe White .15 .07
❑ 142 Jason Bates .15 .07
❑ 143 Vinny Castilla .40 .18
❑ 144 Andres Galarraga .60 .25
❑ 145 Curtis Leskanic .15 .07
❑ 146 Jeff McCurry .15 .07
❑ 147 Mike Munoz .15 .07
❑ 148 Larry Walker .60 .25
❑ 149 Jamey Wright .15 .07
❑ 150 Moises Alou .40 .18
❑ 151 Bobby Bonilla .25 .11
❑ 152 Kevin Brown .40 .18
❑ 153 John Cangelosi .15 .07
❑ 154 Jeff Conine .25 .11
❑ 155 Cliff Floyd .25 .11
❑ 156 Jay Powell .15 .07
❑ 157 Edgar Renteria .25 .11
❑ 158 Tony Saunders .15 .07
❑ 159 Gary Sheffield .40 .18
❑ 160 Jeff Bagwell 1.00 .45
❑ 161 Tim Bogar .15 .07
❑ 162 Tony Eusebio .15 .07
❑ 163 Chris Holt .15 .07
❑ 164 Ray Montgomery .15 .07
❑ 165 Luis Rivera .15 .07
❑ 166 Eric Anthony .15 .07
❑ 167 Brett Butler .25 .11
❑ 168 Juan Castro .15 .07
❑ 169 Tripp Cromer .15 .07
❑ 170 Raul Mondesi .40 .18
❑ 171 Hideo Nomo .75 .35
❑ 172 Mike Piazza 2.00 .90
❑ 173 Tom Prince .15 .07
❑ 174 Adam Riggs .15 .07
❑ 175 Shane Andrews .15 .07
❑ 176 Shayne Bennett .15 .07
❑ 177 Raul Chavez .15 .07
❑ 178 Pedro Martinez .60 .25
❑ 179 Sherman Obando .15 .07
❑ 180 Andy Stankiewicz .15 .07
❑ 181 Alberto Castillo .15 .07
❑ 182 Shawn Gilbert .15 .07
❑ 183 Luis Lopez .15 .07
❑ 184 Roberto Petagine .15 .07
❑ 185 Armando Reynoso .15 .07
❑ 186 Midre Cummings .15 .07
❑ 187 Kevin Jordan .15 .07
❑ 188 Desi Relaford .15 .07
❑ 189 Scott Rolen 1.50 .70
❑ 190 Ken Ryan .15 .07
❑ 191 Kevin Sefcik .15 .07
❑ 192 Emil Brown .25 .11
❑ 193 Lou Collier .15 .07
❑ 194 Francisco Cordova .15 .07
❑ 195 Kevin Elster .15 .07
❑ 196 Mark Smith .15 .07
❑ 197 Marc Wilkins .15 .07
❑ 198 Manny Aybar .25 .11
❑ 199 Jose Bautista .15 .07
❑ 200 David Bell .15 .07
❑ 201 Rigo Beltran .15 .07
❑ 202 Delino DeShields .15 .07
❑ 203 Dennis Eckersley .25 .11
❑ 204 John Mabry .15 .07
❑ 205 Eli Marrero .25 .11
❑ 206 Willie McGee .15 .07
❑ 207 Mark McGwire 4.00 1.80
❑ 208 Ken Caminiti .40 .18
❑ 209 Tony Gwynn 1.50 .70
❑ 210 Chris Jones .15 .07
❑ 211 Craig Shipley .15 .07
❑ 212 Pete Smith .15 .07
❑ 213 Jorge Velandia .15 .07
❑ 214 Dario Veras .15 .07
❑ 215 Rich Aurilia .15 .07
❑ 216 Damon Berryhill .15 .07
❑ 217 Barry Bonds .75 .35
❑ 218 Osvaldo Fernandez .15 .07
❑ 219 Dante Powell .25 .11
❑ 220 Rich Rodriguez .15 .07

1998 Pacific Invincible Interleague Players

	MINT	NRMT
COMPLETE SET (30)	600.00	275.00
COMMON CARD (1A-15N)	3.00	1.35

❑ 1A Roberto Alomar 12.00 5.50
❑ 1N Craig Biggio 12.00 5.50
❑ 2A Cal Ripken 50.00 22.00
❑ 2N Chipper Jones 30.00 13.50
❑ 3A Nomar Garciaparra 40.00 18.00
❑ 3N Scott Rolen 25.00 11.00
❑ 4A Mo Vaughn 15.00 6.75
❑ 4N Andres Galarraga 12.00 5.50
❑ 5A Frank Thomas 40.00 18.00
❑ 5N Tony Gwynn 30.00 13.50
❑ 6A Albert Belle 15.00 6.75
❑ 6N Barry Bonds 15.00 6.75
❑ 7A Hideki Irabu 8.00 3.60
❑ 7N Hideo Nomo 15.00 6.75
❑ 8A Derek Jeter 30.00 13.50
❑ 8N Rey Ordonez 5.00 2.20
❑ 9A Tino Martinez 12.00 5.50
❑ 9N Mark McGwire 80.00 36.00
❑ 10A Alex Rodriguez 40.00 18.00
❑ 10N Edgar Renteria 5.00 2.20
❑ 11A Ken Griffey Jr. 60.00 27.00
❑ 11N Larry Walker 12.00 5.50

		MINT	NRMT
❑ 12A	Randy Johnson	12.00	5.50
❑ 12N	Greg Maddux	40.00	18.00
❑ 13A	Ivan Rodriguez	15.00	6.75
❑ 13N	Mike Piazza	40.00	18.00
❑ 14A	Roger Clemens	25.00	11.00
❑ 14N	Pedro Martinez	12.00	5.50
❑ 15A	Jose Cruz Jr.	12.00	5.50
❑ 15N	Wilton Guerrero	3.00	1.35

1998 Pacific Invincible Moments in Time

	MINT	NRMT
COMPLETE SET (20)	800.00	350.00
COMMON CARD (1-20)	5.00	2.20
❑ 1 Chipper Jones	50.00	22.00
❑ 2 Cal Ripken	80.00	36.00
❑ 3 Frank Thomas	60.00	27.00
❑ 4 David Justice	20.00	9.00
❑ 5 Andres Galarraga	20.00	9.00
❑ 6 Larry Walker	20.00	9.00
❑ 7 Livan Hernandez	8.00	3.60
❑ 8 Wilton Guerrero	5.00	2.20
❑ 9 Hideo Nomo	30.00	13.50
❑ 10 Mike Piazza	60.00	27.00
❑ 11 Pedro Martinez	20.00	9.00
❑ 12 Bernie Williams	20.00	9.00
❑ 13 Ben Grieve	30.00	13.50
❑ 14 Scott Rolen	40.00	18.00
❑ 15 Mark McGwire	120.00	55.00
❑ 16 Tony Gwynn	50.00	22.00
❑ 17 Ken Griffey Jr.	100.00	45.00
❑ 18 Alex Rodriguez	60.00	27.00
❑ 19 Juan Gonzalez	50.00	22.00
❑ 20 Jose Cruz Jr.	20.00	9.00

1998 Pacific Invincible Photoengravings

	MINT	NRMT
COMPLETE SET (18)	200.00	90.00
COMMON CARD (1-18)	4.00	1.80
❑ 1 Greg Maddux	15.00	6.75
❑ 2 Cal Ripken	20.00	9.00
❑ 3 Nomar Garciaparra	15.00	6.75
❑ 4 Frank Thomas	15.00	6.75
❑ 5 Larry Walker	5.00	2.20
❑ 6 Mike Piazza	15.00	6.75
❑ 7 Hideo Nomo	6.00	2.70
❑ 8 Pedro Martinez	5.00	2.20
❑ 9 Derek Jeter	12.00	5.50
❑ 10 Tino Martinez	5.00	2.20
❑ 11 Mark McGwire	30.00	13.50
❑ 12 Tony Gwynn	12.00	5.50
❑ 13 Barry Bonds	6.00	2.70
❑ 14 Ken Griffey Jr.	25.00	11.00
❑ 15 Alex Rodriguez	15.00	6.75
❑ 16 Ivan Rodriguez	6.00	2.70
❑ 17 Roger Clemens	10.00	4.50
❑ 18 Jose Cruz Jr.	4.00	1.80

1998 Pacific Invincible Team Checklists

	MINT	NRMT
COMPLETE SET (30)	200.00	90.00
COMMON CARD (1-30)	2.00	.90
❑ 1 Anaheim Angels Jim Edmonds Tim Salmon Darin Erstad Garret Anderson Rickey Henderson	5.00	2.20
❑ 2 Atlanta Braves Greg Maddux Chipper Jones Javier Lopez Ryan Klesko Andruw Jones	15.00	6.75
❑ 3 Baltimore Orioles Cal Ripken Roberto Alomar Brady Anderson Mike Mussina Rafael Palmeiro	20.00	9.00
❑ 4 Boston Red Sox Nomar Garciaparra Mo Vaughn Steve Avery John Valentin	15.00	6.75
❑ 5 Chicago Cubs Sammy Sosa Mark Grace Ryne Sandberg Jeremi Gonzalez	12.00	5.50
❑ 6 Chicago White Sox Frank Thomas Albert Belle Robin Ventura Ozzie Guillen	15.00	6.75
❑ 7 Cincinnati Reds Barry Larkin Deion Sanders Reggie Sanders Brett Tomko	3.00	1.35
❑ 8 Cleveland Indians Sandy Alomar Manny Ramirez David Justice Jim Thome Omar Vizquel	5.00	2.20
❑ 9 Colorado Rockies Andres Galarraga Larry Walker Vinny Castilla Dante Bichette Ellis Burks	5.00	2.20
❑ 10 Detroit Tigers Justin Thompson Tony Clark Deivi Cruz Bobby Higginson	3.00	1.35
❑ 11 Florida Marlins Gary Sheffield Edgar Renteria Livan Hernandez Charles Johnson Bobby Bonilla	3.00	1.35
❑ 12 Houston Astros Jeff Bagwell Craig Biggio Richard Hidalgo Darryl Kile	8.00	3.60
❑ 13 Kansas City Royals Johnny Damon Jermaine Dye Chili Davis Jose Rosado	2.00	.90
❑ 14 Los Angeles Dodgers Mike Piazza Wilton Guerrero Raul Mondesi Hideo Nomo Ramon Martinez	15.00	6.75
❑ 15 Milwaukee Brewers Dave Nilsson Fernando Vina Jeromy Burnitz Julio Franco Jeff Cirillo	2.00	.90
❑ 16 Minnesota Twins Paul Molitor Chuck Knoblauch Brad Radke Terry Steinbach Marty Cordova	5.00	2.20
❑ 17 Montreal Expos Henry Rodriguez Vladimir Guerrero Pedro Martinez David Segui Mark Grudzielanek	6.00	2.70
❑ 18 New York Mets Carlos Baerga Todd Hundley Rey Ordonez John Olerud Edgardo Alfonzo	2.00	.90
❑ 19 New York Yankees Derek Jeter Tino Martinez Bernie Williams Andy Pettitte Mariano Rivera	12.00	5.50
❑ 20 Oakland Athletics Jose Canseco Ben Grieve Jason Giambi Matt Stairs	8.00	3.60
❑ 21 Philadelphia Phillies Curt Schilling Scott Rolen Gregg Jefferies Len Dykstra Ricky Bottalico	10.00	4.50
❑ 22 Pittsburgh Pirates Al Martin Tony Womack Jose Guillen Esteban Loaiza	2.00	.90
❑ 23 St. Louis Cardinals Mark McGwire Dennis Eckersley Delino DeShields Willie McGee Ray Lankford	30.00	13.50
❑ 24 San Diego Padres Tony Gwynn Ken Caminiti Wally Joyner	12.00	5.50

Steve Finley

	MINT	NRMT
❑ 25 San Francisco Giants	6.00	2.70
Barry Bonds J.T. Snow Stan Javier Rod Beck Jose Vizcaino		
❑ 26 Seattle Mariners	25.00	11.00
Ken Griffey Jr. Alex Rodriguez Edgar Martinez Randy Johnson Jay Buhner		
❑ 27 Texas Rangers	12.00	5.50
Juan Gonzalez Ivan Rodriguez Will Clark John Wetteland Rusty Greer		
❑ 28 Toronto Blue Jays	10.00	4.50
Jose Cruz Jr. Roger Clemens Pat Hentgen Joe Carter		
❑ 29 Arizona Diamond Backs	2.00	.90
Yamil Benitez Devon White Matt Williams Jay Bell		
❑ 30 Tampa Bay Devil Rays	5.00	2.20
Wade Boggs Paul Sorrento Fred McGriff Roberto Hernandez		

1998 Pacific Omega

	MINT	NRMT
COMPLETE SET (250)	40.00	18.00
COMMON CARD (1-250)	.15	.07

Card	MINT	NRMT
❑ 1 Garret Anderson	.25	.11
❑ 2 Gary DiSarcina	.15	.07
❑ 3 Jim Edmonds	.40	.18
❑ 4 Darin Erstad	.75	.35
❑ 5 Cecil Fielder	.25	.11
❑ 6 Chuck Finley	.25	.11
❑ 7 Shigetoshi Hasegawa	.25	.11
❑ 8 Tim Salmon	.60	.25
❑ 9 Brian Anderson	.25	.11
❑ 10 Jay Bell	.25	.11
❑ 11 Andy Benes	.25	.11
❑ 12 Yamil Benitez	.15	.07
❑ 13 Jorge Fabregas	.15	.07
❑ 14 Travis Lee	1.25	.55
❑ 15 Devon White	.25	.11
❑ 16 Matt Williams	.25	.11
❑ 17 Andres Galarraga	.60	.25
❑ 18 Tom Glavine	.60	.25
❑ 19 Andruw Jones	.75	.35
❑ 20 Chipper Jones	1.50	.70
❑ 21 Ryan Klesko	.25	.11
❑ 22 Javy Lopez	.25	.11
❑ 23 Greg Maddux	2.00	.90
❑ 24 Kevin Millwood	1.50	.70
❑ 25 Denny Neagle	.25	.11
❑ 26 John Smoltz	.25	.11
❑ 27 Roberto Alomar	.60	.25
❑ 28 Brady Anderson	.25	.11
❑ 29 Joe Carter	.25	.11
❑ 30 Eric Davis	.25	.11
❑ 31 Jimmy Key	.25	.11
❑ 32 Mike Mussina	.60	.25
❑ 33 Rafael Palmeiro	.40	.18
❑ 34 Cal Ripken	2.50	1.10
❑ 35 B.J. Surhoff	.25	.11
❑ 36 Dennis Eckersley	.25	.11
❑ 37 Nomar Garciaparra	2.00	.90
❑ 38 Reggie Jefferson	.15	.07
❑ 39 Derek Lowe	.15	.07
❑ 40 Pedro Martinez	.60	.25
❑ 41 Brian Rose	.25	.11
❑ 42 John Valentin	.25	.11
❑ 43 Jason Varitek	.15	.07
❑ 44 Mo Vaughn	.75	.35
❑ 45 Jeff Blauser	.15	.07
❑ 46 Jeremi Gonzalez	.25	.11
❑ 47 Mark Grace	.40	.18
❑ 48 Lance Johnson	.15	.07
❑ 49 Kevin Orie	.15	.07
❑ 50 Henry Rodriguez	.25	.11
❑ 51 Sammy Sosa	1.50	.70
❑ 52 Kerry Wood	3.00	1.35
❑ 53 Albert Belle	.60	.25
❑ 54 Mike Cameron	.25	.11
❑ 55 Mike Caruso	.25	.11
❑ 56 Ray Durham	.25	.11
❑ 57 Jaime Navarro	.15	.07
❑ 58 Greg Norton	.15	.07
❑ 59 Magglio Ordonez	.75	.35
❑ 60 Frank Thomas	2.00	.90
❑ 61 Robin Ventura	.25	.11
❑ 62 Bret Boone	.25	.11
❑ 63 Willie Greene	.25	.11
❑ 64 Barry Larkin	.40	.18
❑ 65 Jon Nunnally	.15	.07
❑ 66 Eduardo Perez	.15	.07
❑ 67 Reggie Sanders	.25	.11
❑ 68 Brett Tomko	.25	.11
❑ 69 Sandy Alomar Jr.	.25	.11
❑ 70 Travis Fryman	.25	.11
❑ 71 David Justice	.60	.25
❑ 72 Kenny Lofton	.60	.25
❑ 73 Charles Nagy	.25	.11
❑ 74 Manny Ramirez	.60	.25
❑ 75 Jim Thome	.60	.25
❑ 76 Omar Vizquel	.25	.11
❑ 77 Enrique Wilson	.25	.11
❑ 78 Jaret Wright	.75	.35
❑ 79 Dante Bichette	.25	.11
❑ 80 Ellis Burks	.25	.11
❑ 81 Vinny Castilla	.40	.18
❑ 82 Todd Helton	.75	.35
❑ 83 Darryl Kile	.25	.11
❑ 84 Mike Lansing	.15	.07
❑ 85 Neifi Perez	.25	.11
❑ 86 Larry Walker	.60	.25
❑ 87 Raul Casanova	.15	.07
❑ 88 Tony Clark	.40	.18
❑ 89 Luis Gonzalez	.15	.07
❑ 90 Bobby Higginson	.40	.18
❑ 91 Brian Hunter	.25	.11
❑ 92 Bip Roberts	.15	.07
❑ 93 Justin Thompson	.25	.11
❑ 94 Josh Booty	.15	.07
❑ 95 Craig Counsell	.15	.07
❑ 96 Livan Hernandez	.25	.11
❑ 97 Ryan Jackson	.25	.11
❑ 98 Mark Kotsay	.40	.18
❑ 99 Derrek Lee	.25	.11
❑ 100 Mike Piazza	2.00	.90
❑ 101 Edgar Renteria	.25	.11
❑ 102 Cliff Floyd	.25	.11
❑ 103 Moises Alou	.40	.18
❑ 104 Jeff Bagwell	1.00	.45
❑ 105 Derek Bell	.25	.11
❑ 106 Sean Berry	.15	.07
❑ 107 Craig Biggio	.60	.25
❑ 108 John Halama	.15	.07
❑ 109 Richard Hidalgo	.25	.11
❑ 110 Shane Reynolds	.25	.11
❑ 111 Tim Belcher	.15	.07
❑ 112 Brian Bevil	.15	.07
❑ 113 Jeff Conine	.25	.11
❑ 114 Johnny Damon	.25	.11
❑ 115 Jeff King	.25	.11
❑ 116 Jeff Montgomery	.15	.07
❑ 117 Dean Palmer	.25	.11
❑ 118 Terry Pendleton	.25	.11
❑ 119 Bobby Bonilla	.25	.11
❑ 120 Wilton Guerrero	.15	.07
❑ 121 Todd Hollandsworth	.15	.07
❑ 122 Charles Johnson	.25	.11
❑ 123 Eric Karros	.25	.11
❑ 124 Paul Konerko	.60	.25
❑ 125 Ramon Martinez	.25	.11
❑ 126 Raul Mondesi	.40	.18
❑ 127 Hideo Nomo	.75	.35
❑ 128 Gary Sheffield	.40	.18
❑ 129 Ismael Valdes	.25	.11
❑ 130 Jeromy Burnitz	.25	.11
❑ 131 Jeff Cirillo	.25	.11
❑ 132 Todd Dunn	.15	.07
❑ 133 Marquis Grissom	.25	.11
❑ 134 John Jaha	.15	.07
❑ 135 Scott Karl	.15	.07
❑ 136 Dave Nilsson	.15	.07
❑ 137 Jose Valentin	.15	.07
❑ 138 Fernando Vina	.15	.07
❑ 139 Rick Aguilera	.15	.07
❑ 140 Marty Cordova	.15	.07
❑ 141 Pat Meares	.15	.07
❑ 142 Paul Molitor	.60	.25
❑ 143 David Ortiz	.25	.11
❑ 144 Brad Radke	.25	.11
❑ 145 Terry Steinbach	.25	.11
❑ 146 Todd Walker	.40	.18
❑ 147 Shane Andrews	.15	.07
❑ 148 Brad Fullmer	.25	.11
❑ 149 Mark Grudzielanek	.25	.11
❑ 150 Vladimir Guerrero	1.00	.45
❑ 151 F.P. Santangelo	.15	.07
❑ 152 Jose Vidro	.15	.07
❑ 153 Rondell White	.25	.11
❑ 154 Carlos Baerga	.25	.11
❑ 155 Bernard Gilkey	.15	.07
❑ 156 Todd Hundley	.25	.11
❑ 157 Butch Huskey	.15	.07
❑ 158 Bobby Jones	.15	.07
❑ 159 Brian McRae	.15	.07
❑ 160 John Olerud	.25	.11
❑ 161 Rey Ordonez	.25	.11
❑ 162 Masato Yoshii	.50	.23
❑ 163 David Cone	.40	.18
❑ 164 Hideki Irabu	.40	.18
❑ 165 Derek Jeter	1.50	.70
❑ 166 Chuck Knoblauch	.60	.25
❑ 167 Tino Martinez	.60	.25
❑ 168 Paul O'Neill	.25	.11
❑ 169 Andy Pettitte	.40	.18
❑ 170 Mariano Rivera	.25	.11
❑ 171 Darryl Strawberry	.25	.11
❑ 172 David Wells	.40	.18
❑ 173 Bernie Williams	.60	.25
❑ 174 Ryan Christenson	.25	.11
❑ 175 Jason Giambi	.25	.11
❑ 176 Ben Grieve	1.25	.55
❑ 177 Rickey Henderson	.60	.25
❑ 178 A.J. Hinch	.25	.11
❑ 179 Kenny Rogers	.15	.07
❑ 180 Ricky Bottalico	.25	.11
❑ 181 Rico Brogna	.25	.11
❑ 182 Doug Glanville	.25	.11
❑ 183 Gregg Jefferies	.15	.07
❑ 184 Mike Lieberthal	.15	.07
❑ 185 Scott Rolen	1.50	.70
❑ 186 Curt Schilling	.25	.11
❑ 187 Jermaine Allensworth	.15	.07
❑ 188 Lou Collier	.15	.07
❑ 189 Jose Guillen	.25	.11
❑ 190 Jason Kendall	.25	.11
❑ 191 Al Martin	.15	.07
❑ 192 Tony Womack	.25	.11
❑ 193 Kevin Young	.25	.11
❑ 194 Royce Clayton	.15	.07
❑ 195 Delino DeShields	.15	.07
❑ 196 Gary Gaetti	.15	.07
❑ 197 Ron Gant	.15	.07

❑ 198 Brian Jordan .25 .11
❑ 199 Ray Lankford .25 .11
❑ 200 Mark McGwire 4.00 1.80
❑ 201 Todd Stottlemyre .25 .11
❑ 202 Kevin Brown .40 .18
❑ 203 Ken Caminiti .40 .18
❑ 204 Steve Finley .25 .11
❑ 205 Tony Gwynn 1.50 .70
❑ 206 Carlos Hernandez .15 .07
❑ 207 Wally Joyner .25 .11
❑ 208 Greg Vaughn .25 .11
❑ 209 Barry Bonds .75 .35
❑ 210 Shawn Estes .25 .11
❑ 211 Orel Hershiser .25 .11
❑ 212 Stan Javier .15 .07
❑ 213 Jeff Kent .25 .11
❑ 214 Bill Mueller .25 .11
❑ 215 Robb Nen .25 .11
❑ 216 J.T. Snow .25 .11
❑ 217 Jay Buhner .25 .11
❑ 218 Ken Cloude .25 .11
❑ 219 Joey Cora .25 .11
❑ 220 Ken Griffey Jr. 3.00 1.35
❑ 221 Glenallen Hill .15 .07
❑ 222 Randy Johnson .60 .25
❑ 223 Edgar Martinez .25 .11
❑ 224 Jamie Moyer .15 .07
❑ 225 Alex Rodriguez 2.00 .90
❑ 226 David Segui .25 .11
❑ 227 Dan Wilson .15 .07
❑ 228 Rolando Arrojo 1.00 .45
❑ 229 Wade Boggs .60 .25
❑ 230 Miguel Cairo .25 .11
❑ 231 Roberto Hernandez .15 .07
❑ 232 Quinton McCracken .25 .11
❑ 233 Fred McGriff .40 .18
❑ 234 Paul Sorrento .15 .07
❑ 235 Kevin Stocker .15 .07
❑ 236 Will Clark .60 .25
❑ 237 Juan Gonzalez 1.50 .70
❑ 238 Rusty Greer .25 .11
❑ 239 Rick Helling .25 .11
❑ 240 Roberto Kelly .15 .07
❑ 241 Ivan Rodriguez .75 .35
❑ 242 Aaron Sele .25 .11
❑ 243 John Wetteland .25 .11
❑ 244 Jose Canseco .60 .25
❑ 245 Roger Clemens 1.25 .55
❑ 246 Jose Cruz Jr. .75 .35
❑ 247 Carlos Delgado .25 .11
❑ 248 Alex Gonzalez .15 .07
❑ 249 Ed Sprague .15 .07
❑ 250 Shannon Stewart .25 .11
❑ NNO Tony Gwynn Sample.. 3.00 1.35

1998 Pacific Omega EO Portraits

	MINT	NRMT
COMPLETE SET (20)	400.00	180.00
COMMON CARD (1-20)	10.00	4.50

EO PORTRAIT 1 OF 1 PARALLELS EXIST

❑ 1 Cal Ripken 40.00 18.00
❑ 2 Nomar Garciaparra 30.00 13.50
❑ 3 Mo Vaughn 12.00 5.50
❑ 4 Frank Thomas 30.00 13.50
❑ 5 Manny Ramirez 10.00 4.50
❑ 6 Ben Grieve 15.00 6.75
❑ 7 Ken Griffey Jr. 50.00 22.00
❑ 8 Alex Rodriguez 30.00 13.50
❑ 9 Juan Gonzalez 25.00 11.00
❑ 10 Ivan Rodriguez 12.00 5.50
❑ 11 Travis Lee 15.00 6.75
❑ 12 Greg Maddux 30.00 13.50
❑ 13 Chipper Jones 25.00 11.00
❑ 14 Kerry Wood 40.00 18.00
❑ 15 Larry Walker 10.00 4.50
❑ 16 Jeff Bagwell 15.00 6.75
❑ 17 Mike Piazza 30.00 13.50
❑ 18 Mark McGwire 60.00 27.00
❑ 19 Tony Gwynn 25.00 11.00
❑ 20 Barry Bonds 12.00 5.50

1998 Pacific Omega Face To Face

	MINT	NRMT
COMPLETE SET (10)	300.00	135.00
COMMON CARD (1-10)	12.00	5.50

❑ 1 Alex Rodriguez 40.00 18.00
Nomar Garciaparra
❑ 2 Mark McGwire 60.00 27.00
Ken Griffey Jr.
❑ 3 Mike Piazza 30.00 13.50
Sandy Alomar Jr.
❑ 4 Kerry Wood 40.00 18.00
Roger Clemens
❑ 5 Cal Ripken 40.00 18.00
Paul Molitor
❑ 6 Tony Gwynn 25.00 11.00
Wade Boggs
❑ 7 Frank Thomas 40.00 18.00
Chipper Jones
❑ 8 Travis Lee 25.00 11.00
Ben Grieve
❑ 9 Hideo Nomo 12.00 5.50
Hideki Irabu
❑ 10 Juan Gonzalez 25.00 11.00
Manny Ramirez

1998 Pacific Omega Online Inserts

	MINT	NRMT
COMPLETE SET (36)	200.00	90.00
COMMON CARD (1-36)	1.50	.70

❑ 1 Cal Ripken 15.00 6.75
❑ 2 Nomar Garciaparra 12.00 5.50
❑ 3 Pedro Martinez 4.00 1.80
❑ 4 Mo Vaughn 5.00 2.20
❑ 5 Frank Thomas 12.00 5.50
❑ 6 Sandy Alomar Jr. 1.50 .70
❑ 7 Manny Ramirez 4.00 1.80
❑ 8 Jaret Wright 4.00 1.80
❑ 9 Paul Molitor 4.00 1.80
❑ 10 Derek Jeter 10.00 4.50
❑ 11 Bernie Williams 4.00 1.80
❑ 12 Ben Grieve 6.00 2.70
❑ 13 Ken Griffey Jr. 20.00 9.00
❑ 14 Edgar Martinez 1.50 .70
❑ 15 Alex Rodriguez 12.00 5.50
❑ 16 Wade Boggs 4.00 1.80
❑ 17 Juan Gonzalez 10.00 4.50
❑ 18 Ivan Rodriguez 5.00 2.20
❑ 19 Roger Clemens 8.00 3.60
❑ 20 Travis Lee 6.00 2.70
❑ 21 Matt Williams 1.50 .70
❑ 22 Andres Galarraga 4.00 1.80
❑ 23 Chipper Jones 10.00 4.50
❑ 24 Greg Maddux 12.00 5.50
❑ 25 Sammy Sosa 10.00 4.50
❑ 26 Kerry Wood 15.00 6.75
❑ 27 Barry Larkin 2.50 1.10
❑ 28 Larry Walker 4.00 1.80
❑ 29 Derrek Lee 1.50 .70
❑ 30 Jeff Bagwell 6.00 2.70
❑ 31 Hideo Nomo 5.00 2.20
❑ 32 Mike Piazza 12.00 5.50
❑ 33 Scott Rolen 8.00 3.60
❑ 34 Mark McGwire 25.00 11.00
❑ 35 Tony Gwynn 10.00 4.50
❑ 36 Barry Bonds 5.00 2.20

1998 Pacific Omega Prisms

	MINT	NRMT
COMPLETE SET (20)	200.00	90.00
COMMON CARD (1-20)	2.00	.90

❑ 1 Cal Ripken 20.00 9.00
❑ 2 Nomar Garciaparra 15.00 6.75
❑ 3 Pedro Martinez 5.00 2.20
❑ 4 Frank Thomas 15.00 6.75
❑ 5 Manny Ramirez 5.00 2.20
❑ 6 Brian Giles 2.00 .90
❑ 7 Derek Jeter 12.00 5.50
❑ 8 Ben Grieve 8.00 3.60
❑ 9 Ken Griffey Jr. 25.00 11.00
❑ 10 Alex Rodriguez 15.00 6.75
❑ 11 Juan Gonzalez 12.00 5.50
❑ 12 Travis Lee 8.00 3.60
❑ 13 Chipper Jones 12.00 5.50
❑ 14 Greg Maddux 15.00 6.75
❑ 15 Kerry Wood 20.00 9.00
❑ 16 Larry Walker 5.00 2.20
❑ 17 Hideo Nomo 6.00 2.70
❑ 18 Mike Piazza 15.00 6.75
❑ 19 Mark McGwire 30.00 13.50
❑ 20 Tony Gwynn 12.00 5.50

1998 Pacific Omega Rising Stars

	MINT	NRMT
COMPLETE SET (30)	80.00	36.00
COMMON CARD (1-30)	1.00	.45

*TIER 1: 4X TO 10X BASIC RISING STARS
TIER 1 PRINT RUN 100 SERIAL #'d SETS
TIER 1 CARDS ARE 2/10/16/19/20/25
*TIER 2: 5X TO 12X BASIC RISING STARS
TIER 2 PRINT RUN 75 SERIAL #'d SETS
TIER 2 CARDS ARE 3/12/18/23/26/27
*TIER 3: 6X TO 15X BASIC RISING STARS
TIER 3 PRINT RUN 50 SERIAL #'d SETS
TIER 3 CARDS ARE 1/7/15/17/22/28
*TIER 4: 12.5X TO 30X BASIC RISING STARS
TIER 4 PRINT RUN 25 SERIAL #'d SETS
TIER 4 CARDS ARE 6/9/11/14/21/29
TIER 5 STATED PRINT RUN 1 SET
TIER 5 CARDS ARE 4/5/8/13/24/30
TIER 5 NOT PRICED DUE TO SCARCITY

	MINT	NRMT
❑ 1 Nerio Rodriguez	1.50	.70
Sidney Ponson		
❑ 2 Frank Catalanotto	1.50	.70
Roberto Duran		
Sean Runyan		
❑ 3 Kevin L.Brown	1.00	.45
Carlos Almanzar		
❑ 4 Aaron Boone	1.00	.45
Pat Watkins		
Scott Winchester		
❑ 5 Brian Meadows	1.00	.45
Andy Larkin		
Antonio Alfonseca		
❑ 6 DaRond Stovall	1.00	.45
Trey Moore		
Shayne Bennett		
❑ 7 Felix Martinez	1.00	.45
Larry Sutton		
Brian Bevil		
❑ 8 Homer Bush	1.00	.45
Mike Buddie		
❑ 9 Rich Butler	3.00	1.35
Esteban Yan		
❑ 10 Dave Hollins	1.00	.45
Brian Edmondson		
❑ 11 Lou Collier	1.00	.45
Jose Silva		
Javier Martinez		
❑ 12 Steve Sinclair	1.00	.45
Mark Dalesandro		
❑ 13 Jason Varitek	1.50	.70
Brian Rose		
Brian Shouse		
❑ 14 Mike Caruso	1.50	.70
Jeff Abbott		
Tom Fordham		
❑ 15 Jason Johnson	1.50	.70
Bobby Smith		
❑ 16 Dave Berg	2.50	1.10
Mark Kotsay		
Jesus Sanchez		
❑ 17 Richard Hidalgo	1.50	.70
John Halama		
Trever Miller		
❑ 18 Geoff Jenkins	1.50	.70
Bobby Hughes		
Steve Woodard		
❑ 19 Eli Marrero	1.50	.70
Cliff Politte		
Mike Busby		
❑ 20 Desi Relaford	1.00	.45
Darrin Winston		
❑ 21 Todd Helton	5.00	2.20
Bobby Jones		
❑ 22 Rolando Arrojo	6.00	2.70
Miguel Cairo		
Dan Carlson		
❑ 23 David Ortiz	1.50	.70
Jose Valentin		
Eric Milton		
❑ 24 Magglio Ordonez	4.00	1.80
Greg Norton		
❑ 25 Brad Fullmer	1.50	.70
Javier Vazquez		
Rick DeHart		
❑ 26 Paul Konerko	3.00	1.35
Matt Luke		
❑ 27 Derrek Lee	3.00	1.35
Ryan Jackson		
John Roskos		
❑ 28 Ben Grieve	8.00	3.60
A.J.Hinch		
Ryan Christenson		
❑ 29 Travis Lee	8.00	3.60
Karim Garcia		
Dave Dellucci		
❑ 30 Kerry Wood	20.00	9.00
Marc Pisciotta		

1998 Pacific Online

	MINT	NRMT
COMPLETE SET (800)	150.00	70.00
COMMON CARD (1-780)	.20	.09

	MINT	NRMT
❑ 1 Garret Anderson	.30	.14
❑ 2 Rich DeLucia	.20	.09
❑ 3 Jason Dickson	.30	.14
❑ 4 Gary DiSarcina	.20	.09
❑ 5 Jim Edmonds	.50	.23
❑ 6 Darin Erstad	1.00	.45
❑ 7 Cecil Fielder	.30	.14
❑ 8 Chuck Finley	.30	.14
❑ 9 Carlos Garcia	.20	.09
❑ 10 Shigetoshi Hasegawa	.30	.14
❑ 11 Ken Hill	.20	.09
❑ 12 Dave Hollins	.20	.09
❑ 13 Mike Holtz	.20	.09
❑ 14 Mike James	.20	.09
❑ 15 Norberto Martin	.20	.09
❑ 16 Damon Mashore	.20	.09
❑ 17 Jack McDowell	.20	.09
❑ 18 Phil Nevin	.20	.09
❑ 19 Omar Olivares	.20	.09
❑ 20 Troy Percival	.30	.14
❑ 21 Rich Robertson	.20	.09
❑ 22 Tim Salmon	.75	.35
❑ 23 Craig Shipley	.20	.09
❑ 24 Matt Walbeck	.20	.09
❑ 25 Allen Watson	.20	.09
❑ 26 Jim Edmonds TC	.20	.09
❑ 27 Brian Anderson	.30	.14
❑ 28 Tony Batista	.20	.09
❑ 29 Jay Bell	.30	.14
❑ 30 Andy Benes	.30	.14
❑ 31 Yamil Benitez	.20	.09
❑ 32 Willie Blair	.20	.09
❑ 33 Brent Brede	.20	.09
❑ 34 Scott Brow	.20	.09
❑ 35 Omar Daal	.20	.09
❑ 36 Dave Dellucci	1.00	.45
❑ 37 Edwin Diaz	.20	.09
❑ 38 Jorge Fabregas	.20	.09
❑ 39 Andy Fox	.20	.09
❑ 40 Karim Garcia	.30	.14
❑ 41A T.Lee Fielding	1.50	.70
❑ 41B T.Lee Hitting	1.50	.70
❑ 42 Barry Manuel	.20	.09
❑ 43 Gregg Olson	.20	.09
❑ 44 Felix Rodriguez	.20	.09
❑ 45 Clint Sodowsky	.20	.09
❑ 46 Russ Springer	.20	.09
❑ 47 Andy Stankiewicz	.20	.09
❑ 48 Kelly Stinnett	.20	.09
❑ 49 Jeff Suppan	.20	.09
❑ 50 Devon White	.30	.14
❑ 51 Matt Williams	.30	.14
❑ 52 Travis Lee TC	1.00	.45
❑ 53 Danny Bautista	.20	.09
❑ 54 Rafael Belliard	.20	.09
❑ 55 Adam Butler	.30	.14
❑ 56 Mike Cather	.20	.09
❑ 57 Brian Edmondson	.20	.09
❑ 58 Alan Embree	.20	.09
❑ 59 Andres Galarraga	.75	.35
❑ 60 Tom Glavine	.75	.35
❑ 61 Tony Graffanino	.20	.09
❑ 62 Andruw Jones	1.00	.45
❑ 63A C.Jones Fielding	2.00	.90
❑ 63B C.Jones Hitting	2.00	.90
❑ 64 Ryan Klesko	.30	.14
❑ 65 Keith Lockhart	.20	.09
❑ 66 Javy Lopez	.30	.14
❑ 67A G.Maddux Hitting	2.50	1.10
❑ 67B G.Maddux Pitching	2.50	1.10
❑ 68 Dennis Martinez	.30	.14
❑ 69 Kevin Millwood	2.00	.90
❑ 70 Denny Neagle	.30	.14
❑ 71 Eddie Perez	.20	.09
❑ 72 Curtis Pride	.20	.09
❑ 73 John Smoltz	.30	.14
❑ 74 Michael Tucker	.30	.14
❑ 75 Walt Weiss	.30	.14
❑ 76 Gerald Williams	.20	.09
❑ 77 Mark Wohlers	.20	.09
❑ 78 Chipper Jones TC	1.00	.45
❑ 79 Roberto Alomar	.75	.35
❑ 80 Brady Anderson	.30	.14
❑ 81 Harold Baines	.30	.14
❑ 82 Armando Benitez	.20	.09
❑ 83 Mike Bordick	.20	.09
❑ 84 Joe Carter	.30	.14
❑ 85 Norm Charlton	.20	.09
❑ 86 Eric Davis	.30	.14
❑ 87 Doug Drabek	.20	.09
❑ 88 Scott Erickson	.30	.14
❑ 89 Jeffrey Hammonds	.30	.14
❑ 90 Chris Hoiles	.20	.09
❑ 91 Scott Kamieniecki	.20	.09
❑ 92 Jimmy Key	.30	.14
❑ 93 Terry Mathews	.20	.09
❑ 94 Alan Mills	.20	.09
❑ 95 Mike Mussina	.75	.35
❑ 96 Jesse Orosco	.20	.09
❑ 97 Rafael Palmeiro	.50	.23
❑ 98 Sidney Ponson	.30	.14
❑ 99 Jeff Reboulet	.20	.09
❑ 100 Arthur Rhodes	.20	.09
❑ 101A C.Ripken Hitting	3.00	1.35
❑ 101B C.Ripken	3.00	1.35
Hitting Close-Up		
❑ 102 Nerio Rodriguez	.30	.14
❑ 103 B.J. Surhoff	.30	.14
❑ 104 Lenny Webster	.20	.09
❑ 105 Cal Ripken TC	1.50	.70
❑ 106 Steve Avery	.20	.09
❑ 107 Mike Benjamin	.20	.09
❑ 108 Darren Bragg	.20	.09
❑ 109 Damon Buford	.20	.09

❑ 110 Jim Corsi .20 .09
❑ 111 Dennis Eckersley .30 .14
❑ 112 Rich Garces .20 .09
❑ 113A N.Garciaparra Fielding 2.50 1.10
❑ 113B N.Garciaparra Hitting 2.50 1.10
❑ 114 Tom Gordon .30 .14
❑ 115 Scott Hatteberg .20 .09
❑ 116 Butch Henry .20 .09
❑ 117 Reggie Jefferson .20 .09
❑ 118 Mark Lemke .20 .09
❑ 119 Darren Lewis .20 .09
❑ 120 Jim Leyritz .20 .09
❑ 121 Derek Lowe .20 .09
❑ 122 Pedro Martinez .75 .35
❑ 123 Troy O'Leary .30 .14
❑ 124 Brian Rose .30 .14
❑ 125 Bret Saberhagen .30 .14
❑ 126 Donnie Sadler .30 .14
❑ 127 Brian Shouse .30 .14
❑ 128 John Valentin .30 .14
❑ 129 Jason Varitek .20 .09
❑ 130 Mo Vaughn 1.00 .45
❑ 131 Tim Wakefield .20 .09
❑ 132 John Wasdin .20 .09
❑ 133 Nomar Garciaparra TC 1.25 .55
❑ 134 Terry Adams .20 .09
❑ 135 Manny Alexander .20 .09
❑ 136 Rod Beck .30 .14
❑ 137 Jeff Blauser .20 .09
❑ 138 Brant Brown .30 .14
❑ 139 Mark Clark .20 .09
❑ 140 Jeremi Gonzalez .30 .14
❑ 141 Mark Grace .50 .23
❑ 142 Jose Hernandez .20 .09
❑ 143 Tyler Houston .20 .09
❑ 144 Lance Johnson .20 .09
❑ 145 Sandy Martinez .20 .09
❑ 146 Matt Mieske .20 .09
❑ 147 Mickey Morandini .20 .09
❑ 148 Terry Mulholland .20 .09
❑ 149 Kevin Orie .20 .09
❑ 150 Bob Patterson .20 .09
❑ 151 Marc Pisciotta .20 .09
❑ 152 Henry Rodriguez .30 .14
❑ 153 Scott Servais .20 .09
❑ 154 Sammy Sosa 2.00 .90
❑ 155 Kevin Tapani .20 .09
❑ 156 Steve Trachsel .20 .09
❑ 157A K.Wood Pitching 3.00 1.35
❑ 157B K.Wood 3.00 1.35
Pitching Close-Up
❑ 158 Kerry Wood TC 1.50 .70
❑ 159 Jeff Abbott .30 .14
❑ 160 James Baldwin .30 .14
❑ 161 Albert Belle .75 .35
❑ 162 Jason Bere .20 .09
❑ 163 Mike Cameron .30 .14
❑ 164 Mike Caruso .30 .14
❑ 165 Carlos Castillo .20 .09
❑ 166 Tony Castillo .20 .09
❑ 167 Ray Durham .30 .14
❑ 168 Scott Eyre .20 .09
❑ 169 Tom Fordham .20 .09
❑ 170 Keith Foulke .20 .09
❑ 171 Lou Frazier .20 .09
❑ 172 Matt Karchner .20 .09
❑ 173 Chad Kreuter .20 .09
❑ 174 Jaime Navarro .20 .09
❑ 175 Greg Norton .20 .09
❑ 176 Charlie O'Brien .20 .09
❑ 177 Magglio Ordonez 1.00 .45
❑ 178 Ruben Sierra .20 .09
❑ 179 Bill Simas .20 .09
❑ 180 Mike Sirotka .20 .09
❑ 181 Chris Snopek .20 .09
❑ 182A F.Thomas Batter's Box 2.50 1.10
❑ 182B F.Thomas 2.50 1.10
Swing Through
❑ 183 Robin Ventura .30 .14
❑ 184 Frank Thomas TC 1.25 .55
❑ 185 Stan Belinda .20 .09
❑ 186 Aaron Boone .20 .09
❑ 187 Bret Boone .30 .14
❑ 188 Brook Fordyce .20 .09
❑ 189 Willie Greene .30 .14
❑ 190 Pete Harnisch .20 .09
❑ 191 Lenny Harris .20 .09
❑ 192 Mark Hutton .20 .09
❑ 193 Damian Jackson .20 .09
❑ 194 Ricardo Jordan .20 .09
❑ 195 Barry Larkin .50 .23
❑ 196 Eduardo Perez .20 .09
❑ 197 Pokey Reese .20 .09
❑ 198 Mike Remlinger .20 .09
❑ 199 Reggie Sanders .30 .14
❑ 200 Jeff Shaw .30 .14
❑ 201 Chris Stynes .20 .09
❑ 202 Scott Sullivan .20 .09
❑ 203 Eddie Taubensee .20 .09
❑ 204 Brett Tomko .30 .14
❑ 205 Pat Watkins .20 .09
❑ 206 David Weathers .20 .09
❑ 207 Gabe White .20 .09
❑ 208 Scott Winchester .20 .09
❑ 209 Barry Larkin TC .20 .09
❑ 210 Sandy Alomar Jr. .30 .14
❑ 211 Paul Assenmacher .20 .09
❑ 212 Geronimo Berroa .20 .09
❑ 213 Pat Borders .20 .09
❑ 214 Jeff Branson .20 .09
❑ 215 Dave Burba .20 .09
❑ 216 Bartolo Colon .30 .14
❑ 217 Shawon Dunston .20 .09
❑ 218 Travis Fryman .30 .14
❑ 219 Brian Giles .30 .14
❑ 220 Dwight Gooden .30 .14
❑ 221 Mike Jackson .20 .09
❑ 222 David Justice .75 .35
❑ 223 Kenny Lofton .75 .35
❑ 224 Jose Mesa .20 .09
❑ 225 Alvin Morman .20 .09
❑ 226 Charles Nagy .30 .14
❑ 227 Chad Ogea .20 .09
❑ 228 Eric Plunk .20 .09
❑ 229 Manny Ramirez .75 .35
❑ 230 Paul Shuey .20 .09
❑ 231 Jim Thome .75 .35
❑ 232 Ron Villone .20 .09
❑ 233 Omar Vizquel .30 .14
❑ 234 Enrique Wilson .30 .14
❑ 235 Jaret Wright 1.00 .45
❑ 236 Manny Ramirez TC .30 .14
❑ 237 Pedro Astacio .20 .09
❑ 238 Jason Bates .20 .09
❑ 239 Dante Bichette .30 .14
❑ 240 Ellis Burks .30 .14
❑ 241 Vinny Castilla .50 .23
❑ 242 Greg Colbrunn .20 .09
❑ 243 Mike DeJean .20 .09
❑ 244 Jerry Dipoto .20 .09
❑ 245 Curtis Goodwin .20 .09
❑ 246 Todd Helton 1.00 .45
❑ 247 Bobby Jones .20 .09
❑ 248 Darryl Kile .30 .14
❑ 249 Mike Lansing .20 .09
❑ 250 Curtis Leskanic .20 .09
❑ 251 Nelson Liriano .20 .09
❑ 252 Kirt Manwaring .20 .09
❑ 253 Chuck McElroy .20 .09
❑ 254 Mike Munoz .20 .09
❑ 255 Neifi Perez .30 .14
❑ 256 Jeff Reed .20 .09
❑ 257 Mark Thompson .20 .09
❑ 258 John Vander Wal .20 .09
❑ 259 Dave Veres .20 .09
❑ 260A L.Walker Hitting .75 .35
❑ 260B L.Walker Hitting .75 .35
Close-Up
❑ 261 Jamey Wright .20 .09
❑ 262 Larry Walker TC .30 .14
❑ 263 Kimera Bartee .20 .09
❑ 264 Doug Brocail .20 .09
❑ 265 Raul Casanova .20 .09
❑ 266 Frank Castillo .20 .09
❑ 267 Frank Catalanotto .30 .14
❑ 268 Tony Clark .50 .23
❑ 269 Deivi Cruz .20 .09
❑ 270 Roberto Duran .30 .14
❑ 271 Damion Easley .30 .14
❑ 272 Bryce Florie .20 .09
❑ 273 Luis Gonzalez .20 .09
❑ 274 Bobby Higginson .50 .23
❑ 275 Brian Hunter .30 .14
❑ 276 Todd Jones .20 .09
❑ 277 Greg Keagle .20 .09
❑ 278 Jeff Manto .20 .09
❑ 279 Brian Moehler .20 .09
❑ 280 Joe Oliver .20 .09
❑ 281 Joe Randa .20 .09
❑ 282 Bill Ripken .20 .09
❑ 283 Bip Roberts .20 .09
❑ 284 Sean Runyan .20 .09
❑ 285 A.J. Sager .20 .09
❑ 286 Justin Thompson .30 .14
❑ 287 Tony Clark TC .20 .09
❑ 288 Antonio Alfonseca .20 .09
❑ 289 Dave Berg .20 .09
❑ 290 Josh Booty .20 .09
❑ 291 John Cangelosi .20 .09
❑ 292 Craig Counsell .20 .09
❑ 293 Vic Darensbourg .20 .09
❑ 294 Cliff Floyd .30 .14
❑ 295 Oscar Henriquez .30 .14
❑ 296 Felix Heredia .20 .09
❑ 297 Ryan Jackson .30 .14
❑ 298 Mark Kotsay .50 .23
❑ 299 Andy Larkin .20 .09
❑ 300 Derrek Lee .30 .14
❑ 301 Brian Meadows .20 .09
❑ 302 Rafael Medina .30 .14
❑ 303 Jay Powell .20 .09
❑ 304 Edgar Renteria .30 .14
❑ 305 Jesus Sanchez .50 .23
❑ 306 Rob Stanifer .20 .09
❑ 307 Gregg Zaun .20 .09
❑ 308 Derrek Lee TC .20 .09
❑ 309 Moises Alou .50 .23
❑ 310 Brad Ausmus .20 .09
❑ 311A J.Bagwell Fielding 1.25 .55
❑ 311B J.Bagwell Hitting 1.25 .55
❑ 312 Derek Bell .30 .14
❑ 313 Sean Bergman .20 .09
❑ 314 Sean Berry .20 .09
❑ 315 Craig Biggio .75 .35
❑ 316 Tim Bogar .20 .09
❑ 317 Jose Cabrera .20 .09
❑ 318 Dave Clark .20 .09
❑ 319 Tony Eusebio .20 .09
❑ 320 Carl Everett .20 .09
❑ 321 Ricky Gutierrez .20 .09
❑ 322 John Halama .20 .09
❑ 323 Mike Hampton .20 .09
❑ 324 Doug Henry .20 .09
❑ 325 Richard Hidalgo .30 .14
❑ 326 Jack Howell .20 .09
❑ 327 Jose Lima .20 .09
❑ 328 Mike Magnante .20 .09
❑ 329 Trever Miller .20 .09
❑ 330 C.J. Nitkowski .20 .09
❑ 331 Shane Reynolds .30 .14
❑ 332 Bill Spiers .20 .09
❑ 333 Billy Wagner .30 .14
❑ 334 Jeff Bagwell TC .75 .35
❑ 335 Tim Belcher .20 .09
❑ 336 Brian Bevil .20 .09
❑ 337 Johnny Damon .30 .14
❑ 338 Jermaine Dye .20 .09
❑ 339 Sal Fasano .20 .09
❑ 340 Shane Halter .20 .09
❑ 341 Chris Haney .20 .09
❑ 342 Jed Hansen .20 .09
❑ 343 Jeff King .30 .14
❑ 344 Jeff Montgomery .20 .09
❑ 345 Hal Morris .20 .09
❑ 346 Jose Offerman .20 .09
❑ 347 Dean Palmer .30 .14
❑ 348 Terry Pendleton .30 .14
❑ 349 Hipolito Pichardo .20 .09
❑ 350 Jim Pittsley .20 .09
❑ 351 Pat Rapp .20 .09
❑ 352 Jose Rosado .20 .09
❑ 353 Glendon Rusch .20 .09
❑ 354 Scott Service .20 .09
❑ 355 Larry Sutton .20 .09
❑ 356 Mike Sweeney .20 .09

❑ 357 Joe Vitiello .20 .09
❑ 358 Matt Whisenant .20 .09
❑ 359 Ernie Young .20 .09
❑ 360 Jeff King TC .20 .09
❑ 361 Bobby Bonilla .30 .14
❑ 362 Jim Bruske .20 .09
❑ 363 Juan Castro .20 .09
❑ 364 Roger Cedeno .20 .09
❑ 365 Mike Devereaux .20 .09
❑ 366 Darren Dreifort .30 .14
❑ 367 Jim Eisenreich .20 .09
❑ 368 Wilton Guerrero .20 .09
❑ 369 Mark Guthrie .20 .09
❑ 370 Darren Hall .20 .09
❑ 371 Todd Hollandsworth .20 .09
❑ 372 Thomas Howard .20 .09
❑ 373 Trenidad Hubbard .20 .09
❑ 374 Charles Johnson .30 .14
❑ 375 Eric Karros .30 .14
❑ 376 Paul Konerko .75 .35
❑ 377 Matt Luke .20 .09
❑ 378 Ramon Martinez .30 .14
❑ 379 Raul Mondesi .50 .23
❑ 380 Hideo Nomo 1.00 .45
❑ 381 Antonio Osuna .20 .09
❑ 382 Chan Ho Park .75 .35
❑ 383 Tom Prince .20 .09
❑ 384 Scott Radinsky .20 .09
❑ 385 Gary Sheffield .50 .23
❑ 386 Ismael Valdes .30 .14
❑ 387 Jose Vizcaino .20 .09
❑ 388 Eric Young .30 .14
❑ 389 Gary Sheffield TC .20 .09
❑ 390 Jeromy Burnitz .30 .14
❑ 391 Jeff Cirillo .30 .14
❑ 392 Cal Eldred .20 .09
❑ 393 Chad Fox .20 .09
❑ 394 Marquis Grissom .30 .14
❑ 395 Bob Hamelin .20 .09
❑ 396 Bobby Hughes .20 .09
❑ 397 Darrin Jackson .20 .09
❑ 398 John Jaha .20 .09
❑ 399 Geoff Jenkins .30 .14
❑ 400 Doug Jones .20 .09
❑ 401 Jeff Juden .20 .09
❑ 402 Scott Karl .20 .09
❑ 403 Jesse Levis .20 .09
❑ 404 Mark Loretta .20 .09
❑ 405 Mike Matheny .20 .09
❑ 406 Jose Mercedes .20 .09
❑ 407 Mike Myers .20 .09
❑ 408 Marc Newfield .20 .09
❑ 409 Dave Nilsson .20 .09
❑ 410 Al Reyes .20 .09
❑ 411 Jose Valentin .20 .09
❑ 412 Fernando Vina .20 .09
❑ 413 Paul Wagner .20 .09
❑ 414 Bob Wickman .20 .09
❑ 415 Steve Woodard .30 .14
❑ 416 Marquis Grissom TC .20 .09
❑ 417 Rick Aguilera .20 .09
❑ 418 Ron Coomer .20 .09
❑ 419 Marty Cordova .20 .09
❑ 420 Brent Gates .20 .09
❑ 421 Eddie Guardado .20 .09
❑ 422 Denny Hocking .20 .09
❑ 423 Matt Lawton .30 .14
❑ 424 Pat Meares .20 .09
❑ 425 Orlando Merced .20 .09
❑ 426 Eric Milton .30 .14
❑ 427 Paul Molitor .75 .35
❑ 428 Mike Morgan .20 .09
❑ 429 Dan Naulty .20 .09
❑ 430 Otis Nixon .20 .09
❑ 431 Alex Ochoa .20 .09
❑ 432 David Ortiz .30 .14
❑ 433 Brad Radke .30 .14
❑ 434 Todd Ritchie .20 .09
❑ 435 Frank Rodriguez .20 .09
❑ 436 Terry Steinbach .30 .14
❑ 437 Greg Swindell .20 .09
❑ 438 Bob Tewksbury .20 .09
❑ 439 Mike Trombley .20 .09
❑ 440 Javier Valentin .30 .14
❑ 441 Todd Walker .50 .23
❑ 442 Paul Molitor TC .30 .14
❑ 443 Shane Andrews .20 .09
❑ 444 Miguel Batista .20 .09
❑ 445 Shayne Bennett .20 .09
❑ 446 Rick DeHart .20 .09
❑ 447 Brad Fullmer .30 .14
❑ 448 Mark Grudzielanek .30 .14
❑ 449 Vladimir Guerrero 1.25 .55
❑ 450 Dustin Hermanson .30 .14
❑ 451 Steve Kline .20 .09
❑ 452 Scott Livingstone .20 .09
❑ 453 Mike Maddux .20 .09
❑ 454 Derrick May .20 .09
❑ 455 Ryan McGuire .20 .09
❑ 456 Trey Moore .20 .09
❑ 457 Mike Mordecai .20 .09
❑ 458 Carl Pavano .30 .14
❑ 459 Carlos Perez .30 .14
❑ 460 F.P. Santangelo .20 .09
❑ 461 DaRond Stovall .20 .09
❑ 462 Anthony Telford .20 .09
❑ 463 Ugueth Urbina .30 .14
❑ 464 Marc Valdes .20 .09
❑ 465 Jose Vidro .20 .09
❑ 466 Rondell White .30 .14
❑ 467 Chris Widger .20 .09
❑ 468 Vladimir Guerrero TC .75 .35
❑ 469 Edgardo Alfonzo .30 .14
❑ 470 Carlos Baerga .30 .14
❑ 471 Rich Becker .20 .09
❑ 472 Brian Bohanon .20 .09
❑ 473 Alberto Castillo .20 .09
❑ 474 Dennis Cook .20 .09
❑ 475 John Franco .30 .14
❑ 476 Matt Franco .20 .09
❑ 477 Bernard Gilkey .20 .09
❑ 478 John Hudek .20 .09
❑ 479 Butch Huskey .20 .09
❑ 480 Bobby Jones .20 .09
❑ 481 Al Leiter .30 .14
❑ 482 Luis Lopez .20 .09
❑ 483 Brian McRae .20 .09
❑ 484 Dave Mlicki .20 .09
❑ 485 John Olerud .30 .14
❑ 486 Rey Ordonez .30 .14
❑ 487 Craig Paquette .20 .09
❑ 488A M.Piazza Hitting 2.50 1.10
❑ 488B M.Piazza Hitting Close-Up 2.50 1.10
❑ 489 Todd Pratt .20 .09
❑ 490 Mel Rojas .20 .09
❑ 491 Tim Spehr .20 .09
❑ 492 Turk Wendell .20 .09
❑ 493 Masato Yoshii .60 .25
❑ 494 Mike Piazza TC 1.25 .55
❑ 495 Willie Banks .20 .09
❑ 496 Scott Brosius .30 .14
❑ 497 Mike Buddie .20 .09
❑ 498 Homer Bush .20 .09
❑ 499 David Cone .50 .23
❑ 500 Chad Curtis .20 .09
❑ 501 Chili Davis .30 .14
❑ 502 Joe Girardi .20 .09
❑ 503 Darren Holmes .20 .09
❑ 504 Hideki Irabu .50 .23
❑ 505A D.Jeter Fielding 2.00 .90
❑ 505B D.Jeter Hitting 2.00 .90
❑ 506 Chuck Knoblauch .75 .35
❑ 507 Graeme Lloyd .20 .09
❑ 508 Tino Martinez .75 .35
❑ 509 Ramiro Mendoza .30 .14
❑ 510 Jeff Nelson .20 .09
❑ 511 Paul O'Neill .30 .14
❑ 512 Andy Pettitte .50 .23
❑ 513 Jorge Posada .30 .14
❑ 514 Tim Raines .30 .14
❑ 515 Mariano Rivera .30 .14
❑ 516 Luis Sojo .20 .09
❑ 517 Mike Stanton .20 .09
❑ 518 Darryl Strawberry .30 .14
❑ 519 Dale Sveum .20 .09
❑ 520 David Wells .50 .23
❑ 521 Bernie Williams .75 .35
❑ 522 Bernie Williams TC .30 .14
❑ 523 Kurt Abbott .20 .09
❑ 524 Mike Blowers .20 .09
❑ 525 Rafael Bournigal .20 .09
❑ 526 Tom Candiotti .20 .09
❑ 527 Ryan Christenson .30 .14
❑ 528 Mike Fetters .20 .09
❑ 529 Jason Giambi .30 .14
❑ 530A B.Grieve Running 1.50 .70
❑ 530B B.Grieve,Swinging 1.50 .70
❑ 531 Buddy Groom .20 .09
❑ 532 Jimmy Haynes .20 .09
❑ 533 Rickey Henderson .75 .35
❑ 534 A.J. Hinch .30 .14
❑ 535 Mike Macfarlane .20 .09
❑ 536 Dave Magadan .20 .09
❑ 537 T.J. Mathews .20 .09
❑ 538 Jason McDonald .20 .09
❑ 539 Kevin Mitchell .20 .09
❑ 540 Mike Mohler .20 .09
❑ 541 Mike Oquist .20 .09
❑ 542 Ariel Prieto .20 .09
❑ 543 Kenny Rogers .20 .09
❑ 544 Aaron Small .20 .09
❑ 545 Scott Spiezio .20 .09
❑ 546 Matt Stairs .30 .14
❑ 547 Bill Taylor .20 .09
❑ 548 Dave Telgheder .20 .09
❑ 549 Jack Voigt .20 .09
❑ 550 Ben Grieve TC .75 .35
❑ 551 Bob Abreu .30 .14
❑ 552 Ruben Amaro .20 .09
❑ 553 Alex Arias .20 .09
❑ 554 Matt Beech .20 .09
❑ 555 Ricky Bottalico .30 .14
❑ 556 Billy Brewer .20 .09
❑ 557 Rico Brogna .30 .14
❑ 558 Doug Glanville .30 .14
❑ 559 Wayne Gomes .20 .09
❑ 560 Mike Grace .20 .09
❑ 561 Tyler Green .20 .09
❑ 562 Rex Hudler .20 .09
❑ 563 Gregg Jefferies .20 .09
❑ 564 Kevin Jordan .20 .09
❑ 565 Mark Leiter .20 .09
❑ 566 Mark Lewis .20 .09
❑ 567 Mike Lieberthal .20 .09
❑ 568 Mark Parent .20 .09
❑ 569 Yorkis Perez .20 .09
❑ 570 Desi Relaford .20 .09
❑ 571 Scott Rolen 2.00 .90
❑ 572 Curt Schilling .30 .14
❑ 573 Kevin Sefcik .20 .09
❑ 574 Jerry Spradlin .20 .09
❑ 575 Garrett Stephenson .20 .09
❑ 576 Darrin Winston .20 .09
❑ 577 Scott Rolen TC 1.00 .45
❑ 578 Jermaine Allensworth .20 .09
❑ 579 Jason Christiansen .20 .09
❑ 580 Lou Collier .20 .09
❑ 581 Francisco Cordova .20 .09
❑ 582 Elmer Dessens .20 .09
❑ 583 Freddy Garcia .20 .09
❑ 584 Jose Guillen .30 .14
❑ 585 Jason Kendall .30 .14
❑ 586 Jon Lieber .20 .09
❑ 587 Esteban Loaiza .20 .09
❑ 588 Al Martin .20 .09
❑ 589 Javier Martinez .50 .23
❑ 590 Chris Peters .20 .09
❑ 591 Kevin Polcovich .20 .09
❑ 592 Ricardo Rincon .20 .09
❑ 593 Jason Schmidt .20 .09
❑ 594 Jose Silva .20 .09
❑ 595 Mark Smith .20 .09
❑ 596 Doug Strange .20 .09
❑ 597 Turner Ward .20 .09
❑ 598 Marc Wilkins .20 .09
❑ 599 Mike Williams .20 .09
❑ 600 Tony Womack .30 .14
❑ 601 Kevin Young .30 .14
❑ 602 Tony Womack TC .20 .09
❑ 603 Manny Aybar .30 .14
❑ 604 Kent Bottenfield .20 .09
❑ 605 Jeff Brantley .20 .09
❑ 606 Mike Busby .20 .09
❑ 607 Royce Clayton .20 .09

❑ 608 Delino DeShields .20 .09
❑ 609 John Frascatore .20 .09
❑ 610 Gary Gaetti .20 .09
❑ 611 Ron Gant .20 .09
❑ 612 David Howard .20 .09
❑ 613 Brian Hunter .20 .09
❑ 614 Brian Jordan .30 .14
❑ 615 Tom Lampkin .20 .09
❑ 616 Ray Lankford .30 .14
❑ 617 Braden Looper .30 .14
❑ 618 John Mabry .20 .09
❑ 619 Eli Marrero .30 .14
❑ 620 Willie McGee .20 .09
❑ 621A M.McGwire Fielding .. 5.00 2.20
❑ 621B M.McGwire Hitting 5.00 2.20
❑ 622 Kent Mercker .20 .09
❑ 623 Matt Morris .30 .14
❑ 624 Donovan Osborne .20 .09
❑ 625 Tom Pagnozzi .20 .09
❑ 626 Lance Painter .20 .09
❑ 627 Mark Petkovsek .20 .09
❑ 628 Todd Stottlemyre .30 .14
❑ 629 Mark McGwire TC 2.50 1.10
❑ 630 Andy Ashby .20 .09
❑ 631 Brian Boehringer .20 .09
❑ 632 Kevin Brown .50 .23
❑ 633 Ken Caminiti .50 .23
❑ 634 Steve Finley .30 .14
❑ 635 Ed Giovanola .20 .09
❑ 636 Chris Gomez .20 .09
❑ 637A T. Gwynn Blue Jersey 2.00 .90
❑ 637B T.Gwynn White Jersey 2.00 .90
❑ 638 Joey Hamilton .30 .14
❑ 639 Carlos Hernandez .20 .09
❑ 640 Sterling Hitchcock .30 .14
❑ 641 Trevor Hoffman .30 .14
❑ 642 Wally Joyner .30 .14
❑ 643 Dan Miceli .20 .09
❑ 644 James Mouton .20 .09
❑ 645 Greg Myers .20 .09
❑ 646 Carlos Reyes .20 .09
❑ 647 Andy Sheets .20 .09
❑ 648 Pete Smith .20 .09
❑ 649 Mark Sweeney .20 .09
❑ 650 Greg Vaughn .30 .14
❑ 651 Quilvio Veras .20 .09
❑ 652 Tony Gwynn TC 1.00 .45
❑ 653 Rich Aurilia .20 .09
❑ 654 Marvin Benard .20 .09
❑ 655A B.Bonds Hitting 1.00 .45
❑ 655B B.Bonds Hitting 1.00 .45
Close-Up
❑ 656 Danny Darwin .20 .09
❑ 657 Shawn Estes .30 .14
❑ 658 Mark Gardner .20 .09
❑ 659 Darryl Hamilton .20 .09
❑ 660 Charlie Hayes .20 .09
❑ 661 Orel Hershiser .30 .14
❑ 662 Stan Javier .20 .09
❑ 663 Brian Johnson .20 .09
❑ 664 John Johnstone .20 .09
❑ 665 Jeff Kent .30 .14
❑ 666 Brent Mayne .20 .09
❑ 667 Bill Mueller .30 .14
❑ 668 Robb Nen .30 .14
❑ 669 Jim Poole .20 .09
❑ 670 Steve Reed .20 .09
❑ 671 Rich Rodriguez .20 .09
❑ 672 Kirk Rueter .20 .09
❑ 673 Rey Sanchez .20 .09
❑ 674 J.T. Snow .30 .14
❑ 675 Julian Tavarez .20 .09
❑ 676 Barry Bonds TC .50 .23
❑ 677 Rich Amaral .20 .09
❑ 678 Bobby Ayala .20 .09
❑ 679 Jay Buhner .30 .14
❑ 680 Ken Cloude .30 .14
❑ 681 Joey Cora .30 .14
❑ 682 Russ Davis .30 .14
❑ 683 Rob Ducey .20 .09
❑ 684 Jeff Fassero .20 .09
❑ 685 Tony Fossas .20 .09
❑ 686A K.Griffey Jr. Fielding .. 4.00 1.80
❑ 686B K.Griffey Jr. Hitting 4.00 1.80
❑ 687 Glenallen Hill .20 .09
❑ 688 Jeff Huson .20 .09
❑ 689 Randy Johnson .75 .35
❑ 690 Edgar Martinez .30 .14
❑ 691 John Marzano .20 .09
❑ 692 Jamie Moyer .20 .09
❑ 693A A.Rodriguez Fielding 2.50 1.10
❑ 693B A.Rodriguez Hitting.... 2.50 1.10
❑ 694 David Segui .30 .14
❑ 695 Heathcliff Slocumb .20 .09
❑ 696 Paul Spoljaric .20 .09
❑ 697 Bill Swift .20 .09
❑ 698 Mike Timlin .20 .09
❑ 699 Bob Wells .20 .09
❑ 700 Dan Wilson .20 .09
❑ 701 Ken Griffey Jr. TC 2.00 .90
❑ 702 Wilson Alvarez .30 .14
❑ 703 Rolando Arrojo 1.25 .55
❑ 704A W.Boggs Fielding .75 .35
❑ 704B W.Boggs Hitting .75 .35
❑ 705 Rich Butler .50 .23
❑ 706 Miguel Cairo .30 .14
❑ 707 Mike Difelice .20 .09
❑ 708 John Flaherty .20 .09
❑ 709 Roberto Hernandez .20 .09
❑ 710 Mike Kelly .20 .09
❑ 711 Aaron Ledesma .20 .09
❑ 712 Albie Lopez .20 .09
❑ 713 Dave Martinez .20 .09
❑ 714 Quinton McCracken .30 .14
❑ 715 Fred McGriff .50 .23
❑ 716 Jim Mecir .20 .09
❑ 717 Tony Saunders .20 .09
❑ 718 Bobby Smith .30 .14
❑ 719 Paul Sorrento .20 .09
❑ 720 Dennis Springer .20 .09
❑ 721 Kevin Stocker .20 .09
❑ 722 Ramon Tatis .20 .09
❑ 723 Bubba Trammell .30 .14
❑ 724 Esteban Yan .60 .25
❑ 725 Wade Boggs TC .30 .14
❑ 726 Luis Alicea .20 .09
❑ 727 Scott Bailes .20 .09
❑ 728 John Burkett .20 .09
❑ 729 Domingo Cedeno .20 .09
❑ 730 Will Clark .75 .35
❑ 731 Kevin Elster .20 .09
❑ 732A J.Gonzalez With Bat .. 2.00 .90
❑ 732B J.Gonzalez Without Bat 2.00 .90
❑ 733 Tom Goodwin .20 .09
❑ 734 Rusty Greer .30 .14
❑ 735 Eric Gunderson .20 .09
❑ 736 Bill Haselman .20 .09
❑ 737 Rick Helling .30 .14
❑ 738 Roberto Kelly .20 .09
❑ 739 Mark McLemore .20 .09
❑ 740 Darren Oliver .20 .09
❑ 741 Danny Patterson .20 .09
❑ 742 Roger Pavlik .20 .09
❑ 743A I.Rodriguez Fielding .. 1.00 .45
❑ 743B I.Rodriguez Hitting .... 1.00 .45
❑ 744 Aaron Sele .30 .14
❑ 745 Mike Simms .20 .09
❑ 746 Lee Stevens .20 .09
❑ 747 Fernando Tatis .30 .14
❑ 748 John Wetteland .30 .14
❑ 749 Bobby Witt .20 .09
❑ 750 Juan Gonzalez TC 1.00 .45
❑ 751 Carlos Almanzar .30 .14
❑ 752 Kevin Brown .50 .23
❑ 753 Jose Canseco .75 .35
❑ 754 Chris Carpenter .30 .14
❑ 755 Roger Clemens 1.50 .70
❑ 756 Felipe Crespo .20 .09
❑ 757 Jose Cruz Jr. 1.00 .45
❑ 758 Mark Dalesandro .20 .09
❑ 759 Carlos Delgado .30 .14
❑ 760 Kelvim Escobar .30 .14
❑ 761 Tony Fernandez .20 .09
❑ 762 Darrin Fletcher .20 .09
❑ 763 Alex Gonzalez .20 .09
❑ 764 Craig Grebeck .20 .09
❑ 765 Shawn Green .30 .14
❑ 766 Juan Guzman .20 .09
❑ 767 Erik Hanson .20 .09
❑ 768 Pat Hentgen .30 .14
❑ 769 Randy Myers .30 .14
❑ 770 Robert Person .20 .09
❑ 771 Dan Plesac .20 .09
❑ 772 Paul Quantrill .20 .09
❑ 773 Bill Risley .20 .09
❑ 774 Juan Samuel .20 .09
❑ 775 Steve Sinclair .20 .09
❑ 776 Ed Sprague .20 .09
❑ 777 Mike Stanley .20 .09
❑ 778 Shannon Stewart .30 .14
❑ 779 Woody Williams .20 .09
❑ 780 Roger Clemens TC .75 .35
❑ SAMP Tony Gwynn Sample 3.00 1.35

1998 Pacific Online Web Cards

	MINT	NRMT
COMPLETE SET (800)	750.00	350.00
COMMON CARD (1-780)	.50	.23

*STARS: 1.5X TO 4X BASIC CARDS
*YOUNG STARS: 1.25X TO 3X BASIC CARDS
*ROOKIES: .75X TO 2X BASIC CARDS

1998 Pacific Paramount

	MINT	NRMT
COMPLETE SET (250)	40.00	18.00
COMMON CARD (1-250)	.15	.07

❑ 1 Garret Anderson .25 .11
❑ 2 Gary DiSarcina .15 .07
❑ 3 Jim Edmonds .40 .18
❑ 4 Darin Erstad .75 .35
❑ 5 Cecil Fielder .25 .11
❑ 6 Chuck Finley .25 .11
❑ 7 Todd Greene .25 .11
❑ 8 Shigetoshi Hasegawa .25 .11
❑ 9 Tim Salmon .60 .25
❑ 10 Roberto Alomar .60 .25
❑ 11 Brady Anderson .25 .11
❑ 12 Joe Carter .25 .11
❑ 13 Eric Davis .25 .11
❑ 14 Ozzie Guillen .15 .07
❑ 15 Mike Mussina .60 .25
❑ 16 Rafael Palmeiro .40 .18
❑ 17 Cal Ripken 2.50 1.10
❑ 18 B.J. Surhoff .25 .11
❑ 19 Steve Avery .15 .07
❑ 20 Nomar Garciaparra 2.00 .90

❑ 21 Reggie Jefferson .15 .07
❑ 22 Pedro Martinez .60 .25
❑ 23 Tim Naehring .15 .07
❑ 24 John Valentin .25 .11
❑ 25 Mo Vaughn .75 .35
❑ 26 James Baldwin .25 .11
❑ 27 Albert Belle .60 .25
❑ 28 Ray Durham .25 .11
❑ 29 Benji Gil .15 .07
❑ 30 Jaime Navarro .15 .07
❑ 31 Magglio Ordonez .75 .35
❑ 32 Frank Thomas 2.00 .90
❑ 33 Robin Ventura .25 .11
❑ 34 Sandy Alomar Jr. .25 .11
❑ 35 Geronimo Berroa .15 .07
❑ 36 Travis Fryman .25 .11
❑ 37 David Justice .60 .25
❑ 38 Kenny Lofton .60 .25
❑ 39 Charles Nagy .25 .11
❑ 40 Manny Ramirez .60 .25
❑ 41 Jim Thome .60 .25
❑ 42 Omar Vizquel .25 .11
❑ 43 Jaret Wright .75 .35
❑ 44 Raul Casanova .15 .07
❑ 45 Frank Catalanotto .25 .11
❑ 46 Tony Clark .40 .18
❑ 47 Bobby Higginson .40 .18
❑ 48 Brian Hunter .25 .11
❑ 49 Todd Jones .15 .07
❑ 50 Bip Roberts .15 .07
❑ 51 Justin Thompson .25 .11
❑ 52 Kevin Appier .25 .11
❑ 53 Johnny Damon .25 .11
❑ 54 Jermaine Dye .15 .07
❑ 55 Jeff King .25 .11
❑ 56 Jeff Montgomery .15 .07
❑ 57 Dean Palmer .25 .11
❑ 58 Jose Rosado .15 .07
❑ 59 Larry Sutton .15 .07
❑ 60 Rick Aguilera .15 .07
❑ 61 Marty Cordova .15 .07
❑ 62 Pat Meares .15 .07
❑ 63 Paul Molitor .60 .25
❑ 64 Otis Nixon .15 .07
❑ 65 Brad Radke .25 .11
❑ 66 Terry Steinbach .25 .11
❑ 67 Todd Walker .40 .18
❑ 68 Hideki Irabu .40 .18
❑ 69 Derek Jeter 1.50 .70
❑ 70 Chuck Knoblauch .60 .25
❑ 71 Tino Martinez .60 .25
❑ 72 Paul O'Neill .25 .11
❑ 73 Andy Pettitte .40 .18
❑ 74 Mariano Rivera .25 .11
❑ 75 Bernie Williams .60 .25
❑ 76 Mark Bellhorn .25 .11
❑ 77 Tom Candiotti .15 .07
❑ 78 Jason Giambi .25 .11
❑ 79 Ben Grieve 1.25 .55
❑ 80 Rickey Henderson .60 .25
❑ 81 Jason McDonald .15 .07
❑ 82 Aaron Small .15 .07
❑ 83 Miguel Tejada .25 .11
❑ 84 Jay Buhner .25 .11
❑ 85 Joey Cora .25 .11
❑ 86 Jeff Fassero .15 .07
❑ 87 Ken Griffey Jr. 3.00 1.35
❑ 88 Randy Johnson .60 .25
❑ 89 Edgar Martinez .25 .11
❑ 90 Alex Rodriguez 2.00 .90
❑ 91 David Segui .25 .11
❑ 92 Dan Wilson .15 .07
❑ 93 Wilson Alvarez .25 .11
❑ 94 Wade Boggs .60 .25
❑ 95 Miguel Cairo .25 .11
❑ 96 John Flaherty .15 .07
❑ 97 Dave Martinez .15 .07
❑ 98 Quinton McCracken .25 .11
❑ 99 Fred McGriff .40 .18
❑ 100 Paul Sorrento .15 .07
❑ 101 Kevin Stocker .15 .07
❑ 102 John Burkett .15 .07
❑ 103 Will Clark .60 .25
❑ 104 Juan Gonzalez 1.50 .70
❑ 105 Rusty Greer .25 .11
❑ 106 Roberto Kelly .15 .07
❑ 107 Ivan Rodriguez .75 .35
❑ 108 Fernando Tatis .25 .11
❑ 109 John Wetteland .25 .11
❑ 110 Jose Canseco .60 .25
❑ 111 Roger Clemens 1.25 .55
❑ 112 Jose Cruz Jr. .75 .35
❑ 113 Carlos Delgado .25 .11
❑ 114 Alex Gonzalez .15 .07
❑ 115 Pat Hentgen .25 .11
❑ 116 Ed Sprague .15 .07
❑ 117 Shannon Stewart .25 .11
❑ 118 Brian Anderson .25 .11
❑ 119 Jay Bell .25 .11
❑ 120 Andy Benes .25 .11
❑ 121 Yamil Benitez .15 .07
❑ 122 Jorge Fabregas .15 .07
❑ 123 Travis Lee 1.25 .55
❑ 124 Devon White .25 .11
❑ 125 Matt Williams .25 .11
❑ 126 Bob Wolcott .15 .07
❑ 127 Andres Galarraga .60 .25
❑ 128 Tom Glavine .60 .25
❑ 129 Andruw Jones .75 .35
❑ 130 Chipper Jones 1.50 .70
❑ 131 Ryan Klesko .25 .11
❑ 132 Javy Lopez .25 .11
❑ 133 Greg Maddux 2.00 .90
❑ 134 Denny Neagle .25 .11
❑ 135 John Smoltz .25 .11
❑ 136 Rod Beck .25 .11
❑ 137 Jeff Blauser .15 .07
❑ 138 Mark Grace .40 .18
❑ 139 Lance Johnson .15 .07
❑ 140 Mickey Morandini .15 .07
❑ 141 Kevin Orie .15 .07
❑ 142 Sammy Sosa 1.50 .70
❑ 143 Aaron Boone .15 .07
❑ 144 Bret Boone .25 .11
❑ 145 Dave Burba .15 .07
❑ 146 Lenny Harris .15 .07
❑ 147 Barry Larkin .40 .18
❑ 148 Reggie Sanders .25 .11
❑ 149 Brett Tomko .25 .11
❑ 150 Pedro Astacio .15 .07
❑ 151 Dante Bichette .25 .11
❑ 152 Ellis Burks .25 .11
❑ 153 Vinny Castilla .40 .18
❑ 154 Todd Helton .75 .35
❑ 155 Darryl Kile .25 .11
❑ 156 Jeff Reed .15 .07
❑ 157 Larry Walker .60 .25
❑ 158 Bobby Bonilla .25 .11
❑ 159 Todd Dunwoody .25 .11
❑ 160 Livan Hernandez .25 .11
❑ 161 Charles Johnson .25 .11
❑ 162 Mark Kotsay .40 .18
❑ 163 Derrek Lee .25 .11
❑ 164 Edgar Renteria .25 .11
❑ 165 Gary Sheffield .40 .18
❑ 166 Moises Alou .40 .18
❑ 167 Jeff Bagwell 1.00 .45
❑ 168 Derek Bell .25 .11
❑ 169 Craig Biggio .60 .25
❑ 170 Mike Hampton .15 .07
❑ 171 Richard Hidalgo .25 .11
❑ 172 Chris Holt .15 .07
❑ 173 Shane Reynolds .25 .11
❑ 174 Wilton Guerrero .15 .07
❑ 175 Eric Karros .25 .11
❑ 176 Paul Konerko .60 .25
❑ 177 Ramon Martinez .25 .11
❑ 178 Raul Mondesi .40 .18
❑ 179 Hideo Nomo .75 .35
❑ 180 Chan Ho Park .60 .25
❑ 181 Mike Piazza 2.00 .90
❑ 182 Ismael Valdes .25 .11
❑ 183 Jeromy Burnitz .25 .11
❑ 184 Jeff Cirillo .25 .11
❑ 185 Todd Dunn .15 .07
❑ 186 Marquis Grissom .25 .11
❑ 187 John Jaha .15 .07
❑ 188 Doug Jones .15 .07
❑ 189 Dave Nilsson .15 .07
❑ 190 Jose Valentin .15 .07
❑ 191 Fernando Vina .15 .07
❑ 192 Orlando Cabrera .25 .11
❑ 193 Steve Falteisek .15 .07
❑ 194 Mark Grudzielanek .25 .11
❑ 195 Vladimir Guerrero 1.00 .45
❑ 196 Carlos Perez .25 .11
❑ 197 F.P. Santangelo .15 .07
❑ 198 Jose Vidro .15 .07
❑ 199 Rondell White .25 .11
❑ 200 Edgardo Alfonzo .25 .11
❑ 201 Carlos Baerga .25 .11
❑ 202 John Franco .25 .11
❑ 203 Bernard Gilkey .15 .07
❑ 204 Todd Hundley .25 .11
❑ 205 Butch Huskey .15 .07
❑ 206 Bobby Jones .15 .07
❑ 207 Brian McRae .15 .07
❑ 208 John Olerud .25 .11
❑ 209 Rey Ordonez .25 .11
❑ 210 Ricky Bottalico .25 .11
❑ 211 Bobby Estalella .25 .11
❑ 212 Doug Glanville .25 .11
❑ 213 Gregg Jefferies .15 .07
❑ 214 Mike Lieberthal .15 .07
❑ 215 Desi Relaford .15 .07
❑ 216 Scott Rolen 1.50 .70
❑ 217 Curt Schilling .25 .11
❑ 218 Adrian Brown .25 .11
❑ 219 Emil Brown .25 .11
❑ 220 Francisco Cordova .15 .07
❑ 221 Jose Guillen .25 .11
❑ 222 Al Martin .15 .07
❑ 223 Abraham Nunez .25 .11
❑ 224 Tony Womack .25 .11
❑ 225 Kevin Young .25 .11
❑ 226 Alan Benes .25 .11
❑ 227 Royce Clayton .15 .07
❑ 228 Gary Gaetti .15 .07
❑ 229 Ron Gant .15 .07
❑ 230 Brian Jordan .25 .11
❑ 231 Ray Lankford .25 .11
❑ 232 Mark McGwire 4.00 1.80
❑ 233 Todd Stottlemyre .25 .11
❑ 234 Kevin Brown .40 .18
❑ 235 Ken Caminiti .40 .18
❑ 236 Steve Finley .25 .11
❑ 237 Tony Gwynn 1.50 .70
❑ 238 Wally Joyner .25 .11
❑ 239 Ruben Rivera .25 .11
❑ 240 Greg Vaughn .25 .11
❑ 241 Quilvio Veras .15 .07
❑ 242 Barry Bonds .75 .35
❑ 243 Jacob Cruz .15 .07
❑ 244 Shawn Estes .25 .11
❑ 245 Orel Hershiser .25 .11
❑ 246 Stan Javier .15 .07
❑ 247 Brian Johnson .15 .07
❑ 248 Jeff Kent .25 .11
❑ 249 Robb Nen .25 .11
❑ 250 J.T. Snow .25 .11

1998 Pacific Paramount Holographic Silver

	MINT	NRMT
COMMON CARD (1-250)	15.00	6.75

*STARS: 40X TO 100X BASIC CARDS

*YOUNG STARS: 30X TO 80X BASIC CARDS
*ROOKIES/PROSPECTS: 15X TO 40X BASIC CARDS

1998 Pacific Paramount Platinum Blue

	MINT	NRMT
COMMON CARD (1-250)	10.00	4.50

*STARS: 25X TO 60X BASIC CARDS
*YOUNG STARS: 20X TO 50X BASIC CARDS
*ROOKIES/PROSPECTS: 10X TO 25X BASIC CARDS

1998 Pacific Paramount Cooperstown Bound

	MINT	NRMT
COMPLETE SET (10)	600.00	275.00
COMMON CARD (1-10)	25.00	11.00

*PACIFIC PROOFS: 4X TO 8X BASIC COOP.BOUND
PROOFS: RANDOM INSERTS IN PACKS
PACIFIC PROOFS PRINT RUN 20 SERIAL #'d SETS

	MINT	NRMT
❑ 1 Greg Maddux	80.00	36.00
❑ 2 Cal Ripken	100.00	45.00
❑ 3 Frank Thomas	80.00	36.00
❑ 4 Mike Piazza	80.00	36.00
❑ 5 Paul Molitor	25.00	11.00
❑ 6 Mark McGwire	150.00	70.00
❑ 7 Tony Gwynn	60.00	27.00
❑ 8 Barry Bonds	30.00	13.50
❑ 9 Ken Griffey Jr.	120.00	55.00
❑ 10 Wade Boggs	25.00	11.00

1998 Pacific Paramount Fielder's Choice

	MINT	NRMT
COMPLETE SET (20)	400.00	180.00
COMMON CARD (1-20)	8.00	3.60
❑ 1 Chipper Jones	25.00	11.00
❑ 2 Greg Maddux	30.00	13.50
❑ 3 Cal Ripken	40.00	18.00
❑ 4 Nomar Garciaparra	30.00	13.50
❑ 5 Frank Thomas	30.00	13.50

	MINT	NRMT
❑ 6 David Justice	10.00	4.50
❑ 7 Larry Walker	10.00	4.50
❑ 8 Jeff Bagwell	15.00	6.75
❑ 9 Hideo Nomo	12.00	5.50
❑ 10 Mike Piazza	30.00	13.50
❑ 11 Derek Jeter	25.00	11.00
❑ 12 Ben Grieve	15.00	6.75
❑ 13 Mark McGwire	60.00	27.00
❑ 14 Tony Gwynn	25.00	11.00
❑ 15 Barry Bonds	12.00	5.50
❑ 16 Ken Griffey Jr.	50.00	22.00
❑ 17 Alex Rodriguez	30.00	13.50
❑ 18 Wade Boggs	10.00	4.50
❑ 19 Ivan Rodriguez	12.00	5.50
❑ 20 Jose Cruz Jr.	8.00	3.60

1998 Pacific Paramount Special Delivery

	MINT	NRMT
COMPLETE SET (20)	200.00	90.00
COMMON CARD (1-20)	4.00	1.80
❑ 1 Chipper Jones	12.00	5.50
❑ 2 Greg Maddux	15.00	6.75
❑ 3 Cal Ripken	20.00	9.00
❑ 4 Nomar Garciaparra	15.00	6.75
❑ 5 Pedro Martinez	5.00	2.20
❑ 6 Frank Thomas	15.00	6.75
❑ 7 David Justice	5.00	2.20
❑ 8 Larry Walker	5.00	2.20
❑ 9 Jeff Bagwell	8.00	3.60
❑ 10 Hideo Nomo	6.00	2.70
❑ 11 Mike Piazza	15.00	6.75
❑ 12 Vladimir Guerrero	6.00	2.70
❑ 13 Derek Jeter	12.00	5.50
❑ 14 Ben Grieve	8.00	3.60
❑ 15 Mark McGwire	30.00	13.50
❑ 16 Tony Gwynn	12.00	5.50
❑ 17 Barry Bonds	6.00	2.70
❑ 18 Ken Griffey Jr.	25.00	11.00
❑ 19 Alex Rodriguez	15.00	6.75
❑ 20 Jose Cruz Jr.	5.00	2.20

1998 Pacific Paramount Team Checklists

	MINT	NRMT
COMPLETE SET (30)	150.00	70.00
COMMON CARD (1-30)	1.00	.45

	MINT	NRMT
❑ 1 Tim Salmon	4.00	1.80
❑ 2 Cal Ripken	15.00	6.75
❑ 3 Nomar Garciaparra	12.00	5.50
❑ 4 Frank Thomas	12.00	5.50
❑ 5 Manny Ramirez	4.00	1.80
❑ 6 Tony Clark	2.50	1.10
❑ 7 Dean Palmer	1.50	.70
❑ 8 Paul Molitor	4.00	1.80
❑ 9 Derek Jeter	10.00	4.50
❑ 10 Ben Grieve	6.00	2.70
❑ 11 Ken Griffey Jr.	20.00	9.00
❑ 12 Wade Boggs	4.00	1.80
❑ 13 Ivan Rodriguez	5.00	2.20
❑ 14 Roger Clemens	8.00	3.60
❑ 15 Matt Williams	1.50	.70
❑ 16 Chipper Jones	10.00	4.50
❑ 17 Sammy Sosa	10.00	4.50
❑ 18 Barry Larkin	2.50	1.10
❑ 19 Larry Walker	4.00	1.80
❑ 20 Livan Hernandez	1.50	.70
❑ 21 Jeff Bagwell	6.00	2.70
❑ 22 Mike Piazza	12.00	5.50
❑ 23 John Jaha	1.00	.45
❑ 24 Vladimir Guerrero	5.00	2.20
❑ 25 Todd Hundley	1.50	.70
❑ 26 Scott Rolen	8.00	3.60
❑ 27 Kevin Young	1.50	.70
❑ 28 Mark McGwire	25.00	11.00
❑ 29 Tony Gwynn	10.00	4.50
❑ 30 Barry Bonds	5.00	2.20

1995 Pacific Prisms

	MINT	NRMT
COMPLETE SET (144)	150.00	70.00
COMMON CARD (1-144)	1.00	.45
COMP.TEAM LOGO SET (28)	5.00	2.20
❑ 1 David Justice	3.00	1.35
❑ 2 Ryan Klesko	1.50	.70
❑ 3 Javier Lopez	1.50	.70
❑ 4 Greg Maddux	10.00	4.50
❑ 5 Fred McGriff	2.00	.90
❑ 6 Tony Tarasco	1.00	.45
❑ 7 Jeffrey Hammonds	1.50	.70
❑ 8 Mike Mussina	3.00	1.35
❑ 9 Rafael Palmeiro	2.00	.90
❑ 10 Cal Ripken	12.00	5.50
❑ 11 Lee Smith	1.50	.70
❑ 12 Roger Clemens	6.00	2.70
❑ 13 Scott Cooper	1.00	.45

❑ 14 Mike Greenwell 1.00 .45
❑ 15 Carlos Rodriguez 1.00 .45
❑ 16 Mo Vaughn 4.00 1.80
❑ 17 Chili Davis 1.50 .70
❑ 18 Jim Edmonds UER 2.00 .90
Card incorrectly numbered 21
❑ 19 Jorge Fabregas 1.00 .45
❑ 20 Bo Jackson 1.50 .70
❑ 21 Tim Salmon 3.00 1.35
❑ 22 Mark Grace 2.00 .90
❑ 23 Jose Guzman 1.00 .45
❑ 24 Randy Myers 1.00 .45
❑ 25 Rey Sanchez 1.00 .45
❑ 26 Sammy Sosa 8.00 3.60
❑ 27 Wilson Alvarez 1.50 .70
❑ 28 Julio Franco 1.00 .45
❑ 29 Ozzie Guillen 1.00 .45
❑ 30 Jack McDowell 1.00 .45
❑ 31 Frank Thomas 10.00 4.50
❑ 32 Bret Boone 1.50 .70
❑ 33 Barry Larkin 2.00 .90
❑ 34 Hal Morris 1.00 .45
❑ 35 Jose Rijo 1.00 .45
❑ 36 Deion Sanders 1.50 .70
❑ 37 Carlos Baerga 1.50 .70
❑ 38 Albert Belle 4.00 1.80
❑ 39 Kenny Lofton 3.00 1.35
❑ 40 Dennis Martinez 1.50 .70
❑ 41 Manny Ramirez 3.00 1.35
❑ 42 Omar Vizquel 1.50 .70
❑ 43 Dante Bichette 1.50 .70
❑ 44 Marvin Freeman 1.00 .45
❑ 45 Andres Galarraga 3.00 1.35
❑ 46 Mike Kingery 1.00 .45
❑ 47 Danny Bautista 1.00 .45
❑ 48 Cecil Fielder 1.50 .70
❑ 49 Travis Fryman 1.50 .70
❑ 50 Tony Phillips 1.00 .45
❑ 51 Alan Trammell 1.50 .70
❑ 52 Lou Whitaker 1.50 .70
❑ 53 Alex Arias 1.00 .45
❑ 54 Bret Barberie 1.00 .45
❑ 55 Jeff Conine 1.50 .70
❑ 56 Charles Johnson 1.50 .70
❑ 57 Gary Sheffield 2.00 .90
❑ 58 Jeff Bagwell 5.00 2.20
❑ 59 Craig Biggio 3.00 1.35
❑ 60 Doug Drabek 1.00 .45
❑ 61 Tony Eusebio 1.00 .45
❑ 62 Luis Gonzalez 1.00 .45
❑ 63 David Cone 2.00 .90
❑ 64 Bob Hamelin 1.00 .45
❑ 65 Felix Jose 1.00 .45
❑ 66 Wally Joyner 1.50 .70
❑ 67 Brian McRae 1.00 .45
❑ 68 Brett Butler 1.50 .70
❑ 69 Garey Ingram 1.00 .45
❑ 70 Ramon Martinez 1.50 .70
❑ 71 Raul Mondesi 2.00 .90
❑ 72 Mike Piazza 10.00 4.50
❑ 73 Henry Rodriguez 1.50 .70
❑ 74 Ricky Bones 1.00 .45
❑ 75 Pat Listach 1.00 .45
❑ 76 Dave Nilsson 1.00 .45
❑ 77 Jose Valentin 1.00 .45
❑ 78 Rick Aguilera 1.00 .45
❑ 79 Denny Hocking 1.00 .45
❑ 80 Shane Mack 1.00 .45
❑ 81 Pedro Munoz 1.00 .45
❑ 82 Kirby Puckett 5.00 2.20
❑ 83 Dave Winfield 3.00 1.35
❑ 84 Moises Alou 2.00 .90
❑ 85 Wil Cordero 1.00 .45
❑ 86 Cliff Floyd 1.50 .70
❑ 87 Marquis Grissom 1.50 .70
❑ 88 Pedro J. Martinez 3.00 1.35
❑ 89 Larry Walker 3.00 1.35
❑ 90 Bobby Bonilla 1.50 .70
❑ 91 Jeromy Burnitz 1.50 .70
❑ 92 John Franco 1.50 .70
❑ 93 Jeff Kent 1.50 .70
❑ 94 Jose Vizcaino 1.00 .45
❑ 95 Wade Boggs 3.00 1.35
❑ 96 Jimmy Key 1.50 .70
❑ 97 Don Mattingly 6.00 2.70
❑ 98 Paul O'Neill 1.50 .70
❑ 99 Luis Polonia 1.00 .45
❑ 100 Danny Tartabull 1.00 .45
❑ 101 Geronimo Berroa 1.00 .45
❑ 102 Rickey Henderson 3.00 1.35
❑ 103 Ruben Sierra 1.00 .45
❑ 104 Terry Steinbach 1.50 .70
❑ 105 Darren Daulton 1.50 .70
❑ 106 Mariano Duncan 1.00 .45
❑ 107 Lenny Dykstra 1.50 .70
❑ 108 Mike Lieberthal 1.00 .45
❑ 109 Tony Longmire 1.00 .45
❑ 110 Tom Marsh 1.00 .45
❑ 111 Jay Bell 1.50 .70
❑ 112 Carlos Garcia 1.00 .45
❑ 113 Orlando Merced 1.00 .45
❑ 114 Andy Van Slyke 1.50 .70
❑ 115 Derek Bell 1.50 .70
❑ 116 Tony Gwynn 8.00 3.60
❑ 117 Luis Lopez 1.00 .45
❑ 118 Bip Roberts 1.00 .45
❑ 119 Rod Beck 1.00 .45
❑ 120 Barry Bonds 4.00 1.80
❑ 121 Darryl Strawberry 1.50 .70
❑ 122 Wm. Van Landingham 1.00 .45
❑ 123 Matt Williams 1.50 .70
❑ 124 Jay Buhner 1.50 .70
❑ 125 Felix Fermin 1.00 .45
❑ 126 Ken Griffey Jr. 15.00 6.75
❑ 127 Randy Johnson 3.00 1.35
❑ 128 Edgar Martinez 1.50 .70
❑ 129 Alex Rodriguez 12.00 5.50
❑ 130 Rene Arocha 1.00 .45
❑ 131 Gregg Jefferies 1.00 .45
❑ 132 Mike Perez 1.00 .45
❑ 133 Ozzie Smith 4.00 1.80
❑ 134 Jose Canseco 3.00 1.35
❑ 135 Will Clark 3.00 1.35
❑ 136 Juan Gonzalez 8.00 3.60
❑ 137 Ivan Rodriguez 4.00 1.80
❑ 138 Roberto Alomar 3.00 1.35
❑ 139 Joe Carter 1.50 .70
❑ 140 Carlos Delgado 1.50 .70
❑ 141 Alex Gonzalez 1.00 .45
❑ 142 Juan Guzman 1.00 .45
❑ 143 Paul Molitor 3.00 1.35
❑ 144 John Olerud 1.50 .70
❑ CL1 Checklist .25 .11
❑ CL2 Checklist .25 .11

1996 Pacific Prisms

	MINT	NRMT
COMPLETE SET (144)	150.00	70.00
COMMON CARD (1-144)	.75	.35

❑ P1 Tom Glavine 3.00 1.35
❑ P2 Chipper Jones 8.00 3.60
❑ P3 David Justice 3.00 1.35
❑ P4 Ryan Klesko 1.25 .55
❑ P5 Javy Lopez 1.25 .55
❑ P6 Greg Maddux 10.00 4.50
❑ P7 Fred McGriff 2.00 .90
❑ P8 Frank Castillo .75 .35
❑ P9 Luis Gonzalez .75 .35
❑ P10 Mark Grace 2.00 .90
❑ P11 Brian McRae .75 .35
❑ P12 Jaime Navarro .75 .35
❑ P13 Sammy Sosa 8.00 3.60
❑ P14 Bret Boone 1.25 .55
❑ P15 Ron Gant .75 .35
❑ P16 Barry Larkin 2.00 .90
❑ P17 Reggie Sanders 1.25 .55
❑ P18 Benito Santiago .75 .35
❑ P19 Dante Bichette 1.25 .55
❑ P20 Vinny Castilla 2.00 .90
❑ P21 Andres Galarraga 3.00 1.35
❑ P22 Bryan Rekar .75 .35
❑ P23 Roberto Alomar 3.00 1.35
❑ P24 Jeff Conine 1.25 .55
❑ P25 Andre Dawson 2.00 .90
❑ P26 Charles Johnson 1.25 .55
❑ P27 Gary Sheffield 2.00 .90
❑ P28 Quilvio Veras .75 .35
❑ P29 Jeff Bagwell 5.00 2.20
❑ P30 Derek Bell 1.25 .55
❑ P31 Craig Biggio 3.00 1.35
❑ P32 Tony Eusebio .75 .35
❑ P33 Karim Garcia 1.25 .55
❑ P34 Eric Karros 1.25 .55
❑ P35 Ramon Martinez 1.25 .55
❑ P36 Raul Mondesi 2.00 .90
❑ P37 Hideo Nomo 5.00 2.20
❑ P38 Mike Piazza 10.00 4.50
❑ P39 Ismael Valdes 1.25 .55
❑ P40 Moises Alou 2.00 .90
❑ P41 Wil Cordero .75 .35
❑ P42 Pedro Martinez 3.00 1.35
❑ P43 Mel Rojas .75 .35
❑ P44 David Segui 1.25 .55
❑ P45 Edgardo Alfonzo 1.25 .55
❑ P46 Rico Brogna .75 .35
❑ P47 John Franco 1.25 .55
❑ P48 Jason Isringhausen .75 .35
❑ P49 Jose Vizcaino .75 .35
❑ P50 Ricky Bottalico 1.25 .55
❑ P51 Darren Daulton 1.25 .55
❑ P52 Lenny Dykstra 1.25 .55
❑ P53 Tyler Green .75 .35
❑ P54 Gregg Jefferies .75 .35
❑ P55 Jay Bell 1.25 .55
❑ P56 Jason Christiansen .75 .35
❑ P57 Carlos Garcia .75 .35
❑ P58 Esteban Loaiza .75 .35
❑ P59 Orlando Merced .75 .35
❑ P60 Andujar Cedeno .75 .35
❑ P61 Tony Gwynn 8.00 3.60
❑ P62 Melvin Nieves .75 .35
❑ P63 Phil Plantier .75 .35
❑ P64 Fernando Valenzuela 1.25 .55
❑ P65 Barry Bonds 4.00 1.80
❑ P66 J.R. Phillips .75 .35
❑ P67 Deion Sanders 1.25 .55
❑ P68 Matt Williams 1.25 .55
❑ P69 Bernard Gilkey .75 .35
❑ P70 Tom Henke .75 .35
❑ P71 Brian Jordan 1.25 .55
❑ P72 Ozzie Smith 4.00 1.80
❑ P73 Manny Alexander .75 .35
❑ P74 Bobby Bonilla 1.25 .55
❑ P75 Mike Mussina 3.00 1.35
❑ P76 Rafael Palmeiro 2.00 .90
❑ P77 Cal Ripken 12.00 5.50
❑ P78 Jose Canseco 3.00 1.35
❑ P79 Roger Clemens 6.00 2.70
❑ P80 John Valentin 1.25 .55
❑ P81 Mo Vaughn 4.00 1.80
❑ P82 Tim Wakefield 1.25 .55
❑ P83 Garret Anderson 1.25 .55
❑ P84 Damion Easley 1.25 .55
❑ P85 Jim Edmonds 2.00 .90
❑ P86 Tim Salmon 3.00 1.35
❑ P87 Wilson Alvarez 1.25 .55
❑ P88 Alex Fernandez .75 .35
❑ P89 Ozzie Guillen .75 .35
❑ P90 Roberto Hernandez .75 .35
❑ P91 Frank Thomas 10.00 4.50
❑ P92 Robin Ventura 1.25 .55
❑ P93 Carlos Baerga 1.25 .55
❑ P94 Albert Belle 4.00 1.80
❑ P95 Kenny Lofton 3.00 1.35
❑ P96 Dennis Martinez 1.25 .55
❑ P97 Eddie Murray 3.00 1.35

	MINT	NRMT
☐ P98 Manny Ramirez	3.00	1.35
☐ P99 Omar Vizquel	1.25	.55
☐ P100 Chad Curtis	.75	.35
☐ P101 Cecil Fielder	1.25	.55
☐ P102 Felipe Lira	.75	.35
☐ P103 Alan Trammell	2.00	.90
☐ P104 Kevin Appier	1.25	.55
☐ P105 Johnny Damon	1.25	.55
☐ P106 Gary Gaetti	1.25	.55
☐ P107 Wally Joyner	1.25	.55
☐ P108 Ricky Bones	.75	.35
☐ P109 John Jaha	.75	.35
☐ P110 B.J. Surhoff	1.25	.55
☐ P111 Jose Valentin	.75	.35
☐ P112 Fernando Vina	.75	.35
☐ P113 Marty Cordova	.75	.35
☐ P114 Chuck Knoblauch	3.00	1.35
☐ P115 Scott Leius	.75	.35
☐ P116 Pedro Munoz	.75	.35
☐ P117 Kirby Puckett	5.00	2.20
☐ P118 Wade Boggs	3.00	1.35
☐ P119 Don Mattingly	5.00	2.20
☐ P120 Jack McDowell	.75	.35
☐ P121 Paul O'Neill	1.25	.55
☐ P122 Ruben Rivera	1.25	.55
☐ P123 Bernie Williams	3.00	1.35
☐ P124 Geronimo Berroa	.75	.35
☐ P125 Rickey Henderson	3.00	1.35
☐ P126 Mark McGwire	15.00	6.75
☐ P127 Terry Steinbach	1.25	.55
☐ P128 Danny Tartabull	.75	.35
☐ P129 Jay Buhner	1.25	.55
☐ P130 Joey Cora	1.25	.55
☐ P131 Ken Griffey Jr.	15.00	6.75
☐ P132 Randy Johnson	3.00	1.35
☐ P133 Edgar Martinez	1.25	.55
☐ P134 Tino Martinez	3.00	1.35
☐ P135 Will Clark	3.00	1.35
☐ P136 Juan Gonzalez	8.00	3.60
☐ P137 Dean Palmer	1.25	.55
☐ P138 Ivan Rodriguez	4.00	1.80
☐ P139 Mickey Tettleton	.75	.35
☐ P140 Larry Walker	3.00	1.35
☐ P141 Joe Carter	1.25	.55
☐ P142 Carlos Delgado	1.25	.55
☐ P143 Alex Gonzalez	.75	.35
☐ P144 Paul Molitor	3.00	1.35

1996 Pacific Prisms Fence Busters

	MINT	NRMT
COMPLETE SET (20)	180.00	80.00
COMMON CARD (1-20)	3.00	1.35
☐ FB1 Albert Belle	10.00	4.50
☐ FB2 Dante Bichette	3.00	1.35
☐ FB3 Barry Bonds	10.00	4.50
☐ FB4 Jay Buhner	3.00	1.35
☐ FB5 Jose Canseco	8.00	3.60
☐ FB6 Ken Griffey Jr.	40.00	18.00
☐ FB7 Chipper Jones	20.00	9.00
☐ FB8 Dave Justice	8.00	3.60
☐ FB9 Eric Karros	3.00	1.35
☐ FB10 Edgar Martinez	3.00	1.35
☐ FB11 Mark McGwire	40.00	18.00
☐ FB12 Eddie Murray	8.00	3.60
☐ FB13 Mike Piazza	25.00	11.00
☐ FB14 Kirby Puckett	12.00	5.50
☐ FB15 Cal Ripken	30.00	13.50
☐ FB16 Tim Salmon	8.00	3.60
☐ FB17 Sammy Sosa	20.00	9.00
☐ FB18 Frank Thomas	25.00	11.00
☐ FB19 Mo Vaughn	10.00	4.50
☐ FB20 Larry Walker	8.00	3.60

1996 Pacific Prisms Flame Throwers

	MINT	NRMT
COMPLETE SET (10)	150.00	70.00
COMMON CARD (1-10)	4.00	1.80
☐ FT1 Randy Johnson	15.00	6.75
☐ FT2 Mike Mussina	15.00	6.75
☐ FT3 Roger Clemens	30.00	13.50
☐ FT4 Tom Glavine	15.00	6.75
☐ FT5 Hideo Nomo	25.00	11.00
☐ FT6 Jose Rijo	4.00	1.80
☐ FT7 Greg Maddux	50.00	22.00
☐ FT8 David Cone	10.00	4.50
☐ FT9 Ramon Martinez	6.00	2.70
☐ FT10 Jose Mesa	4.00	1.80

1996 Pacific Prisms Red Hot Stars

	MINT	NRMT
COMPLETE SET (20)	250.00	110.00
COMMON CARD (1-20)	5.00	2.20
☐ RH1 Roberto Alomar	8.00	3.60
☐ RH2 Jose Canseco	8.00	3.60
☐ RH3 Chipper Jones	20.00	9.00
☐ RH4 Mike Piazza	25.00	11.00
☐ RH5 Tim Salmon	8.00	3.60
☐ RH6 Jeff Bagwell	12.00	5.50
☐ RH7 Ken Griffey Jr.	40.00	18.00
☐ RH8 Greg Maddux	25.00	11.00
☐ RH9 Kirby Puckett	12.00	5.50
☐ RH10 Frank Thomas	25.00	11.00
☐ RH11 Albert Belle	10.00	4.50
☐ RH12 Tony Gwynn	20.00	9.00
☐ RH13 Edgar Martinez	5.00	2.20
☐ RH14 Manny Ramirez	8.00	3.60
☐ RH15 Barry Bonds	10.00	4.50
☐ RH16 Wade Boggs	8.00	3.60
☐ RH17 Randy Johnson	8.00	3.60
☐ RH18 Don Mattingly	12.00	5.50
☐ RH19 Cal Ripken	40.00	18.00
☐ RH20 Mo Vaughn	10.00	4.50

1997 Pacific Prisms

	MINT	NRMT
COMPLETE SET (150)	180.00	80.00
COMMON CARD (1-150)	1.00	.45
☐ 1 Chili Davis	1.50	.70
☐ 2 Jim Edmonds	2.00	.90
☐ 3 Darin Erstad	4.00	1.80
☐ 4 Orlando Palmeiro	1.00	.45
☐ 5 Tim Salmon	3.00	1.35
☐ 6 J.T. Snow	1.50	.70
☐ 7 Roberto Alomar	3.00	1.35
☐ 8 Brady Anderson	1.50	.70
☐ 9 Eddie Murray	3.00	1.35
☐ 10 Mike Mussina	3.00	1.35
☐ 11 Rafael Palmeiro	2.00	.90
☐ 12 Cal Ripken	12.00	5.50
☐ 13 Jose Canseco	3.00	1.35
☐ 14 Roger Clemens	6.00	2.70
☐ 15 Nomar Garciaparra	10.00	4.50
☐ 16 Reggie Jefferson	1.00	.45
☐ 17 Mo Vaughn	4.00	1.80
☐ 18 Wilson Alvarez	1.50	.70
☐ 19 Harold Baines	1.50	.70
☐ 20 Alex Fernandez	1.00	.45
☐ 21 Danny Tartabull	1.00	.45
☐ 22 Frank Thomas	10.00	4.50
☐ 23 Robin Ventura	1.50	.70
☐ 24 Sandy Alomar Jr.	1.50	.70
☐ 25 Albert Belle	4.00	1.80
☐ 26 Kenny Lofton	3.00	1.35
☐ 27 Jim Thome	3.00	1.35
☐ 28 Omar Vizquel	1.50	.70
☐ 29 Raul Casanova	1.00	.45
☐ 30 Tony Clark	2.00	.90
☐ 31 Travis Fryman	1.50	.70
☐ 32 Bobby Higginson	2.00	.90
☐ 33 Melvin Nieves	1.00	.45
☐ 34 Justin Thompson	1.50	.70
☐ 35 Johnny Damon	1.50	.70
☐ 36 Tom Goodwin	1.00	.45
☐ 37 Jeff Montgomery	1.00	.45
☐ 38 Jose Offerman	1.00	.45
☐ 39 John Jaha	1.00	.45
☐ 40 Jeff Cirillo	1.50	.70
☐ 41 Dave Nilsson	1.00	.45
☐ 42 Jose Valentin	1.00	.45
☐ 43 Fernando Vina	1.00	.45
☐ 44 Marty Cordova	1.00	.45
☐ 45 Roberto Kelly	1.00	.45
☐ 46 Chuck Knoblauch	3.00	1.35
☐ 47 Paul Molitor	3.00	1.35
☐ 48 Todd Walker	3.00	1.35
☐ 49 Wade Boggs	3.00	1.35
☐ 50 Cecil Fielder	1.50	.70
☐ 51 Derek Jeter	8.00	3.60
☐ 52 Tino Martinez	3.00	1.35
☐ 53 Andy Pettitte	2.00	.90
☐ 54 Mariano Rivera	1.50	.70
☐ 55 Bernie Williams	3.00	1.35
☐ 56 Tony Batista	1.00	.45

❑ 57 Geronimo Berroa	1.00	.45
❑ 58 Jason Giambi	1.50	.70
❑ 59 Mark McGwire	15.00	6.75
❑ 60 Terry Steinbach	1.50	.70
❑ 61 Jay Buhner	1.50	.70
❑ 62 Joey Cora	1.50	.70
❑ 63 Ken Griffey Jr.	15.00	6.75
❑ 64 Edgar Martinez	1.50	.70
❑ 65 Alex Rodriguez	10.00	4.50
❑ 66 Paul Sorrento	1.00	.45
❑ 67 Will Clark	3.00	1.35
❑ 68 Juan Gonzalez	8.00	3.60
❑ 69 Rusty Greer	1.50	.70
❑ 70 Dean Palmer	1.50	.70
❑ 71 Ivan Rodriguez	4.00	1.80
❑ 72 Joe Carter	1.50	.70
❑ 73 Carlos Delgado	1.50	.70
❑ 74 Juan Guzman	1.00	.45
❑ 75 Pat Hentgen	1.50	.70
❑ 76 Ed Sprague	1.00	.45
❑ 77 Jermaine Dye	1.00	.45
❑ 78 Andruw Jones	4.00	1.80
❑ 79 Chipper Jones	8.00	3.60
❑ 80 Ryan Klesko	1.50	.70
❑ 81 Javier Lopez	1.50	.70
❑ 82 Greg Maddux	10.00	4.50
❑ 83 John Smoltz	1.50	.70
❑ 84 Mark Grace	2.00	.90
❑ 85 Luis Gonzalez	1.00	.45
❑ 86 Brooks Kieschnick	1.00	.45
❑ 87 Jaime Navarro	1.00	.45
❑ 88 Ryne Sandberg	4.00	1.80
❑ 89 Sammy Sosa	8.00	3.60
❑ 90 Bret Boone	1.50	.70
❑ 91 Jeff Brantley	1.00	.45
❑ 92 Eric Davis	1.50	.70
❑ 93 Barry Larkin	2.00	.90
❑ 94 Reggie Sanders	1.50	.70
❑ 95 Ellis Burks	1.50	.70
❑ 96 Dante Bichette	1.50	.70
❑ 97 Vinny Castilla	2.00	.90
❑ 98 Andres Galarraga	3.00	1.35
❑ 99 Eric Young	1.50	.70
❑ 100 Kevin Brown	2.00	.90
❑ 101 Jeff Conine	1.50	.70
❑ 102 Charles Johnson	1.50	.70
❑ 103 Edgar Renteria	1.50	.70
❑ 104 Gary Sheffield	2.00	.90
❑ 105 Jeff Bagwell	5.00	2.20
❑ 106 Derek Bell	1.50	.70
❑ 107 Sean Berry	1.00	.45
❑ 108 Craig Biggio	3.00	1.35
❑ 109 Shane Reynolds	1.50	.70
❑ 110 Karim Garcia	1.50	.70
❑ 111 Todd Hollandsworth	1.00	.45
❑ 112 Ramon Martinez	1.50	.70
❑ 113 Raul Mondesi	2.00	.90
❑ 114 Hideo Nomo	4.00	1.80
❑ 115 Mike Piazza	10.00	4.50
❑ 116 Ismael Valdes	1.50	.70
❑ 117 Moises Alou	2.00	.90
❑ 118 Mark Grudzielanek	1.50	.70
❑ 119 Pedro Martinez	3.00	1.35
❑ 120 Henry Rodriguez	1.50	.70
❑ 121 F.P. Santangelo	1.00	.45
❑ 122 Carlos Baerga	1.50	.70
❑ 123 Bernard Gilkey	1.00	.45
❑ 124 Todd Hundley	1.50	.70
❑ 125 Lance Johnson	1.00	.45
❑ 126 Alex Ochoa	1.00	.45
❑ 127 Rey Ordonez	1.50	.70
❑ 128 Lenny Dykstra	1.50	.70
❑ 129 Gregg Jefferies	1.00	.45
❑ 130 Ricky Otero	1.00	.45
❑ 131 Benito Santiago	1.00	.45
❑ 132 Jermaine Allensworth	1.00	.45
❑ 133 Francisco Cordova	1.00	.45
❑ 134 Carlos Garcia	1.00	.45
❑ 135 Jason Kendall	2.00	.90
❑ 136 Al Martin	1.00	.45
❑ 137 Dennis Eckersley	1.50	.70
❑ 138 Ron Gant	1.00	.45
❑ 139 Brian Jordan	1.50	.70
❑ 140 John Mabry	1.00	.45
❑ 141 Ozzie Smith	4.00	1.80
❑ 142 Ken Caminiti	2.00	.90
❑ 143 Steve Finley	1.50	.70
❑ 144 Tony Gwynn	8.00	3.60
❑ 145 Wally Joyner	1.50	.70
❑ 146 Fernando Valenzuela	1.50	.70
❑ 147 Barry Bonds	4.00	1.80
❑ 148 Jacob Cruz	1.00	.45
❑ 149 Osvaldo Fernandez	1.00	.45
❑ 150 Matt Williams	1.50	.70

1997 Pacific Prisms Gate Attractions

	MINT	NRMT
COMPLETE SET (32)	600.00	275.00
COMMON CARD (GA1-GA32)	3.00	1.35
❑ GA1 Roberto Alomar	12.00	5.50
❑ GA2 Brady Anderson	6.00	2.70
❑ GA3 Cal Ripken	50.00	22.00
❑ GA4 Frank Thomas	40.00	18.00
❑ GA5 Kenny Lofton	12.00	5.50
❑ GA6 Omar Vizquel	6.00	2.70
❑ GA7 Paul Molitor	12.00	5.50
❑ GA8 Wade Boggs	12.00	5.50
❑ GA9 Derek Jeter	30.00	13.50
❑ GA10 Andy Pettitte	8.00	3.60
❑ GA11 Bernie Williams	12.00	5.50
❑ GA12 Geronimo Berroa	3.00	1.35
❑ GA13 Mark McGwire	60.00	27.00
❑ GA14 Ken Griffey Jr.	60.00	27.00
❑ GA15 Alex Rodriguez	40.00	18.00
❑ GA16 Juan Gonzalez	30.00	13.50
❑ GA17 Andruw Jones	15.00	6.75
❑ GA18 Chipper Jones	30.00	13.50
❑ GA19 Greg Maddux	40.00	18.00
❑ GA20 Ryne Sandberg	15.00	6.75
❑ GA21 Sammy Sosa	30.00	13.50
❑ GA22 Andres Galarraga	12.00	5.50
❑ GA23 Jeff Bagwell	20.00	9.00
❑ GA24 Todd Hollandsworth	3.00	1.35
❑ GA25 Hideo Nomo	15.00	6.75
❑ GA26 Mike Piazza	40.00	18.00
❑ GA27 Todd Hundley	6.00	2.70
❑ GA28 Lance Johnson	3.00	1.35
❑ GA29 Ozzie Smith	15.00	6.75
❑ GA30 Ken Caminiti	8.00	3.60
❑ GA31 Tony Gwynn	30.00	13.50
❑ GA32 Barry Bonds	15.00	6.75

1997 Pacific Prisms Gems of the Diamond

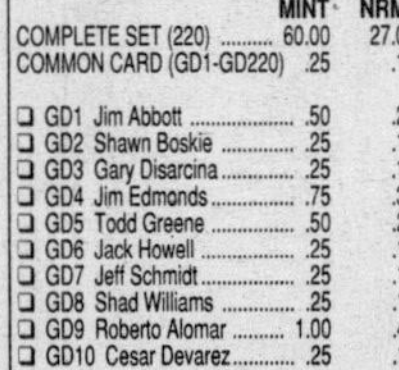

	MINT	NRMT
COMPLETE SET (220)	60.00	27.00
COMMON CARD (GD1-GD220)	.25	.11
❑ GD1 Jim Abbott	.50	.23
❑ GD2 Shawn Boskie	.25	.11
❑ GD3 Gary Disarcina	.25	.11
❑ GD4 Jim Edmonds	.75	.35
❑ GD5 Todd Greene	.50	.23
❑ GD6 Jack Howell	.25	.11
❑ GD7 Jeff Schmidt	.25	.11
❑ GD8 Shad Williams	.25	.11
❑ GD9 Roberto Alomar	1.00	.45
❑ GD10 Cesar Devarez	.25	.11

❑ GD11 Alan Mills	.25	.11
❑ GD12 Eddie Murray	1.00	.45
❑ GD13 Jesse Orosco	.25	.11
❑ GD14 Arthur Rhodes	.25	.11
❑ GD15 Bill Ripken	.25	.11
❑ GD16 Cal Ripken	4.00	1.80
❑ GD17 Mark Smith	.25	.11
❑ GD18 Roger Clemens	2.00	.90
❑ GD19 Vaughn Eshelman	.25	.11
❑ GD20 Rich Garces	.25	.11
❑ GD21 Bill Haselman	.25	.11
❑ GD22 Dwayne Hosey	.25	.11
❑ GD23 Mike Maddux	.25	.11
❑ GD24 Jose Malave	.25	.11
❑ GD25 Aaron Sele	.50	.23
❑ GD26 James Baldwin	.50	.23
❑ GD27 Pat Borders	.25	.11
❑ GD28 Mike Cameron	.50	.23
❑ GD29 Tony Castillo	.25	.11
❑ GD30 Domingo Cedeno	.25	.11
❑ GD31 Greg Norton	.25	.11
❑ GD32 Frank Thomas	3.00	1.35
❑ GD33 Albert Belle	1.25	.55
❑ GD34 Edgar Diaz	.25	.11
❑ GD35 Alan Embree	.25	.11
❑ GD36 Albie Lopez	.25	.11
❑ GD37 Chad Ogea	.25	.11
❑ GD38 Tony Pena	.25	.11
❑ GD39 Joe Roa	.25	.11
❑ GD40 Fausto Cruz	.25	.11
❑ GD41 Joey Eischen	.25	.11
❑ GD42 Travis Fryman	.50	.23
❑ GD43 Mike Myers	.25	.11
❑ GD44 A.J. Sager	.25	.11
❑ GD45 Duane Singleton	.25	.11
❑ GD46 Justin Thompson	.50	.23
❑ GD47 Jeff Granger	.25	.11
❑ GD48 Les Norman	.25	.11
❑ GD49 Jon Nunnally	.25	.11
❑ GD50 Craig Paquette	.25	.11
❑ GD51 Michael Tucker	.50	.23
❑ GD52 Julio Valera	.25	.11
❑ GD53 Kevin Young	.50	.23
❑ GD54 Cal Eldred	.25	.11
❑ GD55 Ramon Garcia	.25	.11
❑ GD56 Marc Newfield	.25	.11
❑ GD57 Al Reyes	.25	.11
❑ GD58 Tim Unroe	.25	.11
❑ GD59 Tim Vanegmond	.25	.11
❑ GD60 Turner Ward	.25	.11
❑ GD61 Bob Wickman	.25	.11
❑ GD62 Chuck Knoblauch	1.00	.45
❑ GD63 Paul Molitor	1.00	.45
❑ GD64 Kirby Puckett	1.50	.70
❑ GD65 Tom Quinlan	.25	.11
❑ GD66 Rich Robertson	.25	.11
❑ GD67 Dave Stevens	.25	.11
❑ GD68 Matt Walbeck	.25	.11
❑ GD69 Wade Boggs	1.00	.45
❑ GD70 Tony Fernandez	.25	.11
❑ GD71 Andy Fox	.25	.11
❑ GD72 Joe Girardi	.25	.11
❑ GD73 Charlie Hayes	.25	.11
❑ GD74 Pat Kelly	.25	.11
❑ GD75 Jeff Nelson	.25	.11
❑ GD76 Melido Perez	.25	.11
❑ GD77 Mark Acre	.25	.11
❑ GD78 Allen Battle	.25	.11

❑ GD79 Rafael Bournigal .... .25 .11
❑ GD80 Mark McGwire 5.00 2.20
❑ GD81 Pedro Munoz .... .25 .11
❑ GD82 Scott Spiezio .... .25 .11
❑ GD83 Don Wengert .... .25 .11
❑ GD84 Steve Wojciechowski .. .25 .11
❑ GD85 Alex Diaz .... .25 .11
❑ GD86 Ken Griffey Jr. 5.00 2.20
❑ GD87 Raul Ibanez .... .25 .11
❑ GD88 Mike Jackson .... .25 .11
❑ GD89 John Marzano .... .25 .11
❑ GD90 Greg McCarthy .... .25 .11
❑ GD91 Alex Rodriguez 3.00 1.35
❑ GD92 Andy Sheets .... .25 .11
❑ GD93 Mac Suzuki .... .25 .11
❑ GD94 Benji Gil .... .25 .11
❑ GD95 Juan Gonzalez 2.50 1.10
❑ GD96 Kevin Gross .... .25 .11
❑ GD97 Gil Heredia .... .25 .11
❑ GD98 Luis Ortiz .... .25 .11
❑ GD99 Jeff Russell .... .25 .11
❑ GD100 Dave Valle .... .25 .11
❑ GD101 Marty Janzen .... .25 .11
❑ GD102 Sandy Martinez .... .25 .11
❑ GD103 Julio Mosquera .... .25 .11
❑ GD104 Otis Nixon .... .25 .11
❑ GD105 Paul Spoljaric .... .25 .11
❑ GD106 Shannon Stewart ...... .50 .23
❑ GD107 Woody Williams .... .25 .11
❑ GD108 Steve Avery .... .25 .11
❑ GD109 Mike Bielecki .... .25 .11
❑ GD110 Pedro Borbon .... .25 .11
❑ GD111 Ed Giovanola .... .25 .11
❑ GD112 Chipper Jones 2.50 1.10
❑ GD113 Greg Maddux 3.00 1.35
❑ GD114 Mike Mordecai .... .25 .11
❑ GD115 Terrell Wade .... .25 .11
❑ GD116 Terry Adams .... .25 .11
❑ GD117 Brian Dorsett .... .25 .11
❑ GD118 Doug Glanville .... .50 .23
❑ GD119 Tyler Houston .... .25 .11
❑ GD120 Robin Jennings .... .25 .11
❑ GD121 Ryne Sandberg ...... 1.25 .55
❑ GD122 Terry Shumpert .... .25 .11
❑ GD123 Amaury Telemaco .... .25 .11
❑ GD124 Steve Trachsel .... .25 .11
❑ GD125 Curtis Goodwin .... .25 .11
❑ GD126 Mike Kelly .... .25 .11
❑ GD127 Chad Mottola .... .25 .11
❑ GD128 Mark Portugal .... .25 .11
❑ GD129 Roger Salkeld .... .25 .11
❑ GD130 John Smiley .... .25 .11
❑ GD131 Lee Smith .... .50 .23
❑ GD132 Roger Bailey .... .25 .11
❑ GD133 Andres Galarraga .. 1.00 .45
❑ GD134 Darren Holmes .... .25 .11
❑ GD135 Curtis Leskanic .... .25 .11
❑ GD136 Mike Munoz .... .25 .11
❑ GD137 Jeff Reed .... .25 .11
❑ GD138 Mark Thompson .... .25 .11
❑ GD139 Jamey Wright .... .25 .11
❑ GD140 Andre Dawson .... .75 .35
❑ GD141 Craig Grebeck .... .25 .11
❑ GD142 Matt Mantei .... .25 .11
❑ GD143 Billy McMillon .... .25 .11
❑ GD144 Kurt Miller .... .25 .11
❑ GD145 Ralph Milliard .... .25 .11
❑ GD146 Bob Natal .... .25 .11
❑ GD147 Joe Siddall .... .25 .11
❑ GD148 Bob Abreu .... .50 .23
❑ GD149 Doug Brocail .... .25 .11
❑ GD150 Danny Darwin .... .25 .11
❑ GD151 Mike Hampton .... .25 .11
❑ GD152 Todd Jones .... .25 .11
❑ GD153 Kirt Manwaring .... .25 .11
❑ GD154 Alvin Morman .... .25 .11
❑ GD155 Billy Ashley .... .25 .11
❑ GD156 Tom Candiotti .... .25 .11
❑ GD157 Darren Dreifort .... .50 .23
❑ GD158 Greg Gagne .... .25 .11
❑ GD159 Wilton Guerrero .... .25 .11
❑ GD160 Hideo Nomo .... 1.25 .55
❑ GD161 Mike Piazza 3.00 1.35
❑ GD162 Tom Prince .... .25 .11
❑ GD163 Todd Worrell .... .25 .11
❑ GD164 Moises Alou .... .75 .35
❑ GD165 Shane Andrews .... .25 .11
❑ GD166 Derek Aucoin .... .25 .11
❑ GD167 Raul Chavez .... .25 .11
❑ GD168 Darrin Fletcher .... .25 .11
❑ GD169 Mark Leiter .... .25 .11
❑ GD170 Henry Rodriguez ...... .50 .23
❑ GD171 Dave Veres .... .25 .11
❑ GD172 Paul Byrd .... .25 .11
❑ GD173 Alberto Castillo .... .25 .11
❑ GD174 Mark Clark .... .25 .11
❑ GD175 Rey Ordonez .... .50 .23
❑ GD176 Roberto Petagine ...... .25 .11
❑ GD177 Andy Tomberlin .... .25 .11
❑ GD178 Derek Wallace .... .25 .11
❑ GD179 Paul Wilson .... .25 .11
❑ GD180 Ruben Amaro Jr. ...... .25 .11
❑ GD181 Toby Borland .... .25 .11
❑ GD182 Rich Hunter .... .25 .11
❑ GD183 Tony Longmire .... .25 .11
❑ GD184 Wendell Magee .... .25 .11
❑ GD185 Bobby Munoz .... .25 .11
❑ GD186 Scott Rolen 2.50 1.10
❑ GD187 Mike Williams .... .25 .11
❑ GD188 Trey Beamon .... .25 .11
❑ GD189 Jason Christiansen .. .25 .11
❑ GD190 Elmer Dessens .... .25 .11
❑ GD191 Angelo Encarnacion .. .25 .11
❑ GD192 Carlos Garcia .... .25 .11
❑ GD193 Mike Kingery .... .25 .11
❑ GD194 Chris Peters .... .25 .11
❑ GD195 Tony Womack .... 1.00 .45
❑ GD196 Brian Barber .... .25 .11
❑ GD197 David Bell .... .25 .11
❑ GD198 Tony Fossas .... .25 .11
❑ GD199 Rick Honeycutt .... .25 .11
❑ GD200 T.J. Mathews .... .25 .11
❑ GD201 Miguel Mejia .... .25 .11
❑ GD202 Donovan Osborne .... .25 .11
❑ GD203 Ozzie Smith .... 1.25 .55
❑ GD204 Andres Berumen ...... .25 .11
❑ GD205 Ken Caminiti .... .75 .35
❑ GD206 Chris Gwynn .... .25 .11
❑ GD207 Tony Gwynn 2.50 1.10
❑ GD208 Rickey Henderson .. 1.00 .45
❑ GD209 Scott Sanders .... .25 .11
❑ GD210 Jason Thompson ...... .25 .11
❑ GD211 Fernando Valenzuela .50 .23
❑ GD212 Tim Worrell .... .25 .11
❑ GD213 Barry Bonds .... 1.25 .55
❑ GD214 Jay Canizaro .... .25 .11
❑ GD215 Doug Creek .... .25 .11
❑ GD216 Jacob Cruz .... .25 .11
❑ GD217 Glenallen Hill .... .25 .11
❑ GD218 Tom Lampkin .... .25 .11
❑ GD219 Jim Poole .... .25 .11
❑ GD220 Desi Wilson .... .25 .11

1997 Pacific Prisms Sizzling Lumber

	MINT	NRMT
COMPLETE SET (36)	400.00	180.00
COMMON CARD (SL1A-SL12B)	2.00	.90

❑ SL1A Cal Ripken 30.00 13.50
❑ SL1B Rafael Palmeiro 5.00 2.20
❑ SL1C Roberto Alomar 8.00 3.60
❑ SL2A Frank Thomas 25.00 11.00
❑ SL2B Robin Ventura 4.00 1.80
❑ SL2C Harold Baines 4.00 1.80
❑ SL3A Albert Belle 10.00 4.50
❑ SL3B Manny Ramirez 8.00 3.60
❑ SL3C Kenny Lofton 8.00 3.60
❑ SL4A Derek Jeter 20.00 9.00
❑ SL4B Bernie Williams 8.00 3.60
❑ SL4C Wade Boggs 8.00 3.60
❑ SL5A Mark McGwire 40.00 18.00
❑ SL5B Jason Giambi 4.00 1.80
❑ SL5C Geronimo Berroa ...... 2.00 .90
❑ SL6A Ken Griffey Jr. 40.00 18.00
❑ SL6B Alex Rodriguez 25.00 11.00
❑ SL6C Jay Buhner 4.00 1.80
❑ SL7A Juan Gonzalez 20.00 9.00
❑ SL7B Dean Palmer 4.00 1.80
❑ SL7C Ivan Rodriguez 10.00 4.50
❑ SL8A Ryan Klesko 4.00 1.80
❑ SL8B Chipper Jones 20.00 9.00
❑ SL8C Andruw Jones 10.00 4.50
❑ SL9A Dante Bichette 4.00 1.80
❑ SL9B Andres Galarraga 8.00 3.60
❑ SL9C Vinny Castilla 5.00 2.20
❑ SL10A Jeff Bagwell 12.00 5.50
❑ SL10B Craig Biggio 8.00 3.60
❑ SL10C Derek Bell 4.00 1.80
❑ SL11A Mike Piazza 25.00 11.00
❑ SL11B Raul Mondesi 5.00 2.20
❑ SL11C Karim Garcia 4.00 1.80
❑ SL12A Tony Gwynn 20.00 9.00
❑ SL12B Ken Caminiti 5.00 2.20
❑ SL12C Greg Vaughn 4.00 1.80

1997 Pacific Prisms Sluggers and Hurlers

	MINT	NRMT
COMPLETE SET (24)	800.00	350.00
COMMON CARD (SH1A-SH12B)	5.00	2.20

❑ SH1A Cal Ripken 80.00 36.00
❑ SH1B Mike Mussina 20.00 9.00
❑ SH2A Jose Canseco 20.00 9.00
❑ SH2B Roger Clemens 40.00 18.00
❑ SH3A Frank Thomas 60.00 27.00
❑ SH3B Wilson Alvarez 8.00 3.60
❑ SH4A Kenny Lofton 20.00 9.00
❑ SH4B Orel Hershiser 8.00 3.60
❑ SH5A Derek Jeter 50.00 22.00
❑ SH5B Andy Pettitte 12.00 5.50
❑ SH6A Ken Griffey Jr. 100.00 45.00
❑ SH6B Randy Johnson 20.00 9.00
❑ SH7A Alex Rodriguez 60.00 27.00
❑ SH7B Jamie Moyer 5.00 2.20
❑ SH8A Andruw Jones 25.00 11.00
❑ SH8B Greg Maddux 60.00 27.00
❑ SH9A Chipper Jones 50.00 22.00
❑ SH9B John Smoltz 8.00 3.60
❑ SH10A Jeff Bagwell 30.00 13.50
❑ SH10B Shane Reynolds 8.00 3.60
❑ SH11A Mike Piazza 60.00 27.00
❑ SH11B Hideo Nomo 30.00 13.50
❑ SH12A Tony Gwynn 50.00 22.00
❑ SH12B Fernando Valenzuela 8.00 3.60

1992 Pinnacle

	MINT	NRMT
COMPLETE SET (620)	40.00	18.00
COMPLETE SERIES 1 (310)	25.00	11.00
COMPLETE SERIES 2 (310)	15.00	6.75
COMMON CARD (1-620)	.10	.05

❑ 1 Frank Thomas	1.25	.55
❑ 2 Benito Santiago	.10	.05
❑ 3 Carlos Baerga	.10	.05
❑ 4 Cecil Fielder	.20	.09
❑ 5 Barry Larkin	.30	.14
❑ 6 Ozzie Smith	.50	.23
❑ 7 Willie McGee	.20	.09
❑ 8 Paul Molitor	.40	.18
❑ 9 Andy Van Slyke	.20	.09
❑ 10 Ryne Sandberg	.50	.23
❑ 11 Kevin Seitzer	.10	.05
❑ 12 Len Dykstra	.20	.09
❑ 13 Edgar Martinez	.30	.14
❑ 14 Ruben Sierra	.10	.05
❑ 15 Howard Johnson	.10	.05
❑ 16 Dave Henderson	.10	.05
❑ 17 Devon White	.10	.05
❑ 18 Terry Pendleton	.10	.05
❑ 19 Steve Finley	.20	.09
❑ 20 Kirby Puckett	.60	.25
❑ 21 Orel Hershiser	.20	.09
❑ 22 Hal Morris	.10	.05
❑ 23 Don Mattingly	.60	.25
❑ 24 Delino DeShields	.20	.09
❑ 25 Dennis Eckersley	.20	.09
❑ 26 Ellis Burks	.20	.09
❑ 27 Jay Buhner	.30	.14
❑ 28 Matt Williams	.30	.14
❑ 29 Lou Whitaker	.20	.09
❑ 30 Alex Fernandez	.20	.09
❑ 31 Albert Belle	.50	.23
❑ 32 Todd Zeile	.10	.05
❑ 33 Tony Pena	.10	.05
❑ 34 Jay Bell	.20	.09
❑ 35 Rafael Palmeiro	.30	.14
❑ 36 Wes Chamberlain	.10	.05
❑ 37 George Bell	.10	.05
❑ 38 Robin Yount	.40	.18
❑ 39 Vince Coleman	.10	.05
❑ 40 Bruce Hurst	.10	.05
❑ 41 Harold Baines	.20	.09
❑ 42 Chuck Finley	.20	.09
❑ 43 Ken Caminiti	.30	.14
❑ 44 Ben McDonald	.10	.05
❑ 45 Roberto Alomar	.40	.18
❑ 46 Chili Davis	.20	.09
❑ 47 Bill Doran	.10	.05
❑ 48 Jerald Clark	.10	.05
❑ 49 Jose Lind	.10	.05
❑ 50 Nolan Ryan	1.50	.70
❑ 51 Phil Plantier	.10	.05
❑ 52 Gary DiSarcina	.10	.05
❑ 53 Kevin Bass	.10	.05
❑ 54 Pat Kelly	.10	.05
❑ 55 Mark Wohlers	.20	.09
❑ 56 Walt Weiss	.10	.05
❑ 57 Lenny Harris	.10	.05
❑ 58 Ivan Calderon	.10	.05
❑ 59 Harold Reynolds	.10	.05
❑ 60 George Brett	.75	.35
❑ 61 Gregg Olson	.10	.05
❑ 62 Orlando Merced	.10	.05
❑ 63 Steve Decker	.10	.05
❑ 64 John Franco	.20	.09
❑ 65 Greg Maddux	1.25	.55
❑ 66 Alex Cole	.10	.05
❑ 67 Dave Hollins	.10	.05
❑ 68 Kent Hrbek	.20	.09
❑ 69 Tom Pagnozzi	.10	.05
❑ 70 Jeff Bagwell	1.00	.45
❑ 71 Jim Gantner	.10	.05
❑ 72 Matt Nokes	.10	.05
❑ 73 Brian Harper	.10	.05
❑ 74 Andy Benes	.20	.09
❑ 75 Tom Glavine	.30	.14
❑ 76 Terry Steinbach	.20	.09
❑ 77 Dennis Martinez	.20	.09
❑ 78 John Olerud	.20	.09
❑ 79 Ozzie Guillen	.10	.05
❑ 80 Darryl Strawberry	.20	.09
❑ 81 Gary Gaetti	.10	.05
❑ 82 Dave Righetti	.10	.05
❑ 83 Chris Hoiles	.10	.05
❑ 84 Andujar Cedeno	.10	.05
❑ 85 Jack Clark	.20	.09
❑ 86 David Howard	.10	.05
❑ 87 Bill Gullickson	.10	.05
❑ 88 Bernard Gilkey	.20	.09
❑ 89 Kevin Elster	.10	.05
❑ 90 Kevin Maas	.10	.05
❑ 91 Mark Lewis	.10	.05
❑ 92 Greg Vaughn	.20	.09
❑ 93 Bret Barberie	.10	.05
❑ 94 Dave Smith	.10	.05
❑ 95 Roger Clemens	.75	.35
❑ 96 Doug Drabek	.10	.05
❑ 97 Omar Vizquel	.20	.09
❑ 98 Jose Guzman	.10	.05
❑ 99 Juan Samuel	.10	.05
❑ 100 Dave Justice	.40	.18
❑ 101 Tom Browning	.10	.05
❑ 102 Mark Gubicza	.10	.05
❑ 103 Mickey Morandini	.10	.05
❑ 104 Ed Whitson	.10	.05
❑ 105 Lance Parrish	.10	.05
❑ 106 Scott Erickson	.20	.09
❑ 107 Jack McDowell	.10	.05
❑ 108 Dave Stieb	.10	.05
❑ 109 Mike Moore	.10	.05
❑ 110 Travis Fryman	.20	.09
❑ 111 Dwight Gooden	.20	.09
❑ 112 Fred McGriff	.30	.14
❑ 113 Alan Trammell	.30	.14
❑ 114 Roberto Kelly	.10	.05
❑ 115 Andre Dawson	.30	.14
❑ 116 Bill Landrum	.10	.05
❑ 117 Brian McRae	.20	.09
❑ 118 B.J. Surhoff	.20	.09
❑ 119 Chuck Knoblauch	.40	.18
❑ 120 Steve Olin	.10	.05
❑ 121 Robin Ventura	.20	.09
❑ 122 Will Clark	.40	.18
❑ 123 Tino Martinez	.40	.18
❑ 124 Dale Murphy	.40	.18
❑ 125 Pete O'Brien	.10	.05
❑ 126 Ray Lankford	.40	.18
❑ 127 Juan Gonzalez	1.25	.55
❑ 128 Ron Gant	.20	.09
❑ 129 Marquis Grissom	.20	.09
❑ 130 Jose Canseco	.40	.18
❑ 131 Mike Greenwell	.10	.05
❑ 132 Mark Langston	.10	.05
❑ 133 Brett Butler	.20	.09
❑ 134 Kelly Gruber	.10	.05
❑ 135 Chris Sabo	.10	.05
❑ 136 Mark Grace	.30	.14
❑ 137 Tony Fernandez	.10	.05
❑ 138 Glenn Davis	.10	.05
❑ 139 Pedro Munoz	.10	.05
❑ 140 Craig Biggio	.40	.18
❑ 141 Pete Schourek	.10	.05
❑ 142 Mike Boddicker	.10	.05
❑ 143 Robby Thompson	.10	.05
❑ 144 Mel Hall	.10	.05
❑ 145 Bryan Harvey	.10	.05
❑ 146 Mike LaValliere	.10	.05
❑ 147 John Kruk	.20	.09
❑ 148 Joe Carter	.20	.09
❑ 149 Greg Olson	.10	.05
❑ 150 Julio Franco	.10	.05
❑ 151 Darryl Hamilton	.10	.05
❑ 152 Felix Fermin	.10	.05
❑ 153 Jose Offerman	.10	.05
❑ 154 Paul O'Neill	.20	.09
❑ 155 Tommy Greene	.10	.05
❑ 156 Ivan Rodriguez	.75	.35
❑ 157 Dave Stewart	.20	.09
❑ 158 Jeff Reardon	.20	.09
❑ 159 Felix Jose	.10	.05
❑ 160 Doug Dascenzo	.10	.05
❑ 161 Tim Wallach	.10	.05
❑ 162 Dan Plesac	.10	.05
❑ 163 Luis Gonzalez	.10	.05
❑ 164 Mike Henneman	.10	.05
❑ 165 Mike Devereaux	.10	.05
❑ 166 Luis Polonia	.10	.05
❑ 167 Mike Sharperson	.10	.05
❑ 168 Chris Donnels	.10	.05
❑ 169 Greg W. Harris	.10	.05
❑ 170 Deion Sanders	.40	.18
❑ 171 Mike Schooler	.10	.05
❑ 172 Jose DeJesus	.10	.05
❑ 173 Jeff Montgomery	.20	.09
❑ 174 Milt Cuyler	.10	.05
❑ 175 Wade Boggs	.40	.18
❑ 176 Kevin Tapani	.10	.05
❑ 177 Bill Spiers	.10	.05
❑ 178 Tim Raines	.20	.09
❑ 179 Randy Milligan	.10	.05
❑ 180 Rob Dibble	.10	.05
❑ 181 Kirt Manwaring	.10	.05
❑ 182 Pascual Perez	.10	.05
❑ 183 Juan Guzman	.10	.05
❑ 184 John Smiley	.10	.05
❑ 185 David Segui	.20	.09
❑ 186 Omar Olivares	.10	.05
❑ 187 Joe Slusarski	.10	.05
❑ 188 Erik Hanson	.10	.05
❑ 189 Mark Portugal	.10	.05
❑ 190 Walt Terrell	.10	.05
❑ 191 John Smoltz	.30	.14
❑ 192 Wilson Alvarez	.20	.09
❑ 193 Jimmy Key	.20	.09
❑ 194 Larry Walker	.40	.18
❑ 195 Lee Smith	.20	.09
❑ 196 Pete Harnisch	.10	.05
❑ 197 Mike Harkey	.10	.05
❑ 198 Frank Tanana	.10	.05
❑ 199 Terry Mulholland	.10	.05
❑ 200 Cal Ripken	1.50	.70
❑ 201 Dave Magadan	.10	.05
❑ 202 Bud Black	.10	.05
❑ 203 Terry Shumpert	.10	.05
❑ 204 Mike Mussina	.60	.25
❑ 205 Mo Vaughn	.60	.25
❑ 206 Steve Farr	.10	.05
❑ 207 Darrin Jackson	.10	.05
❑ 208 Jerry Browne	.10	.05
❑ 209 Jeff Russell	.10	.05
❑ 210 Mike Scioscia	.10	.05
❑ 211 Rick Aguilera	.20	.09
❑ 212 Jaime Navarro	.10	.05
❑ 213 Randy Tomlin	.10	.05
❑ 214 Bobby Thigpen	.10	.05
❑ 215 Mark Gardner	.10	.05
❑ 216 Norm Charlton	.10	.05
❑ 217 Mark McGwire	2.00	.90
❑ 218 Skeeter Barnes	.10	.05
❑ 219 Bob Tewksbury	.10	.05
❑ 220 Junior Felix	.10	.05
❑ 221 Sam Horn	.10	.05
❑ 222 Jody Reed	.10	.05
❑ 223 Luis Sojo	.10	.05
❑ 224 Jerome Walton	.10	.05
❑ 225 Darryl Kile	.20	.09
❑ 226 Mickey Tettleton	.10	.05
❑ 227 Dan Pasqua	.10	.05
❑ 228 Jim Gott	.10	.05
❑ 229 Bernie Williams	.40	.18
❑ 230 Shane Mack	.10	.05

❑	231 Steve Avery	.10	.05
❑	232 Dave Valle	.10	.05
❑	233 Mark Leonard	.10	.05
❑	234 Spike Owen	.10	.05
❑	235 Gary Sheffield	.40	.18
❑	236 Steve Chitren	.10	.05
❑	237 Zane Smith	.10	.05
❑	238 Tom Gordon	.20	.09
❑	239 Jose Oquendo	.10	.05
❑	240 Todd Stottlemyre	.20	.09
❑	241 Darren Daulton	.20	.09
❑	242 Tim Naehring	.20	.09
❑	243 Tony Phillips	.10	.05
❑	244 Shawon Dunston	.10	.05
❑	245 Manuel Lee	.10	.05
❑	246 Mike Pagliarulo	.10	.05
❑	247 Jim Thome	1.00	.45
❑	248 Luis Mercedes	.10	.05
❑	249 Cal Eldred	.10	.05
❑	250 Derek Bell	.20	.09
❑	251 Arthur Rhodes	.10	.05
❑	252 Scott Cooper	.10	.05
❑	253 Roberto Hernandez	.20	.09
❑	254 Mo Sanford	.10	.05
❑	255 Scott Servais	.10	.05
❑	256 Eric Karros	.40	.18
❑	257 Andy Mota	.10	.05
❑	258 Keith Mitchell	.10	.05
❑	259 Joel Johnston	.10	.05
❑	260 John Wehner	.10	.05
❑	261 Gino Minutelli	.10	.05
❑	262 Greg Gagne	.10	.05
❑	263 Stan Royer	.10	.05
❑	264 Carlos Garcia	.10	.05
❑	265 Andy Ashby	.20	.09
❑	266 Kim Batiste	.10	.05
❑	267 Julio Valera	.10	.05
❑	268 Royce Clayton	.10	.05
❑	269 Gary Scott	.10	.05
❑	270 Kirk Dressendorfer	.10	.05
❑	271 Sean Berry	.10	.05
❑	272 Lance Dickson	.10	.05
❑	273 Rob Maurer	.10	.05
❑	274 Scott Brosius	.50	.23
❑	275 Dave Fleming	.10	.05
❑	276 Lenny Webster	.10	.05
❑	277 Mike Humphreys	.10	.05
❑	278 Freddie Benavides	.10	.05
❑	279 Harvey Pulliam	.10	.05
❑	280 Jeff Carter	.10	.05
❑	281 Jim Abbott I Nolan Ryan	.40	.18
❑	282 Wade Boggs I George Brett	.40	.18
❑	283 Ken Griffey Jr. I Rickey Henderson	.75	.35
❑	284 Wally Joyner I Dale Murphy	.20	.09
❑	285 Chuck Knoblauch I Ozzie Smith	.40	.18
❑	286 Robin Ventura I Lou Gehrig	.50	.23
❑	287 Robin Yount SIDE	.20	.09
❑	288 Bob Tewksbury SIDE	.10	.05
❑	289 Kirby Puckett SIDE	.40	.18
❑	290 Kenny Lofton SIDE	.50	.23
❑	291 Jack McDowell SIDE	.10	.05
❑	292 John Burkett SIDE	.10	.05
❑	293 Dwight Smith SIDE	.10	.05
❑	294 Nolan Ryan SIDE	.75	.35
❑	295 Manny Ramirez DP	3.00	1.35
❑	296 Cliff Floyd DP UER (Throws right, not left as indicated on back)	.50	.23
❑	297 Al Shirley DP	.10	.05
❑	298 Brian Barber DP	.10	.05
❑	299 Jon Farrell DP	.10	.05
❑	300 Scott Ruffcorn DP	.10	.05
❑	301 Tyrone Hill DP	.10	.05
❑	302 Benji Gil DP	.10	.05
❑	303 Tyler Green DP	.10	.05
❑	304 Allen Watson DP	.10	.05
❑	305 Jay Buhner SH	.20	.09
❑	306 Roberto Alomar SH	.20	.09
❑	307 Chuck Knoblauch SH	.20	.09
❑	308 Darryl Strawberry SH	.10	.05
❑	309 Danny Tartabull SH	.10	.05
❑	310 Bobby Bonilla SH	.10	.05
❑	311 Mike Felder	.10	.05
❑	312 Storm Davis	.10	.05
❑	313 Tim Teufel	.10	.05
❑	314 Tom Brunansky	.10	.05
❑	315 Rex Hudler	.10	.05
❑	316 Dave Otto	.10	.05
❑	317 Jeff King	.20	.09
❑	318 Dan Gladden	.10	.05
❑	319 Bill Pecota	.10	.05
❑	320 Franklin Stubbs	.10	.05
❑	321 Gary Carter	.40	.18
❑	322 Melido Perez	.10	.05
❑	323 Eric Davis	.20	.09
❑	324 Greg Myers	.10	.05
❑	325 Pete Incaviglia	.10	.05
❑	326 Von Hayes	.10	.05
❑	327 Greg Swindell	.10	.05
❑	328 Steve Sax	.10	.05
❑	329 Chuck McElroy	.10	.05
❑	330 Gregg Jefferies	.10	.05
❑	331 Joe Oliver	.10	.05
❑	332 Paul Faries	.10	.05
❑	333 David West	.10	.05
❑	334 Craig Grebeck	.10	.05
❑	335 Chris Hammond	.10	.05
❑	336 Billy Ripken	.10	.05
❑	337 Scott Sanderson	.10	.05
❑	338 Dick Schofield	.10	.05
❑	339 Bob Milacki	.10	.05
❑	340 Kevin Reimer	.10	.05
❑	341 Jose DeLeon	.10	.05
❑	342 Henry Cotto	.10	.05
❑	343 Daryl Boston	.10	.05
❑	344 Kevin Gross	.10	.05
❑	345 Milt Thompson	.10	.05
❑	346 Luis Rivera	.10	.05
❑	347 Al Osuna	.10	.05
❑	348 Rob Deer	.10	.05
❑	349 Tim Leary	.10	.05
❑	350 Mike Stanton	.10	.05
❑	351 Dean Palmer	.20	.09
❑	352 Trevor Wilson	.10	.05
❑	353 Mark Eichhorn	.10	.05
❑	354 Scott Aldred	.10	.05
❑	355 Mark Whiten	.10	.05
❑	356 Leo Gomez	.10	.05
❑	357 Rafael Belliard	.10	.05
❑	358 Carlos Quintana	.10	.05
❑	359 Mark Davis	.10	.05
❑	360 Chris Nabholz	.10	.05
❑	361 Carlton Fisk	.40	.18
❑	362 Joe Orsulak	.10	.05
❑	363 Eric Anthony	.10	.05
❑	364 Greg Hibbard	.10	.05
❑	365 Scott Leius	.10	.05
❑	366 Hensley Meulens	.10	.05
❑	367 Chris Bosio	.10	.05
❑	368 Brian Downing	.10	.05
❑	369 Sammy Sosa	1.00	.45
❑	370 Stan Belinda	.10	.05
❑	371 Joe Grahe	.10	.05
❑	372 Luis Salazar	.10	.05
❑	373 Lance Johnson	.10	.05
❑	374 Kal Daniels	.10	.05
❑	375 Dave Winfield	.40	.18
❑	376 Brook Jacoby	.10	.05
❑	377 Mariano Duncan	.10	.05
❑	378 Ron Darling	.10	.05
❑	379 Randy Johnson	.40	.18
❑	380 Chito Martinez	.10	.05
❑	381 Andres Galarraga	.40	.18
❑	382 Willie Randolph	.20	.09
❑	383 Charles Nagy	.20	.09
❑	384 Tim Belcher	.10	.05
❑	385 Duane Ward	.10	.05
❑	386 Vicente Palacios	.10	.05
❑	387 Mike Gallego	.10	.05
❑	388 Rich DeLucia	.10	.05
❑	389 Scott Radinsky	.10	.05
❑	390 Damon Berryhill	.10	.05
❑	391 Kirk McCaskill	.10	.05
❑	392 Pedro Guerrero	.10	.05
❑	393 Kevin Mitchell	.20	.09
❑	394 Dickie Thon	.10	.05
❑	395 Bobby Bonilla	.20	.09
❑	396 Bill Wegman	.10	.05
❑	397 Dave Martinez	.10	.05
❑	398 Rick Sutcliffe	.10	.05
❑	399 Larry Andersen	.10	.05
❑	400 Tony Gwynn	1.00	.45
❑	401 Rickey Henderson	.40	.18
❑	402 Greg Cadaret	.10	.05
❑	403 Keith Miller	.10	.05
❑	404 Bip Roberts	.10	.05
❑	405 Kevin Brown	.30	.14
❑	406 Mitch Williams	.10	.05
❑	407 Frank Viola	.10	.05
❑	408 Darren Lewis	.10	.05
❑	409 Bob Welch	.10	.05
❑	410 Bob Walk	.10	.05
❑	411 Todd Frohwirth	.10	.05
❑	412 Brian Hunter	.10	.05
❑	413 Ron Karkovice	.10	.05
❑	414 Mike Morgan	.10	.05
❑	415 Joe Hesketh	.10	.05
❑	416 Don Slaught	.10	.05
❑	417 Tom Henke	.10	.05
❑	418 Kurt Stillwell	.10	.05
❑	419 Hector Villaneuva	.10	.05
❑	420 Glenallen Hill	.10	.05
❑	421 Pat Borders	.10	.05
❑	422 Charlie Hough	.20	.09
❑	423 Charlie Leibrandt	.10	.05
❑	424 Eddie Murray	.40	.18
❑	425 Jesse Barfield	.10	.05
❑	426 Mark Lemke	.10	.05
❑	427 Kevin McReynolds	.10	.05
❑	428 Gilberto Reyes	.10	.05
❑	429 Ramon Martinez	.20	.09
❑	430 Steve Buechele	.10	.05
❑	431 David Wells	.20	.09
❑	432 Kyle Abbott	.10	.05
❑	433 John Habyan	.10	.05
❑	434 Kevin Appier	.20	.09
❑	435 Gene Larkin	.10	.05
❑	436 Sandy Alomar Jr.	.20	.09
❑	437 Mike Jackson	.20	.09
❑	438 Todd Benzinger	.10	.05
❑	439 Teddy Higuera	.10	.05
❑	440 Reggie Sanders	.10	.05
❑	441 Mark Carreon	.10	.05
❑	442 Bret Saberhagen	.20	.09
❑	443 Gene Nelson	.10	.05
❑	444 Jay Howell	.10	.05
❑	445 Roger McDowell	.10	.05
❑	446 Sid Bream	.10	.05
❑	447 Mackey Sasser	.10	.05
❑	448 Bill Swift	.10	.05
❑	449 Hubie Brooks	.10	.05
❑	450 David Cone	.20	.09
❑	451 Bobby Witt	.10	.05
❑	452 Brady Anderson	.30	.14
❑	453 Lee Stevens	.10	.05
❑	454 Luis Aquino	.10	.05
❑	455 Carney Lansford	.20	.09
❑	456 Carlos Hernandez	.10	.05
❑	457 Danny Jackson	.10	.05
❑	458 Gerald Young	.10	.05
❑	459 Tom Candiotti	.10	.05
❑	460 Billy Hatcher	.10	.05
❑	461 John Wetteland	.20	.09
❑	462 Mike Bordick	.10	.05
❑	463 Don Robinson	.10	.05
❑	464 Jeff Johnson	.10	.05
❑	465 Lonnie Smith	.10	.05
❑	466 Paul Assenmacher	.10	.05
❑	467 Alvin Davis	.10	.05
❑	468 Jim Eisenreich	.10	.05
❑	469 Brent Mayne	.10	.05
❑	470 Jeff Brantley	.10	.05
❑	471 Tim Burke	.10	.05
❑	472 Pat Mahomes	.10	.05
❑	473 Ryan Bowen	.10	.05
❑	474 Bryn Smith	.10	.05
❑	475 Mike Flanagan	.10	.05
❑	476 Reggie Jefferson	.20	.09
❑	477 Jeff Blauser	.10	.05

❑ 478 Craig Lefferts .10 .05
❑ 479 Todd Worrell .10 .05
❑ 480 Scott Scudder .10 .05
❑ 481 Kirk Gibson .20 .09
❑ 482 Kenny Rogers .10 .05
❑ 483 Jack Morris .20 .09
❑ 484 Russ Swan .10 .05
❑ 485 Mike Huff .10 .05
❑ 486 Ken Hill .10 .05
❑ 487 Geronimo Pena .10 .05
❑ 488 Charlie O'Brien .10 .05
❑ 489 Mike Maddux .10 .05
❑ 490 Scott Livingstone .10 .05
❑ 491 Carl Willis .10 .05
❑ 492 Kelly Downs .10 .05
❑ 493 Dennis Cook .10 .05
❑ 494 Joe Magrane .10 .05
❑ 495 Bob Kipper .10 .05
❑ 496 Jose Mesa .10 .05
❑ 497 Charlie Hayes .10 .05
❑ 498 Joe Girardi .20 .09
❑ 499 Doug Jones .10 .05
❑ 500 Barry Bonds .50 .23
❑ 501 Bill Krueger .10 .05
❑ 502 Glenn Braggs .10 .05
❑ 503 Eric King .10 .05
❑ 504 Frank Castillo .10 .05
❑ 505 Mike Gardiner .10 .05
❑ 506 Cory Snyder .10 .05
❑ 507 Steve Howe .10 .05
❑ 508 Jose Rijo .10 .05
❑ 509 Sid Fernandez .10 .05
❑ 510 Archi Cianfrocco .10 .05
❑ 511 Mark Guthrie .10 .05
❑ 512 Bob Ojeda .10 .05
❑ 513 John Doherty .10 .05
❑ 514 Dante Bichette .30 .14
❑ 515 Juan Berenguer .10 .05
❑ 516 Jeff M. Robinson .10 .05
❑ 517 Mike Macfarlane .10 .05
❑ 518 Matt Young .10 .05
❑ 519 Otis Nixon .20 .09
❑ 520 Brian Holman .10 .05
❑ 521 Chris Haney .10 .05
❑ 522 Jeff Kent .40 .18
❑ 523 Chad Curtis .40 .18
❑ 524 Vince Horsman .10 .05
❑ 525 Rod Nichols .10 .05
❑ 526 Peter Hoy .10 .05
❑ 527 Shawn Boskie .10 .05
❑ 528 Alejandro Pena .10 .05
❑ 529 Dave Burba .10 .05
❑ 530 Ricky Jordan .10 .05
❑ 531 Dave Silvestri .10 .05
❑ 532 John Patterson UER .10 .05
(Listed as being born in 1960; should be 1967)
❑ 533 Jeff Branson .10 .05
❑ 534 Derrick May .10 .05
❑ 535 Esteban Beltre .10 .05
❑ 536 Jose Melendez .10 .05
❑ 537 Wally Joyner .20 .09
❑ 538 Eddie Taubensee .20 .09
❑ 539 Jim Abbott .20 .09
❑ 540 Brian Williams .10 .05
❑ 541 Donovan Osborne .10 .05
❑ 542 Patrick Lennon .10 .05
❑ 543 Mike Groppuso .10 .05
❑ 544 Jarvis Brown .10 .05
❑ 545 Shawn Livsey .10 .05
❑ 546 Jeff Ware .10 .05
❑ 547 Danny Tartabull .10 .05
❑ 548 Bobby Jones .40 .18
❑ 549 Ken Griffey Jr. 2.50 1.10
❑ 550 Rey Sanchez .10 .05
❑ 551 Pedro Astacio .10 .05
❑ 552 Juan Guerrero .10 .05
❑ 553 Jacob Brumfield .10 .05
❑ 554 Ben Rivera .10 .05
❑ 555 Brian Jordan .75 .35
❑ 556 Denny Neagle .30 .14
❑ 557 Cliff Brantley .10 .05
❑ 558 Anthony Young .10 .05
❑ 559 John Vander Wal .10 .05
❑ 560 Monty Fariss .10 .05
❑ 561 Russ Springer .10 .05
❑ 562 Pat Listach .10 .05
❑ 563 Pat Hentgen .40 .18
❑ 564 Andy Stankiewicz .10 .05
❑ 565 Mike Perez .10 .05
❑ 566 Mike Bielecki .10 .05
❑ 567 Butch Henry .10 .05
❑ 568 Dave Nilsson .20 .09
❑ 569 Scott Hatteberg .10 .05
❑ 570 Ruben Amaro Jr. .10 .05
❑ 571 Todd Hundley .20 .09
❑ 572 Moises Alou .40 .18
❑ 573 Hector Fajardo .10 .05
❑ 574 Todd Van Poppel .10 .05
❑ 575 Willie Banks .10 .05
❑ 576 Bob Zupcic .10 .05
❑ 577 J.J. Johnson .20 .09
❑ 578 John Burkett .10 .05
❑ 579 Trever Miller .10 .05
❑ 580 Scott Bankhead .10 .05
❑ 581 Rich Amaral .10 .05
❑ 582 Kenny Lofton .75 .35
❑ 583 Matt Stairs .40 .18
❑ 584 Don Mattingly .40 .18
Rod Carew IDOLS
❑ 585 Steve Avery .10 .05
Jack Morris IDOLS
❑ 586 Roberto Alomar .30 .14
Sandy Alomar SR. IDOLS
❑ 587 Scott Sanderson .20 .09
Catfish Hunter IDOLS
❑ 588 Dave Justice .40 .18
Willie Stargell IDOLS
❑ 589 Rex Hudler .40 .18
Roger Staubach IDOLS
❑ 590 David Cone .20 .09
Jackie Gleason IDOLS
❑ 591 Tony Gwynn .40 .18
Willie Davis IDOLS
❑ 592 Orel Hershiser SIDE .10 .05
❑ 593 John Wetteland SIDE .10 .05
❑ 594 Tom Glavine SIDE .20 .09
❑ 595 Randy Johnson SIDE .20 .09
❑ 596 Jim Gott SIDE .10 .05
❑ 597 Donald Harris .10 .05
❑ 598 Shawn Hare .10 .05
❑ 599 Chris Gardner .10 .05
❑ 600 Rusty Meacham .10 .05
❑ 601 Benito Santiago .10 .05
❑ 602 Eric Davis SHADE .10 .05
❑ 603 Jose Lind SHADE .10 .05
❑ 604 Dave Justice SHADE .20 .09
❑ 605 Tim Raines SHADE .20 .09
❑ 606 Randy Tomlin GRIP .10 .05
❑ 607 Jack McDowell GRIP .10 .05
❑ 608 Greg Maddux GRIP .60 .25
❑ 609 Charles Nagy GRIP .10 .05
❑ 610 Tom Candiotti GRIP .10 .05
❑ 611 David Cone GRIP .10 .05
❑ 612 Steve Avery GRIP .10 .05
❑ 613 Rod Beck GRIP .20 .09
❑ 614 Rickey Henderson TECH .20 .09
❑ 615 Benito Santiago TECH .10 .05
❑ 616 Ruben Sierra TECH .10 .05
❑ 617 Ryne Sandberg TECH .40 .18
❑ 618 Nolan Ryan TECH .75 .35
❑ 619 Brett Butler TECH .10 .05
❑ 620 Dave Justice TECH .20 .09

1992 Pinnacle Rookie Idols

	MINT	NRMT
COMPLETE SET (18)	120.00	55.00
COMMON PAIR (1-18)	3.00	1.35

❑ 1 Reggie Sanders 4.00 1.80
and Eric Davis
❑ 2 Hector Fajardo 3.00 1.35
and Jim Abbott
❑ 3 Gary Cooper 12.00 5.50
and George Brett
❑ 4 Mark Wohlers 12.00 5.50
and Roger Clemens
❑ 5 Luis Mercedes 3.00 1.35

and Julio Franco
❑ 6 Willie Banks 3.00 1.35
and Doc Gooden
❑ 7 Kenny Lofton 15.00 6.75
and Rickey Henderson
❑ 8 Keith Mitchell 3.00 1.35
and Dave Henderson
❑ 9 Kim Batiste 5.00 2.20
and Barry Larkin
❑ 10 Todd Hundley 8.00 3.60
and Thurman Munson
❑ 11 Eddie Zosky 25.00 11.00
and Cal Ripken
❑ 12 Todd Van Poppel 25.00 11.00
and Nolan Ryan
❑ 13 Jim Thome 25.00 11.00
and Ryne Sandberg
❑ 14 Dave Fleming 3.00 1.35
and Bobby Murcer
❑ 15 Royce Clayton 8.00 3.60
and Ozzie Smith
❑ 16 Donald Harris 3.00 1.35
and Darryl Strawberry
❑ 17 Chad Curtis 6.00 2.70
and Alan Trammell
❑ 18 Derek Bell 6.00 2.70
and Dave Winfield

1992 Pinnacle Slugfest

	MINT	NRMT
COMPLETE SET (15)	40.00	18.00
COMMON CARD (1-15)	.50	.23

❑ 1 Cecil Fielder .75 .35
❑ 2 Mark McGwire 8.00 3.60
❑ 3 Jose Canseco 1.25 .55
❑ 4 Barry Bonds 2.00 .90
❑ 5 David Justice 1.25 .55
❑ 6 Bobby Bonilla .75 .35
❑ 7 Ken Griffey Jr. 10.00 4.50
❑ 8 Ron Gant .75 .35
❑ 9 Ryne Sandberg 2.00 .90
❑ 10 Ruben Sierra .50 .23
❑ 11 Frank Thomas 5.00 2.20
❑ 12 Will Clark 1.25 .55
❑ 13 Kirby Puckett 2.50 1.10
❑ 14 Cal Ripken 6.00 2.70
❑ 15 Jeff Bagwell 4.00 1.80

1992 Pinnacle Team 2000

	MINT	NRMT
COMPLETE SET (80)	30.00	13.50
COMPLETE SERIES 1 (40)	20.00	9.00
COMPLETE SERIES 2 (40)	10.00	4.50
COMMON CARD (1-80)	.15	.07

	MINT	NRMT
❑ 1 Mike Mussina	1.50	.70
❑ 2 Phil Plantier	.15	.07
❑ 3 Frank Thomas	3.00	1.35
❑ 4 Travis Fryman	.25	.11
❑ 5 Kevin Appier	.25	.11
❑ 6 Chuck Knoblauch	1.00	.45
❑ 7 Pat Kelly	.15	.07
❑ 8 Ivan Rodriguez	2.00	.90
❑ 9 Dave Justice	.75	.35
❑ 10 Jeff Bagwell	2.50	1.10
❑ 11 Marquis Grissom	.25	.11
❑ 12 Andy Benes	.25	.11
❑ 13 Gregg Olson	.15	.07
❑ 14 Kevin Morton	.15	.07
❑ 15 Tim Naehring	.25	.11
❑ 16 Dave Hollins	.15	.07
❑ 17 Sandy Alomar Jr.	.25	.11
❑ 18 Albert Belle	1.25	.55
❑ 19 Charles Nagy	.25	.11
❑ 20 Brian McRae	.25	.11
❑ 21 Larry Walker	1.00	.45
❑ 22 Delino DeShields	.25	.11
❑ 23 Jeff Johnson	.15	.07
❑ 24 Bernie Williams	.75	.35
❑ 25 Jose Offerman	.15	.07
❑ 26 Juan Gonzalez	3.00	1.35
❑ 27A Juan Guzman (Pinnacle logo at top)	.25	.11
❑ 27B Juan Guzman (Pinnacle logo at bottom)	.25	.11
❑ 28 Eric Anthony	.15	.07
❑ 29 Brian Hunter	.15	.07
❑ 30 John Smoltz	.40	.18
❑ 31 Deion Sanders	.75	.35
❑ 32 Greg Maddux	3.00	1.35
❑ 33 Andujar Cedeno	.15	.07
❑ 34 Royce Clayton	.15	.07
❑ 35 Kenny Lofton	2.50	1.10
❑ 36 Cal Eldred	.15	.07
❑ 37 Jim Thome	3.00	1.35
❑ 38 Gary DiSarcina	.15	.07
❑ 39 Brian Jordan	1.50	.70
❑ 40 Chad Curtis	.75	.35
❑ 41 Ben McDonald	.15	.07
❑ 42 Jim Abbott	.25	.11
❑ 43 Robin Ventura	.25	.11
❑ 44 Milt Cuyler	.15	.07
❑ 45 Gregg Jefferies	.15	.07
❑ 46 Scott Radinsky	.15	.07
❑ 47 Ken Griffey Jr.	6.00	2.70
❑ 48 Roberto Alomar	1.00	.45
❑ 49 Ramon Martinez	.25	.11
❑ 50 Bret Barberie	.15	.07
❑ 51 Ray Lankford	.75	.35
❑ 52 Leo Gomez	.15	.07
❑ 53 Tommy Greene	.15	.07
❑ 54 Mo Vaughn	1.50	.70
❑ 55 Sammy Sosa	2.00	.90
❑ 56 Carlos Baerga	.15	.07
❑ 57 Mark Lewis	.15	.07
❑ 58 Tom Gordon	.25	.11
❑ 59 Gary Sheffield	.75	.35
❑ 60 Scott Erickson	.25	.11
❑ 61 Pedro Munoz	.15	.07
❑ 62 Tino Martinez	.75	.35
❑ 63 Darren Lewis	.15	.07
❑ 64 Dean Palmer	.25	.11
❑ 65 John Olerud	.25	.11
❑ 66 Steve Avery	.15	.07
❑ 67 Pete Harnisch	.15	.07
❑ 68 Luis Gonzalez	.15	.07
❑ 69 Kim Batiste	.15	.07
❑ 70 Reggie Sanders	.15	.07
❑ 71 Luis Mercedes	.15	.07
❑ 72 Todd Van Poppel	.15	.07
❑ 73 Gary Scott	.15	.07
❑ 74 Monty Fariss	.15	.07
❑ 75 Kyle Abbott	.15	.07
❑ 76 Eric Karros	.75	.35
❑ 77 Mo Sanford	.15	.07
❑ 78 Todd Hundley	.25	.11
❑ 79 Reggie Jefferson	.25	.11
❑ 80 Pat Mahomes	.15	.07

1992 Pinnacle Team Pinnacle

	MINT	NRMT
COMPLETE SET (12)	80.00	36.00
COMMON PAIR (1-12)	3.00	1.35

	MINT	NRMT
❑ 1 Roger Clemens and Ramon Martinez	10.00	4.50
❑ 2 Jim Abbott and Steve Avery	3.00	1.35
❑ 3 Ivan Rodriguez and Benito Santiago	8.00	3.60
❑ 4 Frank Thomas and Will Clark	20.00	9.00
❑ 5 Roberto Alomar and Ryne Sandberg	6.00	2.70
❑ 6 Robin Ventura and Matt Williams	4.00	1.80
❑ 7 Cal Ripken and Barry Larkin	20.00	9.00
❑ 8 Danny Tartabull and Barry Bonds	6.00	2.70
❑ 9 Ken Griffey Jr. and Brett Butler	25.00	11.00
❑ 10 Ruben Sierra and Dave Justice	3.00	1.35
❑ 11 Dennis Eckersley and Rob Dibble	3.00	1.35
❑ 12 Scott Radinsky and John Franco	3.00	1.35

1992 Pinnacle Rookies

	MINT	NRMT
COMP.FACT.SET (30)	4.00	1.80
COMMON CARD (1-30)	.15	.07

	MINT	NRMT
❑ 1 Luis Mercedes	.15	.07
❑ 2 Scott Cooper	.15	.07
❑ 3 Kenny Lofton	1.50	.70
❑ 4 John Doherty	.15	.07
❑ 5 Pat Listach	.15	.07
❑ 6 Andy Stankiewicz	.15	.07
❑ 7 Derek Bell	.40	.18
❑ 8 Gary DiSarcina	.15	.07
❑ 9 Roberto Hernandez	.40	.18
❑ 10 Joel Johnston	.15	.07
❑ 11 Pat Mahomes	.15	.07
❑ 12 Todd Van Poppel	.15	.07
❑ 13 Dave Fleming	.15	.07
❑ 14 Monty Fariss	.15	.07
❑ 15 Gary Scott	.15	.07
❑ 16 Moises Alou	.75	.35
❑ 17 Todd Hundley	.40	.18
❑ 18 Kim Batiste	.15	.07
❑ 19 Denny Neagle	.60	.25
❑ 20 Donovan Osborne	.15	.07
❑ 21 Mark Wohlers	.40	.18
❑ 22 Reggie Sanders	.15	.07
❑ 23 Brian Williams	.15	.07
❑ 24 Eric Karros	.75	.35
❑ 25 Frank Seminara	.15	.07
❑ 26 Royce Clayton	.15	.07
❑ 27 Dave Nilsson	.40	.18
❑ 28 Matt Stairs	.75	.35
❑ 29 Chad Curtis	.75	.35
❑ 30 Carlos Hernandez	.15	.07

1993 Pinnacle

	MINT	NRMT
COMPLETE SET (620)	50.00	22.00
COMPLETE SERIES 1 (310)	25.00	11.00
COMPLETE SERIES 2 (310)	25.00	11.00
COMMON CARD (1-620)	.15	.07

	MINT	NRMT
❑ 1 Gary Sheffield	.60	.25
❑ 2 Cal Eldred	.15	.07
❑ 3 Larry Walker	.60	.25
❑ 4 Deion Sanders	.40	.18
❑ 5 Dave Fleming	.15	.07
❑ 6 Carlos Baerga	.15	.07
❑ 7 Bernie Williams	.60	.25
❑ 8 John Kruk	.30	.14
❑ 9 Jimmy Key	.30	.14
❑ 10 Jeff Bagwell	1.00	.45
❑ 11 Jim Abbott	.30	.14
❑ 12 Terry Steinbach	.15	.07
❑ 13 Bob Tewksbury	.15	.07
❑ 14 Eric Karros	.40	.18
❑ 15 Ryne Sandberg	.75	.35
❑ 16 Will Clark	.60	.25

❑ 17	Edgar Martinez	.40	.18
❑ 18	Eddie Murray	.60	.25
❑ 19	Andy Van Slyke	.30	.14
❑ 20	Cal Ripken Jr.	2.50	1.10
❑ 21	Ivan Rodriguez	.75	.35
❑ 22	Barry Larkin	.40	.18
❑ 23	Don Mattingly	1.00	.45
❑ 24	Gregg Jefferies	.15	.07
❑ 25	Roger Clemens	1.25	.55
❑ 26	Cecil Fielder	.30	.14
❑ 27	Kent Hrbek	.30	.14
❑ 28	Robin Ventura	.30	.14
❑ 29	Rickey Henderson	.60	.25
❑ 30	Roberto Alomar	.60	.25
❑ 31	Luis Polonia	.15	.07
❑ 32	Andujar Cedeno	.15	.07
❑ 33	Pat Listach	.15	.07
❑ 34	Mark Grace	.40	.18
❑ 35	Otis Nixon	.15	.07
❑ 36	Felix Jose	.15	.07
❑ 37	Mike Sharperson	.15	.07
❑ 38	Dennis Martinez	.30	.14
❑ 39	Willie McGee	.30	.14
❑ 40	Kenny Lofton	.60	.25
❑ 41	Randy Johnson	.60	.25
❑ 42	Andy Benes	.30	.14
❑ 43	Bobby Bonilla	.30	.14
❑ 44	Mike Mussina	.60	.25
❑ 45	Len Dykstra	.30	.14
❑ 46	Ellis Burks	.30	.14
❑ 47	Chris Sabo	.15	.07
❑ 48	Jay Bell	.30	.14
❑ 49	Jose Canseco	.60	.25
❑ 50	Craig Biggio	.60	.25
❑ 51	Wally Joyner	.30	.14
❑ 52	Mickey Tettleton	.15	.07
❑ 53	Tim Raines	.30	.14
❑ 54	Brian Harper	.15	.07
❑ 55	Rene Gonzales	.15	.07
❑ 56	Mark Langston	.15	.07
❑ 57	Jack Morris	.30	.14
❑ 58	Mark McGwire	3.00	1.35
❑ 59	Ken Caminiti	.40	.18
❑ 60	Terry Pendleton	.15	.07
❑ 61	Dave Nilsson	.30	.14
❑ 62	Tom Pagnozzi	.15	.07
❑ 63	Mike Morgan	.15	.07
❑ 64	Darryl Strawberry	.30	.14
❑ 65	Charles Nagy	.30	.14
❑ 66	Ken Hill	.15	.07
❑ 67	Matt Williams	.40	.18
❑ 68	Jay Buhner	.40	.18
❑ 69	Vince Coleman	.15	.07
❑ 70	Brady Anderson	.40	.18
❑ 71	Fred McGriff	.40	.18
❑ 72	Ben McDonald	.15	.07
❑ 73	Terry Mulholland	.15	.07
❑ 74	Randy Tomlin	.15	.07
❑ 75	Nolan Ryan	2.50	1.10
❑ 76	Frank Viola UER (Card incorrectly states he has a surgically repaired elbow)	.15	.07
❑ 77	Jose Rijo	.15	.07
❑ 78	Shane Mack	.15	.07
❑ 79	Travis Fryman	.30	.14
❑ 80	Jack McDowell	.15	.07
❑ 81	Mark Gubicza	.15	.07
❑ 82	Matt Nokes	.15	.07
❑ 83	Bert Blyleven	.30	.14
❑ 84	Eric Anthony	.15	.07
❑ 85	Mike Bordick	.15	.07
❑ 86	John Olerud	.40	.18
❑ 87	B.J.Surhoff	.30	.14
❑ 88	Bernard Gilkey	.15	.07
❑ 89	Shawon Dunston	.15	.07
❑ 90	Tom Glavine	.40	.18
❑ 91	Brett Butler	.30	.14
❑ 92	Moises Alou	.30	.14
❑ 93	Albert Belle	.75	.35
❑ 94	Darren Lewis	.15	.07
❑ 95	Omar Vizquel	.30	.14
❑ 96	Dwight Gooden	.30	.14
❑ 97	Gregg Olson	.15	.07
❑ 98	Tony Gwynn	1.50	.70
❑ 99	Darren Daulton	.30	.14
❑ 100	Dennis Eckersley	.30	.14
❑ 101	Rob Dibble	.15	.07
❑ 102	Mike Greenwell	.15	.07
❑ 103	Jose Lind	.15	.07
❑ 104	Julio Franco	.15	.07
❑ 105	Tom Gordon	.30	.14
❑ 106	Scott Livingstone	.15	.07
❑ 107	Chuck Knoblauch	.60	.25
❑ 108	Frank Thomas	2.00	.90
❑ 109	Melido Perez	.15	.07
❑ 110	Ken Griffey Jr.	3.00	1.35
❑ 111	Harold Baines	.30	.14
❑ 112	Gary Gaetti	.15	.07
❑ 113	Pete Harnisch	.15	.07
❑ 114	David Wells	.30	.14
❑ 115	Charlie Leibrandt	.15	.07
❑ 116	Ray Lankford	.40	.18
❑ 117	Kevin Seitzer	.15	.07
❑ 118	Robin Yount	.40	.18
❑ 119	Lenny Harris	.15	.07
❑ 120	Chris James	.15	.07
❑ 121	Delino DeShields	.30	.14
❑ 122	Kirt Manwaring	.15	.07
❑ 123	Glenallen Hill	.15	.07
❑ 124	Hensley Meulens	.15	.07
❑ 125	Darrin Jackson	.15	.07
❑ 126	Todd Hundley	.40	.18
❑ 127	Dave Hollins	.15	.07
❑ 128	Sam Horn	.15	.07
❑ 129	Roberto Hernandez	.30	.14
❑ 130	Vicente Palacios	.15	.07
❑ 131	George Brett	1.25	.55
❑ 132	Dave Martinez	.15	.07
❑ 133	Kevin Appier	.30	.14
❑ 134	Pat Kelly	.15	.07
❑ 135	Pedro Munoz	.15	.07
❑ 136	Mark Carreon	.15	.07
❑ 137	Lance Johnson	.15	.07
❑ 138	Devon White	.15	.07
❑ 139	Julio Valera	.15	.07
❑ 140	Eddie Taubensee	.15	.07
❑ 141	Willie Wilson	.15	.07
❑ 142	Stan Belinda	.15	.07
❑ 143	John Smoltz	.30	.14
❑ 144	Darryl Hamilton	.15	.07
❑ 145	Sammy Sosa	1.50	.70
❑ 146	Carlos Hernandez	.15	.07
❑ 147	Tom Candiotti	.15	.07
❑ 148	Mike Felder	.15	.07
❑ 149	Rusty Meacham	.15	.07
❑ 150	Ivan Calderon	.15	.07
❑ 151	Pete O'Brien	.15	.07
❑ 152	Erik Hanson	.15	.07
❑ 153	Billy Ripken	.15	.07
❑ 154	Kurt Stillwell	.15	.07
❑ 155	Jeff Kent	.30	.14
❑ 156	Mickey Morandini	.15	.07
❑ 157	Randy Milligan	.15	.07
❑ 158	Reggie Sanders	.15	.07
❑ 159	Luis Rivera	.15	.07
❑ 160	Orlando Merced	.15	.07
❑ 161	Dean Palmer	.30	.14
❑ 162	Mike Perez	.15	.07
❑ 163	Scott Erickson	.15	.07
❑ 164	Kevin McReynolds	.15	.07
❑ 165	Kevin Maas	.15	.07
❑ 166	Ozzie Guillen	.15	.07
❑ 167	Rob Deer	.15	.07
❑ 168	Danny Tartabull	.15	.07
❑ 169	Lee Stevens	.15	.07
❑ 170	Dave Henderson	.15	.07
❑ 171	Derek Bell	.30	.14
❑ 172	Steve Finley	.30	.14
❑ 173	Greg Olson	.15	.07
❑ 174	Geronimo Pena	.15	.07
❑ 175	Paul Quantrill	.15	.07
❑ 176	Steve Buechele	.15	.07
❑ 177	Kevin Gross	.15	.07
❑ 178	Tim Wallach	.15	.07
❑ 179	Dave Valle	.15	.07
❑ 180	Dave Silvestri	.15	.07
❑ 181	Bud Black	.15	.07
❑ 182	Henry Rodriguez	.30	.14
❑ 183	Tim Teufel	.15	.07
❑ 184	Mark McLemore	.15	.07
❑ 185	Bret Saberhagen	.30	.14
❑ 186	Chris Hoiles	.15	.07
❑ 187	Ricky Jordan	.15	.07
❑ 188	Don Slaught	.15	.07
❑ 189	Mo Vaughn	.75	.35
❑ 190	Joe Oliver	.15	.07
❑ 191	Juan Gonzalez	1.50	.70
❑ 192	Scott Leius	.15	.07
❑ 193	Milt Cuyler	.15	.07
❑ 194	Chris Haney	.15	.07
❑ 195	Ron Karkovice	.15	.07
❑ 196	Steve Farr	.15	.07
❑ 197	John Orton	.15	.07
❑ 198	Kelly Gruber	.15	.07
❑ 199	Ron Darling	.15	.07
❑ 200	Ruben Sierra	.15	.07
❑ 201	Chuck Finley	.30	.14
❑ 202	Mike Moore	.15	.07
❑ 203	Pat Borders	.15	.07
❑ 204	Sid Bream	.15	.07
❑ 205	Todd Zeile	.15	.07
❑ 206	Rick Wilkins	.15	.07
❑ 207	Jim Gantner	.15	.07
❑ 208	Frank Castillo	.15	.07
❑ 209	Dave Hansen	.15	.07
❑ 210	Trevor Wilson	.15	.07
❑ 211	Sandy Alomar Jr.	.30	.14
❑ 212	Sean Berry	.15	.07
❑ 213	Tino Martinez	.60	.25
❑ 214	Chito Martinez	.15	.07
❑ 215	Dan Walters	.15	.07
❑ 216	John Franco	.30	.14
❑ 217	Glenn Davis	.15	.07
❑ 218	Mariano Duncan	.15	.07
❑ 219	Mike LaValliere	.15	.07
❑ 220	Rafael Palmeiro	.40	.18
❑ 221	Jack Clark	.15	.07
❑ 222	Hal Morris	.15	.07
❑ 223	Ed Sprague	.15	.07
❑ 224	John Valentin	.30	.14
❑ 225	Sam Militello	.15	.07
❑ 226	Bob Wickman	.15	.07
❑ 227	Damion Easley	.30	.14
❑ 228	John Jaha	.15	.07
❑ 229	Bob Ayrault	.15	.07
❑ 230	Mo Sanford	.15	.07
❑ 231	Walt Weiss	.15	.07
❑ 232	Dante Bichette	.30	.14
❑ 233	Steve Decker	.15	.07
❑ 234	Jerald Clark	.15	.07
❑ 235	Bryan Harvey	.15	.07
❑ 236	Joe Girardi	.30	.14
❑ 237	Dave Magadan	.15	.07
❑ 238	David Nied	.15	.07
❑ 239	Eric Wedge	.15	.07
❑ 240	Rico Brogna	.30	.14
❑ 241	J.T.Bruett	.15	.07
❑ 242	Jonathan Hurst	.15	.07
❑ 243	Bret Boone	.30	.14
❑ 244	Manny Alexander	.15	.07
❑ 245	Scooter Tucker	.15	.07
❑ 246	Troy Neel	.15	.07
❑ 247	Eddie Zosky	.15	.07
❑ 248	Melvin Nieves	.15	.07
❑ 249	Ryan Thompson	.15	.07
❑ 250	Shawn Barton	.15	.07
❑ 251	Ryan Klesko	.60	.25
❑ 252	Mike Piazza	3.00	1.35
❑ 253	Steve Hosey	.15	.07
❑ 254	Shane Reynolds	.30	.14
❑ 255	Dan Wilson	.30	.14
❑ 256	Tom Marsh	.15	.07
❑ 257	Barry Manuel	.15	.07
❑ 258	Paul Miller	.15	.07
❑ 259	Pedro Martinez	.75	.35
❑ 260	Steve Cooke	.15	.07
❑ 261	Johnny Guzman	.15	.07
❑ 262	Mike Butcher	.15	.07
❑ 263	Bien Figueroa	.15	.07
❑ 264	Rich Rowland	.15	.07
❑ 265	Shawn Jeter	.15	.07
❑ 266	Gerald Williams	.15	.07
❑ 267	Derek Parks	.15	.07
❑ 268	Henry Mercedes	.15	.07

❑	269	David Hulse	.15	.07
❑	270	Tim Pugh	.15	.07
❑	271	William Suero	.15	.07
❑	272	Ozzie Canseco	.15	.07
❑	273	Fernando Ramsey	.15	.07
❑	274	Bernardo Brito	.15	.07
❑	275	Dave Mlicki	.15	.07
❑	276	Tim Salmon	.60	.25
❑	277	Mike Raczka	.15	.07
❑	278	Ken Ryan	.15	.07
❑	279	Rafael Bournigal	.15	.07
❑	280	Wil Cordero	.15	.07
❑	281	Billy Ashley	.15	.07
❑	282	Paul Wagner	.15	.07
❑	283	Blas Minor	.15	.07
❑	284	Rick Trlicek	.15	.07
❑	285	Willie Greene	.15	.07
❑	286	Ted Wood	.15	.07
❑	287	Phil Clark	.15	.07
❑	288	Jesse Levis	.15	.07
❑	289	Tony Gwynn NT	.75	.35
❑	290	Nolan Ryan NT	1.25	.55
❑	291	Dennis Martinez NT	.15	.07
❑	292	Eddie Murray NT	.30	.14
❑	293	Robin Yount NT	.30	.14
❑	294	George Brett NT	.60	.25
❑	295	Dave Winfield NT	.30	.14
❑	296	Bert Blyleven NT	.15	.07
❑	297	Jeff Bagwell Carl Yastrzemski	.60	.25
❑	298	John Smoltz Jack Morris	.30	.14
❑	299	Larry Walker Mike Bossy	.60	.25
❑	300	Gary Sheffield Barry Larkin	.30	.14
❑	301	Ivan Rodriguez Carlton Fisk	.30	.14
❑	302	Delino DeShields Malcolm X	.60	.25
❑	303	Tim Salmon Dwight Evans	.40	.18
❑	304	Bernard Gilkey HH	.15	.07
❑	305	Cal Ripken Jr. HH	1.25	.55
❑	306	Barry Larkin HH	.40	.18
❑	307	Kent Hrbek HH	.15	.07
❑	308	Rickey Henderson HH	.30	.14
❑	309	Darryl Strawberry HH	.15	.07
❑	310	John Franco HH	.15	.07
❑	311	Todd Stottlemyre	.15	.07
❑	312	Luis Gonzalez	.15	.07
❑	313	Tommy Greene	.15	.07
❑	314	Randy Velarde	.15	.07
❑	315	Steve Avery	.15	.07
❑	316	Jose Oquendo	.15	.07
❑	317	Rey Sanchez	.15	.07
❑	318	Greg Vaughn	.30	.14
❑	319	Orel Hershiser	.30	.14
❑	320	Paul Sorrento	.15	.07
❑	321	Royce Clayton	.15	.07
❑	322	John Vander Wal	.15	.07
❑	323	Henry Cotto	.15	.07
❑	324	Pete Schourek	.15	.07
❑	325	David Segui	.15	.07
❑	326	Arthur Rhodes	.15	.07
❑	327	Bruce Hurst	.15	.07
❑	328	Wes Chamberlain	.15	.07
❑	329	Ozzie Smith	.75	.35
❑	330	Scott Cooper	.15	.07
❑	331	Felix Fermin	.15	.07
❑	332	Mike Macfarlane	.15	.07
❑	333	Dan Gladden	.15	.07
❑	334	Kevin Tapani	.15	.07
❑	335	Steve Sax	.15	.07
❑	336	Jeff Montgomery	.30	.14
❑	337	Gary DiSarcina	.15	.07
❑	338	Lance Blankenship	.15	.07
❑	339	Brian Williams	.15	.07
❑	340	Duane Ward	.15	.07
❑	341	Chuck McElroy	.15	.07
❑	342	Joe Magrane	.15	.07
❑	343	Jaime Navarro	.15	.07
❑	344	Dave Justice	.60	.25
❑	345	Jose Offerman	.15	.07
❑	346	Marquis Grissom	.30	.14
❑	347	Bill Swift	.15	.07
❑	348	Jim Thome	1.25	.55
❑	349	Archi Cianfrocco	.15	.07
❑	350	Anthony Young	.15	.07
❑	351	Leo Gomez	.15	.07
❑	352	Bill Gullickson	.15	.07
❑	353	Alan Trammell	.40	.18
❑	354	Dan Pasqua	.15	.07
❑	355	Jeff King	.30	.14
❑	356	Kevin Brown	.40	.18
❑	357	Tim Belcher	.15	.07
❑	358	Bip Roberts	.15	.07
❑	359	Brent Mayne	.15	.07
❑	360	Rheal Cormier	.15	.07
❑	361	Mark Guthrie	.15	.07
❑	362	Craig Grebeck	.15	.07
❑	363	Andy Stankiewicz	.15	.07
❑	364	Juan Guzman	.15	.07
❑	365	Bobby Witt	.15	.07
❑	366	Mark Portugal	.15	.07
❑	367	Brian McRae	.15	.07
❑	368	Mark Lemke	.15	.07
❑	369	Bill Wegman	.15	.07
❑	370	Donovan Osborne	.15	.07
❑	371	Derrick May	.15	.07
❑	372	Carl Willis	.15	.07
❑	373	Chris Nabholz	.15	.07
❑	374	Mark Lewis	.15	.07
❑	375	John Burkett	.15	.07
❑	376	Luis Mercedes	.15	.07
❑	377	Ramon Martinez	.30	.14
❑	378	Kyle Abbott	.15	.07
❑	379	Mark Wohlers	.15	.07
❑	380	Bob Walk	.15	.07
❑	381	Kenny Rogers	.15	.07
❑	382	Tim Naehring	.15	.07
❑	383	Alex Fernandez	.30	.14
❑	384	Keith Miller	.15	.07
❑	385	Mike Henneman	.15	.07
❑	386	Rick Aguilera	.15	.07
❑	387	George Bell	.15	.07
❑	388	Mike Gallego	.15	.07
❑	389	Howard Johnson	.15	.07
❑	390	Kim Batiste	.15	.07
❑	391	Jerry Browne	.15	.07
❑	392	Damon Berryhill	.15	.07
❑	393	Ricky Bones	.15	.07
❑	394	Omar Olivares	.15	.07
❑	395	Mike Harkey	.15	.07
❑	396	Pedro Astacio	.15	.07
❑	397	John Wetteland	.30	.14
❑	398	Rod Beck	.30	.14
❑	399	Thomas Howard	.15	.07
❑	400	Mike Devereaux	.15	.07
❑	401	Tim Wakefield	.30	.14
❑	402	Curt Schilling	.30	.14
❑	403	Zane Smith	.15	.07
❑	404	Bob Zupcic	.15	.07
❑	405	Tom Browning	.15	.07
❑	406	Tony Phillips	.15	.07
❑	407	John Doherty	.15	.07
❑	408	Pat Mahomes	.15	.07
❑	409	John Habyan	.15	.07
❑	410	Steve Olin	.15	.07
❑	411	Chad Curtis	.30	.14
❑	412	Joe Grahe	.15	.07
❑	413	John Patterson	.15	.07
❑	414	Brian Hunter	.15	.07
❑	415	Doug Henry	.15	.07
❑	416	Lee Smith	.30	.14
❑	417	Bob Scanlan	.15	.07
❑	418	Kent Mercker	.15	.07
❑	419	Mel Rojas	.15	.07
❑	420	Mark Whiten	.15	.07
❑	421	Carlton Fisk	.60	.25
❑	422	Candy Maldonado	.15	.07
❑	423	Doug Drabek	.15	.07
❑	424	Wade Boggs	.60	.25
❑	425	Mark Davis	.15	.07
❑	426	Kirby Puckett	1.00	.45
❑	427	Joe Carter	.30	.14
❑	428	Paul Molitor	.60	.25
❑	429	Eric Davis	.30	.14
❑	430	Darryl Kile	.30	.14
❑	431	Jeff Parrett	.15	.07
❑	432	Jeff Blauser	.15	.07
❑	433	Dan Plesac	.15	.07
❑	434	Andres Galarraga	.60	.25
❑	435	Jim Gott	.15	.07
❑	436	Jose Mesa	.15	.07
❑	437	Ben Rivera	.15	.07
❑	438	Dave Winfield	.40	.18
❑	439	Norm Charlton	.15	.07
❑	440	Chris Bosio	.15	.07
❑	441	Wilson Alvarez	.30	.14
❑	442	Dave Stewart	.30	.14
❑	443	Doug Jones	.15	.07
❑	444	Jeff Russell	.15	.07
❑	445	Ron Gant	.30	.14
❑	446	Paul O'Neill	.30	.14
❑	447	Charlie Hayes	.15	.07
❑	448	Joe Hesketh	.15	.07
❑	449	Chris Hammond	.15	.07
❑	450	Hipolito Pichardo	.15	.07
❑	451	Scott Radinsky	.15	.07
❑	452	Bobby Thigpen	.15	.07
❑	453	Xavier Hernandez	.15	.07
❑	454	Lonnie Smith	.15	.07
❑	455	Jamie Arnold DP	.30	.14
❑	456	B.J. Wallace DP	.15	.07
❑	457	Derek Jeter DP	6.00	2.70
❑	458	Jason Kendall DP	2.00	.90
❑	459	Rick Helling DP	.40	.18
❑	460	Derek Wallace DP	.15	.07
❑	461	Sean Lowe DP	.15	.07
❑	462	Shannon Stewart DP	.50	.23
❑	463	Benji Grigsby DP	.15	.07
❑	464	Todd Steverson DP	.30	.14
❑	465	Dan Serafini DP	.30	.14
❑	466	Michael Tucker DP	.60	.25
❑	467	Chris Roberts DP	.15	.07
❑	468	Pete Janicki DP	.15	.07
❑	469	Jeff Schmidt DP	.15	.07
❑	470	Don Mattingly NT	.60	.25
❑	471	Cal Ripken Jr. NT	1.25	.55
❑	472	Jack Morris NT	.15	.07
❑	473	Terry Pendleton NT	.15	.07
❑	474	Dennis Eckersley NT	.15	.07
❑	475	Carlton Fisk NT	.30	.14
❑	476	Wade Boggs NT	.60	.25
❑	477	Len Dykstra Ken Stabler	.30	.14
❑	478	Danny Tartabull Jose Tartabull	.15	.07
❑	479	Jeff Conine Dale Murphy	.30	.14
❑	480	Gregg Jefferies Ron Cey	.15	.07
❑	481	Paul Molitor Harmon Killebrew	.40	.18
❑	482	John Valentin Dave Concepcion	.15	.07
❑	483	Alex Arias Dave Winfield	.30	.14
❑	484	Barry Bonds HH	.40	.18
❑	485	Doug Drabek HH	.15	.07
❑	486	Dave Winfield HH	.30	.14
❑	487	Brett Butler HH	.15	.07
❑	488	Harold Baines HH	.15	.07
❑	489	David Cone HH	.15	.07
❑	490	Willie McGee HH	.15	.07
❑	491	Robby Thompson	.15	.07
❑	492	Pete Incaviglia	.15	.07
❑	493	Manuel Lee	.15	.07
❑	494	Rafael Belliard	.15	.07
❑	495	Scott Fletcher	.15	.07
❑	496	Jeff Frye	.15	.07
❑	497	Andre Dawson	.40	.18
❑	498	Mike Scioscia	.15	.07
❑	499	Spike Owen	.15	.07
❑	500	Sid Fernandez	.15	.07
❑	501	Joe Orsulak	.15	.07
❑	502	Benito Santiago	.15	.07
❑	503	Dale Murphy	.40	.18
❑	504	Barry Bonds	.75	.35
❑	505	Jose Guzman	.15	.07
❑	506	Tony Pena	.15	.07
❑	507	Greg Swindell	.15	.07
❑	508	Mike Pagliarulo	.15	.07
❑	509	Lou Whitaker	.30	.14

	#	Player	MINT	NRMT
❑	510	Greg Gagne	.15	.07
❑	511	Butch Henry	.15	.07
❑	512	Jeff Brantley	.15	.07
❑	513	Jack Armstrong	.15	.07
❑	514	Danny Jackson	.15	.07
❑	515	Junior Felix	.15	.07
❑	516	Milt Thompson	.15	.07
❑	517	Greg Maddux	2.00	.90
❑	518	Eric Young	.60	.25
❑	519	Jody Reed	.15	.07
❑	520	Roberto Kelly	.15	.07
❑	521	Darren Holmes	.15	.07
❑	522	Craig Lefferts	.15	.07
❑	523	Charlie Hough	.30	.14
❑	524	Bo Jackson	.30	.14
❑	525	Bill Spiers	.15	.07
❑	526	Orestes Destrade	.15	.07
❑	527	Greg Hibbard	.15	.07
❑	528	Roger McDowell	.15	.07
❑	529	Cory Snyder	.15	.07
❑	530	Harold Reynolds	.15	.07
❑	531	Kevin Reimer	.15	.07
❑	532	Rick Sutcliffe	.15	.07
❑	533	Tony Fernandez	.15	.07
❑	534	Tom Brunansky	.15	.07
❑	535	Jeff Reardon	.30	.14
❑	536	Chili Davis	.30	.14
❑	537	Bob Ojeda	.15	.07
❑	538	Greg Colbrunn	.15	.07
❑	539	Phil Plantier	.15	.07
❑	540	Brian Jordan	.30	.14
❑	541	Pete Smith	.15	.07
❑	542	Frank Tanana	.15	.07
❑	543	John Smiley	.15	.07
❑	544	David Cone	.30	.14
❑	545	Daryl Boston	.15	.07
❑	546	Tom Henke	.15	.07
❑	547	Bill Krueger	.15	.07
❑	548	Freddie Benavides	.15	.07
❑	549	Randy Myers	.30	.14
❑	550	Reggie Jefferson	.30	.14
❑	551	Kevin Mitchell	.30	.14
❑	552	Dave Stieb	.30	.14
❑	553	Bret Barberie	.15	.07
❑	554	Tim Crews	.15	.07
❑	555	Doug Dascenzo	.15	.07
❑	556	Alex Cole	.15	.07
❑	557	Jeff Innis	.15	.07
❑	558	Carlos Garcia	.15	.07
❑	559	Steve Howe	.15	.07
❑	560	Kirk McCaskill	.15	.07
❑	561	Frank Seminara	.15	.07
❑	562	Cris Carpenter	.15	.07
❑	563	Mike Stanley	.15	.07
❑	564	Carlos Quintana	.15	.07
❑	565	Mitch Williams	.15	.07
❑	566	Juan Bell	.15	.07
❑	567	Eric Fox	.15	.07
❑	568	Al Leiter	.30	.14
❑	569	Mike Stanton	.15	.07
❑	570	Scott Kamieniecki	.15	.07
❑	571	Ryan Bowen	.15	.07
❑	572	Andy Ashby	.30	.14
❑	573	Bob Welch	.15	.07
❑	574	Scott Sanderson	.15	.07
❑	575	Joe Kmak	.15	.07
❑	576	Scott Pose	.15	.07
❑	577	Ricky Gutierrez	.15	.07
❑	578	Mike Trombley	.15	.07
❑	579	Sterling Hitchcock	.50	.23
❑	580	Rodney Bolton	.15	.07
❑	581	Tyler Green	.15	.07
❑	582	Tim Costo	.15	.07
❑	583	Tim Laker	.15	.07
❑	584	Steve Reed	.15	.07
❑	585	Tom Kramer	.15	.07
❑	586	Robb Nen	.40	.18
❑	587	Jim Tatum	.15	.07
❑	588	Frank Bolick	.15	.07
❑	589	Kevin Young	.15	.07
❑	590	Matt Whiteside	.15	.07
❑	591	Cesar Hernandez	.15	.07
❑	592	Mike Mohler	.15	.07
❑	593	Alan Embree	.15	.07
❑	594	Terry Jorgensen	.15	.07
❑	595	John Cummings	.15	.07
❑	596	Domingo Martinez	.15	.07
❑	597	Benji Gil	.15	.07
❑	598	Todd Pratt	.15	.07
❑	599	Rene Arocha	.15	.07
❑	600	Dennis Moeller	.15	.07
❑	601	Jeff Conine	.15	.07
❑	602	Trevor Hoffman	.60	.25
❑	603	Daniel Smith	.15	.07
❑	604	Lee Tinsley	.30	.14
❑	605	Dan Peltier	.15	.07
❑	606	Billy Brewer	.15	.07
❑	607	Matt Walbeck	.15	.07
❑	608	Richie Lewis	.15	.07
❑	609	J.T. Snow	.75	.35
❑	610	Pat Gomez	.15	.07
❑	611	Phil Hiatt	.15	.07
❑	612	Alex Arias	.15	.07
❑	613	Kevin Rogers	.15	.07
❑	614	Al Martin	.15	.07
❑	615	Greg Gohr	.15	.07
❑	616	Graeme Lloyd	.15	.07
❑	617	Kent Bottenfield	.15	.07
❑	618	Chuck Carr	.15	.07
❑	619	Darrell Sherman	.15	.07
❑	620	Mike Lansing	.30	.14

1993 Pinnacle Expansion Opening Day

	MINT	NRMT
COMPLETE SET (9)	25.00	11.00
COMMON PAIR (1-9)	1.50	.70
❑ 1 Charlie Hough / David Nied	4.00	1.80
❑ 2 Benito Santiago / Joe Girardi	1.50	.70
❑ 3 Orestes Destrade / Andres Galarraga	8.00	3.60
❑ 4 Bret Barberie / Eric Young	4.00	1.80
❑ 5 Dave Magadan / Charlie Hayes	1.50	.70
❑ 6 Walt Weiss / Freddie Benavides	1.50	.70
❑ 7 Jeff Conine / Jerald Clark	6.00	2.70
❑ 8 Scott Pose / Alex Cole	1.50	.70
❑ 9 Junior Felix / Dante Bichette	8.00	3.60

1993 Pinnacle Rookie Team Pinnacle

	MINT	NRMT
COMPLETE SET (10)	100.00	45.00
COMMON PAIR (1-10)	4.00	1.80
❑ 1 Pedro Martinez / Mike Trombley	12.00	5.50
❑ 2 Kevin Rogers / Sterling Hitchcock	4.00	1.80
❑ 3 Mike Piazza / Jesse Levis	50.00	22.00
❑ 4 Ryan Klesko / J.T. Snow	10.00	4.50

	MINT	NRMT
❑ 5 John Patterson / Bret Boone	4.00	1.80
❑ 6 Kevin Young / Domingo Martinez	4.00	1.80
❑ 7 Wil Cordero / Manny Alexander	4.00	1.80
❑ 8 Steve Hosey / Tim Salmon	10.00	4.50
❑ 9 Ryan Thompson / Gerald Williams	4.00	1.80
❑ 10 Melvin Nieves / David Hulse	6.00	2.70

1993 Pinnacle Slugfest

	MINT	NRMT
COMPLETE SET (30)	60.00	27.00
COMMON CARD (1-30)	1.00	.45
❑ 1 Juan Gonzalez	8.00	3.60
❑ 2 Mark McGwire	15.00	6.75
❑ 3 Cecil Fielder	1.50	.70
❑ 4 Joe Carter	1.50	.70
❑ 5 Fred McGriff	2.00	.90
❑ 6 Barry Bonds	4.00	1.80
❑ 7 Gary Sheffield	2.50	1.10
❑ 8 Dave Hollins	1.00	.45
❑ 9 Frank Thomas	10.00	4.50
❑ 10 Danny Tartabull	1.00	.45
❑ 11 Albert Belle	4.00	1.80
❑ 12 Ruben Sierra	1.00	.45
❑ 13 Larry Walker	2.50	1.10
❑ 14 Jeff Bagwell	5.00	2.20
❑ 15 David Justice	2.50	1.10
❑ 16 Kirby Puckett	5.00	2.20
❑ 17 John Kruk	1.50	.70
❑ 18 Howard Johnson	1.00	.45
❑ 19 Darryl Strawberry	1.50	.70
❑ 20 Will Clark	2.50	1.10
❑ 21 Kevin Mitchell	1.50	.70
❑ 22 Mickey Tettleton	1.00	.45
❑ 23 Don Mattingly	5.00	2.20
❑ 24 Jose Canseco	2.50	1.10
❑ 25 George Bell	1.00	.45
❑ 26 Andre Dawson	2.00	.90
❑ 27 Ryne Sandberg	4.00	1.80
❑ 28 Ken Griffey Jr.	15.00	6.75
❑ 29 Carlos Baerga	1.00	.45
❑ 30 Travis Fryman	1.50	.70

1993 Pinnacle Team 2001

	MINT	NRMT
COMPLETE SET (30)	40.00	18.00
COMMON CARD (1-30)	.75	.35
❑ 1 Wil Cordero	.75	.35
❑ 2 Cal Eldred	.75	.35
❑ 3 Mike Mussina	3.00	1.35
❑ 4 Chuck Knoblauch	3.00	1.35
❑ 5 Melvin Nieves	.75	.35
❑ 6 Tim Wakefield	1.25	.55
❑ 7 Carlos Baerga	.75	.35
❑ 8 Bret Boone	1.25	.55
❑ 9 Jeff Bagwell	5.00	2.20
❑ 10 Travis Fryman	1.25	.55
❑ 11 Royce Clayton	.75	.35
❑ 12 Delino DeShields	.75	.35
❑ 13 Juan Gonzalez	8.00	3.60
❑ 14 Pedro Martinez	3.00	1.35
❑ 15 Bernie Williams	3.00	1.35
❑ 16 Billy Ashley	.75	.35
❑ 17 Marquis Grissom	1.25	.55
❑ 18 Kenny Lofton	3.00	1.35
❑ 19 Ray Lankford	1.50	.70
❑ 20 Tim Salmon	3.00	1.35
❑ 21 Steve Hosey	.75	.35
❑ 22 Charles Nagy	1.25	.55
❑ 23 Dave Fleming	.75	.35
❑ 24 Reggie Sanders	.75	.35
❑ 25 Sam Militello	.75	.35
❑ 26 Eric Karros	1.50	.70
❑ 27 Ryan Klesko	3.00	1.35
❑ 28 Dean Palmer	1.25	.55
❑ 29 Ivan Rodriguez	4.00	1.80
❑ 30 Sterling Hitchcock	1.00	.45

1993 Pinnacle Team Pinnacle

	MINT	NRMT
COMPLETE SET (10)	90.00	40.00
COMMON PAIR (1-10/B11)	3.00	1.35
❑ 1 Greg Maddux Mike Mussina	25.00	11.00
❑ 2 Tom Glavine John Smiley	6.00	2.70
❑ 3 Darren Daulton Ivan Rodriguez	10.00	4.50
❑ 4 Fred McGriff Frank Thomas	25.00	11.00
❑ 5 Delino DeShields Carlos Baerga	4.00	1.80
❑ 6 Gary Sheffield Edgar Martinez	8.00	3.60
❑ 7 Ozzie Smith Pat Listach	10.00	4.50
❑ 8 Barry Bonds Juan Gonzalez	20.00	9.00
❑ 9 Andy Van Slyke Kirby Puckett	12.00	5.50
❑ 10 Larry Walker Joe Carter	8.00	3.60
❑ B11 Rob Dibble Rick Aguilera	3.00	1.35

1993 Pinnacle Tribute

	MINT	NRMT
COMPLETE SET (10)	75.00	34.00
COMMON BRETT (1-5)	5.00	2.20
COMMON RYAN (6-10)	10.00	4.50
❑ 1 George Brett Kansas City Royalty	5.00	2.20
❑ 2 George Brett The Chase for .400	5.00	2.20
❑ 3 George Brett Pine Tar Pandemonium	5.00	2.20
❑ 4 George Brett MVP and a World Series& Too	5.00	2.20
❑ 5 George Brett 3,000 or Bust	5.00	2.20
❑ 6 Nolan Ryan The Rookie	10.00	4.50
❑ 7 Nolan Ryan Angel of No Mercy	10.00	4.50
❑ 8 Nolan Ryan Astronomical Success	10.00	4.50
❑ 9 Nolan Ryan 5&000 Ks	10.00	4.50
❑ 10 Nolan Ryan No-Hitter No. 7	10.00	4.50

1994 Pinnacle

	MINT	NRMT
COMPLETE SET (540)	20.00	9.00
COMPLETE SERIES 1 (270)	10.00	4.50
COMPLETE SERIES 2 (270)	10.00	4.50
COMMON CARD (1-540)	.10	.05
❑ 1 Frank Thomas	1.50	.70
❑ 2 Carlos Baerga	.25	.11
❑ 3 Sammy Sosa	1.50	.70
❑ 4 Tony Gwynn	1.25	.55
❑ 5 John Olerud	.25	.11
❑ 6 Ryne Sandberg	.60	.25
❑ 7 Moises Alou	.30	.14
❑ 8 Steve Avery	.10	.05
❑ 9 Tim Salmon	.50	.23
❑ 10 Cecil Fielder	.25	.11
❑ 11 Greg Maddux	1.50	.70
❑ 12 Barry Larkin	.30	.14
❑ 13 Mike Devereaux	.10	.05
❑ 14 Charlie Hayes	.10	.05
❑ 15 Albert Belle	.60	.25
❑ 16 Andy Van Slyke	.25	.11
❑ 17 Mo Vaughn	.60	.25
❑ 18 Brian McRae	.10	.05
❑ 19 Cal Eldred	.10	.05
❑ 20 Craig Biggio	.50	.23
❑ 21 Kirby Puckett	.75	.35
❑ 22 Derek Bell	.25	.11
❑ 23 Don Mattingly	.75	.35
❑ 24 John Burkett	.10	.05
❑ 25 Roger Clemens	1.00	.45
❑ 26 Barry Bonds	.60	.25
❑ 27 Paul Molitor	.50	.23
❑ 28 Mike Piazza	1.50	.70
❑ 29 Robin Ventura	.25	.11
❑ 30 Jeff Conine	.25	.11
❑ 31 Wade Boggs	.50	.23
❑ 32 Dennis Eckersley	.25	.11
❑ 33 Bobby Bonilla	.25	.11
❑ 34 Lenny Dykstra	.25	.11
❑ 35 Manny Alexander	.10	.05
❑ 36 Ray Lankford	.25	.11
❑ 37 Greg Vaughn	.25	.11
❑ 38 Chuck Finley	.25	.11
❑ 39 Todd Benzinger	.10	.05
❑ 40 Dave Justice	.50	.23
❑ 41 Rob Dibble	.10	.05
❑ 42 Tom Henke	.10	.05
❑ 43 David Nied	.10	.05
❑ 44 Sandy Alomar Jr.	.25	.11
❑ 45 Pete Harnisch	.10	.05
❑ 46 Jeff Russell	.10	.05
❑ 47 Terry Mulholland	.10	.05
❑ 48 Kevin Appier	.25	.11
❑ 49 Randy Tomlin	.10	.05
❑ 50 Cal Ripken Jr.	2.00	.90
❑ 51 Andy Benes	.25	.11
❑ 52 Jimmy Key	.25	.11
❑ 53 Kirt Manwaring	.10	.05
❑ 54 Kevin Tapani	.10	.05
❑ 55 Jose Guzman	.10	.05
❑ 56 Todd Stottlemyre	.10	.05
❑ 57 Jack McDowell	.10	.05
❑ 58 Orel Hershiser	.25	.11
❑ 59 Chris Hammond	.10	.05
❑ 60 Chris Nabholz	.10	.05
❑ 61 Ruben Sierra	.10	.05
❑ 62 Dwight Gooden	.25	.11
❑ 63 John Kruk	.25	.11
❑ 64 Omar Vizquel	.25	.11
❑ 65 Tim Naehring	.10	.05
❑ 66 Dwight Smith	.10	.05
❑ 67 Mickey Tettleton	.10	.05
❑ 68 J.T. Snow	.25	.11
❑ 69 Greg McMichael	.10	.05
❑ 70 Kevin Mitchell	.10	.05
❑ 71 Kevin Brown	.25	.11
❑ 72 Scott Cooper	.10	.05
❑ 73 Jim Thome	.60	.25
❑ 74 Joe Girardi	.10	.05
❑ 75 Eric Anthony	.10	.05
❑ 76 Orlando Merced	.10	.05
❑ 77 Felix Jose	.10	.05
❑ 78 Tommy Greene	.10	.05
❑ 79 Bernard Gilkey	.10	.05
❑ 80 Phil Plantier	.10	.05

❑ 81 Danny Tartabull .10 .05
❑ 82 Trevor Wilson .10 .05
❑ 83 Chuck Knoblauch .50 .23
❑ 84 Rick Wilkins .10 .05
❑ 85 Devon White .25 .11
❑ 86 Lance Johnson .10 .05
❑ 87 Eric Karros .25 .11
❑ 88 Gary Sheffield .50 .23
❑ 89 Wil Cordero .10 .05
❑ 90 Ron Darling .10 .05
❑ 91 Darren Daulton .25 .11
❑ 92 Joe Orsulak .10 .05
❑ 93 Steve Cooke .10 .05
❑ 94 Darryl Hamilton .10 .05
❑ 95 Aaron Sele .25 .11
❑ 96 John Doherty .10 .05
❑ 97 Gary DiSarcina .10 .05
❑ 98 Jeff Blauser .10 .05
❑ 99 John Smiley .10 .05
❑ 100 Ken Griffey Jr. 2.50 1.10
❑ 101 Dean Palmer .25 .11
❑ 102 Felix Fermin .10 .05
❑ 103 Jerald Clark .10 .05
❑ 104 Doug Drabek .10 .05
❑ 105 Curt Schilling .25 .11
❑ 106 Jeff Montgomery .10 .05
❑ 107 Rene Arocha .10 .05
❑ 108 Carlos Garcia .10 .05
❑ 109 Wally Whitehurst .10 .05
❑ 110 Jim Abbott .25 .11
❑ 111 Royce Clayton .10 .05
❑ 112 Chris Hoiles .10 .05
❑ 113 Mike Morgan .10 .05
❑ 114 Joe Magrane .10 .05
❑ 115 Tom Candiotti .10 .05
❑ 116 Ron Karkovice .10 .05
❑ 117 Ryan Bowen .10 .05
❑ 118 Rod Beck .10 .05
❑ 119 John Wetteland .25 .11
❑ 120 Terry Steinbach .25 .11
❑ 121 Dave Hollins .10 .05
❑ 122 Jeff Kent .25 .11
❑ 123 Ricky Bones .10 .05
❑ 124 Brian Jordan .25 .11
❑ 125 Chad Kreuter .10 .05
❑ 126 John Valentin .25 .11
❑ 127 Hilly Hathaway .10 .05
❑ 128 Wilson Alvarez .25 .11
❑ 129 Tino Martinez .50 .23
❑ 130 Rodney Bolton .10 .05
❑ 131 David Segui .25 .11
❑ 132 Wayne Kirby .10 .05
❑ 133 Eric Young .10 .05
❑ 134 Scott Servais .10 .05
❑ 135 Scott Radinsky .10 .05
❑ 136 Bret Barberie .10 .05
❑ 137 John Roper .10 .05
❑ 138 Ricky Gutierrez .10 .05
❑ 139 Bernie Williams .50 .23
❑ 140 Bud Black .10 .05
❑ 141 Jose Vizcaino .10 .05
❑ 142 Gerald Williams .10 .05
❑ 143 Duane Ward .10 .05
❑ 144 Danny Jackson .10 .05
❑ 145 Allen Watson .10 .05
❑ 146 Scott Fletcher .10 .05
❑ 147 Delino DeShields .10 .05
❑ 148 Shane Mack .10 .05
❑ 149 Jim Eisenreich .10 .05
❑ 150 Troy Neel .10 .05
❑ 151 Jay Bell .25 .11
❑ 152 B.J. Surhoff .25 .11
❑ 153 Mark Whiten .10 .05
❑ 154 Mike Henneman .10 .05
❑ 155 Todd Hundley .25 .11
❑ 156 Greg Myers .10 .05
❑ 157 Ryan Klesko .25 .11
❑ 158 Dave Fleming .10 .05
❑ 159 Mickey Morandini .10 .05
❑ 160 Blas Minor .10 .05
❑ 161 Reggie Jefferson .10 .05
❑ 162 David Hulse .10 .05
❑ 163 Greg Swindell .10 .05
❑ 164 Roberto Hernandez .10 .05
❑ 165 Brady Anderson .25 .11
❑ 166 Jack Armstrong .10 .05
❑ 167 Phil Clark .10 .05
❑ 168 Melido Perez .10 .05
❑ 169 Darren Lewis .10 .05
❑ 170 Sam Horn .10 .05
❑ 171 Mike Harkey .10 .05
❑ 172 Juan Guzman .10 .05
❑ 173 Bob Natal .10 .05
❑ 174 Deion Sanders .25 .11
❑ 175 Carlos Quintana .10 .05
❑ 176 Mel Rojas .10 .05
❑ 177 Willie Banks .10 .05
❑ 178 Ben Rivera .10 .05
❑ 179 Kenny Lofton .50 .23
❑ 180 Leo Gomez .10 .05
❑ 181 Roberto Mejia .10 .05
❑ 182 Mike Perez .10 .05
❑ 183 Travis Fryman .25 .11
❑ 184 Ben McDonald .10 .05
❑ 185 Steve Frey .10 .05
❑ 186 Kevin Young .10 .05
❑ 187 Dave Magadan .10 .05
❑ 188 Bobby Munoz .10 .05
❑ 189 Pat Rapp .10 .05
❑ 190 Jose Offerman .10 .05
❑ 191 Vinny Castilla .25 .11
❑ 192 Ivan Calderon .10 .05
❑ 193 Ken Caminiti .30 .14
❑ 194 Benji Gil .10 .05
❑ 195 Chuck Carr .10 .05
❑ 196 Derrick May .10 .05
❑ 197 Pat Kelly .10 .05
❑ 198 Jeff Brantley .10 .05
❑ 199 Jose Lind .10 .05
❑ 200 Steve Buechele .10 .05
❑ 201 Wes Chamberlain .10 .05
❑ 202 Eduardo Perez .10 .05
❑ 203 Bret Saberhagen .25 .11
❑ 204 Gregg Jefferies .10 .05
❑ 205 Darrin Fletcher .10 .05
❑ 206 Kent Hrbek .25 .11
❑ 207 Kim Batiste .10 .05
❑ 208 Jeff King .10 .05
❑ 209 Donovan Osborne .10 .05
❑ 210 Dave Nilsson .10 .05
❑ 211 Al Martin .10 .05
❑ 212 Mike Moore .10 .05
❑ 213 Sterling Hitchcock .25 .11
❑ 214 Geronimo Pena .10 .05
❑ 215 Kevin Higgins .10 .05
❑ 216 Norm Charlton .10 .05
❑ 217 Don Slaught .10 .05
❑ 218 Mitch Williams .10 .05
❑ 219 Derek Lilliquist .10 .05
❑ 220 Armando Reynoso .10 .05
❑ 221 Kenny Rogers .10 .05
❑ 222 Doug Jones .10 .05
❑ 223 Luis Aquino .10 .05
❑ 224 Mike Oquist .10 .05
❑ 225 Darryl Scott .10 .05
❑ 226 Kurt Abbott .10 .05
❑ 227 Andy Tomberlin .10 .05
❑ 228 Norberto Martin .10 .05
❑ 229 Pedro Castellano .10 .05
❑ 230 Curtis Pride .10 .05
❑ 231 Jeff McNeely .10 .05
❑ 232 Scott Lydy .10 .05
❑ 233 Darren Oliver .25 .11
❑ 234 Danny Bautista .10 .05
❑ 235 Butch Huskey .25 .11
❑ 236 Chipper Jones 1.50 .70
❑ 237 Eddie Zambrano .10 .05
❑ 238 Domingo Jean .10 .05
❑ 239 Javier Lopez .30 .14
❑ 240 Nigel Wilson .10 .05
❑ 241 Drew Denson .10 .05
❑ 242 Raul Mondesi .50 .23
❑ 243 Luis Ortiz .10 .05
❑ 244 Manny Ramirez .60 .25
❑ 245 Greg Blosser .10 .05
❑ 246 Rondell White .25 .11
❑ 247 Steve Karsay .10 .05
❑ 248 Scott Stahoviak .10 .05
❑ 249 Jose Valentin .10 .05
❑ 250 Marc Newfield .10 .05
❑ 251 Keith Kessinger .10 .05
❑ 252 Carl Everett .10 .05
❑ 253 John O'Donoghue .10 .05
❑ 254 Turk Wendell .10 .05
❑ 255 Scott Ruffcorn .10 .05
❑ 256 Tony Tarasco .10 .05
❑ 257 Andy Cook .10 .05
❑ 258 Matt Mieske .10 .05
❑ 259 Luis Lopez .10 .05
❑ 260 Ramon Caraballo .10 .05
❑ 261 Salomon Torres .10 .05
❑ 262 Brooks Kieschnick .25 .11
❑ 263 Daron Kirkreit .10 .05
❑ 264 Bill Wagner .60 .25
❑ 265 Matt Drews .25 .11
❑ 266 Scott Christman .25 .11
❑ 267 Torii Hunter .10 .05
❑ 268 Jamey Wright .25 .11
❑ 269 Jeff Granger .10 .05
❑ 270 Trot Nixon .60 .25
❑ 271 Randy Myers .10 .05
❑ 272 Trevor Hoffman .25 .11
❑ 273 Bob Wickman .10 .05
❑ 274 Willie McGee .25 .11
❑ 275 Hipolito Pichardo .10 .05
❑ 276 Bobby Witt .10 .05
❑ 277 Gregg Olson .10 .05
❑ 278 Randy Johnson .50 .23
❑ 279 Robb Nen .10 .05
❑ 280 Paul O'Neill .25 .11
❑ 281 Lou Whitaker .25 .11
❑ 282 Chad Curtis .10 .05
❑ 283 Doug Henry .10 .05
❑ 284 Tom Glavine .50 .23
❑ 285 Mike Greenwell .10 .05
❑ 286 Roberto Kelly .10 .05
❑ 287 Roberto Alomar .50 .23
❑ 288 Charlie Hough .10 .05
❑ 289 Alex Fernandez .10 .05
❑ 290 Jeff Bagwell .75 .35
❑ 291 Wally Joyner .25 .11
❑ 292 Andujar Cedeno .10 .05
❑ 293 Rick Aguilera .10 .05
❑ 294 Darryl Strawberry .25 .11
❑ 295 Mike Mussina .50 .23
❑ 296 Jeff Gardner .10 .05
❑ 297 Chris Gwynn .10 .05
❑ 298 Matt Williams .30 .14
❑ 299 Brent Gates .10 .05
❑ 300 Mark McGwire 2.50 1.10
❑ 301 Jim Deshaies .10 .05
❑ 302 Edgar Martinez .25 .11
❑ 303 Danny Darwin .10 .05
❑ 304 Pat Meares .10 .05
❑ 305 Benito Santiago .10 .05
❑ 306 Jose Canseco .50 .23
❑ 307 Jim Gott .10 .05
❑ 308 Paul Sorrento .10 .05
❑ 309 Scott Kamieniecki .10 .05
❑ 310 Larry Walker .50 .23
❑ 311 Mark Langston .10 .05
❑ 312 John Jaha .10 .05
❑ 313 Stan Javier .10 .05
❑ 314 Hal Morris .10 .05
❑ 315 Robby Thompson .10 .05
❑ 316 Pat Hentgen .25 .11
❑ 317 Tom Gordon .10 .05
❑ 318 Joey Cora .25 .11
❑ 319 Luis Alicea .10 .05
❑ 320 Andre Dawson .30 .14
❑ 321 Darryl Kile .25 .11
❑ 322 Jose Rijo .10 .05
❑ 323 Luis Gonzalez .10 .05
❑ 324 Billy Ashley .10 .05
❑ 325 David Cone .30 .14
❑ 326 Bill Swift .10 .05
❑ 327 Phil Hiatt .10 .05
❑ 328 Craig Paquette .10 .05
❑ 329 Bob Welch .10 .05
❑ 330 Tony Phillips .10 .05
❑ 331 Archi Cianfrocco .10 .05
❑ 332 Dave Winfield .50 .23
❑ 333 David McCarty .10 .05
❑ 334 Al Leiter .25 .11
❑ 335 Tom Browning .10 .05

	Player	Mint	NrMt
❑ 336	Mark Grace	.30	.14
❑ 337	Jose Mesa	.10	.05
❑ 338	Mike Stanley	.10	.05
❑ 339	Roger McDowell	.10	.05
❑ 340	Damion Easley	.25	.11
❑ 341	Angel Miranda	.10	.05
❑ 342	John Smoltz	.25	.11
❑ 343	Jay Buhner	.25	.11
❑ 344	Bryan Harvey	.10	.05
❑ 345	Joe Carter	.25	.11
❑ 346	Dante Bichette	.25	.11
❑ 347	Jason Bere	.10	.05
❑ 348	Frank Viola	.10	.05
❑ 349	Ivan Rodriguez	.60	.25
❑ 350	Juan Gonzalez	1.25	.55
❑ 351	Steve Finley	.25	.11
❑ 352	Mike Felder	.10	.05
❑ 353	Ramon Martinez	.25	.11
❑ 354	Greg Gagne	.10	.05
❑ 355	Ken Hill	.10	.05
❑ 356	Pedro Munoz	.10	.05
❑ 357	Todd Van Poppel	.10	.05
❑ 358	Marquis Grissom	.25	.11
❑ 359	Milt Cuyler	.10	.05
❑ 360	Reggie Sanders	.25	.11
❑ 361	Scott Erickson	.25	.11
❑ 362	Billy Hatcher	.10	.05
❑ 363	Gene Harris	.10	.05
❑ 364	Rene Gonzales	.10	.05
❑ 365	Kevin Rogers	.10	.05
❑ 366	Eric Plunk	.10	.05
❑ 367	Todd Zeile	.10	.05
❑ 368	John Franco	.25	.11
❑ 369	Brett Butler	.25	.11
❑ 370	Bill Spiers	.10	.05
❑ 371	Terry Pendleton	.10	.05
❑ 372	Chris Bosio	.10	.05
❑ 373	Orestes Destrade	.10	.05
❑ 374	Dave Stewart	.25	.11
❑ 375	Darren Holmes	.10	.05
❑ 376	Doug Strange	.10	.05
❑ 377	Brian Turang	.10	.05
❑ 378	Carl Willis	.10	.05
❑ 379	Mark McLemore	.10	.05
❑ 380	Bobby Jones	.10	.05
❑ 381	Scott Sanders	.10	.05
❑ 382	Kirk Rueter	.10	.05
❑ 383	Randy Velarde	.10	.05
❑ 384	Fred McGriff	.30	.14
❑ 385	Charles Nagy	.25	.11
❑ 386	Rich Amaral	.10	.05
❑ 387	Geronimo Berroa	.10	.05
❑ 388	Eric Davis	.25	.11
❑ 389	Ozzie Smith	.60	.25
❑ 390	Alex Arias	.10	.05
❑ 391	Brad Ausmus	.10	.05
❑ 392	Cliff Floyd	.25	.11
❑ 393	Roger Salkeld	.10	.05
❑ 394	Jim Edmonds	.50	.23
❑ 395	Jeromy Burnitz	.25	.11
❑ 396	Dave Staton	.10	.05
❑ 397	Rob Butler	.10	.05
❑ 398	Marcos Armas	.10	.05
❑ 399	Darrell Whitmore	.10	.05
❑ 400	Ryan Thompson	.10	.05
❑ 401	Ross Powell	.10	.05
❑ 402	Joe Oliver	.10	.05
❑ 403	Paul Carey	.10	.05
❑ 404	Bob Hamelin	.10	.05
❑ 405	Chris Turner	.10	.05
❑ 406	Nate Minchey	.10	.05
❑ 407	Lonnie Maclin	.10	.05
❑ 408	Harold Baines	.25	.11
❑ 409	Brian Williams	.10	.05
❑ 410	Johnny Ruffin	.10	.05
❑ 411	Julian Tavarez	.25	.11
❑ 412	Mark Hutton	.10	.05
❑ 413	Carlos Delgado	.30	.14
❑ 414	Chris Gomez	.10	.05
❑ 415	Mike Hampton	.10	.05
❑ 416	Alex Diaz	.10	.05
❑ 417	Jeffrey Hammonds	.25	.11
❑ 418	Jayhawk Owens	.10	.05
❑ 419	J.R. Phillips	.10	.05
❑ 420	Cory Bailey	.10	.05
❑ 421	Denny Hocking	.10	.05
❑ 422	Jon Shave	.10	.05
❑ 423	Damon Buford	.10	.05
❑ 424	Troy O'Leary	.25	.11
❑ 425	Tripp Cromer	.10	.05
❑ 426	Albie Lopez	.10	.05
❑ 427	Tony Fernandez	.10	.05
❑ 428	Ozzie Guillen	.10	.05
❑ 429	Alan Trammell	.30	.14
❑ 430	John Wasdin	.25	.11
❑ 431	Marc Valdes	.10	.05
❑ 432	Brian Anderson	.30	.14
❑ 433	Matt Brunson	.10	.05
❑ 434	Wayne Gomes	.10	.05
❑ 435	Jay Powell	.25	.11
❑ 436	Kirk Presley	.25	.11
❑ 437	Jon Ratliff	.25	.11
❑ 438	Derrek Lee	1.50	.70
❑ 439	Tom Pagnozzi	.10	.05
❑ 440	Kent Mercker	.10	.05
❑ 441	Phil Leftwich	.10	.05
❑ 442	Jamie Moyer	.10	.05
❑ 443	John Flaherty	.10	.05
❑ 444	Mark Wohlers	.10	.05
❑ 445	Jose Bautista	.10	.05
❑ 446	Andres Galarraga	.50	.23
❑ 447	Mark Lemke	.10	.05
❑ 448	Tim Wakefield	.25	.11
❑ 449	Pat Listach	.10	.05
❑ 450	Rickey Henderson	.50	.23
❑ 451	Mike Gallego	.10	.05
❑ 452	Bob Tewksbury	.10	.05
❑ 453	Kirk Gibson	.25	.11
❑ 454	Pedro Astacio	.10	.05
❑ 455	Mike Lansing	.25	.11
❑ 456	Sean Berry	.10	.05
❑ 457	Bob Walk	.10	.05
❑ 458	Chili Davis	.25	.11
❑ 459	Ed Sprague	.10	.05
❑ 460	Kevin Stocker	.10	.05
❑ 461	Mike Stanton	.10	.05
❑ 462	Tim Raines	.25	.11
❑ 463	Mike Bordick	.10	.05
❑ 464	David Wells	.30	.14
❑ 465	Tim Laker	.10	.05
❑ 466	Cory Snyder	.10	.05
❑ 467	Alex Cole	.10	.05
❑ 468	Pete Incaviglia	.10	.05
❑ 469	Roger Pavlik	.10	.05
❑ 470	Greg W. Harris	.10	.05
❑ 471	Xavier Hernandez	.10	.05
❑ 472	Erik Hanson	.10	.05
❑ 473	Jesse Orosco	.10	.05
❑ 474	Greg Colbrunn	.10	.05
❑ 475	Harold Reynolds	.10	.05
❑ 476	Greg A. Harris	.10	.05
❑ 477	Pat Borders	.10	.05
❑ 478	Melvin Nieves	.10	.05
❑ 479	Mariano Duncan	.10	.05
❑ 480	Greg Hibbard	.10	.05
❑ 481	Tim Pugh	.10	.05
❑ 482	Bobby Ayala	.10	.05
❑ 483	Sid Fernandez	.10	.05
❑ 484	Tim Wallach	.10	.05
❑ 485	Randy Milligan	.10	.05
❑ 486	Walt Weiss	.10	.05
❑ 487	Matt Walbeck	.10	.05
❑ 488	Mike Macfarlane	.10	.05
❑ 489	Jerry Browne	.10	.05
❑ 490	Chris Sabo	.10	.05
❑ 491	Tim Belcher	.10	.05
❑ 492	Spike Owen	.10	.05
❑ 493	Rafael Palmeiro	.30	.14
❑ 494	Brian Harper	.10	.05
❑ 495	Eddie Murray	.50	.23
❑ 496	Ellis Burks	.25	.11
❑ 497	Karl Rhodes	.10	.05
❑ 498	Otis Nixon	.10	.05
❑ 499	Lee Smith	.25	.11
❑ 500	Bip Roberts	.10	.05
❑ 501	Pedro Martinez	.60	.25
❑ 502	Brian Hunter	.10	.05
❑ 503	Tyler Green	.10	.05
❑ 504	Bruce Hurst	.10	.05
❑ 505	Alex Gonzalez	.10	.05
❑ 506	Mark Portugal	.10	.05
❑ 507	Bob Ojeda	.10	.05
❑ 508	Dave Henderson	.10	.05
❑ 509	Bo Jackson	.25	.11
❑ 510	Bret Boone	.25	.11
❑ 511	Mark Eichhorn	.10	.05
❑ 512	Luis Polonia	.10	.05
❑ 513	Will Clark	.50	.23
❑ 514	Dave Valle	.10	.05
❑ 515	Dan Wilson	.10	.05
❑ 516	Dennis Martinez	.25	.11
❑ 517	Jim Leyritz	.25	.11
❑ 518	Howard Johnson	.10	.05
❑ 519	Jody Reed	.10	.05
❑ 520	Julio Franco	.10	.05
❑ 521	Jeff Reardon	.25	.11
❑ 522	Willie Greene	.25	.11
❑ 523	Shawon Dunston	.10	.05
❑ 524	Keith Mitchell	.10	.05
❑ 525	Rick Helling	.25	.11
❑ 526	Mark Kiefer	.10	.05
❑ 527	Chan Ho Park	2.00	.90
❑ 528	Tony Longmire	.10	.05
❑ 529	Rich Becker	.10	.05
❑ 530	Tim Hyers	.10	.05
❑ 531	Darrin Jackson	.10	.05
❑ 532	Jack Morris	.25	.11
❑ 533	Rick White	.10	.05
❑ 534	Mike Kelly	.10	.05
❑ 535	James Mouton	.10	.05
❑ 536	Steve Trachsel	.10	.05
❑ 537	Tony Eusebio	.10	.05
❑ 538	Kelly Stinnett	.10	.05
❑ 539	Paul Spoljaric	.10	.05
❑ 540	Darren Dreifort	.25	.11
❑ SR1	C.Delgado Super Rook.	3.00	1.35

1994 Pinnacle Rookie Team Pinnacle

	MINT	NRMT
COMPLETE SET (9)	60.00	27.00
COMMON PAIR (1-9)	4.00	1.80

	Players	MINT	NRMT
❑ 1	Carlos Delgado Javier Lopez	10.00	4.50
❑ 2	Bob Hamelin J.R. Phillips	4.00	1.80
❑ 3	Jon Shave Keith Kessinger	4.00	1.80
❑ 4	Luis Ortiz Butch Huskey	6.00	2.70
❑ 5	Kurt Abbott Chipper Jones	30.00	13.50
❑ 6	Manny Ramirez Rondell White	10.00	4.50
❑ 7	Jeffrey Hammonds Cliff Floyd	10.00	4.50
❑ 8	Marc Newfield Nigel Wilson	4.00	1.80
❑ 9	Mark Hutton Salomon Torres	4.00	1.80

1994 Pinnacle Run Creators

	MINT	NRMT
COMPLETE SET (44)	80.00	36.00
COMPLETE SERIES 1 (22)	50.00	22.00
COMPLETE SERIES 2 (22)	30.00	13.50
COMMON CARD (RC1-RC44)	.75	.35

❑ RC1 John Olerud	1.25	.55
❑ RC2 Frank Thomas	12.00	5.50
❑ RC3 Ken Griffey Jr.	20.00	9.00
❑ RC4 Paul Molitor	3.00	1.35
❑ RC5 Rafael Palmeiro	2.00	.90
❑ RC6 Roberto Alomar	3.00	1.35
❑ RC7 Juan Gonzalez	10.00	4.50
❑ RC8 Albert Belle	3.00	1.35
❑ RC9 Travis Fryman	1.25	.55
❑ RC10 Rickey Henderson	3.00	1.35
❑ RC11 Tony Phillips	.75	.35
❑ RC12 Mo Vaughn	3.00	1.35
❑ RC13 Tim Salmon	3.00	1.35
❑ RC14 Kenny Lofton	3.00	1.35
❑ RC15 Carlos Baerga	1.25	.55
❑ RC16 Greg Vaughn	1.25	.55
❑ RC17 Jay Buhner	1.25	.55
❑ RC18 Chris Hoiles	.75	.35
❑ RC19 Mickey Tettleton	.75	.35
❑ RC20 Kirby Puckett	6.00	2.70
❑ RC21 Danny Tartabull	.75	.35
❑ RC22 Devon White	1.25	.55
❑ RC23 Barry Bonds	3.00	1.35
❑ RC24 Lenny Dykstra	1.25	.55
❑ RC25 John Kruk	1.25	.55
❑ RC26 Fred McGriff	2.00	.90
❑ RC27 Gregg Jefferies	.75	.35
❑ RC28 Mike Piazza	12.00	5.50
❑ RC29 Jeff Blauser	.75	.35
❑ RC30 Andres Galarraga	3.00	1.35
❑ RC31 Darren Daulton	1.25	.55
❑ RC32 Dave Justice	3.00	1.35
❑ RC33 Craig Biggio	3.00	1.35
❑ RC34 Mark Grace	2.00	.90
❑ RC35 Tony Gwynn	8.00	3.60
❑ RC36 Jeff Bagwell	6.00	2.70
❑ RC37 Jay Bell	1.25	.55
❑ RC38 Marquis Grissom	1.25	.55
❑ RC39 Matt Williams	2.00	.90
❑ RC40 Charlie Hayes	.75	.35
❑ RC41 Dante Bichette	1.25	.55
❑ RC42 Bernard Gilkey	.75	.35
❑ RC43 Brett Butler	1.25	.55
❑ RC44 Rick Wilkins	.75	.35

1994 Pinnacle Team Pinnacle

	MINT	NRMT
COMPLETE SET (9)	120.00	55.00
COMMON PAIR (1-9)	6.00	2.70

❑ 1 Jeff Bagwell / Frank Thomas	25.00	11.00
❑ 2 Carlos Baerga / Robby Thompson	6.00	2.70
❑ 3 Matt Williams / Dean Palmer	10.00	4.50
❑ 4 Cal Ripken Jr. / Jay Bell	25.00	11.00
❑ 5 Ivan Rodriguez / Mike Piazza	20.00	9.00
❑ 6 Lenny Dykstra / Ken Griffey Jr.	30.00	13.50
❑ 7 Juan Gonzalez / Barry Bonds	20.00	9.00
❑ 8 Tim Salmon / Dave Justice	20.00	9.00
❑ 9 Greg Maddux / Jack McDowell	20.00	9.00

1994 Pinnacle Tribute

	MINT	NRMT
COMPLETE SET (18)	100.00	45.00
COMPLETE SERIES 1 (9)	30.00	13.50
COMPLETE SERIES 2 (9)	70.00	32.00
COMMON CARD (TR1-TR18)	1.00	.45

❑ TR1 Paul Molitor	4.00	1.80
❑ TR2 Jim Abbott	1.50	.70
❑ TR3 Dave Winfield	4.00	1.80
❑ TR4 Bo Jackson	1.50	.70
❑ TR5 David Justice	4.00	1.80
❑ TR6 Len Dykstra	1.50	.70
❑ TR7 Mike Piazza	12.00	5.50
❑ TR8 Barry Bonds	4.00	1.80
❑ TR9 Randy Johnson	4.00	1.80
❑ TR10 Ozzie Smith	5.00	2.20
❑ TR11 Mark Whiten	1.00	.45
❑ TR12 Greg Maddux	12.00	5.50
❑ TR13 Cal Ripken Jr.	15.00	6.75
❑ TR14 Frank Thomas	12.00	5.50
❑ TR15 Juan Gonzalez	10.00	4.50
❑ TR16 Roberto Alomar	4.00	1.80
❑ TR17 Ken Griffey Jr.	20.00	9.00
❑ TR18 Lee Smith	1.50	.70

1995 Pinnacle

	MINT	NRMT
COMPLETE SET (450)	30.00	13.50
COMPLETE SERIES 1 (225)	15.00	6.75
COMPLETE SERIES 2 (225)	15.00	6.75
COMMON CARD (1-450)	.15	.07

❑ 1 Jeff Bagwell	.75	.35
❑ 2 Roger Clemens	1.00	.45
❑ 3 Mark Whiten	.15	.07
❑ 4 Shawon Dunston	.15	.07
❑ 5 Bobby Bonilla	.30	.14
❑ 6 Kevin Tapani	.15	.07
❑ 7 Eric Karros	.30	.14
❑ 8 Cliff Floyd	.30	.14
❑ 9 Pat Kelly	.15	.07
❑ 10 Jeffrey Hammonds	.30	.14
❑ 11 Jeff Conine	.30	.14
❑ 12 Fred McGriff	.40	.18
❑ 13 Chris Bosio	.15	.07
❑ 14 Mike Mussina	.60	.25
❑ 15 Danny Bautista	.15	.07
❑ 16 Mickey Morandini	.15	.07
❑ 17 Chuck Finley	.30	.14
❑ 18 Jim Thome	.60	.25
❑ 19 Luis Ortiz	.15	.07
❑ 20 Walt Weiss	.15	.07
❑ 21 Don Mattingly	.75	.35
❑ 22 Bob Hamelin	.15	.07
❑ 23 Melido Perez	.15	.07
❑ 24 Keith Mitchell	.15	.07
❑ 25 John Smoltz	.30	.14
❑ 26 Hector Carrasco	.15	.07
❑ 27 Pat Hentgen	.30	.14
❑ 28 Derrick May	.15	.07
❑ 29 Mike Kingery	.15	.07
❑ 30 Chuck Carr	.15	.07
❑ 31 Billy Ashley	.15	.07
❑ 32 Todd Hundley	.30	.14
❑ 33 Luis Gonzalez	.15	.07
❑ 34 Marquis Grissom	.30	.14
❑ 35 Jeff King	.15	.07
❑ 36 Eddie Williams	.15	.07
❑ 37 Tom Pagnozzi	.15	.07
❑ 38 Chris Hoiles	.15	.07
❑ 39 Sandy Alomar Jr.	.30	.14
❑ 40 Mike Greenwell	.15	.07
❑ 41 Lance Johnson	.15	.07
❑ 42 Junior Felix	.15	.07
❑ 43 Felix Jose	.15	.07
❑ 44 Scott Leius	.15	.07
❑ 45 Ruben Sierra	.15	.07
❑ 46 Kevin Seitzer	.15	.07
❑ 47 Wade Boggs	.60	.25
❑ 48 Reggie Jefferson	.15	.07
❑ 49 Jose Canseco	.60	.25
❑ 50 David Justice	.60	.25
❑ 51 John Smiley	.15	.07
❑ 52 Joe Carter	.30	.14
❑ 53 Rick Wilkins	.15	.07
❑ 54 Ellis Burks	.30	.14
❑ 55 Dave Weathers	.15	.07
❑ 56 Pedro Astacio	.15	.07
❑ 57 Ryan Thompson	.15	.07
❑ 58 James Mouton	.15	.07
❑ 59 Mel Rojas	.15	.07
❑ 60 Orlando Merced	.15	.07
❑ 61 Matt Williams	.30	.14
❑ 62 Bernard Gilkey	.15	.07
❑ 63 J.R. Phillips	.15	.07
❑ 64 Lee Smith	.30	.14
❑ 65 Jim Edmonds	.40	.18
❑ 66 Darrin Jackson	.15	.07
❑ 67 Scott Cooper	.15	.07
❑ 68 Ron Karkovice	.15	.07
❑ 69 Chris Gomez	.15	.07
❑ 70 Kevin Appier	.30	.14
❑ 71 Bobby Jones	.15	.07

#	Player	Price 1	Price 2
❑ 72	Doug Drabek	.15	.07
❑ 73	Matt Mieske	.15	.07
❑ 74	Sterling Hitchcock	.30	.14
❑ 75	John Valentin	.30	.14
❑ 76	Reggie Sanders	.30	.14
❑ 77	Wally Joyner	.30	.14
❑ 78	Turk Wendell	.15	.07
❑ 79	Charlie Hayes	.15	.07
❑ 80	Bret Barberie	.15	.07
❑ 81	Troy Neel	.15	.07
❑ 82	Ken Caminiti	.40	.18
❑ 83	Milt Thompson	.15	.07
❑ 84	Paul Sorrento	.15	.07
❑ 85	Trevor Hoffman	.30	.14
❑ 86	Jay Bell	.30	.14
❑ 87	Mark Portugal	.15	.07
❑ 88	Sid Fernandez	.15	.07
❑ 89	Charles Nagy	.30	.14
❑ 90	Jeff Montgomery	.15	.07
❑ 91	Chuck Knoblauch	.60	.25
❑ 92	Jeff Frye	.15	.07
❑ 93	Tony Gwynn	1.25	.55
❑ 94	John Olerud	.30	.14
❑ 95	David Nied	.15	.07
❑ 96	Chris Hammond	.15	.07
❑ 97	Edgar Martinez	.30	.14
❑ 98	Kevin Stocker	.15	.07
❑ 99	Jeff Fassero	.15	.07
❑ 100	Curt Schilling	.30	.14
❑ 101	Dave Clark	.15	.07
❑ 102	Delino DeShields	.15	.07
❑ 103	Leo Gomez	.15	.07
❑ 104	Dave Hollins	.15	.07
❑ 105	Tim Naehring	.15	.07
❑ 106	Otis Nixon	.15	.07
❑ 107	Ozzie Guillen	.15	.07
❑ 108	Jose Lind	.15	.07
❑ 109	Stan Javier	.15	.07
❑ 110	Greg Vaughn	.30	.14
❑ 111	Chipper Jones	1.25	.55
❑ 112	Ed Sprague	.15	.07
❑ 113	Mike Macfarlane	.15	.07
❑ 114	Steve Finley	.30	.14
❑ 115	Ken Hill	.15	.07
❑ 116	Carlos Garcia	.15	.07
❑ 117	Lou Whitaker	.30	.14
❑ 118	Todd Zeile	.15	.07
❑ 119	Gary Sheffield	.40	.18
❑ 120	Ben McDonald	.15	.07
❑ 121	Pete Harnisch	.15	.07
❑ 122	Ivan Rodriguez	.60	.25
❑ 123	Wilson Alvarez	.30	.14
❑ 124	Travis Fryman	.30	.14
❑ 125	Pedro Munoz	.15	.07
❑ 126	Mark Lemke	.15	.07
❑ 127	Jose Valentin	.15	.07
❑ 128	Ken Griffey Jr.	2.50	1.10
❑ 129	Omar Vizquel	.30	.14
❑ 130	Milt Cuyler	.15	.07
❑ 131	Steve Trachsel	.15	.07
❑ 132	Alex Rodriguez	2.00	.90
❑ 133	Garret Anderson	.30	.14
❑ 134	Armando Benitez	.15	.07
❑ 135	Shawn Green	.30	.14
❑ 136	Jorge Fabregas	.15	.07
❑ 137	Orlando Miller	.15	.07
❑ 138	Rikkert Faneyte	.15	.07
❑ 139	Ismael Valdes	.30	.14
❑ 140	Jose Oliva	.15	.07
❑ 141	Aaron Small	.15	.07
❑ 142	Tim Davis	.15	.07
❑ 143	Ricky Bottalico	.30	.14
❑ 144	Mike Matheny	.15	.07
❑ 145	Roberto Petagine	.15	.07
❑ 146	Fausto Cruz	.15	.07
❑ 147	Bryce Florie	.15	.07
❑ 148	Jose Lima	.15	.07
❑ 149	John Hudek	.15	.07
❑ 150	Duane Singleton	.15	.07
❑ 151	John Mabry	.15	.07
❑ 152	Robert Eenhoorn	.15	.07
❑ 153	Jon Lieber	.15	.07
❑ 154	Garey Ingram	.15	.07
❑ 155	Paul Shuey	.15	.07
❑ 156	Mike Lieberthal	.15	.07
❑ 157	Steve Dunn	.15	.07
❑ 158	Charles Johnson	.30	.14
❑ 159	Ernie Young	.15	.07
❑ 160	Jose Martinez	.15	.07
❑ 161	Kurt Miller	.15	.07
❑ 162	Joey Eischen	.15	.07
❑ 163	Dave Stevens	.15	.07
❑ 164	Brian L.Hunter	.30	.14
❑ 165	Jeff Cirillo	.30	.14
❑ 166	Mark Smith	.15	.07
❑ 167	McKay Christensen	.30	.14
❑ 168	C.J. Nitkowski	.15	.07
❑ 169	Antone Williamson	.15	.07
❑ 170	Paul Konerko	1.25	.55
❑ 171	Scott Elarton	.60	.25
❑ 172	Jacob Shumate	.15	.07
❑ 173	Terrence Long	.30	.14
❑ 174	Mark Johnson	.15	.07
❑ 175	Ben Grieve	3.00	1.35
❑ 176	Jayson Peterson	.15	.07
❑ 177	Checklist	.15	.07
❑ 178	Checklist	.15	.07
❑ 179	Checklist	.15	.07
❑ 180	Checklist	.15	.07
❑ 181	Brian Anderson	.30	.14
❑ 182	Steve Buechele	.15	.07
❑ 183	Mark Clark	.15	.07
❑ 184	Cecil Fielder	.30	.14
❑ 185	Steve Avery	.15	.07
❑ 186	Devon White	.30	.14
❑ 187	Craig Shipley	.15	.07
❑ 188	Brady Anderson	.30	.14
❑ 189	Kenny Lofton	.60	.25
❑ 190	Alex Cole	.15	.07
❑ 191	Brent Gates	.15	.07
❑ 192	Dean Palmer	.30	.14
❑ 193	Alex Gonzalez	.15	.07
❑ 194	Steve Cooke	.15	.07
❑ 195	Ray Lankford	.30	.14
❑ 196	Mark McGwire	2.50	1.10
❑ 197	Marc Newfield	.15	.07
❑ 198	Pat Rapp	.15	.07
❑ 199	Darren Lewis	.15	.07
❑ 200	Carlos Baerga	.30	.14
❑ 201	Rickey Henderson	.60	.25
❑ 202	Kurt Abbott	.15	.07
❑ 203	Kirt Manwaring	.15	.07
❑ 204	Cal Ripken	2.00	.90
❑ 205	Darren Daulton	.30	.14
❑ 206	Greg Colbrunn	.15	.07
❑ 207	Darryl Hamilton	.15	.07
❑ 208	Bo Jackson	.30	.14
❑ 209	Tony Phillips	.15	.07
❑ 210	Geronimo Berroa	.15	.07
❑ 211	Rich Becker	.15	.07
❑ 212	Tony Tarasco	.15	.07
❑ 213	Karl Rhodes	.15	.07
❑ 214	Phil Plantier	.15	.07
❑ 215	J.T. Snow	.30	.14
❑ 216	Mo Vaughn	.60	.25
❑ 217	Greg Gagne	.15	.07
❑ 218	Ricky Bones	.15	.07
❑ 219	Mike Bordick	.15	.07
❑ 220	Chad Curtis	.15	.07
❑ 221	Royce Clayton	.15	.07
❑ 222	Roberto Alomar	.60	.25
❑ 223	Jose Rijo	.15	.07
❑ 224	Ryan Klesko	.30	.14
❑ 225	Mark Langston	.15	.07
❑ 226	Frank Thomas	1.50	.70
❑ 227	Juan Gonzalez	1.25	.55
❑ 228	Ron Gant	.15	.07
❑ 229	Javier Lopez	.30	.14
❑ 230	Sammy Sosa	1.25	.55
❑ 231	Kevin Brown	.40	.18
❑ 232	Gary DiSarcina	.15	.07
❑ 233	Albert Belle	.75	.35
❑ 234	Jay Buhner	.30	.14
❑ 235	Pedro J. Martinez	.60	.25
❑ 236	Bob Tewksbury	.15	.07
❑ 237	Mike Piazza	1.50	.70
❑ 238	Darryl Kile	.30	.14
❑ 239	Bryan Harvey	.15	.07
❑ 240	Andres Galarraga	.60	.25
❑ 241	Jeff Blauser	.15	.07
❑ 242	Jeff Kent	.30	.14
❑ 243	Bobby Munoz	.15	.07
❑ 244	Greg Maddux	1.50	.70
❑ 245	Paul O'Neill	.30	.14
❑ 246	Lenny Dykstra	.30	.14
❑ 247	Todd Van Poppel	.15	.07
❑ 248	Bernie Williams	.60	.25
❑ 249	Glenallen Hill	.15	.07
❑ 250	Duane Ward	.15	.07
❑ 251	Dennis Eckersley	.30	.14
❑ 252	Pat Mahomes	.15	.07
❑ 253	Rusty Greer	.60	.25
❑ 254	Roberto Kelly	.15	.07
❑ 255	Randy Myers	.15	.07
❑ 256	Scott Ruffcorn	.15	.07
❑ 257	Robin Ventura	.30	.14
❑ 258	Eduardo Perez	.15	.07
❑ 259	Aaron Sele	.30	.14
❑ 260	Paul Molitor	.60	.25
❑ 261	Juan Guzman	.15	.07
❑ 262	Darren Oliver	.15	.07
❑ 263	Mike Stanley	.15	.07
❑ 264	Tom Glavine	.60	.25
❑ 265	Rico Brogna	.15	.07
❑ 266	Craig Biggio	.60	.25
❑ 267	Darrell Whitmore	.15	.07
❑ 268	Jimmy Key	.30	.14
❑ 269	Will Clark	.60	.25
❑ 270	David Cone	.40	.18
❑ 271	Brian Jordan	.30	.14
❑ 272	Barry Bonds	.60	.25
❑ 273	Danny Tartabull	.15	.07
❑ 274	Ramon J.Martinez	.30	.14
❑ 275	Al Martin	.15	.07
❑ 276	Fred McGriff SM	.15	.07
❑ 277	Carlos Delgado SM	.15	.07
❑ 278	Juan Gonzalez SM	.60	.25
❑ 279	Shawn Green SM	.15	.07
❑ 280	Carlos Baerga SM	.15	.07
❑ 281	Cliff Floyd SM	.15	.07
❑ 282	Ozzie Smith SM	.60	.25
❑ 283	Alex Rodriguez SM	1.00	.45
❑ 284	Kenny Lofton SM	.30	.14
❑ 285	Dave Justice SM	.30	.14
❑ 286	Tim Salmon SM	.30	.14
❑ 287	Manny Ramirez SM	.30	.14
❑ 288	Will Clark SM	.30	.14
❑ 289	Garret Anderson SM	.15	.07
❑ 290	Billy Ashley SM	.15	.07
❑ 291	Tony Gwynn SM	.60	.25
❑ 292	Raul Mondesi SM	.15	.07
❑ 293	Rafael Palmeiro SM	.15	.07
❑ 294	Matt Williams SM	.15	.07
❑ 295	Don Mattingly SM	.60	.25
❑ 296	Kirby Puckett SM	.60	.25
❑ 297	Paul Molitor SM	.30	.14
❑ 298	Albert Belle SM	.30	.14
❑ 299	Barry Bonds SM	.40	.18
❑ 300	Mike Piazza SM	.75	.35
❑ 301	Jeff Bagwell SM	.60	.25
❑ 302	Frank Thomas SM	.75	.35
❑ 303	Chipper Jones SM	.60	.25
❑ 304	Ken Griffey Jr. SM	1.25	.55
❑ 305	Cal Ripken Jr. SM	1.00	.45
❑ 306	Eric Anthony	.15	.07
❑ 307	Todd Benzinger	.15	.07
❑ 308	Jacob Brumfield	.15	.07
❑ 309	Wes Chamberlain	.15	.07
❑ 310	Tino Martinez	.60	.25
❑ 311	Roberto Mejia	.15	.07
❑ 312	Jose Offerman	.15	.07
❑ 313	David Segui	.30	.14
❑ 314	Eric Young	.15	.07
❑ 315	Rey Sanchez	.15	.07
❑ 316	Raul Mondesi	.40	.18
❑ 317	Bret Boone	.30	.14
❑ 318	Andre Dawson	.40	.18
❑ 319	Brian McRae	.15	.07
❑ 320	Dave Nilsson	.15	.07
❑ 321	Moises Alou	.40	.18
❑ 322	Don Slaught	.15	.07
❑ 323	Dave McCarty	.15	.07
❑ 324	Mike Huff	.15	.07
❑ 325	Rick Aguilera	.15	.07
❑ 326	Rod Beck	.15	.07

❑ 327 Kenny Rogers .15 .07
❑ 328 Andy Benes .30 .14
❑ 329 Allen Watson .15 .07
❑ 330 Randy Johnson .60 .25
❑ 331 Willie Greene .30 .14
❑ 332 Hal Morris .15 .07
❑ 333 Ozzie Smith .60 .25
❑ 334 Jason Bere .15 .07
❑ 335 Scott Erickson .30 .14
❑ 336 Dante Bichette .30 .14
❑ 337 Willie Banks .15 .07
❑ 338 Eric Davis .30 .14
❑ 339 Rondell White .30 .14
❑ 340 Kirby Puckett .75 .35
❑ 341 Deion Sanders .30 .14
❑ 342 Eddie Murray .60 .25
❑ 343 Mike Harkey .15 .07
❑ 344 Joey Hamilton .30 .14
❑ 345 Roger Salkeld .15 .07
❑ 346 Wil Cordero .15 .07
❑ 347 John Wetteland .30 .14
❑ 348 Geronimo Pena .15 .07
❑ 349 Kirk Gibson .30 .14
❑ 350 Manny Ramirez .60 .25
❑ 351 Wm.VanLandingham .15 .07
❑ 352 B.J. Surhoff .30 .14
❑ 353 Ken Ryan .15 .07
❑ 354 Terry Steinbach .30 .14
❑ 355 Bret Saberhagen .30 .14
❑ 356 John Jaha .15 .07
❑ 357 Joe Girardi .15 .07
❑ 358 Steve Karsay .15 .07
❑ 359 Alex Fernandez .15 .07
❑ 360 Salomon Torres .15 .07
❑ 361 John Burkett .15 .07
❑ 362 Derek Bell .30 .14
❑ 363 Tom Henke .15 .07
❑ 364 Gregg Jefferies .15 .07
❑ 365 Jack McDowell .15 .07
❑ 366 Andujar Cedeno .15 .07
❑ 367 Dave Winfield .60 .25
❑ 368 Carl Everett .15 .07
❑ 369 Danny Jackson .15 .07
❑ 370 Jeromy Burnitz .30 .14
❑ 371 Mark Grace .40 .18
❑ 372 Larry Walker .60 .25
❑ 373 Bill Swift .15 .07
❑ 374 Dennis Martinez .30 .14
❑ 375 Mickey Tettleton .15 .07
❑ 376 Mel Nieves .15 .07
❑ 377 Cal Eldred .15 .07
❑ 378 Orel Hershiser .30 .14
❑ 379 David Wells .40 .18
❑ 380 Gary Gaetti .30 .14
❑ 381 Jeromy Burnitz .30 .14
❑ 382 Barry Larkin .40 .18
❑ 383 Jason Jacome .15 .07
❑ 384 Tim Wallach .15 .07
❑ 385 Robby Thompson .15 .07
❑ 386 Frank Viola .15 .07
❑ 387 Dave Stewart .30 .14
❑ 388 Bip Roberts .15 .07
❑ 389 Ron Darling .15 .07
❑ 390 Carlos Delgado .30 .14
❑ 391 Tim Salmon .60 .25
❑ 392 Alan Trammell .30 .14
❑ 393 Kevin Foster .15 .07
❑ 394 Jim Abbott .30 .14
❑ 395 John Kruk .30 .14
❑ 396 Andy Van Slyke .30 .14
❑ 397 Dave Magadan .15 .07
❑ 398 Rafael Palmeiro .40 .18
❑ 399 Mike Devereaux .15 .07
❑ 400 Benito Santiago .15 .07
❑ 401 Brett Butler .30 .14
❑ 402 John Franco .30 .14
❑ 403 Matt Walbeck .15 .07
❑ 404 Terry Pendleton .15 .07
❑ 405 Chris Sabo .15 .07
❑ 406 Andrew Lorraine .15 .07
❑ 407 Dan Wilson .15 .07
❑ 408 Mike Lansing .15 .07
❑ 409 Ray McDavid .15 .07
❑ 410 Shane Andrews .15 .07
❑ 411 Tom Gordon .15 .07
❑ 412 Chad Ogea .15 .07
❑ 413 James Baldwin .30 .14
❑ 414 Russ Davis .30 .14
❑ 415 Ray Holbert .15 .07
❑ 416 Ray Durham .30 .14
❑ 417 Matt Nokes .15 .07
❑ 418 Rod Henderson .15 .07
❑ 419 Gabe White .15 .07
❑ 420 Todd Hollandsworth .15 .07
❑ 421 Midre Cummings .15 .07
❑ 422 Harold Baines .30 .14
❑ 423 Troy Percival .30 .14
❑ 424 Joe Vitiello .15 .07
❑ 425 Andy Ashby .15 .07
❑ 426 Michael Tucker .30 .14
❑ 427 Mark Gubicza .15 .07
❑ 428 Jim Bullinger .15 .07
❑ 429 Jose Malave .15 .07
❑ 430 Pete Schourek .15 .07
❑ 431 Bobby Ayala .15 .07
❑ 432 Marvin Freeman .15 .07
❑ 433 Pat Listach .15 .07
❑ 434 Eddie Taubensee .15 .07
❑ 435 Steve Howe .15 .07
❑ 436 Kent Mercker .15 .07
❑ 437 Hector Fajardo .15 .07
❑ 438 Scott Kamieniecki .15 .07
❑ 439 Robb Nen .15 .07
❑ 440 Mike Kelly .15 .07
❑ 441 Tom Candiotti .15 .07
❑ 442 Albie Lopez .15 .07
❑ 443 Jeff Granger .15 .07
❑ 444 Rich Aude .15 .07
❑ 445 Luis Polonia .15 .07
❑ 446 Frank Thomas CL .75 .35
❑ 447 Ken Griffey Jr. CL 1.25 .55
❑ 448 Mike Piazza CL .75 .35
❑ 449 Jeff Bagwell CL .60 .25
❑ 450 Jeff Bagwel CL 1.25 .55
Frank Thomas
Ken Griffey Jr.
Mike Piazza

1995 Pinnacle ETA

	MINT	NRMT
COMPLETE SET (6)	25.00	11.00
COMMON CARD (1-6)	2.00	.90

❑ 1 Ben Grieve 15.00 6.75
❑ 2 Alex Ochoa 2.00 .90
❑ 3 Joe Vitiello 2.00 .90
❑ 4 Johnny Damon 3.00 1.35
❑ 5 Trey Beamon 2.00 .90
❑ 6 Brooks Kieschnick 2.00 .90

1995 Pinnacle Gate Attractions

	MINT	NRMT
COMPLETE SET (18)	120.00	55.00
COMMON CARD (GA1-GA18)	2.00	.90

❑ GA1 Ken Griffey Jr. 25.00 11.00
❑ GA2 Frank Thomas 15.00 6.75
❑ GA3 Cal Ripken 20.00 9.00
❑ GA4 Jeff Bagwell 8.00 3.60
❑ GA5 Mike Piazza 15.00 6.75

❑ GA6 Barry Bonds 5.00 2.20
❑ GA7 Kirby Puckett 5.00 2.20
❑ GA8 Albert Belle 5.00 2.20
❑ GA9 Tony Gwynn 12.00 5.50
❑ GA10 Raul Mondesi 3.00 1.35
❑ GA11 Will Clark 5.00 2.20
❑ GA12 Don Mattingly 5.00 2.20
❑ GA13 Roger Clemens 10.00 4.50
❑ GA14 Paul Molitor 5.00 2.20
❑ GA15 Matt Williams 2.00 .90
❑ GA16 Greg Maddux 15.00 6.75
❑ GA17 Kenny Lofton 5.00 2.20
❑ GA18 Cliff Floyd 2.00 .90

1995 Pinnacle New Blood

	MINT	NRMT
COMPLETE SET (9)	80.00	36.00
COMMON CARD (NB1-NB9)	2.50	1.10

❑ NB1 Alex Rodriguez 30.00 13.50
❑ NB2 Shawn Green 4.00 1.80
❑ NB3 Brian Hunter 4.00 1.80
❑ NB4 Garret Anderson 4.00 1.80
❑ NB5 Charles Johnson 4.00 1.80
❑ NB6 Chipper Jones 25.00 11.00
❑ NB7 Carlos Delgado 4.00 1.80
❑ NB8 Billy Ashley 2.50 1.10
❑ NB9 J.R. Phillips UER 2.50 1.10
Dodgers logo on back
Phillips played for the Giants

1995 Pinnacle Performers

	MINT	NRMT
COMPLETE SERIES 1 (18)	100.00	45.00
COMMON CARD (1-18)	1.50	.70

❑ PP1 Frank Thomas 20.00 9.00
❑ PP2 Albert Belle 8.00 3.60
❑ PP3 Barry Bonds 8.00 3.60
❑ PP4 Juan Gonzalez 15.00 6.75
❑ PP5 Andres Galarraga 6.00 2.70
❑ PP6 Raul Mondesi 4.00 1.80
❑ PP7 Paul Molitor 6.00 2.70
❑ PP8 Tim Salmon 6.00 2.70
❑ PP9 Mike Piazza 20.00 9.00

		MINT	NRMT
❑ PP10	Gregg Jefferies	1.50	.70
❑ PP11	Will Clark	6.00	2.70
❑ PP12	Greg Maddux	20.00	9.00
❑ PP13	Manny Ramirez	6.00	2.70
❑ PP14	Kirby Puckett	10.00	4.50
❑ PP15	Shawn Green	2.50	1.10
❑ PP16	Rafael Palmeiro	4.00	1.80
❑ PP17	Paul O'Neill	2.50	1.10
❑ PP18	Jason Bere	1.50	.70

1995 Pinnacle Pin Redemption

	MINT	NRMT
COMPLETE SET (18)	80.00	36.00
COMMON CARD (1-18)	1.50	.70

		MINT	NRMT
❑ 1	Greg Maddux	10.00	4.50
❑ 2	Mike Mussina	3.00	1.35
❑ 3	Mike Piazza	10.00	4.50
❑ 4	Carlos Delgado	1.50	.70
❑ 5	Jeff Bagwell	6.00	2.70
❑ 6	Frank Thomas	10.00	4.50
❑ 7	Craig Biggio	3.00	1.35
❑ 8	Roberto Alomar	3.00	1.35
❑ 9	Ozzie Smith	3.00	1.35
❑ 10	Cal Ripken Jr.	12.00	5.50
❑ 11	Matt Williams	1.50	.70
❑ 12	Travis Fryman	1.50	.70
❑ 13	Barry Bonds	3.00	1.35
❑ 14	Ken Griffey Jr.	15.00	6.75
❑ 15	Dave Justice	3.00	1.35
❑ 16	Albert Belle	3.00	1.35
❑ 17	Tony Gwynn	8.00	3.60
❑ 18	Kirby Puckett	3.00	1.35

1995 Pinnacle Red Hot

	MINT	NRMT
COMPLETE SET (25)	80.00	36.00
COMMON CARD (RH1-RH25)	1.00	.45
COMP.WHITE SET (25)	300.00	135.00

*WHITE HOT: 8X TO 20X RED HOTS
W.HOT SER.2 STATED ODDS 1:36 HOBBY

		MINT	NRMT
❑ RH1	Cal Ripken Jr.	12.00	5.50
❑ RH2	Ken Griffey Jr.	15.00	6.75
❑ RH3	Frank Thomas	10.00	4.50
❑ RH4	Jeff Bagwell	5.00	2.20
❑ RH5	Mike Piazza	10.00	4.50
❑ RH6	Barry Bonds	3.00	1.35
❑ RH7	Albert Belle	3.00	1.35
❑ RH8	Tony Gwynn	8.00	3.60
❑ RH9	Kirby Puckett	3.00	1.35
❑ RH10	Don Mattingly	5.00	2.20
❑ RH11	Matt Williams	1.50	.70
❑ RH12	Greg Maddux	10.00	4.50
❑ RH13	Raul Mondesi	2.00	.90
❑ RH14	Paul Molitor	3.00	1.35
❑ RH15	Manny Ramirez	3.00	1.35
❑ RH16	Joe Carter	1.50	.70
❑ RH17	Will Clark	3.00	1.35
❑ RH18	Roger Clemens	6.00	2.70
❑ RH19	Tim Salmon	3.00	1.35
❑ RH20	Dave Justice	3.00	1.35
❑ RH21	Kenny Lofton	3.00	1.35
❑ RH22	Deion Sanders	1.50	.70
❑ RH23	Roberto Alomar	3.00	1.35
❑ RH24	Cliff Floyd	1.50	.70
❑ RH25	Carlos Baerga	1.00	.45

1995 Pinnacle Team Pinnacle

	MINT	NRMT
COMPLETE SET (9)	200.00	90.00
COMMON CARD (1-9)	5.00	2.20

		MINT	NRMT
❑ TP1	Mike Mussina Greg Maddux	30.00	13.50
❑ TP2	Carlos Delgado Mike Piazza	30.00	13.50
❑ TP3	Frank Thomas Jeff Bagwell	30.00	13.50
❑ TP4	Roberto Alomar Craig Biggio	10.00	4.50
❑ TP5	Cal Ripken Ozzie Smith	40.00	18.00
❑ TP6	Travis Fryman Matt Williams	5.00	2.20
❑ TP7	Ken Griffey Jr. Barry Bonds	50.00	22.00
❑ TP8	Albert Belle David Justice	12.00	5.50
❑ TP9	Kirby Puckett Tony Gwynn	25.00	11.00

1995 Pinnacle Upstarts

	MINT	NRMT
COMPLETE SET (30)	50.00	22.00
COMMON CARD (US1-US30)	1.00	.45

		MINT	NRMT
❑ US1	Frank Thomas	12.00	5.50
❑ US2	Roberto Alomar	4.00	1.80
❑ US3	Mike Piazza	12.00	5.50
❑ US4	Javier Lopez	1.50	.70
❑ US5	Albert Belle	4.00	1.80
❑ US6	Carlos Delgado	1.50	.70
❑ US7	Brent Gates	1.00	.45
❑ US8	Tim Salmon	4.00	1.80
❑ US9	Raul Mondesi	2.50	1.10
❑ US10	Juan Gonzalez	10.00	4.50
❑ US11	Manny Ramirez	4.00	1.80
❑ US12	Sammy Sosa	4.00	1.80
❑ US13	Jeff Kent	1.50	.70
❑ US14	Melvin Nieves	1.00	.45
❑ US15	Rondell White	1.50	.70
❑ US16	Shawn Green	1.50	.70
❑ US17	Bernie Williams	4.00	1.80
❑ US18	Aaron Sele	1.50	.70
❑ US19	Jason Bere	1.00	.45
❑ US20	Joey Hamilton	1.50	.70
❑ US21	Mike Kelly	1.00	.45
❑ US22	Wil Cordero	1.00	.45
❑ US23	Moises Alou	2.50	1.10
❑ US24	Roberto Kelly	1.00	.45
❑ US25	Deion Sanders	1.50	.70
❑ US26	Steve Karsay	1.00	.45
❑ US27	Bret Boone	1.50	.70
❑ US28	Willie Greene	1.50	.70
❑ US29	Billy Ashley	1.00	.45
❑ US30	Brian Anderson	1.50	.70

1996 Pinnacle

	MINT	NRMT
COMPLETE SET (400)	30.00	13.50
COMPLETE SERIES 1 (200)	15.00	6.75
COMPLETE SERIES 2 (200)	15.00	6.75
COMMON CARD (1-399)	.10	.05

		MINT	NRMT
❑ 1	Greg Maddux	1.25	.55
❑ 2	Bill Pulsipher	.10	.05
❑ 3	Dante Bichette	.15	.07
❑ 4	Mike Piazza	1.25	.55
❑ 5	Garret Anderson	.15	.07
❑ 6	Steve Finley	.15	.07

❑ 7	Andy Benes	.15	.07
❑ 8	Chuck Knoblauch	.40	.18
❑ 9	Tom Gordon	.10	.05
❑ 10	Jeff Bagwell	.60	.25
❑ 11	Wil Cordero	.10	.05
❑ 12	John Mabry	.10	.05
❑ 13	Jeff Frye	.10	.05
❑ 14	Travis Fryman	.15	.07
❑ 15	John Wetteland	.15	.07
❑ 16	Jason Bates	.10	.05
❑ 17	Danny Tartabull	.10	.05
❑ 18	Charles Nagy	.15	.07
❑ 19	Robin Ventura	.15	.07
❑ 20	Reggie Sanders	.15	.07
❑ 21	Dave Clark	.10	.05
❑ 22	Jaime Navarro	.10	.05
❑ 23	Joey Hamilton	.15	.07
❑ 24	Al Leiter	.15	.07
❑ 25	Deion Sanders	.15	.07
❑ 26	Tim Salmon	.40	.18
❑ 27	Tino Martinez	.40	.18
❑ 28	Mike Greenwell	.10	.05
❑ 29	Phil Plantier	.10	.05
❑ 30	Bobby Bonilla	.15	.07
❑ 31	Kenny Rogers	.10	.05
❑ 32	Chili Davis	.15	.07
❑ 33	Joe Carter	.15	.07
❑ 34	Mike Mussina	.40	.18
❑ 35	Matt Mieske	.10	.05
❑ 36	Jose Canseco	.40	.18
❑ 37	Brad Radke	.15	.07
❑ 38	Juan Gonzalez	1.00	.45
❑ 39	David Segui	.15	.07
❑ 40	Alex Fernandez	.10	.05
❑ 41	Jeff Kent	.15	.07
❑ 42	Todd Zeile	.10	.05
❑ 43	Darryl Strawberry	.15	.07
❑ 44	Jose Rijo	.10	.05
❑ 45	Ramon Martinez	.15	.07
❑ 46	Manny Ramirez	.40	.18
❑ 47	Gregg Jefferies	.10	.05
❑ 48	Bryan Rekar	.10	.05
❑ 49	Jeff King	.10	.05
❑ 50	John Olerud	.15	.07
❑ 51	Marc Newfield	.10	.05
❑ 52	Charles Johnson	.15	.07
❑ 53	Robby Thompson	.10	.05
❑ 54	Brian L. Hunter	.15	.07
❑ 55	Mike Blowers	.10	.05
❑ 56	Keith Lockhart	.10	.05
❑ 57	Ray Lankford	.15	.07
❑ 58	Tim Wallach	.10	.05
❑ 59	Ivan Rodriguez	.50	.23
❑ 60	Ed Sprague	.10	.05
❑ 61	Paul Molitor	.40	.18
❑ 62	Eric Karros	.15	.07
❑ 63	Glenallen Hill	.10	.05
❑ 64	Jay Bell	.15	.07
❑ 65	Tom Pagnozzi	.10	.05
❑ 66	Greg Colbrunn	.10	.05
❑ 67	Edgar Martinez	.15	.07
❑ 68	Paul Sorrento	.10	.05
❑ 69	Kirt Manwaring	.10	.05
❑ 70	Pete Schourek	.10	.05
❑ 71	Orlando Merced	.10	.05
❑ 72	Shawon Dunston	.10	.05
❑ 73	Ricky Bottalico	.15	.07
❑ 74	Brady Anderson	.15	.07
❑ 75	Steve Ontiveros	.10	.05
❑ 76	Jim Abbott	.15	.07
❑ 77	Carl Everett	.10	.05
❑ 78	Mo Vaughn	.50	.23
❑ 79	Pedro Martinez	.40	.18
❑ 80	Harold Baines	.15	.07
❑ 81	Alan Trammell	.40	.18
❑ 82	Steve Avery	.10	.05
❑ 83	Jeff Cirillo	.15	.07
❑ 84	John Valentin	.15	.07
❑ 85	Bernie Williams	.40	.18
❑ 86	Andre Dawson	.40	.18
❑ 87	Dave Winfield	.40	.18
❑ 88	B.J. Surhoff	.15	.07
❑ 89	Jeff Blauser	.10	.05
❑ 90	Barry Larkin	.40	.18
❑ 91	Cliff Floyd	.15	.07
❑ 92	Sammy Sosa	1.00	.45
❑ 93	Andres Galarraga	.40	.18
❑ 94	Dave Nilsson	.10	.05
❑ 95	James Mouton	.10	.05
❑ 96	Marquis Grissom	.15	.07
❑ 97	Matt Williams	.15	.07
❑ 98	John Jaha	.10	.05
❑ 99	Don Mattingly	.60	.25
❑ 100	Tim Naehring	.10	.05
❑ 101	Kevin Appier	.15	.07
❑ 102	Bobby Higginson	.40	.18
❑ 103	Andy Pettitte	.40	.18
❑ 104	Ozzie Smith	.50	.23
❑ 105	Kenny Lofton	.40	.18
❑ 106	Ken Caminiti	.40	.18
❑ 107	Walt Weiss	.10	.05
❑ 108	Jack McDowell	.10	.05
❑ 109	Brian McRae	.10	.05
❑ 110	Gary Gaetti	.15	.07
❑ 111	Curtis Goodwin	.10	.05
❑ 112	Dennis Martinez	.15	.07
❑ 113	Omar Vizquel	.15	.07
❑ 114	Chipper Jones	1.00	.45
❑ 115	Mark Gubicza	.10	.05
❑ 116	Ruben Sierra	.10	.05
❑ 117	Eddie Murray	.40	.18
❑ 118	Chad Curtis	.10	.05
❑ 119	Hal Morris	.10	.05
❑ 120	Ben McDonald	.10	.05
❑ 121	Marty Cordova	.10	.05
❑ 122	Ken Griffey Jr. UER	2.00	.90
	Card says Ken homered		
	from both sides		
	He is only a left hitter		
❑ 123	Gary Sheffield	.40	.18
❑ 124	Charlie Hayes	.10	.05
❑ 125	Shawn Green	.15	.07
❑ 126	Jason Giambi	.15	.07
❑ 127	Mark Langston	.10	.05
❑ 128	Mark Whiten	.10	.05
❑ 129	Greg Vaughn	.15	.07
❑ 130	Mark McGwire	2.00	.90
❑ 131	Hideo Nomo	.60	.25
❑ 132	Eric Karros	.75	.35
	Mike Piazza		
	Raul Mondesi		
	Hideo Nomo		
❑ 133	Jason Bere	.10	.05
❑ 134	Ken Griffey Jr. NAT	1.00	.45
❑ 135	Frank Thomas NAT	.60	.25
❑ 136	Cal Ripken NAT	.75	.35
❑ 137	Albert Belle NAT	.40	.18
❑ 138	Mike Piazza NAT	.60	.25
❑ 139	Dante Bichette NAT	.10	.05
❑ 140	Sammy Sosa NAT	.50	.23
❑ 141	Mo Vaughn NAT	.40	.18
❑ 142	Tim Salmon NAT	.15	.07
❑ 143	Reggie Sanders NAT	.10	.05
❑ 144	Cecil Fielder NAT	.10	.05
❑ 145	Jim Edmonds NAT	.10	.05
❑ 146	Rafael Palmeiro NAT	.10	.05
❑ 147	Edgar Martinez NAT	.10	.05
❑ 148	Barry Bonds NAT	.40	.18
❑ 149	Manny Ramirez NAT	.15	.07
❑ 150	Larry Walker NAT	.15	.07
❑ 151	Jeff Bagwell NAT	.40	.18
❑ 152	Ron Gant NAT	.10	.05
❑ 153	Andres Galarraga NAT	.15	.07
❑ 154	Eddie Murray NAT	.15	.07
❑ 155	Kirby Puckett NAT	.40	.18
❑ 156	Will Clark NAT	.15	.07
❑ 157	Don Mattingly NAT	.40	.18
❑ 158	Mark McGwire NAT	1.00	.45
❑ 159	Dean Palmer NAT	.10	.05
❑ 160	Matt Williams NAT	.10	.05
❑ 161	Fred McGriff NAT	.10	.05
❑ 162	Joe Carter NAT	.10	.05
❑ 163	Juan Gonzalez NAT	.50	.23
❑ 164	Alex Ochoa	.10	.05
❑ 165	Ruben Rivera	.15	.07
❑ 166	Tony Clark	.40	.18
❑ 167	Brian Barber	.10	.05
❑ 168	Matt Lawton	.40	.18
❑ 169	Terrell Wade	.10	.05
❑ 170	Johnny Damon	.15	.07
❑ 171	Derek Jeter	1.25	.55
❑ 172	Phil Nevin	.10	.05
❑ 173	Robert Perez	.10	.05
❑ 174	C.J. Nitkowski	.10	.05
❑ 175	Joe Vitiello	.10	.05
❑ 176	Roger Cedeno	.10	.05
❑ 177	Ron Coomer	.10	.05
❑ 178	Chris Widger	.10	.05
❑ 179	Jimmy Haynes	.10	.05
❑ 180	Mike Sweeney	.40	.18
❑ 181	Howard Battle	.10	.05
❑ 182	John Wasdin	.10	.05
❑ 183	Jim Pittsley	.10	.05
❑ 184	Bob Wolcott	.10	.05
❑ 185	LaTroy Hawkins	.10	.05
❑ 186	Nigel Wilson	.10	.05
❑ 187	Dustin Hermanson	.15	.07
❑ 188	Chris Snopek	.10	.05
❑ 189	Mariano Rivera	.15	.07
❑ 190	Jose Herrera	.10	.05
❑ 191	Chris Stynes	.10	.05
❑ 192	Larry Thomas	.10	.05
❑ 193	David Bell	.10	.05
❑ 194	Frank Thomas CL	.60	.25
❑ 195	Ken Griffey Jr. CL	1.00	.45
❑ 196	Cal Ripken CL	.75	.35
❑ 197	Jeff Bagwell CL	.40	.18
❑ 198	Mike Piazza CL	.60	.25
❑ 199	Barry Bonds CL	.40	.18
❑ 200	Garret Anderson CL	.40	.18
	Chipper Jones		
❑ 201	Frank Thomas	1.25	.55
❑ 202	Michael Tucker	.15	.07
❑ 203	Kirby Puckett	.60	.25
❑ 204	Alex Gonzalez	.10	.05
❑ 205	Tony Gwynn	1.00	.45
❑ 206	Moises Alou	.40	.18
❑ 207	Albert Belle	.75	.35
❑ 208	Barry Bonds	.50	.23
❑ 209	Fred McGriff	.40	.18
❑ 210	Dennis Eckersley	.15	.07
❑ 211	Craig Biggio	.40	.18
❑ 212	David Cone	.40	.18
❑ 213	Will Clark	.40	.18
❑ 214	Cal Ripken	1.50	.70
❑ 215	Wade Boggs	.40	.18
❑ 216	Pete Schourek	.10	.05
❑ 217	Darren Daulton	.15	.07
❑ 218	Carlos Baerga	.15	.07
❑ 219	Larry Walker	.40	.18
❑ 220	Denny Neagle	.15	.07
❑ 221	Jim Edmonds	.40	.18
❑ 222	Lee Smith	.15	.07
❑ 223	Jason Isringhausen	.10	.05
❑ 224	Jay Buhner	.15	.07
❑ 225	John Olerud	.15	.07
❑ 226	Jeff Conine	.15	.07
❑ 227	Dean Palmer	.15	.07
❑ 228	Jim Abbott	.15	.07
❑ 229	Raul Mondesi	.40	.18
❑ 230	Tom Glavine	.40	.18
❑ 231	Kevin Seitzer	.10	.05
❑ 232	Lenny Dykstra	.15	.07
❑ 233	Brian Jordan	.15	.07
❑ 234	Rondell White	.15	.07
❑ 235	Bret Boone	.15	.07
❑ 236	Randy Johnson	.40	.18
❑ 237	Paul O'Neill	.15	.07
❑ 238	Jim Thome	.40	.18
❑ 239	Edgardo Alfonzo	.15	.07
❑ 240	Terry Pendleton	.10	.05
❑ 241	Harold Baines	.15	.07
❑ 242	Roberto Alomar	.40	.18
❑ 243	Mark Grace	.40	.18
❑ 244	Derek Bell	.15	.07
❑ 245	Vinny Castilla	.40	.18
❑ 246	Cecil Fielder	.15	.07
❑ 247	Roger Clemens	.75	.35
❑ 248	Orel Hershiser	.15	.07
❑ 249	J.T. Snow	.15	.07
❑ 250	Rafael Palmeiro	.40	.18
❑ 251	Bret Saberhagen	.15	.07
❑ 252	Todd Hollandsworth	.10	.05
❑ 253	Ryan Klesko	.15	.07
❑ 254	Greg Maddux HH	.60	.25

❑ 255 Ken Griffey Jr. HH 1.00 .45
❑ 256 Hideo Nomo HH .75 .35
❑ 257 Frank Thomas HH .60 .25
❑ 258 Cal Ripken HH .75 .35
❑ 259 Jeff Bagwell HH .40 .18
❑ 260 Barry Bonds HH .40 .18
❑ 261 Mo Vaughn HH .40 .18
❑ 262 Albert Belle HH .40 .18
❑ 263 Sammy Sosa HH .50 .23
❑ 264 Reggie Sanders HH .10 .05
❑ 265 Mike Piazza HH .60 .25
❑ 266 Chipper Jones HH .50 .23
❑ 267 Tony Gwynn HH .50 .23
❑ 268 Kirby Puckett HH .40 .18
❑ 269 Wade Boggs HH .15 .07
❑ 270 Will Clark HH .15 .07
❑ 271 Gary Sheffield HH .10 .05
❑ 272 Dante Bichette HH .10 .05
❑ 273 Randy Johnson HH .15 .07
❑ 274 Matt Williams HH .10 .05
❑ 275 Alex Rodriguez HH .60 .25
❑ 276 Tim Salmon HH .15 .07
❑ 277 Johnny Damon HH .10 .05
❑ 278 Manny Ramirez HH .15 .07
❑ 279 Derek Jeter HH .60 .25
❑ 280 Eddie Murray HH .15 .07
❑ 281 Ozzie Smith HH .40 .18
❑ 282 Garret Anderson HH .10 .05
❑ 283 Raul Mondesi HH .10 .05
❑ 284 Terry Steinbach .15 .07
❑ 285 Carlos Garcia .10 .05
❑ 286 Dave Justice .40 .18
❑ 287 Eric Anthony .10 .05
❑ 288 Benji Gil .10 .05
❑ 289 Bob Hamelin .10 .05
❑ 290 Dwayne Hosey .10 .05
❑ 291 Andy Pettitte HH .10 .05
❑ 292 Rod Beck .10 .05
❑ 293 Shane Andrews .10 .05
❑ 294 Julian Tavarez .10 .05
❑ 295 Willie Greene .15 .07
❑ 296 Ismael Valdes .15 .07
❑ 297 Glenallen Hill .10 .05
❑ 298 Troy Percival .15 .07
❑ 299 Ray Durham .15 .07
❑ 300 Jeff Conine 300 .10 .05
❑ 301 Ken Griffey Jr. 300 1.00 .45
❑ 302 Will Clark 300 .15 .07
❑ 303 Mike Greenwell 300 .10 .05
❑ 304 Carlos Baerga 300 .10 .05
❑ 305A Paul Molitor 300 .15 .07
❑ 305B Jeff Bagwell 300 .40 .18
❑ 306 Mark Grace 300 .10 .05
❑ 307 Don Mattingly 300 .40 .18
❑ 308 Hal Morris 300 .10 .05
❑ 309 Butch Huskey .10 .05
❑ 310 Ozzie Guillen .10 .05
❑ 311 Erik Hanson .10 .05
❑ 312 Kenny Lofton 300 .15 .07
❑ 313 Edgar Martinez 300 .10 .05
❑ 314 Kurt Abbott .10 .05
❑ 315 John Smoltz .15 .07
❑ 316 Ariel Prieto .10 .05
❑ 317 Mark Carreon .10 .05
❑ 318 Kirby Puckett 300 .40 .18
❑ 319 Carlos Perez .15 .07
❑ 320 Gary DiSarcina .10 .05
❑ 321 Trevor Hoffman .15 .07
❑ 322 Mike Piazza 300 .60 .25
❑ 323 Frank Thomas 300 .60 .25
❑ 324 Juan Acevedo .10 .05
❑ 325 Bip Roberts .10 .05
❑ 326 Javier Lopez .15 .07
❑ 327 Benito Santiago .10 .05
❑ 328 Mark Lewis .10 .05
❑ 329 Royce Clayton .10 .05
❑ 330 Tom Gordon .10 .05
❑ 331 Ben McDonald .10 .05
❑ 332 Dan Wilson .10 .05
❑ 333 Ron Gant .10 .05
❑ 334 Wade Boggs 300 .15 .07
❑ 335 Paul Molitor .40 .18
❑ 336 Tony Gwynn 300 .50 .23
❑ 337 Sean Berry .10 .05
❑ 338 Rickey Henderson .40 .18
❑ 339 Wil Cordero .10 .05
❑ 340 Kent Mercker .10 .05
❑ 341 Kenny Rogers .10 .05
❑ 342 Ryne Sandberg .50 .23
❑ 343 Charlie Hayes .10 .05
❑ 344 Andy Benes .15 .07
❑ 345 Sterling Hitchcock .15 .07
❑ 346 Bernard Gilkey .10 .05
❑ 347 Julio Franco .10 .05
❑ 348 Ken Hill .10 .05
❑ 349 Russ Davis .15 .07
❑ 350 Mike Blowers .10 .05
❑ 351 B.J. Surhoff .15 .07
❑ 352 Lance Johnson .10 .05
❑ 353 Darryl Hamilton .10 .05
❑ 354 Shawon Dunston .10 .05
❑ 355 Rick Aguilera .10 .05
❑ 356 Danny Tartabull .10 .05
❑ 357 Todd Stottlemyre .10 .05
❑ 358 Mike Bordick .10 .05
❑ 359 Jack McDowell .10 .05
❑ 360 Todd Zeile .10 .05
❑ 361 Tino Martinez .40 .18
❑ 362 Greg Gagne .10 .05
❑ 363 Mike Kelly .10 .05
❑ 364 Tim Raines .15 .07
❑ 365 Ernie Young .10 .05
❑ 366 Mike Stanley .10 .05
❑ 367 Wally Joyner .15 .07
❑ 368 Karim Garcia .15 .07
❑ 369 Paul Wilson .10 .05
❑ 370 Sal Fasano .10 .05
❑ 371 Jason Schmidt .10 .05
❑ 372 Livan Hernandez .75 .35
❑ 373 George Arias .10 .05
❑ 374 Steve Gibralter .10 .05
❑ 375 Jermaine Dye .10 .05
❑ 376 Jason Kendall .40 .18
❑ 377 Brooks Kieschnick .10 .05
❑ 378 Jeff Ware .10 .05
❑ 379 Alan Benes .15 .07
❑ 380 Rey Ordonez .15 .07
❑ 381 Jay Powell .10 .05
❑ 382 Osvaldo Fernandez .10 .05
❑ 383 Wilton Guerrero .30 .14
❑ 384 Eric Owens .10 .05
❑ 385 George Williams .10 .05
❑ 386 Chan Ho Park .40 .18
❑ 387 Jeff Suppan .10 .05
❑ 388 F.P. Santangelo .10 .05
❑ 389 Terry Adams .10 .05
❑ 390 Bob Abreu .15 .07
❑ 391 Quinton McCracken .15 .07
❑ 392 Mike Busby .10 .05
❑ 393 Cal Ripken CL .75 .35
❑ 394 Ken Griffey Jr. CL 1.00 .45
❑ 395 Frank Thomas CL .60 .25
❑ 396 Chipper Jones CL .50 .23
❑ 397 Greg Maddux CL .60 .25
❑ 398 Mike Piazza CL .60 .25
❑ 399 Ken Griffey Jr CL .75 .35
Cal Ripken Jr.
Chipper Jones
Frank Thomas
Greg Maddux
Mike Piazza
❑ CR1 Cal Ripken Tribute 15.00 6.75

1996 Pinnacle Christie Brinkley Collection

	MINT	NRMT
COMPLETE SET (16)	60.00	27.00
COMMON CARD (1-16)	1.50	.70

❑ 1 Greg Maddux 12.00 5.50
❑ 2 Ryan Klesko 2.00 .90
❑ 3 Dave Justice 5.00 2.20
❑ 4 Tom Glavine 5.00 2.20
❑ 5 Chipper Jones 15.00 6.75
❑ 6 Fred McGriff 3.00 1.35
❑ 7 Javier Lopez 2.00 .90
❑ 8 Marquis Grissom 2.00 .90

❑ 9 Jason Schmidt 1.50 .70
❑ 10 Albert Belle 6.00 2.70
❑ 11 Manny Ramirez 5.00 2.20
❑ 12 Carlos Baerga 2.00 .90
❑ 13 Sandy Alomar 2.00 .90
❑ 14 Jim Thome 5.00 2.20
❑ 15 Julio Franco 1.50 .70
❑ 16 Kenny Lofton 5.00 2.20
❑ PCB Christie Brinkley Promo 6.00 2.70
On the Beach

1996 Pinnacle Essence of the Game

	MINT	NRMT
COMPLETE SET (18)	150.00	70.00
COMMON CARD (1-18)	2.00	.90

❑ 1 Cal Ripken 20.00 9.00
❑ 2 Greg Maddux 15.00 6.75
❑ 3 Frank Thomas 15.00 6.75
❑ 4 Matt Williams 2.50 1.10
❑ 5 Chipper Jones 12.00 5.50
❑ 6 Reggie Sanders 2.00 .90
❑ 7 Ken Griffey Jr. 25.00 11.00
❑ 8 Kirby Puckett 8.00 3.60
❑ 9 Hideo Nomo 8.00 3.60
❑ 10 Mike Piazza 15.00 6.75
❑ 11 Jeff Bagwell 8.00 3.60
❑ 12 Mo Vaughn 6.00 2.70
❑ 13 Albert Belle 6.00 2.70
❑ 14 Tim Salmon 5.00 2.20
❑ 15 Don Mattingly 8.00 3.60
❑ 16 Will Clark 5.00 2.20
❑ 17 Eddie Murray 5.00 2.20
❑ 18 Barry Bonds 6.00 2.70

1996 Pinnacle First Rate

	MINT	NRMT
COMPLETE SET (18)	120.00	55.00
COMMON CARD (1-18)	2.00	.90

❑ 1 Ken Griffey Jr. 30.00 13.50
❑ 2 Frank Thomas 20.00 9.00
❑ 3 Mo Vaughn 8.00 3.60
❑ 4 Chipper Jones 15.00 6.75
❑ 5 Alex Rodriguez 20.00 9.00

	MINT	NRMT
❑ 6 Kirby Puckett	10.00	4.50
❑ 7 Gary Sheffield	3.00	1.35
❑ 8 Matt Williams	2.00	.90
❑ 9 Barry Bonds	8.00	3.60
❑ 10 Craig Biggio	6.00	2.70
❑ 11 Robin Ventura	2.00	.90
❑ 12 Michael Tucker	2.00	.90
❑ 13 Derek Jeter	15.00	6.75
❑ 14 Manny Ramirez	6.00	2.70
❑ 15 Barry Larkin	3.00	1.35
❑ 16 Shawn Green	2.00	.90
❑ 17 Will Clark	6.00	2.70
❑ 18 Mark McGwire	30.00	13.50

1996 Pinnacle Power

	MINT	NRMT
COMPLETE SET (20)	120.00	55.00
COMMON CARD (1-20)	2.00	.90
❑ 1 Frank Thomas	20.00	9.00
❑ 2 Mo Vaughn	8.00	3.60
❑ 3 Ken Griffey Jr.	30.00	13.50
❑ 4 Matt Williams	2.50	1.10
❑ 5 Barry Bonds	8.00	3.60
❑ 6 Reggie Sanders	2.50	1.10
❑ 7 Mike Piazza	20.00	9.00
❑ 8 Jim Edmonds	3.00	1.35
❑ 9 Dante Bichette	2.50	1.10
❑ 10 Sammy Sosa	15.00	6.75
❑ 11 Jeff Bagwell	10.00	4.50
❑ 12 Fred McGriff	3.00	1.35
❑ 13 Albert Belle	8.00	3.60
❑ 14 Tim Salmon	6.00	2.70
❑ 15 Joe Carter	2.50	1.10
❑ 16 Manny Ramirez	6.00	2.70
❑ 17 Eddie Murray	6.00	2.70
❑ 18 Cecil Fielder	2.00	.90
❑ 19 Larry Walker	6.00	2.70
❑ 20 Juan Gonzalez	15.00	6.75

1996 Pinnacle Project Stardom

	MINT	NRMT
COMPLETE SET (18)	150.00	70.00
COMMON CARD (1-18)	3.00	1.35
❑ 1 Paul Wilson	3.00	1.35
❑ 2 Derek Jeter	25.00	11.00
❑ 3 Karim Garcia	4.00	1.80
❑ 4 Johnny Damon	4.00	1.80
❑ 5 Alex Rodriguez	30.00	13.50
❑ 6 Chipper Jones	25.00	11.00
❑ 7 Charles Johnson	4.00	1.80
❑ 8 Bob Abreu	4.00	1.80
❑ 9 Alan Benes	4.00	1.80
❑ 10 Richard Hidalgo	4.00	1.80
❑ 11 Brooks Kieschnick	3.00	1.35
❑ 12 Garret Anderson	4.00	1.80
❑ 13 Livan Hernandez	10.00	4.50
❑ 14 Manny Ramirez	10.00	4.50
❑ 15 Jermaine Dye	3.00	1.35
❑ 16 Todd Hollandsworth	3.00	1.35
❑ 17 Raul Mondesi	6.00	2.70
❑ 18 Ryan Klesko	4.00	1.80

1996 Pinnacle Skylines

	MINT	NRMT
COMPLETE SET (18)	250.00	110.00
COMMON CARD (1-18)	6.00	2.70
❑ 1 Ken Griffey Jr.	50.00	22.00
❑ 2 Frank Thomas	30.00	13.50
❑ 3 Greg Maddux	30.00	13.50
❑ 4 Cal Ripken	40.00	18.00
❑ 5 Albert Belle	12.00	5.50
❑ 6 Mo Vaughn	12.00	5.50
❑ 7 Mike Piazza	30.00	13.50
❑ 8 Wade Boggs	10.00	4.50
❑ 9 Will Clark	10.00	4.50
❑ 10 Barry Bonds	12.00	5.50
❑ 11 Gary Sheffield	6.00	2.70
❑ 12 Hideo Nomo	20.00	9.00
❑ 13 Tony Gwynn	25.00	11.00
❑ 14 Kirby Puckett	15.00	6.75
❑ 15 Chipper Jones	25.00	11.00
❑ 16 Jeff Bagwell	15.00	6.75
❑ 17 Manny Ramirez	10.00	4.50
❑ 18 Raul Mondesi	6.00	2.70

1996 Pinnacle Slugfest

	MINT	NRMT
COMPLETE SET (18)	200.00	90.00
COMMON CARD (1-18)	3.00	1.35
❑ 1 Frank Thomas	25.00	11.00
❑ 2 Ken Griffey Jr.	40.00	18.00
❑ 3 Jeff Bagwell	12.00	5.50
❑ 4 Barry Bonds	10.00	4.50
❑ 5 Mo Vaughn	10.00	4.50
❑ 6 Albert Belle	10.00	4.50
❑ 7 Mike Piazza	25.00	11.00
❑ 8 Matt Williams	4.00	1.80
❑ 9 Dante Bichette	4.00	1.80
❑ 10 Sammy Sosa	20.00	9.00
❑ 11 Gary Sheffield	5.00	2.20
❑ 12 Reggie Sanders	3.00	1.35
❑ 13 Manny Ramirez	8.00	3.60
❑ 14 Eddie Murray	8.00	3.60
❑ 15 Juan Gonzalez	20.00	9.00
❑ 16 Dean Palmer	4.00	1.80
❑ 17 Rafael Palmeiro	5.00	2.20
❑ 18 Cecil Fielder	4.00	1.80

1996 Pinnacle Team Pinnacle

	MINT	NRMT
COMPLETE SET (9)	150.00	70.00
COMMON CARD (1-9)	4.00	1.80
❑ 1 Frank Thomas Jeff Bagwell	20.00	9.00
❑ 2 Chuck Knoblauch Craig Biggio	6.00	2.70
❑ 3 Jim Thome Matt Williams	4.00	1.80
❑ 4 Barry Larkin Cal Ripken	25.00	11.00
❑ 5 Barry Bonds Tim Salmon	8.00	3.60
❑ 6 Ken Griffey Jr. Reggie Sanders	30.00	13.50
❑ 7 Albert Belle Sammy Sosa	12.00	5.50
❑ 8 Ivan Rodriguez Mike Piazza	20.00	9.00
❑ 9 Greg Maddux Randy Johnson	20.00	9.00

1996 Pinnacle Team Spirit

	MINT	NRMT
COMPLETE SET (12)	250.00	110.00
COMMON CARD (1-12)	3.00	1.35

❑ 1 Greg Maddux	25.00	11.00
❑ 2 Ken Griffey Jr.	40.00	18.00
❑ 3 Derek Jeter	20.00	9.00
❑ 4 Mike Piazza	25.00	11.00
❑ 5 Cal Ripken	30.00	13.50
❑ 6 Frank Thomas	25.00	11.00
❑ 7 Jeff Bagwell	12.00	5.50
❑ 8 Mo Vaughn	10.00	4.50
❑ 9 Albert Belle	10.00	4.50
❑ 10 Chipper Jones	20.00	9.00
❑ 11 Johnny Damon	3.00	1.35
❑ 12 Barry Bonds	10.00	4.50

1996 Pinnacle Team Tomorrow

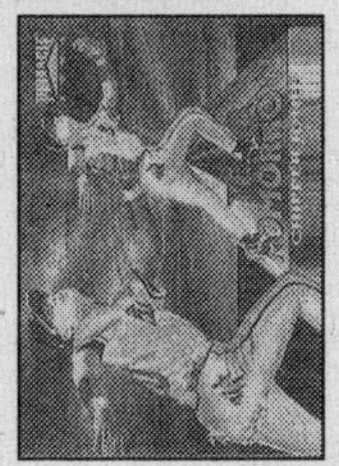

	MINT	NRMT
COMPLETE SET (10)	100.00	45.00
COMMON CARD (1-10)	3.00	1.35
❑ 1 Ruben Rivera	3.00	1.35
❑ 2 Johnny Damon	4.00	1.80
❑ 3 Raul Mondesi	6.00	2.70
❑ 4 Manny Ramirez	8.00	3.60
❑ 5 Hideo Nomo	12.00	5.50
❑ 6 Chipper Jones	20.00	9.00
❑ 7 Garret Anderson	4.00	1.80
❑ 8 Alex Rodriguez	25.00	11.00
❑ 9 Derek Jeter	20.00	9.00
❑ 10 Karim Garcia	3.00	1.35

1997 Pinnacle

	MINT	NRMT
COMPLETE SET (200)	20.00	9.00
COMMON CARD (1-200)	.15	.07
❑ 1 Cecil Fielder	.30	.14
❑ 2 Garret Anderson	.30	.14
❑ 3 Charles Nagy	.30	.14
❑ 4 Darryl Hamilton	.15	.07
❑ 5 Greg Myers	.15	.07
❑ 6 Eric Davis	.30	.14
❑ 7 Jeff Frye	.15	.07
❑ 8 Marquis Grissom	.30	.14
❑ 9 Curt Schilling	.30	.14
❑ 10 Jeff Fassero	.15	.07
❑ 11 Alan Benes	.30	.14
❑ 12 Orlando Miller	.15	.07
❑ 13 Alex Fernandez	.15	.07
❑ 14 Andy Pettitte	.40	.18
❑ 15 Andre Dawson	.40	.18
❑ 16 Mark Grudzielanek	.30	.14
❑ 17 Joe Vitiello	.15	.07
❑ 18 Juan Gonzalez	1.50	.70
❑ 19 Mark Whiten	.15	.07
❑ 20 Lance Johnson	.15	.07
❑ 21 Trevor Hoffman	.30	.14
❑ 22 Marc Newfield	.15	.07
❑ 23 Jim Eisenreich	.15	.07
❑ 24 Joe Carter	.30	.14
❑ 25 Jose Canseco	.60	.25
❑ 26 Bill Swift	.15	.07
❑ 27 Ellis Burks	.30	.14
❑ 28 Ben McDonald	.15	.07
❑ 29 Edgar Martinez	.30	.14
❑ 30 Jamie Moyer	.15	.07
❑ 31 Chan Ho Park	.60	.25
❑ 32 Carlos Delgado	.30	.14
❑ 33 Kevin Mitchell	.15	.07
❑ 34 Carlos Garcia	.15	.07
❑ 35 Darryl Strawberry	.30	.14
❑ 36 Jim Thome	.60	.25
❑ 37 Jose Offerman	.15	.07
❑ 38 Ryan Klesko	.30	.14
❑ 39 Ruben Sierra	.15	.07
❑ 40 Devon White	.30	.14
❑ 41 Brian Jordan	.30	.14
❑ 42 Tony Gwynn	1.50	.70
❑ 43 Rafael Palmeiro	.40	.18
❑ 44 Dante Bichette	.30	.14
❑ 45 Scott Stahoviak	.15	.07
❑ 46 Roger Cedeno	.15	.07
❑ 47 Ivan Rodriguez	.75	.35
❑ 48 Bob Abreu	.30	.14
❑ 49 Darryl Kile	.30	.14
❑ 50 Darren Dreifort	.30	.14
❑ 51 Shawon Dunston	.15	.07
❑ 52 Mark McGwire	3.00	1.35
❑ 53 Tim Salmon	.60	.25
❑ 54 Gene Schall	.15	.07
❑ 55 Roger Clemens	1.25	.55
❑ 56 Rondell White	.30	.14
❑ 57 Ed Sprague	.15	.07
❑ 58 Craig Paquette	.15	.07
❑ 59 David Segui	.30	.14
❑ 60 Jaime Navarro	.15	.07
❑ 61 Tom Glavine	.60	.25
❑ 62 Jeff Brantley	.15	.07
❑ 63 Kimera Bartee	.15	.07
❑ 64 Fernando Vina	.15	.07
❑ 65 Eddie Murray	.60	.25
❑ 66 Lenny Dykstra	.30	.14
❑ 67 Kevin Elster	.15	.07
❑ 68 Vinny Castilla	.40	.18
❑ 69 Mike Fetters	.15	.07
❑ 70 Brett Butler	.30	.14
❑ 71 Robby Thompson	.15	.07
❑ 72 Reggie Jefferson	.15	.07
❑ 73 Todd Hundley	.30	.14
❑ 74 Jeff King	.15	.07
❑ 75 Ernie Young	.15	.07
❑ 76 Jeff Bagwell	1.00	.45
❑ 77 Dan Wilson	.15	.07
❑ 78 Paul Molitor	.60	.25
❑ 79 Kevin Seitzer	.15	.07
❑ 80 Kevin Brown	.40	.18
❑ 81 Ron Gant	.15	.07
❑ 82 Dwight Gooden	.30	.14
❑ 83 Todd Stottlemyre	.15	.07
❑ 84 Ken Caminiti	.40	.18
❑ 85 James Baldwin	.30	.14
❑ 86 Jermaine Dye	.15	.07
❑ 87 Harold Baines	.30	.14
❑ 88 Pat Hentgen	.30	.14
❑ 89 Frank Rodriguez	.15	.07
❑ 90 Mark Johnson	.15	.07
❑ 91 Jason Kendall	.40	.18
❑ 92 Alex Rodriguez	2.00	.90
❑ 93 Alan Trammell	.30	.14
❑ 94 Scott Brosius	.30	.14
❑ 95 Delino DeShields	.15	.07
❑ 96 Chipper Jones	1.50	.70
❑ 97 Barry Bonds	.75	.35
❑ 98 Brady Anderson	.30	.14
❑ 99 Ryne Sandberg	.75	.35
❑ 100 Albert Belle	.75	.35
❑ 101 Jeff Cirillo	.30	.14
❑ 102 Frank Thomas	2.00	.90
❑ 103 Mike Piazza	2.00	.90
❑ 104 Rickey Henderson	.60	.25
❑ 105 Rey Ordonez	.30	.14
❑ 106 Mark Grace	.40	.18
❑ 107 Terry Steinbach	.30	.14
❑ 108 Ray Durham	.30	.14
❑ 109 Barry Larkin	.40	.18
❑ 110 Tony Clark	.40	.18
❑ 111 Bernie Williams	.60	.25
❑ 112 John Smoltz	.30	.14
❑ 113 Moises Alou	.40	.18
❑ 114 Alex Gonzalez	.15	.07
❑ 115 Rico Brogna	.15	.07
❑ 116 Eric Karros	.30	.14
❑ 117 Jeff Conine	.30	.14
❑ 118 Todd Hollandsworth	.15	.07
❑ 119 Troy Percival	.30	.14
❑ 120 Paul Wilson	.15	.07
❑ 121 Orel Hershiser	.30	.14
❑ 122 Ozzie Smith	.75	.35
❑ 123 Dave Hollins	.15	.07
❑ 124 Ken Hill	.15	.07
❑ 125 Rick Wilkins	.15	.07
❑ 126 Scott Servais	.15	.07
❑ 127 Fernando Valenzuela	.30	.14
❑ 128 Mariano Rivera	.30	.14
❑ 129 Mark Loretta	.15	.07
❑ 130 Shane Reynolds	.30	.14
❑ 131 Darren Oliver	.15	.07
❑ 132 Steve Trachsel	.15	.07
❑ 133 Darren Bragg	.15	.07
❑ 134 Jason Dickson	.30	.14
❑ 135 Darrin Fletcher	.15	.07
❑ 136 Gary Gaetti	.15	.07
❑ 137 Joey Cora	.30	.14
❑ 138 Terry Pendleton	.15	.07
❑ 139 Derek Jeter	2.00	.90
❑ 140 Danny Tartabull	.15	.07
❑ 141 John Flaherty	.15	.07
❑ 142 B.J. Surhoff	.30	.14
❑ 143 Mike Sweeney	.15	.07
❑ 144 Chad Mottola	.15	.07
❑ 145 Andujar Cedeno	.15	.07
❑ 146 Tim Belcher	.15	.07
❑ 147 Mark Thompson	.15	.07
❑ 148 Rafael Bournigal	.15	.07
❑ 149 Marty Cordova	.15	.07
❑ 150 Osvaldo Fernandez	.15	.07
❑ 151 Mike Stanley	.15	.07
❑ 152 Ricky Bottalico	.30	.14
❑ 153 Donne Wall	.15	.07
❑ 154 Omar Vizquel	.30	.14
❑ 155 Mike Mussina	.60	.25
❑ 156 Brant Brown	.30	.14
❑ 157 F.P. Santangelo	.15	.07
❑ 158 Ryan Hancock	.15	.07
❑ 159 Jeff D'Amico	.15	.07
❑ 160 Luis Castillo	.30	.14
❑ 161 Darin Erstad	1.00	.45
❑ 162 Ugueth Urbina	.30	.14
❑ 163 Andruw Jones	1.00	.45
❑ 164 Steve Gibralter	.15	.07
❑ 165 Robin Jennings	.15	.07
❑ 166 Mike Cameron	.30	.14

❑ 167 George Arias .15 .07
❑ 168 Chris Stynes .15 .07
❑ 169 Justin Thompson .30 .14
❑ 170 Jamey Wright .15 .07
❑ 171 Todd Walker .60 .25
❑ 172 Nomar Garciaparra 2.00 .90
❑ 173 Jose Paniagua .15 .07
❑ 174 Marvin Benard .15 .07
❑ 175 Rocky Coppinger .15 .07
❑ 176 Quinton McCracken .30 .14
❑ 177 Amaury Telemaco .15 .07
❑ 178 Neifi Perez .15 .07
❑ 179 Todd Greene .30 .14
❑ 180 Jason Thompson .15 .07
❑ 181 Wilton Guerrero .15 .07
❑ 182 Edgar Renteria .30 .14
❑ 183 Billy Wagner .30 .14
❑ 184 Alex Ochoa .15 .07
❑ 185 Dmitri Young .30 .14
❑ 186 Kenny Lofton CT .75 .35
❑ 187 Andres Galarraga CT .30 .14
❑ 188 Chuck Knoblauch CT .30 .14
❑ 189 Greg Maddux CT 2.00 .90
❑ 190 Mo Vaughn CT .75 .35
❑ 191 Cal Ripken CT 2.50 1.10
❑ 192 Hideo Nomo CT .75 .35
❑ 193 Ken Griffey Jr. CT 3.00 1.35
❑ 194 Sammy Sosa CT 1.50 .70
❑ 195 Jay Buhner CT .15 .07
❑ 196 Manny Ramirez CT .30 .14
❑ 197 Matt Williams CT .15 .07
❑ 198 Andruw Jones CL .30 .14
❑ 199 Darin Erstad CL .60 .25
❑ 200 Trey Beamon CL .15 .07

1997 Pinnacle Artist's Proofs

	MINT	NRMT
COMPLETE SET (200)	3000.00	1350.00
COMP.BRONZE SET (125)	800.00	350.00
COMMON BRONZE	6.00	2.70
COMP.SILVER SET (50)	1000.00	450.00
COMMON SILVER	8.00	3.60
COMP.GOLD SET (25)	1200.00	550.00
COMMON GOLD	10.00	4.50

❑ PP1 Cecil Fielder B 10.00 4.50
❑ PP2 Garret Anderson B 10.00 4.50
❑ PP3 Charles Nagy B 10.00 4.50
❑ PP4 Darryl Hamilton B 6.00 2.70
❑ PP5 Greg Myers B 6.00 2.70
❑ PP6 Eric Davis B 10.00 4.50
❑ PP7 Jeff Frye B 6.00 2.70
❑ PP8 Marquis Grissom S 12.00 5.50
❑ PP9 Curt Schilling B 10.00 4.50
❑ PP10 Jeff Fassero B 6.00 2.70
❑ PP11 Alan Benes S 12.00 5.50
❑ PP12 Orlando Miller B 6.00 2.70
❑ PP13 Alex Fernandez B 6.00 2.70
❑ PP14 Andy Pettitte G 25.00 11.00
❑ PP15 Andre Dawson B 15.00 6.75
❑ PP16 Mark Grudzielanek B 10.00 4.50
❑ PP17 Joe Vitiello B 6.00 2.70
❑ PP18 Juan Gonzalez G 100.00 45.00
❑ PP19 Mark Whiten B 6.00 2.70
❑ PP20 Lance Johnson B 6.00 2.70
❑ PP21 Trevor Hoffman B 10.00 4.50
❑ PP22 Marc Newfield B 6.00 2.70
❑ PP23 Jim Eisenreich B 6.00 2.70
❑ PP24 Joe Carter S 12.00 5.50
❑ PP25 Jose Canseco S 30.00 13.50
❑ PP26 Bill Swift B 6.00 2.70
❑ PP27 Ellis Burks B 10.00 4.50
❑ PP28 Ben McDonald B 6.00 2.70
❑ PP29 Edgar Martinez S 12.00 5.50
❑ PP30 Jamie Moyer B 6.00 2.70
❑ PP31 Chan Ho Park S 30.00 13.50
❑ PP32 Carlos Delgado S 12.00 5.50
❑ PP33 Kevin Mitchell B 6.00 2.70
❑ PP34 Carlos Garcia B 6.00 2.70
❑ PP35 Darryl Strawberry G 15.00 6.75
❑ PP36 Jim Thome G 40.00 18.00
❑ PP37 Jose Offerman B 6.00 2.70
❑ PP38 Ryan Klesko S 12.00 5.50
❑ PP39 Ruben Sierra B 6.00 2.70
❑ PP40 Devon White B 10.00 4.50
❑ PP41 Brian Jordan G 15.00 6.75
❑ PP42 Tony Gwynn S 80.00 36.00
❑ PP43 Rafael Palmeiro S 20.00 9.00
❑ PP44 Dante Bichette B 10.00 4.50
❑ PP45 Scott Stahoviak B 6.00 2.70
❑ PP46 Roger Cedeno B 6.00 2.70
❑ PP47 Ivan Rodriguez G 50.00 22.00
❑ PP48 Bob Abreu S 12.00 5.50
❑ PP49 Darryl Kile B 10.00 4.50
❑ PP50 Darren Dreifort B 10.00 4.50
❑ PP51 Shawon Dunston B 6.00 2.70
❑ PP52 Mark McGwire S 150.00 70.00
❑ PP53 Tim Salmon S 30.00 13.50
❑ PP54 Gene Schall B 6.00 2.70
❑ PP55 Roger Clemens B 50.00 22.00
❑ PP56 Rondell White S 12.00 5.50
❑ PP57 Ed Sprague B 6.00 2.70
❑ PP58 Craig Paquette B 6.00 2.70
❑ PP59 David Segui B 10.00 4.50
❑ PP60 Jaime Navarro B 6.00 2.70
❑ PP61 Tom Glavine S 30.00 13.50
❑ PP62 Jeff Brantley B 6.00 2.70
❑ PP63 Kimera Bartee B 6.00 2.70
❑ PP64 Fernando Vina B 6.00 2.70
❑ PP65 Eddie Murray S 30.00 13.50
❑ PP66 Lenny Dykstra B 10.00 4.50
❑ PP67 Kevin Elster B 6.00 2.70
❑ PP68 Vinny Castilla B 15.00 6.75
❑ PP69 Mike Fetters S 8.00 3.60
❑ PP70 Brett Butler B 10.00 4.50
❑ PP71 Robby Thompson B 6.00 2.70
❑ PP72 Reggie Jefferson B 6.00 2.70
❑ PP73 Todd Hundley S 12.00 5.50
❑ PP74 Jeff King B 6.00 2.70
❑ PP75 Ernie Young S 8.00 3.60
❑ PP76 Jeff Bagwell G 60.00 27.00
❑ PP77 Dan Wilson B 6.00 2.70
❑ PP78 Paul Molitor G 40.00 18.00
❑ PP79 Kevin Seitzer B 6.00 2.70
❑ PP80 Kevin Brown S 20.00 9.00
❑ PP81 Ron Gant S 8.00 3.60
❑ PP82 Dwight Gooden S 12.00 5.50
❑ PP83 Todd Stottlemyre B 6.00 2.70
❑ PP84 Ken Caminiti G 25.00 11.00
❑ PP85 James Baldwin B 10.00 4.50
❑ PP86 Jermaine Dye S 8.00 3.60
❑ PP87 Harold Baines B 10.00 4.50
❑ PP88 Pat Hentgen B 10.00 4.50
❑ PP89 Frank Rodriguez B 6.00 2.70
❑ PP90 Mark Johnson B 6.00 2.70
❑ PP91 Jason Kendall S 20.00 9.00
❑ PP92 Alex Rodriguez G 120.00 55.00
❑ PP93 Alan Trammell B 10.00 4.50
❑ PP94 Scott Brosius B 10.00 4.50
❑ PP95 Delino DeShields B 6.00 2.70
❑ PP96 Chipper Jones S 80.00 36.00
❑ PP97 Barry Bonds S 40.00 18.00
❑ PP98 Brady Anderson S 12.00 5.50
❑ PP99 Ryne Sandberg S 40.00 18.00
❑ PP100 Albert Belle G 40.00 18.00
❑ PP101 Jeff Cirillo B 10.00 4.50
❑ PP102 Frank Thomas G 120.00 55.00
❑ PP103 Mike Piazza S 100.00 45.00
❑ PP104 Rickey Henderson B 25.00 11.00
❑ PP105 Rey Ordonez S 12.00 5.50
❑ PP106 Mark Grace S 20.00 9.00
❑ PP107 Terry Steinbach B 10.00 4.50
❑ PP108 Ray Durham B 10.00 4.50
❑ PP109 Barry Larkin S 20.00 9.00
❑ PP110 Tony Clark S 20.00 9.00
❑ PP111 Bernie Williams G 40.00 18.00
❑ PP112 John Smoltz G 15.00 6.75
❑ PP113 Moises Alou B 15.00 6.75
❑ PP114 Alex Gonzalez B 6.00 2.70
❑ PP115 Rico Brogna B 6.00 2.70
❑ PP116 Eric Karros B 10.00 4.50
❑ PP117 Jeff Conine S 12.00 5.50
❑ PP118 Todd Hollandsworth G 10.00 4.50
❑ PP119 Troy Percival S 12.00 5.50
❑ PP120 Paul Wilson S 8.00 3.60
❑ PP121 Orel Hershiser B 10.00 4.50
❑ PP122 Ozzie Smith S 40.00 18.00
❑ PP123 Dave Hollins B 6.00 2.70
❑ PP124 Ken Hill B 6.00 2.70
❑ PP125 Rick Wilkins B 6.00 2.70
❑ PP126 Scott Servais B 6.00 2.70
❑ PP127 F. Valenzuela B 10.00 4.50
❑ PP128 Mariano Rivera G 15.00 6.75
❑ PP129 Mark Loretta B 6.00 2.70
❑ PP130 Shane Reynolds S 12.00 5.50
❑ PP131 Darren Oliver B 6.00 2.70
❑ PP132 Steve Trachsel B 6.00 2.70
❑ PP133 Darren Bragg B 6.00 2.70
❑ PP134 Jason Dickson B 10.00 4.50
❑ PP135 Darren Fletcher B 6.00 2.70
❑ PP136 Gary Gaetti B 6.00 2.70
❑ PP137 Joey Cora B 10.00 4.50
❑ PP138 Terry Pendleton B 6.00 2.70
❑ PP139 Derek Jeter G 100.00 45.00
❑ PP140 Danny Tartabull B 6.00 2.70
❑ PP141 John Flaherty B 6.00 2.70
❑ PP142 B.J. Surhoff B 10.00 4.50
❑ PP143 Mark Sweeney B 6.00 2.70
❑ PP144 Chad Mottola B 6.00 2.70
❑ PP145 Andujar Cedeno B 6.00 2.70
❑ PP146 Tim Belcher B 6.00 2.70
❑ PP147 Mark Thompson B 6.00 2.70
❑ PP148 Rafael Bournigal B 6.00 2.70
❑ PP149 Marty Cordova S 8.00 3.60
❑ PP150 Osvaldo Fernandez B 6.00 2.70
❑ PP151 Mike Stanley B 6.00 2.70
❑ PP152 Ricky Bottalico B 10.00 4.50
❑ PP153 Donne Wall B 6.00 2.70
❑ PP154 Omar Vizquel B 10.00 4.50
❑ PP155 Mike Mussina S 30.00 13.50
❑ PP156 Brant Brown B 10.00 4.50
❑ PP157 F.P. Santangelo S 8.00 3.60
❑ PP158 Ryan Hancock B 6.00 2.70
❑ PP159 Jeff D'Amico B 6.00 2.70
❑ PP160 Luis Castillo B 10.00 4.50
❑ PP161 Darin Erstad G 50.00 22.00
❑ PP162 Ugueth Urbina B 10.00 4.50
❑ PP163 Andruw Jones G 50.00 22.00
❑ PP164 Steve Gibralter B 6.00 2.70
❑ PP165 Robin Jennings S 8.00 3.60
❑ PP166 Mike Cameron B 10.00 4.50
❑ PP167 George Arias S 8.00 3.60
❑ PP168 Chris Stynes B 6.00 2.70
❑ PP169 Justin Thompson B 10.00 4.50
❑ PP170 Jamey Wright B 6.00 2.70
❑ PP171 Todd Walker G 40.00 18.00
❑ PP172 Nomar Garciaparra B 80.00 36.00
❑ PP173 Jose Paniagua B 6.00 2.70
❑ PP174 Marvin Benard B 6.00 2.70
❑ PP175 Rocky Coppinger B 6.00 2.70
❑ PP176 Quinton McCracken B 10.00 4.50
❑ PP177 Amaury Telemaco B 6.00 2.70
❑ PP178 Neifi Perez B 6.00 2.70
❑ PP179 Todd Greene B 10.00 4.50
❑ PP180 Jason Thompson B 6.00 2.70
❑ PP181 Wilton Guerrero B 6.00 2.70
❑ PP182 Edgar Renteria S 12.00 5.50
❑ PP183 Billy Wagner S 12.00 5.50
❑ PP184 Alex Ochoa G 10.00 4.50
❑ PP185 Dmitri Young B 10.00 4.50
❑ PP186 Kenny Lofton CT B 25.00 11.00
❑ PP187 A. Galarraga CT B 25.00 11.00
❑ PP188 C. Knoblauch CT G 40.00 18.00
❑ PP189 Greg Maddux CT S 100.00 45.00
❑ PP190 Mo Vaughn CT S 40.00 18.00
❑ PP191 Cal Ripken CT G 150.00 70.00
❑ PP192 Hideo Nomo CT S 50.00 22.00
❑ PP193 Ken Griffey Jr. CT G 200.00 90.00
❑ PP194 Sammy Sosa CT S 80.00 36.00
❑ PP195 Jay Buhner CT S 12.00 5.50
❑ PP196 Manny Ramirez CT G 40.00 18.00
❑ PP197 Matt Williams CT B 10.00 4.50
❑ PP198 Andruw Jones CL B 40.00 18.00
❑ PP199 Darin Erstad CL B 25.00 11.00
❑ PP200 Trey Beamon CL B 6.00 2.70

1997 Pinnacle Cardfrontations

	MINT	NRMT
COMPLETE SET (20)	250.00	110.00
COMMON CARD (1-20)	4.00	1.80

		MINT	NRMT
❑ 1	Greg Maddux Mike Piazza	30.00	13.50
❑ 2	Tom Glavine Ken Caminiti	6.00	2.70
❑ 3	Randy Johnson Cal Ripken	30.00	13.50
❑ 4	Kevin Appier Mark McGwire	40.00	18.00
❑ 5	Andy Pettitte Juan Gonzalez	20.00	9.00
❑ 6	Pat Hentgen Albert Belle	12.00	5.50
❑ 7	Hideo Nomo Chipper Jones	20.00	9.00
❑ 8	Ismael Valdes Sammy Sosa	20.00	9.00
❑ 9	Mike Mussina Manny Ramirez	8.00	3.60
❑ 10	David Cone Jay Buhner	6.00	2.70
❑ 11	Mark Wohlers Gary Sheffield	8.00	3.60
❑ 12	Alan Benes Barry Bonds	10.00	4.50
❑ 13	Roger Clemens Ivan Rodriguez	15.00	6.75
❑ 14	Mariano Rivera Ken Griffey Jr.	40.00	18.00
❑ 15	Dwight Gooden Frank Thomas	25.00	11.00
❑ 16	John Wetteland Darin Erstad	10.00	4.50
❑ 17	John Smoltz Brian Jordan	4.00	1.80
❑ 18	Kevin Brown Jeff Bagwell	12.00	5.50
❑ 19	Jack McDowell Alex Rodriguez	25.00	11.00
❑ 20	Charles Nagy Bernie Williams	8.00	3.60

1997 Pinnacle Home/Away

	MINT	NRMT
COMPLETE SET (24)	400.00	180.00
COMMON CARD (1-24)	6.00	2.70

		MINT	NRMT
❑ 1	Chipper Jones Away	15.00	6.75
❑ 2	Chipper Jones Home	15.00	6.75
❑ 3	Ken Griffey Jr. Away	30.00	13.50
❑ 4	Ken Griffey Jr. Home	30.00	13.50
❑ 5	Mike Piazza Away	20.00	9.00
❑ 6	Mike Piazza Home	20.00	9.00
❑ 7	Frank Thomas Away	20.00	9.00
❑ 8	Frank Thomas Home	20.00	9.00
❑ 9	Jeff Bagwell Away	10.00	4.50
❑ 10	Jeff Bagwell Home	10.00	4.50
❑ 11	Alex Rodriguez Away	20.00	9.00
❑ 12	Alex Rodriguez Home	20.00	9.00
❑ 13	Barry Bonds Away	8.00	3.60
❑ 14	Barry Bonds Home	8.00	3.60
❑ 15	Mo Vaughn Away	8.00	3.60
❑ 16	Mo Vaughn Home	8.00	3.60
❑ 17	Derek Jeter Away	15.00	6.75
❑ 18	Derek Jeter Home	15.00	6.75
❑ 19	Mark McGwire Away	30.00	13.50
❑ 20	Mark McGwire Home	30.00	13.50
❑ 21	Cal Ripken Away	25.00	11.00
❑ 22	Cal Ripken Home	25.00	11.00
❑ 23	Albert Belle Away	8.00	3.60
❑ 24	Albert Belle Home	6.00	2.70

1997 Pinnacle Passport to the Majors

	MINT	NRMT
COMPLETE SET (25)	250.00	110.00
COMMON CARD (1-25)	1.50	.70

		MINT	NRMT
❑ 1	Greg Maddux	20.00	9.00
❑ 2	Ken Griffey Jr.	30.00	13.50
❑ 3	Frank Thomas	20.00	9.00
❑ 4	Cal Ripken	25.00	11.00
❑ 5	Mike Piazza	20.00	9.00
❑ 6	Alex Rodriguez	20.00	9.00
❑ 7	Mo Vaughn	8.00	3.60
❑ 8	Chipper Jones	15.00	6.75
❑ 9	Roberto Alomar	6.00	2.70
❑ 10	Edgar Martinez	3.00	1.35
❑ 11	Javier Lopez	3.00	1.35
❑ 12	Ivan Rodriguez	8.00	3.60
❑ 13	Juan Gonzalez	15.00	6.75
❑ 14	Carlos Baerga	3.00	1.35
❑ 15	Sammy Sosa	15.00	6.75
❑ 16	Manny Ramirez	6.00	2.70
❑ 17	Raul Mondesi	5.00	2.20
❑ 18	Henry Rodriguez	3.00	1.35
❑ 19	Rafael Palmeiro	5.00	2.20
❑ 20	Rey Ordonez	3.00	1.35
❑ 21	Hideo Nomo	8.00	3.60
❑ 22	Mac Suzuki	1.50	.70
❑ 23	Chan Ho Park	6.00	2.70
❑ 24	Larry Walker	6.00	2.70
❑ 25	Ruben Rivera	3.00	1.35

1997 Pinnacle Shades

	MINT	NRMT
COMPLETE SET (10)	80.00	36.00
COMMON CARD (1-10)	2.00	.90

		MINT	NRMT
❑ 1	Ken Griffey Jr.	20.00	9.00
❑ 2	Juan Gonzalez	10.00	4.50
❑ 3	John Smoltz	2.00	.90
❑ 4	Gary Sheffield	2.50	1.10
❑ 5	Cal Ripken	15.00	6.75
❑ 6	Mo Vaughn	5.00	2.20

		MINT	NRMT
❑ 7	Brian Jordan	2.00	.90
❑ 8	Mike Piazza	12.00	5.50
❑ 9	Frank Thomas	12.00	5.50
❑ 10	Alex Rodriguez	12.00	5.50

1997 Pinnacle Team Pinnacle

	MINT	NRMT
COMPLETE SET (10)	200.00	90.00
COMMON CARD (1-10)	8.00	3.60

		MINT	NRMT
❑ 1	Frank Thomas Jeff Bagwell	30.00	13.50
❑ 2	Chuck Knoblauch Eric Young	10.00	4.50
❑ 3	Ken Caminiti Jim Thome	10.00	4.50
❑ 4	Alex Rodriguez Chipper Jones	40.00	18.00
❑ 5	Mike Piazza Ivan Rodriguez	40.00	18.00
❑ 6	Albert Belle Barry Bonds	12.00	5.50
❑ 7	Ken Griffey Jr. Ellis Burks	50.00	22.00
❑ 8	Juan Gonzalez Gary Sheffield	25.00	11.00
❑ 9	John Smoltz Andy Pettitte	8.00	3.60
❑ 10	Frank Thomas Jeff Bagwell Chuck Knoblauch Eric Young Ken Caminiti Jim Thome Alex Rodriguez Chipper Jones Mike Piazza Ivan Rodriguez Albert Belle Barry Bonds Ken Griffey Jr. Ellis Burks Juan Gonzalez Gary Sheffield John Smoltz Andy Pettitte	25.00	11.00

1998 Pinnacle

		MINT	NRMT
COMPLETE SET (200)		30.00	13.50
COMMON CARD (1-200)		.15	.07
1	Tony Gwynn	1.50	.70
2	Pedro Martinez	.60	.25
3	Kenny Lofton	.60	.25
4	Curt Schilling	.25	.11
5	Shawn Estes	.25	.11
6	Tom Glavine	.60	.25
7	Mike Piazza	2.00	.90
8	Ray Lankford	.25	.11
9	Barry Larkin	.40	.18
10	Tony Womack	.25	.11
11	Jeff Blauser	.15	.07
12	Rod Beck	.25	.11
13	Larry Walker	.60	.25
14	Greg Maddux	2.00	.90
15	Mark Grace	.40	.18
16	Ken Caminiti	.40	.18
17	Bobby Jones	.15	.07
18	Chipper Jones	1.50	.70
19	Javier Lopez	.25	.11
20	Moises Alou	.40	.18
21	Royce Clayton	.15	.07
22	Darryl Kile	.25	.11
23	Barry Bonds	.75	.35
24	Steve Finley	.25	.11
25	Andres Galarraga	.60	.25
26	Denny Neagle	.25	.11
27	Todd Hundley	.25	.11
28	Jeff Bagwell	1.00	.45
29	Andy Pettitte	.40	.18
30	Darin Erstad	.75	.35
31	Carlos Delgado	.25	.11
32	Matt Williams	.25	.11
33	Will Clark	.60	.25
34	Vinny Castilla	.40	.18
35	Brad Radke	.25	.11
36	John Olerud	.25	.11
37	Andruw Jones	.75	.35
38	Jason Giambi	.25	.11
39	Scott Rolen	1.50	.70
40	Gary Sheffield	.40	.18
41	Jimmy Key	.25	.11
42	Kevin Appier	.25	.11
43	Wade Boggs	.60	.25
44	Hideo Nomo	.75	.35
45	Manny Ramirez	.60	.25
46	Wilton Guerrero	.15	.07
47	Travis Fryman	.25	.11
48	Chili Davis	.25	.11
49	Jeromy Burnitz	.25	.11
50	Craig Biggio	.60	.25
51	Tim Salmon	.60	.25
52	Jose Cruz Jr.	.75	.35
53	Sammy Sosa	1.50	.70
54	Hideki Irabu	.40	.18
55	Chan Ho Park	.60	.25
56	Robin Ventura	.25	.11
57	Jose Guillen	.25	.11
58	Deion Sanders	.25	.11
59	Jose Canseco	.60	.25
60	Jay Buhner	.25	.11
61	Rafael Palmeiro	.40	.18
62	Vladimir Guerrero	1.00	.45
63	Mark McGwire	4.00	1.80
64	Derek Jeter	1.50	.70
65	Bobby Bonilla	.25	.11
66	Raul Mondesi	.40	.18
67	Paul Molitor	.60	.25
68	Joe Carter	.25	.11
69	Marquis Grissom	.25	.11
70	Juan Gonzalez	1.50	.70
71	Kevin Orie	.15	.07
72	Rusty Greer	.25	.11
73	Henry Rodriguez	.25	.11
74	Fernando Tatis	.25	.11
75	John Valentin	.25	.11
76	Matt Morris	.25	.11
77	Ray Durham	.25	.11
78	Geronimo Berroa	.15	.07
79	Scott Brosius	.25	.11
80	Willie Greene	.25	.11
81	Rondell White	.25	.11
82	Doug Drabek	.15	.07
83	Derek Bell	.25	.11
84	Butch Huskey	.15	.07
85	Doug Jones	.15	.07
86	Jeff Kent	.25	.11
87	Jim Edmonds	.40	.18
88	Mark McLemore	.15	.07
89	Todd Zeile	.25	.11
90	Edgardo Alfonzo	.25	.11
91	Carlos Baerga	.25	.11
92	Jorge Fabregas	.15	.07
93	Alan Benes	.25	.11
94	Troy Percival	.25	.11
95	Edgar Renteria	.25	.11
96	Jeff Fassero	.15	.07
97	Reggie Sanders	.25	.11
98	Dean Palmer	.25	.11
99	J.T. Snow	.25	.11
100	Dave Nilsson	.15	.07
101	Dan Wilson	.15	.07
102	Robb Nen	.25	.11
103	Damion Easley	.25	.11
104	Kevin Foster	.15	.07
105	Jose Offerman	.15	.07
106	Steve Cooke	.15	.07
107	Matt Stairs	.25	.11
108	Darryl Hamilton	.15	.07
109	Steve Karsay	.15	.07
110	Gary DiSarcina	.15	.07
111	Dante Bichette	.25	.11
112	Billy Wagner	.25	.11
113	David Segui	.25	.11
114	Bobby Higginson	.40	.18
115	Jeffrey Hammonds	.25	.11
116	Kevin Brown	.40	.18
117	Paul Sorrento	.15	.07
118	Mark Leiter	.15	.07
119	Charles Nagy	.25	.11
120	Danny Patterson	.15	.07
121	Brian McRae	.15	.07
122	Jay Bell	.25	.11
123	Jamie Moyer	.15	.07
124	Carl Everett	.15	.07
125	Greg Colbrunn	.15	.07
126	Jason Kendall	.25	.11
127	Luis Sojo	.15	.07
128	Mike Lieberthal	.15	.07
129	Reggie Jefferson	.15	.07
130	Cal Eldred	.15	.07
131	Orel Hershiser	.25	.11
132	Doug Glanville	.25	.11
133	Willie Blair	.15	.07
134	Neifi Perez	.25	.11
135	Sean Berry	.15	.07
136	Chuck Finley	.25	.11
137	Alex Gonzalez	.15	.07
138	Dennis Eckersley	.25	.11
139	Kenny Rogers	.15	.07
140	Troy O'Leary	.25	.11
141	Roger Bailey	.15	.07
142	Yamil Benitez	.15	.07
143	Wally Joyner	.25	.11
144	Bobby Witt	.15	.07
145	Pete Schourek	.15	.07
146	Terry Steinbach	.25	.11
147	B.J. Surhoff	.25	.11
148	Esteban Loaiza	.15	.07
149	Heathcliff Slocumb	.15	.07
150	Ed Sprague	.15	.07
151	Gregg Jefferies	.15	.07
152	Scott Erickson	.25	.11
153	Jaime Navarro	.15	.07
154	David Wells	.40	.18
155	Alex Fernandez	.15	.07
156	Tim Belcher	.15	.07
157	Mark Grudzielanek	.25	.11
158	Scott Hatteberg	.15	.07
159	Paul Konerko	.60	.25
160	Ben Grieve	1.25	.55
161	Abraham Nunez	.25	.11
162	Shannon Stewart	.25	.11
163	Jaret Wright	.75	.35
164	Derrek Lee	.25	.11
165	Todd Dunwoody	.25	.11
166	Steve Woodard	.25	.11
167	Ryan McGuire	.15	.07
168	Jeremi Gonzalez	.25	.11
169	Mark Kotsay	.40	.18
170	Brett Tomko	.25	.11
171	Bobby Estalella	.25	.11
172	Livan Hernandez	.25	.11
173	Todd Helton	.75	.35
174	Garrett Stephenson	.15	.07
175	Pokey Reese	.15	.07
176	Tony Saunders	.15	.07
177	Antone Williamson	.15	.07
178	Bartolo Colon	.25	.11
179	Karim Garcia	.25	.11
180	Juan Encarnacion	.25	.11
181	Jacob Cruz	.15	.07
182	Alex Rodriguez FV	1.00	.45
183	Cal Ripken FV Roberto Alomar	1.00	.45
184	Roger Clemens FV	.60	.25
185	Derek Jeter FV	.75	.35
186	Frank Thomas FV	1.00	.45
187	Ken Griffey Jr. FV	1.50	.70
188	Mark McGwire GJ	2.00	.90
189	Tino Martinez GJ	.25	.11
190	Larry Walker GJ	.25	.11
191	Brady Anderson GJ	.15	.07
192	Jeff Bagwell GJ	.60	.25
193	Ken Griffey Jr. GJ	1.50	.70
194	Chipper Jones GJ	.75	.35
195	Ray Lankford GJ	.15	.07
196	Jim Thome GJ	.25	.11
197	Nomar Garciaparra GJ	1.00	.45
198	AS HR Contestants Brady Anderson Jeff Bagwell Nomar Garciaparra Ken Griffey Jr. Chipper Jones Ray Lankford Tino Martinez Mark McGwire Jim Thome Larry Walker	.75	.35
199	Tino Martinez CL	.25	.11
200	Jacob's Field CL	.15	.07

1998 Pinnacle Hit It Here

	MINT	NRMT
COMPLETE SET (10)	80.00	36.00
COMMON CARD (1-10)	3.00	1.35
❑ 1 Larry Walker	4.00	1.80
❑ 2 Ken Griffey Jr.	20.00	9.00
❑ 3 Mike Piazza	12.00	5.50
❑ 4 Frank Thomas	12.00	5.50
❑ 5 Barry Bonds	5.00	2.20
❑ 6 Albert Belle	5.00	2.20
❑ 7 Tino Martinez	3.00	1.35
❑ 8 Mark McGwire	25.00	11.00
❑ 9 Juan Gonzalez	10.00	4.50
❑ 10 Jeff Bagwell	6.00	2.70

1998 Pinnacle Power Pack Jumbos

	MINT	NRMT
COMPLETE SET (24)	30.00	13.50
COMMON CARD (1-24)	.40	.18
❑ 1 Alex Rodriguez FV	2.50	1.10
❑ 2 Cal Ripken Roberto Alomar FV	2.50	1.10
❑ 3 Roger Clemens FV	1.50	.70
❑ 4 Derek Jeter FV	2.00	.90
❑ 5 Frank Thomas FV	2.50	1.10
❑ 6 Ken Griffey Jr. FV	4.00	1.80
❑ 7 Mark McGwire GJ	5.00	2.20
❑ 8 Tino Martinez GJ	.75	.35
❑ 9 Larry Walker GJ	.75	.35
❑ 10 Brady Anderson GJ	.40	.18
❑ 11 Jeff Bagwell GJ	1.25	.55
❑ 12 Ken Griffey Jr. GJ	4.00	1.80
❑ 13 Chipper Jones GJ	2.00	.90
❑ 14 Ray Lankford GJ	.40	.18
❑ 15 Jim Thome GJ	.75	.35
❑ 16 Nomar Garciaparra GJ	2.50	1.10
❑ 17 Mike Piazza	2.50	1.10
❑ 18 Andruw Jones	1.00	.45
❑ 19 Greg Maddux	2.50	1.10
❑ 20 Tony Gwynn	2.00	.90
❑ 21 Larry Walker	.75	.35
❑ 22 Jeff Bagwell	1.25	.55
❑ 23 Chipper Jones	2.00	.90
❑ 24 Scott Rolen	2.00	.90

1998 Pinnacle Spellbound

	MINT	NRMT
COMPLETE SET (50)	600.00	275.00
COMMON M.MCGWIRE	30.00	13.50
COMMON R.CLEMENS	10.00	4.50
COMMON F.THOMAS	15.00	6.75
COMMON S.ROLEN	10.00	4.50
COMMON K.GRIFFEY	25.00	11.00
COMMON L.WALKER	5.00	2.20
COMMON N.GARCIAPARRA	15.00	6.75
COMMON C.RIPKEN	20.00	9.00
COMMON T.GWYNN	12.00	5.50
❑ 1 Mark McGwire M	30.00	13.50
❑ 2 Mark McGwire C	30.00	13.50
❑ 3 Mark McGwire G	30.00	13.50
❑ 4 Mark McGwire W	30.00	13.50

	MINT	NRMT
❑ 5 Mark McGwire I	30.00	13.50
❑ 6 Mark McGwire R	30.00	13.50
❑ 7 Mark McGwire E	30.00	13.50
❑ 8 Roger Clemens R	10.00	4.50
❑ 9 Roger Clemens O	10.00	4.50
❑ 10 Roger Clemens C	10.00	4.50
❑ 11 Roger Clemens K	10.00	4.50
❑ 12 Roger Clemens E	10.00	4.50
❑ 13 Roger Clemens T	10.00	4.50
❑ 14 Frank Thomas B	15.00	6.75
❑ 15 Frank Thomas I	15.00	6.75
❑ 16 Frank Thomas G	15.00	6.75
❑ 17 Frank Thomas H	15.00	6.75
❑ 18 Frank Thomas U	15.00	6.75
❑ 19 Frank Thomas R	15.00	6.75
❑ 20 Frank Thomas T	15.00	6.75
❑ 21 Scott Rolen R	10.00	4.50
❑ 22 Scott Rolen O	10.00	4.50
❑ 23 Scott Rolen L	10.00	4.50
❑ 24 Scott Rolen E	10.00	4.50
❑ 25 Scott Rolen N	10.00	4.50
❑ 26 Ken Griffey Jr. G	25.00	11.00
❑ 27 Ken Griffey Jr. R	25.00	11.00
❑ 28 Ken Griffey Jr. I	25.00	11.00
❑ 29 Ken Griffey Jr. F	25.00	11.00
❑ 30 Ken Griffey Jr. F	25.00	11.00
❑ 31 Ken Griffey Jr. E	25.00	11.00
❑ 32 Ken Griffey Jr. Y	25.00	11.00
❑ 33 Larry Walker W	5.00	2.20
❑ 34 Larry Walker A	5.00	2.20
❑ 35 Larry Walker L	5.00	2.20
❑ 36 Larry Walker K	5.00	2.20
❑ 37 Larry Walker E	5.00	2.20
❑ 38 Larry Walker R	5.00	2.20
❑ 39 Nomar Garciaparra N	15.00	6.75
❑ 40 Nomar Garciaparra O	15.00	6.75
❑ 41 Nomar Garciaparra M	15.00	6.75
❑ 42 Nomar Garciaparra A	15.00	6.75
❑ 43 Nomar Garciaparra R	15.00	6.75
❑ 44 Cal Ripken C	20.00	9.00
❑ 45 Cal Ripken A	20.00	9.00
❑ 46 Cal Ripken L	20.00	9.00
❑ 47 Tony Gwynn T	12.00	5.50
❑ 48 Tony Gwynn O	12.00	5.50
❑ 49 Tony Gwynn N	12.00	5.50
❑ 50 Tony Gwynn Y	12.00	5.50

1996 Pinnacle Aficionado

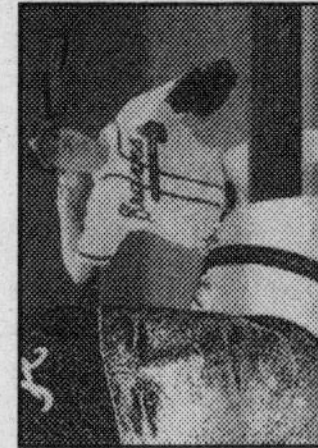

	MINT	NRMT
COMPLETE SET (200)	50.00	22.00
COMMON CARD (1-200)	.25	.11
❑ 1 Jack McDowell	.25	.11
❑ 2 Jay Bell	.50	.23
❑ 3 Rafael Palmeiro	.75	.35
❑ 4 Wally Joyner	.50	.23
❑ 5 Ozzie Smith	1.25	.55
❑ 6 Mark McGwire	5.00	2.20
❑ 7 Kevin Seitzer	.25	.11
❑ 8 Fred McGriff	.75	.35
❑ 9 Roger Clemens	2.00	.90
❑ 10 Randy Johnson	1.00	.45
❑ 11 Cecil Fielder	.50	.23
❑ 12 David Cone	.75	.35
❑ 13 Chili Davis	.50	.23
❑ 14 Andres Galarraga	1.00	.45
❑ 15 Joe Carter	.50	.23
❑ 16 Ryne Sandberg	1.25	.55
❑ 17 Paul O'Neill	.50	.23
❑ 18 Cal Ripken	4.00	1.80
❑ 19 Wade Boggs	1.00	.45
❑ 20 Greg Gagne	.25	.11
❑ 21 Edgar Martinez	.50	.23
❑ 22 Greg Maddux	3.00	1.35
❑ 23 Ken Caminiti	.75	.35
❑ 24 Kirby Puckett	1.50	.70
❑ 25 Craig Biggio	1.00	.45
❑ 26 Will Clark	1.00	.45
❑ 27 Ron Gant	.25	.11
❑ 28 Eddie Murray	1.00	.45
❑ 29 Lance Johnson	.25	.11
❑ 30 Tony Gwynn	2.50	1.10
❑ 31 Dante Bichette	.50	.23
❑ 32 Darren Daulton	.50	.23
❑ 33 Danny Tartabull	.25	.11
❑ 34 Jeff King	.25	.11
❑ 35 Tom Glavine	1.00	.45
❑ 36 Rickey Henderson	1.00	.45
❑ 37 Jose Canseco	1.00	.45
❑ 38 Barry Larkin	.75	.35
❑ 39 Dennis Martinez	.50	.23
❑ 40 Ruben Sierra	.25	.11
❑ 41 Bobby Bonilla	.50	.23
❑ 42 Jeff Conine	.50	.23
❑ 43 Lee Smith	.50	.23
❑ 44 Charlie Hayes	.25	.11
❑ 45 Walt Weiss	.25	.11
❑ 46 Jay Buhner	.50	.23
❑ 47 Kenny Rogers	.25	.11
❑ 48 Paul Molitor	1.00	.45
❑ 49 Hal Morris	.25	.11
❑ 50 Todd Stottlemyre	.25	.11
❑ 51 Mike Stanley	.25	.11
❑ 52 Mark Grace	.75	.35
❑ 53 Lenny Dykstra	.50	.23
❑ 54 Andre Dawson	.75	.35
❑ 55 Dennis Eckersley	.50	.23
❑ 56 Ben McDonald	.25	.11
❑ 57 Ray Lankford	.50	.23
❑ 58 Mo Vaughn	1.25	.55
❑ 59 Frank Thomas	3.00	1.35
❑ 60 Julio Franco	.25	.11
❑ 61 Jim Abbott	.50	.23
❑ 62 Greg Vaughn	.50	.23
❑ 63 Marquis Grissom	.50	.23
❑ 64 Tino Martinez	1.00	.45
❑ 65 Kevin Appier	.50	.23
❑ 66 Matt Williams	.50	.23
❑ 67 Sammy Sosa	2.50	1.10
❑ 68 Larry Walker	1.00	.45
❑ 69 Ivan Rodriguez	1.25	.55
❑ 70 Eric Karros	.50	.23
❑ 71 Bernie Williams	1.00	.45
❑ 72 Carlos Baerga	.50	.23
❑ 73 Jeff Bagwell	1.50	.70
❑ 74 Pete Schourek	.25	.11
❑ 75 Ken Griffey Jr.	5.00	2.20
❑ 76 Bernard Gilkey	.25	.11
❑ 77 Albert Belle	1.25	.55
❑ 78 Chuck Knoblauch	1.00	.45
❑ 79 John Smoltz	.50	.23
❑ 80 Barry Bonds	1.25	.55
❑ 81 Vinny Castilla	.75	.35

❑ 82 John Olerud	.50	.23
❑ 83 Mike Mussina	1.00	.45
❑ 84 Alex Fernandez	.25	.11
❑ 85 Shawon Dunston	.25	.11
❑ 86 Travis Fryman	.50	.23
❑ 87 Moises Alou	.75	.35
❑ 88 Dean Palmer	.50	.23
❑ 89 Gregg Jefferies	.25	.11
❑ 90 Jim Thome	1.00	.45
❑ 91 Dave Justice	1.00	.45
❑ 92 B.J. Surhoff	.50	.23
❑ 93 Ramon Martinez	.50	.23
❑ 94 Gary Sheffield	.75	.35
❑ 95 Andy Benes	.50	.23
❑ 96 Reggie Sanders	.50	.23
❑ 97 Roberto Alomar	1.00	.45
❑ 98 Omar Vizquel	.50	.23
❑ 99 Juan Gonzalez	2.50	1.10
❑ 100 Robin Ventura	.50	.23
❑ 101 Jason Isringhausen	.25	.11
❑ 102 Greg Colbrunn	.25	.11
❑ 103 Brian Jordan	.50	.23
❑ 104 Shawn Green	.50	.23
❑ 105 Brian Hunter	.50	.23
❑ 106 Rondell White	.50	.23
❑ 107 Ryan Klesko	.50	.23
❑ 108 Sterling Hitchcock	.50	.23
❑ 109 Manny Ramirez	1.00	.45
❑ 110 Bret Boone	.50	.23
❑ 111 Michael Tucker	.50	.23
❑ 112 Julian Tavarez	.25	.11
❑ 113 Benji Gil	.25	.11
❑ 114 Kenny Lofton	1.00	.45
❑ 115 Mike Kelly	.25	.11
❑ 116 Ray Durham	.50	.23
❑ 117 Trevor Hoffman	.50	.23
❑ 118 Butch Huskey	.25	.11
❑ 119 Phil Nevin	.25	.11
❑ 120 Pedro Martinez	1.00	.45
❑ 121 Wil Cordero	.25	.11
❑ 122 Tim Salmon	1.00	.45
❑ 123 Jim Edmonds	.75	.35
❑ 124 Mike Piazza	3.00	1.35
❑ 125 Rico Brogna	.25	.11
❑ 126 John Mabry	.25	.11
❑ 127 Chipper Jones	1.50	.70
❑ 128 Johnny Damon	.50	.23
❑ 129 Raul Mondesi	.75	.35
❑ 130 Denny Neagle	.50	.23
❑ 131 Marc Newfield	.25	.11
❑ 132 Hideo Nomo	1.50	.70
❑ 133 Joe Vitiello	.25	.11
❑ 134 Garret Anderson	.50	.23
❑ 135 Dave Nilsson	.25	.11
❑ 136 Alex Rodriguez	3.00	1.35
❑ 137 Russ Davis	.50	.23
❑ 138 Frank Rodriguez	.25	.11
❑ 139 Royce Clayton	.25	.11
❑ 140 John Valentin	.50	.23
❑ 141 Marty Cordova	.25	.11
❑ 142 Alex Gonzalez	.25	.11
❑ 143 Carlos Delgado	.50	.23
❑ 144 Willie Greene	.50	.23
❑ 145 Cliff Floyd	.50	.23
❑ 146 Bobby Higginson	1.00	.45
❑ 147 J.T. Snow	.50	.23
❑ 148 Derek Bell	.50	.23
❑ 149 Edgardo Alfonzo	.50	.23
❑ 150 Charles Johnson	.50	.23
❑ 151 Hideo Nomo GR	1.25	.55
❑ 152 Larry Walker GR	.50	.23
❑ 153 Bob Abreu GR	.25	.11
❑ 154 Karim Garcia GR	.25	.11
❑ 155 Dave Nilsson GR	.25	.11
❑ 156 Chan Ho Park GR	.50	.23
❑ 157 Dennis Martinez GR	.25	.11
❑ 158 Sammy Sosa GR	1.25	.55
❑ 159 Rey Ordonez GR	.25	.11
❑ 160 Roberto Alomar GR	.50	.23
❑ 161 George Arias	.25	.11
❑ 162 Jason Schmidt	.25	.11
❑ 163 Derek Jeter	3.00	1.35
❑ 164 Chris Snopek	.25	.11
❑ 165 Todd Hollandsworth	.25	.11
❑ 166 Sal Fasano	.25	.11
❑ 167 Jay Powell	.25	.11
❑ 168 Paul Wilson	.25	.11
❑ 169 Jim Pittsley	.25	.11
❑ 170 LaTroy Hawkins	.25	.11
❑ 171 Bob Abreu	.50	.23
❑ 172 Mike Grace	.25	.11
❑ 173 Karim Garcia	.50	.23
❑ 174 Richard Hidalgo	.50	.23
❑ 175 Felipe Crespo	.25	.11
❑ 176 Terrell Wade	.25	.11
❑ 177 Steve Gibralter	.25	.11
❑ 178 Jermaine Dye	.25	.11
❑ 179 Alan Benes	.50	.23
❑ 180 Wilton Guerrero	.75	.35
❑ 181 Brooks Kieschnick	.25	.11
❑ 182 Roger Cedeno	.25	.11
❑ 183 Osvaldo Fernandez	.25	.11
❑ 184 Matt Lawton	1.00	.45
❑ 185 George Williams	.25	.11
❑ 186 Jimmy Haynes	.25	.11
❑ 187 Mike Busby	.25	.11
❑ 188 Chan Ho Park	1.00	.45
❑ 189 Marc Barcelo	.25	.11
❑ 190 Jason Kendall	1.00	.45
❑ 191 Rey Ordonez	.50	.23
❑ 192 Tyler Houston	.25	.11
❑ 193 John Wasdin	.25	.11
❑ 194 Jeff Suppan	.25	.11
❑ 195 Jeff Ware	.25	.11
❑ 196 Ken Griffey Jr. CL	2.50	1.10
❑ 197 Albert Belle CL	.75	.35
❑ 198 Mike Piazza CL	1.50	.70
❑ 199 Greg Maddux CL	1.50	.70
❑ 200 Frank Thomas CL	1.50	.70

1996 Pinnacle Aficionado Magic Numbers

	MINT	NRMT
COMPLETE SET (10)	200.00	90.00
COMMON CARD (1-10)	6.00	2.70
❑ 1 Ken Griffey Jr.	50.00	22.00
❑ 2 Greg Maddux	30.00	13.50
❑ 3 Frank Thomas	30.00	13.50
❑ 4 Mo Vaughn	12.00	5.50
❑ 5 Jeff Bagwell	15.00	6.75
❑ 6 Chipper Jones	25.00	11.00
❑ 7 Albert Belle	12.00	5.50
❑ 8 Cal Ripken	40.00	18.00
❑ 9 Matt Williams	6.00	2.70
❑ 10 Sammy Sosa	25.00	11.00

1996 Pinnacle Aficionado Rivals

	MINT	NRMT
COMPLETE SET (24)	250.00	110.00
COMMON CARD (1-24)	8.00	3.60
❑ 1 Ken Griffey Frank Thomas	20.00	9.00
❑ 2 Frank Thomas Cal Ripken	15.00	6.75
❑ 3 Cal Ripken Mo Vaughn	10.00	4.50
❑ 4 Mo Vaughn Ken Griffey Jr.	15.00	6.75
❑ 5 Ken Griffey Jr. Cal Ripken	25.00	11.00
❑ 6 Frank Thomas Mo Vaughn	10.00	4.50
❑ 7 Cal Ripken Ken Griffey Jr.	25.00	11.00
❑ 8 Mo Vaughn Frank Thomas	10.00	4.50
❑ 9 Ken Griffey Jr. Mo Vaughn	15.00	6.75
❑ 10 Frank Thomas Ken Griffey Jr.	20.00	9.00
❑ 11 Cal Ripken Frank Thomas	15.00	6.75
❑ 12 Mo Vaughn Cal Ripken	10.00	4.50
❑ 13 Mike Piazza Jeff Bagwell	8.00	3.60
❑ 14 Jeff Bagwell Barry Bonds	8.00	3.60
❑ 15 Jeff Bagwell Mike Piazza	8.00	3.60
❑ 16 Tony Gwynn Mike Piazza	8.00	3.60
❑ 17 Mike Piazza Barry Bonds	8.00	3.60
❑ 18 Jeff Bagwell Tony Gwynn	8.00	3.60
❑ 19 Barry Bonds Mike Piazza	8.00	3.60
❑ 20 Tony Gwynn Jeff Bagwell	8.00	3.60
❑ 21 Mike Piazza Tony Gwynn	8.00	3.60
❑ 22 Barry Bonds Jeff Bagwell	8.00	3.60
❑ 23 Tony Gwynn Barry Bonds	8.00	3.60
❑ 24 Barry Bonds Tony Gwynn	8.00	3.60

1996 Pinnacle Aficionado Slick Picks

	MINT	NRMT
COMPLETE SET (32)	200.00	90.00
COMMON CARD (1-32)	2.00	.90

#	Player	MINT	NRMT
❑ 1	Mike Piazza	15.00	6.75
❑ 2	Cal Ripken	20.00	9.00
❑ 3	Ken Griffey Jr.	25.00	11.00
❑ 4	Paul Wilson	2.00	.90
❑ 5	Frank Thomas	15.00	6.75
❑ 6	Mo Vaughn	6.00	2.70
❑ 7	Barry Bonds	6.00	2.70
❑ 8	Albert Belle	6.00	2.70
❑ 9	Jeff Bagwell	8.00	3.60
❑ 10	Dante Bichette	2.50	1.10
❑ 11	Hideo Nomo	8.00	3.60
❑ 12	Raul Mondesi	3.00	1.35
❑ 13	Manny Ramirez	5.00	2.20
❑ 14	Greg Maddux	15.00	6.75
❑ 15	Tony Gwynn	12.00	5.50
❑ 16	Ryne Sandberg	6.00	2.70
❑ 17	Reggie Sanders	2.50	1.10
❑ 18	Derek Jeter	12.00	5.50
❑ 19	Johnny Damon	2.50	1.10
❑ 20	Alex Rodriguez	15.00	6.75
❑ 21	Ryan Klesko	2.50	1.10
❑ 22	Jim Thome	5.00	2.20
❑ 23	Kenny Lofton	5.00	2.20
❑ 24	Tino Martinez	5.00	2.20
❑ 25	Randy Johnson	5.00	2.20
❑ 26	Wade Boggs	5.00	2.20
❑ 27	Juan Gonzalez	12.00	5.50
❑ 28	Kirby Puckett	8.00	3.60
❑ 29	Tim Salmon	5.00	2.20
❑ 30	Chipper Jones	12.00	5.50
❑ 31	Garret Anderson	2.50	1.10
❑ 32	Eddie Murray	5.00	2.20

1997 Pinnacle Certified

	MINT	NRMT
COMPLETE SET (150)	40.00	18.00
COMMON CARD (1-150)	.25	.11

#	Player	MINT	NRMT
❑ 1	Barry Bonds	1.25	.55
❑ 2	Mo Vaughn	1.25	.55
❑ 3	Matt Williams	.50	.23
❑ 4	Ryne Sandberg	1.25	.55
❑ 5	Jeff Bagwell	1.50	.70
❑ 6	Alan Benes	.50	.23
❑ 7	John Wetteland	.50	.23
❑ 8	Fred McGriff	.75	.35
❑ 9	Craig Biggio	1.00	.45
❑ 10	Bernie Williams	1.00	.45
❑ 11	Brian Hunter	.50	.23
❑ 12	Sandy Alomar Jr.	.50	.23
❑ 13	Ray Lankford	.50	.23
❑ 14	Ryan Klesko	.50	.23
❑ 15	Jermaine Dye	.25	.11
❑ 16	Andy Benes	.50	.23
❑ 17	Albert Belle	1.25	.55
❑ 18	Tony Clark	.75	.35
❑ 19	Dean Palmer	.50	.23
❑ 20	Bernard Gilkey	.25	.11
❑ 21	Ken Caminiti	.75	.35
❑ 22	Alex Rodriguez	3.00	1.35
❑ 23	Tim Salmon	1.00	.45
❑ 24	Larry Walker	1.00	.45
❑ 25	Barry Larkin	.75	.35
❑ 26	Mike Piazza	3.00	1.35
❑ 27	Brady Anderson	.50	.23
❑ 28	Cal Ripken	4.00	1.80
❑ 29	Charles Nagy	.50	.23
❑ 30	Paul Molitor	1.00	.45
❑ 31	Darin Erstad	1.50	.70
❑ 32	Rey Ordonez	.50	.23
❑ 33	Wally Joyner	.50	.23
❑ 34	David Cone	.75	.35
❑ 35	Sammy Sosa	2.50	1.10
❑ 36	Dante Bichette	.50	.23
❑ 37	Eric Karros	.50	.23
❑ 38	Omar Vizquel	.50	.23
❑ 39	Roger Clemens	2.00	.90
❑ 40	Joe Carter	.50	.23
❑ 41	Frank Thomas	3.00	1.35
❑ 42	Javy Lopez	.50	.23
❑ 43	Mike Mussina	1.00	.45
❑ 44	Gary Sheffield	.75	.35
❑ 45	Tony Gwynn	2.50	1.10
❑ 46	Jason Kendall	.75	.35
❑ 47	Jim Thome	1.00	.45
❑ 48	Andres Galarraga	1.00	.45
❑ 49	Mark McGwire	5.00	2.20
❑ 50	Troy Percival	.50	.23
❑ 51	Derek Jeter	3.00	1.35
❑ 52	Todd Hollandsworth	.25	.11
❑ 53	Ken Griffey Jr.	5.00	2.20
❑ 54	Randy Johnson	1.00	.45
❑ 55	Pat Hentgen	.50	.23
❑ 56	Rusty Greer	.50	.23
❑ 57	John Jaha	.25	.11
❑ 58	Kenny Lofton	1.00	.45
❑ 59	Chipper Jones	2.50	1.10
❑ 60	Robb Nen	.25	.11
❑ 61	Rafael Palmeiro	.75	.35
❑ 62	Mariano Rivera	.50	.23
❑ 63	Hideo Nomo	1.25	.55
❑ 64	Greg Vaughn	.50	.23
❑ 65	Ron Gant	.25	.11
❑ 66	Eddie Murray	1.00	.45
❑ 67	John Smoltz	.50	.23
❑ 68	Manny Ramirez	1.00	.45
❑ 69	Juan Gonzalez	2.50	1.10
❑ 70	F.P. Santangelo	.25	.11
❑ 71	Moises Alou	.75	.35
❑ 72	Alex Ochoa	.25	.11
❑ 73	Chuck Knoblauch	1.00	.45
❑ 74	Raul Mondesi	.75	.35
❑ 75	J.T. Snow	.50	.23
❑ 76	Rickey Henderson	1.00	.45
❑ 77	Bobby Bonilla	.50	.23
❑ 78	Wade Boggs	1.00	.45
❑ 79	Ivan Rodriguez	1.25	.55
❑ 80	Brian Jordan	.50	.23
❑ 81	Al Leiter	.50	.23
❑ 82	Jay Buhner	.50	.23
❑ 83	Greg Maddux	3.00	1.35
❑ 84	Edgar Martinez	.50	.23
❑ 85	Kevin Brown	.75	.35
❑ 86	Eric Young	.50	.23
❑ 87	Todd Hundley	.50	.23
❑ 88	Ellis Burks	.50	.23
❑ 89	Marquis Grissom	.50	.23
❑ 90	Jose Canseco	1.00	.45
❑ 91	Henry Rodriguez	.50	.23
❑ 92	Andy Pettitte	.75	.35
❑ 93	Mark Grudzielanek	.50	.23
❑ 94	Dwight Gooden	.50	.23
❑ 95	Roberto Alomar	1.00	.45
❑ 96	Paul Wilson	.25	.11
❑ 97	Will Clark	1.00	.45
❑ 98	Rondell White	.50	.23
❑ 99	Charles Johnson	.50	.23
❑ 100	Jim Edmonds	.75	.35
❑ 101	Jason Giambi	.50	.23
❑ 102	Billy Wagner	.50	.23
❑ 103	Edgar Renteria	.50	.23
❑ 104	Johnny Damon	.50	.23
❑ 105	Jason Isringhausen	.25	.11
❑ 106	Andruw Jones	1.50	.70
❑ 107	Jose Guillen	1.00	.45
❑ 108	Kevin Orie	.25	.11
❑ 109	Brian Giles	1.00	.45
❑ 110	Danny Patterson	.25	.11
❑ 111	Vladimir Guerrero	2.00	.90
❑ 112	Scott Rolen	2.50	1.10
❑ 113	Damon Mashore	.25	.11
❑ 114	Nomar Garciaparra	3.00	1.35
❑ 115	Todd Walker	1.00	.45
❑ 116	Wilton Guerrero	.25	.11
❑ 117	Bob Abreu	.50	.23
❑ 118	Brooks Kieschnick	.25	.11
❑ 119	Pokey Reese	.25	.11
❑ 120	Todd Greene	.50	.23
❑ 121	Dmitri Young	.50	.23
❑ 122	Raul Casanova	.25	.11
❑ 123	Glendon Rusch	.25	.11
❑ 124	Jason Dickson	.50	.23
❑ 125	Jorge Posada	.50	.23
❑ 126	Rod Myers	.50	.23
❑ 127	Bubba Trammell	.60	.25
❑ 128	Scott Spiezio	.25	.11
❑ 129	Hideki Irabu	2.50	1.10
❑ 130	Wendell Magee	.25	.11
❑ 131	Bartolo Colon	.50	.23
❑ 132	Chris Holt	.25	.11
❑ 133	Calvin Maduro	.25	.11
❑ 134	Ray Montgomery	.25	.11
❑ 135	Shannon Stewart	.50	.23
❑ 136	Ken Griffey Jr. CERT	2.50	1.10
❑ 137	Vladimir Guerrero CERT	1.00	.45
❑ 138	Roger Clemens CERT	1.00	.45
❑ 139	Mark McGwire CERT	2.50	1.10
❑ 140	Albert Belle CERT	.50	.23
❑ 141	Derek Jeter CERT	1.50	.70
❑ 142	Juan Gonzalez CERT	1.25	.55
❑ 143	Greg Maddux CERT	1.50	.70
❑ 144	Alex Rodriguez CERT	1.50	.70
❑ 145	Jeff Bagwell CERT	1.00	.45
❑ 146	Cal Ripken CERT	2.00	.90
❑ 147	Tony Gwynn CERT	1.25	.55
❑ 148	Frank Thomas CERT	1.50	.70
❑ 149	Hideo Nomo CERT	1.00	.45
❑ 150	Andruw Jones CERT	.50	.23
❑ 151	Jose Cruz Jr. Blue Jays	8.00	3.60

1997 Pinnacle Certified Mirror Blue

	MINT	NRMT
COMMON CARD (1-150)	20.00	9.00

*STARS: 30X TO 80X BASIC CARDS
*YOUNG STARS: 25X TO 60X BASIC CARDS
*ROOKIES: 15X TO 40X BASIC CARDS

1997 Pinnacle Certified Mirror Gold

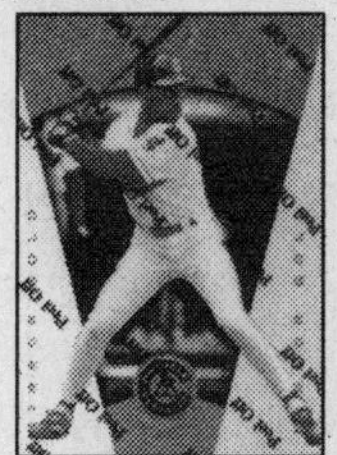

	MINT	NRMT
COMMON CARD (1-150)	60.00	27.00

*STARS: 125X TO 250X BASIC CARDS
*YOUNG STARS: 100X TO 200X BASIC CARDS
*ROOKIES: 60X TO 120X BASIC CARDS

1997 Pinnacle Certified Mirror Red

	MINT	NRMT
COMMON CARD (1-150)	12.00	5.50

*STARS: 20X TO 50X BASIC CARDS
*YOUNG STARS: 15X TO 40X BASIC CARDS
*ROOKIES: 10X TO 25X BASIC CARDS

1997 Pinnacle Certified Certified Team

	MINT	NRMT
COMPLETE SET (20)	300.00	135.00
COMMON CARD (1-20)	4.00	1.80
COMP.GOLD SET (20)	1000.00	450.00

*GOLD TEAM: 1.25X TO 3X BASIC CARDS
GOLD TEAM STATED ODDS 1:119 HOBBY
GOLD TEAM PRINT RUN 475 SERIAL #'d SETS
*MIRROR GOLD: 12.5X TO 30X BASIC CARDS
MIR.GOLD: RANDOM INSERTS IN PACKS
MIR.GOLD PRINT RUN 25 SETS

Card	MINT	NRMT
❑ 1 Frank Thomas	25.00	11.00
❑ 2 Jeff Bagwell	12.00	5.50
❑ 3 Derek Jeter	20.00	9.00
❑ 4 Chipper Jones	20.00	9.00
❑ 5 Alex Rodriguez	25.00	11.00
❑ 6 Ken Caminiti	5.00	2.20
❑ 7 Cal Ripken	30.00	13.50
❑ 8 Mo Vaughn	10.00	4.50
❑ 9 Ivan Rodriguez	10.00	4.50
❑ 10 Mike Piazza	25.00	11.00
❑ 11 Juan Gonzalez	20.00	9.00
❑ 12 Barry Bonds	10.00	4.50
❑ 13 Ken Griffey Jr.	40.00	18.00
❑ 14 Andruw Jones	10.00	4.50
❑ 15 Albert Belle	10.00	4.50
❑ 16 Gary Sheffield	5.00	2.20
❑ 17 Andy Pettitte	5.00	2.20
❑ 18 Hideo Nomo	10.00	4.50
❑ 19 Greg Maddux	25.00	11.00
❑ 20 John Smoltz	4.00	1.80

1997 Pinnacle Certified Lasting Impressions

	MINT	NRMT
COMPLETE SET (20)	225.00	100.00
COMMON CARD (1-20)	4.00	1.80

Card	MINT	NRMT
❑ 1 Cal Ripken	30.00	13.50
❑ 2 Ken Griffey Jr.	40.00	18.00
❑ 3 Mo Vaughn	10.00	4.50
❑ 4 Brian Jordan	4.00	1.80
❑ 5 Mark McGwire	40.00	18.00
❑ 6 Chuck Knoblauch	8.00	3.60
❑ 7 Sammy Sosa	20.00	9.00
❑ 8 Brady Anderson	4.00	1.80
❑ 9 Frank Thomas	25.00	11.00
❑ 10 Tony Gwynn	20.00	9.00
❑ 11 Roger Clemens	15.00	6.75
❑ 12 Alex Rodriguez	25.00	11.00
❑ 13 Paul Molitor	8.00	3.60
❑ 14 Kenny Lofton	8.00	3.60
❑ 15 John Smoltz	4.00	1.80
❑ 16 Roberto Alomar	8.00	3.60
❑ 17 Randy Johnson	8.00	3.60
❑ 18 Ryne Sandberg	10.00	4.50
❑ 19 Manny Ramirez	8.00	3.60
❑ 20 Mike Mussina	8.00	3.60

1997 Pinnacle Inside

	MINT	NRMT
COMPLETE SET (150)	40.00	18.00
COMMON CARD (1-150)	.20	.09

Card	MINT	NRMT
❑ 1 David Cone	.50	.23
❑ 2 Sammy Sosa	2.00	.90
❑ 3 Joe Carter	.40	.18
❑ 4 Juan Gonzalez	2.00	.90
❑ 5 Hideo Nomo	1.00	.45
❑ 6 Moises Alou	.50	.23
❑ 7 Marc Newfield	.20	.09
❑ 8 Alex Rodriguez	2.50	1.10
❑ 9 Kimera Bartee	.20	.09
❑ 10 Chuck Knoblauch	.75	.35
❑ 11 Jason Isringhausen	.20	.09
❑ 12 Jermaine Allensworth	.20	.09
❑ 13 Frank Thomas	2.50	1.10
❑ 14 Paul Molitor	.75	.35
❑ 15 John Mabry	.20	.09
❑ 16 Greg Maddux	2.50	1.10
❑ 17 Rafael Palmeiro	.50	.23
❑ 18 Brian Jordan	.40	.18
❑ 19 Ken Griffey Jr.	4.00	1.80
❑ 20 Brady Anderson	.40	.18
❑ 21 Ruben Sierra	.20	.09
❑ 22 Travis Fryman	.40	.18
❑ 23 Cal Ripken	3.00	1.35
❑ 24 Will Clark	.75	.35
❑ 25 Todd Hollandsworth	.20	.09
❑ 26 Kevin Brown	.50	.23
❑ 27 Mike Piazza	2.50	1.10
❑ 28 Craig Biggio	.75	.35
❑ 29 Paul Wilson	.20	.09
❑ 30 Andres Galarraga	.75	.35
❑ 31 Chipper Jones	2.00	.90
❑ 32 Jason Giambi	.40	.18
❑ 33 Ernie Young	.20	.09
❑ 34 Marty Cordova	.20	.09
❑ 35 Albert Belle	1.00	.45
❑ 36 Roger Clemens	1.50	.70
❑ 37 Ryne Sandberg	1.00	.45
❑ 38 Henry Rodriguez	.40	.18
❑ 39 Jay Buhner	.40	.18
❑ 40 Raul Mondesi	.50	.23
❑ 41 Jeff Fassero	.20	.09
❑ 42 Edgar Martinez	.40	.18
❑ 43 Trey Beamon	.20	.09
❑ 44 Mo Vaughn	1.00	.45
❑ 45 Gary Sheffield	.50	.23
❑ 46 Ray Durham	.40	.18
❑ 47 Brett Butler	.40	.18
❑ 48 Ivan Rodriguez	1.00	.45
❑ 49 Fred McGriff	.50	.23
❑ 50 Dean Palmer	.40	.18
❑ 51 Rickey Henderson	.75	.35
❑ 52 Andy Pettitte	.50	.23
❑ 53 Bobby Bonilla	.40	.18
❑ 54 Shawn Green	.40	.18
❑ 55 Tino Martinez	.75	.35
❑ 56 Tony Gwynn	2.00	.90
❑ 57 Tom Glavine	.75	.35
❑ 58 Eric Young	.40	.18
❑ 59 Kevin Appier	.40	.18
❑ 60 Barry Bonds	1.00	.45
❑ 61 Wade Boggs	.75	.35
❑ 62 Jason Kendall	.50	.23
❑ 63 Jeff Bagwell	1.25	.55
❑ 64 Jeff Conine	.40	.18
❑ 65 Greg Vaughn	.40	.18
❑ 66 Eric Karros	.40	.18
❑ 67 Manny Ramirez	.75	.35
❑ 68 John Smoltz	.40	.18
❑ 69 Terrell Wade	.20	.09
❑ 70 John Wetteland	.40	.18
❑ 71 Kenny Lofton	.75	.35
❑ 72 Jim Thome	.75	.35
❑ 73 Bill Pulsipher	.20	.09
❑ 74 Darryl Strawberry	.40	.18
❑ 75 Roberto Alomar	.75	.35
❑ 76 Bobby Higginson	.50	.23
❑ 77 James Baldwin	.40	.18
❑ 78 Mark McGwire	4.00	1.80
❑ 79 Jose Canseco	.75	.35
❑ 80 Mark Grudzielanek	.40	.18
❑ 81 Ryan Klesko	.40	.18
❑ 82 Javy Lopez	.40	.18
❑ 83 Ken Caminiti	.50	.23
❑ 84 Dave Nilsson	.20	.09
❑ 85 Tim Salmon	.75	.35
❑ 86 Cecil Fielder	.40	.18
❑ 87 Derek Jeter	2.50	1.10
❑ 88 Garret Anderson	.40	.18
❑ 89 Dwight Gooden	.40	.18
❑ 90 Carlos Delgado	.40	.18
❑ 91 Ugueth Urbina	.40	.18
❑ 92 Chan Ho Park	.75	.35
❑ 93 Eddie Murray	.75	.35
❑ 94 Alex Ochoa	.20	.09
❑ 95 Rusty Greer	.40	.18
❑ 96 Mark Grace	.50	.23
❑ 97 Pat Hentgen	.40	.18
❑ 98 John Jaha	.20	.09
❑ 99 Charles Johnson	.40	.18
❑ 100 Jermaine Dye	.20	.09
❑ 101 Quinton McCracken	.40	.18
❑ 102 Troy Percival	.40	.18
❑ 103 Shane Reynolds	.40	.18
❑ 104 Rondell White	.40	.18
❑ 105 Charles Nagy	.40	.18
❑ 106 Alan Benes	.40	.18
❑ 107 Tom Goodwin	.20	.09
❑ 108 Ron Gant	.20	.09
❑ 109 Dan Wilson	.20	.09
❑ 110 Darin Erstad	1.25	.55
❑ 111 Matt Williams	.40	.18
❑ 112 Barry Larkin	.50	.23
❑ 113 Mariano Rivera	.40	.18
❑ 114 Larry Walker	.75	.35
❑ 115 Jim Edmonds	.50	.23
❑ 116 Michael Tucker	.40	.18
❑ 117 Todd Hundley	.40	.18
❑ 118 Alex Fernandez	.20	.09
❑ 119 J.T. Snow	.40	.18
❑ 120 Ellis Burks	.40	.18
❑ 121 Steve Finley	.40	.18
❑ 122 Mike Mussina	.75	.35
❑ 123 Curtis Pride	.20	.09
❑ 124 Derek Bell	.40	.18
❑ 125 Dante Bichette	.40	.18
❑ 126 Terry Steinbach	.40	.18
❑ 127 Randy Johnson	.75	.35
❑ 128 Andruw Jones	1.25	.55
❑ 129 Vladimir Guerrero	1.50	.70
❑ 130 Ruben Rivera	.40	.18
❑ 131 Billy Wagner	.40	.18
❑ 132 Scott Rolen	2.00	.90

	MINT	NRMT
❑ 133 Rey Ordonez	.40	.18
❑ 134 Karim Garcia	.40	.18
❑ 135 George Arias	.20	.09
❑ 136 Todd Greene	.40	.18
❑ 137 Robin Jennings	.20	.09
❑ 138 Raul Casanova	.20	.09
❑ 139 Steve Gibralter	.20	.09
❑ 140 Edgar Renteria	.40	.18
❑ 141 Chad Mottola	.20	.09
❑ 142 Dmitri Young	.40	.18
❑ 143 Tony Clark	.50	.23
❑ 144 Todd Walker	.75	.35
❑ 145 Kevin Brown	.50	.23
❑ 146 Nomar Garciaparra	2.50	1.10
❑ 147 Neifi Perez	.20	.09
❑ 148 Derek Jeter CL Todd Hollandsworth	.75	.35
❑ 149 Pat Hentgen CL John Smoltz	.20	.09
❑ 150 Juan Gonzalez CL Ken Caminiti	.75	.35

1997 Pinnacle Inside Diamond Edition

	MINT	NRMT
COMMON CARD (1-150)	12.00	5.50

*STARS: 30X TO 60X BASIC CARDS
*YOUNG STARS: 25X TO 50X BASIC CARDS

1997 Pinnacle Inside 40 Something

	MINT	NRMT
COMPLETE SET (16)	400.00	180.00
COMMON CARD (1-16)	8.00	3.60
❑ 1 Juan Gonzalez	50.00	22.00
❑ 2 Barry Bonds	25.00	11.00
❑ 3 Ken Caminiti	12.00	5.50
❑ 4 Mark McGwire	100.00	45.00
❑ 5 Todd Hundley	8.00	3.60
❑ 6 Albert Belle	25.00	11.00
❑ 7 Ellis Burks	8.00	3.60
❑ 8 Jay Buhner	8.00	3.60
❑ 9 Brady Anderson	8.00	3.60
❑ 10 Vinny Castilla	12.00	5.50
❑ 11 Mo Vaughn	25.00	11.00
❑ 12 Ken Griffey Jr.	100.00	45.00
❑ 13 Sammy Sosa	50.00	22.00
❑ 14 Andres Galarraga	20.00	9.00
❑ 15 Gary Sheffield	12.00	5.50
❑ 16 Frank Thomas	60.00	27.00

1997 Pinnacle Inside Cans

	MINT	NRMT
COMPLETE SET (24)	25.00	11.00
COMMON CAN (1-24)	.30	.14
COMMON SEALED CAN	3.00	1.35

*SEALED: .75X TO 2X BASE HI ON 1.50+ CANS

	MINT	NRMT
❑ 1 Kenny Lofton	.60	.25
❑ 2 Frank Thomas	2.00	.90
❑ 3 John Smoltz	.30	.14
❑ 4 Manny Ramirez	.60	.25
❑ 5 Alex Rodriguez	2.00	.90
❑ 6 Barry Bonds	.75	.35
❑ 7 Mo Vaughn	.75	.35
❑ 8 Ken Griffey Jr.	3.00	1.35
❑ 9 Albert Belle	.60	.25
❑ 10 Greg Maddux	2.00	.90
❑ 11 Juan Gonzalez	1.50	.70
❑ 12 Andy Pettitte	.40	.18
❑ 13 Jeff Bagwell	1.00	.45
❑ 14 Ryan Klesko	.30	.14
❑ 15 Chipper Jones	1.50	.70
❑ 16 Derek Jeter	2.00	.90
❑ 17 Ivan Rodriguez	.75	.35
❑ 18 Andruw Jones	1.25	.55
❑ 19 Mike Piazza	2.00	.90
❑ 20 Hideo Nomo	1.50	.70
❑ 21 Ken Caminiti	.40	.18
❑ 22 Cal Ripken	2.50	1.10
❑ 23 Mark McGwire	3.00	1.35
❑ 24 Tony Gwynn	1.50	.70

1997 Pinnacle Inside Dueling Dugouts

	MINT	NRMT
COMPLETE SET (20)	500.00	220.00
COMMON CARD (1-20)	8.00	3.60
❑ 1 Alex Rodriguez Cal Ripken	60.00	27.00
❑ 2 Jeff Bagwell Ken Caminiti	15.00	6.75
❑ 3 Barry Bonds Albert Belle	12.00	5.50
❑ 4 Mike Piazza Ivan Rodriguez	40.00	18.00
❑ 5 Chuck Knoblauch Roberto Alomar	10.00	4.50
❑ 6 Ken Griffey Jr. Andruw Jones	60.00	27.00
❑ 7 Chipper Jones Jim Thome	25.00	11.00
❑ 8 Frank Thomas Mo Vaughn	40.00	18.00
❑ 9 Fred McGriff Mark McGwire	50.00	22.00
❑ 10 Brian Jordan Tony Gwynn	25.00	11.00
❑ 11 Barry Larkin Derek Jeter	25.00	11.00
❑ 12 Kenny Lofton Bernie Williams	10.00	4.50
❑ 13 Juan Gonzalez Manny Ramirez	25.00	11.00
❑ 14 Will Clark Rafael Palmeiro	8.00	3.60
❑ 15 Greg Maddux Roger Clemens	40.00	18.00
❑ 16 John Smoltz Andy Pettitte	10.00	4.50
❑ 17 Mariano Rivera John Wetteland	8.00	3.60
❑ 18 Hideo Nomo Mike Mussina	12.00	5.50
❑ 19 Todd Hollandsworth Darin Erstad	12.00	5.50
❑ 20 Vladimir Guerrero Karim Garcia	15.00	6.75

1998 Pinnacle Inside

	MINT	NRMT
COMPLETE SET (150)	40.00	18.00
COMMON CARD (1-150)	.20	.09
❑ 1 Darin Erstad	1.00	.45
❑ 2 Derek Jeter	2.00	.90
❑ 3 Alex Rodriguez	2.50	1.10
❑ 4 Bobby Higginson	.50	.23
❑ 5 Nomar Garciaparra	2.50	1.10
❑ 6 Kenny Lofton	.75	.35
❑ 7 Ivan Rodriguez	1.00	.45
❑ 8 Cal Ripken	3.00	1.35
❑ 9 Todd Hundley	.30	.14
❑ 10 Chipper Jones	2.00	.90
❑ 11 Barry Larkin	.50	.23
❑ 12 Roberto Alomar	.75	.35
❑ 13 Mo Vaughn	1.00	.45
❑ 14 Sammy Sosa	2.00	.90
❑ 15 Sandy Alomar Jr.	.30	.14
❑ 16 Albert Belle	1.00	.45
❑ 17 Scott Rolen	2.00	.90
❑ 18 Pokey Reese	.20	.09
❑ 19 Ryan Klesko	.30	.14
❑ 20 Andres Galarraga	.75	.35
❑ 21 Justin Thompson	.30	.14
❑ 22 Gary Sheffield	.50	.23
❑ 23 David Justice	.75	.35
❑ 24 Ken Griffey Jr.	4.00	1.80
❑ 25 Andruw Jones	1.00	.45
❑ 26 Jeff Bagwell	1.25	.55
❑ 27 Vladimir Guerrero	1.25	.55
❑ 28 Mike Piazza	2.50	1.10
❑ 29 Chuck Knoblauch	.75	.35
❑ 30 Rondell White	.30	.14
❑ 31 Greg Maddux	2.50	1.10
❑ 32 Andy Pettitte	.50	.23
❑ 33 Larry Walker	.75	.35
❑ 34 Bobby Estalella	.30	.14
❑ 35 Frank Thomas	2.50	1.10
❑ 36 Tony Womack	.30	.14
❑ 37 Tony Gwynn	2.00	.90
❑ 38 Barry Bonds	1.00	.45
❑ 39 Randy Johnson	.75	.35
❑ 40 Mark McGwire	5.00	2.20
❑ 41 Juan Gonzalez	2.00	.90

❑ 42 Tim Salmon .75 .35
❑ 43 John Smoltz .30 .14
❑ 44 Rafael Palmeiro .50 .23
❑ 45 Mark Grace .50 .23
❑ 46 Mike Cameron .30 .14
❑ 47 Jim Thome .75 .35
❑ 48 Neifi Perez .30 .14
❑ 49 Kevin Brown .50 .23
❑ 50 Craig Biggio .75 .35
❑ 51 Bernie Williams .75 .35
❑ 52 Hideo Nomo 1.00 .45
❑ 53 Bob Abreu .30 .14
❑ 54 Edgardo Alfonzo .30 .14
❑ 55 Wade Boggs .75 .35
❑ 56 Jose Guillen .30 .14
❑ 57 Ken Caminiti .50 .23
❑ 58 Paul Molitor .75 .35
❑ 59 Shawn Estes .30 .14
❑ 60 Edgar Martinez .30 .14
❑ 61 Livan Hernandez .30 .14
❑ 62 Ray Lankford .30 .14
❑ 63 Rusty Greer .30 .14
❑ 64 Jim Edmonds .50 .23
❑ 65 Tom Glavine .75 .35
❑ 66 Alan Benes .30 .14
❑ 67 Will Clark .75 .35
❑ 68 Garret Anderson .30 .14
❑ 69 Javier Lopez .30 .14
❑ 70 Mike Mussina .75 .35
❑ 71 Kevin Orie .20 .09
❑ 72 Matt Williams .30 .14
❑ 73 Bobby Bonilla .30 .14
❑ 74 Ruben Rivera .30 .14
❑ 75 Jason Giambi .30 .14
❑ 76 Todd Walker .50 .23
❑ 77 Tino Martinez .75 .35
❑ 78 Matt Morris .30 .14
❑ 79 Fernando Tatis .30 .14
❑ 80 Todd Greene .30 .14
❑ 81 Fred McGriff .50 .23
❑ 82 Brady Anderson .30 .14
❑ 83 Mark Kotsay .50 .23
❑ 84 Raul Mondesi .50 .23
❑ 85 Moises Alou .50 .23
❑ 86 Roger Clemens 1.50 .70
❑ 87 Wilton Guerrero .20 .09
❑ 88 Shannon Stewart .30 .14
❑ 89 Chan Ho Park .75 .35
❑ 90 Carlos Delgado .30 .14
❑ 91 Jose Cruz Jr. 1.00 .45
❑ 92 Shawn Green .30 .14
❑ 93 Robin Ventura .30 .14
❑ 94 Reggie Sanders .30 .14
❑ 95 Orel Hershiser .30 .14
❑ 96 Dante Bichette .30 .14
❑ 97 Charles Johnson .30 .14
❑ 98 Pedro Martinez .75 .35
❑ 99 Mariano Rivera .30 .14
❑ 100 Joe Randa .20 .09
❑ 101 Jeff Kent .30 .14
❑ 102 Jay Buhner .30 .14
❑ 103 Brian Jordan .30 .14
❑ 104 Jason Kendall .30 .14
❑ 105 Scott Spiezio .20 .09
❑ 106 Desi Relaford .20 .09
❑ 107 Bernard Gilkey .20 .09
❑ 108 Manny Ramirez .75 .35
❑ 109 Tony Clark .50 .23
❑ 110 Eric Young .30 .14
❑ 111 Johnny Damon .30 .14
❑ 112 Glendon Rusch .20 .09
❑ 113 Ben Grieve 1.50 .70
❑ 114 Homer Bush .20 .09
❑ 115 Miguel Tejada .30 .14
❑ 116 Lou Collier .20 .09
❑ 117 Derrek Lee .30 .14
❑ 118 Jacob Cruz .20 .09
❑ 119 Raul Ibanez .20 .09
❑ 120 Ryan McGuire .20 .09
❑ 121 Antone Williamson .20 .09
❑ 122 Abraham Nunez .30 .14
❑ 123 Jeff Abbott .30 .14
❑ 124 Brett Tomko .30 .14
❑ 125 Richie Sexson .50 .23
❑ 126 Todd Helton 1.00 .45
❑ 127 Juan Encarnacion .30 .14
❑ 128 Richard Hidalgo .30 .14
❑ 129 Paul Konerko .75 .35
❑ 130 Brad Fullmer .30 .14
❑ 131 Jeremi Gonzalez .30 .14
❑ 132 Jaret Wright 1.00 .45
❑ 133 Derek Jeter IT 1.00 .45
❑ 134 Frank Thomas IT 1.25 .55
❑ 135 Nomar Garciaparra IT 1.25 .55
❑ 136 Kenny Lofton IT .30 .14
❑ 137 Jeff Bagwell IT .75 .35
❑ 138 Todd Hundley IT .20 .09
❑ 139 Alex Rodriguez IT 1.25 .55
❑ 140 Ken Griffey Jr. IT 2.00 .90
❑ 141 Sammy Sosa IT 1.00 .45
❑ 142 Greg Maddux IT 1.25 .55
❑ 143 Albert Belle IT .30 .14
❑ 144 Cal Ripken IT 1.50 .70
❑ 145 Mark McGwire IT 2.50 1.10
❑ 146 Chipper Jones IT 1.00 .45
❑ 147 Charles Johnson IT .20 .09
❑ 148 Ken Griffey Jr. CL 2.00 .90
❑ 149 Jose Cruz Jr. CL .30 .14
❑ 150 Larry Walker CL .30 .14

1998 Pinnacle Inside Diamond Edition

	MINT	NRMT
COMMON CARD (1-150)	15.00	6.75

*STARS: 30X TO 80X BASIC CARDS
*YOUNG STARS: 25X TO 60X BASIC CARDS

1998 Pinnacle Inside Behind the Numbers

	MINT	NRMT
COMPLETE SET (20)	300.00	135.00
COMMON CARD (1-20)	4.00	1.80

❑ 1 Ken Griffey Jr. 40.00 18.00
❑ 2 Cal Ripken 30.00 13.50
❑ 3 Alex Rodriguez 25.00 11.00
❑ 4 Jose Cruz Jr. 8.00 3.60
❑ 5 Mike Piazza 25.00 11.00
❑ 6 Nomar Garciaparra 25.00 11.00
❑ 7 Scott Rolen 15.00 6.75
❑ 8 Andruw Jones 8.00 3.60
❑ 9 Frank Thomas 25.00 11.00
❑ 10 Mark McGwire 50.00 22.00
❑ 11 Ivan Rodriguez 10.00 4.50
❑ 12 Greg Maddux 25.00 11.00
❑ 13 Roger Clemens 15.00 6.75
❑ 14 Derek Jeter 20.00 9.00
❑ 15 Tony Gwynn 20.00 9.00
❑ 16 Ben Grieve 12.00 5.50
❑ 17 Jeff Bagwell 12.00 5.50
❑ 18 Chipper Jones 20.00 9.00
❑ 19 Hideo Nomo 10.00 4.50
❑ 20 Sandy Alomar Jr. 4.00 1.80

1998 Pinnacle Inside Cans

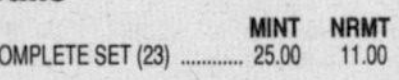

	MINT	NRMT
COMPLETE SET (23)	25.00	11.00

COMMON CAN (1-23)	.50	.23
COMP.GOLD CAN SET (23)	250.00	110.00

*GOLD CANS: 3X TO 8X HI COLUMN

COMMON GOLD SEALED CAN	12.00	5.50

*GOLD SEALED: 4X TO 10X HI ON 1.50+ CANS
GOLD CAN STATED ODDS 1:24 HOBBY

❑ 1 Roger Clemens 1.25 .55
❑ 2 Jose Cruz Jr. .75 .35
❑ 3 Nomar Garciaparra ROY 2.00 .90
❑ 4 Juan Gonzalez 1.50 .70
❑ 5 Ben Grieve 1.25 .55
❑ 6 Ken Griffey Jr. 3.00 1.35
❑ 7 Vladimir Guerrero 1.00 .45
❑ 8 Tony Gwynn 1.50 .70
❑ 9 Derek Jeter 1.50 .70
❑ 10 Andruw Jones .75 .35
❑ 11 Chipper Jones 1.50 .70
❑ 12 Greg Maddux 2.00 .90
❑ 13 Mark McGwire 4.00 1.80
❑ 14 Hideo Nomo .75 .35
❑ 15 Mike Piazza 2.00 .90
❑ 16 Cal Ripken 2.50 1.10
❑ 17 Alex Rodriguez 2.00 .90
❑ 18 Scott Rolen ROY 1.50 .70
❑ 19 Frank Thomas 2.00 .90
❑ 20 Larry Walker MVP .60 .25
❑ 21 Arizona Diamondbacks 1.00 .45
❑ 22 Florida Marlins Champs .50 .23
❑ 23 Tampa Bay Devil Rays 1.00 .45

1998 Pinnacle Inside Stand-Up Guys

	MINT	NRMT
COMPLETE SET (50)	80.00	36.00
COMMON CARD (1AB-25CD)	1.25	.55

❑ 1AB Mike Piazza 8.00 3.60
Ken Griffey Jr.
Tony Gwynn
Cal Ripken
❑ 1CD Ken Griffey Jr. 8.00 3.60
Tony Gwynn
Cal Ripken
Mike Piazza
❑ 2AB Nomar Garciaparra 5.00 2.20
Andruw Jones
Scott Rolen

Alex Rodriguez
❑ 2CD Andruw Jones 5.00 2.20
Scott Rolen
Alex Rodriguez
Nomar Garciaparra
❑ 3AB Chipper Jones 5.00 2.20
Andruw Jones
Javy Lopez
Greg Maddux
❑ 3CD Andruw Jones 5.00 2.20
Javy Lopez
Greg Maddux
Chipper Jones
❑ 4AB Alex Rodriguez............ 6.00 2.70
Jay Buhner
Ken Griffey Jr.
Randy Johnson
❑ 4CD Jay Buhner.................. 6.00 2.70
Ken Griffey Jr.
Randy Johnson
Alex Rodriguez
❑ 5AB Mo Vaughn.................. 8.00 3.60
Frank Thomas
Mark McGwire
Jeff Bagwell
❑ 5CD Frank Thomas 8.00 3.60
Mark McGwire
Jeff Bagwell
Mo Vaughn
❑ 6AB Barry Larkin 5.00 2.20
Nomar Garciaparra
Alex Rodriguez
Derek Jeter
❑ 6CD Nomar Garciaparra 5.00 2.20
Alex Rodriguez
Derek Jeter
Barry Larkin
❑ 7AB Javy Lopez.................. 3.00 1.35
Mike Piazza
Charles Johnson
Ivan Rodriguez
❑ 7CD Mike Piazza 3.00 1.35
Charles Johnson
Ivan Rodriguez
Javy Lopez
❑ 8AB Scott Rolen.................. 5.00 2.20
Cal Ripken
Ken Caminiti
Chipper Jones
❑ 8CD Cal Ripken 5.00 2.20
Ken Caminiti
Chipper Jones
Scott Rolen
❑ 9AB Jose Guillen 2.50 1.10
Jose Cruz Jr.
Andruw Jones
Vladimir Guerrero
❑ 9CD Jose Cruz Jr. 2.50 1.10
Andruw Jones
Vladimir Guerrero
Jose Guillen
❑ 10AB Neifi Perez .... 1.25 .55
Larry Walker
Ellis Burks
Dante Bichette
❑ 10CD Larry Walker............. 1.25 .55
Ellis Burks
Dante Bichette
Neifi Perez
❑ 11AB Manny Ramirez 3.00 1.35
Juan Gonzalez
Vladimir Guerrero
Sammy Sosa
❑ 11CD Juan Gonzalez.......... 3.00 1.35
Vladimir Guerrero
Sammy Sosa
Manny Ramirez
❑ 12AB Randy Johnson 5.00 2.20
Greg Maddux
Hideo Nomo
Roger Clemens
❑ 12CD Greg Maddux............ 5.00 2.20
Hideo Nomo
Roger Clemens
Randy Johnson
❑ 13AB Fernando Tatis.......... 3.00 1.35
Ben Grieve
Jose Cruz Jr.
Paul Konerko
❑ 13CD Ben Grieve................ 3.00 1.35
Jose Cruz Jr.
Paul Konerko
Fernando Tatis
❑ 14AB Craig Biggio .... 2.00 .90
Ryne Sandberg
Roberto Alomar
Chuck Knoblauch
❑ 14CD Ryne Sandberg .... 2.00 .90
Roberto Alomar
Chuck Knoblauch
Craig Biggio
❑ 15AB Roberto Alomar 4.00 1.80
Cal Ripken
Rafael Palmeiro
Brady Anderson
❑ 15CD Cal Ripken 4.00 1.80
Rafael Palmeiro
Brady Anderson
Roberto Alomar
❑ 16AB Garret Anderson........ 1.50 .70
Darin Erstad
Tim Salmon
Jim Edmonds
❑ 16CD Darin Erstad............. 1.50 .70
Tim Salmon
Jim Edmonds
Garret Anderson
❑ 17AB Eric Karros 4.00 1.80
Mike Piazza
Raul Mondesi
Hideo Nomo
❑ 17CD Mike Piazza 4.00 1.80
Raul Mondesi
Hideo Nomo
Eric Karros
❑ 18AB Rusty Greer 2.50 1.10
Ivan Rodriguez
Will Clark
Juan Gonzalez
❑ 18CD Ivan Rodriguez.......... 2.50 1.10
Will Clark
Juan Gonzalez
Rusty Greer
❑ 19AB Andy Pettitte............. 2.50 1.10
Derek Jeter
Tino Martinez
Bernie Williams
❑ 19CD Derek Jeter 2.50 1.10
Tino Martinez
Bernie Williams
Andy Pettitte
❑ 20AB Bernie Williams.......... 5.00 2.20
Kenny Lofton
Brady Anderson
Ken Griffey Jr.
❑ 20CD Kenny Lofton 5.00 2.20
Brady Anderson
Ken Griffey Jr.
Bernie Williams
❑ 21AB Rickey Henderson .... 2.00 .90
Paul Molitor
Ryne Sandberg
Eddie Murray
❑ 21CD Paul Molitor .... 2.00 .90
Ryne Sandberg
Eddie Murray
Rickey Henderson
❑ 22AB Mark McGwire 8.00 3.60
Tony Clark
Jeff Bagwell
Frank Thomas
❑ 22CD Tony Clark 8.00 3.60
Jeff Bagwell
Frank Thomas
Mark McGwire
❑ 23AB Sandy Alomar............ 1.50 .70
Manny Ramirez
David Justice
Jim Thome
❑ 23CD Manny Ramirez .... 1.50 .70
David Justice
Jim Thome
Sandy Alomar
❑ 24AB Dante Bichette 2.50 1.10
Barry Bonds
Jeff Bagwell
Albert Belle
❑ 24CD Barry Bonds 2.50 1.10
Jeff Bagwell
Albert Belle
Dante Bichette
❑ 25AB Andruw Jones............ 8.00 3.60
Ken Griffey Jr.
Alex Rodriguez
Frank Thomas
❑ 25CD Ken Griffey Jr. 8.00 3.60
Alex Rodriguez
Frank Thomas
Andruw Jones

1997 Pinnacle Mint

	MINT	NRMT
COMP.DIE CUT SET (30)	15.00	6.75
COMMON DIE CUT (1-30)..........	.15	.07

❑ 1 Ken Griffey Jr. .... 2.00 .90
❑ 2 Frank Thomas.................. 1.25 .55
❑ 3 Alex Rodriguez .... 1.25 .55
❑ 4 Cal Ripken......................... 1.50 .70
❑ 5 Mo Vaughn .... .50 .23
❑ 6 Juan Gonzalez .... 1.00 .45
❑ 7 Mike Piazza....................... 1.25 .55
❑ 8 Albert Belle .... .50 .23
❑ 9 Chipper Jones.................. 1.00 .45
❑ 10 Andruw Jones .... .60 .25
❑ 11 Greg Maddux .... 1.25 .55
❑ 12 Hideo Nomo .... .50 .23
❑ 13 Jeff Bagwell....................... .60 .25
❑ 14 Manny Ramirez.................. .40 .18
❑ 15 Mark McGwire.................. 2.00 .90
❑ 16 Derek Jeter .... 1.25 .55
❑ 17 Sammy Sosa................... 1.00 .45
❑ 18 Barry Bonds .... .50 .23
❑ 19 Chuck Knoblauch .... .40 .18
❑ 20 Dante Bichette.................. .15 .07
❑ 21 Tony Gwynn .... 1.00 .45
❑ 22 Ken Caminiti .... .25 .11
❑ 23 Gary Sheffield .... .25 .11
❑ 24 Tim Salmon........................ .40 .18
❑ 25 Ivan Rodriguez .... .50 .23
❑ 26 Henry Rodriguez................ .15 .07
❑ 27 Barry Larkin....................... .25 .11
❑ 28 Ryan Klesko .... .15 .07
❑ 29 Brian Jordan .... .15 .07
❑ 30 Jay Buhner .... .15 .07
❑ P28 Ryan Klesko Promo .... 2.00 .90

1997 Pinnacle Mint Coins Brass

	MINT	NRMT
COMP.BRASS SET (30)	50.00	22.00
COMMON BRASS (1-30)............	.40	.18

❑ 1 Ken Griffey Jr. 5.00 2.20
❑ 2 Frank Thomas.................. 3.00 1.35
❑ 3 Alex Rodriguez 3.00 1.35
❑ 4 Cal Ripken......................... 4.00 1.80

	MINT	NRMT
❑ 5 Mo Vaughn	1.25	.55
❑ 6 Juan Gonzalez	2.50	1.10
❑ 7 Mike Piazza	3.00	1.35
❑ 8 Albert Belle	1.50	.70
❑ 9 Chipper Jones	2.50	1.10
❑ 10 Andruw Jones	1.50	.70
❑ 11 Greg Maddux	3.00	1.35
❑ 12 Hideo Nomo	1.25	.55
❑ 13 Jeff Bagwell	1.50	.70
❑ 14A Manny Ramirez COR	1.00	.45
❑ 14B Manny Ramirez ERR	8.00	3.60
says "Fine Silver" on back		
❑ 15 Mark McGwire	5.00	2.20
❑ 16 Derek Jeter	3.00	1.35
❑ 17 Sammy Sosa	2.50	1.10
❑ 18 Barry Bonds	1.25	.55
❑ 19 Chuck Knoblauch	1.00	.45
❑ 20 Dante Bichette	.40	.18
❑ 21 Tony Gwynn	2.50	1.10
❑ 22 Ken Caminiti	.60	.25
❑ 23 Gary Sheffield	.60	.25
❑ 24 Tim Salmon	1.00	.45
❑ 25 Ivan Rodriguez	1.25	.55
❑ 26 Henry Rodriguez	.40	.18
❑ 27 Barry Larkin	.60	.25
❑ 28 Ryan Klesko	.40	.18
❑ 29 Brian Jordan	.40	.18
❑ 30 Jay Buhner	.40	.18
❑ P28 Ryan Klesko Promo	2.00	.90

1998 Pinnacle Mint

	MINT	NRMT
COMP.DIE CUT SET (30)	20.00	9.00
COMMON DIE CUT (1-30)	.20	.09
❑ 1 Jeff Bagwell	.75	.35
❑ 2 Albert Belle	.60	.25
❑ 3 Barry Bonds	.60	.25
❑ 4 Tony Clark	.30	.14
❑ 5 Roger Clemens	1.00	.45
❑ 6 Juan Gonzalez	1.25	.55
❑ 7 Ken Griffey Jr.	2.50	1.10
❑ 8 Tony Gwynn	1.25	.55
❑ 9 Derek Jeter	1.25	.55
❑ 10 Randy Johnson	.50	.23
❑ 11 Chipper Jones	1.25	.55
❑ 12 Greg Maddux	1.50	.70
❑ 13 Tino Martinez	.50	.23
❑ 14 Mark McGwire	3.00	1.35
❑ 15 Hideo Nomo	.60	.25
❑ 16 Andy Pettitte	.30	.14
❑ 17 Mike Piazza	1.50	.70
❑ 18 Cal Ripken Jr.	2.00	.90
❑ 19 Alex Rodriguez	1.50	.70
❑ 20 Ivan Rodriguez	.60	.25
❑ 21 Sammy Sosa	1.25	.55
❑ 22 Frank Thomas	1.50	.70
❑ 23 Mo Vaughn	.60	.25
❑ 24 Larry Walker	.50	.23
❑ 25 Jose Cruz Jr.	.60	.25
❑ 26 Nomar Garciaparra	1.50	.70
❑ 27 Vladimir Guerrero	.75	.35
❑ 28 Livan Hernandez	.20	.09
❑ 29 Andruw Jones	.60	.25
❑ 30 Scott Rolen	1.25	.55

1998 Pinnacle Mint Coins Brass

	MINT	NRMT
COMP.BRASS SET (30)	80.00	36.00
COMMON BRASS (1-30)	.60	.25
❑ 1 Jeff Bagwell	2.50	1.10
❑ 2 Albert Belle	2.00	.90
❑ 3 Barry Bonds	2.00	.90
❑ 4 Tony Clark	1.00	.45
❑ 5 Roger Clemens	3.00	1.35
❑ 6 Juan Gonzalez	4.00	1.80
❑ 7 Ken Griffey Jr.	8.00	3.60
❑ 8 Tony Gwynn	4.00	1.80
❑ 9 Derek Jeter	4.00	1.80
❑ 10 Randy Johnson	1.50	.70
❑ 11 Chipper Jones	4.00	1.80
❑ 12 Greg Maddux	5.00	2.20
❑ 13 Tino Martinez	1.50	.70
❑ 14 Mark McGwire	10.00	4.50
❑ 15 Hideo Nomo	2.00	.90
❑ 16 Andy Pettitte	1.00	.45
❑ 17 Mike Piazza	5.00	2.20
❑ 18 Cal Ripken Jr.	6.00	2.70
❑ 19 Alex Rodriguez	5.00	2.20
❑ 20 Ivan Rodriguez	2.00	.90
❑ 21 Sammy Sosa	4.00	1.80
❑ 22 Frank Thomas	5.00	2.20
❑ 23 Mo Vaughn	2.00	.90
❑ 24 Larry Walker	1.50	.70
❑ 25 Jose Cruz Jr.	2.00	.90
❑ 26 Nomar Garciaparra	5.00	2.20
❑ 27 Vladimir Guerrero	2.50	1.10
❑ 28 Livan Hernandez	.60	.25
❑ 29 Andruw Jones	2.00	.90
❑ 30 Scott Rolen	4.00	1.80

1998 Pinnacle Mint Mint Gems

	MINT	NRMT
COMPLETE SET (6)	50.00	22.00
COMMON CARD (1-6)	4.00	1.80
❑ 1 Ken Griffey Jr.	20.00	9.00
❑ 2 Larry Walker	4.00	1.80
❑ 3 Roger Clemens	8.00	3.60
❑ 4 Pedro Martinez	4.00	1.80
❑ 5 Nomar Garciaparra	12.00	5.50
❑ 6 Scott Rolen	10.00	4.50

1998 Pinnacle Performers

	MINT	NRMT
COMPLETE SET (150)	25.00	11.00
COMMON CARD (1-150)	.10	.05
❑ 1 Ken Griffey Jr.	2.00	.90
❑ 2 Frank Thomas	1.25	.55
❑ 3 Cal Ripken	1.50	.70
❑ 4 Alex Rodriguez	1.25	.55
❑ 5 Greg Maddux	1.25	.55
❑ 6 Mike Piazza	1.25	.55
❑ 7 Chipper Jones	1.00	.45
❑ 8 Tony Gwynn	1.00	.45
❑ 9 Derek Jeter	1.00	.45
❑ 10 Jeff Bagwell	.60	.25
❑ 11 Juan Gonzalez	1.00	.45
❑ 12 Nomar Garciaparra	1.25	.55
❑ 13 Andruw Jones	.50	.23
❑ 14 Hideo Nomo	.50	.23
❑ 15 Roger Clemens	.75	.35
❑ 16 Mark McGwire	2.50	1.10
❑ 17 Scott Rolen	1.00	.45
❑ 18 Vladimir Guerrero	.60	.25
❑ 19 Barry Bonds	.50	.23
❑ 20 Darin Erstad	.50	.23
❑ 21 Albert Belle	.40	.18
❑ 22 Kenny Lofton	.40	.18
❑ 23 Mo Vaughn	.50	.23
❑ 24 Tony Clark	.25	.11
❑ 25 Ivan Rodriguez	.50	.23
❑ 26 Jose Cruz Jr.	.50	.23
❑ 27 Larry Walker	.40	.18
❑ 28 Jaret Wright	.50	.23
❑ 29 Andy Pettitte	.25	.11
❑ 30 Roberto Alomar	.40	.18
❑ 31 Randy Johnson	.40	.18
❑ 32 Manny Ramirez	.40	.18
❑ 33 Paul Molitor	.40	.18
❑ 34 Mike Mussina	.40	.18
❑ 35 Jim Thome	.40	.18
❑ 36 Tino Martinez	.40	.18
❑ 37 Gary Sheffield	.25	.11
❑ 38 Chuck Knoblauch	.40	.18
❑ 39 Bernie Williams	.40	.18
❑ 40 Tim Salmon	.40	.18
❑ 41 Sammy Sosa	1.00	.45
❑ 42 Wade Boggs	.40	.18
❑ 43 Will Clark	.40	.18
❑ 44 Andres Galarraga	.40	.18
❑ 45 Raul Mondesi	.25	.11
❑ 46 Rickey Henderson	.40	.18
❑ 47 Jose Canseco	.40	.18
❑ 48 Pedro Martinez	.40	.18
❑ 49 Jay Buhner	.15	.07

❑ 50	Ryan Klesko	.15	.07
❑ 51	Barry Larkin	.25	.11
❑ 52	Charles Johnson	.15	.07
❑ 53	Tom Glavine	.40	.18
❑ 54	Edgar Martinez	.15	.07
❑ 55	Fred McGriff	.25	.11
❑ 56	Moises Alou	.25	.11
❑ 57	Dante Bichette	.15	.07
❑ 58	Jim Edmonds	.25	.11
❑ 59	Mark Grace	.25	.11
❑ 60	Chan Ho Park	.40	.18
❑ 61	Justin Thompson	.15	.07
❑ 62	John Smoltz	.15	.07
❑ 63	Craig Biggio	.40	.18
❑ 64	Ken Caminiti	.25	.11
❑ 65	Richard Hidalgo	.15	.07
❑ 66	Carlos Delgado	.15	.07
❑ 67	David Justice	.40	.18
❑ 68	J.T. Snow	.15	.07
❑ 69	Jason Giambi	.15	.07
❑ 70	Garret Anderson	.15	.07
❑ 71	Rondell White	.15	.07
❑ 72	Matt Williams	.15	.07
❑ 73	Brady Anderson	.15	.07
❑ 74	Eric Karros	.15	.07
❑ 75	Javier Lopez	.15	.07
❑ 76	Pat Hentgen	.15	.07
❑ 77	Todd Hundley	.15	.07
❑ 78	Ray Lankford	.15	.07
❑ 79	Denny Neagle	.15	.07
❑ 80	Sandy Alomar Jr.	.15	.07
❑ 81	Jason Kendall	.15	.07
❑ 82	Omar Vizquel	.15	.07
❑ 83	Kevin Brown	.25	.11
❑ 84	Kevin Appier	.15	.07
❑ 85	Al Martin	.10	.05
❑ 86	Rusty Greer	.15	.07
❑ 87	Bobby Bonilla	.15	.07
❑ 88	Shawn Estes	.15	.07
❑ 89	Rafael Palmeiro	.25	.11
❑ 90	Edgar Renteria	.15	.07
❑ 91	Alan Benes	.15	.07
❑ 92	Bobby Higginson	.25	.11
❑ 93	Mark Grudzielanek	.15	.07
❑ 94	Jose Guillen	.15	.07
❑ 95	Neifi Perez	.15	.07
❑ 96	Jeff Abbott	.15	.07
❑ 97	Todd Walker	.25	.11
❑ 98	Eric Young	.15	.07
❑ 99	Brett Tomko	.15	.07
❑ 100	Mike Cameron	.15	.07
❑ 101	Karim Garcia	.15	.07
❑ 102	Brian Jordan	.15	.07
❑ 103	Jeff Suppan	.10	.05
❑ 104	Robin Ventura	.15	.07
❑ 105	Henry Rodriguez	.15	.07
❑ 106	Shannon Stewart	.15	.07
❑ 107	Kevin Orie	.10	.05
❑ 108	Bartolo Colon	.15	.07
❑ 109	Bob Abreu	.15	.07
❑ 110	Vinny Castilla	.25	.11
❑ 111	Livan Hernandez	.15	.07
❑ 112	Derrek Lee	.15	.07
❑ 113	Mark Kotsay	.25	.11
❑ 114	Todd Greene	.15	.07
❑ 115	Edgardo Alfonzo	.15	.07
❑ 116	A.J. Hinch	.15	.07
❑ 117	Paul Konerko	.40	.18
❑ 118	Todd Helton	.50	.23
❑ 119	Miguel Tejada	.15	.07
❑ 120	Fernando Tatis	.15	.07
❑ 121	Ben Grieve	.75	.35
❑ 122	Travis Lee	.75	.35
❑ 123	Kerry Wood	2.00	.90
❑ 124	Eli Marrero	.15	.07
❑ 125	David Ortiz	.15	.07
❑ 126	Juan Encarnacion	.15	.07
❑ 127	Brad Fullmer	.15	.07
❑ 128	Richie Sexson	.25	.11
❑ 129	Aaron Boone	.10	.05
❑ 130	Enrique Wilson	.15	.07
❑ 131	Javier Valentin	.15	.07
❑ 132	Abraham Nunez	.15	.07
❑ 133	Ricky Ledee	.15	.07
❑ 134	Carl Pavano	.15	.07
❑ 135	Bobby Estalella	.15	.07
❑ 136	Homer Bush	.10	.05
❑ 137	Brian Rose	.15	.07
❑ 138	Ken Griffey Jr. FA	1.00	.45
❑ 139	Frank Thomas FA	.60	.25
❑ 140	Cal Ripken FA	.75	.35
❑ 141	Alex Rodriguez FA	.60	.25
❑ 142	Greg Maddux FA	.60	.25
❑ 143	Chipper Jones FA	.50	.23
❑ 144	Mike Piazza FA	.60	.25
❑ 145	Tony Gwynn FA	.50	.23
❑ 146	Derek Jeter FA	.50	.23
❑ 147	Jeff Bagwell FA	.40	.18
❑ 148	Checklist	.10	.05
❑ 149	Checklist	.10	.05
❑ 150	Checklist	.10	.05

1998 Pinnacle Performers Big Bang

	MINT	NRMT
COMPLETE SET (20)	350.00	160.00
COMMON CARD (1-20)	6.00	2.70
❑ 1 Ken Griffey Jr.	50.00	22.00
❑ 2 Frank Thomas	30.00	13.50
❑ 3 Mike Piazza	30.00	13.50
❑ 4 Chipper Jones	25.00	11.00
❑ 5 Alex Rodriguez	30.00	13.50
❑ 6 Nomar Garciaparra	30.00	13.50
❑ 7 Jeff Bagwell	15.00	6.75
❑ 8 Cal Ripken	40.00	18.00
❑ 9 Albert Belle	10.00	4.50
❑ 10 Mark McGwire	60.00	27.00
❑ 11 Juan Gonzalez	25.00	11.00
❑ 12 Larry Walker	10.00	4.50
❑ 13 Tino Martinez	10.00	4.50
❑ 14 Jim Thome	10.00	4.50
❑ 15 Manny Ramirez	10.00	4.50
❑ 16 Barry Bonds	12.00	5.50
❑ 17 Mo Vaughn	12.00	5.50
❑ 18 Jose Cruz Jr.	10.00	4.50
❑ 19 Tony Clark	6.00	2.70
❑ 20 Andruw Jones	10.00	4.50

1998 Pinnacle Performers Big Bang Seasonal Outburst

	MINT	NRMT
COMMON CARD (1-20)	60.00	27.00
❑ 1 Ken Griffey Jr./56	400.00	180.00
❑ 2 Frank Thomas/35	300.00	135.00
❑ 3 Mike Piazza/40	250.00	110.00
❑ 4 Chipper Jones/21	500.00	220.00
❑ 5 Alex Rodriguez/23	500.00	220.00
❑ 6 Nomar Garciaparra/30	300.00	135.00
❑ 7 Jeff Bagwell/43	120.00	55.00
❑ 8 Cal Ripken/17	1000.00	450.00
❑ 9 Albert Belle/30	100.00	45.00
❑ 10 Mark McGwire/58	500.00	220.00
❑ 11 Juan Gonzalez/42	200.00	90.00
❑ 12 Larry Walker/49	80.00	36.00
❑ 13 Tino Martinez/44	60.00	27.00
❑ 14 Jim Thome/40	80.00	36.00
❑ 15 Manny Ramirez/26	120.00	55.00
❑ 16 Barry Bonds/40	100.00	45.00
❑ 17 Mo Vaughn/35	120.00	55.00
❑ 18 Jose Cruz Jr./26	120.00	55.00
❑ 19 Tony Clark/32	60.00	27.00
❑ 20 Andruw Jones/18	250.00	110.00

1998 Pinnacle Performers Launching Pad

	MINT	NRMT
COMPLETE SET (20)	100.00	45.00
COMMON CARD (1-20)	1.50	.70
❑ 1 Ben Grieve	4.00	1.80
❑ 2 Ken Griffey Jr.	12.00	5.50
❑ 3 Derek Jeter	6.00	2.70
❑ 4 Frank Thomas	8.00	3.60
❑ 5 Travis Lee	4.00	1.80
❑ 6 Vladimir Guerrero	3.00	1.35
❑ 7 Tony Gwynn	6.00	2.70
❑ 8 Jose Cruz Jr.	2.50	1.10
❑ 9 Cal Ripken	10.00	4.50
❑ 10 Chipper Jones	6.00	2.70
❑ 11 Scott Rolen	5.00	2.20
❑ 12 Andruw Jones	2.50	1.10
❑ 13 Ivan Rodriguez	3.00	1.35
❑ 14 Todd Helton	2.50	1.10
❑ 15 Nomar Garciaparra	8.00	3.60
❑ 16 Mark McGwire	15.00	6.75
❑ 17 Gary Sheffield	1.50	.70
❑ 18 Bernie Williams	2.50	1.10
❑ 19 Alex Rodriguez	8.00	3.60
❑ 20 Mike Piazza	8.00	3.60

1998 Pinnacle Performers Power Trip

	MINT	NRMT
COMPLETE SET (10)	100.00	45.00
COMMON CARD (1-10)	6.00	2.70
❑ 1 Frank Thomas	12.00	5.50
❑ 2 Alex Rodriguez	12.00	5.50
❑ 3 Nomar Garciaparra	12.00	5.50
❑ 4 Jeff Bagwell	6.00	2.70
❑ 5 Cal Ripken	15.00	6.75
❑ 6 Mike Piazza	12.00	5.50

Card	MINT	NRMT
❑ 7 Chipper Jones	10.00	4.50
❑ 8 Ken Griffey Jr.	20.00	9.00
❑ 9 Mark McGwire	25.00	11.00
❑ 10 Juan Gonzalez	10.00	4.50

1998 Pinnacle Performers Swing for the Fences

	MINT	NRMT
COMPLETE SET (50)	50.00	22.00
COMMON CARD (1-50)	.40	.18
❑ 1 Brady Anderson	.40	.18
❑ 2 Albert Belle	1.00	.45
❑ 3 Jay Buhner	.40	.18
❑ 4 Jose Canseco	1.00	.45
❑ 5 Tony Clark	.60	.25
❑ 6 Jose Cruz Jr.	1.25	.55
❑ 7 Jim Edmonds	.60	.25
❑ 8 Cecil Fielder	.40	.18
❑ 9 Travis Fryman	.40	.18
❑ 10 Nomar Garciaparra	3.00	1.35
❑ 11 Juan Gonzalez	2.50	1.10
❑ 12 Ken Griffey Jr.	5.00	2.20
❑ 13 David Justice	1.00	.45
❑ 14 Travis Lee	2.00	.90
❑ 15 Edgar Martinez	.40	.18
❑ 16 Tino Martinez	1.00	.45
❑ 17 Rafael Palmeiro	.60	.25
❑ 18 Manny Ramirez	1.00	.45
❑ 19 Cal Ripken	4.00	1.80
❑ 20 Alex Rodriguez	3.00	1.35
❑ 21 Tim Salmon	1.00	.45
❑ 22 Frank Thomas	3.00	1.35
❑ 23 Jim Thome	1.00	.45
❑ 24 Mo Vaughn	1.25	.55
❑ 25 Bernie Williams	1.00	.45
❑ 26 Fred McGriff	.60	.25
❑ 27 Jeff Bagwell	1.50	.70
❑ 28 Dante Bichette	.40	.18
❑ 29 Barry Bonds	1.25	.55
❑ 30 Ellis Burks	.40	.18
❑ 31 Ken Caminiti	.60	.25
❑ 32 Vinny Castilla	.60	.25
❑ 33 Andres Galarraga	1.00	.45
❑ 34 Vladimir Guerrero	1.50	.70
❑ 35 Todd Helton	1.25	.55
❑ 36 Todd Hundley	.40	.18
❑ 37 Andruw Jones	1.25	.55
❑ 38 Chipper Jones	2.50	1.10
❑ 39 Eric Karros	.40	.18
❑ 40 Ryan Klesko	.40	.18
❑ 41 Ray Lankford	.40	.18
❑ 42 Mark McGwire	6.00	2.70
❑ 43 Raul Mondesi	.60	.25
❑ 44 Mike Piazza	3.00	1.35
❑ 45 Scott Rolen	2.50	1.10
❑ 46 Gary Sheffield	.60	.25
❑ 47 Sammy Sosa	2.50	1.10
❑ 48 Larry Walker	1.00	.45
❑ 49 Matt Williams	.40	.18
❑ 50 Wild Card	.40	.18

1998 Pinnacle Plus

	MINT	NRMT
COMPLETE SET (200)	30.00	13.50
COMMON CARD (1-200)	.10	.05
❑ 1 Roberto Alomar	.50	.23
❑ 2 Sandy Alomar Jr.	.20	.09
❑ 3 Brady Anderson	.20	.09
❑ 4 Albert Belle	.50	.23
❑ 5 Jeff Cirillo	.20	.09
❑ 6 Roger Clemens	1.00	.45
❑ 7 David Cone	.30	.14
❑ 8 Nomar Garciaparra	1.50	.70
❑ 9 Ken Griffey Jr.	2.50	1.10
❑ 10 Jason Dickson	.20	.09
❑ 11 Edgar Martinez	.20	.09
❑ 12 Tino Martinez	.50	.23
❑ 13 Randy Johnson	.50	.23
❑ 14 Mark McGwire	3.00	1.35
❑ 15 David Justice	.50	.23
❑ 16 Mike Mussina	.50	.23
❑ 17 Chuck Knoblauch	.50	.23
❑ 18 Joey Cora	.20	.09
❑ 19 Pat Hentgen	.20	.09
❑ 20 Randy Myers	.20	.09
❑ 21 Cal Ripken	2.00	.90
❑ 22 Mariano Rivera	.20	.09
❑ 23 Jose Rosado	.10	.05
❑ 24 Frank Thomas	1.50	.70
❑ 25 Alex Rodriguez	1.50	.70
❑ 26 Justin Thompson	.20	.09
❑ 27 Ivan Rodriguez	.60	.25
❑ 28 Bernie Williams	.50	.23
❑ 29 Pedro Martinez	.50	.23
❑ 30 Tony Clark	.30	.14
❑ 31 Garret Anderson	.20	.09
❑ 32 Travis Fryman	.20	.09
❑ 33 Mike Piazza	1.50	.70
❑ 34 Carl Pavano	.20	.09
❑ 35 Kevin Millwood	1.25	.55
❑ 36 Miguel Tejada	.20	.09
❑ 37 Willie Blair	.10	.05
❑ 38 Devon White	.20	.09
❑ 39 Andres Galarraga	.50	.23
❑ 40 Barry Larkin	.30	.14
❑ 41 Al Leiter	.20	.09
❑ 42 Moises Alou	.30	.14
❑ 43 Eric Young	.20	.09
❑ 44 John Jaha	.10	.05
❑ 45 Bernard Gilkey	.10	.05
❑ 46 Freddy Garcia	.10	.05
❑ 47 Ruben Rivera	.20	.09
❑ 48 Robb Nen	.20	.09
❑ 49 Ray Lankford	.20	.09
❑ 50 Kenny Lofton	.50	.23
❑ 51 Joe Carter	.20	.09
❑ 52 Jason McDonald	.10	.05
❑ 53 Quinton McCracken	.20	.09
❑ 54 Kerry Wood	2.50	1.10
❑ 55 Mike Lansing	.10	.05
❑ 56 Chipper Jones	1.25	.55
❑ 57 Barry Bonds	.60	.25
❑ 58 Brad Fullmer	.20	.09
❑ 59 Jeff Bagwell	.75	.35
❑ 60 Rondell White	.20	.09
❑ 61 Geronimo Berroa	.10	.05
❑ 62 Magglio Ordonez	.60	.25
❑ 63 Dwight Gooden	.20	.09
❑ 64 Brian Hunter	.20	.09
❑ 65 Todd Walker	.30	.14
❑ 66 Frank Catalanotto	.25	.11
❑ 67 Tony Saunders	.10	.05
❑ 68 Travis Lee	1.00	.45
❑ 69 Michael Tucker	.20	.09
❑ 70 Reggie Sanders	.20	.09
❑ 71 Derrek Lee	.20	.09
❑ 72 Larry Walker	.50	.23
❑ 73 Marquis Grissom	.20	.09
❑ 74 Craig Biggio	.50	.23
❑ 75 Kevin Brown	.30	.14
❑ 76 J.T. Snow	.20	.09
❑ 77 Eric Davis	.20	.09
❑ 78 Jeff Abbott	.20	.09
❑ 79 Jermaine Dye	.10	.05
❑ 80 Otis Nixon	.10	.05
❑ 81 Curt Schilling	.20	.09
❑ 82 Enrique Wilson	.20	.09
❑ 83 Tony Gwynn	1.25	.55
❑ 84 Orlando Cabrera	.20	.09
❑ 85 Ramon Martinez	.20	.09
❑ 86 Greg Vaughn	.20	.09
❑ 87 Alan Benes	.20	.09
❑ 88 Dennis Eckersley	.20	.09
❑ 89 Jim Thome	.50	.23
❑ 90 Juan Encarnacion	.20	.09
❑ 91 Jeff King	.20	.09
❑ 92 Shannon Stewart	.20	.09
❑ 93 Roberto Hernandez	.10	.05
❑ 94 Raul Ibanez	.10	.05
❑ 95 Darryl Kile	.20	.09
❑ 96 Charles Johnson	.20	.09
❑ 97 Rich Becker	.10	.05
❑ 98 Hal Morris	.10	.05
❑ 99 Ismael Valdes	.20	.09
❑ 100 Orel Hershiser	.20	.09
❑ 101 Mo Vaughn	.60	.25
❑ 102 Aaron Boone	.10	.05
❑ 103 Jeff Conine	.20	.09
❑ 104 Paul O'Neill	.20	.09
❑ 105 Tom Candiotti	.10	.05
❑ 106 Wilson Alvarez	.20	.09
❑ 107 Mike Stanley	.10	.05
❑ 108 Carlos Delgado	.20	.09
❑ 109 Tony Batista	.10	.05
❑ 110 Dante Bichette	.20	.09
❑ 111 Henry Rodriguez	.20	.09
❑ 112 Karim Garcia	.20	.09
❑ 113 Shane Reynolds	.20	.09
❑ 114 Ken Caminiti	.30	.14
❑ 115 Jose Silva	.10	.05
❑ 116 Juan Gonzalez	1.25	.55
❑ 117 Brian Jordan	.20	.09
❑ 118 Jim Leyritz	.10	.05
❑ 119 Manny Ramirez	.50	.23
❑ 120 Fred McGriff	.30	.14
❑ 121 Brooks Kieschnick	.10	.05
❑ 122 Sean Casey	.20	.09
❑ 123 John Smoltz	.20	.09
❑ 124 Rusty Greer	.20	.09
❑ 125 Cecil Fielder	.20	.09
❑ 126 Mike Cameron	.20	.09
❑ 127 Reggie Jefferson	.10	.05
❑ 128 Bobby Higginson	.30	.14
❑ 129 Kevin Appier	.20	.09
❑ 130 Robin Ventura	.20	.09
❑ 131 Ben Grieve	1.00	.45
❑ 132 Wade Boggs	.50	.23

Card	MINT	NRMT
❑ 133 Jose Cruz Jr.	.60	.25
❑ 134 Jeff Suppan	.10	.05
❑ 135 Vinny Castilla	.30	.14
❑ 136 Sammy Sosa	1.25	.55
❑ 137 Mark Wohlers	.10	.05
❑ 138 Jay Bell	.20	.09
❑ 139 Brett Tomko	.20	.09
❑ 140 Gary Sheffield	.30	.14
❑ 141 Tim Salmon	.50	.23
❑ 142 Jaret Wright	.60	.25
❑ 143 Kenny Rogers	.10	.05
❑ 144 Brian Anderson	.20	.09
❑ 145 Darrin Fletcher	.10	.05
❑ 146 John Flaherty	.10	.05
❑ 147 Dmitri Young	.20	.09
❑ 148 Andruw Jones	.60	.25
❑ 149 Matt Williams	.20	.09
❑ 150 Bobby Bonilla	.20	.09
❑ 151 Mike Hampton	.10	.05
❑ 152 Al Martin	.10	.05
❑ 153 Mark Grudzielanek	.20	.09
❑ 154 Dave Nilsson	.10	.05
❑ 155 Roger Cedeno	.10	.05
❑ 156 Greg Maddux	1.50	.70
❑ 157 Mark Kotsay	.30	.14
❑ 158 Steve Finley	.20	.09
❑ 159 Wilson Delgado	.20	.09
❑ 160 Ron Gant	.10	.05
❑ 161 Jim Edmonds	.30	.14
❑ 162 Jeff Blauser	.10	.05
❑ 163 Dave Burba	.10	.05
❑ 164 Pedro Astacio	.10	.05
❑ 165 Livan Hernandez	.20	.09
❑ 166 Neifi Perez	.20	.09
❑ 167 Ryan Klesko	.20	.09
❑ 168 Fernando Tatis	.20	.09
❑ 169 Richard Hidalgo	.20	.09
❑ 170 Carlos Perez	.20	.09
❑ 171 Bob Abreu	.20	.09
❑ 172 Francisco Cordova	.10	.05
❑ 173 Todd Helton	.60	.25
❑ 174 Doug Glanville	.20	.09
❑ 175 Brian Rose	.20	.09
❑ 176 Yamil Benitez	.10	.05
❑ 177 Darin Erstad	.60	.25
❑ 178 Scott Rolen	1.25	.55
❑ 179 John Wetteland	.20	.09
❑ 180 Paul Sorrento	.10	.05
❑ 181 Walt Weiss	.20	.09
❑ 182 Vladimir Guerrero	.75	.35
❑ 183 Ken Griffey Jr. NAT	1.25	.55
❑ 184 Alex Rodriguez NAT	.75	.35
❑ 185 Cal Ripken NAT	1.00	.45
❑ 186 Frank Thomas NAT	.75	.35
❑ 187 Chipper Jones NAT	.60	.25
❑ 188 Hideo Nomo NAT	.50	.23
❑ 189 Nomar Garciaparra NAT	.75	.35
❑ 190 Mike Piazza NAT	.75	.35
❑ 191 Greg Maddux NAT	.75	.35
❑ 192 Tony Gwynn NAT	.60	.25
❑ 193 Mark McGwire NAT	1.50	.70
❑ 194 Roger Clemens NAT	.50	.23
❑ 195 Mike Piazza FV	.75	.35
❑ 196 Mark McGwire FV	1.50	.70
❑ 197 Chipper Jones FV	.60	.25
❑ 198 Larry Walker FV	.20	.09
❑ 199 Hideo Nomo FV	.50	.23
❑ 200 Barry Bonds FV	.30	.14

1998 Pinnacle Plus Artist's Proofs

	MINT	NRMT
COMPLETE SET (60)	600.00	275.00
COMMON CARD (PP1-PP)	5.00	2.20

Card	MINT	NRMT
❑ PP1 Roberto Alomar	12.00	5.50
❑ PP2 Albert Belle	12.00	5.50
❑ PP3 Roger Clemens	25.00	11.00
❑ PP4 Nomar Garciaparra	40.00	18.00
❑ PP5 Ken Griffey Jr.	60.00	27.00
❑ PP6 Tino Martinez	12.00	5.50
❑ PP7 Randy Johnson	12.00	5.50
❑ PP8 Mark McGwire	80.00	36.00
❑ PP9 David Justice	12.00	5.50

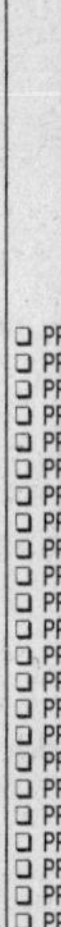

Card	MINT	NRMT
❑ PP10 Chuck Knoblauch	12.00	5.50
❑ PP11 Cal Ripken	50.00	22.00
❑ PP12 Frank Thomas	40.00	18.00
❑ PP13 Alex Rodriguez	40.00	18.00
❑ PP14 Ivan Rodriguez	15.00	6.75
❑ PP15 Bernie Williams	12.00	5.50
❑ PP16 Pedro Martinez	12.00	5.50
❑ PP17 Tony Clark	8.00	3.60
❑ PP18 Mike Piazza	40.00	18.00
❑ PP19 Miguel Tejada	5.00	2.20
❑ PP20 Andres Galarraga	12.00	5.50
❑ PP21 Barry Larkin	8.00	3.60
❑ PP22 Kenny Lofton	12.00	5.50
❑ PP23 Chipper Jones	30.00	13.50
❑ PP24 Barry Bonds	15.00	6.75
❑ PP25 Brad Fullmer	5.00	2.20
❑ PP26 Jeff Bagwell	20.00	9.00
❑ PP27 Todd Walker	8.00	3.60
❑ PP28 Travis Lee	20.00	9.00
❑ PP29 Larry Walker	12.00	5.50
❑ PP30 Craig Biggio	12.00	5.50
❑ PP31 Tony Gwynn	30.00	13.50
❑ PP32 Jim Thome	12.00	5.50
❑ PP33 Juan Encarnacion	5.00	2.20
❑ PP34 Mo Vaughn	15.00	6.75
❑ PP35 Karim Garcia	5.00	2.20
❑ PP36 Ken Caminiti	8.00	3.60
❑ PP37 Juan Gonzalez	30.00	13.50
❑ PP38 Manny Ramirez	12.00	5.50
❑ PP39 Fred McGriff	8.00	3.60
❑ PP40 Rusty Greer	5.00	2.20
❑ PP41 Bobby Higginson	8.00	3.60
❑ PP42 Ben Grieve	20.00	9.00
❑ PP43 Wade Boggs	12.00	5.50
❑ PP44 Jose Cruz Jr.	12.00	5.50
❑ PP45 Sammy Sosa	30.00	13.50
❑ PP46 Gary Sheffield	8.00	3.60
❑ PP47 Tim Salmon	12.00	5.50
❑ PP48 Jaret Wright	12.00	5.50
❑ PP49 Andruw Jones	12.00	5.50
❑ PP50 Matt Williams	5.00	2.20
❑ PP51 Greg Maddux	40.00	18.00
❑ PP52 Jim Edmonds	8.00	3.60
❑ PP53 Livan Hernandez	5.00	2.20
❑ PP54 Neifi Perez	5.00	2.20
❑ PP55 Fernando Tatis	5.00	2.20
❑ PP56 Richard Hidalgo	5.00	2.20
❑ PP57 Todd Helton	12.00	5.50
❑ PP58 Darin Erstad	12.00	5.50
❑ PP59 Scott Rolen	25.00	11.00
❑ PP60 Vladimir Guerrero	15.00	6.75

1998 Pinnacle Plus All-Star Epix

	MINT	NRMT
COMPLETE SET (24)	400.00	180.00
COMMON CARD (1-24)	5.00	2.20

Card	MINT	NRMT
❑ 1 Ken Griffey Jr. MOM	40.00	18.00
❑ 2 Juan Gonzalez MOM	20.00	9.00
❑ 3 Jeff Bagwell MOM	12.00	5.50
❑ 4 Ivan Rodriguez MOM	10.00	4.50
❑ 5 Nomar Garciaparra MOM	25.00	11.00
❑ 6 Ryne Sandberg MOM	10.00	4.50
❑ 7 Frank Thomas MOM	25.00	11.00
❑ 8 Derek Jeter MOM	20.00	9.00

Card	MINT	NRMT
❑ 9 Tony Gwynn MOM	20.00	9.00
❑ 10 Albert Belle MOM	10.00	4.50
❑ 11 Scott Rolen MOM	15.00	6.75
❑ 12 Barry Larkin MOM	5.00	2.20
❑ 13 Alex Rodriguez MOM	25.00	11.00
❑ 14 Cal Ripken MOM	30.00	13.50
❑ 15 Chipper Jones MOM	20.00	9.00
❑ 16 Roger Clemens MOM	15.00	6.75
❑ 17 Mo Vaughn MOM	10.00	4.50
❑ 18 Mark McGwire MOM	50.00	22.00
❑ 19 Mike Piazza MOM	25.00	11.00
❑ 20 Andruw Jones MOM	8.00	3.60
❑ 21 Greg Maddux MOM	25.00	11.00
❑ 22 Barry Bonds MOM	10.00	4.50
❑ 23 Paul Molitor MOM	8.00	3.60
❑ 24 Hideo Nomo MOM	10.00	4.50

1998 Pinnacle Plus Lasting Memories

	MINT	NRMT
COMPLETE SET (30)	60.00	27.00
COMMON CARD (1-30)	.50	.23

Card	MINT	NRMT
❑ 1 Nomar Garciaparra	4.00	1.80
❑ 2 Ken Griffey Jr.	6.00	2.70
❑ 3 Livan Hernandez	.50	.23
❑ 4 Hideo Nomo	1.50	.70
❑ 5 Ben Grieve	2.50	1.10
❑ 6 Scott Rolen	3.00	1.35
❑ 7 Roger Clemens	2.50	1.10
❑ 8 Cal Ripken	5.00	2.20
❑ 9 Mo Vaughn	1.50	.70
❑ 10 Frank Thomas	4.00	1.80
❑ 11 Mark McGwire	8.00	3.60
❑ 12 Barry Larkin	.75	.35
❑ 13 Matt Williams	.50	.23
❑ 14 Jose Cruz Jr.	1.50	.70
❑ 15 Andruw Jones	1.50	.70
❑ 16 Mike Piazza	4.00	1.80
❑ 17 Jeff Bagwell	2.00	.90
❑ 18 Chipper Jones	4.00	1.80
❑ 19 Juan Gonzalez	3.00	1.35
❑ 20 Kenny Lofton	1.25	.55
❑ 21 Greg Maddux	4.00	1.80
❑ 22 Ivan Rodriguez	1.50	.70
❑ 23 Alex Rodriguez	4.00	1.80
❑ 24 Derek Jeter	3.00	1.35
❑ 25 Albert Belle	1.25	.55
❑ 26 Barry Bonds	1.50	.70

		MINT	NRMT
❑ 27	Larry Walker	1.25	.55
❑ 28	Sammy Sosa	3.00	1.35
❑ 29	Tony Gwynn	3.00	1.35
❑ 30	Randy Johnson	1.25	.55

1998 Pinnacle Plus Piece of the Game

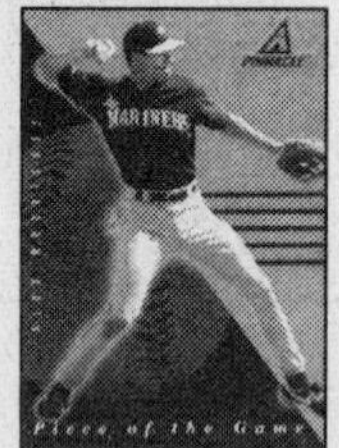

	MINT	NRMT
COMPLETE SET (10)	80.00	36.00
COMMON CARD (1-10)	4.00	1.80

		MINT	NRMT
❑ 1	Ken Griffey Jr.	20.00	9.00
❑ 2	Frank Thomas	12.00	5.50
❑ 3	Alex Rodriguez	12.00	5.50
❑ 4	Chipper Jones	10.00	4.50
❑ 5	Cal Ripken	15.00	6.75
❑ 6	Mike Piazza	12.00	5.50
❑ 7	Greg Maddux	12.00	5.50
❑ 8	Juan Gonzalez	10.00	4.50
❑ 9	Nomar Garciaparra	12.00	5.50
❑ 10	Larry Walker	4.00	1.80

1998 Pinnacle Plus Team Pinnacle

	MINT	NRMT
COMPLETE SET (15)	400.00	180.00
COMMON CARD (1-15)	15.00	6.75
COMP.GOLD SET (15)	1000.00	450.00

*GOLD: 1X TO 2.5X BASIC TEAM PINNACLE
GOLD STATED ODDS 1:199 HOBBY
*MIRROR: 7.5X TO 15X BASIC TEAM PINNACLE
MIRROR: RANDOM INSERTS IN PACKS

		MINT	NRMT
❑ 1	Mike Piazza / Ivan Rodriguez	40.00	18.00
❑ 2	Mark McGwire / Mo Vaughn	60.00	27.00
❑ 3	Roberto Alomar / Craig Biggio	15.00	6.75
❑ 4	Alex Rodriguez / Barry Larkin	40.00	18.00
❑ 5	Cal Ripken / Chipper Jones	50.00	22.00
❑ 6	Ken Griffey Jr. / Larry Walker	50.00	22.00
❑ 7	Juan Gonzalez / Tony Gwynn	40.00	18.00
❑ 8	Albert Belle / Barry Bonds	20.00	9.00
❑ 9	Kenny Lofton / Andruw Jones	15.00	6.75
❑ 10	Tino Martinez / Jeff Bagwell	25.00	11.00
❑ 11	F.Thomas/A.Galarraga	40.00	18.00
❑ 12	R.Clemens/G.Maddux	40.00	18.00
❑ 13	P.Martinez/H.Nomo	25.00	11.00
❑ 14	N.Garciaparra/S.Rolen	40.00	18.00
❑ 15	B.Grieve/P.Konerko	20.00	9.00

1998 Pinnacle Plus Yardwork

	MINT	NRMT
COMPLETE SET (15)	40.00	18.00
COMMON CARD (1-15)	1.00	.45

		MINT	NRMT
❑ 1	Mo Vaughn	2.00	.90
❑ 2	Frank Thomas	5.00	2.20
❑ 3	Albert Belle	1.50	.70
❑ 4	Nomar Garciaparra	5.00	2.20
❑ 5	Tony Clark	1.00	.45
❑ 6	Tino Martinez	1.50	.70
❑ 7	Ken Griffey Jr.	8.00	3.60
❑ 8	Juan Gonzalez	4.00	1.80
❑ 9	Sammy Sosa	4.00	1.80
❑ 10	Jose Cruz Jr.	2.00	.90
❑ 11	Jeff Bagwell	2.50	1.10
❑ 12	Mike Piazza	5.00	2.20
❑ 13	Larry Walker	1.50	.70
❑ 14	Mark McGwire	10.00	4.50
❑ 15	Barry Bonds	2.00	.90

1997 Pinnacle Totally Certified Platinum Gold

	MINT	NRMT
COMMON CARD (1-150)	60.00	27.00

*STARS: 25X TO 50X PLAT. RED
*YOUNG STARS: 20X TO 40X PLAT. RED

		MINT	NRMT
❑ 1	Barry Bonds	300.00	135.00
❑ 2	Mo Vaughn	300.00	135.00
❑ 4	Ryne Sandberg	300.00	135.00
❑ 5	Jeff Bagwell	400.00	180.00
❑ 17	Albert Belle	400.00	180.00
❑ 22	Alex Rodriguez	800.00	350.00
❑ 26	Mike Piazza	800.00	350.00
❑ 28	Cal Ripken	1000.00	450.00
❑ 31	Darin Erstad	300.00	135.00
❑ 39	Roger Clemens	500.00	220.00
❑ 41	Frank Thomas	800.00	350.00
❑ 45	Tony Gwynn	600.00	275.00
❑ 49	Mark McGwire	1200.00	550.00
❑ 51	Derek Jeter	600.00	275.00
❑ 53	Ken Griffey Jr.	1200.00	550.00
❑ 59	Chipper Jones	600.00	275.00
❑ 63	Hideo Nomo	400.00	180.00
❑ 69	Juan Gonzalez	600.00	275.00
❑ 79	Ivan Rodriguez	300.00	135.00
❑ 83	Greg Maddux	800.00	350.00
❑ 106	Andruw Jones	300.00	135.00
❑ 111	Vladimir Guerrero	400.00	180.00
❑ 112	Scott Rolen	500.00	220.00
❑ 114	Nomar Garciaparra	800.00	350.00
❑ 136	Ken Griffey Jr. CERT	600.00	275.00
❑ 139	Mark McGwire CERT	600.00	275.00
❑ 141	Derek Jeter CERT	300.00	135.00
❑ 142	Juan Gonzalez CERT	300.00	135.00
❑ 143	Greg Maddux CERT	400.00	180.00
❑ 144	Alex Rodriguez CERT	400.00	180.00
❑ 146	Cal Ripken CERT	500.00	220.00
❑ 147	Tony Gwynn CERT	300.00	135.00
❑ 148	Frank Thomas CERT	400.00	180.00
❑ 149	Hideo Nomo CERT	250.00	110.00

1997 Pinnacle Totally Certified Platinum Red

	MINT	NRMT
COMPLETE SET (150)	300.00	135.00
COMMON CARD (1-150)	1.25	.55

		MINT	NRMT
❑ 1	Barry Bonds	6.00	2.70
❑ 2	Mo Vaughn	6.00	2.70
❑ 3	Matt Williams	2.50	1.10
❑ 4	Ryne Sandberg	6.00	2.70
❑ 5	Jeff Bagwell	8.00	3.60
❑ 6	Alan Benes	2.50	1.10
❑ 7	John Wetteland	2.50	1.10
❑ 8	Fred McGriff	4.00	1.80
❑ 9	Craig Biggio	5.00	2.20
❑ 10	Bernie Williams	5.00	2.20
❑ 11	Brian Hunter	2.50	1.10
❑ 12	Sandy Alomar Jr.	2.50	1.10
❑ 13	Ray Lankford	2.50	1.10
❑ 14	Ryan Klesko	2.50	1.10
❑ 15	Jermaine Dye	1.25	.55
❑ 16	Andy Benes	2.50	1.10
❑ 17	Albert Belle	5.00	2.20
❑ 18	Tony Clark	4.00	1.80
❑ 19	Dean Palmer	2.50	1.10
❑ 20	Bernard Gilkey	1.25	.55
❑ 21	Ken Caminiti	4.00	1.80
❑ 22	Alex Rodriguez	15.00	6.75
❑ 23	Tim Salmon	5.00	2.20
❑ 24	Larry Walker	5.00	2.20
❑ 25	Barry Larkin	4.00	1.80
❑ 26	Mike Piazza	15.00	6.75
❑ 27	Brady Anderson	2.50	1.10
❑ 28	Cal Ripken	20.00	9.00
❑ 29	Charles Nagy	2.50	1.10
❑ 30	Paul Molitor	5.00	2.20
❑ 31	Darin Erstad	6.00	2.70
❑ 32	Rey Ordonez	2.50	1.10
❑ 33	Wally Joyner	2.50	1.10
❑ 34	David Cone	4.00	1.80
❑ 35	Sammy Sosa	12.00	5.50
❑ 36	Dante Bichette	2.50	1.10
❑ 37	Eric Karros	2.50	1.10
❑ 38	Omar Vizquel	2.50	1.10
❑ 39	Roger Clemens	10.00	4.50
❑ 40	Joe Carter	2.50	1.10
❑ 41	Frank Thomas	15.00	6.75
❑ 42	Javy Lopez	2.50	1.10
❑ 43	Mike Mussina	5.00	2.20
❑ 44	Gary Sheffield	4.00	1.80
❑ 45	Tony Gwynn	12.00	5.50
❑ 46	Jason Kendall	4.00	1.80
❑ 47	Jim Thome	5.00	2.20
❑ 48	Andres Galarraga	5.00	2.20
❑ 49	Mark McGwire	25.00	11.00

❑ 50	Troy Percival	2.50	1.10
❑ 51	Derek Jeter	12.00	5.50
❑ 52	Todd Hollandsworth	1.25	.55
❑ 53	Ken Griffey Jr.	25.00	11.00
❑ 54	Randy Johnson	5.00	2.20
❑ 55	Pat Hentgen	2.50	1.10
❑ 56	Rusty Greer	2.50	1.10
❑ 57	John Jaha	1.25	.55
❑ 58	Kenny Lofton	5.00	2.20
❑ 59	Chipper Jones	12.00	5.50
❑ 60	Robb Nen	1.25	.55
❑ 61	Rafael Palmeiro	4.00	1.80
❑ 62	Mariano Rivera	2.50	1.10
❑ 63	Hideo Nomo	6.00	2.70
❑ 64	Greg Vaughn	2.50	1.10
❑ 65	Ron Gant	1.25	.55
❑ 66	Eddie Murray	5.00	2.20
❑ 67	John Smoltz	2.50	1.10
❑ 68	Manny Ramirez	5.00	2.20
❑ 69	Juan Gonzalez	12.00	5.50
❑ 70	F.P. Santangelo	1.25	.55
❑ 71	Moises Alou	4.00	1.80
❑ 72	Alex Ochoa	1.25	.55
❑ 73	Chuck Knoblauch	5.00	2.20
❑ 74	Raul Mondesi	4.00	1.80
❑ 75	J.T. Snow	2.50	1.10
❑ 76	Rickey Henderson	5.00	2.20
❑ 77	Bobby Bonilla	2.50	1.10
❑ 78	Wade Boggs	5.00	2.20
❑ 79	Ivan Rodriguez	6.00	2.70
❑ 80	Brian Jordan	2.50	1.10
❑ 81	Al Leiter	2.50	1.10
❑ 82	Jay Buhner	2.50	1.10
❑ 83	Greg Maddux	15.00	6.75
❑ 84	Edgar Martinez	2.50	1.10
❑ 85	Kevin Brown	4.00	1.80
❑ 86	Eric Young	2.50	1.10
❑ 87	Todd Hundley	2.50	1.10
❑ 88	Ellis Burks	2.50	1.10
❑ 89	Marquis Grissom	2.50	1.10
❑ 90	Jose Canseco	5.00	2.20
❑ 91	Henry Rodriguez	2.50	1.10
❑ 92	Andy Pettitte	4.00	1.80
❑ 93	Mark Grudzielanek	2.50	1.10
❑ 94	Dwight Gooden	2.50	1.10
❑ 95	Roberto Alomar	5.00	2.20
❑ 96	Paul Wilson	1.25	.55
❑ 97	Will Clark	5.00	2.20
❑ 98	Rondell White	2.50	1.10
❑ 99	Charles Johnson	2.50	1.10
❑ 100	Jim Edmonds	4.00	1.80
❑ 101	Jason Giambi	2.50	1.10
❑ 102	Billy Wagner	2.50	1.10
❑ 103	Edgar Renteria	2.50	1.10
❑ 104	Johnny Damon	2.50	1.10
❑ 105	Jason Isringhausen	1.25	.55
❑ 106	Andruw Jones	6.00	2.70
❑ 107	Jose Guillen	5.00	2.20
❑ 108	Kevin Orie	1.25	.55
❑ 109	Brian Giles	6.00	2.70
❑ 110	Danny Patterson	1.25	.55
❑ 111	Vladimir Guerrero	8.00	3.60
❑ 112	Scott Rolen	10.00	4.50
❑ 113	Damon Mashore	1.25	.55
❑ 114	Nomar Garciaparra	15.00	6.75
❑ 115	Todd Walker	5.00	2.20
❑ 116	Wilton Guerrero	1.25	.55
❑ 117	Bob Abreu	2.50	1.10
❑ 118	Brooks Kieschnick	1.25	.55
❑ 119	Pokey Reese	1.25	.55
❑ 120	Todd Greene	2.50	1.10
❑ 121	Dmitri Young	2.50	1.10
❑ 122	Raul Casanova	1.25	.55
❑ 123	Glendon Rusch	1.25	.55
❑ 124	Jason Dickson	2.50	1.10
❑ 125	Jorge Posada	2.50	1.10
❑ 126	Rod Myers	2.50	1.10
❑ 127	Bubba Trammell	3.00	1.35
❑ 128	Scott Spiezio	1.25	.55
❑ 129	Hideki Irabu	12.00	5.50
❑ 130	Wendell Magee	1.25	.55
❑ 131	Bartolo Colon	2.50	1.10
❑ 132	Chris Holt	1.25	.55
❑ 133	Calvin Maduro	1.25	.55
❑ 134	Ray Montgomery	1.25	.55
❑ 135	Shannon Stewart	2.50	1.10
❑ 136	Ken Griffey Jr. CERT	12.00	5.50
❑ 137	Vladimir Guerrero CERT	5.00	2.20
❑ 138	Roger Clemens CERT	5.00	2.20
❑ 139	Mark McGwire CERT	12.00	5.50
❑ 140	Albert Belle CERT	2.50	1.10
❑ 141	Derek Jeter CERT	6.00	2.70
❑ 142	Juan Gonzalez CERT	6.00	2.70
❑ 143	Greg Maddux CERT	8.00	3.60
❑ 144	Alex Rodriguez CERT	8.00	3.60
❑ 145	Jeff Bagwell CERT	5.00	2.20
❑ 146	Cal Ripken CERT	10.00	4.50
❑ 147	Tony Gwynn CERT	6.00	2.70
❑ 148	Frank Thomas CERT	8.00	3.60
❑ 149	Hideo Nomo CERT	8.00	3.60
❑ 150	Andruw Jones CERT	2.50	1.10

1997 Pinnacle X-Press

	MINT	NRMT
COMPLETE SET (150)	20.00	9.00
COMMON CARD (1-150)	.10	.05

❑ 1	Larry Walker	.40	.18
❑ 2	Andy Pettitte	.30	.14
❑ 3	Matt Williams	.20	.09
❑ 4	Juan Gonzalez	1.00	.45
❑ 5	Frank Thomas	1.25	.55
❑ 6	Kenny Lofton	.40	.18
❑ 7	Ken Griffey Jr.	2.00	.90
❑ 8	Andres Galarraga	.40	.18
❑ 9	Greg Maddux	1.25	.55
❑ 10	Hideo Nomo	.50	.23
❑ 11	Cecil Fielder	.20	.09
❑ 12	Jose Canseco	.40	.18
❑ 13	Tony Gwynn	1.00	.45
❑ 14	Eddie Murray	.40	.18
❑ 15	Alex Rodriguez	1.25	.55
❑ 16	Mike Piazza	1.25	.55
❑ 17	Ken Hill	.10	.05
❑ 18	Chuck Knoblauch	.40	.18
❑ 19	Ellis Burks	.20	.09
❑ 20	Rafael Palmeiro	.30	.14
❑ 21	Vinny Castilla	.30	.14
❑ 22	Rusty Greer	.20	.09
❑ 23	Chipper Jones	1.00	.45
❑ 24	Rey Ordonez	.20	.09
❑ 25	Mariano Rivera	.20	.09
❑ 26	Garret Anderson	.20	.09
❑ 27	Edgar Martinez	.20	.09
❑ 28	Dante Bichette	.20	.09
❑ 29	Todd Hundley	.20	.09
❑ 30	Barry Bonds	.50	.23
❑ 31	Barry Larkin	.30	.14
❑ 32	Derek Jeter	1.25	.55
❑ 33	Marquis Grissom	.20	.09
❑ 34	Dave Justice	.40	.18
❑ 35	Ivan Rodriguez	.50	.23
❑ 36	Jay Buhner	.20	.09
❑ 37	Fred McGriff	.30	.14
❑ 38	Brady Anderson	.20	.09
❑ 39	Tony Clark	.30	.14
❑ 40	Eric Young	.20	.09
❑ 41	Charles Nagy	.20	.09
❑ 42	Mark McGwire	2.00	.90
❑ 43	Paul O'Neill	.20	.09
❑ 44	Tino Martinez	.40	.18
❑ 45	Ryne Sandberg	.50	.23
❑ 46	Bernie Williams	.40	.18
❑ 47	Albert Belle	.50	.23
❑ 48	Jeff Cirillo	.20	.09
❑ 49	Tim Salmon	.40	.18
❑ 50	Steve Finley	.20	.09
❑ 51	Lance Johnson	.10	.05
❑ 52	John Smoltz	.20	.09
❑ 53	Javier Lopez	.20	.09
❑ 54	Roger Clemens	.75	.35
❑ 55	Kevin Appier	.20	.09
❑ 56	Ken Caminiti	.30	.14
❑ 57	Cal Ripken	1.50	.70
❑ 58	Moises Alou	.30	.14
❑ 59	Marty Cordova	.10	.05
❑ 60	David Cone	.30	.14
❑ 61	Manny Ramirez	.40	.18
❑ 62	Ray Durham	.20	.09
❑ 63	Jermaine Dye	.10	.05
❑ 64	Craig Biggio	.40	.18
❑ 65	Will Clark	.40	.18
❑ 66	Omar Vizquel	.20	.09
❑ 67	Bernard Gilkey	.10	.05
❑ 68	Greg Vaughn	.20	.09
❑ 69	Wade Boggs	.40	.18
❑ 70	Dave Nilsson	.10	.05
❑ 71	Mark Grace	.30	.14
❑ 72	Dean Palmer	.20	.09
❑ 73	Sammy Sosa	1.00	.45
❑ 74	Mike Mussina	.40	.18
❑ 75	Alex Fernandez	.10	.05
❑ 76	Henry Rodriguez	.20	.09
❑ 77	Travis Fryman	.20	.09
❑ 78	Jeff Bagwell	.60	.25
❑ 79	Pat Hentgen	.20	.09
❑ 80	Gary Sheffield	.30	.14
❑ 81	Jim Edmonds	.30	.14
❑ 82	Darin Erstad	.60	.25
❑ 83	Mark Grudzielanek	.20	.09
❑ 84	Jim Thome	.40	.18
❑ 85	Bobby Higginson	.30	.14
❑ 86	Al Martin	.10	.05
❑ 87	Jason Giambi	.20	.09
❑ 88	Mo Vaughn	.50	.23
❑ 89	Jeff Conine	.20	.09
❑ 90	Edgar Renteria	.20	.09
❑ 91	Andy Ashby	.10	.05
❑ 92	Ryan Klesko	.20	.09
❑ 93	John Jaha	.10	.05
❑ 94	Paul Molitor	.40	.18
❑ 95	Brian Hunter	.20	.09
❑ 96	Randy Johnson	.40	.18
❑ 97	Joey Hamilton	.20	.09
❑ 98	Billy Wagner	.20	.09
❑ 99	John Wetteland	.20	.09
❑ 100	Jeff Fassero	.10	.05
❑ 101	Rondell White	.20	.09
❑ 102	Kevin Brown	.30	.14
❑ 103	Andy Benes	.20	.09
❑ 104	Raul Mondesi	.30	.14
❑ 105	Todd Hollandsworth	.10	.05
❑ 106	Alex Ochoa	.10	.05
❑ 107	Bobby Bonilla	.20	.09
❑ 108	Brian Jordan	.20	.09
❑ 109	Tom Glavine	.40	.18
❑ 110	Ron Gant	.10	.05
❑ 111	Jason Kendall	.30	.14
❑ 112	Roberto Alomar	.40	.18
❑ 113	Troy Percival	.20	.09
❑ 114	Michael Tucker	.20	.09
❑ 115	Joe Carter	.20	.09
❑ 116	Andruw Jones	.60	.25
❑ 117	Nomar Garciaparra	1.25	.55
❑ 118	Todd Walker	.40	.18
❑ 119	Jose Guillen	.40	.18
❑ 120	Bubba Trammell	.25	.11
❑ 121	Wilton Guerrero	.10	.05
❑ 122	Bob Abreu	.20	.09
❑ 123	Vladimir Guerrero	.75	.35
❑ 124	Dmitri Young	.20	.09
❑ 125	Kevin Orie	.10	.05
❑ 126	Jose Cruz Jr.	1.50	.70
❑ 127	Brooks Kieschnick	.10	.05
❑ 128	Scott Spiezio	.10	.05
❑ 129	Brian Giles	.50	.23
❑ 130	Jason Dickson	.20	.09

		MINT	NRMT
❑ 131	Damon Mashore	.10	.05
❑ 132	Wendell Magee	.10	.05
❑ 133	Matt Morris	.20	.09
❑ 134	Scott Rolen	1.00	.45
❑ 135	Shannon Stewart	.20	.09
❑ 136	Deivi Cruz	.30	.14
❑ 137	Hideki Irabu	1.00	.45
❑ 138	Larry Walker PP	.20	.09
❑ 139	Ken Griffey Jr. PP	1.00	.45
❑ 140	Frank Thomas PP	.60	.25
❑ 141	Ivan Rodriguez PP	.30	.14
❑ 142	Randy Johnson PP	.20	.09
❑ 143	Mark McGwire PP	1.00	.45
❑ 144	Tino Martinez PP	.20	.09
❑ 145	Tony Clark PP	.10	.05
❑ 146	Mike Piazza PP	.60	.25
❑ 147	Alex Rodriguez PP	.60	.25
❑ 148	Roger Clemens CL	.40	.18
❑ 149	Greg Maddux CL	.60	.25
❑ 150	Hideo Nomo CL	.50	.23

1997 Pinnacle X-Press Far and Away

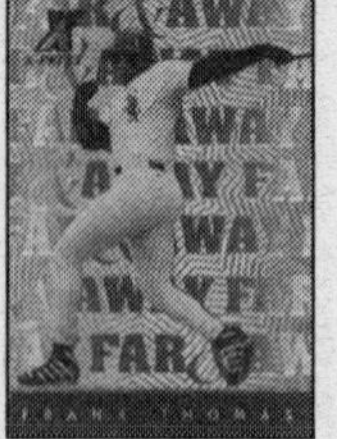

	MINT	NRMT
COMPLETE SET (18)	120.00	55.00
COMMON CARD (1-18)	2.50	1.10

		MINT	NRMT
❑ 1	Albert Belle	5.00	2.20
❑ 2	Mark McGwire	20.00	9.00
❑ 3	Frank Thomas	12.00	5.50
❑ 4	Mo Vaughn	5.00	2.20
❑ 5	Jeff Bagwell	6.00	2.70
❑ 6	Juan Gonzalez	10.00	4.50
❑ 7	Mike Piazza	12.00	5.50
❑ 8	Andruw Jones	6.00	2.70
❑ 9	Chipper Jones	10.00	4.50
❑ 10	Gary Sheffield	2.50	1.10
❑ 11	Sammy Sosa	10.00	4.50
❑ 12	Darin Erstad	6.00	2.70
❑ 13	Jay Buhner	2.50	1.10
❑ 14	Ken Griffey Jr.	20.00	9.00
❑ 15	Ken Caminiti	2.50	1.10
❑ 16	Brady Anderson	2.50	1.10
❑ 17	Manny Ramirez	4.00	1.80
❑ 18	Alex Rodriguez	12.00	5.50

1997 Pinnacle X-Press Melting Pot

	MINT	NRMT
COMPLETE SET (20)	800.00	350.00
COMMON CARD (1-20)	6.00	2.70

		MINT	NRMT
❑ 1	Jose Guillen	25.00	11.00
❑ 2	Vladimir Guerrero	40.00	18.00
❑ 3	Andruw Jones	30.00	13.50
❑ 4	Larry Walker	25.00	11.00
❑ 5	Manny Ramirez	25.00	11.00
❑ 6	Ken Griffey Jr.	120.00	55.00
❑ 7	Alex Rodriguez	80.00	36.00
❑ 8	Frank Thomas	80.00	36.00
❑ 9	Juan Gonzalez	60.00	27.00
❑ 10	Ivan Rodriguez	30.00	13.50
❑ 11	Hideo Nomo	50.00	22.00
❑ 12	Rafael Palmeiro	15.00	6.75
❑ 13	Dave Nilsson	6.00	2.70
❑ 14	Nomar Garciaparra	80.00	36.00
❑ 15	Wilton Guerrero	6.00	2.70
❑ 16	Sammy Sosa	60.00	27.00
❑ 17	Edgar Renteria	10.00	4.50
❑ 18	Cal Ripken	100.00	45.00
❑ 19	Derek Jeter	60.00	27.00
❑ 20	Rey Ordonez	10.00	4.50

1997 Pinnacle X-Press Metal Works

	MINT	NRMT
COMPLETE SET (20)	120.00	55.00
COMMON CARD (1-20)	3.00	1.35

*SILVER: 3X TO 8X BRONZE CARDS
SILVER ODDS 1:54 MASTER DECKS
SILVER REDEMPTION ODDS 1:470 HOBBY
SILVER PRINT RUN 400 SERIAL #'d SETS
*GOLD: 6X TO 15X BRONZE CARDS
GOLD ODDS 1:108 MASTER DECKS
GOLD REDEMPTION ODDS 1:950 HOBBY
GOLD PRINT RUN 200 SERIAL #'d SETS
BRONZE CARDS PRICED BELOW

		MINT	NRMT
❑ 1	Ken Griffey Jr.	15.00	6.75
❑ 2	Frank Thomas	10.00	4.50
❑ 3	Andruw Jones	4.00	1.80
❑ 4	Alex Rodriguez	10.00	4.50
❑ 5	Derek Jeter	8.00	3.60
❑ 6	Cal Ripken	12.00	5.50
❑ 7	Mike Piazza	10.00	4.50
❑ 8	Chipper Jones	8.00	3.60
❑ 9	Juan Gonzalez	8.00	3.60
❑ 10	Greg Maddux	10.00	4.50
❑ 11	Tony Gwynn	8.00	3.60
❑ 12	Jeff Bagwell	5.00	2.20
❑ 13	Albert Belle	6.00	2.70
❑ 14	Mark McGwire	15.00	6.75
❑ 15	Nomar Garciaparra	10.00	4.50
❑ 16	Mo Vaughn	4.00	1.80
❑ 17	Andy Pettitte	3.00	1.35
❑ 18	Manny Ramirez	4.00	1.80
❑ 19	Kenny Lofton	4.00	1.80
❑ 20	Roger Clemens	6.00	2.70
❑ NNO	Silver Redemption Card	40.00	18.00
❑ NNO	Gold Redemption Card	80.00	36.00

1997 Pinnacle X-Press Swing for the Fences

	MINT	NRMT
COMPLETE SET (60)	60.00	27.00
COMMON CARD	.25	.11
COMP.UPGRADE SET (60)	200.00	90.00
COMMON UPGRADE	1.50	.70

*UPG.STARS: 2.5X TO 6X BASE CARD HI
*UPG.YOUNG STARS: 2X TO 5X BASE HI
TEN UPGRADES VIA MAIL PER WINNER
UPGRADE EXCH.DEADLINE: 3/1/98

		MINT	NRMT
❑ 1	Sandy Alomar Jr.	.50	.23
❑ 2	Moises Alou	.75	.35
❑ 3	Brady Anderson	.50	.23
❑ 4	Jeff Bagwell	1.50	.70
❑ 5	Derek Bell	.50	.23
❑ 6	Jay Bell	.50	.23
❑ 7	Albert Belle	1.25	.55
❑ 8	Geronimo Berroa	.25	.11
❑ 9	Dante Bichette	.50	.23
❑ 10	Barry Bonds	1.25	.55
❑ 11	Bobby Bonilla	.50	.23
❑ 12	Jay Buhner	.50	.23
❑ 13	Ellis Burks	.50	.23
❑ 14	Ken Caminiti	.75	.35
❑ 15	Jose Canseco	1.00	.45
❑ 16	Joe Carter	.50	.23
❑ 17	Vinny Castilla	.75	.35
❑ 18	Tony Clark	.75	.35
❑ 19	Carlos Delgado	.50	.23
❑ 20	Jim Edmonds	.75	.35
❑ 21	Cecil Fielder	.50	.23
❑ 22	Andres Galarraga	1.00	.45
❑ 23	Ron Gant	.25	.11
❑ 24	Bernard Gilkey	.25	.11
❑ 25	Juan Gonzalez	2.50	1.10
❑ 26	Ken Griffey Jr. W	15.00	6.75
❑ 27	Vladimir Guerrero	2.00	.90
❑ 28	Todd Hundley	.50	.23
❑ 29	John Jaha	.25	.11
❑ 30	Andruw Jones	1.00	.45
❑ 31	Chipper Jones	2.50	1.10
❑ 32	David Justice	1.00	.45
❑ 33	Jeff Kent	.50	.23
❑ 34	Ryan Klesko	.50	.23
❑ 35	Barry Larkin	.75	.35
❑ 36	Mike Lieberthal	.25	.11
❑ 37	Javier Lopez	.50	.23
❑ 38	Edgar Martinez	.50	.23
❑ 39	Tino Martinez	1.00	.45
❑ 40	Fred McGriff	.75	.35
❑ 41	Mark McGwire W	15.00	6.75
❑ 42	Raul Mondesi	.75	.35
❑ 43	Tim Naehring	.25	.11
❑ 44	Dave Nilsson	.25	.11
❑ 45	Rafael Palmeiro	.75	.35
❑ 46	Dean Palmer	.50	.23
❑ 47	Mike Piazza	3.00	1.35
❑ 48	Cal Ripken	4.00	1.80
❑ 49	Henry Rodriguez	.50	.23
❑ 50	Tim Salmon	1.00	.45
❑ 51	Gary Sheffield	.75	.35
❑ 52	Sammy Sosa	2.50	1.10
❑ 53	Terry Steinbach	.50	.23
❑ 54	Frank Thomas	3.00	1.35

		MINT	NRMT
❑ 55	Jim Thome	1.00	.45
❑ 56	Mo Vaughn	1.25	.55
❑ 57	Larry Walker W	3.00	1.35
❑ 58	Rondell White	.50	.23
❑ 59	Matt Williams	.50	.23
❑ 60	Todd Zeile	.25	.11
❑ NNO	A.Jones AU EXCH	40.00	18.00

1998 Revolution

	MINT	NRMT
COMPLETE SET (150)	125.00	55.00
COMMON CARD (1-150)	.50	.23

		MINT	NRMT
❑ 1	Garret Anderson	.75	.35
❑ 2	Jim Edmonds	1.25	.55
❑ 3	Darin Erstad	2.50	1.10
❑ 4	Chuck Finley	.75	.35
❑ 5	Tim Salmon	2.00	.90
❑ 6	Jay Bell	.75	.35
❑ 7	Travis Lee	4.00	1.80
❑ 8	Devon White	.75	.35
❑ 9	Matt Williams	.75	.35
❑ 10	Andres Galarraga	2.00	.90
❑ 11	Tom Glavine	2.00	.90
❑ 12	Andruw Jones	2.50	1.10
❑ 13	Chipper Jones	5.00	2.20
❑ 14	Ryan Klesko	.75	.35
❑ 15	Javy Lopez	.75	.35
❑ 16	Greg Maddux	6.00	2.70
❑ 17	Walt Weiss	.75	.35
❑ 18	Roberto Alomar	2.00	.90
❑ 19	Joe Carter	.75	.35
❑ 20	Mike Mussina	2.00	.90
❑ 21	Rafael Palmeiro	1.25	.55
❑ 22	Cal Ripken	8.00	3.60
❑ 23	B.J. Surhoff	.75	.35
❑ 24	Nomar Garciaparra	6.00	2.70
❑ 25	Reggie Jefferson	.50	.23
❑ 26	Pedro Martinez	2.00	.90
❑ 27	Troy O'Leary	.75	.35
❑ 28	Mo Vaughn	2.50	1.10
❑ 29	Mark Grace	1.25	.55
❑ 30	Mickey Morandini	.50	.23
❑ 31	Henry Rodriguez	.75	.35
❑ 32	Sammy Sosa	5.00	2.20
❑ 33	Kerry Wood	10.00	4.50
❑ 34	Albert Belle	2.00	.90
❑ 35	Ray Durham	.75	.35
❑ 36	Maggio Ordonez	2.50	1.10
❑ 37	Frank Thomas	6.00	2.70
❑ 38	Robin Ventura	.75	.35
❑ 39	Bret Boone	.75	.35
❑ 40	Barry Larkin	1.25	.55
❑ 41	Reggie Sanders	.75	.35
❑ 42	Brett Tomko	.75	.35
❑ 43	Sandy Alomar Jr.	.75	.35
❑ 44	David Justice	2.00	.90
❑ 45	Kenny Lofton	2.00	.90
❑ 46	Manny Ramirez	2.00	.90
❑ 47	Jim Thome	2.00	.90
❑ 48	Omar Vizquel	.75	.35
❑ 49	Jaret Wright	2.50	1.10
❑ 50	Dante Bichette	.75	.35
❑ 51	Ellis Burks	.75	.35
❑ 52	Vinny Castilla	1.25	.55
❑ 53	Todd Helton	2.50	1.10
❑ 54	Larry Walker	2.00	.90
❑ 55	Tony Clark	1.25	.55
❑ 56	Deivi Cruz	.50	.23
❑ 57	Damion Easley	.75	.35
❑ 58	Bobby Higginson	1.25	.55
❑ 59	Brian Hunter	.75	.35
❑ 60	Cliff Floyd	.75	.35
❑ 61	Livan Hernandez	.75	.35
❑ 62	Derrek Lee	.75	.35
❑ 63	Edgar Renteria	.75	.35
❑ 64	Moises Alou	1.25	.55
❑ 65	Jeff Bagwell	3.00	1.35
❑ 66	Derek Bell	.75	.35
❑ 67	Craig Biggio	2.00	.90
❑ 68	Richard Hidalgo	.75	.35
❑ 69	Johnny Damon	.75	.35
❑ 70	Jeff King	.75	.35
❑ 71	Hal Morris	.50	.23
❑ 72	Dean Palmer	.75	.35
❑ 73	Bobby Bonilla	.75	.35
❑ 74	Charles Johnson	.75	.35
❑ 75	Eric Karros	.75	.35
❑ 76	Raul Mondesi	1.25	.55
❑ 77	Gary Sheffield	1.25	.55
❑ 78	Jeromy Burnitz	.75	.35
❑ 79	Marquis Grissom	.75	.35
❑ 80	Dave Nilsson	.50	.23
❑ 81	Fernando Vina	.50	.23
❑ 82	Marty Cordova	.50	.23
❑ 83	Pat Meares	.50	.23
❑ 84	Paul Molitor	2.00	.90
❑ 85	Brad Radke	.75	.35
❑ 86	Terry Steinbach	.75	.35
❑ 87	Todd Walker	1.25	.55
❑ 88	Brad Fullmer	.75	.35
❑ 89	Vladimir Guerrero	3.00	1.35
❑ 90	Carl Pavano	.75	.35
❑ 91	Rondell White	.75	.35
❑ 92	Bernard Gilkey	.50	.23
❑ 93	Hideo Nomo	2.50	1.10
❑ 94	John Olerud	.75	.35
❑ 95	Rey Ordonez	.75	.35
❑ 96	Mike Piazza	6.00	2.70
❑ 97	Masato Yoshii	1.50	.70
❑ 98	Hideki Irabu	1.25	.55
❑ 99	Derek Jeter	5.00	2.20
❑ 100	Chuck Knoblauch	2.00	.90
❑ 101	Tino Martinez	2.00	.90
❑ 102	Paul O'Neill	.75	.35
❑ 103	Darryl Strawberry	.75	.35
❑ 104	Bernie Williams	2.00	.90
❑ 105	Jason Giambi	.75	.35
❑ 106	Ben Grieve	4.00	1.80
❑ 107	Rickey Henderson	2.00	.90
❑ 108	Matt Stairs	.75	.35
❑ 109	Doug Glanville	.75	.35
❑ 110	Desi Relaford	.50	.23
❑ 111	Scott Rolen	5.00	2.20
❑ 112	Curt Schilling	.75	.35
❑ 113	Jason Kendall	.75	.35
❑ 114	Al Martin	.50	.23
❑ 115	Jason Schmidt	.50	.23
❑ 116	Kevin Young	.75	.35
❑ 117	Delino DeShields	.50	.23
❑ 118	Gary Gaetti	.50	.23
❑ 119	Brian Jordan	.75	.35
❑ 120	Ray Lankford	.75	.35
❑ 121	Mark McGwire	12.00	5.50
❑ 122	Kevin Brown	1.25	.55
❑ 123	Steve Finley	.75	.35
❑ 124	Tony Gwynn	5.00	2.20
❑ 125	Wally Joyner	.75	.35
❑ 126	Greg Vaughn	.75	.35
❑ 127	Barry Bonds	2.50	1.10
❑ 128	Orel Hershiser	.75	.35
❑ 129	Jeff Kent	.75	.35
❑ 130	Bill Mueller	.75	.35
❑ 131	Jay Buhner	.75	.35
❑ 132	Ken Griffey Jr.	10.00	4.50
❑ 133	Randy Johnson	2.00	.90
❑ 134	Edgar Martinez	.75	.35
❑ 135	Alex Rodriguez	6.00	2.70
❑ 136	David Segui	.75	.35
❑ 137	Rolando Arrojo	3.00	1.35
❑ 138	Wade Boggs	2.00	.90
❑ 139	Quinton McCracken	.75	.35
❑ 140	Fred McGriff	1.25	.55
❑ 141	Will Clark	2.00	.90
❑ 142	Juan Gonzalez	5.00	2.20
❑ 143	Tom Goodwin	.50	.23
❑ 144	Ivan Rodriguez	2.50	1.10
❑ 145	Aaron Sele	.75	.35
❑ 146	John Wetteland	.75	.35
❑ 147	Jose Canseco	2.00	.90
❑ 148	Roger Clemens	4.00	1.80
❑ 149	Jose Cruz Jr.	2.50	1.10
❑ 150	Carlos Delgado	.75	.35

1998 Revolution Shadow Series

	MINT	NRMT
COMMON CARD (1-150)	15.00	6.75

*STARS: 12.5X TO 30X BASIC CARDS
*YOUNG STARS: 10X TO 25X BASIC CARDS
*PROSPECTS: 8X TO 20X BASIC CARDS
*ROOKIES: 6X TO 15X BASIC CARDS

1998 Revolution Foul Pole

	MINT	NRMT
COMPLETE SET (20)	500.00	220.00
COMMON CARD (1-20)	8.00	3.60

		MINT	NRMT
❑ 1	Cal Ripken	50.00	22.00
❑ 2	Nomar Garciaparra	40.00	18.00
❑ 3	Mo Vaughn	15.00	6.75
❑ 4	Frank Thomas	40.00	18.00
❑ 5	Manny Ramirez	12.00	5.50
❑ 6	Bernie Williams	12.00	5.50
❑ 7	Ben Grieve	20.00	9.00
❑ 8	Ken Griffey Jr.	60.00	27.00
❑ 9	Alex Rodriguez	40.00	18.00
❑ 10	Juan Gonzalez	30.00	13.50
❑ 11	Ivan Rodriguez	15.00	6.75
❑ 12	Travis Lee	20.00	9.00
❑ 13	Chipper Jones	30.00	13.50
❑ 14	Sammy Sosa	30.00	13.50
❑ 15	Vinny Castilla	8.00	3.60
❑ 16	Moises Alou	8.00	3.60
❑ 17	Gary Sheffield	8.00	3.60
❑ 18	Mike Piazza	40.00	18.00
❑ 19	Mark McGwire	80.00	36.00
❑ 20	Barry Bonds	15.00	6.75

1998 Revolution Major League Icons

	MINT	NRMT
COMPLETE SET (10)	600.00	275.00
COMMON CARD (1-10)	50.00	22.00
❑ 1 Cal Ripken	80.00	36.00
❑ 2 Nomar Garciaparra	60.00	27.00
❑ 3 Frank Thomas	60.00	27.00
❑ 4 Ken Griffey Jr.	100.00	45.00
❑ 5 Alex Rodriguez	60.00	27.00
❑ 6 Chipper Jones	50.00	22.00
❑ 7 Kerry Wood	80.00	36.00
❑ 8 Mike Piazza	60.00	27.00
❑ 9 Mark McGwire	120.00	55.00
❑ 10 Tony Gwynn	50.00	22.00

1998 Revolution Prime Time Performers

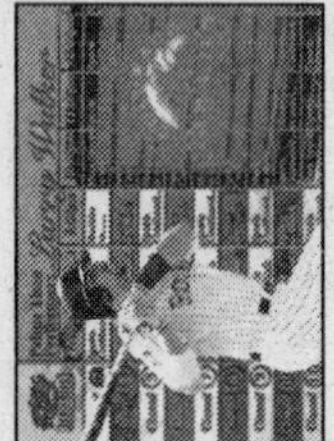

	MINT	NRMT
COMPLETE SET (20)	300.00	135.00
COMMON CARDS (1-20)	4.00	1.80
❑ 1 Cal Ripken	25.00	11.00
❑ 2 Nomar Garciaparra	20.00	9.00
❑ 3 Frank Thomas	20.00	9.00
❑ 4 Jim Thome	6.00	2.70
❑ 5 Hideki Irabu	4.00	1.80
❑ 6 Derek Jeter	15.00	6.75
❑ 7 Ben Grieve	10.00	4.50
❑ 8 Ken Griffey Jr.	30.00	13.50
❑ 9 Alex Rodriguez	20.00	9.00
❑ 10 Juan Gonzalez	15.00	6.75
❑ 11 Ivan Rodriguez	8.00	3.60
❑ 12 Travis Lee	10.00	4.50
❑ 13 Chipper Jones	15.00	6.75
❑ 14 Greg Maddux	20.00	9.00
❑ 15 Kerry Wood	25.00	11.00
❑ 16 Larry Walker	6.00	2.70
❑ 17 Jeff Bagwell	10.00	4.50
❑ 18 Mike Piazza	20.00	9.00
❑ 19 Mark McGwire	40.00	18.00
❑ 20 Tony Gwynn	15.00	6.75

1998 Revolution Rookies and Hardball Heroes

	MINT	NRMT
COMPLETE SET (30)	120.00	55.00
COMMON CARD (1-30)	.75	.35

*GOLD 1-20: 10X TO 25X BASIC ROOK/HARDBALL

	MINT	NRMT
❑ 1 Justin Baughman	1.00	.45
❑ 2 Jarrod Washburn	1.00	.45
❑ 3 Travis Lee	5.00	2.20
❑ 4 Kerry Wood	12.00	5.50
❑ 5 Magglio Ordonez	2.00	.90
❑ 6 Todd Helton	3.00	1.35
❑ 7 Derrek Lee	1.00	.45
❑ 8 Richard Hidalgo	1.00	.45
❑ 9 Mike Caruso	1.00	.45
❑ 10 David Ortiz	1.00	.45
❑ 11 Brad Fullmer	1.00	.45
❑ 12 Masato Yoshii	2.50	1.10
❑ 13 Orlando Hernandez	8.00	3.60
❑ 14 Ricky Ledee	1.00	.45
❑ 15 Ben Grieve	5.00	2.20
❑ 16 Carlton Loewer	1.00	.45
❑ 17 Desi Relaford	.75	.35
❑ 18 Ruben Rivera	1.00	.45
❑ 19 Rolando Arrojo	2.50	1.10
❑ 20 Matt Perisho	.75	.35
❑ 21 Chipper Jones	8.00	3.60
❑ 22 Greg Maddux	10.00	4.50
❑ 23 Cal Ripken Jr.	12.00	5.50
❑ 24 Nomar Garciaparra	10.00	4.50
❑ 25 Frank Thomas	10.00	4.50
❑ 26 Mark McGwire	20.00	9.00
❑ 27 Tony Gwynn	8.00	3.60
❑ 28 Ken Griffey Jr.	15.00	6.75
❑ 29 Alex Rodriguez	10.00	4.50
❑ 30 Juan Gonzalez	8.00	3.60

1998 Revolution Showstoppers

	MINT	NRMT
COMPLETE SET (36)	300.00	135.00
COMMON CARD (1-36)	3.00	1.35
❑ 1 Cal Ripken	20.00	9.00
❑ 2 Nomar Garciaparra	15.00	6.75
❑ 3 Pedro Martinez	5.00	2.20
❑ 4 Mo Vaughn	6.00	2.70
❑ 5 Frank Thomas	15.00	6.75
❑ 6 Manny Ramirez	5.00	2.20
❑ 7 Jim Thome	5.00	2.20
❑ 8 Jaret Wright	5.00	2.20
❑ 9 Paul Molitor	5.00	2.20
❑ 10 Orlando Hernandez	12.00	5.50
❑ 11 Derek Jeter	12.00	5.50
❑ 12 Bernie Williams	5.00	2.20
❑ 13 Ben Grieve	8.00	3.60
❑ 14 Ken Griffey Jr.	25.00	11.00
❑ 15 Alex Rodriguez	15.00	6.75
❑ 16 Wade Boggs	5.00	2.20
❑ 17 Juan Gonzalez	12.00	5.50
❑ 18 Ivan Rodriguez	6.00	2.70
❑ 19 Jose Canseco	5.00	2.20
❑ 20 Roger Clemens	10.00	4.50
❑ 21 Travis Lee	8.00	3.60
❑ 22 Andres Galarraga	5.00	2.20
❑ 23 Chipper Jones	12.00	5.50
❑ 24 Greg Maddux	15.00	6.75
❑ 25 Sammy Sosa	12.00	5.50
❑ 26 Kerry Wood	20.00	9.00
❑ 27 Vinny Castilla	3.00	1.35
❑ 28 Larry Walker	5.00	2.20
❑ 29 Moises Alou	3.00	1.35
❑ 30 Raul Mondesi	3.00	1.35
❑ 31 Gary Sheffield	3.00	1.35
❑ 32 Hideki Irabu	3.00	1.35
❑ 33 Mike Piazza	15.00	6.75
❑ 34 Mark McGwire	30.00	13.50
❑ 35 Tony Gwynn	12.00	5.50
❑ 36 Barry Bonds	6.00	2.70

1988 Score

	MINT	NRMT
COMPLETE SET (660)	10.00	4.50
COMP.FACT.SET (660)	12.00	5.50
COMMON CARD (1-660)	.05	.02
❑ 1 Don Mattingly	.30	.14
❑ 2 Wade Boggs	.20	.09
❑ 3 Tim Raines	.10	.05
❑ 4 Andre Dawson	.20	.09
❑ 5 Mark McGwire	2.00	.90
❑ 6 Kevin Seitzer	.10	.05
❑ 7 Wally Joyner	.15	.07
❑ 8 Jesse Barfield	.05	.02
❑ 9 Pedro Guerrero	.05	.02
❑ 10 Eric Davis	.10	.05
❑ 11 George Brett	.40	.18
❑ 12 Ozzie Smith	.25	.11
❑ 13 Rickey Henderson	.20	.09
❑ 14 Jim Rice	.10	.05
❑ 15 Matt Nokes	.05	.02
❑ 16 Mike Schmidt	.25	.11
❑ 17 Dave Parker	.10	.05
❑ 18 Eddie Murray	.20	.09
❑ 19 Andres Galarraga	.20	.09
❑ 20 Tony Fernandez	.05	.02
❑ 21 Kevin McReynolds	.05	.02
❑ 22 B.J. Surhoff	.10	.05
❑ 23 Pat Tabler	.05	.02
❑ 24 Kirby Puckett	.30	.14
❑ 25 Benny Santiago	.05	.02

Card	Player	Price	Price
❑ 26	Ryne Sandberg	.25	.11
❑ 27	Kelly Downs (Will Clark in background& out of focus)	.10	.05
❑ 28	Jose Cruz	.05	.02
❑ 29	Pete O'Brien	.05	.02
❑ 30	Mark Langston	.05	.02
❑ 31	Lee Smith	.10	.05
❑ 32	Juan Samuel	.05	.02
❑ 33	Kevin Bass	.05	.02
❑ 34	R.J. Reynolds	.05	.02
❑ 35	Steve Sax	.05	.02
❑ 36	John Kruk	.10	.05
❑ 37	Alan Trammell	.15	.07
❑ 38	Chris Bosio	.05	.02
❑ 39	Brook Jacoby	.05	.02
❑ 40	Willie McGee UER (Excited misspelled as excitd)	.10	.05
❑ 41	Dave Magadan	.05	.02
❑ 42	Fred Lynn	.05	.02
❑ 43	Kent Hrbek	.10	.05
❑ 44	Brian Downing	.05	.02
❑ 45	Jose Canseco	.20	.09
❑ 46	Jim Presley	.05	.02
❑ 47	Mike Stanley	.10	.05
❑ 48	Tony Pena	.05	.02
❑ 49	David Cone	.25	.11
❑ 50	Rick Sutcliffe	.05	.02
❑ 51	Doug Drabek	.05	.02
❑ 52	Bill Doran	.05	.02
❑ 53	Mike Scioscia	.05	.02
❑ 54	Candy Maldonado	.05	.02
❑ 55	Dave Winfield	.20	.09
❑ 56	Lou Whitaker	.10	.05
❑ 57	Tom Henke	.05	.02
❑ 58	Ken Gerhart	.05	.02
❑ 59	Glenn Braggs	.05	.02
❑ 60	Julio Franco	.05	.02
❑ 61	Charlie Leibrandt	.05	.02
❑ 62	Gary Gaetti	.10	.05
❑ 63	Bob Boone	.10	.05
❑ 64	Luis Polonia	.05	.02
❑ 65	Dwight Evans	.10	.05
❑ 66	Phil Bradley	.05	.02
❑ 67	Mike Boddicker	.05	.02
❑ 68	Vince Coleman	.05	.02
❑ 69	Howard Johnson	.05	.02
❑ 70	Tim Wallach	.05	.02
❑ 71	Keith Moreland	.05	.02
❑ 72	Barry Larkin	.20	.09
❑ 73	Alan Ashby	.05	.02
❑ 74	Rick Rhoden	.05	.02
❑ 75	Darrell Evans	.10	.05
❑ 76	Dave Stieb	.05	.02
❑ 77	Dan Plesac	.05	.02
❑ 78	Will Clark UER (Born 3/17/64& should be 3/13/64)	.25	.11
❑ 79	Frank White	.10	.05
❑ 80	Joe Carter	.20	.09
❑ 81	Mike Witt	.05	.02
❑ 82	Terry Steinbach	.10	.05
❑ 83	Alvin Davis	.05	.02
❑ 84	Tommy Herr (Will Clark shown sliding into second)	.10	.05
❑ 85	Vance Law	.05	.02
❑ 86	Kal Daniels	.05	.02
❑ 87	Rick Honeycutt UER (Wrong years for stats on back)	.05	.02
❑ 88	Alfredo Griffin	.05	.02
❑ 89	Bret Saberhagen	.10	.05
❑ 90	Bert Blyleven	.10	.05
❑ 91	Jeff Reardon	.10	.05
❑ 92	Cory Snyder	.05	.02
❑ 93A	Greg Walker ERR (93 of 66)	2.00	.90
❑ 93B	Greg Walker COR (93 of 660)	.05	.02
❑ 94	Joe Magrane	.05	.02
❑ 95	Rob Deer	.05	.02
❑ 96	Ray Knight	.05	.02
❑ 97	Casey Candaele	.05	.02
❑ 98	John Cerutti	.05	.02
❑ 99	Buddy Bell	.10	.05
❑ 100	Jack Clark	.10	.05
❑ 101	Eric Bell	.05	.02
❑ 102	Willie Wilson	.05	.02
❑ 103	Dave Schmidt	.05	.02
❑ 104	Dennis Eckersley UER (Complete games stats are wrong)	.10	.05
❑ 105	Don Sutton	.20	.09
❑ 106	Danny Tartabull	.05	.02
❑ 107	Fred McGriff	.20	.09
❑ 108	Les Straker	.05	.02
❑ 109	Lloyd Moseby	.05	.02
❑ 110	Roger Clemens	.40	.18
❑ 111	Glenn Hubbard	.05	.02
❑ 112	Ken Williams	.05	.02
❑ 113	Ruben Sierra	.05	.02
❑ 114	Stan Jefferson	.05	.02
❑ 115	Milt Thompson	.05	.02
❑ 116	Bobby Bonilla	.15	.07
❑ 117	Wayne Tolleson	.05	.02
❑ 118	Matt Williams	.50	.23
❑ 119	Chet Lemon	.05	.02
❑ 120	Dale Sveum	.05	.02
❑ 121	Dennis Boyd	.05	.02
❑ 122	Brett Butler	.10	.05
❑ 123	Terry Kennedy	.05	.02
❑ 124	Jack Howell	.05	.02
❑ 125	Curt Young	.05	.02
❑ 126A	Dave Valle ERR (Misspelled Dale on card front)	.10	.05
❑ 126B	Dave Valle COR	.05	.02
❑ 127	Curt Wilkerson	.05	.02
❑ 128	Tim Teufel	.05	.02
❑ 129	Ozzie Virgil	.05	.02
❑ 130	Brian Fisher	.05	.02
❑ 131	Lance Parrish	.05	.02
❑ 132	Tom Browning	.05	.02
❑ 133A	Larry Andersen ERR (Misspelled Anderson on card front)	.10	.05
❑ 133B	Larry Andersen COR	.05	.02
❑ 134A	Bob Brenly ERR (Misspelled Brenley on card front)	.10	.05
❑ 134B	Bob Brenly COR	.05	.02
❑ 135	Mike Marshall	.05	.02
❑ 136	Gerald Perry	.05	.02
❑ 137	Bobby Meacham	.05	.02
❑ 138	Larry Herndon	.05	.02
❑ 139	Fred Manrique	.05	.02
❑ 140	Charlie Hough	.10	.05
❑ 141	Ron Darling	.05	.02
❑ 142	Herm Winningham	.05	.02
❑ 143	Mike Diaz	.05	.02
❑ 144	Mike Jackson	.20	.09
❑ 145	Denny Walling	.05	.02
❑ 146	Robby Thompson	.05	.02
❑ 147	Franklin Stubbs	.05	.02
❑ 148	Albert Hall	.05	.02
❑ 149	Bobby Witt	.05	.02
❑ 150	Lance McCullers	.05	.02
❑ 151	Scott Bradley	.05	.02
❑ 152	Mark McLemore	.05	.02
❑ 153	Tim Laudner	.05	.02
❑ 154	Greg Swindell	.05	.02
❑ 155	Marty Barrett	.05	.02
❑ 156	Mike Heath	.05	.02
❑ 157	Gary Ward	.05	.02
❑ 158A	Lee Mazzilli ERR (Misspelled Mazilli on card front)	.10	.05
❑ 158B	Lee Mazzilli COR	.05	.02
❑ 159	Tom Foley	.05	.02
❑ 160	Robin Yount	.20	.09
❑ 161	Steve Bedrosian	.05	.02
❑ 162	Bob Walk	.05	.02
❑ 163	Nick Esasky	.05	.02
❑ 164	Ken Caminiti	.75	.35
❑ 165	Jose Uribe	.05	.02
❑ 166	Dave Anderson	.05	.02
❑ 167	Ed Whitson	.05	.02
❑ 168	Ernie Whitt	.05	.02
❑ 169	Cecil Cooper	.10	.05
❑ 170	Mike Pagliarulo	.05	.02
❑ 171	Pat Sheridan	.05	.02
❑ 172	Chris Bando	.05	.02
❑ 173	Lee Lacy	.05	.02
❑ 174	Steve Lombardozzi	.05	.02
❑ 175	Mike Greenwell	.05	.02
❑ 176	Greg Minton	.05	.02
❑ 177	Moose Haas	.05	.02
❑ 178	Mike Kingery	.05	.02
❑ 179	Greg A. Harris	.05	.02
❑ 180	Bo Jackson	.20	.09
❑ 181	Carmelo Martinez	.05	.02
❑ 182	Alex Trevino	.05	.02
❑ 183	Ron Oester	.05	.02
❑ 184	Danny Darwin	.05	.02
❑ 185	Mike Krukow	.05	.02
❑ 186	Rafael Palmeiro	.20	.09
❑ 187	Tim Burke	.05	.02
❑ 188	Roger McDowell	.05	.02
❑ 189	Garry Templeton	.05	.02
❑ 190	Terry Pendleton	.10	.05
❑ 191	Larry Parrish	.05	.02
❑ 192	Rey Quinones	.05	.02
❑ 193	Joaquin Andujar	.05	.02
❑ 194	Tom Brunansky	.05	.02
❑ 195	Donnie Moore	.05	.02
❑ 196	Dan Pasqua	.05	.02
❑ 197	Jim Gantner	.05	.02
❑ 198	Mark Eichhorn	.05	.02
❑ 199	John Grubb	.05	.02
❑ 200	Bill Ripken	.05	.02
❑ 201	Sam Horn	.05	.02
❑ 202	Todd Worrell	.10	.05
❑ 203	Terry Leach	.05	.02
❑ 204	Garth Iorg	.05	.02
❑ 205	Brian Dayett	.05	.02
❑ 206	Bo Diaz	.05	.02
❑ 207	Craig Reynolds	.05	.02
❑ 208	Brian Holton	.05	.02
❑ 209	Marvell Wynne UER (Misspelled Marvelle on card front)	.05	.02
❑ 210	Dave Concepcion	.10	.05
❑ 211	Mike Davis	.05	.02
❑ 212	Devon White	.10	.05
❑ 213	Mickey Brantley	.05	.02
❑ 214	Greg Gagne	.05	.02
❑ 215	Oddibe McDowell	.05	.02
❑ 216	Jimmy Key	.10	.05
❑ 217	Dave Bergman	.05	.02
❑ 218	Calvin Schiraldi	.05	.02
❑ 219	Larry Sheets	.05	.02
❑ 220	Mike Easler	.05	.02
❑ 221	Kurt Stillwell	.05	.02
❑ 222	Chuck Jackson	.05	.02
❑ 223	Dave Martinez	.05	.02
❑ 224	Tim Leary	.05	.02
❑ 225	Steve Garvey	.15	.07
❑ 226	Greg Mathews	.05	.02
❑ 227	Doug Sisk	.05	.02
❑ 228	Dave Henderson (Wearing Red Sox uniform; Red Sox logo on back)	.05	.02
❑ 229	Jimmy Dwyer	.05	.02
❑ 230	Larry Owen	.05	.02
❑ 231	Andre Thornton	.10	.05
❑ 232	Mark Salas	.05	.02
❑ 233	Tom Brookens	.05	.02
❑ 234	Greg Brock	.05	.02
❑ 235	Rance Mulliniks	.05	.02
❑ 236	Bob Brower	.05	.02
❑ 237	Joe Niekro	.05	.02
❑ 238	Scott Bankhead	.05	.02
❑ 239	Doug DeCinces	.05	.02
❑ 240	Tommy John	.10	.05
❑ 241	Rich Gedman	.05	.02
❑ 242	Ted Power	.05	.02
❑ 243	Dave Meads	.05	.02
❑ 244	Jim Sundberg	.05	.02
❑ 245	Ken Oberkfell	.05	.02
❑ 246	Jimmy Jones	.05	.02
❑ 247	Ken Landreaux	.05	.02
❑ 248	Jose Oquendo	.05	.02
❑ 249	John Mitchell	.05	.02

- ❑ 250 Don Baylor .10 .05
- ❑ 251 Scott Fletcher .05 .02
- ❑ 252 Al Newman .05 .02
- ❑ 253 Carney Lansford .10 .05
- ❑ 254 Johnny Ray .05 .02
- ❑ 255 Gary Pettis .05 .02
- ❑ 256 Ken Phelps .05 .02
- ❑ 257 Rick Leach .05 .02
- ❑ 258 Tim Stoddard .05 .02
- ❑ 259 Ed Romero .05 .02
- ❑ 260 Sid Bream .05 .02
- ❑ 261A Tom Niedenfuer ERR .10 .05 (Misspelled Neidenfuer on card front)
- ❑ 261B Tom Niedenfuer COR .05 .02
- ❑ 262 Rick Dempsey .05 .02
- ❑ 263 Lonnie Smith .05 .02
- ❑ 264 Bob Forsch .05 .02
- ❑ 265 Barry Bonds .50 .23
- ❑ 266 Willie Randolph .10 .05
- ❑ 267 Mike Ramsey .05 .02
- ❑ 268 Don Slaught .05 .02
- ❑ 269 Mickey Tettleton .10 .05
- ❑ 270 Jerry Reuss .05 .02
- ❑ 271 Marc Sullivan .05 .02
- ❑ 272 Jim Morrison .05 .02
- ❑ 273 Steve Balboni .05 .02
- ❑ 274 Dick Schofield .05 .02
- ❑ 275 John Tudor .05 .02
- ❑ 276 Gene Larkin .05 .02
- ❑ 277 Harold Reynolds .10 .05
- ❑ 278 Jerry Browne .05 .02
- ❑ 279 Willie Upshaw .05 .02
- ❑ 280 Ted Higuera .05 .02
- ❑ 281 Terry McGriff .05 .02
- ❑ 282 Terry Puhl .05 .02
- ❑ 283 Mark Wasinger .05 .02
- ❑ 284 Luis Salazar .05 .02
- ❑ 285 Ted Simmons .10 .05
- ❑ 286 John Shelby .05 .02
- ❑ 287 John Smiley .10 .05
- ❑ 288 Curt Ford .05 .02
- ❑ 289 Steve Crawford .05 .02
- ❑ 290 Dan Quisenberry .05 .02
- ❑ 291 Alan Wiggins .05 .02
- ❑ 292 Randy Bush .05 .02
- ❑ 293 John Candelaria .05 .02
- ❑ 294 Tony Phillips .05 .02
- ❑ 295 Mike Morgan .05 .02
- ❑ 296 Bill Wegman .05 .02
- ❑ 297A Terry Francona ERR .10 .05 (Misspelled Franconia on card front)
- ❑ 297B Terry Francona COR .05 .02
- ❑ 298 Mickey Hatcher .05 .02
- ❑ 299 Andres Thomas .05 .02
- ❑ 300 Bob Stanley .05 .02
- ❑ 301 Al Pedrique .05 .02
- ❑ 302 Jim Lindeman .05 .02
- ❑ 303 Wally Backman .05 .02
- ❑ 304 Paul O'Neill .15 .07
- ❑ 305 Hubie Brooks .05 .02
- ❑ 306 Steve Buechele .05 .02
- ❑ 307 Bobby Thigpen .05 .02
- ❑ 308 George Hendrick .05 .02
- ❑ 309 John Moses .05 .02
- ❑ 310 Ron Guidry .05 .02
- ❑ 311 Bill Schroeder .05 .02
- ❑ 312 Jose Nunez .05 .02
- ❑ 313 Bud Black .05 .02
- ❑ 314 Joe Sambito .05 .02
- ❑ 315 Scott McGregor .05 .02
- ❑ 316 Rafael Santana .05 .02
- ❑ 317 Frank Williams .05 .02
- ❑ 318 Mike Fitzgerald .05 .02
- ❑ 319 Rick Mahler .05 .02
- ❑ 320 Jim Gott .05 .02
- ❑ 321 Mariano Duncan .05 .02
- ❑ 322 Jose Guzman .05 .02
- ❑ 323 Lee Guetterman .05 .02
- ❑ 324 Dan Gladden .05 .02
- ❑ 325 Gary Carter .15 .07
- ❑ 326 Tracy Jones .05 .02
- ❑ 327 Floyd Youmans .05 .02
- ❑ 328 Bill Dawley .05 .02
- ❑ 329 Paul Noce .05 .02
- ❑ 330 Angel Salazar .05 .02
- ❑ 331 Goose Gossage .15 .07
- ❑ 332 George Frazier .05 .02
- ❑ 333 Ruppert Jones .05 .02
- ❑ 334 Billy Joe Robidoux .05 .02
- ❑ 335 Mike Scott .05 .02
- ❑ 336 Randy Myers .15 .07
- ❑ 337 Bob Sebra .05 .02
- ❑ 338 Eric Show .05 .02
- ❑ 339 Mitch Williams .05 .02
- ❑ 340 Paul Molitor .20 .09
- ❑ 341 Gus Polidor .05 .02
- ❑ 342 Steve Trout .05 .02
- ❑ 343 Jerry Don Gleaton .05 .02
- ❑ 344 Bob Knepper .05 .02
- ❑ 345 Mitch Webster .05 .02
- ❑ 346 John Morris .05 .02
- ❑ 347 Andy Hawkins .05 .02
- ❑ 348 Dave Leiper .05 .02
- ❑ 349 Ernest Riles .05 .02
- ❑ 350 Dwight Gooden .10 .05
- ❑ 351 Dave Righetti .05 .02
- ❑ 352 Pat Dodson .05 .02
- ❑ 353 John Habyan .05 .02
- ❑ 354 Jim Deshaies .05 .02
- ❑ 355 Butch Wynegar .05 .02
- ❑ 356 Bryn Smith .05 .02
- ❑ 357 Matt Young .05 .02
- ❑ 358 Tom Pagnozzi .10 .05
- ❑ 359 Floyd Rayford .05 .02
- ❑ 360 Darryl Strawberry .10 .05
- ❑ 361 Sal Butera .05 .02
- ❑ 362 Domingo Ramos .05 .02
- ❑ 363 Chris Brown .05 .02
- ❑ 364 Jose Gonzalez .05 .02
- ❑ 365 Dave Smith .05 .02
- ❑ 366 Andy McGaffigan .05 .02
- ❑ 367 Stan Javier .05 .02
- ❑ 368 Henry Cotto .05 .02
- ❑ 369 Mike Birkbeck .05 .02
- ❑ 370 Len Dykstra .10 .05
- ❑ 371 Dave Collins .05 .02
- ❑ 372 Spike Owen .05 .02
- ❑ 373 Geno Petralli .05 .02
- ❑ 374 Ron Karkovice .05 .02
- ❑ 375 Shane Rawley .05 .02
- ❑ 376 DeWayne Buice .05 .02
- ❑ 377 Bill Pecota .05 .02
- ❑ 378 Leon Durham .05 .02
- ❑ 379 Ed Olwine .05 .02
- ❑ 380 Bruce Hurst .05 .02
- ❑ 381 Bob McClure .05 .02
- ❑ 382 Mark Thurmond .05 .02
- ❑ 383 Buddy Biancalana .05 .02
- ❑ 384 Tim Conroy .05 .02
- ❑ 385 Tony Gwynn .50 .23
- ❑ 386 Greg Gross .05 .02
- ❑ 387 Barry Lyons .05 .02
- ❑ 388 Mike Felder .05 .02
- ❑ 389 Pat Clements .05 .02
- ❑ 390 Ken Griffey .10 .05
- ❑ 391 Mark Davis .05 .02
- ❑ 392 Jose Rijo .05 .02
- ❑ 393 Mike Young .05 .02
- ❑ 394 Willie Fraser .05 .02
- ❑ 395 Dion James .05 .02
- ❑ 396 Steve Shields .05 .02
- ❑ 397 Randy St.Claire .05 .02
- ❑ 398 Danny Jackson .05 .02
- ❑ 399 Cecil Fielder .15 .07
- ❑ 400 Keith Hernandez .10 .05
- ❑ 401 Don Carman .05 .02
- ❑ 402 Chuck Crim .05 .02
- ❑ 403 Rob Woodward .05 .02
- ❑ 404 Junior Ortiz .05 .02
- ❑ 405 Glenn Wilson .05 .02
- ❑ 406 Ken Howell .05 .02
- ❑ 407 Jeff Kunkel .05 .02
- ❑ 408 Jeff Reed .05 .02
- ❑ 409 Chris James .05 .02
- ❑ 410 Zane Smith .05 .02
- ❑ 411 Ken Dixon .05 .02
- ❑ 412 Ricky Horton .05 .02
- ❑ 413 Frank DiPino .05 .02
- ❑ 414 Shane Mack .05 .02
- ❑ 415 Danny Cox .05 .02
- ❑ 416 Andy Van Slyke .10 .05
- ❑ 417 Danny Heep .05 .02
- ❑ 418 John Cangelosi .05 .02
- ❑ 419A John Christensen ERR .10 .05 (Christiansen on card front)
- ❑ 419B John Christensen COR .05 .02
- ❑ 420 Joey Cora .25 .11
- ❑ 421 Mike LaValliere .05 .02
- ❑ 422 Kelly Gruber .05 .02
- ❑ 423 Bruce Benedict .05 .02
- ❑ 424 Len Matuszek .05 .02
- ❑ 425 Kent Tekulve .05 .02
- ❑ 426 Rafael Ramirez .05 .02
- ❑ 427 Mike Flanagan .05 .02
- ❑ 428 Mike Gallego .05 .02
- ❑ 429 Juan Castillo .05 .02
- ❑ 430 Neal Heaton .05 .02
- ❑ 431 Phil Garner .05 .02
- ❑ 432 Mike Dunne .05 .02
- ❑ 433 Wallace Johnson .05 .02
- ❑ 434 Jack O'Connor .05 .02
- ❑ 435 Steve Jeltz .05 .02
- ❑ 436 Donell Nixon .05 .02
- ❑ 437 Jack Lazorko .05 .02
- ❑ 438 Keith Comstock .05 .02
- ❑ 439 Jeff D. Robinson .05 .02
- ❑ 440 Graig Nettles .10 .05
- ❑ 441 Mel Hall .05 .02
- ❑ 442 Gerald Young .05 .02
- ❑ 443 Gary Redus .05 .02
- ❑ 444 Charlie Moore .05 .02
- ❑ 445 Bill Madlock .10 .05
- ❑ 446 Mark Clear .05 .02
- ❑ 447 Greg Booker .05 .02
- ❑ 448 Rick Schu .05 .02
- ❑ 449 Ron Kittle .05 .02
- ❑ 450 Dale Murphy .20 .09
- ❑ 451 Bob Dernier .05 .02
- ❑ 452 Dale Mohorcic .05 .02
- ❑ 453 Rafael Belliard .05 .02
- ❑ 454 Charlie Puleo .05 .02
- ❑ 455 Dwayne Murphy .05 .02
- ❑ 456 Jim Eisenreich .20 .09
- ❑ 457 David Palmer .05 .02
- ❑ 458 Dave Stewart .10 .05
- ❑ 459 Pascual Perez .05 .02
- ❑ 460 Glenn Davis .05 .02
- ❑ 461 Dan Petry .05 .02
- ❑ 462 Jim Winn .05 .02
- ❑ 463 Darrell Miller .05 .02
- ❑ 464 Mike Moore .05 .02
- ❑ 465 Mike LaCoss .05 .02
- ❑ 466 Steve Farr .05 .02
- ❑ 467 Jerry Mumphrey .05 .02
- ❑ 468 Kevin Gross .05 .02
- ❑ 469 Bruce Bochy .05 .02
- ❑ 470 Orel Hershiser .10 .05
- ❑ 471 Eric King .05 .02
- ❑ 472 Ellis Burks .40 .18
- ❑ 473 Darren Daulton .10 .05
- ❑ 474 Mookie Wilson .10 .05
- ❑ 475 Frank Viola .05 .02
- ❑ 476 Ron Robinson .05 .02
- ❑ 477 Bob Melvin .05 .02
- ❑ 478 Jeff Musselman .05 .02
- ❑ 479 Charlie Kerfeld .05 .02
- ❑ 480 Richard Dotson .05 .02
- ❑ 481 Kevin Mitchell .10 .05
- ❑ 482 Gary Roenicke .05 .02
- ❑ 483 Tim Flannery .05 .02
- ❑ 484 Rich Yett .05 .02
- ❑ 485 Pete Incaviglia .05 .02
- ❑ 486 Rick Cerone .05 .02
- ❑ 487 Tony Armas .05 .02
- ❑ 488 Jerry Reed .05 .02
- ❑ 489 Dave Lopes .10 .05
- ❑ 490 Frank Tanana .05 .02
- ❑ 491 Mike Loynd .05 .02
- ❑ 492 Bruce Ruffin .05 .02
- ❑ 493 Chris Speier .05 .02
- ❑ 494 Tom Hume .05 .02
- ❑ 495 Jesse Orosco .05 .02

❑ 496 Robbie Wine UER .05 .02
(Misspelled Robby on card front)
❑ 497 Jeff Montgomery .20 .09
❑ 498 Jeff Dedmon .05 .02
❑ 499 Luis Aguayo .05 .02
❑ 500 Reggie Jackson .20 .09
(Oakland A's)
❑ 501 Reggie Jackson .20 .09
(Baltimore Orioles)
❑ 502 Reggie Jackson .20 .09
(New York Yankees)
❑ 503 Reggie Jackson .20 .09
(California Angels)
❑ 504 Reggie Jackson .20 .09
(Oakland A's)
❑ 505 Billy Hatcher .05 .02
❑ 506 Ed Lynch .05 .02
❑ 507 Willie Hernandez .05 .02
❑ 508 Jose DeLeon .05 .02
❑ 509 Joel Youngblood .05 .02
❑ 510 Bob Welch .05 .02
❑ 511 Steve Ontiveros .05 .02
❑ 512 Randy Ready .05 .02
❑ 513 Juan Nieves .05 .02
❑ 514 Jeff Russell .05 .02
❑ 515 Von Hayes .05 .02
❑ 516 Mark Gubicza .05 .02
❑ 517 Ken Dayley .05 .02
❑ 518 Don Aase .05 .02
❑ 519 Rick Reuschel .05 .02
❑ 520 Mike Henneman .10 .05
❑ 521 Rick Aguilera .10 .05
❑ 522 Jay Howell .05 .02
❑ 523 Ed Correa .05 .02
❑ 524 Manny Trillo .05 .02
❑ 525 Kirk Gibson .10 .05
❑ 526 Wally Ritchie .05 .02
❑ 527 Al Nipper .05 .02
❑ 528 Atlee Hammaker .05 .02
❑ 529 Shawon Dunston .05 .02
❑ 530 Jim Clancy .05 .02
❑ 531 Tom Paciorek .10 .05
❑ 532 Joel Skinner .05 .02
❑ 533 Scott Garrelts .05 .02
❑ 534 Tom O'Malley .05 .02
❑ 535 John Franco .10 .05
❑ 536 Paul Kilgus .05 .02
❑ 537 Darrell Porter .05 .02
❑ 538 Walt Terrell .05 .02
❑ 539 Bill Long .05 .02
❑ 540 George Bell .05 .02
❑ 541 Jeff Sellers .05 .02
❑ 542 Joe Boever .05 .02
❑ 543 Steve Howe .05 .02
❑ 544 Scott Sanderson .05 .02
❑ 545 Jack Morris .10 .05
❑ 546 Todd Benzinger .05 .02
❑ 547 Steve Henderson .05 .02
❑ 548 Eddie Milner .05 .02
❑ 549 Jeff M. Robinson .05 .02
❑ 550 Cal Ripken .75 .35
❑ 551 Jody Davis .05 .02
❑ 552 Kirk McCaskill .05 .02
❑ 553 Craig Lefferts .05 .02
❑ 554 Darnell Coles .05 .02
❑ 555 Phil Niekro .20 .09
❑ 556 Mike Aldrete .05 .02
❑ 557 Pat Perry .05 .02
❑ 558 Juan Agosto .05 .02
❑ 559 Rob Murphy .05 .02
❑ 560 Dennis Rasmussen .05 .02
❑ 561 Manny Lee .05 .02
❑ 562 Jeff Blauser .25 .11
❑ 563 Bob Ojeda .05 .02
❑ 564 Dave Dravecky .10 .05
❑ 565 Gene Garber .05 .02
❑ 566 Ron Roenicke .05 .02
❑ 567 Tommy Hinzo .05 .02
❑ 568 Eric Nolte .05 .02
❑ 569 Ed Hearn .05 .02
❑ 570 Mark Davidson .05 .02
❑ 571 Jim Walewander .05 .02
❑ 572 Donnie Hill UER .05 .02
(84 Stolen Base total listed as 7)
❑ 573 Jamie Moyer .05 .02
❑ 574 Ken Schrom .05 .02
❑ 575 Nolan Ryan .75 .35
❑ 576 Jim Acker .05 .02
❑ 577 Jamie Quirk .05 .02
❑ 578 Jay Aldrich .05 .02
❑ 579 Claudell Washington .05 .02
❑ 580 Jeff Leonard .05 .02
❑ 581 Carmen Castillo .05 .02
❑ 582 Daryl Boston .05 .02
❑ 583 Jeff DeWillis .05 .02
❑ 584 John Marzano .05 .02
❑ 585 Bill Gullickson .05 .02
❑ 586 Andy Allanson .05 .02
❑ 587 Lee Tunnell UER .05 .02
(1987 stat line reads .4.84 ERA)
❑ 588 Gene Nelson .05 .02
❑ 589 Dave LaPoint .05 .02
❑ 590 Harold Baines .10 .05
❑ 591 Bill Buckner .10 .05
❑ 592 Carlton Fisk .20 .09
❑ 593 Rick Manning .05 .02
❑ 594 Doug Jones .20 .09
❑ 595 Tom Candiotti .05 .02
❑ 596 Steve Lake .05 .02
❑ 597 Jose Lind .05 .02
❑ 598 Ross Jones .05 .02
❑ 599 Gary Matthews .05 .02
❑ 600 Fernando Valenzuela .10 .05
❑ 601 Dennis Martinez .10 .05
❑ 602 Les Lancaster .05 .02
❑ 603 Ozzie Guillen .05 .02
❑ 604 Tony Bernazard .05 .02
❑ 605 Chili Davis .15 .07
❑ 606 Roy Smalley .05 .02
❑ 607 Ivan Calderon .05 .02
❑ 608 Jay Tibbs .05 .02
❑ 609 Guy Hoffman .05 .02
❑ 610 Doyle Alexander .05 .02
❑ 611 Mike Bielecki .05 .02
❑ 612 Shawn Hillegas .05 .02
❑ 613 Keith Atherton .05 .02
❑ 614 Eric Plunk .05 .02
❑ 615 Sid Fernandez .05 .02
❑ 616 Dennis Lamp .05 .02
❑ 617 Dave Engle .05 .02
❑ 618 Harry Spilman .05 .02
❑ 619 Don Robinson .05 .02
❑ 620 John Farrell .05 .02
❑ 621 Nelson Liriano .05 .02
❑ 622 Floyd Bannister .05 .02
❑ 623 Randy Milligan .05 .02
❑ 624 Kevin Elster .05 .02
❑ 625 Jody Reed .10 .05
❑ 626 Shawn Abner .05 .02
❑ 627 Kirt Manwaring .05 .02
❑ 628 Pete Stanicek .05 .02
❑ 629 Rob Ducey .05 .02
❑ 630 Steve Kiefer .05 .02
❑ 631 Gary Thurman .05 .02
❑ 632 Darrel Akerfelds .05 .02
❑ 633 Dave Clark .05 .02
❑ 634 Roberto Kelly .20 .09
❑ 635 Keith Hughes .05 .02
❑ 636 John Davis .05 .02
❑ 637 Mike Devereaux .10 .05
❑ 638 Tom Glavine 1.00 .45
❑ 639 Keith A. Miller .05 .02
❑ 640 Chris Gwynn UER .10 .05
(Wrong batting and throwing on back)
❑ 641 Tim Crews .05 .02
❑ 642 Mackey Sasser .05 .02
❑ 643 Vicente Palacios .05 .02
❑ 644 Kevin Romine .05 .02
❑ 645 Gregg Jefferies .25 .11
❑ 646 Jeff Treadway .05 .02
❑ 647 Ron Gant .25 .11
❑ 648 Mark McGwire and .75 .35
Matt Nokes
(Rookie Sluggers)
❑ 649 Eric Davis and .10 .05
Tim Raines
(Speed and Power)
❑ 650 Don Mattingly and .15 .07
Jack Clark
❑ 651 Tony Fernandez& .25 .11
Alan Trammell& and
Cal Ripken
❑ 652 Vince Coleman HL .05 .02
100 Stolen Bases
❑ 653 Kirby Puckett HL .20 .09
10 Hits in a Row
❑ 654 Benito Santiago HL .05 .02
Hitting Streak
❑ 655 Juan Nieves HL .05 .02
No Hitter
❑ 656 Steve Bedrosian HL .05 .02
Saves Record
❑ 657 Mike Schmidt HL .15 .07
500 Homers
❑ 658 Don Mattingly HL .15 .07
Home Run Streak
❑ 659 Mark McGwire HL 1.00 .45
Rookie HR Record
❑ 660 Paul Molitor HL .15 .07
Hitting Streak

1988 Score Glossy

	MINT	NRMT
COMP.FACT.SET (660)	300.00	135.00
COMMON CARD (1-660)	.50	.23

*STARS: 15X TO 30X BASIC CARDS
*ROOKIES: 15X TO 30X BASIC CARDS

1988 Score Rookie/Traded

	MINT	NRMT
COMP.FACT.SET (110)	50.00	22.00
COMMON CARD (1T-110T)	.25	.11

❑ 1T Jack Clark .75 .35
❑ 2T Danny Jackson .25 .11
❑ 3T Brett Butler .75 .35
❑ 4T Kurt Stillwell .25 .11
❑ 5T Tom Brunansky .25 .11
❑ 6T Dennis Lamp .25 .11
❑ 7T Jose DeLeon .25 .11
❑ 8T Tom Herr .25 .11
❑ 9T Keith Moreland .25 .11
❑ 10T Kirk Gibson 3.00 1.35
❑ 11T Bud Black .25 .11
❑ 12T Rafael Ramirez .25 .11
❑ 13T Luis Salazar .25 .11
❑ 14T Goose Gossage 1.50 .70
❑ 15T Bob Welch .25 .11
❑ 16T Vance Law .25 .11
❑ 17T Ray Knight .25 .11
❑ 18T Dan Quisenberry .25 .11
❑ 19T Don Slaught .25 .11
❑ 20T Lee Smith .75 .35
❑ 21T Rick Cerone .25 .11
❑ 22T Pat Tabler .25 .11
❑ 23T Larry McWilliams .25 .11
❑ 24T Ricky Horton .25 .11
❑ 25T Graig Nettles .75 .35
❑ 26T Dan Petry .25 .11
❑ 27T Jose Rijo .25 .11
❑ 28T Chili Davis 1.50 .70
❑ 29T Dickie Thon .25 .11

Card	Player	MINT	NRMT
❑ 30T	Mackey Sasser	.25	.11
❑ 31T	Mickey Tettleton	.75	.35
❑ 32T	Rick Dempsey	.25	.11
❑ 33T	Ron Hassey	.25	.11
❑ 34T	Phil Bradley	.25	.11
❑ 35T	Jay Howell	.25	.11
❑ 36T	Bill Buckner	.75	.35
❑ 37T	Alfredo Griffin	.25	.11
❑ 38T	Gary Pettis	.25	.11
❑ 39T	Calvin Schiraldi	.25	.11
❑ 40T	John Candelaria	.25	.11
❑ 41T	Joe Orsulak	.25	.11
❑ 42T	Willie Upshaw	.25	.11
❑ 43T	Herm Winningham	.25	.11
❑ 44T	Ron Kittle	.25	.11
❑ 45T	Bob Dernier	.25	.11
❑ 46T	Steve Balboni	.25	.11
❑ 47T	Steve Shields	.25	.11
❑ 48T	Henry Cotto	.25	.11
❑ 49T	Dave Henderson	.25	.11
❑ 50T	Dave Parker	.75	.35
❑ 51T	Mike Young	.25	.11
❑ 52T	Mark Salas	.25	.11
❑ 53T	Mike Davis	.25	.11
❑ 54T	Rafael Santana	.25	.11
❑ 55T	Don Baylor	.75	.35
❑ 56T	Dan Pasqua	.25	.11
❑ 57T	Ernest Riles	.25	.11
❑ 58T	Glenn Hubbard	.25	.11
❑ 59T	Mike Smithson	.25	.11
❑ 60T	Richard Dotson	.25	.11
❑ 61T	Jerry Reuss	.25	.11
❑ 62T	Mike Jackson	3.00	1.35
❑ 63T	Floyd Bannister	.25	.11
❑ 64T	Jesse Orosco	.25	.11
❑ 65T	Larry Parrish	.25	.11
❑ 66T	Jeff Bittiger	.25	.11
❑ 67T	Ray Hayward	.25	.11
❑ 68T	Ricky Jordan	.75	.35
❑ 69T	Tommy Gregg	.25	.11
❑ 70T	Brady Anderson	5.00	2.20
❑ 71T	Jeff Montgomery	3.00	1.35
❑ 72T	Darryl Hamilton	.75	.35
❑ 73T	Cecil Espy	.25	.11
❑ 74T	Greg Briley	.25	.11
❑ 75T	Joey Meyer	.25	.11
❑ 76T	Mike Macfarlane	.25	.11
❑ 77T	Oswald Peraza	.25	.11
❑ 78T	Jack Armstrong	.25	.11
❑ 79T	Don Heinkel	.25	.11
❑ 80T	Mark Grace	8.00	3.60
❑ 81T	Steve Curry	.25	.11
❑ 82T	Damon Berryhill	.25	.11
❑ 83T	Steve Ellsworth	.25	.11
❑ 84T	Pete Smith	.25	.11
❑ 85T	Jack McDowell	3.00	1.35
❑ 86T	Rob Dibble	.75	.35
❑ 87T	Bryan Harvey UER (Games Pitched 47& Innings 5)	.75	.35
❑ 88T	John Dopson	.25	.11
❑ 89T	Dave Gallagher	.25	.11
❑ 90T	Todd Stottlemyre	2.00	.90
❑ 91T	Mike Schooler	.25	.11
❑ 92T	Don Gordon	.25	.11
❑ 93T	Sil Campusano	.25	.11
❑ 94T	Jeff Pico	.25	.11
❑ 95T	Jay Buhner	6.00	2.70
❑ 96T	Nelson Santovenia	.25	.11
❑ 97T	Al Leiter	3.00	1.35
❑ 98T	Luis Alicea	.75	.35
❑ 99T	Pat Borders	.75	.35
❑ 100T	Chris Sabo	.75	.35
❑ 101T	Tim Belcher	.75	.35
❑ 102T	Walt Weiss	2.00	.90
❑ 103T	Craig Biggio	15.00	6.75
❑ 104T	Don August	.25	.11
❑ 105T	Roberto Alomar	20.00	9.00
❑ 106T	Todd Burns	.25	.11
❑ 107T	John Costello	.25	.11
❑ 108T	Melido Perez	.25	.11
❑ 109T	Darrin Jackson	.25	.11
❑ 110T	Orestes Destrade	.75	.35

1988 Score Rookie/Traded Glossy

	MINT	NRMT
COMP.FACT.SET (110)	150.00	70.00
COMMON CARD (1T-110T)	.50	.23

*STARS: 1.5X TO 3X BASIC CARDS
*ROOKIES: 1.5X TO 3X BASIC CARDS

1989 Score

	MINT	NRMT
COMPLETE SET (660)	8.00	3.60
COMP.FACT.SET (660)	8.00	3.60
COMMON CARD (1-660)	.05	.02

Card	Player	MINT	NRMT
❑ 1	Jose Canseco	.20	.09
❑ 2	Andre Dawson	.20	.09
❑ 3	Mark McGwire UER	1.25	.55
❑ 4	Benito Santiago	.05	.02
❑ 5	Rick Reuschel	.05	.02
❑ 6	Fred McGriff	.20	.09
❑ 7	Kal Daniels	.05	.02
❑ 8	Gary Gaetti	.10	.05
❑ 9	Ellis Burks	.05	.02
❑ 10	Darryl Strawberry	.10	.05
❑ 11	Julio Franco	.05	.02
❑ 12	Lloyd Moseby	.05	.02
❑ 13	Jeff Pico	.05	.02
❑ 14	Johnny Ray	.05	.02
❑ 15	Cal Ripken	.75	.35
❑ 16	Dick Schofield	.05	.02
❑ 17	Mel Hall	.05	.02
❑ 18	Bill Ripken	.05	.02
❑ 19	Brook Jacoby	.05	.02
❑ 20	Kirby Puckett	.40	.18
❑ 21	Bill Doran	.05	.02
❑ 22	Pete O'Brien	.05	.02
❑ 23	Matt Nokes	.05	.02
❑ 24	Brian Fisher	.05	.02
❑ 25	Jack Clark	.05	.02
❑ 26	Gary Pettis	.05	.02
❑ 27	Dave Valle	.05	.02
❑ 28	Willie Wilson	.05	.02
❑ 29	Curt Young	.05	.02
❑ 30	Dale Murphy	.20	.09
❑ 31	Barry Larkin	.20	.09
❑ 32	Dave Stewart	.10	.05
❑ 33	Mike LaValliere	.05	.02
❑ 34	Glenn Hubbard	.05	.02
❑ 35	Ryne Sandberg	.25	.11
❑ 36	Tony Pena	.05	.02
❑ 37	Greg Walker	.05	.02
❑ 38	Von Hayes	.05	.02
❑ 39	Kevin Mitchell	.10	.05
❑ 40	Tim Raines	.10	.05
❑ 41	Keith Hernandez	.10	.05
❑ 42	Keith Moreland	.05	.02
❑ 43	Ruben Sierra	.05	.02
❑ 44	Chet Lemon	.05	.02
❑ 45	Willie Randolph	.10	.05
❑ 46	Andy Allanson	.05	.02
❑ 47	Candy Maldonado	.05	.02
❑ 48	Sid Bream	.05	.02
❑ 49	Denny Walling	.05	.02
❑ 50	Dave Winfield	.20	.09
❑ 51	Alvin Davis	.05	.02
❑ 52	Cory Snyder	.05	.02
❑ 53	Hubie Brooks	.05	.02
❑ 54	Chili Davis	.10	.05
❑ 55	Kevin Seitzer	.05	.02
❑ 56	Jose Uribe	.05	.02
❑ 57	Tony Fernandez	.05	.02
❑ 58	Tim Teufel	.05	.02
❑ 59	Oddibe McDowell	.05	.02
❑ 60	Les Lancaster	.05	.02
❑ 61	Billy Hatcher	.05	.02
❑ 62	Dan Gladden	.05	.02
❑ 63	Marty Barrett	.05	.02
❑ 64	Nick Esasky	.05	.02
❑ 65	Wally Joyner	.10	.05
❑ 66	Mike Greenwell	.05	.02
❑ 67	Ken Williams	.05	.02
❑ 68	Bob Horner	.05	.02
❑ 69	Steve Sax	.05	.02
❑ 70	Rickey Henderson	.20	.09
❑ 71	Mitch Webster	.05	.02
❑ 72	Rob Deer	.05	.02
❑ 73	Jim Presley	.05	.02
❑ 74	Albert Hall	.05	.02
❑ 75	George Brett COR (At age 35)	.40	.18
❑ 75A	George Brett ERR (At age 33)	.75	.35
❑ 76	Brian Downing	.05	.02
❑ 77	Dave Martinez	.05	.02
❑ 78	Scott Fletcher	.05	.02
❑ 79	Phil Bradley	.05	.02
❑ 80	Ozzie Smith	.25	.11
❑ 81	Larry Sheets	.05	.02
❑ 82	Mike Aldrete	.05	.02
❑ 83	Darnell Coles	.05	.02
❑ 84	Len Dykstra	.10	.05
❑ 85	Jim Rice	.10	.05
❑ 86	Jeff Treadway	.05	.02
❑ 87	Jose Lind	.05	.02
❑ 88	Willie McGee	.10	.05
❑ 89	Mickey Brantley	.05	.02
❑ 90	Tony Gwynn	.50	.23
❑ 91	R.J. Reynolds	.05	.02
❑ 92	Milt Thompson	.05	.02
❑ 93	Kevin McReynolds	.05	.02
❑ 94	Eddie Murray UER ('86 batting .205& should be .305)	.20	.09
❑ 95	Lance Parrish	.05	.02
❑ 96	Ron Kittle	.05	.02
❑ 97	Gerald Young	.05	.02
❑ 98	Ernie Whitt	.05	.02
❑ 99	Jeff Reed	.05	.02
❑ 100	Don Mattingly	.30	.14
❑ 101	Gerald Perry	.05	.02
❑ 102	Vance Law	.05	.02
❑ 103	John Shelby	.05	.02
❑ 104	Chris Sabo	.05	.02
❑ 105	Danny Tartabull	.05	.02
❑ 106	Glenn Wilson	.05	.02
❑ 107	Mark Davidson	.05	.02
❑ 108	Dave Parker	.10	.05
❑ 109	Eric Davis	.10	.05
❑ 110	Alan Trammell	.05	.02
❑ 111	Ozzie Virgil	.05	.02
❑ 112	Frank Tanana	.05	.02
❑ 113	Rafael Ramirez	.05	.02
❑ 114	Dennis Martinez	.10	.05
❑ 115	Jose DeLeon	.05	.02
❑ 116	Bob Ojeda	.05	.02
❑ 117	Doug Drabek	.05	.02
❑ 118	Andy Hawkins	.05	.02
❑ 119	Greg Maddux	.75	.35
❑ 120	Cecil Fielder UER (Reversed Photo on back)	.10	.05
❑ 121	Mike Scioscia	.05	.02
❑ 122	Dan Petry	.05	.02
❑ 123	Terry Kennedy	.05	.02
❑ 124	Kelly Downs	.05	.02
❑ 125	Greg Gross UER (Gregg on back)	.05	.02
❑ 126	Fred Lynn	.05	.02
❑ 127	Barry Bonds	.40	.18
❑ 128	Harold Baines	.10	.05
❑ 129	Doyle Alexander	.05	.02
❑ 130	Kevin Elster	.05	.02
❑ 131	Mike Heath	.05	.02

1988 Score

❑ 132 Teddy Higuera .05 .02
❑ 133 Charlie Leibrandt .05 .02
❑ 134 Tim Laudner .05 .02
❑ 135A Ray Knight ERR .20 .09
(Reverse negative)
❑ 135B Ray Knight COR .05 .02
❑ 136 Howard Johnson .05 .02
❑ 137 Terry Pendleton .10 .05
❑ 138 Andy McGaffigan .05 .02
❑ 139 Ken Oberkfell .05 .02
❑ 140 Butch Wynegar .05 .02
❑ 141 Rob Murphy .05 .02
❑ 142 Rich Renteria .05 .02
❑ 143 Jose Guzman .05 .02
❑ 144 Andres Galarraga .20 .09
❑ 145 Ricky Horton .05 .02
❑ 146 Frank DiPino .05 .02
❑ 147 Glenn Braggs .05 .02
❑ 148 John Kruk .10 .05
❑ 149 Mike Schmidt .25 .11
❑ 150 Lee Smith .10 .05
❑ 151 Robin Yount .20 .09
❑ 152 Mark Eichhorn .05 .02
❑ 153 DeWayne Buice .05 .02
❑ 154 B.J. Surhoff .10 .05
❑ 155 Vince Coleman .05 .02
❑ 156 Tony Phillips .05 .02
❑ 157 Willie Fraser .05 .02
❑ 158 Lance McCullers .05 .02
❑ 159 Greg Gagne .05 .02
❑ 160 Jesse Barfield .05 .02
❑ 161 Mark Langston .05 .02
❑ 162 Kurt Stillwell .05 .02
❑ 163 Dion James .05 .02
❑ 164 Glenn Davis .05 .02
❑ 165 Walt Weiss .05 .02
❑ 166 Dave Concepcion .10 .05
❑ 167 Alfredo Griffin .05 .02
❑ 168 Don Heinkel .05 .02
❑ 169 Luis Rivera .05 .02
❑ 170 Shane Rawley .05 .02
❑ 171 Darrell Evans .10 .05
❑ 172 Robby Thompson .05 .02
❑ 173 Jody Davis .05 .02
❑ 174 Andy Van Slyke .10 .05
❑ 175 Wade Boggs UER .20 .09
(Bio says .364&
should be .356)
❑ 176 Garry Templeton .05 .02
('85 stats
off-centered)
❑ 177 Gary Redus .05 .02
❑ 178 Craig Lefferts .05 .02
❑ 179 Carney Lansford .10 .05
❑ 180 Ron Darling .05 .02
❑ 181 Kirk McCaskill .05 .02
❑ 182 Tony Armas .05 .02
❑ 183 Steve Farr .05 .02
❑ 184 Tom Brunansky .05 .02
❑ 185 Bryan Harvey UER .05 .02
('87 games 47&
should be 3)
❑ 186 Mike Marshall .05 .02
❑ 187 Bo Diaz .05 .02
❑ 188 Willie Upshaw .05 .02
❑ 189 Mike Pagliarulo .05 .02
❑ 190 Mike Krukow .05 .02
❑ 191 Tommy Herr .05 .02
❑ 192 Jim Pankovits .05 .02
❑ 193 Dwight Evans .10 .05
❑ 194 Kelly Gruber .05 .02
❑ 195 Bobby Bonilla .05 .02
❑ 196 Wallace Johnson .05 .02
❑ 197 Dave Stieb .05 .02
❑ 198 Pat Borders .10 .05
❑ 199 Rafael Palmeiro .20 .09
❑ 200 Dwight Gooden .10 .05
❑ 201 Pete Incaviglia .05 .02
❑ 202 Chris James .05 .02
❑ 203 Marvell Wynne .05 .02
❑ 204 Pat Sheridan .05 .02
❑ 205 Don Baylor .10 .05
❑ 206 Paul O'Neill .10 .05
❑ 207 Pete Smith .05 .02
❑ 208 Mark McLemore .05 .02
❑ 209 Henry Cotto .05 .02
❑ 210 Kirk Gibson .10 .05
❑ 211 Claudell Washington .05 .02
❑ 212 Randy Bush .05 .02
❑ 213 Joe Carter .05 .02
❑ 214 Bill Buckner .10 .05
❑ 215 Bert Blyleven UER .10 .05
(Wrong birth year)
❑ 216 Brett Butler .10 .05
❑ 217 Lee Mazzilli .05 .02
❑ 218 Spike Owen .05 .02
❑ 219 Bill Swift .05 .02
❑ 220 Tim Wallach .05 .02
❑ 221 David Cone .20 .09
❑ 222 Don Carman .05 .02
❑ 223 Rich Gossage .10 .05
❑ 224 Bob Walk .05 .02
❑ 225 Dave Righetti .05 .02
❑ 226 Kevin Bass .05 .02
❑ 227 Kevin Gross .05 .02
❑ 228 Tim Burke .05 .02
❑ 229 Rick Mahler .05 .02
❑ 230 Lou Whitaker UER .10 .05
(252 games in '85&
should be 152)
❑ 231 Luis Alicea .05 .02
❑ 232 Roberto Alomar .30 .14
❑ 233 Bob Boone .10 .05
❑ 234 Dickie Thon .05 .02
❑ 235 Shawon Dunston .05 .02
❑ 236 Pete Stanicek .05 .02
❑ 237 Craig Biggio .75 .35
(Inconsistent design&
portrait on front)
❑ 238 Dennis Boyd .05 .02
❑ 239 Tom Candiotti .05 .02
❑ 240 Gary Carter .05 .02
❑ 241 Mike Stanley .05 .02
❑ 242 Ken Phelps .05 .02
❑ 243 Chris Bosio .05 .02
❑ 244 Les Straker .05 .02
❑ 245 Dave Smith .05 .02
❑ 246 John Candelaria .05 .02
❑ 247 Joe Orsulak .05 .02
❑ 248 Storm Davis .05 .02
❑ 249 Floyd Bannister UER .05 .02
(ML Batting Record)
❑ 250 Jack Morris .10 .05
❑ 251 Bret Saberhagen .10 .05
❑ 252 Tom Niedenfuer .05 .02
❑ 253 Neal Heaton .05 .02
❑ 254 Eric Show .05 .02
❑ 255 Juan Samuel .05 .02
❑ 256 Dale Sveum .05 .02
❑ 257 Jim Gott .05 .02
❑ 258 Scott Garrelts .05 .02
❑ 259 Larry McWilliams .05 .02
❑ 260 Steve Bedrosian .05 .02
❑ 261 Jack Howell .05 .02
❑ 262 Jay Tibbs .05 .02
❑ 263 Jamie Moyer .05 .02
❑ 264 Doug Sisk .05 .02
❑ 265 Todd Worrell .05 .02
❑ 266 John Farrell .05 .02
❑ 267 Dave Collins .05 .02
❑ 268 Sid Fernandez .05 .02
❑ 269 Tom Brookens .05 .02
❑ 270 Shane Mack .05 .02
❑ 271 Paul Kilgus .05 .02
❑ 272 Chuck Crim .05 .02
❑ 273 Bob Knepper .05 .02
❑ 274 Mike Moore .05 .02
❑ 275 Guillermo Hernandez .05 .02
❑ 276 Dennis Eckersley .05 .02
❑ 277 Graig Nettles .10 .05
❑ 278 Rich Dotson .05 .02
❑ 279 Larry Herndon .05 .02
❑ 280 Gene Larkin .05 .02
❑ 281 Roger McDowell .05 .02
❑ 282 Greg Swindell .05 .02
❑ 283 Juan Agosto .05 .02
❑ 284 Jeff M. Robinson .05 .02
❑ 285 Mike Dunne .05 .02
❑ 286 Greg Mathews .05 .02
❑ 287 Kent Tekulve .05 .02
❑ 288 Jerry Mumphrey .05 .02
❑ 289 Jack McDowell .10 .05
❑ 290 Frank Viola .05 .02
❑ 291 Mark Gubicza .05 .02
❑ 292 Dave Schmidt .05 .02
❑ 293 Mike Henneman .05 .02
❑ 294 Jimmy Jones .05 .02
❑ 295 Charlie Hough .10 .05
❑ 296 Rafael Santana .05 .02
❑ 297 Chris Speier .05 .02
❑ 298 Mike Witt .05 .02
❑ 299 Pascual Perez .05 .02
❑ 300 Nolan Ryan .75 .35
❑ 301 Mitch Williams .05 .02
❑ 302 Mookie Wilson .10 .05
❑ 303 Mackey Sasser .05 .02
❑ 304 John Cerutti .05 .02
❑ 305 Jeff Reardon .10 .05
❑ 306 Randy Myers UER .10 .05
(6 hits in '87&
should be 61)
❑ 307 Greg Brock .05 .02
❑ 308 Bob Welch .05 .02
❑ 309 Jeff D. Robinson .05 .02
❑ 310 Harold Reynolds .05 .02
❑ 311 Jim Walewander .05 .02
❑ 312 Dave Magadan .05 .02
❑ 313 Jim Gantner .05 .02
❑ 314 Walt Terrell .05 .02
❑ 315 Wally Backman .05 .02
❑ 316 Luis Salazar .05 .02
❑ 317 Rick Rhoden .05 .02
❑ 318 Tom Henke .05 .02
❑ 319 Mike Macfarlane .05 .02
❑ 320 Dan Plesac .05 .02
❑ 321 Calvin Schiraldi .05 .02
❑ 322 Stan Javier .05 .02
❑ 323 Devon White .10 .05
❑ 324 Scott Bradley .05 .02
❑ 325 Bruce Hurst .05 .02
❑ 326 Manny Lee .05 .02
❑ 327 Rick Aguilera .10 .05
❑ 328 Bruce Ruffin .05 .02
❑ 329 Ed Whitson .05 .02
❑ 330 Bo Jackson .05 .02
❑ 331 Ivan Calderon .05 .02
❑ 332 Mickey Hatcher .05 .02
❑ 333 Barry Jones .05 .02
❑ 334 Ron Hassey .05 .02
❑ 335 Bill Wegman .05 .02
❑ 336 Damon Berryhill .05 .02
❑ 337 Steve Ontiveros .05 .02
❑ 338 Dan Pasqua .05 .02
❑ 339 Bill Pecota .05 .02
❑ 340 Greg Cadaret .05 .02
❑ 341 Scott Bankhead .05 .02
❑ 342 Ron Guidry .10 .05
❑ 343 Danny Heep .05 .02
❑ 344 Bob Brower .05 .02
❑ 345 Rich Gedman .05 .02
❑ 346 Nelson Santovenia .05 .02
❑ 347 George Bell .05 .02
❑ 348 Ted Power .05 .02
❑ 349 Mark Grant .05 .02
❑ 350 Roger Clemens COR .40 .18
(78 career wins)
❑ 350A Roger Clemens ERR 2.00 .90
(778 career wins)
❑ 351 Bill Long .05 .02
❑ 352 Jay Bell .05 .02
❑ 353 Steve Balboni .05 .02
❑ 354 Bob Kipper .05 .02
❑ 355 Steve Jeltz .05 .02
❑ 356 Jesse Orosco .05 .02
❑ 357 Bob Dernier .05 .02
❑ 358 Mickey Tettleton .10 .05
❑ 359 Duane Ward .05 .02
❑ 360 Darrin Jackson .05 .02
❑ 361 Rey Quinones .05 .02
❑ 362 Mark Grace .20 .09
❑ 363 Steve Lake .05 .02
❑ 364 Pat Perry .05 .02
❑ 365 Terry Steinbach .10 .05
❑ 366 Alan Ashby .05 .02
❑ 367 Jeff Montgomery .10 .05

❑ 368	Steve Buechele	.05	.02
❑ 369	Chris Brown	.05	.02
❑ 370	Orel Hershiser	.10	.05
❑ 371	Todd Benzinger	.05	.02
❑ 372	Ron Gant	.10	.05
❑ 373	Paul Assenmacher	.05	.02
❑ 374	Joey Meyer	.05	.02
❑ 375	Neil Allen	.05	.02
❑ 376	Mike Davis	.05	.02
❑ 377	Jeff Parrett	.05	.02
❑ 378	Jay Howell	.05	.02
❑ 379	Rafael Belliard	.05	.02
❑ 380	Luis Polonia UER (2 triples in '87& should be 10)	.05	.02
❑ 381	Keith Atherton	.05	.02
❑ 382	Kent Hrbek	.10	.05
❑ 383	Bob Stanley	.05	.02
❑ 384	Dave LaPoint	.05	.02
❑ 385	Rance Mulliniks	.05	.02
❑ 386	Melido Perez	.05	.02
❑ 387	Doug Jones	.05	.02
❑ 388	Steve Lyons	.05	.02
❑ 389	Alejandro Pena	.05	.02
❑ 390	Frank White	.10	.05
❑ 391	Pat Tabler	.05	.02
❑ 392	Eric Plunk	.05	.02
❑ 393	Mike Maddux	.05	.02
❑ 394	Allan Anderson	.05	.02
❑ 395	Bob Brenly	.05	.02
❑ 396	Rick Cerone	.05	.02
❑ 397	Scott Terry	.05	.02
❑ 398	Mike Jackson	.05	.02
❑ 399	Bobby Thigpen UER (Bio says 37 saves in '88& should be 34)	.05	.02
❑ 400	Don Sutton	.20	.09
❑ 401	Cecil Espy	.05	.02
❑ 402	Junior Ortiz	.05	.02
❑ 403	Mike Smithson	.05	.02
❑ 404	Bud Black	.05	.02
❑ 405	Tom Foley	.05	.02
❑ 406	Andres Thomas	.05	.02
❑ 407	Rick Sutcliffe	.05	.02
❑ 408	Brian Harper	.05	.02
❑ 409	John Smiley	.05	.02
❑ 410	Juan Nieves	.05	.02
❑ 411	Shawn Abner	.05	.02
❑ 412	Wes Gardner	.05	.02
❑ 413	Darren Daulton	.10	.05
❑ 414	Juan Berenguer	.05	.02
❑ 415	Charles Hudson	.05	.02
❑ 416	Rick Honeycutt	.05	.02
❑ 417	Greg Booker	.05	.02
❑ 418	Tim Belcher	.05	.02
❑ 419	Don August	.05	.02
❑ 420	Dale Mohorcic	.05	.02
❑ 421	Steve Lombardozzi	.05	.02
❑ 422	Atlee Hammaker	.05	.02
❑ 423	Jerry Don Gleaton	.05	.02
❑ 424	Scott Bailes	.05	.02
❑ 425	Bruce Sutter	.05	.02
❑ 426	Randy Ready	.05	.02
❑ 427	Jerry Reed	.05	.02
❑ 428	Bryn Smith	.05	.02
❑ 429	Tim Leary	.05	.02
❑ 430	Mark Clear	.05	.02
❑ 431	Terry Leach	.05	.02
❑ 432	John Moses	.05	.02
❑ 433	Ozzie Guillen	.05	.02
❑ 434	Gene Nelson	.05	.02
❑ 435	Gary Ward	.05	.02
❑ 436	Luis Aguayo	.05	.02
❑ 437	Fernando Valenzuela	.10	.05
❑ 438	Jeff Russell UER (Saves total does not add up correctly)	.05	.02
❑ 439	Cecilio Guante	.05	.02
❑ 440	Don Robinson	.05	.02
❑ 441	Rick Anderson	.05	.02
❑ 442	Tom Glavine	.20	.09
❑ 443	Daryl Boston	.05	.02
❑ 444	Joe Price	.05	.02
❑ 445	Stewart Cliburn	.05	.02
❑ 446	Manny Trillo	.05	.02
❑ 447	Joel Skinner	.05	.02
❑ 448	Charlie Puleo	.05	.02
❑ 449	Carlton Fisk	.20	.09
❑ 450	Will Clark	.20	.09
❑ 451	Otis Nixon	.10	.05
❑ 452	Rick Schu	.05	.02
❑ 453	Todd Stottlemyre UER (ML Batting Record)	.05	.02
❑ 454	Tim Birtsas	.05	.02
❑ 455	Dave Gallagher	.05	.02
❑ 456	Barry Lyons	.05	.02
❑ 457	Fred Manrique	.05	.02
❑ 458	Ernest Riles	.05	.02
❑ 459	Doug Jennings	.05	.02
❑ 460	Joe Magrane	.05	.02
❑ 461	Jamie Quirk	.05	.02
❑ 462	Jack Armstrong	.05	.02
❑ 463	Bobby Witt	.05	.02
❑ 464	Keith A. Miller	.05	.02
❑ 465	Todd Burns	.05	.02
❑ 466	John Dopson	.05	.02
❑ 467	Rich Yett	.05	.02
❑ 468	Craig Reynolds	.05	.02
❑ 469	Dave Bergman	.05	.02
❑ 470	Rex Hudler	.05	.02
❑ 471	Eric King	.05	.02
❑ 472	Joaquin Andujar	.05	.02
❑ 473	Sil Campusano	.05	.02
❑ 474	Terry Mulholland	.05	.02
❑ 475	Mike Flanagan	.05	.02
❑ 476	Greg A. Harris	.05	.02
❑ 477	Tommy John	.10	.05
❑ 478	Dave Anderson	.05	.02
❑ 479	Fred Toliver	.05	.02
❑ 480	Jimmy Key	.10	.05
❑ 481	Donell Nixon	.05	.02
❑ 482	Mark Portugal	.05	.02
❑ 483	Tom Pagnozzi	.05	.02
❑ 484	Jeff Kunkel	.05	.02
❑ 485	Frank Williams	.05	.02
❑ 486	Jody Reed	.05	.02
❑ 487	Roberto Kelly	.10	.05
❑ 488	Shawn Hillegas UER (165 innings in '87, should be 165.2)	.05	.02
❑ 489	Jerry Reuss	.05	.02
❑ 490	Mark Davis	.05	.02
❑ 491	Jeff Sellers	.05	.02
❑ 492	Zane Smith	.05	.02
❑ 493	Al Newman	.05	.02
❑ 494	Mike Young	.05	.02
❑ 495	Larry Parrish	.05	.02
❑ 496	Herm Winningham	.05	.02
❑ 497	Carmen Castillo	.05	.02
❑ 498	Joe Hesketh	.05	.02
❑ 499	Darrell Miller	.05	.02
❑ 500	Mike LaCoss	.05	.02
❑ 501	Charlie Lea	.05	.02
❑ 502	Bruce Benedict	.05	.02
❑ 503	Chuck Finley	.10	.05
❑ 504	Brad Wellman	.05	.02
❑ 505	Tim Crews	.05	.02
❑ 506	Ken Gerhart	.05	.02
❑ 507A	Brian Holton ERR (Born 1/25/65 Denver, should be 11/29/59 in McKeesport)	.05	.02
❑ 507B	Brian Holton COR	2.00	.90
❑ 508	Dennis Lamp	.05	.02
❑ 509	Bobby Meacham UER ('84 games 099)	.05	.02
❑ 510	Tracy Jones	.05	.02
❑ 511	Mike R. Fitzgerald	.05	.02
❑ 512	Jeff Bittiger	.05	.02
❑ 513	Tim Flannery	.05	.02
❑ 514	Ray Hayward	.05	.02
❑ 515	Dave Leiper	.05	.02
❑ 516	Rod Scurry	.05	.02
❑ 517	Carmelo Martinez	.05	.02
❑ 518	Curtis Wilkerson	.05	.02
❑ 519	Stan Jefferson	.05	.02
❑ 520	Dan Quisenberry	.05	.02
❑ 521	Lloyd McClendon	.05	.02
❑ 522	Steve Trout	.05	.02
❑ 523	Larry Andersen	.05	.02
❑ 524	Don Aase	.05	.02
❑ 525	Bob Forsch	.05	.02
❑ 526	Geno Petralli	.05	.02
❑ 527	Angel Salazar	.05	.02
❑ 528	Mike Schooler	.05	.02
❑ 529	Jose Oquendo	.05	.02
❑ 530	Jay Buhner UER (Wearing 43 on front, listed as 34 on back)	.20	.09
❑ 531	Tom Bolton	.05	.02
❑ 532	Al Nipper	.05	.02
❑ 533	Dave Henderson	.05	.02
❑ 534	John Costello	.05	.02
❑ 535	Donnie Moore	.05	.02
❑ 536	Mike Laga	.05	.02
❑ 537	Mike Gallego	.05	.02
❑ 538	Jim Clancy	.05	.02
❑ 539	Joel Youngblood	.05	.02
❑ 540	Rick Leach	.05	.02
❑ 541	Kevin Romine	.05	.02
❑ 542	Mark Salas	.05	.02
❑ 543	Greg Minton	.05	.02
❑ 544	Dave Palmer	.05	.02
❑ 545	Dwayne Murphy UER (Game-sinning)	.05	.02
❑ 546	Jim Deshaies	.05	.02
❑ 547	Don Gordon	.05	.02
❑ 548	Ricky Jordan	.10	.05
❑ 549	Mike Boddicker	.05	.02
❑ 550	Mike Scott	.05	.02
❑ 551	Jeff Ballard	.05	.02
❑ 552A	Jose Rijo ERR (Uniform listed as 27 on back)	.20	.09
❑ 552B	Jose Rijo COR (Uniform listed as 24 on back)	.20	.09
❑ 553	Danny Darwin	.05	.02
❑ 554	Tom Browning	.05	.02
❑ 555	Danny Jackson	.05	.02
❑ 556	Rick Dempsey	.05	.02
❑ 557	Jeffrey Leonard	.05	.02
❑ 558	Jeff Musselman	.05	.02
❑ 559	Ron Robinson	.05	.02
❑ 560	John Tudor	.05	.02
❑ 561	Don Slaught UER (237 games in 1987)	.05	.02
❑ 562	Dennis Rasmussen	.05	.02
❑ 563	Brady Anderson	.40	.18
❑ 564	Pedro Guerrero	.05	.02
❑ 565	Paul Molitor	.20	.09
❑ 566	Terry Clark	.05	.02
❑ 567	Terry Puhl	.05	.02
❑ 568	Mike Campbell	.05	.02
❑ 569	Paul Mirabella	.05	.02
❑ 570	Jeff Hamilton	.05	.02
❑ 571	Oswald Peraza	.05	.02
❑ 572	Bob McClure	.05	.02
❑ 573	Jose Bautista	.05	.02
❑ 574	Alex Trevino	.05	.02
❑ 575	John Franco	.10	.05
❑ 576	Mark Parent	.05	.02
❑ 577	Nelson Liriano	.05	.02
❑ 578	Steve Shields	.05	.02
❑ 579	Odell Jones	.05	.02
❑ 580	Al Leiter	.20	.09
❑ 581	Dave Stapleton	.05	.02
❑ 582	World Series '88 Orel Hershiser Jose Canseco Kirk Gibson Dave Stewart	.10	.05
❑ 583	Donnie Hill	.05	.02
❑ 584	Chuck Jackson	.05	.02
❑ 585	Rene Gonzales	.05	.02
❑ 586	Tracy Woodson	.05	.02
❑ 587	Jim Adduci	.05	.02
❑ 588	Mario Soto	.05	.02
❑ 589	Jeff Blauser	.10	.05
❑ 590	Jim Traber	.05	.02
❑ 591	Jon Perlman	.05	.02
❑ 592	Mark Williamson	.05	.02
❑ 593	Dave Meads	.05	.02
❑ 594	Jim Eisenreich	.05	.02
❑ 595A	Paul Gibson P1	1.00	.45

Card	Player	MINT	NRMT
❑ 595B	Paul Gibson P2	.05	.02
	(Airbrushed leg on player in background)		
❑ 596	Mike Birkbeck	.05	.02
❑ 597	Terry Francona	.10	.05
❑ 598	Paul Zuvella	.05	.02
❑ 599	Franklin Stubbs	.05	.02
❑ 600	Gregg Jefferies	.10	.05
❑ 601	John Cangelosi	.05	.02
❑ 602	Mike Sharperson	.05	.02
❑ 603	Mike Diaz	.05	.02
❑ 604	Gary Varsho	.05	.02
❑ 605	Terry Blocker	.05	.02
❑ 606	Charlie O'Brien	.05	.02
❑ 607	Jim Eppard	.05	.02
❑ 608	John Davis	.05	.02
❑ 609	Ken Griffey Sr.	.05	.02
❑ 610	Buddy Bell	.10	.05
❑ 611	Ted Simmons UER	.10	.05
	('78 stats Cardinal)		
❑ 612	Matt Williams	.20	.09
❑ 613	Danny Cox	.05	.02
❑ 614	Al Pedrique	.05	.02
❑ 615	Ron Oester	.05	.02
❑ 616	John Smoltz	.50	.23
❑ 617	Bob Melvin	.05	.02
❑ 618	Rob Dibble	.10	.05
❑ 619	Kirt Manwaring	.05	.02
❑ 620	Felix Fermin	.05	.02
❑ 621	Doug Dascenzo	.05	.02
❑ 622	Bill Brennan	.05	.02
❑ 623	Carlos Quintana	.05	.02
❑ 624	Mike Harkey UER	.05	.02
	(13 and 31 walks in '88& should be 35 and 33)		
❑ 625	Gary Sheffield	.60	.25
❑ 626	Tom Prince	.05	.02
❑ 627	Steve Searcy	.05	.02
❑ 628	Charlie Hayes	.20	.09
	(Listed as outfielder)		
❑ 629	Felix Jose UER	.05	.02
	(Modesto misspelled as Modesta)		
❑ 630	Sandy Alomar Jr.	.40	.18
	(Inconsistent design& portrait on front)		
❑ 631	Derek Lilliquist	.05	.02
❑ 632	Geronimo Berroa	.05	.02
❑ 633	Luis Medina	.05	.02
❑ 634	Tom Gordon UER	.20	.09
	(Height 6'0")		
❑ 635	Ramon Martinez	.25	.11
❑ 636	Craig Worthington	.05	.02
❑ 637	Edgar Martinez	.20	.09
❑ 638	Chad Kreuter	.05	.02
❑ 639	Ron Jones	.05	.02
❑ 640	Van Snider	.05	.02
❑ 641	Lance Blankenship	.05	.02
❑ 642	Dwight Smith UER	.10	.05
	(10 HR's in '87& should be-18)		
❑ 643	Cameron Drew	.05	.02
❑ 644	Jerald Clark	.05	.02
❑ 645	Randy Johnson	1.25	.55
❑ 646	Norm Charlton	.10	.05
❑ 647	Todd Frohwirth UER	.05	.02
	(Southpaw on back)		
❑ 648	Luis De Los Santos	.05	.02
❑ 649	Tim Jones	.05	.02
❑ 650	Dave West UER	.05	.02
	(ML hits 3& should be 6)		
❑ 651	Bob Milacki	.05	.02
❑ 652	Wrigley Field HL	.10	.05
	(Let There Be Lights)		
❑ 653	Orel Hershiser HL	.10	.05
	(The Streak)		
❑ 654A	Wade Boggs HL ERR	1.50	.70
	(Wade Whacks 'Em) ("seaason" on back)		
❑ 654B	Wade Boggs HL COR	.10	.05
	(Wade Whacks 'Em)		
❑ 655	Jose Canseco HL	.10	.05
	(One of a Kind)		
❑ 656	Doug Jones HL	.05	.02
	(Doug Sets Saves)		
❑ 657	Rickey Henderson HL	.10	.05
	(Rickey Rocks 'Em)		
❑ 658	Tom Browning HL	.05	.02
	(Tom Perfect Pitches)		
❑ 659	Mike Greenwell HL	.05	.02
	(Greenwell Gamers)		
❑ 660	Boston Red Sox HL	.05	.02
	(Joe Morgan MG& Sox Sock 'Em)		

1989 Score Rookie/Traded

	MINT	NRMT
COMP.FACT.SET (110)	25.00	11.00
COMMON CARD (1T-110T)	.05	.02

Card	Player	MINT	NRMT
❑ 1T	Rafael Palmeiro	.20	.09
❑ 2T	Nolan Ryan	1.50	.70
❑ 3T	Jack Clark	.05	.02
❑ 4T	Dave LaPoint	.05	.02
❑ 5T	Mike Moore	.05	.02
❑ 6T	Pete O'Brien	.05	.02
❑ 7T	Jeffrey Leonard	.05	.02
❑ 8T	Rob Murphy	.05	.02
❑ 9T	Tom Herr	.05	.02
❑ 10T	Claudell Washington	.05	.02
❑ 11T	Mike Pagliarulo	.05	.02
❑ 12T	Steve Lake	.05	.02
❑ 13T	Spike Owen	.05	.02
❑ 14T	Andy Hawkins	.05	.02
❑ 15T	Todd Benzinger	.05	.02
❑ 16T	Mookie Wilson	.10	.05
❑ 17T	Bert Blyleven	.10	.05
❑ 18T	Jeff Treadway	.05	.02
❑ 19T	Bruce Hurst	.05	.02
❑ 20T	Steve Sax	.05	.02
❑ 21T	Juan Samuel	.05	.02
❑ 22T	Jesse Barfield	.05	.02
❑ 23T	Carmen Castillo	.05	.02
❑ 24T	Terry Leach	.05	.02
❑ 25T	Mark Langston	.05	.02
❑ 26T	Eric King	.05	.02
❑ 27T	Steve Balboni	.05	.02
❑ 28T	Len Dykstra	.10	.05
❑ 29T	Keith Moreland	.05	.02
❑ 30T	Terry Kennedy	.05	.02
❑ 31T	Eddie Murray	.20	.09
❑ 32T	Mitch Williams	.05	.02
❑ 33T	Jeff Parrett	.05	.02
❑ 34T	Wally Backman	.05	.02
❑ 35T	Julio Franco	.05	.02
❑ 36T	Lance Parrish	.05	.02
❑ 37T	Nick Esasky	.05	.02
❑ 38T	Luis Polonia	.05	.02
❑ 39T	Kevin Gross	.05	.02
❑ 40T	John Dopson	.05	.02
❑ 41T	Willie Randolph	.10	.05
❑ 42T	Jim Clancy	.05	.02
❑ 43T	Tracy Jones	.05	.02
❑ 44T	Phil Bradley	.05	.02
❑ 45T	Milt Thompson	.05	.02
❑ 46T	Chris James	.05	.02
❑ 47T	Scott Fletcher	.05	.02
❑ 48T	Kal Daniels	.05	.02
❑ 49T	Steve Bedrosian	.05	.02
❑ 50T	Rickey Henderson	.20	.09
❑ 51T	Dion James	.05	.02
❑ 52T	Tim Leary	.05	.02
❑ 53T	Roger McDowell	.05	.02
❑ 54T	Mel Hall	.05	.02
❑ 55T	Dickie Thon	.05	.02
❑ 56T	Zane Smith	.05	.02
❑ 57T	Danny Heep	.05	.02
❑ 58T	Bob McClure	.05	.02
❑ 59T	Brian Holton	.05	.02
❑ 60T	Randy Ready	.05	.02
❑ 61T	Bob Melvin	.05	.02
❑ 62T	Harold Baines	.10	.05
❑ 63T	Lance McCullers	.05	.02
❑ 64T	Jody Davis	.05	.02
❑ 65T	Darrell Evans	.10	.05
❑ 66T	Joel Youngblood	.05	.02
❑ 67T	Frank Viola	.05	.02
❑ 68T	Mike Aldrete	.05	.02
❑ 69T	Greg Cadaret	.05	.02
❑ 70T	John Kruk	.10	.05
❑ 71T	Pat Sheridan	.05	.02
❑ 72T	Oddibe McDowell	.05	.02
❑ 73T	Tom Brookens	.05	.02
❑ 74T	Bob Boone	.10	.05
❑ 75T	Walt Terrell	.05	.02
❑ 76T	Joel Skinner	.05	.02
❑ 77T	Randy Johnson	2.00	.90
❑ 78T	Felix Fermin	.05	.02
❑ 79T	Rick Mahler	.05	.02
❑ 80T	Richard Dotson	.05	.02
❑ 81T	Cris Carpenter	.05	.02
❑ 82T	Bill Spiers	.05	.02
❑ 83T	Junior Felix	.05	.02
❑ 84T	Joe Girardi	.30	.14
❑ 85T	Jerome Walton	.20	.09
❑ 86T	Greg Litton	.05	.02
❑ 87T	Greg W.Harris	.05	.02
❑ 88T	Jim Abbott	.20	.09
❑ 89T	Kevin Brown	1.00	.45
❑ 90T	John Wetteland	.25	.11
❑ 91T	Gary Wayne	.05	.02
❑ 92T	Rich Monteleone	.05	.02
❑ 93T	Bob Geren	.05	.02
❑ 94T	Clay Parker	.05	.02
❑ 95T	Steve Finley	.25	.11
❑ 96T	Gregg Olson	.20	.09
❑ 97T	Ken Patterson	.05	.02
❑ 98T	Ken Hill	.20	.09
❑ 99T	Scott Scudder	.05	.02
❑ 100T	Ken Griffey Jr.	20.00	9.00
❑ 101T	Jeff Brantley	.05	.02
❑ 102T	Donn Pall	.05	.02
❑ 103T	Carlos Martinez	.05	.02
❑ 104T	Joe Oliver	.10	.05
❑ 105T	Omar Vizquel	.40	.18
❑ 106T	Joey Belle	6.00	2.70
❑ 107T	Kenny Rogers	.20	.09
❑ 108T	Mark Carreon	.05	.02
❑ 109T	Rolando Roomes	.05	.02
❑ 110T	Pete Harnisch	.10	.05

1990 Score

	MINT	NRMT
COMPLETE SET (704)	12.00	5.50
COMP.RETAIL SET (704)	12.00	5.50

COMP.HOBBY SET (714)	15.00	6.75
COMMON CARD (1-704)	.05	.02

❑	1	Don Mattingly	.30	.14
❑	2	Cal Ripken	.75	.35
❑	3	Dwight Evans	.10	.05
❑	4	Barry Bonds	.25	.11
❑	5	Kevin McReynolds	.05	.02
❑	6	Ozzie Guillen	.05	.02
❑	7	Terry Kennedy	.05	.02
❑	8	Bryan Harvey	.05	.02
❑	9	Alan Trammell	.15	.07
❑	10	Cory Snyder	.05	.02
❑	11	Jody Reed	.05	.02
❑	12	Roberto Alomar	.25	.11
❑	13	Pedro Guerrero	.05	.02
❑	14	Gary Redus	.05	.02
❑	15	Marty Barrett	.05	.02
❑	16	Ricky Jordan	.05	.02
❑	17	Joe Magrane	.05	.02
❑	18	Sid Fernandez	.05	.02
❑	19	Richard Dotson	.05	.02
❑	20	Jack Clark	.10	.05
❑	21	Bob Walk	.05	.02
❑	22	Ron Karkovice	.05	.02
❑	23	Lenny Harris	.05	.02
❑	24	Phil Bradley	.05	.02
❑	25	Andres Galarraga	.20	.09
❑	26	Brian Downing	.05	.02
❑	27	Dave Martinez	.05	.02
❑	28	Eric King	.05	.02
❑	29	Barry Lyons	.05	.02
❑	30	Dave Schmidt	.05	.02
❑	31	Mike Boddicker	.05	.02
❑	32	Tom Foley	.05	.02
❑	33	Brady Anderson	.20	.09
❑	34	Jim Presley	.05	.02
❑	35	Lance Parrish	.05	.02
❑	36	Von Hayes	.05	.02
❑	37	Lee Smith	.10	.05
❑	38	Herm Winningham	.05	.02
❑	39	Alejandro Pena	.05	.02
❑	40	Mike Scott	.05	.02
❑	41	Joe Orsulak	.05	.02
❑	42	Rafael Ramirez	.05	.02
❑	43	Gerald Young	.05	.02
❑	44	Dick Schofield	.05	.02
❑	45	Dave Smith	.05	.02
❑	46	Dave Magadan	.05	.02
❑	47	Dennis Martinez	.10	.05
❑	48	Greg Minton	.05	.02
❑	49	Milt Thompson	.05	.02
❑	50	Orel Hershiser	.10	.05
❑	51	Bip Roberts	.05	.02
❑	52	Jerry Browne	.05	.02
❑	53	Bob Ojeda	.05	.02
❑	54	Fernando Valenzuela	.10	.05
❑	55	Matt Nokes	.05	.02
❑	56	Brook Jacoby	.05	.02
❑	57	Frank Tanana	.05	.02
❑	58	Scott Fletcher	.05	.02
❑	59	Ron Oester	.05	.02
❑	60	Bob Boone	.10	.05
❑	61	Dan Gladden	.05	.02
❑	62	Darnell Coles	.05	.02
❑	63	Gregg Olson	.05	.02
❑	64	Todd Burns	.05	.02
❑	65	Todd Benzinger	.05	.02
❑	66	Dale Murphy	.20	.09
❑	67	Mike Flanagan	.05	.02
❑	68	Jose Oquendo	.05	.02
❑	69	Cecil Espy	.05	.02
❑	70	Chris Sabo	.05	.02
❑	71	Shane Rawley	.05	.02
❑	72	Tom Brunansky	.05	.02
❑	73	Vance Law	.05	.02
❑	74	B.J. Surhoff	.10	.05
❑	75	Lou Whitaker	.10	.05
❑	76	Ken Caminiti UER Euclid and Ohio should be Hanford and California	.20	.09
❑	77	Nelson Liriano	.05	.02
❑	78	Tommy Gregg	.05	.02
❑	79	Don Slaught	.05	.02
❑	80	Eddie Murray	.20	.09
❑	81	Joe Boever	.05	.02
❑	82	Charlie Leibrandt	.05	.02
❑	83	Jose Lind	.05	.02
❑	84	Tony Phillips	.05	.02
❑	85	Mitch Webster	.05	.02
❑	86	Dan Plesac	.05	.02
❑	87	Rick Mahler	.05	.02
❑	88	Steve Lyons	.05	.02
❑	89	Tony Fernandez	.05	.02
❑	90	Ryne Sandberg	.25	.11
❑	91	Nick Esasky	.05	.02
❑	92	Luis Salazar	.05	.02
❑	93	Pete Incaviglia	.05	.02
❑	94	Ivan Calderon	.05	.02
❑	95	Jeff Treadway	.05	.02
❑	96	Kurt Stillwell	.05	.02
❑	97	Gary Sheffield	.20	.09
❑	98	Jeffrey Leonard	.05	.02
❑	99	Andres Thomas	.05	.02
❑	100	Roberto Kelly	.05	.02
❑	101	Alvaro Espinoza	.05	.02
❑	102	Greg Gagne	.05	.02
❑	103	John Farrell	.05	.02
❑	104	Willie Wilson	.05	.02
❑	105	Glenn Braggs	.05	.02
❑	106	Chet Lemon	.05	.02
❑	107A	Jamie Moyer ERR (Scintilating)	.05	.02
❑	107B	Jamie Moyer COR (Scintillating)	.10	.05
❑	108	Chuck Crim	.05	.02
❑	109	Dave Valle	.05	.02
❑	110	Walt Weiss	.05	.02
❑	111	Larry Sheets	.05	.02
❑	112	Don Robinson	.05	.02
❑	113	Danny Heep	.05	.02
❑	114	Carmelo Martinez	.05	.02
❑	115	Dave Gallagher	.05	.02
❑	116	Mike LaValliere	.05	.02
❑	117	Bob McClure	.05	.02
❑	118	Rene Gonzales	.05	.02
❑	119	Mark Parent	.05	.02
❑	120	Wally Joyner	.10	.05
❑	121	Mark Gubicza	.05	.02
❑	122	Tony Pena	.05	.02
❑	123	Carmen Castillo	.05	.02
❑	124	Howard Johnson	.05	.02
❑	125	Steve Sax	.05	.02
❑	126	Tim Belcher	.05	.02
❑	127	Tim Burke	.05	.02
❑	128	Al Newman	.05	.02
❑	129	Dennis Rasmussen	.05	.02
❑	130	Doug Jones	.05	.02
❑	131	Fred Lynn	.05	.02
❑	132	Jeff Hamilton	.05	.02
❑	133	German Gonzalez	.05	.02
❑	134	John Morris	.05	.02
❑	135	Dave Parker	.10	.05
❑	136	Gary Pettis	.05	.02
❑	137	Dennis Boyd	.05	.02
❑	138	Candy Maldonado	.05	.02
❑	139	Rick Cerone	.05	.02
❑	140	George Brett	.40	.18
❑	141	Dave Clark	.05	.02
❑	142	Dickie Thon	.05	.02
❑	143	Junior Ortiz	.05	.02
❑	144	Don August	.05	.02
❑	145	Gary Gaetti	.10	.05
❑	146	Kirt Manwaring	.05	.02
❑	147	Jeff Reed	.05	.02
❑	148	Jose Alvarez	.05	.02
❑	149	Mike Schooler	.05	.02
❑	150	Mark Grace	.20	.09
❑	151	Geronimo Berroa	.05	.02
❑	152	Barry Jones	.05	.02
❑	153	Geno Petralli	.05	.02
❑	154	Jim Deshaies	.05	.02
❑	155	Barry Larkin	.20	.09
❑	156	Alfredo Griffin	.05	.02
❑	157	Tom Henke	.05	.02
❑	158	Mike Jeffcoat	.05	.02
❑	159	Bob Welch	.05	.02
❑	160	Julio Franco	.05	.02
❑	161	Henry Cotto	.05	.02
❑	162	Terry Steinbach	.10	.05
❑	163	Damon Berryhill	.05	.02
❑	164	Tim Crews	.05	.02
❑	165	Tom Browning	.05	.02
❑	166	Fred Manrique	.05	.02
❑	167	Harold Reynolds	.05	.02
❑	168A	Ron Hassey ERR (27 on back)	.05	.02
❑	168B	Ron Hassey COR (24 on back)	.50	.23
❑	169	Shawon Dunston	.05	.02
❑	170	Bobby Bonilla	.10	.05
❑	171	Tommy Herr	.05	.02
❑	172	Mike Heath	.05	.02
❑	173	Rich Gedman	.05	.02
❑	174	Bill Ripken	.05	.02
❑	175	Pete O'Brien	.05	.02
❑	176A	Lloyd McClendon ERR (Uniform number on back listed as 1)	.50	.23
❑	176B	Lloyd McClendon COR (Uniform number on back listed as 10)	.05	.02
❑	177	Brian Holton	.05	.02
❑	178	Jeff Blauser	.05	.02
❑	179	Jim Eisenreich	.05	.02
❑	180	Bert Blyleven	.10	.05
❑	181	Rob Murphy	.05	.02
❑	182	Bill Doran	.05	.02
❑	183	Curt Ford	.05	.02
❑	184	Mike Henneman	.05	.02
❑	185	Eric Davis	.10	.05
❑	186	Lance McCullers	.05	.02
❑	187	Steve Davis	.05	.02
❑	188	Bill Wegman	.05	.02
❑	189	Brian Harper	.05	.02
❑	190	Mike Moore	.05	.02
❑	191	Dale Mohorcic	.05	.02
❑	192	Tim Wallach	.05	.02
❑	193	Keith Hernandez	.10	.05
❑	194	Dave Righetti	.05	.02
❑	195A	Bret Saberhagen ERR (Joke)	.10	.05
❑	195B	Bret Saberhagen COR (Joker)	.10	.05
❑	196	Paul Kilgus	.05	.02
❑	197	Bud Black	.05	.02
❑	198	Juan Samuel	.05	.02
❑	199	Kevin Seitzer	.05	.02
❑	200	Darryl Strawberry	.10	.05
❑	201	Dave Stieb	.10	.05
❑	202	Charlie Hough	.10	.05
❑	203	Jack Morris	.10	.05
❑	204	Rance Mulliniks	.05	.02
❑	205	Alvin Davis	.05	.02
❑	206	Jack Howell	.05	.02
❑	207	Ken Patterson	.05	.02
❑	208	Terry Pendleton	.10	.05
❑	209	Craig Lefferts	.05	.02
❑	210	Kevin Brown UER (First mention of '89 Rangers should be '88)	.20	.09
❑	211	Dan Petry	.05	.02
❑	212	Dave Leiper	.05	.02
❑	213	Daryl Boston	.05	.02
❑	214	Kevin Hickey	.05	.02
❑	215	Mike Krukow	.05	.02
❑	216	Terry Francona	.10	.05
❑	217	Kirk McCaskill	.05	.02
❑	218	Scott Bailes	.05	.02
❑	219	Bob Forsch	.05	.02
❑	220A	Mike Aldrete ERR (25 on back)	.05	.02
❑	220B	Mike Aldrete COR (24 on back)	.10	.05
❑	221	Steve Buechele	.05	.02
❑	222	Jesse Barfield	.05	.02
❑	223	Juan Berenguer	.05	.02
❑	224	Andy McGaffigan	.05	.02
❑	225	Pete Smith	.05	.02
❑	226	Mike Witt	.05	.02
❑	227	Jay Howell	.05	.02
❑	228	Scott Bradley	.05	.02
❑	229	Jerome Walton	.05	.02
❑	230	Greg Swindell	.05	.02
❑	231	Atlee Hammaker	.05	.02

❑ 232A Mike Devereaux ERR .. .05 .02
(RF on front)
❑ 232B Mike Devereaux COR .. .50 .23
(CF on front)
❑ 233 Ken Hill .15 .07
❑ 234 Craig Worthington .05 .02
❑ 235 Scott Terry .05 .02
❑ 236 Brett Butler .10 .05
❑ 237 Doyle Alexander .05 .02
❑ 238 Dave Anderson .05 .02
❑ 239 Bob Milacki .05 .02
❑ 240 Dwight Smith .05 .02
❑ 241 Otis Nixon .10 .05
❑ 242 Pat Tabler .05 .02
❑ 243 Derek Lilliquist .05 .02
❑ 244 Danny Tartabull .05 .02
❑ 245 Wade Boggs .20 .09
❑ 246 Scott Garrelts .05 .02
(Should say Relief Pitcher on front)
❑ 247 Spike Owen .05 .02
❑ 248 Norm Charlton .05 .02
❑ 249 Gerald Perry .05 .02
❑ 250 Nolan Ryan .75 .35
❑ 251 Kevin Gross .05 .02
❑ 252 Randy Milligan .05 .02
❑ 253 Mike LaCoss .05 .02
❑ 254 Dave Bergman .05 .02
❑ 255 Tony Gwynn .50 .23
❑ 256 Felix Fermin .05 .02
❑ 257 Greg W. Harris .05 .02
❑ 258 Junior Felix .05 .02
❑ 259 Mark Davis .05 .02
❑ 260 Vince Coleman .05 .02
❑ 261 Paul Gibson .05 .02
❑ 262 Mitch Williams .05 .02
❑ 263 Jeff Russell .05 .02
❑ 264 Omar Vizquel .20 .09
❑ 265 Andre Dawson .20 .09
❑ 266 Storm Davis .05 .02
❑ 267 Guillermo Hernandez .... .05 .02
❑ 268 Mike Felder .05 .02
❑ 269 Tom Candiotti .05 .02
❑ 270 Bruce Hurst .05 .02
❑ 271 Fred McGriff .20 .09
❑ 272 Glenn Davis .05 .02
❑ 273 John Franco .10 .05
❑ 274 Rich Yett .05 .02
❑ 275 Craig Biggio .20 .09
❑ 276 Gene Larkin .05 .02
❑ 277 Rob Dibble .05 .02
❑ 278 Randy Bush .05 .02
❑ 279 Kevin Bass .05 .02
❑ 280A Bo Jackson ERR .20 .09
(Watham)
❑ 280B Bo Jackson COR .10 .05
(Wathan)
❑ 281 Wally Backman .05 .02
❑ 282 Larry Andersen .05 .02
❑ 283 Chris Bosio .05 .02
❑ 284 Juan Agosto .05 .02
❑ 285 Ozzie Smith .25 .11
❑ 286 George Bell .05 .02
❑ 287 Rex Hudler .05 .02
❑ 288 Pat Borders .05 .02
❑ 289 Danny Jackson .05 .02
❑ 290 Carlton Fisk .20 .09
❑ 291 Tracy Jones .05 .02
❑ 292 Allan Anderson .05 .02
❑ 293 Johnny Ray .05 .02
❑ 294 Lee Guetterman .05 .02
❑ 295 Paul O'Neill .10 .05
❑ 296 Carney Lansford .10 .05
❑ 297 Tom Brookens .05 .02
❑ 298 Claudell Washington ...... .05 .02
❑ 299 Hubie Brooks .05 .02
❑ 300 Will Clark .20 .09
❑ 301 Kenny Rogers .10 .05
❑ 302 Darrell Evans .10 .05
❑ 303 Greg Briley .05 .02
❑ 304 Donn Pall .05 .02
❑ 305 Teddy Higuera .05 .02
❑ 306 Dan Pasqua .05 .02
❑ 307 Dave Winfield .20 .09
❑ 308 Dennis Powell .05 .02
❑ 309 Jose DeLeon .05 .02
❑ 310 Roger Clemens UER .40 .18
(Dominate, should say dominant)
❑ 311 Melido Perez .05 .02
❑ 312 Devon White .05 .02
❑ 313 Dwight Gooden .10 .05
❑ 314 Carlos Martinez .05 .02
❑ 315 Dennis Eckersley .15 .07
❑ 316 Clay Parker UER .05 .02
(Height 6'11")
❑ 317 Rick Honeycutt .05 .02
❑ 318 Tim Laudner .05 .02
❑ 319 Joe Carter .10 .05
❑ 320 Robin Yount .20 .09
❑ 321 Felix Jose .05 .02
❑ 322 Mickey Tettleton .10 .05
❑ 323 Mike Gallego .05 .02
❑ 324 Edgar Martinez .20 .09
❑ 325 Dave Henderson .05 .02
❑ 326 Chili Davis .10 .05
❑ 327 Steve Balboni .05 .02
❑ 328 Jody Davis .05 .02
❑ 329 Shawn Hillegas .05 .02
❑ 330 Jim Abbott .15 .07
❑ 331 John Dopson .05 .02
❑ 332 Mark Williamson .05 .02
❑ 333 Jeff D. Robinson .05 .02
❑ 334 John Smiley .05 .02
❑ 335 Bobby Thigpen .05 .02
❑ 336 Garry Templeton .05 .02
❑ 337 Marvell Wynne .05 .02
❑ 338A Ken Griffey Sr. ERR .... .05 .02
(Uniform number on back listed as 25)
❑ 338B Ken Griffey Sr. COR .... .50 .23
(Uniform number on back listed as 30)
❑ 339 Steve Finley .20 .09
❑ 340 Ellis Burks .15 .07
❑ 341 Frank Williams .05 .02
❑ 342 Mike Morgan .05 .02
❑ 343 Kevin Mitchell .05 .02
❑ 344 Joel Youngblood .05 .02
❑ 345 Mike Greenwell .05 .02
❑ 346 Glenn Wilson .05 .02
❑ 347 John Costello .05 .02
❑ 348 Wes Gardner .05 .02
❑ 349 Jeff Ballard .05 .02
❑ 350 Mark Thurmond UER .... .05 .02
(ERA is 192, should be 1.92)
❑ 351 Randy Myers .10 .05
❑ 352 Shawn Abner .05 .02
❑ 353 Jesse Orosco .05 .02
❑ 354 Greg Walker .05 .02
❑ 355 Pete Harnisch .05 .02
❑ 356 Steve Farr .05 .02
❑ 357 Dave LaPoint .05 .02
❑ 358 Willie Fraser .05 .02
❑ 359 Mickey Hatcher .05 .02
❑ 360 Rickey Henderson .20 .09
❑ 361 Mike Fitzgerald .05 .02
❑ 362 Bill Schroeder .05 .02
❑ 363 Mark Carreon .05 .02
❑ 364 Ron Jones .05 .02
❑ 365 Jeff Montgomery .10 .05
❑ 366 Bill Krueger .05 .02
❑ 367 John Cangelosi .05 .02
❑ 368 Jose Gonzalez .05 .02
❑ 369 Greg Hibbard .05 .02
❑ 370 John Smoltz .20 .09
❑ 371 Jeff Brantley .05 .02
❑ 372 Frank White .10 .05
❑ 373 Ed Whitson .05 .02
❑ 374 Willie McGee .10 .05
❑ 375 Jose Canseco .20 .09
❑ 376 Randy Ready .05 .02
❑ 377 Don Aase .05 .02
❑ 378 Tony Armas .05 .02
❑ 379 Steve Bedrosian .05 .02
❑ 380 Chuck Finley .10 .05
❑ 381 Kent Hrbek .10 .05
❑ 382 Jim Gantner .05 .02
❑ 383 Mel Hall .05 .02
❑ 384 Mike Marshall .05 .02
❑ 385 Mark McGwire 1.00 .45
❑ 386 Wayne Tolleson .05 .02
❑ 387 Brian Holman .05 .02
❑ 388 John Wetteland .20 .09
❑ 389 Darren Daulton .10 .05
❑ 390 Rob Deer .05 .02
❑ 391 John Moses .05 .02
❑ 392 Todd Worrell .05 .02
❑ 393 Chuck Cary .05 .02
❑ 394 Stan Javier .05 .02
❑ 395 Willie Randolph .10 .05
❑ 396 Bill Buckner .05 .02
❑ 397 Robby Thompson .05 .02
❑ 398 Mike Scioscia .05 .02
❑ 399 Lonnie Smith .05 .02
❑ 400 Kirby Puckett .30 .14
❑ 401 Mark Langston .05 .02
❑ 402 Danny Darwin .05 .02
❑ 403 Greg Maddux .60 .25
❑ 404 Lloyd Moseby .05 .02
❑ 405 Rafael Palmeiro .20 .09
❑ 406 Chad Kreuter .05 .02
❑ 407 Jimmy Key .10 .05
❑ 408 Tim Birtsas .05 .02
❑ 409 Tim Raines .10 .05
❑ 410 Dave Stewart .10 .05
❑ 411 Eric Yelding .05 .02
❑ 412 Kent Anderson .05 .02
❑ 413 Les Lancaster .05 .02
❑ 414 Rick Dempsey .05 .02
❑ 415 Randy Johnson .30 .14
❑ 416 Gary Carter .20 .09
❑ 417 Rolando Roomes .05 .02
❑ 418 Dan Schatzeder .05 .02
❑ 419 Bryn Smith .05 .02
❑ 420 Ruben Sierra .05 .02
❑ 421 Steve Jeltz .05 .02
❑ 422 Ken Oberkfell .05 .02
❑ 423 Sid Bream .05 .02
❑ 424 Jim Clancy .05 .02
❑ 425 Kelly Gruber .05 .02
❑ 426 Rick Leach .05 .02
❑ 427 Len Dykstra .10 .05
❑ 428 Jeff Pico .05 .02
❑ 429 John Cerutti .05 .02
❑ 430 David Cone .20 .09
❑ 431 Jeff Kunkel .05 .02
❑ 432 Luis Aquino .05 .02
❑ 433 Ernie Whitt .05 .02
❑ 434 Bo Diaz .05 .02
❑ 435 Steve Lake .05 .02
❑ 436 Pat Perry .05 .02
❑ 437 Mike Davis .05 .02
❑ 438 Cecilio Guante .05 .02
❑ 439 Duane Ward .05 .02
❑ 440 Andy Van Slyke .10 .05
❑ 441 Gene Nelson .05 .02
❑ 442 Luis Polonia .05 .02
❑ 443 Kevin Elster .05 .02
❑ 444 Keith Moreland .05 .02
❑ 445 Roger McDowell .05 .02
❑ 446 Ron Darling .05 .02
❑ 447 Ernest Riles .05 .02
❑ 448 Mookie Wilson .10 .05
❑ 449A Billy Spiers ERR .20 .09
(No birth year)
❑ 449B Billy Spiers COR .05 .02
(Born in 1966)
❑ 450 Rick Sutcliffe .05 .02
❑ 451 Nelson Santovenia .05 .02
❑ 452 Andy Allanson .05 .02
❑ 453 Bob Melvin .05 .02
❑ 454 Benito Santiago .05 .02
❑ 455 Jose Uribe .05 .02
❑ 456 Bill Landrum .05 .02
❑ 457 Bobby Witt .05 .02
❑ 458 Kevin Romine .05 .02
❑ 459 Lee Mazzilli .05 .02
❑ 460 Paul Molitor .20 .09
❑ 461 Ramon Martinez .15 .07
❑ 462 Frank DiPino .05 .02
❑ 463 Walt Terrell .05 .02
❑ 464 Bob Geren .05 .02
❑ 465 Rick Reuschel .05 .02

❑ 466 Mark Grant .05 .02
❑ 467 John Kruk .10 .05
❑ 468 Gregg Jefferies .10 .05
❑ 469 R.J. Reynolds .05 .02
❑ 470 Harold Baines .10 .05
❑ 471 Dennis Lamp .05 .02
❑ 472 Tom Gordon .15 .07
❑ 473 Terry Puhl .05 .02
❑ 474 Curt Wilkerson .05 .02
❑ 475 Dan Quisenberry .05 .02
❑ 476 Oddibe McDowell .05 .02
❑ 477A Zane Smith ERR .05 .02
(Career ERA .393)
❑ 477B Zane Smith COR .05 .02
(career ERA 3.93)
❑ 478 Franklin Stubbs .05 .02
❑ 479 Wallace Johnson .05 .02
❑ 480 Jay Tibbs .05 .02
❑ 481 Tom Glavine .20 .09
❑ 482 Manny Lee .05 .02
❑ 483 Joe Hesketh UER .05 .02
(Says Rookiess on back& should say Rookies)
❑ 484 Mike Bielecki .05 .02
❑ 485 Greg Brock .05 .02
❑ 486 Pascual Perez .05 .02
❑ 487 Kirk Gibson .10 .05
❑ 488 Scott Sanderson .05 .02
❑ 489 Domingo Ramos .05 .02
❑ 490 Kal Daniels .05 .02
❑ 491A David Wells ERR .75 .35
(Reverse negative photo on card back)
❑ 491B David Wells COR .15 .07
❑ 492 Jerry Reed .05 .02
❑ 493 Eric Show .05 .02
❑ 494 Mike Pagliarulo .05 .02
❑ 495 Ron Robinson .05 .02
❑ 496 Brad Komminsk .05 .02
❑ 497 Greg Litton .05 .02
❑ 498 Chris James .05 .02
❑ 499 Luis Quinones .05 .02
❑ 500 Frank Viola .05 .02
❑ 501 Tim Teufel UER .05 .02
(Twins '85, the s is lower case, should be upper case)
❑ 502 Terry Leach .05 .02
❑ 503 Matt Williams UER .20 .09
(Wearing 10 on front, listed as 9 on back)
❑ 504 Tim Leary .05 .02
❑ 505 Doug Drabek .05 .02
❑ 506 Mariano Duncan .05 .02
❑ 507 Charlie Hayes .05 .02
❑ 508 Joey Belle 1.00 .45
❑ 509 Pat Sheridan .05 .02
❑ 510 Mackey Sasser .05 .02
❑ 511 Jose Rijo .05 .02
❑ 512 Mike Smithson .05 .02
❑ 513 Gary Ward .05 .02
❑ 514 Dion James .05 .02
❑ 515 Jim Gott .05 .02
❑ 516 Drew Hall .05 .02
❑ 517 Doug Bair .05 .02
❑ 518 Scott Scudder .05 .02
❑ 519 Rick Aguilera .10 .05
❑ 520 Rafael Belliard .05 .02
❑ 521 Jay Buhner .20 .09
❑ 522 Jeff Reardon .10 .05
❑ 523 Steve Rosenberg .05 .02
❑ 524 Randy Velarde .05 .02
❑ 525 Jeff Musselman .05 .02
❑ 526 Bill Long .05 .02
❑ 527 Gary Wayne .05 .02
❑ 528 Dave Johnson (P) .05 .02
❑ 529 Ron Kittle .05 .02
❑ 530 Erik Hanson UER .05 .02
(5th line on back says seson, should say season)
❑ 531 Steve Wilson .05 .02
❑ 532 Joey Meyer .05 .02
❑ 533 Curt Young .05 .02
❑ 534 Kelly Downs .05 .02
❑ 535 Joe Girardi .15 .07
❑ 536 Lance Blankenship .05 .02
❑ 537 Greg Mathews .05 .02
❑ 538 Donell Nixon .05 .02
❑ 539 Mark Knudson .05 .02
❑ 540 Jeff Wetherby .05 .02
❑ 541 Darrin Jackson .05 .02
❑ 542 Terry Mulholland .05 .02
❑ 543 Eric Hetzel .05 .02
❑ 544 Rick Reed .05 .02
❑ 545 Dennis Cook .05 .02
❑ 546 Mike Jackson .10 .05
❑ 547 Brian Fisher .05 .02
❑ 548 Gene Harris .05 .02
❑ 549 Jeff King .10 .05
❑ 550 Dave Dravecky .20 .09
❑ 551 Randy Kutcher .05 .02
❑ 552 Mark Portugal .05 .02
❑ 553 Jim Corsi .05 .02
❑ 554 Todd Stottlemyre .10 .05
❑ 555 Scott Bankhead .05 .02
❑ 556 Ken Dayley .05 .02
❑ 557 Rick Wrona .05 .02
❑ 558 Sammy Sosa 5.00 2.20
❑ 559 Keith Miller .05 .02
❑ 560 Ken Griffey Jr. 2.00 .90
❑ 561A Ryne Sandberg HL ERR 6.00 2.70
(Position on front listed as 3B)
❑ 561B Ryne Sandberg HL COR .20 .09
❑ 562 Billy Hatcher .05 .02
❑ 563 Jay Bell .10 .05
❑ 564 Jack Daugherty .05 .02
❑ 565 Rich Monteleone .05 .02
❑ 566 Bo Jackson AS-MVP .10 .05
❑ 567 Tony Fossas .05 .02
❑ 568 Roy Smith .05 .02
❑ 569 Jaime Navarro .05 .02
❑ 570 Lance Johnson .05 .02
❑ 571 Mike Dyer .05 .02
❑ 572 Kevin Ritz .05 .02
❑ 573 Dave West .05 .02
❑ 574 Gary Mielke .05 .02
❑ 575 Scott Lusader .05 .02
❑ 576 Joe Oliver .05 .02
❑ 577 Sandy Alomar Jr. .15 .07
❑ 578 Andy Benes UER .20 .09
(Extra comma between day and year)
❑ 579 Tim Jones .05 .02
❑ 580 Randy McCament .05 .02
❑ 581 Curt Schilling .20 .09
❑ 582 John Orton .05 .02
❑ 583A Milt Cuyler ERR .50 .23
(998 games)
❑ 583B Milt Cuyler COR .05 .02
(98 games; the extra 9 was ghosted out and may still be visible)
❑ 584 Eric Anthony .05 .02
❑ 585 Greg Vaughn .40 .18
❑ 586 Deion Sanders .20 .09
❑ 587 Jose DeJesus .05 .02
❑ 588 Chip Hale .05 .02
❑ 589 John Olerud .50 .23
❑ 590 Steve Olin .10 .05
❑ 591 Marquis Grissom .25 .11
❑ 592 Moises Alou .75 .35
❑ 593 Mark Lemke .05 .02
❑ 594 Dean Palmer .25 .11
❑ 595 Robin Ventura .20 .09
❑ 596 Tino Martinez .40 .18
❑ 597 Mike Huff .05 .02
❑ 598 Scott Hemond .05 .02
❑ 599 Wally Whitehurst .05 .02
❑ 600 Todd Zeile .10 .05
❑ 601 Glenallen Hill .05 .02
❑ 602 Hal Morris .05 .02
❑ 603 Juan Bell .05 .02
❑ 604 Bobby Rose .05 .02
❑ 605 Matt Merullo .05 .02
❑ 606 Kevin Maas .10 .05
❑ 607 Randy Nosek .05 .02
❑ 608A Billy Bates .05 .02
(Text mentions 12 triples in tenth line)
❑ 608B Billy Bates .05 .02
(Text has no mention of triples)
❑ 609 Mike Stanton .05 .02
❑ 610 Mauro Gozzo .05 .02
❑ 611 Charles Nagy .20 .09
❑ 612 Scott Coolbaugh .05 .02
❑ 613 Jose Vizcaino .20 .09
❑ 614 Greg Smith .05 .02
❑ 615 Jeff Huson .05 .02
❑ 616 Mickey Weston .05 .02
❑ 617 John Pawlowski .05 .02
❑ 618A Joe Skalski ERR .05 .02
(27 on back)
❑ 618B Joe Skalski COR .50 .23
(67 on back)
❑ 619 Bernie Williams 1.25 .55
❑ 620 Shawn Holman .05 .02
❑ 621 Gary Eave .05 .02
❑ 622 Darrin Fletcher UER .10 .05
(Elmherst& should be Elmhurst)
❑ 623 Pat Combs .05 .02
❑ 624 Mike Blowers .10 .05
❑ 625 Kevin Appier .15 .07
❑ 626 Pat Austin .05 .02
❑ 627 Kelly Mann .05 .02
❑ 628 Matt Kinzer .05 .02
❑ 629 Chris Hammond .05 .02
❑ 630 Dean Wilkins .05 .02
❑ 631 Larry Walker UER 1.00 .45
(Uniform number 55 on front and 33 on back; Home is Maple Ridge& not Maple River)
❑ 632 Blaine Beatty .05 .02
❑ 633A Tommy Barrett ERR .05 .02
(29 on back)
❑ 633B Tommy Barrett COR .50 .23
(14 on back)
❑ 634 Stan Belinda .05 .02
❑ 635 Mike (Tex) Smith .05 .02
❑ 636 Hensley Meulens .05 .02
❑ 637 Juan Gonzalez UER 3.00 1.35
(Sarasots on back& should be Sarasota)
❑ 638 Lenny Webster .05 .02
❑ 639 Mark Gardner .05 .02
❑ 640 Tommy Greene .05 .02
❑ 641 Mike Hartley .05 .02
❑ 642 Phil Stephenson .05 .02
❑ 643 Kevin Mmahat .05 .02
❑ 644 Ed Whited .05 .02
❑ 645 Delino DeShields .20 .09
❑ 646 Kevin Blankenship .05 .02
❑ 647 Paul Sorrento .20 .09
❑ 648 Mike Roesler .05 .02
❑ 649 Jason Grimsley .05 .02
❑ 650 Dave Justice .75 .35
❑ 651 Scott Cooper .05 .02
❑ 652 Dave Eiland .05 .02
❑ 653 Mike Munoz .05 .02
❑ 654 Jeff Fischer .05 .02
❑ 655 Terry Jorgensen .05 .02
❑ 656 George Canale .05 .02
❑ 657 Brian DuBois UER .05 .02
(Misspelled Dubois on card)
❑ 658 Carlos Quintana .05 .02
❑ 659 Luis de los Santos .05 .02
❑ 660 Jerald Clark .05 .02
❑ 661 Donald Harris DC .05 .02
❑ 662 Paul Coleman DC .05 .02
❑ 663 Frank Thomas DC 3.00 1.35
❑ 664 Brent Mayne DC .05 .02
❑ 665 Eddie Zosky DC .05 .02
❑ 666 Steve Hosey DC .05 .02
❑ 667 Scott Bryant DC .05 .02
❑ 668 Tom Goodwin DC .20 .09
❑ 669 Cal Eldred DC .10 .05
❑ 670 Earl Cunningham DC .05 .02
❑ 671 Alan Zinter DC .05 .02
❑ 672 Chuck Knoblauch DC .75 .35
❑ 673 Kyle Abbott DC .05 .02

	Card	MINT	NRMT
❑	674 Roger Salkeld DC	.05	.02
❑	675 Maurice Vaughn DC	1.50	.70
❑	676 Keith(Kiki) Jones DC	.05	.02
❑	677 Tyler Houston DC	.20	.09
❑	678 Jeff Jackson DC	.05	.02
❑	679 Greg Gohr DC	.05	.02
❑	680 Ben McDonald DC	.10	.05
❑	681 Greg Blosser DC	.05	.02
❑	682 Willie Greene DC UER Name spelled as Green	.25	.11
❑	683A Wade Boggs DT ERR (Text says 215 hits in '89& should be 205)	.10	.05
❑	683B Wade Boggs DT COR (Text says 205 hits in '89)	.10	.05
❑	684 Will Clark DT	.10	.05
❑	685 Tony Gwynn DT UER (Text reads battling instead of batting)	.25	.11
❑	686 Rickey Henderson DT	.10	.05
❑	687 Bo Jackson DT	.10	.05
❑	688 Mark Langston DT	.05	.02
❑	689 Barry Larkin DT	.10	.05
❑	690 Kirby Puckett DT	.20	.09
❑	691 Ryne Sandberg DT	.20	.09
❑	692 Mike Scott DT	.05	.02
❑	693A Terry Steinbach DT ERR (cathers)	.05	.02
❑	693B Terry Steinbach DT COR (catchers)	.05	.02
❑	694 Bobby Thigpen DT	.05	.02
❑	695 Mitch Williams DT	.05	.02
❑	696 Nolan Ryan HL	.40	.18
❑	697 Bo Jackson FB/BB	.50	.23
❑	698 Rickey Henderson ALCS-MVP	.10	.05
❑	699 Will Clark NLCS-MVP	.10	.05
❑	700 WS Games 1/2 (Dave Stewart Mike Moore)	.10	.05
❑	701 Lights Out: Candlestick 5:04pm (10/17/89)	.20	.09
❑	702 WS Game 3 Bashers Blast Giants (Carney Lansford, Rickey Henderson, Jose Canseco, Dave Henderson)	.20	.09
❑	703 WS Game 4/Wrap-up A's Sweep Battle of the Bay (A's Celebrate)	.05	.02
❑	704 Wade Boggs HL Wade Raps 200	.10	.05

1990 Score Rookie Dream Team

		MINT	NRMT
	COMPLETE SET (10)	4.00	1.80
	COMMON CARD (B1-B10)	.25	.11
❑	B1 A.Bartlett Giamatti COMM MEM	.50	.23
❑	B2 Pat Combs	.25	.11
❑	B3 Todd Zeile	.30	.14
❑	B4 Luis de los Santos	.25	.11
❑	B5 Mark Lemke	.25	.11
❑	B6 Robin Ventura	.50	.23
❑	B7 Jeff Huson	.25	.11
❑	B8 Greg Vaughn	.50	.23
❑	B9 Marquis Grissom	1.25	.55
❑	B10 Eric Anthony	.25	.11

1990 Score Rookie/Traded

		MINT	NRMT
	COMP.FACT.SET (110)	5.00	2.20
	COMMON CARD (1T-110T)	.05	.02
❑	1T Dave Winfield	.20	.09
❑	2T Kevin Bass	.05	.02
❑	3T Nick Esasky	.05	.02
❑	4T Mitch Webster	.05	.02
❑	5T Pascual Perez	.05	.02
❑	6T Gary Pettis	.05	.02
❑	7T Tony Pena	.05	.02
❑	8T Candy Maldonado	.05	.02
❑	9T Cecil Fielder	.10	.05
❑	10T Carmelo Martinez	.05	.02
❑	11T Mark Langston	.05	.02
❑	12T Dave Parker	.10	.05
❑	13T Don Slaught	.05	.02
❑	14T Tony Phillips	.05	.02
❑	15T John Franco	.10	.05
❑	16T Randy Myers	.10	.05
❑	17T Jeff Reardon	.10	.05
❑	18T Sandy Alomar Jr.	.15	.07
❑	19T Joe Carter	.10	.05
❑	20T Fred Lynn	.05	.02
❑	21T Storm Davis	.05	.02
❑	22T Craig Lefferts	.05	.02
❑	23T Pete O'Brien	.05	.02
❑	24T Dennis Boyd	.05	.02
❑	25T Lloyd Moseby	.05	.02
❑	26T Mark Davis	.05	.02
❑	27T Tim Leary	.05	.02
❑	28T Gerald Perry	.05	.02
❑	29T Don Aase	.05	.02
❑	30T Ernie Whitt	.05	.02
❑	31T Dale Murphy	.20	.09
❑	32T Alejandro Pena	.05	.02
❑	33T Juan Samuel	.05	.02
❑	34T Hubie Brooks	.05	.02
❑	35T Gary Carter	.20	.09
❑	36T Jim Presley	.05	.02
❑	37T Wally Backman	.05	.02
❑	38T Matt Nokes	.05	.02
❑	39T Dan Petry	.05	.02
❑	40T Franklin Stubbs	.05	.02
❑	41T Jeff Huson	.05	.02
❑	42T Billy Hatcher	.05	.02
❑	43T Terry Leach	.05	.02
❑	44T Phil Bradley	.05	.02
❑	45T Claudell Washington	.05	.02
❑	46T Luis Polonia	.05	.02
❑	47T Daryl Boston	.05	.02
❑	48T Lee Smith	.10	.05
❑	49T Tom Brunansky	.05	.02
❑	50T Mike Witt	.05	.02
❑	51T Willie Randolph	.10	.05
❑	52T Stan Javier	.05	.02
❑	53T Brad Komminsk	.05	.02
❑	54T John Candelaria	.05	.02
❑	55T Bryn Smith	.05	.02
❑	56T Glenn Braggs	.05	.02
❑	57T Keith Hernandez	.10	.05
❑	58T Ken Oberkfell	.05	.02
❑	59T Steve Jeltz	.05	.02
❑	60T Chris James	.05	.02
❑	61T Scott Sanderson	.05	.02
❑	62T Bill Long	.05	.02
❑	63T Rick Cerone	.05	.02
❑	64T Scott Bailes	.05	.02
❑	65T Larry Sheets	.05	.02
❑	66T Junior Ortiz	.05	.02
❑	67T Francisco Cabrera	.05	.02
❑	68T Gary DiSarcina	.20	.09
❑	69T Greg Olson	.05	.02
❑	70T Beau Allred	.05	.02
❑	71T Oscar Azocar	.05	.02
❑	72T Kent Mercker	.05	.02
❑	73T John Burkett	.10	.05
❑	74T Carlos Baerga	.25	.11
❑	75T Dave Hollins	.20	.09
❑	76T Todd Hundley	.40	.18
❑	77T Rick Parker	.05	.02
❑	78T Steve Cummings	.05	.02
❑	79T Bill Sampen	.05	.02
❑	80T Jerry Kutzler	.05	.02
❑	81T Derek Bell	.40	.18
❑	82T Kevin Tapani	.10	.05
❑	83T Jim Leyritz	.20	.09
❑	84T Ray Lankford	.50	.23
❑	85T Wayne Edwards	.05	.02
❑	86T Frank Thomas	3.00	1.35
❑	87T Tim Naehring	.20	.09
❑	88T Willie Blair	.05	.02
❑	89T Alan Mills	.05	.02
❑	90T Scott Radinsky	.05	.02
❑	91T Howard Farmer	.05	.02
❑	92T Julio Machado	.05	.02
❑	93T Rafael Valdez	.05	.02
❑	94T Shawn Boskie	.05	.02
❑	95T David Segui	.25	.11
❑	96T Chris Hoiles	.20	.09
❑	97T D.J. Dozier	.10	.05
❑	98T Hector Villanueva	.05	.02
❑	99T Eric Gunderson	.05	.02
❑	100T Eric Lindros	1.50	.70
❑	101T Dave Otto	.05	.02
❑	102T Dana Kiecker	.05	.02
❑	103T Tim Drummond	.05	.02
❑	104T Mickey Pina	.05	.02
❑	105T Craig Grebeck	.05	.02
❑	106T Bernard Gilkey	.25	.11
❑	107T Tim Layana	.05	.02
❑	108T Scott Chiamparino	.05	.02
❑	109T Steve Avery	.05	.02
❑	110T Terry Shumpert	.05	.02

1991 Score

		MINT	NRMT
	COMPLETE SET (893)	10.00	4.50
	COMP.FACT.SET (900)	20.00	9.00
	COMMON CARD (1-893)	.05	.02
❑	1 Jose Canseco	.20	.09

❑ 2	Ken Griffey Jr.	1.50	.70
❑ 3	Ryne Sandberg	.25	.11
❑ 4	Nolan Ryan	.75	.35
❑ 5	Bo Jackson	.10	.05
❑ 6	Bret Saberhagen UER (In bio& missed misspelled as mised)	.05	.02
❑ 7	Will Clark	.20	.09
❑ 8	Ellis Burks	.10	.05
❑ 9	Joe Carter	.10	.05
❑ 10	Rickey Henderson	.20	.09
❑ 11	Ozzie Guillen	.05	.02
❑ 12	Wade Boggs	.20	.09
❑ 13	Jerome Walton	.05	.02
❑ 14	John Franco	.10	.05
❑ 15	Ricky Jordan UER (League misspelled as legue)	.05	.02
❑ 16	Wally Backman	.05	.02
❑ 17	Rob Dibble	.05	.02
❑ 18	Glenn Braggs	.05	.02
❑ 19	Cory Snyder	.05	.02
❑ 20	Kal Daniels	.05	.02
❑ 21	Mark Langston	.05	.02
❑ 22	Kevin Gross	.05	.02
❑ 23	Don Mattingly UER (First line& ' is missing from Yankee)	.30	.14
❑ 24	Dave Righetti	.05	.02
❑ 25	Roberto Alomar	.20	.09
❑ 26	Robby Thompson	.05	.02
❑ 27	Jack McDowell	.05	.02
❑ 28	Bip Roberts UER (Bio reads playd)	.05	.02
❑ 29	Jay Howell	.05	.02
❑ 30	Dave Stieb UER (17 wins in bio& 18 in stats)	.05	.02
❑ 31	Johnny Ray	.05	.02
❑ 32	Steve Sax	.05	.02
❑ 33	Terry Mulholland	.05	.02
❑ 34	Lee Guetterman	.05	.02
❑ 35	Tim Raines	.10	.05
❑ 36	Scott Fletcher	.05	.02
❑ 37	Lance Parrish	.05	.02
❑ 38	Tony Phillips UER (Born 4/15 should be 4/25)	.05	.02
❑ 39	Todd Stottlemyre	.10	.05
❑ 40	Alan Trammell	.15	.07
❑ 41	Todd Burns	.05	.02
❑ 42	Mookie Wilson	.10	.05
❑ 43	Chris Bosio	.05	.02
❑ 44	Jeffrey Leonard	.05	.02
❑ 45	Doug Jones	.05	.02
❑ 46	Mike Scott UER (In first line& dominate should read dominating)	.05	.02
❑ 47	Andy Hawkins	.05	.02
❑ 48	Harold Reynolds	.05	.02
❑ 49	Paul Molitor	.20	.09
❑ 50	John Farrell	.05	.02
❑ 51	Danny Darwin	.05	.02
❑ 52	Jeff Blauser	.05	.02
❑ 53	John Tudor UER (41 wins in '81)	.05	.02
❑ 54	Milt Thompson	.05	.02
❑ 55	Dave Justice	.25	.11
❑ 56	Greg Olson	.05	.02
❑ 57	Willie Blair	.05	.02
❑ 58	Rick Parker	.05	.02
❑ 59	Shawn Boskie	.05	.02
❑ 60	Kevin Tapani	.05	.02
❑ 61	Dave Hollins	.05	.02
❑ 62	Scott Radinsky	.05	.02
❑ 63	Francisco Cabrera	.05	.02
❑ 64	Tim Layana	.05	.02
❑ 65	Jim Leyritz	.10	.05
❑ 66	Wayne Edwards	.05	.02
❑ 67	Lee Stevens	.05	.02
❑ 68	Bill Sampen UER (Fourth line& long is spelled along)	.05	.02
❑ 69	Craig Grebeck UER (Born in Cerritos& not Johnstown)	.05	.02
❑ 70	John Burkett	.05	.02
❑ 71	Hector Villanueva	.05	.02
❑ 72	Oscar Azocar	.05	.02
❑ 73	Alan Mills	.05	.02
❑ 74	Carlos Baerga	.10	.05
❑ 75	Charles Nagy	.20	.09
❑ 76	Tim Drummond	.05	.02
❑ 77	Dana Kiecker	.05	.02
❑ 78	Tom Edens	.05	.02
❑ 79	Kent Mercker	.05	.02
❑ 80	Steve Avery	.05	.02
❑ 81	Lee Smith	.10	.05
❑ 82	Dave Martinez	.05	.02
❑ 83	Dave Winfield	.20	.09
❑ 84	Bill Spiers	.05	.02
❑ 85	Dan Pasqua	.05	.02
❑ 86	Randy Milligan	.05	.02
❑ 87	Tracy Jones	.05	.02
❑ 88	Greg Myers	.05	.02
❑ 89	Keith Hernandez	.10	.05
❑ 90	Todd Benzinger	.05	.02
❑ 91	Mike Jackson	.10	.05
❑ 92	Mike Stanley	.05	.02
❑ 93	Candy Maldonado	.05	.02
❑ 94	John Kruk UER (No decimal point before 1990 BA)	.10	.05
❑ 95	Cal Ripken UER (Genius spelled genuis)	.75	.35
❑ 96	Willie Fraser	.05	.02
❑ 97	Mike Felder	.05	.02
❑ 98	Bill Landrum	.05	.02
❑ 99	Chuck Crim	.05	.02
❑ 100	Chuck Finley	.10	.05
❑ 101	Kirt Manwaring	.05	.02
❑ 102	Jaime Navarro	.05	.02
❑ 103	Dickie Thon	.05	.02
❑ 104	Brian Downing	.05	.02
❑ 105	Jim Abbott	.10	.05
❑ 106	Tom Brookens	.05	.02
❑ 107	Darryl Hamilton UER (Bio info is for Jeff Hamilton)	.05	.02
❑ 108	Bryan Harvey	.05	.02
❑ 109	Greg A. Harris UER (Shown pitching lefty& bio says righty)	.05	.02
❑ 110	Greg Swindell	.05	.02
❑ 111	Juan Berenguer	.05	.02
❑ 112	Mike Heath	.05	.02
❑ 113	Scott Bradley	.05	.02
❑ 114	Jack Morris	.10	.05
❑ 115	Barry Jones	.05	.02
❑ 116	Kevin Romine	.05	.02
❑ 117	Garry Templeton	.05	.02
❑ 118	Scott Sanderson	.05	.02
❑ 119	Roberto Kelly	.05	.02
❑ 120	George Brett	.40	.18
❑ 121	Oddibe McDowell	.05	.02
❑ 122	Jim Acker	.05	.02
❑ 123	Bill Swift UER (Born 12/27/61, should be 10/27)	.05	.02
❑ 124	Eric King	.05	.02
❑ 125	Jay Buhner	.20	.09
❑ 126	Matt Young	.05	.02
❑ 127	Alvaro Espinoza	.05	.02
❑ 128	Greg Hibbard	.05	.02
❑ 129	Jeff M. Robinson	.05	.02
❑ 130	Mike Greenwell	.05	.02
❑ 131	Dion James	.05	.02
❑ 132	Donn Pall UER (1988 ERA in stats 0.00)	.05	.02
❑ 133	Lloyd Moseby	.05	.02
❑ 134	Randy Velarde	.05	.02
❑ 135	Allan Anderson	.05	.02
❑ 136	Mark Davis	.05	.02
❑ 137	Eric Davis	.10	.05
❑ 138	Phil Stephenson	.05	.02
❑ 139	Felix Fermin	.05	.02
❑ 140	Pedro Guerrero	.05	.02
❑ 141	Charlie Hough	.10	.05
❑ 142	Mike Henneman	.05	.02
❑ 143	Jeff Montgomery	.10	.05
❑ 144	Lenny Harris	.05	.02
❑ 145	Bruce Hurst	.05	.02
❑ 146	Eric Anthony	.05	.02
❑ 147	Paul Assenmacher	.05	.02
❑ 148	Jesse Barfield	.05	.02
❑ 149	Carlos Quintana	.05	.02
❑ 150	Dave Stewart	.10	.05
❑ 151	Roy Smith	.05	.02
❑ 152	Paul Gibson	.05	.02
❑ 153	Mickey Hatcher	.05	.02
❑ 154	Jim Eisenreich	.05	.02
❑ 155	Kenny Rogers	.05	.02
❑ 156	Dave Schmidt	.05	.02
❑ 157	Lance Johnson	.05	.02
❑ 158	Dave West	.05	.02
❑ 159	Steve Balboni	.05	.02
❑ 160	Jeff Brantley	.05	.02
❑ 161	Craig Biggio	.20	.09
❑ 162	Brook Jacoby	.05	.02
❑ 163	Dan Gladden	.05	.02
❑ 164	Jeff Reardon UER (Total IP shown as 943.2, should be 943.1)	.10	.05
❑ 165	Mark Carreon	.05	.02
❑ 166	Mel Hall	.05	.02
❑ 167	Gary Mielke	.05	.02
❑ 168	Cecil Fielder	.10	.05
❑ 169	Darrin Jackson	.05	.02
❑ 170	Rick Aguilera	.10	.05
❑ 171	Walt Weiss	.05	.02
❑ 172	Steve Farr	.05	.02
❑ 173	Jody Reed	.05	.02
❑ 174	Mike Jeffcoat	.05	.02
❑ 175	Mark Grace	.20	.09
❑ 176	Larry Sheets	.05	.02
❑ 177	Bill Gullickson	.05	.02
❑ 178	Chris Gwynn	.05	.02
❑ 179	Melido Perez	.05	.02
❑ 180	Sid Fernandez UER (779 runs in 1990)	.05	.02
❑ 181	Tim Burke	.05	.02
❑ 182	Gary Pettis	.05	.02
❑ 183	Rob Murphy	.05	.02
❑ 184	Craig Lefferts	.05	.02
❑ 185	Howard Johnson	.05	.02
❑ 186	Ken Caminiti	.20	.09
❑ 187	Tim Belcher	.05	.02
❑ 188	Greg Cadaret	.05	.02
❑ 189	Matt Williams	.20	.09
❑ 190	Dave Magadan	.05	.02
❑ 191	Geno Petralli	.05	.02
❑ 192	Jeff D. Robinson	.05	.02
❑ 193	Jim Deshaies	.05	.02
❑ 194	Willie Randolph	.10	.05
❑ 195	George Bell	.05	.02
❑ 196	Hubie Brooks	.05	.02
❑ 197	Tom Gordon	.10	.05
❑ 198	Mike Fitzgerald	.05	.02
❑ 199	Mike Pagliarulo	.05	.02
❑ 200	Kirby Puckett	.30	.14
❑ 201	Shawon Dunston	.05	.02
❑ 202	Dennis Boyd	.05	.02
❑ 203	Junior Felix UER (Text has him in NL)	.05	.02
❑ 204	Alejandro Pena	.05	.02
❑ 205	Pete Smith	.05	.02
❑ 206	Tom Glavine UER (Lefty spelled leftie)	.20	.09
❑ 207	Luis Salazar	.05	.02
❑ 208	John Smoltz	.20	.09
❑ 209	Doug Dascenzo	.05	.02
❑ 210	Tim Wallach	.05	.02
❑ 211	Greg Gagne	.05	.02
❑ 212	Mark Gubicza	.05	.02
❑ 213	Mark Parent	.05	.02
❑ 214	Ken Oberkfell	.05	.02
❑ 215	Gary Carter	.20	.09
❑ 216	Rafael Palmeiro	.20	.09
❑ 217	Tom Niedenfuer	.05	.02
❑ 218	Dave LaPoint	.05	.02
❑ 219	Jeff Treadway	.05	.02
❑ 220	Mitch Williams UER ('89 ERA shown as 2.76, should be 2.64)	.05	.02
❑ 221	Jose DeLeon	.05	.02

❑ 222 Mike LaValliere .05 .02
❑ 223 Darrel Akerfelds .05 .02
❑ 224A Kent Anderson ERR .10 .05
(First line& flachy
should read flashy)
❑ 224B Kent Anderson COR .10 .05
(Corrected in
factory sets)
❑ 225 Dwight Evans .10 .05
❑ 226 Gary Redus .05 .02
❑ 227 Paul O'Neill .10 .05
❑ 228 Marty Barrett .05 .02
❑ 229 Tom Browning .05 .02
❑ 230 Terry Pendleton .10 .05
❑ 231 Jack Armstrong .05 .02
❑ 232 Mike Boddicker .05 .02
❑ 233 Neal Heaton .05 .02
❑ 234 Marquis Grissom .20 .09
❑ 235 Bert Blyleven .10 .05
❑ 236 Curt Young .05 .02
❑ 237 Don Carman .05 .02
❑ 238 Charlie Hayes .05 .02
❑ 239 Mark Knudson .05 .02
❑ 240 Todd Zeile .10 .05
❑ 241 Larry Walker UER .30 .14
(Maple River, should
be Maple Ridge)
❑ 242 Jerald Clark .05 .02
❑ 243 Jeff Ballard .05 .02
❑ 244 Jeff King .10 .05
❑ 245 Tom Brunansky .05 .02
❑ 246 Darren Daulton .10 .05
❑ 247 Scott Terry .05 .02
❑ 248 Rob Deer .05 .02
❑ 249 Brady Anderson UER .20 .09
(1990 Hagerstown 1 hit,
should say 13 hits)
❑ 250 Len Dykstra .10 .05
❑ 251 Greg W. Harris .05 .02
❑ 252 Mike Hartley .05 .02
❑ 253 Joey Cora .10 .05
❑ 254 Ivan Calderon .05 .02
❑ 255 Ted Power .05 .02
❑ 256 Sammy Sosa 1.00 .45
❑ 257 Steve Buechele .05 .02
❑ 258 Mike Devereaux UER .05 .02
(No comma between
city and state)
❑ 259 Brad Komminsk UER .05 .02
(Last text line,
Ba should be BA)
❑ 260 Teddy Higuera .05 .02
❑ 261 Shawn Abner .05 .02
❑ 262 Dave Valle .05 .02
❑ 263 Jeff Huson .05 .02
❑ 264 Edgar Martinez .20 .09
❑ 265 Carlton Fisk .20 .09
❑ 266 Steve Finley .20 .09
❑ 267 John Wetteland .20 .09
❑ 268 Kevin Appier .10 .05
❑ 269 Steve Lyons .05 .02
❑ 270 Mickey Tettleton .10 .05
❑ 271 Luis Rivera .05 .02
❑ 272 Steve Jeltz .05 .02
❑ 273 R.J. Reynolds .05 .02
❑ 274 Carlos Martinez .05 .02
❑ 275 Dan Plesac .05 .02
❑ 276 Mike Morgan UER .05 .02
(Total IP shown as
1149.1& should be 1149)
❑ 277 Jeff Russell .05 .02
❑ 278 Pete Incaviglia .05 .02
❑ 279 Kevin Seitzer UER .05 .02
(Bio has 200 hits twice
and .300 four times&
should be once and
three times)
❑ 280 Bobby Thigpen .05 .02
❑ 281 Stan Javier UER .05 .02
(Born 1/9&
should say 9/1)
❑ 282 Henry Cotto .05 .02
❑ 283 Gary Wayne .05 .02
❑ 284 Shane Mack .05 .02
❑ 285 Brian Holman .05 .02
❑ 286 Gerald Perry .05 .02
❑ 287 Steve Crawford .05 .02
❑ 288 Nelson Liriano .05 .02
❑ 289 Don Aase .05 .02
❑ 290 Randy Johnson .25 .11
❑ 291 Harold Baines .10 .05
❑ 292 Kent Hrbek .10 .05
❑ 293A Les Lancaster ERR .05 .02
(No comma between
Dallas and Texas)
❑ 293B Les Lancaster COR .05 .02
(Corrected in
factory sets)
❑ 294 Jeff Musselman .05 .02
❑ 295 Kurt Stillwell .05 .02
❑ 296 Stan Belinda .05 .02
❑ 297 Lou Whitaker .10 .05
❑ 298 Glenn Wilson .05 .02
❑ 299 Omar Vizquel UER .20 .09
(Born 5/15& should be
4/24& there is a decimal
before GP total for '90)
❑ 300 Ramon Martinez .10 .05
❑ 301 Dwight Smith .05 .02
❑ 302 Tim Crews .05 .02
❑ 303 Lance Blankenship .05 .02
❑ 304 Sid Bream .05 .02
❑ 305 Rafael Ramirez .05 .02
❑ 306 Steve Wilson .05 .02
❑ 307 Mackey Sasser .05 .02
❑ 308 Franklin Stubbs .05 .02
❑ 309 Jack Daugherty UER .05 .02
(Born 6/3/60,
should say July)
❑ 310 Eddie Murray .20 .09
❑ 311 Bob Welch .05 .02
❑ 312 Brian Harper .05 .02
❑ 313 Lance McCullers .05 .02
❑ 314 Dave Smith .05 .02
❑ 315 Bobby Bonilla .10 .05
❑ 316 Jerry Don Gleaton .05 .02
❑ 317 Greg Maddux .60 .25
❑ 318 Keith Miller .05 .02
❑ 319 Mark Portugal .05 .02
❑ 320 Robin Ventura .20 .09
❑ 321 Bob Ojeda .05 .02
❑ 322 Mike Harkey .05 .02
❑ 323 Jay Bell .10 .05
❑ 324 Mark McGwire 1.00 .45
❑ 325 Gary Gaetti .10 .05
❑ 326 Jeff Pico .05 .02
❑ 327 Kevin McReynolds .05 .02
❑ 328 Frank Tanana .05 .02
❑ 329 Eric Yelding UER .05 .02
(Listed as 6'3"
should be 5'11")
❑ 330 Barry Bonds .25 .11
❑ 331 Brian McRae UER .20 .09
(No comma between
city and state)
❑ 332 Pedro Munoz .05 .02
❑ 333 Daryl Irvine .05 .02
❑ 334 Chris Hoiles .05 .02
❑ 335 Thomas Howard .05 .02
❑ 336 Jeff Schulz .05 .02
❑ 337 Jeff Manto .05 .02
❑ 338 Beau Allred .05 .02
❑ 339 Mike Bordick .20 .09
❑ 340 Todd Hundley .20 .09
❑ 341 Jim Vatcher UER .05 .02
(Height 6'9",
should be 5'9")
❑ 342 Luis Sojo .05 .02
❑ 343 Jose Offerman UER .05 .02
(Born 1969& should
say 1968)
❑ 344 Pete Coachman .05 .02
❑ 345 Mike Benjamin .05 .02
❑ 346 Ozzie Canseco .05 .02
❑ 347 Tim McIntosh .05 .02
❑ 348 Phil Plantier .05 .02
❑ 349 Terry Shumpert .05 .02
❑ 350 Darren Lewis .10 .05
❑ 351 David Walsh .05 .02
❑ 352A Scott Chiamparino .10 .05
ERR (Bats left&
should be right)
❑ 352B Scott Chiamparino .10 .05
COR (corrected in
factory sets)
❑ 353 Julio Valera .05 .02
UER (Progressed mis-
spelled as progessed)
❑ 354 Anthony Telford .05 .02
❑ 355 Kevin Wickander .05 .02
❑ 356 Tim Naehring .10 .05
❑ 357 Jim Poole .05 .02
❑ 358 Mark Whiten UER .05 .02
(Shown hitting lefty&
bio says righty)
❑ 359 Terry Wells .05 .02
❑ 360 Rafael Valdez .05 .02
❑ 361 Mel Stottlemyre Jr. .05 .02
❑ 362 David Segui .10 .05
❑ 363 Paul Abbott .05 .02
❑ 364 Steve Howard .05 .02
❑ 365 Karl Rhodes .05 .02
❑ 366 Rafael Novoa .05 .02
❑ 367 Joe Grahe .05 .02
❑ 368 Darren Reed .05 .02
❑ 369 Jeff McKnight .05 .02
❑ 370 Scott Leius .05 .02
❑ 371 Mark Dewey .05 .02
❑ 372 Mark Lee UER .05 .02
(Shown hitting lefty&
bio says righty& born
in Dakota& should
say North Dakota)
❑ 373 Rosario Rodriguez .05 .02
(Shown hitting lefty&
bio says righty) UER
❑ 374 Chuck McElroy .05 .02
❑ 375 Mike Bell .05 .02
❑ 376 Mickey Morandini .05 .02
❑ 377 Bill Haselman .05 .02
❑ 378 Dave Pavlas .05 .02
❑ 379 Derrick May .05 .02
❑ 380 Jeromy Burnitz FDP .40 .18
❑ 381 Donald Peters FDP .05 .02
❑ 382 Alex Fernandez FDP .10 .05
❑ 383 Mike Mussina FDP 1.25 .55
❑ 384 Dan Smith FDP .05 .02
❑ 385 Lance Dickson FDP .05 .02
❑ 386 Carl Everett FDP .20 .09
❑ 387 Thomas Nevers FDP .05 .02
❑ 388 Adam Hyzdu FDP .05 .02
❑ 389 Todd Van Poppel FDP .05 .02
❑ 390 Rondell White FDP .40 .18
❑ 391 Marc Newfield FDP .10 .05
❑ 392 Julio Franco AS .05 .02
❑ 393 Wade Boggs AS .10 .05
❑ 394 Ozzie Guillen AS .05 .02
❑ 395 Cecil Fielder AS .05 .02
❑ 396 Ken Griffey Jr. AS .75 .35
❑ 397 Rickey Henderson AS .10 .05
❑ 398 Jose Canseco AS .10 .05
❑ 399 Roger Clemens AS .20 .09
❑ 400 Sandy Alomar Jr. AS .05 .02
❑ 401 Bobby Thigpen AS .05 .02
❑ 402 Bobby Bonilla MB .05 .02
❑ 403 Eric Davis MB .05 .02
❑ 404 Fred McGriff MB .10 .05
❑ 405 Glenn Davis MB .05 .02
❑ 406 Kevin Mitchell MB .05 .02
❑ 407 Rob Dibble KM .05 .02
❑ 408 Ramon Martinez KM .05 .02
❑ 409 David Cone KM .05 .02
❑ 410 Bobby Witt KM .05 .02
❑ 411 Mark Langston KM .05 .02
❑ 412 Bo Jackson RIF .10 .05
❑ 413 Shawon Dunston RIF .05 .02
UER (In the baseball&
should say in baseball)
❑ 414 Jesse Barfield RIF .05 .02
❑ 415 Ken Caminiti RIF .10 .05
❑ 416 Benito Santiago RIF .05 .02
❑ 417 Nolan Ryan HL .40 .18
❑ 418 Bobby Thigpen HL UER .05 .02
(Back refers to Hal
McRae Jr.& should
say Brian McRae)

❑ 419 Ramon Martinez HL .05 .02
❑ 420 Bo Jackson HL .10 .05
❑ 421 Carlton Fisk HL .10 .05
❑ 422 Jimmy Key .10 .05
❑ 423 Junior Noboa .05 .02
❑ 424 Al Newman .05 .02
❑ 425 Pat Borders .05 .02
❑ 426 Von Hayes .05 .02
❑ 427 Tim Teufel .05 .02
❑ 428 Eric Plunk UER .05 .02
(Text says Eric's had&
no apostrophe needed)
❑ 429 John Moses .05 .02
❑ 430 Mike Witt .05 .02
❑ 431 Otis Nixon .10 .05
❑ 432 Tony Fernandez .05 .02
❑ 433 Rance Mulliniks .05 .02
❑ 434 Dan Petry .05 .02
❑ 435 Bob Geren .05 .02
❑ 436 Steve Frey .05 .02
❑ 437 Jamie Moyer .05 .02
❑ 438 Junior Ortiz .05 .02
❑ 439 Tom O'Malley .05 .02
❑ 440 Pat Combs .05 .02
❑ 441 Jose Canseco DT .10 .05
❑ 442 Alfredo Griffin .05 .02
❑ 443 Andres Galarraga .20 .09
❑ 444 Bryn Smith .05 .02
❑ 445 Andre Dawson .20 .09
❑ 446 Juan Samuel .05 .02
❑ 447 Mike Aldrete .05 .02
❑ 448 Ron Gant .10 .05
❑ 449 Fernando Valenzuela .10 .05
❑ 450 Vince Coleman UER .05 .02
(Should say topped
majors in steals four
times& not three times)
❑ 451 Kevin Mitchell .05 .02
❑ 452 Spike Owen .05 .02
❑ 453 Mike Bielecki .05 .02
❑ 454 Dennis Martinez .10 .05
❑ 455 Brett Butler .10 .05
❑ 456 Ron Darling .05 .02
❑ 457 Dennis Rasmussen .05 .02
❑ 458 Ken Howell .05 .02
❑ 459 Steve Bedrosian .05 .02
❑ 460 Frank Viola .05 .02
❑ 461 Jose Lind .05 .02
❑ 462 Chris Sabo .05 .02
❑ 463 Dante Bichette .20 .09
❑ 464 Rick Mahler .05 .02
❑ 465 John Smiley .05 .02
❑ 466 Devon White .05 .02
❑ 467 John Orton .05 .02
❑ 468 Mike Stanton .05 .02
❑ 469 Billy Hatcher .05 .02
❑ 470 Wally Joyner .10 .05
❑ 471 Gene Larkin .05 .02
❑ 472 Doug Drabek .05 .02
❑ 473 Gary Sheffield .20 .09
❑ 474 David Wells .10 .05
❑ 475 Andy Van Slyke .10 .05
❑ 476 Mike Gallego .05 .02
❑ 477 B.J. Surhoff .10 .05
❑ 478 Gene Nelson .05 .02
❑ 479 Mariano Duncan .05 .02
❑ 480 Fred McGriff .20 .09
❑ 481 Jerry Browne .05 .02
❑ 482 Alvin Davis .05 .02
❑ 483 Bill Wegman .05 .02
❑ 484 Dave Parker .10 .05
❑ 485 Dennis Eckersley .10 .05
❑ 486 Erik Hanson UER .05 .02
(Basketball misspelled
as baseketball)
❑ 487 Bill Ripken .05 .02
❑ 488 Tom Candiotti .05 .02
❑ 489 Mike Schooler .05 .02
❑ 490 Gregg Olson .05 .02
❑ 491 Chris James .05 .02
❑ 492 Pete Harnisch .05 .02
❑ 493 Julio Franco .05 .02
❑ 494 Greg Briley .05 .02
❑ 495 Ruben Sierra .05 .02
❑ 496 Steve Olin .05 .02
❑ 497 Mike Fetters .05 .02
❑ 498 Mark Williamson .05 .02
❑ 499 Bob Tewksbury .05 .02
❑ 500 Tony Gwynn .50 .23
❑ 501 Randy Myers .10 .05
❑ 502 Keith Comstock .05 .02
❑ 503 Craig Worthington UER .05 .02
(DeCinces misspelled
DiCinces on back)
❑ 504 Mark Eichhorn UER .05 .02
(Stats incomplete&
doesn't have '89
Braves stint)
❑ 505 Barry Larkin .20 .09
❑ 506 Dave Johnson .05 .02
❑ 507 Bobby Witt .05 .02
❑ 508 Joe Orsulak .05 .02
❑ 509 Pete O'Brien .05 .02
❑ 510 Brad Arnsberg .05 .02
❑ 511 Storm Davis .05 .02
❑ 512 Bob Milacki .05 .02
❑ 513 Bill Pecota .05 .02
❑ 514 Glenallen Hill .05 .02
❑ 515 Danny Tartabull .05 .02
❑ 516 Mike Moore .05 .02
❑ 517 Ron Robinson UER .05 .02
(577 K's in 1990)
❑ 518 Mark Gardner .05 .02
❑ 519 Rick Wrona .05 .02
❑ 520 Mike Scioscia .05 .02
❑ 521 Frank Wills .05 .02
❑ 522 Greg Brock .05 .02
❑ 523 Jack Clark .10 .05
❑ 524 Bruce Ruffin .05 .02
❑ 525 Robin Yount .20 .09
❑ 526 Tom Foley .05 .02
❑ 527 Pat Perry .05 .02
❑ 528 Greg Vaughn .20 .09
❑ 529 Wally Whitehurst .05 .02
❑ 530 Norm Charlton .05 .02
❑ 531 Marvell Wynne .05 .02
❑ 532 Jim Gantner .05 .02
❑ 533 Greg Litton .05 .02
❑ 534 Manny Lee .05 .02
❑ 535 Scott Bailes .05 .02
❑ 536 Charlie Leibrandt .05 .02
❑ 537 Roger McDowell .05 .02
❑ 538 Andy Benes .10 .05
❑ 539 Rick Honeycutt .05 .02
❑ 540 Dwight Gooden .10 .05
❑ 541 Scott Garrelts .05 .02
❑ 542 Dave Clark .05 .02
❑ 543 Lonnie Smith .05 .02
❑ 544 Rick Reuschel .05 .02
❑ 545 Delino DeShields UER .10 .05
(Rockford misspelled
as Rock Ford in '88)
❑ 546 Mike Sharperson .05 .02
❑ 547 Mike Kingery .05 .02
❑ 548 Terry Kennedy .05 .02
❑ 549 David Cone .10 .05
❑ 550 Orel Hershiser .10 .05
❑ 551 Matt Nokes .05 .02
❑ 552 Eddie Williams .05 .02
❑ 553 Frank DiPino .05 .02
❑ 554 Fred Lynn .05 .02
❑ 555 Alex Cole .05 .02
❑ 556 Terry Leach .05 .02
❑ 557 Chet Lemon .05 .02
❑ 558 Paul Mirabella .05 .02
❑ 559 Bill Long .05 .02
❑ 560 Phil Bradley .05 .02
❑ 561 Duane Ward .05 .02
❑ 562 Dave Bergman .05 .02
❑ 563 Eric Show .05 .02
❑ 564 Xavier Hernandez .05 .02
❑ 565 Jeff Parrett .05 .02
❑ 566 Chuck Cary .05 .02
❑ 567 Ken Hill .10 .05
❑ 568 Bob Welch Hand .05 .02
(Complement should be
compliment) UER
❑ 569 John Mitchell .05 .02
❑ 570 Travis Fryman .20 .09
❑ 571 Derek Lilliquist .05 .02
❑ 572 Steve Lake .05 .02
❑ 573 John Barfield .05 .02
❑ 574 Randy Bush .05 .02
❑ 575 Joe Magrane .05 .02
❑ 576 Eddie Diaz .05 .02
❑ 577 Casey Candaele .05 .02
❑ 578 Jesse Orosco .05 .02
❑ 579 Tom Henke .05 .02
❑ 580 Rick Cerone UER .05 .02
(Actually his third
go-round with Yankees)
❑ 581 Drew Hall .05 .02
❑ 582 Tony Castillo .05 .02
❑ 583 Jimmy Jones .05 .02
❑ 584 Rick Reed .05 .02
❑ 585 Joe Girardi .10 .05
❑ 586 Jeff Gray .05 .02
❑ 587 Luis Polonia .05 .02
❑ 588 Joe Klink .05 .02
❑ 589 Rex Hudler .05 .02
❑ 590 Kirk McCaskill .05 .02
❑ 591 Juan Agosto .05 .02
❑ 592 Wes Gardner .05 .02
❑ 593 Rich Rodriguez .05 .02
❑ 594 Mitch Webster .05 .02
❑ 595 Kelly Gruber .05 .02
❑ 596 Dale Mohorcic .05 .02
❑ 597 Willie McGee .10 .05
❑ 598 Bill Krueger .05 .02
❑ 599 Bob Walk UER .05 .02
(Cards says he's 33&
but actually he's 34)
❑ 600 Kevin Maas .05 .02
❑ 601 Danny Jackson .05 .02
❑ 602 Craig McMurtry UER .05 .02
(Anonymously misspelled
anonimously)
❑ 603 Curtis Wilkerson .05 .02
❑ 604 Adam Peterson .05 .02
❑ 605 Sam Horn .05 .02
❑ 606 Tommy Gregg .05 .02
❑ 607 Ken Dayley .05 .02
❑ 608 Carmelo Castillo .05 .02
❑ 609 John Shelby .05 .02
❑ 610 Don Slaught .05 .02
❑ 611 Calvin Schiraldi .05 .02
❑ 612 Dennis Lamp .05 .02
❑ 613 Andres Thomas .05 .02
❑ 614 Jose Gonzalez .05 .02
❑ 615 Randy Ready .05 .02
❑ 616 Kevin Bass .05 .02
❑ 617 Mike Marshall .05 .02
❑ 618 Daryl Boston .05 .02
❑ 619 Andy McGaffigan .05 .02
❑ 620 Joe Oliver .05 .02
❑ 621 Jim Gott .05 .02
❑ 622 Jose Oquendo .05 .02
❑ 623 Jose DeJesus .05 .02
❑ 624 Mike Brumley .05 .02
❑ 625 John Olerud .10 .05
❑ 626 Ernest Riles .05 .02
❑ 627 Gene Harris .05 .02
❑ 628 Jose Uribe .05 .02
❑ 629 Darnell Coles .05 .02
❑ 630 Carney Lansford .10 .05
❑ 631 Tim Leary .05 .02
❑ 632 Tim Hulett .05 .02
❑ 633 Kevin Elster .05 .02
❑ 634 Tony Fossas .05 .02
❑ 635 Francisco Oliveras .05 .02
❑ 636 Bob Patterson .05 .02
❑ 637 Gary Ward .05 .02
❑ 638 Rene Gonzales .05 .02
❑ 639 Don Robinson .05 .02
❑ 640 Darryl Strawberry .10 .05
❑ 641 Dave Anderson .05 .02
❑ 642 Scott Scudder .05 .02
❑ 643 Reggie Harris UER .05 .02
(Hepatitis misspelled
as hepititis)
❑ 644 Dave Henderson .05 .02
❑ 645 Ben McDonald .05 .02
❑ 646 Bob Kipper .05 .02
❑ 647 Hal Morris UER .05 .02
(It's should be its)

❑ 648 Tim Birtsas .05 .02
❑ 649 Steve Searcy .05 .02
❑ 650 Dale Murphy .20 .09
❑ 651 Ron Oester .05 .02
❑ 652 Mike LaCoss .05 .02
❑ 653 Ron Jones .05 .02
❑ 654 Kelly Downs .05 .02
❑ 655 Roger Clemens .40 .18
❑ 656 Herm Winningham .05 .02
❑ 657 Trevor Wilson .05 .02
❑ 658 Jose Rijo .05 .02
❑ 659 Dann Bilardello UER .05 .02
(Bio has 13 games& 1 hit& and 32 AB& stats show 19& 2& and 37)
❑ 660 Gregg Jefferies .05 .02
❑ 661 Doug Drabek AS UER .05 .02
(Through is misspelled though)
❑ 662 Randy Myers AS .05 .02
❑ 663 Benny Santiago AS .05 .02
❑ 664 Will Clark AS .10 .05
❑ 665 Ryne Sandberg AS .20 .09
❑ 666 Barry Larkin AS UER .10 .05
(Line 13& coolly misspelled cooly)
❑ 667 Matt Williams AS .10 .05
❑ 668 Barry Bonds AS .20 .09
❑ 669 Eric Davis AS .05 .02
❑ 670 Bobby Bonilla AS .05 .02
❑ 671 Chipper Jones FDP 4.00 1.80
❑ 672 Eric Christopherson FDP .05 .02
❑ 673 Robbie Beckett FDP .05 .02
❑ 674 Shane Andrews FDP .10 .05
❑ 675 Steve Karsay FDP .10 .05
❑ 676 Aaron Holbert FDP .05 .02
❑ 677 Donovan Osborne FDP .10 .05
❑ 678 Todd Ritchie FDP .05 .02
❑ 679 Ron Walden FDP .05 .02
❑ 680 Tim Costo FDP .05 .02
❑ 681 Dan Wilson FDP .25 .11
❑ 682 Kurt Miller FDP .05 .02
❑ 683 Mike Lieberthal FDP .20 .09
❑ 684 Roger Clemens KM .20 .09
❑ 685 Doc Gooden KM .05 .02
❑ 686 Nolan Ryan KM .40 .18
❑ 687 Frank Viola KM .05 .02
❑ 688 Erik Hanson KM .05 .02
❑ 689 Matt Williams MB .10 .05
❑ 690 Jose Canseco MB UER .10 .05
(Mammoth misspelled as monmouth)
❑ 691 Darryl Strawberry MB .05 .02
❑ 692 Bo Jackson MB .10 .05
❑ 693 Cecil Fielder MB .05 .02
❑ 694 Sandy Alomar Jr. RF .05 .02
❑ 695 Cory Snyder RF .05 .02
❑ 696 Eric Davis RF .05 .02
❑ 697 Ken Griffey Jr. RF .75 .35
❑ 698 Andy Van Slyke RF UER .05 .02
(Line 2& outfielders does not need)
❑ 699 Mark Langston NH Mike Witt .05 .02
❑ 700 Randy Johnson NH .20 .09
❑ 701 Nolan Ryan NH .40 .18
❑ 702 Dave Stewart NH .05 .02
❑ 703 Fernando Valenzuela NH .05 .02
❑ 704 Andy Hawkins NH .05 .02
❑ 705 Melido Perez NH .05 .02
❑ 706 Terry Mulholland NH .05 .02
❑ 707 Dave Stieb NH .05 .02
❑ 708 Brian Barnes .05 .02
❑ 709 Bernard Gilkey .10 .05
❑ 710 Steve Decker .05 .02
❑ 711 Paul Faries .05 .02
❑ 712 Paul Marak .05 .02
❑ 713 Wes Chamberlain .05 .02
❑ 714 Kevin Belcher .05 .02
❑ 715 Dan Boone UER .05 .02
(IP adds up to 101, but card has 101.2)
❑ 716 Steve Adkins .05 .02
❑ 717 Geronimo Pena .05 .02
❑ 718 Howard Farmer .05 .02
❑ 719 Mark Leonard .05 .02
❑ 720 Tom Lampkin .05 .02
❑ 721 Mike Gardiner .05 .02
❑ 722 Jeff Conine .25 .11
❑ 723 Efrain Valdez .05 .02
❑ 724 Chuck Malone .05 .02
❑ 725 Leo Gomez .05 .02
❑ 726 Paul McClellan .05 .02
❑ 727 Mark Leiter .05 .02
❑ 728 Rich DeLucia UER .05 .02
(Line 2, all told is written alltold)
❑ 729 Mel Rojas .10 .05
❑ 730 Hector Wagner .05 .02
❑ 731 Ray Lankford .20 .09
❑ 732 Turner Ward .05 .02
❑ 733 Gerald Alexander .05 .02
❑ 734 Scott Anderson .05 .02
❑ 735 Tony Perezchica .05 .02
❑ 736 Jimmy Kremers .05 .02
❑ 737 American Flag .20 .09
(Pray for Peace)
❑ 738 Mike York .05 .02
❑ 739 Mike Rochford .05 .02
❑ 740 Scott Aldred .05 .02
❑ 741 Rico Brogna .15 .07
❑ 742 Dave Burba .05 .02
❑ 743 Ray Stephens .05 .02
❑ 744 Eric Gunderson .05 .02
❑ 745 Troy Afenir .05 .02
❑ 746 Jeff Shaw .05 .02
❑ 747 Orlando Merced .10 .05
❑ 748 Omar Olivares UER .05 .02
(Line 9& league is misspelled legaue)
❑ 749 Jerry Kutzler .05 .02
❑ 750 Mo Vaughn UER .40 .18
(44 SB's in 1990)
❑ 751 Matt Stark .05 .02
❑ 752 Randy Hennis .05 .02
❑ 753 Andujar Cedeno .05 .02
❑ 754 Kelvin Torve .05 .02
❑ 755 Joe Kraemer .05 .02
❑ 756 Phil Clark .05 .02
❑ 757 Ed Vosberg .05 .02
❑ 758 Mike Perez .05 .02
❑ 759 Scott Lewis .05 .02
❑ 760 Steve Chitren .05 .02
❑ 761 Ray Young .05 .02
❑ 762 Andres Santana .05 .02
❑ 763 Rodney McCray .05 .02
❑ 764 Sean Berry UER .10 .05
(Name misspelled Barry on card front)
❑ 765 Brent Mayne .05 .02
❑ 766 Mike Simms .05 .02
❑ 767 Glenn Sutko .05 .02
❑ 768 Gary DiSarcina .05 .02
❑ 769 George Brett HL .20 .09
❑ 770 Cecil Fielder HL .05 .02
❑ 771 Jim Presley .05 .02
❑ 772 John Dopson .05 .02
❑ 773 Bo Jackson Breaker .15 .07
❑ 774 Brent Knackert UER .05 .02
(Born in 1954& shown throwing righty& but bio says lefty)
❑ 775 Bill Doran UER .05 .02
(Reds in NL East)
❑ 776 Dick Schofield .05 .02
❑ 777 Nelson Santovenia .05 .02
❑ 778 Mark Guthrie .05 .02
❑ 779 Mark Lemke .05 .02
❑ 780 Terry Steinbach .10 .05
❑ 781 Tom Bolton .05 .02
❑ 782 Randy Tomlin .05 .02
❑ 783 Jeff Kunkel .05 .02
❑ 784 Felix Jose .05 .02
❑ 785 Rick Sutcliffe .05 .02
❑ 786 John Cerutti .05 .02
❑ 787 Jose Vizcaino UER .05 .02
(Offerman& not Opperman)
❑ 788 Curt Schilling .20 .09
❑ 789 Ed Whitson .05 .02
❑ 790 Tony Pena .05 .02
❑ 791 John Candelaria .05 .02
❑ 792 Carmelo Martinez .05 .02
❑ 793 Sandy Alomar Jr. UER .10 .05
(Indian's should say Indians')
❑ 794 Jim Neidlinger .05 .02
❑ 795 Barry Larkin WS and Chris Sabo .10 .05
❑ 796 Paul Sorrento .10 .05
❑ 797 Tom Pagnozzi .05 .02
❑ 798 Tino Martinez .20 .09
❑ 799 Scott Ruskin UER .05 .02
(Text says first three seasons but lists averages for four)
❑ 800 Kirk Gibson .10 .05
❑ 801 Walt Terrell .05 .02
❑ 802 John Russell .05 .02
❑ 803 Chili Davis .10 .05
❑ 804 Chris Nabholz .05 .02
❑ 805 Juan Gonzalez .75 .35
❑ 806 Ron Hassey .05 .02
❑ 807 Todd Worrell .05 .02
❑ 808 Tommy Greene .05 .02
❑ 809 Joel Skinner UER .05 .02
(Joel& not Bob& was drafted in 1979)
❑ 810 Benito Santiago .05 .02
❑ 811 Pat Tabler UER .05 .02
(Line 3& always misspelled alway)
❑ 812 Scott Erickson UER .10 .05
(Record spelled rcord)
❑ 813 Moises Alou .20 .09
❑ 814 Dale Sveum .05 .02
❑ 815 Ryne Sandberg MANYR .20 .09
❑ 816 Rick Dempsey .05 .02
❑ 817 Scott Bankhead .05 .02
❑ 818 Jason Grimsley .05 .02
❑ 819 Doug Jennings .05 .02
❑ 820 Tom Herr .05 .02
❑ 821 Rob Ducey .05 .02
❑ 822 Luis Quinones .05 .02
❑ 823 Greg Minton .05 .02
❑ 824 Mark Grant .05 .02
❑ 825 Ozzie Smith UER .25 .11
(Shortstop misspelled shortsop)
❑ 826 Dave Eiland .05 .02
❑ 827 Danny Heep .05 .02
❑ 828 Hensley Meulens .05 .02
❑ 829 Charlie O'Brien .05 .02
❑ 830 Glenn Davis .05 .02
❑ 831 John Marzano UER .05 .02
(International misspelled Internaional)
❑ 832 Steve Ontiveros .05 .02
❑ 833 Ron Karkovice .05 .02
❑ 834 Jerry Goff .05 .02
❑ 835 Ken Griffey Sr. .05 .02
❑ 836 Kevin Reimer .05 .02
❑ 837 Randy Kutcher UER .05 .02
(Infectious misspelled infectous)
❑ 838 Mike Blowers .05 .02
❑ 839 Mike Macfarlane .05 .02
❑ 840 Frank Thomas UER 1.00 .45
(1989 Sarasota stats& 15 games but 188 AB)
❑ 841 The Griffeys .75 .35
Ken Griffey Jr.
Ken Griffey Sr.
❑ 842 Jack Howell .05 .02
❑ 843 Goose Gozzo .05 .02
❑ 844 Gerald Young .05 .02
❑ 845 Zane Smith .05 .02
❑ 846 Kevin Brown .15 .07
❑ 847 Sil Campusano .05 .02
❑ 848 Larry Andersen .05 .02
❑ 849 Cal Ripken FRAN .40 .18
❑ 850 Roger Clemens FRAN .20 .09
❑ 851 Sandy Alomar Jr. FRAN .05 .02
❑ 852 Alan Trammell FRAN .10 .05
❑ 853 George Brett FRAN .20 .09

Card	Player	Mint	Nrmt
❑ 854	Robin Yount FRAN	.10	.05
❑ 855	Kirby Puckett FRAN	.20	.09
❑ 856	Don Mattingly FRAN	.20	.09
❑ 857	Rickey Henderson FRAN	.10	.05
❑ 858	Ken Griffey Jr. FRAN	.75	.35
❑ 859	Ruben Sierra FRAN	.05	.02
❑ 860	John Olerud FRAN	.10	.05
❑ 861	Dave Justice FRAN	.10	.05
❑ 862	Ryne Sandberg FRAN	.20	.09
❑ 863	Eric Davis FRAN	.05	.02
❑ 864	Darryl Strawberry FRAN	.05	.02
❑ 865	Tim Wallach FRAN	.05	.02
❑ 866	Doc Gooden FRAN	.05	.02
❑ 867	Len Dykstra FRAN	.05	.02
❑ 868	Barry Bonds FRAN	.20	.09
❑ 869	Todd Zeile FRAN UER (Powerful misspelled as poweful)	.05	.02
❑ 870	Benito Santiago FRAN	.05	.02
❑ 871	Will Clark FRAN	.10	.05
❑ 872	Craig Biggio FRAN	.10	.05
❑ 873	Wally Joyner FRAN	.05	.02
❑ 874	Frank Thomas FRAN	.50	.23
❑ 875	Rickey Henderson MVP	.10	.05
❑ 876	Barry Bonds MVP	.20	.09
❑ 877	Bob Welch CY	.05	.02
❑ 878	Doug Drabek CY	.05	.02
❑ 879	Sandy Alomar Jr ROY	.10	.05
❑ 880	Dave Justice ROY	.10	.05
❑ 881	Damon Berryhill	.05	.02
❑ 882	Frank Viola DT	.05	.02
❑ 883	Dave Stewart DT	.05	.02
❑ 884	Doug Jones DT	.05	.02
❑ 885	Randy Myers DT	.05	.02
❑ 886	Will Clark DT	.10	.05
❑ 887	Roberto Alomar DT	.10	.05
❑ 888	Barry Larkin DT	.10	.05
❑ 889	Wade Boggs DT	.10	.05
❑ 890	Rickey Henderson DT	.10	.05
❑ 891	Kirby Puckett DT	.30	.14
❑ 892	Ken Griffey Jr DT	1.50	.70
❑ 893	Benny Santiago DT	.05	.02

1991 Score Cooperstown

	MINT	NRMT
COMPLETE SET (7)	10.00	4.50
COMMON CARD (B1-B7)	.50	.23

Card	Player	Mint	Nrmt
❑ B1	Wade Boggs	.50	.23
❑ B2	Barry Larkin	.50	.23
❑ B3	Ken Griffey Jr.	6.00	2.70
❑ B4	Rickey Henderson	.50	.23
❑ B5	George Brett	1.50	.70
❑ B6	Will Clark	.50	.23
❑ B7	Nolan Ryan	3.00	1.35

1991 Score Hot Rookies

	MINT	NRMT
COMPLETE SET (10)	12.00	5.50
COMMON CARD (1-10)	.50	.23

Card	Player	Mint	Nrmt
❑ 1	Dave Justice	2.00	.90
❑ 2	Kevin Maas	.50	.23
❑ 3	Hal Morris	.50	.23
❑ 4	Frank Thomas	6.00	2.70
❑ 5	Jeff Conine	1.00	.45
❑ 6	Sandy Alomar Jr.	.75	.35
❑ 7	Ray Lankford	1.50	.70
❑ 8	Steve Decker	.50	.23
❑ 9	Juan Gonzalez	5.00	2.20
❑ 10	Jose Offerman	.50	.23

1991 Score Mantle

	MINT	NRMT
COMPLETE SET (7)	200.00	90.00
COMMON MANTLE (1-7)	30.00	13.50
*PROMO CARDS: 1X BASIC CARDS		

Card	Player	Mint	Nrmt
❑ 1	Mickey Mantle The Rookie (With Billy Martin)	30.00	13.50
❑ 2	Mickey Mantle Triple Crown	30.00	13.50
❑ 3	Mickey Mantle World Series	30.00	13.50
❑ 4	Mickey Mantle Going, Going, Gone	30.00	13.50
❑ 5	Mickey Mantle Speed and Grace	30.00	13.50
❑ 6	Mickey Mantle A True Yankee	30.00	13.50
❑ 7	Mickey Mantle Twilight	30.00	13.50
❑ AU0	Mickey Mantle AU (Autographed with certified signature)	500.00	220.00

1991 Score Rookie/Traded

	MINT	NRMT
COMP.FACT.SET (110)	4.00	1.80
COMMON CARD (1T-110T)	.05	.02

Card	Player	Mint	Nrmt
❑ 1T	Bo Jackson	.10	.05
❑ 2T	Mike Flanagan	.05	.02
❑ 3T	Pete Incaviglia	.05	.02
❑ 4T	Jack Clark	.10	.05
❑ 5T	Hubie Brooks	.05	.02
❑ 6T	Ivan Calderon	.05	.02
❑ 7T	Glenn Davis	.05	.02
❑ 8T	Wally Backman	.05	.02
❑ 9T	Dave Smith	.05	.02
❑ 10T	Tim Raines	.10	.05
❑ 11T	Joe Carter	.10	.05
❑ 12T	Sid Bream	.05	.02
❑ 13T	George Bell	.05	.02
❑ 14T	Steve Bedrosian	.05	.02
❑ 15T	Willie Wilson	.05	.02
❑ 16T	Darryl Strawberry	.10	.05
❑ 17T	Danny Jackson	.05	.02
❑ 18T	Kirk Gibson	.10	.05
❑ 19T	Willie McGee	.10	.05
❑ 20T	Junior Felix	.05	.02
❑ 21T	Steve Farr	.05	.02
❑ 22T	Pat Tabler	.05	.02
❑ 23T	Brett Butler	.10	.05
❑ 24T	Danny Darwin	.05	.02
❑ 25T	Mickey Tettleton	.10	.05
❑ 26T	Gary Carter	.20	.09
❑ 27T	Mitch Williams	.05	.02
❑ 28T	Candy Maldonado	.05	.02
❑ 29T	Otis Nixon	.10	.05
❑ 30T	Brian Downing	.05	.02
❑ 31T	Tom Candiotti	.05	.02
❑ 32T	John Candelaria	.05	.02
❑ 33T	Rob Murphy	.05	.02
❑ 34T	Deion Sanders	.10	.05
❑ 35T	Willie Randolph	.10	.05
❑ 36T	Pete Harnisch	.05	.02
❑ 37T	Dante Bichette	.20	.09
❑ 38T	Garry Templeton	.05	.02
❑ 39T	Gary Gaetti	.10	.05
❑ 40T	John Cerutti	.05	.02
❑ 41T	Rick Cerone	.05	.02
❑ 42T	Mike Pagliarulo	.05	.02
❑ 43T	Ron Hassey	.05	.02
❑ 44T	Roberto Alomar	.20	.09
❑ 45T	Mike Boddicker	.05	.02
❑ 46T	Bud Black	.05	.02
❑ 47T	Rob Deer	.05	.02
❑ 48T	Devon White	.05	.02
❑ 49T	Luis Sojo	.05	.02
❑ 50T	Terry Pendleton	.10	.05
❑ 51T	Kevin Gross	.05	.02
❑ 52T	Mike Huff	.05	.02
❑ 53T	Dave Righetti	.05	.02
❑ 54T	Matt Young	.05	.02
❑ 55T	Earnest Riles	.05	.02
❑ 56T	Bill Gullickson	.05	.02
❑ 57T	Vince Coleman	.05	.02
❑ 58T	Fred McGriff	.20	.09
❑ 59T	Franklin Stubbs	.05	.02
❑ 60T	Eric King	.05	.02
❑ 61T	Cory Snyder	.05	.02
❑ 62T	Dwight Evans	.10	.05
❑ 63T	Gerald Perry	.05	.02
❑ 64T	Eric Show	.05	.02
❑ 65T	Shawn Hillegas	.05	.02
❑ 66T	Tony Fernandez	.05	.02
❑ 67T	Tim Teufel	.05	.02
❑ 68T	Mitch Webster	.05	.02
❑ 69T	Mike Heath	.05	.02
❑ 70T	Chili Davis	.10	.05
❑ 71T	Larry Andersen	.05	.02
❑ 72T	Gary Varsho	.05	.02
❑ 73T	Juan Berenguer	.05	.02
❑ 74T	Jack Morris	.10	.05
❑ 75T	Barry Jones	.05	.02
❑ 76T	Rafael Belliard	.05	.02
❑ 77T	Steve Buechele	.05	.02
❑ 78T	Scott Sanderson	.05	.02

❑ 79T Bob Ojeda .05 .02
❑ 80T Curt Schilling .20 .09
❑ 81T Brian Drahman .05 .02
❑ 82T Ivan Rodriguez 1.50 .70
❑ 83T David Howard .05 .02
❑ 84T Heathcliff Slocumb .20 .09
❑ 85T Mike Timlin .05 .02
❑ 86T Darryl Kile .20 .09
❑ 87T Pete Schourek .10 .05
❑ 88T Bruce Walton .05 .02
❑ 89T Al Osuna .05 .02
❑ 90T Gary Scott .05 .02
❑ 91T Doug Simons .05 .02
❑ 92T Chris Jones .05 .02
❑ 93T Chuck Knoblauch .25 .11
❑ 94T Dana Allison .05 .02
❑ 95T Erik Pappas .05 .02
❑ 96T Jeff Bagwell 2.00 .90
❑ 97T Kirk Dressendorfer .05 .02
❑ 98T Freddie Benavides .05 .02
❑ 99T Luis Gonzalez .20 .09
❑ 100T Wade Taylor .05 .02
❑ 101T Ed Sprague .05 .02
❑ 102T Bob Scanlan .05 .02
❑ 103T Rick Wilkins .05 .02
❑ 104T Chris Donnels .05 .02
❑ 105T Joe Slusarski .05 .02
❑ 106T Mark Lewis .05 .02
❑ 107T Pat Kelly .05 .02
❑ 108T John Briscoe .05 .02
❑ 109T Luis Lopez .05 .02
❑ 110T Jeff Johnson .05 .02

1992 Score

	MINT	NRMT
COMPLETE SET (893)	15.00	6.75
COMP.FACT.SET (910)	20.00	9.00
COMPLETE SERIES 1 (442)	8.00	3.60
COMPLETE SERIES 2 (451)	8.00	3.60
COMMON CARD (1-893)	.05	.02

❑ 1 Ken Griffey Jr. 1.25 .55
❑ 2 Nolan Ryan .75 .35
❑ 3 Will Clark .20 .09
❑ 4 Dave Justice .20 .09
❑ 5 Dave Henderson .05 .02
❑ 6 Bret Saberhagen .10 .05
❑ 7 Fred McGriff .15 .07
❑ 8 Erik Hanson .05 .02
❑ 9 Darryl Strawberry .10 .05
❑ 10 Dwight Gooden .10 .05
❑ 11 Juan Gonzalez .60 .25
❑ 12 Mark Langston .05 .02
❑ 13 Lonnie Smith .05 .02
❑ 14 Jeff Montgomery .10 .05
❑ 15 Roberto Alomar .20 .09
❑ 16 Delino DeShields .10 .05
❑ 17 Steve Bedrosian .05 .02
❑ 18 Terry Pendleton .05 .02
❑ 19 Mark Carreon .05 .02
❑ 20 Mark McGwire 1.00 .45
❑ 21 Roger Clemens .40 .18
❑ 22 Chuck Crim .05 .02
❑ 23 Don Mattingly .30 .14
❑ 24 Dickie Thon .05 .02
❑ 25 Ron Gant .10 .05
❑ 26 Milt Cuyler .05 .02
❑ 27 Mike Macfarlane .05 .02
❑ 28 Dan Gladden .05 .02
❑ 29 Melido Perez .05 .02
❑ 30 Willie Randolph .10 .05
❑ 31 Albert Belle .25 .11
❑ 32 Dave Winfield .20 .09
❑ 33 Jimmy Jones .05 .02
❑ 34 Kevin Gross .05 .02
❑ 35 Andres Galarraga .20 .09
❑ 36 Mike Devereaux .05 .02
❑ 37 Chris Bosio .05 .02
❑ 38 Mike LaValliere .05 .02
❑ 39 Gary Gaetti .05 .02
❑ 40 Felix Jose .05 .02
❑ 41 Alvaro Espinoza .05 .02
❑ 42 Rick Aguilera .10 .05
❑ 43 Mike Gallego .05 .02
❑ 44 Eric Davis .10 .05
❑ 45 George Bell .05 .02
❑ 46 Tom Brunansky .05 .02
❑ 47 Steve Farr .05 .02
❑ 48 Duane Ward .05 .02
❑ 49 David Wells .10 .05
❑ 50 Cecil Fielder .10 .05
❑ 51 Walt Weiss .05 .02
❑ 52 Todd Zeile .05 .02
❑ 53 Doug Jones .05 .02
❑ 54 Bob Walk .05 .02
❑ 55 Rafael Palmeiro .15 .07
❑ 56 Rob Deer .05 .02
❑ 57 Paul O'Neill .10 .05
❑ 58 Jeff Reardon .10 .05
❑ 59 Randy Ready .05 .02
❑ 60 Scott Erickson .10 .05
❑ 61 Paul Molitor .20 .09
❑ 62 Jack McDowell .05 .02
❑ 63 Jim Acker .05 .02
❑ 64 Jay Buhner .15 .07
❑ 65 Travis Fryman .10 .05
❑ 66 Marquis Grissom .10 .05
❑ 67 Mike Harkey .05 .02
❑ 68 Luis Polonia .05 .02
❑ 69 Ken Caminiti .15 .07
❑ 70 Chris Sabo .05 .02
❑ 71 Gregg Olson .05 .02
❑ 72 Carlton Fisk .20 .09
❑ 73 Juan Samuel .05 .02
❑ 74 Todd Stottlemyre .10 .05
❑ 75 Andre Dawson .15 .07
❑ 76 Alvin Davis .05 .02
❑ 77 Bill Doran .05 .02
❑ 78 B.J. Surhoff .10 .05
❑ 79 Kirk McCaskill .05 .02
❑ 80 Dale Murphy .20 .09
❑ 81 Jose DeLeon .05 .02
❑ 82 Alex Fernandez .10 .05
❑ 83 Ivan Calderon .05 .02
❑ 84 Brent Mayne .05 .02
❑ 85 Jody Reed .05 .02
❑ 86 Randy Tomlin .05 .02
❑ 87 Randy Milligan .05 .02
❑ 88 Pascual Perez .05 .02
❑ 89 Hensley Meulens .05 .02
❑ 90 Joe Carter .10 .05
❑ 91 Mike Moore .05 .02
❑ 92 Ozzie Guillen .05 .02
❑ 93 Shawn Hillegas .05 .02
❑ 94 Chili Davis .10 .05
❑ 95 Vince Coleman .05 .02
❑ 96 Jimmy Key .10 .05
❑ 97 Billy Ripken .05 .02
❑ 98 Dave Smith .05 .02
❑ 99 Tom Bolton .05 .02
❑ 100 Barry Larkin .15 .07
❑ 101 Kenny Rogers .05 .02
❑ 102 Mike Boddicker .05 .02
❑ 103 Kevin Elster .05 .02
❑ 104 Ken Hill .05 .02
❑ 105 Charlie Leibrandt .05 .02
❑ 106 Pat Combs .05 .02
❑ 107 Hubie Brooks .05 .02
❑ 108 Julio Franco .05 .02
❑ 109 Vicente Palacios .05 .02
❑ 110 Kal Daniels .05 .02
❑ 111 Bruce Hurst .05 .02
❑ 112 Willie McGee .10 .05
❑ 113 Ted Power .05 .02
❑ 114 Milt Thompson .05 .02
❑ 115 Doug Drabek .05 .02
❑ 116 Rafael Belliard .05 .02
❑ 117 Scott Garrelts .05 .02
❑ 118 Terry Mulholland .05 .02
❑ 119 Jay Howell .05 .02
❑ 120 Danny Jackson .05 .02
❑ 121 Scott Ruskin .05 .02
❑ 122 Robin Ventura .10 .05
❑ 123 Bip Roberts .05 .02
❑ 124 Jeff Russell .05 .02
❑ 125 Hal Morris .05 .02
❑ 126 Teddy Higuera .05 .02
❑ 127 Luis Sojo .05 .02
❑ 128 Carlos Baerga .05 .02
❑ 129 Jeff Ballard .05 .02
❑ 130 Tom Gordon .10 .05
❑ 131 Sid Bream .05 .02
❑ 132 Rance Mulliniks .05 .02
❑ 133 Andy Benes .10 .05
❑ 134 Mickey Tettleton .05 .02
❑ 135 Rich DeLucia .05 .02
❑ 136 Tom Pagnozzi .05 .02
❑ 137 Harold Baines .10 .05
❑ 138 Danny Darwin .05 .02
❑ 139 Kevin Bass .05 .02
❑ 140 Chris Nabholz .05 .02
❑ 141 Pete O'Brien .05 .02
❑ 142 Jeff Treadway .05 .02
❑ 143 Mickey Morandini .05 .02
❑ 144 Eric King .05 .02
❑ 145 Danny Tartabull .05 .02
❑ 146 Lance Johnson .05 .02
❑ 147 Casey Candaele .05 .02
❑ 148 Felix Fermin .05 .02
❑ 149 Rich Rodriguez .05 .02
❑ 150 Dwight Evans .10 .05
❑ 151 Joe Klink .05 .02
❑ 152 Kevin Reimer .05 .02
❑ 153 Orlando Merced .05 .02
❑ 154 Mel Hall .05 .02
❑ 155 Randy Myers .10 .05
❑ 156 Greg A. Harris .05 .02
❑ 157 Jeff Brantley .05 .02
❑ 158 Jim Eisenreich .05 .02
❑ 159 Luis Rivera .05 .02
❑ 160 Cris Carpenter .05 .02
❑ 161 Bruce Ruffin .05 .02
❑ 162 Omar Vizquel .10 .05
❑ 163 Gerald Alexander .05 .02
❑ 164 Mark Guthrie .05 .02
❑ 165 Scott Lewis .05 .02
❑ 166 Bill Sampen .05 .02
❑ 167 Dave Anderson .05 .02
❑ 168 Kevin McReynolds .05 .02
❑ 169 Jose Vizcaino .05 .02
❑ 170 Bob Geren .05 .02
❑ 171 Mike Morgan .05 .02
❑ 172 Jim Gott .05 .02
❑ 173 Mike Pagliarulo .05 .02
❑ 174 Mike Jeffcoat .05 .02
❑ 175 Craig Lefferts .05 .02
❑ 176 Steve Finley .10 .05
❑ 177 Wally Backman .05 .02
❑ 178 Kent Mercker .05 .02
❑ 179 John Cerutti .05 .02
❑ 180 Jay Bell .10 .05
❑ 181 Dale Sveum .05 .02
❑ 182 Greg Gagne .05 .02
❑ 183 Donnie Hill .05 .02
❑ 184 Rex Hudler .05 .02
❑ 185 Pat Kelly .05 .02
❑ 186 Jeff D. Robinson .05 .02
❑ 187 Jeff Gray .05 .02
❑ 188 Jerry Willard .05 .02
❑ 189 Carlos Quintana .05 .02
❑ 190 Dennis Eckersley .10 .05
❑ 191 Kelly Downs .05 .02
❑ 192 Gregg Jefferies .05 .02
❑ 193 Darrin Fletcher .05 .02
❑ 194 Mike Jackson .10 .05
❑ 195 Eddie Murray .20 .09
❑ 196 Bill Landrum .05 .02

❑ 197 Eric Yelding .05 .02
❑ 198 Devon White .05 .02
❑ 199 Larry Walker .20 .09
❑ 200 Ryne Sandberg .25 .11
❑ 201 Dave Magadan .05 .02
❑ 202 Steve Chitren .05 .02
❑ 203 Scott Fletcher .05 .02
❑ 204 Dwayne Henry .05 .02
❑ 205 Scott Coolbaugh .05 .02
❑ 206 Tracy Jones .05 .02
❑ 207 Von Hayes .05 .02
❑ 208 Bob Melvin .05 .02
❑ 209 Scott Scudder .05 .02
❑ 210 Luis Gonzalez .05 .02
❑ 211 Scott Sanderson .05 .02
❑ 212 Chris Donnels .05 .02
❑ 213 Heathcliff Slocumb .05 .02
❑ 214 Mike Timlin .05 .02
❑ 215 Brian Harper .05 .02
❑ 216 Juan Berenguer UER .05 .02
(Decimal point missing in IP total)
❑ 217 Mike Henneman .05 .02
❑ 218 Bill Spiers .05 .02
❑ 219 Scott Terry .05 .02
❑ 220 Frank Viola .05 .02
❑ 221 Mark Eichhorn .05 .02
❑ 222 Ernest Riles .05 .02
❑ 223 Ray Lankford .20 .09
❑ 224 Pete Harnisch .05 .02
❑ 225 Bobby Bonilla .10 .05
❑ 226 Mike Scioscia .05 .02
❑ 227 Joel Skinner .05 .02
❑ 228 Brian Holman .05 .02
❑ 229 Gilberto Reyes .05 .02
❑ 230 Matt Williams .15 .07
❑ 231 Jaime Navarro .05 .02
❑ 232 Jose Rijo .05 .02
❑ 233 Atlee Hammaker .05 .02
❑ 234 Tim Teufel .05 .02
❑ 235 John Kruk .10 .05
❑ 236 Kurt Stillwell .05 .02
❑ 237 Dan Pasqua .05 .02
❑ 238 Tim Crews .05 .02
❑ 239 Dave Gallagher .05 .02
❑ 240 Leo Gomez .05 .02
❑ 241 Steve Avery .05 .02
❑ 242 Bill Gullickson .05 .02
❑ 243 Mark Portugal .05 .02
❑ 244 Lee Guetterman .05 .02
❑ 245 Benito Santiago .05 .02
❑ 246 Jim Gantner .05 .02
❑ 247 Robby Thompson .05 .02
❑ 248 Terry Shumpert .05 .02
❑ 249 Mike Bell .05 .02
❑ 250 Harold Reynolds .05 .02
❑ 251 Mike Felder .05 .02
❑ 252 Bill Pecota .05 .02
❑ 253 Bill Krueger .05 .02
❑ 254 Alfredo Griffin .05 .02
❑ 255 Lou Whitaker .10 .05
❑ 256 Roy Smith .05 .02
❑ 257 Jerald Clark .05 .02
❑ 258 Sammy Sosa .50 .23
❑ 259 Tim Naehring .10 .05
❑ 260 Dave Righetti .05 .02
❑ 261 Paul Gibson .05 .02
❑ 262 Chris James .05 .02
❑ 263 Larry Andersen .05 .02
❑ 264 Storm Davis .05 .02
❑ 265 Jose Lind .05 .02
❑ 266 Greg Hibbard .05 .02
❑ 267 Norm Charlton .05 .02
❑ 268 Paul Kilgus .05 .02
❑ 269 Greg Maddux .60 .25
❑ 270 Ellis Burks .10 .05
❑ 271 Frank Tanana .05 .02
❑ 272 Gene Larkin .05 .02
❑ 273 Ron Hassey .05 .02
❑ 274 Jeff M. Robinson .05 .02
❑ 275 Steve Howe .05 .02
❑ 276 Daryl Boston .05 .02
❑ 277 Mark Lee .05 .02
❑ 278 Jose Segura .05 .02
❑ 279 Lance Blankenship .05 .02
❑ 280 Don Slaught .05 .02
❑ 281 Russ Swan .05 .02
❑ 282 Bob Tewksbury .05 .02
❑ 283 Geno Petralli .05 .02
❑ 284 Shane Mack .05 .02
❑ 285 Bob Scanlan .05 .02
❑ 286 Tim Leary .05 .02
❑ 287 John Smoltz .15 .07
❑ 288 Pat Borders .05 .02
❑ 289 Mark Davidson .05 .02
❑ 290 Sam Horn .05 .02
❑ 291 Lenny Harris .05 .02
❑ 292 Franklin Stubbs .05 .02
❑ 293 Thomas Howard .05 .02
❑ 294 Steve Lyons .05 .02
❑ 295 Francisco Oliveras .05 .02
❑ 296 Terry Leach .05 .02
❑ 297 Barry Jones .05 .02
❑ 298 Lance Parrish .05 .02
❑ 299 Wally Whitehurst .05 .02
❑ 300 Bob Welch .05 .02
❑ 301 Charlie Hayes .05 .02
❑ 302 Charlie Hough .10 .05
❑ 303 Gary Redus .05 .02
❑ 304 Scott Bradley .05 .02
❑ 305 Jose Oquendo .05 .02
❑ 306 Pete Incaviglia .05 .02
❑ 307 Marvin Freeman .05 .02
❑ 308 Gary Pettis .05 .02
❑ 309 Joe Slusarski .05 .02
❑ 310 Kevin Seitzer .05 .02
❑ 311 Jeff Reed .05 .02
❑ 312 Pat Tabler .05 .02
❑ 313 Mike Maddux .05 .02
❑ 314 Bob Milacki .05 .02
❑ 315 Eric Anthony .05 .02
❑ 316 Dante Bichette .15 .07
❑ 317 Steve Decker .05 .02
❑ 318 Jack Clark .10 .05
❑ 319 Doug Dascenzo .05 .02
❑ 320 Scott Leius .05 .02
❑ 321 Jim Lindeman .05 .02
❑ 322 Bryan Harvey .05 .02
❑ 323 Spike Owen .05 .02
❑ 324 Roberto Kelly .05 .02
❑ 325 Stan Belinda .05 .02
❑ 326 Joey Cora .10 .05
❑ 327 Jeff Innis .05 .02
❑ 328 Willie Wilson .05 .02
❑ 329 Juan Agosto .05 .02
❑ 330 Charles Nagy .10 .05
❑ 331 Scott Bailes .05 .02
❑ 332 Pete Schourek .05 .02
❑ 333 Mike Flanagan .05 .02
❑ 334 Omar Olivares .05 .02
❑ 335 Dennis Lamp .05 .02
❑ 336 Tommy Greene .05 .02
❑ 337 Randy Velarde .05 .02
❑ 338 Tom Lampkin .05 .02
❑ 339 John Russell .05 .02
❑ 340 Bob Kipper .05 .02
❑ 341 Todd Burns .05 .02
❑ 342 Ron Jones .05 .02
❑ 343 Dave Valle .05 .02
❑ 344 Mike Heath .05 .02
❑ 345 John Olerud .10 .05
❑ 346 Gerald Young .05 .02
❑ 347 Ken Patterson .05 .02
❑ 348 Les Lancaster .05 .02
❑ 349 Steve Crawford .05 .02
❑ 350 John Candelaria .05 .02
❑ 351 Mike Aldrete .05 .02
❑ 352 Mariano Duncan .05 .02
❑ 353 Julio Machado .05 .02
❑ 354 Ken Williams .05 .02
❑ 355 Walt Terrell .05 .02
❑ 356 Mitch Williams .05 .02
❑ 357 Al Newman .05 .02
❑ 358 Bud Black .05 .02
❑ 359 Joe Hesketh .05 .02
❑ 360 Paul Assenmacher .05 .02
❑ 361 Bo Jackson .10 .05
❑ 362 Jeff Blauser .05 .02
❑ 363 Mike Brumley .05 .02
❑ 364 Jim Deshaies .05 .02
❑ 365 Brady Anderson .15 .07
❑ 366 Chuck McElroy .05 .02
❑ 367 Matt Merullo .05 .02
❑ 368 Tim Belcher .05 .02
❑ 369 Luis Aquino .05 .02
❑ 370 Joe Oliver .05 .02
❑ 371 Greg Swindell .05 .02
❑ 372 Lee Stevens .05 .02
❑ 373 Mark Knudson .05 .02
❑ 374 Bill Wegman .05 .02
❑ 375 Jerry Don Gleaton .05 .02
❑ 376 Pedro Guerrero .05 .02
❑ 377 Randy Bush .05 .02
❑ 378 Greg W. Harris .05 .02
❑ 379 Eric Plunk .05 .02
❑ 380 Jose DeJesus .05 .02
❑ 381 Bobby Witt .05 .02
❑ 382 Curtis Wilkerson .05 .02
❑ 383 Gene Nelson .05 .02
❑ 384 Wes Chamberlain .05 .02
❑ 385 Tom Henke .05 .02
❑ 386 Mark Lemke .05 .02
❑ 387 Greg Briley .05 .02
❑ 388 Rafael Ramirez .05 .02
❑ 389 Tony Fossas .05 .02
❑ 390 Henry Cotto .05 .02
❑ 391 Tim Hulett .05 .02
❑ 392 Dean Palmer .10 .05
❑ 393 Glenn Braggs .05 .02
❑ 394 Mark Salas .05 .02
❑ 395 Rusty Meacham .05 .02
❑ 396 Andy Ashby .10 .05
❑ 397 Jose Melendez .05 .02
❑ 398 Warren Newson .05 .02
❑ 399 Frank Castillo .05 .02
❑ 400 Chito Martinez .05 .02
❑ 401 Bernie Williams .20 .09
❑ 402 Derek Bell .10 .05
❑ 403 Javier Ortiz .05 .02
❑ 404 Tim Sherrill .05 .02
❑ 405 Rob MacDonald .05 .02
❑ 406 Phil Plantier .05 .02
❑ 407 Troy Afenir .05 .02
❑ 408 Gino Minutelli .05 .02
❑ 409 Reggie Jefferson .10 .05
❑ 410 Mike Remlinger .05 .02
❑ 411 Carlos Rodriguez .05 .02
❑ 412 Joe Redfield .05 .02
❑ 413 Alonzo Powell .05 .02
❑ 414 Scott Livingstone UER .05 .02
(Travis Fryman& not Woody& should be referenced on back)
❑ 415 Scott Kamieniecki .05 .02
❑ 416 Tim Spehr .05 .02
❑ 417 Brian Hunter .05 .02
❑ 418 Ced Landrum .05 .02
❑ 419 Bret Barberie .05 .02
❑ 420 Kevin Morton .05 .02
❑ 421 Doug Henry .05 .02
❑ 422 Doug Piatt .05 .02
❑ 423 Pat Rice .05 .02
❑ 424 Juan Guzman .05 .02
❑ 425 Nolan Ryan NH .40 .18
❑ 426 Tommy Greene NH .05 .02
❑ 427 Bob Milacki and Mike Flanagan NH .05 .02
(Mark Williamson and Gregg Olson)
❑ 428 Wilson Alvarez NH .05 .02
❑ 429 Otis Nixon HL .05 .02
❑ 430 Rickey Henderson HL .10 .05
❑ 431 Cecil Fielder AS .05 .02
❑ 432 Julio Franco AS .05 .02
❑ 433 Cal Ripken AS .20 .09
❑ 434 Wade Boggs AS .20 .09
❑ 435 Joe Carter AS .05 .02
❑ 436 Ken Griffey Jr. AS .60 .25
❑ 437 Ruben Sierra AS .05 .02
❑ 438 Scott Erickson AS .05 .02
❑ 439 Tom Henke AS .05 .02
❑ 440 Terry Steinbach AS .05 .02
❑ 441 Rickey Henderson DT .10 .05
❑ 442 Ryne Sandberg DT .25 .11
❑ 443 Otis Nixon .10 .05

❑ 444 Scott Radinsky .05 .02
❑ 445 Mark Grace .15 .07
❑ 446 Tony Pena .05 .02
❑ 447 Billy Hatcher .05 .02
❑ 448 Glenallen Hill .05 .02
❑ 449 Chris Gwynn .05 .02
❑ 450 Tom Glavine .15 .07
❑ 451 John Habyan .05 .02
❑ 452 Al Osuna .05 .02
❑ 453 Tony Phillips .05 .02
❑ 454 Greg Cadaret .05 .02
❑ 455 Rob Dibble .05 .02
❑ 456 Rick Honeycutt .05 .02
❑ 457 Jerome Walton .05 .02
❑ 458 Mookie Wilson .10 .05
❑ 459 Mark Gubicza .05 .02
❑ 460 Craig Biggio .20 .09
❑ 461 Dave Cochrane .05 .02
❑ 462 Keith Miller .05 .02
❑ 463 Alex Cole .05 .02
❑ 464 Pete Smith .05 .02
❑ 465 Brett Butler .10 .05
❑ 466 Jeff Huson .05 .02
❑ 467 Steve Lake .05 .02
❑ 468 Lloyd Moseby .05 .02
❑ 469 Tim McIntosh .05 .02
❑ 470 Dennis Martinez .10 .05
❑ 471 Greg Myers .05 .02
❑ 472 Mackey Sasser .05 .02
❑ 473 Junior Ortiz .05 .02
❑ 474 Greg Olson .05 .02
❑ 475 Steve Sax .05 .02
❑ 476 Ricky Jordan .05 .02
❑ 477 Max Venable .05 .02
❑ 478 Brian McRae .10 .05
❑ 479 Doug Simons .05 .02
❑ 480 Rickey Henderson .20 .09
❑ 481 Gary Varsho .05 .02
❑ 482 Carl Willis .05 .02
❑ 483 Rick Wilkins .05 .02
❑ 484 Donn Pall .05 .02
❑ 485 Edgar Martinez .15 .07
❑ 486 Tom Foley .05 .02
❑ 487 Mark Williamson .05 .02
❑ 488 Jack Armstrong .05 .02
❑ 489 Gary Carter .20 .09
❑ 490 Ruben Sierra .05 .02
❑ 491 Gerald Perry .05 .02
❑ 492 Rob Murphy .05 .02
❑ 493 Zane Smith .05 .02
❑ 494 Darryl Kile .10 .05
❑ 495 Kelly Gruber .05 .02
❑ 496 Jerry Browne .05 .02
❑ 497 Darryl Hamilton .05 .02
❑ 498 Mike Stanton .05 .02
❑ 499 Mark Leonard .05 .02
❑ 500 Jose Canseco .20 .09
❑ 501 Dave Martinez .05 .02
❑ 502 Jose Guzman .05 .02
❑ 503 Terry Kennedy .05 .02
❑ 504 Ed Sprague .05 .02
❑ 505 Frank Thomas UER .60 .25
(His Gulf Coast League stats are wrong)
❑ 506 Darren Daulton .10 .05
❑ 507 Kevin Tapani .05 .02
❑ 508 Luis Salazar .05 .02
❑ 509 Paul Faries .05 .02
❑ 510 Sandy Alomar Jr. .10 .05
❑ 511 Jeff King .10 .05
❑ 512 Gary Thurman .05 .02
❑ 513 Chris Hammond .05 .02
❑ 514 Pedro Munoz .05 .02
❑ 515 Alan Trammell .15 .07
❑ 516 Geronimo Pena .05 .02
❑ 517 Rodney McCray UER .05 .02
(Stole 6 bases in 1990& not 5; career totals are correct at 7)
❑ 518 Manny Lee .05 .02
❑ 519 Junior Felix .05 .02
❑ 520 Kirk Gibson .10 .05
❑ 521 Darrin Jackson .05 .02
❑ 522 John Burkett .05 .02
❑ 523 Jeff Johnson .05 .02
❑ 524 Jim Corsi .05 .02
❑ 525 Robin Yount .20 .09
❑ 526 Jamie Quirk .05 .02
❑ 527 Bob Ojeda .05 .02
❑ 528 Mark Lewis .05 .02
❑ 529 Bryn Smith .05 .02
❑ 530 Kent Hrbek .10 .05
❑ 531 Dennis Boyd .05 .02
❑ 532 Ron Karkovice .05 .02
❑ 533 Don August .05 .02
❑ 534 Todd Frohwirth .05 .02
❑ 535 Wally Joyner .10 .05
❑ 536 Dennis Rasmussen .05 .02
❑ 537 Andy Allanson .05 .02
❑ 538 Goose Gossage .10 .05
❑ 539 John Marzano .05 .02
❑ 540 Cal Ripken .75 .35
❑ 541 Bill Swift UER .05 .02
(Brewers logo on front)
❑ 542 Kevin Appier .10 .05
❑ 543 Dave Bergman .05 .02
❑ 544 Bernard Gilkey .10 .05
❑ 545 Mike Greenwell .05 .02
❑ 546 Jose Uribe .05 .02
❑ 547 Jesse Orosco .05 .02
❑ 548 Bob Patterson .05 .02
❑ 549 Mike Stanley .05 .02
❑ 550 Howard Johnson .05 .02
❑ 551 Joe Orsulak .05 .02
❑ 552 Dick Schofield .05 .02
❑ 553 Dave Hollins .05 .02
❑ 554 David Segui .10 .05
❑ 555 Barry Bonds .25 .11
❑ 556 Mo Vaughn .30 .14
❑ 557 Craig Wilson .05 .02
❑ 558 Bobby Rose .05 .02
❑ 559 Rod Nichols .05 .02
❑ 560 Len Dykstra .10 .05
❑ 561 Craig Grebeck .05 .02
❑ 562 Darren Lewis .05 .02
❑ 563 Todd Benzinger .05 .02
❑ 564 Ed Whitson .05 .02
❑ 565 Jesse Barfield .05 .02
❑ 566 Lloyd McClendon .05 .02
❑ 567 Dan Plesac .05 .02
❑ 568 Danny Cox .05 .02
❑ 569 Skeeter Barnes .05 .02
❑ 570 Bobby Thigpen .05 .02
❑ 571 Deion Sanders .20 .09
❑ 572 Chuck Knoblauch .20 .09
❑ 573 Matt Nokes .05 .02
❑ 574 Herm Winningham .05 .02
❑ 575 Tom Candiotti .05 .02
❑ 576 Jeff Bagwell .50 .23
❑ 577 Brook Jacoby .05 .02
❑ 578 Chico Walker .05 .02
❑ 579 Brian Downing .05 .02
❑ 580 Dave Stewart .10 .05
❑ 581 Francisco Cabrera .05 .02
❑ 582 Rene Gonzales .05 .02
❑ 583 Stan Javier .05 .02
❑ 584 Randy Johnson .20 .09
❑ 585 Chuck Finley .10 .05
❑ 586 Mark Gardner .05 .02
❑ 587 Mark Whiten .05 .02
❑ 588 Garry Templeton .05 .02
❑ 589 Gary Sheffield .20 .09
❑ 590 Ozzie Smith .25 .11
❑ 591 Candy Maldonado .05 .02
❑ 592 Mike Sharperson .05 .02
❑ 593 Carlos Martinez .05 .02
❑ 594 Scott Bankhead .05 .02
❑ 595 Tim Wallach .05 .02
❑ 596 Tino Martinez .20 .09
❑ 597 Roger McDowell .05 .02
❑ 598 Cory Snyder .05 .02
❑ 599 Andujar Cedeno .05 .02
❑ 600 Kirby Puckett .30 .14
❑ 601 Rick Parker .05 .02
❑ 602 Todd Hundley .10 .05
❑ 603 Greg Litton .05 .02
❑ 604 Dave Johnson .05 .02
❑ 605 John Franco .10 .05
❑ 606 Mike Fetters .05 .02
❑ 607 Luis Alicea .05 .02
❑ 608 Trevor Wilson .05 .02
❑ 609 Rob Ducey .05 .02
❑ 610 Ramon Martinez .10 .05
❑ 611 Dave Burba .05 .02
❑ 612 Dwight Smith .05 .02
❑ 613 Kevin Maas .05 .02
❑ 614 John Costello .05 .02
❑ 615 Glenn Davis .05 .02
❑ 616 Shawn Abner .05 .02
❑ 617 Scott Hemond .05 .02
❑ 618 Tom Prince .05 .02
❑ 619 Wally Ritchie .05 .02
❑ 620 Jim Abbott .10 .05
❑ 621 Charlie O'Brien .05 .02
❑ 622 Jack Daugherty .05 .02
❑ 623 Tommy Gregg .05 .02
❑ 624 Jeff Shaw .05 .02
❑ 625 Tony Gwynn .50 .23
❑ 626 Mark Leiter .05 .02
❑ 627 Jim Clancy .05 .02
❑ 628 Tim Layana .05 .02
❑ 629 Jeff Schaefer .05 .02
❑ 630 Lee Smith .10 .05
❑ 631 Wade Taylor .05 .02
❑ 632 Mike Simms .05 .02
❑ 633 Terry Steinbach .10 .05
❑ 634 Shawon Dunston .05 .02
❑ 635 Tim Raines .10 .05
❑ 636 Kirt Manwaring .05 .02
❑ 637 Warren Cromartie .05 .02
❑ 638 Luis Quinones .05 .02
❑ 639 Greg Vaughn .10 .05
❑ 640 Kevin Mitchell .10 .05
❑ 641 Chris Hoiles .05 .02
❑ 642 Tom Browning .05 .02
❑ 643 Mitch Webster .05 .02
❑ 644 Steve Olin .05 .02
❑ 645 Tony Fernandez .05 .02
❑ 646 Juan Bell .05 .02
❑ 647 Joe Boever .05 .02
❑ 648 Carney Lansford .10 .05
❑ 649 Mike Benjamin .05 .02
❑ 650 George Brett .40 .18
❑ 651 Tim Burke .05 .02
❑ 652 Jack Morris .10 .05
❑ 653 Orel Hershiser .10 .05
❑ 654 Mike Schooler .05 .02
❑ 655 Andy Van Slyke .10 .05
❑ 656 Dave Stieb .05 .02
❑ 657 Dave Clark .05 .02
❑ 658 Ben McDonald .05 .02
❑ 659 John Smiley .05 .02
❑ 660 Wade Boggs .20 .09
❑ 661 Eric Bullock .05 .02
❑ 662 Eric Show .05 .02
❑ 663 Lenny Webster .05 .02
❑ 664 Mike Huff .05 .02
❑ 665 Rick Sutcliffe .05 .02
❑ 666 Jeff Manto .05 .02
❑ 667 Mike Fitzgerald .05 .02
❑ 668 Matt Young .05 .02
❑ 669 Dave West .05 .02
❑ 670 Mike Hartley .05 .02
❑ 671 Curt Schilling .15 .07
❑ 672 Brian Bohanon .05 .02
❑ 673 Cecil Espy .05 .02
❑ 674 Joe Grahe .05 .02
❑ 675 Sid Fernandez .05 .02
❑ 676 Edwin Nunez .05 .02
❑ 677 Hector Villanueva .05 .02
❑ 678 Sean Berry .05 .02
❑ 679 Dave Eiland .05 .02
❑ 680 Dave Cone .10 .05
❑ 681 Mike Bordick .05 .02
❑ 682 Tony Castillo .05 .02
❑ 683 John Barfield .05 .02
❑ 684 Jeff Hamilton .05 .02
❑ 685 Ken Dayley .05 .02
❑ 686 Carmelo Martinez .05 .02
❑ 687 Mike Capel .05 .02
❑ 688 Scott Chiamparino .05 .02
❑ 689 Rich Gedman .05 .02
❑ 690 Rich Monteleone .05 .02
❑ 691 Alejandro Pena .05 .02
❑ 692 Oscar Azocar .05 .02

❑ 693 Jim Poole .05 .02
❑ 694 Mike Gardiner .05 .02
❑ 695 Steve Buechele .05 .02
❑ 696 Rudy Seanez .05 .02
❑ 697 Paul Abbott .05 .02
❑ 698 Steve Searcy .05 .02
❑ 699 Jose Offerman .05 .02
❑ 700 Ivan Rodriguez .40 .18
❑ 701 Joe Girardi .10 .05
❑ 702 Tony Perezchica .05 .02
❑ 703 Paul McClellan .05 .02
❑ 704 David Howard .05 .02
❑ 705 Dan Petry .05 .02
❑ 706 Jack Howell .05 .02
❑ 707 Jose Mesa .05 .02
❑ 708 Randy St. Claire .05 .02
❑ 709 Kevin Brown .15 .07
❑ 710 Ron Darling .05 .02
❑ 711 Jason Grimsley .05 .02
❑ 712 John Orton .05 .02
❑ 713 Shawn Boskie .05 .02
❑ 714 Pat Clements .05 .02
❑ 715 Brian Barnes .05 .02
❑ 716 Luis Lopez .05 .02
❑ 717 Bob McClure .05 .02
❑ 718 Mark Davis .05 .02
❑ 719 Dann Bilardello .05 .02
❑ 720 Tom Edens .05 .02
❑ 721 Willie Fraser .05 .02
❑ 722 Curt Young .05 .02
❑ 723 Neal Heaton .05 .02
❑ 724 Craig Worthington .05 .02
❑ 725 Mel Rojas .05 .02
❑ 726 Daryl Irvine .05 .02
❑ 727 Roger Mason .05 .02
❑ 728 Kirk Dressendorfer .05 .02
❑ 729 Scott Aldred .05 .02
❑ 730 Willie Blair .05 .02
❑ 731 Allan Anderson .05 .02
❑ 732 Dana Kiecker .05 .02
❑ 733 Jose Gonzalez .05 .02
❑ 734 Brian Drahman .05 .02
❑ 735 Brad Komminsk .05 .02
❑ 736 Arthur Rhodes .05 .02
❑ 737 Terry Mathews .05 .02
❑ 738 Jeff Fassero .10 .05
❑ 739 Mike Magnante .05 .02
❑ 740 Kip Gross .05 .02
❑ 741 Jim Hunter .05 .02
❑ 742 Jose Mota .05 .02
❑ 743 Joe Bitker .05 .02
❑ 744 Tim Mauser .05 .02
❑ 745 Ramon Garcia .05 .02
❑ 746 Rod Beck .20 .09
❑ 747 Jim Austin .05 .02
❑ 748 Keith Mitchell .05 .02
❑ 749 Wayne Rosenthal .05 .02
❑ 750 Bryan Hickerson .05 .02
❑ 751 Bruce Egloff .05 .02
❑ 752 John Wehner .05 .02
❑ 753 Darren Holmes .05 .02
❑ 754 Dave Hansen .05 .02
❑ 755 Mike Mussina .30 .14
❑ 756 Anthony Young .05 .02
❑ 757 Ron Tingley .05 .02
❑ 758 Ricky Bones .05 .02
❑ 759 Mark Wohlers .10 .05
❑ 760 Wilson Alvarez .10 .05
❑ 761 Harvey Pulliam .05 .02
❑ 762 Ryan Bowen .05 .02
❑ 763 Terry Bross .05 .02
❑ 764 Joel Johnston .05 .02
❑ 765 Terry McDaniel .05 .02
❑ 766 Esteban Beltre .05 .02
❑ 767 Rob Maurer .05 .02
❑ 768 Ted Wood .05 .02
❑ 769 Mo Sanford .05 .02
❑ 770 Jeff Carter .05 .02
❑ 771 Gil Heredia .05 .02
❑ 772 Monty Fariss .05 .02
❑ 773 Will Clark AS .10 .05
❑ 774 Ryne Sandberg AS .20 .09
❑ 775 Barry Larkin AS .15 .07
❑ 776 Howard Johnson AS .05 .02
❑ 777 Barry Bonds AS .20 .09
❑ 778 Brett Butler AS .05 .02
❑ 779 Tony Gwynn AS .25 .11
❑ 780 Ramon Martinez AS .05 .02
❑ 781 Lee Smith AS .05 .02
❑ 782 Mike Scioscia AS .05 .02
❑ 783 Dennis Martinez HL UER .05 .02
(Card has both 13th and 15th perfect game in Major League history)
❑ 784 Dennis Martinez NH .05 .02
❑ 785 Mark Gardner NH .05 .02
❑ 786 Bret Saberhagen NH .05 .02
❑ 787 Kent Mercker NH .05 .02
Mark Wohlers
Alejandro Pena
❑ 788 Cal Ripken MVP .20 .09
❑ 789 Terry Pendleton MVP .05 .02
❑ 790 Roger Clemens CY .20 .09
❑ 791 Tom Glavine CY .10 .05
❑ 792 Chuck Knoblauch ROY .10 .05
❑ 793 Jeff Bagwell ROY .25 .11
❑ 794 Cal Ripken MANYR .20 .09
❑ 795 David Cone HL .05 .02
❑ 796 Kirby Puckett HL .20 .09
❑ 797 Steve Avery HL .05 .02
❑ 798 Jack Morris HL .05 .02
❑ 799 Allen Watson DC .05 .02
❑ 800 Manny Ramirez DC 1.50 .70
❑ 801 Cliff Floyd DC .25 .11
❑ 802 Al Shirley DC .05 .02
❑ 803 Brian Barber DC .05 .02
❑ 804 Jon Farrell DC .05 .02
❑ 805 Brent Gates DC .05 .02
❑ 806 Scott Ruffcorn DC .05 .02
❑ 807 Tyrone Hill DC .05 .02
❑ 808 Benji Gil DC .05 .02
❑ 809 Aaron Sele DC .25 .11
❑ 810 Tyler Green DC .05 .02
❑ 811 Chris Jones .05 .02
❑ 812 Steve Wilson .05 .02
❑ 813 Freddie Benavides .05 .02
❑ 814 Don Wakamatsu .05 .02
❑ 815 Mike Humphreys .05 .02
❑ 816 Scott Servais .05 .02
❑ 817 Rico Rossy .05 .02
❑ 818 John Ramos .05 .02
❑ 819 Rob Mallicoat .05 .02
❑ 820 Milt Hill .05 .02
❑ 821 Carlos Garcia .05 .02
❑ 822 Stan Royer .05 .02
❑ 823 Jeff Plympton .05 .02
❑ 824 Braulio Castillo .05 .02
❑ 825 David Haas .05 .02
❑ 826 Luis Mercedes .05 .02
❑ 827 Eric Karros .20 .09
❑ 828 Shawn Hare .05 .02
❑ 829 Reggie Sanders .05 .02
❑ 830 Tom Goodwin .10 .05
❑ 831 Dan Gakeler .05 .02
❑ 832 Stacy Jones .05 .02
❑ 833 Kim Batiste .05 .02
❑ 834 Cal Eldred .05 .02
❑ 835 Chris George .05 .02
❑ 836 Wayne Housie .05 .02
❑ 837 Mike Ignasiak .05 .02
❑ 838 Josias Manzanillo .05 .02
❑ 839 Jim Olander .05 .02
❑ 840 Gary Cooper .05 .02
❑ 841 Royce Clayton .05 .02
❑ 842 Hector Fajardo .05 .02
❑ 843 Blaine Beatty .05 .02
❑ 844 Jorge Pedre .05 .02
❑ 845 Kenny Lofton .40 .18
❑ 846 Scott Brosius .25 .11
❑ 847 Chris Cron .05 .02
❑ 848 Denis Boucher .05 .02
❑ 849 Kyle Abbott .05 .02
❑ 850 Robert Zupcic .05 .02
❑ 851 Rheal Cormier .05 .02
❑ 852 Jim Lewis .05 .02
❑ 853 Anthony Telford .05 .02
❑ 854 Cliff Brantley .05 .02
❑ 855 Kevin Campbell .05 .02
❑ 856 Craig Shipley .05 .02
❑ 857 Chuck Carr .05 .02
❑ 858 Tony Eusebio .10 .05
❑ 859 Jim Thome .50 .23
❑ 860 Vinny Castilla 2.00 .90
❑ 861 Dann Howitt .05 .02
❑ 862 Kevin Ward .05 .02
❑ 863 Steve Wapnick .05 .02
❑ 864 Rod Brewer .05 .02
❑ 865 Todd Van Poppel .05 .02
❑ 866 Jose Hernandez .05 .02
❑ 867 Amalio Carreno .05 .02
❑ 868 Calvin Jones .05 .02
❑ 869 Jeff Gardner .05 .02
❑ 870 Jarvis Brown .05 .02
❑ 871 Eddie Taubensee .10 .05
❑ 872 Andy Mota .05 .02
❑ 873 Chris Haney .05 .02
❑ 874 Roberto Hernandez .10 .05
❑ 875 Laddie Renfroe .05 .02
❑ 876 Scott Cooper .05 .02
❑ 877 Armando Reynoso .05 .02
❑ 878 Ty Cobb MEMO .25 .11
❑ 879 Babe Ruth MEMO .40 .18
❑ 880 Honus Wagner MEMO .20 .09
❑ 881 Lou Gehrig MEMO .25 .11
❑ 882 Satchel Paige MEMO .20 .09
❑ 883 Will Clark DT .10 .05
❑ 884 Cal Ripken DT 2.00 .90
❑ 885 Wade Boggs DT .10 .05
❑ 886 Kirby Puckett DT .30 .14
❑ 887 Tony Gwynn DT .50 .23
❑ 888 Craig Biggio DT .10 .05
❑ 889 Scott Erickson DT .05 .02
❑ 890 Tom Glavine DT .10 .05
❑ 891 Rob Dibble DT .05 .02
❑ 892 Mitch Williams DT .05 .02
❑ 893 Frank Thomas DT .60 .25
❑ X672 Chuck Knoblauch AU 60.00 27.00
(1990 Score card& autographed with special hologram on back)

1992 Score DiMaggio

	MINT	NRMT
COMPLETE SET (5)	150.00	70.00
COMMON DIMAGGIO (1-5)	30.00	13.50

❑ 1 Joe DiMaggio 30.00 13.50
The Minors
❑ 2 Joe DiMaggio 30.00 13.50
The Rookie
❑ 3 Joe DiMaggio 30.00 13.50
The MVP
❑ 4 Joe DiMaggio 30.00 13.50
The Streak
❑ 5 Joe DiMaggio 30.00 13.50
The Legend
❑ AU0 Joe DiMaggio AU 550.00 250.00
(Autographed with certified signature)

1992 Score Factory Inserts

	MINT	NRMT
COMPLETE SET (17)	6.00	2.70
COMMON CARD (B1-B17)	.25	.11

❑ B1 Greg Gagne WS .25 .11

❑ B2 Scott Leius WS	.25	.11
❑ B3 Mark Lemke WS David Justice	.50	.23
❑ B4 Lonnie Smith WS Brian Harper	.25	.11
❑ B5 David Justice WS	1.00	.45
❑ B6 Kirby Puckett WS	2.50	1.10
❑ B7 Gene Larkin WS	.25	.11
❑ B8 Carlton Fisk	1.00	.45
❑ B9 Ozzie Smith	2.00	.90
❑ B10 Dave Winfield	1.00	.45
❑ B11 Robin Yount	1.00	.45
❑ B12 Joe DiMaggio	1.50	.70
❑ B13 Joe DiMaggio	1.50	.70
❑ B14 Joe DiMaggio	1.50	.70
❑ B15 Carl Yastrzemski	.25	.11
❑ B16 Carl Yastrzemski	.25	.11
❑ B17 Carl Yastrzemski	.25	.11

1992 Score Franchise

	MINT	NRMT
COMPLETE SET (4)	30.00	13.50
COMMON CARD (1-4)	4.00	1.80
❑ 1 Stan Musial	5.00	2.20
❑ 2 Mickey Mantle	12.00	5.50
❑ 3 Carl Yastrzemski	4.00	1.80
❑ 4 The Franchise Players Stan Musial Mickey Mantle Carl Yastrzemski	10.00	4.50
❑ AU1 Stan Musial (Autographed with certified signature)	150.00	70.00
❑ AU2 Mickey Mantle (Autographed with certified signature)	500.00	220.00
❑ AU3 Carl Yastrzemski (Autographed with certified signature)	120.00	55.00
❑ AU4 Franchise Players Stan Musial Mickey Mantle Carl Yastrzemski (Autographed with certified signatures of all three)	1500.00	700.00

1992 Score Hot Rookies

	MINT	NRMT
COMPLETE SET (10)	12.00	5.50
COMMON CARD (1-10)	.50	.23
❑ 1 Cal Eldred	.50	.23
❑ 2 Royce Clayton	.50	.23
❑ 3 Kenny Lofton	5.00	2.20
❑ 4 Todd Van Poppel	.50	.23
❑ 5 Scott Cooper	.50	.23
❑ 6 Todd Hundley	1.00	.45
❑ 7 Tino Martinez	3.00	1.35
❑ 8 Anthony Telford	.50	.23
❑ 9 Derek Bell	1.00	.45
❑ 10 Reggie Jefferson	1.00	.45

1992 Score Impact Players

	MINT	NRMT
COMPLETE SET (90)	20.00	9.00
COMPLETE SERIES 1 (45)	14.00	6.25
COMPLETE SERIES 2 (45)	6.00	2.70
COMMON CARD (1-90)	.10	.05
❑ 1 Chuck Knoblauch	.40	.18
❑ 2 Jeff Bagwell	1.50	.70
❑ 3 Juan Guzman	.10	.05
❑ 4 Milt Cuyler	.10	.05
❑ 5 Ivan Rodriguez	1.25	.55
❑ 6 Rich DeLucia	.10	.05
❑ 7 Orlando Merced	.10	.05
❑ 8 Ray Lankford	.40	.18
❑ 9 Brian Hunter	.10	.05
❑ 10 Roberto Alomar	.40	.18
❑ 11 Wes Chamberlain	.10	.05
❑ 12 Steve Avery	.10	.05
❑ 13 Scott Erickson	.20	.09
❑ 14 Jim Abbott	.20	.09
❑ 15 Mark Whiten	.10	.05
❑ 16 Leo Gomez	.10	.05
❑ 17 Doug Henry	.10	.05
❑ 18 Brent Mayne	.10	.05
❑ 19 Charles Nagy	.20	.09
❑ 20 Phil Plantier	.10	.05
❑ 21 Mo Vaughn	1.00	.45
❑ 22 Craig Biggio	.40	.18
❑ 23 Derek Bell	.20	.09
❑ 24 Royce Clayton	.10	.05
❑ 25 Gary Cooper	.10	.05
❑ 26 Scott Cooper	.10	.05
❑ 27 Juan Gonzalez	2.00	.90
❑ 28 Ken Griffey Jr.	4.00	1.80
❑ 29 Larry Walker	.40	.18
❑ 30 John Smoltz	.30	.14
❑ 31 Todd Hundley	.20	.09
❑ 32 Kenny Lofton	1.50	.70
❑ 33 Andy Mota	.10	.05
❑ 34 Todd Zeile	.10	.05
❑ 35 Arthur Rhodes	.10	.05
❑ 36 Jim Thome	2.00	.90
❑ 37 Todd Van Poppel	.10	.05
❑ 38 Mark Wohlers	.20	.09
❑ 39 Anthony Young	.10	.05
❑ 40 Sandy Alomar Jr.	.20	.09
❑ 41 John Olerud	.20	.09
❑ 42 Robin Ventura	.20	.09
❑ 43 Frank Thomas	2.00	.90
❑ 44 Dave Justice	.40	.18
❑ 45 Hal Morris	.10	.05
❑ 46 Ruben Sierra	.10	.05
❑ 47 Travis Fryman	.20	.09
❑ 48 Mike Mussina	1.00	.45
❑ 49 Tom Glavine	.30	.14
❑ 50 Barry Larkin	.30	.14
❑ 51 Will Clark UER Career Totals spelled To als	.40	.18
❑ 52 Jose Canseco	.40	.18
❑ 53 Bo Jackson	.20	.09
❑ 54 Dwight Gooden	.20	.09
❑ 55 Barry Bonds	.75	.35
❑ 56 Fred McGriff	.30	.14
❑ 57 Roger Clemens	1.25	.55
❑ 58 Benito Santiago	.10	.05
❑ 59 Darryl Strawberry	.20	.09
❑ 60 Cecil Fielder	.20	.09
❑ 61 John Franco	.20	.09
❑ 62 Matt Williams	.30	.14
❑ 63 Marquis Grissom	.20	.09
❑ 64 Danny Tartabull	.10	.05
❑ 65 Ron Gant	.20	.09
❑ 66 Paul O'Neill	.20	.09
❑ 67 Devon White	.10	.05
❑ 68 Rafael Palmeiro	.30	.14
❑ 69 Tom Gordon	.20	.09
❑ 70 Shawon Dunston	.10	.05
❑ 71 Rob Dibble	.10	.05
❑ 72 Eddie Zosky	.10	.05
❑ 73 Jack McDowell	.10	.05
❑ 74 Len Dykstra	.20	.09
❑ 75 Ramon Martinez	.20	.09
❑ 76 Reggie Sanders	.10	.05
❑ 77 Greg Maddux	2.00	.90
❑ 78 Ellis Burks	.20	.09
❑ 79 John Smiley	.10	.05
❑ 80 Roberto Kelly	.10	.05
❑ 81 Ben McDonald	.10	.05
❑ 82 Mark Lewis	.10	.05
❑ 83 Jose Rijo	.10	.05
❑ 84 Ozzie Guillen	.10	.05
❑ 85 Lance Dickson	.10	.05
❑ 86 Kim Batiste	.10	.05
❑ 87 Gregg Olson	.10	.05
❑ 88 Andy Benes	.20	.09
❑ 89 Cal Eldred	.10	.05
❑ 90 David Cone	.20	.09

1992 Score Rookie/Traded

	MINT	NRMT
COMP.FACT.SET (110)	15.00	6.75
COMMON CARD (1T-110T)	.15	.07
❑ 1T Gary Sheffield	.60	.25
❑ 2T Kevin Seitzer	.15	.07
❑ 3T Danny Tartabull	.15	.07
❑ 4T Steve Sax	.15	.07
❑ 5T Bobby Bonilla	.30	.14
❑ 6T Frank Viola	.15	.07
❑ 7T Dave Winfield	.60	.25
❑ 8T Rick Sutcliffe	.15	.07
❑ 9T Jose Canseco	.60	.25
❑ 10T Greg Swindell	.15	.07
❑ 11T Eddie Murray	.60	.25
❑ 12T Randy Myers	.30	.14

❑ 13T	Wally Joyner	.30	.14
❑ 14T	Kenny Lofton	4.00	1.80
❑ 15T	Jack Morris	.30	.14
❑ 16T	Charlie Hayes	.15	.07
❑ 17T	Pete Incaviglia	.15	.07
❑ 18T	Kevin Mitchell	.30	.14
❑ 19T	Kurt Stillwell	.15	.07
❑ 20T	Bret Saberhagen	.30	.14
❑ 21T	Steve Buechele	.15	.07
❑ 22T	John Smiley	.15	.07
❑ 23T	Sammy Sosa	4.00	1.80
❑ 24T	George Bell	.15	.07
❑ 25T	Curt Schilling	1.00	.45
❑ 26T	Dick Schofield	.15	.07
❑ 27T	David Cone	.30	.14
❑ 28T	Dan Gladden	.15	.07
❑ 29T	Kirk McCaskill	.15	.07
❑ 30T	Mike Gallego	.15	.07
❑ 31T	Kevin McReynolds	.15	.07
❑ 32T	Bill Swift	.15	.07
❑ 33T	Dave Martinez	.15	.07
❑ 34T	Storm Davis	.15	.07
❑ 35T	Willie Randolph	.30	.14
❑ 36T	Melido Perez	.15	.07
❑ 37T	Mark Carreon	.15	.07
❑ 38T	Doug Jones	.15	.07
❑ 39T	Gregg Jefferies	.15	.07
❑ 40T	Mike Jackson	.30	.14
❑ 41T	Dickie Thon	.15	.07
❑ 42T	Eric King	.15	.07
❑ 43T	Herm Winningham	.15	.07
❑ 44T	Derek Lilliquist	.15	.07
❑ 45T	Dave Anderson	.15	.07
❑ 46T	Jeff Reardon	.30	.14
❑ 47T	Scott Bankhead	.15	.07
❑ 48T	Cory Snyder	.15	.07
❑ 49T	Al Newman	.15	.07
❑ 50T	Keith Miller	.15	.07
❑ 51T	Dave Burba	.15	.07
❑ 52T	Bill Pecota	.15	.07
❑ 53T	Chuck Crim	.15	.07
❑ 54T	Mariano Duncan	.15	.07
❑ 55T	Dave Gallagher	.15	.07
❑ 56T	Chris Gwynn	.15	.07
❑ 57T	Scott Ruskin	.15	.07
❑ 58T	Jack Armstrong	.15	.07
❑ 59T	Gary Carter	.60	.25
❑ 60T	Andres Galarraga	.60	.25
❑ 61T	Ken Hill	.15	.07
❑ 62T	Eric Davis	.30	.14
❑ 63T	Ruben Sierra	.15	.07
❑ 64T	Darrin Fletcher	.15	.07
❑ 65T	Tim Belcher	.15	.07
❑ 66T	Mike Morgan	.15	.07
❑ 67T	Scott Scudder	.15	.07
❑ 68T	Tom Candiotti	.15	.07
❑ 69T	Hubie Brooks	.15	.07
❑ 70T	Kal Daniels	.15	.07
❑ 71T	Bruce Ruffin	.15	.07
❑ 72T	Billy Hatcher	.15	.07
❑ 73T	Bob Melvin	.15	.07
❑ 74T	Lee Guetterman	.15	.07
❑ 75T	Rene Gonzales	.15	.07
❑ 76T	Kevin Bass	.15	.07
❑ 77T	Tom Bolton	.15	.07
❑ 78T	John Wetteland	.30	.14
❑ 79T	Bip Roberts	.15	.07
❑ 80T	Pat Listach	.15	.07
❑ 81T	John Doherty	.15	.07
❑ 82T	Sam Militello	.15	.07
❑ 83T	Brian Jordan	1.50	.70
❑ 84T	Jeff Kent	1.00	.45
❑ 85T	Dave Fleming	.15	.07
❑ 86T	Jeff Tackett	.15	.07
❑ 87T	Chad Curtis	.60	.25
❑ 88T	Eric Fox	.15	.07
❑ 89T	Denny Neagle	.75	.35
❑ 90T	Donovan Osborne	.15	.07
❑ 91T	Carlos Hernandez	.15	.07
❑ 92T	Tim Wakefield	1.00	.45
❑ 93T	Tim Salmon	4.00	1.80
❑ 94T	Dave Nilsson	.30	.14
❑ 95T	Mike Perez	.15	.07
❑ 96T	Pat Hentgen	.60	.25
❑ 97T	Frank Seminara	.15	.07
❑ 98T	Ruben Amaro Jr.	.15	.07
❑ 99T	Archi Cianfrocco	.15	.07
❑ 100T	Andy Stankiewicz	.15	.07
❑ 101T	Jim Bullinger	.15	.07
❑ 102T	Pat Mahomes	.15	.07
❑ 103T	Hipolito Pichardo	.15	.07
❑ 104T	Bret Boone	.30	.14
❑ 105T	John Vander Wal	.15	.07
❑ 106T	Vince Horsman	.15	.07
❑ 107T	James Austin	.15	.07
❑ 108T	Brian Williams	.15	.07
❑ 109T	Dan Walters	.15	.07
❑ 110T	Wil Cordero	.15	.07

1993 Score

	MINT	NRMT
COMPLETE SET (660)	40.00	18.00
COMMON CARD (1-660)	.10	.05

❑ 1	Ken Griffey Jr.	2.00	.90
❑ 2	Gary Sheffield	.40	.18
❑ 3	Frank Thomas	1.25	.55
❑ 4	Ryne Sandberg	.50	.23
❑ 5	Larry Walker	.40	.18
❑ 6	Cal Ripken Jr.	1.50	.70
❑ 7	Roger Clemens	.75	.35
❑ 8	Bobby Bonilla	.20	.09
❑ 9	Carlos Baerga	.10	.05
❑ 10	Darren Daulton	.20	.09
❑ 11	Travis Fryman	.20	.09
❑ 12	Andy Van Slyke	.20	.09
❑ 13	Jose Canseco	.40	.18
❑ 14	Roberto Alomar	.40	.18
❑ 15	Tom Glavine	.30	.14
❑ 16	Barry Larkin	.30	.14
❑ 17	Gregg Jefferies	.10	.05
❑ 18	Craig Biggio	.40	.18
❑ 19	Shane Mack	.10	.05
❑ 20	Brett Butler	.20	.09
❑ 21	Dennis Eckersley	.20	.09
❑ 22	Will Clark	.40	.18
❑ 23	Don Mattingly	.60	.25
❑ 24	Tony Gwynn	1.00	.45
❑ 25	Ivan Rodriguez	.50	.23
❑ 26	Shawon Dunston	.10	.05
❑ 27	Mike Mussina	.40	.18
❑ 28	Marquis Grissom	.20	.09
❑ 29	Charles Nagy	.20	.09
❑ 30	Len Dykstra	.20	.09
❑ 31	Cecil Fielder	.20	.09
❑ 32	Jay Bell	.20	.09
❑ 33	B.J. Surhoff	.20	.09
❑ 34	Bob Tewksbury	.10	.05
❑ 35	Danny Tartabull	.10	.05
❑ 36	Terry Pendleton	.10	.05
❑ 37	Jack Morris	.20	.09
❑ 38	Hal Morris	.10	.05
❑ 39	Luis Polonia	.10	.05
❑ 40	Ken Caminiti	.30	.14
❑ 41	Robin Ventura	.20	.09
❑ 42	Darryl Strawberry	.20	.09
❑ 43	Wally Joyner	.20	.09
❑ 44	Fred McGriff	.30	.14
❑ 45	Kevin Tapani	.10	.05
❑ 46	Matt Williams	.30	.14
❑ 47	Robin Yount	.30	.14
❑ 48	Ken Hill	.10	.05
❑ 49	Edgar Martinez	.30	.14
❑ 50	Mark Grace	.30	.14
❑ 51	Juan Gonzalez	1.00	.45
❑ 52	Curt Schilling	.20	.09
❑ 53	Dwight Gooden	.20	.09
❑ 54	Chris Hoiles	.10	.05
❑ 55	Frank Viola	.10	.05
❑ 56	Ray Lankford	.30	.14
❑ 57	George Brett	.75	.35
❑ 58	Kenny Lofton	.35	.16
❑ 59	Nolan Ryan	1.50	.70
❑ 60	Mickey Tettleton	.10	.05
❑ 61	John Smoltz	.20	.09
❑ 62	Howard Johnson	.10	.05
❑ 63	Eric Karros	.30	.14
❑ 64	Rick Aguilera	.10	.05
❑ 65	Steve Finley	.20	.09
❑ 66	Mark Langston	.10	.05
❑ 67	Bill Swift	.10	.05
❑ 68	John Olerud	.30	.14
❑ 69	Kevin McReynolds	.10	.05
❑ 70	Jack McDowell	.10	.05
❑ 71	Rickey Henderson	.40	.18
❑ 72	Brian Harper	.10	.05
❑ 73	Mike Morgan	.10	.05
❑ 74	Rafael Palmeiro	.30	.14
❑ 75	Dennis Martinez	.20	.09
❑ 76	Tino Martinez	.40	.18
❑ 77	Eddie Murray	.40	.18
❑ 78	Ellis Burks	.20	.09
❑ 79	John Kruk	.20	.09
❑ 80	Gregg Olson	.10	.05
❑ 81	Bernard Gilkey	.10	.05
❑ 82	Milt Cuyler	.10	.05
❑ 83	Mike LaValliere	.10	.05
❑ 84	Albert Belle	.50	.23
❑ 85	Bip Roberts	.10	.05
❑ 86	Melido Perez	.10	.05
❑ 87	Otis Nixon	.10	.05
❑ 88	Bill Spiers	.10	.05
❑ 89	Jeff Bagwell	.60	.25
❑ 90	Orel Hershiser	.20	.09
❑ 91	Andy Benes	.20	.09
❑ 92	Devon White	.10	.05
❑ 93	Willie McGee	.20	.09
❑ 94	Ozzie Guillen	.10	.05
❑ 95	Ivan Calderon	.10	.05
❑ 96	Keith Miller	.10	.05
❑ 97	Steve Buechele	.10	.05
❑ 98	Kent Hrbek	.20	.09
❑ 99	Dave Hollins	.10	.05
❑ 100	Mike Bordick	.10	.05
❑ 101	Randy Tomlin	.10	.05
❑ 102	Omar Vizquel	.20	.09
❑ 103	Lee Smith	.20	.09
❑ 104	Leo Gomez	.10	.05
❑ 105	Jose Rijo	.10	.05
❑ 106	Mark Whiten	.10	.05
❑ 107	Dave Justice	.40	.18
❑ 108	Eddie Taubensee	.10	.05
❑ 109	Lance Johnson	.10	.05
❑ 110	Felix Jose	.10	.05
❑ 111	Mike Harkey	.10	.05
❑ 112	Randy Milligan	.10	.05
❑ 113	Anthony Young	.10	.05
❑ 114	Rico Brogna	.20	.09
❑ 115	Bret Saberhagen	.20	.09
❑ 116	Sandy Alomar	.20	.09

❑ 117 Terry Mulholland .10 .05
❑ 118 Darryl Hamilton .10 .05
❑ 119 Todd Zeile .10 .05
❑ 120 Bernie Williams .40 .18
❑ 121 Zane Smith .10 .05
❑ 122 Derek Bell .20 .09
❑ 123 Deion Sanders .30 .14
❑ 124 Luis Sojo .10 .05
❑ 125 Joe Oliver .10 .05
❑ 126 Craig Grebeck .10 .05
❑ 127 Andujar Cedeno .10 .05
❑ 128 Brian McRae .10 .05
❑ 129 Jose Offerman .10 .05
❑ 130 Pedro Munoz .10 .05
❑ 131 Bud Black .10 .05
❑ 132 Mo Vaughn .50 .23
❑ 133 Bruce Hurst .10 .05
❑ 134 Dave Henderson .10 .05
❑ 135 Tom Pagnozzi .10 .05
❑ 136 Erik Hanson .10 .05
❑ 137 Orlando Merced .10 .05
❑ 138 Dean Palmer .20 .09
❑ 139 John Franco .20 .09
❑ 140 Brady Anderson .30 .14
❑ 141 Ricky Jordan .10 .05
❑ 142 Jeff Blauser .10 .05
❑ 143 Sammy Sosa 1.00 .45
❑ 144 Bob Walk .10 .05
❑ 145 Delino DeShields .20 .09
❑ 146 Kevin Brown .30 .14
❑ 147 Mark Lemke .10 .05
❑ 148 Chuck Knoblauch .40 .18
❑ 149 Chris Sabo .10 .05
❑ 150 Bobby Witt .10 .05
❑ 151 Luis Gonzalez .10 .05
❑ 152 Ron Karkovice .10 .05
❑ 153 Jeff Brantley .10 .05
❑ 154 Kevin Appier .20 .09
❑ 155 Darrin Jackson .10 .05
❑ 156 Kelly Gruber .10 .05
❑ 157 Royce Clayton .10 .05
❑ 158 Chuck Finley .20 .09
❑ 159 Jeff King .20 .09
❑ 160 Greg Vaughn .20 .09
❑ 161 Geronimo Pena .10 .05
❑ 162 Steve Farr .10 .05
❑ 163 Jose Oquendo .10 .05
❑ 164 Mark Lewis .10 .05
❑ 165 John Wetteland .20 .09
❑ 166 Mike Henneman .10 .05
❑ 167 Todd Hundley .30 .14
❑ 168 Wes Chamberlain .10 .05
❑ 169 Steve Avery .10 .05
❑ 170 Mike Devereaux .10 .05
❑ 171 Reggie Sanders .10 .05
❑ 172 Jay Buhner .30 .14
❑ 173 Eric Anthony .10 .05
❑ 174 John Burkett .10 .05
❑ 175 Tom Candiotti .10 .05
❑ 176 Phil Plantier .10 .05
❑ 177 Doug Henry .10 .05
❑ 178 Scott Leius .10 .05
❑ 179 Kirt Manwaring .10 .05
❑ 180 Jeff Parrett .10 .05
❑ 181 Don Slaught .10 .05
❑ 182 Scott Radinsky .10 .05
❑ 183 Luis Alicea .10 .05
❑ 184 Tom Gordon .20 .09
❑ 185 Rick Wilkins .10 .05
❑ 186 Todd Stottlemyre .10 .05
❑ 187 Moises Alou .20 .09
❑ 188 Joe Grahe .10 .05
❑ 189 Jeff Kent .20 .09
❑ 190 Bill Wegman .10 .05
❑ 191 Kim Batiste .10 .05
❑ 192 Matt Nokes .10 .05
❑ 193 Mark Wohlers .10 .05
❑ 194 Paul Sorrento .10 .05
❑ 195 Chris Hammond .10 .05
❑ 196 Scott Livingstone .10 .05
❑ 197 Doug Jones .10 .05
❑ 198 Scott Cooper .10 .05
❑ 199 Ramon Martinez .20 .09
❑ 200 Dave Valle .10 .05
❑ 201 Mariano Duncan .10 .05
❑ 202 Ben McDonald .10 .05
❑ 203 Darren Lewis .10 .05
❑ 204 Kenny Rogers .10 .05
❑ 205 Manuel Lee .10 .05
❑ 206 Scott Erickson .10 .05
❑ 207 Dan Gladden .10 .05
❑ 208 Bob Welch .10 .05
❑ 209 Greg Olson .10 .05
❑ 210 Dan Pasqua .10 .05
❑ 211 Tim Wallach .10 .05
❑ 212 Jeff Montgomery .20 .09
❑ 213 Derrick May .10 .05
❑ 214 Ed Sprague .10 .05
❑ 215 David Haas .10 .05
❑ 216 Darrin Fletcher .10 .05
❑ 217 Brian Jordan .20 .09
❑ 218 Jaime Navarro .10 .05
❑ 219 Randy Velarde .10 .05
❑ 220 Ron Gant .20 .09
❑ 221 Paul Quantrill .10 .05
❑ 222 Damion Easley .20 .09
❑ 223 Charlie Hough .20 .09
❑ 224 Brad Brink .10 .05
❑ 225 Barry Manuel .10 .05
❑ 226 Kevin Koslofski .10 .05
❑ 227 Ryan Thompson .10 .05
❑ 228 Mike Munoz .10 .05
❑ 229 Dan Wilson .20 .09
❑ 230 Peter Hoy .10 .05
❑ 231 Pedro Astacio .10 .05
❑ 232 Matt Stairs .10 .05
❑ 233 Jeff Reboulet .10 .05
❑ 234 Manny Alexander .10 .05
❑ 235 Willie Banks .10 .05
❑ 236 John Jaha .10 .05
❑ 237 Scooter Tucker .10 .05
❑ 238 Russ Springer .10 .05
❑ 239 Paul Miller .10 .05
❑ 240 Dan Peltier .10 .05
❑ 241 Ozzie Canseco .10 .05
❑ 242 Ben Rivera .10 .05
❑ 243 John Valentin .20 .09
❑ 244 Henry Rodriguez .20 .09
❑ 245 Derek Parks .10 .05
❑ 246 Carlos Garcia .10 .05
❑ 247 Tim Pugh .10 .05
❑ 248 Melvin Nieves .10 .05
❑ 249 Rich Amaral .10 .05
❑ 250 Willie Greene .10 .05
❑ 251 Tim Scott .10 .05
❑ 252 Dave Silvestri .10 .05
❑ 253 Rob Mallicoat .10 .05
❑ 254 Donald Harris .10 .05
❑ 255 Craig Colbert .10 .05
❑ 256 Jose Guzman .10 .05
❑ 257 Domingo Martinez .10 .05
❑ 258 William Suero .10 .05
❑ 259 Juan Guerrero .10 .05
❑ 260 J.T. Snow .50 .23
❑ 261 Tony Pena .10 .05
❑ 262 Tim Fortugno .10 .05
❑ 263 Tom Marsh .10 .05
❑ 264 Kurt Knudsen .10 .05
❑ 265 Tim Costo .10 .05
❑ 266 Steve Shifflett .10 .05
❑ 267 Billy Ashley .10 .05
❑ 268 Jerry Nielsen .10 .05
❑ 269 Pete Young .10 .05
❑ 270 Johnny Guzman .10 .05
❑ 271 Greg Colbrunn .10 .05
❑ 272 Jeff Nelson .10 .05
❑ 273 Kevin Young .10 .05
❑ 274 Jeff Frye .10 .05
❑ 275 J.T. Bruett .10 .05
❑ 276 Todd Pratt .10 .05
❑ 277 Mike Butcher .10 .05
❑ 278 John Flaherty .10 .05
❑ 279 John Patterson .10 .05
❑ 280 Eric Hillman .10 .05
❑ 281 Bien Figueroa .10 .05
❑ 282 Shane Reynolds .20 .09
❑ 283 Rich Rowland .10 .05
❑ 284 Steve Foster .10 .05
❑ 285 Dave Mlicki .10 .05
❑ 286 Mike Piazza 2.00 .90
❑ 287 Mike Trombley .10 .05
❑ 288 Jim Pena .10 .05
❑ 289 Bob Ayrault .10 .05
❑ 290 Henry Mercedes .10 .05
❑ 291 Bob Wickman .10 .05
❑ 292 Jacob Brumfield .10 .05
❑ 293 David Hulse .10 .05
❑ 294 Ryan Klesko .40 .18
❑ 295 Doug Linton .10 .05
❑ 296 Steve Cooke .10 .05
❑ 297 Eddie Zosky .10 .05
❑ 298 Gerald Williams .10 .05
❑ 299 Jonathan Hurst .10 .05
❑ 300 Larry Carter .10 .05
❑ 301 William Pennyfeather .10 .05
❑ 302 Cesar Hernandez .10 .05
❑ 303 Steve Hosey .10 .05
❑ 304 Blas Minor .10 .05
❑ 305 Jeff Grotewald .10 .05
❑ 306 Bernardo Brito .10 .05
❑ 307 Rafael Bournigal .10 .05
❑ 308 Jeff Branson .10 .05
❑ 309 Tom Quinlan .10 .05
❑ 310 Pat Gomez .10 .05
❑ 311 Sterling Hitchcock .40 .18
❑ 312 Kent Bottenfield .10 .05
❑ 313 Alan Trammell .30 .14
❑ 314 Cris Colon .10 .05
❑ 315 Paul Wagner .10 .05
❑ 316 Matt Maysey .10 .05
❑ 317 Mike Stanton .10 .05
❑ 318 Rick Trlicek .10 .05
❑ 319 Kevin Rogers .10 .05
❑ 320 Mark Clark .10 .05
❑ 321 Pedro Martinez .50 .23
❑ 322 Al Martin .10 .05
❑ 323 Mike Macfarlane .10 .05
❑ 324 Rey Sanchez .10 .05
❑ 325 Roger Pavlik .10 .05
❑ 326 Troy Neel .10 .05
❑ 327 Kerry Woodson .10 .05
❑ 328 Wayne Kirby .10 .05
❑ 329 Ken Ryan .10 .05
❑ 330 Jesse Levis .10 .05
❑ 331 James Austin .10 .05
❑ 332 Dan Walters .10 .05
❑ 333 Brian Williams .10 .05
❑ 334 Wil Cordero .10 .05
❑ 335 Bret Boone .20 .09
❑ 336 Hipolito Pichardo .10 .05
❑ 337 Pat Mahomes .10 .05
❑ 338 Andy Stankiewicz .10 .05
❑ 339 Jim Bullinger .10 .05
❑ 340 Archi Cianfrocco .10 .05
❑ 341 Ruben Amaro Jr. .10 .05
❑ 342 Frank Seminara .10 .05
❑ 343 Pat Hentgen .30 .14
❑ 344 Dave Nilsson .20 .09
❑ 345 Mike Perez .10 .05
❑ 346 Tim Salmon .40 .18
❑ 347 Tim Wakefield .20 .09
❑ 348 Carlos Hernandez .10 .05
❑ 349 Donovan Osborne .10 .05
❑ 350 Denny Neagle .20 .09
❑ 351 Sam Militello .10 .05
❑ 352 Eric Fox .10 .05
❑ 353 John Doherty .10 .05
❑ 354 Chad Curtis .20 .09
❑ 355 Jeff Tackett .10 .05
❑ 356 Dave Fleming .10 .05
❑ 357 Pat Listach .10 .05
❑ 358 Kevin Wickander .10 .05
❑ 359 John Vander Wal .10 .05
❑ 360 Arthur Rhodes .10 .05
❑ 361 Bob Scanlan .10 .05
❑ 362 Bob Zupcic .10 .05
❑ 363 Mel Rojas .10 .05
❑ 364 Jim Thome .75 .35
❑ 365 Bill Pecota .10 .05
❑ 366 Mark Carreon .10 .05
❑ 367 Mitch Williams .10 .05
❑ 368 Cal Eldred .10 .05
❑ 369 Stan Belinda .10 .05
❑ 370 Pat Kelly .10 .05
❑ 371 Rheal Cormier .10 .05

❑	372	Juan Guzman	.10	.05
❑	373	Damon Berryhill	.10	.05
❑	374	Gary DiSarcina	.10	.05
❑	375	Norm Charlton	.10	.05
❑	376	Roberto Hernandez	.20	.09
❑	377	Scott Kamieniecki	.10	.05
❑	378	Rusty Meacham	.10	.05
❑	379	Kurt Stillwell	.10	.05
❑	380	Lloyd McClendon	.10	.05
❑	381	Mark Leonard	.10	.05
❑	382	Jerry Browne	.10	.05
❑	383	Glenn Davis	.10	.05
❑	384	Randy Johnson	.40	.18
❑	385	Mike Greenwell	.10	.05
❑	386	Scott Chiamparino	.10	.05
❑	387	George Bell	.10	.05
❑	388	Steve Olin	.10	.05
❑	389	Chuck McElroy	.10	.05
❑	390	Mark Gardner	.10	.05
❑	391	Rod Beck	.20	.09
❑	392	Dennis Rasmussen	.10	.05
❑	393	Charlie Leibrandt	.10	.05
❑	394	Julio Franco	.10	.05
❑	395	Pete Harnisch	.10	.05
❑	396	Sid Bream	.10	.05
❑	397	Milt Thompson	.10	.05
❑	398	Glenallen Hill	.10	.05
❑	399	Chico Walker	.10	.05
❑	400	Alex Cole	.10	.05
❑	401	Trevor Wilson	.10	.05
❑	402	Jeff Conine	.10	.05
❑	403	Kyle Abbott	.10	.05
❑	404	Tom Browning	.10	.05
❑	405	Jerald Clark	.10	.05
❑	406	Vince Horsman	.10	.05
❑	407	Kevin Mitchell	.20	.09
❑	408	Pete Smith	.10	.05
❑	409	Jeff Innis	.10	.05
❑	410	Mike Timlin	.10	.05
❑	411	Charlie Hayes	.10	.05
❑	412	Alex Fernandez	.20	.09
❑	413	Jeff Russell	.10	.05
❑	414	Jody Reed	.10	.05
❑	415	Mickey Morandini	.10	.05
❑	416	Darnell Coles	.10	.05
❑	417	Xavier Hernandez	.10	.05
❑	418	Steve Sax	.10	.05
❑	419	Joe Girardi	.20	.09
❑	420	Mike Fetters	.10	.05
❑	421	Danny Jackson	.10	.05
❑	422	Jim Gott	.10	.05
❑	423	Tim Belcher	.10	.05
❑	424	Jose Mesa	.10	.05
❑	425	Junior Felix	.10	.05
❑	426	Thomas Howard	.10	.05
❑	427	Julio Valera	.10	.05
❑	428	Dante Bichette	.20	.09
❑	429	Mike Sharperson	.10	.05
❑	430	Darryl Kile	.20	.09
❑	431	Lonnie Smith	.10	.05
❑	432	Monty Fariss	.10	.05
❑	433	Reggie Jefferson	.20	.09
❑	434	Bob McClure	.10	.05
❑	435	Craig Lefferts	.10	.05
❑	436	Duane Ward	.10	.05
❑	437	Shawn Abner	.10	.05
❑	438	Roberto Kelly	.10	.05
❑	439	Paul O'Neill	.20	.09
❑	440	Alan Mills	.10	.05
❑	441	Roger Mason	.10	.05
❑	442	Gary Pettis	.10	.05
❑	443	Steve Lake	.10	.05
❑	444	Gene Larkin	.10	.05
❑	445	Larry Andersen	.10	.05
❑	446	Doug Dascenzo	.10	.05
❑	447	Daryl Boston	.10	.05
❑	448	John Candelaria	.10	.05
❑	449	Storm Davis	.10	.05
❑	450	Tom Edens	.10	.05
❑	451	Mike Maddux	.10	.05
❑	452	Tim Naehring	.10	.05
❑	453	John Orton	.10	.05
❑	454	Joey Cora	.20	.09
❑	455	Chuck Crim	.10	.05
❑	456	Dan Plesac	.10	.05
❑	457	Mike Bielecki	.10	.05
❑	458	Terry Jorgensen	.10	.05
❑	459	John Habyan	.10	.05
❑	460	Pete O'Brien	.10	.05
❑	461	Jeff Treadway	.10	.05
❑	462	Frank Castillo	.10	.05
❑	463	Jimmy Jones	.10	.05
❑	464	Tommy Greene	.10	.05
❑	465	Tracy Woodson	.10	.05
❑	466	Rich Rodriguez	.10	.05
❑	467	Joe Hesketh	.10	.05
❑	468	Greg Myers	.10	.05
❑	469	Kirk McCaskill	.10	.05
❑	470	Ricky Bones	.10	.05
❑	471	Lenny Webster	.10	.05
❑	472	Francisco Cabrera	.10	.05
❑	473	Turner Ward	.10	.05
❑	474	Dwayne Henry	.10	.05
❑	475	Al Osuna	.10	.05
❑	476	Craig Wilson	.10	.05
❑	477	Chris Nabholz	.10	.05
❑	478	Rafael Belliard	.10	.05
❑	479	Terry Leach	.10	.05
❑	480	Tim Teufel	.10	.05
❑	481	Dennis Eckersley AW	.10	.05
❑	482	Barry Bonds AW	.30	.14
❑	483	Dennis Eckersley AW	.10	.05
❑	484	Greg Maddux AW	.60	.25
❑	485	Pat Listach AW	.10	.05
❑	486	Eric Karros AW	.10	.05
❑	487	Jamie Arnold DP	.20	.09
❑	488	B.J. Wallace DP	.10	.05
❑	489	Derek Jeter DP	4.00	1.80
❑	490	Jason Kendall DP	1.25	.55
❑	491	Rick Helling DP	.30	.14
❑	492	Derek Wallace DP	.10	.05
❑	493	Sean Lowe DP	.10	.05
❑	494	Shannon Stewart DP	.30	.14
❑	495	Benji Grigsby DP	.10	.05
❑	496	Todd Steverson DP	.20	.09
❑	497	Dan Serafini DP	.20	.09
❑	498	Michael Tucker DP	.40	.18
❑	499	Chris Roberts DP	.10	.05
❑	500	Pete Janicki DP	.10	.05
❑	501	Jeff Schmidt DP	.10	.05
❑	502	Edgar Martinez AS	.20	.09
❑	503	Omar Vizquel AS	.20	.09
❑	504	Ken Griffey Jr. AS	1.00	.45
❑	505	Kirby Puckett AS	.40	.18
❑	506	Joe Carter AS	.10	.05
❑	507	Ivan Rodriguez AS	.40	.18
❑	508	Jack Morris AS	.10	.05
❑	509	Dennis Eckersley AS	.10	.05
❑	510	Frank Thomas AS	.60	.25
❑	511	Roberto Alomar AS	.40	.18
❑	512	Mickey Morandini AS	.10	.05
❑	513	Dennis Eckersley HL	.10	.05
❑	514	Jeff Reardon HL	.10	.05
❑	515	Danny Tartabull HL	.10	.05
❑	516	Bip Roberts HL	.10	.05
❑	517	George Brett HL	.40	.18
❑	518	Robin Yount HL	.30	.14
❑	519	Kevin Gross HL	.10	.05
❑	520	Ed Sprague WS	.10	.05
❑	521	Dave Winfield WS	.20	.09
❑	522	Ozzie Smith AS	.40	.18
❑	523	Barry Bonds AS	.40	.18
❑	524	Andy Van Slyke AS	.10	.05
❑	525	Tony Gwynn AS	.50	.23
❑	526	Darren Daulton AS	.10	.05
❑	527	Greg Maddux AS	.60	.25
❑	528	Fred McGriff AS	.30	.14
❑	529	Lee Smith AS	.10	.05
❑	530	Ryne Sandberg AS	.30	.14
❑	531	Gary Sheffield AS	.20	.09
❑	532	Ozzie Smith DT	.40	.18
❑	533	Kirby Puckett DT	.40	.18
❑	534	Gary Sheffield DT	.20	.09
❑	535	Andy Van Slyke DT	.10	.05
❑	536	Ken Griffey Jr. DT	1.00	.45
❑	537	Ivan Rodriguez DT	.40	.18
❑	538	Charles Nagy DT	.10	.05
❑	539	Tom Glavine DT	.20	.09
❑	540	Dennis Eckersley DT	.10	.05
❑	541	Frank Thomas DT	.60	.25
❑	542	Roberto Alomar DT	.20	.09
❑	543	Sean Berry	.10	.05
❑	544	Mike Schooler	.10	.05
❑	545	Chuck Carr	.10	.05
❑	546	Lenny Harris	.10	.05
❑	547	Gary Scott	.10	.05
❑	548	Derek Lilliquist	.10	.05
❑	549	Brian Hunter	.10	.05
❑	550	Kirby Puckett MOY	.40	.18
❑	551	Jim Eisenreich	.10	.05
❑	552	Andre Dawson	.30	.14
❑	553	David Nied	.10	.05
❑	554	Spike Owen	.10	.05
❑	555	Greg Gagne	.10	.05
❑	556	Sid Fernandez	.10	.05
❑	557	Mark McGwire	2.00	.90
❑	558	Bryan Harvey	.10	.05
❑	559	Harold Reynolds	.10	.05
❑	560	Barry Bonds	.50	.23
❑	561	Eric Wedge	.10	.05
❑	562	Ozzie Smith	.50	.23
❑	563	Rick Sutcliffe	.10	.05
❑	564	Jeff Reardon	.20	.09
❑	565	Alex Arias	.10	.05
❑	566	Greg Swindell	.10	.05
❑	567	Brook Jacoby	.10	.05
❑	568	Pete Incaviglia	.10	.05
❑	569	Butch Henry	.10	.05
❑	570	Eric Davis	.20	.09
❑	571	Kevin Seitzer	.10	.05
❑	572	Tony Fernandez	.10	.05
❑	573	Steve Reed	.10	.05
❑	574	Cory Snyder	.10	.05
❑	575	Joe Carter	.20	.09
❑	576	Greg Maddux	1.25	.55
❑	577	Bert Blyleven UER (Should say 3701 career strikeouts)	.20	.09
❑	578	Kevin Bass	.10	.05
❑	579	Carlton Fisk	.40	.18
❑	580	Doug Drabek	.10	.05
❑	581	Mark Gubicza	.10	.05
❑	582	Bobby Thigpen	.10	.05
❑	583	Chili Davis	.20	.09
❑	584	Scott Bankhead	.10	.05
❑	585	Harold Baines	.20	.09
❑	586	Eric Young	.40	.18
❑	587	Lance Parrish	.10	.05
❑	588	Juan Bell	.10	.05
❑	589	Bob Ojeda	.10	.05
❑	590	Joe Orsulak	.10	.05
❑	591	Benito Santiago	.10	.05
❑	592	Wade Boggs	.40	.18
❑	593	Robby Thompson	.10	.05
❑	594	Eric Plunk	.10	.05
❑	595	Hensley Meulens	.10	.05
❑	596	Lou Whitaker	.20	.09
❑	597	Dale Murphy	.30	.14
❑	598	Paul Molitor	.40	.18
❑	599	Greg W. Harris	.10	.05
❑	600	Darren Holmes	.10	.05
❑	601	Dave Martinez	.10	.05
❑	602	Tom Henke	.10	.05
❑	603	Mike Benjamin	.10	.05
❑	604	Rene Gonzales	.10	.05
❑	605	Roger McDowell	.10	.05
❑	606	Kirby Puckett	.60	.25
❑	607	Randy Myers	.20	.09
❑	608	Ruben Sierra	.10	.05
❑	609	Wilson Alvarez	.20	.09
❑	610	David Segui	.10	.05
❑	611	Juan Samuel	.10	.05
❑	612	Tom Brunansky	.10	.05
❑	613	Willie Randolph	.20	.09
❑	614	Tony Phillips	.10	.05
❑	615	Candy Maldonado	.10	.05
❑	616	Chris Bosio	.10	.05
❑	617	Bret Barberie	.10	.05
❑	618	Scott Sanderson	.10	.05
❑	619	Ron Darling	.10	.05
❑	620	Dave Winfield	.30	.14
❑	621	Mike Felder	.10	.05
❑	622	Greg Hibbard	.10	.05
❑	623	Mike Scioscia	.10	.05
❑	624	John Smiley	.10	.05

❑ 625 Alejandro Pena	.10	.05
❑ 626 Terry Steinbach	.10	.05
❑ 627 Freddie Benavides	.10	.05
❑ 628 Kevin Reimer	.10	.05
❑ 629 Braulio Castillo	.10	.05
❑ 630 Dave Stieb	.20	.09
❑ 631 Dave Magadan	.10	.05
❑ 632 Scott Fletcher	.10	.05
❑ 633 Cris Carpenter	.10	.05
❑ 634 Kevin Maas	.10	.05
❑ 635 Todd Worrell	.10	.05
❑ 636 Rob Deer	.10	.05
❑ 637 Dwight Smith	.10	.05
❑ 638 Chito Martinez	.10	.05
❑ 639 Jimmy Key	.20	.09
❑ 640 Greg A. Harris	.10	.05
❑ 641 Mike Moore	.10	.05
❑ 642 Pat Borders	.10	.05
❑ 643 Bill Gullickson	.10	.05
❑ 644 Gary Gaetti	.10	.05
❑ 645 David Howard	.10	.05
❑ 646 Jim Abbott	.20	.09
❑ 647 Willie Wilson	.10	.05
❑ 648 David Wells	.20	.09
❑ 649 Andres Galarraga	.40	.18
❑ 650 Vince Coleman	.10	.05
❑ 651 Rob Dibble	.10	.05
❑ 652 Frank Tanana	.10	.05
❑ 653 Steve Decker	.10	.05
❑ 654 David Cone	.20	.09
❑ 655 Jack Armstrong	.10	.05
❑ 656 Dave Stewart	.20	.09
❑ 657 Billy Hatcher	.10	.05
❑ 658 Tim Raines	.20	.09
❑ 659 Walt Weiss	.10	.05
❑ 660 Jose Lind	.10	.05

1993 Score Franchise

	MINT	NRMT
COMPLETE SET (28)	120.00	55.00
COMMON CARD (1-28)	1.50	.70
❑ 1 Cal Ripken	25.00	11.00
❑ 2 Roger Clemens	12.00	5.50
❑ 3 Mark Langston	1.50	.70
❑ 4 Frank Thomas	20.00	9.00
❑ 5 Carlos Baerga	1.50	.70
❑ 6 Cecil Fielder	2.50	1.10
❑ 7 Gregg Jefferies	1.50	.70
❑ 8 Robin Yount	4.00	1.80
❑ 9 Kirby Puckett	10.00	4.50
❑ 10 Don Mattingly	10.00	4.50
❑ 11 Dennis Eckersley	2.50	1.10
❑ 12 Ken Griffey Jr.	30.00	13.50
❑ 13 Juan Gonzalez	15.00	6.75
❑ 14 Roberto Alomar	6.00	2.70
❑ 15 Terry Pendleton	1.50	.70
❑ 16 Ryne Sandberg	8.00	3.60
❑ 17 Barry Larkin	4.00	1.80
❑ 18 Jeff Bagwell	10.00	4.50
❑ 19 Brett Butler	2.50	1.10
❑ 20 Larry Walker	6.00	2.70
❑ 21 Bobby Bonilla	2.50	1.10
❑ 22 Darren Daulton	2.50	1.10
❑ 23 Andy Van Slyke	1.50	.70
❑ 24 Ray Lankford	4.00	1.80
❑ 25 Gary Sheffield	6.00	2.70
❑ 26 Will Clark	6.00	2.70
❑ 27 Bryan Harvey	1.50	.70
❑ 28 David Nied	1.50	.70

1993 Score Gold Dream Team

	MINT	NRMT
COMPLETE SET (12)	5.00	2.20
COMMON CARD (1-11)	.20	.09
❑ 1 Ozzie Smith	.75	.35
❑ 2 Kirby Puckett	.75	.35
❑ 3 Gary Sheffield	.40	.18
❑ 4 Andy Van Slyke	.20	.09
❑ 5 Ken Griffey Jr.	2.50	1.10
❑ 6 Ivan Rodriguez	.40	.18
❑ 7 Charles Nagy	.20	.09
❑ 8 Tom Glavine	.30	.14
❑ 9 Dennis Eckersley	.20	.09
❑ 10 Frank Thomas	1.25	.55
❑ 11 Roberto Alomar	.40	.18
❑ NNO Header Card	1.00	.45

1994 Score

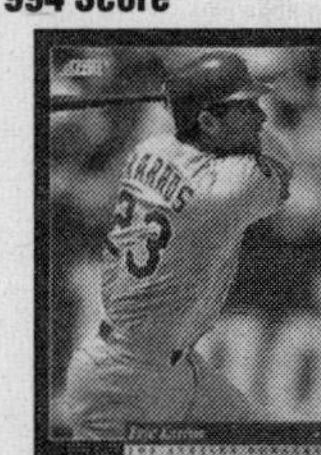

	MINT	NRMT
COMPLETE SET (660)	24.00	11.00
COMPLETE SERIES 1 (330)	12.00	5.50
COMPLETE SERIES 2 (330)	12.00	5.50
COMMON CARD (1-660)	.10	.05
❑ 1 Barry Bonds	.50	.23
❑ 2 John Olerud	.20	.09
❑ 3 Ken Griffey Jr.	2.00	.90
❑ 4 Jeff Bagwell	.60	.25
❑ 5 John Burkett	.10	.05
❑ 6 Jack McDowell	.10	.05
❑ 7 Albert Belle	.50	.23
❑ 8 Andres Galarraga	.40	.18
❑ 9 Mike Mussina	.40	.18
❑ 10 Will Clark	.40	.18
❑ 11 Travis Fryman	.20	.09
❑ 12 Tony Gwynn	1.00	.45
❑ 13 Robin Yount	.40	.18
❑ 14 Dave Magadan	.10	.05
❑ 15 Paul O'Neill	.20	.09
❑ 16 Ray Lankford	.20	.09
❑ 17 Damion Easley	.20	.09
❑ 18 Andy Van Slyke	.20	.09
❑ 19 Brian McRae	.10	.05
❑ 20 Ryne Sandberg	.50	.23
❑ 21 Kirby Puckett	.60	.25
❑ 22 Dwight Gooden	.20	.09
❑ 23 Don Mattingly	.60	.25
❑ 24 Kevin Mitchell	.10	.05
❑ 25 Roger Clemens	.75	.35
❑ 26 Eric Karros	.20	.09
❑ 27 Juan Gonzalez	1.00	.45
❑ 28 John Kruk	.20	.09
❑ 29 Gregg Jefferies	.10	.05
❑ 30 Tom Glavine	.40	.18
❑ 31 Ivan Rodriguez	.50	.23
❑ 32 Jay Bell	.20	.09
❑ 33 Randy Johnson	.40	.18
❑ 34 Darren Daulton	.20	.09
❑ 35 Rickey Henderson	.40	.18
❑ 36 Eddie Murray	.40	.18
❑ 37 Brian Harper	.10	.05
❑ 38 Delino DeShields	.10	.05
❑ 39 Jose Lind	.10	.05
❑ 40 Benito Santiago	.10	.05
❑ 41 Frank Thomas	1.25	.55
❑ 42 Mark Grace	.30	.14
❑ 43 Roberto Alomar	.40	.18
❑ 44 Andy Benes	.20	.09
❑ 45 Luis Polonia	.10	.05
❑ 46 Brett Butler	.20	.09
❑ 47 Terry Steinbach	.20	.09
❑ 48 Craig Biggio	.40	.18
❑ 49 Greg Vaughn	.20	.09
❑ 50 Charlie Hayes	.10	.05
❑ 51 Mickey Tettleton	.10	.05
❑ 52 Jose Rijo	.10	.05
❑ 53 Carlos Baerga	.20	.09
❑ 54 Jeff Blauser	.10	.05
❑ 55 Leo Gomez	.10	.05
❑ 56 Bob Tewksbury	.10	.05
❑ 57 Mo Vaughn	.50	.23
❑ 58 Orlando Merced	.10	.05
❑ 59 Tino Martinez	.40	.18
❑ 60 Lenny Dykstra	.20	.09
❑ 61 Jose Canseco	.40	.18
❑ 62 Tony Fernandez	.10	.05
❑ 63 Donovan Osborne	.10	.05
❑ 64 Ken Hill	.10	.05
❑ 65 Kent Hrbek	.20	.09
❑ 66 Bryan Harvey	.10	.05
❑ 67 Wally Joyner	.20	.09
❑ 68 Derrick May	.10	.05
❑ 69 Lance Johnson	.10	.05
❑ 70 Willie McGee	.20	.09
❑ 71 Mark Langston	.10	.05
❑ 72 Terry Pendleton	.10	.05
❑ 73 Joe Carter	.20	.09
❑ 74 Barry Larkin	.30	.14
❑ 75 Jimmy Key	.20	.09
❑ 76 Joe Girardi	.10	.05
❑ 77 B.J. Surhoff	.20	.09
❑ 78 Pete Harnisch	.10	.05
❑ 79 Lou Whitaker UER (Milt Cuyler pictured on front)	.20	.09
❑ 80 Cory Snyder	.10	.05
❑ 81 Kenny Lofton	.40	.18
❑ 82 Fred McGriff	.30	.14
❑ 83 Mike Greenwell	.10	.05
❑ 84 Mike Perez	.10	.05
❑ 85 Cal Ripken	1.50	.70
❑ 86 Don Slaught	.10	.05
❑ 87 Omar Vizquel	.20	.09
❑ 88 Curt Schilling	.20	.09
❑ 89 Chuck Knoblauch	.40	.18
❑ 90 Moises Alou	.30	.14
❑ 91 Greg Gagne	.10	.05
❑ 92 Bret Saberhagen	.20	.09
❑ 93 Ozzie Guillen	.10	.05
❑ 94 Matt Williams	.30	.14
❑ 95 Chad Curtis	.10	.05
❑ 96 Mike Harkey	.10	.05
❑ 97 Devon White	.20	.09
❑ 98 Walt Weiss	.10	.05
❑ 99 Kevin Brown	.20	.09
❑ 100 Gary Sheffield	.40	.18
❑ 101 Wade Boggs	.40	.18

❑	102	Orel Hershiser	.20	.09
❑	103	Tony Phillips	.10	.05
❑	104	Andujar Cedeno	.10	.05
❑	105	Bill Spiers	.10	.05
❑	106	Otis Nixon	.10	.05
❑	107	Felix Fermin	.10	.05
❑	108	Bip Roberts	.10	.05
❑	109	Dennis Eckersley	.20	.09
❑	110	Dante Bichette	.20	.09
❑	111	Ben McDonald	.10	.05
❑	112	Jim Poole	.10	.05
❑	113	John Dopson	.10	.05
❑	114	Rob Dibble	.10	.05
❑	115	Jeff Treadway	.10	.05
❑	116	Ricky Jordan	.10	.05
❑	117	Mike Henneman	.10	.05
❑	118	Willie Blair	.10	.05
❑	119	Doug Henry	.10	.05
❑	120	Gerald Perry	.10	.05
❑	121	Greg Myers	.10	.05
❑	122	John Franco	.20	.09
❑	123	Roger Mason	.10	.05
❑	124	Chris Hammond	.10	.05
❑	125	Hubie Brooks	.10	.05
❑	126	Kent Mercker	.10	.05
❑	127	Jim Abbott	.20	.09
❑	128	Kevin Bass	.10	.05
❑	129	Rick Aguilera	.10	.05
❑	130	Mitch Webster	.10	.05
❑	131	Eric Plunk	.10	.05
❑	132	Mark Carreon	.10	.05
❑	133	Dave Stewart	.20	.09
❑	134	Willie Wilson	.10	.05
❑	135	Dave Fleming	.10	.05
❑	136	Jeff Tackett	.10	.05
❑	137	Geno Petralli	.10	.05
❑	138	Gene Harris	.10	.05
❑	139	Scott Bankhead	.10	.05
❑	140	Trevor Wilson	.10	.05
❑	141	Alvaro Espinoza	.10	.05
❑	142	Ryan Bowen	.10	.05
❑	143	Mike Moore	.10	.05
❑	144	Bill Pecota	.10	.05
❑	145	Jaime Navarro	.10	.05
❑	146	Jack Daugherty	.10	.05
❑	147	Bob Wickman	.10	.05
❑	148	Chris Jones	.10	.05
❑	149	Todd Stottlemyre	.10	.05
❑	150	Brian Williams	.10	.05
❑	151	Chuck Finley	.20	.09
❑	152	Lenny Harris	.10	.05
❑	153	Alex Fernandez	.10	.05
❑	154	Candy Maldonado	.10	.05
❑	155	Jeff Montgomery	.10	.05
❑	156	David West	.30	.14
❑	157	Mark Williamson	.10	.05
❑	158	Milt Thompson	.10	.05
❑	159	Ron Darling	.10	.05
❑	160	Stan Belinda	.10	.05
❑	161	Henry Cotto	.10	.05
❑	162	Mel Rojas	.10	.05
❑	163	Doug Strange	.10	.05
❑	164	Rene Arocha	.10	.05
❑	165	Tim Hulett	.10	.05
❑	166	Steve Avery	.10	.05
❑	167	Jim Thome	.50	.23
❑	168	Tom Browning	.10	.05
❑	169	Mario Diaz	.10	.05
❑	170	Steve Reed	.10	.05
❑	171	Scott Livingstone	.10	.05
❑	172	Chris Donnels	.10	.05
❑	173	John Jaha	.10	.05
❑	174	Carlos Hernandez	.10	.05
❑	175	Dion James	.10	.05
❑	176	Bud Black	.10	.05
❑	177	Tony Castillo	.10	.05
❑	178	Jose Guzman	.10	.05
❑	179	Torey Lovullo	.10	.05
❑	180	John Vander Wal	.10	.05
❑	181	Mike LaValliere	.10	.05
❑	182	Sid Fernandez	.10	.05
❑	183	Brent Mayne	.10	.05
❑	184	Terry Mulholland	.10	.05
❑	185	Willie Banks	.10	.05
❑	186	Steve Cooke	.10	.05
❑	187	Brent Gates	.10	.05
❑	188	Erik Pappas	.10	.05
❑	189	Bill Haselman	.10	.05
❑	190	Fernando Valenzuela	.20	.09
❑	191	Gary Redus	.10	.05
❑	192	Danny Darwin	.10	.05
❑	193	Mark Portugal	.10	.05
❑	194	Derek Lilliquist	.10	.05
❑	195	Charlie O'Brien	.10	.05
❑	196	Matt Nokes	.10	.05
❑	197	Danny Sheaffer	.10	.05
❑	198	Bill Gullickson	.10	.05
❑	199	Alex Arias	.10	.05
❑	200	Mike Fetters	.10	.05
❑	201	Brian Jordan	.20	.09
❑	202	Joe Grahe	.10	.05
❑	203	Tom Candiotti	.10	.05
❑	204	Jeremy Hernandez	.10	.05
❑	205	Mike Stanton	.10	.05
❑	206	David Howard	.10	.05
❑	207	Darren Holmes	.10	.05
❑	208	Rick Honeycutt	.10	.05
❑	209	Danny Jackson	.10	.05
❑	210	Rich Amaral	.10	.05
❑	211	Blas Minor	.10	.05
❑	212	Kenny Rogers	.10	.05
❑	213	Jim Leyritz	.20	.09
❑	214	Mike Morgan	.10	.05
❑	215	Dan Gladden	.10	.05
❑	216	Randy Velarde	.10	.05
❑	217	Mitch Williams	.10	.05
❑	218	Hipolito Pichardo	.10	.05
❑	219	Dave Burba	.10	.05
❑	220	Wilson Alvarez	.20	.09
❑	221	Bob Zupcic	.10	.05
❑	222	Francisco Cabrera	.10	.05
❑	223	Julio Valera	.10	.05
❑	224	Paul Assenmacher	.10	.05
❑	225	Jeff Branson	.10	.05
❑	226	Todd Frohwirth	.10	.05
❑	227	Armando Reynoso	.10	.05
❑	228	Rich Rowland	.10	.05
❑	229	Freddie Benavides	.10	.05
❑	230	Wayne Kirby	.10	.05
❑	231	Darryl Kile	.20	.09
❑	232	Skeeter Barnes	.10	.05
❑	233	Ramon Martinez	.20	.09
❑	234	Tom Gordon	.10	.05
❑	235	Dave Gallagher	.10	.05
❑	236	Ricky Bones	.10	.05
❑	237	Larry Andersen	.10	.05
❑	238	Pat Meares	.10	.05
❑	239	Zane Smith	.10	.05
❑	240	Tim Leary	.10	.05
❑	241	Phil Clark	.10	.05
❑	242	Danny Cox	.10	.05
❑	243	Mike Jackson	.10	.05
❑	244	Mike Gallego	.10	.05
❑	245	Lee Smith	.20	.09
❑	246	Todd Jones	.10	.05
❑	247	Steve Bedrosian	.10	.05
❑	248	Troy Neel	.10	.05
❑	249	Jose Bautista	.10	.05
❑	250	Steve Frey	.10	.05
❑	251	Jeff Reardon	.20	.09
❑	252	Stan Javier	.10	.05
❑	253	Mo Sanford	.10	.05
❑	254	Steve Sax	.10	.05
❑	255	Luis Aquino	.10	.05
❑	256	Domingo Jean	.10	.05
❑	257	Scott Servais	.10	.05
❑	258	Brad Pennington	.10	.05
❑	259	Dave Hansen	.10	.05
❑	260	Goose Gossage	.20	.09
❑	261	Jeff Fassero	.10	.05
❑	262	Junior Ortiz	.10	.05
❑	263	Anthony Young	.10	.05
❑	264	Chris Bosio	.10	.05
❑	265	Ruben Amaro Jr.	.10	.05
❑	266	Mark Eichhorn	.10	.05
❑	267	Dave Clark	.10	.05
❑	268	Gary Thurman	.10	.05
❑	269	Les Lancaster	.10	.05
❑	270	Jamie Moyer	.10	.05
❑	271	Ricky Gutierrez	.10	.05
❑	272	Greg A.Harris	.10	.05
❑	273	Mike Benjamin	.10	.05
❑	274	Gene Nelson	.10	.05
❑	275	Damon Berryhill	.10	.05
❑	276	Scott Radinsky	.10	.05
❑	277	Mike Aldrete	.10	.05
❑	278	Jerry DiPoto	.10	.05
❑	279	Chris Haney	.10	.05
❑	280	Richie Lewis	.10	.05
❑	281	Jarvis Brown	.10	.05
❑	282	Juan Bell	.10	.05
❑	283	Joe Klink	.10	.05
❑	284	Graeme Lloyd	.10	.05
❑	285	Casey Candaele	.10	.05
❑	286	Bob MacDonald	.10	.05
❑	287	Mike Sharperson	.10	.05
❑	288	Gene Larkin	.10	.05
❑	289	Brian Barnes	.10	.05
❑	290	David McCarty	.10	.05
❑	291	Jeff Innis	.10	.05
❑	292	Bob Patterson	.10	.05
❑	293	Ben Rivera	.10	.05
❑	294	John Habyan	.10	.05
❑	295	Rich Rodriguez	.10	.05
❑	296	Edwin Nunez	.10	.05
❑	297	Rod Brewer	.10	.05
❑	298	Mike Timlin	.10	.05
❑	299	Jesse Orosco	.10	.05
❑	300	Gary Gaetti	.20	.09
❑	301	Todd Benzinger	.10	.05
❑	302	Jeff Nelson	.10	.05
❑	303	Rafael Belliard	.10	.05
❑	304	Matt Whiteside	.10	.05
❑	305	Vinny Castilla	.20	.09
❑	306	Matt Turner	.10	.05
❑	307	Eduardo Perez	.10	.05
❑	308	Joel Johnston	.10	.05
❑	309	Chris Gomez	.10	.05
❑	310	Pat Rapp	.10	.05
❑	311	Jim Tatum	.10	.05
❑	312	Kirk Rueter	.10	.05
❑	313	John Flaherty	.10	.05
❑	314	Tom Kramer	.10	.05
❑	315	Mark Whiten	.10	.05
❑	316	Chris Bosio	.10	.05
❑	317	Baltimore Orioles CL	.10	.05
❑	318	Boston Red Sox CL UER (Viola listed as 316; should be 331)	.10	.05
❑	319	California Angels CL	.10	.05
❑	320	Chicago White Sox CL	.10	.05
❑	321	Cleveland Indians CL	.10	.05
❑	322	Detroit Tigers CL	.10	.05
❑	323	Kansas City Royals CL	.10	.05
❑	324	Milwaukee Brewers CL	.10	.05
❑	325	Minnesota Twins CL	.10	.05
❑	326	New York Yankees CL	.10	.05
❑	327	Oakland Athletics CL	.10	.05
❑	328	Seattle Mariners CL	.10	.05
❑	329	Texas Rangers CL	.10	.05
❑	330	Toronto Blue Jays CL	.10	.05
❑	331	Frank Viola	.10	.05
❑	332	Ron Gant	.20	.09
❑	333	Charles Nagy	.20	.09
❑	334	Roberto Kelly	.10	.05
❑	335	Brady Anderson	.20	.09
❑	336	Alex Cole	.10	.05
❑	337	Alan Trammell	.30	.14
❑	338	Derek Bell	.20	.09
❑	339	Bernie Williams	.40	.18
❑	340	Jose Offerman	.10	.05
❑	341	Bill Wegman	.10	.05
❑	342	Ken Caminiti	.30	.14
❑	343	Pat Borders	.10	.05
❑	344	Kirt Manwaring	.10	.05
❑	345	Chili Davis	.20	.09
❑	346	Steve Buechele	.10	.05
❑	347	Robin Ventura	.20	.09
❑	348	Teddy Higuera	.10	.05
❑	349	Jerry Browne	.10	.05
❑	350	Scott Kamieniecki	.10	.05
❑	351	Kevin Tapani	.10	.05
❑	352	Marquis Grissom	.20	.09
❑	353	Jay Buhner	.20	.09
❑	354	Dave Hollins	.10	.05

❑ 355 Dan Wilson .10 .05
❑ 356 Bob Walk .10 .05
❑ 357 Chris Hoiles .10 .05
❑ 358 Todd Zeile .10 .05
❑ 359 Kevin Appier .20 .09
❑ 360 Chris Sabo .10 .05
❑ 361 David Segui .20 .09
❑ 362 Jerald Clark .10 .05
❑ 363 Tony Pena .10 .05
❑ 364 Steve Finley .20 .09
❑ 365 Roger Pavlik .10 .05
❑ 366 John Smoltz .20 .09
❑ 367 Scott Fletcher .10 .05
❑ 368 Jody Reed .10 .05
❑ 369 David Wells .30 .14
❑ 370 Jose Vizcaino .10 .05
❑ 371 Pat Listach .10 .05
❑ 372 Orestes Destrade .10 .05
❑ 373 Danny Tartabull .10 .05
❑ 374 Greg W. Harris .10 .05
❑ 375 Juan Guzman .10 .05
❑ 376 Larry Walker .40 .18
❑ 377 Gary DiSarcina .10 .05
❑ 378 Bobby Bonilla .20 .09
❑ 379 Tim Raines .20 .09
❑ 380 Tommy Greene .10 .05
❑ 381 Chris Gwynn .10 .05
❑ 382 Jeff King .10 .05
❑ 383 Shane Mack .10 .05
❑ 384 Ozzie Smith .50 .23
❑ 385 Eddie Zambrano .10 .05
❑ 386 Mike Devereaux .10 .05
❑ 387 Erik Hanson .10 .05
❑ 388 Scott Cooper .10 .05
❑ 389 Dean Palmer .20 .09
❑ 390 John Wetteland .20 .09
❑ 391 Reggie Jefferson .10 .05
❑ 392 Mark Lemke .10 .05
❑ 393 Cecil Fielder .20 .09
❑ 394 Reggie Sanders .20 .09
❑ 395 Darryl Hamilton .10 .05
❑ 396 Daryl Boston .10 .05
❑ 397 Pat Kelly .10 .05
❑ 398 Joe Orsulak .10 .05
❑ 399 Ed Sprague .10 .05
❑ 400 Eric Anthony .10 .05
❑ 401 Scott Sanderson .10 .05
❑ 402 Jim Gott .10 .05
❑ 403 Ron Karkovice .10 .05
❑ 404 Phil Plantier .10 .05
❑ 405 David Cone .30 .14
❑ 406 Robby Thompson .10 .05
❑ 407 Dave Winfield .40 .18
❑ 408 Dwight Smith .10 .05
❑ 409 Ruben Sierra .10 .05
❑ 410 Jack Armstrong .10 .05
❑ 411 Mike Felder .10 .05
❑ 412 Wil Cordero .10 .05
❑ 413 Julio Franco .10 .05
❑ 414 Howard Johnson .10 .05
❑ 415 Mark McLemore .10 .05
❑ 416 Pete Incaviglia .10 .05
❑ 417 John Valentin .20 .09
❑ 418 Tim Wakefield .20 .09
❑ 419 Jose Mesa .10 .05
❑ 420 Bernard Gilkey .10 .05
❑ 421 Kirk Gibson .20 .09
❑ 422 Dave Justice .40 .18
❑ 423 Tom Brunansky .10 .05
❑ 424 John Smiley .10 .05
❑ 425 Kevin Maas .10 .05
❑ 426 Doug Drabek .10 .05
❑ 427 Paul Molitor .40 .18
❑ 428 Darryl Strawberry .20 .09
❑ 429 Tim Naehring .10 .05
❑ 430 Bill Swift .10 .05
❑ 431 Ellis Burks .20 .09
❑ 432 Greg Hibbard .10 .05
❑ 433 Felix Jose .10 .05
❑ 434 Bret Barberie .10 .05
❑ 435 Pedro Munoz .10 .05
❑ 436 Darrin Fletcher .10 .05
❑ 437 Bobby Witt .10 .05
❑ 438 Wes Chamberlain .10 .05
❑ 439 Mackey Sasser .10 .05
❑ 440 Mark Whiten .10 .05
❑ 441 Harold Reynolds .10 .05
❑ 442 Greg Olson .10 .05
❑ 443 Billy Hatcher .10 .05
❑ 444 Joe Oliver .10 .05
❑ 445 Sandy Alomar Jr. .20 .09
❑ 446 Tim Wallach .10 .05
❑ 447 Karl Rhodes .10 .05
❑ 448 Royce Clayton .10 .05
❑ 449 Cal Eldred .10 .05
❑ 450 Rick Wilkins .10 .05
❑ 451 Mike Stanley .10 .05
❑ 452 Charlie Hough .10 .05
❑ 453 Jack Morris .20 .09
❑ 454 Jon Ratliff .20 .09
❑ 455 Rene Gonzales .10 .05
❑ 456 Eddie Taubensee .10 .05
❑ 457 Roberto Hernandez .10 .05
❑ 458 Todd Hundley .20 .09
❑ 459 Mike Macfarlane .10 .05
❑ 460 Mickey Morandini .10 .05
❑ 461 Scott Erickson .20 .09
❑ 462 Lonnie Smith .10 .05
❑ 463 Dave Henderson .10 .05
❑ 464 Ryan Klesko .20 .09
❑ 465 Edgar Martinez .20 .09
❑ 466 Tom Pagnozzi .10 .05
❑ 467 Charlie Leibrandt .10 .05
❑ 468 Brian Anderson .30 .14
❑ 469 Harold Baines .20 .09
❑ 470 Tim Belcher .10 .05
❑ 471 Andre Dawson .30 .14
❑ 472 Eric Young .10 .05
❑ 473 Paul Sorrento .10 .05
❑ 474 Luis Gonzalez .10 .05
❑ 475 Rob Deer .10 .05
❑ 476 Mike Piazza 1.25 .55
❑ 477 Kevin Reimer .10 .05
❑ 478 Jeff Gardner .10 .05
❑ 479 Melido Perez .10 .05
❑ 480 Darren Lewis .10 .05
❑ 481 Duane Ward .10 .05
❑ 482 Rey Sanchez .10 .05
❑ 483 Mark Lewis .10 .05
❑ 484 Jeff Conine .20 .09
❑ 485 Joey Cora .20 .09
❑ 486 Trot Nixon .50 .23
❑ 487 Kevin McReynolds .10 .05
❑ 488 Mike Lansing .20 .09
❑ 489 Mike Pagliarulo .10 .05
❑ 490 Mariano Duncan .10 .05
❑ 491 Mike Bordick .10 .05
❑ 492 Kevin Young .10 .05
❑ 493 Dave Valle .10 .05
❑ 494 Wayne Gomes .10 .05
❑ 495 Rafael Palmeiro .30 .14
❑ 496 Deion Sanders .20 .09
❑ 497 Rick Sutcliffe .10 .05
❑ 498 Randy Milligan .10 .05
❑ 499 Carlos Quintana .10 .05
❑ 500 Chris Turner .10 .05
❑ 501 Thomas Howard .10 .05
❑ 502 Greg Swindell .10 .05
❑ 503 Chad Kreuter .10 .05
❑ 504 Eric Davis .20 .09
❑ 505 Dickie Thon .10 .05
❑ 506 Matt Drews .20 .09
❑ 507 Spike Owen .10 .05
❑ 508 Rod Beck .10 .05
❑ 509 Pat Hentgen .20 .09
❑ 510 Sammy Sosa 1.00 .45
❑ 511 J.T. Snow .20 .09
❑ 512 Chuck Carr .10 .05
❑ 513 Bo Jackson .20 .09
❑ 514 Dennis Martinez .20 .09
❑ 515 Phil Hiatt .10 .05
❑ 516 Jeff Kent .20 .09
❑ 517 Brooks Kieschnick .20 .09
❑ 518 Kirk Presley .20 .09
❑ 519 Kevin Seitzer .10 .05
❑ 520 Carlos Garcia .10 .05
❑ 521 Mike Blowers .10 .05
❑ 522 Luis Alicea .10 .05
❑ 523 David Hulse .10 .05
❑ 524 Greg Maddux UER 1.25 .55
(career strikeout totals listed as 113; should be 1134)
❑ 525 Gregg Olson .10 .05
❑ 526 Hal Morris .10 .05
❑ 527 Daron Kirkreit .10 .05
❑ 528 David Nied .10 .05
❑ 529 Jeff Russell .10 .05
❑ 530 Kevin Gross .10 .05
❑ 531 John Doherty .10 .05
❑ 532 Matt Brunson .10 .05
❑ 533 Dave Nilsson .10 .05
❑ 534 Randy Myers .10 .05
❑ 535 Steve Farr .10 .05
❑ 536 Billy Wagner .50 .23
❑ 537 Darnell Coles .10 .05
❑ 538 Frank Tanana .10 .05
❑ 539 Tim Salmon .40 .18
❑ 540 Kim Batiste .10 .05
❑ 541 George Bell .10 .05
❑ 542 Tom Henke .10 .05
❑ 543 Sam Horn .10 .05
❑ 544 Doug Jones .10 .05
❑ 545 Scott Leius .10 .05
❑ 546 Al Martin .10 .05
❑ 547 Bob Welch .10 .05
❑ 548 Scott Christman .20 .09
❑ 549 Norm Charlton .10 .05
❑ 550 Mark McGwire 2.00 .90
❑ 551 Greg McMichael .10 .05
❑ 552 Tim Costo .10 .05
❑ 553 Rodney Bolton .10 .05
❑ 554 Pedro Martinez .50 .23
❑ 555 Marc Valdes .10 .05
❑ 556 Darrell Whitmore .10 .05
❑ 557 Tim Bogar .10 .05
❑ 558 Steve Karsay .10 .05
❑ 559 Danny Bautista .10 .05
❑ 560 Jeffrey Hammonds .20 .09
❑ 561 Aaron Sele .20 .09
❑ 562 Russ Springer .10 .05
❑ 563 Jason Bere .10 .05
❑ 564 Billy Brewer .10 .05
❑ 565 Sterling Hitchcock .20 .09
❑ 566 Bobby Munoz .10 .05
❑ 567 Craig Paquette .10 .05
❑ 568 Bret Boone .20 .09
❑ 569 Dan Peltier .10 .05
❑ 570 Jeromy Burnitz .20 .09
❑ 571 John Wasdin .20 .09
❑ 572 Chipper Jones 1.25 .55
❑ 573 Jamey Wright .20 .09
❑ 574 Jeff Granger .10 .05
❑ 575 Jay Powell .20 .09
❑ 576 Ryan Thompson .10 .05
❑ 577 Lou Frazier .10 .05
❑ 578 Paul Wagner .10 .05
❑ 579 Brad Ausmus .10 .05
❑ 580 Jack Voigt .10 .05
❑ 581 Kevin Rogers .10 .05
❑ 582 Damon Buford .10 .05
❑ 583 Paul Quantrill .10 .05
❑ 584 Marc Newfield .10 .05
❑ 585 Derrek Lee 1.25 .55
❑ 586 Shane Reynolds .20 .09
❑ 587 Cliff Floyd .20 .09
❑ 588 Jeff Schwarz .10 .05
❑ 589 Ross Powell .10 .05
❑ 590 Gerald Williams .10 .05
❑ 591 Mike Trombley .10 .05
❑ 592 Ken Ryan .10 .05
❑ 593 John O'Donoghue .10 .05
❑ 594 Rod Correia .10 .05
❑ 595 Darrell Sherman .10 .05
❑ 596 Steve Scarsone .10 .05
❑ 597 Sherman Obando .10 .05
❑ 598 Kurt Abbott .10 .05
❑ 599 Dave Telgheder .10 .05
❑ 600 Rick Trlicek .10 .05
❑ 601 Carl Everett .10 .05
❑ 602 Luis Ortiz .10 .05
❑ 603 Larry Luebbers .10 .05
❑ 604 Kevin Roberson .10 .05
❑ 605 Butch Huskey .20 .09
❑ 606 Benji Gil .10 .05
❑ 607 Todd Van Poppel .10 .05
❑ 608 Mark Hutton .10 .05

❑ 609 Chip Hale	.10	.05
❑ 610 Matt Maysey	.10	.05
❑ 611 Scott Ruffcorn	.10	.05
❑ 612 Hilly Hathaway	.10	.05
❑ 613 Allen Watson	.10	.05
❑ 614 Carlos Delgado	.30	.14
❑ 615 Roberto Mejia	.10	.05
❑ 616 Turk Wendell	.10	.05
❑ 617 Tony Tarasco	.10	.05
❑ 618 Raul Mondesi	.40	.18
❑ 619 Kevin Stocker	.10	.05
❑ 620 Javier Lopez	.30	.14
❑ 621 Keith Kessinger	.10	.05
❑ 622 Bob Hamelin	.10	.05
❑ 623 John Roper	.10	.05
❑ 624 Lenny Dykstra WS	.10	.05
❑ 625 Joe Carter WS	.10	.05
❑ 626 Jim Abbott HL	.10	.05
❑ 627 Lee Smith HL	.10	.05
❑ 628 Ken Griffey Jr. HL	1.00	.45
❑ 629 Dave Winfield HL	.20	.09
❑ 630 Darryl Kile HL	.10	.05
❑ 631 Frank Thomas AL MVP	.60	.25
❑ 632 Barry Bonds NL MVP	.40	.18
❑ 633 Jack McDowell AL CY	.10	.05
❑ 634 Greg Maddux NL CY	.60	.25
❑ 635 Tim Salmon AL ROY	.20	.09
❑ 636 Mike Piazza NL ROY	.60	.25
❑ 637 Brian Turang	.10	.05
❑ 638 Rondell White	.20	.09
❑ 639 Nigel Wilson	.10	.05
❑ 640 Torii Hunter	.10	.05
❑ 641 Salomon Torres	.10	.05
❑ 642 Kevin Higgins	.10	.05
❑ 643 Eric Wedge	.10	.05
❑ 644 Roger Salkeld	.10	.05
❑ 645 Manny Ramirez	.50	.23
❑ 646 Jeff McNeely	.10	.05
❑ 647 Atlanta Braves CL	.10	.05
❑ 648 Chicago Cubs CL	.10	.05
❑ 649 Cincinnati Reds CL	.10	.05
❑ 650 Colorado Rockies CL	.10	.05
❑ 651 Florida Marlins CL	.10	.05
❑ 652 Houston Astros CL	.10	.05
❑ 653 Los Angeles Dodgers CL	.10	.05
❑ 654 Montreal Expos CL	.10	.05
❑ 655 New York Mets CL	.10	.05
❑ 656 Philadelphia Phillies CL	.10	.05
❑ 657 Pittsburgh Pirates CL	.10	.05
❑ 658 St. Louis Cardinals CL	.10	.05
❑ 659 San Diego Padres CL	.10	.05
❑ 660 San Francisco Giants CL	.10	.05

1994 Score Boys of Summer

	MINT	NRMT
COMPLETE SET (60)	120.00	55.00
COMPLETE SERIES 1 (30)	50.00	22.00
COMPLETE SERIES 2 (30)	70.00	32.00
COMMON CARD (1-60)	1.50	.70

❑ 1 Jeff Conine	3.00	1.35
❑ 2 Aaron Sele	3.00	1.35
❑ 3 Kevin Stocker	1.50	.70
❑ 4 Pat Meares	1.50	.70
❑ 5 Jeromy Burnitz	3.00	1.35
❑ 6 Mike Piazza	25.00	11.00
❑ 7 Allen Watson	1.50	.70
❑ 8 Jeffrey Hammonds	3.00	1.35
❑ 9 Kevin Roberson	1.50	.70
❑ 10 Hilly Hathaway	1.50	.70
❑ 11 Kirk Rueter	1.50	.70
❑ 12 Eduardo Perez	1.50	.70
❑ 13 Ricky Gutierrez	1.50	.70
❑ 14 Domingo Jean	1.50	.70
❑ 15 David Nied	1.50	.70
❑ 16 Wayne Kirby	1.50	.70
❑ 17 Mike Lansing	3.00	1.35
❑ 18 Jason Bere	1.50	.70
❑ 19 Brent Gates	1.50	.70
❑ 20 Javier Lopez	5.00	2.20
❑ 21 Greg McMichael	1.50	.70
❑ 22 David Hulse	1.50	.70
❑ 23 Roberto Mejia	1.50	.70
❑ 24 Tim Salmon	6.00	2.70
❑ 25 Rene Arocha	1.50	.70
❑ 26 Bret Boone	3.00	1.35
❑ 27 David McCarty	1.50	.70
❑ 28 Todd Van Poppel	1.50	.70
❑ 29 Lance Painter	1.50	.70
❑ 30 Erik Pappas	1.50	.70
❑ 31 Chuck Carr	1.50	.70
❑ 32 Mark Hutton	1.50	.70
❑ 33 Jeff McNeely	1.50	.70
❑ 34 Willie Greene	3.00	1.35
❑ 35 Nigel Wilson	1.50	.70
❑ 36 Rondell White	3.00	1.35
❑ 37 Brian Turang	1.50	.70
❑ 38 Manny Ramirez	10.00	4.50
❑ 39 Salomon Torres	1.50	.70
❑ 40 Melvin Nieves	1.50	.70
❑ 41 Ryan Klesko	4.00	1.80
❑ 42 Keith Kessinger	1.50	.70
❑ 43 Brad Ausmus	1.50	.70
❑ 44 Bob Hamelin	1.50	.70
❑ 45 Carlos Delgado	5.00	2.20
❑ 46 Marc Newfield	1.50	.70
❑ 47 Raul Mondesi	6.00	2.70
❑ 48 Tim Costo	1.50	.70
❑ 49 Pedro Martinez	8.00	3.60
❑ 50 Steve Karsay	1.50	.70
❑ 51 Danny Bautista	1.50	.70
❑ 52 Butch Huskey	3.00	1.35
❑ 53 Kurt Abbott	1.50	.70
❑ 54 Darrell Sherman	1.50	.70
❑ 55 Damon Buford	1.50	.70
❑ 56 Ross Powell	1.50	.70
❑ 57 Darrell Whitmore	1.50	.70
❑ 58 Chipper Jones	25.00	11.00
❑ 59 Jeff Granger	1.50	.70
❑ 60 Cliff Floyd	3.00	1.35

1994 Score Cycle

	MINT	NRMT
COMPLETE SET (20)	150.00	70.00
COMMON CARD (TC1-TC20)	2.50	1.10

❑ TC1 Brett Butler	4.00	1.80
❑ TC2 Kenny Lofton	10.00	4.50
❑ TC3 Paul Molitor	10.00	4.50
❑ TC4 Carlos Baerga	4.00	1.80
❑ TC5 Gregg Jefferies Tony Phillips	2.50	1.10
❑ TC6 John Olerud	4.00	1.80
❑ TC7 Charlie Hayes	2.50	1.10
❑ TC8 Lenny Dykstra	4.00	1.80
❑ TC9 Dante Bichette	4.00	1.80
❑ TC10 Devon White	4.00	1.80
❑ TC11 Lance Johnson	2.50	1.10
❑ TC12 Joey Cora Steve Finley	2.50	1.10
❑ TC13 Tony Fernandez	2.50	1.10
❑ TC14 David Hulse Brett Butler	2.50	1.10
❑ TC15 Jay Bell Brian McRae Mickey Morandini	2.50	1.10
❑ TC16 Juan Gonzalez Barry Bonds	20.00	9.00
❑ TC17 Ken Griffey Jr.	50.00	22.00
❑ TC18 Frank Thomas	30.00	13.50
❑ TC19 Dave Justice	10.00	4.50
❑ TC20 Matt Williams Albert Belle	10.00	4.50

1994 Score Dream Team

	MINT	NRMT
COMPLETE SET (10)	60.00	27.00
COMMON CARD (1-10)	2.50	1.10

❑ 1 Mike Mussina	10.00	4.50
❑ 2 Tom Glavine	10.00	4.50
❑ 3 Don Mattingly	15.00	6.75
❑ 4 Carlos Baerga	4.00	1.80
❑ 5 Barry Larkin	6.00	2.70
❑ 6 Matt Williams	6.00	2.70
❑ 7 Juan Gonzalez	25.00	11.00
❑ 8 Andy Van Slyke	4.00	1.80
❑ 9 Larry Walker	10.00	4.50
❑ 10 Mike Stanley	2.50	1.10

1994 Score Gold Stars

	MINT	NRMT
COMPLETE SET (60)	250.00	110.00
COMPLETE NL SERIES (30)	100.00	45.00
COMPLETE AL SERIES (30)	150.00	70.00
COMMON CARD (1-60)	1.50	.70

❑ 1 Barry Bonds	8.00	3.60
❑ 2 Orlando Merced	1.50	.70
❑ 3 Mark Grace	4.00	1.80
❑ 4 Darren Daulton	2.50	1.10

❑ 5 Jeff Blauser	1.50	.70
❑ 6 Deion Sanders	2.50	1.10
❑ 7 John Kruk	2.50	1.10
❑ 8 Jeff Bagwell	10.00	4.50
❑ 9 Gregg Jefferies	1.50	.70
❑ 10 Matt Williams	4.00	1.80
❑ 11 Andres Galarraga	6.00	2.70
❑ 12 Jay Bell	2.50	1.10
❑ 13 Mike Piazza	20.00	9.00
❑ 14 Ron Gant	2.50	1.10
❑ 15 Barry Larkin	4.00	1.80
❑ 16 Tom Glavine	6.00	2.70
❑ 17 Lenny Dykstra	2.50	1.10
❑ 18 Fred McGriff	4.00	1.80
❑ 19 Andy Van Slyke	2.50	1.10
❑ 20 Gary Sheffield	6.00	2.70
❑ 21 John Burkett	1.50	.70
❑ 22 Dante Bichette	2.50	1.10
❑ 23 Tony Gwynn	15.00	6.75
❑ 24 Dave Justice	6.00	2.70
❑ 25 Marquis Grissom	2.50	1.10
❑ 26 Bobby Bonilla	2.50	1.10
❑ 27 Larry Walker	6.00	2.70
❑ 28 Brett Butler	2.50	1.10
❑ 29 Robby Thompson	1.50	.70
❑ 30 Jeff Conine	2.50	1.10
❑ 31 Joe Carter	2.50	1.10
❑ 32 Ken Griffey Jr.	30.00	13.50
❑ 33 Juan Gonzalez	15.00	6.75
❑ 34 Rickey Henderson	6.00	2.70
❑ 35 Bo Jackson	2.50	1.10
❑ 36 Cal Ripken	25.00	11.00
❑ 37 John Olerud	2.50	1.10
❑ 38 Carlos Baerga	2.50	1.10
❑ 39 Jack McDowell	1.50	.70
❑ 40 Cecil Fielder	2.50	1.10
❑ 41 Kenny Lofton	6.00	2.70
❑ 42 Roberto Alomar	6.00	2.70
❑ 43 Randy Johnson	6.00	2.70
❑ 44 Tim Salmon	6.00	2.70
❑ 45 Frank Thomas	20.00	9.00
❑ 46 Albert Belle	8.00	3.60
❑ 47 Greg Vaughn	2.50	1.10
❑ 48 Travis Fryman	2.50	1.10
❑ 49 Don Mattingly	10.00	4.50
❑ 50 Wade Boggs	6.00	2.70
❑ 51 Mo Vaughn	8.00	3.60
❑ 52 Kirby Puckett	10.00	4.50
❑ 53 Devon White	2.50	1.10
❑ 54 Tony Phillips	1.50	.70
❑ 55 Brian Harper	1.50	.70
❑ 56 Chad Curtis	1.50	.70
❑ 57 Paul Molitor	6.00	2.70
❑ 58 Ivan Rodriguez	8.00	3.60
❑ 59 Rafael Palmeiro	4.00	1.80
❑ 60 Brian McRae	1.50	.70

1994 Score Rookie/Traded

	MINT	NRMT
COMPLETE SET (165)	10.00	4.50
COMMON CARD (RT1-RT165)	.10	.05

Card	MINT	NRMT
❑ RT1 Will Clark	.40	.18
❑ RT2 Lee Smith	.20	.09
❑ RT3 Bo Jackson	.20	.09
❑ RT4 Ellis Burks	.20	.09
❑ RT5 Eddie Murray	.40	.18
❑ RT6 Delino DeShields	.10	.05
❑ RT7 Erik Hanson	.10	.05
❑ RT8 Rafael Palmeiro	.30	.14
❑ RT9 Luis Polonia	.10	.05
❑ RT10 Omar Vizquel	.20	.09
❑ RT11 Kurt Abbott	.10	.05
❑ RT12 Vince Coleman	.10	.05
❑ RT13 Rickey Henderson	.40	.18
❑ RT14 Terry Mulholland	.10	.05
❑ RT15 Greg Hibbard	.10	.05
❑ RT16 Walt Weiss	.10	.05
❑ RT17 Chris Sabo	.10	.05
❑ RT18 Dave Henderson	.10	.05
❑ RT19 Rick Sutcliffe	.10	.05
❑ RT20 Harold Reynolds	.10	.05
❑ RT21 Jack Morris	.20	.09
❑ RT22 Dan Wilson	.10	.05
❑ RT23 Dave Magadan	.10	.05
❑ RT24 Dennis Martinez	.20	.09
❑ RT25 Wes Chamberlain	.10	.05
❑ RT26 Otis Nixon	.10	.05
❑ RT27 Eric Anthony	.10	.05
❑ RT28 Randy Milligan	.10	.05
❑ RT29 Julio Franco	.10	.05
❑ RT30 Kevin McReynolds	.10	.05
❑ RT31 Anthony Young	.10	.05
❑ RT32 Brian Harper	.10	.05
❑ RT33 Gene Harris	.10	.05
❑ RT34 Eddie Taubensee	.10	.05
❑ RT35 David Segui	.20	.09
❑ RT36 Stan Javier	.10	.05
❑ RT37 Felix Fermin	.10	.05
❑ RT38 Darrin Jackson	.10	.05
❑ RT39 Tony Fernandez	.10	.05
❑ RT40 Jose Vizcaino	.10	.05
❑ RT41 Willie Banks	.10	.05
❑ RT42 Brian Hunter	.10	.05
❑ RT43 Reggie Jefferson	.10	.05
❑ RT44 Junior Felix	.10	.05
❑ RT45 Jack Armstrong	.10	.05
❑ RT46 Bip Roberts	.10	.05
❑ RT47 Jerry Browne	.10	.05
❑ RT48 Marvin Freeman	.10	.05
❑ RT49 Jody Reed	.10	.05
❑ RT50 Alex Cole	.10	.05
❑ RT51 Sid Fernandez	.10	.05
❑ RT52 Pete Smith	.10	.05
❑ RT53 Xavier Hernandez	.10	.05
❑ RT54 Scott Sanderson	.10	.05
❑ RT55 Turner Ward	.10	.05
❑ RT56 Rex Hudler	.10	.05
❑ RT57 Deion Sanders	.20	.09
❑ RT58 Sid Bream	.10	.05
❑ RT59 Tony Pena	.10	.05
❑ RT60 Bret Boone	.20	.09
❑ RT61 Bobby Ayala	.10	.05
❑ RT62 Pedro Martinez	.50	.23
❑ RT63 Howard Johnson	.10	.05
❑ RT64 Mark Portugal	.10	.05
❑ RT65 Roberto Kelly	.10	.05
❑ RT66 Spike Owen	.10	.05
❑ RT67 Jeff Treadway	.10	.05
❑ RT68 Mike Harkey	.10	.05
❑ RT69 Doug Jones	.10	.05
❑ RT70 Steve Farr	.10	.05
❑ RT71 Billy Taylor	.10	.05
❑ RT72 Manny Ramirez	.50	.23
❑ RT73 Bob Hamelin	.10	.05
❑ RT74 Steve Karsay	.10	.05
❑ RT75 Ryan Klesko	.20	.09
❑ RT76 Cliff Floyd	.20	.09
❑ RT77 Jeffrey Hammonds	.20	.09
❑ RT78 Javier Lopez	.30	.14
❑ RT79 Roger Salkeld	.10	.05
❑ RT80 Hector Carrasco	.10	.05
❑ RT81 Gerald Williams	.10	.05
❑ RT82 Raul Mondesi	.40	.18
❑ RT83 Sterling Hitchcock	.20	.09
❑ RT84 Danny Bautista	.10	.05
❑ RT85 Chris Turner	.10	.05
❑ RT86 Shane Reynolds	.20	.09
❑ RT87 Rondell White	.20	.09
❑ RT88 Salomon Torres	.10	.05
❑ RT89 Turk Wendell	.10	.05
❑ RT90 Tony Tarasco	.10	.05
❑ RT91 Shawn Green	.20	.09
❑ RT92 Greg Colbrunn	.10	.05
❑ RT93 Eddie Zambrano	.10	.05
❑ RT94 Rich Becker	.10	.05
❑ RT95 Chris Gomez	.10	.05
❑ RT96 John Patterson	.10	.05
❑ RT97 Derek Parks	.10	.05
❑ RT98 Rich Rowland	.10	.05
❑ RT99 James Mouton	.10	.05
❑ RT100 Tim Hyers	.10	.05
❑ RT101 Jose Valentin	.10	.05
❑ RT102 Carlos Delgado	.30	.14
❑ RT103 Robert Eenhoorn	.10	.05
❑ RT104 John Hudek	.10	.05
❑ RT105 Domingo Cedeno	.10	.05
❑ RT106 Denny Hocking	.10	.05
❑ RT107 Greg Pirkl	.10	.05
❑ RT108 Mark Smith	.10	.05
❑ RT109 Paul Shuey	.10	.05
❑ RT110 Jorge Fabregas	.10	.05
❑ RT111 Rikkert Faneyte	.10	.05
❑ RT112 Rob Butler	.10	.05
❑ RT113 Darren Oliver	.20	.09
❑ RT114 Troy O'Leary	.20	.09
❑ RT115 Scott Brow	.10	.05
❑ RT116 Tony Eusebio	.10	.05
❑ RT117 Carlos Reyes	.10	.05
❑ RT118 J.R. Phillips	.10	.05
❑ RT119 Alex Diaz	.10	.05
❑ RT120 Charles Johnson	.20	.09
❑ RT121 Nate Minchey	.10	.05
❑ RT122 Scott Sanders	.10	.05
❑ RT123 Daryl Boston	.10	.05
❑ RT124 Joey Hamilton	.40	.18
❑ RT125 Brian Anderson	.30	.14
❑ RT126 Dan Miceli	.10	.05
❑ RT127 Tom Brunansky	.10	.05
❑ RT128 Dave Staton	.10	.05
❑ RT129 Mike Oquist	.10	.05
❑ RT130 John Mabry	.10	.05
❑ RT131 Norberto Martin	.10	.05
❑ RT132 Hector Fajardo	.10	.05
❑ RT133 Mark Hutton	.10	.05
❑ RT134 Fernando Vina	.10	.05
❑ RT135 Lee Tinsley	.10	.05
❑ RT136 Chan Ho Park	1.50	.70
❑ RT137 Paul Spoljaric	.10	.05
❑ RT138 Matias Carrillo	.10	.05
❑ RT139 Mark Kiefer	.10	.05
❑ RT140 Stan Royer	.10	.05
❑ RT141 Bryan Eversgerd	.10	.05
❑ RT142 Brian L.Hunter	.20	.09
❑ RT143 Joe Hall	.10	.05
❑ RT144 Johnny Ruffin	.10	.05
❑ RT145 Alex Gonzalez	.10	.05
❑ RT146 Keith Lockhart	.10	.05
❑ RT147 Tom Marsh	.10	.05
❑ RT148 Tony Longmire	.10	.05
❑ RT149 Keith Mitchell	.10	.05
❑ RT150 Melvin Nieves	.10	.05
❑ RT151 Kelly Stinnett	.10	.05
❑ RT152 Miguel Jimenez	.10	.05
❑ RT153 Jeff Juden	.10	.05
❑ RT154 Matt Walbeck	.10	.05
❑ RT155 Marc Newfield	.10	.05
❑ RT156 Matt Mieske	.10	.05
❑ RT157 Marcus Moore	.10	.05
❑ RT158 Jose Lima SP	1.00	.45
❑ RT159 Mike Kelly	.10	.05
❑ RT160 Jim Edmonds	.40	.18
❑ RT161 Steve Trachsel	.10	.05
❑ RT162 Greg Blosser	.10	.05
❑ RT163 Marc Acre	.10	.05
❑ RT164 AL Checklist	.10	.05
❑ RT165 NL Checklist	.10	.05
❑ HC1 Alex Rodriguez Call-Up Redemption	100.00	45.00

1994 Score Rookie/Traded Changing Places

	MINT	NRMT
COMPLETE SET (10)	30.00	13.50
COMMON CARD (CP1-CP10)	2.50	1.10
❑ CP1 Will Clark	8.00	3.60
❑ CP2 Rafael Palmeiro	4.00	1.80
❑ CP3 Roberto Kelly	2.50	1.10
❑ CP4 Bo Jackson	4.00	1.80
❑ CP5 Otis Nixon	2.50	1.10
❑ CP6 Rickey Henderson	8.00	3.60
❑ CP7 Ellis Burks	4.00	1.80
❑ CP8 Lee Smith	4.00	1.80
❑ CP9 Delino DeShields	2.50	1.10
❑ CP10 Deion Sanders	4.00	1.80

1994 Score Rookie/Traded Super Rookies

	MINT	NRMT
COMPLETE SET (18)	60.00	27.00
COMMON CARD (SU1-SU18)	2.50	1.10
❑ SU1 Carlos Delgado	6.00	2.70
❑ SU2 Manny Ramirez	12.00	5.50
❑ SU3 Ryan Klesko	5.00	2.20
❑ SU4 Raul Mondesi	8.00	3.60
❑ SU5 Bob Hamelin	2.50	1.10
❑ SU6 Steve Karsay	2.50	1.10
❑ SU7 Jeffrey Hammonds	4.00	1.80
❑ SU8 Cliff Floyd	4.00	1.80
❑ SU9 Kurt Abbott	2.50	1.10
❑ SU10 Marc Newfield	2.50	1.10
❑ SU11 Javier Lopez	6.00	2.70
❑ SU12 Rich Becker	2.50	1.10
❑ SU13 Greg Pirkl	2.50	1.10
❑ SU14 Rondell White	4.00	1.80
❑ SU15 James Mouton	2.50	1.10
❑ SU16 Tony Tarasco	2.50	1.10
❑ SU17 Brian Anderson	6.00	2.70
❑ SU18 Jim Edmonds	8.00	3.60

1995 Score

	MINT	NRMT
COMPLETE SET (605)	24.00	11.00
COMPLETE SERIES 1 (330)	12.00	5.50
COMPLETE SERIES 2 (275)	12.00	5.50
COMMON CARD (1-605)	.10	.05
❑ 1 Frank Thomas	1.25	.55
❑ 2 Roberto Alomar	.40	.18
❑ 3 Cal Ripken	1.50	.70
❑ 4 Jose Canseco	.40	.18
❑ 5 Matt Williams	.20	.09
❑ 6 Esteban Beltre	.10	.05
❑ 7 Domingo Cedeno	.10	.05
❑ 8 John Valentin	.20	.09
❑ 9 Glenallen Hill	.10	.05
❑ 10 Rafael Belliard	.10	.05
❑ 11 Randy Myers	.10	.05
❑ 12 Mo Vaughn	.50	.23
❑ 13 Hector Carrasco	.10	.05
❑ 14 Chili Davis	.20	.09
❑ 15 Dante Bichette	.20	.09
❑ 16 Darrin Jackson	.10	.05
❑ 17 Mike Piazza	1.25	.55
❑ 18 Junior Felix	.10	.05
❑ 19 Moises Alou	.30	.14
❑ 20 Mark Gubicza	.10	.05
❑ 21 Bret Saberhagen	.20	.09
❑ 22 Lenny Dykstra	.20	.09
❑ 23 Steve Howe	.10	.05
❑ 24 Mark Dewey	.10	.05
❑ 25 Brian Harper	.10	.05
❑ 26 Ozzie Smith	.50	.23
❑ 27 Scott Erickson	.20	.09
❑ 28 Tony Gwynn	1.00	.45
❑ 29 Bob Welch	.10	.05
❑ 30 Barry Bonds	.50	.23
❑ 31 Leo Gomez	.10	.05
❑ 32 Greg Maddux	1.25	.55
❑ 33 Mike Greenwell	.10	.05
❑ 34 Sammy Sosa	1.00	.45
❑ 35 Darnell Coles	.10	.05
❑ 36 Tommy Greene	.10	.05
❑ 37 Will Clark	.40	.18
❑ 38 Steve Ontiveros	.10	.05
❑ 39 Stan Javier	.10	.05
❑ 40 Bip Roberts	.10	.05
❑ 41 Paul O'Neill	.20	.09
❑ 42 Bill Haselman	.10	.05
❑ 43 Shane Mack	.10	.05
❑ 44 Orlando Merced	.10	.05
❑ 45 Kevin Seitzer	.10	.05
❑ 46 Trevor Hoffman	.20	.09
❑ 47 Greg Gagne	.10	.05
❑ 48 Jeff Kent	.20	.09
❑ 49 Tony Phillips	.10	.05
❑ 50 Ken Hill	.10	.05
❑ 51 Carlos Baerga	.20	.09
❑ 52 Henry Rodriguez	.20	.09
❑ 53 Scott Sanderson	.10	.05
❑ 54 Jeff Conine	.20	.09
❑ 55 Chris Turner	.10	.05
❑ 56 Ken Caminiti	.30	.14
❑ 57 Harold Baines	.20	.09
❑ 58 Charlie Hayes	.10	.05
❑ 59 Roberto Kelly	.10	.05
❑ 60 John Olerud	.20	.09
❑ 61 Tim Davis	.10	.05
❑ 62 Rich Rowland	.10	.05
❑ 63 Rey Sanchez	.10	.05
❑ 64 Junior Ortiz	.10	.05
❑ 65 Ricky Gutierrez	.10	.05
❑ 66 Rex Hudler	.10	.05
❑ 67 Johnny Ruffin	.10	.05
❑ 68 Jay Buhner	.20	.09
❑ 69 Tom Pagnozzi	.10	.05
❑ 70 Julio Franco	.10	.05
❑ 71 Eric Young	.10	.05
❑ 72 Mike Bordick	.10	.05
❑ 73 Don Slaught	.10	.05
❑ 74 Goose Gossage	.20	.09
❑ 75 Lonnie Smith	.10	.05
❑ 76 Jimmy Key	.20	.09
❑ 77 Dave Hollins	.10	.05
❑ 78 Mickey Tettleton	.10	.05
❑ 79 Luis Gonzalez	.10	.05
❑ 80 Dave Winfield	.40	.18
❑ 81 Ryan Thompson	.10	.05
❑ 82 Felix Jose	.10	.05
❑ 83 Rusty Meacham	.10	.05
❑ 84 Darryl Hamilton	.10	.05
❑ 85 John Wetteland	.20	.09
❑ 86 Tom Brunansky	.10	.05
❑ 87 Mark Lemke	.10	.05
❑ 88 Spike Owen	.10	.05
❑ 89 Shawon Dunston	.10	.05
❑ 90 Wilson Alvarez	.20	.09
❑ 91 Lee Smith	.20	.09
❑ 92 Scott Kamieniecki	.10	.05
❑ 93 Jacob Brumfield	.10	.05
❑ 94 Kirk Gibson	.20	.09
❑ 95 Joe Girardi	.10	.05
❑ 96 Mike Macfarlane	.10	.05
❑ 97 Greg Colbrunn	.10	.05
❑ 98 Ricky Bones	.10	.05
❑ 99 Delino DeShields	.10	.05
❑ 100 Pat Meares	.10	.05
❑ 101 Jeff Fassero	.10	.05
❑ 102 Jim Leyritz	.20	.09
❑ 103 Gary Redus	.10	.05
❑ 104 Terry Steinbach	.20	.09
❑ 105 Kevin McReynolds	.10	.05
❑ 106 Felix Fermin	.10	.05
❑ 107 Danny Jackson	.10	.05
❑ 108 Chris James	.10	.05
❑ 109 Jeff King	.10	.05
❑ 110 Pat Hentgen	.20	.09
❑ 111 Gerald Perry	.10	.05
❑ 112 Tim Raines	.20	.09
❑ 113 Eddie Williams	.10	.05
❑ 114 Jamie Moyer	.10	.05
❑ 115 Bud Black	.10	.05
❑ 116 Chris Gomez	.10	.05
❑ 117 Luis Lopez	.10	.05
❑ 118 Roger Clemens	.75	.35
❑ 119 Javier Lopez	.20	.09
❑ 120 Dave Nilsson	.10	.05
❑ 121 Karl Rhodes	.10	.05
❑ 122 Rick Aguilera	.10	.05
❑ 123 Tony Fernandez	.10	.05
❑ 124 Bernie Williams	.40	.18
❑ 125 James Mouton	.10	.05
❑ 126 Mark Langston	.10	.05
❑ 127 Mike Lansing	.10	.05
❑ 128 Tino Martinez	.40	.18
❑ 129 Joe Orsulak	.10	.05
❑ 130 David Hulse	.10	.05
❑ 131 Pete Incaviglia	.10	.05
❑ 132 Mark Clark	.10	.05
❑ 133 Tony Eusebio	.10	.05
❑ 134 Chuck Finley	.20	.09
❑ 135 Lou Frazier	.10	.05
❑ 136 Craig Grebeck	.10	.05
❑ 137 Kelly Stinnett	.10	.05
❑ 138 Paul Shuey	.10	.05
❑ 139 David Nied	.10	.05
❑ 140 Billy Brewer	.10	.05
❑ 141 Dave Weathers	.10	.05
❑ 142 Scott Leius	.10	.05
❑ 143 Brian Jordan	.20	.09
❑ 144 Melido Perez	.10	.05
❑ 145 Tony Tarasco	.10	.05

146	Dan Wilson	.10	.05
147	Rondell White	.20	.09
148	Mike Henneman	.10	.05
149	Brian Johnson	.10	.05
150	Tom Henke	.10	.05
151	John Patterson	.10	.05
152	Bobby Witt	.10	.05
153	Eddie Taubensee	.10	.05
154	Pat Borders	.10	.05
155	Ramon Martinez	.20	.09
156	Mike Kingery	.10	.05
157	Zane Smith	.10	.05
158	Benito Santiago	.10	.05
159	Matias Carrillo	.10	.05
160	Scott Brosius	.20	.09
161	Dave Clark	.10	.05
162	Mark McLemore	.10	.05
163	Curt Schilling	.20	.09
164	J.T. Snow	.20	.09
165	Rod Beck	.10	.05
166	Scott Fletcher	.10	.05
167	Bob Tewksbury	.10	.05
168	Mike LaValliere	.10	.05
169	Dave Hansen	.10	.05
170	Pedro Martinez	.40	.18
171	Kirk Rueter	.10	.05
172	Jose Lind	.10	.05
173	Luis Alicea	.10	.05
174	Mike Moore	.10	.05
175	Andy Ashby	.10	.05
176	Jody Reed	.10	.05
177	Darryl Kile	.20	.09
178	Carl Willis	.10	.05
179	Jeromy Burnitz	.20	.09
180	Mike Gallego	.10	.05
181	Bill VanLandingham	.10	.05
182	Sid Fernandez	.10	.05
183	Kim Batiste	.10	.05
184	Greg Myers	.10	.05
185	Steve Avery	.10	.05
186	Steve Farr	.10	.05
187	Robb Nen	.10	.05
188	Dan Pasqua	.10	.05
189	Bruce Ruffin	.10	.05
190	Jose Valentin	.10	.05
191	Willie Banks	.10	.05
192	Mike Aldrete	.10	.05
193	Randy Milligan	.10	.05
194	Steve Karsay	.10	.05
195	Mike Stanley	.10	.05
196	Jose Mesa	.10	.05
197	Tom Browning	.10	.05
198	John Vander Wal	.10	.05
199	Kevin Brown	.30	.14
200	Mike Oquist	.10	.05
201	Greg Swindell	.10	.05
202	Eddie Zambrano	.10	.05
203	Joe Boever	.10	.05
204	Gary Varsho	.10	.05
205	Chris Gwynn	.10	.05
206	David Howard	.10	.05
207	Jerome Walton	.10	.05
208	Danny Darwin	.10	.05
209	Darryl Strawberry	.20	.09
210	Todd Van Poppel	.10	.05
211	Scott Livingstone	.10	.05
212	Dave Fleming	.10	.05
213	Todd Worrell	.10	.05
214	Carlos Delgado	.20	.09
215	Bill Pecota	.10	.05
216	Jim Lindeman	.10	.05
217	Rick White	.10	.05
218	Jose Oquendo	.10	.05
219	Tony Castillo	.10	.05
220	Fernando Vina	.10	.05
221	Jeff Bagwell	.60	.25
222	Randy Johnson	.40	.18
223	Albert Belle	.50	.23
224	Chuck Carr	.10	.05
225	Mark Leiter	.10	.05
226	Hal Morris	.10	.05
227	Robin Ventura	.20	.09
228	Mike Munoz	.10	.05
229	Jim Thome	.40	.18
230	Mario Diaz	.10	.05
231	John Doherty	.10	.05
232	Bobby Jones	.10	.05
233	Raul Mondesi	.30	.14
234	Ricky Jordan	.10	.05
235	John Jaha	.10	.05
236	Carlos Garcia	.10	.05
237	Kirby Puckett	.60	.25
238	Orel Hershiser	.20	.09
239	Don Mattingly	.60	.25
240	Sid Bream	.10	.05
241	Brent Gates	.10	.05
242	Tony Longmire	.10	.05
243	Robby Thompson	.10	.05
244	Rick Sutcliffe	.10	.05
245	Dean Palmer	.20	.09
246	Marquis Grissom	.20	.09
247	Paul Molitor	.40	.18
248	Mark Carreon	.10	.05
249	Jack Voigt	.10	.05
250	Greg McMichael UER (photo on front is Mike Stanton)	.10	.05
251	Damon Berryhill	.10	.05
252	Brian Dorsett	.10	.05
253	Jim Edmonds	.30	.14
254	Barry Larkin	.30	.14
255	Jack McDowell	.10	.05
256	Wally Joyner	.20	.09
257	Eddie Murray	.40	.18
258	Lenny Webster	.10	.05
259	Milt Cuyler	.10	.05
260	Todd Benzinger	.10	.05
261	Vince Coleman	.10	.05
262	Todd Stottlemyre	.10	.05
263	Turner Ward	.10	.05
264	Ray Lankford	.20	.09
265	Matt Walbeck	.10	.05
266	Deion Sanders	.20	.09
267	Gerald Williams	.10	.05
268	Jim Gott	.10	.05
269	Jeff Frye	.10	.05
270	Jose Rijo	.10	.05
271	Dave Justice	.40	.18
272	Ismael Valdes	.20	.09
273	Ben McDonald	.10	.05
274	Darren Lewis	.10	.05
275	Graeme Lloyd	.10	.05
276	Luis Ortiz	.10	.05
277	Julian Tavarez	.10	.05
278	Mark Dalesandro	.10	.05
279	Brett Merriman	.10	.05
280	Ricky Bottalico	.20	.09
281	Robert Eenhoorn	.10	.05
282	Rikkert Faneyte	.10	.05
283	Mike Kelly	.10	.05
284	Mark Smith	.10	.05
285	Turk Wendell	.10	.05
286	Greg Blosser	.10	.05
287	Garey Ingram	.10	.05
288	Jorge Fabregas	.10	.05
289	Blaise Ilsley	.10	.05
290	Joe Hall	.10	.05
291	Orlando Miller	.10	.05
292	Jose Lima	.10	.05
293	Greg O'Halloran	.10	.05
294	Mark Kiefer	.10	.05
295	Jose Oliva	.10	.05
296	Rich Becker	.10	.05
297	Brian L. Hunter	.20	.09
298	Dave Silvestri	.10	.05
299	Armando Benitez	.10	.05
300	Darren Dreifort	.20	.09
301	John Mabry	.10	.05
302	Greg Pirkl	.10	.05
303	J.R. Phillips	.10	.05
304	Shawn Green	.20	.09
305	Roberto Petagine	.10	.05
306	Keith Lockhart	.10	.05
307	Jonathan Hurst	.10	.05
308	Paul Spoljaric	.10	.05
309	Mike Lieberthal	.10	.05
310	Garret Anderson	.20	.09
311	John Johnstone	.10	.05
312	Alex Rodriguez	1.50	.70
313	Kent Mercker HL	.10	.05
314	John Valentin HL	.10	.05
315	Kenny Rogers HL	.10	.05
316	Fred McGriff HL	.10	.05
317	Team Checklists	.10	.05
318	Team Checklists	.10	.05
319	Team Checklists	.10	.05
320	Team Checklists	.10	.05
321	Team Checklists	.10	.05
322	Team Checklists	.10	.05
323	Team Checklists	.10	.05
324	Team Checklists	.10	.05
325	Team Checklists	.10	.05
326	Team Checklists	.10	.05
327	Team Checklists	.10	.05
328	Team Checklists	.10	.05
329	Team Checklists	.10	.05
330	Team Checklists	.10	.05
331	Pedro Munoz	.10	.05
332	Ryan Klesko	.20	.09
333	Andre Dawson	.30	.14
334	Derrick May	.10	.05
335	Aaron Sele	.20	.09
336	Kevin Mitchell	.10	.05
337	Steve Trachsel	.10	.05
338	Andres Galarraga	.40	.18
339	Terry Pendleton	.10	.05
340	Gary Sheffield	.30	.14
341	Travis Fryman	.20	.09
342	Bo Jackson	.20	.09
343	Gary Gaetti	.20	.09
344	Brett Butler	.20	.09
345	B.J. Surhoff	.20	.09
346	Larry Walker	.40	.18
347	Kevin Tapani	.10	.05
348	Rick Wilkins	.10	.05
349	Wade Boggs	.40	.18
350	Mariano Duncan	.10	.05
351	Ruben Sierra	.10	.05
352	Andy Van Slyke	.20	.09
353	Reggie Jefferson	.10	.05
354	Gregg Jefferies	.10	.05
355	Tim Naehring	.10	.05
356	John Roper	.10	.05
357	Joe Carter	.20	.09
358	Kurt Abbott	.10	.05
359	Lenny Harris	.10	.05
360	Lance Johnson	.10	.05
361	Brian Anderson	.20	.09
362	Jim Eisenreich	.10	.05
363	Jerry Browne	.10	.05
364	Mark Grace	.30	.14
365	Devon White	.20	.09
366	Reggie Sanders	.20	.09
367	Ivan Rodriguez	.50	.23
368	Kirt Manwaring	.10	.05
369	Pat Kelly	.10	.05
370	Ellis Burks	.20	.09
371	Charles Nagy	.20	.09
372	Kevin Bass	.10	.05
373	Lou Whitaker	.20	.09
374	Rene Arocha	.10	.05
375	Derek Parks	.10	.05
376	Mark Whiten	.10	.05
377	Mark McGwire	2.00	.90
378	Doug Drabek	.10	.05
379	Greg Vaughn	.20	.09
380	Al Martin	.10	.05
381	Ron Darling	.10	.05
382	Tim Wallach	.10	.05
383	Alan Trammell	.20	.09
384	Randy Velarde	.10	.05
385	Chris Sabo	.10	.05
386	Wil Cordero	.10	.05
387	Darrin Fletcher	.10	.05
388	David Segui	.20	.09
389	Steve Buechele	.10	.05
390	Dave Gallagher	.10	.05
391	Thomas Howard	.10	.05
392	Chad Curtis	.10	.05
393	Cal Eldred	.10	.05
394	Jason Bere	.10	.05
395	Bret Barberie	.10	.05
396	Paul Sorrento	.10	.05
397	Steve Finley	.20	.09
398	Cecil Fielder	.20	.09
399	Eric Karros	.20	.09

No.	Player	MINT	NRMT
❑ 400	Jeff Montgomery	.10	.05
❑ 401	Cliff Floyd	.20	.09
❑ 402	Matt Mieske	.10	.05
❑ 403	Brian Hunter	.10	.05
❑ 404	Alex Cole	.10	.05
❑ 405	Kevin Stocker	.10	.05
❑ 406	Eric Davis	.20	.09
❑ 407	Marvin Freeman	.10	.05
❑ 408	Dennis Eckersley	.20	.09
❑ 409	Todd Zeile	.10	.05
❑ 410	Keith Mitchell	.10	.05
❑ 411	Andy Benes	.20	.09
❑ 412	Juan Bell	.10	.05
❑ 413	Royce Clayton	.10	.05
❑ 414	Ed Sprague	.10	.05
❑ 415	Mike Mussina	.40	.18
❑ 416	Todd Hundley	.20	.09
❑ 417	Pat Listach	.10	.05
❑ 418	Joe Oliver	.10	.05
❑ 419	Rafael Palmeiro	.30	.14
❑ 420	Tim Salmon	.40	.18
❑ 421	Brady Anderson	.20	.09
❑ 422	Kenny Lofton	.40	.18
❑ 423	Craig Biggio	.40	.18
❑ 424	Bobby Bonilla	.20	.09
❑ 425	Kenny Rogers	.10	.05
❑ 426	Derek Bell	.20	.09
❑ 427	Scott Cooper	.10	.05
❑ 428	Ozzie Guillen	.10	.05
❑ 429	Omar Vizquel	.20	.09
❑ 430	Phil Plantier	.10	.05
❑ 431	Chuck Knoblauch	.40	.18
❑ 432	Darren Daulton	.20	.09
❑ 433	Bob Hamelin	.10	.05
❑ 434	Tom Glavine	.40	.18
❑ 435	Walt Weiss	.10	.05
❑ 436	Jose Vizcaino	.10	.05
❑ 437	Ken Griffey Jr.	2.00	.90
❑ 438	Jay Bell	.20	.09
❑ 439	Juan Gonzalez	1.00	.45
❑ 440	Jeff Blauser	.10	.05
❑ 441	Rickey Henderson	.40	.18
❑ 442	Bobby Ayala	.10	.05
❑ 443	David Cone	.30	.14
❑ 444	Pedro J. Martinez	.40	.18
❑ 445	Manny Ramirez	.40	.18
❑ 446	Mark Portugal	.10	.05
❑ 447	Damion Easley	.20	.09
❑ 448	Gary DiSarcina	.10	.05
❑ 449	Roberto Hernandez	.10	.05
❑ 450	Jeffrey Hammonds	.20	.09
❑ 451	Jeff Treadway	.10	.05
❑ 452	Jim Abbott	.20	.09
❑ 453	Carlos Rodriguez	.10	.05
❑ 454	Joey Cora	.20	.09
❑ 455	Bret Boone	.20	.09
❑ 456	Danny Tartabull	.10	.05
❑ 457	John Franco	.20	.09
❑ 458	Roger Salkeld	.10	.05
❑ 459	Fred McGriff	.30	.14
❑ 460	Pedro Astacio	.10	.05
❑ 461	Jon Lieber	.10	.05
❑ 462	Luis Polonia	.10	.05
❑ 463	Geronimo Pena	.10	.05
❑ 464	Tom Gordon	.10	.05
❑ 465	Brad Ausmus	.10	.05
❑ 466	Willie McGee	.20	.09
❑ 467	Doug Jones	.10	.05
❑ 468	John Smoltz	.20	.09
❑ 469	Troy Neel	.10	.05
❑ 470	Luis Sojo	.10	.05
❑ 471	John Smiley	.10	.05
❑ 472	Rafael Bournigal	.10	.05
❑ 473	Bill Taylor	.10	.05
❑ 474	Juan Guzman	.10	.05
❑ 475	Dave Magadan	.10	.05
❑ 476	Mike Devereaux	.10	.05
❑ 477	Andujar Cedeno	.10	.05
❑ 478	Edgar Martinez	.20	.09
❑ 479	Milt Thompson	.10	.05
❑ 480	Allen Watson	.10	.05
❑ 481	Ron Karkovice	.10	.05
❑ 482	Joey Hamilton	.20	.09
❑ 483	Vinny Castilla	.30	.14
❑ 484	Tim Belcher	.10	.05
❑ 485	Bernard Gilkey	.10	.05
❑ 486	Scott Servais	.10	.05
❑ 487	Cory Snyder	.10	.05
❑ 488	Mel Rojas	.10	.05
❑ 489	Carlos Reyes	.10	.05
❑ 490	Chip Hale	.10	.05
❑ 491	Bill Swift	.10	.05
❑ 492	Pat Rapp	.10	.05
❑ 493	Brian McRae	.10	.05
❑ 494	Mickey Morandini	.10	.05
❑ 495	Tony Pena	.10	.05
❑ 496	Danny Bautista	.10	.05
❑ 497	Armando Reynoso	.10	.05
❑ 498	Ken Ryan	.10	.05
❑ 499	Billy Ripken	.10	.05
❑ 500	Pat Mahomes	.10	.05
❑ 501	Mark Acre	.10	.05
❑ 502	Geronimo Berroa	.10	.05
❑ 503	Norberto Martin	.10	.05
❑ 504	Chad Kreuter	.10	.05
❑ 505	Howard Johnson	.10	.05
❑ 506	Eric Anthony	.10	.05
❑ 507	Mark Wohlers	.10	.05
❑ 508	Scott Sanders	.10	.05
❑ 509	Pete Harnisch	.10	.05
❑ 510	Wes Chamberlain	.10	.05
❑ 511	Tom Candiotti	.10	.05
❑ 512	Albie Lopez	.10	.05
❑ 513	Denny Neagle	.20	.09
❑ 514	Sean Berry	.10	.05
❑ 515	Billy Hatcher	.10	.05
❑ 516	Todd Jones	.10	.05
❑ 517	Wayne Kirby	.10	.05
❑ 518	Butch Henry	.10	.05
❑ 519	Sandy Alomar Jr.	.20	.09
❑ 520	Kevin Appier	.20	.09
❑ 521	Roberto Mejia	.10	.05
❑ 522	Steve Cooke	.10	.05
❑ 523	Terry Shumpert	.10	.05
❑ 524	Mike Jackson	.10	.05
❑ 525	Kent Mercker	.10	.05
❑ 526	David Wells	.30	.14
❑ 527	Juan Samuel	.10	.05
❑ 528	Salomon Torres	.10	.05
❑ 529	Duane Ward	.10	.05
❑ 530	Rob Dibble	.10	.05
❑ 531	Mike Blowers	.10	.05
❑ 532	Mark Eichhorn	.10	.05
❑ 533	Alex Diaz	.10	.05
❑ 534	Dan Miceli	.10	.05
❑ 535	Jeff Branson	.10	.05
❑ 536	Dave Stevens	.10	.05
❑ 537	Charlie O'Brien	.10	.05
❑ 538	Shane Reynolds	.20	.09
❑ 539	Rich Amaral	.10	.05
❑ 540	Rusty Greer	.40	.18
❑ 541	Alex Arias	.10	.05
❑ 542	Eric Plunk	.10	.05
❑ 543	John Hudek	.10	.05
❑ 544	Kirk McCaskill	.10	.05
❑ 545	Jeff Reboulet	.10	.05
❑ 546	Sterling Hitchcock	.20	.09
❑ 547	Warren Newson	.10	.05
❑ 548	Bryan Harvey	.10	.05
❑ 549	Mike Huff	.10	.05
❑ 550	Lance Parrish	.10	.05
❑ 551	Ken Griffey Jr. HIT	1.00	.45
❑ 552	Matt Williams HIT	.10	.05
❑ 553	Roberto Alomar HIT UER (Card says he's a NL All-Star He plays in the AL)	.20	.09
❑ 554	Jeff Bagwell HIT	.40	.18
❑ 555	Dave Justice HIT	.20	.09
❑ 556	Cal Ripken Jr. HIT	.75	.35
❑ 557	Albert Belle HIT	.20	.09
❑ 558	Mike Piazza HIT	.60	.25
❑ 559	Kirby Puckett HIT	.40	.18
❑ 560	Wade Boggs HIT	.20	.09
❑ 561	Tony Gwynn HIT UER card has him winning AL batting titles he's played whole career in the NL	.50	.23
❑ 562	Barry Bonds HIT	.30	.14
❑ 563	Mo Vaughn HIT	.30	.14
❑ 564	Don Mattingly HIT	.40	.18
❑ 565	Carlos Baerga HIT	.10	.05
❑ 566	Paul Molitor HIT	.20	.09
❑ 567	Raul Mondesi HIT	.10	.05
❑ 568	Manny Ramirez HIT	.20	.09
❑ 569	Alex Rodriguez HIT	.75	.35
❑ 570	Will Clark HIT	.20	.09
❑ 571	Frank Thomas HIT	.60	.25
❑ 572	Moises Alou HIT	.10	.05
❑ 573	Jeff Conine HIT	.10	.05
❑ 574	Joe Ausanio	.10	.05
❑ 575	Charles Johnson	.20	.09
❑ 576	Ernie Young	.10	.05
❑ 577	Jeff Granger	.10	.05
❑ 578	Robert Perez	.10	.05
❑ 579	Melvin Nieves	.10	.05
❑ 580	Gar Finnvold	.10	.05
❑ 581	Duane Singleton	.10	.05
❑ 582	Chan Ho Park	.50	.23
❑ 583	Fausto Cruz	.10	.05
❑ 584	Dave Staton	.10	.05
❑ 585	Denny Hocking	.10	.05
❑ 586	Nate Minchey	.10	.05
❑ 587	Marc Newfield	.10	.05
❑ 588	Jayhawk Owens UER Front Photo is Jim Tatum	.10	.05
❑ 589	Darren Bragg	.10	.05
❑ 590	Kevin King	.10	.05
❑ 591	Kurt Miller	.10	.05
❑ 592	Aaron Small	.10	.05
❑ 593	Troy O'Leary	.20	.09
❑ 594	Phil Stidham	.10	.05
❑ 595	Steve Dunn	.10	.05
❑ 596	Cory Bailey	.10	.05
❑ 597	Alex Gonzalez	.10	.05
❑ 598	Jim Bowie	.10	.05
❑ 599	Jeff Cirillo	.20	.09
❑ 600	Mark Hutton	.10	.05
❑ 601	Russ Davis	.20	.09
❑ 602	Checklist	.10	.05
❑ 603	Checklist	.10	.05
❑ 604	Checklist	.10	.05
❑ 605	Checklist	.10	.05
❑ RG1	R.Klesko Rook.Great.	1.00	.45
❑ SG1	Ryan Klesko AU6100	10.00	4.50
❑ NNO	Trade Hall of Gold	1.00	.45

1995 Score Airmail

	MINT	NRMT
COMPLETE SET (18)	50.00	22.00
COMMON CARD (1-18)	2.00	.90

No.	Player	MINT	NRMT
❑ AM1	Bob Hamelin	2.00	.90
❑ AM2	John Mabry	2.00	.90
❑ AM3	Marc Newfield	2.00	.90
❑ AM4	Jose Oliva	2.00	.90
❑ AM5	Charles Johnson	3.00	1.35
❑ AM6	Russ Davis	3.00	1.35
❑ AM7	Ernie Young	2.00	.90
❑ AM8	Billy Ashley	2.00	.90
❑ AM9	Ryan Klesko	3.00	1.35
❑ AM10	J.R. Phillips	2.00	.90
❑ AM11	Cliff Floyd	3.00	1.35
❑ AM12	Carlos Delgado	3.00	1.35
❑ AM13	Melvin Nieves	2.00	.90
❑ AM14	Raul Mondesi	4.00	1.80
❑ AM15	Manny Ramirez	6.00	2.70
❑ AM16	Mike Kelly	2.00	.90
❑ AM17	Alex Rodriguez	30.00	13.50

		MINT	NRMT
❑ AM18	Rusty Greer	6.00	2.70

1995 Score Double Gold Champs

	MINT	NRMT
COMPLETE SET (12)	100.00	45.00
COMMON CARD (1-12)	2.50	1.10

		MINT	NRMT
❑ GC1	Frank Thomas	12.00	5.50
❑ GC2	Ken Griffey Jr.	20.00	9.00
❑ GC3	Barry Bonds	4.00	1.80
❑ GC4	Tony Gwynn	10.00	4.50
❑ GC5	Don Mattingly	6.00	2.70
❑ GC6	Greg Maddux	12.00	5.50
❑ GC7	Roger Clemens	8.00	3.60
❑ GC8	Kenny Lofton	4.00	1.80
❑ GC9	Jeff Bagwell	6.00	2.70
❑ GC10	Matt Williams	2.50	1.10
❑ GC11	Kirby Puckett	4.00	1.80
❑ GC12	Cal Ripken	15.00	6.75

1995 Score Draft Picks

	MINT	NRMT
COMPLETE SET (18)	40.00	18.00
COMMON CARD (DP1-DP18)	1.00	.45

		MINT	NRMT
❑ DP1	McKay Christensen	1.50	.70
❑ DP2	Bret Wagner	1.00	.45
❑ DP3	Paul Wilson	1.00	.45
❑ DP4	C.J. Nitkowski	1.00	.45
❑ DP5	Josh Booty	2.00	.90
❑ DP6	Antone Williamson	1.00	.45
❑ DP7	Paul Konerko	8.00	3.60
❑ DP8	Scott Elarton	2.00	.90
❑ DP9	Jacob Shumate	1.00	.45
❑ DP10	Terrence Long	1.50	.70
❑ DP11	Mark Johnson	1.00	.45
❑ DP12	Ben Grieve	20.00	9.00
❑ DP13	Doug Million	1.00	.45
❑ DP14	Jayson Peterson	1.00	.45
❑ DP15	Dustin Hermanson	1.50	.70
❑ DP16	Matt Smith	1.00	.45
❑ DP17	Kevin Witt	3.00	1.35
❑ DP18	Brian Buchanan	1.00	.45

1995 Score Dream Team

	MINT	NRMT
COMPLETE SET (12)	150.00	70.00
COMMON CARD (DG1-DG12)	2.50	1.10

		MINT	NRMT
❑ DG1	Frank Thomas	25.00	11.00
❑ DG2	Roberto Alomar	8.00	3.60
❑ DG3	Cal Ripken	30.00	13.50
❑ DG4	Matt Williams	2.50	1.10
❑ DG5	Mike Piazza	25.00	11.00
❑ DG6	Albert Belle	8.00	3.60
❑ DG7	Ken Griffey Jr.	40.00	18.00
❑ DG8	Tony Gwynn	20.00	9.00
❑ DG9	Paul Molitor	8.00	3.60
❑ DG10	Jimmy Key	2.50	1.10
❑ DG11	Greg Maddux	25.00	11.00
❑ DG12	Lee Smith	2.50	1.10

1995 Score Hall of Gold

	MINT	NRMT
COMPLETE SET (110)	80.00	36.00
COMPLETE SERIES 1 (55)	50.00	22.00
COMPLETE SERIES 2 (55)	30.00	13.50
COMMON CARD (HG1-HG110)	.50	.23

		MINT	NRMT
❑ HG1	Ken Griffey Jr.	12.00	5.50
❑ HG2	Matt Williams	1.00	.45
❑ HG3	Roberto Alomar	2.00	.90
❑ HG4	Jeff Bagwell	4.00	1.80
❑ HG5	Dave Justice	2.00	.90
❑ HG6	Cal Ripken	10.00	4.50
❑ HG7	Randy Johnson	2.00	.90
❑ HG8	Barry Larkin	1.50	.70
❑ HG9	Albert Belle	2.00	.90
❑ HG10	Mike Piazza	8.00	3.60
❑ HG11	Kirby Puckett	2.00	.90
❑ HG12	Moises Alou	1.50	.70
❑ HG13	Jose Canseco	2.00	.90
❑ HG14	Tony Gwynn	6.00	2.70
❑ HG15	Roger Clemens	4.00	1.80
❑ HG16	Barry Bonds	2.00	.90
❑ HG17	Mo Vaughn	2.00	.90
❑ HG18	Greg Maddux	8.00	3.60
❑ HG19	Dante Bichette	1.00	.45
❑ HG20	Will Clark	2.00	.90
❑ HG21	Lenny Dykstra	1.00	.45
❑ HG22	Don Mattingly	3.00	1.35
❑ HG23	Carlos Baerga	1.00	.45
❑ HG24	Ozzie Smith	2.00	.90
❑ HG25	Paul Molitor	2.00	.90
❑ HG26	Paul O'Neill	1.00	.45
❑ HG27	Deion Sanders	1.00	.45
❑ HG28	Jeff Conine	1.00	.45
❑ HG29	John Olerud	1.00	.45
❑ HG30	Jose Rijo	.50	.23
❑ HG31	Sammy Sosa	8.00	3.60
❑ HG32	Robin Ventura	1.00	.45
❑ HG33	Raul Mondesi	1.50	.70
❑ HG34	Eddie Murray	2.00	.90
❑ HG35	Marquis Grissom	1.00	.45
❑ HG36	Darryl Strawberry	1.00	.45
❑ HG37	Dave Nilsson	.50	.23
❑ HG38	Manny Ramirez	2.00	.90
❑ HG39	Delino DeShields	.50	.23
❑ HG40	Lee Smith	1.00	.45
❑ HG41	Alex Rodriguez	12.00	5.50
❑ HG42	Julio Franco	.50	.23
❑ HG43	Bret Saberhagen	1.00	.45
❑ HG44	Ken Hill	.50	.23
❑ HG45	Roberto Kelly	.50	.23
❑ HG46	Hal Morris	.50	.23
❑ HG47	Jimmy Key	1.00	.45
❑ HG48	Terry Steinbach	1.00	.45
❑ HG49	Mickey Tettleton	.50	.23
❑ HG50	Tony Phillips	.50	.23
❑ HG51	Carlos Garcia	.50	.23
❑ HG52	Jim Edmonds	1.50	.70
❑ HG53	Rod Beck	.50	.23
❑ HG54	Shane Mack	.50	.23
❑ HG55	Ken Caminiti	1.50	.70
❑ HG56	Frank Thomas	10.00	4.50
❑ HG57	Kenny Lofton	2.00	.90
❑ HG58	Juan Gonzalez	8.00	3.60
❑ HG59	Jason Bere	.50	.23
❑ HG60	Joe Carter	1.00	.45
❑ HG61	Gary Sheffield	1.50	.70
❑ HG62	Andres Galarraga	2.00	.90
❑ HG63	Ellis Burks	1.00	.45
❑ HG64	Bobby Bonilla	1.00	.45
❑ HG65	Tom Glavine	2.00	.90
❑ HG66	John Smoltz	1.00	.45
❑ HG67	Fred McGriff	1.50	.70
❑ HG68	Craig Biggio	2.00	.90
❑ HG69	Reggie Sanders	1.00	.45
❑ HG70	Kevin Mitchell	.50	.23
❑ HG71	Larry Walker	2.00	.90
❑ HG72	Carlos Delgado	1.00	.45
❑ HG73	Alex Gonzalez	.50	.23
❑ HG74	Ivan Rodriguez	2.00	.90
❑ HG75	Ryan Klesko	1.00	.45
❑ HG76	John Kruk	1.00	.45
❑ HG77	Brian McRae	.50	.23
❑ HG78	Tim Salmon	2.00	.90
❑ HG79	Travis Fryman	1.00	.45
❑ HG80	Chuck Knoblauch	2.00	.90
❑ HG81	Jay Bell	1.00	.45
❑ HG82	Cecil Fielder	1.00	.45
❑ HG83	Cliff Floyd	1.00	.45
❑ HG84	Ruben Sierra	.50	.23
❑ HG85	Mike Mussina	2.00	.90
❑ HG86	Mark Grace	1.50	.70
❑ HG87	Dennis Eckersley	1.00	.45
❑ HG88	Dennis Martinez	1.00	.45
❑ HG89	Rafael Palmeiro	1.50	.70
❑ HG90	Ben McDonald	.50	.23
❑ HG91	Dave Hollins	.50	.23
❑ HG92	Steve Avery	.50	.23
❑ HG93	David Cone	1.50	.70
❑ HG94	Darren Daulton	1.00	.45
❑ HG95	Bret Boone	1.00	.45
❑ HG96	Wade Boggs	2.00	.90
❑ HG97	Doug Drabek	.50	.23
❑ HG98	Andy Benes	1.00	.45
❑ HG99	Jim Thome	2.00	.90
❑ HG100	Chili Davis	1.00	.45
❑ HG101	Jeffrey Hammonds	1.00	.45
❑ HG102	Rickey Henderson	2.00	.90
❑ HG103	Brett Butler	1.00	.45
❑ HG104	Tim Wallach	.50	.23
❑ HG105	Wil Cordero	.50	.23
❑ HG106	Mark Whiten	.50	.23
❑ HG107	Bob Hamelin	.50	.23
❑ HG108	Rondell White	1.00	.45
❑ HG109	Devon White	1.00	.45
❑ HG110	Tony Tarasco	.50	.23

1995 Score Rookie Dream Team

	MINT	NRMT
COMPLETE SET (12)	60.00	27.00
COMMON CARD (1-12)	2.50	1.10
❑ RDT1 J.R. Phillips	2.50	1.10
❑ RDT2 Alex Gonzalez	2.50	1.10
❑ RDT3 Alex Rodriguez	40.00	18.00
❑ RDT4 Jose Oliva	2.50	1.10
❑ RDT5 Charles Johnson	4.00	1.80
❑ RDT6 Shawn Green	4.00	1.80
❑ RDT7 Brian Hunter	4.00	1.80
❑ RDT8 Garret Anderson	4.00	1.80
❑ RDT9 Julian Tavarez	2.50	1.10
❑ RDT10 Jose Lima	2.50	1.10
❑ RDT11 Armando Benitez	2.50	1.10
❑ RDT12 Ricky Bottalico	4.00	1.80

1995 Score Rules

	MINT	NRMT
COMPLETE SET (30)	120.00	55.00
COMMON CARD (SR1-SR30)	1.00	.45
❑ SR1 Ken Griffey Jr.	20.00	9.00
❑ SR2 Frank Thomas	12.00	5.50
❑ SR3 Mike Piazza	12.00	5.50
❑ SR4 Jeff Bagwell	6.00	2.70
❑ SR5 Alex Rodriguez	15.00	6.75
❑ SR6 Albert Belle	3.00	1.35
❑ SR7 Matt Williams	2.00	.90
❑ SR8 Roberto Alomar	3.00	1.35
❑ SR9 Barry Bonds	3.00	1.35
❑ SR10 Raul Mondesi	2.50	1.10
❑ SR11 Jose Canseco	3.00	1.35
❑ SR12 Kirby Puckett	3.00	1.35
❑ SR13 Fred McGriff	2.50	1.10
❑ SR14 Kenny Lofton	3.00	1.35
❑ SR15 Greg Maddux	12.00	5.50
❑ SR16 Juan Gonzalez	10.00	4.50
❑ SR17 Cliff Floyd	2.00	.90
❑ SR18 Cal Ripken Jr.	15.00	6.75
❑ SR19 Will Clark	3.00	1.35
❑ SR20 Tim Salmon	3.00	1.35
❑ SR21 Paul O'Neill	2.00	.90
❑ SR22 Jason Bere	1.00	.45
❑ SR23 Tony Gwynn	12.00	5.50
❑ SR24 Manny Ramirez	3.00	1.35
❑ SR25 Don Mattingly	6.00	2.70
❑ SR26 Dave Justice	3.00	1.35
❑ SR27 Javier Lopez	2.00	.90
❑ SR28 Ryan Klesko	2.00	.90
❑ SR29 Carlos Delgado	2.00	.90
❑ SR30 Mike Mussina	3.00	1.35

1996 Score

	MINT	NRMT
COMPLETE SET (517)	24.00	11.00
COMPLETE SERIES 1 (275)	12.00	5.50
COMPLETE SERIES 2 (242)	12.00	5.50
COMMON CARD (1-517)	.10	.05
❑ 1 Will Clark	.40	.18
❑ 2 Rich Becker	.10	.05
❑ 3 Ryan Klesko	.20	.09
❑ 4 Jim Edmonds	.30	.14
❑ 5 Barry Larkin	.30	.14
❑ 6 Jim Thome	.40	.18
❑ 7 Raul Mondesi	.30	.14
❑ 8 Don Mattingly	.60	.25
❑ 9 Jeff Conine	.20	.09
❑ 10 Rickey Henderson	.40	.18
❑ 11 Chad Curtis	.10	.05
❑ 12 Darren Daulton	.20	.09
❑ 13 Larry Walker	.40	.18
❑ 14 Carlos Garcia	.10	.05
❑ 15 Carlos Baerga	.20	.09
❑ 16 Tony Gwynn	1.00	.45
❑ 17 Jon Nunnally	.10	.05
❑ 18 Deion Sanders	.20	.09
❑ 19 Mark Grace	.30	.14
❑ 20 Alex Rodriguez	1.25	.55
❑ 21 Frank Thomas	1.25	.55
❑ 22 Brian Jordan	.20	.09
❑ 23 J.T. Snow	.20	.09
❑ 24 Shawn Green	.20	.09
❑ 25 Tim Wakefield	.20	.09
❑ 26 Curtis Goodwin	.10	.05
❑ 27 John Smoltz	.20	.09
❑ 28 Devon White	.20	.09
❑ 29 Johnny Damon	.20	.09
❑ 30 Tim Salmon	.40	.18
❑ 31 Rafael Palmeiro	.30	.14
❑ 32 Bernard Gilkey	.10	.05
❑ 33 John Valentin	.20	.09
❑ 34 Randy Johnson	.40	.18
❑ 35 Garret Anderson	.20	.09
❑ 36 Rikkert Faneyte	.10	.05
❑ 37 Ray Durham	.20	.09
❑ 38 Bip Roberts	.10	.05
❑ 39 Jaime Navarro	.10	.05
❑ 40 Mark Johnson	.10	.05
❑ 41 Darren Lewis	.10	.05
❑ 42 Tyler Green	.10	.05
❑ 43 Bill Pulsipher	.10	.05
❑ 44 Jason Giambi	.20	.09
❑ 45 Kevin Ritz	.10	.05
❑ 46 Jack McDowell	.10	.05
❑ 47 Felipe Lira	.10	.05
❑ 48 Rico Brogna	.10	.05
❑ 49 Terry Pendleton	.10	.05
❑ 50 Rondell White	.20	.09
❑ 51 Andre Dawson	.30	.14
❑ 52 Kirby Puckett	.60	.25
❑ 53 Wally Joyner	.20	.09
❑ 54 B.J. Surhoff	.20	.09
❑ 55 Randy Velarde	.10	.05
❑ 56 Greg Vaughn	.20	.09
❑ 57 Roberto Alomar	.40	.18
❑ 58 David Justice	.40	.18
❑ 59 Kevin Seitzer	.10	.05
❑ 60 Cal Ripken	1.50	.70
❑ 61 Ozzie Smith	.50	.23
❑ 62 Mo Vaughn	.50	.23
❑ 63 Ricky Bones	.10	.05
❑ 64 Gary DiSarcina	.10	.05
❑ 65 Matt Williams	.20	.09
❑ 66 Wilson Alvarez	.20	.09
❑ 67 Lenny Dykstra	.20	.09
❑ 68 Brian McRae	.10	.05
❑ 69 Todd Stottlemyre	.10	.05
❑ 70 Bret Boone	.20	.09
❑ 71 Sterling Hitchcock	.20	.09
❑ 72 Albert Belle	.50	.23
❑ 73 Todd Hundley	.20	.09
❑ 74 Vinny Castilla	.30	.14
❑ 75 Moises Alou	.30	.14
❑ 76 Cecil Fielder	.20	.09
❑ 77 Brad Radke	.20	.09
❑ 78 Quilvio Veras	.10	.05
❑ 79 Eddie Murray	.40	.18
❑ 80 James Mouton	.10	.05
❑ 81 Pat Listach	.10	.05
❑ 82 Mark Gubicza	.10	.05
❑ 83 Dave Winfield	.40	.18
❑ 84 Fred McGriff	.30	.14
❑ 85 Darryl Hamilton	.10	.05
❑ 86 Jeffrey Hammonds	.20	.09
❑ 87 Pedro Munoz	.10	.05
❑ 88 Craig Biggio	.40	.18
❑ 89 Cliff Floyd	.20	.09
❑ 90 Tim Naehring	.10	.05
❑ 91 Brett Butler	.20	.09
❑ 92 Kevin Foster	.10	.05
❑ 93 Pat Kelly	.10	.05
❑ 94 John Smiley	.10	.05
❑ 95 Terry Steinbach	.20	.09
❑ 96 Orel Hershiser	.20	.09
❑ 97 Darrin Fletcher	.10	.05
❑ 98 Walt Weiss	.10	.05
❑ 99 John Wetteland	.20	.09
❑ 100 Alan Trammell	.30	.14
❑ 101 Steve Avery	.10	.05
❑ 102 Tony Eusebio	.10	.05
❑ 103 Sandy Alomar Jr.	.20	.09
❑ 104 Joe Girardi	.10	.05
❑ 105 Rick Aguilera	.10	.05
❑ 106 Tony Tarasco	.10	.05
❑ 107 Chris Hammond	.10	.05
❑ 108 Mike Macfarlane	.10	.05
❑ 109 Doug Drabek	.10	.05
❑ 110 Derek Bell	.20	.09
❑ 111 Ed Sprague	.10	.05
❑ 112 Todd Hollandsworth	.10	.05
❑ 113 Otis Nixon	.10	.05
❑ 114 Keith Lockhart	.10	.05
❑ 115 Donovan Osborne	.10	.05
❑ 116 Dave Magadan	.10	.05
❑ 117 Edgar Martinez	.20	.09
❑ 118 Chuck Carr	.10	.05
❑ 119 J.R. Phillips	.10	.05
❑ 120 Sean Bergman	.10	.05
❑ 121 Andujar Cedeno	.10	.05
❑ 122 Eric Young	.10	.05
❑ 123 Al Martin	.10	.05
❑ 124 Mark Lemke	.10	.05
❑ 125 Jim Eisenreich	.10	.05
❑ 126 Benito Santiago	.10	.05
❑ 127 Ariel Prieto	.10	.05
❑ 128 Jim Bullinger	.10	.05
❑ 129 Russ Davis	.20	.09
❑ 130 Jim Abbott	.20	.09
❑ 131 Jason Isringhausen	.10	.05
❑ 132 Carlos Perez	.20	.09
❑ 133 David Segui	.20	.09
❑ 134 Troy O'Leary	.20	.09
❑ 135 Pat Meares	.10	.05
❑ 136 Chris Hoiles	.10	.05
❑ 137 Ismael Valdes	.20	.09
❑ 138 Jose Oliva	.10	.05

❑ 139 Carlos Delgado .20 .09
❑ 140 Tom Goodwin .10 .05
❑ 141 Bob Tewksbury .10 .05
❑ 142 Chris Gomez .10 .05
❑ 143 Jose Oquendo .10 .05
❑ 144 Mark Lewis .10 .05
❑ 145 Salomon Torres .10 .05
❑ 146 Luis Gonzalez .10 .05
❑ 147 Mark Carreon .10 .05
❑ 148 Lance Johnson .10 .05
❑ 149 Melvin Nieves .10 .05
❑ 150 Lee Smith .20 .09
❑ 151 Jacob Brumfield .10 .05
❑ 152 Armando Benitez .10 .05
❑ 153 Curt Schilling .20 .09
❑ 154 Javier Lopez .20 .09
❑ 155 Frank Rodriguez .10 .05
❑ 156 Alex Gonzalez .10 .05
❑ 157 Todd Worrell .10 .05
❑ 158 Benji Gil .10 .05
❑ 159 Greg Gagne .10 .05
❑ 160 Tom Henke .10 .05
❑ 161 Randy Myers .10 .05
❑ 162 Joey Cora .20 .09
❑ 163 Scott Ruffcorn .10 .05
❑ 164 W. VanLandingham .10 .05
❑ 165 Tony Phillips .10 .05
❑ 166 Eddie Williams .10 .05
❑ 167 Bobby Bonilla .20 .09
❑ 168 Denny Neagle .20 .09
❑ 169 Troy Percival .20 .09
❑ 170 Billy Ashley .10 .05
❑ 171 Andy Van Slyke .10 .05
❑ 172 Jose Offerman .10 .05
❑ 173 Mark Parent .10 .05
❑ 174 Edgardo Alfonzo .20 .09
❑ 175 Trevor Hoffman .20 .09
❑ 176 David Cone .30 .14
❑ 177 Dan Wilson .10 .05
❑ 178 Steve Ontiveros .10 .05
❑ 179 Dean Palmer .20 .09
❑ 180 Mike Kelly .10 .05
❑ 181 Jim Leyritz .10 .05
❑ 182 Ron Karkovice .10 .05
❑ 183 Kevin Brown .40 .18
❑ 184 Jose Valentin .10 .05
❑ 185 Jorge Fabregas .10 .05
❑ 186 Jose Mesa .10 .05
❑ 187 Brent Mayne .10 .05
❑ 188 Carl Everett .10 .05
❑ 189 Paul Sorrento .10 .05
❑ 190 Pete Schourek .10 .05
❑ 191 Scott Kamieniecki .10 .05
❑ 192 Roberto Hernandez .10 .05
❑ 193 Randy Johnson RR .20 .09
❑ 194 Greg Maddux RR .60 .25
❑ 195 Hideo Nomo RR .50 .23
❑ 196 David Cone RR .10 .05
❑ 197 Mike Mussina RR .20 .09
❑ 198 Andy Benes RR .10 .05
❑ 199 Kevin Appier RR .10 .05
❑ 200 John Smoltz RR .10 .05
❑ 201 John Wetteland RR .10 .05
❑ 202 Mark Wohlers RR .10 .05
❑ 203 Stan Belinda .10 .05
❑ 204 Brian Anderson .20 .09
❑ 205 Mike Devereaux .10 .05
❑ 206 Mark Wohlers .10 .05
❑ 207 Omar Vizquel .20 .09
❑ 208 Jose Rijo .10 .05
❑ 209 Willie Blair .10 .05
❑ 210 Jamie Moyer .10 .05
❑ 211 Craig Shipley .10 .05
❑ 212 Shane Reynolds .20 .09
❑ 213 Chad Fonville .10 .05
❑ 214 Jose Vizcaino .10 .05
❑ 215 Sid Fernandez .10 .05
❑ 216 Andy Ashby .10 .05
❑ 217 Frank Castillo .10 .05
❑ 218 Kevin Tapani .10 .05
❑ 219 Kent Mercker .10 .05
❑ 220 Karim Garcia .20 .09
❑ 221 Antonio Osuna .10 .05
❑ 222 Tim Unroe .10 .05
❑ 223 Johnny Damon .20 .09
❑ 224 LaTroy Hawkins .10 .05
❑ 225 Mariano Rivera .20 .09
❑ 226 Jose Alberro .10 .05
❑ 227 Angel Martinez .10 .05
❑ 228 Jason Schmidt .10 .05
❑ 229 Tony Clark .40 .18
❑ 230 Kevin Jordan UER .10 .05
Ricky Jordan pictured on both sides
❑ 231 Mark Thompson .10 .05
❑ 232 Jim Dougherty .10 .05
❑ 233 Roger Cedeno .10 .05
❑ 234 Ugueth Urbina .20 .09
❑ 235 Ricky Otero .10 .05
❑ 236 Mark Smith .10 .05
❑ 237 Brian Barber .10 .05
❑ 238 Kevin Flora .10 .05
❑ 239 Joe Rosselli .10 .05
❑ 240 Derek Jeter 1.25 .55
❑ 241 Michael Tucker .20 .09
❑ 242 Ben Blomdahl .10 .05
❑ 243 Joe Vitiello .10 .05
❑ 244 Todd Steverson .10 .05
❑ 245 James Baldwin .20 .09
❑ 246 Alan Embree .10 .05
❑ 247 Shannon Penn .10 .05
❑ 248 Chris Stynes .10 .05
❑ 249 Oscar Munoz .10 .05
❑ 250 Jose Herrera .10 .05
❑ 251 Scott Sullivan .10 .05
❑ 252 Reggie Williams .10 .05
❑ 253 Mark Grudzielanek .20 .09
❑ 254 Steve Rodriguez .10 .05
❑ 255 Terry Bradshaw .10 .05
❑ 256 F.P. Santangelo .10 .05
❑ 257 Lyle Mouton .10 .05
❑ 258 George Williams .10 .05
❑ 259 Larry Thomas .10 .05
❑ 260 Rudy Pemberton .10 .05
❑ 261 Jim Pittsley .10 .05
❑ 262 Les Norman .10 .05
❑ 263 Ruben Rivera .20 .09
❑ 264 Cesar Devarez .10 .05
❑ 265 Greg Zaun .10 .05
❑ 266 Dustin Hermanson .20 .09
❑ 267 John Frascatore .10 .05
❑ 268 Joe Randa .10 .05
❑ 269 Jeff Bagwell CL .40 .18
❑ 270 Mike Piazza CL .60 .25
❑ 271 Dante Bichette CL .10 .05
❑ 272 Frank Thomas CL .60 .25
❑ 273 Ken Griffey Jr. CL 1.00 .45
❑ 274 Cal Ripken CL .75 .35
❑ 275 Greg Maddux CL .50 .23
Albert Belle
❑ 276 Greg Maddux 1.25 .55
❑ 277 Pedro Martinez .40 .18
❑ 278 Bobby Higginson .40 .18
❑ 279 Ray Lankford .20 .09
❑ 280 Shawon Dunston .10 .05
❑ 281 Gary Sheffield .30 .14
❑ 282 Ken Griffey Jr. 2.00 .90
❑ 283 Paul Molitor .40 .18
❑ 284 Kevin Appier .20 .09
❑ 285 Chuck Knoblauch .40 .18
❑ 286 Alex Fernandez .10 .05
❑ 287 Steve Finley .20 .09
❑ 288 Jeff Blauser .10 .05
❑ 289 Charles Johnson .20 .09
❑ 290 John Franco .20 .09
❑ 291 Mark Langston .10 .05
❑ 292 Bret Saberhagen .20 .09
❑ 293 John Mabry .10 .05
❑ 294 Ramon Martinez .20 .09
❑ 295 Mike Blowers .10 .05
❑ 296 Paul O'Neill .20 .09
❑ 297 Dave Nilsson .10 .05
❑ 298 Dante Bichette .20 .09
❑ 299 Marty Cordova .10 .05
❑ 300 Jay Bell .20 .09
❑ 301 Mike Mussina .40 .18
❑ 302 Ivan Rodriguez .50 .23
❑ 303 Jose Canseco .40 .18
❑ 304 Jeff Bagwell .60 .25
❑ 305 Manny Ramirez .40 .18
❑ 306 Dennis Martinez .20 .09
❑ 307 Charlie Hayes .10 .05
❑ 308 Joe Carter .20 .09
❑ 309 Travis Fryman .20 .09
❑ 310 Mark McGwire 2.00 .90
❑ 311 Reggie Sanders UER .20 .09
Photo on front is John Roper
❑ 312 Julian Tavarez .10 .05
❑ 313 Jeff Montgomery .10 .05
❑ 314 Andy Benes .20 .09
❑ 315 John Jaha .10 .05
❑ 316 Jeff Kent .20 .09
❑ 317 Mike Piazza 1.25 .55
❑ 318 Erik Hanson .10 .05
❑ 319 Kenny Rogers .10 .05
❑ 320 Hideo Nomo .60 .25
❑ 321 Gregg Jefferies .10 .05
❑ 322 Chipper Jones 1.00 .45
❑ 323 Jay Buhner .20 .09
❑ 324 Dennis Eckersley .20 .09
❑ 325 Kenny Lofton .40 .18
❑ 326 Robin Ventura .20 .09
❑ 327 Tom Glavine .40 .18
❑ 328 Tim Salmon .40 .18
❑ 329 Andres Galarraga .40 .18
❑ 330 Hal Morris .10 .05
❑ 331 Brady Anderson .20 .09
❑ 332 Chili Davis .20 .09
❑ 333 Roger Clemens .75 .35
❑ 334 Marquis Grissom .20 .09
❑ 335 Mike Greenwell UER .10 .05
Name spelled Jeff on Front
❑ 336 Sammy Sosa 1.00 .45
❑ 337 Ron Gant .10 .05
❑ 338 Ken Caminiti .30 .14
❑ 339 Danny Tartabull .10 .05
❑ 340 Barry Bonds .50 .23
❑ 341 Ben McDonald .10 .05
❑ 342 Ruben Sierra .10 .05
❑ 343 Bernie Williams .40 .18
❑ 344 Wil Cordero .10 .05
❑ 345 Wade Boggs .40 .18
❑ 346 Gary Gaetti .20 .09
❑ 347 Greg Colbrunn .10 .05
❑ 348 Juan Gonzalez 1.00 .45
❑ 349 Marc Newfield .10 .05
❑ 350 Charles Nagy .20 .09
❑ 351 Robby Thompson .10 .05
❑ 352 Roberto Petagine .10 .05
❑ 353 Darryl Strawberry .20 .09
❑ 354 Tino Martinez .40 .18
❑ 355 Eric Karros .20 .09
❑ 356 Cal Ripken SS .75 .35
❑ 357 Cecil Fielder SS .10 .05
❑ 358 Kirby Puckett SS .40 .18
❑ 359 Jim Edmonds SS .10 .05
❑ 360 Matt Williams SS .10 .05
❑ 361 Alex Rodriguez SS .60 .25
❑ 362 Barry Larkin SS .10 .05
❑ 363 Rafael Palmeiro SS .10 .05
❑ 364 David Cone SS .10 .05
❑ 365 Roberto Alomar SS .20 .09
❑ 366 Eddie Murray SS .20 .09
❑ 367 Randy Johnson SS .20 .09
❑ 368 Ryan Klesko SS .10 .05
❑ 369 Raul Mondesi SS .10 .05
❑ 370 Mo Vaughn SS .30 .14
❑ 371 Will Clark SS .20 .09
❑ 372 Carlos Baerga SS .10 .05
❑ 373 Frank Thomas SS .60 .25
❑ 374 Larry Walker SS .20 .09
❑ 375 Garret Anderson SS .10 .05
❑ 376 Edgar Martinez SS .10 .05
❑ 377 Don Mattingly SS .30 .14
❑ 378 Tony Gwynn SS .50 .23
❑ 379 Albert Belle SS .30 .14
❑ 380 Jason Isringhausen SS .10 .05
❑ 381 Ruben Rivera SS .10 .05
❑ 382 Johnny Damon SS .10 .05
❑ 383 Karim Garcia SS .10 .05
❑ 384 Derek Jeter SS .60 .25
❑ 385 David Justice SS .20 .09
❑ 386 Royce Clayton .10 .05
❑ 387 Mark Whiten .10 .05
❑ 388 Mickey Tettleton .10 .05
❑ 389 Steve Trachsel .10 .05

❑ 390 Danny Bautista .10 .05
❑ 391 Midre Cummings .10 .05
❑ 392 Scott Leius .10 .05
❑ 393 Manny Alexander .10 .05
❑ 394 Brent Gates .10 .05
❑ 395 Rey Sanchez .10 .05
❑ 396 Andy Pettitte .30 .14
❑ 397 Jeff Cirillo .20 .09
❑ 398 Kurt Abbott .10 .05
❑ 399 Lee Tinsley .10 .05
❑ 400 Paul Assenmacher .10 .05
❑ 401 Scott Erickson .20 .09
❑ 402 Todd Zeile .10 .05
❑ 403 Tom Pagnozzi .10 .05
❑ 404 Ozzie Guillen .10 .05
❑ 405 Jeff Frye .10 .05
❑ 406 Kirt Manwaring .10 .05
❑ 407 Chad Ogea .10 .05
❑ 408 Harold Baines .20 .09
❑ 409 Jason Bere .10 .05
❑ 410 Chuck Finley .20 .09
❑ 411 Jeff Fassero .10 .05
❑ 412 Joey Hamilton .20 .09
❑ 413 John Olerud .20 .09
❑ 414 Kevin Stocker .10 .05
❑ 415 Eric Anthony .10 .05
❑ 416 Aaron Sele .20 .09
❑ 417 Chris Bosio .10 .05
❑ 418 Michael Mimbs .10 .05
❑ 419 Orlando Miller .10 .05
❑ 420 Stan Javier .10 .05
❑ 421 Matt Mieske .10 .05
❑ 422 Jason Bates .10 .05
❑ 423 Orlando Merced .10 .05
❑ 424 John Flaherty .10 .05
❑ 425 Reggie Jefferson .10 .05
❑ 426 Scott Stahoviak .10 .05
❑ 427 John Burkett .10 .05
❑ 428 Rod Beck .10 .05
❑ 429 Bill Swift .10 .05
❑ 430 Scott Cooper .10 .05
❑ 431 Mel Rojas .10 .05
❑ 432 Todd Van Poppel .10 .05
❑ 433 Bobby Jones .10 .05
❑ 434 Mike Harkey .10 .05
❑ 435 Sean Berry .10 .05
❑ 436 Glenallen Hill .10 .05
❑ 437 Ryan Thompson .10 .05
❑ 438 Luis Alicea .10 .05
❑ 439 Esteban Loaiza .10 .05
❑ 440 Jeff Reboulet .10 .05
❑ 441 Vince Coleman .10 .05
❑ 442 Ellis Burks .20 .09
❑ 443 Allen Battle .10 .05
❑ 444 Jimmy Key .20 .09
❑ 445 Ricky Bottalico .20 .09
❑ 446 Delino DeShields .10 .05
❑ 447 Albie Lopez .10 .05
❑ 448 Mark Petkovsek .10 .05
❑ 449 Tim Raines .20 .09
❑ 450 Bryan Harvey .10 .05
❑ 451 Pat Hentgen .20 .09
❑ 452 Tim Laker .10 .05
❑ 453 Tom Gordon .10 .05
❑ 454 Phil Plantier .10 .05
❑ 455 Ernie Young .10 .05
❑ 456 Pete Harnisch .10 .05
❑ 457 Roberto Kelly .10 .05
❑ 458 Mark Portugal .10 .05
❑ 459 Mark Leiter .10 .05
❑ 460 Tony Pena .10 .05
❑ 461 Roger Pavlik .10 .05
❑ 462 Jeff King .10 .05
❑ 463 Bryan Rekar .10 .05
❑ 464 Al Leiter .20 .09
❑ 465 Phil Nevin .10 .05
❑ 466 Jose Lima .10 .05
❑ 467 Mike Stanley .10 .05
❑ 468 David McCarty .10 .05
❑ 469 Herb Perry .10 .05
❑ 470 Geronimo Berroa .10 .05
❑ 471 David Wells .30 .14
❑ 472 Vaughn Eshelman .10 .05
❑ 473 Greg Swindell .10 .05
❑ 474 Steve Sparks .10 .05
❑ 475 Luis Sojo .10 .05
❑ 476 Derrick May .10 .05
❑ 477 Joe Oliver .10 .05
❑ 478 Alex Arias .10 .05
❑ 479 Brad Ausmus .10 .05
❑ 480 Gabe White .10 .05
❑ 481 Pat Rapp .10 .05
❑ 482 Damon Buford .10 .05
❑ 483 Turk Wendell .10 .05
❑ 484 Jeff Brantley .10 .05
❑ 485 Curtis Leskanic .10 .05
❑ 486 Robb Nen .10 .05
❑ 487 Lou Whitaker .20 .09
❑ 488 Melido Perez .10 .05
❑ 489 Luis Polonia .10 .05
❑ 490 Scott Brosius .20 .09
❑ 491 Robert Perez .10 .05
❑ 492 Mike Sweeney .30 .14
❑ 493 Mark Loretta .10 .05
❑ 494 Alex Ochoa .10 .05
❑ 495 Matt Lawton .40 .18
❑ 496 Shawn Estes .20 .09
❑ 497 John Wasdin .10 .05
❑ 498 Marc Kroon .10 .05
❑ 499 Chris Snopek .10 .05
❑ 500 Jeff Suppan .10 .05
❑ 501 Terrell Wade .10 .05
❑ 502 Marvin Benard .10 .05
❑ 503 Chris Widger .10 .05
❑ 504 Quinton McCracken .20 .09
❑ 505 Bob Wolcott .10 .05
❑ 506 C.J. Nitkowski .10 .05
❑ 507 Aaron Ledesma .10 .05
❑ 508 Scott Hatteberg .10 .05
❑ 509 Jimmy Haynes .10 .05
❑ 510 Howard Battle .10 .05
❑ 511 Marty Cordova CL .10 .05
❑ 512 Randy Johnson CL .20 .09
❑ 513 Mo Vaughn CL .30 .14
❑ 514 Chan Ho Park CL .20 .09
❑ 515 Greg Maddux CL .60 .25
❑ 516 Barry Larkin CL .10 .05
❑ 517 Tom Glavine CL .20 .09
❑ NNO Cal Ripken 2131 20.00 9.00

1996 Score All-Stars

	MINT	NRMT
COMPLETE SET (20)	60.00	27.00
COMMON CARD (1-20)	.75	.35

❑ 1 Frank Thomas 10.00 4.50
❑ 2 Albert Belle 2.50 1.10
❑ 3 Ken Griffey Jr. 15.00 6.75
❑ 4 Cal Ripken 12.00 5.50
❑ 5 Mo Vaughn 2.50 1.10
❑ 6 Matt Williams 1.25 .55
❑ 7 Barry Bonds 2.50 1.10
❑ 8 Dante Bichette 1.25 .55
❑ 9 Tony Gwynn 8.00 3.60
❑ 10 Greg Maddux 10.00 4.50
❑ 11 Randy Johnson 2.50 1.10
❑ 12 Hideo Nomo 5.00 2.20
❑ 13 Tim Salmon 2.50 1.10
❑ 14 Jeff Bagwell 5.00 2.20
❑ 15 Edgar Martinez 1.25 .55
❑ 16 Reggie Sanders .75 .35
❑ 17 Larry Walker 2.50 1.10
❑ 18 Chipper Jones 8.00 3.60
❑ 19 Manny Ramirez 2.50 1.10
❑ 20 Eddie Murray 2.50 1.10

1996 Score Big Bats

	MINT	NRMT
COMPLETE SET (20)	100.00	45.00
COMMON CARD (1-20)	1.50	.70

❑ 1 Cal Ripken 15.00 6.75
❑ 2 Ken Griffey Jr. 20.00 9.00
❑ 3 Frank Thomas 12.00 5.50
❑ 4 Jeff Bagwell 6.00 2.70
❑ 5 Mike Piazza 12.00 5.50
❑ 6 Barry Bonds 5.00 2.20
❑ 7 Matt Williams 2.50 1.10
❑ 8 Raul Mondesi 2.50 1.10
❑ 9 Tony Gwynn 10.00 4.50
❑ 10 Albert Belle 6.00 2.70
❑ 11 Manny Ramirez 4.00 1.80
❑ 12 Carlos Baerga 2.50 1.10
❑ 13 Mo Vaughn 5.00 2.20
❑ 14 Derek Bell 2.50 1.10
❑ 15 Larry Walker 4.00 1.80
❑ 16 Kenny Lofton 4.00 1.80
❑ 17 Edgar Martinez 2.50 1.10
❑ 18 Reggie Sanders 1.50 .70
❑ 19 Eddie Murray 4.00 1.80
❑ 20 Chipper Jones 10.00 4.50

1996 Score Diamond Aces

	MINT	NRMT
COMPLETE SET (30)	120.00	55.00
COMMON CARD (1-30)	1.50	.70

❑ 1 Hideo Nomo 6.00 2.70
❑ 2 Brian L.Hunter 2.50 1.10
❑ 3 Ray Durham 2.50 1.10
❑ 4 Frank Thomas 12.00 5.50
❑ 5 Cal Ripken 15.00 6.75
❑ 6 Barry Bonds 5.00 2.20
❑ 7 Greg Maddux 12.00 5.50
❑ 8 Chipper Jones 10.00 4.50
❑ 9 Raul Mondesi 2.50 1.10
❑ 10 Mike Piazza 12.00 5.50
❑ 11 Derek Jeter 10.00 4.50
❑ 12 Bill Pulsipher 1.50 .70

❑ 13 Larry Walker	4.00	1.80
❑ 14 Ken Griffey Jr.	20.00	9.00
❑ 15 Alex Rodriguez	12.00	5.50
❑ 16 Manny Ramirez	4.00	1.80
❑ 17 Mo Vaughn	5.00	2.20
❑ 18 Reggie Sanders	2.50	1.10
❑ 19 Derek Bell	2.50	1.10
❑ 20 Jim Edmonds	2.50	1.10
❑ 21 Albert Belle	6.00	2.70
❑ 22 Eddie Murray	4.00	1.80
❑ 23 Tony Gwynn	10.00	4.50
❑ 24 Jeff Bagwell	6.00	2.70
❑ 25 Carlos Baerga	2.50	1.10
❑ 26 Matt Williams	2.50	1.10
❑ 27 Garret Anderson	2.50	1.10
❑ 28 Todd Hollandsworth	1.50	.70
❑ 29 Johnny Damon	2.50	1.10
❑ 30 Tim Salmon	4.00	1.80

1996 Score Dream Team

	MINT	NRMT
COMPLETE SET (9)	80.00	36.00
COMMON CARD (1-9)	1.50	.70
❑ 1 Cal Ripken	15.00	6.75
❑ 2 Frank Thomas	12.00	5.50
❑ 3 Carlos Baerga	1.50	.70
❑ 4 Matt Williams	2.00	.90
❑ 5 Mike Piazza	12.00	5.50
❑ 6 Barry Bonds	5.00	2.20
❑ 7 Ken Griffey Jr.	20.00	9.00
❑ 8 Manny Ramirez	4.00	1.80
❑ 9 Greg Maddux	12.00	5.50

1996 Score Dugout Collection

	MINT	NRMT
COMPLETE SERIES 1 (110)	50.00	22.00
COMPLETE SERIES 2 (110)	50.00	22.00
COMMON CARD (A1-B110)	.40	.18
COMP.AP SER.1 (110)	350.00	160.00
COMP.AP SER.2 (110)	350.00	160.00

*ART.PRF.STARS: 2.5X TO 6X BASIC CARDS
*ART.PRF.YOUNG STARS: 2X TO 5X BASIC CARDS
AP STATED ODDS 1:36 HOB/RET

❑ A1 Will Clark	1.50	.70
❑ A2 Rich Becker	.40	.18
❑ A3 Ryan Klesko	.60	.25
❑ A4 Jim Edmonds	1.00	.45
❑ A5 Barry Larkin	1.00	.45
❑ A6 Jim Thome	1.50	.70
❑ A7 Raul Mondesi	1.00	.45
❑ A8 Don Mattingly	2.50	1.10
❑ A9 Jeff Conine	.60	.25
❑ A10 Rickey Henderson	1.50	.70
❑ A11 Chad Curtis	.40	.18
❑ A12 Darren Daulton	.60	.25
❑ A13 Larry Walker	1.50	.70
❑ A14 Carlos Baerga	.60	.25
❑ A15 Tony Gwynn	4.00	1.80
❑ A16 Jon Nunnally	.40	.18
❑ A17 Deion Sanders	.60	.25
❑ A18 Mark Grace	1.00	.45
❑ A19 Alex Rodriguez	6.00	2.70
❑ A20 Frank Thomas	5.00	2.20
❑ A21 Brian Jordan	.60	.25
❑ A22 J.T. Snow	.60	.25
❑ A23 Shawn Green	.60	.25
❑ A24 Tim Wakefield	.60	.25
❑ A25 Curtis Goodwin	.40	.18
❑ A26 John Smoltz	.60	.25
❑ A27 Devon White	.60	.25
❑ A28 Brian L.Hunter	.60	.25
❑ A29 Rusty Greer	1.00	.45
❑ A30 Rafael Palmeiro	1.00	.45
❑ A31 Bernard Gilkey	.40	.18
❑ A32 John Valentin	.60	.25
❑ A33 Randy Johnson	1.50	.70
❑ A34 Garret Anderson	.60	.25
❑ A35 Ray Durham	.60	.25
❑ A36 Bip Roberts	.40	.18
❑ A37 Tyler Green	.40	.18
❑ A38 Bill Pulsipher	.40	.18
❑ A39 Jason Giambi	.60	.25
❑ A40 Jack McDowell	.40	.18
❑ A41 Rico Brogna	.40	.18
❑ A42 Terry Pendleton	.40	.18
❑ A43 Rondell White	.60	.25
❑ A44 Andre Dawson	1.00	.45
❑ A45 Kirby Puckett	2.50	1.10
❑ A46 Wally Joyner	.60	.25
❑ A47 B.J. Surhoff	.60	.25
❑ A48 Randy Velarde	.40	.18
❑ A49 Greg Vaughn	.60	.25
❑ A50 Roberto Alomar	1.50	.70
❑ A51 David Justice	1.50	.70
❑ A52 Cal Ripken	6.00	2.70
❑ A53 Ozzie Smith	2.00	.90
❑ A54 Mo Vaughn	2.00	.90
❑ A55 Gary DiSarcina	.40	.18
❑ A56 Matt Williams	.60	.25
❑ A57 Lenny Dykstra	.60	.25
❑ A58 Bret Boone	.60	.25
❑ A59 Albert Belle	2.00	.90
❑ A60 Vinny Castilla	1.00	.45
❑ A61 Moises Alou	1.00	.45
❑ A62 Cecil Fielder	.60	.25
❑ A63 Brad Radke	.60	.25
❑ A64 Quilvio Veras	.40	.18
❑ A65 Eddie Murray	1.50	.70
❑ A66 Dave Winfield	1.50	.70
❑ A67 Fred McGriff	1.00	.45
❑ A68 Craig Biggio	1.50	.70
❑ A69 Cliff Floyd	.60	.25
❑ A70 Tim Naehring	.40	.18
❑ A71 John Wetteland	.60	.25
❑ A72 Alan Trammell	1.00	.45
❑ A73 Steve Avery	.40	.18
❑ A74 Rick Aguilera	.40	.18
❑ A75 Derek Bell	.60	.25
❑ A76 Todd Hollandsworth	.40	.18
❑ A77 Edgar Martinez	.60	.25
❑ A78 Mark Lemke	.40	.18
❑ A79 Ariel Prieto	.40	.18
❑ A80 Russ Davis	.60	.25
❑ A81 Jim Abbott	.60	.25
❑ A82 Jason Isringhausen	.40	.18
❑ A83 Carlos Perez	.60	.25
❑ A84 David Segui	.60	.25
❑ A85 Troy O'Leary	.60	.25
❑ A86 Ismael Valdes	.60	.25
❑ A87 Carlos Delgado	.60	.25
❑ A88 Lee Smith	.60	.25
❑ A89 Javier Lopez	.60	.25
❑ A90 Frank Rodriguez	.40	.18
❑ A91 Alex Gonzalez	.40	.18
❑ A92 Benji Gil	.40	.18
❑ A93 Greg Gagne	.40	.18
❑ A94 Randy Myers	.40	.18
❑ A95 Bobby Bonilla	.60	.25
❑ A96 Billy Ashley	.40	.18
❑ A97 Andy Van Slyke	.40	.18
❑ A98 Edgardo Alfonzo	.60	.25
❑ A99 David Cone	1.00	.45
❑ A100 Dean Palmer	.60	.25
❑ A101 Jose Mesa	.40	.18
❑ A102 Karim Garcia	.60	.25
❑ A103 Johnny Damon	.60	.25
❑ A104 LaTroy Hawkins	.40	.18
❑ A105 Mark Smith	.40	.18
❑ A106 Derek Jeter	4.00	1.80
❑ A107 Michael Tucker	.60	.25
❑ A108 Joe Vitiello	.40	.18
❑ A109 Ruben Rivera	.60	.25
❑ A110 Greg Zaun	.40	.18
❑ B1 Greg Maddux	5.00	2.20
❑ B2 Pedro Martinez	1.50	.70
❑ B3 Bobby Higginson	1.50	.70
❑ B4 Ray Lankford	.60	.25
❑ B5 Shawon Dunston	.40	.18
❑ B6 Gary Sheffield	1.00	.45
❑ B7 Ken Griffey Jr.	8.00	3.60
❑ B8 Paul Molitor	1.50	.70
❑ B9 Kevin Appier	.60	.25
❑ B10 Chuck Knoblauch	1.50	.70
❑ B11 Alex Fernandez	.40	.18
❑ B12 Steve Finley	.60	.25
❑ B13 Jeff Blauser	.40	.18
❑ B14 Charles Johnson	.60	.25
❑ B15 John Franco	.60	.25
❑ B16 Mark Langston	.40	.18
❑ B17 Bret Saberhagen	.60	.25
❑ B18 John Mabry	.40	.18
❑ B19 Ramon Martinez	.60	.25
❑ B20 Mike Blowers	.40	.18
❑ B21 Paul O'Neill	.60	.25
❑ B22 Dave Nilsson	.40	.18
❑ B23 Dante Bichette	.60	.25
❑ B24 Marty Cordova	.40	.18
❑ B25 Jay Bell	.60	.25
❑ B26 Mike Mussina	1.50	.70
❑ B27 Ivan Rodriguez	2.00	.90
❑ B28 Jose Canseco	1.50	.70
❑ B29 Jeff Bagwell	2.50	1.10
❑ B30 Manny Ramirez	1.50	.70
❑ B31 Dennis Martinez	.60	.25
❑ B32 Charlie Hayes	.40	.18
❑ B33 Joe Carter	.60	.25
❑ B34 Travis Fryman	.60	.25
❑ B35 Mark McGwire	8.00	3.60
❑ B36 Reggie Sanders	.60	.25
❑ B37 Julian Tavarez	.40	.18
❑ B38 Jeff Montgomery	.40	.18
❑ B39 Andy Benes	.60	.25
❑ B40 John Jaha	.40	.18
❑ B41 Jeff Kent	.60	.25
❑ B42 Mike Piazza	5.00	2.20
❑ B43 Erik Hanson	.40	.18
❑ B44 Kenny Rogers	.40	.18
❑ B45 Hideo Nomo	2.50	1.10
❑ B46 Gregg Jefferies	.40	.18
❑ B47 Chipper Jones	5.00	2.20
❑ B48 Jay Buhner	.60	.25
❑ B49 Dennis Eckersley	.60	.25
❑ B50 Kenny Lofton	1.50	.70
❑ B51 Robin Ventura	.60	.25
❑ B52 Tom Glavine	1.50	.70
❑ B53 Tim Salmon	1.50	.70
❑ B54 Andres Galarraga	1.50	.70
❑ B55 Hal Morris	.40	.18
❑ B56 Brady Anderson	.60	.25
❑ B57 Chili Davis	.60	.25
❑ B58 Roger Clemens	3.00	1.35
❑ B59 Marquis Grissom	.60	.25
❑ B60 Mike Greenwell UER (Front says Jeff Greenwell	.40	.18

❑ B61 Sammy Sosa 4.00 1.80
❑ B62 Ron Gant .... .40 .18
❑ B63 Ken Caminiti .... 1.00 .45
❑ B64 Danny Tartabull .... .40 .18
❑ B65 Barry Bonds .... 2.00 .90
❑ B66 Ben McDonald .... .40 .18
❑ B67 Ruben Sierra............... .40 .18
❑ B68 Bernie Williams .... 1.50 .70
❑ B69 Wil Cordero .... .40 .18
❑ B70 Wade Boggs .... 1.50 .70
❑ B71 Gary Gaetti .... .60 .25
❑ B72 Greg Colbrunn .... .40 .18
❑ B73 Juan Gonzalez 4.00 1.80
❑ B74 Marc Newfield .... .40 .18
❑ B75 Charles Nagy .... .60 .25
❑ B76 Robby Thompson .... .40 .18
❑ B77 Roberto Petagine .... .40 .18
❑ B78 Darryl Strawberry .... .60 .25
❑ B79 Tino Martinez .... 1.50 .70
❑ B80 Eric Karros .... .60 .25
❑ B81 Cal Ripken SS 3.00 1.35
❑ B82 Cecil Fielder SS .... .40 .18
❑ B83 Kirby Puckett SS.......... 1.50 .70
❑ B84 Jim Edmonds SS .... .40 .18
❑ B85 Matt Williams SS............ .40 .18
❑ B86 Alex Rodriguez SS 3.00 1.35
❑ B87 Barry Larkin SS............. .40 .18
❑ B88 Rafael Palmeiro SS ...... .40 .18
❑ B89 David Cone SS .... .40 .18
❑ B90 Roberto Alomar SS........ .60 .25
❑ B91 Eddie Murray SS............ .60 .25
❑ B92 Randy Johnson SS .... .60 .25
❑ B93 Ryan Klesko SS .... .40 .18
❑ B94 Raul Mondesi SS .... .40 .18
❑ B95 Mo Vaughn SS .... 1.50 .70
❑ B96 Will Clark SS.................. .60 .25
❑ B97 Carlos Baerga SS .... .40 .18
❑ B98 Frank Thomas SS........ 2.50 1.10
❑ B99 Larry Walker SS .... .60 .25
❑ B100 Garret Anderson SS .... .40 .18
❑ B101 Edgar Martinez SS ...... .40 .18
❑ B102 Don Mattingly SS ...... 1.00 .45
❑ B103 Tony Gwynn SS .... 2.00 .90
❑ B104 Albert Belle SS .... 1.00 .45
❑ B105 Jason Isringhausen SS .40 .18
❑ B106 Ruben Rivera SS .... .40 .18
❑ B107 Johnny Damon SS ...... .40 .18
❑ B108 Karim Garcia SS........... .40 .18
❑ B109 Derek Jeter SS .... 2.00 .90
❑ B110 David Justice SS.......... .60 .25

1996 Score Future Franchise

	MINT	NRMT
COMPLETE SET (16)	100.00	45.00
COMMON CARD (1-16)...........	3.00	1.35

❑ 1 Jason Isringhausen.......... 3.00 1.35
❑ 2 Chipper Jones............... 20.00 9.00
❑ 3 Derek Jeter 20.00 9.00
❑ 4 Alex Rodriguez 25.00 11.00
❑ 5 Alex Ochoa 3.00 1.35
❑ 6 Manny Ramirez................ 8.00 3.60
❑ 7 Johnny Damon 4.00 1.80
❑ 8 Ruben Rivera 4.00 1.80
❑ 9 Karim Garcia 4.00 1.80
❑ 10 Garret Anderson 4.00 1.80
❑ 11 Marty Cordova............... 3.00 1.35
❑ 12 Bill Pulsipher 3.00 1.35
❑ 13 Hideo Nomo 12.00 5.50
❑ 14 Marc Newfield 3.00 1.35
❑ 15 Charles Johnson 4.00 1.80
❑ 16 Raul Mondesi 5.00 2.20

1996 Score Gold Stars

	MINT	NRMT
COMPLETE SET (30)	50.00	22.00
COMMON CARD (1-30).............	.50	.23

❑ 1 Ken Griffey Jr. 10.00 4.50
❑ 2 Frank Thomas................. 6.00 2.70
❑ 3 Reggie Sanders .... 1.00 .45
❑ 4 Tim Salmon .... 2.00 .90
❑ 5 Mike Piazza...................... 6.00 2.70
❑ 6 Tony Gwynn 5.00 2.20
❑ 7 Gary Sheffield .... 1.50 .70
❑ 8 Matt Williams................... 1.00 .45
❑ 9 Bernie Williams .... 2.00 .90
❑ 10 Jason Isringhausen.......... .50 .23
❑ 11 Albert Belle .... 2.00 .90
❑ 12 Chipper Jones............... 5.00 2.20
❑ 13 Edgar Martinez .... 1.00 .45
❑ 14 Barry Larkin................... 1.50 .70
❑ 15 Barry Bonds .... 2.00 .90
❑ 16 Jeff Bagwell................... 3.00 1.35
❑ 17 Greg Maddux 6.00 2.70
❑ 18 Mo Vaughn .... 2.00 .90
❑ 19 Ryan Klesko .... 1.00 .45
❑ 20 Sammy Sosa.................. 5.00 2.20
❑ 21 Darren Daulton .... 1.00 .45
❑ 22 Ivan Rodriguez .... 2.00 .90
❑ 23 Dante Bichette............... 1.00 .45
❑ 24 Hideo Nomo 3.00 1.35
❑ 25 Cal Ripken...................... 8.00 3.60
❑ 26 Rafael Palmeiro.............. 1.50 .70
❑ 27 Larry Walker .... 2.00 .90
❑ 28 Carlos Baerga .... 1.00 .45
❑ 29 Randy Johnson .... 2.00 .90
❑ 30 Manny Ramirez............. 2.00 .90

1996 Score Numbers Game

	MINT	NRMT
COMPLETE SET (30)	60.00	27.00
COMMON CARD (1-30)..............	.50	.23

❑ 1 Cal Ripken....................... 8.00 3.60
❑ 2 Frank Thomas................. 6.00 2.70
❑ 3 Ken Griffey Jr. 10.00 4.50
❑ 4 Mike Piazza...................... 6.00 2.70
❑ 5 Barry Bonds .... 2.00 .90
❑ 6 Greg Maddux 6.00 2.70
❑ 7 Jeff Bagwell..................... 3.00 1.35
❑ 8 Derek Bell .... 1.00 .45
❑ 9 Tony Gwynn 5.00 2.20
❑ 10 Hideo Nomo 3.00 1.35
❑ 11 Raul Mondesi .... 1.50 .70
❑ 12 Manny Ramirez............. 2.00 .90
❑ 13 Albert Belle .... 2.00 .90
❑ 14 Matt Williams................. 1.00 .45
❑ 15 Jim Edmonds .... 1.50 .70
❑ 16 Edgar Martinez .... 1.00 .45
❑ 17 Mo Vaughn .... 2.00 .90
❑ 18 Reggie Sanders .... .50 .23
❑ 19 Chipper Jones............... 5.00 2.20
❑ 20 Larry Walker .... 2.00 .90
❑ 21 Juan Gonzalez 5.00 2.20
❑ 22 Kenny Lofton................. 2.00 .90
❑ 23 Don Mattingly 4.00 1.80
❑ 24 Ivan Rodriguez .... 2.00 .90
❑ 25 Randy Johnson .... 2.00 .90
❑ 26 Derek Jeter 6.00 2.70
❑ 27 J.T. Snow .... 1.00 .45
❑ 28 Will Clark........................ 2.00 .90
❑ 29 Rafael Palmeiro.............. 1.50 .70
❑ 30 Alex Rodriguez 6.00 2.70

1996 Score Power Pace

	MINT	NRMT
COMPLETE SET (18)	60.00	27.00
COMMON CARD (1-18)...........	1.25	.55

❑ 1 Mark McGwire............... 15.00 6.75
❑ 2 Albert Belle 6.00 2.70
❑ 3 Jay Buhner .... 1.25 .55
❑ 4 Frank Thomas............... 10.00 4.50
❑ 5 Matt Williams................... 1.25 .55
❑ 6 Gary Sheffield .... 2.00 .90
❑ 7 Mike Piazza................... 10.00 4.50
❑ 8 Larry Walker 3.00 1.35
❑ 9 Mo Vaughn 4.00 1.80
❑ 10 Rafael Palmeiro.............. 2.00 .90
❑ 11 Dante Bichette............... 1.25 .55
❑ 12 Ken Griffey Jr. 15.00 6.75
❑ 13 Barry Bonds 4.00 1.80
❑ 14 Manny Ramirez............. 3.00 1.35
❑ 15 Sammy Sosa.................. 8.00 3.60
❑ 16 Tim Salmon.................... 3.00 1.35
❑ 17 Dave Justice 3.00 1.35
❑ 18 Eric Karros .... 1.25 .55

1996 Score Reflextions

	MINT	NRMT
COMPLETE SET (20)	100.00	45.00
COMMON CARD (1-20)............	1.25	.55

❑ 1 Cal Ripken...................... 15.00 6.75
Chipper Jones
❑ 2 Ken Griffey Jr. 20.00 9.00
Alex Rodriguez

		MINT	NRMT
❑ 3	Frank Thomas / Mo Vaughn	10.00	4.50
❑ 4	Kenny Lofton / Brian L.Hunter	3.00	1.35
❑ 5	Don Mattingly / J.T.Snow	5.00	2.20
❑ 6	Manny Ramirez / Raul Mondesi	3.00	1.35
❑ 7	Tony Gwynn / Garret Anderson	8.00	3.60
❑ 8	Roberto Alomar / Carlos Baerga	2.00	.90
❑ 9	Andre Dawson / Larry Walker	2.00	.90
❑ 10	Barry Larkin / Derek Jeter	8.00	3.60
❑ 11	Barry Bonds / Reggie Sanders	4.00	1.80
❑ 12	Mike Piazza / Albert Belle	10.00	4.50
❑ 13	Wade Boggs / Edgar Martinez	3.00	1.35
❑ 14	David Cone / John Smoltz	1.25	.55
❑ 15	Will Clark / Jeff Bagwell	5.00	2.20
❑ 16	Mark McGwire / Cecil Fielder	15.00	6.75
❑ 17	Greg Maddux / Mike Mussina	10.00	4.50
❑ 18	Randy Johnson / Hideo Nomo	5.00	2.20
❑ 19	Jim Thome / Dean Palmer	3.00	1.35
❑ 20	Chuck Knoblauch / Craig Biggio	3.00	1.35

1996 Score Titanic Taters

	MINT	NRMT
COMPLETE SET (18)	80.00	36.00
COMMON CARD (1-18)	1.50	.70

		MINT	NRMT
❑ 1	Albert Belle	6.00	2.70
❑ 2	Frank Thomas	12.00	5.50
❑ 3	Mo Vaughn	5.00	2.20
❑ 4	Ken Griffey Jr.	20.00	9.00
❑ 5	Matt Williams	2.00	.90
❑ 6	Mark McGwire	20.00	9.00
❑ 7	Dante Bichette	2.00	.90
❑ 8	Tim Salmon	4.00	1.80
❑ 9	Jeff Bagwell	6.00	2.70
❑ 10	Rafael Palmeiro	2.50	1.10
❑ 11	Mike Piazza	12.00	5.50
❑ 12	Cecil Fielder	1.50	.70
❑ 13	Larry Walker	4.00	1.80
❑ 14	Sammy Sosa	10.00	4.50
❑ 15	Manny Ramirez	4.00	1.80
❑ 16	Gary Sheffield	2.50	1.10
❑ 17	Barry Bonds	5.00	2.20
❑ 18	Jay Buhner	2.00	.90

1997 Score

	MINT	NRMT
COMPLETE SET (551)	40.00	18.00
COMP.FACT.SET (551)	40.00	18.00
COMPLETE SERIES 1 (330)	15.00	6.75
COMPLETE SERIES 2 (221)	25.00	11.00
COMMON CARD (1-551)	.10	.05

		MINT	NRMT
❑ 1	Jeff Bagwell	.60	.25
❑ 2	Mickey Tettleton	.10	.05
❑ 3	Johnny Damon	.20	.09
❑ 4	Jeff Conine	.20	.09
❑ 5	Bernie Williams	.40	.18
❑ 6	Will Clark	.40	.18
❑ 7	Ryan Klesko	.20	.09
❑ 8	Cecil Fielder	.20	.09
❑ 9	Paul Wilson	.10	.05
❑ 10	Gregg Jefferies	.10	.05
❑ 11	Chili Davis	.20	.09
❑ 12	Albert Belle	.50	.23
❑ 13	Ken Hill	.10	.05
❑ 14	Cliff Floyd	.20	.09
❑ 15	Jaime Navarro	.10	.05
❑ 16	Ismael Valdes	.20	.09
❑ 17	Jeff King	.10	.05
❑ 18	Chris Bosio	.10	.05
❑ 19	Reggie Sanders	.20	.09
❑ 20	Darren Daulton	.20	.09
❑ 21	Ken Caminiti	.30	.14
❑ 22	Mike Piazza	1.25	.55
❑ 23	Chad Mottola	.10	.05
❑ 24	Darin Erstad	.60	.25
❑ 25	Dante Bichette	.20	.09
❑ 26	Frank Thomas	1.25	.55
❑ 27	Ben McDonald	.10	.05
❑ 28	Raul Casanova	.10	.05
❑ 29	Kevin Ritz	.10	.05
❑ 30	Garret Anderson	.20	.09
❑ 31	Jason Kendall	.30	.14
❑ 32	Billy Wagner	.20	.09
❑ 33	Dave Justice	.40	.18
❑ 34	Marty Cordova	.10	.05
❑ 35	Derek Jeter	1.25	.55
❑ 36	Trevor Hoffman	.20	.09
❑ 37	Geronimo Berroa	.10	.05
❑ 38	Walt Weiss	.10	.05
❑ 39	Kirt Manwaring	.10	.05
❑ 40	Alex Gonzalez	.10	.05
❑ 41	Sean Berry	.10	.05
❑ 42	Kevin Appier	.20	.09
❑ 43	Rusty Greer	.20	.09
❑ 44	Pete Incaviglia	.10	.05
❑ 45	Rafael Palmeiro	.30	.14
❑ 46	Eddie Murray	.40	.18
❑ 47	Moises Alou	.30	.14
❑ 48	Mark Lewis	.10	.05
❑ 49	Hal Morris	.10	.05
❑ 50	Edgar Renteria	.20	.09
❑ 51	Rickey Henderson	.40	.18
❑ 52	Pat Listach	.10	.05
❑ 53	John Wasdin	.10	.05
❑ 54	James Baldwin	.20	.09
❑ 55	Brian Jordan	.20	.09
❑ 56	Edgar Martinez	.20	.09
❑ 57	Wil Cordero	.10	.05
❑ 58	Danny Tartabull	.10	.05
❑ 59	Keith Lockhart	.10	.05
❑ 60	Rico Brogna	.10	.05
❑ 61	Ricky Bottalico	.20	.09
❑ 62	Terry Pendleton	.10	.05
❑ 63	Bret Boone	.20	.09
❑ 64	Charlie Hayes	.10	.05
❑ 65	Marc Newfield	.10	.05
❑ 66	Sterling Hitchcock	.20	.09
❑ 67	Roberto Alomar	.40	.18
❑ 68	John Jaha	.10	.05
❑ 69	Greg Colbrunn	.10	.05
❑ 70	Sal Fasano	.10	.05
❑ 71	Brooks Kieschnick	.10	.05
❑ 72	Pedro Martinez	.40	.18
❑ 73	Kevin Elster	.10	.05
❑ 74	Ellis Burks	.20	.09
❑ 75	Chuck Finley	.20	.09
❑ 76	John Olerud	.20	.09
❑ 77	Jay Bell	.20	.09
❑ 78	Allen Watson	.10	.05
❑ 79	Darryl Strawberry	.20	.09
❑ 80	Orlando Miller	.10	.05
❑ 81	Jose Herrera	.10	.05
❑ 82	Andy Pettitte	.30	.14
❑ 83	Juan Guzman	.10	.05
❑ 84	Alan Benes	.20	.09
❑ 85	Jack McDowell	.10	.05
❑ 86	Ugueth Urbina	.20	.09
❑ 87	Rocky Coppinger	.10	.05
❑ 88	Jeff Cirillo	.20	.09
❑ 89	Tom Glavine	.40	.18
❑ 90	Robby Thompson	.10	.05
❑ 91	Barry Bonds	.50	.23
❑ 92	Carlos Delgado	.20	.09
❑ 93	Mo Vaughn	.50	.23
❑ 94	Ryne Sandberg	.50	.23
❑ 95	Alex Rodriguez	1.25	.55
❑ 96	Brady Anderson	.20	.09
❑ 97	Scott Brosius	.20	.09
❑ 98	Dennis Eckersley	.20	.09
❑ 99	Brian McRae	.10	.05
❑ 100	Rey Ordonez	.20	.09
❑ 101	John Valentin	.20	.09
❑ 102	Brett Butler	.20	.09
❑ 103	Eric Karros	.20	.09
❑ 104	Harold Baines	.20	.09
❑ 105	Javier Lopez	.20	.09
❑ 106	Alan Trammell	.20	.09
❑ 107	Jim Thome	.40	.18
❑ 108	Frank Rodriguez	.10	.05
❑ 109	Bernard Gilkey	.10	.05
❑ 110	Reggie Jefferson	.10	.05
❑ 111	Scott Stahoviak	.10	.05
❑ 112	Steve Gibralter	.10	.05
❑ 113	Todd Hollandsworth	.10	.05
❑ 114	Ruben Rivera	.20	.09
❑ 115	Dennis Martinez	.20	.09
❑ 116	Mariano Rivera	.20	.09
❑ 117	John Smoltz	.20	.09
❑ 118	John Mabry	.10	.05
❑ 119	Tom Gordon	.10	.05
❑ 120	Alex Ochoa	.10	.05
❑ 121	Jamey Wright	.10	.05
❑ 122	Dave Nilsson	.10	.05
❑ 123	Bobby Bonilla	.20	.09
❑ 124	Al Leiter	.20	.09
❑ 125	Rick Aguilera	.10	.05
❑ 126	Jeff Brantley	.10	.05
❑ 127	Kevin Brown	.30	.14
❑ 128	George Arias	.10	.05
❑ 129	Darren Oliver	.10	.05
❑ 130	Bill Pulsipher	.10	.05
❑ 131	Roberto Hernandez	.10	.05

❑	132	Delino DeShields	.10	.05
❑	133	Mark Grudzielanek	.20	.09
❑	134	John Wetteland	.20	.09
❑	135	Carlos Baerga	.20	.09
❑	136	Paul Sorrento	.10	.05
❑	137	Leo Gomez	.10	.05
❑	138	Andy Ashby	.10	.05
❑	139	Julio Franco	.20	.09
❑	140	Brian Hunter	.20	.09
❑	141	Jermaine Dye	.10	.05
❑	142	Tony Clark	.30	.14
❑	143	Ruben Sierra	.10	.05
❑	144	Donovan Osborne	.10	.05
❑	145	Mark McLemore	.10	.05
❑	146	Terry Steinbach	.20	.09
❑	147	Bob Wells	.10	.05
❑	148	Chan Ho Park	.40	.18
❑	149	Tim Salmon	.40	.18
❑	150	Paul O'Neill	.20	.09
❑	151	Cal Ripken	1.50	.70
❑	152	Wally Joyner	.20	.09
❑	153	Omar Vizquel	.20	.09
❑	154	Mike Mussina	.40	.18
❑	155	Andres Galarraga	.40	.18
❑	156	Ken Griffey Jr.	2.00	.90
❑	157	Kenny Lofton	.40	.18
❑	158	Ray Durham	.20	.09
❑	159	Hideo Nomo	.50	.23
❑	160	Ozzie Guillen	.10	.05
❑	161	Roger Pavlik	.10	.05
❑	162	Manny Ramirez	.40	.18
❑	163	Mark Lemke	.10	.05
❑	164	Mike Stanley	.10	.05
❑	165	Chuck Knoblauch	.40	.18
❑	166	Kimera Bartee	.10	.05
❑	167	Wade Boggs	.40	.18
❑	168	Jay Buhner	.20	.09
❑	169	Eric Young	.20	.09
❑	170	Jose Canseco	.40	.18
❑	171	Dwight Gooden	.20	.09
❑	172	Fred McGriff	.30	.14
❑	173	Sandy Alomar Jr.	.20	.09
❑	174	Andy Benes	.20	.09
❑	175	Dean Palmer	.20	.09
❑	176	Larry Walker	.40	.18
❑	177	Charles Nagy	.20	.09
❑	178	David Cone	.30	.14
❑	179	Mark Grace	.30	.14
❑	180	Robin Ventura	.20	.09
❑	181	Roger Clemens	.75	.35
❑	182	Bobby Witt	.10	.05
❑	183	Vinny Castilla	.30	.14
❑	184	Gary Sheffield	.30	.14
❑	185	Dan Wilson	.10	.05
❑	186	Roger Cedeno	.10	.05
❑	187	Mark McGwire	2.00	.90
❑	188	Darren Bragg	.10	.05
❑	189	Quinton McCracken	.20	.09
❑	190	Randy Myers	.10	.05
❑	191	Jeromy Burnitz	.20	.09
❑	192	Randy Johnson	.40	.18
❑	193	Chipper Jones	1.00	.45
❑	194	Greg Vaughn	.20	.09
❑	195	Travis Fryman	.20	.09
❑	196	Tim Naehring	.10	.05
❑	197	B.J. Surhoff	.20	.09
❑	198	Juan Gonzalez	1.00	.45
❑	199	Terrell Wade	.10	.05
❑	200	Jeff Frye	.10	.05
❑	201	Joey Cora	.20	.09
❑	202	Raul Mondesi	.30	.14
❑	203	Ivan Rodriguez	.50	.23
❑	204	Armando Reynoso	.10	.05
❑	205	Jeffrey Hammonds	.20	.09
❑	206	Darren Dreifort	.20	.09
❑	207	Kevin Seitzer	.10	.05
❑	208	Tino Martinez	.40	.18
❑	209	Jim Bruske	.10	.05
❑	210	Jeff Suppan	.10	.05
❑	211	Mark Carreon	.10	.05
❑	212	Wilson Alvarez	.20	.09
❑	213	John Burkett	.10	.05
❑	214	Tony Phillips	.10	.05
❑	215	Greg Maddux	1.25	.55
❑	216	Mark Whiten	.10	.05
❑	217	Curtis Pride	.10	.05
❑	218	Lyle Mouton	.10	.05
❑	219	Todd Hundley	.20	.09
❑	220	Greg Gagne	.10	.05
❑	221	Rich Amaral	.10	.05
❑	222	Tom Goodwin	.10	.05
❑	223	Chris Hoiles	.10	.05
❑	224	Jayhawk Owens	.10	.05
❑	225	Kenny Rogers	.10	.05
❑	226	Mike Greenwell	.10	.05
❑	227	Mark Wohlers	.10	.05
❑	228	Henry Rodriguez	.20	.09
❑	229	Robert Perez	.10	.05
❑	230	Jeff Kent	.20	.09
❑	231	Darryl Hamilton	.10	.05
❑	232	Alex Fernandez	.10	.05
❑	233	Ron Karkovice	.10	.05
❑	234	Jimmy Haynes	.10	.05
❑	235	Craig Biggio	.40	.18
❑	236	Ray Lankford	.20	.09
❑	237	Lance Johnson	.10	.05
❑	238	Matt Williams	.20	.09
❑	239	Chad Curtis	.10	.05
❑	240	Mark Thompson	.10	.05
❑	241	Jason Giambi	.20	.09
❑	242	Barry Larkin	.30	.14
❑	243	Paul Molitor	.40	.18
❑	244	Sammy Sosa	1.00	.45
❑	245	Kevin Tapani	.10	.05
❑	246	Marquis Grissom	.20	.09
❑	247	Joe Carter	.20	.09
❑	248	Ramon Martinez	.20	.09
❑	249	Tony Gwynn	1.00	.45
❑	250	Andy Fox	.10	.05
❑	251	Troy O'Leary	.20	.09
❑	252	Warren Newson	.10	.05
❑	253	Troy Percival	.20	.09
❑	254	Jamie Moyer	.10	.05
❑	255	Danny Graves	.10	.05
❑	256	David Wells	.30	.14
❑	257	Todd Zeile	.10	.05
❑	258	Raul Ibanez	.10	.05
❑	259	Tyler Houston	.10	.05
❑	260	LaTroy Hawkins	.10	.05
❑	261	Joey Hamilton	.20	.09
❑	262	Mike Sweeney	.10	.05
❑	263	Brant Brown	.20	.09
❑	264	Pat Hentgen	.20	.09
❑	265	Mark Johnson	.10	.05
❑	266	Robb Nen	.10	.05
❑	267	Justin Thompson	.20	.09
❑	268	Ron Gant	.10	.05
❑	269	Jeff D'Amico	.10	.05
❑	270	Shawn Estes	.20	.09
❑	271	Derek Bell	.20	.09
❑	272	Fernando Valenzuela	.20	.09
❑	273	Tom Pagnozzi	.10	.05
❑	274	John Burke	.10	.05
❑	275	Ed Sprague	.10	.05
❑	276	F.P. Santangelo	.10	.05
❑	277	Todd Greene	.20	.09
❑	278	Butch Huskey	.10	.05
❑	279	Steve Finley	.20	.09
❑	280	Eric Davis	.20	.09
❑	281	Shawn Green	.20	.09
❑	282	Al Martin	.10	.05
❑	283	Michael Tucker	.20	.09
❑	284	Shane Reynolds	.20	.09
❑	285	Matt Mieske	.10	.05
❑	286	Jose Rosado	.10	.05
❑	287	Mark Langston	.20	.09
❑	288	Ralph Milliard	.10	.05
❑	289	Mike Lansing	.10	.05
❑	290	Scott Servais	.10	.05
❑	291	Royce Clayton	.10	.05
❑	292	Mike Grace	.10	.05
❑	293	James Mouton	.10	.05
❑	294	Charles Johnson	.20	.09
❑	295	Gary Gaetti	.10	.05
❑	296	Kevin Mitchell	.10	.05
❑	297	Carlos Garcia	.10	.05
❑	298	Desi Relaford	.10	.05
❑	299	Jason Thompson	.10	.05
❑	300	Osvaldo Fernandez	.10	.05
❑	301	Fernando Vina	.10	.05
❑	302	Jose Offerman	.10	.05
❑	303	Yamil Benitez	.10	.05
❑	304	J.T. Snow	.20	.09
❑	305	Rafael Bournigal	.10	.05
❑	306	Jason Isringhausen	.10	.05
❑	307	Bobby Higginson	.30	.14
❑	308	Nerio Rodriguez	.25	.11
❑	309	Brian Giles	.50	.23
❑	310	Andruw Jones	.60	.25
❑	311	Tony Graffanino	.10	.05
❑	312	Arquimedez Pozo	.10	.05
❑	313	Jermaine Allensworth	.10	.05
❑	314	Jeff Darwin	.10	.05
❑	315	George Williams	.10	.05
❑	316	Karim Garcia	.20	.09
❑	317	Trey Beamon	.10	.05
❑	318	Mac Suzuki	.10	.05
❑	319	Robin Jennings	.10	.05
❑	320	Danny Patterson	.10	.05
❑	321	Damon Mashore	.10	.05
❑	322	Wendell Magee	.10	.05
❑	323	Dax Jones	.10	.05
❑	324	Kevin Brown	.30	.14
❑	325	Marvin Benard	.10	.05
❑	326	Mike Cameron	.20	.09
❑	327	Marcus Jensen	.10	.05
❑	328	Eddie Murray CL	.20	.09
❑	329	Paul Molitor CL	.20	.09
❑	330	Todd Hundley CL	.10	.05
❑	331	Norm Charlton	.10	.05
❑	332	Bruce Ruffin	.10	.05
❑	333	John Wetteland	.20	.09
❑	334	Marquis Grissom	.20	.09
❑	335	Sterling Hitchcock	.20	.09
❑	336	John Olerud	.20	.09
❑	337	David Wells	.30	.14
❑	338	Chili Davis	.20	.09
❑	339	Mark Lewis	.10	.05
❑	340	Kenny Lofton	.40	.18
❑	341	Alex Fernandez	.10	.05
❑	342	Ruben Sierra	.10	.05
❑	343	Delino DeShields	.10	.05
❑	344	John Wasdin	.10	.05
❑	345	Dennis Martinez	.20	.09
❑	346	Kevin Elster	.10	.05
❑	347	Bobby Bonilla	.20	.09
❑	348	Jaime Navarro	.10	.05
❑	349	Chad Curtis	.10	.05
❑	350	Terry Steinbach	.20	.09
❑	351	Ariel Prieto	.10	.05
❑	352	Jeff Kent	.20	.09
❑	353	Carlos Garcia	.10	.05
❑	354	Mark Whiten	.10	.05
❑	355	Todd Zeile	.10	.05
❑	356	Eric Davis	.20	.09
❑	357	Greg Colbrunn	.10	.05
❑	358	Moises Alou	.30	.14
❑	359	Allen Watson	.10	.05
❑	360	Jose Canseco	.40	.18
❑	361	Matt Williams	.20	.09
❑	362	Jeff King	.10	.05
❑	363	Darryl Hamilton	.10	.05
❑	364	Mark Clark	.10	.05
❑	365	J.T. Snow	.20	.09
❑	366	Kevin Mitchell	.10	.05
❑	367	Orlando Miller	.10	.05
❑	368	Rico Brogna	.10	.05
❑	369	Mike James	.10	.05
❑	370	Brad Ausmus	.10	.05
❑	371	Darryl Kile	.20	.09
❑	372	Edgardo Alfonzo	.20	.09
❑	373	Julian Tavarez	.10	.05
❑	374	Darren Lewis	.10	.05
❑	375	Steve Karsay	.10	.05
❑	376	Lee Stevens	.10	.05
❑	377	Albie Lopez	.10	.05
❑	378	Orel Hershiser	.20	.09
❑	379	Lee Smith	.20	.09
❑	380	Rick Helling	.20	.09
❑	381	Carlos Perez	.20	.09
❑	382	Tony Tarasco	.10	.05
❑	383	Melvin Nieves	.10	.05
❑	384	Benji Gil	.10	.05
❑	385	Devon White	.20	.09
❑	386	Armando Benitez	.10	.05

❏ 387	Bill Swift	.10	.05
❏ 388	John Smiley	.10	.05
❏ 389	Midre Cummings	.10	.05
❏ 390	Tim Belcher	.10	.05
❏ 391	Tim Raines	.20	.09
❏ 392	Todd Worrell	.10	.05
❏ 393	Quilvio Veras	.10	.05
❏ 394	Matt Lawton	.20	.09
❏ 395	Aaron Sele	.20	.09
❏ 396	Bip Roberts	.10	.05
❏ 397	Denny Neagle	.20	.09
❏ 398	Tyler Green	.10	.05
❏ 399	Hipolito Pichardo	.10	.05
❏ 400	Scott Erickson	.20	.09
❏ 401	Bobby Jones	.10	.05
❏ 402	Jim Edmonds	.30	.14
❏ 403	Chad Ogea	.10	.05
❏ 404	Cal Eldred	.10	.05
❏ 405	Pat Listach	.10	.05
❏ 406	Todd Stottlemyre	.10	.05
❏ 407	Phil Nevin	.10	.05
❏ 408	Otis Nixon	.10	.05
❏ 409	Billy Ashley	.10	.05
❏ 410	Jimmy Key	.20	.09
❏ 411	Mike Timlin	.10	.05
❏ 412	Joe Vitiello	.10	.05
❏ 413	Rondell White	.20	.09
❏ 414	Jeff Fassero	.10	.05
❏ 415	Rex Hudler	.10	.05
❏ 416	Curt Schilling	.20	.09
❏ 417	Rich Becker	.10	.05
❏ 418	William Van Landingham	.10	.05
❏ 419	Chris Snopek	.10	.05
❏ 420	David Segui	.20	.09
❏ 421	Eddie Murray	.40	.18
❏ 422	Shane Andrews	.10	.05
❏ 423	Gary DiSarcina	.10	.05
❏ 424	Brian Hunter	.20	.09
❏ 425	Willie Greene	.20	.09
❏ 426	Felipe Crespo	.10	.05
❏ 427	Jason Bates	.10	.05
❏ 428	Albert Belle	.50	.23
❏ 429	Rey Sanchez	.10	.05
❏ 430	Roger Clemens	.75	.35
❏ 431	Deion Sanders	.20	.09
❏ 432	Ernie Young	.10	.05
❏ 433	Jay Bell	.20	.09
❏ 434	Jeff Blauser	.10	.05
❏ 435	Lenny Dykstra	.20	.09
❏ 436	Chuck Carr	.10	.05
❏ 437	Russ Davis	.20	.09
❏ 438	Carl Everett	.10	.05
❏ 439	Damion Easley	.20	.09
❏ 440	Pat Kelly	.10	.05
❏ 441	Pat Rapp	.10	.05
❏ 442	Dave Justice	.40	.18
❏ 443	Graeme Lloyd	.10	.05
❏ 444	Damon Buford	.10	.05
❏ 445	Jose Valentin	.10	.05
❏ 446	Jason Schmidt	.10	.05
❏ 447	Dave Martinez	.10	.05
❏ 448	Danny Tartabull	.10	.05
❏ 449	Jose Vizcaino	.10	.05
❏ 450	Steve Avery	.10	.05
❏ 451	Mike Devereaux	.10	.05
❏ 452	Jim Eisenreich	.10	.05
❏ 453	Mark Leiter	.10	.05
❏ 454	Roberto Kelly	.10	.05
❏ 455	Benito Santiago	.10	.05
❏ 456	Steve Trachsel	.10	.05
❏ 457	Gerald Williams	.10	.05
❏ 458	Pete Schourek	.10	.05
❏ 459	Esteban Loaiza	.10	.05
❏ 460	Mel Rojas	.10	.05
❏ 461	Tim Wakefield	.20	.09
❏ 462	Tony Fernandez	.10	.05
❏ 463	Doug Drabek	.10	.05
❏ 464	Joe Girardi	.10	.05
❏ 465	Mike Bordick	.10	.05
❏ 466	Jim Leyritz	.10	.05
❏ 467	Erik Hanson	.10	.05
❏ 468	Michael Tucker	.20	.09
❏ 469	Tony Womack	.30	.14
❏ 470	Doug Glanville	.20	.09
❏ 471	Rudy Pemberton	.10	.05
❏ 472	Keith Lockhart	.10	.05
❏ 473	Nomar Garciaparra	1.25	.55
❏ 474	Scott Rolen	1.00	.45
❏ 475	Jason Dickson	.20	.09
❏ 476	Glendon Rusch	.10	.05
❏ 477	Todd Walker	.40	.18
❏ 478	Dmitri Young	.20	.09
❏ 479	Rod Myers	.20	.09
❏ 480	Wilton Guerrero	.10	.05
❏ 481	Jorge Posada	.20	.09
❏ 482	Brant Brown	.20	.09
❏ 483	Bubba Trammell	.25	.11
❏ 484	Jose Guillen	.40	.18
❏ 485	Scott Spiezio	.10	.05
❏ 486	Bob Abreu	.20	.09
❏ 487	Chris Holt	.10	.05
❏ 488	Deivi Cruz	.30	.14
❏ 489	Vladimir Guerrero	.75	.35
❏ 490	Julio Santana	.10	.05
❏ 491	Ray Montgomery	.10	.05
❏ 492	Kevin Orie	.10	.05
❏ 493	Todd Hundley GY	.10	.05
❏ 494	Tim Salmon GY	.20	.09
❏ 495	Albert Belle GY	.20	.09
❏ 496	Manny Ramirez GY	.20	.09
❏ 497	Rafael Palmeiro GY	.10	.05
❏ 498	Juan Gonzalez GY	.50	.23
❏ 499	Ken Griffey Jr. GY	1.00	.45
❏ 500	Andruw Jones GY	.50	.23
❏ 501	Mike Piazza GY	.60	.25
❏ 502	Jeff Bagwell GY	.40	.18
❏ 503	Bernie Williams GY	.20	.09
❏ 504	Barry Bonds GY	.20	.09
❏ 505	Ken Caminiti GY	.10	.05
❏ 506	Darin Erstad GY	.40	.18
❏ 507	Alex Rodriguez GY	.60	.25
❏ 508	Frank Thomas GY	.60	.25
❏ 509	Chipper Jones GY	.50	.23
❏ 510	Mo Vaughn GY	.30	.14
❏ 511	Mark McGwire GY	1.00	.45
❏ 512	Fred McGriff GY	.10	.05
❏ 513	Jay Buhner GY	.10	.05
❏ 514	Jim Thome GY	.20	.09
❏ 515	Gary Sheffield GY	.10	.05
❏ 516	Dean Palmer GY	.20	.09
❏ 517	Henry Rodriguez GY	.10	.05
❏ 518	Andy Pettitte RF	.10	.05
❏ 519	Mike Mussina RF	.20	.09
❏ 520	Greg Maddux RF	.60	.25
❏ 521	John Smoltz RF	.10	.05
❏ 522	Hideo Nomo RF	.50	.23
❏ 523	Troy Percival RF	.10	.05
❏ 524	John Wetteland RF	.10	.05
❏ 525	Roger Clemens RF	.40	.18
❏ 526	Charles Nagy RF	.10	.05
❏ 527	Mariano Rivera RF	.10	.05
❏ 528	Tom Glavine RF	.20	.09
❏ 529	Randy Johnson RF	.20	.09
❏ 530	Jason Isringhausen RF	.10	.05
❏ 531	Alex Fernandez RF	.10	.05
❏ 532	Kevin Brown RF	.10	.05
❏ 533	Chuck Knoblauch TG	.20	.09
❏ 534	Rusty Greer TG	.10	.05
❏ 535	Tony Gwynn TG	.50	.23
❏ 536	Ryan Klesko TG	.10	.05
❏ 537	Ryne Sandberg TG	.40	.18
❏ 538	Barry Larkin TG	.10	.05
❏ 539	Will Clark TG	.40	.18
❏ 540	Kenny Lofton TG	.20	.09
❏ 541	Paul Molitor TG	.20	.09
❏ 542	Roberto Alomar TG	.20	.09
❏ 543	Rey Ordonez TG	.10	.05
❏ 544	Jason Giambi TG	.10	.05
❏ 545	Derek Jeter TG	.60	.25
❏ 546	Cal Ripken TG	.75	.35
❏ 547	Ivan Rodriguez TG	.30	.14
❏ 548	Ken Griffey Jr. CL	1.00	.45
❏ 549	Frank Thomas CL	.60	.25
❏ 550	Mike Piazza CL	.60	.25
❏ 551A	Hideki Irabu SP	12.00	5.50
❏ 551B	Hideki Irabu Japenese SP	12.00	5.50

1997 Score Blast Masters

	MINT	NRMT
COMPLETE SET (18)	100.00	45.00
COMMON CARD (1-18)	2.00	.90
❏ 1 Mo Vaughn	5.00	2.20
❏ 2 Mark McGwire	20.00	9.00
❏ 3 Juan Gonzalez	10.00	4.50
❏ 4 Albert Belle	6.00	2.70
❏ 5 Barry Bonds	5.00	2.20
❏ 6 Ken Griffey Jr.	20.00	9.00
❏ 7 Andruw Jones	5.00	2.20
❏ 8 Chipper Jones	10.00	4.50
❏ 9 Mike Piazza	12.00	5.50
❏ 10 Jeff Bagwell	6.00	2.70
❏ 11 Dante Bichette	2.00	.90
❏ 12 Alex Rodriguez	12.00	5.50
❏ 13 Gary Sheffield	3.00	1.35
❏ 14 Ken Caminiti	3.00	1.35
❏ 15 Sammy Sosa	10.00	4.50
❏ 16 Vladimir Guerrero	6.00	2.70
❏ 17 Brian Jordan	2.00	.90
❏ 18 Tim Salmon	4.00	1.80

1997 Score Franchise

	MINT	NRMT
COMPLETE SET (9)	100.00	45.00
COMMON CARD (1-9)	2.50	1.10
COMP.GLOWING SET (9)	250.00	110.00

*GLOWING: 1X TO 2.5X BASIC FRANCHISE
GLOW.SER.1 ODDS 1:240H/R, 1:79J, 1:120M

	MINT	NRMT
❏ 1 Ken Griffey Jr.	25.00	11.00
❏ 2 John Smoltz	2.50	1.10
❏ 3 Cal Ripken	20.00	9.00
❏ 4 Chipper Jones	12.00	5.50
❏ 5 Mike Piazza	15.00	6.75
❏ 6 Albert Belle	8.00	3.60
❏ 7 Frank Thomas	15.00	6.75
❏ 8 Sammy Sosa	12.00	5.50
❏ 9 Roberto Alomar	5.00	2.20

1997 Score Heart of the Order

	MINT	NRMT
COMPLETE SET (36)	100.00	45.00
COMMON CARD (1-36)	.75	.35
❑ 1 Will Clark	3.00	1.35
❑ 2 Ivan Rodriguez	4.00	1.80
❑ 3 Juan Gonzalez	8.00	3.60
❑ 4 Frank Thomas	10.00	4.50
❑ 5 Albert Belle	5.00	2.20
❑ 6 Robin Ventura	1.25	.55
❑ 7 Alex Rodriguez	10.00	4.50
❑ 8 Jay Buhner	1.25	.55
❑ 9 Ken Griffey Jr.	15.00	6.75
❑ 10 Rafael Palmeiro	2.00	.90
❑ 11 Roberto Alomar	3.00	1.35
❑ 12 Cal Ripken	12.00	5.50
❑ 13 Manny Ramirez	3.00	1.35
❑ 14 Matt Williams	1.25	.55
❑ 15 Jim Thome	3.00	1.35
❑ 16 Derek Jeter	8.00	3.60
❑ 17 Wade Boggs	3.00	1.35
❑ 18 Bernie Williams	3.00	1.35
❑ 19 Chipper Jones	8.00	3.60
❑ 20 Andruw Jones	4.00	1.80
❑ 21 Ryan Klesko	1.25	.55
❑ 22 Mike Piazza	10.00	4.50
❑ 23 Wilton Guerrero	.75	.35
❑ 24 Raul Mondesi	2.00	.90
❑ 25 Tony Gwynn	8.00	3.60
❑ 26 Greg Vaughn	1.25	.55
❑ 27 Ken Caminiti	2.00	.90
❑ 28 Brian Jordan	1.25	.55
❑ 29 Ron Gant	.75	.35
❑ 30 Dmitri Young	1.25	.55
❑ 31 Darin Erstad	4.00	1.80
❑ 32 Tim Salmon	3.00	1.35
❑ 33 Jim Edmonds	2.00	.90
❑ 34 Chuck Knoblauch	3.00	1.35
❑ 35 Paul Molitor	3.00	1.35
❑ 36 Todd Walker	3.00	1.35

1997 Score Highlight Zone

	MINT	NRMT
COMPLETE SET (18)	200.00	90.00
COMMON CARD (1-18)	4.00	1.80
❑ 1 Frank Thomas	20.00	9.00
❑ 2 Ken Griffey Jr.	30.00	13.50
❑ 3 Mo Vaughn	8.00	3.60
❑ 4 Albert Belle	8.00	3.60
❑ 5 Mike Piazza	20.00	9.00
❑ 6 Barry Bonds	8.00	3.60
❑ 7 Greg Maddux	20.00	9.00
❑ 8 Sammy Sosa	15.00	6.75
❑ 9 Jeff Bagwell	10.00	4.50
❑ 10 Alex Rodriguez	20.00	9.00
❑ 11 Chipper Jones	15.00	6.75
❑ 12 Brady Anderson	4.00	1.80
❑ 13 Ozzie Smith	8.00	3.60
❑ 14 Edgar Martinez	4.00	1.80
❑ 15 Cal Ripken	25.00	11.00
❑ 16 Ryan Klesko	4.00	1.80
❑ 17 Randy Johnson	6.00	2.70
❑ 18 Eddie Murray	6.00	2.70

1997 Score Pitcher Perfect

	MINT	NRMT
COMPLETE SET (15)	60.00	27.00
COMMON CARD (1-15)	1.00	.45
❑ 1 Cal Ripken	10.00	4.50
❑ 2 Alex Rodriguez	8.00	3.60
❑ 3 Alex Rodriguez Cal Ripken	12.00	5.50
❑ 4 Edgar Martinez	1.00	.45
❑ 5 Ivan Rodriguez	3.00	1.35
❑ 6 Mark McGwire	12.00	5.50
❑ 7 Tim Salmon	2.50	1.10
❑ 8 Chili Davis	1.00	.45
❑ 9 Joe Carter	1.00	.45
❑ 10 Frank Thomas	8.00	3.60
❑ 11 Will Clark	2.50	1.10
❑ 12 Mo Vaughn	3.00	1.35
❑ 13 Wade Boggs	2.50	1.10
❑ 14 Ken Griffey Jr.	12.00	5.50
❑ 15 Randy Johnson	2.50	1.10

1997 Score Stand and Deliver

	MINT	NRMT
COMPLETE SET (24)	350.00	160.00
COMMON CARD (1-24)	2.50	1.10
❑ 1 Andruw Jones	12.00	5.50
❑ 2 Greg Maddux	30.00	13.50
❑ 3 Chipper Jones	25.00	11.00
❑ 4 John Smoltz	5.00	2.20
❑ 5 Ken Griffey Jr.	50.00	22.00
❑ 6 Alex Rodriguez	30.00	13.50
❑ 7 Jay Buhner	5.00	2.20
❑ 8 Randy Johnson	10.00	4.50
❑ 9 Derek Jeter	25.00	11.00
❑ 10 Andy Pettitte	6.00	2.70
❑ 11 Bernie Williams	10.00	4.50
❑ 12 Mariano Rivera	5.00	2.20
❑ 13 Mike Piazza	30.00	13.50
❑ 14 Hideo Nomo	12.00	5.50
❑ 15 Raul Mondesi	6.00	2.70
❑ 16 Todd Hollandsworth	2.50	1.10
❑ 17 Manny Ramirez	10.00	4.50
❑ 18 Jim Thome	10.00	4.50
❑ 19 Dave Justice	10.00	4.50
❑ 20 Matt Williams	5.00	2.20
❑ 21 Juan Gonzalez W	25.00	11.00
❑ 22 Jeff Bagwell W	15.00	6.75
❑ 23 Cal Ripken W	40.00	18.00
❑ 24 Frank Thomas W	30.00	13.50

1997 Score Stellar Season

	MINT	NRMT
COMPLETE SET (18)	80.00	36.00
COMMON CARD (1-18)	.75	.35
❑ 1 Juan Gonzalez	8.00	3.60
❑ 2 Chuck Knoblauch	3.00	1.35
❑ 3 Jeff Bagwell	5.00	2.20
❑ 4 John Smoltz	1.50	.70
❑ 5 Mark McGwire	15.00	6.75
❑ 6 Ken Griffey Jr.	15.00	6.75
❑ 7 Frank Thomas	10.00	4.50
❑ 8 Alex Rodriguez	10.00	4.50
❑ 9 Mike Piazza	10.00	4.50
❑ 10 Albert Belle	5.00	2.20
❑ 11 Roberto Alomar	3.00	1.35
❑ 12 Sammy Sosa	8.00	3.60
❑ 13 Mo Vaughn	4.00	1.80
❑ 14 Brady Anderson	1.50	.70
❑ 15 Henry Rodriguez	.75	.35
❑ 16 Eric Young	.75	.35
❑ 17 Gary Sheffield	2.00	.90
❑ 18 Ryan Klesko	1.50	.70

1997 Score Titanic Taters

	MINT	NRMT
COMPLETE SET (18)	120.00	55.00
COMMON CARD (1-18)	2.50	1.10
❑ 1 Mark McGwire	25.00	11.00
❑ 2 Mike Piazza	15.00	6.75
❑ 3 Ken Griffey Jr.	25.00	11.00
❑ 4 Juan Gonzalez	12.00	5.50
❑ 5 Frank Thomas	15.00	6.75
❑ 6 Albert Belle	6.00	2.70
❑ 7 Sammy Sosa	12.00	5.50
❑ 8 Jeff Bagwell	8.00	3.60
❑ 9 Todd Hundley	2.50	1.10

Card	MINT	NRMT
❑ 10 Ryan Klesko	2.50	1.10
❑ 11 Brady Anderson	2.50	1.10
❑ 12 Mo Vaughn	6.00	2.70
❑ 13 Jay Buhner	2.50	1.10
❑ 14 Chipper Jones	12.00	5.50
❑ 15 Barry Bonds	6.00	2.70
❑ 16 Gary Sheffield	3.00	1.35
❑ 17 Alex Rodriguez	15.00	6.75
❑ 18 Cecil Fielder	2.50	1.10

1998 Score

	MINT	NRMT
COMPLETE SET (270)	40.00	18.00
COMMON CARD (1-270)	.10	.05
❑ 1 Andruw Jones	.50	.23
❑ 2 Dan Wilson	.10	.05
❑ 3 Hideo Nomo	.50	.23
❑ 4 Chuck Carr	.10	.05
❑ 5 Barry Bonds	.50	.23
❑ 6 Jack McDowell	.10	.05
❑ 7 Albert Belle	.50	.23
❑ 8 Francisco Cordova	.10	.05
❑ 9 Greg Maddux	1.25	.55
❑ 10 Alex Rodriguez	1.25	.55
❑ 11 Steve Avery	.10	.05
❑ 12 Chuck McElroy	.10	.05
❑ 13 Larry Walker	.40	.18
❑ 14 Hideki Irabu	.25	.11
❑ 15 Roberto Alomar	.40	.18
❑ 16 Neifi Perez	.15	.07
❑ 17 Jim Thome	.40	.18
❑ 18 Rickey Henderson	.40	.18
❑ 19 Andres Galarraga	.40	.18
❑ 20 Jeff Fassero	.10	.05
❑ 21 Kevin Young	.15	.07
❑ 22 Derek Jeter	1.00	.45
❑ 23 Andy Benes	.15	.07
❑ 24 Mike Piazza	1.25	.55
❑ 25 Todd Stottlemyre	.15	.07
❑ 26 Michael Tucker	.15	.07
❑ 27 Denny Neagle	.15	.07
❑ 28 Javier Lopez	.15	.07
❑ 29 Aaron Sele	.15	.07
❑ 30 Ryan Klesko	.15	.07
❑ 31 Dennis Eckersley	.15	.07
❑ 32 Quinton McCracken	.15	.07
❑ 33 Brian Anderson	.15	.07
❑ 34 Ken Griffey Jr.	2.00	.90
❑ 35 Shawn Estes	.15	.07
❑ 36 Tim Wakefield	.10	.05
❑ 37 Jimmy Key	.15	.07
❑ 38 Jeff Bagwell	.60	.25
❑ 39 Edgardo Alfonzo	.15	.07
❑ 40 Mike Cameron	.15	.07
❑ 41 Mark McGwire	2.50	1.10
❑ 42 Tino Martinez	.40	.18
❑ 43 Cal Ripken	1.50	.70
❑ 44 Curtis Goodwin	.10	.05
❑ 45 Bobby Ayala	.10	.05
❑ 46 Sandy Alomar Jr.	.15	.07
❑ 47 Bobby Jones	.10	.05
❑ 48 Omar Vizquel	.15	.07
❑ 49 Roger Clemens	.75	.35
❑ 50 Tony Gwynn	1.00	.45
❑ 51 Chipper Jones	1.00	.45
❑ 52 Ron Coomer	.10	.05
❑ 53 Dmitri Young	.15	.07
❑ 54 Brian Giles	.15	.07
❑ 55 Steve Finley	.15	.07
❑ 56 David Cone	.25	.11
❑ 57 Andy Pettitte	.25	.11
❑ 58 Wilton Guerrero	.10	.05
❑ 59 Deion Sanders	.15	.07
❑ 60 Carlos Delgado	.15	.07
❑ 61 Jason Giambi	.15	.07
❑ 62 Ozzie Guillen	.10	.05
❑ 63 Jay Bell	.15	.07
❑ 64 Barry Larkin	.25	.11
❑ 65 Sammy Sosa	1.00	.45
❑ 66 Bernie Williams	.40	.18
❑ 67 Terry Steinbach	.15	.07
❑ 68 Scott Rolen	1.00	.45
❑ 69 Melvin Nieves	.10	.05
❑ 70 Craig Biggio	.40	.18
❑ 71 Todd Greene	.15	.07
❑ 72 Greg Gagne	.10	.05
❑ 73 Shigetoshi Hasegawa	.15	.07
❑ 74 Mark McLemore	.10	.05
❑ 75 Darren Bragg	.10	.05
❑ 76 Brett Butler	.15	.07
❑ 77 Ron Gant	.10	.05
❑ 78 Mike Difelice	.10	.05
❑ 79 Charles Nagy	.15	.07
❑ 80 Scott Hatteberg	.10	.05
❑ 81 Brady Anderson	.15	.07
❑ 82 Jay Buhner	.15	.07
❑ 83 Todd Hollandsworth	.10	.05
❑ 84 Geronimo Berroa	.10	.05
❑ 85 Jeff Suppan	.10	.05
❑ 86 Pedro Martinez	.40	.18
❑ 87 Roger Cedeno	.10	.05
❑ 88 Ivan Rodriguez	.50	.23
❑ 89 Jaime Navarro	.10	.05
❑ 90 Chris Hoiles	.10	.05
❑ 91 Nomar Garciaparra	1.25	.55
❑ 92 Rafael Palmeiro	.25	.11
❑ 93 Darin Erstad	.50	.23
❑ 94 Kenny Lofton	.40	.18
❑ 95 Mike Timlin	.10	.05
❑ 96 Chris Clemons	.10	.05
❑ 97 Vinny Castilla	.25	.11
❑ 98 Charlie Hayes	.10	.05
❑ 99 Lyle Mouton	.10	.05
❑ 100 Jason Dickson	.15	.07
❑ 101 Justin Thompson	.15	.07
❑ 102 Pat Kelly	.10	.05
❑ 103 Chan Ho Park	.40	.18
❑ 104 Ray Lankford	.15	.07
❑ 105 Frank Thomas	1.25	.55
❑ 106 Jermaine Allensworth	.10	.05
❑ 107 Doug Drabek	.10	.05
❑ 108 Todd Hundley	.15	.07
❑ 109 Carl Everett	.10	.05
❑ 110 Edgar Martinez	.15	.07
❑ 111 Robin Ventura	.15	.07
❑ 112 John Wetteland	.15	.07
❑ 113 Mariano Rivera	.15	.07
❑ 114 Jose Rosado	.10	.05
❑ 115 Ken Caminiti	.25	.11
❑ 116 Paul O'Neill	.15	.07
❑ 117 Tim Salmon	.40	.18
❑ 118 Eduardo Perez	.10	.05
❑ 119 Mike Jackson	.10	.05
❑ 120 John Smoltz	.15	.07
❑ 121 Brant Brown	.15	.07
❑ 122 John Mabry	.10	.05
❑ 123 Chuck Knoblauch	.40	.18
❑ 124 Reggie Sanders	.15	.07
❑ 125 Ken Hill	.10	.05
❑ 126 Mike Mussina	.40	.18
❑ 127 Chad Curtis	.10	.05
❑ 128 Todd Worrell	.10	.05
❑ 129 Chris Widger	.10	.05
❑ 130 Damon Mashore	.10	.05
❑ 131 Kevin Brown	.25	.11
❑ 132 Bip Roberts	.10	.05
❑ 133 Tim Naehring	.10	.05
❑ 134 Dave Martinez	.10	.05
❑ 135 Jeff Blauser	.10	.05
❑ 136 David Justice	.40	.18
❑ 137 Dave Hollins	.10	.05
❑ 138 Pat Hentgen	.15	.07
❑ 139 Darren Daulton	.15	.07
❑ 140 Ramon Martinez	.15	.07
❑ 141 Raul Casanova	.10	.05
❑ 142 Tom Glavine	.40	.18
❑ 143 J.T. Snow	.15	.07
❑ 144 Tony Graffanino	.10	.05
❑ 145 Randy Johnson	.40	.18
❑ 146 Orlando Merced	.10	.05
❑ 147 Jeff Juden	.10	.05
❑ 148 Darryl Kile	.15	.07
❑ 149 Ray Durham	.15	.07
❑ 150 Alex Fernandez	.10	.05
❑ 151 Joey Cora	.15	.07
❑ 152 Royce Clayton	.10	.05
❑ 153 Randy Myers	.15	.07
❑ 154 Charles Johnson	.15	.07
❑ 155 Alan Benes	.15	.07
❑ 156 Mike Bordick	.10	.05
❑ 157 Heathcliff Slocumb	.10	.05
❑ 158 Roger Bailey	.10	.05
❑ 159 Reggie Jefferson	.10	.05
❑ 160 Ricky Bottalico	.15	.07
❑ 161 Scott Erickson	.15	.07
❑ 162 Matt Williams	.15	.07
❑ 163 Robb Nen	.15	.07
❑ 164 Matt Stairs	.15	.07
❑ 165 Ismael Valdes	.15	.07
❑ 166 Lee Stevens	.10	.05
❑ 167 Gary DiSarcina	.10	.05
❑ 168 Brad Radke	.15	.07
❑ 169 Mike Lansing	.10	.05
❑ 170 Armando Benitez	.10	.05
❑ 171 Mike James	.10	.05
❑ 172 Russ Davis	.15	.07
❑ 173 Lance Johnson	.10	.05
❑ 174 Joey Hamilton	.15	.07
❑ 175 John Valentin	.15	.07
❑ 176 David Segui	.15	.07
❑ 177 David Wells	.25	.11
❑ 178 Delino DeShields	.10	.05
❑ 179 Eric Karros	.15	.07
❑ 180 Jim Leyritz	.10	.05
❑ 181 Raul Mondesi	.25	.11
❑ 182 Travis Fryman	.15	.07
❑ 183 Todd Zeile	.15	.07
❑ 184 Brian Jordan	.15	.07
❑ 185 Rey Ordonez	.15	.07
❑ 186 Jim Edmonds	.25	.11
❑ 187 Terrell Wade	.10	.05
❑ 188 Marquis Grissom	.15	.07
❑ 189 Chris Snopek	.10	.05
❑ 190 Shane Reynolds	.15	.07
❑ 191 Jeff Frye	.10	.05
❑ 192 Paul Sorrento	.10	.05
❑ 193 James Baldwin	.15	.07
❑ 194 Brian McRae	.10	.05
❑ 195 Fred McGriff	.25	.11
❑ 196 Troy Percival	.15	.07
❑ 197 Rich Amaral	.10	.05
❑ 198 Juan Guzman	.10	.05
❑ 199 Cecil Fielder	.15	.07
❑ 200 Willie Blair	.10	.05
❑ 201 Chili Davis	.15	.07
❑ 202 Gary Gaetti	.10	.05
❑ 203 B.J. Surhoff	.15	.07
❑ 204 Steve Cooke	.10	.05
❑ 205 Chuck Finley	.15	.07

Card	MINT	NRMT
❑ 206 Jeff Kent	.15	.07
❑ 207 Ben McDonald	.10	.05
❑ 208 Jeffrey Hammonds	.15	.07
❑ 209 Tom Goodwin	.10	.05
❑ 210 Billy Ashley	.10	.05
❑ 211 Wil Cordero	.10	.05
❑ 212 Shawon Dunston	.10	.05
❑ 213 Tony Phillips	.10	.05
❑ 214 Jamie Moyer	.10	.05
❑ 215 John Jaha	.10	.05
❑ 216 Troy O'Leary	.15	.07
❑ 217 Brad Ausmus	.10	.05
❑ 218 Garret Anderson	.15	.07
❑ 219 Wilson Alvarez	.15	.07
❑ 220 Kent Mercker	.10	.05
❑ 221 Wade Boggs	.40	.18
❑ 222 Mark Wohlers	.10	.05
❑ 223 Kevin Appier	.15	.07
❑ 224 Tony Fernandez	.10	.05
❑ 225 Ugueth Urbina	.15	.07
❑ 226 Gregg Jefferies	.10	.05
❑ 227 Mo Vaughn	.50	.23
❑ 228 Arthur Rhodes	.10	.05
❑ 229 Jorge Fabregas	.10	.05
❑ 230 Mark Gardner	.10	.05
❑ 231 Shane Mack	.10	.05
❑ 232 Jorge Posada	.15	.07
❑ 233 Jose Cruz Jr.	.50	.23
❑ 234 Paul Konerko	.40	.18
❑ 235 Derrek Lee	.15	.07
❑ 236 Steve Woodard	.15	.07
❑ 237 Todd Dunwoody	.15	.07
❑ 238 Fernando Tatis	.15	.07
❑ 239 Jacob Cruz	.10	.05
❑ 240 Pokey Reese	.10	.05
❑ 241 Mark Kotsay	.25	.11
❑ 242 Matt Morris	.15	.07
❑ 243 Antone Williamson	.10	.05
❑ 244 Ben Grieve	.75	.35
❑ 245 Ryan McGuire	.10	.05
❑ 246 Lou Collier	.10	.05
❑ 247 Shannon Stewart	.15	.07
❑ 248 Brett Tomko	.15	.07
❑ 249 Bobby Estalella	.15	.07
❑ 250 Livan Hernandez	.15	.07
❑ 251 Todd Helton	.50	.23
❑ 252 Jaret Wright	.50	.23
❑ 253 Darryl Hamilton IM	.10	.05
❑ 254 Stan Javier IM	.10	.05
❑ 255 Glenallen Hill IM	.10	.05
❑ 256 Mark Gardner IM	.10	.05
❑ 257 Cal Ripken IM	.75	.35
❑ 258 Mike Mussina IM	.15	.07
❑ 259 Mike Piazza IM	.60	.25
❑ 260 Sammy Sosa IM	.50	.23
❑ 261 Todd Hundley IM	.10	.05
❑ 262 Eric Karros IM	.10	.05
❑ 263 Denny Neagle IM	.10	.05
❑ 264 Jeromy Burnitz IM	.10	.05
❑ 265 Greg Maddux IM	.60	.25
❑ 266 Tony Clark IM	.10	.05
❑ 267 Vladimir Guerrero IM	.40	.18
❑ 268 Cal Ripken Jr. CL	.75	.35
❑ 269 Ken Griffey Jr. CL	1.00	.45
❑ 270 Mark McGwire CL	1.25	.55
❑ NNO Checklist All-Star Edition	.25	.11
❑ NNO Checklist Regular Issue	.10	.05

1998 Score All Score Team

	MINT	NRMT
COMPLETE SET (20)	120.00	55.00
COMMON CARD (1-20)	1.50	.70

Card	MINT	NRMT
❑ 1 Mike Piazza	12.00	5.50
❑ 2 Ivan Rodriguez	5.00	2.20
❑ 3 Frank Thomas	12.00	5.50
❑ 4 Mark McGwire	25.00	11.00
❑ 5 Ryne Sandberg	5.00	2.20
❑ 6 Roberto Alomar	4.00	1.80
❑ 7 Cal Ripken	15.00	6.75
❑ 8 Barry Larkin	2.50	1.10
❑ 9 Paul Molitor	4.00	1.80
❑ 10 Travis Fryman	1.50	.70

Card	MINT	NRMT
❑ 11 Kirby Puckett	6.00	2.70
❑ 12 Tony Gwynn	10.00	4.50
❑ 13 Ken Griffey Jr.	20.00	9.00
❑ 14 Juan Gonzalez	10.00	4.50
❑ 15 Barry Bonds	5.00	2.20
❑ 16 Andruw Jones	4.00	1.80
❑ 17 Roger Clemens	8.00	3.60
❑ 18 Randy Johnson	4.00	1.80
❑ 19 Greg Maddux	12.00	5.50
❑ 20 Dennis Eckersley	1.50	.70

1998 Score Complete Players

	MINT	NRMT
COMPLETE SET (30)	200.00	90.00
COMMON CARD (1A-10C)	3.00	1.35

Card	MINT	NRMT
❑ 1A Ken Griffey Jr.	15.00	6.75
❑ 1B Ken Griffey Jr.	15.00	6.75
❑ 1C Ken Griffey Jr.	15.00	6.75
❑ 2A Mark McGwire	20.00	9.00
❑ 2B Mark McGwire	20.00	9.00
❑ 2C Mark McGwire	20.00	9.00
❑ 3A Derek Jeter	8.00	3.60
❑ 3B Derek Jeter	8.00	3.60
❑ 3C Derek Jeter	8.00	3.60
❑ 4A Cal Ripken	12.00	5.50
❑ 4B Cal Ripken Jr.	12.00	5.50
❑ 4C Cal Ripken Jr.	12.00	5.50
❑ 5A Mike Piazza	10.00	4.50
❑ 5B Mike Piazza	10.00	4.50
❑ 5C Mike Piazza	10.00	4.50
❑ 6A Darin Erstad	3.00	1.35
❑ 6B Darin Erstad	3.00	1.35
❑ 6C Darin Erstad	3.00	1.35
❑ 7A Frank Thomas	10.00	4.50
❑ 7B Frank Thomas	10.00	4.50
❑ 7C Frank Thomas	10.00	4.50
❑ 8A Andruw Jones	3.00	1.35
❑ 8B Andruw Jones	3.00	1.35
❑ 8C Andruw Jones	3.00	1.35
❑ 9A Nomar Garciaparra	10.00	4.50
❑ 9B Nomar Garciaparra	10.00	4.50
❑ 9C Nomar Garciaparra	10.00	4.50
❑ 10A Manny Ramirez	3.00	1.35
❑ 10B Manny Ramirez	3.00	1.35
❑ 10C Manny Ramirez	3.00	1.35

1998 Score First Pitch

	MINT	NRMT
COMPLETE SET (20)	80.00	36.00
COMMON CARD (1-20)	2.00	.90

Card	MINT	NRMT
❑ 1 Ken Griffey Jr.	10.00	4.50
❑ 2 Frank Thomas	6.00	2.70
❑ 3 Alex Rodriguez	6.00	2.70
❑ 4 Cal Ripken	8.00	3.60
❑ 5 Chipper Jones	5.00	2.20
❑ 6 Juan Gonzalez	5.00	2.20
❑ 7 Derek Jeter	5.00	2.20
❑ 8 Mike Piazza	6.00	2.70
❑ 9 Andruw Jones	2.00	.90
❑ 10 Nomar Garciaparra	6.00	2.70
❑ 11 Barry Bonds	2.50	1.10
❑ 12 Jeff Bagwell	3.00	1.35
❑ 13 Scott Rolen	4.00	1.80
❑ 14 Hideo Nomo	2.50	1.10
❑ 15 Roger Clemens	4.00	1.80
❑ 16 Mark McGwire	12.00	5.50
❑ 17 Greg Maddux	6.00	2.70
❑ 18 Albert Belle	2.00	.90
❑ 19 Ivan Rodriguez	2.50	1.10
❑ 20 Mo Vaughn	2.50	1.10

1998 Score Loaded Lineup

	MINT	NRMT
COMPLETE SET (10)	80.00	36.00
COMMON CARD (LL1-LL10)	3.00	1.35

Card	MINT	NRMT
❑ LL1 Chuck Knoblauch	4.00	1.80
❑ LL2 Tony Gwynn	10.00	4.50
❑ LL3 Frank Thomas	12.00	5.50
❑ LL4 Ken Griffey Jr.	20.00	9.00
❑ LL5 Mike Piazza	12.00	5.50
❑ LL6 Barry Bonds	5.00	2.20
❑ LL7 Cal Ripken	15.00	6.75
❑ LL8 Paul Molitor	3.00	1.35
❑ LL9 Nomar Garciaparra	12.00	5.50
❑ LL10 Greg Maddux	12.00	5.50

1998 Score New Season

	MINT	NRMT
COMPLETE SET (15)	80.00	36.00
COMMON CARD (NS1-NS15)	1.50	.70

Card	MINT	NRMT
❑ NS1 Kenny Lofton	3.00	1.35

Card	Player	MINT	NRMT
❑ NS2	Nomar Garciaparra	10.00	4.50
❑ NS3	Todd Helton	3.00	1.35
❑ NS4	Miguel Tejada	1.50	.70
❑ NS5	Jaret Wright	3.00	1.35
❑ NS6	Alex Rodriguez	10.00	4.50
❑ NS7	Vladimir Guerrero	4.00	1.80
❑ NS8	Ken Griffey Jr.	15.00	6.75
❑ NS9	Ben Grieve	5.00	2.20
❑ NS10	Travis Lee	5.00	2.20
❑ NS11	Jose Cruz Jr.	3.00	1.35
❑ NS12	Paul Konerko	3.00	1.35
❑ NS13	Frank Thomas	10.00	4.50
❑ NS14	Chipper Jones	8.00	3.60
❑ NS15	Cal Ripken	12.00	5.50

1998 Score Rookie Traded

	MINT	NRMT
COMPLETE SET (270)	30.00	13.50
COMMON SP (1-50)	.40	.18
COMMON CARD (51-270)	.10	.05

Card	Player	MINT	NRMT
❑ 1	Tony Clark	.40	.18
❑ 2	Juan Gonzalez	1.50	.70
❑ 3	Frank Thomas	2.00	.90
❑ 4	Greg Maddux	2.00	.90
❑ 5	Barry Larkin	.40	.18
❑ 6	Derek Jeter	1.50	.70
❑ 7	Randy Johnson	.60	.25
❑ 8	Roger Clemens	1.25	.55
❑ 9	Tony Gwynn	1.50	.70
❑ 10	Barry Bonds	.75	.35
❑ 11	Jim Edmonds	.40	.18
❑ 12	Bernie Williams	.60	.25
❑ 13	Ken Griffey Jr.	3.00	1.35
❑ 14	Tim Salmon	.60	.25
❑ 15	Mo Vaughn	.75	.35
❑ 16	David Justice	.60	.25
❑ 17	Jose Cruz Jr.	.75	.35
❑ 18	Andruw Jones	.75	.35
❑ 19	Sammy Sosa	1.50	.70
❑ 20	Jeff Bagwell	1.00	.45
❑ 21	Scott Rolen	1.50	.70
❑ 22	Darin Erstad	.75	.35
❑ 23	Andy Pettitte	.40	.18
❑ 24	Mike Mussina	.60	.25
❑ 25	Mark McGwire	4.00	1.80
❑ 26	Hideo Nomo	.75	.35
❑ 27	Chipper Jones	1.50	.70
❑ 28	Cal Ripken	2.50	1.10
❑ 29	Chuck Knoblauch	.60	.25
❑ 30	Alex Rodriguez	2.00	.90
❑ 31	Jim Thome	.60	.25
❑ 32	Mike Piazza	2.00	.90
❑ 33	Ivan Rodriguez	.75	.35
❑ 34	Roberto Alomar	.60	.25
❑ 35	Nomar Garciaparra	2.00	.90
❑ 36	Albert Belle	.60	.25
❑ 37	Vladimir Guerrero	1.00	.45
❑ 38	Raul Mondesi	.40	.18
❑ 39	Larry Walker	.60	.25
❑ 40	Manny Ramirez	.60	.25
❑ 41	Tino Martinez	.60	.25
❑ 42	Craig Biggio	.60	.25
❑ 43	Jay Buhner	.40	.18
❑ 44	Kenny Lofton	.60	.25
❑ 45	Pedro Martinez	.60	.25
❑ 46	Edgar Martinez	.40	.18
❑ 47	Gary Sheffield	.40	.18
❑ 48	Jose Guillen	.40	.18
❑ 49	Ken Caminiti	.40	.18
❑ 50	Bobby Higginson	.40	.18
❑ 51	Alan Benes	.15	.07
❑ 52	Shawn Green	.15	.07
❑ 53	Ron Coomer	.10	.05
❑ 54	Charles Nagy	.15	.07
❑ 55	Steve Karsay	.10	.05
❑ 56	Matt Morris	.15	.07
❑ 57	Bobby Jones	.10	.05
❑ 58	Jason Kendall	.15	.07
❑ 59	Jeff Conine	.15	.07
❑ 60	Joe Girardi	.10	.05
❑ 61	Mark Kotsay	.25	.11
❑ 62	Eric Karros	.15	.07
❑ 63	Bartolo Colon	.15	.07
❑ 64	Mariano Rivera	.15	.07
❑ 65	Alex Gonzalez	.10	.05
❑ 66	Scott Spiezio	.10	.05
❑ 67	Luis Castillo	.15	.07
❑ 68	Joey Cora	.15	.07
❑ 69	Mark McLemore	.10	.05
❑ 70	Reggie Jefferson	.10	.05
❑ 71	Lance Johnson	.10	.05
❑ 72	Damian Jackson	.10	.05
❑ 73	Jeff D'Amico	.10	.05
❑ 74	David Ortiz	.15	.07
❑ 75	J.T. Snow	.15	.07
❑ 76	Todd Hundley	.15	.07
❑ 77	Billy Wagner	.15	.07
❑ 78	Vinny Castilla	.25	.11
❑ 79	Ismael Valdes	.15	.07
❑ 80	Neifi Perez	.15	.07
❑ 81	Derek Bell	.15	.07
❑ 82	Ryan Klesko	.15	.07
❑ 83	Rey Ordonez	.15	.07
❑ 84	Carlos Garcia	.10	.05
❑ 85	Curt Schilling	.15	.07
❑ 86	Robin Ventura	.15	.07
❑ 87	Pat Hentgen	.15	.07
❑ 88	Glendon Rusch	.10	.05
❑ 89	Hideki Irabu	.25	.11
❑ 90	Antone Williamson	.10	.05
❑ 91	Denny Neagle	.15	.07
❑ 92	Kevin Orie	.10	.05
❑ 93	Reggie Sanders	.15	.07
❑ 94	Brady Anderson	.15	.07
❑ 95	Andy Benes	.15	.07
❑ 96	John Valentin	.15	.07
❑ 97	Bobby Bonilla	.15	.07
❑ 98	Walt Weiss	.15	.07
❑ 99	Robin Jennings	.10	.05
❑ 100	Marty Cordova	.10	.05
❑ 101	Brad Ausmus	.10	.05
❑ 102	Brian Rose	.15	.07
❑ 103	Calvin Maduro	.10	.05
❑ 104	Raul Casanova	.10	.05
❑ 105	Jeff King	.15	.07
❑ 106	Sandy Alomar Jr.	.15	.07
❑ 107	Tim Naehring	.10	.05
❑ 108	Mike Cameron	.15	.07
❑ 109	Omar Vizquel	.15	.07
❑ 110	Brad Radke	.15	.07
❑ 111	Jeff Fassero	.10	.05
❑ 112	Deivi Cruz	.10	.05
❑ 113	Dave Hollins	.10	.05
❑ 114	Dean Palmer	.15	.07
❑ 115	Esteban Loaiza	.10	.05
❑ 116	Brian Giles	.15	.07
❑ 117	Steve Finley	.15	.07
❑ 118	Jose Canseco	.40	.18
❑ 119	Al Martin	.10	.05
❑ 120	Eric Young	.15	.07
❑ 121	Curtis Goodwin	.10	.05
❑ 122	Ellis Burks	.15	.07
❑ 123	Mike Hampton	.10	.05
❑ 124	Lou Collier	.10	.05
❑ 125	John Olerud	.15	.07
❑ 126	Ramon Martinez	.15	.07
❑ 127	Todd Dunwoody	.15	.07
❑ 128	Jermaine Allensworth	.10	.05
❑ 129	Eduardo Perez	.10	.05
❑ 130	Dante Bichette	.15	.07
❑ 131	Edgar Renteria	.15	.07
❑ 132	Bob Abreu	.15	.07
❑ 133	Rondell White	.15	.07
❑ 134	Michael Coleman	.15	.07
❑ 135	Jason Giambi	.15	.07
❑ 136	Brant Brown	.15	.07
❑ 137	Michael Tucker	.15	.07
❑ 138	Dave Nilsson	.10	.05
❑ 139	Benito Santiago	.10	.05
❑ 140	Ray Durham	.15	.07
❑ 141	Jeff Kent	.15	.07
❑ 142	Matt Stairs	.15	.07
❑ 143	Kevin Young	.15	.07
❑ 144	Eric Davis	.15	.07
❑ 145	John Wetteland	.15	.07
❑ 146	Esteban Yan	.30	.14
❑ 147	Wilton Guerrero	.10	.05
❑ 148	Moises Alou	.25	.11
❑ 149	Edgardo Alfonzo	.15	.07
❑ 150	Andy Ashby	.10	.05
❑ 151	Todd Walker	.25	.11
❑ 152	Jermaine Dye	.10	.05
❑ 153	Brian Hunter	.15	.07
❑ 154	Shawn Estes	.15	.07
❑ 155	Bernard Gilkey	.10	.05
❑ 156	Tony Womack	.15	.07
❑ 157	John Smoltz	.15	.07
❑ 158	Delino DeShields	.10	.05
❑ 159	Jacob Cruz	.10	.05
❑ 160	Javier Valentin	.15	.07
❑ 161	Chris Hoiles	.10	.05
❑ 162	Garret Anderson	.15	.07
❑ 163	Dan Wilson	.10	.05
❑ 164	Paul O'Neill	.15	.07
❑ 165	Matt Williams	.15	.07
❑ 166	Travis Fryman	.15	.07
❑ 167	Javier Lopez	.15	.07
❑ 168	Ray Lankford	.15	.07
❑ 169	Bobby Estalella	.15	.07
❑ 170	Henry Rodriguez	.15	.07
❑ 171	Quinton McCracken	.15	.07
❑ 172	Jaret Wright	.50	.23
❑ 173	Darryl Kile	.15	.07
❑ 174	Wade Boggs	.40	.18
❑ 175	Orel Hershiser	.15	.07
❑ 176	B.J. Surhoff	.15	.07
❑ 177	Fernando Tatis	.15	.07
❑ 178	Carlos Delgado	.15	.07
❑ 179	Jorge Fabregas	.10	.05
❑ 180	Tony Saunders	.10	.05
❑ 181	Devon White	.15	.07
❑ 182	Dmitri Young	.15	.07
❑ 183	Ryan McGuire	.10	.05
❑ 184	Mark Bellhorn	.15	.07
❑ 185	Joe Carter	.15	.07
❑ 186	Kevin Stocker	.10	.05
❑ 187	Mike Lansing	.10	.05
❑ 188	Jason Dickson	.15	.07
❑ 189	Charles Johnson	.15	.07
❑ 190	Will Clark	.40	.18
❑ 191	Shannon Stewart	.15	.07
❑ 192	Johnny Damon	.15	.07
❑ 193	Todd Greene	.15	.07
❑ 194	Carlos Baerga	.15	.07
❑ 195	David Cone	.25	.11
❑ 196	Pokey Reese	.10	.05
❑ 197	Livan Hernandez	.15	.07

		MINT	NRMT
❑ 198	Tom Glavine	.40	.18
❑ 199	Geronimo Berroa	.10	.05
❑ 200	Darryl Hamilton	.10	.05
❑ 201	Terry Steinbach	.15	.07
❑ 202	Robb Nen	.15	.07
❑ 203	Ron Gant	.10	.05
❑ 204	Rafael Palmeiro	.25	.11
❑ 205	Rickey Henderson	.40	.18
❑ 206	Justin Thompson	.15	.07
❑ 207	Jeff Suppan	.10	.05
❑ 208	Kevin Brown	.25	.11
❑ 209	Jimmy Key	.15	.07
❑ 210	Brian Jordan	.15	.07
❑ 211	Aaron Sele	.15	.07
❑ 212	Fred McGriff	.25	.11
❑ 213	Jay Bell	.15	.07
❑ 214	Andres Galarraga	.40	.18
❑ 215	Mark Grace	.25	.11
❑ 216	Brett Tomko	.15	.07
❑ 217	Francisco Cordova	.10	.05
❑ 218	Rusty Greer	.15	.07
❑ 219	Bubba Trammell	.15	.07
❑ 220	Derrek Lee	.15	.07
❑ 221	Brian Anderson	.15	.07
❑ 222	Mark Grudzielanek	.15	.07
❑ 223	Marquis Grissom	.15	.07
❑ 224	Gary DiSarcina	.10	.05
❑ 225	Jim Leyritz	.10	.05
❑ 226	Jeffrey Hammonds	.15	.07
❑ 227	Karim Garcia	.15	.07
❑ 228	Chan Ho Park	.40	.18
❑ 229	Brooks Kieschnick	.10	.05
❑ 230	Trey Beamon	.10	.05
❑ 231	Kevin Appier	.15	.07
❑ 232	Wally Joyner	.15	.07
❑ 233	Richie Sexson	.25	.11
❑ 234	Frank Catalanotto	.25	.11
❑ 235	Rafael Medina	.15	.07
❑ 236	Travis Lee	.75	.35
❑ 237	Eli Marrero	.15	.07
❑ 238	Carl Pavano	.15	.07
❑ 239	Enrique Wilson	.15	.07
❑ 240	Richard Hidalgo	.15	.07
❑ 241	Todd Helton	.50	.23
❑ 242	Ben Grieve	.75	.35
❑ 243	Mario Valdez	.15	.07
❑ 244	Magglio Ordonez	.50	.23
❑ 245	Juan Encarnacion	.15	.07
❑ 246	Russell Branyan	.15	.07
❑ 247	Sean Casey	.15	.07
❑ 248	Abraham Nunez	.15	.07
❑ 249	Brad Fullmer	.15	.07
❑ 250	Paul Konerko	.40	.18
❑ 251	Miguel Tejada	.15	.07
❑ 252	Mike Lowell	.40	.18
❑ 253	Ken Griffey Jr. ST	1.00	.45
❑ 254	Frank Thomas ST	.60	.25
❑ 255	Alex Rodriguez ST	.60	.25
❑ 256	Jose Cruz Jr. ST	.25	.11
❑ 257	Jeff Bagwell ST	.40	.18
❑ 258	Chipper Jones ST	.50	.23
❑ 259	Mo Vaughn ST	.25	.11
❑ 260	Nomar Garciaparra ST	.60	.25
❑ 261	Jim Thome ST	.15	.07
❑ 262	Derek Jeter ST	.50	.23
❑ 263	Mike Piazza ST	.60	.25
❑ 264	Tony Gwynn ST	.50	.23
❑ 265	Scott Rolen ST	.50	.23
❑ 266	Andruw Jones ST	.25	.11
❑ 267	Cal Ripken ST	.75	.35
❑ 268	Checklist 1	.10	.05
❑ 269	Checklist 2	.10	.05
❑ 270	Checklist 3	.10	.05
❑ S250	Paul Konerko AU500	30.00	13.50

1998 Score Rookie Traded Complete Players

	MINT	NRMT
COMPLETE SET (30)	100.00	45.00
COMMON CARD (1A-10C)	1.50	.70

		MINT	NRMT
❑ 1A	Ken Griffey Jr.	8.00	3.60
❑ 1B	Ken Griffey Jr.	8.00	3.60
❑ 1C	Ken Griffey Jr.	8.00	3.60
❑ 2A	Larry Walker	1.50	.70
❑ 2B	Larry Walker	1.50	.70
❑ 2C	Larry Walker	1.50	.70
❑ 3A	Alex Rodriguez	5.00	2.20
❑ 3B	Alex Rodriguez	5.00	2.20
❑ 3C	Alex Rodriguez	5.00	2.20
❑ 4A	Jose Cruz Jr.	2.00	.90
❑ 4B	Jose Cruz Jr.	2.00	.90
❑ 4C	Jose Cruz Jr.	2.00	.90
❑ 5A	Jeff Bagwell	2.50	1.10
❑ 5B	Jeff Bagwell	2.50	1.10
❑ 5C	Jeff Bagwell	2.50	1.10
❑ 6A	Greg Maddux	5.00	2.20
❑ 6B	Greg Maddux	5.00	2.20
❑ 6C	Greg Maddux	5.00	2.20
❑ 7A	Ivan Rodriguez	2.00	.90
❑ 7B	Ivan Rodriguez	2.00	.90
❑ 7C	Ivan Rodriguez	2.00	.90
❑ 8A	Roger Clemens	3.00	1.35
❑ 8B	Roger Clemens	3.00	1.35
❑ 8C	Roger Clemens	3.00	1.35
❑ 9A	Chipper Jones	4.00	1.80
❑ 9B	Chipper Jones	4.00	1.80
❑ 9C	Chipper Jones	4.00	1.80
❑ 10A	Hideo Nomo	2.00	.90
❑ 10B	Hideo Nomo	2.00	.90
❑ 10C	Hideo Nomo	2.00	.90

1998 Score Rookie Traded Star Gazing

	MINT	NRMT
COMPLETE SET (20)	150.00	70.00
COMMON CARD (1-20)	2.50	1.10

		MINT	NRMT
❑ 1	Ken Griffey Jr.	20.00	9.00
❑ 2	Frank Thomas	12.00	5.50
❑ 3	Chipper Jones	10.00	4.50
❑ 4	Mark McGwire	25.00	11.00
❑ 5	Cal Ripken	15.00	6.75
❑ 6	Mike Piazza	12.00	5.50
❑ 7	Nomar Garciaparra	12.00	5.50
❑ 8	Derek Jeter	10.00	4.50
❑ 9	Juan Gonzalez	10.00	4.50
❑ 10	Vladimir Guerrero	5.00	2.20
❑ 11	Alex Rodriguez	12.00	5.50
❑ 12	Tony Gwynn	10.00	4.50
❑ 13	Andruw Jones	4.00	1.80
❑ 14	Scott Rolen	8.00	3.60
❑ 15	Jose Cruz Jr.	4.00	1.80
❑ 16	Mo Vaughn	5.00	2.20
❑ 17	Bernie Williams	4.00	1.80
❑ 18	Greg Maddux	12.00	5.50
❑ 19	Tony Clark	2.50	1.10
❑ 20	Ben Grieve	6.00	2.70

1993 Select

	MINT	NRMT
COMPLETE SET (405)	30.00	13.50
COMMON CARD (1-405)	.15	.07

		MINT	NRMT
❑ 1	Barry Bonds	.75	.35
❑ 2	Ken Griffey Jr.	3.00	1.35
❑ 3	Will Clark	.60	.25
❑ 4	Kirby Puckett	1.00	.45
❑ 5	Tony Gwynn	1.50	.70
❑ 6	Frank Thomas	2.00	.90
❑ 7	Tom Glavine	.40	.18
❑ 8	Roberto Alomar	.60	.25
❑ 9	Andre Dawson	.40	.18
❑ 10	Ron Darling	.15	.07
❑ 11	Bobby Bonilla	.30	.14
❑ 12	Danny Tartabull	.15	.07
❑ 13	Darren Daulton	.30	.14
❑ 14	Roger Clemens	1.25	.55
❑ 15	Ozzie Smith	.75	.35
❑ 16	Mark McGwire	3.00	1.35
❑ 17	Terry Pendleton	.15	.07
❑ 18	Cal Ripken	2.50	1.10
❑ 19	Fred McGriff	.40	.18
❑ 20	Cecil Fielder	.30	.14
❑ 21	Darryl Strawberry	.30	.14
❑ 22	Robin Yount	.40	.18
❑ 23	Barry Larkin	.40	.18
❑ 24	Don Mattingly	1.00	.45
❑ 25	Craig Biggio	.60	.25
❑ 26	Sandy Alomar Jr.	.30	.14
❑ 27	Larry Walker	.60	.25
❑ 28	Junior Felix	.15	.07
❑ 29	Eddie Murray	.60	.25
❑ 30	Robin Ventura	.30	.14
❑ 31	Greg Maddux	2.00	.90
❑ 32	Dave Winfield	.40	.18
❑ 33	John Kruk	.30	.14
❑ 34	Wally Joyner	.30	.14
❑ 35	Andy Van Slyke	.30	.14
❑ 36	Chuck Knoblauch	.60	.25
❑ 37	Tom Pagnozzi	.15	.07
❑ 38	Dennis Eckersley	.30	.14
❑ 39	Dave Justice	.60	.25
❑ 40	Juan Gonzalez	1.50	.70
❑ 41	Gary Sheffield	.60	.25
❑ 42	Paul Molitor	.60	.25
❑ 43	Delino DeShields	.30	.14
❑ 44	Travis Fryman	.30	.14
❑ 45	Hal Morris	.15	.07
❑ 46	Greg Olson	.15	.07
❑ 47	Ken Caminiti	.40	.18
❑ 48	Wade Boggs	.60	.25
❑ 49	Orel Hershiser	.30	.14
❑ 50	Albert Belle	.75	.35
❑ 51	Bill Swift	.15	.07
❑ 52	Mark Langston	.15	.07

❑ 53 Joe Girardi .30 .14
❑ 54 Keith Miller .15 .07
❑ 55 Gary Carter .40 .18
❑ 56 Brady Anderson .40 .18
❑ 57 Dwight Gooden .30 .14
❑ 58 Julio Franco .15 .07
❑ 59 Lenny Dykstra .30 .14
❑ 60 Mickey Tettleton .15 .07
❑ 61 Randy Tomlin .15 .07
❑ 62 B.J. Surhoff .30 .14
❑ 63 Todd Zeile .15 .07
❑ 64 Roberto Kelly .15 .07
❑ 65 Rob Dibble .15 .07
❑ 66 Leo Gomez .15 .07
❑ 67 Doug Jones .15 .07
❑ 68 Ellis Burks .30 .14
❑ 69 Mike Scioscia .15 .07
❑ 70 Charles Nagy .30 .14
❑ 71 Cory Snyder .15 .07
❑ 72 Devon White .15 .07
❑ 73 Mark Grace .40 .18
❑ 74 Luis Polonia .15 .07
❑ 75 John Smiley 2X .15 .07
❑ 76 Carlton Fisk .60 .25
❑ 77 Luis Sojo .15 .07
❑ 78 George Brett 1.25 .55
❑ 79 Mitch Williams .15 .07
❑ 80 Kent Hrbek .30 .14
❑ 81 Jay Bell .30 .14
❑ 82 Edgar Martinez .40 .18
❑ 83 Lee Smith .30 .14
❑ 84 Deion Sanders .40 .18
❑ 85 Bill Gullickson .15 .07
❑ 86 Paul O'Neill .30 .14
❑ 87 Kevin Seitzer .15 .07
❑ 88 Steve Finley .30 .14
❑ 89 Mel Hall .15 .07
❑ 90 Nolan Ryan 2.50 1.10
❑ 91 Eric Davis .30 .14
❑ 92 Mike Mussina .60 .25
❑ 93 Tony Fernandez .15 .07
❑ 94 Frank Viola .15 .07
❑ 95 Matt Williams .40 .18
❑ 96 Joe Carter .30 .14
❑ 97 Ryne Sandberg .75 .35
❑ 98 Jim Abbott .30 .14
❑ 99 Marquis Grissom .30 .14
❑ 100 George Bell .15 .07
❑ 101 Howard Johnson .15 .07
❑ 102 Kevin Appier .30 .14
❑ 103 Dale Murphy .40 .18
❑ 104 Shane Mack .15 .07
❑ 105 Jose Lind .15 .07
❑ 106 Rickey Henderson .60 .25
❑ 107 Bob Tewksbury .15 .07
❑ 108 Kevin Mitchell .30 .14
❑ 109 Steve Avery .15 .07
❑ 110 Candy Maldonado .15 .07
❑ 111 Bip Roberts .15 .07
❑ 112 Lou Whitaker .30 .14
❑ 113 Jeff Bagwell 1.00 .45
❑ 114 Dante Bichette .30 .14
❑ 115 Brett Butler .30 .14
❑ 116 Melido Perez .15 .07
❑ 117 Andy Benes .30 .14
❑ 118 Randy Johnson .60 .25
❑ 119 Willie McGee .30 .14
❑ 120 Jody Reed .15 .07
❑ 121 Shawon Dunston .15 .07
❑ 122 Carlos Baerga .15 .07
❑ 123 Bret Saberhagen .30 .14
❑ 124 John Olerud .40 .18
❑ 125 Ivan Calderon .15 .07
❑ 126 Bryan Harvey .15 .07
❑ 127 Terry Mulholland .15 .07
❑ 128 Ozzie Guillen .15 .07
❑ 129 Steve Buechele .15 .07
❑ 130 Kevin Tapani .15 .07
❑ 131 Felix Jose .15 .07
❑ 132 Terry Steinbach .15 .07
❑ 133 Ron Gant .30 .14
❑ 134 Harold Reynolds .15 .07
❑ 135 Chris Sabo .15 .07
❑ 136 Ivan Rodriguez .75 .35
❑ 137 Eric Anthony .15 .07
❑ 138 Mike Henneman .15 .07
❑ 139 Robby Thompson .15 .07
❑ 140 Scott Fletcher .15 .07
❑ 141 Bruce Hurst .15 .07
❑ 142 Kevin Maas .15 .07
❑ 143 Tom Candiotti .15 .07
❑ 144 Chris Hoiles .15 .07
❑ 145 Mike Morgan .15 .07
❑ 146 Mark Whiten .15 .07
❑ 147 Dennis Martinez .30 .14
❑ 148 Tony Pena .15 .07
❑ 149 Dave Magadan .15 .07
❑ 150 Mark Lewis .15 .07
❑ 151 Mariano Duncan .15 .07
❑ 152 Gregg Jefferies .15 .07
❑ 153 Doug Drabek .15 .07
❑ 154 Brian Harper .15 .07
❑ 155 Ray Lankford .40 .18
❑ 156 Carney Lansford .30 .14
❑ 157 Mike Sharperson .15 .07
❑ 158 Jack Morris .30 .14
❑ 159 Otis Nixon .15 .07
❑ 160 Steve Sax .15 .07
❑ 161 Mark Lemke .15 .07
❑ 162 Rafael Palmeiro .40 .18
❑ 163 Jose Rijo .15 .07
❑ 164 Omar Vizquel .30 .14
❑ 165 Sammy Sosa 1.50 .70
❑ 166 Milt Cuyler .15 .07
❑ 167 John Franco .30 .14
❑ 168 Darryl Hamilton .15 .07
❑ 169 Ken Hill .15 .07
❑ 170 Mike Devereaux .15 .07
❑ 171 Don Slaught .15 .07
❑ 172 Steve Farr .15 .07
❑ 173 Bernard Gilkey .15 .07
❑ 174 Mike Fetters .15 .07
❑ 175 Vince Coleman .15 .07
❑ 176 Kevin McReynolds .15 .07
❑ 177 John Smoltz .30 .14
❑ 178 Greg Gagne .15 .07
❑ 179 Greg Swindell .15 .07
❑ 180 Juan Guzman .15 .07
❑ 181 Kal Daniels .15 .07
❑ 182 Rick Sutcliffe .15 .07
❑ 183 Orlando Merced .15 .07
❑ 184 Bill Wegman .15 .07
❑ 185 Mark Gardner .15 .07
❑ 186 Rob Deer .15 .07
❑ 187 Dave Hollins .15 .07
❑ 188 Jack Clark .15 .07
❑ 189 Brian Hunter .15 .07
❑ 190 Tim Wallach .15 .07
❑ 191 Tim Belcher .15 .07
❑ 192 Walt Weiss .15 .07
❑ 193 Kurt Stillwell .15 .07
❑ 194 Charlie Hayes .15 .07
❑ 195 Willie Randolph .30 .14
❑ 196 Jack McDowell .15 .07
❑ 197 Jose Offerman .15 .07
❑ 198 Chuck Finley .30 .14
❑ 199 Darrin Jackson .15 .07
❑ 200 Kelly Gruber .15 .07
❑ 201 John Wetteland .30 .14
❑ 202 Jay Buhner .40 .18
❑ 203 Mike LaValliere .15 .07
❑ 204 Kevin Brown .40 .18
❑ 205 Luis Gonzalez .15 .07
❑ 206 Rick Aguilera .15 .07
❑ 207 Norm Charlton .15 .07
❑ 208 Mike Bordick .15 .07
❑ 209 Charlie Leibrandt .15 .07
❑ 210 Tom Brunansky .15 .07
❑ 211 Tom Henke .15 .07
❑ 212 Randy Milligan .15 .07
❑ 213 Ramon Martinez .30 .14
❑ 214 Mo Vaughn .75 .35
❑ 215 Randy Myers .30 .14
❑ 216 Greg Hibbard .15 .07
❑ 217 Wes Chamberlain .15 .07
❑ 218 Tony Phillips .15 .07
❑ 219 Pete Harnisch .15 .07
❑ 220 Mike Gallego .15 .07
❑ 221 Bud Black .15 .07
❑ 222 Greg Vaughn .30 .14
❑ 223 Milt Thompson .15 .07
❑ 224 Ben McDonald .15 .07
❑ 225 Billy Hatcher .15 .07
❑ 226 Paul Sorrento .15 .07
❑ 227 Mark Gubicza .15 .07
❑ 228 Mike Greenwell .15 .07
❑ 229 Curt Schilling .30 .14
❑ 230 Alan Trammell .40 .18
❑ 231 Zane Smith .15 .07
❑ 232 Bobby Thigpen .15 .07
❑ 233 Greg Olson .15 .07
❑ 234 Joe Orsulak .15 .07
❑ 235 Joe Oliver .15 .07
❑ 236 Tim Raines .30 .14
❑ 237 Juan Samuel .15 .07
❑ 238 Chili Davis .30 .14
❑ 239 Spike Owen .15 .07
❑ 240 Dave Stewart .30 .14
❑ 241 Jim Eisenreich .15 .07
❑ 242 Phil Plantier .15 .07
❑ 243 Sid Fernandez .15 .07
❑ 244 Dan Gladden .15 .07
❑ 245 Mickey Morandini .15 .07
❑ 246 Tino Martinez .60 .25
❑ 247 Kirt Manwaring .15 .07
❑ 248 Dean Palmer .30 .14
❑ 249 Tom Browning .15 .07
❑ 250 Brian McRae .15 .07
❑ 251 Scott Leius .15 .07
❑ 252 Bert Blyleven .30 .14
❑ 253 Scott Erickson .15 .07
❑ 254 Bob Welch .15 .07
❑ 255 Pat Kelly .15 .07
❑ 256 Felix Fermin .15 .07
❑ 257 Harold Baines .30 .14
❑ 258 Duane Ward .15 .07
❑ 259 Bill Spiers .15 .07
❑ 260 Jaime Navarro .15 .07
❑ 261 Scott Sanderson .15 .07
❑ 262 Gary Gaetti .15 .07
❑ 263 Bob Ojeda .15 .07
❑ 264 Jeff Montgomery .30 .14
❑ 265 Scott Bankhead .15 .07
❑ 266 Lance Johnson .15 .07
❑ 267 Rafael Belliard .15 .07
❑ 268 Kevin Reimer .15 .07
❑ 269 Benito Santiago .15 .07
❑ 270 Mike Moore .15 .07
❑ 271 Dave Fleming .15 .07
❑ 272 Moises Alou .30 .14
❑ 273 Pat Listach .15 .07
❑ 274 Reggie Sanders .15 .07
❑ 275 Kenny Lofton .60 .25
❑ 276 Donovan Osborne .15 .07
❑ 277 Rusty Meacham .15 .07
❑ 278 Eric Karros .40 .18
❑ 279 Andy Stankiewicz .15 .07
❑ 280 Brian Jordan .30 .14
❑ 281 Gary DiSarcina .15 .07
❑ 282 Mark Wohlers .15 .07
❑ 283 Dave Nilsson .30 .14
❑ 284 Anthony Young .15 .07
❑ 285 Jim Bullinger .15 .07
❑ 286 Derek Bell .30 .14
❑ 287 Brian Williams .15 .07
❑ 288 Julio Valera .15 .07
❑ 289 Dan Walters .15 .07
❑ 290 Chad Curtis .30 .14
❑ 291 Michael Tucker DP .60 .25
❑ 292 Bob Zupcic .15 .07
❑ 293 Todd Hundley .40 .18
❑ 294 Jeff Tackett .15 .07
❑ 295 Greg Colbrunn .15 .07
❑ 296 Cal Eldred .15 .07
❑ 297 Chris Roberts DP .15 .07
❑ 298 John Doherty .15 .07
❑ 299 Denny Neagle .30 .14
❑ 300 Arthur Rhodes .15 .07
❑ 301 Mark Clark .15 .07
❑ 302 Scott Cooper .15 .07
❑ 303 Jamie Arnold DP .30 .14
❑ 304 Jim Thome 1.25 .55
❑ 305 Frank Seminara .15 .07
❑ 306 Kurt Knudsen .15 .07
❑ 307 Tim Wakefield .30 .14

	MINT	NRMT
❑ 308 John Jaha	.15	.07
❑ 309 Pat Hentgen	.40	.18
❑ 310 B.J. Wallace DP	.15	.07
❑ 311 Roberto Hernandez	.30	.14
❑ 312 Hipolito Pichardo	.15	.07
❑ 313 Eric Fox	.15	.07
❑ 314 Willie Banks	.15	.07
❑ 315 Sam Militello	.15	.07
❑ 316 Vince Horsman	.15	.07
❑ 317 Carlos Hernandez	.15	.07
❑ 318 Jeff Kent	.30	.14
❑ 319 Mike Perez	.15	.07
❑ 320 Scott Livingstone	.15	.07
❑ 321 Jeff Conine	.15	.07
❑ 322 James Austin	.15	.07
❑ 323 John Vander Wal	.15	.07
❑ 324 Pat Mahomes	.15	.07
❑ 325 Pedro Astacio	.15	.07
❑ 326 Bret Boone UER (Misspelled Brett)	.30	.14
❑ 327 Matt Stairs	.15	.07
❑ 328 Damion Easley	.30	.14
❑ 329 Ben Rivera	.15	.07
❑ 330 Reggie Jefferson	.30	.14
❑ 331 Luis Mercedes	.15	.07
❑ 332 Kyle Abbott	.15	.07
❑ 333 Eddie Taubensee	.15	.07
❑ 334 Tim McIntosh	.15	.07
❑ 335 Phil Clark	.15	.07
❑ 336 Wil Cordero	.15	.07
❑ 337 Russ Springer	.15	.07
❑ 338 Craig Colbert	.15	.07
❑ 339 Tim Salmon	.60	.25
❑ 340 Braulio Castillo	.15	.07
❑ 341 Donald Harris	.15	.07
❑ 342 Eric Young	.60	.25
❑ 343 Bob Wickman	.15	.07
❑ 344 John Valentin	.30	.14
❑ 345 Dan Wilson	.30	.14
❑ 346 Steve Hosey	.15	.07
❑ 347 Mike Piazza	3.00	1.35
❑ 348 Willie Greene	.15	.07
❑ 349 Tom Goodwin	.15	.07
❑ 350 Eric Hillman	.15	.07
❑ 351 Steve Reed	.15	.07
❑ 352 Dan Serafini DP	.30	.14
❑ 353 Todd Steverson DP	.30	.14
❑ 354 Benji Grigsby DP	.15	.07
❑ 355 Shannon Stewart DP	.50	.23
❑ 356 Sean Lowe DP	.15	.07
❑ 357 Derek Wallace DP	.15	.07
❑ 358 Rick Helling DP	.40	.18
❑ 359 Jason Kendall DP	2.00	.90
❑ 360 Derek Jeter DP	6.00	2.70
❑ 361 David Cone	.30	.14
❑ 362 Jeff Reardon	.30	.14
❑ 363 Bobby Witt	.15	.07
❑ 364 Jose Canseco	.60	.25
❑ 365 Jeff Russell	.15	.07
❑ 366 Ruben Sierra	.15	.07
❑ 367 Alan Mills	.15	.07
❑ 368 Matt Nokes	.15	.07
❑ 369 Pat Borders	.15	.07
❑ 370 Pedro Munoz	.15	.07
❑ 371 Danny Jackson	.15	.07
❑ 372 Geronimo Pena	.15	.07
❑ 373 Craig Lefferts	.15	.07
❑ 374 Joe Grahe	.15	.07
❑ 375 Roger McDowell	.15	.07
❑ 376 Jimmy Key	.30	.14
❑ 377 Steve Olin	.15	.07
❑ 378 Glenn Davis	.15	.07
❑ 379 Rene Gonzales	.15	.07
❑ 380 Manuel Lee	.15	.07
❑ 381 Ron Karkovice	.15	.07
❑ 382 Sid Bream	.15	.07
❑ 383 Gerald Williams	.15	.07
❑ 384 Lenny Harris	.15	.07
❑ 385 J.T. Snow	.75	.35
❑ 386 Dave Stieb	.30	.14
❑ 387 Kirk McCaskill	.15	.07
❑ 388 Lance Parrish	.15	.07
❑ 389 Craig Grebeck	.15	.07
❑ 390 Rick Wilkins	.15	.07
❑ 391 Manny Alexander	.15	.07
❑ 392 Mike Schooler	.15	.07
❑ 393 Bernie Williams	.60	.25
❑ 394 Kevin Koslofski	.15	.07
❑ 395 Willie Wilson	.15	.07
❑ 396 Jeff Parrett	.15	.07
❑ 397 Mike Harkey	.15	.07
❑ 398 Frank Tanana	.15	.07
❑ 399 Doug Henry	.15	.07
❑ 400 Royce Clayton	.15	.07
❑ 401 Eric Wedge	.15	.07
❑ 402 Derrick May	.15	.07
❑ 403 Carlos Garcia	.15	.07
❑ 404 Henry Rodriguez	.30	.14
❑ 405 Ryan Klesko	.60	.25

1993 Select Aces

	MINT	NRMT
COMPLETE SET (24)	80.00	36.00
COMMON CARD (1-24)	3.00	1.35
❑ 1 Roger Clemens	20.00	9.00
❑ 2 Tom Glavine	6.00	2.70
❑ 3 Jack McDowell	3.00	1.35
❑ 4 Greg Maddux	30.00	13.50
❑ 5 Jack Morris	4.00	1.80
❑ 6 Dennis Martinez	4.00	1.80
❑ 7 Kevin Brown	6.00	2.70
❑ 8 Dwight Gooden	4.00	1.80
❑ 9 Kevin Appier	4.00	1.80
❑ 10 Mike Morgan	3.00	1.35
❑ 11 Juan Guzman	3.00	1.35
❑ 12 Charles Nagy	4.00	1.80
❑ 13 John Smiley	3.00	1.35
❑ 14 Ken Hill	3.00	1.35
❑ 15 Bob Tewksbury	3.00	1.35
❑ 16 Doug Drabek	3.00	1.35
❑ 17 John Smoltz	4.00	1.80
❑ 18 Greg Swindell	3.00	1.35
❑ 19 Bruce Hurst	3.00	1.35
❑ 20 Mike Mussina	10.00	4.50
❑ 21 Cal Eldred	3.00	1.35
❑ 22 Melido Perez	3.00	1.35
❑ 23 Dave Fleming	3.00	1.35
❑ 24 Kevin Tapani	3.00	1.35

1993 Select Chase Rookies

	MINT	NRMT
COMPLETE SET (21)	100.00	45.00
COMMON CARD (1-21)	4.00	1.80
❑ 1 Pat Listach	4.00	1.80
❑ 2 Moises Alou	8.00	3.60
❑ 3 Reggie Sanders	4.00	1.80
❑ 4 Kenny Lofton	25.00	11.00
❑ 5 Eric Karros	12.00	5.50
❑ 6 Brian Williams	4.00	1.80
❑ 7 Donovan Osborne	4.00	1.80
❑ 8 Sam Militello	4.00	1.80
❑ 9 Chad Curtis	8.00	3.60
❑ 10 Bob Zupcic	4.00	1.80
❑ 11 Tim Salmon	25.00	11.00
❑ 12 Jeff Conine	4.00	1.80
❑ 13 Pedro Astacio	4.00	1.80
❑ 14 Arthur Rhodes	4.00	1.80
❑ 15 Cal Eldred	4.00	1.80
❑ 16 Tim Wakefield	8.00	3.60
❑ 17 Andy Stankiewicz	4.00	1.80
❑ 18 Wil Cordero	4.00	1.80
❑ 19 Todd Hundley	12.00	5.50
❑ 20 Dave Fleming	4.00	1.80
❑ 21 Bret Boone	8.00	3.60

1993 Select Chase Stars

	MINT	NRMT
COMPLETE SET (24)	150.00	70.00
COMMON CARD (1-24)	2.00	.90
❑ 1 Fred McGriff	4.00	1.80
❑ 2 Ryne Sandberg	10.00	4.50
❑ 3 Ozzie Smith	10.00	4.50
❑ 4 Gary Sheffield	5.00	2.20
❑ 5 Darren Daulton	3.00	1.35
❑ 6 Andy Van Slyke	2.00	.90
❑ 7 Barry Bonds	10.00	4.50
❑ 8 Tony Gwynn	20.00	9.00
❑ 9 Greg Maddux	25.00	11.00
❑ 10 Tom Glavine	4.00	1.80
❑ 11 John Franco	3.00	1.35
❑ 12 Lee Smith	3.00	1.35
❑ 13 Cecil Fielder	3.00	1.35
❑ 14 Roberto Alomar	5.00	2.20
❑ 15 Cal Ripken	30.00	13.50
❑ 16 Edgar Martinez	4.00	1.80
❑ 17 Ivan Rodriguez	10.00	4.50
❑ 18 Kirby Puckett	12.00	5.50
❑ 19 Ken Griffey Jr.	40.00	18.00
❑ 20 Joe Carter	3.00	1.35
❑ 21 Roger Clemens	15.00	6.75
❑ 22 Dave Fleming	2.00	.90
❑ 23 Paul Molitor	5.00	2.20
❑ 24 Dennis Eckersley	3.00	1.35

1993 Select Stat Leaders

	MINT	NRMT
COMPLETE SET (90)	10.00	4.50
COMMON CARD (1-90)	.10	.05
❑ 1 Edgar Martinez	.30	.14
❑ 2 Kirby Puckett	.60	.25
❑ 3 Frank Thomas	1.25	.55
❑ 4 Gary Sheffield	.40	.18

❑ 5	Andy Van Slyke	.10	.05
❑ 6	John Kruk	.20	.09
❑ 7	Kirby Puckett	.60	.25
❑ 8	Carlos Baerga	.10	.05
❑ 9	Paul Molitor	.40	.18
❑ 10	Terry Pendleton Andy Van Slyke	.10	.05
❑ 11	Ryne Sandberg	.50	.23
❑ 12	Mark Grace	.30	.14
❑ 13	Frank Thomas Edgar Martinez	.75	.35
❑ 14	Don Mattingly Robin Yount	.40	.18
❑ 15	Ken Griffey	2.00	.90
❑ 16	Andy Van Slyke	.10	.05
❑ 17	Mariano Duncan Will Clark Ray Lankford	.20	.09
❑ 18	Marquis Grissom Terry Pendleton	.20	.09
❑ 19	Lance Johnson	.10	.05
❑ 20	Mike Devereaux	.10	.05
❑ 21	Brady Anderson	.20	.09
❑ 22	Deion Sanders	.30	.14
❑ 23	Steve Finley	.20	.09
❑ 24	Andy Van Slyke	.10	.05
❑ 25	Juan Gonzalez	1.00	.45
❑ 26	Mark McGwire	1.50	.70
❑ 27	Cecil Fielder	.20	.09
❑ 28	Fred McGriff	.30	.14
❑ 29	Barry Bonds	.50	.23
❑ 30	Gary Sheffield	.40	.18
❑ 31	Cecil Fielder	.20	.09
❑ 32	Joe Carter	.20	.09
❑ 33	Frank Thomas	1.25	.55
❑ 34	Darren Daulton	.20	.09
❑ 35	Terry Pendleton	.10	.05
❑ 36	Fred McGriff	.30	.14
❑ 37	Tony Phillips	.10	.05
❑ 38	Frank Thomas	1.25	.55
❑ 39	Roberto Alomar	.40	.18
❑ 40	Barry Bonds	.50	.23
❑ 41	Dave Hollins	.10	.05
❑ 42	Andy Van Slyke	.10	.05
❑ 43	Mark McGwire	1.50	.70
❑ 44	Edgar Martinez	.30	.14
❑ 45	Frank Thomas	1.25	.55
❑ 46	Barry Bonds	.50	.23
❑ 47	Gary Sheffield	.40	.18
❑ 48	Fred McGriff	.30	.14
❑ 49	Frank Thomas	1.25	.55
❑ 50	Danny Tartabull	.10	.05
❑ 51	Roberto Alomar	.40	.18
❑ 52	Barry Bonds	.50	.23
❑ 53	John Kruk	.20	.09
❑ 54	Brett Butler	.20	.09
❑ 55	Kenny Lofton	.35	.16
❑ 56	Pat Listach	.10	.05
❑ 57	Brady Anderson	.20	.09
❑ 58	Marquis Grissom	.20	.09
❑ 59	Delino DeShields	.10	.05
❑ 60	Bip Roberts Steve Finley	.10	.05
❑ 61	Jack McDowell	.10	.05
❑ 62	Kevin Brown Roger Clemens	.40	.18
❑ 63	Charles Nagy Melido Perez	.10	.05
❑ 64	Terry Mulholland	.10	.05
❑ 65	Curt Schilling Doug Drabek	.10	.05
❑ 66	Greg Maddux John Smoltz	.75	.35
❑ 67	Dennis Eckersley	.20	.09
❑ 68	Rick Aguilera	.10	.05
❑ 69	Jeff Montgomery	.20	.09
❑ 70	Lee Smith	.20	.09
❑ 71	Randy Myers	.20	.09
❑ 72	John Wetteland	.20	.09
❑ 73	Randy Johnson	.40	.18
❑ 74	Melido Perez	.10	.05
❑ 75	Roger Clemens	1.00	.45
❑ 76	John Smoltz	.20	.09
❑ 77	David Cone	.20	.09
❑ 78	Greg Maddux	1.25	.55
❑ 79	Roger Clemens	1.00	.45
❑ 80	Kevin Appier	.20	.09
❑ 81	Mike Mussina	.40	.18
❑ 82	Bill Swift	.10	.05
❑ 83	Bob Tewksbury	.10	.05
❑ 84	Greg Maddux	1.25	.55
❑ 85	Jack Morris Kevin Brown	.20	.09
❑ 86	Jack McDowell	.10	.05
❑ 87	Roger Clemens Mike Mussina	.40	.18
❑ 88	Tom Glavine Greg Maddux	.75	.35
❑ 89	Ken Hill Bob Tewksbury	.10	.05
❑ 90	Mike Morgan Dennis Martinez	.10	.05

1993 Select Triple Crown

		MINT	NRMT
COMPLETE SET (3)		80.00	36.00
COMMON CARD (1-3)		15.00	6.75
❑ 1	Mickey Mantle	60.00	27.00
❑ 2	Carl Yastrzemski	15.00	6.75
❑ 3	Frank Robinson	15.00	6.75

1993 Select Rookie/Traded

		MINT	NRMT
COMPLETE SET (150)		15.00	6.75
COMMON CARD (1T-150T)		.30	.14
❑ 1T	Rickey Henderson	1.25	.55
❑ 2T	Rob Deer	.30	.14
❑ 3T	Tim Belcher	.30	.14
❑ 4T	Gary Sheffield	1.25	.55
❑ 5T	Fred McGriff	.75	.35
❑ 6T	Mark Whiten	.30	.14
❑ 7T	Jeff Russell	.30	.14
❑ 8T	Harold Baines	.50	.23
❑ 9T	Dave Winfield	.75	.35
❑ 10T	Ellis Burks	.50	.23
❑ 11T	Andre Dawson	.75	.35
❑ 12T	Gregg Jefferies	.30	.14
❑ 13T	Jimmy Key	.50	.23
❑ 14T	Harold Reynolds	.30	.14
❑ 15T	Tom Henke	.30	.14
❑ 16T	Paul Molitor	1.25	.55
❑ 17T	Wade Boggs	1.25	.55
❑ 18T	David Cone	.50	.23
❑ 19T	Tony Fernandez	.30	.14
❑ 20T	Roberto Kelly	.30	.14
❑ 21T	Paul O'Neill	.50	.23
❑ 22T	Jose Lind	.30	.14
❑ 23T	Barry Bonds	1.50	.70
❑ 24T	Dave Stewart	.50	.23
❑ 25T	Randy Myers	.50	.23
❑ 26T	Benito Santiago	.30	.14
❑ 27T	Tim Wallach	.30	.14
❑ 28T	Greg Gagne	.30	.14
❑ 29T	Kevin Mitchell	.50	.23
❑ 30T	Jim Abbott	.50	.23
❑ 31T	Lee Smith	.50	.23
❑ 32T	Bobby Munoz	.30	.14
❑ 33T	Mo Sanford	.30	.14
❑ 34T	John Roper	.30	.14
❑ 35T	David Hulse	.30	.14
❑ 36T	Pedro Martinez	1.50	.70
❑ 37T	Chuck Carr	.30	.14
❑ 38T	Armando Reynoso	.30	.14
❑ 39T	Ryan Thompson	.30	.14
❑ 40T	Carlos Garcia	.30	.14
❑ 41T	Matt Whiteside	.30	.14
❑ 42T	Benji Gil	.30	.14
❑ 43T	Rodney Bolton	.30	.14
❑ 44T	J.T. Snow	1.25	.55
❑ 45T	David McCarty	.30	.14
❑ 46T	Paul Quantrill	.30	.14
❑ 47T	Al Martin	.30	.14
❑ 48T	Lance Painter	.30	.14
❑ 49T	Lou Frazier	.30	.14
❑ 50T	Eduardo Perez	.30	.14
❑ 51T	Kevin Young	.30	.14
❑ 52T	Mike Trombley	.30	.14
❑ 53T	Sterling Hitchcock	2.00	.90
❑ 54T	Tim Bogar	.30	.14
❑ 55T	Hilly Hathaway	.30	.14
❑ 56T	Wayne Kirby	.30	.14
❑ 57T	Craig Paquette	.30	.14
❑ 58T	Bret Boone	.50	.23
❑ 59T	Greg McMichael	.30	.14
❑ 60T	Mike Lansing	.50	.23
❑ 61T	Brent Gates	.30	.14
❑ 62T	Rene Arocha	.30	.14
❑ 63T	Ricky Gutierrez	.30	.14
❑ 64T	Kevin Rogers	.30	.14
❑ 65T	Ken Ryan	.30	.14
❑ 66T	Phil Hiatt	.30	.14
❑ 67T	Pat Meares	.30	.14
❑ 68T	Troy Neel	.30	.14
❑ 69T	Steve Cooke	.30	.14
❑ 70T	Sherman Obando	.30	.14
❑ 71T	Blas Minor	.30	.14
❑ 72T	Angel Miranda	.30	.14
❑ 73T	Tom Kramer	.30	.14
❑ 74T	Chip Hale	.30	.14
❑ 75T	Brad Pennington	.30	.14
❑ 76T	Graeme Lloyd	.30	.14
❑ 77T	Darrell Whitmore	.30	.14
❑ 78T	David Nied	.30	.14
❑ 79T	Todd Van Poppel	.30	.14
❑ 80T	Chris Gomez	.50	.23
❑ 81T	Jason Bere	.30	.14

❑ 82T Jeffrey Hammonds .... .50 .23
❑ 83T Brad Ausmus .... .30 .14
❑ 84T Kevin Stocker .... .30 .14
❑ 85T Jeromy Burnitz .... .50 .23
❑ 86T Aaron Sele .... 1.25 .55
❑ 87T Roberto Mejia .... .30 .14
❑ 88T Kirk Rueter .... 1.00 .45
❑ 89T Kevin Roberson .... .30 .14
❑ 90T Allen Watson .... .30 .14
❑ 91T Charlie Leibrandt .... .30 .14
❑ 92T Eric Davis .... .50 .23
❑ 93T Jody Reed .... .30 .14
❑ 94T Danny Jackson .... .30 .14
❑ 95T Gary Gaetti .... .30 .14
❑ 96T Norm Charlton .... .30 .14
❑ 97T Doug Drabek .... .30 .14
❑ 98T Scott Fletcher .... .30 .14
❑ 99T Greg Swindell .... .30 .14
❑ 100T John Smiley .... .30 .14
❑ 101T Kevin Reimer .... .30 .14
❑ 102T Andres Galarraga ...... 1.25 .55
❑ 103T Greg Hibbard .... .30 .14
❑ 104T Chris Hammond .... .30 .14
❑ 105T Darnell Coles .... .30 .14
❑ 106T Mike Felder .... .30 .14
❑ 107T Jose Guzman .... .30 .14
❑ 108T Chris Bosio .... .30 .14
❑ 109T Spike Owen .... .30 .14
❑ 110T Felix Jose .... .30 .14
❑ 111T Cory Snyder .... .30 .14
❑ 112T Craig Lefferts .... .30 .14
❑ 113T David Wells .... .50 .23
❑ 114T Pete Incaviglia .... .30 .14
❑ 115T Mike Pagliarulo .... .30 .14
❑ 116T Dave Magadan .... .30 .14
❑ 117T Charlie Hough .... .50 .23
❑ 118T Ivan Calderon .... .30 .14
❑ 119T Manuel Lee .... .30 .14
❑ 120T Bob Patterson .... .30 .14
❑ 121T Bob Ojeda .... .30 .14
❑ 122T Scott Bankhead .... .30 .14
❑ 123T Greg Maddux 4.00 1.80
❑ 124T Chili Davis .... .50 .23
❑ 125T Milt Thompson .... .30 .14
❑ 126T Dave Martinez .... .30 .14
❑ 127T Frank Tanana .... .30 .14
❑ 128T Phil Plantier .... .30 .14
❑ 129T Juan Samuel .... .30 .14
❑ 130T Eric Young .... 1.25 .55
❑ 131T Joe Orsulak .... .30 .14
❑ 132T Derek Bell .... .50 .23
❑ 133T Darrin Jackson .... .30 .14
❑ 134T Tom Brunansky .... .30 .14
❑ 135T Jeff Reardon .... .50 .23
❑ 136T Kevin Higgins .... .30 .14
❑ 137T Joel Johnston .... .30 .14
❑ 138T Rick Trlicek .... .30 .14
❑ 139T Richie Lewis .... .30 .14
❑ 140T Jeff Gardner .... .30 .14
❑ 141T Jack Voigt .... .30 .14
❑ 142T Rod Correia .... .30 .14
❑ 143T Billy Brewer .... .30 .14
❑ 144T Terry Jorgensen .... .30 .14
❑ 145T Rich Amaral .... .30 .14
❑ 146T Sean Berry .... .30 .14
❑ 147T Dan Peltier .... .30 .14
❑ 148T Paul Wagner .... .30 .14
❑ 149T Damon Buford .... .30 .14
❑ 150T Wil Cordero .... .30 .14
❑ NR1 Nolan Ryan Tribute .. 40.00 18.00
❑ ROY1 Tim Salmon AL ROY 10.00 4.50
❑ ROY2 Mike Piazza NL ROY 40.00 18.00

1993 Select Rookie/Traded All-Star Rookies

	MINT	NRMT
COMPLETE SET (10)	100.00	45.00
COMMON CARD (1-10)	3.00	1.35

❑ 1 Jeff Conine 3.00 1.35
❑ 2 Brent Gates 3.00 1.35
❑ 3 Mike Lansing 6.00 2.70

❑ 4 Kevin Stocker 3.00 1.35
❑ 5 Mike Piazza 60.00 27.00
❑ 6 Jeffrey Hammonds 6.00 2.70
❑ 7 David Hulse 3.00 1.35
❑ 8 Tim Salmon 15.00 6.75
❑ 9 Rene Arocha 3.00 1.35
❑ 10 Greg McMichael 3.00 1.35

1994 Select

	MINT	NRMT
COMPLETE SET (420)	25.00	11.00
COMPLETE SERIES 1 (210) ..	15.00	6.75
COMPLETE SERIES 2 (210) ..	10.00	4.50
COMMON CARD (1-420)	.15	.07

❑ 1 Ken Griffey Jr. 3.00 1.35
❑ 2 Greg Maddux .... 2.00 .90
❑ 3 Paul Molitor .... .60 .25
❑ 4 Mike Piazza .... 2.00 .90
❑ 5 Jay Bell .... .30 .14
❑ 6 Frank Thomas .... 2.00 .90
❑ 7 Barry Larkin .... .40 .18
❑ 8 Paul O'Neill .... .30 .14
❑ 9 Darren Daulton .... .30 .14
❑ 10 Mike Greenwell .... .15 .07
❑ 11 Chuck Carr .... .15 .07
❑ 12 Joe Carter .... .30 .14
❑ 13 Lance Johnson .... .15 .07
❑ 14 Jeff Blauser .... .15 .07
❑ 15 Chris Hoiles .... .15 .07
❑ 16 Rick Wilkins .... .15 .07
❑ 17 Kirby Puckett .... 1.00 .45
❑ 18 Larry Walker .... .60 .25
❑ 19 Randy Johnson .... .60 .25
❑ 20 Bernard Gilkey .... .15 .07
❑ 21 Devon White .... .30 .14
❑ 22 Randy Myers .... .15 .07
❑ 23 Don Mattingly .... 1.00 .45
❑ 24 John Kruk .... .30 .14
❑ 25 Ozzie Guillen .... .15 .07
❑ 26 Jeff Conine .... .30 .14
❑ 27 Mike Macfarlane .... .15 .07
❑ 28 Dave Hollins .... .15 .07
❑ 29 Chuck Knoblauch .... .60 .25
❑ 30 Ozzie Smith .... .75 .35
❑ 31 Harold Baines .... .30 .14
❑ 32 Ryne Sandberg .... .75 .35
❑ 33 Ron Karkovice .... .15 .07
❑ 34 Terry Pendleton .... .15 .07
❑ 35 Wally Joyner .... .30 .14
❑ 36 Mike Mussina .... .60 .25
❑ 37 Felix Jose .... .15 .07
❑ 38 Derrick May .... .15 .07
❑ 39 Scott Cooper .... .15 .07
❑ 40 Jose Rijo .... .15 .07
❑ 41 Robin Ventura .... .30 .14
❑ 42 Charlie Hayes .... .15 .07
❑ 43 Jimmy Key .... .30 .14
❑ 44 Eric Karros .... .30 .14
❑ 45 Ruben Sierra .... .15 .07
❑ 46 Ryan Thompson .... .15 .07
❑ 47 Brian McRae .... .15 .07
❑ 48 Pat Hentgen .... .30 .14
❑ 49 John Valentin .... .30 .14
❑ 50 Al Martin .... .15 .07
❑ 51 Jose Lind .... .15 .07
❑ 52 Kevin Stocker .... .15 .07
❑ 53 Mike Gallego .... .15 .07
❑ 54 Dwight Gooden .... .30 .14
❑ 55 Brady Anderson .... .30 .14
❑ 56 Jeff King .... .15 .07
❑ 57 Mark McGwire 3.00 1.35
❑ 58 Sammy Sosa .... 1.50 .70
❑ 59 Ryan Bowen .... .15 .07
❑ 60 Mark Lemke .... .15 .07
❑ 61 Roger Clemens .... 1.25 .55
❑ 62 Brian Jordan .... .30 .14
❑ 63 Andres Galarraga .... .60 .25
❑ 64 Kevin Appier .... .30 .14
❑ 65 Don Slaught .... .15 .07
❑ 66 Mike Blowers .... .15 .07
❑ 67 Wes Chamberlain .... .15 .07
❑ 68 Troy Neel .... .15 .07
❑ 69 John Wetteland .... .30 .14
❑ 70 Joe Girardi .... .15 .07
❑ 71 Reggie Sanders .... .30 .14
❑ 72 Edgar Martinez .... .30 .14
❑ 73 Todd Hundley .... .30 .14
❑ 74 Pat Borders .... .15 .07
❑ 75 Roberto Mejia .... .15 .07
❑ 76 David Cone .... .40 .18
❑ 77 Tony Gwynn .... 1.50 .70
❑ 78 Jim Abbott .... .30 .14
❑ 79 Jay Buhner .... .30 .14
❑ 80 Mark McLemore .... .15 .07
❑ 81 Wil Cordero .... .15 .07
❑ 82 Pedro Astacio .... .15 .07
❑ 83 Bob Tewksbury .... .15 .07
❑ 84 Dave Winfield .... .60 .25
❑ 85 Jeff Kent .... .30 .14
❑ 86 Todd Van Poppel .... .15 .07
❑ 87 Steve Avery .... .15 .07
❑ 88 Mike Lansing .... .30 .14
❑ 89 Lenny Dykstra .... .30 .14
❑ 90 Jose Guzman .... .15 .07
❑ 91 Brian R. Hunter .... .15 .07
❑ 92 Tim Raines .... .30 .14
❑ 93 Andre Dawson .... .40 .18
❑ 94 Joe Orsulak .... .15 .07
❑ 95 Ricky Jordan .... .15 .07
❑ 96 Billy Hatcher .... .15 .07
❑ 97 Jack McDowell .... .15 .07
❑ 98 Tom Pagnozzi .... .15 .07
❑ 99 Darryl Strawberry .... .30 .14
❑ 100 Mike Stanley .... .15 .07
❑ 101 Bret Saberhagen .... .30 .14
❑ 102 Willie Greene .... .30 .14
❑ 103 Bryan Harvey .... .15 .07
❑ 104 Tim Bogar .... .15 .07
❑ 105 Jack Voigt .... .15 .07
❑ 106 Brad Ausmus .... .15 .07
❑ 107 Ramon Martinez .... .30 .14
❑ 108 Mike Perez .... .15 .07
❑ 109 Jeff Montgomery .... .15 .07
❑ 110 Danny Darwin .... .15 .07
❑ 111 Wilson Alvarez .... .30 .14
❑ 112 Kevin Mitchell .... .15 .07
❑ 113 David Nied .... .15 .07
❑ 114 Rich Amaral .... .15 .07
❑ 115 Stan Javier .... .15 .07
❑ 116 Mo Vaughn .... .75 .35
❑ 117 Ben McDonald .... .15 .07
❑ 118 Tom Gordon .... .15 .07
❑ 119 Carlos Garcia .... .15 .07
❑ 120 Phil Plantier .... .15 .07

❑ 121 Mike Morgan .15 .07
❑ 122 Pat Meares .15 .07
❑ 123 Kevin Young .15 .07
❑ 124 Jeff Fassero .15 .07
❑ 125 Gene Harris .15 .07
❑ 126 Bob Welch .15 .07
❑ 127 Walt Weiss .15 .07
❑ 128 Bobby Witt .15 .07
❑ 129 Andy Van Slyke .30 .14
❑ 130 Steve Cooke .15 .07
❑ 131 Mike Devereaux .15 .07
❑ 132 Joey Cora .30 .14
❑ 133 Bret Barberie .15 .07
❑ 134 Orel Hershiser .30 .14
❑ 135 Ed Sprague .15 .07
❑ 136 Shawon Dunston .15 .07
❑ 137 Alex Arias .15 .07
❑ 138 Archi Cianfrocco .15 .07
❑ 139 Tim Wallach .15 .07
❑ 140 Bernie Williams .60 .25
❑ 141 Karl Rhodes .15 .07
❑ 142 Pat Kelly .15 .07
❑ 143 Dave Magadan .15 .07
❑ 144 Kevin Tapani .15 .07
❑ 145 Eric Young .15 .07
❑ 146 Derek Bell .30 .14
❑ 147 Dante Bichette .30 .14
❑ 148 Geronimo Pena .15 .07
❑ 149 Joe Oliver .15 .07
❑ 150 Orestes Destrade .15 .07
❑ 151 Tim Naehring .15 .07
❑ 152 Ray Lankford .30 .14
❑ 153 Phil Clark .15 .07
❑ 154 David McCarty .15 .07
❑ 155 Tommy Greene .15 .07
❑ 156 Wade Boggs .60 .25
❑ 157 Kevin Gross .15 .07
❑ 158 Hal Morris .15 .07
❑ 159 Moises Alou .40 .18
❑ 160 Rick Aguilera .15 .07
❑ 161 Curt Schilling .30 .14
❑ 162 Chip Hale .15 .07
❑ 163 Tino Martinez .60 .25
❑ 164 Mark Whiten .15 .07
❑ 165 Dave Stewart .30 .14
❑ 166 Steve Buechele .15 .07
❑ 167 Bobby Jones .15 .07
❑ 168 Darrin Fletcher .15 .07
❑ 169 John Smiley .15 .07
❑ 170 Cory Snyder .15 .07
❑ 171 Scott Erickson .30 .14
❑ 172 Kirk Rueter .15 .07
❑ 173 Dave Fleming .15 .07
❑ 174 John Smoltz .30 .14
❑ 175 Ricky Gutierrez .15 .07
❑ 176 Mike Bordick .15 .07
❑ 177 Chan Ho Park 2.00 .90
❑ 178 Alex Gonzalez .15 .07
❑ 179 Steve Karsay .15 .07
❑ 180 Jeffrey Hammonds .30 .14
❑ 181 Manny Ramirez .75 .35
❑ 182 Salomon Torres .15 .07
❑ 183 Raul Mondesi .60 .25
❑ 184 James Mouton .15 .07
❑ 185 Cliff Floyd .30 .14
❑ 186 Danny Bautista .15 .07
❑ 187 Kurt Abbott .15 .07
❑ 188 Javier Lopez .40 .18
❑ 189 John Patterson .15 .07
❑ 190 Greg Blosser .15 .07
❑ 191 Bob Hamelin .15 .07
❑ 192 Tony Eusebio .15 .07
❑ 193 Carlos Delgado .40 .18
❑ 194 Chris Gomez .15 .07
❑ 195 Kelly Stinnett .15 .07
❑ 196 Shane Reynolds .30 .14
❑ 197 Ryan Klesko .30 .14
❑ 198 Jim Edmonds UER .60 .25
Mark Dalesandro
pictured on front
❑ 199 James Hurst .15 .07
❑ 200 Dave Staton .15 .07
❑ 201 Rondell White .30 .14
❑ 202 Keith Mitchell .15 .07
❑ 203 Darren Oliver .30 .14
❑ 204 Mike Matheny .15 .07
❑ 205 Chris Turner .15 .07
❑ 206 Matt Mieske .15 .07
❑ 207 NL Team Checklist .15 .07
❑ 208 NL Team Checklist .15 .07
❑ 209 AL Team Checklist .15 .07
❑ 210 AL Team Checklist .15 .07
❑ 211 Barry Bonds .75 .35
❑ 212 Juan Gonzalez 1.50 .70
❑ 213 Jim Eisenreich .15 .07
❑ 214 Ivan Rodriguez .75 .35
❑ 215 Tony Phillips .15 .07
❑ 216 John Jaha .15 .07
❑ 217 Lee Smith .30 .14
❑ 218 Bip Roberts .15 .07
❑ 219 Dave Hansen .15 .07
❑ 220 Pat Listach .15 .07
❑ 221 Willie McGee .30 .14
❑ 222 Damion Easley .30 .14
❑ 223 Dean Palmer .30 .14
❑ 224 Mike Moore .15 .07
❑ 225 Brian Harper .15 .07
❑ 226 Gary DiSarcina .15 .07
❑ 227 Delino DeShields .15 .07
❑ 228 Otis Nixon .15 .07
❑ 229 Roberto Alomar .60 .25
❑ 230 Mark Grace .40 .18
❑ 231 Kenny Lofton .60 .25
❑ 232 Gregg Jefferies .15 .07
❑ 233 Cecil Fielder .30 .14
❑ 234 Jeff Bagwell 1.00 .45
❑ 235 Albert Belle .75 .35
❑ 236 Dave Justice .60 .25
❑ 237 Tom Henke .15 .07
❑ 238 Bobby Bonilla .30 .14
❑ 239 John Olerud .30 .14
❑ 240 Robby Thompson .15 .07
❑ 241 Dave Valle .15 .07
❑ 242 Marquis Grissom .30 .14
❑ 243 Greg Swindell .15 .07
❑ 244 Todd Zeile .15 .07
❑ 245 Dennis Eckersley .30 .14
❑ 246 Jose Offerman .15 .07
❑ 247 Greg McMichael .15 .07
❑ 248 Tim Belcher .15 .07
❑ 249 Cal Ripken Jr. 2.50 1.10
❑ 250 Tom Glavine .60 .25
❑ 251 Luis Polonia .15 .07
❑ 252 Bill Swift .15 .07
❑ 253 Juan Guzman .15 .07
❑ 254 Rickey Henderson .60 .25
❑ 255 Terry Mulholland .15 .07
❑ 256 Gary Sheffield .60 .25
❑ 257 Terry Steinbach .30 .14
❑ 258 Brett Butler .30 .14
❑ 259 Jason Bere .15 .07
❑ 260 Doug Strange .15 .07
❑ 261 Kent Hrbek .30 .14
❑ 262 Graeme Lloyd .15 .07
❑ 263 Lou Frazier .15 .07
❑ 264 Charles Nagy .30 .14
❑ 265 Bret Boone .30 .14
❑ 266 Kirk Gibson .30 .14
❑ 267 Kevin Brown .30 .14
❑ 268 Fred McGriff .40 .18
❑ 269 Matt Williams .40 .18
❑ 270 Greg Gagne .15 .07
❑ 271 Mariano Duncan .15 .07
❑ 272 Jeff Russell .15 .07
❑ 273 Eric Davis .30 .14
❑ 274 Shane Mack .15 .07
❑ 275 Jose Vizcaino .15 .07
❑ 276 Jose Canseco .60 .25
❑ 277 Roberto Hernandez .15 .07
❑ 278 Royce Clayton .15 .07
❑ 279 Carlos Baerga .30 .14
❑ 280 Pete Incaviglia .15 .07
❑ 281 Brent Gates .15 .07
❑ 282 Jeromy Burnitz .30 .14
❑ 283 Chili Davis .30 .14
❑ 284 Pete Harnisch .15 .07
❑ 285 Alan Trammell .40 .18
❑ 286 Eric Anthony .15 .07
❑ 287 Ellis Burks .30 .14
❑ 288 Julio Franco .15 .07
❑ 289 Jack Morris .30 .14
❑ 290 Erik Hanson .15 .07
❑ 291 Chuck Finley .30 .14
❑ 292 Reggie Jefferson .15 .07
❑ 293 Kevin McReynolds .15 .07
❑ 294 Greg Hibbard .15 .07
❑ 295 Travis Fryman .30 .14
❑ 296 Craig Biggio .60 .25
❑ 297 Kenny Rogers .15 .07
❑ 298 Dave Henderson .15 .07
❑ 299 Jim Thome .75 .35
❑ 300 Rene Arocha .15 .07
❑ 301 Pedro Munoz .15 .07
❑ 302 David Hulse .15 .07
❑ 303 Greg Vaughn .30 .14
❑ 304 Darren Lewis .15 .07
❑ 305 Deion Sanders .30 .14
❑ 306 Danny Tartabull .15 .07
❑ 307 Darryl Hamilton .15 .07
❑ 308 Andujar Cedeno .15 .07
❑ 309 Tim Salmon .60 .25
❑ 310 Tony Fernandez .15 .07
❑ 311 Alex Fernandez .15 .07
❑ 312 Roberto Kelly .15 .07
❑ 313 Harold Reynolds .15 .07
❑ 314 Chris Sabo .15 .07
❑ 315 Howard Johnson .15 .07
❑ 316 Mark Portugal .15 .07
❑ 317 Rafael Palmeiro .40 .18
❑ 318 Pete Smith .15 .07
❑ 319 Will Clark .60 .25
❑ 320 Henry Rodriguez .30 .14
❑ 321 Omar Vizquel .30 .14
❑ 322 David Segui .30 .14
❑ 323 Lou Whitaker .30 .14
❑ 324 Felix Fermin .15 .07
❑ 325 Spike Owen .15 .07
❑ 326 Darryl Kile .30 .14
❑ 327 Chad Kreuter .15 .07
❑ 328 Rod Beck .15 .07
❑ 329 Eddie Murray .60 .25
❑ 330 B.J. Surhoff .30 .14
❑ 331 Mickey Tettleton .15 .07
❑ 332 Pedro Martinez .75 .35
❑ 333 Roger Pavlik .15 .07
❑ 334 Eddie Taubensee .15 .07
❑ 335 John Doherty .15 .07
❑ 336 Jody Reed .15 .07
❑ 337 Aaron Sele .30 .14
❑ 338 Leo Gomez .15 .07
❑ 339 Dave Nilsson .15 .07
❑ 340 Rob Dibble .15 .07
❑ 341 John Burkett .15 .07
❑ 342 Wayne Kirby .15 .07
❑ 343 Dan Wilson .15 .07
❑ 344 Armando Reynoso .15 .07
❑ 345 Chad Curtis .15 .07
❑ 346 Dennis Martinez .30 .14
❑ 347 Cal Eldred .15 .07
❑ 348 Luis Gonzalez .15 .07
❑ 349 Doug Drabek .15 .07
❑ 350 Jim Leyritz .30 .14
❑ 351 Mark Langston .15 .07
❑ 352 Darrin Jackson .15 .07
❑ 353 Sid Fernandez .15 .07
❑ 354 Benito Santiago .15 .07
❑ 355 Kevin Seitzer .15 .07
❑ 356 Bo Jackson .30 .14
❑ 357 David Wells .40 .18
❑ 358 Paul Sorrento .15 .07
❑ 359 Ken Caminiti .40 .18
❑ 360 Eduardo Perez .15 .07
❑ 361 Orlando Merced .15 .07
❑ 362 Steve Finley .30 .14
❑ 363 Andy Benes .30 .14
❑ 364 Manuel Lee .15 .07
❑ 365 Todd Benzinger .15 .07
❑ 366 Sandy Alomar Jr. .30 .14
❑ 367 Rex Hudler .15 .07
❑ 368 Mike Henneman .15 .07
❑ 369 Vince Coleman .15 .07
❑ 370 Kirt Manwaring .15 .07
❑ 371 Ken Hill .15 .07
❑ 372 Glenallen Hill .15 .07
❑ 373 Sean Berry .15 .07

		MINT	NRMT
❑ 374	Geronimo Berroa	.15	.07
❑ 375	Duane Ward	.15	.07
❑ 376	Allen Watson	.15	.07
❑ 377	Marc Newfield	.15	.07
❑ 378	Dan Miceli	.15	.07
❑ 379	Denny Hocking	.15	.07
❑ 380	Mark Kiefer	.15	.07
❑ 381	Tony Tarasco	.15	.07
❑ 382	Tony Longmire	.15	.07
❑ 383	Brian Anderson	.40	.18
❑ 384	Fernando Vina	.15	.07
❑ 385	Hector Carrasco	.15	.07
❑ 386	Mike Kelly	.15	.07
❑ 387	Greg Colbrunn	.15	.07
❑ 388	Roger Salkeld	.15	.07
❑ 389	Steve Trachsel	.15	.07
❑ 390	Rich Becker	.15	.07
❑ 391	Billy Taylor	.15	.07
❑ 392	Rich Rowland	.15	.07
❑ 393	Carl Everett	.15	.07
❑ 394	Johnny Ruffin	.15	.07
❑ 395	Keith Lockhart	.15	.07
❑ 396	J.R. Phillips	.15	.07
❑ 397	Sterling Hitchcock	.30	.14
❑ 398	Jorge Fabregas	.15	.07
❑ 399	Jeff Granger	.15	.07
❑ 400	Eddie Zambrano	.15	.07
❑ 401	Rikkert Faneyte	.15	.07
❑ 402	Gerald Williams	.15	.07
❑ 403	Joey Hamilton	.60	.25
❑ 404	Joe Hall	.15	.07
❑ 405	John Hudek	.15	.07
❑ 406	Roberto Petagine	.15	.07
❑ 407	Charles Johnson	.30	.14
❑ 408	Mark Smith	.15	.07
❑ 409	Jeff Juden	.15	.07
❑ 410	Carlos Pulido	.15	.07
❑ 411	Paul Shuey	.15	.07
❑ 412	Rob Butler	.15	.07
❑ 413	Mark Acre	.15	.07
❑ 414	Greg Pirkl	.15	.07
❑ 415	Melvin Nieves	.15	.07
❑ 416	Tim Hyers	.15	.07
❑ 417	NL Checklist	.15	.07
❑ 418	NL Checklist	.15	.07
❑ 419	AL Checklist	.15	.07
❑ 420	AL Checklist	.15	.07
❑ RY1	Carlos Delgado	3.00	1.35
❑ SS1	Cal Ripken Jr. Salute	25.00	11.00
❑ SS2	Dave Winfield Salute	5.00	2.20
❑ MVP1	Paul Molitor	6.00	2.70

1994 Select Crown Contenders

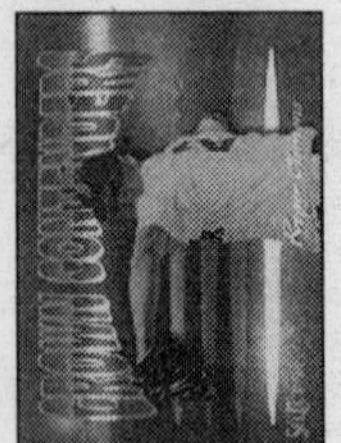

	MINT	NRMT
COMPLETE SET (10)	80.00	36.00
COMMON CARD (CC1-CC10)	1.50	.70

		MINT	NRMT
❑ CC1	Lenny Dykstra	1.50	.70
❑ CC2	Greg Maddux	12.00	5.50
❑ CC3	Roger Clemens	8.00	3.60
❑ CC4	Randy Johnson	5.00	2.20
❑ CC5	Frank Thomas	12.00	5.50
❑ CC6	Barry Bonds	5.00	2.20
❑ CC7	Juan Gonzalez	10.00	4.50
❑ CC8	John Olerud	1.50	.70
❑ CC9	Mike Piazza	12.00	5.50
❑ CC10	Ken Griffey Jr.	20.00	9.00

1994 Select Rookie Surge

	MINT	NRMT
COMPLETE SET (18)	80.00	36.00
COMPLETE SERIES 1 (9)	30.00	13.50
COMPLETE SERIES 2 (9)	50.00	22.00
COMMON CARD (RS1-RS18)	2.50	1.10

		MINT	NRMT
❑ RS1	Cliff Floyd	5.00	2.20
❑ RS2	Bob Hamelin	2.50	1.10
❑ RS3	Ryan Klesko	8.00	3.60
❑ RS4	Carlos Delgado	10.00	4.50
❑ RS5	Jeffrey Hammonds	5.00	2.20
❑ RS6	Rondell White	5.00	2.20
❑ RS7	Salomon Torres	2.50	1.10
❑ RS8	Steve Karsay	2.50	1.10
❑ RS9	Javier Lopez	10.00	4.50
❑ RS10	Manny Ramirez	20.00	9.00
❑ RS11	Tony Tarasco	2.50	1.10
❑ RS12	Kurt Abbott	2.50	1.10
❑ RS13	Chan Ho Park	20.00	9.00
❑ RS14	Rich Becker	2.50	1.10
❑ RS15	James Mouton	2.50	1.10
❑ RS16	Alex Gonzalez	2.50	1.10
❑ RS17	Raul Mondesi	12.00	5.50
❑ RS18	Steve Trachsel	2.50	1.10

1994 Select Skills

	MINT	NRMT
COMPLETE SET (10)	60.00	27.00
COMMON CARD (SK1-SK10)	4.00	1.80

		MINT	NRMT
❑ SK1	Randy Johnson	10.00	4.50
❑ SK2	Barry Larkin	6.00	2.70
❑ SK3	Lenny Dykstra	4.00	1.80
❑ SK4	Kenny Lofton	10.00	4.50
❑ SK5	Juan Gonzalez	25.00	11.00
❑ SK6	Barry Bonds	12.00	5.50
❑ SK7	Marquis Grissom	4.00	1.80
❑ SK8	Ivan Rodriguez	12.00	5.50
❑ SK9	Larry Walker	10.00	4.50
❑ SK10	Travis Fryman	4.00	1.80

1995 Select

	MINT	NRMT
COMPLETE SET (250)	15.00	6.75
COMMON CARD (1-250)	.10	.05

		MINT	NRMT
❑ 1	Cal Ripken Jr.	1.50	.70
❑ 2	Robin Ventura	.20	.09
❑ 3	Al Martin	.10	.05
❑ 4	Jeff Frye	.10	.05
❑ 5	Darryl Strawberry	.20	.09
❑ 6	Chan Ho Park	.50	.23
❑ 7	Steve Avery	.10	.05
❑ 8	Bret Boone	.20	.09
❑ 9	Danny Tartabull	.10	.05
❑ 10	Dante Bichette	.20	.09
❑ 11	Rondell White	.20	.09
❑ 12	Dave McCarty	.10	.05
❑ 13	Bernard Gilkey	.10	.05
❑ 14	Mark McGwire	2.00	.90
❑ 15	Ruben Sierra	.10	.05
❑ 16	Wade Boggs	.40	.18
❑ 17	Mike Piazza	1.25	.55
❑ 18	Jeffrey Hammonds	.20	.09
❑ 19	Mike Mussina	.40	.18
❑ 20	Darryl Kile	.20	.09
❑ 21	Greg Maddux	1.25	.55
❑ 22	Frank Thomas	1.25	.55
❑ 23	Kevin Appier	.20	.09
❑ 24	Jay Bell	.20	.09
❑ 25	Kirk Gibson	.20	.09
❑ 26	Pat Hentgen	.20	.09
❑ 27	Joey Hamilton	.20	.09
❑ 28	Bernie Williams	.40	.18
❑ 29	Aaron Sele	.20	.09
❑ 30	Delino DeShields	.10	.05
❑ 31	Danny Bautista	.10	.05
❑ 32	Jim Thome	.40	.18
❑ 33	Rikkert Faneyte	.10	.05
❑ 34	Roberto Alomar	.40	.18
❑ 35	Paul Molitor	.40	.18
❑ 36	Allen Watson	.10	.05
❑ 37	Jeff Bagwell	.60	.25
❑ 38	Jay Buhner	.20	.09
❑ 39	Marquis Grissom	.20	.09
❑ 40	Jim Edmonds	.30	.14
❑ 41	Ryan Klesko	.20	.09
❑ 42	Fred McGriff	.30	.14
❑ 43	Tony Tarasco	.10	.05
❑ 44	Darren Daulton	.20	.09
❑ 45	Marc Newfield	.10	.05
❑ 46	Barry Bonds	.50	.23
❑ 47	Bobby Bonilla	.20	.09
❑ 48	Greg Pirkl	.10	.05
❑ 49	Steve Karsay	.10	.05
❑ 50	Bob Hamelin	.10	.05
❑ 51	Javier Lopez	.20	.09
❑ 52	Barry Larkin	.30	.14
❑ 53	Kevin Young	.10	.05
❑ 54	Sterling Hitchcock	.20	.09
❑ 55	Tom Glavine	.40	.18
❑ 56	Carlos Delgado	.20	.09
❑ 57	Darren Oliver	.10	.05
❑ 58	Cliff Floyd	.20	.09
❑ 59	Tim Salmon	.40	.18
❑ 60	Albert Belle	.50	.23
❑ 61	Salomon Torres	.10	.05
❑ 62	Gary Sheffield	.30	.14

Card	MINT	NRMT
❑ 63 Ivan Rodriguez	.50	.23
❑ 64 Charles Nagy	.20	.09
❑ 65 Eduardo Perez	.10	.05
❑ 66 Terry Steinbach	.20	.09
❑ 67 Dave Justice	.40	.18
❑ 68 Jason Bere	.10	.05
❑ 69 Dave Nilsson	.10	.05
❑ 70 Brian Anderson	.20	.09
❑ 71 Billy Ashley	.10	.05
❑ 72 Roger Clemens	.75	.35
❑ 73 Jimmy Key	.20	.09
❑ 74 Wally Joyner	.20	.09
❑ 75 Andy Benes	.20	.09
❑ 76 Ray Lankford	.20	.09
❑ 77 Jeff Kent	.20	.09
❑ 78 Moises Alou	.30	.14
❑ 79 Kirby Puckett	.60	.25
❑ 80 Joe Carter	.20	.09
❑ 81 Manny Ramirez	.40	.18
❑ 82 J.R. Phillips	.10	.05
❑ 83 Matt Mieske	.10	.05
❑ 84 John Olerud	.20	.09
❑ 85 Andres Galarraga	.40	.18
❑ 86 Juan Gonzalez	1.00	.45
❑ 87 Pedro Martinez	.40	.18
❑ 88 Dean Palmer	.20	.09
❑ 89 Ken Griffey Jr.	2.00	.90
❑ 90 Brian Jordan	.20	.09
❑ 91 Hal Morris	.10	.05
❑ 92 Lenny Dykstra	.20	.09
❑ 93 Wil Cordero	.10	.05
❑ 94 Tony Gwynn	1.00	.45
❑ 95 Alex Gonzalez	.10	.05
❑ 96 Cecil Fielder	.20	.09
❑ 97 Mo Vaughn	.50	.23
❑ 98 John Valentin	.20	.09
❑ 99 Will Clark	.40	.18
❑ 100 Geronimo Pena	.10	.05
❑ 101 Don Mattingly	.60	.25
❑ 102 Charles Johnson	.20	.09
❑ 103 Raul Mondesi	.30	.14
❑ 104 Reggie Sanders	.20	.09
❑ 105 Royce Clayton	.10	.05
❑ 106 Reggie Jefferson	.10	.05
❑ 107 Craig Biggio	.40	.18
❑ 108 Jack McDowell	.10	.05
❑ 109 James Mouton	.10	.05
❑ 110 Mike Greenwell	.10	.05
❑ 111 David Cone	.30	.14
❑ 112 Matt Williams	.20	.09
❑ 113 Garret Anderson	.20	.09
❑ 114 Carlos Garcia	.10	.05
❑ 115 Alex Fernandez	.10	.05
❑ 116 Deion Sanders	.20	.09
❑ 117 Chili Davis	.20	.09
❑ 118 Mike Kelly	.10	.05
❑ 119 Jeff Conine	.20	.09
❑ 120 Kenny Lofton	.40	.18
❑ 121 Rafael Palmeiro	.30	.14
❑ 122 Chuck Knoblauch	.40	.18
❑ 123 Ozzie Smith	.50	.23
❑ 124 Carlos Baerga	.20	.09
❑ 125 Brett Butler	.20	.09
❑ 126 Sammy Sosa	1.00	.45
❑ 127 Ellis Burks	.20	.09
❑ 128 Bret Saberhagen	.20	.09
❑ 129 Doug Drabek	.10	.05
❑ 130 Dennis Martinez	.20	.09
❑ 131 Paul O'Neill	.20	.09
❑ 132 Travis Fryman	.20	.09
❑ 133 Brent Gates	.10	.05
❑ 134 Rickey Henderson	.40	.18
❑ 135 Randy Johnson	.40	.18
❑ 136 Mark Langston	.10	.05
❑ 137 Greg Colbrunn	.10	.05
❑ 138 Jose Rijo	.10	.05
❑ 139 Bryan Harvey	.10	.05
❑ 140 Dennis Eckersley	.20	.09
❑ 141 Ron Gant	.10	.05
❑ 142 Carl Everett	.10	.05
❑ 143 Jeff Granger	.10	.05
❑ 144 Ben McDonald	.10	.05
❑ 145 Kurt Abbott UER (Mariners logo on front	.10	.05
❑ 146 Jim Abbott	.20	.09
❑ 147 Jason Jacome	.10	.05
❑ 148 Rico Brogna	.10	.05
❑ 149 Cal Eldred	.10	.05
❑ 150 Rich Becker	.10	.05
❑ 151 Pete Harnisch	.10	.05
❑ 152 Roberto Petagine	.10	.05
❑ 153 Jacob Brumfield	.10	.05
❑ 154 Todd Hundley	.20	.09
❑ 155 Roger Cedeno	.10	.05
❑ 156 Harold Baines	.20	.09
❑ 157 Steve Dunn	.10	.05
❑ 158 Tim Belk	.10	.05
❑ 159 Marty Cordova	.10	.05
❑ 160 Russ Davis	.20	.09
❑ 161 Jose Malave	.10	.05
❑ 162 Brian Hunter	.20	.09
❑ 163 Andy Pettitte	.40	.18
❑ 164 Brooks Kieschnick	.10	.05
❑ 165 Midre Cummings	.10	.05
❑ 166 Frank Rodriguez	.10	.05
❑ 167 Chad Mottola	.10	.05
❑ 168 Brian Barber	.10	.05
❑ 169 Tim Unroe	.10	.05
❑ 170 Shane Andrews	.10	.05
❑ 171 Kevin Flora	.10	.05
❑ 172 Ray Durham	.20	.09
❑ 173 Chipper Jones	1.00	.45
❑ 174 Butch Huskey	.10	.05
❑ 175 Ray McDavid	.10	.05
❑ 176 Jeff Cirillo	.20	.09
❑ 177 Terry Pendleton	.10	.05
❑ 178 Scott Ruffcorn	.10	.05
❑ 179 Ray Holbert	.10	.05
❑ 180 Joe Randa	.10	.05
❑ 181 Jose Oliva	.10	.05
❑ 182 Andy Van Slyke	.20	.09
❑ 183 Albie Lopez	.10	.05
❑ 184 Chad Curtis	.10	.05
❑ 185 Ozzie Guillen	.10	.05
❑ 186 Chad Ogea	.10	.05
❑ 187 Dan Wilson	.10	.05
❑ 188 Tony Fernandez	.10	.05
❑ 189 John Smoltz	.20	.09
❑ 190 Willie Greene	.20	.09
❑ 191 Darren Lewis	.10	.05
❑ 192 Orlando Miller	.10	.05
❑ 193 Kurt Miller	.10	.05
❑ 194 Andrew Lorraine	.10	.05
❑ 195 Ernie Young	.10	.05
❑ 196 Jimmy Haynes	.10	.05
❑ 197 Raul Casanova	.10	.05
❑ 198 Joe Vitiello	.10	.05
❑ 199 Brad Woodall	.10	.05
❑ 200 Juan Acevedo	.10	.05
❑ 201 Michael Tucker	.20	.09
❑ 202 Shawn Green	.20	.09
❑ 203 Alex Rodriguez	1.50	.70
❑ 204 Julian Tavarez	.10	.05
❑ 205 Jose Lima	.10	.05
❑ 206 Wilson Alvarez	.20	.09
❑ 207 Rich Aude	.10	.05
❑ 208 Armando Benitez	.10	.05
❑ 209 Dwayne Hosey	.10	.05
❑ 210 Gabe White	.10	.05
❑ 211 Joey Eischen	.10	.05
❑ 212 Bill Pulsipher	.10	.05
❑ 213 Robby Thompson	.10	.05
❑ 214 Toby Borland	.10	.05
❑ 215 Rusty Greer	.40	.18
❑ 216 Fausto Cruz	.10	.05
❑ 217 Luis Ortiz	.10	.05
❑ 218 Duane Singleton	.10	.05
❑ 219 Troy Percival	.20	.09
❑ 220 Gregg Jefferies	.10	.05
❑ 221 Mark Grace	.30	.14
❑ 222 Mickey Tettleton	.10	.05
❑ 223 Phil Plantier	.10	.05
❑ 224 Larry Walker	.40	.18
❑ 225 Ken Caminiti	.30	.14
❑ 226 Dave Winfield	.40	.18
❑ 227 Brady Anderson	.20	.09
❑ 228 Kevin Brown	.30	.14
❑ 229 Andujar Cedeno	.10	.05
❑ 230 Roberto Kelly	.10	.05
❑ 231 Jose Canseco	.40	.18
❑ 232 Scott Ruffcorn ST	.10	.05
❑ 233 Billy Ashley ST	.10	.05
❑ 234 J.R. Phillips ST	.10	.05
❑ 235 Chipper Jones ST	.50	.23
❑ 236 Charles Johnson ST	.10	.05
❑ 237 Midre Cummings ST	.10	.05
❑ 238 Brian L.Hunter ST	.10	.05
❑ 239 Garret Anderson ST	.10	.05
❑ 240 Shawn Green ST	.10	.05
❑ 241 Alex Rodriguez ST	.75	.35
❑ 242 Frank Thomas CL	.60	.25
❑ 243 Ken Griffey Jr. CL	1.00	.45
❑ 244 Albert Belle CL	.20	.09
❑ 245 Cal Ripken Jr. CL	.75	.35
❑ 246 Barry Bonds CL	.30	.14
❑ 247 Raul Mondesi CL	.10	.05
❑ 248 Mike Piazza CL	.60	.25
❑ 249 Jeff Bagwell CL	.40	.18
❑ 250 Jeff Bagwell Ken Griffey Jr. Frank Thomas Mike Piazza CL	1.25	.55
❑ 251S Hideo Nomo	1.50	.70

1995 Select Big Sticks

	MINT	NRMT
COMPLETE SET (12)	150.00	70.00
COMMON CARD (1-12)	4.00	1.80
❑ BS1 Frank Thomas	20.00	9.00
❑ BS2 Ken Griffey Jr.	30.00	13.50
❑ BS3 Cal Ripken Jr.	25.00	11.00
❑ BS4 Mike Piazza	20.00	9.00
❑ BS5 Don Mattingly	10.00	4.50
❑ BS6 Will Clark	6.00	2.70
❑ BS7 Tony Gwynn	15.00	6.75
❑ BS8 Jeff Bagwell	10.00	4.50
❑ BS9 Barry Bonds	8.00	3.60
❑ BS10 Paul Molitor	6.00	2.70
❑ BS11 Matt Williams	4.00	1.80
❑ BS12 Albert Belle	8.00	3.60

1995 Select Can't Miss

	MINT	NRMT
COMPLETE SET (12)	50.00	22.00
COMMON CARD (1-12)	2.00	.90
❑ CM1 Cliff Floyd	2.50	1.10
❑ CM2 Ryan Klesko	2.50	1.10

❑ CM3 Charles Johnson 2.50 1.10
❑ CM4 Raul Mondesi.............. 3.00 1.35
❑ CM5 Manny Ramirez 5.00 2.20
❑ CM6 Billy Ashley .... 2.00 .90
❑ CM7 Alex Gonzalez .... 2.00 .90
❑ CM8 Carlos Delgado 2.50 1.10
❑ CM9 Garret Anderson 2.50 1.10
❑ CM10 Alex Rodriguez 20.00 9.00
❑ CM11 Chipper Jones 15.00 6.75
❑ CM12 Shawn Green............ 2.50 1.10

1995 Select Sure Shots

	MINT	NRMT
COMPLETE SET (10)	50.00	22.00
COMMON CARD (1-10)	2.00	.90

❑ SS1 Ben Grieve 30.00 13.50
❑ SS2 Kevin Witt 5.00 2.20
❑ SS3 Mark Farris .... 2.00 .90
❑ SS4 Paul Konerko 12.00 5.50
❑ SS5 Dustin Hermanson 3.00 1.35
❑ SS6 Ramon Castro 3.00 1.35
❑ SS7 McKay Christensen 3.00 1.35
❑ SS8 Brian Buchanan .... 2.00 .90
❑ SS9 Paul Wilson .... 2.00 .90
❑ SS10 Terrence Long 3.00 1.35

1996 Select

	MINT	NRMT
COMPLETE SET (200)	15.00	6.75
COMMON CARD (1-200)	.10	.05

❑ 1 Wade Boggs .... .40 .18
❑ 2 Shawn Green .... .20 .09
❑ 3 Andres Galarraga .... .40 .18
❑ 4 Bill Pulsipher .... .10 .05
❑ 5 Chuck Knoblauch .... .40 .18
❑ 6 Ken Griffey Jr. .... 2.00 .90
❑ 7 Greg Maddux .... 1.25 .55
❑ 8 Manny Ramirez .... .40 .18
❑ 9 Ivan Rodriguez .... .50 .23
❑ 10 Tim Salmon .... .40 .18
❑ 11 Frank Thomas .... 1.25 .55
❑ 12 Jeff Bagwell .... .60 .25
❑ 13 Travis Fryman .... .20 .09
❑ 14 Kenny Lofton .... .40 .18
❑ 15 Matt Williams .... .20 .09
❑ 16 Jay Bell .... .20 .09
❑ 17 Ken Caminiti .... .30 .14
❑ 18 Ray Lankford .... .20 .09
❑ 19 Cal Ripken .... 1.50 .70
❑ 20 Roger Clemens .... .75 .35
❑ 21 Carlos Baerga .... .20 .09
❑ 22 Mike Piazza .... 1.25 .55
❑ 23 Gregg Jefferies .... .10 .05
❑ 24 Reggie Sanders .... .20 .09
❑ 25 Rondell White .... .20 .09
❑ 26 Sammy Sosa .... 1.00 .45
❑ 27 Kevin Appier .... .20 .09
❑ 28 Kevin Seitzer .... .10 .05
❑ 29 Gary Sheffield .... .30 .14
❑ 30 Mike Mussina .... .40 .18
❑ 31 Mark McGwire .... 2.00 .90
❑ 32 Barry Larkin .... .30 .14
❑ 33 Marc Newfield .... .10 .05
❑ 34 Ismael Valdes .... .20 .09
❑ 35 Marty Cordova .... .10 .05
❑ 36 Albert Belle .... .50 .23
❑ 37 Johnny Damon .... .20 .09
❑ 38 Garret Anderson .... .20 .09
❑ 39 Cecil Fielder .... .20 .09
❑ 40 John Mabry .... .10 .05
❑ 41 Chipper Jones .... 1.00 .45
❑ 42 Omar Vizquel .... .20 .09
❑ 43 Jose Rijo .... .10 .05
❑ 44 Charles Johnson .... .20 .09
❑ 45 Alex Rodriguez .... 1.25 .55
❑ 46 Rico Brogna .... .10 .05
❑ 47 Joe Carter .... .20 .09
❑ 48 Mo Vaughn .... .50 .23
❑ 49 Moises Alou .... .30 .14
❑ 50 Raul Mondesi .... .30 .14
❑ 51 Robin Ventura .... .20 .09
❑ 52 Jim Thome .... .40 .18
❑ 53 David Justice .... .40 .18
❑ 54 Jeff King .... .10 .05
❑ 55 Brian L.Hunter .... .20 .09
❑ 56 Juan Gonzalez .... 1.00 .45
❑ 57 John Olerud .... .20 .09
❑ 58 Rafael Palmeiro .... .30 .14
❑ 59 Tony Gwynn .... 1.00 .45
❑ 60 Eddie Murray .... .40 .18
❑ 61 Jason Isringhausen .... .10 .05
❑ 62 Dante Bichette .... .20 .09
❑ 63 Randy Johnson .... .40 .18
❑ 64 Kirby Puckett .... .60 .25
❑ 65 Jim Edmonds .... .30 .14
❑ 66 David Cone .... .30 .14
❑ 67 Ozzie Smith .... .50 .23
❑ 68 Fred McGriff .... .30 .14
❑ 69 Darren Daulton .... .20 .09
❑ 70 Edgar Martinez .... .20 .09
❑ 71 J.T. Snow .... .20 .09
❑ 72 Butch Huskey .... .10 .05
❑ 73 Hideo Nomo .... .60 .25
❑ 74 Pedro Martinez .... .40 .18
❑ 75 Bobby Bonilla .... .20 .09
❑ 76 Jeff Conine .... .20 .09
❑ 77 Ryan Klesko .... .20 .09
❑ 78 Bernie Williams .... .40 .18
❑ 79 Andre Dawson .... .30 .14
❑ 80 Trevor Hoffman .... .20 .09
❑ 81 Mark Grace .... .30 .14
❑ 82 Benji Gil .... .10 .05
❑ 83 Eric Karros .... .20 .09
❑ 84 Pete Schourek .... .10 .05
❑ 85 Edgardo Alfonzo .... .20 .09
❑ 86 Jay Buhner .... .20 .09
❑ 87 Vinny Castilla .... .30 .14
❑ 88 Bret Boone .... .20 .09
❑ 89 Ray Durham .... .20 .09
❑ 90 Brian Jordan .... .20 .09
❑ 91 Jose Canseco .... .40 .18
❑ 92 Paul O'Neill .... .20 .09
❑ 93 Chili Davis .... .20 .09
❑ 94 Tom Glavine .... .40 .18
❑ 95 Julian Tavarez .... .10 .05
❑ 96 Derek Bell .... .20 .09
❑ 97 Will Clark .... .40 .18
❑ 98 Larry Walker .... .40 .18
❑ 99 Denny Neagle .... .20 .09
❑ 100 Alex Fernandez .... .10 .05
❑ 101 Barry Bonds .... .50 .23
❑ 102 Ben McDonald .... .10 .05
❑ 103 Andy Pettitte .... .30 .14
❑ 104 Tino Martinez .... .40 .18
❑ 105 Sterling Hitchcock .... .20 .09
❑ 106 Royce Clayton .... .10 .05
❑ 107 Jim Abbott .... .20 .09
❑ 108 Rickey Henderson .... .40 .18
❑ 109 Ramon Martinez .... .20 .09
❑ 110 Paul Molitor .... .40 .18
❑ 111 Dennis Eckersley .... .20 .09
❑ 112 Alex Gonzalez .... .10 .05
❑ 113 Marquis Grissom .... .20 .09
❑ 114 Greg Vaughn .... .20 .09
❑ 115 Lance Johnson .... .10 .05
❑ 116 Todd Stottlemyre .... .10 .05
❑ 117 Jack McDowell .... .10 .05
❑ 118 Ruben Sierra .... .10 .05
❑ 119 Brady Anderson .... .20 .09
❑ 120 Julio Franco .... .10 .05
❑ 121 Brooks Kieschnick .... .10 .05
❑ 122 Roberto Alomar .... .40 .18
❑ 123 Greg Gagne .... .10 .05
❑ 124 Wally Joyner .... .20 .09
❑ 125 John Smoltz .... .20 .09
❑ 126 John Valentin .... .20 .09
❑ 127 Russ Davis .... .20 .09
❑ 128 Joe Vitiello .... .10 .05
❑ 129 Shawon Dunston .... .10 .05
❑ 130 Frank Rodriguez .... .10 .05
❑ 131 Charlie Hayes .... .10 .05
❑ 132 Andy Benes .... .20 .09
❑ 133 B.J. Surhoff .... .20 .09
❑ 134 Dave Nilsson .... .10 .05
❑ 135 Carlos Delgado .... .20 .09
❑ 136 Walt Weiss .... .10 .05
❑ 137 Mike Stanley .... .10 .05
❑ 138 Greg Colbrunn .... .10 .05
❑ 139 Mike Kelly .... .10 .05
❑ 140 Ryne Sandberg .... .50 .23
❑ 141 Lee Smith .... .20 .09
❑ 142 Dennis Martinez .... .20 .09
❑ 143 Bernard Gilkey .... .10 .05
❑ 144 Lenny Dykstra .... .20 .09
❑ 145 Danny Tartabull .... .10 .05
❑ 146 Dean Palmer .... .20 .09
❑ 147 Craig Biggio .... .40 .18
❑ 148 Juan Acevedo .... .10 .05
❑ 149 Michael Tucker .... .20 .09
❑ 150 Bobby Higginson .... .40 .18
❑ 151 Ken Griffey Jr. LUL .... 1.00 .45
❑ 152 Frank Thomas LUL .... .60 .25
❑ 153 Cal Ripken LUL .... .75 .35
❑ 154 Albert Belle LUL .... .30 .14
❑ 155 Mike Piazza LUL .... .60 .25
❑ 156 Barry Bonds LUL .... .30 .14
❑ 157 Sammy Sosa LUL .... .50 .23
❑ 158 Mo Vaughn LUL .... .30 .14
❑ 159 Greg Maddux LUL .... .60 .25
❑ 160 Jeff Bagwell LUL .... .40 .18
❑ 161 Derek Jeter .... 1.25 .55
❑ 162 Paul Wilson .... .10 .05
❑ 163 Chris Snopek .... .10 .05
❑ 164 Jason Schmidt .... .10 .05
❑ 165 Jimmy Haynes .... .10 .05
❑ 166 George Arias .... .10 .05
❑ 167 Steve Gibralter .... .10 .05
❑ 168 Bob Wolcott .... .10 .05
❑ 169 Jason Kendall .... .40 .18
❑ 170 Greg Zaun .... .10 .05
❑ 171 Quinton McCracken .... .20 .09
❑ 172 Alan Benes .... .20 .09
❑ 173 Rey Ordonez .... .20 .09
❑ 174 Livan Hernandez .... .75 .35
❑ 175 Osvaldo Fernandez .... .10 .05
❑ 176 Marc Barcelo .... .10 .05
❑ 177 Sal Fasano .... .10 .05
❑ 178 Mike Grace .... .10 .05
❑ 179 Chan Ho Park .... .40 .18
❑ 180 Robert Perez .... .10 .05
❑ 181 Todd Hollandsworth .... .10 .05
❑ 182 Wilton Guerrero .... .30 .14
❑ 183 John Wasdin .... .10 .05
❑ 184 Jim Pittsley .... .10 .05
❑ 185 LaTroy Hawkins .... .10 .05
❑ 186 Jay Powell .... .10 .05
❑ 187 Felipe Crespo .... .10 .05

		MINT	NRMT
❑ 188	Jermaine Dye	.10	.05
❑ 189	Bob Abreu	.20	.09
❑ 190	Matt Luke	.10	.05
❑ 191	Richard Hidalgo	.20	.09
❑ 192	Karim Garcia	.20	.09
❑ 193	Marvin Benard	.10	.05
❑ 194	Andy Fox	.10	.05
❑ 195	Terrell Wade	.10	.05
❑ 196	Frank Thomas CL	.60	.25
❑ 197	Ken Griffey Jr. CL	1.00	.45
❑ 198	Greg Maddux CL	.60	.25
❑ 199	Mike Piazza CL	.60	.25
❑ 200	Cal Ripken CL	.75	.35

1996 Select Claim To Fame

	MINT	NRMT
COMPLETE SET (20)	250.00	110.00
COMMON CARD (1-20)	3.00	1.35

❑ 1	Cal Ripken	30.00	13.50
❑ 2	Greg Maddux	25.00	11.00
❑ 3	Ken Griffey Jr.	40.00	18.00
❑ 4	Frank Thomas	25.00	11.00
❑ 5	Mo Vaughn	10.00	4.50
❑ 6	Albert Belle	10.00	4.50
❑ 7	Jeff Bagwell	12.00	5.50
❑ 8	Sammy Sosa	20.00	9.00
❑ 9	Reggie Sanders	3.00	1.35
❑ 10	Hideo Nomo	12.00	5.50
❑ 11	Chipper Jones	20.00	9.00
❑ 12	Mike Piazza	25.00	11.00
❑ 13	Matt Williams	4.00	1.80
❑ 14	Tony Gwynn	20.00	9.00
❑ 15	Johnny Damon	4.00	1.80
❑ 16	Dante Bichette	4.00	1.80
❑ 17	Kirby Puckett	12.00	5.50
❑ 18	Barry Bonds	10.00	4.50
❑ 19	Randy Johnson	8.00	3.60
❑ 20	Eddie Murray	8.00	3.60

1996 Select En Fuego

	MINT	NRMT
COMPLETE SET (25)	250.00	110.00
COMMON CARD (1-25)	2.50	1.10

❑ 1	Ken Griffey Jr.	30.00	13.50
❑ 2	Frank Thomas	20.00	9.00
❑ 3	Cal Ripken	25.00	11.00
❑ 4	Greg Maddux	20.00	9.00
❑ 5	Jeff Bagwell	10.00	4.50
❑ 6	Barry Bonds	8.00	3.60
❑ 7	Mo Vaughn	8.00	3.60
❑ 8	Albert Belle	8.00	3.60
❑ 9	Sammy Sosa	15.00	6.75
❑ 10	Reggie Sanders	2.50	1.10
❑ 11	Mike Piazza	20.00	9.00
❑ 12	Chipper Jones	15.00	6.75
❑ 13	Tony Gwynn	15.00	6.75
❑ 14	Kirby Puckett	10.00	4.50
❑ 15	Wade Boggs	6.00	2.70
❑ 16	Dan Patrick ANN	6.00	2.70
❑ 17	Gary Sheffield	4.00	1.80
❑ 18	Dante Bichette	3.00	1.35
❑ 19	Randy Johnson	6.00	2.70
❑ 20	Matt Williams	3.00	1.35
❑ 21	Alex Rodriguez	20.00	9.00
❑ 22	Tim Salmon	6.00	2.70
❑ 23	Johnny Damon	3.00	1.35
❑ 24	Manny Ramirez	6.00	2.70
❑ 25	Hideo Nomo	10.00	4.50

1996 Select Team Nucleus

	MINT	NRMT
COMPLETE SET (28)	80.00	36.00
COMMON CARD (1-28)	2.00	.90

❑ 1	Albert Belle Manny Ramirez Carlos Baerga	4.00	1.80
❑ 2	Ray Lankford Brian Jordan Ozzie Smith	3.00	1.35
❑ 3	Jay Bell Jeff King Denny Neagle	2.00	.90
❑ 4	Dante Bichette Andres Galarraga Larry Walker	3.00	1.35
❑ 5	Mark McGwire Mike Bordick Terry Steinbach	15.00	6.75
❑ 6	Bernie Williams Wade Boggs David Cone	3.00	1.35
❑ 7	Joe Carter Alex Gonzalez Shawn Green	2.00	.90
❑ 8	Roger Clemens Mo Vaughn Jose Canseco	6.00	2.70
❑ 9	Ken Griffey Jr. Edgar Martinez Randy Johnson	15.00	6.75
❑ 10	Gregg Jefferies Darren Daulton Len Dykstra	2.00	.90
❑ 11	Mike Piazza Raul Mondesi Hideo Nomo	10.00	4.50
❑ 12	Greg Maddux Chipper Jones Ryan Klesko	12.00	5.50
❑ 13	Cecil Fielder Travis Fryman Phil Nevin	2.00	.90
❑ 14	Ivan Rodriguez Will Clark Juan Gonzalez	8.00	3.60
❑ 15	Ryne Sandberg Sammy Sosa Mark Grace	8.00	3.60
❑ 16	Gary Sheffield Charles Johnson Andre Dawson	3.00	1.35
❑ 17	Johnny Damon Michael Tucker Kevin Appier	2.00	.90
❑ 18	Barry Bonds Matt Williams Rod Beck	3.00	1.35
❑ 19	Kirby Puckett Chuck Knoblauch Marty Cordova	6.00	2.70
❑ 20	Cal Ripken Barry Bonilla Mike Mussina	12.00	5.50
❑ 21	Jason Isringhausen Bill Pulsipher Rico Brogna	2.00	.90
❑ 22	Tony Gwynn Ken Caminiti Mark Newfield	8.00	3.60
❑ 23	Tim Salmon Garret Anderson Jim Edmonds	3.00	1.35
❑ 24	Moises Alou Rondell White Cliff Floyd	2.00	.90
❑ 25	Barry Larkin Reggie Sanders Bret Boone	2.50	1.10
❑ 26	Jeff Bagwell Craig Biggio Derek Bell	6.00	2.70
❑ 27	Frank Thomas Robin Ventura Alex Fernandez	10.00	4.50
❑ 28	John Jaha Greg Vaughn Kevin Seitzer	2.00	.90

1997 Select

	MINT	NRMT
COMPLETE SET (200)	80.00	36.00
COMPLETE SERIES 1 (150)	50.00	22.00
COMMON RED (1-150)	.15	.07
COMMON BLUE (1-150)	.30	.14
COMPLETE HI SERIES (50)	30.00	13.50
COMMON HI SERIES (151-200)	.30	.14

❑ 1	Juan Gonzalez B	3.00	1.35
❑ 2	Mo Vaughn B	1.50	.70
❑ 3	Tony Gwynn R	1.50	.70
❑ 4	Manny Ramirez B	1.25	.55
❑ 5	Jose Canseco R	.60	.25
❑ 6	David Cone R	.40	.18
❑ 7	Chan Ho Park R	.60	.25
❑ 8	Frank Thomas B	4.00	1.80
❑ 9	Todd Hollandsworth R	.15	.07

❑ 10 Marty Cordova R .15 .07
❑ 11 Gary Sheffield B .75 .35
❑ 12 John Smoltz B .60 .25
❑ 13 Mark Grudzielanek R .30 .14
❑ 14 Sammy Sosa B 3.00 1.35
❑ 15 Paul Molitor R .60 .25
❑ 16 Kevin Brown R .40 .18
❑ 17 Albert Belle B 1.50 .70
❑ 18 Eric Young R .30 .14
❑ 19 John Wetteland R .30 .14
❑ 20 Ryan Klesko B .60 .25
❑ 21 Joe Carter R .30 .14
❑ 22 Alex Ochoa R .15 .07
❑ 23 Greg Maddux B 4.00 1.80
❑ 24 Roger Clemens B 2.50 1.10
❑ 25 Ivan Rodriguez B 1.50 .70
❑ 26 Barry Bonds B 1.50 .70
❑ 27 Kenny Lofton B 1.25 .55
❑ 28 Javy Lopez R .30 .14
❑ 29 Hideo Nomo B 1.50 .70
❑ 30 Rusty Greer R .30 .14
❑ 31 Rafael Palmeiro R .40 .18
❑ 32 Mike Piazza B 4.00 1.80
❑ 33 Ryne Sandberg .75 .35
❑ 34 Wade Boggs R .60 .25
❑ 35 Jim Thome B 1.25 .55
❑ 36 Ken Caminiti B .75 .35
❑ 37 Mark Grace R .40 .18
❑ 38 Brian Jordan B .60 .25
❑ 39 Craig Biggio R .60 .25
❑ 40 Henry Rodriguez R .30 .14
❑ 41 Dean Palmer R .30 .14
❑ 42 Jason Kendall R .40 .18
❑ 43 Bill Pulsipher R .15 .07
❑ 44 Tim Salmon B 1.25 .55
❑ 45 Marc Newfield R .15 .07
❑ 46 Pat Hentgen R .30 .14
❑ 47 Ken Griffey Jr. B 6.00 2.70
❑ 48 Paul Wilson R .15 .07
❑ 49 Jay Buhner B .60 .25
❑ 50 Rickey Henderson R .60 .25
❑ 51 Jeff Bagwell B 2.00 .90
❑ 52 Cecil Fielder R .30 .14
❑ 53 Alex Rodriguez B 4.00 1.80
❑ 54 John Jaha R .15 .07
❑ 55 Brady Anderson B .60 .25
❑ 56 Andres Galarraga R .60 .25
❑ 57 Raul Mondesi R .40 .18
❑ 58 Andy Pettitte R .40 .18
❑ 59 Roberto Alomar B 1.25 .55
❑ 60 Derek Jeter B 4.00 1.80
❑ 61 Charles Johnson R .30 .14
❑ 62 Travis Fryman R .30 .14
❑ 63 Chipper Jones B 3.00 1.35
❑ 64 Edgar Martinez R .30 .14
❑ 65 Bobby Bonilla R .30 .14
❑ 66 Greg Vaughn R .30 .14
❑ 67 Bobby Higginson R .40 .18
❑ 68 Garret Anderson R .30 .14
❑ 69 Chuck Knoblauch B 1.25 .55
❑ 70 Jermaine Dye R .15 .07
❑ 71 Cal Ripken B 5.00 2.20
❑ 72 Jason Giambi R .30 .14
❑ 73 Trey Beamon R .15 .07
❑ 74 Shawn Green R .30 .14
❑ 75 Mark McGwire B 6.00 2.70
❑ 76 Carlos Delgado R .30 .14
❑ 77 Jason Isringhausen R .15 .07
❑ 78 Randy Johnson B 1.25 .55
❑ 79 Troy Percival B .60 .25
❑ 80 Ron Gant R .15 .07
❑ 81 Ellis Burks R .30 .14
❑ 82 Mike Mussina B 1.25 .55
❑ 83 Todd Hundley R .30 .14
❑ 84 Jim Edmonds R .40 .18
❑ 85 Charles Nagy R .30 .14
❑ 86 Dante Bichette B .60 .25
❑ 87 Mariano Rivera R .30 .14
❑ 88 Matt Williams B .60 .25
❑ 89 Rondell White R .30 .14
❑ 90 Steve Finley R .30 .14
❑ 91 Alex Fernandez R .15 .07
❑ 92 Barry Larkin R .40 .18
❑ 93 Tom Goodwin R .15 .07
❑ 94 Will Clark R .60 .25
❑ 95 Michael Tucker R .30 .14
❑ 96 Derek Bell R .30 .14
❑ 97 Larry Walker R .60 .25
❑ 98 Alan Benes R .30 .14
❑ 99 Tom Glavine R .60 .25
❑ 100 Darin Erstad B 2.00 .90
❑ 101 Andruw Jones B 2.00 .90
❑ 102 Scott Rolen 1.50 .70
❑ 103 Todd Walker B 1.25 .55
❑ 104 Dmitri Young R .30 .14
❑ 105 Vladimir Guerrero B 2.50 1.10
❑ 106 Nomar Garciaparra 2.00 .90
❑ 107 Danny Patterson R .15 .07
❑ 108 Karim Garcia R .30 .14
❑ 109 Todd Greene R .30 .14
❑ 110 Ruben Rivera R .30 .14
❑ 111 Raul Casanova R .15 .07
❑ 112 Mike Cameron R .30 .14
❑ 113 Bartolo Colon R .30 .14
❑ 114 Rod Myers R .30 .14
❑ 115 Todd Dunn R .15 .07
❑ 116 Torii Hunter R .15 .07
❑ 117 Jason Dickson R .30 .14
❑ 118 Eugene Kingsale R .30 .14
❑ 119 Rafael Medina R .30 .14
❑ 120 Raul Ibanez R .15 .07
❑ 121 Bobby Henley R .15 .07
❑ 122 Scott Spiezio R .15 .07
❑ 123 Bobby Smith R .15 .07
❑ 124 J.J. Johnson R .15 .07
❑ 125 Bubba Trammell R RC .40 .18
❑ 126 Jeff Abbott R .30 .14
❑ 127 Neifi Perez R .15 .07
❑ 128 Derrek Lee R .40 .18
❑ 129 Kevin Brown C R .15 .07
❑ 130 Mendy Lopez R .15 .07
❑ 131 Kevin Orie R .15 .07
❑ 132 Ryan Jones R .15 .07
❑ 133 Juan Encarnacion R .30 .14
❑ 134 Jose Guillen B 1.25 .55
❑ 135 Greg Norton R .15 .07
❑ 136 Richie Sexson R .40 .18
❑ 137 Jay Payton R .15 .07
❑ 138 Bob Abreu R .30 .14
❑ 139 Ron Belliard R .30 .14
❑ 140 Wilton Guerrero B .30 .14
❑ 141 Alex Rodriguez SS B 2.00 .90
❑ 142 Juan Gonzalez SS B 1.50 .70
❑ 143 Ken Caminiti SS B .30 .14
❑ 144 Frank Thomas SS B 2.00 .90
❑ 145 Ken Griffey Jr. SS B 3.00 1.35
❑ 146 John Smoltz SS B .30 .14
❑ 147 Mike Piazza SS B 2.00 .90
❑ 148 Derek Jeter SS B 2.00 .90
❑ 149 Frank Thomas CL R 1.00 .45
❑ 150 Ken Griffey Jr. CL R 1.50 .70
❑ 151 Jose Cruz Jr. 6.00 2.70
❑ 152 Moises Alou .75 .35
❑ 153 Hideki Irabu 4.00 1.80
❑ 154 Glendon Rusch .30 .14
❑ 155 Ron Coomer .30 .14
❑ 156 Jeremi Gonzalez 1.00 .45
❑ 157 Fernando Tatis 2.50 1.10
❑ 158 John Olerud .60 .25
❑ 159 Rickey Henderson 1.25 .55
❑ 160 Shannon Stewart .60 .25
❑ 161 Kevin Polcovich .30 .14
❑ 162 Jose Rosado .30 .14
❑ 163 Ray Lankford .60 .25
❑ 164 David Justice 1.25 .55
❑ 165 Mark Kotsay 4.00 1.80
❑ 166 Deivi Cruz 1.25 .55
❑ 167 Billy Wagner .60 .25
❑ 168 Jacob Cruz .30 .14
❑ 169 Matt Morris .60 .25
❑ 170 Brian Banks .30 .14
❑ 171 Brett Tomko .60 .25
❑ 172 Todd Helton 2.50 1.10
❑ 173 Eric Young .60 .25
❑ 174 Bernie Williams 1.25 .55
❑ 175 Jeff Fassero .30 .14
❑ 176 Ryan McGuire .30 .14
❑ 177 Darryl Kile .60 .25
❑ 178 Kelvim Escobar 1.50 .70
❑ 179 Dave Nilsson .30 .14
❑ 180 Geronimo Berroa .30 .14
❑ 181 Livan Hernandez .60 .25
❑ 182 Tony Womack 1.25 .55
❑ 183 Deion Sanders .60 .25
❑ 184 Jeff Kent .60 .25
❑ 185 Brian Hunter .60 .25
❑ 186 Jose Malave .30 .14
❑ 187 Steve Woodard .75 .35
❑ 188 Brad Radke .60 .25
❑ 189 Todd Dunwoody .60 .25
❑ 190 Joey Hamilton .60 .25
❑ 191 Denny Neagle .60 .25
❑ 192 Bobby Jones .30 .14
❑ 193 Tony Clark .75 .35
❑ 194 Jaret Wright 10.00 4.50
❑ 195 Matt Stairs .60 .25
❑ 196 Francisco Cordova .30 .14
❑ 197 Justin Thompson .60 .25
❑ 198 Pokey Reese .30 .14
❑ 199 Garrett Stephenson .30 .14
❑ 200 Carl Everett .30 .14
❑ P3 Tony Gwynn PROMO 2.00 .90
❑ P23 Greg Maddux PROMO 2.50 1.10
❑ P47 Ken Griffey Jr. PROMO 3.00 1.35

1997 Select Rookie Autographs

	MINT	NRMT
COMPLETE SET (4)	80.00	36.00
COMMON CARD	10.00	4.50
❑ 1 Jose Guillen	20.00	9.00
❑ 2 Wilton Guerrero	10.00	4.50
❑ 3 Andruw Jones	40.00	18.00
❑ 4 Todd Walker	25.00	11.00

1997 Select Rookie Revolution

	MINT	NRMT
COMPLETE SET (20)	150.00	70.00
COMMON CARD (1-20)	2.50	1.10
❑ 1 Andruw Jones	15.00	6.75
❑ 2 Derek Jeter	30.00	13.50
❑ 3 Todd Hollandsworth	2.50	1.10
❑ 4 Edgar Renteria	5.00	2.20
❑ 5 Jason Kendall	6.00	2.70

	MINT	NRMT
❑ 6 Rey Ordonez	5.00	2.20
❑ 7 F.P. Santangelo	2.50	1.10
❑ 8 Jermaine Dye	2.50	1.10
❑ 9 Alex Ochoa	2.50	1.10
❑ 10 Vladimir Guererro	20.00	9.00
❑ 11 Dmitri Young	5.00	2.20
❑ 12 Todd Walker	15.00	6.75
❑ 13 Scott Rolen	25.00	11.00
❑ 14 Nomar Garciaparra	30.00	13.50
❑ 15 Ruben Rivera	5.00	2.20
❑ 16 Darin Erstad	15.00	6.75
❑ 17 Todd Greene	5.00	2.20
❑ 18 Mariano Rivera	5.00	2.20
❑ 19 Trey Beamon	2.50	1.10
❑ 20 Karim Garcia	5.00	2.20

1997 Select Tools of the Trade

	MINT	NRMT
COMPLETE SET (25)	150.00	70.00
COMMON CARD (1-25)	1.50	.70

	MINT	NRMT
❑ 1 Ken Griffey Jr. / Andruw Jones	20.00	9.00
❑ 2 Greg Maddux / Andy Pettitte	10.00	4.50
❑ 3 Cal Ripken / Chipper Jones	15.00	6.75
❑ 4 Mike Piazza / Jason Kendall	10.00	4.50
❑ 5 Albert Belle / Karim Garcia	4.00	1.80
❑ 6 Mo Vaughn / Dmitri Young	4.00	1.80
❑ 7 Juan Gonzalez / Vladimir Guerrero	10.00	4.50
❑ 8 Tony Gwynn / Jermaine Dye	8.00	3.60
❑ 9 Barry Bonds / Alex Ochoa	4.00	1.80
❑ 10 Jeff Bagwell / Jason Giambi	5.00	2.20
❑ 11 Kenny Lofton / Darin Erstad	4.00	1.80
❑ 12 Gary Sheffield / Manny Ramirez	3.00	1.35
❑ 13 Tim Salmon / Todd Hollandsworth	3.00	1.35
❑ 14 Sammy Sosa / Ruben Rivera	8.00	3.60
❑ 15 Paul Molitor / George Arias	3.00	1.35
❑ 16 Jim Thome / Todd Walker	3.00	1.35
❑ 17 Wade Boggs / Scott Rolen	6.00	2.70
❑ 18 Ryne Sandberg / Chuck Knoblauch	4.00	1.80
❑ 19 Mark McGwire / Frank Thomas	20.00	9.00
❑ 20 Ivan Rodriguez / Charles Johnson	4.00	1.80
❑ 21 Brian Jordan / Rusty Greer	1.50	.70
❑ 22 Roger Clemens / Troy Percival	6.00	2.70
❑ 23 John Smoltz / Mike Mussina	3.00	1.35
❑ 24 Alex Rodriguez / Rey Ordonez	10.00	4.50
❑ 25 Derek Jeter / Nomar Garciaparra	12.00	5.50

1995 Select Certified

	MINT	NRMT
COMPLETE SET (135)	40.00	18.00
COMMON CARD (1-135)	.25	.11

	MINT	NRMT
❑ 1 Barry Bonds	1.25	.55
❑ 2 Reggie Sanders	.50	.23
❑ 3 Terry Steinbach	.50	.23
❑ 4 Eduardo Perez	.25	.11
❑ 5 Frank Thomas	3.00	1.35
❑ 6 Wil Cordero	.25	.11
❑ 7 John Olerud	.50	.23
❑ 8 Deion Sanders	.50	.23
❑ 9 Mike Mussina	1.00	.45
❑ 10 Mo Vaughn	1.25	.55
❑ 11 Will Clark	1.00	.45
❑ 12 Chili Davis	.50	.23
❑ 13 Jimmy Key	.50	.23
❑ 14 Eddie Murray	1.00	.45
❑ 15 Bernard Gilkey	.25	.11
❑ 16 David Cone	.75	.35
❑ 17 Tim Salmon	1.00	.45
❑ 19 Steve Ontiveros	.25	.11
❑ 20 Andres Galarraga	1.00	.45
❑ 21 Don Mattingly	1.50	.70
❑ 22 Kevin Appier	.50	.23
❑ 23 Paul Molitor	1.00	.45
❑ 24 Edgar Martinez	.50	.23
❑ 25 Andy Benes	.50	.23
❑ 26 Rafael Palmeiro	.75	.35
❑ 27 Barry Larkin	.75	.35
❑ 28 Gary Sheffield	.75	.35
❑ 29 Wally Joyner	.50	.23
❑ 30 Wade Boggs	1.00	.45
❑ 31 Rico Brogna	.25	.11
❑ 32 Eddie Murray 3000th Hit	.50	.23
❑ 33 Kirby Puckett	1.50	.70
❑ 34 Bobby Bonilla	.50	.23
❑ 35 Hal Morris	.25	.11
❑ 36 Moises Alou	.75	.35
❑ 37 Javier Lopez	.50	.23
❑ 38 Chuck Knoblauch	1.00	.45
❑ 39 Mike Piazza	3.00	1.35
❑ 40 Travis Fryman	.50	.23
❑ 41 Rickey Henderson	1.00	.45
❑ 42 Jim Thome	1.00	.45
❑ 43 Carlos Baerga	.50	.23
❑ 44 Dean Palmer	.50	.23
❑ 45 Kirk Gibson	.50	.23
❑ 46 Bret Saberhagen	.50	.23
❑ 47 Cecil Fielder	.50	.23
❑ 48 Manny Ramirez	1.00	.45
❑ 49 Derek Bell	.50	.23
❑ 50 Mark McGwire	5.00	2.20
❑ 51 Jim Edmonds	.75	.35
❑ 52 Robin Ventura	.50	.23
❑ 53 Ryan Klesko	.50	.23
❑ 54 Jeff Bagwell	1.50	.70
❑ 55 Ozzie Smith	1.25	.55
❑ 56 Albert Belle	1.25	.55
❑ 57 Darren Daulton	.50	.23
❑ 58 Jeff Conine	.50	.23
❑ 59 Greg Maddux	3.00	1.35
❑ 60 Lenny Dykstra	.50	.23
❑ 61 Randy Johnson	1.00	.45
❑ 62 Fred McGriff	.75	.35
❑ 63 Ray Lankford	.50	.23
❑ 64 David Justice	1.00	.45
❑ 65 Paul O'Neill	.50	.23
❑ 66 Tony Gwynn	2.50	1.10
❑ 67 Matt Williams	.50	.23
❑ 68 Dante Bichette	.50	.23
❑ 69 Craig Biggio	1.00	.45
❑ 70 Ken Griffey Jr.	5.00	2.20
❑ 71 J.T. Snow	.50	.23
❑ 72 Cal Ripken	4.00	1.80
❑ 73 Jay Bell	.50	.23
❑ 74 Joe Carter	.50	.23
❑ 75 Roberto Alomar	1.00	.45
❑ 76 Benji Gil	.25	.11
❑ 77 Ivan Rodriguez	1.25	.55
❑ 78 Raul Mondesi	.75	.35
❑ 79 Cliff Floyd	.50	.23
❑ 80 Eric Karros / Mike Piazza / Raul Mondesi	1.00	.45
❑ 81 Royce Clayton	.25	.11
❑ 82 Billy Ashley	.25	.11
❑ 83 Joey Hamilton	.50	.23
❑ 84 Sammy Sosa	2.50	1.10
❑ 85 Jason Bere	.25	.11
❑ 86 Dennis Martinez	.50	.23
❑ 87 Greg Vaughn	.50	.23
❑ 88 Roger Clemens	2.00	.90
❑ 89 Larry Walker	1.00	.45
❑ 90 Mark Grace	.75	.35
❑ 91 Kenny Lofton	1.00	.45
❑ 92 Carlos Perez	.75	.35
❑ 93 Roger Cedeno	.25	.11
❑ 94 Scott Ruffcorn	.25	.11
❑ 95 Jim Pittsley	.25	.11
❑ 96 Andy Pettitte	1.00	.45
❑ 97 James Baldwin	.50	.23
❑ 98 Hideo Nomo	4.00	1.80
❑ 99 Ismael Valdes	.50	.23
❑ 100 Armando Benitez	.25	.11
❑ 101 Jose Malave	.25	.11
❑ 102 Bob Higginson	2.50	1.10
❑ 103 LaTroy Hawkins	.25	.11
❑ 104 Russ Davis	.50	.23
❑ 105 Shawn Green	.50	.23
❑ 106 Joe Vitiello	.25	.11
❑ 107 Chipper Jones	2.50	1.10
❑ 108 Shane Andrews	.25	.11
❑ 109 Jose Oliva	.25	.11
❑ 110 Ray Durham	.50	.23
❑ 111 Jon Nunnally	.25	.11
❑ 112 Alex Gonzalez	.25	.11
❑ 113 Vaughn Eshelman	.25	.11
❑ 114 Marty Cordova	.25	.11
❑ 115 Mark Grudzielanek	.75	.35
❑ 116 Brian L.Hunter	.50	.23
❑ 117 Charles Johnson	.50	.23
❑ 118 Alex Rodriguez	4.00	1.80
❑ 119 David Bell	.25	.11
❑ 120 Todd Hollandsworth	.25	.11
❑ 121 Joe Randa	.25	.11
❑ 122 Derek Jeter	3.00	1.35
❑ 123 Frank Rodriguez	.25	.11
❑ 124 Curtis Goodwin	.25	.11
❑ 125 Bill Pulsipher	.25	.11
❑ 126 John Mabry	.25	.11
❑ 127 Julian Tavarez	.25	.11
❑ 128 Edgardo Alfonzo	.50	.23
❑ 129 Orlando Miller	.25	.11
❑ 130 Juan Acevedo	.25	.11
❑ 131 Jeff Cirillo	.50	.23
❑ 132 Roberto Petagine	.25	.11
❑ 133 Antonio Osuna	.25	.11
❑ 134 Michael Tucker	.50	.23
❑ 135 Garret Anderson	.50	.23
❑ 2131 Cal Ripken TRIB	4.00	1.80

1995 Select Certified Future

	MINT	NRMT
COMPLETE SET (10)	60.00	27.00
COMMON CARD (1-10)	2.00	.90
❑ 1 Chipper Jones	15.00	6.75
❑ 2 Curtis Goodwin	2.00	.90
❑ 3 Hideo Nomo	12.00	5.50
❑ 4 Shawn Green	3.00	1.35
❑ 5 Ray Durham	3.00	1.35
❑ 6 Todd Hollandsworth	2.00	.90
❑ 7 Brian L.Hunter	3.00	1.35
❑ 8 Carlos Delgado	3.00	1.35
❑ 9 Michael Tucker UER (Front photo is Jon Nunnally)	3.00	1.35
❑ 10 Alex Rodriguez	20.00	9.00

1995 Select Certified Gold Team

	MINT	NRMT
COMPLETE SET (12)	300.00	135.00
COMMON CARD (1-12)	8.00	3.60
❑ 1 Ken Griffey Jr.	60.00	27.00
❑ 2 Frank Thomas	40.00	18.00
❑ 3 Cal Ripken	50.00	22.00
❑ 4 Jeff Bagwell	20.00	9.00
❑ 5 Mike Piazza	40.00	18.00
❑ 6 Barry Bonds	15.00	6.75
❑ 7 Matt Williams	8.00	3.60
❑ 8 Don Mattingly	20.00	9.00
❑ 9 Will Clark	8.00	3.60
❑ 10 Tony Gwynn	30.00	13.50
❑ 11 Kirby Puckett	20.00	9.00
❑ 12 Jose Canseco	8.00	3.60

1995 Select Certified Potential Unlimited 1975

	MINT	NRMT
COMPLETE SET (20)	250.00	110.00
COMMON CARD (1-20)	5.00	2.20
COMP.903 SET (20)	300.00	135.00

*903 CARDS: .5X TO 1.2X 1975 CARDS

ONE 903 CARD PER SEALED BOX
STATED PRINT RUN 903 SETS

	MINT	NRMT
❑ 1 Cliff Floyd	8.00	3.60
❑ 2 Manny Ramirez	15.00	6.75
❑ 3 Raul Mondesi	10.00	4.50
❑ 4 Scott Ruffcorn	5.00	2.20
❑ 5 Billy Ashley	5.00	2.20
❑ 6 Alex Gonzalez	5.00	2.20
❑ 7 Midre Cummings	5.00	2.20
❑ 8 Charles Johnson	8.00	3.60
❑ 9 Garret Anderson	8.00	3.60
❑ 10 Hideo Nomo	40.00	18.00
❑ 11 Chipper Jones	50.00	22.00
❑ 12 Curtis Goodwin	5.00	2.20
❑ 13 Frank Rodriguez	5.00	2.20
❑ 14 Shawn Green	8.00	3.60
❑ 15 Ray Durham	8.00	3.60
❑ 16 Todd Hollandsworth	5.00	2.20
❑ 17 Brian L.Hunter	8.00	3.60
❑ 18 Carlos Delgado	8.00	3.60
❑ 19 Michael Tucker	8.00	3.60
❑ 20 Alex Rodriguez	60.00	27.00

1996 Select Certified

	MINT	NRMT
COMPLETE SET (144)	40.00	18.00
COMMON CARD (1-144)	.25	.11
❑ 1 Frank Thomas	3.00	1.35
❑ 2 Tino Martinez	1.00	.45
❑ 3 Gary Sheffield	.75	.35
❑ 4 Kenny Lofton	1.00	.45
❑ 5 Joe Carter	.50	.23
❑ 6 Alex Rodriguez	3.00	1.35
❑ 7 Chipper Jones	2.50	1.10
❑ 8 Roger Clemens	2.00	.90
❑ 9 Jay Bell	.50	.23
❑ 10 Eddie Murray	1.00	.45
❑ 11 Will Clark	1.00	.45
❑ 12 Mike Mussina	1.00	.45
❑ 13 Hideo Nomo	1.50	.70
❑ 14 Andres Galarraga	1.00	.45
❑ 15 Marc Newfield	.25	.11
❑ 16 Jason Isringhausen	.25	.11
❑ 17 Randy Johnson	1.00	.45
❑ 18 Chuck Knoblauch	1.00	.45
❑ 19 J.T. Snow	.50	.23
❑ 20 Mark McGwire	5.00	2.20
❑ 21 Tony Gwynn	2.50	1.10
❑ 22 Albert Belle	1.25	.55
❑ 23 Gregg Jefferies	.25	.11
❑ 24 Reggie Sanders	.50	.23
❑ 25 Bernie Williams	1.00	.45
❑ 26 Ray Lankford	.50	.23
❑ 27 Johnny Damon	.50	.23
❑ 28 Ryne Sandberg	1.25	.55
❑ 29 Rondell White	.50	.23
❑ 30 Mike Piazza	3.00	1.35
❑ 31 Barry Bonds	1.25	.55
❑ 32 Greg Maddux	3.00	1.35
❑ 33 Craig Biggio	1.00	.45
❑ 34 John Valentin	.50	.23
❑ 35 Ivan Rodriguez	1.25	.55
❑ 36 Rico Brogna	.25	.11
❑ 37 Tim Salmon	1.00	.45
❑ 38 Sterling Hitchcock	.50	.23
❑ 39 Charles Johnson	.50	.23
❑ 40 Travis Fryman	.50	.23
❑ 41 Barry Larkin	.75	.35
❑ 42 Tom Glavine	1.00	.45
❑ 43 Marty Cordova	.25	.11
❑ 44 Shawn Green	.50	.23
❑ 45 Ben McDonald	.25	.11
❑ 46 Robin Ventura	.50	.23
❑ 47 Ken Griffey Jr.	5.00	2.20
❑ 48 Orlando Merced	.25	.11
❑ 49 Paul O'Neill	.50	.23
❑ 50 Ozzie Smith	1.25	.55
❑ 51 Manny Ramirez	1.00	.45
❑ 52 Ismael Valdes	.50	.23
❑ 53 Cal Ripken	4.00	1.80
❑ 54 Jeff Bagwell	1.50	.70
❑ 55 Greg Vaughn	.50	.23
❑ 56 Juan Gonzalez	2.50	1.10
❑ 57 Raul Mondesi	.75	.35
❑ 58 Carlos Baerga	.50	.23
❑ 59 Sammy Sosa	2.50	1.10
❑ 60 Mike Kelly	.25	.11
❑ 61 Edgar Martinez	.50	.23
❑ 62 Kirby Puckett	1.50	.70
❑ 63 Cecil Fielder	.50	.23
❑ 64 David Cone	.75	.35
❑ 65 Moises Alou	.75	.35
❑ 66 Fred McGriff	.75	.35
❑ 67 Mo Vaughn	1.25	.55
❑ 68 Edgardo Alfonzo	.50	.23
❑ 69 Jim Thome	1.00	.45
❑ 70 Rickey Henderson	1.00	.45
❑ 71 Dante Bichette	.50	.23
❑ 72 Lenny Dykstra	.50	.23
❑ 73 Benji Gil	.25	.11
❑ 74 Wade Boggs	1.00	.45
❑ 75 Jim Edmonds	.75	.35
❑ 76 Michael Tucker	.50	.23
❑ 77 Carlos Delgado	.50	.23
❑ 78 Butch Huskey	.25	.11
❑ 79 Billy Ashley	.25	.11
❑ 80 Dean Palmer	.50	.23
❑ 81 Paul Molitor	1.00	.45
❑ 82 Ryan Klesko	.50	.23
❑ 83 Brian L.Hunter	.50	.23
❑ 84 Jay Buhner	.50	.23
❑ 85 Larry Walker	1.00	.45
❑ 86 Mike Bordick	.25	.11
❑ 87 Matt Williams	.50	.23
❑ 88 Jack McDowell	.25	.11
❑ 89 Hal Morris	.25	.11
❑ 90 Brian Jordan	.50	.23
❑ 91 Andy Pettitte	.75	.35
❑ 92 Melvin Nieves	.25	.11
❑ 93 Pedro Martinez	1.00	.45
❑ 94 Mark Grace	.75	.35
❑ 95 Garret Anderson	.50	.23
❑ 96 Andre Dawson	.75	.35
❑ 97 Ray Durham	.50	.23
❑ 98 Jose Canseco	1.00	.45
❑ 99 Roberto Alomar	1.00	.45
❑ 100 Derek Jeter	3.00	1.35
❑ 101 Alan Benes	.50	.23
❑ 102 Karim Garcia	.50	.23
❑ 103 Robin Jennings	.25	.11
❑ 104 Bob Abreu	.50	.23
❑ 105 Sal Fasano UER (name on front is Livan Hernandez)	.25	.11

		MINT	NRMT
❑ 106	Steve Gibralter	.25	.11
❑ 107	Jermaine Dye	.25	.11
❑ 108	Jason Kendall	1.00	.45
❑ 109	Mike Grace	.25	.11
❑ 110	Jason Schmidt	.25	.11
❑ 111	Paul Wilson	.25	.11
❑ 112	Rey Ordonez	.50	.23
❑ 113	Wilton Guerrero	.75	.35
❑ 114	Brooks Kieschnick	.25	.11
❑ 115	George Arias	.25	.11
❑ 116	Osvaldo Fernandez	.25	.11
❑ 117	Todd Hollandsworth	.25	.11
❑ 118	John Wasdin	.25	.11
❑ 119	Eric Owens	.25	.11
❑ 120	Chan Ho Park	1.00	.45
❑ 121	Mark Loretta	.25	.11
❑ 122	Richard Hidalgo	.50	.23
❑ 123	Jeff Suppan	.25	.11
❑ 124	Jim Pittsley	.25	.11
❑ 125	LaTroy Hawkins	.25	.11
❑ 126	Chris Snopek	.25	.11
❑ 127	Justin Thompson	.50	.23
❑ 128	Jay Powell	.25	.11
❑ 129	Alex Ochoa	.25	.11
❑ 130	Felipe Crespo	.25	.11
❑ 131	Matt Lawton	1.00	.45
❑ 132	Jimmy Haynes	.25	.11
❑ 133	Terrell Wade	.25	.11
❑ 134	Ruben Rivera	.50	.23
❑ 135	Frank Thomas PP	1.50	.70
❑ 136	Ken Griffey Jr. PP	2.50	1.10
❑ 137	Greg Maddux PP	1.50	.70
❑ 138	Mike Piazza PP	1.50	.70
❑ 139	Cal Ripken PP	2.00	.90
❑ 140	Albert Belle PP	.75	.35
❑ 141	Mo Vaughn PP	.75	.35
❑ 142	Chipper Jones PP	1.25	.55
❑ 143	Hideo Nomo PP	1.25	.55
❑ 144	Ryan Klesko PP	.25	.11

1996 Select Certified Mirror Blue

	MINT	NRMT
COMMON CARD (1-144)	25.00	11.00

*STARS: 40X TO 100X BASIC CARDS
*PP STARS 135-144: 30X TO 80X BASIC CARDS
*YOUNG STARS: 30X TO 80X BASIC CARDS
*ROOKIES: 20X TO 50X BASIC CARDS

1996 Select Certified Mirror Gold

	MINT	NRMT
COMMON CARD (1-144)	100.00	45.00
MINOR STARS	150.00	70.00
SEMISTARS	250.00	110.00
UNLISTED STARS	300.00	135.00

*STARS: 200X TO 400X BASIC CARDS
*PP STARS 135-144: 150X TO 300X BASIC
*YOUNG STARS: 150X TO 300X BASIC CARDS
*ROOKIES: 75X TO 150X BASIC CARDS

1996 Select Certified Mirror Red

	MINT	NRMT
COMMON CARD (1-144)	15.00	6.75

*STARS: 25X TO 60X BASIC CARDS
*YOUNG STARS: 20X TO 50X BASIC CARDS
*ROOKIES: 12.5X TO 30X BASIC CARDS

1996 Select Certified Interleague Preview

	MINT	NRMT
COMPLETE SET (25)	300.00	135.00
COMMON CARD (1-25)	6.00	2.70

		MINT	NRMT
❑ 1	Ken Griffey Jr.	40.00	18.00
	Hideo Nomo		
❑ 2	Greg Maddux	25.00	11.00
	Mo Vaughn		
❑ 3	Frank Thomas	40.00	18.00
	Sammy Sosa		
❑ 4	Mike Piazza	25.00	11.00
	Jim Edmonds		
❑ 5	Ryan Klesko	15.00	6.75
	Roger Clemens		
❑ 6	Derek Jeter	20.00	9.00
	Rey Ordonez		
❑ 7	Johnny Damon	6.00	2.70
	Ray Lankford		
❑ 8	Manny Ramirez	8.00	3.60
	Reggie Sanders		
❑ 9	Barry Bonds	10.00	4.50
	Jay Buhner		
❑ 10	Jason Isringhausen	6.00	2.70
	Wade Boggs		
❑ 11	David Cone	20.00	9.00
	Chipper Jones		
❑ 12	Jeff Bagwell	12.00	5.50
	Will Clark		
❑ 13	Tony Gwynn	20.00	9.00
	Randy Johnson		
❑ 14	Cal Ripken	30.00	13.50
	Tom Glavine		
❑ 15	Kirby Puckett	12.00	5.50
	Andy Benes		
❑ 16	Gary Sheffield	8.00	3.60
	Mike Mussina		
❑ 17	Raul Mondesi	8.00	3.60
	Tim Salmon		
❑ 18	Rondell White	6.00	2.70
	Carlos Delgado		
❑ 19	Cecil Fielder	10.00	4.50
	Ryne Sandberg		
❑ 20	Kenny Lofton	8.00	3.60
	Brian L.Hunter		
❑ 21	Paul Wilson	6.00	2.70
	Paul O'Neill		
❑ 22	Ismael Valdes	6.00	2.70
	Edgar Martinez		
❑ 23	Matt Williams	40.00	18.00
	Mark McGwire		
❑ 24	Albert Belle	10.00	4.50
	Barry Larkin		
❑ 25	Brady Anderson	8.00	3.60
	Marquis Grissom		

1996 Select Certified Select Few

	MINT	NRMT
COMPLETE SET (18)	250.00	110.00
COMMON CARD (1-18)	5.00	2.20

		MINT	NRMT
❑ 1	Sammy Sosa	20.00	9.00
❑ 2	Derek Jeter	20.00	9.00
❑ 3	Ken Griffey Jr.	40.00	18.00
❑ 4	Albert Belle	10.00	4.50
❑ 5	Cal Ripken	30.00	13.50
❑ 6	Greg Maddux	25.00	11.00
❑ 7	Frank Thomas	25.00	11.00
❑ 8	Mo Vaughn	10.00	4.50
❑ 9	Chipper Jones	20.00	9.00
❑ 10	Mike Piazza	25.00	11.00
❑ 11	Ryan Klesko	5.00	2.20
❑ 12	Hideo Nomo	12.00	5.50
❑ 13	Alan Benes	5.00	2.20
❑ 14	Manny Ramirez	8.00	3.60
❑ 15	Gary Sheffield	6.00	2.70
❑ 16	Barry Bonds	10.00	4.50
❑ 17	Matt Williams	5.00	2.20
❑ 18	Johnny Damon	5.00	2.20

1998 SkyBox Dugout Axcess

	MINT	NRMT
COMPLETE SET (150)	20.00	9.00
COMMON CARD (1-150)	.10	.05

		MINT	NRMT
❑ 1	Travis Lee	.75	.35
❑ 2	Matt Williams	.15	.07
❑ 3	Andy Benes	.15	.07
❑ 4	Chipper Jones	1.00	.45
❑ 5	Ryan Klesko	.15	.07
❑ 6	Greg Maddux	1.25	.55
❑ 7	Sammy Sosa	1.00	.45
❑ 8	Henry Rodriguez	.15	.07
❑ 9	Mark Grace	.25	.11
❑ 10	Barry Larkin	.25	.11
❑ 11	Bret Boone	.15	.07
❑ 12	Reggie Sanders	.15	.07
❑ 13	Vinny Castilla	.25	.11
❑ 14	Larry Walker	.40	.18
❑ 15	Darryl Kile	.15	.07
❑ 16	Charles Johnson	.15	.07
❑ 17	Edgar Renteria	.15	.07
❑ 18	Gary Sheffield	.25	.11
❑ 19	Jeff Bagwell	.60	.25
❑ 20	Craig Biggio	.40	.18
❑ 21	Moises Alou	.25	.11
❑ 22	Mike Piazza	1.25	.55
❑ 23	Hideo Nomo	.50	.23
❑ 24	Raul Mondesi	.25	.11
❑ 25	John Jaha	.10	.05
❑ 26	Jeff Cirillo	.15	.07
❑ 27	Jeromy Burnitz	.15	.07
❑ 28	Mark Grudzielanek	.15	.07
❑ 29	Vladimir Guerrero	.60	.25
❑ 30	Rondell White	.15	.07
❑ 31	Edgardo Alfonzo	.15	.07
❑ 32	Rey Ordonez	.15	.07
❑ 33	Bernard Gilkey	.10	.05
❑ 34	Scott Rolen	1.00	.45
❑ 35	Curt Schilling	.15	.07

❑ 36	Ricky Bottalico	.15	.07
❑ 37	Tony Womack	.15	.07
❑ 38	Al Martin	.10	.05
❑ 39	Jason Kendall	.15	.07
❑ 40	Ron Gant	.10	.05
❑ 41	Mark McGwire	2.50	1.10
❑ 42	Ray Lankford	.15	.07
❑ 43	Tony Gwynn	1.00	.45
❑ 44	Ken Caminiti	.25	.11
❑ 45	Kevin Brown	.25	.11
❑ 46	Barry Bonds	.50	.23
❑ 47	J.T. Snow	.15	.07
❑ 48	Shawn Estes	.15	.07
❑ 49	Jim Edmonds	.25	.11
❑ 50	Tim Salmon	.40	.18
❑ 51	Jason Dickson	.15	.07
❑ 52	Cal Ripken	1.50	.70
❑ 53	Mike Mussina	.40	.18
❑ 54	Roberto Alomar	.40	.18
❑ 55	Mo Vaughn	.50	.23
❑ 56	Pedro Martinez	.40	.18
❑ 57	Nomar Garciaparra	1.25	.55
❑ 58	Albert Belle	.40	.18
❑ 59	Frank Thomas	1.25	.55
❑ 60	Robin Ventura	.15	.07
❑ 61	Jim Thome	.40	.18
❑ 62	Sandy Alomar Jr.	.15	.07
❑ 63	Jaret Wright	.50	.23
❑ 64	Bobby Higginson	.25	.11
❑ 65	Tony Clark	.25	.11
❑ 66	Justin Thompson	.15	.07
❑ 67	Dean Palmer	.15	.07
❑ 68	Kevin Appier	.15	.07
❑ 69	Johnny Damon	.15	.07
❑ 70	Paul Molitor	.40	.18
❑ 71	Marty Cordova	.10	.05
❑ 72	Brad Radke	.15	.07
❑ 73	Derek Jeter	1.00	.45
❑ 74	Bernie Williams	.40	.18
❑ 75	Andy Pettitte	.25	.11
❑ 76	Matt Stairs	.15	.07
❑ 77	Ben Grieve	.75	.35
❑ 78	Jason Giambi	.15	.07
❑ 79	Randy Johnson	.40	.18
❑ 80	Ken Griffey Jr.	2.00	.90
❑ 81	Alex Rodriguez	1.25	.55
❑ 82	Fred McGriff	.25	.11
❑ 83	Wade Boggs	.40	.18
❑ 84	Wilson Alvarez	.15	.07
❑ 85	Juan Gonzalez	1.00	.45
❑ 86	Ivan Rodriguez	.50	.23
❑ 87	Fernando Tatis	.15	.07
❑ 88	Roger Clemens	.75	.35
❑ 89	Jose Cruz Jr.	.50	.23
❑ 90	Shawn Green	.15	.07
❑ 91	Jeff Suppan	.10	.05
❑ 92	Eli Marrero	.15	.07
❑ 93	Mike Lowell	.40	.18
❑ 94	Ben Grieve	.75	.35
❑ 95	Cliff Politte	.15	.07
❑ 96	Rolando Arrojo	.60	.25
❑ 97	Mike Caruso	.15	.07
❑ 98	Miguel Tejada	.15	.07
❑ 99	Rod Myers	.10	.05
❑ 100	Juan Encarnacion	.15	.07
❑ 101	Enrique Wilson	.15	.07
❑ 102	Brian Giles	.15	.07
❑ 103	Magglio Ordonez	.50	.23
❑ 104	Brian Rose	.15	.07
❑ 105	Ryan Jackson	.25	.11
❑ 106	Mark Kotsay	.25	.11
❑ 107	Desi Relaford	.10	.05
❑ 108	A.J. Hinch	.15	.07
❑ 109	Eric Milton	.15	.07
❑ 110	Ricky Ledee	.15	.07
❑ 111	Karim Garcia	.15	.07
❑ 112	Derrek Lee	.15	.07
❑ 113	Brad Fullmer	.15	.07
❑ 114	Travis Lee	.75	.35
❑ 115	Greg Norton	.10	.05
❑ 116	Rich Butler	.25	.11
❑ 117	Masato Yoshii	.40	.18
❑ 118	Paul Konerko	.40	.18
❑ 119	Richard Hidalgo	.15	.07
❑ 120	Todd Helton	.50	.23
❑ 121	Nomar Garciaparra 7TH	.60	.25
❑ 122	Scott Rolen 7TH	.50	.23
❑ 123	Cal Ripken 7TH	.75	.35
❑ 124	Derek Jeter 7TH	.50	.23
❑ 125	Mike Piazza 7TH	.60	.25
❑ 126	Tony Gwynn 7TH	.50	.23
❑ 127	Mark McGwire 7TH	1.25	.55
❑ 128	Kenny Lofton 7TH	.15	.07
❑ 129	Greg Maddux 7TH	.60	.25
❑ 130	Jeff Bagwell 7TH	.40	.18
❑ 131	Randy Johnson 7TH	.15	.07
❑ 132	Alex Rodriguez 7TH	.60	.25
❑ 133	Mo Vaughn NAME	.25	.11
❑ 134	Chipper Jones NAME	.50	.23
❑ 135	Juan Gonzalez NAME	.50	.23
❑ 136	Tony Clark NAME	.10	.05
❑ 137	Fred McGriff NAME	.10	.05
❑ 138	Roger Clemens NAME	.40	.18
❑ 139	Ken Griffey Jr. NAME	1.00	.45
❑ 140	Ivan Rodriguez NAME	.25	.11
❑ 141	Vinny Castilla TRIV	.10	.05
❑ 142	Livan Hernandez TRIV	.10	.05
❑ 143	Jose Cruz Jr. TRIV	.25	.11
❑ 144	Andruw Jones TRIV	.25	.11
❑ 145	Rafael Palmeiro TRIV	.10	.05
❑ 146	Chuck Knoblauch TRIV	.15	.07
❑ 147	Jay Buhner TRIV	.10	.05
❑ 148	Andres Galarraga TRIV	.15	.07
❑ 149	Frank Thomas TRIV	.60	.25
❑ 150	Todd Hundley TRIV	.10	.05
❑ NNO	Alex Rodriguez Sample	3.00	1.35

1998 SkyBox Dugout Axcess Inside Axcess

	MINT	NRMT
COMMON CARD (1-150)	20.00	9.00

*STARS: 80X TO 200X BASIC CARDS
*YOUNG STARS: 60X TO 150X BASIC CARDS
*ROOKIES/PROSPECTS: 40X TO 100X BASIC CARDS

❑ 9999 >>>HEADERS ONLY<<<

1998 SkyBox Dugout Axcess Autograph Redemptions

	MINT	NRMT
COMMON CARD	15.00	6.75
❑ 1 Jay Buhner Ball	20.00	9.00
❑ 2 Roger Clemens Ball	120.00	55.00
❑ 3 Jose Cruz Jr. Ball	30.00	13.50
❑ 4 Darin Erstad Glove		
❑ 5 Nomar Garciaparra Ball	120.00	55.00
❑ 6 Tony Gwynn Ball	100.00	45.00
❑ 7 Roberto Hernandez Ball	15.00	6.75
❑ 8 Todd Hollandsworth Glove		
❑ 9 Greg Maddux Ball	150.00	70.00
❑ 10 Alex Ochoa Glove		
❑ 11 Alex Rodriguez Ball	150.00	70.00
❑ 12 Scott Rolen Ball	80.00	36.00
❑ 13 Scott Rolen Glove		
❑ 14 Todd Walker Glove		
❑ 15 Tony Womack Ball	15.00	6.75

1998 SkyBox Dugout Axcess Dishwashers

	MINT	NRMT
COMPLETE SET (10)	12.00	5.50
COMMON CARD (D1-D10)	.50	.23
❑ D1 Greg Maddux	4.00	1.80
❑ D2 Kevin Brown	.75	.35
❑ D3 Pedro Martinez	1.25	.55
❑ D4 Randy Johnson	1.25	.55
❑ D5 Curt Schilling	.50	.23
❑ D6 John Smoltz	.50	.23
❑ D7 Darryl Kile	.50	.23
❑ D8 Roger Clemens	2.50	1.10
❑ D9 Andy Pettitte	.75	.35
❑ D10 Mike Mussina	1.25	.55

1998 SkyBox Dugout Axcess Double Header

	MINT	NRMT
COMPLETE SET (20)	5.00	2.20
COMMON CARD (DH1-DH20)	.15	.07
❑ DH1 Jeff Bagwell	.30	.14
❑ DH2 Albert Belle	.20	.09
❑ DH3 Barry Bonds	.25	.11
❑ DH4 Derek Jeter	.50	.23
❑ DH5 Tony Clark	.15	.07
❑ DH6 Nomar Garciaparra	.60	.25

	Card	Player	MINT	NRMT
❑	DH7	Juan Gonzalez	.50	.23
❑	DH8	Ken Griffey Jr.	1.00	.45
❑	DH9	Chipper Jones	.50	.23
❑	DH10	Kenny Lofton	.20	.09
❑	DH11	Mark McGwire	1.25	.55
❑	DH12	Mo Vaughn	.25	.11
❑	DH13	Mike Piazza	.60	.25
❑	DH14	Cal Ripken	.75	.35
❑	DH15	Ivan Rodriguez	.25	.11
❑	DH16	Scott Rolen	.50	.23
❑	DH17	Frank Thomas	.60	.25
❑	DH18	Tony Gwynn	.50	.23
❑	DH19	Travis Lee	.40	.18
❑	DH20	Jose Cruz Jr.	.25	.11

1998 SkyBox Dugout Axcess Frequent Flyers

	MINT	NRMT
COMPLETE SET (10)	4.00	1.80
COMMON CARD (FF1-FF10)	.20	.09

	Card	Player	MINT	NRMT
❑	FF1	Brian Hunter	.30	.14
❑	FF2	Kenny Lofton	.60	.25
❑	FF3	Chuck Knoblauch	.60	.25
❑	FF4	Tony Womack	.30	.14
❑	FF5	Marquis Grissom	.30	.14
❑	FF6	Craig Biggio	.60	.25
❑	FF7	Barry Bonds	1.00	.45
❑	FF8	Tom Goodwin	.20	.09
❑	FF9	Delino DeShields UER front DeSheilds	.20	.09
❑	FF10	Eric Young	.30	.14

1998 SkyBox Dugout Axcess Gronks

	MINT	NRMT
COMPLETE SET (10)	150.00	70.00
COMMON CARD (G1-G10)	5.00	2.20

	Card	Player	MINT	NRMT
❑	G1	Jeff Bagwell	12.00	5.50
❑	G2	Albert Belle	8.00	3.60
❑	G3	Juan Gonzalez	20.00	9.00
❑	G4	Ken Griffey Jr.	40.00	18.00
❑	G5	Mark McGwire	50.00	22.00
❑	G6	Mike Piazza	25.00	11.00
❑	G7	Frank Thomas	25.00	11.00
❑	G8	Mo Vaughn	10.00	4.50
❑	G9	Ken Caminiti	5.00	2.20
❑	G10	Tony Clark	5.00	2.20

1998 SkyBox Dugout Axcess SuperHeroes

	MINT	NRMT
COMPLETE SET (10)	50.00	22.00
COMMON CARD (SH1-SH10)	2.50	1.10

	Card	Player	MINT	NRMT
❑	SH1	Barry Bonds	4.00	1.80
❑	SH2	Andres Galarraga	2.50	1.10
❑	SH3	Ken Griffey Jr.	15.00	6.75
❑	SH4	Chipper Jones	8.00	3.60
❑	SH5	Andruw Jones	3.00	1.35
❑	SH6	Hideo Nomo	4.00	1.80
❑	SH7	Cal Ripken	12.00	5.50
❑	SH8	Alex Rodriguez	10.00	4.50
❑	SH9	Frank Thomas	10.00	4.50
❑	SH10	Mo Vaughn	4.00	1.80

1993 SP

	MINT	NRMT
COMPLETE SET (290)	80.00	36.00
COMMON CARD (1-270)	.25	.11

	Card	Player	MINT	NRMT
❑	1	Roberto Alomar AS	1.50	.70
❑	2	Wade Boggs AS	1.50	.70
❑	3	Joe Carter AS	.25	.11
❑	4	Ken Griffey Jr. AS	8.00	3.60
❑	5	Mark Langston AS	.25	.11
❑	6	John Olerud AS	1.00	.45
❑	7	Kirby Puckett AS	2.50	1.10
❑	8	Cal Ripken Jr. AS	6.00	2.70
❑	9	Ivan Rodriguez AS	2.00	.90
❑	10	Barry Bonds AS	2.00	.90
❑	11	Darren Daulton AS	.50	.23
❑	12	Marquis Grissom AS	.50	.23
❑	13	David Justice AS	1.50	.70
❑	14	John Kruk AS	.50	.23
❑	15	Barry Larkin AS	1.00	.45
❑	16	Terry Mulholland AS	.25	.11
❑	17	Ryne Sandberg AS	2.00	.90
❑	18	Gary Sheffield AS	.50	.23
❑	19	Chad Curtis	.50	.23
❑	20	Chili Davis	.50	.23
❑	21	Gary DiSarcina	.25	.11
❑	22	Damion Easley	.50	.23
❑	23	Chuck Finley	.50	.23
❑	24	Luis Polonia	.25	.11
❑	25	Tim Salmon	1.50	.70
❑	26	J.T. Snow	2.00	.90
❑	27	Russ Springer	.25	.11
❑	28	Jeff Bagwell	2.50	1.10
❑	29	Craig Biggio	1.50	.70
❑	30	Ken Caminiti	1.00	.45
❑	31	Andujar Cedeno	.25	.11
❑	32	Doug Drabek	.25	.11
❑	33	Steve Finley	.50	.23
❑	34	Luis Gonzalez	.25	.11
❑	35	Pete Harnisch	.25	.11
❑	36	Darryl Kile	.50	.23
❑	37	Mike Bordick	.25	.11
❑	38	Dennis Eckersley	.50	.23
❑	39	Brent Gates	.25	.11
❑	40	Rickey Henderson	1.50	.70
❑	41	Mark McGwire	8.00	3.60
❑	42	Craig Paquette	.25	.11
❑	43	Ruben Sierra	.25	.11
❑	44	Terry Steinbach	.25	.11
❑	45	Todd Van Poppel	.25	.11
❑	46	Pat Borders	.25	.11
❑	47	Tony Fernandez	.25	.11
❑	48	Juan Guzman	.25	.11
❑	49	Pat Hentgen	1.00	.45
❑	50	Paul Molitor	1.50	.70
❑	51	Jack Morris	.50	.23
❑	52	Ed Sprague	.25	.11
❑	53	Duane Ward	.25	.11
❑	54	Devon White	.25	.11
❑	55	Steve Avery	.25	.11
❑	56	Jeff Blauser	.25	.11
❑	57	Ron Gant	.50	.23
❑	58	Tom Glavine	1.00	.45
❑	59	Greg Maddux	5.00	2.20
❑	60	Fred McGriff	1.00	.45
❑	61	Terry Pendleton	.25	.11
❑	62	Deion Sanders	1.00	.45
❑	63	John Smoltz	.50	.23
❑	64	Cal Eldred	.25	.11
❑	65	Darryl Hamilton	.25	.11
❑	66	John Jaha	.25	.11
❑	67	Pat Listach	.25	.11
❑	68	Jaime Navarro	.25	.11
❑	69	Kevin Reimer	.25	.11
❑	70	B.J. Surhoff	.50	.23
❑	71	Greg Vaughn	.50	.23
❑	72	Robin Yount	1.00	.45
❑	73	Rene Arocha	.25	.11
❑	74	Bernard Gilkey	.25	.11
❑	75	Gregg Jefferies	.25	.11
❑	76	Ray Lankford	1.00	.45
❑	77	Tom Pagnozzi	.25	.11
❑	78	Lee Smith	.50	.23
❑	79	Ozzie Smith	2.00	.90
❑	80	Bob Tewksbury	.25	.11
❑	81	Mark Whiten	.25	.11
❑	82	Steve Buechele	.25	.11
❑	83	Mark Grace	1.00	.45
❑	84	Jose Guzman	.25	.11
❑	85	Derrick May	.25	.11
❑	86	Mike Morgan	.25	.11
❑	87	Randy Myers	.50	.23
❑	88	Kevin Roberson	.25	.11
❑	89	Sammy Sosa	4.00	1.80
❑	90	Rick Wilkins	.25	.11
❑	91	Brett Butler	.50	.23
❑	92	Eric Davis	.50	.23
❑	93	Orel Hershiser	.50	.23
❑	94	Eric Karros	1.00	.45
❑	95	Ramon Martinez	.50	.23
❑	96	Raul Mondesi	2.00	.90
❑	97	Jose Offerman	.25	.11
❑	98	Mike Piazza	8.00	3.60
❑	99	Darryl Strawberry	.50	.23
❑	100	Moises Alou	.50	.23
❑	101	Wil Cordero	.25	.11
❑	102	Delino DeShields	.50	.23
❑	103	Darrin Fletcher	.25	.11
❑	104	Ken Hill	.25	.11
❑	105	Mike Lansing	.50	.23
❑	106	Dennis Martinez	.50	.23
❑	107	Larry Walker	1.50	.70
❑	108	John Wetteland	.50	.23

Card	MINT	NRMT
❑ 109 Rod Beck	.50	.23
❑ 110 John Burkett	.25	.11
❑ 111 Will Clark	1.50	.70
❑ 112 Royce Clayton	.25	.11
❑ 113 Darren Lewis	.25	.11
❑ 114 Willie McGee	.50	.23
❑ 115 Bill Swift	.25	.11
❑ 116 Robby Thompson	.25	.11
❑ 117 Matt Williams	1.00	.45
❑ 118 Sandy Alomar Jr.	.50	.23
❑ 119 Carlos Baerga	.25	.11
❑ 120 Albert Belle	2.00	.90
❑ 121 Reggie Jefferson	.50	.23
❑ 122 Wayne Kirby	.25	.11
❑ 123 Kenny Lofton	2.00	.90
❑ 124 Carlos Martinez	.25	.11
❑ 125 Charles Nagy	.50	.23
❑ 126 Paul Sorrento	.25	.11
❑ 127 Rich Amaral	.25	.11
❑ 128 Jay Buhner	1.00	.45
❑ 129 Norm Charlton	.25	.11
❑ 130 Dave Fleming	.25	.11
❑ 131 Erik Hanson	.25	.11
❑ 132 Randy Johnson	1.50	.70
❑ 133 Edgar Martinez	1.00	.45
❑ 134 Tino Martinez	1.50	.70
❑ 135 Omar Vizquel	.50	.23
❑ 136 Bret Barberie	.25	.11
❑ 137 Chuck Carr	.25	.11
❑ 138 Jeff Conine	.25	.11
❑ 139 Orestes Destrade	.25	.11
❑ 140 Chris Hammond	.25	.11
❑ 141 Bryan Harvey	.25	.11
❑ 142 Benito Santiago	.25	.11
❑ 143 Walt Weiss	.25	.11
❑ 144 Darrell Whitmore	.25	.11
❑ 145 Tim Bogar	.25	.11
❑ 146 Bobby Bonilla	.50	.23
❑ 147 Jeromy Burnitz	.50	.23
❑ 148 Vince Coleman	.25	.11
❑ 149 Dwight Gooden	.50	.23
❑ 150 Todd Hundley	1.00	.45
❑ 151 Howard Johnson	.25	.11
❑ 152 Eddie Murray	1.50	.70
❑ 153 Bret Saberhagen	.50	.23
❑ 154 Brady Anderson	1.00	.45
❑ 155 Mike Devereaux	.25	.11
❑ 156 Jeffrey Hammonds	.50	.23
❑ 157 Chris Hoiles	.25	.11
❑ 158 Ben McDonald	.25	.11
❑ 159 Mark McLemore	.25	.11
❑ 160 Mike Mussina	1.50	.70
❑ 161 Gregg Olson	.25	.11
❑ 162 David Segui	.25	.11
❑ 163 Derek Bell	.50	.23
❑ 164 Andy Benes	.50	.23
❑ 165 Archi Cianfrocco	.25	.11
❑ 166 Ricky Gutierrez	.25	.11
❑ 167 Tony Gwynn	4.00	1.80
❑ 168 Gene Harris	.25	.11
❑ 169 Trevor Hoffman	1.50	.70
❑ 170 Ray McDavid	.25	.11
❑ 171 Phil Plantier	.25	.11
❑ 172 Mariano Duncan	.25	.11
❑ 173 Len Dykstra	.50	.23
❑ 174 Tommy Greene	.25	.11
❑ 175 Dave Hollins	.25	.11
❑ 176 Pete Incaviglia	.25	.11
❑ 177 Mickey Morandini	.25	.11
❑ 178 Curt Schilling	.50	.23
❑ 179 Kevin Stocker	.25	.11
❑ 180 Mitch Williams	.25	.11
❑ 181 Stan Belinda	.25	.11
❑ 182 Jay Bell	.50	.23
❑ 183 Steve Cooke	.25	.11
❑ 184 Carlos Garcia	.25	.11
❑ 185 Jeff King	.50	.23
❑ 186 Orlando Merced	.25	.11
❑ 187 Don Slaught	.25	.11
❑ 188 Andy Van Slyke	.50	.23
❑ 189 Kevin Young	.25	.11
❑ 190 Kevin Brown	1.00	.45
❑ 191 Jose Canseco	1.50	.70
❑ 192 Julio Franco	.25	.11
❑ 193 Benji Gil	.25	.11
❑ 194 Juan Gonzalez	4.00	1.80
❑ 195 Tom Henke	.25	.11
❑ 196 Rafael Palmeiro	1.00	.45
❑ 197 Dean Palmer	.50	.23
❑ 198 Nolan Ryan	6.00	2.70
❑ 199 Roger Clemens	3.00	1.35
❑ 200 Scott Cooper	.25	.11
❑ 201 Andre Dawson	1.00	.45
❑ 202 Mike Greenwell	.25	.11
❑ 203 Carlos Quintana	.25	.11
❑ 204 Jeff Russell	.25	.11
❑ 205 Aaron Sele	1.50	.70
❑ 206 Mo Vaughn	2.00	.90
❑ 207 Frank Viola	.25	.11
❑ 208 Rob Dibble	.25	.11
❑ 209 Roberto Kelly	.25	.11
❑ 210 Kevin Mitchell	.50	.23
❑ 211 Hal Morris	.25	.11
❑ 212 Joe Oliver	.25	.11
❑ 213 Jose Rijo	.25	.11
❑ 214 Bip Roberts	.25	.11
❑ 215 Chris Sabo	.25	.11
❑ 216 Reggie Sanders	.25	.11
❑ 217 Dante Bichette	.50	.23
❑ 218 Jerald Clark	.25	.11
❑ 219 Alex Cole	.25	.11
❑ 220 Andres Galarraga	1.50	.70
❑ 221 Joe Girardi	.50	.23
❑ 222 Charlie Hayes	.25	.11
❑ 223 Roberto Mejia	.25	.11
❑ 224 Armando Reynoso	.25	.11
❑ 225 Eric Young	1.50	.70
❑ 226 Kevin Appier	.50	.23
❑ 227 George Brett	3.00	1.35
❑ 228 David Cone	.50	.23
❑ 229 Phil Hiatt	.25	.11
❑ 230 Felix Jose	.25	.11
❑ 231 Wally Joyner	.50	.23
❑ 232 Mike Macfarlane	.25	.11
❑ 233 Brian McRae	.25	.11
❑ 234 Jeff Montgomery	.50	.23
❑ 235 Rob Deer	.25	.11
❑ 236 Cecil Fielder	.50	.23
❑ 237 Travis Fryman	.50	.23
❑ 238 Mike Henneman	.25	.11
❑ 239 Tony Phillips	.25	.11
❑ 240 Mickey Tettleton	.25	.11
❑ 241 Alan Trammell	1.00	.45
❑ 242 David Wells	.50	.23
❑ 243 Lou Whitaker	.50	.23
❑ 244 Rick Aguilera	.25	.11
❑ 245 Scott Erickson	.25	.11
❑ 246 Brian Harper	.25	.11
❑ 247 Kent Hrbek	.50	.23
❑ 248 Chuck Knoblauch	1.50	.70
❑ 249 Shane Mack	.25	.11
❑ 250 David McCarty	.25	.11
❑ 251 Pedro Munoz	.25	.11
❑ 252 Dave Winfield	1.00	.45
❑ 253 Alex Fernandez	.50	.23
❑ 254 Ozzie Guillen	.25	.11
❑ 255 Bo Jackson	.50	.23
❑ 256 Lance Johnson	.25	.11
❑ 257 Ron Karkovice	.25	.11
❑ 258 Jack McDowell	.25	.11
❑ 259 Tim Raines	.50	.23
❑ 260 Frank Thomas	5.00	2.20
❑ 261 Robin Ventura	.50	.23
❑ 262 Jim Abbott	.50	.23
❑ 263 Steve Farr	.25	.11
❑ 264 Jimmy Key	.50	.23
❑ 265 Don Mattingly	2.50	1.10
❑ 266 Paul O'Neill	.50	.23
❑ 267 Mike Stanley	.25	.11
❑ 268 Danny Tartabull	.25	.11
❑ 269 Bob Wickman	.25	.11
❑ 270 Bernie Williams	1.50	.70
❑ 271 Jason Bere FOIL	.50	.23
❑ 272 Roger Cedeno FOIL	1.00	.45
❑ 273 Johnny Damon FOIL	3.00	1.35
❑ 274 Russ Davis FOIL	2.00	.90
❑ 275 Carlos Delgado FOIL	2.00	.90
❑ 276 Carl Everett FOIL	.50	.23
❑ 277 Cliff Floyd FOIL	1.50	.70
❑ 278 Alex Gonzalez FOIL	1.00	.45
❑ 279 Derek Jeter FOIL	50.00	22.00
❑ 280 Chipper Jones FOIL	10.00	4.50
❑ 281 Javier Lopez FOIL	2.00	.90
❑ 282 Chad Mottola FOIL	.50	.23
❑ 283 Marc Newfield FOIL	.50	.23
❑ 284 Eduardo Perez FOIL	.50	.23
❑ 285 Manny Ramirez FOIL	4.00	1.80
❑ 286 Todd Steverson FOIL	.50	.23
❑ 287 Michael Tucker FOIL	1.50	.70
❑ 288 Allen Watson FOIL	.50	.23
❑ 289 Rondell White FOIL	1.00	.45
❑ 290 Dmitri Young FOIL	2.00	.90

1993 SP Platinum Power

	MINT	NRMT
COMPLETE SET (20)	100.00	45.00
COMMON CARD (PP1-PP20)	1.25	.55
❑ PP1 Albert Belle	8.00	3.60
❑ PP2 Barry Bonds	6.00	2.70
❑ PP3 Joe Carter	2.00	.90
❑ PP4 Will Clark	5.00	2.20
❑ PP5 Darren Daulton	2.00	.90
❑ PP6 Cecil Fielder	2.00	.90
❑ PP7 Ron Gant	2.00	.90
❑ PP8 Juan Gonzalez	12.00	5.50
❑ PP9 Ken Griffey Jr.	25.00	11.00
❑ PP10 Dave Hollins	1.25	.55
❑ PP11 David Justice	5.00	2.20
❑ PP12 Fred McGriff	3.00	1.35
❑ PP13 Mark McGwire	25.00	11.00
❑ PP14 Dean Palmer	2.00	.90
❑ PP15 Mike Piazza	20.00	9.00
❑ PP16 Tim Salmon	6.00	2.70
❑ PP17 Ryne Sandberg	6.00	2.70
❑ PP18 Gary Sheffield	5.00	2.20
❑ PP19 Frank Thomas	15.00	6.75
❑ PP20 Matt Williams	3.00	1.35

1994 SP Previews

	MINT	NRMT
COMPLETE SET (15)	180.00	80.00
COMPLETE CENTRAL (5)	80.00	36.00
COMPLETE EAST (5)	40.00	18.00
COMPLETE WEST (5)	60.00	27.00
COMMON CARD	1.50	.70

❑ CR1 Jeff Bagwell 10.00 4.50
❑ CR2 Michael Jordan 40.00 18.00
❑ CR3 Kirby Puckett 10.00 4.50
❑ CR4 Manny Ramirez 8.00 3.60
❑ CR5 Frank Thomas 20.00 9.00
❑ ER1 Roberto Alomar 6.00 2.70
❑ ER2 Cliff Floyd .... 1.50 .70
❑ ER3 Javier Lopez 4.00 1.80
❑ ER4 Don Mattingly 10.00 4.50
❑ ER5 Cal Ripken 25.00 11.00
❑ WR1 Barry Bonds 8.00 3.60
❑ WR2 Juan Gonzalez 15.00 6.75
❑ WR3 Ken Griffey Jr. 30.00 13.50
❑ WR4 Mike Piazza 20.00 9.00
❑ WR5 Tim Salmon 6.00 2.70

1994 SP

	MINT	NRMT
COMPLETE SET (200)	90.00	40.00
COMMON CARD (21-200)	.20	.09

❑ 1 Mike Bell FOIL .... .20 .09
❑ 2 D.J. Boston FOIL .... .50 .23
❑ 3 Johnny Damon FOIL .... .40 .18
❑ 4 Brad Fullmer FOIL 4.00 1.80
❑ 5 Joey Hamilton FOIL .... .75 .35
❑ 6 Todd Hollandsworth FOIL .. .50 .23
❑ 7 Brian L. Hunter FOIL .... .40 .18
❑ 8 LaTroy Hawkins FOIL .... .50 .23
❑ 9 Brooks Kieschnick FOIL .... .50 .23
❑ 10 Derrek Lee FOIL 4.00 1.80
❑ 11 Trot Nixon FOIL .... 2.00 .90
❑ 12 Alex Ochoa FOIL .... .50 .23
❑ 13 Chan Ho Park FOIL 5.00 2.20
❑ 14 Kirk Presley FOIL .... .40 .18
❑ 15 Alex Rodriguez FOIL 70.00 32.00
❑ 16 Jose Silva FOIL .... .50 .23
❑ 17 Terrell Wade FOIL .... .50 .23
❑ 18 Billy Wagner FOIL .... 2.00 .90
❑ 19 Glenn Williams FOIL .... .75 .35
❑ 20 Preston Wilson FOIL .... .40 .18
❑ 21 Brian Anderson .... 1.00 .45
❑ 22 Chad Curtis .... .20 .09
❑ 23 Chili Davis .... .40 .18
❑ 24 Bo Jackson .... .40 .18
❑ 25 Mark Langston .... .20 .09
❑ 26 Tim Salmon .... .75 .35
❑ 27 Jeff Bagwell .... 1.25 .55
❑ 28 Craig Biggio .... .75 .35
❑ 29 Ken Caminiti .... .60 .25
❑ 30 Doug Drabek .... .20 .09
❑ 31 John Hudek .... .20 .09
❑ 32 Greg Swindell .... .20 .09
❑ 33 Brent Gates .... .20 .09
❑ 34 Rickey Henderson .... .75 .35
❑ 35 Steve Karsay .... .20 .09
❑ 36 Mark McGwire 4.00 1.80
❑ 37 Ruben Sierra .... .20 .09
❑ 38 Terry Steinbach .... .40 .18
❑ 39 Roberto Alomar .... .75 .35
❑ 40 Joe Carter .... .40 .18
❑ 41 Carlos Delgado .... .60 .25
❑ 42 Alex Gonzalez .... .20 .09
❑ 43 Juan Guzman .... .20 .09
❑ 44 Paul Molitor .... .75 .35
❑ 45 John Olerud .... .40 .18
❑ 46 Devon White .... .40 .18
❑ 47 Steve Avery .... .20 .09
❑ 48 Jeff Blauser .... .20 .09
❑ 49 Tom Glavine .... .75 .35
❑ 50 David Justice .... .75 .35
❑ 51 Roberto Kelly .... .20 .09
❑ 52 Ryan Klesko .... .40 .18
❑ 53 Javier Lopez .... .60 .25
❑ 54 Greg Maddux 2.50 1.10
❑ 55 Fred McGriff .... .60 .25
❑ 56 Ricky Bones .... .20 .09
❑ 57 Cal Eldred .... .20 .09
❑ 58 Brian Harper .... .20 .09
❑ 59 Pat Listach .... .20 .09
❑ 60 B.J. Surhoff .... .40 .18
❑ 61 Greg Vaughn .... .40 .18
❑ 62 Bernard Gilkey .... .20 .09
❑ 63 Gregg Jefferies .... .20 .09
❑ 64 Ray Lankford .... .40 .18
❑ 65 Ozzie Smith .... 1.00 .45
❑ 66 Bob Tewksbury .... .20 .09
❑ 67 Mark Whiten .... .20 .09
❑ 68 Todd Zeile .... .20 .09
❑ 69 Mark Grace .... .60 .25
❑ 70 Randy Myers .... .20 .09
❑ 71 Ryne Sandberg .... 1.00 .45
❑ 72 Sammy Sosa .... 2.00 .90
❑ 73 Steve Trachsel .... .20 .09
❑ 74 Rick Wilkins .... .20 .09
❑ 75 Brett Butler .... .40 .18
❑ 76 Delino DeShields .... .20 .09
❑ 77 Orel Hershiser .... .40 .18
❑ 78 Eric Karros .... .40 .18
❑ 79 Raul Mondesi .... .75 .35
❑ 80 Mike Piazza 2.50 1.10
❑ 81 Tim Wallach .... .20 .09
❑ 82 Moises Alou .... .60 .25
❑ 83 Cliff Floyd .... .40 .18
❑ 84 Marquis Grissom .... .40 .18
❑ 85 Pedro Martinez .... 1.00 .45
❑ 86 Larry Walker .... .75 .35
❑ 87 John Wetteland .... .40 .18
❑ 88 Rondell White .... .40 .18
❑ 89 Rod Beck .... .20 .09
❑ 90 Barry Bonds .... 1.00 .45
❑ 91 John Burkett .... .20 .09
❑ 92 Royce Clayton .... .20 .09
❑ 93 Billy Swift .... .20 .09
❑ 94 Robby Thompson .... .20 .09
❑ 95 Matt Williams .... .60 .25
❑ 96 Carlos Baerga .... .40 .18
❑ 97 Albert Belle .... 1.00 .45
❑ 98 Kenny Lofton .... .75 .35
❑ 99 Dennis Martinez .... .40 .18
❑ 100 Eddie Murray .... .75 .35
❑ 101 Manny Ramirez .... 1.00 .45
❑ 102 Eric Anthony .... .20 .09
❑ 103 Chris Bosio .... .20 .09
❑ 104 Jay Buhner .... .40 .18
❑ 105 Ken Griffey Jr. 4.00 1.80
❑ 106 Randy Johnson .... .75 .35
❑ 107 Edgar Martinez .... .40 .18
❑ 108 Chuck Carr .... .20 .09
❑ 109 Jeff Conine .... .40 .18
❑ 110 Carl Everett .... .20 .09
❑ 111 Chris Hammond .... .20 .09
❑ 112 Bryan Harvey .... .20 .09
❑ 113 Charles Johnson .... .40 .18
❑ 114 Gary Sheffield .... .75 .35
❑ 115 Bobby Bonilla .... .40 .18
❑ 116 Dwight Gooden .... .40 .18
❑ 117 Todd Hundley .... .40 .18
❑ 118 Bobby Jones .... .20 .09
❑ 119 Jeff Kent .... .40 .18
❑ 120 Bret Saberhagen .... .40 .18
❑ 121 Jeffrey Hammonds .... .40 .18
❑ 122 Chris Hoiles .... .20 .09
❑ 123 Ben McDonald .... .20 .09
❑ 124 Mike Mussina .... .75 .35
❑ 125 Rafael Palmeiro .... .60 .25
❑ 126 Cal Ripken Jr. 3.00 1.35
❑ 127 Lee Smith .... .40 .18
❑ 128 Derek Bell .... .40 .18
❑ 129 Andy Benes .... .40 .18
❑ 130 Tony Gwynn .... 2.00 .90
❑ 131 Trevor Hoffman .... .40 .18
❑ 132 Phil Plantier .... .20 .09
❑ 133 Bip Roberts .... .20 .09
❑ 134 Darren Daulton .... .40 .18
❑ 135 Lenny Dykstra .... .40 .18
❑ 136 Dave Hollins .... .20 .09
❑ 137 Danny Jackson .... .20 .09
❑ 138 John Kruk .... .40 .18
❑ 139 Kevin Stocker .... .20 .09
❑ 140 Jay Bell .... .40 .18
❑ 141 Carlos Garcia .... .20 .09
❑ 142 Jeff King .... .20 .09
❑ 143 Orlando Merced .... .20 .09
❑ 144 Andy Van Slyke .... .40 .18
❑ 145 Rick White .... .20 .09
❑ 146 Jose Canseco .... .75 .35
❑ 147 Will Clark .... .75 .35
❑ 148 Juan Gonzalez .... 2.00 .90
❑ 149 Rick Helling .... .40 .18
❑ 150 Dean Palmer .... .40 .18
❑ 151 Ivan Rodriguez .... 1.00 .45
❑ 152 Roger Clemens .... 1.50 .70
❑ 153 Scott Cooper .... .20 .09
❑ 154 Andre Dawson .... .60 .25
❑ 155 Mike Greenwell .... .20 .09
❑ 156 Aaron Sele .... .40 .18
❑ 157 Mo Vaughn .... 1.00 .45
❑ 158 Bret Boone .... .40 .18
❑ 159 Barry Larkin .... .60 .25
❑ 160 Kevin Mitchell .... .20 .09
❑ 161 Jose Rijo .... .20 .09
❑ 162 Deion Sanders .... .40 .18
❑ 163 Reggie Sanders .... .40 .18
❑ 164 Dante Bichette .... .40 .18
❑ 165 Ellis Burks .... .40 .18
❑ 166 Andres Galarraga .... .75 .35
❑ 167 Charlie Hayes .... .20 .09
❑ 168 David Nied .... .20 .09
❑ 169 Walt Weiss .... .20 .09
❑ 170 Kevin Appier .... .40 .18
❑ 171 David Cone .... .60 .25
❑ 172 Jeff Granger .... .20 .09
❑ 173 Felix Jose .... .20 .09
❑ 174 Wally Joyner .... .40 .18
❑ 175 Brian McRae .... .20 .09
❑ 176 Cecil Fielder .... .40 .18
❑ 177 Travis Fryman .... .40 .18
❑ 178 Mike Henneman .... .20 .09
❑ 179 Tony Phillips .... .20 .09
❑ 180 Mickey Tettleton .... .20 .09
❑ 181 Alan Trammell .... .60 .25
❑ 182 Rick Aguilera .... .20 .09
❑ 183 Rich Becker .... .20 .09
❑ 184 Scott Erickson .... .40 .18
❑ 185 Chuck Knoblauch .... .75 .35
❑ 186 Kirby Puckett .... 1.25 .55
❑ 187 Dave Winfield .... .75 .35
❑ 188 Wilson Alvarez .... .40 .18
❑ 189 Jason Bere .... .20 .09
❑ 190 Alex Fernandez .... .20 .09
❑ 191 Julio Franco .... .20 .09
❑ 192 Jack McDowell .... .20 .09
❑ 193 Frank Thomas 2.50 1.10
❑ 194 Robin Ventura .... .40 .18
❑ 195 Jim Abbott .... .40 .18
❑ 196 Wade Boggs .... .75 .35
❑ 197 Jimmy Key .... .40 .18
❑ 198 Don Mattingly .... 1.25 .55
❑ 199 Paul O'Neill .... .40 .18
❑ 200 Danny Tartabull .... .20 .09
❑ P24 Ken Griffey Jr. Promo .. 3.00 1.35

1994 SP Holoviews

	MINT	NRMT
COMPLETE SET (38)	150.00	70.00
COMMON CARD (1-38)	1.50	.70
COMP.HOLO.DC SET (38)	1200.00	550.00

*DIE CUT STARS: 2X TO 5X BASIC HOLOVIEWS
DIE CUT STATED ODDS 1:75

❑ 1 Roberto Alomar 5.00 2.20
❑ 2 Kevin Appier 3.00 1.35
❑ 3 Jeff Bagwell 8.00 3.60
❑ 4 Jose Canseco 5.00 2.20
❑ 5 Roger Clemens 10.00 4.50

		MINT	NRMT
❑ 6	Carlos Delgado	3.00	1.35
❑ 7	Cecil Fielder	3.00	1.35
❑ 8	Cliff Floyd	3.00	1.35
❑ 9	Travis Fryman	3.00	1.35
❑ 10	Andres Galarraga	5.00	2.20
❑ 11	Juan Gonzalez	12.00	5.50
❑ 12	Ken Griffey Jr.	25.00	11.00
❑ 13	Tony Gwynn	12.00	5.50
❑ 14	Jeffrey Hammonds	3.00	1.35
❑ 15	Bo Jackson	3.00	1.35
❑ 16	Michael Jordan	40.00	18.00
❑ 17	David Justice	5.00	2.20
❑ 18	Steve Karsay	1.50	.70
❑ 19	Jeff Kent	3.00	1.35
❑ 20	Brooks Kieschnick	3.00	1.35
❑ 21	Ryan Klesko	3.00	1.35
❑ 22	John Kruk	3.00	1.35
❑ 23	Barry Larkin	3.00	1.35
❑ 24	Pat Listach	1.50	.70
❑ 25	Don Mattingly	8.00	3.60
❑ 26	Mark McGwire	25.00	11.00
❑ 27	Raul Mondesi	5.00	2.20
❑ 28	Trot Nixon	3.00	1.35
❑ 29	Mike Piazza	15.00	6.75
❑ 30	Kirby Puckett	8.00	3.60
❑ 31	Manny Ramirez	6.00	2.70
❑ 32	Cal Ripken	20.00	9.00
❑ 33	Alex Rodriguez	40.00	18.00
❑ 34	Tim Salmon	5.00	2.20
❑ 35	Gary Sheffield	5.00	2.20
❑ 36	Ozzie Smith	6.00	2.70
❑ 37	Sammy Sosa	12.00	5.50
❑ 38	Andy Van Slyke	3.00	1.35

1995 SP

	MINT	NRMT
COMPLETE SET (207)	40.00	18.00
COMMON CARD (1-207)	.20	.09

		MINT	NRMT
❑ 1	Cal Ripken Salute	3.00	1.35
❑ 2	Nolan Ryan Salute	3.00	1.35
❑ 3	George Brett Salute	1.50	.70
❑ 4	Mike Schmidt Salute	1.00	.45
❑ 5	Dustin Hermanson FOIL	.40	.18
❑ 6	Antonio Osuna FOIL	.25	.11
❑ 7	Mark Grudzielanek FOIL	.60	.25
❑ 8	Ray Durham FOIL	.40	.18
❑ 9	Ugueth Urbina FOIL	.20	.09
❑ 10	Ruben Rivera FOIL	.40	.18
❑ 11	Curtis Goodwin FOIL	.25	.11
❑ 12	Jimmy Hurst FOIL	.20	.09
❑ 13	Jose Malave FOIL	.25	.11
❑ 14	Hideo Nomo FOIL	3.00	1.35
❑ 15	Juan Acevedo FOIL	.25	.11
❑ 16	Tony Clark FOIL	.75	.35
❑ 17	Jim Pittsley FOIL	.20	.09
❑ 18	Freddy Garcia FOIL	.20	.09
❑ 19	Carlos Perez FOIL	.60	.25
❑ 20	Raul Casanova FOIL	.20	.09
❑ 21	Quilvio Veras FOIL	.20	.09
❑ 22	Edgardo Alfonzo FOIL	.40	.18
❑ 23	Marty Cordova FOIL	.20	.09
❑ 24	C.J. Nitkowski FOIL	.25	.11
❑ 25	Wade Boggs CL	.40	.18
❑ 26	Dave Winfield CL	.40	.18
❑ 27	Eddie Murray CL	.40	.18
❑ 28	David Justice	.75	.35
❑ 29	Marquis Grissom	.40	.18
❑ 30	Fred McGriff	.60	.25
❑ 31	Greg Maddux	2.50	1.10
❑ 32	Tom Glavine	.75	.35
❑ 33	Steve Avery	.20	.09
❑ 34	Chipper Jones	2.00	.90
❑ 35	Sammy Sosa	2.00	.90
❑ 36	Jaime Navarro	.20	.09
❑ 37	Randy Myers	.20	.09
❑ 38	Mark Grace	.60	.25
❑ 39	Todd Zeile	.20	.09
❑ 40	Brian McRae	.20	.09
❑ 41	Reggie Sanders	.40	.18
❑ 42	Ron Gant	.20	.09
❑ 43	Deion Sanders	.40	.18
❑ 44	Bret Boone	.40	.18
❑ 45	Barry Larkin	.60	.25
❑ 46	Jose Rijo	.20	.09
❑ 47	Jason Bates	.20	.09
❑ 48	Andres Galarraga	.75	.35
❑ 49	Bill Swift	.20	.09
❑ 50	Larry Walker	.75	.35
❑ 51	Vinny Castilla	.60	.25
❑ 52	Dante Bichette	.40	.18
❑ 53	Jeff Conine	.40	.18
❑ 54	John Burkett	.20	.09
❑ 55	Gary Sheffield	.60	.25
❑ 56	Andre Dawson	.60	.25
❑ 57	Terry Pendleton	.20	.09
❑ 58	Charles Johnson	.40	.18
❑ 59	Brian L. Hunter	.40	.18
❑ 60	Jeff Bagwell	1.25	.55
❑ 61	Craig Biggio	.75	.35
❑ 62	Phil Nevin	.20	.09
❑ 63	Doug Drabek	.20	.09
❑ 64	Derek Bell	.40	.18
❑ 65	Raul Mondesi	.60	.25
❑ 66	Eric Karros	.40	.18
❑ 67	Roger Cedeno	.20	.09
❑ 68	Delino DeShields	.20	.09
❑ 69	Ramon Martinez	.40	.18
❑ 70	Mike Piazza	2.50	1.10
❑ 71	Billy Ashley	.20	.09
❑ 72	Jeff Fassero	.20	.09
❑ 73	Shane Andrews	.20	.09
❑ 74	Wil Cordero	.20	.09
❑ 75	Tony Tarasco	.20	.09
❑ 76	Rondell White	.40	.18
❑ 77	Pedro J. Martinez	.75	.35
❑ 78	Moises Alou	.60	.25
❑ 79	Rico Brogna	.20	.09
❑ 80	Bobby Bonilla	.40	.18
❑ 81	Jeff Kent	.40	.18
❑ 82	Brett Butler	.40	.18
❑ 83	Bobby Jones	.20	.09
❑ 84	Bill Pulsipher	.20	.09
❑ 85	Bret Saberhagen	.40	.18
❑ 86	Gregg Jefferies	.20	.09
❑ 87	Lenny Dykstra	.40	.18
❑ 88	Dave Hollins	.20	.09
❑ 89	Charlie Hayes	.20	.09
❑ 90	Darren Daulton	.40	.18
❑ 91	Curt Schilling	.40	.18
❑ 92	Heathcliff Slocumb	.20	.09
❑ 93	Carlos Garcia	.20	.09
❑ 94	Denny Neagle	.40	.18
❑ 95	Jay Bell	.40	.18
❑ 96	Orlando Merced	.20	.09
❑ 97	Dave Clark	.20	.09
❑ 98	Bernard Gilkey	.20	.09
❑ 99	Scott Cooper	.20	.09
❑ 100	Ozzie Smith	1.00	.45
❑ 101	Tom Henke	.20	.09
❑ 102	Ken Hill	.20	.09
❑ 103	Brian Jordan	.40	.18
❑ 104	Ray Lankford	.40	.18
❑ 105	Tony Gwynn	2.00	.90
❑ 106	Andy Benes	.40	.18
❑ 107	Ken Caminiti	.60	.25
❑ 108	Steve Finley	.40	.18
❑ 109	Joey Hamilton	.40	.18
❑ 110	Bip Roberts	.20	.09
❑ 111	Eddie Williams	.20	.09
❑ 112	Rod Beck	.20	.09
❑ 113	Matt Williams	.40	.18
❑ 114	Glenallen Hill	.20	.09
❑ 115	Barry Bonds	1.00	.45
❑ 116	Robby Thompson	.20	.09
❑ 117	Mark Portugal	.20	.09
❑ 118	Brady Anderson	.40	.18
❑ 119	Mike Mussina	.75	.35
❑ 120	Rafael Palmeiro	.60	.25
❑ 121	Chris Hoiles	.20	.09
❑ 122	Harold Baines	.40	.18
❑ 123	Jeffrey Hammonds	.40	.18
❑ 124	Tim Naehring	.20	.09
❑ 125	Mo Vaughn	1.00	.45
❑ 126	Mike Macfarlane	.20	.09
❑ 127	Roger Clemens	1.50	.70
❑ 128	John Valentin	.40	.18
❑ 129	Aaron Sele	.40	.18
❑ 130	Jose Canseco	.75	.35
❑ 131	J.T. Snow	.40	.18
❑ 132	Mark Langston	.20	.09
❑ 133	Chili Davis	.40	.18
❑ 134	Chuck Finley	.40	.18
❑ 135	Tim Salmon	.75	.35
❑ 136	Tony Phillips	.20	.09
❑ 137	Jason Bere	.20	.09
❑ 138	Robin Ventura	.40	.18
❑ 139	Tim Raines	.40	.18
❑ 140	Frank Thomas COR	2.50	1.10
❑ 140A	Frank Thomas ERR	8.00	3.60
❑ 141	Alex Fernandez	.20	.09
❑ 142	Jim Abbott	.40	.18
❑ 143	Wilson Alvarez	.40	.18
❑ 144	Carlos Baerga	.40	.18
❑ 145	Albert Belle	1.00	.45
❑ 146	Jim Thome	.75	.35
❑ 147	Dennis Martinez	.40	.18
❑ 148	Eddie Murray	.75	.35
❑ 149	Dave Winfield	.75	.35
❑ 150	Kenny Lofton	.75	.35
❑ 151	Manny Ramirez	.75	.35
❑ 152	Chad Curtis	.20	.09
❑ 153	Lou Whitaker	.40	.18
❑ 154	Alan Trammell	.40	.18
❑ 155	Cecil Fielder	.40	.18
❑ 156	Kirk Gibson	.40	.18
❑ 157	Michael Tucker	.40	.18
❑ 158	Jon Nunnally	.20	.09
❑ 159	Wally Joyner	.40	.18
❑ 160	Kevin Appier	.40	.18
❑ 161	Jeff Montgomery	.20	.09
❑ 162	Greg Gagne	.20	.09
❑ 163	Ricky Bones	.20	.09
❑ 164	Cal Eldred	.20	.09
❑ 165	Greg Vaughn	.40	.18
❑ 166	Kevin Seitzer	.20	.09
❑ 167	Jose Valentin	.20	.09
❑ 168	Joe Oliver	.20	.09
❑ 169	Rick Aguilera	.20	.09
❑ 170	Kirby Puckett	1.25	.55
❑ 171	Scott Stahoviak	.20	.09
❑ 172	Kevin Tapani	.20	.09
❑ 173	Chuck Knoblauch	.75	.35
❑ 174	Rich Becker	.20	.09
❑ 175	Don Mattingly	1.25	.55
❑ 176	Jack McDowell	.20	.09
❑ 177	Jimmy Key	.40	.18
❑ 178	Paul O'Neill	.40	.18
❑ 179	John Wetteland	.40	.18
❑ 180	Wade Boggs	.75	.35

		MINT	NRMT
❑ 181	Derek Jeter	2.50	1.10
❑ 182	Rickey Henderson	.75	.35
❑ 183	Terry Steinbach	.40	.18
❑ 184	Ruben Sierra	.20	.09
❑ 185	Mark McGwire	4.00	1.80
❑ 186	Todd Stottlemyre	.20	.09
❑ 187	Dennis Eckersley	.40	.18
❑ 188	Alex Rodriguez	3.00	1.35
❑ 189	Randy Johnson	.75	.35
❑ 190	Ken Griffey Jr.	4.00	1.80
❑ 191	Tino Martinez UER Mike Blowers pictured on back	.40	.18
❑ 192	Jay Buhner	.40	.18
❑ 193	Edgar Martinez	.40	.18
❑ 194	Mickey Tettleton	.20	.09
❑ 195	Juan Gonzalez	2.00	.90
❑ 196	Benji Gil	.20	.09
❑ 197	Dean Palmer	.40	.18
❑ 198	Ivan Rodriguez	1.00	.45
❑ 199	Kenny Rogers	.20	.09
❑ 200	Will Clark	.75	.35
❑ 201	Roberto Alomar	.75	.35
❑ 202	David Cone	.60	.25
❑ 203	Paul Molitor	.75	.35
❑ 204	Shawn Green	.40	.18
❑ 205	Joe Carter	.40	.18
❑ 206	Alex Gonzalez	.20	.09
❑ 207	Pat Hentgen	.40	.18
❑ P100	Ken Griffey Jr. Promo	.20	.09
❑ AU190	Ken Griffey Jr. AU	200.00	90.00

1995 SP Platinum Power

	MINT	NRMT
COMPLETE SET (20)	20.00	9.00
COMMON CARD (PP1-PP20)	.25	.11

		MINT	NRMT
❑ PP1	Jeff Bagwell	1.50	.70
❑ PP2	Barry Bonds	1.00	.45
❑ PP3	Ron Gant	.25	.11
❑ PP4	Fred McGriff	.75	.35
❑ PP5	Raul Mondesi	.75	.35
❑ PP6	Mike Piazza	3.00	1.35
❑ PP7	Larry Walker	1.00	.45
❑ PP8	Matt Williams	.50	.23
❑ PP9	Albert Belle	1.00	.45
❑ PP10	Cecil Fielder	.50	.23
❑ PP11	Juan Gonzalez	2.50	1.10
❑ PP12	Ken Griffey Jr.	5.00	2.20
❑ PP13	Mark McGwire	5.00	2.20
❑ PP14	Eddie Murray	1.00	.45
❑ PP15	Manny Ramirez	1.00	.45
❑ PP16	Cal Ripken	4.00	1.80
❑ PP17	Tim Salmon	1.00	.45
❑ PP18	Frank Thomas	3.00	1.35
❑ PP19	Jim Thome	1.00	.45
❑ PP20	Mo Vaughn	1.00	.45

1995 SP Special FX

	MINT	NRMT
COMPLETE SET (48)	800.00	350.00
COMMON CARD (1-48)	5.00	2.20

		MINT	NRMT
❑ 1	Jose Canseco	15.00	6.75
❑ 2	Roger Clemens	30.00	13.50
❑ 3	Mo Vaughn	20.00	9.00
❑ 4	Tim Salmon	15.00	6.75
❑ 5	Chuck Finley	12.00	5.50
❑ 6	Robin Ventura	12.00	5.50
❑ 7	Jason Bere	5.00	2.20
❑ 8	Carlos Baerga	12.00	5.50
❑ 9	Albert Belle	25.00	11.00
❑ 10	Kenny Lofton	15.00	6.75
❑ 11	Manny Ramirez	15.00	6.75
❑ 12	Jeff Montgomery	5.00	2.20
❑ 13	Kirby Puckett	25.00	11.00
❑ 14	Wade Boggs	15.00	6.75
❑ 15	Don Mattingly	25.00	11.00
❑ 16	Cal Ripken	60.00	27.00
❑ 17	Ruben Sierra	5.00	2.20
❑ 18	Ken Griffey Jr.	80.00	36.00
❑ 19	Randy Johnson	15.00	6.75
❑ 20	Alex Rodriguez	60.00	27.00
❑ 21	Will Clark	15.00	6.75
❑ 22	Juan Gonzalez	40.00	18.00
❑ 23	Roberto Alomar	15.00	6.75
❑ 24	Joe Carter	12.00	5.50
❑ 25	Alex Gonzalez	5.00	2.20
❑ 26	Paul Molitor	15.00	6.75
❑ 27	Ryan Klesko	12.00	5.50
❑ 28	Fred McGriff	10.00	4.50
❑ 29	Greg Maddux	50.00	22.00
❑ 30	Sammy Sosa	40.00	18.00
❑ 31	Bret Boone	12.00	5.50
❑ 32	Barry Larkin	10.00	4.50
❑ 33	Reggie Sanders	12.00	5.50
❑ 34	Dante Bichette	12.00	5.50
❑ 35	Andres Galarraga	15.00	6.75
❑ 36	Charles Johnson	12.00	5.50
❑ 37	Gary Sheffield	10.00	4.50
❑ 38	Jeff Bagwell	25.00	11.00
❑ 39	Craig Biggio	15.00	6.75
❑ 40	Eric Karros	12.00	5.50
❑ 41	Billy Ashley	5.00	2.20
❑ 42	Raul Mondesi	10.00	4.50
❑ 43	Mike Piazza	50.00	22.00
❑ 44	Rondell White	12.00	5.50
❑ 45	Bret Saberhagen	12.00	5.50
❑ 46	Tony Gwynn	40.00	18.00
❑ 47	Melvin Nieves	5.00	2.20
❑ 48	Matt Williams	12.00	5.50

1996 SP

	MINT	NRMT
COMPLETE SET (188)	40.00	18.00
COMMON CARDS (1-188)	.20	.09

		MINT	NRMT
❑ 1	Rey Ordonez FOIL	.40	.18
❑ 2	George Arias FOIL	.20	.09
❑ 3	Osvaldo Fernandez FOIL	.20	.09
❑ 4	Darin Erstad FOIL	20.00	9.00
❑ 5	Paul Wilson FOIL	.20	.09
❑ 6	Richard Hidalgo FOIL	.40	.18
❑ 7	Justin Thompson FOIL	.40	.18
❑ 8	Jimmy Haynes FOIL	.20	.09
❑ 9	Edgar Renteria FOIL	.40	.18
❑ 10	Ruben Rivera FOIL	.40	.18
❑ 11	Chris Snopek FOIL	.20	.09
❑ 12	Billy Wagner FOIL	.40	.18
❑ 13	Mike Grace FOIL	.20	.09
❑ 14	Todd Greene FOIL	.40	.18
❑ 15	Karim Garcia FOIL	.40	.18
❑ 16	John Wasdin FOIL	.20	.09
❑ 17	Jason Kendall FOIL	.75	.35
❑ 18	Bob Abreu FOIL	.40	.18
❑ 19	Jermaine Dye FOIL	.20	.09
❑ 20	Jason Schmidt FOIL	.20	.09
❑ 21	Javy Lopez	.40	.18
❑ 22	Ryan Klesko	.40	.18
❑ 23	Tom Glavine	.75	.35
❑ 24	John Smoltz	.40	.18
❑ 25	Greg Maddux	2.50	1.10
❑ 26	Chipper Jones	2.00	.90
❑ 27	Fred McGriff	.60	.25
❑ 28	David Justice	.75	.35
❑ 29	Roberto Alomar	.75	.35
❑ 30	Cal Ripken	3.00	1.35
❑ 31	B.J. Surhoff	.40	.18
❑ 32	Bobby Bonilla	.40	.18
❑ 33	Mike Mussina	.75	.35
❑ 34	Randy Myers	.20	.09
❑ 35	Rafael Palmeiro	.60	.25
❑ 36	Brady Anderson	.40	.18
❑ 37	Tim Naehring	.20	.09
❑ 38	Jose Canseco	.75	.35
❑ 39	Roger Clemens	1.50	.70
❑ 40	Mo Vaughn	1.00	.45
❑ 41	Jose Valentin	.20	.09
❑ 42	Kevin Mitchell	.20	.09
❑ 43	Chili Davis	.40	.18
❑ 44	Garret Anderson	.40	.18
❑ 45	Tim Salmon	.75	.35
❑ 46	Chuck Finley	.40	.18
❑ 47	Troy Percival	.40	.18
❑ 48	Jim Abbott	.40	.18
❑ 49	J.T. Snow	.40	.18
❑ 50	Jim Edmonds	.60	.25
❑ 51	Sammy Sosa	2.00	.90
❑ 52	Brian McRae	.20	.09
❑ 53	Ryne Sandberg	1.00	.45
❑ 54	Jaime Navarro	.20	.09
❑ 55	Mark Grace	.60	.25
❑ 56	Harold Baines	.40	.18
❑ 57	Robin Ventura	.40	.18
❑ 58	Tony Phillips	.20	.09
❑ 59	Alex Fernandez	.20	.09
❑ 60	Frank Thomas	2.50	1.10
❑ 61	Ray Durham	.40	.18
❑ 62	Bret Boone	.40	.18
❑ 63	Reggie Sanders	.40	.18
❑ 64	Pete Schourek	.20	.09
❑ 65	Barry Larkin	.60	.25
❑ 66	John Smiley	.20	.09
❑ 67	Carlos Baerga	.40	.18
❑ 68	Jim Thome	.75	.35
❑ 69	Eddie Murray	.75	.35
❑ 70	Albert Belle	1.00	.45
❑ 71	Dennis Martinez	.40	.18
❑ 72	Jack McDowell	.20	.09
❑ 73	Kenny Lofton	.75	.35
❑ 74	Manny Ramirez	.75	.35
❑ 75	Dante Bichette	.40	.18
❑ 76	Vinny Castilla	.60	.25
❑ 77	Andres Galarraga	.75	.35
❑ 78	Walt Weiss	.20	.09
❑ 79	Ellis Burks	.40	.18
❑ 80	Larry Walker	.75	.35
❑ 81	Cecil Fielder	.40	.18
❑ 82	Melvin Nieves	.20	.09
❑ 83	Travis Fryman	.40	.18
❑ 84	Chad Curtis	.20	.09
❑ 85	Alan Trammell	.60	.25

❑	86 Gary Sheffield	.60	.25
❑	87 Charles Johnson	.40	.18
❑	88 Andre Dawson	.60	.25
❑	89 Jeff Conine	.40	.18
❑	90 Greg Colbrunn	.20	.09
❑	91 Derek Bell	.40	.18
❑	92 Brian L.Hunter	.40	.18
❑	93 Doug Drabek	.20	.09
❑	94 Craig Biggio	.75	.35
❑	95 Jeff Bagwell	1.25	.55
❑	96 Kevin Appier	.40	.18
❑	97 Jeff Montgomery	.20	.09
❑	98 Michael Tucker	.40	.18
❑	99 Bip Roberts	.20	.09
❑	100 Johnny Damon	.40	.18
❑	101 Eric Karros	.40	.18
❑	102 Raul Mondesi	.60	.25
❑	103 Ramon Martinez	.40	.18
❑	104 Ismael Valdes	.40	.18
❑	105 Mike Piazza	2.50	1.10
❑	106 Hideo Nomo	1.25	.55
❑	107 Chan Ho Park	.75	.35
❑	108 Ben McDonald	.20	.09
❑	109 Kevin Seitzer	.20	.09
❑	110 Greg Vaughn	.40	.18
❑	111 Jose Valentin	.20	.09
❑	112 Rick Aguilera	.20	.09
❑	113 Marty Cordova	.20	.09
❑	114 Brad Radke	.40	.18
❑	115 Kirby Puckett	1.25	.55
❑	116 Chuck Knoblauch	.75	.35
❑	117 Paul Molitor	.75	.35
❑	118 Pedro Martinez	.75	.35
❑	119 Mike Lansing	.20	.09
❑	120 Rondell White	.40	.18
❑	121 Moises Alou	.60	.25
❑	122 Mark Grudzielanek	.40	.18
❑	123 Jeff Fassero	.20	.09
❑	124 Rico Brogna	.20	.09
❑	125 Jason Isringhausen	.20	.09
❑	126 Jeff Kent	.40	.18
❑	127 Bernard Gilkey	.20	.09
❑	128 Todd Hundley	.40	.18
❑	129 David Cone	.60	.25
❑	130 Andy Pettitte	.60	.25
❑	131 Wade Boggs	.75	.35
❑	132 Paul O'Neill	.40	.18
❑	133 Ruben Sierra	.20	.09
❑	134 John Wetteland	.40	.18
❑	135 Derek Jeter	2.50	1.10
❑	136 Geronimo Berroa	.20	.09
❑	137 Terry Steinbach	.40	.18
❑	138 Ariel Prieto	.20	.09
❑	139 Scott Brosius	.40	.18
❑	140 Mark McGwire	4.00	1.80
❑	141 Lenny Dykstra	.40	.18
❑	142 Todd Zeile	.20	.09
❑	143 Benito Santiago	.20	.09
❑	144 Mickey Morandini	.20	.09
❑	145 Gregg Jefferies	.20	.09
❑	146 Denny Neagle	.40	.18
❑	147 Orlando Merced	.20	.09
❑	148 Charlie Hayes	.20	.09
❑	149 Carlos Garcia	.20	.09
❑	150 Jay Bell	.40	.18
❑	151 Ray Lankford	.40	.18
❑	152 Alan Benes Andy Benes	.40	.18
❑	153 Dennis Eckersley	.40	.18
❑	154 Gary Gaetti	.40	.18
❑	155 Ozzie Smith	1.00	.45
❑	156 Ron Gant	.20	.09
❑	157 Brian Jordan	.40	.18
❑	158 Ken Caminiti	.60	.25
❑	159 Rickey Henderson	.75	.35
❑	160 Tony Gwynn	1.50	.70
❑	161 Wally Joyner	.40	.18
❑	162 Andy Ashby	.20	.09
❑	163 Steve Finley	.40	.18
❑	164 Glenallen Hill	.20	.09
❑	165 Matt Williams	.40	.18
❑	166 Barry Bonds	1.00	.45
❑	167 William VanLandingham	.20	.09
❑	168 Rod Beck	.20	.09
❑	169 Randy Johnson	.75	.35
❑	170 Ken Griffey Jr.	4.00	1.80
❑	171 Alex Rodriguez	2.50	1.10
❑	172 Edgar Martinez	.40	.18
❑	173 Jay Buhner	.40	.18
❑	174 Russ Davis	.40	.18
❑	175 Juan Gonzalez	2.00	.90
❑	176 Mickey Tettleton	.20	.09
❑	177 Will Clark	.75	.35
❑	178 Ken Hill	.20	.09
❑	179 Dean Palmer	.40	.18
❑	180 Ivan Rodriguez	1.00	.45
❑	181 Carlos Delgado	.40	.18
❑	182 Alex Gonzalez	.20	.09
❑	183 Shawn Green	.40	.18
❑	184 Juan Guzman	.20	.09
❑	185 Joe Carter	.40	.18
❑	186 Hideo Nomo CL UER Checklist lists Livan Hernandez as #4	1.00	.45
❑	187 Cal Ripken CL	1.50	.70
❑	188 Ken Griffey Jr. CL	2.00	.90

1996 SP Baseball Heroes

	MINT	NRMT
COMPLETE SET (10)	250.00	110.00
COMMON CARD (82-90/HDR)	10.00	4.50
❑ 82 Frank Thomas	30.00	13.50
❑ 83 Albert Belle	12.00	5.50
❑ 84 Barry Bonds	12.00	5.50
❑ 85 Chipper Jones	25.00	11.00
❑ 86 Hideo Nomo	15.00	6.75
❑ 87 Mike Piazza	30.00	13.50
❑ 88 Manny Ramirez	10.00	4.50
❑ 89 Greg Maddux	30.00	13.50
❑ 90 Ken Griffey Jr.	50.00	22.00
❑ NNO Ken Griffey Jr. HDR	50.00	22.00

1996 SP Marquee Matchups

	MINT	NRMT
COMPLETE SET (20)	40.00	18.00
COMMON CARD (MM1-MM20)	.50	.23
COMP.DIE CUT SET (20)	200.00	90.00

*DC STARS: 4X TO 10X BASIC CARDS
DC STATED ODDS 1:61

❑ MM1 Ken Griffey Jr.	8.00	3.60
❑ MM2 Hideo Nomo	2.50	1.10
❑ MM3 Derek Jeter	5.00	2.20
❑ MM4 Rey Ordonez	.50	.23
❑ MM5 Tim Salmon	1.50	.70
❑ MM6 Mike Piazza	5.00	2.20
❑ MM7 Mark McGwire	8.00	3.60
❑ MM8 Barry Bonds	2.00	.90
❑ MM9 Cal Ripken	6.00	2.70
❑ MM10 Greg Maddux	5.00	2.20
❑ MM11 Albert Belle	1.50	.70
❑ MM12 Barry Larkin	1.00	.45
❑ MM13 Jeff Bagwell	2.50	1.10
❑ MM14 Juan Gonzalez	4.00	1.80
❑ MM15 Frank Thomas	5.00	2.20
❑ MM16 Sammy Sosa	4.00	1.80
❑ MM17 Mike Mussina	1.50	.70
❑ MM18 Chipper Jones	4.00	1.80
❑ MM19 Roger Clemens	3.00	1.35
❑ MM20 Fred McGriff	1.00	.45

1996 SP Special FX

	MINT	NRMT
COMPLETE SET (48)	175.00	80.00
COMMON CARD (1-48)	1.50	.70
COMP.DIE CUT SET (48)	800.00	350.00

*DIE CUT STARS: 2X TO 5X BASIC SPECIAL FX
DC STATED ODDS 1:75

❑ 1 Greg Maddux	12.00	5.50
❑ 2 Eric Karros	2.00	.90
❑ 3 Mike Piazza	12.00	5.50
❑ 4 Raul Mondesi	2.50	1.10
❑ 5 Hideo Nomo	6.00	2.70
❑ 6 Jim Edmonds	2.50	1.10
❑ 7 Jason Isringhausen	1.50	.70
❑ 8 Jay Buhner	2.00	.90
❑ 9 Barry Larkin	2.50	1.10
❑ 10 Ken Griffey Jr.	20.00	9.00
❑ 11 Gary Sheffield	2.50	1.10
❑ 12 Craig Biggio	4.00	1.80
❑ 13 Paul Wilson	1.50	.70
❑ 14 Rondell White	2.00	.90
❑ 15 Chipper Jones	10.00	4.50
❑ 16 Kirby Puckett	6.00	2.70
❑ 17 Ron Gant	1.50	.70
❑ 18 Wade Boggs	4.00	1.80
❑ 19 Fred McGriff	2.50	1.10
❑ 20 Cal Ripken	15.00	6.75
❑ 21 Jason Kendall	4.00	1.80
❑ 22 Johnny Damon	2.00	.90
❑ 23 Kenny Lofton	4.00	1.80
❑ 24 Roberto Alomar	4.00	1.80
❑ 25 Barry Bonds	5.00	2.20
❑ 26 Dante Bichette	2.00	.90
❑ 27 Mark McGwire	20.00	9.00
❑ 28 Rafael Palmeiro	2.50	1.10
❑ 29 Juan Gonzalez	10.00	4.50
❑ 30 Albert Belle	5.00	2.20
❑ 31 Randy Johnson	4.00	1.80
❑ 32 Jose Canseco	4.00	1.80
❑ 33 Sammy Sosa	10.00	4.50
❑ 34 Eddie Murray	4.00	1.80
❑ 35 Frank Thomas	12.00	5.50
❑ 36 Tom Glavine	4.00	1.80
❑ 37 Matt Williams	2.00	.90

		MINT	NRMT
❑	38 Roger Clemens	8.00	3.60
❑	39 Paul Molitor	4.00	1.80
❑	40 Tony Gwynn	10.00	4.50
❑	41 Mo Vaughn	5.00	2.20
❑	42 Tim Salmon	4.00	1.80
❑	43 Manny Ramirez	4.00	1.80
❑	44 Jeff Bagwell	6.00	2.70
❑	45 Edgar Martinez	2.00	.90
❑	46 Rey Ordonez	2.00	.90
❑	47 Osvaldo Fernandez	1.50	.70
❑	48 Derek Jeter	10.00	4.50

1997 SP

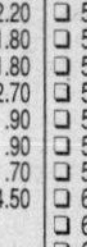
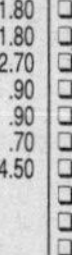
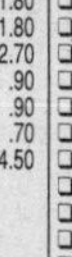
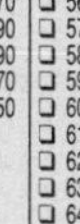

	MINT	NRMT
COMPLETE SET (184)	60.00	27.00
COMMON CARD (1-159/181-184)	.20	.09
COMMON SP (160-180)	.30	.14

		MINT	NRMT
❑	1 Andruw Jones FOIL	1.25	.55
❑	2 Kevin Orie FOIL	.20	.09
❑	3 Nomar Garciaparra FOIL	2.50	1.10
❑	4 Jose Guillen FOIL	.75	.35
❑	5 Todd Walker FOIL	.75	.35
❑	6 Derrick Gibson FOIL	.50	.23
❑	7 Aaron Boone FOIL	.20	.09
❑	8 Bartolo Colon FOIL	.40	.18
❑	9 Derrek Lee FOIL	.50	.23
❑	10 Vladimir Guerrero FOIL	1.50	.70
❑	11 Wilton Guerrero FOIL	.20	.09
❑	12 Luis Castillo FOIL	.40	.18
❑	13 Jason Dickson FOIL	.40	.18
❑	14 Bubba Trammell FOIL	.50	.23
❑	15 Jose Cruz Jr. FOIL	3.00	1.35
❑	16 Eddie Murray	.75	.35
❑	17 Darin Erstad	1.25	.55
❑	18 Garret Anderson	.40	.18
❑	19 Jim Edmonds	.50	.23
❑	20 Tim Salmon	.75	.35
❑	21 Chuck Finley	.40	.18
❑	22 John Smoltz	.40	.18
❑	23 Greg Maddux	2.50	1.10
❑	24 Kenny Lofton	.75	.35
❑	25 Chipper Jones	2.00	.90
❑	26 Ryan Klesko	.40	.18
❑	27 Javier Lopez	.40	.18
❑	28 Fred McGriff	.50	.23
❑	29 Roberto Alomar	.75	.35
❑	30 Rafael Palmeiro	.50	.23
❑	31 Mike Mussina	.75	.35
❑	32 Brady Anderson	.40	.18
❑	33 Rocky Coppinger	.20	.09
❑	34 Cal Ripken	3.00	1.35
❑	35 Mo Vaughn	1.00	.45
❑	36 Steve Avery	.20	.09
❑	37 Tom Gordon	.20	.09
❑	38 Tim Naehring	.20	.09
❑	39 Troy O'Leary	.40	.18
❑	40 Sammy Sosa	2.00	.90
❑	41 Brian McRae	.20	.09
❑	42 Mel Rojas	.20	.09
❑	43 Ryne Sandberg	1.00	.45
❑	44 Mark Grace	.50	.23
❑	45 Albert Belle	1.00	.45
❑	46 Robin Ventura	.40	.18
❑	47 Roberto Hernandez	.20	.09
❑	48 Ray Durham	.40	.18
❑	49 Harold Baines	.40	.18
❑	50 Frank Thomas	2.50	1.10
❑	51 Bret Boone	.40	.18
❑	52 Reggie Sanders	.40	.18
❑	53 Deion Sanders	.40	.18
❑	54 Hal Morris	.20	.09
❑	55 Barry Larkin	.50	.23
❑	56 Jim Thome	.75	.35
❑	57 Marquis Grissom	.40	.18
❑	58 David Justice	.75	.35
❑	59 Charles Nagy	.40	.18
❑	60 Manny Ramirez	.75	.35
❑	61 Matt Williams	.40	.18
❑	62 Jack McDowell	.20	.09
❑	63 Vinny Castilla	.50	.23
❑	64 Dante Bichette	.40	.18
❑	65 Andres Galarraga	.75	.35
❑	66 Ellis Burks	.40	.18
❑	67 Larry Walker	.75	.35
❑	68 Eric Young	.40	.18
❑	69 Brian L. Hunter	.40	.18
❑	70 Travis Fryman	.40	.18
❑	71 Tony Clark	.50	.23
❑	72 Bobby Higginson	.50	.23
❑	73 Melvin Nieves	.20	.09
❑	74 Jeff Conine	.40	.18
❑	75 Gary Sheffield	.50	.23
❑	76 Moises Alou	.50	.23
❑	77 Edgar Renteria	.40	.18
❑	78 Alex Fernandez	.20	.09
❑	79 Charles Johnson	.40	.18
❑	80 Bobby Bonilla	.40	.18
❑	81 Darryl Kile	.40	.18
❑	82 Derek Bell	.40	.18
❑	83 Shane Reynolds	.40	.18
❑	84 Craig Biggio	.75	.35
❑	85 Jeff Bagwell	1.25	.55
❑	86 Billy Wagner	.40	.18
❑	87 Chili Davis	.40	.18
❑	88 Kevin Appier	.40	.18
❑	89 Jay Bell	.40	.18
❑	90 Johnny Damon	.40	.18
❑	91 Jeff King	.20	.09
❑	92 Hideo Nomo	1.00	.45
❑	93 Todd Hollandsworth	.20	.09
❑	94 Eric Karros	.40	.18
❑	95 Mike Piazza	2.50	1.10
❑	96 Ramon Martinez	.40	.18
❑	97 Todd Worrell	.20	.09
❑	98 Raul Mondesi	.50	.23
❑	99 Dave Nilsson	.20	.09
❑	100 John Jaha	.20	.09
❑	101 Jose Valentin	.20	.09
❑	102 Jeff Cirillo	.40	.18
❑	103 Jeff D'Amico	.20	.09
❑	104 Ben McDonald	.20	.09
❑	105 Paul Molitor	.75	.35
❑	106 Rich Becker	.20	.09
❑	107 Frank Rodriguez	.20	.09
❑	108 Marty Cordova	.20	.09
❑	109 Terry Steinbach	.40	.18
❑	110 Chuck Knoblauch	.75	.35
❑	111 Mark Grudzielanek	.40	.18
❑	112 Mike Lansing	.20	.09
❑	113 Pedro J. Martinez	.75	.35
❑	114 Henry Rodriguez	.40	.18
❑	115 Rondell White	.40	.18
❑	116 Rey Ordonez	.40	.18
❑	117 Carlos Baerga	.40	.18
❑	118 Lance Johnson	.20	.09
❑	119 Bernard Gilkey	.20	.09
❑	120 Todd Hundley	.40	.18
❑	121 John Franco	.40	.18
❑	122 Bernie Williams	.75	.35
❑	123 David Cone	.50	.23
❑	124 Cecil Fielder	.40	.18
❑	125 Derek Jeter	2.50	1.10
❑	126 Tino Martinez	.75	.35
❑	127 Mariano Rivera	.40	.18
❑	128 Andy Pettitte	.50	.23
❑	129 Wade Boggs	.75	.35
❑	130 Mark McGwire	4.00	1.80
❑	131 Jose Canseco	.75	.35
❑	132 Geronimo Berroa	.20	.09
❑	133 Jason Giambi	.40	.18
❑	134 Ernie Young	.20	.09
❑	135 Scott Rolen	2.00	.90
❑	136 Ricky Bottalico	.40	.18
❑	137 Curt Schilling	.40	.18
❑	138 Gregg Jefferies	.20	.09
❑	139 Mickey Morandini	.20	.09
❑	140 Jason Kendall	.50	.23
❑	141 Kevin Elster	.20	.09
❑	142 Al Martin	.20	.09
❑	143 Joe Randa	.20	.09
❑	144 Jason Schmidt	.20	.09
❑	145 Ray Lankford	.40	.18
❑	146 Brian Jordan	.40	.18
❑	147 Andy Benes	.40	.18
❑	148 Alan Benes	.40	.18
❑	149 Gary Gaetti	.20	.09
❑	150 Ron Gant	.20	.09
❑	151 Dennis Eckersley	.40	.18
❑	152 Rickey Henderson	.75	.35
❑	153 Joey Hamilton	.40	.18
❑	154 Ken Caminiti	.50	.23
❑	155 Tony Gwynn	2.00	.90
❑	156 Steve Finley	.40	.18
❑	157 Trevor Hoffman	.40	.18
❑	158 Greg Vaughn	.40	.18
❑	159 J.T. Snow	.40	.18
❑	160 Barry Bonds SP	1.50	.70
❑	161 Glenallen Hill SP	.30	.14
❑	162 Bill VanLandingham SP	.30	.14
❑	163 Jeff Kent SP	.50	.23
❑	164 Jay Buhner SP	.50	.23
❑	165 Ken Griffey Jr. SP	6.00	2.70
❑	166 Alex Rodriguez SP	4.00	1.80
❑	167 Randy Johnson SP	1.25	.55
❑	168 Edgar Martinez SP	.50	.23
❑	169 Dan Wilson SP	.30	.14
❑	170 Ivan Rodriguez SP	1.50	.70
❑	171 Roger Pavlik SP	.30	.14
❑	172 Will Clark SP	1.25	.55
❑	173 Dean Palmer SP	.50	.23
❑	174 Rusty Greer SP	.50	.23
❑	175 Juan Gonzalez SP	3.00	1.35
❑	176 John Wetteland SP	.50	.23
❑	177 Joe Carter SP	.50	.23
❑	178 Ed Sprague SP	.30	.14
❑	179 Carlos Delgado SP	.50	.23
❑	180 Roger Clemens SP	2.50	1.10
❑	181 Juan Guzman	.30	.14
❑	182 Pat Hentgen	.50	.23
❑	183 Ken Griffey Jr. CL	3.00	1.35
❑	184 Hideki Irabu	2.00	.90

1997 SP Game Film

	MINT	NRMT
COMPLETE SET (10)	800.00	350.00
COMMON CARD (GF1-GF10)	40.00	18.00

		MINT	NRMT
❑	GF1 Alex Rodriguez	100.00	45.00
❑	GF2 Frank Thomas	100.00	45.00
❑	GF3 Andruw Jones	40.00	18.00
❑	GF4 Cal Ripken	120.00	55.00
❑	GF5 Mike Piazza	100.00	45.00
❑	GF6 Derek Jeter	80.00	36.00
❑	GF7 Mark McGwire	150.00	70.00
❑	GF8 Chipper Jones	80.00	36.00
❑	GF9 Barry Bonds	40.00	18.00
❑	GF10 Ken Griffey Jr.	150.00	70.00

1997 SP Griffey Heroes

	MINT	NRMT
COMPLETE SET (10)	250.00	110.00
COMMON CARD (91-100)	30.00	13.50
❑ 91 Ken Griffey Jr.	30.00	13.50
❑ 92 Ken Griffey Jr.	30.00	13.50
❑ 93 Ken Griffey Jr.	30.00	13.50
❑ 94 Ken Griffey Jr.	30.00	13.50
❑ 95 Ken Griffey Jr.	30.00	13.50
❑ 96 Ken Griffey Jr.	30.00	13.50
❑ 97 Ken Griffey Jr.	30.00	13.50
❑ 98 Ken Griffey Jr.	30.00	13.50
❑ 99 Ken Griffey Jr.	30.00	13.50
❑ 100 Ken Griffey Jr.	30.00	13.50

1997 SP Inside Info

	MINT	NRMT
COMPLETE SET (25)	300.00	135.00
COMMON CARD (1-25)	3.00	1.35
❑ 1 Ken Griffey Jr.	30.00	13.50
❑ 2 Mark McGwire	30.00	13.50
❑ 3 Kenny Lofton	6.00	2.70
❑ 4 Paul Molitor	6.00	2.70
❑ 5 Frank Thomas	20.00	9.00
❑ 6 Greg Maddux	20.00	9.00
❑ 7 Mo Vaughn	8.00	3.60
❑ 8 Cal Ripken	25.00	11.00
❑ 9 Jeff Bagwell	10.00	4.50
❑ 10 Alex Rodriguez	20.00	9.00
❑ 11 John Smoltz	3.00	1.35
❑ 12 Manny Ramirez	6.00	2.70
❑ 13 Sammy Sosa	15.00	6.75
❑ 14 Vladimir Guerrero	10.00	4.50
❑ 15 Albert Belle	8.00	3.60
❑ 16 Mike Piazza	20.00	9.00
❑ 17 Derek Jeter	15.00	6.75
❑ 18 Scott Rolen	12.00	5.50
❑ 19 Tony Gwynn	15.00	6.75
❑ 20 Barry Bonds	8.00	3.60
❑ 21 Ken Caminiti	4.00	1.80
❑ 22 Chipper Jones	15.00	6.75
❑ 23 Juan Gonzalez	15.00	6.75
❑ 24 Roger Clemens	12.00	5.50
❑ 25 Andruw Jones	8.00	3.60

1997 SP Marquee Matchups

	MINT	NRMT
COMPLETE SET (20)	50.00	22.00
COMMON CARD (MM1-MM20)	1.00	.45
❑ MM1 Ken Griffey Jr.	8.00	3.60
❑ MM2 Andres Galarraga	1.50	.70
❑ MM3 Barry Bonds	2.00	.90
❑ MM4 Mark McGwire	8.00	3.60
❑ MM5 Mike Piazza	5.00	2.20
❑ MM6 Tim Salmon	1.50	.70
❑ MM7 Tony Gwynn	4.00	1.80
❑ MM8 Alex Rodriguez	5.00	2.20
❑ MM9 Chipper Jones	4.00	1.80
❑ MM10 Derek Jeter	5.00	2.20
❑ MM11 Manny Ramirez	1.50	.70
❑ MM12 Jeff Bagwell	2.50	1.10
❑ MM13 Greg Maddux	5.00	2.20
❑ MM14 Cal Ripken	6.00	2.70
❑ MM15 Mo Vaughn	2.00	.90
❑ MM16 Gary Sheffield	1.00	.45
❑ MM17 Jim Thome	1.50	.70
❑ MM18 Barry Larkin	1.00	.45
❑ MM19 Frank Thomas	5.00	2.20
❑ MM20 Sammy Sosa	4.00	1.80

1997 SP Special FX

	MINT	NRMT
COMPLETE SET (48)	300.00	135.00
COMMON CARD (1-47/49)	2.50	1.10
❑ 1 Ken Griffey Jr.	25.00	11.00
❑ 2 Frank Thomas	15.00	6.75
❑ 3 Barry Bonds	6.00	2.70
❑ 4 Albert Belle	6.00	2.70
❑ 5 Mike Piazza	15.00	6.75
❑ 6 Greg Maddux	15.00	6.75
❑ 7 Chipper Jones	12.00	5.50
❑ 8 Cal Ripken	20.00	9.00
❑ 9 Jeff Bagwell	8.00	3.60
❑ 10 Alex Rodriguez	15.00	6.75
❑ 11 Mark McGwire	25.00	11.00
❑ 12 Kenny Lofton	5.00	2.20
❑ 13 Juan Gonzalez	12.00	5.50
❑ 14 Mo Vaughn	6.00	2.70
❑ 15 John Smoltz	2.50	1.10
❑ 16 Derek Jeter	12.00	5.50
❑ 17 Tony Gwynn	12.00	5.50
❑ 18 Ivan Rodriguez	6.00	2.70
❑ 19 Barry Larkin	3.00	1.35
❑ 20 Sammy Sosa	12.00	5.50
❑ 21 Mike Mussina	5.00	2.20
❑ 22 Gary Sheffield	3.00	1.35
❑ 23 Brady Anderson	2.50	1.10
❑ 24 Roger Clemens	10.00	4.50
❑ 25 Ken Caminiti	3.00	1.35
❑ 26 Roberto Alomar	5.00	2.20
❑ 27 Hideo Nomo	6.00	2.70
❑ 28 Bernie Williams	5.00	2.20
❑ 29 Todd Hundley	2.50	1.10
❑ 30 Manny Ramirez	5.00	2.20
❑ 31 Eric Karros	2.50	1.10
❑ 32 Tim Salmon	5.00	2.20
❑ 33 Jay Buhner	2.50	1.10
❑ 34 Andy Pettitte	3.00	1.35
❑ 35 Jim Thome	5.00	2.20
❑ 36 Ryne Sandberg	6.00	2.70
❑ 37 Matt Williams	2.50	1.10
❑ 38 Ryan Klesko	2.50	1.10
❑ 39 Jose Canseco	5.00	2.20
❑ 40 Paul Molitor	5.00	2.20
❑ 41 Eddie Murray	5.00	2.20
❑ 42 Darin Erstad	6.00	2.70
❑ 43 Todd Walker	5.00	2.20
❑ 44 Wade Boggs	5.00	2.20
❑ 45 Andruw Jones	6.00	2.70
❑ 46 Scott Rolen	10.00	4.50
❑ 47 Vladimir Guerrero	8.00	3.60
❑ 49 Alex Rodriguez '96	20.00	9.00

1997 SP SPx Force

	MINT	NRMT
COMPLETE SET (10)	750.00	350.00
COMMON CARD (1-10)	50.00	22.00
❑ 1 Ken Griffey Jr. Jay Buhner Andres Galarraga Dante Bichette	120.00	55.00
❑ 2 Albert Belle Brady Anderson Mark McGwire Cecil Fielder	120.00	55.00
❑ 3 Mo Vaughn Ken Caminiti Frank Thomas Jeff Bagwell	80.00	36.00
❑ 4 Gary Sheffield Sammy Sosa Barry Bonds Jose Canseco	60.00	27.00
❑ 5 Greg Maddux Roger Clemens John Smoltz Randy Johnson	80.00	36.00
❑ 6 Alex Rodriguez Derek Jeter Chipper Jones Rey Ordonez	80.00	36.00
❑ 7 Todd Hollandsworth Mike Piazza Raul Mondesi Hideo Nomo	60.00	27.00
❑ 8 Juan Gonzalez Manny Ramirez Roberto Alomar	60.00	27.00

		MINT	NRMT
	Ivan Rodriguez		
❑ 9	Tony Gwynn	60.00	27.00
	Wade Boggs		
	Eddie Murray		
	Paul Molitor		
❑ 10	Andruw Jones	50.00	22.00
	Vladimir Guerrero		
	Todd Walker		
	Scott Rolen		

1997 SP SPx Force Autographs

	MINT	NRMT
COMPLETE SET (10)	2500.00	1100.00
COMMON CARD (1-10)	80.00	36.00
❑ 1 Ken Griffey Jr. AU	800.00	350.00
❑ 2 Albert Belle AU	150.00	70.00
❑ 3 Mo Vaughn AU EXCH	150.00	70.00
❑ 4 Gary Sheffield AU	100.00	45.00
❑ 5 Greg Maddux AU	400.00	180.00
❑ 6 Alex Rodriguez AU	400.00	180.00
❑ 7 Todd Hollandsworth AU	80.00	36.00
❑ 8 Roberto Alomar AU	150.00	70.00
❑ 9 Tony Gwynn AU	300.00	135.00
❑ 10 Andruw Jones AU	150.00	70.00

1997 SP Vintage Autographs

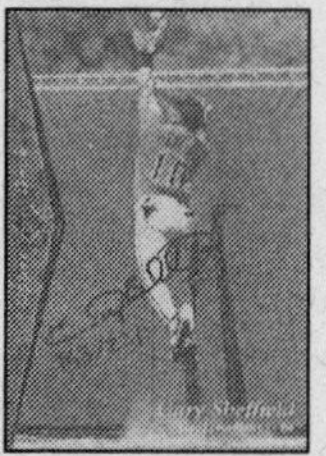

	MINT	NRMT
COMMON CARD (1-31)	25.00	11.00
❑ 1 Jeff Bagwell '93/7		
❑ 2 Jeff Bagwell '95/173	150.00	70.00
❑ 3 Jeff Bagwell '96/292	120.00	55.00
❑ 4 Jeff Bagwell '96 MM/23	400.00	180.00
❑ 5 Jay Buhner '95/57	100.00	45.00
❑ 6 Jay Buhner '96/79	100.00	45.00
❑ 7 Jay Buhner '96 FX/27	150.00	70.00
❑ 8 Ken Griffey Jr. '93/16	2500.00	1100.00
❑ 9 Ken Griffey Jr. '93 PP/5		
❑ 10 Ken Griffey Jr. '94/103	1000.00	450.00
❑ 11 Ken Griffey Jr. '95/38	1500.00	700.00
❑ 12 Ken Griffey Jr. '96/312	500.00	220.00
❑ 13 Tony Gwynn '93/17	800.00	350.00
❑ 14 Tony Gwynn '94/367	200.00	90.00
❑ 15 Tony Gwynn '94 HV/31	500.00	220.00
❑ 16 Tony Gwynn '95/64	400.00	180.00
❑ 17 Tony Gwynn '96/20	600.00	275.00
❑ 18 T. Hollandsworth '94/167	25.00	11.00
❑ 19 Chipper Jones '93/34	500.00	220.00
❑ 20 Chipper Jones '95/60	400.00	180.00
❑ 21 Chipper Jones '96/102	300.00	135.00
❑ 22 R.Ordonez '96/111	30.00	13.50
❑ 23 Rey Ordonez '96 MM/40	50.00	22.00
❑ 24 Alex Rodriguez '94/94	400.00	180.00
❑ 25 Alex Rodriguez '95/63	500.00	220.00
❑ 26 Alex Rodriguez '96/73	500.00	220.00
❑ 27 Gary Sheffield '94/130	80.00	36.00
❑ 28 Gary Sheffield '94 HVDC/4		
❑ 29 Gary Sheffield '95/221	60.00	27.00
❑ 30 Gary Sheffield '96/58	100.00	45.00
❑ 31 Mo Vaughn '97/293	80.00	36.00

1998 SP Authentic

	MINT	NRMT
COMPLETE SET (198)	85.00	38.00
COMMON CARD (1-198)	.25	.11
❑ 1 Travis Lee	2.00	.90
❑ 2 Mike Caruso	.40	.18
❑ 3 Kerry Wood	5.00	2.20
❑ 4 Mark Kotsay	.60	.25
❑ 5 Magglio Ordonez	1.25	.55
❑ 6 Scott Elarton	.40	.18
❑ 7 Carl Pavano	.40	.18
❑ 8 A.J. Hinch	.40	.18
❑ 9 Rolando Arrojo	1.50	.70
❑ 10 Ben Grieve	2.00	.90
❑ 11 Gabe Alvarez	.40	.18
❑ 12 Mike Kinkade	.75	.35
❑ 13 Bruce Chen	.40	.18
❑ 14 Juan Encarnacion	.40	.18
❑ 15 Todd Helton	1.25	.55
❑ 16 Aaron Boone	.25	.11
❑ 17 Sean Casey	.40	.18
❑ 18 Ramon Hernandez	.40	.18
❑ 19 Daryle Ward	.40	.18
❑ 20 Paul Konerko	1.00	.45
❑ 21 David Ortiz	.40	.18
❑ 22 Derrek Lee	.40	.18
❑ 23 Brad Fullmer	.40	.18
❑ 24 Javier Vazquez	.40	.18
❑ 25 Miguel Tejada	.40	.18
❑ 26 Dave Dellucci	1.25	.55
❑ 27 Alex Gonzalez	.40	.18
❑ 28 Matt Clement	.40	.18
❑ 29 Masato Yoshii	.75	.35
❑ 30 Russell Branyan	.40	.18
❑ 31 Chuck Finley	.40	.18
❑ 32 Jim Edmonds	.60	.25
❑ 33 Darin Erstad	1.25	.55
❑ 34 Jason Dickson	.40	.18
❑ 35 Tim Salmon	1.00	.45
❑ 36 Cecil Fielder	.40	.18
❑ 37 Todd Greene	.40	.18
❑ 38 Andy Benes	.40	.18
❑ 39 Jay Bell	.40	.18
❑ 40 Matt Williams	.40	.18
❑ 41 Brian Anderson	.40	.18
❑ 42 Karim Garcia	.40	.18
❑ 43 Javy Lopez	.40	.18
❑ 44 Tom Glavine	1.00	.45
❑ 45 Greg Maddux	3.00	1.35
❑ 46 Andruw Jones	1.25	.55
❑ 47 Chipper Jones	2.50	1.10
❑ 48 Ryan Klesko	.40	.18
❑ 49 John Smoltz	.40	.18
❑ 50 Andres Galarraga	1.00	.45
❑ 51 Rafael Palmeiro	.60	.25
❑ 52 Mike Mussina	1.00	.45
❑ 53 Roberto Alomar	1.00	.45
❑ 54 Joe Carter	.40	.18
❑ 55 Cal Ripken	4.00	1.80
❑ 56 Brady Anderson	.40	.18
❑ 57 Mo Vaughn	1.25	.55
❑ 58 John Valentin	.40	.18
❑ 59 Dennis Eckersley	.40	.18
❑ 60 Nomar Garciaparra	3.00	1.35
❑ 61 Pedro Martinez	1.00	.45
❑ 62 Jeff Blauser	.25	.11
❑ 63 Kevin Orie	.25	.11
❑ 64 Henry Rodriguez	.40	.18
❑ 65 Mark Grace	.60	.25
❑ 66 Albert Belle	1.00	.45
❑ 67 Mike Cameron	.40	.18
❑ 68 Robin Ventura	.40	.18
❑ 69 Frank Thomas	3.00	1.35
❑ 70 Barry Larkin	.60	.25
❑ 71 Brett Tomko	.40	.18
❑ 72 Willie Greene	.40	.18
❑ 73 Reggie Sanders	.40	.18
❑ 74 Sandy Alomar Jr.	.40	.18
❑ 75 Kenny Lofton	1.00	.45
❑ 76 Jaret Wright	1.25	.55
❑ 77 David Justice	1.00	.45
❑ 78 Omar Vizquel	.40	.18
❑ 79 Manny Ramirez	1.00	.45
❑ 80 Jim Thome	1.00	.45
❑ 81 Travis Fryman	.40	.18
❑ 82 Neifi Perez	.40	.18
❑ 83 Mike Lansing	.25	.11
❑ 84 Vinny Castilla	.60	.25
❑ 85 Larry Walker	1.00	.45
❑ 86 Dante Bichette	.40	.18
❑ 87 Darryl Kile	.40	.18
❑ 88 Justin Thompson	.40	.18
❑ 89 Damion Easley	.40	.18
❑ 90 Tony Clark	.60	.25
❑ 91 Bobby Higginson	.60	.25
❑ 92 Brian Hunter	.40	.18
❑ 93 Edgar Renteria	.40	.18
❑ 94 Craig Counsell	.25	.11
❑ 95 Mike Piazza	3.00	1.35
❑ 96 Livan Hernandez	.40	.18
❑ 97 Todd Zeile	.40	.18
❑ 98 Richard Hidalgo	.40	.18
❑ 99 Moises Alou	.60	.25
❑ 100 Jeff Bagwell	1.50	.70
❑ 101 Mike Hampton	.25	.11
❑ 102 Craig Biggio	1.00	.45
❑ 103 Dean Palmer	.40	.18
❑ 104 Tim Belcher	.25	.11
❑ 105 Jeff King	.40	.18
❑ 106 Jeff Conine	.40	.18
❑ 107 Johnny Damon	.40	.18
❑ 108 Hideo Nomo	1.25	.55
❑ 109 Raul Mondesi	.60	.25
❑ 110 Gary Sheffield	.60	.25
❑ 111 Ramon Martinez	.40	.18
❑ 112 Chan Ho Park	1.00	.45
❑ 113 Eric Young	.40	.18
❑ 114 Charles Johnson	.40	.18
❑ 115 Eric Karros	.40	.18
❑ 116 Bobby Bonilla	.40	.18
❑ 117 Jeromy Burnitz	.40	.18
❑ 118 Cal Eldred	.25	.11
❑ 119 Jeff D'Amico	.25	.11
❑ 120 Marquis Grissom	.40	.18
❑ 121 Dave Nilsson	.25	.11
❑ 122 Brad Radke	.40	.18
❑ 123 Marty Cordova	.25	.11
❑ 124 Ron Coomer	.25	.11
❑ 125 Paul Molitor	1.00	.45
❑ 126 Todd Walker	.60	.25
❑ 127 Rondell White	.40	.18
❑ 128 Mark Grudzielanek	.40	.18
❑ 129 Carlos Perez	.40	.18
❑ 130 Vladimir Guerrero	1.50	.70
❑ 131 Dustin Hermanson	.40	.18
❑ 132 Butch Huskey	.25	.11
❑ 133 John Franco	.40	.18
❑ 134 Rey Ordonez	.40	.18
❑ 135 Todd Hundley	.40	.18
❑ 136 Edgardo Alfonzo	.40	.18
❑ 137 Bobby Jones	.25	.11
❑ 138 John Olerud	.40	.18
❑ 139 Chili Davis	.40	.18
❑ 140 Tino Martinez	1.00	.45
❑ 141 Andy Pettitte	.60	.25
❑ 142 Chuck Knoblauch	1.00	.45
❑ 143 Bernie Williams	1.00	.45
❑ 144 David Cone	.60	.25
❑ 145 Derek Jeter	2.50	1.10
❑ 146 Paul O'Neill	.40	.18
❑ 147 Rickey Henderson	1.00	.45

❑ 148	Jason Giambi	.40	.18
❑ 149	Kenny Rogers	.25	.11
❑ 150	Scott Rolen	2.50	1.10
❑ 151	Curt Schilling	.40	.18
❑ 152	Ricky Bottalico	.40	.18
❑ 153	Mike Lieberthal	.25	.11
❑ 154	Francisco Cordova	.25	.11
❑ 155	Jose Guillen	.40	.18
❑ 156	Jason Schmidt	.25	.11
❑ 157	Jason Kendall	.40	.18
❑ 158	Kevin Young	.40	.18
❑ 159	Delino DeShields	.25	.11
❑ 160	Mark McGwire	6.00	2.70
❑ 161	Ray Lankford	.40	.18
❑ 162	Brian Jordan	.40	.18
❑ 163	Ron Gant	.25	.11
❑ 164	Todd Stottlemyre	.40	.18
❑ 165	Ken Caminiti	.60	.25
❑ 166	Kevin Brown	.60	.25
❑ 167	Trevor Hoffman	.40	.18
❑ 168	Steve Finley	.40	.18
❑ 169	Wally Joyner	.40	.18
❑ 170	Tony Gwynn	2.50	1.10
❑ 171	Shawn Estes	.40	.18
❑ 172	J.T. Snow	.40	.18
❑ 173	Jeff Kent	.40	.18
❑ 174	Robb Nen	.40	.18
❑ 175	Barry Bonds	1.25	.55
❑ 176	Randy Johnson	1.00	.45
❑ 177	Edgar Martinez	.40	.18
❑ 178	Jay Buhner	.40	.18
❑ 179	Alex Rodriguez	3.00	1.35
❑ 180	Ken Griffey Jr.	5.00	2.20
❑ 181	Ken Cloude	.40	.18
❑ 182	Wade Boggs	1.00	.45
❑ 183	Tony Saunders	.25	.11
❑ 184	Wilson Alvarez	.40	.18
❑ 185	Fred McGriff	.60	.25
❑ 186	Roberto Hernandez	.25	.11
❑ 187	Kevin Stocker	.25	.11
❑ 188	Fernando Tatis	.40	.18
❑ 189	Will Clark	1.00	.45
❑ 190	Juan Gonzalez	2.50	1.10
❑ 191	Rusty Greer	.40	.18
❑ 192	Ivan Rodriguez	1.25	.55
❑ 193	Jose Canseco	1.00	.45
❑ 194	Carlos Delgado	.40	.18
❑ 195	Roger Clemens	2.00	.90
❑ 196	Pat Hentgen	.40	.18
❑ 197	Randy Myers	.40	.18
❑ 198	Ken Griffey Jr. CL	2.50	1.10
❑ S123	Ken Griffey Jr. Sample	5.00	2.20

1998 SP Authentic Chirography

		MINT	NRMT
COMPLETE SET (30)		2000.00	900.00
COMMON CARD		30.00	13.50
❑ AJ	Andruw Jones	50.00	22.00
❑ AR	Alex Rodriguez SP800	150.00	70.00
❑ BG	Ben Grieve	80.00	36.00
❑ CJ	Charles Johnson	30.00	13.50
❑ CP	Chipper Jones SP800	120.00	55.00
❑ DE	Darin Erstad	50.00	22.00
❑ GS	Gary Sheffield	30.00	13.50
❑ IR	Ivan Rodriguez	60.00	27.00
❑ JC	Jose Cruz Jr.	50.00	22.00
❑ JW	Jaret Wright	50.00	22.00
❑ KG	Ken Griffey Jr. SP400 EXCH	300.00	135.00
❑ LH	Livan Hernandez	30.00	13.50
❑ MK	Mark Kotsay	30.00	13.50
❑ MM	Mike Mussina	50.00	22.00
❑ MT	Miguel Tejada	30.00	13.50
❑ MV	Mo Vaughn SP800	60.00	27.00
❑ NG	Nomar Garciaparra SP400	150.00	70.00
❑ PK	Paul Konerko	30.00	13.50
❑ PM	Paul Molitor SP800	60.00	27.00
❑ RA	Roberto Alomar SP800	60.00	27.00
❑ RB	Russell Branyan	30.00	13.50
❑ RC	Roger Clemens SP400	150.00	70.00
❑ RL	Ray Lankford	30.00	13.50
❑ SC	Sean Casey	30.00	13.50
❑ SR	Scott Rolen	80.00	36.00
❑ TC	Tony Clark	30.00	13.50
❑ TG	Tony Gwynn SP850	120.00	55.00
❑ TH	Todd Helton	50.00	22.00
❑ TL	Travis Lee	80.00	36.00
❑ VG	Vladimir Guerrero	60.00	27.00

1998 SP Authentic Sheer Dominance

		MINT	NRMT
COMPLETE SET (42)		150.00	70.00
COMMON CARD (SD1-SD42)		1.00	.45
❑ SD1	Ken Griffey Jr.	12.00	5.50
❑ SD2	Rickey Henderson	2.50	1.10
❑ SD3	Jaret Wright	2.50	1.10
❑ SD4	Craig Biggio	2.50	1.10
❑ SD5	Travis Lee	4.00	1.80
❑ SD6	Kenny Lofton	2.50	1.10
❑ SD7	Raul Mondesi	1.50	.70
❑ SD8	Cal Ripken	10.00	4.50
❑ SD9	Matt Williams	1.00	.45
❑ SD10	Mark McGwire	15.00	6.75
❑ SD11	Alex Rodriguez	8.00	3.60
❑ SD12	Fred McGriff	1.50	.70
❑ SD13	Scott Rolen	5.00	2.20
❑ SD14	Paul Molitor	2.50	1.10
❑ SD15	Nomar Garciaparra	8.00	3.60
❑ SD16	Vladimir Guerrero	3.00	1.35
❑ SD17	Andruw Jones	2.50	1.10
❑ SD18	Manny Ramirez	2.50	1.10
❑ SD19	Tony Gwynn	6.00	2.70
❑ SD20	Barry Bonds	3.00	1.35
❑ SD21	Ben Grieve	4.00	1.80
❑ SD22	Ivan Rodriguez	3.00	1.35
❑ SD23	Jose Cruz Jr.	2.50	1.10
❑ SD24	Pedro Martinez	2.50	1.10
❑ SD25	Chipper Jones	6.00	2.70
❑ SD26	Albert Belle	2.50	1.10
❑ SD27	Todd Helton	2.50	1.10
❑ SD28	Paul Konerko	2.50	1.10
❑ SD29	Sammy Sosa	6.00	2.70
❑ SD30	Frank Thomas	8.00	3.60
❑ SD31	Greg Maddux	8.00	3.60
❑ SD32	Randy Johnson	2.50	1.10
❑ SD33	Larry Walker	2.50	1.10
❑ SD34	Roberto Alomar	2.50	1.10
❑ SD35	Roger Clemens	5.00	2.20
❑ SD36	Mo Vaughn	3.00	1.35
❑ SD37	Jim Thome	2.50	1.10
❑ SD38	Jeff Bagwell	4.00	1.80
❑ SD39	Tino Martinez	2.50	1.10
❑ SD40	Mike Piazza	8.00	3.60
❑ SD41	Derek Jeter	6.00	2.70
❑ SD42	Juan Gonzalez	6.00	2.70

1998 SP Authentic Trade Cards

		MINT	NRMT
COMMON CARD		40.00	18.00

GRIFFEY GLOVE/JERS.TOO SCARCE TO PRICE

		MINT	NRMT
❑ 1	Roberto Alomar Ball 100	80.00	36.00
❑ 2	Albert Belle Ball 100	80.00	36.00
❑ 3	Jay Buhner Jersey Card 125	100.00	45.00
❑ 4	Ken Griffey Jr. 300 Card 1000 made	40.00	18.00
❑ 5	Ken Griffey Jr. Auto Glove 30		
❑ 6	Ken Griffey Jr. Auto Jersey 30		
❑ 7	Ken Griffey Jr. Jersey Card 125	600.00	275.00
❑ 8	Ken Griffey Jr. Standee 200	80.00	36.00
❑ 9	Tony Gwynn Jersey Card 415	150.00	70.00
❑ 10	Brian Jordan Ball 50	50.00	22.00
❑ 11	Greg Maddux Jersey Card 125	300.00	135.00
❑ 12	Raul Mondesi Ball 100	50.00	22.00
❑ 13	Alex Rodriguez Jersey Card 125	300.00	135.00
❑ 14	Gary Sheffield Jersey Card 125	100.00	45.00
❑ 15	Robin Ventura Ball 50	50.00	22.00

1995 SP Championship

	MINT	NRMT
COMPLETE SET (200)	40.00	18.00
COMMON CARD (1-200)	.20	.09

Card	MINT	NRMT
❑ 1 Hideo Nomo	3.00	1.35
❑ 2 Roger Cedeno	.20	.09
❑ 3 Curtis Goodwin	.20	.09
❑ 4 Jon Nunnally	.20	.09
❑ 5 Bill Pulsipher	.20	.09
❑ 6 Garret Anderson	.40	.18
❑ 7 Dustin Hermanson	.40	.18
❑ 8 Marty Cordova	.20	.09
❑ 9 Ruben Rivera	.40	.18
❑ 10 Ariel Prieto	.20	.09
❑ 11 Edgardo Alfonzo	.40	.18
❑ 12 Ray Durham	.40	.18
❑ 13 Quilvio Veras	.20	.09
❑ 14 Ugueth Urbina	.20	.09
❑ 15 Carlos Perez	.60	.25
❑ 16 Glenn Dishman	.40	.18
❑ 17 Jeff Suppan	.40	.18
❑ 18 Jason Bates	.20	.09
❑ 19 Jason Isringhausen	.40	.18
❑ 20 Derek Jeter	2.50	1.10
❑ 21 Fred McGriff MLP	.20	.09
❑ 22 Marquis Grissom	.40	.18
❑ 23 Fred McGriff	.60	.25
❑ 24 Tom Glavine	.75	.35
❑ 25 Greg Maddux	2.50	1.10
❑ 26 Chipper Jones	2.00	.90
❑ 27 Sammy Sosa MLP	1.00	.45
❑ 28 Randy Myers	.20	.09
❑ 29 Mark Grace	.60	.25
❑ 30 Sammy Sosa	2.00	.90
❑ 31 Todd Zeile	.20	.09
❑ 32 Brian McRae	.20	.09
❑ 33 Ron Gant MLP	.20	.09
❑ 34 Reggie Sanders	.40	.18
❑ 35 Ron Gant	.20	.09
❑ 36 Barry Larkin	.60	.25
❑ 37 Bret Boone	.40	.18
❑ 38 John Smiley	.20	.09
❑ 39 Larry Walker MLP	.40	.18
❑ 40 Andres Galarraga	.75	.35
❑ 41 Bill Swift	.20	.09
❑ 42 Larry Walker	.75	.35
❑ 43 Vinny Castilla	.60	.25
❑ 44 Dante Bichette	.40	.18
❑ 45 Jeff Conine MLP	.20	.09
❑ 46 Charles Johnson	.40	.18
❑ 47 Gary Sheffield	.60	.25
❑ 48 Andre Dawson	.60	.25
❑ 49 Jeff Conine	.40	.18
❑ 50 Jeff Bagwell MLP	.75	.35
❑ 51 Phil Nevin	.20	.09
❑ 52 Craig Biggio	.75	.35
❑ 53 Brian L. Hunter	.40	.18
❑ 54 Doug Drabek	.20	.09
❑ 55 Jeff Bagwell	1.25	.55
❑ 56 Derek Bell	.40	.18
❑ 57 Mike Piazza MLP	1.25	.55
❑ 58 Raul Mondesi	.60	.25
❑ 59 Eric Karros	.40	.18
❑ 60 Mike Piazza	2.50	1.10
❑ 61 Ramon Martinez	.40	.18
❑ 62 Billy Ashley	.20	.09
❑ 63 Rondell White MLP	.20	.09
❑ 64 Jeff Fassero	.20	.09
❑ 65 Moises Alou	.60	.25
❑ 66 Tony Tarasco	.20	.09
❑ 67 Rondell White	.40	.18
❑ 68 Pedro J. Martinez	.75	.35
❑ 69 Bobby Jones MLP	.20	.09
❑ 70 Bobby Bonilla	.40	.18
❑ 71 Bobby Jones	.20	.09
❑ 72 Bret Saberhagen	.40	.18
❑ 73 Darren Daulton MLP	.20	.09
❑ 74 Darren Daulton	.40	.18
❑ 75 Gregg Jefferies	.20	.09
❑ 76 Tyler Green	.20	.09
❑ 77 Heathcliff Slocumb	.20	.09
❑ 78 Lenny Dykstra	.40	.18
❑ 79 Jay Bell MLP	.40	.18
❑ 80 Denny Neagle	.40	.18
❑ 81 Orlando Merced	.20	.09
❑ 82 Jay Bell	.40	.18
❑ 83 Ozzie Smith MLP	.75	.35
❑ 84 Ken Hill	.20	.09
❑ 85 Ozzie Smith	1.00	.45
❑ 86 Bernard Gilkey	.20	.09
❑ 87 Ray Lankford	.40	.18
❑ 88 Tony Gwynn MLP	1.00	.45
❑ 89 Ken Caminiti	.60	.25
❑ 90 Tony Gwynn	2.00	.90
❑ 91 Joey Hamilton	.40	.18
❑ 92 Bip Roberts	.20	.09
❑ 93 Deion Sanders MLP	.20	.09
❑ 94 Glenallen Hill	.20	.09
❑ 95 Matt Williams	.40	.18
❑ 96 Barry Bonds	1.00	.45
❑ 97 Rod Beck	.20	.09
❑ 98 Eddie Murray CL	.40	.18
❑ 99 Cal Ripken Jr. CL	1.50	.70
❑ 100 Roberto Alomar OL	.75	.35
❑ 101 George Brett OL	1.50	.70
❑ 102 Joe Carter OL	.20	.09
❑ 103 Will Clark OL	.40	.18
❑ 104 Dennis Eckersley OL	.20	.09
❑ 105 Whitey Ford OL	.75	.35
❑ 106 Steve Garvey OL	.40	.18
❑ 107 Kirk Gibson OL	.20	.09
❑ 108 Orel Hershiser OL	.20	.09
❑ 109 Reggie Jackson OL	1.00	.45
❑ 110 Paul Molitor OL	.40	.18
❑ 111 Kirby Puckett OL	1.25	.55
❑ 112 Mike Schmidt OL	1.00	.45
❑ 113 Dave Stewart OL	.20	.09
❑ 114 Alan Trammell OL	.40	.18
❑ 115 Cal Ripken Jr. MLP	1.50	.70
❑ 116 Brady Anderson	.40	.18
❑ 117 Mike Mussina	.75	.35
❑ 118 Rafael Palmeiro	.60	.25
❑ 119 Chris Hoiles	.20	.09
❑ 120 Cal Ripken	3.00	1.35
❑ 121 Mo Vaughn MLP	.60	.25
❑ 122 Roger Clemens	1.50	.70
❑ 123 Tim Naehring	.20	.09
❑ 124 John Valentin	.40	.18
❑ 125 Mo Vaughn	1.00	.45
❑ 126 Tim Wakefield	.40	.18
❑ 127 Jose Canseco	.75	.35
❑ 128 Rick Aguilera	.20	.09
❑ 129 Chili Davis MLP	.20	.09
❑ 130 Lee Smith	.40	.18
❑ 131 Jim Edmonds	.60	.25
❑ 132 Chuck Finley	.40	.18
❑ 133 Chili Davis	.40	.18
❑ 134 J.T. Snow	.40	.18
❑ 135 Tim Salmon	.75	.35
❑ 136 Frank Thomas MLP	1.25	.55
❑ 137 Jason Bere	.20	.09
❑ 138 Robin Ventura	.40	.18
❑ 139 Tim Raines	.40	.18
❑ 140 Frank Thomas	2.50	1.10
❑ 141 Alex Fernandez	.20	.09
❑ 142 Eddie Murray MLP	.40	.18
❑ 143 Carlos Baerga	.40	.18
❑ 144 Eddie Murray	.75	.35
❑ 145 Albert Belle	1.00	.45
❑ 146 Jim Thome	.75	.35
❑ 147 Dennis Martinez	.40	.18
❑ 148 Dave Winfield	.75	.35
❑ 149 Kenny Lofton	.75	.35
❑ 150 Manny Ramirez	.75	.35
❑ 151 Cecil Fielder MLP	.20	.09
❑ 152 Lou Whitaker	.40	.18
❑ 153 Alan Trammell	.40	.18
❑ 154 Kirk Gibson	.40	.18
❑ 155 Cecil Fielder	.40	.18
❑ 156 Bobby Higginson	2.00	.90
❑ 157 Kevin Appier MLP	.20	.09
❑ 158 Wally Joyner	.40	.18
❑ 159 Jeff Montgomery	.20	.09
❑ 160 Kevin Appier	.40	.18
❑ 161 Gary Gaetti	.40	.18
❑ 162 Greg Gagne	.20	.09
❑ 163 Ricky Bones MLP	.20	.09
❑ 164 Greg Vaughn	.40	.18
❑ 165 Kevin Seitzer	.20	.09
❑ 166 Ricky Bones	.20	.09
❑ 167 Kirby Puckett MLP	.75	.35
❑ 168 Pedro Munoz	.20	.09
❑ 169 Chuck Knoblauch	.75	.35
❑ 170 Kirby Puckett	1.25	.55
❑ 171 Don Mattingly MLP	.75	.35
❑ 172 Wade Boggs	.75	.35
❑ 173 Paul O'Neill	.40	.18
❑ 174 John Wetteland	.40	.18
❑ 175 Don Mattingly	1.25	.55
❑ 176 Jack McDowell	.20	.09
❑ 177 Mark McGwire MLP	2.00	.90
❑ 178 Rickey Henderson	.75	.35
❑ 179 Terry Steinbach	.40	.18
❑ 180 Ruben Sierra	.20	.09
❑ 181 Mark McGwire	4.00	1.80
❑ 182 Dennis Eckersley	.40	.18
❑ 183 Ken Griffey Jr. MLP	2.00	.90
❑ 184 Alex Rodriguez	3.00	1.35
❑ 185 Ken Griffey Jr.	4.00	1.80
❑ 186 Randy Johnson	.75	.35
❑ 187 Jay Buhner	.40	.18
❑ 188 Edgar Martinez	.40	.18
❑ 189 Will Clark MLP	.40	.18
❑ 190 Juan Gonzalez	2.00	.90
❑ 191 Benji Gil	.20	.09
❑ 192 Ivan Rodriguez	1.00	.45
❑ 193 Kenny Rogers	.20	.09
❑ 194 Will Clark	.75	.35
❑ 195 Paul Molitor MLP	.40	.18
❑ 196 Roberto Alomar	.75	.35
❑ 197 David Cone	.60	.25
❑ 198 Paul Molitor	.75	.35
❑ 199 Shawn Green	.40	.18
❑ 200 Joe Carter	.40	.18
❑ CR1 Cal Ripken, Jr. Tribute	15.00	6.75
❑ CR1 Cal Ripken 2131 DC	50.00	22.00

1995 SP Championship Classic Performances

	MINT	NRMT
COMPLETE SET (10)	40.00	18.00
COMMON CARD (CP1-CP10)	2.00	.90

Card	MINT	NRMT
❑ CP1 Reggie Jackson	5.00	2.20
❑ CP2 Nolan Ryan	15.00	6.75
❑ CP3 Kirk Gibson	2.00	.90
❑ CP4 Joe Carter	2.00	.90
❑ CP5 George Brett	8.00	3.60
❑ CP6 Roberto Alomar	4.00	1.80
❑ CP7 Ozzie Smith	5.00	2.20
❑ CP8 Kirby Puckett	6.00	2.70
❑ CP9 Bret Saberhagen	2.00	.90
❑ CP10 Steve Garvey	2.00	.90

1995 SP Championship Fall Classic

	MINT	NRMT
COMPLETE SET (9)	120.00	55.00
COMMON CARD (1-9)	4.00	1.80
COMP.DIE CUT SET (9)	200.00	90.00

*DIECUTS: .6X TO 1.5X BASIC FALL CLASSIC
DC STATED ODDS 1:75

Card	MINT	NRMT
❑ 1 Ken Griffey Jr.	30.00	13.50
❑ 2 Frank Thomas	20.00	9.00

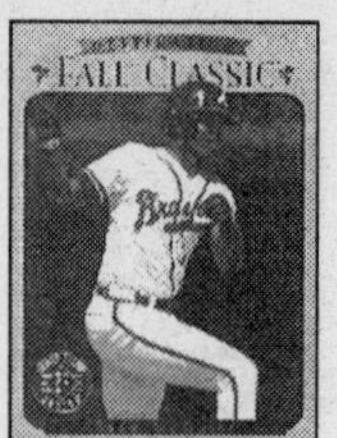

Card	MINT	NRMT
❑ 3 Albert Belle	8.00	3.60
❑ 4 Mike Piazza	20.00	9.00
❑ 5 Don Mattingly	10.00	4.50
❑ 6 Hideo Nomo	12.00	5.50
❑ 7 Greg Maddux	20.00	9.00
❑ 8 Fred McGriff	4.00	1.80
❑ 9 Barry Bonds	8.00	3.60

1994 Sportflics

	MINT	NRMT
COMPLETE SET (193)	25.00	11.00
COMMON CARD (1-193)	.15	.07

Card	MINT	NRMT
❑ 1 Lenny Dykstra	.30	.14
❑ 2 Mike Stanley	.15	.07
❑ 3 Alex Fernandez	.15	.07
❑ 4 Mark McGwire UER (name spelled McGuire on front)	3.00	1.35
❑ 5 Eric Karros	.30	.14
❑ 6 Dave Justice	.60	.25
❑ 7 Jeff Bagwell	1.00	.45
❑ 8 Darren Lewis	.15	.07
❑ 9 David McCarty	.15	.07
❑ 10 Albert Belle	.75	.35
❑ 11 Ben McDonald	.15	.07
❑ 12 Joe Carter	.30	.14
❑ 13 Benito Santiago	.15	.07
❑ 14 Rob Dibble	.15	.07
❑ 15 Roger Clemens	1.25	.55
❑ 16 Travis Fryman	.30	.14
❑ 17 Doug Drabek	.15	.07
❑ 18 Jay Buhner	.30	.14
❑ 19 Orlando Merced	.15	.07
❑ 20 Ryan Klesko	.30	.14
❑ 21 Chuck Finley	.30	.14
❑ 22 Dante Bichette	.30	.14
❑ 23 Wally Joyner	.30	.14
❑ 24 Robin Yount	.60	.25
❑ 25 Tony Gwynn	1.50	.70
❑ 26 Allen Watson	.15	.07
❑ 27 Rick Wilkins	.15	.07
❑ 28 Gary Sheffield	.60	.25
❑ 29 John Burkett	.15	.07
❑ 30 Randy Johnson	.60	.25
❑ 31 Roberto Alomar	.60	.25
❑ 32 Fred McGriff	.40	.18
❑ 33 Ozzie Guillen	.15	.07
❑ 34 Jimmy Key	.30	.14
❑ 35 Juan Gonzalez	1.50	.70
❑ 36 Wil Cordero	.15	.07
❑ 37 Aaron Sele	.30	.14
❑ 38 Mark Langston	.15	.07
❑ 39 David Cone	.40	.18
❑ 40 John Jaha	.15	.07
❑ 41 Ozzie Smith	.75	.35
❑ 42 Kirby Puckett	1.00	.45
❑ 43 Kenny Lofton	.60	.25
❑ 44 Mike Mussina	.60	.25
❑ 45 Ryne Sandberg	.75	.35
❑ 46 Robby Thompson	.15	.07
❑ 47 Bryan Harvey	.15	.07
❑ 48 Marquis Grissom	.30	.14
❑ 49 Bobby Bonilla	.30	.14
❑ 50 Dennis Eckersley	.30	.14
❑ 51 Curt Schilling	.30	.14
❑ 52 Andy Benes	.30	.14
❑ 53 Greg Maddux	2.00	.90
❑ 54 Bill Swift	.15	.07
❑ 55 Andres Galarraga	.60	.25
❑ 56 Tony Phillips	.15	.07
❑ 57 Darryl Hamilton	.15	.07
❑ 58 Duane Ward	.15	.07
❑ 59 Bernie Williams	.60	.25
❑ 60 Steve Avery	.15	.07
❑ 61 Eduardo Perez	.15	.07
❑ 62 Jeff Conine	.30	.14
❑ 63 Dave Winfield	.60	.25
❑ 64 Phil Plantier	.15	.07
❑ 65 Ray Lankford	.30	.14
❑ 66 Robin Ventura	.30	.14
❑ 67 Mike Piazza	2.00	.90
❑ 68 Jason Bere	.15	.07
❑ 69 Cal Ripken	2.50	1.10
❑ 70 Frank Thomas	2.00	.90
❑ 71 Carlos Baerga	.30	.14
❑ 72 Darryl Kile	.30	.14
❑ 73 Ruben Sierra	.15	.07
❑ 74 Gregg Jefferies UER (Name spelled Jeffries on front)	.15	.07
❑ 75 John Olerud	.30	.14
❑ 76 Andy Van Slyke	.30	.14
❑ 77 Larry Walker	.60	.25
❑ 78 Cecil Fielder	.30	.14
❑ 79 Andre Dawson	.40	.18
❑ 80 Tom Glavine	.60	.25
❑ 81 Sammy Sosa	1.50	.70
❑ 82 Charlie Hayes	.15	.07
❑ 83 Chuck Knoblauch	.60	.25
❑ 84 Kevin Appier	.30	.14
❑ 85 Dean Palmer	.30	.14
❑ 86 Royce Clayton	.15	.07
❑ 87 Moises Alou	.40	.18
❑ 88 Ivan Rodriguez	.75	.35
❑ 89 Tim Salmon	.60	.25
❑ 90 Ron Gant	.30	.14
❑ 91 Barry Bonds	.75	.35
❑ 92 Jack McDowell	.15	.07
❑ 93 Alan Trammell	.40	.18
❑ 94 Doc Gooden	.30	.14
❑ 95 Jay Bell	.30	.14
❑ 96 Devon White	.30	.14
❑ 97 Wilson Alvarez	.30	.14
❑ 98 Jim Thome	.75	.35
❑ 99 Ramon Martinez	.30	.14
❑ 100 Kent Hrbek	.30	.14
❑ 101 John Kruk	.30	.14
❑ 102 Wade Boggs	.60	.25
❑ 103 Greg Vaughn	.30	.14
❑ 104 Tom Henke	.15	.07
❑ 105 Brian Jordan	.30	.14
❑ 106 Paul Molitor	.60	.25
❑ 107 Cal Eldred	.15	.07
❑ 108 Deion Sanders	.30	.14
❑ 109 Barry Larkin	.40	.18
❑ 110 Mike Greenwell	.15	.07
❑ 111 Jeff Blauser	.15	.07
❑ 112 Jose Rijo	.15	.07
❑ 113 Pete Harnisch	.15	.07
❑ 114 Chris Hoiles	.15	.07
❑ 115 Edgar Martinez	.30	.14
❑ 116 Juan Guzman	.15	.07
❑ 117 Todd Zeile	.15	.07
❑ 118 Danny Tartabull	.15	.07
❑ 119 Chad Curtis	.15	.07
❑ 120 Mark Grace	.40	.18
❑ 121 J.T. Snow	.30	.14
❑ 122 Mo Vaughn	.75	.35
❑ 123 Lance Johnson	.15	.07
❑ 124 Eric Davis	.30	.14
❑ 125 Orel Hershiser	.30	.14
❑ 126 Kevin Mitchell	.15	.07
❑ 127 Don Mattingly	1.00	.45
❑ 128 Darren Daulton	.30	.14
❑ 129 Rod Beck	.15	.07
❑ 130 Charles Nagy	.30	.14
❑ 131 Mickey Tettleton	.15	.07
❑ 132 Kevin Brown	.30	.14
❑ 133 Pat Hentgen	.30	.14
❑ 134 Terry Mulholland	.15	.07
❑ 135 Steve Finley	.30	.14
❑ 136 John Smoltz	.30	.14
❑ 137 Frank Viola	.15	.07
❑ 138 Jim Abbott	.30	.14
❑ 139 Matt Williams	.40	.18
❑ 140 Bernard Gilkey	.15	.07
❑ 141 Jose Canseco	.60	.25
❑ 142 Mark Whiten	.15	.07
❑ 143 Ken Griffey Jr.	3.00	1.35
❑ 144 Rafael Palmeiro	.40	.18
❑ 145 Dave Hollins	.15	.07
❑ 146 Will Clark	.60	.25
❑ 147 Paul O'Neill	.30	.14
❑ 148 Bobby Jones	.15	.07
❑ 149 Butch Huskey	.30	.14
❑ 150 Jeffrey Hammonds	.30	.14
❑ 151 Manny Ramirez	.75	.35
❑ 152 Bob Hamelin	.15	.07
❑ 153 Kurt Abbott	.15	.07
❑ 154 Scott Stahoviak	.15	.07
❑ 155 Steve Hosey	.15	.07
❑ 156 Salomon Torres	.15	.07
❑ 157 Sterling Hitchcock	.30	.14
❑ 158 Nigel Wilson	.15	.07
❑ 159 Luis Lopez	.15	.07
❑ 160 Chipper Jones	2.00	.90
❑ 161 Norberto Martin	.15	.07
❑ 162 Raul Mondesi	.60	.25
❑ 163 Steve Karsay	.15	.07
❑ 164 J.R. Phillips	.15	.07
❑ 165 Marc Newfield	.15	.07
❑ 166 Mark Hutton	.15	.07
❑ 167 Curtis Pride	.15	.07
❑ 168 Carl Everett	.15	.07
❑ 169 Scott Ruffcorn	.15	.07
❑ 170 Turk Wendell	.15	.07
❑ 171 Jeff McNeely	.15	.07
❑ 172 Javier Lopez	.40	.18
❑ 173 Cliff Floyd	.30	.14
❑ 174 Rondell White	.30	.14
❑ 175 Scott Lydy	.15	.07
❑ 176 Frank Thomas AS	1.00	.45
❑ 177 Roberto Alomar AS	.30	.14
❑ 178 Travis Fryman AS	.15	.07
❑ 179 Cal Ripken AS	1.25	.55
❑ 180 Chris Hoiles AS	.15	.07
❑ 181 Ken Griffey Jr. AS	1.50	.70
❑ 182 Juan Gonzalez AS	.75	.35
❑ 183 Joe Carter AS	.15	.07
❑ 184 Jack McDowell AS	.15	.07
❑ 185 Fred McGriff AS	.15	.07
❑ 186 Robby Thompson AS	.15	.07
❑ 187 Matt Williams AS	.15	.07
❑ 188 Jay Bell AS	.15	.07
❑ 189 Mike Piazza AS	1.00	.45
❑ 190 Barry Bonds AS	.60	.25
❑ 191 Lenny Dykstra AS	.15	.07
❑ 192 Dave Justice AS	.30	.14
❑ 193 Greg Maddux AS	1.00	.45
❑ NNO Cliff Floyd Special	2.00	.90
❑ NNO Paul Molitor Special	8.00	3.60

1994 Sportflics Movers

	MINT	NRMT
COMPLETE SET (12)	50.00	22.00
COMMON CARD (MM1-MM12)	1.00	.45

Card	MINT	NRMT
❑ MM1 Gregg Jefferies	1.00	.45
❑ MM2 Ryne Sandberg	8.00	3.60
❑ MM3 Cecil Fielder	2.00	.90
❑ MM4 Kirby Puckett	8.00	3.60

❑ MM5 Tony Gwynn	12.00	5.50
❑ MM6 Andres Galarraga	5.00	2.20
❑ MM7 Sammy Sosa	10.00	4.50
❑ MM8 Rickey Henderson	5.00	2.20
❑ MM9 Don Mattingly	6.00	2.70
❑ MM10 Joe Carter	2.00	.90
❑ MM11 Carlos Baerga	2.00	.90
❑ MM12 Lenny Dykstra	2.00	.90

1994 Sportflics Shakers

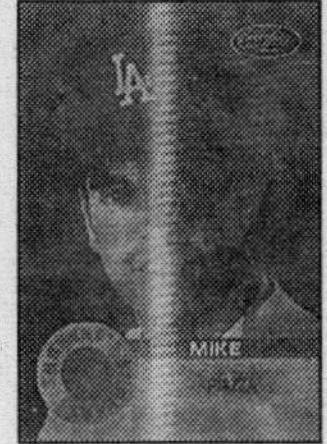

	MINT	NRMT
COMPLETE SET (12)	70.00	32.00
COMMON CARD (SH1-SH12)	1.50	.70
❑ SH1 Kenny Lofton	6.00	2.70
❑ SH2 Tim Salmon	6.00	2.70
❑ SH3 Jeff Bagwell	10.00	4.50
❑ SH4 Jason Bere	1.50	.70
❑ SH5 Salomon Torres	1.50	.70
❑ SH6 Rondell White	2.50	1.10
❑ SH7 Javier Lopez	4.00	1.80
❑ SH8 Dean Palmer	2.50	1.10
❑ SH9 Jim Thome	6.00	2.70
❑ SH10 J.T. Snow	2.50	1.10
❑ SH11 Mike Piazza	20.00	9.00
❑ SH12 Manny Ramirez	8.00	3.60

1994 Sportflics Rookie/Traded

	MINT	NRMT
COMPLETE SET (150)	25.00	11.00
COMMON CARD (1-150)	.25	.11
❑ 1 Will Clark	1.00	.45
❑ 2 Sid Fernandez	.25	.11
❑ 3 Joe Magrane	.25	.11
❑ 4 Pete Smith	.25	.11
❑ 5 Roberto Kelly	.25	.11
❑ 6 Delino DeShields	.25	.11
❑ 7 Brian Harper	.25	.11
❑ 8 Darrin Jackson	.25	.11
❑ 9 Omar Vizquel	.50	.23
❑ 10 Luis Polonia	.25	.11
❑ 11 Reggie Jefferson	.25	.11
❑ 12 Geronimo Berroa	.25	.11
❑ 13 Mike Harkey	.25	.11
❑ 14 Bret Boone	.50	.23
❑ 15 Dave Henderson	.25	.11
❑ 16 Pedro Martinez	1.25	.55
❑ 17 Jose Vizcaino	.25	.11
❑ 18 Xavier Hernandez	.25	.11
❑ 19 Eddie Taubensee	.25	.11
❑ 20 Ellis Burks	.50	.23
❑ 21 Turner Ward	.25	.11
❑ 22 Terry Mulholland	.25	.11
❑ 23 Howard Johnson	.25	.11
❑ 24 Vince Coleman	.25	.11
❑ 25 Deion Sanders	.50	.23
❑ 26 Rafael Palmeiro	.75	.35
❑ 27 Dave Weathers	.25	.11
❑ 28 Kent Mercker	.25	.11
❑ 29 Gregg Olson	.25	.11
❑ 30 Cory Bailey	.25	.11
❑ 31 Brian L.Hunter	.50	.23
❑ 32 Garey Ingram	.25	.11
❑ 33 Daniel Smith	.25	.11
❑ 34 Denny Hocking	.25	.11
❑ 35 Charles Johnson	.50	.23
❑ 36 Otis Nixon	.25	.11
❑ 37 Hector Fajardo	.25	.11
❑ 38 Lee Smith	.50	.23
❑ 39 Phil Stidham	.25	.11
❑ 40 Melvin Nieves	.25	.11
❑ 41 Julio Franco	.25	.11
❑ 42 Greg Gohr	.25	.11
❑ 43 Steve Dunn	.25	.11
❑ 44 Tony Fernandez	.25	.11
❑ 45 Toby Borland	.25	.11
❑ 46 Paul Shuey	.25	.11
❑ 47 Shawn Hare	.25	.11
❑ 48 Shawn Green	.50	.23
❑ 49 Julian Tavarez	.50	.23
❑ 50 Ernie Young	.25	.11
❑ 51 Chris Sabo	.25	.11
❑ 52 Greg O'Halloran	.25	.11
❑ 53 Donnie Elliott	.25	.11
❑ 54 Jim Converse	.25	.11
❑ 55 Ray Holbert	.25	.11
❑ 56 Keith Lockhart	.25	.11
❑ 57 Tony Longmire	.25	.11
❑ 58 Jorge Fabregas	.25	.11
❑ 59 Ravelo Manzanillo	.25	.11
❑ 60 Marcus Moore	.25	.11
❑ 61 Carlos Rodriguez	.25	.11
❑ 62 Mark Portugal	.25	.11
❑ 63 Yorkis Perez	.25	.11
❑ 64 Dan Miceli	.25	.11
❑ 65 Chris Turner	.25	.11
❑ 66 Mike Oquist	.25	.11
❑ 67 Tom Quinlan	.25	.11
❑ 68 Matt Walbeck	.25	.11
❑ 69 Dave Staton	.25	.11
❑ 70 Wm.VanLandingham	.25	.11
❑ 71 Dave Stevens	.25	.11
❑ 72 Domingo Cedeno	.25	.11
❑ 73 Alex Diaz	.25	.11
❑ 74 Darren Bragg	.25	.11
❑ 75 James Hurst	.25	.11
❑ 76 Alex Gonzalez	.25	.11
❑ 77 Steve Dreyer	.25	.11
❑ 78 Robert Eenhoorn	.25	.11
❑ 79 Derek Parks	.25	.11
❑ 80 Jose Valentin	.25	.11
❑ 81 Wes Chamberlain	.25	.11
❑ 82 Tony Tarasco	.25	.11
❑ 83 Steve Traschel	.25	.11
❑ 84 Willie Banks	.25	.11
❑ 85 Rob Butler	.25	.11
❑ 86 Miguel Jimenez	.25	.11
❑ 87 Gerald Williams	.25	.11
❑ 88 Aaron Small	.25	.11
❑ 89 Matt Mieske	.25	.11
❑ 90 Tim Hyers	.25	.11
❑ 91 Eddie Murray	1.00	.45
❑ 92 Dennis Martinez	.50	.23
❑ 93 Tony Eusebio	.25	.11
❑ 94 Brian Anderson	.75	.35
❑ 95 Blaise Ilsley	.25	.11
❑ 96 Johnny Ruffin	.25	.11
❑ 97 Carlos Reyes	.25	.11
❑ 98 Greg Pirkl	.25	.11
❑ 99 Jack Morris	.50	.23
❑ 100 John Mabry	.25	.11
❑ 101 Mike Kelly	.25	.11
❑ 102 Rich Becker	.25	.11
❑ 103 Chris Gomez	.25	.11
❑ 104 Jim Edmonds	1.00	.45
❑ 105 Rich Rowland	.25	.11
❑ 106 Damon Buford	.25	.11
❑ 107 Mark Kiefer	.25	.11
❑ 108 Matias Carrillo	.25	.11
❑ 109 James Mouton	.25	.11
❑ 110 Kelly Stinnett	.25	.11
❑ 111 Billy Ashley	.25	.11
❑ 112 Fausto Cruz	.25	.11
❑ 113 Roberto Petagine	.25	.11
❑ 114 Joe Hall	.25	.11
❑ 115 Brian Johnson	.25	.11
❑ 116 Kevin Jarvis	.25	.11
❑ 117 Tim Davis	.25	.11
❑ 118 John Patterson	.25	.11
❑ 119 Stan Royer	.25	.11
❑ 120 Jeff Juden	.25	.11
❑ 121 Bryan Eversgerd	.25	.11
❑ 122 Chan Ho Park	3.00	1.35
❑ 123 Shane Reynolds	.50	.23
❑ 124 Danny Bautista	.25	.11
❑ 125 Rikkert Faneyte	.25	.11
❑ 126 Carlos Pulido	.25	.11
❑ 127 Mike Matheny	.25	.11
❑ 128 Hector Carrasco	.25	.11
❑ 129 Eddie Zambrano	.25	.11
❑ 130 Lee Tinsley	.25	.11
❑ 131 Roger Salkeld	.25	.11
❑ 132 Carlos Delgado	.75	.35
❑ 133 Troy O'Leary	.50	.23
❑ 134 Keith Mitchell	.25	.11
❑ 135 Lance Painter	.25	.11
❑ 136 Nate Minchey	.25	.11
❑ 137 Eric Anthony	.25	.11
❑ 138 Rafael Bournigal	.25	.11
❑ 139 Joey Hamilton	1.00	.45
❑ 140 Bobby Munoz	.25	.11
❑ 141 Rex Hudler	.25	.11
❑ 142 Alex Cole	.25	.11
❑ 143 Stan Javier	.25	.11
❑ 144 Jose Oliva	.25	.11
❑ 145 Tom Brunansky	.25	.11
❑ 146 Greg Colbrunn	.25	.11
❑ 147 Luis S.Lopez	.25	.11
❑ 148 Alex Rodriguez	15.00	6.75
❑ 149 Darryl Strawberry	.50	.23
❑ 150 Bo Jackson	.50	.23
❑ RO1 R.Klesko ROY M.Ramirez	8.00	3.60

1994 Sportflics Rookie/Traded Artist's Proofs

	MINT	NRMT
COMPLETE SET (150)	2000.00	900.00
COMMON CARD (1-150)	10.00	4.50
SEMISTARS	25.00	11.00
UNLISTED STARS	30.00	13.50

*STARS: 40X TO 80X BASIC CARDS
*YOUNG STARS: 25X TO 50X BASIC CARDS
*ROOKIES: 12X to 20X BASIC CARDS

1994 Sportflics Rookie/Traded Going Going Gone

	MINT	NRMT
COMPLETE SET (12)	90.00	40.00
COMMON CARD (GG1-GG12)	2.00	.90
❑ GG1 Gary Sheffield	5.00	2.20
❑ GG2 Matt Williams	4.00	1.80
❑ GG3 Juan Gonzalez	12.00	5.50
❑ GG4 Ken Griffey Jr.	25.00	11.00
❑ GG5 Mike Piazza	15.00	6.75
❑ GG6 Frank Thomas	15.00	6.75
❑ GG7 Tim Salmon	5.00	2.20
❑ GG8 Barry Bonds	5.00	2.20
❑ GG9 Fred McGriff	4.00	1.80
❑ GG10 Cecil Fielder	2.00	.90
❑ GG11 Albert Belle	6.00	2.70
❑ GG12 Joe Carter	3.00	1.35

1994 Sportflics Rookie/Traded Rookie Starflics

	MINT	NRMT
COMPLETE SET (18)	150.00	70.00
COMMON CARD (TR1-TR18)	5.00	2.20
❑ TR1 John Hudek	5.00	2.20
❑ TR2 Manny Ramirez	25.00	11.00
❑ TR3 Jeffrey Hammonds	8.00	3.60
❑ TR4 Carlos Delgado	12.00	5.50
❑ TR5 Javier Lopez	12.00	5.50
❑ TR6 Alex Gonzalez	5.00	2.20
❑ TR7 Raul Mondesi	15.00	6.75
❑ TR8 Bob Hamelin	5.00	2.20
❑ TR9 Ryan Klesko	10.00	4.50
❑ TR10 Brian Anderson	12.00	5.50
❑ TR11 Alex Rodriguez	80.00	36.00
❑ TR12 Cliff Floyd	8.00	3.60
❑ TR13 Chan Ho Park	25.00	11.00
❑ TR14 Steve Karsay	5.00	2.20
❑ TR15 Rondell White	8.00	3.60
❑ TR16 Shawn Green	8.00	3.60
❑ TR17 Rich Becker	5.00	2.20
❑ TR18 Charles Johnson	8.00	3.60

1995 Sportflix

	MINT	NRMT
COMPLETE SET (170)	20.00	9.00
COMMON CARD (1-170)	.15	.07
❑ 1 Ken Griffey Jr.	3.00	1.35
❑ 2 Jeffrey Hammonds	.30	.14
❑ 3 Fred McGriff	.40	.18
❑ 4 Rickey Henderson	.60	.25
❑ 5 Derrick May	.15	.07
❑ 6 Robin Ventura	.30	.14
❑ 7 Royce Clayton	.15	.07
❑ 8 Paul Molitor	.60	.25
❑ 9 Charlie Hayes	.15	.07
❑ 10 David Nied	.15	.07
❑ 11 Ellis Burks	.30	.14
❑ 12 Bernard Gilkey	.15	.07
❑ 13 Don Mattingly	1.00	.45
❑ 14 Albert Belle	.75	.35
❑ 15 Doug Drabek	.15	.07
❑ 16 Tony Gwynn	1.50	.70
❑ 17 Delino DeShields	.15	.07
❑ 18 Bobby Bonilla	.30	.14
❑ 19 Cliff Floyd	.30	.14
❑ 20 Frank Thomas	2.00	.90
❑ 21 Raul Mondesi	.40	.18
❑ 22 Dave Nilsson	.15	.07
❑ 23 Todd Zeile	.15	.07
❑ 24 Bernie Williams	.60	.25
❑ 25 Kirby Puckett	1.00	.45
❑ 26 David Cone	.40	.18
❑ 27 Darren Daulton	.30	.14
❑ 28 Marquis Grissom	.30	.14
❑ 29 Randy Johnson	.60	.25
❑ 30 Jeff Kent	.30	.14
❑ 31 Orlando Merced	.15	.07
❑ 32 Dave Justice	.60	.25
❑ 33 Ivan Rodriguez	.75	.35
❑ 34 Kirk Gibson	.30	.14
❑ 35 Alex Fernandez	.15	.07
❑ 36 Rick Wilkins	.15	.07
❑ 37 Andy Benes	.30	.14
❑ 38 Bret Saberhagen	.30	.14
❑ 39 Billy Ashley	.15	.07
❑ 40 Jose Rijo	.15	.07
❑ 41 Matt Williams	.30	.14
❑ 42 Lenny Dykstra	.30	.14
❑ 43 Jay Bell	.30	.14
❑ 44 Reggie Jefferson	.15	.07
❑ 45 Greg Maddux	2.00	.90
❑ 46 Gary Sheffield	.40	.18
❑ 47 Bret Boone	.30	.14
❑ 48 Jeff Bagwell	1.00	.45
❑ 49 Ben McDonald	.15	.07
❑ 50 Eric Karros	.30	.14
❑ 51 Roger Clemens	1.25	.55
❑ 52 Sammy Sosa	1.50	.70
❑ 53 Barry Bonds	.75	.35
❑ 54 Joey Hamilton	.30	.14
❑ 55 Brian Jordan	.30	.14
❑ 56 Wil Cordero	.15	.07
❑ 57 Aaron Sele	.30	.14
❑ 58 Paul O'Neill	.30	.14
❑ 59 Carlos Garcia	.15	.07
❑ 60 Mike Mussina	.60	.25
❑ 61 John Olerud	.30	.14
❑ 62 Kevin Appier	.30	.14
❑ 63 Matt Mieske	.15	.07
❑ 64 Carlos Baerga	.30	.14
❑ 65 Ryan Klesko	.30	.14
❑ 66 Jimmy Key	.30	.14
❑ 67 James Mouton	.15	.07
❑ 68 Tim Salmon	.60	.25
❑ 69 Hal Morris	.15	.07
❑ 70 Albie Lopez	.15	.07
❑ 71 Dave Hollins	.15	.07
❑ 72 Greg Colbrunn	.15	.07
❑ 73 Juan Gonzalez	1.50	.70
❑ 74 Wally Joyner	.30	.14
❑ 75 Bob Hamelin	.15	.07
❑ 76 Brady Anderson	.30	.14
❑ 77 Deion Sanders	.30	.14
❑ 78 Javier Lopez	.30	.14
❑ 79 Brian McRae	.15	.07
❑ 80 Craig Biggio	.60	.25
❑ 81 Kenny Lofton	.60	.25
❑ 82 Cecil Fielder	.30	.14
❑ 83 Mike Piazza	2.00	.90
❑ 84 Rafael Palmeiro	.40	.18
❑ 85 Jim Thome	.60	.25
❑ 86 Ruben Sierra	.15	.07
❑ 87 Mark Langston	.15	.07
❑ 88 John Valentin	.30	.14
❑ 89 Shawon Dunston	.15	.07
❑ 90 Travis Fryman	.30	.14
❑ 91 Chuck Knoblauch	.60	.25
❑ 92 Dean Palmer	.30	.14
❑ 93 Robby Thompson	.15	.07
❑ 94 Barry Larkin	.40	.18
❑ 95 Darren Lewis	.15	.07
❑ 96 Andres Galarraga	.60	.25
❑ 97 Tony Phillips	.15	.07
❑ 98 Mo Vaughn	.75	.35
❑ 99 Pedro Martinez	.60	.25
❑ 100 Chad Curtis	.15	.07
❑ 101 Brent Gates	.15	.07
❑ 102 Pat Hentgen	.30	.14
❑ 103 Rico Brogna	.15	.07
❑ 104 Carlos Delgado	.30	.14
❑ 105 Manny Ramirez	.60	.25
❑ 106 Mike Greenwell	.15	.07
❑ 107 Wade Boggs	.60	.25
❑ 108 Ozzie Smith	.75	.35
❑ 109 Rusty Greer	.60	.25
❑ 110 Willie Greene	.30	.14
❑ 111 Chili Davis	.30	.14
❑ 112 Reggie Sanders	.30	.14
❑ 113 Roberto Kelly	.15	.07
❑ 114 Tom Glavine	.60	.25
❑ 115 Moises Alou	.40	.18
❑ 116 Dennis Eckersley	.30	.14
❑ 117 Danny Tartabull	.15	.07
❑ 118 Jeff Conine	.30	.14
❑ 119 Will Clark	.60	.25
❑ 120 Joe Carter	.30	.14
❑ 121 Mark McGwire	3.00	1.35
❑ 122 Cal Ripken Jr.	2.50	1.10
❑ 123 Danny Jackson	.15	.07
❑ 124 Phil Plantier	.15	.07
❑ 125 Dante Bichette	.30	.14
❑ 126 Jack McDowell	.15	.07
❑ 127 Jose Canseco	.60	.25
❑ 128 Roberto Alomar	.60	.25
❑ 129 Rondell White	.30	.14
❑ 130 Ray Lankford	.30	.14
❑ 131 Ryan Thompson	.15	.07
❑ 132 Ken Caminiti	.40	.18
❑ 133 Gregg Jefferies	.15	.07
❑ 134 Omar Vizquel	.30	.14
❑ 135 Mark Grace	.40	.18
❑ 136 Derek Bell	.30	.14
❑ 137 Mickey Tettleton	.15	.07
❑ 138 Wilson Alvarez	.30	.14
❑ 139 Larry Walker	.60	.25
❑ 140 Bo Jackson	.30	.14
❑ 141 Alex Rodriguez	2.50	1.10
❑ 142 Orlando Miller	.15	.07
❑ 143 Shawn Green	.30	.14
❑ 144 Steve Dunn	.15	.07
❑ 145 Midre Cummings	.15	.07
❑ 146 Chan Ho Park	.75	.35
❑ 147 Jose Oliva	.15	.07

		MINT	NRMT
❑ 148	Armando Benitez	.15	.07
❑ 149	J.R. Phillips	.15	.07
❑ 150	Charles Johnson	.30	.14
❑ 151	Garret Anderson	.30	.14
❑ 152	Russ Davis	.30	.14
❑ 153	Brian L.Hunter	.30	.14
❑ 154	Ernie Young	.15	.07
❑ 155	Marc Newfield	.15	.07
❑ 156	Greg Pirkl	.15	.07
❑ 157	Scott Ruffcorn	.15	.07
❑ 158	Rikkert Faneyte	.15	.07
❑ 159	Duane Singleton	.15	.07
❑ 160	Gabe White	.15	.07
❑ 161	Alex Gonzalez	.15	.07
❑ 162	Chipper Jones	1.50	.70
❑ 163	Mike Kelly	.15	.07
❑ 164	Kurt Miller	.15	.07
❑ 165	Roberto Petagine	.15	.07
❑ 166	Jeff Bagwell CL	.60	.25
❑ 167	Mike Piazza CL	1.00	.45
❑ 168	Ken Griffey Jr. CL	1.50	.70
❑ 169	Frank Thomas CL	1.00	.45
❑ 170	Barry Bonds CL Cal Ripken	1.25	.55

1995 Sportflix Detonators

	MINT	NRMT
COMPLETE SET (9)	30.00	13.50
COMMON CARD (1-9)	1.00	.45

		MINT	NRMT
❑ DE1	Jeff Bagwell	3.00	1.35
❑ DE2	Matt Williams	1.25	.55
❑ DE3	Ken Griffey Jr.	10.00	4.50
❑ DE4	Frank Thomas	6.00	2.70
❑ DE5	Mike Piazza	6.00	2.70
❑ DE6	Barry Bonds	2.00	.90
❑ DE7	Albert Belle	2.00	.90
❑ DE8	Cliff Floyd	1.00	.45
❑ DE9	Juan Gonzalez	5.00	2.20

1995 Sportflix Double Take

	MINT	NRMT
COMPLETE SET (12)	120.00	55.00
COMMON CARD (1-12)	4.00	1.80

		MINT	NRMT
❑ 1	Jeff Bagwell Frank Thomas	20.00	9.00
❑ 2	Will Clark Fred McGriff	4.00	1.80
❑ 3	Roberto Alomar Jeff Kent	4.00	1.80
❑ 4	Matt Williams Wade Boggs	4.00	1.80
❑ 5	Cal Ripken Jr. Ozzie Smith	20.00	9.00
❑ 6	Alex Rodriguez Wil Cordero	20.00	9.00
❑ 7	Mike Piazza Carlos Delgado	15.00	6.75
❑ 8	Kenny Lofton Dave Justice	6.00	2.70
❑ 9	Barry Bonds Ken Griffey Jr.	25.00	11.00
❑ 10	Albert Belle Raul Mondesi	6.00	2.70
❑ 11	Tony Gwynn Kirby Puckett	15.00	6.75
❑ 12	Jimmy Key Greg Maddux	12.00	5.50

1995 Sportflix Hammer Team

	MINT	NRMT
COMPLETE SET (18)	25.00	11.00
COMMON CARD (1-18)	.75	.35

		MINT	NRMT
❑ HT1	Ken Griffey Jr.	5.00	2.20
❑ HT2	Frank Thomas	3.00	1.35
❑ HT3	Jeff Bagwell	1.50	.70
❑ HT4	Mike Piazza	3.00	1.35
❑ HT5	Cal Ripken Jr.	4.00	1.80
❑ HT6	Albert Belle	1.00	.45
❑ HT7	Barry Bonds	1.00	.45
❑ HT8	Don Mattingly	1.50	.70
❑ HT9	Will Clark	1.00	.45
❑ HT10	Tony Gwynn	2.50	1.10
❑ HT11	Matt Williams	.75	.35
❑ HT12	Kirby Puckett	1.00	.45
❑ HT13	Manny Ramirez	1.00	.45
❑ HT14	Fred McGriff	.75	.35
❑ HT15	Juan Gonzalez	2.50	1.10
❑ HT16	Kenny Lofton	1.00	.45
❑ HT17	Raul Mondesi	.75	.35
❑ HT18	Tim Salmon	1.00	.45

1995 Sportflix ProMotion

	MINT	NRMT
COMPLETE SET (12)	120.00	55.00
COMMPN CARD (PM1-PM12)	4.00	1.80

		MINT	NRMT
❑ PM1	Ken Griffey Jr.	30.00	13.50
❑ PM2	Frank Thomas	20.00	9.00
❑ PM3	Cal Ripken Jr.	25.00	11.00
❑ PM4	Jeff Bagwell	10.00	4.50
❑ PM5	Mike Piazza	20.00	9.00
❑ PM6	Matt Williams	4.00	1.80
❑ PM7	Albert Belle	10.00	4.50
❑ PM8	Jose Canseco	6.00	2.70
❑ PM9	Don Mattingly	10.00	4.50

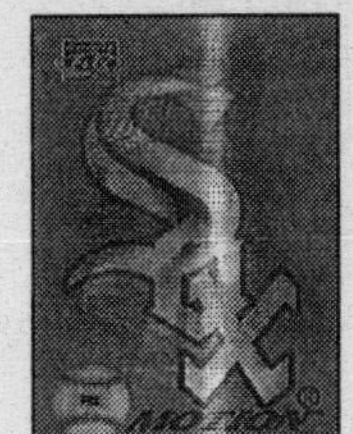

		MINT	NRMT
❑ PM10	Barry Bonds	8.00	3.60
❑ PM11	Will Clark	6.00	2.70
❑ PM12	Kirby Puckett	10.00	4.50

1996 Sportflix

	MINT	NRMT
COMPLETE SET (144)	25.00	11.00
COMMON CARD (1-144)	.15	.07

		MINT	NRMT
❑ 1	Wade Boggs	.60	.25
❑ 2	Tim Salmon	.60	.25
❑ 3	Will Clark	.60	.25
❑ 4	Dante Bichette	.30	.14
❑ 5	Barry Bonds	.75	.35
❑ 6	Kirby Puckett	1.00	.45
❑ 7	Albert Belle	.75	.35
❑ 8	Greg Maddux	2.00	.90
❑ 9	Tony Gwynn	1.50	.70
❑ 10	Mike Piazza	2.00	.90
❑ 11	Ivan Rodriguez	.75	.35
❑ 12	Marty Cordova	.15	.07
❑ 13	Frank Thomas	2.00	.90
❑ 14	Raul Mondesi	.40	.18
❑ 15	Johnny Damon	.30	.14
❑ 16	Mark McGwire	3.00	1.35
❑ 17	Len Dykstra	.30	.14
❑ 18	Ken Griffey Jr.	3.00	1.35
❑ 19	Chipper Jones	1.50	.70
❑ 20	Alex Rodriguez	2.00	.90
❑ 21	Jeff Bagwell	1.00	.45
❑ 22	Jim Edmonds	.40	.18
❑ 23	Edgar Martinez	.30	.14
❑ 24	David Cone	.40	.18
❑ 25	Tom Glavine	.60	.25
❑ 26	Eddie Murray	.60	.25
❑ 27	Paul Molitor	.60	.25
❑ 28	Ryan Klesko	.30	.14
❑ 29	Rafael Palmeiro	.40	.18
❑ 30	Manny Ramirez	.60	.25
❑ 31	Mo Vaughn	.75	.35
❑ 32	Rico Brogna	.15	.07
❑ 33	Marc Newfield	.15	.07
❑ 34	J.T. Snow	.30	.14
❑ 35	Reggie Sanders	.30	.14
❑ 36	Fred McGriff	.40	.18
❑ 37	Craig Biggio	.60	.25
❑ 38	Jeff King	.15	.07
❑ 39	Kenny Lofton	.60	.25
❑ 40	Gary Gaetti	.30	.14
❑ 41	Eric Karros	.30	.14

❑ 42	Jason Isringhausen	.15	.07
❑ 43	B.J. Surhoff	.30	.14
❑ 44	Michael Tucker	.30	.14
❑ 45	Gary Sheffield	.40	.18
❑ 46	Chili Davis	.30	.14
❑ 47	Bobby Bonilla	.30	.14
❑ 48	Hideo Nomo	1.00	.45
❑ 49	Ray Durham	.30	.14
❑ 50	Phil Nevin	.15	.07
❑ 51	Randy Johnson	.60	.25
❑ 52	Bill Pulsipher	.15	.07
❑ 53	Ozzie Smith	.75	.35
❑ 54	Cal Ripken	2.50	1.10
❑ 55	Cecil Fielder	.30	.14
❑ 56	Matt Williams	.30	.14
❑ 57	Sammy Sosa	1.50	.70
❑ 58	Roger Clemens	1.25	.55
❑ 59	Brian L.Hunter	.30	.14
❑ 60	Barry Larkin	.40	.18
❑ 61	Charles Johnson	.30	.14
❑ 62	David Justice	.60	.25
❑ 63	Garret Anderson	.30	.14
❑ 64	Rondell White	.30	.14
❑ 65	Derek Bell	.30	.14
❑ 66	Andres Galarraga	.60	.25
❑ 67	Moises Alou	.40	.18
❑ 68	Travis Fryman	.30	.14
❑ 69	Pedro J. Martinez	.60	.25
❑ 70	Carlos Baerga	.30	.14
❑ 71	John Valentin	.30	.14
❑ 72	Larry Walker	.60	.25
❑ 73	Roberto Alomar	.60	.25
❑ 74	Mike Mussina	.60	.25
❑ 75	Kevin Appier	.30	.14
❑ 76	Bernie Williams	.60	.25
❑ 77	Ray Lankford	.30	.14
❑ 78	Gregg Jefferies	.15	.07
❑ 79	Robin Ventura	.30	.14
❑ 80	Kenny Rogers	.15	.07
❑ 81	Paul O'Neill	.30	.14
❑ 82	Mark Grace	.40	.18
❑ 83	Deion Sanders	.30	.14
❑ 84	Tino Martinez	.60	.25
❑ 85	Joe Carter	.30	.14
❑ 86	Pete Schourek	.15	.07
❑ 87	Jack McDowell	.15	.07
❑ 88	John Mabry	.15	.07
❑ 89	Darren Daulton	.30	.14
❑ 90	Jim Thome	.60	.25
❑ 91	Jay Buhner	.30	.14
❑ 92	Jay Bell	.30	.14
❑ 93	Kevin Seitzer	.15	.07
❑ 94	Jose Canseco	.60	.25
❑ 95	Juan Gonzalez	1.50	.70
❑ 96	Jeff Conine	.30	.14
❑ 97	Chipper Jones UC3	.75	.35
❑ 98	Ken Griffey Jr. UC3	1.50	.70
❑ 99	Frank Thomas UC3	1.00	.45
❑ 100	Cal Ripken UC3	1.25	.55
❑ 101	Albert Belle UC3	.40	.18
❑ 102	Mike Piazza UC3	1.00	.45
❑ 103	Dante Bichette UC3	.15	.07
❑ 104	Sammy Sosa UC3	.75	.35
❑ 105	Mo Vaughn UC3	.40	.18
❑ 106	Tim Salmon UC3	.30	.14
❑ 107	Reggie Sanders UC3	.15	.07
❑ 108	Gary Sheffield UC3	.15	.07
❑ 109	Ruben Rivera UC3	.15	.07
❑ 110	Rafael Palmeiro UC3	.15	.07
❑ 111	Edgar Martinez UC3	.15	.07
❑ 112	Barry Bonds UC3	.40	.18
❑ 113	Manny Ramirez UC3	.30	.14
❑ 114	Larry Walker UC3	.30	.14
❑ 115	Jeff Bagwell UC3	.60	.25
❑ 116	Matt Williams UC3	.15	.07
❑ 117	Mark McGwire UC3	1.50	.70
❑ 118	Johnny Damon UC3	.15	.07
❑ 119	Eddie Murray UC3	.30	.14
❑ 120	Jay Buhner UC3	.15	.07
❑ 121	Tim Unroe	.15	.07
❑ 122	Todd Hollandsworth	.15	.07
❑ 123	Tony Clark	.60	.25
❑ 124	Roger Cedeno	.15	.07
❑ 125	Jim Pittsley	.15	.07
❑ 126	Ruben Rivera	.30	.14
❑ 127	Bob Wolcott	.15	.07
❑ 128	Chan Ho Park	.60	.25
❑ 129	Chris Snopek	.15	.07
❑ 130	Alex Ochoa	.15	.07
❑ 131	Yamil Benitez	.15	.07
❑ 132	Jimmy Haynes	.15	.07
❑ 133	Dustin Hermanson	.30	.14
❑ 134	Shawn Estes	.40	.18
❑ 135	Howard Battle	.15	.07
❑ 136	Matt Lawton	.60	.25
❑ 137	Terrell Wade	.15	.07
❑ 138	Jason Schmidt	.15	.07
❑ 139	Derek Jeter	2.00	.90
❑ 140	Shannon Stewart	.30	.14
❑ 141	Chris Stynes	.15	.07
❑ 142	Ken Griffey Jr. CL	1.50	.70
❑ 143	Greg Maddux CL	1.00	.45
❑ 144	Cal Ripken CL	1.25	.55

1996 Sportflix Double Take

		MINT	NRMT
COMPLETE SET (12)		120.00	55.00
COMMON CARD (1-12)		5.00	2.20
❑ 1	Barry Larkin Cal Ripken	15.00	6.75
❑ 2	Roberto Alomar Craig Biggio	5.00	2.20
❑ 3	Chipper Jones Matt Williams	10.00	4.50
❑ 4	Ken Griffey Ruben Rivera	20.00	9.00
❑ 5	Greg Maddux Hideo Nomo	12.00	5.50
❑ 6	Frank Thomas Mo Vaughn	12.00	5.50
❑ 7	Ivan Rodriguez Mike Piazza	12.00	5.50
❑ 8	Albert Belle Barry Bonds	5.00	2.20
❑ 9	Alex Rodriguez Derek Jeter	20.00	9.00
❑ 10	Kirby Puckett Tony Gwynn	12.00	5.50
❑ 11	Sammy Sosa Manny Ramirez	10.00	4.50
❑ 12	Jeff Bagwell Rico Brogna	6.00	2.70

1996 Sportflix Hit Parade

		MINT	NRMT
COMPLETE SET (16)		100.00	45.00
COMMON CARD (1-16)		2.50	1.10
❑ 1	Ken Griffey Jr.	20.00	9.00
❑ 2	Cal Ripken	15.00	6.75
❑ 3	Frank Thomas	12.00	5.50
❑ 4	Mike Piazza	12.00	5.50
❑ 5	Mo Vaughn	5.00	2.20
❑ 6	Albert Belle	5.00	2.20
❑ 7	Jeff Bagwell	8.00	3.60
❑ 8	Matt Williams	2.50	1.10
❑ 9	Sammy Sosa	10.00	4.50

❑ 10	Kirby Puckett	8.00	3.60
❑ 11	Dante Bichette	2.50	1.10
❑ 12	Gary Sheffield	3.00	1.35
❑ 13	Tony Gwynn	10.00	4.50
❑ 14	Wade Boggs	4.00	1.80
❑ 15	Chipper Jones	10.00	4.50
❑ 16	Barry Bonds	5.00	2.20

1996 Sportflix Power Surge

		MINT	NRMT
COMPLETE SET (24)		150.00	70.00
COMMON CARD (1-24)		1.50	.70
❑ 1	Chipper Jones	15.00	6.75
❑ 2	Ken Griffey Jr.	30.00	13.50
❑ 3	Frank Thomas	20.00	9.00
❑ 4	Cal Ripken	25.00	11.00
❑ 5	Albert Belle	10.00	4.50
❑ 6	Mike Piazza	20.00	9.00
❑ 7	Dante Bichette	2.50	1.10
❑ 8	Sammy Sosa	15.00	6.75
❑ 9	Mo Vaughn	8.00	3.60
❑ 10	Tim Salmon	6.00	2.70
❑ 11	Reggie Sanders	2.50	1.10
❑ 12	Gary Sheffield	4.00	1.80
❑ 13	Ruben Rivera	1.50	.70
❑ 14	Rafael Palmeiro	4.00	1.80
❑ 15	Edgar Martinez	2.50	1.10
❑ 16	Barry Bonds	8.00	3.60
❑ 17	Manny Ramirez	6.00	2.70
❑ 18	Larry Walker	6.00	2.70
❑ 19	Jeff Bagwell	10.00	4.50
❑ 20	Matt Williams	2.50	1.10
❑ 21	Mark McGwire	30.00	13.50
❑ 22	Johnny Damon	1.50	.70
❑ 23	Eddie Murray	6.00	2.70
❑ 24	Jay Buhner	2.50	1.10

1996 Sportflix ProMotion

		MINT	NRMT
COMPLETE SET (20)		80.00	36.00
COMMON CARD (1-20)		1.00	.45
❑ 1	Cal Ripken	12.00	5.50
❑ 2	Greg Maddux	10.00	4.50

No.	Player	MINT	NRMT
❑ 3	Mo Vaughn	3.00	1.35
❑ 4	Albert Belle	3.00	1.35
❑ 5	Mike Piazza	10.00	4.50
❑ 6	Ken Griffey Jr.	15.00	6.75
❑ 7	Frank Thomas	10.00	4.50
❑ 8	Jeff Bagwell	5.00	2.20
❑ 9	Hideo Nomo	5.00	2.20
❑ 10	Chipper Jones	8.00	3.60
❑ 11	Tony Gwynn	8.00	3.60
❑ 12	Don Mattingly	5.00	2.20
❑ 13	Dante Bichette	1.50	.70
❑ 14	Matt Williams	1.50	.70
❑ 15	Manny Ramirez	3.00	1.35
❑ 16	Barry Bonds	3.00	1.35
❑ 17	Reggie Sanders	1.00	.45
❑ 18	Tim Salmon	3.00	1.35
❑ 19	Ruben Rivera	1.50	.70
❑ 20	Garret Anderson	1.50	.70

1997 Sports Illustrated

	MINT	NRMT
COMPLETE SET (180)	40.00	18.00
COMMON CARD (1-180)	.15	.07

No.	Player	MINT	NRMT
❑ 1	Bob Abreu	.30	.14
❑ 2	Jaime Bluma	.15	.07
❑ 3	Emil Brown	.40	.18
❑ 4	Jose Cruz Jr.	2.50	1.10
❑ 5	Jason Dickson	.30	.14
❑ 6	Nomar Garciaparra	2.00	.90
❑ 7	Todd Greene	.30	.14
❑ 8	Vladimir Guerrero	1.25	.55
❑ 9	Wilton Guerrero	.15	.07
❑ 10	Jose Guillen	.60	.25
❑ 11	Hideki Irabu	1.50	.70
❑ 12	Russ Johnson	.15	.07
❑ 13	Andruw Jones	1.00	.45
❑ 14	Damon Mashore	.15	.07
❑ 15	Jason McDonald	.15	.07
❑ 16	Ryan McGuire	.15	.07
❑ 17	Matt Morris	.30	.14
❑ 18	Kevin Orie	.15	.07
❑ 19	Dante Powell	.30	.14
❑ 20	Pokey Reese	.15	.07
❑ 21	Joe Roa	.15	.07
❑ 22	Scott Rolen	1.50	.70
❑ 23	Glendon Rusch	.15	.07
❑ 24	Scott Spiezio	.15	.07
❑ 25	Bubba Trammell	.40	.18
❑ 26	Todd Walker	.60	.25
❑ 27	Jamey Wright	.15	.07
❑ 28	Ken Griffey Jr. SH	1.50	.70
❑ 29	Tino Martinez SH	.30	.14
❑ 30	Roger Clemens SH	.60	.25
❑ 31	Hideki Irabu SH	.60	.25
❑ 32	Kevin Brown SH	.15	.07
❑ 33	Chipper Jones SH Cal Ripken	1.50	.70
❑ 34	Sandy Alomar SH	.15	.07
❑ 35	Ken Caminiti SH	.15	.07
❑ 36	Randy Johnson SH	.30	.14
❑ 37	Andy Ashby IB	.15	.07
❑ 38	Jay Buhner IB	.15	.07
❑ 39	Joe Carter IB	.15	.07
❑ 40	Darren Daulton IB	.15	.07
❑ 41	Jeff Fassero IB	.15	.07
❑ 42	Andres Galarraga IB	.30	.14
❑ 43	Rusty Greer IB	.15	.07
❑ 44	Marquis Grissom IB	.15	.07
❑ 45	Joey Hamilton IB	.15	.07
❑ 46	Jimmy Key IB	.15	.07
❑ 47	Ryan Klesko IB	.15	.07
❑ 48	Eddie Murray IB	.30	.14
❑ 49	Charles Nagy IB	.15	.07
❑ 50	Dave Nilsson IB	.15	.07
❑ 51	Ricardo Rincon IB	.15	.07
❑ 52	Billy Wagner IB	.15	.07
❑ 53	Dan Wilson IB	.15	.07
❑ 54	Dmitri Young IB	.15	.07
❑ 55	Roberto Alomar SIV	.30	.14
❑ 56	Sandy Alomar Jr. SIV	.15	.07
❑ 57	Scott Brosius SIV	.15	.07
❑ 58	Tony Clark SIV	.15	.07
❑ 59	Carlos Delgado SIV	.15	.07
❑ 60	Jermaine Dye SIV	.15	.07
❑ 61	Darin Erstad SIV	.60	.25
❑ 62	Derek Jeter SIV	1.00	.45
❑ 63	Jason Kendall SIV	.15	.07
❑ 64	Hideo Nomo SIV	.60	.25
❑ 65	Rey Ordonez SIV	.15	.07
❑ 66	Andy Pettitte SIV	.15	.07
❑ 67	Manny Ramirez SIV	.30	.14
❑ 68	Edgar Renteria SIV	.15	.07
❑ 69	Shane Reynolds SIV	.15	.07
❑ 70	Alex Rodriguez SIV	1.00	.45
❑ 71	Ivan Rodriguez SIV	.40	.18
❑ 72	Jose Rosado SIV	.15	.07
❑ 73	John Smoltz	.30	.14
❑ 74	Tom Glavine	.60	.25
❑ 75	Greg Maddux	2.00	.90
❑ 76	Chipper Jones	1.50	.70
❑ 77	Kenny Lofton	.60	.25
❑ 78	Fred McGriff	.40	.18
❑ 79	Kevin Brown	.40	.18
❑ 80	Alex Fernandez	.15	.07
❑ 81	Al Leiter	.30	.14
❑ 82	Bobby Bonilla	.30	.14
❑ 83	Gary Sheffield	.40	.18
❑ 84	Moises Alou	.40	.18
❑ 85	Henry Rodriguez	.30	.14
❑ 86	Mark Grudzielanek	.30	.14
❑ 87	Pedro Martinez	.60	.25
❑ 88	Todd Hundley	.30	.14
❑ 89	Bernard Gilkey	.15	.07
❑ 90	Bobby Jones	.15	.07
❑ 91	Curt Schilling	.30	.14
❑ 92	Ricky Bottalico	.30	.14
❑ 93	Mike Lieberthal	.15	.07
❑ 94	Sammy Sosa	1.50	.70
❑ 95	Ryne Sandberg	.75	.35
❑ 96	Mark Grace	.40	.18
❑ 97	Deion Sanders	.30	.14
❑ 98	Reggie Sanders	.30	.14
❑ 99	Barry Larkin	.40	.18
❑ 100	Craig Biggio	.60	.25
❑ 101	Jeff Bagwell	1.00	.45
❑ 102	Derek Bell	.30	.14
❑ 103	Brian Jordan	.30	.14
❑ 104	Ray Lankford	.30	.14
❑ 105	Ron Gant	.15	.07
❑ 106	Al Martin	.15	.07
❑ 107	Kevin Elster	.15	.07
❑ 108	Jermaine Allensworth	.15	.07
❑ 109	Vinny Castilla	.40	.18
❑ 110	Dante Bichette	.30	.14
❑ 111	Larry Walker	.60	.25
❑ 112	Mike Piazza	2.00	.90
❑ 113	Eric Karros	.30	.14
❑ 114	Todd Hollandsworth	.15	.07
❑ 115	Raul Mondesi	.40	.18
❑ 116	Hideo Nomo	.75	.35
❑ 117	Ramon Martinez	.30	.14
❑ 118	Ken Caminiti	.40	.18
❑ 119	Tony Gwynn	1.50	.70
❑ 120	Steve Finley	.30	.14
❑ 121	Barry Bonds	.75	.35
❑ 122	J.T. Snow	.30	.14
❑ 123	Rod Beck	.15	.07
❑ 124	Cal Ripken	2.50	1.10
❑ 125	Mike Mussina	.60	.25
❑ 126	Brady Anderson	.30	.14
❑ 127	Bernie Williams	.60	.25
❑ 128	Derek Jeter	2.00	.90
❑ 129	Tino Martinez	.60	.25
❑ 130	Andy Pettitte	.40	.18
❑ 131	David Cone	.40	.18
❑ 132	Mariano Rivera	.30	.14
❑ 133	Roger Clemens	1.25	.55
❑ 134	Pat Hentgen	.30	.14
❑ 135	Juan Guzman	.15	.07
❑ 136	Bob Higginson	.40	.18
❑ 137	Tony Clark	.40	.18
❑ 138	Travis Fryman	.30	.14
❑ 139	Mo Vaughn	.75	.35
❑ 140	Tim Naehring	.15	.07
❑ 141	John Valentin	.30	.14
❑ 142	Matt Williams	.30	.14
❑ 143	David Justice	.60	.25
❑ 144	Jim Thome	.60	.25
❑ 145	Chuck Knoblauch	.60	.25
❑ 146	Paul Molitor	.60	.25
❑ 147	Marty Cordova	.15	.07
❑ 148	Frank Thomas	2.00	.90
❑ 149	Albert Belle	.75	.35
❑ 150	Robin Ventura	.30	.14
❑ 151	John Jaha	.15	.07
❑ 152	Jeff Cirillo	.30	.14
❑ 153	Jose Valentin	.15	.07
❑ 154	Jay Bell	.30	.14
❑ 155	Jeff King	.15	.07
❑ 156	Kevin Appier	.30	.14
❑ 157	Ken Griffey Jr.	3.00	1.35
❑ 158	Alex Rodriguez	2.00	.90
❑ 159	Randy Johnson	.60	.25
❑ 160	Juan Gonzalez	1.50	.70
❑ 161	Will Clark	.60	.25
❑ 162	Dean Palmer	.30	.14
❑ 163	Tim Salmon	.60	.25
❑ 164	Jim Edmonds	.40	.18
❑ 165	Jim Leyritz	.15	.07
❑ 166	Jose Canseco	.60	.25
❑ 167	Jason Giambi	.30	.14
❑ 168	Mark McGwire	3.00	1.35
❑ 169	Barry Bonds CC	.30	.14
❑ 170	Alex Rodriguez CC	1.00	.45
❑ 171	Roger Clemens CC	.60	.25
❑ 172	Ken Griffey Jr. CC	1.50	.70
❑ 173	Greg Maddux CC	1.00	.45
❑ 174	Mike Piazza CC	1.00	.45
❑ 175	Will Clark CC Mark McGwire	1.50	.70
❑ 176	Hideo Nomo CC	.60	.25
❑ 177	Cal Ripken CC	1.25	.55
❑ 178	Ken Griffey Jr. CC Frank Thomas	2.00	.90
❑ 179	Alex Rodriguez CC Derek Jeter	1.25	.55
❑ 180	John Wetteland CC	.15	.07
❑ P158	Alex Rodriguez Promo	1.00	.45
❑ NNO	Jose Cruz Jr. CL	.50	.23

1997 Sports Illustrated Extra Edition

	MINT	NRMT
COMPLETE SET (180)	2500.00	1100.00
COMMON CARD (1-180)	5.00	2.20
MINOR STARS	8.00	3.60
SEMISTARS	12.00	5.50
UNLISTED STARS	20.00	9.00

*STARS: 15X TO 30X BASIC CARDS
*YOUNG STARS: 12.5X TO 25X BASIC CARDS
*ROOKIES: 7.5X TO 15X BASIC CARDS

1997 Sports Illustrated Autographed Mini-Covers

	MINT	NRMT
COMPLETE SET (6)	1000.00	450.00
COMMON CARD (1-6)	80.00	36.00

	MINT	NRMT
❑ 1 Alex Rodriguez	250.00	110.00
❑ 2 Cal Ripken	300.00	135.00
❑ 3 Kirby Puckett	120.00	55.00
❑ 4 Willie Mays	200.00	90.00
❑ 5 Frank Robinson	80.00	36.00
❑ 6 Hank Aaron	150.00	70.00

1997 Sports Illustrated Cooperstown Collection

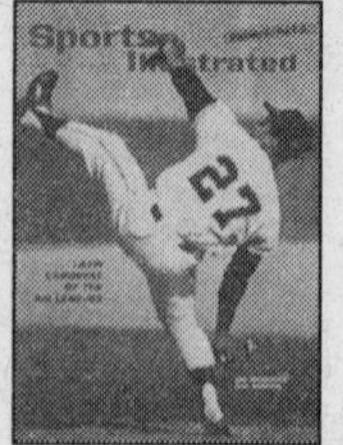

	MINT	NRMT
COMPLETE SET (12)	60.00	27.00
COMMON CARD (1-12)	5.00	2.20

	MINT	NRMT
❑ 1 Hank Aaron	10.00	4.50
❑ 2 Yogi Berra	6.00	2.70
❑ 3 Lou Brock	5.00	2.20
❑ 4 Rod Carew	5.00	2.20
❑ 5 Juan Marichal	5.00	2.20
❑ 6 Al Kaline	6.00	2.70
❑ 7 Joe Morgan	5.00	2.20
❑ 8 Brooks Robinson	5.00	2.20
❑ 9 Willie Stargell	5.00	2.20
❑ 10 Kirby Puckett	8.00	3.60
❑ 11 Willie Mays	12.00	5.50
❑ 12 Frank Robinson	5.00	2.20

1997 Sports Illustrated Great Shots

	MINT	NRMT
COMPLETE SET (25)	8.00	3.60
COMMON CARD (1-25)	.20	.09

	MINT	NRMT
❑ 1 Chipper Jones	1.00	.45
❑ 2 Ryan Klesko	.20	.09
❑ 3 Kenny Lofton	.40	.18
❑ 4 Greg Maddux	1.25	.55
❑ 5 John Smoltz	.20	.09
❑ 6 Roberto Alomar	.40	.18
❑ 7 Cal Ripken	1.50	.70
❑ 8 Mo Vaughn	.50	.23
❑ 9 Albert Belle	.40	.18
❑ 10 Frank Thomas	1.25	.55
❑ 11 Ryne Sandberg	.50	.23
❑ 12 Deion Sanders	.20	.09
❑ 13 Vinny Castilla Andres Galarraga	.30	.14
❑ 14 Eric Karros	.20	.09
❑ 15 Mike Piazza	1.25	.55
❑ 16 Derek Jeter	1.50	.70
❑ 17 Mark McGwire	2.00	.90
❑ 18 Darren Daulton	.20	.09
❑ 19 Andy Ashby	.20	.09
❑ 20 Barry Bonds	.50	.23
❑ 21 Jay Buhner	.20	.09
❑ 22 Randy Johnson	.40	.18
❑ 23 Alex Rodriguez	1.25	.55
❑ 24 Juan Gonzalez	1.00	.45
❑ 25 Ken Griffey Jr.	2.00	.90

1998 Sports Illustrated

	MINT	NRMT
COMPLETE SET (200)	40.00	18.00
COMMON CARD (1-200)	.15	.07

COMPLETE SET DOES NOT INCLUDE SP #201

	MINT	NRMT
❑ 1 Edgardo Alfonzo	.25	.11
❑ 2 Roberto Alomar	.60	.25
❑ 3 Sandy Alomar	.25	.11
❑ 4 Moises Alou	.40	.18
❑ 5 Brady Anderson	.25	.11
❑ 6 Garret Anderson	.25	.11
❑ 7 Kevin Appier	.25	.11
❑ 8 Jeff Bagwell	1.00	.45
❑ 9 Jay Bell	.25	.11
❑ 10 Albert Belle	.75	.35
❑ 11 Dante Bichette	.25	.11
❑ 12 Craig Biggio	.60	.25
❑ 13 Barry Bonds	.75	.35
❑ 14 Bobby Bonilla	.25	.11
❑ 15 Kevin Brown	.40	.18
❑ 16 Jay Buhner	.25	.11
❑ 17 Ellis Burks	.25	.11
❑ 18 Mike Cameron	.25	.11
❑ 19 Ken Caminiti	.40	.18
❑ 20 Jose Canseco	.60	.25
❑ 21 Joe Carter	.25	.11
❑ 22 Vinny Castilla	.40	.18
❑ 23 Jeff Cirillo	.25	.11
❑ 24 Tony Clark	.40	.18
❑ 25 Will Clark	.60	.25
❑ 26 Roger Clemens	1.25	.55
❑ 27 David Cone	.40	.18
❑ 28 Jose Cruz Jr.	.75	.35
❑ 29 Carlos Delgado	.25	.11
❑ 30 Jason Dickson	.25	.11
❑ 31 Dennis Eckersley	.25	.11
❑ 32 Jim Edmonds	.40	.18
❑ 33 Scott Erickson	.25	.11
❑ 34 Darin Erstad	.75	.35
❑ 35 Shawn Estes	.25	.11
❑ 36 Jeff Fassero	.15	.07
❑ 37 Alex Fernandez	.15	.07
❑ 38 Chuck Finley	.25	.11
❑ 39 Steve Finley	.25	.11
❑ 40 Travis Fryman	.25	.11
❑ 41 Andres Galarraga	.60	.25
❑ 42 Ron Gant	.15	.07
❑ 43 Nomar Garciaparra	2.00	.90
❑ 44 Jason Giambi	.25	.11
❑ 45 Tom Glavine	.60	.25
❑ 46 Juan Gonzalez	1.50	.70
❑ 47 Mark Grace	.40	.18
❑ 48 Willie Greene	.25	.11
❑ 49 Rusty Greer	.25	.11
❑ 50 Ben Grieve	1.25	.55
❑ 51 Ken Griffey Jr.	3.00	1.35
❑ 52 Mark Grudzielanek	.25	.11
❑ 53 Vladimir Guerrero	1.00	.45
❑ 54 Juan Guzman	.15	.07
❑ 55 Tony Gwynn	1.50	.70
❑ 56 Joey Hamilton	.25	.11
❑ 57 Rickey Henderson	.60	.25
❑ 58 Pat Hentgen	.25	.11
❑ 59 Livan Hernandez	.25	.11
❑ 60 Bobby Higginson	.40	.18
❑ 61 Todd Hundley	.25	.11
❑ 62 Hideki Irabu	.40	.18
❑ 63 John Jaha	.15	.07
❑ 64 Derek Jeter	1.50	.70
❑ 65 Charles Johnson	.25	.11
❑ 66 Randy Johnson	.60	.25
❑ 67 Andruw Jones	.75	.35
❑ 68 Bobby Jones	.15	.07
❑ 69 Chipper Jones	1.50	.70
❑ 70 Brian Jordan	.25	.11
❑ 71 David Justice	.60	.25
❑ 72 Eric Karros	.25	.11
❑ 73 Jeff Kent	.25	.11
❑ 74 Jimmy Key	.25	.11
❑ 75 Darryl Kile	.25	.11
❑ 76 Jeff King	.25	.11
❑ 77 Ryan Klesko	.25	.11
❑ 78 Chuck Knoblauch	.60	.25
❑ 79 Ray Lankford	.25	.11
❑ 80 Barry Larkin	.40	.18
❑ 81 Kenny Lofton	.60	.25
❑ 82 Greg Maddux	2.00	.90
❑ 83 Al Martin	.15	.07
❑ 84 Edgar Martinez	.25	.11
❑ 85 Pedro Martinez	.60	.25
❑ 86 Tino Martinez	.60	.25
❑ 87 Mark McGwire	4.00	1.80
❑ 88 Paul Molitor	.60	.25
❑ 89 Raul Mondesi	.40	.18
❑ 90 Jamie Moyer	.15	.07
❑ 91 Mike Mussina	.60	.25
❑ 92 Tim Naehring	.15	.07
❑ 93 Charles Nagy	.25	.11
❑ 94 Denny Neagle	.25	.11
❑ 95 Dave Nilsson	.15	.07
❑ 96 Hideo Nomo	.75	.35
❑ 97 Rey Ordonez	.25	.11
❑ 98 Dean Palmer	.25	.11
❑ 99 Rafael Palmeiro	.40	.18
❑ 100 Andy Pettitte	.40	.18
❑ 101 Mike Piazza	2.00	.90
❑ 102 Brad Radke	.25	.11
❑ 103 Manny Ramirez	.60	.25
❑ 104 Edgar Renteria	.25	.11
❑ 105 Cal Ripken	2.50	1.10
❑ 106 Alex Rodriguez	2.00	.90
❑ 107 Henry Rodriguez	.25	.11
❑ 108 Ivan Rodriguez	.75	.35
❑ 109 Scott Rolen	1.50	.70
❑ 110 Tim Salmon	.60	.25
❑ 111 Curt Schilling	.25	.11
❑ 112 Gary Sheffield	.40	.18
❑ 113 John Smoltz	.25	.11
❑ 114 J.T. Snow	.25	.11
❑ 115 Sammy Sosa	1.50	.70
❑ 116 Matt Stairs	.25	.11
❑ 117 Shannon Stewart	.25	.11
❑ 118 Frank Thomas	2.00	.90
❑ 119 Jim Thome	.60	.25
❑ 120 Justin Thompson	.25	.11

❑ 121 Mo Vaughn .75 .35
❑ 122 Robin Ventura .25 .11
❑ 123 Larry Walker .60 .25
❑ 124 Rondell White .25 .11
❑ 125 Bernie Williams .60 .25
❑ 126 Matt Williams .25 .11
❑ 127 Tony Womack .25 .11
❑ 128 Jaret Wright .75 .35
❑ 129 Edgar Renteria BB .15 .07
❑ 130 Kenny Lofton BB .25 .11
❑ 131 Tony Gwynn BB .75 .35
❑ 132 Mark McGwire BB 2.00 .90
❑ 133 Craig Biggio BB .25 .11
❑ 134 Charles Johnson BB .15 .07
❑ 135 J.T. Snow BB .15 .07
❑ 136 Ken Caminiti BB .15 .07
❑ 137 Vladimir Guerrero BB .40 .18
❑ 138 Jim Edmonds BB .15 .07
❑ 139 Randy Johnson BB .25 .11
❑ 140 Darryl Kile BB .15 .07
❑ 141 John Smoltz BB .15 .07
❑ 142 Greg Maddux BB 1.00 .45
❑ 143 Andy Pettitte BB .15 .07
❑ 144 Ken Griffey Jr. BB 1.50 .70
❑ 145 Mike Piazza BB 1.00 .45
❑ 146 Todd Greene BB .15 .07
❑ 147 Vinny Castilla BB .15 .07
❑ 148 Derek Jeter BB .75 .35
❑ 149 Robert Machado OW .15 .07
❑ 150 Mike Gulan OW .15 .07
❑ 151 Randall Simon OW .25 .11
❑ 152 Michael Coleman OW .25 .11
❑ 153 Brian Rose OW .25 .11
❑ 154 Scott Eyre OW .15 .07
❑ 155 Magglio Ordonez OW .75 .35
❑ 156 Todd Helton OW .75 .35
❑ 157 Juan Encarnacion OW .25 .11
❑ 158 Mark Kotsay OW .40 .18
❑ 159 Josh Booty OW .15 .07
❑ 160 Melvin Rosario OW .15 .07
❑ 161 Shane Halter OW .15 .07
❑ 162 Paul Konerko OW .60 .25
❑ 163 Henry Blanco OW .15 .07
❑ 164 Antone Williamson OW .15 .07
❑ 165 Brad Fullmer OW .25 .11
❑ 166 Ricky Ledee OW .25 .11
❑ 167 Ben Grieve OW 1.25 .55
❑ 168 Frank Catalanotto OW .25 .11
❑ 169 Bobby Estalella OW .25 .11
❑ 170 Dennis Reyes OW .25 .11
❑ 171 Kevin Polcovich OW .15 .07
❑ 172 Jacob Cruz OW .15 .07
❑ 173 Ken Cloude OW .25 .11
❑ 174 Eli Marrero OW .25 .11
❑ 175 Fernando Tatis OW .25 .11
❑ 176 Tom Evans OW .25 .11
❑ 177 Rafael Palmeiro .60 .25
Chipper Jones '97
❑ 178 Eric Davis .15 .07
'97 Returns From Cancer
❑ 179 Roger Clemens .60 .25
'97 Triple Crown/200 Wins
❑ 180 Brett Butler .25 .11
Eddie Murray
'97 Retirees
❑ 181 Frank Thomas 1.00 .45
'97 Batting Title
❑ 182 Curt Schilling .15 .07
'97 Sets Strikeout Record
❑ 183 Jeff Bagwell .60 .25
'97 1B Goes 30-30
❑ 184 Mark McGwire 2.00 .90
Ken Griffey Jr.
'97 Chase Maris
❑ 185 Kevin Brown .15 .07
'97 No-Hitter
❑ 186 Francisco Cordova .15 .07
Ricardo Rincon
'97 No-Hitter
❑ 187 Charles Johnson .15 .07
'97 Errorless Streak
❑ 188 Hideki Irabu .15 .07
'97 Debuts
❑ 189 Tony Gwynn .75 .35
'97 8th Batting Title
❑ 190 Sandy Alomar .15 .07
'97 All-Star MVP
❑ 191 Ken Griffey Jr. 1.50 .70
'97 AL MVP
❑ 192 Larry Walker .25 .11
'97 NL MVP
❑ 193 Roger Clemens .60 .25
'97 AL Cy Young Award
❑ 194 Pedro Martinez .25 .11
'97 NL Cy Young Award
❑ 195 Nomar Garciaparra 1.00 .45
'97 AL ROY
❑ 196 Scott Rolen .75 .35
'97 NL ROY
❑ 197 Brian Anderson .15 .07
'97 Arizona 1st Draft Pick
❑ 198 Tony Saunders .15 .07
'97 TB 1st Draft Pick
❑ 199 Florida Celebration .25 .11
'97 World Series Champs
❑ 200 Livan Hernandez .15 .07
'97 World Series MVP
❑ 201 Travis Lee OW SP 10.00 4.50
❑ P106 Alex Rodriguez PROMO 3.00 1.35
❑ NNO Alex Rodriguez CL .50 .23

1998 Sports Illustrated Extra Edition

	MINT	NRMT
COMPLETE SET (201)	4000.00	1800.00
COMMON CARD (1-201)	8.00	3.60

*STARS: 20X TO 50X BASIC CARDS
*YOUNG STARS: 15X TO 40X BASIC CARDS
*ROOKIES/PROSPECTS: 8X TO 20X BASIC CARDS

❑ 201 Travis Lee OW 50.00 22.00

1998 Sports Illustrated Autographs

	MINT	NRMT
COMPLETE SET (6)	400.00	180.00
COMMON CARD	40.00	18.00

❑ 1 Lou Brock/500 80.00 36.00
❑ 2 Jose Cruz Jr./250 60.00 27.00
❑ 3 Rollie Fingers/500 40.00 18.00
❑ 4 Ben Grieve EXCH/250 100.00 45.00
❑ 5 Paul Konerko EXCH/250 40.00 18.00
❑ 6 Brooks Robinson/500 80.00 36.00

1998 Sports Illustrated Covers

	MINT	NRMT
COMPLETE SET (10)	30.00	13.50
COMMON CARD (C1-C10)	1.00	.45

❑ C1 Ken Griffey 8.00 3.60
Mike Piazza
❑ C2 Derek Jeter 5.00 2.20
❑ C3 Ken Griffey Jr. 10.00 4.50
❑ C4 Cal Ripken 8.00 3.60
❑ C5 Manny Ramirez 2.00 .90

❑ C6 Jay Buhner 1.00 .45
❑ C7 Matt Williams 1.00 .45
❑ C8 Randy Johnson 2.00 .90
❑ C9 Deion Sanders 1.00 .45
❑ C10 Jose Canseco 2.00 .90

1998 Sports Illustrated Editor's Choice

	MINT	NRMT
COMPLETE SET (10)	120.00	55.00
COMMON CARD (EC1-EC10)	5.00	2.20

❑ EC1 Ken Griffey Jr. 25.00 11.00
❑ EC2 Alex Rodriguez 15.00 6.75
❑ EC3 Frank Thomas 15.00 6.75
❑ EC4 Mark McGwire 30.00 13.50
❑ EC5 Greg Maddux 15.00 6.75
❑ EC6 Derek Jeter 12.00 5.50
❑ EC7 Cal Ripken 20.00 9.00
❑ EC8 Nomar Garciaparra 15.00 6.75
❑ EC9 Jeff Bagwell 8.00 3.60
❑ EC10 Jose Cruz Jr. 5.00 2.20

1998 Sports Illustrated Opening Day Mini Posters

	MINT	NRMT
COMPLETE SET (30)	10.00	4.50
COMMON CARD (OD1-OD30)	.10	.05

Card	Player	Mint	Nrmt
❑ OD1	Tim Salmon	.40	.18
❑ OD2	Matt Williams	.15	.07
❑ OD3	John Smoltz Greg Maddux	1.00	.45
❑ OD4	Cal Ripken	1.50	.70
❑ OD5	Nomar Garciaparra	1.25	.55
❑ OD6	Sammy Sosa	1.00	.45
❑ OD7	Frank Thomas	1.25	.55
❑ OD8	Barry Larkin	.25	.11
❑ OD9	David Justice	.40	.18
❑ OD10	Larry Walker	.40	.18
❑ OD11	Tony Clark	.25	.11
❑ OD12	Livan Hernandez	.15	.07
❑ OD13	Jeff Bagwell	.60	.25
❑ OD14	Kevin Appier	.15	.07
❑ OD15	Mike Piazza	1.25	.55
❑ OD16	Fernando Vina	.10	.05
❑ OD17	Paul Molitor	.40	.18
❑ OD18	Vladimir Guerrero	.60	.25
❑ OD19	Rey Ordonez	.15	.07
❑ OD20	Bernie Williams	.40	.18
❑ OD21	Matt Stairs	.15	.07
❑ OD22	Curt Schilling	.15	.07
❑ OD23	Tony Womack	.15	.07
❑ OD24	Mark McGwire	2.50	1.10
❑ OD25	Tony Gwynn	1.00	.45
❑ OD26	Barry Bonds	.50	.23
❑ OD27	Ken Griffey Jr.	2.00	.90
❑ OD28	Fred McGriff	.25	.11
❑ OD29	Juan Gonzalez Ivan Rodriguez	.75	.35
❑ OD30	Roger Clemens	.75	.35

1998 Sports Illustrated Then and Now

	MINT	NRMT
COMPLETE SET (150)	40.00	18.00
COMMON CARD (1-150)	.15	.07

Card	Player	Mint	Nrmt
❑ 1	Luis Aparicio	.40	.18
❑ 2	Richie Ashburn	.40	.18
❑ 3	Ernie Banks	.75	.35
❑ 4	Yogi Berra	.75	.35
❑ 5	Lou Boudreau	.30	.14
❑ 6	Lou Brock	.60	.25
❑ 7	Jim Bunning	.30	.14
❑ 8	Rod Carew	.60	.25
❑ 9	Bob Feller	.60	.25
❑ 10	Rollie Fingers	.30	.14
❑ 11	Bob Gibson	.60	.25
❑ 12	Ferguson Jenkins	.30	.14
❑ 13	Al Kaline	.75	.35
❑ 14	George Kell	.30	.14
❑ 15	Harmon Killebrew	.60	.25
❑ 16	Ralph Kiner	.40	.18
❑ 17	Tommy Lasorda	.30	.14
❑ 18	Juan Marichal	.30	.14
❑ 19	Eddie Mathews	.60	.25
❑ 20	Willie Mays	1.50	.70
❑ 21	Willie McCovey	.60	.25
❑ 22	Joe Morgan	.60	.25
❑ 23	Gaylord Perry	.30	.14
❑ 24	Kirby Puckett	1.00	.45
❑ 25	Pee Wee Reese	.40	.18
❑ 26	Phil Rizzuto	.40	.18
❑ 27	Robin Roberts	.30	.14
❑ 28	Brooks Robinson	.60	.25
❑ 29	Frank Robinson	.60	.25
❑ 30	Red Schoendienst	.30	.14
❑ 31	Enos Slaughter	.30	.14
❑ 32	Warren Spahn	.60	.25
❑ 33	Willie Stargell	.40	.18
❑ 34	Earl Weaver	.30	.14
❑ 35	Billy Williams	.60	.25
❑ 36	Early Wynn	.30	.14
❑ 37	Rickey Henderson HIST	.30	.14
❑ 38	Greg Maddux HIST	1.00	.45
❑ 39	Mike Mussina HIST	.30	.14
❑ 40	Cal Ripken HIST	1.25	.55
❑ 41	Albert Belle HIST	.30	.14
❑ 42	Frank Thomas HIST	1.00	.45
❑ 43	Jeff Bagwell HIST	.60	.25
❑ 44	Paul Molitor HIST	.30	.14
❑ 45	Chuck Knoblauch HIST	.30	.14
❑ 46	Todd Hundley HIST	.15	.07
❑ 47	Bernie Williams HIST	.30	.14
❑ 48	Tony Gwynn HIST	.75	.35
❑ 49	Barry Bonds HIST	.40	.18
❑ 50	Ken Griffey Jr. HIST	1.50	.70
❑ 51	Randy Johnson HIST	.30	.14
❑ 52	Mark McGwire HIST	2.00	.90
❑ 53	Roger Clemens HIST	.60	.25
❑ 54	Jose Cruz Jr. HIST	.40	.18
❑ 55	Roberto Alomar	.60	.25
❑ 56	Sandy Alomar	.30	.14
❑ 57	Brady Anderson	.30	.14
❑ 58	Kevin Appier	.30	.14
❑ 59	Jeff Bagwell	1.00	.45
❑ 60	Albert Belle	.75	.35
❑ 61	Dante Bichette	.30	.14
❑ 62	Craig Biggio	.60	.25
❑ 63	Barry Bonds	.75	.35
❑ 64	Kevin Brown	.40	.18
❑ 65	Jay Buhner	.30	.14
❑ 66	Ellis Burks	.30	.14
❑ 67	Ken Caminiti	.40	.18
❑ 68	Jose Canseco	.60	.25
❑ 69	Joe Carter	.30	.14
❑ 70	Vinny Castilla	.40	.18
❑ 71	Tony Clark	.40	.18
❑ 72	Roger Clemens	1.25	.55
❑ 73	David Cone	.40	.18
❑ 74	Jose Cruz Jr.	.75	.35
❑ 75	Jason Dickson	.30	.14
❑ 76	Jim Edmonds	.40	.18
❑ 77	Scott Erickson	.30	.14
❑ 78	Darin Erstad	.75	.35
❑ 79	Alex Fernandez	.15	.07
❑ 80	Steve Finley	.30	.14
❑ 81	Travis Fryman	.30	.14
❑ 82	Andres Galarraga	.60	.25
❑ 83	Nomar Garciaparra	2.00	.90
❑ 84	Tom Glavine	.60	.25
❑ 85	Juan Gonzalez	1.50	.70
❑ 86	Mark Grace	.40	.18
❑ 87	Willie Greene	.30	.14
❑ 88	Ken Griffey Jr.	3.00	1.35
❑ 89	Vladimir Guerrero	1.00	.45
❑ 90	Tony Gwynn	1.50	.70
❑ 91	Livan Hernandez	.30	.14
❑ 92	Bobby Higginson	.40	.18
❑ 93	Derek Jeter	1.50	.70
❑ 94	Charles Johnson	.30	.14
❑ 95	Randy Johnson	.60	.25
❑ 96	Andruw Jones	.75	.35
❑ 97	Chipper Jones	1.50	.70
❑ 98	David Justice	.60	.25
❑ 99	Eric Karros	.30	.14
❑ 100	Jason Kendall	.30	.14
❑ 101	Jimmy Key	.30	.14
❑ 102	Darryl Kile	.30	.14
❑ 103	Chuck Knoblauch	.60	.25
❑ 104	Ray Lankford	.30	.14
❑ 105	Barry Larkin	.40	.18
❑ 106	Kenny Lofton	.60	.25
❑ 107	Greg Maddux	2.00	.90
❑ 108	Al Martin	.15	.07
❑ 109	Edgar Martinez	.30	.14
❑ 110	Pedro Martinez	.60	.25
❑ 111	Ramon Martinez	.30	.14
❑ 112	Tino Martinez	.60	.25
❑ 113	Mark McGwire	4.00	1.80
❑ 114	Raul Mondesi	.40	.18
❑ 115	Matt Morris	.30	.14
❑ 116	Charles Nagy	.30	.14
❑ 117	Denny Neagle	.30	.14
❑ 118	Hideo Nomo	.75	.35
❑ 119	Dean Palmer	.30	.14
❑ 120	Andy Pettitte	.40	.18
❑ 121	Mike Piazza	2.00	.90
❑ 122	Manny Ramirez	.60	.25
❑ 123	Edgar Renteria	.30	.14
❑ 124	Cal Ripken	2.50	1.10
❑ 125	Alex Rodriguez	2.00	.90
❑ 126	Henry Rodriguez	.30	.14
❑ 127	Ivan Rodriguez	.75	.35
❑ 128	Scott Rolen	1.50	.70
❑ 129	Tim Salmon	.60	.25
❑ 130	Curt Schilling	.30	.14
❑ 131	Gary Sheffield	.40	.18
❑ 132	John Smoltz	.30	.14
❑ 133	Sammy Sosa	1.50	.70
❑ 134	Frank Thomas	2.00	.90
❑ 135	Jim Thome	.60	.25
❑ 136	Mo Vaughn	.75	.35
❑ 137	Robin Ventura	.30	.14
❑ 138	Larry Walker	.60	.25
❑ 139	Bernie Williams	.60	.25
❑ 140	Matt Williams	.30	.14
❑ 141	Jaret Wright	.75	.35
❑ 142	Michael Coleman	.30	.14
❑ 143	Juan Encarnacion	.30	.14
❑ 144	Brad Fullmer	.30	.14
❑ 145	Ben Grieve	1.25	.55
❑ 146	Todd Helton	.75	.35
❑ 147	Paul Konerko	.60	.25
❑ 148	Derrek Lee	.30	.14
❑ 149	Magglio Ordonez	.75	.35
❑ 150	Enrique Wilson	.30	.14
❑ P125	Alex Rodriguez PROMO	3.00	1.35
❑ NNO	Alex Rodriguez CL	.50	.23

1998 Sports Illustrated Then and Now Extra Edition

	MINT	NRMT
COMPLETE SET (150)	2000.00	900.00
COMMON CARD (1-150)	5.00	2.20

*STARS: 12.5X TO 30X BASIC CARDS
*YOUNG STARS: 10X TO 25X BASIC CARDS
*ROOKIES: 5X TO 12X BASIC CARDS

1998 Sports Illustrated Then and Now Art of the Game

	MINT	NRMT
COMPLETE SET (8)	25.00	11.00
COMMON CARD (AG1-AG8)	.50	.23

Card	Player	Mint	Nrmt
❑ AG1	Ken Griffey Jr.	8.00	3.60
❑ AG2	Alex Rodriguez	5.00	2.20
❑ AG3	Mike Piazza	5.00	2.20
❑ AG4	Brooks Robinson	1.50	.70
❑ AG5	David Justice	1.50	.70

		MINT	NRMT
❑ AG6	Cal Ripken	6.00	2.70
❑ AG7	Prospect 'n Prospector	.50	.23
❑ AG8	Barry Bonds	2.00	.90

1998 Sports Illustrated Then and Now Autographs

	MINT	NRMT
COMPLETE SET (6)	750.00	350.00
COMMON CARD (1-6)	80.00	36.00

		MINT	NRMT
❑ 1	Roger Clemens/250	150.00	70.00
❑ 2	Bob Gibson/500	80.00	36.00
❑ 3	Tony Gwynn/250	150.00	70.00
❑ 4	Harmon Killebrew/500	80.00	36.00
❑ 5	Willie Mays/250	200.00	90.00
❑ 6	Scott Rolen/250	120.00	55.00

1998 Sports Illustrated Then and Now Covers

	MINT	NRMT
COMPLETE SET (12)	80.00	36.00
COMMON CARD (C1-C12)	4.00	1.80

		MINT	NRMT
❑ C1	Lou Brock	4.00	1.80
❑ C2	Kirby Puckett	6.00	2.70
❑ C3	Harmon Killebrew	4.00	1.80
❑ C4	Eddie Mathews	4.00	1.80
❑ C5	Willie Mays	10.00	4.50
❑ C6	Frank Robinson	4.00	1.80
❑ C7	Cal Ripken	15.00	6.75
❑ C8	Roger Clemens	8.00	3.60
❑ C9	Ken Griffey Jr.	20.00	9.00
❑ C10	Mark McGwire	25.00	11.00
❑ C11	Tony Gwynn	10.00	4.50
❑ C12	Ivan Rodriguez	5.00	2.20

1998 Sports Illustrated Then and Now Great Shots

	MINT	NRMT
COMPLETE SET (25)	10.00	4.50
COMMON CARD (1-25)	.25	.11

		MINT	NRMT
❑ 1	Ken Griffey Jr.	2.00	.90
❑ 2	Frank Thomas	1.25	.55
❑ 3	Alex Rodriguez	1.25	.55
❑ 4	Andruw Jones	.50	.23
❑ 5	Chipper Jones	1.00	.45
❑ 6	Cal Ripken	1.50	.70
❑ 7	Mark McGwire	2.50	1.10
❑ 8	Derek Jeter	1.00	.45
❑ 9	Greg Maddux	1.25	.55
❑ 10	Jeff Bagwell	.60	.25
❑ 11	Mike Piazza	1.25	.55
❑ 12	Scott Rolen	1.00	.45
❑ 13	Nomar Garciaparra	1.25	.55
❑ 14	Jose Cruz Jr.	.50	.23
❑ 15	Charles Johnson	.25	.11
❑ 16	Fergie Jenkins	.25	.11
❑ 17	Lou Brock	.40	.18
❑ 18	Bob Gibson	.40	.18
❑ 19	Harmon Killebrew	.40	.18
❑ 20	Juan Marichal	.25	.11
❑ 21	Brooks Robinson Frank Robinson	.25	.11
❑ 22	Rod Carew	.40	.18
❑ 23	Yogi Berra	.50	.23
❑ 24	Willie Mays	1.00	.45
❑ 25	Kirby Puckett	.60	.25

1998 Sports Illustrated Then and Now Road to Cooperstown

	MINT	NRMT
COMPLETE SET (10)	100.00	45.00
COMMON CARD (RC1-RC10)	5.00	2.20

		MINT	NRMT
❑ RC1	Barry Bonds	6.00	2.70
❑ RC2	Roger Clemens	10.00	4.50
❑ RC3	Ken Griffey Jr.	25.00	11.00
❑ RC4	Tony Gwynn	12.00	5.50
❑ RC5	Rickey Henderson	5.00	2.20
❑ RC6	Greg Maddux	15.00	6.75
❑ RC7	Paul Molitor	5.00	2.20
❑ RC8	Mike Piazza	15.00	6.75
❑ RC9	Cal Ripken	20.00	9.00
❑ RC10	Frank Thomas	15.00	6.75

1998 Sports Illustrated World Series Fever

	MINT	NRMT
COMPLETE SET (150)	45.00	20.00
COMMON CARD (1-150)	.15	.07

		MINT	NRMT
❑ 1	Mickey Mantle COV	3.00	1.35
❑ 2	W.S. Preview COV	.15	.07
❑ 3	W.S. Preview COV	.15	.07
❑ 4	Chicago (AL) COV	.15	.07
❑ 5	W.S. Preview COV	.15	.07
❑ 6	Lou Brock COV	.60	.25
❑ 7	Brooks Robinson COV	.60	.25
❑ 8	Frank Robinson COV	.60	.25
❑ 9	L.A. Oakland COV	.15	.07
❑ 10	Reggie Jackson COV	.75	.35
❑ 11	Kansas City COV	.15	.07
❑ 12	Minnesota COV	.15	.07
❑ 13	Orel Hershiser COV	.15	.07
❑ 14	Rickey Henderson COV	.40	.18
❑ 15	Minnesota COV	.15	.07
❑ 16	Toronto COV	.15	.07
❑ 17	Joe Carter COV	.15	.07
❑ 18	Atlanta COV	.15	.07
❑ 19	New York Yankees COV	.15	.07
❑ 20	Edgar Renteria COV	.15	.07
❑ 21	Bill Mazeroski MM	.25	.11
❑ 22	Joe Carter MM	.25	.11
❑ 23	Carlton Fisk MM	.60	.25
❑ 24	Bucky Dent MM	.25	.11
❑ 25	Mookie Wilson MM	.15	.07
❑ 26	Enos Slaughter MM	.25	.11
❑ 27	Mickey Lolich MM	.15	.07
❑ 28	Bobby Richardson MM	.25	.11
❑ 29	Kirk Gibson MM	.25	.11
❑ 30	Edgar Renteria MM	.15	.07
❑ 31	Albert Belle	.60	.25
❑ 32	Kevin Brown	.40	.18
❑ 33	Brian Rose	.25	.11
❑ 34	Ron Gant	.15	.07
❑ 35	Jeromy Burnitz	.25	.11
❑ 36	Andres Galarraga	.60	.25
❑ 37	Jim Edmonds	.40	.18
❑ 38	Jose Cruz Jr.	.75	.35
❑ 39	Mark Grudzielanek	.25	.11
❑ 40	Shawn Estes	.25	.11
❑ 41	Mark Grace	.40	.18
❑ 42	Nomar Garciaparra	2.00	.90
❑ 43	Juan Gonzalez	1.50	.70
❑ 44	Tom Glavine	.60	.25
❑ 45	Brady Anderson	.25	.11
❑ 46	Tony Clark	.40	.18
❑ 47	Jeff Cirillo	.25	.11
❑ 48	Dante Bichette	.25	.11
❑ 49	Ben Grieve	1.25	.55
❑ 50	Ken Griffey Jr.	3.00	1.35
❑ 51	Edgardo Alfonzo	.25	.11
❑ 52	Roger Clemens	1.25	.55
❑ 53	Pat Hentgen	.25	.11
❑ 54	Todd Helton	.75	.35
❑ 55	Andy Benes	.25	.11
❑ 56	Tony Gwynn	1.50	.70
❑ 57	Andruw Jones	.75	.35
❑ 58	Bobby Higginson	.40	.18
❑ 59	Bobby Jones	.15	.07
❑ 60	Darryl Kile	.25	.11

❑ 61 Chan Ho Park	.60	.25
❑ 62 Charles Johnson	.25	.11
❑ 63 Rusty Greer	.25	.11
❑ 64 Travis Fryman	.25	.11
❑ 65 Derek Jeter	1.50	.70
❑ 66 Jay Buhner	.25	.11
❑ 67 Chuck Knoblauch	.60	.25
❑ 68 David Justice	.60	.25
❑ 69 Brian Hunter	.25	.11
❑ 70 Eric Karros	.25	.11
❑ 71 Edgar Martinez	.25	.11
❑ 72 Chipper Jones	1.50	.70
❑ 73 Barry Larkin	.40	.18
❑ 74 Mike Lansing	.15	.07
❑ 75 Craig Biggio	.60	.25
❑ 76 Al Martin	.15	.07
❑ 77 Barry Bonds	.75	.35
❑ 78 Randy Johnson	.60	.25
❑ 79 Ryan Klesko	.25	.11
❑ 80 Mark McGwire	4.00	1.80
❑ 81 Fred McGriff	.40	.18
❑ 82 Javy Lopez	.25	.11
❑ 83 Kenny Lofton	.60	.25
❑ 84 Sandy Alomar	.25	.11
❑ 85 Matt Morris	.25	.11
❑ 86 Paul Konerko	.60	.25
❑ 87 Ray Lankford	.25	.11
❑ 88 Kerry Wood	3.00	1.35
❑ 89 Roberto Alomar	.60	.25
❑ 90 Greg Maddux	2.00	.90
❑ 91 Travis Lee	1.25	.55
❑ 92 Moises Alou	.40	.18
❑ 93 Dean Palmer	.25	.11
❑ 94 Hideo Nomo	.75	.35
❑ 95 Ken Caminiti	.40	.18
❑ 96 Pedro Martinez	.60	.25
❑ 97 Raul Mondesi	.40	.18
❑ 98 Denny Neagle	.25	.11
❑ 99 Tino Martinez	.60	.25
❑ 100 Mike Mussina	.60	.25
❑ 101 Kevin Appier	.25	.11
❑ 102 Vinny Castilla	.40	.18
❑ 103 Jeff Bagwell	1.00	.45
❑ 104 Paul O'Neill	.25	.11
❑ 105 Rey Ordonez	.25	.11
❑ 106 Vladimir Guerrero	1.00	.45
❑ 107 Rafael Palmeiro	.40	.18
❑ 108 Alex Rodriguez	2.00	.90
❑ 109 Andy Pettitte	.40	.18
❑ 110 Carl Pavano	.25	.11
❑ 111 Henry Rodriguez	.25	.11
❑ 112 Gary Sheffield	.40	.18
❑ 113 Curt Schilling	.25	.11
❑ 114 John Smoltz	.25	.11
❑ 115 Reggie Sanders	.25	.11
❑ 116 Scott Rolen	1.50	.70
❑ 117 Mike Piazza	2.00	.90
❑ 118 Manny Ramirez	.60	.25
❑ 119 Cal Ripken	2.50	1.10
❑ 120 Brad Radke	.25	.11
❑ 121 Tim Salmon	.60	.25
❑ 122 Brett Tomko	.25	.11
❑ 123 Robin Ventura	.25	.11
❑ 124 Mo Vaughn	.75	.35
❑ 125 A.J. Hinch	.25	.11
❑ 126 Derrek Lee	.25	.11
❑ 127 Orlando Hernandez	3.00	1.35
❑ 128 Aramis Ramirez	.60	.25
❑ 129 Frank Thomas	2.00	.90
❑ 130 J.T. Snow	.25	.11
❑ 131 Magglio Ordonez	.75	.35
❑ 132 Bobby Bonilla	.25	.11
❑ 133 Marquis Grissom	.25	.11
❑ 134 Jim Thome	.60	.25
❑ 135 Justin Thompson	.25	.11
❑ 136 Matt Williams	.25	.11
❑ 137 Matt Stairs	.25	.11
❑ 138 Wade Boggs	.60	.25
❑ 139 Chuck Finley	.25	.11
❑ 140 Jaret Wright	.75	.35
❑ 141 Ivan Rodriguez	.75	.35
❑ 142 Brad Fullmer	.25	.11
❑ 143 Bernie Williams	.60	.25
❑ 144 Jason Giambi	.25	.11
❑ 145 Larry Walker	.60	.25
❑ 146 Tony Womack	.25	.11
❑ 147 Sammy Sosa	1.50	.70
❑ 148 Rondell White	.25	.11
❑ 149 Todd Stottlemyre	.25	.11
❑ 150 Shane Reynolds	.25	.11
❑ P8 Cal Ripken Promo	3.00	1.35

1998 Sports Illustrated World Series Fever Extra Edition

	MINT	NRMT
COMMON CARD (1-150)	15.00	6.75

*STARS: 40X TO 100X BASIC CARDS
*YOUNG STARS: 30X TO 80X BASIC CARDS
*PROSPECTS: 25X TO 60X BASIC CARDS
*ROOKIES: 20X TO 50X BASIC CARDS

1998 Sports Illustrated World Series Fever Autumn Excellence

	MINT	NRMT
COMPLETE SET (10)	80.00	36.00
COMMON CARD (1-10)	2.50	1.10
❑ 1 Willie Mays	12.00	5.50
❑ 2 Kirby Puckett	8.00	3.60
❑ 3 Babe Ruth	20.00	9.00
❑ 4 Reggie Jackson	6.00	2.70
❑ 5 Whitey Ford	5.00	2.20
❑ 6 Lou Brock	4.00	1.80
❑ 7 Mickey Mantle	25.00	11.00
❑ 8 Yogi Berra	8.00	3.60
❑ 9 Bob Gibson	4.00	1.80
❑ 10 Don Larsen	2.50	1.10

1998 Sports Illustrated World Series Fever MVP Collection

	MINT	NRMT
COMPLETE SET (10)	8.00	3.60
COMMON CARD (1-10)	1.00	.45
❑ 1 Frank Robinson	2.00	.90
❑ 2 Brooks Robinson	1.50	.70

❑ 3 Willie Stargell	1.50	.70
❑ 4 Bret Saberhagen	1.00	.45
❑ 5 Rollie Fingers	1.00	.45
❑ 6 Orel Hershiser	1.00	.45
❑ 7 Paul Molitor	2.00	.90
❑ 8 Tom Glavine	1.50	.70
❑ 9 John Wetteland	1.00	.45
❑ 10 Livan Hernandez	1.00	.45

1998 Sports Illustrated World Series Fever Reggie Jackson's Picks

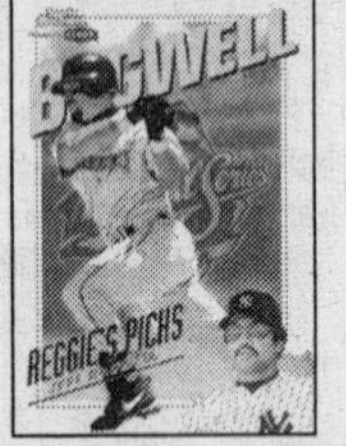

	MINT	NRMT
COMPLETE SET (15)	60.00	27.00
COMMON CARD (1-15)	1.00	.45
❑ 1 Paul O'Neill	1.00	.45
❑ 2 Barry Bonds	2.50	1.10
❑ 3 Ken Griffey Jr.	10.00	4.50
❑ 4 Juan Gonzalez	5.00	2.20
❑ 5 Greg Maddux	6.00	2.70
❑ 6 Mike Piazza	6.00	2.70
❑ 7 Larry Walker	2.00	.90
❑ 8 Mo Vaughn	2.50	1.10
❑ 9 Roger Clemens	4.00	1.80
❑ 10 John Smoltz	1.00	.45
❑ 11 Alex Rodriguez	6.00	2.70
❑ 12 Frank Thomas	6.00	2.70
❑ 13 Mark McGwire	12.00	5.50
❑ 14 Jeff Bagwell	3.00	1.35
❑ 15 Randy Johnson	2.00	.90

1996 SPx

	MINT	NRMT
COMPLETE SET (60)	80.00	36.00
COMMON CARD (1-60)	1.00	.45
❑ 1 Greg Maddux	6.00	2.70
❑ 2 Chipper Jones	5.00	2.20
❑ 3 Fred McGriff	1.50	.70
❑ 4 Tom Glavine	2.00	.90
❑ 5 Cal Ripken	8.00	3.60
❑ 6 Roberto Alomar	2.00	.90
❑ 7 Rafael Palmeiro	1.50	.70
❑ 8 Jose Canseco	2.00	.90
❑ 9 Roger Clemens	4.00	1.80
❑ 10 Mo Vaughn	2.50	1.10

Card	MINT	NRMT
❑ 11 Jim Edmonds	1.50	.70
❑ 12 Tim Salmon	2.00	.90
❑ 13 Sammy Sosa	5.00	2.20
❑ 14 Ryne Sandberg	2.50	1.10
❑ 15 Mark Grace	1.50	.70
❑ 16 Frank Thomas	6.00	2.70
❑ 17 Barry Larkin	1.50	.70
❑ 18 Kenny Lofton	2.00	.90
❑ 19 Albert Belle	2.00	.90
❑ 20 Eddie Murray	2.00	.90
❑ 21 Manny Ramirez	2.00	.90
❑ 22 Dante Bichette	1.25	.55
❑ 23 Larry Walker	2.00	.90
❑ 24 Vinny Castilla	1.50	.70
❑ 25 Andres Galarraga	2.00	.90
❑ 26 Cecil Fielder	1.25	.55
❑ 27 Gary Sheffield	1.50	.70
❑ 28 Craig Biggio	2.00	.90
❑ 29 Jeff Bagwell	3.00	1.35
❑ 30 Derek Bell	1.25	.55
❑ 31 Johnny Damon	1.25	.55
❑ 32 Eric Karros	1.25	.55
❑ 33 Mike Piazza	6.00	2.70
❑ 34 Raul Mondesi	1.50	.70
❑ 35 Hideo Nomo	3.00	1.35
❑ 36 Kirby Puckett	3.00	1.35
❑ 37 Paul Molitor	2.00	.90
❑ 38 Marty Cordova	1.00	.45
❑ 39 Rondell White	1.25	.55
❑ 40 Jason Isringhausen	1.00	.45
❑ 41 Paul Wilson	1.00	.45
❑ 42 Rey Ordonez	1.25	.55
❑ 43 Derek Jeter	6.00	2.70
❑ 44 Wade Boggs	2.00	.90
❑ 45 Mark McGwire	10.00	4.50
❑ 46 Jason Kendall	2.00	.90
❑ 47 Ron Gant	1.00	.45
❑ 48 Ozzie Smith	2.50	1.10
❑ 49 Tony Gwynn	5.00	2.20
❑ 50 Ken Caminiti	1.50	.70
❑ 51 Barry Bonds	2.50	1.10
❑ 52 Matt Williams	1.25	.55
❑ 53 Osvaldo Fernandez	1.00	.45
❑ 54 Jay Buhner	1.25	.55
❑ 55 Ken Griffey Jr.	10.00	4.50
❑ 56 Randy Johnson	2.00	.90
❑ 57 Alex Rodriguez	6.00	2.70
❑ 58 Juan Gonzalez	5.00	2.20
❑ 59 Joe Carter	1.25	.55
❑ 60 Carlos Delgado	1.25	.55
❑ KG1 Ken Griffey Jr. Comm.	15.00	6.75
❑ MP1 Mike Piazza Trib.	8.00	3.60
❑ KGAU Ken Griffey Jr. Auto.	350.00	160.00
❑ MPAU Mike Piazza Auto.	225.00	100.00

1996 SPx Bound for Glory

	MINT	NRMT
COMPLETE SET (10)	100.00	45.00
COMMON CARD (1-10)	5.00	2.20

Card	MINT	NRMT
❑ 1 Ken Griffey Jr.	25.00	11.00
❑ 2 Frank Thomas	15.00	6.75
❑ 3 Barry Bonds	6.00	2.70
❑ 4 Cal Ripken	20.00	9.00
❑ 5 Greg Maddux	15.00	6.75

Card	MINT	NRMT
❑ 6 Chipper Jones	12.00	5.50
❑ 7 Roberto Alomar	5.00	2.20
❑ 8 Manny Ramirez	5.00	2.20
❑ 9 Tony Gwynn	12.00	5.50
❑ 10 Mike Piazza	15.00	6.75

1997 SPx

	MINT	NRMT
COMPLETE SET (50)	60.00	27.00
COMMON CARD (1-50)	.50	.23

Card	MINT	NRMT
❑ 1 Eddie Murray	1.25	.55
❑ 2 Darin Erstad	2.00	.90
❑ 3 Tim Salmon	1.25	.55
❑ 4 Andruw Jones	2.00	.90
❑ 5 Chipper Jones	3.00	1.35
❑ 6 John Smoltz	.50	.23
❑ 7 Greg Maddux	4.00	1.80
❑ 8 Kenny Lofton	1.25	.55
❑ 9 Roberto Alomar	1.25	.55
❑ 10 Rafael Palmeiro	.75	.35
❑ 11 Brady Anderson	.50	.23
❑ 12 Cal Ripken	5.00	2.20
❑ 13 Nomar Garciaparra	4.00	1.80
❑ 14 Mo Vaughn	1.50	.70
❑ 15 Ryne Sandberg	1.50	.70
❑ 16 Sammy Sosa	3.00	1.35
❑ 17 Frank Thomas	4.00	1.80
❑ 18 Albert Belle	1.50	.70
❑ 19 Barry Larkin	.75	.35
❑ 20 Deion Sanders	.50	.23
❑ 21 Manny Ramirez	1.25	.55
❑ 22 Jim Thome	1.25	.55
❑ 23 Dante Bichette	.50	.23
❑ 24 Andres Galarraga	1.25	.55
❑ 25 Larry Walker	1.25	.55
❑ 26 Gary Sheffield	.75	.35
❑ 27 Jeff Bagwell	2.00	.90
❑ 28 Raul Mondesi	.75	.35
❑ 29 Hideo Nomo	1.50	.70
❑ 30 Mike Piazza	4.00	1.80
❑ 31 Paul Molitor	1.25	.55
❑ 32 Todd Walker	1.25	.55
❑ 33 Vladimir Guerrero	2.50	1.10
❑ 34 Todd Hundley	.50	.23
❑ 35 Andy Pettitte	.75	.35
❑ 36 Derek Jeter	4.00	1.80
❑ 37 Jose Canseco	1.25	.55
❑ 38 Mark McGwire	6.00	2.70
❑ 39 Scott Rolen	3.00	1.35
❑ 40 Ron Gant	.50	.23
❑ 41 Ken Caminiti	.75	.35
❑ 42 Tony Gwynn	3.00	1.35
❑ 43 Barry Bonds	1.50	.70
❑ 44 Jay Buhner	.50	.23
❑ 45 Ken Griffey Jr.	6.00	2.70
❑ 46 Alex Rodriguez	4.00	1.80
❑ 47 Jose Cruz Jr.	5.00	2.20
❑ 48 Juan Gonzalez	3.00	1.35
❑ 49 Ivan Rodriguez	1.50	.70
❑ 50 Roger Clemens	2.50	1.10
❑ S45 Ken Griffey Jr. SAMPLE	3.00	1.35

1997 SPx Grand Finale

	MINT	NRMT
COMPLETE SET (50)	7500.00	3400.00
COMMON CARD (1-50)	25.00	11.00
MINOR STARS	40.00	18.00
SEMISTARS	60.00	27.00
UNLISTED STARS	100.00	45.00

*STARS: 40X TO 80X BASIC CARDS
*YOUNG STARS: 30X TO 60X BASIC CARDS
*ROOKIES: 20X TO 40X BASIC CARDS

1997 SPx Bound for Glory

	MINT	NRMT
COMPLETE SET (20)	500.00	220.00
COMMON CARD (1-20)	10.00	4.50

Card	MINT	NRMT
❑ 1 Andruw Jones	15.00	6.75
❑ 2 Chipper Jones	30.00	13.50
❑ 3 Greg Maddux	40.00	18.00
❑ 4 Kenny Lofton	12.00	5.50
❑ 5 Cal Ripken	50.00	22.00
❑ 6 Mo Vaughn	15.00	6.75
❑ 7 Frank Thomas	40.00	18.00
❑ 8 Albert Belle	15.00	6.75
❑ 9 Manny Ramirez	12.00	5.50
❑ 10 Gary Sheffield	10.00	4.50
❑ 11 Jeff Bagwell	20.00	9.00
❑ 12 Mike Piazza	40.00	18.00
❑ 13 Derek Jeter	30.00	13.50
❑ 14 Mark McGwire	60.00	27.00
❑ 15 Tony Gwynn	30.00	13.50
❑ 16 Ken Caminiti	10.00	4.50
❑ 17 Barry Bonds	15.00	6.75
❑ 18 Alex Rodriguez	40.00	18.00
❑ 19 Ken Griffey Jr.	60.00	27.00
❑ 20 Juan Gonzalez	30.00	13.50

1997 SPx Bound for Glory Supreme Signatures

	MINT	NRMT
COMPLETE SET (5)	1200.00	550.00
COMMON CARD (1-5)	60.00	27.00

Card	MINT	NRMT
❑ 1 Jeff Bagwell	150.00	70.00
❑ 2 Ken Griffey Jr.	500.00	220.00
❑ 3 Andruw Jones	120.00	55.00
❑ 4 Alex Rodriguez	300.00	135.00
❑ 5 Gary Sheffield	60.00	27.00

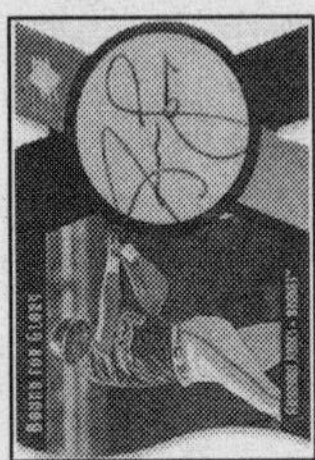

1997 SPx Cornerstones of the Game

	MINT	NRMT
COMPLETE SET (10)	700.00	325.00
COMMON CARD (1-10)	40.00	18.00
❑ 1 Ken Griffey Jr. Barry Bonds	120.00	55.00
❑ 2 Frank Thomas Albert Belle	60.00	27.00
❑ 3 Chipper Jones Greg Maddux	80.00	36.00
❑ 4 Tony Gwynn Paul Molitor	50.00	22.00
❑ 5 Andruw Jones Vladimir Guerrero	40.00	18.00
❑ 6 Jeff Bagwell Ryne Sandberg	40.00	18.00
❑ 7 Mike Piazza Ivan Rodriguez	60.00	27.00
❑ 8 Cal Ripken Eddie Murray	80.00	36.00
❑ 9 Mo Vaughn Mark McGwire	100.00	45.00
❑ 10 Alex Rodriguez Derek Jeter	80.00	36.00

1998 SPx Finite

	MINT	NRMT
COMPLETE SET (360)	1000.00	450.00
COMP.YM SER.1 (30)	80.00	36.00
COMMON YM (1-30)	.75	.35
COMP.PE SER.1 (20)	150.00	70.00
COMMON PE (31-50)	2.00	.90
COMP.BASIC SER.1 (90)	100.00	45.00
COMMON CARD (51-140)	.50	.23
COMP.SF SER.1 (30)	120.00	55.00
COMMON SF (141-170)	1.00	.45
COMP.HG SER.1 (10)	200.00	90.00
COMMON HG (171-180)	10.00	4.50
COMP.YM SER.2 (30)	60.00	27.00
COMMON YM (181-210)	.75	.35
COMP.PP SER.2 (30)	100.00	45.00
COMMON PP (211-240)	1.00	.45
COMP.BASIC SER.2 (90)	60.00	27.00
COMMON CARD (241-330)	.50	.23
COMP.TW SER.2 (20)	40.00	18.00
COMMON TW (331-350)	1.25	.55
COMP.CG SER.2 (10)	200.00	90.00
COMMON CG (351-360)	10.00	4.50
❑ 1 Nomar Garciaparra YM	12.00	5.50
❑ 2 Miguel Tejada YM	1.25	.55
❑ 3 Mike Cameron YM	1.25	.55
❑ 4 Ken Cloude YM	1.25	.55
❑ 5 Jaret Wright YM	4.00	1.80
❑ 6 Mark Kotsay YM	2.00	.90
❑ 7 Craig Counsell YM	.75	.35
❑ 8 Jose Guillen YM	1.25	.55
❑ 9 Neifi Perez YM	1.25	.55
❑ 10 Jose Cruz Jr. YM	4.00	1.80
❑ 11 Brett Tomko YM	1.25	.55
❑ 12 Matt Morris YM	1.25	.55
❑ 13 Justin Thompson YM	1.25	.55
❑ 14 Jeremi Gonzalez YM	1.25	.55
❑ 15 Scott Rolen YM	8.00	3.60
❑ 16 Vladimir Guerrero YM	5.00	2.20
❑ 17 Brad Fullmer YM	1.25	.55
❑ 18 Brian Giles YM	1.25	.55
❑ 19 Todd Dunwoody YM	1.25	.55
❑ 20 Ben Grieve YM	6.00	2.70
❑ 21 Juan Encarnacion YM	1.25	.55
❑ 22 Aaron Boone YM	.75	.35
❑ 23 Richie Sexson YM	2.00	.90
❑ 24 Richard Hidalgo YM	1.25	.55
❑ 25 Andruw Jones YM	4.00	1.80
❑ 26 Todd Helton YM	4.00	1.80
❑ 27 Paul Konerko YM	3.00	1.35
❑ 28 Dante Powell YM	1.25	.55
❑ 29 Eli Marrero YM	1.25	.55
❑ 30 Derek Jeter YM	10.00	4.50
❑ 31 Mike Piazza PE	15.00	6.75
❑ 32 Tony Clark PE	3.00	1.35
❑ 33 Larry Walker PE	5.00	2.20
❑ 34 Jim Thome PE	5.00	2.20
❑ 35 Juan Gonzalez PE	12.00	5.50
❑ 36 Jeff Bagwell PE	8.00	3.60
❑ 37 Jay Buhner PE	2.00	.90
❑ 38 Tim Salmon PE	5.00	2.20
❑ 39 Albert Belle PE	5.00	2.20
❑ 40 Mark McGwire PE	30.00	13.50
❑ 41 Sammy Sosa PE	12.00	5.50
❑ 42 Mo Vaughn PE	6.00	2.70
❑ 43 Manny Ramirez PE	5.00	2.20
❑ 44 Tino Martinez PE	5.00	2.20
❑ 45 Frank Thomas PE	15.00	6.75
❑ 46 Nomar Garciaparra PE	15.00	6.75
❑ 47 Alex Rodriguez PE	15.00	6.75
❑ 48 Chipper Jones PE	12.00	5.50
❑ 49 Barry Bonds PE	6.00	2.70
❑ 50 Ken Griffey Jr. PE	25.00	11.00
❑ 51 Jason Dickson	.75	.35
❑ 52 Jim Edmonds	1.25	.55
❑ 53 Darin Erstad	2.50	1.10
❑ 54 Tim Salmon	2.00	.90
❑ 55 Chipper Jones	5.00	2.20
❑ 56 Ryan Klesko	.75	.35
❑ 57 Tom Glavine	2.00	.90
❑ 58 Denny Neagle	.75	.35
❑ 59 John Smoltz	.75	.35
❑ 60 Javy Lopez	.75	.35
❑ 61 Roberto Alomar	2.00	.90
❑ 62 Rafael Palmeiro	1.25	.55
❑ 63 Mike Mussina	2.00	.90
❑ 64 Cal Ripken	8.00	3.60
❑ 65 Mo Vaughn	2.50	1.10
❑ 66 Tim Naehring	.50	.23
❑ 67 John Valentin	.75	.35
❑ 68 Mark Grace	1.25	.55
❑ 69 Kevin Orie	.50	.23
❑ 70 Sammy Sosa	5.00	2.20
❑ 71 Albert Belle	2.00	.90
❑ 72 Frank Thomas	6.00	2.70
❑ 73 Robin Ventura	.75	.35
❑ 74 David Justice	2.00	.90
❑ 75 Kenny Lofton	2.00	.90
❑ 76 Omar Vizquel	.75	.35
❑ 77 Manny Ramirez	2.00	.90
❑ 78 Jim Thome	2.00	.90
❑ 79 Dante Bichette	.75	.35
❑ 80 Larry Walker	2.00	.90
❑ 81 Vinny Castilla	1.25	.55
❑ 82 Ellis Burks	.75	.35
❑ 83 Bobby Higginson	1.25	.55
❑ 84 Brian Hunter	.75	.35
❑ 85 Tony Clark	1.25	.55
❑ 86 Mike Hampton	.50	.23
❑ 87 Jeff Bagwell	3.00	1.35
❑ 88 Craig Biggio	2.00	.90
❑ 89 Derek Bell	.75	.35
❑ 90 Mike Piazza	6.00	2.70
❑ 91 Ramon Martinez	.75	.35
❑ 92 Raul Mondesi	1.25	.55
❑ 93 Hideo Nomo	2.50	1.10
❑ 94 Eric Karros	.75	.35
❑ 95 Paul Molitor	2.00	.90
❑ 96 Marty Cordova	.50	.23
❑ 97 Brad Radke	.75	.35
❑ 98 Mark Grudzielanek	.75	.35
❑ 99 Carlos Perez	.75	.35
❑ 100 Rondell White	.75	.35
❑ 101 Todd Hundley	.75	.35
❑ 102 Edgardo Alfonzo	.75	.35
❑ 103 John Franco	.75	.35
❑ 104 John Olerud	.75	.35
❑ 105 Tino Martinez	2.00	.90
❑ 106 David Cone	1.25	.55
❑ 107 Paul O'Neill	.75	.35
❑ 108 Andy Pettitte	1.25	.55
❑ 109 Bernie Williams	2.00	.90
❑ 110 Rickey Henderson	2.00	.90
❑ 111 Jason Giambi	.75	.35
❑ 112 Matt Stairs	.75	.35
❑ 113 Gregg Jefferies	.50	.23
❑ 114 Rico Brogna	.75	.35
❑ 115 Curt Schilling	.75	.35
❑ 116 Jason Schmidt	.50	.23
❑ 117 Jose Guillen	.75	.35
❑ 118 Kevin Young	.75	.35
❑ 119 Ray Lankford	.75	.35
❑ 120 Mark McGwire	12.00	5.50
❑ 121 Delino DeShields	.50	.23
❑ 122 Ken Caminiti	1.25	.55
❑ 123 Tony Gwynn	5.00	2.20
❑ 124 Trevor Hoffman	.75	.35
❑ 125 Barry Bonds	2.50	1.10
❑ 126 Jeff Kent	.75	.35
❑ 127 Shawn Estes	.75	.35
❑ 128 J.T. Snow	.75	.35
❑ 129 Jay Buhner	.75	.35
❑ 130 Ken Griffey Jr.	10.00	4.50
❑ 131 Dan Wilson	.50	.23
❑ 132 Edgar Martinez	.75	.35
❑ 133 Alex Rodriguez	6.00	2.70
❑ 134 Rusty Greer	.75	.35
❑ 135 Juan Gonzalez	5.00	2.20
❑ 136 Fernando Tatis	.75	.35
❑ 137 Ivan Rodriguez	2.50	1.10
❑ 138 Carlos Delgado	.75	.35
❑ 139 Pat Hentgen	.75	.35
❑ 140 Roger Clemens	4.00	1.80
❑ 141 Chipper Jones SF	6.00	2.70
❑ 142 Greg Maddux SF	8.00	3.60
❑ 143 Rafael Palmeiro SF	1.50	.70
❑ 144 Mike Mussina SF	2.50	1.10
❑ 145 Cal Ripken SF	10.00	4.50
❑ 146 Nomar Garciaparra SF	8.00	3.60
❑ 147 Mo Vaughn SF	3.00	1.35

❑ 148 Sammy Sosa SF 6.00 2.70
❑ 149 Albert Belle SF 2.50 1.10
❑ 150 Frank Thomas SF 8.00 3.60
❑ 151 Jim Thome SF 2.50 1.10
❑ 152 Kenny Lofton SF 2.50 1.10
❑ 153 Manny Ramirez SF 2.50 1.10
❑ 154 Larry Walker SF 2.50 1.10
❑ 155 Jeff Bagwell SF 4.00 1.80
❑ 156 Craig Biggio SF 2.50 1.10
❑ 157 Mike Piazza SF 8.00 3.60
❑ 158 Paul Molitor SF 2.50 1.10
❑ 159 Derek Jeter SF 6.00 2.70
❑ 160 Tino Martinez SF 2.50 1.10
❑ 161 Curt Schilling SF 1.00 .45
❑ 162 Mark McGwire SF 15.00 6.75
❑ 163 Tony Gwynn SF 6.00 2.70
❑ 164 Barry Bonds SF 3.00 1.35
❑ 165 Ken Griffey Jr. SF 12.00 5.50
❑ 166 Randy Johnson SF 2.50 1.10
❑ 167 Alex Rodriguez SF 8.00 3.60
❑ 168 Juan Gonzalez SF 6.00 2.70
❑ 169 Ivan Rodriguez SF 3.00 1.35
❑ 170 Roger Clemens SF 5.00 2.20
❑ 171 Greg Maddux HG 25.00 11.00
❑ 172 Cal Ripken HG 30.00 13.50
❑ 173 Frank Thomas HG 25.00 11.00
❑ 174 Jeff Bagwell HG 12.00 5.50
❑ 175 Mike Piazza HG 25.00 11.00
❑ 176 Mark McGwire HG 50.00 22.00
❑ 177 Barry Bonds HG 10.00 4.50
❑ 178 Ken Griffey Jr. HG 40.00 18.00
❑ 179 Alex Rodriguez HG 25.00 11.00
❑ 180 Roger Clemens HG 15.00 6.75
❑ 181 Mike Caruso YM 1.25 .55
❑ 182 David Ortiz YM 1.25 .55
❑ 183 Gabe Alvarez YM 1.25 .55
❑ 184 Gary Matthews Jr. YM 2.50 1.10
❑ 185 Kerry Wood YM 15.00 6.75
❑ 186 Carl Pavano YM 1.25 .55
❑ 187 Alex Gonzalez YM 1.25 .55
❑ 188 Masato Yoshii YM 2.50 1.10
❑ 189 Larry Sutton YM .75 .35
❑ 190 Russell Branyan YM 1.25 .55
❑ 191 Bruce Chen YM 1.25 .55
❑ 192 Rolando Arrojo YM 5.00 2.20
❑ 193 Ryan Christenson YM 1.25 .55
❑ 194 Cliff Politte YM 1.25 .55
❑ 195 A.J. Hinch YM 1.25 .55
❑ 196 Kevin Witt YM 1.25 .55
❑ 197 Daryle Ward YM 1.25 .55
❑ 198 Corey Koskie YM 3.00 1.35
❑ 199 Mike Lowell YM 3.00 1.35
❑ 200 Travis Lee YM 6.00 2.70
❑ 201 Kevin Millwood YM 8.00 3.60
❑ 202 Robert Smith YM 1.25 .55
❑ 203 Magglio Ordonez YM 4.00 1.80
❑ 204 Eric Milton YM 1.25 .55
❑ 205 Geoff Jenkins YM 1.25 .55
❑ 206 Rich Butler YM 2.00 .90
❑ 207 Mike Kinkade YM 2.50 1.10
❑ 208 Braden Looper YM 1.25 .55
❑ 209 Matt Clement YM 1.25 .55
❑ 210 Derrek Lee YM 1.25 .55
❑ 211 Randy Johnson PP 2.50 1.10
❑ 212 John Smoltz PP 1.00 .45
❑ 213 Roger Clemens PP 5.00 2.20
❑ 214 Curt Schilling PP 1.00 .45
❑ 215 Pedro Martinez PP 2.50 1.10
❑ 216 Vinny Castilla PP 1.50 .70
❑ 217 Jose Cruz Jr. PP 2.50 1.10
❑ 218 Jim Thome PP 2.50 1.10
❑ 219 Alex Rodriguez PP 8.00 3.60
❑ 220 Frank Thomas PP 8.00 3.60
❑ 221 Tim Salmon PP 2.50 1.10
❑ 222 Larry Walker PP 2.50 1.10
❑ 223 Albert Belle PP 2.50 1.10
❑ 224 Manny Ramirez PP 2.50 1.10
❑ 225 Mark McGwire PP 15.00 6.75
❑ 226 Mo Vaughn PP 3.00 1.35
❑ 227 Andres Galarraga PP 2.50 1.10
❑ 228 Scott Rolen PP 5.00 2.20
❑ 229 Travis Lee PP 4.00 1.80
❑ 230 Mike Piazza PP 8.00 3.60
❑ 231 Nomar Garciaparra PP 8.00 3.60
❑ 232 Andruw Jones PP 2.50 1.10
❑ 233 Barry Bonds PP 3.00 1.35
❑ 234 Jeff Bagwell PP 4.00 1.80
❑ 235 Juan Gonzalez PP 6.00 2.70
❑ 236 Tino Martinez PP 2.50 1.10
❑ 237 Vladimir Guerrero PP 3.00 1.35
❑ 238 Rafael Palmeiro PP 1.50 .70
❑ 239 Russell Branyan PP 1.00 .45
❑ 240 Ken Griffey Jr. PP 12.00 5.50
❑ 241 Cecil Fielder .75 .35
❑ 242 Chuck Finley .75 .35
❑ 243 Jay Bell .75 .35
❑ 244 Andy Benes .75 .35
❑ 245 Matt Williams .75 .35
❑ 246 Brian Anderson .75 .35
❑ 247 Dave Dellucci 2.50 1.10
❑ 248 Andres Galarraga 2.00 .90
❑ 249 Andruw Jones 2.50 1.10
❑ 250 Greg Maddux 6.00 2.70
❑ 251 Brady Anderson .75 .35
❑ 252 Joe Carter .75 .35
❑ 253 Eric Davis .75 .35
❑ 254 Pedro Martinez 2.00 .90
❑ 255 Nomar Garciaparra 6.00 2.70
❑ 256 Dennis Eckersley .75 .35
❑ 257 Henry Rodriguez .75 .35
❑ 258 Jeff Blauser .50 .23
❑ 259 Jaime Navarro .50 .23
❑ 260 Ray Durham .75 .35
❑ 261 Chris Stynes .50 .23
❑ 262 Willie Greene .75 .35
❑ 263 Reggie Sanders .75 .35
❑ 264 Bret Boone .75 .35
❑ 265 Barry Larkin 1.25 .55
❑ 266 Travis Fryman .75 .35
❑ 267 Charles Nagy .75 .35
❑ 268 Sandy Alomar Jr. .75 .35
❑ 269 Darryl Kile .75 .35
❑ 270 Mike Lansing .50 .23
❑ 271 Pedro Astacio .50 .23
❑ 272 Damion Easley .75 .35
❑ 273 Joe Randa .50 .23
❑ 274 Luis Gonzalez .50 .23
❑ 275 Mike Piazza 6.00 2.70
❑ 276 Todd Zeile .75 .35
❑ 277 Edgar Renteria .75 .35
❑ 278 Livan Hernandez .75 .35
❑ 279 Cliff Floyd .75 .35
❑ 280 Moises Alou 1.25 .55
❑ 281 Billy Wagner .75 .35
❑ 282 Jeff King .75 .35
❑ 283 Hal Morris .50 .23
❑ 284 Johnny Damon .75 .35
❑ 285 Dean Palmer .75 .35
❑ 286 Tim Belcher .50 .23
❑ 287 Eric Young .75 .35
❑ 288 Bobby Bonilla .75 .35
❑ 289 Gary Sheffield 1.25 .55
❑ 290 Chan Ho Park 2.00 .90
❑ 291 Charles Johnson .75 .35
❑ 292 Jeff Cirillo .75 .35
❑ 293 Jeromy Burnitz .75 .35
❑ 294 Jose Valentin .50 .23
❑ 295 Marquis Grissom .75 .35
❑ 296 Todd Walker 1.25 .55
❑ 297 Terry Steinbach .75 .35
❑ 298 Rick Aguilera .50 .23
❑ 299 Vladimir Guerrero 3.00 1.35
❑ 300 Rey Ordonez .75 .35
❑ 301 Butch Huskey .50 .23
❑ 302 Bernard Gilkey .50 .23
❑ 303 Mariano Rivera .75 .35
❑ 304 Chuck Knoblauch 2.00 .90
❑ 305 Derek Jeter 5.00 2.20
❑ 306 Ricky Bottalico .75 .35
❑ 307 Bob Abreu .75 .35
❑ 308 Scott Rolen 5.00 2.20
❑ 309 Al Martin .50 .23
❑ 310 Jason Kendall .75 .35
❑ 311 Brian Jordan .75 .35
❑ 312 Ron Gant .50 .23
❑ 313 Todd Stottlemyre .75 .35
❑ 314 Greg Vaughn .75 .35
❑ 315 Kevin Brown 1.25 .55
❑ 316 Wally Joyner .75 .35
❑ 317 Robb Nen .75 .35
❑ 318 Orel Hershiser .75 .35
❑ 319 Russ Davis .75 .35
❑ 320 Randy Johnson 2.00 .90
❑ 321 Quinton McCracken .75 .35
❑ 322 Tony Saunders .50 .23
❑ 323 Wilson Alvarez .75 .35
❑ 324 Wade Boggs 2.00 .90
❑ 325 Fred McGriff 1.25 .55
❑ 326 Lee Stevens .50 .23
❑ 327 John Wetteland .75 .35
❑ 328 Jose Canseco 2.00 .90
❑ 329 Randy Myers .75 .35
❑ 330 Jose Cruz Jr. 2.50 1.10
❑ 331 Matt Williams TW 2.00 .90
❑ 332 Andres Galarraga TW 5.00 2.20
❑ 333 Walt Weiss TW 2.00 .90
❑ 334 Joe Carter TW 2.00 .90
❑ 335 Pedro Martinez TW 5.00 2.20
❑ 336 Henry Rodriguez TW 2.00 .90
❑ 337 Travis Fryman TW 2.00 .90
❑ 338 Darryl Kile TW 2.00 .90
❑ 339 Mike Lansing TW 1.25 .55
❑ 340 Mike Piazza TW 15.00 6.75
❑ 341 Moises Alou TW 3.00 1.35
❑ 342 Charles Johnson TW 2.00 .90
❑ 343 Chuck Knoblauch TW 5.00 2.20
❑ 344 Rickey Henderson TW 5.00 2.20
❑ 345 Kevin Brown TW 3.00 1.35
❑ 346 Orel Hershiser TW 2.00 .90
❑ 347 Wade Boggs TW 5.00 2.20
❑ 348 Fred McGriff TW 3.00 1.35
❑ 349 Jose Canseco TW 5.00 2.20
❑ 350 Gary Sheffield TW 3.00 1.35
❑ 351 Travis Lee CG 12.00 5.50
❑ 352 Nomar Garciaparra CG 25.00 11.00
❑ 353 Frank Thomas CG 25.00 11.00
❑ 354 Cal Ripken CG 30.00 13.50
❑ 355 Mark McGwire CG 50.00 22.00
❑ 356 Mike Piazza CG 25.00 11.00
❑ 357 Alex Rodriguez CG 25.00 11.00
❑ 358 Barry Bonds CG 10.00 4.50
❑ 359 Tony Gwynn CG 20.00 9.00
❑ 360 Ken Griffey Jr. CG 40.00 18.00

1998 SPx Finite Radiance

	MINT	NRMT
COMPLETE SET (360)	4500.00	2000.00
COMP.YM SER.1 (30)	150.00	70.00
COMMON YM (1-30)	1.50	.70
*YOUTH: .75X TO 2X BASIC YOUTH		
COMP.PE SER.1 (20)	500.00	220.00
COMMON PE (31-50)	10.00	4.50
*PE RADIANCE: 1.25X TO 3X BASIC POW.EXP.		
EXCHANGE DEADLINE 6/2/99		
COMP.BASIC SER.1 (90)	200.00	90.00
COMMON CARD (51-140)	1.00	.45
*BASIC RADIANCE: .75X TO 2X BASIC CARDS		
COMP.SF SER.1 (30)	250.00	110.00
COMMON SF (141-170)	2.00	.90
*SF RADIANCE: .75X TO 2X BASIC SF		
COMP.HG SER.1 (10)	1500.00	700.00
COMMON HG (171-180)	80.00	36.00
*HG RADIANCE: 3X TO 8X BASIC HEROES OF GAME		
COMP.YM SER.2 (30)	120.00	55.00

	MINT	NRMT
COMMON YM (181-210)	1.50	.70
*YM RADIANCE: .75X TO 2X BASIC YM		
COMP.PP SER.2 (30)	200.00	90.00
COMMON PP (211-240)	1.25	.55
*PP RADIANCE: .75X TO 2X BASIC PP		
COMP.BASIC SER.2 (90)	120.00	55.00
COMMON CARD (241-330)	1.00	.45
*BASIC RADIANCE: .75X TO 2X BASIC CARDS		
COMP.TW SER.2 (20)	120.00	55.00
COMMON TW (331-350)	4.00	1.80
*TW RADIANCE: 1.25X TO 3X BASIC TW		
COMP.CG SER.2 (10)	1500.00	700.00
COMMON CG (351-360)	80.00	36.00
*CG RADIANCE: 3X TO 8X BASIC CG		

1998 SPx Finite Spectrum

	MINT	NRMT
COMP.YM SER.1 (30)	250.00	110.00
COMMON YM (1-30)	2.50	1.10
*YM SPECTRUM: 1.25X TO 3X BASIC YM		
COMP.PE SER.1 (20)	3000.00	1350.00
COMMON PE (31-50)	60.00	27.00
*PE SPECTRUM: 8X TO 20X BASIC PE		
COMP.BASIC SER.1 (90)	300.00	135.00
COMMON CARD (51-140)	1.50	.70
*BASIC SPECTRUM: 1.25X TO 3X BASIC CARDS		
COMP.SF SER.1 (30)	400.00	180.00
COMMON SF (141-170)	3.00	1.35
*SF SPECTRUM: 1.25X TO 3X BASIC SF		
COMMON HG (171-180)		
HG NOT PRICED DUE TO SCARCITY		
COMP.YM SER.2 (30)	200.00	90.00
COMMON YM (181-210)	2.50	1.10
*YM SPECTRUM: 1.25X TO 3X BASIC YM		
COMP.PP SER.2 (30)	300.00	135.00
COMMON PP (211-240)	2.00	.90
*PP SPECTRUM: 1.25X TO 3X BASIC PP		
COMP.BASIC SER.2 (90)	200.00	90.00
COMMON CARD (241-330)	1.50	.70
*BASIC SPECTRUM: 1.25X TO 3X BASIC CARDS		
COMP.TW SET (20)	800.00	350.00
COMMON CARD (331-350)	25.00	11.00
*TW SPECTRUM: 8X TO 20X BASIC TW		
COMMON CG (351-360)		
*CG SPECTRUM: X TO X BASIC CG		
CG NOT PRICED DUE TO SCARCITY		

1998 SPx Finite Home Run Hysteria

	MINT	NRMT
COMPLETE SET (10)	1800.00	800.00
COMMON CARD (HR1-HR10)	40.00	18.00
❑ HR1 Ken Griffey Jr.	400.00	180.00
❑ HR2 Mark McGwire	500.00	220.00
❑ HR3 Sammy Sosa	200.00	90.00
❑ HR4 Albert Belle	80.00	36.00
❑ HR5 Alex Rodriguez	250.00	110.00
❑ HR6 Greg Vaughn	40.00	18.00
❑ HR7 Andres Galarraga	60.00	27.00
❑ HR8 Vinny Castilla	50.00	22.00
❑ HR9 Juan Gonzalez	200.00	90.00
❑ HR10 Chipper Jones	200.00	90.00

1991 Stadium Club

	MINT	NRMT
COMPLETE SET (600)	80.00	36.00
COMPLETE SERIES 1 (300) ..	50.00	22.00
COMPLETE SERIES 2 (300) ..	30.00	13.50
COMMON CARD (1-600)	.25	.11
❑ 1 Dave Stewart TUX	1.00	.45
❑ 2 Wally Joyner	.50	.23
❑ 3 Shawon Dunston	.25	.11
❑ 4 Darren Daulton	.50	.23
❑ 5 Will Clark	1.00	.45
❑ 6 Sammy Sosa	5.00	2.20
❑ 7 Dan Plesac	.25	.11
❑ 8 Marquis Grissom	1.00	.45
❑ 9 Erik Hanson	.25	.11
❑ 10 Geno Petralli	.25	.11
❑ 11 Jose Rijo	.25	.11
❑ 12 Carlos Quintana	.25	.11
❑ 13 Junior Ortiz	.25	.11
❑ 14 Bob Walk	.25	.11
❑ 15 Mike Macfarlane	.25	.11
❑ 16 Eric Yelding	.25	.11
❑ 17 Bryn Smith	.25	.11
❑ 18 Bip Roberts	.25	.11
❑ 19 Mike Scioscia	.25	.11
❑ 20 Mark Williamson	.25	.11
❑ 21 Don Mattingly	1.50	.70
❑ 22 John Franco	.50	.23
❑ 23 Chet Lemon	.25	.11
❑ 24 Tom Henke	.25	.11
❑ 25 Jerry Browne	.25	.11
❑ 26 Dave Justice	1.25	.55
❑ 27 Mark Langston	.25	.11
❑ 28 Damon Berryhill	.25	.11
❑ 29 Kevin Bass	.25	.11
❑ 30 Scott Fletcher	.25	.11
❑ 31 Moises Alou	2.00	.90
❑ 32 Dave Valle	.25	.11
❑ 33 Jody Reed	.25	.11
❑ 34 Dave West	.25	.11
❑ 35 Kevin McReynolds	.25	.11
❑ 36 Pat Combs	.25	.11
❑ 37 Eric Davis	.50	.23
❑ 38 Bret Saberhagen	.50	.23
❑ 39 Stan Javier	.25	.11
❑ 40 Chuck Cary	.25	.11
❑ 41 Tony Phillips	.25	.11
❑ 42 Lee Smith	.50	.23
❑ 43 Tim Teufel	.25	.11
❑ 44 Lance Dickson	.25	.11
❑ 45 Greg Litton	.25	.11
❑ 46 Teddy Higuera	.25	.11
❑ 47 Edgar Martinez	1.00	.45
❑ 48 Steve Avery	.25	.11
❑ 49 Walt Weiss	.25	.11
❑ 50 David Segui	.50	.23
❑ 51 Andy Benes	.50	.23
❑ 52 Karl Rhodes	.25	.11
❑ 53 Neal Heaton	.25	.11
❑ 54 Danny Gladden	.25	.11
❑ 55 Luis Rivera	.25	.11
❑ 56 Kevin Brown	.75	.35
❑ 57 Frank Thomas	5.00	2.20
❑ 58 Terry Mulholland	.25	.11
❑ 59 Dick Schofield	.25	.11
❑ 60 Ron Darling	.25	.11
❑ 61 Sandy Alomar Jr.	.50	.23
❑ 62 Dave Stieb	.50	.23
❑ 63 Alan Trammell	.75	.35
❑ 64 Matt Nokes	.25	.11
❑ 65 Lenny Harris	.25	.11
❑ 66 Milt Thompson	.25	.11
❑ 67 Storm Davis	.25	.11
❑ 68 Joe Oliver	.25	.11
❑ 69 Andres Galarraga	1.00	.45
❑ 70 Ozzie Guillen	.25	.11
❑ 71 Ken Howell	.25	.11
❑ 72 Garry Templeton	.25	.11
❑ 73 Derrick May	.25	.11
❑ 74 Xavier Hernandez	.25	.11
❑ 75 Dave Parker	.50	.23
❑ 76 Rick Aguilera	.50	.23
❑ 77 Robby Thompson	.25	.11
❑ 78 Pete Incaviglia	.25	.11
❑ 79 Bob Welch	.25	.11
❑ 80 Randy Milligan	.25	.11
❑ 81 Chuck Finley	.50	.23
❑ 82 Alvin Davis	.25	.11
❑ 83 Tim Naehring	.50	.23
❑ 84 Jay Bell	.50	.23
❑ 85 Joe Magrane	.25	.11
❑ 86 Howard Johnson	.25	.11
❑ 87 Jack McDowell	.25	.11
❑ 88 Kevin Seitzer	.25	.11
❑ 89 Bruce Ruffin	.25	.11
❑ 90 Fernando Valenzuela	.50	.23
❑ 91 Terry Kennedy	.25	.11
❑ 92 Barry Larkin	1.00	.45
❑ 93 Larry Walker	1.50	.70
❑ 94 Luis Salazar	.25	.11
❑ 95 Gary Sheffield	1.00	.45
❑ 96 Bobby Witt	.25	.11
❑ 97 Lonnie Smith	.25	.11
❑ 98 Bryan Harvey	.25	.11
❑ 99 Mookie Wilson	.50	.23
❑ 100 Dwight Gooden	.50	.23
❑ 101 Lou Whitaker	.50	.23
❑ 102 Ron Karkovice	.25	.11
❑ 103 Jesse Barfield	.25	.11
❑ 104 Jose DeJesus	.25	.11
❑ 105 Benito Santiago	.25	.11
❑ 106 Brian Holman	.25	.11
❑ 107 Rafael Ramirez	.25	.11
❑ 108 Ellis Burks	.50	.23
❑ 109 Mike Bielecki	.25	.11
❑ 110 Kirby Puckett	1.50	.70
❑ 111 Terry Shumpert	.25	.11
❑ 112 Chuck Crim	.25	.11
❑ 113 Todd Benzinger	.25	.11
❑ 114 Brian Barnes	.25	.11
❑ 115 Carlos Baerga	.50	.23
❑ 116 Kal Daniels	.25	.11
❑ 117 Dave Johnson	.25	.11
❑ 118 Andy Van Slyke	.50	.23
❑ 119 John Burkett	.25	.11
❑ 120 Rickey Henderson	1.00	.45
❑ 121 Tim Jones	.25	.11
❑ 122 Daryl Irvine	.25	.11
❑ 123 Ruben Sierra	.25	.11
❑ 124 Jim Abbott	.50	.23
❑ 125 Daryl Boston	.25	.11
❑ 126 Greg Maddux	3.00	1.35
❑ 127 Von Hayes	.25	.11

❑ 128 Mike Fitzgerald .25 .11
❑ 129 Wayne Edwards .25 .11
❑ 130 Greg Briley .25 .11
❑ 131 Rob Dibble .25 .11
❑ 132 Gene Larkin .25 .11
❑ 133 David Wells .50 .23
❑ 134 Steve Balboni .25 .11
❑ 135 Greg Vaughn 1.00 .45
❑ 136 Mark Davis .25 .11
❑ 137 Dave Rhode .25 .11
❑ 138 Eric Show .25 .11
❑ 139 Bobby Bonilla .50 .23
❑ 140 Dana Kiecker .25 .11
❑ 141 Gary Pettis .25 .11
❑ 142 Dennis Boyd .25 .11
❑ 143 Mike Benjamin .25 .11
❑ 144 Luis Polonia .25 .11
❑ 145 Doug Jones .25 .11
❑ 146 Al Newman .25 .11
❑ 147 Alex Fernandez .50 .23
❑ 148 Bill Doran .25 .11
❑ 149 Kevin Elster .25 .11
❑ 150 Len Dykstra .50 .23
❑ 151 Mike Gallego .25 .11
❑ 152 Tim Belcher .25 .11
❑ 153 Jay Buhner 1.00 .45
❑ 154 Ozzie Smith UER 1.25 .55
(Rookie card is 1979&
but card back says '78)
❑ 155 Jose Canseco 1.00 .45
❑ 156 Gregg Olson .25 .11
❑ 157 Charlie O'Brien .25 .11
❑ 158 Frank Tanana .25 .11
❑ 159 George Brett 2.00 .90
❑ 160 Jeff Huson .25 .11
❑ 161 Kevin Tapani .25 .11
❑ 162 Jerome Walton .25 .11
❑ 163 Charlie Hayes .25 .11
❑ 164 Chris Bosio .25 .11
❑ 165 Chris Sabo .25 .11
❑ 166 Lance Parrish .25 .11
❑ 167 Don Robinson .25 .11
❑ 168 Manny Lee .25 .11
❑ 169 Dennis Rasmussen .25 .11
❑ 170 Wade Boggs 1.00 .45
❑ 171 Bob Geren .25 .11
❑ 172 Mackey Sasser .25 .11
❑ 173 Julio Franco .25 .11
❑ 174 Otis Nixon .50 .23
❑ 175 Bert Blyleven .50 .23
❑ 176 Craig Biggio 1.00 .45
❑ 177 Eddie Murray 1.00 .45
❑ 178 Randy Tomlin .25 .11
❑ 179 Tino Martinez 1.00 .45
❑ 180 Carlton Fisk 1.00 .45
❑ 181 Dwight Smith .25 .11
❑ 182 Scott Garrelts .25 .11
❑ 183 Jim Gantner .25 .11
❑ 184 Dickie Thon .25 .11
❑ 185 John Farrell .25 .11
❑ 186 Cecil Fielder .50 .23
❑ 187 Glenn Braggs .25 .11
❑ 188 Allan Anderson .25 .11
❑ 189 Kurt Stillwell .25 .11
❑ 190 Jose Oquendo .25 .11
❑ 191 Joe Orsulak .25 .11
❑ 192 Ricky Jordan .25 .11
❑ 193 Kelly Downs .25 .11
❑ 194 Delino DeShields .50 .23
❑ 195 Omar Vizquel 1.00 .45
❑ 196 Mark Carreon .25 .11
❑ 197 Mike Harkey .25 .11
❑ 198 Jack Howell .25 .11
❑ 199 Lance Johnson .25 .11
❑ 200 Nolan Ryan TUX 4.00 1.80
❑ 201 John Marzano .25 .11
❑ 202 Doug Drabek .25 .11
❑ 203 Mark Lemke .25 .11
❑ 204 Steve Sax .25 .11
❑ 205 Greg Harris .25 .11
❑ 206 B.J. Surhoff .50 .23
❑ 207 Todd Burns .25 .11
❑ 208 Jose Gonzalez .25 .11
❑ 209 Mike Scott .25 .11
❑ 210 Dave Magadan .25 .11
❑ 211 Dante Bichette 1.00 .45
❑ 212 Trevor Wilson .25 .11
❑ 213 Hector Villanueva .25 .11
❑ 214 Dan Pasqua .25 .11
❑ 215 Greg Colbrunn .25 .11
❑ 216 Mike Jeffcoat .25 .11
❑ 217 Harold Reynolds .25 .11
❑ 218 Paul O'Neill .50 .23
❑ 219 Mark Guthrie .25 .11
❑ 220 Barry Bonds 1.25 .55
❑ 221 Jimmy Key .50 .23
❑ 222 Billy Ripken .25 .11
❑ 223 Tom Pagnozzi .25 .11
❑ 224 Bo Jackson .50 .23
❑ 225 Sid Fernandez .25 .11
❑ 226 Mike Marshall .25 .11
❑ 227 John Kruk .50 .23
❑ 228 Mike Fetters .25 .11
❑ 229 Eric Anthony .25 .11
❑ 230 Ryne Sandberg 1.25 .55
❑ 231 Carney Lansford .50 .23
❑ 232 Melido Perez .25 .11
❑ 233 Jose Lind .25 .11
❑ 234 Darryl Hamilton .25 .11
❑ 235 Tom Browning .25 .11
❑ 236 Spike Owen .25 .11
❑ 237 Juan Gonzalez 8.00 3.60
❑ 238 Felix Fermin .25 .11
❑ 239 Keith Miller .25 .11
❑ 240 Mark Gubicza .25 .11
❑ 241 Kent Anderson .25 .11
❑ 242 Alvaro Espinoza .25 .11
❑ 243 Dale Murphy 1.00 .45
❑ 244 Orel Hershiser .50 .23
❑ 245 Paul Molitor 1.00 .45
❑ 246 Eddie Whitson .25 .11
❑ 247 Joe Girardi .50 .23
❑ 248 Kent Hrbek .50 .23
❑ 249 Bill Sampen .25 .11
❑ 250 Kevin Mitchell .25 .11
❑ 251 Mariano Duncan .25 .11
❑ 252 Scott Bradley .25 .11
❑ 253 Mike Greenwell .25 .11
❑ 254 Tom Gordon .50 .23
❑ 255 Todd Zeile .50 .23
❑ 256 Bobby Thigpen .25 .11
❑ 257 Gregg Jefferies .25 .11
❑ 258 Kenny Rogers .25 .11
❑ 259 Shane Mack .25 .11
❑ 260 Zane Smith .25 .11
❑ 261 Mitch Williams .25 .11
❑ 262 Jim Deshaies .25 .11
❑ 263 Dave Winfield 1.00 .45
❑ 264 Ben McDonald .25 .11
❑ 265 Randy Ready .25 .11
❑ 266 Pat Borders .25 .11
❑ 267 Jose Uribe .25 .11
❑ 268 Derek Lilliquist .25 .11
❑ 269 Greg Brock .25 .11
❑ 270 Ken Griffey Jr. 8.00 3.60
❑ 271 Jeff Gray .25 .11
❑ 272 Danny Tartabull .25 .11
❑ 273 Denny Martinez .50 .23
❑ 274 Robin Ventura 1.00 .45
❑ 275 Randy Myers .50 .23
❑ 276 Jack Daugherty .25 .11
❑ 277 Greg Gagne .25 .11
❑ 278 Jay Howell .25 .11
❑ 279 Mike LaValliere .25 .11
❑ 280 Rex Hudler .25 .11
❑ 281 Mike Simms .25 .11
❑ 282 Kevin Maas .25 .11
❑ 283 Jeff Ballard .25 .11
❑ 284 Dave Henderson .25 .11
❑ 285 Pete O'Brien .25 .11
❑ 286 Brook Jacoby .25 .11
❑ 287 Mike Henneman .25 .11
❑ 288 Greg Olson .25 .11
❑ 289 Greg Myers .25 .11
❑ 290 Mark Grace 1.00 .45
❑ 291 Shawn Abner .25 .11
❑ 292 Frank Viola .25 .11
❑ 293 Lee Stevens .25 .11
❑ 294 Jason Grimsley .25 .11
❑ 295 Matt Williams 1.00 .45
❑ 296 Ron Robinson .25 .11
❑ 297 Tom Brunansky .25 .11
❑ 298 Checklist 1-100 .25 .11
❑ 299 Checklist 101-200 .25 .11
❑ 300 Checklist 201-300 .25 .11
❑ 301 Darryl Strawberry .50 .23
❑ 302 Bud Black .25 .11
❑ 303 Harold Baines .50 .23
❑ 304 Roberto Alomar 1.00 .45
❑ 305 Norm Charlton .25 .11
❑ 306 Gary Thurman .25 .11
❑ 307 Mike Felder .25 .11
❑ 308 Tony Gwynn 2.50 1.10
❑ 309 Roger Clemens 2.00 .90
❑ 310 Andre Dawson 1.00 .45
❑ 311 Scott Radinsky .25 .11
❑ 312 Bob Melvin .25 .11
❑ 313 Kirk McCaskill .25 .11
❑ 314 Pedro Guerrero .25 .11
❑ 315 Walt Terrell .25 .11
❑ 316 Sam Horn .25 .11
❑ 317 Wes Chamberlain UER .25 .11
(Card listed as 1989
Debut card, should be 1990)
❑ 318 Pedro Munoz .25 .11
❑ 319 Roberto Kelly .25 .11
❑ 320 Mark Portugal .25 .11
❑ 321 Tim McIntosh .25 .11
❑ 322 Jesse Orosco .25 .11
❑ 323 Gary Green .25 .11
❑ 324 Greg Harris .25 .11
❑ 325 Hubie Brooks .25 .11
❑ 326 Chris Nabholz .25 .11
❑ 327 Terry Pendleton .50 .23
❑ 328 Eric King .25 .11
❑ 329 Chili Davis .50 .23
❑ 330 Anthony Telford .25 .11
❑ 331 Kelly Gruber .25 .11
❑ 332 Dennis Eckersley .50 .23
❑ 333 Mel Hall .25 .11
❑ 334 Bob Kipper .25 .11
❑ 335 Willie McGee .50 .23
❑ 336 Steve Olin .25 .11
❑ 337 Steve Buechele .25 .11
❑ 338 Scott Leius .25 .11
❑ 339 Hal Morris .25 .11
❑ 340 Jose Offerman .25 .11
❑ 341 Kent Mercker .25 .11
❑ 342 Ken Griffey Sr. .25 .11
❑ 343 Pete Harnisch .25 .11
❑ 344 Kirk Gibson .50 .23
❑ 345 Dave Smith .25 .11
❑ 346 Dave Martinez .25 .11
❑ 347 Atlee Hammaker .25 .11
❑ 348 Brian Downing .25 .11
❑ 349 Todd Hundley 1.50 .70
❑ 350 Candy Maldonado .25 .11
❑ 351 Dwight Evans .50 .23
❑ 352 Steve Searcy .25 .11
❑ 353 Gary Gaetti .50 .23
❑ 354 Jeff Reardon .50 .23
❑ 355 Travis Fryman 1.50 .70
❑ 356 Dave Righetti .25 .11
❑ 357 Fred McGriff 1.00 .45
❑ 358 Don Slaught .25 .11
❑ 359 Gene Nelson .25 .11
❑ 360 Billy Spiers .25 .11
❑ 361 Lee Guetterman .25 .11
❑ 362 Darren Lewis .50 .23
❑ 363 Duane Ward .25 .11
❑ 364 Lloyd Moseby .25 .11
❑ 365 John Smoltz 1.00 .45
❑ 366 Felix Jose .25 .11
❑ 367 David Cone .50 .23
❑ 368 Wally Backman .25 .11
❑ 369 Jeff Montgomery .50 .23
❑ 370 Rich Garces .25 .11
❑ 371 Billy Hatcher .25 .11
❑ 372 Bill Swift .25 .11
❑ 373 Jim Eisenreich .25 .11
❑ 374 Rob Ducey .25 .11
❑ 375 Tim Crews .25 .11
❑ 376 Steve Finley 1.00 .45
❑ 377 Jeff Blauser .25 .11
❑ 378 Willie Wilson .25 .11

❑ 379 Gerald Perry .25 .11
❑ 380 Jose Mesa .25 .11
❑ 381 Pat Kelly .25 .11
❑ 382 Matt Merullo .25 .11
❑ 383 Ivan Calderon .25 .11
❑ 384 Scott Chiamparino .25 .11
❑ 385 Lloyd McClendon .25 .11
❑ 386 Dave Bergman .25 .11
❑ 387 Ed Sprague .25 .11
❑ 388 Jeff Bagwell 5.00 2.20
❑ 389 Brett Butler .50 .23
❑ 390 Larry Andersen .25 .11
❑ 391 Glenn Davis .25 .11
❑ 392 Alex Cole UER .25 .11
(Front photo actually Otis Nixon)
❑ 393 Mike Heath .25 .11
❑ 394 Danny Darwin .25 .11
❑ 395 Steve Lake .25 .11
❑ 396 Tim Layana .25 .11
❑ 397 Terry Leach .25 .11
❑ 398 Bill Wegman .25 .11
❑ 399 Mark McGwire 5.00 2.20
❑ 400 Mike Boddicker .25 .11
❑ 401 Steve Howe .25 .11
❑ 402 Bernard Gilkey .50 .23
❑ 403 Thomas Howard .25 .11
❑ 404 Rafael Belliard .25 .11
❑ 405 Tom Candiotti .25 .11
❑ 406 Rene Gonzales .25 .11
❑ 407 Chuck McElroy .25 .11
❑ 408 Paul Sorrento .50 .23
❑ 409 Randy Johnson 1.25 .55
❑ 410 Brady Anderson 1.00 .45
❑ 411 Dennis Cook .25 .11
❑ 412 Mickey Tettleton .50 .23
❑ 413 Mike Stanton .25 .11
❑ 414 Ken Oberkfell .25 .11
❑ 415 Rick Honeycutt .25 .11
❑ 416 Nelson Santovenia .25 .11
❑ 417 Bob Tewksbury .25 .11
❑ 418 Brent Mayne .25 .11
❑ 419 Steve Farr .25 .11
❑ 420 Phil Stephenson .25 .11
❑ 421 Jeff Russell .25 .11
❑ 422 Chris James .25 .11
❑ 423 Tim Leary .25 .11
❑ 424 Gary Carter 1.00 .45
❑ 425 Glenallen Hill .25 .11
❑ 426 Matt Young UER .25 .11
(Card mentions 83T/Tr as RC& but 84T shown)
❑ 427 Sid Bream .25 .11
❑ 428 Greg Swindell .25 .11
❑ 429 Scott Aldred .25 .11
❑ 430 Cal Ripken 4.00 1.80
❑ 431 Bill Landrum .25 .11
❑ 432 Earnest Riles .25 .11
❑ 433 Danny Jackson .25 .11
❑ 434 Casey Candaele .25 .11
❑ 435 Ken Hill .50 .23
❑ 436 Jaime Navarro .25 .11
❑ 437 Lance Blankenship .25 .11
❑ 438 Randy Velarde .25 .11
❑ 439 Frank DiPino .25 .11
❑ 440 Carl Nichols .25 .11
❑ 441 Jeff M. Robinson .25 .11
❑ 442 Deion Sanders .50 .23
❑ 443 Vicente Palacios .25 .11
❑ 444 Devon White .25 .11
❑ 445 John Cerutti .25 .11
❑ 446 Tracy Jones .25 .11
❑ 447 Jack Morris .50 .23
❑ 448 Mitch Webster .25 .11
❑ 449 Bob Ojeda .25 .11
❑ 450 Oscar Azocar .25 .11
❑ 451 Luis Aquino .25 .11
❑ 452 Mark Whiten .25 .11
❑ 453 Stan Belinda .25 .11
❑ 454 Ron Gant .50 .23
❑ 455 Jose DeLeon .25 .11
❑ 456 Mark Salas UER .25 .11
(Back has 85T photo& but calls it 86T)
❑ 457 Junior Felix .25 .11
❑ 458 Wally Whitehurst .25 .11
❑ 459 Phil Plantier .25 .11
❑ 460 Juan Berenguer .25 .11
❑ 461 Franklin Stubbs .25 .11
❑ 462 Joe Boever .25 .11
❑ 463 Tim Wallach .25 .11
❑ 464 Mike Moore .25 .11
❑ 465 Albert Belle 1.25 .55
❑ 466 Mike Witt .25 .11
❑ 467 Craig Worthington .25 .11
❑ 468 Jerald Clark .25 .11
❑ 469 Scott Terry .25 .11
❑ 470 Milt Cuyler .25 .11
❑ 471 John Smiley .25 .11
❑ 472 Charles Nagy 1.00 .45
❑ 473 Alan Mills .25 .11
❑ 474 John Russell .25 .11
❑ 475 Bruce Hurst .25 .11
❑ 476 Andujar Cedeno .25 .11
❑ 477 Dave Eiland .25 .11
❑ 478 Brian McRae 1.00 .45
❑ 479 Mike LaCoss .25 .11
❑ 480 Chris Gwynn .25 .11
❑ 481 Jamie Moyer .25 .11
❑ 482 John Olerud .50 .23
❑ 483 Efrain Valdez .25 .11
❑ 484 Sil Campusano .25 .11
❑ 485 Pascual Perez .25 .11
❑ 486 Gary Redus .25 .11
❑ 487 Andy Hawkins .25 .11
❑ 488 Cory Snyder .25 .11
❑ 489 Chris Hoiles .25 .11
❑ 490 Ron Hassey .25 .11
❑ 491 Gary Wayne .25 .11
❑ 492 Mark Lewis .25 .11
❑ 493 Scott Coolbaugh .25 .11
❑ 494 Gerald Young .25 .11
❑ 495 Juan Samuel .25 .11
❑ 496 Willie Fraser .25 .11
❑ 497 Jeff Treadway .25 .11
❑ 498 Vince Coleman .25 .11
❑ 499 Cris Carpenter .25 .11
❑ 500 Jack Clark .50 .23
❑ 501 Kevin Appier .50 .23
❑ 502 Rafael Palmeiro 1.00 .45
❑ 503 Hensley Meulens .25 .11
❑ 504 George Bell .25 .11
❑ 505 Tony Pena .25 .11
❑ 506 Roger McDowell .25 .11
❑ 507 Luis Sojo .25 .11
❑ 508 Mike Schooler .25 .11
❑ 509 Robin Yount 1.00 .45
❑ 510 Jack Armstrong .25 .11
❑ 511 Rick Cerone .25 .11
❑ 512 Curt Wilkerson .25 .11
❑ 513 Joe Carter .50 .23
❑ 514 Tim Burke .25 .11
❑ 515 Tony Fernandez .25 .11
❑ 516 Ramon Martinez .50 .23
❑ 517 Tim Hulett .25 .11
❑ 518 Terry Steinbach .50 .23
❑ 519 Pete Smith .25 .11
❑ 520 Ken Caminiti 1.00 .45
❑ 521 Shawn Boskie .25 .11
❑ 522 Mike Pagliarulo .25 .11
❑ 523 Tim Raines .50 .23
❑ 524 Alfredo Griffin .25 .11
❑ 525 Henry Cotto .25 .11
❑ 526 Mike Stanley .25 .11
❑ 527 Charlie Leibrandt .25 .11
❑ 528 Jeff King .50 .23
❑ 529 Eric Plunk .25 .11
❑ 530 Tom Lampkin .25 .11
❑ 531 Steve Bedrosian .25 .11
❑ 532 Tom Herr .25 .11
❑ 533 Craig Lefferts .25 .11
❑ 534 Jeff Reed .25 .11
❑ 535 Mickey Morandini .25 .11
❑ 536 Greg Cadaret .25 .11
❑ 537 Ray Lankford 2.00 .90
❑ 538 John Candelaria .25 .11
❑ 539 Rob Deer .25 .11
❑ 540 Brad Arnsberg .25 .11
❑ 541 Mike Sharperson .25 .11
❑ 542 Jeff D. Robinson .25 .11
❑ 543 Mo Vaughn 5.00 2.20
❑ 544 Jeff Parrett .25 .11
❑ 545 Willie Randolph .50 .23
❑ 546 Herm Winningham .25 .11
❑ 547 Jeff Innis .25 .11
❑ 548 Chuck Knoblauch 2.50 1.10
❑ 549 Tommy Greene UER .25 .11
(Born in North Carolina, not South Carolina)
❑ 550 Jeff Hamilton .25 .11
❑ 551 Barry Jones .25 .11
❑ 552 Ken Dayley .25 .11
❑ 553 Rick Dempsey .25 .11
❑ 554 Greg Smith .25 .11
❑ 555 Mike Devereaux .25 .11
❑ 556 Keith Comstock .25 .11
❑ 557 Paul Faries .25 .11
❑ 558 Tom Glavine 1.00 .45
❑ 559 Craig Grebeck .25 .11
❑ 560 Scott Erickson .50 .23
❑ 561 Joel Skinner .25 .11
❑ 562 Mike Morgan .25 .11
❑ 563 Dave Gallagher .25 .11
❑ 564 Todd Stottlemyre .50 .23
❑ 565 Rich Rodriguez .25 .11
❑ 566 Craig Wilson .25 .11
❑ 567 Jeff Brantley .25 .11
❑ 568 Scott Kamieniecki .25 .11
❑ 569 Steve Decker .25 .11
❑ 570 Juan Agosto .25 .11
❑ 571 Tommy Gregg .25 .11
❑ 572 Kevin Wickander .25 .11
❑ 573 Jamie Quirk UER .25 .11
(Rookie card is 1976, but card back is 1990)
❑ 574 Jerry Don Gleaton .25 .11
❑ 575 Chris Hammond .25 .11
❑ 576 Luis Gonzalez 1.00 .45
❑ 577 Russ Swan .25 .11
❑ 578 Jeff Conine 1.00 .45
❑ 579 Charlie Hough .50 .23
❑ 580 Jeff Kunkel .25 .11
❑ 581 Darrel Akerfelds .25 .11
❑ 582 Jeff Manto .25 .11
❑ 583 Alejandro Pena .25 .11
❑ 584 Mark Davidson .25 .11
❑ 585 Bob MacDonald .25 .11
❑ 586 Paul Assenmacher .25 .11
❑ 587 Dan Wilson 1.00 .45
❑ 588 Tom Bolton .25 .11
❑ 589 Brian Harper .25 .11
❑ 590 John Habyan .25 .11
❑ 591 John Orton .25 .11
❑ 592 Mark Gardner .25 .11
❑ 593 Turner Ward .25 .11
❑ 594 Bob Patterson .25 .11
❑ 595 Ed Nunez .25 .11
❑ 596 Gary Scott UER .25 .11
(Major League Batting Record should be Minor League)
❑ 597 Scott Bankhead .25 .11
❑ 598 Checklist 301-400 .25 .11
❑ 599 Checklist 401-500 .25 .11
❑ 600 Checklist 501-600 .25 .11

1992 Stadium Club Dome

	MINT	NRMT
COMP.FACT.SET (200)	15.00	6.75
COMMON CARD (1-200)	.10	.05

❑ 1 Terry Adams .20 .09
❑ 2 Tommy Adams .10 .05
❑ 3 Rick Aguilera .20 .09
❑ 4 Ron Allen .10 .05
❑ 5 Roberto Alomar .40 .18
❑ 6 Sandy Alomar .20 .09
❑ 7 Greg Anthony .10 .05
❑ 8 James Austin .10 .05
❑ 9 Steve Avery .10 .05
❑ 10 Harold Baines .20 .09
❑ 11 Brian Barber .10 .05
❑ 12 Jon Barnes .10 .05

❑ 13 George Bell	.10	.05
❑ 14 Doug Bennett	.10	.05
❑ 15 Sean Bergman	.10	.05
❑ 16 Craig Biggio	.40	.18
❑ 17 Bill Bliss	.10	.05
❑ 18 Wade Boggs	.40	.18
❑ 19 Bobby Bonilla	.20	.09
❑ 20 Russell Brock	.10	.05
❑ 21 Tarrik Brock	.10	.05
❑ 22 Tom Browning	.10	.05
❑ 23 Brett Butler	.20	.09
❑ 24 Ivan Calderon	.10	.05
❑ 25 Joe Carter	.20	.09
❑ 26 Joe Caruso	.10	.05
❑ 27 Dan Cholowsky	.10	.05
❑ 28 Will Clark	.40	.18
❑ 29 Roger Clemens	.75	.35
❑ 30 Shawn Curran	.10	.05
❑ 31 Chris Curtis	.10	.05
❑ 32 Chili Davis	.20	.09
❑ 33 Andre Dawson	.30	.14
❑ 34 Joe DeBerry	.10	.05
❑ 35 John Dettmer	.10	.05
❑ 36 Rob Dibble	.10	.05
❑ 37 John Donati	.10	.05
❑ 38 Dave Doorneweerd	.10	.05
❑ 39 Darren Dreifort	.20	.09
❑ 40 Mike Durant	.10	.05
❑ 41 Chris Durkin	.10	.05
❑ 42 Dennis Eckersley	.20	.09
❑ 43 Brian Edmondson	.10	.05
❑ 44 Vaughn Eshelman	.10	.05
❑ 45 Shawn Estes	.50	.23
❑ 46 Jorge Fabregas	.10	.05
❑ 47 Jon Farrell	.10	.05
❑ 48 Cecil Fielder	.20	.09
❑ 49 Carlton Fisk	.40	.18
❑ 50 Tim Flannelly	.10	.05
❑ 51 Cliff Floyd	.75	.35
❑ 52 Julio Franco	.10	.05
❑ 53 Greg Gagne	.10	.05
❑ 54 Chris Gambs	.10	.05
❑ 55 Ron Gant	.20	.09
❑ 56 Brent Gates	.10	.05
❑ 57 Dwayne Gerald	.10	.05
❑ 58 Jason Giambi	.50	.23
❑ 59 Benji Gil	.10	.05
❑ 60 Mark Gipner	.10	.05
❑ 61 Danny Gladden	.10	.05
❑ 62 Tom Glavine	.30	.14
❑ 63 Jimmy Gonzalez	.10	.05
❑ 64 Jeff Granger	.20	.09
❑ 65 Dan Grapenthien	.10	.05
❑ 66 Dennis Gray	.10	.05
❑ 67 Shawn Green	1.50	.70
❑ 68 Tyler Green	.10	.05
❑ 69 Todd Greene	.20	.09
❑ 70 Ken Griffey Jr.	2.00	.90
❑ 71 Kelly Gruber	.10	.05
❑ 72 Ozzie Guillen	.10	.05
❑ 73 Tony Gwynn	1.00	.45
❑ 74 Shane Halter	.10	.05
❑ 75 Jeffrey Hammonds	.40	.18
❑ 76 Larry Hanlon	.10	.05
❑ 77 Pete Harnisch	.10	.05
❑ 78 Mike Harrison	.10	.05
❑ 79 Bryan Harvey	.10	.05
❑ 80 Scott Hatteberg	.10	.05
❑ 81 Rick Helling	.40	.18
❑ 82 Dave Henderson	.10	.05
❑ 83 Rickey Henderson	.40	.18
❑ 84 Tyrone Hill	.10	.05
❑ 85 Todd Hollandsworth	.40	.18
❑ 86 Brian Holliday	.10	.05
❑ 87 Terry Horn	.10	.05
❑ 88 Jeff Hostetler	.10	.05
❑ 89 Kent Hrbek	.20	.09
❑ 90 Mark Hubbard	.10	.05
❑ 91 Charles Johnson	.75	.35
❑ 92 Howard Johnson	.10	.05
❑ 93 Todd Johnson	.10	.05
❑ 94 Bobby Jones	.40	.18
❑ 95 Dan Jones	.10	.05
❑ 96 Felix Jose	.10	.05
❑ 97 David Justice	.40	.18
❑ 98 Jimmy Key	.20	.09
❑ 99 Marc Kroon	.10	.05
❑ 100 John Kruk	.20	.09
❑ 101 Mark Langston	.10	.05
❑ 102 Barry Larkin	.30	.14
❑ 103 Mike LaValliere	.10	.05
❑ 104 Scott Leius	.10	.05
❑ 105 Mark Lemke	.10	.05
❑ 106 Donnie Leshnock	.10	.05
❑ 107 Jimmy Lewis	.10	.05
❑ 108 Shane Livesy	.10	.05
❑ 109 Ryan Long	.10	.05
❑ 110 Trevor Mallory	.10	.05
❑ 111 Denny Martinez	.20	.09
❑ 112 Justin Mashore	.10	.05
❑ 113 Jason McDonald	.20	.09
❑ 114 Jack McDowell	.10	.05
❑ 115 Tom McKinnon	.10	.05
❑ 116 Billy McMillon	.10	.05
❑ 117 Buck McNabb	.20	.09
❑ 118 Jim Mecir	.10	.05
❑ 119 Dan Melendez	.10	.05
❑ 120 Shawn Miller	.10	.05
❑ 121 Trever Miller	.10	.05
❑ 122 Paul Molitor	.40	.18
❑ 123 Vincent Moore	.10	.05
❑ 124 Mike Morgan	.10	.05
❑ 125 Jack Morris WS	.10	.05
❑ 126 Jack Morris AS	.10	.05
❑ 127 Sean Mulligan	.10	.05
❑ 128 Eddie Murray AS	.40	.18
❑ 129 Mike Neill	.10	.05
❑ 130 Phil Nevin	.10	.05
❑ 131 Mark O'Brien	.10	.05
❑ 132 Alex Ochoa	.30	.14
❑ 133 Chad Ogea	.40	.18
❑ 134 Greg Olson	.10	.05
❑ 135 Paul O'Neill	.20	.09
❑ 136 Jared Osentowski	.10	.05
❑ 137 Mike Pagliarulo	.10	.05
❑ 138 Rafael Palmeiro	.30	.14
❑ 139 Rodney Pedraza	.10	.05
❑ 140 Tony Phillips (P)	.10	.05
❑ 141 Scott Pisciotta	.10	.05
❑ 142 Christopher Pritchett	.10	.05
❑ 143 Jason Pruitt	.10	.05
❑ 144 Kirby Puckett WS UER (Championship series AB and BA is wrong)	.60	.25
❑ 145 Kirby Puckett AS	.60	.25
❑ 146 Manny Ramirez	10.00	4.50
❑ 147 Eddie Ramos	.10	.05
❑ 148 Mark Ratekin	.10	.05
❑ 149 Jeff Reardon	.20	.09
❑ 150 Sean Rees	.10	.05
❑ 151 Calvin Reese	.40	.18
❑ 152 Desmond Relaford	.50	.23
❑ 153 Eric Richardson	.10	.05
❑ 154 Cal Ripken	1.50	.70
❑ 155 Chris Roberts	.10	.05
❑ 156 Mike Robertson	.10	.05
❑ 157 Steve Rodriguez	.10	.05
❑ 158 Mike Rossiter	.10	.05
❑ 159 Scott Ruffcorn	.10	.05
❑ 160 Chris Sabo	.10	.05
❑ 161 Juan Samuel	.10	.05
❑ 162 Ryne Sandberg UER (On 5th line& prior misspelled as prilor)	.50	.23
❑ 163 Scott Sanderson	.10	.05
❑ 164 Benny Santiago	.10	.05
❑ 165 Gene Schall	.10	.05
❑ 166 Chad Schoenvogel	.10	.05
❑ 167 Chris Seelbach	.10	.05
❑ 168 Aaron Sele	.75	.35
❑ 169 Basil Shabazz	.10	.05
❑ 170 Al Shirley	.10	.05
❑ 171 Paul Shuey	.10	.05
❑ 172 Ruben Sierra	.10	.05
❑ 173 John Smiley	.10	.05
❑ 174 Lee Smith	.20	.09
❑ 175 Ozzie Smith	.50	.23
❑ 176 Tim Smith	.10	.05
❑ 177 Zane Smith	.10	.05
❑ 178 John Smoltz	.30	.14
❑ 179 Scott Stahoviak	.10	.05
❑ 180 Kennie Steenstra	.10	.05
❑ 181 Kevin Stocker	.10	.05
❑ 182 Chris Stynes	.40	.18
❑ 183 Danny Tartabull	.10	.05
❑ 184 Brien Taylor	.10	.05
❑ 185 Todd Taylor	.10	.05
❑ 186 Larry Thomas	.10	.05
❑ 187 Ozzie Timmons (See also 188)	.20	.09
❑ 188 David Tuttle UER (Mistakenly numbered as 187 on card)	.10	.05
❑ 189 Andy Van Slyke	.20	.09
❑ 190 Frank Viola	.10	.05
❑ 191 Michael Walkden	.10	.05
❑ 192 Jeff Ware	.10	.05
❑ 193 Allen Watson	.10	.05
❑ 194 Steve Whitaker	.10	.05
❑ 195 Jerry Willard	.10	.05
❑ 196 Craig Wilson	.10	.05
❑ 197 Chris Wimmer	.10	.05
❑ 198 Steve Wojciechowski	.10	.05
❑ 199 Joel Wolfe	.10	.05
❑ 200 Ivan Zweig	.10	.05

1992 Stadium Club

	MINT	NRMT
COMPLETE SET (900)	50.00	22.00
COMPLETE SERIES 1 (300)	18.00	8.00
COMPLETE SERIES 2 (300)	18.00	8.00
COMPLETE SERIES 3 (300)	18.00	8.00
COMMON CARD (1-900)	.10	.05
❑ 1 Cal Ripken UER (Misspelled Ripkin on card back)	1.50	.70
❑ 2 Eric Yelding	.10	.05
❑ 3 Geno Petralli	.10	.05
❑ 4 Wally Backman	.10	.05
❑ 5 Milt Cuyler	.10	.05
❑ 6 Kevin Bass	.10	.05
❑ 7 Dante Bichette	.30	.14
❑ 8 Ray Lankford	.40	.18
❑ 9 Mel Hall	.10	.05
❑ 10 Joe Carter	.20	.09
❑ 11 Juan Samuel	.10	.05
❑ 12 Jeff Montgomery	.20	.09
❑ 13 Glenn Braggs	.10	.05
❑ 14 Henry Cotto	.10	.05
❑ 15 Deion Sanders	.40	.18

❑ 16 Dick Schofield .10 .05
❑ 17 David Cone .20 .09
❑ 18 Chili Davis .20 .09
❑ 19 Tom Foley .10 .05
❑ 20 Ozzie Guillen .10 .05
❑ 21 Luis Salazar .10 .05
❑ 22 Terry Steinbach .20 .09
❑ 23 Chris James .10 .05
❑ 24 Jeff King .20 .09
❑ 25 Carlos Quintana .10 .05
❑ 26 Mike Maddux .10 .05
❑ 27 Tommy Greene .10 .05
❑ 28 Jeff Russell .10 .05
❑ 29 Steve Finley .20 .09
❑ 30 Mike Flanagan .10 .05
❑ 31 Darren Lewis .10 .05
❑ 32 Mark Lee .10 .05
❑ 33 Willie Fraser .10 .05
❑ 34 Mike Henneman .10 .05
❑ 35 Kevin Maas .10 .05
❑ 36 Dave Hansen .10 .05
❑ 37 Erik Hanson .10 .05
❑ 38 Bill Doran .10 .05
❑ 39 Mike Boddicker .10 .05
❑ 40 Vince Coleman .10 .05
❑ 41 Devon White .10 .05
❑ 42 Mark Gardner .10 .05
❑ 43 Scott Lewis .10 .05
❑ 44 Juan Berenguer .10 .05
❑ 45 Carney Lansford .20 .09
❑ 46 Curt Wilkerson .10 .05
❑ 47 Shane Mack .10 .05
❑ 48 Bip Roberts .10 .05
❑ 49 Greg A. Harris .10 .05
❑ 50 Ryne Sandberg .50 .23
❑ 51 Mark Whiten .10 .05
❑ 52 Jack McDowell .10 .05
❑ 53 Jimmy Jones .10 .05
❑ 54 Steve Lake .10 .05
❑ 55 Bud Black .10 .05
❑ 56 Dave Valle .10 .05
❑ 57 Kevin Reimer .10 .05
❑ 58 Rich Gedman UER .10 .05
(Wrong BARS chart used)
❑ 59 Travis Fryman .20 .09
❑ 60 Steve Avery .10 .05
❑ 61 Francisco de la Rosa .10 .05
❑ 62 Scott Hemond .10 .05
❑ 63 Hal Morris .10 .05
❑ 64 Hensley Meulens .10 .05
❑ 65 Frank Castillo .10 .05
❑ 66 Gene Larkin .10 .05
❑ 67 Jose DeLeon .10 .05
❑ 68 Al Osuna .10 .05
❑ 69 Dave Cochrane .10 .05
❑ 70 Robin Ventura .20 .09
❑ 71 John Cerutti .10 .05
❑ 72 Kevin Gross .10 .05
❑ 73 Ivan Calderon .10 .05
❑ 74 Mike Macfarlane .10 .05
❑ 75 Stan Belinda .10 .05
❑ 76 Shawn Hillegas .10 .05
❑ 77 Pat Borders .10 .05
❑ 78 Jim Vatcher .10 .05
❑ 79 Bobby Rose .10 .05
❑ 80 Roger Clemens .75 .35
❑ 81 Craig Worthington .10 .05
❑ 82 Jeff Treadway .10 .05
❑ 83 Jamie Quirk .10 .05
❑ 84 Randy Bush .10 .05
❑ 85 Anthony Young .10 .05
❑ 86 Trevor Wilson .10 .05
❑ 87 Jaime Navarro .10 .05
❑ 88 Les Lancaster .10 .05
❑ 89 Pat Kelly .10 .05
❑ 90 Alvin Davis .10 .05
❑ 91 Larry Andersen .10 .05
❑ 92 Rob Deer .10 .05
❑ 93 Mike Sharperson .10 .05
❑ 94 Lance Parrish .10 .05
❑ 95 Cecil Espy .10 .05
❑ 96 Tim Spehr .10 .05
❑ 97 Dave Stieb .10 .05
❑ 98 Terry Mulholland .10 .05
❑ 99 Dennis Boyd .10 .05
❑ 100 Barry Larkin .30 .14
❑ 101 Ryan Bowen .10 .05
❑ 102 Felix Fermin .10 .05
❑ 103 Luis Alicea .10 .05
❑ 104 Tim Hulett .10 .05
❑ 105 Rafael Belliard .10 .05
❑ 106 Mike Gallego .10 .05
❑ 107 Dave Righetti .10 .05
❑ 108 Jeff Schaefer .10 .05
❑ 109 Ricky Bones .10 .05
❑ 110 Scott Erickson .20 .09
❑ 111 Matt Nokes .10 .05
❑ 112 Bob Scanlan .10 .05
❑ 113 Tom Candiotti .10 .05
❑ 114 Sean Berry .10 .05
❑ 115 Kevin Morton .10 .05
❑ 116 Scott Fletcher .10 .05
❑ 117 B.J. Surhoff .20 .09
❑ 118 Dave Magadan UER .10 .05
(Born Tampa, not Tamps)
❑ 119 Bill Gullickson .10 .05
❑ 120 Marquis Grissom .20 .09
❑ 121 Lenny Harris .10 .05
❑ 122 Wally Joyner .20 .09
❑ 123 Kevin Brown .30 .14
❑ 124 Braulio Castillo .10 .05
❑ 125 Eric King .10 .05
❑ 126 Mark Portugal .10 .05
❑ 127 Calvin Jones .10 .05
❑ 128 Mike Heath .10 .05
❑ 129 Todd Van Poppel .10 .05
❑ 130 Benny Santiago .10 .05
❑ 131 Gary Thurman .10 .05
❑ 132 Joe Girardi .20 .09
❑ 133 Dave Eiland .10 .05
❑ 134 Orlando Merced .10 .05
❑ 135 Joe Orsulak .10 .05
❑ 136 John Burkett .10 .05
❑ 137 Ken Dayley .10 .05
❑ 138 Ken Hill .10 .05
❑ 139 Walt Terrell .10 .05
❑ 140 Mike Scioscia .10 .05
❑ 141 Junior Felix .10 .05
❑ 142 Ken Caminiti .30 .14
❑ 143 Carlos Baerga .10 .05
❑ 144 Tony Fossas .10 .05
❑ 145 Craig Grebeck .10 .05
❑ 146 Scott Bradley .10 .05
❑ 147 Kent Mercker .10 .05
❑ 148 Derrick May .10 .05
❑ 149 Jerald Clark .10 .05
❑ 150 George Brett .75 .35
❑ 151 Luis Quinones .10 .05
❑ 152 Mike Pagliarulo .10 .05
❑ 153 Jose Guzman .10 .05
❑ 154 Charlie O'Brien .10 .05
❑ 155 Darren Holmes .10 .05
❑ 156 Joe Boever .10 .05
❑ 157 Rich Monteleone .10 .05
❑ 158 Reggie Harris .10 .05
❑ 159 Roberto Alomar .40 .18
❑ 160 Robby Thompson .10 .05
❑ 161 Chris Hoiles .10 .05
❑ 162 Tom Pagnozzi .10 .05
❑ 163 Omar Vizquel .20 .09
❑ 164 John Candelaria .10 .05
❑ 165 Terry Shumpert .10 .05
❑ 166 Andy Mota .10 .05
❑ 167 Scott Bailes .10 .05
❑ 168 Jeff Blauser .10 .05
❑ 169 Steve Olin .10 .05
❑ 170 Doug Drabek .10 .05
❑ 171 Dave Bergman .10 .05
❑ 172 Eddie Whitson .10 .05
❑ 173 Gilberto Reyes .10 .05
❑ 174 Mark Grace .30 .14
❑ 175 Paul O'Neill .20 .09
❑ 176 Greg Cadaret .10 .05
❑ 177 Mark Williamson .10 .05
❑ 178 Casey Candaele .10 .05
❑ 179 Candy Maldonado .10 .05
❑ 180 Lee Smith .20 .09
❑ 181 Harold Reynolds .10 .05
❑ 182 David Justice .40 .18
❑ 183 Lenny Webster .10 .05
❑ 184 Donn Pall .10 .05
❑ 185 Gerald Alexander .10 .05
❑ 186 Jack Clark .20 .09
❑ 187 Stan Javier .10 .05
❑ 188 Ricky Jordan .10 .05
❑ 189 Franklin Stubbs .10 .05
❑ 190 Dennis Eckersley .20 .09
❑ 191 Danny Tartabull .10 .05
❑ 192 Pete O'Brien .10 .05
❑ 193 Mark Lewis .10 .05
❑ 194 Mike Felder .10 .05
❑ 195 Mickey Tettleton .10 .05
❑ 196 Dwight Smith .10 .05
❑ 197 Shawn Abner .10 .05
❑ 198 Jim Leyritz UER .10 .05
(Career totals less than 1991 totals)
❑ 199 Mike Devereaux .10 .05
❑ 200 Craig Biggio .40 .18
❑ 201 Kevin Elster .10 .05
❑ 202 Rance Mulliniks .10 .05
❑ 203 Tony Fernandez .10 .05
❑ 204 Allan Anderson .10 .05
❑ 205 Herm Winningham .10 .05
❑ 206 Tim Jones .10 .05
❑ 207 Ramon Martinez .20 .09
❑ 208 Teddy Higuera .10 .05
❑ 209 John Kruk .20 .09
❑ 210 Jim Abbott .20 .09
❑ 211 Dean Palmer .20 .09
❑ 212 Mark Davis .10 .05
❑ 213 Jay Buhner .30 .14
❑ 214 Jesse Barfield .10 .05
❑ 215 Kevin Mitchell .20 .09
❑ 216 Mike LaValliere .10 .05
❑ 217 Mark Wohlers .20 .09
❑ 218 Dave Henderson .10 .05
❑ 219 Dave Smith .10 .05
❑ 220 Albert Belle .50 .23
❑ 221 Spike Owen .10 .05
❑ 222 Jeff Gray .10 .05
❑ 223 Paul Gibson .10 .05
❑ 224 Bobby Thigpen .10 .05
❑ 225 Mike Mussina .60 .25
❑ 226 Darrin Jackson .10 .05
❑ 227 Luis Gonzalez .10 .05
❑ 228 Greg Briley .10 .05
❑ 229 Brent Mayne .10 .05
❑ 230 Paul Molitor .40 .18
❑ 231 Al Leiter .20 .09
❑ 232 Andy Van Slyke .20 .09
❑ 233 Ron Tingley .10 .05
❑ 234 Bernard Gilkey .20 .09
❑ 235 Kent Hrbek .20 .09
❑ 236 Eric Karros .40 .18
❑ 237 Randy Velarde .10 .05
❑ 238 Andy Allanson .10 .05
❑ 239 Willie McGee .20 .09
❑ 240 Juan Gonzalez 1.25 .55
❑ 241 Karl Rhodes .10 .05
❑ 242 Luis Mercedes .10 .05
❑ 243 Billy Swift .10 .05
❑ 244 Tommy Gregg .10 .05
❑ 245 David Howard .10 .05
❑ 246 Dave Hollins .10 .05
❑ 247 Kip Gross .10 .05
❑ 248 Walt Weiss .10 .05
❑ 249 Mackey Sasser .10 .05
❑ 250 Cecil Fielder .20 .09
❑ 251 Jerry Browne .10 .05
❑ 252 Doug Dascenzo .10 .05
❑ 253 Darryl Hamilton .10 .05
❑ 254 Dann Bilardello .10 .05
❑ 255 Luis Rivera .10 .05
❑ 256 Larry Walker .40 .18
❑ 257 Ron Karkovice .10 .05
❑ 258 Bob Tewksbury .10 .05
❑ 259 Jimmy Key .20 .09
❑ 260 Bernie Williams .40 .18
❑ 261 Gary Wayne .10 .05
❑ 262 Mike Simms UER .10 .05
(Reversed negative)
❑ 263 John Orton .10 .05
❑ 264 Marvin Freeman .10 .05
❑ 265 Mike Jeffcoat .10 .05

❑ 266 Roger Mason .10 .05
❑ 267 Edgar Martinez .30 .14
❑ 268 Henry Rodriguez .40 .18
❑ 269 Sam Horn .10 .05
❑ 270 Brian McRae .20 .09
❑ 271 Kirt Manwaring .10 .05
❑ 272 Mike Bordick .10 .05
❑ 273 Chris Sabo .10 .05
❑ 274 Jim Olander .10 .05
❑ 275 Greg W. Harris .10 .05
❑ 276 Dan Gakeler .10 .05
❑ 277 Bill Sampen .10 .05
❑ 278 Joel Skinner .10 .05
❑ 279 Curt Schilling .30 .14
❑ 280 Dale Murphy .40 .18
❑ 281 Lee Stevens .10 .05
❑ 282 Lonnie Smith .10 .05
❑ 283 Manuel Lee .10 .05
❑ 284 Shawn Boskie .10 .05
❑ 285 Kevin Seitzer .10 .05
❑ 286 Stan Royer .10 .05
❑ 287 John Dopson .10 .05
❑ 288 Scott Bullett .10 .05
❑ 289 Ken Patterson .10 .05
❑ 290 Todd Hundley .20 .09
❑ 291 Tim Leary .10 .05
❑ 292 Brett Butler .20 .09
❑ 293 Gregg Olson .10 .05
❑ 294 Jeff Brantley .10 .05
❑ 295 Brian Holman .10 .05
❑ 296 Brian Harper .10 .05
❑ 297 Brian Bohanon .10 .05
❑ 298 Checklist 1-100 .10 .05
❑ 299 Checklist 101-200 .10 .05
❑ 300 Checklist 201-300 .10 .05
❑ 301 Frank Thomas 1.25 .55
❑ 302 Lloyd McClendon .10 .05
❑ 303 Brady Anderson .30 .14
❑ 304 Julio Valera .10 .05
❑ 305 Mike Aldrete .10 .05
❑ 306 Joe Oliver .10 .05
❑ 307 Todd Stottlemyre .20 .09
❑ 308 Rey Sanchez .10 .05
❑ 309 Gary Sheffield UER .40 .18
(Listed as 5'1", should be 5'11")
❑ 310 Andujar Cedeno .10 .05
❑ 311 Kenny Rogers .10 .05
❑ 312 Bruce Hurst .10 .05
❑ 313 Mike Schooler .10 .05
❑ 314 Mike Benjamin .10 .05
❑ 315 Chuck Finley .20 .09
❑ 316 Mark Lemke .10 .05
❑ 317 Scott Livingstone .10 .05
❑ 318 Chris Nabholz .10 .05
❑ 319 Mike Humphreys .10 .05
❑ 320 Pedro Guerrero .10 .05
❑ 321 Willie Banks .10 .05
❑ 322 Tom Goodwin .20 .09
❑ 323 Hector Wagner .10 .05
❑ 324 Wally Ritchie .10 .05
❑ 325 Mo Vaughn .60 .25
❑ 326 Joe Klink .10 .05
❑ 327 Cal Eldred .10 .05
❑ 328 Daryl Boston .10 .05
❑ 329 Mike Huff .10 .05
❑ 330 Jeff Bagwell 1.00 .45
❑ 331 Bob Milacki .10 .05
❑ 332 Tom Prince .10 .05
❑ 333 Pat Tabler .10 .05
❑ 334 Ced Landrum .10 .05
❑ 335 Reggie Jefferson .20 .09
❑ 336 Mo Sanford .10 .05
❑ 337 Kevin Ritz .10 .05
❑ 338 Gerald Perry .10 .05
❑ 339 Jeff Hamilton .10 .05
❑ 340 Tim Wallach .10 .05
❑ 341 Jeff Huson .10 .05
❑ 342 Jose Melendez .10 .05
❑ 343 Willie Wilson .10 .05
❑ 344 Mike Stanton .10 .05
❑ 345 Joel Johnston .10 .05
❑ 346 Lee Guetterman .10 .05
❑ 347 Francisco Oliveras .10 .05
❑ 348 Dave Burba .10 .05
❑ 349 Tim Crews .10 .05
❑ 350 Scott Leius .10 .05
❑ 351 Danny Cox .10 .05
❑ 352 Wayne Housie .10 .05
❑ 353 Chris Donnels .10 .05
❑ 354 Chris George .10 .05
❑ 355 Gerald Young .10 .05
❑ 356 Roberto Hernandez .20 .09
❑ 357 Neal Heaton .10 .05
❑ 358 Todd Frohwirth .10 .05
❑ 359 Jose Vizcaino .10 .05
❑ 360 Jim Thome 1.00 .45
❑ 361 Craig Wilson .10 .05
❑ 362 Dave Haas .10 .05
❑ 363 Billy Hatcher .10 .05
❑ 364 John Barfield .10 .05
❑ 365 Luis Aquino .10 .05
❑ 366 Charlie Leibrandt .10 .05
❑ 367 Howard Farmer .10 .05
❑ 368 Bryn Smith .10 .05
❑ 369 Mickey Morandini .10 .05
❑ 370 Jose Canseco .40 .18
(See also 597)
❑ 371 Jose Uribe .10 .05
❑ 372 Bob MacDonald .10 .05
❑ 373 Luis Sojo .10 .05
❑ 374 Craig Shipley .10 .05
❑ 375 Scott Bankhead .10 .05
❑ 376 Greg Gagne .10 .05
❑ 377 Scott Cooper .10 .05
❑ 378 Jose Offerman .10 .05
❑ 379 Billy Spiers .10 .05
❑ 380 John Smiley .10 .05
❑ 381 Jeff Carter .10 .05
❑ 382 Heathcliff Slocumb .10 .05
❑ 383 Jeff Tackett .10 .05
❑ 384 John Kiely .10 .05
❑ 385 John Vander Wal .10 .05
❑ 386 Omar Olivares .10 .05
❑ 387 Ruben Sierra .10 .05
❑ 388 Tom Gordon .20 .09
❑ 389 Charles Nagy .20 .09
❑ 390 Dave Stewart .20 .09
❑ 391 Pete Harnisch .10 .05
❑ 392 Tim Burke .10 .05
❑ 393 Roberto Kelly .10 .05
❑ 394 Freddie Benavides .10 .05
❑ 395 Tom Glavine .30 .14
❑ 396 Wes Chamberlain .10 .05
❑ 397 Eric Gunderson .10 .05
❑ 398 Dave West .10 .05
❑ 399 Ellis Burks .20 .09
❑ 400 Ken Griffey Jr. 2.50 1.10
❑ 401 Thomas Howard .10 .05
❑ 402 Juan Guzman .10 .05
❑ 403 Mitch Webster .10 .05
❑ 404 Matt Merullo .10 .05
❑ 405 Steve Buechele .10 .05
❑ 406 Danny Jackson .10 .05
❑ 407 Felix Jose .10 .05
❑ 408 Doug Piatt .10 .05
❑ 409 Jim Eisenreich .10 .05
❑ 410 Bryan Harvey .10 .05
❑ 411 Jim Austin .10 .05
❑ 412 Jim Poole .10 .05
❑ 413 Glenallen Hill .10 .05
❑ 414 Gene Nelson .10 .05
❑ 415 Ivan Rodriguez .75 .35
❑ 416 Frank Tanana .10 .05
❑ 417 Steve Decker .10 .05
❑ 418 Jason Grimsley .10 .05
❑ 419 Tim Layana .10 .05
❑ 420 Don Mattingly .60 .25
❑ 421 Jerome Walton .10 .05
❑ 422 Rob Ducey .10 .05
❑ 423 Andy Benes .20 .09
❑ 424 John Marzano .10 .05
❑ 425 Gene Harris .10 .05
❑ 426 Tim Raines .20 .09
❑ 427 Bret Barberie .10 .05
❑ 428 Harvey Pulliam .10 .05
❑ 429 Cris Carpenter .10 .05
❑ 430 Howard Johnson .10 .05
❑ 431 Orel Hershiser .20 .09
❑ 432 Brian Hunter .10 .05
❑ 433 Kevin Tapani .10 .05
❑ 434 Rick Reed .10 .05
❑ 435 Ron Witmeyer .20 .09
❑ 436 Gary Gaetti .10 .05
❑ 437 Alex Cole .10 .05
❑ 438 Chito Martinez .10 .05
❑ 439 Greg Litton .10 .05
❑ 440 Julio Franco .10 .05
❑ 441 Mike Munoz .10 .05
❑ 442 Erik Pappas .10 .05
❑ 443 Pat Combs .10 .05
❑ 444 Lance Johnson .10 .05
❑ 445 Ed Sprague .10 .05
❑ 446 Mike Greenwell .10 .05
❑ 447 Milt Thompson .10 .05
❑ 448 Mike Magnante .10 .05
❑ 449 Chris Haney .10 .05
❑ 450 Robin Yount .40 .18
❑ 451 Rafael Ramirez .10 .05
❑ 452 Gino Minutelli .10 .05
❑ 453 Tom Lampkin .10 .05
❑ 454 Tony Perezchica .10 .05
❑ 455 Dwight Gooden .20 .09
❑ 456 Mark Guthrie .10 .05
❑ 457 Jay Howell .10 .05
❑ 458 Gary DiSarcina .10 .05
❑ 459 John Smoltz .30 .14
❑ 460 Will Clark .40 .18
❑ 461 Dave Otto .10 .05
❑ 462 Rob Maurer .10 .05
❑ 463 Dwight Evans .20 .09
❑ 464 Tom Brunansky .10 .05
❑ 465 Shawn Hare .10 .05
❑ 466 Geronimo Pena .10 .05
❑ 467 Alex Fernandez .20 .09
❑ 468 Greg Myers .10 .05
❑ 469 Jeff Fassero .20 .09
❑ 470 Len Dykstra .20 .09
❑ 471 Jeff Johnson .10 .05
❑ 472 Russ Swan .10 .05
❑ 473 Archie Corbin .10 .05
❑ 474 Chuck McElroy .10 .05
❑ 475 Mark McGwire 2.00 .90
❑ 476 Wally Whitehurst .10 .05
❑ 477 Tim McIntosh .10 .05
❑ 478 Sid Bream .10 .05
❑ 479 Jeff Juden .10 .05
❑ 480 Carlton Fisk .40 .18
❑ 481 Jeff Plympton .10 .05
❑ 482 Carlos Martinez .10 .05
❑ 483 Jim Gott .10 .05
❑ 484 Bob McClure .10 .05
❑ 485 Tim Teufel .10 .05
❑ 486 Vicente Palacios .10 .05
❑ 487 Jeff Reed .10 .05
❑ 488 Tony Phillips .10 .05
❑ 489 Mel Rojas .10 .05
❑ 490 Ben McDonald .10 .05
❑ 491 Andres Santana .10 .05
❑ 492 Chris Beasley .10 .05
❑ 493 Mike Timlin .10 .05
❑ 494 Brian Downing .10 .05
❑ 495 Kirk Gibson .20 .09
❑ 496 Scott Sanderson .10 .05
❑ 497 Nick Esasky .10 .05
❑ 498 Johnny Guzman .10 .05
❑ 499 Mitch Williams .10 .05
❑ 500 Kirby Puckett .60 .25
❑ 501 Mike Harkey .10 .05
❑ 502 Jim Gantner .10 .05
❑ 503 Bruce Egloff .10 .05
❑ 504 Josias Manzanillo .10 .05
❑ 505 Delino DeShields .20 .09
❑ 506 Rheal Cormier .10 .05
❑ 507 Jay Bell .20 .09
❑ 508 Rich Rowland .10 .05
❑ 509 Scott Servais .10 .05
❑ 510 Terry Pendleton .10 .05
❑ 511 Rich DeLucia .10 .05
❑ 512 Warren Newson .10 .05
❑ 513 Paul Faries .10 .05
❑ 514 Kal Daniels .10 .05
❑ 515 Jarvis Brown .10 .05
❑ 516 Rafael Palmeiro .30 .14
❑ 517 Kelly Downs .10 .05

❑ 518 Steve Chitren .10 .05
❑ 519 Moises Alou .40 .18
❑ 520 Wade Boggs .40 .18
❑ 521 Pete Schourek .10 .05
❑ 522 Scott Terry .10 .05
❑ 523 Kevin Appier .20 .09
❑ 524 Gary Redus .10 .05
❑ 525 George Bell .10 .05
❑ 526 Jeff Kaiser .10 .05
❑ 527 Alvaro Espinoza .10 .05
❑ 528 Luis Polonia .10 .05
❑ 529 Darren Daulton .20 .09
❑ 530 Norm Charlton .10 .05
❑ 531 John Olerud .20 .09
❑ 532 Dan Plesac .10 .05
❑ 533 Billy Ripken .10 .05
❑ 534 Rod Nichols .10 .05
❑ 535 Joey Cora .20 .09
❑ 536 Harold Baines .20 .09
❑ 537 Bob Ojeda .10 .05
❑ 538 Mark Leonard .10 .05
❑ 539 Danny Darwin .10 .05
❑ 540 Shawon Dunston .10 .05
❑ 541 Pedro Munoz .10 .05
❑ 542 Mark Gubicza .10 .05
❑ 543 Kevin Baez .10 .05
❑ 544 Todd Zeile .10 .05
❑ 545 Don Slaught .10 .05
❑ 546 Tony Eusebio .20 .09
❑ 547 Alonzo Powell .10 .05
❑ 548 Gary Pettis .10 .05
❑ 549 Brian Barnes .10 .05
❑ 550 Lou Whitaker .20 .09
❑ 551 Keith Mitchell .10 .05
❑ 552 Oscar Azocar .10 .05
❑ 553 Stu Cole .10 .05
❑ 554 Steve Wapnick .10 .05
❑ 555 Derek Bell .20 .09
❑ 556 Luis Lopez .10 .05
❑ 557 Anthony Telford .10 .05
❑ 558 Tim Mauser .10 .05
❑ 559 Glen Sutko .10 .05
❑ 560 Darryl Strawberry .20 .09
❑ 561 Tom Bolton .10 .05
❑ 562 Cliff Young .10 .05
❑ 563 Bruce Walton .10 .05
❑ 564 Chico Walker .10 .05
❑ 565 John Franco .20 .09
❑ 566 Paul McClellan .10 .05
❑ 567 Paul Abbott .10 .05
❑ 568 Gary Varsho .10 .05
❑ 569 Carlos Maldonado .10 .05
❑ 570 Kelly Gruber .10 .05
❑ 571 Jose Oquendo .10 .05
❑ 572 Steve Frey .10 .05
❑ 573 Tino Martinez .40 .18
❑ 574 Bill Haselman .10 .05
❑ 575 Eric Anthony .10 .05
❑ 576 John Habyan .10 .05
❑ 577 Jeff McNeely .10 .05
❑ 578 Chris Bosio .10 .05
❑ 579 Joe Grahe .10 .05
❑ 580 Fred McGriff .30 .14
❑ 581 Rick Honeycutt .10 .05
❑ 582 Matt Williams .30 .14
❑ 583 Cliff Brantley .10 .05
❑ 584 Rob Dibble .10 .05
❑ 585 Skeeter Barnes .10 .05
❑ 586 Greg Hibbard .10 .05
❑ 587 Randy Milligan .10 .05
❑ 588 Checklist 301-400 .10 .05
❑ 589 Checklist 401-500 .10 .05
❑ 590 Checklist 501-600 .10 .05
❑ 591 Frank Thomas MC .60 .25
❑ 592 David Justice MC .20 .09
❑ 593 Roger Clemens MC .40 .18
❑ 594 Steve Avery MC .10 .05
❑ 595 Cal Ripken MC 1.25 .55
❑ 596 Barry Larkin MC UER .20 .09
(Ranked in AL, should be NL)
❑ 597 Jose Canseco MC UER .20 .09
(Mistakenly numbered 370 on card back)
❑ 598 Will Clark MC .20 .09
❑ 599 Cecil Fielder MC .10 .05
❑ 600 Ryne Sandberg MC .40 .18
❑ 601 Chuck Knoblauch MC .20 .09
❑ 602 Dwight Gooden MC .10 .05
❑ 603 Ken Griffey Jr. MC 1.25 .55
❑ 604 Barry Bonds MC .40 .18
❑ 605 Nolan Ryan MC 1.25 .55
❑ 606 Jeff Bagwell MC .50 .23
❑ 607 Robin Yount MC .20 .09
❑ 608 Bobby Bonilla MC .10 .05
❑ 609 George Brett MC .40 .18
❑ 610 Howard Johnson MC .10 .05
❑ 611 Esteban Beltre .10 .05
❑ 612 Mike Christopher .10 .05
❑ 613 Troy Afenir .10 .05
❑ 614 Mariano Duncan .10 .05
❑ 615 Doug Henry .10 .05
❑ 616 Doug Jones .10 .05
❑ 617 Alvin Davis .10 .05
❑ 618 Craig Lefferts .10 .05
❑ 619 Kevin McReynolds .10 .05
❑ 620 Barry Bonds .50 .23
❑ 621 Turner Ward .10 .05
❑ 622 Joe Magrane .10 .05
❑ 623 Mark Parent .10 .05
❑ 624 Tom Browning .10 .05
❑ 625 John Smiley .10 .05
❑ 626 Steve Wilson .10 .05
❑ 627 Mike Gallego .10 .05
❑ 628 Sammy Sosa 1.00 .45
❑ 629 Rico Rossy .10 .05
❑ 630 Royce Clayton .10 .05
❑ 631 Clay Parker .10 .05
❑ 632 Pete Smith .10 .05
❑ 633 Jeff McKnight .10 .05
❑ 634 Jack Daugherty .10 .05
❑ 635 Steve Sax .10 .05
❑ 636 Joe Hesketh .10 .05
❑ 637 Vince Horsman .10 .05
❑ 638 Eric King .10 .05
❑ 639 Joe Boever .10 .05
❑ 640 Jack Morris .20 .09
❑ 641 Arthur Rhodes .10 .05
❑ 642 Bob Melvin .10 .05
❑ 643 Rick Wilkins .10 .05
❑ 644 Scott Scudder .10 .05
❑ 645 Bip Roberts .10 .05
❑ 646 Julio Valera .10 .05
❑ 647 Kevin Campbell .10 .05
❑ 648 Steve Searcy .10 .05
❑ 649 Scott Kamieniecki .10 .05
❑ 650 Kurt Stillwell .10 .05
❑ 651 Bob Welch .10 .05
❑ 652 Andres Galarraga .40 .18
❑ 653 Mike Jackson .20 .09
❑ 654 Bo Jackson .20 .09
❑ 655 Sid Fernandez .10 .05
❑ 656 Mike Bielecki .10 .05
❑ 657 Jeff Reardon .20 .09
❑ 658 Wayne Rosenthal .10 .05
❑ 659 Eric Bullock .10 .05
❑ 660 Eric Davis .20 .09
❑ 661 Randy Tomlin .10 .05
❑ 662 Tom Edens .10 .05
❑ 663 Rob Murphy .10 .05
❑ 664 Leo Gomez .10 .05
❑ 665 Greg Maddux 1.25 .55
❑ 666 Greg Vaughn .20 .09
❑ 667 Wade Taylor .10 .05
❑ 668 Brad Arnsberg .10 .05
❑ 669 Mike Moore .10 .05
❑ 670 Mark Langston .10 .05
❑ 671 Barry Jones .10 .05
❑ 672 Bill Landrum .10 .05
❑ 673 Greg Swindell .10 .05
❑ 674 Wayne Edwards .10 .05
❑ 675 Greg Olson .10 .05
❑ 676 Bill Pulsipher .20 .09
❑ 677 Bobby Witt .10 .05
❑ 678 Mark Carreon .10 .05
❑ 679 Patrick Lennon .10 .05
❑ 680 Ozzie Smith .50 .23
❑ 681 John Briscoe .10 .05
❑ 682 Matt Young .10 .05
❑ 683 Jeff Conine .20 .09
❑ 684 Phil Stephenson .10 .05
❑ 685 Ron Darling .10 .05
❑ 686 Bryan Hickerson .10 .05
❑ 687 Dale Sveum .10 .05
❑ 688 Kirk McCaskill .10 .05
❑ 689 Rich Amaral .10 .05
❑ 690 Danny Tartabull .10 .05
❑ 691 Donald Harris .10 .05
❑ 692 Doug Davis .10 .05
❑ 693 John Farrell .10 .05
❑ 694 Paul Gibson .10 .05
❑ 695 Kenny Lofton .75 .35
❑ 696 Mike Fetters .10 .05
❑ 697 Rosario Rodriguez .10 .05
❑ 698 Chris Jones .10 .05
❑ 699 Jeff Manto .10 .05
❑ 700 Rick Sutcliffe .10 .05
❑ 701 Scott Bankhead .10 .05
❑ 702 Donnie Hill .10 .05
❑ 703 Todd Worrell .10 .05
❑ 704 Rene Gonzales .10 .05
❑ 705 Rick Cerone .10 .05
❑ 706 Tony Pena .10 .05
❑ 707 Paul Sorrento .10 .05
❑ 708 Gary Scott .10 .05
❑ 709 Junior Noboa .10 .05
❑ 710 Wally Joyner .20 .09
❑ 711 Charlie Hayes .10 .05
❑ 712 Rich Rodriguez .10 .05
❑ 713 Rudy Seanez .10 .05
❑ 714 Jim Bullinger .10 .05
❑ 715 Jeff M. Robinson .10 .05
❑ 716 Jeff Branson .10 .05
❑ 717 Andy Ashby .20 .09
❑ 718 Dave Burba .10 .05
❑ 719 Rich Gossage .20 .09
❑ 720 Randy Johnson .40 .18
❑ 721 David Wells .20 .09
❑ 722 Paul Kilgus .10 .05
❑ 723 Dave Martinez .10 .05
❑ 724 Denny Neagle .30 .14
❑ 725 Andy Stankiewicz .10 .05
❑ 726 Rick Aguilera .20 .09
❑ 727 Junior Ortiz .10 .05
❑ 728 Storm Davis .10 .05
❑ 729 Don Robinson .10 .05
❑ 730 Ron Gant .20 .09
❑ 731 Paul Assenmacher .10 .05
❑ 732 Mike Gardiner .10 .05
❑ 733 Milt Hill .10 .05
❑ 734 Jeremy Hernandez .10 .05
❑ 735 Ken Hill .10 .05
❑ 736 Xavier Hernandez .10 .05
❑ 737 Gregg Jefferies .10 .05
❑ 738 Dick Schofield .10 .05
❑ 739 Ron Robinson .10 .05
❑ 740 Sandy Alomar .20 .09
❑ 741 Mike Stanley .10 .05
❑ 742 Butch Henry .10 .05
❑ 743 Floyd Bannister .10 .05
❑ 744 Brian Drahman .10 .05
❑ 745 Dave Winfield .40 .18
❑ 746 Bob Walk .10 .05
❑ 747 Chris James .10 .05
❑ 748 Don Prybylinski .10 .05
❑ 749 Dennis Rasmussen .10 .05
❑ 750 Rickey Henderson .40 .18
❑ 751 Chris Hammond .10 .05
❑ 752 Bob Kipper .10 .05
❑ 753 Dave Rohde .10 .05
❑ 754 Hubie Brooks .10 .05
❑ 755 Bret Saberhagen .20 .09
❑ 756 Jeff D. Robinson .10 .05
❑ 757 Pat Listach .10 .05
❑ 758 Bill Wegman .10 .05
❑ 759 John Wetteland .20 .09
❑ 760 Phil Plantier .10 .05
❑ 761 Wilson Alvarez .20 .09
❑ 762 Scott Aldred .10 .05
❑ 763 Armando Reynoso .10 .05
❑ 764 Todd Benzinger .10 .05
❑ 765 Kevin Mitchell .20 .09
❑ 766 Gary Sheffield .40 .18
❑ 767 Allan Anderson .10 .05
❑ 768 Rusty Meacham .10 .05

❑ 769 Rick Parker .10 .05
❑ 770 Nolan Ryan 1.50 .70
❑ 771 Jeff Ballard .10 .05
❑ 772 Cory Snyder .10 .05
❑ 773 Denis Boucher .10 .05
❑ 774 Jose Gonzalez .10 .05
❑ 775 Juan Guerrero .10 .05
❑ 776 Ed Nunez .10 .05
❑ 777 Scott Ruskin .10 .05
❑ 778 Terry Leach .10 .05
❑ 779 Carl Willis .10 .05
❑ 780 Bobby Bonilla .20 .09
❑ 781 Duane Ward .10 .05
❑ 782 Joe Slusarski .10 .05
❑ 783 David Segui .20 .09
❑ 784 Kirk Gibson .20 .09
❑ 785 Frank Viola .10 .05
❑ 786 Keith Miller .10 .05
❑ 787 Mike Morgan .10 .05
❑ 788 Kim Batiste .10 .05
❑ 789 Sergio Valdez .10 .05
❑ 790 Eddie Taubensee .20 .09
❑ 791 Jack Armstrong .10 .05
❑ 792 Scott Fletcher .10 .05
❑ 793 Steve Farr .10 .05
❑ 794 Dan Pasqua .10 .05
❑ 795 Eddie Murray .40 .18
❑ 796 John Morris .10 .05
❑ 797 Francisco Cabrera .10 .05
❑ 798 Mike Perez .10 .05
❑ 799 Ted Wood .10 .05
❑ 800 Jose Rijo .10 .05
❑ 801 Danny Gladden .10 .05
❑ 802 Archi Cianfrocco .10 .05
❑ 803 Monty Fariss .10 .05
❑ 804 Roger McDowell .10 .05
❑ 805 Randy Myers .20 .09
❑ 806 Kirk Dressendorfer .10 .05
❑ 807 Zane Smith .10 .05
❑ 808 Glenn Davis .10 .05
❑ 809 Torey Lovullo .10 .05
❑ 810 Andre Dawson .30 .14
❑ 811 Bill Pecota .10 .05
❑ 812 Ted Power .10 .05
❑ 813 Willie Blair .10 .05
❑ 814 Dave Fleming .10 .05
❑ 815 Chris Gwynn .10 .05
❑ 816 Jody Reed .10 .05
❑ 817 Mark Dewey .10 .05
❑ 818 Kyle Abbott .10 .05
❑ 819 Tom Henke .10 .05
❑ 820 Kevin Seitzer .10 .05
❑ 821 Al Newman .10 .05
❑ 822 Tim Sherrill .10 .05
❑ 823 Chuck Crim .10 .05
❑ 824 Darren Reed .10 .05
❑ 825 Tony Gwynn 1.00 .45
❑ 826 Steve Foster .10 .05
❑ 827 Steve Howe .10 .05
❑ 828 Brook Jacoby .10 .05
❑ 829 Rodney McCray .10 .05
❑ 830 Chuck Knoblauch .40 .18
❑ 831 John Wehner .10 .05
❑ 832 Scott Garrelts .10 .05
❑ 833 Alejandro Pena .10 .05
❑ 834 Jeff Parrett UER .10 .05
(Kentucky)
❑ 835 Juan Bell .10 .05
❑ 836 Lance Dickson .10 .05
❑ 837 Darryl Kile .20 .09
❑ 838 Efrain Valdez .10 .05
❑ 839 Bob Zupcic .10 .05
❑ 840 George Bell .10 .05
❑ 841 Dave Gallagher .10 .05
❑ 842 Tim Belcher .10 .05
❑ 843 Jeff Shaw .10 .05
❑ 844 Mike Fitzgerald .10 .05
❑ 845 Gary Carter .40 .18
❑ 846 John Russell .10 .05
❑ 847 Eric Hillman .10 .05
❑ 848 Mike Witt .10 .05
❑ 849 Curt Wilkerson .10 .05
❑ 850 Alan Trammell .30 .14
❑ 851 Rex Hudler .10 .05
❑ 852 Mike Walkden .10 .05
❑ 853 Kevin Ward .10 .05
❑ 854 Tim Naehring .20 .09
❑ 855 Bill Swift .10 .05
❑ 856 Damon Berryhill .10 .05
❑ 857 Mark Eichhorn .10 .05
❑ 858 Hector Villanueva .10 .05
❑ 859 Jose Lind .10 .05
❑ 860 Denny Martinez .20 .09
❑ 861 Bill Krueger .10 .05
❑ 862 Mike Kingery .10 .05
❑ 863 Jeff Innis .10 .05
❑ 864 Derek Lilliquist .10 .05
❑ 865 Reggie Sanders .10 .05
❑ 866 Ramon Garcia .10 .05
❑ 867 Bruce Ruffin .10 .05
❑ 868 Dickie Thon .10 .05
❑ 869 Melido Perez .10 .05
❑ 870 Ruben Amaro .10 .05
❑ 871 Alan Mills .10 .05
❑ 872 Matt Sinatro .10 .05
❑ 873 Eddie Zosky .10 .05
❑ 874 Pete Incaviglia .10 .05
❑ 875 Tom Candiotti .10 .05
❑ 876 Bob Patterson .10 .05
❑ 877 Neal Heaton .10 .05
❑ 878 Terrel Hansen .10 .05
❑ 879 Dave Eiland .10 .05
❑ 880 Von Hayes .10 .05
❑ 881 Tim Scott .10 .05
❑ 882 Otis Nixon .20 .09
❑ 883 Herm Winningham .10 .05
❑ 884 Dion James .10 .05
❑ 885 Dave Wainhouse .10 .05
❑ 886 Frank DiPino .10 .05
❑ 887 Dennis Cook .10 .05
❑ 888 Jose Mesa .10 .05
❑ 889 Mark Leiter .10 .05
❑ 890 Willie Randolph .20 .09
❑ 891 Craig Colbert .10 .05
❑ 892 Dwayne Henry .10 .05
❑ 893 Jim Lindeman .10 .05
❑ 894 Charlie Hough .20 .09
❑ 895 Gil Heredia .10 .05
❑ 896 Scott Chiamparino .10 .05
❑ 897 Lance Blankenship .10 .05
❑ 898 Checklist 601-700 .10 .05
❑ 899 Checklist 701-800 .10 .05
❑ 900 Checklist 801-900 .10 .05

1992 Stadium Club First Draft Picks

	MINT	NRMT
COMPLETE SET (3)	16.00	7.25
COMMON CARD (1-3)	1.00	.45
❑ 1 Chipper Jones	15.00	6.75
❑ 2 Brien Taylor	1.00	.45
❑ 3 Phil Nevin	2.00	.90

1993 Stadium Club Murphy

	MINT	NRMT
COMP.FACT.SET (212)	50.00	22.00
COMPLETE SET (200)	25.00	11.00
COMMON CARD (1-200)	.15	.07

❑ 1 Dave Winfield .40 .18
❑ 2 Juan Guzman .15 .07
❑ 3 Tony Gwynn 1.50 .70
❑ 4 Chris Roberts .15 .07
❑ 5 Benny Santiago .15 .07
❑ 6 Sherard Clinkscales .15 .07
❑ 7 Jon Nunnally .30 .14
❑ 8 Chuck Knoblauch .60 .25
❑ 9 Bob Wolcott .30 .14
❑ 10 Steve Rodriguez .15 .07
❑ 11 Mark Williams .15 .07
❑ 12 Danny Clyburn .50 .23
❑ 13 Darren Dreifort .15 .07
❑ 14 Andy Van Slyke .30 .14
❑ 15 Wade Boggs .60 .25
❑ 16 Scott Patton .15 .07
❑ 17 Gary Sheffield .60 .25
❑ 18 Ron Villone .15 .07
❑ 19 Roberto Alomar .60 .25
❑ 20 Marc Valdes .15 .07
❑ 21 Daron Kirkreit .15 .07
❑ 22 Jeff Granger .15 .07
❑ 23 Levon Largusa .15 .07
❑ 24 Jimmy Key .30 .14
❑ 25 Kevin Pearson .15 .07
❑ 26 Michael Moore .15 .07
❑ 27 Preston Wilson 1.50 .70
❑ 28 Kirby Puckett 1.00 .45
❑ 29 Tim Crabtree .15 .07
❑ 30 Bip Roberts .15 .07
❑ 31 Kelly Gruber .15 .07
❑ 32 Tony Fernandez .15 .07
❑ 33 Jason Angel .15 .07
❑ 34 Calvin Murray .15 .07
❑ 35 Chad McConnell .15 .07
❑ 36 Jason Moler .15 .07
❑ 37 Mark Lemke .15 .07
❑ 38 Tom Knauss .15 .07
❑ 39 Larry Mitchell .15 .07
❑ 40 Doug Mirabelli .15 .07
❑ 41 Everett Stull II .15 .07
❑ 42 Chris Wimmer .15 .07
❑ 43 Dan Serafini .50 .23
❑ 44 Ryne Sandberg .75 .35
❑ 45 Steve Lyons .15 .07
❑ 46 Ryan Freeburg .15 .07
❑ 47 Ruben Sierra .15 .07
❑ 48 David Mysel .15 .07
❑ 49 Joe Hamilton .15 .07
❑ 50 Steve Rodriguez .15 .07
❑ 51 Tim Wakefield .30 .14
❑ 52 Scott Gentile .15 .07
❑ 53 Doug Jones .15 .07
❑ 54 Willie Brown .15 .07
❑ 55 Chad Mottola .15 .07
❑ 56 Ken Griffey Jr. 3.00 1.35
❑ 57 Jon Lieber .15 .07
❑ 58 Denny Martinez .30 .14
❑ 59 Joe Petcka .15 .07
❑ 60 Benji Simonton .15 .07
❑ 61 Brett Backlund .15 .07
❑ 62 Damon Berryhill .15 .07
❑ 63 Juan Guzman .15 .07
❑ 64 Doug Hecker .15 .07
❑ 65 Jamie Arnold .30 .14
❑ 66 Bob Tewksbury .15 .07
❑ 67 Tim Leger .15 .07
❑ 68 Todd Etler .15 .07

❑ 69 Lloyd McClendon	.15	.07
❑ 70 Kurt Ehmann	.15	.07
❑ 71 Rick Magdaleno	.15	.07
❑ 72 Tom Pagnozzi	.15	.07
❑ 73 Jeffrey Hammonds	.30	.14
❑ 74 Joe Carter	.30	.14
❑ 75 Chris Holt	.15	.07
❑ 76 Charles Johnson	1.00	.45
❑ 77 Bob Walk	.15	.07
❑ 78 Fred McGriff	.40	.18
❑ 79 Tom Evans	1.00	.45
❑ 80 Scott Klingenbeck	.15	.07
❑ 81 Chad McConnell	.15	.07
❑ 82 Chris Eddy	.15	.07
❑ 83 Phil Nevin	.15	.07
❑ 84 John Kruk	.30	.14
❑ 85 Tony Sheffield	.15	.07
❑ 86 John Smoltz	.30	.14
❑ 87 Trevor Humphry	.15	.07
❑ 88 Charles Nagy	.30	.14
❑ 89 Sean Runyan	.15	.07
❑ 90 Mike Gulan	.15	.07
❑ 91 Darren Daulton	.30	.14
❑ 92 Otis Nixon	.15	.07
❑ 93 Nomar Garciaparra	25.00	11.00
❑ 94 Larry Walker	.60	.25
❑ 95 Hut Smith	.15	.07
❑ 96 Rick Helling	.40	.18
❑ 97 Roger Clemens	1.25	.55
❑ 98 Ron Gant	.30	.14
❑ 99 Kenny Felder	.15	.07
❑ 100 Steve Murphy	.15	.07
❑ 101 Mike Smith	.15	.07
❑ 102 Terry Pendleton	.15	.07
❑ 103 Tim Davis	.15	.07
❑ 104 Jeff Patzke	.30	.14
❑ 105 Craig Wilson	.15	.07
❑ 106 Tom Glavine	.40	.18
❑ 107 Mark Langston	.15	.07
❑ 108 Mark Thompson	.15	.07
❑ 109 Eric Owens	.15	.07
❑ 110 Keith Johnson	.15	.07
❑ 111 Robin Ventura	.30	.14
❑ 112 Ed Sprague	.15	.07
❑ 113 Jeff Schmidt	.15	.07
❑ 114 Don Wengert	.15	.07
❑ 115 Craig Biggio	.60	.25
❑ 116 Kenny Carlyle	.15	.07
❑ 117 Derek Jeter	25.00	11.00
❑ 118 Manuel Lee	.15	.07
❑ 119 Jeff Haas	.15	.07
❑ 120 Roger Bailey	.15	.07
❑ 121 Sean Lowe	.15	.07
❑ 122 Rick Aguilera	.15	.07
❑ 123 Sandy Alomar	.30	.14
❑ 124 Derek Wallace	.15	.07
❑ 125 B.J. Wallace	.15	.07
❑ 126 Greg Maddux	2.00	.90
❑ 127 Tim Moore	.15	.07
❑ 128 Lee Smith	.30	.14
❑ 129 Todd Steverson	.30	.14
❑ 130 Chris Widger	.15	.07
❑ 131 Paul Molitor	.60	.25
❑ 132 Chris Smith	.15	.07
❑ 133 Chris Gomez	.30	.14
❑ 134 Jimmy Baron	.15	.07
❑ 135 John Smoltz	.30	.14
❑ 136 Pat Borders	.15	.07
❑ 137 Donnie Leshnock	.15	.07
❑ 138 Gus Gandarillos	.15	.07
❑ 139 Will Clark	.60	.25
❑ 140 Ryan Luzinski	.15	.07
❑ 141 Cal Ripken	2.50	1.10
❑ 142 B.J. Wallace	.15	.07
❑ 143 Trey Beamon	.50	.23
❑ 144 Norm Charlton	.15	.07
❑ 145 Mike Mussina	.60	.25
❑ 146 Billy Owens	.15	.07
❑ 147 Ozzie Smith	.75	.35
❑ 148 Jason Kendall	5.00	2.20
❑ 149 Mike Matthews	.15	.07
❑ 150 David Spykstra	.15	.07
❑ 151 Benji Grigsby	.15	.07
❑ 152 Sean Smith	.15	.07
❑ 153 Mark McGwire	3.00	1.35
❑ 154 David Cone	.30	.14
❑ 155 Shon Walker	.15	.07
❑ 156 Jason Giambi	.60	.25
❑ 157 Jack McDowell	.15	.07
❑ 158 Paxton Briley	.15	.07
❑ 159 Edgar Martinez	.40	.18
❑ 160 Brian Sackinsky	.15	.07
❑ 161 Barry Bonds	.75	.35
❑ 162 Roberto Kelly	.15	.07
❑ 163 Jeff Alkire	.15	.07
❑ 164 Mike Sharperson	.15	.07
❑ 165 Jamie Taylor	.15	.07
❑ 166 John Saffer	.15	.07
❑ 167 Jerry Browne	.15	.07
❑ 168 Travis Fryman	.30	.14
❑ 169 Brady Anderson	.40	.18
❑ 170 Chris Roberts	.15	.07
❑ 171 Lloyd Peever	.15	.07
❑ 172 Francisco Cabrera	.15	.07
❑ 173 Ramiro Martinez	.15	.07
❑ 174 Jeff Alkire	.15	.07
❑ 175 Ivan Rodriguez	.75	.35
❑ 176 Kevin Brown	.40	.18
❑ 177 Chad Roper	.15	.07
❑ 178 Rod Henderson	.15	.07
❑ 179 Dennis Eckersley	.30	.14
❑ 180 Shannon Stewart	1.50	.70
❑ 181 DeShawn Warren	.15	.07
❑ 182 Lonnie Smith	.15	.07
❑ 183 Willie Adams	.15	.07
❑ 184 Jeff Montgomery	.30	.14
❑ 185 Damon Hollins	.50	.23
❑ 186 Byron Mathews	.15	.07
❑ 187 Harold Baines	.30	.14
❑ 188 Rick Greene	.15	.07
❑ 189 Carlos Baerga	.15	.07
❑ 190 Brandon Cromer	.15	.07
❑ 191 Roberto Alomar	.60	.25
❑ 192 Rich Ireland	.15	.07
❑ 193 Steve Montgomery	.15	.07
❑ 194 Brant Brown	2.00	.90
❑ 195 Ritchie Moody	.15	.07
❑ 196 Michael Tucker	.60	.25
❑ 197 Jason Varitek	.60	.25
❑ 198 David Manning	.15	.07
❑ 199 Marquis Riley	.15	.07
❑ 200 Jason Giambi	.60	.25

1993 Stadium Club

	MINT	NRMT
COMPLETE SET (750)	60.00	27.00
COMPLETE SERIES 1 (300)	20.00	9.00
COMPLETE SERIES 2 (300)	25.00	11.00
COMPLETE SERIES 3 (150)	15.00	6.75
COMMON CARD (1-750)	.15	.07

❑ 1 Pat Borders	.15	.07
❑ 2 Greg Maddux	2.00	.90
❑ 3 Daryl Boston	.15	.07
❑ 4 Bob Ayrault	.15	.07
❑ 5 Tony Phillips IF	.15	.07
❑ 6 Damion Easley	.30	.14
❑ 7 Kip Gross	.15	.07
❑ 8 Jim Thome	1.25	.55
❑ 9 Tim Belcher	.15	.07
❑ 10 Gary Wayne	.15	.07
❑ 11 Sam Militello	.15	.07
❑ 12 Mike Magnante	.15	.07
❑ 13 Tim Wakefield	.30	.14
❑ 14 Tim Hulett	.15	.07
❑ 15 Rheal Cormier	.15	.07
❑ 16 Juan Guerrero	.15	.07
❑ 17 Rich Gossage	.30	.14
❑ 18 Tim Laker	.15	.07
❑ 19 Darrin Jackson	.15	.07
❑ 20 Jack Clark	.15	.07
❑ 21 Roberto Hernandez	.30	.14
❑ 22 Dean Palmer	.30	.14
❑ 23 Harold Reynolds	.15	.07
❑ 24 Dan Plesac	.15	.07
❑ 25 Brent Mayne	.15	.07
❑ 26 Pat Hentgen	.40	.18
❑ 27 Luis Sojo	.15	.07
❑ 28 Ron Gant	.30	.14
❑ 29 Paul Gibson	.15	.07
❑ 30 Bip Roberts	.15	.07
❑ 31 Mickey Tettleton	.15	.07
❑ 32 Randy Velarde	.15	.07
❑ 33 Brian McRae	.15	.07
❑ 34 Wes Chamberlain	.15	.07
❑ 35 Wayne Kirby	.15	.07
❑ 36 Rey Sanchez	.15	.07
❑ 37 Jesse Orosco	.15	.07
❑ 38 Mike Stanton	.15	.07
❑ 39 Royce Clayton	.15	.07
❑ 40 Cal Ripken UER (Place of birth Havre de Grave; should be Havre de Grace)	2.50	1.10
❑ 41 John Dopson	.15	.07
❑ 42 Gene Larkin	.15	.07
❑ 43 Tim Raines	.30	.14
❑ 44 Randy Myers	.30	.14
❑ 45 Clay Parker	.15	.07
❑ 46 Mike Scioscia	.15	.07
❑ 47 Pete Incaviglia	.15	.07
❑ 48 Todd Van Poppel	.15	.07
❑ 49 Ray Lankford	.40	.18
❑ 50 Eddie Murray	.60	.25
❑ 51 Barry Bonds COR	.75	.35
❑ 51A Barry Bonds ERR (Missing four stars over name to indicate NL MVP)	.75	.35
❑ 52 Gary Thurman	.15	.07
❑ 53 Bob Wickman	.15	.07
❑ 54 Joey Cora	.30	.14
❑ 55 Kenny Rogers	.15	.07
❑ 56 Mike Devereaux	.15	.07
❑ 57 Kevin Seitzer	.15	.07
❑ 58 Rafael Belliard	.15	.07
❑ 59 David Wells	.30	.14
❑ 60 Mark Clark	.15	.07
❑ 61 Carlos Baerga	.15	.07
❑ 62 Scott Brosius	.15	.07
❑ 63 Jeff Grotewold	.15	.07
❑ 64 Rick Wrona	.15	.07
❑ 65 Kurt Knudsen	.15	.07
❑ 66 Lloyd McClendon	.15	.07
❑ 67 Omar Vizquel	.30	.14
❑ 68 Jose Vizcaino	.15	.07
❑ 69 Rob Ducey	.15	.07
❑ 70 Casey Candaele	.15	.07
❑ 71 Ramon Martinez	.30	.14
❑ 72 Todd Hundley	.40	.18
❑ 73 John Marzano	.15	.07
❑ 74 Derek Parks	.15	.07
❑ 75 Jack McDowell	.15	.07
❑ 76 Tim Scott	.15	.07
❑ 77 Mike Mussina	.60	.25
❑ 78 Delino DeShields	.30	.14
❑ 79 Chris Bosio	.15	.07
❑ 80 Mike Bordick	.15	.07
❑ 81 Rod Beck	.30	.14
❑ 82 Ted Power	.15	.07
❑ 83 John Kruk	.30	.14
❑ 84 Steve Shifflett	.15	.07
❑ 85 Danny Tartabull	.15	.07
❑ 86 Mike Greenwell	.15	.07
❑ 87 Jose Melendez	.15	.07
❑ 88 Craig Wilson	.15	.07
❑ 89 Melvin Nieves	.15	.07
❑ 90 Ed Sprague	.15	.07
❑ 91 Willie McGee	.30	.14

❑ 92 Joe Orsulak .15 .07
❑ 93 Jeff King .30 .14
❑ 94 Dan Pasqua .15 .07
❑ 95 Brian Harper .15 .07
❑ 96 Joe Oliver .15 .07
❑ 97 Shane Turner .15 .07
❑ 98 Lenny Harris .15 .07
❑ 99 Jeff Parrett .15 .07
❑ 100 Luis Polonia .15 .07
❑ 101 Kent Bottenfield .15 .07
❑ 102 Albert Belle .75 .35
❑ 103 Mike Maddux .15 .07
❑ 104 Randy Tomlin .15 .07
❑ 105 Andy Stankiewicz .15 .07
❑ 106 Rico Rossy .15 .07
❑ 107 Joe Hesketh .15 .07
❑ 108 Dennis Powell .15 .07
❑ 109 Derrick May .15 .07
❑ 110 Pete Harnisch .15 .07
❑ 111 Kent Mercker .15 .07
❑ 112 Scott Fletcher .15 .07
❑ 113 Rex Hudler .15 .07
❑ 114 Chico Walker .15 .07
❑ 115 Rafael Palmeiro .40 .18
❑ 116 Mark Leiter .15 .07
❑ 117 Pedro Munoz .15 .07
❑ 118 Jim Bullinger .15 .07
❑ 119 Ivan Calderon .15 .07
❑ 120 Mike Timlin .15 .07
❑ 121 Rene Gonzales .15 .07
❑ 122 Greg Vaughn .30 .14
❑ 123 Mike Flanagan .15 .07
❑ 124 Mike Hartley .15 .07
❑ 125 Jeff Montgomery .30 .14
❑ 126 Mike Gallego .15 .07
❑ 127 Don Slaught .15 .07
❑ 128 Charlie O'Brien .15 .07
❑ 129 Jose Offerman .15 .07
(Can be found with home town missing on back)
❑ 130 Mark Wohlers .15 .07
❑ 131 Eric Fox .15 .07
❑ 132 Doug Strange .15 .07
❑ 133 Jeff Frye .15 .07
❑ 134 Wade Boggs UER .60 .25
(Redundantly lists lefty breakdown)
❑ 135 Lou Whitaker .30 .14
❑ 136 Craig Grebeck .15 .07
❑ 137 Rich Rodriguez .15 .07
❑ 138 Jay Bell .30 .14
❑ 139 Felix Fermin .15 .07
❑ 140 Denny Martinez .30 .14
❑ 141 Eric Anthony .15 .07
❑ 142 Roberto Alomar .60 .25
❑ 143 Darren Lewis .15 .07
❑ 144 Mike Blowers .15 .07
❑ 145 Scott Bankhead .15 .07
❑ 146 Jeff Reboulet .15 .07
❑ 147 Frank Viola .15 .07
❑ 148 Bill Pecota .15 .07
❑ 149 Carlos Hernandez .15 .07
❑ 150 Bobby Witt .15 .07
❑ 151 Sid Bream .15 .07
❑ 152 Todd Zeile .15 .07
❑ 153 Dennis Cook .15 .07
❑ 154 Brian Bohanon .15 .07
❑ 155 Pat Kelly .15 .07
❑ 156 Milt Cuyler .15 .07
❑ 157 Juan Bell .15 .07
❑ 158 Randy Milligan .15 .07
❑ 159 Mark Gardner .15 .07
❑ 160 Pat Tabler .15 .07
❑ 161 Jeff Reardon .30 .14
❑ 162 Ken Patterson .15 .07
❑ 163 Bobby Bonilla .30 .14
❑ 164 Tony Pena .15 .07
❑ 165 Greg Swindell .15 .07
❑ 166 Kirk McCaskill .15 .07
❑ 167 Doug Drabek .15 .07
❑ 168 Franklin Stubbs .15 .07
❑ 169 Ron Tingley .15 .07
❑ 170 Willie Banks .15 .07
❑ 171 Sergio Valdez .15 .07
❑ 172 Mark Lemke .15 .07
❑ 173 Robin Yount .40 .18
❑ 174 Storm Davis .15 .07
❑ 175 Dan Walters .15 .07
❑ 176 Steve Farr .15 .07
❑ 177 Curt Wilkerson .15 .07
❑ 178 Luis Alicea .15 .07
❑ 179 Russ Swan .15 .07
❑ 180 Mitch Williams .15 .07
❑ 181 Wilson Alvarez .30 .14
❑ 182 Carl Willis .15 .07
❑ 183 Craig Biggio .60 .25
❑ 184 Sean Berry .15 .07
❑ 185 Trevor Wilson .15 .07
❑ 186 Jeff Tackett .15 .07
❑ 187 Ellis Burks .30 .14
❑ 188 Jeff Branson .15 .07
❑ 189 Matt Nokes .15 .07
❑ 190 John Smiley .15 .07
❑ 191 Danny Gladden .15 .07
❑ 192 Mike Boddicker .15 .07
❑ 193 Roger Pavlik .15 .07
❑ 194 Paul Sorrento .15 .07
❑ 195 Vince Coleman .15 .07
❑ 196 Gary DiSarcina .15 .07
❑ 197 Rafael Bournigal .15 .07
❑ 198 Mike Schooler .15 .07
❑ 199 Scott Ruskin .15 .07
❑ 200 Frank Thomas 2.00 .90
❑ 201 Kyle Abbott .15 .07
❑ 202 Mike Perez .15 .07
❑ 203 Andre Dawson .40 .18
❑ 204 Bill Swift .15 .07
❑ 205 Alejandro Pena .15 .07
❑ 206 Dave Winfield .40 .18
❑ 207 Andujar Cedeno .15 .07
❑ 208 Terry Steinbach .15 .07
❑ 209 Chris Hammond .15 .07
❑ 210 Todd Burns .15 .07
❑ 211 Hipolito Pichardo .15 .07
❑ 212 John Kiely .15 .07
❑ 213 Tim Teufel .15 .07
❑ 214 Lee Guetterman .15 .07
❑ 215 Geronimo Pena .15 .07
❑ 216 Brett Butler .30 .14
❑ 217 Bryan Hickerson .15 .07
❑ 218 Rick Trlicek .15 .07
❑ 219 Lee Stevens .15 .07
❑ 220 Roger Clemens 1.25 .55
❑ 221 Carlton Fisk .60 .25
❑ 222 Chili Davis .30 .14
❑ 223 Walt Terrell .15 .07
❑ 224 Jim Eisenreich .15 .07
❑ 225 Ricky Bones .15 .07
❑ 226 Henry Rodriguez .30 .14
❑ 227 Ken Hill .15 .07
❑ 228 Rick Wilkins .15 .07
❑ 229 Ricky Jordan .15 .07
❑ 230 Bernard Gilkey .15 .07
❑ 231 Tim Fortugno .15 .07
❑ 232 Geno Petralli .15 .07
❑ 233 Jose Rijo .15 .07
❑ 234 Jim Leyritz .15 .07
❑ 235 Kevin Campbell .15 .07
❑ 236 Al Osuna .15 .07
❑ 237 Pete Smith .15 .07
❑ 238 Pete Schourek .15 .07
❑ 239 Moises Alou .30 .14
❑ 240 Donn Pall .15 .07
❑ 241 Denny Neagle .30 .14
❑ 242 Dan Peltier .15 .07
❑ 243 Scott Scudder .15 .07
❑ 244 Juan Guzman .15 .07
❑ 245 Dave Burba .15 .07
❑ 246 Rick Sutcliffe .15 .07
❑ 247 Tony Fossas .15 .07
❑ 248 Mike Munoz .15 .07
❑ 249 Tim Salmon .60 .25
❑ 250 Rob Murphy .15 .07
❑ 251 Roger McDowell .15 .07
❑ 252 Lance Parrish .15 .07
❑ 253 Cliff Brantley .15 .07
❑ 254 Scott Leius .15 .07
❑ 255 Carlos Martinez .15 .07
❑ 256 Vince Horsman .15 .07
❑ 257 Oscar Azocar .15 .07
❑ 258 Craig Shipley .15 .07
❑ 259 Ben McDonald .15 .07
❑ 260 Jeff Brantley .15 .07
❑ 261 Damon Berryhill .15 .07
❑ 262 Joe Grahe .15 .07
❑ 263 Dave Hansen .15 .07
❑ 264 Rich Amaral .15 .07
❑ 265 Tim Pugh .15 .07
❑ 266 Dion James .15 .07
❑ 267 Frank Tanana .15 .07
❑ 268 Stan Belinda .15 .07
❑ 269 Jeff Kent .30 .14
❑ 270 Bruce Ruffin .15 .07
❑ 271 Xavier Hernandez .15 .07
❑ 272 Darrin Fletcher .15 .07
❑ 273 Tino Martinez .60 .25
❑ 274 Benny Santiago .15 .07
❑ 275 Scott Radinsky .15 .07
❑ 276 Mariano Duncan .15 .07
❑ 277 Kenny Lofton .60 .25
❑ 278 Dwight Smith .15 .07
❑ 279 Joe Carter .30 .14
❑ 280 Tim Jones .15 .07
❑ 281 Jeff Huson .15 .07
❑ 282 Phil Plantier .15 .07
❑ 283 Kirby Puckett 1.00 .45
❑ 284 Johnny Guzman .15 .07
❑ 285 Mike Morgan .15 .07
❑ 286 Chris Sabo .15 .07
❑ 287 Matt Williams .40 .18
❑ 288 Checklist 1-100 .15 .07
❑ 289 Checklist 101-200 .15 .07
❑ 290 Checklist 201-300 .15 .07
❑ 291 Dennis Eckersley MC .15 .07
❑ 292 Eric Karros MC .15 .07
❑ 293 Pat Listach MC .15 .07
❑ 294 Andy Van Slyke MC .15 .07
❑ 295 Robin Ventura MC .30 .14
❑ 296 Tom Glavine MC .30 .14
❑ 297 Juan Gonzalez MC UER .75 .35
(Misspelled Gonzales)
❑ 298 Travis Fryman MC .15 .07
❑ 299 Larry Walker MC .60 .25
❑ 300 Gary Sheffield MC .30 .14
❑ 301 Chuck Finley .30 .14
❑ 302 Luis Gonzalez .15 .07
❑ 303 Darryl Hamilton .15 .07
❑ 304 Bien Figueroa .15 .07
❑ 305 Ron Darling .15 .07
❑ 306 Jonathan Hurst .15 .07
❑ 307 Mike Sharperson .15 .07
❑ 308 Mike Christopher .15 .07
❑ 309 Marvin Freeman .15 .07
❑ 310 Jay Buhner .40 .18
❑ 311 Butch Henry .15 .07
❑ 312 Greg W. Harris .15 .07
❑ 313 Darren Daulton .30 .14
❑ 314 Chuck Knoblauch .60 .25
❑ 315 Greg A. Harris .15 .07
❑ 316 John Franco .30 .14
❑ 317 John Wehner .15 .07
❑ 318 Donald Harris .15 .07
❑ 319 Benny Santiago .15 .07
❑ 320 Larry Walker .60 .25
❑ 321 Randy Knorr .15 .07
❑ 322 Ramon Martinez .30 .14
❑ 323 Mike Stanley .15 .07
❑ 324 Bill Wegman .15 .07
❑ 325 Tom Candiotti .15 .07
❑ 326 Glenn Davis .15 .07
❑ 327 Chuck Crim .15 .07
❑ 328 Scott Livingstone .15 .07
❑ 329 Eddie Taubensee .15 .07
❑ 330 George Bell .15 .07
❑ 331 Edgar Martinez .40 .18
❑ 332 Paul Assenmacher .15 .07
❑ 333 Steve Hosey .15 .07
❑ 334 Mo Vaughn .75 .35
❑ 335 Bret Saberhagen .30 .14
❑ 336 Mike Trombley .15 .07
❑ 337 Mark Lewis .15 .07
❑ 338 Terry Pendleton .15 .07
❑ 339 Dave Hollins .15 .07
❑ 340 Jeff Conine .15 .07
❑ 341 Bob Tewksbury .15 .07

❑ 342 Billy Ashley .15 .07
❑ 343 Zane Smith .15 .07
❑ 344 John Wetteland .30 .14
❑ 345 Chris Hoiles .15 .07
❑ 346 Frank Castillo .15 .07
❑ 347 Bruce Hurst .15 .07
❑ 348 Kevin McReynolds .15 .07
❑ 349 Dave Henderson .15 .07
❑ 350 Ryan Bowen .15 .07
❑ 351 Sid Fernandez .15 .07
❑ 352 Mark Whiten .15 .07
❑ 353 Nolan Ryan 2.50 1.10
❑ 354 Rick Aguilera .15 .07
❑ 355 Mark Langston .15 .07
❑ 356 Jack Morris .30 .14
❑ 357 Rob Deer .15 .07
❑ 358 Dave Fleming .15 .07
❑ 359 Lance Johnson .15 .07
❑ 360 Joe Millette .15 .07
❑ 361 Wil Cordero .15 .07
❑ 362 Chito Martinez .15 .07
❑ 363 Scott Servais .15 .07
❑ 364 Bernie Williams .60 .25
❑ 365 Pedro Martinez .75 .35
❑ 366 Ryne Sandberg .75 .35
❑ 367 Brad Ausmus .15 .07
❑ 368 Scott Cooper .15 .07
❑ 369 Rob Dibble .15 .07
❑ 370 Walt Weiss .15 .07
❑ 371 Mark Davis .15 .07
❑ 372 Orlando Merced .15 .07
❑ 373 Mike Jackson .15 .07
❑ 374 Kevin Appier .30 .14
❑ 375 Esteban Beltre .15 .07
❑ 376 Joe Slusarski .15 .07
❑ 377 William Suero .15 .07
❑ 378 Pete O'Brien .15 .07
❑ 379 Alan Embree .15 .07
❑ 380 Lenny Webster .15 .07
❑ 381 Eric Davis .30 .14
❑ 382 Duane Ward .15 .07
❑ 383 John Habyan .15 .07
❑ 384 Jeff Bagwell 1.00 .45
❑ 385 Ruben Amaro .15 .07
❑ 386 Julio Valera .15 .07
❑ 387 Robin Ventura .30 .14
❑ 388 Archi Cianfrocco .15 .07
❑ 389 Skeeter Barnes .15 .07
❑ 390 Tim Costo .15 .07
❑ 391 Luis Mercedes .15 .07
❑ 392 Jeremy Hernandez .15 .07
❑ 393 Shawon Dunston .15 .07
❑ 394 Andy Van Slyke .30 .14
❑ 395 Kevin Maas .15 .07
❑ 396 Kevin Brown .40 .18
❑ 397 J.T. Bruett .15 .07
❑ 398 Darryl Strawberry .30 .14
❑ 399 Tom Pagnozzi .15 .07
❑ 400 Sandy Alomar Jr. .30 .14
❑ 401 Keith Miller .15 .07
❑ 402 Rich DeLucia .15 .07
❑ 403 Shawn Abner .15 .07
❑ 404 Howard Johnson .15 .07
❑ 405 Mike Benjamin .15 .07
❑ 406 Roberto Mejia .15 .07
❑ 407 Mike Butcher .15 .07
❑ 408 Deion Sanders UER .40 .18
(Braves on front and Yankees on back)
❑ 409 Todd Stottlemyre .15 .07
❑ 410 Scott Kamieniecki .15 .07
❑ 411 Doug Jones .15 .07
❑ 412 John Burkett .15 .07
❑ 413 Lance Blankenship .15 .07
❑ 414 Jeff Parrett .15 .07
❑ 415 Barry Larkin .40 .18
❑ 416 Alan Trammell .40 .18
❑ 417 Mark Kiefer .15 .07
❑ 418 Gregg Olson .15 .07
❑ 419 Mark Grace .40 .18
❑ 420 Shane Mack .15 .07
❑ 421 Bob Walk .15 .07
❑ 422 Curt Schilling .30 .14
❑ 423 Erik Hanson .15 .07
❑ 424 George Brett 1.25 .55
❑ 425 Reggie Jefferson .30 .14
❑ 426 Mark Portugal .15 .07
❑ 427 Ron Karkovice .15 .07
❑ 428 Matt Young .15 .07
❑ 429 Troy Neel .15 .07
❑ 430 Hector Fajardo .15 .07
❑ 431 Dave Righetti .15 .07
❑ 432 Pat Listach .15 .07
❑ 433 Jeff Innis .15 .07
❑ 434 Bob MacDonald .15 .07
❑ 435 Brian Jordan .30 .14
❑ 436 Jeff Blauser .15 .07
❑ 437 Mike Myers .15 .07
❑ 438 Frank Seminara .15 .07
❑ 439 Rusty Meacham .15 .07
❑ 440 Greg Briley .15 .07
❑ 441 Derek Lilliquist .15 .07
❑ 442 John Vander Wal .15 .07
❑ 443 Scott Erickson .15 .07
❑ 444 Bob Scanlan .15 .07
❑ 445 Todd Frohwirth .15 .07
❑ 446 Tom Goodwin .15 .07
❑ 447 William Pennyfeather .15 .07
❑ 448 Travis Fryman .30 .14
❑ 449 Mickey Morandini .15 .07
❑ 450 Greg Olson .15 .07
❑ 451 Trevor Hoffman .60 .25
❑ 452 Dave Magadan .15 .07
❑ 453 Shawn Jeter .15 .07
❑ 454 Andres Galarraga .60 .25
❑ 455 Ted Wood .15 .07
❑ 456 Freddie Benavides .15 .07
❑ 457 Junior Felix .15 .07
❑ 458 Alex Cole .15 .07
❑ 459 John Orton .15 .07
❑ 460 Eddie Zosky .15 .07
❑ 461 Dennis Eckersley .30 .14
❑ 462 Lee Smith .30 .14
❑ 463 John Smoltz .30 .14
❑ 464 Ken Caminiti .40 .18
❑ 465 Melido Perez .15 .07
❑ 466 Tom Marsh .15 .07
❑ 467 Jeff Nelson .15 .07
❑ 468 Jesse Levis .15 .07
❑ 469 Chris Nabholz .15 .07
❑ 470 Mike Macfarlane .15 .07
❑ 471 Reggie Sanders .15 .07
❑ 472 Chuck McElroy .15 .07
❑ 473 Kevin Gross .15 .07
❑ 474 Matt Whiteside .15 .07
❑ 475 Cal Eldred .15 .07
❑ 476 Dave Gallagher .15 .07
❑ 477 Len Dykstra .30 .14
❑ 478 Mark McGwire 3.00 1.35
❑ 479 David Segui .15 .07
❑ 480 Mike Henneman .15 .07
❑ 481 Bret Barberie .15 .07
❑ 482 Steve Sax .15 .07
❑ 483 Dave Valle .15 .07
❑ 484 Danny Darwin .15 .07
❑ 485 Devon White .15 .07
❑ 486 Eric Plunk .15 .07
❑ 487 Jim Gott .15 .07
❑ 488 Scooter Tucker .15 .07
❑ 489 Omar Olivares .15 .07
❑ 490 Greg Myers .15 .07
❑ 491 Brian Hunter .15 .07
❑ 492 Kevin Tapani .15 .07
❑ 493 Rich Monteleone .15 .07
❑ 494 Steve Buechele .15 .07
❑ 495 Bo Jackson .30 .14
❑ 496 Mike LaValliere .15 .07
❑ 497 Mark Leonard .15 .07
❑ 498 Daryl Boston .15 .07
❑ 499 Jose Canseco .60 .25
❑ 500 Brian Barnes .15 .07
❑ 501 Randy Johnson .60 .25
❑ 502 Tim McIntosh .15 .07
❑ 503 Cecil Fielder .30 .14
❑ 504 Derek Bell .30 .14
❑ 505 Kevin Koslofski .15 .07
❑ 506 Darren Holmes .15 .07
❑ 507 Brady Anderson .40 .18
❑ 508 John Valentin .30 .14
❑ 509 Jerry Browne .15 .07
❑ 510 Fred McGriff .40 .18
❑ 511 Pedro Astacio .15 .07
❑ 512 Gary Gaetti .15 .07
❑ 513 John Burke .15 .07
❑ 514 Dwight Gooden .30 .14
❑ 515 Thomas Howard .15 .07
❑ 516 Darrell Whitmore UER .15 .07
(11 games played in 1992; should be 121)
❑ 517 Ozzie Guillen .15 .07
❑ 518 Darryl Kile .30 .14
❑ 519 Rich Rowland .15 .07
❑ 520 Carlos Delgado .60 .25
❑ 521 Doug Henry .15 .07
❑ 522 Greg Colbrunn .15 .07
❑ 523 Tom Gordon .30 .14
❑ 524 Ivan Rodriguez .75 .35
❑ 525 Kent Hrbek .30 .14
❑ 526 Eric Young .60 .25
❑ 527 Rod Brewer .15 .07
❑ 528 Eric Karros .40 .18
❑ 529 Marquis Grissom .30 .14
❑ 530 Rico Brogna .30 .14
❑ 531 Sammy Sosa 1.50 .70
❑ 532 Bret Boone .30 .14
❑ 533 Luis Rivera .15 .07
❑ 534 Hal Morris .15 .07
❑ 535 Monty Fariss .15 .07
❑ 536 Leo Gomez .15 .07
❑ 537 Wally Joyner .30 .14
❑ 538 Tony Gwynn 1.50 .70
❑ 539 Mike Williams .15 .07
❑ 540 Juan Gonzalez 1.50 .70
❑ 541 Ryan Klesko .60 .25
❑ 542 Ryan Thompson .15 .07
❑ 543 Chad Curtis .30 .14
❑ 544 Orel Hershiser .30 .14
❑ 545 Carlos Garcia .15 .07
❑ 546 Bob Welch .15 .07
❑ 547 Vinny Castilla .75 .35
❑ 548 Ozzie Smith .75 .35
❑ 549 Luis Salazar .15 .07
❑ 550 Mark Guthrie .15 .07
❑ 551 Charles Nagy .30 .14
❑ 552 Alex Fernandez .30 .14
❑ 553 Mel Rojas .15 .07
❑ 554 Orestes Destrade .15 .07
❑ 555 Mark Gubicza .15 .07
❑ 556 Steve Finley .30 .14
❑ 557 Don Mattingly 1.00 .45
❑ 558 Rickey Henderson .60 .25
❑ 559 Tommy Greene .15 .07
❑ 560 Arthur Rhodes .15 .07
❑ 561 Alfredo Griffin .15 .07
❑ 562 Will Clark .60 .25
❑ 563 Bob Zupcic .15 .07
❑ 564 Chuck Carr .15 .07
❑ 565 Henry Cotto .15 .07
❑ 566 Billy Spiers .15 .07
❑ 567 Jack Armstrong .15 .07
❑ 568 Kurt Stillwell .15 .07
❑ 569 David McCarty .15 .07
❑ 570 Joe Vitiello .15 .07
❑ 571 Gerald Williams .15 .07
❑ 572 Dale Murphy .40 .18
❑ 573 Scott Aldred .15 .07
❑ 574 Bill Gullickson .15 .07
❑ 575 Bobby Thigpen .15 .07
❑ 576 Glenallen Hill .15 .07
❑ 577 Dwayne Henry .15 .07
❑ 578 Calvin Jones .15 .07
❑ 579 Al Martin .15 .07
❑ 580 Ruben Sierra .15 .07
❑ 581 Andy Benes .30 .14
❑ 582 Anthony Young .15 .07
❑ 583 Shawn Boskie .15 .07
❑ 584 Scott Pose .15 .07
❑ 585 Mike Piazza 3.00 1.35
❑ 586 Donovan Osborne .15 .07
❑ 587 James Austin .15 .07
❑ 588 Checklist 301-400 .15 .07
❑ 589 Checklist 401-500 .15 .07
❑ 590 Checklist 501-600 .15 .07
❑ 591 Ken Griffey Jr. MC 1.50 .70
❑ 592 Ivan Rodriguez MC .60 .25

❑ 593 Carlos Baerga MC	.15	.07
❑ 594 Fred McGriff MC	.30	.14
❑ 595 Mark McGwire MC	1.50	.70
❑ 596 Roberto Alomar MC	.30	.14
❑ 597 Kirby Puckett MC	.60	.25
❑ 598 Marquis Grissom MC	.15	.07
❑ 599 John Smoltz MC	.15	.07
❑ 600 Ryne Sandberg MC	.40	.18
❑ 601 Wade Boggs	.60	.25
❑ 602 Jeff Reardon	.30	.14
❑ 603 Billy Ripken	.15	.07
❑ 604 Bryan Harvey	.15	.07
❑ 605 Carlos Quintana	.15	.07
❑ 606 Greg Hibbard	.15	.07
❑ 607 Ellis Burks	.30	.14
❑ 608 Greg Swindell	.15	.07
❑ 609 Dave Winfield	.40	.18
❑ 610 Charlie Hough	.30	.14
❑ 611 Chili Davis	.30	.14
❑ 612 Jody Reed	.15	.07
❑ 613 Mark Williamson	.15	.07
❑ 614 Phil Plantier	.15	.07
❑ 615 Jim Abbott	.30	.14
❑ 616 Dante Bichette	.30	.14
❑ 617 Mark Eichhorn	.15	.07
❑ 618 Gary Sheffield	.60	.25
❑ 619 Richie Lewis	.15	.07
❑ 620 Joe Girardi	.30	.14
❑ 621 Jaime Navarro	.15	.07
❑ 622 Willie Wilson	.15	.07
❑ 623 Scott Fletcher	.15	.07
❑ 624 Bud Black	.15	.07
❑ 625 Tom Brunansky	.15	.07
❑ 626 Steve Avery	.15	.07
❑ 627 Paul Molitor	.60	.25
❑ 628 Gregg Jefferies	.15	.07
❑ 629 Dave Stewart	.30	.14
❑ 630 Javier Lopez	.60	.25
❑ 631 Greg Gagne	.15	.07
❑ 632 Roberto Kelly	.15	.07
❑ 633 Mike Fetters	.15	.07
❑ 634 Ozzie Canseco	.15	.07
❑ 635 Jeff Russell	.15	.07
❑ 636 Pete Incaviglia	.15	.07
❑ 637 Tom Henke	.15	.07
❑ 638 Chipper Jones	3.00	1.35
❑ 639 Jimmy Key	.30	.14
❑ 640 Dave Martinez	.15	.07
❑ 641 Dave Stieb	.30	.14
❑ 642 Milt Thompson	.15	.07
❑ 643 Alan Mills	.15	.07
❑ 644 Tony Fernandez	.15	.07
❑ 645 Randy Bush	.15	.07
❑ 646 Joe Magrane	.15	.07
❑ 647 Ivan Calderon	.15	.07
❑ 648 Jose Guzman	.15	.07
❑ 649 John Olerud	.40	.18
❑ 650 Tom Glavine	.40	.18
❑ 651 Julio Franco	.15	.07
❑ 652 Armando Reynoso	.15	.07
❑ 653 Felix Jose	.15	.07
❑ 654 Ben Rivera	.15	.07
❑ 655 Andre Dawson	.40	.18
❑ 656 Mike Harkey	.15	.07
❑ 657 Kevin Seitzer	.15	.07
❑ 658 Lonnie Smith	.15	.07
❑ 659 Norm Charlton	.15	.07
❑ 660 David Justice	.60	.25
❑ 661 Fernando Valenzuela	.30	.14
❑ 662 Dan Wilson	.30	.14
❑ 663 Mark Gardner	.15	.07
❑ 664 Doug Dascenzo	.15	.07
❑ 665 Greg Maddux	2.00	.90
❑ 666 Harold Baines	.30	.14
❑ 667 Randy Myers	.30	.14
❑ 668 Harold Reynolds	.15	.07
❑ 669 Candy Maldonado	.15	.07
❑ 670 Al Leiter	.30	.14
❑ 671 Jerald Clark	.15	.07
❑ 672 Doug Drabek	.15	.07
❑ 673 Kirk Gibson	.30	.14
❑ 674 Steve Reed	.15	.07
❑ 675 Mike Felder	.15	.07
❑ 676 Ricky Gutierrez	.15	.07
❑ 677 Spike Owen	.15	.07
❑ 678 Otis Nixon	.15	.07
❑ 679 Scott Sanderson	.15	.07
❑ 680 Mark Carreon	.15	.07
❑ 681 Troy Percival	.40	.18
❑ 682 Kevin Stocker	.15	.07
❑ 683 Jim Converse	.15	.07
❑ 684 Barry Bonds	.75	.35
❑ 685 Greg Gohr	.15	.07
❑ 686 Tim Wallach	.15	.07
❑ 687 Matt Mieske	.15	.07
❑ 688 Robby Thompson	.15	.07
❑ 689 Brien Taylor	.15	.07
❑ 690 Kirt Manwaring	.15	.07
❑ 691 Mike Lansing	.30	.14
❑ 692 Steve Decker	.15	.07
❑ 693 Mike Moore	.15	.07
❑ 694 Kevin Mitchell	.30	.14
❑ 695 Phil Hiatt	.15	.07
❑ 696 Tony Tarasco	.15	.07
❑ 697 Benji Gil	.15	.07
❑ 698 Jeff Juden	.15	.07
❑ 699 Kevin Reimer	.15	.07
❑ 700 Andy Ashby	.30	.14
❑ 701 John Jaha	.15	.07
❑ 702 Tim Bogar	.15	.07
❑ 703 David Cone	.30	.14
❑ 704 Willie Greene	.15	.07
❑ 705 David Hulse	.15	.07
❑ 706 Cris Carpenter	.15	.07
❑ 707 Ken Griffey Jr.	3.00	1.35
❑ 708 Steve Bedrosian	.15	.07
❑ 709 Dave Nilsson	.30	.14
❑ 710 Paul Wagner	.15	.07
❑ 711 B.J. Surhoff	.30	.14
❑ 712 Rene Arocha	.15	.07
❑ 713 Manuel Lee	.15	.07
❑ 714 Brian Williams	.15	.07
❑ 715 Sherman Obando	.15	.07
❑ 716 Terry Mulholland	.15	.07
❑ 717 Paul O'Neill	.30	.14
❑ 718 David Nied	.15	.07
❑ 719 J.T. Snow	.75	.35
❑ 720 Nigel Wilson	.15	.07
❑ 721 Mike Bielecki	.15	.07
❑ 722 Kevin Young	.15	.07
❑ 723 Charlie Leibrandt	.15	.07
❑ 724 Frank Bolick	.15	.07
❑ 725 Jon Shave	.15	.07
❑ 726 Steve Cooke	.15	.07
❑ 727 Domingo Martinez	.15	.07
❑ 728 Todd Worrell	.15	.07
❑ 729 Jose Lind	.15	.07
❑ 730 Jim Tatum	.15	.07
❑ 731 Mike Hampton	.40	.18
❑ 732 Mike Draper	.15	.07
❑ 733 Henry Mercedes	.15	.07
❑ 734 John Johnstone	.15	.07
❑ 735 Mitch Webster	.15	.07
❑ 736 Russ Springer	.15	.07
❑ 737 Rob Natal	.15	.07
❑ 738 Steve Howe	.15	.07
❑ 739 Darrell Sherman	.15	.07
❑ 740 Pat Mahomes	.15	.07
❑ 741 Alex Arias	.15	.07
❑ 742 Damon Buford	.15	.07
❑ 743 Charlie Hayes	.15	.07
❑ 744 Guillermo Velasquez	.15	.07
❑ 745 Checklist 601-750 UER (650 Tom Glavine)	.15	.07
❑ 746 Frank Thomas MC	1.00	.45
❑ 747 Barry Bonds MC	.40	.18
❑ 748 Roger Clemens MC	.60	.25
❑ 749 Joe Carter MC	.15	.07
❑ 750 Greg Maddux MC	1.00	.45

1993 Stadium Club Inserts

	MINT	NRMT
COMPLETE SET (10)	16.00	7.25
COMPLETE SERIES 1 (4)	5.00	2.20
COMPLETE SERIES 2 (4)	10.00	4.50
COMPLETE SERIES 3 (2)	2.00	.90
COMMON SER.1 CARD (A1-A4)	.50	.23
COMMON SER.2 CARD (B1-B4)	1.25	.55
COMMON SER.3 CARD (C1-C2)	.50	.23
❑ A1 Robin Yount 3000 Hit Club	1.00	.45
❑ A2 George Brett 3000 Hit Club	4.00	1.80
❑ A3 David Nied First Draft Pick of the Rockies	.50	.23
❑ A4 Nigel Wilson 1st DP Marlins	.50	.23
❑ B1 Will Clark Mark McGwire Pacific Terrific	4.00	1.80
❑ B2 Dwight Gooden Don Mattingly Broadway Stars NY	1.25	.55
❑ B3 Ryne Sandberg Frank Thomas Second City Sluggers	3.00	1.35
❑ B4 Darryl Strawberry Ken Griffey Jr. Pacific Terrific	4.00	1.80
❑ C1 David Nied UER Colorado Rockies Firsts (Misspelled pitch-hitter on back)	.50	.23
❑ C2 Charlie Hough Florida Marlins Firsts	.50	.23

1993 Stadium Club Master Photos

	MINT	NRMT
COMPLETE SET (30)	24.00	11.00
COMPLETE SERIES 1 (12)	6.00	2.70
COMPLETE SERIES 2 (12)	8.00	3.60
COMPLETE SERIES 3 (6)	10.00	4.50
COMMON CARD	.25	.11
❑ 1 Carlos Baerga	.25	.11
❑ 2 Delino DeShields	.25	.11
❑ 3 Brian McRae	.25	.11
❑ 4 Sam Militello	.25	.11
❑ 5 Joe Oliver	.25	.11
❑ 6 Kirby Puckett	1.50	.70
❑ 7 Cal Ripken	4.00	1.80
❑ 8 Bip Roberts	.25	.11
❑ 9 Mike Scioscia	.25	.11
❑ 10 Rick Sutcliffe	.25	.11

	Card	MINT	NRMT
❑	11 Danny Tartabull	.25	.11
❑	12 Tim Wakefield	.50	.23
❑	13 George Brett	2.00	.90
❑	14 Jose Canseco	1.00	.45
❑	15 Will Clark	1.00	.45
❑	16 Travis Fryman	.50	.23
❑	17 Dwight Gooden	.50	.23
❑	18 Mark Grace	.75	.35
❑	19 Rickey Henderson	1.00	.45
❑	20 Mark McGwire MC	2.00	.90
❑	21 Nolan Ryan	4.00	1.80
❑	22 Ruben Sierra	.25	.11
❑	23 Darryl Strawberry	.50	.23
❑	24 Larry Walker	1.00	.45
❑	25 Barry Bonds	1.25	.55
❑	26 Ken Griffey Jr.	5.00	2.20
❑	27 Greg Maddux	3.00	1.35
❑	28 David Nied	.25	.11
❑	29 J.T. Snow	1.00	.45
❑	30 Brien Taylor	.25	.11

1994 Stadium Club

	MINT	NRMT
COMPLETE SET (720)	55.00	25.00
COMPLETE SERIES 1 (270)	20.00	9.00
COMPLETE SERIES 2 (270)	20.00	9.00
COMPLETE SERIES 3 (180)	15.00	6.75
COMMON CARD (1-720)	.15	.07

	Card	MINT	NRMT
❑	1 Robin Yount	.60	.25
❑	2 Rick Wilkins	.15	.07
❑	3 Steve Scarsone	.15	.07
❑	4 Gary Sheffield	.60	.25
❑	5 George Brett UER	1.25	.55
	(birthdate listed as 1963; should be 1953)		
❑	6 Al Martin	.15	.07
❑	7 Joe Oliver	.15	.07
❑	8 Stan Belinda	.15	.07
❑	9 Denny Hocking	.15	.07
❑	10 Roberto Alomar	.60	.25
❑	11 Luis Polonia	.15	.07
❑	12 Scott Hemond	.15	.07
❑	13 Jody Reed	.15	.07
❑	14 Mel Rojas	.15	.07
❑	15 Junior Ortiz	.15	.07
❑	16 Harold Baines	.30	.14
❑	17 Brad Pennington	.15	.07
❑	18 Jay Bell	.30	.14
❑	19 Tom Henke	.15	.07
❑	20 Jeff Branson	.15	.07
❑	21 Roberto Mejia	.15	.07
❑	22 Pedro Munoz	.15	.07
❑	23 Matt Nokes	.15	.07
❑	24 Jack McDowell	.15	.07
❑	25 Cecil Fielder	.30	.14
❑	26 Tony Fossas	.15	.07
❑	27 Jim Eisenreich	.15	.07
❑	28 Anthony Young	.15	.07
❑	29 Chuck Carr	.15	.07
❑	30 Jeff Treadway	.15	.07
❑	31 Chris Nabholz	.15	.07
❑	32 Tom Candiotti	.15	.07
❑	33 Mike Maddux	.15	.07
❑	34 Nolan Ryan	2.50	1.10
❑	35 Luis Gonzalez	.15	.07
❑	36 Tim Salmon	.60	.25
❑	37 Mark Whiten	.15	.07
❑	38 Roger McDowell	.15	.07
❑	39 Royce Clayton	.15	.07
❑	40 Troy Neel	.15	.07
❑	41 Mike Harkey	.15	.07
❑	42 Darrin Fletcher	.15	.07
❑	43 Wayne Kirby	.15	.07
❑	44 Rich Amaral	.15	.07
❑	45 Robb Nen UER	.15	.07
	(Nenn on back)		
❑	46 Tim Teufel	.15	.07
❑	47 Steve Cooke	.15	.07
❑	48 Jeff McNeely	.15	.07
❑	49 Jeff Montgomery	.15	.07
❑	50 Skeeter Barnes	.15	.07
❑	51 Scott Stahoviak	.15	.07
❑	52 Pat Kelly	.15	.07
❑	53 Brady Anderson	.30	.14
❑	54 Mariano Duncan	.15	.07
❑	55 Brian Bohanon	.15	.07
❑	56 Jerry Spradlin	.15	.07
❑	57 Ron Karkovice	.15	.07
❑	58 Jeff Gardner	.15	.07
❑	59 Bobby Bonilla	.30	.14
❑	60 Tino Martinez	.60	.25
❑	61 Todd Benzinger	.15	.07
❑	62 Steve Trachsel	.15	.07
❑	63 Brian Jordan	.30	.14
❑	64 Steve Bedrosian	.15	.07
❑	65 Brent Gates	.15	.07
❑	66 Shawn Green	.30	.14
❑	67 Sean Berry	.15	.07
❑	68 Joe Klink	.15	.07
❑	69 Fernando Valenzuela	.30	.14
❑	70 Andy Tomberlin	.15	.07
❑	71 Tony Pena	.15	.07
❑	72 Eric Young	.15	.07
❑	73 Chris Gomez	.15	.07
❑	74 Paul O'Neill	.30	.14
❑	75 Ricky Gutierrez	.15	.07
❑	76 Brad Holman	.15	.07
❑	77 Lance Painter	.15	.07
❑	78 Mike Butcher	.15	.07
❑	79 Sid Bream	.15	.07
❑	80 Sammy Sosa	1.50	.70
❑	81 Felix Fermin	.15	.07
❑	82 Todd Hundley	.30	.14
❑	83 Kevin Higgins	.15	.07
❑	84 Todd Pratt	.15	.07
❑	85 Ken Griffey Jr.	3.00	1.35
❑	86 John O'Donoghue	.15	.07
❑	87 Rick Renteria	.15	.07
❑	88 John Burkett	.15	.07
❑	89 Jose Vizcaino	.15	.07
❑	90 Kevin Seitzer	.15	.07
❑	91 Bobby Witt	.15	.07
❑	92 Chris Turner	.15	.07
❑	93 Omar Vizquel	.30	.14
❑	94 David Justice	.60	.25
❑	95 David Segui	.30	.14
❑	96 Dave Hollins	.15	.07
❑	97 Doug Strange	.15	.07
❑	98 Jerald Clark	.15	.07
❑	99 Mike Moore	.15	.07
❑	100 Joey Cora	.30	.14
❑	101 Scott Kamieniecki	.15	.07
❑	102 Andy Benes	.30	.14
❑	103 Chris Bosio	.15	.07
❑	104 Rey Sanchez	.15	.07
❑	105 John Jaha	.15	.07
❑	106 Otis Nixon	.15	.07
❑	107 Rickey Henderson	.60	.25
❑	108 Jeff Bagwell	1.00	.45
❑	109 Gregg Jefferies	.15	.07
❑	110 Roberto Alomar	.40	.18
	Paul Molitor		
	John Olerud		
❑	111 Ron Gant	.30	.14
	David Justice		
	Fred McGriff		
❑	112 Juan Gonzalez	.40	.18
	Rafael Palmeiro		
	Dean Palmer		
❑	113 Greg Swindell	.15	.07
❑	114 Bill Haselman	.15	.07
❑	115 Phil Plantier	.15	.07
❑	116 Ivan Rodriguez	.75	.35
❑	117 Kevin Tapani	.15	.07
❑	118 Mike LaValliere	.15	.07
❑	119 Tim Costo	.15	.07
❑	120 Mickey Morandini	.15	.07
❑	121 Brett Butler	.30	.14
❑	122 Tom Pagnozzi	.15	.07
❑	123 Ron Gant	.30	.14
❑	124 Damion Easley	.30	.14
❑	125 Dennis Eckersley	.30	.14
❑	126 Matt Mieske	.15	.07
❑	127 Cliff Floyd	.30	.14
❑	128 Julian Tavarez	.30	.14
❑	129 Arthur Rhodes	.15	.07
❑	130 Dave West	.15	.07
❑	131 Tim Naehring	.15	.07
❑	132 Freddie Benavides	.15	.07
❑	133 Paul Assenmacher	.15	.07
❑	134 David McCarty	.15	.07
❑	135 Jose Lind	.15	.07
❑	136 Reggie Sanders	.30	.14
❑	137 Don Slaught	.15	.07
❑	138 Andujar Cedeno	.15	.07
❑	139 Rob Deer	.15	.07
❑	140 Mike Piazza UER	2.00	.90
	(listed as outfielder)		
❑	141 Moises Alou	.40	.18
❑	142 Tom Foley	.15	.07
❑	143 Benito Santiago	.15	.07
❑	144 Sandy Alomar	.30	.14
❑	145 Carlos Hernandez	.15	.07
❑	146 Luis Alicea	.15	.07
❑	147 Tom Lampkin	.15	.07
❑	148 Ryan Klesko	.30	.14
❑	149 Juan Guzman	.15	.07
❑	150 Scott Servais	.15	.07
❑	151 Tony Gwynn	1.50	.70
❑	152 Tim Wakefield	.30	.14
❑	153 David Nied	.15	.07
❑	154 Chris Haney	.15	.07
❑	155 Danny Bautista	.15	.07
❑	156 Randy Velarde	.15	.07
❑	157 Darrin Jackson	.15	.07
❑	158 J.R. Phillips	.15	.07
❑	159 Greg Gagne	.15	.07
❑	160 Luis Aquino	.15	.07
❑	161 John Vander Wal	.15	.07
❑	162 Randy Myers	.15	.07
❑	163 Ted Power	.15	.07
❑	164 Scott Brosius	.30	.14
❑	165 Len Dykstra	.30	.14
❑	166 Jacob Brumfield	.15	.07
❑	167 Bo Jackson	.30	.14
❑	168 Eddie Taubensee	.15	.07
❑	169 Carlos Baerga	.30	.14
❑	170 Tim Bogar	.15	.07
❑	171 Jose Canseco	.60	.25
❑	172 Greg Blosser UER	.15	.07
	(Gregg on front)		
❑	173 Chili Davis	.30	.14
❑	174 Randy Knorr	.15	.07
❑	175 Mike Perez	.15	.07
❑	176 Henry Rodriguez	.30	.14
❑	177 Brian Turang	.15	.07
❑	178 Roger Pavlik	.15	.07
❑	179 Aaron Sele	.30	.14
❑	180 Fred McGriff	.40	.18
	Gary Sheffield		
❑	181 J.T. Snow	.60	.25
	Tim Salmon		
❑	182 Roberto Hernandez	.15	.07
❑	183 Jeff Reboulet	.15	.07
❑	184 John Doherty	.15	.07
❑	185 Danny Sheaffer	.15	.07
❑	186 Bip Roberts	.15	.07
❑	187 Denny Martinez	.30	.14
❑	188 Darryl Hamilton	.15	.07
❑	189 Eduardo Perez	.15	.07
❑	190 Pete Harnisch	.15	.07
❑	191 Rich Gossage	.30	.14
❑	192 Mickey Tettleton	.15	.07
❑	193 Lenny Webster	.15	.07
❑	194 Lance Johnson	.15	.07
❑	195 Don Mattingly	1.00	.45

❑ 196 Gregg Olson .15 .07
❑ 197 Mark Gubicza .15 .07
❑ 198 Scott Fletcher .15 .07
❑ 199 Jon Shave .15 .07
❑ 200 Tim Mauser .15 .07
❑ 201 Jeromy Burnitz .30 .14
❑ 202 Rob Dibble .15 .07
❑ 203 Will Clark .60 .25
❑ 204 Steve Buechele .15 .07
❑ 205 Brian Williams .15 .07
❑ 206 Carlos Garcia .15 .07
❑ 207 Mark Clark .15 .07
❑ 208 Rafael Palmeiro .40 .18
❑ 209 Eric Davis .30 .14
❑ 210 Pat Meares .15 .07
❑ 211 Chuck Finley .30 .14
❑ 212 Jason Bere .15 .07
❑ 213 Gary DiSarcina .15 .07
❑ 214 Tony Fernandez .15 .07
❑ 215 B.J. Surhoff .30 .14
❑ 216 Lee Guetterman .15 .07
❑ 217 Tim Wallach .15 .07
❑ 218 Kirt Manwaring .15 .07
❑ 219 Albert Belle .75 .35
❑ 220 Doc Gooden .30 .14
❑ 221 Archi Cianfrocco .15 .07
❑ 222 Terry Mulholland .15 .07
❑ 223 Hipolito Pichardo .15 .07
❑ 224 Kent Hrbek .30 .14
❑ 225 Craig Grebeck .15 .07
❑ 226 Todd Jones .15 .07
❑ 227 Mike Bordick .15 .07
❑ 228 John Olerud .30 .14
❑ 229 Jeff Blauser .15 .07
❑ 230 Alex Arias .15 .07
❑ 231 Bernard Gilkey .15 .07
❑ 232 Denny Neagle .30 .14
❑ 233 Pedro Borbon .15 .07
❑ 234 Dick Schofield .15 .07
❑ 235 Matias Carrillo .15 .07
❑ 236 Juan Bell .15 .07
❑ 237 Mike Hampton .15 .07
❑ 238 Barry Bonds .75 .35
❑ 239 Cris Carpenter .15 .07
❑ 240 Eric Karros .30 .14
❑ 241 Greg McMichael .15 .07
❑ 242 Pat Hentgen .30 .14
❑ 243 Tim Pugh .15 .07
❑ 244 Vinny Castilla .30 .14
❑ 245 Charlie Hough .15 .07
❑ 246 Bobby Munoz .15 .07
❑ 247 Kevin Baez .15 .07
❑ 248 Todd Frohwirth .15 .07
❑ 249 Charlie Hayes .15 .07
❑ 250 Mike Macfarlane .15 .07
❑ 251 Danny Darwin .15 .07
❑ 252 Ben Rivera .15 .07
❑ 253 Dave Henderson .15 .07
❑ 254 Steve Avery .15 .07
❑ 255 Tim Belcher .15 .07
❑ 256 Dan Plesac .15 .07
❑ 257 Jim Thome .75 .35
❑ 258 Albert Belle HR .40 .18
❑ 259 Barry Bonds HR .60 .25
❑ 260 Ron Gant HR .15 .07
❑ 261 Juan Gonzalez HR .75 .35
❑ 262 Ken Griffey Jr. HR 1.50 .70
❑ 263 David Justice HR .30 .14
❑ 264 Fred McGriff HR .15 .07
❑ 265 Rafael Palmeiro HR .15 .07
❑ 266 Mike Piazza HR 1.00 .45
❑ 267 Frank Thomas HR 1.00 .45
❑ 268 Matt Williams HR .15 .07
❑ 269 Checklist 1-135 .15 .07
❑ 270 Checklist 136-270 .15 .07
❑ 271 Mike Stanley .15 .07
❑ 272 Tony Tarasco .15 .07
❑ 273 Teddy Higuera .15 .07
❑ 274 Ryan Thompson .15 .07
❑ 275 Rick Aguilera .15 .07
❑ 276 Ramon Martinez .30 .14
❑ 277 Orlando Merced .15 .07
❑ 278 Guillermo Velasquez .15 .07
❑ 279 Mark Hutton .15 .07
❑ 280 Larry Walker .60 .25

❑ 281 Kevin Gross .15 .07
❑ 282 Jose Offerman .15 .07
❑ 283 Jim Leyritz .30 .14
❑ 284 Jamie Moyer .15 .07
❑ 285 Frank Thomas 2.00 .90
❑ 286 Derek Bell .30 .14
❑ 287 Derrick May .15 .07
❑ 288 Dave Winfield .60 .25
❑ 289 Curt Schilling .30 .14
❑ 290 Carlos Quintana .15 .07
❑ 291 Bob Natal .15 .07
❑ 292 David Cone .40 .18
❑ 293 Al Osuna .15 .07
❑ 294 Bob Hamelin .15 .07
❑ 295 Chad Curtis .15 .07
❑ 296 Danny Jackson .15 .07
❑ 297 Bob Welch .15 .07
❑ 298 Felix Jose .15 .07
❑ 299 Jay Buhner .30 .14
❑ 300 Joe Carter .30 .14
❑ 301 Kenny Lofton .60 .25
❑ 302 Kirk Rueter .15 .07
❑ 303 Kim Batiste .15 .07
❑ 304 Mike Morgan .15 .07
❑ 305 Pat Borders .15 .07
❑ 306 Rene Arocha .15 .07
❑ 307 Ruben Sierra .15 .07
❑ 308 Steve Finley .30 .14
❑ 309 Travis Fryman .30 .14
❑ 310 Zane Smith .15 .07
❑ 311 Willie Wilson .15 .07
❑ 312 Trevor Hoffman .30 .14
❑ 313 Terry Pendleton .15 .07
❑ 314 Salomon Torres .15 .07
❑ 315 Robin Ventura .30 .14
❑ 316 Randy Tomlin .15 .07
❑ 317 Dave Stewart .30 .14
❑ 318 Mike Benjamin .15 .07
❑ 319 Matt Turner .15 .07
❑ 320 Manny Ramirez .75 .35
❑ 321 Kevin Young .15 .07
❑ 322 Ken Caminiti .40 .18
❑ 323 Joe Girardi .15 .07
❑ 324 Jeff McKnight .15 .07
❑ 325 Gene Harris .15 .07
❑ 326 Devon White .30 .14
❑ 327 Darryl Kile .30 .14
❑ 328 Craig Paquette .15 .07
❑ 329 Cal Eldred .15 .07
❑ 330 Bill Swift .15 .07
❑ 331 Alan Trammell .40 .18
❑ 332 Armando Reynoso .15 .07
❑ 333 Brent Mayne .15 .07
❑ 334 Chris Donnels .15 .07
❑ 335 Darryl Strawberry .30 .14
❑ 336 Dean Palmer .30 .14
❑ 337 Frank Castillo .15 .07
❑ 338 Jeff King .15 .07
❑ 339 John Franco .30 .14
❑ 340 Kevin Appier .30 .14
❑ 341 Lance Blankenship .15 .07
❑ 342 Mark McLemore .15 .07
❑ 343 Pedro Astacio .15 .07
❑ 344 Rich Batchelor .15 .07
❑ 345 Ryan Bowen .15 .07
❑ 346 Terry Steinbach .30 .14
❑ 347 Troy O'Leary .30 .14
❑ 348 Willie Blair .15 .07
❑ 349 Wade Boggs .60 .25
❑ 350 Tim Raines .30 .14
❑ 351 Scott Livingstone .15 .07
❑ 352 Rod Correia .15 .07
❑ 353 Ray Lankford .30 .14
❑ 354 Pat Listach .15 .07
❑ 355 Milt Thompson .15 .07
❑ 356 Miguel Jimenez .15 .07
❑ 357 Marc Newfield .15 .07
❑ 358 Mark McGwire 3.00 1.35
❑ 359 Kirby Puckett 1.00 .45
❑ 360 Kent Mercker .15 .07
❑ 361 John Kruk .30 .14
❑ 362 Jeff Kent .30 .14
❑ 363 Hal Morris .15 .07
❑ 364 Edgar Martinez .30 .14
❑ 365 Dave Magadan .15 .07

❑ 366 Dante Bichette .30 .14
❑ 367 Chris Hammond .15 .07
❑ 368 Bret Saberhagen .30 .14
❑ 369 Billy Ripken .15 .07
❑ 370 Bill Gullickson .15 .07
❑ 371 Andre Dawson .40 .18
❑ 372 Roberto Kelly .15 .07
❑ 373 Cal Ripken 2.50 1.10
❑ 374 Craig Biggio .60 .25
❑ 375 Dan Pasqua .15 .07
❑ 376 Dave Nilsson .15 .07
❑ 377 Duane Ward .15 .07
❑ 378 Greg Vaughn .30 .14
❑ 379 Jeff Fassero .15 .07
❑ 380 Jerry DiPoto .15 .07
❑ 381 John Patterson .15 .07
❑ 382 Kevin Brown .30 .14
❑ 383 Kevin Roberson .15 .07
❑ 384 Joe Orsulak .15 .07
❑ 385 Hilly Hathaway .15 .07
❑ 386 Mike Greenwell .15 .07
❑ 387 Orestes Destrade .15 .07
❑ 388 Mike Gallego .15 .07
❑ 389 Ozzie Guillen .15 .07
❑ 390 Raul Mondesi .60 .25
❑ 391 Scott Lydy .15 .07
❑ 392 Tom Urbani .15 .07
❑ 393 Wil Cordero .15 .07
❑ 394 Tony Longmire .15 .07
❑ 395 Todd Zeile .15 .07
❑ 396 Scott Cooper .15 .07
❑ 397 Ryne Sandberg .75 .35
❑ 398 Ricky Bones .15 .07
❑ 399 Phil Clark .15 .07
❑ 400 Orel Hershiser .30 .14
❑ 401 Mike Henneman .15 .07
❑ 402 Mark Lemke .15 .07
❑ 403 Mark Grace .40 .18
❑ 404 Ken Ryan .15 .07
❑ 405 John Smoltz .30 .14
❑ 406 Jeff Conine .30 .14
❑ 407 Greg Harris .15 .07
❑ 408 Doug Drabek .15 .07
❑ 409 Dave Fleming .15 .07
❑ 410 Danny Tartabull .15 .07
❑ 411 Chad Kreuter .15 .07
❑ 412 Brad Ausmus .15 .07
❑ 413 Ben McDonald .15 .07
❑ 414 Barry Larkin .40 .18
❑ 415 Bret Barberie .15 .07
❑ 416 Chuck Knoblauch .60 .25
❑ 417 Ozzie Smith .75 .35
❑ 418 Ed Sprague .15 .07
❑ 419 Matt Williams .40 .18
❑ 420 Jeremy Hernandez .15 .07
❑ 421 Jose Bautista .15 .07
❑ 422 Kevin Mitchell .15 .07
❑ 423 Manuel Lee .15 .07
❑ 424 Mike Devereaux .15 .07
❑ 425 Omar Olivares .15 .07
❑ 426 Rafael Belliard .15 .07
❑ 427 Richie Lewis .15 .07
❑ 428 Ron Darling .15 .07
❑ 429 Shane Mack .15 .07
❑ 430 Tim Hulett .15 .07
❑ 431 Wally Joyner .30 .14
❑ 432 Wes Chamberlain .15 .07
❑ 433 Tom Browning .15 .07
❑ 434 Scott Radinsky .15 .07
❑ 435 Rondell White .30 .14
❑ 436 Rod Beck .15 .07
❑ 437 Rheal Cormier .15 .07
❑ 438 Randy Johnson .60 .25
❑ 439 Pete Schourek .15 .07
❑ 440 Mo Vaughn .75 .35
❑ 441 Mike Timlin .15 .07
❑ 442 Mark Langston .15 .07
❑ 443 Lou Whitaker .30 .14
❑ 444 Kevin Stocker .15 .07
❑ 445 Ken Hill .15 .07
❑ 446 John Wetteland .30 .14
❑ 447 J.T. Snow .30 .14
❑ 448 Erik Pappas .15 .07
❑ 449 David Hulse .15 .07
❑ 450 Darren Daulton .30 .14

❑ 451	Chris Hoiles	.15	.07
❑ 452	Bryan Harvey	.15	.07
❑ 453	Darren Lewis	.15	.07
❑ 454	Andres Galarraga	.60	.25
❑ 455	Joe Hesketh	.15	.07
❑ 456	Jose Valentin	.15	.07
❑ 457	Dan Peltier	.15	.07
❑ 458	Joe Boever	.15	.07
❑ 459	Kevin Rogers	.15	.07
❑ 460	Craig Shipley	.15	.07
❑ 461	Alvaro Espinoza	.15	.07
❑ 462	Wilson Alvarez	.30	.14
❑ 463	Cory Snyder	.15	.07
❑ 464	Candy Maldonado	.15	.07
❑ 465	Blas Minor	.15	.07
❑ 466	Rod Bolton	.15	.07
❑ 467	Kenny Rogers	.15	.07
❑ 468	Greg Myers	.15	.07
❑ 469	Jimmy Key	.30	.14
❑ 470	Tony Castillo	.15	.07
❑ 471	Mike Stanton	.15	.07
❑ 472	Deion Sanders	.30	.14
❑ 473	Tito Navarro	.15	.07
❑ 474	Mike Gardiner	.15	.07
❑ 475	Steve Reed	.15	.07
❑ 476	John Roper	.15	.07
❑ 477	Mike Trombley	.15	.07
❑ 478	Charles Nagy	.30	.14
❑ 479	Larry Casian	.15	.07
❑ 480	Eric Hillman	.15	.07
❑ 481	Bill Wertz	.15	.07
❑ 482	Jeff Schwarz	.15	.07
❑ 483	John Valentin	.30	.14
❑ 484	Carl Willis	.15	.07
❑ 485	Gary Gaetti	.30	.14
❑ 486	Bill Pecota	.15	.07
❑ 487	John Smiley	.15	.07
❑ 488	Mike Mussina	.60	.25
❑ 489	Mike Ignasiak	.15	.07
❑ 490	Billy Brewer	.15	.07
❑ 491	Jack Voigt	.15	.07
❑ 492	Mike Munoz	.15	.07
❑ 493	Lee Tinsley	.15	.07
❑ 494	Bob Wickman	.15	.07
❑ 495	Roger Salkeld	.15	.07
❑ 496	Thomas Howard	.15	.07
❑ 497	Mark Davis	.15	.07
❑ 498	Dave Clark	.15	.07
❑ 499	Turk Wendell	.15	.07
❑ 500	Rafael Bournigal	.15	.07
❑ 501	Chip Hale	.15	.07
❑ 502	Matt Whiteside	.15	.07
❑ 503	Brian Koelling	.15	.07
❑ 504	Jeff Reed	.15	.07
❑ 505	Paul Wagner	.15	.07
❑ 506	Torey Lovullo	.15	.07
❑ 507	Curtis Leskanic	.15	.07
❑ 508	Derek Lilliquist	.15	.07
❑ 509	Joe Magrane	.15	.07
❑ 510	Mackey Sasser	.15	.07
❑ 511	Lloyd McClendon	.15	.07
❑ 512	Jayhawk Owens	.15	.07
❑ 513	Woody Williams	.15	.07
❑ 514	Gary Redus	.15	.07
❑ 515	Tim Spehr	.15	.07
❑ 516	Jim Abbott	.30	.14
❑ 517	Lou Frazier	.15	.07
❑ 518	Erik Plantenberg	.15	.07
❑ 519	Tim Worrell	.15	.07
❑ 520	Brian McRae	.15	.07
❑ 521	Chan Ho Park	2.50	1.10
❑ 522	Mark Wohlers	.15	.07
❑ 523	Geronimo Pena	.15	.07
❑ 524	Andy Ashby	.15	.07
❑ 525	Tim Raines TALE	.15	.07
❑ 526	Paul Molitor TALE	.30	.14
❑ 527	Joe Carter DL	.15	.07
❑ 528	Frank Thomas DL UER (listed as third in RBI in 1993; was actually second)	1.00	.45
❑ 529	Ken Griffey Jr. DL	1.50	.70
❑ 530	David Justice DL	.30	.14
❑ 531	Gregg Jefferies DL	.15	.07
❑ 532	Barry Bonds DL	.60	.25
❑ 533	John Kruk QS	.15	.07
❑ 534	Roger Clemens QS	.60	.25
❑ 535	Cecil Fielder QS	.15	.07
❑ 536	Ruben Sierra QS	.15	.07
❑ 537	Tony Gwynn QS	.75	.35
❑ 538	Tom Glavine QS	.30	.14
❑ 539	Checklist 271-405 UER (number on back is 269)	.15	.07
❑ 540	Checklist 406-540 UER (numbered 270 on back)	.15	.07
❑ 541	Ozzie Smith ATL	.60	.25
❑ 542	Eddie Murray ATL	.30	.14
❑ 543	Lee Smith ATL	.15	.07
❑ 544	Greg Maddux	2.00	.90
❑ 545	Denis Boucher	.15	.07
❑ 546	Mark Gardner	.15	.07
❑ 547	Bo Jackson	.30	.14
❑ 548	Eric Anthony	.15	.07
❑ 549	Delino DeShields	.15	.07
❑ 550	Turner Ward	.15	.07
❑ 551	Scott Sanderson	.15	.07
❑ 552	Hector Carrasco	.15	.07
❑ 553	Tony Phillips	.15	.07
❑ 554	Melido Perez	.15	.07
❑ 555	Mike Felder	.15	.07
❑ 556	Jack Morris	.30	.14
❑ 557	Rafael Palmeiro	.40	.18
❑ 558	Shane Reynolds	.30	.14
❑ 559	Pete Incaviglia	.15	.07
❑ 560	Greg Harris	.15	.07
❑ 561	Matt Walbeck	.15	.07
❑ 562	Todd Van Poppel	.15	.07
❑ 563	Todd Stottlemyre	.15	.07
❑ 564	Ricky Bones	.15	.07
❑ 565	Mike Jackson	.15	.07
❑ 566	Kevin McReynolds	.15	.07
❑ 567	Melvin Nieves	.15	.07
❑ 568	Juan Gonzalez	1.50	.70
❑ 569	Frank Viola	.15	.07
❑ 570	Vince Coleman	.15	.07
❑ 571	Brian Anderson	.40	.18
❑ 572	Omar Vizquel	.30	.14
❑ 573	Bernie Williams	.60	.25
❑ 574	Tom Glavine	.60	.25
❑ 575	Mitch Williams	.15	.07
❑ 576	Shawon Dunston	.15	.07
❑ 577	Mike Lansing	.30	.14
❑ 578	Greg Pirkl	.15	.07
❑ 579	Sid Fernandez	.15	.07
❑ 580	Doug Jones	.15	.07
❑ 581	Walt Weiss	.15	.07
❑ 582	Tim Belcher	.15	.07
❑ 583	Alex Fernandez	.15	.07
❑ 584	Alex Cole	.15	.07
❑ 585	Greg Cadaret	.15	.07
❑ 586	Bob Tewksbury	.15	.07
❑ 587	Dave Hansen	.15	.07
❑ 588	Kurt Abbott	.15	.07
❑ 589	Rick White	.15	.07
❑ 590	Kevin Bass	.15	.07
❑ 591	Geronimo Berroa	.15	.07
❑ 592	Jaime Navarro	.15	.07
❑ 593	Steve Farr	.15	.07
❑ 594	Jack Armstrong	.15	.07
❑ 595	Steve Howe	.15	.07
❑ 596	Jose Rijo	.15	.07
❑ 597	Otis Nixon	.15	.07
❑ 598	Robby Thompson	.15	.07
❑ 599	Kelly Stinnett	.15	.07
❑ 600	Carlos Delgado	.40	.18
❑ 601	Brian Johnson	.15	.07
❑ 602	Gregg Olson	.15	.07
❑ 603	Jim Edmonds	.60	.25
❑ 604	Mike Blowers	.15	.07
❑ 605	Lee Smith	.30	.14
❑ 606	Pat Rapp	.15	.07
❑ 607	Mike Magnante	.15	.07
❑ 608	Karl Rhodes	.15	.07
❑ 609	Jeff Juden	.15	.07
❑ 610	Rusty Meacham	.15	.07
❑ 611	Pedro Martinez	.60	.25
❑ 612	Todd Worrell	.15	.07
❑ 613	Stan Javier	.15	.07
❑ 614	Mike Hampton	.15	.07
❑ 615	Jose Guzman	.15	.07
❑ 616	Xavier Hernandez	.15	.07
❑ 617	David Wells	.40	.18
❑ 618	John Habyan	.15	.07
❑ 619	Chris Nabholz	.15	.07
❑ 620	Bobby Jones	.15	.07
❑ 621	Chris James	.15	.07
❑ 622	Ellis Burks	.30	.14
❑ 623	Erik Hanson	.15	.07
❑ 624	Pat Meares	.15	.07
❑ 625	Harold Reynolds	.15	.07
❑ 626	Bob Hamelin RR	.15	.07
❑ 627	Manny Ramirez RR	.40	.18
❑ 628	Ryan Klesko RR	.15	.07
❑ 629	Carlos Delgado RR	.15	.07
❑ 630	Javier Lopez RR	.15	.07
❑ 631	Steve Karsay RR	.15	.07
❑ 632	Rick Helling RR	.15	.07
❑ 633	Steve Trachsel RR	.15	.07
❑ 634	Hector Carrasco RR	.15	.07
❑ 635	Andy Stankiewicz	.15	.07
❑ 636	Paul Sorrento	.15	.07
❑ 637	Scott Erickson	.30	.14
❑ 638	Chipper Jones	2.00	.90
❑ 639	Luis Polonia	.15	.07
❑ 640	Howard Johnson	.15	.07
❑ 641	John Dopson	.15	.07
❑ 642	Jody Reed	.15	.07
❑ 643	Lonnie Smith UER (Card numbered 543)	.15	.07
❑ 644	Mark Portugal	.15	.07
❑ 645	Paul Molitor	.60	.25
❑ 646	Paul Assenmacher	.15	.07
❑ 647	Hubie Brooks	.15	.07
❑ 648	Gary Wayne	.15	.07
❑ 649	Sean Berry	.15	.07
❑ 650	Roger Clemens	1.25	.55
❑ 651	Brian L.Hunter	.30	.14
❑ 652	Wally Whitehurst	.15	.07
❑ 653	Allen Watson	.15	.07
❑ 654	Rickey Henderson	.60	.25
❑ 655	Sid Bream	.15	.07
❑ 656	Dan Wilson	.15	.07
❑ 657	Ricky Jordan	.15	.07
❑ 658	Sterling Hitchcock	.30	.14
❑ 659	Darrin Jackson	.15	.07
❑ 660	Junior Felix	.15	.07
❑ 661	Tom Brunansky	.15	.07
❑ 662	Jose Vizcaino	.15	.07
❑ 663	Mark Leiter	.15	.07
❑ 664	Gil Heredia	.15	.07
❑ 665	Fred McGriff	.40	.18
❑ 666	Will Clark	.60	.25
❑ 667	Al Leiter	.30	.14
❑ 668	James Mouton	.15	.07
❑ 669	Billy Bean	.15	.07
❑ 670	Scott Leius	.15	.07
❑ 671	Bret Boone	.30	.14
❑ 672	Darren Holmes	.15	.07
❑ 673	Dave Weathers	.15	.07
❑ 674	Eddie Murray	.60	.25
❑ 675	Felix Fermin	.15	.07
❑ 676	Chris Sabo	.15	.07
❑ 677	Billy Spiers	.15	.07
❑ 678	Aaron Sele	.30	.14
❑ 679	Juan Samuel	.15	.07
❑ 680	Julio Franco	.15	.07
❑ 681	Heathcliff Slocumb	.15	.07
❑ 682	Denny Martinez	.30	.14
❑ 683	Jerry Browne	.15	.07
❑ 684	Pedro Martinez	.60	.25
❑ 685	Rex Hudler	.15	.07
❑ 686	Willie McGee	.30	.14
❑ 687	Andy Van Slyke	.30	.14
❑ 688	Pat Mahomes	.15	.07
❑ 689	Dave Henderson	.15	.07
❑ 690	Tony Eusebio	.15	.07
❑ 691	Rick Sutcliffe	.15	.07
❑ 692	Willie Banks	.15	.07
❑ 693	Alan Mills	.15	.07
❑ 694	Jeff Treadway	.15	.07
❑ 695	Alex Gonzalez	.15	.07
❑ 696	David Segui	.30	.14
❑ 697	Rick Helling	.30	.14
❑ 698	Bip Roberts	.15	.07
❑ 699	Jeff Cirillo	.75	.35
❑ 700	Terry Mulholland	.15	.07

Card	MINT	NRMT
❑ 701 Marvin Freeman	.15	.07
❑ 702 Jason Bere	.15	.07
❑ 703 Javier Lopez	.40	.18
❑ 704 Greg Hibbard	.15	.07
❑ 705 Tommy Greene	.15	.07
❑ 706 Marquis Grissom	.30	.14
❑ 707 Brian Harper	.15	.07
❑ 708 Steve Karsay	.15	.07
❑ 709 Jeff Brantley	.15	.07
❑ 710 Jeff Russell	.15	.07
❑ 711 Bryan Hickerson	.15	.07
❑ 712 Jim Pittsley	.30	.14
❑ 713 Bobby Ayala	.15	.07
❑ 714 John Smoltz	.30	.14
❑ 715 Jose Rijo	.15	.07
❑ 716 Greg Maddux	1.00	.45
❑ 717 Matt Williams	.40	.18
❑ 718 Frank Thomas	1.00	.45
❑ 719 Ryne Sandberg	.60	.25
❑ 720 Checklist	.15	.07

1994 Stadium Club Dugout Dirt

	MINT	NRMT
COMPLETE SET (12)	10.00	4.50
COMPLETE SERIES 1 (4)	5.00	2.20
COMPLETE SERIES 2 (4)	3.00	1.35
COMPLETE SERIES 3 (4)	3.00	1.35
COMMON CARD (DD1-DD12)	.15	.07
❑ DD1 Mike Piazza	2.00	.90
❑ DD2 Dave Winfield	.60	.25
❑ DD3 John Kruk	.15	.07
❑ DD4 Cal Ripken	2.50	1.10
❑ DD5 Jack McDowell	.15	.07
❑ DD6 Barry Bonds	.60	.25
❑ DD7 Ken Griffey Jr.	3.00	1.35
❑ DD8 Tim Salmon	.60	.25
❑ DD9 Frank Thomas	2.00	.90
❑ DD10 Jeff Kent	.25	.11
❑ DD11 Randy Johnson	.60	.25
❑ DD12 Darren Daulton	.25	.11

1994 Stadium Club Finest

	MINT	NRMT
COMPLETE SET (10)	30.00	13.50
COMMON CARD (F1-F10)	1.00	.45

*JUMBOS: 2X TO 5X BASIC FINEST

Card	MINT	NRMT
❑ F1 Jeff Bagwell	3.00	1.35
❑ F2 Albert Belle	2.00	.90
❑ F3 Barry Bonds	2.00	.90
❑ F4 Juan Gonzalez	5.00	2.20
❑ F5 Ken Griffey Jr.	10.00	4.50
❑ F6 Marquis Grissom	1.00	.45
❑ F7 David Justice	2.00	.90
❑ F8 Mike Piazza	6.00	2.70
❑ F9 Tim Salmon	2.00	.90
❑ F10 Frank Thomas	6.00	2.70

1994 Stadium Club Super Teams

	MINT	NRMT
COMPLETE SET (28)	50.00	22.00
COMMON TEAM (1-28)	1.00	.45
❑ ST1 Atlanta Braves (Jeff Blauser Terry Pendleton)	10.00	4.50
❑ ST2 Chicago Cubs (Sammy Sosa Derrick May)	1.00	.45
❑ ST3 Cincinnati Reds (Reggie Sanders Barry Larkin)	2.00	.90
❑ ST4 Colorado Rockies (Vinny Castilla Eric Young)	1.00	.45
❑ ST5 Florida Marlins (Alex Arias)	1.00	.45
❑ ST6 Houston Astros (Eric Anthony Steve Finley)	1.00	.45
❑ ST7 Los Angeles Dodgers (Mike Piazza)	6.00	2.70
❑ ST8 Montreal Expos (Marquis Grissom)	1.00	.45
❑ ST9 New York Mets (Bobby Bonilla)	1.00	.45
❑ ST10 Philadelphia Phillies (Mickey Morandini)	1.00	.45
❑ ST11 Pittsburgh Pirates (Andy Van Slyke Jay Bell)	1.00	.45
❑ ST12 St. Louis Cardinals (Todd Zeile Gregg Jefferies)	1.00	.45
❑ ST13 San Diego Padres (Ricky Gutierrez)	1.00	.45
❑ ST14 San Francisco Giants (Matt Williams Kirt Manwaring)	2.00	.90
❑ ST15 Baltimore Orioles (Cal Ripken)	8.00	3.60
❑ ST16 Boston Red Sox (Luis Rivera John Valentin)	2.00	.90
❑ ST17 California Angels (Tim Salmon)	1.00	.45
❑ ST18 Chicago White Sox (Joey Cora)	1.00	.45
❑ ST19 Cleveland Indians (Kenny Lofton Carlos Baerga Albert Belle)	3.00	1.35
❑ ST20 Detroit Tigers (Alan Trammell Tony Phillips)	1.00	.45
❑ ST21 Kansas City Royals Jose Lind Curt Wilkerson)	1.00	.45
❑ ST22 Milwaukee Brewers (Julio Navarro John Jaha Cal Eldred)	1.00	.45
❑ ST23 Minnesota Twins (Kirby Puckett Kent Hrbek)	4.00	1.80
❑ ST24 New York Yankees Don Mattingly Bernie Williams)	3.00	1.35
❑ ST25 Oakland Athletics (Mike Bordick Brent Gates)	1.00	.45
❑ ST26 Seattle Mariners (Jay Buhner Mike Blowers)	2.00	.90
❑ ST27 Texas Rangers (Ivan Rodriguez Dean Palmer Jose Canseco Juan Gonzalez)	5.00	2.20
❑ ST28 Toronto Blue Jays (John Olerud)	1.00	.45

1995 Stadium Club

	MINT	NRMT
COMPLETE SET (630)	60.00	27.00
COMPLETE SERIES 1 (270)	25.00	11.00
COMPLETE SERIES 2 (225)	20.00	9.00
COMPLETE SERIES 3 (135)	15.00	6.75
COMMON CARD (1-630)	.15	.07
❑ 1 Cal Ripken	2.50	1.10
❑ 2 Bo Jackson	.30	.14
❑ 3 Bryan Harvey	.15	.07
❑ 4 Curt Schilling	.30	.14
❑ 5 Bruce Ruffin	.15	.07
❑ 6 Travis Fryman	.30	.14
❑ 7 Jim Abbott	.30	.14
❑ 8 David McCarty	.15	.07
❑ 9 Gary Gaetti	.30	.14
❑ 10 Roger Clemens	1.25	.55
❑ 11 Carlos Garcia	.15	.07
❑ 12 Lee Smith	.30	.14
❑ 13 Bobby Ayala	.15	.07
❑ 14 Charles Nagy	.30	.14
❑ 15 Lou Frazier	.15	.07
❑ 16 Rene Arocha	.15	.07
❑ 17 Carlos Delgado	.30	.14
❑ 18 Steve Finley	.30	.14
❑ 19 Ryan Klesko	.30	.14
❑ 20 Cal Eldred	.15	.07
❑ 21 Rey Sanchez	.15	.07
❑ 22 Ken Hill	.15	.07
❑ 23 Benito Santiago	.15	.07
❑ 24 Julian Tavarez	.15	.07
❑ 25 Jose Vizcaino	.15	.07
❑ 26 Andy Benes	.30	.14
❑ 27 Mariano Duncan	.15	.07
❑ 28 Checklist A	.15	.07

❑ 29 Shawon Dunston .15 .07
❑ 30 Rafael Palmeiro .40 .18
❑ 31 Dean Palmer .30 .14
❑ 32 Andres Galarraga .60 .25
❑ 33 Joey Cora .30 .14
❑ 34 Mickey Tettleton .15 .07
❑ 35 Barry Larkin .40 .18
❑ 36 Carlos Baerga .30 .14
❑ 37 Orel Hershiser .30 .14
❑ 38 Jody Reed .15 .07
❑ 39 Paul Molitor .60 .25
❑ 40 Jim Edmonds .40 .18
❑ 41 Bob Tewksbury .15 .07
❑ 42 John Patterson .15 .07
❑ 43 Ray McDavid .15 .07
❑ 44 Zane Smith .15 .07
❑ 45 Bret Saberhagen SE .30 .14
❑ 46 Greg Maddux SE 1.00 .45
❑ 47 Frank Thomas SE 1.00 .45
❑ 48 Carlos Baerga SE .15 .07
❑ 49 Billy Spiers .15 .07
❑ 50 Stan Javier .15 .07
❑ 51 Rex Hudler .15 .07
❑ 52 Denny Hocking .15 .07
❑ 53 Todd Worrell .15 .07
❑ 54 Mark Clark .15 .07
❑ 55 Hipolito Pichardo .15 .07
❑ 56 Bob Wickman .15 .07
❑ 57 Raul Mondesi .40 .18
❑ 58 Steve Cooke .15 .07
❑ 59 Rod Beck .15 .07
❑ 60 Tim Davis .15 .07
❑ 61 Jeff Kent .30 .14
❑ 62 John Valentin .30 .14
❑ 63 Alex Arias .15 .07
❑ 64 Steve Reed .15 .07
❑ 65 Ozzie Smith .75 .35
❑ 66 Terry Pendleton .15 .07
❑ 67 Kenny Rogers .15 .07
❑ 68 Vince Coleman .15 .07
❑ 69 Tom Pagnozzi .15 .07
❑ 70 Roberto Alomar .60 .25
❑ 71 Darrin Jackson .15 .07
❑ 72 Dennis Eckersley .30 .14
❑ 73 Jay Buhner .30 .14
❑ 74 Darren Lewis .15 .07
❑ 75 Dave Weathers .15 .07
❑ 76 Matt Walbeck .15 .07
❑ 77 Brad Ausmus .15 .07
❑ 78 Danny Bautista .15 .07
❑ 79 Bob Hamelin .15 .07
❑ 80 Steve Trachsel .15 .07
❑ 81 Ken Ryan .15 .07
❑ 82 Chris Turner .15 .07
❑ 83 David Segui .30 .14
❑ 84 Ben McDonald .15 .07
❑ 85 Wade Boggs .60 .25
❑ 86 John VanderWal .15 .07
❑ 87 Sandy Alomar Jr. .30 .14
❑ 88 Ron Karkovice .15 .07
❑ 89 Doug Jones .15 .07
❑ 90 Gary Sheffield .40 .18
❑ 91 Ken Caminiti .40 .18
❑ 92 Chris Bosio .15 .07
❑ 93 Kevin Tapani .15 .07
❑ 94 Walt Weiss .15 .07
❑ 95 Erik Hanson .15 .07
❑ 96 Ruben Sierra .15 .07
❑ 97 Nomar Garciaparra 4.00 1.80
❑ 98 Terrence Long .30 .14
❑ 99 Jacob Shumate .15 .07
❑ 100 Paul Wilson .15 .07
❑ 101 Kevin Witt .75 .35
❑ 102 Paul Konerko 1.50 .70
❑ 103 Ben Grieve 4.00 1.80
❑ 104 Mark Johnson .15 .07
❑ 105 Cade Gaspar .30 .14
❑ 106 Mark Farris .15 .07
❑ 107 Dustin Hermanson .30 .14
❑ 108 Scott Elarton .75 .35
❑ 109 Doug Million .15 .07
❑ 110 Matt Smith .15 .07
❑ 111 Brian Buchanan .30 .14
❑ 112 Jayson Peterson .15 .07
❑ 113 Bret Wagner .15 .07
❑ 114 C.J. Nitkowski .15 .07
❑ 115 Ramon Castro .30 .14
❑ 116 Rafael Bournigal .15 .07
❑ 117 Jeff Fassero .15 .07
❑ 118 Bobby Bonilla .30 .14
❑ 119 Ricky Gutierrez .15 .07
❑ 120 Roger Pavlik .15 .07
❑ 121 Mike Greenwell .15 .07
❑ 122 Deion Sanders .30 .14
❑ 123 Charlie Hayes .15 .07
❑ 124 Paul O'Neill .30 .14
❑ 125 Jay Bell .30 .14
❑ 126 Royce Clayton .15 .07
❑ 127 Willie Banks .15 .07
❑ 128 Mark Wohlers .15 .07
❑ 129 Todd Jones .15 .07
❑ 130 Todd Stottlemyre .15 .07
❑ 131 Will Clark .60 .25
❑ 132 Wilson Alvarez .30 .14
❑ 133 Chili Davis .30 .14
❑ 134 Dave Burba .15 .07
❑ 135 Chris Hoiles .15 .07
❑ 136 Jeff Blauser .15 .07
❑ 137 Jeff Reboulet .15 .07
❑ 138 Bret Saberhagen .30 .14
❑ 139 Kirk Rueter .15 .07
❑ 140 Dave Nilsson .15 .07
❑ 141 Pat Borders .15 .07
❑ 142 Ron Darling .15 .07
❑ 143 Derek Bell .30 .14
❑ 144 Dave Hollins .15 .07
❑ 145 Juan Gonzalez 1.50 .70
❑ 146 Andre Dawson .40 .18
❑ 147 Jim Thome .60 .25
❑ 148 Larry Walker .60 .25
❑ 149 Mike Piazza 2.00 .90
❑ 150 Mike Perez .15 .07
❑ 151 Steve Avery .15 .07
❑ 152 Dan Wilson .15 .07
❑ 153 Andy Van Slyke .30 .14
❑ 154 Junior Felix .15 .07
❑ 155 Jack McDowell .15 .07
❑ 156 Danny Tartabull .15 .07
❑ 157 Willie Blair .15 .07
❑ 158 Wm.VanLandingham .15 .07
❑ 159 Robb Nen .15 .07
❑ 160 Lee Tinsley .15 .07
❑ 161 Ismael Valdes .30 .14
❑ 162 Juan Guzman .15 .07
❑ 163 Scott Servais .15 .07
❑ 164 Cliff Floyd .30 .14
❑ 165 Allen Watson .15 .07
❑ 166 Eddie Taubensee .15 .07
❑ 167 Scott Hemond .15 .07
❑ 168 Jeff Tackett .15 .07
❑ 169 Chad Curtis .15 .07
❑ 170 Rico Brogna .15 .07
❑ 171 Luis Polonia .15 .07
❑ 172 Checklist B .15 .07
❑ 173 Lance Johnson .15 .07
❑ 174 Sammy Sosa 1.50 .70
❑ 175 Mike Macfarlane .15 .07
❑ 176 Darryl Hamilton .15 .07
❑ 177 Rick Aguilera .15 .07
❑ 178 Dave West .15 .07
❑ 179 Mike Gallego .15 .07
❑ 180 Marc Newfield .15 .07
❑ 181 Steve Buechele .15 .07
❑ 182 David Wells .40 .18
❑ 183 Tom Glavine .60 .25
❑ 184 Joe Girardi .15 .07
❑ 185 Craig Biggio .60 .25
❑ 186 Eddie Murray .60 .25
❑ 187 Kevin Gross .15 .07
❑ 188 Sid Fernandez .15 .07
❑ 189 John Franco .30 .14
❑ 190 Bernard Gilkey .15 .07
❑ 191 Matt Williams .30 .14
❑ 192 Darrin Fletcher .15 .07
❑ 193 Jeff Conine .30 .14
❑ 194 Ed Sprague .15 .07
❑ 195 Eduardo Perez .15 .07
❑ 196 Scott Livingstone .15 .07
❑ 197 Ivan Rodriguez .75 .35
❑ 198 Orlando Merced .15 .07
❑ 199 Ricky Bones .15 .07
❑ 200 Javier Lopez .30 .14
❑ 201 Miguel Jimenez .15 .07
❑ 202 Terry McGriff .15 .07
❑ 203 Mike Lieberthal .15 .07
❑ 204 David Cone .40 .18
❑ 205 Todd Hundley .30 .14
❑ 206 Ozzie Guillen .15 .07
❑ 207 Alex Cole .15 .07
❑ 208 Tony Phillips .15 .07
❑ 209 Jim Eisenreich .15 .07
❑ 210 Greg Vaughn BES .15 .07
❑ 211 Barry Larkin BES .15 .07
❑ 212 Don Mattingly BES .60 .25
❑ 213 Mark Grace BES .15 .07
❑ 214 Jose Canseco BES .30 .14
❑ 215 Joe Carter BES .15 .07
❑ 216 David Cone BES .15 .07
❑ 217 Sandy Alomar Jr. BES .15 .07
❑ 218 Al Martin BES .15 .07
❑ 219 Roberto Kelly BES .15 .07
❑ 220 Paul Sorrento .15 .07
❑ 221 Tony Fernandez .15 .07
❑ 222 Stan Belinda .15 .07
❑ 223 Mike Stanley .15 .07
❑ 224 Doug Drabek .15 .07
❑ 225 Todd Van Poppel .15 .07
❑ 226 Matt Mieske .15 .07
❑ 227 Tino Martinez .60 .25
❑ 228 Andy Ashby .15 .07
❑ 229 Midre Cummings .15 .07
❑ 230 Jeff Frye .15 .07
❑ 231 Hal Morris .15 .07
❑ 232 Jose Lind .15 .07
❑ 233 Shawn Green .30 .14
❑ 234 Rafael Belliard .15 .07
❑ 235 Randy Myers .15 .07
❑ 236 Frank Thomas CE 1.00 .45
❑ 237 Darren Daulton CE .15 .07
❑ 238 Sammy Sosa CE .75 .35
❑ 239 Cal Ripken CE 1.25 .55
❑ 240 Jeff Bagwell CE .60 .25
❑ 241 Ken Griffey Jr. 3.00 1.35
❑ 242 Brett Butler .30 .14
❑ 243 Derrick May .15 .07
❑ 244 Pat Listach .15 .07
❑ 245 Mike Bordick .15 .07
❑ 246 Mark Langston .15 .07
❑ 247 Randy Velarde .15 .07
❑ 248 Julio Franco .15 .07
❑ 249 Chuck Knoblauch .60 .25
❑ 250 Bill Gullickson .15 .07
❑ 251 Dave Henderson .15 .07
❑ 252 Bret Boone .30 .14
❑ 253 Al Martin .15 .07
❑ 254 Armando Benitez .15 .07
❑ 255 Wil Cordero .15 .07
❑ 256 Al Leiter .30 .14
❑ 257 Luis Gonzalez .15 .07
❑ 258 Charlie O'Brien .15 .07
❑ 259 Tim Wallach .15 .07
❑ 260 Scott Sanders .15 .07
❑ 261 Tom Henke .15 .07
❑ 262 Otis Nixon .15 .07
❑ 263 Darren Daulton .30 .14
❑ 264 Manny Ramirez .60 .25
❑ 265 Bret Barberie .15 .07
❑ 266 Mel Rojas .15 .07
❑ 267 John Burkett .15 .07
❑ 268 Brady Anderson .30 .14
❑ 269 John Roper .15 .07
❑ 270 Shane Reynolds .30 .14
❑ 271 Barry Bonds .75 .35
❑ 272 Alex Fernandez .15 .07
❑ 273 Brian McRae .15 .07
❑ 274 Todd Zeile .15 .07
❑ 275 Greg Swindell .15 .07
❑ 276 Johnny Ruffin .15 .07
❑ 277 Troy Neel .15 .07
❑ 278 Eric Karros .30 .14
❑ 279 John Hudek .15 .07
❑ 280 Thomas Howard .15 .07
❑ 281 Joe Carter .30 .14
❑ 282 Mike Devereaux .15 .07
❑ 283 Butch Henry .15 .07

❑ 284 Reggie Jefferson .15 .07
❑ 285 Mark Lemke .15 .07
❑ 286 Jeff Montgomery .15 .07
❑ 287 Ryan Thompson .15 .07
❑ 288 Paul Shuey .15 .07
❑ 289 Mark McGwire 3.00 1.35
❑ 290 Bernie Williams .60 .25
❑ 291 Mickey Morandini .15 .07
❑ 292 Scott Leius .15 .07
❑ 293 David Hulse .15 .07
❑ 294 Greg Gagne .15 .07
❑ 295 Moises Alou .40 .18
❑ 296 Geronimo Berroa .15 .07
❑ 297 Eddie Zambrano .15 .07
❑ 298 Alan Trammell .30 .14
❑ 299 Don Slaught .15 .07
❑ 300 Jose Rijo .15 .07
❑ 301 Joe Ausanio .15 .07
❑ 302 Tim Raines .30 .14
❑ 303 Melido Perez .15 .07
❑ 304 Kent Mercker .15 .07
❑ 305 James Mouton .15 .07
❑ 306 Luis Lopez .15 .07
❑ 307 Mike Kingery .15 .07
❑ 308 Willie Greene .30 .14
❑ 309 Cecil Fielder .30 .14
❑ 310 Scott Kamieniecki .15 .07
❑ 311 Mike Greenwell BES .15 .07
❑ 312 Bobby Bonilla BES .15 .07
❑ 313 Andres Galarraga BES .60 .25
❑ 314 Cal Ripken BES 1.25 .55
❑ 315 Matt Williams BES .15 .07
❑ 316 Tom Pagnozzi BES .15 .07
❑ 317 Len Dykstra BES .15 .07
❑ 318 Frank Thomas BES 1.00 .45
❑ 319 Kirby Puckett BES .60 .25
❑ 320 Mike Piazza BES 1.00 .45
❑ 321 Jason Jacome .15 .07
❑ 322 Brian Hunter .15 .07
❑ 323 Brent Gates .15 .07
❑ 324 Jim Converse .15 .07
❑ 325 Damion Easley .30 .14
❑ 326 Dante Bichette .30 .14
❑ 327 Kurt Abbott .15 .07
❑ 328 Scott Cooper .15 .07
❑ 329 Mike Henneman .15 .07
❑ 330 Orlando Miller .15 .07
❑ 331 John Kruk .30 .14
❑ 332 Jose Oliva .15 .07
❑ 333 Reggie Sanders .30 .14
❑ 334 Omar Vizquel .30 .14
❑ 335 Devon White .30 .14
❑ 336 Mike Morgan .15 .07
❑ 337 J.R. Phillips .15 .07
❑ 338 Gary DiSarcina .15 .07
❑ 339 Joey Hamilton .30 .14
❑ 340 Randy Johnson .60 .25
❑ 341 Jim Leyritz .30 .14
❑ 342 Bobby Jones .15 .07
❑ 343 Jaime Navarro .15 .07
❑ 344 Bip Roberts .15 .07
❑ 345 Steve Karsay .15 .07
❑ 346 Kevin Stocker .15 .07
❑ 347 Jose Canseco .60 .25
❑ 348 Bill Wegman .15 .07
❑ 349 Rondell White .30 .14
❑ 350 Mo Vaughn .75 .35
❑ 351 Joe Orsulak .15 .07
❑ 352 Pat Meares .15 .07
❑ 353 Albie Lopez .15 .07
❑ 354 Edgar Martinez .30 .14
❑ 355 Brian Jordan .30 .14
❑ 356 Tommy Greene .15 .07
❑ 357 Chuck Carr .15 .07
❑ 358 Pedro Astacio .15 .07
❑ 359 Russ Davis .30 .14
❑ 360 Chris Hammond .15 .07
❑ 361 Gregg Jefferies .15 .07
❑ 362 Shane Mack .15 .07
❑ 363 Fred McGriff .40 .18
❑ 364 Pat Rapp .15 .07
❑ 365 Bill Swift .15 .07
❑ 366 Checklist .15 .07
❑ 367 Robin Ventura .30 .14
❑ 368 Bobby Witt .15 .07
❑ 369 Karl Rhodes .15 .07
❑ 370 Eddie Williams .15 .07
❑ 371 John Jaha .15 .07
❑ 372 Steve Howe .15 .07
❑ 373 Leo Gomez .15 .07
❑ 374 Hector Fajardo .15 .07
❑ 375 Jeff Bagwell 1.00 .45
❑ 376 Mark Acre .15 .07
❑ 377 Wayne Kirby .15 .07
❑ 378 Mark Portugal .15 .07
❑ 379 Jesus Tavarez .15 .07
❑ 380 Jim Lindeman .15 .07
❑ 381 Don Mattingly 1.00 .45
❑ 382 Trevor Hoffman .30 .14
❑ 383 Chris Gomez .15 .07
❑ 384 Garret Anderson .30 .14
❑ 385 Bobby Munoz .15 .07
❑ 386 Jon Lieber .15 .07
❑ 387 Rick Helling .30 .14
❑ 388 Marvin Freeman .15 .07
❑ 389 Juan Castillo .15 .07
❑ 390 Jeff Cirillo .30 .14
❑ 391 Sean Berry .15 .07
❑ 392 Hector Carrasco .15 .07
❑ 393 Mark Grace .40 .18
❑ 394 Pat Kelly .15 .07
❑ 395 Tim Naehring .15 .07
❑ 396 Greg Pirkl .15 .07
❑ 397 John Smoltz .30 .14
❑ 398 Robby Thompson .15 .07
❑ 399 Rick White .15 .07
❑ 400 Frank Thomas 2.00 .90
❑ 401 Jeff Conine CS .15 .07
❑ 402 Jose Valentin CS .15 .07
❑ 403 Carlos Baerga CS .15 .07
❑ 404 Rick Aguilera CS .15 .07
❑ 405 Wilson Alvarez CS .15 .07
❑ 406 Juan Gonzalez CS .75 .35
❑ 407 Barry Larkin CS .15 .07
❑ 408 Ken Hill CS .15 .07
❑ 409 Chuck Carr CS .15 .07
❑ 410 Tim Raines CS .15 .07
❑ 411 Bryan Eversgerd .15 .07
❑ 412 Phil Plantier .15 .07
❑ 413 Josias Manzanillo .15 .07
❑ 414 Roberto Kelly .15 .07
❑ 415 Rickey Henderson .60 .25
❑ 416 John Smiley .15 .07
❑ 417 Kevin Brown .40 .18
❑ 418 Jimmy Key .30 .14
❑ 419 Wally Joyner .30 .14
❑ 420 Roberto Hernandez .15 .07
❑ 421 Felix Fermin .15 .07
❑ 422 Checklist .15 .07
❑ 423 Greg Vaughn .30 .14
❑ 424 Ray Lankford .30 .14
❑ 425 Greg Maddux 2.00 .90
❑ 426 Mike Mussina .60 .25
❑ 427 Geronimo Pena .15 .07
❑ 428 David Nied .15 .07
❑ 429 Scott Erickson .30 .14
❑ 430 Kevin Mitchell .15 .07
❑ 431 Mike Lansing .15 .07
❑ 432 Brian Anderson .30 .14
❑ 433 Jeff King .15 .07
❑ 434 Ramon Martinez .30 .14
❑ 435 Kevin Seitzer .15 .07
❑ 436 Salomon Torres .15 .07
❑ 437 Brian L.Hunter .30 .14
❑ 438 Melvin Nieves .15 .07
❑ 439 Mike Kelly .15 .07
❑ 440 Marquis Grissom .30 .14
❑ 441 Chuck Finley .30 .14
❑ 442 Len Dykstra .30 .14
❑ 443 Ellis Burks .30 .14
❑ 444 Harold Baines .30 .14
❑ 445 Kevin Appier .30 .14
❑ 446 David Justice .60 .25
❑ 447 Darryl Kile .30 .14
❑ 448 John Olerud .30 .14
❑ 449 Greg McMichael .15 .07
❑ 450 Kirby Puckett 1.00 .45
❑ 451 Jose Valentin .15 .07
❑ 452 Rick Wilkins .15 .07
❑ 453 Arthur Rhodes .15 .07
❑ 454 Pat Hentgen .30 .14
❑ 455 Tom Gordon .15 .07
❑ 456 Tom Candiotti .15 .07
❑ 457 Jason Bere .15 .07
❑ 458 Wes Chamberlain .15 .07
❑ 459 Greg Colbrunn .15 .07
❑ 460 John Doherty .15 .07
❑ 461 Kevin Foster .15 .07
❑ 462 Mark Whiten .15 .07
❑ 463 Terry Steinbach .30 .14
❑ 464 Aaron Sele .30 .14
❑ 465 Kirt Manwaring .15 .07
❑ 466 Darren Hall .15 .07
❑ 467 Delino DeShields .15 .07
❑ 468 Andujar Cedeno .15 .07
❑ 469 Billy Ashley .15 .07
❑ 470 Kenny Lofton .60 .25
❑ 471 Pedro Munoz .15 .07
❑ 472 John Wetteland .30 .14
❑ 473 Tim Salmon .60 .25
❑ 474 Denny Neagle .30 .14
❑ 475 Tony Gwynn 1.50 .70
❑ 476 Vinny Castilla .40 .18
❑ 477 Steve Dreyer .15 .07
❑ 478 Jeff Shaw .15 .07
❑ 479 Chad Ogea .15 .07
❑ 480 Scott Ruffcorn .15 .07
❑ 481 Lou Whitaker .30 .14
❑ 482 J.T. Snow .30 .14
❑ 483 Rich Rowland .15 .07
❑ 484 Denny Martinez .30 .14
❑ 485 Pedro Martinez .60 .25
❑ 486 Rusty Greer .60 .25
❑ 487 Dave Fleming .15 .07
❑ 488 John Dettmer .15 .07
❑ 489 Albert Belle .75 .35
❑ 490 Ravelo Manzanillo .15 .07
❑ 491 Henry Rodriguez .30 .14
❑ 492 Andrew Lorraine .15 .07
❑ 493 Dwayne Hosey .15 .07
❑ 494 Mike Blowers .15 .07
❑ 495 Turner Ward .15 .07
❑ 496 Fred McGriff EC .15 .07
❑ 497 Sammy Sosa EC .75 .35
❑ 498 Barry Larkin EC .15 .07
❑ 499 Andres Galarraga EC .60 .25
❑ 500 Gary Sheffield EC .15 .07
❑ 501 Jeff Bagwell EC .60 .25
❑ 502 Mike Piazza EC 1.00 .45
❑ 503 Moises Alou EC .15 .07
❑ 504 Bobby Bonilla EC .15 .07
❑ 505 Darren Daulton EC .15 .07
❑ 506 Jeff King EC .15 .07
❑ 507 Ray Lankford EC .15 .07
❑ 508 Tony Gwynn EC .75 .35
❑ 509 Barry Bonds EC .40 .18
❑ 510 Cal Ripken EC 1.25 .55
❑ 511 Mo Vaughn EC .40 .18
❑ 512 Tim Salmon EC .30 .14
❑ 513 Frank Thomas EC 1.00 .45
❑ 514 Albert Belle EC .60 .25
❑ 515 Cecil Fielder EC .15 .07
❑ 516 Kevin Appier EC .15 .07
❑ 517 Greg Vaughn EC .15 .07
❑ 518 Kirby Puckett EC .60 .25
❑ 519 Paul O'Neill EC .15 .07
❑ 520 Ruben Sierra EC .15 .07
❑ 521 Ken Griffey Jr. EC 1.50 .70
❑ 522 Will Clark EC .30 .14
❑ 523 Joe Carter EC .15 .07
❑ 524 Antonio Osuna .15 .07
❑ 525 Glenallen Hill .15 .07
❑ 526 Alex Gonzalez .15 .07
❑ 527 Dave Stewart .30 .14
❑ 528 Ron Gant .15 .07
❑ 529 Jason Bates .15 .07
❑ 530 Mike Macfarlane .15 .07
❑ 531 Esteban Loaiza .15 .07
❑ 532 Joe Randa .15 .07
❑ 533 Dave Winfield .60 .25
❑ 534 Danny Darwin .15 .07
❑ 535 Pete Harnisch .15 .07
❑ 536 Joey Cora .30 .14
❑ 537 Jaime Navarro .15 .07
❑ 538 Marty Cordova .15 .07

539	Andujar Cedeno	.15	.07
540	Mickey Tettleton	.15	.07
541	Andy Van Slyke	.30	.14
542	Carlos Perez	.50	.23
543	Chipper Jones	1.50	.70
544	Tony Fernandez	.15	.07
545	Tom Henke	.15	.07
546	Pat Borders	.15	.07
547	Chad Curtis	.15	.07
548	Ray Durham	.30	.14
549	Joe Oliver	.15	.07
550	Jose Mesa	.15	.07
551	Steve Finley	.30	.14
552	Otis Nixon	.15	.07
553	Jacob Brumfield	.15	.07
554	Bill Swift	.15	.07
555	Quilvio Veras	.15	.07
556	Hideo Nomo UER Wins and IP totals reversed	2.50	1.10
557	Joe Vitiello	.15	.07
558	Mike Perez	.15	.07
559	Charlie Hayes	.15	.07
560	Brad Radke	.75	.35
561	Darren Bragg	.15	.07
562	Orel Hershiser	.30	.14
563	Edgardo Alfonzo	.30	.14
564	Doug Jones	.15	.07
565	Andy Pettitte	.60	.25
566	Benito Santiago	.15	.07
567	John Burkett	.15	.07
568	Brad Clontz	.15	.07
569	Jim Abbott	.30	.14
570	Joe Rosselli	.15	.07
571	Mark Grudzielanek	.50	.23
572	Dustin Hermanson	.30	.14
573	Benji Gil	.15	.07
574	Mark Whiten	.15	.07
575	Mike Ignasiak	.15	.07
576	Kevin Ritz	.15	.07
577	Paul Quantrill	.15	.07
578	Andre Dawson	.40	.18
579	Jerald Clark	.15	.07
580	Frank Rodriguez	.15	.07
581	Mark Kiefer	.15	.07
582	Trevor Wilson	.15	.07
583	Gary Wilson	.15	.07
584	Andy Stankiewicz	.15	.07
585	Felipe Lira	.15	.07
586	Mike Mimbs	.15	.07
587	Jon Nunnally	.15	.07
588	Tomas Perez	.30	.14
589	Checklist	.15	.07
590	Todd Hollandsworth	.15	.07
591	Roberto Petagine	.15	.07
592	Mariano Rivera	.60	.25
593	Mark McLemore	.15	.07
594	Bobby Witt	.15	.07
595	Jose Offerman	.15	.07
596	Jason Christiansen	.15	.07
597	Jeff Manto	.15	.07
598	Jim Dougherty	.15	.07
599	Juan Acevedo	.15	.07
600	Troy O'Leary	.30	.14
601	Ron Villone	.15	.07
602	Tripp Cromer	.15	.07
603	Steve Scarsone	.15	.07
604	Lance Parrish	.15	.07
605	Ozzie Timmons	.15	.07
606	Ray Holbert	.15	.07
607	Tony Phillips	.15	.07
608	Phil Plantier	.15	.07
609	Shane Andrews	.15	.07
610	Heathcliff Slocumb	.15	.07
611	Bobby Higginson	1.50	.70
612	Bob Tewksbury	.15	.07
613	Terry Pendleton	.15	.07
614	Scott Cooper TA	.15	.07
615	John Wetteland TA	.15	.07
616	Ken Hill TA	.15	.07
617	Marquis Grissom TA	.15	.07
618	Larry Walker TA	.30	.14
619	Derek Bell TA	.15	.07
620	David Cone TA	.15	.07
621	Ken Caminiti TA	.15	.07
622	Jack McDowell TA	.15	.07
623	Vaughn Eshelman TA	.15	.07
624	Brian McRae TA	.15	.07
625	Gregg Jefferies TA	.15	.07
626	Kevin Brown TA	.15	.07
627	Lee Smith TA	.15	.07
628	Tony Tarasco TA	.15	.07
629	Brett Butler TA	.15	.07
630	Jose Canseco TA	.30	.14

1995 Stadium Club Clear Cut

	MINT	NRMT
COMPLETE SET (28)	80.00	36.00
COMPLETE SET (14)	40.00	18.00
COMPLETE SERIES 2 (14)	40.00	18.00
COMMON CARD (CC1-CC28)	1.50	.70

CC1	Mike Piazza	15.00	6.75
CC2	Ruben Sierra	1.50	.70
CC3	Tony Gwynn	12.00	5.50
CC4	Frank Thomas	15.00	6.75
CC5	Fred McGriff	4.00	1.80
CC6	Rafael Palmeiro	4.00	1.80
CC7	Bobby Bonilla	2.50	1.10
CC8	Chili Davis	2.50	1.10
CC9	Hal Morris	1.50	.70
CC10	Jose Canseco	5.00	2.20
CC11	Jay Bell	2.50	1.10
CC12	Kirby Puckett	5.00	2.20
CC13	Gary Sheffield	4.00	1.80
CC14	Bob Hamelin	1.50	.70
CC15	Jeff Bagwell	8.00	3.60
CC16	Albert Belle	5.00	2.20
CC17	Sammy Sosa	12.00	5.50
CC18	Ken Griffey Jr.	25.00	11.00
CC19	Todd Zeile	1.50	.70
CC20	Mo Vaughn	5.00	2.20
CC21	Moises Alou	4.00	1.80
CC22	Paul O'Neill	2.50	1.10
CC23	Andres Galarraga	5.00	2.20
CC24	Greg Vaughn	2.50	1.10
CC25	Len Dykstra	2.50	1.10
CC26	Joe Carter	2.50	1.10
CC27	Barry Bonds	5.00	2.20
CC28	Cecil Fielder	2.50	1.10

1995 Stadium Club Crunch Time

	MINT	NRMT
COMPLETE SET (20)	40.00	18.00
COMMON CARD (1-20)	.50	.23

1	Jeff Bagwell	3.00	1.35
2	Kirby Puckett	2.00	.90
3	Frank Thomas	6.00	2.70
4	Albert Belle	2.00	.90
5	Julio Franco	.50	.23
6	Jose Canseco	2.00	.90
7	Paul Molitor	2.00	.90
8	Joe Carter	1.00	.45
9	Ken Griffey Jr.	10.00	4.50
10	Larry Walker	2.00	.90
11	Dante Bichette	1.00	.45
12	Carlos Baerga	1.00	.45
13	Fred McGriff	1.50	.70
14	Ruben Sierra	.50	.23
15	Will Clark	2.00	.90
16	Moises Alou	1.50	.70
17	Rafael Palmeiro	1.50	.70
18	Travis Fryman	1.00	.45
19	Barry Bonds	2.00	.90
20	Cal Ripken	8.00	3.60

1995 Stadium Club Crystal Ball

	MINT	NRMT
COMPLETE SET (15)	60.00	27.00
COMMON CARD (CB1-CB15)	2.00	.90

CB1	Chipper Jones	25.00	11.00
CB2	Dustin Hermanson	3.00	1.35
CB3	Ray Durham	3.00	1.35
CB4	Phil Nevin	2.00	.90
CB5	Billy Ashley	2.00	.90
CB6	Shawn Green	3.00	1.35
CB7	Jason Bates	2.00	.90
CB8	Benji Gil	2.00	.90
CB9	Marty Cordova	2.00	.90
CB10	Quilvio Veras	2.00	.90
CB11	Mark Grudzielanek	6.00	2.70
CB12	Ruben Rivera	3.00	1.35
CB13	Bill Pulsipher	2.00	.90
CB14	Derek Jeter	25.00	11.00
CB15	LaTroy Hawkins	2.00	.90

1995 Stadium Club Power Zone

	MINT	NRMT
COMPLETE SET (12)	80.00	36.00
COMMON CARD (PZ1-PZ12)	2.50	1.10

PZ1	Jeff Bagwell	10.00	4.50
PZ2	Albert Belle	8.00	3.60
PZ3	Barry Bonds	8.00	3.60
PZ4	Joe Carter	2.50	1.10
PZ5	Cecil Fielder	2.50	1.10
PZ6	Andres Galarraga	6.00	2.70
PZ7	Ken Griffey Jr.	30.00	13.50
PZ8	Paul Molitor	6.00	2.70
PZ9	Fred McGriff	4.00	1.80
PZ10	Rafael Palmeiro	4.00	1.80
PZ11	Frank Thomas	20.00	9.00
PZ12	Matt Williams	2.50	1.10

1995 Stadium Club Ring Leaders

	MINT	NRMT
COMPLETE SET (40)	160.00	70.00
COMPLETE SERIES 1 (20)	80.00	36.00
COMPLETE SERIES 2 (20)	80.00	36.00
COMMON CARD (RL1-RL40)	1.50	.70

❏ RL1 Jeff Bagwell	10.00	4.50
❏ RL2 Mark McGwire	30.00	13.50
❏ RL3 Ozzie Smith	8.00	3.60
❏ RL4 Paul Molitor	6.00	2.70
❏ RL5 Darryl Strawberry	2.50	1.10
❏ RL6 Eddie Murray	6.00	2.70
❏ RL7 Tony Gwynn	15.00	6.75
❏ RL8 Jose Canseco	6.00	2.70
❏ RL9 Howard Johnson	1.50	.70
❏ RL10 Andre Dawson	4.00	1.80
❏ RL11 Matt Williams	2.50	1.10
❏ RL12 Tim Raines	2.50	1.10
❏ RL13 Fred McGriff	4.00	1.80
❏ RL14 Ken Griffey Jr.	30.00	13.50
❏ RL15 Gary Sheffield	4.00	1.80
❏ RL16 Dennis Eckersley	2.50	1.10
❏ RL17 Kevin Mitchell	1.50	.70
❏ RL18 Will Clark	6.00	2.70
❏ RL19 Darren Daulton	2.50	1.10
❏ RL20 Paul O'Neill	2.50	1.10
❏ RL21 Julio Franco	1.50	.70
❏ RL22 Albert Belle	8.00	3.60
❏ RL23 Juan Gonzalez	15.00	6.75
❏ RL24 Kirby Puckett	10.00	4.50
❏ RL25 Joe Carter	2.50	1.10
❏ RL26 Frank Thomas	20.00	9.00
❏ RL27 Cal Ripken	25.00	11.00
❏ RL28 John Olerud	2.50	1.10
❏ RL29 Ruben Sierra	1.50	.70
❏ RL30 Barry Bonds	8.00	3.60
❏ RL31 Cecil Fielder	2.50	1.10
❏ RL32 Roger Clemens	12.00	5.50
❏ RL33 Don Mattingly	10.00	4.50
❏ RL34 Terry Pendleton	1.50	.70
❏ RL35 Rickey Henderson	6.00	2.70
❏ RL36 Dave Winfield	6.00	2.70
❏ RL37 Edgar Martinez	2.50	1.10
❏ RL38 Wade Boggs	6.00	2.70
❏ RL39 Willie McGee	2.50	1.10
❏ RL40 Andres Galarraga	6.00	2.70

1995 Stadium Club Super Skills

	MINT	NRMT
COMPLETE SET (20)	70.00	32.00
COMPLETE SERIES 1 (9)	30.00	13.50
COMPLETE SERIES 2 (11)	40.00	18.00
COMMON CARD (SS1-SS20)	1.50	.70

❏ SS1 Roberto Alomar	5.00	2.20
❏ SS2 Barry Bonds	5.00	2.20
❏ SS3 Jay Buhner	2.50	1.10
❏ SS4 Chuck Carr	1.50	.70
❏ SS5 Don Mattingly	6.00	2.70
❏ SS6 Raul Mondesi	4.00	1.80
❏ SS7 Tim Salmon	5.00	2.20
❏ SS8 Deion Sanders	2.50	1.10
❏ SS9 Devon White	2.50	1.10
❏ SS10 Mark Whiten	1.50	.70
❏ SS11 Ken Griffey Jr.	25.00	11.00
❏ SS12 Marquis Grissom	2.50	1.10
❏ SS13 Paul O'Neill	2.50	1.10
❏ SS14 Kenny Lofton	5.00	2.20
❏ SS15 Larry Walker	5.00	2.20
❏ SS16 Scott Cooper	1.50	.70
❏ SS17 Barry Larkin	4.00	1.80
❏ SS18 Matt Williams	2.50	1.10
❏ SS19 John Wetteland	2.50	1.10
❏ SS20 Randy Johnson	5.00	2.20

1995 Stadium Club Virtual Extremists

	MINT	NRMT
COMPLETE SET (10)	120.00	55.00
COMMON CARD (VRE1-VRE10)	2.50	1.10

❏ VRE1 Barry Bonds	10.00	4.50
❏ VRE2 Ken Griffey Jr.	40.00	18.00
❏ VRE3 Jeff Bagwell	12.00	5.50
❏ VRE4 Albert Belle	10.00	4.50
❏ VRE5 Frank Thomas	25.00	11.00
❏ VRE6 Tony Gwynn	20.00	9.00
❏ VRE7 Kenny Lofton	8.00	3.60
❏ VRE8 Deion Sanders	4.00	1.80
❏ VRE9 Ken Hill	2.50	1.10
❏ VRE10 Jimmy Key	4.00	1.80

1996 Stadium Club

	MINT	NRMT
COMPLETE SET (450)	80.00	36.00
COMP.CEREAL SET (454)	80.00	36.00
COMPLETE SERIES 1 (225)	40.00	18.00
COMPLETE SERIES 2 (225)	40.00	18.00
COMMON (1-180/271-450)	.15	.07
COMMON TSC SP (181-270)	.25	.11

❏ 1 Hideo Nomo	1.00	.45
❏ 2 Paul Molitor	.60	.25
❏ 3 Garret Anderson	.30	.14
❏ 4 Jose Mesa	.15	.07
❏ 5 Vinny Castilla	.40	.18
❏ 6 Mike Mussina	.60	.25
❏ 7 Ray Durham	.30	.14
❏ 8 Jack McDowell	.15	.07
❏ 9 Juan Gonzalez	1.50	.70
❏ 10 Chipper Jones	1.50	.70
❏ 11 Deion Sanders	.30	.14
❏ 12 Rondell White	.30	.14
❏ 13 Tom Henke	.15	.07
❏ 14 Derek Bell	.30	.14
❏ 15 Randy Myers	.15	.07
❏ 16 Randy Johnson	.60	.25
❏ 17 Len Dykstra	.30	.14
❏ 18 Bill Pulsipher	.15	.07
❏ 19 Greg Colbrunn	.15	.07
❏ 20 David Wells	.40	.18
❏ 21 Chad Curtis	.15	.07
❏ 22 Roberto Hernandez	.15	.07
❏ 23 Kirby Puckett	1.00	.45
❏ 24 Joe Vitiello	.15	.07
❏ 25 Roger Clemens	1.25	.55
❏ 26 Al Martin	.15	.07
❏ 27 Chad Ogea	.15	.07
❏ 28 David Segui	.30	.14
❏ 29 Joey Hamilton	.30	.14
❏ 30 Dan Wilson	.15	.07
❏ 31 Chad Fonville	.15	.07
❏ 32 Bernard Gilkey	.15	.07
❏ 33 Kevin Seitzer	.15	.07
❏ 34 Shawn Green	.30	.14
❏ 35 Rick Aguilera	.15	.07
❏ 36 Gary DiSarcina	.15	.07
❏ 37 Jaime Navarro	.15	.07
❏ 38 Doug Jones	.15	.07
❏ 39 Brent Gates	.15	.07
❏ 40 Dean Palmer	.30	.14
❏ 41 Pat Rapp	.15	.07
❏ 42 Tony Clark	.60	.25
❏ 43 Bill Swift	.15	.07
❏ 44 Randy Velarde	.15	.07
❏ 45 Matt Williams	.30	.14
❏ 46 John Mabry	.15	.07
❏ 47 Mike Fetters	.15	.07
❏ 48 Orlando Miller	.15	.07
❏ 49 Tom Glavine	.60	.25
❏ 50 Delino DeShields	.15	.07
❏ 51 Scott Erickson	.30	.14
❏ 52 Andy Van Slyke	.15	.07
❏ 53 Jim Bullinger	.15	.07
❏ 54 Lyle Mouton	.15	.07
❏ 55 Bret Saberhagen	.30	.14
❏ 56 Benito Santiago	.15	.07
❏ 57 Dan Miceli	.15	.07
❏ 58 Carl Everett	.15	.07

59	Rod Beck	.15	.07
60	Phil Nevin	.15	.07
61	Jason Giambi	.30	.14
62	Paul Menhart	.15	.07
63	Eric Karros	.30	.14
64	Allen Watson	.15	.07
65	Jeff Cirillo	.30	.14
66	Lee Smith	.30	.14
67	Sean Berry	.15	.07
68	Luis Sojo	.15	.07
69	Jeff Montgomery	.15	.07
70	Todd Hundley	.30	.14
71	John Burkett	.15	.07
72	Mark Gubicza	.15	.07
73	Don Mattingly	1.00	.45
74	Jeff Brantley	.15	.07
75	Matt Walbeck	.15	.07
76	Steve Parris	.15	.07
77	Ken Caminiti	.40	.18
78	Kirt Manwaring	.15	.07
79	Greg Vaughn	.30	.14
80	Pedro Martinez	.60	.25
81	Benji Gil	.15	.07
82	Heathcliff Slocumb	.15	.07
83	Joe Girardi	.15	.07
84	Sean Bergman	.15	.07
85	Matt Karchner	.15	.07
86	Butch Huskey	.15	.07
87	Mike Morgan	.15	.07
88	Todd Worrell	.15	.07
89	Mike Bordick	.15	.07
90	Bip Roberts	.15	.07
91	Mike Hampton	.15	.07
92	Troy O'Leary	.30	.14
93	Wally Joyner	.30	.14
94	Dave Stevens	.15	.07
95	Cecil Fielder	.30	.14
96	Wade Boggs	.60	.25
97	Hal Morris	.15	.07
98	Mickey Tettleton	.15	.07
99	Jeff Kent	.30	.14
100	Denny Martinez	.30	.14
101	Luis Gonzalez	.15	.07
102	John Jaha	.15	.07
103	Javier Lopez	.30	.14
104	Mark McGwire	3.00	1.35
105	Ken Griffey Jr.	3.00	1.35
106	Darren Daulton	.30	.14
107	Bryan Rekar	.15	.07
108	Mike Macfarlane	.15	.07
109	Gary Gaetti	.30	.14
110	Shane Reynolds	.30	.14
111	Pat Meares	.15	.07
112	Jason Schmidt	.15	.07
113	Otis Nixon	.15	.07
114	John Franco	.30	.14
115	Marc Newfield	.15	.07
116	Andy Benes	.30	.14
117	Ozzie Guillen	.15	.07
118	Brian Jordan	.30	.14
119	Terry Pendleton	.15	.07
120	Chuck Finley	.30	.14
121	Scott Stahoviak	.15	.07
122	Sid Fernandez	.15	.07
123	Derek Jeter	2.00	.90
124	John Smiley	.15	.07
125	David Bell	.15	.07
126	Brett Butler	.30	.14
127	Doug Drabek	.15	.07
128	J.T. Snow	.30	.14
129	Joe Carter	.30	.14
130	Dennis Eckersley	.30	.14
131	Marty Cordova	.15	.07
132	Greg Maddux	2.00	.90
133	Tom Goodwin	.15	.07
134	Andy Ashby	.15	.07
135	Paul Sorrento	.15	.07
136	Ricky Bones	.15	.07
137	Shawon Dunston	.15	.07
138	Moises Alou	.40	.18
139	Mickey Morandini	.15	.07
140	Ramon Martinez	.30	.14
141	Royce Clayton	.15	.07
142	Brad Ausmus	.15	.07
143	Kenny Rogers	.15	.07
144	Tim Naehring	.15	.07
145	Chris Gomez	.15	.07
146	Bobby Bonilla	.30	.14
147	Wilson Alvarez	.30	.14
148	Johnny Damon	.30	.14
149	Pat Hentgen	.30	.14
150	Andres Galarraga	.60	.25
151	David Cone	.40	.18
152	Lance Johnson	.15	.07
153	Carlos Garcia	.15	.07
154	Doug Johns	.15	.07
155	Midre Cummings	.15	.07
156	Steve Sparks	.15	.07
157	Sandy Martinez	.15	.07
158	Wm. Van Landingham	.15	.07
159	David Justice	.60	.25
160	Mark Grace	.40	.18
161	Robb Nen	.15	.07
162	Mike Greenwell	.15	.07
163	Brad Radke	.30	.14
164	Edgardo Alfonzo	.30	.14
165	Mark Leiter	.15	.07
166	Walt Weiss	.15	.07
167	Mel Rojas	.15	.07
168	Bret Boone	.30	.14
169	Ricky Bottalico	.30	.14
170	Bobby Higginson	.60	.25
171	Trevor Hoffman	.30	.14
172	Jay Bell	.30	.14
173	Gabe White	.15	.07
174	Curtis Goodwin	.15	.07
175	Tyler Green	.15	.07
176	Roberto Alomar	.60	.25
177	Sterling Hitchcock	.30	.14
178	Ryan Klesko	.30	.14
179	Donne Wall	.15	.07
180	Brian McRae	.15	.07
181	Will Clark TSC SP	.75	.35
182	Frank Thomas TSC SP	2.50	1.10
183	Jeff Bagwell TSC SP	1.25	.55
184	Mo Vaughn TSC SP	1.00	.45
185	Tino Martinez TSC SP	.75	.35
186	Craig Biggio TSC SP	.75	.35
187	C. Knoblauch TSC SP	.75	.35
188	Carlos Baerga TSC SP	.40	.18
189	Quilvio Veras TSC SP	.25	.11
190	Luis Alicea TSC SP	.25	.11
191	Jim Thome TSC SP	.75	.35
192	Mike Blowers TSC SP	.25	.11
193	Robin Ventura TSC SP	.40	.18
194	Jeff King TSC SP	.25	.11
195	Tony Phillips TSC SP	.25	.11
196	John Valentin TSC SP	.40	.18
197	Barry Larkin TSC SP	.50	.23
198	Cal Ripken TSC SP	3.00	1.35
199	Omar Vizquel TSC SP	.40	.18
200	Kurt Abbott TSC SP	.25	.11
201	Albert Belle TSC SP	1.00	.45
202	Barry Bonds TSC SP	1.00	.45
203	Ron Gant TSC SP	.25	.11
204	Dante Bichette TSC SP	.40	.18
205	Jeff Conine TSC SP	.40	.18
206	Jim Edmonds TSC SP UER Greg Myers pictured on front	.50	.23
207	Stan Javier TSC SP	.25	.11
208	Kenny Lofton TSC SP	.75	.35
209	Ray Lankford TSC SP	.40	.18
210	Bernie Williams TSC SP	.75	.35
211	Jay Buhner TSC SP	.40	.18
212	Paul O'Neill TSC SP	.40	.18
213	Tim Salmon TSC SP	.75	.35
214	Reggie Sanders TSC SP	.25	.11
215	Manny Ramirez TSC SP	.75	.35
216	Mike Piazza TSC SP	2.50	1.10
217	Mike Stanley TSC SP	.25	.11
218	Tony Eusebio TSC SP	.25	.11
219	Chris Hoiles TSC SP	.25	.11
220	Ron Karkovice TSC SP	.25	.11
221	Edgar Martinez TSC SP	.40	.18
222	Chili Davis TSC SP	.40	.18
223	Jose Canseco TSC SP	.75	.35
224	Eddie Murray TSC SP	.75	.35
225	Geronimo Berroa TSC SP	.25	.11
226	Chipper Jones TSC SP	2.00	.90
227	Garret Anderson TSC SP	.40	.18
228	Marty Cordova TSC SP	.25	.11
229	Jon Nunnally TSC SP	.25	.11
230	Brian L.Hunter TSC SP	.40	.18
231	Shawn Green TSC SP	.40	.18
232	Ray Durham TSC SP	.40	.18
233	Alex Gonzalez TSC SP	.25	.11
234	Bobby Higginson TSC SP	.75	.35
235	Randy Johnson TSC SP	.75	.35
236	Al Leiter TSC SP	.40	.18
237	Tom Glavine TSC SP	.75	.35
238	Kenny Rogers TSC SP	.25	.11
239	Mike Hampton TSC SP	.25	.11
240	David Wells TSC SP	.50	.23
241	Jim Abbott TSC SP	.40	.18
242	Denny Neagle TSC SP	.40	.18
243	Wilson Alvarez TSC SP	.40	.18
244	John Smiley TSC SP	.25	.11
245	Greg Maddux TSC SP	2.50	1.10
246	Andy Ashby TSC SP	.25	.11
247	Hideo Nomo TSC SP	1.25	.55
248	Pat Rapp TSC SP	.25	.11
249	Tim Wakefield TSC SP	.40	.18
250	John Smoltz TSC SP	.40	.18
251	Joey Hamilton TSC SP	.40	.18
252	Frank Castillo TSC SP	.25	.11
253	Denny Martinez TSC SP	.40	.18
254	Jaime Navarro TSC SP	.25	.11
255	Karim Garcia TSC SP	.40	.18
256	Bob Abreu TSC SP	.40	.18
257	Butch Huskey TSC SP	.15	.07
258	Ruben Rivera TSC SP	.40	.18
259	Johnny Damon TSC SP	.40	.18
260	Derek Jeter TSC SP	2.50	1.10
261	D. Eckersley TSC SP	.40	.18
262	Jose Mesa TSC SP	.25	.11
263	Tom Henke TSC SP	.25	.11
264	Rick Aguilera TSC SP	.25	.11
265	Randy Myers TSC SP	.25	.11
266	John Franco TSC SP	.40	.18
267	Jeff Brantley TSC SP	.25	.11
268	John Wetteland TSC SP	.40	.18
269	Mark Wohlers TSC SP	.25	.11
270	Rod Beck TSC SP	.25	.11
271	Barry Larkin	.40	.18
272	Paul O'Neill	.30	.14
273	Bobby Jones	.15	.07
274	Will Clark	.60	.25
275	Steve Avery	.15	.07
276	Jim Edmonds	.40	.18
277	John Olerud	.30	.14
278	Carlos Perez	.30	.14
279	Chris Hoiles	.15	.07
280	Jeff Conine	.30	.14
281	Jim Eisenreich	.15	.07
282	Jason Jacome	.15	.07
283	Ray Lankford	.30	.14
284	John Wasdin	.15	.07
285	Frank Thomas	2.00	.90
286	Jason Isringhausen	.15	.07
287	Glenallen Hill	.15	.07
288	Esteban Loaiza	.15	.07
289	Bernie Williams	.60	.25
290	Curtis Leskanic	.15	.07
291	Scott Cooper	.15	.07
292	Curt Schilling	.30	.14
293	Eddie Murray	.60	.25
294	Rick Krivda	.15	.07
295	Domingo Cedeno	.15	.07
296	Jeff Fassero	.15	.07
297	Albert Belle	.75	.35
298	Craig Biggio	.60	.25
299	Fernando Vina	.15	.07
300	Edgar Martinez	.30	.14
301	Tony Gwynn	1.50	.70
302	Felipe Lira	.15	.07
303	Mo Vaughn	.75	.35
304	Alex Fernandez	.15	.07
305	Keith Lockhart	.15	.07
306	Roger Pavlik	.15	.07
307	Lee Tinsley	.15	.07
308	Omar Vizquel	.30	.14
309	Scott Servais	.15	.07
310	Danny Tartabull	.15	.07
311	Chili Davis	.30	.14

	Card	Player	Mint	NRMT
❑	312	Cal Eldred	.15	.07
❑	313	Roger Cedeno	.15	.07
❑	314	Chris Hammond	.15	.07
❑	315	Rusty Greer	.40	.18
❑	316	Brady Anderson	.30	.14
❑	317	Ron Villone	.15	.07
❑	318	Mark Carreon	.15	.07
❑	319	Larry Walker	.60	.25
❑	320	Pete Harnisch	.15	.07
❑	321	Robin Ventura	.30	.14
❑	322	Tim Belcher	.15	.07
❑	323	Tony Tarasco	.15	.07
❑	324	Juan Guzman	.15	.07
❑	325	Kenny Lofton	.60	.25
❑	326	Kevin Foster	.15	.07
❑	327	Wil Cordero	.15	.07
❑	328	Troy Percival	.30	.14
❑	329	Turk Wendell	.15	.07
❑	330	Thomas Howard	.15	.07
❑	331	Carlos Baerga	.30	.14
❑	332	B.J. Surhoff	.30	.14
❑	333	Jay Buhner	.30	.14
❑	334	Andujar Cedeno	.15	.07
❑	335	Jeff King	.15	.07
❑	336	Dante Bichette	.30	.14
❑	337	Alan Trammell	.40	.18
❑	338	Scott Leius	.15	.07
❑	339	Chris Snopek	.15	.07
❑	340	Roger Bailey	.15	.07
❑	341	Jacob Brumfield	.15	.07
❑	342	Jose Canseco	.60	.25
❑	343	Rafael Palmeiro	.40	.18
❑	344	Quilvio Veras	.15	.07
❑	345	Darrin Fletcher	.15	.07
❑	346	Carlos Delgado	.30	.14
❑	347	Tony Eusebio	.15	.07
❑	348	Ismael Valdes	.30	.14
❑	349	Terry Steinbach	.30	.14
❑	350	Orel Hershiser	.30	.14
❑	351	Kurt Abbott	.15	.07
❑	352	Jody Reed	.15	.07
❑	353	David Howard	.15	.07
❑	354	Ruben Sierra	.15	.07
❑	355	John Ericks	.15	.07
❑	356	Buck Showalter MG	.15	.07
❑	357	Jim Thome	.60	.25
❑	358	Geronimo Berroa	.15	.07
❑	359	Robby Thompson	.15	.07
❑	360	Jose Vizcaino	.15	.07
❑	361	Jeff Frye	.15	.07
❑	362	Kevin Appier	.30	.14
❑	363	Pat Kelly	.15	.07
❑	364	Ron Gant	.15	.07
❑	365	Luis Alicea	.15	.07
❑	366	Armando Benitez	.15	.07
❑	367	Rico Brogna	.15	.07
❑	368	Manny Ramirez	.60	.25
❑	369	Mike Lansing	.15	.07
❑	370	Sammy Sosa	1.50	.70
❑	371	Don Wengert	.15	.07
❑	372	Dave Nilsson	.15	.07
❑	373	Sandy Alomar	.30	.14
❑	374	Joey Cora	.30	.14
❑	375	Larry Thomas	.15	.07
❑	376	John Valentin	.30	.14
❑	377	Kevin Ritz	.15	.07
❑	378	Steve Finley	.30	.14
❑	379	Frank Rodriguez	.15	.07
❑	380	Ivan Rodriguez	.75	.35
❑	381	Alex Ochoa	.15	.07
❑	382	Mark Lemke	.15	.07
❑	383	Scott Brosius	.30	.14
❑	384	James Mouton	.15	.07
❑	385	Mark Langston	.15	.07
❑	386	Ed Sprague	.15	.07
❑	387	Joe Oliver	.15	.07
❑	388	Steve Ontiveros	.15	.07
❑	389	Rey Sanchez	.15	.07
❑	390	Mike Henneman	.15	.07
❑	391	Jose Valentin	.15	.07
❑	392	Tom Candiotti	.15	.07
❑	393	Damon Buford	.15	.07
❑	394	Erik Hanson	.15	.07
❑	395	Mark Smith	.15	.07
❑	396	Pete Schourek	.15	.07
❑	397	John Flaherty	.15	.07
❑	398	Dave Martinez	.15	.07
❑	399	Tommy Greene	.15	.07
❑	400	Gary Sheffield	.40	.18
❑	401	Glenn Dishman	.15	.07
❑	402	Barry Bonds	.75	.35
❑	403	Tom Pagnozzi	.15	.07
❑	404	Todd Stottlemyre	.15	.07
❑	405	Tim Salmon	.60	.25
❑	406	John Hudek	.15	.07
❑	407	Fred McGriff	.40	.18
❑	408	Orlando Merced	.15	.07
❑	409	Brian Barber	.15	.07
❑	410	Ryan Thompson	.15	.07
❑	411	Mariano Rivera	.30	.14
❑	412	Eric Young	.15	.07
❑	413	Chris Bosio	.15	.07
❑	414	Chuck Knoblauch	.60	.25
❑	415	Jamie Moyer	.15	.07
❑	416	Chan Ho Park	.60	.25
❑	417	Mark Portugal	.15	.07
❑	418	Tim Raines	.30	.14
❑	419	Antonio Osuna	.15	.07
❑	420	Todd Zeile	.15	.07
❑	421	Steve Wojciechowski	.15	.07
❑	422	Marquis Grissom	.30	.14
❑	423	Norm Charlton	.15	.07
❑	424	Cal Ripken	2.50	1.10
❑	425	Gregg Jefferies	.15	.07
❑	426	Mike Stanton	.15	.07
❑	427	Tony Fernandez	.15	.07
❑	428	Jose Rijo	.15	.07
❑	429	Jeff Bagwell	1.00	.45
❑	430	Raul Mondesi	.40	.18
❑	431	Travis Fryman	.30	.14
❑	432	Ron Karkovice	.15	.07
❑	433	Alan Benes	.30	.14
❑	434	Tony Phillips	.15	.07
❑	435	Reggie Sanders	.30	.14
❑	436	Andy Pettitte	.40	.18
❑	437	Matt Lawton	.60	.25
❑	438	Jeff Blauser	.15	.07
❑	439	Michael Tucker	.30	.14
❑	440	Mark Loretta	.15	.07
❑	441	Charlie Hayes	.15	.07
❑	442	Mike Piazza	2.00	.90
❑	443	Shane Andrews	.15	.07
❑	444	Jeff Suppan	.15	.07
❑	445	Steve Rodriguez	.15	.07
❑	446	Mike Matheny	.15	.07
❑	447	Trenidad Hubbard	.15	.07
❑	448	Denny Hocking	.15	.07
❑	449	Mark Grudzielanek	.30	.14
❑	450	Joe Randa	.15	.07

1996 Stadium Club Bash and Burn

		MINT	NRMT
COMPLETE SET (10)		30.00	13.50
COMMON CARD (BB1-BB10)		1.25	.55
❑ BB1	Sammy Sosa	15.00	6.75
❑ BB2	Barry Bonds	8.00	3.60
❑ BB3	Reggie Sanders	3.00	1.35
❑ BB4	Craig Biggio	5.00	2.20
❑ BB5	Raul Mondesi	2.50	1.10
❑ BB6	Ron Gant	1.25	.55
❑ BB7	Ray Lankford	3.00	1.35
❑ BB8	Glenallen Hill	1.25	.55
❑ BB9	Chad Curtis	1.25	.55
❑ BB10	John Valentin	3.00	1.35

1996 Stadium Club Extreme Players Bronze

	MINT	NRMT
COMP.BRONZE SET (179)	250.00	110.00
COMP.BRONZE SER.1 (90)	125.00	55.00
COMP.BRONZE SER.2 (89)	125.00	55.00
COMMON BRONZE	.75	.35

*SILVER SINGLES: .6X VALUE
SILVER STATED ODDS 1:24
*GOLD SINGLES: 1.25X VALUE
GOLD STATED ODDS 1:48
BRONZE WINNERS LISTED BELOW
SKIP-NUMBERED SET

	Card	Player	Mint	NRMT
❑	1	Hideo Nomo	5.00	2.20
❑	3	Garret Anderson	1.25	.55
❑	4	Jose Mesa	.75	.35
❑	5	Vinny Castilla	2.00	.90
❑	6	Mike Mussina	3.00	1.35
❑	7	Ray Durham	1.25	.55
❑	8	Jack McDowell	.75	.35
❑	9	Juan Gonzalez	8.00	3.60
❑	10	Chipper Jones	10.00	4.50
❑	11	Deion Sanders	1.25	.55
❑	12	Rondell White	1.25	.55
❑	13	Tom Henke	.75	.35
❑	14	Derek Bell	1.25	.55
❑	15	Randy Myers	.75	.35
❑	16	Randy Johnson	3.00	1.35
❑	17	Len Dykstra	1.25	.55
❑	18	Bill Pulsipher	.75	.35
❑	21	Chad Curtis	.75	.35
❑	22	Roberto Hernandez	.75	.35
❑	23	Kirby Puckett	5.00	2.20
❑	25	Roger Clemens	6.00	2.70
❑	31	Chad Fonville	.75	.35
❑	32	Bernard Gilkey	.75	.35
❑	34	Shawn Green	1.25	.55
❑	35	Rick Aguilera	.75	.35
❑	40	Dean Palmer	1.25	.55
❑	45	Matt Williams	1.25	.55
❑	49	Tom Glavine	3.00	1.35
❑	50	Delino DeShields	.75	.35
❑	56	Benito Santiago	.75	.35
❑	59	Rod Beck	.75	.35
❑	63	Eric Karros	1.25	.55
❑	66	Lee Smith	1.25	.55
❑	69	Jeff Montgomery	.75	.35
❑	70	Todd Hundley	1.25	.55
❑	73	Don Mattingly	5.00	2.20
❑	77	Ken Caminiti W	4.00	1.80
❑	80	Pedro Martinez	3.00	1.35
❑	82	Heathcliff Slocumb	.75	.35
❑	83	Joe Girardi	.75	.35
❑	88	Todd Worrell W	1.50	.70
❑	90	Bip Roberts	.75	.35
❑	95	Cecil Fielder	1.25	.55
❑	96	Wade Boggs	3.00	1.35
❑	98	Mickey Tettleton	.75	.35
❑	99	Jeff Kent	1.25	.55

	No.	Player	MINT	NRMT
❑	100	Denny Martinez	1.25	.55
❑	101	Luis Gonzalez	.75	.35
❑	103	Javy Lopez	1.25	.55
❑	104	Mark McGwire	15.00	6.75
❑	105	Ken Griffey Jr. W	30.00	13.50
❑	106	Darren Daulton	1.25	.55
❑	108	Mike Macfarlane	.75	.35
❑	110	Shane Reynolds	1.25	.55
❑	114	John Franco	1.25	.55
❑	116	Andy Benes	1.25	.55
❑	118	Brian Jordan	1.25	.55
❑	119	Terry Pendleton	.75	.35
❑	120	Chuck Finley	1.25	.55
❑	123	Derek Jeter	8.00	3.60
❑	124	John Smiley	.75	.35
❑	126	Brett Butler	1.25	.55
❑	127	Doug Drabek	.75	.35
❑	128	J.T. Snow	1.25	.55
❑	129	Joe Carter	1.25	.55
❑	130	Dennis Eckersley	1.25	.55
❑	131	Marty Cordova	.75	.35
❑	132	Greg Maddux W	20.00	9.00
❑	135	Paul Sorrento	.75	.35
❑	137	Shawon Dunston	.75	.35
❑	138	Moises Alou	2.00	.90
❑	140	Ramon Martinez	1.25	.55
❑	141	Royce Clayton	.75	.35
❑	143	Kenny Rogers	.75	.35
❑	144	Tim Naehring	.75	.35
❑	145	Chris Gomez	.75	.35
❑	146	Bobby Bonilla	1.25	.55
❑	148	Johnny Damon	1.25	.55
❑	150	Andres Galarraga W	5.00	2.20
❑	151	David Cone	2.00	.90
❑	152	Lance Johnson	.75	.35
❑	159	David Justice	3.00	1.35
❑	160	Mark Grace	2.00	.90
❑	161	Robb Nen	.75	.35
❑	162	Mike Greenwell	.75	.35
❑	167	Mel Rojas	.75	.35
❑	168	Bret Boone	1.25	.55
❑	172	Jay Bell	1.25	.55
❑	176	Roberto Alomar	3.00	1.35
❑	178	Ryan Klesko	1.25	.55
❑	271	Barry Larkin W	4.00	1.80
❑	272	Paul O'Neill	1.25	.55
❑	274	Will Clark	3.00	1.35
❑	275	Steve Avery	.75	.35
❑	276	Jim Edmonds	2.00	.90
❑	277	John Olerud	1.25	.55
❑	279	Chris Hoiles	.75	.35
❑	280	Jeff Conine	1.25	.55
❑	283	Ray Lankford	1.25	.55
❑	285	Frank Thomas	10.00	4.50
❑	286	Jason Isringhausen	.75	.35
❑	287	Glenallen Hill	.75	.35
❑	289	Bernie Williams	3.00	1.35
❑	290	Eddie Murray	3.00	1.35
❑	296	Jeff Fassero	.75	.35
❑	297	Albert Belle	4.00	1.80
❑	298	Craig Biggio	3.00	1.35
❑	300	Edgar Martinez	1.25	.55
❑	301	Tony Gwynn	8.00	3.60
❑	303	Mo Vaughn	4.00	1.80
❑	304	Alex Fernandez	.75	.35
❑	308	Omar Vizquel	1.25	.55
❑	310	Danny Tartabull	.75	.35
❑	316	Brady Anderson	1.25	.55
❑	319	Larry Walker	3.00	1.35
❑	321	Robin Ventura	1.25	.55
❑	325	Kenny Lofton	3.00	1.35
❑	327	Wil Cordero	.75	.35
❑	328	Troy Percival	1.25	.55
❑	331	Carlos Baerga	1.25	.55
❑	333	Jay Buhner	1.25	.55
❑	335	Jeff King	.75	.35
❑	336	Dante Bichette	1.25	.55
❑	337	Alan Trammell	2.00	.90
❑	342	Jose Canseco	3.00	1.35
❑	343	Rafael Palmeiro	2.00	.90
❑	344	Quilvio Veras	.75	.35
❑	345	Darrin Fletcher	.75	.35
❑	347	Tony Eusebio	.75	.35
❑	348	Ismael Valdes	1.25	.55
❑	349	Terry Steinbach	1.25	.55
❑	350	Orel Hershiser	1.25	.55
❑	351	Kurt Abbott	.75	.35
❑	354	Ruben Sierra	.75	.35
❑	357	Jim Thome	3.00	1.35
❑	358	Geronimo Berroa	.75	.35
❑	359	Robby Thompson	.75	.35
❑	360	Jose Vizcaino	.75	.35
❑	362	Kevin Appier	1.25	.55
❑	364	Ron Gant	.75	.35
❑	367	Rico Brogna	.75	.35
❑	368	Manny Ramirez	3.00	1.35
❑	370	Sammy Sosa	8.00	3.60
❑	373	Sandy Alomar	1.25	.55
❑	378	Steve Finley	1.25	.55
❑	380	Ivan Rodriguez	4.00	1.80
❑	382	Mark Lemke	.75	.35
❑	385	Mark Langston	.75	.35
❑	386	Ed Sprague	.75	.35
❑	388	Steve Ontiveros	.75	.35
❑	392	Tom Candiotti	.75	.35
❑	394	Erik Hanson	.75	.35
❑	396	Pete Schourek	.75	.35
❑	400	Gary Sheffield W	4.00	1.80
❑	402	Barry Bonds W	8.00	3.60
❑	403	Tom Pagnozzi	.75	.35
❑	404	Todd Stottlemyre	.75	.35
❑	405	Tim Salmon	3.00	1.35
❑	407	Fred McGriff	2.00	.90
❑	408	Orlando Merced	.75	.35
❑	412	Eric Young	.75	.35
❑	414	Chuck Knoblauch W	5.00	2.20
❑	417	Mark Portugal	.75	.35
❑	418	Tim Raines	1.25	.55
❑	420	Todd Zeile	.75	.35
❑	422	Marquis Grissom	1.25	.55
❑	423	Norm Charlton	.75	.35
❑	424	Cal Ripken	12.00	5.50
❑	425	Gregg Jefferies	.75	.35
❑	428	Jose Rijo	.75	.35
❑	429	Jeff Bagwell	5.00	2.20
❑	430	Raul Mondesi	2.00	.90
❑	431	Travis Fryman	1.25	.55
❑	434	Tony Phillips	.75	.35
❑	435	Reggie Sanders	1.25	.55
❑	436	Andy Pettitte	2.00	.90
❑	438	Jeff Blauser	.75	.35
❑	441	Charlie Hayes	.75	.35
❑	442	Mike Piazza W	20.00	9.00

1996 Stadium Club Extreme Winners Bronze

	MINT	NRMT
COMPLETE SET (10)	25.00	11.00
COMMON CARD (EW1-EW10)	.50	.23

	No.	Player	MINT	NRMT
❑	EW1	Greg Maddux	6.00	2.70
❑	EW2	Mike Piazza	6.00	2.70
❑	EW3	Andres Galarraga	2.00	.90
❑	EW4	Chuck Knoblauch	2.00	.90
❑	EW5	Ken Caminiti	1.00	.45
❑	EW6	Barry Larkin	1.00	.45
❑	EW7	Barry Bonds	2.50	1.10
❑	EW8	Ken Griffey Jr.	10.00	4.50
❑	EW9	Gary Sheffield	1.00	.45
❑	EW10	Todd Worrell	.50	.23

1996 Stadium Club Mantle

	MINT	NRMT
COMPLETE SET (19)	170.00	75.00
COMPLETE SERIES 1 (9)	110.00	50.00
COMPLETE SERIES 2 (10)	60.00	27.00
COMMON CARD (MM1-MM9)	15.00	6.75
COMMON CARD (MM10-MM19)	8.00	3.60

	No.	Player	MINT	NRMT
❑	MM1	Mickey Mantle Batting Follow Through, 1950	15.00	6.75
❑	MM2	Mickey Mantle	15.00	6.75
❑	MM3	Mickey Mantle Locker room shot, 1951	15.00	6.75
❑	MM4	Mickey Mantle	15.00	6.75
❑	MM5	Mickey Mantle	15.00	6.75
❑	MM6	Mickey Mantle	15.00	6.75
❑	MM7	Mickey Mantle	15.00	6.75
❑	MM8	Mickey Mantle	15.00	6.75
❑	MM9	Mickey Mantle Batting both ways, 1959	15.00	6.75
❑	MM10	Mickey Mantle	8.00	3.60
❑	MM11	Mickey Mantle Beating out hit, 1961	8.00	3.60
❑	MM12	Mickey Mantle Roger Maris, 1961	8.00	3.60
❑	MM13	Mickey Mantle	8.00	3.60
❑	MM14	Mickey Mantle	8.00	3.60
❑	MM15	Mickey Mantle Smiling Pose, 1964	8.00	3.60
❑	MM16	Mickey Mantle	8.00	3.60
❑	MM17	Mickey Mantle	8.00	3.60
❑	MM18	Mickey Mantle	8.00	3.60
❑	MM19	Mickey Mantle	8.00	3.60

1996 Stadium Club Megaheroes

	MINT	NRMT
COMPLETE SET (10)	50.00	22.00
COMMON CARD (MH1-MH10)	1.00	.45

	No.	Player	MINT	NRMT
❑	MH1	Frank Thomas	12.00	5.50
❑	MH2	Ken Griffey Jr.	20.00	9.00
❑	MH3	Hideo Nomo	6.00	2.70
❑	MH4	Ozzie Smith	5.00	2.20
❑	MH5	Will Clark	4.00	1.80
❑	MH6	Jack McDowell	1.00	.45

		MINT	NRMT
❑ MH7	Andres Galarraga	4.00	1.80
❑ MH8	Roger Clemens	8.00	3.60
❑ MH9	Deion Sanders	2.00	.90
❑ MH10	Mo Vaughn	5.00	2.20

1996 Stadium Club Metalists

	MINT	NRMT
COMPLETE SET (8)	50.00	22.00
COMMON CARD (M1-M8)	1.50	.70
❑ M1 Jeff Bagwell	6.00	2.70
❑ M2 Barry Bonds	5.00	2.20
❑ M3 Jose Canseco	3.00	1.35
❑ M4 Roger Clemens	8.00	3.60
❑ M5 Dennis Eckersley	1.50	.70
❑ M6 Greg Maddux	12.00	5.50
❑ M7 Cal Ripken	15.00	6.75
❑ M8 Frank Thomas	12.00	5.50

1996 Stadium Club Midsummer Matchups

	MINT	NRMT
COMPLETE SET (10)	60.00	27.00
COMMON CARD (M1-M10)	2.00	.90
❑ MM1 Hideo Nomo Randy Johnson	6.00	2.70
❑ MM2 Mike Piazza Ivan Rodriguez	12.00	5.50
❑ MM3 Fred McGriff Frank Thomas	12.00	5.50
❑ MM4 Craig Biggio Carlos Baerga	2.00	.90
❑ MM5 Vinny Castilla Wade Boggs	4.00	1.80
❑ MM6 Barry Larkin Cal Ripken	15.00	6.75
❑ MM7 Barry Bonds Albert Belle	5.00	2.20
❑ MM8 Len Dykstra Kenny Lofton	5.00	2.20
❑ MM9 Tony Gwynn Kirby Puckett	12.00	5.50
❑ MM10 Ron Gant Edgar Martinez	2.50	1.10

1996 Stadium Club Power Packed

	MINT	NRMT
COMPLETE SET (15)	80.00	36.00
COMMON CARD (PP1-PP15)	2.00	.90
❑ PP1 Albert Belle	6.00	2.70
❑ PP2 Mark McGwire	25.00	11.00
❑ PP3 Jose Canseco	5.00	2.20
❑ PP4 Mike Piazza	15.00	6.75
❑ PP5 Ron Gant	2.00	.90
❑ PP6 Ken Griffey Jr.	25.00	11.00
❑ PP7 Mo Vaughn	6.00	2.70
❑ PP8 Cecil Fielder	2.50	1.10
❑ PP9 Tim Salmon	5.00	2.20
❑ PP10 Frank Thomas	15.00	6.75
❑ PP11 Juan Gonzalez	12.00	5.50
❑ PP12 Andres Galarraga	5.00	2.20
❑ PP13 Fred McGriff	3.00	1.35
❑ PP14 Jay Buhner	2.50	1.10
❑ PP15 Dante Bichette	2.50	1.10

1996 Stadium Club Power Streak

	MINT	NRMT
COMPLETE SET (15)	60.00	27.00
COMMON CARD (PS1-PS15)	1.25	.55
❑ PS1 Randy Johnson	5.00	2.20
❑ PS2 Hideo Nomo	8.00	3.60
❑ PS3 Albert Belle	6.00	2.70
❑ PS4 Dante Bichette	2.00	.90
❑ PS5 Jay Buhner	2.00	.90
❑ PS6 Frank Thomas	15.00	6.75
❑ PS7 Mark McGwire	25.00	11.00
❑ PS8 Rafael Palmeiro	3.00	1.35
❑ PS9 Mo Vaughn	6.00	2.70
❑ PS10 Sammy Sosa	12.00	5.50
❑ PS11 Larry Walker	5.00	2.20
❑ PS12 Gary Gaetti	1.25	.55
❑ PS13 Tim Salmon	5.00	2.20
❑ PS14 Barry Bonds	6.00	2.70
❑ PS15 Jim Edmonds	3.00	1.35

1996 Stadium Club Prime Cuts

	MINT	NRMT
COMPLETE SET (8)	60.00	27.00
COMMON CARD (PC1-PC8)	2.50	1.10
❑ PC1 Albert Belle	5.00	2.20
❑ PC2 Barry Bonds	5.00	2.20
❑ PC3 Ken Griffey Jr.	20.00	9.00
❑ PC4 Tony Gwynn	10.00	4.50
❑ PC5 Edgar Martinez	2.50	1.10
❑ PC6 Rafael Palmeiro	3.00	1.35
❑ PC7 Mike Piazza	12.00	5.50
❑ PC8 Frank Thomas	12.00	5.50

1996 Stadium Club TSC Awards

	MINT	NRMT
COMPLETE SET (10)	40.00	18.00
COMMON CARD (1-10)	1.00	.45
❑ 1 Cal Ripken	12.00	5.50
❑ 2 Albert Belle	3.00	1.35
❑ 3 Tom Glavine	3.00	1.35
❑ 4 Jeff Conine	1.50	.70
❑ 5 Ken Griffey Jr.	15.00	6.75
❑ 6 Hideo Nomo	5.00	2.20
❑ 7 Greg Maddux	10.00	4.50
❑ 8 Chipper Jones	8.00	3.60
❑ 9 Randy Johnson	3.00	1.35
❑ 10 Jose Mesa	1.00	.45

1997 Stadium Club

	MINT	NRMT
COMPLETE SET (390)	90.00	40.00
COMPLETE SERIES 1 (195)	45.00	20.00
COMPLETE SERIES 2 (195)	45.00	20.00
COMMON (1-180/196-375)	.15	.07
COM.SP (181-195/376-390)	.30	.14
❑ 1 Chipper Jones	1.50	.70
❑ 2 Gary Sheffield	.40	.18
❑ 3 Kenny Lofton	.60	.25
❑ 4 Brian Jordan	.30	.14
❑ 5 Mark McGwire	3.00	1.35
❑ 6 Charles Nagy	.30	.14
❑ 7 Tim Salmon	.60	.25

❑ 8 Cal Ripken 2.50 1.10
❑ 9 Jeff Conine .30 .14
❑ 10 Paul Molitor .60 .25
❑ 11 Mariano Rivera .30 .14
❑ 12 Pedro Martinez .60 .25
❑ 13 Jeff Bagwell 1.00 .45
❑ 14 Bobby Bonilla .30 .14
❑ 15 Barry Bonds .75 .35
❑ 16 Ryan Klesko .30 .14
❑ 17 Barry Larkin .40 .18
❑ 18 Jim Thome .60 .25
❑ 19 Jay Buhner .30 .14
❑ 20 Juan Gonzalez 1.50 .70
❑ 21 Mike Mussina .60 .25
❑ 22 Kevin Appier .30 .14
❑ 23 Eric Karros .30 .14
❑ 24 Steve Finley .30 .14
❑ 25 Ed Sprague .15 .07
❑ 26 Bernard Gilkey .15 .07
❑ 27 Tony Phillips .15 .07
❑ 28 Henry Rodriguez .30 .14
❑ 29 John Smoltz .30 .14
❑ 30 Dante Bichette .30 .14
❑ 31 Mike Piazza 2.00 .90
❑ 32 Paul O'Neill .30 .14
❑ 33 Billy Wagner .30 .14
❑ 34 Reggie Sanders .30 .14
❑ 35 John Jaha .15 .07
❑ 36 Eddie Murray .60 .25
❑ 37 Eric Young .30 .14
❑ 38 Roberto Hernandez .15 .07
❑ 39 Pat Hentgen .30 .14
❑ 40 Sammy Sosa 1.50 .70
❑ 41 Todd Hundley .30 .14
❑ 42 Mo Vaughn .75 .35
❑ 43 Robin Ventura .30 .14
❑ 44 Mark Grudzielanek .30 .14
❑ 45 Shane Reynolds .30 .14
❑ 46 Andy Pettitte .40 .18
❑ 47 Fred McGriff .40 .18
❑ 48 Rey Ordonez .30 .14
❑ 49 Will Clark .60 .25
❑ 50 Ken Griffey Jr. 3.00 1.35
❑ 51 Todd Worrell .15 .07
❑ 52 Rusty Greer .30 .14
❑ 53 Mark Grace .40 .18
❑ 54 Tom Glavine .60 .25
❑ 55 Derek Jeter 2.00 .90
❑ 56 Rafael Palmeiro .40 .18
❑ 57 Bernie Williams .60 .25
❑ 58 Marty Cordova .15 .07
❑ 59 Andres Galarraga .60 .25
❑ 60 Ken Caminiti .40 .18
❑ 61 Garret Anderson .30 .14
❑ 62 Denny Martinez .30 .14
❑ 63 Mike Greenwell .15 .07
❑ 64 David Segui .30 .14
❑ 65 Julio Franco .30 .14
❑ 66 Rickey Henderson .60 .25
❑ 67 Ozzie Guillen .15 .07
❑ 68 Pete Harnisch .15 .07
❑ 69 Chan Ho Park .60 .25
❑ 70 Harold Baines .30 .14
❑ 71 Mark Clark .15 .07
❑ 72 Steve Avery .15 .07
❑ 73 Brian Hunter .30 .14
❑ 74 Pedro Astacio .15 .07
❑ 75 Jack McDowell .15 .07
❑ 76 Gregg Jefferies .15 .07
❑ 77 Jason Kendall .40 .18
❑ 78 Todd Walker .60 .25
❑ 79 B.J. Surhoff .30 .14
❑ 80 Moises Alou .40 .18
❑ 81 Fernando Vina .15 .07
❑ 82 Darryl Strawberry .30 .14
❑ 83 Jose Rosado .15 .07
❑ 84 Chris Gomez .15 .07
❑ 85 Chili Davis .30 .14
❑ 86 Alan Benes .30 .14
❑ 87 Todd Hollandsworth .15 .07
❑ 88 Jose Vizcaino .15 .07
❑ 89 Edgardo Alfonzo .30 .14
❑ 90 Ruben Rivera .30 .14
❑ 91 Donovan Osborne .15 .07
❑ 92 Doug Glanville .30 .14
❑ 93 Gary DiSarcina .15 .07
❑ 94 Brooks Kieschnick .15 .07
❑ 95 Bobby Jones .15 .07
❑ 96 Raul Casanova .15 .07
❑ 97 Jermaine Allensworth .15 .07
❑ 98 Kenny Rogers .15 .07
❑ 99 Mark McLemore .15 .07
❑ 100 Jeff Fassero .15 .07
❑ 101 Sandy Alomar Jr. .30 .14
❑ 102 Chuck Finley .30 .14
❑ 103 Eric Owens .15 .07
❑ 104 Billy McMillon .15 .07
❑ 105 Dwight Gooden .30 .14
❑ 106 Sterling Hitchcock .30 .14
❑ 107 Doug Drabek .15 .07
❑ 108 Paul Wilson .15 .07
❑ 109 Chris Snopek .15 .07
❑ 110 Al Leiter .30 .14
❑ 111 Bob Tewksbury .15 .07
❑ 112 Todd Greene .30 .14
❑ 113 Jose Valentin .15 .07
❑ 114 Delino DeShields .15 .07
❑ 115 Mike Bordick .15 .07
❑ 116 Pat Meares .15 .07
❑ 117 Mariano Duncan .15 .07
❑ 118 Steve Trachsel .15 .07
❑ 119 Luis Castillo .30 .14
❑ 120 Andy Benes .30 .14
❑ 121 Donne Wall .15 .07
❑ 122 Alex Gonzalez .15 .07
❑ 123 Dan Wilson .15 .07
❑ 124 Omar Vizquel .30 .14
❑ 125 Devon White .30 .14
❑ 126 Darryl Hamilton .15 .07
❑ 127 Orlando Merced .15 .07
❑ 128 Royce Clayton .15 .07
❑ 129 William VanLandingham .15 .07
❑ 130 Terry Steinbach .30 .14
❑ 131 Jeff Blauser .15 .07
❑ 132 Jeff Cirillo .30 .14
❑ 133 Roger Pavlik .15 .07
❑ 134 Danny Tartabull .15 .07
❑ 135 Jeff Montgomery .15 .07
❑ 136 Bobby Higginson .40 .18
❑ 137 Mike Grace .15 .07
❑ 138 Kevin Elster .15 .07
❑ 139 Brian Giles .75 .35
❑ 140 Rod Beck .15 .07
❑ 141 Ismael Valdes .30 .14
❑ 142 Scott Brosius .30 .14
❑ 143 Mike Fetters .15 .07
❑ 144 Gary Gaetti .15 .07
❑ 145 Mike Lansing .15 .07
❑ 146 Glenallen Hill .15 .07
❑ 147 Shawn Green .30 .14
❑ 148 Mel Rojas .15 .07
❑ 149 Joey Cora .30 .14
❑ 150 John Smiley .15 .07
❑ 151 Marvin Benard .15 .07
❑ 152 Curt Schilling .30 .14
❑ 153 Dave Nilsson .15 .07
❑ 154 Edgar Renteria .30 .14
❑ 155 Joey Hamilton .30 .14
❑ 156 Carlos Garcia .15 .07
❑ 157 Nomar Garciaparra 2.00 .90
❑ 158 Kevin Ritz .15 .07
❑ 159 Keith Lockhart .15 .07
❑ 160 Justin Thompson .30 .14
❑ 161 Terry Adams .15 .07
❑ 162 Jamey Wright .15 .07
❑ 163 Otis Nixon .15 .07
❑ 164 Michael Tucker .30 .14
❑ 165 Mike Stanley .15 .07
❑ 166 Ben McDonald .15 .07
❑ 167 John Mabry .15 .07
❑ 168 Troy O'Leary .30 .14
❑ 169 Mel Nieves .15 .07
❑ 170 Bret Boone .30 .14
❑ 171 Mike Timlin .15 .07
❑ 172 Scott Rolen 1.50 .70
❑ 173 Reggie Jefferson .15 .07
❑ 174 Neifi Perez .15 .07
❑ 175 Brian McRae .15 .07
❑ 176 Tom Goodwin .15 .07
❑ 177 Aaron Sele .30 .14
❑ 178 Benito Santiago .15 .07
❑ 179 Frank Rodriguez .15 .07
❑ 180 Eric Davis .30 .14
❑ 181 Andruw Jones 2000 SP 2.00 .90
❑ 182 Todd Walker 2000 SP 1.25 .55
❑ 183 Wes Helms 2000 SP .75 .35
❑ 184 Nelson Figueroa 2000 SP .50 .23
❑ 185 V. Guerrero 2000 SP 2.50 1.10
❑ 186 Billy McMillon 2000 SP .30 .14
❑ 187 Todd Helton 2000 SP 2.50 1.10
❑ 188 N. Garciaparra 2000 SP 4.00 1.80
❑ 189 K. Maeda 2000 SP .50 .23
❑ 190 Russell Branyan 2000 SP 1.50 .70
❑ 191 Glendon Rusch 2000 SP .30 .14
❑ 192 Bartolo Colon 2000 SP .50 .23
❑ 193 Scott Rolen 2000 SP 3.00 1.35
❑ 194 A. Echevarria 2000 SP .30 .14
❑ 195 Bob Abreu 2000 SP .50 .23
❑ 196 Greg Maddux 2.00 .90
❑ 197 Joe Carter .30 .14
❑ 198 Alex Ochoa .15 .07
❑ 199 Ellis Burks .30 .14
❑ 200 Ivan Rodriguez .75 .35
❑ 201 Marquis Grissom .30 .14
❑ 202 Trevor Hoffman .30 .14
❑ 203 Matt Williams .30 .14
❑ 204 Carlos Delgado .30 .14
❑ 205 Ramon Martinez .30 .14
❑ 206 Chuck Knoblauch .60 .25
❑ 207 Juan Guzman .15 .07
❑ 208 Derek Bell .30 .14
❑ 209 Roger Clemens 1.25 .55
❑ 210 Vladimir Guerrero 1.25 .55
❑ 211 Cecil Fielder .30 .14
❑ 212 Hideo Nomo .60 .25
❑ 213 Frank Thomas 2.00 .90
❑ 214 Greg Vaughn .30 .14
❑ 215 Javy Lopez .30 .14
❑ 216 Raul Mondesi .40 .18
❑ 217 Wade Boggs .60 .25
❑ 218 Carlos Baerga .30 .14
❑ 219 Tony Gwynn 1.50 .70
❑ 220 Tino Martinez .60 .25
❑ 221 Vinny Castilla .40 .18
❑ 222 Lance Johnson .15 .07
❑ 223 David Justice .60 .25
❑ 224 Rondell White .30 .14
❑ 225 Dean Palmer .30 .14
❑ 226 Jim Edmonds .40 .18
❑ 227 Albert Belle 1.00 .45
❑ 228 Alex Fernandez .15 .07
❑ 229 Ryne Sandberg .75 .35
❑ 230 Jose Mesa .15 .07
❑ 231 David Cone .40 .18
❑ 232 Troy Percival .30 .14
❑ 233 Edgar Martinez .30 .14
❑ 234 Jose Canseco .60 .25
❑ 235 Kevin Brown .40 .18
❑ 236 Ray Lankford .30 .14
❑ 237 Karim Garcia .30 .14
❑ 238 J.T. Snow .30 .14
❑ 239 Dennis Eckersley .30 .14
❑ 240 Roberto Alomar .60 .25
❑ 241 John Valentin .30 .14
❑ 242 Ron Gant .15 .07
❑ 243 Geronimo Berroa .15 .07
❑ 244 Manny Ramirez .60 .25
❑ 245 Travis Fryman .30 .14

❑ 246 Denny Neagle .30 .14
❑ 247 Randy Johnson .60 .25
❑ 248 Darin Erstad 1.00 .45
❑ 249 Mark Wohlers .15 .07
❑ 250 Ken Hill .15 .07
❑ 251 Larry Walker .60 .25
❑ 252 Craig Biggio .60 .25
❑ 253 Brady Anderson .30 .14
❑ 254 John Wetteland .30 .14
❑ 255 Andruw Jones 1.00 .45
❑ 256 Turk Wendell .15 .07
❑ 257 Jason Isringhausen .15 .07
❑ 258 Jaime Navarro .15 .07
❑ 259 Sean Berry .15 .07
❑ 260 Albie Lopez .15 .07
❑ 261 Jay Bell .30 .14
❑ 262 Bobby Witt .15 .07
❑ 263 Tony Clark .40 .18
❑ 264 Tim Wakefield .30 .14
❑ 265 Brad Radke .30 .14
❑ 266 Tim Belcher .15 .07
❑ 267 Nerio Rodriguez .50 .23
❑ 268 Roger Cedeno .15 .07
❑ 269 Tim Naehring .15 .07
❑ 270 Kevin Tapani .15 .07
❑ 271 Joe Randa .15 .07
❑ 272 Randy Myers .15 .07
❑ 273 Dave Burba .15 .07
❑ 274 Mike Sweeney .15 .07
❑ 275 Danny Graves .15 .07
❑ 276 Chad Mottola .15 .07
❑ 277 Ruben Sierra .15 .07
❑ 278 Norm Charlton .15 .07
❑ 279 Scott Servais .15 .07
❑ 280 Jacob Cruz .15 .07
❑ 281 Mike Macfarlane .15 .07
❑ 282 Rich Becker .15 .07
❑ 283 Shannon Stewart .30 .14
❑ 284 Gerald Williams .15 .07
❑ 285 Jody Reed .15 .07
❑ 286 Jeff D'Amico .15 .07
❑ 287 Walt Weiss .15 .07
❑ 288 Jim Leyritz .15 .07
❑ 289 Francisco Cordova .15 .07
❑ 290 F.P. Santangelo .15 .07
❑ 291 Scott Erickson .30 .14
❑ 292 Hal Morris .15 .07
❑ 293 Ray Durham .30 .14
❑ 294 Andy Ashby .15 .07
❑ 295 Darryl Kile .30 .14
❑ 296 Jose Paniagua .15 .07
❑ 297 Mickey Tettleton .15 .07
❑ 298 Joe Girardi .15 .07
❑ 299 Rocky Coppinger .15 .07
❑ 300 Bob Abreu .30 .14
❑ 301 John Olerud .30 .14
❑ 302 Paul Shuey .15 .07
❑ 303 Jeff Brantley .15 .07
❑ 304 Bob Wells .15 .07
❑ 305 Kevin Seitzer .15 .07
❑ 306 Shawon Dunston .15 .07
❑ 307 Jose Herrera .15 .07
❑ 308 Butch Huskey .15 .07
❑ 309 Jose Offerman .15 .07
❑ 310 Rick Aguilera .15 .07
❑ 311 Greg Gagne .15 .07
❑ 312 John Burkett .15 .07
❑ 313 Mark Thompson .15 .07
❑ 314 Alvaro Espinoza .15 .07
❑ 315 Todd Stottlemyre .15 .07
❑ 316 Al Martin .15 .07
❑ 317 James Baldwin .30 .14
❑ 318 Cal Eldred .15 .07
❑ 319 Sid Fernandez .15 .07
❑ 320 Mickey Morandini .15 .07
❑ 321 Robb Nen .15 .07
❑ 322 Mark Lemke .15 .07
❑ 323 Pete Schourek .15 .07
❑ 324 Marcus Jensen .15 .07
❑ 325 Rich Aurilia .15 .07
❑ 326 Jeff King .15 .07
❑ 327 Scott Stahoviak .15 .07
❑ 328 Ricky Otero .15 .07
❑ 329 Antonio Osuna .15 .07
❑ 330 Chris Hoiles .15 .07
❑ 331 Luis Gonzalez .15 .07
❑ 332 Wil Cordero .15 .07
❑ 333 Johnny Damon .30 .14
❑ 334 Mark Langston .30 .14
❑ 335 Orlando Miller .15 .07
❑ 336 Jason Giambi .30 .14
❑ 337 Damian Jackson .15 .07
❑ 338 David Wells .40 .18
❑ 339 Bip Roberts .15 .07
❑ 340 Matt Ruebel .15 .07
❑ 341 Tom Candiotti .15 .07
❑ 342 Wally Joyner .30 .14
❑ 343 Jimmy Key .30 .14
❑ 344 Tony Batista .15 .07
❑ 345 Paul Sorrento .15 .07
❑ 346 Ron Karkovice .15 .07
❑ 347 Wilson Alvarez .30 .14
❑ 348 John Flaherty .15 .07
❑ 349 Rey Sanchez .15 .07
❑ 350 John Vander Wal .15 .07
❑ 351 Jermaine Dye .15 .07
❑ 352 Mike Hampton .15 .07
❑ 353 Greg Colbrunn .15 .07
❑ 354 Heathcliff Slocumb .15 .07
❑ 355 Ricky Bottalico .30 .14
❑ 356 Marty Janzen .15 .07
❑ 357 Orel Hershiser .30 .14
❑ 358 Rex Hudler .15 .07
❑ 359 Amaury Telemaco .15 .07
❑ 360 Darrin Fletcher .15 .07
❑ 361 Brant Brown UER .30 .14
Card numbered 351
❑ 362 Russ Davis .30 .14
❑ 363 Allen Watson .15 .07
❑ 364 Mike Lieberthal .15 .07
❑ 365 Dave Stevens .15 .07
❑ 366 Jay Powell .15 .07
❑ 367 Tony Fossas .15 .07
❑ 368 Bob Wolcott .15 .07
❑ 369 Mark Loretta .15 .07
❑ 370 Shawn Estes .30 .14
❑ 371 Sandy Martinez .15 .07
❑ 372 Wendell Magee Jr. .15 .07
❑ 373 John Franco .30 .14
❑ 374 Tom Pagnozzi UER .15 .07
misnumbered as 274
❑ 375 Willie Adams .15 .07
❑ 376 Chipper Jones SS SP 3.00 1.35
❑ 377 Mo Vaughn SS SP 1.50 .70
❑ 378 Frank Thomas SS SP 4.00 1.80
❑ 379 Albert Belle SS SP 1.50 .70
❑ 380 Andres Galarraga SS SP 1.25 .55
❑ 381 Gary Sheffield SS SP .75 .35
❑ 382 Jeff Bagwell SS SP 2.00 .90
❑ 383 Mike Piazza SS SP 4.00 1.80
❑ 384 Mark McGwire SS SP 6.00 2.70
❑ 385 Ken Griffey Jr. SS SP 6.00 2.70
❑ 386 Barry Bonds SS SP 1.50 .70
❑ 387 Juan Gonzalez SS SP 3.00 1.35
❑ 388 Brady Anderson SS SP .50 .23
❑ 389 Ken Caminiti SS SP .75 .35
❑ 390 Jay Buhner SS SP .50 .23

1997 Stadium Club Co-Signers

	MINT	NRMT
COMPLETE SET (10)	600.00	275.00
COMPLETE SERIES 1 (5)	300.00	135.00
COMPLETE SERIES 2 (5)	300.00	135.00
COMMON CARD (CO1-CO10)	20.00	9.00

❑ CO1 Andy Pettitte 120.00 55.00
Derek Jeter
❑ CO2 Paul Wilson 25.00 11.00
Todd Hundley
❑ CO3 Jermaine Dye 20.00 9.00
Mark Wohlers
❑ CO4 Scott Rolen 100.00 45.00
Gregg Jefferies
❑ CO5 Todd Hollandsworth 40.00 18.00
Jason Kendall
❑ CO6 Alan Benes 40.00 18.00
Robin Ventura
❑ CO7 Eric Karros 50.00 22.00
Raul Mondesi
❑ CO8 Rey Ordonez 120.00 55.00
Nomar Garciaparra
❑ CO9 Rondell White 25.00 11.00
Marty Cordova
❑ CO10 Tony Gwynn 120.00 55.00
Karim Garcia

1997 Stadium Club Firebrand Redemption

	MINT	NRMT
COMPLETE SET (12)	150.00	70.00
COMMON CARD (F1-F12)	3.00	1.35

*WOOD CARDS: 1.25X BASIC CARDS
ONE WOOD CARD VIA MAIL PER EXCH.CARD

❑ F1 Jeff Bagwell 10.00 4.50
❑ F2 Albert Belle 8.00 3.60
❑ F3 Barry Bonds 8.00 3.60
❑ F4 Andres Galarraga 6.00 2.70
❑ F5 Ken Griffey Jr. 30.00 13.50
❑ F6 Brady Anderson 3.00 1.35
❑ F7 Mark McGwire 30.00 13.50
❑ F8 Chipper Jones 15.00 6.75
❑ F9 Frank Thomas 20.00 9.00
❑ F10 Mike Piazza 20.00 9.00
❑ F11 Mo Vaughn 8.00 3.60
❑ F12 Juan Gonzalez 15.00 6.75

1997 Stadium Club Instavision

	MINT	NRMT
COMPLETE SET (22)	60.00	27.00
COMPLETE SERIES 1 (10)	30.00	13.50
COMPLETE SERIES 2 (12)	30.00	13.50
COMMON CARD (I1-I22)	2.00	.90

❑ I1 Eddie Murray 4.00 1.80
❑ I2 Paul Molitor 4.00 1.80
❑ I3 Todd Hundley 2.00 .90
❑ I4 Roger Clemens 8.00 3.60
❑ I5 Barry Bonds 5.00 2.20
❑ I6 Mark McGwire 20.00 9.00
❑ I7 Brady Anderson 2.00 .90
❑ I8 Barry Larkin 3.00 1.35
❑ I9 Ken Caminiti 3.00 1.35
❑ I10 Hideo Nomo 5.00 2.20
❑ I14 Albert Belle 6.00 2.70

1997 Stadium Club Millennium

	MINT	NRMT
COMPLETE SET (40)	250.00	110.00
COMPLETE SERIES 1 (20)	100.00	45.00
COMPLETE SERIES 2 (20)	150.00	70.00
COMMON CARD (M1-M40)	2.00	.90
❑ M1 Derek Jeter	20.00	9.00
❑ M2 Mark Grudzielanek	4.00	1.80
❑ M3 Jacob Cruz	2.00	.90
❑ M4 Ray Durham	4.00	1.80
❑ M5 Tony Clark	5.00	2.20
❑ M6 Chipper Jones	20.00	9.00
❑ M7 Luis Castillo	4.00	1.80
❑ M8 Carlos Delgado	4.00	1.80
❑ M9 Brant Brown	4.00	1.80
❑ M10 Jason Kendall	5.00	2.20
❑ M11 Alan Benes	4.00	1.80
❑ M12 Rey Ordonez	4.00	1.80
❑ M13 Justin Thompson	4.00	1.80
❑ M14 Jermaine Allensworth	2.00	.90
❑ M15 Brian Hunter	4.00	1.80
❑ M16 Marty Cordova	2.00	.90
❑ M17 Edgar Renteria	4.00	1.80
❑ M18 Karim Garcia	4.00	1.80
❑ M19 Todd Greene	4.00	1.80
❑ M20 Paul Wilson	2.00	.90

1997 Stadium Club Patent Leather

	MINT	NRMT
COMPLETE SET (13)	120.00	55.00
COMMON CARD (PL1-PL13)	2.00	.90
❑ PL1 Ivan Rodriguez	10.00	4.50
❑ PL2 Ken Caminiti	5.00	2.20
❑ PL3 Barry Bonds	10.00	4.50
❑ PL4 Ken Griffey Jr.	40.00	18.00
❑ PL5 Greg Maddux	25.00	11.00
❑ PL6 Craig Biggio	8.00	3.60
❑ PL7 Andres Galarraga	8.00	3.60
❑ PL8 Kenny Lofton	8.00	3.60
❑ PL9 Barry Larkin	5.00	2.20
❑ PL10 Mark Grace	5.00	2.20
❑ PL11 Rey Ordonez	2.00	.90
❑ PL12 Roberto Alomar	8.00	3.60
❑ PL13 Derek Jeter	20.00	9.00

1997 Stadium Club Pure Gold

	MINT	NRMT
COMPLETE SET (20)	450.00	200.00
COMPLETE SERIES 1 (10)	200.00	90.00
COMPLETE SERIES 2 (10)	250.00	110.00
COMMON CARD (PG1-PG20)	6.00	2.70
❑ PG1 Brady Anderson	6.00	2.70
❑ PG2 Albert Belle	15.00	6.75
❑ PG3 Dante Bichette	6.00	2.70
❑ PG4 Barry Bonds	15.00	6.75
❑ PG5 Jay Buhner	6.00	2.70
❑ PG6 Tony Gwynn	30.00	13.50
❑ PG7 Chipper Jones	30.00	13.50
❑ PG8 Mark McGwire	60.00	27.00
❑ PG9 Gary Sheffield	10.00	4.50
❑ PG10 Frank Thomas	40.00	18.00
❑ PG11 Juan Gonzalez	30.00	13.50
❑ PG12 Ken Caminiti	8.00	3.60
❑ PG13 Kenny Lofton	12.00	5.50
❑ PG14 Jeff Bagwell	20.00	9.00
❑ PG15 Ken Griffey Jr.	60.00	27.00
❑ PG16 Cal Ripken	50.00	22.00
❑ PG17 Mo Vaughn	15.00	6.75
❑ PG18 Mike Piazza	40.00	18.00
❑ PG19 Derek Jeter	30.00	13.50
❑ PG20 Andres Galarraga	12.00	5.50

1998 Stadium Club

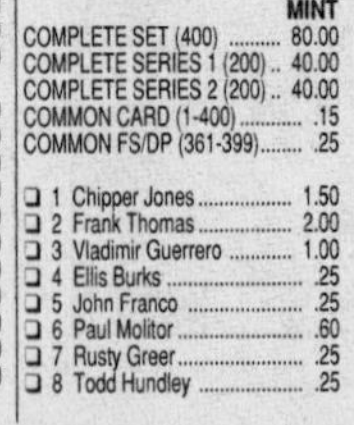

	MINT	NRMT
COMPLETE SET (400)	80.00	36.00
COMPLETE SERIES 1 (200)	40.00	18.00
COMPLETE SERIES 2 (200)	40.00	18.00
COMMON CARD (1-400)	.15	.07
COMMON FS/DP (361-399)	.25	.11
❑ 1 Chipper Jones	1.50	.70
❑ 2 Frank Thomas	2.00	.90
❑ 3 Vladimir Guerrero	1.00	.45
❑ 4 Ellis Burks	.25	.11
❑ 5 John Franco	.25	.11
❑ 6 Paul Molitor	.60	.25
❑ 7 Rusty Greer	.25	.11
❑ 8 Todd Hundley	.25	.11
❑ 9 Brett Tomko	.25	.11
❑ 10 Eric Karros	.25	.11
❑ 11 Mike Cameron	.25	.11
❑ 12 Jim Edmonds	.40	.18
❑ 13 Bernie Williams	.60	.25
❑ 14 Denny Neagle	.25	.11
❑ 15 Jason Dickson	.25	.11
❑ 16 Sammy Sosa	1.50	.70
❑ 17 Brian Jordan	.25	.11
❑ 18 Jose Vidro	.15	.07
❑ 19 Scott Spiezio	.15	.07
❑ 20 Jay Buhner	.25	.11
❑ 21 Jim Thome	.60	.25
❑ 22 Sandy Alomar	.25	.11
❑ 23 Livan Hernandez	.25	.11
❑ 24 Roberto Alomar	.60	.25
❑ 25 Chris Gomez	.15	.07
❑ 26 John Wetteland	.25	.11
❑ 27 Willie Greene	.25	.11
❑ 28 Gregg Jefferies	.15	.07
❑ 29 Johnny Damon	.25	.11
❑ 30 Barry Larkin	.40	.18
❑ 31 Chuck Knoblauch	.60	.25
❑ 32 Mo Vaughn	.75	.35
❑ 33 Tony Clark	.40	.18
❑ 34 Marty Cordova	.15	.07
❑ 35 Vinny Castilla	.40	.18
❑ 36 Jeff King	.25	.11
❑ 37 Reggie Jefferson	.15	.07
❑ 38 Mariano Rivera	.25	.11
❑ 39 Jermaine Allensworth	.15	.07
❑ 40 Livan Hernandez	.25	.11
❑ 41 Heathcliff Slocumb	.15	.07
❑ 42 Jacob Cruz	.15	.07
❑ 43 Barry Bonds	.75	.35
❑ 44 Dave Magadan	.15	.07
❑ 45 Chan Ho Park	.60	.25
❑ 46 Jeremi Gonzalez	.25	.11
❑ 47 Jeff Cirillo	.25	.11
❑ 48 Delino DeShields	.15	.07
❑ 49 Craig Biggio	.60	.25
❑ 50 Benito Santiago	.15	.07
❑ 51 Mark Clark	.15	.07
❑ 52 Fernando Vina	.15	.07
❑ 53 F.P. Santangelo	.15	.07
❑ 54 Pep Harris	.15	.07
❑ 55 Edgar Renteria	.25	.11
❑ 56 Jeff Bagwell	1.00	.45
❑ 57 Jimmy Key	.25	.11
❑ 58 Bartolo Colon	.25	.11
❑ 59 Curt Schilling	.25	.11
❑ 60 Steve Finley	.25	.11
❑ 61 Andy Ashby	.15	.07
❑ 62 John Burkett	.15	.07
❑ 63 Orel Hershiser	.25	.11
❑ 64 Pokey Reese	.15	.07
❑ 65 Scott Servais	.15	.07
❑ 66 Todd Jones	.15	.07
❑ 67 Javy Lopez	.25	.11
❑ 68 Robin Ventura	.25	.11
❑ 69 Miguel Tejada	.25	.11
❑ 70 Raul Casanova	.15	.07
❑ 71 Reggie Sanders	.25	.11
❑ 72 Edgardo Alfonzo	.25	.11
❑ 73 Dean Palmer	.25	.11
❑ 74 Todd Stottlemyre	.25	.11
❑ 75 David Wells	.40	.18
❑ 76 Troy Percival	.25	.11

❑ 77 Albert Belle .75 .35
❑ 78 Pat Hentgen .25 .11
❑ 79 Brian Hunter .25 .11
❑ 80 Richard Hidalgo .25 .11
❑ 81 Darren Oliver .15 .07
❑ 82 Mark Wohlers .15 .07
❑ 83 Cal Ripken 2.50 1.10
❑ 84 Hideo Nomo .75 .35
❑ 85 Derrek Lee .25 .11
❑ 86 Stan Javier .15 .07
❑ 87 Rey Ordonez .25 .11
❑ 88 Randy Johnson .60 .25
❑ 89 Jeff Kent .25 .11
❑ 90 Brian McRae .15 .07
❑ 91 Manny Ramirez .60 .25
❑ 92 Trevor Hoffman .25 .11
❑ 93 Doug Glanville .25 .11
❑ 94 Todd Walker .40 .18
❑ 95 Andy Benes .25 .11
❑ 96 Jason Schmidt .15 .07
❑ 97 Mike Matheny .15 .07
❑ 98 Tim Naehring .15 .07
❑ 99 Keith Lockhart .15 .07
❑ 100 Jose Rosado .15 .07
❑ 101 Roger Clemens 1.25 .55
❑ 102 Pedro Astacio .15 .07
❑ 103 Mark Bellhorn .25 .11
❑ 104 Paul O'Neill .25 .11
❑ 105 Darin Erstad .75 .35
❑ 106 Mike Lieberthal .15 .07
❑ 107 Wilson Alvarez .25 .11
❑ 108 Mike Mussina .60 .25
❑ 109 George Williams .15 .07
❑ 110 Cliff Floyd .25 .11
❑ 111 Shawn Estes .25 .11
❑ 112 Mark Grudzielanek .25 .11
❑ 113 Tony Gwynn 1.50 .70
❑ 114 Alan Benes .25 .11
❑ 115 Terry Steinbach .25 .11
❑ 116 Greg Maddux 2.00 .90
❑ 117 Andy Pettitte .40 .18
❑ 118 Dave Nilsson .15 .07
❑ 119 Deivi Cruz .15 .07
❑ 120 Carlos Delgado .25 .11
❑ 121 Scott Hatteberg .15 .07
❑ 122 John Olerud .25 .11
❑ 123 Todd Dunwoody .25 .11
❑ 124 Garret Anderson .25 .11
❑ 125 Royce Clayton .15 .07
❑ 126 Dante Powell .25 .11
❑ 127 Tom Glavine .60 .25
❑ 128 Gary DiSarcina .15 .07
❑ 129 Terry Adams .15 .07
❑ 130 Raul Mondesi .40 .18
❑ 131 Dan Wilson .15 .07
❑ 132 Al Martin .15 .07
❑ 133 Mickey Morandini .15 .07
❑ 134 Rafael Palmeiro .40 .18
❑ 135 Juan Encarnacion .25 .11
❑ 136 Jim Pittsley .15 .07
❑ 137 Magglio Ordonez .75 .35
❑ 138 Will Clark .60 .25
❑ 139 Todd Helton .75 .35
❑ 140 Kelvim Escobar .25 .11
❑ 141 Esteban Loaiza .15 .07
❑ 142 John Jaha .15 .07
❑ 143 Jeff Fassero .15 .07
❑ 144 Harold Baines .25 .11
❑ 145 Butch Huskey .15 .07
❑ 146 Pat Meares .15 .07
❑ 147 Brian Giles .25 .11
❑ 148 Ramiro Mendoza .25 .11
❑ 149 John Smoltz .25 .11
❑ 150 Felix Martinez .15 .07
❑ 151 Jose Valentin .15 .07
❑ 152 Brad Rigby .15 .07
❑ 153 Ed Sprague .15 .07
❑ 154 Mike Hampton .15 .07
❑ 155 Carlos Perez .25 .11
❑ 156 Ray Lankford .25 .11
❑ 157 Bobby Bonilla .25 .11
❑ 158 Bill Mueller .25 .11
❑ 159 Jeffrey Hammonds .25 .11
❑ 160 Charles Nagy .25 .11
❑ 161 Rich Loiselle .40 .18
❑ 162 Al Leiter .25 .11
❑ 163 Larry Walker .60 .25
❑ 164 Chris Hoiles .15 .07
❑ 165 Jeff Montgomery .15 .07
❑ 166 Francisco Cordova .15 .07
❑ 167 James Baldwin .25 .11
❑ 168 Mark McLemore .15 .07
❑ 169 Kevin Appier .25 .11
❑ 170 Jamey Wright .15 .07
❑ 171 Nomar Garciaparra 2.00 .90
❑ 172 Matt Franco .15 .07
❑ 173 Armando Benitez .15 .07
❑ 174 Jeromy Burnitz .25 .11
❑ 175 Ismael Valdes .25 .11
❑ 176 Lance Johnson .15 .07
❑ 177 Paul Sorrento .15 .07
❑ 178 Rondell White .25 .11
❑ 179 Kevin Elster .15 .07
❑ 180 Jason Giambi .25 .11
❑ 181 Carlos Baerga .25 .11
❑ 182 Russ Davis .25 .11
❑ 183 Ryan McGuire .15 .07
❑ 184 Eric Young .25 .11
❑ 185 Ron Gant .15 .07
❑ 186 Manny Alexander .15 .07
❑ 187 Scott Karl .15 .07
❑ 188 Brady Anderson .25 .11
❑ 189 Randall Simon .25 .11
❑ 190 Tim Belcher .15 .07
❑ 191 Jaret Wright .75 .35
❑ 192 Dante Bichette .25 .11
❑ 193 John Valentin .25 .11
❑ 194 Darren Bragg .15 .07
❑ 195 Mike Sweeney .15 .07
❑ 196 Craig Counsell .15 .07
❑ 197 Jaime Navarro .15 .07
❑ 198 Todd Dunn .15 .07
❑ 199 Ken Griffey Jr. 3.00 1.35
❑ 200 Juan Gonzalez 1.50 .70
❑ 201 Billy Wagner .25 .11
❑ 202 Tino Martinez .60 .25
❑ 203 Mark McGwire 4.00 1.80
❑ 204 Jeff D'Amico .15 .07
❑ 205 Rico Brogna .25 .11
❑ 206 Todd Hollandsworth .15 .07
❑ 207 Chad Curtis .15 .07
❑ 208 Tom Goodwin .15 .07
❑ 209 Neifi Perez .25 .11
❑ 210 Derek Bell .25 .11
❑ 211 Quilvio Veras .15 .07
❑ 212 Greg Vaughn .25 .11
❑ 213 Kirk Rueter .15 .07
❑ 214 Arthur Rhodes .15 .07
❑ 215 Cal Eldred .15 .07
❑ 216 Bill Taylor .15 .07
❑ 217 Todd Greene .25 .11
❑ 218 Mario Valdez .25 .11
❑ 219 Ricky Bottalico .25 .11
❑ 220 Frank Rodriguez .15 .07
❑ 221 Rich Becker .15 .07
❑ 222 Roberto Duran .25 .11
❑ 223 Ivan Rodriguez .75 .35
❑ 224 Mike Jackson .15 .07
❑ 225 Deion Sanders .25 .11
❑ 226 Tony Womack .25 .11
❑ 227 Mark Kotsay .40 .18
❑ 228 Steve Trachsel .15 .07
❑ 229 Ryan Klesko .25 .11
❑ 230 Ken Cloude .25 .11
❑ 231 Luis Gonzalez .15 .07
❑ 232 Gary Gaetti .15 .07
❑ 233 Michael Tucker .25 .11
❑ 234 Shawn Green .25 .11
❑ 235 Ariel Prieto .15 .07
❑ 236 Kirt Manwaring .15 .07
❑ 237 Omar Vizquel .25 .11
❑ 238 Matt Beech .15 .07
❑ 239 Justin Thompson .25 .11
❑ 240 Bret Boone .25 .11
❑ 241 Derek Jeter 1.50 .70
❑ 242 Ken Caminiti .40 .18
❑ 243 Jose Offerman .15 .07
❑ 244 Kevin Tapani .15 .07
❑ 245 Jason Kendall .25 .11
❑ 246 Jose Guillen .25 .11
❑ 247 Mike Bordick .15 .07
❑ 248 Dustin Hermanson .25 .11
❑ 249 Darrin Fletcher .15 .07
❑ 250 Dave Hollins .15 .07
❑ 251 Ramon Martinez .25 .11
❑ 252 Hideki Irabu .40 .18
❑ 253 Mark Grace .40 .18
❑ 254 Jason Isringhausen .15 .07
❑ 255 Jose Cruz Jr. .75 .35
❑ 256 Brian Johnson .15 .07
❑ 257 Brad Ausmus .15 .07
❑ 258 Andruw Jones .75 .35
❑ 259 Doug Jones .15 .07
❑ 260 Jeff Shaw .25 .11
❑ 261 Chuck Finley .25 .11
❑ 262 Gary Sheffield .40 .18
❑ 263 David Segui .25 .11
❑ 264 John Smiley .15 .07
❑ 265 Tim Salmon .60 .25
❑ 266 J.T. Snow .25 .11
❑ 267 Alex Fernandez .15 .07
❑ 268 Matt Stairs .25 .11
❑ 269 B.J. Surhoff .25 .11
❑ 270 Keith Foulke .15 .07
❑ 271 Edgar Martinez .25 .11
❑ 272 Shannon Stewart .25 .11
❑ 273 Eduardo Perez .15 .07
❑ 274 Wally Joyner .25 .11
❑ 275 Kevin Young .25 .11
❑ 276 Eli Marrero .25 .11
❑ 277 Brad Radke .25 .11
❑ 278 Jamie Moyer .15 .07
❑ 279 Joe Girardi .15 .07
❑ 280 Troy O'Leary .25 .11
❑ 281 Jeff Frye .15 .07
❑ 282 Jose Offerman .15 .07
❑ 283 Scott Erickson .25 .11
❑ 284 Sean Berry .15 .07
❑ 285 Shigetoshi Hasegawa .25 .11
❑ 286 Felix Heredia .15 .07
❑ 287 Willie McGee .15 .07
❑ 288 Alex Rodriguez 2.00 .90
❑ 289 Ugueth Urbina .25 .11
❑ 290 Jon Lieber .15 .07
❑ 291 Fernando Tatis .25 .11
❑ 292 Chris Stynes .15 .07
❑ 293 Bernard Gilkey .15 .07
❑ 294 Joey Hamilton .25 .11
❑ 295 Matt Karchner .15 .07
❑ 296 Paul Wilson .15 .07
❑ 297 Damion Easley .25 .11
❑ 298 Kevin Millwood 1.50 .70
❑ 299 Ellis Burks .25 .11
❑ 300 Jerry DiPoto .15 .07
❑ 301 Jermaine Dye .15 .07
❑ 302 Travis Lee 2.00 .90
❑ 303 Ron Coomer .15 .07
❑ 304 Matt Williams .25 .11
❑ 305 Bobby Higginson .40 .18
❑ 306 Jorge Fabregas .15 .07
❑ 307 Jon Nunnally .15 .07
❑ 308 Jay Bell .25 .11
❑ 309 Jason Schmidt .15 .07
❑ 310 Andy Benes .25 .11
❑ 311 Sterling Hitchcock .25 .11
❑ 312 Jeff Suppan .15 .07
❑ 313 Shane Reynolds .25 .11
❑ 314 Willie Blair .15 .07
❑ 315 Scott Rolen 1.50 .70
❑ 316 Wilson Alvarez .25 .11
❑ 317 David Justice .60 .25
❑ 318 Fred McGriff .40 .18
❑ 319 Bobby Jones .15 .07
❑ 320 Wade Boggs .60 .25
❑ 321 Tim Wakefield .15 .07
❑ 322 Tony Saunders .15 .07
❑ 323 David Cone .40 .18
❑ 324 Roberto Hernandez .15 .07
❑ 325 Jose Canseco .60 .25
❑ 326 Kevin Stocker .15 .07
❑ 327 Gerald Williams .15 .07
❑ 328 Quinton McCracken .25 .11
❑ 329 Mark Gardner .15 .07
❑ 330 Ben Grieve 1.25 .55
❑ 331 Kevin Brown .40 .18

		MINT	NRMT
❑ 332	Mike Lowell	.60	.25
❑ 333	Jed Hansen	.15	.07
❑ 334	Abraham Nunez	.25	.11
❑ 335	John Thomson	.15	.07
❑ 336	Masato Yoshii	.50	.23
❑ 337	Mike Piazza	2.00	.90
❑ 338	Brad Fullmer	.25	.11
❑ 339	Ray Durham	.25	.11
❑ 340	Kerry Wood	5.00	2.20
❑ 341	Kevin Polcovich	.15	.07
❑ 342	Russ Johnson	.15	.07
❑ 343	Darryl Hamilton	.15	.07
❑ 344	David Ortiz	.25	.11
❑ 345	Kevin Orie	.15	.07
❑ 346	Mike Caruso	.25	.11
❑ 347	Juan Guzman	.15	.07
❑ 348	Ruben Rivera	.25	.11
❑ 349	Rick Aguilera	.15	.07
❑ 350	Bobby Estalella	.25	.11
❑ 351	Bobby Witt	.15	.07
❑ 352	Paul Konerko	.60	.25
❑ 353	Matt Morris	.25	.11
❑ 354	Carl Pavano	.25	.11
❑ 355	Todd Zeile	.25	.11
❑ 356	Kevin Brown TR	.25	.11
❑ 357	Alex Gonzalez	.15	.07
❑ 358	Chuck Knoblauch TR	.25	.11
❑ 359	Joey Cora	.25	.11
❑ 360	Mike Lansing TR	.15	.07
❑ 361	Adrian Beltre	1.25	.55
❑ 362	Dennis Eckersley TR	.25	.11
❑ 363	A.J. Hinch	.40	.18
❑ 364	Kenny Lofton TR	.40	.18
❑ 365	Alex Gonzalez	.40	.18
❑ 366	Henry Rodriguez TR	.15	.07
❑ 367	Mike Stoner	1.00	.45
❑ 368	Darryl Kile TR	.25	.11
❑ 369	Kevin McGlinchy	.25	.11
❑ 370	Walt Weiss TR	.25	.11
❑ 371	Kris Benson	.40	.18
❑ 372	Cecil Fielder TR	.25	.11
❑ 373	Dermal Brown	.40	.18
❑ 374	Rod Beck TR	.25	.11
❑ 375	Eric Milton	.40	.18
❑ 376	Travis Fryman TR	.25	.11
❑ 377	Preston Wilson	.40	.18
❑ 378	Chili Davis TR	.25	.11
❑ 379	Travis Lee	2.00	.90
❑ 380	Jim Leyritz TR	.15	.07
❑ 381	Vernon Wells	.60	.25
❑ 382	Joe Carter TR	.25	.11
❑ 383	J.J. Davis	.40	.18
❑ 384	Marquis Grissom TR	.25	.11
❑ 385	Mike Cuddyer	1.50	.70
❑ 386	Rickey Henderson TR	.50	.23
❑ 387	Chris Enochs	1.25	.55
❑ 388	Andres Galarraga TR	.60	.25
❑ 389	Jason Dellaero	.40	.18
❑ 390	Robb Nen TR	.25	.11
❑ 391	Mark Mangum	.40	.18
❑ 392	Jeff Blauser TR	.15	.07
❑ 393	Adam Kennedy	.40	.18
❑ 394	Bob Abreu TR	.25	.11
❑ 395	Jack Cust	1.50	.70
❑ 396	Jose Vizcaino TR	.15	.07
❑ 397	Jon Garland	.40	.18
❑ 398	Pedro Martinez TR	.40	.18
❑ 399	Aaron Akin	.25	.11
❑ 400	Jeff Conine TR	.25	.11
❑ NNO	Ripken Sound Chip 1	20.00	9.00
❑ NNO	Ripken Sound Chip 2	20.00	9.00

1998 Stadium Club First Day Issue

	MINT	NRMT
COMMON CARD (1-400)	8.00	3.60

*STARS: 20X TO 50X BASIC CARDS
*YOUNG STARS: 15X TO 40X BASIC CARDS
*ROOKIES: 12.5X TO 30X BASIC CARDS
*FS/DP PROSPECTS: 10X TO 25X BASIC CARDS
*FS/DP ROOKIES: 8X TO 20X BASIC CARDS

1998 Stadium Club One Of A Kind

	MINT	NRMT
COMMON CARD (1-400)	10.00	4.50

*STARS: 25X TO 60X BASIC CARDS
*YOUNG STARS: 20X TO 50X BASIC CARDS
*ROOKIES: 15X TO 40X BASIC CARDS
*ROOKIES/PROSPECTS: 12.5X TO 30X BASIC CARDS
*FS/DP ROOK/PROSP: 10X TO 25X BASIC CARDS

1998 Stadium Club Bowman Previews

		MINT	NRMT
COMPLETE SET (10)		40.00	18.00
COMMON CARD (BP1-BP10)		2.00	.90
❑ BP1	Nomar Garciaparra	6.00	2.70
❑ BP2	Scott Rolen	5.00	2.20
❑ BP3	Ken Griffey Jr.	10.00	4.50
❑ BP4	Frank Thomas	6.00	2.70
❑ BP5	Larry Walker	2.00	.90
❑ BP6	Mike Piazza	6.00	2.70
❑ BP7	Chipper Jones	5.00	2.20
❑ BP8	Tino Martinez	2.00	.90
❑ BP9	Mark McGwire	12.00	5.50
❑ BP10	Barry Bonds	2.50	1.10

1998 Stadium Club Bowman Prospect Previews

		MINT	NRMT
COMPLETE SET (10)		15.00	6.75
COMMON CARD (BP1-BP10)		1.00	.45
❑ BP1	Ben Grieve	5.00	2.20
❑ BP2	Brad Fullmer	1.00	.45
❑ BP3	Ryan Anderson	5.00	2.20
❑ BP4	Mark Kotsay	1.50	.70
❑ BP5	Bobby Estalella	1.00	.45
❑ BP6	Juan Encarnacion	1.00	.45
❑ BP7	Todd Helton	3.00	1.35
❑ BP8	Mike Lowell	2.50	1.10
❑ BP9	A.J. Hinch	1.00	.45
❑ BP10	Richard Hidalgo	1.00	.45

1998 Stadium Club Co-Signers

		MINT	NRMT
COMMON CARD (CS1-CS36)		50.00	22.00
❑ CS1	Nomar Garciaparra A Scott Rolen	800.00	350.00
❑ CS2	Nomar Garciaparra B Derek Jeter	300.00	135.00
❑ CS3	Nomar Garciaparra C Eric Karros	120.00	55.00
❑ CS4	Scott Rolen C Derek Jeter	150.00	70.00
❑ CS5	Scott Rolen B Eric Karros	200.00	90.00
❑ CS6	Derek Jeter A Eric Karros	500.00	220.00
❑ CS7	Travis Lee B Jose Cruz Jr.	200.00	90.00
❑ CS8	Travis Lee C Mark Kotsay	100.00	45.00
❑ CS9	Travis Lee A Paul Konerko	400.00	180.00
❑ CS10	Jose Cruz Jr. A Mark Kotsay	250.00	110.00
❑ CS11	Jose Cruz Jr. C Paul Konerko	80.00	36.00
❑ CS12	Mark Kotsay B Paul Konerko	80.00	36.00
❑ CS13	Tony Gwynn A Larry Walker	600.00	275.00
❑ CS14	Tony Gwynn C Mark Grudzielanek	120.00	55.00
❑ CS15	Tony Gwynn B Andres Galarraga	250.00	110.00
❑ CS16	Larry Walker B Mark Grudzielanek	100.00	45.00
❑ CS17	Larry Walker C Andres Galarraga	80.00	36.00
❑ CS18	Mark Grudzielanek A Andres Galarraga	150.00	70.00
❑ CS19	Sandy Alomar A Roberto Alomar	500.00	220.00
❑ CS20	Sandy Alomar C Andy Pettitte	50.00	22.00
❑ CS21	Sandy Alomar B Tino Martinez	80.00	36.00
❑ CS22	Roberto Alomar B Andy Pettitte	120.00	55.00
❑ CS23	Roberto Alomar C Tino Martinez	60.00	27.00
❑ CS24	Andy Pettitte A Tino Martinez	250.00	110.00
❑ CS25	Tony Clark A Todd Hundley	150.00	70.00
❑ CS26	Tony Clark B Tim Salmon	100.00	45.00
❑ CS27	Tony Clark C Robin Ventura	50.00	22.00
❑ CS28	Todd Hundley C Tim Salmon	50.00	22.00
❑ CS29	Todd Hundley B Robin Ventura	50.00	22.00
❑ CS30	Tim Salmon A Robin Ventura	200.00	90.00
❑ CS31	Roger Clemens B Randy Johnson	250.00	110.00

- ❑ CS32 Roger Clemens A.. 500.00 220.00
  Jaret Wright
- ❑ CS33 Roger Clemens C.. 100.00 45.00
  Matt Morris
- ❑ CS34 Randy Johnson C.... 80.00 36.00
  Jaret Wright
- ❑ CS35 Randy Johnson A.. 200.00 90.00
  Matt Morris
- ❑ CS36 Jaret Wright B 100.00 45.00
  Matt Morris

1998 Stadium Club In The Wings

	MINT	NRMT
COMPLETE SET (15)	60.00	27.00
COMMON CARD (W1-W15)	2.00	.90

- ❑ W1 Juan Encarnacion 3.00 1.35
- ❑ W2 Brad Fullmer 3.00 1.35
- ❑ W3 Ben Grieve..................... 15.00 6.75
- ❑ W4 Todd Helton 10.00 4.50
- ❑ W5 Richard Hidalgo 3.00 1.35
- ❑ W6 Russ Johnson .... 2.00 .90
- ❑ W7 Paul Konerko 8.00 3.60
- ❑ W8 Mark Kotsay.................. 5.00 2.20
- ❑ W9 Derrek Lee..................... 3.00 1.35
- ❑ W10 Travis Lee 15.00 6.75
- ❑ W11 Eli Marrero.................. 3.00 1.35
- ❑ W12 David Ortiz.................. 3.00 1.35
- ❑ W13 Randall Simon 3.00 1.35
- ❑ W14 Shannon Stewart 3.00 1.35
- ❑ W15 Fernando Tatis............ 3.00 1.35

1998 Stadium Club Never Compromise

	MINT	NRMT
COMPLETE SET (20)	100.00	45.00
COMMON CARD (NC1-NC20)	2.00	.90

- ❑ NC1 Cal Ripken 12.00 5.50
- ❑ NC2 Ivan Rodriguez............ 4.00 1.80
- ❑ NC3 Ken Griffey Jr. 15.00 6.75
- ❑ NC4 Frank Thomas 10.00 4.50
- ❑ NC5 Tony Gwynn................ 8.00 3.60
- ❑ NC6 Mike Piazza 10.00 4.50
- ❑ NC7 Randy Johnson 3.00 1.35
- ❑ NC8 Greg Maddux 10.00 4.50
- ❑ NC9 Roger Clemens 6.00 2.70
- ❑ NC10 Derek Jeter 8.00 3.60
- ❑ NC11 Chipper Jones 8.00 3.60
- ❑ NC12 Barry Bonds 4.00 1.80
- ❑ NC13 Larry Walker.............. 3.00 1.35
- ❑ NC14 Jeff Bagwell 5.00 2.20
- ❑ NC15 Barry Larkin .... 2.00 .90
- ❑ NC16 Ken Caminiti............... 2.00 .90
- ❑ NC17 Mark McGwire 20.00 9.00
- ❑ NC18 Manny Ramirez 3.00 1.35
- ❑ NC19 Tim Salmon 3.00 1.35
- ❑ NC20 Paul Molitor 3.00 1.35

1998 Stadium Club Playing With Passion

	MINT	NRMT
COMPLETE SET (10)	30.00	13.50
COMMON CARD (P1-P10)	1.25	.55

- ❑ P1 Bernie Williams.............. 2.00 .90
- ❑ P2 Jim Edmonds .... 1.25 .55
- ❑ P3 Chipper Jones............... 5.00 2.20
- ❑ P4 Cal Ripken 8.00 3.60
- ❑ P5 Craig Biggio .... 2.00 .90
- ❑ P6 Juan Gonzalez 5.00 2.20
- ❑ P7 Alex Rodriguez 6.00 2.70
- ❑ P8 Tino Martinez .... 2.00 .90
- ❑ P9 Mike Piazza 6.00 2.70
- ❑ P10 Ken Griffey Jr............. 10.00 4.50

1998 Stadium Club Royal Court

	MINT	NRMT
COMPLETE SET (15)	200.00	90.00
COMMON CARD (RC1-RC15)	4.00	1.80

- ❑ RC1 Ken Griffey Jr. 30.00 13.50
- ❑ RC2 Frank Thomas 20.00 9.00
- ❑ RC3 Mike Piazza 20.00 9.00
- ❑ RC4 Chipper Jones 15.00 6.75
- ❑ RC5 Mark McGwire 40.00 18.00
- ❑ RC6 Cal Ripken 20.00 9.00
- ❑ RC7 Jeff Bagwell 10.00 4.50
- ❑ RC8 Barry Bonds 8.00 3.60
- ❑ RC9 Juan Gonzalez 15.00 6.75
- ❑ RC10 Alex Rodriguez........ 20.00 9.00
- ❑ RC11 Travis Lee 10.00 4.50
- ❑ RC12 Paul Konerko 6.00 2.70
- ❑ RC13 Todd Helton 6.00 2.70
- ❑ RC14 Ben Grieve.............. 10.00 4.50
- ❑ RC15 Mark Kotsay 4.00 1.80

1998 Stadium Club Triumvirate Luminous

	MINT	NRMT
COMPLETE SET (54)	1000.00	450.00
COMPLETE SERIES 1 (24)	400.00	180.00
COMPLETE SERIES 2 (30)	600.00	275.00
COMMON CARD (T1A-T18C)	5.00	2.20

- ❑ T1A Chipper Jones 30.00 13.50
- ❑ T1B Andruw Jones........... 12.00 5.50
- ❑ T1C Kenny Lofton 12.00 5.50
- ❑ T2A Derek Jeter................ 30.00 13.50
- ❑ T2B Bernie Williams.......... 12.00 5.50
- ❑ T2C Tino Martinez 12.00 5.50
- ❑ T3A Jay Buhner 5.00 2.20
- ❑ T3B Edgar Martinez 5.00 2.20
- ❑ T3C Ken Griffey Jr. 60.00 27.00
- ❑ T4A Albert Belle 15.00 6.75
- ❑ T4B Robin Ventura.............. 5.00 2.20
- ❑ T4C Frank Thomas 40.00 18.00
- ❑ T5A Brady Anderson 5.00 2.20
- ❑ T5B Cal Ripken 50.00 22.00
- ❑ T5C Rafael Palmeiro 8.00 3.60
- ❑ T6A Mike Piazza 40.00 18.00
- ❑ T6B Raul Mondesi 8.00 3.60
- ❑ T6C Eric Karros 5.00 2.20
- ❑ T7A Vinny Castilla 8.00 3.60
- ❑ T7B Andres Galarraga...... 12.00 5.50
- ❑ T7C Larry Walker............. 12.00 5.50
- ❑ T8A Jim Thome 12.00 5.50
- ❑ T8B Manny Ramirez 12.00 5.50
- ❑ T8C David Justice 12.00 5.50
- ❑ T9A Mike Mussina 12.00 5.50
- ❑ T9B Greg Maddux 40.00 18.00
- ❑ T9C Randy Johnson 12.00 5.50
- ❑ T10A Mike Piazza 40.00 18.00
- ❑ T10B Sandy Alomar........... 5.00 2.20
- ❑ T10C Ivan Rodriguez 15.00 6.75
- ❑ T11A Mark McGwire 80.00 36.00
- ❑ T11B Tino Martinez 12.00 5.50
- ❑ T11C Frank Thomas 40.00 18.00
- ❑ T12A Roberto Alomar 12.00 5.50
- ❑ T12B Chuck Knoblauch 12.00 5.50
- ❑ T12C Craig Biggio 12.00 5.50
- ❑ T13A Cal Ripken 50.00 22.00
- ❑ T13B Chipper Jones 30.00 13.50
- ❑ T13C Ken Caminiti............. 8.00 3.60
- ❑ T14A Derek Jeter............. 25.00 11.00
- ❑ T14B Nomar Garciaparra.. 40.00 18.00
- ❑ T14C Alex Rodriguez........ 40.00 18.00
- ❑ T15A Barry Bonds 15.00 6.75
- ❑ T15B David Justice 12.00 5.50
- ❑ T15C Albert Belle 12.00 5.50
- ❑ T16A Bernie Williams........ 12.00 5.50
- ❑ T16B Ken Griffey Jr........... 60.00 27.00
- ❑ T16C Ray Lankford 5.00 2.20
- ❑ T17A Tim Salmon 12.00 5.50
- ❑ T17B Larry Walker........... 12.00 5.50
- ❑ T17C Tony Gwynn 25.00 11.00
- ❑ T18A Paul Molitor............. 12.00 5.50
- ❑ T18B Edgar Martinez 5.00 2.20
- ❑ T18C Juan Gonzalez 30.00 13.50

1991 Studio Previews

	MINT	NRMT
COMPLETE SET (18)	20.00	9.00
COMMON CARD (1-17)	1.00	.45

	MINT	NRMT
❑ 1 Juan Bell	1.00	.45
❑ 2 Roger Clemens	10.00	4.50
❑ 3 Dave Parker	2.00	.90
❑ 4 Tim Raines	2.00	.90
❑ 5 Kevin Seitzer	1.00	.45
❑ 6 Ted Higuera	1.00	.45
❑ 7 Bernie Williams	8.00	3.60
❑ 8 Harold Baines	2.00	.90
❑ 9 Gary Pettis	1.00	.45
❑ 10 Dave Justice	5.00	2.20
❑ 11 Eric Davis	2.00	.90
❑ 12 Andujar Cedeno	1.00	.45
❑ 13 Tom Foley	1.00	.45
❑ 14 Dwight Gooden	2.00	.90
❑ 15 Doug Drabek	1.00	.45
❑ 16 Steve Decker	1.00	.45
❑ 17 Joe Torre MG	2.00	.90
❑ NNO Title card	1.00	.45

1991 Studio

	MINT	NRMT
COMPLETE SET (264)	15.00	6.75
COMMON CARD (1-263)	.10	.05

	MINT	NRMT
❑ 1 Glenn Davis	.10	.05
❑ 2 Dwight Evans	.20	.09
❑ 3 Leo Gomez	.10	.05
❑ 4 Chris Hoiles	.10	.05
❑ 5 Sam Horn	.10	.05
❑ 6 Ben McDonald	.10	.05
❑ 7 Randy Milligan	.10	.05
❑ 8 Gregg Olson	.10	.05
❑ 9 Cal Ripken	1.50	.70
❑ 10 David Segui	.20	.09
❑ 11 Wade Boggs	.40	.18
❑ 12 Ellis Burks	.20	.09
❑ 13 Jack Clark	.20	.09
❑ 14 Roger Clemens	.75	.35
❑ 15 Mike Greenwell	.10	.05
❑ 16 Tim Naehring	.20	.09
❑ 17 Tony Pena	.10	.05
❑ 18 Phil Plantier	.10	.05
❑ 19 Jeff Reardon	.20	.09
❑ 20 Mo Vaughn	.75	.35
❑ 21 Jimmy Reese CO	.20	.09
❑ 22 Jim Abbott UER (Born in 1967, not 1969)	.20	.09
❑ 23 Bert Blyleven	.20	.09
❑ 24 Chuck Finley	.20	.09
❑ 25 Gary Gaetti	.20	.09
❑ 26 Wally Joyner	.20	.09
❑ 27 Mark Langston	.10	.05
❑ 28 Kirk McCaskill	.10	.05
❑ 29 Lance Parrish	.10	.05
❑ 30 Dave Winfield	.40	.18
❑ 31 Alex Fernandez	.20	.09
❑ 32 Carlton Fisk	.40	.18
❑ 33 Scott Fletcher	.10	.05
❑ 34 Greg Hibbard	.10	.05
❑ 35 Charlie Hough	.20	.09
❑ 36 Jack McDowell	.10	.05
❑ 37 Tim Raines	.20	.09
❑ 38 Sammy Sosa	2.00	.90
❑ 39 Bobby Thigpen	.10	.05
❑ 40 Frank Thomas	2.00	.90
❑ 41 Sandy Alomar Jr.	.20	.09
❑ 42 John Farrell	.10	.05
❑ 43 Glenallen Hill	.10	.05
❑ 44 Brook Jacoby	.10	.05
❑ 45 Chris James	.10	.05
❑ 46 Doug Jones	.10	.05
❑ 47 Eric King	.10	.05
❑ 48 Mark Lewis	.10	.05
❑ 49 Greg Swindell UER (Photo actually Turner Ward)	.10	.05
❑ 50 Mark Whiten	.10	.05
❑ 51 Milt Cuyler	.10	.05
❑ 52 Rob Deer	.10	.05
❑ 53 Cecil Fielder	.20	.09
❑ 54 Travis Fryman	.40	.18
❑ 55 Bill Gullickson	.10	.05
❑ 56 Lloyd Moseby	.10	.05
❑ 57 Frank Tanana	.10	.05
❑ 58 Mickey Tettleton	.20	.09
❑ 59 Alan Trammell	.30	.14
❑ 60 Lou Whitaker	.20	.09
❑ 61 Mike Boddicker	.10	.05
❑ 62 George Brett	.75	.35
❑ 63 Jeff Conine	.50	.23
❑ 64 Warren Cromartie	.10	.05
❑ 65 Storm Davis	.10	.05
❑ 66 Kirk Gibson	.20	.09
❑ 67 Mark Gubicza	.10	.05
❑ 68 Brian McRae	.40	.18
❑ 69 Bret Saberhagen	.20	.09
❑ 70 Kurt Stillwell	.10	.05
❑ 71 Tim McIntosh	.10	.05
❑ 72 Candy Maldonado	.10	.05
❑ 73 Paul Molitor	.40	.18
❑ 74 Willie Randolph	.20	.09
❑ 75 Ron Robinson	.10	.05
❑ 76 Gary Sheffield	.40	.18
❑ 77 Franklin Stubbs	.10	.05
❑ 78 B.J. Surhoff	.20	.09
❑ 79 Greg Vaughn	.40	.18
❑ 80 Robin Yount	.40	.18
❑ 81 Rick Aguilera	.20	.09
❑ 82 Steve Bedrosian	.10	.05
❑ 83 Scott Erickson	.20	.09
❑ 84 Greg Gagne	.10	.05
❑ 85 Dan Gladden	.10	.05
❑ 86 Brian Harper	.10	.05
❑ 87 Kent Hrbek	.20	.09
❑ 88 Shane Mack	.10	.05
❑ 89 Jack Morris	.20	.09
❑ 90 Kirby Puckett	.60	.25
❑ 91 Jesse Barfield	.10	.05
❑ 92 Steve Farr	.10	.05
❑ 93 Steve Howe	.10	.05
❑ 94 Roberto Kelly	.10	.05
❑ 95 Tim Leary	.10	.05
❑ 96 Kevin Maas	.10	.05
❑ 97 Don Mattingly	.60	.25
❑ 98 Hensley Meulens	.10	.05
❑ 99 Scott Sanderson	.10	.05
❑ 100 Steve Sax	.10	.05
❑ 101 Jose Canseco	.40	.18
❑ 102 Dennis Eckersley	.20	.09
❑ 103 Dave Henderson	.10	.05
❑ 104 Rickey Henderson	.40	.18
❑ 105 Rick Honeycutt	.10	.05
❑ 106 Mark McGwire	2.00	.90
❑ 107 Dave Stewart UER (No-hitter against Toronto& not Texas)	.10	.05
❑ 108 Eric Show	.10	.05
❑ 109 Todd Van Poppel	.10	.05
❑ 110 Bob Welch	.10	.05
❑ 111 Alvin Davis	.10	.05
❑ 112 Ken Griffey Jr.	3.00	1.35
❑ 113 Ken Griffey Sr.	.10	.05
❑ 114 Erik Hanson UER (Misspelled Eric)	.10	.05
❑ 115 Brian Holman	.10	.05
❑ 116 Randy Johnson	.50	.23
❑ 117 Edgar Martinez	.40	.18
❑ 118 Tino Martinez	.40	.18
❑ 119 Harold Reynolds	.10	.05
❑ 120 David Valle	.10	.05
❑ 121 Kevin Belcher	.10	.05
❑ 122 Scott Chiamparino	.10	.05
❑ 123 Julio Franco	.10	.05
❑ 124 Juan Gonzalez	1.50	.70
❑ 125 Rich Gossage	.20	.09
❑ 126 Jeff Kunkel	.10	.05
❑ 127 Rafael Palmeiro	.40	.18
❑ 128 Nolan Ryan	1.50	.70
❑ 129 Ruben Sierra	.10	.05
❑ 130 Bobby Witt	.10	.05
❑ 131 Roberto Alomar	.40	.18
❑ 132 Tom Candiotti	.10	.05
❑ 133 Joe Carter	.20	.09
❑ 134 Ken Dayley	.10	.05
❑ 135 Kelly Gruber	.10	.05
❑ 136 John Olerud	.20	.09
❑ 137 Dave Stieb	.20	.09
❑ 138 Turner Ward	.10	.05
❑ 139 Devon White	.10	.05
❑ 140 Mookie Wilson	.20	.09
❑ 141 Steve Avery	.10	.05
❑ 142 Sid Bream	.10	.05
❑ 143 Nick Esasky UER (Homers abbreviated RH)	.10	.05
❑ 144 Ron Gant	.20	.09
❑ 145 Tom Glavine	.40	.18
❑ 146 David Justice	.50	.23
❑ 147 Kelly Mann	.10	.05
❑ 148 Terry Pendleton	.20	.09
❑ 149 John Smoltz	.40	.18
❑ 150 Jeff Treadway	.10	.05
❑ 151 George Bell	.10	.05
❑ 152 Shawn Boskie	.10	.05
❑ 153 Andre Dawson	.40	.18
❑ 154 Lance Dickson	.10	.05
❑ 155 Shawon Dunston	.10	.05
❑ 156 Joe Girardi	.20	.09
❑ 157 Mark Grace	.40	.18
❑ 158 Ryne Sandberg	.50	.23
❑ 159 Gary Scott	.10	.05
❑ 160 Dave Smith	.10	.05
❑ 161 Tom Browning	.10	.05
❑ 162 Eric Davis	.20	.09
❑ 163 Rob Dibble	.10	.05
❑ 164 Mariano Duncan	.10	.05
❑ 165 Chris Hammond	.10	.05
❑ 166 Billy Hatcher	.10	.05
❑ 167 Barry Larkin	.40	.18
❑ 168 Hal Morris	.10	.05
❑ 169 Paul O'Neill	.20	.09
❑ 170 Chris Sabo	.10	.05
❑ 171 Eric Anthony	.10	.05
❑ 172 Jeff Bagwell	2.50	1.10
❑ 173 Craig Biggio	.40	.18
❑ 174 Ken Caminiti	.40	.18
❑ 175 Jim Deshaies	.10	.05
❑ 176 Steve Finley	.40	.18
❑ 177 Pete Harnisch	.10	.05
❑ 178 Darryl Kile	.40	.18
❑ 179 Curt Schilling	.40	.18
❑ 180 Mike Scott	.10	.05
❑ 181 Brett Butler	.20	.09
❑ 182 Gary Carter	.40	.18
❑ 183 Orel Hershiser	.20	.09

	Card	Mint	NrMt
❑	184 Ramon Martinez	.20	.09
❑	185 Eddie Murray	.40	.18
❑	186 Jose Offerman	.10	.05
❑	187 Bob Ojeda	.10	.05
❑	188 Juan Samuel	.10	.05
❑	189 Mike Scioscia	.10	.05
❑	190 Darryl Strawberry	.20	.09
❑	191 Moises Alou	.40	.18
❑	192 Brian Barnes	.10	.05
❑	193 Oil Can Boyd	.10	.05
❑	194 Ivan Calderon	.10	.05
❑	195 Delino DeShields	.20	.09
❑	196 Mike Fitzgerald	.10	.05
❑	197 Andres Galarraga	.40	.18
❑	198 Marquis Grissom	.40	.18
❑	199 Bill Sampen	.10	.05
❑	200 Tim Wallach	.10	.05
❑	201 Daryl Boston	.10	.05
❑	202 Vince Coleman	.10	.05
❑	203 John Franco	.20	.09
❑	204 Dwight Gooden	.20	.09
❑	205 Tom Herr	.10	.05
❑	206 Gregg Jefferies	.10	.05
❑	207 Howard Johnson	.10	.05
❑	208 Dave Magadan UER (Born 1862& should be 1962)	.10	.05
❑	209 Kevin McReynolds	.10	.05
❑	210 Frank Viola	.10	.05
❑	211 Wes Chamberlain	.10	.05
❑	212 Darren Daulton	.20	.09
❑	213 Len Dykstra	.20	.09
❑	214 Charlie Hayes	.10	.05
❑	215 Ricky Jordan	.10	.05
❑	216 Steve Lake (Pictured with parrot on his shoulder)	.20	.09
❑	217 Roger McDowell	.10	.05
❑	218 Mickey Morandini	.10	.05
❑	219 Terry Mulholland	.10	.05
❑	220 Dale Murphy	.40	.18
❑	221 Jay Bell	.20	.09
❑	222 Barry Bonds	.50	.23
❑	223 Bobby Bonilla	.20	.09
❑	224 Doug Drabek	.10	.05
❑	225 Bill Landrum	.10	.05
❑	226 Mike LaValliere	.10	.05
❑	227 Jose Lind	.10	.05
❑	228 Don Slaught	.10	.05
❑	229 John Smiley	.10	.05
❑	230 Andy Van Slyke	.20	.09
❑	231 Bernard Gilkey	.20	.09
❑	232 Pedro Guerrero	.10	.05
❑	233 Rex Hudler	.10	.05
❑	234 Ray Lankford	.40	.18
❑	235 Joe Magrane	.10	.05
❑	236 Jose Oquendo	.10	.05
❑	237 Lee Smith	.20	.09
❑	238 Ozzie Smith	.50	.23
❑	239 Milt Thompson	.10	.05
❑	240 Todd Zeile	.20	.09
❑	241 Larry Andersen	.10	.05
❑	242 Andy Benes	.20	.09
❑	243 Paul Faries	.10	.05
❑	244 Tony Fernandez	.10	.05
❑	245 Tony Gwynn	1.00	.45
❑	246 Atlee Hammaker	.10	.05
❑	247 Fred McGriff	.40	.18
❑	248 Bip Roberts	.10	.05
❑	249 Bentio Santiago	.10	.05
❑	250 Ed Whitson	.10	.05
❑	251 Dave Anderson	.10	.05
❑	252 Mike Benjamin	.10	.05
❑	253 John Burkett UER (Front photo actually Trevor Wilson)	.10	.05
❑	254 Will Clark	.40	.18
❑	255 Scott Garrelts	.10	.05
❑	256 Willie McGee	.20	.09
❑	257 Kevin Mitchell	.10	.05
❑	258 Dave Righetti	.10	.05
❑	259 Matt Williams	.40	.18
❑	260 Bud Black Steve Decker	.10	.05
❑	261 Sparky Anderson MG CL	.20	.09
❑	262 Tom Lasorda MG CL	.30	.14
❑	263 Tony LaRussa MG CL	.20	.09
❑	NNO Title Card	.10	.05

1992 Studio

	MINT	NRMT
COMPLETE SET (264)	15.00	6.75
COMMON CARD (1-264)	.05	.02

	Card	Mint	NrMt
❑	1 Steve Avery	.05	.02
❑	2 Sid Bream	.05	.02
❑	3 Ron Gant	.10	.05
❑	4 Tom Glavine	.20	.09
❑	5 David Justice	.30	.14
❑	6 Mark Lemke	.05	.02
❑	7 Greg Olson	.05	.02
❑	8 Terry Pendleton	.05	.02
❑	9 Deion Sanders	.30	.14
❑	10 John Smoltz	.20	.09
❑	11 Doug Dascenzo	.05	.02
❑	12 Andre Dawson	.20	.09
❑	13 Joe Girardi	.10	.05
❑	14 Mark Grace	.20	.09
❑	15 Greg Maddux	1.00	.45
❑	16 Chuck McElroy	.05	.02
❑	17 Mike Morgan	.05	.02
❑	18 Ryne Sandberg	.40	.18
❑	19 Gary Scott	.05	.02
❑	20 Sammy Sosa	.75	.35
❑	21 Norm Charlton	.05	.02
❑	22 Rob Dibble	.05	.02
❑	23 Barry Larkin	.20	.09
❑	24 Hal Morris	.05	.02
❑	25 Paul O'Neill	.10	.05
❑	26 Jose Rijo	.05	.02
❑	27 Bip Roberts	.05	.02
❑	28 Chris Sabo	.05	.02
❑	29 Reggie Sanders	.05	.02
❑	30 Greg Swindell	.05	.02
❑	31 Jeff Bagwell	.75	.35
❑	32 Craig Biggio	.30	.14
❑	33 Ken Caminiti	.20	.09
❑	34 Andujar Cedeno	.05	.02
❑	35 Steve Finley	.10	.05
❑	36 Pete Harnisch	.05	.02
❑	37 Butch Henry	.05	.02
❑	38 Doug Jones	.05	.02
❑	39 Darryl Kile	.10	.05
❑	40 Eddie Taubensee	.10	.05
❑	41 Brett Butler	.10	.05
❑	42 Tom Candiotti	.05	.02
❑	43 Eric Davis	.10	.05
❑	44 Orel Hershiser	.10	.05
❑	45 Eric Karros	.30	.14
❑	46 Ramon Martinez	.10	.05
❑	47 Jose Offerman	.05	.02
❑	48 Mike Scioscia	.05	.02
❑	49 Mike Sharperson	.05	.02
❑	50 Darryl Strawberry	.10	.05
❑	51 Bret Barberie	.05	.02
❑	52 Ivan Calderon	.05	.02
❑	53 Gary Carter	.30	.14
❑	54 Delino DeShields	.10	.05
❑	55 Marquis Grissom	.10	.05
❑	56 Ken Hill	.05	.02
❑	57 Dennis Martinez	.10	.05
❑	58 Spike Owen	.05	.02
❑	59 Larry Walker	.30	.14
❑	60 Tim Wallach	.05	.02
❑	61 Bobby Bonilla	.10	.05
❑	62 Tim Burke	.05	.02
❑	63 Vince Coleman	.05	.02
❑	64 John Franco	.10	.05
❑	65 Dwight Gooden	.10	.05
❑	66 Todd Hundley	.10	.05
❑	67 Howard Johnson	.05	.02
❑	68 Eddie Murray UER (He's not all-time switch homer leader, but he has most games with homers from both sides)	.30	.14
❑	69 Bret Saberhagen	.10	.05
❑	70 Anthony Young	.05	.02
❑	71 Kim Batiste	.05	.02
❑	72 Wes Chamberlain	.05	.02
❑	73 Darren Daulton	.10	.05
❑	74 Mariano Duncan	.05	.02
❑	75 Len Dykstra	.10	.05
❑	76 John Kruk	.10	.05
❑	77 Mickey Morandini	.05	.02
❑	78 Terry Mulholland	.05	.02
❑	79 Dale Murphy	.30	.14
❑	80 Mitch Williams	.05	.02
❑	81 Jay Bell	.10	.05
❑	82 Barry Bonds	.40	.18
❑	83 Steve Buechele	.05	.02
❑	84 Doug Drabek	.05	.02
❑	85 Mike LaValliere	.05	.02
❑	86 Jose Lind	.05	.02
❑	87 Denny Neagle	.20	.09
❑	88 Randy Tomlin	.05	.02
❑	89 Andy Van Slyke	.10	.05
❑	90 Gary Varsho	.05	.02
❑	91 Pedro Guerrero	.05	.02
❑	92 Rex Hudler	.05	.02
❑	93 Brian Jordan	.60	.25
❑	94 Felix Jose	.05	.02
❑	95 Donovan Osborne	.05	.02
❑	96 Tom Pagnozzi	.05	.02
❑	97 Lee Smith	.10	.05
❑	98 Ozzie Smith	.40	.18
❑	99 Todd Worrell	.05	.02
❑	100 Todd Zeile	.05	.02
❑	101 Andy Benes	.10	.05
❑	102 Jerald Clark	.05	.02
❑	103 Tony Fernandez	.05	.02
❑	104 Tony Gwynn	.75	.35
❑	105 Greg W. Harris	.05	.02
❑	106 Fred McGriff	.20	.09
❑	107 Benito Santiago	.05	.02
❑	108 Gary Sheffield	.30	.14
❑	109 Kurt Stillwell	.05	.02
❑	110 Tim Teufel	.05	.02
❑	111 Kevin Bass	.05	.02
❑	112 Jeff Brantley	.05	.02
❑	113 John Burkett	.05	.02
❑	114 Will Clark	.30	.14
❑	115 Royce Clayton	.05	.02
❑	116 Mike Jackson	.10	.05
❑	117 Darren Lewis	.05	.02
❑	118 Bill Swift	.05	.02
❑	119 Robby Thompson	.05	.02
❑	120 Matt Williams	.20	.09
❑	121 Brady Anderson	.20	.09
❑	122 Glenn Davis	.05	.02
❑	123 Mike Devereaux	.05	.02
❑	124 Chris Hoiles	.05	.02
❑	125 Sam Horn	.05	.02
❑	126 Ben McDonald	.05	.02
❑	127 Mike Mussina	.50	.23
❑	128 Gregg Olson	.05	.02
❑	129 Cal Ripken Jr.	1.25	.55
❑	130 Rick Sutcliffe	.05	.02
❑	131 Wade Boggs	.30	.14
❑	132 Roger Clemens	.60	.25
❑	133 Greg A. Harris	.05	.02
❑	134 Tim Naehring	.10	.05
❑	135 Tony Pena	.05	.02
❑	136 Phil Plantier	.05	.02
❑	137 Jeff Reardon	.10	.05
❑	138 Jody Reed	.05	.02
❑	139 Mo Vaughn	.50	.23

	Card	MINT	NRMT
❑ 140	Frank Viola	.05	.02
❑ 141	Jim Abbott	.10	.05
❑ 142	Hubie Brooks	.05	.02
❑ 143	Chad Curtis	.30	.14
❑ 144	Gary DiSarcina	.05	.02
❑ 145	Chuck Finley	.10	.05
❑ 146	Bryan Harvey	.05	.02
❑ 147	Von Hayes	.05	.02
❑ 148	Mark Langston	.05	.02
❑ 149	Lance Parrish	.05	.02
❑ 150	Lee Stevens	.05	.02
❑ 151	George Bell	.05	.02
❑ 152	Alex Fernandez	.10	.05
❑ 153	Greg Hibbard	.05	.02
❑ 154	Lance Johnson	.05	.02
❑ 155	Kirk McCaskill	.05	.02
❑ 156	Tim Raines	.10	.05
❑ 157	Steve Sax	.05	.02
❑ 158	Bobby Thigpen	.05	.02
❑ 159	Frank Thomas	1.00	.45
❑ 160	Robin Ventura	.10	.05
❑ 161	Sandy Alomar Jr.	.10	.05
❑ 162	Jack Armstrong	.05	.02
❑ 163	Carlos Baerga	.05	.02
❑ 164	Albert Belle	.40	.18
❑ 165	Alex Cole	.05	.02
❑ 166	Glenallen Hill	.05	.02
❑ 167	Mark Lewis	.05	.02
❑ 168	Kenny Lofton	.60	.25
❑ 169	Paul Sorrento	.05	.02
❑ 170	Mark Whiten	.05	.02
❑ 171	Milt Cuyler	.05	.02
❑ 172	Rob Deer	.05	.02
❑ 173	Cecil Fielder	.10	.05
❑ 174	Travis Fryman	.10	.05
❑ 175	Mike Henneman	.05	.02
❑ 176	Tony Phillips	.05	.02
❑ 177	Frank Tanana	.05	.02
❑ 178	Mickey Tettleton	.05	.02
❑ 179	Alan Trammell	.20	.09
❑ 180	Lou Whitaker	.10	.05
❑ 181	George Brett	.60	.25
❑ 182	Tom Gordon	.10	.05
❑ 183	Mark Gubicza	.05	.02
❑ 184	Gregg Jefferies	.05	.02
❑ 185	Wally Joyner	.10	.05
❑ 186	Brent Mayne	.05	.02
❑ 187	Brian McRae	.10	.05
❑ 188	Kevin McReynolds	.05	.02
❑ 189	Keith Miller	.05	.02
❑ 190	Jeff Montgomery	.10	.05
❑ 191	Dante Bichette	.20	.09
❑ 192	Ricky Bones	.05	.02
❑ 193	Scott Fletcher	.05	.02
❑ 194	Paul Molitor	.30	.14
❑ 195	Jaime Navarro	.05	.02
❑ 196	Franklin Stubbs	.05	.02
❑ 197	B.J. Surhoff	.10	.05
❑ 198	Greg Vaughn	.10	.05
❑ 199	Bill Wegman	.05	.02
❑ 200	Robin Yount	.30	.14
❑ 201	Rick Aguilera	.10	.05
❑ 202	Scott Erickson	.10	.05
❑ 203	Greg Gagne	.05	.02
❑ 204	Brian Harper	.05	.02
❑ 205	Kent Hrbek	.10	.05
❑ 206	Scott Leius	.05	.02
❑ 207	Shane Mack	.05	.02
❑ 208	Pat Mahomes	.05	.02
❑ 209	Kirby Puckett	.50	.23
❑ 210	John Smiley	.05	.02
❑ 211	Mike Gallego	.05	.02
❑ 212	Charlie Hayes	.05	.02
❑ 213	Pat Kelly	.05	.02
❑ 214	Roberto Kelly	.05	.02
❑ 215	Kevin Maas	.05	.02
❑ 216	Don Mattingly	.50	.23
❑ 217	Matt Nokes	.05	.02
❑ 218	Melido Perez	.05	.02
❑ 219	Scott Sanderson	.05	.02
❑ 220	Danny Tartabull	.05	.02
❑ 221	Harold Baines	.10	.05
❑ 222	Jose Canseco	.30	.14
❑ 223	Dennis Eckersley	.10	.05
❑ 224	Dave Henderson	.05	.02
❑ 225	Carney Lansford	.10	.05
❑ 226	Mark McGwire	1.50	.70
❑ 227	Mike Moore	.05	.02
❑ 228	Randy Ready	.05	.02
❑ 229	Terry Steinbach	.10	.05
❑ 230	Dave Stewart	.10	.05
❑ 231	Jay Buhner	.20	.09
❑ 232	Ken Griffey Jr.	2.00	.90
❑ 233	Erik Hanson	.05	.02
❑ 234	Randy Johnson	.30	.14
❑ 235	Edgar Martinez	.20	.09
❑ 236	Tino Martinez	.30	.14
❑ 237	Kevin Mitchell	.10	.05
❑ 238	Pete O'Brien	.05	.02
❑ 239	Harold Reynolds	.05	.02
❑ 240	David Valle	.05	.02
❑ 241	Julio Franco	.05	.02
❑ 242	Juan Gonzalez	1.00	.45
❑ 243	Jose Guzman	.05	.02
❑ 244	Rafael Palmeiro	.20	.09
❑ 245	Dean Palmer	.10	.05
❑ 246	Ivan Rodriguez	.60	.25
❑ 247	Jeff Russell	.05	.02
❑ 248	Nolan Ryan	1.25	.55
❑ 249	Ruben Sierra	.05	.02
❑ 250	Dickie Thon	.05	.02
❑ 251	Roberto Alomar	.30	.14
❑ 252	Derek Bell	.10	.05
❑ 253	Pat Borders	.05	.02
❑ 254	Joe Carter	.10	.05
❑ 255	Kelly Gruber	.05	.02
❑ 256	Juan Guzman	.05	.02
❑ 257	Jack Morris	.10	.05
❑ 258	John Olerud	.10	.05
❑ 259	Devon White	.05	.02
❑ 260	Dave Winfield	.30	.14
❑ 261	Checklist	.05	.02
❑ 262	Checklist	.05	.02
❑ 263	Checklist	.05	.02
❑ 264	History Card	.05	.02

1992 Studio Heritage

	MINT	NRMT
COMPLETE SET (14)	25.00	11.00
COMP.FOIL SET (8)	15.00	6.75
COMP.JUMBO SET (6)	10.00	4.50
COMMON CARD (BC1-BC14)	.75	.35

	Card	MINT	NRMT
❑ BC1	Ryne Sandberg	2.00	.90
❑ BC2	Carlton Fisk	1.50	.70
❑ BC3	Wade Boggs	1.50	.70
❑ BC4	Jose Canseco	1.50	.70
❑ BC5	Don Mattingly	2.50	1.10
❑ BC6	Darryl Strawberry	1.00	.45
❑ BC7	Cal Ripken	6.00	2.70
❑ BC8	Will Clark	1.50	.70
❑ BC9	Andre Dawson	1.25	.55
❑ BC10	Andy Van Slyke	.75	.35
❑ BC11	Paul Molitor	1.50	.70
❑ BC12	Jeff Bagwell	4.00	1.80
❑ BC13	Darren Daulton	1.00	.45
❑ BC14	Kirby Puckett	2.50	1.10

1993 Studio

	MINT	NRMT
COMPLETE SET (220)	20.00	9.00
COMMON CARD (1-220)	.10	.05

	Card	MINT	NRMT
❑ 1	Dennis Eckersley	.25	.11
❑ 2	Chad Curtis	.25	.11
❑ 3	Eric Anthony	.10	.05
❑ 4	Roberto Alomar	.50	.23
❑ 5	Steve Avery	.10	.05
❑ 6	Cal Eldred	.10	.05
❑ 7	Bernard Gilkey	.10	.05
❑ 8	Steve Buechele	.10	.05
❑ 9	Brett Butler	.25	.11
❑ 10	Terry Mulholland	.10	.05
❑ 11	Moises Alou	.25	.11
❑ 12	Barry Bonds	.60	.25
❑ 13	Sandy Alomar Jr.	.25	.11
❑ 14	Chris Bosio	.10	.05
❑ 15	Scott Sanderson	.10	.05
❑ 16	Bobby Bonilla	.25	.11
❑ 17	Brady Anderson	.30	.14
❑ 18	Derek Bell	.25	.11
❑ 19	Wes Chamberlain	.10	.05
❑ 20	Jay Bell	.25	.11
❑ 21	Kevin Brown	.30	.14
❑ 22	Roger Clemens	1.00	.45
❑ 23	Roberto Kelly	.10	.05
❑ 24	Dante Bichette	.25	.11
❑ 25	George Brett	1.00	.45
❑ 26	Rob Deer	.10	.05
❑ 27	Brian Harper	.10	.05
❑ 28	George Bell	.10	.05
❑ 29	Jim Abbott	.25	.11
❑ 30	Dave Henderson	.10	.05
❑ 31	Wade Boggs	.50	.23
❑ 32	Chili Davis	.25	.11
❑ 33	Ellis Burks	.25	.11
❑ 34	Jeff Bagwell	.75	.35
❑ 35	Kent Hrbek	.25	.11
❑ 36	Pat Borders	.10	.05
❑ 37	Cecil Fielder	.25	.11
❑ 38	Sid Bream	.10	.05
❑ 39	Greg Gagne	.10	.05
❑ 40	Darryl Hamilton	.10	.05
❑ 41	Jerald Clark	.10	.05
❑ 42	Mark Grace	.30	.14
❑ 43	Barry Larkin	.30	.14
❑ 44	John Burkett	.10	.05
❑ 45	Scott Cooper	.10	.05
❑ 46	Mike Lansing	.25	.11
❑ 47	Jose Canseco	.50	.23
❑ 48	Will Clark	.50	.23
❑ 49	Carlos Garcia	.10	.05
❑ 50	Carlos Baerga	.10	.05
❑ 51	Darren Daulton	.25	.11
❑ 52	Jay Buhner	.30	.14
❑ 53	Andy Benes	.25	.11
❑ 54	Jeff Conine	.10	.05
❑ 55	Mike Devereaux	.10	.05
❑ 56	Vince Coleman	.10	.05
❑ 57	Terry Steinbach	.10	.05
❑ 58	J.T. Snow	.60	.25
❑ 59	Greg Swindell	.10	.05
❑ 60	Devon White	.10	.05
❑ 61	John Smoltz	.25	.11
❑ 62	Todd Zeile	.10	.05
❑ 63	Rick Wilkins	.10	.05
❑ 64	Tim Wallach	.10	.05
❑ 65	John Wetteland	.25	.11
❑ 66	Matt Williams	.30	.14

❑ 67 Paul Sorrento .10 .05
❑ 68 David Valle .10 .05
❑ 69 Walt Weiss .10 .05
❑ 70 John Franco .25 .11
❑ 71 Nolan Ryan 2.00 .90
❑ 72 Frank Viola .10 .05
❑ 73 Chris Sabo .10 .05
❑ 74 David Nied .10 .05
❑ 75 Kevin McReynolds .10 .05
❑ 76 Lou Whitaker .25 .11
❑ 77 Dave Winfield .30 .14
❑ 78 Robin Ventura .25 .11
❑ 79 Spike Owen .10 .05
❑ 80 Cal Ripken Jr. 2.00 .90
❑ 81 Dan Walters .10 .05
❑ 82 Mitch Williams .10 .05
❑ 83 Tim Wakefield .25 .11
❑ 84 Rickey Henderson .50 .23
❑ 85 Gary DiSarcina .10 .05
❑ 86 Craig Biggio .50 .23
❑ 87 Joe Carter .25 .11
❑ 88 Ron Gant .25 .11
❑ 89 John Jaha .10 .05
❑ 90 Gregg Jefferies .10 .05
❑ 91 Jose Guzman .10 .05
❑ 92 Eric Karros .30 .14
❑ 93 Wil Cordero .10 .05
❑ 94 Royce Clayton .10 .05
❑ 95 Albert Belle .60 .25
❑ 96 Ken Griffey Jr. 2.50 1.10
❑ 97 Orestes Destrade .10 .05
❑ 98 Tony Fernandez .10 .05
❑ 99 Leo Gomez .10 .05
❑ 100 Tony Gwynn 1.25 .55
❑ 101 Len Dykstra .25 .11
❑ 102 Jeff King .25 .11
❑ 103 Julio Franco .10 .05
❑ 104 Andre Dawson .30 .14
❑ 105 Randy Milligan .10 .05
❑ 106 Alex Cole .10 .05
❑ 107 Phil Hiatt .10 .05
❑ 108 Travis Fryman .25 .11
❑ 109 Chuck Knoblauch .50 .23
❑ 110 Bo Jackson .25 .11
❑ 111 Pat Kelly .10 .05
❑ 112 Bret Saberhagen .25 .11
❑ 113 Ruben Sierra .10 .05
❑ 114 Tim Salmon .50 .23
❑ 115 Doug Jones .10 .05
❑ 116 Ed Sprague .10 .05
❑ 117 Terry Pendleton .10 .05
❑ 118 Robin Yount .30 .14
❑ 119 Mark Whiten .10 .05
❑ 120 Checklist 1-110 .10 .05
❑ 121 Sammy Sosa 1.25 .55
❑ 122 Darryl Strawberry .25 .11
❑ 123 Larry Walker .50 .23
❑ 124 Robby Thompson .10 .05
❑ 125 Carlos Martinez .10 .05
❑ 126 Edgar Martinez .30 .14
❑ 127 Benito Santiago .10 .05
❑ 128 Howard Johnson .10 .05
❑ 129 Harold Reynolds .10 .05
❑ 130 Craig Shipley .10 .05
❑ 131 Curt Schilling .25 .11
❑ 132 Andy Van Slyke .25 .11
❑ 133 Ivan Rodriguez .60 .25
❑ 134 Mo Vaughn .60 .25
❑ 135 Bip Roberts .10 .05
❑ 136 Charlie Hayes .10 .05
❑ 137 Brian McRae .10 .05
❑ 138 Mickey Tettleton .10 .05
❑ 139 Frank Thomas 1.50 .70
❑ 140 Paul O'Neill .25 .11
❑ 141 Mark McGwire 2.50 1.10
❑ 142 Damion Easley .25 .11
❑ 143 Ken Caminiti .30 .14
❑ 144 Juan Guzman .10 .05
❑ 145 Tom Glavine .30 .14
❑ 146 Pat Listach .10 .05
❑ 147 Lee Smith .25 .11
❑ 148 Derrick May .10 .05
❑ 149 Ramon Martinez .25 .11
❑ 150 Delino DeShields .25 .11
❑ 151 Kirt Manwaring .10 .05
❑ 152 Reggie Jefferson .25 .11
❑ 153 Randy Johnson .50 .23
❑ 154 Dave Magadan .10 .05
❑ 155 Dwight Gooden .25 .11
❑ 156 Chris Hoiles .10 .05
❑ 157 Fred McGriff .30 .14
❑ 158 Dave Hollins .10 .05
❑ 159 Al Martin .10 .05
❑ 160 Juan Gonzalez 1.25 .55
❑ 161 Mike Greenwell .10 .05
❑ 162 Kevin Mitchell .25 .11
❑ 163 Andres Galarraga .50 .23
❑ 164 Wally Joyner .25 .11
❑ 165 Kirk Gibson .25 .11
❑ 166 Pedro Munoz .10 .05
❑ 167 Ozzie Guillen .10 .05
❑ 168 Jimmy Key .25 .11
❑ 169 Kevin Seitzer .10 .05
❑ 170 Luis Polonia .10 .05
❑ 171 Luis Gonzalez .10 .05
❑ 172 Paul Molitor .50 .23
❑ 173 David Justice .50 .23
❑ 174 B.J. Surhoff .25 .11
❑ 175 Ray Lankford .30 .14
❑ 176 Ryne Sandberg .60 .25
❑ 177 Jody Reed .10 .05
❑ 178 Marquis Grissom .25 .11
❑ 179 Willie McGee .25 .11
❑ 180 Kenny Lofton .50 .23
❑ 181 Junior Felix .10 .05
❑ 182 Jose Offerman .10 .05
❑ 183 John Kruk .25 .11
❑ 184 Orlando Merced .10 .05
❑ 185 Rafael Palmeiro .30 .14
❑ 186 Billy Hatcher .10 .05
❑ 187 Joe Oliver .10 .05
❑ 188 Joe Girardi .25 .11
❑ 189 Jose Lind .10 .05
❑ 190 Harold Baines .25 .11
❑ 191 Mike Pagliarulo .10 .05
❑ 192 Lance Johnson .10 .05
❑ 193 Don Mattingly .75 .35
❑ 194 Doug Drabek .10 .05
❑ 195 John Olerud .30 .14
❑ 196 Greg Maddux 1.50 .70
❑ 197 Greg Vaughn .25 .11
❑ 198 Tom Pagnozzi .10 .05
❑ 199 Willie Wilson .10 .05
❑ 200 Jack McDowell .10 .05
❑ 201 Mike Piazza 2.50 1.10
❑ 202 Mike Mussina .50 .23
❑ 203 Charles Nagy .25 .11
❑ 204 Tino Martinez .50 .23
❑ 205 Charlie Hough .25 .11
❑ 206 Todd Hundley .30 .14
❑ 207 Gary Sheffield .50 .23
❑ 208 Mickey Morandini .10 .05
❑ 209 Don Slaught .10 .05
❑ 210 Dean Palmer .25 .11
❑ 211 Jose Rijo .10 .05
❑ 212 Vinny Castilla .75 .35
❑ 213 Tony Phillips .10 .05
❑ 214 Kirby Puckett .75 .35
❑ 215 Tim Raines .25 .11
❑ 216 Otis Nixon .10 .05
❑ 217 Ozzie Smith .60 .25
❑ 218 Jose Vizcaino .10 .05
❑ 219 Randy Tomlin .10 .05
❑ 220 Checklist 111-220 .10 .05

1993 Studio Heritage

	MINT	NRMT
COMPLETE SET (12)	30.00	13.50
COMMON CARD (1-12)	1.00	.45

❑ 1 George Brett 6.00 2.70
❑ 2 Juan Gonzalez 8.00 3.60
❑ 3 Roger Clemens 6.00 2.70
❑ 4 Mark McGwire 15.00 6.75
❑ 5 Mark Grace 2.00 .90
❑ 6 Ozzie Smith 4.00 1.80
❑ 7 Barry Larkin 2.00 .90
❑ 8 Frank Thomas 10.00 4.50
❑ 9 Carlos Baerga 1.00 .45
❑ 10 Eric Karros 2.00 .90

❑ 11 J.T. Snow 1.50 .70
❑ 12 John Kruk 1.50 .70

1993 Studio Silhouettes

	MINT	NRMT
COMPLETE SET (10)	25.00	11.00
COMMON CARD (1-10)	.50	.23

❑ 1 Frank Thomas 5.00 2.20
❑ 2 Barry Bonds 2.00 .90
❑ 3 Jeff Bagwell 2.50 1.10
❑ 4 Juan Gonzalez 4.00 1.80
❑ 5 Travis Fryman .75 .35
❑ 6 J.T. Snow 1.00 .45
❑ 7 John Kruk .75 .35
❑ 8 Jeff Blauser .50 .23
❑ 9 Mike Piazza 8.00 3.60
❑ 10 Nolan Ryan 6.00 2.70

1993 Studio Superstars on Canvas

	MINT	NRMT
COMPLETE SET (10)	35.00	16.00
COMMON CARD (1-10)	1.50	.70

❑ 1 Ken Griffey Jr. 15.00 6.75
❑ 2 Jose Canseco 3.00 1.35
❑ 3 Mark McGwire 15.00 6.75
❑ 4 Mike Mussina 3.00 1.35
❑ 5 Joe Carter 1.50 .70
❑ 6 Frank Thomas 10.00 4.50

	MINT	NRMT
❑ 7 Darren Daulton	1.50	.70
❑ 8 Mark Grace	2.00	.90
❑ 9 Andres Galarraga	3.00	1.35
❑ 10 Barry Bonds	4.00	1.80

1993 Studio Thomas

	MINT	NRMT
COMPLETE SET (5)	30.00	13.50
COMMON THOMAS (1-5)	6.00	2.70
❑ 1 Frank Thomas Childhood	6.00	2.70
❑ 2 Frank Thomas Baseball Memories	6.00	2.70
❑ 3 Frank Thomas Family	6.00	2.70
❑ 4 Frank Thomas Performance	6.00	2.70
❑ 5 Frank Thomas Role Model	6.00	2.70

1994 Studio

	MINT	NRMT
COMPLETE SET (220)	15.00	6.75
COMMON CARD (1-220)	.15	.07
❑ 1 Dennis Eckersley	.30	.14
❑ 2 Brent Gates	.15	.07
❑ 3 Rickey Henderson	.60	.25
❑ 4 Mark McGwire	3.00	1.35
❑ 5 Troy Neel	.15	.07
❑ 6 Ruben Sierra	.15	.07
❑ 7 Terry Steinbach	.30	.14
❑ 8 Chad Curtis	.15	.07
❑ 9 Chili Davis	.30	.14
❑ 10 Gary DiSarcina	.15	.07
❑ 11 Damion Easley	.30	.14
❑ 12 Bo Jackson	.30	.14
❑ 13 Mark Langston	.15	.07
❑ 14 Eduardo Perez	.15	.07
❑ 15 Tim Salmon	.60	.25
❑ 16 Jeff Bagwell	1.00	.45
❑ 17 Craig Biggio	.60	.25
❑ 18 Ken Caminiti	.40	.18
❑ 19 Andujar Cedeno	.15	.07
❑ 20 Doug Drabek	.15	.07
❑ 21 Steve Finley	.30	.14
❑ 22 Luis Gonzalez	.15	.07
❑ 23 Darryl Kile	.30	.14
❑ 24 Roberto Alomar	.60	.25
❑ 25 Pat Borders	.15	.07
❑ 26 Joe Carter	.30	.14
❑ 27 Carlos Delgado	.40	.18
❑ 28 Pat Hentgen	.30	.14
❑ 29 Paul Molitor	.60	.25
❑ 30 John Olerud	.30	.14
❑ 31 Ed Sprague	.15	.07
❑ 32 Devon White	.30	.14
❑ 33 Steve Avery	.15	.07
❑ 34 Tom Glavine	.60	.25
❑ 35 David Justice	.60	.25
❑ 36 Roberto Kelly	.15	.07
❑ 37 Ryan Klesko	.30	.14
❑ 38 Javier Lopez	.40	.18
❑ 39 Greg Maddux	2.00	.90
❑ 40 Fred McGriff	.40	.18
❑ 41 Terry Pendleton	.15	.07
❑ 42 Ricky Bones	.15	.07
❑ 43 Darryl Hamilton	.15	.07
❑ 44 Brian Harper	.15	.07
❑ 45 John Jaha	.15	.07
❑ 46 Dave Nilsson	.15	.07
❑ 47 Kevin Seitzer	.15	.07
❑ 48 Greg Vaughn	.30	.14
❑ 49 Turner Ward	.15	.07
❑ 50 Bernard Gilkey	.15	.07
❑ 51 Gregg Jefferies	.15	.07
❑ 52 Ray Lankford	.30	.14
❑ 53 Tom Pagnozzi	.15	.07
❑ 54 Ozzie Smith	.75	.35
❑ 55 Bob Tewksbury	.15	.07
❑ 56 Mark Whiten	.15	.07
❑ 57 Todd Zeile	.15	.07
❑ 58 Steve Buechele	.15	.07
❑ 59 Shawon Dunston	.15	.07
❑ 60 Mark Grace	.40	.18
❑ 61 Derrick May	.15	.07
❑ 62 Karl Rhodes	.15	.07
❑ 63 Ryne Sandberg	.75	.35
❑ 64 Sammy Sosa	1.50	.70
❑ 65 Rick Wilkins	.15	.07
❑ 66 Brett Butler	.30	.14
❑ 67 Delino DeShields	.15	.07
❑ 68 Orel Hershiser	.30	.14
❑ 69 Eric Karros	.30	.14
❑ 70 Raul Mondesi	.60	.25
❑ 71 Jose Offerman	.15	.07
❑ 72 Mike Piazza	2.00	.90
❑ 73 Tim Wallach	.15	.07
❑ 74 Moises Alou	.40	.18
❑ 75 Sean Berry	.15	.07
❑ 76 Wil Cordero	.15	.07
❑ 77 Cliff Floyd	.30	.14
❑ 78 Marquis Grissom	.30	.14
❑ 79 Ken Hill	.15	.07
❑ 80 Larry Walker	.60	.25
❑ 81 John Wetteland	.30	.14
❑ 82 Rod Beck	.15	.07
❑ 83 Barry Bonds	.75	.35
❑ 84 Royce Clayton	.15	.07
❑ 85 Darren Lewis	.15	.07
❑ 86 Willie McGee	.30	.14
❑ 87 Bill Swift	.15	.07
❑ 88 Robby Thompson	.15	.07
❑ 89 Matt Williams	.40	.18
❑ 90 Sandy Alomar Jr.	.30	.14
❑ 91 Carlos Baerga	.30	.14
❑ 92 Albert Belle	.75	.35
❑ 93 Kenny Lofton	.60	.25
❑ 94 Eddie Murray	.60	.25
❑ 95 Manny Ramirez	.75	.35
❑ 96 Paul Sorrento	.15	.07
❑ 97 Jim Thome	.75	.35
❑ 98 Rich Amaral	.15	.07
❑ 99 Eric Anthony	.15	.07
❑ 100 Jay Buhner	.30	.14
❑ 101 Ken Griffey Jr.	3.00	1.35
❑ 102 Randy Johnson	.60	.25
❑ 103 Edgar Martinez	.30	.14
❑ 104 Tino Martinez	.60	.25
❑ 105 Kurt Abbott	.15	.07
❑ 106 Bret Barberie	.15	.07
❑ 107 Chuck Carr	.15	.07
❑ 108 Jeff Conine	.30	.14
❑ 109 Chris Hammond	.15	.07
❑ 110 Bryan Harvey	.15	.07
❑ 111 Benito Santiago	.15	.07
❑ 112 Gary Sheffield	.60	.25
❑ 113 Bobby Bonilla	.30	.14
❑ 114 Dwight Gooden	.30	.14
❑ 115 Todd Hundley	.30	.14
❑ 116 Bobby Jones	.15	.07
❑ 117 Jeff Kent	.30	.14
❑ 118 Kevin McReynolds	.15	.07
❑ 119 Bret Saberhagen	.30	.14
❑ 120 Ryan Thompson	.15	.07
❑ 121 Harold Baines	.30	.14
❑ 122 Mike Devereaux	.15	.07
❑ 123 Jeffrey Hammonds	.30	.14
❑ 124 Ben McDonald	.15	.07
❑ 125 Mike Mussina	.60	.25
❑ 126 Rafael Palmeiro	.40	.18
❑ 127 Cal Ripken Jr.	2.50	1.10
❑ 128 Lee Smith	.30	.14
❑ 129 Brad Ausmus	.15	.07
❑ 130 Derek Bell	.30	.14
❑ 131 Andy Benes	.30	.14
❑ 132 Tony Gwynn	1.50	.70
❑ 133 Trevor Hoffman	.30	.14
❑ 134 Scott Livingstone	.15	.07
❑ 135 Phil Plantier	.15	.07
❑ 136 Darren Daulton	.30	.14
❑ 137 Mariano Duncan	.15	.07
❑ 138 Lenny Dykstra	.30	.14
❑ 139 Dave Hollins	.15	.07
❑ 140 Pete Incaviglia	.15	.07
❑ 141 Danny Jackson	.15	.07
❑ 142 John Kruk	.30	.14
❑ 143 Kevin Stocker	.15	.07
❑ 144 Jay Bell	.30	.14
❑ 145 Carlos Garcia	.15	.07
❑ 146 Jeff King	.15	.07
❑ 147 Al Martin	.15	.07
❑ 148 Orlando Merced	.15	.07
❑ 149 Don Slaught	.15	.07
❑ 150 Andy Van Slyke	.30	.14
❑ 151 Kevin Brown	.30	.14
❑ 152 Jose Canseco	.60	.25
❑ 153 Will Clark	.60	.25
❑ 154 Juan Gonzalez	1.50	.70
❑ 155 David Hulse	.15	.07
❑ 156 Dean Palmer	.30	.14
❑ 157 Ivan Rodriguez	.75	.35
❑ 158 Kenny Rogers	.15	.07
❑ 159 Roger Clemens	1.25	.55
❑ 160 Scott Cooper	.15	.07
❑ 161 Andre Dawson	.40	.18
❑ 162 Mike Greenwell	.15	.07
❑ 163 Otis Nixon	.15	.07
❑ 164 Aaron Sele	.30	.14
❑ 165 John Valentin	.30	.14
❑ 166 Mo Vaughn	.75	.35
❑ 167 Bret Boone	.30	.14
❑ 168 Barry Larkin	.40	.18
❑ 169 Kevin Mitchell	.15	.07
❑ 170 Hal Morris	.15	.07
❑ 171 Jose Rijo	.15	.07
❑ 172 Deion Sanders	.30	.14
❑ 173 Reggie Sanders	.30	.14
❑ 174 John Smiley	.15	.07
❑ 175 Dante Bichette	.30	.14
❑ 176 Ellis Burks	.30	.14
❑ 177 Andres Galarraga	.60	.25
❑ 178 Joe Girardi	.15	.07
❑ 179 Charlie Hayes	.15	.07
❑ 180 Roberto Mejia	.15	.07
❑ 181 Walt Weiss	.15	.07
❑ 182 David Cone	.40	.18
❑ 183 Gary Gaetti	.30	.14
❑ 184 Greg Gagne	.15	.07
❑ 185 Felix Jose	.15	.07
❑ 186 Wally Joyner	.30	.14
❑ 187 Mike Macfarlane	.15	.07
❑ 188 Brian McRae	.15	.07
❑ 189 Eric Davis	.30	.14
❑ 190 Cecil Fielder	.30	.14
❑ 191 Travis Fryman	.30	.14
❑ 192 Tony Phillips	.15	.07
❑ 193 Mickey Tettleton	.15	.07

Card	MINT	NRMT
❑ 194 Alan Trammell	.40	.18
❑ 195 Lou Whitaker	.30	.14
❑ 196 Kent Hrbek	.30	.14
❑ 197 Chuck Knoblauch	.60	.25
❑ 198 Shane Mack	.15	.07
❑ 199 Pat Meares	.15	.07
❑ 200 Kirby Puckett	1.00	.45
❑ 201 Matt Walbeck	.15	.07
❑ 202 Dave Winfield	.60	.25
❑ 203 Wilson Alvarez	.30	.14
❑ 204 Alex Fernandez	.15	.07
❑ 205 Julio Franco	.15	.07
❑ 206 Ozzie Guillen	.15	.07
❑ 207 Jack McDowell	.15	.07
❑ 208 Tim Raines	.30	.14
❑ 209 Frank Thomas	2.00	.90
❑ 210 Robin Ventura	.30	.14
❑ 211 Jim Abbott	.30	.14
❑ 212 Wade Boggs	.60	.25
❑ 213 Pat Kelly	.15	.07
❑ 214 Jimmy Key	.30	.14
❑ 215 Don Mattingly	1.00	.45
❑ 216 Paul O'Neill	.30	.14
❑ 217 Mike Stanley	.15	.07
❑ 218 Danny Tartabull	.15	.07
❑ 219 Checklist	.15	.07
❑ 220 Checklist	.15	.07

1994 Studio Editor's Choice

	MINT	NRMT
COMPLETE SET (8)	40.00	18.00
COMMON CARD (1-8)	1.50	.70
❑ 1 Barry Bonds	3.00	1.35
❑ 2 Frank Thomas	10.00	4.50
❑ 3 Ken Griffey Jr.	15.00	6.75
❑ 4 Andres Galarraga	3.00	1.35
❑ 5 Juan Gonzalez	8.00	3.60
❑ 6 Tim Salmon	3.00	1.35
❑ 7 Paul O'Neill	1.50	.70
❑ 8 Mike Piazza	10.00	4.50

1994 Studio Heritage

	MINT	NRMT
COMPLETE SET (8)	15.00	6.75
COMMON CARD (1-8)	.50	.23
❑ 1 Barry Bonds	1.50	.70
❑ 2 Frank Thomas	5.00	2.20
❑ 3 Joe Carter	.75	.35
❑ 4 Don Mattingly	2.50	1.10
❑ 5 Ryne Sandberg	2.00	.90
❑ 6 Javier Lopez	1.00	.45
❑ 7 Gregg Jefferies	.50	.23
❑ 8 Mike Mussina	1.50	.70

1994 Studio Series Stars

	MINT	NRMT
COMPLETE SET (10)	150.00	70.00
COMMON CARD (1-10)	3.00	1.35
COMP.GOLD SET (10)	300.00	135.00

*GOLD: 1X TO 2X BASIC SERIES STARS
GOLD STATED ODDS 1:120
GOLD PRINT RUN 5000 SERIAL #'d SETS

Card	MINT	NRMT
❑ 1 Tony Gwynn	15.00	6.75
❑ 2 Barry Bonds	8.00	3.60
❑ 3 Frank Thomas	20.00	9.00
❑ 4 Ken Griffey Jr.	30.00	13.50
❑ 5 Joe Carter	3.00	1.35
❑ 6 Mike Piazza	20.00	9.00
❑ 7 Cal Ripken Jr.	25.00	11.00
❑ 8 Greg Maddux	20.00	9.00
❑ 9 Juan Gonzalez	15.00	6.75
❑ 10 Don Mattingly	10.00	4.50

1995 Studio

	MINT	NRMT
COMPLETE SET (200)	60.00	27.00
COMMON CARD (1-200)	.20	.09
❑ 1 Frank Thomas	2.50	1.10
❑ 2 Jeff Bagwell	1.25	.55
❑ 3 Don Mattingly	1.25	.55
❑ 4 Mike Piazza	2.50	1.10
❑ 5 Ken Griffey Jr.	4.00	1.80
❑ 6 Greg Maddux	2.50	1.10
❑ 7 Barry Bonds	1.00	.45
❑ 8 Cal Ripken Jr.	3.00	1.35
❑ 9 Jose Canseco	.75	.35
❑ 10 Paul Molitor	.75	.35
❑ 11 Kenny Lofton	.75	.35
❑ 12 Will Clark	.75	.35
❑ 13 Tim Salmon	.75	.35
❑ 14 Joe Carter	.40	.18
❑ 15 Albert Belle	1.00	.45
❑ 16 Roger Clemens	1.50	.70
❑ 17 Roberto Alomar	.75	.35
❑ 18 Alex Rodriguez	3.00	1.35
❑ 19 Raul Mondesi	.60	.25
❑ 20 Deion Sanders	.40	.18
❑ 21 Juan Gonzalez	2.00	.90
❑ 22 Kirby Puckett	1.25	.55
❑ 23 Fred McGriff	.60	.25
❑ 24 Matt Williams	.40	.18
❑ 25 Tony Gwynn	2.00	.90
❑ 26 Cliff Floyd	.40	.18
❑ 27 Travis Fryman	.40	.18
❑ 28 Shawn Green	.40	.18
❑ 29 Mike Mussina	.75	.35
❑ 30 Bob Hamelin	.20	.09
❑ 31 David Justice	.75	.35
❑ 32 Manny Ramirez	.75	.35
❑ 33 David Cone	.60	.25
❑ 34 Marquis Grissom	.40	.18
❑ 35 Moises Alou	.60	.25
❑ 36 Carlos Baerga	.40	.18
❑ 37 Barry Larkin	.60	.25
❑ 38 Robin Ventura	.40	.18
❑ 39 Mo Vaughn	1.00	.45
❑ 40 Jeffrey Hammonds	.40	.18
❑ 41 Ozzie Smith	1.00	.45
❑ 42 Andres Galarraga	.75	.35
❑ 43 Carlos Delgado	.40	.18
❑ 44 Lenny Dykstra	.40	.18
❑ 45 Cecil Fielder	.40	.18
❑ 46 Wade Boggs	.75	.35
❑ 47 Gregg Jefferies	.20	.09
❑ 48 Randy Johnson	.75	.35
❑ 49 Rafael Palmeiro	.60	.25
❑ 50 Craig Biggio	.75	.35
❑ 51 Steve Avery	.20	.09
❑ 52 Ricky Bottalico	.40	.18
❑ 53 Chris Gomez	.20	.09
❑ 54 Carlos Garcia	.20	.09
❑ 55 Brian Anderson	.40	.18
❑ 56 Wilson Alvarez	.40	.18
❑ 57 Roberto Kelly	.20	.09
❑ 58 Larry Walker	.75	.35
❑ 59 Dean Palmer	.40	.18
❑ 60 Rick Aguilera	.20	.09
❑ 61 Javier Lopez	.40	.18
❑ 62 Shawon Dunston	.20	.09
❑ 63 Wm. VanLandingham	.20	.09
❑ 64 Jeff Kent	.40	.18
❑ 65 David McCarty	.20	.09
❑ 66 Armando Benitez	.20	.09
❑ 67 Brett Butler	.40	.18
❑ 68 Bernard Gilkey	.20	.09
❑ 69 Joey Hamilton	.40	.18
❑ 70 Chad Curtis	.20	.09
❑ 71 Dante Bichette	.40	.18
❑ 72 Chuck Carr	.20	.09
❑ 73 Pedro Martinez	.75	.35
❑ 74 Ramon Martinez	.40	.18
❑ 75 Rondell White	.40	.18
❑ 76 Alex Fernandez	.20	.09
❑ 77 Dennis Martinez	.40	.18
❑ 78 Sammy Sosa	2.00	.90
❑ 79 Bernie Williams	.75	.35
❑ 80 Lou Whitaker	.40	.18
❑ 81 Kurt Abbott	.20	.09
❑ 82 Tino Martinez	.75	.35
❑ 83 Willie Greene	.40	.18
❑ 84 Garret Anderson	.40	.18
❑ 85 Jose Rijo	.20	.09
❑ 86 Jeff Montgomery	.20	.09
❑ 87 Mark Langston	.20	.09
❑ 88 Reggie Sanders	.40	.18
❑ 89 Rusty Greer	.75	.35
❑ 90 Delino DeShields	.20	.09
❑ 91 Jason Bere	.20	.09
❑ 92 Lee Smith	.40	.18
❑ 93 Devon White	.40	.18
❑ 94 John Wetteland	.40	.18
❑ 95 Luis Gonzalez	.20	.09
❑ 96 Greg Vaughn	.40	.18
❑ 97 Lance Johnson	.20	.09
❑ 98 Alan Trammell	.40	.18

❑ 99	Bret Saberhagen	.40	.18
❑ 100	Jack McDowell	.20	.09
❑ 101	Trevor Hoffman	.40	.18
❑ 102	Dave Nilsson	.20	.09
❑ 103	Bryan Harvey	.20	.09
❑ 104	Chuck Knoblauch	.75	.35
❑ 105	Bobby Bonilla	.40	.18
❑ 106	Hal Morris	.20	.09
❑ 107	Mark Whiten	.20	.09
❑ 108	Phil Plantier	.20	.09
❑ 109	Ryan Klesko	.40	.18
❑ 110	Greg Gagne	.20	.09
❑ 111	Ruben Sierra	.20	.09
❑ 112	J.R. Phillips	.20	.09
❑ 113	Terry Steinbach	.40	.18
❑ 114	Jay Buhner	.40	.18
❑ 115	Ken Caminiti	.60	.25
❑ 116	Gary DiSarcina	.20	.09
❑ 117	Ivan Rodriguez	1.00	.45
❑ 118	Bip Roberts	.20	.09
❑ 119	Jay Bell	.40	.18
❑ 120	Ken Hill	.20	.09
❑ 121	Mike Greenwell	.20	.09
❑ 122	Rick Wilkins	.20	.09
❑ 123	Rickey Henderson	.75	.35
❑ 124	Dave Hollins	.20	.09
❑ 125	Terry Pendleton	.20	.09
❑ 126	Rich Becker	.20	.09
❑ 127	Billy Ashley	.20	.09
❑ 128	Derek Bell	.40	.18
❑ 129	Dennis Eckersley	.40	.18
❑ 130	Andujar Cedeno	.20	.09
❑ 131	John Jaha	.20	.09
❑ 132	Chuck Finley	.40	.18
❑ 133	Steve Finley	.40	.18
❑ 134	Danny Tartabull	.20	.09
❑ 135	Jeff Conine	.40	.18
❑ 136	Jon Lieber	.20	.09
❑ 137	Jim Abbott	.40	.18
❑ 138	Steve Trachsel	.20	.09
❑ 139	Bret Boone	.40	.18
❑ 140	Charles Johnson	.40	.18
❑ 141	Mark McGwire	4.00	1.80
❑ 142	Eddie Murray	.75	.35
❑ 143	Doug Drabek	.20	.09
❑ 144	Steve Cooke	.20	.09
❑ 145	Kevin Seitzer	.20	.09
❑ 146	Rod Beck	.20	.09
❑ 147	Eric Karros	.40	.18
❑ 148	Tim Raines	.40	.18
❑ 149	Joe Girardi	.20	.09
❑ 150	Aaron Sele	.40	.18
❑ 151	Robby Thompson	.20	.09
❑ 152	Chan Ho Park	1.00	.45
❑ 153	Ellis Burks	.40	.18
❑ 154	Brian McRae	.20	.09
❑ 155	Jimmy Key	.40	.18
❑ 156	Rico Brogna	.20	.09
❑ 157	Ozzie Guillen	.20	.09
❑ 158	Chili Davis	.40	.18
❑ 159	Darren Daulton	.40	.18
❑ 160	Chipper Jones	2.00	.90
❑ 161	Walt Weiss	.20	.09
❑ 162	Paul O'Neill	.40	.18
❑ 163	Al Martin	.20	.09
❑ 164	John Valentin	.40	.18
❑ 165	Tim Wallach	.20	.09
❑ 166	Scott Erickson	.40	.18
❑ 167	Ryan Thompson	.20	.09
❑ 168	Todd Zeile	.20	.09
❑ 169	Scott Cooper	.20	.09
❑ 170	Matt Mieske	.20	.09
❑ 171	Allen Watson	.20	.09
❑ 172	Brian L.Hunter	.40	.18
❑ 173	Kevin Stocker	.20	.09
❑ 174	Cal Eldred	.20	.09
❑ 175	Tony Phillips	.20	.09
❑ 176	Ben McDonald	.20	.09
❑ 177	Mark Grace	.60	.25
❑ 178	Midre Cummings	.20	.09
❑ 179	Orlando Merced	.20	.09
❑ 180	Jeff King	.20	.09
❑ 181	Gary Sheffield	.60	.25
❑ 182	Tom Glavine	.75	.35
❑ 183	Edgar Martinez	.40	.18
❑ 184	Steve Karsay	.20	.09
❑ 185	Pat Listach	.20	.09
❑ 186	Wil Cordero	.20	.09
❑ 187	Brady Anderson	.40	.18
❑ 188	Bobby Jones	.20	.09
❑ 189	Andy Benes	.40	.18
❑ 190	Ray Lankford	.40	.18
❑ 191	John Doherty	.20	.09
❑ 192	Wally Joyner	.40	.18
❑ 193	Jim Thome	.75	.35
❑ 194	Royce Clayton	.20	.09
❑ 195	John Olerud	.40	.18
❑ 196	Steve Buechele	.20	.09
❑ 197	Harold Baines	.40	.18
❑ 198	Geronimo Berroa	.20	.09
❑ 199	Checklist	.20	.09
❑ 200	Checklist	.20	.09

1996 Studio

	MINT	NRMT
COMPLETE SET (150)	15.00	6.75
COMMON CARD (1-150)	.15	.07

❑ 1	Cal Ripken	2.00	.90
❑ 2	Alex Gonzalez	.15	.07
❑ 3	Roger Cedeno	.15	.07
❑ 4	Todd Hollandsworth	.15	.07
❑ 5	Gregg Jefferies	.15	.07
❑ 6	Ryne Sandberg	.60	.25
❑ 7	Eric Karros	.25	.11
❑ 8	Jeff Conine	.25	.11
❑ 9	Rafael Palmeiro	.40	.18
❑ 10	Bip Roberts	.15	.07
❑ 11	Roger Clemens	1.00	.45
❑ 12	Tom Glavine	.50	.23
❑ 13	Jason Giambi	.25	.11
❑ 14	Rey Ordonez	.25	.11
❑ 15	Chan Ho Park	.50	.23
❑ 16	Vinny Castilla	.40	.18
❑ 17	Butch Huskey	.15	.07
❑ 18	Greg Maddux	1.50	.70
❑ 19	Bernard Gilkey	.15	.07
❑ 20	Marquis Grissom	.25	.11
❑ 21	Chuck Knoblauch	.50	.23
❑ 22	Ozzie Smith	.60	.25
❑ 23	Garret Anderson	.25	.11
❑ 24	J.T. Snow	.25	.11
❑ 25	John Valentin	.25	.11
❑ 26	Barry Larkin	.40	.18
❑ 27	Bobby Bonilla	.25	.11
❑ 28	Todd Zeile	.15	.07
❑ 29	Roberto Alomar	.50	.23
❑ 30	Ramon Martinez	.25	.11
❑ 31	Jeff King	.15	.07
❑ 32	Dennis Eckersley	.25	.11
❑ 33	Derek Jeter	1.50	.70
❑ 34	Edgar Martinez	.25	.11
❑ 35	Geronimo Berroa	.15	.07
❑ 36	Hal Morris	.15	.07
❑ 37	Troy Percival	.25	.11
❑ 38	Jason Isringhausen	.15	.07
❑ 39	Greg Vaughn	.25	.11
❑ 40	Robin Ventura	.25	.11
❑ 41	Craig Biggio	.50	.23
❑ 42	Will Clark	.50	.23
❑ 43	Sammy Sosa	1.25	.55
❑ 44	Bernie Williams	.50	.23
❑ 45	Kenny Lofton	.50	.23
❑ 46	Wade Boggs	.50	.23
❑ 47	Javy Lopez	.25	.11
❑ 48	Reggie Sanders	.25	.11
❑ 49	Jeff Bagwell	.75	.35
❑ 50	Fred McGriff	.40	.18
❑ 51	Charles Johnson	.25	.11
❑ 52	Darren Daulton	.25	.11
❑ 53	Jose Canseco	.50	.23
❑ 54	Cecil Fielder	.25	.11
❑ 55	Hideo Nomo	.75	.35
❑ 56	Tim Salmon	.50	.23
❑ 57	Carlos Delgado	.25	.11
❑ 58	David Cone	.40	.18
❑ 59	Tim Raines	.25	.11
❑ 60	Lyle Mouton	.15	.07
❑ 61	Wally Joyner	.25	.11
❑ 62	Bret Boone	.25	.11
❑ 63	Raul Mondesi	.40	.18
❑ 64	Gary Sheffield	.40	.18
❑ 65	Alex Rodriguez	1.50	.70
❑ 66	Russ Davis	.25	.11
❑ 67	Checklist	.15	.07
❑ 68	Marty Cordova	.15	.07
❑ 69	Ruben Sierra	.15	.07
❑ 70	Jose Mesa	.15	.07
❑ 71	Matt Williams	.25	.11
❑ 72	Chipper Jones	1.25	.55
❑ 73	Randy Johnson	.50	.23
❑ 74	Kirby Puckett	.75	.35
❑ 75	Jim Edmonds	.40	.18
❑ 76	Barry Bonds	.60	.25
❑ 77	David Segui	.25	.11
❑ 78	Larry Walker	.50	.23
❑ 79	Jason Kendall	.50	.23
❑ 80	Mike Piazza	1.50	.70
❑ 81	Brian L.Hunter	.25	.11
❑ 82	Julio Franco	.15	.07
❑ 83	Jay Bell	.25	.11
❑ 84	Kevin Seitzer	.15	.07
❑ 85	John Smoltz	.25	.11
❑ 86	Joe Carter	.25	.11
❑ 87	Ray Durham	.25	.11
❑ 88	Carlos Baerga	.25	.11
❑ 89	Ron Gant	.15	.07
❑ 90	Orlando Merced	.15	.07
❑ 91	Lee Smith	.25	.11
❑ 92	Pedro Martinez	.50	.23
❑ 93	Frank Thomas	1.50	.70
❑ 94	Al Martin	.15	.07
❑ 95	Chad Curtis	.15	.07
❑ 96	Eddie Murray	.50	.23
❑ 97	Rusty Greer	.40	.18
❑ 98	Jay Buhner	.25	.11
❑ 99	Rico Brogna	.15	.07
❑ 100	Todd Hundley	.25	.11
❑ 101	Moises Alou	.40	.18
❑ 102	Chili Davis	.25	.11
❑ 103	Ismael Valdes	.25	.11
❑ 104	Mo Vaughn	.60	.25
❑ 105	Juan Gonzalez	1.25	.55
❑ 106	Mark Grudzielanek	.25	.11
❑ 107	Derek Bell	.25	.11
❑ 108	Shawn Green	.25	.11
❑ 109	David Justice	.50	.23
❑ 110	Paul O'Neill	.25	.11
❑ 111	Kevin Appier	.25	.11
❑ 112	Ray Lankford	.25	.11
❑ 113	Travis Fryman	.25	.11
❑ 114	Manny Ramirez	.50	.23
❑ 115	Brooks Kieschnick	.15	.07
❑ 116	Ken Griffey Jr.	2.50	1.10
❑ 117	Jeffrey Hammonds	.25	.11
❑ 118	Mark McGwire	2.50	1.10
❑ 119	Denny Neagle	.25	.11
❑ 120	Quilvio Veras	.15	.07
❑ 121	Alan Benes	.25	.11
❑ 122	Rondell White	.25	.11
❑ 123	Osvaldo Fernandez	.15	.07
❑ 124	Andres Galarraga	.50	.23
❑ 125	Johnny Damon	.25	.11
❑ 126	Lenny Dykstra	.25	.11
❑ 127	Jason Schmidt	.15	.07
❑ 128	Mike Mussina	.50	.23
❑ 129	Ken Caminiti	.40	.18

		MINT	NRMT
❑ 130	Michael Tucker	.25	.11
❑ 131	LaTroy Hawkins	.15	.07
❑ 132	Checklist	.15	.07
❑ 133	Delino DeShields	.15	.07
❑ 134	Dave Nilsson	.15	.07
❑ 135	Jack McDowell	.15	.07
❑ 136	Joey Hamilton	.25	.11
❑ 137	Dante Bichette	.25	.11
❑ 138	Paul Molitor	.50	.23
❑ 139	Ivan Rodriguez	.60	.25
❑ 140	Mark Grace	.40	.18
❑ 141	Paul Wilson	.15	.07
❑ 142	Orel Hershiser	.25	.11
❑ 143	Albert Belle	.60	.25
❑ 144	Tino Martinez	.50	.23
❑ 145	Tony Gwynn	1.25	.55
❑ 146	George Arias	.15	.07
❑ 147	Brian Jordan	.25	.11
❑ 148	Brian McRae	.15	.07
❑ 149	Rickey Henderson	.50	.23
❑ 150	Ryan Klesko	.25	.11

1996 Studio Hit Parade

	MINT	NRMT
COMPLETE SET (10)	100.00	45.00
COMMON CARD (1-10)	4.00	1.80
❑ 1 Tony Gwynn	12.00	5.50
❑ 2 Ken Griffey Jr.	25.00	11.00
❑ 3 Frank Thomas	15.00	6.75
❑ 4 Jeff Bagwell	8.00	3.60
❑ 5 Kirby Puckett	8.00	3.60
❑ 6 Mike Piazza	15.00	6.75
❑ 7 Barry Bonds	6.00	2.70
❑ 8 Albert Belle	6.00	2.70
❑ 9 Tim Salmon	4.00	1.80
❑ 10 Mo Vaughn	6.00	2.70

1996 Studio Masterstrokes

	MINT	NRMT
COMPLETE SET (8)	150.00	70.00
COMMON CARD (1-8)	8.00	3.60
❑ 1 Tony Gwynn	20.00	9.00
❑ 2 Mike Piazza	25.00	11.00
❑ 3 Jeff Bagwell	12.00	5.50
❑ 4 Manny Ramirez	8.00	3.60
❑ 5 Cal Ripken	30.00	13.50
❑ 6 Frank Thomas	25.00	11.00
❑ 7 Ken Griffey Jr.	40.00	18.00
❑ 8 Greg Maddux	25.00	11.00
❑ P2 Mike Piazza Promo	5.00	2.20

1996 Studio Stained Glass Stars

	MINT	NRMT
COMPLETE SET (12)	100.00	45.00
COMMON CARD (1-12)	3.00	1.35
❑ 1 Cal Ripken	12.00	5.50
❑ 2 Ken Griffey Jr.	15.00	6.75
❑ 3 Frank Thomas	10.00	4.50
❑ 4 Greg Maddux	10.00	4.50
❑ 5 Chipper Jones	8.00	3.60
❑ 6 Mike Piazza	10.00	4.50
❑ 7 Albert Belle	3.00	1.35
❑ 8 Jeff Bagwell	5.00	2.20
❑ 9 Hideo Nomo	5.00	2.20
❑ 10 Barry Bonds	3.00	1.35
❑ 11 Manny Ramirez	3.00	1.35
❑ 12 Kenny Lofton	3.00	1.35

1997 Studio

	MINT	NRMT
COMPLETE SET (165)	50.00	22.00
COMMON CARD (1-165)	.15	.07
❑ 1 Frank Thomas	2.00	.90
❑ 2 Gary Sheffield	.40	.18
❑ 3 Jason Isringhausen	.15	.07
❑ 4 Ron Gant	.15	.07
❑ 5 Andy Pettitte	.40	.18
❑ 6 Todd Hollandsworth	.15	.07
❑ 7 Troy Percival	.30	.14
❑ 8 Mark McGwire	3.00	1.35
❑ 9 Barry Larkin	.40	.18
❑ 10 Ken Caminiti	.40	.18
❑ 11 Paul Molitor	.60	.25
❑ 12 Travis Fryman	.30	.14
❑ 13 Kevin Brown	.40	.18
❑ 14 Robin Ventura	.30	.14
❑ 15 Andres Galarraga	.60	.25
❑ 16 Ken Griffey Jr.	3.00	1.35
❑ 17 Roger Clemens	1.25	.55
❑ 18 Alan Benes	.30	.14
❑ 19 Dave Justice	.60	.25
❑ 20 Damon Buford	.15	.07
❑ 21 Mike Piazza	2.00	.90
❑ 22 Ray Durham	.30	.14
❑ 23 Billy Wagner	.30	.14
❑ 24 Dean Palmer	.30	.14
❑ 25 David Cone	.40	.18
❑ 26 Ruben Sierra	.15	.07
❑ 27 Henry Rodriguez	.30	.14
❑ 28 Ray Lankford	.30	.14
❑ 29 Jamey Wright	.15	.07
❑ 30 Brady Anderson	.30	.14
❑ 31 Tino Martinez	.60	.25
❑ 32 Manny Ramirez	.60	.25
❑ 33 Jeff Conine	.30	.14
❑ 34 Dante Bichette	.30	.14
❑ 35 Jose Canseco	.60	.25
❑ 36 Mo Vaughn	.75	.35
❑ 37 Sammy Sosa	1.50	.70
❑ 38 Mark Grudzielanek	.30	.14
❑ 39 Mike Mussina	.60	.25
❑ 40 Bill Pulsipher	.15	.07
❑ 41 Ryne Sandberg	.75	.35
❑ 42 Rickey Henderson	.60	.25
❑ 43 Alex Rodriguez	2.00	.90
❑ 44 Eddie Murray	.60	.25
❑ 45 Ernie Young	.15	.07
❑ 46 Joey Hamilton	.30	.14
❑ 47 Wade Boggs	.60	.25
❑ 48 Rusty Greer	.30	.14
❑ 49 Carlos Delgado	.30	.14
❑ 50 Ellis Burks	.30	.14
❑ 51 Cal Ripken	2.50	1.10
❑ 52 Alex Fernandez	.15	.07
❑ 53 Wally Joyner	.30	.14
❑ 54 James Baldwin	.30	.14
❑ 55 Juan Gonzalez	1.50	.70
❑ 56 John Smoltz	.30	.14
❑ 57 Omar Vizquel	.30	.14
❑ 58 Shane Reynolds	.30	.14
❑ 59 Barry Bonds	.75	.35
❑ 60 Jason Kendall	.40	.18
❑ 61 Marty Cordova	.15	.07
❑ 62 Charles Johnson	.30	.14
❑ 63 John Jaha	.15	.07
❑ 64 Chan Ho Park	.60	.25
❑ 65 Jermaine Allensworth	.15	.07
❑ 66 Mark Grace	.40	.18
❑ 67 Tim Salmon	.60	.25
❑ 68 Edgar Martinez	.30	.14
❑ 69 Marquis Grissom	.30	.14
❑ 70 Craig Biggio	.60	.25
❑ 71 Bobby Higginson	.40	.18
❑ 72 Kevin Seitzer	.15	.07
❑ 73 Hideo Nomo	.75	.35
❑ 74 Dennis Eckersley	.30	.14
❑ 75 Bobby Bonilla	.30	.14
❑ 76 Dwight Gooden	.30	.14
❑ 77 Jeff Cirillo	.30	.14
❑ 78 Brian McRae	.15	.07
❑ 79 Chipper Jones	1.50	.70
❑ 80 Jeff Fassero	.15	.07
❑ 81 Fred McGriff	.40	.18
❑ 82 Garret Anderson	.30	.14
❑ 83 Eric Karros	.30	.14
❑ 84 Derek Bell	.30	.14
❑ 85 Kenny Lofton	.60	.25
❑ 86 John Mabry	.15	.07
❑ 87 Pat Hentgen	.30	.14
❑ 88 Greg Maddux	2.00	.90
❑ 89 Jason Giambi	.30	.14
❑ 90 Al Martin	.15	.07
❑ 91 Derek Jeter	2.00	.90
❑ 92 Rey Ordonez	.30	.14
❑ 93 Will Clark	.60	.25
❑ 94 Kevin Appier	.30	.14
❑ 95 Roberto Alomar	.60	.25
❑ 96 Joe Carter	.30	.14
❑ 97 Bernie Williams	.60	.25
❑ 98 Albert Belle	.75	.35
❑ 99 Greg Vaughn	.30	.14
❑ 100 Tony Clark	.40	.18
❑ 101 Matt Williams	.30	.14
❑ 102 Jeff Bagwell	1.00	.45
❑ 103 Reggie Sanders	.30	.14

❑ 104 Mariano Rivera .30 .14
❑ 105 Larry Walker .60 .25
❑ 106 Shawn Green .30 .14
❑ 107 Alex Ochoa .15 .07
❑ 108 Ivan Rodriguez .75 .35
❑ 109 Eric Young .30 .14
❑ 110 Javier Lopez .30 .14
❑ 111 Brian Hunter .30 .14
❑ 112 Raul Mondesi SP 2.50 1.10
❑ 113 Randy Johnson .60 .25
❑ 114 Tony Phillips .15 .07
❑ 115 Carlos Garcia .15 .07
❑ 116 Moises Alou .40 .18
❑ 117 Paul O'Neill .30 .14
❑ 118 Jim Thome .60 .25
❑ 119 Jermaine Dye .15 .07
❑ 120 Wilson Alvarez .30 .14
❑ 121 Rondell White .30 .14
❑ 122 Michael Tucker .30 .14
❑ 123 Mike Lansing .15 .07
❑ 124 Tony Gwynn 1.50 .70
❑ 125 Ryan Klesko .30 .14
❑ 126 Jim Edmonds .40 .18
❑ 127 Chuck Knoblauch .60 .25
❑ 128 Rafael Palmeiro .40 .18
❑ 129 Jay Buhner .30 .14
❑ 130 Tom Glavine .60 .25
❑ 131 Julio Franco .30 .14
❑ 132 Cecil Fielder .30 .14
❑ 133 Paul Wilson SP 2.00 .90
❑ 134 Deion Sanders .30 .14
❑ 135 Alex Gonzalez .15 .07
❑ 136 Charles Nagy .30 .14
❑ 137 Andy Ashby SP 2.00 .90
❑ 138 Edgar Renteria .30 .14
❑ 139 Pedro Martinez .60 .25
❑ 140 Brian Jordan .30 .14
❑ 141 Todd Hundley .30 .14
❑ 142 Marc Newfield .15 .07
❑ 143 Darryl Strawberry .30 .14
❑ 144 Dan Wilson .15 .07
❑ 145 Brian Giles .75 .35
❑ 146 F.P. Santangelo .15 .07
❑ 147 Shannon Stewart SP 2.00 .90
❑ 148 Scott Spiezio .15 .07
❑ 149 Andruw Jones 1.00 .45
❑ 150 Karim Garcia .30 .14
❑ 151 Vladimir Guerrero 1.25 .55
❑ 152 George Arias .15 .07
❑ 153 Brooks Kieschnick .15 .07
❑ 154 Todd Walker .60 .25
❑ 155 Scott Rolen 1.50 .70
❑ 156 Todd Greene .30 .14
❑ 157 Dmitri Young .30 .14
❑ 158 Ruben Rivera .30 .14
❑ 159 Bartolo Colon .30 .14
❑ 160 Nomar Garciaparra 2.00 .90
❑ 161 Bob Abreu SP 2.00 .90
❑ 162 Darin Erstad 1.00 .45
❑ 163 Ken Griffey Jr. CL 1.50 .70
❑ 164 Frank Thomas CL 1.00 .45
❑ 165 Alex Rodriguez CL 1.00 .45

1997 Studio Autographs

	MINT	NRMT
COMPLETE SET (3)	200.00	90.00
COMMON CARD	30.00	13.50

❑ 12 Todd Walker/1250 30.00 13.50
❑ 21 Vladimir Guerrero/500 100.00 45.00
❑ 24 Scott Rolen/1000 100.00 45.00

1997 Studio Hard Hats

	MINT	NRMT
COMPLETE SET (24)	180.00	80.00
COMMON CARD (1-24)	2.00	.90

❑ 1 Ivan Rodriguez 6.00 2.70
❑ 2 Albert Belle 8.00 3.60
❑ 3 Ken Griffey Jr. 25.00 11.00
❑ 4 Chuck Knoblauch 5.00 2.20
❑ 5 Frank Thomas 15.00 6.75
❑ 6 Cal Ripken 20.00 9.00
❑ 7 Todd Walker 5.00 2.20
❑ 8 Alex Rodriguez 15.00 6.75
❑ 9 Jim Thome 5.00 2.20
❑ 10 Mike Piazza 15.00 6.75
❑ 11 Barry Larkin 4.00 1.80
❑ 12 Chipper Jones 12.00 5.50
❑ 13 Derek Jeter 12.00 5.50
❑ 14 Matt Williams 2.50 1.10
❑ 15 Jason Giambi 2.50 1.10
❑ 16 Tim Salmon 5.00 2.20
❑ 17 Brady Anderson 2.50 1.10
❑ 18 Rondell White 2.50 1.10
❑ 19 Bernie Williams 5.00 2.20
❑ 20 Juan Gonzalez 12.00 5.50
❑ 21 Karim Garcia 2.00 .90
❑ 22 Scott Rolen 12.00 5.50
❑ 23 Darin Erstad 8.00 3.60
❑ 24 Brian Jordan 2.50 1.10

1997 Studio Master Strokes

	MINT	NRMT
COMPLETE SET (24)	600.00	275.00
COMMON CARD (1-24)	10.00	4.50
COMP. 8 X 10 SET (24)	250.00	110.00
COMMON 8 X 10 (1-24)	4.00	1.80

*8 X 10'S: .15X TO .4X BASIC MASTER STROKE
8 X 10: RANDOM INSERTS IN PACKS
8 X 10 PRINT RUN 5000 SERIAL #'d SETS

❑ 1 Derek Jeter 30.00 13.50
❑ 2 Jeff Bagwell 20.00 9.00
❑ 3 Ken Griffey Jr. 60.00 27.00
❑ 4 Barry Bonds 15.00 6.75
❑ 5 Frank Thomas 40.00 18.00
❑ 6 Andy Pettitte 12.00 5.50
❑ 7 Mo Vaughn 15.00 6.75
❑ 8 Alex Rodriguez 40.00 18.00
❑ 9 Andruw Jones 15.00 6.75
❑ 10 Kenny Lofton 12.00 5.50
❑ 11 Cal Ripken 50.00 22.00
❑ 12 Greg Maddux 40.00 18.00
❑ 13 Manny Ramirez 12.00 5.50
❑ 14 Mike Piazza 40.00 18.00
❑ 15 Vladimir Guerrero 20.00 9.00
❑ 16 Albert Belle 20.00 9.00
❑ 17 Chipper Jones 30.00 13.50
❑ 18 Hideo Nomo 15.00 6.75
❑ 19 Sammy Sosa 30.00 13.50
❑ 20 Tony Gwynn 30.00 13.50
❑ 21 Gary Sheffield 10.00 4.50
❑ 22 Mark McGwire 60.00 27.00
❑ 23 Juan Gonzalez 30.00 13.50
❑ 24 Paul Molitor 12.00 5.50

1997 Studio Portraits 8x10

	MINT	NRMT
COMPLETE SET (24)	25.00	11.00
COMMON CARD (1-24)	.50	.23

❑ 1 Ken Griffey Jr. 6.00 2.70
❑ 2 Frank Thomas 4.00 1.80
❑ 3 Alex Rodriguez 4.00 1.80
❑ 4 Andruw Jones 2.50 1.10
❑ 5 Cal Ripken 5.00 2.20
❑ 6 Greg Maddux 4.00 1.80
❑ 7 Mike Piazza 4.00 1.80
❑ 8 Chipper Jones 3.00 1.35
❑ 9 Albert Belle 1.25 .55
❑ 10 Derek Jeter 4.00 1.80
❑ 11 Juan Gonzalez 3.00 1.35
❑ 12 Todd Walker 1.25 .55
❑ 13 Mark McGwire 6.00 2.70
❑ 14 Barry Bonds 1.50 .70
❑ 15 Jeff Bagwell 2.00 .90
❑ 16 Manny Ramirez 1.25 .55
❑ 17 Kenny Lofton 1.50 .70
❑ 18 Mo Vaughn 1.50 .70
❑ 19 Hideo Nomo 3.00 1.35
❑ 20 Tony Gwynn 3.00 1.35
❑ 21 Vladimir Guerrero 2.50 1.10
❑ 22 Gary Sheffield .50 .23
❑ 23 Ryne Sandberg 1.50 .70
❑ 24 Scott Rolen 3.00 1.35

1998 Studio

	MINT	NRMT
COMPLETE SET (220)	50.00	22.00
COMMON (1-214/CL1-CL6)	.15	.07

❑ 1 Tony Clark .40 .18
❑ 2 Jose Cruz Jr. .75 .35
❑ 3 Ivan Rodriguez .75 .35
❑ 4 Mo Vaughn .75 .35
❑ 5 Kenny Lofton .60 .25
❑ 6 Will Clark .60 .25
❑ 7 Barry Larkin .40 .18

❑ 8 Jay Bell .25 .11
❑ 9 Kevin Young .25 .11
❑ 10 Francisco Cordova .15 .07
❑ 11 Justin Thompson .25 .11
❑ 12 Paul Molitor .60 .25
❑ 13 Jeff Bagwell 1.00 .45
❑ 14 Jose Canseco .60 .25
❑ 15 Scott Rolen 1.50 .70
❑ 16 Wilton Guerrero .15 .07
❑ 17 Shannon Stewart .25 .11
❑ 18 Hideki Irabu .40 .18
❑ 19 Michael Tucker .25 .11
❑ 20 Joe Carter .25 .11
❑ 21 Gabe Alvarez .25 .11
❑ 22 Ricky Ledee .25 .11
❑ 23 Karim Garcia .25 .11
❑ 24 Eli Marrero .25 .11
❑ 25 Scott Elarton .25 .11
❑ 26 Mario Valdez .25 .11
❑ 27 Ben Grieve 1.25 .55
❑ 28 Paul Konerko .60 .25
❑ 29 Esteban Yan .50 .23
❑ 30 Esteban Loaiza .15 .07
❑ 31 Delino DeShields .15 .07
❑ 32 Bernie Williams .60 .25
❑ 33 Joe Randa .15 .07
❑ 34 Randy Johnson .60 .25
❑ 35 Brett Tomko .25 .11
❑ 36 Todd Erdos .25 .11
❑ 37 Bobby Higginson .40 .18
❑ 38 Jason Kendall .25 .11
❑ 39 Ray Lankford .25 .11
❑ 40 Mark Grace .40 .18
❑ 41 Andy Pettitte .40 .18
❑ 42 Alex Rodriguez 2.00 .90
❑ 43 Hideo Nomo .75 .35
❑ 44 Sammy Sosa 1.50 .70
❑ 45 J.T. Snow .25 .11
❑ 46 Jason Varitek .15 .07
❑ 47 Vinny Castilla .40 .18
❑ 48 Neifi Perez .25 .11
❑ 49 Todd Walker .40 .18
❑ 50 Mike Cameron .25 .11
❑ 51 Jeffrey Hammonds .25 .11
❑ 52 Deivi Cruz .15 .07
❑ 53 Brian Hunter .25 .11
❑ 54 Al Martin .15 .07
❑ 55 Ron Coomer .15 .07
❑ 56 Chan Ho Park .60 .25
❑ 57 Pedro Martinez .60 .25
❑ 58 Darin Erstad .75 .35
❑ 59 Albert Belle .60 .25
❑ 60 Nomar Garciaparra 2.00 .90
❑ 61 Tony Gwynn 1.50 .70
❑ 62 Mike Piazza 2.00 .90
❑ 63 Todd Helton .75 .35
❑ 64 David Ortiz .25 .11
❑ 65 Todd Dunwoody .25 .11
❑ 66 Orlando Cabrera .25 .11
❑ 67 Ken Cloude .25 .11
❑ 68 Andy Benes .25 .11
❑ 69 Mariano Rivera .25 .11
❑ 70 Cecil Fielder .25 .11
❑ 71 Brian Jordan .25 .11
❑ 72 Darryl Kile .25 .11
❑ 73 Reggie Jefferson .15 .07
❑ 74 Shawn Estes .25 .11
❑ 75 Bobby Bonilla .25 .11
❑ 76 Denny Neagle .25 .11
❑ 77 Robin Ventura .25 .11
❑ 78 Omar Vizquel .25 .11
❑ 79 Craig Biggio .60 .25
❑ 80 Moises Alou .40 .18
❑ 81 Garret Anderson .25 .11
❑ 82 Eric Karros .25 .11
❑ 83 Dante Bichette .25 .11
❑ 84 Charles Johnson .25 .11
❑ 85 Rusty Greer .25 .11
❑ 86 Travis Fryman .25 .11
❑ 87 Fernando Tatis .25 .11
❑ 88 Wilson Alvarez .25 .11
❑ 89 Carl Pavano .25 .11
❑ 90 Brian Rose .25 .11
❑ 91 Geoff Jenkins .25 .11
❑ 92 Magglio Ordonez .75 .35
❑ 93 David Segui .25 .11
❑ 94 David Cone .40 .18
❑ 95 John Smoltz .25 .11
❑ 96 Jim Thome .60 .25
❑ 97 Gary Sheffield .40 .18
❑ 98 Barry Bonds .75 .35
❑ 99 Andres Galarraga .60 .25
❑ 100 Brad Fullmer .25 .11
❑ 101 Bobby Estalella .25 .11
❑ 102 Enrique Wilson .25 .11
❑ 103 Frank Catalanotto .25 .11
❑ 104 Mike Lowell .60 .25
❑ 105 Kevin Orie .15 .07
❑ 106 Matt Morris .25 .11
❑ 107 Pokey Reese .15 .07
❑ 108 Shawn Green .25 .11
❑ 109 Tony Womack .25 .11
❑ 110 Ken Caminiti .40 .18
❑ 111 Roberto Alomar .60 .25
❑ 112 Ken Griffey Jr. 3.00 1.35
❑ 113 Cal Ripken 2.50 1.10
❑ 114 Lou Collier .15 .07
❑ 115 Larry Walker .60 .25
❑ 116 Fred McGriff .40 .18
❑ 117 Jim Edmonds .40 .18
❑ 118 Edgar Martinez .25 .11
❑ 119 Matt Williams .25 .11
❑ 120 Ismael Valdes .25 .11
❑ 121 Bartolo Colon .25 .11
❑ 122 Jeff Cirillo .25 .11
❑ 123 Steve Woodard .25 .11
❑ 124 Kevin Millwood 1.50 .70
❑ 125 Derrick Gibson .25 .11
❑ 126 Jacob Cruz .15 .07
❑ 127 Russell Branyan .25 .11
❑ 128 Sean Casey .25 .11
❑ 129 Derrek Lee .25 .11
❑ 130 Paul O'Neill .25 .11
❑ 131 Brad Radke .25 .11
❑ 132 Kevin Appier .25 .11
❑ 133 John Olerud .25 .11
❑ 134 Alan Benes .25 .11
❑ 135 Todd Greene .25 .11
❑ 136 Carlos Mendoza .25 .11
❑ 137 Wade Boggs .60 .25
❑ 138 Jose Guillen .25 .11
❑ 139 Tino Martinez .60 .25
❑ 140 Aaron Boone .15 .07
❑ 141 Abraham Nunez .25 .11
❑ 142 Preston Wilson .25 .11
❑ 143 Randall Simon .25 .11
❑ 144 Dennis Reyes .25 .11
❑ 145 Mark Kotsay .40 .18
❑ 146 Richard Hidalgo .25 .11
❑ 147 Travis Lee 1.25 .55
❑ 148 Hanley Frias .25 .11
❑ 149 Ruben Rivera .25 .11
❑ 150 Rafael Medina .25 .11
❑ 151 Dave Nilsson .15 .07
❑ 152 Curt Schilling .25 .11
❑ 153 Brady Anderson .25 .11
❑ 154 Carlos Delgado .25 .11
❑ 155 Jason Giambi .25 .11
❑ 156 Pat Hentgen .25 .11
❑ 157 Tom Glavine .60 .25
❑ 158 Ryan Klesko .25 .11
❑ 159 Chipper Jones 1.50 .70
❑ 160 Juan Gonzalez 1.50 .70
❑ 161 Mark McGwire 4.00 1.80
❑ 162 Vladimir Guerrero 1.00 .45
❑ 163 Derek Jeter 1.50 .70
❑ 164 Manny Ramirez .60 .25
❑ 165 Mike Mussina .60 .25
❑ 166 Rafael Palmeiro .40 .18
❑ 167 Henry Rodriguez .25 .11
❑ 168 Jeff Suppan .15 .07
❑ 169 Eric Milton .25 .11
❑ 170 Scott Spiezio .15 .07
❑ 171 Wilson Delgado .25 .11
❑ 172 Bubba Trammell .25 .11
❑ 173 Ellis Burks .25 .11
❑ 174 Jason Dickson .25 .11
❑ 175 Butch Huskey .15 .07
❑ 176 Edgardo Alfonzo .25 .11
❑ 177 Eric Young .25 .11
❑ 178 Marquis Grissom .25 .11
❑ 179 Lance Johnson .15 .07
❑ 180 Kevin Brown .40 .18
❑ 181 Sandy Alomar Jr. .25 .11
❑ 182 Todd Hundley .25 .11
❑ 183 Rondell White .25 .11
❑ 184 Javier Lopez .25 .11
❑ 185 Damian Jackson .15 .07
❑ 186 Raul Mondesi .40 .18
❑ 187 Rickey Henderson .60 .25
❑ 188 David Justice .60 .25
❑ 189 Jay Buhner .25 .11
❑ 190 Jaret Wright .75 .35
❑ 191 Miguel Tejada .25 .11
❑ 192 Ron Wright .25 .11
❑ 193 Livan Hernandez .25 .11
❑ 194 A.J. Hinch .25 .11
❑ 195 Richie Sexson .40 .18
❑ 196 Bob Abreu .25 .11
❑ 197 Louis Castillo .15 .07
❑ 198 Michael Coleman .25 .11
❑ 199 Greg Maddux 2.00 .90
❑ 200 Frank Thomas 2.00 .90
❑ 201 Andruw Jones .75 .35
❑ 202 Roger Clemens 1.25 .55
❑ 203 Tim Salmon .60 .25
❑ 204 Chuck Knoblauch .60 .25
❑ 205 Wes Helms .25 .11
❑ 206 Juan Encarnacion .25 .11
❑ 207 Russ Davis .25 .11
❑ 208 John Valentin .25 .11
❑ 209 Tony Saunders .15 .07
❑ 210 Mike Sweeney .15 .07
❑ 211 Steve Finley .25 .11
❑ 212 Dave Dellucci .75 .35
❑ 213 Edgar Renteria .25 .11
❑ 214 Jeremi Gonzalez .25 .11
❑ CL1 Jeff Bagwell CL .60 .25
❑ CL2 Mike Piazza CL 1.00 .45
❑ CL3 Greg Maddux CL 1.00 .45
❑ CL4 Cal Ripken CL 1.25 .55
❑ CL5 Frank Thomas CL 1.00 .45
❑ CL6 Ken Griffey Jr. CL 1.50 .70

1998 Studio Autographs 8 x 10

	MINT	NRMT
COMPLETE SET (3)	250.00	110.00
COMMON CARD (1-3)	50.00	22.00

❑ 1 Travis Lee/500 120.00 55.00
❑ 2 Todd Helton/1000 50.00 22.00
❑ 3 Ben Grieve/1000 80.00 36.00

1998 Studio Freeze Frame

	MINT	NRMT
COMPLETE SET (30)	300.00	135.00
COMMON CARD (1-30)	2.50	1.10

❑ 1 Ken Griffey Jr. 30.00 13.50
❑ 2 Derek Jeter 15.00 6.75
❑ 3 Ben Grieve 10.00 4.50
❑ 4 Cal Ripken 25.00 11.00
❑ 5 Alex Rodriguez 20.00 9.00

	MINT	NRMT
❑ 6 Greg Maddux	20.00	9.00
❑ 7 David Justice	6.00	2.70
❑ 8 Mike Piazza	20.00	9.00
❑ 9 Chipper Jones	15.00	6.75
❑ 10 Randy Johnson	6.00	2.70
❑ 11 Jeff Bagwell	10.00	4.50
❑ 12 Nomar Garciaparra	20.00	9.00
❑ 13 Andruw Jones	6.00	2.70
❑ 14 Frank Thomas	20.00	9.00
❑ 15 Scott Rolen	12.00	5.50
❑ 16 Barry Bonds	8.00	3.60
❑ 17 Kenny Lofton	6.00	2.70
❑ 18 Ivan Rodriguez	8.00	3.60
❑ 19 Chuck Knoblauch	6.00	2.70
❑ 20 Jose Cruz Jr.	6.00	2.70
❑ 21 Bernie Williams	6.00	2.70
❑ 22 Tony Gwynn	15.00	6.75
❑ 23 Juan Gonzalez	15.00	6.75
❑ 24 Gary Sheffield	4.00	1.80
❑ 25 Roger Clemens	12.00	5.50
❑ 26 Travis Lee	10.00	4.50
❑ 27 Brad Fullmer	2.50	1.10
❑ 28 Tim Salmon	6.00	2.70
❑ 29 Raul Mondesi	4.00	1.80
❑ 30 Roberto Alomar	6.00	2.70

1998 Studio Hit Parade

	MINT	NRMT
COMPLETE SET (20)	120.00	55.00
COMMON CARD (1-20)	3.00	1.35

	MINT	NRMT
❑ 1 Tony Gwynn	12.00	5.50
❑ 2 Larry Walker	5.00	2.20
❑ 3 Mike Piazza	15.00	6.75
❑ 4 Frank Thomas	15.00	6.75
❑ 5 Manny Ramirez	5.00	2.20
❑ 6 Ken Griffey Jr.	25.00	11.00
❑ 7 Todd Helton	5.00	2.20
❑ 8 Vladimir Guerrero	6.00	2.70
❑ 9 Albert Belle	6.00	2.70
❑ 10 Jeff Bagwell	8.00	3.60
❑ 11 Juan Gonzalez	12.00	5.50
❑ 12 Jim Thome	5.00	2.20
❑ 13 Scott Rolen	10.00	4.50
❑ 14 Tino Martinez	5.00	2.20
❑ 15 Mark McGwire	30.00	13.50
❑ 16 Barry Bonds	6.00	2.70
❑ 17 Tony Clark	3.00	1.35
❑ 18 Mo Vaughn	6.00	2.70
❑ 19 Darin Erstad	5.00	2.20
❑ 20 Paul Konerko	5.00	2.20

1998 Studio Masterstrokes

	MINT	NRMT
COMPLETE SET (20)	800.00	350.00
COMMON CARD (1-20)	15.00	6.75

	MINT	NRMT
❑ 1 Travis Lee	25.00	11.00
❑ 2 Kenny Lofton	15.00	6.75
❑ 3 Mo Vaughn	20.00	9.00
❑ 4 Ivan Rodriguez	20.00	9.00
❑ 5 Roger Clemens	30.00	13.50
❑ 6 Mark McGwire	100.00	45.00
❑ 7 Hideo Nomo	25.00	11.00
❑ 8 Andruw Jones	15.00	6.75
❑ 9 Nomar Garciaparra	50.00	22.00
❑ 10 Juan Gonzalez	40.00	18.00
❑ 11 Jeff Bagwell	25.00	11.00
❑ 12 Derek Jeter	40.00	18.00
❑ 13 Tony Gwynn	40.00	18.00
❑ 14 Chipper Jones	40.00	18.00
❑ 15 Mike Piazza	50.00	22.00
❑ 16 Greg Maddux	50.00	22.00
❑ 17 Alex Rodriguez	50.00	22.00
❑ 18 Cal Ripken	60.00	27.00
❑ 19 Frank Thomas	50.00	22.00
❑ 20 Ken Griffey Jr.	80.00	36.00

1998 Studio Portraits 8 x 10

	MINT	NRMT
COMPLETE SET (36)	40.00	18.00
COMMON CARD (1-36)	.75	.35

	MINT	NRMT
❑ 1 Travis Lee	2.00	.90
❑ 2 Todd Helton	1.25	.55
❑ 3 Ben Grieve	2.00	.90
❑ 4 Paul Konerko	1.25	.55
❑ 5 Jeff Bagwell	1.50	.70
❑ 6 Derek Jeter	2.00	.90
❑ 7 Ivan Rodriguez	1.25	.55
❑ 8 Cal Ripken	4.00	1.80
❑ 9 Mike Piazza	3.00	1.35
❑ 10 Chipper Jones	2.50	1.10
❑ 11 Frank Thomas	3.00	1.35
❑ 12 Tony Gwynn	2.00	.90
❑ 13 Nomar Garciaparra	3.00	1.35
❑ 14 Juan Gonzalez	2.00	.90
❑ 15 Greg Maddux	3.00	1.35
❑ 16 Hideo Nomo	1.25	.55
❑ 17 Scott Rolen	2.00	.90
❑ 18 Barry Bonds	1.25	.55
❑ 19 Ken Griffey Jr.	5.00	2.20
❑ 20 Alex Rodriguez	3.00	1.35
❑ 21 Roger Clemens	2.00	.90
❑ 22 Mark McGwire	6.00	2.70
❑ 23 Jose Cruz Jr.	1.25	.55
❑ 24 Andruw Jones	1.25	.55
❑ 25 Tino Martinez	1.25	.55
❑ 26 Mo Vaughn	1.25	.55
❑ 27 Vladimir Guerrero	1.50	.70
❑ 28 Tony Clark	.75	.35
❑ 29 Andy Pettitte	.75	.35
❑ 30 Jaret Wright	1.25	.55
❑ 31 Paul Molitor	1.25	.55
❑ 32 Darin Erstad	1.25	.55
❑ 33 Larry Walker	1.25	.55
❑ 34 Chuck Knoblauch	1.25	.55
❑ 35 Barry Larkin	.75	.35
❑ 36 Kenny Lofton	1.25	.55

1998 Studio MLB 99

MINT NRMT

PLEASE SEE 1998 DONRUSS MLB 99

1995 Summit

	MINT	NRMT
COMPLETE SET (200)	20.00	9.00
COMMON CARD (1-200)	.10	.05

	MINT	NRMT
❑ 1 Ken Griffey Jr.	2.50	1.10
❑ 2 Alex Fernandez	.10	.05
❑ 3 Fred McGriff	.40	.18
❑ 4 Ben McDonald	.10	.05
❑ 5 Rafael Palmeiro	.40	.18
❑ 6 Tony Gwynn	1.25	.55
❑ 7 Jim Thome	.50	.23
❑ 8 Ken Hill	.10	.05
❑ 9 Barry Bonds	.60	.25
❑ 10 Barry Larkin	.40	.18
❑ 11 Albert Belle	.60	.25
❑ 12 Billy Ashley	.10	.05
❑ 13 Matt Williams	.25	.11
❑ 14 Andy Benes	.25	.11
❑ 15 Midre Cummings	.10	.05
❑ 16 J.R. Phillips	.10	.05
❑ 17 Edgar Martinez	.25	.11

❑ 18 Manny Ramirez .50 .23
❑ 19 Jose Canseco .50 .23
❑ 20 Chili Davis .25 .11
❑ 21 Don Mattingly .75 .35
❑ 22 Bernie Williams .50 .23
❑ 23 Tom Glavine .50 .23
❑ 24 Robin Ventura .25 .11
❑ 25 Jeff Conine .25 .11
❑ 26 Mark Grace .40 .18
❑ 27 Mark McGwire 2.50 1.10
❑ 28 Carlos Delgado .25 .11
❑ 29 Greg Colbrunn .10 .05
❑ 30 Greg Maddux 1.50 .70
❑ 31 Craig Biggio .50 .23
❑ 32 Kirby Puckett .75 .35
❑ 33 Derek Bell .25 .11
❑ 34 Lenny Dykstra .25 .11
❑ 35 Tim Salmon .50 .23
❑ 36 Deion Sanders .25 .11
❑ 37 Moises Alou .40 .18
❑ 38 Ray Lankford .25 .11
❑ 39 Willie Greene .25 .11
❑ 40 Ozzie Smith .60 .25
❑ 41 Roger Clemens 1.00 .45
❑ 42 Andres Galarraga .50 .23
❑ 43 Gary Sheffield .40 .18
❑ 44 Sammy Sosa 1.25 .55
❑ 45 Larry Walker .50 .23
❑ 46 Kevin Appier .25 .11
❑ 47 Raul Mondesi .40 .18
❑ 48 Kenny Lofton .50 .23
❑ 49 Darryl Hamilton .10 .05
❑ 50 Roberto Alomar .50 .23
❑ 51 Hal Morris .10 .05
❑ 52 Cliff Floyd .25 .11
❑ 53 Brent Gates .10 .05
❑ 54 Rickey Henderson .50 .23
❑ 55 John Olerud .25 .11
❑ 56 Gregg Jefferies .10 .05
❑ 57 Cecil Fielder .25 .11
❑ 58 Paul Molitor .50 .23
❑ 59 Bret Boone .25 .11
❑ 60 Greg Vaughn .25 .11
❑ 61 Wally Joyner .25 .11
❑ 62 Jeffrey Hammonds .25 .11
❑ 63 James Mouton .10 .05
❑ 64 Omar Vizquel .25 .11
❑ 65 Wade Boggs .50 .23
❑ 66 Terry Steinbach .25 .11
❑ 67 Wil Cordero .10 .05
❑ 68 Joey Hamilton .25 .11
❑ 69 Rico Brogna .10 .05
❑ 70 Darren Daulton .25 .11
❑ 71 Chuck Knoblauch .50 .23
❑ 72 Bob Hamelin .10 .05
❑ 73 Carl Everett .10 .05
❑ 74 Joe Carter .25 .11
❑ 75 Dave Winfield .50 .23
❑ 76 Bobby Bonilla .25 .11
❑ 77 Paul O'Neill .25 .11
❑ 78 Javier Lopez .25 .11
❑ 79 Cal Ripken 2.00 .90
❑ 80 David Cone .40 .18
❑ 81 Bernard Gilkey .10 .05
❑ 82 Ivan Rodriguez .60 .25
❑ 83 Dean Palmer .25 .11
❑ 84 Jason Bere .10 .05
❑ 85 Will Clark .50 .23
❑ 86 Scott Cooper .10 .05
❑ 87 Royce Clayton .10 .05
❑ 88 Mike Piazza 1.50 .70
❑ 89 Ryan Klesko .25 .11
❑ 90 Juan Gonzalez 1.25 .55
❑ 91 Travis Fryman .25 .11
❑ 92 Frank Thomas 1.50 .70
❑ 93 Eduardo Perez .10 .05
❑ 94 Mo Vaughn .60 .25
❑ 95 Jay Bell .25 .11
❑ 96 Jeff Bagwell .75 .35
❑ 97 Randy Johnson .50 .23
❑ 98 Jimmy Key .25 .11
❑ 99 Dennis Eckersley .25 .11
❑ 100 Carlos Baerga .25 .11
❑ 101 Eddie Murray .50 .23
❑ 102 Mike Mussina .50 .23
❑ 103 Brian Anderson .25 .11
❑ 104 Jeff Cirillo .25 .11
❑ 105 Dante Bichette .25 .11
❑ 106 Bret Saberhagen .25 .11
❑ 107 Jeff Kent .25 .11
❑ 108 Ruben Sierra .10 .05
❑ 109 Kirk Gibson .25 .11
❑ 110 Steve Karsay .10 .05
❑ 111 David Justice .50 .23
❑ 112 Benji Gil .10 .05
❑ 113 Vaughn Eshelman .10 .05
❑ 114 Carlos Perez .40 .18
❑ 115 Chipper Jones 1.25 .55
❑ 116 Shane Andrews .10 .05
❑ 117 Orlando Miller .10 .05
❑ 118 Scott Ruffcorn .10 .05
❑ 119 Jose Oliva .10 .05
❑ 120 Joe Vitiello .10 .05
❑ 121 Jon Nunnally .10 .05
❑ 122 Garret Anderson .25 .11
❑ 123 Curtis Goodwin .10 .05
❑ 124 Mark Grudzielanek .40 .18
❑ 125 Alex Gonzalez .10 .05
❑ 126 David Bell .10 .05
❑ 127 Dustin Hermanson .25 .11
❑ 128 Dave Nilsson .10 .05
❑ 129 Wilson Heredia .10 .05
❑ 130 Charles Johnson .25 .11
❑ 131 Frank Rodriguez .10 .05
❑ 132 Alex Ochoa .10 .05
❑ 133 Alex Rodriguez 2.00 .90
❑ 134 Bobby Higginson 1.25 .55
❑ 135 Edgardo Alfonzo .25 .11
❑ 136 Armando Benitez .10 .05
❑ 137 Rich Aude .10 .05
❑ 138 Tim Naehring .10 .05
❑ 139 Joe Randa .10 .05
❑ 140 Quilvio Veras .10 .05
❑ 141 Hideo Nomo 2.00 .90
❑ 142 Ray Holbert .10 .05
❑ 143 Michael Tucker .25 .11
❑ 144 Chad Mottola .10 .05
❑ 145 John Valentin .25 .11
❑ 146 James Baldwin .25 .11
❑ 147 Esteban Loaiza .10 .05
❑ 148 Marty Cordova .10 .05
❑ 149 Juan Acevedo .10 .05
❑ 150 Tim Unroe UER .10 .05
Cardinals logo
❑ 151 Brad Clontz UER .10 .05
A's logo
❑ 152 Steve Rodriguez UER .10 .05
Yankees logo
❑ 153 Rudy Pemberton UER .10 .05
Dodgers logo
❑ 154 Ozzie Timmons UER .10 .05
Tigers logo
❑ 155 Ricky Otero .10 .05
❑ 156 Allen Battle .10 .05
❑ 157 Joe Rosselli .10 .05
❑ 158 Roberto Petagine .10 .05
❑ 159 Todd Hollandsworth .10 .05
❑ 160 Shannon Penn UER .10 .05
Cubs logo
❑ 161 Antonio Osuna UER .10 .05
Tigers logo
❑ 162 Russ Davis UER .25 .11
Red Sox logo
❑ 163 Jason Giambi UER .25 .11
two errors: front photo actually Brent Gates
also Braves logo
❑ 164 Terry Bradshaw UER .10 .05
Brewers logo
❑ 165 Ray Durham .25 .11
❑ 166 Todd Steverson .10 .05
❑ 167 Tim Belk .10 .05
❑ 168 Andy Pettitte .50 .23
❑ 169 Roger Cedeno .10 .05
❑ 170 Jose Parra .10 .05
❑ 171 Scott Sullivan .10 .05
❑ 172 LaTroy Hawkins .10 .05
❑ 173 Jeff McCurry .10 .05
❑ 174 Ken Griffey Jr. BS 1.25 .55
❑ 175 Frank Thomas BS .75 .35
❑ 176 Cal Ripken Jr. BS 1.00 .45
❑ 177 Jeff Bagwell BS .50 .23
❑ 178 Mike Piazza BS .75 .35
❑ 179 Barry Bonds BS .40 .18
❑ 180 Matt Williams BS .10 .05
❑ 181 Don Mattingly BS .50 .23
❑ 182 Will Clark BS .25 .11
❑ 183 Tony Gwynn BS .60 .25
❑ 184 Kirby Puckett BS .50 .23
❑ 185 Jose Canseco BS .25 .11
❑ 186 Paul Molitor BS .25 .11
❑ 187 Albert Belle BS .25 .11
❑ 188 Joe Carter BS .10 .05
❑ 189 Greg Maddux SD .75 .35
❑ 190 Roger Clemens SD .50 .23
❑ 191 David Cone SD .10 .05
❑ 192 Mike Mussina SD .25 .11
❑ 193 Randy Johnson SD .25 .11
❑ 194 Frank Thomas CL .75 .35
❑ 195 Ken Griffey Jr. CL 1.25 .55
❑ 196 Cal Ripken CL 1.00 .45
❑ 197 Jeff Bagwell CL .60 .25
❑ 198 Mike Piazza CL .75 .35
❑ 199 Barry Bonds CL .40 .18
❑ 200 Mo Vaughn CL .40 .18
Matt Williams

1995 Summit Big Bang

	MINT	NRMT
COMPLETE SET (20)	250.00	110.00
COMMON CARD (BB1-BB20)	5.00	2.20

❑ BB1 Ken Griffey Jr. 50.00 22.00
❑ BB2 Frank Thomas 30.00 13.50
❑ BB3 Cal Ripken 40.00 18.00
❑ BB4 Jeff Bagwell 15.00 6.75
❑ BB5 Mike Piazza 30.00 13.50
❑ BB6 Barry Bonds 12.00 5.50
❑ BB7 Matt Williams 5.00 2.20
❑ BB8 Don Mattingly 15.00 6.75
❑ BB9 Will Clark 10.00 4.50
❑ BB10 Tony Gwynn 25.00 11.00
❑ BB11 Kirby Puckett 15.00 6.75
❑ BB12 Jose Canseco 10.00 4.50
❑ BB13 Paul Molitor 10.00 4.50
❑ BB14 Albert Belle 15.00 6.75
❑ BB15 Joe Carter 5.00 2.20
❑ BB16 Rafael Palmeiro 6.00 2.70
❑ BB17 Fred McGriff 6.00 2.70
❑ BB18 David Justice 10.00 4.50
❑ BB19 Tim Salmon 10.00 4.50
❑ BB20 Mo Vaughn 12.00 5.50

1995 Summit New Age

	MINT	NRMT
COMPLETE SET (15)	60.00	27.00
COMMON CARD (NA1-NA15)	1.50	.70

❑ NA1 Cliff Floyd 2.00 .90
❑ NA2 Manny Ramirez 6.00 2.70
❑ NA3 Raul Mondesi 3.00 1.35
❑ NA4 Alex Rodriguez 25.00 11.00
❑ NA5 Billy Ashley 1.50 .70
❑ NA6 Alex Gonzalez 1.50 .70
❑ NA7 Michael Tucker 2.00 .90
❑ NA8 Charles Johnson 2.00 .90

❑ NA9 Carlos Delgado	2.00	.90
❑ NA10 Benji Gil	1.50	.70
❑ NA11 Chipper Jones	20.00	9.00
❑ NA12 Todd Hollandsworth	1.50	.70
❑ NA13 Frankie Rodriguez	1.50	.70
❑ NA14 Shawn Green	2.00	.90
❑ NA15 Ray Durham	2.00	.90

1995 Summit 21 Club

	MINT	NRMT
COMPLETE SET (9)	25.00	11.00
COMMON CARD (TC1-TC9)	3.00	1.35
❑ TC1 Bob Abreu	5.00	2.20
❑ TC2 Pokey Reese	3.00	1.35
❑ TC3 Edgardo Alfonzo	4.00	1.80
❑ TC4 Jim Pittsley	3.00	1.35
❑ TC5 Ruben Rivera	4.00	1.80
❑ TC6 Chan Ho Park	4.00	1.80
❑ TC7 Julian Tavarez	3.00	1.35
❑ TC8 Ismael Valdes	4.00	1.80
❑ TC9 Dmitri Young	4.00	1.80

1996 Summit

	MINT	NRMT
COMPLETE SET (200)	25.00	11.00
COMMON CARD (1-200)	.15	.07
❑ 1 Mike Piazza	2.00	.90
❑ 2 Matt Williams	.30	.14
❑ 3 Tino Martinez	.60	.25
❑ 4 Reggie Sanders	.30	.14
❑ 5 Ray Durham	.30	.14
❑ 6 Brad Radke	.30	.14
❑ 7 Jeff Bagwell	1.00	.45
❑ 8 Ron Gant	.15	.07
❑ 9 Lance Johnson	.15	.07
❑ 10 Kevin Seitzer	.15	.07
❑ 11 Dante Bichette	.30	.14
❑ 12 Ivan Rodriguez	.75	.35
❑ 13 Jim Abbott	.30	.14
❑ 14 Greg Colbrunn	.15	.07
❑ 15 Rondell White	.30	.14
❑ 16 Shawn Green	.30	.14
❑ 17 Gregg Jefferies	.15	.07
❑ 18 Omar Vizquel	.30	.14
❑ 19 Cal Ripken	2.50	1.10
❑ 20 Mark McGwire	3.00	1.35
❑ 21 Wally Joyner	.30	.14
❑ 22 Chili Davis	.30	.14
❑ 23 Jose Canseco	.60	.25
❑ 24 Royce Clayton	.15	.07
❑ 25 Jay Bell	.30	.14
❑ 26 Travis Fryman	.30	.14
❑ 27 Jeff King	.15	.07
❑ 28 Todd Hundley	.30	.14
❑ 29 Joe Vitiello	.15	.07
❑ 30 Russ Davis	.30	.14
❑ 31 Mo Vaughn	.75	.35
❑ 32 Raul Mondesi	.40	.18
❑ 33 Ray Lankford	.30	.14
❑ 34 Mike Stanley	.15	.07
❑ 35 B.J. Surhoff	.30	.14
❑ 36 Greg Vaughn	.30	.14
❑ 37 Todd Stottlemyre	.15	.07
❑ 38 Carlos Delgado	.30	.14
❑ 39 Kenny Lofton	.60	.25
❑ 40 Hideo Nomo	1.00	.45
❑ 41 Sterling Hitchcock	.30	.14
❑ 42 Pete Schourek	.15	.07
❑ 43 Edgardo Alfonzo	.30	.14
❑ 44 Ken Hill	.15	.07
❑ 45 Ken Caminiti	.40	.18
❑ 46 Bobby Higginson	.60	.25
❑ 47 Michael Tucker	.30	.14
❑ 48 David Cone	.40	.18
❑ 49 Cecil Fielder	.30	.14
❑ 50 Brian L. Hunter	.30	.14
❑ 51 Charles Johnson	.30	.14
❑ 52 Bobby Bonilla	.30	.14
❑ 53 Eddie Murray	.60	.25
❑ 54 Kenny Rogers	.15	.07
❑ 55 Jim Edmonds	.40	.18
❑ 56 Trevor Hoffman	.30	.14
❑ 57 Kevin Mitchell UER	.15	.07
❑ 58 Ruben Sierra	.15	.07
❑ 59 Benji Gil	.15	.07
❑ 60 Juan Gonzalez	1.50	.70
❑ 61 Larry Walker	.60	.25
❑ 62 Jack McDowell	.15	.07
❑ 63 Shawon Dunston	.15	.07
❑ 64 Andy Benes	.30	.14
❑ 65 Jay Buhner	.30	.14
❑ 66 Rickey Henderson	.60	.25
❑ 67 Alex Gonzalez	.15	.07
❑ 68 Mike Kelly	.15	.07
❑ 69 Fred McGriff	.40	.18
❑ 70 Ryne Sandberg	.75	.35
❑ 71 Ernie Young	.15	.07
❑ 72 Kevin Appier	.30	.14
❑ 73 Moises Alou	.40	.18
❑ 74 John Jaha	.15	.07
❑ 75 J.T. Snow	.30	.14
❑ 76 Jim Thome	.60	.25
❑ 77 Kirby Puckett	1.00	.45
❑ 78 Hal Morris	.15	.07
❑ 79 Robin Ventura	.30	.14
❑ 80 Ben McDonald	.15	.07
❑ 81 Tim Salmon	.60	.25
❑ 82 Albert Belle	.75	.35
❑ 83 Marquis Grissom	.30	.14
❑ 84 Alex Rodriguez	2.00	.90
❑ 85 Manny Ramirez	.60	.25
❑ 86 Ken Griffey Jr.	3.00	1.35
❑ 87 Sammy Sosa	1.50	.70
❑ 88 Frank Thomas	2.00	.90
❑ 89 Lee Smith	.30	.14
❑ 90 Marty Cordova	.15	.07
❑ 91 Greg Maddux	2.00	.90
❑ 92 Lenny Dykstra	.30	.14
❑ 93 Butch Huskey	.15	.07
❑ 94 Garret Anderson	.30	.14
❑ 95 Mike Bordick	.15	.07
❑ 96 Dave Justice	.60	.25
❑ 97 Chad Curtis	.15	.07
❑ 98 Carlos Baerga	.30	.14
❑ 99 Jason Isringhausen	.15	.07
❑ 100 Gary Sheffield	.40	.18
❑ 101 Roger Clemens	1.25	.55
❑ 102 Ozzie Smith	.75	.35
❑ 103 Ramon Martinez	.30	.14
❑ 104 Paul O'Neill	.30	.14
❑ 105 Will Clark	.60	.25
❑ 106 Tom Glavine	.60	.25
❑ 107 Barry Bonds	.75	.35
❑ 108 Barry Larkin	.40	.18
❑ 109 Derek Bell	.30	.14
❑ 110 Randy Johnson	.60	.25
❑ 111 Jeff Conine	.30	.14
❑ 112 John Mabry	.15	.07
❑ 113 Julian Tavarez	.15	.07
❑ 114 Gary DiSarcina	.15	.07
❑ 115 Andres Galarraga	.60	.25
❑ 116 Marc Newfield	.15	.07
❑ 117 Frank Rodriguez	.15	.07
❑ 118 Brady Anderson	.30	.14
❑ 119 Mike Mussina	.60	.25
❑ 120 Orlando Merced	.15	.07
❑ 121 Melvin Nieves	.15	.07
❑ 122 Brian Jordan	.30	.14
❑ 123 Rafael Palmeiro	.40	.18
❑ 124 Johnny Damon	.30	.14
❑ 125 Wil Cordero	.15	.07
❑ 126 Chipper Jones	1.50	.70
❑ 127 Eric Karros	.30	.14
❑ 128 Darren Daulton	.30	.14
❑ 129 Vinny Castilla	.40	.18
❑ 130 Joe Carter	.30	.14
❑ 131 Bernie Williams	.60	.25
❑ 132 Bernard Gilkey	.15	.07
❑ 133 Bret Boone	.30	.14
❑ 134 Tony Gwynn	1.50	.70
❑ 135 Dave Nilsson	.15	.07
❑ 136 Ryan Klesko	.30	.14
❑ 137 Paul Molitor	.60	.25
❑ 138 John Olerud	.30	.14
❑ 139 Craig Biggio	.60	.25
❑ 140 John Valentin	.30	.14
❑ 141 Chuck Knoblauch	.60	.25
❑ 142 Edgar Martinez	.30	.14
❑ 143 Rico Brogna	.15	.07
❑ 144 Dean Palmer	.30	.14
❑ 145 Mark Grace	.40	.18
❑ 146 Roberto Alomar	.60	.25
❑ 147 Alex Fernandez	.15	.07
❑ 148 Andre Dawson	.40	.18
❑ 149 Wade Boggs	.60	.25
❑ 150 Mark Lewis	.15	.07
❑ 151 Gary Gaetti	.30	.14
❑ 152 Paul Wilson	.40	.18
Roger Clemens ❑ 153 Rey Ordonez	.30	.14
Ozzie Smith ❑ 154 Derek Jeter	1.00	.45
Cal Ripken ❑ 155 Andy Benes	.15	.07
Alan Benes ❑ 156 Jason Kendall	.75	.35
Mike Piazza ❑ 157 Ryan Klesko	.75	.35
Frank Thomas ❑ 158 Johnny Damon	1.00	.45
Ken Griffey Jr. ❑ 159 Karim Garcia	.30	.14
Sammy Sosa ❑ 160 Raul Mondesi	.30	.14
Tim Salmon ❑ 161 Chipper Jones	.75	.35
Matt Williams ❑ 162 Rey Ordonez	.30	.14
❑ 163 Bob Wolcott	.15	.07

❑ 164 Brooks Kieschnick	.15	.07
❑ 165 Steve Gibralter	.15	.07
❑ 166 Bob Abreu	.30	.14
❑ 167 Greg Zaun	.15	.07
❑ 168 Tavo Alvarez	.15	.07
❑ 169 Sal Fasano	.15	.07
❑ 170 George Arias	.15	.07
❑ 171 Derek Jeter	2.00	.90
❑ 172 Livan Hernandez	1.25	.55
❑ 173 Alan Benes	.30	.14
❑ 174 George Williams	.15	.07
❑ 175 John Wasdin	.15	.07
❑ 176 Chan Ho Park	.60	.25
❑ 177 Paul Wilson	.15	.07
❑ 178 Jeff Suppan	.15	.07
❑ 179 Quinton McCracken	.30	.14
❑ 180 Wilton Guerrero	.50	.23
❑ 181 Eric Owens	.15	.07
❑ 182 Felipe Crespo	.15	.07
❑ 183 LaTroy Hawkins	.15	.07
❑ 184 Jason Schmidt	.15	.07
❑ 185 Terrell Wade	.15	.07
❑ 186 Mike Grace	.15	.07
❑ 187 Chris Snopek	.15	.07
❑ 188 Jason Kendall	.60	.25
❑ 189 Todd Hollandsworth	.15	.07
❑ 190 Jim Pittsley	.15	.07
❑ 191 Jermaine Dye	.15	.07
❑ 192 Mike Busby	.15	.07
❑ 193 Richard Hidalgo	.30	.14
❑ 194 Tyler Houston	.15	.07
❑ 195 Jimmy Haynes	.15	.07
❑ 196 Karim Garcia	.30	.14
❑ 197 Ken Griffey Jr. CL	1.50	.70
❑ 198 Frank Thomas CL	1.00	.45
❑ 199 Greg Maddux CL	1.00	.45
❑ 200 Cal Ripken CL	1.25	.55

1996 Summit Ballparks

	MINT	NRMT
COMPLETE SET (18)	150.00	70.00
COMMON CARD (1-18)	1.25	.55

Card	MINT	NRMT
❑ 1 Cal Ripken	20.00	9.00
❑ 2 Albert Belle	6.00	2.70
❑ 3 Dante Bichette	2.00	.90
❑ 4 Mo Vaughn	6.00	2.70
❑ 5 Ken Griffey Jr.	25.00	11.00
❑ 6 Derek Jeter	12.00	5.50
❑ 7 Juan Gonzalez	12.00	5.50
❑ 8 Greg Maddux	15.00	6.75
❑ 9 Frank Thomas	15.00	6.75
❑ 10 Ryne Sandberg	6.00	2.70
❑ 11 Mike Piazza	15.00	6.75
❑ 12 Johnny Damon	2.00	.90
❑ 13 Barry Bonds	6.00	2.70
❑ 14 Jeff Bagwell	8.00	3.60
❑ 15 Paul Wilson	1.25	.55
❑ 16 Tim Salmon	5.00	2.20
❑ 17 Kirby Puckett	8.00	3.60
❑ 18 Tony Gwynn	12.00	5.50

1996 Summit Big Bang

	MINT	NRMT
COMPLETE SET (16)	750.00	350.00
COMMON CARD (1-16)	10.00	4.50

*MIRAGE: 1X BASIC BIG BANG
MIRAGE STATED ODDS 1:72
MIRAGE PRINT RUN 600 SERIAL #'d SETS

Card	MINT	NRMT
❑ 1 Frank Thomas	80.00	36.00
❑ 2 Ken Griffey Jr.	120.00	55.00
❑ 3 Albert Belle	30.00	13.50
❑ 4 Mo Vaughn	30.00	13.50
❑ 5 Barry Bonds	30.00	13.50
❑ 6 Cal Ripken	100.00	45.00
❑ 7 Jeff Bagwell	40.00	18.00
❑ 8 Mike Piazza	80.00	36.00
❑ 9 Ryan Klesko	15.00	6.75
❑ 10 Manny Ramirez	25.00	11.00
❑ 11 Tim Salmon	25.00	11.00
❑ 12 Dante Bichette	10.00	4.50
❑ 13 Sammy Sosa	60.00	27.00
❑ 14 Raul Mondesi	15.00	6.75
❑ 15 Chipper Jones	60.00	27.00
❑ 16 Garret Anderson	10.00	4.50

1996 Summit Hitters Inc.

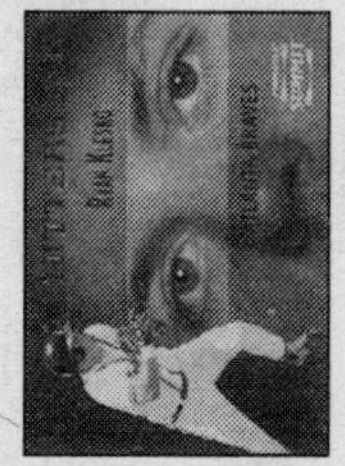

	MINT	NRMT
COMPLETE SET (16)	250.00	110.00
COMMON CARD (1-16)	5.00	2.20

Card	MINT	NRMT
❑ 1 Tony Gwynn	20.00	9.00
❑ 2 Mo Vaughn	10.00	4.50
❑ 3 Tim Salmon	8.00	3.60
❑ 4 Ken Griffey Jr.	40.00	18.00
❑ 5 Sammy Sosa	20.00	9.00
❑ 6 Frank Thomas	25.00	11.00
❑ 7 Wade Boggs	8.00	3.60
❑ 8 Albert Belle	10.00	4.50
❑ 9 Cal Ripken	30.00	13.50
❑ 10 Manny Ramirez	8.00	3.60
❑ 11 Ryan Klesko	5.00	2.20
❑ 12 Dante Bichette	5.00	2.20
❑ 13 Mike Piazza	25.00	11.00
❑ 14 Chipper Jones	20.00	9.00
❑ 15 Ryne Sandberg	10.00	4.50
❑ 16 Matt Williams	5.00	2.20

1996 Summit Positions

	MINT	NRMT
COMPLETE SET (9)	325.00	145.00
COMMON CARD (1-9)	15.00	6.75

Card	MINT	NRMT
❑ 1 Jeff Bagwell Mo Vaughn Frank Thomas	50.00	22.00
❑ 2 Roberto Alomar Craig Biggio Chuck Knoblauch	15.00	6.75
❑ 3 Matt Williams Jim Thome Chipper Jones	40.00	18.00
❑ 4 Barry Larkin Cal Ripken Alex Rodriguez	80.00	36.00
❑ 5 Mike Piazza Ivan Rodriguez Charles Johnson	40.00	18.00
❑ 6 Hideo Nomo Greg Maddux Randy Johnson	50.00	22.00
❑ 7 Barry Bonds Albert Belle Ryan Klesko	20.00	9.00
❑ 8 Johnny Damon Jim Edmonds Ken Griffey Jr.	60.00	27.00
❑ 9 Manny Ramirez Gary Sheffield Sammy Sosa	30.00	13.50

1952 Topps

	NRMT	VG-E
COMPLETE SET (407)	65000.00	29200.00
COMMON CARD (1-80)	60.00	27.00
*RED/BLACK BACKS 1-80 SAME VALUE		
COMMON CARD (81-250)	40.00	18.00
COMMON CARD (251-310)	50.00	22.00
COMMON CARD (311-407)	250.00	110.00
WRAPPER (1-cent)	250.00	110.00
WRAPPER (5-cent)	100.00	45.00

Card	NRMT	VG-E
❑ 1 Andy Pafko	2000.00	200.00
❑ 2 Pete Runnels	125.00	55.00
❑ 3 Hank Thompson	70.00	32.00
❑ 4 Don Lenhardt	60.00	27.00
❑ 5 Larry Jansen	60.00	27.00
❑ 6 Grady Hatton	60.00	27.00
❑ 7 Wayne Terwilliger	60.00	27.00
❑ 8 Fred Marsh	60.00	27.00
❑ 9 Robert Hogue	60.00	27.00
❑ 10 Al Rosen	60.00	27.00
❑ 11 Phil Rizzuto	200.00	90.00

❑	12 Monty Basgall	60.00	27.00
❑	13 Johnny Wyrostek	60.00	27.00
❑	14 Bob Elliott	70.00	32.00
❑	15 Johnny Pesky	60.00	27.00
❑	16 Gene Hermanski	60.00	27.00
❑	17 Jim Hegan	70.00	32.00
❑	18 Merrill Combs	60.00	27.00
❑	19 Johnny Bucha	60.00	27.00
❑	20 Billy Loes	125.00	55.00
❑	21 Ferris Fain	70.00	32.00
❑	22 Dom DiMaggio	80.00	36.00
❑	23 Billy Goodman	70.00	32.00
❑	24 Luke Easter	60.00	27.00
❑	25 Johnny Groth	60.00	27.00
❑	26 Monte Irvin	125.00	55.00
❑	27 Sam Jethroe	70.00	32.00
❑	28 Jerry Priddy	60.00	27.00
❑	29 Ted Kluszewski	100.00	45.00
❑	30 Mel Parnell	70.00	32.00
❑	31 Gus Zernial	80.00	36.00
	Posed with seven baseballs		
❑	32 Eddie Robinson	60.00	27.00
❑	33 Warren Spahn	200.00	90.00
❑	34 Elmer Valo	60.00	27.00
❑	35 Hank Sauer	60.00	27.00
❑	36 Gil Hodges	175.00	80.00
❑	37 Duke Snider	275.00	125.00
❑	38 Wally Westlake	60.00	27.00
❑	39 Dizzy Trout	70.00	32.00
❑	40 Irv Noren	70.00	32.00
❑	41 Bob Wellman	60.00	27.00
❑	42 Lou Kretlow	60.00	27.00
❑	43 Ray Scarborough	60.00	27.00
❑	44 Con Dempsey	60.00	27.00
❑	45 Eddie Joost	60.00	27.00
❑	46 Gordon Goldsberry	60.00	27.00
❑	47 Willie Jones	70.00	32.00
❑	48A Joe Page COR	75.00	34.00
❑	48B Joe Page ERR	300.00	135.00
	(Bio for Sain)		
❑	49A Johnny Sain COR	75.00	34.00
❑	49B Johnny Sain ERR	275.00	125.00
	(Bio for Page)		
❑	50 Marv Rickert	60.00	27.00
❑	51 Jim Russell	60.00	27.00
❑	52 Don Mueller	70.00	32.00
❑	53 Chris Van Cuyk	60.00	27.00
❑	54 Leo Kiely	60.00	27.00
❑	55 Ray Boone	60.00	27.00
❑	56 Tommy Glaviano	60.00	27.00
❑	57 Ed Lopat	80.00	36.00
❑	58 Bob Mahoney	60.00	27.00
❑	59 Robin Roberts	150.00	70.00
❑	60 Sid Hudson	60.00	27.00
❑	61 Tookie Gilbert	60.00	27.00
❑	62 Chuck Stobbs	60.00	27.00
❑	63 Howie Pollet	60.00	27.00
❑	64 Roy Sievers	60.00	27.00
❑	65 Enos Slaughter	150.00	70.00
❑	66 Preacher Roe	80.00	36.00
❑	67 Allie Reynolds	80.00	36.00
❑	68 Cliff Chambers	60.00	27.00
❑	69 Virgil Stallcup	60.00	27.00
❑	70 Al Zarilla	60.00	27.00
❑	71 Tom Upton	60.00	27.00
❑	72 Karl Olson	60.00	27.00
❑	73 Bill Werle	60.00	27.00
❑	74 Andy Hansen	60.00	27.00
❑	75 Wes Westrum	70.00	32.00
❑	76 Eddie Stanky	60.00	27.00
❑	77 Bob Kennedy	70.00	32.00
❑	78 Ellis Kinder	60.00	27.00
❑	79 Gerry Staley	60.00	27.00
❑	80 Herman Wehmeier	60.00	27.00
❑	81 Vernon Law	50.00	22.00
❑	82 Duane Pillette	40.00	18.00
❑	83 Billy Johnson	40.00	18.00
❑	84 Vern Stephens	50.00	22.00
❑	85 Bob Kuzava	50.00	22.00
❑	86 Ted Gray	40.00	18.00
❑	87 Dale Coogan	40.00	18.00
❑	88 Bob Feller	200.00	90.00
❑	89 Johnny Lipon	40.00	18.00
❑	90 Mickey Grasso	40.00	18.00
❑	91 Red Schoendienst	80.00	36.00
❑	92 Dale Mitchell	50.00	22.00
❑	93 Al Sima	40.00	18.00
❑	94 Sam Mele	40.00	18.00
❑	95 Ken Holcombe	40.00	18.00
❑	96 Willard Marshall	40.00	18.00
❑	97 Earl Torgeson	40.00	18.00
❑	98 Billy Pierce	50.00	22.00
❑	99 Gene Woodling	60.00	27.00
❑	100 Del Rice	40.00	18.00
❑	101 Max Lanier	40.00	18.00
❑	102 Bill Kennedy	40.00	18.00
❑	103 Cliff Mapes	40.00	18.00
❑	104 Don Kolloway	40.00	18.00
❑	105 Johnny Pramesa	40.00	18.00
❑	106 Mickey Vernon	60.00	27.00
❑	107 Connie Ryan	40.00	18.00
❑	108 Jim Konstanty	60.00	27.00
❑	109 Ted Wilks	40.00	18.00
❑	110 Dutch Leonard	40.00	18.00
❑	111 Peanuts Lowrey	40.00	18.00
❑	112 Hank Majeski	40.00	18.00
❑	113 Dick Sisler	50.00	22.00
❑	114 Willard Ramsdell	40.00	18.00
❑	115 Red Munger	40.00	18.00
❑	116 Carl Scheib	40.00	18.00
❑	117 Sherm Lollar	50.00	22.00
❑	118 Ken Raffensberger	40.00	18.00
❑	119 Mickey McDermott	40.00	18.00
❑	120 Bob Chakales	40.00	18.00
❑	121 Gus Niarhos	40.00	18.00
❑	122 Jackie Jensen	80.00	36.00
❑	123 Eddie Yost	50.00	22.00
❑	124 Monte Kennedy	40.00	18.00
❑	125 Bill Rigney	40.00	18.00
❑	126 Fred Hutchinson	50.00	22.00
❑	127 Paul Minner	40.00	18.00
❑	128 Don Bollweg	40.00	18.00
❑	129 Johnny Mize	90.00	40.00
❑	130 Sheldon Jones	40.00	18.00
❑	131 Morrie Martin	40.00	18.00
❑	132 Clyde Kluttz	40.00	18.00
❑	133 Al Widmar	40.00	18.00
❑	134 Joe Tipton	40.00	18.00
❑	135 Dixie Howell	40.00	18.00
❑	136 Johnny Schmitz	40.00	18.00
❑	137 Roy McMillan	50.00	22.00
❑	138 Bill MacDonald	40.00	18.00
❑	139 Ken Wood	40.00	18.00
❑	140 Johnny Antonelli	50.00	22.00
❑	141 Clint Hartung	40.00	18.00
❑	142 Harry Perkowski	40.00	18.00
❑	143 Les Moss	40.00	18.00
❑	144 Ed Blake	40.00	18.00
❑	145 Joe Haynes	40.00	18.00
❑	146 Frank House	40.00	18.00
❑	147 Bob Young	40.00	18.00
❑	148 Johnny Klippstein	40.00	18.00
❑	149 Dick Kryhoski	40.00	18.00
❑	150 Ted Beard	40.00	18.00
❑	151 Wally Post	50.00	22.00
❑	152 Al Evans	40.00	18.00
❑	153 Bob Rush	40.00	18.00
❑	154 Joe Muir	40.00	18.00
❑	155 Frank Overmire	40.00	18.00
❑	156 Frank Hiller	40.00	18.00
❑	157 Bob Usher	40.00	18.00
❑	158 Eddie Waitkus	40.00	18.00
❑	159 Saul Rogovin	40.00	18.00
❑	160 Owen Friend	40.00	18.00
❑	161 Bud Byerly	40.00	18.00
❑	162 Del Crandall	50.00	22.00
❑	163 Stan Rojek	40.00	18.00
❑	164 Walt Dubiel	40.00	18.00
❑	165 Eddie Kazak	40.00	18.00
❑	166 Paul LaPalme	40.00	18.00
❑	167 Bill Howerton	40.00	18.00
❑	168 Charlie Silvera	60.00	27.00
❑	169 Howie Judson	40.00	18.00
❑	170 Gus Bell	50.00	22.00
❑	171 Ed Erautt	40.00	18.00
❑	172 Eddie Miksis	40.00	18.00
❑	173 Roy Smalley	40.00	18.00
❑	174 Clarence Marshall	40.00	18.00
❑	175 Billy Martin	300.00	135.00
❑	176 Hank Edwards	40.00	18.00
❑	177 Bill Wight	40.00	18.00
❑	178 Cass Michaels	40.00	18.00
❑	179 Frank Smith	40.00	18.00
❑	180 Charlie Maxwell	50.00	22.00
❑	181 Bob Swift	40.00	18.00
❑	182 Billy Hitchcock	40.00	18.00
❑	183 Erv Dusak	40.00	18.00
❑	184 Bob Ramazzotti	40.00	18.00
❑	185 Bill Nicholson	50.00	22.00
❑	186 Walt Masterson	40.00	18.00
❑	187 Bob Miller	40.00	18.00
❑	188 Clarence Podbielan	40.00	18.00
❑	189 Pete Reiser	60.00	27.00
❑	190 Don Johnson	40.00	18.00
❑	191 Yogi Berra	375.00	170.00
❑	192 Myron Ginsberg	40.00	18.00
❑	193 Harry Simpson	50.00	22.00
❑	194 Joe Hatton	40.00	18.00
❑	195 Minnie Minoso	150.00	70.00
❑	196 Solly Hemus	60.00	27.00
❑	197 George Strickland	40.00	18.00
❑	198 Phil Haugstad	40.00	18.00
❑	199 George Zuverink	40.00	18.00
❑	200 Ralph Houk	80.00	36.00
❑	201 Alex Kellner	40.00	18.00
❑	202 Joe Collins	65.00	29.00
❑	203 Curt Simmons	60.00	27.00
❑	204 Ron Northey	40.00	18.00
❑	205 Clyde King	60.00	27.00
❑	206 Joe Ostrowski	40.00	18.00
❑	207 Mickey Harris	40.00	18.00
❑	208 Marlin Stuart	40.00	18.00
❑	209 Howie Fox	40.00	18.00
❑	210 Dick Fowler	40.00	18.00
❑	211 Ray Coleman	40.00	18.00
❑	212 Ned Garver	40.00	18.00
❑	213 Nippy Jones	40.00	18.00
❑	214 Johnny Hopp	50.00	22.00
❑	215 Hank Bauer	65.00	29.00
❑	216 Richie Ashburn	175.00	80.00
❑	217 Snuffy Stirnweiss	50.00	22.00
❑	218 Clyde McCullough	40.00	18.00
❑	219 Bobby Shantz	60.00	27.00
❑	220 Joe Presko	40.00	18.00
❑	221 Granny Hamner	40.00	18.00
❑	222 Hoot Evers	40.00	18.00
❑	223 Del Ennis	50.00	22.00
❑	224 Bruce Edwards	40.00	18.00
❑	225 Frank Baumholtz	40.00	18.00
❑	226 Dave Philley	40.00	18.00
❑	227 Joe Garagiola	80.00	36.00
❑	228 Al Brazle	40.00	18.00
❑	229 Gene Bearden UER	40.00	18.00
	(Misspelled Beardon)		
❑	230 Matt Batts	40.00	18.00
❑	231 Sam Zoldak	40.00	18.00
❑	232 Billy Cox	50.00	22.00
❑	233 Bob Friend	60.00	27.00
❑	234 Steve Souchock	40.00	18.00
❑	235 Walt Dropo	40.00	18.00
❑	236 Ed Fitzgerald	40.00	18.00
❑	237 Jerry Coleman	65.00	29.00
❑	238 Art Houtteman	40.00	18.00
❑	239 Rocky Bridges	50.00	22.00
❑	240 Jack Phillips	40.00	18.00
❑	241 Tommy Byrne	40.00	18.00
❑	242 Tom Poholsky	40.00	18.00
❑	243 Larry Doby	80.00	36.00
❑	244 Vic Wertz	40.00	18.00
❑	245 Sherry Robertson	40.00	18.00
❑	246 George Kell	80.00	36.00
❑	247 Randy Gumpert	40.00	18.00
❑	248 Frank Shea	40.00	18.00
❑	249 Bobby Adams	40.00	18.00
❑	250 Carl Erskine	100.00	45.00
❑	251 Chico Carrasquel	50.00	22.00
❑	252 Vern Bickford	50.00	22.00
❑	253 Johnny Berardino	75.00	34.00
❑	254 Joe Dobson	50.00	22.00
❑	255 Clyde Vollmer	50.00	22.00
❑	256 Pete Suder	50.00	22.00
❑	257 Bobby Avila	60.00	27.00
❑	258 Steve Gromek	50.00	22.00
❑	259 Bob Addis	50.00	22.00
❑	260 Pete Castiglione	50.00	22.00

No.	Player	NRMT	VG-E
261	Willie Mays	2500.00	1100.00
262	Virgil Trucks	60.00	27.00
263	Harry Brecheen	60.00	27.00
264	Roy Hartsfield	50.00	22.00
265	Chuck Diering	50.00	22.00
266	Murry Dickson	50.00	22.00
267	Sid Gordon	60.00	27.00
268	Bob Lemon	150.00	70.00
269	Willard Nixon	50.00	22.00
270	Lou Brissie	50.00	22.00
271	Jim Delsing	50.00	22.00
272	Mike Garcia	60.00	27.00
273	Erv Palica	50.00	22.00
274	Ralph Branca	125.00	55.00
275	Pat Mullin	50.00	22.00
276	Jim Wilson	50.00	22.00
277	Early Wynn	150.00	70.00
278	Allie Clark	50.00	22.00
279	Eddie Stewart	50.00	22.00
280	Cloyd Boyer	60.00	27.00
281	Tommy Brown SP	60.00	27.00
282	Birdie Tebbetts SP	75.00	34.00
283	Phil Masi SP	60.00	27.00
284	Hank Arft SP	60.00	27.00
285	Cliff Fannin SP	60.00	27.00
286	Joe DeMaestri SP	60.00	27.00
287	Steve Bilko SP	60.00	27.00
288	Chet Nichols SP	60.00	27.00
289	Tommy Holmes SP	75.00	34.00
290	Joe Astroth SP	60.00	27.00
291	Gil Coan SP	60.00	27.00
292	Floyd Baker SP	60.00	27.00
293	Sibby Sisti SP	60.00	27.00
294	Walker Cooper SP	60.00	27.00
295	Phil Cavarretta SP	75.00	34.00
296	Red Rolfe MG SP	60.00	27.00
297	Andy Seminick SP	60.00	27.00
298	Bob Ross SP	60.00	27.00
299	Ray Murray SP	60.00	27.00
300	Barney McCosky SP	60.00	27.00
301	Bob Porterfield	50.00	22.00
302	Max Surkont	50.00	22.00
303	Harry Dorish	50.00	22.00
304	Sam Dente	50.00	22.00
305	Paul Richards MG	60.00	27.00
306	Lou Sleater	50.00	22.00
307	Frank Campos	50.00	22.00
308	Luis Aloma	50.00	22.00
309	Jim Busby	50.00	22.00
310	George Metkovich	60.00	27.00
311	Mickey Mantle	20000.00	9000.00
312	Jackie Robinson DP	1500.00	700.00
313	Bobby Thomson DP	300.00	135.00
314	Roy Campanella	2000.00	900.00
315	Leo Durocher MG	400.00	180.00
316	Dave Williams	300.00	135.00
317	Conrado Marrero	300.00	135.00
318	Harold Gregg	250.00	110.00
319	Al Walker	250.00	110.00
320	John Rutherford	300.00	135.00
321	Joe Black	350.00	160.00
322	Randy Jackson	250.00	110.00
323	Bubba Church	250.00	110.00
324	Warren Hacker	250.00	110.00
325	Bill Serena	250.00	110.00
326	George Shuba	400.00	180.00
327	Al Wilson	250.00	110.00
328	Bob Borkowski	250.00	110.00
329	Ike Delock	250.00	110.00
330	Turk Lown	250.00	110.00
331	Tom Morgan	250.00	110.00
332	Anthony Bartirome	250.00	110.00
333	Pee Wee Reese	1600.00	700.00
334	Wilmer Mizell	300.00	135.00
335	Ted Lepcio	250.00	110.00
336	Dave Koslo	250.00	110.00
337	Jim Hearn	250.00	110.00
338	Sal Yvars	250.00	110.00
339	Russ Meyer	250.00	110.00
340	Bob Hooper	250.00	110.00
341	Hal Jeffcoat	250.00	110.00
342	Clem Labine	400.00	180.00
343	Dick Gernert	250.00	110.00
344	Ewell Blackwell	300.00	135.00
345	Sammy White	250.00	110.00
346	George Spencer	250.00	110.00
347	Joe Adcock	300.00	135.00
348	Robert Kelly	250.00	110.00
349	Bob Cain	250.00	110.00
350	Cal Abrams	250.00	110.00
351	Alvin Dark	300.00	135.00
352	Karl Drews	250.00	110.00
353	Bobby Del Greco	250.00	110.00
354	Fred Hatfield	250.00	110.00
355	Bobby Morgan	250.00	110.00
356	Toby Atwell	250.00	110.00
357	Smoky Burgess	300.00	135.00
358	John Kucab	250.00	110.00
359	Dee Fondy	250.00	110.00
360	George Crowe	300.00	135.00
361	William Posedel CO	250.00	110.00
362	Ken Heintzelman	250.00	110.00
363	Dick Rozek	250.00	110.00
364	Clyde Sukeforth CO	250.00	110.00
365	Cookie Lavagetto CO	375.00	170.00
366	Dave Madison	250.00	110.00
367	Ben Thorpe	250.00	110.00
368	Ed Wright	250.00	110.00
369	Dick Groat	350.00	160.00
370	Billy Hoeft	300.00	135.00
371	Bobby Hofman	250.00	110.00
372	Gil McDougald	375.00	170.00
373	Jim Turner CO	400.00	180.00
374	John Benton	250.00	110.00
375	John Merson	250.00	110.00
376	Faye Throneberry	250.00	110.00
377	Chuck Dressen MG	375.00	170.00
378	Leroy Fusselman	250.00	110.00
379	Joe Rossi	250.00	110.00
380	Clem Koshorek	250.00	110.00
381	Milton Stock CO	250.00	110.00
382	Sam Jones	350.00	160.00
383	Del Wilber	250.00	110.00
384	Frank Crosetti CO	400.00	180.00
385	Herman Franks CO	250.00	110.00
386	John Yuhas	250.00	110.00
387	Billy Meyer MG	250.00	110.00
388	Bob Chipman	250.00	110.00
389	Ben Wade	250.00	110.00
390	Glenn Nelson	250.00	110.00
391	Ben Chapman UER CO (Photo actually Sam Chapman)	250.00	110.00
392	Hoyt Wilhelm	750.00	350.00
393	Ebba St.Claire	250.00	110.00
394	Billy Herman CO	400.00	180.00
395	Jake Pitler CO	325.00	145.00
396	Dick Williams	400.00	180.00
397	Forrest Main	250.00	110.00
398	Hal Rice	250.00	110.00
399	Jim Fridley	250.00	110.00
400	Bill Dickey CO	800.00	350.00
401	Bob Schultz	250.00	110.00
402	Earl Harrist	250.00	110.00
403	Bill Miller	250.00	110.00
404	Dick Brodowski	250.00	110.00
405	Eddie Pellagrini	250.00	110.00
406	Joe Nuxhall	350.00	160.00
407	Eddie Mathews	4000.00	1000.00

1953 Topps

	NRMT	VG-E
COMPLETE SET (274)	13500.00	6100.00
COMMON CARD (1-165)	30.00	13.50
COMMON CARD (166-220)	25.00	11.00
COMMON DP (1-220)	15.00	6.75
COMMON CARD (221-280)	100.00	45.00
WRAPPER (1-CENT, DATED)	200.00	90.00
WRAPPER (1-CENT, UNDATED)	300.00	135.00
WRAPPER (5-CENT, DATED)	400.00	180.00
WRAPPER (5-CENT, UNDATED)	350.00	160.00

No.	Player	NRMT	VG-E
1	Jackie Robinson DP	500.00	140.00
2	Luke Easter DP	20.00	9.00
3	George Crowe	30.00	13.50
4	Ben Wade	30.00	13.50
5	Joe Dobson	30.00	13.50
6	Sam Jones	40.00	18.00
7	Bob Borkowski DP	15.00	6.75
8	Clem Koshorek DP	15.00	6.75
9	Joe Collins	40.00	18.00
10	Smoky Burgess SP	70.00	32.00
11	Sal Yvars	30.00	13.50
12	Howie Judson DP	15.00	6.75
13	Conrado Marrero DP	15.00	6.75
14	Clem Labine DP	20.00	9.00
15	Bobo Newsom DP	30.00	13.50
16	Peanuts Lowrey DP	15.00	6.75
17	Billy Hitchcock	30.00	13.50
18	Ted Lepcio DP	30.00	13.50
19	Mel Parnell DP	30.00	13.50
20	Hank Thompson	40.00	18.00
21	Billy Johnson	30.00	13.50
22	Howie Fox	30.00	13.50
23	Toby Atwell DP	15.00	6.75
24	Ferris Fain	40.00	18.00
25	Ray Boone	40.00	18.00
26	Dale Mitchell DP	20.00	9.00
27	Roy Campanella DP	175.00	80.00
28	Eddie Pellagrini	30.00	13.50
29	Hal Jeffcoat	30.00	13.50
30	Willard Nixon	30.00	13.50
31	Ewell Blackwell	50.00	22.00
32	Clyde Vollmer	30.00	13.50
33	Bob Kennedy DP	15.00	6.75
34	George Shuba	40.00	18.00
35	Irv Noren DP	15.00	6.75
36	Johnny Groth DP	15.00	6.75
37	Eddie Mathews DP	100.00	45.00
38	Jim Hearn DP	15.00	6.75
39	Eddie Miksis	30.00	13.50
40	John Lipon	30.00	13.50
41	Enos Slaughter	80.00	36.00
42	Gus Zernial DP	30.00	13.50
43	Gil McDougald	50.00	22.00
44	Ellis Kinder SP	35.00	16.00
45	Grady Hatton DP	15.00	6.75
46	Johnny Klippstein DP	15.00	6.75
47	Bubba Church DP	15.00	6.75
48	Bob Del Greco DP	15.00	6.75
49	Faye Throneberry DP	15.00	6.75
50	Chuck Dressen MG DP	22.50	10.00
51	Frank Campos DP	15.00	6.75
52	Ted Gray DP	15.00	6.75
53	Sherm Lollar DP	30.00	13.50
54	Bob Feller DP	100.00	45.00
55	Maurice McDermott DP	15.00	6.75
56	Gerry Staley DP	15.00	6.75
57	Carl Scheib	30.00	13.50
58	George Metkovich	30.00	13.50
59	Karl Drews DP	15.00	6.75
60	Cloyd Boyer DP	15.00	6.75
61	Early Wynn SP	100.00	45.00
62	Monte Irvin DP	35.00	16.00
63	Gus Niarhos DP	15.00	6.75
64	Dave Philley	30.00	13.50
65	Earl Harrist	30.00	13.50
66	Minnie Minoso	50.00	22.00
67	Roy Sievers DP	30.00	13.50
68	Del Rice	30.00	13.50
69	Dick Brodowski	30.00	13.50
70	Ed Yuhas	30.00	13.50
71	Tony Bartirome	30.00	13.50
72	Fred Hutchinson MG SP	50.00	22.00
73	Eddie Robinson	30.00	13.50
74	Joe Rossi	30.00	13.50

Card	NRMT	VG-E
❑ 75 Mike Garcia	40.00	18.00
❑ 76 Pee Wee Reese	150.00	70.00
❑ 77 Johnny Mize DP	50.00	22.00
❑ 78 Red Schoendienst	60.00	27.00
❑ 79 Johnny Wyrostek	30.00	13.50
❑ 80 Jim Hegan	40.00	18.00
❑ 81 Joe Black SP	70.00	32.00
❑ 82 Mickey Mantle	3000.00	1350.00
❑ 83 Howie Pollet	30.00	13.50
❑ 84 Bob Hooper DP	15.00	6.75
❑ 85 Bobby Morgan DP	15.00	6.75
❑ 86 Billy Martin	125.00	55.00
❑ 87 Ed Lopat	50.00	22.00
❑ 88 Willie Jones DP	15.00	6.75
❑ 89 Chuck Stobbs DP	15.00	6.75
❑ 90 Hank Edwards DP	15.00	6.75
❑ 91 Ebba St.Claire DP	15.00	6.75
❑ 92 Paul Minner DP	15.00	6.75
❑ 93 Hal Rice DP	15.00	6.75
❑ 94 Bill Kennedy DP	15.00	6.75
❑ 95 Willard Marshall DP	15.00	6.75
❑ 96 Virgil Trucks	40.00	18.00
❑ 97 Don Kolloway DP	15.00	6.75
❑ 98 Cal Abrams DP	15.00	6.75
❑ 99 Dave Madison	30.00	13.50
❑ 100 Bill Miller	30.00	13.50
❑ 101 Ted Wilks	30.00	13.50
❑ 102 Connie Ryan DP	15.00	6.75
❑ 103 Joe Astroth DP	15.00	6.75
❑ 104 Yogi Berra	200.00	90.00
❑ 105 Joe Nuxhall DP	30.00	13.50
❑ 106 Johnny Antonelli	40.00	18.00
❑ 107 Danny O'Connell DP	15.00	6.75
❑ 108 Bob Porterfield DP	15.00	6.75
❑ 109 Alvin Dark	40.00	18.00
❑ 110 Herman Wehmeier DP	15.00	6.75
❑ 111 Hank Sauer DP	20.00	9.00
❑ 112 Ned Garver DP	15.00	6.75
❑ 113 Jerry Priddy	30.00	13.50
❑ 114 Phil Rizzuto	160.00	70.00
❑ 115 George Spencer	30.00	13.50
❑ 116 Frank Smith DP	15.00	6.75
❑ 117 Sid Gordon DP	15.00	6.75
❑ 118 Gus Bell DP	20.00	9.00
❑ 119 Johnny Sain SP	50.00	22.00
❑ 120 Davey Williams	40.00	18.00
❑ 121 Walt Dropo	40.00	18.00
❑ 122 Elmer Valo	30.00	13.50
❑ 123 Tommy Byrne DP	15.00	6.75
❑ 124 Sibby Sisti DP	15.00	6.75
❑ 125 Dick Williams DP	22.50	10.00
❑ 126 Bill Connelly DP	15.00	6.75
❑ 127 Clint Courtney DP	15.00	6.75
❑ 128 Wilmer Mizell DP (Inconsistent design, logo on front with black birds)	20.00	9.00
❑ 129 Keith Thomas	30.00	13.50
❑ 130 Turk Lown DP	15.00	6.75
❑ 131 Harry Byrd DP	15.00	6.75
❑ 132 Tom Morgan	30.00	13.50
❑ 133 Gil Coan	30.00	13.50
❑ 134 Rube Walker	40.00	18.00
❑ 135 Al Rosen DP	25.00	11.00
❑ 136 Ken Heintzelman DP	15.00	6.75
❑ 137 John Rutherford DP	15.00	6.75
❑ 138 George Kell	60.00	27.00
❑ 139 Sammy White	30.00	13.50
❑ 140 Tommy Glaviano	30.00	13.50
❑ 141 Allie Reynolds DP	25.00	11.00
❑ 142 Vic Wertz	40.00	18.00
❑ 143 Billy Pierce	50.00	22.00
❑ 144 Bob Schultz DP	15.00	6.75
❑ 145 Harry Dorish DP	15.00	6.75
❑ 146 Granny Hamner	30.00	13.50
❑ 147 Warren Spahn	150.00	70.00
❑ 148 Mickey Grasso	30.00	13.50
❑ 149 Dom DiMaggio DP	35.00	16.00
❑ 150 Harry Simpson DP	15.00	6.75
❑ 151 Hoyt Wilhelm	80.00	36.00
❑ 152 Bob Adams DP	15.00	6.75
❑ 153 Andy Seminick DP	15.00	6.75
❑ 154 Dick Groat	40.00	18.00
❑ 155 Dutch Leonard	30.00	13.50
❑ 156 Jim Rivera DP	30.00	13.50
❑ 157 Bob Addis DP	15.00	6.75
❑ 158 Johnny Logan	35.00	16.00
❑ 159 Wayne Terwilliger DP	15.00	6.75
❑ 160 Bob Young	30.00	13.50
❑ 161 Vern Bickford DP	15.00	6.75
❑ 162 Ted Kluszewski	50.00	22.00
❑ 163 Fred Hatfield DP	15.00	6.75
❑ 164 Frank Shea DP	15.00	6.75
❑ 165 Billy Hoeft	30.00	13.50
❑ 166 Billy Hunter	25.00	11.00
❑ 167 Art Schult	25.00	11.00
❑ 168 Willard Schmidt	25.00	11.00
❑ 169 Dizzy Trout	40.00	18.00
❑ 170 Bill Werle	25.00	11.00
❑ 171 Bill Glynn	25.00	11.00
❑ 172 Rip Repulski	25.00	11.00
❑ 173 Preston Ward	25.00	11.00
❑ 174 Billy Loes	40.00	18.00
❑ 175 Ron Kline	25.00	11.00
❑ 176 Don Hoak	40.00	18.00
❑ 177 Jim Dyck	25.00	11.00
❑ 178 Jim Waugh	25.00	11.00
❑ 179 Gene Hermanski	25.00	11.00
❑ 180 Virgil Stallcup	25.00	11.00
❑ 181 Al Zarilla	25.00	11.00
❑ 182 Bobby Hofman	25.00	11.00
❑ 183 Stu Miller	40.00	18.00
❑ 184 Hal Brown	25.00	11.00
❑ 185 Jim Pendleton	25.00	11.00
❑ 186 Charlie Bishop	25.00	11.00
❑ 187 Jim Fridley	25.00	11.00
❑ 188 Andy Carey	40.00	18.00
❑ 189 Ray Jablonski	25.00	11.00
❑ 190 Dixie Walker CO	40.00	18.00
❑ 191 Ralph Kiner	80.00	36.00
❑ 192 Wally Westlake	25.00	11.00
❑ 193 Mike Clark	25.00	11.00
❑ 194 Eddie Kazak	25.00	11.00
❑ 195 Ed McGhee	25.00	11.00
❑ 196 Bob Keegan	25.00	11.00
❑ 197 Del Crandall	40.00	18.00
❑ 198 Forrest Main	25.00	11.00
❑ 199 Marion Fricano	25.00	11.00
❑ 200 Gordon Goldsberry	25.00	11.00
❑ 201 Paul LaPalme	25.00	11.00
❑ 202 Carl Sawatski	25.00	11.00
❑ 203 Cliff Fannin	25.00	11.00
❑ 204 Dick Bokelman	25.00	11.00
❑ 205 Vern Benson	25.00	11.00
❑ 206 Ed Bailey	25.00	11.00
❑ 207 Whitey Ford	160.00	70.00
❑ 208 Jim Wilson	25.00	11.00
❑ 209 Jim Greengrass	25.00	11.00
❑ 210 Bob Cerv	40.00	18.00
❑ 211 J.W. Porter	25.00	11.00
❑ 212 Jack Dittmer	25.00	11.00
❑ 213 Ray Scarborough	25.00	11.00
❑ 214 Bill Bruton	40.00	18.00
❑ 215 Gene Conley	40.00	18.00
❑ 216 Jim Hughes	25.00	11.00
❑ 217 Murray Wall	25.00	11.00
❑ 218 Les Fusselman	25.00	11.00
❑ 219 Pete Runnels UER (Photo actually Don Johnson)	40.00	18.00
❑ 220 Satchel Paige UER (Misspelled Satchell on card front)	450.00	200.00
❑ 221 Bob Milliken	100.00	45.00
❑ 222 Vic Janowicz DP	60.00	27.00
❑ 223 Johnny O'Brien DP	50.00	22.00
❑ 224 Lou Sleater DP	100.00	45.00
❑ 225 Bobby Shantz	120.00	55.00
❑ 226 Ed Erautt	100.00	45.00
❑ 227 Morrie Martin	100.00	45.00
❑ 228 Hal Newhouser	150.00	70.00
❑ 229 Rocky Krsnich	100.00	45.00
❑ 230 Johnny Lindell DP	50.00	22.00
❑ 231 Solly Hemus DP	50.00	22.00
❑ 232 Dick Kokos	100.00	45.00
❑ 233 Al Aber	100.00	45.00
❑ 234 Ray Murray DP	50.00	22.00
❑ 235 John Hetki DP	50.00	22.00
❑ 236 Harry Perkowski DP	50.00	22.00
❑ 237 Bud Podbielan DP	50.00	22.00
❑ 238 Cal Hogue DP	50.00	22.00
❑ 239 Jim Delsing	100.00	45.00
❑ 240 Fred Marsh	100.00	45.00
❑ 241 Al Sima DP	50.00	22.00
❑ 242 Charlie Silvera	120.00	55.00
❑ 243 Carlos Bernier DP	50.00	22.00
❑ 244 Willie Mays	2700.00	1200.00
❑ 245 Bill Norman CO	100.00	45.00
❑ 246 Roy Face DP	80.00	36.00
❑ 247 Mike Sandlock DP	50.00	22.00
❑ 248 Gene Stephens DP	50.00	22.00
❑ 249 Eddie O'Brien	100.00	45.00
❑ 250 Bob Wilson	100.00	45.00
❑ 251 Sid Hudson	100.00	45.00
❑ 252 Hank Foiles	100.00	45.00
❑ 253 Does not exist		
❑ 254 Preacher Roe DP	80.00	36.00
❑ 255 Dixie Howell	100.00	45.00
❑ 256 Les Peden	100.00	45.00
❑ 257 Bob Boyd	100.00	45.00
❑ 258 Jim Gilliam	300.00	135.00
❑ 259 Roy McMillan DP	100.00	45.00
❑ 260 Sam Calderone	100.00	45.00
❑ 261 Does not exist		
❑ 262 Bob Oldis	100.00	45.00
❑ 263 Johnny Podres	300.00	135.00
❑ 264 Gene Woodling DP	100.00	45.00
❑ 265 Jackie Jensen	125.00	55.00
❑ 266 Bob Cain	100.00	45.00
❑ 267 Does not exist		
❑ 268 Does not exist		
❑ 269 Duane Pillette	100.00	45.00
❑ 270 Vern Stephens	120.00	55.00
❑ 271 Does not exist		
❑ 272 Bill Antonello	100.00	45.00
❑ 273 Harvey Haddix	125.00	55.00
❑ 274 John Riddle CO	100.00	45.00
❑ 275 Does not exist		
❑ 276 Ken Raffensberger	100.00	45.00
❑ 277 Don Lund	100.00	45.00
❑ 278 Willie Miranda	100.00	45.00
❑ 279 Joe Coleman DP	50.00	22.00
❑ 280 Milt Bolling	350.00	57.50

1954 Topps

	NRMT	VG-E
COMPLETE SET (250)	7500.00	3400.00
COMMON (1-50/76-250)	15.00	6.75
COMMON CARD (51-75)	25.00	11.00
WRAPPER (1-CENT, DATED)	200.00	90.00
WRAPPER (1-CENT, UNDATED)	150.00	70.00
WRAPPER (5-CENT, DATED)	300.00	135.00
WRAPPER (5-CENT, UNDATED)	250.00	110.00

Card	NRMT	VG-E
❑ 1 Ted Williams	650.00	230.00
❑ 2 Gus Zernial	25.00	11.00
❑ 3 Monte Irvin	40.00	18.00
❑ 4 Hank Sauer	25.00	11.00
❑ 5 Ed Lopat	25.00	11.00
❑ 6 Pete Runnels	25.00	11.00
❑ 7 Ted Kluszewski	40.00	18.00
❑ 8 Bob Young	15.00	6.75
❑ 9 Harvey Haddix	25.00	11.00
❑ 10 Jackie Robinson	325.00	145.00
❑ 11 Paul Leslie Smith	15.00	6.75
❑ 12 Del Crandall	25.00	11.00
❑ 13 Billy Martin	70.00	32.00

	No.	Player	NRMT	VG-E
❑	14	Preacher Roe	25.00	11.00
❑	15	Al Rosen	25.00	11.00
❑	16	Vic Janowicz	25.00	11.00
❑	17	Phil Rizzuto	75.00	34.00
❑	18	Walt Dropo	25.00	11.00
❑	19	Johnny Lipon	15.00	6.75
❑	20	Warren Spahn	75.00	34.00
❑	21	Bobby Shantz	25.00	11.00
❑	22	Jim Greengrass	15.00	6.75
❑	23	Luke Easter	25.00	11.00
❑	24	Granny Hamner	15.00	6.75
❑	25	Harvey Kuenn	40.00	18.00
❑	26	Ray Jablonski	15.00	6.75
❑	27	Ferris Fain	25.00	11.00
❑	28	Paul Minner	15.00	6.75
❑	29	Jim Hegan	25.00	11.00
❑	30	Eddie Mathews	75.00	34.00
❑	31	Johnny Klippstein	15.00	6.75
❑	32	Duke Snider	150.00	70.00
❑	33	Johnny Schmitz	15.00	6.75
❑	34	Jim Rivera	15.00	6.75
❑	35	Jim Gilliam	40.00	18.00
❑	36	Hoyt Wilhelm	50.00	22.00
❑	37	Whitey Ford	100.00	45.00
❑	38	Eddie Stanky MG	25.00	11.00
❑	39	Sherm Lollar	25.00	11.00
❑	40	Mel Parnell	25.00	11.00
❑	41	Willie Jones	15.00	6.75
❑	42	Don Mueller	25.00	11.00
❑	43	Dick Groat	25.00	11.00
❑	44	Ned Garver	15.00	6.75
❑	45	Richie Ashburn	70.00	32.00
❑	46	Ken Raffensberger	15.00	6.75
❑	47	Ellis Kinder	15.00	6.75
❑	48	Billy Hunter	25.00	11.00
❑	49	Ray Murray	15.00	6.75
❑	50	Yogi Berra	160.00	70.00
❑	51	Johnny Lindell	25.00	11.00
❑	52	Vic Power	35.00	16.00
❑	53	Jack Dittmer	25.00	11.00
❑	54	Vern Stephens	30.00	13.50
❑	55	Phil Cavarretta MG	30.00	13.50
❑	56	Willie Miranda	25.00	11.00
❑	57	Luis Aloma	25.00	11.00
❑	58	Bob Wilson	25.00	11.00
❑	59	Gene Conley	30.00	13.50
❑	60	Frank Baumholtz	25.00	11.00
❑	61	Bob Cain	25.00	11.00
❑	62	Eddie Robinson	25.00	11.00
❑	63	Johnny Pesky	30.00	13.50
❑	64	Hank Thompson	25.00	11.00
❑	65	Bob Swift CO	25.00	11.00
❑	66	Ted Lepcio	25.00	11.00
❑	67	Jim Willis	25.00	11.00
❑	68	Sam Calderone	25.00	11.00
❑	69	Bud Podbielan	25.00	11.00
❑	70	Larry Doby	50.00	22.00
❑	71	Frank Smith	25.00	11.00
❑	72	Preston Ward	25.00	11.00
❑	73	Wayne Terwilliger	25.00	11.00
❑	74	Bill Taylor	25.00	11.00
❑	75	Fred Haney MG	25.00	11.00
❑	76	Bob Scheffing CO	15.00	6.75
❑	77	Ray Boone	25.00	11.00
❑	78	Ted Kazanski	15.00	6.75
❑	79	Andy Pafko	25.00	11.00
❑	80	Jackie Jensen	25.00	11.00
❑	81	Dave Hoskins	15.00	6.75
❑	82	Milt Bolling	15.00	6.75
❑	83	Joe Collins	25.00	11.00
❑	84	Dick Cole	15.00	6.75
❑	85	Bob Turley	30.00	13.50
❑	86	Billy Herman CO	25.00	11.00
❑	87	Roy Face	25.00	11.00
❑	88	Matt Batts	15.00	6.75
❑	89	Howie Pollet	15.00	6.75
❑	90	Willie Mays	500.00	220.00
❑	91	Bob Oldis	15.00	6.75
❑	92	Wally Westlake	15.00	6.75
❑	93	Sid Hudson	15.00	6.75
❑	94	Ernie Banks	750.00	350.00
❑	95	Hal Rice	15.00	6.75
❑	96	Charlie Silvera	25.00	11.00
❑	97	Jerald Hal Lane	15.00	6.75
❑	98	Joe Black	30.00	13.50
❑	99	Bobby Hofman	15.00	6.75
❑	100	Bob Keegan	15.00	6.75
❑	101	Gene Woodling	25.00	11.00
❑	102	Gil Hodges	70.00	32.00
❑	103	Jim Lemon	15.00	6.75
❑	104	Mike Sandlock	15.00	6.75
❑	105	Andy Carey	25.00	11.00
❑	106	Dick Kokos	15.00	6.75
❑	107	Duane Pillette	15.00	6.75
❑	108	Thornton Kipper	15.00	6.75
❑	109	Bill Bruton	25.00	11.00
❑	110	Harry Dorish	15.00	6.75
❑	111	Jim Delsing	15.00	6.75
❑	112	Bill Renna	15.00	6.75
❑	113	Bob Boyd	15.00	6.75
❑	114	Dean Stone	15.00	6.75
❑	115	Rip Repulski	15.00	6.75
❑	116	Steve Bilko	15.00	6.75
❑	117	Solly Hemus	15.00	6.75
❑	118	Carl Scheib	15.00	6.75
❑	119	Johnny Antonelli	25.00	11.00
❑	120	Roy McMillan	25.00	11.00
❑	121	Clem Labine	25.00	11.00
❑	122	Johnny Logan	25.00	11.00
❑	123	Bobby Adams	15.00	6.75
❑	124	Marion Fricano	15.00	6.75
❑	125	Harry Perkowski	15.00	6.75
❑	126	Ben Wade	15.00	6.75
❑	127	Steve O'Neill MG	15.00	6.75
❑	128	Hank Aaron	1500.00	700.00
❑	129	Forrest Jacobs	15.00	6.75
❑	130	Hank Bauer	25.00	11.00
❑	131	Reno Bertoia	15.00	6.75
❑	132	Tommy Lasorda	200.00	90.00
❑	133	Del Baker CO	15.00	6.75
❑	134	Cal Hogue	15.00	6.75
❑	135	Joe Presko	15.00	6.75
❑	136	Connie Ryan	15.00	6.75
❑	137	Wally Moon	30.00	13.50
❑	138	Bob Borkowski	15.00	6.75
❑	139	The O'Briens Johnny O'Brien Eddie O'Brien	40.00	18.00
❑	140	Tom Wright	15.00	6.75
❑	141	Joey Jay	25.00	11.00
❑	142	Tom Poholsky	15.00	6.75
❑	143	Rollie Hemsley CO	15.00	6.75
❑	144	Bill Werle	15.00	6.75
❑	145	Elmer Valo	15.00	6.75
❑	146	Don Johnson	15.00	6.75
❑	147	Johnny Riddle CO	15.00	6.75
❑	148	Bob Trice	15.00	6.75
❑	149	Al Robertson	15.00	6.75
❑	150	Dick Kryhoski	15.00	6.75
❑	151	Alex Grammas	15.00	6.75
❑	152	Michael Blyzka	15.00	6.75
❑	153	Al Walker	15.00	6.75
❑	154	Mike Fornieles	15.00	6.75
❑	155	Bob Kennedy	25.00	11.00
❑	156	Joe Coleman	15.00	6.75
❑	157	Don Lenhardt	15.00	6.75
❑	158	Peanuts Lowrey	15.00	6.75
❑	159	Dave Philley	15.00	6.75
❑	160	Ralph Kress CO	15.00	6.75
❑	161	John Hetki	15.00	6.75
❑	162	Herman Wehmeier	15.00	6.75
❑	163	Frank House	15.00	6.75
❑	164	Stu Miller	25.00	11.00
❑	165	Jim Pendleton	15.00	6.75
❑	166	Johnny Podres	30.00	13.50
❑	167	Don Lund	15.00	6.75
❑	168	Morrie Martin	15.00	6.75
❑	169	Jim Hughes	25.00	11.00
❑	170	James(Dusty) Rhodes	25.00	11.00
❑	171	Leo Kiely	15.00	6.75
❑	172	Harold Brown	15.00	6.75
❑	173	Jack Harshman	15.00	6.75
❑	174	Tom Qualters	15.00	6.75
❑	175	Frank Leja	25.00	11.00
❑	176	Robert Keely CO	15.00	6.75
❑	177	Bob Milliken	15.00	6.75
❑	178	Bill Glynn	15.00	6.75
❑	179	Gair Allie	15.00	6.75
❑	180	Wes Westrum	25.00	11.00
❑	181	Mel Roach	15.00	6.75
❑	182	Chuck Harmon	15.00	6.75
❑	183	Earle Combs CO	25.00	11.00
❑	184	Ed Bailey	15.00	6.75
❑	185	Chuck Stobbs	15.00	6.75
❑	186	Karl Olson	15.00	6.75
❑	187	Heinie Manush CO	25.00	11.00
❑	188	Dave Jolly	15.00	6.75
❑	189	Bob Ross	15.00	6.75
❑	190	Ray Herbert	15.00	6.75
❑	191	John(Dick) Schofield	25.00	11.00
❑	192	Ellis Deal CO	15.00	6.75
❑	193	Johnny Hopp CO	25.00	11.00
❑	194	Bill Sarni	15.00	6.75
❑	195	Billy Consolo	15.00	6.75
❑	196	Stan Jok	15.00	6.75
❑	197	Lynwood Rowe CO ("Schoolboy")	25.00	11.00
❑	198	Carl Sawatski	15.00	6.75
❑	199	Glenn(Rocky) Nelson	15.00	6.75
❑	200	Larry Jansen	25.00	11.00
❑	201	Al Kaline	750.00	350.00
❑	202	Bob Purkey	25.00	11.00
❑	203	Harry Brecheen CO	25.00	11.00
❑	204	Angel Scull	15.00	6.75
❑	205	Johnny Sain	30.00	13.50
❑	206	Ray Crone	15.00	6.75
❑	207	Tom Oliver CO	15.00	6.75
❑	208	Grady Hatton	15.00	6.75
❑	209	Chuck Thompson	15.00	6.75
❑	210	Bob Buhl	25.00	11.00
❑	211	Don Hoak	25.00	11.00
❑	212	Bob Micelotta	15.00	6.75
❑	213	Johnny Fitzpatrick CO	15.00	6.75
❑	214	Arnie Portocarrero	15.00	6.75
❑	215	Ed McGhee	15.00	6.75
❑	216	Al Sima	15.00	6.75
❑	217	Paul Schreiber CO	15.00	6.75
❑	218	Fred Marsh	15.00	6.75
❑	219	Chuck Kress	15.00	6.75
❑	220	Ruben Gomez	25.00	11.00
❑	221	Dick Brodowski	15.00	6.75
❑	222	Bill Wilson	15.00	6.75
❑	223	Joe Haynes CO	15.00	6.75
❑	224	Dick Weik	15.00	6.75
❑	225	Don Liddle	15.00	6.75
❑	226	Jehosie Heard	15.00	6.75
❑	227	Colonel Mills CO	15.00	6.75
❑	228	Gene Hermanski	15.00	6.75
❑	229	Bob Talbot	15.00	6.75
❑	230	Bob Kuzava	25.00	11.00
❑	231	Roy Smalley	15.00	6.75
❑	232	Lou Limmer	15.00	6.75
❑	233	Augie Galan CO	15.00	6.75
❑	234	Jerry Lynch	15.00	6.75
❑	235	Vern Law	25.00	11.00
❑	236	Paul Penson	15.00	6.75
❑	237	Mike Ryba CO	15.00	6.75
❑	238	Al Aber	15.00	6.75
❑	239	Bill Skowron	100.00	45.00
❑	240	Sam Mele	25.00	11.00
❑	241	Robert Miller	15.00	6.75
❑	242	Curt Roberts	15.00	6.75
❑	243	Ray Blades CO	15.00	6.75
❑	244	Leroy Wheat	15.00	6.75
❑	245	Roy Sievers	25.00	11.00
❑	246	Howie Fox	15.00	6.75
❑	247	Ed Mayo CO	15.00	6.75
❑	248	Al Smith	25.00	11.00
❑	249	Wilmer Mizell	25.00	11.00
❑	250	Ted Williams	800.00	325.00

1955 Topps

	NRMT	VG-E
COMPLETE SET (206)	7200.00	3200.00
COMMON CARD (1-150)	12.00	5.50
COMMON CARD (151-160)	20.00	9.00
COMMON CARD (161-210)	30.00	13.50
WRAPPER (1-CENT, DATED)	150.00	70.00
WRAPPER (1-CENT, UNDATED)	50.00	22.00
WRAPPER (5-CENT, DATED)	150.00	70.00
WRAPPER (5-CENT, DATED)	100.00	45.00

	No.	Player	NRMT	VG-E
❑	1	Dusty Rhodes	50.00	10.00
❑	2	Ted Williams	475.00	210.00
❑	3	Art Fowler	15.00	6.75

- ❑ 4 Al Kaline 175.00 80.00
- ❑ 5 Jim Gilliam 25.00 11.00
- ❑ 6 Stan Hack MG 18.00 8.00
- ❑ 7 Jim Hegan 15.00 6.75
- ❑ 8 Harold Smith 12.00 5.50
- ❑ 9 Robert Miller 12.00 5.50
- ❑ 10 Bob Keegan 12.00 5.50
- ❑ 11 Ferris Fain 15.00 6.75
- ❑ 12 Vernon(Jake) Thies 12.00 5.50
- ❑ 13 Fred Marsh 12.00 5.50
- ❑ 14 Jim Finigan 12.00 5.50
- ❑ 15 Jim Pendleton 12.00 5.50
- ❑ 16 Roy Sievers 15.00 6.75
- ❑ 17 Bobby Hofman 12.00 5.50
- ❑ 18 Russ Kemmerer 12.00 5.50
- ❑ 19 Billy Herman CO 18.00 8.00
- ❑ 20 Andy Carey 15.00 6.75
- ❑ 21 Alex Grammas 12.00 5.50
- ❑ 22 Bill Skowron 20.00 9.00
- ❑ 23 Jack Parks 12.00 5.50
- ❑ 24 Hal Newhouser 18.00 8.00
- ❑ 25 Johnny Podres 20.00 9.00
- ❑ 26 Dick Groat 18.00 8.00
- ❑ 27 Billy Gardner 15.00 6.75
- ❑ 28 Ernie Banks 175.00 80.00
- ❑ 29 Herman Wehmeier 12.00 5.50
- ❑ 30 Vic Power 15.00 6.75
- ❑ 31 Warren Spahn 90.00 40.00
- ❑ 32 Warren McGhee 12.00 5.50
- ❑ 33 Tom Qualters 12.00 5.50
- ❑ 34 Wayne Terwilliger 12.00 5.50
- ❑ 35 Dave Jolly 12.00 5.50
- ❑ 36 Leo Kiely 12.00 5.50
- ❑ 37 Joe Cunningham 15.00 6.75
- ❑ 38 Bob Turley 18.00 8.00
- ❑ 39 Bill Glynn 12.00 5.50
- ❑ 40 Don Hoak 15.00 6.75
- ❑ 41 Chuck Stobbs 12.00 5.50
- ❑ 42 John(Windy) McCall 12.00 5.50
- ❑ 43 Harvey Haddix 18.00 8.00
- ❑ 44 Harold Valentine 12.00 5.50
- ❑ 45 Hank Sauer 18.00 8.00
- ❑ 46 Ted Kazanski 12.00 5.50
- ❑ 47 Hank Aaron UER 350.00 160.00
  (Birth incorrectly listed as 2/10)
- ❑ 48 Bob Kennedy 15.00 6.75
- ❑ 49 J.W. Porter 12.00 5.50
- ❑ 50 Jackie Robinson 300.00 135.00
- ❑ 51 Jim Hughes 15.00 6.75
- ❑ 52 Bill Tremel 12.00 5.50
- ❑ 53 Bill Taylor 12.00 5.50
- ❑ 54 Lou Limmer 12.00 5.50
- ❑ 55 Rip Repulski 12.00 5.50
- ❑ 56 Ray Jablonski 12.00 5.50
- ❑ 57 Billy O'Dell 12.00 5.50
- ❑ 58 Jim Rivera 12.00 5.50
- ❑ 59 Gair Allie 12.00 5.50
- ❑ 60 Dean Stone 12.00 5.50
- ❑ 61 Forrest Jacobs 12.00 5.50
- ❑ 62 Thornton Kipper 12.00 5.50
- ❑ 63 Joe Collins 15.00 6.75
- ❑ 64 Gus Triandos 18.00 8.00
- ❑ 65 Ray Boone 18.00 8.00
- ❑ 66 Ron Jackson 12.00 5.50
- ❑ 67 Wally Moon 18.00 8.00
- ❑ 68 Jim Davis 12.00 5.50
- ❑ 69 Ed Bailey 15.00 6.75
- ❑ 70 Al Rosen 18.00 8.00
- ❑ 71 Ruben Gomez 12.00 5.50
- ❑ 72 Karl Olson 12.00 5.50
- ❑ 73 Jack Shepard 12.00 5.50
- ❑ 74 Bob Borkowski 12.00 5.50
- ❑ 75 Sandy Amoros 30.00 13.50
- ❑ 76 Howie Pollet 12.00 5.50
- ❑ 77 Arnie Portocarrero 12.00 5.50
- ❑ 78 Gordon Jones 12.00 5.50
- ❑ 79 Clyde(Danny) Schell 12.00 5.50
- ❑ 80 Bob Grim 18.00 8.00
- ❑ 81 Gene Conley 15.00 6.75
- ❑ 82 Chuck Harmon 12.00 5.50
- ❑ 83 Tom Brewer 12.00 5.50
- ❑ 84 Camilo Pascual 18.00 8.00
- ❑ 85 Don Mossi 18.00 8.00
- ❑ 86 Bill Wilson 12.00 5.50
- ❑ 87 Frank House 12.00 5.50
- ❑ 88 Bob Skinner 18.00 8.00
- ❑ 89 Joe Frazier 15.00 6.75
- ❑ 90 Karl Spooner 15.00 6.75
- ❑ 91 Milt Bolling 12.00 5.50
- ❑ 92 Don Zimmer 30.00 13.50
- ❑ 93 Steve Bilko 12.00 5.50
- ❑ 94 Reno Bertoia 12.00 5.50
- ❑ 95 Preston Ward 12.00 5.50
- ❑ 96 Chuck Bishop 12.00 5.50
- ❑ 97 Carlos Paula 12.00 5.50
- ❑ 98 John Riddle CO 12.00 5.50
- ❑ 99 Frank Leja 12.00 5.50
- ❑ 100 Monte Irvin 35.00 16.00
- ❑ 101 Johnny Gray 12.00 5.50
- ❑ 102 Wally Westlake 12.00 5.50
- ❑ 103 Chuck White 12.00 5.50
- ❑ 104 Jack Harshman 12.00 5.50
- ❑ 105 Chuck Diering 12.00 5.50
- ❑ 106 Frank Sullivan 12.00 5.50
- ❑ 107 Curt Roberts 12.00 5.50
- ❑ 108 Al Walker 15.00 6.75
- ❑ 109 Ed Lopat 18.00 8.00
- ❑ 110 Gus Zernial 15.00 6.75
- ❑ 111 Bob Milliken 15.00 6.75
- ❑ 112 Nelson King 12.00 5.50
- ❑ 113 Harry Brecheen CO 15.00 6.75
- ❑ 114 Louis Ortiz 12.00 5.50
- ❑ 115 Ellis Kinder 12.00 5.50
- ❑ 116 Tom Hurd 12.00 5.50
- ❑ 117 Mel Roach 12.00 5.50
- ❑ 118 Bob Purkey 12.00 5.50
- ❑ 119 Bob Lennon 12.00 5.50
- ❑ 120 Ted Kluszewski 40.00 18.00
- ❑ 121 Bill Renna 12.00 5.50
- ❑ 122 Carl Sawatski 12.00 5.50
- ❑ 123 Sandy Koufax 900.00 400.00
- ❑ 124 Harmon Killebrew 250.00 110.00
- ❑ 125 Ken Boyer 60.00 27.00
- ❑ 126 Dick Hall 12.00 5.50
- ❑ 127 Dale Long 18.00 8.00
- ❑ 128 Ted Lepcio 12.00 5.50
- ❑ 129 Elvin Tappe 12.00 5.50
- ❑ 130 Mayo Smith MG 12.00 5.50
- ❑ 131 Grady Hatton 12.00 5.50
- ❑ 132 Bob Trice 12.00 5.50
- ❑ 133 Dave Hoskins 12.00 5.50
- ❑ 134 Joey Jay 15.00 6.75
- ❑ 135 Johnny O'Brien 15.00 6.75
- ❑ 136 Veston(Bunky) Stewart 12.00 5.50
- ❑ 137 Harry Elliott 12.00 5.50
- ❑ 138 Ray Herbert 12.00 5.50
- ❑ 139 Steve Kraly 12.00 5.50
- ❑ 140 Mel Parnell 15.00 6.75
- ❑ 141 Tom Wright 12.00 5.50
- ❑ 142 Jerry Lynch 15.00 6.75
- ❑ 143 John(Dick) Schofield 15.00 6.75
- ❑ 144 John(Joe) Amalfitano 12.00 5.50
- ❑ 145 Elmer Valo 12.00 5.50
- ❑ 146 Dick Donovan 12.00 5.50
- ❑ 147 Hugh Pepper 12.00 5.50
- ❑ 148 Hector Brown 12.00 5.50
- ❑ 149 Ray Crone 12.00 5.50
- ❑ 150 Mike Higgins MG 12.00 5.50
- ❑ 151 Ralph Kress CO 20.00 9.00
- ❑ 152 Harry Agganis 70.00 32.00
- ❑ 153 Bud Podbielan 20.00 9.00
- ❑ 154 Willie Miranda 20.00 9.00
- ❑ 155 Eddie Mathews 90.00 40.00
- ❑ 156 Joe Black 35.00 16.00
- ❑ 157 Robert Miller 20.00 9.00
- ❑ 158 Tommy Carroll 20.00 9.00
- ❑ 159 Johnny Schmitz 20.00 9.00
- ❑ 160 Ray Narleski 20.00 9.00
- ❑ 161 Chuck Tanner 35.00 16.00
- ❑ 162 Joe Coleman 30.00 13.50
- ❑ 163 Faye Throneberry 30.00 13.50
- ❑ 164 Roberto Clemente 2200.00 1000.00
- ❑ 165 Don Johnson 30.00 13.50
- ❑ 166 Hank Bauer 45.00 20.00
- ❑ 167 Thomas Casagrande 30.00 13.50
- ❑ 168 Duane Pillette 30.00 13.50
- ❑ 169 Bob Oldis 30.00 13.50
- ❑ 170 Jim Pearce DP 15.00 6.75
- ❑ 171 Dick Brodowski 30.00 13.50
- ❑ 172 Frank Baumholtz DP 15.00 6.75
- ❑ 173 Bob Kline 30.00 13.50
- ❑ 174 Rudy Minarcin 30.00 13.50
- ❑ 175 Does not exist
- ❑ 176 Norm Zauchin 30.00 13.50
- ❑ 177 Al Robertson 30.00 13.50
- ❑ 178 Bobby Adams 30.00 13.50
- ❑ 179 Jim Bolger 30.00 13.50
- ❑ 180 Clem Labine 45.00 20.00
- ❑ 181 Roy McMillan 40.00 18.00
- ❑ 182 Humberto Robinson 30.00 13.50
- ❑ 183 Anthony Jacobs 30.00 13.50
- ❑ 184 Harry Perkowski DP 15.00 6.75
- ❑ 185 Don Ferrarese 30.00 13.50
- ❑ 186 Does not exist
- ❑ 187 Gil Hodges 135.00 60.00
- ❑ 188 Charlie Silvera DP 15.00 6.75
- ❑ 189 Phil Rizzuto 135.00 60.00
- ❑ 190 Gene Woodling 40.00 18.00
- ❑ 191 Eddie Stanky MG 40.00 18.00
- ❑ 192 Jim Delsing 30.00 13.50
- ❑ 193 Johnny Sain 45.00 20.00
- ❑ 194 Willie Mays 400.00 180.00
- ❑ 195 Ed Roebuck 45.00 20.00
- ❑ 196 Gale Wade 30.00 13.50
- ❑ 197 Al Smith 40.00 18.00
- ❑ 198 Yogi Berra 200.00 90.00
- ❑ 199 Odbert Hamric 40.00 18.00
- ❑ 200 Jackie Jensen 35.00 16.00
- ❑ 201 Sherman Lollar ! 20.00 9.00
- ❑ 202 Jim Owens 30.00 13.50
- ❑ 203 Does not exist
- ❑ 204 Frank Smith 30.00 13.50
- ❑ 205 Gene Freese 30.00 13.50
- ❑ 206 Pete Daley 30.00 13.50
- ❑ 207 Billy Consolo 30.00 13.50
- ❑ 208 Ray Moore 30.00 13.50
- ❑ 209 Does not exist
- ❑ 210 Duke Snider 450.00 135.00

1956 Topps

	NRMT	VG-E
COMPLETE SET (340)	7000.00	3200.00
COMMON CARD (1-100)	10.00	4.50
COMMON CARD (101-180)	12.00	5.50
COMMON CARD (261-340)	12.00	5.50
COMMON CARD (181-260)	15.00	6.75
WRAPPER (1-CENT)	250.00	110.00
WRAPPER (1-CENT, REPEAT)	100.00	45.00
WRAPPER (5-CENT)	200.00	90.00

❑	1	William Harridge PRES	100.00	28.00
❑	2	Warren Giles PRES	25.00	11.00
❑	3	Elmer Valo	10.00	4.50
❑	4	Carlos Paula	10.00	4.50
❑	5	Ted Williams	325.00	145.00
❑	6	Ray Boone	16.00	7.25
❑	7	Ron Negray	10.00	4.50
❑	8	Walter Alston MG	40.00	18.00
❑	9	Ruben Gomez DP	9.00	4.00
❑	10	Warren Spahn	75.00	34.00
❑	11A	Chicago Cubs (Centered)	30.00	13.50
❑	11B	Cubs Team (Dated 1955)	80.00	36.00
❑	11C	Cubs Team (Name at far left)	30.00	13.50
❑	12	Andy Carey	15.00	6.75
❑	13	Roy Face	16.00	7.25
❑	14	Ken Boyer DP	16.00	7.25
❑	15	Ernie Banks DP	80.00	36.00
❑	16	Hector Lopez	16.00	7.25
❑	17	Gene Conley	15.00	6.75
❑	18	Dick Donovan	10.00	4.50
❑	19	Chuck Diering	10.00	4.50
❑	20	Al Kaline	100.00	45.00
❑	21	Joe Collins DP	15.00	6.75
❑	22	Jim Finigan	10.00	4.50
❑	23	Fred Marsh	10.00	4.50
❑	24	Dick Groat	16.00	7.25
❑	25	Ted Kluszewski	35.00	16.00
❑	26	Grady Hatton	10.00	4.50
❑	27	Nelson Burbrink	10.00	4.50
❑	28	Bobby Hofman	10.00	4.50
❑	29	Jack Harshman	10.00	4.50
❑	30	Jackie Robinson DP	175.00	80.00
❑	31	Hank Aaron UER (Small photo actually Willie Mays)	275.00	125.00
❑	32	Frank House	10.00	4.50
❑	33	Roberto Clemente	450.00	200.00
❑	34	Tom Brewer	10.00	4.50
❑	35	Al Rosen	16.00	7.25
❑	36	Rudy Minarcin	10.00	4.50
❑	37	Alex Grammas	10.00	4.50
❑	38	Bob Kennedy	15.00	6.75
❑	39	Don Mossi	15.00	6.75
❑	40	Bob Turley	16.00	7.25
❑	41	Hank Sauer	16.00	7.25
❑	42	Sandy Amoros	16.00	7.25
❑	43	Ray Moore	10.00	4.50
❑	44	Windy McCall	10.00	4.50
❑	45	Gus Zernial	15.00	6.75
❑	46	Gene Freese DP	9.00	4.00
❑	47	Art Fowler	10.00	4.50
❑	48	Jim Hegan	15.00	6.75
❑	49	Pedro Ramos	10.00	4.50
❑	50	Dusty Rhodes	16.00	7.25
❑	51	Ernie Oravetz	10.00	4.50
❑	52	Bob Grim	15.00	6.75
❑	53	Arnie Portocarrero	10.00	4.50
❑	54	Bob Keegan	10.00	4.50
❑	55	Wally Moon	16.00	7.25
❑	56	Dale Long	15.00	6.75
❑	57	Duke Maas	10.00	4.50
❑	58	Ed Roebuck	15.00	6.75
❑	59	Jose Santiago	10.00	4.50
❑	60	Mayo Smith MG DP	9.00	4.00
❑	61	Bill Skowron	16.00	7.25
❑	62	Hal Smith	10.00	4.50
❑	63	Roger Craig	16.00	7.25
❑	64	Luis Arroyo	10.00	4.50
❑	65	Johnny O'Brien	15.00	6.75
❑	66	Bob Speake	10.00	4.50
❑	67	Vic Power	15.00	6.75
❑	68	Chuck Stobbs	10.00	4.50
❑	69	Chuck Tanner	16.00	7.25
❑	70	Jim Rivera	10.00	4.50
❑	71	Frank Sullivan	10.00	4.50
❑	72A	Phillies Team (Centered)	30.00	13.50
❑	72B	Phillies Team (Dated 1955)	80.00	36.00
❑	72C	Phillies Team (Name at far left)	30.00	13.50
❑	73	Wayne Terwilliger	10.00	4.50
❑	74	Jim King	10.00	4.50
❑	75	Roy Sievers DP	15.00	6.75
❑	76	Ray Crone	10.00	4.50
❑	77	Harvey Haddix	16.00	7.25
❑	78	Herman Wehmeier	10.00	4.50
❑	79	Sandy Koufax	350.00	160.00
❑	80	Gus Triandos DP	10.00	4.50
❑	81	Wally Westlake	10.00	4.50
❑	82	Bill Renna	10.00	4.50
❑	83	Karl Spooner	15.00	6.75
❑	84	Babe Birrer	10.00	4.50
❑	85A	Cleveland Indians (Centered)	30.00	13.50
❑	85B	Indians Team (Dated 1955)	80.00	36.00
❑	85C	Indians Team (Name at far left)	30.00	13.50
❑	86	Ray Jablonski DP	9.00	4.00
❑	87	Dean Stone	10.00	4.50
❑	88	Johnny Kucks	15.00	6.75
❑	89	Norm Zauchin	10.00	4.50
❑	90A	Cincinnati Redlegs Team (Centered)	30.00	13.50
❑	90B	Reds Team (Dated 1955)	80.00	36.00
❑	90C	Reds Team (Name at far left)	30.00	13.50
❑	91	Gail Harris	10.00	4.50
❑	92	Bob(Red) Wilson	10.00	4.50
❑	93	George Susce	10.00	4.50
❑	94	Ron Kline	10.00	4.50
❑	95A	Milwaukee Braves Team (Centered)	42.00	19.00
❑	95B	Braves Team (Dated 1955)	80.00	36.00
❑	95C	Braves Team (Name at far left)	42.00	19.00
❑	96	Bill Tremel	10.00	4.50
❑	97	Jerry Lynch	15.00	6.75
❑	98	Camilo Pascual	15.00	6.75
❑	99	Don Zimmer	15.00	6.75
❑	100A	Baltimore Orioles Team (centered)	35.00	16.00
❑	100B	Orioles Team (Dated 1955)	80.00	36.00
❑	100C	Orioles Team (Name at far left)	35.00	16.00
❑	101	Roy Campanella	150.00	70.00
❑	102	Jim Davis	12.00	5.50
❑	103	Willie Miranda	12.00	5.50
❑	104	Bob Lennon	12.00	5.50
❑	105	Al Smith	12.00	5.50
❑	106	Joe Astroth	12.00	5.50
❑	107	Eddie Mathews	70.00	32.00
❑	108	Laurin Pepper	12.00	5.50
❑	109	Enos Slaughter	35.00	16.00
❑	110	Yogi Berra	150.00	70.00
❑	111	Boston Red Sox Team Card	40.00	18.00
❑	112	Dee Fondy	12.00	5.50
❑	113	Phil Rizzuto	100.00	45.00
❑	114	Jim Owens	12.00	5.50
❑	115	Jackie Jensen	15.00	6.75
❑	116	Eddie O'Brien	12.00	5.50
❑	117	Virgil Trucks	15.00	6.75
❑	118	Nellie Fox	50.00	22.00
❑	119	Larry Jackson	15.00	6.75
❑	120	Richie Ashburn	50.00	22.00
❑	121	Pittsburgh Pirates Team Card	25.00	11.00
❑	122	Willard Nixon	12.00	5.50
❑	123	Roy McMillan	15.00	6.75
❑	124	Don Kaiser	12.00	5.50
❑	125	Minnie Minoso	35.00	16.00
❑	126	Jim Brady	12.00	5.50
❑	127	Willie Jones	15.00	6.75
❑	128	Eddie Yost	15.00	6.75
❑	129	Jake Martin	12.00	5.50
❑	130	Willie Mays	300.00	135.00
❑	131	Bob Roselli	12.00	5.50
❑	132	Bobby Avila	12.00	5.50
❑	133	Ray Narleski	12.00	5.50
❑	134	St. Louis Cardinals Team Card	25.00	11.00
❑	135	Mickey Mantle	1400.00	650.00
❑	136	Johnny Logan	15.00	6.75
❑	137	Al Silvera	12.00	5.50
❑	138	Johnny Antonelli	15.00	6.75
❑	139	Tommy Carroll	12.00	5.50
❑	140	Herb Score	60.00	27.00
❑	141	Joe Frazier	12.00	5.50
❑	142	Gene Baker	12.00	5.50
❑	143	Jim Piersall	15.00	6.75
❑	144	Leroy Powell	12.00	5.50
❑	145	Gil Hodges	50.00	22.00
❑	146	Washington Nationals Team Card	25.00	11.00
❑	147	Earl Torgeson	12.00	5.50
❑	148	Alvin Dark	16.00	7.25
❑	149	Dixie Howell	12.00	5.50
❑	150	Duke Snider	100.00	45.00
❑	151	Spook Jacobs	15.00	6.75
❑	152	Billy Hoeft	15.00	6.75
❑	153	Frank Thomas	15.00	6.75
❑	154	Dave Pope	12.00	5.50
❑	155	Harvey Kuenn	16.00	7.25
❑	156	Wes Westrum	15.00	6.75
❑	157	Dick Brodowski	12.00	5.50
❑	158	Wally Post	15.00	6.75
❑	159	Clint Courtney	12.00	5.50
❑	160	Billy Pierce	15.00	6.75
❑	161	Joe DeMaestri	12.00	5.50
❑	162	Dave(Gus) Bell	15.00	6.75
❑	163	Gene Woodling	15.00	6.75
❑	164	Harmon Killebrew	100.00	45.00
❑	165	Red Schoendienst	35.00	16.00
❑	166	Brooklyn Dodgers Team Card	250.00	110.00
❑	167	Harry Dorish	12.00	5.50
❑	168	Sammy White	12.00	5.50
❑	169	Bob Nelson	12.00	5.50
❑	170	Bill Virdon	15.00	6.75
❑	171	Jim Wilson	12.00	5.50
❑	172	Frank Torre	15.00	6.75
❑	173	Johnny Podres	22.50	10.00
❑	174	Glen Gorbous	12.00	5.50
❑	175	Del Crandall	15.00	6.75
❑	176	Alex Kellner	12.00	5.50
❑	177	Hank Bauer	22.50	10.00
❑	178	Joe Black	16.00	7.25
❑	179	Harry Chiti	12.00	5.50
❑	180	Robin Roberts	40.00	18.00
❑	181	Billy Martin	60.00	27.00
❑	182	Paul Minner	15.00	6.75
❑	183	Stan Lopata	15.00	6.75
❑	184	Don Bessent	15.00	6.75
❑	185	Bill Bruton	20.00	9.00
❑	186	Ron Jackson	15.00	6.75
❑	187	Early Wynn	40.00	18.00
❑	188	Chicago White Sox Team Card	40.00	18.00
❑	189	Ned Garver	15.00	6.75
❑	190	Carl Furillo	35.00	16.00
❑	191	Frank Lary	20.00	9.00
❑	192	Smoky Burgess	20.00	9.00
❑	193	Wilmer Mizell	20.00	9.00
❑	194	Monte Irvin	35.00	16.00
❑	195	George Kell	35.00	16.00
❑	196	Tom Poholsky	15.00	6.75
❑	197	Granny Hamner	15.00	6.75
❑	198	Ed Fitzgerald	15.00	6.75
❑	199	Hank Thompson	20.00	9.00
❑	200	Bob Feller	100.00	45.00
❑	201	Rip Repulski	15.00	6.75
❑	202	Jim Hearn	15.00	6.75
❑	203	Bill Tuttle	15.00	6.75
❑	204	Art Swanson	15.00	6.75
❑	205	Whitey Lockman	20.00	9.00
❑	206	Erv Palica	15.00	6.75
❑	207	Jim Small	15.00	6.75
❑	208	Elston Howard	50.00	22.00
❑	209	Max Surkont	15.00	6.75
❑	210	Mike Garcia	20.00	9.00
❑	211	Murry Dickson	15.00	6.75
❑	212	Johnny Temple	15.00	6.75
❑	213	Detroit Tigers Team Card	60.00	27.00
❑	214	Bob Rush	15.00	6.75
❑	215	Tommy Byrne	20.00	9.00

❑ 216 Jerry Schoonmaker 15.00 6.75
❑ 217 Billy Klaus 15.00 6.75
❑ 218 Joe Nuxhall UER 20.00 9.00
(Misspelled Nuxall)
❑ 219 Lew Burdette 20.00 9.00
❑ 220 Del Ennis 20.00 9.00
❑ 221 Bob Friend 20.00 9.00
❑ 222 Dave Philley 15.00 6.75
❑ 223 Randy Jackson 15.00 6.75
❑ 224 Bud Podbielan 15.00 6.75
❑ 225 Gil McDougald 30.00 13.50
❑ 226 New York Giants 80.00 36.00
Team Card
❑ 227 Russ Meyer 15.00 6.75
❑ 228 Mickey Vernon 20.00 9.00
❑ 229 Harry Brecheen CO 20.00 9.00
❑ 230 Chico Carrasquel 15.00 6.75
❑ 231 Bob Hale 15.00 6.75
❑ 232 Toby Atwell 15.00 6.75
❑ 233 Carl Erskine 35.00 16.00
❑ 234 Pete Runnels 15.00 6.75
❑ 235 Don Newcombe 50.00 22.00
❑ 236 Kansas City Athletics 30.00 13.50
Team Card
❑ 237 Jose Valdivielso 15.00 6.75
❑ 238 Walt Dropo 20.00 9.00
❑ 239 Harry Simpson 15.00 6.75
❑ 240 Whitey Ford 100.00 45.00
❑ 241 Don Mueller UER 20.00 9.00
(6" tall)
❑ 242 Hershell Freeman 15.00 6.75
❑ 243 Sherm Lollar 20.00 9.00
❑ 244 Bob Buhl 20.00 9.00
❑ 245 Billy Goodman 20.00 9.00
❑ 246 Tom Gorman 15.00 6.75
❑ 247 Bill Sarni 15.00 6.75
❑ 248 Bob Porterfield 15.00 6.75
❑ 249 Johnny Klippstein 15.00 6.75
❑ 250 Larry Doby 35.00 16.00
❑ 251 New York Yankees 275.00 125.00
Team Card UER
(Don Larsen misspelled
as Larson on front)
❑ 252 Vern Law 20.00 9.00
❑ 253 Irv Noren 15.00 6.75
❑ 254 George Crowe 15.00 6.75
❑ 255 Bob Lemon 35.00 16.00
❑ 256 Tom Hurd 15.00 6.75
❑ 257 Bobby Thomson 35.00 16.00
❑ 258 Art Ditmar 15.00 6.75
❑ 259 Sam Jones 20.00 9.00
❑ 260 Pee Wee Reese 120.00 55.00
❑ 261 Bobby Shantz 15.00 6.75
❑ 262 Howie Pollet 12.00 5.50
❑ 263 Bob Miller 12.00 5.50
❑ 264 Ray Monzant 12.00 5.50
❑ 265 Sandy Consuegra 12.00 5.50
❑ 266 Don Ferrarese 12.00 5.50
❑ 267 Bob Nieman 12.00 5.50
❑ 268 Dale Mitchell 16.00 7.25
❑ 269 Jack Meyer 12.00 5.50
❑ 270 Billy Loes 15.00 6.75
❑ 271 Foster Castleman 12.00 5.50
❑ 272 Danny O'Connell 12.00 5.50
❑ 273 Walker Cooper 12.00 5.50
❑ 274 Frank Baumholtz 12.00 5.50
❑ 275 Jim Greengrass 12.00 5.50
❑ 276 George Zuverink 12.00 5.50
❑ 277 Daryl Spencer 12.00 5.50
❑ 278 Chet Nichols 12.00 5.50
❑ 279 Johnny Groth 12.00 5.50
❑ 280 Jim Gilliam 35.00 16.00
❑ 281 Art Houtteman 12.00 5.50
❑ 282 Warren Hacker 12.00 5.50
❑ 283 Hal Smith 12.00 5.50
❑ 284 Ike Delock 12.00 5.50
❑ 285 Eddie Miksis 12.00 5.50
❑ 286 Bill Wight 12.00 5.50
❑ 287 Bobby Adams 12.00 5.50
❑ 288 Bob Cerv 40.00 18.00
❑ 289 Hal Jeffcoat 12.00 5.50
❑ 290 Curt Simmons 15.00 6.75
❑ 291 Frank Kellert 12.00 5.50
❑ 292 Luis Aparicio 150.00 70.00
❑ 293 Stu Miller 15.00 6.75
❑ 294 Ernie Johnson 15.00 6.75
❑ 295 Clem Labine 18.00 8.00
❑ 296 Andy Seminick 12.00 5.50
❑ 297 Bob Skinner 15.00 6.75
❑ 298 Johnny Schmitz 12.00 5.50
❑ 299 Charlie Neal 35.00 16.00
❑ 300 Vic Wertz 16.00 7.25
❑ 301 Marv Grissom 12.00 5.50
❑ 302 Eddie Robinson 12.00 5.50
❑ 303 Jim Dyck 12.00 5.50
❑ 304 Frank Malzone 16.00 7.25
❑ 305 Brooks Lawrence 12.00 5.50
❑ 306 Curt Roberts 12.00 5.50
❑ 307 Hoyt Wilhelm 35.00 16.00
❑ 308 Chuck Harmon 12.00 5.50
❑ 309 Don Blasingame 16.00 7.25
❑ 310 Steve Gromek 12.00 5.50
❑ 311 Hal Naragon 12.00 5.50
❑ 312 Andy Pafko 16.00 7.25
❑ 313 Gene Stephens 12.00 5.50
❑ 314 Hobie Landrith 12.00 5.50
❑ 315 Milt Bolling 12.00 5.50
❑ 316 Jerry Coleman 18.00 8.00
❑ 317 Al Aber 12.00 5.50
❑ 318 Fred Hatfield 12.00 5.50
❑ 319 Jack Crimian 12.00 5.50
❑ 320 Joe Adcock 16.00 7.25
❑ 321 Jim Konstanty 15.00 6.75
❑ 322 Karl Olson 12.00 5.50
❑ 323 Willard Schmidt 12.00 5.50
❑ 324 Rocky Bridges 15.00 6.75
❑ 325 Don Liddle 12.00 5.50
❑ 326 Connie Johnson 12.00 5.50
❑ 327 Bob Wiesler 12.00 5.50
❑ 328 Preston Ward 12.00 5.50
❑ 329 Lou Berberet 12.00 5.50
❑ 330 Jim Busby 12.00 5.50
❑ 331 Dick Hall 12.00 5.50
❑ 332 Don Larsen 60.00 27.00
❑ 333 Rube Walker 12.00 5.50
❑ 334 Bob Miller 12.00 5.50
❑ 335 Don Hoak 15.00 6.75
❑ 336 Ellis Kinder 12.00 5.50
❑ 337 Bobby Morgan 12.00 5.50
❑ 338 Jim Delsing 12.00 5.50
❑ 339 Rance Pless 12.00 5.50
❑ 340 Mickey McDermott 60.00 12.00
❑ NNO Checklist 1/3 275.00 90.00
❑ NNO Checklist 2/4 275.00 90.00

1957 Topps

	NRMT	VG-E
COMPLETE SET (407)	7000.00	3200.00
COMMON CARD (1-88)	10.00	4.50
COMMON CARD (89-176)	8.00	3.60
COMMON CARD (177-264)	8.00	3.60
COMMON CARD (265-352)	20.00	9.00
COMMON CARD (353-407)	8.00	3.60
COMMON DP (265-352)	14.00	6.25
WRAPPER (1-CENT)	300.00	135.00
WRAPPER (5-CENT)	200.00	90.00

❑ 1 Ted Williams 500.00 150.00
❑ 2 Yogi Berra 135.00 60.00
❑ 3 Dale Long 15.00 6.75
❑ 4 Johnny Logan 15.00 6.75
❑ 5 Sal Maglie 18.00 8.00
❑ 6 Hector Lopez 15.00 6.75
❑ 7 Luis Aparicio 35.00 16.00
❑ 8 Don Mossi 15.00 6.75
❑ 9 Johnny Temple 15.00 6.75
❑ 10 Willie Mays 225.00 100.00
❑ 11 George Zuverink 10.00 4.50
❑ 12 Dick Groat 14.00 6.25
❑ 13 Wally Burnette 10.00 4.50
❑ 14 Bob Nieman 10.00 4.50
❑ 15 Robin Roberts 35.00 16.00
❑ 16 Walt Moryn 10.00 4.50
❑ 17 Billy Gardner 10.00 4.50
❑ 18 Don Drysdale 200.00 90.00
❑ 19 Bob Wilson 10.00 4.50
❑ 20 Hank Aaron UER 200.00 90.00
(Reverse negative
photo on front)
❑ 21 Frank Sullivan 10.00 4.50
❑ 22 Jerry Snyder UER 10.00 4.50
(Photo actually
Ed Fitzgerald)
❑ 23 Sherm Lollar 15.00 6.75
❑ 24 Bill Mazeroski 70.00 32.00
❑ 25 Whitey Ford 70.00 32.00
❑ 26 Bob Boyd 10.00 4.50
❑ 27 Ted Kazanski 10.00 4.50
❑ 28 Gene Conley 15.00 6.75
❑ 29 Whitey Herzog 25.00 11.00
❑ 30 Pee Wee Reese 60.00 27.00
❑ 31 Ron Northey 10.00 4.50
❑ 32 Hershell Freeman 10.00 4.50
❑ 33 Jim Small 10.00 4.50
❑ 34 Tom Sturdivant 15.00 6.75
❑ 35 Frank Robinson 200.00 90.00
❑ 36 Bob Grim 10.00 4.50
❑ 37 Frank Torre 15.00 6.75
❑ 38 Nellie Fox 45.00 20.00
❑ 39 Al Worthington 10.00 4.50
❑ 40 Early Wynn 30.00 13.50
❑ 41 Hal W. Smith 10.00 4.50
❑ 42 Dee Fondy 10.00 4.50
❑ 43 Connie Johnson 10.00 4.50
❑ 44 Joe DeMaestri 10.00 4.50
❑ 45 Carl Furillo 20.00 9.00
❑ 46 Robert J. Miller 10.00 4.50
❑ 47 Don Blasingame 10.00 4.50
❑ 48 Bill Bruton 15.00 6.75
❑ 49 Daryl Spencer 10.00 4.50
❑ 50 Herb Score 20.00 9.00
❑ 51 Clint Courtney 10.00 4.50
❑ 52 Lee Walls 10.00 4.50
❑ 53 Clem Labine 18.00 8.00
❑ 54 Elmer Valo 10.00 4.50
❑ 55 Ernie Banks 120.00 55.00
❑ 56 Dave Sisler 10.00 4.50
❑ 57 Jim Lemon 15.00 6.75
❑ 58 Ruben Gomez 10.00 4.50
❑ 59 Dick Williams 14.00 6.25
❑ 60 Billy Hoeft 15.00 6.75
❑ 61 Dusty Rhodes 14.00 6.25
❑ 62 Billy Martin 45.00 20.00
❑ 63 Ike Delock 10.00 4.50
❑ 64 Pete Runnels 15.00 6.75
❑ 65 Wally Moon 14.00 6.25
❑ 66 Brooks Lawrence 10.00 4.50
❑ 67 Chico Carrasquel 10.00 4.50
❑ 68 Ray Crone 10.00 4.50
❑ 69 Roy McMillan 15.00 6.75
❑ 70 Richie Ashburn 45.00 20.00
❑ 71 Murry Dickson 10.00 4.50
❑ 72 Bill Tuttle 10.00 4.50
❑ 73 George Crowe 10.00 4.50
❑ 74 Vito Valentinetti 10.00 4.50
❑ 75 Jimmy Piersall 14.00 6.25
❑ 76 Roberto Clemente 300.00 135.00
❑ 77 Paul Foytack 10.00 4.50
❑ 78 Vic Wertz 14.00 6.25
❑ 79 Lindy McDaniel 14.00 6.25
❑ 80 Gil Hodges 45.00 20.00
❑ 81 Herman Wehmeier 10.00 4.50
❑ 82 Elston Howard 20.00 9.00
❑ 83 Lou Skizas 10.00 4.50
❑ 84 Moe Drabowsky 15.00 6.75
❑ 85 Larry Doby 20.00 9.00
❑ 86 Bill Sarni 10.00 4.50

❑ 87 Tom Gorman 10.00 4.50
❑ 88 Harvey Kuenn 14.00 6.25
❑ 89 Roy Sievers 15.00 6.75
❑ 90 Warren Spahn 70.00 32.00
❑ 91 Mack Burk 8.00 3.60
❑ 92 Mickey Vernon 15.00 6.75
❑ 93 Hal Jeffcoat 8.00 3.60
❑ 94 Bobby Del Greco 8.00 3.60
❑ 95 Mickey Mantle 1000.00 450.00
❑ 96 Hank Aguirre 8.00 3.60
❑ 97 New York Yankees 80.00 36.00
Team Card
❑ 98 Alvin Dark 14.00 6.25
❑ 99 Bob Keegan 8.00 3.60
❑ 100 League Presidents 14.00 6.25
Warren Giles
Will Harridge
❑ 101 Chuck Stobbs 8.00 3.60
❑ 102 Ray Boone 14.00 6.25
❑ 103 Joe Nuxhall 14.00 6.25
❑ 104 Hank Foiles 8.00 3.60
❑ 105 Johnny Antonelli 14.00 6.25
❑ 106 Ray Moore 8.00 3.60
❑ 107 Jim Rivera 8.00 3.60
❑ 108 Tommy Byrne 15.00 6.75
❑ 109 Hank Thompson 8.00 3.60
❑ 110 Bill Virdon 15.00 6.75
❑ 111 Hal R. Smith 8.00 3.60
❑ 112 Tom Brewer 8.00 3.60
❑ 113 Wilmer Mizell 15.00 6.75
❑ 114 Milwaukee Braves 22.00 10.00
Team Card
❑ 115 Jim Gilliam 14.00 6.25
❑ 116 Mike Fornieles 8.00 3.60
❑ 117 Joe Adcock 14.00 6.25
❑ 118 Bob Porterfield 8.00 3.60
❑ 119 Stan Lopata 8.00 3.60
❑ 120 Bob Lemon 25.00 11.00
❑ 121 Clete Boyer 20.00 9.00
❑ 122 Ken Boyer 18.00 8.00
❑ 123 Steve Ridzik 8.00 3.60
❑ 124 Dave Philley 8.00 3.60
❑ 125 Al Kaline 100.00 45.00
❑ 126 Bob Wiesler 8.00 3.60
❑ 127 Bob Buhl 15.00 6.75
❑ 128 Ed Bailey 15.00 6.75
❑ 129 Saul Rogovin 8.00 3.60
❑ 130 Don Newcombe 20.00 9.00
❑ 131 Milt Bolling 8.00 3.60
❑ 132 Art Ditmar 15.00 6.75
❑ 133 Del Crandall 15.00 6.75
❑ 134 Don Kaiser 8.00 3.60
❑ 135 Bill Skowron 18.00 8.00
❑ 136 Jim Hegan 15.00 6.75
❑ 137 Bob Rush 8.00 3.60
❑ 138 Minnie Minoso 20.00 9.00
❑ 139 Lou Kretlow 8.00 3.60
❑ 140 Frank Thomas 15.00 6.75
❑ 141 Al Aber 8.00 3.60
❑ 142 Charley Thompson 8.00 3.60
❑ 143 Andy Pafko 14.00 6.25
❑ 144 Ray Narleski 8.00 3.60
❑ 145 Al Smith 8.00 3.60
❑ 146 Don Ferrarese 8.00 3.60
❑ 147 Al Walker 8.00 3.60
❑ 148 Don Mueller 15.00 6.75
❑ 149 Bob Kennedy 15.00 6.75
❑ 150 Bob Friend 14.00 6.25
❑ 151 Willie Miranda 8.00 3.60
❑ 152 Jack Harshman 8.00 3.60
❑ 153 Karl Olson 8.00 3.60
❑ 154 Red Schoendienst 25.00 11.00
❑ 155 Jim Brosnan 15.00 6.75
❑ 156 Gus Triandos 15.00 6.75
❑ 157 Wally Post 15.00 6.75
❑ 158 Curt Simmons 15.00 6.75
❑ 159 Solly Drake 8.00 3.60
❑ 160 Billy Pierce 15.00 6.75
❑ 161 Pittsburgh Pirates 20.00 9.00
Team Card
❑ 162 Jack Meyer 8.00 3.60
❑ 163 Sammy White 8.00 3.60
❑ 164 Tommy Carroll 8.00 3.60
❑ 165 Ted Kluszewski 60.00 27.00
❑ 166 Roy Face 15.00 6.75
❑ 167 Vic Power 15.00 6.75
❑ 168 Frank Lary 15.00 6.75
❑ 169 Herb Plews 8.00 3.60
❑ 170 Duke Snider 100.00 45.00
❑ 171 Boston Red Sox 20.00 9.00
Team Card
❑ 172 Gene Woodling 15.00 6.75
❑ 173 Roger Craig 14.00 6.25
❑ 174 Willie Jones 8.00 3.60
❑ 175 Don Larsen 25.00 11.00
❑ 176A Gene Baker ERR .. 350.00 160.00
(Misspelled Bakep
on card back)
❑ 176B Gene Baker COR 15.00 6.75
❑ 177 Eddie Yost 15.00 6.75
❑ 178 Don Bessent 8.00 3.60
❑ 179 Ernie Oravetz 8.00 3.60
❑ 180 Gus Bell 15.00 6.75
❑ 181 Dick Donovan 8.00 3.60
❑ 182 Hobie Landrith 8.00 3.60
❑ 183 Chicago Cubs 20.00 9.00
Team Card
❑ 184 Tito Francona 8.00 3.60
❑ 185 Johnny Kucks 15.00 6.75
❑ 186 Jim King 8.00 3.60
❑ 187 Virgil Trucks 15.00 6.75
❑ 188 Felix Mantilla 15.00 6.75
❑ 189 Willard Nixon 8.00 3.60
❑ 190 Randy Jackson 8.00 3.60
❑ 191 Joe Margoneri 8.00 3.60
❑ 192 Jerry Coleman 15.00 6.75
❑ 193 Del Rice 8.00 3.60
❑ 194 Hal Brown 8.00 3.60
❑ 195 Bobby Avila 8.00 3.60
❑ 196 Larry Jackson 15.00 6.75
❑ 197 Hank Sauer 15.00 6.75
❑ 198 Detroit Tigers 20.00 9.00
Team Card
❑ 199 Vern Law 15.00 6.75
❑ 200 Gil McDougald 18.00 8.00
❑ 201 Sandy Amoros 15.00 6.75
❑ 202 Dick Gernert 8.00 3.60
❑ 203 Hoyt Wilhelm 25.00 11.00
❑ 204 Kansas City Athletics 20.00 9.00
Team Card
❑ 205 Charlie Maxwell 15.00 6.75
❑ 206 Willard Schmidt 8.00 3.60
❑ 207 Gordon(Billy) Hunter 8.00 3.60
❑ 208 Lou Burdette 14.00 6.25
❑ 209 Bob Skinner 15.00 6.75
❑ 210 Roy Campanella 125.00 55.00
❑ 211 Camilo Pascual 15.00 6.75
❑ 212 Rocky Colavito 160.00 70.00
❑ 213 Les Moss 8.00 3.60
❑ 214 Philadelphia Phillies .. 20.00 9.00
Team Card
❑ 215 Enos Slaughter 25.00 11.00
❑ 216 Marv Grissom 8.00 3.60
❑ 217 Gene Stephens 8.00 3.60
❑ 218 Ray Jablonski 8.00 3.60
❑ 219 Tom Acker 8.00 3.60
❑ 220 Jackie Jensen 15.00 6.75
❑ 221 Dixie Howell 8.00 3.60
❑ 222 Alex Grammas 8.00 3.60
❑ 223 Frank House 8.00 3.60
❑ 224 Marv Blaylock 8.00 3.60
❑ 225 Harry Simpson 8.00 3.60
❑ 226 Preston Ward 8.00 3.60
❑ 227 Gerry Staley 8.00 3.60
❑ 228 Smoky Burgess UER 15.00 6.75
(Misspelled Smokey
on card back)
❑ 229 George Susce 8.00 3.60
❑ 230 George Kell 25.00 11.00
❑ 231 Solly Hemus 8.00 3.60
❑ 232 Whitey Lockman 15.00 6.75
❑ 233 Art Fowler 8.00 3.60
❑ 234 Dick Cole 8.00 3.60
❑ 235 Tom Poholsky 8.00 3.60
❑ 236 Joe Ginsberg 8.00 3.60
❑ 237 Foster Castleman 8.00 3.60
❑ 238 Eddie Robinson 8.00 3.60
❑ 239 Tom Morgan 8.00 3.60
❑ 240 Hank Bauer 14.00 6.25
❑ 241 Joe Lonnett 8.00 3.60
❑ 242 Charlie Neal 14.00 6.25
❑ 243 St. Louis Cardinals 20.00 9.00
Team Card
❑ 244 Billy Loes 15.00 6.75
❑ 245 Rip Repulski 8.00 3.60
❑ 246 Jose Valdivielso 8.00 3.60
❑ 247 Turk Lown 8.00 3.60
❑ 248 Jim Finigan 8.00 3.60
❑ 249 Dave Pope 8.00 3.60
❑ 250 Eddie Mathews 45.00 20.00
❑ 251 Baltimore Orioles 15.00 6.75
Team Card
❑ 252 Carl Erskine 14.00 6.25
❑ 253 Gus Zernial 15.00 6.75
❑ 254 Ron Negray 8.00 3.60
❑ 255 Charlie Silvera 15.00 6.75
❑ 256 Ron Kline 8.00 3.60
❑ 257 Walt Dropo 8.00 3.60
❑ 258 Steve Gromek 8.00 3.60
❑ 259 Eddie O'Brien 8.00 3.60
❑ 260 Del Ennis 15.00 6.75
❑ 261 Bob Chakales 8.00 3.60
❑ 262 Bobby Thomson 15.00 6.75
❑ 263 George Strickland 8.00 3.60
❑ 264 Bob Turley 15.00 6.75
❑ 265 Harvey Haddix DP 14.00 6.25
❑ 266 Ken Kuhn DP 14.00 6.25
❑ 267 Danny Kravitz 20.00 9.00
❑ 268 Jack Collum 20.00 9.00
❑ 269 Bob Cerv 25.00 11.00
❑ 270 Washington Senators 50.00 22.00
Team Card
❑ 271 Danny O'Connell DP .. 14.00 6.25
❑ 272 Bobby Shantz 25.00 11.00
❑ 273 Jim Davis 20.00 9.00
❑ 274 Don Hoak 20.00 9.00
❑ 275 Cleveland Indians 50.00 22.00
Team Card UER
(Text on back credits Tribe
with winning AL title in '28.
The Yankees won that year.)
❑ 276 Jim Pyburn 20.00 9.00
❑ 277 Johnny Podres DP 45.00 20.00
❑ 278 Fred Hatfield DP 14.00 6.25
❑ 279 Bob Thurman 20.00 9.00
❑ 280 Alex Kellner 20.00 9.00
❑ 281 Gail Harris 20.00 9.00
❑ 282 Jack Dittmer DP 14.00 6.25
❑ 283 Wes Covington DP 14.00 6.25
❑ 284 Don Zimmer 35.00 16.00
❑ 285 Ned Garver 20.00 9.00
❑ 286 Bobby Richardson 125.00 55.00
❑ 287 Sam Jones 20.00 9.00
❑ 288 Ted Lepcio 20.00 9.00
❑ 289 Jim Bolger DP 14.00 6.25
❑ 290 Andy Carey DP 30.00 13.50
❑ 291 Windy McCall 20.00 9.00
❑ 292 Billy Klaus 20.00 9.00
❑ 293 Ted Abernathy 20.00 9.00
❑ 294 Rocky Bridges DP 14.00 6.25
❑ 295 Joe Collins DP 30.00 13.50
❑ 296 Johnny Klippstein 20.00 9.00
❑ 297 Jack Crimian 20.00 9.00
❑ 298 Irv Noren DP 14.00 6.25
❑ 299 Chuck Harmon 20.00 9.00
❑ 300 Mike Garcia 30.00 13.50
❑ 301 Sammy Esposito DP .. 20.00 9.00
❑ 302 Sandy Koufax DP 250.00 110.00
❑ 303 Billy Goodman 30.00 13.50
❑ 304 Joe Cunningham 30.00 13.50
❑ 305 Chico Fernandez 20.00 9.00
❑ 306 Darrell Johnson DP 14.00 6.25
❑ 307 Jack D. Phillips DP 14.00 6.25
❑ 308 Dick Hall 20.00 9.00
❑ 309 Jim Busby DP 14.00 6.25
❑ 310 Max Surkont DP 14.00 6.25
❑ 311 Al Pilarcik DP 14.00 6.25
❑ 312 Tony Kubek DP 60.00 27.00
❑ 313 Mel Parnell 15.00 6.75
❑ 314 Ed Bouchee DP 14.00 6.25
❑ 315 Lou Berberet DP 14.00 6.25
❑ 316 Billy O'Dell 20.00 9.00
❑ 317 New York Giants 70.00 32.00
Team Card
❑ 318 Mickey McDermott 20.00 9.00

	Card	NRMT	VG-E
❑ 319	Gino Cimoli	20.00	9.00
❑ 320	Neil Chrisley	20.00	9.00
❑ 321	John(Red) Murff	20.00	9.00
❑ 322	Cincinnati Reds Team Card	70.00	32.00
❑ 323	Wes Westrum	30.00	13.50
❑ 324	Brooklyn Dodgers Team Card	125.00	55.00
❑ 325	Frank Bolling	20.00	9.00
❑ 326	Pedro Ramos	20.00	9.00
❑ 327	Jim Pendleton	20.00	9.00
❑ 328	Brooks Robinson	400.00	180.00
❑ 329	Chicago White Sox Team Card	50.00	22.00
❑ 330	Jim Wilson	20.00	9.00
❑ 331	Ray Katt	20.00	9.00
❑ 332	Bob Bowman	20.00	9.00
❑ 333	Ernie Johnson	20.00	9.00
❑ 334	Jerry Schoonmaker	20.00	9.00
❑ 335	Granny Hamner	20.00	9.00
❑ 336	Haywood Sullivan	25.00	11.00
❑ 337	Rene Valdes	20.00	9.00
❑ 338	Jim Bunning	140.00	65.00
❑ 339	Bob Speake	20.00	9.00
❑ 340	Bill Wight	20.00	9.00
❑ 341	Don Gross	20.00	9.00
❑ 342	Gene Mauch	25.00	11.00
❑ 343	Taylor Phillips	20.00	9.00
❑ 344	Paul LaPalme	20.00	9.00
❑ 345	Paul Smith	20.00	9.00
❑ 346	Dick Littlefield	20.00	9.00
❑ 347	Hal Naragon	20.00	9.00
❑ 348	Jim Hearn	20.00	9.00
❑ 349	Nellie King	20.00	9.00
❑ 350	Eddie Miksis	20.00	9.00
❑ 351	Dave Hillman	20.00	9.00
❑ 352	Ellis Kinder	20.00	9.00
❑ 353	Cal Neeman	8.00	3.60
❑ 354	W. (Rip) Coleman	8.00	3.60
❑ 355	Frank Malzone	15.00	6.75
❑ 356	Faye Throneberry	8.00	3.60
❑ 357	Earl Torgeson	8.00	3.60
❑ 358	Jerry Lynch	15.00	6.75
❑ 359	Tom Cheney	8.00	3.60
❑ 360	Johnny Groth	8.00	3.60
❑ 361	Curt Barclay	8.00	3.60
❑ 362	Roman Mejias	15.00	6.75
❑ 363	Eddie Kasko	8.00	3.60
❑ 364	Cal McLish	15.00	6.75
❑ 365	Ozzie Virgil	8.00	3.60
❑ 366	Ken Lehman	8.00	3.60
❑ 367	Ed Fitzgerald	8.00	3.60
❑ 368	Bob Purkey	8.00	3.60
❑ 369	Milt Graff	8.00	3.60
❑ 370	Warren Hacker	8.00	3.60
❑ 371	Bob Lennon	8.00	3.60
❑ 372	Norm Zauchin	8.00	3.60
❑ 373	Pete Whisenant	8.00	3.60
❑ 374	Don Cardwell	8.00	3.60
❑ 375	Jim Landis	15.00	6.75
❑ 376	Don Elston	8.00	3.60
❑ 377	Andre Rodgers	8.00	3.60
❑ 378	Elmer Singleton	8.00	3.60
❑ 379	Don Lee	8.00	3.60
❑ 380	Walker Cooper	8.00	3.60
❑ 381	Dean Stone	8.00	3.60
❑ 382	Jim Brideweser	8.00	3.60
❑ 383	Juan Pizarro	8.00	3.60
❑ 384	Bobby G. Smith	8.00	3.60
❑ 385	Art Houtteman	8.00	3.60
❑ 386	Lyle Luttrell	8.00	3.60
❑ 387	Jack Sanford	15.00	6.75
❑ 388	Pete Daley	8.00	3.60
❑ 389	Dave Jolly	8.00	3.60
❑ 390	Reno Bertoia	8.00	3.60
❑ 391	Ralph Terry	15.00	6.75
❑ 392	Chuck Tanner	14.00	6.25
❑ 393	Raul Sanchez	8.00	3.60
❑ 394	Luis Arroyo	15.00	6.75
❑ 395	Bubba Phillips	8.00	3.60
❑ 396	Casey Wise	8.00	3.60
❑ 397	Roy Smalley	8.00	3.60
❑ 398	Al Cicotte	15.00	6.75
❑ 399	Billy Consolo	8.00	3.60
❑ 400	Dodgers' Sluggers Carl Furillo Gil Hodges Roy Campanella Duke Snider	250.00	110.00
❑ 401	Earl Battey	14.00	6.25
❑ 402	Jim Pisoni	8.00	3.60
❑ 403	Dick Hyde	8.00	3.60
❑ 404	Harry Anderson	8.00	3.60
❑ 405	Duke Maas	8.00	3.60
❑ 406	Bob Hale	8.00	3.60
❑ 407	Yankee Power Hitters Mickey Mantle Yogi Berra	500.00	150.00
❑ NNO1	Checklist 1/2	250.00	75.00
❑ NNO2	Checklist 2/3	400.00	100.00
❑ NNO3	Checklist 3/4	750.00	170.00
❑ NNO4	Checklist 4/5	900.00	200.00
❑ NNO5	Saturday, May 4th Boston Red Sox vs. Cleveland Indians Cincinnati Redlegs vs. New York Giants	90.00	22.00
❑ NNO6	Saturday, May 25th Detroit Tigers vs. Kansas City Athletics Pittsburgh Pirates vs. Philadelphia Phillies	90.00	22.00
❑ NNO7	Saturday, June 22nd Brooklyn Dodgers vs. St. Louis Cardinals Chicago White Sox vs. New York Yankees	120.00	30.00
❑ NNO8	Saturday, July 19th Milwaukee Braves vs. New York Giants Baltimore Orioles vs. Kansas City Athletics	120.00	30.00
❑ NNO9	Lucky Penny Charm and Key Chain offer card	100.00	45.00

1958 Topps

	NRMT	VG-E
COMPLETE SET (494)	4800.00	2200.00
COMMON CARD (1-110)	12.00	5.50
COMMON CARD (111-495)	8.00	3.60
WRAPPER (1-CENT)	100.00	45.00
WRAPPER (5-CENT)	125.00	55.00

	Card	NRMT	VG-E
❑ 1	Ted Williams	425.00	150.00
❑ 2A	Bob Lemon	35.00	16.00
❑ 2B	Bob Lemon YT	60.00	27.00
❑ 3	Alex Kellner	12.00	5.50
❑ 4	Hank Foiles	12.00	5.50
❑ 5	Willie Mays	225.00	100.00
❑ 6	George Zuverink	12.00	5.50
❑ 7	Dale Long	15.00	6.75
❑ 8A	Eddie Kasko	12.00	5.50
❑ 8B	Eddie Kasko YL	45.00	20.00
❑ 9	Hank Bauer	15.00	6.75
❑ 10	Lou Burdette	15.00	6.75
❑ 11A	Jim Rivera	12.00	5.50
❑ 11B	Jim Rivera YT	45.00	20.00
❑ 12	George Crowe	12.00	5.50
❑ 13A	Billy Hoeft	12.00	5.50
❑ 13B	Billy Hoeft YL	45.00	20.00
❑ 14	Rip Repulski	12.00	5.50
❑ 15	Jim Lemon	15.00	6.75
❑ 16	Charlie Neal	15.00	6.75
❑ 17	Felix Mantilla	12.00	5.50
❑ 18	Frank Sullivan	12.00	5.50
❑ 19	New York Giants Team Card (Checklist on back)	40.00	8.00
❑ 20A	Gil McDougald	18.00	8.00
❑ 20B	Gil McDougald YL	60.00	27.00
❑ 21	Curt Barclay	12.00	5.50
❑ 22	Hal Naragon	12.00	5.50
❑ 23A	Bill Tuttle	12.00	5.50
❑ 23B	Bill Tuttle YL	45.00	20.00
❑ 24A	Hobie Landrith	12.00	5.50
❑ 24B	Hobie Landrith YL	45.00	20.00
❑ 25	Don Drysdale	85.00	38.00
❑ 26	Ron Jackson	12.00	5.50
❑ 27	Bud Freeman	12.00	5.50
❑ 28	Jim Busby	12.00	5.50
❑ 29	Ted Lepcio	12.00	5.50
❑ 30A	Hank Aaron	200.00	90.00
❑ 30B	Hank Aaron YL	425.00	190.00
❑ 31	Tex Clevenger	12.00	5.50
❑ 32A	J.W. Porter	12.00	5.50
❑ 32B	J.W. Porter YL	45.00	20.00
❑ 33A	Cal Neeman	12.00	5.50
❑ 33B	Cal Neeman YT	45.00	20.00
❑ 34	Bob Thurman	12.00	5.50
❑ 35A	Don Mossi	15.00	6.75
❑ 35B	Don Mossi YT	45.00	20.00
❑ 36	Ted Kazanski	12.00	5.50
❑ 37	Mike McCormick UER (Photo actually Ray Monzant)	15.00	6.75
❑ 38	Dick Gernert	12.00	5.50
❑ 39	Bob Martyn	12.00	5.50
❑ 40	George Kell	18.00	8.00
❑ 41	Dave Hillman	12.00	5.50
❑ 42	John Roseboro	24.00	11.00
❑ 43	Sal Maglie	15.00	6.75
❑ 44	Washington Senators Team Card (Checklist on back)	20.00	4.00
❑ 45	Dick Groat	15.00	6.75
❑ 46A	Lou Sleater	12.00	5.50
❑ 46B	Lou Sleater YL	45.00	20.00
❑ 47	Roger Maris	450.00	200.00
❑ 48	Chuck Harmon	12.00	5.50
❑ 49	Smoky Burgess	15.00	6.75
❑ 50A	Billy Pierce	15.00	6.75
❑ 50B	Billy Pierce YT	50.00	22.00
❑ 51	Del Rice	12.00	5.50
❑ 52A	Bob Clemente	275.00	125.00
❑ 52B	Bob Clemente YT	450.00	200.00
❑ 53A	Morrie Martin	12.00	5.50
❑ 53B	Morrie Martin YL	45.00	20.00
❑ 54	Norm Siebern	20.00	9.00
❑ 55	Chico Carrasquel	12.00	5.50
❑ 56	Bill Fischer	12.00	5.50
❑ 57A	Tim Thompson	12.00	5.50
❑ 57B	Tim Thompson YL	45.00	20.00
❑ 58A	Art Schult	12.00	5.50
❑ 58B	Art Schult YT	45.00	20.00
❑ 59	Dave Sisler	12.00	5.50
❑ 60A	Del Ennis	15.00	6.75
❑ 60B	Del Ennis YL	50.00	22.00
❑ 61A	Darrell Johnson	12.00	5.50
❑ 61B	Darrell Johnson YL	45.00	20.00
❑ 62	Joe DeMaestri	12.00	5.50
❑ 63	Joe Nuxhall	15.00	6.75
❑ 64	Joe Lonnett	12.00	5.50
❑ 65A	Von McDaniel	12.00	5.50
❑ 65B	Von McDaniel YL	45.00	20.00
❑ 66	Lee Walls	12.00	5.50
❑ 67	Joe Ginsberg	12.00	5.50
❑ 68	Daryl Spencer	12.00	5.50
❑ 69	Wally Burnette	12.00	5.50
❑ 70A	Al Kaline	100.00	45.00
❑ 70B	Al Kaline YL	180.00	80.00
❑ 71	Dodgers Team (Checklist on back)	60.00	12.00
❑ 72	Bud Byerly	12.00	5.50
❑ 73	Pete Daley	12.00	5.50
❑ 74	Roy Face	15.00	6.75
❑ 75	Gus Bell	15.00	6.75
❑ 76A	Dick Farrell	12.00	5.50

❑	76B	Dick Farrell YT	45.00	20.00
❑	77A	Don Zimmer	15.00	6.75
❑	77B	Don Zimmer YT	50.00	22.00
❑	78A	Ernie Johnson	15.00	6.75
❑	78B	Ernie Johnson YL	50.00	22.00
❑	79A	Dick Williams	15.00	6.75
❑	79B	Dick Williams YT	50.00	22.00
❑	80	Dick Drott	12.00	5.50
❑	81A	Steve Boros	12.00	5.50
❑	81B	Steve Boros YT	45.00	20.00
❑	82	Ron Kline	12.00	5.50
❑	83	Bob Hazle	12.00	5.50
❑	84	Billy O'Dell	12.00	5.50
❑	85A	Luis Aparicio	30.00	13.50
❑	85B	Luis Aparicio YT	70.00	32.00
❑	86	Valmy Thomas	12.00	5.50
❑	87	Johnny Kucks	12.00	5.50
❑	88	Duke Snider	75.00	34.00
❑	89	Billy Klaus	12.00	5.50
❑	90	Robin Roberts	30.00	13.50
❑	91	Chuck Tanner	15.00	6.75
❑	92A	Clint Courtney	12.00	5.50
❑	92B	Clint Courtney YL	45.00	20.00
❑	93	Sandy Amoros	15.00	6.75
❑	94	Bob Skinner	15.00	6.75
❑	95	Frank Bolling	12.00	5.50
❑	96	Joe Durham	12.00	5.50
❑	97A	Larry Jackson	12.00	5.50
❑	97B	Larry Jackson YL	45.00	20.00
❑	98A	Billy Hunter	12.00	5.50
❑	98B	Billy Hunter YL	45.00	20.00
❑	99	Bobby Adams	12.00	5.50
❑	100A	Early Wynn	25.00	11.00
❑	100B	Early Wynn YT	60.00	27.00
❑	101A	Bobby Richardson	24.00	11.00
❑	101B	Bobby Richardson YL	55.00	25.00
❑	102	George Strickland	12.00	5.50
❑	103	Jerry Lynch	15.00	6.75
❑	104	Jim Pendleton	12.00	5.50
❑	105	Billy Gardner	12.00	5.50
❑	106	Dick Schofield	15.00	6.75
❑	107	Ossie Virgil	12.00	5.50
❑	108A	Jim Landis	12.00	5.50
❑	108B	Jim Landis YT	45.00	20.00
❑	109	Herb Plews	12.00	5.50
❑	110	Johnny Logan	15.00	6.75
❑	111	Stu Miller	10.00	4.50
❑	112	Gus Zernial	10.00	4.50
❑	113	Jerry Walker	8.00	3.60
❑	114	Irv Noren	10.00	4.50
❑	115	Jim Bunning	25.00	11.00
❑	116	Dave Philley	8.00	3.60
❑	117	Frank Torre	10.00	4.50
❑	118	Harvey Haddix	10.00	4.50
❑	119	Harry Chiti	8.00	3.60
❑	120	Johnny Podres	12.00	5.50
❑	121	Eddie Miksis	8.00	3.60
❑	122	Walt Moryn	8.00	3.60
❑	123	Dick Tomanek	8.00	3.60
❑	124	Bobby Usher	8.00	3.60
❑	125	Alvin Dark	10.00	4.50
❑	126	Stan Palys	8.00	3.60
❑	127	Tom Sturdivant	10.00	4.50
❑	128	Willie Kirkland	8.00	3.60
❑	129	Jim Derrington	8.00	3.60
❑	130	Jackie Jensen	10.00	4.50
❑	131	Bob Henrich	8.00	3.60
❑	132	Vern Law	10.00	4.50
❑	133	Russ Nixon	8.00	3.60
❑	134	Philadelphia Phillies Team Card (Checklist on back)	15.00	3.00
❑	135	Mike(Moe) Drabowsky	10.00	4.50
❑	136	Jim Finigan	8.00	3.60
❑	137	Russ Kemmerer	8.00	3.60
❑	138	Earl Torgeson	8.00	3.60
❑	139	George Brunet	8.00	3.60
❑	140	Wes Covington	10.00	4.50
❑	141	Ken Lehman	8.00	3.60
❑	142	Enos Slaughter	25.00	11.00
❑	143	Billy Muffett	8.00	3.60
❑	144	Bobby Morgan	8.00	3.60
❑	145	Never issued		
❑	146	Dick Gray	8.00	3.60
❑	147	Don McMahon	8.00	3.60
❑	148	Billy Consolo	8.00	3.60
❑	149	Tom Acker	8.00	3.60
❑	150	Mickey Mantle	800.00	350.00
❑	151	Buddy Pritchard	8.00	3.60
❑	152	Johnny Antonelli	10.00	4.50
❑	153	Les Moss	8.00	3.60
❑	154	Harry Byrd	8.00	3.60
❑	155	Hector Lopez	10.00	4.50
❑	156	Dick Hyde	8.00	3.60
❑	157	Dee Fondy	8.00	3.60
❑	158	Cleveland Indians Team Card (Checklist on back)	15.00	3.00
❑	159	Taylor Phillips	8.00	3.60
❑	160	Don Hoak	10.00	4.50
❑	161	Don Larsen	14.00	6.25
❑	162	Gil Hodges	30.00	13.50
❑	163	Jim Wilson	8.00	3.60
❑	164	Bob Taylor	8.00	3.60
❑	165	Bob Nieman	8.00	3.60
❑	166	Danny O'Connell	8.00	3.60
❑	167	Frank Baumann	8.00	3.60
❑	168	Joe Cunningham	8.00	3.60
❑	169	Ralph Terry	10.00	4.50
❑	170	Vic Wertz	10.00	4.50
❑	171	Harry Anderson	8.00	3.60
❑	172	Don Gross	8.00	3.60
❑	173	Eddie Yost	8.00	3.60
❑	174	Athletics Team (Checklist on back)	15.00	3.00
❑	175	Marv Throneberry	16.00	7.25
❑	176	Bob Buhl	10.00	4.50
❑	177	Al Smith	8.00	3.60
❑	178	Ted Kluszewski	16.00	7.25
❑	179	Willie Miranda	8.00	3.60
❑	180	Lindy McDaniel	10.00	4.50
❑	181	Willie Jones	8.00	3.60
❑	182	Joe Caffie	8.00	3.60
❑	183	Dave Jolly	8.00	3.60
❑	184	Elvin Tappe	8.00	3.60
❑	185	Ray Boone	10.00	4.50
❑	186	Jack Meyer	8.00	3.60
❑	187	Sandy Koufax	225.00	100.00
❑	188	Milt Bolling UER (Photo actually Lou Berberet)	8.00	3.60
❑	189	George Susce	8.00	3.60
❑	190	Red Schoendienst	18.00	8.00
❑	191	Art Ceccarelli	8.00	3.60
❑	192	Milt Graff	8.00	3.60
❑	193	Jerry Lumpe	8.00	3.60
❑	194	Roger Craig	10.00	4.50
❑	195	Whitey Lockman	10.00	4.50
❑	196	Mike Garcia	10.00	4.50
❑	197	Haywood Sullivan	10.00	4.50
❑	198	Bill Virdon	10.00	4.50
❑	199	Don Blasingame	8.00	3.60
❑	200	Bob Keegan	8.00	3.60
❑	201	Jim Bolger	8.00	3.60
❑	202	Woody Held	8.00	3.60
❑	203	Al Walker	8.00	3.60
❑	204	Leo Kiely	8.00	3.60
❑	205	Johnny Temple	10.00	4.50
❑	206	Bob Shaw	8.00	3.60
❑	207	Solly Hemus	8.00	3.60
❑	208	Cal McLish	8.00	3.60
❑	209	Bob Anderson	8.00	3.60
❑	210	Wally Moon	10.00	4.50
❑	211	Pete Burnside	8.00	3.60
❑	212	Bubba Phillips	8.00	3.60
❑	213	Red Wilson	8.00	3.60
❑	214	Willard Schmidt	8.00	3.60
❑	215	Jim Gilliam	14.00	6.25
❑	216	St. Louis Cardinals Team Card (Checklist on back)	15.00	3.00
❑	217	Jack Harshman	8.00	3.60
❑	218	Dick Rand	8.00	3.60
❑	219	Camilo Pascual	10.00	4.50
❑	220	Tom Brewer	8.00	3.60
❑	221	Jerry Kindall	8.00	3.60
❑	222	Bud Daley	8.00	3.60
❑	223	Andy Pafko	10.00	4.50
❑	224	Bob Grim	10.00	4.50
❑	225	Billy Goodman	10.00	4.50
❑	226	Bob Smith	8.00	3.60
❑	227	Gene Stephens	8.00	3.60
❑	228	Duke Maas	8.00	3.60
❑	229	Frank Zupo	8.00	3.60
❑	230	Richie Ashburn	30.00	13.50
❑	231	Lloyd Merritt	8.00	3.60
❑	232	Reno Bertoia	8.00	3.60
❑	233	Mickey Vernon	10.00	4.50
❑	234	Carl Sawatski	8.00	3.60
❑	235	Tom Gorman	8.00	3.60
❑	236	Ed Fitzgerald	8.00	3.60
❑	237	Bill Wight	8.00	3.60
❑	238	Bill Mazeroski	24.00	11.00
❑	239	Chuck Stobbs	8.00	3.60
❑	240	Bill Skowron	16.00	7.25
❑	241	Dick Littlefield	8.00	3.60
❑	242	Johnny Klippstein	8.00	3.60
❑	243	Larry Raines	8.00	3.60
❑	244	Don Demeter	8.00	3.60
❑	245	Frank Lary	10.00	4.50
❑	246	New York Yankees Team Card (Checklist on back)	100.00	20.00
❑	247	Casey Wise	8.00	3.60
❑	248	Herman Wehmeier	8.00	3.60
❑	249	Ray Moore	8.00	3.60
❑	250	Roy Sievers	10.00	4.50
❑	251	Warren Hacker	8.00	3.60
❑	252	Bob Trowbridge	8.00	3.60
❑	253	Don Mueller	10.00	4.50
❑	254	Alex Grammas	8.00	3.60
❑	255	Bob Turley	10.00	4.50
❑	256	Chicago White Sox Team Card (Checklist on back)	15.00	3.00
❑	257	Hal Smith	8.00	3.60
❑	258	Carl Erskine	14.00	6.25
❑	259	Al Pilarcik	8.00	3.60
❑	260	Frank Malzone	10.00	4.50
❑	261	Turk Lown	8.00	3.60
❑	262	Johnny Groth	8.00	3.60
❑	263	Eddie Bressoud	10.00	4.50
❑	264	Jack Sanford	10.00	4.50
❑	265	Pete Runnels	10.00	4.50
❑	266	Connie Johnson	8.00	3.60
❑	267	Sherm Lollar	10.00	4.50
❑	268	Granny Hamner	8.00	3.60
❑	269	Paul Smith	8.00	3.60
❑	270	Warren Spahn	50.00	22.00
❑	271	Billy Martin	30.00	13.50
❑	272	Ray Crone	8.00	3.60
❑	273	Hal Smith	8.00	3.60
❑	274	Rocky Bridges	8.00	3.60
❑	275	Elston Howard	16.00	7.25
❑	276	Bobby Avila	8.00	3.60
❑	277	Virgil Trucks	10.00	4.50
❑	278	Mack Burk	8.00	3.60
❑	279	Bob Boyd	8.00	3.60
❑	280	Jim Piersall	10.00	4.50
❑	281	Sammy Taylor	8.00	3.60
❑	282	Paul Foytack	8.00	3.60
❑	283	Ray Shearer	8.00	3.60
❑	284	Ray Katt	8.00	3.60
❑	285	Frank Robinson	100.00	45.00
❑	286	Gino Cimoli	8.00	3.60
❑	287	Sam Jones	10.00	4.50
❑	288	Harmon Killebrew	85.00	38.00
❑	289	Lou Burdette Bobby Shantz	10.00	4.50
❑	290	Dick Donovan	8.00	3.60
❑	291	Don Landrum	8.00	3.60
❑	292	Ned Garver	8.00	3.60
❑	293	Gene Freese	8.00	3.60
❑	294	Hal Jeffcoat	8.00	3.60
❑	295	Minnie Minoso	14.00	6.25
❑	296	Ryne Duren	16.00	7.25
❑	297	Don Buddin	8.00	3.60
❑	298	Jim Hearn	8.00	3.60
❑	299	Harry Simpson	8.00	3.60
❑	300	Will Harridge PRES Warren Giles	14.00	6.25
❑	301	Randy Jackson	8.00	3.60
❑	302	Mike Baxes	8.00	3.60
❑	303	Neil Chrisley	8.00	3.60
❑	304	Harvey Kuenn Al Kaline	20.00	9.00

No.	Card	NRMT	VG-E
❑ 305	Clem Labine	10.00	4.50
❑ 306	Whammy Douglas	8.00	3.60
❑ 307	Brooks Robinson	100.00	45.00
❑ 308	Paul Giel	10.00	4.50
❑ 309	Gail Harris	8.00	3.60
❑ 310	Ernie Banks	100.00	45.00
❑ 311	Bob Purkey	8.00	3.60
❑ 312	Boston Red Sox	15.00	3.00
	Team Card		
	(Checklist on back)		
❑ 313	Bob Rush	8.00	3.60
❑ 314	Duke Snider	30.00	13.50
	Walt Alston MG		
❑ 315	Bob Friend	10.00	4.50
❑ 316	Tito Francona	10.00	4.50
❑ 317	Albie Pearson	10.00	4.50
❑ 318	Frank House	8.00	3.60
❑ 319	Lou Skizas	8.00	3.60
❑ 320	Whitey Ford	50.00	22.00
❑ 321	Sluggers Supreme	70.00	32.00
	Ted Kluszewski		
	Ted Williams		
❑ 322	Harding Peterson	10.00	4.50
❑ 323	Elmer Valo	8.00	3.60
❑ 324	Hoyt Wilhelm	18.00	8.00
❑ 325	Joe Adcock	10.00	4.50
❑ 326	Bob Miller	8.00	3.60
❑ 327	Chicago Cubs	15.00	3.00
	Team Card		
	(Checklist on back)		
❑ 328	Ike Delock	8.00	3.60
❑ 329	Bob Cerv	10.00	4.50
❑ 330	Ed Bailey	10.00	4.50
❑ 331	Pedro Ramos	8.00	3.60
❑ 332	Jim King	8.00	3.60
❑ 333	Andy Carey	10.00	4.50
❑ 334	Bob Friend	10.00	4.50
	Billy Pierce		
❑ 335	Ruben Gomez	8.00	3.60
❑ 336	Bert Hamric	8.00	3.60
❑ 337	Hank Aguirre	8.00	3.60
❑ 338	Walt Dropo	10.00	4.50
❑ 339	Fred Hatfield	8.00	3.60
❑ 340	Don Newcombe	14.00	6.25
❑ 341	Pittsburgh Pirates	15.00	3.00
	Team Card		
	(Checklist on back)		
❑ 342	Jim Brosnan	10.00	4.50
❑ 343	Orlando Cepeda	90.00	40.00
❑ 344	Bob Porterfield	8.00	3.60
❑ 345	Jim Hegan	10.00	4.50
❑ 346	Steve Bilko	8.00	3.60
❑ 347	Don Rudolph	8.00	3.60
❑ 348	Chico Fernandez	8.00	3.60
❑ 349	Murry Dickson	8.00	3.60
❑ 350	Ken Boyer	16.00	7.25
❑ 351	Braves Fence Busters	35.00	16.00
	Del Crandall		
	Eddie Mathews		
	Hank Aaron		
	Joe Adcock		
❑ 352	Herb Score	14.00	6.25
❑ 353	Stan Lopata	8.00	3.60
❑ 354	Art Ditmar	10.00	4.50
❑ 355	Bill Bruton	10.00	4.50
❑ 356	Bob Malkmus	8.00	3.60
❑ 357	Danny McDevitt	8.00	3.60
❑ 358	Gene Baker	8.00	3.60
❑ 359	Billy Loes	10.00	4.50
❑ 360	Roy McMillan	10.00	4.50
❑ 361	Mike Fornieles	8.00	3.60
❑ 362	Ray Jablonski	8.00	3.60
❑ 363	Don Elston	8.00	3.60
❑ 364	Earl Battey	8.00	3.60
❑ 365	Tom Morgan	8.00	3.60
❑ 366	Gene Green	8.00	3.60
❑ 367	Jack Urban	8.00	3.60
❑ 368	Rocky Colavito	50.00	22.00
❑ 369	Ralph Lumenti	8.00	3.60
❑ 370	Yogi Berra	90.00	40.00
❑ 371	Marty Keough	8.00	3.60
❑ 372	Don Cardwell	8.00	3.60
❑ 373	Joe Pignatano	8.00	3.60
❑ 374	Brooks Lawrence	8.00	3.60
❑ 375	Pee Wee Reese	50.00	22.00
❑ 376	Charley Rabe	8.00	3.60
❑ 377A	Milwaukee Braves	15.00	6.75
	Team Card		
	(Alphabetical)		
❑ 377B	Milwaukee Team	100.00	20.00
	numerical checklist		
❑ 378	Hank Sauer	10.00	4.50
❑ 379	Ray Herbert	8.00	3.60
❑ 380	Charlie Maxwell	10.00	4.50
❑ 381	Hal Brown	8.00	3.60
❑ 382	Al Cicotte	8.00	3.60
❑ 383	Lou Berberet	8.00	3.60
❑ 384	John Goryl	8.00	3.60
❑ 385	Wilmer Mizell	10.00	4.50
❑ 386	Birdie's Sluggers	14.00	6.25
	Ed Bailey		
	Birdie Tebbetts MG		
	Frank Robinson		
❑ 387	Wally Post	10.00	4.50
❑ 388	Billy Moran	8.00	3.60
❑ 389	Bill Taylor	8.00	3.60
❑ 390	Del Crandall	10.00	4.50
❑ 391	Dave Melton	8.00	3.60
❑ 392	Bennie Daniels	8.00	3.60
❑ 393	Tony Kubek	18.00	8.00
❑ 394	Jim Grant	8.00	3.60
❑ 395	Willard Nixon	8.00	3.60
❑ 396	Dutch Dotterer	8.00	3.60
❑ 397A	Detroit Tigers	15.00	6.75
	Team Card		
	(Alphabetical)		
❑ 397B	Detroit Team	100.00	20.00
	numerical checklist		
❑ 398	Gene Woodling	10.00	4.50
❑ 399	Marv Grissom	8.00	3.60
❑ 400	Nellie Fox	30.00	13.50
❑ 401	Don Bessent	8.00	3.60
❑ 402	Bobby Gene Smith	8.00	3.60
❑ 403	Steve Korcheck	8.00	3.60
❑ 404	Curt Simmons	10.00	4.50
❑ 405	Ken Aspromonte	8.00	3.60
❑ 406	Vic Power	10.00	4.50
❑ 407	Carlton Willey	10.00	4.50
❑ 408A	Baltimore Orioles	15.00	6.75
	Team Card		
	(Alphabetical)		
❑ 408B	Baltimore Team	100.00	20.00
	numerical checklist		
❑ 409	Frank Thomas	10.00	4.50
❑ 410	Murray Wall	8.00	3.60
❑ 411	Tony Taylor	10.00	4.50
❑ 412	Gerry Staley	8.00	3.60
❑ 413	Jim Davenport	8.00	3.60
❑ 414	Sammy White	8.00	3.60
❑ 415	Bob Bowman	8.00	3.60
❑ 416	Foster Castleman	8.00	3.60
❑ 417	Carl Furillo	14.00	6.25
❑ 418	Mickey Mantle	275.00	125.00
	Hank Aaron		
❑ 419	Bobby Shantz	10.00	4.50
❑ 420	Vada Pinson	40.00	18.00
❑ 421	Dixie Howell	8.00	3.60
❑ 422	Norm Zauchin	8.00	3.60
❑ 423	Phil Clark	8.00	3.60
❑ 424	Larry Doby	14.00	6.25
❑ 425	Sammy Esposito	8.00	3.60
❑ 426	Johnny O'Brien	10.00	4.50
❑ 427	Al Worthington	8.00	3.60
❑ 428A	Cincinnati Reds	15.00	6.75
	Team Card		
	(Alphabetical)		
❑ 428B	Cincinnati Team	100.00	20.00
	numerical checklist		
❑ 429	Gus Triandos	10.00	4.50
❑ 430	Bobby Thomson	10.00	4.50
❑ 431	Gene Conley	10.00	4.50
❑ 432	John Powers	8.00	3.60
❑ 433A	Pancho Herrer ERR	650.00	300.00
❑ 433B	Pancho Herrera COR	10.00	4.50
❑ 434	Harvey Kuenn	10.00	4.50
❑ 435	Ed Roebuck	10.00	4.50
❑ 436	Willie Mays	75.00	34.00
	Duke Snider		
❑ 437	Bob Speake	8.00	3.60
❑ 438	Whitey Herzog	10.00	4.50
❑ 439	Ray Narleski	8.00	3.60
❑ 440	Eddie Mathews	40.00	18.00
❑ 441	Jim Marshall	10.00	4.50
❑ 442	Phil Paine	8.00	3.60
❑ 443	Billy Harrell SP	20.00	9.00
❑ 444	Danny Kravitz	8.00	3.60
❑ 445	Bob Smith	8.00	3.60
❑ 446	Carroll Hardy SP	20.00	9.00
❑ 447	Ray Monzant	8.00	3.60
❑ 448	Charlie Lau	12.00	5.50
❑ 449	Gene Fodge	8.00	3.60
❑ 450	Preston Ward SP	20.00	9.00
❑ 451	Joe Taylor	8.00	3.60
❑ 452	Roman Mejias	8.00	3.60
❑ 453	Tom Qualters	8.00	3.60
❑ 454	Harry Hanebrink	8.00	3.60
❑ 455	Hal Griggs	8.00	3.60
❑ 456	Dick Brown	8.00	3.60
❑ 457	Milt Pappas	12.00	5.50
❑ 458	Julio Becquer	8.00	3.60
❑ 459	Ron Blackburn	8.00	3.60
❑ 460	Chuck Essegian	8.00	3.60
❑ 461	Ed Mayer	8.00	3.60
❑ 462	Gary Geiger SP	20.00	9.00
❑ 463	Vito Valentinetti	8.00	3.60
❑ 464	Curt Flood	30.00	13.50
❑ 465	Arnie Portocarrero	8.00	3.60
❑ 466	Pete Whisenant	8.00	3.60
❑ 467	Glen Hobbie	8.00	3.60
❑ 468	Bob Schmidt	8.00	3.60
❑ 469	Don Ferrarese	8.00	3.60
❑ 470	R.C. Stevens	8.00	3.60
❑ 471	Lenny Green	8.00	3.60
❑ 472	Joey Jay	10.00	4.50
❑ 473	Bill Renna	8.00	3.60
❑ 474	Roman Semproch	8.00	3.60
❑ 475	Fred Haney AS MG and	20.00	6.00
	Casey Stengel AS MG		
	(Checklist back)		
❑ 476	Stan Musial AS TP	40.00	18.00
❑ 477	Bill Skowron AS	10.00	4.50
❑ 478	Johnny Temple AS	8.00	3.60
❑ 479	Nellie Fox AS	18.00	8.00
❑ 480	Eddie Mathews AS	20.00	9.00
❑ 481	Frank Malzone AS	8.00	3.60
❑ 482	Ernie Banks AS	35.00	16.00
❑ 483	Luis Aparicio AS	18.00	8.00
❑ 484	Frank Robinson AS	24.00	11.00
❑ 485	Ted Williams AS	125.00	55.00
❑ 486	Willie Mays AS	50.00	22.00
❑ 487	Mickey Mantle AS TP	175.00	80.00
❑ 488	Hank Aaron AS	50.00	22.00
❑ 489	Jackie Jensen AS	10.00	4.50
❑ 490	Ed Bailey AS	8.00	3.60
❑ 491	Sherm Lollar AS	8.00	3.60
❑ 492	Bob Friend AS	8.00	3.60
❑ 493	Bob Turley AS	10.00	4.50
❑ 494	Warren Spahn AS	24.00	11.00
❑ 495	Herb Score AS	16.00	3.20
❑ xx	Contest Cards	70.00	32.00

1959 Topps

	NRMT	VG-E
COMPLETE SET (572)	4500.00	2000.00
COMMON CARD (1-110)	6.00	2.70
COMMON CARD (111-506)	4.00	1.80
COMMON CARD (507-572)	16.00	7.25

	Card	Price 1	Price 2
	WRAPPER (1-CENT)	125.00	55.00
	WRAPPER (5-CENT)	100.00	45.00
❑	1 Ford Frick COMM	50.00	13.50
❑	2 Eddie Yost	8.00	3.60
❑	3 Don McMahon	8.00	3.60
❑	4 Albie Pearson	8.00	3.60
❑	5 Dick Donovan	8.00	3.60
❑	6 Alex Grammas	6.00	2.70
❑	7 Al Pilarcik	6.00	2.70
❑	8 Phillies Team	65.00	13.00
	(Checklist on back)		
❑	9 Paul Giel	8.00	3.60
❑	10 Mickey Mantle	600.00	275.00
❑	11 Billy Hunter	8.00	3.60
❑	12 Vern Law	8.00	3.60
❑	13 Dick Gernert	6.00	2.70
❑	14 Pete Whisenant	6.00	2.70
❑	15 Dick Drott	6.00	2.70
❑	16 Joe Pignatano	6.00	2.70
❑	17 Frank Thomas	8.00	3.60
	Danny Murtaugh MG		
	Ted Kluszewski		
❑	18 Jack Urban	6.00	2.70
❑	19 Eddie Bressoud	6.00	2.70
❑	20 Duke Snider	50.00	22.00
❑	21 Connie Johnson	6.00	2.70
❑	22 Al Smith	8.00	3.60
❑	23 Murry Dickson	8.00	3.60
❑	24 Red Wilson	6.00	2.70
❑	25 Don Hoak	8.00	3.60
❑	26 Chuck Stobbs	6.00	2.70
❑	27 Andy Pafko	8.00	3.60
❑	28 Al Worthington	6.00	2.70
❑	29 Jim Bolger	6.00	2.70
❑	30 Nellie Fox	30.00	13.50
❑	31 Ken Lehman	6.00	2.70
❑	32 Don Buddin	6.00	2.70
❑	33 Ed Fitzgerald	6.00	2.70
❑	34 Al Kaline	20.00	9.00
	Charley Maxwell		
❑	35 Ted Kluszewski	16.00	7.25
❑	36 Hank Aguirre	6.00	2.70
❑	37 Gene Green	6.00	2.70
❑	38 Morrie Martin	6.00	2.70
❑	39 Ed Bouchee	6.00	2.70
❑	40A Warren Spahn ERR	75.00	34.00
	(Born 1931)		
❑	40B Warren Spahn ERR	100.00	45.00
	(Born 1931, but three		
	is partially obscured)		
❑	40C Warren Spahn COR	50.00	22.00
	(Born 1921)		
❑	41 Bob Martyn	6.00	2.70
❑	42 Murray Wall	6.00	2.70
❑	43 Steve Bilko	6.00	2.70
❑	44 Vito Valentinetti	6.00	2.70
❑	45 Andy Carey	8.00	3.60
❑	46 Bill R. Henry	6.00	2.70
❑	47 Jim Finigan	6.00	2.70
❑	48 Orioles Team	25.00	5.00
	(Checklist on back)		
❑	49 Bill Hall	6.00	2.70
❑	50 Willie Mays	125.00	55.00
❑	51 Rip Coleman	6.00	2.70
❑	52 Coot Veal	6.00	2.70
❑	53 Stan Williams	8.00	3.60
❑	54 Mel Roach	6.00	2.70
❑	55 Tom Brewer	6.00	2.70
❑	56 Carl Sawatski	6.00	2.70
❑	57 Al Cicotte	6.00	2.70
❑	58 Eddie Miksis	6.00	2.70
❑	59 Irv Noren	8.00	3.60
❑	60 Bob Turley	8.00	3.60
❑	61 Dick Brown	6.00	2.70
❑	62 Tony Taylor	8.00	3.60
❑	63 Jim Hearn	6.00	2.70
❑	64 Joe DeMaestri	6.00	2.70
❑	65 Frank Torre	8.00	3.60
❑	66 Joe Ginsberg	6.00	2.70
❑	67 Brooks Lawrence	6.00	2.70
❑	68 Dick Schofield	8.00	3.60
❑	69 Giants Team	25.00	5.00
	(Checklist on back)		
❑	70 Harvey Kuenn	8.00	3.60
❑	71 Don Bessent	6.00	2.70
❑	72 Bill Renna	6.00	2.70
❑	73 Ron Jackson	8.00	3.60
❑	74 Jim Lemon	8.00	3.60
	Cookie Lavagetto MG		
	Roy Sievers		
❑	75 Sam Jones	8.00	3.60
❑	76 Bobby Richardson	20.00	9.00
❑	77 John Goryl	6.00	2.70
❑	78 Pedro Ramos	6.00	2.70
❑	79 Harry Chiti	6.00	2.70
❑	80 Minnie Minoso	10.00	4.50
❑	81 Hal Jeffcoat	6.00	2.70
❑	82 Bob Boyd	6.00	2.70
❑	83 Bob Smith	6.00	2.70
❑	84 Reno Bertoia	6.00	2.70
❑	85 Harry Anderson	6.00	2.70
❑	86 Bob Keegan	8.00	3.60
❑	87 Danny O'Connell	6.00	2.70
❑	88 Herb Score	10.00	4.50
❑	89 Billy Gardner	6.00	2.70
❑	90 Bill Skowron	16.00	7.25
❑	91 Herb Moford	6.00	2.70
❑	92 Dave Philley	6.00	2.70
❑	93 Julio Becquer	6.00	2.70
❑	94 White Sox Team	40.00	8.00
	(Checklist on back)		
❑	95 Carl Willey	6.00	2.70
❑	96 Lou Berberet	6.00	2.70
❑	97 Jerry Lynch	8.00	3.60
❑	98 Arnie Portocarrero	6.00	2.70
❑	99 Ted Kazanski	6.00	2.70
❑	100 Bob Cerv	8.00	3.60
❑	101 Alex Kellner	6.00	2.70
❑	102 Felipe Alou	30.00	13.50
❑	103 Billy Goodman	8.00	3.60
❑	104 Del Rice	8.00	3.60
❑	105 Lee Walls	6.00	2.70
❑	106 Hal Woodeshick	6.00	2.70
❑	107 Norm Larker	8.00	3.60
❑	108 Zack Monroe	8.00	3.60
❑	109 Bob Schmidt	6.00	2.70
❑	110 George Witt	8.00	3.60
❑	111 Redlegs Team	12.00	2.40
	(Checklist on back)		
❑	112 Billy Consolo	4.00	1.80
❑	113 Taylor Phillips	4.00	1.80
❑	114 Earl Battey	8.00	3.60
❑	115 Mickey Vernon	8.00	3.60
❑	116 Bob Allison RP	12.00	5.50
❑	117 John Blanchard RP	8.00	3.60
❑	118 John Buzhardt RP	4.00	1.80
❑	119 John Callison RP	12.00	5.50
❑	120 Chuck Coles RP	4.00	1.80
❑	121 Bob Conley RP	4.00	1.80
❑	122 Bennie Daniels RP	4.00	1.80
❑	123 Don Dillard RP	4.00	1.80
❑	124 Dan Dobbek RP	4.00	1.80
❑	125 Ron Fairly RP	8.00	3.60
❑	126 Ed Haas RP	4.00	1.80
❑	127 Kent Hadley RP	4.00	1.80
❑	128 Bob Hartman RP	4.00	1.80
❑	129 Frank Herrera RP	4.00	1.80
❑	130 Lou Jackson RP	4.00	1.80
❑	131 Deron Johnson RP	8.00	3.60
❑	132 Don Lee RP	4.00	1.80
❑	133 Bob Lillis RP	4.00	1.80
❑	134 Jim McDaniel RP	4.00	1.80
❑	135 Gene Oliver RP	4.00	1.80
❑	136 Jim O'Toole RP	4.00	1.80
❑	137 Dick Ricketts RP	4.00	1.80
❑	138 John Romano RP	4.00	1.80
❑	139 Ed Sadowski RP	4.00	1.80
❑	140 Charlie Secrest RP	4.00	1.80
❑	141 Joe Shipley RP	4.00	1.80
❑	142 Dick Stigman RP	4.00	1.80
❑	143 Willie Tasby RP	4.00	1.80
❑	144 Jerry Walker RP	4.00	1.80
❑	145 Dom Zanni RP	4.00	1.80
❑	146 Jerry Zimmerman RP	4.00	1.80
❑	147 Cubs Clubbers	25.00	11.00
	Dale Long		
	Ernie Banks		
	Walt Moryn		
❑	148 Mike McCormick	8.00	3.60
❑	149 Jim Bunning	20.00	9.00
❑	150 Stan Musial	125.00	55.00
❑	151 Bob Malkmus	4.00	1.80
❑	152 Johnny Klippstein	4.00	1.80
❑	153 Jim Marshall	4.00	1.80
❑	154 Ray Herbert	4.00	1.80
❑	155 Enos Slaughter	20.00	9.00
❑	156 Ace Hurlers	12.00	5.50
	Billy Pierce		
	Robin Roberts		
❑	157 Felix Mantilla	4.00	1.80
❑	158 Walt Dropo	4.00	1.80
❑	159 Bob Shaw	8.00	3.60
❑	160 Dick Groat	8.00	3.60
❑	161 Frank Baumann	4.00	1.80
❑	162 Bobby G. Smith	4.00	1.80
❑	163 Sandy Koufax	150.00	70.00
❑	164 Johnny Groth	4.00	1.80
❑	165 Bill Bruton	4.00	1.80
❑	166 Destruction Crew	30.00	13.50
	Minnie Minoso		
	Rocky Colavito		
	(Misspelled Colovito		
	on card back)		
	Larry Doby		
❑	167 Duke Maas	4.00	1.80
❑	168 Carroll Hardy	4.00	1.80
❑	169 Ted Abernathy	4.00	1.80
❑	170 Gene Woodling	8.00	3.60
❑	171 Willard Schmidt	4.00	1.80
❑	172 Athletics Team	12.00	2.40
	(Checklist on back)		
❑	173 Bill Monbouquette	8.00	3.60
❑	174 Jim Pendleton	4.00	1.80
❑	175 Dick Farrell	8.00	3.60
❑	176 Preston Ward	4.00	1.80
❑	177 John Briggs	4.00	1.80
❑	178 Ruben Amaro	8.00	3.60
❑	179 Don Rudolph	4.00	1.80
❑	180 Yogi Berra	75.00	34.00
❑	181 Bob Porterfield	4.00	1.80
❑	182 Milt Graff	4.00	1.80
❑	183 Stu Miller	8.00	3.60
❑	184 Harvey Haddix	8.00	3.60
❑	185 Jim Busby	4.00	1.80
❑	186 Mudcat Grant	8.00	3.60
❑	187 Bubba Phillips	8.00	3.60
❑	188 Juan Pizarro	4.00	1.80
❑	189 Neil Chrisley	4.00	1.80
❑	190 Bill Virdon	8.00	3.60
❑	191 Russ Kemmerer	4.00	1.80
❑	192 Charlie Beamon	4.00	1.80
❑	193 Sammy Taylor	4.00	1.80
❑	194 Jim Brosnan	8.00	3.60
❑	195 Rip Repulski	4.00	1.80
❑	196 Billy Moran	4.00	1.80
❑	197 Ray Semproch	4.00	1.80
❑	198 Jim Davenport	8.00	3.60
❑	199 Leo Kiely	4.00	1.80
❑	200 Warren Giles NL PRES	8.00	3.60
❑	201 Tom Acker	4.00	1.80
❑	202 Roger Maris	125.00	55.00
❑	203 Ossie Virgil	4.00	1.80
❑	204 Casey Wise	4.00	1.80
❑	205 Don Larsen	8.00	3.60
❑	206 Carl Furillo	8.00	3.60
❑	207 George Strickland	4.00	1.80
❑	208 Willie Jones	4.00	1.80
❑	209 Lenny Green	4.00	1.80
❑	210 Ed Bailey	4.00	1.80
❑	211 Bob Blaylock	4.00	1.80
❑	212 Hank Aaron	75.00	34.00
	Eddie Mathews		
❑	213 Jim Rivera	8.00	3.60
❑	214 Marcelino Solis	4.00	1.80
❑	215 Jim Lemon	8.00	3.60
❑	216 Andre Rodgers	4.00	1.80
❑	217 Carl Erskine	8.00	3.60
❑	218 Roman Mejias	4.00	1.80
❑	219 George Zuverink	4.00	1.80
❑	220 Frank Malzone	8.00	3.60
❑	221 Bob Bowman	4.00	1.80
❑	222 Bobby Shantz	4.00	1.80
❑	223 Cardinals Team	12.00	2.40
	(Checklist on back)		

❑ 224 Claude Osteen 8.00 3.60
❑ 225 Johnny Logan 8.00 3.60
❑ 226 Art Ceccarelli 4.00 1.80
❑ 227 Hal W. Smith 4.00 1.80
❑ 228 Don Gross 4.00 1.80
❑ 229 Vic Power 8.00 3.60
❑ 230 Bill Fischer 4.00 1.80
❑ 231 Ellis Burton 4.00 1.80
❑ 232 Eddie Kasko 4.00 1.80
❑ 233 Paul Foytack 4.00 1.80
❑ 234 Chuck Tanner 8.00 3.60
❑ 235 Valmy Thomas 4.00 1.80
❑ 236 Ted Bowsfield 4.00 1.80
❑ 237 Run Preventers 12.00 5.50
Gil McDougald
Bob Turley
Bobby Richardson
❑ 238 Gene Baker 4.00 1.80
❑ 239 Bob Trowbridge 4.00 1.80
❑ 240 Hank Bauer 8.00 3.60
❑ 241 Billy Muffett 4.00 1.80
❑ 242 Ron Samford 4.00 1.80
❑ 243 Marv Grissom 4.00 1.80
❑ 244 Ted Gray 4.00 1.80
❑ 245 Ned Garver 4.00 1.80
❑ 246 J.W. Porter 4.00 1.80
❑ 247 Don Ferrarese 4.00 1.80
❑ 248 Red Sox Team 12.00 2.40
(Checklist on back)
❑ 249 Bobby Adams 4.00 1.80
❑ 250 Billy O'Dell 4.00 1.80
❑ 251 Clete Boyer 8.00 3.60
❑ 252 Ray Boone 8.00 3.60
❑ 253 Seth Morehead 4.00 1.80
❑ 254 Zeke Bella 4.00 1.80
❑ 255 Del Ennis 8.00 3.60
❑ 256 Jerry Davie 4.00 1.80
❑ 257 Leon Wagner 8.00 3.60
❑ 258 Fred Kipp 4.00 1.80
❑ 259 Jim Pisoni 4.00 1.80
❑ 260 Early Wynn UER 16.00 7.25
(1957 Cleevland)
❑ 261 Gene Stephens 4.00 1.80
❑ 262 Johnny Podres 16.00 7.25
Clem Labine
Don Drysdale
❑ 263 Bud Daley 4.00 1.80
❑ 264 Chico Carrasquel 4.00 1.80
❑ 265 Ron Kline 4.00 1.80
❑ 266 Woody Held 4.00 1.80
❑ 267 John Romonosky 4.00 1.80
❑ 268 Tito Francona 8.00 3.60
❑ 269 Jack Meyer 4.00 1.80
❑ 270 Gil Hodges 25.00 11.00
❑ 271 Orlando Pena 4.00 1.80
❑ 272 Jerry Lumpe 4.00 1.80
❑ 273 Joey Jay 8.00 3.60
❑ 274 Jerry Kindall 8.00 3.60
❑ 275 Jack Sanford 8.00 3.60
❑ 276 Pete Daley 4.00 1.80
❑ 277 Turk Lown 8.00 3.60
❑ 278 Chuck Essegian 4.00 1.80
❑ 279 Ernie Johnson 4.00 1.80
❑ 280 Frank Bolling 4.00 1.80
❑ 281 Walt Craddock 4.00 1.80
❑ 282 R.C. Stevens 4.00 1.80
❑ 283 Russ Heman 4.00 1.80
❑ 284 Steve Korcheck 4.00 1.80
❑ 285 Joe Cunningham 4.00 1.80
❑ 286 Dean Stone 4.00 1.80
❑ 287 Don Zimmer 8.00 3.60
❑ 288 Dutch Dotterer 4.00 1.80
❑ 289 Johnny Kucks 8.00 3.60
❑ 290 Wes Covington 4.00 1.80
❑ 291 Pedro Ramos 4.00 1.80
Camilo Pascual
❑ 292 Dick Williams 8.00 3.60
❑ 293 Ray Moore 4.00 1.80
❑ 294 Hank Foiles 4.00 1.80
❑ 295 Billy Martin 25.00 11.00
❑ 296 Ernie Broglio 4.00 1.80
❑ 297 Jackie Brandt 4.00 1.80
❑ 298 Tex Clevenger 4.00 1.80
❑ 299 Billy Klaus 4.00 1.80
❑ 300 Richie Ashburn 25.00 11.00
❑ 301 Earl Averill 4.00 1.80
❑ 302 Don Mossi 8.00 3.60
❑ 303 Marty Keough 4.00 1.80
❑ 304 Cubs Team 12.00 2.40
(Checklist on back)
❑ 305 Curt Raydon 4.00 1.80
❑ 306 Jim Gilliam 8.00 3.60
❑ 307 Curt Barclay 4.00 1.80
❑ 308 Norm Siebern 4.00 1.80
❑ 309 Sal Maglie 8.00 3.60
❑ 310 Luis Aparicio 20.00 9.00
❑ 311 Norm Zauchin 4.00 1.80
❑ 312 Don Newcombe 8.00 3.60
❑ 313 Frank House 4.00 1.80
❑ 314 Don Cardwell 4.00 1.80
❑ 315 Joe Adcock 8.00 3.60
❑ 316A Ralph Lumenti UER 4.00 1.80
(Option)
(Photo actually
Camilo Pascual)
❑ 316B Ralph Lumenti UER 80.00 36.00
(No option)
(Photo actually
Camilo Pascual)
❑ 317 Willie Mays 70.00 32.00
Richie Ashburn
❑ 318 Rocky Bridges 4.00 1.80
❑ 319 Dave Hillman 4.00 1.80
❑ 320 Bob Skinner 8.00 3.60
❑ 321A Bob Giallombardo 4.00 1.80
(Option)
❑ 321B Bob Giallombardo 80.00 36.00
(No option)
❑ 322A Harry Hanebrink 4.00 1.80
(Traded)
❑ 322B Harry Hanebrink 80.00 36.00
(No trade)
❑ 323 Frank Sullivan 4.00 1.80
❑ 324 Don Demeter 4.00 1.80
❑ 325 Ken Boyer 10.00 4.50
❑ 326 Marv Throneberry 8.00 3.60
❑ 327 Gary Bell 4.00 1.80
❑ 328 Lou Skizas 4.00 1.80
❑ 329 Tigers Team 12.00 2.40
(Checklist on back)
❑ 330 Gus Triandos 8.00 3.60
❑ 331 Steve Boros 4.00 1.80
❑ 332 Ray Monzant 4.00 1.80
❑ 333 Harry Simpson 4.00 1.80
❑ 334 Glen Hobbie 4.00 1.80
❑ 335 Johnny Temple 8.00 3.60
❑ 336A Billy Loes 8.00 3.60
(With traded line)
❑ 336B Billy Loes 80.00 36.00
(No trade)
❑ 337 George Crowe 4.00 1.80
❑ 338 Sparky Anderson 60.00 27.00
❑ 339 Roy Face 8.00 3.60
❑ 340 Roy Sievers 8.00 3.60
❑ 341 Tom Qualters 4.00 1.80
❑ 342 Ray Jablonski 4.00 1.80
❑ 343 Billy Hoeft 4.00 1.80
❑ 344 Russ Nixon 4.00 1.80
❑ 345 Gil McDougald 8.00 3.60
❑ 346 Dave Sisler 4.00 1.80
Tom Brewer
❑ 347 Bob Buhl 4.00 1.80
❑ 348 Ted Lepcio 4.00 1.80
❑ 349 Hoyt Wilhelm 16.00 7.25
❑ 350 Ernie Banks 75.00 34.00
❑ 351 Earl Torgeson 4.00 1.80
❑ 352 Robin Roberts 20.00 9.00
❑ 353 Curt Flood 8.00 3.60
❑ 354 Pete Burnside 4.00 1.80
❑ 355 Jimmy Piersall 8.00 3.60
❑ 356 Bob Mabe 4.00 1.80
❑ 357 Dick Stuart 8.00 3.60
❑ 358 Ralph Terry 8.00 3.60
❑ 359 Bill White 20.00 9.00
❑ 360 Al Kaline 60.00 27.00
❑ 361 Willard Nixon 4.00 1.80
❑ 362A Dolan Nichols 4.00 1.80
(With option line)
❑ 362B Dolan Nichols 80.00 36.00
(No option)
❑ 363 Bobby Avila 4.00 1.80
❑ 364 Danny McDevitt 4.00 1.80
❑ 365 Gus Bell 8.00 3.60
❑ 366 Humberto Robinson 4.00 1.80
❑ 367 Cal Neeman 4.00 1.80
❑ 368 Don Mueller 8.00 3.60
❑ 369 Dick Tomanek 4.00 1.80
❑ 370 Pete Runnels 8.00 3.60
❑ 371 Dick Brodowski 4.00 1.80
❑ 372 Jim Hegan 8.00 3.60
❑ 373 Herb Plews 4.00 1.80
❑ 374 Art Ditmar 8.00 3.60
❑ 375 Bob Nieman 4.00 1.80
❑ 376 Hal Naragon 4.00 1.80
❑ 377 John Antonelli 8.00 3.60
❑ 378 Gail Harris 4.00 1.80
❑ 379 Bob Miller 4.00 1.80
❑ 380 Hank Aaron 125.00 55.00
❑ 381 Mike Baxes 4.00 1.80
❑ 382 Curt Simmons 8.00 3.60
❑ 383 Words of Wisdom 14.00 6.25
Don Larsen
Casey Stengel MG
❑ 384 Dave Sisler 4.00 1.80
❑ 385 Sherm Lollar 8.00 3.60
❑ 386 Jim Delsing 4.00 1.80
❑ 387 Don Drysdale 35.00 16.00
❑ 388 Bob Will 4.00 1.80
❑ 389 Joe Nuxhall 8.00 3.60
❑ 390 Orlando Cepeda 16.00 7.25
❑ 391 Milt Pappas 8.00 3.60
❑ 392 Whitey Herzog 8.00 3.60
❑ 393 Frank Lary 8.00 3.60
❑ 394 Randy Jackson 4.00 1.80
❑ 395 Elston Howard 10.00 4.50
❑ 396 Bob Rush 4.00 1.80
❑ 397 Senators Team 12.00 2.40
(Checklist on back)
❑ 398 Wally Post 8.00 3.60
❑ 399 Larry Jackson 4.00 1.80
❑ 400 Jackie Jensen 8.00 3.60
❑ 401 Ron Blackburn 4.00 1.80
❑ 402 Hector Lopez 8.00 3.60
❑ 403 Clem Labine 8.00 3.60
❑ 404 Hank Sauer 8.00 3.60
❑ 405 Roy McMillan 8.00 3.60
❑ 406 Solly Drake 4.00 1.80
❑ 407 Moe Drabowsky 8.00 3.60
❑ 408 Nellie Fox 35.00 16.00
Luis Aparicio
❑ 409 Gus Zernial 8.00 3.60
❑ 410 Billy Pierce 8.00 3.60
❑ 411 Whitey Lockman 8.00 3.60
❑ 412 Stan Lopata 4.00 1.80
❑ 413 Camilo Pascual UER 8.00 3.60
(Listed as Camillo
on front and Pasqual
on back)
❑ 414 Dale Long 8.00 3.60
❑ 415 Bill Mazeroski 12.00 5.50
❑ 416 Haywood Sullivan 8.00 3.60
❑ 417 Virgil Trucks 8.00 3.60
❑ 418 Gino Cimoli 4.00 1.80
❑ 419 Braves Team 12.00 2.40
(Checklist on back)
❑ 420 Rocky Colavito 30.00 13.50
❑ 421 Herman Wehmeier 4.00 1.80
❑ 422 Hobie Landrith 4.00 1.80
❑ 423 Bob Grim 8.00 3.60
❑ 424 Ken Aspromonte 4.00 1.80
❑ 425 Del Crandall 8.00 3.60
❑ 426 Gerry Staley 8.00 3.60
❑ 427 Charlie Neal 8.00 3.60
❑ 428 Ron Kline 4.00 1.80
Bob Friend
Vernon Law
Roy Face
❑ 429 Bobby Thomson 8.00 3.60
❑ 430 Whitey Ford 50.00 22.00
❑ 431 Whammy Douglas 4.00 1.80
❑ 432 Smoky Burgess 8.00 3.60
❑ 433 Billy Harrell 4.00 1.80
❑ 434 Hal Griggs 4.00 1.80
❑ 435 Frank Robinson 50.00 22.00
❑ 436 Granny Hamner 4.00 1.80

No.	Player	NRMT	VG-E
437	Ike Delock	4.00	1.80
438	Sammy Esposito	4.00	1.80
439	Brooks Robinson	50.00	22.00
440	Lou Burdette	8.00	3.60
	(Posing as if lefthanded)		
441	John Roseboro	8.00	3.60
442	Ray Narleski	4.00	1.80
443	Daryl Spencer	4.00	1.80
444	Ron Hansen	8.00	3.60
445	Cal McLish	4.00	1.80
446	Rocky Nelson	4.00	1.80
447	Bob Anderson	4.00	1.80
448	Vada Pinson UER	10.00	4.50
	(Born: 8/8/38 should be 8/11/38)		
449	Tom Gorman	4.00	1.80
450	Eddie Mathews	35.00	16.00
451	Jimmy Constable	4.00	1.80
452	Chico Fernandez	4.00	1.80
453	Les Moss	4.00	1.80
454	Phil Clark	4.00	1.80
455	Larry Doby	8.00	3.60
456	Jerry Casale	4.00	1.80
457	Dodgers Team	30.00	6.00
	(Checklist on back)		
458	Gordon Jones	4.00	1.80
459	Bill Tuttle	4.00	1.80
460	Bob Friend	8.00	3.60
461	Mickey Mantle HL	130.00	57.50
462	Rocky Colavito HL	16.00	7.25
463	Al Kaline HL	25.00	11.00
464	Willie Mays HL	40.00	18.00
	54 World Series Catch		
465	Roy Sievers HL	8.00	3.60
466	Billy Pierce HL	8.00	3.60
467	Hank Aaron HL	30.00	13.50
468	Duke Snider HL	18.00	8.00
469	Ernie Banks HL	18.00	8.00
470	Stan Musial HL	25.00	11.00
	3,000 Hits		
471	Tom Sturdivant	4.00	1.80
472	Gene Freese	4.00	1.80
473	Mike Fornieles	4.00	1.80
474	Moe Thacker	4.00	1.80
475	Jack Harshman	4.00	1.80
476	Indians Team	12.00	2.40
	(Checklist on back)		
477	Barry Latman	4.00	1.80
478	Bob Clemente	225.00	100.00
479	Lindy McDaniel	8.00	3.60
480	Red Schoendienst	16.00	7.25
481	Charlie Maxwell	8.00	3.60
482	Russ Meyer	4.00	1.80
483	Clint Courtney	4.00	1.80
484	Willie Kirkland	4.00	1.80
485	Ryne Duren	8.00	3.60
486	Sammy White	4.00	1.80
487	Hal Brown	4.00	1.80
488	Walt Moryn	4.00	1.80
489	John Powers	4.00	1.80
490	Frank Thomas	8.00	3.60
491	Don Blasingame	4.00	1.80
492	Gene Conley	8.00	3.60
493	Jim Landis	8.00	3.60
494	Don Pavletich	4.00	1.80
495	Johnny Podres	8.00	3.60
496	Wayne Terwilliger UER	4.00	1.80
	(Athlftics on front)		
497	Hal R. Smith	4.00	1.80
498	Dick Hyde	4.00	1.80
499	Johnny O'Brien	8.00	3.60
500	Vic Wertz	8.00	3.60
501	Bob Tiefenauer	4.00	1.80
502	Alvin Dark	8.00	3.60
503	Jim Owens	4.00	1.80
504	Ossie Alvarez	4.00	1.80
505	Tony Kubek	12.00	5.50
506	Bob Purkey	4.00	1.80
507	Bob Hale	16.00	7.25
508	Art Fowler	16.00	7.25
509	Norm Cash	65.00	29.00
510	Yankees Team	125.00	25.00
	(Checklist on back)		
511	George Susce	16.00	7.25
512	George Altman	16.00	7.25
513	Tommy Carroll	16.00	7.25
514	Bob Gibson	250.00	110.00
515	Harmon Killebrew	125.00	55.00
516	Mike Garcia	20.00	9.00
517	Joe Koppe	16.00	7.25
518	Mike Cueller UER	30.00	13.50
	(Sic, Cuellar)		
519	Pete Runnels	20.00	9.00
	Dick Gernert		
	Frank Malzone		
520	Don Elston	16.00	7.25
521	Gary Geiger	16.00	7.25
522	Gene Snyder	16.00	7.25
523	Harry Bright	16.00	7.25
524	Larry Osborne	16.00	7.25
525	Jim Coates	20.00	9.00
526	Bob Speake	16.00	7.25
527	Solly Hemus	16.00	7.25
528	Pirates Team	70.00	14.00
	(Checklist on back)		
529	George Bamberger	25.00	11.00
530	Wally Moon	20.00	9.00
531	Ray Webster	16.00	7.25
532	Mark Freeman	16.00	7.25
533	Darrell Johnson	20.00	9.00
534	Faye Throneberry	16.00	7.25
535	Ruben Gomez	16.00	7.25
536	Danny Kravitz	16.00	7.25
537	Rudolph Arias	16.00	7.25
538	Chick King	16.00	7.25
539	Gary Blaylock	16.00	7.25
540	Willie Miranda	16.00	7.25
541	Bob Thurman	16.00	7.25
542	Jim Perry	30.00	13.50
543	Bob Skinner	175.00	80.00
	Bill Virdon		
	Roberto Clemente		
544	Lee Tate	16.00	7.25
545	Tom Morgan	16.00	7.25
546	Al Schroll	16.00	7.25
547	Jim Baxes	16.00	7.25
548	Elmer Singleton	16.00	7.25
549	Howie Nunn	16.00	7.25
550	Roy Campanella	160.00	70.00
	(Symbol of Courage)		
551	Fred Haney AS MG	16.00	7.25
552	Casey Stengel AS MG	30.00	13.50
553	Orlando Cepeda AS	25.00	11.00
554	Bill Skowron AS	25.00	11.00
555	Bill Mazeroski AS	25.00	11.00
556	Nellie Fox AS	40.00	18.00
557	Ken Boyer AS	25.00	11.00
558	Frank Malzone AS	16.00	7.25
559	Ernie Banks AS	65.00	29.00
560	Luis Aparicio AS	30.00	13.50
561	Hank Aaron AS	125.00	55.00
562	Al Kaline AS	65.00	29.00
563	Willie Mays AS	125.00	55.00
564	Mickey Mantle AS	300.00	135.00
565	Wes Covington AS	16.00	7.25
566	Roy Sievers AS	16.00	7.25
567	Del Crandall AS	16.00	7.25
568	Gus Triandos AS	16.00	7.25
569	Bob Friend AS	16.00	7.25
570	Bob Turley AS	16.00	7.25
571	Warren Spahn AS	40.00	18.00
572	Billy Pierce AS	30.00	9.50

1960 Topps

	NRMT	VG-E
COMPLETE SET (572)	3500.00	1600.00
COMMON CARD (1-440)	4.00	1.80
COMMON CARD (441-506)	7.00	3.10
COMMON CARD (507-572)	16.00	7.25
WRAPPER (1-CENT)	900.00	400.00
WRAPPER (1-CENT REPEAT)	500.00	220.00
WRAPPER (5-CENT)	40.00	18.00

No.	Player	NRMT	VG-E
1	Early Wynn	30.00	7.50
2	Roman Mejias	4.00	1.80
3	Joe Adcock	6.00	2.70
4	Bob Purkey	4.00	1.80
5	Wally Moon	6.00	2.70
6	Lou Berberet	4.00	1.80
7	Master and Mentor	25.00	11.00
	Willie Mays		
	Bill Rigney MG		
8	Bud Daley	4.00	1.80
9	Faye Throneberry	4.00	1.80
10	Ernie Banks	50.00	22.00
11	Norm Siebern	4.00	1.80
12	Milt Pappas	6.00	2.70
13	Wally Post	6.00	2.70
14	Jim Grant	6.00	2.70
15	Pete Runnels	6.00	2.70
16	Ernie Broglio	6.00	2.70
17	Johnny Callison	6.00	2.70
18	Dodgers Team	50.00	10.00
	(Checklist on back)		
19	Felix Mantilla	4.00	1.80
20	Roy Face	6.00	2.70
21	Dutch Dotterer	4.00	1.80
22	Rocky Bridges	4.00	1.80
23	Eddie Fisher	4.00	1.80
24	Dick Gray	4.00	1.80
25	Roy Sievers	6.00	2.70
26	Wayne Terwilliger	4.00	1.80
27	Dick Drott	4.00	1.80
28	Brooks Robinson	50.00	22.00
29	Clem Labine	6.00	2.70
30	Tito Francona	4.00	1.80
31	Sammy Esposito	4.00	1.80
32	Sophomore Stalwarts	4.00	1.80
	Jim O'Toole		
	Vada Pinson		
33	Tom Morgan	4.00	1.80
34	Sparky Anderson	14.00	6.25
35	Whitey Ford	50.00	22.00
36	Russ Nixon	4.00	1.80
37	Bill Bruton	4.00	1.80
38	Jerry Casale	4.00	1.80
39	Earl Averill	4.00	1.80
40	Joe Cunningham	4.00	1.80
41	Barry Latman	4.00	1.80
42	Hobie Landrith	4.00	1.80
43	Senators Team	9.00	1.80
	(Checklist on back)		
44	Bobby Locke	4.00	1.80
45	Roy McMillan	6.00	2.70
46	Jerry Fisher	4.00	1.80
47	Don Zimmer	6.00	2.70
48	Hal W. Smith	4.00	1.80
49	Curt Raydon	4.00	1.80
50	Al Kaline	50.00	22.00
51	Jim Coates	6.00	2.70
52	Dave Philley	4.00	1.80
53	Jackie Brandt	4.00	1.80
54	Mike Fornieles	4.00	1.80
55	Bill Mazeroski	10.00	4.50
56	Steve Korcheck	4.00	1.80
57	Win Savers	4.00	1.80
	Turk Lown		
	Gerry Staley		
58	Gino Cimoli	4.00	1.80
59	Juan Pizarro	4.00	1.80
60	Gus Triandos	6.00	2.70
61	Eddie Kasko	4.00	1.80
62	Roger Craig	6.00	2.70
63	George Strickland	4.00	1.80
64	Jack Meyer	4.00	1.80
65	Elston Howard	7.00	3.10
66	Bob Trowbridge	4.00	1.80

❑ 67 Jose Pagan 4.00 1.80
❑ 68 Dave Hillman 4.00 1.80
❑ 69 Billy Goodman 6.00 2.70
❑ 70 Lew Burdette 6.00 2.70
❑ 71 Marty Keough 4.00 1.80
❑ 72 Tigers Team 20.00 4.00
(Checklist on back)
❑ 73 Bob Gibson 50.00 22.00
❑ 74 Walt Moryn 4.00 1.80
❑ 75 Vic Power 6.00 2.70
❑ 76 Bill Fischer 4.00 1.80
❑ 77 Hank Foiles 4.00 1.80
❑ 78 Bob Grim 4.00 1.80
❑ 79 Walt Dropo 4.00 1.80
❑ 80 Johnny Antonelli 6.00 2.70
❑ 81 Russ Snyder 4.00 1.80
❑ 82 Ruben Gomez 4.00 1.80
❑ 83 Tony Kubek 7.00 3.10
❑ 84 Hal R. Smith 4.00 1.80
❑ 85 Frank Lary 6.00 2.70
❑ 86 Dick Gernert 4.00 1.80
❑ 87 John Romonosky 4.00 1.80
❑ 88 John Roseboro 6.00 2.70
❑ 89 Hal Brown 4.00 1.80
❑ 90 Bobby Avila 4.00 1.80
❑ 91 Bennie Daniels 4.00 1.80
❑ 92 Whitey Herzog 6.00 2.70
❑ 93 Art Schult 4.00 1.80
❑ 94 Leo Kiely 4.00 1.80
❑ 95 Frank Thomas 6.00 2.70
❑ 96 Ralph Terry 6.00 2.70
❑ 97 Ted Lepcio 4.00 1.80
❑ 98 Gordon Jones 4.00 1.80
❑ 99 Lenny Green 4.00 1.80
❑ 100 Nellie Fox 20.00 9.00
❑ 101 Bob Miller 4.00 1.80
❑ 102 Kent Hadley 4.00 1.80
❑ 103 Dick Farrell 6.00 2.70
❑ 104 Dick Schofield 6.00 2.70
❑ 105 Larry Sherry 6.00 2.70
❑ 106 Billy Gardner 4.00 1.80
❑ 107 Carlton Willey 4.00 1.80
❑ 108 Pete Daley 4.00 1.80
❑ 109 Clete Boyer 6.00 2.70
❑ 110 Cal McLish 4.00 1.80
❑ 111 Vic Wertz 6.00 2.70
❑ 112 Jack Harshman 4.00 1.80
❑ 113 Bob Skinner 4.00 1.80
❑ 114 Ken Aspromonte 4.00 1.80
❑ 115 Fork and Knuckler 7.00 3.10
Roy Face
Hoyt Wilhelm
❑ 116 Jim Rivera 4.00 1.80
❑ 117 Tom Borland RP 4.00 1.80
❑ 118 Bob Bruce RP 4.00 1.80
❑ 119 Chico Cardenas RP 6.00 2.70
❑ 120 Duke Carmel RP 4.00 1.80
❑ 121 Camilo Carreon RP 4.00 1.80
❑ 122 Don Dillard RP 4.00 1.80
❑ 123 Dan Dobbek RP 4.00 1.80
❑ 124 Jim Donohue RP 4.00 1.80
❑ 125 Dick Ellsworth RP 6.00 2.70
❑ 126 Chuck Estrada RP 4.00 1.80
❑ 127 Ron Hansen RP 6.00 2.70
❑ 128 Bill Harris RP 4.00 1.80
❑ 129 Bob Hartman RP 4.00 1.80
❑ 130 Frank Herrera RP 4.00 1.80
❑ 131 Ed Hobaugh RP 4.00 1.80
❑ 132 Frank Howard RP 25.00 11.00
❑ 133 Manuel Javier RP 6.00 2.70
(Sic, Julian)
❑ 134 Deron Johnson RP 6.00 2.70
❑ 135 Ken Johnson RP 4.00 1.80
❑ 136 Jim Kaat RP 40.00 18.00
❑ 137 Lou Klimchock RP 4.00 1.80
❑ 138 Art Mahaffey RP 6.00 2.70
❑ 139 Carl Mathias RP 4.00 1.80
❑ 140 Julio Navarro RP 4.00 1.80
❑ 141 Jim Proctor RP 4.00 1.80
❑ 142 Bill Short RP 4.00 1.80
❑ 143 Al Spangler RP 4.00 1.80
❑ 144 Al Stieglitz RP 4.00 1.80
❑ 145 Jim Umbricht RP 4.00 1.80
❑ 146 Ted Wieand RP 4.00 1.80
❑ 147 Bob Will RP 4.00 1.80
❑ 148 Carl Yastrzemski RP 125.00 55.00
❑ 149 Bob Nieman 4.00 1.80
❑ 150 Billy Pierce 6.00 2.70
❑ 151 Giants Team 9.00 1.80
(Checklist on back)
❑ 152 Gail Harris 4.00 1.80
❑ 153 Bobby Thomson 6.00 2.70
❑ 154 Jim Davenport 6.00 2.70
❑ 155 Charlie Neal 6.00 2.70
❑ 156 Art Ceccarelli 4.00 1.80
❑ 157 Rocky Nelson 6.00 2.70
❑ 158 Wes Covington 6.00 2.70
❑ 159 Jim Piersall 6.00 2.70
❑ 160 Rival All-Stars 140.00 65.00
Mickey Mantle
Ken Boyer
❑ 161 Ray Narleski 4.00 1.80
❑ 162 Sammy Taylor 4.00 1.80
❑ 163 Hector Lopez 6.00 2.70
❑ 164 Reds Team 9.00 1.80
(Checklist on back)
❑ 165 Jack Sanford 6.00 2.70
❑ 166 Chuck Essegian 4.00 1.80
❑ 167 Valmy Thomas 4.00 1.80
❑ 168 Alex Grammas 4.00 1.80
❑ 169 Jake Striker 4.00 1.80
❑ 170 Del Crandall 6.00 2.70
❑ 171 Johnny Groth 4.00 1.80
❑ 172 Willie Kirkland 4.00 1.80
❑ 173 Billy Martin 20.00 9.00
❑ 174 Indians Team 9.00 1.80
(Checklist on back)
❑ 175 Pedro Ramos 4.00 1.80
❑ 176 Vada Pinson 6.00 2.70
❑ 177 Johnny Kucks 4.00 1.80
❑ 178 Woody Held 4.00 1.80
❑ 179 Rip Coleman 4.00 1.80
❑ 180 Harry Simpson 4.00 1.80
❑ 181 Billy Loes 6.00 2.70
❑ 182 Glen Hobbie 4.00 1.80
❑ 183 Eli Grba 4.00 1.80
❑ 184 Gary Geiger 4.00 1.80
❑ 185 Jim Owens 4.00 1.80
❑ 186 Dave Sisler 4.00 1.80
❑ 187 Jay Hook 4.00 1.80
❑ 188 Dick Williams 6.00 2.70
❑ 189 Don McMahon 4.00 1.80
❑ 190 Gene Woodling 6.00 2.70
❑ 191 Johnny Klippstein 4.00 1.80
❑ 192 Danny O'Connell 4.00 1.80
❑ 193 Dick Hyde 4.00 1.80
❑ 194 Bobby Gene Smith 4.00 1.80
❑ 195 Lindy McDaniel 6.00 2.70
❑ 196 Andy Carey 6.00 2.70
❑ 197 Ron Kline 4.00 1.80
❑ 198 Jerry Lynch 6.00 2.70
❑ 199 Dick Donovan 6.00 2.70
❑ 200 Willie Mays 90.00 40.00
❑ 201 Larry Osborne 4.00 1.80
❑ 202 Fred Kipp 4.00 1.80
❑ 203 Sammy White 4.00 1.80
❑ 204 Ryne Duren 6.00 2.70
❑ 205 Johnny Logan 6.00 2.70
❑ 206 Claude Osteen 6.00 2.70
❑ 207 Bob Boyd 4.00 1.80
❑ 208 White Sox Team 9.00 1.80
(Checklist on back)
❑ 209 Ron Blackburn 4.00 1.80
❑ 210 Harmon Killebrew 25.00 11.00
❑ 211 Taylor Phillips 4.00 1.80
❑ 212 Walter Alston MG 12.00 5.50
❑ 213 Chuck Dressen MG 6.00 2.70
❑ 214 Jimmy Dykes MG 6.00 2.70
❑ 215 Bob Elliott MG 6.00 2.70
❑ 216 Joe Gordon MG 6.00 2.70
❑ 217 Charlie Grimm MG 6.00 2.70
❑ 218 Solly Hemus MG 4.00 1.80
❑ 219 Fred Hutchinson MG 6.00 2.70
❑ 220 Billy Jurges MG 4.00 1.80
❑ 221 Cookie Lavagetto MG 4.00 1.80
❑ 222 Al Lopez MG 6.00 2.70
❑ 223 Danny Murtaugh MG 6.00 2.70
❑ 224 Paul Richards MG 6.00 2.70
❑ 225 Bill Rigney MG 4.00 1.80
❑ 226 Eddie Sawyer MG 4.00 1.80
❑ 227 Casey Stengel MG 15.00 6.75
❑ 228 Ernie Johnson 6.00 2.70
❑ 229 Joe M. Morgan 4.00 1.80
❑ 230 Mound Magicians 12.00 5.50
Lou Burdette
Warren Spahn
Bob Buhl
❑ 231 Hal Naragon 4.00 1.80
❑ 232 Jim Busby 4.00 1.80
❑ 233 Don Elston 4.00 1.80
❑ 234 Don Demeter 4.00 1.80
❑ 235 Gus Bell 6.00 2.70
❑ 236 Dick Ricketts 4.00 1.80
❑ 237 Elmer Valo 4.00 1.80
❑ 238 Danny Kravitz 4.00 1.80
❑ 239 Joe Shipley 4.00 1.80
❑ 240 Luis Aparicio 15.00 6.75
❑ 241 Albie Pearson 6.00 2.70
❑ 242 Cardinals Team 9.00 1.80
(Checklist on back)
❑ 243 Bubba Phillips 4.00 1.80
❑ 244 Hal Griggs 4.00 1.80
❑ 245 Eddie Yost 6.00 2.70
❑ 246 Lee Maye 6.00 2.70
❑ 247 Gil McDougald 6.00 2.70
❑ 248 Del Rice 4.00 1.80
❑ 249 Earl Wilson 6.00 2.70
❑ 250 Stan Musial 80.00 36.00
❑ 251 Bob Malkmus 4.00 1.80
❑ 252 Ray Herbert 4.00 1.80
❑ 253 Eddie Bressoud 4.00 1.80
❑ 254 Arnie Portocarrero 4.00 1.80
❑ 255 Jim Gilliam 6.00 2.70
❑ 256 Dick Brown 4.00 1.80
❑ 257 Gordy Coleman 4.00 1.80
❑ 258 Dick Groat 6.00 2.70
❑ 259 George Altman 4.00 1.80
❑ 260 Power Plus 14.00 6.25
Rocky Colavito
Tito Francona
❑ 261 Pete Burnside 4.00 1.80
❑ 262 Hank Bauer 6.00 2.70
❑ 263 Darrell Johnson 4.00 1.80
❑ 264 Robin Roberts 15.00 6.75
❑ 265 Rip Repulski 4.00 1.80
❑ 266 Joey Jay 6.00 2.70
❑ 267 Jim Marshall 4.00 1.80
❑ 268 Al Worthington 4.00 1.80
❑ 269 Gene Green 4.00 1.80
❑ 270 Bob Turley 6.00 2.70
❑ 271 Julio Becquer 4.00 1.80
❑ 272 Fred Green 6.00 2.70
❑ 273 Neil Chrisley 4.00 1.80
❑ 274 Tom Acker 4.00 1.80
❑ 275 Curt Flood 6.00 2.70
❑ 276 Ken McBride 4.00 1.80
❑ 277 Harry Bright 4.00 1.80
❑ 278 Stan Williams 6.00 2.70
❑ 279 Chuck Tanner 6.00 2.70
❑ 280 Frank Sullivan 4.00 1.80
❑ 281 Ray Boone 6.00 2.70
❑ 282 Joe Nuxhall 6.00 2.70
❑ 283 John Blanchard 6.00 2.70
❑ 284 Don Gross 4.00 1.80
❑ 285 Harry Anderson 4.00 1.80
❑ 286 Ray Semproch 4.00 1.80
❑ 287 Felipe Alou 6.00 2.70
❑ 288 Bob Mabe 4.00 1.80
❑ 289 Willie Jones 4.00 1.80
❑ 290 Jerry Lumpe 4.00 1.80
❑ 291 Bob Keegan 4.00 1.80
❑ 292 Dodger Backstops 6.00 2.70
Joe Pignatano
John Roseboro
❑ 293 Gene Conley 6.00 2.70
❑ 294 Tony Taylor 6.00 2.70
❑ 295 Gil Hodges 20.00 9.00
❑ 296 Nelson Chittum 4.00 1.80
❑ 297 Reno Bertoia 4.00 1.80
❑ 298 George Witt 4.00 1.80
❑ 299 Earl Torgeson 4.00 1.80
❑ 300 Hank Aaron 80.00 36.00
❑ 301 Jerry Davie 4.00 1.80
❑ 302 Phillies Team 9.00 1.80
(Checklist on back)

	No.	Card	Price	Price
❑	303	Billy O'Dell	4.00	1.80
❑	304	Joe Ginsberg	4.00	1.80
❑	305	Richie Ashburn	20.00	9.00
❑	306	Frank Baumann	4.00	1.80
❑	307	Gene Oliver	4.00	1.80
❑	308	Dick Hall	4.00	1.80
❑	309	Bob Hale	4.00	1.80
❑	310	Frank Malzone	6.00	2.70
❑	311	Raul Sanchez	4.00	1.80
❑	312	Charley Lau	6.00	2.70
❑	313	Turk Lown	4.00	1.80
❑	314	Chico Fernandez	4.00	1.80
❑	315	Bobby Shantz	6.00	2.70
❑	316	Willie McCovey	115.00	52.50
❑	317	Pumpsie Green	6.00	2.70
❑	318	Jim Baxes	6.00	2.70
❑	319	Joe Koppe	6.00	2.70
❑	320	Bob Allison	6.00	2.70
❑	321	Ron Fairly	6.00	2.70
❑	322	Willie Tasby	6.00	2.70
❑	323	John Romano	6.00	2.70
❑	324	Jim Perry	6.00	2.70
❑	325	Jim O'Toole	6.00	2.70
❑	326	Bob Clemente	225.00	100.00
❑	327	Ray Sadecki	4.00	1.80
❑	328	Earl Battey	4.00	1.80
❑	329	Zack Monroe	4.00	1.80
❑	330	Harvey Kuenn	6.00	2.70
❑	331	Henry Mason	4.00	1.80
❑	332	Yankees Team	80.00	16.00
		(Checklist on back)		
❑	333	Danny McDevitt	4.00	1.80
❑	334	Ted Abernathy	4.00	1.80
❑	335	Red Schoendienst	12.00	5.50
❑	336	Ike Delock	4.00	1.80
❑	337	Cal Neeman	4.00	1.80
❑	338	Ray Monzant	4.00	1.80
❑	339	Harry Chiti	4.00	1.80
❑	340	Harvey Haddix	6.00	2.70
❑	341	Carroll Hardy	4.00	1.80
❑	342	Casey Wise	4.00	1.80
❑	343	Sandy Koufax	150.00	70.00
❑	344	Clint Courtney	4.00	1.80
❑	345	Don Newcombe	6.00	2.70
❑	346	J.C. Martin UER	6.00	2.70
		(Face actually		
		Gary Peters)		
❑	347	Ed Bouchee	4.00	1.80
❑	348	Barry Shetrone	4.00	1.80
❑	349	Moe Drabowsky	6.00	2.70
❑	350	Mickey Mantle	475.00	210.00
❑	351	Don Nottebart	4.00	1.80
❑	352	Cincy Clouters	8.00	3.60
		Gus Bell		
		Frank Robinson		
		Jerry Lynch		
❑	353	Don Larsen	6.00	2.70
❑	354	Bob Lillis	4.00	1.80
❑	355	Bill White	6.00	2.70
❑	356	Joe Amalfitano	4.00	1.80
❑	357	Al Schroll	4.00	1.80
❑	358	Joe DeMaestri	4.00	1.80
❑	359	Buddy Gilbert	4.00	1.80
❑	360	Herb Score	6.00	2.70
❑	361	Bob Oldis	4.00	1.80
❑	362	Russ Kemmerer	4.00	1.80
❑	363	Gene Stephens	4.00	1.80
❑	364	Paul Foytack	4.00	1.80
❑	365	Minnie Minoso	7.00	3.10
❑	366	Dallas Green	8.00	3.60
❑	367	Bill Tuttle	4.00	1.80
❑	368	Daryl Spencer	4.00	1.80
❑	369	Billy Hoeft	4.00	1.80
❑	370	Bill Skowron	7.00	3.10
❑	371	Bud Byerly	4.00	1.80
❑	372	Frank House	4.00	1.80
❑	373	Don Hoak	6.00	2.70
❑	374	Bob Buhl	6.00	2.70
❑	375	Dale Long	6.00	2.70
❑	376	John Briggs	4.00	1.80
❑	377	Roger Maris	90.00	40.00
❑	378	Stu Miller	6.00	2.70
❑	379	Red Wilson	4.00	1.80
❑	380	Bob Shaw	4.00	1.80
❑	381	Braves Team	9.00	1.80
		(Checklist on back)		
❑	382	Ted Bowsfield	4.00	1.80
❑	383	Leon Wagner	4.00	1.80
❑	384	Don Cardwell	4.00	1.80
❑	385	Charlie Neal WS	6.00	2.70
❑	386	Charlie Neal WS	6.00	2.70
❑	387	Carl Furillo WS	6.00	2.70
❑	388	Gil Hodges WS	10.00	4.50
❑	389	Luis Aparicio WS	12.00	5.50
		Maury Wills		
❑	390	World Series Game 6	6.00	2.70
❑	391	World Series Summary	6.00	2.70
		The Champs Celebrate		
❑	392	Tex Clevenger	4.00	1.80
❑	393	Smoky Burgess	6.00	2.70
❑	394	Norm Larker	6.00	2.70
❑	395	Hoyt Wilhelm	15.00	6.75
❑	396	Steve Bilko	4.00	1.80
❑	397	Don Blasingame	4.00	1.80
❑	398	Mike Cuellar	6.00	2.70
❑	399	Young Hill Stars	6.00	2.70
		Milt Pappas		
		Jack Fisher		
		Jerry Walker		
❑	400	Rocky Colavito	20.00	9.00
❑	401	Bob Duliba	4.00	1.80
❑	402	Dick Stuart	6.00	2.70
❑	403	Ed Sadowski	4.00	1.80
❑	404	Bob Rush	4.00	1.80
❑	405	Bobby Richardson	14.00	6.25
❑	406	Billy Klaus	4.00	1.80
❑	407	Gary Peters UER	6.00	2.70
		(Face actually		
		J.C. Martin)		
❑	408	Carl Furillo	6.00	2.70
❑	409	Ron Samford	4.00	1.80
❑	410	Sam Jones	6.00	2.70
❑	411	Ed Bailey	4.00	1.80
❑	412	Bob Anderson	4.00	1.80
❑	413	Athletics Team	9.00	1.80
		(Checklist on back)		
❑	414	Don Williams	4.00	1.80
❑	415	Bob Cerv	4.00	1.80
❑	416	Humberto Robinson	4.00	1.80
❑	417	Chuck Cottier	4.00	1.80
❑	418	Don Mossi	6.00	2.70
❑	419	George Crowe	4.00	1.80
❑	420	Eddie Mathews	30.00	13.50
❑	421	Duke Maas	4.00	1.80
❑	422	John Powers	4.00	1.80
❑	423	Ed Fitzgerald	4.00	1.80
❑	424	Pete Whisenant	4.00	1.80
❑	425	Johnny Podres	6.00	2.70
❑	426	Ron Jackson	4.00	1.80
❑	427	Al Grunwald	4.00	1.80
❑	428	Al Smith	4.00	1.80
❑	429	AL Kings	12.00	5.50
		Nellie Fox		
		Harvey Kuenn		
❑	430	Art Ditmar	4.00	1.80
❑	431	Andre Rodgers	4.00	1.80
❑	432	Chuck Stobbs	4.00	1.80
❑	433	Irv Noren	4.00	1.80
❑	434	Brooks Lawrence	4.00	1.80
❑	435	Gene Freese	4.00	1.80
❑	436	Marv Throneberry	6.00	2.70
❑	437	Bob Friend	6.00	2.70
❑	438	Jim Coker	4.00	1.80
❑	439	Tom Brewer	4.00	1.80
❑	440	Jim Lemon	6.00	2.70
❑	441	Gary Bell	7.00	3.10
❑	442	Joe Pignatano	7.00	3.10
❑	443	Charlie Maxwell	7.00	3.10
❑	444	Jerry Kindall	7.00	3.10
❑	445	Warren Spahn	50.00	22.00
❑	446	Ellis Burton	7.00	3.10
❑	447	Ray Moore	7.00	3.10
❑	448	Jim Gentile	20.00	9.00
❑	449	Jim Brosnan	7.00	3.10
❑	450	Orlando Cepeda	18.00	8.00
❑	451	Curt Simmons	7.00	3.10
❑	452	Ray Webster	7.00	3.10
❑	453	Vern Law	10.00	4.50
❑	454	Hal Woodeshick	7.00	3.10
❑	455	Baltimore Coaches	7.00	3.10
		Eddie Robinson		
		Harry Brecheen		
		Luman Harris		
❑	456	Red Sox Coaches	10.00	4.50
		Rudy York		
		Billy Herman		
		Sal Maglie		
		Del Baker		
❑	457	Cubs Coaches	7.00	3.10
		Charlie Root		
		Lou Klein		
		Elvin Tappe		
❑	458	White Sox Coaches	7.00	3.10
		Johnny Cooney		
		Don Gutteridge		
		Tony Cuccinello		
		Ray Berres		
❑	459	Reds Coaches	7.00	3.10
		Reggie Otero		
		Cot Deal		
		Wally Moses		
❑	460	Indians Coaches	10.00	4.50
		Mel Harder		
		Jo-Jo White		
		Bob Lemon		
		Ralph(Red) Kress		
❑	461	Tigers Coaches	10.00	4.50
		Tom Ferrick		
		Luke Appling		
		Billy Hitchcock		
❑	462	Athletics Coaches	7.00	3.10
		Fred Fitzsimmons		
		Don Heffner		
		Walker Cooper		
❑	463	Dodgers Coaches	7.00	3.10
		Bobby Bragan		
		Pete Reiser		
		Joe Becker		
		Greg Mulleavy		
❑	464	Braves Coaches	7.00	3.10
		Bob Scheffing		
		Whitlow Wyatt		
		Andy Pafko		
		George Myatt		
❑	465	Yankees Coaches	12.00	5.50
		Bill Dickey		
		Ralph Houk		
		Frank Crosetti		
		Ed Lopat		
❑	466	Phillies Coaches	7.00	3.10
		Ken Silvestri		
		Dick Carter		
		Andy Cohen		
❑	467	Pirates Coaches	7.00	3.10
		Mickey Vernon		
		Frank Oceak		
		Sam Narron		
		Bill Burwell		
❑	468	Cardinals Coaches	7.00	3.10
		Johnny Keane		
		Howie Pollet		
		Ray Katt		
		Harry Walker		
❑	469	Giants Coaches	7.00	3.10
		Wes Westrum		
		Salty Parker		
		Bill Posedel		
❑	470	Senators Coaches	7.00	3.10
		Bob Swift		
		Ellis Clary		
		Sam Mele		
❑	471	Ned Garver	7.00	3.10
❑	472	Alvin Dark	7.00	3.10
❑	473	Al Cicotte	7.00	3.10
❑	474	Haywood Sullivan	7.00	3.10
❑	475	Don Drysdale	35.00	16.00
❑	476	Lou Johnson	7.00	3.10
❑	477	Don Ferrarese	7.00	3.10
❑	478	Frank Torre	7.00	3.10
❑	479	Georges Maranda	7.00	3.10
❑	480	Yogi Berra	70.00	32.00
❑	481	Wes Stock	7.00	3.10
❑	482	Frank Bolling	7.00	3.10
❑	483	Camilo Pascual	7.00	3.10
❑	484	Pirates Team	50.00	10.00
		(Checklist on back)		
❑	485	Ken Boyer	14.00	6.25

	Card	NRMT	VG-E
❑	486 Bobby Del Greco	7.00	3.10
❑	487 Tom Sturdivant	7.00	3.10
❑	488 Norm Cash	20.00	9.00
❑	489 Steve Ridzik	7.00	3.10
❑	490 Frank Robinson	50.00	22.00
❑	491 Mel Roach	7.00	3.10
❑	492 Larry Jackson	7.00	3.10
❑	493 Duke Snider	50.00	22.00
❑	494 Orioles Team (Checklist on back)	25.00	5.00
❑	495 Sherm Lollar	7.00	3.10
❑	496 Bill Virdon	10.00	4.50
❑	497 John Tsitouris	7.00	3.10
❑	498 Al Pilarcik	7.00	3.10
❑	499 Johnny James	7.00	3.10
❑	500 Johnny Temple	7.00	3.10
❑	501 Bob Schmidt	7.00	3.10
❑	502 Jim Bunning	20.00	9.00
❑	503 Don Lee	7.00	3.10
❑	504 Seth Morehead	7.00	3.10
❑	505 Ted Kluszewski	20.00	9.00
❑	506 Lee Walls	7.00	3.10
❑	507 Dick Stigman	16.00	7.25
❑	508 Billy Consolo	16.00	7.25
❑	509 Tommy Davis	25.00	11.00
❑	510 Gerry Staley	16.00	7.25
❑	511 Ken Walters	16.00	7.25
❑	512 Joe Gibbon	16.00	7.25
❑	513 Chicago Cubs Team Card (Checklist on back)	30.00	6.00
❑	514 Steve Barber	16.00	7.25
❑	515 Stan Lopata	16.00	7.25
❑	516 Marty Kutyna	16.00	7.25
❑	517 Charlie James	16.00	7.25
❑	518 Tony Gonzalez	16.00	7.25
❑	519 Ed Roebuck	16.00	7.25
❑	520 Don Buddin	16.00	7.25
❑	521 Mike Lee	16.00	7.25
❑	522 Ken Hunt	20.00	9.00
❑	523 Clay Dalrymple	16.00	7.25
❑	524 Bill Henry	16.00	7.25
❑	525 Marv Breeding	16.00	7.25
❑	526 Paul Giel	16.00	7.25
❑	527 Jose Valdivielso	16.00	7.25
❑	528 Ben Johnson	16.00	7.25
❑	529 Norm Sherry	20.00	9.00
❑	530 Mike McCormick	16.00	7.25
❑	531 Sandy Amoros	16.00	7.25
❑	532 Mike Garcia	16.00	7.25
❑	533 Lu Clinton	16.00	7.25
❑	534 Ken MacKenzie	16.00	7.25
❑	535 Whitey Lockman	16.00	7.25
❑	536 Wynn Hawkins	16.00	7.25
❑	537 Boston Red Sox Team Card (Checklist on back)	30.00	6.00
❑	538 Frank Barnes	16.00	7.25
❑	539 Gene Baker	16.00	7.25
❑	540 Jerry Walker	16.00	7.25
❑	541 Tony Curry	16.00	7.25
❑	542 Ken Hamlin	16.00	7.25
❑	543 Elio Chacon	16.00	7.25
❑	544 Bill Monbouquette	16.00	7.25
❑	545 Carl Sawatski	16.00	7.25
❑	546 Hank Aguirre	16.00	7.25
❑	547 Bob Aspromonte	16.00	7.25
❑	548 Don Mincher	16.00	7.25
❑	549 John Buzhardt	16.00	7.25
❑	550 Jim Landis	16.00	7.25
❑	551 Ed Rakow	16.00	7.25
❑	552 Walt Bond	16.00	7.25
❑	553 Bill Skowron AS	20.00	9.00
❑	554 Willie McCovey AS	30.00	13.50
❑	555 Nellie Fox AS	30.00	13.50
❑	556 Charlie Neal AS	16.00	7.25
❑	557 Frank Malzone AS	16.00	7.25
❑	558 Eddie Mathews AS	30.00	13.50
❑	559 Luis Aparicio AS	30.00	13.50
❑	560 Ernie Banks AS	60.00	27.00
❑	561 Al Kaline AS	60.00	27.00
❑	562 Joe Cunningham AS	16.00	7.25
❑	563 Mickey Mantle AS	325.00	145.00
❑	564 Willie Mays AS	125.00	55.00
❑	565 Roger Maris AS	90.00	40.00
❑	566 Hank Aaron AS	100.00	45.00
❑	567 Sherm Lollar AS	16.00	7.25
❑	568 Del Crandall AS	16.00	7.25
❑	569 Camilo Pascual AS	16.00	7.25
❑	570 Don Drysdale AS	30.00	13.50
❑	571 Billy Pierce AS	16.00	7.25
❑	572 Johnny Antonelli AS	30.00	9.00
❑	NNO Iron-on team transfer	4.00	1.80

1961 Topps

	NRMT	VG-E
COMPLETE SET (587)	4800.00	2200.00
COMMON CARD (1-370)	3.00	1.35
COMMON CARD (371-446)	4.00	1.80
COMMON CARD (447-522)	7.00	3.10
COMMON CARD (523-589)	30.00	13.50
NOT ISSUED (587/588)		
WRAPPER (1-CENT)	200.00	90.00
WRAPPER (1-CENT, REPEAT)	100.00	45.00
WRAPPER (5-CENT)	40.00	18.00

	Card	NRMT	VG-E
❑	1 Dick Groat	30.00	6.00
❑	2 Roger Maris	175.00	80.00
❑	3 John Buzhardt	3.00	1.35
❑	4 Lenny Green	3.00	1.35
❑	5 John Romano	3.00	1.35
❑	6 Ed Roebuck	3.00	1.35
❑	7 White Sox Team	8.00	3.60
❑	8 Dick Williams	6.00	2.70
❑	9 Bob Purkey	3.00	1.35
❑	10 Brooks Robinson	40.00	18.00
❑	11 Curt Simmons	6.00	2.70
❑	12 Moe Thacker	3.00	1.35
❑	13 Chuck Cottier	3.00	1.35
❑	14 Don Mossi	6.00	2.70
❑	15 Willie Kirkland	3.00	1.35
❑	16 Billy Muffett	3.00	1.35
❑	17 Checklist 1	12.00	2.40
❑	18 Jim Grant	6.00	2.70
❑	19 Clete Boyer	7.00	3.10
❑	20 Robin Roberts	15.00	6.75
❑	21 Zorro Versalles UER (First name should be Zoilo)	7.00	3.10
❑	22 Clem Labine	6.00	2.70
❑	23 Don Demeter	3.00	1.35
❑	24 Ken Johnson	3.00	1.35
❑	25 Reds' Heavy Artillery Vada Pinson Gus Bell Frank Robinson	8.00	3.60
❑	26 Wes Stock	3.00	1.35
❑	27 Jerry Kindall	3.00	1.35
❑	28 Hector Lopez	6.00	2.70
❑	29 Don Nottebart	3.00	1.35
❑	30 Nellie Fox	15.00	6.75
❑	31 Bob Schmidt	3.00	1.35
❑	32 Ray Sadecki	3.00	1.35
❑	33 Gary Geiger	3.00	1.35
❑	34 Wynn Hawkins	3.00	1.35
❑	35 Ron Santo	40.00	18.00
❑	36 Jack Kralick	3.00	1.35
❑	37 Charley Maxwell	6.00	2.70
❑	38 Bob Lillis	3.00	1.35
❑	39 Leo Posada	3.00	1.35
❑	40 Bob Turley	6.00	2.70
❑	41 NL Batting Leaders Dick Groat Norm Larker Willie Mays Roberto Clemente	35.00	16.00
❑	42 AL Batting Leaders Pete Runnels Al Smith Minnie Minoso Bill Skowron	8.00	3.60
❑	43 NL Home Run Leaders Ernie Banks Hank Aaron Ed Mathews Ken Boyer	30.00	13.50
❑	44 AL Home Run Leaders Mickey Mantle Roger Maris Jim Lemon Rocky Colavito	100.00	45.00
❑	45 NL ERA Leaders Mike McCormick Ernie Broglio Don Drysdale Bob Friend Stan Williams	8.00	3.60
❑	46 AL ERA Leaders Frank Baumann Jim Bunning Art Ditmar Hal Brown	8.00	3.60
❑	47 NL Pitching Leaders Ernie Broglio Warren Spahn Vern Law Lou Burdette	8.00	3.60
❑	48 AL Pitching Leaders Chuck Estrada Jim Perry UER (Listed as an Oriole) Bud Daley Art Ditmar Frank Lary Milt Pappas	8.00	3.60
❑	49 NL Strikeout Leaders Don Drysdale Sandy Koufax Sam Jones Ernie Broglio	20.00	9.00
❑	50 AL Strikeout Leaders Jim Bunning Pedro Ramos Early Wynn Frank Lary	8.00	3.60
❑	51 Detroit Tigers Team Card	8.00	3.60
❑	52 George Crowe	3.00	1.35
❑	53 Russ Nixon	3.00	1.35
❑	54 Earl Francis	3.00	1.35
❑	55 Jim Davenport	6.00	2.70
❑	56 Russ Kemmerer	3.00	1.35
❑	57 Marv Throneberry	7.00	3.10
❑	58 Joe Schaffernoth	3.00	1.35
❑	59 Jim Woods	3.00	1.35
❑	60 Woody Held	3.00	1.35
❑	61 Ron Piche	3.00	1.35
❑	62 Al Pilarcik	3.00	1.35
❑	63 Jim Kaat	8.00	3.60
❑	64 Alex Grammas	3.00	1.35
❑	65 Ted Kluszewski	8.00	3.60
❑	66 Bill Henry	3.00	1.35
❑	67 Ossie Virgil	3.00	1.35
❑	68 Deron Johnson	6.00	2.70
❑	69 Earl Wilson	6.00	2.70
❑	70 Bill Virdon	6.00	2.70
❑	71 Jerry Adair	3.00	1.35
❑	72 Stu Miller	6.00	2.70
❑	73 Al Spangler	3.00	1.35
❑	74 Joe Pignatano	3.00	1.35
❑	75 Lindy Shows Larry Lindy McDaniel Larry Jackson	6.00	2.70
❑	76 Harry Anderson	3.00	1.35
❑	77 Dick Stigman	3.00	1.35
❑	78 Lee Walls	3.00	1.35
❑	79 Joe Ginsberg	3.00	1.35

No.	Card	Price 1	Price 2
80	Harmon Killebrew	20.00	9.00
81	Tracy Stallard	3.00	1.35
82	Joe Christopher	3.00	1.35
83	Bob Bruce	3.00	1.35
84	Lee Maye	3.00	1.35
85	Jerry Walker	3.00	1.35
86	Los Angeles Dodgers Team Card	8.00	3.60
87	Joe Amalfitano	3.00	1.35
88	Richie Ashburn	15.00	6.75
89	Billy Martin	15.00	6.75
90	Gerry Staley	3.00	1.35
91	Walt Moryn	3.00	1.35
92	Hal Naragon	3.00	1.35
93	Tony Gonzalez	3.00	1.35
94	Johnny Kucks	3.00	1.35
95	Norm Cash	7.00	3.10
96	Billy O'Dell	3.00	1.35
97	Jerry Lynch	6.00	2.70
98A	Checklist 2 (Red "Checklist" 98 black on white)	70.00	14.00
98B	Checklist 2 (Yellow "Checklist" 98 black on white)	70.00	14.00
98C	Checklist 2 (Yellow "Checklist" 98 white on black no copyright)	70.00	14.00
99	Don Buddin UER (66 HR's)	3.00	1.35
100	Harvey Haddix	7.00	3.10
101	Bubba Phillips	3.00	1.35
102	Gene Stephens	3.00	1.35
103	Ruben Amaro	3.00	1.35
104	John Blanchard	6.00	2.70
105	Carl Willey	3.00	1.35
106	Whitey Herzog	3.00	1.35
107	Seth Morehead	3.00	1.35
108	Dan Dobbek	3.00	1.35
109	Johnny Podres	7.00	3.10
110	Vada Pinson	7.00	3.10
111	Jack Meyer	3.00	1.35
112	Chico Fernandez	3.00	1.35
113	Mike Fornieles	3.00	1.35
114	Hobie Landrith	3.00	1.35
115	Johnny Antonelli	6.00	2.70
116	Joe DeMaestri	3.00	1.35
117	Dale Long	6.00	2.70
118	Chris Cannizzaro	3.00	1.35
119	A's Big Armor Norm Siebern Hank Bauer Jerry Lumpe	6.00	2.70
120	Eddie Mathews	30.00	13.50
121	Eli Grba	6.00	2.70
122	Chicago Cubs Team Card	8.00	3.60
123	Billy Gardner	3.00	1.35
124	J.C. Martin	3.00	1.35
125	Steve Barber	3.00	1.35
126	Dick Stuart	6.00	2.70
127	Ron Kline	3.00	1.35
128	Rip Repulski	3.00	1.35
129	Ed Hobaugh	3.00	1.35
130	Norm Larker	3.00	1.35
131	Paul Richards MG	6.00	2.70
132	Al Lopez MG	6.00	2.70
133	Ralph Houk MG	6.00	2.70
134	Mickey Vernon MG	6.00	2.70
135	Fred Hutchinson MG	6.00	2.70
136	Walter Alston MG	7.00	3.10
137	Chuck Dressen MG	6.00	2.70
138	Danny Murtaugh MG	7.00	3.10
139	Solly Hemus MG	6.00	2.70
140	Gus Triandos	6.00	2.70
141	Billy Williams	60.00	27.00
142	Luis Arroyo	6.00	2.70
143	Russ Snyder	3.00	1.35
144	Jim Coker	3.00	1.35
145	Bob Buhl	6.00	2.70
146	Marty Keough	3.00	1.35
147	Ed Rakow	3.00	1.35
148	Julian Javier	6.00	2.70
149	Bob Oldis	3.00	1.35
150	Willie Mays	100.00	45.00
151	Jim Donohue	3.00	1.35
152	Earl Torgeson	3.00	1.35
153	Don Lee	3.00	1.35
154	Bobby Del Greco	3.00	1.35
155	Johnny Temple	6.00	2.70
156	Ken Hunt	6.00	2.70
157	Cal McLish	3.00	1.35
158	Pete Daley	3.00	1.35
159	Orioles Team	8.00	3.60
160	Whitey Ford UER (Incorrectly listed as 5'0" tall)	40.00	18.00
161	Sherman Jones UER (Photo actually Eddie Fisher)	3.00	1.35
162	Jay Hook	3.00	1.35
163	Ed Sadowski	3.00	1.35
164	Felix Mantilla	3.00	1.35
165	Gino Cimoli	3.00	1.35
166	Danny Kravitz	3.00	1.35
167	San Francisco Giants Team Card	8.00	3.60
168	Tommy Davis	7.00	3.10
169	Don Elston	3.00	1.35
170	Al Smith	3.00	1.35
171	Paul Foytack	3.00	1.35
172	Don Dillard	3.00	1.35
173	Beantown Bombers Frank Malzone Vic Wertz Jackie Jensen	6.00	2.70
174	Ray Semproch	3.00	1.35
175	Gene Freese	3.00	1.35
176	Ken Aspromonte	3.00	1.35
177	Don Larsen	7.00	3.10
178	Bob Nieman	3.00	1.35
179	Joe Koppe	3.00	1.35
180	Bobby Richardson	12.00	5.50
181	Fred Green	3.00	1.35
182	Dave Nicholson	3.00	1.35
183	Andre Rodgers	3.00	1.35
184	Steve Bilko	6.00	2.70
185	Herb Score	7.00	3.10
186	Elmer Valo	6.00	2.70
187	Billy Klaus	3.00	1.35
188	Jim Marshall	3.00	1.35
189A	Checklist 3 (Copyright symbol almost adjacent to 263 Ken Hamlin)	70.00	14.00
189B	Checklist 3 (Copyright symbol adjacent to 264 Glen Hobbie)	70.00	14.00
190	Stan Williams	6.00	2.70
191	Mike de la Hoz	3.00	1.35
192	Dick Brown	3.00	1.35
193	Gene Conley	6.00	2.70
194	Gordy Coleman	6.00	2.70
195	Jerry Casale	3.00	1.35
196	Ed Bouchee	3.00	1.35
197	Dick Hall	3.00	1.35
198	Carl Sawatski	3.00	1.35
199	Bob Boyd	3.00	1.35
200	Warren Spahn	30.00	13.50
201	Pete Whisenant	3.00	1.35
202	Al Neiger	3.00	1.35
203	Eddie Bressoud	3.00	1.35
204	Bob Skinner	6.00	2.70
205	Billy Pierce	6.00	2.70
206	Gene Green	3.00	1.35
207	Dodger Southpaws Sandy Koufax Johnny Podres	30.00	13.50
208	Larry Osborne	3.00	1.35
209	Ken McBride	3.00	1.35
210	Pete Runnels	6.00	2.70
211	Bob Gibson	40.00	18.00
212	Haywood Sullivan	6.00	2.70
213	Bill Stafford	3.00	1.35
214	Danny Murphy	3.00	1.35
215	Gus Bell	6.00	2.70
216	Ted Bowsfield	3.00	1.35
217	Mel Roach	3.00	1.35
218	Hal Brown	3.00	1.35
219	Gene Mauch MG	6.00	2.70
220	Alvin Dark MG	6.00	2.70
221	Mike Higgins MG	3.00	1.35
222	Jimmy Dykes MG	6.00	2.70
223	Bob Scheffing MG	3.00	1.35
224	Joe Gordon MG	6.00	2.70
225	Bill Rigney MG	6.00	2.70
226	Cookie Lavagetto MG	6.00	2.70
227	Juan Pizarro	3.00	1.35
228	New York Yankees Team Card	70.00	32.00
229	Rudy Hernandez	3.00	1.35
230	Don Hoak	6.00	2.70
231	Dick Drott	3.00	1.35
232	Bill White	7.00	3.10
233	Joey Jay	6.00	2.70
234	Ted Lepcio	3.00	1.35
235	Camilo Pascual	6.00	2.70
236	Don Gile	3.00	1.35
237	Billy Loes	6.00	2.70
238	Jim Gilliam	7.00	3.10
239	Dave Sisler	3.00	1.35
240	Ron Hansen	3.00	1.35
241	Al Cicotte	3.00	1.35
242	Hal Smith	3.00	1.35
243	Frank Lary	6.00	2.70
244	Chico Cardenas	6.00	2.70
245	Joe Adcock	7.00	3.10
246	Bob Davis	3.00	1.35
247	Billy Goodman	6.00	2.70
248	Ed Keegan	3.00	1.35
249	Cincinnati Reds Team Card	6.00	2.70
250	Buc Hill Aces Vern Law Roy Face	6.00	2.70
251	Bill Bruton	3.00	1.35
252	Bill Short	3.00	1.35
253	Sammy Taylor	3.00	1.35
254	Ted Sadowski	3.00	1.35
255	Vic Power	6.00	2.70
256	Billy Hoeft	3.00	1.35
257	Carroll Hardy	3.00	1.35
258	Jack Sanford	6.00	2.70
259	John Schaive	3.00	1.35
260	Don Drysdale	30.00	13.50
261	Charlie Lau	6.00	2.70
262	Tony Curry	3.00	1.35
263	Ken Hamlin	3.00	1.35
264	Glen Hobbie	3.00	1.35
265	Tony Kubek	8.00	3.60
266	Lindy McDaniel	6.00	2.70
267	Norm Siebern	3.00	1.35
268	Ike Delock	3.00	1.35
269	Harry Chiti	3.00	1.35
270	Bob Friend	7.00	3.10
271	Jim Landis	3.00	1.35
272	Tom Morgan	3.00	1.35
273A	Checklist 4 (Copyright symbol adjacent to 336 Don Mincher)	16.00	3.20
273B	Checklist 4 (Copyright symbol adjacent to 339 Gene Baker)	16.00	3.20
274	Gary Bell	3.00	1.35
275	Gene Woodling	6.00	2.70
276	Ray Rippelmeyer	3.00	1.35
277	Hank Foiles	3.00	1.35
278	Don McMahon	3.00	1.35
279	Jose Pagan	3.00	1.35
280	Frank Howard	8.00	3.60
281	Frank Sullivan	3.00	1.35
282	Faye Throneberry	3.00	1.35
283	Bob Anderson	3.00	1.35
284	Dick Gernert	3.00	1.35
285	Sherm Lollar	6.00	2.70
286	George Witt	3.00	1.35
287	Carl Yastrzemski	50.00	22.00
288	Albie Pearson	6.00	2.70
289	Ray Moore	3.00	1.35
290	Stan Musial	100.00	45.00
291	Tex Clevenger	3.00	1.35

❑ 292 Jim Baumer 3.00 1.35
❑ 293 Tom Sturdivant 3.00 1.35
❑ 294 Don Blasingame 3.00 1.35
❑ 295 Milt Pappas 6.00 2.70
❑ 296 Wes Covington 6.00 2.70
❑ 297 Athletics Team 16.00 7.25
❑ 298 Jim Golden 3.00 1.35
❑ 299 Clay Dalrymple 3.00 1.35
❑ 300 Mickey Mantle 500.00 220.00
❑ 301 Chet Nichols 3.00 1.35
❑ 302 Al Heist 3.00 1.35
❑ 303 Gary Peters 6.00 2.70
❑ 304 Rocky Nelson 3.00 1.35
❑ 305 Mike McCormick 6.00 2.70
❑ 306 Bill Virdon WS 8.00 3.60
❑ 307 Mickey Mantle WS .. 100.00 45.00
❑ 308 Bobby Richardson WS 12.00 5.50
❑ 309 Gino Cimoli WS 8.00 3.60
❑ 310 Roy Face WS 8.00 3.60
❑ 311 Whitey Ford WS 16.00 7.25
❑ 312 Bill Mazeroski WS 20.00 9.00
Mazeroski Homer Wins it
❑ 313 World Series Summary 16.00 7.25
Pirates Celebrate
❑ 314 Bob Miller 3.00 1.35
❑ 315 Earl Battey 6.00 2.70
❑ 316 Bobby Gene Smith 3.00 1.35
❑ 317 Jim Brewer 3.00 1.35
❑ 318 Danny O'Connell 3.00 1.35
❑ 319 Valmy Thomas 3.00 1.35
❑ 320 Lou Burdette 7.00 3.10
❑ 321 Marv Breeding 3.00 1.35
❑ 322 Bill Kunkel 6.00 2.70
❑ 323 Sammy Esposito 3.00 1.35
❑ 324 Hank Aguirre 3.00 1.35
❑ 325 Wally Moon 6.00 2.70
❑ 326 Dave Hillman 3.00 1.35
❑ 327 Matty Alou 10.00 4.50
❑ 328 Jim O'Toole 6.00 2.70
❑ 329 Julio Becquer 3.00 1.35
❑ 330 Rocky Colavito 20.00 9.00
❑ 331 Ned Garver 3.00 1.35
❑ 332 Dutch Dotterer UER 3.00 1.35
(Photo actually
Tommy Dotterer
Dutch's brother)
❑ 333 Fritz Brickell 3.00 1.35
❑ 334 Walt Bond 3.00 1.35
❑ 335 Frank Bolling 3.00 1.35
❑ 336 Don Mincher 6.00 2.70
❑ 337 Al's Aces 7.00 3.10
Early Wynn
Al Lopez
Herb Score
❑ 338 Don Landrum 3.00 1.35
❑ 339 Gene Baker 3.00 1.35
❑ 340 Vic Wertz 6.00 2.70
❑ 341 Jim Owens 3.00 1.35
❑ 342 Clint Courtney 3.00 1.35
❑ 343 Earl Robinson 3.00 1.35
❑ 344 Sandy Koufax 125.00 55.00
❑ 345 Jimmy Piersall 7.00 3.10
❑ 346 Howie Nunn 3.00 1.35
❑ 347 St. Louis Cardinals 6.00 2.70
Team Card
❑ 348 Steve Boros 3.00 1.35
❑ 349 Danny McDevitt 3.00 1.35
❑ 350 Ernie Banks 45.00 20.00
❑ 351 Jim King 3.00 1.35
❑ 352 Bob Shaw 3.00 1.35
❑ 353 Howie Bedell 3.00 1.35
❑ 354 Billy Harrell 3.00 1.35
❑ 355 Bob Allison 7.00 3.10
❑ 356 Ryne Duren 3.00 1.35
❑ 357 Daryl Spencer 3.00 1.35
❑ 358 Earl Averill 6.00 2.70
❑ 359 Dallas Green 3.00 1.35
❑ 360 Frank Robinson 40.00 18.00
❑ 361A Checklist 5 10.00 2.00
(No ad on back)
❑ 361B Checklist 5 10.00 2.00
(Special Feature
ad on back)
❑ 362 Frank Funk 3.00 1.35
❑ 363 John Roseboro 7.00 3.10
❑ 364 Moe Drabowsky 6.00 2.70
❑ 365 Jerry Lumpe 3.00 1.35
❑ 366 Eddie Fisher 3.00 1.35
❑ 367 Jim Rivera 3.00 1.35
❑ 368 Bennie Daniels 3.00 1.35
❑ 369 Dave Philley 3.00 1.35
❑ 370 Roy Face 6.00 2.70
❑ 371 Bill Skowron SP 60.00 27.00
❑ 372 Bob Hendley 4.00 1.80
❑ 373 Boston Red Sox 6.00 2.70
Team Card
❑ 374 Paul Giel 4.00 1.80
❑ 375 Ken Boyer 10.00 4.50
❑ 376 Mike Roarke 4.00 1.80
❑ 377 Ruben Gomez 4.00 1.80
❑ 378 Wally Post 6.00 2.70
❑ 379 Bobby Shantz 4.00 1.80
❑ 380 Minnie Minoso 8.00 3.60
❑ 381 Dave Wickersham 4.00 1.80
❑ 382 Frank Thomas 6.00 2.70
❑ 383 Frisco First Liners 6.00 2.70
Mike McCormick
Jack Sanford
Billy O'Dell
❑ 384 Chuck Essegian 4.00 1.80
❑ 385 Jim Perry 6.00 2.70
❑ 386 Joe Hicks 4.00 1.80
❑ 387 Duke Maas 4.00 1.80
❑ 388 Bob Clemente 175.00 80.00
❑ 389 Ralph Terry 6.00 2.70
❑ 390 Del Crandall 6.00 2.70
❑ 391 Winston Brown 4.00 1.80
❑ 392 Reno Bertoia 4.00 1.80
❑ 393 Batter Bafflers 4.00 1.80
Don Cardwell
Glen Hobbie
❑ 394 Ken Walters 4.00 1.80
❑ 395 Chuck Estrada 6.00 2.70
❑ 396 Bob Aspromonte 4.00 1.80
❑ 397 Hal Woodeshick 4.00 1.80
❑ 398 Hank Bauer 7.00 3.10
❑ 399 Cliff Cook 4.00 1.80
❑ 400 Vern Law 6.00 2.70
❑ 401 Babe Ruth HL 50.00 22.00
60th HR
❑ 402 Don Larsen HL SP 30.00 13.50
WS Perfect Game
❑ 403 Joe Oeschger HL 6.00 2.70
Leon Cadore
26 Inning Tie
❑ 404 Rogers Hornsby HL 10.00 4.50
.424 Season BA
❑ 405 Lou Gehrig HL 80.00 36.00
Consecutive Game Streak
❑ 406 Mickey Mantle HL 100.00 45.00
565 foot HR
❑ 407 Jack Chesbro HL 6.00 2.70
41 victories
❑ 408 C. Mathewson HL SP 20.00 9.00
267 Strikeouts
❑ 409 Walter Johnson SL 12.00 5.50
3 Shutouts in 4 days
❑ 410 Harvey Haddix HL 6.00 2.70
12 Perfect Innings
❑ 411 Tony Taylor 6.00 2.70
❑ 412 Larry Sherry 6.00 2.70
❑ 413 Eddie Yost 6.00 2.70
❑ 414 Dick Donovan 6.00 2.70
❑ 415 Hank Aaron 90.00 40.00
❑ 416 Dick Howser 10.00 4.50
❑ 417 Juan Marichal SP 125.00 55.00
❑ 418 Ed Bailey 6.00 2.70
❑ 419 Tom Borland 4.00 1.80
❑ 420 Ernie Broglio 6.00 2.70
❑ 421 Ty Cline SP 9.00 4.00
❑ 422 Bud Daley 4.00 1.80
❑ 423 Charlie Neal SP 9.00 4.00
❑ 424 Turk Lown 4.00 1.80
❑ 425 Yogi Berra 80.00 36.00
❑ 426 Milwaukee Braves 12.00 5.50
Team Card
(Back numbered 463)
❑ 427 Dick Ellsworth 6.00 2.70
❑ 428 Ray Barker SP 9.00 4.00
❑ 429 Al Kaline 45.00 20.00
❑ 430 Bill Mazeroski SP 60.00 27.00
❑ 431 Chuck Stobbs 4.00 1.80
❑ 432 Coot Veal 6.00 2.70
❑ 433 Art Mahaffey 4.00 1.80
❑ 434 Tom Brewer 4.00 1.80
❑ 435 Orlando Cepeda UER 14.00 6.25
(San Francis on
card front)
❑ 436 Jim Maloney SP 20.00 9.00
❑ 437A Checklist 6 10.00 2.00
440 Louis Aparicio
❑ 437B Checklist 6 10.00 2.00
440 Luis Aparicio
❑ 438 Curt Flood 8.00 3.60
❑ 439 Phil Regan 6.00 2.70
❑ 440 Luis Aparicio 15.00 6.75
❑ 441 Dick Bertell 4.00 1.80
❑ 442 Gordon Jones 4.00 1.80
❑ 443 Duke Snider 40.00 18.00
❑ 444 Joe Nuxhall 6.00 2.70
❑ 445 Frank Malzone 6.00 2.70
❑ 446 Bob Taylor 4.00 1.80
❑ 447 Harry Bright 7.00 3.10
❑ 448 Del Rice 7.00 3.10
❑ 449 Bob Bolin 7.00 3.10
❑ 450 Jim Lemon 7.00 3.10
❑ 451 Power for Ernie 7.00 3.10
Daryl Spencer
Bill White
Ernie Broglio
❑ 452 Bob Allen 7.00 3.10
❑ 453 Dick Schofield 7.00 3.10
❑ 454 Pumpsie Green 7.00 3.10
❑ 455 Early Wynn 15.00 6.75
❑ 456 Hal Bevan 7.00 3.10
❑ 457 Johnny James 7.00 3.10
(Listed as Angel,
but wearing Yankee
uniform and cap)
❑ 458 Willie Tasby 7.00 3.10
❑ 459 Terry Fox 7.00 3.10
❑ 460 Gil Hodges 20.00 9.00
❑ 461 Smoky Burgess 10.00 4.50
❑ 462 Lou Klimchock 7.00 3.10
❑ 463 Jack Fisher 7.00 3.10
(See also 426)
❑ 464 Lee Thomas 10.00 4.50
(Pictured with Yankee
cap but listed as
Los Angeles Angel)
❑ 465 Roy McMillan 7.00 3.10
❑ 466 Ron Moeller 7.00 3.10
❑ 467 Cleveland Indians 7.50 3.40
Team Card
❑ 468 John Callison 10.00 4.50
❑ 469 Ralph Lumenti 7.00 3.10
❑ 470 Roy Sievers 10.00 4.50
❑ 471 Phil Rizzuto MVP 20.00 9.00
❑ 472 Yogi Berra MVP 60.00 27.00
❑ 473 Bob Shantz MVP 7.00 3.10
❑ 474 Al Rosen MVP 10.00 4.50
❑ 475 Mickey Mantle MVP 200.00 90.00
❑ 476 Jackie Jensen MVP 10.00 4.50
❑ 477 Nellie Fox MVP 18.00 8.00
❑ 478 Roger Maris MVP 60.00 27.00
❑ 479 Jim Konstanty MVP 7.00 3.10
❑ 480 Roy Campanella MVP 35.00 16.00
❑ 481 Hank Sauer MVP 7.00 3.10
❑ 482 Willie Mays MVP 50.00 22.00
❑ 483 Don Newcombe MVP 10.00 4.50
❑ 484 Hank Aaron MVP 50.00 22.00
❑ 485 Ernie Banks MVP 35.00 16.00
❑ 486 Dick Groat MVP 10.00 4.50
❑ 487 Gene Oliver 7.00 3.10
❑ 488 Joe McClain 10.00 4.50
❑ 489 Walt Dropo 7.00 3.10
❑ 490 Jim Bunning 16.00 7.25
❑ 491 Philadelphia Phillies 7.50 3.40
Team Card
❑ 492 Ron Fairly 10.00 4.50
❑ 493 Don Zimmer UER 10.00 4.50
(Brooklyn A.L.)
❑ 494 Tom Cheney 7.00 3.10
❑ 495 Elston Howard 12.00 5.50
❑ 496 Ken MacKenzie 7.00 3.10

❑ 497	Willie Jones	7.00	3.10
❑ 498	Ray Herbert	7.00	3.10
❑ 499	Chuck Schilling	7.00	3.10
❑ 500	Harvey Kuenn	10.00	4.50
❑ 501	John DeMerit	7.00	3.10
❑ 502	Clarence Coleman	10.00	4.50
❑ 503	Tito Francona	7.00	3.10
❑ 504	Billy Consolo	7.00	3.10
❑ 505	Red Schoendienst	14.00	6.25
❑ 506	Willie Davis	16.00	7.25
❑ 507	Pete Burnside	7.00	3.10
❑ 508	Rocky Bridges	7.00	3.10
❑ 509	Camilo Carreon	7.00	3.10
❑ 510	Art Ditmar	7.00	3.10
❑ 511	Joe M. Morgan	7.00	3.10
❑ 512	Bob Will	7.00	3.10
❑ 513	Jim Brosnan	7.00	3.10
❑ 514	Jake Wood	7.00	3.10
❑ 515	Jackie Brandt	7.00	3.10
❑ 516	Checklist 7	10.00	2.00
❑ 517	Willie McCovey	50.00	22.00
❑ 518	Andy Carey	7.00	3.10
❑ 519	Jim Pagliaroni	7.00	3.10
❑ 520	Joe Cunningham	7.00	3.10
❑ 521	Brother Battery	7.00	3.10
	Norm Sherry		
	Larry Sherry		
❑ 522	Dick Farrell UER	7.00	3.10
	(Phillies cap but listed on Dodgers)		
❑ 523	Joe Gibbon	30.00	13.50
❑ 524	Johnny Logan	30.00	13.50
❑ 525	Ron Perranoski	40.00	18.00
❑ 526	R.C. Stevens	30.00	13.50
❑ 527	Gene Leek	30.00	13.50
❑ 528	Pedro Ramos	30.00	13.50
❑ 529	Bob Roselli	30.00	13.50
❑ 530	Bob Malkmus	30.00	13.50
❑ 531	Jim Coates	40.00	18.00
❑ 532	Bob Hale	30.00	13.50
❑ 533	Jack Curtis	30.00	13.50
❑ 534	Eddie Kasko	30.00	13.50
❑ 535	Larry Jackson	30.00	13.50
❑ 536	Bill Tuttle	30.00	13.50
❑ 537	Bobby Locke	30.00	13.50
❑ 538	Chuck Hiller	30.00	13.50
❑ 539	Johnny Klippstein	30.00	13.50
❑ 540	Jackie Jensen	40.00	18.00
❑ 541	Roland Sheldon	40.00	18.00
❑ 542	Minnesota Twins Team Card	70.00	32.00
❑ 543	Roger Craig	40.00	18.00
❑ 544	George Thomas	30.00	13.50
❑ 545	Hoyt Wilhelm	50.00	22.00
❑ 546	Marty Kutyna	30.00	13.50
❑ 547	Leon Wagner	30.00	13.50
❑ 548	Ted Wills	30.00	13.50
❑ 549	Hal R. Smith	30.00	13.50
❑ 550	Frank Baumann	30.00	13.50
❑ 551	George Altman	30.00	13.50
❑ 552	Jim Archer	30.00	13.50
❑ 553	Bill Fischer	30.00	13.50
❑ 554	Pittsburgh Pirates Team Card	70.00	32.00
❑ 555	Sam Jones	30.00	13.50
❑ 556	Ken R. Hunt	30.00	13.50
❑ 557	Jose Valdivielso	30.00	13.50
❑ 558	Don Ferrarese	30.00	13.50
❑ 559	Jim Gentile	60.00	27.00
❑ 560	Barry Latman	30.00	13.50
❑ 561	Charley James	30.00	13.50
❑ 562	Bill Monbouquette	30.00	13.50
❑ 563	Bob Cerv	45.00	20.00
❑ 564	Don Cardwell	30.00	13.50
❑ 565	Felipe Alou	40.00	18.00
❑ 566	Paul Richards AS MG	30.00	13.50
❑ 567	Danny Murtaugh AS MG	30.00	13.50
❑ 568	Bill Skowron AS	40.00	18.00
❑ 569	Frank Herrera AS	30.00	13.50
❑ 570	Nellie Fox AS	50.00	22.00
❑ 571	Bill Mazeroski AS	40.00	18.00
❑ 572	Brooks Robinson AS	90.00	40.00
❑ 573	Ken Boyer AS	40.00	18.00
❑ 574	Luis Aparicio AS	45.00	20.00
❑ 575	Ernie Banks AS	90.00	40.00
❑ 576	Roger Maris AS	175.00	80.00
❑ 577	Hank Aaron AS	160.00	70.00
❑ 578	Mickey Mantle AS	425.00	190.00
❑ 579	Willie Mays AS	160.00	70.00
❑ 580	Al Kaline AS	90.00	40.00
❑ 581	Frank Robinson AS	90.00	40.00
❑ 582	Earl Battey AS	30.00	13.50
❑ 583	Del Crandall AS	30.00	13.50
❑ 584	Jim Perry AS	30.00	13.50
❑ 585	Bob Friend AS	30.00	13.50
❑ 586	Whitey Ford AS	90.00	40.00
❑ 589	Warren Spahn AS	100.00	30.00

1962 Topps

	NRMT	VG-E
COMPLETE SET (598)	4600.00	2100.00
COMMON CARD (1-370)	5.00	2.20
COMMON CARD (371-446)	6.00	2.70
COMMON CARD (447-522)	12.00	5.50
COMMON CARD (523-598)	20.00	9.00
WRAPPER (1-CENT)	100.00	45.00
WRAPPER (5-CENT)	30.00	13.50

❑ 1	Roger Maris	250.00	60.00
❑ 2	Jim Brosnan	5.00	2.20
❑ 3	Pete Runnels	5.00	2.20
❑ 4	John DeMerit	8.00	3.60
❑ 5	Sandy Koufax UER	160.00	70.00
	(Struck ou 18)		
❑ 6	Marv Breeding	5.00	2.20
❑ 7	Frank Thomas	10.00	4.50
❑ 8	Ray Herbert	5.00	2.20
❑ 9	Jim Davenport	8.00	3.60
❑ 10	Bob Clemente	250.00	110.00
❑ 11	Tom Morgan	5.00	2.20
❑ 12	Harry Craft MG	8.00	3.60
❑ 13	Dick Howser	8.00	3.60
❑ 14	Bill White	8.00	3.60
❑ 15	Dick Donovan	5.00	2.20
❑ 16	Darrell Johnson	5.00	2.20
❑ 17	Johnny Callison	8.00	3.60
❑ 18	Managers' Dream	200.00	90.00
	Mickey Mantle		
	Willie Mays		
❑ 19	Ray Washburn	5.00	2.20
❑ 20	Rocky Colavito	15.00	6.75
❑ 21	Jim Kaat	8.00	3.60
❑ 22A	Checklist 1 ERR	12.00	2.40
	(121-176 on back)		
❑ 22B	Checklist 1 COR	12.00	2.40
❑ 23	Norm Larker	5.00	2.20
❑ 24	Tigers Team	10.00	4.50
❑ 25	Ernie Banks	45.00	20.00
❑ 26	Chris Cannizzaro	8.00	3.60
❑ 27	Chuck Cottier	5.00	2.20
❑ 28	Minnie Minoso	10.00	4.50
❑ 29	Casey Stengel MG	20.00	9.00
❑ 30	Eddie Mathews	25.00	11.00
❑ 31	Tom Tresh	20.00	9.00
❑ 32	John Roseboro	8.00	3.60
❑ 33	Don Larsen	8.00	3.60
❑ 34	Johnny Temple	8.00	3.60
❑ 35	Don Schwall	8.00	3.60
❑ 36	Don Leppert	5.00	2.20
❑ 37	Tribe Hill Trio	5.00	2.20
	Barry Latman		
	Dick Stigman		
	Jim Perry		
❑ 38	Gene Stephens	5.00	2.20
❑ 39	Joe Koppe	5.00	2.20
❑ 40	Orlando Cepeda	14.00	6.25
❑ 41	Cliff Cook	5.00	2.20
❑ 42	Jim King	5.00	2.20
❑ 43	Los Angeles Dodgers Team Card	10.00	4.50
❑ 44	Don Taussig	5.00	2.20
❑ 45	Brooks Robinson	45.00	20.00
❑ 46	Jack Baldschun	5.00	2.20
❑ 47	Bob Will	5.00	2.20
❑ 48	Ralph Terry	8.00	3.60
❑ 49	Hal Jones	5.00	2.20
❑ 50	Stan Musial	100.00	45.00
❑ 51	AL Batting Leaders	8.00	3.60
	Norm Cash		
	Jim Piersall		
	Al Kaline		
	Elston Howard		
❑ 52	NL Batting Leaders	20.00	9.00
	Bob Clemente		
	Vada Pinson		
	Ken Boyer		
	Wally Moon		
❑ 53	AL Home Run Leaders	110.00	50.00
	Roger Maris		
	Mickey Mantle		
	Jim Gentile		
	Harmon Killebrew		
❑ 54	NL Home Run Leaders	20.00	9.00
	Orlando Cepeda		
	Willie Mays		
	Frank Robinson		
❑ 55	AL ERA Leaders	8.00	3.60
	Dick Donovan		
	Bill Stafford		
	Don Mossi		
	Milt Pappas		
❑ 56	NL ERA Leaders	8.00	3.60
	Warren Spahn		
	Jim O'Toole		
	Curt Simmons		
	Mike McCormick		
❑ 57	AL Wins Leaders	8.00	3.60
	Whitey Ford		
	Frank Lary		
	Steve Barber		
	Jim Bunning		
❑ 58	NL Wins Leaders	8.00	3.60
	Warren Spahn		
	Joe Jay		
	Jim O'Toole		
❑ 59	AL Strikeout Leaders	8.00	3.60
	Camilo Pascual		
	Whitey Ford		
	Jim Bunning		
	Juan Pizzaro		
❑ 60	NL Strikeout Leaders	20.00	9.00
	Sandy Koufax		
	Stan Williams		
	Don Drysdale		
	Jim O'Toole		
❑ 61	Cardinals Team	10.00	4.50
❑ 62	Steve Boros	5.00	2.20
❑ 63	Tony Cloninger	8.00	3.60
❑ 64	Russ Snyder	5.00	2.20
❑ 65	Bobby Richardson	12.00	5.50
❑ 66	Cuno Barragan	5.00	2.20
❑ 67	Harvey Haddix	8.00	3.60
❑ 68	Ken Hunt	5.00	2.20
❑ 69	Phil Ortega	5.00	2.20
❑ 70	Harmon Killebrew	25.00	11.00
❑ 71	Dick LeMay	5.00	2.20
❑ 72	Bob's Pupils	5.00	2.20
	Steve Boros		
	Bob Scheffing MG		
	Jake Wood		
❑ 73	Nellie Fox	20.00	9.00
❑ 74	Bob Lillis	8.00	3.60
❑ 75	Milt Pappas	8.00	3.60
❑ 76	Howie Bedell	5.00	2.20
❑ 77	Tony Taylor	8.00	3.60
❑ 78	Gene Green	5.00	2.20
❑ 79	Ed Hobaugh	5.00	2.20

❑	80 Vada Pinson	8.00	3.60
❑	81 Jim Pagliaroni	5.00	2.20
❑	82 Deron Johnson	8.00	3.60
❑	83 Larry Jackson	5.00	2.20
❑	84 Lenny Green	5.00	2.20
❑	85 Gil Hodges	20.00	9.00
❑	86 Donn Clendenon	8.00	3.60
❑	87 Mike Roarke	5.00	2.20
❑	88 Ralph Houk MG	8.00	3.60
	(Berra in background)		
❑	89 Barney Schultz	5.00	2.20
❑	90 Jimmy Piersall	8.00	3.60
❑	91 J.C. Martin	5.00	2.20
❑	92 Sam Jones	5.00	2.20
❑	93 John Blanchard	8.00	3.60
❑	94 Jay Hook	8.00	3.60
❑	95 Don Hoak	8.00	3.60
❑	96 Eli Grba	5.00	2.20
❑	97 Tito Francona	5.00	2.20
❑	98 Checklist 2	12.00	2.40
❑	99 John (Boog) Powell	30.00	13.50
❑	100 Warren Spahn	30.00	13.50
❑	101 Carroll Hardy	5.00	2.20
❑	102 Al Schroll	5.00	2.20
❑	103 Don Blasingame	5.00	2.20
❑	104 Ted Savage	5.00	2.20
❑	105 Don Mossi	8.00	3.60
❑	106 Carl Sawatski	5.00	2.20
❑	107 Mike McCormick	8.00	3.60
❑	108 Willie Davis	8.00	3.60
❑	109 Bob Shaw	5.00	2.20
❑	110 Bill Skowron	8.00	3.60
❑	111 Dallas Green	8.00	3.60
❑	112 Hank Foiles	5.00	2.20
❑	113 Chicago White Sox	10.00	4.50
	Team Card		
❑	114 Howie Koplitz	5.00	2.20
❑	115 Bob Skinner	8.00	3.60
❑	116 Herb Score	8.00	3.60
❑	117 Gary Geiger	5.00	2.20
❑	118 Julian Javier	8.00	3.60
❑	119 Danny Murphy	5.00	2.20
❑	120 Bob Purkey	5.00	2.20
❑	121 Billy Hitchcock MG	5.00	2.20
❑	122 Norm Bass	5.00	2.20
❑	123 Mike de la Hoz	5.00	2.20
❑	124 Bill Pleis	5.00	2.20
❑	125 Gene Woodling	8.00	3.60
❑	126 Al Cicotte	5.00	2.20
❑	127 Pride of A's	5.00	2.20
	Norm Siebern		
	Hank Bauer MG		
	Jerry Lumpe		
❑	128 Art Fowler	5.00	2.20
❑	129A Lee Walls	5.00	2.20
	(Facing right)		
❑	129B Lee Walls	25.00	11.00
	(Facing left)		
❑	130 Frank Bolling	5.00	2.20
❑	131 Pete Richert	5.00	2.20
❑	132A Angels Team	10.00	4.50
	(Without photo)		
❑	132B Angels Team	25.00	11.00
	(With photo)		
❑	133 Felipe Alou	8.00	3.60
❑	134A Billy Hoeft	5.00	2.20
	(Facing right)		
❑	134B Billy Hoeft	25.00	11.00
	(Facing straight)		
❑	135 Babe Ruth Special 1	20.00	9.00
	Babe as a Boy		
❑	136 Babe Ruth Special 2	20.00	9.00
	Babe Joins Yanks		
❑	137 Babe Ruth Special 3	20.00	9.00
	With Miller Huggins		
❑	138 Babe Ruth Special 4	20.00	9.00
	Famous Slugger		
❑	139A Babe Ruth Special 5	30.00	13.50
	Babe Hits 60		
❑	139B Hal Reniff PORT	12.00	5.50
❑	139C Hal Reniff	65.00	29.00
	(Pitching)		
❑	140 Babe Ruth Special 6	50.00	22.00
	With Lou Gehrig		
❑	141 Babe Ruth Special 7	20.00	9.00
	Twilight Years		
❑	142 Babe Ruth Special 8	20.00	9.00
	Coaching Dodgers		
❑	143 Babe Ruth Special 9	20.00	9.00
	Greatest Sports Hero		
❑	144 Babe Ruth Special 10	20.00	9.00
	Farewell Speech		
❑	145 Barry Latman	5.00	2.20
❑	146 Don Demeter	5.00	2.20
❑	147A Bill Kunkel PORT	5.00	2.20
❑	147B Bill Kunkel	25.00	11.00
	(Pitching pose)		
❑	148 Wally Post	5.00	2.20
❑	149 Bob Duliba	5.00	2.20
❑	150 Al Kaline	45.00	20.00
❑	151 Johnny Klippstein	5.00	2.20
❑	152 Mickey Vernon MG	8.00	3.60
❑	153 Pumpsie Green	6.00	2.70
❑	154 Lee Thomas	6.00	2.70
❑	155 Stu Miller	6.00	2.70
❑	156 Merritt Ranew	5.00	2.20
❑	157 Wes Covington	8.00	3.60
❑	158 Braves Team	10.00	4.50
❑	159 Hal Reniff	8.00	3.60
❑	160 Dick Stuart	8.00	3.60
❑	161 Frank Baumann	5.00	2.20
❑	162 Sammy Drake	5.00	2.20
❑	163 Hot Corner Guard	8.00	3.60
	Billy Gardner		
	Cletis Boyer		
❑	164 Hal Naragon	5.00	2.20
❑	165 Jackie Brandt	5.00	2.20
❑	166 Don Lee	5.00	2.20
❑	167 Tim McCarver	30.00	13.50
❑	168 Leo Posada	5.00	2.20
❑	169 Bob Cerv	8.00	3.60
❑	170 Ron Santo	14.00	6.25
❑	171 Dave Sisler	5.00	2.20
❑	172 Fred Hutchinson MG	8.00	3.60
❑	173 Chico Fernandez	5.00	2.20
❑	174A Carl Willey	5.00	2.20
	(Capless)		
❑	174B Carl Willey	25.00	11.00
	(With cap)		
❑	175 Frank Howard	8.00	3.60
❑	176A Eddie Yost PORT	5.00	2.20
❑	176B Eddie Yost BATTING	25.00	11.00
❑	177 Bobby Shantz	8.00	3.60
❑	178 Camilo Carreon	5.00	2.20
❑	179 Tom Sturdivant	5.00	2.20
❑	180 Bob Allison	8.00	3.60
❑	181 Paul Brown	5.00	2.20
❑	182 Bob Nieman	5.00	2.20
❑	183 Roger Craig	8.00	3.60
❑	184 Haywood Sullivan	8.00	3.60
❑	185 Roland Sheldon	8.00	3.60
❑	186 Mack Jones	5.00	2.20
❑	187 Gene Conley	5.00	2.20
❑	188 Chuck Hiller	5.00	2.20
❑	189 Dick Hall	5.00	2.20
❑	190A Wally Moon PORT	5.00	2.20
❑	190B Wally Moon BATTING	28.00	12.50
❑	191 Jim Brewer	5.00	2.20
❑	192A Checklist 3	12.00	2.40
	(Without comma)		
❑	192B Checklist 3	16.00	3.20
	(Comma after Checklist)		
❑	193 Eddie Kasko	5.00	2.20
❑	194 Dean Chance	8.00	3.60
❑	195 Joe Cunningham	5.00	2.20
❑	196 Terry Fox	5.00	2.20
❑	197 Daryl Spencer	5.00	2.20
❑	198 Johnny Keane MG	5.00	2.20
❑	199 Gaylord Perry	80.00	36.00
❑	200 Mickey Mantle	450.00	200.00
❑	201 Ike Delock	5.00	2.20
❑	202 Carl Warwick	5.00	2.20
❑	203 Jack Fisher	5.00	2.20
❑	204 Johnny Weekly	5.00	2.20
❑	205 Gene Freese	5.00	2.20
❑	206 Senators Team	10.00	4.50
❑	207 Pete Burnside	5.00	2.20
❑	208 Billy Martin	20.00	9.00
❑	209 Jim Fregosi	14.00	6.25
❑	210 Roy Face	8.00	3.60
❑	211 Midway Masters	5.00	2.20
	Frank Bolling		
	Roy McMillan		
❑	212 Jim Owens	5.00	2.20
❑	213 Richie Ashburn	20.00	9.00
❑	214 Dom Zanni	5.00	2.20
❑	215 Woody Held	5.00	2.20
❑	216 Ron Kline	5.00	2.20
❑	217 Walter Alston MG	8.00	3.60
❑	218 Joe Torre	40.00	18.00
❑	219 Al Downing	8.00	3.60
❑	220 Roy Sievers	8.00	3.60
❑	221 Bill Short	5.00	2.20
❑	222 Jerry Zimmerman	5.00	2.20
❑	223 Alex Grammas	5.00	2.20
❑	224 Don Rudolph	5.00	2.20
❑	225 Frank Malzone	8.00	3.60
❑	226 San Francisco Giants	10.00	4.50
	Team Card		
❑	227 Bob Tiefenauer	5.00	2.20
❑	228 Dale Long	8.00	3.60
❑	229 Jesus McFarlane	5.00	2.20
❑	230 Camilo Pascual	8.00	3.60
❑	231 Ernie Bowman	5.00	2.20
❑	232 World Series Game 1	10.00	4.50
	Yanks win opener		
❑	233 Joey Jay WS	10.00	4.50
❑	234 Roger Maris WS	25.00	11.00
❑	235 Whitey Ford WS	10.00	4.50
	sets new mark		
❑	236 World Series Game 5	10.00	4.50
	Yanks crush Reds		
❑	237 World Series Summary	10.00	4.50
	Yanks celebrate		
❑	238 Norm Sherry	5.00	2.20
❑	239 Cecil Butler	5.00	2.20
❑	240 George Altman	5.00	2.20
❑	241 Johnny Kucks	5.00	2.20
❑	242 Mel McGaha MG	5.00	2.20
❑	243 Robin Roberts	15.00	6.75
❑	244 Don Gile	5.00	2.20
❑	245 Ron Hansen	5.00	2.20
❑	246 Art Ditmar	5.00	2.20
❑	247 Joe Pignatano	5.00	2.20
❑	248 Bob Aspromonte	8.00	3.60
❑	249 Ed Keegan	5.00	2.20
❑	250 Norm Cash	8.00	3.60
❑	251 New York Yankees	60.00	27.00
	Team Card		
❑	252 Earl Francis	5.00	2.20
❑	253 Harry Chiti MG	5.00	2.20
❑	254 Gordon Windhorn	5.00	2.20
❑	255 Juan Pizarro	5.00	2.20
❑	256 Elio Chacon	8.00	3.60
❑	257 Jack Spring	5.00	2.20
❑	258 Marty Keough	5.00	2.20
❑	259 Lou Klimchock	5.00	2.20
❑	260 Billy Pierce	8.00	3.60
❑	261 George Alusik	5.00	2.20
❑	262 Bob Schmidt	5.00	2.20
❑	263 The Right Pitch	5.00	2.20
	Bob Purkey		
	Jim Turner CO		
	Joe Jay		
❑	264 Dick Ellsworth	8.00	3.60
❑	265 Joe Adcock	8.00	3.60
❑	266 John Anderson	5.00	2.20
❑	267 Dan Dobbek	5.00	2.20
❑	268 Ken McBride	5.00	2.20
❑	269 Bob Oldis	5.00	2.20
❑	270 Dick Groat	8.00	3.60
❑	271 Ray Rippelmeyer	5.00	2.20
❑	272 Earl Robinson	5.00	2.20
❑	273 Gary Bell	5.00	2.20
❑	274 Sammy Taylor	5.00	2.20
❑	275 Norm Siebern	5.00	2.20
❑	276 Hal Kolstad	5.00	2.20
❑	277 Checklist 4	16.00	3.20
❑	278 Ken Johnson	8.00	3.60
❑	279 Hobie Landrith UER	8.00	3.60
	(Wrong birthdate)		
❑	280 Johnny Podres	8.00	3.60
❑	281 Jake Gibbs	8.00	3.60
❑	282 Dave Hillman	5.00	2.20
❑	283 Charlie Smith	5.00	2.20

❑ 284 Ruben Amaro 5.00 2.20
❑ 285 Curt Simmons 8.00 3.60
❑ 286 Al Lopez MG 8.00 3.60
❑ 287 George Witt 5.00 2.20
❑ 288 Billy Williams 30.00 13.50
❑ 289 Mike Krsnich 5.00 2.20
❑ 290 Jim Gentile 8.00 3.60
❑ 291 Hal Stowe 5.00 2.20
❑ 292 Jerry Kindall 5.00 2.20
❑ 293 Bob Miller 8.00 3.60
❑ 294 Phillies Team 10.00 4.50
❑ 295 Vern Law 8.00 3.60
❑ 296 Ken Hamlin 5.00 2.20
❑ 297 Ron Perranoski 8.00 3.60
❑ 298 Bill Tuttle 5.00 2.20
❑ 299 Don Wert 5.00 2.20
❑ 300 Willie Mays 150.00 70.00
❑ 301 Galen Cisco 5.00 2.20
❑ 302 Johnny Edwards 5.00 2.20
❑ 303 Frank Torre 8.00 3.60
❑ 304 Dick Farrell 8.00 3.60
❑ 305 Jerry Lumpe 5.00 2.20
❑ 306 Redbird Rippers 5.00 2.20
Lindy McDaniel
Larry Jackson
❑ 307 Jim Grant 8.00 3.60
❑ 308 Neil Chrisley 8.00 3.60
❑ 309 Moe Morhardt 5.00 2.20
❑ 310 Whitey Ford 45.00 20.00
❑ 311 Tony Kubek IA 8.00 3.60
❑ 312 Warren Spahn IA 14.00 6.25
❑ 313 Roger Maris IA 40.00 18.00
Blasts 61th
❑ 314 Rocky Colavito IA 12.00 5.50
❑ 315 Whitey Ford IA 15.00 6.75
❑ 316 Harmon Killebrew IA 15.00 6.75
❑ 317 Stan Musial IA 20.00 9.00
❑ 318 Mickey Mantle IA 150.00 70.00
❑ 319 Mike McCormick IA 5.00 2.20
❑ 320 Hank Aaron 140.00 65.00
❑ 321 Lee Stange 5.00 2.20
❑ 322 Alvin Dark MG 8.00 3.60
❑ 323 Don Landrum 5.00 2.20
❑ 324 Joe McClain 5.00 2.20
❑ 325 Luis Aparicio 15.00 6.75
❑ 326 Tom Parsons 5.00 2.20
❑ 327 Ozzie Virgil 5.00 2.20
❑ 328 Ken Walters 5.00 2.20
❑ 329 Bob Bolin 5.00 2.20
❑ 330 John Romano 5.00 2.20
❑ 331 Moe Drabowsky 8.00 3.60
❑ 332 Don Buddin 5.00 2.20
❑ 333 Frank Cipriani 5.00 2.20
❑ 334 Boston Red Sox 10.00 4.50
Team Card
❑ 335 Bill Bruton 5.00 2.20
❑ 336 Billy Muffett 5.00 2.20
❑ 337 Jim Marshall 8.00 3.60
❑ 338 Billy Gardner 5.00 2.20
❑ 339 Jose Valdivielso 5.00 2.20
❑ 340 Don Drysdale 45.00 20.00
❑ 341 Mike Hershberger 5.00 2.20
❑ 342 Ed Rakow 5.00 2.20
❑ 343 Albie Pearson 8.00 3.60
❑ 344 Ed Bauta 5.00 2.20
❑ 345 Chuck Schilling 5.00 2.20
❑ 346 Jack Kralick 5.00 2.20
❑ 347 Chuck Hinton 5.00 2.20
❑ 348 Larry Burright 8.00 3.60
❑ 349 Paul Foytack 5.00 2.20
❑ 350 Frank Robinson 45.00 20.00
❑ 351 Braves' Backstops 8.00 3.60
Joe Torre
Del Crandall
❑ 352 Frank Sullivan 5.00 2.20
❑ 353 Bill Mazeroski 10.00 4.50
❑ 354 Roman Mejias 8.00 3.60
❑ 355 Steve Barber 5.00 2.20
❑ 356 Tom Haller 5.00 2.20
❑ 357 Jerry Walker 5.00 2.20
❑ 358 Tommy Davis 8.00 3.60
❑ 359 Bobby Locke 5.00 2.20
❑ 360 Yogi Berra 75.00 34.00
❑ 361 Bob Hendley 5.00 2.20
❑ 362 Ty Cline 5.00 2.20
❑ 363 Bob Roselli 5.00 2.20
❑ 364 Ken Hunt 5.00 2.20
❑ 365 Charlie Neal 8.00 3.60
❑ 366 Phil Regan 8.00 3.60
❑ 367 Checklist 5 16.00 3.20
❑ 368 Bob Tillman 5.00 2.20
❑ 369 Ted Bowsfield 5.00 2.20
❑ 370 Ken Boyer 8.00 3.60
❑ 371 Earl Battey 6.00 2.70
❑ 372 Jack Curtis 6.00 2.70
❑ 373 Al Heist 6.00 2.70
❑ 374 Gene Mauch MG 10.00 4.50
❑ 375 Ron Fairly 10.00 4.50
❑ 376 Bud Daley 8.00 3.60
❑ 377 John Orsino 6.00 2.70
❑ 378 Bennie Daniels 6.00 2.70
❑ 379 Chuck Essegian 6.00 2.70
❑ 380 Lou Burdette 10.00 4.50
❑ 381 Chico Cardenas 10.00 4.50
❑ 382 Dick Williams 8.00 3.60
❑ 383 Ray Sadecki 6.00 2.70
❑ 384 K.C. Athletics 10.00 4.50
Team Card
❑ 385 Early Wynn 15.00 6.75
❑ 386 Don Mincher 8.00 3.60
❑ 387 Lou Brock 125.00 55.00
❑ 388 Ryne Duren 8.00 3.60
❑ 389 Smoky Burgess 10.00 4.50
❑ 390 Orlando Cepeda AS 10.00 4.50
❑ 391 Bill Mazeroski AS 10.00 4.50
❑ 392 Ken Boyer AS 8.00 3.60
❑ 393 Roy McMillan AS 6.00 2.70
❑ 394 Hank Aaron AS 45.00 20.00
❑ 395 Willie Mays AS 50.00 22.00
❑ 396 Frank Robinson AS 16.00 7.25
❑ 397 John Roseboro AS 6.00 2.70
❑ 398 Don Drysdale AS 16.00 7.25
❑ 399 Warren Spahn AS 16.00 7.25
❑ 400 Elston Howard 10.00 4.50
❑ 401 AL/NL Homer Kings 60.00 27.00
Roger Maris
Orlando Cepeda
❑ 402 Gino Cimoli 6.00 2.70
❑ 403 Chet Nichols 6.00 2.70
❑ 404 Tim Harkness 8.00 3.60
❑ 405 Jim Perry 8.00 3.60
❑ 406 Bob Taylor 6.00 2.70
❑ 407 Hank Aguirre 6.00 2.70
❑ 408 Gus Bell 8.00 3.60
❑ 409 Pittsburgh Pirates 10.00 4.50
Team Card
❑ 410 Al Smith 6.00 2.70
❑ 411 Danny O'Connell 6.00 2.70
❑ 412 Charlie James 6.00 2.70
❑ 413 Matty Alou 10.00 4.50
❑ 414 Joe Gaines 6.00 2.70
❑ 415 Bill Virdon 10.00 4.50
❑ 416 Bob Scheffing MG 6.00 2.70
❑ 417 Joe Azcue 6.00 2.70
❑ 418 Andy Carey 6.00 2.70
❑ 419 Bob Bruce 8.00 3.60
❑ 420 Gus Triandos 8.00 3.60
❑ 421 Ken MacKenzie 8.00 3.60
❑ 422 Steve Bilko 6.00 2.70
❑ 423 Rival League 10.00 4.50
Relief Aces:
Roy Face
Hoyt Wilhelm
❑ 424 Al McBean 6.00 2.70
❑ 425 Carl Yastrzemski 125.00 55.00
❑ 426 Bob Farley 6.00 2.70
❑ 427 Jake Wood 6.00 2.70
❑ 428 Joe Hicks 6.00 2.70
❑ 429 Billy O'Dell 6.00 2.70
❑ 430 Tony Kubek 10.00 4.50
❑ 431 Bob Rodgers 8.00 3.60
❑ 432 Jim Pendleton 6.00 2.70
❑ 433 Jim Archer 6.00 2.70
❑ 434 Clay Dalrymple 6.00 2.70
❑ 435 Larry Sherry 8.00 3.60
❑ 436 Felix Mantilla 8.00 3.60
❑ 437 Ray Moore 6.00 2.70
❑ 438 Dick Brown 6.00 2.70
❑ 439 Jerry Buchek 6.00 2.70
❑ 440 Joey Jay 6.00 2.70
❑ 441 Checklist 6 16.00 7.25
❑ 442 Wes Stock 6.00 2.70
❑ 443 Del Crandall 8.00 3.60
❑ 444 Ted Wills 6.00 2.70
❑ 445 Vic Power 8.00 3.60
❑ 446 Don Elston 6.00 2.70
❑ 447 Willie Kirkland 12.00 5.50
❑ 448 Joe Gibbon 12.00 5.50
❑ 449 Jerry Adair 12.00 5.50
❑ 450 Jim O'Toole 15.00 6.75
❑ 451 Jose Tartabull 16.00 7.25
❑ 452 Earl Averill Jr. 12.00 5.50
❑ 453 Cal McLish 12.00 5.50
❑ 454 Floyd Robinson 12.00 5.50
❑ 455 Luis Arroyo 15.00 6.75
❑ 456 Joe Amalfitano 15.00 6.75
❑ 457 Lou Clinton 12.00 5.50
❑ 458A Bob Buhl 15.00 6.75
(Braves emblem
on cap)
❑ 458B Bob Buhl 50.00 22.00
(No emblem on cap)
❑ 459 Ed Bailey 12.00 5.50
❑ 460 Jim Bunning 18.00 8.00
❑ 461 Ken Hubbs 35.00 16.00
❑ 462A Willie Tasby 12.00 5.50
(Senators emblem
on cap)
❑ 462B Willie Tasby 50.00 22.00
(No emblem on cap)
❑ 463 Hank Bauer MG 16.00 7.25
❑ 464 Al Jackson 12.00 5.50
❑ 465 Reds Team 20.00 9.00
❑ 466 Norm Cash AS 15.00 6.75
❑ 467 Chuck Schilling AS 12.00 5.50
❑ 468 Brooks Robinson AS 25.00 11.00
❑ 469 Luis Aparicio AS 16.00 7.25
❑ 470 Al Kaline AS 25.00 11.00
❑ 471 Mickey Mantle AS 200.00 90.00
❑ 472 Rocky Colavito AS 16.00 7.25
❑ 473 Elston Howard AS 15.00 6.75
❑ 474 Frank Lary AS 12.00 5.50
❑ 475 Whitey Ford AS 16.00 7.25
❑ 476 Orioles Team 20.00 9.00
❑ 477 Andre Rodgers 12.00 5.50
❑ 478 Don Zimmer 20.00 9.00
(Shown with Mets cap,
but listed as with
Cincinnati)
❑ 479 Joel Horlen 12.00 5.50
❑ 480 Harvey Kuenn 16.00 7.25
❑ 481 Vic Wertz 16.00 7.25
❑ 482 Sam Mele MG 12.00 5.50
❑ 483 Don McMahon 12.00 5.50
❑ 484 Dick Schofield 12.00 5.50
❑ 485 Pedro Ramos 12.00 5.50
❑ 486 Jim Gilliam 16.00 7.25
❑ 487 Jerry Lynch 12.00 5.50
❑ 488 Hal Brown 12.00 5.50
❑ 489 Julio Gotay 12.00 5.50
❑ 490 Clete Boyer UER 16.00 7.25
Reversed Negative
❑ 491 Leon Wagner 12.00 5.50
❑ 492 Hal W. Smith 15.00 6.75
❑ 493 Danny McDevitt 12.00 5.50
❑ 494 Sammy White 12.00 5.50
❑ 495 Don Cardwell 12.00 5.50
❑ 496 Wayne Causey 12.00 5.50
❑ 497 Ed Bouchee 15.00 6.75
❑ 498 Jim Donohue 12.00 5.50
❑ 499 Zoilo Versalles 15.00 6.75
❑ 500 Duke Snider 50.00 22.00
❑ 501 Claude Osteen 15.00 6.75
❑ 502 Hector Lopez 15.00 6.75
❑ 503 Danny Murtaugh MG 15.00 6.75
❑ 504 Eddie Bressoud 12.00 5.50
❑ 505 Juan Marichal 45.00 20.00
❑ 506 Charlie Maxwell 15.00 6.75
❑ 507 Ernie Broglio 15.00 6.75
❑ 508 Gordy Coleman 15.00 6.75
❑ 509 Dave Giusti 16.00 7.25
❑ 510 Jim Lemon 12.00 5.50
❑ 511 Bubba Phillips 12.00 5.50
❑ 512 Mike Fornieles 12.00 5.50
❑ 513 Whitey Herzog 16.00 7.25

❑ 514 Sherm Lollar 15.00 6.75
❑ 515 Stan Williams 15.00 6.75
❑ 516 Checklist 7.................. 45.00 9.00
❑ 517 Dave Wickersham...... 12.00 5.50
❑ 518 Lee Maye 12.00 5.50
❑ 519 Bob Johnson 12.00 5.50
❑ 520 Bob Friend.................. 16.00 7.25
❑ 521 Jacke Davis UER 12.00 5.50
(Listed as OF on
front and P on back)
❑ 522 Lindy McDaniel 15.00 6.75
❑ 523 Russ Nixon SP 35.00 16.00
❑ 524 Howie Nunn SP.......... 35.00 16.00
❑ 525 George Thomas 20.00 9.00
❑ 526 Hal Woodeshick SP .. 35.00 16.00
❑ 527 Dick McAuliffe 25.00 11.00
❑ 528 Turk Lown 20.00 9.00
❑ 529 John Schaive SP........ 35.00 16.00
❑ 530 Bob Gibson SP 150.00 70.00
❑ 531 Bobby G. Smith.......... 20.00 9.00
❑ 532 Dick Stigman.............. 20.00 9.00
❑ 533 Charley Lau SP.......... 35.00 16.00
❑ 534 Tony Gonzalez SP 35.00 16.00
❑ 535 Ed Roebuck................ 20.00 9.00
❑ 536 Dick Gernert 20.00 9.00
❑ 537 Cleveland Indians 50.00 22.00
Team Card
❑ 538 Jack Sanford 20.00 9.00
❑ 539 Billy Moran 20.00 9.00
❑ 540 Jim Landis SP............ 35.00 16.00
❑ 541 Don Nottebart SP 35.00 16.00
❑ 542 Dave Philley 20.00 9.00
❑ 543 Bob Allen SP.............. 35.00 16.00
❑ 544 Willie McCovey SP .. 100.00 45.00
❑ 545 Hoyt Wilhelm SP 50.00 22.00
❑ 546 Moe Thacker SP 35.00 16.00
❑ 547 Don Ferrarese............ 20.00 9.00
❑ 548 Bobby Del Greco........ 20.00 9.00
❑ 549 Bill Rigney MG SP...... 35.00 16.00
❑ 550 Art Mahaffey SP 35.00 16.00
❑ 551 Harry Bright................ 20.00 9.00
❑ 552 Chicago Cubs SP 60.00 27.00
Team Card
❑ 553 Jim Coates 20.00 9.00
❑ 554 Bubba Morton SP 35.00 16.00
❑ 555 John Buzhardt SP 35.00 16.00
❑ 556 Al Spangler 20.00 9.00
❑ 557 Bob Anderson SP 35.00 16.00
❑ 558 John Goryl.................. 20.00 9.00
❑ 559 Mike Higgins MG........ 20.00 9.00
❑ 560 Chuck Estrada SP...... 35.00 16.00
❑ 561 Gene Oliver SP 35.00 16.00
❑ 562 Bill Henry.................... 20.00 9.00
❑ 563 Ken Aspromonte 20.00 9.00
❑ 564 Bob Grim.................... 20.00 9.00
❑ 565 Jose Pagan 20.00 9.00
❑ 566 Marty Kutyna SP........ 35.00 16.00
❑ 567 Tracy Stallard SP 35.00 16.00
❑ 568 Jim Golden 20.00 9.00
❑ 569 Ed Sadowski SP 35.00 16.00
❑ 570 Bill Stafford SP 35.00 16.00
❑ 571 Billy Klaus SP 35.00 16.00
❑ 572 Bob G. Miller SP 35.00 16.00
❑ 573 Johnny Logan 20.00 9.00
❑ 574 Dean Stone 20.00 9.00
❑ 575 Red Schoendienst SP 50.00 22.00
❑ 576 Russ Kemmerer SP .. 35.00 16.00
❑ 577 Dave Nicholson SP 35.00 16.00
❑ 578 Jim Duffalo 20.00 9.00
❑ 579 Jim Schaffer SP 35.00 16.00
❑ 580 Bill Monbouquette 20.00 9.00
❑ 581 Mel Roach.................. 20.00 9.00
❑ 582 Ron Piche 20.00 9.00
❑ 583 Larry Osborne 20.00 9.00
❑ 584 Minnesota Twins SP .. 60.00 27.00
Team Card
❑ 585 Glen Hobbie SP 35.00 16.00
❑ 586 Sammy Esposito SP .. 35.00 16.00
❑ 587 Frank Funk SP 35.00 16.00
❑ 588 Birdie Tebbetts MG 20.00 9.00
❑ 589 Bob Turley.................. 30.00 13.50
❑ 590 Curt Flood 30.00 13.50
❑ 591 Rookie Pitchers SP 70.00 32.00
Sam McDowell
Ron Taylor
Ron Nischwitz
Art Quirk
Dick Radatz
❑ 592 Rookie Pitchers SP 70.00 32.00
Dan Pfister
Bo Belinsky
Dave Stenhouse
Jim Bouton
Joe Bonikowski
❑ 593 Rookie Pitchers SP 40.00 18.00
Jack Lamabe
Craig Anderson
Jack Hamilton
Bob Moorhead
Bob Veale
❑ 594 Rookie Catchers SP .. 75.00 34.00
Doc Edwards
Ken Retzer
Bob Uecker
Doug Camilli
Don Pavletich
❑ 595 Rookie Infielders SP .. 40.00 18.00
Bob Sadowski
Felix Torres
Marlan Coughtry
Ed Charles
❑ 596 Rookie Infielders SP .. 70.00 32.00
Bernie Allen
Joe Pepitone
Phil Linz
Rich Rollins
❑ 597 Rookie Infielders SP .. 40.00 18.00
Jim McKnight
Rod Kanehl
Amado Samuel
Denis Menke
❑ 598 Rookie Outfielders SP 80.00 23.00
Al Luplow
Manny Jimenez
Howie Goss
Jim Hickman
Ed Olivares

1963 Topps

	NRMT	VG-E
COMPLETE SET (576)	5000.00	2200.00
COMMON CARD (1-196)	4.00	1.80
COMMON CARD (197-283)	5.00	2.20
COMMON CARD (284-370)	5.00	2.20
COMMON CARD (371-446)	5.00	2.20
COMMON CARD (447-522)	25.00	11.00
COMMON CARD (523-576)	15.00	6.75
WRAPPER (1-CENT)	40.00	18.00
WRAPPER (5-CENT)	30.00	13.50

❑ 1 NL Batting Leaders 40.00 8.00
Tommy Davis
Frank Robinson
Stan Musial
Hank Aaron
Bill White
❑ 2 AL Batting Leaders 50.00 22.00
Pete Runnels
Mickey Mantle
Floyd Robinson
Norm Siebern
Chuck Hinton
❑ 3 NL Home Run Leaders .. 30.00 13.50
Willie Mays
Hank Aaron
Frank Robinson
Orlando Cepeda
Ernie Banks
❑ 4 AL Home Run Leaders .. 20.00 9.00
Harmon Killebrew
Norm Cash
Rocky Colavito
Roger Maris
Jim Gentile
Leon Wagner
❑ 5 NL ERA Leaders 20.00 9.00
Sandy Koufax
Bob Shaw
Bob Purkey
Bob Gibson
Don Drysdale
❑ 6 AL ERA Leaders 10.00 4.50
Hank Aguirre
Robin Roberts
Whitey Ford
Eddie Fisher
Dean Chance
❑ 7 NL Pitching Leaders 10.00 4.50
Don Drysdale
Jack Sanford
Bob Purkey
Billy O'Dell
Art Mahaffey
Joe Jay
❑ 8 AL Pitching Leaders 8.00 3.60
Ralph Terry
Dick Donovan
Ray Herbert
Jim Bunning
Camilo Pascual
❑ 9 NL Strikeout Leaders 20.00 9.00
Don Drysdale
Sandy Koufax
Bob Gibson
Billy O'Dell
Dick Farrell
❑ 10 AL Strikeout Leaders...... 8.00 3.60
Camilo Pascual
Jim Bunning
Ralph Terry
Juan Pizarro
Jim Kaat
❑ 11 Lee Walls 4.00 1.80
❑ 12 Steve Barber.................. 4.00 1.80
❑ 13 Philadelphia Phillies 8.00 3.60
Team Card
❑ 14 Pedro Ramos 4.00 1.80
❑ 15 Ken Hubbs UER 10.00 4.50
(No position listed
on front of card)
❑ 16 Al Smith.......................... 4.00 1.80
❑ 17 Ryne Duren 8.00 3.60
❑ 18 Buc Blasters 70.00 32.00
Smoky Burgess
Dick Stuart
Bob Clemente
Bob Skinner
❑ 19 Pete Burnside 4.00 1.80
❑ 20 Tony Kubek.................... 8.00 3.60
❑ 21 Marty Keough 4.00 1.80
❑ 22 Curt Simmons 8.00 3.60
❑ 23 Ed Lopat MG.................. 8.00 3.60
❑ 24 Bob Bruce 4.00 1.80
❑ 25 Al Kaline 45.00 20.00
❑ 26 Ray Moore...................... 4.00 1.80
❑ 27 Choo Choo Coleman...... 8.00 3.60
❑ 28 Mike Fornieles................ 4.00 1.80
❑ 29A 1962 Rookie Stars 8.00 3.60
Sammy Ellis
Ray Culp
John Boozer
Jesse Gonder
❑ 29B 1963 Rookie Stars 4.00 1.80
Sammy Ellis
Ray Culp
John Boozer
Jesse Gonder
❑ 30 Harvey Kuenn 8.00 3.60

❑	31 Cal Koonce	4.00	1.80
❑	32 Tony Gonzalez	4.00	1.80
❑	33 Bo Belinsky	8.00	3.60
❑	34 Dick Schofield	4.00	1.80
❑	35 John Buzhardt	4.00	1.80
❑	36 Jerry Kindall	4.00	1.80
❑	37 Jerry Lynch	4.00	1.80
❑	38 Bud Daley	8.00	3.60
❑	39 Angels Team	8.00	3.60
❑	40 Vic Power	8.00	3.60
❑	41 Charley Lau	8.00	3.60
❑	42 Stan Williams	8.00	3.60
	(Listed as Yankee on card but LA cap)		
❑	43 Veteran Masters	8.00	3.60
	Casey Stengel MG		
	Gene Woodling		
❑	44 Terry Fox	4.00	1.80
❑	45 Bob Aspromonte	4.00	1.80
❑	46 Tommie Aaron	8.00	3.60
❑	47 Don Lock	4.00	1.80
❑	48 Birdie Tebbetts MG	8.00	3.60
❑	49 Dal Maxvill	8.00	3.60
❑	50 Billy Pierce	8.00	3.60
❑	51 George Alusik	4.00	1.80
❑	52 Chuck Schilling	4.00	1.80
❑	53 Joe Moeller	8.00	3.60
❑	54A 1962 Rookie Stars	15.00	6.75
	Nelson Mathews		
	Harry Fanok		
	Jack Cullen		
	Dave DeBusschere		
❑	54B 1963 Rookie Stars	8.00	3.60
	Nelson Mathews		
	Harry Fanok		
	Jack Cullen		
	Dave DeBusschere		
❑	55 Bill Virdon	8.00	3.60
❑	56 Dennis Bennett	4.00	1.80
❑	57 Billy Moran	4.00	1.80
❑	58 Bob Will	4.00	1.80
❑	59 Craig Anderson	4.00	1.80
❑	60 Elston Howard	8.00	3.60
❑	61 Ernie Bowman	4.00	1.80
❑	62 Bob Hendley	4.00	1.80
❑	63 Reds Team	8.00	3.60
❑	64 Dick McAuliffe	8.00	3.60
❑	65 Jackie Brandt	4.00	1.80
❑	66 Mike Joyce	4.00	1.80
❑	67 Ed Charles	4.00	1.80
❑	68 Friendly Foes	25.00	11.00
	Duke Snider		
	Gil Hodges		
❑	69 Bud Zipfel	4.00	1.80
❑	70 Jim O'Toole	8.00	3.60
❑	71 Bobby Wine	8.00	3.60
❑	72 Johnny Romano	4.00	1.80
❑	73 Bobby Bragan MG	8.00	3.60
❑	74 Denny Lemaster	4.00	1.80
❑	75 Bob Allison	8.00	3.60
❑	76 Earl Wilson	8.00	3.60
❑	77 Al Spangler	4.00	1.80
❑	78 Marv Throneberry	8.00	3.60
❑	79 Checklist 1	10.00	2.00
❑	80 Jim Gilliam	8.00	3.60
❑	81 Jim Schaffer	4.00	1.80
❑	82 Ed Rakow	4.00	1.80
❑	83 Charley James	4.00	1.80
❑	84 Ron Kline	4.00	1.80
❑	85 Tom Haller	8.00	3.60
❑	86 Charley Maxwell	8.00	3.60
❑	87 Bob Veale	8.00	3.60
❑	88 Ron Hansen	4.00	1.80
❑	89 Dick Stigman	4.00	1.80
❑	90 Gordy Coleman	8.00	3.60
❑	91 Dallas Green	8.00	3.60
❑	92 Hector Lopez	8.00	3.60
❑	93 Galen Cisco	4.00	1.80
❑	94 Bob Schmidt	4.00	1.80
❑	95 Larry Jackson	4.00	1.80
❑	96 Lou Clinton	4.00	1.80
❑	97 Bob Duliba	4.00	1.80
❑	98 George Thomas	4.00	1.80
❑	99 Jim Umbricht	4.00	1.80
❑	100 Joe Cunningham	4.00	1.80
❑	101 Joe Gibbon	4.00	1.80
❑	102A Checklist 2	10.00	2.00
	(Red on yellow)		
❑	102B Checklist 2	10.00	2.00
	(White on red)		
❑	103 Chuck Essegian	4.00	1.80
❑	104 Lew Krausse	4.00	1.80
❑	105 Ron Fairly	8.00	3.60
❑	106 Bobby Bolin	4.00	1.80
❑	107 Jim Hickman	8.00	3.60
❑	108 Hoyt Wilhelm	10.00	4.50
❑	109 Lee Maye	4.00	1.80
❑	110 Rich Rollins	8.00	3.60
❑	111 Al Jackson	4.00	1.80
❑	112 Dick Brown	4.00	1.80
❑	113 Don Landrum UER	4.00	1.80
	(Photo actually Ron Santo)		
❑	114 Dan Osinski	4.00	1.80
❑	115 Carl Yastrzemski	40.00	18.00
❑	116 Jim Brosnan	8.00	3.60
❑	117 Jacke Davis	4.00	1.80
❑	118 Sherm Lollar	4.00	1.80
❑	119 Bob Lillis	4.00	1.80
❑	120 Roger Maris	50.00	22.00
❑	121 Jim Hannan	4.00	1.80
❑	122 Julio Gotay	4.00	1.80
❑	123 Frank Howard	8.00	3.60
❑	124 Dick Howser	8.00	3.60
❑	125 Robin Roberts	14.00	6.25
❑	126 Bob Uecker	14.00	6.25
❑	127 Bill Tuttle	4.00	1.80
❑	128 Matty Alou	8.00	3.60
❑	129 Gary Bell	4.00	1.80
❑	130 Dick Groat	8.00	3.60
❑	131 Washington Senators	8.00	3.60
	Team Card		
❑	132 Jack Hamilton	4.00	1.80
❑	133 Gene Freese	4.00	1.80
❑	134 Bob Scheffing MG	4.00	1.80
❑	135 Richie Ashburn	20.00	9.00
❑	136 Ike Delock	4.00	1.80
❑	137 Mack Jones	4.00	1.80
❑	138 Pride of NL	70.00	32.00
	Willie Mays		
	Stan Musial		
❑	139 Earl Averill	4.00	1.80
❑	140 Frank Lary	8.00	3.60
❑	141 Manny Mota	8.00	3.60
❑	142 Whitey Ford WS	10.00	4.50
❑	143 Jack Sanford WS	8.00	3.60
❑	144 Roger Maris WS	12.00	5.50
❑	145 Chuck Hiller WS	8.00	3.60
❑	146 Tom Tresh WS	8.00	3.60
❑	147 Billy Pierce WS	8.00	3.60
❑	148 Ralph Terry WS	8.00	3.60
❑	149 Marv Breeding	4.00	1.80
❑	150 Johnny Podres	8.00	3.60
❑	151 Pirates Team	8.00	3.60
❑	152 Ron Nischwitz	4.00	1.80
❑	153 Hal Smith	4.00	1.80
❑	154 Walter Alston MG	8.00	3.60
❑	155 Bill Stafford	4.00	1.80
❑	156 Roy McMillan	8.00	3.60
❑	157 Diego Segui	8.00	3.60
❑	158 Rookie Stars	8.00	3.60
	Rogelio Alvares		
	Dave Roberts		
	Tommy Harper		
	Bob Saverine		
❑	159 Jim Pagliaroni	4.00	1.80
❑	160 Juan Pizarro	4.00	1.80
❑	161 Frank Torre	8.00	3.60
❑	162 Twins Team	8.00	3.60
❑	163 Don Larsen	8.00	3.60
❑	164 Bubba Morton	4.00	1.80
❑	165 Jim Kaat	8.00	3.60
❑	166 Johnny Keane MG	4.00	1.80
❑	167 Jim Fregosi	8.00	3.60
❑	168 Russ Nixon	4.00	1.80
❑	169 Rookie Stars	25.00	11.00
	Dick Egan		
	Julio Navarro		
	Tommie Sisk		
	Gaylord Perry		
❑	170 Joe Adcock	8.00	3.60
❑	171 Steve Hamilton	4.00	1.80
❑	172 Gene Oliver	4.00	1.80
❑	173 Bombers' Best	175.00	80.00
	Tom Tresh		
	Mickey Mantle		
	Bobby Richardson		
❑	174 Larry Burright	4.00	1.80
❑	175 Bob Buhl	8.00	3.60
❑	176 Jim King	4.00	1.80
❑	177 Bubba Phillips	4.00	1.80
❑	178 Johnny Edwards	4.00	1.80
❑	179 Ron Piche	4.00	1.80
❑	180 Bill Skowron	8.00	3.60
❑	181 Sammy Esposito	4.00	1.80
❑	182 Albie Pearson	8.00	3.60
❑	183 Joe Pepitone	8.00	3.60
❑	184 Vern Law	8.00	3.60
❑	185 Chuck Hiller	4.00	1.80
❑	186 Jerry Zimmerman	4.00	1.80
❑	187 Willie Kirkland	4.00	1.80
❑	188 Eddie Bressoud	4.00	1.80
❑	189 Dave Giusti	8.00	3.60
❑	190 Minnie Minoso	8.00	3.60
❑	191 Checklist 3	10.00	2.00
❑	192 Clay Dalrymple	4.00	1.80
❑	193 Andre Rodgers	4.00	1.80
❑	194 Joe Nuxhall	8.00	3.60
❑	195 Manny Jimenez	4.00	1.80
❑	196 Doug Camilli	4.00	1.80
❑	197 Roger Craig	8.00	3.60
❑	198 Lenny Green	5.00	2.20
❑	199 Joe Amalfitano	5.00	2.20
❑	200 Mickey Mantle	500.00	220.00
❑	201 Cecil Butler	5.00	2.20
❑	202 Boston Red Sox	8.00	3.60
	Team Card		
❑	203 Chico Cardenas	8.00	3.60
❑	204 Don Nottebart	5.00	2.20
❑	205 Luis Aparicio	15.00	6.75
❑	206 Ray Washburn	5.00	2.20
❑	207 Ken Hunt	5.00	2.20
❑	208 Rookie Stars	5.00	2.20
	Ron Herbel		
	John Miller		
	Wally Wolf		
	Ron Taylor		
❑	209 Hobie Landrith	5.00	2.20
❑	210 Sandy Koufax !	175.00	80.00
❑	211 Fred Whitfield	5.00	2.20
❑	212 Glen Hobbie	5.00	2.20
❑	213 Billy Hitchcock MG	5.00	2.20
❑	214 Orlando Pena	5.00	2.20
❑	215 Bob Skinner	8.00	3.60
❑	216 Gene Conley	8.00	3.60
❑	217 Joe Christopher	5.00	2.20
❑	218 Tiger Twirlers	8.00	3.60
	Frank Lary		
	Don Mossi		
	Jim Bunning		
❑	219 Chuck Cottier	5.00	2.20
❑	220 Camilo Pascual	8.00	3.60
❑	221 Cookie Rojas	8.00	3.60
❑	222 Cubs Team	8.00	3.60
❑	223 Eddie Fisher	5.00	2.20
❑	224 Mike Roarke	5.00	2.20
❑	225 Joey Jay	5.00	2.20
❑	226 Julian Javier	8.00	3.60
❑	227 Jim Grant	8.00	3.60
❑	228 Rookie Stars	40.00	18.00
	Max Alvis		
	Bob Bailey		
	Tony Oliva		
	(Listed as Pedro)		
	Ed Kranepool		
❑	229 Willie Davis	8.00	3.60
❑	230 Pete Runnels	8.00	3.60
❑	231 Eli Grba UER	5.00	2.20
	(Large photo is Ryne Duren)		
❑	232 Frank Malzone	8.00	3.60
❑	233 Casey Stengel MG	20.00	9.00
❑	234 Dave Nicholson	5.00	2.20
❑	235 Billy O'Dell	5.00	2.20
❑	236 Bill Bryan	5.00	2.20

237	Jim Coates	8.00	3.60
238	Lou Johnson	5.00	2.20
239	Harvey Haddix	8.00	3.60
240	Rocky Colavito	15.00	6.75
241	Bob Smith	5.00	2.20
242	Power Plus	60.00	27.00
	Ernie Banks		
	Hank Aaron		
243	Don Leppert	5.00	2.20
244	John Tsitouris	5.00	2.20
245	Gil Hodges	20.00	9.00
246	Lee Stange	5.00	2.20
247	Yankees Team	40.00	18.00
248	Tito Francona	5.00	2.20
249	Leo Burke	5.00	2.20
250	Stan Musial	125.00	55.00
251	Jack Lamabe	5.00	2.20
252	Ron Santo	10.00	4.50
253	Rookie Stars	5.00	2.20
	Len Gabrielson		
	Pete Jernigan		
	John Wojcik		
	Deacon Jones		
254	Mike Hershberger	5.00	2.20
255	Bob Shaw	5.00	2.20
256	Jerry Lumpe	5.00	2.20
257	Hank Aguirre	5.00	2.20
258	Alvin Dark MG	8.00	3.60
259	Johnny Logan	8.00	3.60
260	Jim Gentile	8.00	3.60
261	Bob Miller	5.00	2.20
262	Ellis Burton	5.00	2.20
263	Dave Stenhouse	5.00	2.20
264	Phil Linz	5.00	2.20
265	Vada Pinson	8.00	3.60
266	Bob Allen	5.00	2.20
267	Carl Sawatski	5.00	2.20
268	Don Demeter	5.00	2.20
269	Don Mincher	5.00	2.20
270	Felipe Alou	8.00	3.60
271	Dean Stone	5.00	2.20
272	Danny Murphy	5.00	2.20
273	Sammy Taylor	5.00	2.20
274	Checklist 4	10.00	2.00
275	Eddie Mathews	20.00	9.00
276	Barry Shetrone	5.00	2.20
277	Dick Farrell	5.00	2.20
278	Chico Fernandez	5.00	2.20
279	Wally Moon	8.00	3.60
280	Bob Rodgers	5.00	2.20
281	Tom Sturdivant	5.00	2.20
282	Bobby Del Greco	5.00	2.20
283	Roy Sievers	8.00	3.60
284	Dave Sisler	5.00	2.20
285	Dick Stuart	8.00	3.60
286	Stu Miller	8.00	3.60
287	Dick Bertell	5.00	2.20
288	Chicago White Sox	8.00	3.60
	Team Card		
289	Hal Brown	5.00	2.20
290	Bill White	8.00	3.60
291	Don Rudolph	5.00	2.20
292	Pumpsie Green	8.00	3.60
293	Bill Pleis	5.00	2.20
294	Bill Rigney MG	5.00	2.20
295	Ed Roebuck	5.00	2.20
296	Doc Edwards	5.00	2.20
297	Jim Golden	5.00	2.20
298	Don Dillard	5.00	2.20
299	Rookie Stars	8.00	3.60
	Dave Morehead		
	Bob Dustal		
	Tom Butters		
	Dan Schneider		
300	Willie Mays	135.00	60.00
301	Bill Fischer	5.00	2.20
302	Whitey Herzog	8.00	3.60
303	Earl Francis	5.00	2.20
304	Harry Bright	5.00	2.20
305	Don Hoak	5.00	2.20
306	Star Receivers	8.00	3.60
	Earl Battey		
	Elston Howard		
307	Chet Nichols	5.00	2.20
308	Camilo Carreon	5.00	2.20
309	Jim Brewer	5.00	2.20
310	Tommy Davis	8.00	3.60
311	Joe McClain	5.00	2.20
312	Houston Colts	25.00	11.00
	Team Card		
313	Ernie Broglio	5.00	2.20
314	John Goryl	5.00	2.20
315	Ralph Terry	8.00	3.60
316	Norm Sherry	8.00	3.60
317	Sam McDowell	8.00	3.60
318	Gene Mauch MG	8.00	3.60
319	Joe Gaines	5.00	2.20
320	Warren Spahn	40.00	18.00
321	Gino Cimoli	5.00	2.20
322	Bob Turley	8.00	3.60
323	Bill Mazeroski	10.00	4.50
324	Rookie Stars	8.00	3.60
	George Williams		
	Pete Ward		
	Phil Roof		
	Vic Davalillo		
325	Jack Sanford	5.00	2.20
326	Hank Foiles	5.00	2.20
327	Paul Foytack	5.00	2.20
328	Dick Williams	8.00	3.60
329	Lindy McDaniel	8.00	3.60
330	Chuck Hinton	5.00	2.20
331	Series Foes	8.00	3.60
	Bill Stafford		
	Bill Pierce		
332	Joel Horlen	8.00	3.60
333	Carl Warwick	5.00	2.20
334	Wynn Hawkins	5.00	2.20
335	Leon Wagner	5.00	2.20
336	Ed Bauta	5.00	2.20
337	Dodgers Team	25.00	11.00
338	Russ Kemmerer	5.00	2.20
339	Ted Bowsfield	5.00	2.20
340	Yogi Berra P/CO	70.00	32.00
341	Jack Baldschun	5.00	2.20
342	Gene Woodling	8.00	3.60
343	Johnny Pesky MG	8.00	3.60
344	Don Schwall	5.00	2.20
345	Brooks Robinson	60.00	27.00
346	Billy Hoeft	5.00	2.20
347	Joe Torre	14.00	6.25
348	Vic Wertz	8.00	3.60
349	Zoilo Versalles	8.00	3.60
350	Bob Purkey	5.00	2.20
351	Al Luplow	5.00	2.20
352	Ken Johnson	5.00	2.20
353	Billy Williams	30.00	13.50
354	Dom Zanni	5.00	2.20
355	Dean Chance	8.00	3.60
356	John Schaive	5.00	2.20
357	George Altman	5.00	2.20
358	Milt Pappas	8.00	3.60
359	Haywood Sullivan	8.00	3.60
360	Don Drysdale	40.00	18.00
361	Clete Boyer	8.00	3.60
362	Checklist 5	10.00	2.00
363	Dick Radatz	8.00	3.60
364	Howie Goss	5.00	2.20
365	Jim Bunning	15.00	6.75
366	Tony Taylor	8.00	3.60
367	Tony Cloninger	5.00	2.20
368	Ed Bailey	5.00	2.20
369	Jim Lemon	5.00	2.20
370	Dick Donovan	5.00	2.20
371	Rod Kanehl	8.00	3.60
372	Don Lee	5.00	2.20
373	Jim Campbell	5.00	2.20
374	Claude Osteen	8.00	3.60
375	Ken Boyer	8.00	3.60
376	John Wyatt	5.00	2.20
377	Baltimore Orioles	10.00	4.50
	Team Card		
378	Bill Henry	5.00	2.20
379	Bob Anderson	5.00	2.20
380	Ernie Banks UER	75.00	34.00
	(Back has career Major and Minor, but he never played in Minors)		
381	Frank Baumann	5.00	2.20
382	Ralph Houk MG	8.00	3.60
383	Pete Richert	5.00	2.20
384	Bob Tillman	5.00	2.20
385	Art Mahaffey	5.00	2.20
386	Rookie Stars	5.00	2.20
	Ed Kirkpatrick		
	John Bateman		
	Larry Bearnarth		
	Garry Roggenburk		
387	Al McBean	5.00	2.20
388	Jim Davenport	8.00	3.60
389	Frank Sullivan	5.00	2.20
390	Hank Aaron	125.00	55.00
391	Bill Dailey	5.00	2.20
392	Tribe Thumpers	5.00	2.20
	Johnny Romano		
	Tito Francona		
393	Ken MacKenzie	8.00	3.60
394	Tim McCarver	14.00	6.25
395	Don McMahon	5.00	2.20
396	Joe Koppe	5.00	2.20
397	Kansas City Athletics	8.00	3.60
	Team Card		
398	Boog Powell	25.00	11.00
399	Dick Ellsworth	5.00	2.20
400	Frank Robinson	60.00	27.00
401	Jim Bouton	14.00	6.25
402	Mickey Vernon MG	8.00	3.60
403	Ron Perranoski	8.00	3.60
404	Bob Oldis	5.00	2.20
405	Floyd Robinson	5.00	2.20
406	Howie Koplitz	5.00	2.20
407	Rookie Stars	5.00	2.20
	Frank Kostro		
	Chico Ruiz		
	Larry Elliot		
	Dick Simpson		
408	Billy Gardner	5.00	2.20
409	Roy Face	8.00	3.60
410	Earl Battey	5.00	2.20
411	Jim Constable	5.00	2.20
412	Dodger Big Three	40.00	18.00
	Johnny Podres		
	Don Drysdale		
	Sandy Koufax		
413	Jerry Walker	5.00	2.20
414	Ty Cline	5.00	2.20
415	Bob Gibson	60.00	27.00
416	Alex Grammas	5.00	2.20
417	Giants Team	8.00	3.60
418	John Orsino	5.00	2.20
419	Tracy Stallard	5.00	2.20
420	Bobby Richardson	14.00	6.25
421	Tom Morgan	5.00	2.20
422	Fred Hutchinson MG	8.00	3.60
423	Ed Hobaugh	5.00	2.20
424	Charlie Smith	5.00	2.20
425	Smoky Burgess	8.00	3.60
426	Barry Latman	5.00	2.20
427	Bernie Allen	5.00	2.20
428	Carl Boles	5.00	2.20
429	Lou Burdette	8.00	3.60
430	Norm Siebern	5.00	2.20
431A	Checklist 6	10.00	2.00
	(White on red)		
431B	Checklist 6	30.00	6.00
	(Black on orange)		
432	Roman Mejias	5.00	2.20
433	Denis Menke	5.00	2.20
434	John Callison	8.00	3.60
435	Woody Held	5.00	2.20
436	Tim Harkness	8.00	3.60
437	Bill Bruton	5.00	2.20
438	Wes Stock	5.00	2.20
439	Don Zimmer	8.00	3.60
440	Juan Marichal	30.00	13.50
441	Lee Thomas	8.00	3.60
442	J.C. Hartman	5.00	2.20
443	Jimmy Piersall	8.00	3.60
444	Jim Maloney	8.00	3.60
445	Norm Cash	8.00	3.60
446	Whitey Ford	40.00	18.00
447	Felix Mantilla	25.00	11.00
448	Jack Kralick	25.00	11.00
449	Jose Tartabull	25.00	11.00
450	Bob Friend	30.00	13.50

❑ 451 Indians Team 40.00 18.00
❑ 452 Barney Schultz 25.00 11.00
❑ 453 Jake Wood 25.00 11.00
❑ 454A Art Fowler 25.00 11.00
(Card number on
white background)
❑ 454B Art Fowler 30.00 13.50
(Card number on
orange background)
❑ 455 Ruben Amaro 25.00 11.00
❑ 456 Jim Coker 25.00 11.00
❑ 457 Tex Clevenger 25.00 11.00
❑ 458 Al Lopez MG 30.00 13.50
❑ 459 Dick LeMay 25.00 11.00
❑ 460 Del Crandall 30.00 13.50
❑ 461 Norm Bass 25.00 11.00
❑ 462 Wally Post 25.00 11.00
❑ 463 Joe Schaffernoth 25.00 11.00
❑ 464 Ken Aspromonte 25.00 11.00
❑ 465 Chuck Estrada 25.00 11.00
❑ 466 Rookie Stars SP 60.00 27.00
Nate Oliver
Tony Martinez
Bill Freehan
Jerry Robinson
❑ 467 Phil Ortega 25.00 11.00
❑ 468 Carroll Hardy 30.00 13.50
❑ 469 Jay Hook 30.00 13.50
❑ 470 Tom Tresh SP 60.00 27.00
❑ 471 Ken Retzer 25.00 11.00
❑ 472 Lou Brock 100.00 45.00
❑ 473 New York Mets 100.00 45.00
Team Card
❑ 474 Jack Fisher 25.00 11.00
❑ 475 Gus Triandos 30.00 13.50
❑ 476 Frank Funk 25.00 11.00
❑ 477 Donn Clendenon 30.00 13.50
❑ 478 Paul Brown 25.00 11.00
❑ 479 Ed Brinkman 25.00 11.00
❑ 480 Bill Monbouquette 25.00 11.00
❑ 481 Bob Taylor 25.00 11.00
❑ 482 Felix Torres 25.00 11.00
❑ 483 Jim Owens UER 25.00 11.00
(Stat column for Wins
has an R instead)
❑ 484 Dale Long SP 30.00 13.50
❑ 485 Jim Landis 25.00 11.00
❑ 486 Ray Sadecki 25.00 11.00
❑ 487 John Roseboro 30.00 13.50
❑ 488 Jerry Adair 25.00 11.00
❑ 489 Paul Toth 25.00 11.00
❑ 490 Willie McCovey 125.00 55.00
❑ 491 Harry Craft MG 25.00 11.00
❑ 492 Dave Wickersham 25.00 11.00
❑ 493 Walt Bond 25.00 11.00
❑ 494 Phil Regan 25.00 11.00
❑ 495 Frank Thomas SP 30.00 13.50
❑ 496 Rookie Stars 30.00 13.50
Steve Dalkowski
Fred Newman
Jack Smith
Carl Bouldin
❑ 497 Bennie Daniels 25.00 11.00
❑ 498 Eddie Kasko 25.00 11.00
❑ 499 J.C. Martin 25.00 11.00
❑ 500 Harmon Killebrew SP 150.00 70.00
❑ 501 Joe Azcue 25.00 11.00
❑ 502 Daryl Spencer 25.00 11.00
❑ 503 Braves Team 40.00 18.00
❑ 504 Bob Johnson 25.00 11.00
❑ 505 Curt Flood 30.00 13.50
❑ 506 Gene Green 25.00 11.00
❑ 507 Roland Sheldon 30.00 13.50
❑ 508 Ted Savage 25.00 11.00
❑ 509A Checklist 7 .... 40.00 8.00
(Copyright centered)
❑ 509B Checklist 7 .... 40.00 8.00
(Copyright to right)
❑ 510 Ken McBride 25.00 11.00
❑ 511 Charlie Neal 30.00 13.50
❑ 512 Cal McLish 25.00 11.00
❑ 513 Gary Geiger 25.00 11.00
❑ 514 Larry Osborne 25.00 11.00
❑ 515 Don Elston 25.00 11.00
❑ 516 Purnell Goldy 25.00 11.00
❑ 517 Hal Woodeshick 25.00 11.00
❑ 518 Don Blasingame 25.00 11.00
❑ 519 Claude Raymond 25.00 11.00
❑ 520 Orlando Cepeda 30.00 13.50
❑ 521 Dan Pfister 25.00 11.00
❑ 522 Rookie Stars 30.00 13.50
Mel Nelson
Gary Peters
Jim Roland
Art Quirk
❑ 523 Bill Kunkel 15.00 6.75
❑ 524 Cardinals Team 30.00 13.50
❑ 525 Nellie Fox 50.00 22.00
❑ 526 Dick Hall 15.00 6.75
❑ 527 Ed Sadowski 15.00 6.75
❑ 528 Carl Willey 15.00 6.75
❑ 529 Wes Covington 15.00 6.75
❑ 530 Don Mossi 20.00 9.00
❑ 531 Sam Mele MG 15.00 6.75
❑ 532 Steve Boros 15.00 6.75
❑ 533 Bobby Shantz 20.00 9.00
❑ 534 Ken Walters 15.00 6.75
❑ 535 Jim Perry 20.00 9.00
❑ 536 Norm Larker 15.00 6.75
❑ 537 Rookie Stars 900.00 400.00
Pedro Gonzalez
Ken McMullen
Al Weis
Pete Rose
❑ 538 George Brunet 15.00 6.75
❑ 539 Wayne Causey 15.00 6.75
❑ 540 Bob Clemente 375.00 170.00
❑ 541 Ron Moeller 15.00 6.75
❑ 542 Lou Klimchock 15.00 6.75
❑ 543 Russ Snyder 15.00 6.75
❑ 544 Rookie Stars 40.00 18.00
Duke Carmel
Bill Haas
Rusty Staub
Dick Phillips
❑ 545 Jose Pagan 15.00 6.75
❑ 546 Hal Reniff 20.00 9.00
❑ 547 Gus Bell 15.00 6.75
❑ 548 Tom Satriano 15.00 6.75
❑ 549 Rookie Stars 15.00 6.75
Marcelino Lopez
Pete Lovrich
Paul Ratliff
Elmo Plaskett
❑ 550 Duke Snider 75.00 34.00
❑ 551 Billy Klaus 15.00 6.75
❑ 552 Detroit Tigers 50.00 22.00
Team Card
❑ 553 Rookie Stars 125.00 55.00
Brock Davis
Jim Gosger
Willie Stargell
John Herrnstein
❑ 554 Hank Fischer 15.00 6.75
❑ 555 John Blanchard 20.00 9.00
❑ 556 Al Worthington 15.00 6.75
❑ 557 Cuno Barragan 15.00 6.75
❑ 558 Rookie Stars 20.00 9.00
Bill Faul
Ron Hunt
Al Moran
Bob Lipski
❑ 559 Danny Murtaugh MG.. 15.00 6.75
❑ 560 Ray Herbert 15.00 6.75
❑ 561 Mike De La Hoz 15.00 6.75
❑ 562 Rookie Stars 25.00 11.00
Randy Cardinal
Dave McNally
Ken Rowe
Don Rowe
❑ 563 Mike McCormick 15.00 6.75
❑ 564 George Banks 15.00 6.75
❑ 565 Larry Sherry 15.00 6.75
❑ 566 Cliff Cook 15.00 6.75
❑ 567 Jim Duffalo 15.00 6.75
❑ 568 Bob Sadowski 15.00 6.75
❑ 569 Luis Arroyo 20.00 9.00
❑ 570 Frank Bolling 15.00 6.75
❑ 571 Johnny Klippstein 15.00 6.75
❑ 572 Jack Spring 15.00 6.75
❑ 573 Coot Veal 15.00 6.75
❑ 574 Hal Kolstad 15.00 6.75
❑ 575 Don Cardwell 15.00 6.75
❑ 576 Johnny Temple 25.00 9.50

1964 Topps

	NRMT	VG-E
COMPLETE SET (587)	3000.00	1350.00
COMMON CARD (1-196)	3.00	1.35
COMMON CARD (197-370)	4.00	1.80
COMMON CARD (371-522)	7.00	3.10
COMMON CARD (523-587)	16.00	7.25
WRAPPER (1-CENT)	100.00	45.00
WRAPPER (1-CENT, REPEAT)	125.00	55.00
WRAPPER (5-CENT)	30.00	13.50
WRAPPER (5-CENT, COIN)	40.00	18.00

❑ 1 NL ERA Leaders 30.00 9.00
Sandy Koufax
Dick Ellsworth
Bob Friend
❑ 2 AL ERA Leaders 6.00 2.70
Gary Peters
Juan Pizarro
Camilo Pascual
❑ 3 NL Pitching Leaders 20.00 9.00
Sandy Koufax
Juan Marichal
Warren Spahn
Jim Maloney
❑ 4 AL Pitching Leaders 10.00 4.50
Whitey Ford
Camilo Pascual
Jim Bouton
❑ 5 NL Strikeout Leaders 15.00 6.75
Sandy Koufax
Jim Maloney
Don Drysdale
❑ 6 AL Strikeout Leaders 6.00 2.70
Camilo Pascual
Jim Bunning
Dick Stigman
❑ 7 NL Batting Leaders 20.00 9.00
Tommy Davis
Bob Clemente
Dick Groat
Hank Aaron
❑ 8 AL Batting Leaders 15.00 6.75
Carl Yastrzemski
Al Kaline
Rich Rollins
❑ 9 NL Home Run Leaders .. 30.00 13.50
Hank Aaron
Willie McCovey
Willie Mays
Orlando Cepeda
❑ 10 AL Home Run Leaders 10.00 4.50
Harmon Killebrew
Dick Stuart
Bob Allison
❑ 11 NL RBI Leaders 15.00 6.75
Hank Aaron
Ken Boyer
Bill White
❑ 12 AL RBI Leaders 10.00 4.50
Dick Stuart
Al Kaline

		Harmon Killebrew		
❑	13	Hoyt Wilhelm	10.00	4.50
❑	14	Dodgers Rookies	3.00	1.35
		Dick Nen		
		Nick Willhite		
❑	15	Zoilo Versalles	6.00	2.70
❑	16	John Boozer	3.00	1.35
❑	17	Willie Kirkland	3.00	1.35
❑	18	Billy O'Dell	3.00	1.35
❑	19	Don Wert	3.00	1.35
❑	20	Bob Friend	6.00	2.70
❑	21	Yogi Berra MG	30.00	13.50
❑	22	Jerry Adair	3.00	1.35
❑	23	Chris Zachary	3.00	1.35
❑	24	Carl Sawatski	3.00	1.35
❑	25	Bill Monbouquette	3.00	1.35
❑	26	Gino Cimoli	3.00	1.35
❑	27	New York Mets	8.00	3.60
		Team Card		
❑	28	Claude Osteen	6.00	2.70
❑	29	Lou Brock	35.00	16.00
❑	30	Ron Perranoski	6.00	2.70
❑	31	Dave Nicholson	3.00	1.35
❑	32	Dean Chance	6.00	2.70
❑	33	Reds Rookies	6.00	2.70
		Sammy Ellis		
		Mel Queen		
❑	34	Jim Perry	6.00	2.70
❑	35	Eddie Mathews	20.00	9.00
❑	36	Hal Reniff	3.00	1.35
❑	37	Smoky Burgess	6.00	2.70
❑	38	Jim Wynn	7.00	3.10
❑	39	Hank Aguirre	3.00	1.35
❑	40	Dick Groat	6.00	2.70
❑	41	Friendly Foes	8.00	3.60
		Willie McCovey		
		Leon Wagner		
❑	42	Moe Drabowsky	6.00	2.70
❑	43	Roy Sievers	6.00	2.70
❑	44	Duke Carmel	3.00	1.35
❑	45	Milt Pappas	6.00	2.70
❑	46	Ed Brinkman	3.00	1.35
❑	47	Giants Rookies	6.00	2.70
		Jesus Alou		
		Ron Herbel		
❑	48	Bob Perry	3.00	1.35
❑	49	Bill Henry	3.00	1.35
❑	50	Mickey Mantle	300.00	135.00
❑	51	Pete Richert	3.00	1.35
❑	52	Chuck Hinton	3.00	1.35
❑	53	Denis Menke	3.00	1.35
❑	54	Sam Mele MG	3.00	1.35
❑	55	Ernie Banks	35.00	16.00
❑	56	Hal Brown	3.00	1.35
❑	57	Tim Harkness	3.00	1.35
❑	58	Don Demeter	3.00	1.35
❑	59	Ernie Broglio	3.00	1.35
❑	60	Frank Malzone	6.00	2.70
❑	61	Angel Backstops	6.00	2.70
		Bob Rodgers		
		Ed Sadowski		
❑	62	Ted Savage	3.00	1.35
❑	63	John Orsino	3.00	1.35
❑	64	Ted Abernathy	3.00	1.35
❑	65	Felipe Alou	6.00	2.70
❑	66	Eddie Fisher	3.00	1.35
❑	67	Tigers Team	8.00	3.60
❑	68	Willie Davis	6.00	2.70
❑	69	Clete Boyer	6.00	2.70
❑	70	Joe Torre	8.00	3.60
❑	71	Jack Spring	3.00	1.35
❑	72	Chico Cardenas	6.00	2.70
❑	73	Jimmie Hall	6.00	2.70
❑	74	Pirates Rookies	3.00	1.35
		Bob Priddy		
		Tom Butters		
❑	75	Wayne Causey	3.00	1.35
❑	76	Checklist 1	8.00	1.60
❑	77	Jerry Walker	3.00	1.35
❑	78	Merritt Ranew	3.00	1.35
❑	79	Bob Heffner	3.00	1.35
❑	80	Vada Pinson	6.00	2.70
❑	81	All-Star Vets	10.00	4.50
		Nellie Fox		
		Harmon Killebrew		
❑	82	Jim Davenport	6.00	2.70
❑	83	Gus Triandos	6.00	2.70
❑	84	Carl Willey	3.00	1.35
❑	85	Pete Ward	3.00	1.35
❑	86	Al Downing	6.00	2.70
❑	87	St. Louis Cardinals	8.00	3.60
		Team Card		
❑	88	John Roseboro	6.00	2.70
❑	89	Boog Powell	6.00	2.70
❑	90	Earl Battey	3.00	1.35
❑	91	Bob Bailey	6.00	2.70
❑	92	Steve Ridzik	3.00	1.35
❑	93	Gary Geiger	3.00	1.35
❑	94	Braves Rookies	3.00	1.35
		Jim Britton		
		Larry Maxie		
❑	95	George Altman	3.00	1.35
❑	96	Bob Buhl	6.00	2.70
❑	97	Jim Fregosi	6.00	2.70
❑	98	Bill Bruton	3.00	1.35
❑	99	Al Stanek	3.00	1.35
❑	100	Elston Howard	6.00	2.70
❑	101	Walt Alston MG	6.00	2.70
❑	102	Checklist 2	8.00	1.60
❑	103	Curt Flood	6.00	2.70
❑	104	Art Mahaffey	6.00	2.70
❑	105	Woody Held	3.00	1.35
❑	106	Joe Nuxhall	6.00	2.70
❑	107	White Sox Rookies	3.00	1.35
		Bruce Howard		
		Frank Kreutzer		
❑	108	John Wyatt	3.00	1.35
❑	109	Rusty Staub	6.00	2.70
❑	110	Albie Pearson	6.00	2.70
❑	111	Don Elston	3.00	1.35
❑	112	Bob Tillman	3.00	1.35
❑	113	Grover Powell	3.00	1.35
❑	114	Don Lock	3.00	1.35
❑	115	Frank Bolling	3.00	1.35
❑	116	Twins Rookies	12.00	5.50
		Jay Ward		
		Tony Oliva		
❑	117	Earl Francis	3.00	1.35
❑	118	John Blanchard	6.00	2.70
❑	119	Gary Kolb	3.00	1.35
❑	120	Don Drysdale	20.00	9.00
❑	121	Pete Runnels	6.00	2.70
❑	122	Don McMahon	3.00	1.35
❑	123	Jose Pagan	3.00	1.35
❑	124	Orlando Pena	3.00	1.35
❑	125	Pete Rose	140.00	65.00
❑	126	Russ Snyder	3.00	1.35
❑	127	Angels Rookies	3.00	1.35
		Aubrey Gatewood		
		Dick Simpson		
❑	128	Mickey Lolich	20.00	9.00
❑	129	Amado Samuel	3.00	1.35
❑	130	Gary Peters	6.00	2.70
❑	131	Steve Boros	3.00	1.35
❑	132	Braves Team	8.00	3.60
❑	133	Jim Grant	6.00	2.70
❑	134	Don Zimmer	6.00	2.70
❑	135	Johnny Callison	6.00	2.70
❑	136	Sandy Koufax WS	20.00	9.00
		strikes out 15		
❑	137	Tommy Davis WS	8.00	3.60
❑	138	Ron Fairly WS	8.00	3.60
❑	139	Frank Howard WS	8.00	3.60
❑	140	World Series Summary	8.00	3.60
		Dodgers celebrate		
❑	141	Danny Murtaugh MG	6.00	2.70
❑	142	John Bateman	3.00	1.35
❑	143	Bubba Phillips	3.00	1.35
❑	144	Al Worthington	3.00	1.35
❑	145	Norm Siebern	3.00	1.35
❑	146	Indians Rookies	30.00	13.50
		Tommy John		
		Bob Chance		
❑	147	Ray Sadecki	3.00	1.35
❑	148	J.C. Martin	3.00	1.35
❑	149	Paul Foytack	3.00	1.35
❑	150	Willie Mays	100.00	45.00
❑	151	Athletics Team	8.00	3.60
❑	152	Denny Lemaster	3.00	1.35
❑	153	Dick Williams	6.00	2.70
❑	154	Dick Tracewski	6.00	2.70
❑	155	Duke Snider	30.00	13.50
❑	156	Bill Dailey	3.00	1.35
❑	157	Gene Mauch MG	6.00	2.70
❑	158	Ken Johnson	3.00	1.35
❑	159	Charlie Dees	3.00	1.35
❑	160	Ken Boyer	6.00	2.70
❑	161	Dave McNally	6.00	2.70
❑	162	Hitting Area	6.00	2.70
		Dick Sisler CO		
		Vada Pinson		
❑	163	Donn Clendenon	6.00	2.70
❑	164	Bud Daley	3.00	1.35
❑	165	Jerry Lumpe	3.00	1.35
❑	166	Marty Keough	3.00	1.35
❑	167	Senators Rookies	30.00	13.50
		Mike Brumley		
		Lou Piniella		
❑	168	Al Weis	3.00	1.35
❑	169	Del Crandall	6.00	2.70
❑	170	Dick Radatz	6.00	2.70
❑	171	Ty Cline	3.00	1.35
❑	172	Indians Team	8.00	3.60
❑	173	Ryne Duren	6.00	2.70
❑	174	Doc Edwards	3.00	1.35
❑	175	Billy Williams	12.00	5.50
❑	176	Tracy Stallard	3.00	1.35
❑	177	Harmon Killebrew	20.00	9.00
❑	178	Hank Bauer MG	6.00	2.70
❑	179	Carl Warwick	3.00	1.35
❑	180	Tommy Davis	6.00	2.70
❑	181	Dave Wickersham	3.00	1.35
❑	182	Sox Sockers	15.00	6.75
		Carl Yastrzemski		
		Chuck Schilling		
❑	183	Ron Taylor	3.00	1.35
❑	184	Al Luplow	3.00	1.35
❑	185	Jim O'Toole	6.00	2.70
❑	186	Roman Mejias	3.00	1.35
❑	187	Ed Roebuck	3.00	1.35
❑	188	Checklist 3	8.00	1.60
❑	189	Bob Hendley	3.00	1.35
❑	190	Bobby Richardson	8.00	3.60
❑	191	Clay Dalrymple	6.00	2.70
❑	192	Cubs Rookies	3.00	1.35
		John Boccabella		
		Billy Cowan		
❑	193	Jerry Lynch	3.00	1.35
❑	194	John Goryl	3.00	1.35
❑	195	Floyd Robinson	3.00	1.35
❑	196	Jim Gentile	3.00	1.35
❑	197	Frank Lary	6.00	2.70
❑	198	Len Gabrielson	4.00	1.80
❑	199	Joe Azcue	4.00	1.80
❑	200	Sandy Koufax	100.00	45.00
❑	201	Orioles Rookies	6.00	2.70
		Sam Bowens		
		Wally Bunker		
❑	202	Galen Cisco	6.00	2.70
❑	203	John Kennedy	6.00	2.70
❑	204	Matty Alou	6.00	2.70
❑	205	Nellie Fox	14.00	6.25
❑	206	Steve Hamilton	6.00	2.70
❑	207	Fred Hutchinson MG	6.00	2.70
❑	208	Wes Covington	6.00	2.70
❑	209	Bob Allen	4.00	1.80
❑	210	Carl Yastrzemski	35.00	16.00
❑	211	Jim Coker	4.00	1.80
❑	212	Pete Lovrich	4.00	1.80
❑	213	Angels Team	8.00	3.60
❑	214	Ken McMullen	6.00	2.70
❑	215	Ray Herbert	4.00	1.80
❑	216	Mike de la Hoz	4.00	1.80
❑	217	Jim King	4.00	1.80
❑	218	Hank Fischer	4.00	1.80
❑	219	Young Aces	6.00	2.70
		Al Downing		
		Jim Bouton		
❑	220	Dick Ellsworth	6.00	2.70
❑	221	Bob Saverine	4.00	1.80
❑	222	Billy Pierce	6.00	2.70
❑	223	George Banks	4.00	1.80
❑	224	Tommie Sisk	4.00	1.80
❑	225	Roger Maris	60.00	27.00
❑	226	Colts Rookies	7.00	3.10
		Jerry Grote		

	Larry Yellen		
❑ 227	Barry Latman	4.00	1.80
❑ 228	Felix Mantilla	4.00	1.80
❑ 229	Charley Lau	6.00	2.70
❑ 230	Brooks Robinson	35.00	16.00
❑ 231	Dick Calmus	4.00	1.80
❑ 232	Al Lopez MG	6.00	2.70
❑ 233	Hal Smith	4.00	1.80
❑ 234	Gary Bell	4.00	1.80
❑ 235	Ron Hunt	4.00	1.80
❑ 236	Bill Faul	4.00	1.80
❑ 237	Cubs Team	8.00	3.60
❑ 238	Roy McMillan	6.00	2.70
❑ 239	Herm Starrette	4.00	1.80
❑ 240	Bill White	6.00	2.70
❑ 241	Jim Owens	4.00	1.80
❑ 242	Harvey Kuenn	6.00	2.70
❑ 243	Phillies Rookies	30.00	13.50
	Richie Allen		
	John Herrnstein		
❑ 244	Tony LaRussa	30.00	13.50
❑ 245	Dick Stigman	4.00	1.80
❑ 246	Manny Mota	6.00	2.70
❑ 247	Dave DeBusschere	6.00	2.70
❑ 248	Johnny Pesky MG	6.00	2.70
❑ 249	Doug Camilli	4.00	1.80
❑ 250	Al Kaline	40.00	18.00
❑ 251	Choo Choo Coleman	6.00	2.70
❑ 252	Ken Aspromonte	4.00	1.80
❑ 253	Wally Post	6.00	2.70
❑ 254	Don Hoak	6.00	2.70
❑ 255	Lee Thomas	6.00	2.70
❑ 256	Johnny Weekly	4.00	1.80
❑ 257	San Francisco Giants	8.00	3.60
	Team Card		
❑ 258	Garry Roggenburk	4.00	1.80
❑ 259	Harry Bright	4.00	1.80
❑ 260	Frank Robinson	35.00	16.00
❑ 261	Jim Hannan	4.00	1.80
❑ 262	Cards Rookies	8.00	3.60
	Mike Shannon		
	Harry Fanok		
❑ 263	Chuck Estrada	4.00	1.80
❑ 264	Jim Landis	4.00	1.80
❑ 265	Jim Bunning	14.00	6.25
❑ 266	Gene Freese	4.00	1.80
❑ 267	Wilbur Wood	7.00	3.10
❑ 268	Bill's Got It	6.00	2.70
	Danny Murtaugh MG		
	Bill Virdon		
❑ 269	Ellis Burton	4.00	1.80
❑ 270	Rich Rollins	6.00	2.70
❑ 271	Bob Sadowski	4.00	1.80
❑ 272	Jake Wood	4.00	1.80
❑ 273	Mel Nelson	4.00	1.80
❑ 274	Checklist 4	8.00	1.60
❑ 275	John Tsitouris	4.00	1.80
❑ 276	Jose Tartabull	6.00	2.70
❑ 277	Ken Retzer	4.00	1.80
❑ 278	Bobby Shantz	6.00	2.70
❑ 279	Joe Koppe UER	4.00	1.80
	(Glove on wrong hand)		
❑ 280	Juan Marichal	12.00	5.50
❑ 281	Yankees Rookies	6.00	2.70
	Jake Gibbs		
	Tom Metcalf		
❑ 282	Bob Bruce	4.00	1.80
❑ 283	Tom McCraw	4.00	1.80
❑ 284	Dick Schofield	4.00	1.80
❑ 285	Robin Roberts	14.00	6.25
❑ 286	Don Landrum	4.00	1.80
❑ 287	Red Sox Rookies	50.00	22.00
	Tony Conigliaro		
	Bill Spanswick		
❑ 288	Al Moran	4.00	1.80
❑ 289	Frank Funk	4.00	1.80
❑ 290	Bob Allison	6.00	2.70
❑ 291	Phil Ortega	4.00	1.80
❑ 292	Mike Roarke	4.00	1.80
❑ 293	Phillies Team	8.00	3.60
❑ 294	Ken L. Hunt	4.00	1.80
❑ 295	Roger Craig	6.00	2.70
❑ 296	Ed Kirkpatrick	4.00	1.80
❑ 297	Ken MacKenzie	4.00	1.80
❑ 298	Harry Craft MG	4.00	1.80
❑ 299	Bill Stafford	4.00	1.80
❑ 300	Hank Aaron	90.00	40.00
❑ 301	Larry Brown	4.00	1.80
❑ 302	Dan Pfister	4.00	1.80
❑ 303	Jim Campbell	4.00	1.80
❑ 304	Bob Johnson	4.00	1.80
❑ 305	Jack Lamabe	4.00	1.80
❑ 306	Giant Gunners	35.00	16.00
	Willie Mays		
	Orlando Cepeda		
❑ 307	Joe Gibbon	4.00	1.80
❑ 308	Gene Stephens	4.00	1.80
❑ 309	Paul Toth	4.00	1.80
❑ 310	Jim Gilliam	6.00	2.70
❑ 311	Tom Brown	6.00	2.70
❑ 312	Tigers Rookies	4.00	1.80
	Fritz Fisher		
	Fred Gladding		
❑ 313	Chuck Hiller	4.00	1.80
❑ 314	Jerry Buchek	4.00	1.80
❑ 315	Bo Belinsky	6.00	2.70
❑ 316	Gene Oliver	4.00	1.80
❑ 317	Al Smith	4.00	1.80
❑ 318	Minnesota Twins	8.00	3.60
	Team Card		
❑ 319	Paul Brown	4.00	1.80
❑ 320	Rocky Colavito	14.00	6.25
❑ 321	Bob Lillis	4.00	1.80
❑ 322	George Brunet	4.00	1.80
❑ 323	John Buzhardt	4.00	1.80
❑ 324	Casey Stengel MG	15.00	6.75
❑ 325	Hector Lopez	6.00	2.70
❑ 326	Ron Brand	4.00	1.80
❑ 327	Don Blasingame	4.00	1.80
❑ 328	Bob Shaw	4.00	1.80
❑ 329	Russ Nixon	4.00	1.80
❑ 330	Tommy Harper	6.00	2.70
❑ 331	AL Bombers	150.00	70.00
	Roger Maris		
	Norm Cash		
	Mickey Mantle		
	Al Kaline		
❑ 332	Ray Washburn	4.00	1.80
❑ 333	Billy Moran	4.00	1.80
❑ 334	Lew Krausse	4.00	1.80
❑ 335	Don Mossi	6.00	2.70
❑ 336	Andre Rodgers	4.00	1.80
❑ 337	Dodgers Rookies	6.00	2.70
	Al Ferrara		
	Jeff Torborg		
❑ 338	Jack Kralick	4.00	1.80
❑ 339	Walt Bond	4.00	1.80
❑ 340	Joe Cunningham	4.00	1.80
❑ 341	Jim Roland	4.00	1.80
❑ 342	Willie Stargell	30.00	13.50
❑ 343	Senators Team	8.00	3.60
❑ 344	Phil Linz	6.00	2.70
❑ 345	Frank Thomas	6.00	2.70
❑ 346	Joey Jay	4.00	1.80
❑ 347	Bobby Wine	6.00	2.70
❑ 348	Ed Lopat MG	6.00	2.70
❑ 349	Art Fowler	4.00	1.80
❑ 350	Willie McCovey	20.00	9.00
❑ 351	Dan Schneider	4.00	1.80
❑ 352	Eddie Bressoud	4.00	1.80
❑ 353	Wally Moon	6.00	2.70
❑ 354	Dave Giusti	4.00	1.80
❑ 355	Vic Power	6.00	2.70
❑ 356	Reds Rookies	6.00	2.70
	Bill McCool		
	Chico Ruiz		
❑ 357	Charley James	4.00	1.80
❑ 358	Ron Kline	4.00	1.80
❑ 359	Jim Schaffer	4.00	1.80
❑ 360	Joe Pepitone	7.00	3.10
❑ 361	Jay Hook	4.00	1.80
❑ 362	Checklist 5	8.00	1.60
❑ 363	Dick McAuliffe	6.00	2.70
❑ 364	Joe Gaines	4.00	1.80
❑ 365	Cal McLish	6.00	2.70
❑ 366	Nelson Mathews	4.00	1.80
❑ 367	Fred Whitfield	4.00	1.80
❑ 368	White Sox Rookies	6.00	2.70
	Fritz Ackley		
	Don Buford		
❑ 369	Jerry Zimmerman	4.00	1.80
❑ 370	Hal Woodeshick	4.00	1.80
❑ 371	Frank Howard	10.00	4.50
❑ 372	Howie Koplitz	7.00	3.10
❑ 373	Pirates Team	15.00	6.75
❑ 374	Bobby Bolin	7.00	3.10
❑ 375	Ron Santo	10.00	4.50
❑ 376	Dave Morehead	7.00	3.10
❑ 377	Bob Skinner	7.00	3.10
❑ 378	Braves Rookies	10.00	4.50
	Woody Woodward		
	Jack Smith		
❑ 379	Tony Gonzalez	7.00	3.10
❑ 380	Whitey Ford	35.00	16.00
❑ 381	Bob Taylor	7.00	3.10
❑ 382	Wes Stock	7.00	3.10
❑ 383	Bill Rigney MG	7.00	3.10
❑ 384	Ron Hansen	7.00	3.10
❑ 385	Curt Simmons	10.00	4.50
❑ 386	Lenny Green	7.00	3.10
❑ 387	Terry Fox	7.00	3.10
❑ 388	A's Rookies	10.00	4.50
	John O'Donoghue		
	George Williams		
❑ 389	Jim Umbricht	10.00	4.50
	(Card back mentions		
	his death)		
❑ 390	Orlando Cepeda	10.00	4.50
❑ 391	Sam McDowell	10.00	4.50
❑ 392	Jim Pagliaroni	7.00	3.10
❑ 393	Casey Teaches	10.00	4.50
	Casey Stengel MG		
	Ed Kranepool		
❑ 394	Bob Miller	7.00	3.10
❑ 395	Tom Tresh	10.00	4.50
❑ 396	Dennis Bennett	7.00	3.10
❑ 397	Chuck Cottier	7.00	3.10
❑ 398	Mets Rookies	7.00	3.10
	Bill Haas		
	Dick Smith		
❑ 399	Jackie Brandt	7.00	3.10
❑ 400	Warren Spahn	40.00	18.00
❑ 401	Charlie Maxwell	7.00	3.10
❑ 402	Tom Sturdivant	7.00	3.10
❑ 403	Reds Team	15.00	6.75
❑ 404	Tony Martinez	7.00	3.10
❑ 405	Ken McBride	7.00	3.10
❑ 406	Al Spangler	7.00	3.10
❑ 407	Bill Freehan	10.00	4.50
❑ 408	Cubs Rookies	7.00	3.10
	Jim Stewart		
	Fred Burdette		
❑ 409	Bill Fischer	7.00	3.10
❑ 410	Dick Stuart	10.00	4.50
❑ 411	Lee Walls	7.00	3.10
❑ 412	Ray Culp	10.00	4.50
❑ 413	Johnny Keane MG	7.00	3.10
❑ 414	Jack Sanford	7.00	3.10
❑ 415	Tony Kubek	10.00	4.50
❑ 416	Lee Maye	7.00	3.10
❑ 417	Don Cardwell	7.00	3.10
❑ 418	Orioles Rookies	10.00	4.50
	Darold Knowles		
	Les Narum		
❑ 419	Ken Harrelson	14.00	6.25
❑ 420	Jim Maloney	10.00	4.50
❑ 421	Camilo Carreon	7.00	3.10
❑ 422	Jack Fisher	7.00	3.10
❑ 423	Tops in NL	125.00	55.00
	Hank Aaron		
	Willie Mays		
❑ 424	Dick Bertell	7.00	3.10
❑ 425	Norm Cash	10.00	4.50
❑ 426	Bob Rodgers	7.00	3.10
❑ 427	Don Rudolph	7.00	3.10
❑ 428	Red Sox Rookies	7.00	3.10
	Archie Skeen		
	Pete Smith		
	(Back states Archie		
	has retired)		
❑ 429	Tim McCarver	10.00	4.50
❑ 430	Juan Pizarro	7.00	3.10
❑ 431	George Alusik	7.00	3.10
❑ 432	Ruben Amaro	10.00	4.50
❑ 433	Yankees Team	40.00	18.00

No.	Card	NRMT	VG-E
❑ 434	Don Nottebart	7.00	3.10
❑ 435	Vic Davalillo	7.00	3.10
❑ 436	Charlie Neal	10.00	4.50
❑ 437	Ed Bailey	7.00	3.10
❑ 438	Checklist 6	25.00	5.00
❑ 439	Harvey Haddix	10.00	4.50
❑ 440	Bob Clemente UER	250.00	110.00
	(1960 Pittsburfh)		
❑ 441	Bob Duliba	7.00	3.10
❑ 442	Pumpsie Green	10.00	4.50
❑ 443	Chuck Dressen MG	10.00	4.50
❑ 444	Larry Jackson	7.00	3.10
❑ 445	Bill Skowron	10.00	4.50
❑ 446	Julian Javier	10.00	4.50
❑ 447	Ted Bowsfield	7.00	3.10
❑ 448	Cookie Rojas	10.00	4.50
❑ 449	Deron Johnson	10.00	4.50
❑ 450	Steve Barber	7.00	3.10
❑ 451	Joe Amalfitano	7.00	3.10
❑ 452	Giants Rookies	10.00	4.50
	Gil Garrido		
	Jim Ray Hart		
❑ 453	Frank Baumann	7.00	3.10
❑ 454	Tommie Aaron	10.00	4.50
❑ 455	Bernie Allen	7.00	3.10
❑ 456	Dodgers Rookies	10.00	4.50
	Wes Parker		
	John Werhas		
❑ 457	Jesse Gonder	7.00	3.10
❑ 458	Ralph Terry	10.00	4.50
❑ 459	Red Sox Rookies	7.00	3.10
	Pete Charton		
	Dalton Jones		
❑ 460	Bob Gibson	35.00	16.00
❑ 461	George Thomas	7.00	3.10
❑ 462	Birdie Tebbetts MG	7.00	3.10
❑ 463	Don Leppert	7.00	3.10
❑ 464	Dallas Green	10.00	4.50
❑ 465	Mike Hershberger	7.00	3.10
❑ 466	A's Rookies	10.00	4.50
	Dick Green		
	Aurelio Monteagudo		
❑ 467	Bob Aspromonte	7.00	3.10
❑ 468	Gaylord Perry	40.00	18.00
❑ 469	Cubs Rookies	10.00	4.50
	Fred Norman		
	Sterling Slaughter		
❑ 470	Jim Bouton	10.00	4.50
❑ 471	Gates Brown	10.00	4.50
❑ 472	Vern Law	10.00	4.50
❑ 473	Baltimore Orioles	15.00	6.75
	Team Card		
❑ 474	Larry Sherry	10.00	4.50
❑ 475	Ed Charles	7.00	3.10
❑ 476	Braves Rookies	14.00	6.25
	Rico Carty		
	Dick Kelley		
❑ 477	Mike Joyce	7.00	3.10
❑ 478	Dick Howser	10.00	4.50
❑ 479	Cardinals Rookies	7.00	3.10
	Dave Bakenhaster		
	Johnny Lewis		
❑ 480	Bob Purkey	7.00	3.10
❑ 481	Chuck Schilling	7.00	3.10
❑ 482	Phillies Rookies	10.00	4.50
	John Briggs		
	Danny Cater		
❑ 483	Fred Valentine	7.00	3.10
❑ 484	Bill Pleis	7.00	3.10
❑ 485	Tom Haller	7.00	3.10
❑ 486	Bob Kennedy MG	7.00	3.10
❑ 487	Mike McCormick	7.00	3.10
❑ 488	Yankees Rookies	10.00	4.50
	Pete Mikkelsen		
	Bob Meyer		
❑ 489	Julio Navarro	7.00	3.10
❑ 490	Ron Fairly	10.00	4.50
❑ 491	Ed Rakow	7.00	3.10
❑ 492	Colts Rookies	7.00	3.10
	Jim Beauchamp		
	Mike White		
❑ 493	Don Lee	7.00	3.10
❑ 494	Al Jackson	7.00	3.10
❑ 495	Bill Virdon	10.00	4.50
❑ 496	White Sox Team	15.00	6.75
❑ 497	Jeoff Long	7.00	3.10
❑ 498	Dave Stenhouse	7.00	3.10
❑ 499	Indians Rookies	7.00	3.10
	Chico Salmon		
	Gordon Seyfried		
❑ 500	Camilo Pascual	10.00	4.50
❑ 501	Bob Veale	10.00	4.50
❑ 502	Angels Rookies	7.00	3.10
	Bobby Knoop		
	Bob Lee		
❑ 503	Earl Wilson	7.00	3.10
❑ 504	Claude Raymond	7.00	3.10
❑ 505	Stan Williams	7.00	3.10
❑ 506	Bobby Bragan MG	7.00	3.10
❑ 507	Johnny Edwards	7.00	3.10
❑ 508	Diego Segui	7.00	3.10
❑ 509	Pirates Rookies	10.00	4.50
	Gene Alley		
	Orlando McFarlane		
❑ 510	Lindy McDaniel	10.00	4.50
❑ 511	Lou Jackson	10.00	4.50
❑ 512	Tigers Rookies	14.00	6.25
	Willie Horton		
	Joe Sparma		
❑ 513	Don Larsen	10.00	4.50
❑ 514	Jim Hickman	10.00	4.50
❑ 515	Johnny Romano	7.00	3.10
❑ 516	Twins Rookies	7.00	3.10
	Jerry Arrigo		
	Dwight Siebler		
❑ 517A	Checklist 7 ERR	25.00	5.00
	(Incorrect numbering		
	sequence on back)		
❑ 517B	Checklist 7 COR	15.00	3.00
	(Correct numbering		
	on back)		
❑ 518	Carl Bouldin	7.00	3.10
❑ 519	Charlie Smith	7.00	3.10
❑ 520	Jack Baldschun	10.00	4.50
❑ 521	Tom Satriano	7.00	3.10
❑ 522	Bob Tiefenauer	7.00	3.10
❑ 523	Lou Burdette UER	20.00	9.00
	(Pitching lefty)		
❑ 524	Reds Rookies	16.00	7.25
	Jim Dickson		
	Bobby Klaus		
❑ 525	Al McBean	16.00	7.25
❑ 526	Lou Clinton	16.00	7.25
❑ 527	Larry Bearnarth	16.00	7.25
❑ 528	A's Rookies	20.00	9.00
	Dave Duncan		
	Tommie Reynolds		
❑ 529	Alvin Dark MG	20.00	9.00
❑ 530	Leon Wagner	16.00	7.25
❑ 531	Los Angeles Dodgers	25.00	11.00
	Team Card		
❑ 532	Twins Rookies	16.00	7.25
	Bud Bloomfield		
	(Bloomfield photo		
	actually Jay Ward)		
	Joe Nossek		
❑ 533	Johnny Klippstein	16.00	7.25
❑ 534	Gus Bell	16.00	7.25
❑ 535	Phil Regan	16.00	7.25
❑ 536	Mets Rookies	16.00	7.25
	Larry Elliot		
	John Stephenson		
❑ 537	Dan Osinski	16.00	7.25
❑ 538	Minnie Minoso	20.00	9.00
❑ 539	Roy Face	20.00	9.00
❑ 540	Luis Aparicio	25.00	11.00
❑ 541	Braves Rookies	100.00	45.00
	Phil Roof		
	Phil Niekro		
❑ 542	Don Mincher	16.00	7.25
❑ 543	Bob Uecker	40.00	18.00
❑ 544	Colts Rookies	16.00	7.25
	Steve Hertz		
	Joe Hoerner		
❑ 545	Max Alvis	16.00	7.25
❑ 546	Joe Christopher	16.00	7.25
❑ 547	Gil Hodges MG	25.00	11.00
❑ 548	NL Rookies	16.00	7.25
	Wayne Schurr		
	Paul Speckenbach		
❑ 549	Joe Moeller	16.00	7.25
❑ 550	Ken Hubbs MEM	35.00	16.00
❑ 551	Billy Hoeft	16.00	7.25
❑ 552	Indians Rookies	16.00	7.25
	Tom Kelley		
	Sonny Siebert		
❑ 553	Jim Brewer	16.00	7.25
❑ 554	Hank Foiles	16.00	7.25
❑ 555	Lee Stange	16.00	7.25
❑ 556	Mets Rookies	16.00	7.25
	Steve Dillon		
	Ron Locke		
❑ 557	Leo Burke	16.00	7.25
❑ 558	Don Schwall	16.00	7.25
❑ 559	Dick Phillips	16.00	7.25
❑ 560	Dick Farrell	16.00	7.25
❑ 561	Phillies Rookies UER	20.00	9.00
	Dave Bennett		
	(19 ... is 18)		
	Rick Wise		
❑ 562	Pedro Ramos	16.00	7.25
❑ 563	Dal Maxvill	16.00	7.25
❑ 564	AL Rookies	16.00	7.25
	Joe McCabe		
	Jerry McNertney		
❑ 565	Stu Miller	16.00	7.25
❑ 566	Ed Kranepool	20.00	9.00
❑ 567	Jim Kaat	20.00	9.00
❑ 568	NL Rookies	16.00	7.25
	Phil Gagliano		
	Cap Peterson		
❑ 569	Fred Newman	16.00	7.25
❑ 570	Bill Mazeroski	20.00	9.00
❑ 571	Gene Conley	16.00	7.25
❑ 572	AL Rookies	16.00	7.25
	Dave Gray		
	Dick Egan		
❑ 573	Jim Duffalo	16.00	7.25
❑ 574	Manny Jimenez	16.00	7.25
❑ 575	Tony Cloninger	16.00	7.25
❑ 576	Mets Rookies	16.00	7.25
	Jerry Hinsley		
	Bill Wakefield		
❑ 577	Gordy Coleman	16.00	7.25
❑ 578	Glen Hobbie	16.00	7.25
❑ 579	Red Sox Team	25.00	11.00
❑ 580	Johnny Podres	20.00	9.00
❑ 581	Yankees Rookies	20.00	9.00
	Pedro Gonzalez		
	Archie Moore		
❑ 582	Rod Kanehl	20.00	9.00
❑ 583	Tito Francona	16.00	7.25
❑ 584	Joel Horlen	16.00	7.25
❑ 585	Tony Taylor	20.00	9.00
❑ 586	Jimmy Piersall	20.00	9.00
❑ 587	Bennie Daniels !	20.00	8.00

1965 Topps

	NRMT	VG-E
COMPLETE SET (598)	3500.00	1600.00
COMMON CARD (1-196)	2.00	.90
COMMON CARD (197-283)	2.50	1.10
COMMON CARD (284-370)	4.00	1.80
COMMON CARD (371-598)	7.00	3.10
WRAPPER (1-CENT)	125.00	55.00
WRAPPER (5-CENT)	100.00	45.00

❑ 1 AL Batting Leaders 20.00 6.00
Tony Oliva
Elston Howard
Brooks Robinson
❑ 2 NL Batting Leaders 25.00 11.00
Bob Clemente
Hank Aaron
Rico Carty
❑ 3 AL Home Run Leaders .. 40.00 18.00
Harmon Killebrew
Mickey Mantle
Boog Powell
❑ 4 NL Home Run Leaders .. 15.00 6.75
Willie Mays
Billy Williams
Jim Ray Hart
Orlando Cepeda
Johnny Callison
❑ 5 AL RBI Leaders............. 40.00 18.00
Brooks Robinson
Harmon Killebrew
Mickey Mantle
Dick Stuart
❑ 6 NL RBI Leaders............. 12.00 5.50
Ken Boyer
Willie Mays
Ron Santo
❑ 7 AL ERA Leaders 4.00 1.80
Dean Chance
Joel Horlen
❑ 8 NL ERA Leaders 20.00 9.00
Sandy Koufax
Don Drysdale
❑ 9 AL Pitching Leaders 4.00 1.80
Dean Chance
Gary Peters
Dave Wickersham
Juan Pizarro
Wally Bunker
❑ 10 NL Pitching Leaders 4.00 1.80
Larry Jackson
Ray Sadecki
Juan Marichal
❑ 11 AL Strikeout Leaders...... 4.00 1.80
Al Downing
Dean Chance
Camilo Pascual
❑ 12 NL Strikeout Leaders 8.00 3.60
Bob Veale
Don Drysdale
Bob Gibson
❑ 13 Pedro Ramos 4.00 1.80
❑ 14 Len Gabrielson .... 2.00 .90
❑ 15 Robin Roberts 10.00 4.50
❑ 16 Houston Rookie DP...... 70.00 32.00
Joe Morgan
Sonny Jackson
❑ 17 Johnny Romano .... 2.00 .90
❑ 18 Bill McCool .... 2.00 .90
❑ 19 Gates Brown 4.00 1.80
❑ 20 Jim Bunning 10.00 4.50
❑ 21 Don Blasingame .... 2.00 .90
❑ 22 Charlie Smith................. 2.00 .90
❑ 23 Bob Tiefenauer .... 2.00 .90
❑ 24 Minnesota Twins 4.00 1.80
Team Card
❑ 25 Al McBean...................... 2.00 .90
❑ 26 Bobby Knoop.................. 2.00 .90
❑ 27 Dick Bertell .... 2.00 .90
❑ 28 Barney Schultz .... 2.00 .90
❑ 29 Felix Mantilla .... 2.00 .90
❑ 30 Jim Bouton 6.00 2.70
❑ 31 Mike White .... 2.00 .90
❑ 32 Herman Franks MG........ 2.00 .90
❑ 33 Jackie Brandt .... 2.00 .90
❑ 34 Cal Koonce .... 2.00 .90
❑ 35 Ed Charles .... 2.00 .90
❑ 36 Bobby Wine..................... 2.00 .90
❑ 37 Fred Gladding................. 2.00 .90
❑ 38 Jim King .... 2.00 .90
❑ 39 Gerry Arrigo.................... 2.00 .90
❑ 40 Frank Howard 5.00 2.20
❑ 41 White Sox Rookies .... 2.00 .90
Bruce Howard
Marv Staehle
❑ 42 Earl Wilson 4.00 1.80
❑ 43 Mike Shannon 4.00 1.80
(Name in red, other
Cardinals in yellow)
❑ 44 Wade Blasingame.......... 2.00 .90
❑ 45 Roy McMillan.................. 4.00 1.80
❑ 46 Bob Lee.......................... 2.00 .90
❑ 47 Tommy Harper 4.00 1.80
❑ 48 Claude Raymond 4.00 1.80
❑ 49 Orioles Rookies.............. 4.00 1.80
Curt Blefary
John Miller
❑ 50 Juan Marichal 10.00 4.50
❑ 51 Bill Bryan .... 2.00 .90
❑ 52 Ed Roebuck..................... 2.00 .90
❑ 53 Dick McAuliffe 4.00 1.80
❑ 54 Joe Gibbon .... 2.00 .90
❑ 55 Tony Conigliaro............ 15.00 6.75
❑ 56 Ron Kline........................ 2.00 .90
❑ 57 Cardinals Team.............. 4.00 1.80
❑ 58 Fred Talbot .... 2.00 .90
❑ 59 Nate Oliver .... 2.00 .90
❑ 60 Jim O'Toole..................... 4.00 1.80
❑ 61 Chris Cannizzaro............ 2.00 .90
❑ 62 Jim Kaat UER DP 6.00 2.70
(Misspelled Katt)
❑ 63 Ty Cline.......................... 2.00 .90
❑ 64 Lou Burdette 5.00 2.20
❑ 65 Tony Kubek..................... 5.00 2.20
❑ 66 Bill Rigney MG .... 2.00 .90
❑ 67 Harvey Haddix................ 4.00 1.80
❑ 68 Del Crandall 4.00 1.80
❑ 69 Bill Virdon 4.00 1.80
❑ 70 Bill Skowron 5.00 2.20
❑ 71 John O'Donoghue .... 2.00 .90
❑ 72 Tony Gonzalez .... 2.00 .90
❑ 73 Dennis Ribant .... 2.00 .90
❑ 74 Red Sox Rookies 10.00 4.50
Rico Petrocelli
Jerry Stephenson
❑ 75 Deron Johnson 4.00 1.80
❑ 76 Sam McDowell 4.00 1.80
❑ 77 Doug Camilli .... 2.00 .90
❑ 78 Dal Maxvill..................... 2.00 .90
❑ 79A Checklist 1 .... 10.00 2.00
(61 Cannizzaro)
❑ 79B Checklist 1 .... 10.00 2.00
(61 C.Cannizzaro)
❑ 80 Turk Farrell .... 2.00 .90
❑ 81 Don Buford 4.00 1.80
❑ 82 Braves Rookies.............. 6.00 2.70
Santos Alomar
John Braun
❑ 83 George Thomas .... 2.00 .90
❑ 84 Ron Herbel .... 2.00 .90
❑ 85 Willie Smith .... 2.00 .90
❑ 86 Les Narum...................... 2.00 .90
❑ 87 Nelson Mathews .... 2.00 .90
❑ 88 Jack Lamabe.................. 2.00 .90
❑ 89 Mike Hershberger .... 2.00 .90
❑ 90 Rich Rollins 4.00 1.80
❑ 91 Cubs Team 4.00 1.80
❑ 92 Dick Howser 4.00 1.80
❑ 93 Jack Fisher .... 2.00 .90
❑ 94 Charlie Lau 4.00 1.80
❑ 95 Bill Mazeroski DP 5.00 2.20
❑ 96 Sonny Siebert 4.00 1.80
❑ 97 Pedro Gonzalez .... 2.00 .90
❑ 98 Bob Miller .... 2.00 .90
❑ 99 Gil Hodges MG 7.00 3.10
❑ 100 Ken Boyer 5.00 2.20
❑ 101 Fred Newman .... 2.00 .90
❑ 102 Steve Boros.................. 2.00 .90
❑ 103 Harvey Kuenn 4.00 1.80
❑ 104 Checklist 2.............. 10.00 2.00
❑ 105 Chico Salmon .... 2.00 .90
❑ 106 Gene Oliver................... 2.00 .90
❑ 107 Phillies Rookies............ 4.00 1.80
Pat Corrales
Costen Shockley
❑ 108 Don Mincher .... 2.00 .90
❑ 109 Walt Bond .... 2.00 .90
❑ 110 Ron Santo 6.00 2.70
❑ 111 Lee Thomas 4.00 1.80
❑ 112 Derrell Griffith .... 2.00 .90
❑ 113 Steve Barber .... 2.00 .90
❑ 114 Jim Hickman 4.00 1.80
❑ 115 Bobby Richardson........ 6.00 2.70
❑ 116 Cardinals Rookies......... 4.00 1.80
Dave Dowling
Bob Tolan
❑ 117 Wes Stock .... 2.00 .90
❑ 118 Hal Lanier 4.00 1.80
❑ 119 John Kennedy .... 2.00 .90
❑ 120 Frank Robinson.......... 35.00 16.00
❑ 121 Gene Alley.................... 4.00 1.80
❑ 122 Bill Pleis........................ 2.00 .90
❑ 123 Frank Thomas............... 4.00 1.80
❑ 124 Tom Satriano................. 2.00 .90
❑ 125 Juan Pizarro .... 2.00 .90
❑ 126 Dodgers Team 6.00 2.70
❑ 127 Frank Lary..................... 2.00 .90
❑ 128 Vic Davalillo.................. 2.00 .90
❑ 129 Bennie Daniels .... 2.00 .90
❑ 130 Al Kaline 35.00 16.00
❑ 131 Johnny Keane MG .... 2.00 .90
❑ 132 Mike Shannon WS 6.00 2.70
❑ 133 Mel Stottlemyre WS 6.00 2.70
❑ 134 Mickey Mantle WS 75.00 34.00
Mantle's Clutch HR
❑ 135 Ken Boyer WS............... 6.00 2.70
❑ 136 Tim McCarver WS......... 6.00 2.70
❑ 137 Jim Bouton WS 6.00 2.70
❑ 138 Bob Gibson WS.......... 12.00 5.50
❑ 139 World Series Summary 4.00 1.80
Cards celebrate
❑ 140 Dean Chance 5.00 2.20
❑ 141 Charlie James............... 2.00 .90
❑ 142 Bill Monbouquette .... 2.00 .90
❑ 143 Pirates Rookies............ 2.00 .90
John Gelnar
Jerry May
❑ 144 Ed Kranepool 4.00 1.80
❑ 145 Luis Tiant.................... 12.00 5.50
❑ 146 Ron Hansen .... 2.00 .90
❑ 147 Dennis Bennett .... 2.00 .90
❑ 148 Willie Kirkland .... 2.00 .90
❑ 149 Wayne Schurr .... 2.00 .90
❑ 150 Brooks Robinson........ 35.00 16.00
❑ 151 Athletics Team 4.00 1.80
❑ 152 Phil Ortega .... 2.00 .90
❑ 153 Norm Cash 5.00 2.20
❑ 154 Bob Humphreys .... 2.00 .90
❑ 155 Roger Maris............... 60.00 27.00
❑ 156 Bob Sadowski .... 2.00 .90
❑ 157 Zoilo Versalles.............. 4.00 1.80
❑ 158 Dick Sisler .... 2.00 .90
❑ 159 Jim Duffalo .... 2.00 .90
❑ 160 Bob Clemente UER.. 160.00 70.00
(1960 Pittsburfh)
❑ 161 Frank Baumann............ 2.00 .90
❑ 162 Russ Nixon .... 2.00 .90
❑ 163 Johnny Briggs .... 2.00 .90
❑ 164 Al Spangler .... 2.00 .90
❑ 165 Dick Ellsworth .... 2.00 .90
❑ 166 Indians Rookies............ 5.00 2.20
George Culver
Tommie Agee
❑ 167 Bill Wakefield................ 2.00 .90
❑ 168 Dick Green .... 2.00 .90
❑ 169 Dave Vineyard.............. 2.00 .90
❑ 170 Hank Aaron 90.00 40.00
❑ 171 Jim Roland .... 2.00 .90
❑ 172 Jimmy Piersall.............. 5.00 2.20
❑ 173 Detroit Tigers................ 4.00 1.80
Team Card
❑ 174 Joey Jay .... 2.00 .90
❑ 175 Bob Aspromonte .... 2.00 .90
❑ 176 Willie McCovey 20.00 9.00
❑ 177 Pete Mikkelsen .... 2.00 .90
❑ 178 Dalton Jones .... 2.00 .90
❑ 179 Hal Woodeshick .... 2.00 .90
❑ 180 Bob Allison 4.00 1.80
❑ 181 Senators Rookies .... 2.00 .90
Don Loun
Joe McCabe
❑ 182 Mike de la Hoz .... 2.00 .90
❑ 183 Dave Nicholson............ 2.00 .90
❑ 184 John Boozer .... 2.00 .90
❑ 185 Max Alvis...................... 2.00 .90

❑	186	Billy Cowan	2.00	.90
❑	187	Casey Stengel MG	15.00	6.75
❑	188	Sam Bowens	2.00	.90
❑	189	Checklist 3	10.00	2.00
❑	190	Bill White	5.00	2.20
❑	191	Phil Regan	4.00	1.80
❑	192	Jim Coker	2.00	.90
❑	193	Gaylord Perry	15.00	6.75
❑	194	Rookie Stars	2.00	.90
		Bill Kelso		
		Rick Reichardt		
❑	195	Bob Veale	4.00	1.80
❑	196	Ron Fairly	5.00	2.20
❑	197	Diego Segui	2.50	1.10
❑	198	Smoky Burgess	4.00	1.80
❑	199	Bob Heffner	2.50	1.10
❑	200	Joe Torre	6.00	2.70
❑	201	Twins Rookies	4.00	1.80
		Sandy Valdespino		
		Cesar Tovar		
❑	202	Leo Burke	2.50	1.10
❑	203	Dallas Green	4.00	1.80
❑	204	Russ Snyder	2.50	1.10
❑	205	Warren Spahn	30.00	13.50
❑	206	Willie Horton	4.00	1.80
❑	207	Pete Rose	130.00	57.50
❑	208	Tommy John	8.00	3.60
❑	209	Pirates Team	6.00	2.70
❑	210	Jim Fregosi	5.00	2.20
❑	211	Steve Ridzik	2.50	1.10
❑	212	Ron Brand	2.50	1.10
❑	213	Jim Davenport	2.50	1.10
❑	214	Bob Purkey	2.50	1.10
❑	215	Pete Ward	2.50	1.10
❑	216	Al Worthington	2.50	1.10
❑	217	Walter Alston MG	5.00	2.20
❑	218	Dick Schofield	2.50	1.10
❑	219	Bob Meyer	2.50	1.10
❑	220	Billy Williams	10.00	4.50
❑	221	John Tsitouris	2.50	1.10
❑	222	Bob Tillman	2.50	1.10
❑	223	Dan Osinski	2.50	1.10
❑	224	Bob Chance	2.50	1.10
❑	225	Bo Belinsky	4.00	1.80
❑	226	Yankees Rookies	4.00	1.80
		Elvio Jimenez		
		Jake Gibbs		
❑	227	Bobby Klaus	2.50	1.10
❑	228	Jack Sanford	2.50	1.10
❑	229	Lou Clinton	2.50	1.10
❑	230	Ray Sadecki	2.50	1.10
❑	231	Jerry Adair	2.50	1.10
❑	232	Steve Blass	4.00	1.80
❑	233	Don Zimmer	4.00	1.80
❑	234	White Sox Team	4.00	1.80
❑	235	Chuck Hinton	2.50	1.10
❑	236	Denny McLain	30.00	13.50
❑	237	Bernie Allen	2.50	1.10
❑	238	Joe Moeller	2.50	1.10
❑	239	Doc Edwards	2.50	1.10
❑	240	Bob Bruce	2.50	1.10
❑	241	Mack Jones	2.50	1.10
❑	242	George Brunet	2.50	1.10
❑	243	Reds Rookies	4.00	1.80
		Ted Davidson		
		Tommy Helms		
❑	244	Lindy McDaniel	4.00	1.80
❑	245	Joe Pepitone	3.50	1.55
❑	246	Tom Butters	4.00	1.80
❑	247	Wally Moon	4.00	1.80
❑	248	Gus Triandos	4.00	1.80
❑	249	Dave McNally	4.00	1.80
❑	250	Willie Mays	100.00	45.00
❑	251	Billy Herman MG	5.00	2.20
❑	252	Pete Richert	2.50	1.10
❑	253	Danny Cater	2.50	1.10
❑	254	Roland Sheldon	2.50	1.10
❑	255	Camilo Pascual	4.00	1.80
❑	256	Tito Francona	2.50	1.10
❑	257	Jim Wynn	5.00	2.20
❑	258	Larry Bearnarth	2.50	1.10
❑	259	Tigers Rookies	7.00	3.10
		Jim Northrup		
		Ray Oyler		
❑	260	Don Drysdale	20.00	9.00
❑	261	Duke Carmel	2.50	1.10
❑	262	Bud Daley	2.50	1.10
❑	263	Marty Keough	2.50	1.10
❑	264	Bob Buhl	4.00	1.80
❑	265	Jim Pagliaroni	2.50	1.10
❑	266	Bert Campaneris	10.00	4.50
❑	267	Senators Team	4.00	1.80
❑	268	Ken McBride	2.50	1.10
❑	269	Frank Bolling	2.50	1.10
❑	270	Milt Pappas	4.00	1.80
❑	271	Don Wert	2.50	1.10
❑	272	Chuck Schilling	2.50	1.10
❑	273	Checklist 4	10.00	2.00
❑	274	Lum Harris MG	2.50	1.10
❑	275	Dick Groat	5.00	2.20
❑	276	Hoyt Wilhelm	10.00	4.50
❑	277	Johnny Lewis	2.50	1.10
❑	278	Ken Retzer	2.50	1.10
❑	279	Dick Tracewski	2.50	1.10
❑	280	Dick Stuart	4.00	1.80
❑	281	Bill Stafford	2.50	1.10
❑	282	Giants Rookies	40.00	18.00
		Dick Estelle		
		Masanori Murakami		
❑	283	Fred Whitfield	2.50	1.10
❑	284	Nick Willhite	4.00	1.80
❑	285	Ron Hunt	4.00	1.80
❑	286	Athletics Rookies	4.00	1.80
		Jim Dickson		
		Aurelio Monteagudo		
❑	287	Gary Kolb	4.00	1.80
❑	288	Jack Hamilton	4.00	1.80
❑	289	Gordy Coleman	6.00	2.70
❑	290	Wally Bunker	6.00	2.70
❑	291	Jerry Lynch	4.00	1.80
❑	292	Larry Yellen	4.00	1.80
❑	293	Angels Team	10.00	4.50
❑	294	Tim McCarver	8.00	3.60
❑	295	Dick Radatz	6.00	2.70
❑	296	Tony Taylor	6.00	2.70
❑	297	Dave DeBusschere	8.00	3.60
❑	298	Jim Stewart	4.00	1.80
❑	299	Jerry Zimmerman	4.00	1.80
❑	300	Sandy Koufax	120.00	55.00
❑	301	Birdie Tebbetts MG	6.00	2.70
❑	302	Al Stanek	4.00	1.80
❑	303	John Orsino	4.00	1.80
❑	304	Dave Stenhouse	4.00	1.80
❑	305	Rico Carty	6.00	2.70
❑	306	Bubba Phillips	4.00	1.80
❑	307	Barry Latman	4.00	1.80
❑	308	Mets Rookies	6.00	2.70
		Cleon Jones		
		Tom Parsons		
❑	309	Steve Hamilton	6.00	2.70
❑	310	Johnny Callison	6.00	2.70
❑	311	Orlando Pena	4.00	1.80
❑	312	Joe Nuxhall	4.00	1.80
❑	313	Jim Schaffer	4.00	1.80
❑	314	Sterling Slaughter	4.00	1.80
❑	315	Frank Malzone	6.00	2.70
❑	316	Reds Team	10.00	4.50
❑	317	Don McMahon	4.00	1.80
❑	318	Matty Alou	8.00	3.60
❑	319	Ken McMullen	4.00	1.80
❑	320	Bob Gibson	40.00	18.00
❑	321	Rusty Staub	8.00	3.60
❑	322	Rick Wise	6.00	2.70
❑	323	Hank Bauer MG	6.00	2.70
❑	324	Bobby Locke	4.00	1.80
❑	325	Donn Clendenon	6.00	2.70
❑	326	Dwight Siebler	4.00	1.80
❑	327	Denis Menke	4.00	1.80
❑	328	Eddie Fisher	4.00	1.80
❑	329	Hawk Taylor	4.00	1.80
❑	330	Whitey Ford	35.00	16.00
❑	331	Dodgers Rookies	6.00	2.70
		Al Ferrara		
		John Purdin		
❑	332	Ted Abernathy	4.00	1.80
❑	333	Tom Reynolds	4.00	1.80
❑	334	Vic Roznovsky	4.00	1.80
❑	335	Mickey Lolich	8.00	3.60
❑	336	Woody Held	4.00	1.80
❑	337	Mike Cuellar	6.00	2.70
❑	338	Philadelphia Phillies	10.00	4.50
		Team Card		
❑	339	Ryne Duren	6.00	2.70
❑	340	Tony Oliva	20.00	9.00
❑	341	Bob Bolin	4.00	1.80
❑	342	Bob Rodgers	6.00	2.70
❑	343	Mike McCormick	6.00	2.70
❑	344	Wes Parker	6.00	2.70
❑	345	Floyd Robinson	4.00	1.80
❑	346	Bobby Bragan MG	4.00	1.80
❑	347	Roy Face	6.00	2.70
❑	348	George Banks	4.00	1.80
❑	349	Larry Miller	4.00	1.80
❑	350	Mickey Mantle	550.00	250.00
❑	351	Jim Perry	6.00	2.70
❑	352	Alex Johnson	6.00	2.70
❑	353	Jerry Lumpe	4.00	1.80
❑	354	Cubs Rookies	4.00	1.80
		Billy Ott		
		Jack Warner		
❑	355	Vada Pinson	8.00	3.60
❑	356	Bill Spanswick	4.00	1.80
❑	357	Carl Warwick	4.00	1.80
❑	358	Albie Pearson	6.00	2.70
❑	359	Ken Johnson	4.00	1.80
❑	360	Orlando Cepeda	8.00	3.60
❑	361	Checklist 5	15.00	3.00
❑	362	Don Schwall	4.00	1.80
❑	363	Bob Johnson	4.00	1.80
❑	364	Galen Cisco	4.00	1.80
❑	365	Jim Gentile	6.00	2.70
❑	366	Dan Schneider	4.00	1.80
❑	367	Leon Wagner	4.00	1.80
❑	368	White Sox Rookies	6.00	2.70
		Ken Berry		
		Joel Gibson		
❑	369	Phil Linz	6.00	2.70
❑	370	Tommy Davis	6.00	2.70
❑	371	Frank Kreutzer	7.00	3.10
❑	372	Clay Dalrymple	7.00	3.10
❑	373	Curt Simmons	7.00	3.10
❑	374	Angels Rookies	7.00	3.10
		Jose Cardenal		
		Dick Simpson		
❑	375	Dave Wickersham	7.00	3.10
❑	376	Jim Landis	7.00	3.10
❑	377	Willie Stargell	30.00	13.50
❑	378	Chuck Estrada	7.00	3.10
❑	379	Giants Team	15.00	6.75
❑	380	Rocky Colavito	18.00	8.00
❑	381	Al Jackson	7.00	3.10
❑	382	J.C. Martin	7.00	3.10
❑	383	Felipe Alou	10.00	4.50
❑	384	Johnny Klippstein	7.00	3.10
❑	385	Carl Yastrzemski	70.00	32.00
❑	386	Cubs Rookies	7.00	3.10
		Paul Jaeckel		
		Fred Norman		
❑	387	Johnny Podres	10.00	4.50
❑	388	John Blanchard	15.00	6.75
❑	389	Don Larsen	10.00	4.50
❑	390	Bill Freehan	10.00	4.50
❑	391	Mel McGaha MG	7.00	3.10
❑	392	Bob Friend	15.00	6.75
❑	393	Ed Kirkpatrick	7.00	3.10
❑	394	Jim Hannan	7.00	3.10
❑	395	Jim Ray Hart	7.00	3.10
❑	396	Frank Bertaina	7.00	3.10
❑	397	Jerry Buchek	7.00	3.10
❑	398	Reds Rookies	15.00	6.75
		Dan Neville		
		Art Shamsky		
❑	399	Ray Herbert	7.00	3.10
❑	400	Harmon Killebrew	40.00	18.00
❑	401	Carl Willey	7.00	3.10
❑	402	Joe Amalfitano	7.00	3.10
❑	403	Boston Red Sox	15.00	6.75
		Team Card		
❑	404	Stan Williams	7.00	3.10
		(Listed as Indian		
		but Yankee cap)		
❑	405	John Roseboro	15.00	6.75
❑	406	Ralph Terry	15.00	6.75
❑	407	Lee Maye	7.00	3.10
❑	408	Larry Sherry	7.00	3.10

❑ 409 Astros Rookies 10.00 4.50
Jim Beauchamp
Larry Dierker
❑ 410 Luis Aparicio 12.00 5.50
❑ 411 Roger Craig................ 15.00 6.75
❑ 412 Bob Bailey.................. 7.00 3.10
❑ 413 Hal Reniff 7.00 3.10
❑ 414 Al Lopez MG 10.00 4.50
❑ 415 Curt Flood 10.00 4.50
❑ 416 Jim Brewer 7.00 3.10
❑ 417 Ed Brinkman 7.00 3.10
❑ 418 Johnny Edwards 7.00 3.10
❑ 419 Ruben Amaro 7.00 3.10
❑ 420 Larry Jackson 7.00 3.10
❑ 421 Twins Rookies.............. 7.00 3.10
Gary Dotter
Jay Ward
❑ 422 Aubrey Gatewood 7.00 3.10
❑ 423 Jesse Gonder 7.00 3.10
❑ 424 Gary Bell 7.00 3.10
❑ 425 Wayne Causey 7.00 3.10
❑ 426 Braves Team.............. 25.00 11.00
❑ 427 Bob Saverine................ 7.00 3.10
❑ 428 Bob Shaw 7.00 3.10
❑ 429 Don Demeter................ 7.00 3.10
❑ 430 Gary Peters.................. 7.00 3.10
❑ 431 Cards Rookies............ 10.00 4.50
Nelson Briles
Wayne Spiezio
❑ 432 Jim Grant.................... 15.00 6.75
❑ 433 John Bateman.............. 7.00 3.10
❑ 434 Dave Morehead............ 7.00 3.10
❑ 435 Willie Davis 10.00 4.50
❑ 436 Don Elston.................... 7.00 3.10
❑ 437 Chico Cardenas 15.00 6.75
❑ 438 Harry Walker MG 7.00 3.10
❑ 439 Moe Drabowsky 15.00 6.75
❑ 440 Tom Tresh.................. 10.00 4.50
❑ 441 Denny Lemaster 7.00 3.10
❑ 442 Vic Power 7.00 3.10
❑ 443 Checklist 6................ 25.00 5.00
❑ 444 Bob Hendley 7.00 3.10
❑ 445 Don Lock 7.00 3.10
❑ 446 Art Mahaffey 7.00 3.10
❑ 447 Julian Javier 15.00 6.75
❑ 448 Lee Stange 7.00 3.10
❑ 449 Mets Rookies 7.00 3.10
Jerry Hinsley
Gary Kroll
❑ 450 Elston Howard............ 10.00 4.50
❑ 451 Jim Owens 7.00 3.10
❑ 452 Gary Geiger.................. 7.00 3.10
❑ 453 Dodgers Rookies........ 15.00 6.75
Willie Crawford
John Werhas
❑ 454 Ed Rakow 7.00 3.10
❑ 455 Norm Siebern 7.00 3.10
❑ 456 Bill Henry...................... 7.00 3.10
❑ 457 Bob Kennedy MG 15.00 6.75
❑ 458 John Buzhardt.............. 7.00 3.10
❑ 459 Frank Kostro 7.00 3.10
❑ 460 Richie Allen 40.00 18.00
❑ 461 Braves Rookies.......... 60.00 27.00
Clay Carroll
Phil Niekro
❑ 462 Lew Krausse UER........ 7.00 3.10
(Photo actually
Pete Lovrich)
❑ 463 Manny Mota 10.00 4.50
❑ 464 Ron Piche 7.00 3.10
❑ 465 Tom Haller.................. 15.00 6.75
❑ 466 Senators Rookies 7.00 3.10
Pete Craig
Dick Nen
❑ 467 Ray Washburn 7.00 3.10
❑ 468 Larry Brown.................. 7.00 3.10
❑ 469 Don Nottebart 7.00 3.10
❑ 470 Yogi Berra P/CO 50.00 22.00
❑ 471 Billy Hoeft 7.00 3.10
❑ 472 Don Pavletich UER 7.00 3.10
Listed as a pitcher
❑ 473 Orioles Rookies.......... 16.00 7.25
Paul Blair
Dave Johnson
❑ 474 Cookie Rojas.............. 15.00 6.75
❑ 475 Clete Boyer 10.00 4.50
❑ 476 Billy O'Dell.................... 7.00 3.10
❑ 477 Cards Rookies.......... 250.00 110.00
Fritz Ackley
Steve Carlton
❑ 478 Wilbur Wood 10.00 4.50
❑ 479 Ken Harrelson 10.00 4.50
❑ 480 Joel Horlen 7.00 3.10
❑ 481 Cleveland Indians 25.00 11.00
Team Card
❑ 482 Bob Priddy.................... 7.00 3.10
❑ 483 George Smith 7.00 3.10
❑ 484 Ron Perranoski 15.00 6.75
❑ 485 Nellie Fox P/CO 16.00 7.25
❑ 486 Angels Rookies 7.00 3.10
Tom Egan
Pat Rogan
❑ 487 Woody Woodward...... 15.00 6.75
❑ 488 Ted Wills 7.00 3.10
❑ 489 Gene Mauch MG........ 15.00 6.75
❑ 490 Earl Battey.................... 7.00 3.10
❑ 491 Tracy Stallard 7.00 3.10
❑ 492 Gene Freese 7.00 3.10
❑ 493 Tigers Rookies 7.00 3.10
Bill Roman
Bruce Brubaker
❑ 494 Jay Ritchie.................... 7.00 3.10
❑ 495 Joe Christopher............ 7.00 3.10
❑ 496 Joe Cunningham.......... 7.00 3.10
❑ 497 Giants Rookies 15.00 6.75
Ken Henderson
Jack Hiatt
❑ 498 Gene Stephens 7.00 3.10
❑ 499 Stu Miller 15.00 6.75
❑ 500 Eddie Mathews 35.00 16.00
❑ 501 Indians Rookies............ 7.00 3.10
Ralph Gagliano
Jim Rittwage
❑ 502 Don Cardwell................ 7.00 3.10
❑ 503 Phil Gagliano................ 7.00 3.10
❑ 504 Jerry Grote 15.00 6.75
❑ 505 Ray Culp 7.00 3.10
❑ 506 Sam Mele MG 7.00 3.10
❑ 507 Sammy Ellis 7.00 3.10
❑ 508 Checklist 7.................. 25.00 5.00
❑ 509 Red Sox Rookies 7.00 3.10
Bob Guindon
Gerry Vezendy
❑ 510 Ernie Banks................ 80.00 36.00
❑ 511 Ron Locke 7.00 3.10
❑ 512 Cap Peterson 7.00 3.10
❑ 513 New York Yankees 40.00 18.00
Team Card
❑ 514 Joe Azcue 7.00 3.10
❑ 515 Vern Law.................... 15.00 6.75
❑ 516 Al Weis 7.00 3.10
❑ 517 Angels Rookies 15.00 6.75
Paul Schaal
Jack Warner
❑ 518 Ken Rowe 7.00 3.10
❑ 519 Bob Uecker UER........ 30.00 13.50
(Posing as a left-
handed batter)
❑ 520 Tony Cloninger 7.00 3.10
❑ 521 Phillies Rookies............ 7.00 3.10
Dave Bennett
Morrie Stevens
❑ 522 Hank Aguirre 7.00 3.10
❑ 523 Mike Brumley SP........ 12.00 5.50
❑ 524 Dave Giusti SP 12.00 5.50
❑ 525 Eddie Bressoud............ 7.00 3.10
❑ 526 Athletics Rookies SP .. 80.00 36.00
Rene Lachemann
Johnny Odom
Jim Hunter UER
(Tim on back)
Skip Lockwood
❑ 527 Jeff Torborg SP 16.00 7.25
❑ 528 George Altman 7.00 3.10
❑ 529 Jerry Fosnow SP........ 12.00 5.50
❑ 530 Jim Maloney 15.00 6.75
❑ 531 Chuck Hiller.................. 7.00 3.10
❑ 532 Hector Lopez.............. 15.00 6.75
❑ 533 Mets Rookies SP........ 25.00 11.00
Dan Napoleon
Ron Swoboda
Tug McGraw
Jim Bethke
❑ 534 John Herrnstein............ 7.00 3.10
❑ 535 Jack Kralick SP 12.00 5.50
❑ 536 Andre Rodgers SP 12.00 5.50
❑ 537 Angels Rookies 7.00 3.10
Marcelino Lopez
Phil Roof
Rudy May
❑ 538 Chuck Dressen SP MG 15.00 6.75
❑ 539 Herm Starrette.............. 7.00 3.10
❑ 540 Lou Brock SP 50.00 22.00
❑ 541 White Sox Rookies 7.00 3.10
Greg Bollo
Bob Locker
❑ 542 Lou Klimchock.............. 7.00 3.10
❑ 543 Ed Connolly SP 12.00 5.50
❑ 544 Howie Reed.................. 7.00 3.10
❑ 545 Jesus Alou SP............ 14.00 6.25
❑ 546 Indians Rookies............ 7.00 3.10
Bill Davis
Mike Hedlund
Ray Barker
Floyd Weaver
❑ 547 Jake Wood SP 12.00 5.50
❑ 548 Dick Stigman................ 7.00 3.10
❑ 549 Cubs Rookies SP 20.00 9.00
Roberto Pena
Glenn Beckert
❑ 550 Mel Stottlemyre SP 30.00 13.50
❑ 551 New York Mets SP 30.00 13.50
Team Card
❑ 552 Julio Gotay 7.00 3.10
❑ 553 Astros Rookies 7.00 3.10
Dan Coombs
Gene Ratliff
Jack McClure
❑ 554 Chico Ruiz SP............ 12.00 5.50
❑ 555 Jack Baldschun SP 12.00 5.50
❑ 556 Red Schoendienst...... 24.00 11.00
SP MG
❑ 557 Jose Santiago 7.00 3.10
❑ 558 Tommie Sisk 7.00 3.10
❑ 559 Ed Bailey SP 12.00 5.50
❑ 560 Boog Powell SP 24.00 11.00
❑ 561 Dodgers Rookies........ 10.00 4.50
Dennis Daboll
Mike Kekich
Hector Valle
Jim Lefebvre
❑ 562 Billy Moran 7.00 3.10
❑ 563 Julio Navarro................ 7.00 3.10
❑ 564 Mel Nelson 7.00 3.10
❑ 565 Ernie Broglio SP 12.00 5.50
❑ 566 Yankees Rookies SP 15.00 6.75
Gil Blanco
Ross Moschitto
Art Lopez
❑ 567 Tommie Aaron.............. 7.00 3.10
❑ 568 Ron Taylor SP............ 12.00 5.50
❑ 569 Gino Cimoli SP 12.00 5.50
❑ 570 Claude Osteen SP 15.00 6.75
❑ 571 Ossie Virgil SP 12.00 5.50
❑ 572 Baltimore Orioles SP.. 30.00 13.50
Team Card
❑ 573 Red Sox Rookies SP.. 24.00 11.00
Jim Lonborg
Gerry Moses
Bill Schlesinger
Mike Ryan
❑ 574 Roy Sievers................ 15.00 6.75
❑ 575 Jose Pagan 7.00 3.10
❑ 576 Terry Fox SP.............. 12.00 5.50
❑ 577 AL Rookie Stars SP .. 15.00 6.75
Darold Knowles
Don Buschhorn
Richie Scheinblum
❑ 578 Camilo Carreon SP.... 12.00 5.50
❑ 579 Dick Smith SP 12.00 5.50
❑ 580 Jimmie Hall SP 12.00 5.50
❑ 581 NL Rookie Stars SP 100.00 45.00
Tony Perez
Dave Ricketts
Kevin Collins
❑ 582 Bob Schmidt SP 12.00 5.50

	NRMT	VG-E
❑ 583 Wes Covington SP	12.00	5.50
❑ 584 Harry Bright	15.00	6.75
❑ 585 Hank Fischer	7.00	3.10
❑ 586 Tom McCraw SP	12.00	5.50
❑ 587 Joe Sparma	7.00	3.10
❑ 588 Lenny Green	7.00	3.10
❑ 589 Giants Rookies SP	12.00	5.50
Frank Linzy		
Bob Schroder		
❑ 590 John Wyatt	7.00	3.10
❑ 591 Bob Skinner SP	12.00	5.50
❑ 592 Frank Bork SP	12.00	5.50
❑ 593 Tigers Rookies SP	12.00	5.50
Jackie Moore		
John Sullivan		
❑ 594 Joe Gaines	7.00	3.10
❑ 595 Don Lee	7.00	3.10
❑ 596 Don Landrum SP	12.00	5.50
❑ 597 Twins Rookies	7.00	3.10
Joe Nossek		
John Sevcik		
Dick Reese		
❑ 598 Al Downing SP	24.00	7.25

1966 Topps

	NRMT	VG-E
COMPLETE SET (598)	4000.00	1800.00
COMMON CARD (1-109)	1.50	.70
COMMON CARD (110-283)	2.00	.90
COMMON CARD (284-370)	3.00	1.35
COMMON CARD (371-446)	5.00	2.20
COMMON CARD (447-522)	9.00	4.00
COMMON CARD (523-598)	15.00	6.75
COMMON SP (523-598)	30.00	13.50
WRAPPER (5-CENT)	25.00	11.00

	NRMT	VG-E
❑ 1 Willie Mays	135.00	42.50
❑ 2 Ted Abernathy	1.50	.70
❑ 3 Sam Mele MG	1.50	.70
❑ 4 Ray Culp	1.50	.70
❑ 5 Jim Fregosi	4.00	1.80
❑ 6 Chuck Schilling	1.50	.70
❑ 7 Tracy Stallard	1.50	.70
❑ 8 Floyd Robinson	1.50	.70
❑ 9 Clete Boyer	4.00	1.80
❑ 10 Tony Cloninger	1.50	.70
❑ 11 Senators Rookies	1.50	.70
Brant Alyea		
Pete Craig		
❑ 12 John Tsitouris	1.50	.70
❑ 13 Lou Johnson	4.00	1.80
❑ 14 Norm Siebern	1.50	.70
❑ 15 Vern Law	4.00	1.80
❑ 16 Larry Brown	1.50	.70
❑ 17 John Stephenson	1.50	.70
❑ 18 Roland Sheldon	1.50	.70
❑ 19 San Francisco Giants	6.00	2.70
Team Card		
❑ 20 Willie Horton	4.00	1.80
❑ 21 Don Nottebart	1.50	.70
❑ 22 Joe Nossek	1.50	.70
❑ 23 Jack Sanford	1.50	.70
❑ 24 Don Kessinger	6.00	2.70
❑ 25 Pete Ward	1.50	.70
❑ 26 Ray Sadecki	1.50	.70
❑ 27 Orioles Rookies	1.50	.70
Darold Knowles		
Andy Etchebarren		
❑ 28 Phil Niekro	20.00	9.00
❑ 29 Mike Brumley	1.50	.70
❑ 30 Pete Rose DP	35.00	16.00
❑ 31 Jack Cullen	4.00	1.80
❑ 32 Adolfo Phillips	1.50	.70
❑ 33 Jim Pagliaroni	1.50	.70
❑ 34 Checklist 1	6.00	1.20
❑ 35 Ron Swoboda	4.00	1.80
❑ 36 Jim Hunter UER	20.00	9.00
(Stats say 1963 and 1964, should be 1964 and 1965)		
❑ 37 Billy Herman MG	4.00	1.80
❑ 38 Ron Nischwitz	1.50	.70
❑ 39 Ken Henderson	1.50	.70
❑ 40 Jim Grant	1.50	.70
❑ 41 Don LeJohn	1.50	.70
❑ 42 Aubrey Gatewood	1.50	.70
❑ 43A Don Landrum	4.00	1.80
(Dark button on pants showing)		
❑ 43B Don Landrum	20.00	9.00
(Button on pants partially airbrushed)		
❑ 43C Don Landrum	4.00	1.80
(Button on pants not showing)		
❑ 44 Indians Rookies	1.50	.70
Bill Davis		
Tom Kelley		
❑ 45 Jim Gentile	4.00	1.80
❑ 46 Howie Koplitz	1.50	.70
❑ 47 J.C. Martin	1.50	.70
❑ 48 Paul Blair	4.00	1.80
❑ 49 Woody Woodward	4.00	1.80
❑ 50 Mickey Mantle DP	200.00	90.00
❑ 51 Gordon Richardson	1.50	.70
❑ 52 Power Plus	4.00	1.80
Wes Covington		
Johnny Callison		
❑ 53 Bob Duliba	1.50	.70
❑ 54 Jose Pagan	1.50	.70
❑ 55 Ken Harrelson	4.00	1.80
❑ 56 Sandy Valdespino	1.50	.70
❑ 57 Jim Lefebvre	4.00	1.80
❑ 58 Dave Wickersham	1.50	.70
❑ 59 Reds Team	6.00	2.70
❑ 60 Curt Flood	4.00	1.80
❑ 61 Bob Bolin	1.50	.70
❑ 62A Merritt Ranew	4.00	1.80
(With sold line)		
❑ 62B Merritt Ranew	30.00	13.50
(Without sold line)		
❑ 63 Jim Stewart	1.50	.70
❑ 64 Bob Bruce	1.50	.70
❑ 65 Leon Wagner	1.50	.70
❑ 66 Al Weis	1.50	.70
❑ 67 Mets Rookies	4.00	1.80
Cleon Jones		
Dick Selma		
❑ 68 Hal Reniff	1.50	.70
❑ 69 Ken Hamlin	1.50	.70
❑ 70 Carl Yastrzemski	25.00	11.00
❑ 71 Frank Carpin	1.50	.70
❑ 72 Tony Perez	25.00	11.00
❑ 73 Jerry Zimmerman	1.50	.70
❑ 74 Don Mossi	4.00	1.80
❑ 75 Tommy Davis	4.00	1.80
❑ 76 Red Schoendienst MG	4.00	1.80
❑ 77 John Orsino	1.50	.70
❑ 78 Frank Linzy	1.50	.70
❑ 79 Joe Pepitone	2.50	1.10
❑ 80 Richie Allen	5.00	2.20
❑ 81 Ray Oyler	1.50	.70
❑ 82 Bob Hendley	1.50	.70
❑ 83 Albie Pearson	4.00	1.80
❑ 84 Braves Rookies	1.50	.70
Jim Beauchamp		
Dick Kelley		
❑ 85 Eddie Fisher	1.50	.70
❑ 86 John Bateman	1.50	.70
❑ 87 Dan Napoleon	1.50	.70
❑ 88 Fred Whitfield	1.50	.70
❑ 89 Ted Davidson	1.50	.70
❑ 90 Luis Aparicio	7.00	3.10
❑ 91A Bob Uecker TR	10.00	4.50
❑ 91B Bob Uecker NTR	40.00	18.00
❑ 92 Yankees Team	14.00	6.25
❑ 93 Jim Lonborg	4.00	1.80
❑ 94 Matty Alou	4.00	1.80
❑ 95 Pete Richert	1.50	.70
❑ 96 Felipe Alou	4.00	1.80
❑ 97 Jim Merritt	1.50	.70
❑ 98 Don Demeter	1.50	.70
❑ 99 Buc Belters	6.00	2.70
Willie Stargell		
Donn Clendenon		
❑ 100 Sandy Koufax	75.00	34.00
❑ 101A Checklist 2	16.00	3.20
(115 W. Spahn) ERR		
❑ 101B Checklist 2	10.00	2.00
(115 Bill Henry) COR		
❑ 102 Ed Kirkpatrick	1.50	.70
❑ 103A Dick Groat TR	4.00	1.80
❑ 103B Dick Groat NTR	40.00	18.00
❑ 104A Alex Johnson TR	4.00	1.80
❑ 104B Alex Johnson NTR	30.00	13.50
❑ 105 Milt Pappas	4.00	1.80
❑ 106 Rusty Staub	4.00	1.80
❑ 107 A's Rookies	1.50	.70
Larry Stahl		
Ron Tompkins		
❑ 108 Bobby Klaus	1.50	.70
❑ 109 Ralph Terry	4.00	1.80
❑ 110 Ernie Banks	30.00	13.50
❑ 111 Gary Peters	2.00	.90
❑ 112 Manny Mota	4.00	1.80
❑ 113 Hank Aguirre	2.00	.90
❑ 114 Jim Gosger	2.00	.90
❑ 115 Bill Henry	2.00	.90
❑ 116 Walter Alston MG	4.00	1.80
❑ 117 Jake Gibbs	4.00	1.80
❑ 118 Mike McCormick	4.00	1.80
❑ 119 Art Shamsky	2.00	.90
❑ 120 Harmon Killebrew	15.00	6.75
❑ 121 Ray Herbert	2.00	.90
❑ 122 Joe Gaines	2.00	.90
❑ 123 Pirates Rookies	2.00	.90
Frank Bork		
Jerry May		
❑ 124 Tug McGraw	4.00	1.80
❑ 125 Lou Brock	20.00	9.00
❑ 126 Jim Palmer UER	100.00	45.00
(Described as a lefthander on card back)		
❑ 127 Ken Berry	2.00	.90
❑ 128 Jim Landis	2.00	.90
❑ 129 Jack Kralick	2.00	.90
❑ 130 Joe Torre	4.00	1.80
❑ 131 Angels Team	6.00	2.70
❑ 132 Orlando Cepeda	5.00	2.20
❑ 133 Don McMahon	2.00	.90
❑ 134 Wes Parker	4.00	1.80
❑ 135 Dave Morehead	2.00	.90
❑ 136 Woody Held	2.00	.90
❑ 137 Pat Corrales	4.00	1.80
❑ 138 Roger Repoz	2.00	.90
❑ 139 Cubs Rookies	2.00	.90
Byron Browne		
Don Young		
❑ 140 Jim Maloney	4.00	1.80
❑ 141 Tom McCraw	2.00	.90
❑ 142 Don Dennis	2.00	.90
❑ 143 Jose Tartabull	4.00	1.80
❑ 144 Don Schwall	2.00	.90
❑ 145 Bill Freehan	4.00	1.80
❑ 146 George Altman	2.00	.90
❑ 147 Lum Harris MG	2.00	.90
❑ 148 Bob Johnson	2.00	.90
❑ 149 Dick Nen	2.00	.90
❑ 150 Rocky Colavito	8.00	3.60
❑ 151 Gary Wagner	2.00	.90
❑ 152 Frank Malzone	4.00	1.80
❑ 153 Rico Carty	4.00	1.80
❑ 154 Chuck Hiller	2.00	.90
❑ 155 Marcelino Lopez	2.00	.90
❑ 156 Double Play Combo	2.00	.90
Dick Schofield		
Hal Lanier		

	No.	Card	NRMT	VG-E
❑	157	Rene Lachemann	2.00	.90
❑	158	Jim Brewer	2.00	.90
❑	159	Chico Ruiz	2.00	.90
❑	160	Whitey Ford	25.00	11.00
❑	161	Jerry Lumpe	2.00	.90
❑	162	Lee Maye	2.00	.90
❑	163	Tito Francona	2.00	.90
❑	164	White Sox Rookies	4.00	1.80
		Tommie Agee		
		Marv Staehle		
❑	165	Don Lock	2.00	.90
❑	166	Chris Krug	2.00	.90
❑	167	Boog Powell	5.00	2.20
❑	168	Dan Osinski	2.00	.90
❑	169	Duke Sims	2.00	.90
❑	170	Cookie Rojas	4.00	1.80
❑	171	Nick Willhite	2.00	.90
❑	172	Mets Team	6.00	2.70
❑	173	Al Spangler	2.00	.90
❑	174	Ron Taylor	2.00	.90
❑	175	Bert Campaneris	4.00	1.80
❑	176	Jim Davenport	2.00	.90
❑	177	Hector Lopez	2.00	.90
❑	178	Bob Tillman	2.00	.90
❑	179	Cards Rookies	4.00	1.80
		Dennis Aust		
		Bob Tolan		
❑	180	Vada Pinson	4.00	1.80
❑	181	Al Worthington	2.00	.90
❑	182	Jerry Lynch	2.00	.90
❑	183A	Checklist 3	8.00	1.60
		(Large print on front)		
❑	183B	Checklist 3	8.00	1.60
		(Small print on front)		
❑	184	Denis Menke	2.00	.90
❑	185	Bob Buhl	4.00	1.80
❑	186	Ruben Amaro	2.00	.90
❑	187	Chuck Dressen MG	4.00	1.80
❑	188	Al Luplow	2.00	.90
❑	189	John Roseboro	4.00	1.80
❑	190	Jimmie Hall	2.00	.90
❑	191	Darrell Sutherland	2.00	.90
❑	192	Vic Power	4.00	1.80
❑	193	Dave McNally	4.00	1.80
❑	194	Senators Team	6.00	2.70
❑	195	Joe Morgan	14.00	6.25
❑	196	Don Pavletich	2.00	.90
❑	197	Sonny Siebert	2.00	.90
❑	198	Mickey Stanley	4.00	1.80
❑	199	Chisox Clubbers	4.00	1.80
		Bill Skowron		
		Johnny Romano		
		Floyd Robinson		
❑	200	Eddie Mathews	15.00	6.75
❑	201	Jim Dickson	2.00	.90
❑	202	Clay Dalrymple	2.00	.90
❑	203	Jose Santiago	2.00	.90
❑	204	Cubs Team	6.00	2.70
❑	205	Tom Tresh	4.00	1.80
❑	206	Al Jackson	2.00	.90
❑	207	Frank Quilici	2.00	.90
❑	208	Bob Miller	2.00	.90
❑	209	Tigers Rookies	4.00	1.80
		Fritz Fisher		
		John Hiller		
❑	210	Bill Mazeroski	5.00	2.20
❑	211	Frank Kreutzer	2.00	.90
❑	212	Ed Kranepool	4.00	1.80
❑	213	Fred Newman	2.00	.90
❑	214	Tommy Harper	4.00	1.80
❑	215	NL Batting Leaders	50.00	22.00
		Bob Clemente		
		Hank Aaron		
		Willie Mays		
❑	216	AL Batting Leaders	6.00	2.70
		Tony Oliva		
		Carl Yastrzemski		
		Vic Davalillo		
❑	217	NL Home Run Leaders	20.00	9.00
		Willie Mays		
		Willie McCovey		
		Billy Williams		
❑	218	AL Home Run Leaders	4.00	1.80
		Tony Conigliaro		
		Norm Cash		
		Willie Horton		
❑	219	NL RBI Leaders	12.00	5.50
		Deron Johnson		
		Frank Robinson		
		Willie Mays		
❑	220	AL RBI Leaders	4.00	1.80
		Rocky Colavito		
		Willie Horton		
		Tony Oliva		
❑	221	NL ERA Leaders	12.00	5.50
		Sandy Koufax		
		Juan Marichal		
		Vern Law		
❑	222	AL ERA Leaders	4.00	1.80
		Sam McDowell		
		Eddie Fisher		
		Sonny Siebert		
❑	223	NL Pitching Leaders	12.00	5.50
		Sandy Koufax		
		Tony Cloninger		
		Don Drysdale		
❑	224	AL Pitching Leaders	4.00	1.80
		Jim Grant		
		Mel Stottlemyre		
		Jim Kaat		
❑	225	NL Strikeout Leaders	12.00	5.50
		Sandy Koufax		
		Bob Veale		
		Bob Gibson		
❑	226	AL Strikeout Leaders	4.00	1.80
		Sam McDowell		
		Mickey Lolich		
		Dennis McLain		
		Sonny Siebert		
❑	227	Russ Nixon	2.00	.90
❑	228	Larry Dierker	4.00	1.80
❑	229	Hank Bauer MG	4.00	1.80
❑	230	Johnny Callison	4.00	1.80
❑	231	Floyd Weaver	2.00	.90
❑	232	Glenn Beckert	4.00	1.80
❑	233	Dom Zanni	2.00	.90
❑	234	Yankees Rookies	8.00	3.60
		Rich Beck		
		Roy White		
❑	235	Don Cardwell	2.00	.90
❑	236	Mike Hershberger	2.00	.90
❑	237	Billy O'Dell	2.00	.90
❑	238	Dodgers Team	6.00	2.70
❑	239	Orlando Pena	2.00	.90
❑	240	Earl Battey	2.00	.90
❑	241	Dennis Ribant	2.00	.90
❑	242	Jesus Alou	2.00	.90
❑	243	Nelson Briles	4.00	1.80
❑	244	Astros Rookies	2.00	.90
		Chuck Harrison		
		Sonny Jackson		
❑	245	John Buzhardt	2.00	.90
❑	246	Ed Bailey	2.00	.90
❑	247	Carl Warwick	2.00	.90
❑	248	Pete Mikkelsen	2.00	.90
❑	249	Bill Rigney MG	2.00	.90
❑	250	Sammy Ellis	2.00	.90
❑	251	Ed Brinkman	2.00	.90
❑	252	Denny Lemaster	2.00	.90
❑	253	Don Wert	2.00	.90
❑	254	Phillies Rookies	70.00	32.00
		Ferguson Jenkins		
		Bill Sorrell		
❑	255	Willie Stargell	20.00	9.00
❑	256	Lew Krausse	2.00	.90
❑	257	Jeff Torborg	4.00	1.80
❑	258	Dave Giusti	2.00	.90
❑	259	Boston Red Sox	6.00	2.70
		Team Card		
❑	260	Bob Shaw	2.00	.90
❑	261	Ron Hansen	2.00	.90
❑	262	Jack Hamilton	2.00	.90
❑	263	Tom Egan	2.00	.90
❑	264	Twins Rookies	2.00	.90
		Andy Kosco		
		Ted Uhlaender		
❑	265	Stu Miller	4.00	1.80
❑	266	Pedro Gonzalez UER	2.00	.90
		(Misspelled Gonzales on card back)		
❑	267	Joe Sparma	2.00	.90
❑	268	John Blanchard	2.00	.90
❑	269	Don Heffner MG	2.00	.90
❑	270	Claude Osteen	4.00	1.80
❑	271	Hal Lanier	2.00	.90
❑	272	Jack Baldschun	2.00	.90
❑	273	Astro Aces	4.00	1.80
		Bob Aspromonte		
		Rusty Staub		
❑	274	Buster Narum	2.00	.90
❑	275	Tim McCarver	4.00	1.80
❑	276	Jim Bouton	4.00	1.80
❑	277	George Thomas	2.00	.90
❑	278	Cal Koonce	2.00	.90
❑	279A	Checklist 4	8.00	1.60
		(Player's cap black)		
❑	279B	Checklist 4	8.00	1.60
		(Player's cap red)		
❑	280	Bobby Knoop	2.00	.90
❑	281	Bruce Howard	2.00	.90
❑	282	Johnny Lewis	2.00	.90
❑	283	Jim Perry	4.00	1.80
❑	284	Bobby Wine	3.00	1.35
❑	285	Luis Tiant	6.00	2.70
❑	286	Gary Geiger	3.00	1.35
❑	287	Jack Aker	3.00	1.35
❑	288	Dodgers Rookies	50.00	22.00
		Bill Singer		
		Don Sutton		
❑	289	Larry Sherry	3.00	1.35
❑	290	Ron Santo	6.00	2.70
❑	291	Moe Drabowsky	5.00	2.20
❑	292	Jim Coker	3.00	1.35
❑	293	Mike Shannon	5.00	2.20
❑	294	Steve Ridzik	3.00	1.35
❑	295	Jim Ray Hart	5.00	2.20
❑	296	Johnny Keane MG	5.00	2.20
❑	297	Jim Owens	3.00	1.35
❑	298	Rico Petrocelli	6.00	2.70
❑	299	Lou Burdette	6.00	2.70
❑	300	Bob Clemente	150.00	70.00
❑	301	Greg Bollo	3.00	1.35
❑	302	Ernie Bowman	3.00	1.35
❑	303	Cleveland Indians	5.00	2.20
		Team Card		
❑	304	John Herrnstein	3.00	1.35
❑	305	Camilo Pascual	5.00	2.20
❑	306	Ty Cline	3.00	1.35
❑	307	Clay Carroll	5.00	2.20
❑	308	Tom Haller	5.00	2.20
❑	309	Diego Segui	3.00	1.35
❑	310	Frank Robinson	30.00	13.50
❑	311	Reds Rookies	5.00	2.20
		Tommy Helms		
		Dick Simpson		
❑	312	Bob Saverine	3.00	1.35
❑	313	Chris Zachary	3.00	1.35
❑	314	Hector Valle	3.00	1.35
❑	315	Norm Cash	6.00	2.70
❑	316	Jack Fisher	3.00	1.35
❑	317	Dalton Jones	3.00	1.35
❑	318	Harry Walker MG	3.00	1.35
❑	319	Gene Freese	3.00	1.35
❑	320	Bob Gibson	25.00	11.00
❑	321	Rick Reichardt	3.00	1.35
❑	322	Bill Faul	3.00	1.35
❑	323	Ray Barker	3.00	1.35
❑	324	John Boozer	3.00	1.35
❑	325	Vic Davalillo	3.00	1.35
❑	326	Braves Team	5.00	2.20
❑	327	Bernie Allen	3.00	1.35
❑	328	Jerry Grote	5.00	2.20
❑	329	Pete Charton	3.00	1.35
❑	330	Ron Fairly	5.00	2.20
❑	331	Ron Herbel	3.00	1.35
❑	332	Bill Bryan	3.00	1.35
❑	333	Senators Rookies	3.00	1.35
		Joe Coleman		
		Jim French		
❑	334	Marty Keough	3.00	1.35
❑	335	Juan Pizarro	3.00	1.35
❑	336	Gene Alley	5.00	2.20
❑	337	Fred Gladding	3.00	1.35
❑	338	Dal Maxvill	3.00	1.35
❑	339	Del Crandall	5.00	2.20

	No.	Card	Price	Price
❑	340	Dean Chance	5.00	2.20
❑	341	Wes Westrum MG	5.00	2.20
❑	342	Bob Humphreys	3.00	1.35
❑	343	Joe Christopher	3.00	1.35
❑	344	Steve Blass	5.00	2.20
❑	345	Bob Allison	5.00	2.20
❑	346	Mike de la Hoz	3.00	1.35
❑	347	Phil Regan	5.00	2.20
❑	348	Orioles Team	8.00	3.60
❑	349	Cap Peterson	3.00	1.35
❑	350	Mel Stottlemyre	6.00	2.70
❑	351	Fred Valentine	3.00	1.35
❑	352	Bob Aspromonte	3.00	1.35
❑	353	Al McBean	3.00	1.35
❑	354	Smoky Burgess	5.00	2.20
❑	355	Wade Blasingame	3.00	1.35
❑	356	Red Sox Rookies	3.00	1.35
		Owen Johnson		
		Ken Sanders		
❑	357	Gerry Arrigo	3.00	1.35
❑	358	Charlie Smith	3.00	1.35
❑	359	Johnny Briggs	3.00	1.35
❑	360	Ron Hunt	3.00	1.35
❑	361	Tom Satriano	3.00	1.35
❑	362	Gates Brown	5.00	2.20
❑	363	Checklist 5	8.00	1.60
❑	364	Nate Oliver	3.00	1.35
❑	365	Roger Maris	40.00	18.00
❑	366	Wayne Causey	3.00	1.35
❑	367	Mel Nelson	3.00	1.35
❑	368	Charlie Lau	5.00	2.20
❑	369	Jim King	3.00	1.35
❑	370	Chico Cardenas	3.00	1.35
❑	371	Lee Stange	5.00	2.20
❑	372	Harvey Kuenn	8.00	3.60
❑	373	Giants Rookies	8.00	3.60
		Jack Hiatt		
		Dick Estelle		
❑	374	Bob Locker	5.00	2.20
❑	375	Donn Clendenon	8.00	3.60
❑	376	Paul Schaal	5.00	2.20
❑	377	Turk Farrell	5.00	2.20
❑	378	Dick Tracewski	5.00	2.20
❑	379	Cardinal Team	10.00	4.50
❑	380	Tony Conigliaro	10.00	4.50
❑	381	Hank Fischer	5.00	2.20
❑	382	Phil Roof	5.00	2.20
❑	383	Jackie Brandt	5.00	2.20
❑	384	Al Downing	8.00	3.60
❑	385	Ken Boyer	8.00	3.60
❑	386	Gil Hodges MG	8.00	3.60
❑	387	Howie Reed	5.00	2.20
❑	388	Don Mincher	5.00	2.20
❑	389	Jim O'Toole	8.00	3.60
❑	390	Brooks Robinson	45.00	20.00
❑	391	Chuck Hinton	5.00	2.20
❑	392	Cubs Rookies	8.00	3.60
		Bill Hands		
		Randy Hundley		
❑	393	George Brunet	5.00	2.20
❑	394	Ron Brand	5.00	2.20
❑	395	Len Gabrielson	5.00	2.20
❑	396	Jerry Stephenson	5.00	2.20
❑	397	Bill White	8.00	3.60
❑	398	Danny Cater	5.00	2.20
❑	399	Ray Washburn	5.00	2.20
❑	400	Zoilo Versalles	8.00	3.60
❑	401	Ken McMullen	5.00	2.20
❑	402	Jim Hickman	5.00	2.20
❑	403	Fred Talbot	5.00	2.20
❑	404	Pittsburgh Pirates	10.00	4.50
		Team Card		
❑	405	Elston Howard	8.00	3.60
❑	406	Joey Jay	5.00	2.20
❑	407	John Kennedy	5.00	2.20
❑	408	Lee Thomas	8.00	3.60
❑	409	Billy Hoeft	5.00	2.20
❑	410	Al Kaline	35.00	16.00
❑	411	Gene Mauch MG	5.00	2.20
❑	412	Sam Bowens	5.00	2.20
❑	413	Johnny Romano	5.00	2.20
❑	414	Dan Coombs	5.00	2.20
❑	415	Max Alvis	5.00	2.20
❑	416	Phil Ortega	5.00	2.20
❑	417	Angels Rookies	5.00	2.20
		Jim McGlothlin		
		Ed Sukla		
❑	418	Phil Gagliano	5.00	2.20
❑	419	Mike Ryan	5.00	2.20
❑	420	Juan Marichal	14.00	6.25
❑	421	Roy McMillan	8.00	3.60
❑	422	Ed Charles	5.00	2.20
❑	423	Ernie Broglio	5.00	2.20
❑	424	Reds Rookies	10.00	4.50
		Lee May		
		Darrell Osteen		
❑	425	Bob Veale	8.00	3.60
❑	426	White Sox Team	8.00	3.60
❑	427	John Miller	5.00	2.20
❑	428	Sandy Alomar	8.00	3.60
❑	429	Bill Monbouquette	5.00	2.20
❑	430	Don Drysdale	20.00	9.00
❑	431	Walt Bond	5.00	2.20
❑	432	Bob Heffner	5.00	2.20
❑	433	Alvin Dark MG	8.00	3.60
❑	434	Willie Kirkland	5.00	2.20
❑	435	Jim Bunning	14.00	6.25
❑	436	Julian Javier	8.00	3.60
❑	437	Al Stanek	5.00	2.20
❑	438	Willie Smith	5.00	2.20
❑	439	Pedro Ramos	5.00	2.20
❑	440	Deron Johnson	8.00	3.60
❑	441	Tommie Sisk	5.00	2.20
❑	442	Orioles Rookies	5.00	2.20
		Ed Barnowski		
		Eddie Watt		
❑	443	Bill Wakefield	5.00	2.20
❑	444	Checklist 6	8.00	1.60
❑	445	Jim Kaat	10.00	4.50
❑	446	Mack Jones	5.00	2.20
❑	447	Dick Ellsworth UER	12.00	5.50
		(Photo actually		
		Ken Hubbs)		
❑	448	Eddie Stanky MG	9.00	4.00
❑	449	Joe Moeller	9.00	4.00
❑	450	Tony Oliva	12.00	5.50
❑	451	Barry Latman	9.00	4.00
❑	452	Joe Azcue	9.00	4.00
❑	453	Ron Kline	9.00	4.00
❑	454	Jerry Buchek	9.00	4.00
❑	455	Mickey Lolich	12.00	5.50
❑	456	Red Sox Rookies	9.00	4.00
		Darrell Brandon		
		Joe Foy		
❑	457	Joe Gibbon	9.00	4.00
❑	458	Manny Jiminez	9.00	4.00
❑	459	Bill McCool	9.00	4.00
❑	460	Curt Blefary	9.00	4.00
❑	461	Roy Face	15.00	6.75
❑	462	Bob Rodgers	9.00	4.00
❑	463	Philadelphia Phillies	15.00	6.75
		Team Card		
❑	464	Larry Bearnarth	9.00	4.00
❑	465	Don Buford	9.00	4.00
❑	466	Ken Johnson	9.00	4.00
❑	467	Vic Roznovsky	9.00	4.00
❑	468	Johnny Podres	12.00	5.50
❑	469	Yankees Rookies	25.00	11.00
		Bobby Murcer		
		Dooley Womack		
❑	470	Sam McDowell	15.00	6.75
❑	471	Bob Skinner	9.00	4.00
❑	472	Terry Fox	9.00	4.00
❑	473	Rich Rollins	9.00	4.00
❑	474	Dick Schofield	9.00	4.00
❑	475	Dick Radatz	9.00	4.00
❑	476	Bobby Bragan MG	9.00	4.00
❑	477	Steve Barber	9.00	4.00
❑	478	Tony Gonzalez	9.00	4.00
❑	479	Jim Hannan	9.00	4.00
❑	480	Dick Stuart	9.00	4.00
❑	481	Bob Lee	9.00	4.00
❑	482	Cubs Rookies	9.00	4.00
		John Boccabella		
		Dave Dowling		
❑	483	Joe Nuxhall	9.00	4.00
❑	484	Wes Covington	9.00	4.00
❑	485	Bob Bailey	9.00	4.00
❑	486	Tommy John	12.00	5.50
❑	487	Al Ferrara	9.00	4.00
❑	488	George Banks	9.00	4.00
❑	489	Curt Simmons	9.00	4.00
❑	490	Bobby Richardson	12.00	5.50
❑	491	Dennis Bennett	9.00	4.00
❑	492	Athletics Team	15.00	6.75
❑	493	Johnny Klippstein	9.00	4.00
❑	494	Gordy Coleman	9.00	4.00
❑	495	Dick McAuliffe	15.00	6.75
❑	496	Lindy McDaniel	9.00	4.00
❑	497	Chris Cannizzaro	9.00	4.00
❑	498	Pirates Rookies	9.00	4.00
		Luke Walker		
		Woody Fryman		
❑	499	Wally Bunker	9.00	4.00
❑	500	Hank Aaron	125.00	55.00
❑	501	John O'Donoghue	9.00	4.00
❑	502	Lenny Green UER	9.00	4.00
		(Born: aJn. 6, 1933)		
❑	503	Steve Hamilton	15.00	6.75
❑	504	Grady Hatton MG	9.00	4.00
❑	505	Jose Cardenal	9.00	4.00
❑	506	Bo Belinsky	15.00	6.75
❑	507	Johnny Edwards	9.00	4.00
❑	508	Steve Hargan	9.00	4.00
❑	509	Jake Wood	9.00	4.00
❑	510	Hoyt Wilhelm	16.00	7.25
❑	511	Giants Rookies	9.00	4.00
		Bob Barton		
		Tito Fuentes		
❑	512	Dick Stigman	9.00	4.00
❑	513	Camilo Carreon	9.00	4.00
❑	514	Hal Woodeshick	9.00	4.00
❑	515	Frank Howard	14.00	6.25
❑	516	Eddie Bressoud	9.00	4.00
❑	517A	Checklist 7	15.00	3.00
		529 White Sox Rookies		
		544 Cardinals Rookies		
❑	517B	Checklist 7	15.00	3.00
		529 W. Sox Rookies		
		544 Cards Rookies		
❑	518	Braves Rookies	9.00	4.00
		Herb Hippauf		
		Arnie Umbach		
❑	519	Bob Friend	15.00	6.75
❑	520	Jim Wynn	15.00	6.75
❑	521	John Wyatt	9.00	4.00
❑	522	Phil Linz	9.00	4.00
❑	523	Bob Sadowski	15.00	6.75
❑	524	Giants Rookies SP	30.00	13.50
		Ollie Brown		
		Don Mason		
❑	525	Gary Bell SP	30.00	13.50
❑	526	Twins Team SP	100.00	45.00
❑	527	Julio Navarro	15.00	6.75
❑	528	Jesse Gonder SP	30.00	13.50
❑	529	White Sox Rookies	15.00	6.75
		Lee Elia		
		Dennis Higgins		
		Bill Voss		
❑	530	Robin Roberts	60.00	27.00
❑	531	Joe Cunningham	15.00	6.75
❑	532	Aurelio Monteagudo SP	30.00	13.50
❑	533	Jerry Adair SP	30.00	13.50
❑	534	Mets Rookies	15.00	6.75
		Dave Eilers		
		Rob Gardner		
❑	535	Willie Davis SP	40.00	18.00
❑	536	Dick Egan	15.00	6.75
❑	537	Herman Franks MG	15.00	6.75
❑	538	Bob Allen SP	30.00	13.50
❑	539	Astros Rookies	15.00	6.75
		Bill Heath		
		Carroll Sembera		
❑	540	Denny McLain SP	80.00	36.00
❑	541	Gene Oliver SP	30.00	13.50
❑	542	George Smith	15.00	6.75
❑	543	Roger Craig SP	35.00	16.00
❑	544	Cardinals Rookies SP	30.00	13.50
		Joe Hoerner		
		George Kernek		
		Jimy Williams UER		
		(Misspelled Jimmy		
		on card)		
❑	545	Dick Green SP	30.00	13.50
❑	546	Dwight Siebler	15.00	6.75
❑	547	Horace Clarke SP	40.00	18.00

Card	NRMT	VG-E
❑ 548 Gary Kroll SP	30.00	13.50
❑ 549 Senators Rookies	15.00	6.75
Al Closter		
Casey Cox		
❑ 550 Willie McCovey SP	90.00	40.00
❑ 551 Bob Purkey SP	30.00	13.50
❑ 552 Birdie Tebbetts MG SP	30.00	13.50
❑ 553 Rookie Stars	15.00	6.75
Pat Garrett		
Jackie Warner		
❑ 554 Jim Northrup SP	30.00	13.50
❑ 555 Ron Perranoski SP	30.00	13.50
❑ 556 Mel Queen SP	30.00	13.50
❑ 557 Felix Mantilla SP	30.00	13.50
❑ 558 Red Sox Rookies	20.00	9.00
Guido Grilli		
Pete Magrini		
George Scott		
❑ 559 Roberto Pena SP	30.00	13.50
❑ 560 Joel Horlen	8.00	3.60
❑ 561 ChooChoo Coleman SP	35.00	16.00
❑ 562 Russ Snyder	15.00	6.75
❑ 563 Twins Rookies	15.00	6.75
Pete Cimino		
Cesar Tovar		
❑ 564 Bob Chance SP	30.00	13.50
❑ 565 Jimmy Piersall SP	40.00	18.00
❑ 566 Mike Cuellar SP	35.00	16.00
❑ 567 Dick Howser SP	40.00	18.00
❑ 568 Athletics Rookies	15.00	6.75
Paul Lindblad		
Ron Stone		
❑ 569 Orlando McFarlane SP	30.00	13.50
❑ 570 Art Mahaffey SP	30.00	13.50
❑ 571 Dave Roberts SP	30.00	13.50
❑ 572 Bob Priddy	15.00	6.75
❑ 573 Derrell Griffith	15.00	6.75
❑ 574 Mets Rookies	15.00	6.75
Bill Hepler		
Bill Murphy		
❑ 575 Earl Wilson	15.00	6.75
❑ 576 Dave Nicholson SP	30.00	13.50
❑ 577 Jack Lamabe SP	30.00	13.50
❑ 578 Chi Chi Olivo SP	30.00	13.50
❑ 579 Orioles Rookies	20.00	9.00
Frank Bertaina		
Gene Brabender		
Dave Johnson		
❑ 580 Billy Williams SP	70.00	32.00
❑ 581 Tony Martinez	15.00	6.75
❑ 582 Garry Roggenburk	15.00	6.75
❑ 583 Tigers Team SP UER	125.00	55.00
(Text on back states Tigers finished third in 1966 instead of fourth.)		
❑ 584 Yankees Rookies	15.00	6.75
Frank Fernandez		
Fritz Peterson		
❑ 585 Tony Taylor	25.00	11.00
❑ 586 Claude Raymond SP	30.00	13.50
❑ 587 Dick Bertell	15.00	6.75
❑ 588 Athletics Rookies	15.00	6.75
Chuck Dobson		
Ken Suarez		
❑ 589 Lou Klimchock SP	35.00	16.00
❑ 590 Bill Skowron SP	40.00	18.00
❑ 591 NL Rookies SP	40.00	18.00
Bart Shirley		
Grant Jackson		
❑ 592 Andre Rodgers	15.00	6.75
❑ 593 Doug Camilli SP	30.00	13.50
❑ 594 Chico Salmon	15.00	6.75
❑ 595 Larry Jackson	15.00	6.75
❑ 596 Astros Rookies SP	35.00	16.00
Nate Colbert		
Greg Sims		
❑ 597 John Sullivan	15.00	6.75
❑ 598 Gaylord Perry SP	200.00	57.50

1967 Topps

	NRMT	VG-E
COMPLETE SET (609)	4600.00	2100.00
COMMON CARD (1-109)	1.50	.70
COMMON CARD (110-283)	2.00	.90
COMMON CARD (284-370)	2.50	1.10
COMMON CARD (371-457)	4.00	1.80
COMMON CARD (458-533)	6.00	2.70
COMMON CARD (534-609)	16.00	7.25
COMMON DP (534-609)	9.00	4.00
WRAPPER (5-CENT)	25.00	11.00

Card	NRMT	VG-E
❑ 1 The Champs DP	20.00	6.00
Frank Robinson		
Hank Bauer MG		
Brooks Robinson		
❑ 2 Jack Hamilton	1.50	.70
❑ 3 Duke Sims	1.50	.70
❑ 4 Hal Lanier	1.50	.70
❑ 5 Whitey Ford UER	20.00	9.00
(1953 listed as 1933 in stats on back)		
❑ 6 Dick Simpson	1.50	.70
❑ 7 Don McMahon	1.50	.70
❑ 8 Chuck Harrison	1.50	.70
❑ 9 Ron Hansen	1.50	.70
❑ 10 Matty Alou	2.50	1.10
❑ 11 Barry Moore	1.50	.70
❑ 12 Dodgers Rookies	2.50	1.10
Jim Campanis		
Bill Singer		
❑ 13 Joe Sparma	1.50	.70
❑ 14 Phil Linz	4.00	1.80
❑ 15 Earl Battey	1.50	.70
❑ 16 Bill Hands	1.50	.70
❑ 17 Jim Gosger	1.50	.70
❑ 18 Gene Oliver	1.50	.70
❑ 19 Jim McGlothlin	1.50	.70
❑ 20 Orlando Cepeda	6.00	2.70
❑ 21 Dave Bristol MG	1.50	.70
❑ 22 Gene Brabender	1.50	.70
❑ 23 Larry Elliot	1.50	.70
❑ 24 Bob Allen	1.50	.70
❑ 25 Elston Howard	4.00	1.80
❑ 26A Bob Priddy NTR	30.00	13.50
❑ 26B Bob Priddy TR	4.00	1.80
❑ 27 Bob Saverine	1.50	.70
❑ 28 Barry Latman	1.50	.70
❑ 29 Tom McCraw	1.50	.70
❑ 30 Al Kaline DP	15.00	6.75
❑ 31 Jim Brewer	1.50	.70
❑ 32 Bob Bailey	4.00	1.80
❑ 33 Athletic Rookies	5.00	2.20
Sal Bando		
Randy Schwartz		
❑ 34 Pete Cimino	1.50	.70
❑ 35 Rico Carty	4.00	1.80
❑ 36 Bob Tillman	1.50	.70
❑ 37 Rick Wise	4.00	1.80
❑ 38 Bob Johnson	1.50	.70
❑ 39 Curt Simmons	2.50	1.10
❑ 40 Rick Reichardt	1.50	.70
❑ 41 Joe Hoerner	1.50	.70
❑ 42 Mets Team	10.00	4.50
❑ 43 Chico Salmon	1.50	.70
❑ 44 Joe Nuxhall	4.00	1.80
❑ 45 Roger Maris	35.00	16.00
❑ 46 Lindy McDaniel	4.00	1.80
❑ 47 Ken McMullen	1.50	.70
❑ 48 Bill Freehan	2.50	1.10
❑ 49 Roy Face	2.50	1.10
❑ 50 Tony Oliva	6.00	2.70
❑ 51 Astros Rookies	1.50	.70
Dave Adlesh		
Wes Bales		
❑ 52 Dennis Higgins	1.50	.70
❑ 53 Clay Dalrymple	1.50	.70
❑ 54 Dick Green	1.50	.70
❑ 55 Don Drysdale	16.00	7.25
❑ 56 Jose Tartabull	4.00	1.80
❑ 57 Pat Jarvis	1.50	.70
❑ 58A Paul Schaal Green Bat	1.50	.70
❑ 58B Paul Schall Normal Colored Bat	1.50	.70
❑ 59 Ralph Terry	4.00	1.80
❑ 60 Luis Aparicio	6.00	2.70
❑ 61 Gordy Coleman	4.00	1.80
❑ 62 Frank Robinson CL	30.00	6.00
❑ 63 Cards' Clubbers	10.00	4.50
Lou Brock		
Curt Flood		
❑ 64 Fred Valentine	1.50	.70
❑ 65 Tom Haller	4.00	1.80
❑ 66 Manny Mota	2.50	1.10
❑ 67 Ken Berry	1.50	.70
❑ 68 Bob Buhl	4.00	1.80
❑ 69 Vic Davalillo	1.50	.70
❑ 70 Ron Santo	4.00	1.80
❑ 71 Camilo Pascual	2.50	1.10
❑ 72 Tigers Rookies	1.50	.70
George Korince		
(Photo actually James Murray Brown)		
John (Tom) Matchick		
❑ 73 Rusty Staub	4.00	1.80
❑ 74 Wes Stock	1.50	.70
❑ 75 George Scott	2.50	1.10
❑ 76 Jim Barbieri	1.50	.70
❑ 77 Dooley Womack	4.00	1.80
❑ 78 Pat Corrales	4.00	1.80
❑ 79 Bubba Morton	1.50	.70
❑ 80 Jim Maloney	4.00	1.80
❑ 81 Eddie Stanky MG	2.50	1.10
❑ 82 Steve Barber	1.50	.70
❑ 83 Ollie Brown	1.50	.70
❑ 84 Tommie Sisk	1.50	.70
❑ 85 Johnny Callison	2.50	1.10
❑ 86A Mike McCormick NTR	30.00	13.50
(Senators on front and Senators on back)		
❑ 86B Mike McCormick TR	4.00	1.80
(Traded line at end of bio; Senators on front, but Giants on back)		
❑ 87 George Altman	1.50	.70
❑ 88 Mickey Lolich	4.00	1.80
❑ 89 Felix Millan	2.50	1.10
❑ 90 Jim Nash	1.50	.70
❑ 91 Johnny Lewis	1.50	.70
❑ 92 Ray Washburn	1.50	.70
❑ 93 Yankees Rookies	4.00	1.80
Stan Bahnsen		
Bobby Murcer		
❑ 94 Ron Fairly	2.50	1.10
❑ 95 Sonny Siebert	1.50	.70
❑ 96 Art Shamsky	1.50	.70
❑ 97 Mike Cuellar	4.00	1.80
❑ 98 Rich Rollins	1.50	.70
❑ 99 Lee Stange	1.50	.70
❑ 100 Frank Robinson DP	14.00	6.25
❑ 101 Ken Johnson	1.50	.70
❑ 102 Philadelphia Phillies Team Card	4.00	1.80
❑ 103 Mickey Mantle CL	20.00	4.00
❑ 104 Minnie Rojas	1.50	.70
❑ 105 Ken Boyer	2.50	1.10
❑ 106 Randy Hundley	4.00	1.80
❑ 107 Joel Horlen	1.50	.70
❑ 108 Alex Johnson	4.00	1.80
❑ 109 Tribe Thumpers	5.00	2.20
Rocky Colavito		
Leon Wagner		
❑ 110 Jack Aker	4.00	1.80
❑ 111 John Kennedy	2.00	.90
❑ 112 Dave Wickersham	2.00	.90
❑ 113 Dave Nicholson	2.00	.90

❑ 114 Jack Baldschun 2.00 .90
❑ 115 Paul Casanova 2.00 .90
❑ 116 Herman Franks MG 2.00 .90
❑ 117 Darrell Brandon 2.00 .90
❑ 118 Bernie Allen 2.00 .90
❑ 119 Wade Blasingame 2.00 .90
❑ 120 Floyd Robinson 2.00 .90
❑ 121 Eddie Bressoud 2.00 .90
❑ 122 George Brunet 2.00 .90
❑ 123 Pirates Rookies 2.00 .90
Jim Price
Luke Walker
❑ 124 Jim Stewart 2.00 .90
❑ 125 Moe Drabowsky 4.00 1.80
❑ 126 Tony Taylor 2.00 .90
❑ 127 John O'Donoghue 2.00 .90
❑ 128 Ed Spiezio 2.00 .90
❑ 129 Phil Roof 2.00 .90
❑ 130 Phil Regan 4.00 1.80
❑ 131 Yankees Team 10.00 4.50
❑ 132 Ozzie Virgil 2.00 .90
❑ 133 Ron Kline 2.00 .90
❑ 134 Gates Brown 3.00 1.35
❑ 135 Deron Johnson 4.00 1.80
❑ 136 Carroll Sembera 2.00 .90
❑ 137 Twins Rookies 2.00 .90
Ron Clark
Jim Ollum
❑ 138 Dick Kelley 2.00 .90
❑ 139 Dalton Jones 4.00 1.80
❑ 140 Willie Stargell 20.00 9.00
❑ 141 John Miller 2.00 .90
❑ 142 Jackie Brandt 2.00 .90
❑ 143 Sox Sockers 2.00 .90
Pete Ward
Don Buford
❑ 144 Bill Hepler 2.00 .90
❑ 145 Larry Brown 2.00 .90
❑ 146 Steve Carlton 75.00 34.00
❑ 147 Tom Egan 2.00 .90
❑ 148 Adolfo Phillips 2.00 .90
❑ 149 Joe Moeller 2.00 .90
❑ 150 Mickey Mantle 300.00 135.00
❑ 151 Moe Drabowsky WS 4.00 1.80
❑ 152 Jim Palmer WS 8.00 3.60
❑ 153 Paul Blair WS 4.00 1.80
❑ 154 Brooks Robinson WS 4.00 1.80
Dave McNally
❑ 155 World Series Summary 4.00 1.80
Winners celebrate
❑ 156 Ron Herbel 2.00 .90
❑ 157 Danny Cater 2.00 .90
❑ 158 Jimmie Coker 2.00 .90
❑ 159 Bruce Howard 2.00 .90
❑ 160 Willie Davis 3.00 1.35
❑ 161 Dick Williams MG 3.00 1.35
❑ 162 Billy O'Dell 2.00 .90
❑ 163 Vic Roznovsky 2.00 .90
❑ 164 Dwight Siebler UER 2.00 .90
(Last line of stats
shows 1960 Minnesota)
❑ 165 Cleon Jones 4.00 1.80
❑ 166 Eddie Mathews 15.00 6.75
❑ 167 Senators Rookies 2.00 .90
Joe Coleman
Tim Cullen
❑ 168 Ray Culp 2.00 .90
❑ 169 Horace Clarke 4.00 1.80
❑ 170 Dick McAuliffe 3.00 1.35
❑ 171 Cal Koonce 2.00 .90
❑ 172 Bill Heath 2.00 .90
❑ 173 St. Louis Cardinals 4.00 1.80
Team Card
❑ 174 Dick Radatz 4.00 1.80
❑ 175 Bobby Knoop 2.00 .90
❑ 176 Sammy Ellis 2.00 .90
❑ 177 Tito Fuentes 2.00 .90
❑ 178 John Buzhardt 2.00 .90
❑ 179 Braves Rookies 2.00 .90
Charles Vaughan
Cecil Upshaw
❑ 180 Curt Blefary 2.00 .90
❑ 181 Terry Fox 2.00 .90
❑ 182 Ed Charles 2.00 .90
❑ 183 Jim Pagliaroni 2.00 .90
❑ 184 George Thomas 2.00 .90
❑ 185 Ken Holtzman 3.00 1.35
❑ 186 Mets Maulers 3.00 1.35
Ed Kranepool
Ron Swoboda
❑ 187 Pedro Ramos 2.00 .90
❑ 188 Ken Harrelson 3.00 1.35
❑ 189 Chuck Hinton 2.00 .90
❑ 190 Turk Farrell 2.00 .90
❑ 191A Willie Mays CL 10.00 2.00
214 Tom Kelley
❑ 191B Willie Mays CL 12.00 2.40
214 Dick Kelley
❑ 192 Fred Gladding 2.00 .90
❑ 193 Jose Cardenal 3.00 1.35
❑ 194 Bob Allison 3.00 1.35
❑ 195 Al Jackson 2.00 .90
❑ 196 Johnny Romano 2.00 .90
❑ 197 Ron Perranoski 3.00 1.35
❑ 198 Chuck Hiller 2.00 .90
❑ 199 Billy Hitchcock MG 2.00 .90
❑ 200 Willie Mays UER 80.00 36.00
('63 Sna Francisco
on card back stats)
❑ 201 Hal Reniff 4.00 1.80
❑ 202 Johnny Edwards 2.00 .90
❑ 203 Al McBean 2.00 .90
❑ 204 Orioles Rookies 3.00 1.35
Mike Epstein
Tom Phoebus
❑ 205 Dick Groat 3.00 1.35
❑ 206 Dennis Bennett 2.00 .90
❑ 207 John Orsino 2.00 .90
❑ 208 Jack Lamabe 2.00 .90
❑ 209 Joe Nossek 2.00 .90
❑ 210 Bob Gibson 20.00 9.00
❑ 211 Twins Team 4.00 1.80
❑ 212 Chris Zachary 2.00 .90
❑ 213 Jay Johnstone 3.00 1.35
❑ 214 Dick Kelley 2.00 .90
❑ 215 Ernie Banks 20.00 9.00
❑ 216 Bengal Belters 10.00 4.50
Norm Cash
Al Kaline
❑ 217 Rob Gardner 2.00 .90
❑ 218 Wes Parker 3.00 1.35
❑ 219 Clay Carroll 4.00 1.80
❑ 220 Jim Ray Hart 3.00 1.35
❑ 221 Woody Fryman 4.00 1.80
❑ 222 Reds Rookies 3.00 1.35
Darrell Osteen
Lee May
❑ 223 Mike Ryan 4.00 1.80
❑ 224 Walt Bond 2.00 .90
❑ 225 Mel Stottlemyre 3.00 1.35
❑ 226 Julian Javier 3.00 1.35
❑ 227 Paul Lindblad 2.00 .90
❑ 228 Gil Hodges MG 5.00 2.20
❑ 229 Larry Jackson 2.00 .90
❑ 230 Boog Powell 6.00 2.70
❑ 231 John Bateman 2.00 .90
❑ 232 Don Buford 2.00 .90
❑ 233 AL ERA Leaders 4.00 1.80
Gary Peters
Joel Horlen
Steve Hargan
❑ 234 NL ERA Leaders 15.00 6.75
Sandy Koufax
Mike Cuellar
Juan Marichal
❑ 235 AL Pitching Leaders 6.00 2.70
Jim Kaat
Denny McLain
Earl Wilson
❑ 236 NL Pitching Leaders 25.00 11.00
Sandy Koufax
Juan Marichal
Bob Gibson
Gaylord Perry
❑ 237 AL Strikeout Leaders 6.00 2.70
Sam McDowell
Jim Kaat
Earl Wilson
❑ 238 NL Strikeout Leaders 12.00 5.50
Sandy Koufax
Jim Bunning
Bob Veale
❑ 239 AL Batting Leaders 9.00 4.00
Frank Robinson
Tony Oliva
Al Kaline
❑ 240 NL Batting Leaders 6.00 2.70
Matty Alou
Felipe Alou
Rico Carty
❑ 241 AL RBI Leaders 9.00 4.00
Frank Robinson
Harmon Killebrew
Boog Powell
❑ 242 NL RBI Leaders 25.00 11.00
Hank Aaron
Bob Clemente
Richie Allen
❑ 243 AL Home Run Leaders 9.00 4.00
Frank Robinson
Harmon Killebrew
Boog Powell
❑ 244 NL Home Run Leaders 20.00 9.00
Hank Aaron
Richie Allen
Willie Mays
❑ 245 Curt Flood 3.00 1.35
❑ 246 Jim Perry 3.00 1.35
❑ 247 Jerry Lumpe 2.00 .90
❑ 248 Gene Mauch MG 3.00 1.35
❑ 249 Nick Willhite 2.00 .90
❑ 250 Hank Aaron UER 80.00 36.00
(Second 1961 in stats
should be 1962)
❑ 251 Woody Held 2.00 .90
❑ 252 Bob Bolin 2.00 .90
❑ 253 Indians Rookies 2.00 .90
Bill Davis
Gus Gil
❑ 254 Milt Pappas 3.00 1.35
(No facsimile auto-
graph on card front)
❑ 255 Frank Howard 4.00 1.80
❑ 256 Bob Hendley 2.00 .90
❑ 257 Charlie Smith 2.00 .90
❑ 258 Lee Maye 2.00 .90
❑ 259 Don Dennis 2.00 .90
❑ 260 Jim Lefebvre 3.00 1.35
❑ 261 John Wyatt 2.00 .90
❑ 262 Athletics Team 4.00 1.80
❑ 263 Hank Aguirre 2.00 .90
❑ 264 Ron Swoboda 3.00 1.35
❑ 265 Lou Burdette 3.00 1.35
❑ 266 Pitt Power 5.00 2.20
Willie Stargell
Donn Clendenon
❑ 267 Don Schwall 2.00 .90
❑ 268 Johnny Briggs 2.00 .90
❑ 269 Don Nottebart 2.00 .90
❑ 270 Zoilo Versalles 2.00 .90
❑ 271 Eddie Watt 2.00 .90
❑ 272 Cubs Rookies 4.00 1.80
Bill Connors
Dave Dowling
❑ 273 Dick Lines 2.00 .90
❑ 274 Bob Aspromonte 2.00 .90
❑ 275 Fred Whitfield 2.00 .90
❑ 276 Bruce Brubaker 2.00 .90
❑ 277 Steve Whitaker 4.00 1.80
❑ 278 Jim Kaat CL 30.00 6.00
❑ 279 Frank Linzy 2.00 .90
❑ 280 Tony Conigliaro 10.00 4.50
❑ 281 Bob Rodgers 2.00 .90
❑ 282 John Odom 2.00 .90
❑ 283 Gene Alley 4.00 1.80
❑ 284 Johnny Podres 3.00 1.35
❑ 285 Lou Brock 20.00 9.00
❑ 286 Wayne Causey 2.50 1.10
❑ 287 Mets Rookies 2.50 1.10
Greg Goossen
Bart Shirley
❑ 288 Denny Lemaster 2.50 1.10
❑ 289 Tom Tresh 3.50 1.55
❑ 290 Bill White 3.00 1.35
❑ 291 Jim Hannan 2.50 1.10
❑ 292 Don Pavletich 2.50 1.10

No.	Player	NRMT	VG-E
❑ 293	Ed Kirkpatrick	2.50	1.10
❑ 294	Walter Alston MG	4.00	1.80
❑ 295	Sam McDowell	5.00	2.20
❑ 296	Glenn Beckert	5.00	2.20
❑ 297	Dave Morehead	5.00	2.20
❑ 298	Ron Davis	2.50	1.10
❑ 299	Norm Siebern	2.50	1.10
❑ 300	Jim Kaat	6.00	2.70
❑ 301	Jesse Gonder	2.50	1.10
❑ 302	Orioles Team	6.00	2.70
❑ 303	Gil Blanco	2.50	1.10
❑ 304	Phil Gagliano	2.50	1.10
❑ 305	Earl Wilson	5.00	2.20
❑ 306	Bud Harrelson	6.00	2.70
❑ 307	Jim Beauchamp	2.50	1.10
❑ 308	Al Downing	5.00	2.20
❑ 309	Hurlers Beware	5.00	2.20
	Johnny Callison		
	Richie Allen		
❑ 310	Gary Peters	2.50	1.10
❑ 311	Ed Brinkman	2.50	1.10
❑ 312	Don Mincher	2.50	1.10
❑ 313	Bob Lee	2.50	1.10
❑ 314	Red Sox Rookies	8.00	3.60
	Mike Andrews		
	Reggie Smith		
❑ 315	Billy Williams	10.00	4.50
❑ 316	Jack Kralick	2.50	1.10
❑ 317	Cesar Tovar	3.00	1.35
❑ 318	Dave Giusti	2.50	1.10
❑ 319	Paul Blair	5.00	2.20
❑ 320	Gaylord Perry	15.00	6.75
❑ 321	Mayo Smith MG	2.50	1.10
❑ 322	Jose Pagan	2.50	1.10
❑ 323	Mike Hershberger	2.50	1.10
❑ 324	Hal Woodeshick	2.50	1.10
❑ 325	Chico Cardenas	5.00	2.20
❑ 326	Bob Uecker	10.00	4.50
❑ 327	California Angels	6.00	2.70
	Team Card		
❑ 328	Clete Boyer UER	5.00	2.20
	(Stats only go up		
	through 1965)		
❑ 329	Charlie Lau	5.00	2.20
❑ 330	Claude Osteen	5.00	2.20
❑ 331	Joe Foy	5.00	2.20
❑ 332	Jesus Alou	2.50	1.10
❑ 333	Ferguson Jenkins	20.00	9.00
❑ 334	Twin Terrors	6.00	2.70
	Bob Allison		
	Harmon Killebrew		
❑ 335	Bob Veale	5.00	2.20
❑ 336	Joe Azcue	2.50	1.10
❑ 337	Joe Morgan	15.00	6.75
❑ 338	Bob Locker	2.50	1.10
❑ 339	Chico Ruiz	2.50	1.10
❑ 340	Joe Pepitone	3.50	1.55
❑ 341	Giants Rookies	2.50	1.10
	Dick Dietz		
	Bill Sorrell		
❑ 342	Hank Fischer	2.50	1.10
❑ 343	Tom Satriano	2.50	1.10
❑ 344	Ossie Chavarria	2.50	1.10
❑ 345	Stu Miller	5.00	2.20
❑ 346	Jim Hickman	2.50	1.10
❑ 347	Grady Hatton MG	2.50	1.10
❑ 348	Tug McGraw	3.00	1.35
❑ 349	Bob Chance	2.50	1.10
❑ 350	Joe Torre	5.00	2.20
❑ 351	Vern Law	5.00	2.20
❑ 352	Ray Oyler	2.50	1.10
❑ 353	Bill McCool	2.50	1.10
❑ 354	Cubs Team	6.00	2.70
❑ 355	Carl Yastrzemski	50.00	22.00
❑ 356	Larry Jaster	2.50	1.10
❑ 357	Bill Skowron	3.00	1.35
❑ 358	Ruben Amaro	2.50	1.10
❑ 359	Dick Ellsworth	2.50	1.10
❑ 360	Leon Wagner	2.50	1.10
❑ 361	Roberto Clemente CL	15.00	3.00
❑ 362	Darold Knowles	2.50	1.10
❑ 363	Dave Johnson	5.00	2.20
❑ 364	Claude Raymond	2.50	1.10
❑ 365	John Roseboro	5.00	2.20
❑ 366	Andy Kosco	2.50	1.10
❑ 367	Angels Rookies	2.50	1.10
	Bill Kelso		
	Don Wallace		
❑ 368	Jack Hiatt	2.50	1.10
❑ 369	Jim Hunter	15.00	6.75
❑ 370	Tommy Davis	3.00	1.35
❑ 371	Jim Lonborg	8.00	3.60
❑ 372	Mike de la Hoz	4.00	1.80
❑ 373	White Sox Rookies DP	4.00	1.80
	Duane Josephson		
	Fred Klages		
❑ 374A	Mel Queen ERR DP	20.00	9.00
	(Incomplete stat		
	line on back)		
❑ 374B	Mel Queen COR DP	4.00	1.80
	(Complete stat		
	line on back)		
❑ 375	Jake Gibbs	8.00	3.60
❑ 376	Don Lock DP	4.00	1.80
❑ 377	Luis Tiant	8.00	3.60
❑ 378	Detroit Tigers	8.00	3.60
	Team Card UER		
	(Willie Horton with		
	262 RBI's in 1966)		
❑ 379	Jerry May DP	4.00	1.80
❑ 380	Dean Chance DP	4.00	1.80
❑ 381	Dick Schofield DP	4.00	1.80
❑ 382	Dave McNally	8.00	3.60
❑ 383	Ken Henderson DP	4.00	1.80
❑ 384	Cardinals Rookies	4.00	1.80
	Jim Cosman		
	Dick Hughes		
❑ 385	Jim Fregosi	8.00	3.60
	(Batting wrong)		
❑ 386	Dick Selma DP	4.00	1.80
❑ 387	Cap Peterson DP	4.00	1.80
❑ 388	Arnold Earley DP	4.00	1.80
❑ 389	Alvin Dark MG DP	8.00	3.60
❑ 390	Jim Wynn DP	8.00	3.60
❑ 391	Wilbur Wood DP	8.00	3.60
❑ 392	Tommy Harper DP	8.00	3.60
❑ 393	Jim Bouton DP	8.00	3.60
❑ 394	Jake Wood DP	4.00	1.80
❑ 395	Chris Short	8.00	3.60
❑ 396	Atlanta Aces	4.00	1.80
	Denis Menke		
	Tony Cloninger		
❑ 397	Willie Smith DP	4.00	1.80
❑ 398	Jeff Torborg	8.00	3.60
❑ 399	Al Worthington DP	4.00	1.80
❑ 400	Bob Clemente DP	100.00	45.00
❑ 401	Jim Coates	4.00	1.80
❑ 402A	Phillies Rookies DP	20.00	9.00
	Grant Jackson		
	Billy Wilson		
	Incomplete stat line		
❑ 402B	Phillies Rookies DP	8.00	3.60
	Grant Jackson		
	Billy Wilson		
❑ 403	Dick Nen	4.00	1.80
❑ 404	Nelson Briles	8.00	3.60
❑ 405	Russ Snyder	4.00	1.80
❑ 406	Lee Elia DP	4.00	1.80
❑ 407	Reds Team	8.00	3.60
❑ 408	Jim Northrup DP	8.00	3.60
❑ 409	Ray Sadecki	4.00	1.80
❑ 410	Lou Johnson DP	4.00	1.80
❑ 411	Dick Howser DP	4.00	1.80
❑ 412	Astros Rookies	8.00	3.60
	Norm Miller		
	Doug Rader		
❑ 413	Jerry Grote	4.00	1.80
❑ 414	Casey Cox	4.00	1.80
❑ 415	Sonny Jackson	4.00	1.80
❑ 416	Roger Repoz	4.00	1.80
❑ 417A	Bob Bruce ERR DP	30.00	13.50
	(RBAVES on back)		
❑ 417B	Bob Bruce COR DP	4.00	1.80
❑ 418	Sam Mele MG	4.00	1.80
❑ 419	Don Kessinger DP	8.00	3.60
❑ 420	Denny McLain	6.00	2.70
❑ 421	Dal Maxvill DP	4.00	1.80
❑ 422	Hoyt Wilhelm	10.00	4.50
❑ 423	Fence Busters DP	25.00	11.00
	Willie Mays		
	Willie McCovey		
❑ 424	Pedro Gonzalez	4.00	1.80
❑ 425	Pete Mikkelsen	4.00	1.80
❑ 426	Lou Clinton	4.00	1.80
❑ 427A	Ruben Gomez ERR DP	20.00	9.00
	(Incomplete stat		
	line on back)		
❑ 427B	Ruben Gomez COR DP	4.00	1.80
	(Complete stat		
	line on back)		
❑ 428	Dodgers Rookies DP	8.00	3.60
	Tom Hutton		
	Gene Michael		
❑ 429	Garry Roggenburk DP	4.00	1.80
❑ 430	Pete Rose	75.00	34.00
❑ 431	Ted Uhlaender	4.00	1.80
❑ 432	Jimmie Hall DP	4.00	1.80
❑ 433	Al Luplow DP	4.00	1.80
❑ 434	Eddie Fisher DP	4.00	1.80
❑ 435	Mack Jones DP	4.00	1.80
❑ 436	Pete Ward	4.00	1.80
❑ 437	Senators Team	8.00	3.60
❑ 438	Chuck Dobson	4.00	1.80
❑ 439	Byron Browne	4.00	1.80
❑ 440	Steve Hargan	4.00	1.80
❑ 441	Jim Davenport	4.00	1.80
❑ 442	Yankees Rookies DP	8.00	3.60
	Bill Robinson		
	Joe Verbanic		
❑ 443	Tito Francona DP	4.00	1.80
❑ 444	George Smith	4.00	1.80
❑ 445	Don Sutton	25.00	11.00
❑ 446	Russ Nixon DP	4.00	1.80
❑ 447A	Bo Belinsky ERR DP	5.00	2.20
	(Incomplete stat		
	line on back)		
❑ 447B	Bo Belinsky COR DP	8.00	3.60
	(Complete stat		
	line on back)		
❑ 448	Harry Walker DP MG	4.00	1.80
❑ 449	Orlando Pena	4.00	1.80
❑ 450	Richie Allen	9.00	4.00
❑ 451	Fred Newman DP	4.00	1.80
❑ 452	Ed Kranepool	8.00	3.60
❑ 453	Aurelio Monteagudo DP	4.00	1.80
❑ 454A	Juan Marichal CL	8.00	1.60
	Missing left ear		
❑ 454B	Juan Marichal CL	8.00	1.60
	left ear showing		
❑ 455	Tommie Agee	8.00	3.60
❑ 456	Phil Niekro	16.00	7.25
❑ 457	Andy Etchebarren DP	8.00	3.60
❑ 458	Lee Thomas	6.00	2.70
❑ 459	Senators Rookies	6.00	2.70
	Dick Bosman		
	Pete Craig		
❑ 460	Harmon Killebrew	60.00	27.00
❑ 461	Bob Miller	6.00	2.70
❑ 462	Bob Barton	6.00	2.70
❑ 463	Hill Aces	12.00	5.50
	Sam McDowell		
	Sonny Siebert		
❑ 464	Dan Coombs	6.00	2.70
❑ 465	Willie Horton	12.00	5.50
❑ 466	Bobby Wine	6.00	2.70
❑ 467	Jim O'Toole	6.00	2.70
❑ 468	Ralph Houk MG	6.00	2.70
❑ 469	Len Gabrielson	6.00	2.70
❑ 470	Bob Shaw	6.00	2.70
❑ 471	Rene Lachemann	6.00	2.70
❑ 472	Rookies Pirates	6.00	2.70
	John Gelnar		
	George Spriggs		
❑ 473	Jose Santiago	6.00	2.70
❑ 474	Bob Tolan	6.00	2.70
❑ 475	Jim Palmer	80.00	36.00
❑ 476	Tony Perez SP	70.00	32.00
❑ 477	Braves Team	15.00	6.75
❑ 478	Bob Humphreys	6.00	2.70
❑ 479	Gary Bell	6.00	2.70
❑ 480	Willie McCovey	35.00	16.00
❑ 481	Leo Durocher MG	15.00	6.75
❑ 482	Bill Monbouquette	6.00	2.70
❑ 483	Jim Landis	6.00	2.70
❑ 484	Jerry Adair	6.00	2.70
❑ 485	Tim McCarver	20.00	9.00

❑ 486 Twins Rookies 6.00 2.70
Rich Reese
Bill Whitby
❑ 487 Tommie Reynolds 6.00 2.70
❑ 488 Gerry Arrigo 6.00 2.70
❑ 489 Doug Clemens 6.00 2.70
❑ 490 Tony Cloninger 6.00 2.70
❑ 491 Sam Bowens 6.00 2.70
❑ 492 Pittsburgh Pirates 15.00 6.75
Team Card
❑ 493 Phil Ortega 6.00 2.70
❑ 494 Bill Rigney MG 6.00 2.70
❑ 495 Fritz Peterson 6.00 2.70
❑ 496 Orlando McFarlane 6.00 2.70
❑ 497 Ron Campbell 6.00 2.70
❑ 498 Larry Dierker 12.00 5.50
❑ 499 Indians Rookies 6.00 2.70
George Culver
Jose Vidal
❑ 500 Juan Marichal 25.00 11.00
❑ 501 Jerry Zimmerman 6.00 2.70
❑ 502 Derrell Griffith 6.00 2.70
❑ 503 Los Angeles Dodgers 15.00 6.75
Team Card
❑ 504 Orlando Martinez 6.00 2.70
❑ 505 Tommy Helms 12.00 5.50
❑ 506 Smoky Burgess 6.00 2.70
❑ 507 Orioles Rookies 6.00 2.70
Ed Barnowski
Larry Haney
❑ 508 Dick Hall 6.00 2.70
❑ 509 Jim King 6.00 2.70
❑ 510 Bill Mazeroski 15.00 6.75
❑ 511 Don Wert 6.00 2.70
❑ 512 Red Schoendienst MG 15.00 6.75
❑ 513 Marcelino Lopez 6.00 2.70
❑ 514 John Werhas 6.00 2.70
❑ 515 Bert Campaneris 9.00 4.00
❑ 516 Giants Team 15.00 6.75
❑ 517 Fred Talbot 6.00 2.70
❑ 518 Denis Menke 6.00 2.70
❑ 519 Ted Davidson 6.00 2.70
❑ 520 Max Alvis 6.00 2.70
❑ 521 Bird Bombers 12.00 5.50
Boog Powell
Curt Blefary
❑ 522 John Stephenson 6.00 2.70
❑ 523 Jim Merritt 6.00 2.70
❑ 524 Felix Mantilla 6.00 2.70
❑ 525 Ron Hunt 6.00 2.70
❑ 526 Tigers Rookies 6.00 2.70
Pat Dobson
George Korince
(See 67T-72)
❑ 527 Dennis Ribant 6.00 2.70
❑ 528 Rico Petrocelli 10.00 4.50
❑ 529 Gary Wagner 6.00 2.70
❑ 530 Felipe Alou 12.00 5.50
❑ 531 Brooks Robinson CL .. 14.00 2.80
❑ 532 Jim Hicks 6.00 2.70
❑ 533 Jack Fisher 6.00 2.70
❑ 534 Hank Bauer MG DP 9.00 4.00
❑ 535 Donn Clendenon 18.00 8.00
❑ 536 Cubs Rookies 35.00 16.00
Joe Niekro
Paul Popovich
❑ 537 Chuck Estrada DP 9.00 4.00
❑ 538 J.C. Martin 16.00 7.25
❑ 539 Dick Egan DP 9.00 4.00
❑ 540 Norm Cash 35.00 16.00
❑ 541 Joe Gibbon 16.00 7.25
❑ 542 Athletics Rookies DP .. 15.00 6.75
Rick Monday
Tony Pierce
❑ 543 Dan Schneider 16.00 7.25
❑ 544 Cleveland Indians 30.00 13.50
Team Card
❑ 545 Jim Grant 16.00 7.25
❑ 546 Woody Woodward 18.00 8.00
❑ 547 Red Sox Rookies DP .. 9.00 4.00
Russ Gibson
Bill Rohr
❑ 548 Tony Gonzalez DP 9.00 4.00
❑ 549 Jack Sanford 16.00 7.25
❑ 550 Vada Pinson DP 10.00 4.50

❑ 551 Doug Camilli DP 9.00 4.00
❑ 552 Ted Savage 16.00 7.25
❑ 553 Yankees Rookies 30.00 13.50
Mike Hegan
Thad Tillotson
❑ 554 Andre Rodgers DP 9.00 4.00
❑ 555 Don Cardwell 18.00 8.00
❑ 556 Al Weis DP 9.00 4.00
❑ 557 Al Ferrara 16.00 7.25
❑ 558 Orioles Rookies 50.00 22.00
Mark Belanger
Bill Dillman
❑ 559 Dick Tracewski DP 9.00 4.00
❑ 560 Jim Bunning 70.00 32.00
❑ 561 Sandy Alomar 20.00 9.00
❑ 562 Steve Blass DP 9.00 4.00
❑ 563 Joe Adcock 20.00 9.00
❑ 564 Astros Rookies DP 9.00 4.00
Alonzo Harris
Aaron Pointer
❑ 565 Lew Krausse 16.00 7.25
❑ 566 Gary Geiger DP 9.00 4.00
❑ 567 Steve Hamilton 25.00 11.00
❑ 568 John Sullivan 25.00 11.00
❑ 569 AL Rookies DP 250.00 110.00
Rod Carew
Hank Allen
❑ 570 Maury Wills 90.00 40.00
❑ 571 Larry Sherry 16.00 7.25
❑ 572 Don Demeter 16.00 7.25
❑ 573 Chicago White Sox 30.00 13.50
Team Card UER
(Indians team
stats on back)
❑ 574 Jerry Buchek 16.00 7.25
❑ 575 Dave Boswell 16.00 7.25
❑ 576 NL Rookies 25.00 11.00
Ramon Hernandez
Norm Gigon
❑ 577 Bill Short 16.00 7.25
❑ 578 John Boccabella 16.00 7.25
❑ 579 Bill Henry 16.00 7.25
❑ 580 Rocky Colavito 100.00 45.00
❑ 581 Mets Rookies 850.00 375.00
Bill Denehy
Tom Seaver
❑ 582 Jim Owens DP 9.00 4.00
❑ 583 Ray Barker 25.00 11.00
❑ 584 Jimmy Piersall 35.00 16.00
❑ 585 Wally Bunker 16.00 7.25
❑ 586 Manny Jimenez 16.00 7.25
❑ 587 NL Rookies 35.00 16.00
Don Shaw
Gary Sutherland
❑ 588 Johnny Klippstein DP .. 9.00 4.00
❑ 589 Dave Ricketts DP 9.00 4.00
❑ 590 Pete Richert 16.00 7.25
❑ 591 Ty Cline 16.00 7.25
❑ 592 NL Rookies 25.00 11.00
Jim Shellenback
Ron Willis
❑ 593 Wes Westrum MG 25.00 11.00
❑ 594 Dan Osinski 18.00 8.00
❑ 595 Cookie Rojas 18.00 8.00
❑ 596 Galen Cisco DP 10.00 4.50
❑ 597 Ted Abernathy 16.00 7.25
❑ 598 White Sox Rookies 18.00 8.00
Walt Williams
Ed Stroud
❑ 599 Bob Duliba DP 9.00 4.00
❑ 600 Brooks Robinson 275.00 125.00
❑ 601 Bill Bryan DP 9.00 4.00
❑ 602 Juan Pizarro 25.00 11.00
❑ 603 Athletics Rookies 25.00 11.00
Tim Talton
Ramon Webster
❑ 604 Red Sox Team 125.00 55.00
❑ 605 Mike Shannon 50.00 22.00
❑ 606 Ron Taylor 18.00 8.00
❑ 607 Mickey Stanley 40.00 18.00
❑ 608 Cubs Rookies DP 9.00 4.00
Rich Nye
John Upham
❑ 609 Tommy John 70.00 23.00

1968 Topps

	NRMT	VG-E
COMPLETE SET (598)	3000.00	1350.00
COMMON CARD (1-457)	1.75	.80
COMMON CARD (458-598)	3.50	1.55
WRAPPER (5-CENT)	25.00	11.00

❑ 1 NL Batting Leaders 30.00 12.00
Bob Clemente
Tony Gonzalez
Matty Alou
❑ 2 AL Batting Leaders 14.00 6.25
Carl Yastrzemski
Frank Robinson
Al Kaline
❑ 3 NL RBI Leaders 20.00 9.00
Orlando Cepeda
Bob Clemente
Hank Aaron
❑ 4 AL RBI Leaders 12.00 5.50
Carl Yastrzemski
Harmon Killebrew
Frank Robinson
❑ 5 NL Home Run Leaders 8.00 3.60
Hank Aaron
Jim Wynn
Ron Santo
Willie McCovey
❑ 6 AL Home Run Leaders 8.00 3.60
Carl Yastrzemski
Harmon Killebrew
Frank Howard
❑ 7 NL ERA Leaders 3.50 1.55
Phil Niekro
Jim Bunning
Chris Short
❑ 8 AL ERA Leaders 3.50 1.55
Joel Horlen
Gary Peters
Sonny Siebert
❑ 9 NL Pitching Leaders 5.00 2.20
Mike McCormick
Ferguson Jenkins
Jim Bunning
Claude Osteen
❑ 10A AL Pitching Leaders 4.00 1.80
Jim Lonborg ERR
(Misspelled Lonberg
on card back)
Earl Wilson
Dean Chance
❑ 10B AL Pitching Leaders 4.00 1.80
Jim Lonborg COR
Earl Wilson
Dean Chance
❑ 11 NL Strikeout Leaders 6.00 2.70
Jim Bunning
Ferguson Jenkins
Gaylord Perry
❑ 12 AL Strikeout Leaders 3.50 1.55
Jim Lonborg UER
(Misspelled Longberg
on card back)
Sam McDowell
Dean Chance
❑ 13 Chuck Hartenstein .... 1.75 .80
❑ 14 Jerry McNertney .... 1.75 .80

❑ 15 Ron Hunt 1.75 .80
❑ 16 Indians Rookies 5.00 2.20
Lou Piniella
Richie Scheinblum
❑ 17 Dick Hall 1.75 .80
❑ 18 Mike Hershberger 1.75 .80
❑ 19 Juan Pizarro 1.75 .80
❑ 20 Brooks Robinson 25.00 11.00
❑ 21 Ron Davis 1.75 .80
❑ 22 Pat Dobson 4.00 1.80
❑ 23 Chico Cardenas 4.00 1.80
❑ 24 Bobby Locke 1.75 .80
❑ 25 Julian Javier 4.00 1.80
❑ 26 Darrell Brandon 1.75 .80
❑ 27 Gil Hodges MG 8.00 3.60
❑ 28 Ted Uhlaender 1.75 .80
❑ 29 Joe Verbanic 1.75 .80
❑ 30 Joe Torre 5.00 2.20
❑ 31 Ed Stroud 1.75 .80
❑ 32 Joe Gibbon 1.75 .80
❑ 33 Pete Ward 1.75 .80
❑ 34 Al Ferrara 1.75 .80
❑ 35 Steve Hargan 1.75 .80
❑ 36 Pirates Rookies 4.00 1.80
Bob Moose
Bob Robertson
❑ 37 Billy Williams 8.00 3.60
❑ 38 Tony Pierce 1.75 .80
❑ 39 Cookie Rojas 4.00 1.80
❑ 40 Denny McLain 10.00 4.50
❑ 41 Julio Gotay 1.75 .80
❑ 42 Larry Haney 1.75 .80
❑ 43 Gary Bell 1.75 .80
❑ 44 Frank Kostro 1.75 .80
❑ 45 Tom Seaver 50.00 22.00
❑ 46 Dave Ricketts 1.75 .80
❑ 47 Ralph Houk MG 4.00 1.80
❑ 48 Ted Davidson 1.75 .80
❑ 49A Eddie Brinkman 1.75 .80
(White team name)
❑ 49B Eddie Brinkman 50.00 22.00
(Yellow team name)
❑ 50 Willie Mays 60.00 27.00
❑ 51 Bob Locker 1.75 .80
❑ 52 Hawk Taylor 1.75 .80
❑ 53 Gene Alley 4.00 1.80
❑ 54 Stan Williams 4.00 1.80
❑ 55 Felipe Alou 5.00 2.20
❑ 56 Orioles Rookies 1.75 .80
Dave Leonhard
Dave May
❑ 57 Dan Schneider 1.75 .80
❑ 58 Eddie Mathews 15.00 6.75
❑ 59 Don Lock 1.75 .80
❑ 60 Ken Holtzman 4.00 1.80
❑ 61 Reggie Smith 3.00 1.35
❑ 62 Chuck Dobson 1.75 .80
❑ 63 Dick Kenworthy 1.75 .80
❑ 64 Jim Merritt 1.75 .80
❑ 65 John Roseboro 4.00 1.80
❑ 66A Casey Cox 1.75 .80
(White team name)
❑ 66B Casey Cox 100.00 45.00
(Yellow team name)
❑ 67 Jim Kaat CL 6.00 1.20
❑ 68 Ron Willis 1.75 .80
❑ 69 Tom Tresh 2.50 1.10
❑ 70 Bob Veale 4.00 1.80
❑ 71 Vern Fuller 1.75 .80
❑ 72 Tommy John 6.00 2.70
❑ 73 Jim Ray Hart 4.00 1.80
❑ 74 Milt Pappas 4.00 1.80
❑ 75 Don Mincher 1.75 .80
❑ 76 Braves Rookies 4.00 1.80
Jim Britton
Ron Reed
❑ 77 Don Wilson 4.00 1.80
❑ 78 Jim Northrup 5.00 2.20
❑ 79 Ted Kubiak 1.75 .80
❑ 80 Rod Carew 50.00 22.00
❑ 81 Larry Jackson 1.75 .80
❑ 82 Sam Bowens 1.75 .80
❑ 83 John Stephenson 1.75 .80
❑ 84 Bob Tolan 4.00 1.80
❑ 85 Gaylord Perry 8.00 3.60
❑ 86 Willie Stargell 8.00 3.60
❑ 87 Dick Williams MG 4.00 1.80
❑ 88 Phil Regan 4.00 1.80
❑ 89 Jake Gibbs 4.00 1.80
❑ 90 Vada Pinson 3.00 1.35
❑ 91 Jim Ollom 1.75 .80
❑ 92 Ed Kranepool 4.00 1.80
❑ 93 Tony Cloninger 1.75 .80
❑ 94 Lee Maye 1.75 .80
❑ 95 Bob Aspromonte 1.75 .80
❑ 96 Senator Rookies 1.75 .80
Frank Coggins
Dick Nold
❑ 97 Tom Phoebus 1.75 .80
❑ 98 Gary Sutherland 1.75 .80
❑ 99 Rocky Colavito 8.00 3.60
❑ 100 Bob Gibson 25.00 11.00
❑ 101 Glenn Beckert 4.00 1.80
❑ 102 Jose Cardenal 4.00 1.80
❑ 103 Don Sutton 6.00 2.70
❑ 104 Dick Dietz 1.75 .80
❑ 105 Al Downing 4.00 1.80
❑ 106 Dalton Jones 1.75 .80
❑ 107A Juan Marichal CL 6.00 1.20
Tan wide mesh
❑ 107B Juan Marichal CL 6.00 1.20
Brown fine mesh
❑ 108 Don Pavletich 1.75 .80
❑ 109 Bert Campaneris 4.00 1.80
❑ 110 Hank Aaron 60.00 27.00
❑ 111 Rich Reese 1.75 .80
❑ 112 Woody Fryman 1.75 .80
❑ 113 Tigers Rookies 2.50 1.10
Tom Matchick
Daryl Patterson
❑ 114 Ron Swoboda 4.00 1.80
❑ 115 Sam McDowell 4.00 1.80
❑ 116 Ken McMullen 1.75 .80
❑ 117 Larry Jaster 1.75 .80
❑ 118 Mark Belanger 4.00 1.80
❑ 119 Ted Savage 1.75 .80
❑ 120 Mel Stottlemyre 5.00 2.20
❑ 121 Jimmie Hall 1.75 .80
❑ 122 Gene Mauch MG 4.00 1.80
❑ 123 Jose Santiago 1.75 .80
❑ 124 Nate Oliver 1.75 .80
❑ 125 Joel Horlen 1.75 .80
❑ 126 Bobby Etheridge 1.75 .80
❑ 127 Paul Lindblad 1.75 .80
❑ 128 Astros Rookies 1.75 .80
Tom Dukes
Alonzo Harris
❑ 129 Mickey Stanley 5.00 2.20
❑ 130 Tony Perez 8.00 3.60
❑ 131 Frank Bertaina 1.75 .80
❑ 132 Bud Harrelson 4.00 1.80
❑ 133 Fred Whitfield 1.75 .80
❑ 134 Pat Jarvis 1.75 .80
❑ 135 Paul Blair 4.00 1.80
❑ 136 Randy Hundley 4.00 1.80
❑ 137 Twins Team 4.00 1.80
❑ 138 Ruben Amaro 1.75 .80
❑ 139 Chris Short 1.75 .80
❑ 140 Tony Conigliaro 8.00 3.60
❑ 141 Dal Maxvill 1.75 .80
❑ 142 White Sox Rookies 1.75 .80
Buddy Bradford
Bill Voss
❑ 143 Pete Cimino 1.75 .80
❑ 144 Joe Morgan 12.00 5.50
❑ 145 Don Drysdale 12.00 5.50
❑ 146 Sal Bando 4.00 1.80
❑ 147 Frank Linzy 1.75 .80
❑ 148 Dave Bristol MG 1.75 .80
❑ 149 Bob Saverine 1.75 .80
❑ 150 Bob Clemente 75.00 34.00
❑ 151 Lou Brock WS 10.00 4.50
❑ 152 Carl Yastrzemski WS 10.00 4.50
❑ 153 Nellie Briles WS 4.50 2.00
❑ 154 Bob Gibson WS 10.00 4.50
❑ 155 Jim Lonborg WS 4.50 2.00
❑ 156 Rico Petrocelli WS 4.50 2.00
❑ 157 World Series Game 7 4.50 2.00
St. Louis wins it
❑ 158 World Series Summary 4.50 2.00
Cardinals celebrate
❑ 159 Don Kessinger 4.00 1.80
❑ 160 Earl Wilson 4.00 1.80
❑ 161 Norm Miller 1.75 .80
❑ 162 Cards Rookies 4.00 1.80
Hal Gilson
Mike Torrez
❑ 163 Gene Brabender 1.75 .80
❑ 164 Ramon Webster 1.75 .80
❑ 165 Tony Oliva 5.00 2.20
❑ 166 Claude Raymond 1.75 .80
❑ 167 Elston Howard 5.00 2.20
❑ 168 Dodgers Team 4.00 1.80
❑ 169 Bob Bolin 1.75 .80
❑ 170 Jim Fregosi 4.00 1.80
❑ 171 Don Nottebart 1.75 .80
❑ 172 Walt Williams 1.75 .80
❑ 173 John Boozer 1.75 .80
❑ 174 Bob Tillman 1.75 .80
❑ 175 Maury Wills 6.00 2.70
❑ 176 Bob Allen 1.75 .80
❑ 177 Mets Rookies 900.00 400.00
Jerry Koosman
Nolan Ryan
❑ 178 Don Wert 4.00 1.80
❑ 179 Bill Stoneman 1.75 .80
❑ 180 Curt Flood 3.00 1.35
❑ 181 Jerry Zimmerman 1.75 .80
❑ 182 Dave Giusti 1.75 .80
❑ 183 Bob Kennedy MG 4.00 1.80
❑ 184 Lou Johnson 4.00 1.80
❑ 185 Tom Haller 1.75 .80
❑ 186 Eddie Watt 1.75 .80
❑ 187 Sonny Jackson 1.75 .80
❑ 188 Cap Peterson 1.75 .80
❑ 189 Bill Landis 1.75 .80
❑ 190 Bill White 3.00 1.35
❑ 191 Dan Frisella 1.75 .80
❑ 192A Carl Yastrzemski CL 8.00 1.60
Special Baseball Playing Card
❑ 192B Carl Yastrzemski CL 8.00 1.60
Special Baseball
Playing Card Game
❑ 193 Jack Hamilton 1.75 .80
❑ 194 Don Buford 1.75 .80
❑ 195 Joe Pepitone 2.50 1.10
❑ 196 Gary Nolan 4.00 1.80
❑ 197 Larry Brown 1.75 .80
❑ 198 Roy Face 4.00 1.80
❑ 199 A's Rookies 1.75 .80
Roberto Rodriquez
Darrell Osteen
❑ 200 Orlando Cepeda 6.00 2.70
❑ 201 Mike Marshall 3.00 1.35
❑ 202 Adolfo Phillips 1.75 .80
❑ 203 Dick Kelley 1.75 .80
❑ 204 Andy Etchebarren 1.75 .80
❑ 205 Juan Marichal 8.00 3.60
❑ 206 Cal Ermer MG 1.75 .80
❑ 207 Carroll Sembera 1.75 .80
❑ 208 Willie Davis 2.50 1.10
❑ 209 Tim Cullen 1.75 .80
❑ 210 Gary Peters 1.75 .80
❑ 211 J.C. Martin 1.75 .80
❑ 212 Dave Morehead 1.75 .80
❑ 213 Chico Ruiz 1.75 .80
❑ 214 Yankees Rookies 4.00 1.80
Stan Bahnsen
Frank Fernandez
❑ 215 Jim Bunning 7.00 3.10
❑ 216 Bubba Morton 1.75 .80
❑ 217 Dick Farrell 1.75 .80
❑ 218 Ken Suarez 1.75 .80
❑ 219 Rob Gardner 1.75 .80
❑ 220 Harmon Killebrew 15.00 6.75
❑ 221 Braves Team 4.00 1.80
❑ 222 Jim Hardin 1.75 .80
❑ 223 Ollie Brown 1.75 .80
❑ 224 Jack Aker 1.75 .80
❑ 225 Richie Allen 6.00 2.70
❑ 226 Jimmie Price 1.75 .80
❑ 227 Joe Hoerner 1.75 .80
❑ 228 Dodgers Rookies 4.00 1.80
Jack Billingham
Jim Fairey
❑ 229 Fred Klages 1.75 .80

❑ 230	Pete Rose	35.00	16.00
❑ 231	Dave Baldwin	1.75	.80
❑ 232	Denis Menke	1.75	.80
❑ 233	George Scott	4.00	1.80
❑ 234	Bill Monbouquette	1.75	.80
❑ 235	Ron Santo	5.00	2.20
❑ 236	Tug McGraw	5.00	2.20
❑ 237	Alvin Dark MG	4.00	1.80
❑ 238	Tom Satriano	1.75	.80
❑ 239	Bill Henry	1.75	.80
❑ 240	Al Kaline	25.00	11.00
❑ 241	Felix Millan	1.75	.80
❑ 242	Moe Drabowsky	4.00	1.80
❑ 243	Rich Rollins	1.75	.80
❑ 244	John Donaldson	1.75	.80
❑ 245	Tony Gonzalez	1.75	.80
❑ 246	Fritz Peterson	4.00	1.80
❑ 247	Reds Rookies	125.00	55.00
	Johnny Bench		
	Ron Tompkins		
❑ 248	Fred Valentine	1.75	.80
❑ 249	Bill Singer	1.75	.80
❑ 250	Carl Yastrzemski	25.00	11.00
❑ 251	Manny Sanguillen	6.00	2.70
❑ 252	Angels Team	4.00	1.80
❑ 253	Dick Hughes	1.75	.80
❑ 254	Cleon Jones	4.00	1.80
❑ 255	Dean Chance	4.00	1.80
❑ 256	Norm Cash	6.00	2.70
❑ 257	Phil Niekro	8.00	3.60
❑ 258	Cubs Rookies	1.75	.80
	Jose Arcia		
	Bill Schlesinger		
❑ 259	Ken Boyer	3.00	1.35
❑ 260	Jim Wynn	4.00	1.80
❑ 261	Dave Duncan	4.00	1.80
❑ 262	Rick Wise	4.00	1.80
❑ 263	Horace Clarke	4.00	1.80
❑ 264	Ted Abernathy	1.75	.80
❑ 265	Tommy Davis	4.00	1.80
❑ 266	Paul Popovich	1.75	.80
❑ 267	Herman Franks MG	1.75	.80
❑ 268	Bob Humphreys	1.75	.80
❑ 269	Bob Tiefenauer	1.75	.80
❑ 270	Matty Alou	4.00	1.80
❑ 271	Bobby Knoop	1.75	.80
❑ 272	Ray Culp	1.75	.80
❑ 273	Dave Johnson	4.00	1.80
❑ 274	Mike Cuellar	4.00	1.80
❑ 275	Tim McCarver	5.00	2.20
❑ 276	Jim Roland	1.75	.80
❑ 277	Jerry Buchek	1.75	.80
❑ 278	Orlando Cepeda CL	6.00	1.20
❑ 279	Bill Hands	1.75	.80
❑ 280	Mickey Mantle	250.00	110.00
❑ 281	Jim Campanis	1.75	.80
❑ 282	Rick Monday	4.00	1.80
❑ 283	Mel Queen	1.75	.80
❑ 284	Johnny Briggs	1.75	.80
❑ 285	Dick McAuliffe	4.00	1.80
❑ 286	Cecil Upshaw	1.75	.80
❑ 287	White Sox Rookies	1.75	.80
	Mickey Abarbanel		
	Cisco Carlos		
❑ 288	Dave Wickersham	1.75	.80
❑ 289	Woody Held	1.75	.80
❑ 290	Willie McCovey	12.00	5.50
❑ 291	Dick Lines	1.75	.80
❑ 292	Art Shamsky	1.75	.80
❑ 293	Bruce Howard	1.75	.80
❑ 294	Red Schoendienst MG	5.00	2.20
❑ 295	Sonny Siebert	1.75	.80
❑ 296	Byron Browne	1.75	.80
❑ 297	Russ Gibson	1.75	.80
❑ 298	Jim Brewer	1.75	.80
❑ 299	Gene Michael	4.00	1.80
❑ 300	Rusty Staub	3.00	1.35
❑ 301	Twins Rookies	1.75	.80
	George Mitterwald		
	Rick Renick		
❑ 302	Gerry Arrigo	1.75	.80
❑ 303	Dick Green	4.00	1.80
❑ 304	Sandy Valdespino	1.75	.80
❑ 305	Minnie Rojas	1.75	.80
❑ 306	Mike Ryan	1.75	.80
❑ 307	John Hiller	4.00	1.80
❑ 308	Pirates Team	4.00	1.80
❑ 309	Ken Henderson	1.75	.80
❑ 310	Luis Aparicio	7.00	3.10
❑ 311	Jack Lamabe	1.75	.80
❑ 312	Curt Blefary	1.75	.80
❑ 313	Al Weis	1.75	.80
❑ 314	Red Sox Rookies	1.75	.80
	Bill Rohr		
	George Spriggs		
❑ 315	Zoilo Versalles	1.75	.80
❑ 316	Steve Barber	1.75	.80
❑ 317	Ron Brand	1.75	.80
❑ 318	Chico Salmon	1.75	.80
❑ 319	George Culver	1.75	.80
❑ 320	Frank Howard	5.00	2.20
❑ 321	Leo Durocher MG	5.00	2.20
❑ 322	Dave Boswell	1.75	.80
❑ 323	Deron Johnson	4.00	1.80
❑ 324	Jim Nash	1.75	.80
❑ 325	Manny Mota	4.00	1.80
❑ 326	Dennis Ribant	1.75	.80
❑ 327	Tony Taylor	4.00	1.80
❑ 328	Angels Rookies	1.75	.80
	Chuck Vinson		
	Jim Weaver		
❑ 329	Duane Josephson	1.75	.80
❑ 330	Roger Maris	35.00	16.00
❑ 331	Dan Osinski	1.75	.80
❑ 332	Doug Rader	4.00	1.80
❑ 333	Ron Herbel	1.75	.80
❑ 334	Orioles Team	4.00	1.80
❑ 335	Bob Allison	4.00	1.80
❑ 336	John Purdin	1.75	.80
❑ 337	Bill Robinson	4.00	1.80
❑ 338	Bob Johnson	1.75	.80
❑ 339	Rich Nye	1.75	.80
❑ 340	Max Alvis	1.75	.80
❑ 341	Jim Lemon MG	1.75	.80
❑ 342	Ken Johnson	1.75	.80
❑ 343	Jim Gosger	1.75	.80
❑ 344	Donn Clendenon	4.00	1.80
❑ 345	Bob Hendley	1.75	.80
❑ 346	Jerry Adair	1.75	.80
❑ 347	George Brunet	1.75	.80
❑ 348	Phillies Rookies	1.75	.80
	Larry Colton		
	Dick Thoenen		
❑ 349	Ed Spiezio	1.75	.80
❑ 350	Hoyt Wilhelm	7.00	3.10
❑ 351	Bob Barton	1.75	.80
❑ 352	Jackie Hernandez	1.75	.80
❑ 353	Mack Jones	1.75	.80
❑ 354	Pete Richert	1.75	.80
❑ 355	Ernie Banks	25.00	11.00
❑ 356A	Ken Holtzman CL	6.00	1.20
	Head centered within circle		
❑ 356B	Ken Holtzman	6.00	1.20
	Head shifted right		
	within circle		
❑ 357	Len Gabrielson	1.75	.80
❑ 358	Mike Epstein	1.75	.80
❑ 359	Joe Moeller	1.75	.80
❑ 360	Willie Horton	5.00	2.20
❑ 361	Harmon Killebrew AS	8.00	3.60
❑ 362	Orlando Cepeda AS	4.00	1.80
❑ 363	Rod Carew AS	8.00	3.60
❑ 364	Joe Morgan AS	8.00	3.60
❑ 365	Brooks Robinson AS	8.00	3.60
❑ 366	Ron Santo AS	3.00	1.35
❑ 367	Jim Fregosi AS	4.00	1.80
❑ 368	Gene Alley AS	4.00	1.80
❑ 369	Carl Yastrzemski AS	10.00	4.50
❑ 370	Hank Aaron AS	20.00	9.00
❑ 371	Tony Oliva AS	3.00	1.35
❑ 372	Lou Brock AS	8.00	3.60
❑ 373	Frank Robinson AS	8.00	3.60
❑ 374	Bob Clemente AS	30.00	13.50
❑ 375	Bill Freehan AS	3.00	1.35
❑ 376	Tim McCarver AS	4.00	1.80
❑ 377	Joel Horlen AS	4.00	1.80
❑ 378	Bob Gibson AS	8.00	3.60
❑ 379	Gary Peters AS	4.00	1.80
❑ 380	Ken Holtzman AS	4.00	1.80
❑ 381	Boog Powell	5.00	2.20
❑ 382	Ramon Hernandez	1.75	.80
❑ 383	Steve Whitaker	1.75	.80
❑ 384	Reds Rookies	6.00	2.70
	Bill Henry		
	Hal McRae		
❑ 385	Jim Hunter	10.00	4.50
❑ 386	Greg Goossen	1.75	.80
❑ 387	Joe Foy	1.75	.80
❑ 388	Ray Washburn	1.75	.80
❑ 389	Jay Johnstone	4.00	1.80
❑ 390	Bill Mazeroski	5.00	2.20
❑ 391	Bob Priddy	1.75	.80
❑ 392	Grady Hatton MG	1.75	.80
❑ 393	Jim Perry	4.00	1.80
❑ 394	Tommie Aaron	4.00	1.80
❑ 395	Camilo Pascual	4.00	1.80
❑ 396	Bobby Wine	1.75	.80
❑ 397	Vic Davalillo	1.75	.80
❑ 398	Jim Grant	1.75	.80
❑ 399	Ray Oyler	4.00	1.80
❑ 400A	Mike McCormick	4.00	1.80
	(Yellow letters)		
❑ 400B	Mike McCormick	150.00	70.00
	(Team name in		
	white letters)		
❑ 401	Mets Team	3.50	1.55
❑ 402	Mike Hegan	4.00	1.80
❑ 403	John Buzhardt	1.75	.80
❑ 404	Floyd Robinson	1.75	.80
❑ 405	Tommy Helms	4.00	1.80
❑ 406	Dick Ellsworth	1.75	.80
❑ 407	Gary Kolb	1.75	.80
❑ 408	Steve Carlton	30.00	13.50
❑ 409	Orioles Rookies	1.75	.80
	Frank Peters		
	Ron Stone		
❑ 410	Ferguson Jenkins	10.00	4.50
❑ 411	Ron Hansen	1.75	.80
❑ 412	Clay Carroll	4.00	1.80
❑ 413	Tom McCraw	1.75	.80
❑ 414	Mickey Lolich	8.00	3.60
❑ 415	Johnny Callison	4.00	1.80
❑ 416	Bill Rigney MG	1.75	.80
❑ 417	Willie Crawford	1.75	.80
❑ 418	Eddie Fisher	1.75	.80
❑ 419	Jack Hiatt	1.75	.80
❑ 420	Cesar Tovar	1.75	.80
❑ 421	Ron Taylor	1.75	.80
❑ 422	Rene Lachemann	1.75	.80
❑ 423	Fred Gladding	1.75	.80
❑ 424	Chicago White Sox	3.50	1.55
	Team Card		
❑ 425	Jim Maloney	4.00	1.80
❑ 426	Hank Allen	1.75	.80
❑ 427	Dick Calmus	1.75	.80
❑ 428	Vic Roznovsky	1.75	.80
❑ 429	Tommie Sisk	1.75	.80
❑ 430	Rico Petrocelli	4.00	1.80
❑ 431	Dooley Womack	1.75	.80
❑ 432	Indians Rookies	1.75	.80
	Bill Davis		
	Jose Vidal		
❑ 433	Bob Rodgers	1.75	.80
❑ 434	Ricardo Joseph	1.75	.80
❑ 435	Ron Perranoski	4.00	1.80
❑ 436	Hal Lanier	1.75	.80
❑ 437	Don Cardwell	1.75	.80
❑ 438	Lee Thomas	4.00	1.80
❑ 439	Lum Harris MG	1.75	.80
❑ 440	Claude Osteen	4.00	1.80
❑ 441	Alex Johnson	4.00	1.80
❑ 442	Dick Bosman	1.75	.80
❑ 443	Joe Azcue	1.75	.80
❑ 444	Jack Fisher	1.75	.80
❑ 445	Mike Shannon	4.00	1.80
❑ 446	Ron Kline	1.75	.80
❑ 447	Tigers Rookies	4.00	1.80
	George Korince		
	Fred Lasher		
❑ 448	Gary Wagner	1.75	.80
❑ 449	Gene Oliver	1.75	.80
❑ 450	Jim Kaat	6.00	2.70
❑ 451	Al Spangler	1.75	.80
❑ 452	Jesus Alou	1.75	.80
❑ 453	Sammy Ellis	1.75	.80

	No.	Player	NRMT	VG-E
❑	454A	Frank Robinson CL Cap complete within circle	6.00	1.20
❑	454B	Frank Robinson CL Cap partially within circle	6.00	1.20
❑	455	Rico Carty	4.00	1.80
❑	456	John O'Donoghue	1.75	.80
❑	457	Jim Lefebvre	4.00	1.80
❑	458	Lew Krausse	6.00	2.70
❑	459	Dick Simpson	3.50	1.55
❑	460	Jim Lonborg	6.00	2.70
❑	461	Chuck Hiller	3.50	1.55
❑	462	Barry Moore	3.50	1.55
❑	463	Jim Schaffer	3.50	1.55
❑	464	Don McMahon	3.50	1.55
❑	465	Tommie Agee	4.00	1.80
❑	466	Bill Dillman	3.50	1.55
❑	467	Dick Howser	6.00	2.70
❑	468	Larry Sherry	3.50	1.55
❑	469	Ty Cline	3.50	1.55
❑	470	Bill Freehan	6.00	2.70
❑	471	Orlando Pena	3.50	1.55
❑	472	Walter Alston MG	6.00	2.70
❑	473	Al Worthington	3.50	1.55
❑	474	Paul Schaal	3.50	1.55
❑	475	Joe Niekro	5.00	2.20
❑	476	Woody Woodward	3.50	1.55
❑	477	Philadelphia Phillies Team Card	6.00	2.70
❑	478	Dave McNally	6.00	2.70
❑	479	Phil Gagliano	3.50	1.55
❑	480	Manager's Dream Tony Oliva Chico Cardenas Bob Clemente	80.00	36.00
❑	481	John Wyatt	3.50	1.55
❑	482	Jose Pagan	3.50	1.55
❑	483	Darold Knowles	3.50	1.55
❑	484	Phil Roof	3.50	1.55
❑	485	Ken Berry	3.50	1.55
❑	486	Cal Koonce	3.50	1.55
❑	487	Lee May	4.00	1.80
❑	488	Dick Tracewski	4.50	2.00
❑	489	Wally Bunker	3.50	1.55
❑	490	Super Stars Harmon Killebrew Willie Mays Mickey Mantle	175.00	80.00
❑	491	Denny Lemaster	3.50	1.55
❑	492	Jeff Torborg	6.00	2.70
❑	493	Jim McGlothlin	3.50	1.55
❑	494	Ray Sadecki	3.50	1.55
❑	495	Leon Wagner	3.50	1.55
❑	496	Steve Hamilton	6.00	2.70
❑	497	Cardinals Team	7.00	3.10
❑	498	Bill Bryan	3.50	1.55
❑	499	Steve Blass	6.00	2.70
❑	500	Frank Robinson	30.00	13.50
❑	501	John Odom	6.00	2.70
❑	502	Mike Andrews	3.50	1.55
❑	503	Al Jackson	3.50	1.55
❑	504	Russ Snyder	3.50	1.55
❑	505	Joe Sparma	10.00	4.50
❑	506	Clarence Jones	4.00	1.80
❑	507	Wade Blasingame	3.50	1.55
❑	508	Duke Sims	3.50	1.55
❑	509	Dennis Higgins	3.50	1.55
❑	510	Ron Fairly	4.00	1.80
❑	511	Bill Kelso	3.50	1.55
❑	512	Grant Jackson	3.50	1.55
❑	513	Hank Bauer MG	6.00	2.70
❑	514	Al McBean	3.50	1.55
❑	515	Russ Nixon	3.50	1.55
❑	516	Pete Mikkelsen	3.50	1.55
❑	517	Diego Segui	6.00	2.70
❑	518A	Clete Boyer CL ERR 539 AL Rookies	12.00	2.40
❑	518B	Clete Boyer CL COR 539 ML Rookies	12.00	2.40
❑	519	Jerry Stephenson	3.50	1.55
❑	520	Lou Brock	25.00	11.00
❑	521	Don Shaw	3.50	1.55
❑	522	Wayne Causey	3.50	1.55
❑	523	John Tsitouris	3.50	1.55
❑	524	Andy Kosco	3.50	1.55
❑	525	Jim Davenport	3.50	1.55
❑	526	Bill Denehy	3.50	1.55
❑	527	Tito Francona	3.50	1.55
❑	528	Tigers Team	70.00	32.00
❑	529	Bruce Von Hoff	3.50	1.55
❑	530	Bird Belters Brooks Robinson Frank Robinson	40.00	18.00
❑	531	Chuck Hinton	3.50	1.55
❑	532	Luis Tiant	6.00	2.70
❑	533	Wes Parker	4.50	2.00
❑	534	Bob Miller	3.50	1.55
❑	535	Danny Cater	6.00	2.70
❑	536	Bill Short	3.50	1.55
❑	537	Norm Siebern	3.50	1.55
❑	538	Manny Jimenez	3.50	1.55
❑	539	Major League Rookies Jim Ray Mike Ferraro	3.50	1.55
❑	540	Nelson Briles	6.00	2.70
❑	541	Sandy Alomar	6.00	2.70
❑	542	John Boccabella	3.50	1.55
❑	543	Bob Lee	3.50	1.55
❑	544	Mayo Smith MG	8.00	3.60
❑	545	Lindy McDaniel	6.00	2.70
❑	546	Roy White	4.50	2.00
❑	547	Dan Coombs	3.50	1.55
❑	548	Bernie Allen	3.50	1.55
❑	549	Orioles Rookies Curt Motton Roger Nelson	3.50	1.55
❑	550	Clete Boyer	6.00	2.70
❑	551	Darrell Sutherland	3.50	1.55
❑	552	Ed Kirkpatrick	3.50	1.55
❑	553	Hank Aguirre	3.50	1.55
❑	554	A's Team	8.00	3.60
❑	555	Jose Tartabull	6.00	2.70
❑	556	Dick Selma	3.50	1.55
❑	557	Frank Quilici	3.50	1.55
❑	558	Johnny Edwards	3.50	1.55
❑	559	Pirates Rookies Carl Taylor Luke Walker	3.50	1.55
❑	560	Paul Casanova	3.50	1.55
❑	561	Lee Elia	3.50	1.55
❑	562	Jim Bouton	6.00	2.70
❑	563	Ed Charles	3.50	1.55
❑	564	Eddie Stanky MG	6.00	2.70
❑	565	Larry Dierker	6.00	2.70
❑	566	Ken Harrelson	6.00	2.70
❑	567	Clay Dalrymple	3.50	1.55
❑	568	Willie Smith	3.50	1.55
❑	569	NL Rookies Ivan Murrell Les Rohr	3.50	1.55
❑	570	Rick Reichardt	3.50	1.55
❑	571	Tony LaRussa	12.00	5.50
❑	572	Don Bosch	3.50	1.55
❑	573	Joe Coleman	3.50	1.55
❑	574	Cincinnati Reds Team Card	8.00	3.60
❑	575	Jim Palmer	35.00	16.00
❑	576	Dave Adlesh	3.50	1.55
❑	577	Fred Talbot	3.50	1.55
❑	578	Orlando Martinez	3.50	1.55
❑	579	NL Rookies Larry Hisle Mike Lum	6.00	2.70
❑	580	Bob Bailey	3.50	1.55
❑	581	Garry Roggenburk	3.50	1.55
❑	582	Jerry Grote	6.00	2.70
❑	583	Gates Brown	8.00	3.60
❑	584	Larry Shepard MG	3.50	1.55
❑	585	Wilbur Wood	6.00	2.70
❑	586	Jim Pagliaroni	6.00	2.70
❑	587	Roger Repoz	3.50	1.55
❑	588	Dick Schofield	3.50	1.55
❑	589	Twins Rookies Ron Clark Moe Ogier	3.50	1.55
❑	590	Tommy Harper	4.00	1.80
❑	591	Dick Nen	3.50	1.55
❑	592	John Bateman	3.50	1.55
❑	593	Lee Stange	3.50	1.55
❑	594	Phil Linz	6.00	2.70
❑	595	Phil Ortega	3.50	1.55
❑	596	Charlie Smith	3.50	1.55
❑	597	Bill McCool	3.50	1.55
❑	598	Jerry May	7.00	2.20

1969 Topps

	NRMT	VG-E
COMPLETE SET (664)	2200.00	1000.00
COMMON (1-218/328-512)	1.50	.70
COMMON CARD (219-327)	2.50	1.10
COMMON CARD (513-588)	2.00	.90
COMMON CARD (589-664)	3.00	1.35
WRAPPER (5-CENT)	20.00	9.00

	No.	Player	NRMT	VG-E
❑	1	AL Batting Leaders Carl Yastrzemski Danny Cater Tony Oliva	15.00	5.25
❑	2	NL Batting Leaders Pete Rose Matty Alou Felipe Alou	7.00	3.10
❑	3	AL RBI Leaders Ken Harrelson Frank Howard Jim Northrup	3.50	1.55
❑	4	NL RBI Leaders Willie McCovey Ron Santo Billy Williams	6.00	2.70
❑	5	AL Home Run Leaders Frank Howard Willie Horton Ken Harrelson	3.50	1.55
❑	6	NL Home Run Leaders Willie McCovey Richie Allen Ernie Banks	6.00	2.70
❑	7	AL ERA Leaders Luis Tiant Sam McDowell Dave McNally	3.50	1.55
❑	8	NL ERA Leaders Bob Gibson Bobby Bolin Bob Veale	5.00	2.20
❑	9	AL Pitching Leaders Denny McLain Dave McNally Luis Tiant Mel Stottlemyre	3.50	1.55
❑	10	NL Pitching Leaders Juan Marichal Bob Gibson Fergie Jenkins	7.00	3.10
❑	11	AL Strikeout Leaders Sam McDowell Denny McLain Luis Tiant	3.50	1.55
❑	12	NL Strikeout Leaders Bob Gibson Fergie Jenkins Bill Singer	4.00	1.80
❑	13	Mickey Stanley	2.50	1.10
❑	14	Al McBean	1.50	.70
❑	15	Boog Powell	3.50	1.55
❑	16	Giants Rookies Cesar Gutierrez	1.50	.70

		Rich Robertson		
❑	17	Mike Marshall	2.50	1.10
❑	18	Dick Schofield	1.50	.70
❑	19	Ken Suarez	1.50	.70
❑	20	Ernie Banks	20.00	9.00
❑	21	Jose Santiago	1.50	.70
❑	22	Jesus Alou	2.50	1.10
❑	23	Lew Krausse	1.50	.70
❑	24	Walt Alston MG	4.00	1.80
❑	25	Roy White	2.50	1.10
❑	26	Clay Carroll	2.50	1.10
❑	27	Bernie Allen	1.50	.70
❑	28	Mike Ryan	1.50	.70
❑	29	Dave Morehead	1.50	.70
❑	30	Bob Allison	2.50	1.10
❑	31	Mets Rookies	2.50	1.10
		Gary Gentry		
		Amos Otis		
❑	32	Sammy Ellis	1.50	.70
❑	33	Wayne Causey	1.50	.70
❑	34	Gary Peters	1.50	.70
❑	35	Joe Morgan	10.00	4.50
❑	36	Luke Walker	1.50	.70
❑	37	Curt Motton	1.50	.70
❑	38	Zoilo Versalles	2.50	1.10
❑	39	Dick Hughes	1.50	.70
❑	40	Mayo Smith MG	1.50	.70
❑	41	Bob Barton	1.50	.70
❑	42	Tommy Harper	2.50	1.10
❑	43	Joe Niekro	2.50	1.10
❑	44	Danny Cater	1.50	.70
❑	45	Maury Wills	3.00	1.35
❑	46	Fritz Peterson	2.50	1.10
❑	47A	Paul Popovich	1.50	.70
		(No helmet emblem)		
❑	47B	Paul Popovich	25.00	11.00
		(C emblem on helmet)		
❑	48	Brant Alyea	1.50	.70
❑	49A	Royals Rookies ERR	25.00	11.00
		Steve Jones		
		E. Rodriquez		
❑	49B	Royals Rookies COR	1.50	.70
		Steve Jones		
		E. Rodriguez		
❑	50	Bob Clemente UER	50.00	22.00
		(Bats Right		
		listed twice)		
❑	51	Woody Fryman	1.50	.70
❑	52	Mike Andrews	1.50	.70
❑	53	Sonny Jackson	1.50	.70
❑	54	Cisco Carlos	1.50	.70
❑	55	Jerry Grote	2.50	1.10
❑	56	Rich Reese	1.50	.70
❑	57	Denny McLain CL	6.00	1.20
❑	58	Fred Gladding	1.50	.70
❑	59	Jay Johnstone	2.50	1.10
❑	60	Nelson Briles	2.50	1.10
❑	61	Jimmie Hall	1.50	.70
❑	62	Chico Salmon	1.50	.70
❑	63	Jim Hickman	2.50	1.10
❑	64	Bill Monbouquette	1.50	.70
❑	65	Willie Davis	2.50	1.10
❑	66	Orioles Rookies	1.50	.70
		Mike Adamson		
		Merv Rettenmund		
❑	67	Bill Stoneman	2.50	1.10
❑	68	Dave Duncan	2.50	1.10
❑	69	Steve Hamilton	2.50	1.10
❑	70	Tommy Helms	2.50	1.10
❑	71	Steve Whitaker	2.50	1.10
❑	72	Ron Taylor	1.50	.70
❑	73	Johnny Briggs	1.50	.70
❑	74	Preston Gomez MG	2.50	1.10
❑	75	Luis Aparicio	5.00	2.20
❑	76	Norm Miller	1.50	.70
❑	77A	Ron Perranoski	2.50	1.10
		(No emblem on cap)		
❑	77B	Ron Perranoski	25.00	11.00
		(LA on cap)		
❑	78	Tom Satriano	1.50	.70
❑	79	Milt Pappas	2.50	1.10
❑	80	Norm Cash	2.50	1.10
❑	81	Mel Queen	1.50	.70
❑	82	Pirates Rookies	8.00	3.60
		Rich Hebner		
		Al Oliver		
❑	83	Mike Ferraro	2.50	1.10
❑	84	Bob Humphreys	1.50	.70
❑	85	Lou Brock	20.00	9.00
❑	86	Pete Richert	1.50	.70
❑	87	Horace Clarke	2.50	1.10
❑	88	Rich Nye	1.50	.70
❑	89	Russ Gibson	1.50	.70
❑	90	Jerry Koosman	2.50	1.10
❑	91	Alvin Dark MG	2.50	1.10
❑	92	Jack Billingham	2.50	1.10
❑	93	Joe Foy	2.50	1.10
❑	94	Hank Aguirre	1.50	.70
❑	95	Johnny Bench	45.00	20.00
❑	96	Denny Lemaster	1.50	.70
❑	97	Buddy Bradford	1.50	.70
❑	98	Dave Giusti	1.50	.70
❑	99A	Twins Rookies	15.00	6.75
		Danny Morris		
		Graig Nettles		
		(No loop)		
❑	99B	Twins Rookies	15.00	6.75
		Danny Morris		
		Graig Nettles		
		(Errant loop in		
		upper left corner		
		of obverse)		
❑	100	Hank Aaron	35.00	16.00
❑	101	Daryl Patterson	1.50	.70
❑	102	Jim Davenport	1.50	.70
❑	103	Roger Repoz	1.50	.70
❑	104	Steve Blass	2.50	1.10
❑	105	Rick Monday	2.50	1.10
❑	106	Jim Hannan	1.50	.70
❑	107A	Bob Gibson CL ERR	6.00	1.20
		161 Jim Purdin		
❑	107B	Bob Gibson CL COR	7.50	1.50
		161 John Purdin		
❑	108	Tony Taylor	2.50	1.10
❑	109	Jim Lonborg	2.50	1.10
❑	110	Mike Shannon	2.50	1.10
❑	111	Johnny Morris	1.50	.70
❑	112	J.C. Martin	2.50	1.10
❑	113	Dave May	1.50	.70
❑	114	Yankees Rookies	2.50	1.10
		Alan Closter		
		John Cumberland		
❑	115	Bill Hands	1.50	.70
❑	116	Chuck Harrison	1.50	.70
❑	117	Jim Fairey	1.50	.70
❑	118	Stan Williams	1.50	.70
❑	119	Doug Rader	2.50	1.10
❑	120	Pete Rose	20.00	9.00
❑	121	Joe Grzenda	1.50	.70
❑	122	Ron Fairly	2.50	1.10
❑	123	Wilbur Wood	2.50	1.10
❑	124	Hank Bauer MG	2.50	1.10
❑	125	Ray Sadecki	1.50	.70
❑	126	Dick Tracewski	1.50	.70
❑	127	Kevin Collins	2.50	1.10
❑	128	Tommie Aaron	2.50	1.10
❑	129	Bill McCool	1.50	.70
❑	130	Carl Yastrzemski	20.00	9.00
❑	131	Chris Cannizzaro	1.50	.70
❑	132	Dave Baldwin	1.50	.70
❑	133	Johnny Callison	2.50	1.10
❑	134	Jim Weaver	1.50	.70
❑	135	Tommy Davis	2.50	1.10
❑	136	Cards Rookies	1.50	.70
		Steve Huntz		
		Mike Torrez		
❑	137	Wally Bunker	1.50	.70
❑	138	John Bateman	1.50	.70
❑	139	Andy Kosco	1.50	.70
❑	140	Jim Lefebvre	2.50	1.10
❑	141	Bill Dillman	1.50	.70
❑	142	Woody Woodward	2.50	1.10
❑	143	Joe Nossek	1.50	.70
❑	144	Bob Hendley	2.50	1.10
❑	145	Max Alvis	1.50	.70
❑	146	Jim Perry	2.50	1.10
❑	147	Leo Durocher MG	4.00	1.80
❑	148	Lee Stange	1.50	.70
❑	149	Ollie Brown	2.50	1.10
❑	150	Denny McLain	4.00	1.80
❑	151A	Clay Dalrymple	1.50	.70
		Portrait, Orioles		
❑	151B	Clay Dalrymple	15.00	6.75
		Catching, Phillies		
❑	152	Tommie Sisk	1.50	.70
❑	153	Ed Brinkman	1.50	.70
❑	154	Jim Britton	1.50	.70
❑	155	Pete Ward	1.50	.70
❑	156	Houston Rookies	1.50	.70
		Hal Gilson		
		Leon McFadden		
❑	157	Bob Rodgers	2.50	1.10
❑	158	Joe Gibbon	1.50	.70
❑	159	Jerry Adair	1.50	.70
❑	160	Vada Pinson	2.50	1.10
❑	161	John Purdin	1.50	.70
❑	162	Bob Gibson WS	8.00	3.60
		Fans 17		
❑	163	Willie Horton WS	6.00	2.70
❑	164	Tim McCarver WS	12.00	5.50
		Roger Maris		
❑	165	Lou Brock WS	8.00	3.60
❑	166	Al Kaline WS	8.00	3.60
❑	167	Jim Northrup WS	6.00	2.70
❑	168	Mickey Lolich WS	8.00	3.60
		Bob Gibson		
❑	169	Dick McAuliffe WS	6.00	2.70
		Denny McLain		
		Willie Horton		
❑	170	Frank Howard	3.00	1.35
❑	171	Glenn Beckert	2.50	1.10
❑	172	Jerry Stephenson	1.50	.70
❑	173	White Sox Rookies	1.50	.70
		Bob Christian		
		Gerry Nyman		
❑	174	Grant Jackson	1.50	.70
❑	175	Jim Bunning	7.00	3.10
❑	176	Joe Azcue	1.50	.70
❑	177	Ron Reed	1.50	.70
❑	178	Ray Oyler	2.50	1.10
❑	179	Don Pavletich	1.50	.70
❑	180	Willie Horton	2.50	1.10
❑	181	Mel Nelson	1.50	.70
❑	182	Bill Rigney MG	1.50	.70
❑	183	Don Shaw	1.50	.70
❑	184	Roberto Pena	1.50	.70
❑	185	Tom Phoebus	1.50	.70
❑	186	Johnny Edwards	1.50	.70
❑	187	Leon Wagner	1.50	.70
❑	188	Rick Wise	2.50	1.10
❑	189	Red Sox Rookies	1.50	.70
		Joe Lahoud		
		John Thibodeau		
❑	190	Willie Mays	45.00	20.00
❑	191	Lindy McDaniel	2.50	1.10
❑	192	Jose Pagan	1.50	.70
❑	193	Don Cardwell	2.50	1.10
❑	194	Ted Uhlaender	1.50	.70
❑	195	John Odom	1.50	.70
❑	196	Lum Harris MG	1.50	.70
❑	197	Dick Selma	1.50	.70
❑	198	Willie Smith	1.50	.70
❑	199	Jim French	1.50	.70
❑	200	Bob Gibson	12.00	5.50
❑	201	Russ Snyder	1.50	.70
❑	202	Don Wilson	2.50	1.10
❑	203	Dave Johnson	2.50	1.10
❑	204	Jack Hiatt	1.50	.70
❑	205	Rick Reichardt	1.50	.70
❑	206	Phillies Rookies	2.50	1.10
		Larry Hisle		
		Barry Lersch		
❑	207	Roy Face	2.50	1.10
❑	208A	Donn Clendenon	2.50	1.10
		Houston		
❑	208B	Donn Clendenon	15.00	6.75
		Expos		
❑	209	Larry Haney UER	1.50	.70
		(Reverse negative)		
❑	210	Felix Millan	1.50	.70
❑	211	Galen Cisco	1.50	.70
❑	212	Tom Tresh	2.50	1.10
❑	213	Gerry Arrigo	1.50	.70
❑	214	Checklist 3	6.00	1.20
		With 69T deckle CL		
		on back (no player)		
❑	215	Rico Petrocelli	2.50	1.10

❑	216	Don Sutton	6.00	2.70
❑	217	John Donaldson	1.50	.70
❑	218	John Roseboro	2.50	1.10
❑	219	Freddie Patek	3.00	1.35
❑	220	Sam McDowell	4.00	1.80
❑	221	Art Shamsky	4.00	1.80
❑	222	Duane Josephson	2.50	1.10
❑	223	Tom Dukes	4.00	1.80
❑	224	Angels Rookies	2.50	1.10
		Bill Harrelson		
		Steve Kealey		
❑	225	Don Kessinger	4.00	1.80
❑	226	Bruce Howard	2.50	1.10
❑	227	Frank Johnson	2.50	1.10
❑	228	Dave Leonhard	2.50	1.10
❑	229	Don Lock	2.50	1.10
❑	230	Rusty Staub UER	4.00	1.80
		For 1966 stats, Houston spelled Huoston		
❑	231	Pat Dobson	4.00	1.80
❑	232	Dave Ricketts	2.50	1.10
❑	233	Steve Barber	4.00	1.80
❑	234	Dave Bristol MG	2.50	1.10
❑	235	Jim Hunter	10.00	4.50
❑	236	Manny Mota	4.00	1.80
❑	237	Bobby Cox	10.00	4.50
❑	238	Ken Johnson	2.50	1.10
❑	239	Bob Taylor	4.00	1.80
❑	240	Ken Harrelson	4.00	1.80
❑	241	Jim Brewer	2.50	1.10
❑	242	Frank Kostro	2.50	1.10
❑	243	Ron Kline	2.50	1.10
❑	244	Indians Rookies	3.00	1.35
		Ray Fosse		
		George Woodson		
❑	245	Ed Charles	4.00	1.80
❑	246	Joe Coleman	2.50	1.10
❑	247	Gene Oliver	2.50	1.10
❑	248	Bob Priddy	2.50	1.10
❑	249	Ed Spiezio	4.00	1.80
❑	250	Frank Robinson	20.00	9.00
❑	251	Ron Herbel	2.50	1.10
❑	252	Chuck Cottier	2.50	1.10
❑	253	Jerry Johnson	2.50	1.10
❑	254	Joe Schultz MG	4.00	1.80
❑	255	Steve Carlton	30.00	13.50
❑	256	Gates Brown	4.00	1.80
❑	257	Jim Ray	2.50	1.10
❑	258	Jackie Hernandez	4.00	1.80
❑	259	Bill Short	2.50	1.10
❑	260	Reggie Jackson	325.00	145.00
❑	261	Bob Johnson	2.50	1.10
❑	262	Mike Kekich	4.00	1.80
❑	263	Jerry May	2.50	1.10
❑	264	Bill Landis	2.50	1.10
❑	265	Chico Cardenas	4.00	1.80
❑	266	Dodger Rookies	4.00	1.80
		Tom Hutton		
		Alan Foster		
❑	267	Vicente Romo	2.50	1.10
❑	268	Al Spangler	2.50	1.10
❑	269	Al Weis	4.00	1.80
❑	270	Mickey Lolich	3.00	1.35
❑	271	Larry Stahl	4.00	1.80
❑	272	Ed Stroud	2.50	1.10
❑	273	Ron Willis	2.50	1.10
❑	274	Clyde King MG	2.50	1.10
❑	275	Vic Davalillo	2.50	1.10
❑	276	Gary Wagner	2.50	1.10
❑	277	Elrod Hendricks	2.50	1.10
❑	278	Gary Geiger UER	2.50	1.10
		(Batting wrong)		
❑	279	Roger Nelson	4.00	1.80
❑	280	Alex Johnson	4.00	1.80
❑	281	Ted Kubiak	2.50	1.10
❑	282	Pat Jarvis	2.50	1.10
❑	283	Sandy Alomar	4.00	1.80
❑	284	Expos Rookies	4.00	1.80
		Jerry Robertson		
		Mike Wegener		
❑	285	Don Mincher	4.00	1.80
❑	286	Dock Ellis	3.00	1.35
❑	287	Jose Tartabull	4.00	1.80
❑	288	Ken Holtzman	4.00	1.80
❑	289	Bart Shirley	2.50	1.10
❑	290	Jim Kaat	4.00	1.80
❑	291	Vern Fuller	2.50	1.10
❑	292	Al Downing	4.00	1.80
❑	293	Dick Dietz	2.50	1.10
❑	294	Jim Lemon MG	2.50	1.10
❑	295	Tony Perez	12.00	5.50
❑	296	Andy Messersmith	4.00	1.80
❑	297	Deron Johnson	2.50	1.10
❑	298	Dave Nicholson	4.00	1.80
❑	299	Mark Belanger	4.00	1.80
❑	300	Felipe Alou	4.00	1.80
❑	301	Darrell Brandon	4.00	1.80
❑	302	Jim Pagliaroni	2.50	1.10
❑	303	Cal Koonce	4.00	1.80
❑	304	Padres Rookies	8.00	3.60
		Bill Davis		
		Clarence Gaston		
❑	305	Dick McAuliffe	4.00	1.80
❑	306	Jim Grant	4.00	1.80
❑	307	Gary Kolb	2.50	1.10
❑	308	Wade Blasingame	2.50	1.10
❑	309	Walt Williams	2.50	1.10
❑	310	Tom Haller	2.50	1.10
❑	311	Sparky Lyle	8.00	3.60
❑	312	Lee Elia	2.50	1.10
❑	313	Bill Robinson	4.00	1.80
❑	314	Don Drysdale CL	6.00	1.20
❑	315	Eddie Fisher	2.50	1.10
❑	316	Hal Lanier	2.50	1.10
❑	317	Bruce Look	2.50	1.10
❑	318	Jack Fisher	2.50	1.10
❑	319	Ken McMullen UER	2.50	1.10
		(Headings on back are for a pitcher)		
❑	320	Dal Maxvill	2.50	1.10
❑	321	Jim McAndrew	4.00	1.80
❑	322	Jose Vidal	4.00	1.80
❑	323	Larry Miller	2.50	1.10
❑	324	Tiger Rookies	4.00	1.80
		Les Cain		
		Dave Campbell		
❑	325	Jose Cardenal	4.00	1.80
❑	326	Gary Sutherland	4.00	1.80
❑	327	Willie Crawford	2.50	1.10
❑	328	Joel Horlen	1.50	.70
❑	329	Rick Joseph	1.50	.70
❑	330	Tony Conigliaro	5.00	2.20
❑	331	Braves Rookies	2.50	1.10
		Gil Garrido		
		Tom House		
❑	332	Fred Talbot	1.50	.70
❑	333	Ivan Murrell	1.50	.70
❑	334	Phil Roof	1.50	.70
❑	335	Bill Mazeroski	3.00	1.35
❑	336	Jim Roland	1.50	.70
❑	337	Marty Martinez	1.50	.70
❑	338	Del Unser	1.50	.70
❑	339	Reds Rookies	1.50	.70
		Steve Mingori		
		Jose Pena		
❑	340	Dave McNally	2.50	1.10
❑	341	Dave Adlesh	1.50	.70
❑	342	Bubba Morton	1.50	.70
❑	343	Dan Frisella	1.50	.70
❑	344	Tom Matchick	1.50	.70
❑	345	Frank Linzy	1.50	.70
❑	346	Wayne Comer	1.50	.70
❑	347	Randy Hundley	2.50	1.10
❑	348	Steve Hargan	1.50	.70
❑	349	Dick Williams MG	2.50	1.10
❑	350	Richie Allen	4.00	1.80
❑	351	Carroll Sembera	1.50	.70
❑	352	Paul Schaal	2.50	1.10
❑	353	Jeff Torborg	2.50	1.10
❑	354	Nate Oliver	1.50	.70
❑	355	Phil Niekro	7.00	3.10
❑	356	Frank Quilici	1.50	.70
❑	357	Carl Taylor	1.50	.70
❑	358	Athletics Rookies	1.50	.70
		George Lauzerique		
		Roberto Rodriquez		
❑	359	Dick Kelley	1.50	.70
❑	360	Jim Wynn	2.50	1.10
❑	361	Gary Holman	1.50	.70
❑	362	Jim Maloney	2.50	1.10
❑	363	Russ Nixon	1.50	.70
❑	364	Tommie Agee	4.00	1.80
❑	365	Jim Fregosi	2.50	1.10
❑	366	Bo Belinsky	2.50	1.10
❑	367	Lou Johnson	2.50	1.10
❑	368	Vic Roznovsky	1.50	.70
❑	369	Bob Skinner MG	2.50	1.10
❑	370	Juan Marichal	8.00	3.60
❑	371	Sal Bando	2.50	1.10
❑	372	Adolfo Phillips	1.50	.70
❑	373	Fred Lasher	1.50	.70
❑	374	Bob Tillman	1.50	.70
❑	375	Harmon Killebrew	15.00	6.75
❑	376	Royals Rookies	1.50	.70
		Mike Fiore		
		Jim Rooker		
❑	377	Gary Bell	2.50	1.10
❑	378	Jose Herrera	1.50	.70
❑	379	Ken Boyer	2.50	1.10
❑	380	Stan Bahnsen	2.50	1.10
❑	381	Ed Kranepool	2.50	1.10
❑	382	Pat Corrales	2.50	1.10
❑	383	Casey Cox	1.50	.70
❑	384	Larry Shepard MG	1.50	.70
❑	385	Orlando Cepeda	3.50	1.55
❑	386	Jim McGlothlin	1.50	.70
❑	387	Bobby Klaus	1.50	.70
❑	388	Tom McCraw	1.50	.70
❑	389	Dan Coombs	1.50	.70
❑	390	Bill Freehan	2.50	1.10
❑	391	Ray Culp	1.50	.70
❑	392	Bob Burda	1.50	.70
❑	393	Gene Brabender	2.50	1.10
❑	394	Pilots Rookies	5.00	2.20
		Lou Piniella		
		Marv Staehle		
❑	395	Chris Short	1.50	.70
❑	396	Jim Campanis	1.50	.70
❑	397	Chuck Dobson	1.50	.70
❑	398	Tito Francona	1.50	.70
❑	399	Bob Bailey	2.50	1.10
❑	400	Don Drysdale	16.00	7.25
❑	401	Jake Gibbs	2.50	1.10
❑	402	Ken Boswell	2.50	1.10
❑	403	Bob Miller	1.50	.70
❑	404	Cubs Rookies	2.50	1.10
		Vic LaRose		
		Gary Ross		
❑	405	Lee May	2.50	1.10
❑	406	Phil Ortega	1.50	.70
❑	407	Tom Egan	1.50	.70
❑	408	Nate Colbert	1.50	.70
❑	409	Bob Moose	1.50	.70
❑	410	Al Kaline	25.00	11.00
❑	411	Larry Dierker	2.50	1.10
❑	412	Mickey Mantle CL DP	15.00	3.00
❑	413	Roland Sheldon	2.50	1.10
❑	414	Duke Sims	1.50	.70
❑	415	Ray Washburn	1.50	.70
❑	416	Willie McCovey AS	7.00	3.10
❑	417	Ken Harrelson AS	2.50	1.10
❑	418	Tommy Helms AS	2.50	1.10
❑	419	Rod Carew AS	10.00	4.50
❑	420	Ron Santo AS	4.00	1.80
❑	421	Brooks Robinson AS	7.00	3.10
❑	422	Don Kessinger AS	2.50	1.10
❑	423	Bert Campaneris AS	4.00	1.80
❑	424	Pete Rose AS	14.00	6.25
❑	425	Carl Yastrzemski AS	10.00	4.50
❑	426	Curt Flood AS	4.00	1.80
❑	427	Tony Oliva AS	4.00	1.80
❑	428	Lou Brock AS	6.00	2.70
❑	429	Willie Horton AS	2.50	1.10
❑	430	Johnny Bench AS	10.00	4.50
❑	431	Bill Freehan AS	4.00	1.80
❑	432	Bob Gibson AS	6.00	2.70
❑	433	Denny McLain AS	2.50	1.10
❑	434	Jerry Koosman AS	3.00	1.35
❑	435	Sam McDowell AS	2.50	1.10
❑	436	Gene Alley	2.50	1.10
❑	437	Luis Alcaraz	1.50	.70
❑	438	Gary Waslewski	1.50	.70
❑	439	White Sox Rookies	1.50	.70
		Ed Herrmann		
		Dan Lazar		

❑ 440A Willie McCovey 15.00 6.75
❑ 440B Willie McCovey WL 100.00 45.00
(McCovey white)
❑ 441A Dennis Higgins .... 1.50 .70
❑ 441B Dennis Higgins WL .. 20.00 9.00
(Higgins white)
❑ 442 Ty Cline .... 1.50 .70
❑ 443 Don Wert .... 1.50 .70
❑ 444A Joe Moeller .... 1.50 .70
❑ 444B Joe Moeller WL 20.00 9.00
(Moeller white)
❑ 445 Bobby Knoop .... 1.50 .70
❑ 446 Claude Raymond .... 1.50 .70
❑ 447A Ralph Houk MG 2.50 1.10
❑ 447B Ralph Houk WL 22.00 10.00
MG (Houk white)
❑ 448 Bob Tolan 2.50 1.10
❑ 449 Paul Lindblad .... 1.50 .70
❑ 450 Billy Williams 7.00 3.10
❑ 451A Rich Rollins 2.50 1.10
❑ 451B Rich Rollins WL 20.00 9.00
(Rich and 3B white)
❑ 452A Al Ferrara .... 1.50 .70
❑ 452B Al Ferrara WL 20.00 9.00
(Al and OF white)
❑ 453 Mike Cuellar 2.50 1.10
❑ 454A Phillies Rookies 2.50 1.10
Larry Colton
Don Money
❑ 454B Phillies Rookies WL 22.00 10.00
Larry Colton
Don Money
(Names in white)
❑ 455 Sonny Siebert .... 1.50 .70
❑ 456 Bud Harrelson 2.50 1.10
❑ 457 Dalton Jones .... 1.50 .70
❑ 458 Curt Blefary .... 1.50 .70
❑ 459 Dave Boswell .... 1.50 .70
❑ 460 Joe Torre 3.50 1.55
❑ 461A Mike Epstein .... 1.50 .70
❑ 461B Mike Epstein WL 20.00 9.00
(Epstein white)
❑ 462 Red Schoendienst 2.50 1.10
MG
❑ 463 Dennis Ribant .... 1.50 .70
❑ 464A Dave Marshall .... 1.50 .70
❑ 464B Dave Marshall WL .. 20.00 9.00
(Marshall white)
❑ 465 Tommy John 4.00 1.80
❑ 466 John Boccabella 2.50 1.10
❑ 467 Tommie Reynolds .... 1.50 .70
❑ 468A Pirates Rookies .... 1.50 .70
Bruce Dal Canton
Bob Robertson
❑ 468B Pirates Rookies WL 20.00 9.00
Bruce Dal Canton
Bob Robertson
(Names in white)
❑ 469 Chico Ruiz .... 1.50 .70
❑ 470A Mel Stottlemyre 2.50 1.10
❑ 470B Mel Stottlemyre WL 30.00 13.50
(Stottlemyre white)
❑ 471A Ted Savage .... 1.50 .70
❑ 471B Ted Savage WL 20.00 9.00
(Savage white)
❑ 472 Jim Price .... 1.50 .70
❑ 473A Jose Arcia .... 1.50 .70
❑ 473B Jose Arcia WL 20.00 9.00
(Jose and 2B white)
❑ 474 Tom Murphy .... 1.50 .70
❑ 475 Tim McCarver 3.00 1.35
❑ 476A Boston Rookies 3.00 1.35
Ken Brett
Gerry Moses
❑ 476B Boston Rookies WL 30.00 13.50
Ken Brett
Gerry Moses
(Names in white)
❑ 477 Jeff James .... 1.50 .70
❑ 478 Don Buford .... 1.50 .70
❑ 479 Richie Scheinblum ...... 1.50 .70
❑ 480 Tom Seaver 80.00 36.00
❑ 481 Bill Melton 2.50 1.10
❑ 482A Jim Gosger .... 1.50 .70
❑ 482B Jim Gosger WL 20.00 9.00
(Jim and OF white)
❑ 483 Ted Abernathy .... 1.50 .70
❑ 484 Joe Gordon MG 2.50 1.10
❑ 485A Gaylord Perry 10.00 4.50
❑ 485B Gaylord Perry WL 85.00 38.00
(Perry white)
❑ 486A Paul Casanova .... 1.50 .70
❑ 486B Paul Casanova WL .. 20.00 9.00
(Casanova white)
❑ 487 Denis Menke .... 1.50 .70
❑ 488 Joe Sparma .... 1.50 .70
❑ 489 Clete Boyer 2.50 1.10
❑ 490 Matty Alou 2.50 1.10
❑ 491A Twins Rookies .... 1.50 .70
Jerry Crider
George Mitterwald
❑ 491B Twins Rookies WL .. 20.00 9.00
Jerry Crider
George Mitterwald
(Names in white)
❑ 492 Tony Cloninger .... 1.50 .70
❑ 493A Wes Parker 2.50 1.10
❑ 493B Wes Parker WL 22.00 10.00
(Parker white)
❑ 494 Ken Berry .... 1.50 .70
❑ 495 Bert Campaneris 2.50 1.10
❑ 496 Larry Jaster .... 1.50 .70
❑ 497 Julian Javier 2.50 1.10
❑ 498 Juan Pizarro 2.50 1.10
❑ 499 Astro Rookies .... 1.50 .70
Don Bryant
Steve Shea
❑ 500A Mickey Mantle UER 350.00 160.00
(No Topps copy-
right on card back)
❑ 500B Mickey Mantle WL 1000.00 450.00
(Mantle in white;
no Topps copyright
on card back) UER
❑ 501A Tony Gonzalez 2.50 1.10
❑ 501B Tony Gonzalez WL .. 22.00 10.00
(Tony and OF white)
❑ 502 Minnie Rojas .... 1.50 .70
❑ 503 Larry Brown .... 1.50 .70
❑ 504 Brooks Robinson CL 7.00 1.40
❑ 505A Bobby Bolin .... 1.50 .70
❑ 505B Bobby Bolin WL 22.00 10.00
(Bolin white)
❑ 506 Paul Blair 2.50 1.10
❑ 507 Cookie Rojas 2.50 1.10
❑ 508 Moe Drabowsky 2.50 1.10
❑ 509 Manny Sanguillen 2.50 1.10
❑ 510 Rod Carew 35.00 16.00
❑ 511A Diego Segui 2.50 1.10
❑ 511B Diego Segui WL 22.00 10.00
(Diego and P white)
❑ 512 Cleon Jones 2.50 1.10
❑ 513 Camilo Pascual 3.00 1.35
❑ 514 Mike Lum .... 2.00 .90
❑ 515 Dick Green .... 2.00 .90
❑ 516 Earl Weaver MG 20.00 9.00
❑ 517 Mike McCormick 3.00 1.35
❑ 518 Fred Whitfield .... 2.00 .90
❑ 519 Yankees Rookies .... 2.00 .90
Jerry Kenney
Len Boehmer
❑ 520 Bob Veale 3.00 1.35
❑ 521 George Thomas .... 2.00 .90
❑ 522 Joe Hoerner .... 2.00 .90
❑ 523 Bob Chance .... 2.00 .90
❑ 524 Expos Rookies 3.00 1.35
Jose Laboy
Floyd Wicker
❑ 525 Earl Wilson 3.00 1.35
❑ 526 Hector Torres .... 2.00 .90
❑ 527 Al Lopez MG 4.00 1.80
❑ 528 Claude Osteen 3.00 1.35
❑ 529 Ed Kirkpatrick 3.00 1.35
❑ 530 Cesar Tovar .... 2.00 .90
❑ 531 Dick Farrell .... 2.00 .90
❑ 532 Bird Hill Aces 3.00 1.35
Tom Phoebus
Jim Hardin
Dave McNally
Mike Cuellar
❑ 533 Nolan Ryan 425.00 190.00
❑ 534 Jerry McNertney 3.00 1.35
❑ 535 Phil Regan 3.00 1.35
❑ 536 Padres Rookies .... 2.00 .90
Danny Breeden
Dave Roberts
❑ 537 Mike Paul .... 2.00 .90
❑ 538 Charlie Smith .... 2.00 .90
❑ 539 Ted Shows How 12.00 5.50
Mike Epstein
Ted Williams MG
❑ 540 Curt Flood 3.00 1.35
❑ 541 Joe Verbanic .... 2.00 .90
❑ 542 Bob Aspromonte .... 2.00 .90
❑ 543 Fred Newman .... 2.00 .90
❑ 544 Tigers Rookies .... 2.00 .90
Mike Kilkenny
Ron Woods
❑ 545 Willie Stargell 12.00 5.50
❑ 546 Jim Nash .... 2.00 .90
❑ 547 Billy Martin MG 6.00 2.70
❑ 548 Bob Locker .... 2.00 .90
❑ 549 Ron Brand .... 2.00 .90
❑ 550 Brooks Robinson 30.00 13.50
❑ 551 Wayne Granger .... 2.00 .90
❑ 552 Dodgers Rookies 3.00 1.35
Ted Sizemore
Bill Sudakis
❑ 553 Ron Davis .... 2.00 .90
❑ 554 Frank Bertaina .... 2.00 .90
❑ 555 Jim Ray Hart 3.00 1.35
❑ 556 A's Stars 3.00 1.35
Sal Bando
Bert Campaneris
Danny Cater
❑ 557 Frank Fernandez .... 2.00 .90
❑ 558 Tom Burgmeier 3.00 1.35
❑ 559 Cardinals Rookies .... 2.00 .90
Joe Hague
Jim Hicks
❑ 560 Luis Tiant 3.00 1.35
❑ 561 Ron Clark .... 2.00 .90
❑ 562 Bob Watson 7.00 3.10
❑ 563 Marty Pattin 3.00 1.35
❑ 564 Gil Hodges MG 10.00 4.50
❑ 565 Hoyt Wilhelm 7.00 3.10
❑ 566 Ron Hansen .... 2.00 .90
❑ 567 Pirates Rookies .... 2.00 .90
Elvio Jimenez
Jim Shellenback
❑ 568 Cecil Upshaw .... 2.00 .90
❑ 569 Billy Harris .... 2.00 .90
❑ 570 Ron Santo 7.00 3.10
❑ 571 Cap Peterson .... 2.00 .90
❑ 572 Giants Heroes 16.00 7.25
Willie McCovey
Juan Marichal
❑ 573 Jim Palmer 35.00 16.00
❑ 574 George Scott 3.00 1.35
❑ 575 Bill Singer 3.00 1.35
❑ 576 Phillies Rookies .... 2.00 .90
Ron Stone
Bill Wilson
❑ 577 Mike Hegan 3.00 1.35
❑ 578 Don Bosch .... 2.00 .90
❑ 579 Dave Nelson .... 2.00 .90
❑ 580 Jim Northrup 3.00 1.35
❑ 581 Gary Nolan 3.00 1.35
❑ 582A Tony Oliva CL 5.00 1.00
White circle on back
❑ 582B Tony Oliva CL 8.00 1.60
Red circle on back
❑ 583 Clyde Wright .... 2.00 .90
❑ 584 Don Mason .... 2.00 .90
❑ 585 Ron Swoboda 3.00 1.35
❑ 586 Tim Cullen .... 2.00 .90
❑ 587 Joe Rudi 7.00 3.10
❑ 588 Bill White 3.00 1.35
❑ 589 Joe Pepitone 4.00 1.80
❑ 590 Rico Carty 5.00 2.20
❑ 591 Mike Hedlund 3.00 1.35
❑ 592 Padres Rookies 5.00 2.20
Rafael Robles
Al Santorini
❑ 593 Don Nottebart 3.00 1.35
❑ 594 Dooley Womack 3.00 1.35

	Card	NRMT	VG-E
❑ 595	Lee Maye	3.00	1.35
❑ 596	Chuck Hartenstein	3.00	1.35
❑ 597	A.L. Rookies	35.00	16.00
	Bob Floyd		
	Larry Burchart		
	Rollie Fingers		
❑ 598	Ruben Amaro	3.00	1.35
❑ 599	John Boozer	3.00	1.35
❑ 600	Tony Oliva	6.00	2.70
❑ 601	Tug McGraw	7.00	3.10
❑ 602	Cubs Rookies	5.00	2.20
	Alec Distaso		
	Don Young		
	Jim Qualls		
❑ 603	Joe Keough	3.00	1.35
❑ 604	Bobby Etheridge	3.00	1.35
❑ 605	Dick Ellsworth	3.00	1.35
❑ 606	Gene Mauch MG	5.00	2.20
❑ 607	Dick Bosman	3.00	1.35
❑ 608	Dick Simpson	3.00	1.35
❑ 609	Phil Gagliano	3.00	1.35
❑ 610	Jim Hardin	3.00	1.35
❑ 611	Braves Rookies	5.00	2.20
	Bob Didier		
	Walt Hriniak		
	Gary Neibauer		
❑ 612	Jack Aker	5.00	2.20
❑ 613	Jim Beauchamp	3.00	1.35
❑ 614	Houston Rookies	3.00	1.35
	Tom Griffin		
	Skip Guinn		
❑ 615	Len Gabrielson	3.00	1.35
❑ 616	Don McMahon	3.00	1.35
❑ 617	Jesse Gonder	3.00	1.35
❑ 618	Ramon Webster	3.00	1.35
❑ 619	Royals Rookies	4.00	1.80
	Bill Butler		
	Pat Kelly		
	Juan Rios		
❑ 620	Dean Chance	4.00	1.80
❑ 621	Bill Voss	3.00	1.35
❑ 622	Dan Osinski	3.00	1.35
❑ 623	Hank Allen	3.00	1.35
❑ 624	NL Rookies	4.00	1.80
	Darrel Chaney		
	Duffy Dyer		
	Terry Harmon		
❑ 625	Mack Jones UER	5.00	2.20
	(Batting wrong)		
❑ 626	Gene Michael	5.00	2.20
❑ 627	George Stone	3.00	1.35
❑ 628	Red Sox Rookies	4.00	1.80
	Bill Conigliaro		
	Syd O'Brien		
	Fred Wenz		
❑ 629	Jack Hamilton	3.00	1.35
❑ 630	Bobby Bonds	35.00	16.00
❑ 631	John Kennedy	5.00	2.20
❑ 632	Jon Warden	3.00	1.35
❑ 633	Harry Walker MG	3.00	1.35
❑ 634	Andy Etchebarren	3.00	1.35
❑ 635	George Culver	3.00	1.35
❑ 636	Woody Held	3.00	1.35
❑ 637	Padres Rookies	4.00	1.80
	Jerry DaVanon		
	Frank Reberger		
	Clay Kirby		
❑ 638	Ed Sprague	3.00	1.35
❑ 639	Barry Moore	3.00	1.35
❑ 640	Ferguson Jenkins	20.00	9.00
❑ 641	NL Rookies	4.00	1.80
	Bobby Darwin		
	John Miller		
	Tommy Dean		
❑ 642	John Hiller	3.00	1.35
❑ 643	Billy Cowan	3.00	1.35
❑ 644	Chuck Hinton	3.00	1.35
❑ 645	George Brunet	3.00	1.35
❑ 646	Expos Rookies	5.00	2.20
	Dan McGinn		
	Carl Morton		
❑ 647	Dave Wickersham	3.00	1.35
❑ 648	Bobby Wine	5.00	2.20
❑ 649	Al Jackson	3.00	1.35
❑ 650	Ted Williams MG	20.00	9.00
❑ 651	Gus Gil	5.00	2.20
❑ 652	Eddie Watt	3.00	1.35
❑ 653	Aurelio Rodriguez UER	5.00	2.20
	(Photo actually		
	Angels' batboy)		
❑ 654	White Sox Rookies	5.00	2.20
	Carlos May		
	Don Secrist		
	Rich Morales		
❑ 655	Mike Hershberger	3.00	1.35
❑ 656	Dan Schneider	3.00	1.35
❑ 657	Bobby Murcer	6.00	2.70
❑ 658	AL Rookies	3.00	1.35
	Tom Hall		
	Bill Burbach		
	Jim Miles		
❑ 659	Johnny Podres	4.00	1.80
❑ 660	Reggie Smith	6.00	2.70
❑ 661	Jim Merritt	3.00	1.35
❑ 662	Royals Rookies	5.00	2.20
	Dick Drago		
	George Spriggs		
	Bob Oliver		
❑ 663	Dick Radatz	5.00	2.20
❑ 664	Ron Hunt	5.00	1.35

1970 Topps

	NRMT	VG-E
COMPLETE SET (720)	1800.00	800.00
COMMON CARD (1-372)	1.00	.45
COMMON CARD (373-459)	1.50	.70
COMMON CARD (460-546)	2.00	.90
COMMON CARD (547-633)	4.00	1.80
COMMON CARD (634-720)	10.00	4.50
WRAPPER (10-CENT)	20.00	9.00

	Card	NRMT	VG-E
❑ 1	New York Mets	20.00	6.25
	Team Card		
❑ 2	Diego Segui	2.00	.90
❑ 3	Darrel Chaney	1.00	.45
❑ 4	Tom Egan	1.00	.45
❑ 5	Wes Parker	1.50	.70
❑ 6	Grant Jackson	1.00	.45
❑ 7	Indians Rookies	1.00	.45
	Gary Boyd		
	Russ Nagelson		
❑ 8	Jose Martinez	1.00	.45
❑ 9	Checklist 1	12.00	2.40
❑ 10	Carl Yastrzemski	15.00	6.75
❑ 11	Nate Colbert	1.00	.45
❑ 12	John Hiller	1.00	.45
❑ 13	Jack Hiatt	1.00	.45
❑ 14	Hank Allen	1.00	.45
❑ 15	Larry Dierker	1.00	.45
❑ 16	Charlie Metro MG	1.00	.45
❑ 17	Hoyt Wilhelm	5.00	2.20
❑ 18	Carlos May	1.00	.45
❑ 19	John Boccabella	1.00	.45
❑ 20	Dave McNally	1.00	.45
❑ 21	A's Rookies	6.00	2.70
	Vida Blue		
	Gene Tenace		
❑ 22	Ray Washburn	1.00	.45
❑ 23	Bill Robinson	2.00	.90
❑ 24	Dick Selma	1.00	.45
❑ 25	Cesar Tovar	1.00	.45
❑ 26	Tug McGraw	2.00	.90
❑ 27	Chuck Hinton	1.00	.45
❑ 28	Billy Wilson	1.00	.45
❑ 29	Sandy Alomar	2.00	.90
❑ 30	Matty Alou	2.00	.90
❑ 31	Marty Pattin	2.00	.90
❑ 32	Harry Walker MG	1.00	.45
❑ 33	Don Wert	1.00	.45
❑ 34	Willie Crawford	1.00	.45
❑ 35	Joel Horlen	1.00	.45
❑ 36	Red Rookies	2.00	.90
	Danny Breeden		
	Bernie Carbo		
❑ 37	Dick Drago	1.00	.45
❑ 38	Mack Jones	1.00	.45
❑ 39	Mike Nagy	1.00	.45
❑ 40	Rich Allen	2.00	.90
❑ 41	George Lauzerique	1.00	.45
❑ 42	Tito Fuentes	1.00	.45
❑ 43	Jack Aker	1.00	.45
❑ 44	Roberto Pena	1.00	.45
❑ 45	Dave Johnson	2.00	.90
❑ 46	Ken Rudolph	1.00	.45
❑ 47	Bob Miller	1.00	.45
❑ 48	Gil Garrido	1.00	.45
❑ 49	Tim Cullen	1.00	.45
❑ 50	Tommie Agee	2.00	.90
❑ 51	Bob Christian	1.00	.45
❑ 52	Bruce Dal Canton	1.00	.45
❑ 53	John Kennedy	1.00	.45
❑ 54	Jeff Torborg	2.00	.90
❑ 55	John Odom	1.00	.45
❑ 56	Phillies Rookies	1.00	.45
	Joe Lis		
	Scott Reid		
❑ 57	Pat Kelly	1.00	.45
❑ 58	Dave Marshall	1.00	.45
❑ 59	Dick Ellsworth	1.00	.45
❑ 60	Jim Wynn	2.00	.90
❑ 61	NL Batting Leaders	12.00	5.50
	Pete Rose		
	Bob Clemente		
	Cleon Jones		
❑ 62	AL Batting Leaders	3.50	1.55
	Rod Carew		
	Reggie Smith		
	Tony Oliva		
❑ 63	NL RBI Leaders	4.00	1.80
	Willie McCovey		
	Ron Santo		
	Tony Perez		
❑ 64	AL RBI Leaders	6.00	2.70
	Harmon Killebrew		
	Boog Powell		
	Reggie Jackson		
❑ 65	NL Home Run Leaders	6.00	2.70
	Willie McCovey		
	Hank Aaron		
	Lee May		
❑ 66	AL Home Run Leaders	6.00	2.70
	Harmon Killebrew		
	Frank Howard		
	Reggie Jackson		
❑ 67	NL ERA Leaders	7.00	3.10
	Juan Marichal		
	Steve Carlton		
	Bob Gibson		
❑ 68	AL ERA Leaders	2.00	.90
	Dick Bosman		
	Jim Palmer		
	Mike Cuellar		
❑ 69	NL Pitching Leaders	7.00	3.10
	Tom Seaver		
	Phil Niekro		
	Fergie Jenkins		
	Juan Marichal		
❑ 70	AL Pitching Leaders	2.00	.90
	Dennis McLain		
	Mike Cuellar		
	Dave Boswell		
	Dave McNally		
	Jim Perry		
	Mel Stottlemyre		
❑ 71	NL Strikeout Leaders	4.00	1.80
	Fergie Jenkins		
	Bob Gibson		
	Bill Singer		

❑ 72 AL Strikeout Leaders...... 2.00 .90
Sam McDowell
Mickey Lolich
Andy Messersmith
❑ 73 Wayne Granger............. 1.00 .45
❑ 74 Angels Rookies............. 1.00 .45
Greg Washburn
Wally Wolf
❑ 75 Jim Kaat .... 2.00 .90
❑ 76 Carl Taylor...................... 1.00 .45
❑ 77 Frank Linzy .... 1.00 .45
❑ 78 Joe Lahoud .... 1.00 .45
❑ 79 Clay Kirby .... 1.00 .45
❑ 80 Don Kessinger.................. 2.00 .90
❑ 81 Dave May .... 1.00 .45
❑ 82 Frank Fernandez.............. 1.00 .45
❑ 83 Don Cardwell.................... 1.00 .45
❑ 84 Paul Casanova .... 1.00 .45
❑ 85 Max Alvis.......................... 1.00 .45
❑ 86 Lum Harris MG .... 1.00 .45
❑ 87 Steve Renko .... 1.00 .45
❑ 88 Pilots Rookies .... 2.00 .90
Miguel Fuentes
Dick Baney
❑ 89 Juan Rios .... 1.00 .45
❑ 90 Tim McCarver .... 2.00 .90
❑ 91 Rich Morales .... 1.00 .45
❑ 92 George Culver.................. 1.00 .45
❑ 93 Rick Renick...................... 1.00 .45
❑ 94 Freddie Patek .... 2.00 .90
❑ 95 Earl Wilson .... 2.00 .90
❑ 96 Cardinals Rookies.......... 2.00 .90
Leron Lee
Jerry Reuss
❑ 97 Joe Moeller .... 1.00 .45
❑ 98 Gates Brown .... 2.00 .90
❑ 99 Bobby Pfeil .... 1.00 .45
❑ 100 Mel Stottlemyre .... 2.00 .90
❑ 101 Bobby Floyd .... 1.00 .45
❑ 102 Joe Rudi .... 2.00 .90
❑ 103 Frank Reberger............ 1.00 .45
❑ 104 Gerry Moses .... 1.00 .45
❑ 105 Tony Gonzalez .... 1.00 .45
❑ 106 Darold Knowles............ 1.00 .45
❑ 107 Bobby Etheridge .... 1.00 .45
❑ 108 Tom Burgmeier .... 1.00 .45
❑ 109 Expos Rookies.............. 1.00 .45
Garry Jestadt
Carl Morton
❑ 110 Bob Moose .... 1.00 .45
❑ 111 Mike Hegan.................. 2.00 .90
❑ 112 Dave Nelson .... 1.00 .45
❑ 113 Jim Ray......................... 1.00 .45
❑ 114 Gene Michael .... 1.00 .45
❑ 115 Alex Johnson................ 2.00 .90
❑ 116 Sparky Lyle .... 2.00 .90
❑ 117 Don Young .... 1.00 .45
❑ 118 George Mitterwald........ 1.00 .45
❑ 119 Chuck Taylor................ 1.00 .45
❑ 120 Sal Bando .... 2.00 .90
❑ 121 Orioles Rookies............ 1.00 .45
Fred Beene
Terry Crowley
❑ 122 George Stone .... 1.00 .45
❑ 123 Don Gutteridge MG...... 1.00 .45
❑ 124 Larry Jaster .... 1.00 .45
❑ 125 Deron Johnson .... 1.00 .45
❑ 126 Marty Martinez .... 1.00 .45
❑ 127 Joe Coleman................ 1.00 .45
❑ 128A Checklist 2 ERR 6.00 1.20
(226 R Perranoski)
❑ 128B Checklist 2 COR 6.00 1.20
(226 R. Perranoski)
❑ 129 Jimmie Price .... 1.00 .45
❑ 130 Ollie Brown .... 1.00 .45
❑ 131 Dodgers Rookies.......... 1.00 .45
Ray Lamb
Bob Stinson
❑ 132 Jim McGlothlin.............. 1.00 .45
❑ 133 Clay Carroll .... 1.00 .45
❑ 134 Danny Walton .... 1.00 .45
❑ 135 Dick Dietz .... 1.00 .45
❑ 136 Steve Hargan .... 1.00 .45
❑ 137 Art Shamsky .... 1.00 .45
❑ 138 Joe Foy .... 1.00 .45
❑ 139 Rich Nye .... 1.00 .45
❑ 140 Reggie Jackson.......... 50.00 22.00
❑ 141 Pirates Rookies........... 2.00 .90
Dave Cash
Johnny Jeter
❑ 142 Fritz Peterson .... 1.00 .45
❑ 143 Phil Gagliano................ 1.00 .45
❑ 144 Ray Culp .... 1.00 .45
❑ 145 Rico Carty .... 2.00 .90
❑ 146 Danny Murphy.............. 1.00 .45
❑ 147 Angel Hermoso .... 1.00 .45
❑ 148 Earl Weaver MG 3.00 1.35
❑ 149 Billy Champion .... 1.00 .45
❑ 150 Harmon Killebrew 8.00 3.60
❑ 151 Dave Roberts .... 1.00 .45
❑ 152 Ike Brown .... 1.00 .45
❑ 153 Gary Gentry.................. 1.00 .45
❑ 154 Senators Rookies .... 1.00 .45
Jim Miles
Jan Dukes
❑ 155 Denis Menke .... 1.00 .45
❑ 156 Eddie Fisher .... 1.00 .45
❑ 157 Manny Mota .... 2.00 .90
❑ 158 Jerry McNertney .... 2.00 .90
❑ 159 Tommy Helms.............. 2.00 .90
❑ 160 Phil Niekro................... 5.00 2.20
❑ 161 Richie Scheinblum ...... 1.00 .45
❑ 162 Jerry Johnson .... 1.00 .45
❑ 163 Syd O'Brien .... 1.00 .45
❑ 164 Ty Cline........................ 1.00 .45
❑ 165 Ed Kirkpatrick .... 1.00 .45
❑ 166 Al Oliver....................... 2.00 .90
❑ 167 Bill Burbach.................. 1.00 .45
❑ 168 Dave Watkins .... 1.00 .45
❑ 169 Tom Hall .... 1.00 .45
❑ 170 Billy Williams 7.00 3.10
❑ 171 Jim Nash .... 1.00 .45
❑ 172 Braves Rookies............ 2.00 .90
Garry Hill
Ralph Garr
❑ 173 Jim Hicks...................... 1.00 .45
❑ 174 Ted Sizemore .... 2.00 .90
❑ 175 Dick Bosman................ 1.00 .45
❑ 176 Jim Ray Hart .... 2.00 .90
❑ 177 Jim Northrup .... 2.00 .90
❑ 178 Denny Lemaster .... 1.00 .45
❑ 179 Ivan Murrell.................. 1.00 .45
❑ 180 Tommy John .... 2.00 .90
❑ 181 Sparky Anderson MG .. 5.00 2.20
❑ 182 Dick Hall .... 1.00 .45
❑ 183 Jerry Grote .... 1.00 .45
❑ 184 Ray Fosse.................... 1.00 .45
❑ 185 Don Mincher .... 2.00 .90
❑ 186 Rick Joseph.................. 1.00 .45
❑ 187 Mike Hedlund .... 1.00 .45
❑ 188 Manny Sanguillen .... 2.00 .90
❑ 189 Yankees Rookies 50.00 22.00
Thurman Munson
Dave McDonald
❑ 190 Joe Torre...................... 2.00 .90
❑ 191 Vicente Romo .... 1.00 .45
❑ 192 Jim Qualls .... 1.00 .45
❑ 193 Mike Wegener.............. 1.00 .45
❑ 194 Chuck Manuel.............. 1.00 .45
❑ 195 Tom Seaver NLCS 15.00 6.75
❑ 196 Ken Boswell NLCS ...... 2.00 .90
❑ 197 Nolan Ryan NLCS...... 30.00 13.50
❑ 198 NL Playoff Summary .. 15.00 6.75
Mets celebrate
(Nolan Ryan)
❑ 199 Mike Cuellar ALCS ...... 2.00 .90
❑ 200 Boog Powell ALCS 4.00 1.80
❑ 201 Boog Powell ALCS ...... 2.00 .90
Andy Etchebarren)
❑ 202 AL Playoff Summary .... 2.00 .90
Orioles celebrate
❑ 203 Rudy May .... 1.00 .45
❑ 204 Len Gabrielson .... 1.00 .45
❑ 205 Bert Campaneris .... 2.00 .90
❑ 206 Clete Boyer .... 2.00 .90
❑ 207 Tigers Rookies .... 1.00 .45
Norman McRae
Bob Reed
❑ 208 Fred Gladding .... 1.00 .45
❑ 209 Ken Suarez .... 1.00 .45
❑ 210 Juan Marichal 7.00 3.10
❑ 211 Ted Williams MG......... 12.00 5.50
❑ 212 Al Santorini .... 1.00 .45
❑ 213 Andy Etchebarren .... 1.00 .45
❑ 214 Ken Boswell .... 1.00 .45
❑ 215 Reggie Smith................ 2.00 .90
❑ 216 Chuck Hartenstein........ 1.00 .45
❑ 217 Ron Hansen .... 1.00 .45
❑ 218 Ron Stone .... 1.00 .45
❑ 219 Jerry Kenney .... 1.00 .45
❑ 220 Steve Carlton 15.00 6.75
❑ 221 Ron Brand.................... 1.00 .45
❑ 222 Jim Rooker .... 2.00 .90
❑ 223 Nate Oliver .... 1.00 .45
❑ 224 Steve Barber .... 2.00 .90
❑ 225 Lee May .... 2.00 .90
❑ 226 Ron Perranoski .... 1.50 .70
❑ 227 Astros Rookies .... 1.50 .70
John Mayberry
Bob Watkins
❑ 228 Aurelio Rodriguez .... 1.00 .45
❑ 229 Rich Robertson .... 1.00 .45
❑ 230 Brooks Robinson........ 15.00 6.75
❑ 231 Luis Tiant...................... 1.50 .70
❑ 232 Bob Didier .... 1.00 .45
❑ 233 Lew Krausse .... 1.00 .45
❑ 234 Tommy Dean................ 1.00 .45
❑ 235 Mike Epstein .... 1.00 .45
❑ 236 Bob Veale .... 1.00 .45
❑ 237 Russ Gibson .... 1.00 .45
❑ 238 Jose Laboy .... 1.00 .45
❑ 239 Ken Berry .... 1.00 .45
❑ 240 Ferguson Jenkins 7.00 3.10
❑ 241 Royals Rookies .... 1.00 .45
Al Fitzmorris
Scott Northey
❑ 242 Walter Alston MG .... 2.00 .90
❑ 243 Joe Sparma.................. 1.00 .45
❑ 244A Checklist 3 .... 6.00 1.20
(Red bat on front)
❑ 244B Checklist 3 .... 6.00 1.20
(Brown bat on front)
❑ 245 Leo Cardenas .... 1.00 .45
❑ 246 Jim McAndrew.............. 1.00 .45
❑ 247 Lou Klimchock.............. 1.00 .45
❑ 248 Jesus Alou.................... 1.00 .45
❑ 249 Bob Locker .... 1.00 .45
❑ 250 Willie McCovey UER .. 10.00 4.50
(1963 San Francisci)
❑ 251 Dick Schofield .... 1.00 .45
❑ 252 Lowell Palmer .... 1.00 .45
❑ 253 Ron Woods .... 1.00 .45
❑ 254 Camilo Pascual .... 1.00 .45
❑ 255 Jim Spencer .... 1.00 .45
❑ 256 Vic Davalillo.................. 1.00 .45
❑ 257 Dennis Higgins .... 1.00 .45
❑ 258 Paul Popovich .... 1.00 .45
❑ 259 Tommie Reynolds .... 1.00 .45
❑ 260 Claude Osteen .... 1.00 .45
❑ 261 Curt Motton .... 1.00 .45
❑ 262 Padres Rookies............ 1.00 .45
Jerry Morales
Jim Williams
❑ 263 Duane Josephson .... 1.00 .45
❑ 264 Rich Hebner .... 1.00 .45
❑ 265 Randy Hundley .... 1.00 .45
❑ 266 Wally Bunker................ 1.00 .45
❑ 267 Twins Rookies.............. 1.00 .45
Herman Hill
Paul Ratliff
❑ 268 Claude Raymond .... 1.00 .45
❑ 269 Cesar Gutierrez............ 1.00 .45
❑ 270 Chris Short .... 1.00 .45
❑ 271 Greg Goossen.............. 1.00 .45
❑ 272 Hector Torres .... 1.00 .45
❑ 273 Ralph Houk MG............ 1.50 .70
❑ 274 Gerry Arrigo.................. 1.00 .45
❑ 275 Duke Sims.................... 1.00 .45
❑ 276 Ron Hunt .... 1.00 .45
❑ 277 Paul Doyle.................... 1.00 .45
❑ 278 Tommie Aaron.............. 1.00 .45
❑ 279 Bill Lee .... 2.00 .90
❑ 280 Donn Clendenon .... 1.00 .45
❑ 281 Casey Cox.................... 1.00 .45
❑ 282 Steve Huntz.................. 1.00 .45

- ❑ 283 Angel Bravo 1.00 .45
- ❑ 284 Jack Baldschun 1.00 .45
- ❑ 285 Paul Blair 2.00 .90
- ❑ 286 Dodgers Rookies 6.00 2.70
  Jack Jenkins
  Bill Buckner
- ❑ 287 Fred Talbot 1.00 .45
- ❑ 288 Larry Hisle 1.00 .45
- ❑ 289 Gene Brabender 1.00 .45
- ❑ 290 Rod Carew 18.00 8.00
- ❑ 291 Leo Durocher MG 3.00 1.35
- ❑ 292 Eddie Leon 1.00 .45
- ❑ 293 Bob Bailey 1.00 .45
- ❑ 294 Jose Azcue 1.00 .45
- ❑ 295 Cecil Upshaw 1.00 .45
- ❑ 296 Woody Woodward 1.00 .45
- ❑ 297 Curt Blefary 1.00 .45
- ❑ 298 Ken Henderson 1.00 .45
- ❑ 299 Buddy Bradford 1.00 .45
- ❑ 300 Tom Seaver 40.00 18.00
- ❑ 301 Chico Salmon 1.00 .45
- ❑ 302 Jeff James 1.00 .45
- ❑ 303 Brant Alyea 1.00 .45
- ❑ 304 Bill Russell 6.00 2.70
- ❑ 305 Don Buford WS 4.00 1.80
- ❑ 306 Donn Clendenon WS 4.00 1.80
- ❑ 307 Tommie Agee WS 4.00 1.80
- ❑ 308 J.C. Martin WS 4.00 1.80
- ❑ 309 Jerry Koosman WS 4.00 1.80
- ❑ 310 World Series Summary 5.00 2.20
  Mets whoop it up
- ❑ 311 Dick Green 1.00 .45
- ❑ 312 Mike Torrez 1.00 .45
- ❑ 313 Mayo Smith MG 1.00 .45
- ❑ 314 Bill McCool 1.00 .45
- ❑ 315 Luis Aparicio 5.00 2.20
- ❑ 316 Skip Guinn 1.00 .45
- ❑ 317 Red Sox Rookies 1.00 .45
  Billy Conigliaro
  Luis Alvarado
- ❑ 318 Willie Smith 1.00 .45
- ❑ 319 Clay Dalrymple 1.00 .45
- ❑ 320 Jim Maloney 1.00 .45
- ❑ 321 Lou Piniella 2.00 .90
- ❑ 322 Luke Walker 1.00 .45
- ❑ 323 Wayne Comer 1.00 .45
- ❑ 324 Tony Taylor 1.00 .45
- ❑ 325 Dave Boswell 1.00 .45
- ❑ 326 Bill Voss 1.00 .45
- ❑ 327 Hal King 1.00 .45
- ❑ 328 George Brunet 1.00 .45
- ❑ 329 Chris Cannizzaro 1.00 .45
- ❑ 330 Lou Brock 10.00 4.50
- ❑ 331 Chuck Dobson 1.00 .45
- ❑ 332 Bobby Wine 1.00 .45
- ❑ 333 Bobby Murcer 2.00 .90
- ❑ 334 Phil Regan 1.00 .45
- ❑ 335 Bill Freehan 2.00 .90
- ❑ 336 Del Unser 1.00 .45
- ❑ 337 Mike McCormick 1.00 .45
- ❑ 338 Paul Schaal 1.00 .45
- ❑ 339 Johnny Edwards 1.00 .45
- ❑ 340 Tony Conigliaro 3.00 1.35
- ❑ 341 Bill Sudakis 1.00 .45
- ❑ 342 Wilbur Wood 1.50 .70
- ❑ 343A Checklist 4 6.00 1.20
  (Red bat on front)
- ❑ 343B Checklist 4 6.00 1.20
  (Brown bat on front)
- ❑ 344 Marcelino Lopez 1.00 .45
- ❑ 345 Al Ferrara 1.00 .45
- ❑ 346 Red Schoendienst MG 2.00 .90
- ❑ 347 Russ Snyder 1.00 .45
- ❑ 348 Mets Rookies 1.50 .70
  Mike Jorgensen
  Jesse Hudson
- ❑ 349 Steve Hamilton 1.00 .45
- ❑ 350 Roberto Clemente 70.00 32.00
- ❑ 351 Tom Murphy 1.00 .45
- ❑ 352 Bob Barton 1.00 .45
- ❑ 353 Stan Williams 1.00 .45
- ❑ 354 Amos Otis 1.50 .70
- ❑ 355 Doug Rader 1.00 .45
- ❑ 356 Fred Lasher 1.00 .45
- ❑ 357 Bob Burda 1.00 .45
- ❑ 358 Pedro Borbon 1.50 .70
- ❑ 359 Phil Roof 1.00 .45
- ❑ 360 Curt Flood 2.00 .90
- ❑ 361 Ray Jarvis 1.00 .45
- ❑ 362 Joe Hague 1.00 .45
- ❑ 363 Tom Shopay 1.00 .45
- ❑ 364 Dan McGinn 1.00 .45
- ❑ 365 Zoilo Versalles 1.00 .45
- ❑ 366 Barry Moore 1.00 .45
- ❑ 367 Mike Lum 1.00 .45
- ❑ 368 Ed Herrmann 1.00 .45
- ❑ 369 Alan Foster 1.00 .45
- ❑ 370 Tommy Harper 2.00 .90
- ❑ 371 Rod Gaspar 1.00 .45
- ❑ 372 Dave Giusti 1.50 .70
- ❑ 373 Roy White 2.00 .90
- ❑ 374 Tommie Sisk 1.50 .70
- ❑ 375 Johnny Callison 2.00 .90
- ❑ 376 Lefty Phillips MG 1.50 .70
- ❑ 377 Bill Butler 1.00 .45
- ❑ 378 Jim Davenport 1.50 .70
- ❑ 379 Tom Tischinski 1.50 .70
- ❑ 380 Tony Perez 7.00 3.10
- ❑ 381 Athletics Rookies 1.50 .70
  Bobby Brooks
  Mike Olivo
- ❑ 382 Jack DiLauro 1.50 .70
- ❑ 383 Mickey Stanley 2.00 .90
- ❑ 384 Gary Neibauer 1.50 .70
- ❑ 385 George Scott 2.00 .90
- ❑ 386 Bill Dillman 1.50 .70
- ❑ 387 Baltimore Orioles 4.00 1.80
  Team Card
- ❑ 388 Byron Browne 1.50 .70
- ❑ 389 Jim Shellenback 1.50 .70
- ❑ 390 Willie Davis 2.00 .90
- ❑ 391 Larry Brown 1.50 .70
- ❑ 392 Walt Hriniak 2.00 .90
- ❑ 393 John Gelnar 1.50 .70
- ❑ 394 Gil Hodges MG 5.00 2.20
- ❑ 395 Walt Williams 1.50 .70
- ❑ 396 Steve Blass 2.00 .90
- ❑ 397 Roger Repoz 1.50 .70
- ❑ 398 Bill Stoneman 1.50 .70
- ❑ 399 New York Yankees 4.00 1.80
  Team Card
- ❑ 400 Denny McLain 2.00 .90
- ❑ 401 Giants Rookies 1.50 .70
  John Harrell
  Bernie Williams
- ❑ 402 Ellie Rodriguez 1.50 .70
- ❑ 403 Jim Bunning 5.00 2.20
- ❑ 404 Rich Reese 1.50 .70
- ❑ 405 Bill Hands 1.50 .70
- ❑ 406 Mike Andrews 1.50 .70
- ❑ 407 Bob Watson 2.00 .90
- ❑ 408 Paul Lindblad 1.50 .70
- ❑ 409 Bob Tolan 2.00 .90
- ❑ 410 Boog Powell 4.00 1.80
- ❑ 411 Los Angeles Dodgers 4.00 1.80
  Team Card
- ❑ 412 Larry Burchart 1.50 .70
- ❑ 413 Sonny Jackson 1.50 .70
- ❑ 414 Paul Edmondson 1.50 .70
- ❑ 415 Julian Javier 2.00 .90
- ❑ 416 Joe Verbanic 1.50 .70
- ❑ 417 John Bateman 1.50 .70
- ❑ 418 John Donaldson 1.50 .70
- ❑ 419 Ron Taylor 1.50 .70
- ❑ 420 Ken McMullen 2.00 .90
- ❑ 421 Pat Dobson 2.00 .90
- ❑ 422 Royals Team 4.00 1.80
- ❑ 423 Jerry May 1.50 .70
- ❑ 424 Mike Kilkenny 1.50 .70
  (Inconsistent design
  card number in
  white circle)
- ❑ 425 Bobby Bonds 6.00 2.70
- ❑ 426 Bill Rigney MG 1.50 .70
- ❑ 427 Fred Norman 1.50 .70
- ❑ 428 Don Buford 1.50 .70
- ❑ 429 Cubs Rookies 1.50 .70
  Randy Bobb
  Jim Cosman
- ❑ 430 Andy Messersmith 2.00 .90
- ❑ 431 Ron Swoboda 2.00 .90
- ❑ 432A Checklist 5 6.00 1.20
  (Baseball in
  yellow letters)
- ❑ 432B Checklist 5 6.00 1.20
  (Baseball in
  white letters)
- ❑ 433 Ron Bryant 1.50 .70
- ❑ 434 Felipe Alou 2.00 .90
- ❑ 435 Nelson Briles 2.00 .90
- ❑ 436 Philadelphia Phillies 4.00 1.80
  Team Card
- ❑ 437 Danny Cater 1.50 .70
- ❑ 438 Pat Jarvis 1.50 .70
- ❑ 439 Lee Maye 1.50 .70
- ❑ 440 Bill Mazeroski 3.00 1.35
- ❑ 441 John O'Donoghue 1.50 .70
- ❑ 442 Gene Mauch MG 2.00 .90
- ❑ 443 Al Jackson 1.50 .70
- ❑ 444 White Sox Rookies 1.50 .70
  Billy Farmer
  John Matias
- ❑ 445 Vada Pinson 2.00 .90
- ❑ 446 Billy Grabarkewitz 1.50 .70
- ❑ 447 Lee Stange 1.50 .70
- ❑ 448 Houston Astros 4.00 1.80
  Team Card
- ❑ 449 Jim Palmer 12.00 5.50
- ❑ 450 Willie McCovey AS 7.00 3.10
- ❑ 451 Boog Powell AS 4.00 1.80
- ❑ 452 Felix Millan AS 2.00 .90
- ❑ 453 Rod Carew AS 7.00 3.10
- ❑ 454 Ron Santo AS 4.00 1.80
- ❑ 455 Brooks Robinson AS 7.00 3.10
- ❑ 456 Don Kessinger AS 2.00 .90
- ❑ 457 Rico Petrocelli AS 4.00 1.80
- ❑ 458 Pete Rose AS 14.00 6.25
- ❑ 459 Reggie Jackson AS 12.00 5.50
- ❑ 460 Matty Alou AS 3.00 1.35
- ❑ 461 Carl Yastrzemski AS 10.00 4.50
- ❑ 462 Hank Aaron AS 15.00 6.75
- ❑ 463 Frank Robinson AS 7.00 3.10
- ❑ 464 Johnny Bench AS 15.00 6.75
- ❑ 465 Bill Freehan AS 3.00 1.35
- ❑ 466 Juan Marichal AS 4.00 1.80
- ❑ 467 Denny McLain AS 3.00 1.35
- ❑ 468 Jerry Koosman AS 3.00 1.35
- ❑ 469 Sam McDowell AS 3.00 1.35
- ❑ 470 Willie Stargell 10.00 4.50
- ❑ 471 Chris Zachary 2.00 .90
- ❑ 472 Braves Team 3.00 1.35
- ❑ 473 Don Bryant 2.00 .90
- ❑ 474 Dick Kelley 2.00 .90
- ❑ 475 Dick McAuliffe 3.00 1.35
- ❑ 476 Don Shaw 2.00 .90
- ❑ 477 Orioles Rookies 2.00 .90
  Al Severinsen
  Roger Freed
- ❑ 478 Bobby Heise 2.00 .90
- ❑ 479 Dick Woodson 2.00 .90
- ❑ 480 Glenn Beckert 3.00 1.35
- ❑ 481 Jose Tartabull 3.00 1.35
- ❑ 482 Tom Hilgendorf 2.00 .90
- ❑ 483 Gail Hopkins 2.00 .90
- ❑ 484 Gary Nolan 3.00 1.35
- ❑ 485 Jay Johnstone 3.00 1.35
- ❑ 486 Terry Harmon 2.00 .90
- ❑ 487 Cisco Carlos 2.00 .90
- ❑ 488 J.C. Martin 2.00 .90
- ❑ 489 Eddie Kasko MG 2.00 .90
- ❑ 490 Bill Singer 3.00 1.35
- ❑ 491 Graig Nettles 6.00 2.70
- ❑ 492 Astros Rookies 2.00 .90
  Keith Lampard
  Scipio Spinks
- ❑ 493 Lindy McDaniel 3.00 1.35
- ❑ 494 Larry Stahl 2.00 .90
- ❑ 495 Dave Morehead 2.00 .90
- ❑ 496 Steve Whitaker 2.00 .90
- ❑ 497 Eddie Watt 2.00 .90
- ❑ 498 Al Weis 2.00 .90
- ❑ 499 Skip Lockwood 3.00 1.35
- ❑ 500 Hank Aaron 50.00 22.00
- ❑ 501 Chicago White Sox 5.00 2.20
  Team Card

❑ 502 Rollie Fingers 10.00 4.50
❑ 503 Dal Maxvill .... 2.00 .90
❑ 504 Don Pavletich .... 2.00 .90
❑ 505 Ken Holtzman 3.00 1.35
❑ 506 Ed Stroud .... 2.00 .90
❑ 507 Pat Corrales 3.00 1.35
❑ 508 Joe Niekro 3.00 1.35
❑ 509 Montreal Expos 3.00 1.35
Team Card
❑ 510 Tony Oliva 3.00 1.35
❑ 511 Joe Hoerner .... 2.00 .90
❑ 512 Billy Harris .... 2.00 .90
❑ 513 Preston Gomez MG .... 2.00 .90
❑ 514 Steve Hovley .... 2.00 .90
❑ 515 Don Wilson 3.00 1.35
❑ 516 Yankees Rookies .... 2.00 .90
John Ellis
Jim Lyttle
❑ 517 Joe Gibbon .... 2.00 .90
❑ 518 Bill Melton .... 2.00 .90
❑ 519 Don McMahon .... 2.00 .90
❑ 520 Willie Horton 3.00 1.35
❑ 521 Cal Koonce .... 2.00 .90
❑ 522 Angels Team 5.00 2.20
❑ 523 Jose Pena .... 2.00 .90
❑ 524 Alvin Dark MG 3.00 1.35
❑ 525 Jerry Adair .... 2.00 .90
❑ 526 Ron Herbel .... 2.00 .90
❑ 527 Don Bosch .... 2.00 .90
❑ 528 Elrod Hendricks .... 2.00 .90
❑ 529 Bob Aspromonte .... 2.00 .90
❑ 530 Bob Gibson 14.00 6.25
❑ 531 Ron Clark .... 2.00 .90
❑ 532 Danny Murtaugh MG 3.00 1.35
❑ 533 Buzz Stephen .... 2.00 .90
❑ 534 Minnesota Twins 5.00 2.20
Team Card
❑ 535 Andy Kosco .... 2.00 .90
❑ 536 Mike Kekich .... 2.00 .90
❑ 537 Joe Morgan 10.00 4.50
❑ 538 Bob Humphreys .... 2.00 .90
❑ 539 Phillies Rookies 6.00 2.70
Denny Doyle
Larry Bowa
❑ 540 Gary Peters .... 2.00 .90
❑ 541 Bill Heath .... 2.00 .90
❑ 542 Checklist 6 .... 8.00 1.60
❑ 543 Clyde Wright .... 2.00 .90
❑ 544 Cincinnati Reds 2.50 1.10
Team Card
❑ 545 Ken Harrelson 3.00 1.35
❑ 546 Ron Reed .... 2.00 .90
❑ 547 Rick Monday 6.00 2.70
❑ 548 Howie Reed 4.00 1.80
❑ 549 St. Louis Cardinals 8.00 3.60
Team Card
❑ 550 Frank Howard 6.00 2.70
❑ 551 Dock Ellis 6.00 2.70
❑ 552 Royals Rookies 4.00 1.80
Don O'Riley
Dennis Paepke
Fred Rico
❑ 553 Jim Lefebvre 6.00 2.70
❑ 554 Tom Timmermann 4.00 1.80
❑ 555 Orlando Cepeda 6.00 2.70
❑ 556 Dave Bristol MG 6.00 2.70
❑ 557 Ed Kranepool 6.00 2.70
❑ 558 Vern Fuller 4.00 1.80
❑ 559 Tommy Davis 6.00 2.70
❑ 560 Gaylord Perry 10.00 4.50
❑ 561 Tom McCraw 4.00 1.80
❑ 562 Ted Abernathy 4.00 1.80
❑ 563 Boston Red Sox 8.00 3.60
Team Card
❑ 564 Johnny Briggs 4.00 1.80
❑ 565 Jim Hunter 10.00 4.50
❑ 566 Gene Alley 6.00 2.70
❑ 567 Bob Oliver 4.00 1.80
❑ 568 Stan Bahnsen 6.00 2.70
❑ 569 Cookie Rojas 6.00 2.70
❑ 570 Jim Fregosi 6.00 2.70
White Chevy Pick-Up in Background
❑ 571 Jim Brewer 4.00 1.80
❑ 572 Frank Quilici MG 4.00 1.80
❑ 573 Padres Rookies 4.00 1.80
Mike Corkins
Rafael Robles
Ron Slocum
❑ 574 Bobby Bolin 6.00 2.70
❑ 575 Cleon Jones 6.00 2.70
❑ 576 Milt Pappas 6.00 2.70
❑ 577 Bernie Allen 4.00 1.80
❑ 578 Tom Griffin 4.00 1.80
❑ 579 Detroit Tigers 8.00 3.60
Team Card
❑ 580 Pete Rose 45.00 20.00
❑ 581 Tom Satriano 4.00 1.80
❑ 582 Mike Paul 4.00 1.80
❑ 583 Hal Lanier 4.00 1.80
❑ 584 Al Downing 6.00 2.70
❑ 585 Rusty Staub 8.00 3.60
❑ 586 Rickey Clark 4.00 1.80
❑ 587 Jose Arcia 4.00 1.80
❑ 588A Checklist 7 ERR 12.00 2.40
(666 Adolfo)
❑ 588B Checklist 7 COR 12.00 2.40
(666 Adolpho)
❑ 589 Joe Keough 4.00 1.80
❑ 590 Mike Cuellar 6.00 2.70
❑ 591 Mike Ryan UER 4.00 1.80
(Pitching Record
header on card back)
❑ 592 Daryl Patterson 4.00 1.80
❑ 593 Chicago Cubs 8.00 3.60
Team Card
❑ 594 Jake Gibbs 4.00 1.80
❑ 595 Maury Wills 8.00 3.60
❑ 596 Mike Hershberger 6.00 2.70
❑ 597 Sonny Siebert 4.00 1.80
❑ 598 Joe Pepitone 6.00 2.70
❑ 599 Senators Rookies 4.00 1.80
Dick Stelmaszek
Gene Martin
Dick Such
❑ 600 Willie Mays 70.00 32.00
❑ 601 Pete Richert 4.00 1.80
❑ 602 Ted Savage 4.00 1.80
❑ 603 Ray Oyler 4.00 1.80
❑ 604 Clarence Gaston 6.00 2.70
❑ 605 Rick Wise 6.00 2.70
❑ 606 Chico Ruiz 4.00 1.80
❑ 607 Gary Waslewski 4.00 1.80
❑ 608 Pittsburgh Pirates 8.00 3.60
Team Card
❑ 609 Buck Martinez 6.00 2.70
(Inconsistent design
card number in
white circle)
❑ 610 Jerry Koosman 8.00 3.60
❑ 611 Norm Cash 5.00 2.20
❑ 612 Jim Hickman 6.00 2.70
❑ 613 Dave Baldwin 6.00 2.70
❑ 614 Mike Shannon 6.00 2.70
❑ 615 Mark Belanger 6.00 2.70
❑ 616 Jim Merritt 4.00 1.80
❑ 617 Jim French 4.00 1.80
❑ 618 Billy Wynne 4.00 1.80
❑ 619 Norm Miller 4.00 1.80
❑ 620 Jim Perry 6.00 2.70
❑ 621 Braves Rookies 10.00 4.50
Mike McQueen
Darrell Evans
Rick Kester
❑ 622 Don Sutton 10.00 4.50
❑ 623 Horace Clarke 6.00 2.70
❑ 624 Clyde King MG 4.00 1.80
❑ 625 Dean Chance 4.00 1.80
❑ 626 Dave Ricketts 4.00 1.80
❑ 627 Gary Wagner 4.00 1.80
❑ 628 Wayne Garrett 4.00 1.80
❑ 629 Merv Rettenmund 4.00 1.80
❑ 630 Ernie Banks 50.00 22.00
❑ 631 Oakland Athletics 8.00 3.60
Team Card
❑ 632 Gary Sutherland 4.00 1.80
❑ 633 Roger Nelson 4.00 1.80
❑ 634 Bud Harrelson 15.00 6.75
❑ 635 Bob Allison 15.00 6.75
❑ 636 Jim Stewart 10.00 4.50
❑ 637 Cleveland Indians 15.00 6.75
Team Card
❑ 638 Frank Bertaina 10.00 4.50
❑ 639 Dave Campbell 10.00 4.50
❑ 640 Al Kaline 50.00 22.00
❑ 641 Al McBean 10.00 4.50
❑ 642 Angels Rookies 10.00 4.50
Greg Garrett
Gordon Lund
Jarvis Tatum
❑ 643 Jose Pagan 10.00 4.50
❑ 644 Gerry Nyman 10.00 4.50
❑ 645 Don Money 15.00 6.75
❑ 646 Jim Britton 10.00 4.50
❑ 647 Tom Matchick 10.00 4.50
❑ 648 Larry Haney 10.00 4.50
❑ 649 Jimmie Hall 10.00 4.50
❑ 650 Sam McDowell 15.00 6.75
❑ 651 Jim Gosger 10.00 4.50
❑ 652 Rich Rollins 15.00 6.75
❑ 653 Moe Drabowsky 10.00 4.50
❑ 654 NL Rookies 12.00 5.50
Oscar Gamble
Boots Day
Angel Mangual
❑ 655 John Roseboro 15.00 6.75
❑ 656 Jim Hardin 10.00 4.50
❑ 657 San Diego Padres 15.00 6.75
Team Card
❑ 658 Ken Tatum 10.00 4.50
❑ 659 Pete Ward 10.00 4.50
❑ 660 Johnny Bench 100.00 45.00
❑ 661 Jerry Robertson 10.00 4.50
❑ 662 Frank Lucchesi MG 10.00 4.50
❑ 663 Tito Francona 10.00 4.50
❑ 664 Bob Robertson 10.00 4.50
❑ 665 Jim Lonborg 15.00 6.75
❑ 666 Adolpho Phillips 10.00 4.50
❑ 667 Bob Meyer 15.00 6.75
❑ 668 Bob Tillman 10.00 4.50
❑ 669 White Sox Rookies 10.00 4.50
Bart Johnson
Dan Lazar
Mickey Scott
❑ 670 Ron Santo 12.00 5.50
❑ 671 Jim Campanis 10.00 4.50
❑ 672 Leon McFadden 10.00 4.50
❑ 673 Ted Uhlaender 10.00 4.50
❑ 674 Dave Leonhard 10.00 4.50
❑ 675 Jose Cardenal 15.00 6.75
❑ 676 Washington Senators 20.00 9.00
Team Card
❑ 677 Woodie Fryman 10.00 4.50
❑ 678 Dave Duncan 15.00 6.75
❑ 679 Ray Sadecki 10.00 4.50
❑ 680 Rico Petrocelli 15.00 6.75
❑ 681 Bob Garibaldi 10.00 4.50
❑ 682 Dalton Jones 10.00 4.50
❑ 683 Reds Rookies 15.00 6.75
Vern Geishert
Hal McRae
Wayne Simpson
❑ 684 Jack Fisher 10.00 4.50
❑ 685 Tom Haller 10.00 4.50
❑ 686 Jackie Hernandez 10.00 4.50
❑ 687 Bob Priddy 10.00 4.50
❑ 688 Ted Kubiak 15.00 6.75
❑ 689 Frank Tepedino 10.00 4.50
❑ 690 Ron Fairly 15.00 6.75
❑ 691 Joe Grzenda 10.00 4.50
❑ 692 Duffy Dyer 10.00 4.50
❑ 693 Bob Johnson 10.00 4.50
❑ 694 Gary Ross 10.00 4.50
❑ 695 Bobby Knoop 10.00 4.50
❑ 696 San Francisco Giants 15.00 6.75
Team Card
❑ 697 Jim Hannan 10.00 4.50
❑ 698 Tom Tresh 15.00 6.75
❑ 699 Hank Aguirre 10.00 4.50
❑ 700 Frank Robinson 50.00 22.00
❑ 701 Jack Billingham 10.00 4.50
❑ 702 AL Rookies 10.00 4.50
Bob Johnson
Ron Klimkowski
Bill Zepp
❑ 703 Lou Marone 10.00 4.50
❑ 704 Frank Baker 10.00 4.50

Card	NRMT	VG-E
❑ 705 Tony Cloninger UER ..	10.00	4.50
(Batter headings on card back)		
❑ 706 John McNamara MG ..	10.00	4.50
❑ 707 Kevin Collins	10.00	4.50
❑ 708 Jose Santiago	10.00	4.50
❑ 709 Mike Fiore	10.00	4.50
❑ 710 Felix Millan	10.00	4.50
❑ 711 Ed Brinkman	10.00	4.50
❑ 712 Nolan Ryan	375.00	170.00
❑ 713 Seattle Pilots	25.00	11.00
Team Card		
❑ 714 Al Spangler	10.00	4.50
❑ 715 Mickey Lolich..............	15.00	6.75
❑ 716 Cardinals Rookies	15.00	6.75
Sal Campisi		
Reggie Cleveland		
Santiago Guzman		
❑ 717 Tom Phoebus	10.00	4.50
❑ 718 Ed Spiezio..................	10.00	4.50
❑ 719 Jim Roland	10.00	4.50
❑ 720 Rick Reichardt............	14.00	4.70

1971 Topps

	NRMT	VG-E
COMPLETE SET (752)	2000.00	900.00
COMMON CARD (1-393)..........	1.50	.70
COMMON CARD (394-523)......	2.50	1.10
COMMON CARD (524-643)......	4.00	1.80
COMMON CARD (644-752)......	8.00	3.60
COMMON SP (644-752)	12.00	5.50
WRAPPER (10-CENT)............	15.00	6.75

Card	NRMT	VG-E
❑ 1 Baltimore Orioles............	15.00	5.00
Team Card		
❑ 2 Dock Ellis	1.50	.70
❑ 3 Dick McAuliffe	1.50	.70
❑ 4 Vic Davalillo......................	1.50	.70
❑ 5 Thurman Munson	18.00	8.00
❑ 6 Ed Spiezio........................	1.50	.70
❑ 7 Jim Holt	1.50	.70
❑ 8 Mike McQueen	1.50	.70
❑ 9 George Scott....................	2.00	.90
❑ 10 Claude Osteen	1.50	.70
❑ 11 Elliott Maddox	2.00	.90
❑ 12 Johnny Callison..............	2.00	.90
❑ 13 White Sox Rookies	1.50	.70
Charlie Brinkman		
Dick Moloney		
❑ 14 Dave Concepcion	18.00	8.00
❑ 15 Andy Messersmith..........	2.00	.90
❑ 16 Ken Singleton	4.00	1.80
❑ 17 Billy Sorrell	1.50	.70
❑ 18 Norm Miller	1.50	.70
❑ 19 Skip Pitlock	1.50	.70
❑ 20 Reggie Jackson............	25.00	11.00
❑ 21 Dan McGinn	1.50	.70
❑ 22 Phil Roof	1.50	.70
❑ 23 Oscar Gamble.................	1.50	.70
❑ 24 Rich Hand	1.50	.70
❑ 25 Clarence Gaston	2.50	1.10
❑ 26 Bert Blyleven..................	8.00	3.60
❑ 27 Pirates Rookies..............	1.50	.70
Fred Cambria		
Gene Clines		
❑ 28 Ron Klimkowski...............	1.50	.70
❑ 29 Don Buford	1.50	.70
❑ 30 Phil Niekro........................	5.00	2.20
❑ 31 Eddie Kasko MG	1.50	.70
❑ 32 Jerry DaVanon	1.50	.70
❑ 33 Del Unser	1.50	.70
❑ 34 Sandy Vance..................	1.50	.70
❑ 35 Lou Piniella	2.50	1.10
❑ 36 Dean Chance	1.50	.70
❑ 37 Rich McKinney	1.50	.70
❑ 38 Jim Colborn.....................	1.50	.70
❑ 39 Tiger Rookies	1.50	.70
Lerrin LaGrow		
Gene Lamont		
❑ 40 Lee May	2.00	.90
❑ 41 Rick Austin	1.50	.70
❑ 42 Boots Day	1.50	.70
❑ 43 Steve Kealey....................	1.50	.70
❑ 44 Johnny Edwards	1.50	.70
❑ 45 Jim Hunter........................	7.00	3.10
❑ 46 Dave Campbell	1.50	.70
❑ 47 Johnny Jeter	1.50	.70
❑ 48 Dave Baldwin	1.50	.70
❑ 49 Don Money	1.50	.70
❑ 50 Willie McCovey	8.00	3.60
❑ 51 Steve Kline	1.50	.70
❑ 52 Braves Rookies..............	1.50	.70
Oscar Brown		
Earl Williams		
❑ 53 Paul Blair........................	2.00	.90
❑ 54 Checklist 1......................	6.00	1.20
❑ 55 Steve Carlton	15.00	6.75
❑ 56 Duane Josephson	1.50	.70
❑ 57 Von Joshua	1.50	.70
❑ 58 Bill Lee	2.00	.90
❑ 59 Gene Mauch MG............	2.00	.90
❑ 60 Dick Bosman....................	1.50	.70
❑ 61 AL Batting Leaders	3.50	1.55
Alex Johnson		
Carl Yastrzemski		
Tony Oliva		
❑ 62 NL Batting Leaders	2.00	.90
Rico Carty		
Joe Torre		
Manny Sanguillen		
❑ 63 AL RBI Leaders..............	2.50	1.10
Frank Howard		
Tony Conigliaro		
Boog Powell		
❑ 64 NL RBI Leaders..............	5.00	2.20
Johnny Bench		
Tony Perez		
Billy Williams		
❑ 65 AL HR Leaders	4.00	1.80
Frank Howard		
Harmon Killebrew		
Carl Yastrzemski		
❑ 66 NL HR Leaders	6.00	2.70
Johnny Bench		
Billy Williams		
Tony Perez		
❑ 67 AL ERA Leaders	3.50	1.55
Diego Segui		
Jim Palmer		
Clyde Wright		
❑ 68 NL ERA Leaders............	3.50	1.55
Tom Seaver		
Wayne Simpson		
Luke Walker		
❑ 69 AL Pitching Leaders	2.00	.90
Mike Cuellar		
Dave McNally		
Jim Perry		
❑ 70 NL Pitching Leaders	6.00	2.70
Bob Gibson		
Gaylord Perry		
Fergie Jenkins		
❑ 71 AL Strikeout Leaders......	2.00	.90
Sam McDowell		
Mickey Lolich		
Bob Johnson		
❑ 72 NL Strikeout Leaders	7.00	3.10
Tom Seaver		
Bob Gibson		
Fergie Jenkins		
❑ 73 George Brunet................	1.50	.70
❑ 74 Twins Rookies................	1.50	.70
Pete Hamm		
Jim Nettles		
❑ 75 Gary Nolan	2.00	.90
❑ 76 Ted Savage......................	1.50	.70
❑ 77 Mike Compton	1.50	.70
❑ 78 Jim Spencer	1.50	.70
❑ 79 Wade Blasingame	1.50	.70
❑ 80 Bill Melton	1.50	.70
❑ 81 Felix Millan	1.50	.70
❑ 82 Casey Cox.........................	1.50	.70
❑ 83 Met Rookies	1.50	.70
Tim Foli		
Randy Bobb		
❑ 84 Marcel Lachemann	1.50	.70
❑ 85 Billy Grabarkewitz	1.50	.70
❑ 86 Mike Kilkenny	1.50	.70
❑ 87 Jack Heidemann	1.50	.70
❑ 88 Hal King...........................	1.50	.70
❑ 89 Ken Brett	1.50	.70
❑ 90 Joe Pepitone	2.50	1.10
❑ 91 Bob Lemon MG	2.50	1.10
❑ 92 Fred Wenz........................	1.50	.70
❑ 93 Senators Rookies	1.50	.70
Norm McRae		
Denny Riddleberger		
❑ 94 Don Hahn	1.50	.70
❑ 95 Luis Tiant..........................	2.50	1.10
❑ 96 Joe Hague........................	1.50	.70
❑ 97 Floyd Wicker	1.50	.70
❑ 98 Joe Decker	1.50	.70
❑ 99 Mark Belanger.................	2.00	.90
❑ 100 Pete Rose	25.00	11.00
❑ 101 Les Cain	1.50	.70
❑ 102 Astros Rookies	2.00	.90
Ken Forsch		
Larry Howard		
❑ 103 Rich Severson...............	1.50	.70
❑ 104 Dan Frisella..................	1.50	.70
❑ 105 Tony Conigliaro	2.50	1.10
❑ 106 Tom Dukes	1.50	.70
❑ 107 Roy Foster......................	1.50	.70
❑ 108 John Cumberland	1.50	.70
❑ 109 Steve Hovley	1.50	.70
❑ 110 Bill Mazeroski	2.50	1.10
❑ 111 Yankee Rookies	1.50	.70
Loyd Colson		
Bobby Mitchell		
❑ 112 Manny Mota	2.00	.90
❑ 113 Jerry Crider	1.50	.70
❑ 114 Billy Conigliaro	2.00	.90
❑ 115 Donn Clendenon	2.00	.90
❑ 116 Ken Sanders	1.50	.70
❑ 117 Ted Simmons	8.00	3.60
❑ 118 Cookie Rojas	2.00	.90
❑ 119 Frank Lucchesi MG......	1.50	.70
❑ 120 Willie Horton	2.50	1.10
❑ 121 Cubs Rookies	1.50	.70
Jim Dunegan		
Roe Skidmore		
❑ 122 Eddie Watt.....................	1.50	.70
❑ 123A Checklist 2	6.00	1.20
(Card number at bottom right)		
❑ 123B Checklist 2	6.00	1.20
(Card number centered)		
❑ 124 Don Gullett	2.00	.90
❑ 125 Ray Fosse....................	2.00	.90
❑ 126 Danny Coombs	1.50	.70
❑ 127 Danny Thompson	2.00	.90
❑ 128 Frank Johnson	1.50	.70
❑ 129 Aurelio Monteagudo	1.50	.70
❑ 130 Denis Menke................	1.50	.70
❑ 131 Curt Blefary	1.50	.70
❑ 132 Jose Laboy	1.50	.70
❑ 133 Mickey Lolich..............	2.50	1.10
❑ 134 Jose Arcia	1.50	.70
❑ 135 Rick Monday	2.50	1.10
❑ 136 Duffy Dyer	1.50	.70
❑ 137 Marcelino Lopez	1.50	.70
❑ 138 Phillies Rookies...........	2.00	.90
Joe Lis		
Willie Montanez		
❑ 139 Paul Casanova	1.50	.70
❑ 140 Gaylord Perry	7.00	3.10
❑ 141 Frank Quilici	1.50	.70

142 Mack Jones	1.50	.70
143 Steve Blass	2.00	.90
144 Jackie Hernandez	1.50	.70
145 Bill Singer	2.00	.90
146 Ralph Houk MG	2.00	.90
147 Bob Priddy	1.50	.70
148 John Mayberry	2.00	.90
149 Mike Hershberger	1.50	.70
150 Sam McDowell	2.50	1.10
151 Tommy Davis	2.00	.90
152 Angels Rookies Lloyd Allen Winston Llenas	1.50	.70
153 Gary Ross	1.50	.70
154 Cesar Gutierrez	1.50	.70
155 Ken Henderson	1.50	.70
156 Bart Johnson	1.50	.70
157 Bob Bailey	1.50	.70
158 Jerry Reuss	2.00	.90
159 Jarvis Tatum	1.50	.70
160 Tom Seaver	20.00	9.00
161 Coin Checklist	6.00	1.20
162 Jack Billingham	1.50	.70
163 Buck Martinez	2.00	.90
164 Reds Rookies Frank Duffy Milt Wilcox	2.00	.90
165 Cesar Tovar	1.50	.70
166 Joe Hoerner	1.50	.70
167 Tom Grieve	2.50	1.10
168 Bruce Dal Canton	1.50	.70
169 Ed Herrmann	1.50	.70
170 Mike Cuellar	2.00	.90
171 Bobby Wine	1.50	.70
172 Duke Sims	1.50	.70
173 Gil Garrido	1.50	.70
174 Dave LaRoche	1.50	.70
175 Jim Hickman	1.50	.70
176 Red Sox Rookies Bob Montgomery Doug Griffin	2.00	.90
177 Hal McRae	2.50	1.10
178 Dave Duncan	1.50	.70
179 Mike Corkins	1.50	.70
180 Al Kaline UER (Home instead of Birth)	20.00	9.00
181 Hal Lanier	1.50	.70
182 Al Downing	2.00	.90
183 Gil Hodges MG	4.00	1.80
184 Stan Bahnsen	1.50	.70
185 Julian Javier	2.00	.90
186 Bob Spence	1.50	.70
187 Ted Abernathy	1.50	.70
188 Dodgers Rookies Bob Valentine Mike Strahler	3.00	1.35
189 George Mitterwald	1.50	.70
190 Bob Tolan	2.00	.90
191 Mike Andrews	1.50	.70
192 Billy Wilson	1.50	.70
193 Bob Grich	4.00	1.80
194 Mike Lum	1.50	.70
195 Boog Powell ALCS	3.00	1.35
196 Dave McNally ALCS	3.00	1.35
197 Jim Palmer ALCS	5.00	2.20
198 AL Playoff Summary Orioles celebrate	2.50	1.10
199 Ty Cline NLCS	2.50	1.10
200 Bobby Tolan NLCS	2.50	1.10
201 Ty Cline NLCS	2.50	1.10
202 NL Playoff Summary Reds celebrate	2.50	1.10
203 Larry Gura	2.00	.90
204 Brewers Rookies Bernie Smith George Kopacz	1.50	.70
205 Gerry Moses	1.50	.70
206 Checklist 3	6.00	1.20
207 Alan Foster	1.50	.70
208 Billy Martin MG	4.00	1.80
209 Steve Renko	1.50	.70
210 Rod Carew	15.00	6.75
211 Phil Hennigan	1.50	.70
212 Rich Hebner	2.00	.90
213 Frank Baker	1.50	.70
214 Al Ferrara	1.50	.70
215 Diego Segui	1.50	.70
216 Cards Rookies Reggie Cleveland Luis Melendez	1.50	.70
217 Ed Stroud	1.50	.70
218 Tony Cloninger	1.50	.70
219 Elrod Hendricks	1.50	.70
220 Ron Santo	2.50	1.10
221 Dave Morehead	1.50	.70
222 Bob Watson	2.50	1.10
223 Cecil Upshaw	1.50	.70
224 Alan Gallagher	1.50	.70
225 Gary Peters	1.50	.70
226 Bill Russell	2.50	1.10
227 Floyd Weaver	1.50	.70
228 Wayne Garrett	1.50	.70
229 Jim Hannan	1.50	.70
230 Willie Stargell	8.00	3.60
231 Indians Rookies Vince Colbert John Lowenstein	1.50	.70
232 John Strohmayer	1.50	.70
233 Larry Bowa	2.50	1.10
234 Jim Lyttle	1.50	.70
235 Nate Colbert	1.50	.70
236 Bob Humphreys	1.50	.70
237 Cesar Cedeno	3.00	1.35
238 Chuck Dobson	1.50	.70
239 Red Schoendienst MG	2.50	1.10
240 Clyde Wright	1.50	.70
241 Dave Nelson	1.50	.70
242 Jim Ray	1.50	.70
243 Carlos May	2.00	.90
244 Bob Tillman	1.50	.70
245 Jim Kaat	2.50	1.10
246 Tony Taylor	2.00	.90
247 Royals Rookies Jerry Cram Paul Splittorff	2.00	.90
248 Hoyt Wilhelm	4.00	1.80
249 Chico Salmon	1.50	.70
250 Johnny Bench	20.00	9.00
251 Frank Reberger	1.50	.70
252 Eddie Leon	1.50	.70
253 Bill Sudakis	1.50	.70
254 Cal Koonce	1.50	.70
255 Bob Robertson	2.00	.90
256 Tony Gonzalez	1.50	.70
257 Nelson Briles	1.50	.70
258 Dick Green	1.50	.70
259 Dave Marshall	1.50	.70
260 Tommy Harper	2.00	.90
261 Darold Knowles	1.50	.70
262 Padres Rookies Jim Williams Dave Robinson	1.50	.70
263 John Ellis	1.50	.70
264 Joe Morgan	8.00	3.60
265 Jim Northrup	2.00	.90
266 Bill Stoneman	1.50	.70
267 Rich Morales	1.50	.70
268 Philadelphia Phillies Team Card	4.00	1.80
269 Gail Hopkins	1.50	.70
270 Rico Carty	2.50	1.10
271 Bill Zepp	1.50	.70
272 Tommy Helms	2.00	.90
273 Pete Richert	1.50	.70
274 Ron Slocum	1.50	.70
275 Vada Pinson	2.50	1.10
276 Giants Rookies Mike Davison George Foster	8.00	3.60
277 Gary Waslewski	1.50	.70
278 Jerry Grote	1.50	.70
279 Lefty Phillips MG	1.50	.70
280 Ferguson Jenkins	7.00	3.10
281 Danny Walton	1.50	.70
282 Jose Pagan	1.50	.70
283 Dick Such	1.50	.70
284 Jim Gosger	1.50	.70
285 Sal Bando	2.50	1.10
286 Jerry McNertney	1.50	.70
287 Mike Fiore	1.50	.70
288 Joe Moeller	1.50	.70
289 Chicago White Sox Team Card	2.00	.90
290 Tony Oliva	2.50	1.10
291 George Culver	1.50	.70
292 Jay Johnstone	2.00	.90
293 Pat Corrales	2.00	.90
294 Steve Dunning	1.50	.70
295 Bobby Bonds	5.00	2.20
296 Tom Timmermann	1.50	.70
297 Johnny Briggs	1.50	.70
298 Jim Nelson	1.50	.70
299 Ed Kirkpatrick	1.50	.70
300 Brooks Robinson	20.00	9.00
301 Earl Wilson	1.50	.70
302 Phil Gagliano	1.50	.70
303 Lindy McDaniel	2.00	.90
304 Ron Brand	1.50	.70
305 Reggie Smith	2.50	1.10
306 Jim Nash	1.50	.70
307 Don Wert	1.50	.70
308 St. Louis Cardinals Team Card	2.00	.90
309 Dick Ellsworth	1.50	.70
310 Tommie Agee	2.50	1.10
311 Lee Stange	1.50	.70
312 Harry Walker MG	1.50	.70
313 Tom Hall	1.50	.70
314 Jeff Torborg	2.00	.90
315 Ron Fairly	2.50	1.10
316 Fred Scherman	1.50	.70
317 Athletic Rookies Jim Driscoll Angel Mangual	1.50	.70
318 Rudy May	1.50	.70
319 Ty Cline	1.50	.70
320 Dave McNally	2.00	.90
321 Tom Matchick	1.50	.70
322 Jim Beauchamp	1.50	.70
323 Billy Champion	1.50	.70
324 Graig Nettles	2.50	1.10
325 Juan Marichal	7.00	3.10
326 Richie Scheinblum	1.50	.70
327 Boog Powell WS	2.50	1.10
328 Don Buford WS	2.50	1.10
329 Frank Robinson WS	5.00	2.20
330 World Series Game 4 Reds stay alive	2.50	1.10
331 Brooks Robinson WS commits robbery	6.00	2.70
332 World Series Summary Orioles celebrate	2.50	1.10
333 Clay Kirby	1.50	.70
334 Roberto Pena	1.50	.70
335 Jerry Koosman	2.50	1.10
336 Detroit Tigers Team Card	2.00	.90
337 Jesus Alou	1.50	.70
338 Gene Tenace	2.00	.90
339 Wayne Simpson	1.50	.70
340 Rico Petrocelli	2.50	1.10
341 Steve Garvey	25.00	11.00
342 Frank Tepedino	1.50	.70
343 Pirates Rookies Ed Acosta Milt May	1.50	.70
344 Ellie Rodriguez	1.50	.70
345 Joel Horlen	1.50	.70
346 Lum Harris MG	1.50	.70
347 Ted Uhlaender	1.50	.70
348 Fred Norman	1.50	.70
349 Rich Reese	1.50	.70
350 Billy Williams	7.00	3.10
351 Jim Shellenback	1.50	.70
352 Denny Doyle	1.50	.70
353 Carl Taylor	1.50	.70
354 Don McMahon	1.50	.70
355 Bud Harrelson (Nolan Ryan in photo)	3.50	1.55
356 Bob Locker	1.50	.70
357 Cincinnati Reds Team Card	2.00	.90
358 Danny Cater	1.50	.70
359 Ron Reed	1.50	.70

❑ 360	Jim Fregosi	2.00	.90
❑ 361	Don Sutton	7.00	3.10
❑ 362	Orioles Rookies	1.50	.70
	Mike Adamson		
	Roger Freed		
❑ 363	Mike Nagy	1.50	.70
❑ 364	Tommy Dean	1.50	.70
❑ 365	Bob Johnson	1.50	.70
❑ 366	Ron Stone	1.50	.70
❑ 367	Dalton Jones	1.50	.70
❑ 368	Bob Veale	2.00	.90
❑ 369	Checklist 4	6.00	1.20
❑ 370	Joe Torre	2.50	1.10
❑ 371	Jack Hiatt	1.50	.70
❑ 372	Lew Krausse	1.50	.70
❑ 373	Tom McCraw	1.50	.70
❑ 374	Clete Boyer	2.00	.90
❑ 375	Steve Hargan	1.50	.70
❑ 376	Expos Rookies	1.50	.70
	Clyde Mashore		
	Ernie McAnally		
❑ 377	Greg Garrett	1.50	.70
❑ 378	Tito Fuentes	1.50	.70
❑ 379	Wayne Granger	1.50	.70
❑ 380	Ted Williams MG	12.00	5.50
❑ 381	Fred Gladding	1.50	.70
❑ 382	Jake Gibbs	1.50	.70
❑ 383	Rod Gaspar	1.50	.70
❑ 384	Rollie Fingers	6.00	2.70
❑ 385	Maury Wills	2.50	1.10
❑ 386	Boston Red Sox	2.00	.90
	Team Card		
❑ 387	Ron Herbel	1.50	.70
❑ 388	Al Oliver	2.50	1.10
❑ 389	Ed Brinkman	1.50	.70
❑ 390	Glenn Beckert	2.00	.90
❑ 391	Twins Rookies	2.00	.90
	Steve Brye		
	Cotton Nash		
❑ 392	Grant Jackson	1.50	.70
❑ 393	Merv Rettenmund	2.00	.90
❑ 394	Clay Carroll	2.50	1.10
❑ 395	Roy White	3.00	1.35
❑ 396	Dick Schofield	2.50	1.10
❑ 397	Alvin Dark MG	3.00	1.35
❑ 398	Howie Reed	2.50	1.10
❑ 399	Jim French	2.50	1.10
❑ 400	Hank Aaron	50.00	22.00
❑ 401	Tom Murphy	2.50	1.10
❑ 402	Los Angeles Dodgers	5.00	2.20
	Team Card		
❑ 403	Joe Coleman	2.50	1.10
❑ 404	Astros Rookies	2.50	1.10
	Buddy Harris		
	Roger Metzger		
❑ 405	Leo Cardenas	2.50	1.10
❑ 406	Ray Sadecki	2.50	1.10
❑ 407	Joe Rudi	3.00	1.35
❑ 408	Rafael Robles	2.50	1.10
❑ 409	Don Pavletich	2.50	1.10
❑ 410	Ken Holtzman	4.00	1.80
❑ 411	George Spriggs	2.50	1.10
❑ 412	Jerry Johnson	2.50	1.10
❑ 413	Pat Kelly	2.50	1.10
❑ 414	Woodie Fryman	2.50	1.10
❑ 415	Mike Hegan	2.50	1.10
❑ 416	Gene Alley	2.50	1.10
❑ 417	Dick Hall	2.50	1.10
❑ 418	Adolfo Phillips	2.50	1.10
❑ 419	Ron Hansen	2.50	1.10
❑ 420	Jim Merritt	2.50	1.10
❑ 421	John Stephenson	2.50	1.10
❑ 422	Frank Bertaina	2.50	1.10
❑ 423	Tigers Rookies	2.50	1.10
	Dennis Saunders		
	Tim Marting		
❑ 424	Roberto Rodriquez	2.50	1.10
❑ 425	Doug Rader	2.50	1.10
❑ 426	Chris Cannizzaro	2.50	1.10
❑ 427	Bernie Allen	2.50	1.10
❑ 428	Jim McAndrew	2.50	1.10
❑ 429	Chuck Hinton	2.50	1.10
❑ 430	Wes Parker	2.50	1.10
❑ 431	Tom Burgmeier	2.50	1.10
❑ 432	Bob Didier	2.50	1.10
❑ 433	Skip Lockwood	2.50	1.10
❑ 434	Gary Sutherland	2.50	1.10
❑ 435	Jose Cardenal	4.00	1.80
❑ 436	Wilbur Wood	2.50	1.10
❑ 437	Danny Murtaugh MG	3.00	1.35
❑ 438	Mike McCormick	4.00	1.80
❑ 439	Phillies Rookies	6.00	2.70
	Greg Luzinski		
	Scott Reid		
❑ 440	Bert Campaneris	3.00	1.35
❑ 441	Milt Pappas	4.00	1.80
❑ 442	California Angels	4.00	1.80
	Team Card		
❑ 443	Rich Robertson	2.50	1.10
❑ 444	Jimmie Price	2.50	1.10
❑ 445	Art Shamsky	2.50	1.10
❑ 446	Bobby Bolin	2.50	1.10
❑ 447	Cesar Geronimo	4.00	1.80
❑ 448	Dave Roberts	2.50	1.10
❑ 449	Brant Alyea	2.50	1.10
❑ 450	Bob Gibson	15.00	6.75
❑ 451	Joe Keough	2.50	1.10
❑ 452	John Boccabella	2.50	1.10
❑ 453	Terry Crowley	2.50	1.10
❑ 454	Mike Paul	2.50	1.10
❑ 455	Don Kessinger	3.00	1.35
❑ 456	Bob Meyer	2.50	1.10
❑ 457	Willie Smith	2.50	1.10
❑ 458	White Sox Rookies	2.50	1.10
	Ron Lolich		
	Dave Lemonds		
❑ 459	Jim Lefebvre	2.50	1.10
❑ 460	Fritz Peterson	2.50	1.10
❑ 461	Jim Ray Hart	2.50	1.10
❑ 462	Washington Senators	5.00	2.20
	Team Card		
❑ 463	Tom Kelley	2.50	1.10
❑ 464	Aurelio Rodriguez	2.50	1.10
❑ 465	Tim McCarver	6.00	2.70
❑ 466	Ken Berry	2.50	1.10
❑ 467	Al Santorini	2.50	1.10
❑ 468	Frank Fernandez	2.50	1.10
❑ 469	Bob Aspromonte	2.50	1.10
❑ 470	Bob Oliver	2.50	1.10
❑ 471	Tom Griffin	2.50	1.10
❑ 472	Ken Rudolph	2.50	1.10
❑ 473	Gary Wagner	2.50	1.10
❑ 474	Jim Fairey	2.50	1.10
❑ 475	Ron Perranoski	2.50	1.10
❑ 476	Dal Maxvill	2.50	1.10
❑ 477	Earl Weaver MG	4.00	1.80
❑ 478	Bernie Carbo	2.50	1.10
❑ 479	Dennis Higgins	2.50	1.10
❑ 480	Manny Sanguillen	3.00	1.35
❑ 481	Daryl Patterson	2.50	1.10
❑ 482	San Diego Padres	5.00	2.20
	Team Card		
❑ 483	Gene Michael	4.00	1.80
❑ 484	Don Wilson	2.50	1.10
❑ 485	Ken McMullen	2.50	1.10
❑ 486	Steve Huntz	2.50	1.10
❑ 487	Paul Schaal	2.50	1.10
❑ 488	Jerry Stephenson	2.50	1.10
❑ 489	Luis Alvarado	2.50	1.10
❑ 490	Deron Johnson	4.00	1.80
❑ 491	Jim Hardin	2.50	1.10
❑ 492	Ken Boswell	2.50	1.10
❑ 493	Dave May	2.50	1.10
❑ 494	Braves Rookies	4.00	1.80
	Ralph Garr		
	Rick Kester		
❑ 495	Felipe Alou	4.00	1.80
❑ 496	Woody Woodward	2.50	1.10
❑ 497	Horacio Pina	2.50	1.10
❑ 498	John Kennedy	2.50	1.10
❑ 499	Checklist 5	6.00	1.20
❑ 500	Jim Perry	4.00	1.80
❑ 501	Andy Etchebarren	2.50	1.10
❑ 502	Chicago Cubs	5.00	2.20
	Team Card		
❑ 503	Gates Brown	4.00	1.80
❑ 504	Ken Wright	2.50	1.10
❑ 505	Ollie Brown	2.50	1.10
❑ 506	Bobby Knoop	2.50	1.10
❑ 507	George Stone	2.50	1.10
❑ 508	Roger Repoz	2.50	1.10
❑ 509	Jim Grant	2.50	1.10
❑ 510	Ken Harrelson	3.00	1.35
❑ 511	Chris Short	4.00	1.80
	(Pete Rose leading off second)		
❑ 512	Red Sox Rookies	2.50	1.10
	Dick Mills		
	Mike Garman		
❑ 513	Nolan Ryan	250.00	110.00
❑ 514	Ron Woods	2.50	1.10
❑ 515	Carl Morton	2.50	1.10
❑ 516	Ted Kubiak	2.50	1.10
❑ 517	Charlie Fox MG	2.50	1.10
❑ 518	Joe Grzenda	2.50	1.10
❑ 519	Willie Crawford	2.50	1.10
❑ 520	Tommy John	5.00	2.20
❑ 521	Leron Lee	2.50	1.10
❑ 522	Minnesota Twins	5.00	2.20
	Team Card		
❑ 523	John Odom	2.50	1.10
❑ 524	Mickey Stanley	5.00	2.20
❑ 525	Ernie Banks	50.00	22.00
❑ 526	Ray Jarvis	4.00	1.80
❑ 527	Cleon Jones	6.00	2.70
❑ 528	Wally Bunker	4.00	1.80
❑ 529	NL Rookie Infielders	5.00	2.20
	Enzo Hernandez		
	Bill Buckner		
	Marty Perez		
❑ 530	Carl Yastrzemski	40.00	18.00
❑ 531	Mike Torrez	4.00	1.80
❑ 532	Bill Rigney MG	4.00	1.80
❑ 533	Mike Ryan	4.00	1.80
❑ 534	Luke Walker	4.00	1.80
❑ 535	Curt Flood	5.00	2.20
❑ 536	Claude Raymond	5.00	2.20
❑ 537	Tom Egan	4.00	1.80
❑ 538	Angel Bravo	4.00	1.80
❑ 539	Larry Brown	4.00	1.80
❑ 540	Larry Dierker	6.00	2.70
❑ 541	Bob Burda	4.00	1.80
❑ 542	Bob Miller	4.00	1.80
❑ 543	New York Yankees	10.00	4.50
	Team Card		
❑ 544	Vida Blue	6.00	2.70
❑ 545	Dick Dietz	4.00	1.80
❑ 546	John Matias	4.00	1.80
❑ 547	Pat Dobson	6.00	2.70
❑ 548	Don Mason	4.00	1.80
❑ 549	Jim Brewer	5.00	2.20
❑ 550	Harmon Killebrew	25.00	11.00
❑ 551	Frank Linzy	4.00	1.80
❑ 552	Buddy Bradford	4.00	1.80
❑ 553	Kevin Collins	4.00	1.80
❑ 554	Lowell Palmer	4.00	1.80
❑ 555	Walt Williams	4.00	1.80
❑ 556	Jim McGlothlin	4.00	1.80
❑ 557	Tom Satriano	4.00	1.80
❑ 558	Hector Torres	4.00	1.80
❑ 559	AL Rookie Pitchers	4.00	1.80
	Terry Cox		
	Bill Gogolewski		
	Gary Jones		
❑ 560	Rusty Staub	5.00	2.20
❑ 561	Syd O'Brien	4.00	1.80
❑ 562	Dave Giusti	4.00	1.80
❑ 563	San Francisco Giants	8.00	3.60
	Team Card		
❑ 564	Al Fitzmorris	4.00	1.80
❑ 565	Jim Wynn	5.00	2.20
❑ 566	Tim Cullen	4.00	1.80
❑ 567	Walt Alston MG	6.00	2.70
❑ 568	Sal Campisi	4.00	1.80
❑ 569	Ivan Murrell	4.00	1.80
❑ 570	Jim Palmer	30.00	13.50
❑ 571	Ted Sizemore	4.00	1.80
❑ 572	Jerry Kenney	4.00	1.80
❑ 573	Ed Kranepool	5.00	2.20
❑ 574	Jim Bunning	7.00	3.10
❑ 575	Bill Freehan	5.00	2.20
❑ 576	Cubs Rookies	4.00	1.80
	Adrian Garrett		
	Brock Davis		
	Garry Jestadt		
❑ 577	Jim Lonborg	5.00	2.20

❑ 578 Ron Hunt 4.00 1.80
❑ 579 Marty Pattin 4.00 1.80
❑ 580 Tony Perez 20.00 9.00
❑ 581 Roger Nelson 4.00 1.80
❑ 582 Dave Cash 6.00 2.70
❑ 583 Ron Cook 4.00 1.80
❑ 584 Cleveland Indians 8.00 3.60
Team Card
❑ 585 Willie Davis 5.00 2.20
❑ 586 Dick Woodson 4.00 1.80
❑ 587 Sonny Jackson 4.00 1.80
❑ 588 Tom Bradley 4.00 1.80
❑ 589 Bob Barton 4.00 1.80
❑ 590 Alex Johnson 6.00 2.70
❑ 591 Jackie Brown 4.00 1.80
❑ 592 Randy Hundley 6.00 2.70
❑ 593 Jack Aker 4.00 1.80
❑ 594 Cards Rookies 5.00 2.20
Bob Chlupsa
Bob Stinson
Al Hrabosky
❑ 595 Dave Johnson 6.00 2.70
❑ 596 Mike Jorgensen 4.00 1.80
❑ 597 Ken Suarez 4.00 1.80
❑ 598 Rick Wise 6.00 2.70
❑ 599 Norm Cash 5.00 2.20
❑ 600 Willie Mays 100.00 45.00
❑ 601 Ken Tatum 4.00 1.80
❑ 602 Marty Martinez 4.00 1.80
❑ 603 Pittsburgh Pirates 8.00 3.60
Team Card
❑ 604 John Gelnar 4.00 1.80
❑ 605 Orlando Cepeda 6.00 2.70
❑ 606 Chuck Taylor 4.00 1.80
❑ 607 Paul Ratliff 4.00 1.80
❑ 608 Mike Wegener 4.00 1.80
❑ 609 Leo Durocher MG 7.00 3.10
❑ 610 Amos Otis 6.00 2.70
❑ 611 Tom Phoebus 4.00 1.80
❑ 612 Indians Rookies 4.00 1.80
Lou Camilli
Ted Ford
Steve Mingori
❑ 613 Pedro Borbon 4.00 1.80
❑ 614 Billy Cowan 4.00 1.80
❑ 615 Mel Stottlemyre 5.00 2.20
❑ 616 Larry Hisle 6.00 2.70
❑ 617 Clay Dalrymple 4.00 1.80
❑ 618 Tug McGraw 5.00 2.20
❑ 619A Checklist 6 ERR 8.00 1.60
(No copyright)
❑ 619B Checklist 6 COR 12.00 2.40
(Copyright on back)
❑ 620 Frank Howard 5.00 2.20
❑ 621 Ron Bryant 4.00 1.80
❑ 622 Joe Lahoud 4.00 1.80
❑ 623 Pat Jarvis 4.00 1.80
❑ 624 Oakland Athletics 8.00 3.60
Team Card
❑ 625 Lou Brock 30.00 13.50
❑ 626 Freddie Patek 6.00 2.70
❑ 627 Steve Hamilton 4.00 1.80
❑ 628 John Bateman 4.00 1.80
❑ 629 John Hiller 6.00 2.70
❑ 630 Roberto Clemente 110.00 50.00
❑ 631 Eddie Fisher 4.00 1.80
❑ 632 Darrel Chaney 4.00 1.80
❑ 633 AL Rookie Outfielders 4.00 1.80
Bobby Brooks
Pete Koegel
Scott Northey
❑ 634 Phil Regan 6.00 2.70
❑ 635 Bobby Murcer 6.00 2.70
❑ 636 Denny Lemaster 4.00 1.80
❑ 637 Dave Bristol MG 4.00 1.80
❑ 638 Stan Williams 4.00 1.80
❑ 639 Tom Haller 4.00 1.80
❑ 640 Frank Robinson 40.00 18.00
❑ 641 New York Mets 15.00 6.75
Team Card
❑ 642 Jim Roland 4.00 1.80
❑ 643 Rick Reichardt 6.00 2.70
❑ 644 Jim Stewart SP 12.00 5.50
❑ 645 Jim Maloney SP 14.00 6.25
❑ 646 Bobby Floyd SP 12.00 5.50
❑ 647 Juan Pizarro 8.00 3.60
❑ 648 Mets Rookies SP 25.00 11.00
Rich Folkers
Ted Martinez
John Matlack
❑ 649 Sparky Lyle SP 18.00 8.00
❑ 650 Rich Allen SP 40.00 18.00
❑ 651 Jerry Robertson SP 12.00 5.50
❑ 652 Atlanta Braves 8.00 3.60
Team Card
❑ 653 Russ Snyder SP 12.00 5.50
❑ 654 Don Shaw SP 12.00 5.50
❑ 655 Mike Epstein SP 12.00 5.50
❑ 656 Gerry Nyman SP 12.00 5.50
❑ 657 Jose Azcue 8.00 3.60
❑ 658 Paul Lindblad SP 12.00 5.50
❑ 659 Byron Browne SP 12.00 5.50
❑ 660 Ray Culp 8.00 3.60
❑ 661 Chuck Tanner MG SP 14.00 6.25
❑ 662 Mike Hedlund SP 12.00 5.50
❑ 663 Marv Staehle 8.00 3.60
❑ 664 Rookie Pitchers SP 14.00 6.25
Archie Reynolds
Bob Reynolds
Ken Reynolds
❑ 665 Ron Swoboda SP 18.00 8.00
❑ 666 Gene Brabender SP 12.00 5.50
❑ 667 Pete Ward 8.00 3.60
❑ 668 Gary Neibauer 8.00 3.60
❑ 669 Ike Brown SP 14.00 6.25
❑ 670 Bill Hands 8.00 3.60
❑ 671 Bill Voss SP 12.00 5.50
❑ 672 Ed Crosby SP 12.00 5.50
❑ 673 Gerry Janeski SP 12.00 5.50
❑ 674 Montreal Expos 12.00 5.50
Team Card
❑ 675 Dave Boswell 8.00 3.60
❑ 676 Tommie Reynolds 8.00 3.60
❑ 677 Jack DiLauro SP 12.00 5.50
❑ 678 George Thomas 8.00 3.60
❑ 679 Don O'Riley 8.00 3.60
❑ 680 Don Mincher SP 12.00 5.50
❑ 681 Bill Butler 8.00 3.60
❑ 682 Terry Harmon 8.00 3.60
❑ 683 Bill Burbach SP 12.00 5.50
❑ 684 Curt Motton 8.00 3.60
❑ 685 Moe Drabowsky 8.00 3.60
❑ 686 Chico Ruiz SP 12.00 5.50
❑ 687 Ron Taylor SP 12.00 5.50
❑ 688 Sparky Anderson MG SP 40.00 18.00
❑ 689 Frank Baker 8.00 3.60
❑ 690 Bob Moose 8.00 3.60
❑ 691 Bobby Heise 8.00 3.60
❑ 692 AL Rookie Pitchers SP 12.00 5.50
Hal Haydel
Rogelio Moret
Wayne Twitchell
❑ 693 Jose Pena SP 12.00 5.50
❑ 694 Rick Renick SP 12.00 5.50
❑ 695 Joe Niekro 9.00 4.00
❑ 696 Jerry Morales 8.00 3.60
❑ 697 Rickey Clark SP 12.00 5.50
❑ 698 M. Brewers SP 20.00 9.00
Team Card
❑ 699 Jim Britton 8.00 3.60
❑ 700 Boog Powell SP 30.00 13.50
❑ 701 Bob Garibaldi 8.00 3.60
❑ 702 Milt Ramirez 8.00 3.60
❑ 703 Mike Kekich 8.00 3.60
❑ 704 J.C. Martin SP 12.00 5.50
❑ 705 Dick Selma SP 12.00 5.50
❑ 706 Joe Foy SP 12.00 5.50
❑ 707 Fred Lasher 8.00 3.60
❑ 708 Russ Nagelson SP 12.00 5.50
❑ 709 Rookie Outfielders SP 100.00 45.00
Dusty Baker
Don Baylor
Tom Paciorek
❑ 710 Sonny Siebert 8.00 3.60
❑ 711 Larry Stahl SP 12.00 5.50
❑ 712 Jose Martinez 8.00 3.60
❑ 713 Mike Marshall SP 14.00 6.25
❑ 714 Dick Williams MG SP 14.00 6.25
❑ 715 Horace Clarke SP 14.00 6.25
❑ 716 Dave Leonhard 8.00 3.60
❑ 717 Tommie Aaron SP 12.00 5.50
❑ 718 Billy Wynne 8.00 3.60
❑ 719 Jerry May SP 12.00 5.50
❑ 720 Matty Alou 9.00 4.00
❑ 721 John Morris 8.00 3.60
❑ 722 Houston Astros SP 20.00 9.00
Team Card
❑ 723 Vicente Romo SP 12.00 5.50
❑ 724 Tom Tischinski SP 12.00 5.50
❑ 725 Gary Gentry SP 12.00 5.50
❑ 726 Paul Popovich 8.00 3.60
❑ 727 Ray Lamb SP 12.00 5.50
❑ 728 NL Rookie Outfielders 8.00 3.60
Wayne Redmond
Keith Lampard
Bernie Williams
❑ 729 Dick Billings 8.00 3.60
❑ 730 Jim Rooker 8.00 3.60
❑ 731 Jim Qualls SP 12.00 5.50
❑ 732 Bob Reed 8.00 3.60
❑ 733 Lee Maye SP 12.00 5.50
❑ 734 Rob Gardner SP 12.00 5.50
❑ 735 Mike Shannon SP 14.00 6.25
❑ 736 Mel Queen SP 12.00 5.50
❑ 737 Preston Gomez SP MG 12.00 5.50
❑ 738 Russ Gibson SP 12.00 5.50
❑ 739 Barry Lersch SP 12.00 5.50
❑ 740 Luis Aparicio SP UER 30.00 13.50
(Led AL in steals from 1965 to 1964, should be 1956 to 1964)
❑ 741 Skip Guinn 8.00 3.60
❑ 742 Kansas City Royals 12.00 5.50
Team Card
❑ 743 John O'Donoghue SP 12.00 5.50
❑ 744 Chuck Manuel SP 12.00 5.50
❑ 745 Sandy Alomar SP 12.00 5.50
❑ 746 Andy Kosco 8.00 3.60
❑ 747 NL Rookie Pitchers 8.00 3.60
Al Severinsen
Scipio Spinks
Balor Moore
❑ 748 John Purdin SP 12.00 5.50
❑ 749 Ken Szotkiewicz 8.00 3.60
❑ 750 Denny McLain SP 25.00 11.00
❑ 751 Al Weis SP 15.00 6.75
❑ 752 Dick Drago 12.00 2.90

1972 Topps

	NRMT	VG-E
COMPLETE SET (787)	1600.00	700.00
COMMON CARD (1-132)	.60	.25
COMMON CARD (133-263)	1.00	.45
COMMON CARD (264-394)	1.25	.55
COMMON CARD (395-525)	1.50	.70
COMMON CARD (526-656)	4.00	1.80
COMMON CARD (657-787)	12.00	5.50
WRAPPER (10-CENT)	15.00	6.75

❑ 1 Pittsburgh Pirates 8.00 2.90
Team Card
❑ 2 Ray Culp .60 .25
❑ 3 Bob Tolan .60 .25
❑ 4 Checklist 1-132 4.00 .80
❑ 5 John Bateman .60 .25
❑ 6 Fred Scherman .60 .25
❑ 7 Enzo Hernandez .60 .25

❑ 8 Ron Swoboda 1.25 .55
❑ 9 Stan Williams .60 .25
❑ 10 Amos Otis 1.25 .55
❑ 11 Bobby Valentine 1.00 .45
❑ 12 Jose Cardenal .60 .25
❑ 13 Joe Grzenda .60 .25
❑ 14 Phillies Rookies .60 .25
Pete Koegel
Mike Anderson
Wayne Twitchell
❑ 15 Walt Williams .60 .25
❑ 16 Mike Jorgensen .60 .25
❑ 17 Dave Duncan .60 .25
❑ 18A Juan Pizarro .60 .25
(Yellow underline
C and S of Cubs)
❑ 18B Juan Pizarro 5.00 2.20
(Green underline
C and S of Cubs)
❑ 19 Billy Cowan .60 .25
❑ 20 Don Wilson .60 .25
❑ 21 Atlanta Braves 1.25 .55
Team Card
❑ 22 Rob Gardner .60 .25
❑ 23 Ted Kubiak .60 .25
❑ 24 Ted Ford .60 .25
❑ 25 Bill Singer .60 .25
❑ 26 Andy Etchebarren .60 .25
❑ 27 Bob Johnson .60 .25
❑ 28 Twins Rookies .60 .25
Bob Gebhard
Steve Brye
Hal Haydel
❑ 29A Bill Bonham .60 .25
(Yellow underline
C and S of Cubs)
❑ 29B Bill Bonham 5.00 2.20
(Green underline
C and S of Cubs)
❑ 30 Rico Petrocelli 1.00 .45
❑ 31 Cleon Jones 1.25 .55
❑ 32 Cleon Jones IA .60 .25
❑ 33 Billy Martin MG 4.00 1.80
❑ 34 Billy Martin IA 2.00 .90
❑ 35 Jerry Johnson .60 .25
❑ 36 Jerry Johnson IA .60 .25
❑ 37 Carl Yastrzemski 10.00 4.50
❑ 38 Carl Yastrzemski IA 6.00 2.70
❑ 39 Bob Barton .60 .25
❑ 40 Bob Barton IA .60 .25
❑ 41 Tommy Davis 1.00 .45
❑ 42 Tommy Davis IA .60 .25
❑ 43 Rick Wise 1.25 .55
❑ 44 Rick Wise IA .60 .25
❑ 45A Glenn Beckert 1.25 .55
(Yellow underline
C and S of Cubs)
❑ 45B Glenn Beckert 5.00 2.20
(Green underline
C and S of Cubs)
❑ 46 Glenn Beckert IA .60 .25
❑ 47 John Ellis .60 .25
❑ 48 John Ellis IA .60 .25
❑ 49 Willie Mays 25.00 11.00
❑ 50 Willie Mays IA 14.00 6.25
❑ 51 Harmon Killebrew 7.00 3.10
❑ 52 Harmon Killebrew IA 3.50 1.55
❑ 53 Bud Harrelson 1.00 .45
❑ 54 Bud Harrelson IA .60 .25
❑ 55 Clyde Wright .60 .25
❑ 56 Rich Chiles .60 .25
❑ 57 Bob Oliver .60 .25
❑ 58 Ernie McAnally .60 .25
❑ 59 Fred Stanley .60 .25
❑ 60 Manny Sanguillen 1.00 .45
❑ 61 Cubs Rookies 1.00 .45
Burt Hooton
Gene Hiser
Earl Stephenson
❑ 62 Angel Mangual .60 .25
❑ 63 Duke Sims .60 .25
❑ 64 Pete Broberg .60 .25
❑ 65 Cesar Cedeno 1.00 .45
❑ 66 Ray Corbin .60 .25
❑ 67 Red Schoendienst MG 1.00 .45
❑ 68 Jim York .60 .25
❑ 69 Roger Freed .60 .25
❑ 70 Mike Cuellar 1.25 .55
❑ 71 California Angels 1.50 .70
Team Card
❑ 72 Bruce Kison .60 .25
❑ 73 Steve Huntz .60 .25
❑ 74 Cecil Upshaw .60 .25
❑ 75 Bert Campaneris 1.00 .45
❑ 76 Don Carrithers .60 .25
❑ 77 Ron Theobald .60 .25
❑ 78 Steve Arlin .60 .25
❑ 79 Red Sox Rookies 60.00 27.00
Mike Garman
Cecil Cooper
Carlton Fisk
❑ 80 Tony Perez 4.00 1.80
❑ 81 Mike Hedlund .60 .25
❑ 82 Ron Woods .60 .25
❑ 83 Dalton Jones .60 .25
❑ 84 Vince Colbert .60 .25
❑ 85 NL Batting Leaders 1.75 .80
Joe Torre
Ralph Garr
Glenn Beckert
❑ 86 AL Batting Leaders 1.75 .80
Tony Oliva
Bobby Murcer
Merv Rettenmund
❑ 87 NL RBI Leaders 3.50 1.55
Joe Torre
Willie Stargell
Hank Aaron
❑ 88 AL RBI Leaders 3.00 1.35
Harmon Killebrew
Frank Robinson
Reggie Smith
❑ 89 NL Home Run Leaders 3.00 1.35
Willie Stargell
Hank Aaron
Lee May
❑ 90 AL Home Run Leaders 2.50 1.10
Bill Melton
Norm Cash
Reggie Jackson
❑ 91 NL ERA Leaders 2.50 1.10
Tom Seaver
Dave Roberts UER
(Photo actually
Danny Coombs)
Don Wilson
❑ 92 AL ERA Leaders 2.50 1.10
Vida Blue
Wilbur Wood
Jim Palmer
❑ 93 NL Pitching Leaders 4.00 1.80
Fergie Jenkins
Steve Carlton
Al Downing
Tom Seaver
❑ 94 AL Pitching Leaders 1.75 .80
Mickey Lolich
Vida Blue
Wilbur Wood
❑ 95 NL Strikeout Leaders 3.00 1.35
Tom Seaver
Fergie Jenkins
Bill Stoneman
❑ 96 AL Strikeout Leaders 1.75 .80
Mickey Lolich
Vida Blue
Joe Coleman
❑ 97 Tom Kelley .60 .25
❑ 98 Chuck Tanner MG 1.00 .45
❑ 99 Ross Grimsley .60 .25
❑ 100 Frank Robinson 8.00 3.60
❑ 101 Astros Rookies 1.50 .70
Bill Greif
J.R. Richard
Ray Busse
❑ 102 Lloyd Allen .60 .25
❑ 103 Checklist 133-263 4.00 .80
❑ 104 Toby Harrah 1.50 .70
❑ 105 Gary Gentry .60 .25
❑ 106 Milwaukee Brewers 1.25 .55
Team Card
❑ 107 Jose Cruz 1.50 .70
❑ 108 Gary Waslewski .60 .25
❑ 109 Jerry May .60 .25
❑ 110 Ron Hunt .60 .25
❑ 111 Jim Grant .60 .25
❑ 112 Greg Luzinski 1.50 .70
❑ 113 Rogelio Moret .60 .25
❑ 114 Bill Buckner 1.50 .70
❑ 115 Jim Fregosi 1.00 .45
❑ 116 Ed Farmer .60 .25
❑ 117A Cleo James .60 .25
(Yellow underline
C and S of Cubs)
❑ 117B Cleo James 5.00 2.20
(Green underline
C and S of Cubs)
❑ 118 Skip Lockwood .60 .25
❑ 119 Marty Perez .60 .25
❑ 120 Bill Freehan 1.00 .45
❑ 121 Ed Sprague .60 .25
❑ 122 Larry Biittner .60 .25
❑ 123 Ed Acosta .60 .25
❑ 124 Yankees Rookies .60 .25
Alan Closter
Rusty Torres
Roger Hambright
❑ 125 Dave Cash 1.25 .55
❑ 126 Bart Johnson .60 .25
❑ 127 Duffy Dyer .60 .25
❑ 128 Eddie Watt .60 .25
❑ 129 Charlie Fox MG .60 .25
❑ 130 Bob Gibson 8.00 3.60
❑ 131 Jim Nettles .60 .25
❑ 132 Joe Morgan 6.00 2.70
❑ 133 Joe Keough 1.00 .45
❑ 134 Carl Morton 1.00 .45
❑ 135 Vada Pinson 1.50 .70
❑ 136 Darrel Chaney 1.00 .45
❑ 137 Dick Williams MG 1.50 .70
❑ 138 Mike Kekich 1.00 .45
❑ 139 Tim McCarver 2.00 .90
❑ 140 Pat Dobson 2.00 .90
❑ 141 Mets Rookies 2.00 .90
Buzz Capra
Lee Stanton
Jon Matlack
❑ 142 Chris Chambliss 4.00 1.80
❑ 143 Garry Jestadt 1.00 .45
❑ 144 Marty Pattin 1.00 .45
❑ 145 Don Kessinger 1.50 .70
❑ 146 Steve Kealey 1.00 .45
❑ 147 Dave Kingman 5.00 2.20
❑ 148 Dick Billings 1.00 .45
❑ 149 Gary Neibauer 1.00 .45
❑ 150 Norm Cash 2.00 .90
❑ 151 Jim Brewer 1.00 .45
❑ 152 Gene Clines 1.00 .45
❑ 153 Rick Auerbach 1.00 .45
❑ 154 Ted Simmons 3.00 1.35
❑ 155 Larry Dierker 2.00 .90
❑ 156 Minnesota Twins 2.00 .90
Team Card
❑ 157 Don Gullett 1.00 .45
❑ 158 Jerry Kenney 1.00 .45
❑ 159 John Boccabella 1.00 .45
❑ 160 Andy Messersmith 2.00 .90
❑ 161 Brock Davis 1.00 .45
❑ 162 Brewers Rookies UER 2.00 .90
Jerry Bell
Darrell Porter
Bob Reynolds
(Porter and Bell
photos switched)
❑ 163 Tug McGraw 2.00 .90
❑ 164 Tug McGraw IA 2.00 .90
❑ 165 Chris Speier 2.00 .90
❑ 166 Chris Speier IA 2.00 .90
❑ 167 Deron Johnson 1.00 .45
❑ 168 Deron Johnson IA 1.00 .45
❑ 169 Vida Blue 2.00 .90
❑ 170 Vida Blue IA 2.00 .90
❑ 171 Darrell Evans 2.00 .90
❑ 172 Darrell Evans IA 2.00 .90
❑ 173 Clay Kirby 1.00 .45
❑ 174 Clay Kirby IA 1.00 .45

175	Tom Haller	1.00	.45
176	Tom Haller IA	1.00	.45
177	Paul Schaal	1.00	.45
178	Paul Schaal IA	1.00	.45
179	Dock Ellis	1.00	.45
180	Dock Ellis IA	1.00	.45
181	Ed Kranepool	1.00	.45
182	Ed Kranepool IA	1.00	.45
183	Bill Melton	1.00	.45
184	Bill Melton IA	1.00	.45
185	Ron Bryant	1.00	.45
186	Ron Bryant IA	1.00	.45
187	Gates Brown	1.00	.45
188	Frank Lucchesi MG	1.00	.45
189	Gene Tenace	1.50	.70
190	Dave Giusti	1.00	.45
191	Jeff Burroughs	2.00	.90
192	Chicago Cubs	2.00	.90
	Team Card		
193	Kurt Bevacqua	1.00	.45
194	Fred Norman	1.00	.45
195	Orlando Cepeda	2.00	.90
196	Mel Queen	1.00	.45
197	Johnny Briggs	1.00	.45
198	Dodgers Rookies	4.00	1.80
	Charlie Hough		
	Bob O'Brien		
	Mike Strahler		
199	Mike Fiore	1.00	.45
200	Lou Brock	7.00	3.10
201	Phil Roof	1.00	.45
202	Scipio Spinks	1.00	.45
203	Ron Blomberg	1.00	.45
204	Tommy Helms	1.00	.45
205	Dick Drago	1.00	.45
206	Dal Maxvill	1.00	.45
207	Tom Egan	1.00	.45
208	Milt Pappas	2.00	.90
209	Joe Rudi	1.50	.70
210	Denny McLain	1.50	.70
211	Gary Sutherland	1.00	.45
212	Grant Jackson	1.00	.45
213	Angels Rookies	1.00	.45
	Billy Parker		
	Art Kusnyer		
	Tom Silverio		
214	Mike McQueen	1.00	.45
215	Alex Johnson	2.00	.90
216	Joe Niekro	2.00	.90
217	Roger Metzger	1.00	.45
218	Eddie Kasko MG	1.00	.45
219	Rennie Stennett	2.00	.90
220	Jim Perry	2.00	.90
221	NL Playoffs	1.50	.70
	Bucs champs		
222	Brooks Robinson ALCS	3.00	1.35
223	Dave McNally WS	1.75	.80
224	Dave Johnson WS	1.75	.80
	Mark Belanger		
225	Manny Sanguillen WS	1.75	.80
226	Roberto Clemente WS	8.00	3.60
227	Nellie Briles WS	1.75	.80
228	Frank Robinson WS	2.50	1.10
	Manny Sanguillen		
229	Steve Blass WS	1.75	.80
230	World Series Summary	1.75	.80
	(Pirates celebrate)		
231	Casey Cox	1.00	.45
232	Giants Rookies	1.00	.45
	Chris Arnold		
	Jim Barr		
	Dave Rader		
233	Jay Johnstone	2.00	.90
234	Ron Taylor	1.00	.45
235	Merv Rettenmund	1.00	.45
236	Jim McGlothlin	1.00	.45
237	New York Yankees	2.00	.90
	Team Card		
238	Leron Lee	1.00	.45
239	Tom Timmermann	1.00	.45
240	Rich Allen	2.00	.90
241	Rollie Fingers	5.00	2.20
242	Don Mincher	2.00	.90
243	Frank Linzy	1.00	.45
244	Steve Braun	1.00	.45

245	Tommie Agee	1.50	.70
246	Tom Burgmeier	1.00	.45
247	Milt May	1.00	.45
248	Tom Bradley	1.00	.45
249	Harry Walker MG	1.00	.45
250	Boog Powell	2.00	.90
251	Checklist 264-394	6.00	1.20
252	Ken Reynolds	1.00	.45
253	Sandy Alomar	1.50	.70
254	Boots Day	1.00	.45
255	Jim Lonborg	2.00	.90
256	George Foster	2.50	1.10
257	Tigers Rookies	1.00	.45
	Jim Foor		
	Tim Hosley		
	Paul Jata		
258	Randy Hundley	1.50	.70
259	Sparky Lyle	2.00	.90
260	Ralph Garr	2.00	.90
261	Steve Mingori	1.00	.45
262	San Diego Padres	2.00	.90
	Team Card		
263	Felipe Alou	1.50	.70
264	Tommy John	1.50	.70
265	Wes Parker	1.50	.70
266	Bobby Bolin	1.25	.55
267	Dave Concepcion	3.00	1.35
268	A's Rookies	1.25	.55
	Dwain Anderson		
	Chris Floethe		
269	Don Hahn	1.25	.55
270	Jim Palmer	8.00	3.60
271	Ken Rudolph	1.25	.55
272	Mickey Rivers	1.50	.70
273	Bobby Floyd	1.25	.55
274	Al Severinsen	1.25	.55
275	Cesar Tovar	1.25	.55
276	Gene Mauch MG	2.00	.90
277	Elliott Maddox	1.25	.55
278	Dennis Higgins	1.25	.55
279	Larry Brown	1.25	.55
280	Willie McCovey	7.00	3.10
281	Bill Parsons	1.25	.55
282	Houston Astros	2.00	.90
	Team Card		
283	Darrell Brandon	1.25	.55
284	Ike Brown	1.25	.55
285	Gaylord Perry	6.00	2.70
286	Gene Alley	2.00	.90
287	Jim Hardin	1.25	.55
288	Johnny Jeter	1.25	.55
289	Syd O'Brien	1.25	.55
290	Sonny Siebert	1.25	.55
291	Hal McRae	1.50	.70
292	Hal McRae IA	2.00	.90
293	Dan Frisella	1.25	.55
294	Dan Frisella IA	1.25	.55
295	Dick Dietz	1.25	.55
296	Dick Dietz IA	1.25	.55
297	Claude Osteen	2.00	.90
298	Claude Osteen IA	1.25	.55
299	Hank Aaron	40.00	18.00
300	Hank Aaron IA	20.00	9.00
301	George Mitterwald	1.25	.55
302	George Mitterwald IA	1.25	.55
303	Joe Pepitone	1.50	.70
304	Joe Pepitone IA	1.25	.55
305	Ken Boswell	1.25	.55
306	Ken Boswell IA	1.25	.55
307	Steve Renko	1.25	.55
308	Steve Renko IA	1.25	.55
309	Roberto Clemente	50.00	22.00
310	Roberto Clemente IA	25.00	11.00
311	Clay Carroll	1.25	.55
312	Clay Carroll IA	1.25	.55
313	Luis Aparicio	4.00	1.80
314	Luis Aparicio IA	1.75	.80
315	Paul Splittorff	1.25	.55
316	Cardinals Rookies	2.00	.90
	Jim Bibby		
	Jorge Roque		
	Santiago Guzman		
317	Rich Hand	1.25	.55
318	Sonny Jackson	1.25	.55
319	Aurelio Rodriguez	1.25	.55

320	Steve Blass	2.00	.90
321	Joe Lahoud	1.25	.55
322	Jose Pena	1.25	.55
323	Earl Weaver MG	1.50	.70
324	Mike Ryan	1.25	.55
325	Mel Stottlemyre	1.50	.70
326	Pat Kelly	1.25	.55
327	Steve Stone	1.50	.70
328	Boston Red Sox	2.00	.90
	Team Card		
329	Roy Foster	1.25	.55
330	Jim Hunter	4.00	1.80
331	Stan Swanson	1.25	.55
332	Buck Martinez	1.25	.55
333	Steve Barber	1.25	.55
334	Rangers Rookies	1.25	.55
	Bill Fahey		
	Jim Mason		
	Tom Ragland		
335	Bill Hands	1.25	.55
336	Marty Martinez	1.25	.55
337	Mike Kilkenny	1.25	.55
338	Bob Grich	1.50	.70
339	Ron Cook	1.25	.55
340	Roy White	1.50	.70
341	Joe Torre KP	1.25	.55
342	Wilbur Wood KP	1.25	.55
343	Willie Stargell KP	1.50	.70
344	Dave McNally KP	1.25	.55
345	Rick Wise KP	1.25	.55
346	Jim Fregosi KP	1.25	.55
347	Tom Seaver KP	3.00	1.35
348	Sal Bando KP	1.25	.55
349	Al Fitzmorris	1.25	.55
350	Frank Howard	1.50	.70
351	Braves Rookies	2.00	.90
	Tom House		
	Rick Kester		
	Jimmy Britton		
352	Dave LaRoche	1.25	.55
353	Art Shamsky	1.25	.55
354	Tom Murphy	1.25	.55
355	Bob Watson	2.00	.90
356	Gerry Moses	1.25	.55
357	Woody Fryman	1.25	.55
358	Sparky Anderson MG	3.00	1.35
359	Don Pavletich	1.25	.55
360	Dave Roberts	1.25	.55
361	Mike Andrews	1.25	.55
362	New York Mets	2.00	.90
	Team Card		
363	Ron Klimkowski	1.25	.55
364	Johnny Callison	2.00	.90
365	Dick Bosman	2.00	.90
366	Jimmy Rosario	1.25	.55
367	Ron Perranoski	2.00	.90
368	Danny Thompson	1.25	.55
369	Jim Lefebvre	2.00	.90
370	Don Buford	1.25	.55
371	Denny Lemaster	1.25	.55
372	Royals Rookies	1.25	.55
	Lance Clemons		
	Monty Montgomery		
373	John Mayberry	2.00	.90
374	Jack Heidemann	1.25	.55
375	Reggie Cleveland	1.25	.55
376	Andy Kosco	1.25	.55
377	Terry Harmon	1.25	.55
378	Checklist 395-525	4.00	.80
379	Ken Berry	1.25	.55
380	Earl Williams	1.25	.55
381	Chicago White Sox	2.00	.90
	Team Card		
382	Joe Gibbon	1.25	.55
383	Brant Alyea	1.25	.55
384	Dave Campbell	2.00	.90
385	Mickey Stanley	2.00	.90
386	Jim Colborn	1.25	.55
387	Horace Clarke	2.00	.90
388	Charlie Williams	1.25	.55
389	Bill Rigney MG	1.25	.55
390	Willie Davis	1.50	.70
391	Ken Sanders	1.25	.55
392	Pirates Rookies	2.00	.90
	Fred Cambria		
	Richie Zisk		

❑	393	Curt Motton	1.25	.55
❑	394	Ken Forsch	2.00	.90
❑	395	Matty Alou	1.75	.80
❑	396	Paul Lindblad	1.50	.70
❑	397	Philadelphia Phillies	2.00	.90
		Team Card		
❑	398	Larry Hisle	2.00	.90
❑	399	Milt Wilcox	1.50	.70
❑	400	Tony Oliva	1.75	.80
❑	401	Jim Nash	1.50	.70
❑	402	Bobby Heise	1.50	.70
❑	403	John Cumberland	1.50	.70
❑	404	Jeff Torborg	2.00	.90
❑	405	Ron Fairly	2.00	.90
❑	406	George Hendrick	1.75	.80
❑	407	Chuck Taylor	1.00	.45
❑	408	Jim Northrup	2.00	.90
❑	409	Frank Baker	1.00	.45
❑	410	Ferguson Jenkins	6.00	2.70
❑	411	Bob Montgomery	1.00	.45
❑	412	Dick Kelley	1.00	.45
❑	413	White Sox Rookies	1.00	.45
		Don Eddy		
		Dave Lemonds		
❑	414	Bob Miller	1.00	.45
❑	415	Cookie Rojas	2.00	.90
❑	416	Johnny Edwards	1.00	.45
❑	417	Tom Hall	1.00	.45
❑	418	Tom Shopay	1.00	.45
❑	419	Jim Spencer	1.00	.45
❑	420	Steve Carlton	18.00	8.00
❑	421	Ellie Rodriguez	1.00	.45
❑	422	Ray Lamb	1.00	.45
❑	423	Oscar Gamble	2.00	.90
❑	424	Bill Gogolewski	1.00	.45
❑	425	Ken Singleton	2.00	.90
❑	426	Ken Singleton IA	1.00	.45
❑	427	Tito Fuentes	1.00	.45
❑	428	Tito Fuentes IA	1.00	.45
❑	429	Bob Robertson	1.00	.45
❑	430	Bob Robertson IA	1.00	.45
❑	431	Clarence Gaston	1.75	.80
❑	432	Clarence Gaston IA	2.00	.90
❑	433	Johnny Bench	25.00	11.00
❑	434	Johnny Bench IA	15.00	6.75
❑	435	Reggie Jackson	25.00	11.00
❑	436	Reggie Jackson IA	12.00	5.50
❑	437	Maury Wills	1.75	.80
❑	438	Maury Wills IA	2.00	.90
❑	439	Billy Williams	6.00	2.70
❑	440	Billy Williams IA	3.00	1.35
❑	441	Thurman Munson	15.00	6.75
❑	442	Thurman Munson IA	8.00	3.60
❑	443	Ken Henderson	1.50	.70
❑	444	Ken Henderson IA	1.50	.70
❑	445	Tom Seaver	30.00	13.50
❑	446	Tom Seaver IA	15.00	6.75
❑	447	Willie Stargell	8.00	3.60
❑	448	Willie Stargell IA	3.00	1.35
❑	449	Bob Lemon MG	1.75	.80
❑	450	Mickey Lolich	1.75	.80
❑	451	Tony LaRussa	3.00	1.35
❑	452	Ed Herrmann	1.50	.70
❑	453	Barry Lersch	1.50	.70
❑	454	Oakland A's	2.00	.90
		Team Card		
❑	455	Tommy Harper	2.00	.90
❑	456	Mark Belanger	2.00	.90
❑	457	Padres Rookies	1.50	.70
		Darcy Fast		
		Derrel Thomas		
		Mike Ivie		
❑	458	Aurelio Monteagudo	1.50	.70
❑	459	Rick Renick	1.50	.70
❑	460	Al Downing	1.50	.70
❑	461	Tim Cullen	1.50	.70
❑	462	Rickey Clark	1.50	.70
❑	463	Bernie Carbo	1.50	.70
❑	464	Jim Roland	1.50	.70
❑	465	Gil Hodges MG	4.00	1.80
❑	466	Norm Miller	1.50	.70
❑	467	Steve Kline	1.50	.70
❑	468	Richie Scheinblum	1.50	.70
❑	469	Ron Herbel	1.50	.70
❑	470	Ray Fosse	1.50	.70
❑	471	Luke Walker	1.50	.70
❑	472	Phil Gagliano	1.50	.70
❑	473	Dan McGinn	1.50	.70
❑	474	Orioles Rookies	15.00	6.75
		Don Baylor		
		Roric Harrison		
		Johnny Oates		
❑	475	Gary Nolan	2.00	.90
❑	476	Lee Richard	1.50	.70
❑	477	Tom Phoebus	1.50	.70
❑	478	Checklist 526-656	6.00	1.20
❑	479	Don Shaw	1.50	.70
❑	480	Lee May	2.00	.90
❑	481	Billy Conigliaro	1.75	.80
❑	482	Joe Hoerner	1.50	.70
❑	483	Ken Suarez	1.50	.70
❑	484	Lum Harris MG	1.50	.70
❑	485	Phil Regan	2.00	.90
❑	486	John Lowenstein	1.50	.70
❑	487	Detroit Tigers	2.00	.90
		Team Card		
❑	488	Mike Nagy	1.50	.70
❑	489	Expos Rookies	1.50	.70
		Terry Humphrey		
		Keith Lampard		
❑	490	Dave McNally	2.00	.90
❑	491	Lou Piniella KP	2.00	.90
❑	492	Mel Stottlemyre KP	2.00	.90
❑	493	Bob Bailey KP	2.00	.90
❑	494	Willie Horton KP	2.00	.90
❑	495	Bill Melton KP	2.00	.90
❑	496	Bud Harrelson KP	2.00	.90
❑	497	Jim Perry KP	2.00	.90
❑	498	Brooks Robinson KP	3.00	1.35
❑	499	Vicente Romo	1.50	.70
❑	500	Joe Torre	1.75	.80
❑	501	Pete Hamm	1.50	.70
❑	502	Jackie Hernandez	1.50	.70
❑	503	Gary Peters	1.50	.70
❑	504	Ed Spiezio	1.50	.70
❑	505	Mike Marshall	1.75	.80
❑	506	Indians Rookies	1.50	.70
		Terry Ley		
		Jim Moyer		
		Dick Tidrow		
❑	507	Fred Gladding	1.50	.70
❑	508	Elrod Hendricks	1.50	.70
❑	509	Don McMahon	1.50	.70
❑	510	Ted Williams MG	12.00	5.50
❑	511	Tony Taylor	2.00	.90
❑	512	Paul Popovich	1.50	.70
❑	513	Lindy McDaniel	2.00	.90
❑	514	Ted Sizemore	1.50	.70
❑	515	Bert Blyleven	3.00	1.35
❑	516	Oscar Brown	1.00	.45
❑	517	Ken Brett	1.00	.45
❑	518	Wayne Garrett	1.00	.45
❑	519	Ted Abernathy	1.00	.45
❑	520	Larry Bowa	1.75	.80
❑	521	Alan Foster	1.00	.45
❑	522	Los Angeles Dodgers	3.00	1.35
		Team Card		
❑	523	Chuck Dobson	1.00	.45
❑	524	Reds Rookies	1.00	.45
		Ed Armbrister		
		Mel Behney		
❑	525	Carlos May	2.00	.90
❑	526	Bob Bailey	6.00	2.70
❑	527	Dave Leonhard	4.00	1.80
❑	528	Ron Stone	4.00	1.80
❑	529	Dave Nelson	6.00	2.70
❑	530	Don Sutton	7.00	3.10
❑	531	Freddie Patek	6.00	2.70
❑	532	Fred Kendall	4.00	1.80
❑	533	Ralph Houk MG	4.50	2.00
❑	534	Jim Hickman	6.00	2.70
❑	535	Ed Brinkman	4.00	1.80
❑	536	Doug Rader	6.00	2.70
❑	537	Bob Locker	4.00	1.80
❑	538	Charlie Sands	4.00	1.80
❑	539	Terry Forster	4.50	2.00
❑	540	Felix Millan	4.00	1.80
❑	541	Roger Repoz	4.00	1.80
❑	542	Jack Billingham	4.00	1.80
❑	543	Duane Josephson	4.00	1.80
❑	544	Ted Martinez	4.00	1.80
❑	545	Wayne Granger	4.00	1.80
❑	546	Joe Hague	4.00	1.80
❑	547	Cleveland Indians	8.00	3.60
		Team Card		
❑	548	Frank Reberger	4.00	1.80
❑	549	Dave May	4.00	1.80
❑	550	Brooks Robinson	25.00	11.00
❑	551	Ollie Brown	4.00	1.80
❑	552	Ollie Brown IA	4.00	1.80
❑	553	Wilbur Wood	4.50	2.00
❑	554	Wilbur Wood IA	4.00	1.80
❑	555	Ron Santo	4.50	2.00
❑	556	Ron Santo IA	6.00	2.70
❑	557	John Odom	4.00	1.80
❑	558	John Odom IA	4.00	1.80
❑	559	Pete Rose	35.00	16.00
❑	560	Pete Rose IA	20.00	9.00
❑	561	Leo Cardenas	4.00	1.80
❑	562	Leo Cardenas IA	4.00	1.80
❑	563	Ray Sadecki	4.00	1.80
❑	564	Ray Sadecki IA	4.00	1.80
❑	565	Reggie Smith	4.50	2.00
❑	566	Reggie Smith IA	4.00	1.80
❑	567	Juan Marichal	12.00	5.50
❑	568	Juan Marichal IA	6.00	2.70
❑	569	Ed Kirkpatrick	4.00	1.80
❑	570	Ed Kirkpatrick IA	4.00	1.80
❑	571	Nate Colbert	4.00	1.80
❑	572	Nate Colbert IA	4.00	1.80
❑	573	Fritz Peterson	4.00	1.80
❑	574	Fritz Peterson IA	4.00	1.80
❑	575	Al Oliver	4.50	2.00
❑	576	Leo Durocher MG	5.00	2.20
❑	577	Mike Paul	6.00	2.70
❑	578	Billy Grabarkewitz	4.00	1.80
❑	579	Doyle Alexander	4.50	2.00
❑	580	Lou Piniella	5.00	2.20
❑	581	Wade Blasingame	4.00	1.80
❑	582	Montreal Expos	8.00	3.60
		Team Card		
❑	583	Darold Knowles	4.00	1.80
❑	584	Jerry McNertney	4.00	1.80
❑	585	George Scott	4.50	2.00
❑	586	Denis Menke	4.00	1.80
❑	587	Billy Wilson	4.00	1.80
❑	588	Jim Holt	4.00	1.80
❑	589	Hal Lanier	4.00	1.80
❑	590	Graig Nettles	4.50	2.00
❑	591	Paul Casanova	4.00	1.80
❑	592	Lew Krausse	4.00	1.80
❑	593	Rich Morales	4.00	1.80
❑	594	Jim Beauchamp	4.00	1.80
❑	595	Nolan Ryan	200.00	90.00
❑	596	Manny Mota	4.50	2.00
❑	597	Jim Magnuson	4.00	1.80
❑	598	Hal King	6.00	2.70
❑	599	Billy Champion	4.00	1.80
❑	600	Al Kaline	25.00	11.00
❑	601	George Stone	4.00	1.80
❑	602	Dave Bristol MG	4.00	1.80
❑	603	Jim Ray	4.00	1.80
❑	604A	Checklist 657-787	12.00	2.40
		(Copyright on back bottom right)		
❑	604B	Checklist 657-787	12.00	2.40
		(Copyright on back bottom left)		
❑	605	Nelson Briles	6.00	2.70
❑	606	Luis Melendez	4.00	1.80
❑	607	Frank Duffy	4.00	1.80
❑	608	Mike Corkins	4.00	1.80
❑	609	Tom Grieve	6.00	2.70
❑	610	Bill Stoneman	6.00	2.70
❑	611	Rich Reese	4.00	1.80
❑	612	Joe Decker	4.00	1.80
❑	613	Mike Ferraro	4.00	1.80
❑	614	Ted Uhlaender	4.00	1.80
❑	615	Steve Hargan	4.00	1.80
❑	616	Joe Ferguson	6.00	2.70
❑	617	Kansas City Royals	8.00	3.60
		Team Card		
❑	618	Rich Robertson	4.00	1.80
❑	619	Rich McKinney	4.00	1.80
❑	620	Phil Niekro	10.00	4.50

❑ 621 Commissioners Award 5.00 2.20
❑ 622 MVP Award 5.00 2.20
❑ 623 Cy Young Award 5.00 2.20
❑ 624 Minor League Player 5.00 2.20
of the Year
❑ 625 Rookie of the Year 5.00 2.20
❑ 626 Babe Ruth Award 5.00 2.20
❑ 627 Moe Drabowsky 4.00 1.80
❑ 628 Terry Crowley 4.00 1.80
❑ 629 Paul Doyle 4.00 1.80
❑ 630 Rich Hebner 6.00 2.70
❑ 631 John Strohmayer 4.00 1.80
❑ 632 Mike Hegan 4.00 1.80
❑ 633 Jack Hiatt 4.00 1.80
❑ 634 Dick Woodson 4.00 1.80
❑ 635 Don Money 6.00 2.70
❑ 636 Bill Lee 6.00 2.70
❑ 637 Preston Gomez MG 4.00 1.80
❑ 638 Ken Wright 4.00 1.80
❑ 639 J.C. Martin 4.00 1.80
❑ 640 Joe Coleman 4.00 1.80
❑ 641 Mike Lum 4.00 1.80
❑ 642 Dennis Riddleberger 4.00 1.80
❑ 643 Russ Gibson 4.00 1.80
❑ 644 Bernie Allen 4.00 1.80
❑ 645 Jim Maloney 6.00 2.70
❑ 646 Chico Salmon 4.00 1.80
❑ 647 Bob Moose 4.00 1.80
❑ 648 Jim Lyttle 4.00 1.80
❑ 649 Pete Richert 4.00 1.80
❑ 650 Sal Bando 4.50 2.00
❑ 651 Cincinnati Reds 7.00 3.10
Team Card
❑ 652 Marcelino Lopez 4.00 1.80
❑ 653 Jim Fairey 4.00 1.80
❑ 654 Horacio Pina 6.00 2.70
❑ 655 Jerry Grote 4.00 1.80
❑ 656 Rudy May 4.00 1.80
❑ 657 Bobby Wine 12.00 5.50
❑ 658 Steve Dunning 12.00 5.50
❑ 659 Bob Aspromonte 12.00 5.50
❑ 660 Paul Blair 15.00 6.75
❑ 661 Bill Virdon MG 13.00 5.75
❑ 662 Stan Bahnsen 12.00 5.50
❑ 663 Fran Healy 15.00 6.75
❑ 664 Bobby Knoop 12.00 5.50
❑ 665 Chris Short 12.00 5.50
❑ 666 Hector Torres 12.00 5.50
❑ 667 Ray Newman 12.00 5.50
❑ 668 Texas Rangers 30.00 13.50
Team Card
❑ 669 Willie Crawford 12.00 5.50
❑ 670 Ken Holtzman 15.00 6.75
❑ 671 Donn Clendenon 15.00 6.75
❑ 672 Archie Reynolds 12.00 5.50
❑ 673 Dave Marshall 12.00 5.50
❑ 674 John Kennedy 12.00 5.50
❑ 675 Pat Jarvis 12.00 5.50
❑ 676 Danny Cater 12.00 5.50
❑ 677 Ivan Murrell 12.00 5.50
❑ 678 Steve Luebber 12.00 5.50
❑ 679 Astros Rookies 12.00 5.50
Bob Fenwick
Bob Stinson
❑ 680 Dave Johnson 15.00 6.75
❑ 681 Bobby Pfeil 12.00 5.50
❑ 682 Mike McCormick 15.00 6.75
❑ 683 Steve Hovley 12.00 5.50
❑ 684 Hal Breeden 12.00 5.50
❑ 685 Joel Horlen 12.00 5.50
❑ 686 Steve Garvey 40.00 18.00
❑ 687 Del Unser 12.00 5.50
❑ 688 St. Louis Cardinals 20.00 9.00
Team Card
❑ 689 Eddie Fisher 12.00 5.50
❑ 690 Willie Montanez 15.00 6.75
❑ 691 Curt Blefary 12.00 5.50
❑ 692 Curt Blefary IA 12.00 5.50
❑ 693 Alan Gallagher 12.00 5.50
❑ 694 Alan Gallagher IA 12.00 5.50
❑ 695 Rod Carew 75.00 34.00
❑ 696 Rod Carew IA 35.00 16.00
❑ 697 Jerry Koosman 15.00 6.75
❑ 698 Jerry Koosman IA 13.00 5.75
❑ 699 Bobby Murcer 15.00 6.75
❑ 700 Bobby Murcer IA 13.00 5.75
❑ 701 Jose Pagan 12.00 5.50
❑ 702 Jose Pagan IA 12.00 5.50
❑ 703 Doug Griffin 12.00 5.50
❑ 704 Doug Griffin IA 12.00 5.50
❑ 705 Pat Corrales 15.00 6.75
❑ 706 Pat Corrales IA 12.00 5.50
❑ 707 Tim Foli 12.00 5.50
❑ 708 Tim Foli IA 12.00 5.50
❑ 709 Jim Kaat 16.00 7.25
❑ 710 Jim Kaat IA 14.00 6.25
❑ 711 Bobby Bonds 20.00 9.00
❑ 712 Bobby Bonds IA 14.00 6.25
❑ 713 Gene Michael 20.00 9.00
❑ 714 Gene Michael IA 15.00 6.75
❑ 715 Mike Epstein 12.00 5.50
❑ 716 Jesus Alou 12.00 5.50
❑ 717 Bruce Dal Canton 12.00 5.50
❑ 718 Del Rice MG 12.00 5.50
❑ 719 Cesar Geronimo 12.00 5.50
❑ 720 Sam McDowell 15.00 6.75
❑ 721 Eddie Leon 12.00 5.50
❑ 722 Bill Sudakis 12.00 5.50
❑ 723 Al Santorini 12.00 5.50
❑ 724 AL Rookie Pitchers 12.00 5.50
John Curtis
Rich Hinton
Mickey Scott
❑ 725 Dick McAuliffe 15.00 6.75
❑ 726 Dick Selma 12.00 5.50
❑ 727 Jose Laboy 12.00 5.50
❑ 728 Gail Hopkins 12.00 5.50
❑ 729 Bob Veale 15.00 6.75
❑ 730 Rick Monday 13.00 5.75
❑ 731 Baltimore Orioles 20.00 9.00
Team Card
❑ 732 George Culver 12.00 5.50
❑ 733 Jim Ray Hart 15.00 6.75
❑ 734 Bob Burda 12.00 5.50
❑ 735 Diego Segui 12.00 5.50
❑ 736 Bill Russell 13.00 5.75
❑ 737 Len Randle 15.00 6.75
❑ 738 Jim Merritt 12.00 5.50
❑ 739 Don Mason 12.00 5.50
❑ 740 Rico Carty 15.00 6.75
❑ 741 Rookie First Basemen 13.00 5.75
Tom Hutton
John Milner
Rick Miller
❑ 742 Jim Rooker 12.00 5.50
❑ 743 Cesar Gutierrez 12.00 5.50
❑ 744 Jim Slaton 12.00 5.50
❑ 745 Julian Javier 15.00 6.75
❑ 746 Lowell Palmer 12.00 5.50
❑ 747 Jim Stewart 12.00 5.50
❑ 748 Phil Hennigan 12.00 5.50
❑ 749 Walter Alston MG 14.00 6.25
❑ 750 Willie Horton 12.00 5.50
❑ 751 Steve Carlton TR 50.00 22.00
❑ 752 Joe Morgan TR 45.00 20.00
❑ 753 Denny McLain TR 20.00 9.00
❑ 754 Frank Robinson TR 45.00 20.00
❑ 755 Jim Fregosi TR 13.00 5.75
❑ 756 Rick Wise TR 15.00 6.75
❑ 757 Jose Cardenal TR 15.00 6.75
❑ 758 Gil Garrido 12.00 5.50
❑ 759 Chris Cannizzaro 12.00 5.50
❑ 760 Bill Mazeroski 18.00 8.00
❑ 761 Rookie Outfielders 25.00 11.00
Ben Oglivie
Ron Cey
Bernie Williams
❑ 762 Wayne Simpson 12.00 5.50
❑ 763 Ron Hansen 12.00 5.50
❑ 764 Dusty Baker 20.00 9.00
❑ 765 Ken McMullen 12.00 5.50
❑ 766 Steve Hamilton 12.00 5.50
❑ 767 Tom McCraw 15.00 6.75
❑ 768 Denny Doyle 12.00 5.50
❑ 769 Jack Aker 12.00 5.50
❑ 770 Jim Wynn 13.00 5.75
❑ 771 San Francisco Giants 20.00 9.00
Team Card
❑ 772 Ken Tatum 12.00 5.50
❑ 773 Ron Brand 12.00 5.50
❑ 774 Luis Alvarado 12.00 5.50
❑ 775 Jerry Reuss 15.00 6.75
❑ 776 Bill Voss 12.00 5.50
❑ 777 Hoyt Wilhelm 25.00 11.00
❑ 778 Twins Rookies 18.00 8.00
Vic Albury
Rick Dempsey
Jim Strickland
❑ 779 Tony Cloninger 12.00 5.50
❑ 780 Dick Green 12.00 5.50
❑ 781 Jim McAndrew 12.00 5.50
❑ 782 Larry Stahl 12.00 5.50
❑ 783 Les Cain 12.00 5.50
❑ 784 Ken Aspromonte 12.00 5.50
❑ 785 Vic Davalillo 12.00 5.50
❑ 786 Chuck Brinkman 12.00 5.50
❑ 787 Ron Reed 16.00 5.50

1973 Topps

	NRMT	VG-E
COMPLETE SET (660)	700.00	325.00
COMMON CARD (1-264)	.50	.23
COMMON CARD (265-396)	.75	.35
COMMON CARD (397-528)	1.25	.55
COMMON CARD (529-660)	3.50	1.55
WRAPPER (10-CENT, BAT)	15.00	6.75
WRAPPER (10-CENT)	15.00	6.75

❑ 1 All-Time HR Leaders 40.00 11.50
Babe Ruth 714
Hank Aaron 673
Willie Mays 654
❑ 2 Rich Hebner 1.50 .70
❑ 3 Jim Lonborg 1.50 .70
❑ 4 John Milner .50 .23
❑ 5 Ed Brinkman .50 .23
❑ 6 Mac Scarce .50 .23
❑ 7 Texas Rangers 1.50 .70
Team Card
❑ 8 Tom Hall .50 .23
❑ 9 Johnny Oates .50 .23
❑ 10 Don Sutton 1.00 .45
❑ 11 Chris Chambliss .75 .35
❑ 12A Padres Leaders 1.50 .70
Don Zimmer MG
Dave Garcia CO
Johnny Podres CO
Bob Skinner CO
Whitey Wietelmann CO
(Podres no right ear)
❑ 12B Padres Leaders 2.50 1.10
(Podres has right ear)
❑ 13 George Hendrick 1.50 .70
❑ 14 Sonny Siebert .50 .23
❑ 15 Ralph Garr 1.50 .70
❑ 16 Steve Braun .50 .23
❑ 17 Fred Gladding .50 .23
❑ 18 Leroy Stanton .50 .23
❑ 19 Tim Foli .50 .23
❑ 20 Stan Bahnsen .50 .23
❑ 21 Randy Hundley 1.50 .70
❑ 22 Ted Abernathy .50 .23
❑ 23 Dave Kingman 1.00 .45
❑ 24 Al Santorini .50 .23
❑ 25 Roy White .75 .35
❑ 26 Pittsburgh Pirates 1.50 .70
Team Card

❑ 27 Bill Gogolewski .50 .23
❑ 28 Hal McRae 1.00 .45
❑ 29 Tony Taylor 1.50 .70
❑ 30 Tug McGraw .75 .35
❑ 31 Buddy Bell 3.00 1.35
❑ 32 Fred Norman .50 .23
❑ 33 Jim Breazeale .50 .23
❑ 34 Pat Dobson .50 .23
❑ 35 Willie Davis .75 .35
❑ 36 Steve Barber .50 .23
❑ 37 Bill Robinson 1.50 .70
❑ 38 Mike Epstein .50 .23
❑ 39 Dave Roberts .50 .23
❑ 40 Reggie Smith .75 .35
❑ 41 Tom Walker .50 .23
❑ 42 Mike Andrews .50 .23
❑ 43 Randy Moffitt .50 .23
❑ 44 Rick Monday .75 .35
❑ 45 Ellie Rodriguez UER .50 .23
(Photo actually
John Felske)
❑ 46 Lindy McDaniel 1.50 .70
❑ 47 Luis Melendez .50 .23
❑ 48 Paul Splittorff .50 .23
❑ 49A Twins Leaders 1.50 .70
Frank Quilici MG
Vern Morgan CO
Bob Rodgers CO
Ralph Rowe CO
Al Worthington CO
(Solid backgrounds)
❑ 49B Twins Leaders 2.50 1.10
(Natural backgrounds)
❑ 50 Roberto Clemente 70.00 32.00
❑ 51 Chuck Seelbach .50 .23
❑ 52 Denis Menke .50 .23
❑ 53 Steve Dunning .50 .23
❑ 54 Checklist 1-132 4.00 .80
❑ 55 Jon Matlack 1.50 .70
❑ 56 Merv Rettenmund .50 .23
❑ 57 Derrel Thomas .50 .23
❑ 58 Mike Paul .50 .23
❑ 59 Steve Yeager 1.50 .70
❑ 60 Ken Holtzman 1.50 .70
❑ 61 Batting Leaders 3.00 1.35
Billy Williams
Rod Carew
❑ 62 Home Run Leaders 2.50 1.10
Johnny Bench
Dick Allen
❑ 63 RBI Leaders 2.50 1.10
Johnny Bench
Dick Allen
❑ 64 Stolen Base Leaders 2.00 .90
Lou Brock
Bert Campaneris
❑ 65 ERA Leaders 2.00 .90
Steve Carlton
Luis Tiant
❑ 66 Victory Leaders 2.00 .90
Steve Carlton
Gaylord Perry
Wilbur Wood
❑ 67 Strikeout Leaders 30.00 13.50
Steve Carlton
Nolan Ryan
❑ 68 Leading Firemen 1.50 .70
Clay Carroll
Sparky Lyle
❑ 69 Phil Gagliano .50 .23
❑ 70 Milt Pappas 1.50 .70
❑ 71 Johnny Briggs .50 .23
❑ 72 Ron Reed .50 .23
❑ 73 Ed Herrmann .50 .23
❑ 74 Billy Champion .50 .23
❑ 75 Vada Pinson 1.00 .45
❑ 76 Doug Rader .50 .23
❑ 77 Mike Torrez 1.50 .70
❑ 78 Richie Scheinblum .50 .23
❑ 79 Jim Willoughby .50 .23
❑ 80 Tony Oliva UER 1.00 .45
(Minnseota on front)
❑ 81A Cubs Leaders 1.50 .70
Whitey Lockman MG
Hank Aguirre CO
Ernie Banks CO
Larry Jansen CO
Pete Reiser CO
(Solid backgrounds)
❑ 81B Cubs Leaders 2.00 .90
(Natural backgrounds)
❑ 82 Fritz Peterson .50 .23
❑ 83 Leron Lee .50 .23
❑ 84 Rollie Fingers 5.00 2.20
❑ 85 Ted Simmons 1.00 .45
❑ 86 Tom McCraw .50 .23
❑ 87 Ken Boswell .50 .23
❑ 88 Mickey Stanley 1.50 .70
❑ 89 Jack Billingham .50 .23
❑ 90 Brooks Robinson 7.00 3.10
❑ 91 Los Angeles Dodgers 1.50 .70
Team Card
❑ 92 Jerry Bell .50 .23
❑ 93 Jesus Alou .50 .23
❑ 94 Dick Billings .50 .23
❑ 95 Steve Blass 1.50 .70
❑ 96 Doug Griffin .50 .23
❑ 97 Willie Montanez 1.50 .70
❑ 98 Dick Woodson .50 .23
❑ 99 Carl Taylor .50 .23
❑ 100 Hank Aaron 25.00 11.00
❑ 101 Ken Henderson .50 .23
❑ 102 Rudy May .50 .23
❑ 103 Celerino Sanchez .50 .23
❑ 104 Reggie Cleveland .50 .23
❑ 105 Carlos May .50 .23
❑ 106 Terry Humphrey .50 .23
❑ 107 Phil Hennigan .50 .23
❑ 108 Bill Russell .75 .35
❑ 109 Doyle Alexander 1.50 .70
❑ 110 Bob Watson 1.50 .70
❑ 111 Dave Nelson .50 .23
❑ 112 Gary Ross .50 .23
❑ 113 Jerry Grote .50 .23
❑ 114 Lynn McGlothen .50 .23
❑ 115 Ron Santo 1.00 .45
❑ 116A Yankees Leaders 1.50 .70
Ralph Houk MG
Jim Hegan CO
Elston Howard CO
Dick Howser CO
Jim Turner CO
(Solid backgrounds)
❑ 116B Yankees Leaders 2.50 1.10
(Natural backgrounds)
❑ 117 Ramon Hernandez .50 .23
❑ 118 John Mayberry 1.50 .70
❑ 119 Larry Bowa .75 .35
❑ 120 Joe Coleman .50 .23
❑ 121 Dave Rader .50 .23
❑ 122 Jim Strickland .50 .23
❑ 123 Sandy Alomar 1.50 .70
❑ 124 Jim Hardin .50 .23
❑ 125 Ron Fairly 1.50 .70
❑ 126 Jim Brewer .50 .23
❑ 127 Milwaukee Brewers 1.50 .70
Team Card
❑ 128 Ted Sizemore .50 .23
❑ 129 Terry Forster 1.50 .70
❑ 130 Pete Rose 14.00 6.25
❑ 131A Red Sox Leaders 1.50 .70
Eddie Kasko MG
Doug Camilli CO
Don Lenhardt CO
Eddie Popowski CO
(No right ear)
Lee Stange CO
❑ 131B Red Sox Leaders 2.50 1.10
(Popowski has right
ear showing)
❑ 132 Matty Alou .75 .35
❑ 133 Dave Roberts .50 .23
❑ 134 Milt Wilcox .50 .23
❑ 135 Lee May UER 1.50 .70
(Career average .000)
❑ 136A Orioles Leaders 2.00 .90
Earl Weaver MG
George Bamberger CO
Jim Frey CO
Billy Hunter CO
George Staller CO
(Orange backgrounds)
❑ 136B Orioles Leaders 3.00 1.35
(Dark pale
backgrounds)
❑ 137 Jim Beauchamp .50 .23
❑ 138 Horacio Pina .50 .23
❑ 139 Carmen Fanzone .50 .23
❑ 140 Lou Piniella 1.00 .45
❑ 141 Bruce Kison .50 .23
❑ 142 Thurman Munson 6.00 2.70
❑ 143 John Curtis .50 .23
❑ 144 Marty Perez .50 .23
❑ 145 Bobby Bonds 1.00 .45
❑ 146 Woodie Fryman .50 .23
❑ 147 Mike Anderson .50 .23
❑ 148 Dave Goltz .50 .23
❑ 149 Ron Hunt .50 .23
❑ 150 Wilbur Wood 1.50 .70
❑ 151 Wes Parker 1.50 .70
❑ 152 Dave May .50 .23
❑ 153 Al Hrabosky 1.50 .70
❑ 154 Jeff Torborg 1.50 .70
❑ 155 Sal Bando 1.50 .70
❑ 156 Cesar Geronimo .50 .23
❑ 157 Denny Riddleberger .50 .23
❑ 158 Houston Astros 1.50 .70
Team Card
❑ 159 Clarence Gaston 1.00 .45
❑ 160 Jim Palmer 7.00 3.10
❑ 161 Ted Martinez .50 .23
❑ 162 Pete Broberg .50 .23
❑ 163 Vic Davalillo .50 .23
❑ 164 Monty Montgomery .50 .23
❑ 165 Luis Aparicio 3.00 1.35
❑ 166 Terry Harmon .50 .23
❑ 167 Steve Stone 1.50 .70
❑ 168 Jim Northrup 1.50 .70
❑ 169 Ron Schueler .50 .23
❑ 170 Harmon Killebrew 5.00 2.20
❑ 171 Bernie Carbo .50 .23
❑ 172 Steve Kline .50 .23
❑ 173 Hal Breeden .50 .23
❑ 174 Rich Gossage 6.00 2.70
❑ 175 Frank Robinson 7.00 3.10
❑ 176 Chuck Taylor .50 .23
❑ 177 Bill Plummer .50 .23
❑ 178 Don Rose .50 .23
❑ 179A A's Leaders 1.50 .70
Dick Williams MG
Jerry Adair CO
Vern Hoscheit CO
Irv Noren CO
Wes Stock CO
(Hoscheit left ear
showing)
❑ 179B A's Leaders 2.50 1.10
(Hoscheit left ear
not showing)
❑ 180 Ferguson Jenkins 5.00 2.20
❑ 181 Jack Brohamer .50 .23
❑ 182 Mike Caldwell 1.50 .70
❑ 183 Don Buford .50 .23
❑ 184 Jerry Koosman 1.00 .45
❑ 185 Jim Wynn .75 .35
❑ 186 Bill Fahey .50 .23
❑ 187 Luke Walker .50 .23
❑ 188 Cookie Rojas 1.50 .70
❑ 189 Greg Luzinski 1.00 .45
❑ 190 Bob Gibson 7.00 3.10
❑ 191 Detroit Tigers 1.50 .70
Team Card
❑ 192 Pat Jarvis .50 .23
❑ 193 Carlton Fisk 7.00 3.10
❑ 194 Jorge Orta .50 .23
❑ 195 Clay Carroll .50 .23
❑ 196 Ken McMullen .50 .23
❑ 197 Ed Goodson .50 .23
❑ 198 Horace Clarke .50 .23
❑ 199 Bert Blyleven 1.00 .45
❑ 200 Billy Williams 5.00 2.20
❑ 201 George Hendrick ALCS 1.50 .70
❑ 202 George Foster NLCS 1.50 .70
❑ 203 Gene Tenace WS 1.50 .70
❑ 204 World Series Game 2 1.50 .70
A's two straight
❑ 205 Tony Perez WS 2.50 1.10

❑ 206 Gene Tenace WS .... 1.50 .70
❑ 207 Blue Moon Odom WS .. 1.50 .70
❑ 208 Johnny Bench WS6...... 5.00 2.20
❑ 209 Bert Campaneris WS .. 1.50 .70
❑ 210 World Series Summary .. .50 .23
World champions:
A's Win
❑ 211 Balor Moore.................. .50 .23
❑ 212 Joe Lahoud .... .50 .23
❑ 213 Steve Garvey 5.00 2.20
❑ 214 Steve Hamilton .... .50 .23
❑ 215 Dusty Baker.................. 1.00 .45
❑ 216 Toby Harrah .... 1.50 .70
❑ 217 Don Wilson .... .50 .23
❑ 218 Aurelio Rodriguez .... .50 .23
❑ 219 St. Louis Cardinals ...... 1.50 .70
Team Card
❑ 220 Nolan Ryan 90.00 40.00
❑ 221 Fred Kendall .... .50 .23
❑ 222 Rob Gardner .... .50 .23
❑ 223 Bud Harrelson .... 1.50 .70
❑ 224 Bill Lee .... 1.50 .70
❑ 225 Al Oliver...................... 1.00 .45
❑ 226 Ray Fosse.................... .50 .23
❑ 227 Wayne Twitchell .... .50 .23
❑ 228 Bobby Darwin .... .50 .23
❑ 229 Roric Harrison .... .50 .23
❑ 230 Joe Morgan 6.00 2.70
❑ 231 Bill Parsons .... .50 .23
❑ 232 Ken Singleton .... 1.50 .70
❑ 233 Ed Kirkpatrick .... .50 .23
❑ 234 Bill North .... .50 .23
❑ 235 Jim Hunter.................. 4.00 1.80
❑ 236 Tito Fuentes .... .50 .23
❑ 237A Braves Leaders......... 1.50 .70
Eddie Mathews MG
Lew Burdette CO
Jim Busby CO
Roy Hartsfield CO
Ken Silvestri CO
(Burdette right ear
showing)
❑ 237B Braves Leaders.......... 3.00 1.35
(Burdette right ear
not showing)
❑ 238 Tony Muser .... .50 .23
❑ 239 Pete Richert .... .50 .23
❑ 240 Bobby Murcer .... .75 .35
❑ 241 Dwain Anderson .... .50 .23
❑ 242 George Culver............... .50 .23
❑ 243 California Angels......... 1.50 .70
Team Card
❑ 244 Ed Acosta .... .50 .23
❑ 245 Carl Yastrzemski 8.00 3.60
❑ 246 Ken Sanders .... .50 .23
❑ 247 Del Unser .... .50 .23
❑ 248 Jerry Johnson .... .50 .23
❑ 249 Larry Biittner .... .50 .23
❑ 250 Manny Sanguillen .... 1.50 .70
❑ 251 Roger Nelson .... .50 .23
❑ 252A Giants Leaders .... 1.50 .70
Charlie Fox MG
Joe Amalfitano CO
Andy Gilbert CO
Don McMahon CO
John McNamara CO
(Orange backgrounds)
❑ 252B Giants Leaders 2.50 1.10
(Dark pale
backgrounds)
❑ 253 Mark Belanger............. 1.50 .70
❑ 254 Bill Stoneman .... .50 .23
❑ 255 Reggie Jackson.......... 12.00 5.50
❑ 256 Chris Zachary .... .50 .23
❑ 257A Mets Leaders 2.50 1.10
Yogi Berra MG
Roy McMillan CO
Joe Pignatano CO
Rube Walker CO
Eddie Yost CO
(Orange backgrounds)
❑ 257B Mets Leaders 5.00 2.20
(Dark pale
backgrounds)
❑ 258 Tommy John .... 1.00 .45
❑ 259 Jim Holt .... .50 .23
❑ 260 Gary Nolan .... 1.50 .70
❑ 261 Pat Kelly .... .50 .23
❑ 262 Jack Aker .... .50 .23
❑ 263 George Scott............... 1.50 .70
❑ 264 Checklist 133-264 .... 4.00 .80
❑ 265 Gene Michael .... 1.50 .70
❑ 266 Mike Lum..................... .50 .23
❑ 267 Lloyd Allen.................... .50 .23
❑ 268 Jerry Morales .... .50 .23
❑ 269 Tim McCarver .... 1.00 .45
❑ 270 Luis Tiant.................... 1.00 .45
❑ 271 Tom Hutton .... .50 .23
❑ 272 Ed Farmer..................... .50 .23
❑ 273 Chris Speier .... .50 .23
❑ 274 Darold Knowles.............. .50 .23
❑ 275 Tony Perez 4.00 1.80
❑ 276 Joe Lovitto.................... .50 .23
❑ 277 Bob Miller .... .50 .23
❑ 278 Baltimore Orioles......... 1.50 .70
Team Card
❑ 279 Mike Strahler................. .50 .23
❑ 280 Al Kaline 7.00 3.10
❑ 281 Mike Jorgensen............. .50 .23
❑ 282 Steve Hovley.................. .50 .23
❑ 283 Ray Sadecki .... .50 .23
❑ 284 Glenn Borgmann............ .50 .23
❑ 285 Don Kessinger................ .50 .23
❑ 286 Frank Linzy .... .50 .23
❑ 287 Eddie Leon .... .50 .23
❑ 288 Gary Gentry................... .50 .23
❑ 289 Bob Oliver .... .50 .23
❑ 290 Cesar Cedeno............. 1.00 .45
❑ 291 Rogelio Moret .... .50 .23
❑ 292 Jose Cruz .... 1.50 .70
❑ 293 Bernie Allen................... .50 .23
❑ 294 Steve Arlin..................... .50 .23
❑ 295 Bert Campaneris .... 1.00 .45
❑ 296 Reds Leaders 2.50 1.10
Sparky Anderson MG
Alex Grammas CO
Ted Kluszewski CO
George Scherger CO
Larry Shepard CO
❑ 297 Walt Williams................. .50 .23
❑ 298 Ron Bryant .... .50 .23
❑ 299 Ted Ford .... .50 .23
❑ 300 Steve Carlton 10.00 4.50
❑ 301 Billy Grabarkewitz .... .50 .23
❑ 302 Terry Crowley .... .50 .23
❑ 303 Nelson Briles.................. .50 .23
❑ 304 Duke Sims..................... .50 .23
❑ 305 Willie Mays 35.00 16.00
❑ 306 Tom Burgmeier .... .50 .23
❑ 307 Boots Day .... .50 .23
❑ 308 Skip Lockwood .... .50 .23
❑ 309 Paul Popovich .... .50 .23
❑ 310 Dick Allen .... 1.50 .70
❑ 311 Joe Decker .... .50 .23
❑ 312 Oscar Brown .... .50 .23
❑ 313 Jim Ray .... .50 .23
❑ 314 Ron Swoboda .... .50 .23
❑ 315 John Odom .... .50 .23
❑ 316 San Diego Padres....... 1.50 .70
Team Card
❑ 317 Danny Cater .... .50 .23
❑ 318 Jim McGlothlin............... .50 .23
❑ 319 Jim Spencer .... .50 .23
❑ 320 Lou Brock 6.00 2.70
❑ 321 Rich Hinton .... .50 .23
❑ 322 Garry Maddox .... 1.00 .45
❑ 323 Tigers Leaders .... 1.50 .70
Billy Martin MG
Art Fowler CO
Charlie Silvera CO
Dick Tracewski CO
❑ 324 Al Downing .... .50 .23
❑ 325 Boog Powell .... 1.00 .45
❑ 326 Darrell Brandon.............. .50 .23
❑ 327 John Lowenstein .... .50 .23
❑ 328 Bill Bonham.................... .50 .23
❑ 329 Ed Kranepool .... .50 .23
❑ 330 Rod Carew 7.00 3.10
❑ 331 Carl Morton .... .50 .23
❑ 332 John Felske.................... .50 .23
❑ 333 Gene Clines .... .50 .23
❑ 334 Freddie Patek .... .50 .23
❑ 335 Bob Tolan .... .50 .23
❑ 336 Tom Bradley .... .50 .23
❑ 337 Dave Duncan .... .50 .23
❑ 338 Checklist 265-396 .... 4.00 .80
❑ 339 Dick Tidrow .... .50 .23
❑ 340 Nate Colbert .... .50 .23
❑ 341 Jim Palmer KP .... 1.50 .70
❑ 342 Sam McDowell KP .... .50 .23
❑ 343 Bobby Murcer KP .... .50 .23
❑ 344 Jim Hunter KP .... 1.50 .70
❑ 345 Chris Speier KP.............. .50 .23
❑ 346 Gaylord Perry KP .... 1.50 .70
❑ 347 Kansas City Royals...... 1.50 .70
Team Card
❑ 348 Rennie Stennett .... .50 .23
❑ 349 Dick McAuliffe .... .50 .23
❑ 350 Tom Seaver............... 12.00 5.50
❑ 351 Jimmy Stewart............... .50 .23
❑ 352 Don Stanhouse .... .50 .23
❑ 353 Steve Brye..................... .50 .23
❑ 354 Billy Parker .... .50 .23
❑ 355 Mike Marshall .... 1.50 .70
❑ 356 White Sox Leaders .... .50 .23
Chuck Tanner MG
Joe Lonnett CO
Jim Mahoney CO
Al Monchak CO
Johnny Sain CO
❑ 357 Ross Grimsley................ .50 .23
❑ 358 Jim Nettles .... .50 .23
❑ 359 Cecil Upshaw .... .50 .23
❑ 360 Joe Rudi UER .... 1.50 .70
(Photo actually
Gene Tenace)
❑ 361 Fran Healy..................... .50 .23
❑ 362 Eddie Watt..................... .50 .23
❑ 363 Jackie Hernandez .... .50 .23
❑ 364 Rick Wise .... .50 .23
❑ 365 Rico Petrocelli .... 1.50 .70
❑ 366 Brock Davis................... .50 .23
❑ 367 Burt Hooton................... .50 .23
❑ 368 Bill Buckner .... 1.00 .45
❑ 369 Lerrin LaGrow .... .50 .23
❑ 370 Willie Stargell 5.00 2.20
❑ 371 Mike Kekich.................... .50 .23
❑ 372 Oscar Gamble................ .50 .23
❑ 373 Clyde Wright .... .50 .23
❑ 374 Darrell Evans.............. 1.00 .45
❑ 375 Larry Dierker .... 1.50 .70
❑ 376 Frank Duffy .... .50 .23
❑ 377 Expos Leaders .... .50 .23
Gene Mauch MG
Dave Bristol CO
Larry Doby CO
Cal McLish CO
Jerry Zimmerman CO
❑ 378 Len Randle .... .50 .23
❑ 379 Cy Acosta .... .50 .23
❑ 380 Johnny Bench 12.00 5.50
❑ 381 Vicente Romo .... .50 .23
❑ 382 Mike Hegan.................... .50 .23
❑ 383 Diego Segui.................... .50 .23
❑ 384 Don Baylor 4.00 1.80
❑ 385 Jim Perry.................... 1.50 .70
❑ 386 Don Money .... .50 .23
❑ 387 Jim Barr.......................... .50 .23
❑ 388 Ben Oglivie .... 1.50 .70
❑ 389 New York Mets 3.00 1.35
Team Card
❑ 390 Mickey Lolich............... 1.00 .45
❑ 391 Lee Lacy .... .50 .23
❑ 392 Dick Drago .... .50 .23
❑ 393 Jose Cardenal................. .50 .23
❑ 394 Sparky Lyle .... 1.00 .45
❑ 395 Roger Metzger .... .50 .23
❑ 396 Grant Jackson................. .50 .23
❑ 397 Dave Cash .... 1.25 .55
❑ 398 Rich Hand .... 1.25 .55
❑ 399 George Foster............. 2.00 .90
❑ 400 Gaylord Perry 5.00 2.20
❑ 401 Clyde Mashore .... 1.25 .55
❑ 402 Jack Hiatt .... 1.25 .55
❑ 403 Sonny Jackson .... 1.25 .55

❑ 404 Chuck Brinkman .... 1.25 .55
❑ 405 Cesar Tovar .... 1.25 .55
❑ 406 Paul Lindblad .... 1.25 .55
❑ 407 Felix Millan .... 1.25 .55
❑ 408 Jim Colborn .... 1.25 .55
❑ 409 Ivan Murrell .... 1.25 .55
❑ 410 Willie McCovey 6.00 2.70
(Bench behind plate)
❑ 411 Ray Corbin .... 1.25 .55
❑ 412 Manny Mota .... 2.00 .90
❑ 413 Tom Timmermann .... 1.25 .55
❑ 414 Ken Rudolph .... 1.25 .55
❑ 415 Marty Pattin .... 1.25 .55
❑ 416 Paul Schaal .... 1.25 .55
❑ 417 Scipio Spinks .... 1.25 .55
❑ 418 Bob Grich .... 2.00 .90
❑ 419 Casey Cox .... 1.25 .55
❑ 420 Tommie Agee .... 1.25 .55
❑ 421A Angels Leaders .... 2.00 .90
Bobby Winkles MG
Tom Morgan CO
Salty Parker CO
Jimmie Reese CO
John Roseboro CO
(Orange backgrounds)
❑ 421B Angels Leaders 3.00 1.35
(Dark pale
backgrounds)
❑ 422 Bob Robertson .... 1.25 .55
❑ 423 Johnny Jeter .... 1.25 .55
❑ 424 Denny Doyle .... 1.25 .55
❑ 425 Alex Johnson .... 1.25 .55
❑ 426 Dave LaRoche .... 1.25 .55
❑ 427 Rick Auerbach .... 1.25 .55
❑ 428 Wayne Simpson .... 1.25 .55
❑ 429 Jim Fairey .... 1.25 .55
❑ 430 Vida Blue .... 2.00 .90
❑ 431 Gerry Moses .... 1.25 .55
❑ 432 Dan Frisella .... 1.25 .55
❑ 433 Willie Horton .... 2.00 .90
❑ 434 San Francisco Giants .. 3.00 1.35
Team Card
❑ 435 Rico Carty .... 2.00 .90
❑ 436 Jim McAndrew .... 1.25 .55
❑ 437 John Kennedy .... 1.25 .55
❑ 438 Enzo Hernandez .... 1.25 .55
❑ 439 Eddie Fisher .... 1.25 .55
❑ 440 Glenn Beckert .... 1.25 .55
❑ 441 Gail Hopkins .... 1.25 .55
❑ 442 Dick Dietz .... 1.25 .55
❑ 443 Danny Thompson .... 1.25 .55
❑ 444 Ken Brett .... 1.25 .55
❑ 445 Ken Berry .... 1.25 .55
❑ 446 Jerry Reuss .... 2.00 .90
❑ 447 Joe Hague .... 1.25 .55
❑ 448 John Hiller .... 1.25 .55
❑ 449A Indians Leaders 4.00 1.80
Ken Aspromonte MG
Rocky Colavito CO
Joe Lutz CO
Warren Spahn CO
(Spahn's right
ear pointed)
❑ 449B Indians Leaders 4.00 1.80
(Spahn's right
ear round)
❑ 450 Joe Torre .... 2.00 .90
❑ 451 John Vukovich .... 1.25 .55
❑ 452 Paul Casanova .... 1.25 .55
❑ 453 Checklist 397-528 .... 3.00 .60
❑ 454 Tom Haller .... 1.25 .55
❑ 455 Bill Melton .... 1.25 .55
❑ 456 Dick Green .... 1.25 .55
❑ 457 John Strohmayer .... 1.25 .55
❑ 458 Jim Mason .... 1.25 .55
❑ 459 Jimmy Howarth .... 1.25 .55
❑ 460 Bill Freehan .... 2.00 .90
❑ 461 Mike Corkins .... 1.25 .55
❑ 462 Ron Blomberg .... 1.25 .55
❑ 463 Ken Tatum .... 1.25 .55
❑ 464 Chicago Cubs 3.00 1.35
Team Card
❑ 465 Dave Giusti .... 1.25 .55
❑ 466 Jose Arcia .... 1.25 .55
❑ 467 Mike Ryan .... 1.25 .55
❑ 468 Tom Griffin .... 1.25 .55
❑ 469 Dan Monzon .... 1.25 .55
❑ 470 Mike Cuellar .... 2.00 .90
❑ 471 Ty Cobb ATL 8.00 3.60
4191 Hits
❑ 472 Lou Gehrig ATL 15.00 6.75
23 Grand Slams
❑ 473 Hank Aaron ATL 10.00 4.50
6172 Total Bases
❑ 474 Babe Ruth ATL 20.00 9.00
2209 RBI
❑ 475 Ty Cobb ATL 8.00 3.60
.367 Batting Average
❑ 476 Walter Johnson ATL 3.00 1.35
113 Shutouts
❑ 477 Cy Young ATL 3.00 1.35
511 Victories
❑ 478 Walter Johnson ATL 3.00 1.35
3508 Strikeouts
❑ 479 Hal Lanier .... 1.25 .55
❑ 480 Juan Marichal 5.00 2.20
❑ 481 Chicago White Sox 3.00 1.35
Team Card
❑ 482 Rick Reuschel 3.00 1.35
❑ 483 Dal Maxvill .... 1.25 .55
❑ 484 Ernie McAnally .... 1.25 .55
❑ 485 Norm Cash .... 2.00 .90
❑ 486A Phillies Leaders .... 2.00 .90
Danny Ozark MG
Carroll Beringer CO
Billy DeMars CO
Ray Rippelmeyer CO
Bobby Wine CO
(Orange backgrounds)
❑ 486B Phillies Leaders 3.00 1.35
(Dark pale
backgrounds)
❑ 487 Bruce Dal Canton .... 1.25 .55
❑ 488 Dave Campbell .... 2.00 .90
❑ 489 Jeff Burroughs .... 2.00 .90
❑ 490 Claude Osteen .... 1.25 .55
❑ 491 Bob Montgomery .... 1.25 .55
❑ 492 Pedro Borbon .... 1.25 .55
❑ 493 Duffy Dyer .... 1.25 .55
❑ 494 Rich Morales .... 1.25 .55
❑ 495 Tommy Helms .... 1.25 .55
❑ 496 Ray Lamb .... 1.25 .55
❑ 497A Cardinals Leaders ...... 2.00 .90
Red Schoendienst MG
Vern Benson CO
George Kissell CO
Barney Schultz CO
(Orange backgrounds)
❑ 497B Cardinals Leaders 3.00 1.35
(Dark pale
backgrounds)
❑ 498 Graig Nettles 3.00 1.35
❑ 499 Bob Moose .... 1.25 .55
❑ 500 Oakland A's 3.00 1.35
Team Card
❑ 501 Larry Gura .... 1.25 .55
❑ 502 Bobby Valentine .... 2.00 .90
❑ 503 Phil Niekro 5.00 2.20
❑ 504 Earl Williams .... 1.25 .55
❑ 505 Bob Bailey .... 1.25 .55
❑ 506 Bart Johnson .... 1.25 .55
❑ 507 Darrel Chaney .... 1.25 .55
❑ 508 Gates Brown .... 1.25 .55
❑ 509 Jim Nash .... 1.25 .55
❑ 510 Amos Otis .... 2.00 .90
❑ 511 Sam McDowell .... 2.00 .90
❑ 512 Dalton Jones .... 1.25 .55
❑ 513 Dave Marshall .... 1.25 .55
❑ 514 Jerry Kenney .... 1.25 .55
❑ 515 Andy Messersmith .... 2.00 .90
❑ 516 Danny Walton .... 1.25 .55
❑ 517A Pirates Leaders .... 2.00 .90
Bill Virdon MG
Don Leppert CO
Bill Mazeroski CO
Dave Ricketts CO
Mel Wright CO
(Mazeroski has
no right ear)
❑ 517B Pirates Leaders 3.00 1.35
(Mazeroski has
right ear)
❑ 518 Bob Veale .... 1.25 .55
❑ 519 Johnny Edwards .... 1.25 .55
❑ 520 Mel Stottlemyre .... 2.00 .90
❑ 521 Atlanta Braves 3.00 1.35
Team Card
❑ 522 Leo Cardenas .... 1.25 .55
❑ 523 Wayne Granger .... 1.25 .55
❑ 524 Gene Tenace .... 2.00 .90
❑ 525 Jim Fregosi .... 2.00 .90
❑ 526 Ollie Brown .... 1.25 .55
❑ 527 Dan McGinn .... 1.25 .55
❑ 528 Paul Blair .... 1.25 .55
❑ 529 Milt May 3.50 1.55
❑ 530 Jim Kaat 5.00 2.20
❑ 531 Ron Woods 3.50 1.55
❑ 532 Steve Mingori 3.50 1.55
❑ 533 Larry Stahl 3.50 1.55
❑ 534 Dave Lemonds 3.50 1.55
❑ 535 Johnny Callison 5.00 2.20
❑ 536 Philadelphia Phillies 5.00 2.20
Team Card
❑ 537 Bill Slayback 3.50 1.55
❑ 538 Jim Ray Hart 5.00 2.20
❑ 539 Tom Murphy 3.50 1.55
❑ 540 Cleon Jones 5.00 2.20
❑ 541 Bob Bolin 3.50 1.55
❑ 542 Pat Corrales 5.00 2.20
❑ 543 Alan Foster 3.50 1.55
❑ 544 Von Joshua 3.50 1.55
❑ 545 Orlando Cepeda 5.00 2.20
❑ 546 Jim York 3.50 1.55
❑ 547 Bobby Heise 3.50 1.55
❑ 548 Don Durham 3.50 1.55
❑ 549 Rangers Leaders 5.00 2.20
Whitey Herzog MG
Chuck Estrada CO
Chuck Hiller CO
Jackie Moore CO
❑ 550 Dave Johnson 5.00 2.20
❑ 551 Mike Kilkenny 3.50 1.55
❑ 552 J.C. Martin 3.50 1.55
❑ 553 Mickey Scott 3.50 1.55
❑ 554 Dave Concepcion 5.00 2.20
❑ 555 Bill Hands 3.50 1.55
❑ 556 New York Yankees 8.00 3.60
Team Card
❑ 557 Bernie Williams 3.50 1.55
❑ 558 Jerry May 3.50 1.55
❑ 559 Barry Lersch 3.50 1.55
❑ 560 Frank Howard 4.00 1.80
❑ 561 Jim Geddes 3.50 1.55
❑ 562 Wayne Garrett 3.50 1.55
❑ 563 Larry Haney 3.50 1.55
❑ 564 Mike Thompson 3.50 1.55
❑ 565 Jim Hickman 3.50 1.55
❑ 566 Lew Krausse 3.50 1.55
❑ 567 Bob Fenwick 3.50 1.55
❑ 568 Ray Newman 3.50 1.55
❑ 569 Dodgers Leaders 5.00 2.20
Walt Alston MG
Red Adams CO
Monty Basgall CO
Jim Gilliam CO
Tom Lasorda CO
❑ 570 Bill Singer 5.00 2.20
❑ 571 Rusty Torres 3.50 1.55
❑ 572 Gary Sutherland 3.50 1.55
❑ 573 Fred Beene 3.50 1.55
❑ 574 Bob Didier 3.50 1.55
❑ 575 Dock Ellis 3.50 1.55
❑ 576 Montreal Expos 6.00 2.70
Team Card
❑ 577 Eric Soderholm 3.50 1.55
❑ 578 Ken Wright 3.50 1.55
❑ 579 Tom Grieve 5.00 2.20
❑ 580 Joe Pepitone 5.00 2.20
❑ 581 Steve Kealey 3.50 1.55
❑ 582 Darrell Porter 5.00 2.20
❑ 583 Bill Grief 3.50 1.55
❑ 584 Chris Arnold 3.50 1.55
❑ 585 Joe Niekro 5.00 2.20
❑ 586 Bill Sudakis 3.50 1.55
❑ 587 Rich McKinney 3.50 1.55
❑ 588 Checklist 529-660 ...... 24.00 4.80

No.	Card	NRMT	VG-E
❑ 589	Ken Forsch	3.50	1.55
❑ 590	Deron Johnson	5.00	2.20
❑ 591	Mike Hedlund	3.50	1.55
❑ 592	John Boccabella	3.50	1.55
❑ 593	Royals Leaders	3.50	1.55
	Jack McKeon MG		
	Galen Cisco CO		
	Harry Dunlop CO		
	Charlie Lau CO		
❑ 594	Vic Harris	3.50	1.55
❑ 595	Don Gullett	5.00	2.20
❑ 596	Boston Red Sox	8.00	3.60
	Team Card		
❑ 597	Mickey Rivers	4.00	1.80
❑ 598	Phil Roof	3.50	1.55
❑ 599	Ed Crosby	3.50	1.55
❑ 600	Dave McNally	5.00	2.20
❑ 601	Rookie Catchers	5.00	2.20
	Sergio Robles		
	George Pena		
	Rick Stelmaszek		
❑ 602	Rookie Pitchers	5.00	2.20
	Mel Behney		
	Ralph Garcia		
	Doug Rau		
❑ 603	Rookie 3rd Basemen	5.00	2.20
	Terry Hughes		
	Bill McNulty		
	Ken Reitz		
❑ 604	Rookie Pitchers	5.00	2.20
	Jesse Jefferson		
	Dennis O'Toole		
	Bob Strampe		
❑ 605	Rookie 1st Basemen	5.00	2.20
	Enos Cabell		
	Pat Bourque		
	Gonzalo Marquez		
❑ 606	Rookie Outfielders	5.00	2.20
	Gary Matthews		
	Tom Paciorek		
	Jorge Roque		
❑ 607	Rookie Shortstops	5.00	2.20
	Pepe Frias		
	Ray Busse		
	Mario Guerrero		
❑ 608	Rookie Pitchers	5.00	2.20
	Steve Busby		
	Dick Colpaert		
	George Medich		
❑ 609	Rookie 2nd Basemen	6.00	2.70
	Larvell Blanks		
	Pedro Garcia		
	Dave Lopes		
❑ 610	Rookie Pitchers	5.00	2.20
	Jimmy Freeman		
	Charlie Hough		
	Hank Webb		
❑ 611	Rookie Outfielders	5.00	2.20
	Rich Coggins		
	Jim Wohlford		
	Richie Zisk		
❑ 612	Rookie Pitchers	5.00	2.20
	Steve Lawson		
	Bob Reynolds		
	Brent Strom		
❑ 613	Rookie Catchers	15.00	6.75
	Bob Boone		
	Skip Jutze		
	Mike Ivie		
❑ 614	Rookie Outfielders	15.00	6.75
	Al Bumbry		
	Dwight Evans		
	Charlie Spikes		
❑ 615	Rookie 3rd Basemen	300.00	135.00
	Ron Cey		
	John Hilton		
	Mike Schmidt		
❑ 616	Rookie Pitchers	5.00	2.20
	Norm Angelini		
	Steve Blateric		
	Mike Garman		
❑ 617	Rich Chiles	3.50	1.55
❑ 618	Andy Etchebarren	3.50	1.55
❑ 619	Billy Wilson	3.50	1.55
❑ 620	Tommy Harper	5.00	2.20
❑ 621	Joe Ferguson	5.00	2.20
❑ 622	Larry Hisle	5.00	2.20
❑ 623	Steve Renko	3.50	1.55
❑ 624	Astros Leaders	6.00	2.70
	Leo Durocher MG		
	Preston Gomez CO		
	Grady Hatton CO		
	Hub Kittle CO		
	Jim Owens CO		
❑ 625	Angel Mangual	3.50	1.55
❑ 626	Bob Barton	3.50	1.55
❑ 627	Luis Alvarado	3.50	1.55
❑ 628	Jim Slaton	3.50	1.55
❑ 629	Cleveland Indians	6.00	2.70
	Team Card		
❑ 630	Denny McLain	8.00	3.60
❑ 631	Tom Matchick	3.50	1.55
❑ 632	Dick Selma	3.50	1.55
❑ 633	Ike Brown	3.50	1.55
❑ 634	Alan Closter	3.50	1.55
❑ 635	Gene Alley	5.00	2.20
❑ 636	Rickey Clark	3.50	1.55
❑ 637	Norm Miller	3.50	1.55
❑ 638	Ken Reynolds	3.50	1.55
❑ 639	Willie Crawford	3.50	1.55
❑ 640	Dick Bosman	3.50	1.55
❑ 641	Cincinnati Reds	8.00	3.60
	Team Card		
❑ 642	Jose Laboy	3.50	1.55
❑ 643	Al Fitzmorris	3.50	1.55
❑ 644	Jack Heidemann	3.50	1.55
❑ 645	Bob Locker	3.50	1.55
❑ 646	Brewers Leaders	3.50	1.55
	Del Crandall MG		
	Harvey Kuenn CO		
	Joe Nossek CO		
	Bob Shaw CO		
	Jim Walton CO		
❑ 647	George Stone	3.50	1.55
❑ 648	Tom Egan	3.50	1.55
❑ 649	Rich Folkers	3.50	1.55
❑ 650	Felipe Alou	4.00	1.80
❑ 651	Don Carrithers	3.50	1.55
❑ 652	Ted Kubiak	3.50	1.55
❑ 653	Joe Hoerner	3.50	1.55
❑ 654	Minnesota Twins	5.00	2.20
	Team Card		
❑ 655	Clay Kirby	3.50	1.55
❑ 656	John Ellis	3.50	1.55
❑ 657	Bob Johnson	3.50	1.55
❑ 658	Elliott Maddox	3.50	1.55
❑ 659	Jose Pagan	3.50	1.55
❑ 660	Fred Scherman	4.00	1.55

1974 Topps

	NRMT	VG-E
COMPLETE SET (660)	600.00	275.00
COMPLETE FACT.SET (660)	600.00	275.00
COMMON CARD (1-660)	.50	.23
WRAPPERS (10-CENTS)	10.00	4.50

No.	Card	NRMT	VG-E
❑ 1	Hank Aaron	40.00	12.00
	All-Time Home Run King		
	(Complete ML record)		
❑ 2	Aaron Special 54-57	6.00	2.70
	(Records on back)		
❑ 3	Aaron Special 58-61	6.00	2.70
	(Memorable homers)		
❑ 4	Aaron Special 62-65	6.00	2.70
	(Life in ML's 1954-63)		
❑ 5	Aaron Special 66-69	6.00	2.70
	(Life in ML's 1964-73)		
❑ 6	Aaron Special 70-73	6.00	2.70
	(Milestone homers)		
❑ 7	Jim Hunter	3.00	1.35
❑ 8	George Theodore	.50	.23
❑ 9	Mickey Lolich	1.00	.45
❑ 10	Johnny Bench	12.00	5.50
❑ 11	Jim Bibby	.50	.23
❑ 12	Dave May	.50	.23
❑ 13	Tom Hilgendorf	.50	.23
❑ 14	Paul Popovich	.50	.23
❑ 15	Joe Torre	2.00	.90
❑ 16	Baltimore Orioles	1.00	.45
	Team Card		
❑ 17	Doug Bird	.50	.23
❑ 18	Gary Thomasson	.50	.23
❑ 19	Gerry Moses	.50	.23
❑ 20	Nolan Ryan	70.00	32.00
❑ 21	Bob Gallagher	.50	.23
❑ 22	Cy Acosta	.50	.23
❑ 23	Craig Robinson	.50	.23
❑ 24	John Hiller	1.00	.45
❑ 25	Ken Singleton	1.00	.45
❑ 26	Bill Campbell	.50	.23
❑ 27	George Scott	1.00	.45
❑ 28	Manny Sanguillen	1.00	.45
❑ 29	Phil Niekro	3.00	1.35
❑ 30	Bobby Bonds	2.00	.90
❑ 31	Astros Leaders	1.00	.45
	Preston Gomez MG		
	Roger Craig CO		
	Hub Kittle CO		
	Grady Hatton CO		
	Bob Lillis CO		
❑ 32A	Johnny Grubb SD	1.00	.45
❑ 32B	Johnny Grubb WAS	6.00	2.70
❑ 33	Don Newhauser	.50	.23
❑ 34	Andy Kosco	.50	.23
❑ 35	Gaylord Perry	3.00	1.35
❑ 36	St. Louis Cardinals	1.00	.45
	Team Card		
❑ 37	Dave Sells	.50	.23
❑ 38	Don Kessinger	1.00	.45
❑ 39	Ken Suarez	.50	.23
❑ 40	Jim Palmer	5.00	2.20
❑ 41	Bobby Floyd	.50	.23
❑ 42	Claude Osteen	1.00	.45
❑ 43	Jim Wynn	1.00	.45
❑ 44	Mel Stottlemyre	1.00	.45
❑ 45	Dave Johnson	1.00	.45
❑ 46	Pat Kelly	.50	.23
❑ 47	Dick Ruthven	.50	.23
❑ 48	Dick Sharon	.50	.23
❑ 49	Steve Renko	.50	.23
❑ 50	Rod Carew	5.00	2.20
❑ 51	Bobby Heise	.50	.23
❑ 52	Al Oliver	.50	.23
❑ 53A	Fred Kendall SD	1.00	.45
❑ 53B	Fred Kendall WAS	6.00	2.70
❑ 54	Elias Sosa	.50	.23
❑ 55	Frank Robinson	6.00	2.70
❑ 56	New York Mets	1.00	.45
	Team Card		
❑ 57	Darold Knowles	.50	.23
❑ 58	Charlie Spikes	.50	.23
❑ 59	Ross Grimsley	.50	.23
❑ 60	Lou Brock	5.00	2.20
❑ 61	Luis Aparicio	3.00	1.35
❑ 62	Bob Locker	.50	.23
❑ 63	Bill Sudakis	.50	.23
❑ 64	Doug Rau	.50	.23
❑ 65	Amos Otis	1.00	.45
❑ 66	Sparky Lyle	1.00	.45
❑ 67	Tommy Helms	.50	.23
❑ 68	Grant Jackson	.50	.23
❑ 69	Del Unser	.50	.23
❑ 70	Dick Allen	2.00	.90
❑ 71	Dan Frisella	.50	.23
❑ 72	Aurelio Rodriguez	.50	.23
❑ 73	Mike Marshall	2.00	.90
❑ 74	Minnesota Twins	1.00	.45
	Team Card		

❑ 75 Jim Colborn .50 .23
❑ 76 Mickey Rivers 1.00 .45
❑ 77A Rich Troedson SD 6.00 2.70
❑ 77B Rich Troedson WAS 1.00 .45
❑ 78 Giants Leaders 1.00 .45
Charlie Fox MG
John McNamara CO
Joe Amalfitano CO
Andy Gilbert CO
Don McMahon CO
❑ 79 Gene Tenace 1.00 .45
❑ 80 Tom Seaver 12.00 5.50
❑ 81 Frank Duffy .50 .23
❑ 82 Dave Giusti .50 .23
❑ 83 Orlando Cepeda 2.00 .90
❑ 84 Rick Wise .50 .23
❑ 85 Joe Morgan 5.00 2.20
❑ 86 Joe Ferguson 1.00 .45
❑ 87 Fergie Jenkins 3.00 1.35
❑ 88 Freddie Patek 1.00 .45
❑ 89 Jackie Brown .50 .23
❑ 90 Bobby Murcer 1.00 .45
❑ 91 Ken Forsch .50 .23
❑ 92 Paul Blair 1.00 .45
❑ 93 Rod Gilbreath .50 .23
❑ 94 Detroit Tigers 1.00 .45
Team Card
❑ 95 Steve Carlton 6.00 2.70
❑ 96 Jerry Hairston .50 .23
❑ 97 Bob Bailey .50 .23
❑ 98 Bert Blyleven 2.00 .90
❑ 99 Brewers Leaders 1.00 .45
Del Crandall MG
Harvey Kuenn CO
Joe Nossek CO
Jim Walton CO
Al Widmar CO
❑ 100 Willie Stargell 4.00 1.80
❑ 101 Bobby Valentine 1.00 .45
❑ 102A Bill Greif SD 1.00 .45
❑ 102B Bill Greif WAS 6.00 2.70
❑ 103 Sal Bando 1.00 .45
❑ 104 Ron Bryant .50 .23
❑ 105 Carlton Fisk 12.00 5.50
❑ 106 Harry Parker .50 .23
❑ 107 Alex Johnson .50 .23
❑ 108 Al Hrabosky 1.00 .45
❑ 109 Bob Grich 1.00 .45
❑ 110 Billy Williams 3.00 1.35
❑ 111 Clay Carroll .50 .23
❑ 112 Dave Lopes 2.00 .90
❑ 113 Dick Drago .50 .23
❑ 114 Angels Team 1.00 .45
❑ 115 Willie Horton 1.00 .45
❑ 116 Jerry Reuss 1.00 .45
❑ 117 Ron Blomberg .50 .23
❑ 118 Bill Lee 1.00 .45
❑ 119 Phillies Leaders 1.00 .45
Danny Ozark MG
Ray Ripplemeyer CO
Bobby Wine CO
Carroll Beringer CO
Billy DeMars CO
❑ 120 Wilbur Wood .50 .23
❑ 121 Larry Lintz .50 .23
❑ 122 Jim Holt .50 .23
❑ 123 Nelson Briles 1.00 .45
❑ 124 Bobby Coluccio .50 .23
❑ 125A Nate Colbert SD 1.00 .45
❑ 125B Nate Colbert WAS 6.00 2.70
❑ 126 Checklist 1-132 3.00 .60
❑ 127 Tom Paciorek 1.00 .45
❑ 128 John Ellis .50 .23
❑ 129 Chris Speier .50 .23
❑ 130 Reggie Jackson 15.00 6.75
❑ 131 Bob Boone 2.00 .90
❑ 132 Felix Millan .50 .23
❑ 133 David Clyde 1.00 .45
❑ 134 Denis Menke .50 .23
❑ 135 Roy White 1.00 .45
❑ 136 Rick Reuschel 1.00 .45
❑ 137 Al Bumbry 1.00 .45
❑ 138 Eddie Brinkman .50 .23
❑ 139 Aurelio Monteagudo .50 .23
❑ 140 Darrell Evans 2.00 .90
❑ 141 Pat Bourque .50 .23
❑ 142 Pedro Garcia .50 .23
❑ 143 Dick Woodson .50 .23
❑ 144 Dodgers Leaders 2.00 .90
Walter Alston MG
Tom Lasorda CO
Jim Gilliam CO
Red Adams CO
Monty Basgall CO
❑ 145 Dock Ellis .50 .23
❑ 146 Ron Fairly 1.00 .45
❑ 147 Bart Johnson .50 .23
❑ 148A Dave Hilton SD 1.00 .45
❑ 148B Dave Hilton WAS 6.00 2.70
❑ 149 Mac Scarce .50 .23
❑ 150 John Mayberry 1.00 .45
❑ 151 Diego Segui .50 .23
❑ 152 Oscar Gamble 1.00 .45
❑ 153 Jon Matlack 1.00 .45
❑ 154 Houston Astros 1.00 .45
Team Card
❑ 155 Bert Campaneris 1.00 .45
❑ 156 Randy Moffitt .50 .23
❑ 157 Vic Harris .50 .23
❑ 158 Jack Billingham .50 .23
❑ 159 Jim Ray Hart 1.00 .45
❑ 160 Brooks Robinson 6.00 2.70
❑ 161 Ray Burris UER 1.00 .45
(Card number is
printed sideways)
❑ 162 Bill Freehan 1.00 .45
❑ 163 Ken Berry .50 .23
❑ 164 Tom House .50 .23
❑ 165 Willie Davis 1.00 .45
❑ 166 Royals Leaders 1.00 .45
Jack McKeon MG
Charlie Lau CO
Harry Dunlop CO
Galen Cisco CO
❑ 167 Luis Tiant 2.00 .90
❑ 168 Danny Thompson .50 .23
❑ 169 Steve Rogers 2.00 .90
❑ 170 Bill Melton .50 .23
❑ 171 Eduardo Rodriguez .50 .23
❑ 172 Gene Clines .50 .23
❑ 173A Randy Jones SD 2.00 .90
❑ 173B Randy Jones WAS 10.00 4.50
❑ 174 Bill Robinson 1.00 .45
❑ 175 Reggie Cleveland .50 .23
❑ 176 John Lowenstein .50 .23
❑ 177 Dave Roberts .50 .23
❑ 178 Garry Maddox 1.00 .45
❑ 179 Mets Leaders 3.00 1.35
Yogi Berra MG
Rube Walker CO
Eddie Yost CO
Roy McMillan CO
Joe Pignatano CO
❑ 180 Ken Holtzman 1.00 .45
❑ 181 Cesar Geronimo .50 .23
❑ 182 Lindy McDaniel 1.00 .45
❑ 183 Johnny Oates 1.00 .45
❑ 184 Texas Rangers 1.00 .45
Team Card
❑ 185 Jose Cardenal .50 .23
❑ 186 Fred Scherman .50 .23
❑ 187 Don Baylor 2.00 .90
❑ 188 Rudy Meoli .50 .23
❑ 189 Jim Brewer .50 .23
❑ 190 Tony Oliva 2.00 .90
❑ 191 Al Fitzmorris .50 .23
❑ 192 Mario Guerrero .50 .23
❑ 193 Tom Walker .50 .23
❑ 194 Darrell Porter 1.00 .45
❑ 195 Carlos May .50 .23
❑ 196 Jim Fregosi 1.00 .45
❑ 197A Vicente Romo SD 1.00 .45
❑ 197B Vicente Romo WAS 6.00 2.70
❑ 198 Dave Cash .50 .23
❑ 199 Mike Kekich .50 .23
❑ 200 Cesar Cedeno 1.00 .45
❑ 201 Batting Leaders 5.00 2.20
Rod Carew
Pete Rose
❑ 202 Home Run Leaders 5.00 2.20
Reggie Jackson
Willie Stargell
❑ 203 RBI Leaders 5.00 2.20
Reggie Jackson
Willie Stargell
❑ 204 Stolen Base Leaders 2.00 .90
Tommy Harper
Lou Brock
❑ 205 Victory Leaders 1.00 .45
Wilbur Wood
Ron Bryant
❑ 206 ERA Leaders 5.00 2.20
Jim Palmer
Tom Seaver
❑ 207 Strikeout Leaders 20.00 9.00
Nolan Ryan
Tom Seaver
❑ 208 Leading Firemen 1.00 .45
John Hiller
Mike Marshall
❑ 209 Ted Sizemore .50 .23
❑ 210 Bill Singer .50 .23
❑ 211 Chicago Cubs Team 1.00 .45
❑ 212 Rollie Fingers 3.00 1.35
❑ 213 Dave Rader .50 .23
❑ 214 Billy Grabarkewitz .50 .23
❑ 215 Al Kaline UER 5.00 2.20
(No copyright on back)
❑ 216 Ray Sadecki .50 .23
❑ 217 Tim Foli .50 .23
❑ 218 Johnny Briggs .50 .23
❑ 219 Doug Griffin .50 .23
❑ 220 Don Sutton 3.00 1.35
❑ 221 White Sox Leaders 1.00 .45
Chuck Tanner MG
Jim Mahoney CO
Alex Monchak CO
Johnny Sain CO
Joe Lonnett CO
❑ 222 Ramon Hernandez .50 .23
❑ 223 Jeff Burroughs 1.00 .45
❑ 224 Roger Metzger .50 .23
❑ 225 Paul Splittorff .50 .23
❑ 226A Padres Team SD 2.00 .90
❑ 226B Padres Team WAS 10.00 4.50
❑ 227 Mike Lum .50 .23
❑ 228 Ted Kubiak .50 .23
❑ 229 Fritz Peterson .50 .23
❑ 230 Tony Perez 3.00 1.35
❑ 231 Dick Tidrow .50 .23
❑ 232 Steve Brye .50 .23
❑ 233 Jim Barr .50 .23
❑ 234 John Milner .50 .23
❑ 235 Dave McNally 1.00 .45
❑ 236 Cardinals Leaders 2.00 .90
Red Schoendienst MG
Barney Schultz CO
George Kissell CO
Johnny Lewis CO
Vern Benson CO
❑ 237 Ken Brett .50 .23
❑ 238 Fran Healy HOR 2.00 .90
(Munson sliding
in background)
❑ 239 Bill Russell 2.00 .90
❑ 240 Joe Coleman .50 .23
❑ 241A Glenn Beckert SD 1.00 .45
❑ 241B Glenn Beckert WAS 6.00 2.70
❑ 242 Bill Gogolewski .50 .23
❑ 243 Bob Oliver .50 .23
❑ 244 Carl Morton .50 .23
❑ 245 Cleon Jones .50 .23
❑ 246 Oakland Athletics 2.00 .90
Team Card
❑ 247 Rick Miller .50 .23
❑ 248 Tom Hall .50 .23
❑ 249 George Mitterwald .50 .23
❑ 250A Willie McCovey SD 6.00 2.70
❑ 250B Willie McCovey WAS 30.00 13.50
❑ 251 Graig Nettles 2.00 .90
❑ 252 Dave Parker 10.00 4.50
❑ 253 John Boccabella .50 .23
❑ 254 Stan Bahnsen .50 .23
❑ 255 Larry Bowa 1.00 .45
❑ 256 Tom Griffin .50 .23
❑ 257 Buddy Bell 2.00 .90

❑ 258 Jerry Morales .50 .23
❑ 259 Bob Reynolds .50 .23
❑ 260 Ted Simmons 2.00 .90
❑ 261 Jerry Bell .50 .23
❑ 262 Ed Kirkpatrick .50 .23
❑ 263 Checklist 133-264 3.00 .60
❑ 264 Joe Rudi 1.00 .45
❑ 265 Tug McGraw 2.00 .90
❑ 266 Jim Northrup 1.00 .45
❑ 267 Andy Messersmith 1.00 .45
❑ 268 Tom Grieve 1.00 .45
❑ 269 Bob Johnson .50 .23
❑ 270 Ron Santo 2.00 .90
❑ 271 Bill Hands .50 .23
❑ 272 Paul Casanova .50 .23
❑ 273 Checklist 265-396 3.00 .60
❑ 274 Fred Beene .50 .23
❑ 275 Ron Hunt .50 .23
❑ 276 Angels Leaders 1.00 .45
Bobby Winkles MG
John Roseboro CO
Tom Morgan CO
Jimmie Reese CO
Salty Parker CO
❑ 277 Gary Nolan 1.00 .45
❑ 278 Cookie Rojas 1.00 .45
❑ 279 Jim Crawford .50 .23
❑ 280 Carl Yastrzemski 6.00 2.70
❑ 281 San Francisco Giants 1.00 .45
Team Card
❑ 282 Doyle Alexander 1.00 .45
❑ 283 Mike Schmidt 50.00 22.00
❑ 284 Dave Duncan 1.00 .45
❑ 285 Reggie Smith 1.00 .45
❑ 286 Tony Muser .50 .23
❑ 287 Clay Kirby .50 .23
❑ 288 Gorman Thomas 2.00 .90
❑ 289 Rick Auerbach .50 .23
❑ 290 Vida Blue 1.00 .45
❑ 291 Don Hahn .50 .23
❑ 292 Chuck Seelbach .50 .23
❑ 293 Milt May .50 .23
❑ 294 Steve Foucault .50 .23
❑ 295 Rick Monday 1.00 .45
❑ 296 Ray Corbin .50 .23
❑ 297 Hal Breeden .50 .23
❑ 298 Roric Harrison .50 .23
❑ 299 Gene Michael 1.00 .45
❑ 300 Pete Rose 15.00 6.75
❑ 301 Bob Montgomery .50 .23
❑ 302 Rudy May .50 .23
❑ 303 George Hendrick 1.00 .45
❑ 304 Don Wilson .50 .23
❑ 305 Tito Fuentes .50 .23
❑ 306 Orioles Leaders 2.00 .90
Earl Weaver MG
Jim Frey CO
George Bamberger CO
Billy Hunter CO
George Staller CO
❑ 307 Luis Melendez .50 .23
❑ 308 Bruce Dal Canton .50 .23
❑ 309A Dave Roberts SD 1.00 .45
❑ 309B Dave Roberts WAS 7.00 3.10
❑ 310 Terry Forster 1.00 .45
❑ 311 Jerry Grote .50 .23
❑ 312 Deron Johnson 1.00 .45
❑ 313 Barry Lersch .50 .23
❑ 314 Milwaukee Brewers 1.00 .45
Team Card
❑ 315 Ron Cey 2.00 .90
❑ 316 Jim Perry 1.00 .45
❑ 317 Richie Zisk 1.00 .45
❑ 318 Jim Merritt .50 .23
❑ 319 Randy Hundley 1.00 .45
❑ 320 Dusty Baker 2.00 .90
❑ 321 Steve Braun .50 .23
❑ 322 Ernie McAnally .50 .23
❑ 323 Richie Scheinblum .50 .23
❑ 324 Steve Kline .50 .23
❑ 325 Tommy Harper 2.00 .90
❑ 326 Reds Leaders 3.00 1.35
Sparky Anderson MG
Larry Shepard CO
George Scherger CO
Alex Grammas CO
Ted Kluszewski CO
❑ 327 Tom Timmermann .50 .23
❑ 328 Skip Jutze .50 .23
❑ 329 Mark Belanger 1.00 .45
❑ 330 Juan Marichal 3.00 1.35
❑ 331 All-Star Catchers 5.00 2.20
Carlton Fisk
Johnny Bench
❑ 332 All-Star 1B 5.00 2.20
Dick Allen
Hank Aaron
❑ 333 All-Star 2B 3.00 1.35
Rod Carew
Joe Morgan
❑ 334 All-Star 3B 3.00 1.35
Brooks Robinson
Ron Santo
❑ 335 All-Star SS 1.00 .45
Bert Campaneris
Chris Speier
❑ 336 All-Star LF 3.00 1.35
Bobby Murcer
Pete Rose
❑ 337 All-Star CF 1.00 .45
Amos Otis
Cesar Cedeno
❑ 338 All-Star RF 5.00 2.20
Reggie Jackson
Billy Williams
❑ 339 All-Star Pitchers 3.00 1.35
Jim Hunter
Rick Wise
❑ 340 Thurman Munson 6.00 2.70
❑ 341 Dan Driessen 1.00 .45
❑ 342 Jim Lonborg 1.00 .45
❑ 343 Royals Team 1.00 .45
❑ 344 Mike Caldwell .50 .23
❑ 345 Bill North .50 .23
❑ 346 Ron Reed .50 .23
❑ 347 Sandy Alomar 1.00 .45
❑ 348 Pete Richert .50 .23
❑ 349 John Vukovich .50 .23
❑ 350 Bob Gibson 5.00 2.20
❑ 351 Dwight Evans 3.00 1.35
❑ 352 Bill Stoneman .50 .23
❑ 353 Rich Coggins .50 .23
❑ 354 Cubs Leaders 1.00 .45
Whitey Lockman MG
J.C. Martin CO
Hank Aguirre CO
Al Spangler CO
Jim Marshall CO
❑ 355 Dave Nelson .50 .23
❑ 356 Jerry Koosman 1.00 .45
❑ 357 Buddy Bradford .50 .23
❑ 358 Dal Maxvill .50 .23
❑ 359 Brent Strom .50 .23
❑ 360 Greg Luzinski 2.00 .90
❑ 361 Don Carrithers .50 .23
❑ 362 Hal King .50 .23
❑ 363 New York Yankees 2.00 .90
Team Card
❑ 364A Cito Gaston SD 2.00 .90
❑ 364B Cito Gaston WAS 8.00 3.60
❑ 365 Steve Busby 1.00 .45
❑ 366 Larry Hisle 1.00 .45
❑ 367 Norm Cash 2.00 .90
❑ 368 Manny Mota 1.00 .45
❑ 369 Paul Lindblad .50 .23
❑ 370 Bob Watson 1.00 .45
❑ 371 Jim Slaton .50 .23
❑ 372 Ken Reitz .50 .23
❑ 373 John Curtis .50 .23
❑ 374 Marty Perez .50 .23
❑ 375 Earl Williams .50 .23
❑ 376 Jorge Orta .50 .23
❑ 377 Ron Woods .50 .23
❑ 378 Burt Hooton 1.00 .45
❑ 379 Rangers Leaders 2.00 .90
Billy Martin MG
Frank Lucchesi CO
Art Fowler CO
Charlie Silvera CO
Jackie Moore CO
❑ 380 Bud Harrelson 1.00 .45
❑ 381 Charlie Sands .50 .23
❑ 382 Bob Moose .50 .23
❑ 383 Philadelphia Phillies 1.00 .45
Team Card
❑ 384 Chris Chambliss 1.00 .45
❑ 385 Don Gullett 1.00 .45
❑ 386 Gary Matthews 2.00 .90
❑ 387A Rich Morales SD 1.00 .45
❑ 387B Rich Morales WAS 7.00 3.10
❑ 388 Phil Roof .50 .23
❑ 389 Gates Brown .50 .23
❑ 390 Lou Piniella 2.00 .90
❑ 391 Billy Champion .50 .23
❑ 392 Dick Green .50 .23
❑ 393 Orlando Pena .50 .23
❑ 394 Ken Henderson .50 .23
❑ 395 Doug Rader .50 .23
❑ 396 Tommy Davis 1.00 .45
❑ 397 George Stone .50 .23
❑ 398 Duke Sims .50 .23
❑ 399 Mike Paul .50 .23
❑ 400 Harmon Killebrew 5.00 2.20
❑ 401 Elliott Maddox .50 .23
❑ 402 Jim Rooker .50 .23
❑ 403 Red Sox Leaders 1.00 .45
Darrell Johnson MG
Eddie Popowski CO
Lee Stange CO
Don Zimmer CO
Don Bryant CO
❑ 404 Jim Howarth .50 .23
❑ 405 Ellie Rodriguez .50 .23
❑ 406 Steve Arlin .50 .23
❑ 407 Jim Wohlford .50 .23
❑ 408 Charlie Hough 2.00 .90
❑ 409 Ike Brown .50 .23
❑ 410 Pedro Borbon .50 .23
❑ 411 Frank Baker .50 .23
❑ 412 Chuck Taylor .50 .23
❑ 413 Don Money 1.00 .45
❑ 414 Checklist 397-526 3.00 .60
❑ 415 Gary Gentry .50 .23
❑ 416 Chicago White Sox 1.00 .45
Team Card
❑ 417 Rich Folkers .50 .23
❑ 418 Walt Williams .50 .23
❑ 419 Wayne Twitchell .50 .23
❑ 420 Ray Fosse .50 .23
❑ 421 Dan Fife .50 .23
❑ 422 Gonzalo Marquez .50 .23
❑ 423 Fred Stanley .50 .23
❑ 424 Jim Beauchamp .50 .23
❑ 425 Pete Broberg .50 .23
❑ 426 Rennie Stennett .50 .23
❑ 427 Bobby Bolin .50 .23
❑ 428 Gary Sutherland .50 .23
❑ 429 Dick Lange .50 .23
❑ 430 Matty Alou 1.00 .45
❑ 431 Gene Garber 1.00 .45
❑ 432 Chris Arnold .50 .23
❑ 433 Lerrin LaGrow .50 .23
❑ 434 Ken McMullen .50 .23
❑ 435 Dave Concepcion 2.00 .90
❑ 436 Don Hood .50 .23
❑ 437 Jim Lyttle .50 .23
❑ 438 Ed Herrmann .50 .23
❑ 439 Norm Miller .50 .23
❑ 440 Jim Kaat 2.00 .90
❑ 441 Tom Ragland .50 .23
❑ 442 Alan Foster .50 .23
❑ 443 Tom Hutton .50 .23
❑ 444 Vic Davalillo .50 .23
❑ 445 George Medich .50 .23
❑ 446 Len Randle .50 .23
❑ 447 Twins Leaders 1.00 .45
Frank Quilici MG
Ralph Rowe CO
Bob Rodgers CO
Vern Morgan CO
❑ 448 Ron Hodges .50 .23
❑ 449 Tom McCraw .50 .23
❑ 450 Rich Hebner 1.00 .45
❑ 451 Tommy John 2.00 .90
❑ 452 Gene Hiser .50 .23
❑ 453 Balor Moore .50 .23

❑ 454 Kurt Bevacqua .50 .23
❑ 455 Tom Bradley .50 .23
❑ 456 Dave Winfield 100.00 45.00
❑ 457 Chuck Goggin .50 .23
❑ 458 Jim Ray .50 .23
❑ 459 Cincinnati Reds 2.00 .90
Team Card
❑ 460 Boog Powell 2.00 .90
❑ 461 John Odom .50 .23
❑ 462 Luis Alvarado .50 .23
❑ 463 Pat Dobson .50 .23
❑ 464 Jose Cruz 2.00 .90
❑ 465 Dick Bosman .50 .23
❑ 466 Dick Billings .50 .23
❑ 467 Winston Llenas .50 .23
❑ 468 Pepe Frias .50 .23
❑ 469 Joe Decker .50 .23
❑ 470 Reggie Jackson ALCS 6.00 2.70
❑ 471 Jon Matlack NLCS 1.00 .45
❑ 472 Darold Knowles WS 1.00 .45
❑ 473 Willie Mays WS 8.00 3.60
❑ 474 Bert Campaneris WS 1.00 .45
❑ 475 Rusty Staub WS 1.00 .45
❑ 476 Cleon Jones WS 1.00 .45
❑ 477 Reggie Jackson WS 6.00 2.70
❑ 478 Bert Campaneris WS 1.00 .45
❑ 479 World Series Summary 1.00 .45
A's celebrate; win
2nd consecutive
championship
❑ 480 Willie Crawford .50 .23
❑ 481 Jerry Terrell .50 .23
❑ 482 Bob Didier .50 .23
❑ 483 Atlanta Braves 1.00 .45
Team Card
❑ 484 Carmen Fanzone .50 .23
❑ 485 Felipe Alou 2.00 .90
❑ 486 Steve Stone 1.00 .45
❑ 487 Ted Martinez .50 .23
❑ 488 Andy Etchebarren .50 .23
❑ 489 Pirates Leaders 1.00 .45
Danny Murtaugh MG
Don Osborn CO
Don Leppert CO
Bill Mazeroski CO
Bob Skinner CO
❑ 490 Vada Pinson 2.00 .90
❑ 491 Roger Nelson .50 .23
❑ 492 Mike Rogodzinski .50 .23
❑ 493 Joe Hoerner .50 .23
❑ 494 Ed Goodson .50 .23
❑ 495 Dick McAuliffe 1.00 .45
❑ 496 Tom Murphy .50 .23
❑ 497 Bobby Mitchell .50 .23
❑ 498 Pat Corrales 1.00 .45
❑ 499 Rusty Torres .50 .23
❑ 500 Lee May 1.00 .45
❑ 501 Eddie Leon .50 .23
❑ 502 Dave LaRoche .50 .23
❑ 503 Eric Soderholm .50 .23
❑ 504 Joe Niekro 1.00 .45
❑ 505 Bill Buckner 1.00 .45
❑ 506 Ed Farmer .50 .23
❑ 507 Larry Stahl .50 .23
❑ 508 Montreal Expos 1.00 .45
Team Card
❑ 509 Jesse Jefferson .50 .23
❑ 510 Wayne Garrett .50 .23
❑ 511 Toby Harrah 1.00 .45
❑ 512 Joe Lahoud .50 .23
❑ 513 Jim Campanis .50 .23
❑ 514 Paul Schaal .50 .23
❑ 515 Willie Montanez .50 .23
❑ 516 Horacio Pina .50 .23
❑ 517 Mike Hegan .50 .23
❑ 518 Derrel Thomas .50 .23
❑ 519 Bill Sharp .50 .23
❑ 520 Tim McCarver 2.00 .90
❑ 521 Indians Leaders 1.00 .45
Ken Aspromonte MG
Clay Bryant CO
Tony Pacheco CO
❑ 522 J.R. Richard 2.00 .90
❑ 523 Cecil Cooper 2.00 .90
❑ 524 Bill Plummer .50 .23
❑ 525 Clyde Wright .50 .23
❑ 526 Frank Tepedino .50 .23
❑ 527 Bobby Darwin .50 .23
❑ 528 Bill Bonham .50 .23
❑ 529 Horace Clarke 1.00 .45
❑ 530 Mickey Stanley 1.00 .45
❑ 531 Expos Leaders 1.00 .45
Gene Mauch MG
Dave Bristol CO
Cal McLish CO
Larry Doby CO
Jerry Zimmerman CO
❑ 532 Skip Lockwood .50 .23
❑ 533 Mike Phillips .50 .23
❑ 534 Eddie Watt .50 .23
❑ 535 Bob Tolan .50 .23
❑ 536 Duffy Dyer .50 .23
❑ 537 Steve Mingori .50 .23
❑ 538 Cesar Tovar .50 .23
❑ 539 Lloyd Allen .50 .23
❑ 540 Bob Robertson .50 .23
❑ 541 Cleveland Indians 1.00 .45
Team Card
❑ 542 Rich Gossage 2.00 .90
❑ 543 Danny Cater .50 .23
❑ 544 Ron Schueler .50 .23
❑ 545 Billy Conigliaro 1.00 .45
❑ 546 Mike Corkins .50 .23
❑ 547 Glenn Borgmann .50 .23
❑ 548 Sonny Siebert .50 .23
❑ 549 Mike Jorgensen .50 .23
❑ 550 Sam McDowell 1.00 .45
❑ 551 Von Joshua .50 .23
❑ 552 Denny Doyle .50 .23
❑ 553 Jim Willoughby .50 .23
❑ 554 Tim Johnson .50 .23
❑ 555 Woodie Fryman .50 .23
❑ 556 Dave Campbell .50 .23
❑ 557 Jim McGlothlin .50 .23
❑ 558 Bill Fahey .50 .23
❑ 559 Darrel Chaney .50 .23
❑ 560 Mike Cuellar 1.00 .45
❑ 561 Ed Kranepool 1.00 .45
❑ 562 Jack Aker .50 .23
❑ 563 Hal McRae 1.00 .45
❑ 564 Mike Ryan .50 .23
❑ 565 Milt Wilcox .50 .23
❑ 566 Jackie Hernandez .50 .23
❑ 567 Boston Red Sox 1.00 .45
Team Card
❑ 568 Mike Torrez 1.00 .45
❑ 569 Rick Dempsey 1.00 .45
❑ 570 Ralph Garr 1.00 .45
❑ 571 Rich Hand .50 .23
❑ 572 Enzo Hernandez .50 .23
❑ 573 Mike Adams .50 .23
❑ 574 Bill Parsons .50 .23
❑ 575 Steve Garvey 4.00 1.80
❑ 576 Scipio Spinks .50 .23
❑ 577 Mike Sadek .50 .23
❑ 578 Ralph Houk MG 1.00 .45
❑ 579 Cecil Upshaw .50 .23
❑ 580 Jim Spencer .50 .23
❑ 581 Fred Norman .50 .23
❑ 582 Bucky Dent 4.00 1.80
❑ 583 Marty Pattin .50 .23
❑ 584 Ken Rudolph .50 .23
❑ 585 Merv Rettenmund .50 .23
❑ 586 Jack Brohamer .50 .23
❑ 587 Larry Christenson .50 .23
❑ 588 Hal Lanier .50 .23
❑ 589 Boots Day .50 .23
❑ 590 Roger Moret .50 .23
❑ 591 Sonny Jackson .50 .23
❑ 592 Ed Bane .50 .23
❑ 593 Steve Yeager 1.00 .45
❑ 594 Leroy Stanton .50 .23
❑ 595 Steve Blass 1.00 .45
❑ 596 Rookie Pitchers .50 .23
Wayne Garland
Fred Holdsworth
Mark Littell
Dick Pole
❑ 597 Rookie Shortstops 1.00 .45
Dave Chalk
John Gamble
Pete MacKanin
Manny Trillo
❑ 598 Rookie Outfielders 12.00 5.50
Dave Augustine
Ken Griffey
Steve Ontiveros
Jim Tyrone
❑ 599A Rookie Pitchers WAS 2.00 .90
Ron Diorio
Dave Freisleben
Frank Riccelli
Greg Shanahan
❑ 599B Rookie Pitchers SD 3.00 1.35
(SD in large print)
❑ 599C Rookie Pitchers SD 5.00 2.20
(SD in small print)
❑ 600 Rookie Infielders 5.00 2.20
Ron Cash
Jim Cox
Bill Madlock
Reggie Sanders
❑ 601 Rookie Outfielders 3.00 1.35
Ed Armbrister
Rich Bladt
Brian Downing
Bake McBride
❑ 602 Rookie Pitchers 1.00 .45
Glen Abbott
Rick Henninger
Craig Swan
Dan Vossler
❑ 603 Rookie Catchers 1.00 .45
Barry Foote
Tom Lundstedt
Charlie Moore
Sergio Robles
❑ 604 Rookie Infielders 5.00 2.20
Terry Hughes
John Knox
Andre Thornton
Frank White
❑ 605 Rookie Pitchers 4.00 1.80
Vic Albury
Ken Frailing
Kevin Kobel
Frank Tanana
❑ 606 Rookie Outfielders 1.00 .45
Jim Fuller
Wilbur Howard
Tommy Smith
Otto Velez
❑ 607 Rookie Shortstops 1.00 .45
Leo Foster
Tom Heintzelman
Dave Rosello
Frank Taveras
❑ 608A Rookie Pitchers: ERR 2.00 .90
Bob Apodaco (sic)
Dick Baney
John D'Acquisto
Mike Wallace
❑ 608B Rookie Pitchers: COR 1.00 .45
Bob Apodaca
Dick Baney
John D'Acquisto
Mike Wallace
❑ 609 Rico Petrocelli 1.00 .45
❑ 610 Dave Kingman 2.00 .90
❑ 611 Rich Stelmaszek .50 .23
❑ 612 Luke Walker .50 .23
❑ 613 Dan Monzon .50 .23
❑ 614 Adrian Devine .50 .23
❑ 615 Johnny Jeter UER .50 .23
(Misspelled Johnnie
on card back)
❑ 616 Larry Gura .50 .23
❑ 617 Ted Ford .50 .23
❑ 618 Jim Mason .50 .23
❑ 619 Mike Anderson .50 .23
❑ 620 Al Downing .50 .23
❑ 621 Bernie Carbo .50 .23
❑ 622 Phil Gagliano .50 .23
❑ 623 Celerino Sanchez .50 .23
❑ 624 Bob Miller .50 .23
❑ 625 Ollie Brown .50 .23

Card	NRMT	VG-E
❑ 626 Pittsburgh Pirates	1.00	.45
Team Card		
❑ 627 Carl Taylor	.50	.23
❑ 628 Ivan Murrell	.50	.23
❑ 629 Rusty Staub	2.00	.90
❑ 630 Tommie Agee	1.00	.45
❑ 631 Steve Barber	.50	.23
❑ 632 George Culver	.50	.23
❑ 633 Dave Hamilton	.50	.23
❑ 634 Braves Leaders	2.00	.90
Eddie Mathews MG		
Herm Starrette CO		
Connie Ryan CO		
Jim Busby CO		
Ken Silvestri CO		
❑ 635 Johnny Edwards	.50	.23
❑ 636 Dave Goltz	.50	.23
❑ 637 Checklist 529-660	3.00	.60
❑ 638 Ken Sanders	.50	.23
❑ 639 Joe Lovitto	.50	.23
❑ 640 Milt Pappas	1.00	.45
❑ 641 Chuck Brinkman	.50	.23
❑ 642 Terry Harmon	.50	.23
❑ 643 Dodgers Team	1.00	.45
❑ 644 Wayne Granger	.50	.23
❑ 645 Ken Boswell	.50	.23
❑ 646 George Foster	2.00	.90
❑ 647 Juan Beniquez	.50	.23
❑ 648 Terry Crowley	.50	.23
❑ 649 Fernando Gonzalez	.50	.23
❑ 650 Mike Epstein	.50	.23
❑ 651 Leron Lee	.50	.23
❑ 652 Gail Hopkins	.50	.23
❑ 653 Bob Stinson	.50	.23
❑ 654A Jesus Alou ERR	1.00	.45
(No position)		
❑ 654B Jesus Alou COR	5.00	2.20
(Outfield)		
❑ 655 Mike Tyson	.50	.23
❑ 656 Adrian Garrett	.50	.23
❑ 657 Jim Shellenback	.50	.23
❑ 658 Lee Lacy	.50	.23
❑ 659 Joe Lis	.50	.23
❑ 660 Larry Dierker	2.00	.50

1974 Topps Traded

	NRMT	VG-E
COMPLETE SET (44)	15.00	6.75
COMMON CARD	.50	.23
❑ 23T Craig Robinson	.50	.23
❑ 42T Claude Osteen	.75	.35
❑ 43T Jim Wynn	.75	.35
❑ 51T Bobby Heise	.50	.23
❑ 59T Ross Grimsley	.50	.23
❑ 62T Bob Locker	.50	.23
❑ 63T Bill Sudakis	.50	.23
❑ 73T Mike Marshall	.75	.35
❑ 123T Nelson Briles	.75	.35
❑ 139T Aurelio Monteagudo	.50	.23
❑ 151T Diego Segui	.50	.23
❑ 165T Willie Davis	.75	.35
❑ 175T Reggie Cleveland	.50	.23
❑ 182T Lindy McDaniel	.75	.35
❑ 186T Fred Scherman	.50	.23
❑ 249T George Mitterwald	.50	.23
❑ 262T Ed Kirkpatrick	.50	.23
❑ 269T Bob Johnson	.50	.23
❑ 270T Ron Santo	1.00	.45
❑ 313T Barry Lersch	.50	.23
❑ 319T Randy Hundley	.75	.35
❑ 330T Juan Marichal	2.00	.90
❑ 348T Pete Richert	.50	.23
❑ 373T John Curtis	.50	.23
❑ 390T Lou Piniella	1.00	.45
❑ 428T Gary Sutherland	.50	.23
❑ 454T Kurt Bevacqua	.50	.23
❑ 458T Jim Ray	.50	.23
❑ 485T Felipe Alou	1.00	.45
❑ 486T Steve Stone	.75	.35
❑ 496T Tom Murphy	.50	.23
❑ 516T Horacio Pina	.50	.23
❑ 534T Eddie Watt	.50	.23
❑ 538T Cesar Tovar	.50	.23
❑ 544T Ron Schueler	.50	.23
❑ 579T Cecil Upshaw	.50	.23
❑ 585T Merv Rettenmund	.50	.23
❑ 612T Luke Walker	.50	.23
❑ 616T Larry Gura	.75	.35
❑ 618T Jim Mason	.50	.23
❑ 630T Tommie Agee	.75	.35
❑ 648T Terry Crowley	.50	.23
❑ 649T Fernando Gonzalez	.50	.23
❑ NNO Traded Checklist	1.50	.30

1975 Topps

	NRMT	VG-E
COMPLETE SET (660)	750.00	350.00
COMMON CARD (1-660)	.50	.23
WRAPPER (15-CENT)	10.00	4.50
❑ 1 Hank Aaron RB	30.00	10.00
Sets Homer Mark		
❑ 2 Lou Brock RB	3.00	1.35
118 Stolen Bases		
❑ 3 Bob Gibson RB	3.00	1.35
3000th Strikeout		
❑ 4 Al Kaline RB	4.00	1.80
3000 Hit Club		
❑ 5 Nolan Ryan RB	40.00	18.00
Fans 300 for		
3rd Year in a Row		
❑ 6 Mike Marshall RB	1.00	.45
Hurls 106 Games		
❑ 7 Steve Busby HL	12.00	5.50
Dick Bosman		
Nolan Ryan		
❑ 8 Rogelio Moret	.50	.23
❑ 9 Frank Tepedino	.50	.23
❑ 10 Willie Davis	1.00	.45
❑ 11 Bill Melton	.50	.23
❑ 12 David Clyde	.50	.23
❑ 13 Gene Locklear	1.00	.45
❑ 14 Milt Wilcox	.50	.23
❑ 15 Jose Cardenal	1.00	.45
❑ 16 Frank Tanana	2.00	.90
❑ 17 Dave Concepcion	2.00	.90
❑ 18 Tigers: Team/Mgr.	2.00	.40
Ralph Houk		
(Checklist back)		
❑ 19 Jerry Koosman	1.00	.45
❑ 20 Thurman Munson	6.00	2.70
❑ 21 Rollie Fingers	3.00	1.35
❑ 22 Dave Cash	.50	.23
❑ 23 Bill Russell	1.00	.45
❑ 24 Al Fitzmorris	.50	.23
❑ 25 Lee May	1.00	.45
❑ 26 Dave McNally	1.00	.45
❑ 27 Ken Reitz	.50	.23
❑ 28 Tom Murphy	.50	.23
❑ 29 Dave Parker	4.00	1.80
❑ 30 Bert Blyleven	2.00	.90
❑ 31 Dave Rader	.50	.23
❑ 32 Reggie Cleveland	.50	.23
❑ 33 Dusty Baker	2.00	.90
❑ 34 Steve Renko	.50	.23
❑ 35 Ron Santo	1.00	.45
❑ 36 Joe Lovitto	.50	.23
❑ 37 Dave Freisleben	.50	.23
❑ 38 Buddy Bell	2.00	.90
❑ 39 Andre Thornton	1.00	.45
❑ 40 Bill Singer	.50	.23
❑ 41 Cesar Geronimo	1.00	.45
❑ 42 Joe Coleman	.50	.23
❑ 43 Cleon Jones	1.00	.45
❑ 44 Pat Dobson	.50	.23
❑ 45 Joe Rudi	1.00	.45
❑ 46 Phillies: Team/Mgr.	2.00	.40
Danny Ozark UER		
(Checklist back)		
(Terry Harmon listed as 339		
instead of 399)		
❑ 47 Tommy John	2.00	.90
❑ 48 Freddie Patek	1.00	.45
❑ 49 Larry Dierker	1.00	.45
❑ 50 Brooks Robinson	6.00	2.70
❑ 51 Bob Forsch	1.00	.45
❑ 52 Darrell Porter	1.00	.45
❑ 53 Dave Giusti	.50	.23
❑ 54 Eric Soderholm	.50	.23
❑ 55 Bobby Bonds	2.00	.90
❑ 56 Rick Wise	1.00	.45
❑ 57 Dave Johnson	1.00	.45
❑ 58 Chuck Taylor	.50	.23
❑ 59 Ken Henderson	.50	.23
❑ 60 Fergie Jenkins	3.00	1.35
❑ 61 Dave Winfield	25.00	11.00
❑ 62 Fritz Peterson	.50	.23
❑ 63 Steve Swisher	.50	.23
❑ 64 Dave Chalk	.50	.23
❑ 65 Don Gullett	1.00	.45
❑ 66 Willie Horton	1.00	.45
❑ 67 Tug McGraw	1.00	.45
❑ 68 Ron Blomberg	.50	.23
❑ 69 John Odom	.50	.23
❑ 70 Mike Schmidt	50.00	22.00
❑ 71 Charlie Hough	1.00	.45
❑ 72 Royals: Team/Mgr.	2.00	.40
Jack McKeon		
(Checklist back)		
❑ 73 J.R. Richard	1.00	.45
❑ 74 Mark Belanger	1.00	.45
❑ 75 Ted Simmons	2.00	.90
❑ 76 Ed Sprague	.50	.23
❑ 77 Richie Zisk	1.00	.45
❑ 78 Ray Corbin	.50	.23
❑ 79 Gary Matthews	1.00	.45
❑ 80 Carlton Fisk	10.00	4.50
❑ 81 Ron Reed	.50	.23
❑ 82 Pat Kelly	.50	.23
❑ 83 Jim Merritt	.50	.23
❑ 84 Enzo Hernandez	.50	.23
❑ 85 Bill Bonham	.50	.23
❑ 86 Joe Lis	.50	.23
❑ 87 George Foster	2.00	.90
❑ 88 Tom Egan	.50	.23
❑ 89 Jim Ray	.50	.23
❑ 90 Rusty Staub	2.00	.90
❑ 91 Dick Green	.50	.23
❑ 92 Cecil Upshaw	.50	.23
❑ 93 Dave Lopes	2.00	.90
❑ 94 Jim Lonborg	1.00	.45
❑ 95 John Mayberry	1.00	.45
❑ 96 Mike Cosgrove	.50	.23
❑ 97 Earl Williams	.50	.23
❑ 98 Rich Folkers	.50	.23
❑ 99 Mike Hegan	.50	.23
❑ 100 Willie Stargell	4.00	1.80
❑ 101 Expos: Team/Mgr.	2.00	.40
Gene Mauch		

(Checklist back)
❑ 102 Joe Decker .50 .23
❑ 103 Rick Miller .50 .23
❑ 104 Bill Madlock 2.00 .90
❑ 105 Buzz Capra .50 .23
❑ 106 Mike Hargrove 3.00 1.35
❑ 107 Jim Barr .50 .23
❑ 108 Tom Hall .50 .23
❑ 109 George Hendrick 1.00 .45
❑ 110 Wilbur Wood .50 .23
❑ 111 Wayne Garrett .50 .23
❑ 112 Larry Hardy .50 .23
❑ 113 Elliott Maddox .50 .23
❑ 114 Dick Lange .50 .23
❑ 115 Joe Ferguson .50 .23
❑ 116 Lerrin LaGrow .50 .23
❑ 117 Orioles: Team/Mgr. 3.00 .60
Earl Weaver
(Checklist back)
❑ 118 Mike Anderson .50 .23
❑ 119 Tommy Helms .50 .23
❑ 120 Steve Busby UER 1.00 .45
(Photo actually
Fran Healy)
❑ 121 Bill North .50 .23
❑ 122 Al Hrabosky 1.00 .45
❑ 123 Johnny Briggs .50 .23
❑ 124 Jerry Reuss 1.00 .45
❑ 125 Ken Singleton 1.00 .45
❑ 126 Checklist 1-132 3.00 .60
❑ 127 Glenn Borgmann .50 .23
❑ 128 Bill Lee 1.00 .45
❑ 129 Rick Monday 1.00 .45
❑ 130 Phil Niekro 3.00 1.35
❑ 131 Toby Harrah 1.00 .45
❑ 132 Randy Moffitt .50 .23
❑ 133 Dan Driessen 1.00 .45
❑ 134 Ron Hodges .50 .23
❑ 135 Charlie Spikes .50 .23
❑ 136 Jim Mason .50 .23
❑ 137 Terry Forster 1.00 .45
❑ 138 Del Unser .50 .23
❑ 139 Horacio Pina .50 .23
❑ 140 Steve Garvey 4.00 1.80
❑ 141 Mickey Stanley 1.00 .45
❑ 142 Bob Reynolds .50 .23
❑ 143 Cliff Johnson 1.00 .45
❑ 144 Jim Wohlford .50 .23
❑ 145 Ken Holtzman 1.00 .45
❑ 146 Padres: Team/Mgr. 2.00 .40
John McNamara
(Checklist back)
❑ 147 Pedro Garcia .50 .23
❑ 148 Jim Rooker .50 .23
❑ 149 Tim Foli .50 .23
❑ 150 Bob Gibson 5.00 2.20
❑ 151 Steve Brye .50 .23
❑ 152 Mario Guerrero .50 .23
❑ 153 Rick Reuschel 1.00 .45
❑ 154 Mike Lum .50 .23
❑ 155 Jim Bibby .50 .23
❑ 156 Dave Kingman 2.00 .90
❑ 157 Pedro Borbon 1.00 .45
❑ 158 Jerry Grote .50 .23
❑ 159 Steve Arlin .50 .23
❑ 160 Graig Nettles 2.00 .90
❑ 161 Stan Bahnsen .50 .23
❑ 162 Willie Montanez .50 .23
❑ 163 Jim Brewer .50 .23
❑ 164 Mickey Rivers 1.00 .45
❑ 165 Doug Rader 1.00 .45
❑ 166 Woodie Fryman .50 .23
❑ 167 Rich Coggins .50 .23
❑ 168 Bill Greif .50 .23
❑ 169 Cookie Rojas 1.00 .45
❑ 170 Bert Campaneris 1.00 .45
❑ 171 Ed Kirkpatrick .50 .23
❑ 172 Red Sox: Team/Mgr. 3.00 .60
Darrell Johnson
(Checklist back)
❑ 173 Steve Rogers 1.00 .45
❑ 174 Bake McBride 1.00 .45
❑ 175 Don Money 1.00 .45
❑ 176 Burt Hooton 1.00 .45
❑ 177 Vic Correll .50 .23
❑ 178 Cesar Tovar .50 .23
❑ 179 Tom Bradley .50 .23
❑ 180 Joe Morgan 5.00 2.20
❑ 181 Fred Beene .50 .23
❑ 182 Don Hahn .50 .23
❑ 183 Mel Stottlemyre 1.00 .45
❑ 184 Jorge Orta .50 .23
❑ 185 Steve Carlton 6.00 2.70
❑ 186 Willie Crawford .50 .23
❑ 187 Denny Doyle .50 .23
❑ 188 Tom Griffin .50 .23
❑ 189 1951 MVP's 3.00 1.35
Larry (Yogi) Berra
Roy Campanella
(Campy never issued)
❑ 190 1952 MVP's 2.00 .90
Bobby Shantz
Hank Sauer
❑ 191 1953 MVP's 2.00 .90
Al Rosen
Roy Campanella
❑ 192 1954 MVP's 4.00 1.80
Yogi Berra
Willie Mays
❑ 193 1955 MVP's UER 3.00 1.35
Yogi Berra
Roy Campanella
(Campy card never
issued, pictured
with LA cap)
❑ 194 1956 MVP's 20.00 9.00
Mickey Mantle
Don Newcombe
❑ 195 1957 MVP's 25.00 11.00
Mickey Mantle
Hank Aaron
❑ 196 1958 MVP's 2.00 .90
Jackie Jensen
Ernie Banks
❑ 197 1959 MVP's 2.00 .90
Nellie Fox
Ernie Banks
❑ 198 1960 MVP's 2.00 .90
Roger Maris
Dick Groat
❑ 199 1961 MVP's 3.00 1.35
Roger Maris
Frank Robinson
❑ 200 1962 MVP's 20.00 9.00
Mickey Mantle
Maury Wills
(Wills never issued)
❑ 201 1963 MVP's 2.00 .90
Elston Howard
Sandy Koufax
❑ 202 1964 MVP's 2.00 .90
Brooks Robinson
Ken Boyer
❑ 203 1965 MVP's 2.00 .90
Zoilo Versalles
Willie Mays
❑ 204 1966 MVP's 8.00 3.60
Frank Robinson
Bob Clemente
❑ 205 1967 MVP's 2.00 .90
Carl Yastrzemski
Orlando Cepeda
❑ 206 1968 MVP's 2.00 .90
Denny McLain
Bob Gibson
❑ 207 1969 MVP's 2.00 .90
Harmon Killebrew
Willie McCovey
❑ 208 1970 MVP's 2.00 .90
Boog Powell
Johnny Bench
❑ 209 1971 MVP's 2.00 .90
Vida Blue
Joe Torre
❑ 210 1972 MVP's 2.00 .90
Rich Allen
Johnny Bench
❑ 211 1973 MVP's 6.00 2.70
Reggie Jackson
Pete Rose
❑ 212 1974 MVP's 2.00 .90
Jeff Burroughs
Steve Garvey
❑ 213 Oscar Gamble 1.00 .45
❑ 214 Harry Parker .50 .23
❑ 215 Bobby Valentine 1.00 .45
❑ 216 Giants: Team/Mgr. 2.00 .40
Wes Westrum
(Checklist back)
❑ 217 Lou Piniella 2.00 .90
❑ 218 Jerry Johnson .50 .23
❑ 219 Ed Herrmann .50 .23
❑ 220 Don Sutton 3.00 1.35
❑ 221 Aurelio Rodriguez .50 .23
❑ 222 Dan Spillner .50 .23
❑ 223 Robin Yount 80.00 36.00
❑ 224 Ramon Hernandez .50 .23
❑ 225 Bob Grich 1.00 .45
❑ 226 Bill Campbell .50 .23
❑ 227 Bob Watson 1.00 .45
❑ 228 George Brett 150.00 70.00
❑ 229 Barry Foote .50 .23
❑ 230 Jim Hunter 3.00 1.35
❑ 231 Mike Tyson .50 .23
❑ 232 Diego Segui .50 .23
❑ 233 Billy Grabarkewitz .50 .23
❑ 234 Tom Grieve 1.00 .45
❑ 235 Jack Billingham 1.00 .45
❑ 236 Angels: Team/Mgr. 2.00 .40
Dick Williams
(Checklist back)
❑ 237 Carl Morton .50 .23
❑ 238 Dave Duncan .50 .23
❑ 239 George Stone .50 .23
❑ 240 Garry Maddox 1.00 .45
❑ 241 Dick Tidrow .50 .23
❑ 242 Jay Johnstone 1.00 .45
❑ 243 Jim Kaat 2.00 .90
❑ 244 Bill Buckner 1.00 .45
❑ 245 Mickey Lolich 2.00 .90
❑ 246 Cardinals: Team/Mgr. 2.00 .40
Red Schoendienst
(Checklist back)
❑ 247 Enos Cabell .50 .23
❑ 248 Randy Jones 2.00 .90
❑ 249 Danny Thompson .50 .23
❑ 250 Ken Brett .50 .23
❑ 251 Fran Healy .50 .23
❑ 252 Fred Scherman .50 .23
❑ 253 Jesus Alou .50 .23
❑ 254 Mike Torrez 1.00 .45
❑ 255 Dwight Evans 2.00 .90
❑ 256 Billy Champion .50 .23
❑ 257 Checklist: 133-264 3.00 .60
❑ 258 Dave LaRoche .50 .23
❑ 259 Len Randle .50 .23
❑ 260 Johnny Bench 12.00 5.50
❑ 261 Andy Hassler .50 .23
❑ 262 Rowland Office .50 .23
❑ 263 Jim Perry 1.00 .45
❑ 264 John Milner .50 .23
❑ 265 Ron Bryant .50 .23
❑ 266 Sandy Alomar 1.00 .45
❑ 267 Dick Ruthven .50 .23
❑ 268 Hal McRae 1.00 .45
❑ 269 Doug Rau .50 .23
❑ 270 Ron Fairly 1.00 .45
❑ 271 Gerry Moses .50 .23
❑ 272 Lynn McGlothen .50 .23
❑ 273 Steve Braun .50 .23
❑ 274 Vicente Romo .50 .23
❑ 275 Paul Blair 1.00 .45
❑ 276 White Sox Team/Mgr. 2.00 .40
Chuck Tanner
(Checklist back)
❑ 277 Frank Taveras .50 .23
❑ 278 Paul Lindblad .50 .23
❑ 279 Milt May .50 .23
❑ 280 Carl Yastrzemski 6.00 2.70
❑ 281 Jim Slaton .50 .23
❑ 282 Jerry Morales .50 .23
❑ 283 Steve Foucault .50 .23
❑ 284 Ken Griffey 4.00 1.80
❑ 285 Ellie Rodriguez .50 .23
❑ 286 Mike Jorgensen .50 .23

❑ 287 Roric Harrison .50 .23
❑ 288 Bruce Ellingsen .50 .23
❑ 289 Ken Rudolph .50 .23
❑ 290 Jon Matlack .50 .23
❑ 291 Bill Sudakis .50 .23
❑ 292 Ron Schueler .50 .23
❑ 293 Dick Sharon .50 .23
❑ 294 Geoff Zahn .50 .23
❑ 295 Vada Pinson 2.00 .90
❑ 296 Alan Foster .50 .23
❑ 297 Craig Kusick .50 .23
❑ 298 Johnny Grubb .50 .23
❑ 299 Bucky Dent 2.00 .90
❑ 300 Reggie Jackson 15.00 6.75
❑ 301 Dave Roberts .50 .23
❑ 302 Rick Burleson 1.00 .45
❑ 303 Grant Jackson .50 .23
❑ 304 Pirates: Team/Mgr. 2.00 .40
Danny Murtaugh
(Checklist back)
❑ 305 Jim Colborn .50 .23
❑ 306 Batting Leaders 2.00 .90
Rod Carew
Ralph Garr
❑ 307 Home Run Leaders 3.00 1.35
Dick Allen
Mike Schmidt
❑ 308 RBI Leaders 2.00 .90
Jeff Burroughs
Johnny Bench
❑ 309 Stolen Base Leaders 2.00 .90
Bill North
Lou Brock
❑ 310 Victory Leaders 2.00 .90
Jim Hunter
Fergie Jenkins
Andy Messersmith
Phil Niekro
❑ 311 ERA Leaders 2.00 .90
Jim Hunter
Buzz Capra
❑ 312 Strikeout Leaders 20.00 9.00
Nolan Ryan
Steve Carlton
❑ 313 Leading Firemen 1.00 .45
Terry Forster
Mike Marshall
❑ 314 Buck Martinez .50 .23
❑ 315 Don Kessinger 1.00 .45
❑ 316 Jackie Brown .50 .23
❑ 317 Joe Lahoud .50 .23
❑ 318 Ernie McAnally .50 .23
❑ 319 Johnny Oates 1.00 .45
❑ 320 Pete Rose 15.00 6.75
❑ 321 Rudy May .50 .23
❑ 322 Ed Goodson .50 .23
❑ 323 Fred Holdsworth .50 .23
❑ 324 Ed Kranepool 1.00 .45
❑ 325 Tony Oliva 2.00 .90
❑ 326 Wayne Twitchell .50 .23
❑ 327 Jerry Hairston .50 .23
❑ 328 Sonny Siebert .50 .23
❑ 329 Ted Kubiak .50 .23
❑ 330 Mike Marshall 1.00 .45
❑ 331 Indians: Team/Mgr. 2.00 .40
Frank Robinson
(Checklist back)
❑ 332 Fred Kendall .50 .23
❑ 333 Dick Drago .50 .23
❑ 334 Greg Gross .50 .23
❑ 335 Jim Palmer 5.00 2.20
❑ 336 Rennie Stennett .50 .23
❑ 337 Kevin Kobel .50 .23
❑ 338 Rich Stelmaszek .50 .23
❑ 339 Jim Fregosi 1.00 .45
❑ 340 Paul Splittorff .50 .23
❑ 341 Hal Breeden .50 .23
❑ 342 Leroy Stanton .50 .23
❑ 343 Danny Frisella .50 .23
❑ 344 Ben Oglivie 1.00 .45
❑ 345 Clay Carroll 1.00 .45
❑ 346 Bobby Darwin .50 .23
❑ 347 Mike Caldwell .50 .23
❑ 348 Tony Muser .50 .23
❑ 349 Ray Sadecki .50 .23
❑ 350 Bobby Murcer 1.00 .45
❑ 351 Bob Boone 2.00 .90
❑ 352 Darold Knowles .50 .23
❑ 353 Luis Melendez .50 .23
❑ 354 Dick Bosman .50 .23
❑ 355 Chris Cannizzaro .50 .23
❑ 356 Rico Petrocelli 1.00 .45
❑ 357 Ken Forsch .50 .23
❑ 358 Al Bumbry 1.00 .45
❑ 359 Paul Popovich .50 .23
❑ 360 George Scott 1.00 .45
❑ 361 Dodgers: Team/Mgr. 2.00 .40
Walter Alston
(Checklist back)
❑ 362 Steve Hargan .50 .23
❑ 363 Carmen Fanzone .50 .23
❑ 364 Doug Bird .50 .23
❑ 365 Bob Bailey .50 .23
❑ 366 Ken Sanders .50 .23
❑ 367 Craig Robinson .50 .23
❑ 368 Vic Albury .50 .23
❑ 369 Merv Rettenmund .50 .23
❑ 370 Tom Seaver 12.00 5.50
❑ 371 Gates Brown .50 .23
❑ 372 John D'Acquisto .50 .23
❑ 373 Bill Sharp .50 .23
❑ 374 Eddie Watt .50 .23
❑ 375 Roy White 1.00 .45
❑ 376 Steve Yeager 1.00 .45
❑ 377 Tom Hilgendorf .50 .23
❑ 378 Derrel Thomas .50 .23
❑ 379 Bernie Carbo .50 .23
❑ 380 Sal Bando 1.00 .45
❑ 381 John Curtis .50 .23
❑ 382 Don Baylor 2.00 .90
❑ 383 Jim York .50 .23
❑ 384 Brewers: Team/Mgr. 2.00 .40
Del Crandall
(Checklist back)
❑ 385 Dock Ellis .50 .23
❑ 386 Checklist: 265-396 3.00 .60
❑ 387 Jim Spencer .50 .23
❑ 388 Steve Stone 1.00 .45
❑ 389 Tony Solaita .50 .23
❑ 390 Ron Cey 2.00 .90
❑ 391 Don DeMola .50 .23
❑ 392 Bruce Bochte 1.00 .45
❑ 393 Gary Gentry .50 .23
❑ 394 Larvell Blanks .50 .23
❑ 395 Bud Harrelson 1.00 .45
❑ 396 Fred Norman 1.00 .45
❑ 397 Bill Freehan 1.00 .45
❑ 398 Elias Sosa .50 .23
❑ 399 Terry Harmon .50 .23
❑ 400 Dick Allen 2.00 .90
❑ 401 Mike Wallace .50 .23
❑ 402 Bob Tolan .50 .23
❑ 403 Tom Buskey .50 .23
❑ 404 Ted Sizemore .50 .23
❑ 405 John Montague .50 .23
❑ 406 Bob Gallagher .50 .23
❑ 407 Herb Washington 2.00 .90
❑ 408 Clyde Wright .50 .23
❑ 409 Bob Robertson .50 .23
❑ 410 Mike Cueller UER 1.00 .45
(Sic, Cuellar)
❑ 411 George Mitterwald .50 .23
❑ 412 Bill Hands .50 .23
❑ 413 Marty Pattin .50 .23
❑ 414 Manny Mota 1.00 .45
❑ 415 John Hiller 1.00 .45
❑ 416 Larry Lintz .50 .23
❑ 417 Skip Lockwood .50 .23
❑ 418 Leo Foster .50 .23
❑ 419 Dave Goltz .50 .23
❑ 420 Larry Bowa 2.00 .90
❑ 421 Mets: Team/Mgr. 3.00 .60
Yogi Berra
(Checklist back)
❑ 422 Brian Downing 1.00 .45
❑ 423 Clay Kirby .50 .23
❑ 424 John Lowenstein .50 .23
❑ 425 Tito Fuentes .50 .23
❑ 426 George Medich .50 .23
❑ 427 Clarence Gaston 1.00 .45
❑ 428 Dave Hamilton .50 .23
❑ 429 Jim Dwyer .50 .23
❑ 430 Luis Tiant 2.00 .90
❑ 431 Rod Gilbreath .50 .23
❑ 432 Ken Berry .50 .23
❑ 433 Larry Demery .50 .23
❑ 434 Bob Locker .50 .23
❑ 435 Dave Nelson .50 .23
❑ 436 Ken Frailing .50 .23
❑ 437 Al Cowens 1.00 .45
❑ 438 Don Carrithers .50 .23
❑ 439 Ed Brinkman .50 .23
❑ 440 Andy Messersmith 1.00 .45
❑ 441 Bobby Heise .50 .23
❑ 442 Maximino Leon .50 .23
❑ 443 Twins: Team/Mgr. 2.00 .40
Frank Quilici
(Checklist back)
❑ 444 Gene Garber 1.00 .45
❑ 445 Felix Millan .50 .23
❑ 446 Bart Johnson .50 .23
❑ 447 Terry Crowley .50 .23
❑ 448 Frank Duffy .50 .23
❑ 449 Charlie Williams .50 .23
❑ 450 Willie McCovey 5.00 2.20
❑ 451 Rick Dempsey 1.00 .45
❑ 452 Angel Mangual .50 .23
❑ 453 Claude Osteen 1.00 .45
❑ 454 Doug Griffin .50 .23
❑ 455 Don Wilson .50 .23
❑ 456 Bob Coluccio .50 .23
❑ 457 Mario Mendoza .50 .23
❑ 458 Ross Grimsley .50 .23
❑ 459 1974 AL Champs 1.00 .45
A's over Orioles
(Second base action
pictured)
❑ 460 Frank Taveras NLCS 2.00 .90
Steve Garvey
❑ 461 Reggie Jackson WS 4.00 1.80
❑ 462 World Series Game 2 1.00 .45
(Dodger dugout)
❑ 463 Rollie Fingers WS 2.00 .90
❑ 464 World Series Game 4 1.00 .45
(A's batter)
❑ 465 Joe Rudi WS 1.00 .45
❑ 466 World Series Summary 2.00 .90
A's do it again;
win third straight
(A's group picture)
❑ 467 Ed Halicki .50 .23
❑ 468 Bobby Mitchell .50 .23
❑ 469 Tom Dettore .50 .23
❑ 470 Jeff Burroughs 1.00 .45
❑ 471 Bob Stinson .50 .23
❑ 472 Bruce Dal Canton .50 .23
❑ 473 Ken McMullen .50 .23
❑ 474 Luke Walker .50 .23
❑ 475 Darrell Evans 1.00 .45
❑ 476 Ed Figueroa .50 .23
❑ 477 Tom Hutton .50 .23
❑ 478 Tom Burgmeier .50 .23
❑ 479 Ken Boswell .50 .23
❑ 480 Carlos May .50 .23
❑ 481 Will McEnaney 1.00 .45
❑ 482 Tom McCraw .50 .23
❑ 483 Steve Ontiveros .50 .23
❑ 484 Glenn Beckert 1.00 .45
❑ 485 Sparky Lyle 1.00 .45
❑ 486 Ray Fosse .50 .23
❑ 487 Astros: Team/Mgr. 2.00 .40
Preston Gomez
(Checklist back)
❑ 488 Bill Travers .50 .23
❑ 489 Cecil Cooper 2.00 .90
❑ 490 Reggie Smith 1.00 .45
❑ 491 Doyle Alexander 1.00 .45
❑ 492 Rich Hebner 1.00 .45
❑ 493 Don Stanhouse .50 .23
❑ 494 Pete LaCock .50 .23
❑ 495 Nelson Briles 1.00 .45
❑ 496 Pepe Frias .50 .23
❑ 497 Jim Nettles .50 .23
❑ 498 Al Downing .50 .23
❑ 499 Marty Perez .50 .23

❑ 500 Nolan Ryan 80.00 36.00
❑ 501 Bill Robinson .... 1.00 .45
❑ 502 Pat Bourque .... .50 .23
❑ 503 Fred Stanley .... .50 .23
❑ 504 Buddy Bradford .... .50 .23
❑ 505 Chris Speier .... .50 .23
❑ 506 Leron Lee .... .50 .23
❑ 507 Tom Carroll .... .50 .23
❑ 508 Bob Hansen .... .50 .23
❑ 509 Dave Hilton .... .50 .23
❑ 510 Vida Blue .... 1.00 .45
❑ 511 Rangers: Team/Mgr. ..... 2.00 .40
Billy Martin
(Checklist back)
❑ 512 Larry Milbourne .... .50 .23
❑ 513 Dick Pole .... .50 .23
❑ 514 Jose Cruz .... 2.00 .90
❑ 515 Manny Sanguillen .... 1.00 .45
❑ 516 Don Hood .... .50 .23
❑ 517 Checklist: 397-528 ...... 3.00 .60
❑ 518 Leo Cardenas .... .50 .23
❑ 519 Jim Todd .... .50 .23
❑ 520 Amos Otis .... 1.00 .45
❑ 521 Dennis Blair .... .50 .23
❑ 522 Gary Sutherland .... .50 .23
❑ 523 Tom Paciorek .... 1.00 .45
❑ 524 John Doherty .... .50 .23
❑ 525 Tom House .... .50 .23
❑ 526 Larry Hisle .... 1.00 .45
❑ 527 Mac Scarce .... .50 .23
❑ 528 Eddie Leon .... .50 .23
❑ 529 Gary Thomasson .... .50 .23
❑ 530 Gaylord Perry 3.00 1.35
❑ 531 Reds: Team/Mgr. .... 4.00 .80
Sparky Anderson
(Checklist back)
❑ 532 Gorman Thomas .... 1.00 .45
❑ 533 Rudy Meoli .... .50 .23
❑ 534 Alex Johnson .... .50 .23
❑ 535 Gene Tenace .... 1.00 .45
❑ 536 Bob Moose .... .50 .23
❑ 537 Tommy Harper .... 1.00 .45
❑ 538 Duffy Dyer .... .50 .23
❑ 539 Jesse Jefferson .... .50 .23
❑ 540 Lou Brock 5.00 2.20
❑ 541 Roger Metzger .... .50 .23
❑ 542 Pete Broberg .... .50 .23
❑ 543 Larry Biittner .... .50 .23
❑ 544 Steve Mingori .... .50 .23
❑ 545 Billy Williams 3.00 1.35
❑ 546 John Knox .... .50 .23
❑ 547 Von Joshua .... .50 .23
❑ 548 Charlie Sands .... .50 .23
❑ 549 Bill Butler .... .50 .23
❑ 550 Ralph Garr .... 1.00 .45
❑ 551 Larry Christenson .... .50 .23
❑ 552 Jack Brohamer .... .50 .23
❑ 553 John Boccabella .... .50 .23
❑ 554 Rich Gossage .... 2.00 .90
❑ 555 Al Oliver .... 2.00 .90
❑ 556 Tim Johnson .... .50 .23
❑ 557 Larry Gura .... .50 .23
❑ 558 Dave Roberts .... .50 .23
❑ 559 Bob Montgomery .... .50 .23
❑ 560 Tony Perez 3.00 1.35
❑ 561 A's: Team/Mgr. .... 2.00 .40
Alvin Dark
(Checklist back)
❑ 562 Gary Nolan .... 1.00 .45
❑ 563 Wilbur Howard .... .50 .23
❑ 564 Tommy Davis .... 1.00 .45
❑ 565 Joe Torre .... 2.00 .90
❑ 566 Ray Burris .... .50 .23
❑ 567 Jim Sundberg .... 2.00 .90
❑ 568 Dale Murray .... .50 .23
❑ 569 Frank White .... 1.00 .45
❑ 570 Jim Wynn .... 1.00 .45
❑ 571 Dave Lemanczyk .... .50 .23
❑ 572 Roger Nelson .... .50 .23
❑ 573 Orlando Pena .... .50 .23
❑ 574 Tony Taylor .... 1.00 .45
❑ 575 Gene Clines .... .50 .23
❑ 576 Phil Roof .... .50 .23
❑ 577 John Morris .... .50 .23
❑ 578 Dave Tomlin .... .50 .23
❑ 579 Skip Pitlock .... .50 .23
❑ 580 Frank Robinson 6.00 2.70
❑ 581 Darrel Chaney .... .50 .23
❑ 582 Eduardo Rodriguez .... .50 .23
❑ 583 Andy Etchebarren .... .50 .23
❑ 584 Mike Garman .... .50 .23
❑ 585 Chris Chambliss .... 1.00 .45
❑ 586 Tim McCarver .... 2.00 .90
❑ 587 Chris Ward .... .50 .23
❑ 588 Rick Auerbach .... .50 .23
❑ 589 Braves: Team/Mgr. ...... 2.00 .40
Clyde King
(Checklist back)
❑ 590 Cesar Cedeno .... 1.00 .45
❑ 591 Glenn Abbott .... .50 .23
❑ 592 Balor Moore .... .50 .23
❑ 593 Gene Lamont .... .50 .23
❑ 594 Jim Fuller .... .50 .23
❑ 595 Joe Niekro .... 1.00 .45
❑ 596 Ollie Brown .... .50 .23
❑ 597 Winston Llenas .... .50 .23
❑ 598 Bruce Kison .... .50 .23
❑ 599 Nate Colbert .... .50 .23
❑ 600 Rod Carew 5.00 2.20
❑ 601 Juan Beniquez .... .50 .23
❑ 602 John Vukovich .... .50 .23
❑ 603 Lew Krausse .... .50 .23
❑ 604 Oscar Zamora .... .50 .23
❑ 605 John Ellis .... .50 .23
❑ 606 Bruce Miller .... .50 .23
❑ 607 Jim Holt .... .50 .23
❑ 608 Gene Michael .... 1.00 .45
❑ 609 Elrod Hendricks .... .50 .23
❑ 610 Ron Hunt .... .50 .23
❑ 611 Yankees: Team/Mgr. .... 2.00 .40
Bill Virdon
(Checklist back)
❑ 612 Terry Hughes .... .50 .23
❑ 613 Bill Parsons .... .50 .23
❑ 614 Rookie Pitchers .... 1.00 .45
Jack Kucek
Dyar Miller
Vern Ruhle
Paul Siebert
❑ 615 Rookie Pitchers .... 2.00 .90
Pat Darcy
Dennis Leonard
Tom Underwood
Hank Webb
❑ 616 Rookie Outfielders...... 12.00 5.50
Dave Augustine
Pepe Mangual
Jim Rice
John Scott
❑ 617 Rookie Infielders .... 2.00 .90
Mike Cubbage
Doug DeCinces
Reggie Sanders
Manny Trillo
❑ 618 Rookie Pitchers .... 1.00 .45
Jamie Easterly
Tom Johnson
Scott McGregor
Rick Rhoden
❑ 619 Rookie Outfielders........ 1.00 .45
Benny Ayala
Nyls Nyman
Tommy Smith
Jerry Turner
❑ 620 Rookie Catcher/OF 20.00 9.00
Gary Carter
Marc Hill
Danny Meyer
Leon Roberts
❑ 621 Rookie Pitchers .... 2.00 .90
John Denny
Rawly Eastwick
Jim Kern
Juan Veintidos
❑ 622 Rookie Outfielders........ 6.00 2.70
Ed Armbrister
Fred Lynn
Tom Poquette
Terry Whitfield UER
(Listed as Ney York)
❑ 623 Rookie Infielders 6.00 2.70
Phil Garner
Keith Hernandez UER
(Sic, bats right)
Bob Sheldon
Tom Veryzer
❑ 624 Rookie Pitchers .... 1.00 .45
Doug Konieczny
Gary Lavelle
Jim Otten
Eddie Solomon
❑ 625 Boog Powell .... 2.00 .90
❑ 626 Larry Haney UER .... .50 .23
(Photo actually
Dave Duncan)
❑ 627 Tom Walker .... .50 .23
❑ 628 Ron LeFlore .... 1.00 .45
❑ 629 Joe Hoerner .... .50 .23
❑ 630 Greg Luzinski .... 2.00 .90
❑ 631 Lee Lacy .... .50 .23
❑ 632 Morris Nettles .... .50 .23
❑ 633 Paul Casanova .... .50 .23
❑ 634 Cy Acosta .... .50 .23
❑ 635 Chuck Dobson .... .50 .23
❑ 636 Charlie Moore .... .50 .23
❑ 637 Ted Martinez .... .50 .23
❑ 638 Cubs: Team/Mgr. .... 2.00 .40
Jim Marshall
(Checklist back)
❑ 639 Steve Kline .... .50 .23
❑ 640 Harmon Killebrew 5.00 2.20
❑ 641 Jim Northrup .... .50 .23
❑ 642 Mike Phillips .... .50 .23
❑ 643 Brent Strom .... .50 .23
❑ 644 Bill Fahey .... .50 .23
❑ 645 Danny Cater .... .50 .23
❑ 646 Checklist: 529-660 ...... 3.00 .60
❑ 647 Claudell Washington .... 2.00 .90
❑ 648 Dave Pagan .... .50 .23
❑ 649 Jack Heidemann .... .50 .23
❑ 650 Dave May .... .50 .23
❑ 651 John Morlan .... .50 .23
❑ 652 Lindy McDaniel .... 1.00 .45
❑ 653 Lee Richard UER .... .50 .23
(Listed as Richards
on card front)
❑ 654 Jerry Terrell .... .50 .23
❑ 655 Rico Carty .... 1.00 .45
❑ 656 Bill Plummer .... .50 .23
❑ 657 Bob Oliver .... .50 .23
❑ 658 Vic Harris .... .50 .23
❑ 659 Bob Apodaca .... .50 .23
❑ 660 Hank Aaron 30.00 9.00

1976 Topps

	NRMT	VG-E
COMPLETE SET (660)	350.00	160.00
COMMON CARD (1-660)	.40	.18

❑ 1 Hank Aaron RB 15.00 4.70
2262 Career RBIs
❑ 2 Bobby Bonds RB .... 1.50 .70
Most leadoff HR's 32;
plus three seasons
30 homers/30 steals
❑ 3 Mickey Lolich RB .... .75 .35
Most Lefthanded Strikeouts: 2679

❑ 4 Dave Lopes RB .75 .35
Most Consecutive SB's: 38
❑ 5 Tom Seaver RB 4.00 1.80
Most Consecutive seasons
with 200 Strikeouts
❑ 6 Rennie Stennett RB .75 .35
7 Hits in a 9 inning game
❑ 7 Jim Umbarger .40 .18
❑ 8 Tito Fuentes .40 .18
❑ 9 Paul Lindblad .40 .18
❑ 10 Lou Brock 4.00 1.80
❑ 11 Jim Hughes .40 .18
❑ 12 Richie Zisk .75 .35
❑ 13 John Wockenfuss .40 .18
❑ 14 Gene Garber .75 .35
❑ 15 George Scott .75 .35
❑ 16 Bob Apodaca .40 .18
❑ 17 New York Yankees 1.50 .30
Team Card;
Billy Martin MG
(Checklist back)
❑ 18 Dale Murray .40 .18
❑ 19 George Brett 50.00 22.00
❑ 20 Bob Watson .75 .35
❑ 21 Dave LaRoche .40 .18
❑ 22 Bill Russell .75 .35
❑ 23 Brian Downing .40 .18
❑ 24 Cesar Geronimo .75 .35
❑ 25 Mike Torrez .75 .35
❑ 26 Andre Thornton .75 .35
❑ 27 Ed Figueroa .40 .18
❑ 28 Dusty Baker 1.50 .70
❑ 29 Rick Burleson .75 .35
❑ 30 John Montefusco .75 .35
❑ 31 Len Randle .40 .18
❑ 32 Danny Frisella .40 .18
❑ 33 Bill North .40 .18
❑ 34 Mike Garman .40 .18
❑ 35 Tony Oliva 1.50 .70
❑ 36 Frank Taveras .40 .18
❑ 37 John Hiller .75 .35
❑ 38 Garry Maddox .75 .35
❑ 39 Pete Broberg .40 .18
❑ 40 Dave Kingman 1.50 .70
❑ 41 Tippy Martinez .75 .35
❑ 42 Barry Foote .40 .18
❑ 43 Paul Splittorff .40 .18
❑ 44 Doug Rader .75 .35
❑ 45 Boog Powell 1.50 .70
❑ 46 Los Angeles Dodgers 1.50 .30
Team Card;
Walter Alston MG
(Checklist back)
❑ 47 Jesse Jefferson .40 .18
❑ 48 Dave Concepcion 1.50 .70
❑ 49 Dave Duncan .40 .18
❑ 50 Fred Lynn 1.50 .70
❑ 51 Ray Burris .40 .18
❑ 52 Dave Chalk .40 .18
❑ 53 Mike Beard .40 .18
❑ 54 Dave Rader .40 .18
❑ 55 Gaylord Perry 2.50 1.10
❑ 56 Bob Tolan .40 .18
❑ 57 Phil Garner .75 .35
❑ 58 Ron Reed .40 .18
❑ 59 Larry Hisle .75 .35
❑ 60 Jerry Reuss .75 .35
❑ 61 Ron LeFlore .75 .35
❑ 62 Johnny Oates .75 .35
❑ 63 Bobby Darwin .40 .18
❑ 64 Jerry Koosman .75 .35
❑ 65 Chris Chambliss .75 .35
❑ 66 Gus Bell FS .75 .35
Buddy Bell
❑ 67 Ray Boone FS .75 .35
Bob Boone
❑ 68 Joe Coleman FS .40 .18
Joe Coleman Jr.
❑ 69 Jim Hegan FS .40 .18
Mike Hegan
❑ 70 Roy Smalley FS .75 .35
Roy Smalley Jr.
❑ 71 Steve Rogers .75 .35
❑ 72 Hal McRae .75 .35
❑ 73 Baltimore Orioles 1.50 .30
Team Card;
Earl Weaver MG
(Checklist back)
❑ 74 Oscar Gamble .75 .35
❑ 75 Larry Dierker .75 .35
❑ 76 Willie Crawford .40 .18
❑ 77 Pedro Borbon .75 .35
❑ 78 Cecil Cooper .75 .35
❑ 79 Jerry Morales .40 .18
❑ 80 Jim Kaat 1.50 .70
❑ 81 Darrell Evans .75 .35
❑ 82 Von Joshua .40 .18
❑ 83 Jim Spencer .40 .18
❑ 84 Brent Strom .40 .18
❑ 85 Mickey Rivers .75 .35
❑ 86 Mike Tyson .40 .18
❑ 87 Tom Burgmeier .40 .18
❑ 88 Duffy Dyer .40 .18
❑ 89 Vern Ruhle .40 .18
❑ 90 Sal Bando .75 .35
❑ 91 Tom Hutton .40 .18
❑ 92 Eduardo Rodriguez .40 .18
❑ 93 Mike Phillips .40 .18
❑ 94 Jim Dwyer .40 .18
❑ 95 Brooks Robinson 5.00 2.20
❑ 96 Doug Bird .40 .18
❑ 97 Wilbur Howard .40 .18
❑ 98 Dennis Eckersley 40.00 18.00
❑ 99 Lee Lacy .40 .18
❑ 100 Jim Hunter 2.50 1.10
❑ 101 Pete LaCock .40 .18
❑ 102 Jim Willoughby .40 .18
❑ 103 Biff Pocoroba .40 .18
❑ 104 Cincinnati Reds 2.50 .50
Team Card;
Sparky Anderson MG
(Checklist back)
❑ 105 Gary Lavelle .40 .18
❑ 106 Tom Grieve .75 .35
❑ 107 Dave Roberts .40 .18
❑ 108 Don Kirkwood .40 .18
❑ 109 Larry Lintz .40 .18
❑ 110 Carlos May .40 .18
❑ 111 Danny Thompson .40 .18
❑ 112 Kent Tekulve 1.50 .70
❑ 113 Gary Sutherland .40 .18
❑ 114 Jay Johnstone .75 .35
❑ 115 Ken Holtzman .75 .35
❑ 116 Charlie Moore .40 .18
❑ 117 Mike Jorgensen .40 .18
❑ 118 Boston Red Sox 1.50 .30
Team Card;
Darrell Johnson MG
(Checklist back)
❑ 119 Checklist 1-132 1.50 .30
❑ 120 Rusty Staub .75 .35
❑ 121 Tony Solaita .40 .18
❑ 122 Mike Cosgrove .40 .18
❑ 123 Walt Williams .40 .18
❑ 124 Doug Rau .40 .18
❑ 125 Don Baylor 1.50 .70
❑ 126 Tom Dettore .40 .18
❑ 127 Larvell Blanks .40 .18
❑ 128 Ken Griffey 2.50 1.10
❑ 129 Andy Etchebarren .40 .18
❑ 130 Luis Tiant 1.50 .70
❑ 131 Bill Stein .40 .18
❑ 132 Don Hood .40 .18
❑ 133 Gary Matthews .75 .35
❑ 134 Mike Ivie .40 .18
❑ 135 Bake McBride .75 .35
❑ 136 Dave Goltz .40 .18
❑ 137 Bill Robinson .75 .35
❑ 138 Lerrin LaGrow .40 .18
❑ 139 Gorman Thomas .75 .35
❑ 140 Vida Blue .75 .35
❑ 141 Larry Parrish 1.50 .70
❑ 142 Dick Drago .40 .18
❑ 143 Jerry Grote .40 .18
❑ 144 Al Fitzmorris .40 .18
❑ 145 Larry Bowa .75 .35
❑ 146 George Medich .40 .18
❑ 147 Houston Astros 1.50 .30
Team Card;
Bill Virdon MG
(Checklist back)
❑ 148 Stan Thomas .40 .18
❑ 149 Tommy Davis .75 .35
❑ 150 Steve Garvey 2.50 1.10
❑ 151 Bill Bonham .40 .18
❑ 152 Leroy Stanton .40 .18
❑ 153 Buzz Capra .40 .18
❑ 154 Bucky Dent .75 .35
❑ 155 Jack Billingham .75 .35
❑ 156 Rico Carty .75 .35
❑ 157 Mike Caldwell .40 .18
❑ 158 Ken Reitz .40 .18
❑ 159 Jerry Terrell .40 .18
❑ 160 Dave Winfield 12.00 5.50
❑ 161 Bruce Kison .40 .18
❑ 162 Jack Pierce .40 .18
❑ 163 Jim Slaton .40 .18
❑ 164 Pepe Mangual .40 .18
❑ 165 Gene Tenace .75 .35
❑ 166 Skip Lockwood .40 .18
❑ 167 Freddie Patek .75 .35
❑ 168 Tom Hilgendorf .40 .18
❑ 169 Graig Nettles 1.50 .70
❑ 170 Rick Wise .40 .18
❑ 171 Greg Gross .40 .18
❑ 172 Texas Rangers 1.50 .30
Team Card;
Frank Lucchesi MG
(Checklist back)
❑ 173 Steve Swisher .40 .18
❑ 174 Charlie Hough .75 .35
❑ 175 Ken Singleton .75 .35
❑ 176 Dick Lange .40 .18
❑ 177 Marty Perez .40 .18
❑ 178 Tom Buskey .40 .18
❑ 179 George Foster 1.50 .70
❑ 180 Rich Gossage 1.50 .70
❑ 181 Willie Montanez .40 .18
❑ 182 Harry Rasmussen .40 .18
❑ 183 Steve Braun .40 .18
❑ 184 Bill Greif .40 .18
❑ 185 Dave Parker 1.50 .70
❑ 186 Tom Walker .40 .18
❑ 187 Pedro Garcia .40 .18
❑ 188 Fred Scherman .40 .18
❑ 189 Claudell Washington .75 .35
❑ 190 Jon Matlack .40 .18
❑ 191 NL Batting Leaders .75 .35
Bill Madlock
Ted Simmons
Manny Sanguillen
❑ 192 AL Batting Leaders 2.50 1.10
Rod Carew
Fred Lynn
Thurman Munson
❑ 193 NL Home Run Leaders 3.00 1.35
Mike Schmidt
Dave Kingman
Greg Luzinski
❑ 194 AL Home Run Leaders 2.50 1.10
Reggie Jackson
George Scott
John Mayberry
❑ 195 NL RBI Leaders 1.50 .70
Greg Luzinski
Johnny Bench
Tony Perez
❑ 196 AL RBI Leaders .75 .35
George Scott
John Mayberry
Fred Lynn
❑ 197 NL Steals Leaders 1.50 .70
Dave Lopes
Joe Morgan
Lou Brock
❑ 198 AL Steals Leaders .75 .35
Mickey Rivers
Claudell Washington
Amos Otis
❑ 199 NL Victory Leaders 1.50 .70
Tom Seaver
Randy Jones
Andy Messersmith
❑ 200 AL Victory Leaders 1.50 .70
Jim Hunter
Jim Palmer
Vida Blue

❑ 201 NL ERA Leaders .... 1.50 .70
Randy Jones
Andy Messersmith
Tom Seaver
❑ 202 AL ERA Leaders 5.00 2.20
Jim Palmer
Jim Hunter
Dennis Eckersley
❑ 203 NL Strikeout Leaders .. 1.50 .70
Tom Seaver
John Montefusco
Andy Messersmith
❑ 204 AL Strikeout Leaders...... .75 .35
Frank Tanana
Bert Blyleven
Gaylord Perry
❑ 205 Leading Firemen .... .75 .35
Al Hrabosky
Rich Gossage
❑ 206 Manny Trillo.................... .40 .18
❑ 207 Andy Hassler.................. .40 .18
❑ 208 Mike Lum......................... .40 .18
❑ 209 Alan Ashby .... .75 .35
❑ 210 Lee May .... .75 .35
❑ 211 Clay Carroll .... .75 .35
❑ 212 Pat Kelly .... .40 .18
❑ 213 Dave Heaverlo .... .40 .18
❑ 214 Eric Soderholm .... .40 .18
❑ 215 Reggie Smith..................... .75 .35
❑ 216 Montreal Expos .... 1.50 .30
Team Card;
Karl Kuehl MG
(Checklist back)
❑ 217 Dave Freisleben .... .40 .18
❑ 218 John Knox .... .40 .18
❑ 219 Tom Murphy .... .40 .18
❑ 220 Manny Sanguillen .... .75 .35
❑ 221 Jim Todd .... .40 .18
❑ 222 Wayne Garrett................... .40 .18
❑ 223 Ollie Brown .... .40 .18
❑ 224 Jim York .... .40 .18
❑ 225 Roy White .... .75 .35
❑ 226 Jim Sundberg .... .75 .35
❑ 227 Oscar Zamora .... .40 .18
❑ 228 John Hale .... .40 .18
❑ 229 Jerry Remy .... .40 .18
❑ 230 Carl Yastrzemski 5.00 2.20
❑ 231 Tom House .... .40 .18
❑ 232 Frank Duffy .... .40 .18
❑ 233 Grant Jackson .... .40 .18
❑ 234 Mike Sadek .... .40 .18
❑ 235 Bert Blyleven .... 1.50 .70
❑ 236 Kansas City Royals ...... 1.50 .30
Team Card;
Whitey Herzog MG
(Checklist back)
❑ 237 Dave Hamilton.................. .40 .18
❑ 238 Larry Biittner .... .40 .18
❑ 239 John Curtis .... .40 .18
❑ 240 Pete Rose 12.00 5.50
❑ 241 Hector Torres .... .40 .18
❑ 242 Dan Meyer......................... .40 .18
❑ 243 Jim Rooker .... .40 .18
❑ 244 Bill Sharp........................... .40 .18
❑ 245 Felix Millan .... .40 .18
❑ 246 Cesar Tovar .... .40 .18
❑ 247 Terry Harmon .... .40 .18
❑ 248 Dick Tidrow .... .40 .18
❑ 249 Cliff Johnson .... .75 .35
❑ 250 Fergie Jenkins 2.50 1.10
❑ 251 Rick Monday .... .75 .35
❑ 252 Tim Nordbrook .... .40 .18
❑ 253 Bill Buckner .... .75 .35
❑ 254 Rudy Meoli .... .40 .18
❑ 255 Fritz Peterson .... .40 .18
❑ 256 Rowland Office .... .40 .18
❑ 257 Ross Grimsley .... .40 .18
❑ 258 Nyls Nyman....................... .40 .18
❑ 259 Darrel Chaney .... .40 .18
❑ 260 Steve Busby .... .40 .18
❑ 261 Gary Thomasson.............. .40 .18
❑ 262 Checklist 133-264 .... 1.50 .30
❑ 263 Lyman Bostock .... 1.50 .70
❑ 264 Steve Renko .... .40 .18
❑ 265 Willie Davis .... .75 .35
❑ 266 Alan Foster .... .40 .18
❑ 267 Aurelio Rodriguez .... .40 .18
❑ 268 Del Unser .... .40 .18
❑ 269 Rick Austin .... .40 .18
❑ 270 Willie Stargell 3.00 1.35
❑ 271 Jim Lonborg .... .75 .35
❑ 272 Rick Dempsey .... .75 .35
❑ 273 Joe Niekro .... .75 .35
❑ 274 Tommy Harper .... .75 .35
❑ 275 Rick Manning .... .40 .18
❑ 276 Mickey Scott .... .40 .18
❑ 277 Chicago Cubs .... 1.50 .30
Team Card;
Jim Marshall MG
(Checklist back)
❑ 278 Bernie Carbo .... .40 .18
❑ 279 Roy Howell .... .40 .18
❑ 280 Burt Hooton .... .75 .35
❑ 281 Dave May .... .40 .18
❑ 282 Dan Osborn .... .40 .18
❑ 283 Merv Rettenmund .... .40 .18
❑ 284 Steve Ontiveros .... .40 .18
❑ 285 Mike Cuellar .... .75 .35
❑ 286 Jim Wohlford .... .40 .18
❑ 287 Pete Mackanin .... .40 .18
❑ 288 Bill Campbell .... .40 .18
❑ 289 Enzo Hernandez .... .40 .18
❑ 290 Ted Simmons .... .75 .35
❑ 291 Ken Sanders .... .40 .18
❑ 292 Leon Roberts .... .40 .18
❑ 293 Bill Castro .... .40 .18
❑ 294 Ed Kirkpatrick .... .40 .18
❑ 295 Dave Cash .... .40 .18
❑ 296 Pat Dobson .... .40 .18
❑ 297 Roger Metzger .... .40 .18
❑ 298 Dick Bosman .... .40 .18
❑ 299 Champ Summers .... .40 .18
❑ 300 Johnny Bench 8.00 3.60
❑ 301 Jackie Brown .... .40 .18
❑ 302 Rick Miller .... .40 .18
❑ 303 Steve Foucault .... .40 .18
❑ 304 California Angels .... 1.50 .30
Team Card;
Dick Williams MG
(Checklist back)
❑ 305 Andy Messersmith .... .75 .35
❑ 306 Rod Gilbreath .... .40 .18
❑ 307 Al Bumbry .... .75 .35
❑ 308 Jim Barr .... .40 .18
❑ 309 Bill Melton .... .40 .18
❑ 310 Randy Jones .... .75 .35
❑ 311 Cookie Rojas .... .75 .35
❑ 312 Don Carrithers .... .40 .18
❑ 313 Dan Ford .... .40 .18
❑ 314 Ed Kranepool .... .40 .18
❑ 315 Al Hrabosky .... .75 .35
❑ 316 Robin Yount 25.00 11.00
❑ 317 John Candelaria .... 1.50 .70
❑ 318 Bob Boone .... 1.50 .70
❑ 319 Larry Gura .... .40 .18
❑ 320 Willie Horton .... .75 .35
❑ 321 Jose Cruz .... 1.50 .70
❑ 322 Glenn Abbott .... .40 .18
❑ 323 Rob Sperring .... .40 .18
❑ 324 Jim Bibby .... .40 .18
❑ 325 Tony Perez 2.50 1.10
❑ 326 Dick Pole .... .40 .18
❑ 327 Dave Moates .... .40 .18
❑ 328 Carl Morton .... .40 .18
❑ 329 Joe Ferguson .... .40 .18
❑ 330 Nolan Ryan 60.00 27.00
❑ 331 San Diego Padres .... 1.50 .30
Team Card;
John McNamara MG
(Checklist back)
❑ 332 Charlie Williams .... .40 .18
❑ 333 Bob Coluccio .... .40 .18
❑ 334 Dennis Leonard .... .75 .35
❑ 335 Bob Grich .... .75 .35
❑ 336 Vic Albury .... .40 .18
❑ 337 Bud Harrelson .... .75 .35
❑ 338 Bob Bailey .... .40 .18
❑ 339 John Denny .... .75 .35
❑ 340 Jim Rice 4.00 1.80
❑ 341 Lou Gehrig ATG 12.00 5.50
❑ 342 Rogers Hornsby ATG .. 3.00 1.35
❑ 343 Pie Traynor ATG .... 1.50 .70
❑ 344 Honus Wagner ATG 5.00 2.20
❑ 345 Babe Ruth ATG 15.00 6.75
❑ 346 Ty Cobb ATG 8.00 3.60
❑ 347 Ted Williams ATG 10.00 4.50
❑ 348 Mickey Cochrane ATG 1.50 .70
❑ 349 Walter Johnson ATG.... 3.00 1.35
❑ 350 Lefty Grove ATG .... 1.50 .70
❑ 351 Randy Hundley .... .75 .35
❑ 352 Dave Giusti .... .40 .18
❑ 353 Sixto Lezcano .... .75 .35
❑ 354 Ron Blomberg .... .40 .18
❑ 355 Steve Carlton 5.00 2.20
❑ 356 Ted Martinez .... .40 .18
❑ 357 Ken Forsch .... .40 .18
❑ 358 Buddy Bell .... .75 .35
❑ 359 Rick Reuschel .... .75 .35
❑ 360 Jeff Burroughs .... .75 .35
❑ 361 Detroit Tigers .... 1.50 .30
Team Card;
Ralph Houk MG
(Checklist back)
❑ 362 Will McEnaney .... .75 .35
❑ 363 Dave Collins .... .75 .35
❑ 364 Elias Sosa .... .40 .18
❑ 365 Carlton Fisk 6.00 2.70
❑ 366 Bobby Valentine .... .75 .35
❑ 367 Bruce Miller .... .40 .18
❑ 368 Wilbur Wood .... .40 .18
❑ 369 Frank White .... .75 .35
❑ 370 Ron Cey .... .75 .35
❑ 371 Elrod Hendricks .... .40 .18
❑ 372 Rick Baldwin .... .40 .18
❑ 373 Johnny Briggs .... .40 .18
❑ 374 Dan Warthen .... .40 .18
❑ 375 Ron Fairly .... .75 .35
❑ 376 Rich Hebner .... .75 .35
❑ 377 Mike Hegan .... .40 .18
❑ 378 Steve Stone .... .75 .35
❑ 379 Ken Boswell .... .40 .18
❑ 380 Bobby Bonds .... 1.50 .70
❑ 381 Denny Doyle .... .40 .18
❑ 382 Matt Alexander .... .40 .18
❑ 383 John Ellis .... .40 .18
❑ 384 Philadelphia Phillies .... 1.50 .30
Team Card;
Danny Ozark MG
(Checklist back)
❑ 385 Mickey Lolich .... .75 .35
❑ 386 Ed Goodson .... .40 .18
❑ 387 Mike Miley .... .40 .18
❑ 388 Stan Perzanowski .... .40 .18
❑ 389 Glenn Adams .... .40 .18
❑ 390 Don Gullett .... .75 .35
❑ 391 Jerry Hairston .... .40 .18
❑ 392 Checklist 265-396 .... 1.50 .30
❑ 393 Paul Mitchell .... .40 .18
❑ 394 Fran Healy .... .40 .18
❑ 395 Jim Wynn .... .75 .35
❑ 396 Bill Lee .... .40 .18
❑ 397 Tim Foli .... .40 .18
❑ 398 Dave Tomlin .... .40 .18
❑ 399 Luis Melendez .... .40 .18
❑ 400 Rod Carew 4.00 1.80
❑ 401 Ken Brett .... .40 .18
❑ 402 Don Money .... .75 .35
❑ 403 Geoff Zahn .... .40 .18
❑ 404 Enos Cabell .... .40 .18
❑ 405 Rollie Fingers 2.50 1.10
❑ 406 Ed Herrmann .... .40 .18
❑ 407 Tom Underwood .... .40 .18
❑ 408 Charlie Spikes .... .40 .18
❑ 409 Dave Lemanczyk .... .40 .18
❑ 410 Ralph Garr .... .75 .35
❑ 411 Bill Singer .... .40 .18
❑ 412 Toby Harrah .... .75 .35
❑ 413 Pete Varney .... .40 .18
❑ 414 Wayne Garland .... .40 .18
❑ 415 Vada Pinson .... 1.50 .70
❑ 416 Tommy John .... 1.50 .70
❑ 417 Gene Clines .... .40 .18
❑ 418 Jose Morales .... .40 .18
❑ 419 Reggie Cleveland .... .40 .18
❑ 420 Joe Morgan 4.00 1.80

❑ 421 Oakland A's .... 1.50 .30
Team Card;
(No MG on front;
checklist back)
❑ 422 Johnny Grubb .... .40 .18
❑ 423 Ed Halicki .... .40 .18
❑ 424 Phil Roof .... .40 .18
❑ 425 Rennie Stennett .... .40 .18
❑ 426 Bob Forsch .... .40 .18
❑ 427 Kurt Bevacqua................ .40 .18
❑ 428 Jim Crawford.................. .40 .18
❑ 429 Fred Stanley .... .40 .18
❑ 430 Jose Cardenal................ .75 .35
❑ 431 Dick Ruthven.................. .40 .18
❑ 432 Tom Veryzer .... .40 .18
❑ 433 Rick Waits .... .40 .18
❑ 434 Morris Nettles .... .40 .18
❑ 435 Phil Niekro.................... 2.50 1.10
❑ 436 Bill Fahey .... .40 .18
❑ 437 Terry Forster .... .40 .18
❑ 438 Doug DeCinces.............. .75 .35
❑ 439 Rick Rhoden .... .75 .35
❑ 440 John Mayberry .... .75 .35
❑ 441 Gary Carter 5.00 2.20
❑ 442 Hank Webb .... .40 .18
❑ 443 San Francisco Giants .. 1.50 .30
Team Card;
(No MG on front;
checklist back)
❑ 444 Gary Nolan .... .75 .35
❑ 445 Rico Petrocelli .... .75 .35
❑ 446 Larry Haney.................... .40 .18
❑ 447 Gene Locklear................ .75 .35
❑ 448 Tom Johnson .... .40 .18
❑ 449 Bob Robertson .... .40 .18
❑ 450 Jim Palmer 4.00 1.80
❑ 451 Buddy Bradford.............. .40 .18
❑ 452 Tom Hausman................. .40 .18
❑ 453 Lou Piniella .... 1.50 .70
❑ 454 Tom Griffin .... .40 .18
❑ 455 Dick Allen .... 1.50 .70
❑ 456 Joe Coleman................... .40 .18
❑ 457 Ed Crosby .... .40 .18
❑ 458 Earl Williams .... .40 .18
❑ 459 Jim Brewer .... .40 .18
❑ 460 Cesar Cedeno................. .75 .35
❑ 461 NL and AL Champs......... .75 .35
Reds sweep Bucs,
Bosox surprise A's
❑ 462 '75 World Series .... .75 .35
Reds Champs
❑ 463 Steve Hargan .... .40 .18
❑ 464 Ken Henderson............... .40 .18
❑ 465 Mike Marshall .... .75 .35
❑ 466 Bob Stinson..................... .40 .18
❑ 467 Woodie Fryman.............. .40 .18
❑ 468 Jesus Alou...................... .40 .18
❑ 469 Rawly Eastwick.............. .75 .35
❑ 470 Bobby Murcer .... .75 .35
❑ 471 Jim Burton....................... .40 .18
❑ 472 Bob Davis .... .40 .18
❑ 473 Paul Blair........................ .75 .35
❑ 474 Ray Corbin .... .40 .18
❑ 475 Joe Rudi .... .75 .35
❑ 476 Bob Moose .... 1.50 .70
❑ 477 Cleveland Indians .... 1.50 .30
Team Card;
Frank Robinson MG
(Checklist back)
❑ 478 Lynn McGlothen .... .40 .18
❑ 479 Bobby Mitchell................ .40 .18
❑ 480 Mike Schmidt............. 25.00 11.00
❑ 481 Rudy May .... .40 .18
❑ 482 Tim Hosley .... .40 .18
❑ 483 Mickey Stanley .... .40 .18
❑ 484 Eric Raich .... .40 .18
❑ 485 Mike Hargrove................ .75 .35
❑ 486 Bruce Dal Canton .... .40 .18
❑ 487 Leron Lee .... .40 .18
❑ 488 Claude Osteen .... .75 .35
❑ 489 Skip Jutze .... .40 .18
❑ 490 Frank Tanana .... .75 .35
❑ 491 Terry Crowley .... .40 .18
❑ 492 Marty Pattin..................... .40 .18
❑ 493 Derrel Thomas .... .40 .18
❑ 494 Craig Swan .... .75 .35
❑ 495 Nate Colbert .... .40 .18
❑ 496 Juan Beniquez .... .40 .18
❑ 497 Joe McIntosh................... .40 .18
❑ 498 Glenn Borgmann............ .40 .18
❑ 499 Mario Guerrero .... .40 .18
❑ 500 Reggie Jackson.......... 12.00 5.50
❑ 501 Billy Champion .... .40 .18
❑ 502 Tim McCarver .... 1.50 .70
❑ 503 Elliott Maddox .... .40 .18
❑ 504 Pittsburgh Pirates .... 1.50 .30
Team Card;
Danny Murtaugh MG
(Checklist back)
❑ 505 Mark Belanger................ .75 .35
❑ 506 George Mitterwald.......... .40 .18
❑ 507 Ray Bare .... .40 .18
❑ 508 Duane Kuiper .... .40 .18
❑ 509 Bill Hands .... .40 .18
❑ 510 Amos Otis .... .75 .35
❑ 511 Jamie Easterley.............. .40 .18
❑ 512 Ellie Rodriguez .... .40 .18
❑ 513 Bart Johnson................... .40 .18
❑ 514 Dan Driessen .... .75 .35
❑ 515 Steve Yeager .... .75 .35
❑ 516 Wayne Granger.............. .40 .18
❑ 517 John Milner .... .40 .18
❑ 518 Doug Flynn .... .40 .18
❑ 519 Steve Brye....................... .40 .18
❑ 520 Willie McCovey 4.00 1.80
❑ 521 Jim Colborn..................... .40 .18
❑ 522 Ted Sizemore .... .40 .18
❑ 523 Bob Montgomery........... .40 .18
❑ 524 Pete Falcone................... .40 .18
❑ 525 Billy Williams 2.50 1.10
❑ 526 Checklist 397-528 .... 1.50 .30
❑ 527 Mike Anderson .... .40 .18
❑ 528 Dock Ellis .... .40 .18
❑ 529 Deron Johnson .... .75 .35
❑ 530 Don Sutton 2.50 1.10
❑ 531 New York Mets .... 1.50 .30
Team Card;
Joe Frazier MG
(Checklist back)
❑ 532 Milt May........................... .40 .18
❑ 533 Lee Richard..................... .40 .18
❑ 534 Stan Bahnsen .... .40 .18
❑ 535 Dave Nelson.................... .40 .18
❑ 536 Mike Thompson.............. .40 .18
❑ 537 Tony Muser..................... .40 .18
❑ 538 Pat Darcy .... .40 .18
❑ 539 John Balaz .... .75 .35
❑ 540 Bill Freehan..................... .75 .35
❑ 541 Steve Mingori .... .40 .18
❑ 542 Keith Hernandez .... 1.50 .70
❑ 543 Wayne Twitchell .... .40 .18
❑ 544 Pepe Frias....................... .40 .18
❑ 545 Sparky Lyle .... .75 .35
❑ 546 Dave Rosello................... .40 .18
❑ 547 Roric Harrison .... .40 .18
❑ 548 Manny Mota .... .75 .35
❑ 549 Randy Tate .... .40 .18
❑ 550 Hank Aaron 25.00 11.00
❑ 551 Jerry DaVanon .... .40 .18
❑ 552 Terry Humphrey .... .40 .18
❑ 553 Randy Moffitt .... .40 .18
❑ 554 Ray Fosse....................... .40 .18
❑ 555 Dyar Miller....................... .40 .18
❑ 556 Minnesota Twins .... 1.50 .30
Team Card;
Gene Mauch MG
(Checklist back)
❑ 557 Dan Spillner.................... .40 .18
❑ 558 Clarence Gaston .... .75 .35
❑ 559 Clyde Wright .... .40 .18
❑ 560 Jorge Orta....................... .40 .18
❑ 561 Tom Carroll..................... .40 .18
❑ 562 Adrian Garrett .... .40 .18
❑ 563 Larry Demery .... .40 .18
❑ 564 Bubble Gum Champ .... 1.50 .70
Kurt Bevacqua
❑ 565 Tug McGraw .... .75 .35
❑ 566 Ken McMullen .... .40 .18
❑ 567 George Stone .... .40 .18
❑ 568 Rob Andrews.................. .40 .18
❑ 569 Nelson Briles .... .75 .35
❑ 570 George Hendrick........... .75 .35
❑ 571 Don DeMola .... .40 .18
❑ 572 Rich Coggins.................. .40 .18
❑ 573 Bill Travers .... .40 .18
❑ 574 Don Kessinger............... .75 .35
❑ 575 Dwight Evans .... 1.50 .70
❑ 576 Maximino Leon .... .40 .18
❑ 577 Marc Hill .... .40 .18
❑ 578 Ted Kubiak .... .40 .18
❑ 579 Clay Kirby .... .40 .18
❑ 580 Bert Campaneris .... .75 .35
❑ 581 St. Louis Cardinals ...... 1.50 .30
Team Card;
Red Schoendienst MG
(Checklist back)
❑ 582 Mike Kekich.................... .40 .18
❑ 583 Tommy Helms................ .40 .18
❑ 584 Stan Wall .... .40 .18
❑ 585 Joe Torre...................... 1.50 .70
❑ 586 Ron Schueler .... .40 .18
❑ 587 Leo Cardenas .... .40 .18
❑ 588 Kevin Kobel.................... .40 .18
❑ 589 Rookie Pitchers .... 1.50 .70
Santo Alcala
Mike Flanagan
Joe Pactwa
Pablo Torrealba
❑ 590 Rookie Outfielders.......... .75 .35
Henry Cruz
Chet Lemon
Ellis Valentine
Terry Whitfield
❑ 591 Rookie Pitchers.............. .75 .35
Steve Grilli
Craig Mitchell
Jose Sosa
George Throop
❑ 592 Rookie Infielders 6.00 2.70
Willie Randolph
Dave McKay
Jerry Royster
Roy Staiger
❑ 593 Rookie Pitchers.............. .75 .35
Larry Anderson
Ken Crosby
Mark Littell
Butch Metzger
❑ 594 Rookie Catchers/OF ...... .75 .35
Andy Merchant
Ed Ott
Royle Stillman
Jerry White
❑ 595 Rookie Pitchers.............. .75 .35
Art DeFillipis
Randy Lerch
Sid Monge
Steve Barr
❑ 596 Rookie Infielders .... .75 .35
Craig Reynolds
Lamar Johnson
Johnnie LeMaster
Jerry Manuel
❑ 597 Rookie Pitchers.............. .75 .35
Don Aase
Jack Kucek
Frank LaCorte
Mike Pazik
❑ 598 Rookie Outfielders.......... .75 .35
Hector Cruz
Jamie Quirk
Jerry Turner
Joe Wallis
❑ 599 Rookie Pitchers........... 6.00 2.70
Rob Dressler
Ron Guidry
Bob McClure
Pat Zachry
❑ 600 Tom Seaver................. 8.00 3.60
❑ 601 Ken Rudolph .... .40 .18
❑ 602 Doug Konieczny .... .40 .18
❑ 603 Jim Holt........................... .40 .18
❑ 604 Joe Lovitto...................... .40 .18
❑ 605 Al Downing .... .40 .18
❑ 606 Milwaukee Brewers...... 1.50 .30
Team Card;

Alex Grammas MG
(Checklist back)
❑ 607 Rich Hinton .40 .18
❑ 608 Vic Correll .40 .18
❑ 609 Fred Norman .75 .35
❑ 610 Greg Luzinski 1.50 .70
❑ 611 Rich Folkers .40 .18
❑ 612 Joe Lahoud .40 .18
❑ 613 Tim Johnson .40 .18
❑ 614 Fernando Arroyo .40 .18
❑ 615 Mike Cubbage .40 .18
❑ 616 Buck Martinez .40 .18
❑ 617 Darold Knowles .40 .18
❑ 618 Jack Brohamer .40 .18
❑ 619 Bill Butler .40 .18
❑ 620 Al Oliver .75 .35
❑ 621 Tom Hall .40 .18
❑ 622 Rick Auerbach .40 .18
❑ 623 Bob Allietta .40 .18
❑ 624 Tony Taylor .75 .35
❑ 625 J.R. Richard .75 .35
❑ 626 Bob Sheldon .40 .18
❑ 627 Bill Plummer .40 .18
❑ 628 John D'Acquisto .40 .18
❑ 629 Sandy Alomar .75 .35
❑ 630 Chris Speier .40 .18
❑ 631 Atlanta Braves 1.50 .30
Team Card;
Dave Bristol MG
(Checklist back)
❑ 632 Rogelio Moret .40 .18
❑ 633 John Stearns .75 .35
❑ 634 Larry Christenson .40 .18
❑ 635 Jim Fregosi .75 .35
❑ 636 Joe Decker .40 .18
❑ 637 Bruce Bochte .40 .18
❑ 638 Doyle Alexander .75 .35
❑ 639 Fred Kendall .40 .18
❑ 640 Bill Madlock 1.50 .70
❑ 641 Tom Paciorek .75 .35
❑ 642 Dennis Blair .40 .18
❑ 643 Checklist 529-660 1.50 .30
❑ 644 Tom Bradley .40 .18
❑ 645 Darrell Porter .75 .35
❑ 646 John Lowenstein .40 .18
❑ 647 Ramon Hernandez .40 .18
❑ 648 Al Cowens .40 .18
❑ 649 Dave Roberts .40 .18
❑ 650 Thurman Munson 5.00 2.20
❑ 651 John Odom .40 .18
❑ 652 Ed Armbrister .40 .18
❑ 653 Mike Norris .75 .35
❑ 654 Doug Griffin .40 .18
❑ 655 Mike Vail .40 .18
❑ 656 Chicago White Sox 1.50 .30
Team Card;
Chuck Tanner MG
(Checklist back)
❑ 657 Roy Smalley .75 .35
❑ 658 Jerry Johnson .40 .18
❑ 659 Ben Oglivie .75 .35
❑ 660 Dave Lopes 1.50 .30

1976 Topps Traded

	NRMT	VG-E
COMPLETE SET (44)	20.00	9.00
COMMON CARD	.25	.11

❑ 27T Ed Figueroa .25 .11
❑ 28T Dusty Baker 1.00 .45
❑ 44T Doug Rader .50 .23
❑ 58T Ron Reed .25 .11
❑ 74T Oscar Gamble 1.00 .45
❑ 80T Jim Kaat 1.00 .45
❑ 83T Jim Spencer .25 .11
❑ 85T Mickey Rivers .50 .23
❑ 99T Lee Lacy .25 .11
❑ 120T Rusty Staub .50 .23
❑ 127T Larvell Blanks .25 .11
❑ 146T George Medich .25 .11
❑ 158T Ken Reitz .25 .11
❑ 208T Mike Lum .25 .11
❑ 211T Clay Carroll .25 .11
❑ 231T Tom House .25 .11
❑ 250T Fergie Jenkins 2.50 1.10
❑ 259T Darrel Chaney .25 .11
❑ 292T Leon Roberts .25 .11
❑ 296T Pat Dobson .25 .11
❑ 309T Bill Melton .25 .11
❑ 338T Bob Bailey .25 .11
❑ 380T Bobby Bonds 1.00 .45
❑ 383T John Ellis .25 .11
❑ 385T Mickey Lolich .50 .23
❑ 401T Ken Brett .25 .11
❑ 410T Ralph Garr .50 .23
❑ 411T Bill Singer .25 .11
❑ 428T Jim Crawford .25 .11
❑ 434T Morris Nettles .25 .11
❑ 464T Ken Henderson .25 .11
❑ 497T Joe McIntosh .25 .11
❑ 524T Pete Falcone .25 .11
❑ 527T Mike Anderson .25 .11
❑ 528T Dock Ellis .25 .11
❑ 532T Milt May .25 .11
❑ 554T Ray Fosse .25 .11
❑ 579T Clay Kirby .25 .11
❑ 583T Tommy Helms .25 .11
❑ 592T Willie Randolph 4.00 1.80
❑ 618T Jack Brohamer .25 .11
❑ 632T Rogelio Moret .25 .11
❑ 649T Dave Roberts .25 .11
❑ NNO Traded Checklist 1.50 .30

1977 Topps

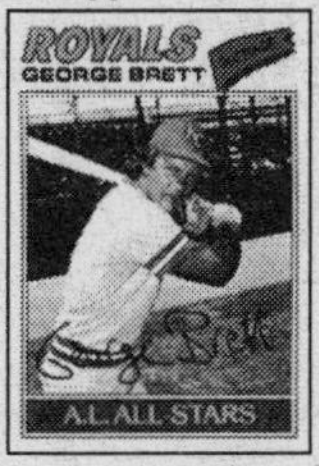

	NRMT	VG-E
COMPLETE SET (660)	250.00	110.00
COMMON CARD (1-660)	.30	.14

❑ 1 Batting Leaders 8.00 2.30
George Brett
Bill Madlock
❑ 2 Home Run Leaders 2.50 1.10
Graig Nettles
Mike Schmidt
❑ 3 RBI Leaders 1.50 .70
Lee May
George Foster
❑ 4 Stolen Base Leaders .75 .35
Bill North
Dave Lopes
❑ 5 Victory Leaders 1.50 .70
Jim Palmer
Randy Jones
❑ 6 Strikeout Leaders 15.00 6.75
Nolan Ryan
Tom Seaver
❑ 7 ERA Leaders .75 .35
Mark Fidrych
John Denny
❑ 8 Leading Firemen .75 .35
Bill Campbell
Rawly Eastwick
❑ 9 Doug Rader .30 .14
❑ 10 Reggie Jackson 10.00 4.50
❑ 11 Rob Dressler .30 .14
❑ 12 Larry Haney .30 .14
❑ 13 Luis Gomez .30 .14
❑ 14 Tommy Smith .30 .14
❑ 15 Don Gullett .75 .35
❑ 16 Bob Jones .30 .14
❑ 17 Steve Stone .75 .35
❑ 18 Indians Team/Mgr. 1.50 .30
Frank Robinson
(Checklist back)
❑ 19 John D'Acquisto .30 .14
❑ 20 Graig Nettles 1.50 .70
❑ 21 Ken Forsch .30 .14
❑ 22 Bill Freehan .75 .35
❑ 23 Dan Driessen .30 .14
❑ 24 Carl Morton .30 .14
❑ 25 Dwight Evans 1.50 .70
❑ 26 Ray Sadecki .30 .14
❑ 27 Bill Buckner .75 .35
❑ 28 Woodie Fryman .30 .14
❑ 29 Bucky Dent .75 .35
❑ 30 Greg Luzinski 1.50 .70
❑ 31 Jim Todd .30 .14
❑ 32 Checklist 1-132 1.50 .30
❑ 33 Wayne Garland .30 .14
❑ 34 Angels Team/Mgr. 1.50 .30
Norm Sherry
(Checklist back)
❑ 35 Rennie Stennett .30 .14
❑ 36 John Ellis .30 .14
❑ 37 Steve Hargan .30 .14
❑ 38 Craig Kusick .30 .14
❑ 39 Tom Griffin .30 .14
❑ 40 Bobby Murcer .75 .35
❑ 41 Jim Kern .30 .14
❑ 42 Jose Cruz .75 .35
❑ 43 Ray Bare .30 .14
❑ 44 Bud Harrelson .75 .35
❑ 45 Rawly Eastwick .30 .14
❑ 46 Buck Martinez .30 .14
❑ 47 Lynn McGlothen .30 .14
❑ 48 Tom Paciorek .75 .35
❑ 49 Grant Jackson .30 .14
❑ 50 Ron Cey .75 .35
❑ 51 Brewers Team/Mgr. 1.50 .30
Alex Grammas
(Checklist back)
❑ 52 Ellis Valentine .30 .14
❑ 53 Paul Mitchell .30 .14
❑ 54 Sandy Alomar .75 .35
❑ 55 Jeff Burroughs .75 .35
❑ 56 Rudy May .30 .14
❑ 57 Marc Hill .30 .14
❑ 58 Chet Lemon .75 .35
❑ 59 Larry Christenson .30 .14
❑ 60 Jim Rice 2.50 1.10
❑ 61 Manny Sanguillen .75 .35
❑ 62 Eric Raich .30 .14
❑ 63 Tito Fuentes .30 .14
❑ 64 Larry Biittner .30 .14
❑ 65 Skip Lockwood .30 .14
❑ 66 Roy Smalley .75 .35
❑ 67 Joaquin Andujar .75 .35
❑ 68 Bruce Bochte .30 .14
❑ 69 Jim Crawford .30 .14
❑ 70 Johnny Bench 6.00 2.70
❑ 71 Dock Ellis .30 .14
❑ 72 Mike Anderson .30 .14
❑ 73 Charlie Williams .30 .14
❑ 74 A's Team/Mgr. 1.50 .30
Jack McKeon
(Checklist back)
❑ 75 Dennis Leonard .75 .35
❑ 76 Tim Foli .30 .14
❑ 77 Dyar Miller .30 .14
❑ 78 Bob Davis .30 .14

	No.	Card	Price	Price
❑	79	Don Money	.75	.35
❑	80	Andy Messersmith	.75	.35
❑	81	Juan Beniquez	.30	.14
❑	82	Jim Rooker	.30	.14
❑	83	Kevin Bell	.30	.14
❑	84	Ollie Brown	.30	.14
❑	85	Duane Kuiper	.30	.14
❑	86	Pat Zachry	.30	.14
❑	87	Glenn Borgmann	.30	.14
❑	88	Stan Wall	.30	.14
❑	89	Butch Hobson	.75	.35
❑	90	Cesar Cedeno	.75	.35
❑	91	John Verhoeven	.30	.14
❑	92	Dave Rosello	.30	.14
❑	93	Tom Poquette	.30	.14
❑	94	Craig Swan	.30	.14
❑	95	Keith Hernandez	.75	.35
❑	96	Lou Piniella	.75	.35
❑	97	Dave Heaverlo	.30	.14
❑	98	Milt May	.30	.14
❑	99	Tom Hausman	.30	.14
❑	100	Joe Morgan	3.00	1.35
❑	101	Dick Bosman	.30	.14
❑	102	Jose Morales	.30	.14
❑	103	Mike Bacsik	.30	.14
❑	104	Omar Moreno	.75	.35
❑	105	Steve Yeager	.75	.35
❑	106	Mike Flanagan	.75	.35
❑	107	Bill Melton	.30	.14
❑	108	Alan Foster	.30	.14
❑	109	Jorge Orta	.30	.14
❑	110	Steve Carlton	4.00	1.80
❑	111	Rico Petrocelli	.75	.35
❑	112	Bill Greif	.30	.14
❑	113	Blue Jays Leaders	1.50	.30
		Roy Hartsfield MG		
		Don Leppert CO		
		Bob Miller CO		
		Jackie Moore CO		
		Harry Warner CO		
		(Checklist back)		
❑	114	Bruce Dal Canton	.30	.14
❑	115	Rick Manning	.30	.14
❑	116	Joe Niekro	.75	.35
❑	117	Frank White	.75	.35
❑	118	Rick Jones	.30	.14
❑	119	John Stearns	.30	.14
❑	120	Rod Carew	3.00	1.35
❑	121	Gary Nolan	.30	.14
❑	122	Ben Oglivie	.75	.35
❑	123	Fred Stanley	.30	.14
❑	124	George Mitterwald	.30	.14
❑	125	Bill Travers	.30	.14
❑	126	Rod Gilbreath	.30	.14
❑	127	Ron Fairly	.75	.35
❑	128	Tommy John	1.50	.70
❑	129	Mike Sadek	.30	.14
❑	130	Al Oliver	.75	.35
❑	131	Orlando Ramirez	.30	.14
❑	132	Chip Lang	.30	.14
❑	133	Ralph Garr	.75	.35
❑	134	Padres Team/Mgr.	1.50	.30
		John McNamara		
		(Checklist back)		
❑	135	Mark Belanger	.75	.35
❑	136	Jerry Mumphrey	.75	.35
❑	137	Jeff Terpko	.30	.14
❑	138	Bob Stinson	.30	.14
❑	139	Fred Norman	.30	.14
❑	140	Mike Schmidt	15.00	6.75
❑	141	Mark Littell	.30	.14
❑	142	Steve Dillard	.30	.14
❑	143	Ed Herrmann	.30	.14
❑	144	Bruce Sutter	2.50	1.10
❑	145	Tom Veryzer	.30	.14
❑	146	Dusty Baker	1.50	.70
❑	147	Jackie Brown	.30	.14
❑	148	Fran Healy	.30	.14
❑	149	Mike Cubbage	.30	.14
❑	150	Tom Seaver	6.00	2.70
❑	151	Johnny LeMaster	.30	.14
❑	152	Gaylord Perry	2.50	1.10
❑	153	Ron Jackson	.30	.14
❑	154	Dave Giusti	.30	.14
❑	155	Joe Rudi	.75	.35
❑	156	Pete Mackanin	.30	.14
❑	157	Ken Brett	.30	.14
❑	158	Ted Kubiak	.30	.14
❑	159	Bernie Carbo	.30	.14
❑	160	Will McEnaney	.30	.14
❑	161	Garry Templeton	1.50	.70
❑	162	Mike Cuellar	.75	.35
❑	163	Dave Hilton	.30	.14
❑	164	Tug McGraw	.75	.35
❑	165	Jim Wynn	.75	.35
❑	166	Bill Campbell	.30	.14
❑	167	Rich Hebner	.75	.35
❑	168	Charlie Spikes	.30	.14
❑	169	Darold Knowles	.30	.14
❑	170	Thurman Munson	4.00	1.80
❑	171	Ken Sanders	.30	.14
❑	172	John Milner	.30	.14
❑	173	Chuck Scrivener	.30	.14
❑	174	Nelson Briles	.75	.35
❑	175	Butch Wynegar	.75	.35
❑	176	Bob Robertson	.30	.14
❑	177	Bart Johnson	.30	.14
❑	178	Bombo Rivera	.30	.14
❑	179	Paul Hartzell	.30	.14
❑	180	Dave Lopes	.75	.35
❑	181	Ken McMullen	.30	.14
❑	182	Dan Spillner	.30	.14
❑	183	Cardinals Team/Mgr.	1.50	.30
		Vern Rapp		
		(Checklist back)		
❑	184	Bo McLaughlin	.30	.14
❑	185	Sixto Lezcano	.30	.14
❑	186	Doug Flynn	.30	.14
❑	187	Dick Pole	.30	.14
❑	188	Bob Tolan	.30	.14
❑	189	Rick Dempsey	.75	.35
❑	190	Ray Burris	.30	.14
❑	191	Doug Griffin	.30	.14
❑	192	Clarence Gaston	.75	.35
❑	193	Larry Gura	.30	.14
❑	194	Gary Matthews	.75	.35
❑	195	Ed Figueroa	.30	.14
❑	196	Len Randle	.30	.14
❑	197	Ed Ott	.30	.14
❑	198	Wilbur Wood	.30	.14
❑	199	Pepe Frias	.30	.14
❑	200	Frank Tanana	.75	.35
❑	201	Ed Kranepool	.30	.14
❑	202	Tom Johnson	.30	.14
❑	203	Ed Armbrister	.30	.14
❑	204	Jeff Newman	.30	.14
❑	205	Pete Falcone	.30	.14
❑	206	Boog Powell	1.50	.70
❑	207	Glenn Abbott	.30	.14
❑	208	Checklist 133-264	1.50	.30
❑	209	Rob Andrews	.30	.14
❑	210	Fred Lynn	.75	.15
❑	211	Giants Team/Mgr.	1.50	.70
		Joe Altobelli		
		(Checklist back)		
❑	212	Jim Mason	.30	.14
❑	213	Maximino Leon	.30	.14
❑	214	Darrell Porter	.75	.35
❑	215	Butch Metzger	.30	.14
❑	216	Doug DeCinces	.75	.35
❑	217	Tom Underwood	.30	.14
❑	218	John Wathan	.30	.14
❑	219	Joe Coleman	.30	.14
❑	220	Chris Chambliss	.75	.35
❑	221	Bob Bailey	.30	.14
❑	222	Francisco Barrios	.30	.14
❑	223	Earl Williams	.30	.14
❑	224	Rusty Torres	.30	.14
❑	225	Bob Apodaca	.30	.14
❑	226	Leroy Stanton	.75	.35
❑	227	Joe Sambito	.30	.14
❑	228	Twins Team/Mgr.	1.50	.30
		Gene Mauch		
		(Checklist back)		
❑	229	Don Kessinger	.75	.35
❑	230	Vida Blue	.75	.35
❑	231	George Brett RB	12.00	5.50
		Most consecutive games 3 or more hits		
❑	232	Minnie Minoso RB	.75	.35
		Oldest to hit safely		
❑	233	Jose Morales RB	.30	.14
		Most pinch-hits season		
❑	234	Nolan Ryan RB	20.00	9.00
		Most seasons, 300 strikeouts		
❑	235	Cecil Cooper	.75	.35
❑	236	Tom Buskey	.30	.14
❑	237	Gene Clines	.30	.14
❑	238	Tippy Martinez	.75	.35
❑	239	Bill Plummer	.30	.14
❑	240	Ron LeFlore	.75	.35
❑	241	Dave Tomlin	.30	.14
❑	242	Ken Henderson	.30	.14
❑	243	Ron Reed	.30	.14
❑	244	John Mayberry	.75	.35
		(Cartoon mentions T206 Wagner)		
❑	245	Rick Rhoden	.75	.35
❑	246	Mike Vail	.30	.14
❑	247	Chris Knapp	.30	.14
❑	248	Wilbur Howard	.30	.14
❑	249	Pete Redfern	.30	.14
❑	250	Bill Madlock	.75	.35
❑	251	Tony Muser	.30	.14
❑	252	Dale Murray	.30	.14
❑	253	John Hale	.30	.14
❑	254	Doyle Alexander	.30	.14
❑	255	George Scott	.75	.35
❑	256	Joe Hoerner	.30	.14
❑	257	Mike Miley	.30	.14
❑	258	Luis Tiant	.75	.35
❑	259	Mets Team/Mgr.	1.50	.30
		Joe Frazier		
		(Checklist back)		
❑	260	J.R. Richard	.75	.35
❑	261	Phil Garner	.75	.35
❑	262	Al Cowens	.30	.14
❑	263	Mike Marshall	.75	.35
❑	264	Tom Hutton	.30	.14
❑	265	Mark Fidrych	4.00	1.80
❑	266	Derrel Thomas	.30	.14
❑	267	Ray Fosse	.30	.14
❑	268	Rick Sawyer	.30	.14
❑	269	Joe Lis	.30	.14
❑	270	Dave Parker	1.50	.70
❑	271	Terry Forster	.30	.14
❑	272	Lee Lacy	.30	.14
❑	273	Eric Soderholm	.30	.14
❑	274	Don Stanhouse	.30	.14
❑	275	Mike Hargrove	.75	.35
❑	276	Chris Chambliss ALCS	1.50	.70
		homer decides it		
❑	277	Pete Rose NLCS	2.00	.90
❑	278	Danny Frisella	.30	.14
❑	279	Joe Wallis	.30	.14
❑	280	Jim Hunter	2.50	1.10
❑	281	Roy Staiger	.30	.14
❑	282	Sid Monge	.30	.14
❑	283	Jerry DaVanon	.30	.14
❑	284	Mike Norris	.30	.14
❑	285	Brooks Robinson	4.00	1.80
❑	286	Johnny Grubb	.30	.06
❑	287	Reds Team/Mgr.	1.50	.70
		Sparky Anderson		
		(Checklist back)		
❑	288	Bob Montgomery	.30	.14
❑	289	Gene Garber	.75	.35
❑	290	Amos Otis	.75	.35
❑	291	Jason Thompson	.75	.35
❑	292	Rogelio Moret	.30	.14
❑	293	Jack Brohamer	.30	.14
❑	294	George Medich	.30	.14
❑	295	Gary Carter	4.00	1.80
❑	296	Don Hood	.30	.14
❑	297	Ken Reitz	.30	.14
❑	298	Charlie Hough	.75	.35
❑	299	Otto Velez	.75	.35
❑	300	Jerry Koosman	.75	.35
❑	301	Toby Harrah	.75	.35
❑	302	Mike Garman	.30	.14
❑	303	Gene Tenace	.75	.35
❑	304	Jim Hughes	.30	.14
❑	305	Mickey Rivers	.75	.35
❑	306	Rick Waits	.30	.14
❑	307	Gary Sutherland	.30	.14
❑	308	Gene Pentz	.30	.14

❑ 309 Red Sox Team/Mgr. .... 1.50 .30
Don Zimmer
(Checklist back)
❑ 310 Larry Bowa .... .75 .35
❑ 311 Vern Ruhle .... .30 .14
❑ 312 Rob Belloir .... .30 .14
❑ 313 Paul Blair .... .75 .35
❑ 314 Steve Mingori .... .30 .14
❑ 315 Dave Chalk .... .30 .14
❑ 316 Steve Rogers .... .30 .14
❑ 317 Kurt Bevacqua .... .30 .14
❑ 318 Duffy Dyer .... .30 .14
❑ 319 Rich Gossage .... 1.50 .70
❑ 320 Ken Griffey .... 1.50 .70
❑ 321 Dave Goltz .... .30 .14
❑ 322 Bill Russell .... .75 .35
❑ 323 Larry Lintz .... .30 .14
❑ 324 John Curtis .... .30 .14
❑ 325 Mike Ivie .... .30 .14
❑ 326 Jesse Jefferson .... .30 .14
❑ 327 Astros Team/Mgr. .... 1.50 .30
Bill Virdon
(Checklist back)
❑ 328 Tommy Boggs .... .30 .14
❑ 329 Ron Hodges .... .30 .14
❑ 330 George Hendrick .... .75 .35
❑ 331 Jim Colborn .... .30 .14
❑ 332 Elliott Maddox .... .30 .14
❑ 333 Paul Reuschel .... .30 .14
❑ 334 Bill Stein .... .30 .14
❑ 335 Bill Robinson .... .75 .35
❑ 336 Denny Doyle .... .30 .14
❑ 337 Ron Schueler .... .30 .14
❑ 338 Dave Duncan .... .30 .14
❑ 339 Adrian Devine .... .30 .14
❑ 340 Hal McRae .... .75 .35
❑ 341 Joe Kerrigan .... .30 .14
❑ 342 Jerry Remy .... .30 .14
❑ 343 Ed Halicki .... .30 .14
❑ 344 Brian Downing .... .75 .35
❑ 345 Reggie Smith .... .75 .35
❑ 346 Bill Singer .... .30 .14
❑ 347 George Foster .... 1.50 .70
❑ 348 Brent Strom .... .30 .14
❑ 349 Jim Holt .... .30 .14
❑ 350 Larry Dierker .... .75 .35
❑ 351 Jim Sundberg .... .75 .35
❑ 352 Mike Phillips .... .30 .14
❑ 353 Stan Thomas .... .30 .14
❑ 354 Pirates Team/Mgr. .... 1.50 .30
Chuck Tanner
(Checklist back)
❑ 355 Lou Brock 3.00 1.35
❑ 356 Checklist 265-396 .... 1.50 .30
❑ 357 Tim McCarver .... 1.50 .70
❑ 358 Tom House .... .30 .14
❑ 359 Willie Randolph .... 1.50 .70
❑ 360 Rick Monday .... .75 .35
❑ 361 Eduardo Rodriguez .... .30 .14
❑ 362 Tommy Davis .... .75 .35
❑ 363 Dave Roberts .... .30 .14
❑ 364 Vic Correll .... .30 .14
❑ 365 Mike Torrez .... .75 .35
❑ 366 Ted Sizemore .... .30 .14
❑ 367 Dave Hamilton .... .30 .14
❑ 368 Mike Jorgensen .... .30 .14
❑ 369 Terry Humphrey .... .30 .14
❑ 370 John Montefusco .... .30 .14
❑ 371 Royals Team/Mgr. .... 1.50 .30
Whitey Herzog
(Checklist back)
❑ 372 Rich Folkers .... .30 .14
❑ 373 Bert Campaneris .... .75 .35
❑ 374 Kent Tekulve .... .75 .35
❑ 375 Larry Hisle .... .75 .35
❑ 376 Nino Espinosa .... .30 .14
❑ 377 Dave McKay .... .30 .14
❑ 378 Jim Umbarger .... .30 .14
❑ 379 Larry Cox .... .30 .14
❑ 380 Lee May .... .75 .35
❑ 381 Bob Forsch .... .30 .14
❑ 382 Charlie Moore .... .30 .14
❑ 383 Stan Bahnsen .... .30 .14
❑ 384 Darrel Chaney .... .30 .14
❑ 385 Dave LaRoche .... .30 .14
❑ 386 Manny Mota .... .75 .35
❑ 387 Yankees Team/Mgr. .... 2.50 .50
Billy Martin
(Checklist back)
❑ 388 Terry Harmon .... .30 .14
❑ 389 Ken Kravec .... .30 .14
❑ 390 Dave Winfield 8.00 3.60
❑ 391 Dan Warthen .... .30 .14
❑ 392 Phil Roof .... .30 .14
❑ 393 John Lowenstein .... .30 .14
❑ 394 Bill Laxton .... .30 .14
❑ 395 Manny Trillo .... .30 .14
❑ 396 Tom Murphy .... .30 .14
❑ 397 Larry Herndon .... .75 .35
❑ 398 Tom Burgmeier .... .30 .14
❑ 399 Bruce Boisclair .... .30 .14
❑ 400 Steve Garvey 2.50 1.10
❑ 401 Mickey Scott .... .30 .14
❑ 402 Tommy Helms .... .30 .14
❑ 403 Tom Grieve .... .75 .35
❑ 404 Eric Rasmussen .... .30 .14
❑ 405 Claudell Washington .... .75 .35
❑ 406 Tim Johnson .... .30 .14
❑ 407 Dave Freisleben .... .30 .14
❑ 408 Cesar Tovar .... .30 .14
❑ 409 Pete Broberg .... .30 .14
❑ 410 Willie Montanez .... .30 .14
❑ 411 Joe Morgan WS 2.50 1.10
Johnny Bench
❑ 412 Johnny Bench WS 2.50 1.10
❑ 413 World Series Summary .. .75 .35
Cincy wins 2nd
straight series
❑ 414 Tommy Harper .... .75 .35
❑ 415 Jay Johnstone .... .75 .35
❑ 416 Chuck Hartenstein .... .30 .14
❑ 417 Wayne Garrett .... .30 .14
❑ 418 White Sox Team/Mgr. .. 1.50 .30
Bob Lemon
(Checklist back)
❑ 419 Steve Swisher .... .30 .14
❑ 420 Rusty Staub .... 1.50 .70
❑ 421 Doug Rau .... .30 .14
❑ 422 Freddie Patek .... .75 .35
❑ 423 Gary Lavelle .... .30 .14
❑ 424 Steve Brye .... .30 .14
❑ 425 Joe Torre .... 1.50 .70
❑ 426 Dick Drago .... .30 .14
❑ 427 Dave Rader .... .30 .14
❑ 428 Rangers Team/Mgr. .... 1.50 .30
Frank Lucchesi
(Checklist back)
❑ 429 Ken Boswell .... .30 .14
❑ 430 Fergie Jenkins 2.50 1.10
❑ 431 Dave Collins UER .... .75 .35
(Photo actually
Bobby Jones)
❑ 432 Buzz Capra .... .30 .14
❑ 433 Nate Colbert TBC .... .30 .14
(5 HR, 13 RBI)
❑ 434 Carl Yastrzemski TBC .. 1.50 .70
'67 Triple Crown
❑ 435 Maury Wills TBC .... .75 .35
104 steals
❑ 436 Bob Keegan TBC .... .30 .14
Majors' only no-hitter
❑ 437 Ralph Kiner TBC .... 1.50 .70
Leads NL in HR's
7th straight year
❑ 438 Marty Perez .... .30 .14
❑ 439 Gorman Thomas .... .75 .35
❑ 440 Jon Matlack .... .30 .14
❑ 441 Larvell Blanks .... .30 .14
❑ 442 Braves Team/Mgr. .... 1.50 .30
Dave Bristol
(Checklist back)
❑ 443 Lamar Johnson .... .30 .14
❑ 444 Wayne Twitchell .... .30 .14
❑ 445 Ken Singleton .... .75 .35
❑ 446 Bill Bonham .... .30 .14
❑ 447 Jerry Turner .... .30 .14
❑ 448 Ellie Rodriguez .... .30 .14
❑ 449 Al Fitzmorris .... .30 .14
❑ 450 Pete Rose 10.00 4.50
❑ 451 Checklist 397-528 .... 1.50 .30
❑ 452 Mike Caldwell .... .30 .14
❑ 453 Pedro Garcia .... .30 .14
❑ 454 Andy Etchebarren .... .30 .14
❑ 455 Rick Wise .... .30 .14
❑ 456 Leon Roberts .... .30 .14
❑ 457 Steve Luebber .... .30 .14
❑ 458 Leo Foster .... .30 .14
❑ 459 Steve Foucault .... .30 .14
❑ 460 Willie Stargell 2.50 1.10
❑ 461 Dick Tidrow .... .30 .14
❑ 462 Don Baylor .... 1.50 .70
❑ 463 Jamie Quirk .... .30 .14
❑ 464 Randy Moffitt .... .30 .14
❑ 465 Rico Carty .... .75 .35
❑ 466 Fred Holdsworth .... .30 .14
❑ 467 Phillies Team/Mgr. .... 1.50 .30
Danny Ozark
(Checklist back)
❑ 468 Ramon Hernandez .... .30 .14
❑ 469 Pat Kelly .... .30 .14
❑ 470 Ted Simmons .... .75 .35
❑ 471 Del Unser .... .30 .14
❑ 472 Rookie Pitchers .... .30 .14
Don Aase
Bob McClure
Gil Patterson
Dave Wehrmeister
❑ 473 Rookie Outfielders 40.00 18.00
Andre Dawson
Gene Richards
John Scott
Denny Walling
❑ 474 Rookie Shortstops .... .75 .35
Bob Bailor
Kiko Garcia
Craig Reynolds
Alex Taveras
❑ 475 Rookie Pitchers .... .75 .35
Chris Batton
Rick Camp
Scott McGregor
Manny Sarmiento
❑ 476 Rookie Catchers 20.00 9.00
Gary Alexander
Rick Cerone
Dale Murphy
Kevin Pasley
❑ 477 Rookie Infielders .... .75 .35
Doug Ault
Rich Dauer
Orlando Gonzalez
Phil Mankowski
❑ 478 Rookie Pitchers .... .75 .35
Jim Gideon
Leon Hooten
Dave Johnson
Mark Lemongello
❑ 479 Rookie Outfielders .... .75 .35
Brian Asselstine
Wayne Gross
Sam Mejias
Alvis Woods
❑ 480 Carl Yastrzemski 4.00 1.80
❑ 481 Roger Metzger .... .30 .14
❑ 482 Tony Solaita .... .30 .14
❑ 483 Richie Zisk .... .30 .14
❑ 484 Burt Hooton .... .75 .35
❑ 485 Roy White .... .75 .35
❑ 486 Ed Bane .... .30 .14
❑ 487 Rookie Pitchers .... .75 .35
Larry Anderson
Ed Glynn
Joe Henderson
Greg Terlecky
❑ 488 Rookie Outfielders 4.00 1.80
Jack Clark
Ruppert Jones
Lee Mazzilli
Dan Thomas
❑ 489 Rookie Pitchers .... .75 .35
Len Barker
Randy Lerch
Greg Minton
Mike Overy
❑ 490 Rookie Shortstops .... .75 .35
Billy Almon

Mickey Klutts
Tommy McMillan
Mark Wagner
❑ 491 Rookie Pitchers 5.00 2.20
Mike Dupree
Dennis Martinez
Craig Mitchell
Bob Sykes
❑ 492 Rookie Outfielders.......... .75 .35
Tony Armas
Steve Kemp
Carlos Lopez
Gary Woods
❑ 493 Rookie Pitchers .... .75 .35
Mike Krukow
Jim Otten
Gary Wheelock
Mike Willis
❑ 494 Rookie Infielders .... 1.50 .70
Juan Bernhardt
Mike Champion
Jim Gantner
Bump Wills
❑ 495 Al Hrabosky .... .30 .14
❑ 496 Gary Thomasson............ .30 .14
❑ 497 Clay Carroll .... .30 .14
❑ 498 Sal Bando .... .75 .35
❑ 499 Pablo Torrealba............. .30 .14
❑ 500 Dave Kingman............. 1.50 .70
❑ 501 Jim Bibby...................... .30 .14
❑ 502 Randy Hundley .... .30 .14
❑ 503 Bill Lee .... .30 .14
❑ 504 Dodgers Team/Mgr. .... 1.50 .30
Tom Lasorda
(Checklist back)
❑ 505 Oscar Gamble .... .75 .35
❑ 506 Steve Grilli..................... .30 .14
❑ 507 Mike Hegan.................... .30 .14
❑ 508 Dave Pagan .... .30 .14
❑ 509 Cookie Rojas.................. .75 .35
❑ 510 John Candelaria .... .30 .14
❑ 511 Bill Fahey .... .30 .14
❑ 512 Jack Billingham .... .30 .14
❑ 513 Jerry Terrell................... .30 .14
❑ 514 Cliff Johnson .... .30 .14
❑ 515 Chris Speier .... .30 .14
❑ 516 Bake McBride .... .75 .35
❑ 517 Pete Vuckovich .... .75 .35
❑ 518 Cubs Team/Mgr. .... 1.50 .30
Herman Franks
(Checklist back)
❑ 519 Don Kirkwood .... .30 .14
❑ 520 Garry Maddox .... .30 .14
❑ 521 Bob Grich .... .75 .35
❑ 522 Enzo Hernandez .... .30 .14
❑ 523 Rollie Fingers 2.50 1.10
❑ 524 Rowland Office .... .30 .14
❑ 525 Dennis Eckersley 6.00 2.70
❑ 526 Larry Parrish .... .75 .35
❑ 527 Dan Meyer..................... .75 .35
❑ 528 Bill Castro .... .30 .14
❑ 529 Jim Essian...................... .30 .14
❑ 530 Rick Reuschel................ .75 .35
❑ 531 Lyman Bostock .... .75 .35
❑ 532 Jim Willoughby .... .30 .14
❑ 533 Mickey Stanley .... .30 .14
❑ 534 Paul Splittorff................. .30 .14
❑ 535 Cesar Geronimo .... .30 .14
❑ 536 Vic Albury .... .30 .14
❑ 537 Dave Roberts .... .30 .14
❑ 538 Frank Taveras................ .30 .14
❑ 539 Mike Wallace.................. .30 .14
❑ 540 Bob Watson.................... .75 .35
❑ 541 John Denny.................... .75 .35
❑ 542 Frank Duffy .... .30 .14
❑ 543 Ron Blomberg .... .30 .14
❑ 544 Gary Ross .... .30 .14
❑ 545 Bob Boone .... .75 .35
❑ 546 Orioles Team/Mgr. ...... 1.50 .30
Earl Weaver
(Checklist back)
❑ 547 Willie McCovey 3.00 1.35
❑ 548 Joel Youngblood .... .30 .14
❑ 549 Jerry Royster.................. .30 .14
❑ 550 Randy Jones .... .30 .14
❑ 551 Bill North .... .30 .14
❑ 552 Pepe Mangual................ .30 .14
❑ 553 Jack Heidemann .... .30 .14
❑ 554 Bruce Kimm.................... .30 .14
❑ 555 Dan Ford .... .30 .14
❑ 556 Doug Bird .... .30 .14
❑ 557 Jerry White .... .30 .14
❑ 558 Elias Sosa .... .30 .14
❑ 559 Alan Bannister................ .30 .14
❑ 560 Dave Concepcion .... 1.50 .70
❑ 561 Pete LaCock .... .30 .14
❑ 562 Checklist 529-660 .... 1.50 .30
❑ 563 Bruce Kison.................... .30 .14
❑ 564 Alan Ashby .... .75 .35
❑ 565 Mickey Lolich.................. .75 .35
❑ 566 Rick Miller .... .30 .14
❑ 567 Enos Cabell.................... .30 .14
❑ 568 Carlos May .... .30 .14
❑ 569 Jim Lonborg .... .75 .35
❑ 570 Bobby Bonds............... 1.50 .70
❑ 571 Darrell Evans.................. .75 .35
❑ 572 Ross Grimsley................ .30 .14
❑ 573 Joe Ferguson .... .30 .14
❑ 574 Aurelio Rodriguez .... .30 .14
❑ 575 Dick Ruthven.................. .30 .14
❑ 576 Fred Kendall .... .30 .14
❑ 577 Jerry Augustine .... .30 .14
❑ 578 Bob Randall.................... .30 .14
❑ 579 Don Carrithers................ .30 .14
❑ 580 George Brett 25.00 11.00
❑ 581 Pedro Borbon .... .30 .14
❑ 582 Ed Kirkpatrick .... .30 .14
❑ 583 Paul Lindblad .... .30 .14
❑ 584 Ed Goodson .... .30 .14
❑ 585 Rick Burleson .... .75 .35
❑ 586 Steve Renko .... .30 .14
❑ 587 Rick Baldwin .... .30 .14
❑ 588 Dave Moates.................. .30 .14
❑ 589 Mike Cosgrove .... .30 .14
❑ 590 Buddy Bell...................... .75 .35
❑ 591 Chris Arnold .... .30 .14
❑ 592 Dan Briggs .... .30 .14
❑ 593 Dennis Blair.................... .30 .14
❑ 594 Biff Pocoroba.................. .30 .14
❑ 595 John Hiller .... .30 .14
❑ 596 Jerry Martin .... .30 .14
❑ 597 Mariners Leaders .... 1.50 .30
Darrell Johnson MG
Don Bryant CO
Jim Busby CO
Vada Pinson CO
Wes Stock CO
(Checklist back)
❑ 598 Sparky Lyle .... .75 .35
❑ 599 Mike Tyson .... .30 .14
❑ 600 Jim Palmer 3.00 1.35
❑ 601 Mike Lum........................ .30 .14
❑ 602 Andy Hassler.................. .30 .14
❑ 603 Willie Davis .... .75 .35
❑ 604 Jim Slaton .... .30 .14
❑ 605 Felix Millan .... .30 .14
❑ 606 Steve Braun .... .30 .14
❑ 607 Larry Demery .... .30 .14
❑ 608 Roy Howell .... .30 .14
❑ 609 Jim Barr.......................... .30 .14
❑ 610 Jose Cardenal................ .75 .35
❑ 611 Dave Lemanczyk............ .30 .14
❑ 612 Barry Foote .... .30 .14
❑ 613 Reggie Cleveland .... .30 .14
❑ 614 Greg Gross .... .30 .14
❑ 615 Phil Niekro.................... 2.50 1.10
❑ 616 Tommy Sandt .... .30 .14
❑ 617 Bobby Darwin .... .30 .14
❑ 618 Pat Dobson .... .30 .14
❑ 619 Johnny Oates .... .75 .35
❑ 620 Don Sutton 2.50 1.10
❑ 621 Tigers Team/Mgr. .... 1.50 .30
Ralph Houk
(Checklist back)
❑ 622 Jim Wohlford.................. .30 .14
❑ 623 Jack Kucek .... .30 .14
❑ 624 Hector Cruz.................... .30 .14
❑ 625 Ken Holtzman .... .75 .35
❑ 626 Al Bumbry .... .75 .35
❑ 627 Bob Myrick .... .30 .14
❑ 628 Mario Guerrero .... .30 .14
❑ 629 Bobby Valentine .... .30 .14
❑ 630 Bert Blyleven .... 1.50 .70
❑ 631 George Brett 8.00 3.60
Ken Brett
❑ 632 Bob Forsch .... .75 .35
Ken Forsch
❑ 633 Lee May .... .75 .35
Carlos May
❑ 634 Paul Reuschel............... .75 .35
Rick Reuschel UER
(Photos switched)
❑ 635 Robin Yount 10.00 4.50
❑ 636 Santo Alcala .... .30 .14
❑ 637 Alex Johnson................. .30 .14
❑ 638 Jim Kaat .... 1.50 .70
❑ 639 Jerry Morales .... .30 .14
❑ 640 Carlton Fisk................. 5.00 2.20
❑ 641 Dan Larson .... .30 .14
❑ 642 Willie Crawford .... .30 .14
❑ 643 Mike Pazik..................... .30 .14
❑ 644 Matt Alexander .... .30 .14
❑ 645 Jerry Reuss................... .75 .35
❑ 646 Andres Mora .... .30 .14
❑ 647 Expos Team/Mgr. .... 1.50 .30
Dick Williams
(Checklist back)
❑ 648 Jim Spencer .... .30 .14
❑ 649 Dave Cash .... .30 .14
❑ 650 Nolan Ryan 50.00 22.00
❑ 651 Von Joshua .... .30 .14
❑ 652 Tom Walker................... .30 .14
❑ 653 Diego Segui................... .75 .35
❑ 654 Ron Pruitt .... .30 .14
❑ 655 Tony Perez 2.50 1.10
❑ 656 Ron Guidry .... 1.50 .70
❑ 657 Mick Kelleher................ .30 .14
❑ 658 Marty Pattin .... .30 .14
❑ 659 Merv Rettenmund .... .30 .14
❑ 660 Willie Horton .... 1.50 .30

1978 Topps

	NRMT	VG-E
COMPLETE SET (726)	250.00	110.00
COMMON CARD (1-726)	.25	.11
COMMON CARD DP	.15	.07

❑ 1 Lou Brock RB .... 3.00 .90
Most lifetime steals
❑ 2 Sparky Lyle RB .... .60 .25
Most career games pure relief
❑ 3 Willie McCovey RB 2.50 1.10
Most times 2 HR's in inning
❑ 4 Brooks Robinson RB........ 2.00 .90
Most consecutive
seasons with one club
❑ 5 Pete Rose RB 3.00 1.35
Most lifetime switch-hitter hits
❑ 6 Nolan Ryan RB 15.00 6.75
Most games 10 or more strikeouts
❑ 7 Reggie Jackson RB.......... 3.00 1.35
Most homers,
one World Series
❑ 8 Mike Sadek .... .25 .11
❑ 9 Doug DeCinces................. .60 .25
❑ 10 Phil Niekro................... 2.50 1.10
❑ 11 Rick Manning .... .25 .11

❑ 12 Don Aase .25 .11
❑ 13 Art Howe .60 .25
❑ 14 Lerrin LaGrow .25 .11
❑ 15 Tony Perez DP 1.25 .55
❑ 16 Roy White .60 .25
❑ 17 Mike Krukow .25 .11
❑ 18 Bob Grich .60 .25
❑ 19 Darrell Porter .60 .25
❑ 20 Pete Rose DP 5.00 2.20
❑ 21 Steve Kemp .25 .11
❑ 22 Charlie Hough .60 .25
❑ 23 Bump Wills .25 .11
❑ 24 Don Money DP .15 .07
❑ 25 Jon Matlack .25 .11
❑ 26 Rich Hebner .60 .25
❑ 27 Geoff Zahn .25 .11
❑ 28 Ed Ott .25 .11
❑ 29 Bob Lacey .25 .11
❑ 30 George Hendrick .60 .25
❑ 31 Glenn Abbott .25 .11
❑ 32 Garry Templeton .60 .25
❑ 33 Dave Lemanczyk .25 .11
❑ 34 Willie McCovey 2.50 1.10
❑ 35 Sparky Lyle .60 .25
❑ 36 Eddie Murray 100.00 45.00
❑ 37 Rick Waits .25 .11
❑ 38 Willie Montanez .25 .11
❑ 39 Floyd Bannister .25 .11
❑ 40 Carl Yastrzemski 3.00 1.35
❑ 41 Burt Hooton .60 .25
❑ 42 Jorge Orta .25 .11
❑ 43 Bill Atkinson .25 .11
❑ 44 Toby Harrah .60 .25
❑ 45 Mark Fidrych 2.50 1.10
❑ 46 Al Cowens .25 .11
❑ 47 Jack Billingham .25 .11
❑ 48 Don Baylor 1.25 .55
❑ 49 Ed Kranepool .60 .25
❑ 50 Rick Reuschel .60 .25
❑ 51 Charlie Moore DP .15 .07
❑ 52 Jim Lonborg .25 .11
❑ 53 Phil Garner DP .25 .11
❑ 54 Tom Johnson .25 .11
❑ 55 Mitchell Page .25 .11
❑ 56 Randy Jones .25 .11
❑ 57 Dan Meyer .25 .11
❑ 58 Bob Forsch .25 .11
❑ 59 Otto Velez .25 .11
❑ 60 Thurman Munson 3.00 1.35
❑ 61 Larvell Blanks .25 .11
❑ 62 Jim Barr .25 .11
❑ 63 Don Zimmer MG .60 .25
❑ 64 Gene Pentz .25 .11
❑ 65 Ken Singleton .60 .25
❑ 66 Chicago White Sox 1.25 .25
Team Card
(Checklist back)
❑ 67 Claudell Washington .60 .25
❑ 68 Steve Foucault DP .15 .07
❑ 69 Mike Vail .25 .11
❑ 70 Rich Gossage 1.25 .55
❑ 71 Terry Humphrey .25 .11
❑ 72 Andre Dawson 10.00 4.50
❑ 73 Andy Hassler .25 .11
❑ 74 Checklist 1-121 1.25 .25
❑ 75 Dick Ruthven .25 .11
❑ 76 Steve Ontiveros .25 .11
❑ 77 Ed Kirkpatrick .25 .11
❑ 78 Pablo Torrealba .25 .11
❑ 79 Darrell Johnson DP MG .15 .07
❑ 80 Ken Griffey 1.25 .55
❑ 81 Pete Redfern .25 .11
❑ 82 San Francisco Giants 1.25 .25
Team Card
(Checklist back)
❑ 83 Bob Montgomery .25 .11
❑ 84 Kent Tekulve .60 .25
❑ 85 Ron Fairly .60 .25
❑ 86 Dave Tomlin .25 .11
❑ 87 John Lowenstein .25 .11
❑ 88 Mike Phillips .25 .11
❑ 89 Ken Clay .25 .11
❑ 90 Larry Bowa 1.25 .55
❑ 91 Oscar Zamora .25 .11
❑ 92 Adrian Devine .25 .11
❑ 93 Bobby Cox DP .25 .11
❑ 94 Chuck Scrivener .25 .11
❑ 95 Jamie Quirk .25 .11
❑ 96 Baltimore Orioles 1.25 .25
Team Card
(Checklist back)
❑ 97 Stan Bahnsen .25 .11
❑ 98 Jim Essian .60 .25
❑ 99 Willie Hernandez 1.25 .55
❑ 100 George Brett 20.00 9.00
❑ 101 Sid Monge .25 .11
❑ 102 Matt Alexander .25 .11
❑ 103 Tom Murphy .25 .11
❑ 104 Lee Lacy .25 .11
❑ 105 Reggie Cleveland .25 .11
❑ 106 Bill Plummer .25 .11
❑ 107 Ed Halicki .25 .11
❑ 108 Von Joshua .25 .11
❑ 109 Joe Torre MG .60 .25
❑ 110 Richie Zisk .25 .11
❑ 111 Mike Tyson .25 .11
❑ 112 Houston Astros 1.25 .25
Team Card
(Checklist back)
❑ 113 Don Carrithers .25 .11
❑ 114 Paul Blair .60 .25
❑ 115 Gary Nolan .25 .11
❑ 116 Tucker Ashford .25 .11
❑ 117 John Montague .25 .11
❑ 118 Terry Harmon .25 .11
❑ 119 Dennis Martinez 2.50 1.10
❑ 120 Gary Carter 2.50 1.10
❑ 121 Alvis Woods .25 .11
❑ 122 Dennis Eckersley 4.00 1.80
❑ 123 Manny Trillo .25 .11
❑ 124 Dave Rozema .25 .11
❑ 125 George Scott .60 .25
❑ 126 Paul Moskau .25 .11
❑ 127 Chet Lemon .60 .25
❑ 128 Bill Russell .60 .25
❑ 129 Jim Colborn .25 .11
❑ 130 Jeff Burroughs .60 .25
❑ 131 Bert Blyleven 1.25 .55
❑ 132 Enos Cabell .25 .11
❑ 133 Jerry Augustine .25 .11
❑ 134 Steve Henderson .25 .11
❑ 135 Ron Guidry DP 1.25 .55
❑ 136 Ted Sizemore .25 .11
❑ 137 Craig Kusick .25 .11
❑ 138 Larry Demery .25 .11
❑ 139 Wayne Gross .25 .11
❑ 140 Rollie Fingers 2.50 1.10
❑ 141 Ruppert Jones .25 .11
❑ 142 John Montefusco .25 .11
❑ 143 Keith Hernandez .60 .25
❑ 144 Jesse Jefferson .25 .11
❑ 145 Rick Monday .60 .25
❑ 146 Doyle Alexander .25 .11
❑ 147 Lee Mazzilli .25 .11
❑ 148 Andre Thornton .60 .25
❑ 149 Dale Murray .25 .11
❑ 150 Bobby Bonds 1.25 .55
❑ 151 Milt Wilcox .25 .11
❑ 152 Ivan DeJesus .25 .11
❑ 153 Steve Stone .60 .25
❑ 154 Cecil Cooper DP .25 .11
❑ 155 Butch Hobson .25 .11
❑ 156 Andy Messersmith .60 .25
❑ 157 Pete LaCock DP .15 .07
❑ 158 Joaquin Andujar .60 .25
❑ 159 Lou Piniella .60 .25
❑ 160 Jim Palmer 2.50 1.10
❑ 161 Bob Boone 1.25 .55
❑ 162 Paul Thormodsgard .25 .11
❑ 163 Bill North .25 .11
❑ 164 Bob Owchinko .25 .11
❑ 165 Rennie Stennett .25 .11
❑ 166 Carlos Lopez .25 .11
❑ 167 Tim Foli .25 .11
❑ 168 Reggie Smith .60 .25
❑ 169 Jerry Johnson .25 .11
❑ 170 Lou Brock 2.50 1.10
❑ 171 Pat Zachry .25 .11
❑ 172 Mike Hargrove .60 .25
❑ 173 Robin Yount UER 8.00 3.60
(Played for Newark
in 1973, not 1971)
❑ 174 Wayne Garland .25 .11
❑ 175 Jerry Morales .25 .11
❑ 176 Milt May .25 .11
❑ 177 Gene Garber DP .25 .11
❑ 178 Dave Chalk .25 .11
❑ 179 Dick Tidrow .25 .11
❑ 180 Dave Concepcion 1.25 .55
❑ 181 Ken Forsch .25 .11
❑ 182 Jim Spencer .25 .11
❑ 183 Doug Bird .25 .11
❑ 184 Checklist 122-242 1.25 .25
❑ 185 Ellis Valentine .25 .11
❑ 186 Bob Stanley DP .25 .11
❑ 187 Jerry Royster DP .15 .07
❑ 188 Al Bumbry .60 .25
❑ 189 Tom Lasorda MG 2.50 1.10
❑ 190 John Candelaria .60 .25
❑ 191 Rodney Scott .25 .11
❑ 192 San Diego Padres 1.25 .25
Team Card
(Checklist back)
❑ 193 Rich Chiles .25 .11
❑ 194 Derrel Thomas .25 .11
❑ 195 Larry Dierker .60 .25
❑ 196 Bob Bailor .25 .11
❑ 197 Nino Espinosa .25 .11
❑ 198 Ron Pruitt .25 .11
❑ 199 Craig Reynolds .25 .11
❑ 200 Reggie Jackson 8.00 3.60
❑ 201 Batting Leaders 1.25 .55
Dave Parker
Rod Carew
❑ 202 Home Run Leaders DP .60 .25
George Foster
Jim Rice
❑ 203 RBI Leaders .60 .25
George Foster
Larry Hisle
❑ 204 Steals Leaders DP .25 .11
Frank Taveras
Freddie Patek
❑ 205 Victory Leaders 2.50 1.10
Steve Carlton
Dave Goltz
Dennis Leonard
Jim Palmer
❑ 206 Strikeout Leaders DP 5.00 2.20
Phil Niekro
Nolan Ryan
❑ 207 ERA Leaders DP .60 .25
John Candelaria
Frank Tanana
❑ 208 Top Firemen 1.25 .55
Rollie Fingers
Bill Campbell
❑ 209 Dock Ellis .25 .11
❑ 210 Jose Cardenal .25 .11
❑ 211 Earl Weaver MG DP 1.25 .55
❑ 212 Mike Caldwell .25 .11
❑ 213 Alan Bannister .25 .11
❑ 214 California Angels 1.25 .25
Team Card
(Checklist back)
❑ 215 Darrell Evans .60 .25
❑ 216 Mike Paxton .25 .11
❑ 217 Rod Gilbreath .25 .11
❑ 218 Marty Pattin .25 .11
❑ 219 Mike Cubbage .25 .11
❑ 220 Pedro Borbon .25 .11
❑ 221 Chris Speier .25 .11
❑ 222 Jerry Martin .25 .11
❑ 223 Bruce Kison .25 .11
❑ 224 Jerry Tabb .25 .11
❑ 225 Don Gullett DP .25 .11
❑ 226 Joe Ferguson .25 .11
❑ 227 Al Fitzmorris .25 .11
❑ 228 Manny Mota DP .25 .11
❑ 229 Leo Foster .25 .11
❑ 230 Al Hrabosky .25 .11
❑ 231 Wayne Nordhagen .25 .11
❑ 232 Mickey Stanley .25 .11
❑ 233 Dick Pole .25 .11
❑ 234 Herman Franks MG .25 .11
❑ 235 Tim McCarver .60 .25

❑	236	Terry Whitfield	.25	.11
❑	237	Rich Dauer	.25	.11
❑	238	Juan Beniquez	.25	.11
❑	239	Dyar Miller	.25	.11
❑	240	Gene Tenace	.60	.25
❑	241	Pete Vuckovich	.60	.25
❑	242	Barry Bonnell DP	.15	.07
❑	243	Bob McClure	.25	.11
❑	244	Montreal Expos Team Card DP (Checklist back)	.60	.12
❑	245	Rick Burleson	.60	.25
❑	246	Dan Driessen	.25	.11
❑	247	Larry Christenson	.25	.11
❑	248	Frank White DP	.60	.25
❑	249	Dave Goltz DP	.15	.07
❑	250	Graig Nettles DP	.60	.25
❑	251	Don Kirkwood	.25	.11
❑	252	Steve Swisher DP	.15	.07
❑	253	Jim Kern	.25	.11
❑	254	Dave Collins	.60	.25
❑	255	Jerry Reuss	.60	.25
❑	256	Joe Altobelli MG	.25	.11
❑	257	Hector Cruz	.25	.11
❑	258	John Hiller	.25	.11
❑	259	Los Angeles Dodgers Team Card (Checklist back)	1.25	.25
❑	260	Bert Campaneris	.60	.25
❑	261	Tim Hosley	.25	.11
❑	262	Rudy May	.25	.11
❑	263	Danny Walton	.25	.11
❑	264	Jamie Easterly	.25	.11
❑	265	Sal Bando DP	.60	.25
❑	266	Bob Shirley	.25	.11
❑	267	Doug Ault	.25	.11
❑	268	Gil Flores	.25	.11
❑	269	Wayne Twitchell	.25	.11
❑	270	Carlton Fisk	3.00	1.35
❑	271	Randy Lerch DP	.15	.07
❑	272	Royle Stillman	.25	.11
❑	273	Fred Norman	.25	.11
❑	274	Freddie Patek	.60	.25
❑	275	Dan Ford	.25	.11
❑	276	Bill Bonham DP	.15	.07
❑	277	Bruce Boisclair	.25	.11
❑	278	Enrique Romo	.25	.11
❑	279	Bill Virdon MG	.25	.11
❑	280	Buddy Bell	.60	.25
❑	281	Eric Rasmussen DP	.15	.07
❑	282	New York Yankees Team Card (Checklist back)	2.50	.50
❑	283	Omar Moreno	.25	.11
❑	284	Randy Moffitt	.25	.11
❑	285	Steve Yeager DP	.60	.25
❑	286	Ben Oglivie	.60	.25
❑	287	Kiko Garcia	.25	.11
❑	288	Dave Hamilton	.25	.11
❑	289	Checklist 243-363	1.25	.25
❑	290	Willie Horton	.60	.25
❑	291	Gary Ross	.25	.11
❑	292	Gene Richards	.25	.11
❑	293	Mike Willis	.25	.11
❑	294	Larry Parrish	.60	.25
❑	295	Bill Lee	.25	.11
❑	296	Biff Pocoroba	.25	.11
❑	297	Warren Brusstar DP	.15	.07
❑	298	Tony Armas	.60	.25
❑	299	Whitey Herzog MG	.60	.25
❑	300	Joe Morgan	2.50	1.10
❑	301	Buddy Schultz	.25	.11
❑	302	Chicago Cubs Team Card (Checklist back)	1.25	.25
❑	303	Sam Hinds	.25	.11
❑	304	John Milner	.25	.11
❑	305	Rico Carty	.60	.25
❑	306	Joe Niekro	.60	.25
❑	307	Glenn Borgmann	.25	.11
❑	308	Jim Rooker	.25	.11
❑	309	Cliff Johnson	.25	.11
❑	310	Don Sutton	2.50	1.10
❑	311	Jose Baez DP	.15	.07
❑	312	Greg Minton	.25	.11
❑	313	Andy Etchebarren	.25	.11
❑	314	Paul Lindblad	.25	.11
❑	315	Mark Belanger	.60	.25
❑	316	Henry Cruz DP	.15	.07
❑	317	Dave Johnson	.25	.11
❑	318	Tom Griffin	.25	.11
❑	319	Alan Ashby	.25	.11
❑	320	Fred Lynn	.60	.25
❑	321	Santo Alcala	.25	.11
❑	322	Tom Paciorek	.60	.25
❑	323	Jim Fregosi DP	.25	.11
❑	324	Vern Rapp MG	.25	.11
❑	325	Bruce Sutter	1.25	.55
❑	326	Mike Lum DP	.15	.07
❑	327	Rick Langford DP	.15	.07
❑	328	Milwaukee Brewers Team Card (Checklist back)	1.25	.25
❑	329	John Verhoeven	.25	.11
❑	330	Bob Watson	.60	.25
❑	331	Mark Littell	.25	.11
❑	332	Duane Kuiper	.25	.11
❑	333	Jim Todd	.25	.11
❑	334	John Stearns	.25	.11
❑	335	Bucky Dent	.60	.25
❑	336	Steve Busby	.25	.11
❑	337	Tom Grieve	.60	.25
❑	338	Dave Heaverlo	.25	.11
❑	339	Mario Guerrero	.25	.11
❑	340	Bake McBride	.60	.25
❑	341	Mike Flanagan	.60	.25
❑	342	Aurelio Rodriguez	.25	.11
❑	343	John Wathan DP	.15	.07
❑	344	Sam Ewing	.25	.11
❑	345	Luis Tiant	.60	.25
❑	346	Larry Biittner	.25	.11
❑	347	Terry Forster	.25	.11
❑	348	Del Unser	.25	.11
❑	349	Rick Camp DP	.15	.07
❑	350	Steve Garvey	2.50	1.10
❑	351	Jeff Torborg	.60	.25
❑	352	Tony Scott	.25	.11
❑	353	Doug Bair	.25	.11
❑	354	Cesar Geronimo	.25	.11
❑	355	Bill Travers	.25	.11
❑	356	New York Mets Team Card (Checklist back)	1.25	.25
❑	357	Tom Poquette	.25	.11
❑	358	Mark Lemongello	.25	.11
❑	359	Marc Hill	.25	.11
❑	360	Mike Schmidt	12.00	5.50
❑	361	Chris Knapp	.25	.11
❑	362	Dave May	.25	.11
❑	363	Bob Randall	.25	.11
❑	364	Jerry Turner	.25	.11
❑	365	Ed Figueroa	.25	.11
❑	366	Larry Milbourne DP	.15	.07
❑	367	Rick Dempsey	.60	.25
❑	368	Balor Moore	.25	.11
❑	369	Tim Nordbrook	.25	.11
❑	370	Rusty Staub	1.25	.55
❑	371	Ray Burris	.25	.11
❑	372	Brian Asselstine	.25	.11
❑	373	Jim Willoughby	.25	.11
❑	374	Jose Morales	.25	.11
❑	375	Tommy John	1.25	.55
❑	376	Jim Wohlford	.25	.11
❑	377	Manny Sarmiento	.25	.11
❑	378	Bobby Winkles MG	.25	.11
❑	379	Skip Lockwood	.25	.11
❑	380	Ted Simmons	.60	.25
❑	381	Philadelphia Phillies Team Card (Checklist back)	1.25	.25
❑	382	Joe Lahoud	.25	.11
❑	383	Mario Mendoza	.25	.11
❑	384	Jack Clark	1.25	.55
❑	385	Tito Fuentes	.25	.11
❑	386	Bob Gorinski	.25	.11
❑	387	Ken Holtzman	.60	.25
❑	388	Bill Fahey DP	.15	.07
❑	389	Julio Gonzalez	.25	.11
❑	390	Oscar Gamble	.60	.25
❑	391	Larry Haney	.25	.11
❑	392	Billy Almon	.25	.11
❑	393	Tippy Martinez	.60	.25
❑	394	Roy Howell DP	.15	.07
❑	395	Jim Hughes	.25	.11
❑	396	Bob Stinson DP	.15	.07
❑	397	Greg Gross	.25	.11
❑	398	Don Hood	.25	.11
❑	399	Pete Mackanin	.25	.11
❑	400	Nolan Ryan	40.00	18.00
❑	401	Sparky Anderson MG	.60	.25
❑	402	Dave Campbell	.25	.11
❑	403	Bud Harrelson	.60	.25
❑	404	Detroit Tigers Team Card (Checklist back)	1.25	.25
❑	405	Rawly Eastwick	.25	.11
❑	406	Mike Jorgensen	.25	.11
❑	407	Odell Jones	.25	.11
❑	408	Joe Zdeb	.25	.11
❑	409	Ron Schueler	.25	.11
❑	410	Bill Madlock	.60	.25
❑	411	Willie Randolph ALCS	.60	.25
❑	412	Davey Lopes NLCS	.60	.25
❑	413	Reggie Jackson WS	3.00	1.35
❑	414	Darold Knowles DP	.15	.07
❑	415	Ray Fosse	.25	.11
❑	416	Jack Brohamer	.25	.11
❑	417	Mike Garman DP	.15	.07
❑	418	Tony Muser	.25	.11
❑	419	Jerry Garvin	.25	.11
❑	420	Greg Luzinski	1.25	.55
❑	421	Junior Moore	.25	.11
❑	422	Steve Braun	.25	.11
❑	423	Dave Rosello	.25	.11
❑	424	Boston Red Sox Team Card (Checklist back)	1.25	.25
❑	425	Steve Rogers DP	.25	.11
❑	426	Fred Kendall	.25	.11
❑	427	Mario Soto	.60	.25
❑	428	Joel Youngblood	.25	.11
❑	429	Mike Barlow	.25	.11
❑	430	Al Oliver	.60	.25
❑	431	Butch Metzger	.25	.11
❑	432	Terry Bulling	.25	.11
❑	433	Fernando Gonzalez	.25	.11
❑	434	Mike Norris	.25	.11
❑	435	Checklist 364-484	1.25	.25
❑	436	Vic Harris DP	.15	.07
❑	437	Bo McLaughlin	.25	.11
❑	438	John Ellis	.25	.11
❑	439	Ken Kravec	.25	.11
❑	440	Dave Lopes	.60	.25
❑	441	Larry Gura	.25	.11
❑	442	Elliott Maddox	.25	.11
❑	443	Darrel Chaney	.25	.11
❑	444	Roy Hartsfield MG	.25	.11
❑	445	Mike Ivie	.25	.11
❑	446	Tug McGraw	.60	.25
❑	447	Leroy Stanton	.25	.11
❑	448	Bill Castro	.25	.11
❑	449	Tim Blackwell DP	.15	.07
❑	450	Tom Seaver	4.00	1.80
❑	451	Minnesota Twins Team Card (Checklist back)	1.25	.25
❑	452	Jerry Mumphrey	.25	.11
❑	453	Doug Flynn	.25	.11
❑	454	Dave LaRoche	.25	.11
❑	455	Bill Robinson	.60	.25
❑	456	Vern Ruhle	.25	.11
❑	457	Bob Bailey	.25	.11
❑	458	Jeff Newman	.25	.11
❑	459	Charlie Spikes	.25	.11
❑	460	Jim Hunter	2.50	1.10
❑	461	Rob Andrews DP	.15	.07
❑	462	Rogelio Moret	.25	.11
❑	463	Kevin Bell	.25	.11
❑	464	Jerry Grote	.25	.11
❑	465	Hal McRae	.60	.25
❑	466	Dennis Blair	.25	.11
❑	467	Alvin Dark MG	.60	.25
❑	468	Warren Cromartie	.60	.25
❑	469	Rick Cerone	.60	.25
❑	470	J.R. Richard	.60	.25

❑ 471 Roy Smalley .60 .25
❑ 472 Ron Reed .25 .11
❑ 473 Bill Buckner .60 .25
❑ 474 Jim Slaton .25 .11
❑ 475 Gary Matthews .60 .25
❑ 476 Bill Stein .25 .11
❑ 477 Doug Capilla .25 .11
❑ 478 Jerry Remy .25 .11
❑ 479 St. Louis Cardinals 1.25 .25
Team Card
(Checklist back)
❑ 480 Ron LeFlore .60 .25
❑ 481 Jackson Todd .25 .11
❑ 482 Rick Miller .25 .11
❑ 483 Ken Macha .25 .11
❑ 484 Jim Norris .25 .11
❑ 485 Chris Chambliss .60 .25
❑ 486 John Curtis .25 .11
❑ 487 Jim Tyrone .25 .11
❑ 488 Dan Spillner .25 .11
❑ 489 Rudy Meoli .25 .11
❑ 490 Amos Otis .60 .25
❑ 491 Scott McGregor .60 .25
❑ 492 Jim Sundberg .60 .25
❑ 493 Steve Renko .25 .11
❑ 494 Chuck Tanner MG .60 .25
❑ 495 Dave Cash .25 .11
❑ 496 Jim Clancy DP .15 .07
❑ 497 Glenn Adams .25 .11
❑ 498 Joe Sambito .25 .11
❑ 499 Seattle Mariners 1.25 .25
Team Card
(Checklist back)
❑ 500 George Foster 1.25 .55
❑ 501 Dave Roberts .25 .11
❑ 502 Pat Rockett .25 .11
❑ 503 Ike Hampton .25 .11
❑ 504 Roger Freed .25 .11
❑ 505 Felix Millan .25 .11
❑ 506 Ron Blomberg .25 .11
❑ 507 Willie Crawford .25 .11
❑ 508 Johnny Oates .60 .25
❑ 509 Brent Strom .25 .11
❑ 510 Willie Stargell 2.00 .90
❑ 511 Frank Duffy .25 .11
❑ 512 Larry Herndon .25 .11
❑ 513 Barry Foote .25 .11
❑ 514 Rob Sperring .25 .11
❑ 515 Tim Corcoran .25 .11
❑ 516 Gary Beare .25 .11
❑ 517 Andres Mora .25 .11
❑ 518 Tommy Boggs DP .15 .07
❑ 519 Brian Downing .60 .25
❑ 520 Larry Hisle .25 .11
❑ 521 Steve Staggs .25 .11
❑ 522 Dick Williams MG .60 .25
❑ 523 Donnie Moore .25 .11
❑ 524 Bernie Carbo .25 .11
❑ 525 Jerry Terrell .25 .11
❑ 526 Cincinnati Reds 1.25 .25
Team Card
(Checklist back)
❑ 527 Vic Correll .25 .11
❑ 528 Rob Picciolo .25 .11
❑ 529 Paul Hartzell .25 .11
❑ 530 Dave Winfield 6.00 2.70
❑ 531 Tom Underwood .25 .11
❑ 532 Skip Jutze .25 .11
❑ 533 Sandy Alomar .60 .25
❑ 534 Wilbur Howard .25 .11
❑ 535 Checklist 485-605 1.25 .25
❑ 536 Roric Harrison .25 .11
❑ 537 Bruce Bochte .25 .11
❑ 538 Johnny LeMaster .25 .11
❑ 539 Vic Davalillo DP .15 .07
❑ 540 Steve Carlton 3.00 1.35
❑ 541 Larry Cox .25 .11
❑ 542 Tim Johnson .25 .11
❑ 543 Larry Harlow DP .15 .07
❑ 544 Len Randle DP .15 .07
❑ 545 Bill Campbell .25 .11
❑ 546 Ted Martinez .25 .11
❑ 547 John Scott .25 .11
❑ 548 Billy Hunter DP MG .15 .07
❑ 549 Joe Kerrigan .25 .11
❑ 550 John Mayberry .60 .25
❑ 551 Atlanta Braves 1.25 .25
Team Card
(Checklist back)
❑ 552 Francisco Barrios .25 .11
❑ 553 Terry Puhl .60 .25
❑ 554 Joe Coleman .25 .11
❑ 555 Butch Wynegar .25 .11
❑ 556 Ed Armbrister .25 .11
❑ 557 Tony Solaita .25 .11
❑ 558 Paul Mitchell .25 .11
❑ 559 Phil Mankowski .25 .11
❑ 560 Dave Parker 1.25 .55
❑ 561 Charlie Williams .25 .11
❑ 562 Glenn Burke .25 .11
❑ 563 Dave Rader .25 .11
❑ 564 Mick Kelleher .25 .11
❑ 565 Jerry Koosman .60 .25
❑ 566 Merv Rettenmund .25 .11
❑ 567 Dick Drago .25 .11
❑ 568 Tom Hutton .25 .11
❑ 569 Lary Sorensen .25 .11
❑ 570 Dave Kingman 1.25 .55
❑ 571 Buck Martinez .25 .11
❑ 572 Rick Wise .25 .11
❑ 573 Luis Gomez .25 .11
❑ 574 Bob Lemon MG 1.25 .55
❑ 575 Pat Dobson .25 .11
❑ 576 Sam Mejias .25 .11
❑ 577 Oakland A's 1.25 .25
Team Card
(Checklist back)
❑ 578 Buzz Capra .25 .11
❑ 579 Rance Mulliniks .25 .11
❑ 580 Rod Carew 2.50 1.10
❑ 581 Lynn McGlothen .25 .11
❑ 582 Fran Healy .25 .11
❑ 583 George Medich .25 .11
❑ 584 John Hale .25 .11
❑ 585 Woodie Fryman DP .15 .07
❑ 586 Ed Goodson .25 .11
❑ 587 John Urrea .25 .11
❑ 588 Jim Mason .25 .11
❑ 589 Bob Knepper .25 .11
❑ 590 Bobby Murcer .60 .25
❑ 591 George Zeber .25 .11
❑ 592 Bob Apodaca .25 .11
❑ 593 Dave Skaggs .25 .11
❑ 594 Dave Freisleben .25 .11
❑ 595 Sixto Lezcano .25 .11
❑ 596 Gary Wheelock .25 .11
❑ 597 Steve Dillard .25 .11
❑ 598 Eddie Solomon .25 .11
❑ 599 Gary Woods .25 .11
❑ 600 Frank Tanana .60 .25
❑ 601 Gene Mauch MG .60 .25
❑ 602 Eric Soderholm .25 .11
❑ 603 Will McEnaney .25 .11
❑ 604 Earl Williams .25 .11
❑ 605 Rick Rhoden .60 .25
❑ 606 Pittsburgh Pirates 1.25 .25
Team Card
(Checklist back)
❑ 607 Fernando Arroyo .25 .11
❑ 608 Johnny Grubb .25 .11
❑ 609 John Denny .25 .11
❑ 610 Garry Maddox .60 .25
❑ 611 Pat Scanlon .25 .11
❑ 612 Ken Henderson .25 .11
❑ 613 Marty Perez .25 .11
❑ 614 Joe Wallis .25 .11
❑ 615 Clay Carroll .25 .11
❑ 616 Pat Kelly .25 .11
❑ 617 Joe Nolan .25 .11
❑ 618 Tommy Helms .25 .11
❑ 619 Thad Bosley DP .15 .07
❑ 620 Willie Randolph 1.25 .55
❑ 621 Craig Swan DP .15 .07
❑ 622 Champ Summers .25 .11
❑ 623 Eduardo Rodriguez .25 .11
❑ 624 Gary Alexander DP .15 .07
❑ 625 Jose Cruz .60 .25
❑ 626 Toronto Blue Jays 1.25 .25
Team Card DP
(Checklist back)
❑ 627 David Johnson .25 .11
❑ 628 Ralph Garr .60 .25
❑ 629 Don Stanhouse .25 .11
❑ 630 Ron Cey 1.25 .55
❑ 631 Danny Ozark MG .25 .11
❑ 632 Rowland Office .25 .11
❑ 633 Tom Veryzer .25 .11
❑ 634 Len Barker .25 .11
❑ 635 Joe Rudi .60 .25
❑ 636 Jim Bibby .25 .11
❑ 637 Duffy Dyer .25 .11
❑ 638 Paul Splittorff .25 .11
❑ 639 Gene Clines .25 .11
❑ 640 Lee May DP .25 .11
❑ 641 Doug Rau .25 .11
❑ 642 Denny Doyle .25 .11
❑ 643 Tom House .25 .11
❑ 644 Jim Dwyer .25 .11
❑ 645 Mike Torrez .60 .25
❑ 646 Rick Auerbach DP .15 .07
❑ 647 Steve Dunning .25 .11
❑ 648 Gary Thomasson .25 .11
❑ 649 Moose Haas .25 .11
❑ 650 Cesar Cedeno .60 .25
❑ 651 Doug Rader .25 .11
❑ 652 Checklist 606-726 1.25 .25
❑ 653 Ron Hodges DP .15 .07
❑ 654 Pepe Frias .25 .11
❑ 655 Lyman Bostock .60 .25
❑ 656 Dave Garcia MG .25 .11
❑ 657 Bombo Rivera .25 .11
❑ 658 Manny Sanguillen .60 .25
❑ 659 Texas Rangers 1.25 .25
Team Card
(Checklist back)
❑ 660 Jason Thompson .60 .25
❑ 661 Grant Jackson .25 .11
❑ 662 Paul Dade .25 .11
❑ 663 Paul Reuschel .25 .11
❑ 664 Fred Stanley .25 .11
❑ 665 Dennis Leonard .60 .25
❑ 666 Billy Smith .25 .11
❑ 667 Jeff Byrd .25 .11
❑ 668 Dusty Baker 1.25 .55
❑ 669 Pete Falcone .25 .11
❑ 670 Jim Rice 1.25 .55
❑ 671 Gary Lavelle .25 .11
❑ 672 Don Kessinger .60 .25
❑ 673 Steve Brye .25 .11
❑ 674 Ray Knight 2.50 1.10
❑ 675 Jay Johnstone .60 .25
❑ 676 Bob Myrick .25 .11
❑ 677 Ed Herrmann .25 .11
❑ 678 Tom Burgmeier .25 .11
❑ 679 Wayne Garrett .25 .11
❑ 680 Vida Blue .60 .25
❑ 681 Rob Belloir .25 .11
❑ 682 Ken Brett .25 .11
❑ 683 Mike Champion .25 .11
❑ 684 Ralph Houk MG .60 .25
❑ 685 Frank Taveras .25 .11
❑ 686 Gaylord Perry 2.50 1.10
❑ 687 Julio Cruz .25 .11
❑ 688 George Mitterwald .25 .11
❑ 689 Cleveland Indians 1.25 .25
Team Card
(Checklist back)
❑ 690 Mickey Rivers .60 .25
❑ 691 Ross Grimsley .25 .11
❑ 692 Ken Reitz .25 .11
❑ 693 Lamar Johnson .25 .11
❑ 694 Elias Sosa .25 .11
❑ 695 Dwight Evans 1.25 .55
❑ 696 Steve Mingori .25 .11
❑ 697 Roger Metzger .25 .11
❑ 698 Juan Bernhardt .25 .11
❑ 699 Jackie Brown .25 .11
❑ 700 Johnny Bench 4.00 1.80
❑ 701 Rookie Pitchers .60 .25
Tom Hume
Larry Landreth
Steve McCatty
Bruce Taylor
❑ 702 Rookie Catchers .60 .25
Bill Nahorodny
Kevin Pasley

Rick Sweet
Don Werner
❑ 703 Rookie Pitchers DP 5.00 2.20
Larry Andersen
Tim Jones
Mickey Mahler
Jack Morris
❑ 704 Rookie 2nd Basemen 10.00 4.50
Garth Iorg
Dave Oliver
Sam Perlozzo
Lou Whitaker
❑ 705 Rookie Outfielders........ 1.25 .55
Dave Bergman
Miguel Dilone
Clint Hurdle
Willie Norwood
❑ 706 Rookie 1st Basemen ...... .60 .25
Wayne Cage
Ted Cox
Pat Putnam
Dave Revering
❑ 707 Rookie Shortstops 80.00 36.00
Mickey Klutts
Paul Molitor
Alan Trammell
U.L. Washington
❑ 708 Rookie Catchers 5.00 2.20
Bo Diaz
Dale Murphy
Lance Parrish
Ernie Whitt
❑ 709 Rookie Pitchers............. .60 .25
Steve Burke
Matt Keough
Lance Rautzhan
Dan Schatzeder
❑ 710 Rookie Outfielders........ 1.25 .55
Dell Alston
Rick Bosetti
Mike Easler
Keith Smith
❑ 711 Rookie Pitchers DP .... .25 .11
Cardell Camper
Dennis Lamp
Craig Mitchell
Roy Thomas
❑ 712 Bobby Valentine .... .60 .25
❑ 713 Bob Davis .... .25 .11
❑ 714 Mike Anderson .... .25 .11
❑ 715 Jim Kaat .... 1.25 .55
❑ 716 Clarence Gaston .... .60 .25
❑ 717 Nelson Briles .... .25 .11
❑ 718 Ron Jackson .... .25 .11
❑ 719 Randy Elliott .... .25 .11
❑ 720 Fergie Jenkins 2.50 1.10
❑ 721 Billy Martin MG .... 1.25 .55
❑ 722 Pete Broberg .... .25 .11
❑ 723 John Wockenfuss .... .25 .11
❑ 724 Kansas City Royals ...... 1.25 .25
Team Card
(Checklist back)
❑ 725 Kurt Bevacqua................ .25 .11
❑ 726 Wilbur Wood .... 1.25 .30

1979 Topps

	NRMT	VG-E
COMPLETE SET (726)	180.00	80.00
COMMON CARD (1-726)	.25	.11
COMMON CARD DP	.10	.05

❑ 1 Batting Leaders .... 2.50 .50
Rod Carew
Dave Parker
❑ 2 Home Run Leaders .... 1.00 .45
Jim Rice
George Foster
❑ 3 RBI Leaders .... 1.00 .45
Jim Rice
George Foster
❑ 4 Stolen Base Leaders .... .50 .23
Ron LeFlore
Omar Moreno
❑ 5 Victory Leaders .... .50 .23
Ron Guidry
Gaylord Perry
❑ 6 Strikeout Leaders 6.00 2.70
Nolan Ryan
J.R. Richard
❑ 7 ERA Leaders..................... .50 .23
Ron Guidry
Craig Swan
❑ 8 Leading Firemen .... 1.00 .45
Rich Gossage
Rollie Fingers
❑ 9 Dave Campbell .... .25 .11
❑ 10 Lee May .... .50 .23
❑ 11 Marc Hill .... .25 .11
❑ 12 Dick Drago .... .25 .11
❑ 13 Paul Dade .... .25 .11
❑ 14 Rafael Landestoy .... .25 .11
❑ 15 Ross Grimsley .... .25 .11
❑ 16 Fred Stanley .... .25 .11
❑ 17 Donnie Moore .... .25 .11
❑ 18 Tony Solaita .... .25 .11
❑ 19 Larry Gura DP .... .10 .05
❑ 20 Joe Morgan DP .... 2.00 .90
❑ 21 Kevin Kobel .... .25 .11
❑ 22 Mike Jorgensen .... .25 .11
❑ 23 Terry Forster .... .25 .11
❑ 24 Paul Molitor 20.00 9.00
❑ 25 Steve Carlton 2.50 1.10
❑ 26 Jamie Quirk .... .25 .11
❑ 27 Dave Goltz .... .25 .11
❑ 28 Steve Brye....................... .25 .11
❑ 29 Rick Langford .... .25 .11
❑ 30 Dave Winfield 5.00 2.20
❑ 31 Tom House DP .... .10 .05
❑ 32 Jerry Mumphrey .... .25 .11
❑ 33 Dave Rozema .... .25 .11
❑ 34 Rob Andrews.................... .25 .11
❑ 35 Ed Figueroa...................... .25 .11
❑ 36 Alan Ashby .... .25 .11
❑ 37 Joe Kerrigan DP .... .10 .05
❑ 38 Bernie Carbo .... .25 .11
❑ 39 Dale Murphy 4.00 1.80
❑ 40 Dennis Eckersley .... 2.00 .90
❑ 41 Twins Team/Mgr. .... 1.00 .20
Gene Mauch
(Checklist back)
❑ 42 Ron Blomberg .... .25 .11
❑ 43 Wayne Twitchell .... .25 .11
❑ 44 Kurt Bevacqua.................. .25 .11
❑ 45 Al Hrabosky...................... .25 .11
❑ 46 Ron Hodges .... .25 .11
❑ 47 Fred Norman .... .25 .11
❑ 48 Merv Rettenmund .... .25 .11
❑ 49 Vern Ruhle .... .25 .11
❑ 50 Steve Garvey DP .... 1.00 .45
❑ 51 Ray Fosse DP .... .10 .05
❑ 52 Randy Lerch .... .25 .11
❑ 53 Mick Kelleher.................... .25 .11
❑ 54 Dell Alston DP .... .10 .05
❑ 55 Willie Stargell .... 1.50 .70
❑ 56 John Hale .... .25 .11
❑ 57 Eric Rasmussen .... .25 .11
❑ 58 Bob Randall DP .... .10 .05
❑ 59 John Denny DP .... .25 .11
❑ 60 Mickey Rivers .... .50 .23
❑ 61 Bo Diaz .... .25 .11
❑ 62 Randy Moffitt.................... .25 .11
❑ 63 Jack Brohamer .... .25 .11
❑ 64 Tom Underwood .... .25 .11
❑ 65 Mark Belanger.................. .50 .23
❑ 66 Tigers Team/Mgr. .... 1.00 .20
Les Moss
(Checklist back)
❑ 67 Jim Mason DP .... .10 .05
❑ 68 Joe Niekro DP .... .25 .11
❑ 69 Elliott Maddox .... .25 .11
❑ 70 John Candelaria .... .50 .23
❑ 71 Brian Downing.................. .50 .23
❑ 72 Steve Mingori .... .25 .11
❑ 73 Ken Henderson .... .25 .11
❑ 74 Shane Rawley .... .25 .11
❑ 75 Steve Yeager .... .50 .23
❑ 76 Warren Cromartie .... .50 .23
❑ 77 Dan Briggs DP .... .10 .05
❑ 78 Elias Sosa .... .25 .11
❑ 79 Ted Cox............................ .25 .11
❑ 80 Jason Thompson.............. .50 .23
❑ 81 Roger Erickson .... .25 .11
❑ 82 Mets Team/Mgr. .... 1.00 .20
Joe Torre
(Checklist back)
❑ 83 Fred Kendall .... .25 .11
❑ 84 Greg Minton .... .25 .11
❑ 85 Gary Matthews .... .50 .23
❑ 86 Rodney Scott................... .25 .11
❑ 87 Pete Falcone..................... .25 .11
❑ 88 Bob Molinaro.................... .25 .11
❑ 89 Dick Tidrow .... .25 .11
❑ 90 Bob Boone .... 1.00 .45
❑ 91 Terry Crowley .... .25 .11
❑ 92 Jim Bibby......................... .25 .11
❑ 93 Phil Mankowski .... .25 .11
❑ 94 Len Barker........................ .25 .11
❑ 95 Robin Yount 6.00 2.70
❑ 96 Indians Team/Mgr. .... 1.00 .20
Jeff Torborg
(Checklist back)
❑ 97 Sam Mejias .... .25 .11
❑ 98 Ray Burris .... .25 .11
❑ 99 John Wathan.................... .50 .23
❑ 100 Tom Seaver DP .... 2.00 .90
❑ 101 Roy Howell .... .25 .11
❑ 102 Mike Anderson .... .25 .11
❑ 103 Jim Todd .... .25 .11
❑ 104 Johnny Oates DP .... .25 .11
❑ 105 Rick Camp DP.............. .10 .05
❑ 106 Frank Duffy .... .25 .11
❑ 107 Jesus Alou DP.............. .10 .05
❑ 108 Eduardo Rodriguez .... .25 .11
❑ 109 Joel Youngblood .... .25 .11
❑ 110 Vida Blue...................... .50 .23
❑ 111 Roger Freed .... .25 .11
❑ 112 Phillies Team/Mgr. ...... 1.00 .20
Danny Ozark
(Checklist back)
❑ 113 Pete Redfern .... .25 .11
❑ 114 Cliff Johnson .... .25 .11
❑ 115 Nolan Ryan 30.00 13.50
❑ 116 Ozzie Smith............. 100.00 45.00
❑ 117 Grant Jackson .... .25 .11
❑ 118 Bud Harrelson .... .50 .23
❑ 119 Don Stanhouse .... .25 .11
❑ 120 Jim Sundberg .... .50 .23
❑ 121 Checklist 1-121 DP .... .50 .10
❑ 122 Mike Paxton .... .25 .11
❑ 123 Lou Whitaker 2.50 1.10
❑ 124 Dan Schatzeder .... .25 .11
❑ 125 Rick Burleson .... .25 .11
❑ 126 Doug Bair .... .25 .11
❑ 127 Thad Bosley .... .25 .11
❑ 128 Ted Martinez .... .25 .11
❑ 129 Marty Pattin DP .... .10 .05
❑ 130 Bob Watson DP .... .25 .11
❑ 131 Jim Clancy .... .25 .11
❑ 132 Rowland Office .... .25 .11
❑ 133 Bill Castro .... .25 .11
❑ 134 Alan Bannister............... .25 .11
❑ 135 Bobby Murcer .... .50 .23
❑ 136 Jim Kaat .... .50 .23
❑ 137 Larry Wolfe DP .... .10 .05
❑ 138 Mark Lee .... .25 .11
❑ 139 Luis Pujols..................... .25 .11

❑ 140 Don Gullett .50 .23
❑ 141 Tom Paciorek .50 .23
❑ 142 Charlie Williams .25 .11
❑ 143 Tony Scott .25 .11
❑ 144 Sandy Alomar .50 .23
❑ 145 Rick Rhoden .25 .11
❑ 146 Duane Kuiper .25 .11
❑ 147 Dave Hamilton .25 .11
❑ 148 Bruce Boisclair .25 .11
❑ 149 Manny Sarmiento .25 .11
❑ 150 Wayne Cage .25 .11
❑ 151 John Hiller .25 .11
❑ 152 Rick Cerone .25 .11
❑ 153 Dennis Lamp .25 .11
❑ 154 Jim Gantner DP .25 .11
❑ 155 Dwight Evans 1.00 .45
❑ 156 Buddy Solomon .25 .11
❑ 157 U.L. Washington UER .25 .11
(Sic, bats left, should be right)
❑ 158 Joe Sambito .25 .11
❑ 159 Roy White .50 .23
❑ 160 Mike Flanagan 1.00 .45
❑ 161 Barry Foote .25 .11
❑ 162 Tom Johnson .25 .11
❑ 163 Glenn Burke .25 .11
❑ 164 Mickey Lolich .50 .23
❑ 165 Frank Taveras .25 .11
❑ 166 Leon Roberts .25 .11
❑ 167 Roger Metzger DP .10 .05
❑ 168 Dave Freisleben .25 .11
❑ 169 Bill Nahorodny .25 .11
❑ 170 Don Sutton 2.00 .90
❑ 171 Gene Clines .25 .11
❑ 172 Mike Bruhert .25 .11
❑ 173 John Lowenstein .25 .11
❑ 174 Rick Auerbach .25 .11
❑ 175 George Hendrick 1.00 .45
❑ 176 Aurelio Rodriguez .25 .11
❑ 177 Ron Reed .25 .11
❑ 178 Alvis Woods .25 .11
❑ 179 Jim Beattie DP .25 .11
❑ 180 Larry Hisle .25 .11
❑ 181 Mike Garman .25 .11
❑ 182 Tim Johnson .25 .11
❑ 183 Paul Splittorff .25 .11
❑ 184 Darrel Chaney .25 .11
❑ 185 Mike Torrez .50 .23
❑ 186 Eric Soderholm .25 .11
❑ 187 Mark Lemongello .25 .11
❑ 188 Pat Kelly .25 .11
❑ 189 Eddie Whitson .25 .11
❑ 190 Ron Cey .50 .23
❑ 191 Mike Norris .25 .11
❑ 192 Cardinals Team/Mgr. 1.00 .20
Ken Boyer
(Checklist back)
❑ 193 Glenn Adams .25 .11
❑ 194 Randy Jones .25 .11
❑ 195 Bill Madlock .50 .23
❑ 196 Steve Kemp DP .25 .11
❑ 197 Bob Apodaca .25 .11
❑ 198 Johnny Grubb .25 .11
❑ 199 Larry Milbourne .25 .11
❑ 200 Johnny Bench DP 2.00 .90
❑ 201 Mike Edwards RB .25 .11
❑ 202 Ron Guidry RB 1.00 .45
❑ 203 J.R. Richard RB .25 .11
❑ 204 Pete Rose RB 2.00 .90
❑ 205 John Stearns RB .25 .11
❑ 206 Sammy Stewart RB .25 .11
❑ 207 Dave Lemanczyk .25 .11
❑ 208 Clarence Gaston .50 .23
❑ 209 Reggie Cleveland .25 .11
❑ 210 Larry Bowa .50 .23
❑ 211 Denny Martinez 2.00 .90
❑ 212 Carney Lansford 1.50 .70
❑ 213 Bill Travers .25 .11
❑ 214 Red Sox Team/Mgr. 1.00 .20
Don Zimmer
(Checklist back)
❑ 215 Willie McCovey 2.00 .90
❑ 216 Wilbur Wood .25 .11
❑ 217 Steve Dillard .25 .11
❑ 218 Dennis Leonard .50 .23
❑ 219 Roy Smalley .50 .23
❑ 220 Cesar Geronimo .25 .11
❑ 221 Jesse Jefferson .25 .11
❑ 222 Bob Beall .25 .11
❑ 223 Kent Tekulve .50 .23
❑ 224 Dave Revering .25 .11
❑ 225 Rich Gossage 1.00 .45
❑ 226 Ron Pruitt .25 .11
❑ 227 Steve Stone .50 .23
❑ 228 Vic Davalillo .25 .11
❑ 229 Doug Flynn .25 .11
❑ 230 Bob Forsch .25 .11
❑ 231 John Wockenfuss .25 .11
❑ 232 Jimmy Sexton .25 .11
❑ 233 Paul Mitchell .25 .11
❑ 234 Toby Harrah .50 .23
❑ 235 Steve Rogers .25 .11
❑ 236 Jim Dwyer .25 .11
❑ 237 Billy Smith .25 .11
❑ 238 Balor Moore .25 .11
❑ 239 Willie Horton .50 .23
❑ 240 Rick Reuschel .50 .23
❑ 241 Checklist 122-242 DP .50 .10
❑ 242 Pablo Torrealba .25 .11
❑ 243 Buck Martinez DP .10 .05
❑ 244 Pirates Team/Mgr. 1.00 .20
Chuck Tanner
(Checklist back)
❑ 245 Jeff Burroughs .50 .23
❑ 246 Darrell Jackson .25 .11
❑ 247 Tucker Ashford DP .10 .05
❑ 248 Pete LaCock .25 .11
❑ 249 Paul Thormodsgard .25 .11
❑ 250 Willie Randolph .50 .23
❑ 251 Jack Morris 2.00 .90
❑ 252 Bob Stinson .25 .11
❑ 253 Rick Wise .25 .11
❑ 254 Luis Gomez .25 .11
❑ 255 Tommy John 1.00 .45
❑ 256 Mike Sadek .25 .11
❑ 257 Adrian Devine .25 .11
❑ 258 Mike Phillips .25 .11
❑ 259 Reds Team/Mgr. 1.00 .20
Sparky Anderson
(Checklist back)
❑ 260 Richie Zisk .25 .11
❑ 261 Mario Guerrero .25 .11
❑ 262 Nelson Briles .25 .11
❑ 263 Oscar Gamble .50 .23
❑ 264 Don Robinson .25 .11
❑ 265 Don Money .25 .11
❑ 266 Jim Willoughby .25 .11
❑ 267 Joe Rudi .50 .23
❑ 268 Julio Gonzalez .25 .11
❑ 269 Woodie Fryman .25 .11
❑ 270 Butch Hobson .50 .23
❑ 271 Rawly Eastwick .25 .11
❑ 272 Tim Corcoran .25 .11
❑ 273 Jerry Terrell .25 .11
❑ 274 Willie Norwood .25 .11
❑ 275 Junior Moore .25 .11
❑ 276 Jim Colborn .25 .11
❑ 277 Tom Grieve .50 .23
❑ 278 Andy Messersmith .50 .23
❑ 279 Jerry Grote DP .10 .05
❑ 280 Andre Thornton .50 .23
❑ 281 Vic Correll DP .10 .05
❑ 282 Blue Jays Team/Mgr. .50 .10
Roy Hartsfield
(Checklist back)
❑ 283 Ken Kravec .25 .11
❑ 284 Johnnie LeMaster .25 .11
❑ 285 Bobby Bonds 1.00 .45
❑ 286 Duffy Dyer .25 .11
❑ 287 Andres Mora .25 .11
❑ 288 Milt Wilcox .25 .11
❑ 289 Jose Cruz 1.00 .45
❑ 290 Dave Lopes .50 .23
❑ 291 Tom Griffin .25 .11
❑ 292 Don Reynolds .25 .11
❑ 293 Jerry Garvin .25 .11
❑ 294 Pepe Frias .25 .11
❑ 295 Mitchell Page .25 .11
❑ 296 Preston Hanna .25 .11
❑ 297 Ted Sizemore .25 .11
❑ 298 Rich Gale .25 .11
❑ 299 Steve Ontiveros .25 .11
❑ 300 Rod Carew 2.00 .90
❑ 301 Tom Hume .25 .11
❑ 302 Braves Team/Mgr. 1.00 .20
Bobby Cox
(Checklist back)
❑ 303 Lary Sorensen DP .10 .05
❑ 304 Steve Swisher .25 .11
❑ 305 Willie Montanez .25 .11
❑ 306 Floyd Bannister .25 .11
❑ 307 Larvell Blanks .25 .11
❑ 308 Bert Blyleven 1.00 .45
❑ 309 Ralph Garr .50 .23
❑ 310 Thurman Munson 2.00 .90
❑ 311 Gary Lavelle .25 .11
❑ 312 Bob Robertson .25 .11
❑ 313 Dyar Miller .25 .11
❑ 314 Larry Harlow .25 .11
❑ 315 Jon Matlack .25 .11
❑ 316 Milt May .25 .11
❑ 317 Jose Cardenal .50 .23
❑ 318 Bob Welch 2.00 .90
❑ 319 Wayne Garrett .25 .11
❑ 320 Carl Yastrzemski 2.50 1.10
❑ 321 Gaylord Perry 2.00 .90
❑ 322 Danny Goodwin .25 .11
❑ 323 Lynn McGlothen .25 .11
❑ 324 Mike Tyson .25 .11
❑ 325 Cecil Cooper .50 .23
❑ 326 Pedro Borbon .25 .11
❑ 327 Art Howe DP .25 .11
❑ 328 Oakland A's Team/Mgr. 1.00 .20
Jack McKeon
(Checklist back)
❑ 329 Joe Coleman .25 .11
❑ 330 George Brett 15.00 6.75
❑ 331 Mickey Mahler .25 .11
❑ 332 Gary Alexander .25 .11
❑ 333 Chet Lemon .50 .23
❑ 334 Craig Swan .25 .11
❑ 335 Chris Chambliss .50 .23
❑ 336 Bobby Thompson .25 .11
❑ 337 John Montague .25 .11
❑ 338 Vic Harris .25 .11
❑ 339 Ron Jackson .25 .11
❑ 340 Jim Palmer 2.00 .90
❑ 341 Willie Upshaw .50 .23
❑ 342 Dave Roberts .25 .11
❑ 343 Ed Glynn .25 .11
❑ 344 Jerry Royster .25 .11
❑ 345 Tug McGraw .50 .23
❑ 346 Bill Buckner .50 .23
❑ 347 Doug Rau .25 .11
❑ 348 Andre Dawson 5.00 2.20
❑ 349 Jim Wright .25 .11
❑ 350 Garry Templeton .50 .23
❑ 351 Wayne Nordhagen DP .10 .05
❑ 352 Steve Renko .25 .11
❑ 353 Checklist 243-363 1.00 .20
❑ 354 Bill Bonham .25 .11
❑ 355 Lee Mazzilli .25 .11
❑ 356 Giants Team/Mgr. 1.00 .20
Joe Altobelli
(Checklist back)
❑ 357 Jerry Augustine .25 .11
❑ 358 Alan Trammell 4.00 1.80
❑ 359 Dan Spillner DP .10 .05
❑ 360 Amos Otis .50 .23
❑ 361 Tom Dixon .25 .11
❑ 362 Mike Cubbage .25 .11
❑ 363 Craig Skok .25 .11
❑ 364 Gene Richards .25 .11
❑ 365 Sparky Lyle .50 .23
❑ 366 Juan Bernhardt .25 .11
❑ 367 Dave Skaggs .25 .11
❑ 368 Don Aase .25 .11
❑ 369A Bump Wills ERR 3.00 1.35
(Blue Jays)
❑ 369B Bump Wills COR 3.00 1.35
(Rangers)
❑ 370 Dave Kingman 1.00 .45
❑ 371 Jeff Holly .25 .11
❑ 372 Lamar Johnson .25 .11
❑ 373 Lance Rautzhan .25 .11

❑ 374 Ed Herrmann .25 .11
❑ 375 Bill Campbell .25 .11
❑ 376 Gorman Thomas .50 .23
❑ 377 Paul Moskau .25 .11
❑ 378 Rob Picciolo DP .10 .05
❑ 379 Dale Murray .25 .11
❑ 380 John Mayberry .50 .23
❑ 381 Astros Team/Mgr. 1.00 .20
Bill Virdon
(Checklist back)
❑ 382 Jerry Martin .25 .11
❑ 383 Phil Garner .50 .23
❑ 384 Tommy Boggs .25 .11
❑ 385 Dan Ford .25 .11
❑ 386 Francisco Barrios .25 .11
❑ 387 Gary Thomasson .25 .11
❑ 388 Jack Billingham .25 .11
❑ 389 Joe Zdeb .25 .11
❑ 390 Rollie Fingers 2.00 .90
❑ 391 Al Oliver .50 .23
❑ 392 Doug Ault .25 .11
❑ 393 Scott McGregor .50 .23
❑ 394 Randy Stein .25 .11
❑ 395 Dave Cash .25 .11
❑ 396 Bill Plummer .25 .11
❑ 397 Sergio Ferrer .25 .11
❑ 398 Ivan DeJesus .25 .11
❑ 399 David Clyde .25 .11
❑ 400 Jim Rice 1.00 .45
❑ 401 Ray Knight .50 .23
❑ 402 Paul Hartzell .25 .11
❑ 403 Tim Foli .25 .11
❑ 404 White Sox Team/Mgr 1.00 .20
Don Kessinger
(Checklist back)
❑ 405 Butch Wynegar DP .10 .05
❑ 406 Joe Wallis DP .10 .05
❑ 407 Pete Vuckovich .50 .23
❑ 408 Charlie Moore DP .10 .05
❑ 409 Willie Wilson 1.50 .70
❑ 410 Darrell Evans 1.00 .45
❑ 411 George Sisler ATL 2.00 .90
Ty Cobb
❑ 412 Hack Wilson ATL 2.00 .90
Hank Aaron
❑ 413 Roger Maris ATL 2.00 .90
Hank Aaron
❑ 414 Rogers Hornsby ATL 2.00 .90
Ty Cobb
❑ 415 Lou Brock ATL 1.00 .45
❑ 416 Jack Chesbro ATL .50 .23
Cy Young
❑ 417 Nolan Ryan ATL DP 4.00 1.80
Walter Johnson
❑ 418 Dutch Leonard ATL DP .25 .11
Walter Johnson
❑ 419 Dick Ruthven .25 .11
❑ 420 Ken Griffey .50 .23
❑ 421 Doug DeCinces .50 .23
❑ 422 Ruppert Jones .25 .11
❑ 423 Bob Montgomery .25 .11
❑ 424 Angels Team/Mgr. 1.00 .20
Jim Fregosi
(Checklist back)
❑ 425 Rick Manning .25 .11
❑ 426 Chris Speier .25 .11
❑ 427 Andy Replogle .25 .11
❑ 428 Bobby Valentine .50 .23
❑ 429 John Urrea DP .10 .05
❑ 430 Dave Parker .50 .23
❑ 431 Glenn Borgmann .25 .11
❑ 432 Dave Heaverlo .25 .11
❑ 433 Larry Biittner .25 .11
❑ 434 Ken Clay .25 .11
❑ 435 Gene Tenace .50 .23
❑ 436 Hector Cruz .25 .11
❑ 437 Rick Williams .25 .11
❑ 438 Horace Speed .25 .11
❑ 439 Frank White .50 .23
❑ 440 Rusty Staub 1.00 .45
❑ 441 Lee Lacy .25 .11
❑ 442 Doyle Alexander .25 .11
❑ 443 Bruce Bochte .25 .11
❑ 444 Aurelio Lopez .25 .11
❑ 445 Steve Henderson .25 .11
❑ 446 Jim Lonborg .50 .23
❑ 447 Manny Sanguillen .50 .23
❑ 448 Moose Haas .25 .11
❑ 449 Bombo Rivera .25 .11
❑ 450 Dave Concepcion 1.00 .45
❑ 451 Royals Team/Mgr. 1.00 .20
Whitey Herzog
(Checklist back)
❑ 452 Jerry Morales .25 .11
❑ 453 Chris Knapp .25 .11
❑ 454 Len Randle .25 .11
❑ 455 Bill Lee DP .10 .05
❑ 456 Chuck Baker .25 .11
❑ 457 Bruce Sutter .50 .23
❑ 458 Jim Essian .25 .11
❑ 459 Sid Monge .25 .11
❑ 460 Graig Nettles 1.00 .45
❑ 461 Jim Barr DP .10 .05
❑ 462 Otto Velez .25 .11
❑ 463 Steve Comer .25 .11
❑ 464 Joe Nolan .25 .11
❑ 465 Reggie Smith .50 .23
❑ 466 Mark Littell .25 .11
❑ 467 Don Kessinger DP .25 .11
❑ 468 Stan Bahnsen DP .10 .05
❑ 469 Lance Parrish 1.00 .45
❑ 470 Garry Maddox DP .25 .11
❑ 471 Joaquin Andujar .50 .23
❑ 472 Craig Kusick .25 .11
❑ 473 Dave Roberts .25 .11
❑ 474 Dick Davis .25 .11
❑ 475 Dan Driessen .25 .11
❑ 476 Tom Poquette .25 .11
❑ 477 Bob Grich .50 .23
❑ 478 Juan Beniquez .25 .11
❑ 479 Padres Team/Mgr. 1.00 .20
Roger Craig
(Checklist back)
❑ 480 Fred Lynn .50 .23
❑ 481 Skip Lockwood .25 .11
❑ 482 Craig Reynolds .25 .11
❑ 483 Checklist 364-484 DP .50 .10
❑ 484 Rick Waits .25 .11
❑ 485 Bucky Dent .50 .23
❑ 486 Bob Knepper .25 .11
❑ 487 Miguel Dilone .25 .11
❑ 488 Bob Owchinko .25 .11
❑ 489 Larry Cox UER .25 .11
(Photo actually
Dave Rader)
❑ 490 Al Cowens .25 .11
❑ 491 Tippy Martinez .25 .11
❑ 492 Bob Bailor .25 .11
❑ 493 Larry Christenson .25 .11
❑ 494 Jerry White .25 .11
❑ 495 Tony Perez 2.00 .90
❑ 496 Barry Bonnell DP .10 .05
❑ 497 Glenn Abbott .25 .11
❑ 498 Rich Chiles .25 .11
❑ 499 Rangers Team/Mgr. 1.00 .20
Pat Corrales
(Checklist back)
❑ 500 Ron Guidry .50 .23
❑ 501 Junior Kennedy .25 .11
❑ 502 Steve Braun .25 .11
❑ 503 Terry Humphrey .25 .11
❑ 504 Larry McWilliams .25 .11
❑ 505 Ed Kranepool .50 .23
❑ 506 John D'Acquisto .25 .11
❑ 507 Tony Armas .50 .23
❑ 508 Charlie Hough .50 .23
❑ 509 Mario Mendoza UER .25 .11
(Career BA .278,
should say .204)
❑ 510 Ted Simmons 1.00 .45
❑ 511 Paul Reuschel DP .10 .05
❑ 512 Jack Clark .50 .23
❑ 513 Dave Johnson .50 .23
❑ 514 Mike Proly .25 .11
❑ 515 Enos Cabell .25 .11
❑ 516 Champ Summers DP .10 .05
❑ 517 Al Bumbry .50 .23
❑ 518 Jim Umbarger .25 .11
❑ 519 Ben Oglivie .50 .23
❑ 520 Gary Carter 2.00 .90
❑ 521 Sam Ewing .25 .11
❑ 522 Ken Holtzman .50 .23
❑ 523 John Milner .25 .11
❑ 524 Tom Burgmeier .25 .11
❑ 525 Freddie Patek .25 .11
❑ 526 Dodgers Team/Mgr. 1.00 .20
Tom Lasorda
(Checklist back)
❑ 527 Lerrin LaGrow .25 .11
❑ 528 Wayne Gross DP .10 .05
❑ 529 Brian Asselstine .25 .11
❑ 530 Frank Tanana .50 .23
❑ 531 Fernando Gonzalez .25 .11
❑ 532 Buddy Schultz .25 .11
❑ 533 Leroy Stanton .25 .11
❑ 534 Ken Forsch .25 .11
❑ 535 Ellis Valentine .25 .11
❑ 536 Jerry Reuss .50 .23
❑ 537 Tom Veryzer .25 .11
❑ 538 Mike Ivie DP .10 .05
❑ 539 John Ellis .25 .11
❑ 540 Greg Luzinski .50 .23
❑ 541 Jim Slaton .25 .11
❑ 542 Rick Bosetti .25 .11
❑ 543 Kiko Garcia .25 .11
❑ 544 Fergie Jenkins 2.00 .90
❑ 545 John Stearns .25 .11
❑ 546 Bill Russell .50 .23
❑ 547 Clint Hurdle .25 .11
❑ 548 Enrique Romo .25 .11
❑ 549 Bob Bailey .25 .11
❑ 550 Sal Bando .50 .23
❑ 551 Cubs Team/Mgr. 1.00 .20
Herman Franks
(Checklist back)
❑ 552 Jose Morales .25 .11
❑ 553 Denny Walling .25 .11
❑ 554 Matt Keough .25 .11
❑ 555 Biff Pocoroba .25 .11
❑ 556 Mike Lum .25 .11
❑ 557 Ken Brett .25 .11
❑ 558 Jay Johnstone .50 .23
❑ 559 Greg Pryor .25 .11
❑ 560 John Montefusco .25 .11
❑ 561 Ed Ott .25 .11
❑ 562 Dusty Baker 1.00 .45
❑ 563 Roy Thomas .25 .11
❑ 564 Jerry Turner .25 .11
❑ 565 Rico Carty .50 .23
❑ 566 Nino Espinosa .25 .11
❑ 567 Richie Hebner .50 .23
❑ 568 Carlos Lopez .25 .11
❑ 569 Bob Sykes .25 .11
❑ 570 Cesar Cedeno .50 .23
❑ 571 Darrell Porter .50 .23
❑ 572 Rod Gilbreath .25 .11
❑ 573 Jim Kern .25 .11
❑ 574 Claudell Washington .50 .23
❑ 575 Luis Tiant .50 .23
❑ 576 Mike Parrott .25 .11
❑ 577 Brewers Team/Mgr. 1.00 .20
George Bamberger
(Checklist back)
❑ 578 Pete Broberg .25 .11
❑ 579 Greg Gross .25 .11
❑ 580 Ron Fairly .50 .23
❑ 581 Darold Knowles .25 .11
❑ 582 Paul Blair .50 .23
❑ 583 Julio Cruz .25 .11
❑ 584 Jim Rooker .25 .11
❑ 585 Hal McRae 1.00 .45
❑ 586 Bob Horner 1.00 .45
❑ 587 Ken Reitz .25 .11
❑ 588 Tom Murphy .25 .11
❑ 589 Terry Whitfield .25 .11
❑ 590 J.R. Richard .50 .23
❑ 591 Mike Hargrove .50 .23
❑ 592 Mike Krukow .25 .11
❑ 593 Rick Dempsey .50 .23
❑ 594 Bob Shirley .25 .11
❑ 595 Phil Niekro 2.00 .90
❑ 596 Jim Wohlford .25 .11
❑ 597 Bob Stanley .25 .11
❑ 598 Mark Wagner .25 .11
❑ 599 Jim Spencer .25 .11

❑ 600 George Foster .50 .23
❑ 601 Dave LaRoche .25 .11
❑ 602 Checklist 485-605 1.00 .20
❑ 603 Rudy May .25 .11
❑ 604 Jeff Newman .25 .11
❑ 605 Rick Monday DP .25 .11
❑ 606 Expos Team/Mgr. 1.00 .20
Dick Williams
(Checklist back)
❑ 607 Omar Moreno .25 .11
❑ 608 Dave McKay .25 .11
❑ 609 Silvio Martinez .25 .11
❑ 610 Mike Schmidt 8.00 3.60
❑ 611 Jim Norris .25 .11
❑ 612 Rick Honeycutt .50 .23
❑ 613 Mike Edwards .25 .11
❑ 614 Willie Hernandez .50 .23
❑ 615 Ken Singleton .50 .23
❑ 616 Billy Almon .25 .11
❑ 617 Terry Puhl .25 .11
❑ 618 Jerry Remy .25 .11
❑ 619 Ken Landreaux .50 .23
❑ 620 Bert Campaneris .50 .23
❑ 621 Pat Zachry .25 .11
❑ 622 Dave Collins .50 .23
❑ 623 Bob McClure .25 .11
❑ 624 Larry Herndon .25 .11
❑ 625 Mark Fidrych 2.00 .90
❑ 626 Yankees Team/Mgr. 1.00 .20
Bob Lemon
(Checklist back)
❑ 627 Gary Serum .25 .11
❑ 628 Del Unser .25 .11
❑ 629 Gene Garber .50 .23
❑ 630 Bake McBride .50 .23
❑ 631 Jorge Orta .25 .11
❑ 632 Don Kirkwood .25 .11
❑ 633 Rob Wilfong DP .10 .05
❑ 634 Paul Lindblad .25 .11
❑ 635 Don Baylor 1.00 .45
❑ 636 Wayne Garland .25 .11
❑ 637 Bill Robinson .50 .23
❑ 638 Al Fitzmorris .25 .11
❑ 639 Manny Trillo .25 .11
❑ 640 Eddie Murray 20.00 9.00
❑ 641 Bobby Castillo .25 .11
❑ 642 Wilbur Howard DP .10 .05
❑ 643 Tom Hausman .25 .11
❑ 644 Manny Mota .50 .23
❑ 645 George Scott DP .25 .11
❑ 646 Rick Sweet .25 .11
❑ 647 Bob Lacey .25 .11
❑ 648 Lou Piniella .50 .23
❑ 649 John Curtis .25 .11
❑ 650 Pete Rose 5.00 2.20
❑ 651 Mike Caldwell .25 .11
❑ 652 Stan Papi .25 .11
❑ 653 Warren Brusstar DP .10 .05
❑ 654 Rick Miller .25 .11
❑ 655 Jerry Koosman .50 .23
❑ 656 Hosken Powell .25 .11
❑ 657 George Medich .25 .11
❑ 658 Taylor Duncan .25 .11
❑ 659 Mariners Team/Mgr. 1.00 .20
Darrell Johnson
(Checklist back)
❑ 660 Ron LeFlore DP .25 .11
❑ 661 Bruce Kison .25 .11
❑ 662 Kevin Bell .25 .11
❑ 663 Mike Vail .25 .11
❑ 664 Doug Bird .25 .11
❑ 665 Lou Brock 2.00 .90
❑ 666 Rich Dauer .25 .11
❑ 667 Don Hood .25 .11
❑ 668 Bill North .25 .11
❑ 669 Checklist 606-726 1.00 .20
❑ 670 Jim Hunter DP 1.00 .45
❑ 671 Joe Ferguson DP .10 .05
❑ 672 Ed Halicki .25 .11
❑ 673 Tom Hutton .25 .11
❑ 674 Dave Tomlin .25 .11
❑ 675 Tim McCarver 1.00 .45
❑ 676 Johnny Sutton .25 .11
❑ 677 Larry Parrish .50 .23
❑ 678 Geoff Zahn .25 .11
❑ 679 Derrel Thomas .25 .11
❑ 680 Carlton Fisk 2.50 1.10
❑ 681 John Henry Johnson .25 .11
❑ 682 Dave Chalk .25 .11
❑ 683 Dan Meyer DP .10 .05
❑ 684 Jamie Easterly DP .10 .05
❑ 685 Sixto Lezcano .25 .11
❑ 686 Ron Schueler DP .10 .05
❑ 687 Rennie Stennett .25 .11
❑ 688 Mike Willis .25 .11
❑ 689 Orioles Team/Mgr. 1.00 .20
Earl Weaver
(Checklist back)
❑ 690 Buddy Bell DP .25 .11
❑ 691 Dock Ellis DP .10 .05
❑ 692 Mickey Stanley .25 .11
❑ 693 Dave Rader .25 .11
❑ 694 Burt Hooton .50 .23
❑ 695 Keith Hernandez 1.00 .45
❑ 696 Andy Hassler .25 .11
❑ 697 Dave Bergman .25 .11
❑ 698 Bill Stein .25 .11
❑ 699 Hal Dues .25 .11
❑ 700 Reggie Jackson DP 2.00 .90
❑ 701 Orioles Prospects .50 .23
Mark Corey
John Flinn
Sammy Stewart
❑ 702 Red Sox Prospects .50 .23
Joel Finch
Garry Hancock
Allen Ripley
❑ 703 Angels Prospects .50 .23
Jim Anderson
Dave Frost
Bob Slater
❑ 704 White Sox Prospects .50 .23
Ross Baumgarten
Mike Colbern
Mike Squires
❑ 705 Indians Prospects 1.00 .45
Alfredo Griffin
Tim Norrid
Dave Oliver
❑ 706 Tigers Prospects .50 .23
Dave Stegman
Dave Tobik
Kip Young
❑ 707 Royals Prospects 1.00 .45
Randy Bass
Jim Gaudet
Randy McGilberry
❑ 708 Brewers Prospects 1.00 .45
Kevin Bass
Eddie Romero
Ned Yost
❑ 709 Twins Prospects .50 .23
Sam Perlozzo
Rick Sofield
Kevin Stanfield
❑ 710 Yankees Prospects .50 .23
Brian Doyle
Mike Heath
Dave Rajsich
❑ 711 A's Prospects 1.00 .45
Dwayne Murphy
Bruce Robinson
Alan Wirth
❑ 712 Mariners Prospects .50 .23
Bud Anderson
Greg Biercevicz
Byron McLaughlin
❑ 713 Rangers Prospects 1.00 .45
Danny Darwin
Pat Putnam
Billy Sample
❑ 714 Blue Jays Prospects .50 .23
Victor Cruz
Pat Kelly
Ernie Whitt
❑ 715 Braves Prospects 1.00 .45
Bruce Benedict
Glenn Hubbard
Larry Whisenton
❑ 716 Cubs Prospects .50 .23
Dave Geisel
Karl Pagel
Scot Thompson
❑ 717 Reds Prospects .50 .23
Mike LaCoss
Ron Oester
Harry Spilman
❑ 718 Astros Prospects .50 .23
Bruce Bochy
Mike Fischlin
Don Pisker
❑ 719 Dodgers Prospects 1.50 .70
Pedro Guerrero
Rudy Law
Joe Simpson
❑ 720 Expos Prospects 1.00 .45
Jerry Fry
Jerry Pirtle
Scott Sanderson
❑ 721 Mets Prospects .50 .23
Juan Berenguer
Dwight Bernard
Dan Norman
❑ 722 Phillies Prospects 1.00 .45
Jim Morrison
Lonnie Smith
Jim Wright
❑ 723 Pirates Prospects .50 .23
Dale Berra
Eugenio Cotes
Ben Wiltbank
❑ 724 Cardinals Prospects 1.00 .45
Tom Bruno
George Frazier
Terry Kennedy
❑ 725 Padres Prospects .50 .23
Jim Beswick
Steve Mura
Broderick Perkins
❑ 726 Giants Prospects .50 .10
Greg Johnston
Joe Strain
John Tamargo

1980 Topps

	NRMT	VG-E
COMPLETE SET (726)	100.00	45.00
COMMON CARD (1-726)	.25	.11
COMMON CARD DP	.10	.05

❑ 1 Lou Brock HL 3.00 .60
Carl Yastrzemski
Enter 3000 hit circle
❑ 2 Willie McCovey HL 1.00 .45
512th homer sets new
mark for NL lefties
❑ 3 Manny Mota HL .25 .11
All-time pinch-hits, 145
❑ 4 Pete Rose HL 2.00 .90
Career Record 10th season
with 200 or more hits
❑ 5 Garry Templeton HL .50 .23
First with 100 hits
from each side of plate
❑ 6 Del Unser HL .50 .23
3 consecutive
pinch homers
❑ 7 Mike Lum .25 .11

❑	8	Craig Swan	.25	.11
❑	9	Steve Braun	.25	.11
❑	10	Dennis Martinez	2.00	.90
❑	11	Jimmy Sexton	.25	.11
❑	12	John Curtis DP	.10	.05
❑	13	Ron Pruitt	.25	.11
❑	14	Dave Cash	.25	.11
❑	15	Bill Campbell	.25	.11
❑	16	Jerry Narron	.25	.11
❑	17	Bruce Sutter	.50	.23
❑	18	Ron Jackson	.25	.11
❑	19	Balor Moore	.25	.11
❑	20	Dan Ford	.25	.11
❑	21	Manny Sarmiento	.25	.11
❑	22	Pat Putnam	.25	.11
❑	23	Derrel Thomas	.25	.11
❑	24	Jim Slaton	.25	.11
❑	25	Lee Mazzilli	.50	.23
❑	26	Marty Pattin	.25	.11
❑	27	Del Unser	.25	.11
❑	28	Bruce Kison	.25	.11
❑	29	Mark Wagner	.25	.11
❑	30	Vida Blue	1.00	.45
❑	31	Jay Johnstone	.50	.23
❑	32	Julio Cruz DP	.10	.05
❑	33	Tony Scott	.25	.11
❑	34	Jeff Newman DP	.10	.05
❑	35	Luis Tiant	.50	.23
❑	36	Rusty Torres	.25	.11
❑	37	Kiko Garcia	.25	.11
❑	38	Dan Spillner DP	.10	.05
❑	39	Rowland Office	.25	.11
❑	40	Carlton Fisk	2.00	.90
❑	41	Rangers Team/Mgr.	1.00	.20
		Pat Corrales		
		(Checklist back)		
❑	42	David Palmer	.25	.11
❑	43	Bombo Rivera	.25	.11
❑	44	Bill Fahey	.25	.11
❑	45	Frank White	1.00	.45
❑	46	Rico Carty	.50	.23
❑	47	Bill Bonham DP	.10	.05
❑	48	Rick Miller	.25	.11
❑	49	Mario Guerrero	.25	.11
❑	50	J.R. Richard	.50	.23
❑	51	Joe Ferguson DP	.10	.05
❑	52	Warren Brusstar	.25	.11
❑	53	Ben Oglivie	.50	.23
❑	54	Dennis Lamp	.25	.11
❑	55	Bill Madlock	.50	.23
❑	56	Bobby Valentine	.50	.23
❑	57	Pete Vuckovich	.25	.11
❑	58	Doug Flynn	.25	.11
❑	59	Eddy Putman	.25	.11
❑	60	Bucky Dent	.50	.23
❑	61	Gary Serum	.25	.11
❑	62	Mike Ivie	.25	.11
❑	63	Bob Stanley	.25	.11
❑	64	Joe Nolan	.25	.11
❑	65	Al Bumbry	.50	.23
❑	66	Royals Team/Mgr.	1.00	.20
		Jim Frey		
		(Checklist back)		
❑	67	Doyle Alexander	.25	.11
❑	68	Larry Harlow	.25	.11
❑	69	Rick Williams	.25	.11
❑	70	Gary Carter	2.00	.90
❑	71	John Milner DP	.10	.05
❑	72	Fred Howard DP	.10	.05
❑	73	Dave Collins	.25	.11
❑	74	Sid Monge	.25	.11
❑	75	Bill Russell	.50	.23
❑	76	John Stearns	.25	.11
❑	77	Dave Stieb	2.00	.90
❑	78	Ruppert Jones	.25	.11
❑	79	Bob Owchinko	.25	.11
❑	80	Ron LeFlore	.50	.23
❑	81	Ted Sizemore	.25	.11
❑	82	Astros Team/Mgr.	1.00	.20
		Bill Virdon		
		(Checklist back)		
❑	83	Steve Trout	.25	.11
❑	84	Gary Lavelle	.25	.11
❑	85	Ted Simmons	.50	.23
❑	86	Dave Hamilton	.25	.11
❑	87	Pepe Frias	.25	.11
❑	88	Ken Landreaux	.25	.11
❑	89	Don Hood	.25	.11
❑	90	Manny Trillo	.50	.23
❑	91	Rick Dempsey	.50	.23
❑	92	Rick Rhoden	.25	.11
❑	93	Dave Roberts DP	.10	.05
❑	94	Neil Allen	.50	.23
❑	95	Cecil Cooper	.50	.23
❑	96	A's Team/Mgr.	1.00	.20
		Jim Marshall		
		(Checklist back)		
❑	97	Bill Lee	.50	.23
❑	98	Jerry Terrell	.25	.11
❑	99	Victor Cruz	.25	.11
❑	100	Johnny Bench	3.00	1.35
❑	101	Aurelio Lopez	.25	.11
❑	102	Rich Dauer	.25	.11
❑	103	Bill Caudill	.25	.11
❑	104	Manny Mota	.50	.23
❑	105	Frank Tanana	.50	.23
❑	106	Jeff Leonard	1.00	.45
❑	107	Francisco Barrios	.25	.11
❑	108	Bob Horner	.50	.23
❑	109	Bill Travers	.25	.11
❑	110	Fred Lynn DP	.50	.23
❑	111	Bob Knepper	.25	.11
❑	112	White Sox Team/Mgr.	1.00	.20
		Tony LaRussa		
		(Checklist back)		
❑	113	Geoff Zahn	.25	.11
❑	114	Juan Beniquez	.25	.11
❑	115	Sparky Lyle	.50	.23
❑	116	Larry Cox	.25	.11
❑	117	Dock Ellis	.25	.11
❑	118	Phil Garner	.50	.23
❑	119	Sammy Stewart	.25	.11
❑	120	Greg Luzinski	.50	.23
❑	121	Checklist 1-121	1.00	.20
❑	122	Dave Rosello DP	.10	.05
❑	123	Lynn Jones	.25	.11
❑	124	Dave Lemanczyk	.25	.11
❑	125	Tony Perez	2.00	.90
❑	126	Dave Tomlin	.25	.11
❑	127	Gary Thomasson	.25	.11
❑	128	Tom Burgmeier	.25	.11
❑	129	Craig Reynolds	.25	.11
❑	130	Amos Otis	.50	.23
❑	131	Paul Mitchell	.25	.11
❑	132	Biff Pocoroba	.25	.11
❑	133	Jerry Turner	.25	.11
❑	134	Matt Keough	.25	.11
❑	135	Bill Buckner	.50	.23
❑	136	Dick Ruthven	.25	.11
❑	137	John Castino	.25	.11
❑	138	Ross Baumgarten	.25	.11
❑	139	Dane Iorg	.25	.11
❑	140	Rich Gossage	1.00	.45
❑	141	Gary Alexander	.25	.11
❑	142	Phil Huffman	.25	.11
❑	143	Bruce Bochte DP	.10	.05
❑	144	Steve Comer	.25	.11
❑	145	Darrell Evans	.50	.23
❑	146	Bob Welch	.50	.23
❑	147	Terry Puhl	.25	.11
❑	148	Manny Sanguillen	.50	.23
❑	149	Tom Hume	.25	.11
❑	150	Jason Thompson	.25	.11
❑	151	Tom Hausman DP	.10	.05
❑	152	John Fulgham	.25	.11
❑	153	Tim Blackwell	.25	.11
❑	154	Lary Sorensen	.25	.11
❑	155	Jerry Remy	.25	.11
❑	156	Tony Brizzolara	.25	.11
❑	157	Willie Wilson DP	.50	.23
❑	158	Rob Picciolo DP	.10	.05
❑	159	Ken Clay	.25	.11
❑	160	Eddie Murray	10.00	4.50
❑	161	Larry Christenson	.25	.11
❑	162	Bob Randall	.25	.11
❑	163	Steve Swisher	.25	.11
❑	164	Greg Pryor	.25	.11
❑	165	Omar Moreno	.25	.11
❑	166	Glenn Abbott	.25	.11
❑	167	Jack Clark	.50	.23
❑	168	Rick Waits	.25	.11
❑	169	Luis Gomez	.25	.11
❑	170	Burt Hooton	.50	.23
❑	171	Fernando Gonzalez	.25	.11
❑	172	Ron Hodges	.25	.11
❑	173	John Henry Johnson	.25	.11
❑	174	Ray Knight	.50	.23
❑	175	Rick Reuschel	.50	.23
❑	176	Champ Summers	.25	.11
❑	177	Dave Heaverlo	.25	.11
❑	178	Tim McCarver	1.00	.45
❑	179	Ron Davis	.25	.11
❑	180	Warren Cromartie	.25	.11
❑	181	Moose Haas	.25	.11
❑	182	Ken Reitz	.25	.11
❑	183	Jim Anderson DP	.10	.05
❑	184	Steve Renko DP	.10	.05
❑	185	Hal McRae	.50	.23
❑	186	Junior Moore	.25	.11
❑	187	Alan Ashby	.25	.11
❑	188	Terry Crowley	.25	.11
❑	189	Kevin Kobel	.25	.11
❑	190	Buddy Bell	.50	.23
❑	191	Ted Martinez	.25	.11
❑	192	Braves Team/Mgr.	1.00	.20
		Bobby Cox		
		(Checklist back)		
❑	193	Dave Goltz	.25	.11
❑	194	Mike Easler	.25	.11
❑	195	John Montefusco	.25	.11
❑	196	Lance Parrish	.50	.23
❑	197	Byron McLaughlin	.25	.11
❑	198	Dell Alston DP	.10	.05
❑	199	Mike LaCoss	.25	.11
❑	200	Jim Rice	.50	.23
❑	201	Batting Leaders	1.00	.45
		Keith Hernandez		
		Fred Lynn		
❑	202	Home Run Leaders	1.00	.45
		Dave Kingman		
		Gorman Thomas		
❑	203	RBI Leaders	2.00	.90
		Dave Winfield		
		Don Baylor		
❑	204	Stolen Base Leaders	.50	.23
		Omar Moreno		
		Willie Wilson		
❑	205	Victory Leaders	1.00	.45
		Joe Niekro		
		Phil Niekro		
		Mike Flanagan		
❑	206	Strikeout Leaders	5.00	2.20
		J.R. Richard		
		Nolan Ryan		
❑	207	ERA Leaders	1.00	.45
		J.R. Richard		
		Ron Guidry		
❑	208	Wayne Cage	.25	.11
❑	209	Von Joshua	.25	.11
❑	210	Steve Carlton	2.00	.90
❑	211	Dave Skaggs DP	.10	.05
❑	212	Dave Roberts	.25	.11
❑	213	Mike Jorgensen DP	.10	.05
❑	214	Angels Team/Mgr.	1.00	.20
		Jim Fregosi		
		(Checklist back)		
❑	215	Sixto Lezcano	.25	.11
❑	216	Phil Mankowski	.25	.11
❑	217	Ed Halicki	.25	.11
❑	218	Jose Morales	.25	.11
❑	219	Steve Mingori	.25	.11
❑	220	Dave Concepcion	1.00	.45
❑	221	Joe Cannon	.25	.11
❑	222	Ron Hassey	.25	.11
❑	223	Bob Sykes	.25	.11
❑	224	Willie Montanez	.25	.11
❑	225	Lou Piniella	1.00	.45
❑	226	Bill Stein	.25	.11
❑	227	Len Barker	.25	.11
❑	228	Johnny Oates	.50	.23
❑	229	Jim Bibby	.25	.11
❑	230	Dave Winfield	4.00	1.80
❑	231	Steve McCatty	.25	.11
❑	232	Alan Trammell	2.50	1.10
❑	233	LaRue Washington	.25	.11

❑ 234 Vern Ruhle .25 .11
❑ 235 Andre Dawson 3.00 1.35
❑ 236 Marc Hill .25 .11
❑ 237 Scott McGregor .50 .23
❑ 238 Rob Wilfong .25 .11
❑ 239 Don Aase .25 .11
❑ 240 Dave Kingman 1.00 .45
❑ 241 Checklist 122-242 1.00 .20
❑ 242 Lamar Johnson .25 .11
❑ 243 Jerry Augustine .25 .11
❑ 244 Cardinals Team/Mgr. 1.00 .20
Ken Boyer
(Checklist back)
❑ 245 Phil Niekro 2.00 .90
❑ 246 Tim Foli DP .10 .05
❑ 247 Frank Riccelli .25 .11
❑ 248 Jamie Quirk .25 .11
❑ 249 Jim Clancy .25 .11
❑ 250 Jim Kaat 1.00 .45
❑ 251 Kip Young .25 .11
❑ 252 Ted Cox .25 .11
❑ 253 John Montague .25 .11
❑ 254 Paul Dade DP .10 .05
❑ 255 Dusty Baker DP .50 .23
❑ 256 Roger Erickson .25 .11
❑ 257 Larry Herndon .25 .11
❑ 258 Paul Moskau .25 .11
❑ 259 Mets Team/Mgr. 1.00 .20
Joe Torre
(Checklist back)
❑ 260 Al Oliver 1.00 .45
❑ 261 Dave Chalk .25 .11
❑ 262 Benny Ayala .25 .11
❑ 263 Dave LaRoche DP .10 .05
❑ 264 Bill Robinson .25 .11
❑ 265 Robin Yount 5.00 2.20
❑ 266 Bernie Carbo .25 .11
❑ 267 Dan Schatzeder .25 .11
❑ 268 Rafael Landestoy .25 .11
❑ 269 Dave Tobik .25 .11
❑ 270 Mike Schmidt DP 3.00 1.35
❑ 271 Dick Drago DP .10 .05
❑ 272 Ralph Garr .50 .23
❑ 273 Eduardo Rodriguez .25 .11
❑ 274 Dale Murphy 2.00 .90
❑ 275 Jerry Koosman .50 .23
❑ 276 Tom Veryzer .25 .11
❑ 277 Rick Bosetti .25 .11
❑ 278 Jim Spencer .25 .11
❑ 279 Rob Andrews .25 .11
❑ 280 Gaylord Perry 2.00 .90
❑ 281 Paul Blair .50 .23
❑ 282 Mariners Team/Mgr. 1.00 .20
Darrell Johnson
(Checklist back)
❑ 283 John Ellis .25 .11
❑ 284 Larry Murray DP .10 .05
❑ 285 Don Baylor 1.00 .45
❑ 286 Darold Knowles DP .10 .05
❑ 287 John Lowenstein .25 .11
❑ 288 Dave Rozema .25 .11
❑ 289 Bruce Bochy .25 .11
❑ 290 Steve Garvey 2.00 .90
❑ 291 Randy Scarberry .25 .11
❑ 292 Dale Berra .25 .11
❑ 293 Elias Sosa .25 .11
❑ 294 Charlie Spikes .25 .11
❑ 295 Larry Gura .25 .11
❑ 296 Dave Rader .25 .11
❑ 297 Tim Johnson .25 .11
❑ 298 Ken Holtzman .50 .23
❑ 299 Steve Henderson .25 .11
❑ 300 Ron Guidry .50 .23
❑ 301 Mike Edwards .25 .11
❑ 302 Dodgers Team/Mgr. 1.00 .20
Tom Lasorda
(Checklist back)
❑ 303 Bill Castro .25 .11
❑ 304 Butch Wynegar .25 .11
❑ 305 Randy Jones .25 .11
❑ 306 Denny Walling .25 .11
❑ 307 Rick Honeycutt .50 .23
❑ 308 Mike Hargrove .50 .23
❑ 309 Larry McWilliams .25 .11
❑ 310 Dave Parker 1.00 .45
❑ 311 Roger Metzger .25 .11
❑ 312 Mike Barlow .25 .11
❑ 313 Johnny Grubb .25 .11
❑ 314 Tim Stoddard .25 .11
❑ 315 Steve Kemp .25 .11
❑ 316 Bob Lacey .25 .11
❑ 317 Mike Anderson DP .10 .05
❑ 318 Jerry Reuss .50 .23
❑ 319 Chris Speier .25 .11
❑ 320 Dennis Eckersley 1.00 .45
❑ 321 Keith Hernandez .50 .23
❑ 322 Claudell Washington .50 .23
❑ 323 Mick Kelleher .25 .11
❑ 324 Tom Underwood .25 .11
❑ 325 Dan Driessen .25 .11
❑ 326 Bo McLaughlin .25 .11
❑ 327 Ray Fosse DP .10 .05
❑ 328 Twins Team/Mgr. 1.00 .20
Gene Mauch
(Checklist back)
❑ 329 Bert Roberge .25 .11
❑ 330 Al Cowens .25 .11
❑ 331 Richie Hebner .50 .23
❑ 332 Enrique Romo .25 .11
❑ 333 Jim Norris DP .10 .05
❑ 334 Jim Beattie .25 .11
❑ 335 Willie McCovey 2.00 .90
❑ 336 George Medich .25 .11
❑ 337 Carney Lansford .50 .23
❑ 338 John Wockenfuss .25 .11
❑ 339 John D'Acquisto .25 .11
❑ 340 Ken Singleton .50 .23
❑ 341 Jim Essian .25 .11
❑ 342 Odell Jones .25 .11
❑ 343 Mike Vail .25 .11
❑ 344 Randy Lerch .25 .11
❑ 345 Larry Parrish .50 .23
❑ 346 Buddy Solomon .25 .11
❑ 347 Harry Chappas .25 .11
❑ 348 Checklist 243-363 1.00 .20
❑ 349 Jack Brohamer .25 .11
❑ 350 George Hendrick .50 .23
❑ 351 Bob Davis .25 .11
❑ 352 Dan Briggs .25 .11
❑ 353 Andy Hassler .25 .11
❑ 354 Rick Auerbach .25 .11
❑ 355 Gary Matthews .50 .23
❑ 356 Padres Team/Mgr. 1.00 .20
Jerry Coleman
(Checklist back)
❑ 357 Bob McClure .25 .11
❑ 358 Lou Whitaker 2.00 .90
❑ 359 Randy Moffitt .25 .11
❑ 360 Darrell Porter DP .25 .11
❑ 361 Wayne Garland .25 .11
❑ 362 Danny Goodwin .25 .11
❑ 363 Wayne Gross .25 .11
❑ 364 Ray Burris .25 .11
❑ 365 Bobby Murcer .50 .23
❑ 366 Rob Dressler .25 .11
❑ 367 Billy Smith .25 .11
❑ 368 Willie Aikens .25 .11
❑ 369 Jim Kern .25 .11
❑ 370 Cesar Cedeno .50 .23
❑ 371 Jack Morris 1.00 .45
❑ 372 Joel Youngblood .25 .11
❑ 373 Dan Petry DP .25 .11
❑ 374 Jim Gantner .50 .23
❑ 375 Ross Grimsley .25 .11
❑ 376 Gary Allenson .25 .11
❑ 377 Junior Kennedy .25 .11
❑ 378 Jerry Mumphrey .25 .11
❑ 379 Kevin Bell .25 .11
❑ 380 Garry Maddox .50 .23
❑ 381 Cubs Team/Mgr. 1.00 .20
Preston Gomez
(Checklist back)
❑ 382 Dave Freisleben .25 .11
❑ 383 Ed Ott .25 .11
❑ 384 Joey McLaughlin .25 .11
❑ 385 Enos Cabell .25 .11
❑ 386 Darrell Jackson .25 .11
❑ 387A Fred Stanley YL 5.00 2.20
❑ 387B Fred Stanley .25 .11
(Red name on front)
❑ 388 Mike Paxton .25 .11
❑ 389 Pete LaCock .25 .11
❑ 390 Fergie Jenkins 2.00 .90
❑ 391 Tony Armas DP .25 .11
❑ 392 Milt Wilcox .25 .11
❑ 393 Ozzie Smith 20.00 9.00
❑ 394 Reggie Cleveland .25 .11
❑ 395 Ellis Valentine .25 .11
❑ 396 Dan Meyer .25 .11
❑ 397 Roy Thomas DP .10 .05
❑ 398 Barry Foote .25 .11
❑ 399 Mike Proly DP .10 .05
❑ 400 George Foster .50 .23
❑ 401 Pete Falcone .25 .11
❑ 402 Merv Rettenmund .25 .11
❑ 403 Pete Redfern DP .10 .05
❑ 404 Orioles Team/Mgr. 1.00 .20
Earl Weaver
(Checklist back)
❑ 405 Dwight Evans .50 .23
❑ 406 Paul Molitor 10.00 4.50
❑ 407 Tony Solaita .25 .11
❑ 408 Bill North .25 .11
❑ 409 Paul Splittorff .25 .11
❑ 410 Bobby Bonds 1.00 .45
❑ 411 Frank LaCorte .25 .11
❑ 412 Thad Bosley .25 .11
❑ 413 Allen Ripley .25 .11
❑ 414 George Scott .50 .23
❑ 415 Bill Atkinson .25 .11
❑ 416 Tom Brookens .25 .11
❑ 417 Craig Chamberlain DP .10 .05
❑ 418 Roger Freed DP .10 .05
❑ 419 Vic Correll .25 .11
❑ 420 Butch Hobson .50 .23
❑ 421 Doug Bird .25 .11
❑ 422 Larry Milbourne .25 .11
❑ 423 Dave Frost .25 .11
❑ 424 Yankees Team/Mgr. 1.00 .20
Dick Howser
(Checklist back)
❑ 425 Mark Belanger .50 .23
❑ 426 Grant Jackson .25 .11
❑ 427 Tom Hutton DP .10 .05
❑ 428 Pat Zachry .25 .11
❑ 429 Duane Kuiper .25 .11
❑ 430 Larry Hisle DP .10 .05
❑ 431 Mike Krukow .25 .11
❑ 432 Willie Norwood .25 .11
❑ 433 Rich Gale .25 .11
❑ 434 Johnnie LeMaster .25 .11
❑ 435 Don Gullett .50 .23
❑ 436 Billy Almon .25 .11
❑ 437 Joe Niekro .50 .23
❑ 438 Dave Revering .25 .11
❑ 439 Mike Phillips .25 .11
❑ 440 Don Sutton 2.00 .90
❑ 441 Eric Soderholm .25 .11
❑ 442 Jorge Orta .25 .11
❑ 443 Mike Parrott .25 .11
❑ 444 Alvis Woods .25 .11
❑ 445 Mark Fidrych 2.00 .90
❑ 446 Duffy Dyer .25 .11
❑ 447 Nino Espinosa .25 .11
❑ 448 Jim Wohlford .25 .11
❑ 449 Doug Bair .25 .11
❑ 450 George Brett 12.00 5.50
❑ 451 Indians Team/Mgr. .50 .10
Dave Garcia
(Checklist back)
❑ 452 Steve Dillard .25 .11
❑ 453 Mike Bacsik .25 .11
❑ 454 Tom Donohue .25 .11
❑ 455 Mike Torrez .25 .11
❑ 456 Frank Taveras .25 .11
❑ 457 Bert Blyleven 1.00 .45
❑ 458 Billy Sample .25 .11
❑ 459 Mickey Lolich DP .25 .11
❑ 460 Willie Randolph .50 .23
❑ 461 Dwayne Murphy .25 .11
❑ 462 Mike Sadek DP .10 .05
❑ 463 Jerry Royster .25 .11
❑ 464 John Denny .25 .11
❑ 465 Rick Monday .25 .11
❑ 466 Mike Squires .25 .11

❑ 467 Jesse Jefferson .25 .11
❑ 468 Aurelio Rodriguez .25 .11
❑ 469 Randy Niemann DP .10 .05
❑ 470 Bob Boone 1.00 .45
❑ 471 Hosken Powell DP .10 .05
❑ 472 Willie Hernandez .50 .23
❑ 473 Bump Wills .25 .11
❑ 474 Steve Busby .25 .11
❑ 475 Cesar Geronimo .25 .11
❑ 476 Bob Shirley .25 .11
❑ 477 Buck Martinez .25 .11
❑ 478 Gil Flores .25 .11
❑ 479 Expos Team/Mgr. 1.00 .20
Dick Williams
(Checklist back)
❑ 480 Bob Watson .50 .23
❑ 481 Tom Paciorek .50 .23
❑ 482 Rickey Henderson UER 60.00 27.00
(7 steals at Modesto,
should be at Fresno)
❑ 483 Bo Diaz .25 .11
❑ 484 Checklist 364-484 1.00 .20
❑ 485 Mickey Rivers .50 .23
❑ 486 Mike Tyson DP .10 .05
❑ 487 Wayne Nordhagen .25 .11
❑ 488 Roy Howell .25 .11
❑ 489 Preston Hanna DP .10 .05
❑ 490 Lee May .50 .23
❑ 491 Steve Mura DP .10 .05
❑ 492 Todd Cruz .25 .11
❑ 493 Jerry Martin .25 .11
❑ 494 Craig Minetto .25 .11
❑ 495 Bake McBride .25 .11
❑ 496 Silvio Martinez .25 .11
❑ 497 Jim Mason .25 .11
❑ 498 Danny Darwin .50 .23
❑ 499 Giants Team/Mgr. 1.00 .20
Dave Bristol
(Checklist back)
❑ 500 Tom Seaver 3.00 1.35
❑ 501 Rennie Stennett .25 .11
❑ 502 Rich Wortham DP .10 .05
❑ 503 Mike Cubbage .25 .11
❑ 504 Gene Garber .50 .23
❑ 505 Bert Campaneris .50 .23
❑ 506 Tom Buskey .25 .11
❑ 507 Leon Roberts .25 .11
❑ 508 U.L. Washington .25 .11
❑ 509 Ed Glynn .25 .11
❑ 510 Ron Cey 1.00 .45
❑ 511 Eric Wilkins .25 .11
❑ 512 Jose Cardenal .25 .11
❑ 513 Tom Dixon DP .10 .05
❑ 514 Steve Ontiveros .25 .11
❑ 515 Mike Caldwell UER .25 .11
1979 loss total reads
96 instead of 6#
❑ 516 Hector Cruz .25 .11
❑ 517 Don Stanhouse .25 .11
❑ 518 Nelson Norman .25 .11
❑ 519 Steve Nicosia .25 .11
❑ 520 Steve Rogers .25 .11
❑ 521 Ken Brett .25 .11
❑ 522 Jim Morrison .25 .11
❑ 523 Ken Henderson .25 .11
❑ 524 Jim Wright DP .10 .05
❑ 525 Clint Hurdle .25 .11
❑ 526 Phillies Team/Mgr. 1.00 .20
Dallas Green
(Checklist back)
❑ 527 Doug Rau DP .10 .05
❑ 528 Adrian Devine .25 .11
❑ 529 Jim Barr .25 .11
❑ 530 Jim Sundberg DP .25 .11
❑ 531 Eric Rasmussen .25 .11
❑ 532 Willie Horton .50 .23
❑ 533 Checklist 485-605 1.00 .20
❑ 534 Andre Thornton .50 .23
❑ 535 Bob Forsch .25 .11
❑ 536 Lee Lacy .25 .11
❑ 537 Alex Trevino .25 .11
❑ 538 Joe Strain .25 .11
❑ 539 Rudy May .25 .11
❑ 540 Pete Rose 3.00 1.35
❑ 541 Miguel Dilone .25 .11
❑ 542 Joe Coleman .25 .11
❑ 543 Pat Kelly .25 .11
❑ 544 Rick Sutcliffe 1.00 .45
❑ 545 Jeff Burroughs .50 .23
❑ 546 Rick Langford .25 .11
❑ 547 John Wathan .25 .11
❑ 548 Dave Rajsich .25 .11
❑ 549 Larry Wolfe .25 .11
❑ 550 Ken Griffey 1.00 .45
❑ 551 Pirates Team/Mgr. 1.00 .20
Chuck Tanner
(Checklist back)
❑ 552 Bill Nahorodny .25 .11
❑ 553 Dick Davis .25 .11
❑ 554 Art Howe .50 .23
❑ 555 Ed Figueroa .25 .11
❑ 556 Joe Rudi .50 .23
❑ 557 Mark Lee .25 .11
❑ 558 Alfredo Griffin .25 .11
❑ 559 Dale Murray .25 .11
❑ 560 Dave Lopes .50 .23
❑ 561 Eddie Whitson .25 .11
❑ 562 Joe Wallis .25 .11
❑ 563 Will McEnaney .25 .11
❑ 564 Rick Manning .25 .11
❑ 565 Dennis Leonard .50 .23
❑ 566 Bud Harrelson .50 .23
❑ 567 Skip Lockwood .25 .11
❑ 568 Gary Roenicke .50 .23
❑ 569 Terry Kennedy .50 .23
❑ 570 Roy Smalley .25 .11
❑ 571 Joe Sambito .25 .11
❑ 572 Jerry Morales DP .10 .05
❑ 573 Kent Tekulve .50 .23
❑ 574 Scot Thompson .25 .11
❑ 575 Ken Kravec .25 .11
❑ 576 Jim Dwyer .25 .11
❑ 577 Blue Jays Team/Mgr. 1.00 .20
Bobby Mattick
(Checklist back)
❑ 578 Scott Sanderson .50 .23
❑ 579 Charlie Moore .25 .11
❑ 580 Nolan Ryan 20.00 9.00
❑ 581 Bob Bailor .25 .11
❑ 582 Brian Doyle .25 .11
❑ 583 Bob Stinson .25 .11
❑ 584 Kurt Bevacqua .25 .11
❑ 585 Al Hrabosky .25 .11
❑ 586 Mitchell Page .25 .11
❑ 587 Garry Templeton .25 .11
❑ 588 Greg Minton .25 .11
❑ 589 Chet Lemon .50 .23
❑ 590 Jim Palmer 2.00 .90
❑ 591 Rick Cerone .25 .11
❑ 592 Jon Matlack .25 .11
❑ 593 Jesus Alou .25 .11
❑ 594 Dick Tidrow .25 .11
❑ 595 Don Money .25 .11
❑ 596 Rick Matula .25 .11
❑ 597 Tom Poquette .25 .11
❑ 598 Fred Kendall DP .10 .05
❑ 599 Mike Norris .25 .11
❑ 600 Reggie Jackson 3.00 1.35
❑ 601 Buddy Schultz .25 .11
❑ 602 Brian Downing .25 .11
❑ 603 Jack Billingham DP .10 .05
❑ 604 Glenn Adams .25 .11
❑ 605 Terry Forster .25 .11
❑ 606 Reds Team/Mgr. 1.00 .20
John McNamara
(Checklist back)
❑ 607 Woodie Fryman .25 .11
❑ 608 Alan Bannister .25 .11
❑ 609 Ron Reed .25 .11
❑ 610 Willie Stargell 2.00 .90
❑ 611 Jerry Garvin DP .10 .05
❑ 612 Cliff Johnson .25 .11
❑ 613 Randy Stein .25 .11
❑ 614 John Hiller .25 .11
❑ 615 Doug DeCinces .50 .23
❑ 616 Gene Richards .25 .11
❑ 617 Joaquin Andujar .50 .23
❑ 618 Bob Montgomery DP .10 .05
❑ 619 Sergio Ferrer .25 .11
❑ 620 Richie Zisk .25 .11
❑ 621 Bob Grich .50 .23
❑ 622 Mario Soto .25 .11
❑ 623 Gorman Thomas .50 .23
❑ 624 Lerrin LaGrow .25 .11
❑ 625 Chris Chambliss .50 .23
❑ 626 Tigers Team/Mgr. 1.00 .20
Sparky Anderson
(Checklist back)
❑ 627 Pedro Borbon .25 .11
❑ 628 Doug Capilla .25 .11
❑ 629 Jim Todd .25 .11
❑ 630 Larry Bowa .50 .23
❑ 631 Mark Littell .25 .11
❑ 632 Barry Bonnell .25 .11
❑ 633 Bob Apodaca .25 .11
❑ 634 Glenn Borgmann DP .10 .05
❑ 635 John Candelaria .50 .23
❑ 636 Toby Harrah .50 .23
❑ 637 Joe Simpson .25 .11
❑ 638 Mark Clear .25 .11
❑ 639 Larry Biittner .25 .11
❑ 640 Mike Flanagan .50 .23
❑ 641 Ed Kranepool .25 .11
❑ 642 Ken Forsch DP .10 .05
❑ 643 John Mayberry .50 .23
❑ 644 Charlie Hough .50 .23
❑ 645 Rick Burleson .25 .11
❑ 646 Checklist 606-726 1.00 .20
❑ 647 Milt May .25 .11
❑ 648 Roy White .25 .11
❑ 649 Tom Griffin .25 .11
❑ 650 Joe Morgan 2.00 .90
❑ 651 Rollie Fingers 2.00 .90
❑ 652 Mario Mendoza .25 .11
❑ 653 Stan Bahnsen .25 .11
❑ 654 Bruce Boisclair DP .10 .05
❑ 655 Tug McGraw .50 .23
❑ 656 Larvell Blanks .25 .11
❑ 657 Dave Edwards .25 .11
❑ 658 Chris Knapp .25 .11
❑ 659 Brewers Team/Mgr. 1.00 .20
George Bamberger
(Checklist back)
❑ 660 Rusty Staub .50 .23
❑ 661 Orioles Rookies .50 .23
Mark Corey
Dave Ford
Wayne Krenchicki
❑ 662 Red Sox Rookies .50 .23
Joel Finch
Mike O'Berry
Chuck Rainey
❑ 663 Angels Rookies 1.00 .45
Ralph Botting
Bob Clark
Dickie Thon
❑ 664 White Sox Rookies .50 .23
Mike Colbern
Guy Hoffman
Dewey Robinson
❑ 665 Indians Rookies 1.00 .45
Larry Andersen
Bobby Cuellar
Sandy Wihtol
❑ 666 Tigers Rookies .50 .23
Mike Chris
Al Greene
Bruce Robbins
❑ 667 Royals Rookies 1.00 .45
Renie Martin
Bill Paschall
Dan Quisenberry
❑ 668 Brewers Rookies .50 .23
Danny Boitano
Willie Mueller
Lenn Sakata
❑ 669 Twins Rookies .50 .23
Dan Graham
Rick Sofield
Gary Ward
❑ 670 Yankees Rookies .50 .23
Bobby Brown
Brad Gulden
Darryl Jones
❑ 671 A's Rookies 2.00 .90
Derek Bryant

Brian Kingman
Mike Morgan
❑ 672 Mariners Rookies .50 .23
Charlie Beamon
Rodney Craig
Rafael Vasquez
❑ 673 Rangers Rookies .50 .23
Brian Allard
Jerry Don Gleaton
Greg Mahlberg
❑ 674 Blue Jays Rookies .50 .23
Butch Edge
Pat Kelly
Ted Wilborn
❑ 675 Braves Rookies .50 .23
Bruce Benedict
Larry Bradford
Eddie Miller
❑ 676 Cubs Rookies .50 .23
Dave Geisel
Steve Macko
Karl Pagel
❑ 677 Reds Rookies .50 .23
Art DeFreites
Frank Pastore
Harry Spilman
❑ 678 Astros Rookies .50 .23
Reggie Baldwin
Alan Knicely
Pete Ladd
❑ 679 Dodgers Rookies 1.00 .45
Joe Beckwith
Mickey Hatcher
Dave Patterson
❑ 680 Expos Rookies 1.00 .45
Tony Bernazard
Randy Miller
John Tamargo
❑ 681 Mets Rookies 2.00 .90
Dan Norman
Jesse Orosco
Mike Scott
❑ 682 Phillies Rookies .50 .23
Ramon Aviles
Dickie Noles
Kevin Saucier
❑ 683 Pirates Rookies .50 .23
Dorian Boyland
Alberto Lois
Harry Saferight
❑ 684 Cardinals Rookies 1.00 .45
George Frazier
Tom Herr
Dan O'Brien
❑ 685 Padres Rookies .50 .23
Tim Flannery
Brian Greer
Jim Wilhelm
❑ 686 Giants Rookies .50 .23
Greg Johnston
Dennis Littlejohn
Phil Nastu
❑ 687 Mike Heath DP .10 .05
❑ 688 Steve Stone .50 .23
❑ 689 Red Sox Team/Mgr. 1.00 .20
Don Zimmer
(Checklist back)
❑ 690 Tommy John 1.00 .45
❑ 691 Ivan DeJesus .25 .11
❑ 692 Rawly Eastwick DP .10 .05
❑ 693 Craig Kusick .25 .11
❑ 694 Jim Rooker .25 .11
❑ 695 Reggie Smith .50 .23
❑ 696 Julio Gonzalez .25 .11
❑ 697 David Clyde .25 .11
❑ 698 Oscar Gamble .50 .23
❑ 699 Floyd Bannister .25 .11
❑ 700 Rod Carew DP 1.00 .45
❑ 701 Ken Oberkfell .25 .11
❑ 702 Ed Farmer .25 .11
❑ 703 Otto Velez .25 .11
❑ 704 Gene Tenace .50 .23
❑ 705 Freddie Patek .25 .11
❑ 706 Tippy Martinez .50 .23
❑ 707 Elliott Maddox .25 .11
❑ 708 Bob Tolan .25 .11
❑ 709 Pat Underwood .25 .11
❑ 710 Graig Nettles 1.00 .45
❑ 711 Bob Galasso .25 .11
❑ 712 Rodney Scott .25 .11
❑ 713 Terry Whitfield .25 .11
❑ 714 Fred Norman .25 .11
❑ 715 Sal Bando .50 .23
❑ 716 Lynn McGlothen .25 .11
❑ 717 Mickey Klutts DP .10 .05
❑ 718 Greg Gross .25 .11
❑ 719 Don Robinson .50 .23
❑ 720 Carl Yastrzemski DP 2.00 .90
❑ 721 Paul Hartzell .25 .11
❑ 722 Jose Cruz .50 .23
❑ 723 Shane Rawley .25 .11
❑ 724 Jerry White .25 .11
❑ 725 Rick Wise .25 .11
❑ 726 Steve Yeager 1.00 .20

1981 Topps

	NRMT	VG-E
COMPLETE SET (726)	40.00	18.00
COMMON CARD (1-726)	.15	.07
COMMON CARD DP	.10	.05

❑ 1 Batting Leaders 2.50 1.10
George Brett
Bill Buckner
❑ 2 Home Run Leaders 1.50 .70
Reggie Jackson
Ben Oglivie
Mike Schmidt
❑ 3 RBI Leaders 1.50 .70
Cecil Cooper
Mike Schmidt
❑ 4 Stolen Base Leaders 1.50 .70
Rickey Henderson
Ron LeFlore
❑ 5 Victory Leaders 1.50 .70
Steve Stone
Steve Carlton
❑ 6 Strikeout Leaders 1.50 .70
Len Barker
Steve Carlton
❑ 7 ERA Leaders .75 .35
Rudy May
Don Sutton
❑ 8 Leading Firemen .75 .35
Dan Quisenberry
Rollie Fingers
Tom Hume
❑ 9 Pete LaCock DP .10 .05
❑ 10 Mike Flanagan .40 .18
❑ 11 Jim Wohlford DP .10 .05
❑ 12 Mark Clear .15 .07
❑ 13 Joe Charboneau 1.50 .70
❑ 14 John Tudor .40 .18
❑ 15 Larry Parrish .15 .07
❑ 16 Ron Davis .15 .07
❑ 17 Cliff Johnson .15 .07
❑ 18 Glenn Adams .15 .07
❑ 19 Jim Clancy .15 .07
❑ 20 Jeff Burroughs .15 .07
❑ 21 Ron Oester .15 .07
❑ 22 Danny Darwin .40 .18
❑ 23 Alex Trevino .15 .07
❑ 24 Don Stanhouse .15 .07
❑ 25 Sixto Lezcano .15 .07
❑ 26 U.L. Washington .15 .07
❑ 27 Champ Summers DP .10 .05
❑ 28 Enrique Romo .15 .07
❑ 29 Gene Tenace .40 .18
❑ 30 Jack Clark .40 .18
❑ 31 Checklist 1-121 DP .15 .07
❑ 32 Ken Oberkfell .15 .07
❑ 33 Rick Honeycutt .15 .07
❑ 34 Aurelio Rodriguez .15 .07
❑ 35 Mitchell Page .15 .07
❑ 36 Ed Farmer .15 .07
❑ 37 Gary Roenicke .15 .07
❑ 38 Win Remmerswaal .15 .07
❑ 39 Tom Veryzer .15 .07
❑ 40 Tug McGraw .40 .18
❑ 41 Ranger Rookies .15 .07
Bob Babcock
John Butcher
Jerry Don Gleaton
❑ 42 Jerry White DP .10 .05
❑ 43 Jose Morales .15 .07
❑ 44 Larry McWilliams .15 .07
❑ 45 Enos Cabell .15 .07
❑ 46 Rick Bosetti .15 .07
❑ 47 Ken Brett .15 .07
❑ 48 Dave Skaggs .15 .07
❑ 49 Bob Shirley .15 .07
❑ 50 Dave Lopes .40 .18
❑ 51 Bill Robinson DP .15 .07
❑ 52 Hector Cruz .15 .07
❑ 53 Kevin Saucier .15 .07
❑ 54 Ivan DeJesus .15 .07
❑ 55 Mike Norris .15 .07
❑ 56 Buck Martinez .15 .07
❑ 57 Dave Roberts .15 .07
❑ 58 Joel Youngblood .15 .07
❑ 59 Dan Petry .15 .07
❑ 60 Willie Randolph .40 .18
❑ 61 Butch Wynegar .15 .07
❑ 62 Joe Pettini .15 .07
❑ 63 Steve Renko DP .10 .05
❑ 64 Brian Asselstine .15 .07
❑ 65 Scott McGregor .15 .07
❑ 66 Royals Rookies .15 .07
Manny Castillo
Tim Ireland
Mike Jones
❑ 67 Ken Kravec .15 .07
❑ 68 Matt Alexander DP .10 .05
❑ 69 Ed Halicki .15 .07
❑ 70 Al Oliver DP .40 .18
❑ 71 Hal Dues .15 .07
❑ 72 Barry Evans DP .10 .05
❑ 73 Doug Bair .15 .07
❑ 74 Mike Hargrove .40 .18
❑ 75 Reggie Smith .40 .18
❑ 76 Mario Mendoza .15 .07
❑ 77 Mike Barlow .15 .07
❑ 78 Steve Dillard .15 .07
❑ 79 Bruce Robbins .15 .07
❑ 80 Rusty Staub .40 .18
❑ 81 Dave Stapleton .15 .07
❑ 82 Astros Rookies DP .15 .07
Danny Heep
Alan Knicely
Bobby Sprowl
❑ 83 Mike Proly .15 .07
❑ 84 Johnnie LeMaster .15 .07
❑ 85 Mike Caldwell .15 .07
❑ 86 Wayne Gross .15 .07
❑ 87 Rick Camp .15 .07
❑ 88 Joe Lefebvre .15 .07
❑ 89 Darrell Jackson .15 .07
❑ 90 Bake McBride .15 .07
❑ 91 Tim Stoddard DP .10 .05
❑ 92 Mike Easler .15 .07
❑ 93 Ed Glynn DP .10 .05
❑ 94 Harry Spilman DP .10 .05
❑ 95 Jim Sundberg .40 .18
❑ 96 A's Rookies .15 .07
Dave Beard
Ernie Camacho
Pat Dempsey

❑ 97	Chris Speier	.15	.07
❑ 98	Clint Hurdle	.15	.07
❑ 99	Eric Wilkins	.15	.07
❑ 100	Rod Carew	1.50	.70
❑ 101	Benny Ayala	.15	.07
❑ 102	Dave Tobik	.15	.07
❑ 103	Jerry Martin	.15	.07
❑ 104	Terry Forster	.15	.07
❑ 105	Jose Cruz	.40	.18
❑ 106	Don Money	.15	.07
❑ 107	Rich Wortham	.15	.07
❑ 108	Bruce Benedict	.15	.07
❑ 109	Mike Scott	.40	.18
❑ 110	Carl Yastrzemski	1.50	.70
❑ 111	Greg Minton	.15	.07
❑ 112	White Sox Rookies	.15	.07
	Rusty Kuntz		
	Fran Mullins		
	Leo Sutherland		
❑ 113	Mike Phillips	.15	.07
❑ 114	Tom Underwood	.15	.07
❑ 115	Roy Smalley	.15	.07
❑ 116	Joe Simpson	.15	.07
❑ 117	Pete Falcone	.15	.07
❑ 118	Kurt Bevacqua	.15	.07
❑ 119	Tippy Martinez	.15	.07
❑ 120	Larry Bowa	.40	.18
❑ 121	Larry Harlow	.15	.07
❑ 122	John Denny	.15	.07
❑ 123	Al Cowens	.15	.07
❑ 124	Jerry Garvin	.15	.07
❑ 125	Andre Dawson	1.50	.70
❑ 126	Charlie Leibrandt	.75	.35
❑ 127	Rudy Law	.15	.07
❑ 128	Gary Allenson DP	.10	.05
❑ 129	Art Howe	.15	.07
❑ 130	Larry Gura	.15	.07
❑ 131	Keith Moreland	.40	.18
❑ 132	Tommy Boggs	.15	.07
❑ 133	Jeff Cox	.15	.07
❑ 134	Steve Mura	.15	.07
❑ 135	Gorman Thomas	.40	.18
❑ 136	Doug Capilla	.15	.07
❑ 137	Hosken Powell	.15	.07
❑ 138	Rich Dotson DP	.15	.07
❑ 139	Oscar Gamble	.15	.07
❑ 140	Bob Forsch	.15	.07
❑ 141	Miguel Dilone	.15	.07
❑ 142	Jackson Todd	.15	.07
❑ 143	Dan Meyer	.15	.07
❑ 144	Allen Ripley	.15	.07
❑ 145	Mickey Rivers	.40	.18
❑ 146	Bobby Castillo	.15	.07
❑ 147	Dale Berra	.15	.07
❑ 148	Randy Niemann	.15	.07
❑ 149	Joe Nolan	.15	.07
❑ 150	Mark Fidrych	1.50	.70
❑ 151	Claudell Washington	.15	.07
❑ 152	John Urrea	.15	.07
❑ 153	Tom Poquette	.15	.07
❑ 154	Rick Langford	.15	.07
❑ 155	Chris Chambliss	.40	.18
❑ 156	Bob McClure	.15	.07
❑ 157	John Wathan	.15	.07
❑ 158	Fergie Jenkins	1.50	.70
❑ 159	Brian Doyle	.15	.07
❑ 160	Garry Maddox	.15	.07
❑ 161	Dan Graham	.15	.07
❑ 162	Doug Corbett	.15	.07
❑ 163	Bill Almon	.15	.07
❑ 164	LaMarr Hoyt	.40	.18
❑ 165	Tony Scott	.15	.07
❑ 166	Floyd Bannister	.15	.07
❑ 167	Terry Whitfield	.15	.07
❑ 168	Don Robinson DP	.10	.05
❑ 169	John Mayberry	.15	.07
❑ 170	Ross Grimsley	.15	.07
❑ 171	Gene Richards	.15	.07
❑ 172	Gary Woods	.15	.07
❑ 173	Bump Wills	.15	.07
❑ 174	Doug Rau	.15	.07
❑ 175	Dave Collins	.15	.07
❑ 176	Mike Krukow	.15	.07
❑ 177	Rick Peters	.15	.07
❑ 178	Jim Essian DP	.10	.05
❑ 179	Rudy May	.15	.07
❑ 180	Pete Rose	2.00	.90
❑ 181	Elias Sosa	.15	.07
❑ 182	Bob Grich	.40	.18
❑ 183	Dick Davis DP	.10	.05
❑ 184	Jim Dwyer	.15	.07
❑ 185	Dennis Leonard	.15	.07
❑ 186	Wayne Nordhagen	.15	.07
❑ 187	Mike Parrott	.15	.07
❑ 188	Doug DeCinces	.40	.18
❑ 189	Craig Swan	.15	.07
❑ 190	Cesar Cedeno	.40	.18
❑ 191	Rick Sutcliffe	.40	.18
❑ 192	Braves Rookies	.40	.18
	Terry Harper		
	Ed Miller		
	Rafael Ramirez		
❑ 193	Pete Vuckovich	.40	.18
❑ 194	Rod Scurry	.15	.07
❑ 195	Rich Murray	.15	.07
❑ 196	Duffy Dyer	.15	.07
❑ 197	Jim Kern	.15	.07
❑ 198	Jerry Dybzinski	.15	.07
❑ 199	Chuck Rainey	.15	.07
❑ 200	George Foster	.40	.18
❑ 201	Johnny Bench RB	.75	.35
	Most homers catchers		
❑ 202	Steve Carlton RB	.75	.35
	Most strikeouts,		
	lefthander, lifetime		
❑ 203	Bill Gullickson RB	.75	.35
	Most SO's, game, rookie		
❑ 204	Ron LeFlore RB	.40	.18
	Rodney Scott RB		
	Most stolen bases		
	teammates, season		
❑ 205	Pete Rose RB	1.50	.70
	Most cons. seasons		
	600 or more at-bats		
❑ 206	Mike Schmidt RB	.75	.35
	Most homers, 3rd baseman, season		
❑ 207	Ozzie Smith RB	2.00	.90
	Most assists,		
	season, shortstop		
❑ 208	Willie Wilson RB	.40	.18
	Most AB's season		
❑ 209	Dickie Thon DP	.40	.18
❑ 210	Jim Palmer	1.50	.70
❑ 211	Derrel Thomas	.15	.07
❑ 212	Steve Nicosia	.15	.07
❑ 213	Al Holland	.15	.07
❑ 214	Angels Rookies	.15	.07
	Ralph Botting		
	Jim Dorsey		
	John Harris		
❑ 215	Larry Hisle	.15	.07
❑ 216	John Henry Johnson	.15	.07
❑ 217	Rich Hebner	.15	.07
❑ 218	Paul Splittorff	.15	.07
❑ 219	Ken Landreaux	.15	.07
❑ 220	Tom Seaver	2.00	.90
❑ 221	Bob Davis	.15	.07
❑ 222	Jorge Orta	.15	.07
❑ 223	Roy Lee Jackson	.15	.07
❑ 224	Pat Zachry	.15	.07
❑ 225	Ruppert Jones	.15	.07
❑ 226	Manny Sanguillen DP	.10	.05
❑ 227	Fred Martinez	.15	.07
❑ 228	Tom Paciorek	.40	.18
❑ 229	Rollie Fingers	1.50	.70
❑ 230	George Hendrick	.40	.18
❑ 231	Joe Beckwith	.15	.07
❑ 232	Mickey Klutts	.15	.07
❑ 233	Skip Lockwood	.15	.07
❑ 234	Lou Whitaker	1.50	.70
❑ 235	Scott Sanderson	.15	.07
❑ 236	Mike Ivie	.15	.07
❑ 237	Charlie Moore	.15	.07
❑ 238	Willie Hernandez	.40	.18
❑ 239	Rick Miller DP	.10	.05
❑ 240	Nolan Ryan	8.00	3.60
❑ 241	Checklist 122-242 DP	.15	.07
❑ 242	Chet Lemon	.15	.07
❑ 243	Sal Butera	.15	.07
❑ 244	Cardinals Rookies	.15	.07
	Tito Landrum		
	Al Olmsted		
	Andy Rincon		
❑ 245	Ed Figueroa	.15	.07
❑ 246	Ed Ott DP	.10	.05
❑ 247	Glenn Hubbard DP	.10	.05
❑ 248	Joey McLaughlin	.15	.07
❑ 249	Larry Cox	.15	.07
❑ 250	Ron Guidry	.40	.18
❑ 251	Tom Brookens	.15	.07
❑ 252	Victor Cruz	.15	.07
❑ 253	Dave Bergman	.15	.07
❑ 254	Ozzie Smith	6.00	2.70
❑ 255	Mark Littell	.15	.07
❑ 256	Bombo Rivera	.15	.07
❑ 257	Rennie Stennett	.15	.07
❑ 258	Joe Price	.15	.07
❑ 259	Mets Rookies	1.50	.70
	Juan Berenguer		
	Hubie Brooks		
	Mookie Wilson		
❑ 260	Ron Cey	.40	.18
❑ 261	Rickey Henderson	4.00	1.80
❑ 262	Sammy Stewart	.15	.07
❑ 263	Brian Downing	.40	.18
❑ 264	Jim Norris	.15	.07
❑ 265	John Candelaria	.40	.18
❑ 266	Tom Herr	.40	.18
❑ 267	Stan Bahnsen	.15	.07
❑ 268	Jerry Royster	.15	.07
❑ 269	Ken Forsch	.15	.07
❑ 270	Greg Luzinski	.40	.18
❑ 271	Bill Castro	.15	.07
❑ 272	Bruce Kimm	.15	.07
❑ 273	Stan Papi	.15	.07
❑ 274	Craig Chamberlain	.15	.07
❑ 275	Dwight Evans	.75	.35
❑ 276	Dan Spillner	.15	.07
❑ 277	Alfredo Griffin	.15	.07
❑ 278	Rick Sofield	.15	.07
❑ 279	Bob Knepper	.15	.07
❑ 280	Ken Griffey	.75	.35
❑ 281	Fred Stanley	.15	.07
❑ 282	Mariners Rookies	.15	.07
	Rick Anderson		
	Greg Biercevicz		
	Rodney Craig		
❑ 283	Billy Sample	.15	.07
❑ 284	Brian Kingman	.15	.07
❑ 285	Jerry Turner	.15	.07
❑ 286	Dave Frost	.15	.07
❑ 287	Lenn Sakata	.15	.07
❑ 288	Bob Clark	.15	.07
❑ 289	Mickey Hatcher	.40	.18
❑ 290	Bob Boone DP	.40	.18
❑ 291	Aurelio Lopez	.15	.07
❑ 292	Mike Squires	.15	.07
❑ 293	Charlie Lea	.15	.07
❑ 294	Mike Tyson DP	.10	.05
❑ 295	Hal McRae	.40	.18
❑ 296	Bill Nahorodny DP	.10	.05
❑ 297	Bob Bailor	.15	.07
❑ 298	Buddy Solomon	.15	.07
❑ 299	Elliott Maddox	.15	.07
❑ 300	Paul Molitor	3.00	1.35
❑ 301	Matt Keough	.15	.07
❑ 302	Dodgers Rookies	3.00	1.35
	Jack Perconte		
	Mike Scioscia		
	Fernando Valenzuela		
❑ 303	Johnny Oates	.40	.18
❑ 304	John Castino	.15	.07
❑ 305	Ken Clay	.15	.07
❑ 306	Juan Beniquez DP	.10	.05
❑ 307	Gene Garber	.15	.07
❑ 308	Rick Manning	.15	.07
❑ 309	Luis Salazar	.15	.07
❑ 310	Vida Blue DP	.15	.07
❑ 311	Freddie Patek	.15	.07
❑ 312	Rick Rhoden	.15	.07
❑ 313	Luis Pujols	.15	.07
❑ 314	Rich Dauer	.15	.07
❑ 315	Kirk Gibson	3.00	1.35
❑ 316	Craig Minetto	.15	.07
❑ 317	Lonnie Smith	.40	.18
❑ 318	Steve Yeager	.15	.07

❑ 319 Rowland Office .15 .07
❑ 320 Tom Burgmeier .15 .07
❑ 321 Leon Durham .40 .18
❑ 322 Neil Allen .15 .07
❑ 323 Jim Morrison DP .10 .05
❑ 324 Mike Willis .15 .07
❑ 325 Ray Knight .40 .18
❑ 326 Biff Pocoroba .15 .07
❑ 327 Moose Haas .15 .07
❑ 328 Twins Rookies .15 .07
Dave Engle
Greg Johnston
Gary Ward
❑ 329 Joaquin Andujar .40 .18
❑ 330 Frank White .40 .18
❑ 331 Dennis Lamp .15 .07
❑ 332 Lee Lacy DP .10 .05
❑ 333 Sid Monge .15 .07
❑ 334 Dane Iorg .15 .07
❑ 335 Rick Cerone .15 .07
❑ 336 Eddie Whitson .15 .07
❑ 337 Lynn Jones .15 .07
❑ 338 Checklist 243-363 .75 .35
❑ 339 John Ellis .15 .07
❑ 340 Bruce Kison .15 .07
❑ 341 Dwayne Murphy .15 .07
❑ 342 Eric Rasmussen DP .10 .05
❑ 343 Frank Taveras .15 .07
❑ 344 Byron McLaughlin .15 .07
❑ 345 Warren Cromartie .15 .07
❑ 346 Larry Christenson DP .10 .05
❑ 347 Harold Baines 2.50 1.10
❑ 348 Bob Sykes .15 .07
❑ 349 Glenn Hoffman .15 .07
❑ 350 J.R. Richard .40 .18
❑ 351 Otto Velez .15 .07
❑ 352 Dick Tidrow DP .10 .05
❑ 353 Terry Kennedy .15 .07
❑ 354 Mario Soto .15 .07
❑ 355 Bob Horner .40 .18
❑ 356 Padres Rookies .15 .07
George Stablein
Craig Stimac
Tom Tellmann
❑ 357 Jim Slaton .15 .07
❑ 358 Mark Wagner .15 .07
❑ 359 Tom Hausman .15 .07
❑ 360 Willie Wilson .40 .18
❑ 361 Joe Strain .15 .07
❑ 362 Bo Diaz .15 .07
❑ 363 Geoff Zahn .15 .07
❑ 364 Mike Davis .15 .07
❑ 365 Graig Nettles DP .40 .18
❑ 366 Mike Ramsey .15 .07
❑ 367 Dennis Martinez .75 .35
❑ 368 Leon Roberts .15 .07
❑ 369 Frank Tanana .40 .18
❑ 370 Dave Winfield 1.50 .70
❑ 371 Charlie Hough .40 .18
❑ 372 Jay Johnstone .40 .18
❑ 373 Pat Underwood .15 .07
❑ 374 Tommy Hutton .15 .07
❑ 375 Dave Concepcion .40 .18
❑ 376 Ron Reed .15 .07
❑ 377 Jerry Morales .15 .07
❑ 378 Dave Rader .15 .07
❑ 379 Lary Sorensen .15 .07
❑ 380 Willie Stargell 1.50 .70
❑ 381 Cubs Rookies .15 .07
Carlos Lezcano
Steve Macko
Randy Martz
❑ 382 Paul Mirabella .15 .07
❑ 383 Eric Soderholm DP .10 .05
❑ 384 Mike Sadek .15 .07
❑ 385 Joe Sambito .15 .07
❑ 386 Dave Edwards .15 .07
❑ 387 Phil Niekro 1.50 .70
❑ 388 Andre Thornton .40 .18
❑ 389 Marty Pattin .15 .07
❑ 390 Cesar Geronimo .15 .07
❑ 391 Dave Lemanczyk DP .10 .05
❑ 392 Lance Parrish .40 .18
❑ 393 Broderick Perkins .15 .07
❑ 394 Woodie Fryman .15 .07
❑ 395 Scot Thompson .15 .07
❑ 396 Bill Campbell .15 .07
❑ 397 Julio Cruz .15 .07
❑ 398 Ross Baumgarten .15 .07
❑ 399 Orioles Rookies 1.50 .70
Mike Boddicker
Mark Corey
Floyd Rayford
❑ 400 Reggie Jackson 2.00 .90
❑ 401 George Brett ALCS 2.00 .90
❑ 402 NL Champs .75 .35
Phillies squeak
past Astros
(Phillies celebrating)
❑ 403 Larry Bowa WS .75 .35
❑ 404 Tug McGraw WS .75 .35
❑ 405 Nino Espinosa .15 .07
❑ 406 Dickie Noles .15 .07
❑ 407 Ernie Whitt .15 .07
❑ 408 Fernando Arroyo .15 .07
❑ 409 Larry Herndon .15 .07
❑ 410 Bert Campaneris .40 .18
❑ 411 Terry Puhl .15 .07
❑ 412 Britt Burns .15 .07
❑ 413 Tony Bernazard .15 .07
❑ 414 John Pacella DP .10 .05
❑ 415 Ben Oglivie .40 .18
❑ 416 Gary Alexander .15 .07
❑ 417 Dan Schatzeder .15 .07
❑ 418 Bobby Brown .15 .07
❑ 419 Tom Hume .15 .07
❑ 420 Keith Hernandez .40 .18
❑ 421 Bob Stanley .15 .07
❑ 422 Dan Ford .15 .07
❑ 423 Shane Rawley .15 .07
❑ 424 Yankees Rookies .15 .07
Tim Lollar
Bruce Robinson
Dennis Werth
❑ 425 Al Bumbry .40 .18
❑ 426 Warren Brusstar .15 .07
❑ 427 John D'Acquisto .15 .07
❑ 428 John Stearns .15 .07
❑ 429 Mick Kelleher .15 .07
❑ 430 Jim Bibby .15 .07
❑ 431 Dave Roberts .15 .07
❑ 432 Len Barker .15 .07
❑ 433 Rance Mulliniks .15 .07
❑ 434 Roger Erickson .15 .07
❑ 435 Jim Spencer .15 .07
❑ 436 Gary Lucas .15 .07
❑ 437 Mike Heath DP .10 .05
❑ 438 John Montefusco .15 .07
❑ 439 Denny Walling .15 .07
❑ 440 Jerry Reuss .40 .18
❑ 441 Ken Reitz .15 .07
❑ 442 Ron Pruitt .15 .07
❑ 443 Jim Beattie DP .10 .05
❑ 444 Garth Iorg .15 .07
❑ 445 Ellis Valentine .15 .07
❑ 446 Checklist 364-484 .75 .35
❑ 447 Junior Kennedy DP .10 .05
❑ 448 Tim Corcoran .15 .07
❑ 449 Paul Mitchell .15 .07
❑ 450 Dave Kingman DP .40 .18
❑ 451 Indians Rookies .15 .07
Chris Bando
Tom Brennan
Sandy Wihtol
❑ 452 Renie Martin .15 .07
❑ 453 Rob Wilfong DP .10 .05
❑ 454 Andy Hassler .15 .07
❑ 455 Rick Burleson .15 .07
❑ 456 Jeff Reardon 1.50 .70
❑ 457 Mike Lum .15 .07
❑ 458 Randy Jones .15 .07
❑ 459 Greg Gross .15 .07
❑ 460 Rich Gossage .75 .35
❑ 461 Dave McKay .15 .07
❑ 462 Jack Brohamer .15 .07
❑ 463 Milt May .15 .07
❑ 464 Adrian Devine .15 .07
❑ 465 Bill Russell .40 .18
❑ 466 Bob Molinaro .15 .07
❑ 467 Dave Stieb .40 .18
❑ 468 John Wockenfuss .15 .07
❑ 469 Jeff Leonard .40 .18
❑ 470 Manny Trillo .15 .07
❑ 471 Mike Vail .15 .07
❑ 472 Dyar Miller DP .10 .05
❑ 473 Jose Cardenal .15 .07
❑ 474 Mike LaCoss .15 .07
❑ 475 Buddy Bell .40 .18
❑ 476 Jerry Koosman .40 .18
❑ 477 Luis Gomez .15 .07
❑ 478 Juan Eichelberger .15 .07
❑ 479 Expos Rookies 3.00 1.35
Tim Raines
Roberto Ramos
Bobby Pate
❑ 480 Carlton Fisk 1.50 .70
❑ 481 Bob Lacey DP .10 .05
❑ 482 Jim Gantner .40 .18
❑ 483 Mike Griffin .15 .07
❑ 484 Max Venable DP .10 .05
❑ 485 Garry Templeton .15 .07
❑ 486 Marc Hill .15 .07
❑ 487 Dewey Robinson .15 .07
❑ 488 Damaso Garcia .15 .07
❑ 489 John Littlefield .15 .07
❑ 490 Eddie Murray 3.00 1.35
❑ 491 Gordy Pladson .15 .07
❑ 492 Barry Foote .15 .07
❑ 493 Dan Quisenberry .40 .18
❑ 494 Bob Walk .40 .18
❑ 495 Dusty Baker .75 .35
❑ 496 Paul Dade .15 .07
❑ 497 Fred Norman .15 .07
❑ 498 Pat Putnam .15 .07
❑ 499 Frank Pastore .15 .07
❑ 500 Jim Rice .40 .18
❑ 501 Tim Foli DP .10 .05
❑ 502 Giants Rookies .15 .07
Chris Bourjos
Al Hargesheimer
Mike Rowland
❑ 503 Steve McCatty .15 .07
❑ 504 Dale Murphy 1.50 .70
❑ 505 Jason Thompson .15 .07
❑ 506 Phil Huffman .15 .07
❑ 507 Jamie Quirk .15 .07
❑ 508 Rob Dressler .15 .07
❑ 509 Pete Mackanin .15 .07
❑ 510 Lee Mazzilli .15 .07
❑ 511 Wayne Garland .15 .07
❑ 512 Gary Thomasson .15 .07
❑ 513 Frank LaCorte .15 .07
❑ 514 George Riley .15 .07
❑ 515 Robin Yount 2.00 .90
❑ 516 Doug Bird .15 .07
❑ 517 Richie Zisk .15 .07
❑ 518 Grant Jackson .15 .07
❑ 519 John Tamargo DP .10 .05
❑ 520 Steve Stone .40 .18
❑ 521 Sam Mejias .15 .07
❑ 522 Mike Colbern .15 .07
❑ 523 John Fulgham .15 .07
❑ 524 Willie Aikens .15 .07
❑ 525 Mike Torrez .15 .07
❑ 526 Phillies Rookies .15 .07
Marty Bystrom
Jay Loviglio
Jim Wright
❑ 527 Danny Goodwin .15 .07
❑ 528 Gary Matthews .40 .18
❑ 529 Dave LaRoche .15 .07
❑ 530 Steve Garvey .75 .35
❑ 531 John Curtis .15 .07
❑ 532 Bill Stein .15 .07
❑ 533 Jesus Figueroa .15 .07
❑ 534 Dave Smith .40 .18
❑ 535 Omar Moreno .15 .07
❑ 536 Bob Owchinko DP .10 .05
❑ 537 Ron Hodges .15 .07
❑ 538 Tom Griffin .15 .07
❑ 539 Rodney Scott .15 .07
❑ 540 Mike Schmidt DP 2.00 .90
❑ 541 Steve Swisher .15 .07
❑ 542 Larry Bradford DP .10 .05
❑ 543 Terry Crowley .15 .07

	No.	Player	NRMT	VG-E
❑	544	Rich Gale	.15	.07
❑	545	Johnny Grubb	.15	.07
❑	546	Paul Moskau	.15	.07
❑	547	Mario Guerrero	.15	.07
❑	548	Dave Goltz	.15	.07
❑	549	Jerry Remy	.15	.07
❑	550	Tommy John	.75	.35
❑	551	Pirates Rookies Vance Law Tony Pena Pascual Perez	1.50	.70
❑	552	Steve Trout	.15	.07
❑	553	Tim Blackwell	.15	.07
❑	554	Bert Blyleven UER (1 is missing from 1980 on card back)	.75	.35
❑	555	Cecil Cooper	.40	.18
❑	556	Jerry Mumphrey	.15	.07
❑	557	Chris Knapp	.15	.07
❑	558	Barry Bonnell	.15	.07
❑	559	Willie Montanez	.15	.07
❑	560	Joe Morgan	1.50	.70
❑	561	Dennis Littlejohn	.15	.07
❑	562	Checklist 485-605	.75	.35
❑	563	Jim Kaat	.40	.18
❑	564	Ron Hassey DP	.10	.05
❑	565	Burt Hooton	.15	.07
❑	566	Del Unser	.15	.07
❑	567	Mark Bomback	.15	.07
❑	568	Dave Revering	.15	.07
❑	569	Al Williams DP	.10	.05
❑	570	Ken Singleton	.40	.18
❑	571	Todd Cruz	.15	.07
❑	572	Jack Morris	1.50	.70
❑	573	Phil Garner	.40	.18
❑	574	Bill Caudill	.15	.07
❑	575	Tony Perez	1.50	.70
❑	576	Reggie Cleveland	.15	.07
❑	577	Blue Jays Rookies Luis Leal Brian Milner Ken Schrom	.15	.07
❑	578	Bill Gullickson	.75	.35
❑	579	Tim Flannery	.15	.07
❑	580	Don Baylor	.75	.35
❑	581	Roy Howell	.15	.07
❑	582	Gaylord Perry	1.50	.70
❑	583	Larry Milbourne	.15	.07
❑	584	Randy Lerch	.15	.07
❑	585	Amos Otis	.40	.18
❑	586	Silvio Martinez	.15	.07
❑	587	Jeff Newman	.15	.07
❑	588	Gary Lavelle	.15	.07
❑	589	Lamar Johnson	.15	.07
❑	590	Bruce Sutter	.40	.18
❑	591	John Lowenstein	.15	.07
❑	592	Steve Comer	.15	.07
❑	593	Steve Kemp	.15	.07
❑	594	Preston Hanna DP	.10	.05
❑	595	Butch Hobson	.15	.07
❑	596	Jerry Augustine	.15	.07
❑	597	Rafael Landestoy	.15	.07
❑	598	George Vukovich DP	.10	.05
❑	599	Dennis Kinney	.15	.07
❑	600	Johnny Bench	2.00	.90
❑	601	Don Aase	.15	.07
❑	602	Bobby Murcer	.40	.18
❑	603	John Verhoeven	.15	.07
❑	604	Rob Picciolo	.15	.07
❑	605	Don Sutton	1.50	.70
❑	606	Reds Rookies DP Bruce Berenyi Geoff Combe Paul Householder	.15	.07
❑	607	David Palmer	.15	.07
❑	608	Greg Pryor	.15	.07
❑	609	Lynn McGlothen	.15	.07
❑	610	Darrell Porter	.15	.07
❑	611	Rick Matula DP	.10	.05
❑	612	Duane Kuiper	.15	.07
❑	613	Jim Anderson	.15	.07
❑	614	Dave Rozema	.15	.07
❑	615	Rick Dempsey	.40	.18
❑	616	Rick Wise	.15	.07
❑	617	Craig Reynolds	.15	.07
❑	618	John Milner	.15	.07
❑	619	Steve Henderson	.15	.07
❑	620	Dennis Eckersley	1.50	.70
❑	621	Tom Donohue	.15	.07
❑	622	Randy Moffitt	.15	.07
❑	623	Sal Bando	.40	.18
❑	624	Bob Welch	.40	.18
❑	625	Bill Buckner	.40	.18
❑	626	Tigers Rookies Dave Steffen Jerry Ujdur Roger Weaver	.15	.07
❑	627	Luis Tiant	.40	.18
❑	628	Vic Correll	.15	.07
❑	629	Tony Armas	.40	.18
❑	630	Steve Carlton	1.50	.70
❑	631	Ron Jackson	.15	.07
❑	632	Alan Bannister	.15	.07
❑	633	Bill Lee	.40	.18
❑	634	Doug Flynn	.15	.07
❑	635	Bobby Bonds	.40	.18
❑	636	Al Hrabosky	.15	.07
❑	637	Jerry Narron	.15	.07
❑	638	Checklist 606-726	.75	.35
❑	639	Carney Lansford	.40	.18
❑	640	Dave Parker	.40	.18
❑	641	Mark Belanger	.40	.18
❑	642	Vern Ruhle	.15	.07
❑	643	Lloyd Moseby	.40	.18
❑	644	Ramon Aviles DP	.10	.05
❑	645	Rick Reuschel	.40	.18
❑	646	Marvis Foley	.15	.07
❑	647	Dick Drago	.15	.07
❑	648	Darrell Evans	.40	.18
❑	649	Manny Sarmiento	.15	.07
❑	650	Bucky Dent	.40	.18
❑	651	Pedro Guerrero	.75	.35
❑	652	John Montague	.15	.07
❑	653	Bill Fahey	.15	.07
❑	654	Ray Burris	.15	.07
❑	655	Dan Driessen	.15	.07
❑	656	Jon Matlack	.15	.07
❑	657	Mike Cubbage DP	.10	.05
❑	658	Milt Wilcox	.15	.07
❑	659	Brewers Rookies John Flinn Ed Romero Ned Yost	.15	.07
❑	660	Gary Carter	1.50	.70
❑	661	Orioles Team/Mgr. Earl Weaver	.75	.35
❑	662	Red Sox Team/Mgr. Ralph Houk	.75	.35
❑	663	Angels Team/Mgr. Jim Fregosi	.75	.35
❑	664	White Sox Team/Mgr. Tony LaRussa	.75	.35
❑	665	Indians Team/Mgr. Dave Garcia	.75	.35
❑	666	Tigers Team/Mgr. Sparky Anderson	.75	.35
❑	667	Royals Team/Mgr. Jim Frey	.75	.35
❑	668	Brewers Team/Mgr. Bob Rodgers	.75	.35
❑	669	Twins Team/Mgr. John Goryl	.75	.35
❑	670	Yankees Team/Mgr. Gene Michael	.75	.35
❑	671	A's Team/Mgr. Billy Martin	.75	.35
❑	672	Mariners Team/Mgr. Maury Wills	.75	.35
❑	673	Rangers Team/Mgr. Don Zimmer	.75	.35
❑	674	Blue Jays Team/Mgr. Bobby Mattick	.75	.35
❑	675	Braves Team/Mgr. Bobby Cox	.75	.35
❑	676	Cubs Team/Mgr. Joe Amalfitano	.75	.35
❑	677	Reds Team/Mgr. John McNamara	.75	.35
❑	678	Astros Team/Mgr. Bill Virdon	.75	.35
❑	679	Dodgers Team/Mgr. Tom Lasorda	.75	.35
❑	680	Expos Team/Mgr. Dick Williams	.75	.35
❑	681	Mets Team/Mgr. Joe Torre	.75	.35
❑	682	Phillies Team/Mgr. Dallas Green	.75	.35
❑	683	Pirates Team/Mgr. Chuck Tanner	.75	.35
❑	684	Cardinals Team/Mgr. Whitey Herzog	.75	.35
❑	685	Padres Team/Mgr. Frank Howard	.75	.35
❑	686	Giants Team/Mgr. Dave Bristol	.75	.35
❑	687	Jeff Jones	.15	.07
❑	688	Kiko Garcia	.15	.07
❑	689	Red Sox Rookies Bruce Hurst Keith MacWhorter Reid Nichols	1.50	.70
❑	690	Bob Watson	.40	.18
❑	691	Dick Ruthven	.15	.07
❑	692	Lenny Randle	.15	.07
❑	693	Steve Howe	.40	.18
❑	694	Bud Harrelson DP	.15	.07
❑	695	Kent Tekulve	.40	.18
❑	696	Alan Ashby	.15	.07
❑	697	Rick Waits	.15	.07
❑	698	Mike Jorgensen	.15	.07
❑	699	Glenn Abbott	.15	.07
❑	700	George Brett	4.00	1.80
❑	701	Joe Rudi	.40	.18
❑	702	George Medich	.15	.07
❑	703	Alvis Woods	.15	.07
❑	704	Bill Travers DP	.10	.05
❑	705	Ted Simmons	.40	.18
❑	706	Dave Ford	.15	.07
❑	707	Dave Cash	.15	.07
❑	708	Doyle Alexander	.15	.07
❑	709	Alan Trammell DP	1.50	.70
❑	710	Ron LeFlore DP	.15	.07
❑	711	Joe Ferguson	.15	.07
❑	712	Bill Bonham	.15	.07
❑	713	Bill North	.15	.07
❑	714	Pete Redfern	.15	.07
❑	715	Bill Madlock	.40	.18
❑	716	Glenn Borgmann	.15	.07
❑	717	Jim Barr DP	.10	.05
❑	718	Larry Biittner	.15	.07
❑	719	Sparky Lyle	.40	.18
❑	720	Fred Lynn	.40	.18
❑	721	Toby Harrah	.40	.18
❑	722	Joe Niekro	.40	.18
❑	723	Bruce Bochte	.15	.07
❑	724	Lou Piniella	.40	.18
❑	725	Steve Rogers	.15	.07
❑	726	Rick Monday	.40	.18

1981 Topps Traded

	NRMT	VG-E
COMPLETE SET (132)	30.00	13.50
COMP.FACT.SET (132)	30.00	13.50
COMMON CARD (727-858)	.25	.11

	No.	Player	NRMT	VG-E
❑	727	Danny Ainge	5.00	2.20

❑ 728 Doyle Alexander .... .25 .11
❑ 729 Gary Alexander .... .25 .11
❑ 730 Bill Almon .... .25 .11
❑ 731 Joaquin Andujar .... 1.00 .45
❑ 732 Bob Bailor .... .25 .11
❑ 733 Juan Beniquez .... .25 .11
❑ 734 Dave Bergman .... .25 .11
❑ 735 Tony Bernazard .... .25 .11
❑ 736 Larry Biittner .... .25 .11
❑ 737 Doug Bird .... .25 .11
❑ 738 Bert Blyleven 3.00 1.35
❑ 739 Mark Bomback .... .25 .11
❑ 740 Bobby Bonds .... 1.00 .45
❑ 741 Rick Bosetti .... .25 .11
❑ 742 Hubie Brooks .... 1.00 .45
❑ 743 Rick Burleson .... .25 .11
❑ 744 Ray Burris .... .25 .11
❑ 745 Jeff Burroughs .... .25 .11
❑ 746 Enos Cabell .... .25 .11
❑ 747 Ken Clay .... .25 .11
❑ 748 Mark Clear .... .25 .11
❑ 749 Larry Cox .... .25 .11
❑ 750 Hector Cruz .... .25 .11
❑ 751 Victor Cruz .... .25 .11
❑ 752 Mike Cubbage .... .25 .11
❑ 753 Dick Davis .... .25 .11
❑ 754 Brian Doyle .... .25 .11
❑ 755 Dick Drago .... .25 .11
❑ 756 Leon Durham .... 1.00 .45
❑ 757 Jim Dwyer .... .25 .11
❑ 758 Dave Edwards UER .... .25 .11
No birthdate on card
❑ 759 Jim Essian .... .25 .11
❑ 760 Bill Fahey .... .25 .11
❑ 761 Rollie Fingers 4.00 1.80
❑ 762 Carlton Fisk 5.00 2.20
❑ 763 Barry Foote .... .25 .11
❑ 764 Ken Forsch .... .25 .11
❑ 765 Kiko Garcia .... .25 .11
❑ 766 Cesar Geronimo .... .25 .11
❑ 767 Gary Gray .... .25 .11
❑ 768 Mickey Hatcher .... 1.00 .45
❑ 769 Steve Henderson .... .25 .11
❑ 770 Marc Hill .... .25 .11
❑ 771 Butch Hobson .... .25 .11
❑ 772 Rick Honeycutt .... .25 .11
❑ 773 Roy Howell .... .25 .11
❑ 774 Mike Ivie .... .25 .11
❑ 775 Roy Lee Jackson .... .25 .11
❑ 776 Cliff Johnson .... .25 .11
❑ 777 Randy Jones .... .25 .11
❑ 778 Ruppert Jones .... .25 .11
❑ 779 Mick Kelleher .... .25 .11
❑ 780 Terry Kennedy .... .25 .11
❑ 781 Dave Kingman 3.00 1.35
❑ 782 Bob Knepper .... .25 .11
❑ 783 Ken Kravec .... .25 .11
❑ 784 Bob Lacey .... .25 .11
❑ 785 Dennis Lamp .... .25 .11
❑ 786 Rafael Landestoy .... .25 .11
❑ 787 Ken Landreaux .... .25 .11
❑ 788 Carney Lansford .... 1.00 .45
❑ 789 Dave LaRoche .... .25 .11
❑ 790 Joe Lefebvre .... .25 .11
❑ 791 Ron LeFlore .... 1.00 .45
❑ 792 Randy Lerch .... .25 .11
❑ 793 Sixto Lezcano .... .25 .11
❑ 794 John Littlefield .... .25 .11
❑ 795 Mike Lum .... .25 .11
❑ 796 Greg Luzinski .... 1.00 .45
❑ 797 Fred Lynn .... 1.00 .45
❑ 798 Jerry Martin .... .25 .11
❑ 799 Buck Martinez .... .25 .11
❑ 800 Gary Matthews .... 1.00 .45
❑ 801 Mario Mendoza .... .25 .11
❑ 802 Larry Milbourne .... .25 .11
❑ 803 Rick Miller .... .25 .11
❑ 804 John Montefusco .... .25 .11
❑ 805 Jerry Morales .... .25 .11
❑ 806 Jose Morales .... .25 .11
❑ 807 Joe Morgan 4.00 1.80
❑ 808 Jerry Mumphrey .... .25 .11
❑ 809 Gene Nelson .... .25 .11
❑ 810 Ed Ott .... .25 .11
❑ 811 Bob Owchinko .... .25 .11
❑ 812 Gaylord Perry 4.00 1.80
❑ 813 Mike Phillips .... .25 .11
❑ 814 Darrell Porter .... .25 .11
❑ 815 Mike Proly .... .25 .11
❑ 816 Tim Raines 6.00 2.70
❑ 817 Lenny Randle .... .25 .11
❑ 818 Doug Rau .... .25 .11
❑ 819 Jeff Reardon 4.00 1.80
❑ 820 Ken Reitz .... .25 .11
❑ 821 Steve Renko .... .25 .11
❑ 822 Rick Reuschel .... 1.00 .45
❑ 823 Dave Revering .... .25 .11
❑ 824 Dave Roberts .... .25 .11
❑ 825 Leon Roberts .... .25 .11
❑ 826 Joe Rudi .... 1.00 .45
❑ 827 Kevin Saucier .... .25 .11
❑ 828 Tony Scott .... .25 .11
❑ 829 Bob Shirley .... .25 .11
❑ 830 Ted Simmons .... 1.00 .45
❑ 831 Lary Sorensen .... .25 .11
❑ 832 Jim Spencer .... .25 .11
❑ 833 Harry Spilman .... .25 .11
❑ 834 Fred Stanley .... .25 .11
❑ 835 Rusty Staub .... 1.00 .45
❑ 836 Bill Stein .... .25 .11
❑ 837 Joe Strain .... .25 .11
❑ 838 Bruce Sutter .... 1.00 .45
❑ 839 Don Sutton 4.00 1.80
❑ 840 Steve Swisher .... .25 .11
❑ 841 Frank Tanana .... 1.00 .45
❑ 842 Gene Tenace .... 1.00 .45
❑ 843 Jason Thompson .... .25 .11
❑ 844 Dickie Thon .... 1.00 .45
❑ 845 Bill Travers .... .25 .11
❑ 846 Tom Underwood .... .25 .11
❑ 847 John Urrea .... .25 .11
❑ 848 Mike Vail .... .25 .11
❑ 849 Ellis Valentine .... .25 .11
❑ 850 Fernando Valenzuela .. 6.00 2.70
❑ 851 Pete Vuckovich .... 1.00 .45
❑ 852 Mark Wagner .... .25 .11
❑ 853 Bob Walk .... 1.00 .45
❑ 854 Claudell Washington .... .25 .11
❑ 855 Dave Winfield 5.00 2.20
❑ 856 Geoff Zahn .... .25 .11
❑ 857 Richie Zisk .... .25 .11
❑ 858 Checklist 727-858 .... .25 .11

1982 Topps

	NRMT	VG-E
COMPLETE SET (792)	100.00	45.00
COMMON CARD (1-792)	.15	.07

❑ 1 Steve Carlton HL .... 1.25 .55
Sets new NL strikeout record
❑ 2 Ron Davis HL .... .15 .07
Fans 8 straight in relief
❑ 3 Tim Raines HL .... .60 .25
71 steals as rookie
❑ 4 Pete Rose HL .... .60 .25
Sets NL hit mark
❑ 5 Nolan Ryan HL 3.00 1.35
Pitches fifth no-hitter
❑ 6 Fernando Valenzuela HL .. .60 .25
8 shutouts as rookie
❑ 7 Scott Sanderson .... .15 .07
❑ 8 Rich Dauer .... .15 .07
❑ 9 Ron Guidry .... .30 .14
❑ 10 Ron Guidry SA .... .15 .07
❑ 11 Gary Alexander .... .15 .07
❑ 12 Moose Haas .... .15 .07
❑ 13 Lamar Johnson .... .15 .07
❑ 14 Steve Howe .... .15 .07
❑ 15 Ellis Valentine .... .15 .07
❑ 16 Steve Comer .... .15 .07
❑ 17 Darrell Evans .... .30 .14
❑ 18 Fernando Arroyo .... .15 .07
❑ 19 Ernie Whitt .... .15 .07
❑ 20 Garry Maddox .... .15 .07
❑ 21 Orioles Rookies 60.00 27.00
Bob Bonner
Cal Ripken
Jeff Schneider
❑ 22 Jim Beattie .... .15 .07
❑ 23 Willie Hernandez .... .30 .14
❑ 24 Dave Frost .... .15 .07
❑ 25 Jerry Remy .... .15 .07
❑ 26 Jorge Orta .... .15 .07
❑ 27 Tom Herr .... .30 .14
❑ 28 John Urrea .... .15 .07
❑ 29 Dwayne Murphy .... .15 .07
❑ 30 Tom Seaver .... 1.50 .70
❑ 31 Tom Seaver SA .... .60 .25
❑ 32 Gene Garber .... .15 .07
❑ 33 Jerry Morales .... .15 .07
❑ 34 Joe Sambito .... .15 .07
❑ 35 Willie Aikens .... .15 .07
❑ 36 Rangers TL .... .60 .25
BA: Al Oliver
Pitching: Doc Medich
❑ 37 Dan Graham .... .15 .07
❑ 38 Charlie Lea .... .15 .07
❑ 39 Lou Whitaker .... 1.25 .55
❑ 40 Dave Parker .... .30 .14
❑ 41 Dave Parker SA .... .15 .07
❑ 42 Rick Sofield .... .15 .07
❑ 43 Mike Cubbage .... .15 .07
❑ 44 Britt Burns .... .15 .07
❑ 45 Rick Cerone .... .15 .07
❑ 46 Jerry Augustine .... .15 .07
❑ 47 Jeff Leonard .... .15 .07
❑ 48 Bobby Castillo .... .15 .07
❑ 49 Alvis Woods .... .15 .07
❑ 50 Buddy Bell .... .30 .14
❑ 51 Cubs Rookies .... .60 .25
Jay Howell
Carlos Lezcano
Ty Waller
❑ 52 Larry Andersen .... .15 .07
❑ 53 Greg Gross .... .15 .07
❑ 54 Ron Hassey .... .15 .07
❑ 55 Rick Burleson .... .15 .07
❑ 56 Mark Littell .... .15 .07
❑ 57 Craig Reynolds .... .15 .07
❑ 58 John D'Acquisto .... .15 .07
❑ 59 Rich Gedman .... .30 .14
❑ 60 Tony Armas .... .15 .07
❑ 61 Tommy Boggs .... .15 .07
❑ 62 Mike Tyson .... .15 .07
❑ 63 Mario Soto .... .15 .07
❑ 64 Lynn Jones .... .15 .07
❑ 65 Terry Kennedy .... .15 .07
❑ 66 Astros TL .... 2.00 .90
BA: Art Howe
Pitching: Nolan Ryan
❑ 67 Rich Gale .... .15 .07
❑ 68 Roy Howell .... .15 .07
❑ 69 Al Williams .... .15 .07
❑ 70 Tim Raines .... 1.25 .55
❑ 71 Roy Lee Jackson .... .15 .07
❑ 72 Rick Auerbach .... .15 .07
❑ 73 Buddy Solomon .... .15 .07
❑ 74 Bob Clark .... .15 .07
❑ 75 Tommy John .... .60 .25
❑ 76 Greg Pryor .... .15 .07
❑ 77 Miguel Dilone .... .15 .07
❑ 78 George Medich .... .15 .07
❑ 79 Bob Bailor .... .15 .07
❑ 80 Jim Palmer .... 1.25 .55
❑ 81 Jim Palmer SA .... .60 .25
❑ 82 Bob Welch .... .30 .14
❑ 83 Yankees Rookies .... .60 .25
Steve Balboni

Andy McGaffigan
Andre Robertson
❑ 84 Rennie Stennett .15 .07
❑ 85 Lynn McGlothen .15 .07
❑ 86 Dane Iorg .15 .07
❑ 87 Matt Keough .15 .07
❑ 88 Biff Pocoroba .15 .07
❑ 89 Steve Henderson .15 .07
❑ 90 Nolan Ryan 6.00 2.70
❑ 91 Carney Lansford .30 .14
❑ 92 Brad Havens .15 .07
❑ 93 Larry Hisle .15 .07
❑ 94 Andy Hassler .15 .07
❑ 95 Ozzie Smith 3.00 1.35
❑ 96 Royals TL 1.25 .55
BA: George Brett
Pitching: Larry Gura
❑ 97 Paul Moskau .15 .07
❑ 98 Terry Bulling .15 .07
❑ 99 Barry Bonnell .15 .07
❑ 100 Mike Schmidt 1.50 .70
❑ 101 Mike Schmidt SA .60 .25
❑ 102 Dan Briggs .15 .07
❑ 103 Bob Lacey .15 .07
❑ 104 Rance Mulliniks .15 .07
❑ 105 Kirk Gibson 1.25 .55
❑ 106 Enrique Romo .15 .07
❑ 107 Wayne Krenchicki .15 .07
❑ 108 Bob Sykes .15 .07
❑ 109 Dave Revering .15 .07
❑ 110 Carlton Fisk 1.25 .55
❑ 111 Carlton Fisk SA .60 .25
❑ 112 Billy Sample .15 .07
❑ 113 Steve McCatty .15 .07
❑ 114 Ken Landreaux .15 .07
❑ 115 Gaylord Perry 1.25 .55
❑ 116 Jim Wohlford .15 .07
❑ 117 Rawly Eastwick .15 .07
❑ 118 Expos Rookies .30 .14
Terry Francona
Brad Mills
Bryn Smith
❑ 119 Joe Pittman .15 .07
❑ 120 Gary Lucas .15 .07
❑ 121 Ed Lynch .15 .07
❑ 122 Jamie Easterly UER .15 .07
(Photo actually
Reggie Cleveland)
❑ 123 Danny Goodwin .15 .07
❑ 124 Reid Nichols .15 .07
❑ 125 Danny Ainge 1.50 .70
❑ 126 Braves TL .60 .25
BA: Claudell Washington
Pitching: Rick Mahler
❑ 127 Lonnie Smith .30 .14
❑ 128 Frank Pastore .15 .07
❑ 129 Checklist 1-132 .60 .25
❑ 130 Julio Cruz .15 .07
❑ 131 Stan Bahnsen .15 .07
❑ 132 Lee May .30 .14
❑ 133 Pat Underwood .15 .07
❑ 134 Dan Ford .15 .07
❑ 135 Andy Rincon .15 .07
❑ 136 Lenn Sakata .15 .07
❑ 137 George Cappuzzello .15 .07
❑ 138 Tony Pena .30 .14
❑ 139 Jeff Jones .15 .07
❑ 140 Ron LeFlore .30 .14
❑ 141 Indians Rookies .30 .14
Chris Bando
Tom Brennan
Von Hayes
❑ 142 Dave LaRoche .15 .07
❑ 143 Mookie Wilson .30 .14
❑ 144 Fred Breining .15 .07
❑ 145 Bob Horner .30 .14
❑ 146 Mike Griffin .15 .07
❑ 147 Denny Walling .15 .07
❑ 148 Mickey Klutts .15 .07
❑ 149 Pat Putnam .15 .07
❑ 150 Ted Simmons .30 .14
❑ 151 Dave Edwards .15 .07
❑ 152 Ramon Aviles .15 .07
❑ 153 Roger Erickson .15 .07
❑ 154 Dennis Werth .15 .07
❑ 155 Otto Velez .15 .07
❑ 156 Oakland A's TL .60 .25
BA: Rickey Henderson
Pitching: Steve McCatty
❑ 157 Steve Crawford .15 .07
❑ 158 Brian Downing .15 .07
❑ 159 Larry Biittner .15 .07
❑ 160 Luis Tiant .30 .14
❑ 161 Batting Leaders .30 .14
Bill Madlock
Carney Lansford
❑ 162 Home Run Leaders 1.25 .55
Mike Schmidt
Tony Armas
Dwight Evans
Bobby Grich
Eddie Murray
❑ 163 RBI Leaders 1.25 .55
Mike Schmidt
Eddie Murray
❑ 164 Stolen Base Leaders 1.25 .55
Tim Raines
Rickey Henderson
❑ 165 Victory Leaders .60 .25
Tom Seaver
Denny Martinez
Steve McCatty
Jack Morris
Pete Vuckovich
❑ 166 Strikeout Leaders .30 .14
Fernando Valenzuela
Len Barker
❑ 167 ERA Leaders 2.00 .90
Nolan Ryan
Steve McCatty
❑ 168 Leading Firemen .60 .25
Bruce Sutter
Rollie Fingers
❑ 169 Charlie Leibrandt .15 .07
❑ 170 Jim Bibby .15 .07
❑ 171 Giants Rookies 2.00 .90
Bob Brenly
Chili Davis
Bob Tufts
❑ 172 Bill Gullickson .15 .07
❑ 173 Jamie Quirk .15 .07
❑ 174 Dave Ford .15 .07
❑ 175 Jerry Mumphrey .15 .07
❑ 176 Dewey Robinson .15 .07
❑ 177 John Ellis .15 .07
❑ 178 Dyar Miller .15 .07
❑ 179 Steve Garvey .60 .25
❑ 180 Steve Garvey SA .30 .14
❑ 181 Silvio Martinez .15 .07
❑ 182 Larry Herndon .15 .07
❑ 183 Mike Proly .15 .07
❑ 184 Mick Kelleher .15 .07
❑ 185 Phil Niekro 1.25 .55
❑ 186 Cardinals TL .60 .25
BA: Keith Hernandez
Pitching: Bob Forsch
❑ 187 Jeff Newman .15 .07
❑ 188 Randy Martz .15 .07
❑ 189 Glenn Hoffman .15 .07
❑ 190 J.R. Richard .30 .14
❑ 191 Tim Wallach .60 .25
❑ 192 Broderick Perkins .15 .07
❑ 193 Darrell Jackson .15 .07
❑ 194 Mike Vail .15 .07
❑ 195 Paul Molitor 1.50 .70
❑ 196 Willie Upshaw .15 .07
❑ 197 Shane Rawley .15 .07
❑ 198 Chris Speier .15 .07
❑ 199 Don Aase .15 .07
❑ 200 George Brett 2.50 1.10
❑ 201 George Brett SA 1.25 .55
❑ 202 Rick Manning .15 .07
❑ 203 Blue Jays Rookies .60 .25
Jesse Barfield
Brian Milner
Boomer Wells
❑ 204 Gary Roenicke .15 .07
❑ 205 Neil Allen .15 .07
❑ 206 Tony Bernazard .15 .07
❑ 207 Rod Scurry .15 .07
❑ 208 Bobby Murcer .30 .14
❑ 209 Gary Lavelle .15 .07
❑ 210 Keith Hernandez .30 .14
❑ 211 Dan Petry .15 .07
❑ 212 Mario Mendoza .15 .07
❑ 213 Dave Stewart 1.50 .70
❑ 214 Brian Asselstine .15 .07
❑ 215 Mike Krukow .15 .07
❑ 216 White Sox TL .60 .25
BA: Chet Lemon
Pitching: Dennis Lamp
❑ 217 Bo McLaughlin .15 .07
❑ 218 Dave Roberts .15 .07
❑ 219 John Curtis .15 .07
❑ 220 Manny Trillo .15 .07
❑ 221 Jim Slaton .15 .07
❑ 222 Butch Wynegar .15 .07
❑ 223 Lloyd Moseby .15 .07
❑ 224 Bruce Bochte .15 .07
❑ 225 Mike Torrez .15 .07
❑ 226 Checklist 133-264 .60 .25
❑ 227 Ray Burris .15 .07
❑ 228 Sam Mejias .15 .07
❑ 229 Geoff Zahn .15 .07
❑ 230 Willie Wilson .30 .14
❑ 231 Phillies Rookies .60 .25
Mark Davis
Bob Dernier
Ozzie Virgil
❑ 232 Terry Crowley .15 .07
❑ 233 Duane Kuiper .15 .07
❑ 234 Ron Hodges .15 .07
❑ 235 Mike Easler .15 .07
❑ 236 John Martin .15 .07
❑ 237 Rusty Kuntz .15 .07
❑ 238 Kevin Saucier .15 .07
❑ 239 Jon Matlack .15 .07
❑ 240 Bucky Dent .30 .14
❑ 241 Bucky Dent SA .15 .07
❑ 242 Milt May .15 .07
❑ 243 Bob Owchinko .15 .07
❑ 244 Rufino Linares .15 .07
❑ 245 Ken Reitz .15 .07
❑ 246 New York Mets TL .60 .25
BA: Hubie Brooks
Pitching: Mike Scott
❑ 247 Pedro Guerrero .30 .14
❑ 248 Frank LaCorte .15 .07
❑ 249 Tim Flannery .15 .07
❑ 250 Tug McGraw .30 .14
❑ 251 Fred Lynn .30 .14
❑ 252 Fred Lynn SA .15 .07
❑ 253 Chuck Baker .15 .07
❑ 254 Jorge Bell 1.25 .55
❑ 255 Tony Perez 1.25 .55
❑ 256 Tony Perez SA .60 .25
❑ 257 Larry Harlow .15 .07
❑ 258 Bo Diaz .15 .07
❑ 259 Rodney Scott .15 .07
❑ 260 Bruce Sutter .30 .14
❑ 261 Tigers Rookies UER .15 .07
Howard Bailey
Marty Castillo
Dave Rucker
(Rucker photo act-
ally Roger Weaver)
❑ 262 Doug Bair .15 .07
❑ 263 Victor Cruz .15 .07
❑ 264 Dan Quisenberry .30 .14
❑ 265 Al Bumbry .15 .07
❑ 266 Rick Leach .15 .07
❑ 267 Kurt Bevacqua .15 .07
❑ 268 Rickey Keeton .15 .07
❑ 269 Jim Essian .15 .07
❑ 270 Rusty Staub .30 .14
❑ 271 Larry Bradford .15 .07
❑ 272 Bump Wills .15 .07
❑ 273 Doug Bird .15 .07
❑ 274 Bob Ojeda .60 .25
❑ 275 Bob Watson .30 .14
❑ 276 Angels TL .60 .25
BA: Rod Carew
Pitching: Ken Forsch
❑ 277 Terry Puhl .15 .07
❑ 278 John Littlefield .15 .07

❑ 279 Bill Russell .30 .14
❑ 280 Ben Oglivie .30 .14
❑ 281 John Verhoeven .15 .07
❑ 282 Ken Macha .15 .07
❑ 283 Brian Allard .15 .07
❑ 284 Bobby Grich .30 .14
❑ 285 Sparky Lyle .30 .14
❑ 286 Bill Fahey .15 .07
❑ 287 Alan Bannister .15 .07
❑ 288 Garry Templeton .15 .07
❑ 289 Bob Stanley .15 .07
❑ 290 Ken Singleton .30 .14
❑ 291 Pirates Rookies .30 .14
Vance Law
Bob Long
Johnny Ray
❑ 292 David Palmer .15 .07
❑ 293 Rob Picciolo .15 .07
❑ 294 Mike LaCoss .15 .07
❑ 295 Jason Thompson .15 .07
❑ 296 Bob Walk .15 .07
❑ 297 Clint Hurdle .15 .07
❑ 298 Danny Darwin .30 .14
❑ 299 Steve Trout .15 .07
❑ 300 Reggie Jackson 1.50 .70
❑ 301 Reggie Jackson SA .60 .25
❑ 302 Doug Flynn .15 .07
❑ 303 Bill Caudill .15 .07
❑ 304 Johnnie LeMaster .15 .07
❑ 305 Don Sutton 1.25 .55
❑ 306 Don Sutton SA .60 .25
❑ 307 Randy Bass .15 .07
❑ 308 Charlie Moore .15 .07
❑ 309 Pete Redfern .15 .07
❑ 310 Mike Hargrove .30 .14
❑ 311 Dodgers TL .60 .25
BA: Dusty Baker
Pitching: Burt Hooton
❑ 312 Lenny Randle .15 .07
❑ 313 John Harris .15 .07
❑ 314 Buck Martinez .15 .07
❑ 315 Burt Hooton .15 .07
❑ 316 Steve Braun .15 .07
❑ 317 Dick Ruthven .15 .07
❑ 318 Mike Heath .15 .07
❑ 319 Dave Rozema .15 .07
❑ 320 Chris Chambliss .30 .14
❑ 321 Chris Chambliss SA .15 .07
❑ 322 Garry Hancock .15 .07
❑ 323 Bill Lee .30 .14
❑ 324 Steve Dillard .15 .07
❑ 325 Jose Cruz .30 .14
❑ 326 Pete Falcone .15 .07
❑ 327 Joe Nolan .15 .07
❑ 328 Ed Farmer .15 .07
❑ 329 U.L. Washington .15 .07
❑ 330 Rick Wise .15 .07
❑ 331 Benny Ayala .15 .07
❑ 332 Don Robinson .15 .07
❑ 333 Brewers Rookies .15 .07
Frank DiPino
Marshall Edwards
Chuck Porter
❑ 334 Aurelio Rodriguez .15 .07
❑ 335 Jim Sundberg .30 .14
❑ 336 Mariners TL .60 .25
BA: Tom Paciorek
Pitching: Glenn Abbott
❑ 337 Pete Rose AS .60 .25
❑ 338 Dave Lopes AS .15 .07
❑ 339 Mike Schmidt AS .60 .25
❑ 340 Dave Concepcion AS .15 .07
❑ 341 Andre Dawson AS .60 .25
❑ 342A George Foster AS .30 .14
(With autograph)
❑ 342B George Foster AS 1.25 .55
(W/o autograph)
❑ 343 Dave Parker AS .15 .07
❑ 344 Gary Carter AS .30 .14
❑ 345 Fernando Valenzuela AS .60 .25
❑ 346 Tom Seaver AS ERR 1.25 .55
("t ed")
❑ 346B Tom Seaver AS COR 1.25 .55
("tied")
❑ 347 Bruce Sutter AS .15 .07
❑ 348 Derrel Thomas .15 .07
❑ 349 George Frazier .15 .07
❑ 350 Thad Bosley .15 .07
❑ 351 Reds Rookies .15 .07
Scott Brown
Geoff Combe
Paul Householder
❑ 352 Dick Davis .15 .07
❑ 353 Jack O'Connor .15 .07
❑ 354 Roberto Ramos .15 .07
❑ 355 Dwight Evans .60 .25
❑ 356 Denny Lewallyn .15 .07
❑ 357 Butch Hobson .15 .07
❑ 358 Mike Parrott .15 .07
❑ 359 Jim Dwyer .15 .07
❑ 360 Len Barker .15 .07
❑ 361 Rafael Landestoy .15 .07
❑ 362 Jim Wright UER .15 .07
(Wrong Jim Wright
pictured)
❑ 363 Bob Molinaro .15 .07
❑ 364 Doyle Alexander .15 .07
❑ 365 Bill Madlock .30 .14
❑ 366 Padres TL .60 .25
BA: Luis Salazar
Pitching: Juan
Eichelberger
❑ 367 Jim Kaat .30 .14
❑ 368 Alex Trevino .15 .07
❑ 369 Champ Summers .15 .07
❑ 370 Mike Norris .15 .07
❑ 371 Jerry Don Gleaton .15 .07
❑ 372 Luis Gomez .15 .07
❑ 373 Gene Nelson .15 .07
❑ 374 Tim Blackwell .15 .07
❑ 375 Dusty Baker .60 .25
❑ 376 Chris Welsh .15 .07
❑ 377 Kiko Garcia .15 .07
❑ 378 Mike Caldwell .15 .07
❑ 379 Rob Wilfong .15 .07
❑ 380 Dave Stieb .30 .14
❑ 381 Red Sox Rookies .30 .14
Bruce Hurst
Dave Schmidt
Julio Valdez
❑ 382 Joe Simpson .15 .07
❑ 383A Pascual Perez ERR .. 5.00 2.20
(No position
on front)
❑ 383B Pascual Perez COR .30 .14
❑ 384 Keith Moreland .15 .07
❑ 385 Ken Forsch .15 .07
❑ 386 Jerry White .15 .07
❑ 387 Tom Veryzer .15 .07
❑ 388 Joe Rudi .15 .07
❑ 389 George Vukovich .15 .07
❑ 390 Eddie Murray 1.50 .70
❑ 391 Dave Tobik .15 .07
❑ 392 Rick Bosetti .15 .07
❑ 393 Al Hrabosky .15 .07
❑ 394 Checklist 265-396 .60 .25
❑ 395 Omar Moreno .15 .07
❑ 396 Twins TL .60 .25
BA: John Castino
Fernando Arroyo
❑ 397 Ken Brett .15 .07
❑ 398 Mike Squires .15 .07
❑ 399 Pat Zachry .15 .07
❑ 400 Johnny Bench 1.50 .70
❑ 401 Johnny Bench SA .60 .25
❑ 402 Bill Stein .15 .07
❑ 403 Jim Tracy .15 .07
❑ 404 Dickie Thon .15 .07
❑ 405 Rick Reuschel .30 .14
❑ 406 Al Holland .15 .07
❑ 407 Danny Boone .15 .07
❑ 408 Ed Romero .15 .07
❑ 409 Don Cooper .15 .07
❑ 410 Ron Cey .30 .14
❑ 411 Ron Cey SA .15 .07
❑ 412 Luis Leal .15 .07
❑ 413 Dan Meyer .15 .07
❑ 414 Elias Sosa .15 .07
❑ 415 Don Baylor .60 .25
❑ 416 Marty Bystrom .15 .07
❑ 417 Pat Kelly .15 .07
❑ 418 Rangers Rookies .15 .07
John Butcher
Bobby Johnson
Dave Schmidt
❑ 419 Steve Stone .30 .14
❑ 420 George Hendrick .15 .07
❑ 421 Mark Clear .15 .07
❑ 422 Cliff Johnson .15 .07
❑ 423 Stan Papi .15 .07
❑ 424 Bruce Benedict .15 .07
❑ 425 John Candelaria .15 .07
❑ 426 Orioles TL .60 .25
BA: Eddie Murray
Pitching: Sammy Stewart
❑ 427 Ron Oester .15 .07
❑ 428 LaMarr Hoyt .15 .07
❑ 429 John Wathan .15 .07
❑ 430 Vida Blue .30 .14
❑ 431 Vida Blue SA .15 .07
❑ 432 Mike Scott .30 .14
❑ 433 Alan Ashby .15 .07
❑ 434 Joe Lefebvre .15 .07
❑ 435 Robin Yount 1.25 .55
❑ 436 Joe Strain .15 .07
❑ 437 Juan Berenguer .15 .07
❑ 438 Pete Mackanin .15 .07
❑ 439 Dave Righetti 1.25 .55
❑ 440 Jeff Burroughs .15 .07
❑ 441 Astros Rookies .15 .07
Danny Heep
Billy Smith
Bobby Sprowl
❑ 442 Bruce Kison .15 .07
❑ 443 Mark Wagner .15 .07
❑ 444 Terry Forster .15 .07
❑ 445 Larry Parrish .15 .07
❑ 446 Wayne Garland .15 .07
❑ 447 Darrell Porter .30 .14
❑ 448 Darrell Porter SA .15 .07
❑ 449 Luis Aguayo .15 .07
❑ 450 Jack Morris .30 .14
❑ 451 Ed Miller .15 .07
❑ 452 Lee Smith 4.00 1.80
❑ 453 Art Howe .30 .14
❑ 454 Rick Langford .15 .07
❑ 455 Tom Burgmeier .15 .07
❑ 456 Chicago Cubs TL .60 .25
BA: Bill Buckner
Pitching: Randy Martz
❑ 457 Tim Stoddard .15 .07
❑ 458 Willie Montanez .15 .07
❑ 459 Bruce Berenyi .15 .07
❑ 460 Jack Clark .30 .14
❑ 461 Rich Dotson .15 .07
❑ 462 Dave Chalk .15 .07
❑ 463 Jim Kern .15 .07
❑ 464 Juan Bonilla .15 .07
❑ 465 Lee Mazzilli .15 .07
❑ 466 Randy Lerch .15 .07
❑ 467 Mickey Hatcher .15 .07
❑ 468 Floyd Bannister .15 .07
❑ 469 Ed Ott .15 .07
❑ 470 John Mayberry .15 .07
❑ 471 Royals Rookies .15 .07
Atlee Hammaker
Mike Jones
Darryl Motley
❑ 472 Oscar Gamble .15 .07
❑ 473 Mike Stanton .15 .07
❑ 474 Ken Oberkfell .15 .07
❑ 475 Alan Trammell 1.25 .55
❑ 476 Brian Kingman .15 .07
❑ 477 Steve Yeager .15 .07
❑ 478 Ray Searage .15 .07
❑ 479 Rowland Office .15 .07
❑ 480 Steve Carlton 1.25 .55
❑ 481 Steve Carlton SA .60 .25
❑ 482 Glenn Hubbard .15 .07
❑ 483 Gary Woods .15 .07
❑ 484 Ivan DeJesus .15 .07
❑ 485 Kent Tekulve .30 .14
❑ 486 Yankees TL .30 .14
BA: Jerry Mumphrey
Pitching: Tommy John

❑	487	Bob McClure	.15	.07
❑	488	Ron Jackson	.15	.07
❑	489	Rick Dempsey	.30	.14
❑	490	Dennis Eckersley	1.25	.55
❑	491	Checklist 397-528	.60	.25
❑	492	Joe Price	.15	.07
❑	493	Chet Lemon	.15	.07
❑	494	Hubie Brooks	.30	.14
❑	495	Dennis Leonard	.15	.07
❑	496	Johnny Grubb	.15	.07
❑	497	Jim Anderson	.15	.07
❑	498	Dave Bergman	.15	.07
❑	499	Paul Mirabella	.15	.07
❑	500	Rod Carew	1.25	.55
❑	501	Rod Carew SA	.60	.25
❑	502	Braves Rookies	2.00	.90
		Steve Bedrosian UER		
		(Photo actually		
		Larry Owen)		
		Brett Butler		
		Larry Owen		
❑	503	Julio Gonzalez	.15	.07
❑	504	Rick Peters	.15	.07
❑	505	Graig Nettles	.30	.14
❑	506	Graig Nettles SA	.15	.07
❑	507	Terry Harper	.15	.07
❑	508	Jody Davis	.15	.07
❑	509	Harry Spilman	.15	.07
❑	510	Fernando Valenzuela	1.25	.55
❑	511	Ruppert Jones	.15	.07
❑	512	Jerry Dybzinski	.15	.07
❑	513	Rick Rhoden	.15	.07
❑	514	Joe Ferguson	.15	.07
❑	515	Larry Bowa	.30	.14
❑	516	Larry Bowa SA	.15	.07
❑	517	Mark Brouhard	.15	.07
❑	518	Garth Iorg	.15	.07
❑	519	Glenn Adams	.15	.07
❑	520	Mike Flanagan	.30	.14
❑	521	Bill Almon	.15	.07
❑	522	Chuck Rainey	.15	.07
❑	523	Gary Gray	.15	.07
❑	524	Tom Hausman	.15	.07
❑	525	Ray Knight	.30	.14
❑	526	Expos TL	.60	.25
		BA: Warren Cromartie		
		Pitching: Bill Gullickson		
❑	527	John Henry Johnson	.15	.07
❑	528	Matt Alexander	.15	.07
❑	529	Allen Ripley	.15	.07
❑	530	Dickie Noles	.15	.07
❑	531	A's Rookies	.15	.07
		Rich Bordi		
		Mark Budaska		
		Kelvin Moore		
❑	532	Toby Harrah	.30	.14
❑	533	Joaquin Andujar	.30	.14
❑	534	Dave McKay	.15	.07
❑	535	Lance Parrish	.60	.25
❑	536	Rafael Ramirez	.15	.07
❑	537	Doug Capilla	.15	.07
❑	538	Lou Piniella	.30	.14
❑	539	Vern Ruhle	.15	.07
❑	540	Andre Dawson	1.25	.55
❑	541	Barry Evans	.15	.07
❑	542	Ned Yost	.15	.07
❑	543	Bill Robinson	.15	.07
❑	544	Larry Christenson	.15	.07
❑	545	Reggie Smith	.30	.14
❑	546	Reggie Smith SA	.15	.07
❑	547	Rod Carew AS	1.25	.55
❑	548	Willie Randolph AS	.30	.14
❑	549	George Brett AS	1.25	.55
❑	550	Bucky Dent AS	.15	.07
❑	551	Reggie Jackson AS	.60	.25
❑	552	Ken Singleton AS	.15	.07
❑	553	Dave Winfield AS	.60	.25
❑	554	Carlton Fisk AS	.60	.25
❑	555	Scott McGregor AS	.15	.07
❑	556	Jack Morris AS	.15	.07
❑	557	Rich Gossage AS	.30	.14
❑	558	John Tudor	.15	.07
❑	559	Indians TL	.30	.14
		BA: Mike Hargrove		
		Pitching: Bert Blyleven		
❑	560	Doug Corbett	.15	.07
❑	561	Cardinals Rookies	.15	.07
		Glenn Brummer		
		Luis DeLeon		
		Gene Roof		
❑	562	Mike O'Berry	.15	.07
❑	563	Ross Baumgarten	.15	.07
❑	564	Doug DeCinces	.30	.14
❑	565	Jackson Todd	.15	.07
❑	566	Mike Jorgensen	.15	.07
❑	567	Bob Babcock	.15	.07
❑	568	Joe Pettini	.15	.07
❑	569	Willie Randolph	.30	.14
❑	570	Willie Randolph SA	.30	.14
❑	571	Glenn Abbott	.15	.07
❑	572	Juan Beniquez	.15	.07
❑	573	Rick Waits	.15	.07
❑	574	Mike Ramsey	.15	.07
❑	575	Al Cowens	.15	.07
❑	576	Giants TL	.60	.25
		BA: Milt May		
		Pitching: Vida Blue		
❑	577	Rick Monday	.15	.07
❑	578	Shooty Babitt	.15	.07
❑	579	Rick Mahler	.15	.07
❑	580	Bobby Bonds	.30	.14
❑	581	Ron Reed	.15	.07
❑	582	Luis Pujols	.15	.07
❑	583	Tippy Martinez	.15	.07
❑	584	Hosken Powell	.15	.07
❑	585	Rollie Fingers	1.25	.55
❑	586	Rollie Fingers SA	.60	.25
❑	587	Tim Lollar	.15	.07
❑	588	Dale Berra	.15	.07
❑	589	Dave Stapleton	.15	.07
❑	590	Al Oliver	.30	.14
❑	591	Al Oliver SA	.15	.07
❑	592	Craig Swan	.15	.07
❑	593	Billy Smith	.15	.07
❑	594	Renie Martin	.15	.07
❑	595	Dave Collins	.15	.07
❑	596	Damaso Garcia	.15	.07
❑	597	Wayne Nordhagen	.15	.07
❑	598	Bob Galasso	.15	.07
❑	599	White Sox Rookies	.15	.07
		Jay Loviglio		
		Reggie Patterson		
		Leo Sutherland		
❑	600	Dave Winfield	1.25	.55
❑	601	Sid Monge	.15	.07
❑	602	Freddie Patek	.15	.07
❑	603	Rich Hebner	.30	.14
❑	604	Orlando Sanchez	.15	.07
❑	605	Steve Rogers	.15	.07
❑	606	Blue Jays TL	.60	.25
		BA: John Mayberry		
		Pitching: Dave Stieb		
❑	607	Leon Durham	.15	.07
❑	608	Jerry Royster	.15	.07
❑	609	Rick Sutcliffe	.30	.14
❑	610	Rickey Henderson	2.50	1.10
❑	611	Joe Niekro	.30	.14
❑	612	Gary Ward	.15	.07
❑	613	Jim Gantner	.30	.14
❑	614	Juan Eichelberger	.15	.07
❑	615	Bob Boone	.30	.14
❑	616	Bob Boone SA	.15	.07
❑	617	Scott McGregor	.15	.07
❑	618	Tim Foli	.15	.07
❑	619	Bill Campbell	.15	.07
❑	620	Ken Griffey	.30	.14
❑	621	Ken Griffey SA	.15	.07
❑	622	Dennis Lamp	.15	.07
❑	623	Mets Rookies	.60	.25
		Ron Gardenhire		
		Terry Leach		
		Tim Leary		
❑	624	Fergie Jenkins	1.25	.55
❑	625	Hal McRae	.30	.14
❑	626	Randy Jones	.15	.07
❑	627	Enos Cabell	.15	.07
❑	628	Bill Travers	.15	.07
❑	629	John Wockenfuss	.15	.07
❑	630	Joe Charboneau	.30	.14
❑	631	Gene Tenace	.30	.14
❑	632	Bryan Clark	.15	.07
❑	633	Mitchell Page	.15	.07
❑	634	Checklist 529-660	.60	.25
❑	635	Ron Davis	.15	.07
❑	636	Phillies TL	1.25	.55
		BA: Pete Rose		
		Pitching: Steve Carlton		
❑	637	Rick Camp	.15	.07
❑	638	John Milner	.15	.07
❑	639	Ken Kravec	.15	.07
❑	640	Cesar Cedeno	.30	.14
❑	641	Steve Mura	.15	.07
❑	642	Mike Scioscia	.30	.14
❑	643	Pete Vuckovich	.15	.07
❑	644	John Castino	.15	.07
❑	645	Frank White	.30	.14
❑	646	Frank White SA	.15	.07
❑	647	Warren Brusstar	.15	.07
❑	648	Jose Morales	.15	.07
❑	649	Ken Clay	.15	.07
❑	650	Carl Yastrzemski	1.25	.55
❑	651	Carl Yastrzemski SA	.60	.25
❑	652	Steve Nicosia	.15	.07
❑	653	Angels Rookies	.60	.25
		Tom Brunansky		
		Luis Sanchez		
		Daryl Sconiers		
❑	654	Jim Morrison	.15	.07
❑	655	Joel Youngblood	.15	.07
❑	656	Eddie Whitson	.15	.07
❑	657	Tom Poquette	.15	.07
❑	658	Tito Landrum	.15	.07
❑	659	Fred Martinez	.15	.07
❑	660	Dave Concepcion	.30	.14
❑	661	Dave Concepcion SA	.15	.07
❑	662	Luis Salazar	.15	.07
❑	663	Hector Cruz	.15	.07
❑	664	Dan Spillner	.15	.07
❑	665	Jim Clancy	.15	.07
❑	666	Tigers TL	.60	.25
		BA: Steve Kemp		
		Pitching: Dan Petry		
❑	667	Jeff Reardon	.60	.25
❑	668	Dale Murphy	1.25	.55
❑	669	Larry Milbourne	.15	.07
❑	670	Steve Kemp	.15	.07
❑	671	Mike Davis	.15	.07
❑	672	Bob Knepper	.15	.07
❑	673	Keith Drumwright	.15	.07
❑	674	Dave Goltz	.15	.07
❑	675	Cecil Cooper	.30	.14
❑	676	Sal Butera	.15	.07
❑	677	Alfredo Griffin	.15	.07
❑	678	Tom Paciorek	.30	.14
❑	679	Sammy Stewart	.15	.07
❑	680	Gary Matthews	.30	.14
❑	681	Dodgers Rookies	1.25	.55
		Mike Marshall		
		Ron Roenicke		
		Steve Sax		
❑	682	Jesse Jefferson	.15	.07
❑	683	Phil Garner	.30	.14
❑	684	Harold Baines	1.25	.55
❑	685	Bert Blyleven	.60	.25
❑	686	Gary Allenson	.15	.07
❑	687	Greg Minton	.15	.07
❑	688	Leon Roberts	.15	.07
❑	689	Lary Sorensen	.15	.07
❑	690	Dave Kingman	.30	.14
❑	691	Dan Schatzeder	.15	.07
❑	692	Wayne Gross	.15	.07
❑	693	Cesar Geronimo	.15	.07
❑	694	Dave Wehrmeister	.15	.07
❑	695	Warren Cromartie	.15	.07
❑	696	Pirates TL	.60	.25
		BA: Bill Madlock		
		Pitching: Eddie Solomon		
❑	697	John Montefusco	.15	.07
❑	698	Tony Scott	.15	.07
❑	699	Dick Tidrow	.15	.07
❑	700	George Foster	.30	.14
❑	701	George Foster SA	.15	.07
❑	702	Steve Renko	.15	.07
❑	703	Brewers TL	.60	.25
		BA: Cecil Cooper		
		Pitching: Pete Vuckovich		

❑ 704 Mickey Rivers .15 .07
❑ 705 Mickey Rivers SA .15 .07
❑ 706 Barry Foote .15 .07
❑ 707 Mark Bomback .15 .07
❑ 708 Gene Richards .15 .07
❑ 709 Don Money .15 .07
❑ 710 Jerry Reuss .30 .14
❑ 711 Mariners Rookies .60 .25
Dave Edler
Dave Henderson
Reggie Walton
❑ 712 Dennis Martinez .60 .25
❑ 713 Del Unser .15 .07
❑ 714 Jerry Koosman .30 .14
❑ 715 Willie Stargell 1.25 .55
❑ 716 Willie Stargell SA .60 .25
❑ 717 Rick Miller .15 .07
❑ 718 Charlie Hough .30 .14
❑ 719 Jerry Narron .15 .07
❑ 720 Greg Luzinski .30 .14
❑ 721 Greg Luzinski SA .15 .07
❑ 722 Jerry Martin .15 .07
❑ 723 Junior Kennedy .15 .07
❑ 724 Dave Rosello .15 .07
❑ 725 Amos Otis .30 .14
❑ 726 Amos Otis SA .15 .07
❑ 727 Sixto Lezcano .15 .07
❑ 728 Aurelio Lopez .15 .07
❑ 729 Jim Spencer .15 .07
❑ 730 Gary Carter 1.25 .55
❑ 731 Padres Rookies .15 .07
Mike Armstrong
Doug Gwosdz
Fred Kuhaulua
❑ 732 Mike Lum .15 .07
❑ 733 Larry McWilliams .15 .07
❑ 734 Mike Ivie .15 .07
❑ 735 Rudy May .15 .07
❑ 736 Jerry Turner .15 .07
❑ 737 Reggie Cleveland .15 .07
❑ 738 Dave Engle .15 .07
❑ 739 Joey McLaughlin .15 .07
❑ 740 Dave Lopes .30 .14
❑ 741 Dave Lopes SA .15 .07
❑ 742 Dick Drago .15 .07
❑ 743 John Stearns .15 .07
❑ 744 Mike Witt .30 .14
❑ 745 Bake McBride .15 .07
❑ 746 Andre Thornton .15 .07
❑ 747 John Lowenstein .15 .07
❑ 748 Marc Hill .15 .07
❑ 749 Bob Shirley .15 .07
❑ 750 Jim Rice .60 .25
❑ 751 Rick Honeycutt .15 .07
❑ 752 Lee Lacy .15 .07
❑ 753 Tom Brookens .15 .07
❑ 754 Joe Morgan 1.25 .55
❑ 755 Joe Morgan SA .60 .25
❑ 756 Reds TL .60 .25
BA: Ken Griffey
Pitching: Tom Seaver
❑ 757 Tom Underwood .15 .07
❑ 758 Claudell Washington .15 .07
❑ 759 Paul Splittorff .15 .07
❑ 760 Bill Buckner .30 .14
❑ 761 Dave Smith .15 .07
❑ 762 Mike Phillips .15 .07
❑ 763 Tom Hume .15 .07
❑ 764 Steve Swisher .15 .07
❑ 765 Gorman Thomas .30 .14
❑ 766 Twins Rookies 1.50 .70
Lenny Faedo
Kent Hrbek
Tim Laudner
❑ 767 Roy Smalley .15 .07
❑ 768 Jerry Garvin .15 .07
❑ 769 Richie Zisk .15 .07
❑ 770 Rich Gossage .60 .25
❑ 771 Rich Gossage SA .30 .14
❑ 772 Bert Campaneris .30 .14
❑ 773 John Denny .15 .07
❑ 774 Jay Johnstone .30 .14
❑ 775 Bob Forsch .15 .07
❑ 776 Mark Belanger .30 .14
❑ 777 Tom Griffin .15 .07
❑ 778 Kevin Hickey .15 .07
❑ 779 Grant Jackson .15 .07
❑ 780 Pete Rose 1.50 .70
❑ 781 Pete Rose SA .60 .25
❑ 782 Frank Taveras .15 .07
❑ 783 Greg Harris .15 .07
❑ 784 Milt Wilcox .15 .07
❑ 785 Dan Driessen .15 .07
❑ 786 Red Sox TL .60 .25
BA: Carney Lansford
Pitching: Mike Torrez
❑ 787 Fred Stanley .15 .07
❑ 788 Woodie Fryman .15 .07
❑ 789 Checklist 661-792 .60 .25
❑ 790 Larry Gura .15 .07
❑ 791 Bobby Brown .15 .07
❑ 792 Frank Tanana .30 .14

1982 Topps Traded

	NRMT	VG-E
COMP.FACT.SET (132)	250.00	110.00
COMMON CARD (1T-132T)	.50	.23

❑ 1T Doyle Alexander .50 .23
❑ 2T Jesse Barfield 1.00 .45
❑ 3T Ross Baumgarten .50 .23
❑ 4T Steve Bedrosian 1.00 .45
❑ 5T Mark Belanger 1.00 .45
❑ 6T Kurt Bevacqua .50 .23
❑ 7T Tim Blackwell .50 .23
❑ 8T Vida Blue 1.00 .45
❑ 9T Bob Boone 1.00 .45
❑ 10T Larry Bowa 1.00 .45
❑ 11T Dan Briggs .50 .23
❑ 12T Bobby Brown .50 .23
❑ 13T Tom Brunansky 1.00 .45
❑ 14T Jeff Burroughs .50 .23
❑ 15T Enos Cabell .50 .23
❑ 16T Bill Campbell .50 .23
❑ 17T Bobby Castillo .50 .23
❑ 18T Bill Caudill .50 .23
❑ 19T Cesar Cedeno 1.00 .45
❑ 20T Dave Collins .50 .23
❑ 21T Doug Corbett .50 .23
❑ 22T Al Cowens .50 .23
❑ 23T Chili Davis 6.00 2.70
❑ 24T Dick Davis .50 .23
❑ 25T Ron Davis .50 .23
❑ 26T Doug DeCinces 1.00 .45
❑ 27T Ivan DeJesus .50 .23
❑ 28T Bob Dernier .50 .23
❑ 29T Bo Diaz .50 .23
❑ 30T Roger Erickson .50 .23
❑ 31T Jim Essian .50 .23
❑ 32T Ed Farmer .50 .23
❑ 33T Doug Flynn .50 .23
❑ 34T Tim Foli .50 .23
❑ 35T Dan Ford .50 .23
❑ 36T George Foster 1.00 .45
❑ 37T Dave Frost .50 .23
❑ 38T Rich Gale .50 .23
❑ 39T Ron Gardenhire .50 .23
❑ 40T Ken Griffey 1.00 .45
❑ 41T Greg Harris .50 .23
❑ 42T Von Hayes 1.00 .45
❑ 43T Larry Herndon .50 .23
❑ 44T Kent Hrbek 2.00 .90
❑ 45T Mike Ivie .50 .23
❑ 46T Grant Jackson .50 .23
❑ 47T Reggie Jackson 10.00 4.50
❑ 48T Ron Jackson .50 .23
❑ 49T Fergie Jenkins 4.00 1.80
❑ 50T Lamar Johnson .50 .23
❑ 51T Randy Johnson .50 .23
❑ 52T Jay Johnstone 1.00 .45
❑ 53T Mick Kelleher .50 .23
❑ 54T Steve Kemp .50 .23
❑ 55T Junior Kennedy .50 .23
❑ 56T Jim Kern .50 .23
❑ 57T Ray Knight 1.00 .45
❑ 58T Wayne Krenchicki .50 .23
❑ 59T Mike Krukow .50 .23
❑ 60T Duane Kuiper .50 .23
❑ 61T Mike LaCoss .50 .23
❑ 62T Chet Lemon .50 .23
❑ 63T Sixto Lezcano .50 .23
❑ 64T Dave Lopes 1.00 .45
❑ 65T Jerry Martin .50 .23
❑ 66T Renie Martin .50 .23
❑ 67T John Mayberry .50 .23
❑ 68T Lee Mazzilli .50 .23
❑ 69T Bake McBride .50 .23
❑ 70T Dan Meyer .50 .23
❑ 71T Larry Milbourne .50 .23
❑ 72T Eddie Milner .50 .23
❑ 73T Sid Monge .50 .23
❑ 74T John Montefusco .50 .23
❑ 75T Jose Morales .50 .23
❑ 76T Keith Moreland .50 .23
❑ 77T Jim Morrison .50 .23
❑ 78T Rance Mulliniks .50 .23
❑ 79T Steve Mura .50 .23
❑ 80T Gene Nelson .50 .23
❑ 81T Joe Nolan .50 .23
❑ 82T Dickie Noles .50 .23
❑ 83T Al Oliver 1.00 .45
❑ 84T Jorge Orta .50 .23
❑ 85T Tom Paciorek 1.00 .45
❑ 86T Larry Parrish .50 .23
❑ 87T Jack Perconte .50 .23
❑ 88T Gaylord Perry 4.00 1.80
❑ 89T Rob Picciolo .50 .23
❑ 90T Joe Pittman .50 .23
❑ 91T Hosken Powell .50 .23
❑ 92T Mike Proly .50 .23
❑ 93T Greg Pryor .50 .23
❑ 94T Charlie Puleo .50 .23
❑ 95T Shane Rawley .50 .23
❑ 96T Johnny Ray 1.00 .45
❑ 97T Dave Revering .50 .23
❑ 98T Cal Ripken 200.00 90.00
❑ 99T Allen Ripley .50 .23
❑ 100T Bill Robinson .50 .23
❑ 101T Aurelio Rodriguez .50 .23
❑ 102T Joe Rudi .50 .23
❑ 103T Steve Sax 4.00 1.80
❑ 104T Dan Schatzeder .50 .23
❑ 105T Bob Shirley .50 .23
❑ 106T Eric Show 1.00 .45
❑ 107T Roy Smalley .50 .23
❑ 108T Lonnie Smith 1.00 .45
❑ 109T Ozzie Smith 25.00 11.00
❑ 110T Reggie Smith 1.00 .45
❑ 111T Lary Sorensen .50 .23
❑ 112T Elias Sosa .50 .23
❑ 113T Mike Stanton .50 .23
❑ 114T Steve Stroughter .50 .23
❑ 115T Champ Summers .50 .23
❑ 116T Rick Sutcliffe 1.00 .45
❑ 117T Frank Tanana 1.00 .45
❑ 118T Frank Taveras .50 .23
❑ 119T Garry Templeton .50 .23
❑ 120T Alex Trevino .50 .23
❑ 121T Jerry Turner .50 .23
❑ 122T Ed VandeBerg .50 .23
❑ 123T Tom Veryzer .50 .23
❑ 124T Ron Washington .50 .23
❑ 125T Bob Watson 1.00 .45
❑ 126T Dennis Werth .50 .23
❑ 127T Eddie Whitson .50 .23
❑ 128T Rob Wilfong .50 .23
❑ 129T Bump Wills .50 .23

❑ 130T Gary Woods .50 .23
❑ 131T Butch Wynegar .50 .23
❑ 132T Checklist: 1-132 .50 .23

1983 Topps

	NRMT	VG-E
COMPLETE SET (792)	120.00	55.00
COMP.FACT SET (792)	.15	.07
COMMON CARD (1-792)	.15	.07

❑ 1 Tony Armas RB .30 .14
❑ 2 Rickey Henderson RB .60 .25
Sets modern SB record
❑ 3 Greg Minton RB .15 .07
269 1/3 homerless innings streak
❑ 4 Lance Parrish RB .15 .07
❑ 5 Manny Trillo RB .15 .07
479 consecutive errorless chances, second baseman
❑ 6 John Wathan RB .15 .07
ML catcher steals, season
❑ 7 Gene Richards .15 .07
❑ 8 Steve Balboni .15 .07
❑ 9 Joey McLaughlin .15 .07
❑ 10 Gorman Thomas .15 .07
❑ 11 Billy Gardner MG .15 .07
❑ 12 Paul Mirabella .15 .07
❑ 13 Larry Herndon .15 .07
❑ 14 Frank LaCorte .15 .07
❑ 15 Ron Cey .30 .14
❑ 16 George Vukovich .15 .07
❑ 17 Kent Tekulve .30 .14
❑ 18 Kent Tekulve SV .15 .07
❑ 19 Oscar Gamble .15 .07
❑ 20 Carlton Fisk 1.25 .55
❑ 21 Baltimore Orioles TL .60 .25
BA: Eddie Murray
ERA: Jim Palmer
❑ 22 Randy Martz .15 .07
❑ 23 Mike Heath .15 .07
❑ 24 Steve Mura .15 .07
❑ 25 Hal McRae .30 .14
❑ 26 Jerry Royster .15 .07
❑ 27 Doug Corbett .15 .07
❑ 28 Bruce Bochte .15 .07
❑ 29 Randy Jones .15 .07
❑ 30 Jim Rice .30 .14
❑ 31 Bill Gullickson .30 .14
❑ 32 Dave Bergman .15 .07
❑ 33 Jack O'Connor .15 .07
❑ 34 Paul Householder .15 .07
❑ 35 Rollie Fingers 1.25 .55
❑ 36 Rollie Fingers SV .60 .25
❑ 37 Darrell Johnson MG .15 .07
❑ 38 Tim Flannery .15 .07
❑ 39 Terry Puhl .15 .07
❑ 40 Fernando Valenzuela .60 .25
❑ 41 Jerry Turner .15 .07
❑ 42 Dale Murray .15 .07
❑ 43 Bob Dernier .15 .07
❑ 44 Don Robinson .15 .07
❑ 45 John Mayberry .15 .07
❑ 46 Richard Dotson .15 .07
❑ 47 Dave McKay .15 .07
❑ 48 Lary Sorensen .15 .07
❑ 49 Willie McGee 1.25 .55
❑ 50 Bob Horner UER .15 .07
('82 RBI total 7)
❑ 51 Chicago Cubs TL .30 .14
BA: Leon Durham
ERA: Fergie Jenkins
❑ 52 Onix Concepcion .15 .07
❑ 53 Mike Witt .15 .07
❑ 54 Jim Maler .15 .07
❑ 55 Mookie Wilson .30 .14
❑ 56 Chuck Rainey .15 .07
❑ 57 Tim Blackwell .15 .07
❑ 58 Al Holland .15 .07
❑ 59 Benny Ayala .15 .07
❑ 60 Johnny Bench 1.50 .70
❑ 61 Johnny Bench SV .60 .25
❑ 62 Bob McClure .15 .07
❑ 63 Rick Monday .15 .07
❑ 64 Bill Stein .15 .07
❑ 65 Jack Morris .30 .14
❑ 66 Bob Lillis MG .15 .07
❑ 67 Sal Butera .15 .07
❑ 68 Eric Show .15 .07
❑ 69 Lee Lacy .15 .07
❑ 70 Steve Carlton 1.25 .55
❑ 71 Steve Carlton SV .60 .25
❑ 72 Tom Paciorek .30 .14
❑ 73 Allen Ripley .15 .07
❑ 74 Julio Gonzalez .15 .07
❑ 75 Amos Otis .30 .14
❑ 76 Rick Mahler .15 .07
❑ 77 Hosken Powell .15 .07
❑ 78 Bill Caudill .15 .07
❑ 79 Mick Kelleher .15 .07
❑ 80 George Foster .30 .14
❑ 81 Yankees TL .30 .14
BA: Jerry Mumphrey
ERA: Dave Righetti
❑ 82 Bruce Hurst .15 .07
❑ 83 Ryne Sandberg 20.00 9.00
❑ 84 Milt May .15 .07
❑ 85 Ken Singleton .15 .07
❑ 86 Tom Hume .15 .07
❑ 87 Joe Rudi .15 .07
❑ 88 Jim Gantner .30 .14
❑ 89 Leon Roberts .15 .07
❑ 90 Jerry Reuss .30 .14
❑ 91 Larry Milbourne .15 .07
❑ 92 Mike LaCoss .15 .07
❑ 93 John Castino .15 .07
❑ 94 Dave Edwards .15 .07
❑ 95 Alan Trammell 1.25 .55
❑ 96 Dick Howser MG .15 .07
❑ 97 Ross Baumgarten .15 .07
❑ 98 Vance Law .15 .07
❑ 99 Dickie Noles .15 .07
❑ 100 Pete Rose 1.50 .70
❑ 101 Pete Rose SV .60 .25
❑ 102 Dave Beard .15 .07
❑ 103 Darrell Porter .15 .07
❑ 104 Bob Walk .15 .07
❑ 105 Don Baylor .60 .25
❑ 106 Gene Nelson .15 .07
❑ 107 Mike Jorgensen .15 .07
❑ 108 Glenn Hoffman .15 .07
❑ 109 Luis Leal .15 .07
❑ 110 Ken Griffey .30 .14
❑ 111 Montreal Expos TL .30 .14
BA: Al Oliver
ERA: Steve Rogers
❑ 112 Bob Shirley .15 .07
❑ 113 Ron Roenicke .15 .07
❑ 114 Jim Slaton .15 .07
❑ 115 Chili Davis 1.25 .55
❑ 116 Dave Schmidt .15 .07
❑ 117 Alan Knicely .15 .07
❑ 118 Chris Welsh .15 .07
❑ 119 Tom Brookens .15 .07
❑ 120 Len Barker .15 .07
❑ 121 Mickey Hatcher .15 .07
❑ 122 Jimmy Smith .15 .07
❑ 123 George Frazier .15 .07
❑ 124 Marc Hill .15 .07
❑ 125 Leon Durham .15 .07
❑ 126 Joe Torre MG .30 .14
❑ 127 Preston Hanna .15 .07
❑ 128 Mike Ramsey .15 .07
❑ 129 Checklist: 1-132 .30 .14
❑ 130 Dave Stieb .30 .14
❑ 131 Ed Ott .15 .07
❑ 132 Todd Cruz .15 .07
❑ 133 Jim Barr .15 .07
❑ 134 Hubie Brooks .30 .14
❑ 135 Dwight Evans .30 .14
❑ 136 Willie Aikens .15 .07
❑ 137 Woodie Fryman .15 .07
❑ 138 Rick Dempsey .30 .14
❑ 139 Bruce Berenyi .15 .07
❑ 140 Willie Randolph .30 .14
❑ 141 Indians TL .30 .14
BA: Toby Harrah
ERA: Rick Sutcliffe
❑ 142 Mike Caldwell .15 .07
❑ 143 Joe Pettini .15 .07
❑ 144 Mark Wagner .15 .07
❑ 145 Don Sutton 1.25 .55
❑ 146 Don Sutton SV .60 .25
❑ 147 Rick Leach .15 .07
❑ 148 Dave Roberts .15 .07
❑ 149 Johnny Ray .15 .07
❑ 150 Bruce Sutter .30 .14
❑ 151 Bruce Sutter SV .15 .07
❑ 152 Jay Johnstone .30 .14
❑ 153 Jerry Koosman .30 .14
❑ 154 Johnnie LeMaster .15 .07
❑ 155 Dan Quisenberry .30 .14
❑ 156 Billy Martin MG .30 .14
❑ 157 Steve Bedrosian .30 .14
❑ 158 Rob Wilfong .15 .07
❑ 159 Mike Stanton .15 .07
❑ 160 Dave Kingman .60 .25
❑ 161 Dave Kingman SV .30 .14
❑ 162 Mark Clear .15 .07
❑ 163 Cal Ripken 12.00 5.50
❑ 164 David Palmer .15 .07
❑ 165 Dan Driessen .15 .07
❑ 166 John Pacella .15 .07
❑ 167 Mark Brouhard .15 .07
❑ 168 Juan Eichelberger .15 .07
❑ 169 Doug Flynn .15 .07
❑ 170 Steve Howe .15 .07
❑ 171 Giants TL .60 .25
BA: Joe Morgan
ERA: Bill Laskey
❑ 172 Vern Ruhle .15 .07
❑ 173 Jim Morrison .15 .07
❑ 174 Jerry Ujdur .15 .07
❑ 175 Bo Diaz .15 .07
❑ 176 Dave Righetti .30 .14
❑ 177 Harold Baines .60 .25
❑ 178 Luis Tiant .30 .14
❑ 179 Luis Tiant SV .15 .07
❑ 180 Rickey Henderson 1.50 .70
❑ 181 Terry Felton .15 .07
❑ 182 Mike Fischlin .15 .07
❑ 183 Ed VandeBerg .15 .07
❑ 184 Bob Clark .15 .07
❑ 185 Tim Lollar .15 .07
❑ 186 Whitey Herzog MG .30 .14
❑ 187 Terry Leach .15 .07
❑ 188 Rick Miller .15 .07
❑ 189 Dan Schatzeder .15 .07
❑ 190 Cecil Cooper .30 .14
❑ 191 Joe Price .15 .07
❑ 192 Floyd Rayford .15 .07
❑ 193 Harry Spilman .15 .07
❑ 194 Cesar Geronimo .15 .07
❑ 195 Bob Stoddard .15 .07
❑ 196 Bill Fahey .15 .07
❑ 197 Jim Eisenreich 1.25 .55
❑ 198 Kiko Garcia .15 .07
❑ 199 Marty Bystrom .15 .07
❑ 200 Rod Carew 1.25 .55
❑ 201 Rod Carew SV .60 .25
❑ 202 Blue Jays TL .30 .14
BA: Damaso Garcia
ERA: Dave Stieb
❑ 203 Mike Morgan .15 .07
❑ 204 Junior Kennedy .15 .07
❑ 205 Dave Parker .30 .14

❑ 206	Ken Oberkfell	.15	.07
❑ 207	Rick Camp	.15	.07
❑ 208	Dan Meyer	.15	.07
❑ 209	Mike Moore	.30	.14
❑ 210	Jack Clark	.30	.14
❑ 211	John Denny	.15	.07
❑ 212	John Stearns	.15	.07
❑ 213	Tom Burgmeier	.15	.07
❑ 214	Jerry White	.15	.07
❑ 215	Mario Soto	.15	.07
❑ 216	Tony LaRussa MG	.30	.14
❑ 217	Tim Stoddard	.15	.07
❑ 218	Roy Howell	.15	.07
❑ 219	Mike Armstrong	.15	.07
❑ 220	Dusty Baker	.30	.14
❑ 221	Joe Niekro	.30	.14
❑ 222	Damaso Garcia	.15	.07
❑ 223	John Montefusco	.15	.07
❑ 224	Mickey Rivers	.15	.07
❑ 225	Enos Cabell	.15	.07
❑ 226	Enrique Romo	.15	.07
❑ 227	Chris Bando	.15	.07
❑ 228	Joaquin Andujar	.15	.07
❑ 229	Phillies TL	.60	.25
	BA: Bo Diaz		
	ERA: Steve Carlton		
❑ 230	Fergie Jenkins	1.25	.55
❑ 231	Fergie Jenkins SV	.60	.25
❑ 232	Tom Brunansky	.30	.14
❑ 233	Wayne Gross	.15	.07
❑ 234	Larry Andersen	.15	.07
❑ 235	Claudell Washington	.15	.07
❑ 236	Steve Renko	.15	.07
❑ 237	Dan Norman	.15	.07
❑ 238	Bud Black	.30	.14
❑ 239	Dave Stapleton	.15	.07
❑ 240	Rich Gossage	.60	.25
❑ 241	Rich Gossage SV	.30	.14
❑ 242	Joe Nolan	.15	.07
❑ 243	Duane Walker	.15	.07
❑ 244	Dwight Bernard	.15	.07
❑ 245	Steve Sax	.30	.14
❑ 246	George Bamberger MG	.15	.07
❑ 247	Dave Smith	.15	.07
❑ 248	Bake McBride	.15	.07
❑ 249	Checklist: 133-264	.30	.14
❑ 250	Bill Buckner	.30	.14
❑ 251	Alan Wiggins	.15	.07
❑ 252	Luis Aguayo	.15	.07
❑ 253	Larry McWilliams	.15	.07
❑ 254	Rick Cerone	.15	.07
❑ 255	Gene Garber	.15	.07
❑ 256	Gene Garber SV	.15	.07
❑ 257	Jesse Barfield	.30	.14
❑ 258	Manny Castillo	.15	.07
❑ 259	Jeff Jones	.15	.07
❑ 260	Steve Kemp	.15	.07
❑ 261	Tigers TL	.30	.14
	BA: Larry Herndon		
	ERA: Dan Petry		
❑ 262	Ron Jackson	.15	.07
❑ 263	Renie Martin	.15	.07
❑ 264	Jamie Quirk	.15	.07
❑ 265	Joel Youngblood	.15	.07
❑ 266	Paul Boris	.15	.07
❑ 267	Terry Francona	.15	.07
❑ 268	Storm Davis	.15	.07
❑ 269	Ron Oester	.15	.07
❑ 270	Dennis Eckersley	1.25	.55
❑ 271	Ed Romero	.15	.07
❑ 272	Frank Tanana	.30	.14
❑ 273	Mark Belanger	.15	.07
❑ 274	Terry Kennedy	.15	.07
❑ 275	Ray Knight	.30	.14
❑ 276	Gene Mauch MG	.15	.07
❑ 277	Rance Mulliniks	.15	.07
❑ 278	Kevin Hickey	.15	.07
❑ 279	Greg Gross	.15	.07
❑ 280	Bert Blyleven	1.25	.55
❑ 281	Andre Robertson	.15	.07
❑ 282	Reggie Smith	1.25	.55
	(Ryne Sandberg ducking back)		
❑ 283	Reggie Smith SV	.15	.07
❑ 284	Jeff Lahti	.15	.07
❑ 285	Lance Parrish	.30	.14
❑ 286	Rick Langford	.15	.07
❑ 287	Bobby Brown	.15	.07
❑ 288	Joe Cowley	.15	.07
❑ 289	Jerry Dybzinski	.15	.07
❑ 290	Jeff Reardon	.30	.14
❑ 291	Pirates TL	.30	.14
	BA: Bill Madlock		
	ERA: John Candelaria		
❑ 292	Craig Swan	.15	.07
❑ 293	Glenn Gulliver	.15	.07
❑ 294	Dave Engle	.15	.07
❑ 295	Jerry Remy	.15	.07
❑ 296	Greg Harris	.15	.07
❑ 297	Ned Yost	.15	.07
❑ 298	Floyd Chiffer	.15	.07
❑ 299	George Wright	.15	.07
❑ 300	Mike Schmidt	1.50	.70
❑ 301	Mike Schmidt SV	.60	.25
❑ 302	Ernie Whitt	.15	.07
❑ 303	Miguel Dilone	.15	.07
❑ 304	Dave Rucker	.15	.07
❑ 305	Larry Bowa	.30	.14
❑ 306	Tom Lasorda MG	.60	.25
❑ 307	Lou Piniella	.30	.14
❑ 308	Jesus Vega	.15	.07
❑ 309	Jeff Leonard	.15	.07
❑ 310	Greg Luzinski	.30	.14
❑ 311	Glenn Brummer	.15	.07
❑ 312	Brian Kingman	.15	.07
❑ 313	Gary Gray	.15	.07
❑ 314	Ken Dayley	.15	.07
❑ 315	Rick Burleson	.15	.07
❑ 316	Paul Splittorff	.15	.07
❑ 317	Gary Rajsich	.15	.07
❑ 318	John Tudor	.15	.07
❑ 319	Lenn Sakata	.15	.07
❑ 320	Steve Rogers	.15	.07
❑ 321	Brewers TL	.60	.25
	BA: Robin Yount		
	ERA: Pete Vuckovich		
❑ 322	Dave Van Gorder	.15	.07
❑ 323	Luis DeLeon	.15	.07
❑ 324	Mike Marshall	.15	.07
❑ 325	Von Hayes	.30	.14
❑ 326	Garth Iorg	.15	.07
❑ 327	Bobby Castillo	.15	.07
❑ 328	Craig Reynolds	.15	.07
❑ 329	Randy Niemann	.15	.07
❑ 330	Buddy Bell	.30	.14
❑ 331	Mike Krukow	.15	.07
❑ 332	Glenn Wilson	.30	.14
❑ 333	Dave LaRoche	.15	.07
❑ 334	Dave LaRoche SV	.15	.07
❑ 335	Steve Henderson	.15	.07
❑ 336	Rene Lachemann MG	.15	.07
❑ 337	Tito Landrum	.15	.07
❑ 338	Bob Owchinko	.15	.07
❑ 339	Terry Harper	.15	.07
❑ 340	Larry Gura	.15	.07
❑ 341	Doug DeCinces	.30	.14
❑ 342	Atlee Hammaker	.15	.07
❑ 343	Bob Bailor	.15	.07
❑ 344	Roger LaFrancois	.15	.07
❑ 345	Jim Clancy	.15	.07
❑ 346	Joe Pittman	.15	.07
❑ 347	Sammy Stewart	.15	.07
❑ 348	Alan Bannister	.15	.07
❑ 349	Checklist: 265-396	.30	.14
❑ 350	Robin Yount	1.25	.55
❑ 351	Reds TL	.30	.14
	BA: Cesar Cedeno		
	ERA: Mario Soto		
❑ 352	Mike Scioscia	.30	.14
❑ 353	Steve Comer	.15	.07
❑ 354	Randy Johnson	.15	.07
❑ 355	Jim Bibby	.15	.07
❑ 356	Gary Woods	.15	.07
❑ 357	Len Matuszek	.15	.07
❑ 358	Jerry Garvin	.15	.07
❑ 359	Dave Collins	.15	.07
❑ 360	Nolan Ryan	6.00	2.70
❑ 361	Nolan Ryan SV	3.00	1.35
❑ 362	Bill Almon	.15	.07
❑ 363	John Stuper	.15	.07
❑ 364	Brett Butler	1.25	.55
❑ 365	Dave Lopes	.30	.14
❑ 366	Dick Williams MG	.15	.07
❑ 367	Bud Anderson	.15	.07
❑ 368	Richie Zisk	.15	.07
❑ 369	Jesse Orosco	.15	.07
❑ 370	Gary Carter	1.25	.55
❑ 371	Mike Richardt	.15	.07
❑ 372	Terry Crowley	.15	.07
❑ 373	Kevin Saucier	.15	.07
❑ 374	Wayne Krenchicki	.15	.07
❑ 375	Pete Vuckovich	.15	.07
❑ 376	Ken Landreaux	.15	.07
❑ 377	Lee May	.30	.14
❑ 378	Lee May SV	.15	.07
❑ 379	Guy Sularz	.15	.07
❑ 380	Ron Davis	.15	.07
❑ 381	Red Sox TL	.30	.14
	BA: Jim Rice		
	ERA: Bob Stanley		
❑ 382	Bob Knepper	.15	.07
❑ 383	Ozzie Virgil	.15	.07
❑ 384	Dave Dravecky	1.25	.55
❑ 385	Mike Easler	.15	.07
❑ 386	Rod Carew AS	.60	.25
❑ 387	Bob Grich AS	.15	.07
❑ 388	George Brett AS	1.25	.55
❑ 389	Robin Yount AS	.60	.25
❑ 390	Reggie Jackson AS	.60	.25
❑ 391	Rickey Henderson AS	.60	.25
❑ 392	Fred Lynn AS	.15	.07
❑ 393	Carlton Fisk AS	.60	.25
❑ 394	Pete Vuckovich AS	.15	.07
❑ 395	Larry Gura AS	.15	.07
❑ 396	Dan Quisenberry AS	.15	.07
❑ 397	Pete Rose AS	.60	.25
❑ 398	Manny Trillo AS	.15	.07
❑ 399	Mike Schmidt AS	.60	.25
❑ 400	Dave Concepcion AS	.15	.07
❑ 401	Dale Murphy AS	.60	.25
❑ 402	Andre Dawson AS	.60	.25
❑ 403	Tim Raines AS	.30	.14
❑ 404	Gary Carter AS	.60	.25
❑ 405	Steve Rogers AS	.15	.07
❑ 406	Steve Carlton AS	.60	.25
❑ 407	Bruce Sutter AS	.15	.07
❑ 408	Rudy May	.15	.07
❑ 409	Marvis Foley	.15	.07
❑ 410	Phil Niekro	1.25	.55
❑ 411	Phil Niekro SV	.60	.25
❑ 412	Rangers TL	.30	.14
	BA: Buddy Bell		
	ERA: Charlie Hough		
❑ 413	Matt Keough	.15	.07
❑ 414	Julio Cruz	.15	.07
❑ 415	Bob Forsch	.15	.07
❑ 416	Joe Ferguson	.15	.07
❑ 417	Tom Hausman	.15	.07
❑ 418	Greg Pryor	.15	.07
❑ 419	Steve Crawford	.15	.07
❑ 420	Al Oliver	.30	.14
❑ 421	Al Oliver SV	.15	.07
❑ 422	George Cappuzzello	.15	.07
❑ 423	Tom Lawless	.15	.07
❑ 424	Jerry Augustine	.15	.07
❑ 425	Pedro Guerrero	.30	.14
❑ 426	Earl Weaver MG	.60	.25
❑ 427	Roy Lee Jackson	.15	.07
❑ 428	Champ Summers	.15	.07
❑ 429	Eddie Whitson	.15	.07
❑ 430	Kirk Gibson	1.25	.55
❑ 431	Gary Gaetti	1.25	.55
❑ 432	Porfirio Altamirano	.15	.07
❑ 433	Dale Berra	.15	.07
❑ 434	Dennis Lamp	.15	.07
❑ 435	Tony Armas	.15	.07
❑ 436	Bill Campbell	.15	.07
❑ 437	Rick Sweet	.15	.07
❑ 438	Dave LaPoint	.15	.07
❑ 439	Rafael Ramirez	.15	.07
❑ 440	Ron Guidry	.30	.14
❑ 441	Astros TL	.30	.14
	BA: Ray Knight		
	ERA: Joe Niekro		
❑ 442	Brian Downing	.15	.07

- ❑ 443 Don Hood .15 .07
- ❑ 444 Wally Backman .15 .07
- ❑ 445 Mike Flanagan .30 .14
- ❑ 446 Reid Nichols .15 .07
- ❑ 447 Bryn Smith .15 .07
- ❑ 448 Darrell Evans .30 .14
- ❑ 449 Eddie Milner .15 .07
- ❑ 450 Ted Simmons .30 .14
- ❑ 451 Ted Simmons SV .15 .07
- ❑ 452 Lloyd Moseby .15 .07
- ❑ 453 Lamar Johnson .15 .07
- ❑ 454 Bob Welch .30 .14
- ❑ 455 Sixto Lezcano .15 .07
- ❑ 456 Lee Elia MG .15 .07
- ❑ 457 Milt Wilcox .15 .07
- ❑ 458 Ron Washington .15 .07
- ❑ 459 Ed Farmer .15 .07
- ❑ 460 Roy Smalley .15 .07
- ❑ 461 Steve Trout .15 .07
- ❑ 462 Steve Nicosia .15 .07
- ❑ 463 Gaylord Perry 1.25 .55
- ❑ 464 Gaylord Perry SV .60 .25
- ❑ 465 Lonnie Smith .15 .07
- ❑ 466 Tom Underwood .15 .07
- ❑ 467 Rufino Linares .15 .07
- ❑ 468 Dave Goltz .15 .07
- ❑ 469 Ron Gardenhire .15 .07
- ❑ 470 Greg Minton .15 .07
- ❑ 471 Kansas City Royals TL .30 .14
  BA: Willie Wilson
  ERA: Vida Blue
- ❑ 472 Gary Allenson .15 .07
- ❑ 473 John Lowenstein .15 .07
- ❑ 474 Ray Burris .15 .07
- ❑ 475 Cesar Cedeno .30 .14
- ❑ 476 Rob Picciolo .15 .07
- ❑ 477 Tom Niedenfuer .15 .07
- ❑ 478 Phil Garner .30 .14
- ❑ 479 Charlie Hough .30 .14
- ❑ 480 Toby Harrah .15 .07
- ❑ 481 Scot Thompson .15 .07
- ❑ 482 Tony Gwynn UER 60.00 27.00
  (No Topps logo under card number on back)
- ❑ 483 Lynn Jones .15 .07
- ❑ 484 Dick Ruthven .15 .07
- ❑ 485 Omar Moreno .15 .07
- ❑ 486 Clyde King MG .15 .07
- ❑ 487 Jerry Hairston .15 .07
- ❑ 488 Alfredo Griffin .15 .07
- ❑ 489 Tom Herr .30 .14
- ❑ 490 Jim Palmer 1.25 .55
- ❑ 491 Jim Palmer SV .60 .25
- ❑ 492 Paul Serna .15 .07
- ❑ 493 Steve McCatty .15 .07
- ❑ 494 Bob Brenly .15 .07
- ❑ 495 Warren Cromartie .15 .07
- ❑ 496 Tom Veryzer .15 .07
- ❑ 497 Rick Sutcliffe .30 .14
- ❑ 498 Wade Boggs 20.00 9.00
- ❑ 499 Jeff Little .15 .07
- ❑ 500 Reggie Jackson 1.50 .70
- ❑ 501 Reggie Jackson SV .60 .25
- ❑ 502 Atlanta Braves TL .30 .14
  BA: Dale Murphy
  ERA: Phil Niekro
- ❑ 503 Moose Haas .15 .07
- ❑ 504 Don Werner .15 .07
- ❑ 505 Garry Templeton .15 .07
- ❑ 506 Jim Gott .15 .07
- ❑ 507 Tony Scott .15 .07
- ❑ 508 Tom Filer .15 .07
- ❑ 509 Lou Whitaker .60 .25
- ❑ 510 Tug McGraw .30 .14
- ❑ 511 Tug McGraw SV .15 .07
- ❑ 512 Doyle Alexander .15 .07
- ❑ 513 Fred Stanley .15 .07
- ❑ 514 Rudy Law .15 .07
- ❑ 515 Gene Tenace .30 .14
- ❑ 516 Bill Virdon MG .15 .07
- ❑ 517 Gary Ward .15 .07
- ❑ 518 Bill Laskey .15 .07
- ❑ 519 Terry Bulling .15 .07
- ❑ 520 Fred Lynn .30 .14
- ❑ 521 Bruce Benedict .15 .07
- ❑ 522 Pat Zachry .15 .07
- ❑ 523 Carney Lansford .30 .14
- ❑ 524 Tom Brennan .15 .07
- ❑ 525 Frank White .30 .14
- ❑ 526 Checklist: 397-528 .30 .14
- ❑ 527 Larry Biittner .15 .07
- ❑ 528 Jamie Easterly .15 .07
- ❑ 529 Tim Laudner .15 .07
- ❑ 530 Eddie Murray 1.50 .70
- ❑ 531 Oakland A's TL .60 .25
  BA: Rickey Henderson
  ERA: Rick Langford
- ❑ 532 Dave Stewart .30 .14
- ❑ 533 Luis Salazar .15 .07
- ❑ 534 John Butcher .15 .07
- ❑ 535 Manny Trillo .15 .07
- ❑ 536 John Wockenfuss .15 .07
- ❑ 537 Rod Scurry .15 .07
- ❑ 538 Danny Heep .15 .07
- ❑ 539 Roger Erickson .15 .07
- ❑ 540 Ozzie Smith 2.50 1.10
- ❑ 541 Britt Burns .15 .07
- ❑ 542 Jody Davis .15 .07
- ❑ 543 Alan Fowlkes .15 .07
- ❑ 544 Larry Whisenton .15 .07
- ❑ 545 Floyd Bannister .15 .07
- ❑ 546 Dave Garcia MG .15 .07
- ❑ 547 Geoff Zahn .15 .07
- ❑ 548 Brian Giles .15 .07
- ❑ 549 Charlie Puleo .15 .07
- ❑ 550 Carl Yastrzemski 1.25 .55
- ❑ 551 Carl Yastrzemski SV .60 .25
- ❑ 552 Tim Wallach .30 .14
- ❑ 553 Dennis Martinez .30 .14
- ❑ 554 Mike Vail .15 .07
- ❑ 555 Steve Yeager .15 .07
- ❑ 556 Willie Upshaw .15 .07
- ❑ 557 Rick Honeycutt .15 .07
- ❑ 558 Dickie Thon .15 .07
- ❑ 559 Pete Redfern .15 .07
- ❑ 560 Ron LeFlore .15 .07
- ❑ 561 Cardinals TL .30 .14
  BA: Lonnie Smith
  ERA: Joaquin Andujar
- ❑ 562 Dave Rozema .15 .07
- ❑ 563 Juan Bonilla .15 .07
- ❑ 564 Sid Monge .15 .07
- ❑ 565 Bucky Dent .30 .14
- ❑ 566 Manny Sarmiento .15 .07
- ❑ 567 Joe Simpson .15 .07
- ❑ 568 Willie Hernandez .30 .14
- ❑ 569 Jack Perconte .15 .07
- ❑ 570 Vida Blue .30 .14
- ❑ 571 Mickey Klutts .15 .07
- ❑ 572 Bob Watson .30 .14
- ❑ 573 Andy Hassler .15 .07
- ❑ 574 Glenn Adams .15 .07
- ❑ 575 Neil Allen .15 .07
- ❑ 576 Frank Robinson MG .60 .25
- ❑ 577 Luis Aponte .15 .07
- ❑ 578 David Green .15 .07
- ❑ 579 Rich Dauer .15 .07
- ❑ 580 Tom Seaver 1.50 .70
- ❑ 581 Tom Seaver SV .60 .25
- ❑ 582 Marshall Edwards .15 .07
- ❑ 583 Terry Forster .15 .07
- ❑ 584 Dave Hostetler .15 .07
- ❑ 585 Jose Cruz .30 .14
- ❑ 586 Frank Viola 1.25 .55
- ❑ 587 Ivan DeJesus .15 .07
- ❑ 588 Pat Underwood .15 .07
- ❑ 589 Alvis Woods .15 .07
- ❑ 590 Tony Pena .15 .07
- ❑ 591 White Sox TL .30 .14
  BA: Greg Luzinski
  ERA: LaMarr Hoyt
- ❑ 592 Shane Rawley .15 .07
- ❑ 593 Broderick Perkins .15 .07
- ❑ 594 Eric Rasmussen .15 .07
- ❑ 595 Tim Raines 1.25 .55
- ❑ 596 Randy Johnson .15 .07
- ❑ 597 Mike Proly .15 .07
- ❑ 598 Dwayne Murphy .15 .07
- ❑ 599 Don Aase .15 .07
- ❑ 600 George Brett 2.50 1.10
- ❑ 601 Ed Lynch .15 .07
- ❑ 602 Rich Gedman .15 .07
- ❑ 603 Joe Morgan 1.25 .55
- ❑ 604 Joe Morgan SV .60 .25
- ❑ 605 Gary Roenicke .15 .07
- ❑ 606 Bobby Cox MG .30 .14
- ❑ 607 Charlie Leibrandt .15 .07
- ❑ 608 Don Money .15 .07
- ❑ 609 Danny Darwin .30 .14
- ❑ 610 Steve Garvey .60 .25
- ❑ 611 Bert Roberge .15 .07
- ❑ 612 Steve Swisher .15 .07
- ❑ 613 Mike Ivie .15 .07
- ❑ 614 Ed Glynn .15 .07
- ❑ 615 Garry Maddox .15 .07
- ❑ 616 Bill Nahorodny .15 .07
- ❑ 617 Butch Wynegar .15 .07
- ❑ 618 LaMarr Hoyt .30 .14
- ❑ 619 Keith Moreland .15 .07
- ❑ 620 Mike Norris .15 .07
- ❑ 621 New York Mets TL .30 .14
  BA: Mookie Wilson
  ERA: Craig Swan
- ❑ 622 Dave Edler .15 .07
- ❑ 623 Luis Sanchez .15 .07
- ❑ 624 Glenn Hubbard .15 .07
- ❑ 625 Ken Forsch .15 .07
- ❑ 626 Jerry Martin .15 .07
- ❑ 627 Doug Bair .15 .07
- ❑ 628 Julio Valdez .15 .07
- ❑ 629 Charlie Lea .15 .07
- ❑ 630 Paul Molitor 1.50 .70
- ❑ 631 Tippy Martinez .15 .07
- ❑ 632 Alex Trevino .15 .07
- ❑ 633 Vicente Romo .15 .07
- ❑ 634 Max Venable .15 .07
- ❑ 635 Graig Nettles .30 .14
- ❑ 636 Graig Nettles SV .15 .07
- ❑ 637 Pat Corrales MG .15 .07
- ❑ 638 Dan Petry .15 .07
- ❑ 639 Art Howe .30 .14
- ❑ 640 Andre Thornton .15 .07
- ❑ 641 Billy Sample .15 .07
- ❑ 642 Checklist: 529-660 .30 .14
- ❑ 643 Bump Wills .15 .07
- ❑ 644 Joe Lefebvre .15 .07
- ❑ 645 Bill Madlock .30 .14
- ❑ 646 Jim Essian .15 .07
- ❑ 647 Bobby Mitchell .15 .07
- ❑ 648 Jeff Burroughs .15 .07
- ❑ 649 Tommy Boggs .15 .07
- ❑ 650 George Hendrick .15 .07
- ❑ 651 Angels TL .60 .25
  BA: Rod Carew
  ERA: Mike Witt
- ❑ 652 Butch Hobson .15 .07
- ❑ 653 Ellis Valentine .15 .07
- ❑ 654 Bob Ojeda .15 .07
- ❑ 655 Al Bumbry .15 .07
- ❑ 656 Dave Frost .15 .07
- ❑ 657 Mike Gates .15 .07
- ❑ 658 Frank Pastore .15 .07
- ❑ 659 Charlie Moore .15 .07
- ❑ 660 Mike Hargrove .30 .14
- ❑ 661 Bill Russell .30 .14
- ❑ 662 Joe Sambito .15 .07
- ❑ 663 Tom O'Malley .15 .07
- ❑ 664 Bob Molinaro .15 .07
- ❑ 665 Jim Sundberg .30 .14
- ❑ 666 Sparky Anderson MG .30 .14
- ❑ 667 Dick Davis .15 .07
- ❑ 668 Larry Christenson .15 .07
- ❑ 669 Mike Squires .15 .07
- ❑ 670 Jerry Mumphrey .15 .07
- ❑ 671 Lenny Faedo .15 .07
- ❑ 672 Jim Kaat .30 .14
- ❑ 673 Jim Kaat SV .15 .07
- ❑ 674 Kurt Bevacqua .15 .07
- ❑ 675 Jim Beattie .15 .07
- ❑ 676 Biff Pocoroba .15 .07
- ❑ 677 Dave Revering .15 .07
- ❑ 678 Juan Beniquez .15 .07
- ❑ 679 Mike Scott .30 .14
- ❑ 680 Andre Dawson 1.25 .55
- ❑ 681 Dodgers Leaders .30 .14
  BA: Pedro Guerrero

ERA: Fernando Valenzuela
❑ 682 Bob Stanley .15 .07
❑ 683 Dan Ford .15 .07
❑ 684 Rafael Landestoy .15 .07
❑ 685 Lee Mazzilli .15 .07
❑ 686 Randy Lerch .15 .07
❑ 687 U.L. Washington .15 .07
❑ 688 Jim Wohlford .15 .07
❑ 689 Ron Hassey .15 .07
❑ 690 Kent Hrbek .30 .14
❑ 691 Dave Tobik .15 .07
❑ 692 Denny Walling .15 .07
❑ 693 Sparky Lyle .30 .14
❑ 694 Sparky Lyle SV .15 .07
❑ 695 Ruppert Jones .15 .07
❑ 696 Chuck Tanner MG .15 .07
❑ 697 Barry Foote .15 .07
❑ 698 Tony Bernazard .15 .07
❑ 699 Lee Smith 1.25 .55
❑ 700 Keith Hernandez .30 .14
❑ 701 Batting Leaders .30 .14
AL: Willie Wilson
NL: Al Oliver
❑ 702 Home Run Leaders .60 .25
AL: Reggie Jackson
AL: Gorman Thomas
NL: Dave Kingman
❑ 703 RBI Leaders .30 .14
AL: Hal McRae
NL: Dale Murphy
NL: Al Oliver
❑ 704 SB Leaders 1.25 .55
AL: Rickey Henderson
NL: Tim Raines
❑ 705 Victory Leaders .60 .25
AL: LaMarr Hoyt
NL: Steve Carlton
❑ 706 Strikeout Leaders .60 .25
AL: Floyd Bannister
NL: Steve Carlton
❑ 707 ERA Leaders .30 .14
AL: Rick Sutcliffe
NL: Steve Rogers
❑ 708 Leading Firemen .30 .14
AL: Dan Quisenberry
NL: Bruce Sutter
❑ 709 Jimmy Sexton .15 .07
❑ 710 Willie Wilson .30 .14
❑ 711 Mariners TL .30 .14
BA: Bruce Bochte
ERA: Jim Beattie
❑ 712 Bruce Kison .15 .07
❑ 713 Ron Hodges .15 .07
❑ 714 Wayne Nordhagen .15 .07
❑ 715 Tony Perez 1.25 .55
❑ 716 Tony Perez SV .60 .25
❑ 717 Scott Sanderson .15 .07
❑ 718 Jim Dwyer .15 .07
❑ 719 Rich Gale .15 .07
❑ 720 Dave Concepcion .30 .14
❑ 721 John Martin .15 .07
❑ 722 Jorge Orta .15 .07
❑ 723 Randy Moffitt .15 .07
❑ 724 Johnny Grubb .15 .07
❑ 725 Dan Spillner .15 .07
❑ 726 Harvey Kuenn MG .15 .07
❑ 727 Chet Lemon .15 .07
❑ 728 Ron Reed .15 .07
❑ 729 Jerry Morales .15 .07
❑ 730 Jason Thompson .15 .07
❑ 731 Al Williams .15 .07
❑ 732 Dave Henderson .15 .07
❑ 733 Buck Martinez .15 .07
❑ 734 Steve Braun .15 .07
❑ 735 Tommy John .60 .25
❑ 736 Tommy John SV .30 .14
❑ 737 Mitchell Page .15 .07
❑ 738 Tim Foli .15 .07
❑ 739 Rick Ownbey .15 .07
❑ 740 Rusty Staub .30 .14
❑ 741 Rusty Staub SV .15 .07
❑ 742 Padres TL .30 .14
BA: Terry Kennedy
ERA: Tim Lollar
❑ 743 Mike Torrez .15 .07
❑ 744 Brad Mills .15 .07
❑ 745 Scott McGregor .15 .07
❑ 746 John Wathan .15 .07
❑ 747 Fred Breining .15 .07
❑ 748 Derrel Thomas .15 .07
❑ 749 Jon Matlack .15 .07
❑ 750 Ben Oglivie .15 .07
❑ 751 Brad Havens .15 .07
❑ 752 Luis Pujols .15 .07
❑ 753 Elias Sosa .15 .07
❑ 754 Bill Robinson .15 .07
❑ 755 John Candelaria .15 .07
❑ 756 Russ Nixon MG .15 .07
❑ 757 Rick Manning .15 .07
❑ 758 Aurelio Rodriguez .15 .07
❑ 759 Doug Bird .15 .07
❑ 760 Dale Murphy 1.25 .55
❑ 761 Gary Lucas .15 .07
❑ 762 Cliff Johnson .15 .07
❑ 763 Al Cowens .15 .07
❑ 764 Pete Falcone .15 .07
❑ 765 Bob Boone .30 .14
❑ 766 Barry Bonnell .15 .07
❑ 767 Duane Kuiper .15 .07
❑ 768 Chris Speier .15 .07
❑ 769 Checklist: 661-792 .30 .14
❑ 770 Dave Winfield 1.25 .55
❑ 771 Twins TL .30 .14
BA: Kent Hrbek
ERA: Bobby Castillo
❑ 772 Jim Kern .15 .07
❑ 773 Larry Hisle .15 .07
❑ 774 Alan Ashby .15 .07
❑ 775 Burt Hooton .15 .07
❑ 776 Larry Parrish .15 .07
❑ 777 John Curtis .15 .07
❑ 778 Rich Hebner .30 .14
❑ 779 Rick Waits .15 .07
❑ 780 Gary Matthews .30 .14
❑ 781 Rick Rhoden .15 .07
❑ 782 Bobby Murcer .30 .14
❑ 783 Bobby Murcer SV .15 .07
❑ 784 Jeff Newman .15 .07
❑ 785 Dennis Leonard .15 .07
❑ 786 Ralph Houk MG .15 .07
❑ 787 Dick Tidrow .15 .07
❑ 788 Dane Iorg .15 .07
❑ 789 Bryan Clark .15 .07
❑ 790 Bob Grich .30 .14
❑ 791 Gary Lavelle .15 .07
❑ 792 Chris Chambliss .30 .14

1983 Topps Traded

	NRMT	VG-E
COMP.FACT.SET (132)	35.00	16.00
COMMON CARD (1T-132T)	.25	.11

❑ 1T Neil Allen .25 .11
❑ 2T Bill Almon .25 .11
❑ 3T Joe Altobelli MG .25 .11
❑ 4T Tony Armas .25 .11
❑ 5T Doug Bair .25 .11
❑ 6T Steve Baker .25 .11
❑ 7T Floyd Bannister .25 .11
❑ 8T Don Baylor 2.00 .90
❑ 9T Tony Bernazard .25 .11
❑ 10T Larry Biittner .25 .11
❑ 11T Dann Bilardello .25 .11
❑ 12T Doug Bird .25 .11
❑ 13T Steve Boros MG .25 .11
❑ 14T Greg Brock .25 .11
❑ 15T Mike C. Brown .25 .11
❑ 16T Tom Burgmeier .25 .11
❑ 17T Randy Bush .25 .11
❑ 18T Bert Campaneris 1.00 .45
❑ 19T Ron Cey 1.00 .45
❑ 20T Chris Codiroli .25 .11
❑ 21T Dave Collins .25 .11
❑ 22T Terry Crowley .25 .11
❑ 23T Julio Cruz .25 .11
❑ 24T Mike Davis .25 .11
❑ 25T Frank DiPino .25 .11
❑ 26T Bill Doran 1.00 .45
❑ 27T Jerry Dybzinski .25 .11
❑ 28T Jamie Easterly .25 .11
❑ 29T Juan Eichelberger .25 .11
❑ 30T Jim Essian .25 .11
❑ 31T Pete Falcone .25 .11
❑ 32T Mike Ferraro MG .25 .11
❑ 33T Terry Forster .25 .11
❑ 34T Julio Franco 4.00 1.80
❑ 35T Rich Gale .25 .11
❑ 36T Kiko Garcia .25 .11
❑ 37T Steve Garvey 2.00 .90
❑ 38T Johnny Grubb .25 .11
❑ 39T Mel Hall 1.00 .45
❑ 40T Von Hayes 1.00 .45
❑ 41T Danny Heep .25 .11
❑ 42T Steve Henderson .25 .11
❑ 43T Keith Hernandez 2.00 .90
❑ 44T Leo Hernandez .25 .11
❑ 45T Willie Hernandez 1.00 .45
❑ 46T Al Holland .25 .11
❑ 47T Frank Howard MG 1.00 .45
❑ 48T Bobby Johnson .25 .11
❑ 49T Cliff Johnson .25 .11
❑ 50T Odell Jones .25 .11
❑ 51T Mike Jorgensen .25 .11
❑ 52T Bob Kearney .25 .11
❑ 53T Steve Kemp .25 .11
❑ 54T Matt Keough .25 .11
❑ 55T Ron Kittle 2.00 .90
❑ 56T Mickey Klutts .25 .11
❑ 57T Alan Knicely .25 .11
❑ 58T Mike Krukow .25 .11
❑ 59T Rafael Landestoy .25 .11
❑ 60T Carney Lansford 1.00 .45
❑ 61T Joe Lefebvre .25 .11
❑ 62T Bryan Little .25 .11
❑ 63T Aurelio Lopez .25 .11
❑ 64T Mike Madden .25 .11
❑ 65T Rick Manning .25 .11
❑ 66T Billy Martin MG 1.00 .45
❑ 67T Lee Mazzilli .25 .11
❑ 68T Andy McGaffigan .25 .11
❑ 69T Craig McMurtry .25 .11
❑ 70T John McNamara MG .25 .11
❑ 71T Orlando Mercado .25 .11
❑ 72T Larry Milbourne .25 .11
❑ 73T Randy Moffitt .25 .11
❑ 74T Sid Monge .25 .11
❑ 75T Jose Morales .25 .11
❑ 76T Omar Moreno .25 .11
❑ 77T Joe Morgan
❑ 78T Mike Morgan .25 .11
❑ 79T Dale Murray .25 .11
❑ 80T Jeff Newman .25 .11
❑ 81T Pete O'Brien 1.00 .45
❑ 82T Jorge Orta .25 .11
❑ 83T Alejandro Pena 1.00 .45
❑ 84T Pascual Perez .25 .11
❑ 85T Tony Perez
❑ 86T Broderick Perkins .25 .11
❑ 87T Tony Phillips 4.00 1.80
❑ 88T Charlie Puleo .25 .11
❑ 89T Pat Putnam .25 .11
❑ 90T Jamie Quirk .25 .11
❑ 91T Doug Rader MG .25 .11
❑ 92T Chuck Rainey .25 .11
❑ 93T Bobby Ramos .25 .11
❑ 94T Gary Redus 1.00 .45
❑ 95T Steve Renko .25 .11

❑ 96T Leon Roberts .25 .11
❑ 97T Aurelio Rodriguez .25 .11
❑ 98T Dick Ruthven .25 .11
❑ 99T Daryl Sconiers .25 .11
❑ 100T Mike Scott 1.00 .45
❑ 101T Tom Seaver 5.00 2.20
❑ 102T John Shelby .25 .11
❑ 103T Bob Shirley .25 .11
❑ 104T Joe Simpson .25 .11
❑ 105T Doug Sisk .25 .11
❑ 106T Mike Smithson .25 .11
❑ 107T Elias Sosa .25 .11
❑ 108T Darryl Strawberry 20.00 9.00
❑ 109T Tom Tellmann .25 .11
❑ 110T Gene Tenace 1.00 .45
❑ 111T Gorman Thomas .25 .11
❑ 112T Dick Tidrow .25 .11
❑ 113T Dave Tobik .25 .11
❑ 114T Wayne Tolleson .25 .11
❑ 115T Mike Torrez .25 .11
❑ 116T Manny Trillo .25 .11
❑ 117T Steve Trout .25 .11
❑ 118T Lee Tunnell .25 .11
❑ 119T Mike Vail .25 .11
❑ 120T Ellis Valentine .25 .11
❑ 121T Tom Veryzer .25 .11
❑ 122T George Vukovich .25 .11
❑ 123T Rick Waits .25 .11
❑ 124T Greg Walker 1.00 .45
❑ 125T Chris Welsh .25 .11
❑ 126T Len Whitehouse .25 .11
❑ 127T Eddie Whitson .25 .11
❑ 128T Jim Wohlford .25 .11
❑ 129T Matt Young .25 .11
❑ 130T Joel Youngblood .25 .11
❑ 131T Pat Zachry .25 .11
❑ 132T Checklist 1T-132T .25 .11

1984 Topps

	NRMT	VG-E
COMPLETE SET (792)	40.00	18.00
COMMON CARD (1-792)	.10	.05

❑ 1 Steve Carlton HL .60 .25
300th win and
all-time SO king
❑ 2 Rickey Henderson HL .40 .18
100 stolen bases
three times
❑ 3 Dan Quisenberry HL .10 .05
Sets save record
❑ 4 Nolan Ryan HL 1.00 .45
Steve Carlton
Gaylord Perry
All surpass Johnson
❑ 5 Dave Righetti HL .20 .09
Bob Forsch
Mike Warren
All pitch no-hitters
❑ 6 Johnny Bench HL .60 .25
Gaylord Perry
Carl Yastrzemski
Superstars retire
❑ 7 Gary Lucas .10 .05
❑ 8 Don Mattingly 8.00 3.60
❑ 9 Jim Gott .10 .05
❑ 10 Robin Yount .60 .25
❑ 11 Minnesota Twins TL .20 .09
Kent Hrbek
Ken Schrom
❑ 12 Billy Sample .10 .05
❑ 13 Scott Holman .10 .05
❑ 14 Tom Brookens .20 .09
❑ 15 Burt Hooton .10 .05
❑ 16 Omar Moreno .10 .05
❑ 17 John Denny .10 .05
❑ 18 Dale Berra .10 .05
❑ 19 Ray Fontenot .10 .05
❑ 20 Greg Luzinski .20 .09
❑ 21 Joe Altobelli MG .10 .05
❑ 22 Bryan Clark .10 .05
❑ 23 Keith Moreland .10 .05
❑ 24 John Martin .10 .05
❑ 25 Glenn Hubbard .10 .05
❑ 26 Bud Black .10 .05
❑ 27 Daryl Sconiers .10 .05
❑ 28 Frank Viola .40 .18
❑ 29 Danny Heep .10 .05
❑ 30 Wade Boggs 1.25 .55
❑ 31 Andy McGaffigan .10 .05
❑ 32 Bobby Ramos .10 .05
❑ 33 Tom Burgmeier .10 .05
❑ 34 Eddie Milner .10 .05
❑ 35 Don Sutton .60 .25
❑ 36 Denny Walling .10 .05
❑ 37 Texas Rangers TL .20 .09
Buddy Bell
Rick Honeycutt
❑ 38 Luis DeLeon .10 .05
❑ 39 Garth Iorg .10 .05
❑ 40 Dusty Baker .20 .09
❑ 41 Tony Bernazard .10 .05
❑ 42 Johnny Grubb .10 .05
❑ 43 Ron Reed .10 .05
❑ 44 Jim Morrison .10 .05
❑ 45 Jerry Mumphrey .10 .05
❑ 46 Ray Smith .10 .05
❑ 47 Rudy Law .10 .05
❑ 48 Julio Franco .40 .18
❑ 49 John Stuper .10 .05
❑ 50 Chris Chambliss .10 .05
❑ 51 Jim Frey MG .10 .05
❑ 52 Paul Splittorff .10 .05
❑ 53 Juan Beniquez .10 .05
❑ 54 Jesse Orosco .10 .05
❑ 55 Dave Concepcion .20 .09
❑ 56 Gary Allenson .10 .05
❑ 57 Dan Schatzeder .10 .05
❑ 58 Max Venable .10 .05
❑ 59 Sammy Stewart .10 .05
❑ 60 Paul Molitor UER .60 .25
('83 stats .272, 613,
167; should be .270,
608, 164)
❑ 61 Chris Codiroli .10 .05
❑ 62 Dave Hostetler .10 .05
❑ 63 Ed VandeBerg .10 .05
❑ 64 Mike Scioscia .10 .05
❑ 65 Kirk Gibson .60 .25
❑ 66 Houston Astros TL 1.00 .45
Jose Cruz
Nolan Ryan
❑ 67 Gary Ward .10 .05
❑ 68 Luis Salazar .10 .05
❑ 69 Rod Scurry .10 .05
❑ 70 Gary Matthews .20 .09
❑ 71 Leo Hernandez .10 .05
❑ 72 Mike Squires .10 .05
❑ 73 Jody Davis .10 .05
❑ 74 Jerry Martin .10 .05
❑ 75 Bob Forsch .10 .05
❑ 76 Alfredo Griffin .10 .05
❑ 77 Brett Butler .40 .18
❑ 78 Mike Torrez .10 .05
❑ 79 Rob Wilfong .10 .05
❑ 80 Steve Rogers .10 .05
❑ 81 Billy Martin MG .20 .09
❑ 82 Doug Bird .10 .05
❑ 83 Richie Zisk .10 .05
❑ 84 Lenny Faedo .10 .05
❑ 85 Atlee Hammaker .10 .05
❑ 86 John Shelby .10 .05
❑ 87 Frank Pastore .10 .05
❑ 88 Rob Picciolo .10 .05
❑ 89 Mike Smithson .10 .05
❑ 90 Pedro Guerrero .20 .09
❑ 91 Dan Spillner .10 .05
❑ 92 Lloyd Moseby .10 .05
❑ 93 Bob Knepper .10 .05
❑ 94 Mario Ramirez .10 .05
❑ 95 Aurelio Lopez .20 .09
❑ 96 Kansas City Royals TL .20 .09
Hal McRae
Larry Gura
❑ 97 LaMarr Hoyt .10 .05
❑ 98 Steve Nicosia .10 .05
❑ 99 Craig Lefferts .10 .05
❑ 100 Reggie Jackson .75 .35
❑ 101 Porfirio Altamirano .10 .05
❑ 102 Ken Oberkfell .10 .05
❑ 103 Dwayne Murphy .10 .05
❑ 104 Ken Dayley .10 .05
❑ 105 Tony Armas .10 .05
❑ 106 Tim Stoddard .10 .05
❑ 107 Ned Yost .10 .05
❑ 108 Randy Moffitt .10 .05
❑ 109 Brad Wellman .10 .05
❑ 110 Ron Guidry .20 .09
❑ 111 Bill Virdon MG .10 .05
❑ 112 Tom Niedenfuer .10 .05
❑ 113 Kelly Paris .10 .05
❑ 114 Checklist 1-132 .20 .09
❑ 115 Andre Thornton .10 .05
❑ 116 George Bjorkman .10 .05
❑ 117 Tom Veryzer .10 .05
❑ 118 Charlie Hough .20 .09
❑ 119 John Wockenfuss .10 .05
❑ 120 Keith Hernandez .20 .09
❑ 121 Pat Sheridan .10 .05
❑ 122 Cecilio Guante .10 .05
❑ 123 Butch Wynegar .10 .05
❑ 124 Damaso Garcia .10 .05
❑ 125 Britt Burns .10 .05
❑ 126 Atlanta Braves TL .40 .18
Dale Murphy
Craig McMurtry
❑ 127 Mike Madden .10 .05
❑ 128 Rick Manning .10 .05
❑ 129 Bill Laskey .10 .05
❑ 130 Ozzie Smith 1.00 .45
❑ 131 Batting Leaders .60 .25
Bill Madlock
Wade Boggs
❑ 132 Home Run Leaders .60 .25
Mike Schmidt
Jim Rice
❑ 133 RBI Leaders .60 .25
Dale Murphy
Cecil Cooper
Jim Rice
❑ 134 Stolen Base Leaders .60 .25
Tim Raines
Rickey Henderson
❑ 135 Victory Leaders .60 .25
John Denny
LaMarr Hoyt
❑ 136 Strikeout Leaders .60 .25
Steve Carlton
Jack Morris
❑ 137 ERA Leaders .20 .09
Atlee Hammaker
Rick Honeycutt
❑ 138 Leading Firemen .20 .09
Al Holland
Dan Quisenberry
❑ 139 Bert Campaneris .20 .09
❑ 140 Storm Davis .10 .05
❑ 141 Pat Corrales MG .10 .05
❑ 142 Rich Gale .10 .05
❑ 143 Jose Morales .10 .05
❑ 144 Brian Harper .20 .09
❑ 145 Gary Lavelle .10 .05
❑ 146 Ed Romero .10 .05
❑ 147 Dan Petry .20 .09
❑ 148 Joe Lefebvre .10 .05
❑ 149 Jon Matlack .10 .05
❑ 150 Dale Murphy .60 .25

❑ 151 Steve Trout .10 .05
❑ 152 Glenn Brummer .10 .05
❑ 153 Dick Tidrow .10 .05
❑ 154 Dave Henderson .20 .09
❑ 155 Frank White .20 .09
❑ 156 Oakland A's TL .60 .25
Rickey Henderson
Tim Conroy
❑ 157 Gary Gaetti .40 .18
❑ 158 John Curtis .10 .05
❑ 159 Darryl Cias .10 .05
❑ 160 Mario Soto .10 .05
❑ 161 Junior Ortiz .10 .05
❑ 162 Bob Ojeda .10 .05
❑ 163 Lorenzo Gray .10 .05
❑ 164 Scott Sanderson .10 .05
❑ 165 Ken Singleton .10 .05
❑ 166 Jamie Nelson .10 .05
❑ 167 Marshall Edwards .10 .05
❑ 168 Juan Bonilla .10 .05
❑ 169 Larry Parrish .10 .05
❑ 170 Jerry Reuss .10 .05
❑ 171 Frank Robinson MG .40 .18
❑ 172 Frank DiPino .10 .05
❑ 173 Marvell Wynne .10 .05
❑ 174 Juan Berenguer .10 .05
❑ 175 Graig Nettles .20 .09
❑ 176 Lee Smith .60 .25
❑ 177 Jerry Hairston .10 .05
❑ 178 Bill Krueger .10 .05
❑ 179 Buck Martinez .10 .05
❑ 180 Manny Trillo .10 .05
❑ 181 Roy Thomas .10 .05
❑ 182 Darryl Strawberry 2.00 .90
❑ 183 Al Williams .10 .05
❑ 184 Mike O'Berry .10 .05
❑ 185 Sixto Lezcano .10 .05
❑ 186 Cardinal TL .20 .09
Lonnie Smith
John Stuper
❑ 187 Luis Aponte .10 .05
❑ 188 Bryan Little .10 .05
❑ 189 Tim Conroy .10 .05
❑ 190 Ben Oglivie .10 .05
❑ 191 Mike Boddicker .10 .05
❑ 192 Nick Esasky .10 .05
❑ 193 Darrell Brown .10 .05
❑ 194 Domingo Ramos .10 .05
❑ 195 Jack Morris .60 .25
❑ 196 Don Slaught .20 .09
❑ 197 Garry Hancock .10 .05
❑ 198 Bill Doran .20 .09
❑ 199 Willie Hernandez .20 .09
❑ 200 Andre Dawson .60 .25
❑ 201 Bruce Kison .10 .05
❑ 202 Bobby Cox MG .20 .09
❑ 203 Matt Keough .10 .05
❑ 204 Bobby Meacham .10 .05
❑ 205 Greg Minton .10 .05
❑ 206 Andy Van Slyke .60 .25
❑ 207 Donnie Moore .10 .05
❑ 208 Jose Oquendo .20 .09
❑ 209 Manny Sarmiento .10 .05
❑ 210 Joe Morgan .60 .25
❑ 211 Rick Sweet .10 .05
❑ 212 Broderick Perkins .10 .05
❑ 213 Bruce Hurst .10 .05
❑ 214 Paul Householder .10 .05
❑ 215 Tippy Martinez .10 .05
❑ 216 White Sox TL .60 .25
Carlton Fisk
Richard Dotson
❑ 217 Alan Ashby .10 .05
❑ 218 Rick Waits .10 .05
❑ 219 Joe Simpson .10 .05
❑ 220 Fernando Valenzuela .20 .09
❑ 221 Cliff Johnson .10 .05
❑ 222 Rick Honeycutt .10 .05
❑ 223 Wayne Krenchicki .10 .05
❑ 224 Sid Monge .10 .05
❑ 225 Lee Mazzilli .10 .05
❑ 226 Juan Eichelberger .10 .05
❑ 227 Steve Braun .10 .05
❑ 228 John Rabb .10 .05
❑ 229 Paul Owens MG .10 .05
❑ 230 Rickey Henderson .60 .25
❑ 231 Gary Woods .10 .05
❑ 232 Tim Wallach .20 .09
❑ 233 Checklist 133-264 .20 .09
❑ 234 Rafael Ramirez .10 .05
❑ 235 Matt Young .10 .05
❑ 236 Ellis Valentine .10 .05
❑ 237 John Castino .10 .05
❑ 238 Reid Nichols .10 .05
❑ 239 Jay Howell .10 .05
❑ 240 Eddie Murray .60 .25
❑ 241 Bill Almon .10 .05
❑ 242 Alex Trevino .10 .05
❑ 243 Pete Ladd .10 .05
❑ 244 Candy Maldonado .10 .05
❑ 245 Rick Sutcliffe .20 .09
❑ 246 New York Mets TL .60 .25
Mookie Wilson
Tom Seaver
❑ 247 Onix Concepcion .10 .05
❑ 248 Bill Dawley .10 .05
❑ 249 Jay Johnstone .20 .09
❑ 250 Bill Madlock .20 .09
❑ 251 Tony Gwynn 4.00 1.80
❑ 252 Larry Christenson .10 .05
❑ 253 Jim Wohlford .10 .05
❑ 254 Shane Rawley .10 .05
❑ 255 Bruce Benedict .10 .05
❑ 256 Dave Geisel .10 .05
❑ 257 Julio Cruz .10 .05
❑ 258 Luis Sanchez .10 .05
❑ 259 Sparky Anderson MG .40 .18
❑ 260 Scott McGregor .10 .05
❑ 261 Bobby Brown .10 .05
❑ 262 Tom Candiotti .60 .25
❑ 263 Jack Fimple .10 .05
❑ 264 Doug Frobel .10 .05
❑ 265 Donnie Hill .10 .05
❑ 266 Steve Lubratich .10 .05
❑ 267 Carmelo Martinez .10 .05
❑ 268 Jack O'Connor .10 .05
❑ 269 Aurelio Rodriguez .10 .05
❑ 270 Jeff Russell .20 .09
❑ 271 Moose Haas .10 .05
❑ 272 Rick Dempsey .10 .05
❑ 273 Charlie Puleo .10 .05
❑ 274 Rick Monday .10 .05
❑ 275 Len Matuszek .10 .05
❑ 276 Angels TL .60 .25
Rod Carew
Geoff Zahn
❑ 277 Eddie Whitson .10 .05
❑ 278 Jorge Bell .40 .18
❑ 279 Ivan DeJesus .10 .05
❑ 280 Floyd Bannister .10 .05
❑ 281 Larry Milbourne .10 .05
❑ 282 Jim Barr .10 .05
❑ 283 Larry Biittner .10 .05
❑ 284 Howard Bailey .10 .05
❑ 285 Darrell Porter .10 .05
❑ 286 Lary Sorensen .10 .05
❑ 287 Warren Cromartie .10 .05
❑ 288 Jim Beattie .10 .05
❑ 289 Randy Johnson .10 .05
❑ 290 Dave Dravecky .20 .09
❑ 291 Chuck Tanner MG .10 .05
❑ 292 Tony Scott .10 .05
❑ 293 Ed Lynch .10 .05
❑ 294 U.L. Washington .10 .05
❑ 295 Mike Flanagan .10 .05
❑ 296 Jeff Newman .10 .05
❑ 297 Bruce Berenyi .10 .05
❑ 298 Jim Gantner .20 .09
❑ 299 John Butcher .10 .05
❑ 300 Pete Rose .75 .35
❑ 301 Frank LaCorte .10 .05
❑ 302 Barry Bonnell .10 .05
❑ 303 Marty Castillo .10 .05
❑ 304 Warren Brusstar .10 .05
❑ 305 Roy Smalley .10 .05
❑ 306 Dodgers TL .20 .09
Pedro Guerrero
Bob Welch
❑ 307 Bobby Mitchell .10 .05
❑ 308 Ron Hassey .10 .05
❑ 309 Tony Phillips .60 .25
❑ 310 Willie McGee .40 .18
❑ 311 Jerry Koosman .20 .09
❑ 312 Jorge Orta .10 .05
❑ 313 Mike Jorgensen .10 .05
❑ 314 Orlando Mercado .10 .05
❑ 315 Bobby Grich .20 .09
❑ 316 Mark Bradley .10 .05
❑ 317 Greg Pryor .10 .05
❑ 318 Bill Gullickson .10 .05
❑ 319 Al Bumbry .20 .09
❑ 320 Bob Stanley .10 .05
❑ 321 Harvey Kuenn MG .20 .09
❑ 322 Ken Schrom .10 .05
❑ 323 Alan Knicely .10 .05
❑ 324 Alejandro Pena .20 .09
❑ 325 Darrell Evans .20 .09
❑ 326 Bob Kearney .10 .05
❑ 327 Ruppert Jones .10 .05
❑ 328 Vern Ruhle .10 .05
❑ 329 Pat Tabler .10 .05
❑ 330 John Candelaria .10 .05
❑ 331 Bucky Dent .20 .09
❑ 332 Kevin Gross .20 .09
❑ 333 Larry Herndon .20 .09
❑ 334 Chuck Rainey .10 .05
❑ 335 Don Baylor .40 .18
❑ 336 Seattle Mariners TL .20 .09
Pat Putnam
Matt Young
❑ 337 Kevin Hagen .10 .05
❑ 338 Mike Warren .10 .05
❑ 339 Roy Lee Jackson .10 .05
❑ 340 Hal McRae .20 .09
❑ 341 Dave Tobik .10 .05
❑ 342 Tim Foli .10 .05
❑ 343 Mark Davis .10 .05
❑ 344 Rick Miller .10 .05
❑ 345 Kent Hrbek .20 .09
❑ 346 Kurt Bevacqua .10 .05
❑ 347 Allan Ramirez .10 .05
❑ 348 Toby Harrah .20 .09
❑ 349 Bob L. Gibson .10 .05
❑ 350 George Foster .20 .09
❑ 351 Russ Nixon MG .10 .05
❑ 352 Dave Stewart .20 .09
❑ 353 Jim Anderson .10 .05
❑ 354 Jeff Burroughs .10 .05
❑ 355 Jason Thompson .10 .05
❑ 356 Glenn Abbott .10 .05
❑ 357 Ron Cey .20 .09
❑ 358 Bob Dernier .10 .05
❑ 359 Jim Acker .10 .05
❑ 360 Willie Randolph .20 .09
❑ 361 Dave Smith .10 .05
❑ 362 David Green .10 .05
❑ 363 Tim Laudner .10 .05
❑ 364 Scott Fletcher .10 .05
❑ 365 Steve Bedrosian .10 .05
❑ 366 Padres TL .20 .09
Terry Kennedy
Dave Dravecky
❑ 367 Jamie Easterly .10 .05
❑ 368 Hubie Brooks .10 .05
❑ 369 Steve McCatty .10 .05
❑ 370 Tim Raines .40 .18
❑ 371 Dave Gumpert .10 .05
❑ 372 Gary Roenicke .10 .05
❑ 373 Bill Scherrer .10 .05
❑ 374 Don Money .10 .05
❑ 375 Dennis Leonard .10 .05
❑ 376 Dave Anderson .10 .05
❑ 377 Danny Darwin .20 .09
❑ 378 Bob Brenly .10 .05
❑ 379 Checklist 265-396 .20 .09
❑ 380 Steve Garvey .40 .18
❑ 381 Ralph Houk MG .20 .09
❑ 382 Chris Nyman .10 .05
❑ 383 Terry Puhl .10 .05
❑ 384 Lee Tunnell .10 .05
❑ 385 Tony Perez .60 .25
❑ 386 George Hendrick AS .10 .05
❑ 387 Johnny Ray AS .10 .05
❑ 388 Mike Schmidt AS .40 .18
❑ 389 Ozzie Smith AS .60 .25

❑ 390	Tim Raines AS	.20	.09
❑ 391	Dale Murphy AS	.40	.18
❑ 392	Andre Dawson AS	.40	.18
❑ 393	Gary Carter AS	.40	.18
❑ 394	Steve Rogers AS	.10	.05
❑ 395	Steve Carlton AS	.40	.18
❑ 396	Jesse Orosco AS	.10	.05
❑ 397	Eddie Murray AS	.40	.18
❑ 398	Lou Whitaker AS	.20	.09
❑ 399	George Brett AS	.60	.25
❑ 400	Cal Ripken AS	2.00	.90
❑ 401	Jim Rice AS	.10	.05
❑ 402	Dave Winfield AS	.40	.18
❑ 403	Lloyd Moseby AS	.10	.05
❑ 404	Ted Simmons AS	.10	.05
❑ 405	LaMarr Hoyt AS	.10	.05
❑ 406	Ron Guidry AS	.10	.05
❑ 407	Dan Quisenberry AS	.10	.05
❑ 408	Lou Piniella	.20	.09
❑ 409	Juan Agosto	.10	.05
❑ 410	Claudell Washington	.10	.05
❑ 411	Houston Jimenez	.10	.05
❑ 412	Doug Rader MG	.10	.05
❑ 413	Spike Owen	.20	.09
❑ 414	Mitchell Page	.10	.05
❑ 415	Tommy John	.40	.18
❑ 416	Dane Iorg	.10	.05
❑ 417	Mike Armstrong	.10	.05
❑ 418	Ron Hodges	.10	.05
❑ 419	John Henry Johnson	.10	.05
❑ 420	Cecil Cooper	.20	.09
❑ 421	Charlie Lea	.10	.05
❑ 422	Jose Cruz	.20	.09
❑ 423	Mike Morgan	.10	.05
❑ 424	Dann Bilardello	.10	.05
❑ 425	Steve Howe	.10	.05
❑ 426	Orioles TL	1.50	.70
	Cal Ripken		
	Mike Boddicker		
❑ 427	Rick Leach	.10	.05
❑ 428	Fred Breining	.10	.05
❑ 429	Randy Bush	.10	.05
❑ 430	Rusty Staub	.20	.09
❑ 431	Chris Bando	.10	.05
❑ 432	Charles Hudson	.10	.05
❑ 433	Rich Hebner	.10	.05
❑ 434	Harold Baines	.40	.18
❑ 435	Neil Allen	.10	.05
❑ 436	Rick Peters	.10	.05
❑ 437	Mike Proly	.10	.05
❑ 438	Biff Pocoroba	.10	.05
❑ 439	Bob Stoddard	.10	.05
❑ 440	Steve Kemp	.10	.05
❑ 441	Bob Lillis MG	.10	.05
❑ 442	Byron McLaughlin	.10	.05
❑ 443	Benny Ayala	.10	.05
❑ 444	Steve Renko	.10	.05
❑ 445	Jerry Remy	.10	.05
❑ 446	Luis Pujols	.10	.05
❑ 447	Tom Brunansky	.20	.09
❑ 448	Ben Hayes	.10	.05
❑ 449	Joe Pettini	.10	.05
❑ 450	Gary Carter	.60	.25
❑ 451	Bob Jones	.10	.05
❑ 452	Chuck Porter	.10	.05
❑ 453	Willie Upshaw	.10	.05
❑ 454	Joe Beckwith	.10	.05
❑ 455	Terry Kennedy	.10	.05
❑ 456	Chicago Cubs TL	.40	.18
	Keith Moreland		
	Fergie Jenkins		
❑ 457	Dave Rozema	.10	.05
❑ 458	Kiko Garcia	.10	.05
❑ 459	Kevin Hickey	.10	.05
❑ 460	Dave Winfield	.60	.25
❑ 461	Jim Maler	.10	.05
❑ 462	Lee Lacy	.10	.05
❑ 463	Dave Engle	.10	.05
❑ 464	Jeff A. Jones	.10	.05
❑ 465	Mookie Wilson	.20	.09
❑ 466	Gene Garber	.10	.05
❑ 467	Mike Ramsey	.10	.05
❑ 468	Geoff Zahn	.10	.05
❑ 469	Tom O'Malley	.10	.05
❑ 470	Nolan Ryan	4.00	1.80
❑ 471	Dick Howser MG	.10	.05
❑ 472	Mike G. Brown	.10	.05
❑ 473	Jim Dwyer	.10	.05
❑ 474	Greg Bargar	.10	.05
❑ 475	Gary Redus	.10	.05
❑ 476	Tom Tellmann	.10	.05
❑ 477	Rafael Landestoy	.10	.05
❑ 478	Alan Bannister	.10	.05
❑ 479	Frank Tanana	.20	.09
❑ 480	Ron Kittle	.10	.05
❑ 481	Mark Thurmond	.10	.05
❑ 482	Enos Cabell	.10	.05
❑ 483	Fergie Jenkins	.60	.25
❑ 484	Ozzie Virgil	.10	.05
❑ 485	Rick Rhoden	.10	.05
❑ 486	N.Y. Yankees TL	.60	.25
	Don Baylor		
	Ron Guidry		
❑ 487	Ricky Adams	.10	.05
❑ 488	Jesse Barfield	.20	.09
❑ 489	Dave Von Ohlen	.10	.05
❑ 490	Cal Ripken	4.00	1.80
❑ 491	Bobby Castillo	.10	.05
❑ 492	Tucker Ashford	.10	.05
❑ 493	Mike Norris	.10	.05
❑ 494	Chili Davis	.40	.18
❑ 495	Rollie Fingers	.60	.25
❑ 496	Terry Francona	.10	.05
❑ 497	Bud Anderson	.10	.05
❑ 498	Rich Gedman	.10	.05
❑ 499	Mike Witt	.10	.05
❑ 500	George Brett	1.25	.55
❑ 501	Steve Henderson	.10	.05
❑ 502	Joe Torre MG	.20	.09
❑ 503	Elias Sosa	.10	.05
❑ 504	Mickey Rivers	.10	.05
❑ 505	Pete Vuckovich	.10	.05
❑ 506	Ernie Whitt	.10	.05
❑ 507	Mike LaCoss	.10	.05
❑ 508	Mel Hall	.20	.09
❑ 509	Brad Havens	.10	.05
❑ 510	Alan Trammell	.60	.25
❑ 511	Marty Bystrom	.10	.05
❑ 512	Oscar Gamble	.10	.05
❑ 513	Dave Beard	.10	.05
❑ 514	Floyd Rayford	.10	.05
❑ 515	Gorman Thomas	.10	.05
❑ 516	Montreal Expos TL	.20	.09
	Al Oliver		
	Charlie Lea		
❑ 517	John Moses	.10	.05
❑ 518	Greg Walker	.20	.09
❑ 519	Ron Davis	.10	.05
❑ 520	Bob Boone	.20	.09
❑ 521	Pete Falcone	.10	.05
❑ 522	Dave Bergman	.10	.05
❑ 523	Glenn Hoffman	.10	.05
❑ 524	Carlos Diaz	.10	.05
❑ 525	Willie Wilson	.10	.05
❑ 526	Ron Oester	.10	.05
❑ 527	Checklist 397-528	.20	.09
❑ 528	Mark Brouhard	.10	.05
❑ 529	Keith Atherton	.10	.05
❑ 530	Dan Ford	.10	.05
❑ 531	Steve Boros MG	.10	.05
❑ 532	Eric Show	.10	.05
❑ 533	Ken Landreaux	.10	.05
❑ 534	Pete O'Brien	.20	.09
❑ 535	Bo Diaz	.10	.05
❑ 536	Doug Bair	.10	.05
❑ 537	Johnny Ray	.10	.05
❑ 538	Kevin Bass	.10	.05
❑ 539	George Frazier	.10	.05
❑ 540	George Hendrick	.10	.05
❑ 541	Dennis Lamp	.10	.05
❑ 542	Duane Kuiper	.10	.05
❑ 543	Craig McMurtry	.10	.05
❑ 544	Cesar Geronimo	.10	.05
❑ 545	Bill Buckner	.20	.09
❑ 546	Indians TL	.20	.09
	Mike Hargrove		
	Lary Sorensen		
❑ 547	Mike Moore	.10	.05
❑ 548	Ron Jackson	.10	.05
❑ 549	Walt Terrell	.10	.05
❑ 550	Jim Rice	.20	.09
❑ 551	Scott Ullger	.10	.05
❑ 552	Ray Burris	.10	.05
❑ 553	Joe Nolan	.10	.05
❑ 554	Ted Power	.10	.05
❑ 555	Greg Brock	.10	.05
❑ 556	Joey McLaughlin	.10	.05
❑ 557	Wayne Tolleson	.10	.05
❑ 558	Mike Davis	.10	.05
❑ 559	Mike Scott	.20	.09
❑ 560	Carlton Fisk	.60	.25
❑ 561	Whitey Herzog MG	.20	.09
❑ 562	Manny Castillo	.10	.05
❑ 563	Glenn Wilson	.20	.09
❑ 564	Al Holland	.10	.05
❑ 565	Leon Durham	.10	.05
❑ 566	Jim Bibby	.10	.05
❑ 567	Mike Heath	.10	.05
❑ 568	Pete Filson	.10	.05
❑ 569	Bake McBride	.10	.05
❑ 570	Dan Quisenberry	.10	.05
❑ 571	Bruce Bochy	.10	.05
❑ 572	Jerry Royster	.10	.05
❑ 573	Dave Kingman	.40	.18
❑ 574	Brian Downing	.10	.05
❑ 575	Jim Clancy	.10	.05
❑ 576	Giants TL	.20	.09
	Jeff Leonard		
	Atlee Hammaker		
❑ 577	Mark Clear	.10	.05
❑ 578	Lenn Sakata	.10	.05
❑ 579	Bob James	.10	.05
❑ 580	Lonnie Smith	.10	.05
❑ 581	Jose DeLeon	.10	.05
❑ 582	Bob McClure	.10	.05
❑ 583	Derrel Thomas	.10	.05
❑ 584	Dave Schmidt	.10	.05
❑ 585	Dan Driessen	.10	.05
❑ 586	Joe Niekro	.20	.09
❑ 587	Von Hayes	.10	.05
❑ 588	Milt Wilcox	.10	.05
❑ 589	Mike Easler	.10	.05
❑ 590	Dave Stieb	.10	.05
❑ 591	Tony LaRussa MG	.20	.09
❑ 592	Andre Robertson	.10	.05
❑ 593	Jeff Lahti	.10	.05
❑ 594	Gene Richards	.10	.05
❑ 595	Jeff Reardon	.20	.09
❑ 596	Ryne Sandberg	2.00	.90
❑ 597	Rick Camp	.10	.05
❑ 598	Rusty Kuntz	.10	.05
❑ 599	Doug Sisk	.10	.05
❑ 600	Rod Carew	.60	.25
❑ 601	John Tudor	.10	.05
❑ 602	John Wathan	.10	.05
❑ 603	Renie Martin	.10	.05
❑ 604	John Lowenstein	.10	.05
❑ 605	Mike Caldwell	.10	.05
❑ 606	Blue Jays TL	.20	.09
	Lloyd Moseby		
	Dave Stieb		
❑ 607	Tom Hume	.10	.05
❑ 608	Bobby Johnson	.10	.05
❑ 609	Dan Meyer	.10	.05
❑ 610	Steve Sax	.20	.09
❑ 611	Chet Lemon	.20	.09
❑ 612	Harry Spilman	.10	.05
❑ 613	Greg Gross	.10	.05
❑ 614	Len Barker	.10	.05
❑ 615	Garry Templeton	.10	.05
❑ 616	Don Robinson	.10	.05
❑ 617	Rick Cerone	.10	.05
❑ 618	Dickie Noles	.10	.05
❑ 619	Jerry Dybzinski	.10	.05
❑ 620	Al Oliver	.20	.09
❑ 621	Frank Howard MG	.20	.09
❑ 622	Al Cowens	.10	.05
❑ 623	Ron Washington	.10	.05
❑ 624	Terry Harper	.10	.05
❑ 625	Larry Gura	.10	.05
❑ 626	Bob Clark	.10	.05
❑ 627	Dave LaPoint	.10	.05
❑ 628	Ed Jurak	.10	.05
❑ 629	Rick Langford	.10	.05
❑ 630	Ted Simmons	.20	.09

Card	NRMT	VG-E
❑ 631 Dennis Martinez	.20	.09
❑ 632 Tom Foley	.10	.05
❑ 633 Mike Krukow	.10	.05
❑ 634 Mike Marshall	.10	.05
❑ 635 Dave Righetti	.20	.09
❑ 636 Pat Putnam	.10	.05
❑ 637 Phillies TL	.20	.09
Gary Matthews		
John Denny		
❑ 638 George Vukovich	.10	.05
❑ 639 Rick Lysander	.10	.05
❑ 640 Lance Parrish	.40	.18
❑ 641 Mike Richardt	.10	.05
❑ 642 Tom Underwood	.10	.05
❑ 643 Mike C. Brown	.10	.05
❑ 644 Tim Lollar	.10	.05
❑ 645 Tony Pena	.10	.05
❑ 646 Checklist 529-660	.20	.09
❑ 647 Ron Roenicke	.10	.05
❑ 648 Len Whitehouse	.10	.05
❑ 649 Tom Herr	.20	.09
❑ 650 Phil Niekro	.60	.25
❑ 651 John McNamara MG	.10	.05
❑ 652 Rudy May	.10	.05
❑ 653 Dave Stapleton	.10	.05
❑ 654 Bob Bailor	.10	.05
❑ 655 Amos Otis	.20	.09
❑ 656 Bryn Smith	.10	.05
❑ 657 Thad Bosley	.10	.05
❑ 658 Jerry Augustine	.10	.05
❑ 659 Duane Walker	.10	.05
❑ 660 Ray Knight	.20	.09
❑ 661 Steve Yeager	.10	.05
❑ 662 Tom Brennan	.10	.05
❑ 663 Johnnie LeMaster	.10	.05
❑ 664 Dave Stegman	.10	.05
❑ 665 Buddy Bell	.20	.09
❑ 666 Detroit Tigers TL	.60	.25
Lou Whitaker		
Jack Morris		
❑ 667 Vance Law	.10	.05
❑ 668 Larry McWilliams	.10	.05
❑ 669 Dave Lopes	.20	.09
❑ 670 Rich Gossage	.40	.18
❑ 671 Jamie Quirk	.10	.05
❑ 672 Ricky Nelson	.10	.05
❑ 673 Mike Walters	.10	.05
❑ 674 Tim Flannery	.10	.05
❑ 675 Pascual Perez	.10	.05
❑ 676 Brian Giles	.10	.05
❑ 677 Doyle Alexander	.10	.05
❑ 678 Chris Speier	.10	.05
❑ 679 Art Howe	.20	.09
❑ 680 Fred Lynn	.20	.09
❑ 681 Tom Lasorda MG	.40	.18
❑ 682 Dan Morogiello	.10	.05
❑ 683 Marty Barrett	.20	.09
❑ 684 Bob Shirley	.10	.05
❑ 685 Willie Aikens	.10	.05
❑ 686 Joe Price	.10	.05
❑ 687 Roy Howell	.10	.05
❑ 688 George Wright	.10	.05
❑ 689 Mike Fischlin	.10	.05
❑ 690 Jack Clark	.20	.09
❑ 691 Steve Lake	.10	.05
❑ 692 Dickie Thon	.10	.05
❑ 693 Alan Wiggins	.10	.05
❑ 694 Mike Stanton	.10	.05
❑ 695 Lou Whitaker	.60	.25
❑ 696 Pirates TL	.20	.09
Bill Madlock		
Rick Rhoden		
❑ 697 Dale Murray	.10	.05
❑ 698 Marc Hill	.10	.05
❑ 699 Dave Rucker	.10	.05
❑ 700 Mike Schmidt	.75	.35
❑ 701 NL Active Batting	.60	.25
Bill Madlock		
Pete Rose		
Dave Parker		
❑ 702 NL Active Hits	.60	.25
Pete Rose		
Rusty Staub		
Tony Perez		
❑ 703 NL Active Home Run	.60	.25
Mike Schmidt		
Tony Perez		
Dave Kingman		
❑ 704 NL Active RBI	.60	.25
Tony Perez		
Rusty Staub		
Al Oliver		
❑ 705 NL Active Steals	.60	.25
Joe Morgan		
Cesar Cedeno		
Larry Bowa		
❑ 706 NL Active Victory	.60	.25
Steve Carlton		
Fergie Jenkins		
Tom Seaver		
❑ 707 NL Active Strikeout	1.50	.70
Steve Carlton		
Nolan Ryan		
Tom Seaver		
❑ 708 NL Active ERA	.60	.25
Tom Seaver		
Steve Carlton		
Steve Rogers		
❑ 709 NL Active Save	.20	.09
Bruce Sutter		
Tug McGraw		
Gene Garber		
❑ 710 AL Active Batting	.60	.25
Rod Carew		
George Brett		
Cecil Cooper		
❑ 711 AL Active Hits	.60	.25
Rod Carew		
Bert Campaneris		
Reggie Jackson		
❑ 712 AL Active Home Run	.60	.25
Reggie Jackson		
Graig Nettles		
Greg Luzinski		
❑ 713 AL Active RBI	.60	.25
Reggie Jackson		
Ted Simmons		
Graig Nettles		
❑ 714 AL Active Steals	.20	.09
Bert Campaneris		
Dave Lopes		
Omar Moreno		
❑ 715 AL Active Victory	.60	.25
Jim Palmer		
Don Sutton		
Tommy John		
❑ 716 AL Active Strikeout	.60	.25
Don Sutton		
Bert Blyleven		
Jerry Koosman		
❑ 717 AL Active ERA	.60	.25
Jim Palmer		
Rollie Fingers		
Ron Guidry		
❑ 718 AL Active Save	.60	.25
Rollie Fingers		
Rich Gossage		
Dan Quisenberry		
❑ 719 Andy Hassler	.10	.05
❑ 720 Dwight Evans	.20	.09
❑ 721 Del Crandall MG	.10	.05
❑ 722 Bob Welch	.10	.05
❑ 723 Rich Dauer	.10	.05
❑ 724 Eric Rasmussen	.10	.05
❑ 725 Cesar Cedeno	.20	.09
❑ 726 Brewers TL	.20	.09
Ted Simmons		
Moose Haas		
❑ 727 Joel Youngblood	.10	.05
❑ 728 Tug McGraw	.20	.09
❑ 729 Gene Tenace	.20	.09
❑ 730 Bruce Sutter	.20	.09
❑ 731 Lynn Jones	.10	.05
❑ 732 Terry Crowley	.10	.05
❑ 733 Dave Collins	.10	.05
❑ 734 Odell Jones	.10	.05
❑ 735 Rick Burleson	.10	.05
❑ 736 Dick Ruthven	.10	.05
❑ 737 Jim Essian	.10	.05
❑ 738 Bill Schroeder	.10	.05
❑ 739 Bob Watson	.20	.09
❑ 740 Tom Seaver	.75	.35
❑ 741 Wayne Gross	.10	.05
❑ 742 Dick Williams MG	.20	.09
❑ 743 Don Hood	.10	.05
❑ 744 Jamie Allen	.10	.05
❑ 745 Dennis Eckersley	.60	.25
❑ 746 Mickey Hatcher	.10	.05
❑ 747 Pat Zachry	.10	.05
❑ 748 Jeff Leonard	.10	.05
❑ 749 Doug Flynn	.10	.05
❑ 750 Jim Palmer	.60	.25
❑ 751 Charlie Moore	.10	.05
❑ 752 Phil Garner	.20	.09
❑ 753 Doug Gwosdz	.10	.05
❑ 754 Kent Tekulve	.20	.09
❑ 755 Garry Maddox	.10	.05
❑ 756 Reds TL	.20	.09
Ron Oester		
Mario Soto		
❑ 757 Larry Bowa	.20	.09
❑ 758 Bill Stein	.10	.05
❑ 759 Richard Dotson	.10	.05
❑ 760 Bob Horner	.10	.05
❑ 761 John Montefusco	.10	.05
❑ 762 Rance Mulliniks	.10	.05
❑ 763 Craig Swan	.10	.05
❑ 764 Mike Hargrove	.20	.09
❑ 765 Ken Forsch	.10	.05
❑ 766 Mike Vail	.10	.05
❑ 767 Carney Lansford	.20	.09
❑ 768 Champ Summers	.10	.05
❑ 769 Bill Caudill	.10	.05
❑ 770 Ken Griffey	.20	.09
❑ 771 Billy Gardner MG	.10	.05
❑ 772 Jim Slaton	.10	.05
❑ 773 Todd Cruz	.10	.05
❑ 774 Tom Gorman	.10	.05
❑ 775 Dave Parker	.20	.09
❑ 776 Craig Reynolds	.10	.05
❑ 777 Tom Paciorek	.20	.09
❑ 778 Andy Hawkins	.10	.05
❑ 779 Jim Sundberg	.20	.09
❑ 780 Steve Carlton	.60	.25
❑ 781 Checklist 661-792	.20	.09
❑ 782 Steve Balboni	.10	.05
❑ 783 Luis Leal	.10	.05
❑ 784 Leon Roberts	.10	.05
❑ 785 Joaquin Andujar	.10	.05
❑ 786 Red Sox TL	.60	.25
Wade Boggs		
Bob Ojeda		
❑ 787 Bill Campbell	.10	.05
❑ 788 Milt May	.10	.05
❑ 789 Bert Blyleven	.20	.09
❑ 790 Doug DeCinces	.10	.05
❑ 791 Terry Forster	.10	.05
❑ 792 Bill Russell	.20	.09

1984 Topps Tiffany

	NRMT	VG-E
COMP.FACT.SET (792)	200.00	90.00
COMMON CARD (1-792)	.40	.18

*STARS: 4X TO 8X BASIC CARDS
*ROOKIES: 4X TO 8X BASIC CARDS

1984 Topps Traded

	NRMT	VG-E
COMP.FACT.SET (132)	40.00	18.00
COMMON CARD (1T-132T)	.40	.18

Card	NRMT	VG-E
❑ 1T Willie Aikens	.40	.18
❑ 2T Luis Aponte	.40	.18
❑ 3T Mike Armstrong	.40	.18
❑ 4T Bob Bailor	.40	.18
❑ 5T Dusty Baker	1.00	.45
❑ 6T Steve Balboni	.40	.18
❑ 7T Alan Bannister	.40	.18
❑ 8T Dave Beard	.40	.18
❑ 9T Joe Beckwith	.40	.18
❑ 10T Bruce Berenyi	.40	.18
❑ 11T Dave Bergman	.40	.18
❑ 12T Tony Bernazard	.40	.18
❑ 13T Yogi Berra MG	2.00	.90
❑ 14T Barry Bonnell	.40	.18
❑ 15T Phil Bradley	1.00	.45
❑ 16T Fred Breining	.40	.18
❑ 17T Bill Buckner	1.00	.45
❑ 18T Ray Burris	.40	.18
❑ 19T John Butcher	.40	.18
❑ 20T Brett Butler	1.25	.55
❑ 21T Enos Cabell	.40	.18
❑ 22T Bill Campbell	.40	.18
❑ 23T Bill Caudill	.40	.18
❑ 24T Bob Clark	.40	.18
❑ 25T Bryan Clark	.40	.18
❑ 26T Jaime Cocanower	.40	.18
❑ 27T Ron Darling	1.25	.55
❑ 28T Alvin Davis	1.00	.45
❑ 29T Ken Dayley	.40	.18
❑ 30T Jeff Dedmon	.40	.18
❑ 31T Bob Dernier	.40	.18
❑ 32T Carlos Diaz	.40	.18
❑ 33T Mike Easler	.40	.18
❑ 34T Dennis Eckersley	1.50	.70
❑ 35T Jim Essian	.40	.18
❑ 36T Darrell Evans	1.00	.45
❑ 37T Mike Fitzgerald	.40	.18
❑ 38T Tim Foli	.40	.18
❑ 39T George Frazier	.40	.18
❑ 40T Rich Gale	.40	.18
❑ 41T Barbaro Garbey	.40	.18
❑ 42T Dwight Gooden	5.00	2.20
❑ 43T Rich Gossage	1.25	.55
❑ 44T Wayne Gross	.40	.18
❑ 45T Mark Gubicza	1.00	.45
❑ 46T Jackie Gutierrez	.40	.18
❑ 47T Mel Hall	1.00	.45
❑ 48T Toby Harrah	1.00	.45
❑ 49T Ron Hassey	.40	.18
❑ 50T Rich Hebner	.40	.18
❑ 51T Willie Hernandez	1.00	.45
❑ 52T Ricky Horton	.40	.18
❑ 53T Art Howe	1.00	.45
❑ 54T Dane Iorg	.40	.18
❑ 55T Brook Jacoby	1.00	.45
❑ 56T Mike Jeffcoat	.40	.18
❑ 57T Dave Johnson MG	1.00	.45
❑ 58T Lynn Jones	.40	.18
❑ 59T Ruppert Jones	.40	.18
❑ 60T Mike Jorgensen	.40	.18
❑ 61T Bob Kearney	.40	.18
❑ 62T Jimmy Key	4.00	1.80
❑ 63T Dave Kingman	1.25	.55
❑ 64T Jerry Koosman	1.00	.45
❑ 65T Wayne Krenchicki	.40	.18
❑ 66T Rusty Kuntz	.40	.18
❑ 67T Rene Lachemann MG	.40	.18
❑ 68T Frank LaCorte	.40	.18
❑ 69T Dennis Lamp	.40	.18
❑ 70T Mark Langston	2.00	.90
❑ 71T Rick Leach	.40	.18
❑ 72T Craig Lefferts	1.00	.45
❑ 73T Gary Lucas	.40	.18
❑ 74T Jerry Martin	.40	.18
❑ 75T Carmelo Martinez	.40	.18
❑ 76T Mike Mason	.40	.18
❑ 77T Gary Matthews	1.00	.45
❑ 78T Andy McGaffigan	.40	.18
❑ 79T Larry Milbourne	.40	.18
❑ 80T Sid Monge	.40	.18
❑ 81T Jackie Moore MG	.40	.18
❑ 82T Joe Morgan	2.50	1.10
❑ 83T Graig Nettles	1.00	.45
❑ 84T Phil Niekro	1.50	.70
❑ 85T Ken Oberkfell	.40	.18
❑ 86T Mike O'Berry	.40	.18
❑ 87T Al Oliver	1.00	.45
❑ 88T Jorge Orta	.40	.18
❑ 89T Amos Otis	1.00	.45
❑ 90T Dave Parker	1.00	.45
❑ 91T Tony Perez	1.50	.70
❑ 92T Gerald Perry	1.00	.45
❑ 93T Gary Pettis	.40	.18
❑ 94T Rob Picciolo	.40	.18
❑ 95T Vern Rapp MG	.40	.18
❑ 96T Floyd Rayford	.40	.18
❑ 97T Randy Ready	1.00	.45
❑ 98T Ron Reed	.40	.18
❑ 99T Gene Richards	.40	.18
❑ 100T Jose Rijo	1.50	.70
❑ 101T Jeff D. Robinson	.40	.18
❑ 102T Ron Romanick	.40	.18
❑ 103T Pete Rose	4.00	1.80
❑ 104T Bret Saberhagen	3.00	1.35
❑ 105T Juan Samuel	1.25	.55
❑ 106T Scott Sanderson	.40	.18
❑ 107T Dick Schofield	1.00	.45
❑ 108T Tom Seaver	4.00	1.80
❑ 109T Jim Slaton	.40	.18
❑ 110T Mike Smithson	.40	.18
❑ 111T Lary Sorensen	.40	.18
❑ 112T Tim Stoddard	.40	.18
❑ 113T Champ Summers	.40	.18
❑ 114T Jim Sundberg	1.00	.45
❑ 115T Rick Sutcliffe	1.25	.55
❑ 116T Craig Swan	.40	.18
❑ 117T Tim Teufel	.40	.18
❑ 118T Derrel Thomas	.40	.18
❑ 119T Gorman Thomas	.40	.18
❑ 120T Alex Trevino	.40	.18
❑ 121T Manny Trillo	.40	.18
❑ 122T John Tudor	.40	.18
❑ 123T Tom Underwood	.40	.18
❑ 124T Mike Vail	.40	.18
❑ 125T Tom Waddell	.40	.18
❑ 126T Gary Ward	.40	.18
❑ 127T Curtis Wilkerson	.40	.18
❑ 128T Frank Williams	.40	.18
❑ 129T Glenn Wilson	.40	.18
❑ 130T John Wockenfuss	.40	.18
❑ 131T Ned Yost	.40	.18
❑ 132T Checklist 1T-132T	.40	.18

1984 Topps Traded Tiffany

	NRMT	VG-E
COMP.FACT.SET (132)	50.00	22.00
COMMON CARD (1T-132T)	.40	.18

*STARS: .75X TO 1.5X BASIC CARDS
*ROOKIES: 1.25X TO 2.5X BASIC CARDS

1985 Topps

	NRMT	VG-E
COMPLETE SET (792)	250.00	110.00
COMP.FACT.SET (792)	300.00	135.00
COMMON CARD (1-792)	.10	.05

Card	NRMT	VG-E
❑ 1 Carlton Fisk RB Longest game by catcher	.20	.09
❑ 2 Steve Garvey RB Consecutive error- less games, 1B	.20	.09
❑ 3 Dwight Gooden RB Most rookie strikeouts	.60	.25
❑ 4 Cliff Johnson RB Most pinch-hit homers	.10	.05
❑ 5 Joe Morgan RB Most homers 2B, lifetime	.20	.09
❑ 6 Pete Rose RB Most career singles	.40	.18
❑ 7 Nolan Ryan RB Most career strikeouts	1.50	.70
❑ 8 Juan Samuel RB Most SB's, rookie season	.10	.05
❑ 9 Bruce Sutter RB Most NL season saves	.10	.05
❑ 10 Don Sutton RB Most seasons 100 or more K's	.20	.09
❑ 11 Ralph Houk MG	.10	.05
❑ 12 Dave Lopes (Now with Cubs on card front)	.20	.09
❑ 13 Tim Lollar	.10	.05
❑ 14 Chris Bando	.10	.05
❑ 15 Jerry Koosman	.10	.05
❑ 16 Bobby Meacham	.10	.05
❑ 17 Mike Scott	.10	.05
❑ 18 Mickey Hatcher	.10	.05
❑ 19 George Frazier	.10	.05
❑ 20 Chet Lemon	.10	.05
❑ 21 Lee Tunnell	.10	.05
❑ 22 Duane Kuiper	.10	.05
❑ 23 Bret Saberhagen	.60	.25
❑ 24 Jesse Barfield	.10	.05
❑ 25 Steve Bedrosian	.10	.05
❑ 26 Roy Smalley	.10	.05
❑ 27 Bruce Berenyi	.10	.05
❑ 28 Dann Bilardello	.10	.05
❑ 29 Odell Jones	.10	.05
❑ 30 Cal Ripken	3.00	1.35
❑ 31 Terry Whitfield	.10	.05
❑ 32 Chuck Porter	.10	.05
❑ 33 Tito Landrum	.10	.05
❑ 34 Ed Nunez	.10	.05
❑ 35 Graig Nettles	.20	.09
❑ 36 Fred Breining	.10	.05
❑ 37 Reid Nichols	.10	.05
❑ 38 Jackie Moore MG	.10	.05
❑ 39 John Wockenfuss	.10	.05
❑ 40 Phil Niekro	.60	.25
❑ 41 Mike Fischlin	.10	.05
❑ 42 Luis Sanchez	.10	.05
❑ 43 Andre David	.10	.05
❑ 44 Dickie Thon	.10	.05
❑ 45 Greg Minton	.10	.05
❑ 46 Gary Woods	.10	.05
❑ 47 Dave Rozema	.10	.05
❑ 48 Tony Fernandez	.20	.09
❑ 49 Butch Davis	.10	.05
❑ 50 John Candelaria	.10	.05
❑ 51 Bob Watson	.20	.09
❑ 52 Jerry Dybzinski	.10	.05
❑ 53 Tom Gorman	.10	.05
❑ 54 Cesar Cedeno	.20	.09
❑ 55 Frank Tanana	.10	.05
❑ 56 Jim Dwyer	.10	.05
❑ 57 Pat Zachry	.10	.05
❑ 58 Orlando Mercado	.10	.05
❑ 59 Rick Waits	.10	.05
❑ 60 George Hendrick	.10	.05
❑ 61 Curt Kaufman	.10	.05
❑ 62 Mike Ramsey	.10	.05
❑ 63 Steve McCatty	.10	.05
❑ 64 Mark Bailey	.10	.05
❑ 65 Bill Buckner	.20	.09
❑ 66 Dick Williams MG	.20	.09
❑ 67 Rafael Santana	.10	.05
❑ 68 Von Hayes	.10	.05
❑ 69 Jim Winn	.10	.05
❑ 70 Don Baylor	.20	.09
❑ 71 Tim Laudner	.10	.05

❑ 72 Rick Sutcliffe .10 .05
❑ 73 Rusty Kuntz .10 .05
❑ 74 Mike Krukow .10 .05
❑ 75 Willie Upshaw .10 .05
❑ 76 Alan Bannister .10 .05
❑ 77 Joe Beckwith .10 .05
❑ 78 Scott Fletcher .10 .05
❑ 79 Rick Mahler .10 .05
❑ 80 Keith Hernandez .20 .09
❑ 81 Lenn Sakata .10 .05
❑ 82 Joe Price .10 .05
❑ 83 Charlie Moore .10 .05
❑ 84 Spike Owen .10 .05
❑ 85 Mike Marshall .10 .05
❑ 86 Don Aase .10 .05
❑ 87 David Green .10 .05
❑ 88 Bryn Smith .10 .05
❑ 89 Jackie Gutierrez .10 .05
❑ 90 Rich Gossage .20 .09
❑ 91 Jeff Burroughs .10 .05
❑ 92 Paul Owens MG .10 .05
❑ 93 Don Schulze .10 .05
❑ 94 Toby Harrah .10 .05
❑ 95 Jose Cruz .20 .09
❑ 96 Johnny Ray .10 .05
❑ 97 Pete Filson .10 .05
❑ 98 Steve Lake .10 .05
❑ 99 Milt Wilcox .10 .05
❑ 100 George Brett 1.25 .55
❑ 101 Jim Acker .10 .05
❑ 102 Tommy Dunbar .10 .05
❑ 103 Randy Lerch .10 .05
❑ 104 Mike Fitzgerald .10 .05
❑ 105 Ron Kittle .10 .05
❑ 106 Pascual Perez .10 .05
❑ 107 Tom Foley .10 .05
❑ 108 Darnell Coles .10 .05
❑ 109 Gary Roenicke .10 .05
❑ 110 Alejandro Pena .10 .05
❑ 111 Doug DeCinces .10 .05
❑ 112 Tom Tellmann .10 .05
❑ 113 Tom Herr .10 .05
❑ 114 Bob James .10 .05
❑ 115 Rickey Henderson .60 .25
❑ 116 Dennis Boyd .10 .05
❑ 117 Greg Gross .10 .05
❑ 118 Eric Show .10 .05
❑ 119 Pat Corrales MG .10 .05
❑ 120 Steve Kemp .10 .05
❑ 121 Checklist: 1-132 .10 .05
❑ 122 Tom Brunansky .20 .09
❑ 123 Dave Smith .10 .05
❑ 124 Rich Hebner .10 .05
❑ 125 Kent Tekulve .10 .05
❑ 126 Ruppert Jones .10 .05
❑ 127 Mark Gubicza .20 .09
❑ 128 Ernie Whitt .10 .05
❑ 129 Gene Garber .10 .05
❑ 130 Al Oliver .20 .09
❑ 131 Buddy Bell FS .20 .09
Gus Bell
❑ 132 Dale Berra FS .20 .09
Yogi Berra
❑ 133 Bob Boone FS .10 .05
Ray Boone
❑ 134 Terry Francona FS .10 .05
Tito Francona
❑ 135 Terry Kennedy FS .10 .05
Bob Kennedy
❑ 136 Jeff Kunkel FS .10 .05
Bill Kunkel
❑ 137 Vance Law FS .20 .09
Vern Law
❑ 138 Dick Schofield FS .10 .05
Dick Schofield
❑ 139 Joel Skinner FS .10 .05
Bob Skinner
❑ 140 Roy Smalley Jr. FS .10 .05
Roy Smalley
❑ 141 Mike Stenhouse FS .10 .05
Dave Stenhouse
❑ 142 Steve Trout FS .10 .05
Dizzy Trout
❑ 143 Ozzie Virgil FS .10 .05
Ossie Virgil
❑ 144 Ron Gardenhire .10 .05
❑ 145 Alvin Davis .20 .09
❑ 146 Gary Redus .10 .05
❑ 147 Bill Swaggerty .10 .05
❑ 148 Steve Yeager .10 .05
❑ 149 Dickie Noles .10 .05
❑ 150 Jim Rice .20 .09
❑ 151 Moose Haas .10 .05
❑ 152 Steve Braun .10 .05
❑ 153 Frank LaCorte .10 .05
❑ 154 Argenis Salazar .10 .05
❑ 155 Yogi Berra MG .40 .18
❑ 156 Craig Reynolds .10 .05
❑ 157 Tug McGraw .20 .09
❑ 158 Pat Tabler .10 .05
❑ 159 Carlos Diaz .10 .05
❑ 160 Lance Parrish .20 .09
❑ 161 Ken Schrom .10 .05
❑ 162 Benny Distefano .10 .05
❑ 163 Dennis Eckersley .60 .25
❑ 164 Jorge Orta .10 .05
❑ 165 Dusty Baker .20 .09
❑ 166 Keith Atherton .10 .05
❑ 167 Rufino Linares .10 .05
❑ 168 Garth Iorg .10 .05
❑ 169 Dan Spillner .10 .05
❑ 170 George Foster .20 .09
❑ 171 Bill Stein .10 .05
❑ 172 Jack Perconte .10 .05
❑ 173 Mike Young .10 .05
❑ 174 Rick Honeycutt .10 .05
❑ 175 Dave Parker .20 .09
❑ 176 Bill Schroeder .10 .05
❑ 177 Dave Von Ohlen .10 .05
❑ 178 Miguel Dilone .10 .05
❑ 179 Tommy John .40 .18
❑ 180 Dave Winfield .60 .25
❑ 181 Roger Clemens 25.00 11.00
❑ 182 Tim Flannery .10 .05
❑ 183 Larry McWilliams .10 .05
❑ 184 Carmen Castillo .10 .05
❑ 185 Al Holland .10 .05
❑ 186 Bob Lillis MG .10 .05
❑ 187 Mike Walters .10 .05
❑ 188 Greg Pryor .10 .05
❑ 189 Warren Brusstar .10 .05
❑ 190 Rusty Staub .20 .09
❑ 191 Steve Nicosia .10 .05
❑ 192 Howard Johnson .20 .09
❑ 193 Jimmy Key .75 .35
❑ 194 Dave Stegman .10 .05
❑ 195 Glenn Hubbard .10 .05
❑ 196 Pete O'Brien .10 .05
❑ 197 Mike Warren .10 .05
❑ 198 Eddie Milner .10 .05
❑ 199 Dennis Martinez .20 .09
❑ 200 Reggie Jackson .75 .35
❑ 201 Burt Hooton .10 .05
❑ 202 Gorman Thomas .10 .05
❑ 203 Bob McClure .10 .05
❑ 204 Art Howe .10 .05
❑ 205 Steve Rogers .10 .05
❑ 206 Phil Garner .20 .09
❑ 207 Mark Clear .10 .05
❑ 208 Champ Summers .10 .05
❑ 209 Bill Campbell .10 .05
❑ 210 Gary Matthews .10 .05
❑ 211 Clay Christiansen .10 .05
❑ 212 George Vukovich .10 .05
❑ 213 Billy Gardner MG .20 .09
❑ 214 John Tudor .10 .05
❑ 215 Bob Brenly .10 .05
❑ 216 Jerry Don Gleaton .10 .05
❑ 217 Leon Roberts .10 .05
❑ 218 Doyle Alexander .10 .05
❑ 219 Gerald Perry .10 .05
❑ 220 Fred Lynn .20 .09
❑ 221 Ron Reed .10 .05
❑ 222 Hubie Brooks .10 .05
❑ 223 Tom Hume .10 .05
❑ 224 Al Cowens .10 .05
❑ 225 Mike Boddicker .10 .05
❑ 226 Juan Beniquez .10 .05
❑ 227 Danny Darwin .20 .09
❑ 228 Dion James .10 .05
❑ 229 Dave LaPoint .10 .05
❑ 230 Gary Carter .60 .25
❑ 231 Dwayne Murphy .10 .05
❑ 232 Dave Beard .10 .05
❑ 233 Ed Jurak .10 .05
❑ 234 Jerry Narron .10 .05
❑ 235 Garry Maddox .10 .05
❑ 236 Mark Thurmond .10 .05
❑ 237 Julio Franco .40 .18
❑ 238 Jose Rijo .40 .18
❑ 239 Tim Teufel .10 .05
❑ 240 Dave Stieb .20 .09
❑ 241 Jim Frey MG .10 .05
❑ 242 Greg Harris .10 .05
❑ 243 Barbaro Garbey .10 .05
❑ 244 Mike Jones .10 .05
❑ 245 Chili Davis .20 .09
❑ 246 Mike Norris .10 .05
❑ 247 Wayne Tolleson .10 .05
❑ 248 Terry Forster .10 .05
❑ 249 Harold Baines .20 .09
❑ 250 Jesse Orosco .10 .05
❑ 251 Brad Gulden .10 .05
❑ 252 Dan Ford .10 .05
❑ 253 Sid Bream .20 .09
❑ 254 Pete Vuckovich .10 .05
❑ 255 Lonnie Smith .10 .05
❑ 256 Mike Stanton .10 .05
❑ 257 Bryan Little UER .10 .05
Name spelled Brian on front
❑ 258 Mike C. Brown .10 .05
❑ 259 Gary Allenson .10 .05
❑ 260 Dave Righetti .20 .09
❑ 261 Checklist: 133-264 .10 .05
❑ 262 Greg Booker .10 .05
❑ 263 Mel Hall .10 .05
❑ 264 Joe Sambito .10 .05
❑ 265 Juan Samuel .10 .05
❑ 266 Frank Viola .20 .09
❑ 267 Henry Cotto .10 .05
❑ 268 Chuck Tanner MG .20 .09
❑ 269 Doug Baker .10 .05
❑ 270 Dan Quisenberry .20 .09
❑ 271 Tim Foli FDP68 .10 .05
❑ 272 Jeff Burroughs FDP69 .10 .05
❑ 273 Bill Almon FDP74 .10 .05
❑ 274 Floyd Bannister FDP76 .10 .05
❑ 275 Harold Baines FDP77 .10 .05
❑ 276 Bob Horner FDP78 .10 .05
❑ 277 Al Chambers FDP79 .10 .05
❑ 278 Darryl Strawberry .20 .09
FDP80
❑ 279 Mike Moore FDP81 .10 .05
❑ 280 Shawon Dunston FDP82 .60 .25
❑ 281 Tim Belcher FDP83 .60 .25
❑ 282 Shawn Abner FDP84 .10 .05
❑ 283 Fran Mullins .10 .05
❑ 284 Marty Bystrom .10 .05
❑ 285 Dan Driessen .10 .05
❑ 286 Rudy Law .10 .05
❑ 287 Walt Terrell .10 .05
❑ 288 Jeff Kunkel .10 .05
❑ 289 Tom Underwood .10 .05
❑ 290 Cecil Cooper .20 .09
❑ 291 Bob Welch .10 .05
❑ 292 Brad Komminsk .10 .05
❑ 293 Curt Young .10 .05
❑ 294 Tom Nieto .10 .05
❑ 295 Joe Niekro .10 .05
❑ 296 Ricky Nelson .10 .05
❑ 297 Gary Lucas .10 .05
❑ 298 Marty Barrett .10 .05
❑ 299 Andy Hawkins .10 .05
❑ 300 Rod Carew .60 .25
❑ 301 John Montefusco .10 .05
❑ 302 Tim Corcoran .10 .05
❑ 303 Mike Jeffcoat .10 .05
❑ 304 Gary Gaetti .20 .09
❑ 305 Dale Berra .10 .05
❑ 306 Rick Reuschel .10 .05
❑ 307 Sparky Anderson MG .20 .09
❑ 308 John Wathan .10 .05
❑ 309 Mike Witt .10 .05
❑ 310 Manny Trillo .10 .05
❑ 311 Jim Gott .10 .05

❑ 312 Marc Hill .10 .05
❑ 313 Dave Schmidt .10 .05
❑ 314 Ron Oester .10 .05
❑ 315 Doug Sisk .10 .05
❑ 316 John Lowenstein .10 .05
❑ 317 Jack Lazorko .10 .05
❑ 318 Ted Simmons .20 .09
❑ 319 Jeff Jones .10 .05
❑ 320 Dale Murphy .60 .25
❑ 321 Ricky Horton .10 .05
❑ 322 Dave Stapleton .10 .05
❑ 323 Andy McGaffigan .10 .05
❑ 324 Bruce Bochy .10 .05
❑ 325 John Denny .10 .05
❑ 326 Kevin Bass .10 .05
❑ 327 Brook Jacoby .10 .05
❑ 328 Bob Shirley .10 .05
❑ 329 Ron Washington .10 .05
❑ 330 Leon Durham .10 .05
❑ 331 Bill Laskey .10 .05
❑ 332 Brian Harper .10 .05
❑ 333 Willie Hernandez .10 .05
❑ 334 Dick Howser MG .20 .09
❑ 335 Bruce Benedict .10 .05
❑ 336 Rance Mulliniks .10 .05
❑ 337 Billy Sample .10 .05
❑ 338 Britt Burns .10 .05
❑ 339 Danny Heep .10 .05
❑ 340 Robin Yount .60 .25
❑ 341 Floyd Rayford .10 .05
❑ 342 Ted Power .10 .05
❑ 343 Bill Russell .20 .09
❑ 344 Dave Henderson .10 .05
❑ 345 Charlie Lea .10 .05
❑ 346 Terry Pendleton .60 .25
❑ 347 Rick Langford .10 .05
❑ 348 Bob Boone .20 .09
❑ 349 Domingo Ramos .10 .05
❑ 350 Wade Boggs .75 .35
❑ 351 Juan Agosto .10 .05
❑ 352 Joe Morgan .60 .25
❑ 353 Julio Solano .10 .05
❑ 354 Andre Robertson .10 .05
❑ 355 Bert Blyleven .20 .09
❑ 356 Dave Meier .10 .05
❑ 357 Rich Bordi .10 .05
❑ 358 Tony Pena .10 .05
❑ 359 Pat Sheridan .10 .05
❑ 360 Steve Carlton .60 .25
❑ 361 Alfredo Griffin .10 .05
❑ 362 Craig McMurtry .10 .05
❑ 363 Ron Hodges .10 .05
❑ 364 Richard Dotson .10 .05
❑ 365 Danny Ozark MG .10 .05
❑ 366 Todd Cruz .10 .05
❑ 367 Keefe Cato .10 .05
❑ 368 Dave Bergman .10 .05
❑ 369 R.J. Reynolds .10 .05
❑ 370 Bruce Sutter .20 .09
❑ 371 Mickey Rivers .10 .05
❑ 372 Roy Howell .10 .05
❑ 373 Mike Moore .10 .05
❑ 374 Brian Downing .10 .05
❑ 375 Jeff Reardon .20 .09
❑ 376 Jeff Newman .10 .05
❑ 377 Checklist: 265-396 .10 .05
❑ 378 Alan Wiggins .10 .05
❑ 379 Charles Hudson .10 .05
❑ 380 Ken Griffey .20 .09
❑ 381 Roy Smith .10 .05
❑ 382 Denny Walling .10 .05
❑ 383 Rick Lysander .10 .05
❑ 384 Jody Davis .10 .05
❑ 385 Jose DeLeon .10 .05
❑ 386 Dan Gladden .20 .09
❑ 387 Buddy Biancalana .10 .05
❑ 388 Bert Roberge .10 .05
❑ 389 Rod Dedeaux OLY CO .20 .09
❑ 390 Sid Akins OLY .10 .05
❑ 391 Flavio Alfaro OLY .10 .05
❑ 392 Don August OLY .10 .05
❑ 393 Scott Bankhead OLY .10 .05
❑ 394 Bob Caffrey OLY .10 .05
❑ 395 Mike Dunne OLY .20 .09
❑ 396 Gary Green OLY .10 .05
❑ 397 John Hoover OLY .10 .05
❑ 398 Shane Mack OLY .60 .25
❑ 399 John Marzano OLY .20 .09
❑ 400 Oddibe McDowell OLY .20 .09
❑ 401 Mark McGwire OLY 200.00 90.00
❑ 402 Pat Pacillo OLY .20 .09
❑ 403 Cory Snyder OLY .40 .18
❑ 404 Billy Swift OLY .40 .18
❑ 405 Tom Veryzer .10 .05
❑ 406 Len Whitehouse .10 .05
❑ 407 Bobby Ramos .10 .05
❑ 408 Sid Monge .10 .05
❑ 409 Brad Wellman .10 .05
❑ 410 Bob Horner .10 .05
❑ 411 Bobby Cox MG .10 .05
❑ 412 Bud Black .10 .05
❑ 413 Vance Law .10 .05
❑ 414 Gary Ward .10 .05
❑ 415 Ron Darling UER .20 .09
(No trivia answer)
❑ 416 Wayne Gross .10 .05
❑ 417 John Franco .60 .25
❑ 418 Ken Landreaux .10 .05
❑ 419 Mike Caldwell .10 .05
❑ 420 Andre Dawson .60 .25
❑ 421 Dave Rucker .10 .05
❑ 422 Carney Lansford .20 .09
❑ 423 Barry Bonnell .10 .05
❑ 424 Al Nipper .10 .05
❑ 425 Mike Hargrove .20 .09
❑ 426 Vern Ruhle .10 .05
❑ 427 Mario Ramirez .10 .05
❑ 428 Larry Andersen .10 .05
❑ 429 Rick Cerone .10 .05
❑ 430 Ron Davis .10 .05
❑ 431 U.L. Washington .10 .05
❑ 432 Thad Bosley .10 .05
❑ 433 Jim Morrison .10 .05
❑ 434 Gene Richards .10 .05
❑ 435 Dan Petry .10 .05
❑ 436 Willie Aikens .10 .05
❑ 437 Al Jones .10 .05
❑ 438 Joe Torre MG .40 .18
❑ 439 Junior Ortiz .10 .05
❑ 440 Fernando Valenzuela .20 .09
❑ 441 Duane Walker .10 .05
❑ 442 Ken Forsch .10 .05
❑ 443 George Wright .10 .05
❑ 444 Tony Phillips .10 .05
❑ 445 Tippy Martinez .10 .05
❑ 446 Jim Sundberg .10 .05
❑ 447 Jeff Lahti .10 .05
❑ 448 Derrel Thomas .10 .05
❑ 449 Phil Bradley .20 .09
❑ 450 Steve Garvey .40 .18
❑ 451 Bruce Hurst .10 .05
❑ 452 John Castino .10 .05
❑ 453 Tom Waddell .10 .05
❑ 454 Glenn Wilson .10 .05
❑ 455 Bob Knepper .10 .05
❑ 456 Tim Foli .10 .05
❑ 457 Cecilio Guante .10 .05
❑ 458 Randy Johnson .10 .05
❑ 459 Charlie Leibrandt .10 .05
❑ 460 Ryne Sandberg 1.25 .55
❑ 461 Marty Castillo .10 .05
❑ 462 Gary Lavelle .10 .05
❑ 463 Dave Collins .10 .05
❑ 464 Mike Mason .10 .05
❑ 465 Bobby Grich .20 .09
❑ 466 Tony LaRussa MG .40 .18
❑ 467 Ed Lynch .10 .05
❑ 468 Wayne Krenchicki .10 .05
❑ 469 Sammy Stewart .10 .05
❑ 470 Steve Sax .10 .05
❑ 471 Pete Ladd .10 .05
❑ 472 Jim Essian .10 .05
❑ 473 Tim Wallach .20 .09
❑ 474 Kurt Kepshire .10 .05
❑ 475 Andre Thornton .10 .05
❑ 476 Jeff Stone .10 .05
❑ 477 Bob Ojeda .10 .05
❑ 478 Kurt Bevacqua .10 .05
❑ 479 Mike Madden .10 .05
❑ 480 Lou Whitaker .40 .18
❑ 481 Dale Murray .10 .05
❑ 482 Harry Spilman .10 .05
❑ 483 Mike Smithson .10 .05
❑ 484 Larry Bowa .20 .09
❑ 485 Matt Young .10 .05
❑ 486 Steve Balboni .10 .05
❑ 487 Frank Williams .10 .05
❑ 488 Joel Skinner .10 .05
❑ 489 Bryan Clark .10 .05
❑ 490 Jason Thompson .10 .05
❑ 491 Rick Camp .10 .05
❑ 492 Dave Johnson MG .20 .09
❑ 493 Orel Hershiser .75 .35
❑ 494 Rich Dauer .10 .05
❑ 495 Mario Soto .10 .05
❑ 496 Donnie Scott .10 .05
❑ 497 Gary Pettis UER .10 .05
(Photo actually Gary's little brother Lynn)
❑ 498 Ed Romero .10 .05
❑ 499 Danny Cox .10 .05
❑ 500 Mike Schmidt .75 .35
❑ 501 Dan Schatzeder .10 .05
❑ 502 Rick Miller .10 .05
❑ 503 Tim Conroy .10 .05
❑ 504 Jerry Willard .10 .05
❑ 505 Jim Beattie .10 .05
❑ 506 Franklin Stubbs .10 .05
❑ 507 Ray Fontenot .10 .05
❑ 508 John Shelby .10 .05
❑ 509 Milt May .10 .05
❑ 510 Kent Hrbek .20 .09
❑ 511 Lee Smith .40 .18
❑ 512 Tom Brookens .10 .05
❑ 513 Lynn Jones .10 .05
❑ 514 Jeff Cornell .10 .05
❑ 515 Dave Concepcion .20 .09
❑ 516 Roy Lee Jackson .10 .05
❑ 517 Jerry Martin .10 .05
❑ 518 Chris Chambliss .10 .05
❑ 519 Doug Rader MG .10 .05
❑ 520 LaMarr Hoyt .10 .05
❑ 521 Rick Dempsey .10 .05
❑ 522 Paul Molitor .60 .25
❑ 523 Candy Maldonado .10 .05
❑ 524 Rob Wilfong .10 .05
❑ 525 Darrell Porter .10 .05
❑ 526 David Palmer .10 .05
❑ 527 Checklist: 397-528 .10 .05
❑ 528 Bill Krueger .10 .05
❑ 529 Rich Gedman .10 .05
❑ 530 Dave Dravecky .20 .09
❑ 531 Joe Lefebvre .10 .05
❑ 532 Frank DiPino .10 .05
❑ 533 Tony Bernazard .10 .05
❑ 534 Brian Dayett .10 .05
❑ 535 Pat Putnam .10 .05
❑ 536 Kirby Puckett 8.00 3.60
❑ 537 Don Robinson .10 .05
❑ 538 Keith Moreland .10 .05
❑ 539 Aurelio Lopez .10 .05
❑ 540 Claudell Washington .10 .05
❑ 541 Mark Davis .10 .05
❑ 542 Don Slaught .10 .05
❑ 543 Mike Squires .10 .05
❑ 544 Bruce Kison .10 .05
❑ 545 Lloyd Moseby .10 .05
❑ 546 Brent Gaff .10 .05
❑ 547 Pete Rose MG .40 .18
❑ 548 Larry Parrish .10 .05
❑ 549 Mike Scioscia .10 .05
❑ 550 Scott McGregor .10 .05
❑ 551 Andy Van Slyke .40 .18
❑ 552 Chris Codiroli .10 .05
❑ 553 Bob Clark .10 .05
❑ 554 Doug Flynn .10 .05
❑ 555 Bob Stanley .10 .05
❑ 556 Sixto Lezcano .10 .05
❑ 557 Len Barker .10 .05
❑ 558 Carmelo Martinez .10 .05
❑ 559 Jay Howell .10 .05
❑ 560 Bill Madlock .20 .09
❑ 561 Darryl Motley .10 .05
❑ 562 Houston Jimenez .10 .05

❑ 563 Dick Ruthven .10 .05
❑ 564 Alan Ashby .10 .05
❑ 565 Kirk Gibson .20 .09
❑ 566 Ed VandeBerg .10 .05
❑ 567 Joel Youngblood .10 .05
❑ 568 Cliff Johnson .10 .05
❑ 569 Ken Oberkfell .10 .05
❑ 570 Darryl Strawberry .60 .25
❑ 571 Charlie Hough .20 .09
❑ 572 Tom Paciorek .20 .09
❑ 573 Jay Tibbs .10 .05
❑ 574 Joe Altobelli MG .10 .05
❑ 575 Pedro Guerrero .20 .09
❑ 576 Jaime Cocanower .10 .05
❑ 577 Chris Speier .10 .05
❑ 578 Terry Francona .10 .05
❑ 579 Ron Romanick .10 .05
❑ 580 Dwight Evans .20 .09
❑ 581 Mark Wagner .10 .05
❑ 582 Ken Phelps .10 .05
❑ 583 Bobby Brown .10 .05
❑ 584 Kevin Gross .10 .05
❑ 585 Butch Wynegar .10 .05
❑ 586 Bill Scherrer .10 .05
❑ 587 Doug Frobel .10 .05
❑ 588 Bobby Castillo .10 .05
❑ 589 Bob Dernier .10 .05
❑ 590 Ray Knight .10 .05
❑ 591 Larry Herndon .10 .05
❑ 592 Jeff D. Robinson .10 .05
❑ 593 Rick Leach .10 .05
❑ 594 Curt Wilkerson .10 .05
❑ 595 Larry Gura .10 .05
❑ 596 Jerry Hairston .10 .05
❑ 597 Brad Lesley .10 .05
❑ 598 Jose Oquendo .10 .05
❑ 599 Storm Davis .10 .05
❑ 600 Pete Rose .75 .35
❑ 601 Tom Lasorda MG .40 .18
❑ 602 Jeff Dedmon .10 .05
❑ 603 Rick Manning .10 .05
❑ 604 Daryl Sconiers .10 .05
❑ 605 Ozzie Smith .75 .35
❑ 606 Rich Gale .10 .05
❑ 607 Bill Almon .10 .05
❑ 608 Craig Lefferts .10 .05
❑ 609 Broderick Perkins .10 .05
❑ 610 Jack Morris .20 .09
❑ 611 Ozzie Virgil .10 .05
❑ 612 Mike Armstrong .10 .05
❑ 613 Terry Puhl .10 .05
❑ 614 Al Williams .10 .05
❑ 615 Marvell Wynne .10 .05
❑ 616 Scott Sanderson .10 .05
❑ 617 Willie Wilson .10 .05
❑ 618 Pete Falcone .10 .05
❑ 619 Jeff Leonard .10 .05
❑ 620 Dwight Gooden 1.00 .45
❑ 621 Marvis Foley .10 .05
❑ 622 Luis Leal .10 .05
❑ 623 Greg Walker .10 .05
❑ 624 Benny Ayala .10 .05
❑ 625 Mark Langston .40 .18
❑ 626 German Rivera .10 .05
❑ 627 Eric Davis 1.25 .55
❑ 628 Rene Lachemann MG .10 .05
❑ 629 Dick Schofield .10 .05
❑ 630 Tim Raines .20 .09
❑ 631 Bob Forsch .10 .05
❑ 632 Bruce Bochte .10 .05
❑ 633 Glenn Hoffman .10 .05
❑ 634 Bill Dawley .10 .05
❑ 635 Terry Kennedy .10 .05
❑ 636 Shane Rawley .10 .05
❑ 637 Brett Butler .20 .09
❑ 638 Mike Pagliarulo .10 .05
❑ 639 Ed Hodge .10 .05
❑ 640 Steve Henderson .10 .05
❑ 641 Rod Scurry .10 .05
❑ 642 Dave Owen .10 .05
❑ 643 Johnny Grubb .10 .05
❑ 644 Mark Huismann .10 .05
❑ 645 Damaso Garcia .10 .05
❑ 646 Scot Thompson .10 .05
❑ 647 Rafael Ramirez .10 .05
❑ 648 Bob Jones .10 .05
❑ 649 Sid Fernandez .20 .09
❑ 650 Greg Luzinski .20 .09
❑ 651 Jeff Russell .10 .05
❑ 652 Joe Nolan .10 .05
❑ 653 Mark Brouhard .10 .05
❑ 654 Dave Anderson .10 .05
❑ 655 Joaquin Andujar .10 .05
❑ 656 Chuck Cottier MG .10 .05
❑ 657 Jim Slaton .10 .05
❑ 658 Mike Stenhouse .10 .05
❑ 659 Checklist: 529-660 .10 .05
❑ 660 Tony Gwynn 2.50 1.10
❑ 661 Steve Crawford .10 .05
❑ 662 Mike Heath .10 .05
❑ 663 Luis Aguayo .10 .05
❑ 664 Steve Farr .20 .09
❑ 665 Don Mattingly 1.50 .70
❑ 666 Mike LaCoss .10 .05
❑ 667 Dave Engle .10 .05
❑ 668 Steve Trout .10 .05
❑ 669 Lee Lacy .10 .05
❑ 670 Tom Seaver .75 .35
❑ 671 Dane Iorg .10 .05
❑ 672 Juan Berenguer .10 .05
❑ 673 Buck Martinez .10 .05
❑ 674 Atlee Hammaker .10 .05
❑ 675 Tony Perez .60 .25
❑ 676 Albert Hall .10 .05
❑ 677 Wally Backman .10 .05
❑ 678 Joey McLaughlin .10 .05
❑ 679 Bob Kearney .10 .05
❑ 680 Jerry Reuss .10 .05
❑ 681 Ben Oglivie .10 .05
❑ 682 Doug Corbett .10 .05
❑ 683 Whitey Herzog MG .20 .09
❑ 684 Bill Doran .10 .05
❑ 685 Bill Caudill .10 .05
❑ 686 Mike Easler .10 .05
❑ 687 Bill Gullickson .10 .05
❑ 688 Len Matuszek .10 .05
❑ 689 Luis DeLeon .10 .05
❑ 690 Alan Trammell .40 .18
❑ 691 Dennis Rasmussen .10 .05
❑ 692 Randy Bush .10 .05
❑ 693 Tim Stoddard .10 .05
❑ 694 Joe Carter .60 .25
❑ 695 Rick Rhoden .10 .05
❑ 696 John Rabb .10 .05
❑ 697 Onix Concepcion .10 .05
❑ 698 Jorge Bell .20 .09
❑ 699 Donnie Moore .10 .05
❑ 700 Eddie Murray .60 .25
❑ 701 Eddie Murray AS .20 .09
❑ 702 Damaso Garcia AS .10 .05
❑ 703 George Brett AS .60 .25
❑ 704 Cal Ripken AS .60 .25
❑ 705 Dave Winfield AS .20 .09
❑ 706 Rickey Henderson AS .20 .09
❑ 707 Tony Armas AS .10 .05
❑ 708 Lance Parrish AS .10 .05
❑ 709 Mike Boddicker AS .10 .05
❑ 710 Frank Viola AS .10 .05
❑ 711 Dan Quisenberry AS .10 .05
❑ 712 Keith Hernandez AS .10 .05
❑ 713 Ryne Sandberg AS .60 .25
❑ 714 Mike Schmidt AS .40 .18
❑ 715 Ozzie Smith AS .40 .18
❑ 716 Dale Murphy AS .20 .09
❑ 717 Tony Gwynn AS .60 .25
❑ 718 Jeff Leonard AS .10 .05
❑ 719 Gary Carter AS .20 .09
❑ 720 Rick Sutcliffe AS .10 .05
❑ 721 Bob Knepper AS .10 .05
❑ 722 Bruce Sutter AS .10 .05
❑ 723 Dave Stewart .20 .09
❑ 724 Oscar Gamble .10 .05
❑ 725 Floyd Bannister .10 .05
❑ 726 Al Bumbry .10 .05
❑ 727 Frank Pastore .10 .05
❑ 728 Bob Bailor .10 .05
❑ 729 Don Sutton .60 .25
❑ 730 Dave Kingman .20 .09
❑ 731 Neil Allen .10 .05
❑ 732 John McNamara MG .10 .05
❑ 733 Tony Scott .10 .05
❑ 734 John Henry Johnson .10 .05
❑ 735 Garry Templeton .10 .05
❑ 736 Jerry Mumphrey .10 .05
❑ 737 Bo Diaz .10 .05
❑ 738 Omar Moreno .10 .05
❑ 739 Ernie Camacho .10 .05
❑ 740 Jack Clark .20 .09
❑ 741 John Butcher .10 .05
❑ 742 Ron Hassey .10 .05
❑ 743 Frank White .20 .09
❑ 744 Doug Bair .10 .05
❑ 745 Buddy Bell .20 .09
❑ 746 Jim Clancy .10 .05
❑ 747 Alex Trevino .10 .05
❑ 748 Lee Mazzilli .10 .05
❑ 749 Julio Cruz .10 .05
❑ 750 Rollie Fingers .60 .25
❑ 751 Kelvin Chapman .10 .05
❑ 752 Bob Owchinko .10 .05
❑ 753 Greg Brock .10 .05
❑ 754 Larry Milbourne .10 .05
❑ 755 Ken Singleton .10 .05
❑ 756 Rob Picciolo .10 .05
❑ 757 Willie McGee .20 .09
❑ 758 Ray Burris .10 .05
❑ 759 Jim Fanning MG .10 .05
❑ 760 Nolan Ryan 3.00 1.35
❑ 761 Jerry Remy .10 .05
❑ 762 Eddie Whitson .10 .05
❑ 763 Kiko Garcia .10 .05
❑ 764 Jamie Easterly .10 .05
❑ 765 Willie Randolph .20 .09
❑ 766 Paul Mirabella .10 .05
❑ 767 Darrell Brown .10 .05
❑ 768 Ron Cey .20 .09
❑ 769 Joe Cowley .10 .05
❑ 770 Carlton Fisk .60 .25
❑ 771 Geoff Zahn .10 .05
❑ 772 Johnnie LeMaster .10 .05
❑ 773 Hal McRae .20 .09
❑ 774 Dennis Lamp .10 .05
❑ 775 Mookie Wilson .20 .09
❑ 776 Jerry Royster .10 .05
❑ 777 Ned Yost .10 .05
❑ 778 Mike Davis .10 .05
❑ 779 Nick Esasky .10 .05
❑ 780 Mike Flanagan .10 .05
❑ 781 Jim Gantner .10 .05
❑ 782 Tom Niedenfuer .10 .05
❑ 783 Mike Jorgensen .10 .05
❑ 784 Checklist: 661-792 .10 .05
❑ 785 Tony Armas .10 .05
❑ 786 Enos Cabell .10 .05
❑ 787 Jim Wohlford .10 .05
❑ 788 Steve Comer .10 .05
❑ 789 Luis Salazar .10 .05
❑ 790 Ron Guidry .20 .09
❑ 791 Ivan DeJesus .10 .05
❑ 792 Darrell Evans .20 .09

1985 Topps Tiffany

	NRMT	VG-E
COMP.FACT.SET (792)	1000.00	450.00
COMMON CARD (1-792)	.40	.18

*STARS: 4X TO 8X BASIC CARDS
*ROOKIES: 4X TO 8X BASIC CARDS

❑ 181 Roger Clemens 100.00 45.00
❑ 401 Mark McGwire OLY 600.00 275.00
❑ 536 Kirby Puckett 50.00 22.00

1985 Topps Traded

	NRMT	VG-E
COMP.FACT.SET (132)	10.00	4.50
COMMON CARD (1T-132T)	.15	.07

❑ 1T Don Aase .15 .07
❑ 2T Bill Almon .15 .07
❑ 3T Benny Ayala .15 .07
❑ 4T Dusty Baker .40 .18
❑ 5T George Bamberger MG .15 .07
❑ 6T Dale Berra .15 .07
❑ 7T Rich Bordi .15 .07

❑ 8T Daryl Boston .15 .07
❑ 9T Hubie Brooks .15 .07
❑ 10T Chris Brown .15 .07
❑ 11T Tom Browning .40 .18
❑ 12T Al Bumbry .15 .07
❑ 13T Ray Burris .15 .07
❑ 14T Jeff Burroughs .15 .07
❑ 15T Bill Campbell .15 .07
❑ 16T Don Carman .15 .07
❑ 17T Gary Carter .75 .35
❑ 18T Bobby Castillo .15 .07
❑ 19T Bill Caudill .15 .07
❑ 20T Rick Cerone .15 .07
❑ 21T Bryan Clark .15 .07
❑ 22T Jack Clark .40 .18
❑ 23T Pat Clements .15 .07
❑ 24T Vince Coleman .75 .35
❑ 25T Dave Collins .15 .07
❑ 26T Danny Darwin .40 .18
❑ 27T Jim Davenport MG .15 .07
❑ 28T Jerry Davis .15 .07
❑ 29T Brian Dayett .15 .07
❑ 30T Ivan DeJesus .15 .07
❑ 31T Ken Dixon .15 .07
❑ 32T Mariano Duncan .75 .35
❑ 33T John Felske MG .15 .07
❑ 34T Mike Fitzgerald .15 .07
❑ 35T Ray Fontenot .15 .07
❑ 36T Greg Gagne .40 .18
❑ 37T Oscar Gamble .15 .07
❑ 38T Scott Garrelts .15 .07
❑ 39T Bob L. Gibson .15 .07
❑ 40T Jim Gott .15 .07
❑ 41T David Green .15 .07
❑ 42T Alfredo Griffin .15 .07
❑ 43T Ozzie Guillen 1.50 .70
❑ 44T Eddie Haas MG .15 .07
❑ 45T Terry Harper .15 .07
❑ 46T Toby Harrah .15 .07
❑ 47T Greg Harris .15 .07
❑ 48T Ron Hassey .15 .07
❑ 49T Rickey Henderson 1.00 .45
❑ 50T Steve Henderson .15 .07
❑ 51T George Hendrick .15 .07
❑ 52T Joe Hesketh .15 .07
❑ 53T Teddy Higuera .40 .18
❑ 54T Donnie Hill .15 .07
❑ 55T Al Holland .15 .07
❑ 56T Burt Hooton .15 .07
❑ 57T Jay Howell .15 .07
❑ 58T Ken Howell .15 .07
❑ 59T LaMarr Hoyt .15 .07
❑ 60T Tim Hulett .15 .07
❑ 61T Bob James .15 .07
❑ 62T Steve Jeltz .15 .07
❑ 63T Cliff Johnson .15 .07
❑ 64T Howard Johnson .40 .18
❑ 65T Ruppert Jones .15 .07
❑ 66T Steve Kemp .15 .07
❑ 67T Bruce Kison .15 .07
❑ 68T Alan Knicely .15 .07
❑ 69T Mike LaCoss .15 .07
❑ 70T Lee Lacy .15 .07
❑ 71T Dave LaPoint .15 .07
❑ 72T Gary Lavelle .15 .07
❑ 73T Vance Law .15 .07
❑ 74T Johnnie LeMaster .15 .07
❑ 75T Sixto Lezcano .15 .07
❑ 76T Tim Lollar .15 .07
❑ 77T Fred Lynn .40 .18
❑ 78T Billy Martin MG .40 .18
❑ 79T Ron Mathis .15 .07
❑ 80T Len Matuszek .15 .07
❑ 81T Gene Mauch MG .40 .18
❑ 82T Oddibe McDowell .40 .18
❑ 83T Roger McDowell .40 .18
❑ 84T John McNamara MG .15 .07
❑ 85T Donnie Moore .15 .07
❑ 86T Gene Nelson .15 .07
❑ 87T Steve Nicosia .15 .07
❑ 88T Al Oliver .40 .18
❑ 89T Joe Orsulak .40 .18
❑ 90T Rob Picciolo .15 .07
❑ 91T Chris Pittaro .15 .07
❑ 92T Jim Presley .40 .18
❑ 93T Rick Reuschel .15 .07
❑ 94T Bert Roberge .15 .07
❑ 95T Bob Rodgers MG .15 .07
❑ 96T Jerry Royster .15 .07
❑ 97T Dave Rozema .15 .07
❑ 98T Dave Rucker .15 .07
❑ 99T Vern Ruhle .15 .07
❑ 100T Paul Runge .15 .07
❑ 101T Mark Salas .15 .07
❑ 102T Luis Salazar .15 .07
❑ 103T Joe Sambito .15 .07
❑ 104T Rick Schu .15 .07
❑ 105T Donnie Scott .15 .07
❑ 106T Larry Sheets .15 .07
❑ 107T Don Slaught .15 .07
❑ 108T Roy Smalley .15 .07
❑ 109T Lonnie Smith .15 .07
❑ 110T Nate Snell UER .15 .07
(Headings on back for a batter)
❑ 111T Chris Speier .15 .07
❑ 112T Mike Stenhouse .15 .07
❑ 113T Tim Stoddard .15 .07
❑ 114T Jim Sundberg .15 .07
❑ 115T Bruce Sutter .40 .18
❑ 116T Don Sutton .75 .35
❑ 117T Kent Tekulve .15 .07
❑ 118T Tom Tellmann .15 .07
❑ 119T Walt Terrell .15 .07
❑ 120T Mickey Tettleton 1.00 .45
❑ 121T Derrel Thomas .15 .07
❑ 122T Rich Thompson .15 .07
❑ 123T Alex Trevino .15 .07
❑ 124T John Tudor .15 .07
❑ 125T Jose Uribe .15 .07
❑ 126T Bobby Valentine MG .15 .07
❑ 127T Dave Von Ohlen .15 .07
❑ 128T U.L. Washington .15 .07
❑ 129T Earl Weaver MG .75 .35
❑ 130T Eddie Whitson .15 .07
❑ 131T Herm Winningham .15 .07
❑ 132T Checklist 1-132 .15 .07

1985 Topps Traded Tiffany

	NRMT	VG-E
COMP.FACT.SET (132)	40.00	18.00
COMMON CARD (1T-132T)	.40	.18

*STARS: 2X TO 4X BASIC CARDS
*ROOKIES: 2X TO 4X BASIC CARDS

1986 Topps

	MINT	NRMT
COMPLETE SET (792)	20.00	9.00
COMP.FACT.SET (792)	25.00	11.00
COMMON CARD (1-792)	.05	.02

❑ 1 Pete Rose .75 .35
❑ 2 Rose Special: '63-'66 .25 .11
❑ 3 Rose Special: '67-'70 .25 .11
❑ 4 Rose Special: '71-'74 .25 .11
❑ 5 Rose Special: '75-'78 .25 .11
❑ 6 Rose Special: '79-'82 .25 .11
❑ 7 Rose Special: '83-'85 .25 .11
❑ 8 Dwayne Murphy .05 .02
❑ 9 Roy Smith .05 .02

❑ 10 Tony Gwynn 1.00 .45
❑ 11 Bob Ojeda .05 .02
❑ 12 Jose Uribe .05 .02
❑ 13 Bob Kearney .05 .02
❑ 14 Julio Cruz .05 .02
❑ 15 Eddie Whitson .05 .02
❑ 16 Rick Schu .05 .02
❑ 17 Mike Stenhouse .05 .02
❑ 18 Brent Gaff .05 .02
❑ 19 Rich Hebner .05 .02
❑ 20 Lou Whitaker .10 .05
❑ 21 George Bamberger MG .05 .02
❑ 22 Duane Walker .05 .02
❑ 23 Manny Lee .05 .02
❑ 24 Len Barker .05 .02
❑ 25 Willie Wilson .05 .02
❑ 26 Frank DiPino .05 .02
❑ 27 Ray Knight .10 .05
❑ 28 Eric Davis .20 .09
❑ 29 Tony Phillips .05 .02
❑ 30 Eddie Murray .40 .18
❑ 31 Jamie Easterly .05 .02
❑ 32 Steve Yeager .05 .02
❑ 33 Jeff Lahti .05 .02
❑ 34 Ken Phelps .05 .02
❑ 35 Jeff Reardon .10 .05
❑ 36 Lance Parrish TL .10 .05
❑ 37 Mark Thurmond .05 .02
❑ 38 Glenn Hoffman .05 .02
❑ 39 Dave Rucker .05 .02
❑ 40 Ken Griffey .10 .05
❑ 41 Brad Wellman .05 .02
❑ 42 Geoff Zahn .05 .02
❑ 43 Dave Engle .05 .02
❑ 44 Lance McCullers .05 .02
❑ 45 Damaso Garcia .05 .02
❑ 46 Billy Hatcher .05 .02
❑ 47 Juan Berenguer .05 .02
❑ 48 Bill Almon .05 .02
❑ 49 Rick Manning .05 .02
❑ 50 Dan Quisenberry .05 .02
❑ 51 Bobby Wine MG ERR .05 .02
(Number of card on back is actually 57)
❑ 52 Chris Welsh .05 .02
❑ 53 Len Dykstra .75 .35
❑ 54 John Franco .40 .18
❑ 55 Fred Lynn .10 .05
❑ 56 Tom Niedenfuer .05 .02
❑ 57 Bill Doran .05 .02
(See also 51)
❑ 58 Bill Krueger .05 .02
❑ 59 Andre Thornton .05 .02
❑ 60 Dwight Evans .10 .05
❑ 61 Karl Best .05 .02
❑ 62 Bob Boone .10 .05
❑ 63 Ron Roenicke .05 .02
❑ 64 Floyd Bannister .05 .02
❑ 65 Dan Driessen .05 .02
❑ 66 Bob Forsch TL .05 .02
❑ 67 Carmelo Martinez .05 .02
❑ 68 Ed Lynch .05 .02
❑ 69 Luis Aguayo .05 .02
❑ 70 Dave Winfield .40 .18
❑ 71 Ken Schrom .05 .02
❑ 72 Shawon Dunston .10 .05
❑ 73 Randy O'Neal .05 .02
❑ 74 Rance Mulliniks .05 .02

❑ 75 Jose DeLeon .05 .02
❑ 76 Dion James .05 .02
❑ 77 Charlie Leibrandt .05 .02
❑ 78 Bruce Benedict .05 .02
❑ 79 Dave Schmidt .05 .02
❑ 80 Darryl Strawberry .40 .18
❑ 81 Gene Mauch MG .10 .05
❑ 82 Tippy Martinez .05 .02
❑ 83 Phil Garner .05 .02
❑ 84 Curt Young .05 .02
❑ 85 Tony Perez .40 .18
(Eric Davis also
shown on card)
❑ 86 Tom Waddell .05 .02
❑ 87 Candy Maldonado .05 .02
❑ 88 Tom Nieto .05 .02
❑ 89 Randy St.Claire .05 .02
❑ 90 Garry Templeton .05 .02
❑ 91 Steve Crawford .05 .02
❑ 92 Al Cowens .05 .02
❑ 93 Scot Thompson .05 .02
❑ 94 Rich Bordi .05 .02
❑ 95 Ozzie Virgil .05 .02
❑ 96 Jim Clancy TL .05 .02
❑ 97 Gary Gaetti .10 .05
❑ 98 Dick Ruthven .05 .02
❑ 99 Buddy Biancalana .05 .02
❑ 100 Nolan Ryan 1.50 .70
❑ 101 Dave Bergman .05 .02
❑ 102 Joe Orsulak .05 .02
❑ 103 Luis Salazar .05 .02
❑ 104 Sid Fernandez .10 .05
❑ 105 Gary Ward .05 .02
❑ 106 Ray Burris .05 .02
❑ 107 Rafael Ramirez .05 .02
❑ 108 Ted Power .05 .02
❑ 109 Len Matuszek .05 .02
❑ 110 Scott McGregor .05 .02
❑ 111 Roger Craig MG .10 .05
❑ 112 Bill Campbell .05 .02
❑ 113 U.L. Washington .05 .02
❑ 114 Mike C. Brown .05 .02
❑ 115 Jay Howell .05 .02
❑ 116 Brook Jacoby .05 .02
❑ 117 Bruce Kison .05 .02
❑ 118 Jerry Royster .05 .02
❑ 119 Barry Bonnell .05 .02
❑ 120 Steve Carlton .40 .18
❑ 121 Nelson Simmons .05 .02
❑ 122 Pete Filson .05 .02
❑ 123 Greg Walker .05 .02
❑ 124 Luis Sanchez .05 .02
❑ 125 Dave Lopes .10 .05
❑ 126 Mookie Wilson TL .05 .02
❑ 127 Jack Howell .05 .02
❑ 128 John Wathan .05 .02
❑ 129 Jeff Dedmon .05 .02
❑ 130 Alan Trammell .20 .09
❑ 131 Checklist: 1-132 .10 .05
❑ 132 Razor Shines .05 .02
❑ 133 Andy McGaffigan .05 .02
❑ 134 Carney Lansford .10 .05
❑ 135 Joe Niekro .05 .02
❑ 136 Mike Hargrove .10 .05
❑ 137 Charlie Moore .05 .02
❑ 138 Mark Davis .05 .02
❑ 139 Daryl Boston .05 .02
❑ 140 John Candelaria .05 .02
❑ 141 Chuck Cottier MG .05 .02
See also 171
❑ 142 Bob Jones .05 .02
❑ 143 Dave Van Gorder .05 .02
❑ 144 Doug Sisk .05 .02
❑ 145 Pedro Guerrero .10 .05
❑ 146 Jack Perconte .05 .02
❑ 147 Larry Sheets .05 .02
❑ 148 Mike Heath .05 .02
❑ 149 Brett Butler .10 .05
❑ 150 Joaquin Andujar .05 .02
❑ 151 Dave Stapleton .05 .02
❑ 152 Mike Morgan .05 .02
❑ 153 Ricky Adams .05 .02
❑ 154 Bert Roberge .05 .02
❑ 155 Bob Grich .10 .05
❑ 156 Richard Dotson TL .05 .02
❑ 157 Ron Hassey .05 .02
❑ 158 Derrel Thomas .05 .02
❑ 159 Orel Hershiser UER .40 .18
(82 Alburquerque)
❑ 160 Chet Lemon .05 .02
❑ 161 Lee Tunnell .05 .02
❑ 162 Greg Gagne .05 .02
❑ 163 Pete Ladd .05 .02
❑ 164 Steve Balboni .05 .02
❑ 165 Mike Davis .05 .02
❑ 166 Dickie Thon .05 .02
❑ 167 Zane Smith .05 .02
❑ 168 Jeff Burroughs .05 .02
❑ 169 George Wright .05 .02
❑ 170 Gary Carter .40 .18
❑ 171 Bob Rodgers MG ERR .05 .02
Number of card on
back actually 141)
❑ 172 Jerry Reed .05 .02
❑ 173 Wayne Gross .05 .02
❑ 174 Brian Snyder .05 .02
❑ 175 Steve Sax .05 .02
❑ 176 Jay Tibbs .05 .02
❑ 177 Joel Youngblood .05 .02
❑ 178 Ivan DeJesus .05 .02
❑ 179 Stu Cliburn .05 .02
❑ 180 Don Mattingly .60 .25
❑ 181 Al Nipper .05 .02
❑ 182 Bobby Brown .05 .02
❑ 183 Larry Andersen .05 .02
❑ 184 Tim Laudner .05 .02
❑ 185 Rollie Fingers .40 .18
❑ 186 Jose Cruz TL .05 .02
❑ 187 Scott Fletcher .05 .02
❑ 188 Bob Dernier .05 .02
❑ 189 Mike Mason .05 .02
❑ 190 George Hendrick .05 .02
❑ 191 Wally Backman .05 .02
❑ 192 Milt Wilcox .05 .02
❑ 193 Daryl Sconiers .05 .02
❑ 194 Craig McMurtry .05 .02
❑ 195 Dave Concepcion .10 .05
❑ 196 Doyle Alexander .05 .02
❑ 197 Enos Cabell .05 .02
❑ 198 Ken Dixon .05 .02
❑ 199 Dick Howser MG .10 .05
❑ 200 Mike Schmidt .50 .23
❑ 201 Vince Coleman RB .10 .05
Most SB's rookie season
❑ 202 Dwight Gooden RB .10 .05
Youngest 20 game
winner
❑ 203 Keith Hernandez RB .05 .02
Most game-winning RBI's
❑ 204 Phil Niekro RB .10 .05
Oldest shutout pitcher
❑ 205 Tony Perez RB .10 .05
Oldest grand slammer
❑ 206 Pete Rose RB .40 .18
Most lifetime hits
❑ 207 Fernando Valenzuela RB .10 .05
Most cons. innings
start of season,
no earned runs
❑ 208 Ramon Romero .05 .02
❑ 209 Randy Ready .05 .02
❑ 210 Calvin Schiraldi .05 .02
❑ 211 Ed Wojna .05 .02
❑ 212 Chris Speier .05 .02
❑ 213 Bob Shirley .05 .02
❑ 214 Randy Bush .05 .02
❑ 215 Frank White .10 .05
❑ 216 Dwayne Murphy TL .05 .02
❑ 217 Bill Scherrer .05 .02
❑ 218 Randy Hunt .05 .02
❑ 219 Dennis Lamp .05 .02
❑ 220 Bob Horner .05 .02
❑ 221 Dave Henderson .05 .02
❑ 222 Craig Gerber .05 .02
❑ 223 Atlee Hammaker .05 .02
❑ 224 Cesar Cedeno .10 .05
❑ 225 Ron Darling .05 .02
❑ 226 Lee Lacy .05 .02
❑ 227 Al Jones .05 .02
❑ 228 Tom Lawless .05 .02
❑ 229 Bill Gullickson .05 .02
❑ 230 Terry Kennedy .05 .02
❑ 231 Jim Frey MG .10 .05
❑ 232 Rick Rhoden .05 .02
❑ 233 Steve Lyons .05 .02
❑ 234 Doug Corbett .05 .02
❑ 235 Butch Wynegar .05 .02
❑ 236 Frank Eufemia .05 .02
❑ 237 Ted Simmons .10 .05
❑ 238 Larry Parrish .05 .02
❑ 239 Joel Skinner .05 .02
❑ 240 Tommy John .40 .18
❑ 241 Tony Fernandez .05 .02
❑ 242 Rich Thompson .05 .02
❑ 243 Johnny Grubb .05 .02
❑ 244 Craig Lefferts .05 .02
❑ 245 Jim Sundberg .05 .02
❑ 246 Steve Carlton TL .10 .05
❑ 247 Terry Harper .05 .02
❑ 248 Spike Owen .05 .02
❑ 249 Rob Deer .10 .05
❑ 250 Dwight Gooden .40 .18
❑ 251 Rich Dauer .05 .02
❑ 252 Bobby Castillo .05 .02
❑ 253 Dann Bilardello .05 .02
❑ 254 Ozzie Guillen .20 .09
❑ 255 Tony Armas .05 .02
❑ 256 Kurt Kepshire .05 .02
❑ 257 Doug DeCinces .05 .02
❑ 258 Tim Burke .05 .02
❑ 259 Dan Pasqua .05 .02
❑ 260 Tony Pena .05 .02
❑ 261 Bobby Valentine MG .10 .05
❑ 262 Mario Ramirez .05 .02
❑ 263 Checklist: 133-264 .10 .05
❑ 264 Darren Daulton .75 .35
❑ 265 Ron Davis .05 .02
❑ 266 Keith Moreland .05 .02
❑ 267 Paul Molitor .40 .18
❑ 268 Mike Scott .05 .02
❑ 269 Dane Iorg .05 .02
❑ 270 Jack Morris .10 .05
❑ 271 Dave Collins .05 .02
❑ 272 Tim Tolman .05 .02
❑ 273 Jerry Willard .05 .02
❑ 274 Ron Gardenhire .05 .02
❑ 275 Charlie Hough .10 .05
❑ 276 Willie Randolph TL .10 .05
❑ 277 Jaime Cocanower .05 .02
❑ 278 Sixto Lezcano .05 .02
❑ 279 Al Pardo .05 .02
❑ 280 Tim Raines .10 .05
❑ 281 Steve Mura .05 .02
❑ 282 Jerry Mumphrey .05 .02
❑ 283 Mike Fischlin .05 .02
❑ 284 Brian Dayett .05 .02
❑ 285 Buddy Bell .10 .05
❑ 286 Luis DeLeon .05 .02
❑ 287 John Christensen .05 .02
❑ 288 Don Aase .05 .02
❑ 289 Johnnie LeMaster .05 .02
❑ 290 Carlton Fisk .40 .18
❑ 291 Tom Lasorda MG .20 .09
❑ 292 Chuck Porter .05 .02
❑ 293 Chris Chambliss .10 .05
❑ 294 Danny Cox .05 .02
❑ 295 Kirk Gibson .10 .05
❑ 296 Geno Petralli .05 .02
❑ 297 Tim Lollar .05 .02
❑ 298 Craig Reynolds .05 .02
❑ 299 Bryn Smith .05 .02
❑ 300 George Brett .75 .35
❑ 301 Dennis Rasmussen .05 .02
❑ 302 Greg Gross .05 .02
❑ 303 Curt Wardle .05 .02
❑ 304 Mike Gallego .10 .05
❑ 305 Phil Bradley .05 .02
❑ 306 Terry Kennedy TL .05 .02
❑ 307 Dave Sax .05 .02
❑ 308 Ray Fontenot .05 .02
❑ 309 John Shelby .05 .02
❑ 310 Greg Minton .05 .02
❑ 311 Dick Schofield .05 .02
❑ 312 Tom Filer .05 .02
❑ 313 Joe DeSa .05 .02

❑ 314	Frank Pastore	.05	.02
❑ 315	Mookie Wilson	.10	.05
❑ 316	Sammy Khalifa	.05	.02
❑ 317	Ed Romero	.05	.02
❑ 318	Terry Whitfield	.05	.02
❑ 319	Rick Camp	.05	.02
❑ 320	Jim Rice	.10	.05
❑ 321	Earl Weaver MG	.40	.18
❑ 322	Bob Forsch	.05	.02
❑ 323	Jerry Davis	.05	.02
❑ 324	Dan Schatzeder	.05	.02
❑ 325	Juan Beniquez	.05	.02
❑ 326	Kent Tekulve	.05	.02
❑ 327	Mike Pagliarulo	.05	.02
❑ 328	Pete O'Brien	.05	.02
❑ 329	Kirby Puckett	1.25	.55
❑ 330	Rick Sutcliffe	.05	.02
❑ 331	Alan Ashby	.05	.02
❑ 332	Darryl Motley	.05	.02
❑ 333	Tom Henke	.10	.05
❑ 334	Ken Oberkfell	.05	.02
❑ 335	Don Sutton	.40	.18
❑ 336	Andre Thornton TL	.10	.05
❑ 337	Darnell Coles	.05	.02
❑ 338	Jorge Bell	.10	.05
❑ 339	Bruce Berenyi	.05	.02
❑ 340	Cal Ripken	1.50	.70
❑ 341	Frank Williams	.05	.02
❑ 342	Gary Redus	.05	.02
❑ 343	Carlos Diaz	.05	.02
❑ 344	Jim Wohlford	.05	.02
❑ 345	Donnie Moore	.05	.02
❑ 346	Bryan Little	.05	.02
❑ 347	Teddy Higuera	.10	.05
❑ 348	Cliff Johnson	.05	.02
❑ 349	Mark Clear	.05	.02
❑ 350	Jack Clark	.10	.05
❑ 351	Chuck Tanner MG	.05	.02
❑ 352	Harry Spilman	.05	.02
❑ 353	Keith Atherton	.05	.02
❑ 354	Tony Bernazard	.05	.02
❑ 355	Lee Smith	.20	.09
❑ 356	Mickey Hatcher	.05	.02
❑ 357	Ed VandeBerg	.05	.02
❑ 358	Rick Dempsey	.05	.02
❑ 359	Mike LaCoss	.05	.02
❑ 360	Lloyd Moseby	.05	.02
❑ 361	Shane Rawley	.05	.02
❑ 362	Tom Paciorek	.10	.05
❑ 363	Terry Forster	.05	.02
❑ 364	Reid Nichols	.05	.02
❑ 365	Mike Flanagan	.05	.02
❑ 366	Dave Concepcion TL	.10	.05
❑ 367	Aurelio Lopez	.05	.02
❑ 368	Greg Brock	.05	.02
❑ 369	Al Holland	.05	.02
❑ 370	Vince Coleman	.40	.18
❑ 371	Bill Stein	.05	.02
❑ 372	Ben Oglivie	.05	.02
❑ 373	Urbano Lugo	.05	.02
❑ 374	Terry Francona	.05	.02
❑ 375	Rich Gedman	.05	.02
❑ 376	Bill Dawley	.05	.02
❑ 377	Joe Carter	.40	.18
❑ 378	Bruce Bochte	.05	.02
❑ 379	Bobby Meacham	.05	.02
❑ 380	LaMarr Hoyt	.05	.02
❑ 381	Ray Miller MG	.05	.02
❑ 382	Ivan Calderon	.10	.05
❑ 383	Chris Brown	.05	.02
❑ 384	Steve Trout	.05	.02
❑ 385	Cecil Cooper	.10	.05
❑ 386	Cecil Fielder	.75	.35
❑ 387	Steve Kemp	.05	.02
❑ 388	Dickie Noles	.05	.02
❑ 389	Glenn Davis	.10	.05
❑ 390	Tom Seaver	.50	.23
❑ 391	Julio Franco	.10	.05
❑ 392	John Russell	.05	.02
❑ 393	Chris Pittaro	.05	.02
❑ 394	Checklist: 265-396	.10	.05
❑ 395	Scott Garrelts	.05	.02
❑ 396	Dwight Evans TL	.10	.05
❑ 397	Steve Buechele	.10	.05
❑ 398	Earnie Riles	.05	.02
❑ 399	Bill Swift	.05	.02
❑ 400	Rod Carew	.40	.18
❑ 401	Fernando Valenzuela TBC '81	.10	.05
❑ 402	Tom Seaver TBC '76	.10	.05
❑ 403	Willie Mays TBC '71	.20	.09
❑ 404	Frank Robinson TBC '66	.10	.05
❑ 405	Roger Maris TBC '61	.10	.05
❑ 406	Scott Sanderson	.05	.02
❑ 407	Sal Butera	.05	.02
❑ 408	Dave Smith	.05	.02
❑ 409	Paul Runge	.05	.02
❑ 410	Dave Kingman	.10	.05
❑ 411	Sparky Anderson MG	.20	.09
❑ 412	Jim Clancy	.05	.02
❑ 413	Tim Flannery	.05	.02
❑ 414	Tom Gorman	.05	.02
❑ 415	Hal McRae	.10	.05
❑ 416	Dennis Martinez	.10	.05
❑ 417	R.J. Reynolds	.05	.02
❑ 418	Alan Knicely	.05	.02
❑ 419	Frank Wills	.05	.02
❑ 420	Von Hayes	.05	.02
❑ 421	David Palmer	.05	.02
❑ 422	Mike Jorgensen	.05	.02
❑ 423	Dan Spillner	.05	.02
❑ 424	Rick Miller	.05	.02
❑ 425	Larry McWilliams	.05	.02
❑ 426	Charlie Moore TL	.05	.02
❑ 427	Joe Cowley	.05	.02
❑ 428	Max Venable	.05	.02
❑ 429	Greg Booker	.05	.02
❑ 430	Kent Hrbek	.10	.05
❑ 431	George Frazier	.05	.02
❑ 432	Mark Bailey	.05	.02
❑ 433	Chris Codiroli	.05	.02
❑ 434	Curt Wilkerson	.05	.02
❑ 435	Bill Caudill	.05	.02
❑ 436	Doug Flynn	.05	.02
❑ 437	Rick Mahler	.05	.02
❑ 438	Clint Hurdle	.05	.02
❑ 439	Rick Honeycutt	.05	.02
❑ 440	Alvin Davis	.05	.02
❑ 441	Whitey Herzog MG	.20	.09
❑ 442	Ron Robinson	.05	.02
❑ 443	Bill Buckner	.10	.05
❑ 444	Alex Trevino	.05	.02
❑ 445	Bert Blyleven	.10	.05
❑ 446	Lenn Sakata	.05	.02
❑ 447	Jerry Don Gleaton	.05	.02
❑ 448	Herm Winningham	.05	.02
❑ 449	Rod Scurry	.05	.02
❑ 450	Graig Nettles	.10	.05
❑ 451	Mark Brown	.05	.02
❑ 452	Bob Clark	.05	.02
❑ 453	Steve Jeltz	.05	.02
❑ 454	Burt Hooton	.05	.02
❑ 455	Willie Randolph	.10	.05
❑ 456	Dale Murphy TL	.10	.05
❑ 457	Mickey Tettleton	.40	.18
❑ 458	Kevin Bass	.05	.02
❑ 459	Luis Leal	.05	.02
❑ 460	Leon Durham	.05	.02
❑ 461	Walt Terrell	.05	.02
❑ 462	Domingo Ramos	.05	.02
❑ 463	Jim Gott	.05	.02
❑ 464	Ruppert Jones	.05	.02
❑ 465	Jesse Orosco	.05	.02
❑ 466	Tom Foley	.05	.02
❑ 467	Bob James	.05	.02
❑ 468	Mike Scioscia	.05	.02
❑ 469	Storm Davis	.05	.02
❑ 470	Bill Madlock	.05	.02
❑ 471	Bobby Cox MG	.10	.05
❑ 472	Joe Hesketh	.05	.02
❑ 473	Mark Brouhard	.05	.02
❑ 474	John Tudor	.05	.02
❑ 475	Juan Samuel	.05	.02
❑ 476	Ron Mathis	.05	.02
❑ 477	Mike Easler	.05	.02
❑ 478	Andy Hawkins	.05	.02
❑ 479	Bob Melvin	.05	.02
❑ 480	Oddibe McDowell	.05	.02
❑ 481	Scott Bradley	.05	.02
❑ 482	Rick Lysander	.05	.02
❑ 483	George Vukovich	.05	.02
❑ 484	Donnie Hill	.05	.02
❑ 485	Gary Matthews	.05	.02
❑ 486	Bobby Grich TL	.05	.02
❑ 487	Bret Saberhagen	.10	.05
❑ 488	Lou Thornton	.05	.02
❑ 489	Jim Winn	.05	.02
❑ 490	Jeff Leonard	.05	.02
❑ 491	Pascual Perez	.05	.02
❑ 492	Kelvin Chapman	.05	.02
❑ 493	Gene Nelson	.05	.02
❑ 494	Gary Roenicke	.05	.02
❑ 495	Mark Langston	.05	.02
❑ 496	Jay Johnstone	.10	.05
❑ 497	John Stuper	.05	.02
❑ 498	Tito Landrum	.05	.02
❑ 499	Bob L. Gibson	.05	.02
❑ 500	Rickey Henderson	.40	.18
❑ 501	Dave Johnson MG	.10	.05
❑ 502	Glen Cook	.05	.02
❑ 503	Mike Fitzgerald	.05	.02
❑ 504	Denny Walling	.05	.02
❑ 505	Jerry Koosman	.10	.05
❑ 506	Bill Russell	.10	.05
❑ 507	Steve Ontiveros	.10	.05
❑ 508	Alan Wiggins	.05	.02
❑ 509	Ernie Camacho	.05	.02
❑ 510	Wade Boggs	.40	.18
❑ 511	Ed Nunez	.05	.02
❑ 512	Thad Bosley	.05	.02
❑ 513	Ron Washington	.05	.02
❑ 514	Mike Jones	.05	.02
❑ 515	Darrell Evans	.10	.05
❑ 516	Greg Minton TL	.05	.02
❑ 517	Milt Thompson	.10	.05
❑ 518	Buck Martinez	.05	.02
❑ 519	Danny Darwin	.05	.02
❑ 520	Keith Hernandez	.10	.05
❑ 521	Nate Snell	.05	.02
❑ 522	Bob Bailor	.05	.02
❑ 523	Joe Price	.05	.02
❑ 524	Darrell Miller	.05	.02
❑ 525	Marvell Wynne	.05	.02
❑ 526	Charlie Lea	.05	.02
❑ 527	Checklist: 397-528	.10	.05
❑ 528	Terry Pendleton	.20	.09
❑ 529	Marc Sullivan	.05	.02
❑ 530	Rich Gossage	.10	.05
❑ 531	Tony LaRussa MG	.10	.05
❑ 532	Don Carman	.05	.02
❑ 533	Billy Sample	.05	.02
❑ 534	Jeff Calhoun	.05	.02
❑ 535	Toby Harrah	.05	.02
❑ 536	Jose Rijo	.05	.02
❑ 537	Mark Salas	.05	.02
❑ 538	Dennis Eckersley	.40	.18
❑ 539	Glenn Hubbard	.05	.02
❑ 540	Dan Petry	.05	.02
❑ 541	Jorge Orta	.05	.02
❑ 542	Don Schulze	.05	.02
❑ 543	Jerry Narron	.05	.02
❑ 544	Eddie Milner	.05	.02
❑ 545	Jimmy Key	.40	.18
❑ 546	Dave Henderson TL	.05	.02
❑ 547	Roger McDowell	.10	.05
❑ 548	Mike Young	.05	.02
❑ 549	Bob Welch	.05	.02
❑ 550	Tom Herr	.05	.02
❑ 551	Dave LaPoint	.05	.02
❑ 552	Marc Hill	.05	.02
❑ 553	Jim Morrison	.05	.02
❑ 554	Paul Householder	.05	.02
❑ 555	Hubie Brooks	.05	.02
❑ 556	John Denny	.05	.02
❑ 557	Gerald Perry	.05	.02
❑ 558	Tim Stoddard	.05	.02
❑ 559	Tommy Dunbar	.05	.02
❑ 560	Dave Righetti	.05	.02
❑ 561	Bob Lillis MG	.05	.02
❑ 562	Joe Beckwith	.05	.02
❑ 563	Alejandro Sanchez	.05	.02
❑ 564	Warren Brusstar	.05	.02
❑ 565	Tom Brunansky	.05	.02
❑ 566	Alfredo Griffin	.05	.02

❑ 567 Jeff Barkley .05 .02
❑ 568 Donnie Scott .05 .02
❑ 569 Jim Acker .05 .02
❑ 570 Rusty Staub .10 .05
❑ 571 Mike Jeffcoat .05 .02
❑ 572 Paul Zuvella .05 .02
❑ 573 Tom Hume .05 .02
❑ 574 Ron Kittle .05 .02
❑ 575 Mike Boddicker .05 .02
❑ 576 Andre Dawson TL .10 .05
❑ 577 Jerry Reuss .05 .02
❑ 578 Lee Mazzilli .05 .02
❑ 579 Jim Slaton .05 .02
❑ 580 Willie McGee .10 .05
❑ 581 Bruce Hurst .05 .02
❑ 582 Jim Gantner .05 .02
❑ 583 Al Bumbry .05 .02
❑ 584 Brian Fisher .05 .02
❑ 585 Garry Maddox .05 .02
❑ 586 Greg Harris .05 .02
❑ 587 Rafael Santana .05 .02
❑ 588 Steve Lake .05 .02
❑ 589 Sid Bream .05 .02
❑ 590 Bob Knepper .05 .02
❑ 591 Jackie Moore MG .05 .02
❑ 592 Frank Tanana .05 .02
❑ 593 Jesse Barfield .05 .02
❑ 594 Chris Bando .05 .02
❑ 595 Dave Parker .10 .05
❑ 596 Onix Concepcion .05 .02
❑ 597 Sammy Stewart .05 .02
❑ 598 Jim Presley .05 .02
❑ 599 Rick Aguilera .40 .18
❑ 600 Dale Murphy .40 .18
❑ 601 Gary Lucas .05 .02
❑ 602 Mariano Duncan .40 .18
❑ 603 Bill Laskey .05 .02
❑ 604 Gary Pettis .05 .02
❑ 605 Dennis Boyd .05 .02
❑ 606 Hal McRae TL .10 .05
❑ 607 Ken Dayley .05 .02
❑ 608 Bruce Bochy .05 .02
❑ 609 Barbaro Garbey .05 .02
❑ 610 Ron Guidry .10 .05
❑ 611 Gary Woods .05 .02
❑ 612 Richard Dotson .05 .02
❑ 613 Roy Smalley .05 .02
❑ 614 Rick Waits .05 .02
❑ 615 Johnny Ray .05 .02
❑ 616 Glenn Brummer .05 .02
❑ 617 Lonnie Smith .05 .02
❑ 618 Jim Pankovits .05 .02
❑ 619 Danny Heep .05 .02
❑ 620 Bruce Sutter .10 .05
❑ 621 John Felske MG .05 .02
❑ 622 Gary Lavelle .05 .02
❑ 623 Floyd Rayford .05 .02
❑ 624 Steve McCatty .05 .02
❑ 625 Bob Brenly .05 .02
❑ 626 Roy Thomas .05 .02
❑ 627 Ron Oester .05 .02
❑ 628 Kirk McCaskill .10 .05
❑ 629 Mitch Webster .05 .02
❑ 630 Fernando Valenzuela .10 .05
❑ 631 Steve Braun .05 .02
❑ 632 Dave Von Ohlen .05 .02
❑ 633 Jackie Gutierrez .05 .02
❑ 634 Roy Lee Jackson .05 .02
❑ 635 Jason Thompson .05 .02
❑ 636 Lee Smith TL .10 .05
❑ 637 Rudy Law .05 .02
❑ 638 John Butcher .05 .02
❑ 639 Bo Diaz .05 .02
❑ 640 Jose Cruz .10 .05
❑ 641 Wayne Tolleson .05 .02
❑ 642 Ray Searage .05 .02
❑ 643 Tom Brookens .05 .02
❑ 644 Mark Gubicza .05 .02
❑ 645 Dusty Baker .10 .05
❑ 646 Mike Moore .05 .02
❑ 647 Mel Hall .05 .02
❑ 648 Steve Bedrosian .05 .02
❑ 649 Ronn Reynolds .05 .02
❑ 650 Dave Stieb .05 .02
❑ 651 Billy Martin MG .10 .05
❑ 652 Tom Browning .05 .02
❑ 653 Jim Dwyer .05 .02
❑ 654 Ken Howell .05 .02
❑ 655 Manny Trillo .05 .02
❑ 656 Brian Harper .05 .02
❑ 657 Juan Agosto .05 .02
❑ 658 Rob Wilfong .05 .02
❑ 659 Checklist: 529-660 .10 .05
❑ 660 Steve Garvey .20 .09
❑ 661 Roger Clemens 1.50 .70
❑ 662 Bill Schroeder .05 .02
❑ 663 Neil Allen .05 .02
❑ 664 Tim Corcoran .05 .02
❑ 665 Alejandro Pena .05 .02
❑ 666 Charlie Hough TL .10 .05
❑ 667 Tim Teufel .05 .02
❑ 668 Cecilio Guante .05 .02
❑ 669 Ron Cey .10 .05
❑ 670 Willie Hernandez .05 .02
❑ 671 Lynn Jones .05 .02
❑ 672 Rob Picciolo .05 .02
❑ 673 Ernie Whitt .05 .02
❑ 674 Pat Tabler .05 .02
❑ 675 Claudell Washington .05 .02
❑ 676 Matt Young .05 .02
❑ 677 Nick Esasky .05 .02
❑ 678 Dan Gladden .05 .02
❑ 679 Britt Burns .05 .02
❑ 680 George Foster .10 .05
❑ 681 Dick Williams MG .10 .05
❑ 682 Junior Ortiz .05 .02
❑ 683 Andy Van Slyke .10 .05
❑ 684 Bob McClure .05 .02
❑ 685 Tim Wallach .05 .02
❑ 686 Jeff Stone .05 .02
❑ 687 Mike Trujillo .05 .02
❑ 688 Larry Herndon .05 .02
❑ 689 Dave Stewart .10 .05
❑ 690 Ryne Sandberg UER .50 .23
(No Topps logo
on front)
❑ 691 Mike Madden .05 .02
❑ 692 Dale Berra .05 .02
❑ 693 Tom Tellmann .05 .02
❑ 694 Garth Iorg .05 .02
❑ 695 Mike Smithson .05 .02
❑ 696 Bill Russell TL .10 .05
❑ 697 Bud Black .05 .02
❑ 698 Brad Komminsk .05 .02
❑ 699 Pat Corrales MG .05 .02
❑ 700 Reggie Jackson .50 .23
❑ 701 Keith Hernandez AS .05 .02
❑ 702 Tom Herr AS .05 .02
❑ 703 Tim Wallach AS .05 .02
❑ 704 Ozzie Smith AS .20 .09
❑ 705 Dale Murphy AS .10 .05
❑ 706 Pedro Guerrero AS .05 .02
❑ 707 Willie McGee AS .05 .02
❑ 708 Gary Carter AS .10 .05
❑ 709 Dwight Gooden AS .10 .05
❑ 710 John Tudor AS .05 .02
❑ 711 Jeff Reardon AS .05 .02
❑ 712 Don Mattingly AS .40 .18
❑ 713 Damaso Garcia AS .05 .02
❑ 714 George Brett AS .40 .18
❑ 715 Cal Ripken AS .75 .35
❑ 716 Rickey Henderson AS .10 .05
❑ 717 Dave Winfield AS .10 .05
❑ 718 George Bell AS .05 .02
❑ 719 Carlton Fisk AS .10 .05
❑ 720 Bret Saberhagen AS .05 .02
❑ 721 Ron Guidry AS .10 .05
❑ 722 Dan Quisenberry AS .05 .02
❑ 723 Marty Bystrom .05 .02
❑ 724 Tim Hulett .05 .02
❑ 725 Mario Soto .05 .02
❑ 726 Rick Dempsey TL .10 .05
❑ 727 David Green .05 .02
❑ 728 Mike Marshall .05 .02
❑ 729 Jim Beattie .05 .02
❑ 730 Ozzie Smith .50 .23
❑ 731 Don Robinson .05 .02
❑ 732 Floyd Youmans .05 .02
❑ 733 Ron Romanick .05 .02
❑ 734 Marty Barrett .05 .02
❑ 735 Dave Dravecky .10 .05
❑ 736 Glenn Wilson .05 .02
❑ 737 Pete Vuckovich .05 .02
❑ 738 Andre Robertson .05 .02
❑ 739 Dave Rozema .05 .02
❑ 740 Lance Parrish .10 .05
❑ 741 Pete Rose MG .40 .18
❑ 742 Frank Viola .10 .05
❑ 743 Pat Sheridan .05 .02
❑ 744 Lary Sorensen .05 .02
❑ 745 Willie Upshaw .05 .02
❑ 746 Denny Gonzalez .05 .02
❑ 747 Rick Cerone .05 .02
❑ 748 Steve Henderson .05 .02
❑ 749 Ed Jurak .05 .02
❑ 750 Gorman Thomas .05 .02
❑ 751 Howard Johnson .10 .05
❑ 752 Mike Krukow .05 .02
❑ 753 Dan Ford .05 .02
❑ 754 Pat Clements .05 .02
❑ 755 Harold Baines .20 .09
❑ 756 Rick Rhoden TL .05 .02
❑ 757 Darrell Porter .10 .05
❑ 758 Dave Anderson .05 .02
❑ 759 Moose Haas .05 .02
❑ 760 Andre Dawson .40 .18
❑ 761 Don Slaught .05 .02
❑ 762 Eric Show .05 .02
❑ 763 Terry Puhl .05 .02
❑ 764 Kevin Gross .05 .02
❑ 765 Don Baylor .20 .09
❑ 766 Rick Langford .05 .02
❑ 767 Jody Davis .05 .02
❑ 768 Vern Ruhle .05 .02
❑ 769 Harold Reynolds .40 .18
❑ 770 Vida Blue .10 .05
❑ 771 John McNamara MG .05 .02
❑ 772 Brian Downing .05 .02
❑ 773 Greg Pryor .05 .02
❑ 774 Terry Leach .05 .02
❑ 775 Al Oliver .10 .05
❑ 776 Gene Garber .05 .02
❑ 777 Wayne Krenchicki .05 .02
❑ 778 Jerry Hairston .05 .02
❑ 779 Rick Reuschel .05 .02
❑ 780 Robin Yount .40 .18
❑ 781 Joe Nolan .05 .02
❑ 782 Ken Landreaux .05 .02
❑ 783 Ricky Horton .05 .02
❑ 784 Alan Bannister .05 .02
❑ 785 Bob Stanley .05 .02
❑ 786 Mickey Hatcher TL .05 .02
❑ 787 Vance Law .05 .02
❑ 788 Marty Castillo .05 .02
❑ 789 Kurt Bevacqua .05 .02
❑ 790 Phil Niekro .40 .18
❑ 791 Checklist: 661-792 .10 .05
❑ 792 Charles Hudson .05 .02

1986 Topps Tiffany

	MINT	NRMT
COMP.FACT.SET (792)	100.00	45.00
COMMON CARD (1-792)	.40	.18
*STARS: 6X TO 12X BASIC CARDS		
*ROOKIES: 6X TO 12X BASIC CARDS		

1986 Topps Traded

	MINT	NRMT
COMP.FACT.SET (132)	10.00	4.50
COMMON CARD (1T-132T)	.05	.02

Card	MINT	NRMT
❑ 1T Andy Allanson	.05	.02
❑ 2T Neil Allen	.05	.02
❑ 3T Joaquin Andujar	.05	.02
❑ 4T Paul Assenmacher	.05	.02
❑ 5T Scott Bailes	.05	.02
❑ 6T Don Baylor	.20	.09
❑ 7T Steve Bedrosian	.05	.02
❑ 8T Juan Beniquez	.05	.02
❑ 9T Juan Berenguer	.05	.02
❑ 10T Mike Bielecki	.05	.02
❑ 11T Barry Bonds	5.00	2.20
❑ 12T Bobby Bonilla	.60	.25
❑ 13T Juan Bonilla	.05	.02
❑ 14T Rich Bordi	.05	.02
❑ 15T Steve Boros MG	.05	.02
❑ 16T Rick Burleson	.05	.02
❑ 17T Bill Campbell	.05	.02
❑ 18T Tom Candiotti	.05	.02
❑ 19T John Cangelosi	.05	.02
❑ 20T Jose Canseco	3.00	1.35
❑ 21T Carmen Castillo	.05	.02
❑ 22T Rick Cerone	.05	.02
❑ 23T John Cerutti	.05	.02
❑ 24T Will Clark	1.50	.70
❑ 25T Mark Clear	.05	.02
❑ 26T Darnell Coles	.05	.02
❑ 27T Dave Collins	.05	.02
❑ 28T Tim Conroy	.05	.02
❑ 29T Joe Cowley	.05	.02
❑ 30T Joel Davis	.05	.02
❑ 31T Rob Deer	.05	.02
❑ 32T John Denny	.05	.02
❑ 33T Mike Easler	.05	.02
❑ 34T Mark Eichhorn	.05	.02
❑ 35T Steve Farr	.05	.02
❑ 36T Scott Fletcher	.05	.02
❑ 37T Terry Forster	.05	.02
❑ 38T Terry Francona	.05	.02
❑ 39T Jim Fregosi MG	.05	.02
❑ 40T Andres Galarraga	1.50	.70
❑ 41T Ken Griffey	.10	.05
❑ 42T Bill Gullickson	.05	.02
❑ 43T Jose Guzman	.05	.02
❑ 44T Moose Haas	.05	.02
❑ 45T Billy Hatcher	.05	.02
❑ 46T Mike Heath	.05	.02
❑ 47T Tom Hume	.05	.02
❑ 48T Pete Incaviglia	.40	.18
❑ 49T Dane Iorg	.05	.02
❑ 50T Bo Jackson	.75	.35
❑ 51T Wally Joyner	.40	.18
❑ 52T Charlie Kerfeld	.05	.02
❑ 53T Eric King	.05	.02
❑ 54T Bob Kipper	.05	.02
❑ 55T Wayne Krenchicki	.05	.02
❑ 56T John Kruk	.40	.18
❑ 57T Mike LaCoss	.05	.02
❑ 58T Pete Ladd	.05	.02
❑ 59T Mike Laga	.05	.02
❑ 60T Hal Lanier MG	.05	.02
❑ 61T Dave LaPoint	.05	.02
❑ 62T Rudy Law	.05	.02
❑ 63T Rick Leach	.05	.02
❑ 64T Tim Leary	.05	.02
❑ 65T Dennis Leonard	.05	.02
❑ 66T Jim Leyland MG	.05	.02
❑ 67T Steve Lyons	.05	.02
❑ 68T Mickey Mahler	.05	.02
❑ 69T Candy Maldonado	.05	.02
❑ 70T Roger Mason	.05	.02
❑ 71T Bob McClure	.05	.02
❑ 72T Andy McGaffigan	.05	.02
❑ 73T Gene Michael MG	.05	.02
❑ 74T Kevin Mitchell	.40	.18
❑ 75T Omar Moreno	.05	.02
❑ 76T Jerry Mumphrey	.05	.02
❑ 77T Phil Niekro	.40	.18
❑ 78T Randy Niemann	.05	.02
❑ 79T Juan Nieves	.05	.02
❑ 80T Otis Nixon	.40	.18
❑ 81T Bob Ojeda	.05	.02
❑ 82T Jose Oquendo	.05	.02
❑ 83T Tom Paciorek	.10	.05
❑ 84T David Palmer	.05	.02
❑ 85T Frank Pastore	.05	.02
❑ 86T Lou Piniella MG	.10	.05
❑ 87T Dan Plesac	.05	.02
❑ 88T Darrell Porter	.10	.05
❑ 89T Rey Quinones	.05	.02
❑ 90T Gary Redus	.05	.02
❑ 91T Bip Roberts	.40	.18
❑ 92T Billy Joe Robidoux	.05	.02
❑ 93T Jeff D. Robinson	.05	.02
❑ 94T Gary Roenicke	.05	.02
❑ 95T Ed Romero	.05	.02
❑ 96T Argenis Salazar	.05	.02
❑ 97T Joe Sambito	.05	.02
❑ 98T Billy Sample	.05	.02
❑ 99T Dave Schmidt	.05	.02
❑ 100T Ken Schrom	.05	.02
❑ 101T Tom Seaver	.50	.23
❑ 102T Ted Simmons	.10	.05
❑ 103T Sammy Stewart	.05	.02
❑ 104T Kurt Stillwell	.05	.02
❑ 105T Franklin Stubbs	.05	.02
❑ 106T Dale Sveum	.05	.02
❑ 107T Chuck Tanner MG	.05	.02
❑ 108T Danny Tartabull	.10	.05
❑ 109T Tim Teufel	.05	.02
❑ 110T Bob Tewksbury	.10	.05
❑ 111T Andres Thomas	.05	.02
❑ 112T Milt Thompson	.05	.02
❑ 113T Robby Thompson	.10	.05
❑ 114T Jay Tibbs	.05	.02
❑ 115T Wayne Tolleson	.05	.02
❑ 116T Alex Trevino	.05	.02
❑ 117T Manny Trillo	.05	.02
❑ 118T Ed VandeBerg	.05	.02
❑ 119T Ozzie Virgil	.05	.02
❑ 120T Bob Walk	.05	.02
❑ 121T Gene Walter	.05	.02
❑ 122T Claudell Washington	.05	.02
❑ 123T Bill Wegman	.05	.02
❑ 124T Dick Williams MG	.10	.05
❑ 125T Mitch Williams	.10	.05
❑ 126T Bobby Witt	.20	.09
❑ 127T Todd Worrell	.40	.18
❑ 128T George Wright	.05	.02
❑ 129T Ricky Wright	.05	.02
❑ 130T Steve Yeager	.05	.02
❑ 131T Paul Zuvella	.05	.02
❑ 132T Checklist 1T-132T	.05	.02

1986 Topps Traded Tiffany

	MINT	NRMT
COMP.FACT.SET (132)	150.00	70.00
COMMON CARD (1T-132T)	.40	.18

*STARS: 6X TO 12X BASIC CARDS
*ROOKIES: 6X TO 12X BASIC CARDS

1987 Topps

	MINT	NRMT
COMPLETE SET (792)	15.00	6.75
COMP.HOBBY SET (792)	25.00	11.00
COMP.X-MAS.SET (792)	25.00	11.00
COMMON CARD (1-792)	.05	.02

Card	MINT	NRMT
❑ 1 Roger Clemens RB	.20	.09
Most K's 9-inning game		
❑ 2 Jim Deshaies RB	.05	.02
Most cons. K's, start of game		
❑ 3 Dwight Evans RB	.10	.05
Earliest home run		
❑ 4 Davey Lopes RB	.05	.02
Most steals season, 40-year-old		
❑ 5 Dave Righetti RB	.05	.02
Most saves season		
❑ 6 Ruben Sierra RB	.05	.02
Youngest player to switch hit HR's, game		
❑ 7 Todd Worrell RB	.05	.02
Most saves rookie season		
❑ 8 Terry Pendleton	.10	.05
❑ 9 Jay Tibbs	.05	.02
❑ 10 Cecil Cooper	.10	.05
❑ 11 Indians Team	.05	.02
(Mound conference)		
❑ 12 Jeff Sellers	.05	.02
❑ 13 Nick Esasky	.05	.02
❑ 14 Dave Stewart	.10	.05
❑ 15 Claudell Washington	.05	.02
❑ 16 Pat Clements	.05	.02
❑ 17 Pete O'Brien	.05	.02
❑ 18 Dick Howser MG	.05	.02
❑ 19 Matt Young	.05	.02
❑ 20 Gary Carter	.15	.07
❑ 21 Mark Davis	.05	.02
❑ 22 Doug DeCinces	.05	.02
❑ 23 Lee Smith	.15	.07
❑ 24 Tony Walker	.05	.02
❑ 25 Bert Blyleven	.10	.05
❑ 26 Greg Brock	.05	.02
❑ 27 Joe Cowley	.05	.02
❑ 28 Rick Dempsey	.10	.05
❑ 29 Jimmy Key	.15	.07
❑ 30 Tim Raines	.10	.05
❑ 31 Braves Team	.05	.02
(Glenn Hubbard and Rafael Ramirez)		
❑ 32 Tim Leary	.05	.02
❑ 33 Andy Van Slyke	.10	.05
❑ 34 Jose Rijo	.05	.02
❑ 35 Sid Bream	.05	.02
❑ 36 Eric King	.05	.02
❑ 37 Marvell Wynne	.05	.02
❑ 38 Dennis Leonard	.05	.02
❑ 39 Marty Barrett	.05	.02
❑ 40 Dave Righetti	.05	.02
❑ 41 Bo Diaz	.05	.02
❑ 42 Gary Redus	.05	.02
❑ 43 Gene Michael MG	.05	.02
❑ 44 Greg Harris	.05	.02
❑ 45 Jim Presley	.05	.02
❑ 46 Dan Gladden	.05	.02
❑ 47 Dennis Powell	.05	.02
❑ 48 Wally Backman	.05	.02
❑ 49 Terry Harper	.05	.02
❑ 50 Dave Smith	.05	.02
❑ 51 Mel Hall	.05	.02
❑ 52 Keith Atherton	.05	.02
❑ 53 Ruppert Jones	.05	.02
❑ 54 Bill Dawley	.05	.02
❑ 55 Tim Wallach	.05	.02
❑ 56 Brewers Team	.05	.02
(Mound conference)		
❑ 57 Scott Nielsen	.05	.02
❑ 58 Thad Bosley	.05	.02
❑ 59 Ken Dayley	.05	.02
❑ 60 Tony Pena	.05	.02
❑ 61 Bobby Thigpen	.10	.05
❑ 62 Bobby Meacham	.05	.02
❑ 63 Fred Toliver	.05	.02
❑ 64 Harry Spilman	.05	.02
❑ 65 Tom Browning	.05	.02
❑ 66 Marc Sullivan	.05	.02
❑ 67 Bill Swift	.05	.02
❑ 68 Tony LaRussa MG	.10	.05
❑ 69 Lonnie Smith	.05	.02
❑ 70 Charlie Hough	.05	.02

❑ 71 Mike Aldrete .10 .05
❑ 72 Walt Terrell .05 .02
❑ 73 Dave Anderson .05 .02
❑ 74 Dan Pasqua .05 .02
❑ 75 Ron Darling .05 .02
❑ 76 Rafael Ramirez .05 .02
❑ 77 Bryan Oelkers .05 .02
❑ 78 Tom Foley .05 .02
❑ 79 Juan Nieves .05 .02
❑ 80 Wally Joyner .20 .09
❑ 81 Padres Team .05 .02
(Andy Hawkins and
Terry Kennedy)
❑ 82 Rob Murphy .05 .02
❑ 83 Mike Davis .05 .02
❑ 84 Steve Lake .05 .02
❑ 85 Kevin Bass .05 .02
❑ 86 Nate Snell .05 .02
❑ 87 Mark Salas .05 .02
❑ 88 Ed Wojna .05 .02
❑ 89 Ozzie Guillen .10 .05
❑ 90 Dave Stieb .05 .02
❑ 91 Harold Reynolds .10 .05
❑ 92A Urbano Lugo .20 .09
ERR (no trademark)
❑ 92B Urbano Lugo COR .05 .02
❑ 93 Jim Leyland MG .10 .05
❑ 94 Calvin Schiraldi .05 .02
❑ 95 Oddibe McDowell .05 .02
❑ 96 Frank Williams .05 .02
❑ 97 Glenn Wilson .05 .02
❑ 98 Bill Scherrer .05 .02
❑ 99 Darryl Motley .05 .02
(Now with Braves
on card front)
❑ 100 Steve Garvey .15 .07
❑ 101 Carl Willis .05 .02
❑ 102 Paul Zuvella .05 .02
❑ 103 Rick Aguilera .10 .05
❑ 104 Billy Sample .05 .02
❑ 105 Floyd Youmans .05 .02
❑ 106 Blue Jays Team .05 .02
(George Bell and
Jesse Barfield)
❑ 107 John Butcher .05 .02
❑ 108 Jim Gantner UER .05 .02
(Brewers logo
reversed)
❑ 109 R.J. Reynolds .05 .02
❑ 110 John Tudor .05 .02
❑ 111 Alfredo Griffin .05 .02
❑ 112 Alan Ashby .05 .02
❑ 113 Neil Allen .05 .02
❑ 114 Billy Beane .05 .02
❑ 115 Donnie Moore .05 .02
❑ 116 Bill Russell .05 .02
❑ 117 Jim Beattie .05 .02
❑ 118 Bobby Valentine MG .05 .02
❑ 119 Ron Robinson .05 .02
❑ 120 Eddie Murray .20 .09
❑ 121 Kevin Romine .05 .02
❑ 122 Jim Clancy .05 .02
❑ 123 John Kruk .20 .09
❑ 124 Ray Fontenot .05 .02
❑ 125 Bob Brenly .05 .02
❑ 126 Mike Loynd .05 .02
❑ 127 Vance Law .05 .02
❑ 128 Checklist 1-132 .05 .02
❑ 129 Rick Cerone .05 .02
❑ 130 Dwight Gooden .15 .07
❑ 131 Pirates Team .05 .02
(Sid Bream and
Tony Pena)
❑ 132 Paul Assenmacher .15 .07
❑ 133 Jose Oquendo .05 .02
❑ 134 Rich Yett .05 .02
❑ 135 Mike Easler .05 .02
❑ 136 Ron Romanick .05 .02
❑ 137 Jerry Willard .05 .02
❑ 138 Roy Lee Jackson .05 .02
❑ 139 Devon White .25 .11
❑ 140 Bret Saberhagen .10 .05
❑ 141 Herm Winningham .05 .02
❑ 142 Rick Sutcliffe .05 .02
❑ 143 Steve Boros MG .05 .02

❑ 144 Mike Scioscia .05 .02
❑ 145 Charlie Kerfeld .05 .02
❑ 146 Tracy Jones .05 .02
❑ 147 Randy Niemann .05 .02
❑ 148 Dave Collins .05 .02
❑ 149 Ray Searage .05 .02
❑ 150 Wade Boggs .20 .09
❑ 151 Mike LaCoss .05 .02
❑ 152 Toby Harrah .05 .02
❑ 153 Duane Ward .10 .05
❑ 154 Tom O'Malley .05 .02
❑ 155 Eddie Whitson .05 .02
❑ 156 Mariners Team .05 .02
(Mound conference)
❑ 157 Danny Darwin .05 .02
❑ 158 Tim Teufel .05 .02
❑ 159 Ed Olwine .05 .02
❑ 160 Julio Franco .10 .05
❑ 161 Steve Ontiveros .05 .02
❑ 162 Mike LaValliere .05 .02
❑ 163 Kevin Gross .05 .02
❑ 164 Sammy Khalifa .05 .02
❑ 165 Jeff Reardon .10 .05
❑ 166 Bob Boone .10 .05
❑ 167 Jim Deshaies .05 .02
❑ 168 Lou Piniella MG .10 .05
❑ 169 Ron Washington .05 .02
❑ 170 Bo Jackson .30 .14
❑ 171 Chuck Cary .05 .02
❑ 172 Ron Oester .05 .02
❑ 173 Alex Trevino .05 .02
❑ 174 Henry Cotto .05 .02
❑ 175 Bob Stanley .05 .02
❑ 176 Steve Buechele .05 .02
❑ 177 Keith Moreland .05 .02
❑ 178 Cecil Fielder .15 .07
❑ 179 Bill Wegman .05 .02
❑ 180 Chris Brown .05 .02
❑ 181 Cardinals Team .05 .02
(Mound conference)
❑ 182 Lee Lacy .05 .02
❑ 183 Andy Hawkins .05 .02
❑ 184 Bobby Bonilla .25 .11
❑ 185 Roger McDowell .05 .02
❑ 186 Bruce Benedict .05 .02
❑ 187 Mark Huismann .05 .02
❑ 188 Tony Phillips .05 .02
❑ 189 Joe Hesketh .05 .02
❑ 190 Jim Sundberg .05 .02
❑ 191 Charles Hudson .05 .02
❑ 192 Cory Snyder .05 .02
❑ 193 Roger Craig MG .05 .02
❑ 194 Kirk McCaskill .05 .02
❑ 195 Mike Pagliarulo .05 .02
❑ 196 Randy O'Neal UER .05 .02
(Wrong ML career
W-L totals)
❑ 197 Mark Bailey .05 .02
❑ 198 Lee Mazzilli .05 .02
❑ 199 Mariano Duncan .05 .02
❑ 200 Pete Rose .25 .11
❑ 201 John Cangelosi .05 .02
❑ 202 Ricky Wright .05 .02
❑ 203 Mike Kingery .05 .02
❑ 204 Sammy Stewart .05 .02
❑ 205 Graig Nettles .10 .05
❑ 206 Twins Team .05 .02
(Frank Viola and
Tim Laudner)
❑ 207 George Frazier .05 .02
❑ 208 John Shelby .05 .02
❑ 209 Rick Schu .05 .02
❑ 210 Lloyd Moseby .05 .02
❑ 211 John Morris .05 .02
❑ 212 Mike Fitzgerald .05 .02
❑ 213 Randy Myers .20 .09
❑ 214 Omar Moreno .05 .02
❑ 215 Mark Langston .05 .02
❑ 216 B.J. Surhoff .20 .09
❑ 217 Chris Codiroli .05 .02
❑ 218 Sparky Anderson MG .10 .05
❑ 219 Cecilio Guante .05 .02
❑ 220 Joe Carter .20 .09
❑ 221 Vern Ruhle .05 .02
❑ 222 Denny Walling .05 .02

❑ 223 Charlie Leibrandt .05 .02
❑ 224 Wayne Tolleson .05 .02
❑ 225 Mike Smithson .05 .02
❑ 226 Max Venable .05 .02
❑ 227 Jamie Moyer .15 .07
❑ 228 Curt Wilkerson .05 .02
❑ 229 Mike Birkbeck .05 .02
❑ 230 Don Baylor .10 .05
❑ 231 Giants Team .05 .02
(Bob Brenly and
Jim Gott)
❑ 232 Reggie Williams .05 .02
❑ 233 Russ Morman .05 .02
❑ 234 Pat Sheridan .05 .02
❑ 235 Alvin Davis .05 .02
❑ 236 Tommy John .10 .05
❑ 237 Jim Morrison .05 .02
❑ 238 Bill Krueger .05 .02
❑ 239 Juan Espino .05 .02
❑ 240 Steve Balboni .05 .02
❑ 241 Danny Heep .05 .02
❑ 242 Rick Mahler .05 .02
❑ 243 Whitey Herzog MG .10 .05
❑ 244 Dickie Noles .05 .02
❑ 245 Willie Upshaw .05 .02
❑ 246 Jim Dwyer .05 .02
❑ 247 Jeff Reed .05 .02
❑ 248 Gene Walter .05 .02
❑ 249 Jim Pankovits .05 .02
❑ 250 Teddy Higuera .05 .02
❑ 251 Rob Wilfong .05 .02
❑ 252 Dennis Martinez .10 .05
❑ 253 Eddie Milner .05 .02
❑ 254 Bob Tewksbury .10 .05
❑ 255 Juan Samuel .05 .02
❑ 256 Royals Team .15 .07
(George Brett and
Frank White)
❑ 257 Bob Forsch .05 .02
❑ 258 Steve Yeager .05 .02
❑ 259 Mike Greenwell .20 .09
❑ 260 Vida Blue .10 .05
❑ 261 Ruben Sierra .10 .05
❑ 262 Jim Winn .05 .02
❑ 263 Stan Javier .05 .02
❑ 264 Checklist 133-264 .05 .02
❑ 265 Darrell Evans .10 .05
❑ 266 Jeff Hamilton .05 .02
❑ 267 Howard Johnson .05 .02
❑ 268 Pat Corrales MG .10 .05
❑ 269 Cliff Speck .05 .02
❑ 270 Jody Davis .05 .02
❑ 271 Mike G. Brown .05 .02
❑ 272 Andres Galarraga .25 .11
❑ 273 Gene Nelson .05 .02
❑ 274 Jeff Hearron UER .05 .02
(Duplicate 1986
stat line on back)
❑ 275 LaMarr Hoyt .05 .02
❑ 276 Jackie Gutierrez .05 .02
❑ 277 Juan Agosto .05 .02
❑ 278 Gary Pettis .05 .02
❑ 279 Dan Plesac .05 .02
❑ 280 Jeff Leonard .05 .02
❑ 281 Reds Team .20 .09
(Pete Rose, Bo Diaz,
and Bill Gullickson)
❑ 282 Jeff Calhoun .05 .02
❑ 283 Doug Drabek .20 .09
❑ 284 John Moses .05 .02
❑ 285 Dennis Boyd .05 .02
❑ 286 Mike Woodard .05 .02
❑ 287 Dave Von Ohlen .05 .02
❑ 288 Tito Landrum .05 .02
❑ 289 Bob Kipper .05 .02
❑ 290 Leon Durham .05 .02
❑ 291 Mitch Williams .10 .05
❑ 292 Franklin Stubbs .05 .02
❑ 293 Bob Rodgers MG .05 .02
❑ 294 Steve Jeltz .05 .02
❑ 295 Len Dykstra .15 .07
❑ 296 Andres Thomas .05 .02
❑ 297 Don Schulze .05 .02
❑ 298 Larry Herndon .05 .02
❑ 299 Joel Davis .05 .02

❑ 300 Reggie Jackson .25 .11
❑ 301 Luis Aquino UER .05 .02
(No trademark
never corrected)
❑ 302 Bill Schroeder .05 .02
❑ 303 Juan Berenguer .05 .02
❑ 304 Phil Garner .05 .02
❑ 305 John Franco .10 .05
❑ 306 Red Sox Team .10 .05
(Tom Seaver,
John McNamara MG,
and Rich Gedman)
❑ 307 Lee Guetterman .05 .02
❑ 308 Don Slaught .05 .02
❑ 309 Mike Young .05 .02
❑ 310 Frank Viola .05 .02
❑ 311 Rickey Henderson .10 .05
TBC '82
❑ 312 Reggie Jackson .20 .09
TBC '77
❑ 313 Roberto Clemente .25 .11
TBC '72
❑ 314 Carl Yastrzemski UER .. .20 .09
TBC '67 (Sic, 112
RBI's on back)
❑ 315 Maury Wills TBC '62 .10 .05
❑ 316 Brian Fisher .05 .02
❑ 317 Clint Hurdle .05 .02
❑ 318 Jim Fregosi MG .05 .02
❑ 319 Greg Swindell .20 .09
❑ 320 Barry Bonds 2.00 .90
❑ 321 Mike Laga .05 .02
❑ 322 Chris Bando .05 .02
❑ 323 Al Newman .05 .02
❑ 324 David Palmer .05 .02
❑ 325 Garry Templeton .05 .02
❑ 326 Mark Gubicza .05 .02
❑ 327 Dale Sveum .05 .02
❑ 328 Bob Welch .05 .02
❑ 329 Ron Roenicke .05 .02
❑ 330 Mike Scott .05 .02
❑ 331 Mets Team .10 .05
(Gary Carter and
Darryl Strawberry)
❑ 332 Joe Price .05 .02
❑ 333 Ken Phelps .05 .02
❑ 334 Ed Correa .05 .02
❑ 335 Candy Maldonado .05 .02
❑ 336 Allan Anderson .05 .02
❑ 337 Darrell Miller .05 .02
❑ 338 Tim Conroy .05 .02
❑ 339 Donnie Hill .05 .02
❑ 340 Roger Clemens .50 .23
❑ 341 Mike C. Brown .05 .02
❑ 342 Bob James .05 .02
❑ 343 Hal Lanier MG .05 .02
❑ 344A Joe Niekro .05 .02
(Copyright inside
righthand border)
❑ 344B Joe Niekro .05 .02
(Copyright outside
righthand border)
❑ 345 Andre Dawson .20 .09
❑ 346 Shawon Dunston .05 .02
❑ 347 Mickey Brantley .05 .02
❑ 348 Carmelo Martinez .05 .02
❑ 349 Storm Davis .05 .02
❑ 350 Keith Hernandez .10 .05
❑ 351 Gene Garber .05 .02
❑ 352 Mike Felder .05 .02
❑ 353 Ernie Camacho .05 .02
❑ 354 Jamie Quirk .05 .02
❑ 355 Don Carman .05 .02
❑ 356 White Sox Team .05 .02
(Mound conference)
❑ 357 Steve Fireovid .05 .02
❑ 358 Sal Butera .05 .02
❑ 359 Doug Corbett .05 .02
❑ 360 Pedro Guerrero .05 .02
❑ 361 Mark Thurmond .05 .02
❑ 362 Luis Quinones .05 .02
❑ 363 Jose Guzman .05 .02
❑ 364 Randy Bush .05 .02
❑ 365 Rick Rhoden .05 .02
❑ 366 Mark McGwire 5.00 2.20

❑ 367 Jeff Lahti .05 .02
❑ 368 John McNamara MG .05 .02
❑ 369 Brian Dayett .05 .02
❑ 370 Fred Lynn .10 .05
❑ 371 Mark Eichhorn .05 .02
❑ 372 Jerry Mumphrey .05 .02
❑ 373 Jeff Dedmon .05 .02
❑ 374 Glenn Hoffman .05 .02
❑ 375 Ron Guidry .10 .05
❑ 376 Scott Bradley .05 .02
❑ 377 John Henry Johnson .05 .02
❑ 378 Rafael Santana .05 .02
❑ 379 John Russell .05 .02
❑ 380 Rich Gossage .10 .05
❑ 381 Expos Team .05 .02
(Mound conference)
❑ 382 Rudy Law .05 .02
❑ 383 Ron Davis .05 .02
❑ 384 Johnny Grubb .05 .02
❑ 385 Orel Hershiser .10 .05
❑ 386 Dickie Thon .05 .02
❑ 387 T.R. Bryden .05 .02
❑ 388 Geno Petralli .05 .02
❑ 389 Jeff D. Robinson .05 .02
❑ 390 Gary Matthews .05 .02
❑ 391 Jay Howell .05 .02
❑ 392 Checklist 265-396 .05 .02
❑ 393 Pete Rose MG .15 .07
❑ 394 Mike Bielecki .05 .02
❑ 395 Damaso Garcia .05 .02
❑ 396 Tim Lollar .05 .02
❑ 397 Greg Walker .05 .02
❑ 398 Brad Havens .05 .02
❑ 399 Curt Ford .05 .02
❑ 400 George Brett .40 .18
❑ 401 Billy Joe Robidoux .05 .02
❑ 402 Mike Trujillo .05 .02
❑ 403 Jerry Royster .05 .02
❑ 404 Doug Sisk .05 .02
❑ 405 Brook Jacoby .05 .02
❑ 406 Yankees Team .20 .09
(Rickey Henderson and
Don Mattingly)
❑ 407 Jim Acker .05 .02
❑ 408 John Mizerock .05 .02
❑ 409 Milt Thompson .05 .02
❑ 410 Fernando Valenzuela .10 .05
❑ 411 Darnell Coles .05 .02
❑ 412 Eric Davis .15 .07
❑ 413 Moose Haas .05 .02
❑ 414 Joe Orsulak .05 .02
❑ 415 Bobby Witt .10 .05
❑ 416 Tom Nieto .05 .02
❑ 417 Pat Perry .05 .02
❑ 418 Dick Williams MG .10 .05
❑ 419 Mark Portugal .10 .05
❑ 420 Will Clark .75 .35
❑ 421 Jose DeLeon .05 .02
❑ 422 Jack Howell .05 .02
❑ 423 Jaime Cocanower .05 .02
❑ 424 Chris Speier .05 .02
❑ 425 Tom Seaver UER .20 .09
Earned Runs amount is wrong
For 86 Red Sox and Career
Also the ERA is wrong for 86 and
career
❑ 426 Floyd Rayford .05 .02
❑ 427 Edwin Nunez .05 .02
❑ 428 Bruce Bochy .05 .02
❑ 429 Tim Pyznarski .05 .02
❑ 430 Mike Schmidt .25 .11
❑ 431 Dodgers Team .05 .02
(Mound conference)
❑ 432 Jim Slaton .05 .02
❑ 433 Ed Hearn .05 .02
❑ 434 Mike Fischlin .05 .02
❑ 435 Bruce Sutter .05 .02
❑ 436 Andy Allanson .05 .02
❑ 437 Ted Power .05 .02
❑ 438 Kelly Downs .05 .02
❑ 439 Karl Best .05 .02
❑ 440 Willie McGee .10 .05
❑ 441 Dave Leiper .05 .02
❑ 442 Mitch Webster .05 .02
❑ 443 John Felske MG .05 .02

❑ 444 Jeff Russell .05 .02
❑ 445 Dave Lopes .10 .05
❑ 446 Chuck Finley .20 .09
❑ 447 Bill Almon .05 .02
❑ 448 Chris Bosio .10 .05
❑ 449 Pat Dodson .05 .02
❑ 450 Kirby Puckett .40 .18
❑ 451 Joe Sambito .05 .02
❑ 452 Dave Henderson .05 .02
❑ 453 Scott Terry .05 .02
❑ 454 Luis Salazar .05 .02
❑ 455 Mike Boddicker .05 .02
❑ 456 A's Team .05 .02
(Mound conference)
❑ 457 Len Matuszek .05 .02
❑ 458 Kelly Gruber .05 .02
❑ 459 Dennis Eckersley .20 .09
❑ 460 Darryl Strawberry .15 .07
❑ 461 Craig McMurtry .05 .02
❑ 462 Scott Fletcher .05 .02
❑ 463 Tom Candiotti .05 .02
❑ 464 Butch Wynegar .05 .02
❑ 465 Todd Worrell .10 .05
❑ 466 Kal Daniels .05 .02
❑ 467 Randy St.Claire .05 .02
❑ 468 George Bamberger MG .. .05 .02
❑ 469 Mike Diaz .05 .02
❑ 470 Dave Dravecky .10 .05
❑ 471 Ronn Reynolds .05 .02
❑ 472 Bill Doran .05 .02
❑ 473 Steve Farr .05 .02
❑ 474 Jerry Narron .05 .02
❑ 475 Scott Garrelts .05 .02
❑ 476 Danny Tartabull .05 .02
❑ 477 Ken Howell .05 .02
❑ 478 Tim Laudner .05 .02
❑ 479 Bob Sebra .05 .02
❑ 480 Jim Rice .10 .05
❑ 481 Phillies Team .05 .02
(Glenn Wilson
Juan Samuel and
Von Hayes)
❑ 482 Daryl Boston .05 .02
❑ 483 Dwight Lowry .05 .02
❑ 484 Jim Traber .05 .02
❑ 485 Tony Fernandez .05 .02
❑ 486 Otis Nixon .15 .07
❑ 487 Dave Gumpert .05 .02
❑ 488 Ray Knight .05 .02
❑ 489 Bill Gullickson .05 .02
❑ 490 Dale Murphy .20 .09
❑ 491 Ron Karkovice .10 .05
❑ 492 Mike Heath .05 .02
❑ 493 Tom Lasorda MG .10 .05
❑ 494 Barry Jones .05 .02
❑ 495 Gorman Thomas .05 .02
❑ 496 Bruce Bochte .05 .02
❑ 497 Dale Mohorcic .05 .02
❑ 498 Bob Kearney .05 .02
❑ 499 Bruce Ruffin .05 .02
❑ 500 Don Mattingly .30 .14
❑ 501 Craig Lefferts .05 .02
❑ 502 Dick Schofield .05 .02
❑ 503 Larry Andersen .05 .02
❑ 504 Mickey Hatcher .05 .02
❑ 505 Bryn Smith .05 .02
❑ 506 Orioles Team .05 .02
(Mound conference)
❑ 507 Dave L. Stapleton .05 .02
❑ 508 Scott Bankhead .05 .02
❑ 509 Enos Cabell .05 .02
❑ 510 Tom Henke .05 .02
❑ 511 Steve Lyons .05 .02
❑ 512 Dave Magadan .10 .05
❑ 513 Carmen Castillo .05 .02
❑ 514 Orlando Mercado .05 .02
❑ 515 Willie Hernandez .05 .02
❑ 516 Ted Simmons .10 .05
❑ 517 Mario Soto .05 .02
❑ 518 Gene Mauch MG .10 .05
❑ 519 Curt Young .05 .02
❑ 520 Jack Clark .10 .05
❑ 521 Rick Reuschel .05 .02
❑ 522 Checklist 397-528 .05 .02
❑ 523 Earnie Riles .05 .02

❑ 524 Bob Shirley .05 .02
❑ 525 Phil Bradley .05 .02
❑ 526 Roger Mason .05 .02
❑ 527 Jim Wohlford .05 .02
❑ 528 Ken Dixon .05 .02
❑ 529 Alvaro Espinoza .05 .02
❑ 530 Tony Gwynn .50 .23
❑ 531 Astros Team .10 .05
(Yogi Berra conference)
❑ 532 Jeff Stone .05 .02
❑ 533 Argenis Salazar .05 .02
❑ 534 Scott Sanderson .05 .02
❑ 535 Tony Armas .05 .02
❑ 536 Terry Mulholland .10 .05
❑ 537 Rance Mulliniks .05 .02
❑ 538 Tom Niedenfuer .05 .02
❑ 539 Reid Nichols .05 .02
❑ 540 Terry Kennedy .05 .02
❑ 541 Rafael Belliard .05 .02
❑ 542 Ricky Horton .05 .02
❑ 543 Dave Johnson MG .10 .05
❑ 544 Zane Smith .05 .02
❑ 545 Buddy Bell .10 .05
❑ 546 Mike Morgan .05 .02
❑ 547 Rob Deer .05 .02
❑ 548 Bill Mooneyham .05 .02
❑ 549 Bob Melvin .05 .02
❑ 550 Pete Incaviglia .10 .05
❑ 551 Frank Wills .05 .02
❑ 552 Larry Sheets .05 .02
❑ 553 Mike Maddux .05 .02
❑ 554 Buddy Biancalana .05 .02
❑ 555 Dennis Rasmussen .05 .02
❑ 556 Angels Team .05 .02
(Rene Lachemann CO, Mike Witt, and Bob Boone)
❑ 557 John Cerutti .05 .02
❑ 558 Greg Gagne .05 .02
❑ 559 Lance McCullers .05 .02
❑ 560 Glenn Davis .05 .02
❑ 561 Rey Quinones .05 .02
❑ 562 Bryan Clutterbuck .05 .02
❑ 563 John Stefero .05 .02
❑ 564 Larry McWilliams .05 .02
❑ 565 Dusty Baker .10 .05
❑ 566 Tim Hulett .05 .02
❑ 567 Greg Mathews .05 .02
❑ 568 Earl Weaver MG .20 .09
❑ 569 Wade Rowdon .05 .02
❑ 570 Sid Fernandez .05 .02
❑ 571 Ozzie Virgil .05 .02
❑ 572 Pete Ladd .05 .02
❑ 573 Hal McRae .10 .05
❑ 574 Manny Lee .05 .02
❑ 575 Pat Tabler .05 .02
❑ 576 Frank Pastore .05 .02
❑ 577 Dann Bilardello .05 .02
❑ 578 Billy Hatcher .05 .02
❑ 579 Rick Burleson .05 .02
❑ 580 Mike Krukow .05 .02
❑ 581 Cubs Team .05 .02
(Ron Cey and Steve Trout)
❑ 582 Bruce Berenyi .05 .02
❑ 583 Junior Ortiz .05 .02
❑ 584 Ron Kittle .05 .02
❑ 585 Scott Bailes .05 .02
❑ 586 Ben Oglivie .05 .02
❑ 587 Eric Plunk .05 .02
❑ 588 Wallace Johnson .05 .02
❑ 589 Steve Crawford .05 .02
❑ 590 Vince Coleman .05 .02
❑ 591 Spike Owen .05 .02
❑ 592 Chris Welsh .05 .02
❑ 593 Chuck Tanner MG .05 .02
❑ 594 Rick Anderson .05 .02
❑ 595 Keith Hernandez AS .05 .02
❑ 596 Steve Sax AS .05 .02
❑ 597 Mike Schmidt AS .15 .07
❑ 598 Ozzie Smith AS .15 .07
❑ 599 Tony Gwynn AS .20 .09
❑ 600 Dave Parker AS .05 .02
❑ 601 Darryl Strawberry AS .10 .05
❑ 602 Gary Carter AS .10 .05
❑ 603A Dwight Gooden AS .15 .07
ERR (no trademark)
❑ 603B Dwight Gooden AS COR .15 .07
❑ 604 Fernando Valenzuela AS .10 .05
❑ 605 Todd Worrell AS .10 .05
❑ 606 Don Mattingly AS COR .20 .09
❑ 606A Don Mattingly AS .75 .35
ERR (no trademark)
❑ 607 Tony Bernazard AS .05 .02
❑ 608 Wade Boggs AS .10 .05
❑ 609 Cal Ripken AS .40 .18
❑ 610 Jim Rice AS .05 .02
❑ 611 Kirby Puckett AS .20 .09
❑ 612 George Bell AS .05 .02
❑ 613 Lance Parrish AS UER .10 .05
(Pitcher heading on back)
❑ 614 Roger Clemens AS .20 .09
❑ 615 Teddy Higuera AS .05 .02
❑ 616 Dave Righetti AS .05 .02
❑ 617 Al Nipper .05 .02
❑ 618 Tom Kelly MG .05 .02
❑ 619 Jerry Reed .05 .02
❑ 620 Jose Canseco .40 .18
❑ 621 Danny Cox .05 .02
❑ 622 Glenn Braggs .05 .02
❑ 623 Kurt Stillwell .05 .02
❑ 624 Tim Burke .05 .02
❑ 625 Mookie Wilson .10 .05
❑ 626 Joel Skinner .05 .02
❑ 627 Ken Oberkfell .05 .02
❑ 628 Bob Walk .05 .02
❑ 629 Larry Parrish .05 .02
❑ 630 John Candelaria .05 .02
❑ 631 Tigers Team .05 .02
(Mound conference)
❑ 632 Rob Woodward .05 .02
❑ 633 Jose Uribe .05 .02
❑ 634 Rafael Palmeiro .60 .25
❑ 635 Ken Schrom .05 .02
❑ 636 Darren Daulton .15 .07
❑ 637 Bip Roberts .20 .09
❑ 638 Rich Bordi .05 .02
❑ 639 Gerald Perry .05 .02
❑ 640 Mark Clear .05 .02
❑ 641 Domingo Ramos .05 .02
❑ 642 Al Pulido .05 .02
❑ 643 Ron Shepherd .05 .02
❑ 644 John Denny .05 .02
❑ 645 Dwight Evans .10 .05
❑ 646 Mike Mason .05 .02
❑ 647 Tom Lawless .05 .02
❑ 648 Barry Larkin .50 .23
❑ 649 Mickey Tettleton .10 .05
❑ 650 Hubie Brooks .05 .02
❑ 651 Benny Distefano .05 .02
❑ 652 Terry Forster .05 .02
❑ 653 Kevin Mitchell .15 .07
❑ 654 Checklist 529-660 .10 .05
❑ 655 Jesse Barfield .05 .02
❑ 656 Rangers Team .05 .02
(Bobby Valentine MG and Ricky Wright)
❑ 657 Tom Waddell .05 .02
❑ 658 Robby Thompson .10 .05
❑ 659 Aurelio Lopez .05 .02
❑ 660 Bob Horner .05 .02
❑ 661 Lou Whitaker .10 .05
❑ 662 Frank DiPino .05 .02
❑ 663 Cliff Johnson .05 .02
❑ 664 Mike Marshall .05 .02
❑ 665 Rod Scurry .05 .02
❑ 666 Von Hayes .05 .02
❑ 667 Ron Hassey .05 .02
❑ 668 Juan Bonilla .05 .02
❑ 669 Bud Black .05 .02
❑ 670 Jose Cruz .10 .05
❑ 671A Ray Soff ERR .05 .02
(No D* before copyright line)
❑ 671B Ray Soff COR .05 .02
(D* before copyright line)
❑ 672 Chili Davis .15 .07
❑ 673 Don Sutton .20 .09
❑ 674 Bill Campbell .05 .02
❑ 675 Ed Romero .05 .02
❑ 676 Charlie Moore .05 .02
❑ 677 Bob Grich .10 .05
❑ 678 Carney Lansford .10 .05
❑ 679 Kent Hrbek .10 .05
❑ 680 Ryne Sandberg .25 .11
❑ 681 George Bell .05 .02
❑ 682 Jerry Reuss .05 .02
❑ 683 Gary Roenicke .05 .02
❑ 684 Kent Tekulve .05 .02
❑ 685 Jerry Hairston .05 .02
❑ 686 Doyle Alexander .05 .02
❑ 687 Alan Trammell .15 .07
❑ 688 Juan Beniquez .05 .02
❑ 689 Darrell Porter .05 .02
❑ 690 Dane Iorg .05 .02
❑ 691 Dave Parker .10 .05
❑ 692 Frank White .10 .05
❑ 693 Terry Puhl .05 .02
❑ 694 Phil Niekro .20 .09
❑ 695 Chico Walker .05 .02
❑ 696 Gary Lucas .05 .02
❑ 697 Ed Lynch .05 .02
❑ 698 Ernie Whitt .05 .02
❑ 699 Ken Landreaux .05 .02
❑ 700 Dave Bergman .05 .02
❑ 701 Willie Randolph .10 .05
❑ 702 Greg Gross .05 .02
❑ 703 Dave Schmidt .05 .02
❑ 704 Jesse Orosco .05 .02
❑ 705 Bruce Hurst .05 .02
❑ 706 Rick Manning .05 .02
❑ 707 Bob McClure .05 .02
❑ 708 Scott McGregor .05 .02
❑ 709 Dave Kingman .10 .05
❑ 710 Gary Gaetti .10 .05
❑ 711 Ken Griffey .10 .05
❑ 712 Don Robinson .05 .02
❑ 713 Tom Brookens .05 .02
❑ 714 Dan Quisenberry .05 .02
❑ 715 Bob Dernier .05 .02
❑ 716 Rick Leach .05 .02
❑ 717 Ed VandeBerg .05 .02
❑ 718 Steve Carlton .20 .09
❑ 719 Tom Hume .05 .02
❑ 720 Richard Dotson .05 .02
❑ 721 Tom Herr .05 .02
❑ 722 Bob Knepper .05 .02
❑ 723 Brett Butler .10 .05
❑ 724 Greg Minton .05 .02
❑ 725 George Hendrick .05 .02
❑ 726 Frank Tanana .05 .02
❑ 727 Mike Moore .05 .02
❑ 728 Tippy Martinez .05 .02
❑ 729 Tom Paciorek .10 .05
❑ 730 Eric Show .05 .02
❑ 731 Dave Concepcion .10 .05
❑ 732 Manny Trillo .05 .02
❑ 733 Bill Caudill .05 .02
❑ 734 Bill Madlock .10 .05
❑ 735 Rickey Henderson .20 .09
❑ 736 Steve Bedrosian .05 .02
❑ 737 Floyd Bannister .05 .02
❑ 738 Jorge Orta .05 .02
❑ 739 Chet Lemon .05 .02
❑ 740 Rich Gedman .05 .02
❑ 741 Paul Molitor .20 .09
❑ 742 Andy McGaffigan .05 .02
❑ 743 Dwayne Murphy .05 .02
❑ 744 Roy Smalley .05 .02
❑ 745 Glenn Hubbard .05 .02
❑ 746 Bob Ojeda .05 .02
❑ 747 Johnny Ray .05 .02
❑ 748 Mike Flanagan .05 .02
❑ 749 Ozzie Smith .25 .11
❑ 750 Steve Trout .05 .02
❑ 751 Garth Iorg .05 .02
❑ 752 Dan Petry .05 .02
❑ 753 Rick Honeycutt .05 .02
❑ 754 Dave LaPoint .05 .02
❑ 755 Luis Aguayo .05 .02
❑ 756 Carlton Fisk .20 .09
❑ 757 Nolan Ryan .75 .35

❑ 758 Tony Bernazard .05 .02
❑ 759 Joel Youngblood .05 .02
❑ 760 Mike Witt .05 .02
❑ 761 Greg Pryor .05 .02
❑ 762 Gary Ward .05 .02
❑ 763 Tim Flannery .05 .02
❑ 764 Bill Buckner .10 .05
❑ 765 Kirk Gibson .10 .05
❑ 766 Don Aase .05 .02
❑ 767 Ron Cey .10 .05
❑ 768 Dennis Lamp .05 .02
❑ 769 Steve Sax .05 .02
❑ 770 Dave Winfield .20 .09
❑ 771 Shane Rawley .05 .02
❑ 772 Harold Baines .10 .05
❑ 773 Robin Yount .20 .09
❑ 774 Wayne Krenchicki .05 .02
❑ 775 Joaquin Andujar .05 .02
❑ 776 Tom Brunansky .05 .02
❑ 777 Chris Chambliss .05 .02
❑ 778 Jack Morris .10 .05
❑ 779 Craig Reynolds .05 .02
❑ 780 Andre Thornton .05 .02
❑ 781 Atlee Hammaker .05 .02
❑ 782 Brian Downing .05 .02
❑ 783 Willie Wilson .10 .05
❑ 784 Cal Ripken .75 .35
❑ 785 Terry Francona .10 .05
❑ 786 Jimy Williams MG .05 .02
❑ 787 Alejandro Pena .05 .02
❑ 788 Tim Stoddard .05 .02
❑ 789 Dan Schatzeder .05 .02
❑ 790 Julio Cruz .05 .02
❑ 791 Lance Parrish UER .10 .05
(No trademark, never corrected)
❑ 792 Checklist 661-792 .05 .02

1987 Topps Tiffany

	MINT	NRMT
COMP.FACT.SET (792)	100.00	45.00
COMMON CARD (1-792)	.15	.07

*STARS: 3X TO 6X BASIC CARDS
*ROOKIES: 6X TO 12X BASIC CARDS

1987 Topps Rookies

	MINT	NRMT
COMPLETE SET (22)	12.00	5.50
COMMON CARD (1-22)	.20	.09

❑ 1 Andy Allanson .20 .09
❑ 2 John Cangelosi .20 .09
❑ 3 Jose Canseco 2.50 1.10
❑ 4 Will Clark 3.00 1.35
❑ 5 Mark Eichhorn .20 .09
❑ 6 Pete Incaviglia .20 .09
❑ 7 Wally Joyner .50 .23
❑ 8 Eric King .20 .09
❑ 9 Dave Magadan .20 .09
❑ 10 John Morris .20 .09
❑ 11 Juan Nieves .20 .09
❑ 12 Rafael Palmeiro 2.00 .90
❑ 13 Billy Joe Robidoux .20 .09
❑ 14 Bruce Ruffin .20 .09
❑ 15 Ruben Sierra .20 .09
❑ 16 Cory Snyder .20 .09
❑ 17 Kurt Stillwell .20 .09
❑ 18 Dale Sveum .20 .09
❑ 19 Danny Tartabull .20 .09
❑ 20 Andres Thomas .20 .09
❑ 21 Robby Thompson .20 .09
❑ 22 Todd Worrell .20 .09

1987 Topps Traded

	MINT	NRMT
COMP.FACT.SET (132)	8.00	3.60
COMMON CARD (1T-132T)	.05	.02

❑ 1T Bill Almon .05 .02
❑ 2T Scott Bankhead .05 .02
❑ 3T Eric Bell .05 .02
❑ 4T Juan Beniquez .05 .02
❑ 5T Juan Berenguer .05 .02
❑ 6T Greg Booker .05 .02
❑ 7T Thad Bosley .05 .02
❑ 8T Larry Bowa MG .15 .07
❑ 9T Greg Brock .05 .02
❑ 10T Bob Brower .05 .02
❑ 11T Jerry Browne .05 .02
❑ 12T Ralph Bryant .05 .02
❑ 13T DeWayne Buice .05 .02
❑ 14T Ellis Burks .75 .35
❑ 15T Ivan Calderon .05 .02
❑ 16T Jeff Calhoun .05 .02
❑ 17T Casey Candaele .05 .02
❑ 18T John Cangelosi .05 .02
❑ 19T Steve Carlton .30 .14
❑ 20T Juan Castillo .05 .02
❑ 21T Rick Cerone .05 .02
❑ 22T Ron Cey .15 .07
❑ 23T John Christensen .05 .02
❑ 24T David Cone 1.50 .70
❑ 25T Chuck Crim .05 .02
❑ 26T Storm Davis .05 .02
❑ 27T Andre Dawson .30 .14
❑ 28T Rick Dempsey .15 .07
❑ 29T Doug Drabek .30 .14
❑ 30T Mike Dunne .05 .02
❑ 31T Dennis Eckersley .30 .14
❑ 32T Lee Elia MG .05 .02
❑ 33T Brian Fisher .05 .02
❑ 34T Terry Francona .15 .07
❑ 35T Willie Fraser .05 .02
❑ 36T Billy Gardner MG .05 .02
❑ 37T Ken Gerhart .05 .02
❑ 38T Dan Gladden .05 .02
❑ 39T Jim Gott .05 .02
❑ 40T Cecilio Guante .05 .02
❑ 41T Albert Hall .05 .02
❑ 42T Terry Harper .05 .02
❑ 43T Mickey Hatcher .05 .02
❑ 44T Brad Havens .05 .02
❑ 45T Neal Heaton .05 .02
❑ 46T Mike Henneman .30 .14
❑ 47T Donnie Hill .05 .02
❑ 48T Guy Hoffman .05 .02
❑ 49T Brian Holton .05 .02
❑ 50T Charles Hudson .05 .02
❑ 51T Danny Jackson .05 .02
❑ 52T Reggie Jackson .40 .18
❑ 53T Chris James .05 .02
❑ 54T Dion James .05 .02
❑ 55T Stan Jefferson .05 .02
❑ 56T Joe Johnson .05 .02
❑ 57T Terry Kennedy .05 .02
❑ 58T Mike Kingery .05 .02
❑ 59T Ray Knight .05 .02
❑ 60T Gene Larkin .05 .02
❑ 61T Mike LaValliere .05 .02
❑ 62T Jack Lazorko .05 .02
❑ 63T Terry Leach .05 .02
❑ 64T Tim Leary .05 .02
❑ 65T Jim Lindeman .05 .02
❑ 66T Steve Lombardozzi .05 .02
❑ 67T Bill Long .05 .02
❑ 68T Barry Lyons .05 .02
❑ 69T Shane Mack .15 .07
❑ 70T Greg Maddux 6.00 2.70
❑ 71T Bill Madlock .15 .07
❑ 72T Joe Magrane .05 .02
❑ 73T Dave Martinez .15 .07
❑ 74T Fred McGriff .40 .18
❑ 75T Mark McLemore .15 .07
❑ 76T Kevin McReynolds .05 .02
❑ 77T Dave Meads .05 .02
❑ 78T Eddie Milner .05 .02
❑ 79T Greg Minton .05 .02
❑ 80T John Mitchell .05 .02
❑ 81T Kevin Mitchell .10 .05
❑ 82T Charlie Moore .05 .02
❑ 83T Jeff Musselman .05 .02
❑ 84T Gene Nelson .05 .02
❑ 85T Graig Nettles .15 .07
❑ 86T Al Newman .05 .02
❑ 87T Reid Nichols .05 .02
❑ 88T Tom Niedenfuer .05 .02
❑ 89T Joe Niekro .05 .02
❑ 90T Tom Nieto .05 .02
❑ 91T Matt Nokes .15 .07
❑ 92T Dickie Noles .05 .02
❑ 93T Pat Pacillo .05 .02
❑ 94T Lance Parrish .15 .07
❑ 95T Tony Pena .05 .02
❑ 96T Luis Polonia .15 .07
❑ 97T Randy Ready .05 .02
❑ 98T Jeff Reardon .15 .07
❑ 99T Gary Redus .05 .02
❑ 100T Jeff Reed .05 .02
❑ 101T Rick Rhoden .05 .02
❑ 102T Cal Ripken Sr. MG .05 .02
❑ 103T Wally Ritchie .05 .02
❑ 104T Jeff M. Robinson .05 .02
❑ 105T Gary Roenicke .05 .02
❑ 106T Jerry Royster .05 .02
❑ 107T Mark Salas .05 .02
❑ 108T Luis Salazar .05 .02
❑ 109T Benny Santiago .15 .07
❑ 110T Dave Schmidt .05 .02
❑ 111T Kevin Seitzer .30 .14
❑ 112T John Shelby .05 .02
❑ 113T Steve Shields .05 .02
❑ 114T John Smiley .15 .07
❑ 115T Chris Speier .05 .02
❑ 116T Mike Stanley .30 .14
❑ 117T Terry Steinbach .30 .14
❑ 118T Les Straker .05 .02
❑ 119T Jim Sundberg .05 .02
❑ 120T Danny Tartabull .05 .02
❑ 121T Tom Trebelhorn MG .05 .02
❑ 122T Dave Valle .05 .02
❑ 123T Ed VandeBerg .05 .02
❑ 124T Andy Van Slyke .15 .07
❑ 125T Gary Ward .05 .02
❑ 126T Alan Wiggins .05 .02
❑ 127T Bill Wilkinson .05 .02
❑ 128T Frank Williams .05 .02
❑ 129T Matt Williams 1.25 .55
❑ 130T Jim Winn .05 .02
❑ 131T Matt Young .05 .02
❑ 132T Checklist 1T-132T .05 .02

1987 Topps Traded Tiffany

	MINT	NRMT
COMP.FACT.SET (132)	50.00	22.00
COMMON CARD (1T-132T)	.15	.07

*STARS: 2.5X TO 5X BASIC CARDS
*ROOKIES: 2.5X TO 5X BASIC CARDS

1988 Topps

	MINT	NRMT
COMPLETE SET (792)	10.00	4.50
COMP.FACT.SET (792)	12.00	5.50
COMMON CARD (1-792)	.05	.02

❑ 1 Vince Coleman RB .05 .02
100 Steals for Third Cons. Season
❑ 2 Don Mattingly RB .15 .07
Six Grand Slams
❑ 3 Mark McGwire RB 1.00 .45
Rookie Homer Record (No white spot)
❑ 3A Mark McGwire RB 1.00 .45

Rookie Homer Record
(White spot behind
left foot)

❑ 4 Eddie Murray RB .10 .05
Switch Home Runs,
Two Straight Games
(No caption on front)
❑ 4A Eddie Murray RB .40 .18
Switch Home Runs,
Two Straight Games
(Caption in box
on card front)
❑ 5 Phil Niekro .10 .05
Joe Niekro RB
Brothers Win Record
❑ 6 Nolan Ryan RB .40 .18
11th 200 K's Season
❑ 7 Benito Santiago RB .05 .02
34-Game Hitting Streak
Rookie Record
❑ 8 Kevin Elster .05 .02
❑ 9 Andy Hawkins .05 .02
❑ 10 Ryne Sandberg .25 .11
❑ 11 Mike Young .05 .02
❑ 12 Bill Schroeder .05 .02
❑ 13 Andres Thomas .05 .02
❑ 14 Sparky Anderson MG .10 .05
❑ 15 Chili Davis .15 .07
❑ 16 Kirk McCaskill .05 .02
❑ 17 Ron Oester .05 .02
❑ 18A Al Leiter ERR .20 .09
(Photo actually
Steve George,
right ear visible)
❑ 18B Al Leiter COR .25 .11
(Left ear visible)
❑ 19 Mark Davidson .05 .02
❑ 20 Kevin Gross .05 .02
❑ 21 Red Sox TL .10 .05
Wade Boggs and
Spike Owen
❑ 22 Greg Swindell .05 .02
❑ 23 Ken Landreaux .05 .02
❑ 24 Jim Deshaies .05 .02
❑ 25 Andres Galarraga .20 .09
❑ 26 Mitch Williams .05 .02
❑ 27 R.J. Reynolds .05 .02
❑ 28 Jose Nunez .05 .02
❑ 29 Argenis Salazar .05 .02
❑ 30 Sid Fernandez .05 .02
❑ 31 Bruce Bochy .05 .02
❑ 32 Mike Morgan .05 .02
❑ 33 Rob Deer .05 .02
❑ 34 Ricky Horton .05 .02
❑ 35 Harold Baines .10 .05
❑ 36 Jamie Moyer .05 .02
❑ 37 Ed Romero .05 .02
❑ 38 Jeff Calhoun .05 .02
❑ 39 Gerald Perry .05 .02
❑ 40 Orel Hershiser .10 .05
❑ 41 Bob Melvin .05 .02
❑ 42 Bill Landrum .05 .02
❑ 43 Dick Schofield .05 .02
❑ 44 Lou Piniella MG .10 .05
❑ 45 Kent Hrbek .10 .05
❑ 46 Darnell Coles .05 .02
❑ 47 Joaquin Andujar .05 .02
❑ 48 Alan Ashby .05 .02
❑ 49 Dave Clark .05 .02
❑ 50 Hubie Brooks .05 .02
❑ 51 Orioles TL .40 .18
Eddie Murray and
Cal Ripken
❑ 52 Don Robinson .05 .02
❑ 53 Curt Wilkerson .05 .02
❑ 54 Jim Clancy .05 .02
❑ 55 Phil Bradley .05 .02
❑ 56 Ed Hearn .05 .02
❑ 57 Tim Crews .05 .02
❑ 58 Dave Magadan .05 .02
❑ 59 Danny Cox .05 .02
❑ 60 Rickey Henderson .20 .09
❑ 61 Mark Knudson .05 .02
❑ 62 Jeff Hamilton .05 .02
❑ 63 Jimmy Jones .05 .02
❑ 64 Ken Caminiti .75 .35
❑ 65 Leon Durham .05 .02
❑ 66 Shane Rawley .05 .02
❑ 67 Ken Oberkfell .05 .02
❑ 68 Dave Dravecky .10 .05
❑ 69 Mike Hart .05 .02
❑ 70 Roger Clemens .40 .18
❑ 71 Gary Pettis .05 .02
❑ 72 Dennis Eckersley .10 .05
❑ 73 Randy Bush .05 .02
❑ 74 Tom Lasorda MG .20 .09
❑ 75 Joe Carter .20 .09
❑ 76 Dennis Martinez .10 .05
❑ 77 Tom O'Malley .05 .02
❑ 78 Dan Petry .05 .02
❑ 79 Ernie Whitt .05 .02
❑ 80 Mark Langston .05 .02
❑ 81 Reds TL .05 .02
Ron Robinson
and John Franco
❑ 82 Darrel Akerfelds .05 .02
❑ 83 Jose Oquendo .05 .02
❑ 84 Cecilio Guante .05 .02
❑ 85 Howard Johnson .05 .02
❑ 86 Ron Karkovice .05 .02
❑ 87 Mike Mason .05 .02
❑ 88 Earnie Riles .05 .02
❑ 89 Gary Thurman .05 .02
❑ 90 Dale Murphy .20 .09
❑ 91 Joey Cora .25 .11
❑ 92 Len Matuszek .05 .02
❑ 93 Bob Sebra .05 .02
❑ 94 Chuck Jackson .05 .02
❑ 95 Lance Parrish .05 .02
❑ 96 Todd Benzinger .05 .02
❑ 97 Scott Garrelts .05 .02
❑ 98 Rene Gonzales .05 .02
❑ 99 Chuck Finley .15 .07
❑ 100 Jack Clark .10 .05
❑ 101 Allan Anderson .05 .02
❑ 102 Barry Larkin .20 .09
❑ 103 Curt Young .05 .02
❑ 104 Dick Williams MG .10 .05
❑ 105 Jesse Orosco .05 .02
❑ 106 Jim Walewander .05 .02
❑ 107 Scott Bailes .05 .02
❑ 108 Steve Lyons .05 .02
❑ 109 Joel Skinner .05 .02
❑ 110 Teddy Higuera .05 .02
❑ 111 Expos TL .05 .02
Hubie Brooks and
Vance Law
❑ 112 Les Lancaster .05 .02
❑ 113 Kelly Gruber .05 .02
❑ 114 Jeff Russell .05 .02
❑ 115 Johnny Ray .05 .02
❑ 116 Jerry Don Gleaton .05 .02
❑ 117 James Steels .05 .02
❑ 118 Bob Welch .05 .02
❑ 119 Robbie Wine .05 .02
❑ 120 Kirby Puckett .30 .14
❑ 121 Checklist 1-132 .05 .02
❑ 122 Tony Bernazard .05 .02
❑ 123 Tom Candiotti .05 .02
❑ 124 Ray Knight .05 .02
❑ 125 Bruce Hurst .05 .02
❑ 126 Steve Jeltz .05 .02
❑ 127 Jim Gott .05 .02
❑ 128 Johnny Grubb .05 .02
❑ 129 Greg Minton .05 .02
❑ 130 Buddy Bell .10 .05
❑ 131 Don Schulze .05 .02
❑ 132 Donnie Hill .05 .02
❑ 133 Greg Mathews .05 .02
❑ 134 Chuck Tanner MG .10 .05
❑ 135 Dennis Rasmussen .05 .02
❑ 136 Brian Dayett .05 .02
❑ 137 Chris Bosio .05 .02
❑ 138 Mitch Webster .05 .02
❑ 139 Jerry Browne .05 .02
❑ 140 Jesse Barfield .05 .02
❑ 141 Royals TL .20 .09
George Brett and
Bret Saberhagen
❑ 142 Andy Van Slyke .10 .05
❑ 143 Mickey Tettleton .10 .05
❑ 144 Don Gordon .05 .02
❑ 145 Bill Madlock .10 .05
❑ 146 Donell Nixon .05 .02
❑ 147 Bill Buckner .10 .05
❑ 148 Carmelo Martinez .05 .02
❑ 149 Ken Howell .05 .02
❑ 150 Eric Davis .10 .05
❑ 151 Bob Knepper .05 .02
❑ 152 Jody Reed .10 .05
❑ 153 John Habyan .05 .02
❑ 154 Jeff Stone .05 .02
❑ 155 Bruce Sutter .10 .05
❑ 156 Gary Matthews .05 .02
❑ 157 Atlee Hammaker .05 .02
❑ 158 Tim Hulett .05 .02
❑ 159 Brad Arnsberg .05 .02
❑ 160 Willie McGee .10 .05
❑ 161 Bryn Smith .05 .02
❑ 162 Mark McLemore .05 .02
❑ 163 Dale Mohorcic .05 .02
❑ 164 Dave Johnson MG .10 .05
❑ 165 Robin Yount .20 .09
❑ 166 Rick Rodriquez .05 .02
❑ 167 Rance Mulliniks .05 .02
❑ 168 Barry Jones .05 .02
❑ 169 Ross Jones .05 .02
❑ 170 Rich Gossage .10 .05
❑ 171 Cubs TL .05 .02
Shawon Dunston
and Manny Trillo
❑ 172 Lloyd McClendon .05 .02
❑ 173 Eric Plunk .05 .02
❑ 174 Phil Garner .05 .02
❑ 175 Kevin Bass .05 .02
❑ 176 Jeff Reed .05 .02
❑ 177 Frank Tanana .05 .02
❑ 178 Dwayne Henry .05 .02
❑ 179 Charlie Puleo .05 .02
❑ 180 Terry Kennedy .05 .02
❑ 181 David Cone .25 .11
❑ 182 Ken Phelps .05 .02
❑ 183 Tom Lawless .05 .02
❑ 184 Ivan Calderon .05 .02
❑ 185 Rick Rhoden .05 .02
❑ 186 Rafael Palmeiro .20 .09
❑ 187 Steve Kiefer .05 .02
❑ 188 John Russell .05 .02
❑ 189 Wes Gardner .05 .02
❑ 190 Candy Maldonado .05 .02
❑ 191 John Cerutti .05 .02
❑ 192 Devon White .10 .05
❑ 193 Brian Fisher .05 .02
❑ 194 Tom Kelly MG .05 .02
❑ 195 Dan Quisenberry .05 .02
❑ 196 Dave Engle .05 .02
❑ 197 Lance McCullers .05 .02
❑ 198 Franklin Stubbs .05 .02
❑ 199 Dave Meads .05 .02
❑ 200 Wade Boggs .20 .09
❑ 201 Rangers TL .05 .02
Bobby Valentine MG
Pete O'Brien,
Pete Incaviglia and
Steve Buechele
❑ 202 Glenn Hoffman .05 .02
❑ 203 Fred Toliver .05 .02
❑ 204 Paul O'Neill .15 .07

❑ 205 Nelson Liriano .05 .02
❑ 206 Domingo Ramos .05 .02
❑ 207 John Mitchell .05 .02
❑ 208 Steve Lake .05 .02
❑ 209 Richard Dotson .05 .02
❑ 210 Willie Randolph .10 .05
❑ 211 Frank DiPino .05 .02
❑ 212 Greg Brock .05 .02
❑ 213 Albert Hall .05 .02
❑ 214 Dave Schmidt .05 .02
❑ 215 Von Hayes .05 .02
❑ 216 Jerry Reuss .05 .02
❑ 217 Harry Spilman .05 .02
❑ 218 Dan Schatzeder .05 .02
❑ 219 Mike Stanley .10 .05
❑ 220 Tom Henke .05 .02
❑ 221 Rafael Belliard .05 .02
❑ 222 Steve Farr .05 .02
❑ 223 Stan Jefferson .05 .02
❑ 224 Tom Trebelhorn MG .05 .02
❑ 225 Mike Scioscia .05 .02
❑ 226 Dave Lopes .10 .05
❑ 227 Ed Correa .05 .02
❑ 228 Wallace Johnson .05 .02
❑ 229 Jeff Musselman .05 .02
❑ 230 Pat Tabler .05 .02
❑ 231 Pirates TL .20 .09
Barry Bonds and
Bobby Bonilla
❑ 232 Bob James .05 .02
❑ 233 Rafael Santana .05 .02
❑ 234 Ken Dayley .05 .02
❑ 235 Gary Ward .05 .02
❑ 236 Ted Power .05 .02
❑ 237 Mike Heath .05 .02
❑ 238 Luis Polonia .05 .02
❑ 239 Roy Smalley .05 .02
❑ 240 Lee Smith .10 .05
❑ 241 Damaso Garcia .05 .02
❑ 242 Tom Niedenfuer .05 .02
❑ 243 Mark Ryal .05 .02
❑ 244 Jeff D. Robinson .05 .02
❑ 245 Rich Gedman .05 .02
❑ 246 Mike Campbell .05 .02
❑ 247 Thad Bosley .05 .02
❑ 248 Storm Davis .05 .02
❑ 249 Mike Marshall .05 .02
❑ 250 Nolan Ryan .75 .35
❑ 251 Tom Foley .05 .02
❑ 252 Bob Brower .05 .02
❑ 253 Checklist 133-264 .05 .02
❑ 254 Lee Elia MG .05 .02
❑ 255 Mookie Wilson .10 .05
❑ 256 Ken Schrom .05 .02
❑ 257 Jerry Royster .05 .02
❑ 258 Ed Nunez .05 .02
❑ 259 Ron Kittle .05 .02
❑ 260 Vince Coleman .05 .02
❑ 261 Giants TL .05 .02
(Five players)
❑ 262 Drew Hall .05 .02
❑ 263 Glenn Braggs .05 .02
❑ 264 Les Straker .05 .02
❑ 265 Bo Diaz .05 .02
❑ 266 Paul Assenmacher .05 .02
❑ 267 Billy Bean .05 .02
❑ 268 Bruce Ruffin .05 .02
❑ 269 Ellis Burks .40 .18
❑ 270 Mike Witt .05 .02
❑ 271 Ken Gerhart .05 .02
❑ 272 Steve Ontiveros .05 .02
❑ 273 Garth Iorg .05 .02
❑ 274 Junior Ortiz .05 .02
❑ 275 Kevin Seitzer .10 .05
❑ 276 Luis Salazar .05 .02
❑ 277 Alejandro Pena .05 .02
❑ 278 Jose Cruz .05 .02
❑ 279 Randy St.Claire .05 .02
❑ 280 Pete Incaviglia .05 .02
❑ 281 Jerry Hairston .05 .02
❑ 282 Pat Perry .05 .02
❑ 283 Phil Lombardi .05 .02
❑ 284 Larry Bowa MG .05 .02
❑ 285 Jim Presley .05 .02
❑ 286 Chuck Crim .05 .02
❑ 287 Manny Trillo .05 .02
❑ 288 Pat Pacillo .05 .02
(Chris Sabo in
background of photo)
❑ 289 Dave Bergman .05 .02
❑ 290 Tony Fernandez .05 .02
❑ 291 Astros TL .05 .02
Billy Hatcher
and Kevin Bass
❑ 292 Carney Lansford .10 .05
❑ 293 Doug Jones .20 .09
❑ 294 Al Pedrique .05 .02
❑ 295 Bert Blyleven .10 .05
❑ 296 Floyd Rayford .05 .02
❑ 297 Zane Smith .05 .02
❑ 298 Milt Thompson .05 .02
❑ 299 Steve Crawford .05 .02
❑ 300 Don Mattingly .30 .14
❑ 301 Bud Black .05 .02
❑ 302 Jose Uribe .05 .02
❑ 303 Eric Show .05 .02
❑ 304 George Hendrick .05 .02
❑ 305 Steve Sax .05 .02
❑ 306 Billy Hatcher .05 .02
❑ 307 Mike Trujillo .05 .02
❑ 308 Lee Mazzilli .05 .02
❑ 309 Bill Long .05 .02
❑ 310 Tom Herr .05 .02
❑ 311 Scott Sanderson .05 .02
❑ 312 Joey Meyer .05 .02
❑ 313 Bob McClure .05 .02
❑ 314 Jimy Williams MG .05 .02
❑ 315 Dave Parker .10 .05
❑ 316 Jose Rijo .05 .02
❑ 317 Tom Nieto .05 .02
❑ 318 Mel Hall .05 .02
❑ 319 Mike Loynd .05 .02
❑ 320 Alan Trammell .15 .07
❑ 321 White Sox TL .10 .05
Harold Baines and
Carlton Fisk
❑ 322 Vicente Palacios .05 .02
❑ 323 Rick Leach .05 .02
❑ 324 Danny Jackson .05 .02
❑ 325 Glenn Hubbard .05 .02
❑ 326 Al Nipper .05 .02
❑ 327 Larry Sheets .05 .02
❑ 328 Greg Cadaret .05 .02
❑ 329 Chris Speier .05 .02
❑ 330 Eddie Whitson .05 .02
❑ 331 Brian Downing .05 .02
❑ 332 Jerry Reed .05 .02
❑ 333 Wally Backman .05 .02
❑ 334 Dave LaPoint .05 .02
❑ 335 Claudell Washington .05 .02
❑ 336 Ed Lynch .05 .02
❑ 337 Jim Gantner .05 .02
❑ 338 Brian Holton UER .05 .02
(1987 ERA .389,
should be 3.89)
❑ 339 Kurt Stillwell .05 .02
❑ 340 Jack Morris .10 .05
❑ 341 Carmen Castillo .05 .02
❑ 342 Larry Andersen .05 .02
❑ 343 Greg Gagne .05 .02
❑ 344 Tony LaRussa MG .10 .05
❑ 345 Scott Fletcher .05 .02
❑ 346 Vance Law .05 .02
❑ 347 Joe Johnson .05 .02
❑ 348 Jim Eisenreich .20 .09
❑ 349 Bob Walk .05 .02
❑ 350 Will Clark .25 .11
❑ 351 Cardinals TL .10 .05
Red Schoendienst CO
and Tony Pena
❑ 352 Billy Ripken .05 .02
❑ 353 Ed Olwine .05 .02
❑ 354 Marc Sullivan .05 .02
❑ 355 Roger McDowell .05 .02
❑ 356 Luis Aguayo .05 .02
❑ 357 Floyd Bannister .05 .02
❑ 358 Rey Quinones .05 .02
❑ 359 Tim Stoddard .05 .02
❑ 360 Tony Gwynn .50 .23
❑ 361 Greg Maddux 1.25 .55
❑ 362 Juan Castillo .05 .02
❑ 363 Willie Fraser .05 .02
❑ 364 Nick Esasky .05 .02
❑ 365 Floyd Youmans .05 .02
❑ 366 Chet Lemon .05 .02
❑ 367 Tim Leary .05 .02
❑ 368 Gerald Young .05 .02
❑ 369 Greg Harris .05 .02
❑ 370 Jose Canseco .20 .09
❑ 371 Joe Hesketh .05 .02
❑ 372 Matt Williams .50 .23
❑ 373 Checklist 265-396 .05 .02
❑ 374 Doc Edwards MG .05 .02
❑ 375 Tom Brunansky .05 .02
❑ 376 Bill Wilkinson .05 .02
❑ 377 Sam Horn .05 .02
❑ 378 Todd Frohwirth .05 .02
❑ 379 Rafael Ramirez .05 .02
❑ 380 Joe Magrane .05 .02
❑ 381 Angels TL .10 .05
Wally Joyner and
Jack Howell
❑ 382 Keith A. Miller .05 .02
❑ 383 Eric Bell .05 .02
❑ 384 Neil Allen .05 .02
❑ 385 Carlton Fisk .20 .09
❑ 386 Don Mattingly AS .15 .07
❑ 387 Willie Randolph AS .05 .02
❑ 388 Wade Boggs AS .10 .05
❑ 389 Alan Trammell AS .10 .05
❑ 390 George Bell AS .05 .02
❑ 391 Kirby Puckett AS .20 .09
❑ 392 Dave Winfield AS .20 .09
❑ 393 Matt Nokes AS .05 .02
❑ 394 Roger Clemens AS .20 .09
❑ 395 Jimmy Key AS .05 .02
❑ 396 Tom Henke AS .05 .02
❑ 397 Jack Clark AS .10 .05
❑ 398 Juan Samuel AS .05 .02
❑ 399 Tim Wallach AS .05 .02
❑ 400 Ozzie Smith AS .15 .07
❑ 401 Andre Dawson AS .20 .09
❑ 402 Tony Gwynn AS .25 .11
❑ 403 Tim Raines AS .05 .02
❑ 404 Benny Santiago AS .05 .02
❑ 405 Dwight Gooden AS .10 .05
❑ 406 Shane Rawley AS .05 .02
❑ 407 Steve Bedrosian AS .05 .02
❑ 408 Dion James .05 .02
❑ 409 Joel McKeon .05 .02
❑ 410 Tony Pena .05 .02
❑ 411 Wayne Tolleson .05 .02
❑ 412 Randy Myers .15 .07
❑ 413 John Christensen .05 .02
❑ 414 John McNamara MG .05 .02
❑ 415 Don Carman .05 .02
❑ 416 Keith Moreland .05 .02
❑ 417 Mark Ciardi .05 .02
❑ 418 Joel Youngblood .05 .02
❑ 419 Scott McGregor .05 .02
❑ 420 Wally Joyner .15 .07
❑ 421 Ed VandeBerg .05 .02
❑ 422 Dave Concepcion .10 .05
❑ 423 John Smiley .10 .05
❑ 424 Dwayne Murphy .05 .02
❑ 425 Jeff Reardon .10 .05
❑ 426 Randy Ready .05 .02
❑ 427 Paul Kilgus .05 .02
❑ 428 John Shelby .05 .02
❑ 429 Tigers TL .10 .05
Alan Trammell and
Kirk Gibson
❑ 430 Glenn Davis .05 .02
❑ 431 Casey Candaele .05 .02
❑ 432 Mike Moore .05 .02
❑ 433 Bill Pecota .05 .02
❑ 434 Rick Aguilera .10 .05
❑ 435 Mike Pagliarulo .05 .02
❑ 436 Mike Bielecki .05 .02
❑ 437 Fred Manrique .05 .02
❑ 438 Rob Ducey .05 .02
❑ 439 Dave Martinez .05 .02
❑ 440 Steve Bedrosian .05 .02
❑ 441 Rick Manning .05 .02
❑ 442 Tom Bolton .05 .02

❑	443	Ken Griffey	.10	.05
❑	444	Cal Ripken Sr. MG UER	.05	.02
		two copyrights		
❑	445	Mike Krukow	.05	.02
❑	446	Doug DeCinces	.05	.02
		(Now with Cardinals on card front)		
❑	447	Jeff Montgomery	.20	.09
❑	448	Mike Davis	.05	.02
❑	449	Jeff M. Robinson	.05	.02
❑	450	Barry Bonds	.50	.23
❑	451	Keith Atherton	.05	.02
❑	452	Willie Wilson	.05	.02
❑	453	Dennis Powell	.05	.02
❑	454	Marvell Wynne	.05	.02
❑	455	Shawn Hillegas	.05	.02
❑	456	Dave Anderson	.05	.02
❑	457	Terry Leach	.05	.02
❑	458	Ron Hassey	.05	.02
❑	459	Yankees TL	.20	.09
		Dave Winfield and Willie Randolph		
❑	460	Ozzie Smith	.25	.11
❑	461	Danny Darwin	.05	.02
❑	462	Don Slaught	.05	.02
❑	463	Fred McGriff	.20	.09
❑	464	Jay Tibbs	.05	.02
❑	465	Paul Molitor	.20	.09
❑	466	Jerry Mumphrey	.05	.02
❑	467	Don Aase	.05	.02
❑	468	Darren Daulton	.10	.05
❑	469	Jeff Dedmon	.05	.02
❑	470	Dwight Evans	.10	.05
❑	471	Donnie Moore	.05	.02
❑	472	Robby Thompson	.05	.02
❑	473	Joe Niekro	.05	.02
❑	474	Tom Brookens	.05	.02
❑	475	Pete Rose MG	.25	.11
❑	476	Dave Stewart	.10	.05
❑	477	Jamie Quirk	.05	.02
❑	478	Sid Bream	.05	.02
❑	479	Brett Butler	.10	.05
❑	480	Dwight Gooden	.10	.05
❑	481	Mariano Duncan	.05	.02
❑	482	Mark Davis	.05	.02
❑	483	Rod Booker	.05	.02
❑	484	Pat Clements	.05	.02
❑	485	Harold Reynolds	.10	.05
❑	486	Pat Keedy	.05	.02
❑	487	Jim Pankovits	.05	.02
❑	488	Andy McGaffigan	.05	.02
❑	489	Dodgers TL	.05	.02
		Pedro Guerrero and Fernando Valenzuela		
❑	490	Larry Parrish	.05	.02
❑	491	B.J. Surhoff	.10	.05
❑	492	Doyle Alexander	.05	.02
❑	493	Mike Greenwell	.05	.02
❑	494	Wally Ritchie	.05	.02
❑	495	Eddie Murray	.20	.09
❑	496	Guy Hoffman	.05	.02
❑	497	Kevin Mitchell	.10	.05
❑	498	Bob Boone	.10	.05
❑	499	Eric King	.05	.02
❑	500	Andre Dawson	.20	.09
❑	501	Tim Birtsas	.05	.02
❑	502	Dan Gladden	.05	.02
❑	503	Junior Noboa	.05	.02
❑	504	Bob Rodgers MG	.05	.02
❑	505	Willie Upshaw	.05	.02
❑	506	John Cangelosi	.05	.02
❑	507	Mark Gubicza	.05	.02
❑	508	Tim Teufel	.05	.02
❑	509	Bill Dawley	.05	.02
❑	510	Dave Winfield	.20	.09
❑	511	Joel Davis	.05	.02
❑	512	Alex Trevino	.05	.02
❑	513	Tim Flannery	.05	.02
❑	514	Pat Sheridan	.05	.02
❑	515	Juan Nieves	.05	.02
❑	516	Jim Sundberg	.05	.02
❑	517	Ron Robinson	.05	.02
❑	518	Greg Gross	.05	.02
❑	519	Mariners TL	.05	.02
		Harold Reynolds and Phil Bradley		
❑	520	Dave Smith	.05	.02
❑	521	Jim Dwyer	.05	.02
❑	522	Bob Patterson	.05	.02
❑	523	Gary Roenicke	.05	.02
❑	524	Gary Lucas	.05	.02
❑	525	Marty Barrett	.05	.02
❑	526	Juan Berenguer	.05	.02
❑	527	Steve Henderson	.05	.02
❑	528A	Checklist 397-528	.20	.09
		ERR (455 S. Carlton)		
❑	528B	Checklist 397-528	.10	.05
		COR (455 S. Hillegas)		
❑	529	Tim Burke	.05	.02
❑	530	Gary Carter	.15	.07
❑	531	Rich Yett	.05	.02
❑	532	Mike Kingery	.05	.02
❑	533	John Farrell	.05	.02
❑	534	John Wathan MG	.05	.02
❑	535	Ron Guidry	.05	.02
❑	536	John Morris	.05	.02
❑	537	Steve Buechele	.05	.02
❑	538	Bill Wegman	.05	.02
❑	539	Mike LaValliere	.05	.02
❑	540	Bret Saberhagen	.10	.05
❑	541	Juan Beniquez	.05	.02
❑	542	Paul Noce	.05	.02
❑	543	Kent Tekulve	.05	.02
❑	544	Jim Traber	.05	.02
❑	545	Don Baylor	.10	.05
❑	546	John Candelaria	.05	.02
❑	547	Felix Fermin	.05	.02
❑	548	Shane Mack	.05	.02
❑	549	Braves TL	.05	.02
		Albert Hall, Dale Murphy, Ken Griffey and Dion James		
❑	550	Pedro Guerrero	.05	.02
❑	551	Terry Steinbach	.10	.05
❑	552	Mark Thurmond	.05	.02
❑	553	Tracy Jones	.05	.02
❑	554	Mike Smithson	.05	.02
❑	555	Brook Jacoby	.05	.02
❑	556	Stan Clarke	.05	.02
❑	557	Craig Reynolds	.05	.02
❑	558	Bob Ojeda	.05	.02
❑	559	Ken Williams	.05	.02
❑	560	Tim Wallach	.05	.02
❑	561	Rick Cerone	.05	.02
❑	562	Jim Lindeman	.05	.02
❑	563	Jose Guzman	.05	.02
❑	564	Frank Lucchesi MG	.05	.02
❑	565	Lloyd Moseby	.05	.02
❑	566	Charlie O'Brien	.05	.02
❑	567	Mike Diaz	.05	.02
❑	568	Chris Brown	.05	.02
❑	569	Charlie Leibrandt	.05	.02
❑	570	Jeffrey Leonard	.05	.02
❑	571	Mark Williamson	.05	.02
❑	572	Chris James	.05	.02
❑	573	Bob Stanley	.05	.02
❑	574	Graig Nettles	.10	.05
❑	575	Don Sutton	.20	.09
❑	576	Tommy Hinzo	.05	.02
❑	577	Tom Browning	.05	.02
❑	578	Gary Gaetti	.10	.05
❑	579	Mets TL	.05	.02
		Gary Carter and Kevin McReynolds		
❑	580	Mark McGwire	2.00	.90
❑	581	Tito Landrum	.05	.02
❑	582	Mike Henneman	.10	.05
❑	583	Dave Valle	.05	.02
❑	584	Steve Trout	.05	.02
❑	585	Ozzie Guillen	.05	.02
❑	586	Bob Forsch	.05	.02
❑	587	Terry Puhl	.05	.02
❑	588	Jeff Parrett	.05	.02
❑	589	Geno Petralli	.05	.02
❑	590	George Bell	.05	.02
❑	591	Doug Drabek	.05	.02
❑	592	Dale Sveum	.05	.02
❑	593	Bob Tewksbury	.05	.02
❑	594	Bobby Valentine MG	.10	.05
❑	595	Frank White	.10	.05
❑	596	John Kruk	.10	.05
❑	597	Gene Garber	.05	.02
❑	598	Lee Lacy	.05	.02
❑	599	Calvin Schiraldi	.05	.02
❑	600	Mike Schmidt	.25	.11
❑	601	Jack Lazorko	.05	.02
❑	602	Mike Aldrete	.05	.02
❑	603	Rob Murphy	.05	.02
❑	604	Chris Bando	.05	.02
❑	605	Kirk Gibson	.10	.05
❑	606	Moose Haas	.05	.02
❑	607	Mickey Hatcher	.05	.02
❑	608	Charlie Kerfeld	.05	.02
❑	609	Twins TL	.10	.05
		Gary Gaetti and Kent Hrbek		
❑	610	Keith Hernandez	.10	.05
❑	611	Tommy John	.10	.05
❑	612	Curt Ford	.05	.02
❑	613	Bobby Thigpen	.05	.02
❑	614	Herm Winningham	.05	.02
❑	615	Jody Davis	.05	.02
❑	616	Jay Aldrich	.05	.02
❑	617	Oddibe McDowell	.05	.02
❑	618	Cecil Fielder	.15	.07
❑	619	Mike Dunne	.05	.02
		(Inconsistent design, black name on front)		
❑	620	Cory Snyder	.05	.02
❑	621	Gene Nelson	.05	.02
❑	622	Kal Daniels	.05	.02
❑	623	Mike Flanagan	.05	.02
❑	624	Jim Leyland MG	.10	.05
❑	625	Frank Viola	.05	.02
❑	626	Glenn Wilson	.05	.02
❑	627	Joe Boever	.05	.02
❑	628	Dave Henderson	.05	.02
❑	629	Kelly Downs	.05	.02
❑	630	Darrell Evans	.10	.05
❑	631	Jack Howell	.05	.02
❑	632	Steve Shields	.05	.02
❑	633	Barry Lyons	.05	.02
❑	634	Jose DeLeon	.05	.02
❑	635	Terry Pendleton	.10	.05
❑	636	Charles Hudson	.05	.02
❑	637	Jay Bell	.25	.11
❑	638	Steve Balboni	.05	.02
❑	639	Brewers TL	.05	.02
		Glenn Braggs and Tony Muser CO		
❑	640	Garry Templeton	.05	.02
		(Inconsistent design, green border)		
❑	641	Rick Honeycutt	.05	.02
❑	642	Bob Dernier	.05	.02
❑	643	Rocky Childress	.05	.02
❑	644	Terry McGriff	.05	.02
❑	645	Matt Nokes	.05	.02
❑	646	Checklist 529-660	.05	.02
❑	647	Pascual Perez	.05	.02
❑	648	Al Newman	.05	.02
❑	649	DeWayne Buice	.05	.02
❑	650	Cal Ripken	.75	.35
❑	651	Mike Jackson	.20	.09
❑	652	Bruce Benedict	.05	.02
❑	653	Jeff Sellers	.05	.02
❑	654	Roger Craig MG	.10	.05
❑	655	Len Dykstra	.10	.05
❑	656	Lee Guetterman	.05	.02
❑	657	Gary Redus	.05	.02
❑	658	Tim Conroy	.05	.02
		(Inconsistent design, name in white)		
❑	659	Bobby Meacham	.05	.02
❑	660	Rick Reuschel	.05	.02
❑	661	Nolan Ryan TBC '83	.40	.18
❑	662	Jim Rice TBC '78	.05	.02
❑	663	Ron Blomberg TBC '73	.05	.02
❑	664	Bob Gibson TBC '68	.20	.09
❑	665	Stan Musial TBC '63	.20	.09
❑	666	Mario Soto	.05	.02
❑	667	Luis Quinones	.05	.02
❑	668	Walt Terrell	.05	.02
❑	669	Phillies TL	.05	.02
		Lance Parrish and Mike Ryan CO		

❑ 670 Dan Plesac .05 .02
❑ 671 Tim Laudner .05 .02
❑ 672 John Davis .05 .02
❑ 673 Tony Phillips .05 .02
❑ 674 Mike Fitzgerald .05 .02
❑ 675 Jim Rice .10 .05
❑ 676 Ken Dixon .05 .02
❑ 677 Eddie Milner .05 .02
❑ 678 Jim Acker .05 .02
❑ 679 Darrell Miller .05 .02
❑ 680 Charlie Hough .10 .05
❑ 681 Bobby Bonilla .15 .07
❑ 682 Jimmy Key .10 .05
❑ 683 Julio Franco .05 .02
❑ 684 Hal Lanier MG .05 .02
❑ 685 Ron Darling .05 .02
❑ 686 Terry Francona .05 .02
❑ 687 Mickey Brantley .05 .02
❑ 688 Jim Winn .05 .02
❑ 689 Tom Pagnozzi .10 .05
❑ 690 Jay Howell .05 .02
❑ 691 Dan Pasqua .05 .02
❑ 692 Mike Birkbeck .05 .02
❑ 693 Benito Santiago .05 .02
❑ 694 Eric Nolte .05 .02
❑ 695 Shawon Dunston .05 .02
❑ 696 Duane Ward .05 .02
❑ 697 Steve Lombardozzi .05 .02
❑ 698 Brad Havens .05 .02
❑ 699 Padres TL .10 .05
Benito Santiago
and Tony Gwynn
❑ 700 George Brett .40 .18
❑ 701 Sammy Stewart .05 .02
❑ 702 Mike Gallego .05 .02
❑ 703 Bob Brenly .05 .02
❑ 704 Dennis Boyd .05 .02
❑ 705 Juan Samuel .05 .02
❑ 706 Rick Mahler .05 .02
❑ 707 Fred Lynn .05 .02
❑ 708 Gus Polidor .05 .02
❑ 709 George Frazier .05 .02
❑ 710 Darryl Strawberry .10 .05
❑ 711 Bill Gullickson .05 .02
❑ 712 John Moses .05 .02
❑ 713 Willie Hernandez .05 .02
❑ 714 Jim Fregosi MG .05 .02
❑ 715 Todd Worrell .10 .05
❑ 716 Lenn Sakata .05 .02
❑ 717 Jay Baller .05 .02
❑ 718 Mike Felder .05 .02
❑ 719 Denny Walling .05 .02
❑ 720 Tim Raines .10 .05
❑ 721 Pete O'Brien .05 .02
❑ 722 Manny Lee .05 .02
❑ 723 Bob Kipper .05 .02
❑ 724 Danny Tartabull .05 .02
❑ 725 Mike Boddicker .05 .02
❑ 726 Alfredo Griffin .05 .02
❑ 727 Greg Booker .05 .02
❑ 728 Andy Allanson .05 .02
❑ 729 Blue Jays TL .10 .05
George Bell and
Fred McGriff
❑ 730 John Franco .10 .05
❑ 731 Rick Schu .05 .02
❑ 732 David Palmer .05 .02
❑ 733 Spike Owen .05 .02
❑ 734 Craig Lefferts .05 .02
❑ 735 Kevin McReynolds .05 .02
❑ 736 Matt Young .05 .02
❑ 737 Butch Wynegar .05 .02
❑ 738 Scott Bankhead .05 .02
❑ 739 Daryl Boston .05 .02
❑ 740 Rick Sutcliffe .05 .02
❑ 741 Mike Easler .05 .02
❑ 742 Mark Clear .05 .02
❑ 743 Larry Herndon .05 .02
❑ 744 Whitey Herzog MG .10 .05
❑ 745 Bill Doran .05 .02
❑ 746 Gene Larkin .05 .02
❑ 747 Bobby Witt .05 .02
❑ 748 Reid Nichols .05 .02
❑ 749 Mark Eichhorn .05 .02
❑ 750 Bo Jackson .20 .09
❑ 751 Jim Morrison .05 .02
❑ 752 Mark Grant .05 .02
❑ 753 Danny Heep .05 .02
❑ 754 Mike LaCoss .05 .02
❑ 755 Ozzie Virgil .05 .02
❑ 756 Mike Maddux .05 .02
❑ 757 John Marzano .05 .02
❑ 758 Eddie Williams .10 .05
❑ 759 A's TL UER .75 .35
Mark McGwire
and Jose Canseco
(two copyrights)
❑ 760 Mike Scott .05 .02
❑ 761 Tony Armas .05 .02
❑ 762 Scott Bradley .05 .02
❑ 763 Doug Sisk .05 .02
❑ 764 Greg Walker .05 .02
❑ 765 Neal Heaton .05 .02
❑ 766 Henry Cotto .05 .02
❑ 767 Jose Lind .05 .02
❑ 768 Dickie Noles .05 .02
(Now with Tigers
on card front)
❑ 769 Cecil Cooper .10 .05
❑ 770 Lou Whitaker .10 .05
❑ 771 Ruben Sierra .05 .02
❑ 772 Sal Butera .05 .02
❑ 773 Frank Williams .05 .02
❑ 774 Gene Mauch MG .10 .05
❑ 775 Dave Stieb .05 .02
❑ 776 Checklist 661-792 .05 .02
❑ 777 Lonnie Smith .05 .02
❑ 778A Keith Comstock ERR 2.00 .90
(White "Padres")
❑ 778B Keith Comstock COR .05 .02
(Blue "Padres")
❑ 779 Tom Glavine 1.00 .45
❑ 780 Fernando Valenzuela .10 .05
❑ 781 Keith Hughes .05 .02
❑ 782 Jeff Ballard .05 .02
❑ 783 Ron Roenicke .05 .02
❑ 784 Joe Sambito .05 .02
❑ 785 Alvin Davis .05 .02
❑ 786 Joe Price .05 .02
(Inconsistent design,
orange team name)
❑ 787 Bill Almon .05 .02
❑ 788 Ray Searage .05 .02
❑ 789 Indians' TL .10 .05
Joe Carter and
Cory Snyder
❑ 790 Dave Righetti .05 .02
❑ 791 Ted Simmons .10 .05
❑ 792 John Tudor .05 .02

1988 Topps Tiffany

	MINT	NRMT
COMP.FACT.SET (792)	80.00	36.00
COMMON CARD (1-792)	.15	.07

*STARS: 5X TO 10X BASIC CARDS
*ROOKIES: 7.5X TO 15X BASIC CARDS

1988 Topps Rookies

	MINT	NRMT
COMPLETE SET (22)	7.00	3.10
COMMON CARD (1-22)	.20	.09

❑ 1 Billy Ripken .20 .09
❑ 2 Ellis Burks .75 .35
❑ 3 Mike Greenwell .20 .09
❑ 4 DeWayne Buice .20 .09
❑ 5 Devon White .40 .18
❑ 6 Fred Manrique .20 .09
❑ 7 Mike Henneman .10 .05
❑ 8 Matt Nokes .20 .09
❑ 9 Kevin Seitzer .10 .05
❑ 10 B.J. Surhoff .10 .05
❑ 11 Casey Candaele .20 .09
❑ 12 Randy Myers .40 .18
❑ 13 Mark McGwire 1.50 .70
❑ 14 Luis Polonia .20 .09
❑ 15 Terry Steinbach .10 .05
❑ 16 Mike Dunne .20 .09
❑ 17 Al Pedrique .20 .09
❑ 18 Benito Santiago .10 .05
❑ 19 Kelly Downs .20 .09
❑ 20 Joe Magrane .20 .09
❑ 21 Jerry Browne .20 .09
❑ 22 Jeff Musselman .20 .09

1988 Topps Traded

	MINT	NRMT
COMP.FACT.SET (132)	10.00	4.50
COMMON CARD (1T-132T)	.10	.05

❑ 1T Jim Abbott OLY .50 .23
❑ 2T Juan Agosto .10 .05
❑ 3T Luis Alicea .20 .09
❑ 4T Roberto Alomar 2.50 1.10
❑ 5T Brady Anderson 1.00 .45
❑ 6T Jack Armstrong .10 .05
❑ 7T Don August .10 .05
❑ 8T Floyd Bannister .10 .05
❑ 9T Bret Barberie OLY .20 .09
❑ 10T Jose Bautista .10 .05
❑ 11T Don Baylor .20 .09
❑ 12T Tim Belcher .20 .09
❑ 13T Buddy Bell .20 .09
❑ 14T Andy Benes OLY .75 .35
❑ 15T Damon Berryhill .10 .05
❑ 16T Bud Black .10 .05
❑ 17T Pat Borders .20 .09
❑ 18T Phil Bradley .10 .05
❑ 19T Jeff Branson OLY .20 .09
❑ 20T Tom Brunansky .10 .05
❑ 21T Jay Buhner 1.25 .55
❑ 22T Brett Butler .20 .09
❑ 23T Jim Campanis OLY .10 .05
❑ 24T Sil Campusano .10 .05
❑ 25T John Candelaria .10 .05
❑ 26T Jose Cecena .10 .05
❑ 27T Rick Cerone .10 .05
❑ 28T Jack Clark .20 .09
❑ 29T Kevin Coffman .10 .05
❑ 30T Pat Combs OLY .10 .05
❑ 31T Henry Cotto .10 .05
❑ 32T Chili Davis .30 .14
❑ 33T Mike Davis .10 .05
❑ 34T Jose DeLeon .10 .05
❑ 35T Richard Dotson .10 .05
❑ 36T Cecil Espy .10 .05
❑ 37T Tom Filer .10 .05
❑ 38T Mike Fiore OLY .10 .05
❑ 39T Ron Gant .50 .23
❑ 40T Kirk Gibson .50 .23
❑ 41T Rich Gossage .20 .09
❑ 42T Mark Grace 1.50 .70
❑ 43T Alfredo Griffin .10 .05
❑ 44T Ty Griffin OLY .10 .05
❑ 45T Bryan Harvey .20 .09
❑ 46T Ron Hassey .10 .05
❑ 47T Ray Hayward .10 .05
❑ 48T Dave Henderson .10 .05
❑ 49T Tom Herr .10 .05
❑ 50T Bob Horner .10 .05
❑ 51T Ricky Horton .10 .05
❑ 52T Jay Howell .10 .05
❑ 53T Glenn Hubbard .10 .05
❑ 54T Jeff Innis .10 .05
❑ 55T Danny Jackson .10 .05
❑ 56T Darrin Jackson .20 .09

Card	Player	MINT	NRMT
❑ 57T	Roberto Kelly	.50	.23
❑ 58T	Ron Kittle	.10	.05
❑ 59T	Ray Knight	.10	.05
❑ 60T	Vance Law	.10	.05
❑ 61T	Jeffrey Leonard	.10	.05
❑ 62T	Mike Macfarlane	.10	.05
❑ 63T	Scotti Madison	.10	.05
❑ 64T	Kirt Manwaring	.10	.05
❑ 65T	Mark Marquess OLY CO	.10	.05
❑ 66T	Tino Martinez OLY	5.00	2.20
❑ 67T	Billy Masse OLY	.10	.05
❑ 68T	Jack McDowell	.50	.23
❑ 69T	Jack McKeon MG	.10	.05
❑ 70T	Larry McWilliams	.10	.05
❑ 71T	Mickey Morandini OLY	.30	.14
❑ 72T	Keith Moreland	.10	.05
❑ 73T	Mike Morgan	.10	.05
❑ 74T	Charles Nagy OLY	.75	.35
❑ 75T	Al Nipper	.10	.05
❑ 76T	Russ Nixon MG	.10	.05
❑ 77T	Jesse Orosco	.10	.05
❑ 78T	Joe Orsulak	.10	.05
❑ 79T	Dave Palmer	.10	.05
❑ 80T	Mark Parent	.10	.05
❑ 81T	Dave Parker	.20	.09
❑ 82T	Dan Pasqua	.10	.05
❑ 83T	Melido Perez	.10	.05
❑ 84T	Steve Peters	.10	.05
❑ 85T	Dan Petry	.10	.05
❑ 86T	Gary Pettis	.10	.05
❑ 87T	Jeff Pico	.10	.05
❑ 88T	Jim Poole OLY	.20	.09
❑ 89T	Ted Power	.10	.05
❑ 90T	Rafael Ramirez	.10	.05
❑ 91T	Dennis Rasmussen	.10	.05
❑ 92T	Jose Rijo	.10	.05
❑ 93T	Ernie Riles	.10	.05
❑ 94T	Luis Rivera	.10	.05
❑ 95T	Doug Robbins OLY	.10	.05
❑ 96T	Frank Robinson MG	.30	.14
❑ 97T	Cookie Rojas MG	.10	.05
❑ 98T	Chris Sabo	.20	.09
❑ 99T	Mark Salas	.10	.05
❑ 100T	Luis Salazar	.10	.05
❑ 101T	Rafael Santana	.10	.05
❑ 102T	Nelson Santovenia	.10	.05
❑ 103T	Mackey Sasser	.10	.05
❑ 104T	Calvin Schiraldi	.10	.05
❑ 105T	Mike Schooler	.10	.05
❑ 106T	Scott Servais OLY	.20	.09
❑ 107T	Dave Silvestri OLY	.10	.05
❑ 108T	Don Slaught	.10	.05
❑ 109T	Joe Slusarski OLY	.10	.05
❑ 110T	Lee Smith	.20	.09
❑ 111T	Pete Smith	.10	.05
❑ 112T	Jim Snyder MG	.10	.05
❑ 113T	Ed Sprague OLY	.50	.23
❑ 114T	Pete Stanicek	.10	.05
❑ 115T	Kurt Stillwell	.10	.05
❑ 116T	Todd Stottlemyre	.50	.23
❑ 117T	Bill Swift	.10	.05
❑ 118T	Pat Tabler	.10	.05
❑ 119T	Scott Terry	.10	.05
❑ 120T	Mickey Tettleton	.20	.09
❑ 121T	Dickie Thon	.10	.05
❑ 122T	Jeff Treadway	.10	.05
❑ 123T	Willie Upshaw	.10	.05
❑ 124T	Robin Ventura OLY	1.50	.70
❑ 125T	Ron Washington	.10	.05
❑ 126T	Walt Weiss	.20	.09
❑ 127T	Bob Welch	.10	.05
❑ 128T	David Wells	2.00	.90
❑ 129T	Glenn Wilson	.10	.05
❑ 130T	Ted Wood OLY	.20	.09
❑ 131T	Don Zimmer MG	.20	.09
❑ 132T	Checklist 1T-132T	.10	.05

1988 Topps Traded Tiffany

	MINT	NRMT
COMP.FACT.SET (132)	50.00	22.00
COMMON CARD (1T-132T)	.15	.07

*STARS: 2X TO 4X BASIC CARDS
*ROOKIES: 3X TO 6X BASIC CARDS

1989 Topps

	MINT	NRMT
COMPLETE SET (792)	12.00	5.50
COMP.FACT.SET (792)	15.00	6.75
COMMON CARD (1-792)	.05	.02

Card	Player	MINT	NRMT
❑ 1	George Bell RB Slams 3 Opening Day HR's	.05	.02
❑ 2	Wade Boggs RB 200 Hits 6th Straight Season	.10	.05
❑ 3	Gary Carter RB Career Putouts Record	.10	.05
❑ 4	Andre Dawson RB Logs Double Figures in HR and SB	.10	.05
❑ 5	Orel Hershiser RB 59 Scoreless Innings	.10	.05
❑ 6	Doug Jones RB UER Earns His 15th Straight Save (Photo actually Chris Codiroli)	.05	.02
❑ 7	Kevin McReynolds RB Steals 21 Without Being Caught	.05	.02
❑ 8	Dave Eiland	.05	.02
❑ 9	Tim Teufel	.05	.02
❑ 10	Andre Dawson	.20	.09
❑ 11	Bruce Sutter	.05	.02
❑ 12	Dale Sveum	.05	.02
❑ 13	Doug Sisk	.05	.02
❑ 14	Tom Kelly MG	.05	.02
❑ 15	Robby Thompson	.05	.02
❑ 16	Ron Robinson	.05	.02
❑ 17	Brian Downing	.05	.02
❑ 18	Rick Rhoden	.05	.02
❑ 19	Greg Gagne	.05	.02
❑ 20	Steve Bedrosian	.05	.02
❑ 21	Chicago White Sox TL Greg Walker	.05	.02
❑ 22	Tim Crews	.05	.02
❑ 23	Mike Fitzgerald	.05	.02
❑ 24	Larry Andersen	.05	.02
❑ 25	Frank White	.10	.05
❑ 26	Dale Mohorcic	.05	.02
❑ 27A	Orestes Destrade (F* next to copyright)	.05	.02
❑ 27B	Orestes Destrade (E*F* next to copyright)	.05	.02
❑ 28	Mike Moore	.05	.02
❑ 29	Kelly Gruber	.05	.02
❑ 30	Dwight Gooden	.10	.05
❑ 31	Terry Francona	.10	.05
❑ 32	Dennis Rasmussen	.05	.02
❑ 33	B.J. Surhoff	.10	.05
❑ 34	Ken Williams	.05	.02
❑ 35	John Tudor UER (With Red Sox in '84, should be Pirates)	.05	.02
❑ 36	Mitch Webster	.05	.02
❑ 37	Bob Stanley	.05	.02
❑ 38	Paul Runge	.05	.02
❑ 39	Mike Maddux	.05	.02
❑ 40	Steve Sax	.05	.02
❑ 41	Terry Mulholland	.05	.02
❑ 42	Jim Eppard	.05	.02
❑ 43	Guillermo Hernandez	.05	.02
❑ 44	Jim Snyder MG	.05	.02
❑ 45	Kal Daniels	.05	.02
❑ 46	Mark Portugal	.05	.02
❑ 47	Carney Lansford	.10	.05
❑ 48	Tim Burke	.05	.02
❑ 49	Craig Biggio	.75	.35
❑ 50	George Bell	.05	.02
❑ 51	California Angels TL Mark McLemore	.05	.02
❑ 52	Bob Brenly	.05	.02
❑ 53	Ruben Sierra	.05	.02
❑ 54	Steve Trout	.05	.02
❑ 55	Julio Franco	.05	.02
❑ 56	Pat Tabler	.05	.02
❑ 57	Alejandro Pena	.05	.02
❑ 58	Lee Mazzilli	.05	.02
❑ 59	Mark Davis	.05	.02
❑ 60	Tom Brunansky	.05	.02
❑ 61	Neil Allen	.05	.02
❑ 62	Alfredo Griffin	.05	.02
❑ 63	Mark Clear	.05	.02
❑ 64	Alex Trevino	.05	.02
❑ 65	Rick Reuschel	.05	.02
❑ 66	Manny Trillo	.05	.02
❑ 67	Dave Palmer	.05	.02
❑ 68	Darrell Miller	.05	.02
❑ 69	Jeff Ballard	.05	.02
❑ 70	Mark McGwire	1.25	.55
❑ 71	Mike Boddicker	.05	.02
❑ 72	John Moses	.05	.02
❑ 73	Pascual Perez	.05	.02
❑ 74	Nick Leyva MG	.05	.02
❑ 75	Tom Henke	.05	.02
❑ 76	Terry Blocker	.05	.02
❑ 77	Doyle Alexander	.05	.02
❑ 78	Jim Sundberg	.05	.02
❑ 79	Scott Bankhead	.05	.02
❑ 80	Cory Snyder	.05	.02
❑ 81	Montreal Expos TL Tim Raines	.10	.05
❑ 82	Dave Leiper	.05	.02
❑ 83	Jeff Blauser	.10	.05
❑ 84	Bill Bene FDP	.05	.02
❑ 85	Kevin McReynolds	.05	.02
❑ 86	Al Nipper	.05	.02
❑ 87	Larry Owen	.05	.02
❑ 88	Darryl Hamilton	.05	.02
❑ 89	Dave LaPoint	.05	.02
❑ 90	Vince Coleman UER (Wrong birth year)	.05	.02
❑ 91	Floyd Youmans	.05	.02
❑ 92	Jeff Kunkel	.05	.02
❑ 93	Ken Howell	.05	.02
❑ 94	Chris Speier	.05	.02
❑ 95	Gerald Young	.05	.02
❑ 96	Rick Cerone	.05	.02
❑ 97	Greg Mathews	.05	.02
❑ 98	Larry Sheets	.05	.02
❑ 99	Sherman Corbett	.05	.02
❑ 100	Mike Schmidt	.25	.11
❑ 101	Les Straker	.05	.02
❑ 102	Mike Gallego	.05	.02
❑ 103	Tim Birtsas	.05	.02
❑ 104	Dallas Green MG	.05	.02
❑ 105	Ron Darling	.05	.02
❑ 106	Willie Upshaw	.05	.02
❑ 107	Jose DeLeon	.05	.02
❑ 108	Fred Manrique	.05	.02
❑ 109	Hipolito Pena	.05	.02
❑ 110	Paul Molitor	.20	.09
❑ 111	Cincinnati Reds TL Eric Davis (Swinging bat)	.05	.02
❑ 112	Jim Presley	.05	.02
❑ 113	Lloyd Moseby	.05	.02
❑ 114	Bob Kipper	.05	.02
❑ 115	Jody Davis	.05	.02
❑ 116	Jeff Montgomery	.10	.05
❑ 117	Dave Anderson	.05	.02
❑ 118	Checklist 1-132	.05	.02
❑ 119	Terry Puhl	.05	.02
❑ 120	Frank Viola	.05	.02
❑ 121	Garry Templeton	.05	.02
❑ 122	Lance Johnson	.10	.05

❑ 123 Spike Owen .05 .02
❑ 124 Jim Traber .05 .02
❑ 125 Mike Krukow .05 .02
❑ 126 Sid Bream .05 .02
❑ 127 Walt Terrell .05 .02
❑ 128 Milt Thompson .05 .02
❑ 129 Terry Clark .05 .02
❑ 130 Gerald Perry .05 .02
❑ 131 Dave Otto .05 .02
❑ 132 Curt Ford .05 .02
❑ 133 Bill Long .05 .02
❑ 134 Don Zimmer MG .05 .02
❑ 135 Jose Rijo .05 .02
❑ 136 Joey Meyer .05 .02
❑ 137 Geno Petralli .05 .02
❑ 138 Wallace Johnson .05 .02
❑ 139 Mike Flanagan .05 .02
❑ 140 Shawon Dunston .05 .02
❑ 141 Cleveland Indians TL .05 .02
Brook Jacoby
❑ 142 Mike Diaz .05 .02
❑ 143 Mike Campbell .05 .02
❑ 144 Jay Bell .15 .07
❑ 145 Dave Stewart .10 .05
❑ 146 Gary Pettis .05 .02
❑ 147 DeWayne Buice .05 .02
❑ 148 Bill Pecota .05 .02
❑ 149 Doug Dascenzo .05 .02
❑ 150 Fernando Valenzuela .10 .05
❑ 151 Terry McGriff .05 .02
❑ 152 Mark Thurmond .05 .02
❑ 153 Jim Pankovits .05 .02
❑ 154 Don Carman .05 .02
❑ 155 Marty Barrett .05 .02
❑ 156 Dave Gallagher .05 .02
❑ 157 Tom Glavine .20 .09
❑ 158 Mike Aldrete .05 .02
❑ 159 Pat Clements .05 .02
❑ 160 Jeffrey Leonard .05 .02
❑ 161 Gregg Olson FDP UER .20 .09
(Born Scribner, NE, should be Omaha, NE)
❑ 162 John Davis .05 .02
❑ 163 Bob Forsch .05 .02
❑ 164 Hal Lanier MG .05 .02
❑ 165 Mike Dunne .05 .02
❑ 166 Doug Jennings .05 .02
❑ 167 Steve Searcy FS .05 .02
❑ 168 Willie Wilson .05 .02
❑ 169 Mike Jackson .15 .07
❑ 170 Tony Fernandez .05 .02
❑ 171 Atlanta Braves TL .05 .02
Andres Thomas
❑ 172 Frank Williams .05 .02
❑ 173 Mel Hall .05 .02
❑ 174 Todd Burns .05 .02
❑ 175 John Shelby .05 .02
❑ 176 Jeff Parrett .05 .02
❑ 177 Monty Fariss FDP .05 .02
❑ 178 Mark Grant .05 .02
❑ 179 Ozzie Virgil .05 .02
❑ 180 Mike Scott .05 .02
❑ 181 Craig Worthington .05 .02
❑ 182 Bob McClure .05 .02
❑ 183 Oddibe McDowell .05 .02
❑ 184 John Costello .05 .02
❑ 185 Claudell Washington .05 .02
❑ 186 Pat Perry .05 .02
❑ 187 Darren Daulton .10 .05
❑ 188 Dennis Lamp .05 .02
❑ 189 Kevin Mitchell .10 .05
❑ 190 Mike Witt .05 .02
❑ 191 Sil Campusano .05 .02
❑ 192 Paul Mirabella .05 .02
❑ 193 Sparky Anderson MG .10 .05
UER (553 Salazer)
❑ 194 Greg W. Harris .05 .02
❑ 195 Ozzie Guillen .05 .02
❑ 196 Denny Walling .05 .02
❑ 197 Neal Heaton .05 .02
❑ 198 Danny Heep .05 .02
❑ 199 Mike Schooler .05 .02
❑ 200 George Brett .40 .18
❑ 201 Blue Jays TL .05 .02
Kelly Gruber
❑ 202 Brad Moore .05 .02
❑ 203 Rob Ducey .05 .02
❑ 204 Brad Havens .05 .02
❑ 205 Dwight Evans .10 .05
❑ 206 Roberto Alomar .30 .14
❑ 207 Terry Leach .05 .02
❑ 208 Tom Pagnozzi .05 .02
❑ 209 Jeff Bittiger .05 .02
❑ 210 Dale Murphy .20 .09
❑ 211 Mike Pagliarulo .05 .02
❑ 212 Scott Sanderson .05 .02
❑ 213 Rene Gonzales .05 .02
❑ 214 Charlie O'Brien .05 .02
❑ 215 Kevin Gross .05 .02
❑ 216 Jack Howell .05 .02
❑ 217 Joe Price .05 .02
❑ 218 Mike LaValliere .05 .02
❑ 219 Jim Clancy .05 .02
❑ 220 Gary Gaetti .10 .05
❑ 221 Cecil Espy .05 .02
❑ 222 Mark Lewis FDP .20 .09
❑ 223 Jay Buhner .20 .09
❑ 224 Tony LaRussa MG .10 .05
❑ 225 Ramon Martinez .25 .11
❑ 226 Bill Doran .05 .02
❑ 227 John Farrell .05 .02
❑ 228 Nelson Santovenia .05 .02
❑ 229 Jimmy Key .10 .05
❑ 230 Ozzie Smith .25 .11
❑ 231 San Diego Padres TL .20 .09
Roberto Alomar
(Gary Carter at plate)
❑ 232 Ricky Horton .05 .02
❑ 233 Gregg Jefferies FS .10 .05
❑ 234 Tom Browning .05 .02
❑ 235 John Kruk .10 .05
❑ 236 Charles Hudson .05 .02
❑ 237 Glenn Hubbard .05 .02
❑ 238 Eric King .05 .02
❑ 239 Tim Laudner .05 .02
❑ 240 Greg Maddux .75 .35
❑ 241 Brett Butler .10 .05
❑ 242 Ed VandeBerg .05 .02
❑ 243 Bob Boone .10 .05
❑ 244 Jim Acker .05 .02
❑ 245 Jim Rice .10 .05
❑ 246 Rey Quinones .05 .02
❑ 247 Shawn Hillegas .05 .02
❑ 248 Tony Phillips .05 .02
❑ 249 Tim Leary .05 .02
❑ 250 Cal Ripken .75 .35
❑ 251 John Dopson .05 .02
❑ 252 Billy Hatcher .05 .02
❑ 253 Jose Alvarez .05 .02
❑ 254 Tom Lasorda MG .20 .09
❑ 255 Ron Guidry .10 .05
❑ 256 Benny Santiago .05 .02
❑ 257 Rick Aguilera .10 .05
❑ 258 Checklist 133-264 .05 .02
❑ 259 Larry McWilliams .05 .02
❑ 260 Dave Winfield .20 .09
❑ 261 St.Louis Cardinals TL .05 .02
Tom Brunansky
(With Luis Alicea)
❑ 262 Jeff Pico .05 .02
❑ 263 Mike Felder .05 .02
❑ 264 Rob Dibble .10 .05
❑ 265 Kent Hrbek .10 .05
❑ 266 Luis Aquino .05 .02
❑ 267 Jeff M. Robinson .05 .02
❑ 268 N. Keith Miller .05 .02
❑ 269 Tom Bolton .05 .02
❑ 270 Wally Joyner .10 .05
❑ 271 Jay Tibbs .05 .02
❑ 272 Ron Hassey .05 .02
❑ 273 Jose Lind .05 .02
❑ 274 Mark Eichhorn .05 .02
❑ 275 Danny Tartabull UER .05 .02
(Born San Juan, PR should be Miami, FL)
❑ 276 Paul Kilgus .05 .02
❑ 277 Mike Davis .05 .02
❑ 278 Andy McGaffigan .05 .02
❑ 279 Scott Bradley .05 .02
❑ 280 Bob Knepper .05 .02
❑ 281 Gary Redus .05 .02
❑ 282 Cris Carpenter .05 .02
❑ 283 Andy Allanson .05 .02
❑ 284 Jim Leyland MG .10 .05
❑ 285 John Candelaria .05 .02
❑ 286 Darrin Jackson .05 .02
❑ 287 Juan Nieves .05 .02
❑ 288 Pat Sheridan .05 .02
❑ 289 Ernie Whitt .05 .02
❑ 290 John Franco .10 .05
❑ 291 New York Mets TL .10 .05
Darryl Strawberry
(With Keith Hernandez and Kevin McReynolds)
❑ 292 Jim Corsi .05 .02
❑ 293 Glenn Wilson .05 .02
❑ 294 Juan Berenguer .05 .02
❑ 295 Scott Fletcher .05 .02
❑ 296 Ron Gant .10 .05
❑ 297 Oswald Peraza .05 .02
❑ 298 Chris James .05 .02
❑ 299 Steve Ellsworth .05 .02
❑ 300 Darryl Strawberry .10 .05
❑ 301 Charlie Leibrandt .05 .02
❑ 302 Gary Ward .05 .02
❑ 303 Felix Fermin .05 .02
❑ 304 Joel Youngblood .05 .02
❑ 305 Dave Smith .05 .02
❑ 306 Tracy Woodson .05 .02
❑ 307 Lance McCullers .05 .02
❑ 308 Ron Karkovice .05 .02
❑ 309 Mario Diaz .05 .02
❑ 310 Rafael Palmeiro .20 .09
❑ 311 Chris Bosio .05 .02
❑ 312 Tom Lawless .05 .02
❑ 313 Dennis Martinez .10 .05
❑ 314 Bobby Valentine MG .05 .02
❑ 315 Greg Swindell .05 .02
❑ 316 Walt Weiss .05 .02
❑ 317 Jack Armstrong .05 .02
❑ 318 Gene Larkin .05 .02
❑ 319 Greg Booker .05 .02
❑ 320 Lou Whitaker .10 .05
❑ 321 Boston Red Sox TL .05 .02
Jody Reed
❑ 322 John Smiley .05 .02
❑ 323 Gary Thurman .05 .02
❑ 324 Bob Milacki .05 .02
❑ 325 Jesse Barfield .05 .02
❑ 326 Dennis Boyd .05 .02
❑ 327 Mark Lemke .15 .07
❑ 328 Rick Honeycutt .05 .02
❑ 329 Bob Melvin .05 .02
❑ 330 Eric Davis .10 .05
❑ 331 Curt Wilkerson .05 .02
❑ 332 Tony Armas .05 .02
❑ 333 Bob Ojeda .05 .02
❑ 334 Steve Lyons .05 .02
❑ 335 Dave Righetti .05 .02
❑ 336 Steve Balboni .05 .02
❑ 337 Calvin Schiraldi .05 .02
❑ 338 Jim Adduci .05 .02
❑ 339 Scott Bailes .05 .02
❑ 340 Kirk Gibson .10 .05
❑ 341 Jim Deshaies .05 .02
❑ 342 Tom Brookens .05 .02
❑ 343 Gary Sheffield FS .60 .25
❑ 344 Tom Trebelhorn MG .05 .02
❑ 345 Charlie Hough .10 .05
❑ 346 Rex Hudler .05 .02
❑ 347 John Cerutti .05 .02
❑ 348 Ed Hearn .05 .02
❑ 349 Ron Jones .05 .02
❑ 350 Andy Van Slyke .10 .05
❑ 351 San Fran. Giants TL .05 .02
Bob Melvin
(With Bill Fahey CO)
❑ 352 Rick Schu .05 .02
❑ 353 Marvell Wynne .05 .02
❑ 354 Larry Parrish .05 .02
❑ 355 Mark Langston .05 .02
❑ 356 Kevin Elster .05 .02
❑ 357 Jerry Reuss .05 .02
❑ 358 Ricky Jordan .10 .05
❑ 359 Tommy John .10 .05

❑ 360	Ryne Sandberg	.25	.11
❑ 361	Kelly Downs	.05	.02
❑ 362	Jack Lazorko	.05	.02
❑ 363	Rich Yett	.05	.02
❑ 364	Rob Deer	.05	.02
❑ 365	Mike Henneman	.05	.02
❑ 366	Herm Winningham	.05	.02
❑ 367	Johnny Paredes	.05	.02
❑ 368	Brian Holton	.05	.02
❑ 369	Ken Caminiti	.20	.09
❑ 370	Dennis Eckersley	.15	.07
❑ 371	Manny Lee	.05	.02
❑ 372	Craig Lefferts	.05	.02
❑ 373	Tracy Jones	.05	.02
❑ 374	John Wathan MG	.05	.02
❑ 375	Terry Pendleton	.10	.05
❑ 376	Steve Lombardozzi	.05	.02
❑ 377	Mike Smithson	.05	.02
❑ 378	Checklist 265-396	.05	.02
❑ 379	Tim Flannery	.05	.02
❑ 380	Rickey Henderson	.20	.09
❑ 381	Baltimore Orioles TL	.05	.02
	Larry Sheets		
❑ 382	John Smoltz	.50	.23
❑ 383	Howard Johnson	.05	.02
❑ 384	Mark Salas	.05	.02
❑ 385	Von Hayes	.05	.02
❑ 386	Andres Galarraga AS	.10	.05
❑ 387	Ryne Sandberg AS	.15	.07
❑ 388	Bobby Bonilla AS	.10	.05
❑ 389	Ozzie Smith AS	.15	.07
❑ 390	Darryl Strawberry AS	.05	.02
❑ 391	Andre Dawson AS	.10	.05
❑ 392	Andy Van Slyke AS	.05	.02
❑ 393	Gary Carter AS	.10	.05
❑ 394	Orel Hershiser AS	.10	.05
❑ 395	Danny Jackson AS	.05	.02
❑ 396	Kirk Gibson AS	.10	.05
❑ 397	Don Mattingly AS	.15	.07
❑ 398	Julio Franco AS	.05	.02
❑ 399	Wade Boggs AS	.10	.05
❑ 400	Alan Trammell AS	.10	.05
❑ 401	Jose Canseco AS	.10	.05
❑ 402	Mike Greenwell AS	.05	.02
❑ 403	Kirby Puckett AS	.20	.09
❑ 404	Bob Boone AS	.05	.02
❑ 405	Roger Clemens AS	.20	.09
❑ 406	Frank Viola AS	.05	.02
❑ 407	Dave Winfield AS	.10	.05
❑ 408	Greg Walker	.05	.02
❑ 409	Ken Dayley	.05	.02
❑ 410	Jack Clark	.05	.02
❑ 411	Mitch Williams	.05	.02
❑ 412	Barry Lyons	.05	.02
❑ 413	Mike Kingery	.05	.02
❑ 414	Jim Fregosi MG	.05	.02
❑ 415	Rich Gossage	.10	.05
❑ 416	Fred Lynn	.05	.02
❑ 417	Mike LaCoss	.05	.02
❑ 418	Bob Dernier	.05	.02
❑ 419	Tom Filer	.05	.02
❑ 420	Joe Carter	.15	.07
❑ 421	Kirk McCaskill	.05	.02
❑ 422	Bo Diaz	.05	.02
❑ 423	Brian Fisher	.05	.02
❑ 424	Luis Polonia UER	.05	.02
	(Wrong birthdate)		
❑ 425	Jay Howell	.05	.02
❑ 426	Dan Gladden	.05	.02
❑ 427	Eric Show	.05	.02
❑ 428	Craig Reynolds	.05	.02
❑ 429	Minnesota Twins TL	.05	.02
	Greg Gagne		
	(Taking throw at 2nd)		
❑ 430	Mark Gubicza	.05	.02
❑ 431	Luis Rivera	.05	.02
❑ 432	Chad Kreuter	.05	.02
❑ 433	Albert Hall	.05	.02
❑ 434	Ken Patterson	.05	.02
❑ 435	Len Dykstra	.10	.05
❑ 436	Bobby Meacham	.05	.02
❑ 437	Andy Benes FDP	.25	.11
❑ 438	Greg Gross	.05	.02
❑ 439	Frank DiPino	.05	.02
❑ 440	Bobby Bonilla	.15	.07
❑ 441	Jerry Reed	.05	.02
❑ 442	Jose Oquendo	.05	.02
❑ 443	Rod Nichols	.05	.02
❑ 444	Moose Stubing MG	.05	.02
❑ 445	Matt Nokes	.05	.02
❑ 446	Rob Murphy	.05	.02
❑ 447	Donell Nixon	.05	.02
❑ 448	Eric Plunk	.05	.02
❑ 449	Carmelo Martinez	.05	.02
❑ 450	Roger Clemens	.40	.18
❑ 451	Mark Davidson	.05	.02
❑ 452	Israel Sanchez	.05	.02
❑ 453	Tom Prince	.05	.02
❑ 454	Paul Assenmacher	.05	.02
❑ 455	Johnny Ray	.05	.02
❑ 456	Tim Belcher	.05	.02
❑ 457	Mackey Sasser	.05	.02
❑ 458	Donn Pall	.05	.02
❑ 459	Seattle Mariners TL	.05	.02
	Dave Valle		
❑ 460	Dave Stieb	.05	.02
❑ 461	Buddy Bell	.10	.05
❑ 462	Jose Guzman	.05	.02
❑ 463	Steve Lake	.05	.02
❑ 464	Bryn Smith	.05	.02
❑ 465	Mark Grace	.20	.09
❑ 466	Chuck Crim	.05	.02
❑ 467	Jim Walewander	.05	.02
❑ 468	Henry Cotto	.05	.02
❑ 469	Jose Bautista	.05	.02
❑ 470	Lance Parrish	.05	.02
❑ 471	Steve Curry	.05	.02
❑ 472	Brian Harper	.05	.02
❑ 473	Don Robinson	.05	.02
❑ 474	Bob Rodgers MG	.05	.02
❑ 475	Dave Parker	.10	.05
❑ 476	Jon Perlman	.05	.02
❑ 477	Dick Schofield	.05	.02
❑ 478	Doug Drabek	.05	.02
❑ 479	Mike Macfarlane	.05	.02
❑ 480	Keith Hernandez	.10	.05
❑ 481	Chris Brown	.05	.02
❑ 482	Steve Peters	.05	.02
❑ 483	Mickey Hatcher	.05	.02
❑ 484	Steve Shields	.05	.02
❑ 485	Hubie Brooks	.05	.02
❑ 486	Jack McDowell	.10	.05
❑ 487	Scott Lusader	.05	.02
❑ 488	Kevin Coffman	.05	.02
	Now with Cubs		
❑ 489	Phila. Phillies TL	.10	.05
	Mike Schmidt		
❑ 490	Chris Sabo	.05	.02
❑ 491	Mike Birkbeck	.05	.02
❑ 492	Alan Ashby	.05	.02
❑ 493	Todd Benzinger	.05	.02
❑ 494	Shane Rawley	.05	.02
❑ 495	Candy Maldonado	.05	.02
❑ 496	Dwayne Henry	.05	.02
❑ 497	Pete Stanicek	.05	.02
❑ 498	Dave Valle	.05	.02
❑ 499	Don Heinkel	.05	.02
❑ 500	Jose Canseco	.20	.09
❑ 501	Vance Law	.05	.02
❑ 502	Duane Ward	.05	.02
❑ 503	Al Newman	.05	.02
❑ 504	Bob Walk	.05	.02
❑ 505	Pete Rose MG	.25	.11
❑ 506	Kirt Manwaring	.05	.02
❑ 507	Steve Farr	.05	.02
❑ 508	Wally Backman	.05	.02
❑ 509	Bud Black	.05	.02
❑ 510	Bob Horner	.05	.02
❑ 511	Richard Dotson	.05	.02
❑ 512	Donnie Hill	.05	.02
❑ 513	Jesse Orosco	.05	.02
❑ 514	Chet Lemon	.05	.02
❑ 515	Barry Larkin	.20	.09
❑ 516	Eddie Whitson	.05	.02
❑ 517	Greg Brock	.05	.02
❑ 518	Bruce Ruffin	.05	.02
❑ 519	New York Yankees TL	.05	.02
	Willie Randolph		
❑ 520	Rick Sutcliffe	.05	.02
❑ 521	Mickey Tettleton	.10	.05
❑ 522	Randy Kramer	.05	.02
❑ 523	Andres Thomas	.05	.02
❑ 524	Checklist 397-528	.05	.02
❑ 525	Chili Davis	.10	.05
❑ 526	Wes Gardner	.05	.02
❑ 527	Dave Henderson	.05	.02
❑ 528	Luis Medina	.05	.02
	(Lower left front		
	has white triangle)		
❑ 529	Tom Foley	.05	.02
❑ 530	Nolan Ryan	.75	.35
❑ 531	Dave Hengel	.05	.02
❑ 532	Jerry Browne	.05	.02
❑ 533	Andy Hawkins	.05	.02
❑ 534	Doc Edwards MG	.05	.02
❑ 535	Todd Worrell UER	.05	.02
	(4 wins in '88,		
	should be 5)		
❑ 536	Joel Skinner	.05	.02
❑ 537	Pete Smith	.05	.02
❑ 538	Juan Castillo	.05	.02
❑ 539	Barry Jones	.05	.02
❑ 540	Bo Jackson	.15	.07
❑ 541	Cecil Fielder	.10	.05
❑ 542	Todd Frohwirth	.05	.02
❑ 543	Damon Berryhill	.05	.02
❑ 544	Jeff Sellers	.05	.02
❑ 545	Mookie Wilson	.10	.05
❑ 546	Mark Williamson	.05	.02
❑ 547	Mark McLemore	.05	.02
❑ 548	Bobby Witt	.05	.02
❑ 549	Chicago Cubs TL	.05	.02
	Jamie Moyer		
	(Pitching)		
❑ 550	Orel Hershiser	.10	.05
❑ 551	Randy Ready	.05	.02
❑ 552	Greg Cadaret	.05	.02
❑ 553	Luis Salazar	.05	.02
❑ 554	Nick Esasky	.05	.02
❑ 555	Bert Blyleven	.10	.05
❑ 556	Bruce Fields	.05	.02
❑ 557	Keith A. Miller	.05	.02
❑ 558	Dan Pasqua	.05	.02
❑ 559	Juan Agosto	.05	.02
❑ 560	Tim Raines	.10	.05
❑ 561	Luis Aguayo	.05	.02
❑ 562	Danny Cox	.05	.02
❑ 563	Bill Schroeder	.05	.02
❑ 564	Russ Nixon MG	.05	.02
❑ 565	Jeff Russell	.05	.02
❑ 566	Al Pedrique	.05	.02
❑ 567	David Wells UER	.20	.09
	(Complete Pitching		
	Recor)		
❑ 568	Mickey Brantley	.05	.02
❑ 569	German Jimenez	.05	.02
❑ 570	Tony Gwynn UER	.50	.23
	('88 average should		
	be italicized as		
	league leader)		
❑ 571	Billy Ripken	.05	.02
❑ 572	Atlee Hammaker	.05	.02
❑ 573	Jim Abbott FDP	.20	.09
❑ 574	Dave Clark	.05	.02
❑ 575	Juan Samuel	.05	.02
❑ 576	Greg Minton	.05	.02
❑ 577	Randy Bush	.05	.02
❑ 578	John Morris	.05	.02
❑ 579	Houston Astros TL	.05	.02
	Glenn Davis		
	(Batting stance)		
❑ 580	Harold Reynolds	.05	.02
❑ 581	Gene Nelson	.05	.02
❑ 582	Mike Marshall	.05	.02
❑ 583	Paul Gibson	.05	.02
❑ 584	Randy Velarde UER	.05	.02
	(Signed 1935,		
	should be 1985)		
❑ 585	Harold Baines	.10	.05
❑ 586	Joe Boever	.05	.02
❑ 587	Mike Stanley	.05	.02
❑ 588	Luis Alicea	.05	.02
❑ 589	Dave Meads	.05	.02
❑ 590	Andres Galarraga	.20	.09
❑ 591	Jeff Musselman	.05	.02

❑ 592 John Cangelosi .05 .02
❑ 593 Drew Hall .05 .02
❑ 594 Jimy Williams MG .05 .02
❑ 595 Teddy Higuera .05 .02
❑ 596 Kurt Stillwell .05 .02
❑ 597 Terry Taylor .05 .02
❑ 598 Ken Gerhart .05 .02
❑ 599 Tom Candiotti .05 .02
❑ 600 Wade Boggs .20 .09
❑ 601 Dave Dravecky .10 .05
❑ 602 Devon White .10 .05
❑ 603 Frank Tanana .05 .02
❑ 604 Paul O'Neill .10 .05
❑ 605A Bob Welch ERR 2.00 .90
(Missing line on back
Complete M.L. Pitching Record
❑ 605B Bob Welch COR .05 .02
❑ 606 Rick Dempsey .05 .02
❑ 607 Willie Ansley FDP .05 .02
❑ 608 Phil Bradley .05 .02
❑ 609 Detroit Tigers TL .05 .02
Frank Tanana
(With Alan Trammell
and Mike Heath)
❑ 610 Randy Myers .10 .05
❑ 611 Don Slaught .05 .02
❑ 612 Dan Quisenberry .05 .02
❑ 613 Gary Varsho .05 .02
❑ 614 Joe Hesketh .05 .02
❑ 615 Robin Yount .20 .09
❑ 616 Steve Rosenberg .05 .02
❑ 617 Mark Parent .05 .02
❑ 618 Rance Mulliniks .05 .02
❑ 619 Checklist 529-660 .05 .02
❑ 620 Barry Bonds .40 .18
❑ 621 Rick Mahler .05 .02
❑ 622 Stan Javier .05 .02
❑ 623 Fred Toliver .05 .02
❑ 624 Jack McKeon MG .05 .02
❑ 625 Eddie Murray .20 .09
❑ 626 Jeff Reed .05 .02
❑ 627 Greg A. Harris .05 .02
❑ 628 Matt Williams .20 .09
❑ 629 Pete O'Brien .05 .02
❑ 630 Mike Greenwell .05 .02
❑ 631 Dave Bergman .05 .02
❑ 632 Bryan Harvey .05 .02
❑ 633 Daryl Boston .05 .02
❑ 634 Marvin Freeman .05 .02
❑ 635 Willie Randolph .10 .05
❑ 636 Bill Wilkinson .05 .02
❑ 637 Carmen Castillo .05 .02
❑ 638 Floyd Bannister .05 .02
❑ 639 Oakland A's TL .05 .02
Walt Weiss
❑ 640 Willie McGee .10 .05
❑ 641 Curt Young .05 .02
❑ 642 Argenis Salazar .05 .02
❑ 643 Louie Meadows .05 .02
❑ 644 Lloyd McClendon .05 .02
❑ 645 Jack Morris .10 .05
❑ 646 Kevin Bass .05 .02
❑ 647 Randy Johnson 1.25 .55
❑ 648 Sandy Alomar FS .40 .18
❑ 649 Stewart Cliburn .05 .02
❑ 650 Kirby Puckett .40 .18
❑ 651 Tom Niedenfuer .05 .02
❑ 652 Rich Gedman .05 .02
❑ 653 Tommy Barrett .05 .02
❑ 654 Whitey Herzog MG .05 .02
❑ 655 Dave Magadan .05 .02
❑ 656 Ivan Calderon .05 .02
❑ 657 Joe Magrane .05 .02
❑ 658 R.J. Reynolds .05 .02
❑ 659 Al Leiter .20 .09
❑ 660 Will Clark .20 .09
❑ 661 Dwight Gooden TBC84 .05 .02
❑ 662 Lou Brock TBC79 .20 .09
❑ 663 Hank Aaron TBC74 .20 .09
❑ 664 Gil Hodges TBC69 .15 .07
❑ 665A Tony Oliva TBC64 2.00 .90
ERR (fabricated card
is enlarged version
of Oliva's 64T card;
Topps copyright
missing)
❑ 665B Tony Oliva TBC64 .10 .05
COR (fabricated
card)
❑ 666 Randy St.Claire .05 .02
❑ 667 Dwayne Murphy .05 .02
❑ 668 Mike Bielecki .05 .02
❑ 669 L.A. Dodgers TL .10 .05
Orel Hershiser
(Mound conference
with Mike Scioscia)
❑ 670 Kevin Seitzer .05 .02
❑ 671 Jim Gantner .05 .02
❑ 672 Allan Anderson .05 .02
❑ 673 Don Baylor .10 .05
❑ 674 Otis Nixon .10 .05
❑ 675 Bruce Hurst .05 .02
❑ 676 Ernie Riles .05 .02
❑ 677 Dave Schmidt .05 .02
❑ 678 Dion James .05 .02
❑ 679 Willie Fraser .05 .02
❑ 680 Gary Carter .15 .07
❑ 681 Jeff D. Robinson .05 .02
❑ 682 Rick Leach .05 .02
❑ 683 Jose Cecena .05 .02
❑ 684 Dave Johnson MG .05 .02
❑ 685 Jeff Treadway .05 .02
❑ 686 Scott Terry .05 .02
❑ 687 Alvin Davis .05 .02
❑ 688 Zane Smith .05 .02
❑ 689A Stan Jefferson .05 .02
(Pink triangle on
front bottom left)
❑ 689B Stan Jefferson .05 .02
(Violet triangle on
front bottom left)
❑ 690 Doug Jones .05 .02
❑ 691 Roberto Kelly UER .05 .02
(83 Oneonita)
❑ 692 Steve Ontiveros .05 .02
❑ 693 Pat Borders .10 .05
❑ 694 Les Lancaster .05 .02
❑ 695 Carlton Fisk .20 .09
❑ 696 Don August .05 .02
❑ 697A Franklin Stubbs .05 .02
(Team name on front
in white)
❑ 697B Franklin Stubbs .05 .02
(Team name on front
in gray)
❑ 698 Keith Atherton .05 .02
❑ 699 Pittsburgh Pirates TL .05 .02
Al Pedrique
(Tony Gwynn sliding)
❑ 700 Don Mattingly .30 .14
❑ 701 Storm Davis .05 .02
❑ 702 Jamie Quirk .05 .02
❑ 703 Scott Garrelts .05 .02
❑ 704 Carlos Quintana .05 .02
❑ 705 Terry Kennedy .05 .02
❑ 706 Pete Incaviglia .05 .02
❑ 707 Steve Jeltz .05 .02
❑ 708 Chuck Finley .10 .05
❑ 709 Tom Herr .05 .02
❑ 710 David Cone .20 .09
❑ 711 Candy Sierra .05 .02
❑ 712 Bill Swift .05 .02
❑ 713 Ty Griffin FDP .05 .02
❑ 714 Joe Morgan MG .05 .02
❑ 715 Tony Pena .05 .02
❑ 716 Wayne Tolleson .05 .02
❑ 717 Jamie Moyer .05 .02
❑ 718 Glenn Braggs .05 .02
❑ 719 Danny Darwin .05 .02
❑ 720 Tim Wallach .05 .02
❑ 721 Ron Tingley .05 .02
❑ 722 Todd Stottlemyre .15 .07
❑ 723 Rafael Belliard .05 .02
❑ 724 Jerry Don Gleaton .05 .02
❑ 725 Terry Steinbach .10 .05
❑ 726 Dickie Thon .05 .02
❑ 727 Joe Orsulak .05 .02
❑ 728 Charlie Puleo .05 .02
❑ 729 Texas Rangers TL .05 .02
Steve Buechele
(Inconsistent design,
team name on front
surrounded by black,
should be white)
❑ 730 Danny Jackson .05 .02
❑ 731 Mike Young .05 .02
❑ 732 Steve Buechele .05 .02
❑ 733 Randy Bockus .05 .02
❑ 734 Jody Reed .05 .02
❑ 735 Roger McDowell .05 .02
❑ 736 Jeff Hamilton .05 .02
❑ 737 Norm Charlton .10 .05
❑ 738 Darnell Coles .05 .02
❑ 739 Brook Jacoby .05 .02
❑ 740 Dan Plesac .05 .02
❑ 741 Ken Phelps .05 .02
❑ 742 Mike Harkey FS .05 .02
❑ 743 Mike Heath .05 .02
❑ 744 Roger Craig MG .05 .02
❑ 745 Fred McGriff .20 .09
❑ 746 German Gonzalez UER .05 .02
(Wrong birthdate)
❑ 747 Wil Tejada .05 .02
❑ 748 Jimmy Jones .05 .02
❑ 749 Rafael Ramirez .05 .02
❑ 750 Bret Saberhagen .10 .05
❑ 751 Ken Oberkfell .05 .02
❑ 752 Jim Gott .05 .02
❑ 753 Jose Uribe .05 .02
❑ 754 Bob Brower .05 .02
❑ 755 Mike Scioscia .05 .02
❑ 756 Scott Medvin .05 .02
❑ 757 Brady Anderson .40 .18
❑ 758 Gene Walter .05 .02
❑ 759 Milwaukee Brewers TL .05 .02
Rob Deer
❑ 760 Lee Smith .10 .05
❑ 761 Dante Bichette .40 .18
❑ 762 Bobby Thigpen .05 .02
❑ 763 Dave Martinez .05 .02
❑ 764 Robin Ventura FDP .40 .18
❑ 765 Glenn Davis .05 .02
❑ 766 Cecilio Guante .05 .02
❑ 767 Mike Capel .05 .02
❑ 768 Bill Wegman .05 .02
❑ 769 Junior Ortiz .05 .02
❑ 770 Alan Trammell .15 .07
❑ 771 Ron Kittle .05 .02
❑ 772 Ron Oester .05 .02
❑ 773 Keith Moreland .05 .02
❑ 774 Frank Robinson MG .20 .09
❑ 775 Jeff Reardon .10 .05
❑ 776 Nelson Liriano .05 .02
❑ 777 Ted Power .05 .02
❑ 778 Bruce Benedict .05 .02
❑ 779 Craig McMurtry .05 .02
❑ 780 Pedro Guerrero .05 .02
❑ 781 Greg Briley .05 .02
❑ 782 Checklist 661-792 .05 .02
❑ 783 Trevor Wilson .05 .02
❑ 784 Steve Avery FDP .20 .09
❑ 785 Ellis Burks .15 .07
❑ 786 Melido Perez .05 .02
❑ 787 Dave West .05 .02
❑ 788 Mike Morgan .05 .02
❑ 789 Kansas City Royals TL .20 .09
Bo Jackson
(Throwing)
❑ 790 Sid Fernandez .05 .02
❑ 791 Jim Lindeman .05 .02
❑ 792 Rafael Santana .05 .02

1989 Topps Tiffany

	MINT	NRMT
COMP.FACT.SET (792)	100.00	45.00
COMMON CARD (1-792)	.20	.09

*STARS: 6X TO 12X BASIC CARDS
*ROOKIES: 7.5X TO 15X BASIC CARDS

1989 Topps Rookies

	MINT	NRMT
COMPLETE SET (22)	7.00	3.10
COMMON CARD (1-22)	.20	.09

❑ 1 Roberto Alomar 1.50 .70
❑ 2 Brady Anderson .50 .23

Card	MINT	NRMT
❑ 3 Tim Belcher	.20	.09
❑ 4 Damon Berryhill	.20	.09
❑ 5 Jay Buhner	.50	.23
❑ 6 Kevin Elster	.10	.05
❑ 7 Cecil Espy	.20	.09
❑ 8 Dave Gallagher	.20	.09
❑ 9 Ron Gant	.75	.35
❑ 10 Paul Gibson	.20	.09
❑ 11 Mark Grace	.75	.35
❑ 12 Darrin Jackson	.20	.09
❑ 13 Gregg Jefferies	.10	.05
❑ 14 Ricky Jordan	.20	.09
❑ 15 Al Leiter	.25	.11
❑ 16 Melido Perez	.20	.09
❑ 17 Chris Sabo	.20	.09
❑ 18 Nelson Santovenia	.20	.09
❑ 19 Mackey Sasser	.20	.09
❑ 20 Gary Sheffield	1.25	.55
❑ 21 Walt Weiss	.20	.09
❑ 22 David Wells	.25	.11

1989 Topps Traded

	MINT	NRMT
COMP.FACT.SET (132)	20.00	9.00
COMMON CARD (1T-132T)	.05	.02

Card	MINT	NRMT
❑ 1T Don Aase	.05	.02
❑ 2T Jim Abbott	.20	.09
❑ 3T Kent Anderson	.05	.02
❑ 4T Keith Atherton	.05	.02
❑ 5T Wally Backman	.05	.02
❑ 6T Steve Balboni	.05	.02
❑ 7T Jesse Barfield	.05	.02
❑ 8T Steve Bedrosian	.05	.02
❑ 9T Todd Benzinger	.05	.02
❑ 10T Geronimo Berroa	.05	.02
❑ 11T Bert Blyleven	.10	.05
❑ 12T Bob Boone	.10	.05
❑ 13T Phil Bradley	.05	.02
❑ 14T Jeff Brantley	.05	.02
❑ 15T Kevin Brown	.60	.25
❑ 16T Jerry Browne	.05	.02
❑ 17T Chuck Cary	.05	.02
❑ 18T Carmen Castillo	.05	.02
❑ 19T Jim Clancy	.05	.02
❑ 20T Jack Clark	.05	.02
❑ 21T Bryan Clutterbuck	.05	.02
❑ 22T Jody Davis	.05	.02
❑ 23T Mike Devereaux	.05	.02
❑ 24T Frank DiPino	.05	.02
❑ 25T Benny Distefano	.05	.02
❑ 26T John Dopson	.05	.02
❑ 27T Len Dykstra	.10	.05
❑ 28T Jim Eisenreich	.05	.02
❑ 29T Nick Esasky	.05	.02
❑ 30T Alvaro Espinoza	.05	.02
❑ 31T Darrell Evans UER (Stat headings on back are for a pitcher)	.10	.05
❑ 32T Junior Felix	.05	.02
❑ 33T Felix Fermin	.05	.02
❑ 34T Julio Franco	.05	.02
❑ 35T Terry Francona	.10	.05
❑ 36T Cito Gaston MG	.10	.05
❑ 37T Bob Geren UER (Photo actually Mike Fennell)	.05	.02
❑ 38T Tom Gordon	.20	.09
❑ 39T Tommy Gregg	.05	.02
❑ 40T Ken Griffey Sr.	.05	.02
❑ 41T Ken Griffey Jr.	15.00	6.75
❑ 42T Kevin Gross	.05	.02
❑ 43T Lee Guetterman	.05	.02
❑ 44T Mel Hall	.05	.02
❑ 45T Erik Hanson	.10	.05
❑ 46T Gene Harris	.05	.02
❑ 47T Andy Hawkins	.05	.02
❑ 48T Rickey Henderson	.20	.09
❑ 49T Tom Herr	.05	.02
❑ 50T Ken Hill	.20	.09
❑ 51T Brian Holman	.05	.02
❑ 52T Brian Holton	.05	.02
❑ 53T Art Howe MG	.05	.02
❑ 54T Ken Howell	.05	.02
❑ 55T Bruce Hurst	.05	.02
❑ 56T Chris James	.05	.02
❑ 57T Randy Johnson	1.25	.55
❑ 58T Jimmy Jones	.05	.02
❑ 59T Terry Kennedy	.05	.02
❑ 60T Paul Kilgus	.05	.02
❑ 61T Eric King	.05	.02
❑ 62T Ron Kittle	.05	.02
❑ 63T John Kruk	.10	.05
❑ 64T Randy Kutcher	.05	.02
❑ 65T Steve Lake	.05	.02
❑ 66T Mark Langston	.05	.02
❑ 67T Dave LaPoint	.05	.02
❑ 68T Rick Leach	.05	.02
❑ 69T Terry Leach	.05	.02
❑ 70T Jim Lefebvre MG	.05	.02
❑ 71T Al Leiter	.20	.09
❑ 72T Jeffrey Leonard	.05	.02
❑ 73T Derek Lilliquist	.05	.02
❑ 74T Rick Mahler	.05	.02
❑ 75T Tom McCarthy	.05	.02
❑ 76T Lloyd McClendon	.05	.02
❑ 77T Lance McCullers	.05	.02
❑ 78T Oddibe McDowell	.05	.02
❑ 79T Roger McDowell	.05	.02
❑ 80T Larry McWilliams	.05	.02
❑ 81T Randy Milligan	.05	.02
❑ 82T Mike Moore	.05	.02
❑ 83T Keith Moreland	.05	.02
❑ 84T Mike Morgan	.05	.02
❑ 85T Jamie Moyer	.05	.02
❑ 86T Rob Murphy	.05	.02
❑ 87T Eddie Murray	.20	.09
❑ 88T Pete O'Brien	.05	.02
❑ 89T Gregg Olson	.20	.09
❑ 90T Steve Ontiveros	.05	.02
❑ 91T Jesse Orosco	.05	.02
❑ 92T Spike Owen	.05	.02
❑ 93T Rafael Palmeiro	.20	.09
❑ 94T Clay Parker	.05	.02
❑ 95T Jeff Parrett	.05	.02
❑ 96T Lance Parrish	.05	.02
❑ 97T Dennis Powell	.05	.02
❑ 98T Rey Quinones	.05	.02
❑ 99T Doug Rader MG	.05	.02
❑ 100T Willie Randolph	.10	.05
❑ 101T Shane Rawley	.05	.02
❑ 102T Randy Ready	.05	.02
❑ 103T Bip Roberts	.10	.05
❑ 104T Kenny Rogers	.20	.09
❑ 105T Ed Romero	.05	.02
❑ 106T Nolan Ryan	1.50	.70
❑ 107T Luis Salazar	.05	.02
❑ 108T Juan Samuel	.05	.02
❑ 109T Alex Sanchez	.05	.02
❑ 110T Deion Sanders	.75	.35
❑ 111T Steve Sax	.05	.02
❑ 112T Rick Schu	.05	.02
❑ 113T Dwight Smith	.10	.05
❑ 114T Lonnie Smith	.05	.02
❑ 115T Billy Spiers	.05	.02
❑ 116T Kent Tekulve	.05	.02
❑ 117T Walt Terrell	.05	.02
❑ 118T Milt Thompson	.05	.02
❑ 119T Dickie Thon	.05	.02
❑ 120T Jeff Torborg MG	.05	.02
❑ 121T Jeff Treadway	.05	.02
❑ 122T Omar Vizquel	.40	.18
❑ 123T Jerome Walton	.20	.09
❑ 124T Gary Ward	.05	.02
❑ 125T Claudell Washington	.05	.02
❑ 126T Curt Wilkerson	.05	.02
❑ 127T Eddie Williams	.05	.02
❑ 128T Frank Williams	.05	.02
❑ 129T Ken Williams	.05	.02
❑ 130T Mitch Williams	.05	.02
❑ 131T Steve Wilson	.05	.02
❑ 132T Checklist 1T-132T	.05	.02

1989 Topps Traded Tiffany

	MINT	NRMT
COMP.FACT.SET (132)	350.00	160.00
COMMON CARD (1T-132T)	.20	.09

*STARS: 6X TO 12X BASIC CARDS
*ROOKIES: 7.5X TO 15X BASIC CARDS

1990 Topps

	MINT	NRMT
COMPLETE SET (792)	20.00	9.00
COMP.FACT.SET (792)	25.00	11.00
COMP.X-MAS.SET (792)	25.00	11.00
COMMON CARD (1-792)	.05	.02

Card	MINT	NRMT
❑ 1 Nolan Ryan	.75	.35
❑ 2 Nolan Ryan Salute New York Mets	.40	.18
❑ 3 Nolan Ryan Salute California Angels	.40	.18
❑ 4 Nolan Ryan Salute Houston Astros	.40	.18
❑ 5 Nolan Ryan Salute Texas Rangers UER (Says Texas Stadium rather than Arlington Stadium)	.40	.18
❑ 6 Vince Coleman RB (50 consecutive SB's	.05	.02
❑ 7 Rickey Henderson RB (40 career leadoff HR's	.10	.05
❑ 8 Cal Ripken RB (20 or more homers for 8 consecutive years, record for shortstops)	.40	.18
❑ 9 Eric Plunk	.05	.02
❑ 10 Barry Larkin	.20	.09
❑ 11 Paul Gibson	.05	.02
❑ 12 Joe Girardi	.15	.07
❑ 13 Mark Williamson	.05	.02
❑ 14 Mike Fetters	.05	.02
❑ 15 Teddy Higuera	.05	.02
❑ 16 Kent Anderson	.05	.02
❑ 17 Kelly Downs	.05	.02
❑ 18 Carlos Quintana	.05	.02
❑ 19 Al Newman	.05	.02
❑ 20 Mark Gubicza	.05	.02
❑ 21 Jeff Torborg MG	.05	.02
❑ 22 Bruce Ruffin	.05	.02
❑ 23 Randy Velarde	.05	.02
❑ 24 Joe Hesketh	.05	.02
❑ 25 Willie Randolph	.10	.05
❑ 26 Don Slaught	.05	.02
❑ 27 Rick Leach	.05	.02
❑ 28 Duane Ward	.05	.02

❑ 29 John Cangelosi .05 .02
❑ 30 David Cone .20 .09
❑ 31 Henry Cotto .05 .02
❑ 32 John Farrell .05 .02
❑ 33 Greg Walker .05 .02
❑ 34 Tony Fossas .05 .02
❑ 35 Benito Santiago .05 .02
❑ 36 John Costello .05 .02
❑ 37 Domingo Ramos .05 .02
❑ 38 Wes Gardner .05 .02
❑ 39 Curt Ford .05 .02
❑ 40 Jay Howell .05 .02
❑ 41 Matt Williams .20 .09
❑ 42 Jeff M. Robinson .05 .02
❑ 43 Dante Bichette .20 .09
❑ 44 Roger Salkeld FDP .05 .02
❑ 45 Dave Parker UER .10 .05
(Born in Jackson, not Calhoun)
❑ 46 Rob Dibble .05 .02
❑ 47 Brian Harper .05 .02
❑ 48 Zane Smith .05 .02
❑ 49 Tom Lawless .05 .02
❑ 50 Glenn Davis .05 .02
❑ 51 Doug Rader MG .05 .02
❑ 52 Jack Daugherty .05 .02
❑ 53 Mike LaCoss .05 .02
❑ 54 Joel Skinner .05 .02
❑ 55 Darrell Evans UER .10 .05
(HR total should be 414, not 424)
❑ 56 Franklin Stubbs .05 .02
❑ 57 Greg Vaughn .40 .18
❑ 58 Keith Miller .05 .02
❑ 59 Ted Power .05 .02
❑ 60 George Brett .40 .18
❑ 61 Deion Sanders .20 .09
❑ 62 Ramon Martinez .15 .07
❑ 63 Mike Pagliarulo .05 .02
❑ 64 Danny Darwin .05 .02
❑ 65 Devon White .05 .02
❑ 66 Greg Litton .05 .02
❑ 67 Scott Sanderson .05 .02
❑ 68 Dave Henderson .05 .02
❑ 69 Todd Frohwirth .05 .02
❑ 70 Mike Greenwell .05 .02
❑ 71 Allan Anderson .05 .02
❑ 72 Jeff Huson .05 .02
❑ 73 Bob Milacki .05 .02
❑ 74 Jeff Jackson FDP .05 .02
❑ 75 Doug Jones .05 .02
❑ 76 Dave Valle .05 .02
❑ 77 Dave Bergman .05 .02
❑ 78 Mike Flanagan .05 .02
❑ 79 Ron Kittle .05 .02
❑ 80 Jeff Russell .05 .02
❑ 81 Bob Rodgers MG .05 .02
❑ 82 Scott Terry .05 .02
❑ 83 Hensley Meulens .05 .02
❑ 84 Ray Searage .05 .02
❑ 85 Juan Samuel .05 .02
❑ 86 Paul Kilgus .05 .02
❑ 87 Rick Luecken .05 .02
❑ 88 Glenn Braggs .05 .02
❑ 89 Clint Zavaras .05 .02
❑ 90 Jack Clark .10 .05
❑ 91 Steve Frey .05 .02
❑ 92 Mike Stanley .05 .02
❑ 93 Shawn Hillegas .05 .02
❑ 94 Herm Winningham .05 .02
❑ 95 Todd Worrell .05 .02
❑ 96 Jody Reed .05 .02
❑ 97 Curt Schilling .20 .09
❑ 98 Jose Gonzalez .05 .02
❑ 99 Rich Monteleone .05 .02
❑ 100 Will Clark .20 .09
❑ 101 Shane Rawley .05 .02
❑ 102 Stan Javier .05 .02
❑ 103 Marvin Freeman .05 .02
❑ 104 Bob Knepper .05 .02
❑ 105 Randy Myers .10 .05
❑ 106 Charlie O'Brien .05 .02
❑ 107 Fred Lynn .05 .02
❑ 108 Rod Nichols .05 .02
❑ 109 Roberto Kelly .05 .02
❑ 110 Tommy Helms MG .05 .02
❑ 111 Ed Whited .05 .02
❑ 112 Glenn Wilson .05 .02
❑ 113 Manny Lee .05 .02
❑ 114 Mike Bielecki .05 .02
❑ 115 Tony Pena .05 .02
❑ 116 Floyd Bannister .05 .02
❑ 117 Mike Sharperson .05 .02
❑ 118 Erik Hanson .05 .02
❑ 119 Billy Hatcher .05 .02
❑ 120 John Franco .10 .05
❑ 121 Robin Ventura .20 .09
❑ 122 Shawn Abner .05 .02
❑ 123 Rich Gedman .05 .02
❑ 124 Dave Dravecky .10 .05
❑ 125 Kent Hrbek .10 .05
❑ 126 Randy Kramer .05 .02
❑ 127 Mike Devereaux .05 .02
❑ 128 Checklist 1 .05 .02
❑ 129 Ron Jones .05 .02
❑ 130 Bert Blyleven .10 .05
❑ 131 Matt Nokes .05 .02
❑ 132 Lance Blankenship .05 .02
❑ 133 Ricky Horton .05 .02
❑ 134 Earl Cunningham FDP .05 .02
❑ 135 Dave Magadan .05 .02
❑ 136 Kevin Brown .20 .09
❑ 137 Marty Pevey .05 .02
❑ 138 Al Leiter .20 .09
❑ 139 Greg Brock .05 .02
❑ 140 Andre Dawson .20 .09
❑ 141 John Hart MG .05 .02
❑ 142 Jeff Wetherby .05 .02
❑ 143 Rafael Belliard .05 .02
❑ 144 Bud Black .05 .02
❑ 145 Terry Steinbach .10 .05
❑ 146 Rob Richie .05 .02
❑ 147 Chuck Finley .10 .05
❑ 148 Edgar Martinez .20 .09
❑ 149 Steve Farr .05 .02
❑ 150 Kirk Gibson .10 .05
❑ 151 Rick Mahler .05 .02
❑ 152 Lonnie Smith .05 .02
❑ 153 Randy Milligan .05 .02
❑ 154 Mike Maddux .05 .02
❑ 155 Ellis Burks .15 .07
❑ 156 Ken Patterson .05 .02
❑ 157 Craig Biggio .20 .09
❑ 158 Craig Lefferts .05 .02
❑ 159 Mike Felder .05 .02
❑ 160 Dave Righetti .05 .02
❑ 161 Harold Reynolds .05 .02
❑ 162 Todd Zeile .10 .05
❑ 163 Phil Bradley .05 .02
❑ 164 Jeff Juden FDP .05 .02
❑ 165 Walt Weiss .05 .02
❑ 166 Bobby Witt .05 .02
❑ 167 Kevin Appier .15 .07
❑ 168 Jose Lind .05 .02
❑ 169 Richard Dotson .05 .02
❑ 170 George Bell .05 .02
❑ 171 Russ Nixon MG .05 .02
❑ 172 Tom Lampkin .05 .02
❑ 173 Tim Belcher .05 .02
❑ 174 Jeff Kunkel .05 .02
❑ 175 Mike Moore .05 .02
❑ 176 Luis Quinones .05 .02
❑ 177 Mike Henneman .05 .02
❑ 178 Chris James .05 .02
❑ 179 Brian Holton .05 .02
❑ 180 Tim Raines .10 .05
❑ 181 Juan Agosto .05 .02
❑ 182 Mookie Wilson .10 .05
❑ 183 Steve Lake .05 .02
❑ 184 Danny Cox .05 .02
❑ 185 Ruben Sierra .05 .02
❑ 186 Dave LaPoint .05 .02
❑ 187 Rick Wrona .05 .02
❑ 188 Mike Smithson .05 .02
❑ 189 Dick Schofield .05 .02
❑ 190 Rick Reuschel .05 .02
❑ 191 Pat Borders .05 .02
❑ 192 Don August .05 .02
❑ 193 Andy Benes .20 .09
❑ 194 Glenallen Hill .05 .02
❑ 195 Tim Burke .05 .02
❑ 196 Gerald Young .05 .02
❑ 197 Doug Drabek .05 .02
❑ 198 Mike Marshall .05 .02
❑ 199 Sergio Valdez .05 .02
❑ 200 Don Mattingly .30 .14
❑ 201 Cito Gaston MG .05 .02
❑ 202 Mike Macfarlane .05 .02
❑ 203 Mike Roesler .05 .02
❑ 204 Bob Dernier .05 .02
❑ 205 Mark Davis .05 .02
❑ 206 Nick Esasky .05 .02
❑ 207 Bob Ojeda .05 .02
❑ 208 Brook Jacoby .05 .02
❑ 209 Greg Mathews .05 .02
❑ 210 Ryne Sandberg .25 .11
❑ 211 John Cerutti .05 .02
❑ 212 Joe Orsulak .05 .02
❑ 213 Scott Bankhead .05 .02
❑ 214 Terry Francona .10 .05
❑ 215 Kirk McCaskill .05 .02
❑ 216 Ricky Jordan .05 .02
❑ 217 Don Robinson .05 .02
❑ 218 Wally Backman .05 .02
❑ 219 Donn Pall .05 .02
❑ 220 Barry Bonds .25 .11
❑ 221 Gary Mielke .05 .02
❑ 222 Kurt Stillwell UER .05 .02
(Graduate misspelled as gradute)
❑ 223 Tommy Gregg .05 .02
❑ 224 Delino DeShields .20 .09
❑ 225 Jim Deshaies .05 .02
❑ 226 Mickey Hatcher .05 .02
❑ 227 Kevin Tapani .10 .05
❑ 228 Dave Martinez .05 .02
❑ 229 David Wells .15 .07
❑ 230 Keith Hernandez .10 .05
❑ 231 Jack McKeon MG .05 .02
❑ 232 Darnell Coles .05 .02
❑ 233 Ken Hill .15 .07
❑ 234 Mariano Duncan .05 .02
❑ 235 Jeff Reardon .10 .05
❑ 236 Hal Morris .05 .02
❑ 237 Kevin Ritz .05 .02
❑ 238 Felix Jose .05 .02
❑ 239 Eric Show .05 .02
❑ 240 Mark Grace .20 .09
❑ 241 Mike Krukow .05 .02
❑ 242 Fred Manrique .05 .02
❑ 243 Barry Jones .05 .02
❑ 244 Bill Schroeder .05 .02
❑ 245 Roger Clemens .40 .18
❑ 246 Jim Eisenreich .05 .02
❑ 247 Jerry Reed .05 .02
❑ 248 Dave Anderson .05 .02
❑ 249 Mike(Texas) Smith .05 .02
❑ 250 Jose Canseco .20 .09
❑ 251 Jeff Blauser .05 .02
❑ 252 Otis Nixon .10 .05
❑ 253 Mark Portugal .05 .02
❑ 254 Francisco Cabrera .05 .02
❑ 255 Bobby Thigpen .05 .02
❑ 256 Marvell Wynne .05 .02
❑ 257 Jose DeLeon .05 .02
❑ 258 Barry Lyons .05 .02
❑ 259 Lance McCullers .05 .02
❑ 260 Eric Davis .10 .05
❑ 261 Whitey Herzog MG .10 .05
❑ 262 Checklist 2 .05 .02
❑ 263 Mel Stottlemyre Jr. .05 .02
❑ 264 Bryan Clutterbuck .05 .02
❑ 265 Pete O'Brien .05 .02
❑ 266 German Gonzalez .05 .02
❑ 267 Mark Davidson .05 .02
❑ 268 Rob Murphy .05 .02
❑ 269 Dickie Thon .05 .02
❑ 270 Dave Stewart .10 .05
❑ 271 Chet Lemon .05 .02
❑ 272 Bryan Harvey .05 .02
❑ 273 Bobby Bonilla .10 .05
❑ 274 Mauro Gozzo .05 .02
❑ 275 Mickey Tettleton .10 .05
❑ 276 Gary Thurman .05 .02
❑ 277 Lenny Harris .05 .02

❑ 278	Pascual Perez	.05	.02
❑ 279	Steve Buechele	.05	.02
❑ 280	Lou Whitaker	.10	.05
❑ 281	Kevin Bass	.05	.02
❑ 282	Derek Lilliquist	.05	.02
❑ 283	Joey Belle	1.00	.45
❑ 284	Mark Gardner	.05	.02
❑ 285	Willie McGee	.10	.05
❑ 286	Lee Guetterman	.05	.02
❑ 287	Vance Law	.05	.02
❑ 288	Greg Briley	.05	.02
❑ 289	Norm Charlton	.05	.02
❑ 290	Robin Yount	.20	.09
❑ 291	Dave Johnson MG	.10	.05
❑ 292	Jim Gott	.05	.02
❑ 293	Mike Gallego	.05	.02
❑ 294	Craig McMurtry	.05	.02
❑ 295	Fred McGriff	.20	.09
❑ 296	Jeff Ballard	.05	.02
❑ 297	Tommy Herr	.05	.02
❑ 298	Dan Gladden	.05	.02
❑ 299	Adam Peterson	.05	.02
❑ 300	Bo Jackson	.10	.05
❑ 301	Don Aase	.05	.02
❑ 302	Marcus Lawton	.05	.02
❑ 303	Rick Cerone	.05	.02
❑ 304	Marty Clary	.05	.02
❑ 305	Eddie Murray	.20	.09
❑ 306	Tom Niedenfuer	.05	.02
❑ 307	Bip Roberts	.05	.02
❑ 308	Jose Guzman	.05	.02
❑ 309	Eric Yelding	.05	.02
❑ 310	Steve Bedrosian	.05	.02
❑ 311	Dwight Smith	.05	.02
❑ 312	Dan Quisenberry	.05	.02
❑ 313	Gus Polidor	.05	.02
❑ 314	Donald Harris FDP	.05	.02
❑ 315	Bruce Hurst	.05	.02
❑ 316	Carney Lansford	.10	.05
❑ 317	Mark Guthrie	.05	.02
❑ 318	Wallace Johnson	.05	.02
❑ 319	Dion James	.05	.02
❑ 320	Dave Stieb	.10	.05
❑ 321	Joe Morgan MG	.05	.02
❑ 322	Junior Ortiz	.05	.02
❑ 323	Willie Wilson	.05	.02
❑ 324	Pete Harnisch	.05	.02
❑ 325	Robby Thompson	.05	.02
❑ 326	Tom McCarthy	.05	.02
❑ 327	Ken Williams	.05	.02
❑ 328	Curt Young	.05	.02
❑ 329	Oddibe McDowell	.05	.02
❑ 330	Ron Darling	.05	.02
❑ 331	Juan Gonzalez	3.00	1.35
❑ 332	Paul O'Neill	.10	.05
❑ 333	Bill Wegman	.05	.02
❑ 334	Johnny Ray	.05	.02
❑ 335	Andy Hawkins	.05	.02
❑ 336	Ken Griffey Jr.	2.00	.90
❑ 337	Lloyd McClendon	.05	.02
❑ 338	Dennis Lamp	.05	.02
❑ 339	Dave Clark	.05	.02
❑ 340	Fernando Valenzuela	.10	.05
❑ 341	Tom Foley	.05	.02
❑ 342	Alex Trevino	.05	.02
❑ 343	Frank Tanana	.05	.02
❑ 344	George Canale	.05	.02
❑ 345	Harold Baines	.10	.05
❑ 346	Jim Presley	.05	.02
❑ 347	Junior Felix	.05	.02
❑ 348	Gary Wayne	.05	.02
❑ 349	Steve Finley	.20	.09
❑ 350	Bret Saberhagen	.10	.05
❑ 351	Roger Craig MG	.05	.02
❑ 352	Bryn Smith	.05	.02
❑ 353	Sandy Alomar Jr. (Not listed as Jr. on card front)	.15	.07
❑ 354	Stan Belinda	.05	.02
❑ 355	Marty Barrett	.05	.02
❑ 356	Randy Ready	.05	.02
❑ 357	Dave West	.05	.02
❑ 358	Andres Thomas	.05	.02
❑ 359	Jimmy Jones	.05	.02
❑ 360	Paul Molitor	.20	.09
❑ 361	Randy McCament	.05	.02
❑ 362	Damon Berryhill	.05	.02
❑ 363	Dan Petry	.05	.02
❑ 364	Rolando Roomes	.05	.02
❑ 365	Ozzie Guillen	.05	.02
❑ 366	Mike Heath	.05	.02
❑ 367	Mike Morgan	.05	.02
❑ 368	Bill Doran	.05	.02
❑ 369	Todd Burns	.05	.02
❑ 370	Tim Wallach	.05	.02
❑ 371	Jimmy Key	.10	.05
❑ 372	Terry Kennedy	.05	.02
❑ 373	Alvin Davis	.05	.02
❑ 374	Steve Cummings	.05	.02
❑ 375	Dwight Evans	.10	.05
❑ 376	Checklist 3 UER (Higuera misalphabetized in Brewer list)	.05	.02
❑ 377	Mickey Weston	.05	.02
❑ 378	Luis Salazar	.05	.02
❑ 379	Steve Rosenberg	.05	.02
❑ 380	Dave Winfield	.20	.09
❑ 381	Frank Robinson MG	.15	.07
❑ 382	Jeff Musselman	.05	.02
❑ 383	John Morris	.05	.02
❑ 384	Pat Combs	.05	.02
❑ 385	Fred McGriff AS	.10	.05
❑ 386	Julio Franco AS	.05	.02
❑ 387	Wade Boggs AS	.10	.05
❑ 388	Cal Ripken AS	.40	.18
❑ 389	Robin Yount AS	.10	.05
❑ 390	Ruben Sierra AS	.05	.02
❑ 391	Kirby Puckett AS	.20	.09
❑ 392	Carlton Fisk AS	.10	.05
❑ 393	Bret Saberhagen AS	.05	.02
❑ 394	Jeff Ballard AS	.05	.02
❑ 395	Jeff Russell AS	.05	.02
❑ 396	A.Bartlett Giamatti COMM MEM	.20	.09
❑ 397	Will Clark AS	.10	.05
❑ 398	Ryne Sandberg AS	.20	.09
❑ 399	Howard Johnson AS	.05	.02
❑ 400	Ozzie Smith AS	.20	.09
❑ 401	Kevin Mitchell AS	.05	.02
❑ 402	Eric Davis AS	.05	.02
❑ 403	Tony Gwynn AS	.25	.11
❑ 404	Craig Biggio AS	.10	.05
❑ 405	Mike Scott AS	.05	.02
❑ 406	Joe Magrane AS	.05	.02
❑ 407	Mark Davis AS	.05	.02
❑ 408	Trevor Wilson	.05	.02
❑ 409	Tom Brunansky	.05	.02
❑ 410	Joe Boever	.05	.02
❑ 411	Ken Phelps	.05	.02
❑ 412	Jamie Moyer	.05	.02
❑ 413	Brian DuBois	.05	.02
❑ 414A	Frank Thomas FDP ERR (Name missing on card front)	1500.00	700.00
❑ 414B	F. Thomas FDP COR	3.00	1.35
❑ 415	Shawon Dunston	.05	.02
❑ 416	Dave Johnson (P)	.05	.02
❑ 417	Jim Gantner	.05	.02
❑ 418	Tom Browning	.05	.02
❑ 419	Beau Allred	.05	.02
❑ 420	Carlton Fisk	.20	.09
❑ 421	Greg Minton	.05	.02
❑ 422	Pat Sheridan	.05	.02
❑ 423	Fred Toliver	.05	.02
❑ 424	Jerry Reuss	.05	.02
❑ 425	Bill Landrum	.05	.02
❑ 426	Jeff Hamilton UER (Stats say he fanned 197 times in 1987, but he only had 147 at bats)	.05	.02
❑ 427	Carmen Castillo	.05	.02
❑ 428	Steve Davis	.05	.02
❑ 429	Tom Kelly MG	.05	.02
❑ 430	Pete Incaviglia	.05	.02
❑ 431	Randy Johnson	.30	.14
❑ 432	Damaso Garcia	.05	.02
❑ 433	Steve Olin	.10	.05
❑ 434	Mark Carreon	.05	.02
❑ 435	Kevin Seitzer	.05	.02
❑ 436	Mel Hall	.05	.02
❑ 437	Les Lancaster	.05	.02
❑ 438	Greg Myers	.05	.02
❑ 439	Jeff Parrett	.05	.02
❑ 440	Alan Trammell	.15	.07
❑ 441	Bob Kipper	.05	.02
❑ 442	Jerry Browne	.05	.02
❑ 443	Cris Carpenter	.05	.02
❑ 444	Kyle Abbott FDP	.05	.02
❑ 445	Danny Jackson	.05	.02
❑ 446	Dan Pasqua	.05	.02
❑ 447	Atlee Hammaker	.05	.02
❑ 448	Greg Gagne	.05	.02
❑ 449	Dennis Rasmussen	.05	.02
❑ 450	Rickey Henderson	.20	.09
❑ 451	Mark Lemke	.05	.02
❑ 452	Luis DeLosSantos	.05	.02
❑ 453	Jody Davis	.05	.02
❑ 454	Jeff King	.10	.05
❑ 455	Jeffrey Leonard	.05	.02
❑ 456	Chris Gwynn	.05	.02
❑ 457	Gregg Jefferies	.10	.05
❑ 458	Bob McClure	.05	.02
❑ 459	Jim Lefebvre MG	.05	.02
❑ 460	Mike Scott	.05	.02
❑ 461	Carlos Martinez	.05	.02
❑ 462	Denny Walling	.05	.02
❑ 463	Drew Hall	.05	.02
❑ 464	Jerome Walton	.05	.02
❑ 465	Kevin Gross	.05	.02
❑ 466	Rance Mulliniks	.05	.02
❑ 467	Juan Nieves	.05	.02
❑ 468	Bill Ripken	.05	.02
❑ 469	John Kruk	.10	.05
❑ 470	Frank Viola	.05	.02
❑ 471	Mike Brumley	.05	.02
❑ 472	Jose Uribe	.05	.02
❑ 473	Joe Price	.05	.02
❑ 474	Rich Thompson	.05	.02
❑ 475	Bob Welch	.05	.02
❑ 476	Brad Komminsk	.05	.02
❑ 477	Willie Fraser	.05	.02
❑ 478	Mike LaValliere	.05	.02
❑ 479	Frank White	.10	.05
❑ 480	Sid Fernandez	.05	.02
❑ 481	Garry Templeton	.05	.02
❑ 482	Steve Carter	.05	.02
❑ 483	Alejandro Pena	.05	.02
❑ 484	Mike Fitzgerald	.05	.02
❑ 485	John Candelaria	.05	.02
❑ 486	Jeff Treadway	.05	.02
❑ 487	Steve Searcy	.05	.02
❑ 488	Ken Oberkfell	.05	.02
❑ 489	Nick Leyva MG	.05	.02
❑ 490	Dan Plesac	.05	.02
❑ 491	Dave Cochrane	.05	.02
❑ 492	Ron Oester	.05	.02
❑ 493	Jason Grimsley	.05	.02
❑ 494	Terry Puhl	.05	.02
❑ 495	Lee Smith	.10	.05
❑ 496	Cecil Espy UER ('88 stats have 3 SB's, should be 33)	.05	.02
❑ 497	Dave Schmidt	.05	.02
❑ 498	Rick Schu	.05	.02
❑ 499	Bill Long	.05	.02
❑ 500	Kevin Mitchell	.05	.02
❑ 501	Matt Young	.05	.02
❑ 502	Mitch Webster	.05	.02
❑ 503	Randy St.Claire	.05	.02
❑ 504	Tom O'Malley	.05	.02
❑ 505	Kelly Gruber	.05	.02
❑ 506	Tom Glavine	.20	.09
❑ 507	Gary Redus	.05	.02
❑ 508	Terry Leach	.05	.02
❑ 509	Tom Pagnozzi	.05	.02
❑ 510	Dwight Gooden	.10	.05
❑ 511	Clay Parker	.05	.02
❑ 512	Gary Pettis	.05	.02
❑ 513	Mark Eichhorn	.05	.02
❑ 514	Andy Allanson	.05	.02
❑ 515	Len Dykstra	.10	.05
❑ 516	Tim Leary	.05	.02
❑ 517	Roberto Alomar	.25	.11
❑ 518	Bill Krueger	.05	.02
❑ 519	Bucky Dent MG	.05	.02

❑	520	Mitch Williams	.05	.02
❑	521	Craig Worthington	.05	.02
❑	522	Mike Dunne	.05	.02
❑	523	Jay Bell	.10	.05
❑	524	Daryl Boston	.05	.02
❑	525	Wally Joyner	.10	.05
❑	526	Checklist 4	.05	.02
❑	527	Ron Hassey	.05	.02
❑	528	Kevin Wickander UER (Monthly scoreboard strikeout total was 2.2, that was his innings pitched total)	.05	.02
❑	529	Greg A. Harris	.05	.02
❑	530	Mark Langston	.05	.02
❑	531	Ken Caminiti	.20	.09
❑	532	Cecilio Guante	.05	.02
❑	533	Tim Jones	.05	.02
❑	534	Louie Meadows	.05	.02
❑	535	John Smoltz	.20	.09
❑	536	Bob Geren	.05	.02
❑	537	Mark Grant	.05	.02
❑	538	Bill Spiers UER (Photo actually George Canale)	.05	.02
❑	539	Neal Heaton	.05	.02
❑	540	Danny Tartabull	.05	.02
❑	541	Pat Perry	.05	.02
❑	542	Darren Daulton	.10	.05
❑	543	Nelson Liriano	.05	.02
❑	544	Dennis Boyd	.05	.02
❑	545	Kevin McReynolds	.05	.02
❑	546	Kevin Hickey	.05	.02
❑	547	Jack Howell	.05	.02
❑	548	Pat Clements	.05	.02
❑	549	Don Zimmer MG	.05	.02
❑	550	Julio Franco	.05	.02
❑	551	Tim Crews	.05	.02
❑	552	Mike(Miss.) Smith	.05	.02
❑	553	Scott Scudder UER (Cedar Rap1ds)	.05	.02
❑	554	Jay Buhner	.20	.09
❑	555	Jack Morris	.10	.05
❑	556	Gene Larkin	.05	.02
❑	557	Jeff Innis	.05	.02
❑	558	Rafael Ramirez	.05	.02
❑	559	Andy McGaffigan	.05	.02
❑	560	Steve Sax	.05	.02
❑	561	Ken Dayley	.05	.02
❑	562	Chad Kreuter	.05	.02
❑	563	Alex Sanchez	.05	.02
❑	564	Tyler Houston FDP	.20	.09
❑	565	Scott Fletcher	.05	.02
❑	566	Mark Knudson	.05	.02
❑	567	Ron Gant	.10	.05
❑	568	John Smiley	.05	.02
❑	569	Ivan Calderon	.05	.02
❑	570	Cal Ripken	.75	.35
❑	571	Brett Butler	.10	.05
❑	572	Greg W. Harris	.05	.02
❑	573	Danny Heep	.05	.02
❑	574	Bill Swift	.05	.02
❑	575	Lance Parrish	.05	.02
❑	576	Mike Dyer	.05	.02
❑	577	Charlie Hayes	.05	.02
❑	578	Joe Magrane	.05	.02
❑	579	Art Howe MG	.05	.02
❑	580	Joe Carter	.10	.05
❑	581	Ken Griffey Sr.	.05	.02
❑	582	Rick Honeycutt	.05	.02
❑	583	Bruce Benedict	.05	.02
❑	584	Phil Stephenson	.05	.02
❑	585	Kal Daniels	.05	.02
❑	586	Edwin Nunez	.05	.02
❑	587	Lance Johnson	.05	.02
❑	588	Rick Rhoden	.05	.02
❑	589	Mike Aldrete	.05	.02
❑	590	Ozzie Smith	.25	.11
❑	591	Todd Stottlemyre	.10	.05
❑	592	R.J. Reynolds	.05	.02
❑	593	Scott Bradley	.05	.02
❑	594	Luis Sojo	.05	.02
❑	595	Greg Swindell	.05	.02
❑	596	Jose DeJesus	.05	.02
❑	597	Chris Bosio	.05	.02
❑	598	Brady Anderson	.20	.09
❑	599	Frank Williams	.05	.02
❑	600	Darryl Strawberry	.10	.05
❑	601	Luis Rivera	.05	.02
❑	602	Scott Garrelts	.05	.02
❑	603	Tony Armas	.05	.02
❑	604	Ron Robinson	.05	.02
❑	605	Mike Scioscia	.05	.02
❑	606	Storm Davis	.05	.02
❑	607	Steve Jeltz	.05	.02
❑	608	Eric Anthony	.05	.02
❑	609	Sparky Anderson MG	.10	.05
❑	610	Pedro Guerrero	.05	.02
❑	611	Walt Terrell	.05	.02
❑	612	Dave Gallagher	.05	.02
❑	613	Jeff Pico	.05	.02
❑	614	Nelson Santovenia	.05	.02
❑	615	Rob Deer	.05	.02
❑	616	Brian Holman	.05	.02
❑	617	Geronimo Berroa	.05	.02
❑	618	Ed Whitson	.05	.02
❑	619	Rob Ducey	.05	.02
❑	620	Tony Castillo	.05	.02
❑	621	Melido Perez	.05	.02
❑	622	Sid Bream	.05	.02
❑	623	Jim Corsi	.05	.02
❑	624	Darrin Jackson	.05	.02
❑	625	Roger McDowell	.05	.02
❑	626	Bob Melvin	.05	.02
❑	627	Jose Rijo	.05	.02
❑	628	Candy Maldonado	.05	.02
❑	629	Eric Hetzel	.05	.02
❑	630	Gary Gaetti	.10	.05
❑	631	John Wetteland	.20	.09
❑	632	Scott Lusader	.05	.02
❑	633	Dennis Cook	.05	.02
❑	634	Luis Polonia	.05	.02
❑	635	Brian Downing	.05	.02
❑	636	Jesse Orosco	.05	.02
❑	637	Craig Reynolds	.05	.02
❑	638	Jeff Montgomery	.10	.05
❑	639	Tony LaRussa MG	.10	.05
❑	640	Rick Sutcliffe	.05	.02
❑	641	Doug Strange	.05	.02
❑	642	Jack Armstrong	.05	.02
❑	643	Alfredo Griffin	.05	.02
❑	644	Paul Assenmacher	.05	.02
❑	645	Jose Oquendo	.05	.02
❑	646	Checklist 5	.05	.02
❑	647	Rex Hudler	.05	.02
❑	648	Jim Clancy	.05	.02
❑	649	Dan Murphy	.05	.02
❑	650	Mike Witt	.05	.02
❑	651	Rafael Santana	.05	.02
❑	652	Mike Boddicker	.05	.02
❑	653	John Moses	.05	.02
❑	654	Paul Coleman FDP	.05	.02
❑	655	Gregg Olson	.05	.02
❑	656	Mackey Sasser	.05	.02
❑	657	Terry Mulholland	.05	.02
❑	658	Donell Nixon	.05	.02
❑	659	Greg Cadaret	.05	.02
❑	660	Vince Coleman	.05	.02
❑	661	Dick Howser TBC'85 UER (Seaver's 300th on 7/11/85, should be 8/4/85)	.05	.02
❑	662	Mike Schmidt TBC'80	.20	.09
❑	663	Fred Lynn TBC'75	.05	.02
❑	664	Johnny Bench TBC'70	.20	.09
❑	665	Sandy Koufax TBC'65	.25	.11
❑	666	Brian Fisher	.05	.02
❑	667	Curt Wilkerson	.05	.02
❑	668	Joe Oliver	.05	.02
❑	669	Tom Lasorda MG	.20	.09
❑	670	Dennis Eckersley	.15	.07
❑	671	Bob Boone	.10	.05
❑	672	Roy Smith	.05	.02
❑	673	Joey Meyer	.05	.02
❑	674	Spike Owen	.05	.02
❑	675	Jim Abbott	.15	.07
❑	676	Randy Kutcher	.05	.02
❑	677	Jay Tibbs	.05	.02
❑	678	Kirt Manwaring UER ('88 Phoenix stats repeated)	.05	.02
❑	679	Gary Ward	.05	.02
❑	680	Howard Johnson	.05	.02
❑	681	Mike Schooler	.05	.02
❑	682	Dann Bilardello	.05	.02
❑	683	Kenny Rogers	.10	.05
❑	684	Julio Machado	.05	.02
❑	685	Tony Fernandez	.05	.02
❑	686	Carmelo Martinez	.05	.02
❑	687	Tim Birtsas	.05	.02
❑	688	Milt Thompson	.05	.02
❑	689	Rich Yett	.05	.02
❑	690	Mark McGwire	1.00	.45
❑	691	Chuck Cary	.05	.02
❑	692	Sammy Sosa	5.00	2.20
❑	693	Calvin Schiraldi	.05	.02
❑	694	Mike Stanton	.05	.02
❑	695	Tom Henke	.05	.02
❑	696	B.J. Surhoff	.10	.05
❑	697	Mike Davis	.05	.02
❑	698	Omar Vizquel	.20	.09
❑	699	Jim Leyland MG	.05	.02
❑	700	Kirby Puckett	.30	.14
❑	701	Bernie Williams	1.25	.55
❑	702	Tony Phillips	.05	.02
❑	703	Jeff Brantley	.05	.02
❑	704	Chip Hale	.05	.02
❑	705	Claudell Washington	.05	.02
❑	706	Geno Petralli	.05	.02
❑	707	Luis Aquino	.05	.02
❑	708	Larry Sheets	.05	.02
❑	709	Juan Berenguer	.05	.02
❑	710	Von Hayes	.05	.02
❑	711	Rick Aguilera	.10	.05
❑	712	Todd Benzinger	.05	.02
❑	713	Tim Drummond	.05	.02
❑	714	Marquis Grissom	.25	.11
❑	715	Greg Maddux	.60	.25
❑	716	Steve Balboni	.05	.02
❑	717	Ron Karkovice	.05	.02
❑	718	Gary Sheffield	.20	.09
❑	719	Wally Whitehurst	.05	.02
❑	720	Andres Galarraga	.20	.09
❑	721	Lee Mazzilli	.05	.02
❑	722	Felix Fermin	.05	.02
❑	723	Jeff D. Robinson	.05	.02
❑	724	Juan Bell	.05	.02
❑	725	Terry Pendleton	.10	.05
❑	726	Gene Nelson	.05	.02
❑	727	Pat Tabler	.05	.02
❑	728	Jim Acker	.05	.02
❑	729	Bobby Valentine MG	.05	.02
❑	730	Tony Gwynn	.50	.23
❑	731	Don Carman	.05	.02
❑	732	Ernest Riles	.05	.02
❑	733	John Dopson	.05	.02
❑	734	Kevin Elster	.05	.02
❑	735	Charlie Hough	.10	.05
❑	736	Rick Dempsey	.05	.02
❑	737	Chris Sabo	.05	.02
❑	738	Gene Harris	.05	.02
❑	739	Dale Sveum	.05	.02
❑	740	Jesse Barfield	.05	.02
❑	741	Steve Wilson	.05	.02
❑	742	Ernie Whitt	.05	.02
❑	743	Tom Candiotti	.05	.02
❑	744	Kelly Mann	.05	.02
❑	745	Hubie Brooks	.05	.02
❑	746	Dave Smith	.05	.02
❑	747	Randy Bush	.05	.02
❑	748	Doyle Alexander	.05	.02
❑	749	Mark Parent UER ('87 BA .80, should be .080)	.05	.02
❑	750	Dale Murphy	.20	.09
❑	751	Steve Lyons	.05	.02
❑	752	Tom Gordon	.15	.07
❑	753	Chris Speier	.05	.02
❑	754	Bob Walk	.05	.02
❑	755	Rafael Palmeiro	.20	.09
❑	756	Ken Howell	.05	.02
❑	757	Larry Walker	1.00	.45
❑	758	Mark Thurmond	.05	.02
❑	759	Tom Trebelhorn MG	.05	.02
❑	760	Wade Boggs	.20	.09
❑	761	Mike Jackson	.10	.05

Card	Mint	NrMt
❑ 762 Doug Dascenzo	.05	.02
❑ 763 Dennis Martinez	.10	.05
❑ 764 Tim Teufel	.05	.02
❑ 765 Chili Davis	.10	.05
❑ 766 Brian Meyer	.05	.02
❑ 767 Tracy Jones	.05	.02
❑ 768 Chuck Crim	.05	.02
❑ 769 Greg Hibbard	.05	.02
❑ 770 Cory Snyder	.05	.02
❑ 771 Pete Smith	.05	.02
❑ 772 Jeff Reed	.05	.02
❑ 773 Dave Leiper	.05	.02
❑ 774 Ben McDonald	.10	.05
❑ 775 Andy Van Slyke	.10	.05
❑ 776 Charlie Leibrandt	.05	.02
❑ 777 Tim Laudner	.05	.02
❑ 778 Mike Jeffcoat	.05	.02
❑ 779 Lloyd Moseby	.05	.02
❑ 780 Orel Hershiser	.10	.05
❑ 781 Mario Diaz	.05	.02
❑ 782 Jose Alvarez	.05	.02
❑ 783 Checklist 6	.05	.02
❑ 784 Scott Bailes	.05	.02
❑ 785 Jim Rice	.10	.05
❑ 786 Eric King	.05	.02
❑ 787 Rene Gonzales	.05	.02
❑ 788 Frank DiPino	.05	.02
❑ 789 John Wathan MG	.05	.02
❑ 790 Gary Carter	.20	.09
❑ 791 Alvaro Espinoza	.05	.02
❑ 792 Gerald Perry	.05	.02

1990 Topps Tiffany

	MINT	NRMT
COMP.FACT.SET (792)	300.00	135.00
COMMON CARD (1-792)	.25	.11

*STARS: 7.5X TO 15X BASIC CARDS
*ROOKIES: 12.5X TO 25X BASIC CARDS

1990 Topps Rookies

	MINT	NRMT
COMPLETE SET (33)	10.00	4.50
COMMON CARD (1-33)	.20	.09

Card	Mint	NrMt
❑ 1 Jim Abbott	.15	.07
❑ 2 Albert Belle	1.00	.45
❑ 3 Andy Benes	.25	.11
❑ 4 Greg Briley	.20	.09
❑ 5 Kevin Brown	.40	.18
❑ 6 Mark Carreon	.20	.09
❑ 7 Mike Devereaux	.20	.09
❑ 8 Junior Felix	.20	.09
❑ 9 Bob Geren	.20	.09
❑ 10 Tom Gordon	.15	.07
❑ 11 Ken Griffey Jr.	3.00	1.35
❑ 12 Pete Harnisch	.20	.09
❑ 13 Greg W. Harris	.20	.09
❑ 14 Greg Hibbard	.20	.09
❑ 15 Ken Hill	.15	.07
❑ 16 Gregg Jefferies	.10	.05
❑ 17 Jeff King	.10	.05
❑ 18 Derek Lilliquist	.20	.09
❑ 19 Carlos Martinez	.20	.09
❑ 20 Ramon Martinez	.15	.07
❑ 21 Bob Milacki	.20	.09
❑ 22 Gregg Olson	.20	.09
❑ 23 Donn Pall	.20	.09
❑ 24 Kenny Rogers	.10	.05
❑ 25 Gary Sheffield	1.00	.45
❑ 26 Dwight Smith	.20	.09
❑ 27 Billy Spiers	.20	.09
❑ 28 Omar Vizquel	.25	.11
❑ 29 Jerome Walton	.20	.09
❑ 30 Dave West	.20	.09
❑ 31 John Wetteland	.25	.11
❑ 32 Steve Wilson	.20	.09
❑ 33 Craig Worthington	.20	.09

1990 Topps Traded

	MINT	NRMT
COMPLETE SET (132)	3.00	1.35
COMP.FACT.SET (132)	3.00	1.35
COMMON CARD (1T-132T)	.05	.02

Card	Mint	NrMt
❑ 1T Darrel Akerfelds	.05	.02
❑ 2T Sandy Alomar Jr.	.15	.07
❑ 3T Brad Arnsberg	.05	.02
❑ 4T Steve Avery	.05	.02
❑ 5T Wally Backman	.05	.02
❑ 6T Carlos Baerga	.25	.11
❑ 7T Kevin Bass	.05	.02
❑ 8T Willie Blair	.05	.02
❑ 9T Mike Blowers	.10	.05
❑ 10T Shawn Boskie	.05	.02
❑ 11T Daryl Boston	.05	.02
❑ 12T Dennis Boyd	.05	.02
❑ 13T Glenn Braggs	.05	.02
❑ 14T Hubie Brooks	.05	.02
❑ 15T Tom Brunansky	.05	.02
❑ 16T John Burkett	.10	.05
❑ 17T Casey Candaele	.05	.02
❑ 18T John Candelaria	.05	.02
❑ 19T Gary Carter	.20	.09
❑ 20T Joe Carter	.10	.05
❑ 21T Rick Cerone	.05	.02
❑ 22T Scott Coolbaugh	.05	.02
❑ 23T Bobby Cox MG	.10	.05
❑ 24T Mark Davis	.05	.02
❑ 25T Storm Davis	.05	.02
❑ 26T Edgar Diaz	.05	.02
❑ 27T Wayne Edwards	.05	.02
❑ 28T Mark Eichhorn	.05	.02
❑ 29T Scott Erickson	.25	.11
❑ 30T Nick Esasky	.05	.02
❑ 31T Cecil Fielder	.10	.05
❑ 32T John Franco	.10	.05
❑ 33T Travis Fryman	.40	.18
❑ 34T Bill Gullickson	.05	.02
❑ 35T Darryl Hamilton	.05	.02
❑ 36T Mike Harkey	.05	.02
❑ 37T Bud Harrelson MG	.05	.02
❑ 38T Billy Hatcher	.05	.02
❑ 39T Keith Hernandez	.10	.05
❑ 40T Joe Hesketh	.05	.02
❑ 41T Dave Hollins	.20	.09
❑ 42T Sam Horn	.05	.02
❑ 43T Steve Howard	.05	.02
❑ 44T Todd Hundley	.40	.18
❑ 45T Jeff Huson	.05	.02
❑ 46T Chris James	.05	.02
❑ 47T Stan Javier	.05	.02
❑ 48T Dave Justice	.75	.35
❑ 49T Jeff Kaiser	.05	.02
❑ 50T Dana Kiecker	.05	.02
❑ 51T Joe Klink	.05	.02
❑ 52T Brent Knackert	.05	.02
❑ 53T Brad Komminsk	.05	.02
❑ 54T Mark Langston	.05	.02
❑ 55T Tim Layana	.05	.02
❑ 56T Rick Leach	.05	.02
❑ 57T Terry Leach	.05	.02
❑ 58T Tim Leary	.05	.02
❑ 59T Craig Lefferts	.05	.02
❑ 60T Charlie Leibrandt	.05	.02
❑ 61T Jim Leyritz	.20	.09
❑ 62T Fred Lynn	.05	.02
❑ 63T Kevin Maas	.10	.05
❑ 64T Shane Mack	.05	.02
❑ 65T Candy Maldonado	.05	.02
❑ 66T Fred Manrique	.05	.02
❑ 67T Mike Marshall	.05	.02
❑ 68T Carmelo Martinez	.05	.02
❑ 69T John Marzano	.05	.02
❑ 70T Ben McDonald	.05	.02
❑ 71T Jack McDowell	.05	.02
❑ 72T John McNamara MG	.05	.02
❑ 73T Orlando Mercado	.05	.02
❑ 74T Stump Merrill MG	.05	.02
❑ 75T Alan Mills	.05	.02
❑ 76T Hal Morris	.05	.02
❑ 77T Lloyd Moseby	.05	.02
❑ 78T Randy Myers	.10	.05
❑ 79T Tim Naehring	.20	.09
❑ 80T Junior Noboa	.05	.02
❑ 81T Matt Nokes	.05	.02
❑ 82T Pete O'Brien	.05	.02
❑ 83T John Olerud	.50	.23
❑ 84T Greg Olson	.05	.02
❑ 85T Junior Ortiz	.05	.02
❑ 86T Dave Parker	.10	.05
❑ 87T Rick Parker	.05	.02
❑ 88T Bob Patterson	.05	.02
❑ 89T Alejandro Pena	.05	.02
❑ 90T Tony Pena	.05	.02
❑ 91T Pascual Perez	.05	.02
❑ 92T Gerald Perry	.05	.02
❑ 93T Dan Petry	.05	.02
❑ 94T Gary Pettis	.05	.02
❑ 95T Tony Phillips	.05	.02
❑ 96T Lou Piniella MG	.10	.05
❑ 97T Luis Polonia	.05	.02
❑ 98T Jim Presley	.05	.02
❑ 99T Scott Radinsky	.05	.02
❑ 100T Willie Randolph	.10	.05
❑ 101T Jeff Reardon	.10	.05
❑ 102T Greg Riddoch MG	.05	.02
❑ 103T Jeff Robinson	.05	.02
❑ 104T Ron Robinson	.05	.02
❑ 105T Kevin Romine	.05	.02
❑ 106T Scott Ruskin	.05	.02
❑ 107T John Russell	.05	.02
❑ 108T Bill Sampen	.05	.02
❑ 109T Juan Samuel	.05	.02
❑ 110T Scott Sanderson	.05	.02
❑ 111T Jack Savage	.05	.02
❑ 112T Dave Schmidt	.05	.02
❑ 113T Red Schoendienst MG	.20	.09
❑ 114T Terry Shumpert	.05	.02
❑ 115T Matt Sinatro	.05	.02
❑ 116T Don Slaught	.05	.02
❑ 117T Bryn Smith	.05	.02
❑ 118T Lee Smith	.10	.05
❑ 119T Paul Sorrento	.20	.09
❑ 120T Franklin Stubbs UER ('84 says '99 and has the same stats as '89, '83 stats are missing)	.05	.02
❑ 121T Russ Swan	.05	.02
❑ 122T Bob Tewksbury	.05	.02
❑ 123T Wayne Tolleson	.05	.02
❑ 124T John Tudor	.05	.02
❑ 125T Randy Veres	.05	.02
❑ 126T Hector Villanueva	.05	.02
❑ 127T Mitch Webster	.05	.02
❑ 128T Ernie Whitt	.05	.02
❑ 129T Frank Wills	.05	.02
❑ 130T Dave Winfield	.20	.09
❑ 131T Matt Young	.05	.02
❑ 132T Checklist 1T-132T	.05	.02

1990 Topps Traded Tiffany

	MINT	NRMT
COMP.FACT.SET (132)	40.00	18.00
COMMON CARD (1T-132T)	.25	.11

*STARS: 7.5X TO 15X BASIC CARDS
*ROOKIES: 12.5X TO 25X BASIC CARDS

1990 Topps Debut '89

	MINT	NRMT
COMP.FACT.SET (152)	30.00	13.50
COMMON CARD (1-152)	.15	.07

Card	Mint	NrMt
❑ 1 Jim Abbott	.50	.23
❑ 2 Beau Allred	.15	.07

❑ 3 Wilson Alvarez .50 .23
❑ 4 Kent Anderson .15 .07
❑ 5 Eric Anthony .15 .07
❑ 6 Kevin Appier .50 .23
❑ 7 Larry Arndt .15 .07
❑ 8 John Barfield .15 .07
❑ 9 Billy Bates .15 .07
❑ 10 Kevin Batiste .15 .07
❑ 11 Blaine Beatty .15 .07
❑ 12 Stan Belinda .15 .07
❑ 13 Juan Bell .15 .07
❑ 14 Joey Belle 6.00 2.70
(Now known as Albert)
❑ 15 Andy Benes .50 .23
❑ 16 Mike Benjamin .15 .07
❑ 17 Geronimo Berroa .25 .11
❑ 18 Mike Blowers .25 .11
❑ 19 Brian Brady .15 .07
❑ 20 Francisco Cabrera .15 .07
❑ 21 George Canale .15 .07
❑ 22 Jose Cano .15 .07
❑ 23 Steve Carter .15 .07
❑ 24 Pat Combs .15 .07
❑ 25 Scott Coolbaugh .15 .07
❑ 26 Steve Cummings .15 .07
❑ 27 Pete Dalena .15 .07
❑ 28 Jeff Datz .15 .07
❑ 29 Bobby Davidson .15 .07
❑ 30 Drew Denson .15 .07
❑ 31 Gary DiSarcina .25 .11
❑ 32 Brian DuBois .15 .07
❑ 33 Mike Dyer .15 .07
❑ 34 Wayne Edwards .15 .07
❑ 35 Junior Felix .15 .07
❑ 36 Mike Fetters .15 .07
❑ 37 Steve Finley .50 .23
❑ 38 Darrin Fletcher .25 .11
❑ 39 LaVel Freeman .15 .07
❑ 40 Steve Frey .15 .07
❑ 41 Mark Gardner .15 .07
❑ 42 Joe Girardi .50 .23
❑ 43 Juan Gonzalez 8.00 3.60
❑ 44 Goose Gozzo .15 .07
❑ 45 Tommy Greene .15 .07
❑ 46 Ken Griffey Jr. 12.00 5.50
❑ 47 Jason Grimsley .15 .07
❑ 48 Marquis Grissom 1.00 .45
❑ 49 Mark Guthrie .15 .07
❑ 50 Chip Hale .15 .07
❑ 51 Jack Hardy .15 .07
❑ 52 Gene Harris .15 .07
❑ 53 Mike Hartley .15 .07
❑ 54 Scott Hemond .15 .07
❑ 55 Xavier Hernandez .15 .07
❑ 56 Eric Hetzel .15 .07
❑ 57 Greg Hibbard .15 .07
❑ 58 Mark Higgins .15 .07
❑ 59 Glenallen Hill .15 .07
❑ 60 Chris Hoiles .40 .18
❑ 61 Shawn Holman .15 .07
❑ 62 Dann Howitt .15 .07
❑ 63 Mike Huff .15 .07
❑ 64 Terry Jorgensen .15 .07
❑ 65 Dave Justice 2.00 .90
❑ 66 Jeff King .40 .18
❑ 67 Matt Kinzer .15 .07
❑ 68 Joe Kraemer .15 .07
❑ 69 Marcus Lawton .15 .07
❑ 70 Derek Lilliquist .15 .07
❑ 71 Scott Little .15 .07
❑ 72 Greg Litton .15 .07
❑ 73 Rick Luecken .15 .07
❑ 74 Julio Machado .15 .07
❑ 75 Tom Magrann .15 .07
❑ 76 Kelly Mann .15 .07
❑ 77 Randy McCament .15 .07
❑ 78 Ben McDonald .15 .07
❑ 79 Chuck McElroy .15 .07
❑ 80 Jeff McKnight .15 .07
❑ 81 Kent Mercker .15 .07
❑ 82 Matt Merullo .15 .07
❑ 83 Hensley Meulens .15 .07
❑ 84 Kevin Mmahat .15 .07
❑ 85 Mike Munoz .15 .07
❑ 86 Dan Murphy .15 .07
❑ 87 Jaime Navarro .25 .11
❑ 88 Randy Nosek .15 .07
❑ 89 John Olerud 1.00 .45
❑ 90 Steve Olin .25 .11
❑ 91 Joe Oliver .15 .07
❑ 92 Francisco Oliveras .15 .07
❑ 93 Gregg Olson .25 .11
❑ 94 John Orton .15 .07
❑ 95 Dean Palmer .50 .23
❑ 96 Ramon Pena .15 .07
❑ 97 Jeff Peterek .15 .07
❑ 98 Marty Pevey .15 .07
❑ 99 Rusty Richards .15 .07
❑ 100 Jeff Richardson .15 .07
❑ 101 Rob Richie .15 .07
❑ 102 Kevin Ritz .15 .07
❑ 103 Rosario Rodriguez .15 .07
❑ 104 Mike Roesler .15 .07
❑ 105 Kenny Rogers .25 .11
❑ 106 Bobby Rose .15 .07
❑ 107 Alex Sanchez .15 .07
❑ 108 Deion Sanders 1.50 .70
❑ 109 Jeff Schaefer .15 .07
❑ 110 Jeff Schulz .15 .07
❑ 111 Mike Schwabe .15 .07
❑ 112 Dick Scott .15 .07
❑ 113 Scott Scudder .15 .07
❑ 114 Rudy Seanez .15 .07
❑ 115 Joe Skalski .15 .07
❑ 116 Dwight Smith .15 .07
❑ 117 Greg Smith .15 .07
❑ 118 Mike Smith .15 .07
❑ 119 Paul Sorrento .50 .23
❑ 120 Sammy Sosa 20.00 9.00
❑ 121 Billy Spiers .15 .07
❑ 122 Mike Stanton .15 .07
❑ 123 Phil Stephenson .15 .07
❑ 124 Doug Strange .15 .07
❑ 125 Russ Swan .15 .07
❑ 126 Kevin Tapani .25 .11
❑ 127 Stu Tate .15 .07
❑ 128 Greg Vaughn 2.50 1.10
❑ 129 Robin Ventura .50 .23
❑ 130 Randy Veres .15 .07
❑ 131 Jose Vizcaino .25 .11
❑ 132 Omar Vizquel .50 .23
❑ 133 Larry Walker 3.00 1.35
❑ 134 Jerome Walton .25 .11
❑ 135 Gary Wayne .15 .07
❑ 136 Lenny Webster .15 .07
❑ 137 Mickey Weston .15 .07
❑ 138 Jeff Wetherby .15 .07
❑ 139 John Wetteland .50 .23
❑ 140 Ed Whited .15 .07
❑ 141 Wally Whitehurst .15 .07
❑ 142 Kevin Wickander .15 .07
❑ 143 Dean Wilkins .15 .07
❑ 144 Dana Williams .15 .07
❑ 145 Paul Wilmet .15 .07
❑ 146 Craig Wilson .15 .07
❑ 147 Matt Winters .15 .07
❑ 148 Eric Yelding .15 .07
❑ 149 Clint Zavaras .15 .07
❑ 150 Todd Zeile .25 .11
❑ 151 Checklist Card .15 .07
❑ 152 Checklist Card .15 .07

1991 Topps

	MINT	NRMT
COMPLETE SET (792)	15.00	6.75
COMP.FACT.SET (792)	20.00	9.00
COMMON CARD (1-792)	.05	.02

❑ 1 Nolan Ryan .75 .35
❑ 2 George Brett RB .20 .09
Batting Title, 3 decades
❑ 3 Carlton Fisk RB .10 .05
Catcher HR Record
❑ 4 Kevin Maas RB .05 .02
Quickest to 10 HR's
❑ 5 Cal Ripken RB .40 .18
Most cons. errorless games
❑ 6 Nolan Ryan RB .40 .18
Oldest pitcher, no-hitter
❑ 7 Ryne Sandberg RB .20 .09
Most cons. errorless games
❑ 8 Bobby Thigpen RB .05 .02
Most saves, season
❑ 9 Darrin Fletcher .05 .02
❑ 10 Gregg Olson .05 .02
❑ 11 Roberto Kelly .05 .02
❑ 12 Paul Assenmacher .05 .02
❑ 13 Mariano Duncan .05 .02
❑ 14 Dennis Lamp .05 .02
❑ 15 Von Hayes .05 .02
❑ 16 Mike Heath .05 .02
❑ 17 Jeff Brantley .05 .02
❑ 18 Nelson Liriano .05 .02
❑ 19 Jeff D. Robinson .05 .02
❑ 20 Pedro Guerrero .05 .02
❑ 21 Joe Morgan MG .05 .02
❑ 22 Storm Davis .05 .02
❑ 23 Jim Gantner .05 .02
❑ 24 Dave Martinez .05 .02
❑ 25 Tim Belcher .05 .02
❑ 26 Luis Sojo UER .05 .02
(Born in Barquisimento, not Carquis)
❑ 27 Bobby Witt .05 .02
❑ 28 Alvaro Espinoza .05 .02
❑ 29 Bob Walk .05 .02
❑ 30 Gregg Jefferies .05 .02
❑ 31 Colby Ward .05 .02
❑ 32 Mike Simms .05 .02
❑ 33 Barry Jones .05 .02
❑ 34 Atlee Hammaker .05 .02
❑ 35 Greg Maddux .60 .25
❑ 36 Donnie Hill .05 .02
❑ 37 Tom Bolton .05 .02
❑ 38 Scott Bradley .05 .02
❑ 39 Jim Neidlinger .05 .02
❑ 40 Kevin Mitchell .05 .02
❑ 41 Ken Dayley .05 .02
❑ 42 Chris Hoiles .05 .02
❑ 43 Roger McDowell .05 .02
❑ 44 Mike Felder .05 .02
❑ 45 Chris Sabo .05 .02
❑ 46 Tim Drummond .05 .02
❑ 47 Brook Jacoby .05 .02
❑ 48 Dennis Boyd .05 .02
❑ 49A Pat Borders ERR .20 .09
(40 steals at Kinston in '86)
❑ 49B Pat Borders COR .05 .02

(0 steals at Kinston in '86)
❑ 50 Bob Welch .05 .02
❑ 51 Art Howe MG .05 .02
❑ 52 Francisco Oliveras .05 .02
❑ 53 Mike Sharperson UER .05 .02
(Born in 1961, not 1960)
❑ 54 Gary Mielke .05 .02
❑ 55 Jeffrey Leonard .05 .02
❑ 56 Jeff Parrett .05 .02
❑ 57 Jack Howell .05 .02
❑ 58 Mel Stottlemyre Jr. .05 .02
❑ 59 Eric Yelding .05 .02
❑ 60 Frank Viola .05 .02
❑ 61 Stan Javier .05 .02
❑ 62 Lee Guetterman .05 .02
❑ 63 Milt Thompson .05 .02
❑ 64 Tom Herr .05 .02
❑ 65 Bruce Hurst .05 .02
❑ 66 Terry Kennedy .05 .02
❑ 67 Rick Honeycutt .05 .02
❑ 68 Gary Sheffield .20 .09
❑ 69 Steve Wilson .05 .02
❑ 70 Ellis Burks .10 .05
❑ 71 Jim Acker .05 .02
❑ 72 Junior Ortiz .05 .02
❑ 73 Craig Worthington .05 .02
❑ 74 Shane Andrews .10 .05
❑ 75 Jack Morris .10 .05
❑ 76 Jerry Browne .05 .02
❑ 77 Drew Hall .05 .02
❑ 78 Geno Petralli .05 .02
❑ 79 Frank Thomas 1.00 .45
❑ 80A Fernando Valenzuela .10 .05
ERR (104 earned runs in '90 tied for league lead)
❑ 80B Fernando Valenzuela .10 .05
COR (104 earned runs in '90 led league, 20 CG's in 1986 now italicized)
❑ 81 Cito Gaston MG .05 .02
❑ 82 Tom Glavine .20 .09
❑ 83 Daryl Boston .05 .02
❑ 84 Bob McClure .05 .02
❑ 85 Jesse Barfield .05 .02
❑ 86 Les Lancaster .05 .02
❑ 87 Tracy Jones .05 .02
❑ 88 Bob Tewksbury .05 .02
❑ 89 Darren Daulton .10 .05
❑ 90 Danny Tartabull .05 .02
❑ 91 Greg Colbrunn .05 .02
❑ 92 Danny Jackson .05 .02
❑ 93 Ivan Calderon .05 .02
❑ 94 John Dopson .05 .02
❑ 95 Paul Molitor .20 .09
❑ 96 Trevor Wilson .05 .02
❑ 97A Brady Anderson ERR .25 .11
(September, 2 RBI and 3 hits, should be 3 RBI and 14 hits
❑ 97B Brady Anderson COR .20 .09
❑ 98 Sergio Valdez .05 .02
❑ 99 Chris Gwynn .05 .02
❑ 100 Don Mattingly COR .30 .14
(101 hits in 1990)
❑ 100A Don Mattingly ERR 1.00 .45
(10 hits in 1990)
❑ 101 Rob Ducey .05 .02
❑ 102 Gene Larkin .05 .02
❑ 103 Tim Costo .05 .02
❑ 104 Don Robinson .05 .02
❑ 105 Kevin McReynolds .05 .02
❑ 106 Ed Nunez .05 .02
❑ 107 Luis Polonia .05 .02
❑ 108 Matt Young .05 .02
❑ 109 Greg Riddoch MG .05 .02
❑ 110 Tom Henke .05 .02
❑ 111 Andres Thomas .05 .02
❑ 112 Frank DiPino .05 .02
❑ 113 Carl Everett .20 .09
❑ 114 Lance Dickson .05 .02
❑ 115 Hubie Brooks .05 .02
❑ 116 Mark Davis .05 .02
❑ 117 Dion James .05 .02
❑ 118 Tom Edens .05 .02
❑ 119 Carl Nichols .05 .02
❑ 120 Joe Carter .10 .05
❑ 121 Eric King .05 .02
❑ 122 Paul O'Neill .10 .05
❑ 123 Greg A. Harris .05 .02
❑ 124 Randy Bush .05 .02
❑ 125 Steve Bedrosian .05 .02
❑ 126 Bernard Gilkey .10 .05
❑ 127 Joe Price .05 .02
❑ 128 Travis Fryman .20 .09
(Front has SS back has SS-3B)
❑ 129 Mark Eichhorn .05 .02
❑ 130 Ozzie Smith .25 .11
❑ 131A Checklist 1 ERR .20 .09
727 Phil Bradley
❑ 131B Checklist 1 COR .05 .02
717 Phil Bradley
❑ 132 Jamie Quirk .05 .02
❑ 133 Greg Briley .05 .02
❑ 134 Kevin Elster .05 .02
❑ 135 Jerome Walton .05 .02
❑ 136 Dave Schmidt .05 .02
❑ 137 Randy Ready .05 .02
❑ 138 Jamie Moyer .05 .02
❑ 139 Jeff Treadway .05 .02
❑ 140 Fred McGriff .20 .09
❑ 141 Nick Leyva MG .05 .02
❑ 142 Curt Wilkerson .05 .02
❑ 143 John Smiley .05 .02
❑ 144 Dave Henderson .05 .02
❑ 145 Lou Whitaker .10 .05
❑ 146 Dan Plesac .05 .02
❑ 147 Carlos Baerga .10 .05
❑ 148 Rey Palacios .05 .02
❑ 149 Al Osuna UER .05 .02
(Shown throwing right, but bio says lefty)
❑ 150 Cal Ripken .75 .35
❑ 151 Tom Browning .05 .02
❑ 152 Mickey Hatcher .05 .02
❑ 153 Bryan Harvey .05 .02
❑ 154 Jay Buhner .20 .09
❑ 155A Dwight Evans ERR .20 .09
(Led league with 162 games in '82)
❑ 155B Dwight Evans COR .10 .05
(Tied for lead with 162 games in '82)
❑ 156 Carlos Martinez .05 .02
❑ 157 John Smoltz .20 .09
❑ 158 Jose Uribe .05 .02
❑ 159 Joe Boever .05 .02
❑ 160 Vince Coleman UER .05 .02
(Wrong birth year, born 9/22/60)
❑ 161 Tim Leary .05 .02
❑ 162 Ozzie Canseco .05 .02
❑ 163 Dave Johnson .05 .02
❑ 164 Edgar Diaz .05 .02
❑ 165 Sandy Alomar Jr. .10 .05
❑ 166 Harold Baines .10 .05
❑ 167A Randy Tomlin ERR .20 .09
(Harriburg)
❑ 167B Randy Tomlin COR .05 .02
(Harrisburg)
❑ 168 John Olerud .10 .05
❑ 169 Luis Aquino .05 .02
❑ 170 Carlton Fisk .20 .09
❑ 171 Tony LaRussa MG .10 .05
❑ 172 Pete Incaviglia .05 .02
❑ 173 Jason Grimsley .05 .02
❑ 174 Ken Caminiti .20 .09
❑ 175 Jack Armstrong .05 .02
❑ 176 John Orton .05 .02
❑ 177 Reggie Harris .05 .02
❑ 178 Dave Valle .05 .02
❑ 179 Pete Harnisch .05 .02
❑ 180 Tony Gwynn .50 .23
❑ 181 Duane Ward .05 .02
❑ 182 Junior Noboa .05 .02
❑ 183 Clay Parker .05 .02
❑ 184 Gary Green .05 .02
❑ 185 Joe Magrane .05 .02
❑ 186 Rod Booker .05 .02
❑ 187 Greg Cadaret .05 .02
❑ 188 Damon Berryhill .05 .02
❑ 189 Daryl Irvine .05 .02
❑ 190 Matt Williams .20 .09
❑ 191 Willie Blair .05 .02
❑ 192 Rob Deer .05 .02
❑ 193 Felix Fermin .05 .02
❑ 194 Xavier Hernandez .05 .02
❑ 195 Wally Joyner .10 .05
❑ 196 Jim Vatcher .05 .02
❑ 197 Chris Nabholz .05 .02
❑ 198 R.J. Reynolds .05 .02
❑ 199 Mike Hartley .05 .02
❑ 200 Darryl Strawberry .10 .05
❑ 201 Tom Kelly MG .05 .02
❑ 202 Jim Leyritz .10 .05
❑ 203 Gene Harris .05 .02
❑ 204 Herm Winningham .05 .02
❑ 205 Mike Perez .05 .02
❑ 206 Carlos Quintana .05 .02
❑ 207 Gary Wayne .05 .02
❑ 208 Willie Wilson .05 .02
❑ 209 Ken Howell .05 .02
❑ 210 Lance Parrish .05 .02
❑ 211 Brian Barnes .05 .02
❑ 212 Steve Finley .20 .09
❑ 213 Frank Wills .05 .02
❑ 214 Joe Girardi .10 .05
❑ 215 Dave Smith .05 .02
❑ 216 Greg Gagne .05 .02
❑ 217 Chris Bosio .05 .02
❑ 218 Rick Parker .05 .02
❑ 219 Jack McDowell .05 .02
❑ 220 Tim Wallach .05 .02
❑ 221 Don Slaught .05 .02
❑ 222 Brian McRae .20 .09
❑ 223 Allan Anderson .05 .02
❑ 224 Juan Gonzalez .75 .35
❑ 225 Randy Johnson .25 .11
❑ 226 Alfredo Griffin .05 .02
❑ 227 Steve Avery UER .05 .02
(Pitched 13 games for Durham in 1989, not 2)
❑ 228 Rex Hudler .05 .02
❑ 229 Rance Mulliniks .05 .02
❑ 230 Sid Fernandez .05 .02
❑ 231 Doug Rader MG .05 .02
❑ 232 Jose DeJesus .05 .02
❑ 233 Al Leiter .10 .05
❑ 234 Scott Erickson .10 .05
❑ 235 Dave Parker .10 .05
❑ 236A Frank Tanana ERR .10 .05
(Tied for lead with 269 K's in '75)
❑ 236B Frank Tanana COR .05 .02
(Led league with 269 K's in '75)
❑ 237 Rick Cerone .05 .02
❑ 238 Mike Dunne .05 .02
❑ 239 Darren Lewis .10 .05
❑ 240 Mike Scott .05 .02
❑ 241 Dave Clark UER .05 .02
(Career totals 19 HR and 5 3B, should be 22 and 3)
❑ 242 Mike LaCoss .05 .02
❑ 243 Lance Johnson .05 .02
❑ 244 Mike Jeffcoat .05 .02
❑ 245 Kal Daniels .05 .02
❑ 246 Kevin Wickander .05 .02
❑ 247 Jody Reed .05 .02
❑ 248 Tom Gordon .10 .05
❑ 249 Bob Melvin .05 .02
❑ 250 Dennis Eckersley .10 .05
❑ 251 Mark Lemke .05 .02
❑ 252 Mel Rojas .10 .05
❑ 253 Garry Templeton .05 .02
❑ 254 Shawn Boskie .05 .02
❑ 255 Brian Downing .05 .02
❑ 256 Greg Hibbard .05 .02
❑ 257 Tom O'Malley .05 .02
❑ 258 Chris Hammond .05 .02
❑ 259 Hensley Meulens .05 .02

❑ 260 Harold Reynolds .05 .02
❑ 261 Bud Harrelson MG .05 .02
❑ 262 Tim Jones .05 .02
❑ 263 Checklist 2 .05 .02
❑ 264 Dave Hollins .05 .02
❑ 265 Mark Gubicza .05 .02
❑ 266 Carmelo Castillo .05 .02
❑ 267 Mark Knudson .05 .02
❑ 268 Tom Brookens .05 .02
❑ 269 Joe Hesketh .05 .02
❑ 270 Mark McGwire COR 1.00 .45
(1987 Slugging Pctg. listed as .618)
❑ 270A Mark McGwire ERR 1.25 .55
(1987 Slugging Pctg. listed as 618)
❑ 271 Omar Olivares .05 .02
❑ 272 Jeff King .10 .05
❑ 273 Johnny Ray .05 .02
❑ 274 Ken Williams .05 .02
❑ 275 Alan Trammell .15 .07
❑ 276 Bill Swift .05 .02
❑ 277 Scott Coolbaugh .05 .02
❑ 278 Alex Fernandez UER .10 .05
(No '90 White Sox stats)
❑ 279A Jose Gonzalez ERR .05 .02
(Photo actually Billy Bean)
❑ 279B Jose Gonzalez COR .05 .02
❑ 280 Bret Saberhagen .10 .05
❑ 281 Larry Sheets .05 .02
❑ 282 Don Carman .05 .02
❑ 283 Marquis Grissom .20 .09
❑ 284 Billy Spiers .05 .02
❑ 285 Jim Abbott .10 .05
❑ 286 Ken Oberkfell .05 .02
❑ 287 Mark Grant .05 .02
❑ 288 Derrick May .05 .02
❑ 289 Tim Birtsas .05 .02
❑ 290 Steve Sax .05 .02
❑ 291 John Wathan MG .05 .02
❑ 292 Bud Black .05 .02
❑ 293 Jay Bell .10 .05
❑ 294 Mike Moore .05 .02
❑ 295 Rafael Palmeiro .20 .09
❑ 296 Mark Williamson .05 .02
❑ 297 Manny Lee .05 .02
❑ 298 Omar Vizquel .20 .09
❑ 299 Scott Radinsky .05 .02
❑ 300 Kirby Puckett .30 .14
❑ 301 Steve Farr .05 .02
❑ 302 Tim Teufel .05 .02
❑ 303 Mike Boddicker .05 .02
❑ 304 Kevin Reimer .05 .02
❑ 305 Mike Scioscia .05 .02
❑ 306A Lonnie Smith ERR .20 .09
(136 games in '90)
❑ 306B Lonnie Smith COR .05 .02
(135 games in '90)
❑ 307 Andy Benes .10 .05
❑ 308 Tom Pagnozzi .05 .02
❑ 309 Norm Charlton .05 .02
❑ 310 Gary Carter .20 .09
❑ 311 Jeff Pico .05 .02
❑ 312 Charlie Hayes .05 .02
❑ 313 Ron Robinson .05 .02
❑ 314 Gary Pettis .05 .02
❑ 315 Roberto Alomar .20 .09
❑ 316 Gene Nelson .05 .02
❑ 317 Mike Fitzgerald .05 .02
❑ 318 Rick Aguilera .10 .05
❑ 319 Jeff McKnight .05 .02
❑ 320 Tony Fernandez .05 .02
❑ 321 Bob Rodgers MG .05 .02
❑ 322 Terry Shumpert .05 .02
❑ 323 Cory Snyder .05 .02
❑ 324A Ron Kittle ERR .20 .09
(Set another standard ...)
❑ 324B Ron Kittle COR .05 .02
(Tied another standard ...)
❑ 325 Brett Butler .10 .05
❑ 326 Ken Patterson .05 .02
❑ 327 Ron Hassey .05 .02
❑ 328 Walt Terrell .05 .02
❑ 329 Dave Justice UER .25 .11
(Drafted third round on card, should say fourth pick)
❑ 330 Dwight Gooden .10 .05
❑ 331 Eric Anthony .05 .02
❑ 332 Kenny Rogers .05 .02
❑ 333 Chipper Jones FDP 4.00 1.80
❑ 334 Todd Benzinger .05 .02
❑ 335 Mitch Williams .05 .02
❑ 336 Matt Nokes .05 .02
❑ 337A Keith Comstock ERR .20 .09
(Cubs logo on front)
❑ 337B Keith Comstock COR .05 .02
(Mariners logo on front)
❑ 338 Luis Rivera .05 .02
❑ 339 Larry Walker .30 .14
❑ 340 Ramon Martinez .10 .05
❑ 341 John Moses .05 .02
❑ 342 Mickey Morandini .05 .02
❑ 343 Jose Oquendo .05 .02
❑ 344 Jeff Russell .05 .02
❑ 345 Len Dykstra .10 .05
❑ 346 Jesse Orosco .05 .02
❑ 347 Greg Vaughn .20 .09
❑ 348 Todd Stottlemyre .10 .05
❑ 349 Dave Gallagher .05 .02
❑ 350 Glenn Davis .05 .02
❑ 351 Joe Torre MG .10 .05
❑ 352 Frank White .10 .05
❑ 353 Tony Castillo .05 .02
❑ 354 Sid Bream .05 .02
❑ 355 Chili Davis .10 .05
❑ 356 Mike Marshall .05 .02
❑ 357 Jack Savage .05 .02
❑ 358 Mark Parent .05 .02
❑ 359 Chuck Cary .05 .02
❑ 360 Tim Raines .10 .05
❑ 361 Scott Garrelts .05 .02
❑ 362 Hector Villenueva .05 .02
❑ 363 Rick Mahler .05 .02
❑ 364 Dan Pasqua .05 .02
❑ 365 Mike Schooler .05 .02
❑ 366A Checklist 3 ERR .20 .09
19 Carl Nichols
❑ 366B Checklist 3 COR .05 .02
119 Carl Nichols
❑ 367 Dave Walsh .05 .02
❑ 368 Felix Jose .05 .02
❑ 369 Steve Searcy .05 .02
❑ 370 Kelly Gruber .05 .02
❑ 371 Jeff Montgomery .10 .05
❑ 372 Spike Owen .05 .02
❑ 373 Darrin Jackson .05 .02
❑ 374 Larry Casian .05 .02
❑ 375 Tony Pena .05 .02
❑ 376 Mike Harkey .05 .02
❑ 377 Rene Gonzales .05 .02
❑ 378A Wilson Alvarez ERR .50 .23
('89 Port Charlotte and '90 Birmingham stat lines omitted)
❑ 378B Wilson Alvarez COR .20 .09
(Text still says 143 K's in 1988, whereas stats say 134)
❑ 379 Randy Velarde .05 .02
❑ 380 Willie McGee .10 .05
❑ 381 Jim Leyland MG .05 .02
❑ 382 Mackey Sasser .05 .02
❑ 383 Pete Smith .05 .02
❑ 384 Gerald Perry .05 .02
❑ 385 Mickey Tettleton .10 .05
❑ 386 Cecil Fielder AS .05 .02
❑ 387 Julio Franco AS .05 .02
❑ 388 Kelly Gruber AS .05 .02
❑ 389 Alan Trammell AS .10 .05
❑ 390 Jose Canseco AS .10 .05
❑ 391 Rickey Henderson AS .10 .05
❑ 392 Ken Griffey Jr. AS .75 .35
❑ 393 Carlton Fisk AS .10 .05
❑ 394 Bob Welch AS .05 .02
❑ 395 Chuck Finley AS .05 .02
❑ 396 Bobby Thigpen AS .05 .02
❑ 397 Eddie Murray AS .10 .05
❑ 398 Ryne Sandberg AS .20 .09
❑ 399 Matt Williams AS .10 .05
❑ 400 Barry Larkin AS .10 .05
❑ 401 Barry Bonds AS .20 .09
❑ 402 Darryl Strawbery AS .05 .02
❑ 403 Bobby Bonilla AS .05 .02
❑ 404 Mike Scioscia AS .05 .02
❑ 405 Doug Drabek AS .05 .02
❑ 406 Frank Viola AS .05 .02
❑ 407 John Franco AS .05 .02
❑ 408 Earnie Riles .05 .02
❑ 409 Mike Stanley .05 .02
❑ 410 Dave Righetti .05 .02
❑ 411 Lance Blankenship .05 .02
❑ 412 Dave Bergman .05 .02
❑ 413 Terry Mulholland .05 .02
❑ 414 Sammy Sosa 1.00 .45
❑ 415 Rick Sutcliffe .05 .02
❑ 416 Randy Milligan .05 .02
❑ 417 Bill Krueger .05 .02
❑ 418 Nick Esasky .05 .02
❑ 419 Jeff Reed .05 .02
❑ 420 Bobby Thigpen .05 .02
❑ 421 Alex Cole .05 .02
❑ 422 Rick Reuschel .05 .02
❑ 423 Rafael Ramirez UER .05 .02
(Born 1959, not 1958)
❑ 424 Calvin Schiraldi .05 .02
❑ 425 Andy Van Slyke .10 .05
❑ 426 Joe Grahe .05 .02
❑ 427 Rick Dempsey .05 .02
❑ 428 John Barfield .05 .02
❑ 429 Stump Merrill MG .05 .02
❑ 430 Gary Gaetti .10 .05
❑ 431 Paul Gibson .05 .02
❑ 432 Delino DeShields .10 .05
❑ 433 Pat Tabler .05 .02
❑ 434 Julio Machado .05 .02
❑ 435 Kevin Maas .05 .02
❑ 436 Scott Bankhead .05 .02
❑ 437 Doug Dascenzo .05 .02
❑ 438 Vicente Palacios .05 .02
❑ 439 Dickie Thon .05 .02
❑ 440 George Bell .05 .02
❑ 441 Zane Smith .05 .02
❑ 442 Charlie O'Brien .05 .02
❑ 443 Jeff Innis .05 .02
❑ 444 Glenn Braggs .05 .02
❑ 445 Greg Swindell .05 .02
❑ 446 Craig Grebeck .05 .02
❑ 447 John Burkett .05 .02
❑ 448 Craig Lefferts .05 .02
❑ 449 Juan Berenguer .05 .02
❑ 450 Wade Boggs .20 .09
❑ 451 Neal Heaton .05 .02
❑ 452 Bill Schroeder .05 .02
❑ 453 Lenny Harris .05 .02
❑ 454A Kevin Appier ERR .10 .05
('90 Omaha stat line omitted)
❑ 454B Kevin Appier COR .10 .05
❑ 455 Walt Weiss .05 .02
❑ 456 Charlie Leibrandt .05 .02
❑ 457 Todd Hundley .20 .09
❑ 458 Brian Holman .05 .02
❑ 459 Tom Trebelhorn MG UER .05 .02
(Pitching and batting columns switched)
❑ 460 Dave Stieb .10 .05
❑ 461 Robin Ventura .20 .09
❑ 462 Steve Frey .05 .02
❑ 463 Dwight Smith .05 .02
❑ 464 Steve Buechele .05 .02
❑ 465 Ken Griffey Sr. .05 .02
❑ 466 Charles Nagy .20 .09
❑ 467 Dennis Cook .05 .02
❑ 468 Tim Hulett .05 .02
❑ 469 Chet Lemon .05 .02
❑ 470 Howard Johnson .05 .02
❑ 471 Mike Lieberthal .20 .09
❑ 472 Kirt Manwaring .05 .02
❑ 473 Curt Young .05 .02
❑ 474 Phil Plantier .05 .02
❑ 475 Teddy Higuera .05 .02

Card	Price	Price
❑ 476 Glenn Wilson	.05	.02
❑ 477 Mike Fetters	.05	.02
❑ 478 Kurt Stillwell	.05	.02
❑ 479 Bob Patterson UER (Has a decimal point between 7 and 9)	.05	.02
❑ 480 Dave Magadan	.05	.02
❑ 481 Eddie Whitson	.05	.02
❑ 482 Tino Martinez	.20	.09
❑ 483 Mike Aldrete	.05	.02
❑ 484 Dave LaPoint	.05	.02
❑ 485 Terry Pendleton	.10	.05
❑ 486 Tommy Greene	.05	.02
❑ 487 Rafael Belliard	.05	.02
❑ 488 Jeff Manto	.05	.02
❑ 489 Bobby Valentine MG	.05	.02
❑ 490 Kirk Gibson	.10	.05
❑ 491 Kurt Miller	.05	.02
❑ 492 Ernie Whitt	.05	.02
❑ 493 Jose Rijo	.05	.02
❑ 494 Chris James	.05	.02
❑ 495 Charlie Hough	.10	.05
❑ 496 Marty Barrett	.05	.02
❑ 497 Ben McDonald	.05	.02
❑ 498 Mark Salas	.05	.02
❑ 499 Melido Perez	.05	.02
❑ 500 Will Clark	.20	.09
❑ 501 Mike Bielecki	.05	.02
❑ 502 Carney Lansford	.10	.05
❑ 503 Roy Smith	.05	.02
❑ 504 Julio Valera	.05	.02
❑ 505 Chuck Finley	.10	.05
❑ 506 Darnell Coles	.05	.02
❑ 507 Steve Jeltz	.05	.02
❑ 508 Mike York	.05	.02
❑ 509 Glenallen Hill	.05	.02
❑ 510 John Franco	.10	.05
❑ 511 Steve Balboni	.05	.02
❑ 512 Jose Mesa	.05	.02
❑ 513 Jerald Clark	.05	.02
❑ 514 Mike Stanton	.05	.02
❑ 515 Alvin Davis	.05	.02
❑ 516 Karl Rhodes	.05	.02
❑ 517 Joe Oliver	.05	.02
❑ 518 Cris Carpenter	.05	.02
❑ 519 Sparky Anderson MG	.10	.05
❑ 520 Mark Grace	.20	.09
❑ 521 Joe Orsulak	.05	.02
❑ 522 Stan Belinda	.05	.02
❑ 523 Rodney McCray	.05	.02
❑ 524 Darrel Akerfelds	.05	.02
❑ 525 Willie Randolph	.10	.05
❑ 526A Moises Alou ERR (37 runs in 2 games for '90 Pirates)	.50	.23
❑ 526B Moises Alou COR (0 runs in 2 games for '90 Pirates)	.20	.09
❑ 527A Checklist 4 ERR 105 Keith Miller 719 Kevin McReynolds	.20	.09
❑ 527B Checklist 4 COR 105 Kevin McReynolds 719 Keith Miller	.05	.02
❑ 528 Denny Martinez	.10	.05
❑ 529 Marc Newfield	.10	.05
❑ 530 Roger Clemens	.40	.18
❑ 531 Dave Rohde	.05	.02
❑ 532 Kirk McCaskill	.05	.02
❑ 533 Oddibe McDowell	.05	.02
❑ 534 Mike Jackson	.10	.05
❑ 535 Ruben Sierra UER (Back reads 100 Runs amd 100 RBI's)	.05	.02
❑ 536 Mike Witt	.05	.02
❑ 537 Jose Lind	.05	.02
❑ 538 Bip Roberts	.05	.02
❑ 539 Scott Terry	.05	.02
❑ 540 George Brett	.40	.18
❑ 541 Domingo Ramos	.05	.02
❑ 542 Rob Murphy	.05	.02
❑ 543 Junior Felix	.05	.02
❑ 544 Alejandro Pena	.05	.02
❑ 545 Dale Murphy	.20	.09
❑ 546 Jeff Ballard	.05	.02
❑ 547 Mike Pagliarulo	.05	.02
❑ 548 Jaime Navarro	.05	.02
❑ 549 John McNamara MG	.05	.02
❑ 550 Eric Davis	.10	.05
❑ 551 Bob Kipper	.05	.02
❑ 552 Jeff Hamilton	.05	.02
❑ 553 Joe Klink	.05	.02
❑ 554 Brian Harper	.05	.02
❑ 555 Turner Ward	.05	.02
❑ 556 Gary Ward	.05	.02
❑ 557 Wally Whitehurst	.05	.02
❑ 558 Otis Nixon	.10	.05
❑ 559 Adam Peterson	.05	.02
❑ 560 Greg Smith	.05	.02
❑ 561 Tim McIntosh	.05	.02
❑ 562 Jeff Kunkel	.05	.02
❑ 563 Brent Knackert	.05	.02
❑ 564 Dante Bichette	.20	.09
❑ 565 Craig Biggio	.20	.09
❑ 566 Craig Wilson	.05	.02
❑ 567 Dwayne Henry	.05	.02
❑ 568 Ron Karkovice	.05	.02
❑ 569 Curt Schilling	.20	.09
❑ 570 Barry Bonds	.25	.11
❑ 571 Pat Combs	.05	.02
❑ 572 Dave Anderson	.05	.02
❑ 573 Rich Rodriguez UER (Stats say drafted 4th, but bio says 9th round)	.05	.02
❑ 574 John Marzano	.05	.02
❑ 575 Robin Yount	.20	.09
❑ 576 Jeff Kaiser	.05	.02
❑ 577 Bill Doran	.05	.02
❑ 578 Dave West	.05	.02
❑ 579 Roger Craig MG	.05	.02
❑ 580 Dave Stewart	.10	.05
❑ 581 Luis Quinones	.05	.02
❑ 582 Marty Clary	.05	.02
❑ 583 Tony Phillips	.05	.02
❑ 584 Kevin Brown	.15	.07
❑ 585 Pete O'Brien	.05	.02
❑ 586 Fred Lynn	.05	.02
❑ 587 Jose Offerman UER (Text says he signed 7/24/86, but bio says 1988)	.05	.02
❑ 588 Mark Whiten	.05	.02
❑ 589 Scott Ruskin	.05	.02
❑ 590 Eddie Murray	.20	.09
❑ 591 Ken Hill	.10	.05
❑ 592 B.J. Surhoff	.10	.05
❑ 593A Mike Walker ERR ('90 Canton-Akron stat line omitted)	.20	.09
❑ 593B Mike Walker COR	.05	.02
❑ 594 Rich Garces	.05	.02
❑ 595 Bill Landrum	.05	.02
❑ 596 Ronnie Walden	.05	.02
❑ 597 Jerry Don Gleaton	.05	.02
❑ 598 Sam Horn	.05	.02
❑ 599A Greg Myers ERR ('90 Syracuse stat line omitted)	.20	.09
❑ 599B Greg Myers COR	.05	.02
❑ 600 Bo Jackson	.10	.05
❑ 601 Bob Ojeda	.05	.02
❑ 602 Casey Candaele	.05	.02
❑ 603A Wes Chamberlain ERR (Photo actually Louie Meadows)	.20	.09
❑ 603B Wes Chamberlain COR	.05	.02
❑ 604 Billy Hatcher	.05	.02
❑ 605 Jeff Reardon	.10	.05
❑ 606 Jim Gott	.05	.02
❑ 607 Edgar Martinez	.20	.09
❑ 608 Todd Burns	.05	.02
❑ 609 Jeff Torborg MG	.05	.02
❑ 610 Andres Galarraga	.20	.09
❑ 611 Dave Eiland	.05	.02
❑ 612 Steve Lyons	.05	.02
❑ 613 Eric Show	.05	.02
❑ 614 Luis Salazar	.05	.02
❑ 615 Bert Blyleven	.10	.05
❑ 616 Todd Zeile	.10	.05
❑ 617 Bill Wegman	.05	.02
❑ 618 Sil Campusano	.05	.02
❑ 619 David Wells	.10	.05
❑ 620 Ozzie Guillen	.05	.02
❑ 621 Ted Power	.05	.02
❑ 622 Jack Daugherty	.05	.02
❑ 623 Jeff Blauser	.05	.02
❑ 624 Tom Candiotti	.05	.02
❑ 625 Terry Steinbach	.10	.05
❑ 626 Gerald Young	.05	.02
❑ 627 Tim Layana	.05	.02
❑ 628 Greg Litton	.05	.02
❑ 629 Wes Gardner	.05	.02
❑ 630 Dave Winfield	.20	.09
❑ 631 Mike Morgan	.05	.02
❑ 632 Lloyd Moseby	.05	.02
❑ 633 Kevin Tapani	.05	.02
❑ 634 Henry Cotto	.05	.02
❑ 635 Andy Hawkins	.05	.02
❑ 636 Geronimo Pena	.05	.02
❑ 637 Bruce Ruffin	.05	.02
❑ 638 Mike Macfarlane	.05	.02
❑ 639 Frank Robinson MG	.15	.07
❑ 640 Andre Dawson	.20	.09
❑ 641 Mike Henneman	.05	.02
❑ 642 Hal Morris	.05	.02
❑ 643 Jim Presley	.05	.02
❑ 644 Chuck Crim	.05	.02
❑ 645 Juan Samuel	.05	.02
❑ 646 Andujar Cedeno	.05	.02
❑ 647 Mark Portugal	.05	.02
❑ 648 Lee Stevens	.05	.02
❑ 649 Bill Sampen	.05	.02
❑ 650 Jack Clark	.10	.05
❑ 651 Alan Mills	.05	.02
❑ 652 Kevin Romine	.05	.02
❑ 653 Anthony Telford	.05	.02
❑ 654 Paul Sorrento	.10	.05
❑ 655 Erik Hanson	.05	.02
❑ 656A Checklist 5 ERR 348 Vicente Palacios 381 Jose Lind 537 Mike LaValliere 665 Jim Leyland	.20	.09
❑ 656B Checklist 5 ERR 433 Vicente Palacios (Palacios should be 438) 537 Jose Lind 665 Mike LaValliere 381 Jim Leyland	.20	.09
❑ 656C Checklist 5 COR 438 Vicente Palacios 537 Jose Lind 665 Mike LaValliere 381 Jim Leyland	.20	.09
❑ 657 Mike Kingery	.05	.02
❑ 658 Scott Aldred	.05	.02
❑ 659 Oscar Azocar	.05	.02
❑ 660 Lee Smith	.10	.05
❑ 661 Steve Lake	.05	.02
❑ 662 Ron Dibble	.05	.02
❑ 663 Greg Brock	.05	.02
❑ 664 John Farrell	.05	.02
❑ 665 Mike LaValliere	.05	.02
❑ 666 Danny Darwin	.05	.02
❑ 667 Kent Anderson	.05	.02
❑ 668 Bill Long	.05	.02
❑ 669 Lou Piniella MG	.10	.05
❑ 670 Rickey Henderson	.20	.09
❑ 671 Andy McGaffigan	.05	.02
❑ 672 Shane Mack	.05	.02
❑ 673 Greg Olson UER (6 RBI in '88 at Tidewater and 2 RBI in '87, should be 48 and 15)	.05	.02
❑ 674A Kevin Gross ERR (89 BB with Phillies in '88 tied for league lead)	.20	.09
❑ 674B Kevin Gross COR (89 BB with Phillies in '88 led league)	.05	.02
❑ 675 Tom Brunansky	.05	.02
❑ 676 Scott Chiamparino	.05	.02
❑ 677 Billy Ripken	.05	.02
❑ 678 Mark Davidson	.05	.02

		MINT	NRMT
❑ 679	Bill Bathe	.05	.02
❑ 680	David Cone	.10	.05
❑ 681	Jeff Schaefer	.05	.02
❑ 682	Ray Lankford	.20	.09
❑ 683	Derek Lilliquist	.05	.02
❑ 684	Milt Cuyler	.05	.02
❑ 685	Doug Drabek	.05	.02
❑ 686	Mike Gallego	.05	.02
❑ 687A	John Cerutti ERR (4.46 ERA in '90)	.20	.09
❑ 687B	John Cerutti COR (4.76 ERA in '90)	.05	.02
❑ 688	Rosario Rodriguez	.05	.02
❑ 689	John Kruk	.10	.05
❑ 690	Orel Hershiser	.10	.05
❑ 691	Mike Blowers	.05	.02
❑ 692A	Efrain Valdez ERR (Born 6/11/66)	.20	.09
❑ 692B	Efrain Valdez COR (Born 7/11/66 and two lines of text added)	.05	.02
❑ 693	Francisco Cabrera	.05	.02
❑ 694	Randy Veres	.05	.02
❑ 695	Kevin Seitzer	.05	.02
❑ 696	Steve Olin	.05	.02
❑ 697	Shawn Abner	.05	.02
❑ 698	Mark Guthrie	.05	.02
❑ 699	Jim Lefebvre MG	.05	.02
❑ 700	Jose Canseco	.20	.09
❑ 701	Pascual Perez	.05	.02
❑ 702	Tim Naehring	.10	.05
❑ 703	Juan Agosto	.05	.02
❑ 704	Devon White	.05	.02
❑ 705	Robby Thompson	.05	.02
❑ 706A	Brad Arnsberg ERR (68.2 IP in '90)	.20	.09
❑ 706B	Brad Arnsberg COR (62.2 IP in '90)	.05	.02
❑ 707	Jim Eisenreich	.05	.02
❑ 708	John Mitchell	.05	.02
❑ 709	Matt Sinatro	.05	.02
❑ 710	Kent Hrbek	.10	.05
❑ 711	Jose DeLeon	.05	.02
❑ 712	Ricky Jordan	.05	.02
❑ 713	Scott Scudder	.05	.02
❑ 714	Marvell Wynne	.05	.02
❑ 715	Tim Burke	.05	.02
❑ 716	Bob Geren	.05	.02
❑ 717	Phil Bradley	.05	.02
❑ 718	Steve Crawford	.05	.02
❑ 719	Keith Miller	.05	.02
❑ 720	Cecil Fielder	.10	.05
❑ 721	Mark Lee	.05	.02
❑ 722	Wally Backman	.05	.02
❑ 723	Candy Maldonado	.05	.02
❑ 724	David Segui	.10	.05
❑ 725	Ron Gant	.10	.05
❑ 726	Phil Stephenson	.05	.02
❑ 727	Mookie Wilson	.10	.05
❑ 728	Scott Sanderson	.05	.02
❑ 729	Don Zimmer MG	.05	.02
❑ 730	Barry Larkin	.20	.09
❑ 731	Jeff Gray	.05	.02
❑ 732	Franklin Stubbs	.05	.02
❑ 733	Kelly Downs	.05	.02
❑ 734	John Russell	.05	.02
❑ 735	Ron Darling	.05	.02
❑ 736	Dick Schofield	.05	.02
❑ 737	Tim Crews	.05	.02
❑ 738	Mel Hall	.05	.02
❑ 739	Russ Swan	.05	.02
❑ 740	Ryne Sandberg	.25	.11
❑ 741	Jimmy Key	.10	.05
❑ 742	Tommy Gregg	.05	.02
❑ 743	Bryn Smith	.05	.02
❑ 744	Nelson Santovenia	.05	.02
❑ 745	Doug Jones	.05	.02
❑ 746	John Shelby	.05	.02
❑ 747	Tony Fossas	.05	.02
❑ 748	Al Newman	.05	.02
❑ 749	Greg W. Harris	.05	.02
❑ 750	Bobby Bonilla	.10	.05
❑ 751	Wayne Edwards	.05	.02
❑ 752	Kevin Bass	.05	.02
❑ 753	Paul Marak UER (Stats say drafted in Jan. but bio says May)	.05	.02
❑ 754	Bill Pecota	.05	.02
❑ 755	Mark Langston	.05	.02
❑ 756	Jeff Huson	.05	.02
❑ 757	Mark Gardner	.05	.02
❑ 758	Mike Devereaux	.05	.02
❑ 759	Bobby Cox MG	.05	.02
❑ 760	Benny Santiago	.05	.02
❑ 761	Larry Andersen	.05	.02
❑ 762	Mitch Webster	.05	.02
❑ 763	Dana Kiecker	.05	.02
❑ 764	Mark Carreon	.05	.02
❑ 765	Shawon Dunston	.05	.02
❑ 766	Jeff Robinson	.05	.02
❑ 767	Dan Wilson	.25	.11
❑ 768	Don Pall	.05	.02
❑ 769	Tim Sherrill	.05	.02
❑ 770	Jay Howell	.05	.02
❑ 771	Gary Redus UER (Born in Tanner, should say Athens)	.05	.02
❑ 772	Kent Mercker UER (Born in Indianapolis, should say Dublin, Ohio)	.05	.02
❑ 773	Tom Foley	.05	.02
❑ 774	Dennis Rasmussen	.05	.02
❑ 775	Julio Franco	.05	.02
❑ 776	Brent Mayne	.05	.02
❑ 777	John Candelaria	.05	.02
❑ 778	Dan Gladden	.05	.02
❑ 779	Carmelo Martinez	.05	.02
❑ 780A	Randy Myers ERR (15 career losses)	.05	.02
❑ 780B	Randy Myers COR (19 career losses)	.05	.02
❑ 781	Darryl Hamilton	.05	.02
❑ 782	Jim Deshaies	.05	.02
❑ 783	Joel Skinner	.05	.02
❑ 784	Willie Fraser	.05	.02
❑ 785	Scott Fletcher	.05	.02
❑ 786	Eric Plunk	.05	.02
❑ 787	Checklist 6	.05	.02
❑ 788	Bob Milacki	.05	.02
❑ 789	Tom Lasorda MG	.20	.09
❑ 790	Ken Griffey Jr.	1.50	.70
❑ 791	Mike Benjamin	.05	.02
❑ 792	Mike Greenwell	.05	.02

1991 Topps Tiffany

	MINT	NRMT
COMP.FACT.SET (792)	300.00	135.00
COMMON CARD (1-792)	.50	.23

*STARS: 15X TO 30X BASIC CARDS
*ROOKIES: 20X TO 40X BASIC CARDS

1991 Topps Rookies

	MINT	NRMT
COMPLETE SET (33)	15.00	6.75
COMMON CARD (1-33)	.25	.11

❑ 1	Sandy Alomar	.20	.09
❑ 2	Kevin Appier	.20	.09
❑ 3	Steve Avery	.25	.11
❑ 4	Carlos Baerga	.20	.09
❑ 5	John Burkett	.25	.11
❑ 6	Alex Cole	.25	.11
❑ 7	Pat Combs	.25	.11
❑ 8	Delino DeShields	.20	.09
❑ 9	Travis Fryman	.35	.16
❑ 10	Marquis Grissom	.50	.23
❑ 11	Mike Harkey	.25	.11
❑ 12	Glenallen Hill	.25	.11
❑ 13	Jeff Huson	.25	.11
❑ 14	Felix Jose	.25	.11
❑ 15	Dave Justice	1.50	.70
❑ 16	Jim Leyritz	.20	.09
❑ 17	Kevin Maas	.25	.11
❑ 18	Ben McDonald	.25	.11
❑ 19	Kent Mercker	.25	.11
❑ 20	Hal Morris	.25	.11
❑ 21	Chris Nabholz	.25	.11
❑ 22	Tim Naehring	.20	.09
❑ 23	Jose Offerman	.25	.11
❑ 24	John Olerud	1.50	.70
❑ 25	Scott Radinsky	.25	.11
❑ 26	Scott Ruskin	.25	.11
❑ 27	Kevin Tapani	.25	.11
❑ 28	Frank Thomas	3.00	1.35
❑ 29	Randy Tomlin	.25	.11
❑ 30	Greg Vaughn	.75	.35
❑ 31	Robin Ventura	.50	.23
❑ 32	Larry Walker	.75	.35
❑ 33	Todd Zeile	.20	.09

1991 Topps Traded

	MINT	NRMT
COMPLETE SET (132)	5.00	2.20
COMP.FACT.SET (132)	5.00	2.20
COMMON CARD (1T-132T)	.05	.02

❑ 1T	Juan Agosto	.05	.02
❑ 2T	Roberto Alomar	.20	.09
❑ 3T	Wally Backman	.05	.02
❑ 4T	Jeff Bagwell	2.00	.90
❑ 5T	Skeeter Barnes	.05	.02
❑ 6T	Steve Bedrosian	.05	.02
❑ 7T	Derek Bell	.20	.09
❑ 8T	George Bell	.05	.02
❑ 9T	Rafael Belliard	.05	.02
❑ 10T	Dante Bichette	.20	.09
❑ 11T	Bud Black	.05	.02
❑ 12T	Mike Boddicker	.05	.02
❑ 13T	Sid Bream	.05	.02
❑ 14T	Hubie Brooks	.05	.02
❑ 15T	Brett Butler	.10	.05
❑ 16T	Ivan Calderon	.05	.02
❑ 17T	John Candelaria	.05	.02
❑ 18T	Tom Candiotti	.05	.02
❑ 19T	Gary Carter	.20	.09
❑ 20T	Joe Carter	.10	.05
❑ 21T	Rick Cerone	.05	.02
❑ 22T	Jack Clark	.10	.05
❑ 23T	Vince Coleman	.05	.02
❑ 24T	Scott Coolbaugh	.05	.02
❑ 25T	Danny Cox	.05	.02
❑ 26T	Danny Darwin	.05	.02
❑ 27T	Chili Davis	.10	.05
❑ 28T	Glenn Davis	.05	.02
❑ 29T	Steve Decker	.05	.02
❑ 30T	Rob Deer	.05	.02
❑ 31T	Rich DeLucia	.05	.02
❑ 32T	John Dettmer USA	.10	.05
❑ 33T	Brian Downing	.05	.02
❑ 34T	Darren Dreifort USA	.50	.23
❑ 35T	Kirk Dressendorfer	.05	.02
❑ 36T	Jim Essian MG	.05	.02
❑ 37T	Dwight Evans	.10	.05
❑ 38T	Steve Farr	.05	.02
❑ 39T	Jeff Fassero	.25	.11
❑ 40T	Junior Felix	.05	.02
❑ 41T	Tony Fernandez	.05	.02
❑ 42T	Steve Finley	.20	.09
❑ 43T	Jim Fregosi MG	.05	.02
❑ 44T	Gary Gaetti	.10	.05
❑ 45T	Jason Giambi USA	1.00	.45
❑ 46T	Kirk Gibson	.10	.05
❑ 47T	Leo Gomez	.05	.02
❑ 48T	Luis Gonzalez	.20	.09
❑ 49T	Jeff Granger USA	.20	.09
❑ 50T	Todd Greene USA	.75	.35
❑ 51T	Jeffrey Hammonds USA	.50	.23

❑ 52T Mike Hargrove MG .05 .02
❑ 53T Pete Harnisch .05 .02
❑ 54T Rick Helling USA UER 1.00 .45
(Misspelled Hellings on card back)
❑ 55T Glenallen Hill .05 .02
❑ 56T Charlie Hough .10 .05
❑ 57T Pete Incaviglia .05 .02
❑ 58T Bo Jackson .10 .05
❑ 59T Danny Jackson .05 .02
❑ 60T Reggie Jefferson .15 .07
❑ 61T Charles Johnson USA 1.25 .55
❑ 62T Jeff Johnson .05 .02
❑ 63T Todd Johnson USA .05 .02
❑ 64T Barry Jones .05 .02
❑ 65T Chris Jones .05 .02
❑ 66T Scott Kamieniecki .05 .02
❑ 67T Pat Kelly .05 .02
❑ 68T Darryl Kile .20 .09
❑ 69T Chuck Knoblauch .25 .11
❑ 70T Bill Krueger .05 .02
❑ 71T Scott Leius .05 .02
❑ 72T Donnie Leshnock USA .05 .02
❑ 73T Mark Lewis .05 .02
❑ 74T Candy Maldonado .05 .02
❑ 75T Jason McDonald USA .15 .07
❑ 76T Willie McGee .10 .05
❑ 77T Fred McGriff .20 .09
❑ 78T Billy McMillon USA .10 .05
❑ 79T Hal McRae MG .05 .02
❑ 80T Dan Melendez USA .05 .02
❑ 81T Orlando Merced .10 .05
❑ 82T Jack Morris .10 .05
❑ 83T Phil Nevin USA .20 .09
❑ 84T Otis Nixon .10 .05
❑ 85T Johnny Oates MG .05 .02
❑ 86T Bob Ojeda .05 .02
❑ 87T Mike Pagliarulo .05 .02
❑ 88T Dean Palmer .10 .05
❑ 89T Dave Parker .10 .05
❑ 90T Terry Pendleton .10 .05
❑ 91T Tony Phillips (P) USA .05 .02
❑ 92T Doug Piatt .05 .02
❑ 93T Ron Polk USA CO .05 .02
❑ 94T Tim Raines .10 .05
❑ 95T Willie Randolph .10 .05
❑ 96T Dave Righetti .05 .02
❑ 97T Ernie Riles .05 .02
❑ 98T Chris Roberts USA .20 .09
❑ 99T Jeff D. Robinson .05 .02
❑ 100T Jeff M. Robinson .05 .02
❑ 101T Ivan Rodriguez 1.50 .70
❑ 102T Steve Rodriguez USA .05 .02
❑ 103T Tom Runnells MG .05 .02
❑ 104T Scott Sanderson .05 .02
❑ 105T Bob Scanlan .05 .02
❑ 106T Pete Schourek .10 .05
❑ 107T Gary Scott .05 .02
❑ 108T Paul Shuey USA .20 .09
❑ 109T Doug Simons .05 .02
❑ 110T Dave Smith .05 .02
❑ 111T Cory Snyder .05 .02
❑ 112T Luis Sojo .05 .02
❑ 113T Kennie Steenstra USA .05 .02
❑ 114T Darryl Strawberry .10 .05
❑ 115T Franklin Stubbs .05 .02
❑ 116T Todd Taylor USA .05 .02
❑ 117T Wade Taylor .05 .02
❑ 118T Garry Templeton .05 .02
❑ 119T Mickey Tettleton .10 .05
❑ 120T Tim Teufel .05 .02
❑ 121T Mike Timlin .05 .02
❑ 122T David Tuttle USA .05 .02
❑ 123T Mo Vaughn .40 .18
❑ 124T Jeff Ware USA .05 .02
❑ 125T Devon White .05 .02
❑ 126T Mark Whiten .05 .02
❑ 127T Mitch Williams .05 .02
❑ 128T Craig Wilson USA .05 .02
❑ 129T Willie Wilson .05 .02
❑ 130T Chris Wimmer USA .05 .02
❑ 131T Ivan Zweig USA .05 .02
❑ 132T Checklist 1T-132T .05 .02

1991 Topps Traded Tiffany

	MINT	NRMT
COMP.FACT.SET (132)	150.00	70.00
COMMON CARD (1T-132T)	.50	.23

*STARS: 15X TO 30X BASIC CARDS
*ROOKIES: 20X TO 40X BASIC CARDS
*USA ROOKIES: 7.5X TO 15X BASIC CARDS

1992 Topps

	MINT	NRMT
COMPLETE SET (792)	25.00	11.00
COMP.FACT.SET (802)	30.00	13.50
COMP.HOLIDAY SET (811)	35.00	16.00
COMMON CARD (1-792)	.05	.02

❑ 1 Nolan Ryan .75 .35
❑ 2 Ricky Henderson RB .10 .05
Most career SB's
(Some cards have print marks that show 1.991 on the front)
❑ 3 Jeff Reardon RB .05 .02
10 seasons, 20 or more saves
❑ 4 Nolan Ryan RB .40 .18
22 cons. 100 K seasons
❑ 5 Dave Winfield RB .15 .07
Oldest player, cycle
❑ 6 Brien Taylor .05 .02
❑ 7 Jim Olander .05 .02
❑ 8 Bryan Hickerson .05 .02
❑ 9 Jon Farrell .05 .02
❑ 10 Wade Boggs .20 .09
❑ 11 Jack McDowell .05 .02
❑ 12 Luis Gonzalez .05 .02
❑ 13 Mike Scioscia .05 .02
❑ 14 Wes Chamberlain .05 .02
❑ 15 Dennis Martinez .10 .05
❑ 16 Jeff Montgomery .10 .05
❑ 17 Randy Milligan .05 .02
❑ 18 Greg Cadaret .05 .02
❑ 19 Jamie Quirk .05 .02
❑ 20 Bip Roberts .05 .02
❑ 21 Buck Rodgers MG .05 .02
❑ 22 Bill Wegman .05 .02
❑ 23 Chuck Knoblauch .20 .09
❑ 24 Randy Myers .10 .05
❑ 25 Ron Gant .10 .05
❑ 26 Mike Bielecki .05 .02
❑ 27 Juan Gonzalez .60 .25
❑ 28 Mike Schooler .05 .02
❑ 29 Mickey Tettleton .05 .02
❑ 30 John Kruk .10 .05
❑ 31 Bryn Smith .05 .02
❑ 32 Chris Nabholz .05 .02
❑ 33 Carlos Baerga .05 .02
❑ 34 Jeff Juden .05 .02
❑ 35 Dave Righetti .05 .02
❑ 36 Scott Ruffcorn .05 .02
❑ 37 Luis Polonia .05 .02
❑ 38 Tom Candiotti .05 .02
❑ 39 Greg Olson .05 .02
❑ 40 Cal Ripken 2.00 .90
❑ 41 Craig Lefferts .05 .02
❑ 42 Mike Macfarlane .05 .02
❑ 43 Jose Lind .05 .02
❑ 44 Rick Aguilera .10 .05
❑ 45 Gary Carter .20 .09
❑ 46 Steve Farr .05 .02
❑ 47 Rex Hudler .05 .02
❑ 48 Scott Scudder .05 .02
❑ 49 Damon Berryhill .05 .02
❑ 50 Ken Griffey Jr. 1.25 .55
❑ 51 Tom Runnells MG .05 .02
❑ 52 Juan Bell .05 .02
❑ 53 Tommy Gregg .05 .02
❑ 54 David Wells .10 .05
❑ 55 Rafael Palmeiro .15 .07
❑ 56 Charlie O'Brien .05 .02
❑ 57 Donn Pall .05 .02
❑ 58 1992 Prospects C .10 .05
Brad Ausmus
Jim Campanis Jr.
Dave Nilsson
Doug Robbins
❑ 59 Mo Vaughn .30 .14
❑ 60 Tony Fernandez .05 .02
❑ 61 Paul O'Neill .10 .05
❑ 62 Gene Nelson .05 .02
❑ 63 Randy Ready .05 .02
❑ 64 Bob Kipper .05 .02
❑ 65 Willie McGee .10 .05
❑ 66 Scott Stahoviak .05 .02
❑ 67 Luis Salazar .05 .02
❑ 68 Marvin Freeman .05 .02
❑ 69 Kenny Lofton .40 .18
❑ 70 Gary Gaetti .05 .02
❑ 71 Erik Hanson .05 .02
❑ 72 Eddie Zosky .05 .02
❑ 73 Brian Barnes .05 .02
❑ 74 Scott Leius .05 .02
❑ 75 Bret Saberhagen .10 .05
❑ 76 Mike Gallego .05 .02
❑ 77 Jack Armstrong .05 .02
❑ 78 Ivan Rodriguez .40 .18
❑ 79 Jesse Orosco .05 .02
❑ 80 David Justice .20 .09
❑ 81 Ced Landrum .05 .02
❑ 82 Doug Simons .05 .02
❑ 83 Tommy Greene .05 .02
❑ 84 Leo Gomez .05 .02
❑ 85 Jose DeLeon .05 .02
❑ 86 Steve Finley .10 .05
❑ 87 Bob MacDonald .05 .02
❑ 88 Darrin Jackson .05 .02
❑ 89 Neal Heaton .05 .02
❑ 90 Robin Yount .20 .09
❑ 91 Jeff Reed .05 .02
❑ 92 Lenny Harris .05 .02
❑ 93 Reggie Jefferson .10 .05
❑ 94 Sammy Sosa .50 .23
❑ 95 Scott Bailes .05 .02
❑ 96 Tom McKinnon .05 .02
❑ 97 Luis Rivera .05 .02
❑ 98 Mike Harkey .05 .02
❑ 99 Jeff Treadway .05 .02
❑ 100 Jose Canseco .20 .09
❑ 101 Omar Vizquel .10 .05
❑ 102 Scott Kamieniecki .05 .02
❑ 103 Ricky Jordan .05 .02
❑ 104 Jeff Ballard .05 .02
❑ 105 Felix Jose .05 .02
❑ 106 Mike Boddicker .05 .02
❑ 107 Dan Pasqua .05 .02
❑ 108 Mike Timlin .05 .02
❑ 109 Roger Craig MG .05 .02
❑ 110 Ryne Sandberg .25 .11
❑ 111 Mark Carreon .05 .02
❑ 112 Oscar Azocar .05 .02
❑ 113 Mike Greenwell .05 .02
❑ 114 Mark Portugal .05 .02
❑ 115 Terry Pendleton .05 .02
❑ 116 Willie Randolph .10 .05
❑ 117 Scott Terry .05 .02
❑ 118 Chili Davis .10 .05
❑ 119 Mark Gardner .05 .02
❑ 120 Alan Trammell .15 .07
❑ 121 Derek Bell .10 .05
❑ 122 Gary Varsho .05 .02
❑ 123 Bob Ojeda .05 .02
❑ 124 Shawn Livsey .05 .02

❑ 125 Chris Hoiles .05 .02
❑ 126 1992 Prospects 1B .25 .11
Ryan Klesko
John Jaha
Rico Brogna
Dave Staton
❑ 127 Carlos Quintana .05 .02
❑ 128 Kurt Stillwell .05 .02
❑ 129 Melido Perez .05 .02
❑ 130 Alvin Davis .05 .02
❑ 131 Checklist 1-132 .05 .02
❑ 132 Eric Show .05 .02
❑ 133 Rance Mulliniks .05 .02
❑ 134 Darryl Kile .10 .05
❑ 135 Von Hayes .05 .02
❑ 136 Bill Doran .05 .02
❑ 137 Jeff D. Robinson .05 .02
❑ 138 Monty Fariss .05 .02
❑ 139 Jeff Innis .05 .02
❑ 140 Mark Grace UER .15 .07
(Home Calie., should be Calif.)
❑ 141 Jim Leyland MG UER .10 .05
(No closed parenthesis after East in 1991)
❑ 142 Todd Van Poppel .05 .02
❑ 143 Paul Gibson .05 .02
❑ 144 Bill Swift .05 .02
❑ 145 Danny Tartabull .05 .02
❑ 146 Al Newman .05 .02
❑ 147 Cris Carpenter .05 .02
❑ 148 Anthony Young .05 .02
❑ 149 Brian Bohanon .05 .02
❑ 150 Roger Clemens UER .40 .18
(League leading ERA in 1990 not italicized)
❑ 151 Jeff Hamilton .05 .02
❑ 152 Charlie Leibrandt .05 .02
❑ 153 Ron Karkovice .05 .02
❑ 154 Hensley Meulens .05 .02
❑ 155 Scott Bankhead .05 .02
❑ 156 Manny Ramirez 1.50 .70
❑ 157 Keith Miller .05 .02
❑ 158 Todd Frohwirth .05 .02
❑ 159 Darrin Fletcher .05 .02
❑ 160 Bobby Bonilla .10 .05
❑ 161 Casey Candaele .05 .02
❑ 162 Paul Faries .05 .02
❑ 163 Dana Kiecker .05 .02
❑ 164 Shane Mack .05 .02
❑ 165 Mark Langston .05 .02
❑ 166 Geronimo Pena .05 .02
❑ 167 Andy Allanson .05 .02
❑ 168 Dwight Smith .05 .02
❑ 169 Chuck Crim .05 .02
❑ 170 Alex Cole .05 .02
❑ 171 Bill Plummer MG .05 .02
❑ 172 Juan Berenguer .05 .02
❑ 173 Brian Downing .05 .02
❑ 174 Steve Frey .05 .02
❑ 175 Orel Hershiser .10 .05
❑ 176 Ramon Garcia .05 .02
❑ 177 Dan Gladden .05 .02
❑ 178 Jim Acker .05 .02
❑ 179 1992 Prospects 2B .05 .02
Bobby DeJardin
Cesar Bernhardt
Armando Moreno
Andy Stankiewicz
❑ 180 Kevin Mitchell .10 .05
❑ 181 Hector Villanueva .05 .02
❑ 182 Jeff Reardon .10 .05
❑ 183 Brent Mayne .05 .02
❑ 184 Jimmy Jones .05 .02
❑ 185 Benito Santiago .05 .02
❑ 186 Cliff Floyd .25 .11
❑ 187 Ernie Riles .05 .02
❑ 188 Jose Guzman .05 .02
❑ 189 Junior Felix .05 .02
❑ 190 Glenn Davis .05 .02
❑ 191 Charlie Hough .10 .05
❑ 192 Dave Fleming .05 .02
❑ 193 Omar Olivares .05 .02
❑ 194 Eric Karros .20 .09
❑ 195 David Cone .10 .05
❑ 196 Frank Castillo .05 .02
❑ 197 Glenn Braggs .05 .02
❑ 198 Scott Aldred .05 .02
❑ 199 Jeff Blauser .05 .02
❑ 200 Len Dykstra .10 .05
❑ 201 Buck Showalter MG .20 .09
❑ 202 Rick Honeycutt .05 .02
❑ 203 Greg Myers .05 .02
❑ 204 Trevor Wilson .05 .02
❑ 205 Jay Howell .05 .02
❑ 206 Luis Sojo .05 .02
❑ 207 Jack Clark .10 .05
❑ 208 Julio Machado .05 .02
❑ 209 Lloyd McClendon .05 .02
❑ 210 Ozzie Guillen .05 .02
❑ 211 Jeremy Hernandez .05 .02
❑ 212 Randy Velarde .05 .02
❑ 213 Les Lancaster .05 .02
❑ 214 Andy Mota .05 .02
❑ 215 Rich Gossage .10 .05
❑ 216 Brent Gates .05 .02
❑ 217 Brian Harper .05 .02
❑ 218 Mike Flanagan .05 .02
❑ 219 Jerry Browne .05 .02
❑ 220 Jose Rijo .05 .02
❑ 221 Skeeter Barnes .05 .02
❑ 222 Jaime Navarro .05 .02
❑ 223 Mel Hall .05 .02
❑ 224 Bret Barberie .05 .02
❑ 225 Roberto Alomar .20 .09
❑ 226 Pete Smith .05 .02
❑ 227 Daryl Boston .05 .02
❑ 228 Eddie Whitson .05 .02
❑ 229 Shawn Boskie .05 .02
❑ 230 Dick Schofield .05 .02
❑ 231 Brian Drahman .05 .02
❑ 232 John Smiley .05 .02
❑ 233 Mitch Webster .05 .02
❑ 234 Terry Steinbach .10 .05
❑ 235 Jack Morris .10 .05
❑ 236 Bill Pecota .05 .02
❑ 237 Jose Hernandez .05 .02
❑ 238 Greg Litton .05 .02
❑ 239 Brian Holman .05 .02
❑ 240 Andres Galarraga .20 .09
❑ 241 Gerald Young .05 .02
❑ 242 Mike Mussina .30 .14
❑ 243 Alvaro Espinoza .05 .02
❑ 244 Darren Daulton .10 .05
❑ 245 John Smoltz .15 .07
❑ 246 Jason Pruitt .05 .02
❑ 247 Chuck Finley .10 .05
❑ 248 Jim Gantner .05 .02
❑ 249 Tony Fossas .05 .02
❑ 250 Ken Griffey Sr. .10 .05
❑ 251 Kevin Elster .05 .02
❑ 252 Dennis Rasmussen .05 .02
❑ 253 Terry Kennedy .05 .02
❑ 254 Ryan Bowen .05 .02
❑ 255 Robin Ventura .10 .05
❑ 256 Mike Aldrete .05 .02
❑ 257 Jeff Russell .05 .02
❑ 258 Jim Lindeman .05 .02
❑ 259 Ron Darling .05 .02
❑ 260 Devon White .05 .02
❑ 261 Tom Lasorda MG .15 .07
❑ 262 Terry Lee .05 .02
❑ 263 Bob Patterson .05 .02
❑ 264 Checklist 133-264 .05 .02
❑ 265 Teddy Higuera .05 .02
❑ 266 Roberto Kelly .05 .02
❑ 267 Steve Bedrosian .05 .02
❑ 268 Brady Anderson .15 .07
❑ 269 Ruben Amaro Jr. .05 .02
❑ 270 Tony Gwynn .50 .23
❑ 271 Tracy Jones .05 .02
❑ 272 Jerry Don Gleaton .05 .02
❑ 273 Craig Grebeck .05 .02
❑ 274 Bob Scanlan .05 .02
❑ 275 Todd Zeile .05 .02
❑ 276 Shawn Green .50 .23
❑ 277 Scott Chiamparino .05 .02
❑ 278 Darryl Hamilton .05 .02
❑ 279 Jim Clancy .05 .02
❑ 280 Carlos Martinez .05 .02
❑ 281 Kevin Appier .10 .05
❑ 282 John Wehner .05 .02
❑ 283 Reggie Sanders .05 .02
❑ 284 Gene Larkin .05 .02
❑ 285 Bob Welch .05 .02
❑ 286 Gilberto Reyes .05 .02
❑ 287 Pete Schourek .05 .02
❑ 288 Andujar Cedeno .05 .02
❑ 289 Mike Morgan .05 .02
❑ 290 Bo Jackson .10 .05
❑ 291 Phil Garner MG .05 .02
❑ 292 Ray Lankford .20 .09
❑ 293 Mike Henneman .05 .02
❑ 294 Dave Valle .05 .02
❑ 295 Alonzo Powell .05 .02
❑ 296 Tom Brunansky .05 .02
❑ 297 Kevin Brown .15 .07
❑ 298 Kelly Gruber .05 .02
❑ 299 Charles Nagy .10 .05
❑ 300 Don Mattingly .30 .14
❑ 301 Kirk McCaskill .05 .02
❑ 302 Joey Cora .10 .05
❑ 303 Dan Plesac .05 .02
❑ 304 Joe Oliver .05 .02
❑ 305 Tom Glavine .15 .07
❑ 306 Al Shirley .05 .02
❑ 307 Bruce Ruffin .05 .02
❑ 308 Craig Shipley .05 .02
❑ 309 Dave Martinez .05 .02
❑ 310 Jose Mesa .05 .02
❑ 311 Henry Cotto .05 .02
❑ 312 Mike LaValliere .05 .02
❑ 313 Kevin Tapani .05 .02
❑ 314 Jeff Huson .05 .02
(Shows Jose Canseco sliding into second)
❑ 315 Juan Samuel .05 .02
❑ 316 Curt Schilling .15 .07
❑ 317 Mike Bordick .05 .02
❑ 318 Steve Howe .05 .02
❑ 319 Tony Phillips .05 .02
❑ 320 George Bell .05 .02
❑ 321 Lou Piniella MG .10 .05
❑ 322 Tim Burke .05 .02
❑ 323 Milt Thompson .05 .02
❑ 324 Danny Darwin .05 .02
❑ 325 Joe Orsulak .05 .02
❑ 326 Eric King .05 .02
❑ 327 Jay Buhner .15 .07
❑ 328 Joel Johnston .05 .02
❑ 329 Franklin Stubbs .05 .02
❑ 330 Will Clark .20 .09
❑ 331 Steve Lake .05 .02
❑ 332 Chris Jones .05 .02
❑ 333 Pat Tabler .05 .02
❑ 334 Kevin Gross .05 .02
❑ 335 Dave Henderson .05 .02
❑ 336 Greg Anthony .05 .02
❑ 337 Alejandro Pena .05 .02
❑ 338 Shawn Abner .05 .02
❑ 339 Tom Browning .05 .02
❑ 340 Otis Nixon .10 .05
❑ 341 Bob Geren .05 .02
❑ 342 Tim Spehr .05 .02
❑ 343 John Vander Wal .05 .02
❑ 344 Jack Daugherty .05 .02
❑ 345 Zane Smith .05 .02
❑ 346 Rheal Cormier .05 .02
❑ 347 Kent Hrbek .10 .05
❑ 348 Rick Wilkins .05 .02
❑ 349 Steve Lyons .05 .02
❑ 350 Gregg Olson .05 .02
❑ 351 Greg Riddoch MG .05 .02
❑ 352 Ed Nunez .05 .02
❑ 353 Braulio Castillo .05 .02
❑ 354 Dave Bergman .05 .02
❑ 355 Warren Newson .05 .02
❑ 356 Luis Quinones .05 .02
❑ 357 Mike Witt .05 .02
❑ 358 Ted Wood .05 .02
❑ 359 Mike Moore .05 .02
❑ 360 Lance Parrish .05 .02
❑ 361 Barry Jones .05 .02
❑ 362 Javier Ortiz .05 .02
❑ 363 John Candelaria .05 .02

❑ 364	Glenallen Hill	.05	.02
❑ 365	Duane Ward	.05	.02
❑ 366	Checklist 265-396	.05	.02
❑ 367	Rafael Belliard	.05	.02
❑ 368	Bill Krueger	.05	.02
❑ 369	Steve Whitaker	.05	.02
❑ 370	Shawon Dunston	.05	.02
❑ 371	Dante Bichette	.15	.07
❑ 372	Kip Gross	.05	.02
❑ 373	Don Robinson	.05	.02
❑ 374	Bernie Williams	.20	.09
❑ 375	Bert Blyleven	.10	.05
❑ 376	Chris Donnels	.05	.02
❑ 377	Bob Zupcic	.05	.02
❑ 378	Joel Skinner	.05	.02
❑ 379	Steve Chitren	.05	.02
❑ 380	Barry Bonds	.25	.11
❑ 381	Sparky Anderson MG	.10	.05
❑ 382	Sid Fernandez	.05	.02
❑ 383	Dave Hollins	.05	.02
❑ 384	Mark Lee	.05	.02
❑ 385	Tim Wallach	.05	.02
❑ 386	Will Clark AS	.10	.05
❑ 387	Ryne Sandberg AS	.20	.09
❑ 388	Howard Johnson AS	.05	.02
❑ 389	Barry Larkin AS	.15	.07
❑ 390	Barry Bonds AS	.20	.09
❑ 391	Ron Gant AS	.05	.02
❑ 392	Bobby Bonilla AS	.05	.02
❑ 393	Craig Biggio AS	.10	.05
❑ 394	Dennis Martinez AS	.05	.02
❑ 395	Tom Glavine AS	.10	.05
❑ 396	Lee Smith AS	.05	.02
❑ 397	Cecil Fielder AS	.05	.02
❑ 398	Julio Franco AS	.05	.02
❑ 399	Wade Boggs AS	.10	.05
❑ 400	Cal Ripken AS	.20	.09
❑ 401	Jose Canseco AS	.10	.05
❑ 402	Joe Carter AS	.10	.05
❑ 403	Ruben Sierra AS	.05	.02
❑ 404	Matt Nokes AS	.05	.02
❑ 405	Roger Clemens AS	.20	.09
❑ 406	Jim Abbott AS	.05	.02
❑ 407	Bryan Harvey AS	.05	.02
❑ 408	Bob Milacki	.05	.02
❑ 409	Geno Petralli	.05	.02
❑ 410	Dave Stewart	.10	.05
❑ 411	Mike Jackson	.10	.05
❑ 412	Luis Aquino	.05	.02
❑ 413	Tim Teufel	.05	.02
❑ 414	Jeff Ware	.05	.02
❑ 415	Jim Deshaies	.05	.02
❑ 416	Ellis Burks	.10	.05
❑ 417	Allan Anderson	.05	.02
❑ 418	Alfredo Griffin	.05	.02
❑ 419	Wally Whitehurst	.05	.02
❑ 420	Sandy Alomar Jr.	.10	.05
❑ 421	Juan Agosto	.05	.02
❑ 422	Sam Horn	.05	.02
❑ 423	Jeff Fassero	.10	.05
❑ 424	Paul McClellan	.05	.02
❑ 425	Cecil Fielder	.10	.05
❑ 426	Tim Raines	.10	.05
❑ 427	Eddie Taubensee	.10	.05
❑ 428	Dennis Boyd	.05	.02
❑ 429	Tony LaRussa MG	.10	.05
❑ 430	Steve Sax	.05	.02
❑ 431	Tom Gordon	.10	.05
❑ 432	Billy Hatcher	.05	.02
❑ 433	Cal Eldred	.05	.02
❑ 434	Wally Backman	.05	.02
❑ 435	Mark Eichhorn	.05	.02
❑ 436	Mookie Wilson	.10	.05
❑ 437	Scott Servais	.05	.02
❑ 438	Mike Maddux	.05	.02
❑ 439	Chico Walker	.05	.02
❑ 440	Doug Drabek	.05	.02
❑ 441	Rob Deer	.05	.02
❑ 442	Dave West	.05	.02
❑ 443	Spike Owen	.05	.02
❑ 444	Tyrone Hill	.05	.02
❑ 445	Matt Williams	.15	.07
❑ 446	Mark Lewis	.05	.02
❑ 447	David Segui	.10	.05
❑ 448	Tom Pagnozzi	.05	.02
❑ 449	Jeff Johnson	.05	.02
❑ 450	Mark McGwire	1.00	.45
❑ 451	Tom Henke	.05	.02
❑ 452	Wilson Alvarez	.10	.05
❑ 453	Gary Redus	.05	.02
❑ 454	Darren Holmes	.05	.02
❑ 455	Pete O'Brien	.05	.02
❑ 456	Pat Combs	.05	.02
❑ 457	Hubie Brooks	.05	.02
❑ 458	Frank Tanana	.05	.02
❑ 459	Tom Kelly MG	.05	.02
❑ 460	Andre Dawson	.15	.07
❑ 461	Doug Jones	.05	.02
❑ 462	Rich Rodriguez	.05	.02
❑ 463	Mike Simms	.05	.02
❑ 464	Mike Jeffcoat	.05	.02
❑ 465	Barry Larkin	.15	.07
❑ 466	Stan Belinda	.05	.02
❑ 467	Lonnie Smith	.05	.02
❑ 468	Greg Harris	.05	.02
❑ 469	Jim Eisenreich	.05	.02
❑ 470	Pedro Guerrero	.05	.02
❑ 471	Jose DeJesus	.05	.02
❑ 472	Rich Rowland	.05	.02
❑ 473	1992 Prospects 3B UER	.20	.09
	Frank Bolick		
	Craig Paquette		
	Tom Redington		
	Paul Russo		
	(Line around top border)		
❑ 474	Mike Rossiter	.05	.02
❑ 475	Robby Thompson	.05	.02
❑ 476	Randy Bush	.05	.02
❑ 477	Greg Hibbard	.05	.02
❑ 478	Dale Sveum	.05	.02
❑ 479	Chito Martinez	.05	.02
❑ 480	Scott Sanderson	.05	.02
❑ 481	Tino Martinez	.20	.09
❑ 482	Jimmy Key	.10	.05
❑ 483	Terry Shumpert	.05	.02
❑ 484	Mike Hartley	.05	.02
❑ 485	Chris Sabo	.05	.02
❑ 486	Bob Walk	.05	.02
❑ 487	John Cerutti	.05	.02
❑ 488	Scott Cooper	.05	.02
❑ 489	Bobby Cox MG	.10	.05
❑ 490	Julio Franco	.05	.02
❑ 491	Jeff Brantley	.05	.02
❑ 492	Mike Devereaux	.05	.02
❑ 493	Jose Offerman	.05	.02
❑ 494	Gary Thurman	.05	.02
❑ 495	Carney Lansford	.10	.05
❑ 496	Joe Grahe	.05	.02
❑ 497	Andy Ashby	.10	.05
❑ 498	Gerald Perry	.05	.02
❑ 499	Dave Otto	.05	.02
❑ 500	Vince Coleman	.05	.02
❑ 501	Rob Mallicoat	.05	.02
❑ 502	Greg Briley	.05	.02
❑ 503	Pascual Perez	.05	.02
❑ 504	Aaron Sele	.25	.11
❑ 505	Bobby Thigpen	.05	.02
❑ 506	Todd Benzinger	.05	.02
❑ 507	Candy Maldonado	.05	.02
❑ 508	Bill Gullickson	.05	.02
❑ 509	Doug Dascenzo	.05	.02
❑ 510	Frank Viola	.05	.02
❑ 511	Kenny Rogers	.05	.02
❑ 512	Mike Heath	.05	.02
❑ 513	Kevin Bass	.05	.02
❑ 514	Kim Batiste	.05	.02
❑ 515	Delino DeShields	.10	.05
❑ 516	Ed Sprague Jr.	.05	.02
❑ 517	Jim Gott	.05	.02
❑ 518	Jose Melendez	.05	.02
❑ 519	Hal McRae MG	.05	.02
❑ 520	Jeff Bagwell	.50	.23
❑ 521	Joe Hesketh	.05	.02
❑ 522	Milt Cuyler	.05	.02
❑ 523	Shawn Hillegas	.05	.02
❑ 524	Don Slaught	.05	.02
❑ 525	Randy Johnson	.20	.09
❑ 526	Doug Piatt	.05	.02
❑ 527	Checklist 397-528	.05	.02
❑ 528	Steve Foster	.05	.02
❑ 529	Joe Girardi	.10	.05
❑ 530	Jim Abbott	.10	.05
❑ 531	Larry Walker	.20	.09
❑ 532	Mike Huff	.05	.02
❑ 533	Mackey Sasser	.05	.02
❑ 534	Benji Gil	.05	.02
❑ 535	Dave Stieb	.05	.02
❑ 536	Willie Wilson	.05	.02
❑ 537	Mark Leiter	.05	.02
❑ 538	Jose Uribe	.05	.02
❑ 539	Thomas Howard	.05	.02
❑ 540	Ben McDonald	.05	.02
❑ 541	Jose Tolentino	.05	.02
❑ 542	Keith Mitchell	.05	.02
❑ 543	Jerome Walton	.05	.02
❑ 544	Cliff Brantley	.05	.02
❑ 545	Andy Van Slyke	.10	.05
❑ 546	Paul Sorrento	.05	.02
❑ 547	Herm Winningham	.05	.02
❑ 548	Mark Guthrie	.05	.02
❑ 549	Joe Torre MG	.10	.05
❑ 550	Darryl Strawberry	.10	.05
❑ 551	1992 Prospects SS UER	1.50	.70
	Wilfredo Cordero		
	Chipper Jones		
	Manny Alexander		
	Alex Arias		
	(No line around		
	top border)		
❑ 552	Dave Gallagher	.05	.02
❑ 553	Edgar Martinez	.15	.07
❑ 554	Donald Harris	.05	.02
❑ 555	Frank Thomas	.60	.25
❑ 556	Storm Davis	.05	.02
❑ 557	Dickie Thon	.05	.02
❑ 558	Scott Garrelts	.05	.02
❑ 559	Steve Olin	.05	.02
❑ 560	Rickey Henderson	.20	.09
❑ 561	Jose Vizcaino	.05	.02
❑ 562	Wade Taylor	.05	.02
❑ 563	Pat Borders	.05	.02
❑ 564	Jimmy Gonzalez	.05	.02
❑ 565	Lee Smith	.10	.05
❑ 566	Bill Sampen	.05	.02
❑ 567	Dean Palmer	.10	.05
❑ 568	Bryan Harvey	.05	.02
❑ 569	Tony Pena	.05	.02
❑ 570	Lou Whitaker	.10	.05
❑ 571	Randy Tomlin	.05	.02
❑ 572	Greg Vaughn	.10	.05
❑ 573	Kelly Downs	.05	.02
❑ 574	Steve Avery UER	.05	.02
	(Should be 13 games		
	for Durham in 1989)		
❑ 575	Kirby Puckett	.30	.14
❑ 576	Heathcliff Slocumb	.05	.02
❑ 577	Kevin Seitzer	.05	.02
❑ 578	Lee Guetterman	.05	.02
❑ 579	Johnny Oates MG	.05	.02
❑ 580	Greg Maddux	.60	.25
❑ 581	Stan Javier	.05	.02
❑ 582	Vicente Palacios	.05	.02
❑ 583	Mel Rojas	.05	.02
❑ 584	Wayne Rosenthal	.05	.02
❑ 585	Lenny Webster	.05	.02
❑ 586	Rod Nichols	.05	.02
❑ 587	Mickey Morandini	.05	.02
❑ 588	Russ Swan	.05	.02
❑ 589	Mariano Duncan	.05	.02
❑ 590	Howard Johnson	.05	.02
❑ 591	1992 Prospects OF	.20	.09
	Jeromy Burnitz		
	Jacob Brumfield		
	Alan Cockrell		
	D.J. Dozier		
❑ 592	Denny Neagle	.15	.07
❑ 593	Steve Decker	.05	.02
❑ 594	Brian Barber	.05	.02
❑ 595	Bruce Hurst	.05	.02
❑ 596	Kent Mercker	.05	.02
❑ 597	Mike Magnante	.05	.02
❑ 598	Jody Reed	.05	.02
❑ 599	Steve Searcy	.05	.02
❑ 600	Paul Molitor	.20	.09
❑ 601	Dave Smith	.05	.02

❑ 602 Mike Fetters .05 .02
❑ 603 Luis Mercedes .05 .02
❑ 604 Chris Gwynn .05 .02
❑ 605 Scott Erickson .10 .05
❑ 606 Brook Jacoby .05 .02
❑ 607 Todd Stottlemyre .10 .05
❑ 608 Scott Bradley .05 .02
❑ 609 Mike Hargrove MG .10 .05
❑ 610 Eric Davis .10 .05
❑ 611 Brian Hunter .05 .02
❑ 612 Pat Kelly .05 .02
❑ 613 Pedro Munoz .05 .02
❑ 614 Al Osuna .05 .02
❑ 615 Matt Merullo .05 .02
❑ 616 Larry Andersen .05 .02
❑ 617 Junior Ortiz .05 .02
❑ 618 1992 Prospects OF .05 .02
Cesar Hernandez
Steve Hosey
Jeff McNeely
Dan Peltier
❑ 619 Danny Jackson .05 .02
❑ 620 George Brett .40 .18
❑ 621 Dan Gakeler .05 .02
❑ 622 Steve Buechele .05 .02
❑ 623 Bob Tewksbury .05 .02
❑ 624 Shawn Estes .25 .11
❑ 625 Kevin McReynolds .05 .02
❑ 626 Chris Haney .05 .02
❑ 627 Mike Sharperson .05 .02
❑ 628 Mark Williamson .05 .02
❑ 629 Wally Joyner .10 .05
❑ 630 Carlton Fisk .20 .09
❑ 631 Armando Reynoso .05 .02
❑ 632 Felix Fermin .05 .02
❑ 633 Mitch Williams .05 .02
❑ 634 Manuel Lee .05 .02
❑ 635 Harold Baines .10 .05
❑ 636 Greg Harris .05 .02
❑ 637 Orlando Merced .05 .02
❑ 638 Chris Bosio .05 .02
❑ 639 Wayne Housie .05 .02
❑ 640 Xavier Hernandez .05 .02
❑ 641 David Howard .05 .02
❑ 642 Tim Crews .05 .02
❑ 643 Rick Cerone .05 .02
❑ 644 Terry Leach .05 .02
❑ 645 Deion Sanders .20 .09
❑ 646 Craig Wilson .05 .02
❑ 647 Marquis Grissom .10 .05
❑ 648 Scott Fletcher .05 .02
❑ 649 Norm Charlton .05 .02
❑ 650 Jesse Barfield .05 .02
❑ 651 Joe Slusarski .05 .02
❑ 652 Bobby Rose .05 .02
❑ 653 Dennis Lamp .05 .02
❑ 654 Allen Watson .05 .02
❑ 655 Brett Butler .10 .05
❑ 656 1992 Prospects OF .20 .09
Rudy Pemberton
Henry Rodriguez
Lee Tinsley
Gerald Williams
❑ 657 Dave Johnson .05 .02
❑ 658 Checklist 529-660 .05 .02
❑ 659 Brian McRae .10 .05
❑ 660 Fred McGriff .15 .07
❑ 661 Bill Landrum .05 .02
❑ 662 Juan Guzman .05 .02
❑ 663 Greg Gagne .05 .02
❑ 664 Ken Hill .05 .02
❑ 665 Dave Haas .05 .02
❑ 666 Tom Foley .05 .02
❑ 667 Roberto Hernandez .10 .05
❑ 668 Dwayne Henry .05 .02
❑ 669 Jim Fregosi MG .05 .02
❑ 670 Harold Reynolds .05 .02
❑ 671 Mark Whiten .05 .02
❑ 672 Eric Plunk .05 .02
❑ 673 Todd Hundley .10 .05
❑ 674 Mo Sanford .05 .02
❑ 675 Bobby Witt .05 .02
❑ 676 1992 Prospects P .05 .02
Sam Militello
Pat Mahomes
Turk Wendell
Roger Salkeld
❑ 677 John Marzano .05 .02
❑ 678 Joe Klink .05 .02
❑ 679 Pete Incaviglia .05 .02
❑ 680 Dale Murphy .20 .09
❑ 681 Rene Gonzales .05 .02
❑ 682 Andy Benes .10 .05
❑ 683 Jim Poole .05 .02
❑ 684 Trever Miller .05 .02
❑ 685 Scott Livingstone .05 .02
❑ 686 Rich DeLucia .05 .02
❑ 687 Harvey Pulliam .05 .02
❑ 688 Tim Belcher .05 .02
❑ 689 Mark Lemke .05 .02
❑ 690 John Franco .10 .05
❑ 691 Walt Weiss .05 .02
❑ 692 Scott Ruskin .05 .02
❑ 693 Jeff King .10 .05
❑ 694 Mike Gardiner .05 .02
❑ 695 Gary Sheffield .20 .09
❑ 696 Joe Boever .05 .02
❑ 697 Mike Felder .05 .02
❑ 698 John Habyan .05 .02
❑ 699 Cito Gaston MG .05 .02
❑ 700 Ruben Sierra .05 .02
❑ 701 Scott Radinsky .05 .02
❑ 702 Lee Stevens .05 .02
❑ 703 Mark Wohlers .10 .05
❑ 704 Curt Young .05 .02
❑ 705 Dwight Evans .10 .05
❑ 706 Rob Murphy .05 .02
❑ 707 Gregg Jefferies .05 .02
❑ 708 Tom Bolton .05 .02
❑ 709 Chris James .05 .02
❑ 710 Kevin Maas .05 .02
❑ 711 Ricky Bones .05 .02
❑ 712 Curt Wilkerson .05 .02
❑ 713 Roger McDowell .05 .02
❑ 714 Calvin Reese .20 .09
❑ 715 Craig Biggio .20 .09
❑ 716 Kirk Dressendorfer .05 .02
❑ 717 Ken Dayley .05 .02
❑ 718 B.J. Surhoff .10 .05
❑ 719 Terry Mulholland .05 .02
❑ 720 Kirk Gibson .10 .05
❑ 721 Mike Pagliarulo .05 .02
❑ 722 Walt Terrell .05 .02
❑ 723 Jose Oquendo .05 .02
❑ 724 Kevin Morton .05 .02
❑ 725 Dwight Gooden .10 .05
❑ 726 Kirt Manwaring .05 .02
❑ 727 Chuck McElroy .05 .02
❑ 728 Dave Burba .05 .02
❑ 729 Art Howe MG .05 .02
❑ 730 Ramon Martinez .10 .05
❑ 731 Donnie Hill .05 .02
❑ 732 Nelson Santovenia .05 .02
❑ 733 Bob Melvin .05 .02
❑ 734 Scott Hatteberg .05 .02
❑ 735 Greg Swindell .05 .02
❑ 736 Lance Johnson .05 .02
❑ 737 Kevin Reimer .05 .02
❑ 738 Dennis Eckersley .10 .05
❑ 739 Rob Ducey .05 .02
❑ 740 Ken Caminiti .15 .07
❑ 741 Mark Gubicza .05 .02
❑ 742 Billy Spiers .05 .02
❑ 743 Darren Lewis .05 .02
❑ 744 Chris Hammond .05 .02
❑ 745 Dave Magadan .05 .02
❑ 746 Bernard Gilkey .10 .05
❑ 747 Willie Banks .05 .02
❑ 748 Matt Nokes .05 .02
❑ 749 Jerald Clark .05 .02
❑ 750 Travis Fryman .10 .05
❑ 751 Steve Wilson .05 .02
❑ 752 Billy Ripken .05 .02
❑ 753 Paul Assenmacher .05 .02
❑ 754 Charlie Hayes .05 .02
❑ 755 Alex Fernandez .10 .05
❑ 756 Gary Pettis .05 .02
❑ 757 Rob Dibble .05 .02
❑ 758 Tim Naehring .10 .05
❑ 759 Jeff Torborg MG .05 .02
❑ 760 Ozzie Smith .25 .11
❑ 761 Mike Fitzgerald .05 .02
❑ 762 John Burkett .05 .02
❑ 763 Kyle Abbott .05 .02
❑ 764 Tyler Green .05 .02
❑ 765 Pete Harnisch .05 .02
❑ 766 Mark Davis .05 .02
❑ 767 Kal Daniels .05 .02
❑ 768 Jim Thome .50 .23
❑ 769 Jack Howell .05 .02
❑ 770 Sid Bream .05 .02
❑ 771 Arthur Rhodes .05 .02
❑ 772 Garry Templeton UER .05 .02
(Stat heading in for pitchers)
❑ 773 Hal Morris .05 .02
❑ 774 Bud Black .05 .02
❑ 775 Ivan Calderon .05 .02
❑ 776 Doug Henry .05 .02
❑ 777 John Olerud .10 .05
❑ 778 Tim Leary .05 .02
❑ 779 Jay Bell .10 .05
❑ 780 Eddie Murray .20 .09
❑ 781 Paul Abbott .05 .02
❑ 782 Phil Plantier .05 .02
❑ 783 Joe Magrane .05 .02
❑ 784 Ken Patterson .05 .02
❑ 785 Albert Belle .25 .11
❑ 786 Royce Clayton .05 .02
❑ 787 Checklist 661-792 .05 .02
❑ 788 Mike Stanton .05 .02
❑ 789 Bobby Valentine MG .05 .02
❑ 790 Joe Carter .10 .05
❑ 791 Danny Cox .05 .02
❑ 792 Dave Winfield .20 .09

1992 Topps Traded

	MINT	NRMT
COMP.FACT.SET (132)	120.00	55.00
COMMON CARD (1T-132T)	.10	.05

❑ 1T Willie Adams USA .10 .05
❑ 2T Jeff Alkire USA .10 .05
❑ 3T Felipe Alou MG .10 .05
❑ 4T Moises Alou 1.00 .45
❑ 5T Ruben Amaro .10 .05
❑ 6T Jack Armstrong .10 .05
❑ 7T Scott Bankhead .10 .05
❑ 8T Tim Belcher .10 .05
❑ 9T George Bell .10 .05
❑ 10T Freddie Benavides .10 .05
❑ 11T Todd Benzinger .10 .05
❑ 12T Joe Boever .10 .05
❑ 13T Ricky Bones .10 .05
❑ 14T Bobby Bonilla .20 .09
❑ 15T Hubie Brooks .10 .05
❑ 16T Jerry Browne .10 .05
❑ 17T Jim Bullinger .10 .05
❑ 18T Dave Burba .10 .05
❑ 19T Kevin Campbell .10 .05
❑ 20T Tom Candiotti .10 .05
❑ 21T Mark Carreon .10 .05
❑ 22T Gary Carter .40 .18
❑ 23T Archi Cianfrocco .10 .05
❑ 24T Phil Clark .10 .05
❑ 25T Chad Curtis .40 .18
❑ 26T Eric Davis .20 .09
❑ 27T Tim Davis USA .10 .05
❑ 28T Gary DiSarcina .10 .05

No.	Player	MINT	NRMT
29T	Darren Dreifort USA	.20	.09
30T	Mariano Duncan	.10	.05
31T	Mike Fitzgerald	.10	.05
32T	John Flaherty	.10	.05
33T	Darrin Fletcher	.10	.05
34T	Scott Fletcher	.10	.05
35T	Ron Fraser CO USA	.10	.05
36T	Andres Galarraga	.40	.18
37T	Dave Gallagher	.10	.05
38T	Mike Gallego	.10	.05
39T	Nomar Garciaparra USA	100.00	45.00
40T	Jason Giambi USA	.50	.23
41T	Danny Gladden	.10	.05
42T	Rene Gonzales	.10	.05
43T	Jeff Granger USA	.20	.09
44T	Rick Greene USA	.10	.05
45T	Jeffrey Hammonds USA	.40	.18
46T	Charlie Hayes	.10	.05
47T	Von Hayes	.10	.05
48T	Rick Helling USA	.40	.18
49T	Butch Henry	.10	.05
50T	Carlos Hernandez	.10	.05
51T	Ken Hill	.10	.05
52T	Butch Hobson	.10	.05
53T	Vince Horsman	.10	.05
54T	Pete Incaviglia	.10	.05
55T	Gregg Jefferies	.10	.05
56T	Charles Johnson USA	.75	.35
57T	Doug Jones	.10	.05
58T	Brian Jordan	2.50	1.10
59T	Wally Joyner	.20	.09
60T	Daron Kirkreit USA	.20	.09
61T	Bill Krueger	.10	.05
62T	Gene Lamont MG	.10	.05
63T	Jim Lefebvre MG	.10	.05
64T	Danny Leon	.10	.05
65T	Pat Listach	.10	.05
66T	Kenny Lofton	1.50	.70
67T	Dave Martinez	.10	.05
68T	Derrick May	.10	.05
69T	Kirk McCaskill	.10	.05
70T	Chad McConnell USA	.20	.09
71T	Kevin McReynolds	.10	.05
72T	Rusty Meacham	.10	.05
73T	Keith Miller	.10	.05
74T	Kevin Mitchell	.20	.09
75T	Jason Moler USA	.10	.05
76T	Mike Morgan	.10	.05
77T	Jack Morris	.20	.09
78T	Calvin Murray USA	.10	.05
79T	Eddie Murray	.40	.18
80T	Randy Myers	.20	.09
81T	Denny Neagle	.30	.14
82T	Phil Nevin USA	.10	.05
83T	Dave Nilsson	.20	.09
84T	Junior Ortiz	.10	.05
85T	Donovan Osborne	.10	.05
86T	Bill Pecota	.10	.05
87T	Melido Perez	.10	.05
88T	Mike Perez	.10	.05
89T	Hipolito Pichardo	.10	.05
90T	Willie Randolph	.20	.09
91T	Darren Reed	.10	.05
92T	Bip Roberts	.10	.05
93T	Chris Roberts USA	.10	.05
94T	Steve Rodriguez USA	.10	.05
95T	Bruce Ruffin	.10	.05
96T	Scott Ruskin	.10	.05
97T	Bret Saberhagen	.20	.09
98T	Rey Sanchez	.10	.05
99T	Steve Sax	.10	.05
100T	Curt Schilling	.30	.14
101T	Dick Schofield	.10	.05
102T	Gary Scott	.10	.05
103T	Kevin Seitzer	.10	.05
104T	Frank Seminara	.10	.05
105T	Gary Sheffield	.40	.18
106T	John Smiley	.10	.05
107T	Cory Snyder	.10	.05
108T	Paul Sorrento	.10	.05
109T	Sammy Sosa	3.00	1.35
110T	Matt Stairs	.40	.18
111T	Andy Stankiewicz	.10	.05
112T	Kurt Stillwell	.10	.05
113T	Rick Sutcliffe	.10	.05
114T	Bill Swift	.10	.05
115T	Jeff Tackett	.10	.05
116T	Danny Tartabull	.10	.05
117T	Eddie Taubensee	.20	.09
118T	Dickie Thon	.10	.05
119T	Michael Tucker USA	1.00	.45
120T	Scooter Tucker	.10	.05
121T	Marc Valdes USA	.10	.05
122T	Julio Valera	.10	.05
123T	Jason Varitek USA	.75	.35
124T	Ron Villone USA	.10	.05
125T	Frank Viola	.10	.05
126T	B.J. Wallace USA	.20	.09
127T	Dan Walters	.10	.05
128T	Craig Wilson USA	.10	.05
129T	Chris Wimmer USA	.10	.05
130T	Dave Winfield	.40	.18
131T	Herm Winningham	.10	.05
132T	Checklist 1T-132T	.10	.05

1993 Topps

	MINT	NRMT
COMPLETE SET (825)	30.00	13.50
COMP.RETAIL.SET (838)	40.00	18.00
COMP.HOBBY.SET (847)	50.00	22.00
COMP.1994 PREPROD. (9)	7.00	3.10
COMPLETE SERIES 1 (396)	15.00	6.75
COMPLETE SERIES 2 (429)	15.00	6.75
COMMON CARD (1-825)	.10	.05

No.	Player	MINT	NRMT
1	Robin Yount	.30	.14
2	Barry Bonds	.50	.23
3	Ryne Sandberg	.50	.23
4	Roger Clemens	.75	.35
5	Tony Gwynn	1.00	.45
6	Jeff Tackett	.10	.05
7	Pete Incaviglia	.10	.05
8	Mark Wohlers	.10	.05
9	Kent Hrbek	.20	.09
10	Will Clark	.40	.18
11	Eric Karros	.30	.14
12	Lee Smith	.20	.09
13	Esteban Beltre	.10	.05
14	Greg Briley	.10	.05
15	Marquis Grissom	.20	.09
16	Dan Plesac	.10	.05
17	Dave Hollins	.10	.05
18	Terry Steinbach	.10	.05
19	Ed Nunez	.10	.05
20	Tim Salmon	.40	.18
21	Luis Salazar	.10	.05
22	Jim Eisenreich	.10	.05
23	Todd Stottlemyre	.10	.05
24	Tim Naehring	.10	.05
25	John Franco	.20	.09
26	Skeeter Barnes	.10	.05
27	Carlos Garcia	.10	.05
28	Joe Orsulak	.10	.05
29	Dwayne Henry	.10	.05
30	Fred McGriff	.30	.14
31	Derek Lilliquist	.10	.05
32	Don Mattingly	.60	.25
33	B.J. Wallace	.10	.05
34	Juan Gonzalez	1.00	.45
35	John Smoltz	.20	.09
36	Scott Servais	.10	.05
37	Lenny Webster	.10	.05
38	Chris James	.10	.05
39	Roger McDowell	.10	.05
40	Ozzie Smith	.50	.23
41	Alex Fernandez	.20	.09
42	Spike Owen	.10	.05
43	Ruben Amaro	.10	.05
44	Kevin Seitzer	.10	.05
45	Dave Fleming	.10	.05
46	Eric Fox	.10	.05
47	Bob Scanlan	.10	.05
48	Bert Blyleven	.20	.09
49	Brian McRae	.10	.05
50	Roberto Alomar	.40	.18
51	Mo Vaughn	.50	.23
52	Bobby Bonilla	.20	.09
53	Frank Tanana	.10	.05
54	Mike LaValliere	.10	.05
55	Mark McLemore	.10	.05
56	Chad Mottola	.10	.05
57	Norm Charlton	.10	.05
58	Jose Melendez	.10	.05
59	Carlos Martinez	.10	.05
60	Roberto Kelly	.10	.05
61	Gene Larkin	.10	.05
62	Rafael Belliard	.10	.05
63	Al Osuna	.10	.05
64	Scott Chiamparino	.10	.05
65	Brett Butler	.20	.09
66	John Burkett	.10	.05
67	Felix Jose	.10	.05
68	Omar Vizquel	.20	.09
69	John Vander Wal	.10	.05
70	Roberto Hernandez	.20	.09
71	Ricky Bones	.10	.05
72	Jeff Grotewold	.10	.05
73	Mike Moore	.10	.05
74	Steve Buechele	.10	.05
75	Juan Guzman	.10	.05
76	Kevin Appier	.20	.09
77	Junior Felix	.10	.05
78	Greg W. Harris	.10	.05
79	Dick Schofield	.10	.05
80	Cecil Fielder	.20	.09
81	Lloyd McClendon	.10	.05
82	David Segui	.10	.05
83	Reggie Sanders	.10	.05
84	Kurt Stillwell	.10	.05
85	Sandy Alomar	.20	.09
86	John Habyan	.10	.05
87	Kevin Reimer	.10	.05
88	Mike Stanton	.10	.05
89	Eric Anthony	.10	.05
90	Scott Erickson	.10	.05
91	Craig Colbert	.10	.05
92	Tom Pagnozzi	.10	.05
93	Pedro Astacio	.10	.05
94	Lance Johnson	.10	.05
95	Larry Walker	.40	.18
96	Russ Swan	.10	.05
97	Scott Fletcher	.10	.05
98	Derek Jeter	4.00	1.80
99	Mike Williams	.10	.05
100	Mark McGwire	2.00	.90
101	Jim Bullinger	.10	.05
102	Brian Hunter	.10	.05
103	Jody Reed	.10	.05
104	Mike Butcher	.10	.05
105	Gregg Jefferies	.10	.05
106	Howard Johnson	.10	.05
107	John Kiely	.10	.05
108	Jose Lind	.10	.05
109	Sam Horn	.10	.05
110	Barry Larkin	.30	.14
111	Bruce Hurst	.10	.05
112	Brian Barnes	.10	.05
113	Thomas Howard	.10	.05
114	Mel Hall	.10	.05
115	Robby Thompson	.10	.05
116	Mark Lemke	.10	.05
117	Eddie Taubensee	.10	.05
118	David Hulse	.10	.05
119	Pedro Munoz	.10	.05
120	Ramon Martinez	.20	.09
121	Todd Worrell	.10	.05
122	Joey Cora	.20	.09

	No.	Player	Price 1	Price 2
❑	123	Moises Alou	.20	.09
❑	124	Franklin Stubbs	.10	.05
❑	125	Pete O'Brien	.10	.05
❑	126	Bob Ayrault	.10	.05
❑	127	Carney Lansford	.20	.09
❑	128	Kal Daniels	.10	.05
❑	129	Joe Grahe	.10	.05
❑	130	Jeff Montgomery	.20	.09
❑	131	Dave Winfield	.30	.14
❑	132	Preston Wilson	.30	.14
❑	133	Steve Wilson	.10	.05
❑	134	Lee Guetterman	.10	.05
❑	135	Mickey Tettleton	.10	.05
❑	136	Jeff King	.20	.09
❑	137	Alan Mills	.10	.05
❑	138	Joe Oliver	.10	.05
❑	139	Gary Gaetti	.10	.05
❑	140	Gary Sheffield	.40	.18
❑	141	Dennis Cook	.10	.05
❑	142	Charlie Hayes	.10	.05
❑	143	Jeff Huson	.10	.05
❑	144	Kent Mercker	.10	.05
❑	145	Eric Young	.40	.18
❑	146	Scott Leius	.10	.05
❑	147	Bryan Hickerson	.10	.05
❑	148	Steve Finley	.20	.09
❑	149	Rheal Cormier	.10	.05
❑	150	Frank Thomas UER (Categories leading league are italicized but not printed in red)	1.25	.55
❑	151	Archi Cianfrocco	.10	.05
❑	152	Rich DeLucia	.10	.05
❑	153	Greg Vaughn	.20	.09
❑	154	Wes Chamberlain	.10	.05
❑	155	Dennis Eckersley	.20	.09
❑	156	Sammy Sosa	1.00	.45
❑	157	Gary DiSarcina	.10	.05
❑	158	Kevin Koslofski	.10	.05
❑	159	Doug Linton	.10	.05
❑	160	Lou Whitaker	.20	.09
❑	161	Chad McConnell	.10	.05
❑	162	Joe Hesketh	.10	.05
❑	163	Tim Wakefield	.20	.09
❑	164	Leo Gomez	.10	.05
❑	165	Jose Rijo	.10	.05
❑	166	Tim Scott	.10	.05
❑	167	Steve Olin UER (Born 10/4/65 should say 10/10/65)	.10	.05
❑	168	Kevin Maas	.10	.05
❑	169	Kenny Rogers	.10	.05
❑	170	David Justice	.40	.18
❑	171	Doug Jones	.10	.05
❑	172	Jeff Reboulet	.10	.05
❑	173	Andres Galarraga	.40	.18
❑	174	Randy Velarde	.10	.05
❑	175	Kirk McCaskill	.10	.05
❑	176	Darren Lewis	.10	.05
❑	177	Lenny Harris	.10	.05
❑	178	Jeff Fassero	.10	.05
❑	179	Ken Griffey Jr.	2.00	.90
❑	180	Darren Daulton	.20	.09
❑	181	John Jaha	.10	.05
❑	182	Ron Darling	.10	.05
❑	183	Greg Maddux	1.25	.55
❑	184	Damion Easley	.20	.09
❑	185	Jack Morris	.20	.09
❑	186	Mike Magnante	.10	.05
❑	187	John Dopson	.10	.05
❑	188	Sid Fernandez	.10	.05
❑	189	Tony Phillips	.10	.05
❑	190	Doug Drabek	.10	.05
❑	191	Sean Lowe	.10	.05
❑	192	Bob Milacki	.10	.05
❑	193	Steve Foster	.10	.05
❑	194	Jerald Clark	.10	.05
❑	195	Pete Harnisch	.10	.05
❑	196	Pat Kelly	.10	.05
❑	197	Jeff Frye	.10	.05
❑	198	Alejandro Pena	.10	.05
❑	199	Junior Ortiz	.10	.05
❑	200	Kirby Puckett	.60	.25
❑	201	Jose Uribe	.10	.05
❑	202	Mike Scioscia	.10	.05
❑	203	Bernard Gilkey	.10	.05
❑	204	Dan Pasqua	.10	.05
❑	205	Gary Carter	.30	.14
❑	206	Henry Cotto	.10	.05
❑	207	Paul Molitor	.40	.18
❑	208	Mike Hartley	.10	.05
❑	209	Jeff Parrett	.10	.05
❑	210	Mark Langston	.10	.05
❑	211	Doug Dascenzo	.10	.05
❑	212	Rick Reed	.10	.05
❑	213	Candy Maldonado	.10	.05
❑	214	Danny Darwin	.10	.05
❑	215	Pat Howell	.10	.05
❑	216	Mark Leiter	.10	.05
❑	217	Kevin Mitchell	.20	.09
❑	218	Ben McDonald	.10	.05
❑	219	Bip Roberts	.10	.05
❑	220	Benny Santiago	.10	.05
❑	221	Carlos Baerga	.10	.05
❑	222	Bernie Williams	.40	.18
❑	223	Roger Pavlik	.10	.05
❑	224	Sid Bream	.10	.05
❑	225	Matt Williams	.30	.14
❑	226	Willie Banks	.10	.05
❑	227	Jeff Bagwell	.60	.25
❑	228	Tom Goodwin	.10	.05
❑	229	Mike Perez	.10	.05
❑	230	Carlton Fisk	.40	.18
❑	231	John Wetteland	.20	.09
❑	232	Tino Martinez	.40	.18
❑	233	Rick Greene	.10	.05
❑	234	Tim McIntosh	.10	.05
❑	235	Mitch Williams	.10	.05
❑	236	Kevin Campbell	.10	.05
❑	237	Jose Vizcaino	.10	.05
❑	238	Chris Donnels	.10	.05
❑	239	Mike Boddicker	.10	.05
❑	240	John Olerud	.30	.14
❑	241	Mike Gardiner	.10	.05
❑	242	Charlie O'Brien	.10	.05
❑	243	Rob Deer	.10	.05
❑	244	Denny Neagle	.20	.09
❑	245	Chris Sabo	.10	.05
❑	246	Gregg Olson	.10	.05
❑	247	Frank Seminara UER (Acquired 12/3/98)	.10	.05
❑	248	Scott Scudder	.10	.05
❑	249	Tim Burke	.10	.05
❑	250	Chuck Knoblauch	.40	.18
❑	251	Mike Bielecki	.10	.05
❑	252	Xavier Hernandez	.10	.05
❑	253	Jose Guzman	.10	.05
❑	254	Cory Snyder	.10	.05
❑	255	Orel Hershiser	.20	.09
❑	256	Wil Cordero	.10	.05
❑	257	Luis Alicea	.10	.05
❑	258	Mike Schooler	.10	.05
❑	259	Craig Grebeck	.10	.05
❑	260	Duane Ward	.10	.05
❑	261	Bill Wegman	.10	.05
❑	262	Mickey Morandini	.10	.05
❑	263	Vince Horsman	.10	.05
❑	264	Paul Sorrento	.10	.05
❑	265	Andre Dawson	.30	.14
❑	266	Rene Gonzales	.10	.05
❑	267	Keith Miller	.10	.05
❑	268	Derek Bell	.20	.09
❑	269	Todd Steverson	.20	.09
❑	270	Frank Viola	.10	.05
❑	271	Wally Whitehurst	.10	.05
❑	272	Kurt Knudsen	.10	.05
❑	273	Dan Walters	.10	.05
❑	274	Rick Sutcliffe	.10	.05
❑	275	Andy Van Slyke	.20	.09
❑	276	Paul O'Neill	.20	.09
❑	277	Mark Whiten	.10	.05
❑	278	Chris Nabholz	.10	.05
❑	279	Todd Burns	.10	.05
❑	280	Tom Glavine	.30	.14
❑	281	Butch Henry	.10	.05
❑	282	Shane Mack	.10	.05
❑	283	Mike Jackson	.10	.05
❑	284	Henry Rodriguez	.20	.09
❑	285	Bob Tewksbury	.10	.05
❑	286	Ron Karkovice	.10	.05
❑	287	Mike Gallego	.10	.05
❑	288	Dave Cochrane	.10	.05
❑	289	Jesse Orosco	.10	.05
❑	290	Dave Stewart	.20	.09
❑	291	Tommy Greene	.10	.05
❑	292	Rey Sanchez	.10	.05
❑	293	Rob Ducey	.10	.05
❑	294	Brent Mayne	.10	.05
❑	295	Dave Stieb	.20	.09
❑	296	Luis Rivera	.10	.05
❑	297	Jeff Innis	.10	.05
❑	298	Scott Livingstone	.10	.05
❑	299	Bob Patterson	.10	.05
❑	300	Cal Ripken	1.50	.70
❑	301	Cesar Hernandez	.10	.05
❑	302	Randy Myers	.20	.09
❑	303	Brook Jacoby	.10	.05
❑	304	Melido Perez	.10	.05
❑	305	Rafael Palmeiro	.30	.14
❑	306	Damon Berryhill	.10	.05
❑	307	Dan Serafini	.20	.09
❑	308	Darryl Kile	.20	.09
❑	309	J.T. Bruett	.10	.05
❑	310	Dave Righetti	.10	.05
❑	311	Jay Howell	.10	.05
❑	312	Geronimo Pena	.10	.05
❑	313	Greg Hibbard	.10	.05
❑	314	Mark Gardner	.10	.05
❑	315	Edgar Martinez	.30	.14
❑	316	Dave Nilsson	.20	.09
❑	317	Kyle Abbott	.10	.05
❑	318	Willie Wilson	.10	.05
❑	319	Paul Assenmacher	.10	.05
❑	320	Tim Fortugno	.10	.05
❑	321	Rusty Meacham	.10	.05
❑	322	Pat Borders	.10	.05
❑	323	Mike Greenwell	.10	.05
❑	324	Willie Randolph	.20	.09
❑	325	Bill Gullickson	.10	.05
❑	326	Gary Varsho	.10	.05
❑	327	Tim Hulett	.10	.05
❑	328	Scott Ruskin	.10	.05
❑	329	Mike Maddux	.10	.05
❑	330	Danny Tartabull	.10	.05
❑	331	Kenny Lofton	.35	.16
❑	332	Geno Petralli	.10	.05
❑	333	Otis Nixon	.10	.05
❑	334	Jason Kendall	1.25	.55
❑	335	Mark Portugal	.10	.05
❑	336	Mike Pagliarulo	.10	.05
❑	337	Kirt Manwaring	.10	.05
❑	338	Bob Ojeda	.10	.05
❑	339	Mark Clark	.10	.05
❑	340	John Kruk	.20	.09
❑	341	Mel Rojas	.10	.05
❑	342	Erik Hanson	.10	.05
❑	343	Doug Henry	.10	.05
❑	344	Jack McDowell	.10	.05
❑	345	Harold Baines	.20	.09
❑	346	Chuck McElroy	.10	.05
❑	347	Luis Sojo	.10	.05
❑	348	Andy Stankiewicz	.10	.05
❑	349	Hipolito Pichardo	.10	.05
❑	350	Joe Carter	.20	.09
❑	351	Ellis Burks	.20	.09
❑	352	Pete Schourek	.10	.05
❑	353	Bubby Groom	.10	.05
❑	354	Jay Bell	.20	.09
❑	355	Brady Anderson	.30	.14
❑	356	Freddie Benavides	.10	.05
❑	357	Phil Stephenson	.10	.05
❑	358	Kevin Wickander	.10	.05
❑	359	Mike Stanley	.10	.05
❑	360	Ivan Rodriguez	.50	.23
❑	361	Scott Bankhead	.10	.05
❑	362	Luis Gonzalez	.10	.05
❑	363	John Smiley	.10	.05
❑	364	Trevor Wilson	.10	.05
❑	365	Tom Candiotti	.10	.05
❑	366	Craig Wilson	.10	.05
❑	367	Steve Sax	.10	.05
❑	368	Delino DeShields	.20	.09
❑	369	Jaime Navarro	.10	.05
❑	370	Dave Valle	.10	.05
❑	371	Mariano Duncan	.10	.05

372	Rod Nichols	.10	.05
373	Mike Morgan	.10	.05
374	Julio Valera	.10	.05
375	Wally Joyner	.20	.09
376	Tom Henke	.10	.05
377	Herm Winningham	.10	.05
378	Orlando Merced	.10	.05
379	Mike Munoz	.10	.05
380	Todd Hundley	.30	.14
381	Mike Flanagan	.10	.05
382	Tim Belcher	.10	.05
383	Jerry Browne	.10	.05
384	Mike Benjamin	.10	.05
385	Jim Leyritz	.10	.05
386	Ray Lankford	.30	.14
387	Devon White	.10	.05
388	Jeremy Hernandez	.10	.05
389	Brian Harper	.10	.05
390	Wade Boggs	.40	.18
391	Derrick May	.10	.05
392	Travis Fryman	.20	.09
393	Ron Gant	.20	.09
394	Checklist 1-132	.10	.05
395	Checklist 133-264 UER (Eckerlsey)	.10	.05
396	Checklist 265-396	.10	.05
397	George Brett	.75	.35
398	Bobby Witt	.10	.05
399	Daryl Boston	.10	.05
400	Bo Jackson	.20	.09
401	Fred McGriff Frank Thomas	.50	.23
402	Ryne Sandberg Carlos Baerga	.20	.09
403	Gary Sheffield Edgar Martinez	.20	.09
404	Barry Larkin Travis Fryman	.20	.09
405	Andy Van Slyke Ken Griffey Jr.	.50	.23
406	Larry Walker Kirby Puckett	.40	.18
407	Barry Bonds Joe Carter	.20	.09
408	Darren Daulton Brian Harper	.20	.09
409	Greg Maddux Roger Clemens	.40	.18
410	Tom Glavine Dave Fleming	.20	.09
411	Lee Smith Dennis Eckersley	.20	.09
412	Jamie McAndrew	.10	.05
413	Pete Smith	.10	.05
414	Juan Guerrero	.10	.05
415	Todd Frohwirth	.10	.05
416	Randy Tomlin	.10	.05
417	B.J. Surhoff	.20	.09
418	Jim Gott	.10	.05
419	Mark Thompson	.10	.05
420	Kevin Tapani	.10	.05
421	Curt Schilling	.20	.09
422	J.T. Snow	.50	.23
423	1993 Prospects Ryan Klesko Ivan Cruz Bubba Smith Larry Sutton	.40	.18
424	John Valentin	.20	.09
425	Joe Girardi	.20	.09
426	Nigel Wilson	.10	.05
427	Bob MacDonald	.10	.05
428	Todd Zeile	.10	.05
429	Milt Cuyler	.10	.05
430	Eddie Murray	.40	.18
431	Rich Amaral	.10	.05
432	Pete Young	.10	.05
433	Roger Bailey and Tom Schmidt	.10	.05
434	Jack Armstrong	.10	.05
435	Willie McGee	.20	.09
436	Greg W. Harris	.10	.05
437	Chris Hammond	.10	.05
438	Ritchie Moody	.10	.05
439	Bryan Harvey	.10	.05
440	Ruben Sierra	.10	.05
441	Don Lemon and Todd Pridy	.10	.05
442	Kevin McReynolds	.10	.05
443	Terry Leach	.10	.05
444	David Nied	.10	.05
445	Dale Murphy	.30	.14
446	Luis Mercedes	.10	.05
447	Keith Shepherd	.10	.05
448	Ken Caminiti	.30	.14
449	James Austin	.10	.05
450	Darryl Strawberry	.20	.09
451	1993 Prospects Ramon Caraballo Jon Shave Brent Gates Quinton McCracken	.20	.09
452	Bob Wickman	.10	.05
453	Victor Cole	.10	.05
454	John Johnstone	.10	.05
455	Chili Davis	.20	.09
456	Scott Taylor	.10	.05
457	Tracy Woodson	.10	.05
458	David Wells	.20	.09
459	Derek Wallace	.10	.05
460	Randy Johnson	.40	.18
461	Steve Reed	.10	.05
462	Felix Fermin	.10	.05
463	Scott Aldred	.10	.05
464	Greg Colbrunn	.10	.05
465	Tony Fernandez	.10	.05
466	Mike Felder	.10	.05
467	Lee Stevens	.10	.05
468	Matt Whiteside	.10	.05
469	Dave Hansen	.10	.05
470	Rob Dibble	.10	.05
471	Dave Gallagher	.10	.05
472	Chris Gwynn	.10	.05
473	Dave Henderson	.10	.05
474	Ozzie Guillen	.10	.05
475	Jeff Reardon	.20	.09
476	Mark Voisard and Will Scalzitti	.10	.05
477	Jimmy Jones	.10	.05
478	Greg Cadaret	.10	.05
479	Todd Pratt	.10	.05
480	Pat Listach	.10	.05
481	Ryan Luzinski	.10	.05
482	Darren Reed	.10	.05
483	Brian Griffiths	.10	.05
484	John Wehner	.10	.05
485	Glenn Davis	.10	.05
486	Eric Wedge	.10	.05
487	Jesse Hollins	.10	.05
488	Manuel Lee	.10	.05
489	Scott Fredrickson	.10	.05
490	Omar Olivares	.10	.05
491	Shawn Hare	.10	.05
492	Tom Lampkin	.10	.05
493	Jeff Nelson	.10	.05
494	1993 Prospects Kevin Young Adell Davenport Eduardo Perez Lou Lucca	.20	.09
495	Ken Hill	.10	.05
496	Reggie Jefferson	.20	.09
497	Matt Petersen and Willie Brown	.10	.05
498	Bud Black	.10	.05
499	Chuck Crim	.10	.05
500	Jose Canseco	.40	.18
501	Johnny Oates MG Bobby Cox MG	.20	.09
502	Butch Hobson MG Jim Lefebvre MG	.10	.05
503	Buck Rodgers MG Tony Perez MG	.20	.09
504	Gene Lamont MG Don Baylor MG	.20	.09
505	Mike Hargrove MG Rene Lachemann MG	.20	.09
506	Sparky Anderson MG Art Howe MG	.20	.09
507	Hal McRae MG Tom Lasorda MG	.20	.09
508	Phil Garner MG Felipe Alou MG	.20	.09
509	Tom Kelly MG Jeff Torborg MG	.10	.05
510	Buck Showalter MG Jim Fregosi MG	.20	.09
511	Tony LaRussa MG Jim Leyland MG	.20	.09
512	Lou Piniella MG Joe Torre MG	.20	.09
513	Kevin Kennedy MG Jim Riggleman MG	.10	.05
514	Cito Gaston MG Dusty Baker MG	.10	.05
515	Greg Swindell	.10	.05
516	Alex Arias	.10	.05
517	Bill Pecota	.10	.05
518	Benji Grigsby UER (Misspelled Bengi on card front)	.10	.05
519	David Howard	.10	.05
520	Charlie Hough	.20	.09
521	Kevin Flora	.10	.05
522	Shane Reynolds	.20	.09
523	Doug Bochtler	.10	.05
524	Chris Hoiles	.10	.05
525	Scott Sanderson	.10	.05
526	Mike Sharperson	.10	.05
527	Mike Fetters	.10	.05
528	Paul Quantrill	.10	.05
529	1993 Prospects Dave Silvestri Chipper Jones Benji Gil Jeff Patzke	2.00	.90
530	Sterling Hitchcock	.40	.18
531	Joe Millette	.10	.05
532	Tom Brunansky	.10	.05
533	Frank Castillo	.10	.05
534	Randy Knorr	.10	.05
535	Jose Oquendo	.10	.05
536	Dave Haas	.10	.05
537	Jason Hutchins and Ryan Turner	.10	.05
538	Jimmy Baron	.10	.05
539	Kerry Woodson	.10	.05
540	Ivan Calderon	.10	.05
541	Denis Boucher	.10	.05
542	Royce Clayton	.10	.05
543	Reggie Williams	.10	.05
544	Steve Decker	.10	.05
545	Dean Palmer	.20	.09
546	Hal Morris	.10	.05
547	Ryan Thompson	.10	.05
548	Lance Blankenship	.10	.05
549	Hensley Meulens	.10	.05
550	Scott Radinsky	.10	.05
551	Eric Young	.40	.18
552	Jeff Blauser	.10	.05
553	Andujar Cedeno	.10	.05
554	Arthur Rhodes	.10	.05
555	Terry Mulholland	.10	.05
556	Darryl Hamilton	.10	.05
557	Pedro Martinez	.50	.23
558	Ryan Whitman and Mark Skeels	.10	.05
559	Jamie Arnold	.20	.09
560	Zane Smith	.10	.05
561	Matt Nokes	.10	.05
562	Bob Zupcic	.10	.05
563	Shawn Boskie	.10	.05
564	Mike Timlin	.10	.05
565	Jerald Clark	.10	.05
566	Rod Brewer	.10	.05
567	Mark Carreon	.10	.05
568	Andy Benes	.20	.09
569	Shawn Barton	.10	.05
570	Tim Wallach	.10	.05
571	Dave Mlicki	.10	.05
572	Trevor Hoffman	.40	.18
573	John Patterson	.10	.05
574	De Shawn Warren	.10	.05
575	Monty Fariss	.10	.05
576	1993 Prospects Darrell Sherman Damon Buford	.20	.09

Cliff Floyd
Michael Moore
❑ 577 Tim Costo .10 .05
❑ 578 Dave Magadan .10 .05
❑ 579 Neil Garret and .20 .09
Jason Bates
❑ 580 Walt Weiss .10 .05
❑ 581 Chris Haney .10 .05
❑ 582 Shawn Abner .10 .05
❑ 583 Marvin Freeman .10 .05
❑ 584 Casey Candaele .10 .05
❑ 585 Ricky Jordan .10 .05
❑ 586 Jeff Tabaka .10 .05
❑ 587 Manny Alexander .10 .05
❑ 588 Mike Trombley .10 .05
❑ 589 Carlos Hernandez .10 .05
❑ 590 Cal Eldred .10 .05
❑ 591 Alex Cole .10 .05
❑ 592 Phil Plantier .10 .05
❑ 593 Brett Merriman .10 .05
❑ 594 Jerry Nielsen .10 .05
❑ 595 Shawon Dunston .10 .05
❑ 596 Jimmy Key .20 .09
❑ 597 Gerald Perry .10 .05
❑ 598 Rico Brogna .20 .09
❑ 599 Clemente Nunez and .10 .05
Daniel Robinson
❑ 600 Bret Saberhagen .20 .09
❑ 601 Craig Shipley .10 .05
❑ 602 Henry Mercedes .10 .05
❑ 603 Jim Thome .75 .35
❑ 604 Rod Beck .20 .09
❑ 605 Chuck Finley .20 .09
❑ 606 J. Owens .10 .05
❑ 607 Dan Smith .10 .05
❑ 608 Bill Doran .10 .05
❑ 609 Lance Parrish .10 .05
❑ 610 Denny Martinez .20 .09
❑ 611 Tom Gordon .20 .09
❑ 612 Byron Mathews .10 .05
❑ 613 Joel Adamson .10 .05
❑ 614 Brian Williams .10 .05
❑ 615 Steve Avery .10 .05
❑ 616 1993 Prospects .40 .18
Matt Mieske
Tracy Sanders
Midre Cummings
Ryan Freeburg
❑ 617 Craig Lefferts .10 .05
❑ 618 Tony Pena .10 .05
❑ 619 Billy Spiers .10 .05
❑ 620 Todd Benzinger .10 .05
❑ 621 Mike Kotarski and .10 .05
Greg Boyd
❑ 622 Ben Rivera .10 .05
❑ 623 Al Martin .10 .05
❑ 624 Sam Militello UER .10 .05
(Profile says drafted
in 1988, bio says
drafted in 1990)
❑ 625 Rick Aguilera .10 .05
❑ 626 Dan Gladden .10 .05
❑ 627 Andres Berumen .10 .05
❑ 628 Kelly Gruber .10 .05
❑ 629 Cris Carpenter .10 .05
❑ 630 Mark Grace .30 .14
❑ 631 Jeff Brantley .10 .05
❑ 632 Chris Widger .10 .05
❑ 633 Three Russians UER .10 .05
Rudolf Razjigaev
Eugneyi Puchkov
Ilya Bogatyrev
Bogatyrev is a shortstop,
card has pitching header
❑ 634 Mo Sanford .10 .05
❑ 635 Albert Belle .50 .23
❑ 636 Tim Teufel .10 .05
❑ 637 Greg Myers .10 .05
❑ 638 Brian Bohanon .10 .05
❑ 639 Mike Bordick .10 .05
❑ 640 Dwight Gooden .20 .09
❑ 641 Pat Leahy and .10 .05
Gavin Baugh
❑ 642 Milt Hill .10 .05
❑ 643 Luis Aquino .10 .05
❑ 644 Dante Bichette .20 .09
❑ 645 Bobby Thigpen .10 .05
❑ 646 Rich Scheid .10 .05
❑ 647 Brian Sackinsky .10 .05
❑ 648 Ryan Hawblitzel .10 .05
❑ 649 Tom Marsh .10 .05
❑ 650 Terry Pendleton .10 .05
❑ 651 Rafael Bournigal .10 .05
❑ 652 Dave West .10 .05
❑ 653 Steve Hosey .10 .05
❑ 654 Gerald Williams .10 .05
❑ 655 Scott Cooper .10 .05
❑ 656 Gary Scott .10 .05
❑ 657 Mike Harkey .10 .05
❑ 658 1993 Prospects .30 .14
Jeromy Burnitz
Melvin Nieves
Rich Becker
Shon Walker
❑ 659 Ed Sprague .10 .05
❑ 660 Alan Trammell .30 .14
❑ 661 Garvin Alston and .20 .09
Michael Case
❑ 662 Donovan Osborne .10 .05
❑ 663 Jeff Gardner .10 .05
❑ 664 Calvin Jones .10 .05
❑ 665 Darrin Fletcher .10 .05
❑ 666 Glenallen Hill .10 .05
❑ 667 Jim Rosenbohm .10 .05
❑ 668 Scott Lewis .10 .05
❑ 669 Kip Yaughn .10 .05
❑ 670 Julio Franco .10 .05
❑ 671 Dave Martinez .10 .05
❑ 672 Kevin Bass .10 .05
❑ 673 Todd Van Poppel .10 .05
❑ 674 Mark Gubicza .10 .05
❑ 675 Tim Raines .20 .09
❑ 676 Rudy Seanez .10 .05
❑ 677 Charlie Leibrandt .10 .05
❑ 678 Randy Milligan .10 .05
❑ 679 Kim Batiste .10 .05
❑ 680 Craig Biggio .40 .18
❑ 681 Darren Holmes .10 .05
❑ 682 John Candelaria .10 .05
❑ 683 Jerry Stafford and .20 .09
Eddie Christian
❑ 684 Pat Mahomes .10 .05
❑ 685 Bob Walk .10 .05
❑ 686 Russ Springer .10 .05
❑ 687 Tony Sheffield .10 .05
❑ 688 Dwight Smith .10 .05
❑ 689 Eddie Zosky .10 .05
❑ 690 Bien Figueroa .10 .05
❑ 691 Jim Tatum .10 .05
❑ 692 Chad Kreuter .10 .05
❑ 693 Rich Rodriguez .10 .05
❑ 694 Shane Turner .10 .05
❑ 695 Kent Bottenfield .10 .05
❑ 696 Jose Mesa .10 .05
❑ 697 Darrell Whitmore .10 .05
❑ 698 Ted Wood .10 .05
❑ 699 Chad Curtis .20 .09
❑ 700 Nolan Ryan 1.50 .70
❑ 701 1993 Prospects 2.00 .90
Mike Piazza
Brook Fordyce
Carlos Delgado
Donnie Leshnock
❑ 702 Tim Pugh .10 .05
❑ 703 Jeff Kent .20 .09
❑ 704 Jon Goodrich and .20 .09
Danny Figueroa
❑ 705 Bob Welch .10 .05
❑ 706 Sherard Clinkscales .10 .05
❑ 707 Donn Pall .10 .05
❑ 708 Greg Olson .10 .05
❑ 709 Jeff Juden .10 .05
❑ 710 Mike Mussina .40 .18
❑ 711 Scott Chiamparino .10 .05
❑ 712 Stan Javier .10 .05
❑ 713 John Doherty .10 .05
❑ 714 Kevin Gross .10 .05
❑ 715 Greg Gagne .10 .05
❑ 716 Steve Cooke .10 .05
❑ 717 Steve Farr .10 .05
❑ 718 Jay Buhner .30 .14
❑ 719 Butch Henry .10 .05
❑ 720 David Cone .20 .09
❑ 721 Rick Wilkins .10 .05
❑ 722 Chuck Carr .10 .05
❑ 723 Kenny Felder .10 .05
❑ 724 Guillermo Velasquez .10 .05
❑ 725 Billy Hatcher .10 .05
❑ 726 Mike Veneziale and .20 .09
Ken Kendrena
❑ 727 Jonathan Hurst .10 .05
❑ 728 Steve Frey .10 .05
❑ 729 Mark Leonard .10 .05
❑ 730 Charles Nagy .20 .09
❑ 731 Donald Harris .10 .05
❑ 732 Travis Buckley .10 .05
❑ 733 Tom Browning .10 .05
❑ 734 Anthony Young .10 .05
❑ 735 Steve Shifflett .10 .05
❑ 736 Jeff Russell .10 .05
❑ 737 Wilson Alvarez .20 .09
❑ 738 Lance Painter .10 .05
❑ 739 Dave Weathers .10 .05
❑ 740 Len Dykstra .20 .09
❑ 741 Mike Devereaux .10 .05
❑ 742 1993 Prospects .10 .05
Rene Arocha
Alan Embree
Brien Taylor
Tim Crabtree
❑ 743 Dave Landaker .10 .05
❑ 744 Chris George .10 .05
❑ 745 Eric Davis .20 .09
❑ 746 Mark Strittmatter and .20 .09
Lamarr Rogers
❑ 747 Carl Willis .10 .05
❑ 748 Stan Belinda .10 .05
❑ 749 Scott Kamieniecki .10 .05
❑ 750 Rickey Henderson .40 .18
❑ 751 Eric Hillman .10 .05
❑ 752 Pat Hentgen .30 .14
❑ 753 Jim Corsi .10 .05
❑ 754 Brian Jordan .20 .09
❑ 755 Bill Swift .10 .05
❑ 756 Mike Henneman .10 .05
❑ 757 Harold Reynolds .10 .05
❑ 758 Sean Berry .10 .05
❑ 759 Charlie Hayes .10 .05
❑ 760 Luis Polonia .10 .05
❑ 761 Darrin Jackson .10 .05
❑ 762 Mark Lewis .10 .05
❑ 763 Rob Maurer .10 .05
❑ 764 Willie Greene .10 .05
❑ 765 Vince Coleman .10 .05
❑ 766 Todd Revenig .10 .05
❑ 767 Rich Ireland .10 .05
❑ 768 Mike Macfarlane .10 .05
❑ 769 Francisco Cabrera .10 .05
❑ 770 Robin Ventura .20 .09
❑ 771 Kevin Ritz .10 .05
❑ 772 Chito Martinez .10 .05
❑ 773 Cliff Brantley .10 .05
❑ 774 Curtis Leskanic .10 .05
❑ 775 Chris Bosio .10 .05
❑ 776 Jose Offerman .10 .05
❑ 777 Mark Guthrie .10 .05
❑ 778 Don Slaught .10 .05
❑ 779 Rich Monteleone .10 .05
❑ 780 Jim Abbott .20 .09
❑ 781 Jack Clark .10 .05
❑ 782 Reynol Mendoza and .20 .09
Dan Roman
❑ 783 Heathcliff Slocumb .10 .05
❑ 784 Jeff Branson .10 .05
❑ 785 Kevin Brown .30 .14
❑ 786 1993 Prospects .20 .09
Mike Christopher
Ken Ryan
Aaron Taylor
Gus Gandarillas
❑ 787 Mike Matthews .10 .05
❑ 788 Mackey Sasser .10 .05
❑ 789 Jeff Conine UER .10 .05
(No inclusion of 1990
stats in career total)

	MINT	NRMT
❑ 790 George Bell	.10	.05
❑ 791 Pat Rapp	.10	.05
❑ 792 Joe Boever	.10	.05
❑ 793 Jim Poole	.10	.05
❑ 794 Andy Ashby	.20	.09
❑ 795 Deion Sanders	.30	.14
❑ 796 Scott Brosius	.10	.05
❑ 797 Brad Pennington	.10	.05
❑ 798 Greg Blosser	.10	.05
❑ 799 Jim Edmonds	1.00	.45
❑ 800 Shawn Jeter	.10	.05
❑ 801 Jesse Levis	.10	.05
❑ 802 Phil Clark UER (Word "a" is missing in sentence beginning with "In 1992 ...")	.10	.05
❑ 803 Ed Pierce	.10	.05
❑ 804 Jose Valentin	.40	.18
❑ 805 Terry Jorgensen	.10	.05
❑ 806 Mark Hutton	.10	.05
❑ 807 Troy Neel	.10	.05
❑ 808 Bret Boone	.20	.09
❑ 809 Cris Colon	.10	.05
❑ 810 Domingo Martinez	.10	.05
❑ 811 Javier Lopez	.40	.18
❑ 812 Matt Walbeck	.10	.05
❑ 813 Dan Wilson	.20	.09
❑ 814 Scooter Tucker	.10	.05
❑ 815 Billy Ashley	.10	.05
❑ 816 Tim Laker	.10	.05
❑ 817 Bobby Jones	.30	.14
❑ 818 Brad Brink	.10	.05
❑ 819 William Pennyfeather	.10	.05
❑ 820 Stan Royer	.10	.05
❑ 821 Doug Brocail	.10	.05
❑ 822 Kevin Rogers	.10	.05
❑ 823 Checklist 397-540	.10	.05
❑ 824 Checklist 541-691	.10	.05
❑ 825 Checklist 692-825	.10	.05

1993 Topps Black Gold

	MINT	NRMT
COMPLETE SET (44)	10.00	4.50
COMPLETE SERIES 1 (22)	4.00	1.80
COMPLETE SERIES 2 (22)	6.00	2.70
COMMON CARD (1-44)	.10	.05

	MINT	NRMT
❑ 1 Barry Bonds	.75	.35
❑ 2 Will Clark	.60	.25
❑ 3 Darren Daulton	.25	.11
❑ 4 Andre Dawson	.40	.18
❑ 5 Delino DeShields	.10	.05
❑ 6 Tom Glavine	.40	.18
❑ 7 Marquis Grissom	.25	.11
❑ 8 Tony Gwynn	1.50	.70
❑ 9 Eric Karros	.40	.18
❑ 10 Ray Lankford	.40	.18
❑ 11 Barry Larkin	.40	.18
❑ 12 Greg Maddux	2.00	.90
❑ 13 Fred McGriff	.40	.18
❑ 14 Joe Oliver	.10	.05
❑ 15 Terry Pendleton	.10	.05
❑ 16 Bip Roberts	.10	.05
❑ 17 Ryne Sandberg	.75	.35
❑ 18 Gary Sheffield	.60	.25
❑ 19 Lee Smith	.25	.11
❑ 20 Ozzie Smith	.75	.35
❑ 21 Andy Van Slyke	.10	.05
❑ 22 Larry Walker	.60	.25
❑ 23 Roberto Alomar	.60	.25
❑ 24 Brady Anderson	.40	.18
❑ 25 Carlos Baerga	.10	.05
❑ 26 Joe Carter	.25	.11
❑ 27 Roger Clemens	1.00	.45
❑ 28 Mike Devereaux	.10	.05
❑ 29 Dennis Eckersley	.25	.11
❑ 30 Cecil Fielder	.25	.11
❑ 31 Travis Fryman	.25	.11
❑ 32 Juan Gonzalez UER (No copyright or licensing on card)	1.50	.70
❑ 33 Ken Griffey Jr.	3.00	1.35
❑ 34 Brian Harper	.10	.05
❑ 35 Pat Listach	.10	.05
❑ 36 Kenny Lofton	.60	.25
❑ 37 Edgar Martinez	.40	.18
❑ 38 Jack McDowell	.10	.05
❑ 39 Mark McGwire	2.50	1.10
❑ 40 Kirby Puckett	1.00	.45
❑ 41 Mickey Tettleton	.10	.05
❑ 42 Frank Thomas UER (No copyright or licensing on card)	2.50	1.10
❑ 43 Robin Ventura	.25	.11
❑ 44 Dave Winfield	.40	.18
❑ A Winner A 1-11	.50	.23
❑ B Winner B 12-22	.50	.23
❑ C Winner C 23-33	.75	.35
❑ D Winner D 34-44	.75	.35
❑ AB Winner AB 1-22 UER (Numbers 10 and 11 have the 1 missing)	1.00	.45
❑ CD Winner C/D 23-44	1.50	.70
❑ ABCD Winner ABCD 1-44	2.50	1.10

1993 Topps Traded

	MINT	NRMT
COMP.FACT.SET (132)	30.00	13.50
COMMON CARD (1T-132T)	.15	.07

	MINT	NRMT
❑ 1T Barry Bonds	.60	.25
❑ 2T Rich Renteria	.15	.07
❑ 3T Aaron Sele	.50	.23
❑ 4T Carlton Loewer USA	1.50	.70
❑ 5T Erik Pappas	.15	.07
❑ 6T Greg McMichael	.15	.07
❑ 7T Freddie Benavides	.15	.07
❑ 8T Kirk Gibson	.25	.11
❑ 9T Tony Fernandez	.15	.07
❑ 10T Jay Gainer	.15	.07
❑ 11T Orestes Destrade	.15	.07
❑ 12T A.J. Hinch USA	4.00	1.80
❑ 13T Bobby Munoz	.15	.07
❑ 14T Tom Henke	.15	.07
❑ 15T Rob Butler	.15	.07
❑ 16T Gary Wayne	.15	.07
❑ 17T David McCarty	.15	.07
❑ 18T Walt Weiss	.15	.07
❑ 19T Todd Helton USA	20.00	9.00
❑ 20T Mark Whiten	.15	.07
❑ 21T Ricky Gutierrez	.15	.07
❑ 22T Dustin Hermanson USA	1.00	.45
❑ 23T Sherman Obando	.15	.07
❑ 24T Mike Piazza	2.50	1.10
❑ 25T Jeff Russell	.15	.07
❑ 26T Jason Bere	.15	.07
❑ 27T Jack Voigt	.15	.07
❑ 28T Chris Bosio	.15	.07
❑ 29T Phil Hiatt	.15	.07
❑ 30T Matt Beaumont USA	.30	.14
❑ 31T Andres Galarraga	.50	.23
❑ 32T Greg Swindell	.15	.07
❑ 33T Vinny Castilla	2.00	.90
❑ 34T Pat Clougherty USA	.15	.07
❑ 35T Greg Briley	.15	.07
❑ 36T Dallas Green MG Davey Johnson MG	.15	.07
❑ 37T Tyler Green	.15	.07
❑ 38T Craig Paquette	.15	.07
❑ 39T Danny Sheaffer	.15	.07
❑ 40T Jim Converse	.15	.07
❑ 41T Terry Harvey USA	.15	.07
❑ 42T Phil Plantier	.15	.07
❑ 43T Doug Saunders	.15	.07
❑ 44T Benny Santiago	.15	.07
❑ 45T Dante Powell USA	1.50	.70
❑ 46T Jeff Parrett	.15	.07
❑ 47T Wade Boggs	.50	.23
❑ 48T Paul Molitor	.50	.23
❑ 49T Turk Wendell	.15	.07
❑ 50T David Wells	.25	.11
❑ 51T Gary Sheffield	.50	.23
❑ 52T Kevin Young	.15	.07
❑ 53T Nelson Liriano	.15	.07
❑ 54T Greg Maddux	1.50	.70
❑ 55T Derek Bell	.25	.11
❑ 56T Matt Turner	.15	.07
❑ 57T Charlie Nelson USA	.15	.07
❑ 58T Mike Hampton	.30	.14
❑ 59T Troy O'Leary	1.50	.70
❑ 60T Benji Gil	.15	.07
❑ 61T Mitch Lyden	.15	.07
❑ 62T J.T. Snow	.50	.23
❑ 63T Damon Buford	.15	.07
❑ 64T Gene Harris	.15	.07
❑ 65T Randy Myers	.25	.11
❑ 66T Felix Jose	.15	.07
❑ 67T Todd Dunn USA	.15	.07
❑ 68T Jimmy Key	.25	.11
❑ 69T Pedro Castellano	.15	.07
❑ 70T Mark Merila USA	.25	.11
❑ 71T Rich Rodriguez	.15	.07
❑ 72T Matt Mieske	.15	.07
❑ 73T Pete Incaviglia	.15	.07
❑ 74T Carl Everett	.25	.11
❑ 75T Jim Abbott	.25	.11
❑ 76T Luis Aquino	.15	.07
❑ 77T Rene Arocha	.15	.07
❑ 78T Jon Shave	.15	.07
❑ 79T Todd Walker USA	10.00	4.50
❑ 80T Jack Armstrong	.15	.07
❑ 81T Jeff Richardson	.15	.07
❑ 82T Blas Minor	.15	.07
❑ 83T Dave Winfield	.30	.14
❑ 84T Paul O'Neill	.25	.11
❑ 85T Steve Reich USA	.15	.07
❑ 86T Chris Hammond	.15	.07
❑ 87T Hilly Hathaway	.15	.07
❑ 88T Fred McGriff	.30	.14
❑ 89T Dave Telgheder	.15	.07
❑ 90T Richie Lewis	.15	.07
❑ 91T Brent Gates	.15	.07
❑ 92T Andre Dawson	.30	.14
❑ 93T Andy Barkett USA	.15	.07
❑ 94T Doug Drabek	.15	.07
❑ 95T Joe Klink	.15	.07
❑ 96T Willie Blair	.15	.07
❑ 97T Danny Graves USA	.15	.07
❑ 98T Pat Meares	.15	.07
❑ 99T Mike Lansing	.25	.11
❑ 100T Marcos Armas	.15	.07
❑ 101T Darren Grass USA	.15	.07
❑ 102T Chris Jones	.15	.07
❑ 103T Ken Ryan	.15	.07
❑ 104T Ellis Burks	.25	.11
❑ 105T Roberto Kelly	.15	.07
❑ 106T Dave Magadan	.15	.07
❑ 107T Paul Wilson USA	.50	.23
❑ 108T Rob Natal	.15	.07

		MINT	NRMT
❑ 109T	Paul Wagner	.15	.07
❑ 110T	Jeromy Burnitz	.25	.11
❑ 111T	Monty Fariss	.15	.07
❑ 112T	Kevin Mitchell	.25	.11
❑ 113T	Scott Pose	.15	.07
❑ 114T	Dave Stewart	.25	.11
❑ 115T	Russ Johnson USA	.50	.23
❑ 116T	Armando Reynoso	.15	.07
❑ 117T	Geronimo Berroa	.15	.07
❑ 118T	Woody Williams	1.00	.45
❑ 119T	Tim Bogar	.15	.07
❑ 120T	Bob Scafa USA	.15	.07
❑ 121T	Henry Cotto	.15	.07
❑ 122T	Gregg Jefferies	.15	.07
❑ 123T	Norm Charlton	.15	.07
❑ 124T	Bret Wagner USA	.50	.23
❑ 125T	David Cone	.25	.11
❑ 126T	Daryl Boston	.15	.07
❑ 127T	Tim Wallach	.15	.07
❑ 128T	Mike Martin USA	.25	.11
❑ 129T	John Cummings	.15	.07
❑ 130T	Ryan Bowen	.15	.07
❑ 131T	John Powell USA	.25	.11
❑ 132T	Checklist 1-132	.15	.07

1994 Topps

	MINT	NRMT
COMPLETE SET (792)	30.00	13.50
COMP.FACT.SET (808)	50.00	22.00
COMP.BAKER SET (818)	50.00	22.00
COMPLETE SERIES 1 (396)	15.00	6.75
COMPLETE SERIES 2 (396)	15.00	6.75
COMMON CARD (1-792)	.10	.05

		MINT	NRMT
❑ 1	Mike Piazza	1.25	.55
❑ 2	Bernie Williams	.40	.18
❑ 3	Kevin Rogers	.10	.05
❑ 4	Paul Carey	.10	.05
❑ 5	Ozzie Guillen	.10	.05
❑ 6	Derrick May	.10	.05
❑ 7	Jose Mesa	.10	.05
❑ 8	Todd Hundley	.20	.09
❑ 9	Chris Haney	.10	.05
❑ 10	John Olerud	.20	.09
❑ 11	Andujar Cedeno	.10	.05
❑ 12	John Smiley	.10	.05
❑ 13	Phil Plantier	.10	.05
❑ 14	Willie Banks	.10	.05
❑ 15	Jay Bell	.20	.09
❑ 16	Doug Henry	.10	.05
❑ 17	Lance Blankenship	.10	.05
❑ 18	Greg W. Harris	.10	.05
❑ 19	Scott Livingstone	.10	.05
❑ 20	Bryan Harvey	.10	.05
❑ 21	Wil Cordero	.10	.05
❑ 22	Roger Pavlik	.10	.05
❑ 23	Mark Lemke	.10	.05
❑ 24	Jeff Nelson	.10	.05
❑ 25	Todd Zeile	.10	.05
❑ 26	Billy Hatcher	.10	.05
❑ 27	Joe Magrane	.10	.05
❑ 28	Tony Longmire	.10	.05
❑ 29	Omar Daal	.10	.05
❑ 30	Kirt Manwaring	.10	.05
❑ 31	Melido Perez	.10	.05
❑ 32	Tim Hulett	.10	.05
❑ 33	Jeff Schwartz	.10	.05
❑ 34	Nolan Ryan	1.50	.70
❑ 35	Jose Guzman	.10	.05
❑ 36	Felix Fermin	.10	.05
❑ 37	Jeff Innis	.10	.05
❑ 38	Brett Mayne	.10	.05
❑ 39	Huck Flener	.10	.05
❑ 40	Jeff Bagwell	.60	.25
❑ 41	Kevin Wickander	.10	.05
❑ 42	Ricky Gutierrez	.10	.05
❑ 43	Pat Mahomes	.10	.05
❑ 44	Jeff King	.10	.05
❑ 45	Cal Eldred	.10	.05
❑ 46	Craig Paquette	.10	.05
❑ 47	Richie Lewis	.10	.05
❑ 48	Tony Phillips	.10	.05
❑ 49	Armando Reynoso	.10	.05
❑ 50	Moises Alou	.30	.14
❑ 51	Manuel Lee	.10	.05
❑ 52	Otis Nixon	.10	.05
❑ 53	Billy Ashley	.10	.05
❑ 54	Mark Whiten	.10	.05
❑ 55	Jeff Russell	.10	.05
❑ 56	Chad Curtis	.10	.05
❑ 57	Kevin Stocker	.10	.05
❑ 58	Mike Jackson	.10	.05
❑ 59	Matt Nokes	.10	.05
❑ 60	Chris Bosio	.10	.05
❑ 61	Damon Buford	.10	.05
❑ 62	Tim Belcher	.10	.05
❑ 63	Glenallen Hill	.10	.05
❑ 64	Bill Wertz	.10	.05
❑ 65	Eddie Murray	.40	.18
❑ 66	Tom Gordon	.10	.05
❑ 67	Alex Gonzalez	.10	.05
❑ 68	Eddie Taubensee	.10	.05
❑ 69	Jacob Brumfield	.10	.05
❑ 70	Andy Benes	.20	.09
❑ 71	Rich Becker	.10	.05
❑ 72	Steve Cooke	.10	.05
❑ 73	Billy Spiers	.10	.05
❑ 74	Scott Brosius	.20	.09
❑ 75	Alan Trammell	.30	.14
❑ 76	Luis Aquino	.10	.05
❑ 77	Jerald Clark	.10	.05
❑ 78	Mel Rojas	.10	.05
❑ 79	Outfield Prospects Billy Masse Stanton Cameron Tim Clark Craig McClure	.30	.14
❑ 80	Jose Canseco	.40	.18
❑ 81	Greg McMichael	.10	.05
❑ 82	Brian Turang	.10	.05
❑ 83	Tom Urbani	.10	.05
❑ 84	Garret Anderson	.40	.18
❑ 85	Tony Pena	.10	.05
❑ 86	Ricky Jordan	.10	.05
❑ 87	Jim Gott	.10	.05
❑ 88	Pat Kelly	.10	.05
❑ 89	Bud Black	.10	.05
❑ 90	Robin Ventura	.20	.09
❑ 91	Rick Sutcliffe	.10	.05
❑ 92	Jose Bautista	.10	.05
❑ 93	Bob Ojeda	.10	.05
❑ 94	Phil Hiatt	.10	.05
❑ 95	Tim Pugh	.10	.05
❑ 96	Randy Knorr	.10	.05
❑ 97	Todd Jones	.10	.05
❑ 98	Ryan Thompson	.10	.05
❑ 99	Tim Mauser	.10	.05
❑ 100	Kirby Puckett	.60	.25
❑ 101	Mark Dewey	.10	.05
❑ 102	B.J. Surhoff	.20	.09
❑ 103	Sterling Hitchcock	.20	.09
❑ 104	Alex Arias	.10	.05
❑ 105	David Wells	.30	.14
❑ 106	Daryl Boston	.10	.05
❑ 107	Mike Stanton	.10	.05
❑ 108	Gary Redus	.10	.05
❑ 109	Delino DeShields	.10	.05
❑ 110	Lee Smith	.20	.09
❑ 111	Greg Litton	.10	.05
❑ 112	Frankie Rodriguez	.10	.05
❑ 113	Russ Springer	.10	.05
❑ 114	Mitch Williams	.10	.05
❑ 115	Eric Karros	.20	.09
❑ 116	Jeff Brantley	.10	.05
❑ 117	Jack Voigt	.10	.05
❑ 118	Jason Bere	.10	.05
❑ 119	Kevin Roberson	.10	.05
❑ 120	Jimmy Key	.20	.09
❑ 121	Reggie Jefferson	.10	.05
❑ 122	Jeromy Burnitz	.20	.09
❑ 123	Billy Brewer	.10	.05
❑ 124	Willie Canate	.10	.05
❑ 125	Greg Swindell	.10	.05
❑ 126	Hal Morris	.10	.05
❑ 127	Brad Ausmus	.10	.05
❑ 128	George Tsamis	.10	.05
❑ 129	Denny Neagle	.20	.09
❑ 130	Pat Listach	.10	.05
❑ 131	Steve Karsay	.10	.05
❑ 132	Bret Barberie	.10	.05
❑ 133	Mark Leiter	.10	.05
❑ 134	Greg Colbrunn	.10	.05
❑ 135	David Nied	.10	.05
❑ 136	Dean Palmer	.20	.09
❑ 137	Steve Avery	.10	.05
❑ 138	Bill Haselman	.10	.05
❑ 139	Tripp Cromer	.10	.05
❑ 140	Frank Viola	.10	.05
❑ 141	Rene Gonzales	.10	.05
❑ 142	Curt Schilling	.20	.09
❑ 143	Tim Wallach	.10	.05
❑ 144	Bobby Munoz	.10	.05
❑ 145	Brady Anderson	.20	.09
❑ 146	Rod Beck	.10	.05
❑ 147	Mike LaValliere	.10	.05
❑ 148	Greg Hibbard	.10	.05
❑ 149	Kenny Lofton	.40	.18
❑ 150	Doc Gooden	.20	.09
❑ 151	Greg Gagne	.10	.05
❑ 152	Ray McDavid	.10	.05
❑ 153	Chris Donnels	.10	.05
❑ 154	Dan Wilson	.10	.05
❑ 155	Todd Stottlemyre	.10	.05
❑ 156	David McCarty	.10	.05
❑ 157	Paul Wagner	.10	.05
❑ 158	Shortstop Prospects Orlando Miller Brandon Wilson Derek Jeter Mike Neal	1.50	.70
❑ 159	Mike Fetters	.10	.05
❑ 160	Scott Lydy	.10	.05
❑ 161	Darrell Whitmore	.10	.05
❑ 162	Bob MacDonald	.10	.05
❑ 163	Vinny Castilla	.20	.09
❑ 164	Denis Boucher	.10	.05
❑ 165	Ivan Rodriguez	.50	.23
❑ 166	Ron Gant	.20	.09
❑ 167	Tim Davis	.10	.05
❑ 168	Steve Dixon	.10	.05
❑ 169	Scott Fletcher	.10	.05
❑ 170	Terry Mulholland	.10	.05
❑ 171	Greg Myers	.10	.05
❑ 172	Brett Butler	.20	.09
❑ 173	Bob Wickman	.10	.05
❑ 174	Dave Martinez	.10	.05
❑ 175	Fernando Valenzuela	.20	.09
❑ 176	Craig Grebeck	.10	.05
❑ 177	Shawn Boskie	.10	.05
❑ 178	Albie Lopez	.10	.05
❑ 179	Butch Huskey	.20	.09
❑ 180	George Brett	.75	.35
❑ 181	Juan Guzman	.10	.05
❑ 182	Eric Anthony	.10	.05
❑ 183	Rob Dibble	.10	.05
❑ 184	Craig Shipley	.10	.05
❑ 185	Kevin Tapani	.10	.05
❑ 186	Marcus Moore	.10	.05
❑ 187	Graeme Lloyd	.10	.05
❑ 188	Mike Bordick	.10	.05
❑ 189	Chris Hammond	.10	.05
❑ 190	Cecil Fielder	.20	.09
❑ 191	Curtis Leskanic	.10	.05
❑ 192	Lou Frazier	.10	.05
❑ 193	Steve Dreyer	.10	.05
❑ 194	Javier Lopez	.30	.14
❑ 195	Edgar Martinez	.20	.09

❑ 196 Allen Watson .10 .05
❑ 197 John Flaherty .10 .05
❑ 198 Kurt Stillwell .10 .05
❑ 199 Danny Jackson .10 .05
❑ 200 Cal Ripken 1.50 .70
❑ 201 Mike Bell FDP .10 .05
❑ 202 Alan Benes FDP .50 .23
❑ 203 Matt Farner FDP .10 .05
❑ 204 Jeff Granger .10 .05
❑ 205 Brooks Kieschnick FDP .20 .09
❑ 206 Jeremy Lee FDP .20 .09
❑ 207 Charles Peterson FDP .20 .09
❑ 208 Alan Rice FDP .20 .09
❑ 209 Billy Wagner FDP .50 .23
❑ 210 Kelly Wunsch FDP .20 .09
❑ 211 Tom Candiotti .10 .05
❑ 212 Domingo Jean .10 .05
❑ 213 John Burkett .10 .05
❑ 214 George Bell .10 .05
❑ 215 Dan Plesac .10 .05
❑ 216 Manny Ramirez .50 .23
❑ 217 Mike Maddux .10 .05
❑ 218 Kevin McReynolds .10 .05
❑ 219 Pat Borders .10 .05
❑ 220 Doug Drabek .10 .05
❑ 221 Larry Luebbers .10 .05
❑ 222 Trevor Hoffman .20 .09
❑ 223 Pat Meares .10 .05
❑ 224 Danny Miceli .10 .05
❑ 225 Greg Vaughn .20 .09
❑ 226 Scott Hemond .10 .05
❑ 227 Pat Rapp .10 .05
❑ 228 Kirk Gibson .20 .09
❑ 229 Lance Painter .10 .05
❑ 230 Larry Walker .40 .18
❑ 231 Benji Gil .10 .05
❑ 232 Mark Wohlers .10 .05
❑ 233 Rich Amaral .10 .05
❑ 234 Eric Pappas .10 .05
❑ 235 Scott Cooper .10 .05
❑ 236 Mike Butcher .10 .05
❑ 237 Outfield Prospects .20 .09
Curtis Pride
Shawn Green
Mark Sweeney
Eddie Davis
❑ 238 Kim Batiste .10 .05
❑ 239 Paul Assenmacher .10 .05
❑ 240 Will Clark .40 .18
❑ 241 Jose Offerman .10 .05
❑ 242 Todd Frohwirth .10 .05
❑ 243 Tim Raines .20 .09
❑ 244 Rick Wilkins .10 .05
❑ 245 Bret Saberhagen .20 .09
❑ 246 Thomas Howard .10 .05
❑ 247 Stan Belinda .10 .05
❑ 248 Rickey Henderson .40 .18
❑ 249 Brian Williams .10 .05
❑ 250 Barry Larkin .30 .14
❑ 251 Jose Valentin .10 .05
❑ 252 Lenny Webster .10 .05
❑ 253 Blas Minor .10 .05
❑ 254 Tim Teufel .10 .05
❑ 255 Bobby Witt .10 .05
❑ 256 Walt Weiss .10 .05
❑ 257 Chad Kreuter .10 .05
❑ 258 Roberto Mejia .10 .05
❑ 259 Cliff Floyd .20 .09
❑ 260 Julio Franco .10 .05
❑ 261 Rafael Belliard .10 .05
❑ 262 Marc Newfield .10 .05
❑ 263 Gerald Perry .10 .05
❑ 264 Ken Ryan .10 .05
❑ 265 Chili Davis .20 .09
❑ 266 Dave West .10 .05
❑ 267 Royce Clayton .10 .05
❑ 268 Pedro Martinez .50 .23
❑ 269 Mark Hutton .10 .05
❑ 270 Frank Thomas 1.25 .55
❑ 271 Brad Pennington .10 .05
❑ 272 Mike Harkey .10 .05
❑ 273 Sandy Alomar .20 .09
❑ 274 Dave Gallagher .10 .05
❑ 275 Wally Joyner .20 .09
❑ 276 Ricky Trlicek .10 .05
❑ 277 Al Osuna .10 .05
❑ 278 Calvin Reese .20 .09
❑ 279 Kevin Higgins .10 .05
❑ 280 Rick Aguilera .10 .05
❑ 281 Orlando Merced .10 .05
❑ 282 Mike Mohler .10 .05
❑ 283 John Jaha .10 .05
❑ 284 Robb Nen .10 .05
❑ 285 Travis Fryman .20 .09
❑ 286 Mark Thompson .10 .05
❑ 287 Mike Lansing .20 .09
❑ 288 Craig Lefferts .10 .05
❑ 289 Damon Berryhill .10 .05
❑ 290 Randy Johnson .40 .18
❑ 291 Jeff Reed .10 .05
❑ 292 Danny Darwin .10 .05
❑ 293 J.T. Snow .20 .09
❑ 294 Tyler Green .10 .05
❑ 295 Chris Hoiles .10 .05
❑ 296 Roger McDowell .10 .05
❑ 297 Spike Owen .10 .05
❑ 298 Salomon Torres .10 .05
❑ 299 Wilson Alvarez .20 .09
❑ 300 Ryne Sandberg .50 .23
❑ 301 Derek Lilliquist .10 .05
❑ 302 Howard Johnson .10 .05
❑ 303 Greg Cadaret .10 .05
❑ 304 Pat Hentgen .20 .09
❑ 305 Craig Biggio .40 .18
❑ 306 Scott Service .10 .05
❑ 307 Melvin Nieves .10 .05
❑ 308 Mike Trombley .10 .05
❑ 309 Carlos Garcia .10 .05
❑ 310 Robin Yount UER .40 .18
(listed with 111 triples in 1988; should be 11)
❑ 311 Marcos Armas .10 .05
❑ 312 Rich Rodriguez .10 .05
❑ 313 Justin Thompson .30 .14
❑ 314 Danny Sheaffer .10 .05
❑ 315 Ken Hill .10 .05
❑ 316 Pitching Prospects .20 .09
Chad Ogea
Duff Brumley
Terrell Wade
Chris Michalak
❑ 317 Cris Carpenter .10 .05
❑ 318 Jeff Blauser .10 .05
❑ 319 Ted Power .10 .05
❑ 320 Ozzie Smith .50 .23
❑ 321 John Dopson .10 .05
❑ 322 Chris Turner .10 .05
❑ 323 Pete Incaviglia .10 .05
❑ 324 Alan Mills .10 .05
❑ 325 Jody Reed .10 .05
❑ 326 Rich Monteleone .10 .05
❑ 327 Mark Carreon .10 .05
❑ 328 Donn Pall .10 .05
❑ 329 Matt Walbeck .10 .05
❑ 330 Charles Nagy .20 .09
❑ 331 Jeff McKnight .10 .05
❑ 332 Jose Lind .10 .05
❑ 333 Mike Timlin .10 .05
❑ 334 Doug Jones .10 .05
❑ 335 Kevin Mitchell .10 .05
❑ 336 Luis Lopez .10 .05
❑ 337 Shane Mack .10 .05
❑ 338 Randy Tomlin .10 .05
❑ 339 Matt Mieske .10 .05
❑ 340 Mark McGwire 2.00 .90
❑ 341 Nigel Wilson .10 .05
❑ 342 Danny Gladden .10 .05
❑ 343 Mo Sanford .10 .05
❑ 344 Sean Berry .10 .05
❑ 345 Kevin Brown .20 .09
❑ 346 Greg Olson .10 .05
❑ 347 Dave Magadan .10 .05
❑ 348 Rene Arocha .10 .05
❑ 349 Carlos Quintana .10 .05
❑ 350 Jim Abbott .20 .09
❑ 351 Gary DiSarcina .10 .05
❑ 352 Ben Rivera .10 .05
❑ 353 Carlos Hernandez .10 .05
❑ 354 Darren Lewis .10 .05
❑ 355 Harold Reynolds .10 .05
❑ 356 Scott Ruffcorn .10 .05
❑ 357 Mark Gubicza .10 .05
❑ 358 Paul Sorrento .10 .05
❑ 359 Anthony Young .10 .05
❑ 360 Mark Grace .30 .14
❑ 361 Rob Butler .10 .05
❑ 362 Kevin Bass .10 .05
❑ 363 Eric Helfand .10 .05
❑ 364 Derek Bell .20 .09
❑ 365 Scott Erickson .20 .09
❑ 366 Al Martin .10 .05
❑ 367 Ricky Bones .10 .05
❑ 368 Jeff Branson .10 .05
❑ 369 Third Base Prospects .40 .18
Luis Ortiz
David Bell
Jason Giambi
George Arias
❑ 370 Benito Santiago .10 .05
(See also 379)
❑ 371 John Doherty .10 .05
❑ 372 Joe Girardi .10 .05
❑ 373 Tim Scott .10 .05
❑ 374 Marvin Freeman .10 .05
❑ 375 Deion Sanders .20 .09
❑ 376 Roger Salkeld .10 .05
❑ 377 Bernard Gilkey .10 .05
❑ 378 Tony Fossas .10 .05
❑ 379 Mark McLemore UER .10 .05
(Card number is 370)
❑ 380 Darren Daulton .20 .09
❑ 381 Chuck Finley .20 .09
❑ 382 Mitch Webster .10 .05
❑ 383 Gerald Williams .10 .05
❑ 384 Frank Thomas AS .60 .25
Fred McGriff AS
❑ 385 Roberto Alomar AS .20 .09
Robby Thompson AS
❑ 386 Wade Boggs AS .20 .09
Matt Williams AS
❑ 387 Cal Ripken AS .50 .23
Jeff Blauser AS
❑ 388 Ken Griffey Jr. AS .50 .23
Len Dykstra AS
❑ 389 Juan Gonzalez AS .40 .18
David Justice AS
❑ 390 George Belle AS .20 .09
Bobby Bonds AS
❑ 391 Mike Stanley AS .40 .18
Mike Piazza AS
❑ 392 Jack McDowell AS .30 .14
Greg Maddux AS
❑ 393 Jimmy Key AS .20 .09
Tom Glavine AS
❑ 394 Jeff Montgomery AS .10 .05
Randy Myers AS
❑ 395 Checklist 1-198 .10 .05
❑ 396 Checklist 199-396 .10 .05
❑ 397 Tim Salmon .40 .18
❑ 398 Todd Benzinger .10 .05
❑ 399 Frank Castillo .10 .05
❑ 400 Ken Griffey Jr. 2.00 .90
❑ 401 John Kruk .20 .09
❑ 402 Dave Telgheder .10 .05
❑ 403 Gary Gaetti .20 .09
❑ 404 Jim Edmonds .40 .18
❑ 405 Don Slaught .10 .05
❑ 406 Jose Oquendo .10 .05
❑ 407 Bruce Ruffin .10 .05
❑ 408 Phil Clark .10 .05
❑ 409 Joe Klink .10 .05
❑ 410 Lou Whitaker .20 .09
❑ 411 Kevin Seitzer .10 .05
❑ 412 Darrin Fletcher .10 .05
❑ 413 Kenny Rogers .10 .05
❑ 414 Bill Pecota .10 .05
❑ 415 Dave Fleming .10 .05
❑ 416 Luis Alicea .10 .05
❑ 417 Paul Quantrill .10 .05
❑ 418 Damion Easley .20 .09
❑ 419 Wes Chamberlain .10 .05
❑ 420 Harold Baines .20 .09
❑ 421 Scott Radinsky .10 .05
❑ 422 Rey Sanchez .10 .05
❑ 423 Junior Ortiz .10 .05

❑ 424 Jeff Kent .20 .09
❑ 425 Brian McRae .10 .05
❑ 426 Ed Sprague .10 .05
❑ 427 Tom Edens .10 .05
❑ 428 Willie Greene .20 .09
❑ 429 Bryan Hickerson .10 .05
❑ 430 Dave Winfield .40 .18
❑ 431 Pedro Astacio .10 .05
❑ 432 Mike Gallego .10 .05
❑ 433 Dave Burba .10 .05
❑ 434 Bob Walk .10 .05
❑ 435 Darryl Hamilton .10 .05
❑ 436 Vince Horsman .10 .05
❑ 437 Bob Natal .10 .05
❑ 438 Mike Henneman .10 .05
❑ 439 Willie Blair .10 .05
❑ 440 Denny Martinez .20 .09
❑ 441 Dan Peltier .10 .05
❑ 442 Tony Tarasco .10 .05
❑ 443 John Cummings .10 .05
❑ 444 Geronimo Pena .10 .05
❑ 445 Aaron Sele .20 .09
❑ 446 Stan Javier .10 .05
❑ 447 Mike Williams .10 .05
❑ 448 First Base Prospects .30 .14
Greg Pirkl
Roberto Petagine
D.J.Boston
Shawn Wooten
❑ 449 Jim Poole .10 .05
❑ 450 Carlos Baerga .20 .09
❑ 451 Bob Scanlan .10 .05
❑ 452 Lance Johnson .10 .05
❑ 453 Eric Hillman .10 .05
❑ 454 Keith Miller .10 .05
❑ 455 Dave Stewart .20 .09
❑ 456 Pete Harnisch .10 .05
❑ 457 Roberto Kelly .10 .05
❑ 458 Tim Worrell .10 .05
❑ 459 Pedro Munoz .10 .05
❑ 460 Orel Hershiser .20 .09
❑ 461 Randy Velarde .10 .05
❑ 462 Trevor Wilson .10 .05
❑ 463 Jerry Goff .10 .05
❑ 464 Bill Wegman .10 .05
❑ 465 Dennis Eckersley .20 .09
❑ 466 Jeff Conine .20 .09
❑ 467 Joe Boever .10 .05
❑ 468 Dante Bichette .20 .09
❑ 469 Jeff Shaw .10 .05
❑ 470 Rafael Palmeiro .30 .14
❑ 471 Phil Leftwich .10 .05
❑ 472 Jay Buhner .20 .09
❑ 473 Bob Tewksbury .10 .05
❑ 474 Tim Naehring .10 .05
❑ 475 Tom Glavine .40 .18
❑ 476 Dave Hollins .10 .05
❑ 477 Arthur Rhodes .10 .05
❑ 478 Joey Cora .20 .09
❑ 479 Mike Morgan .10 .05
❑ 480 Albert Belle .50 .23
❑ 481 John Franco .20 .09
❑ 482 Hipolito Pichardo .10 .05
❑ 483 Duane Ward .10 .05
❑ 484 Luis Gonzalez .10 .05
❑ 485 Joe Oliver .10 .05
❑ 486 Wally Whitehurst .10 .05
❑ 487 Mike Benjamin .10 .05
❑ 488 Eric Davis .20 .09
❑ 489 Scott Kamieniecki .10 .05
❑ 490 Kent Hrbek .20 .09
❑ 491 John Hope .10 .05
❑ 492 Jesse Orosco .10 .05
❑ 493 Troy Neel .10 .05
❑ 494 Ryan Bowen .10 .05
❑ 495 Mickey Tettleton .10 .05
❑ 496 Chris Jones .10 .05
❑ 497 John Wetteland .20 .09
❑ 498 David Hulse .10 .05
❑ 499 Greg Maddux 1.25 .55
❑ 500 Bo Jackson .20 .09
❑ 501 Donovan Osborne .10 .05
❑ 502 Mike Greenwell .10 .05
❑ 503 Steve Frey .10 .05
❑ 504 Jim Eisenreich .10 .05
❑ 505 Robby Thompson .10 .05
❑ 506 Leo Gomez .10 .05
❑ 507 Dave Staton .10 .05
❑ 508 Wayne Kirby .10 .05
❑ 509 Tim Bogar .10 .05
❑ 510 David Cone .30 .14
❑ 511 Devon White .20 .09
❑ 512 Xavier Hernandez .10 .05
❑ 513 Tim Costo .10 .05
❑ 514 Gene Harris .10 .05
❑ 515 Jack McDowell .10 .05
❑ 516 Kevin Gross .10 .05
❑ 517 Scott Leius .10 .05
❑ 518 Lloyd McClendon .10 .05
❑ 519 Alex Diaz .10 .05
❑ 520 Wade Boggs .40 .18
❑ 521 Bob Welch .10 .05
❑ 522 Henry Cotto .10 .05
❑ 523 Mike Moore .10 .05
❑ 524 Tim Laker .10 .05
❑ 525 Andres Galarraga .40 .18
❑ 526 Jamie Moyer .10 .05
❑ 527 Second Base Prospects .20 .09
Norberto Martin
Ruben Santana
Jason Hardtke
Chris Sexton
❑ 528 Sid Bream .10 .05
❑ 529 Erik Hanson .10 .05
❑ 530 Ray Lankford .20 .09
❑ 531 Rob Deer .10 .05
❑ 532 Rod Correia .10 .05
❑ 533 Roger Mason .10 .05
❑ 534 Mike Devereaux .10 .05
❑ 535 Jeff Montgomery .10 .05
❑ 536 Dwight Smith .10 .05
❑ 537 Jeremy Hernandez .10 .05
❑ 538 Ellis Burks .20 .09
❑ 539 Bobby Jones .10 .05
❑ 540 Paul Molitor .40 .18
❑ 541 Jeff Juden .10 .05
❑ 542 Chris Sabo .10 .05
❑ 543 Larry Casian .10 .05
❑ 544 Jeff Gardner .10 .05
❑ 545 Ramon Martinez .20 .09
❑ 546 Paul O'Neill .20 .09
❑ 547 Steve Hosey .10 .05
❑ 548 Dave Nilsson .10 .05
❑ 549 Ron Darling .10 .05
❑ 550 Matt Williams .30 .14
❑ 551 Jack Armstrong .10 .05
❑ 552 Bill Krueger .10 .05
❑ 553 Freddie Benavides .10 .05
❑ 554 Jeff Fassero .10 .05
❑ 555 Chuck Knoblauch .40 .18
❑ 556 Guillermo Velasquez .10 .05
❑ 557 Joel Johnston .10 .05
❑ 558 Tom Lampkin .10 .05
❑ 559 Todd Van Poppel .10 .05
❑ 560 Gary Sheffield .40 .18
❑ 561 Skeeter Barnes .10 .05
❑ 562 Darren Holmes .10 .05
❑ 563 John Vander Wal .10 .05
❑ 564 Mike Ignasiak .10 .05
❑ 565 Fred McGriff .30 .14
❑ 566 Luis Polonia .10 .05
❑ 567 Mike Perez .10 .05
❑ 568 John Valentin .20 .09
❑ 569 Mike Felder .10 .05
❑ 570 Tommy Greene .10 .05
❑ 571 David Segui .20 .09
❑ 572 Roberto Hernandez .10 .05
❑ 573 Steve Wilson .10 .05
❑ 574 Willie McGee .20 .09
❑ 575 Randy Myers .10 .05
❑ 576 Darrin Jackson .10 .05
❑ 577 Eric Plunk .10 .05
❑ 578 Mike Macfarlane .10 .05
❑ 579 Doug Brocail .10 .05
❑ 580 Steve Finley .20 .09
❑ 581 John Roper .10 .05
❑ 582 Danny Cox .10 .05
❑ 583 Chip Hale .10 .05
❑ 584 Scott Bullett .10 .05
❑ 585 Kevin Reimer .10 .05
❑ 586 Brent Gates .10 .05
❑ 587 Matt Turner .10 .05
❑ 588 Rich Rowland .10 .05
❑ 589 Kent Bottenfield .10 .05
❑ 590 Marquis Grissom .20 .09
❑ 591 Doug Strange .10 .05
❑ 592 Jay Howell .10 .05
❑ 593 Omar Vizquel .20 .09
❑ 594 Rheal Cormier .10 .05
❑ 595 Andre Dawson .30 .14
❑ 596 Hilly Hathaway .10 .05
❑ 597 Todd Pratt .10 .05
❑ 598 Mike Mussina .40 .18
❑ 599 Alex Fernandez .10 .05
❑ 600 Don Mattingly .60 .25
❑ 601 Frank Thomas ST .60 .25
❑ 602 Ryne Sandberg ST .30 .14
❑ 603 Wade Boggs ST .40 .18
❑ 604 Cal Ripken ST .75 .35
❑ 605 Barry Bonds ST .40 .18
❑ 606 Ken Griffey Jr. ST 1.00 .45
❑ 607 Kirby Puckett ST .40 .18
❑ 608 Darren Daulton ST .10 .05
❑ 609 Paul Molitor ST .20 .09
❑ 610 Terry Steinbach .20 .09
❑ 611 Todd Worrell .10 .05
❑ 612 Jim Thome .50 .23
❑ 613 Chuck McElroy .10 .05
❑ 614 John Habyan .10 .05
❑ 615 Sid Fernandez .10 .05
❑ 616 Outfield Prospects .20 .09
Eddie Zambrano
Glenn Murray
Chad Mottola
Jermaine Allensworth
❑ 617 Steve Bedrosian .10 .05
❑ 618 Rob Ducey .10 .05
❑ 619 Tom Browning .10 .05
❑ 620 Tony Gwynn 1.00 .45
❑ 621 Carl Willis .10 .05
❑ 622 Kevin Young .10 .05
❑ 623 Rafael Novoa .10 .05
❑ 624 Jerry Browne .10 .05
❑ 625 Charlie Hough .10 .05
❑ 626 Chris Gomez .10 .05
❑ 627 Steve Reed .10 .05
❑ 628 Kirk Rueter .10 .05
❑ 629 Matt Whiteside .10 .05
❑ 630 David Justice .40 .18
❑ 631 Brad Holman .10 .05
❑ 632 Brian Jordan .20 .09
❑ 633 Scott Bankhead .10 .05
❑ 634 Torey Lovullo .10 .05
❑ 635 Len Dykstra .20 .09
❑ 636 Ben McDonald .10 .05
❑ 637 Steve Howe .10 .05
❑ 638 Jose Vizcaino .10 .05
❑ 639 Bill Swift .10 .05
❑ 640 Darryl Strawberry .20 .09
❑ 641 Steve Farr .10 .05
❑ 642 Tom Kramer .10 .05
❑ 643 Joe Orsulak .10 .05
❑ 644 Tom Henke .10 .05
❑ 645 Joe Carter .20 .09
❑ 646 Ken Caminiti .30 .14
❑ 647 Reggie Sanders .20 .09
❑ 648 Andy Ashby .10 .05
❑ 649 Derek Parks .10 .05
❑ 650 Andy Van Slyke .20 .09
❑ 651 Juan Bell .10 .05
❑ 652 Roger Smithberg .10 .05
❑ 653 Chuck Carr .10 .05
❑ 654 Bill Gullickson .10 .05
❑ 655 Charlie Hayes .10 .05
❑ 656 Chris Nabholz .10 .05
❑ 657 Karl Rhodes .10 .05
❑ 658 Pete Smith .10 .05
❑ 659 Bret Boone .20 .09
❑ 660 Gregg Jefferies .10 .05
❑ 661 Bob Zupcic .10 .05
❑ 662 Steve Sax .10 .05
❑ 663 Mariano Duncan .10 .05
❑ 664 Jeff Tackett .10 .05
❑ 665 Mark Lengston .10 .05
❑ 666 Steve Buechele .10 .05

❑ 667 Candy Maldonado	.10	.05
❑ 668 Woody Williams	.10	.05
❑ 669 Tim Wakefield	.20	.09
❑ 670 Danny Tartabull	.10	.05
❑ 671 Charlie O'Brien	.10	.05
❑ 672 Felix Jose	.10	.05
❑ 673 Bobby Ayala	.10	.05
❑ 674 Scott Servais	.10	.05
❑ 675 Roberto Alomar	.40	.18
❑ 676 Pedro Martinez	.40	.18
❑ 677 Eddie Guardado	.10	.05
❑ 678 Mark Lewis	.10	.05
❑ 679 Jaime Navarro	.10	.05
❑ 680 Ruben Sierrra	.10	.05
❑ 681 Rick Renteria	.10	.05
❑ 682 Storm Davis	.10	.05
❑ 683 Cory Snyder	.10	.05
❑ 684 Ron Karkovice	.10	.05
❑ 685 Juan Gonzalez	1.00	.45
❑ 686 Catchers Prospects Chris Howard Carlos Delgado Jason Kendall Paul Bako	.40	.18
❑ 687 John Smoltz	.20	.09
❑ 688 Brian Dorsett	.10	.05
❑ 689 Omar Olivares	.10	.05
❑ 690 Mo Vaughn	.50	.23
❑ 691 Joe Grahe	.10	.05
❑ 692 Mickey Morandini	.10	.05
❑ 693 Tino Martinez	.40	.18
❑ 694 Brian Barnes	.10	.05
❑ 695 Mike Stanley	.10	.05
❑ 696 Mark Clark	.10	.05
❑ 697 Dave Hansen	.10	.05
❑ 698 Willie Wilson	.10	.05
❑ 699 Pete Schourek	.10	.05
❑ 700 Barry Bonds	.50	.23
❑ 701 Kevin Appier	.20	.09
❑ 702 Tony Fernandez	.10	.05
❑ 703 Darryl Kile	.20	.09
❑ 704 Archi Cianfrocco	.10	.05
❑ 705 Jose Rijo	.10	.05
❑ 706 Brian Harper	.10	.05
❑ 707 Zane Smith	.10	.05
❑ 708 Dave Henderson	.10	.05
❑ 709 Angel Miranda UER (no Topps logo on back)	.10	.05
❑ 710 Orestes Destrade	.10	.05
❑ 711 Greg Gohr	.10	.05
❑ 712 Eric Young	.10	.05
❑ 713 Relief Pitchers Prospects Todd Williams Ron Watson Kirk Bullinger Mike Welch	.20	.09
❑ 714 Tim Spehr	.10	.05
❑ 715 Hank Aaron	.50	.23
❑ 716 Nate Minchey	.10	.05
❑ 717 Mike Blowers	.10	.05
❑ 718 Kent Mercker	.10	.05
❑ 719 Tom Pagnozzi	.10	.05
❑ 720 Roger Clemens	.75	.35
❑ 721 Eduardo Perez	.10	.05
❑ 722 Milt Thompson	.10	.05
❑ 723 Gregg Olson	.10	.05
❑ 724 Kirk McCaskill	.10	.05
❑ 725 Sammy Sosa	1.00	.45
❑ 726 Alvaro Espinoza	.10	.05
❑ 727 Henry Rodriguez	.20	.09
❑ 728 Jim Leyritz	.20	.09
❑ 729 Steve Scarsone	.10	.05
❑ 730 Bobby Bonilla	.20	.09
❑ 731 Chris Gwynn	.10	.05
❑ 732 Al Leiter	.20	.09
❑ 733 Bip Roberts	.10	.05
❑ 734 Mark Portugal	.10	.05
❑ 735 Terry Pendleton	.10	.05
❑ 736 Dave Valle	.10	.05
❑ 737 Paul Kilgus	.10	.05
❑ 738 Greg A. Harris	.10	.05
❑ 739 Jon Ratliff DP	.20	.09
❑ 740 Kirk Presley DP	.20	.09
❑ 741 Josue Estrada DP	.20	.09
❑ 742 Wayne Gomes DP	.10	.05
❑ 743 Pat Watkins DP	.20	.09
❑ 744 Jamey Wright DP	.20	.09
❑ 745 Jay Powell DP	.20	.09
❑ 746 Ryan McGuire DP	.20	.09
❑ 747 Marc Barcelo DP	.20	.09
❑ 748 Sloan Smith DP	.20	.09
❑ 749 John Wasdin DP	.20	.09
❑ 750 Marc Vlades	.10	.05
❑ 751 Dan Ehler DP	.20	.09
❑ 752 Andre King DP	.10	.05
❑ 753 Greg Keagle DP	.10	.05
❑ 754 Jason Myers DP	.20	.09
❑ 755 Dax Winslett DP	.20	.09
❑ 756 Casey Whitten DP	.20	.09
❑ 757 Tony Fuduric DP	.10	.05
❑ 758 Greg Norton DP	.20	.09
❑ 759 Jeff D'Amico DP	.20	.09
❑ 760 Ryan Hancock DP	.10	.05
❑ 761 David Cooper DP	.10	.05
❑ 762 Kevin Orie DP	.40	.18
❑ 763 John O'Donoghue Mike Oquist	.10	.05
❑ 764 Cory Bailey Scott Hatteberg	.10	.05
❑ 765 Mark Holzemer Paul Swingle	.10	.05
❑ 766 James Baldwin Rod Bolton	.20	.09
❑ 767 Jerry Di Poto Julian Tavarez	.20	.09
❑ 768 Danny Bautista Sean Bergman	.10	.05
❑ 769 Bob Hamelin Joe Vitiello	.10	.05
❑ 770 Mark Kiefer Troy O'Leary	.20	.09
❑ 771 Denny Hocking Oscar Munoz	.20	.09
❑ 772 Russ Davis Brien Taylor	.20	.09
❑ 773 Kyle Abbott Miguel Jimenez	.10	.05
❑ 774 Kevin King Eric Plantenberg	.10	.05
❑ 775 Jon Shave Desi Wilson	.10	.05
❑ 776 Domingo Cedeno Paul Spoljaric	.10	.05
❑ 777 Chipper Jones Ryan Klesko	1.50	.70
❑ 778 Steve Trachsel Turk Wendell	.10	.05
❑ 779 Johnny Ruffin Jerry Spradlin	.10	.05
❑ 780 Jason Bates John Burke	.10	.05
❑ 781 Carl Everett Dave Weathers	.20	.09
❑ 782 Gary Mota James Mouton	.20	.09
❑ 783 Raul Mondesi Ben Van Ryn	.40	.18
❑ 784 Gabe White Rondell White	.30	.14
❑ 785 Brook Fordyce Bill Pulsipher	.20	.09
❑ 786 Kevin Foster Gene Schall	.10	.05
❑ 787 Rich Aude Midre Cummings	.10	.05
❑ 788 Brian Barber Rich Batchelor	.20	.09
❑ 789 Brian Johnson Scott Sanders	.10	.05
❑ 790 Ricky Faneyte J.R. Phillips	.10	.05
❑ 791 Checklist 3	.10	.05
❑ 792 Checklist 4	.10	.05

1994 Topps Black Gold

	MINT	NRMT
COMPLETE SET (44)	25.00	11.00
COMPLETE SERIES 1 (22)	15.00	6.75
COMPLETE SERIES 2 (22)	10.00	4.50

COMMON CARD (1-44)	.25	.11
❑ 1 Roberto Alomar	.75	.35
❑ 2 Carlos Baerga	.40	.18
❑ 3 Albert Belle	.75	.35
❑ 4 Joe Carter	.40	.18
❑ 5 Cecil Fielder	.40	.18
❑ 6 Travis Fryman	.40	.18
❑ 7 Juan Gonzalez	2.00	.90
❑ 8 Ken Griffey Jr.	4.00	1.80
❑ 9 Chris Hoiles	.25	.11
❑ 10 Randy Johnson	.75	.35
❑ 11 Kenny Lofton	.75	.35
❑ 12 Jack McDowell	.25	.11
❑ 13 Paul Molitor	.75	.35
❑ 14 Jeff Montgomery	.25	.11
❑ 15 John Olerud	.40	.18
❑ 16 Rafael Palmeiro	.50	.23
❑ 17 Kirby Puckett	1.50	.70
❑ 18 Cal Ripken	3.00	1.35
❑ 19 Tim Salmon	.75	.35
❑ 20 Mike Stanley	.25	.11
❑ 21 Frank Thomas	2.50	1.10
❑ 22 Robin Ventura	.40	.18
❑ 23 Jeff Bagwell	1.25	.55
❑ 24 Jay Bell	.40	.18
❑ 25 Craig Biggio	.75	.35
❑ 26 Jeff Blauser	.25	.11
❑ 27 Barry Bonds	.75	.35
❑ 28 Darren Daulton	.40	.18
❑ 29 Len Dykstra	.40	.18
❑ 30 Andres Galarraga	.75	.35
❑ 31 Ron Gant	.40	.18
❑ 32 Tom Glavine	.75	.35
❑ 33 Mark Grace	.50	.23
❑ 34 Marquis Grissom	.40	.18
❑ 35 Gregg Jefferies	.25	.11
❑ 36 David Justice	.75	.35
❑ 37 John Kruk	.40	.18
❑ 38 Greg Maddux	2.50	1.10
❑ 39 Fred McGriff	.50	.23
❑ 40 Randy Myers	.25	.11
❑ 41 Mike Piazza	2.50	1.10
❑ 42 Sammy Sosa	2.00	.90
❑ 43 Robby Thompson	.25	.11
❑ 44 Matt Williams	.50	.23
❑ A Winner A 1-11	1.00	.45
❑ B Winner B 12-22	1.00	.45
❑ C Winner C 23-33	1.00	.45
❑ D Winner D 34-44	1.00	.45
❑ AB Winner AB 1-22	2.00	.90
❑ CD Winner CD 23-44	2.00	.90
❑ ABCD Winner ABCD 1-44	4.00	1.80

1994 Topps Traded

	MINT	NRMT
COMP.FACT.SET (140)	80.00	36.00
COMPLETE SET (132)	75.00	34.00
COMMON CARD (1T-132T)	.15	.07
❑ 1T Paul Wilson	.25	.11
❑ 2T Bill Taylor	.15	.07
❑ 3T Dan Wilson	.15	.07
❑ 4T Mark Smith	.15	.07
❑ 5T Toby Borland	.15	.07
❑ 6T Dave Clark	.15	.07
❑ 7T Denny Martinez	.25	.11

- ❑ 8T Dave Gallagher .15 .07
- ❑ 9T Josias Manzanillo .15 .07
- ❑ 10T Brian Anderson 1.50 .70
- ❑ 11T Damon Berryhill .15 .07
- ❑ 12T Alex Cole .15 .07
- ❑ 13T Jacob Shumate .25 .11
- ❑ 14T Oddibe McDowell .15 .07
- ❑ 15T Willie Banks .15 .07
- ❑ 16T Jerry Browne .15 .07
- ❑ 17T Donnie Elliott .15 .07
- ❑ 18T Ellis Burks .25 .11
- ❑ 19T Chuck McElroy .15 .07
- ❑ 20T Luis Polonia .15 .07
- ❑ 21T Brian Harper .15 .07
- ❑ 22T Mark Portugal .15 .07
- ❑ 23T Dave Henderson .15 .07
- ❑ 24T Mark Acre .15 .07
- ❑ 25T Julio Franco .15 .07
- ❑ 26T Darren Hall .15 .07
- ❑ 27T Eric Anthony .15 .07
- ❑ 28T Sid Fernandez .15 .07
- ❑ 29T Rusty Greer 8.00 3.60
- ❑ 30T Riccardo Ingram .15 .07
- ❑ 31T Gabe White .15 .07
- ❑ 32T Tim Belcher .15 .07
- ❑ 33T Terrence Long 1.50 .70
- ❑ 34T Mark Dalesandro .15 .07
- ❑ 35T Mike Kelly .15 .07
- ❑ 36T Jack Morris .25 .11
- ❑ 37T Jeff Brantley .15 .07
- ❑ 38T Larry Barnes .25 .11
- ❑ 39T Brian R. Hunter .15 .07
- ❑ 40T Otis Nixon .15 .07
- ❑ 41T Bret Wagner .15 .07
- ❑ 42T Pedro Martinez TR .30 .14
  Delino Deshields
- ❑ 43T Heathcliff Slocumb .15 .07
- ❑ 44T Ben Grieve 50.00 22.00
- ❑ 45T John Hudek .15 .07
- ❑ 46T Shawon Dunston .15 .07
- ❑ 47T Greg Colbrunn .15 .07
- ❑ 48T Joey Hamilton .50 .23
- ❑ 49T Marvin Freeman .15 .07
- ❑ 50T Terry Mulholland .15 .07
- ❑ 51T Keith Mitchell .15 .07
- ❑ 52T Dwight Smith .15 .07
- ❑ 53T Shawn Boskie .15 .07
- ❑ 54T Kevin Witt 8.00 3.60
- ❑ 55T Ron Gant .25 .11
- ❑ 56T 1994 Prospects 1.50 .70
  Trenidad Hubbard
  Jason Schmidt
  Larry Sutton
  Stephen Larkin
- ❑ 57T Jody Reed .15 .07
- ❑ 58T Rick Helling .25 .11
- ❑ 59T John Powell .25 .11
- ❑ 60T Eddie Murray .50 .23
- ❑ 61T Joe Hall .15 .07
- ❑ 62T Jorge Fabregas .15 .07
- ❑ 63T Mike Mordecai .15 .07
- ❑ 64T Ed Vosberg .15 .07
- ❑ 65T Rickey Henderson .50 .23
- ❑ 66T Tim Grieve .15 .07
- ❑ 67T Jon Lieber .15 .07
- ❑ 68T Chris Howard .15 .07
- ❑ 69T Matt Walbeck .15 .07
- ❑ 70T Chan Ho Park 10.00 4.50
- ❑ 71T Bryan Eversgerd .15 .07
- ❑ 72T John Dettmer .15 .07
- ❑ 73T Erik Hanson .15 .07
- ❑ 74T Mike Thurman .15 .07
- ❑ 75T Bobby Ayala .15 .07
- ❑ 76T Rafael Palmeiro .30 .14
- ❑ 77T Bret Boone .25 .11
- ❑ 78T Paul Shuey .15 .07
- ❑ 79T Kevin Foster .15 .07
- ❑ 80T Dave Magadan .15 .07
- ❑ 81T Bip Roberts .15 .07
- ❑ 82T Howard Johnson .15 .07
- ❑ 83T Xavier Hernandez .15 .07
- ❑ 84T Ross Powell .15 .07
- ❑ 85T Doug Million .15 .07
- ❑ 86T Geronimo Berroa .15 .07
- ❑ 87T Mark Farris .25 .11
- ❑ 88T Butch Henry .15 .07
- ❑ 89T Junior Felix .15 .07
- ❑ 90T Bo Jackson .25 .11
- ❑ 91T Hector Carrasco .15 .07
- ❑ 92T Charlie O'Brien .15 .07
- ❑ 93T Omar Vizquel .25 .11
- ❑ 94T David Segui .25 .11
- ❑ 95T Dustin Hermanson .25 .11
- ❑ 96T Gar Finnvold .15 .07
- ❑ 97T Dave Stevens .15 .07
- ❑ 98T Corey Pointer .25 .11
- ❑ 99T Felix Fermin .15 .07
- ❑ 100T Lee Smith .25 .11
- ❑ 101T Reid Ryan .25 .11
- ❑ 102T Bobby Munoz .15 .07
- ❑ 103T Deion Sanders TR .25 .11
  Roberto Kelly
- ❑ 104T Turner Ward .15 .07
- ❑ 105T W.VanLandingham .15 .07
- ❑ 106T Vince Coleman .15 .07
- ❑ 107T Stan Javier .15 .07
- ❑ 108T Darrin Jackson .15 .07
- ❑ 109T C.J. Nitkowski .15 .07
- ❑ 110T Anthony Young .15 .07
- ❑ 111T Kurt Miller .15 .07
- ❑ 112T Paul Konerko 20.00 9.00
- ❑ 113T Walt Weiss .15 .07
- ❑ 114T Daryl Boston .15 .07
- ❑ 115T Will Clark .50 .23
- ❑ 116T Matt Smith .25 .11
- ❑ 117T Mark Leiter .15 .07
- ❑ 118T Gregg Olson .15 .07
- ❑ 119T Tony Pena .15 .07
- ❑ 120T Jose Vizcaino .15 .07
- ❑ 121T Rick White .15 .07
- ❑ 122T Rich Rowland .15 .07
- ❑ 123T Jeff Reboulet .15 .07
- ❑ 124T Greg Hibbard .15 .07
- ❑ 125T Chris Sabo .15 .07
- ❑ 126T Doug Jones .15 .07
- ❑ 127T Tony Fernandez .15 .07
- ❑ 128T Carlos Reyes .15 .07
- ❑ 129T Kevin Brown .50 .23
- ❑ 130T Ryne Sandberg 1.00 .45
  Farewell
- ❑ 131T Ryne Sandberg 1.00 .45
  Farewell
- ❑ 132T Checklist 1-132 .15 .07

1994 Topps Traded Finest Inserts

	MINT	NRMT
COMPLETE SET (8)	5.00	2.20
COMMON CARD (1-8)	.30	.14

- ❑ 1 Greg Maddux 1.25 .55
- ❑ 2 Mike Piazza 1.25 .55
- ❑ 3 Matt Williams .30 .14
- ❑ 4 Raul Mondesi .40 .18
- ❑ 5 Ken Griffey Jr. 2.00 .90
- ❑ 6 Kenny Lofton .40 .18
- ❑ 7 Frank Thomas 1.25 .55
- ❑ 8 Manny Ramirez .40 .18

1995 Topps

	MINT	NRMT
COMPLETE SET (660)	50.00	22.00
COMP.HOBBY SET (677)	80.00	36.00
COMP.RETAIL SET (677)	80.00	36.00
COMPLETE SERIES 1 (396)	25.00	11.00
COMPLETE SERIES 2 (264)	25.00	11.00
COMMON CARD (1-660)	.15	.07

- ❑ 1 Frank Thomas 2.00 .90
- ❑ 2 Mickey Morandini .15 .07
- ❑ 3 Babe Ruth 100th B-Day 2.00 .90
- ❑ 4 Scott Cooper .15 .07
- ❑ 5 David Cone .40 .18
- ❑ 6 Jacob Shumate .15 .07
- ❑ 7 Trevor Hoffman .30 .14
- ❑ 8 Shane Mack .15 .07
- ❑ 9 Delino DeShields .15 .07
- ❑ 10 Matt Williams .30 .14
- ❑ 11 Sammy Sosa 1.50 .70
- ❑ 12 Gary DiSarcina .15 .07
- ❑ 13 Kenny Rogers .15 .07
- ❑ 14 Jose Vizcaino .15 .07
- ❑ 15 Lou Whitaker .30 .14
- ❑ 16 Ron Darling .15 .07
- ❑ 17 Dave Nilsson .15 .07
- ❑ 18 Chris Hammond .15 .07
- ❑ 19 Sid Bream .15 .07
- ❑ 20 Denny Martinez .30 .14
- ❑ 21 Orlando Merced .15 .07
- ❑ 22 John Wetteland .30 .14
- ❑ 23 Mike Devereaux .15 .07
- ❑ 24 Rene Arocha .15 .07
- ❑ 25 Jay Buhner .30 .14
- ❑ 26 Darren Holmes .15 .07
- ❑ 27 Hal Morris .15 .07
- ❑ 28 Brian Buchanan .30 .14
- ❑ 29 Keith Miller .15 .07
- ❑ 30 Paul Molitor .60 .25
- ❑ 31 Dave West .15 .07
- ❑ 32 Tony Tarasco .15 .07
- ❑ 33 Scott Sanders .15 .07
- ❑ 34 Eddie Zambrano .15 .07
- ❑ 35 Ricky Bones .15 .07
- ❑ 36 John Valentin .30 .14
- ❑ 37 Kevin Tapani .15 .07
- ❑ 38 Tim Wallach .15 .07
- ❑ 39 Darren Lewis .15 .07
- ❑ 40 Travis Fryman .30 .14

❑ 41 Mark Leiter .15 .07
❑ 42 Jose Bautista .15 .07
❑ 43 Pete Smith .15 .07
❑ 44 Bret Barberie .15 .07
❑ 45 Dennis Eckersley .30 .14
❑ 46 Ken Hill .15 .07
❑ 47 Chad Ogea .15 .07
❑ 48 Pete Harnisch .15 .07
❑ 49 James Baldwin .30 .14
❑ 50 Mike Mussina .60 .25
❑ 51 Al Martin .15 .07
❑ 52 Mark Thompson .15 .07
❑ 53 Matt Smith .15 .07
❑ 54 Joey Hamilton .30 .14
❑ 55 Edgar Martinez .30 .14
❑ 56 John Smiley .15 .07
❑ 57 Rey Sanchez .15 .07
❑ 58 Mike Timlin .15 .07
❑ 59 Ricky Bottalico .30 .14
❑ 60 Jim Abbott .30 .14
❑ 61 Mike Kelly .15 .07
❑ 62 Brian Jordan .30 .14
❑ 63 Ken Ryan .15 .07
❑ 64 Matt Mieske .15 .07
❑ 65 Rick Aguilera .15 .07
❑ 66 Ismael Valdes .30 .14
❑ 67 Royce Clayton .15 .07
❑ 68 Junior Felix .15 .07
❑ 69 Harold Reynolds .15 .07
❑ 70 Juan Gonzalez 1.50 .70
❑ 71 Kelly Stinnett .15 .07
❑ 72 Carlos Reyes .15 .07
❑ 73 Dave Weathers .15 .07
❑ 74 Mel Rojas .15 .07
❑ 75 Doug Drabek .15 .07
❑ 76 Charles Nagy .30 .14
❑ 77 Tim Raines .30 .14
❑ 78 Midre Cummings .15 .07
❑ 79 First Base Prospects .40 .18
Gene Schall
Scott Talanoa
Harold Williams
Ray Brown
❑ 80 Rafael Palmeiro .40 .18
❑ 81 Charlie Hayes .15 .07
❑ 82 Ray Lankford .30 .14
❑ 83 Tim Davis .15 .07
❑ 84 C.J. Nitkowski .15 .07
❑ 85 Andy Ashby .15 .07
❑ 86 Gerald Williams .15 .07
❑ 87 Terry Shumpert .15 .07
❑ 88 Heathcliff Slocumb .15 .07
❑ 89 Domingo Cedeno .15 .07
❑ 90 Mark Grace .40 .18
❑ 91 Brad Woodall .15 .07
❑ 92 Gar Finnvold .15 .07
❑ 93 Jaime Navarro .15 .07
❑ 94 Carlos Hernandez .15 .07
❑ 95 Mark Langston .15 .07
❑ 96 Chuck Carr .15 .07
❑ 97 Mike Gardiner .15 .07
❑ 98 Dave McCarty .15 .07
❑ 99 Cris Carpenter .15 .07
❑ 100 Barry Bonds .75 .35
❑ 101 David Segui .30 .14
❑ 102 Scott Brosius .30 .14
❑ 103 Mariano Duncan .15 .07
❑ 104 Kenny Lofton .60 .25
❑ 105 Ken Caminiti .40 .18
❑ 106 Darrin Jackson .15 .07
❑ 107 Jim Poole .15 .07
❑ 108 Wil Cordero .15 .07
❑ 109 Danny Miceli .15 .07
❑ 110 Walt Weiss .15 .07
❑ 111 Tom Pagnozzi .15 .07
❑ 112 Terrence Long .30 .14
❑ 113 Bret Boone .30 .14
❑ 114 Daryl Boston .15 .07
❑ 115 Wally Joyner .30 .14
❑ 116 Rob Butler .15 .07
❑ 117 Rafael Belliard .15 .07
❑ 118 Luis Lopez .15 .07
❑ 119 Tony Fossas .15 .07
❑ 120 Len Dykstra .30 .14
❑ 121 Mike Morgan .15 .07
❑ 122 Denny Hocking .15 .07
❑ 123 Kevin Gross .15 .07
❑ 124 Todd Benzinger .15 .07
❑ 125 John Doherty .15 .07
❑ 126 Eduardo Perez .15 .07
❑ 127 Dan Smith .15 .07
❑ 128 Joe Orsulak .15 .07
❑ 129 Brent Gates .15 .07
❑ 130 Jeff Conine .30 .14
❑ 131 Doug Henry .15 .07
❑ 132 Paul Sorrento .15 .07
❑ 133 Mike Hampton .15 .07
❑ 134 Tim Spehr .15 .07
❑ 135 Julio Franco .15 .07
❑ 136 Mike Dyer .15 .07
❑ 137 Chris Sabo .15 .07
❑ 138 Rheal Cormier .15 .07
❑ 139 Paul Konerko 1.50 .70
❑ 140 Dante Bichette .30 .14
❑ 141 Chuck McElroy .15 .07
❑ 142 Mike Stanley .15 .07
❑ 143 Bob Hamelin .15 .07
❑ 144 Tommy Greene .15 .07
❑ 145 John Smoltz .30 .14
❑ 146 Ed Sprague .15 .07
❑ 147 Ray McDavid .15 .07
❑ 148 Otis Nixon .15 .07
❑ 149 Turk Wendell .15 .07
❑ 150 Chris James .15 .07
❑ 151 Derek Parks .15 .07
❑ 152 Jose Offerman .15 .07
❑ 153 Tony Clark .60 .25
❑ 154 Chad Curtis .15 .07
❑ 155 Mark Portugal .15 .07
❑ 156 Bill Pulsipher .15 .07
❑ 157 Troy Neel .15 .07
❑ 158 Dave Winfield .60 .25
❑ 159 Bill Wegman .15 .07
❑ 160 Benito Santiago .15 .07
❑ 161 Jose Mesa .15 .07
❑ 162 Luis Gonzalez .15 .07
❑ 163 Alex Fernandez .15 .07
❑ 164 Freddie Benavides .15 .07
❑ 165 Ben McDonald .15 .07
❑ 166 Blas Minor .15 .07
❑ 167 Bret Wagner .15 .07
❑ 168 Mac Suzuki .30 .14
❑ 169 Roberto Mejia .15 .07
❑ 170 Wade Boggs .60 .25
❑ 171 Calvin Reese .15 .07
❑ 172 Hipolito Pichardo .15 .07
❑ 173 Kim Batiste .15 .07
❑ 174 Darren Hall .15 .07
❑ 175 Tom Glavine .60 .25
❑ 176 Phil Plantier .15 .07
❑ 177 Chris Howard .15 .07
❑ 178 Karl Rhodes .15 .07
❑ 179 LaTroy Hawkins .15 .07
❑ 180 Raul Mondesi .40 .18
❑ 181 Jeff Reed .15 .07
❑ 182 Milt Cuyler .15 .07
❑ 183 Jim Edmonds .40 .18
❑ 184 Hector Fajardo .15 .07
❑ 185 Jeff Kent .30 .14
❑ 186 Wilson Alvarez .30 .14
❑ 187 Geronimo Berroa .15 .07
❑ 188 Billy Spiers .15 .07
❑ 189 Derek Lilliquist .15 .07
❑ 190 Craig Biggio .60 .25
❑ 191 Roberto Hernandez .15 .07
❑ 192 Bob Natal .15 .07
❑ 193 Bobby Ayala .15 .07
❑ 194 Travis Miller .15 .07
❑ 195 Bob Tewksbury .15 .07
❑ 196 Rondell White .30 .14
❑ 197 Steve Cooke .15 .07
❑ 198 Jeff Branson .15 .07
❑ 199 Derek Jeter 2.00 .90
❑ 200 Tim Salmon .60 .25
❑ 201 Steve Frey .15 .07
❑ 202 Kent Mercker .15 .07
❑ 203 Randy Johnson .60 .25
❑ 204 Todd Worrell .15 .07
❑ 205 Mo Vaughn .75 .35
❑ 206 Howard Johnson .15 .07
❑ 207 John Wasdin .15 .07
❑ 208 Eddie Williams .15 .07
❑ 209 Tim Belcher .15 .07
❑ 210 Jeff Montgomery .15 .07
❑ 211 Kirt Manwaring .15 .07
❑ 212 Ben Grieve 4.00 1.80
❑ 213 Pat Hentgen .30 .14
❑ 214 Shawon Dunston .15 .07
❑ 215 Mike Greenwell .15 .07
❑ 216 Alex Diaz .15 .07
❑ 217 Pat Mahomes .15 .07
❑ 218 Dave Hansen .15 .07
❑ 219 Kevin Rogers .15 .07
❑ 220 Cecil Fielder .30 .14
❑ 221 Andrew Lorraine .15 .07
❑ 222 Jack Armstrong .15 .07
❑ 223 Todd Hundley .30 .14
❑ 224 Mark Acre .15 .07
❑ 225 Darrell Whitmore .15 .07
❑ 226 Randy Milligan .15 .07
❑ 227 Wayne Kirby .15 .07
❑ 228 Darryl Kile .30 .14
❑ 229 Bob Zupcic .15 .07
❑ 230 Jay Bell .30 .14
❑ 231 Dustin Hermanson .30 .14
❑ 232 Harold Baines .30 .14
❑ 233 Alan Benes .30 .14
❑ 234 Felix Fermin .15 .07
❑ 235 Ellis Burks .30 .14
❑ 236 Jeff Brantley .15 .07
❑ 237 Outfield Prospects 1.00 .45
Brian Hunter
Jose Malave
Karim Garcia
Shane Pullen
❑ 238 Matt Nokes .15 .07
❑ 239 Ben Rivera .15 .07
❑ 240 Joe Carter .30 .14
❑ 241 Jeff Granger .15 .07
❑ 242 Terry Pendelton .15 .07
❑ 243 Melvin Nieves .30 .14
❑ 244 Frankie Rodriguez .15 .07
❑ 245 Darryl Hamilton .15 .07
❑ 246 Brooks Kieschnick .15 .07
❑ 247 Todd Hollandsworth .15 .07
❑ 248 Joe Rosselli .15 .07
❑ 249 Bill Gullickson .15 .07
❑ 250 Chuck Knoblauch .60 .25
❑ 251 Kurt Miller .15 .07
❑ 252 Bobby Jones .15 .07
❑ 253 Lance Blankenship .15 .07
❑ 254 Matt Whiteside .15 .07
❑ 255 Darrin Fletcher .15 .07
❑ 256 Eric Plunk .15 .07
❑ 257 Shane Reynolds .30 .14
❑ 258 Norberto Martin .15 .07
❑ 259 Mike Thurman .15 .07
❑ 260 Andy Van Slyke .30 .14
❑ 261 Dwight Smith .15 .07
❑ 262 Allen Watson .15 .07
❑ 263 Dan Wilson .15 .07
❑ 264 Brent Mayne .15 .07
❑ 265 Bip Roberts .15 .07
❑ 266 Sterling Hitchcock .30 .14
❑ 267 Alex Gonzalez .15 .07
❑ 268 Greg Harris .15 .07
❑ 269 Ricky Jordan .15 .07
❑ 270 Johnny Ruffin .15 .07
❑ 271 Mike Stanton .15 .07
❑ 272 Rich Rowland .15 .07
❑ 273 Steve Trachsel .15 .07
❑ 274 Pedro Munoz .15 .07
❑ 275 Ramon Martinez .30 .14
❑ 276 Dave Henderson .15 .07
❑ 277 Chris Gomez .15 .07
❑ 278 Joe Grahe .15 .07
❑ 279 Rusty Greer .60 .25
❑ 280 John Franco .30 .14
❑ 281 Mike Bordick .15 .07
❑ 282 Jeff D'Amico .30 .14
❑ 283 Dave Magadan .15 .07
❑ 284 Tony Pena .15 .07
❑ 285 Greg Swindell .15 .07
❑ 286 Doug Million .15 .07
❑ 287 Gabe White .15 .07

❑ 288 Trey Beamon .15 .07
❑ 289 Arthur Rhodes .15 .07
❑ 290 Juan Guzman .15 .07
❑ 291 Jose Oquendo .15 .07
❑ 292 Willie Blair .15 .07
❑ 293 Eddie Taubensee .15 .07
❑ 294 Steve Howe .15 .07
❑ 295 Greg Maddux 2.00 .90
❑ 296 Mike Macfarlane .15 .07
❑ 297 Curt Schilling .30 .14
❑ 298 Phil Clark .15 .07
❑ 299 Woody Williams .15 .07
❑ 300 Jose Canseco .60 .25
❑ 301 Aaron Sele .30 .14
❑ 302 Carl Willis .15 .07
❑ 303 Steve Buechele .15 .07
❑ 304 Dave Burba .15 .07
❑ 305 Orel Hershiser .30 .14
❑ 306 Damion Easley .30 .14
❑ 307 Mike Henneman .15 .07
❑ 308 Josias Manzanillo .15 .07
❑ 309 Kevin Seitzer .15 .07
❑ 310 Ruben Sierra .15 .07
❑ 311 Bryan Harvey .15 .07
❑ 312 Jim Thome .60 .25
❑ 313 Ramon Castro .30 .14
❑ 314 Lance Johnson .15 .07
❑ 315 Marquis Grissom .30 .14
❑ 316 Starting Pitcher .40 .18
Prospects
Terrell Wade
Juan Acevedo
Matt Arrandale
Eddie Priest
❑ 317 Paul Wagner .15 .07
❑ 318 Jamie Moyer .15 .07
❑ 319 Todd Zeile .15 .07
❑ 320 Chris Bosio .15 .07
❑ 321 Steve Reed .15 .07
❑ 322 Erik Hanson .15 .07
❑ 323 Luis Polonia .15 .07
❑ 324 Ryan Klesko .30 .14
❑ 325 Kevin Appier .30 .14
❑ 326 Jim Eisenreich .15 .07
❑ 327 Randy Knorr .15 .07
❑ 328 Craig Shipley .15 .07
❑ 329 Tim Naehring .15 .07
❑ 330 Randy Myers .15 .07
❑ 331 Alex Cole .15 .07
❑ 332 Jim Gott .15 .07
❑ 333 Mike Jackson .15 .07
❑ 334 John Flaherty .15 .07
❑ 335 Chili Davis .30 .14
❑ 336 Benji Gil .15 .07
❑ 337 Jason Jacome .15 .07
❑ 338 Stan Javier .15 .07
❑ 339 Mike Fetters .15 .07
❑ 340 Rich Renteria .15 .07
❑ 341 Kevin Witt .75 .35
❑ 342 Scott Servais .15 .07
❑ 343 Craig Grebeck .15 .07
❑ 344 Kirk Rueter .15 .07
❑ 345 Don Slaught .15 .07
❑ 346 Armando Benitez .15 .07
❑ 347 Ozzie Smith .75 .35
❑ 348 Mike Blowers .15 .07
❑ 349 Armando Reynoso .15 .07
❑ 350 Barry Larkin .40 .18
❑ 351 Mike Williams .15 .07
❑ 352 Scott Kamieniecki .15 .07
❑ 353 Gary Gaetti .30 .14
❑ 354 Todd Stottlemyre .15 .07
❑ 355 Fred McGriff .40 .18
❑ 356 Tim Mauser .15 .07
❑ 357 Chris Gwynn .15 .07
❑ 358 Frank Castillo .15 .07
❑ 359 Jeff Reboulet .15 .07
❑ 360 Roger Clemens 1.25 .55
❑ 361 Mark Carreon .15 .07
❑ 362 Chad Kreuter .15 .07
❑ 363 Mark Farris .15 .07
❑ 364 Bob Welch .15 .07
❑ 365 Dean Palmer .30 .14
❑ 366 Jeromy Burnitz .30 .14
❑ 367 B.J. Surhoff .30 .14
❑ 368 Mike Butcher .15 .07
❑ 369 Relief Pitcher .30 .14
Prospects
Brad Clontz
Steve Phoenix
Scott Gentile
Bucky Buckles
❑ 370 Eddie Murray .60 .25
❑ 371 Orlando Miller .15 .07
❑ 372 Ron Karkovice .15 .07
❑ 373 Richie Lewis .15 .07
❑ 374 Lenny Webster .15 .07
❑ 375 Jeff Tackett .15 .07
❑ 376 Tom Urbani .15 .07
❑ 377 Tino Martinez .60 .25
❑ 378 Mark Dewey .15 .07
❑ 379 Charles O'Brien .15 .07
❑ 380 Terry Mulholland .15 .07
❑ 381 Thomas Howard .15 .07
❑ 382 Chris Haney .15 .07
❑ 383 Billy Hatcher .15 .07
❑ 384 Jeff Bagwell AS .60 .25
Frank Thomas AS
❑ 385 Bret Boone AS .15 .07
Carlos Baerga AS
❑ 386 Matt Williams AS .40 .18
Wade Boggs AS
❑ 387 Wil Cordero AS .60 .25
Cal Ripken AS
❑ 388 Barry Bonds AS .75 .35
Ken Griffey AS
❑ 389 Tony Gwynn AS .50 .23
Albert Belle AS
❑ 390 Dante Bichette AS .40 .18
Kirby Puckett AS
❑ 391 Mike Piazza AS .60 .25
Mike Stanley AS
❑ 392 Greg Maddux AS .60 .25
David Cone AS
❑ 393 Danny Jackson AS .15 .07
Jimmy Key AS
❑ 394 John Franco AS .15 .07
Lee Smith AS
❑ 395 Checklist 1-198 .15 .07
❑ 396 Checklist 199-396 .15 .07
❑ 397 Ken Griffey Jr. 3.00 1.35
❑ 398 Rick Heiserman .15 .07
❑ 399 Don Mattingly 1.00 .45
❑ 400 Henry Rodriguez .30 .14
❑ 401 Lenny Harris .15 .07
❑ 402 Ryan Thompson .15 .07
❑ 403 Darren Oliver .15 .07
❑ 404 Omar Vizquel .30 .14
❑ 405 Jeff Bagwell 1.00 .45
❑ 406 Doug Webb .15 .07
❑ 407 Todd Van Poppel .15 .07
❑ 408 Leo Gomez .15 .07
❑ 409 Mark Whiten .15 .07
❑ 410 Pedro Martinez .60 .25
❑ 411 Reggie Sanders .30 .14
❑ 412 Kevin Foster .15 .07
❑ 413 Danny Tartabull .15 .07
❑ 414 Jeff Blauser .15 .07
❑ 415 Mike Magnante .15 .07
❑ 416 Tom Candiotti .15 .07
❑ 417 Rod Beck .15 .07
❑ 418 Jody Reed .15 .07
❑ 419 Vince Coleman .15 .07
❑ 420 Danny Jackson .15 .07
❑ 421 Ryan Nye .30 .14
❑ 422 Larry Walker .60 .25
❑ 423 Russ Johnson DP .30 .14
❑ 424 Pat Borders .15 .07
❑ 425 Lee Smith .30 .14
❑ 426 Paul O'Neill .30 .14
❑ 427 Devon White .30 .14
❑ 428 Jim Bullinger .15 .07
❑ 429 Starting Pitchers .30 .14
Prospects
Greg Hansell
Brian Sackinsky
Carey Paige
Rob Welch
❑ 430 Steve Avery .15 .07
❑ 431 Tony Gwynn 1.50 .70
❑ 432 Pat Meares .15 .07
❑ 433 Bill Swift .15 .07
❑ 434 David Wells .40 .18
❑ 435 John Briscoe .15 .07
❑ 436 Roger Pavlik .15 .07
❑ 437 Jayson Peterson .15 .07
❑ 438 Roberto Alomar .60 .25
❑ 439 Billy Brewer .15 .07
❑ 440 Gary Sheffield .40 .18
❑ 441 Lou Frazier .15 .07
❑ 442 Terry Steinbach .30 .14
❑ 443 Jay Payton .30 .14
❑ 444 Jason Bere .15 .07
❑ 445 Denny Neagle .30 .14
❑ 446 Andres Galarraga .60 .25
❑ 447 Hector Carrasco .15 .07
❑ 448 Bill Risley .15 .07
❑ 449 Andy Benes .30 .14
❑ 450 Jim Leyritz .30 .14
❑ 451 Jose Oliva .15 .07
❑ 452 Greg Vaughn .30 .14
❑ 453 Rich Monteleone .15 .07
❑ 454 Tony Eusebio .15 .07
❑ 455 Chuck Finley .30 .14
❑ 456 Kevin Brown .40 .18
❑ 457 Joe Boever .15 .07
❑ 458 Bobby Munoz .15 .07
❑ 459 Bret Saberhagen .30 .14
❑ 460 Kurt Abbott .15 .07
❑ 461 Bobby Witt .15 .07
❑ 462 Cliff Floyd .30 .14
❑ 463 Mark Clark .15 .07
❑ 464 Andujar Cedeno .15 .07
❑ 465 Marvin Freeman .15 .07
❑ 466 Mike Piazza 2.00 .90
❑ 467 Willie Greene .30 .14
❑ 468 Pat Kelly .15 .07
❑ 469 Carlos Delgado .30 .14
❑ 470 Willie Banks .15 .07
❑ 471 Matt Walbeck .15 .07
❑ 472 Mark McGwire 3.00 1.35
❑ 473 McKay Christensen .30 .14
❑ 474 Alan Trammell .30 .14
❑ 475 Tom Gordon .15 .07
❑ 476 Greg Colbrunn .15 .07
❑ 477 Darren Daulton .30 .14
❑ 478 Albie Lopez .15 .07
❑ 479 Robin Ventura .30 .14
❑ 480 Catcher Prospects .30 .14
Eddie Perez
Jason Kendall
Einar Diaz
Bret Hemphill
❑ 481 Bryan Eversgerd .15 .07
❑ 482 Dave Fleming .15 .07
❑ 483 Scott Livingstone .15 .07
❑ 484 Pete Schourek .15 .07
❑ 485 Bernie Williams .60 .25
❑ 486 Mark Lemke .15 .07
❑ 487 Eric Karros .30 .14
❑ 488 Scott Ruffcorn .15 .07
❑ 489 Billy Ashley .15 .07
❑ 490 Rico Brogna .15 .07
❑ 491 John Burkett .15 .07
❑ 492 Cade Gaspar .30 .14
❑ 493 Jorge Fabregas .15 .07
❑ 494 Greg Gagne .15 .07
❑ 495 Doug Jones .15 .07
❑ 496 Troy O'Leary .30 .14
❑ 497 Pat Rapp .15 .07
❑ 498 Butch Henry .15 .07
❑ 499 John Olerud .30 .14
❑ 500 John Hudek .15 .07
❑ 501 Jeff King .15 .07
❑ 502 Bobby Bonilla .30 .14
❑ 503 Albert Belle .75 .35
❑ 504 Rick Wilkins .15 .07
❑ 505 John Jaha .15 .07
❑ 506 Nigel Wilson .15 .07
❑ 507 Sid Fernandez .15 .07
❑ 508 Deion Sanders .30 .14
❑ 509 Gil Heredia .15 .07
❑ 510 Scott Elarton .75 .35
❑ 511 Melido Perez .15 .07
❑ 512 Greg McMichael .15 .07

❑ 513 Rusty Meacham .15 .07
❑ 514 Shawn Green .30 .14
❑ 515 Carlos Garcia .15 .07
❑ 516 Dave Stevens .15 .07
❑ 517 Eric Young .15 .07
❑ 518 Omar Daal .15 .07
❑ 519 Kirk Gibson .30 .14
❑ 520 Spike Owen .15 .07
❑ 521 Jacob Cruz .75 .35
❑ 522 Sandy Alomar Jr. .30 .14
❑ 523 Steve Bedrosian .15 .07
❑ 524 Ricky Gutierrez .15 .07
❑ 525 Dave Veres .15 .07
❑ 526 Gregg Jefferies .15 .07
❑ 527 Jose Valentin .15 .07
❑ 528 Robb Nen .15 .07
❑ 529 Jose Rijo .15 .07
❑ 530 Sean Berry .15 .07
❑ 531 Mike Gallego .15 .07
❑ 532 Roberto Kelly .15 .07
❑ 533 Kevin Stocker .15 .07
❑ 534 Kirby Puckett 1.00 .45
❑ 535 Chipper Jones 1.50 .70
❑ 536 Russ Davis .30 .14
❑ 537 Jon Lieber .15 .07
❑ 538 Trey Moore .30 .14
❑ 539 Joe Girardi .15 .07
❑ 540 Second Base Prospects .50 .23
Quilvio Veras
Arquimedez Pozo
Miguel Cairo
Jason Camilli
❑ 541 Tony Phillips .15 .07
❑ 542 Brian Anderson .30 .14
❑ 543 Ivan Rodriguez .75 .35
❑ 544 Jeff Cirillo .30 .14
❑ 545 Joey Cora .30 .14
❑ 546 Chris Hoiles .15 .07
❑ 547 Bernard Gilkey .15 .07
❑ 548 Mike Lansing .15 .07
❑ 549 Jimmy Key .30 .14
❑ 550 Mark Wohlers .15 .07
❑ 551 Chris Clemons .30 .14
❑ 552 Vinny Castilla .40 .18
❑ 553 Mark Guthrie .15 .07
❑ 554 Mike Lieberthal .15 .07
❑ 555 Tommy Davis .30 .14
❑ 556 Robby Thompson .15 .07
❑ 557 Danny Bautista .15 .07
❑ 558 Will Clark .60 .25
❑ 559 Rickey Henderson .60 .25
❑ 560 Todd Jones .15 .07
❑ 561 Jack McDowell .15 .07
❑ 562 Carlos Rodriguez .15 .07
❑ 563 Mark Eichhorn .15 .07
❑ 564 Jeff Nelson .15 .07
❑ 565 Eric Anthony .15 .07
❑ 566 Randy Velarde .15 .07
❑ 567 Javier Lopez .30 .14
❑ 568 Kevin Mitchell .15 .07
❑ 569 Steve Karsay .15 .07
❑ 570 Brian Meadows .30 .14
❑ 571 Rey Ordonez .60 .25
Mike Metcalfe
Kevin Orie
Ray Holbert
❑ 572 John Kruk .30 .14
❑ 573 Scott Leius .15 .07
❑ 574 John Patterson .15 .07
❑ 575 Kevin Brown .40 .18
❑ 576 Mike Moore .15 .07
❑ 577 Manny Ramirez .60 .25
❑ 578 Jose Lind .15 .07
❑ 579 Derrick May .15 .07
❑ 580 Cal Eldred .15 .07
❑ 581 Third Base Prospects .30 .14
David Bell
Joel Chelmis
Lino Diaz
Aaron Boone
❑ 582 J.T. Snow .30 .14
❑ 583 Luis Sojo .15 .07
❑ 584 Moises Alou .40 .18
❑ 585 Dave Clark .15 .07
❑ 586 Dave Hollins .15 .07
❑ 587 Nomar Garciaparra 4.00 1.80
❑ 588 Cal Ripken 2.50 1.10
❑ 589 Pedro Astacio .15 .07
❑ 590 J.R. Phillips .15 .07
❑ 591 Jeff Frye .15 .07
❑ 592 Bo Jackson .30 .14
❑ 593 Steve Ontiveros .15 .07
❑ 594 David Nied .15 .07
❑ 595 Brad Ausmus .15 .07
❑ 596 Carlos Baerga .30 .14
❑ 597 James Mouton .15 .07
❑ 598 Ozzie Guillen .15 .07
❑ 599 Outfield Prospects .60 .25
Ozzie Timmons
Curtis Goodwin
Johnny Damon
Jeff Abbott
❑ 600 Yorkis Perez .15 .07
❑ 601 Rich Rodriguez .15 .07
❑ 602 Mark McLemore .15 .07
❑ 603 Jeff Fassero .15 .07
❑ 604 John Roper .15 .07
❑ 605 Mark Johnson .15 .07
❑ 606 Wes Chamberlain .15 .07
❑ 607 Felix Jose .15 .07
❑ 608 Tony Longmire .15 .07
❑ 609 Duane Ward .15 .07
❑ 610 Brett Butler .30 .14
❑ 611 William VanLandingham .15 .07
❑ 612 Mickey Tettleton .15 .07
❑ 613 Brady Anderson .30 .14
❑ 614 Reggie Jefferson .15 .07
❑ 615 Mike Kingery .15 .07
❑ 616 Derek Bell .30 .14
❑ 617 Scott Erickson .30 .14
❑ 618 Bob Wickman .15 .07
❑ 619 Phil Leftwich .15 .07
❑ 620 David Justice .60 .25
❑ 621 Paul Wilson .15 .07
❑ 622 Pedro Martinez .60 .25
❑ 623 Terry Mathews .15 .07
❑ 624 Brian McRae .15 .07
❑ 625 Bruce Ruffin .15 .07
❑ 626 Steve Finley .30 .14
❑ 627 Ron Gant .15 .07
❑ 628 Rafael Bournigal .15 .07
❑ 629 Darryl Strawberry .30 .14
❑ 630 Luis Alicea .15 .07
❑ 631 Orioles Prospects .30 .14
Mark Smith
Scott Klingenbeck
❑ 632 Red Sox Prospects .30 .14
Cory Bailey
Scott Hatteberg
❑ 633 Angels Prospects .30 .14
Todd Greene
Troy Percival
❑ 634 White Sox Prospects .15 .07
Rod Bolton
Olmedo Saenz
❑ 635 Indians Prospects .30 .14
Steve Kline
Herb Perry
❑ 636 Tigers Prospects .15 .07
Sean Bergman
Shannon Penn
❑ 637 Royals Prospects .30 .14
Joe Randa
Joe Vitiello
❑ 638 Brewers Prospects .15 .07
Jose Mercedes
Duane Singleton
❑ 639 Twins Prospects .15 .07
Marc Barcelo
Marty Cordova
❑ 640 Yankees Prospects .75 .35
Andy Pettitte
Ruben Rivera
❑ 641 Athletics Prospects .30 .14
Willie Adams
Scott Spiezio
❑ 642 Mariners Prospects .30 .14
Eddy Diaz
Desi Relaford
❑ 643 Rangers Prospects .15 .07
Terrell Lowery
Jon Shave
❑ 644 Blue Jays Prospects .15 .07
Angel Martinez
Paul Spoljaric
❑ 645 Braves Prospects .30 .14
Tony Graffanino
Damon Hollins
❑ 646 Cubs Prospects .30 .14
Darron Cox
Doug Glanville
❑ 647 Reds Prospects .30 .14
Tim Belk
Pat Watkins
❑ 648 Rockies Propsects .15 .07
Rod Pedraza
Phil Schneider
❑ 649 Marlins Prospects .30 .14
Vic Darensbourg
Marc Valdes
❑ 650 Astros Prospects .15 .07
Rick Huisman
Roberto Petagine
❑ 651 Dodgers Prospects .30 .14
Roger Cedeno
Ron Coomer
❑ 652 Expos Prospects .50 .23
Shane Andrews
Carlos Perez
❑ 653 Mets Prospects .30 .14
Jason Isringhausen
Chris Roberts
❑ 654 Phillies Prospects .30 .14
Wayne Gomes
Kevin Jordan
❑ 655 Pirates Prospects .15 .07
Esteban Loiaza
Steve Pegues
❑ 656 Cardinals Prospects .15 .07
Terry Bradshaw
John Frascatore
❑ 657 Padres Prospects .30 .14
Andres Berumen
Bryce Florie
❑ 658 Giants Prospects .30 .14
Dan Carlson
Keith Williams
❑ 659 Checklist .15 .07
❑ 660 Checklist .15 .07

1995 Topps Finest Inserts

	MINT	NRMT
COMPLETE SET (15)	60.00	27.00
COMMON CARD (1-15)	1.50	.70
❑ 1 Jeff Bagwell	6.00	2.70
❑ 2 Albert Belle	4.00	1.80
❑ 3 Ken Griffey Jr.	20.00	9.00
❑ 4 Frank Thomas	12.00	5.50
❑ 5 Matt Williams	2.00	.90
❑ 6 Dante Bichette	2.00	.90
❑ 7 Barry Bonds	4.00	1.80
❑ 8 Moises Alou	3.00	1.35
❑ 9 Andres Galarraga	4.00	1.80
❑ 10 Kenny Lofton	4.00	1.80
❑ 11 Rafael Palmeiro	3.00	1.35

❑ 12	Tony Gwynn	10.00	4.50
❑ 13	Kirby Puckett	4.00	1.80
❑ 14	Jose Canseco	4.00	1.80
❑ 15	Jeff Conine	1.50	.70

1995 Topps League Leaders

	MINT	NRMT
COMPLETE SET (50)	50.00	22.00
COMPLETE SERIES 1 (25)	20.00	9.00
COMPLETE SERIES 2 (25)	30.00	13.50
COMMON CARD (LL1-LL50)	.50	.23

❑ LL1	Albert Belle	1.25	.55
❑ LL2	Kevin Mitchell	.50	.23
❑ LL3	Wade Boggs	1.25	.55
❑ LL4	Tony Gwynn	3.00	1.35
❑ LL5	Moises Alou	1.00	.45
❑ LL6	Andres Galarraga	1.25	.55
❑ LL7	Matt Williams	.75	.35
❑ LL8	Barry Bonds	1.25	.55
❑ LL9	Frank Thomas	4.00	1.80
❑ LL10	Jose Canseco	1.25	.55
❑ LL11	Jeff Bagwell	2.00	.90
❑ LL12	Kirby Puckett	1.25	.55
❑ LL13	Julio Franco	.50	.23
❑ LL14	Albert Belle	1.25	.55
❑ LL15	Fred McGriff	1.00	.45
❑ LL16	Kenny Lofton	1.25	.55
❑ LL17	Otis Nixon	.50	.23
❑ LL18	Brady Anderson	.75	.35
❑ LL19	Deion Sanders	.75	.35
❑ LL20	Chuck Carr	.50	.23
❑ LL21	Pat Hentgen	.75	.35
❑ LL22	Andy Benes	.75	.35
❑ LL23	Roger Clemens	2.50	1.10
❑ LL24	Greg Maddux	4.00	1.80
❑ LL25	Pedro Martinez	1.25	.55
❑ LL26	Paul O'Neill	.75	.35
❑ LL27	Jeff Bagwell	2.50	1.10
❑ LL28	Frank Thomas	4.00	1.80
❑ LL29	Hal Morris	.50	.23
❑ LL30	Kenny Lofton	1.25	.55
❑ LL31	Ken Griffey Jr.	6.00	2.70
❑ LL32	Jeff Bagwell	2.00	.90
❑ LL33	Albert Belle	1.25	.55
❑ LL34	Fred McGriff	1.00	.45
❑ LL35	Cecil Fielder	.75	.35
❑ LL36	Matt Williams	.75	.35
❑ LL37	Joe Carter	.75	.35
❑ LL38	Dante Bichette	.75	.35
❑ LL39	Frank Thomas	4.00	1.80
❑ LL40	Mike Piazza	4.00	1.80
❑ LL41	Craig Biggio	1.25	.55
❑ LL42	Vince Coleman	.50	.23
❑ LL43	Marquis Grissom	.75	.35
❑ LL44	Chuck Knoblauch	1.25	.55
❑ LL45	Darren Lewis	.50	.23
❑ LL46	Randy Johnson	1.25	.55
❑ LL47	Jose Rijo	.50	.23
❑ LL48	Chuck Finley	.75	.35
❑ LL49	Bret Saberhagen	.75	.35
❑ LL50	Kevin Appier	.75	.35

1995 Topps Traded

	MINT	NRMT
COMPLETE SET (165)	45.00	20.00
COMMON CARD (1T-165T)	.15	.07

❑ 1T	Frank Thomas ATB	1.00	.45
❑ 2T	Ken Griffey Jr. ATB	1.50	.70
❑ 3T	Barry Bonds ATB	.40	.18
❑ 4T	Albert Belle ATB	.30	.14
❑ 5T	Cal Ripken ATB	1.25	.55
❑ 6T	Mike Piazza ATB	1.00	.45
❑ 7T	Tony Gwynn ATB	.75	.35
❑ 8T	Jeff Bagwell ATB	.60	.25
❑ 9T	Mo Vaughn ATB	.40	.18
❑ 10T	Matt Williams ATB	.15	.07
❑ 11T	Ray Durham	.30	.14
❑ 12T	Juan LeBron	3.00	1.35
❑ 13T	Shawn Green	.30	.14
❑ 14T	Kevin Gross	.15	.07
❑ 15T	Jon Nunnally	.15	.07
❑ 16T	Brian Maxcy	.15	.07
❑ 17T	Mark Kiefer	.15	.07
❑ 18T	Carlos Beltran	10.00	4.50
❑ 19T	Mike Mimbs	.15	.07
❑ 20T	Larry Walker	.60	.25
❑ 21T	Chad Curtis	.15	.07
❑ 22T	Jeff Barry	.15	.07
❑ 23T	Joe Oliver	.15	.07
❑ 24T	Tomas Perez	.30	.14
❑ 25T	Michael Barrett	12.00	5.50
❑ 26T	Brian McRae	.15	.07
❑ 27T	Derek Bell	.30	.14
❑ 28T	Ray Durham	.30	.14
❑ 29T	Todd Williams	.15	.07
❑ 30T	Ryan Jaroncyk	.15	.07
❑ 31T	Todd Steverson	.15	.07
❑ 32T	Mike Devereaux	.15	.07
❑ 33T	Rheal Cormier	.15	.07
❑ 34T	Benny Santiago	.15	.07
❑ 35T	Bobby Higginson	1.50	.70
❑ 36T	Jack McDowell	.15	.07
❑ 37T	Mike Macfarlane	.15	.07
❑ 38T	Tony McKnight	.30	.14
❑ 39T	Brian Hunter	.30	.14
❑ 40T	Hideo Nomo	2.50	1.10
❑ 41T	Brett Butler	.30	.14
❑ 42T	Donovan Osborne	.15	.07
❑ 43T	Scott Karl	.15	.07
❑ 44T	Tony Phillips	.15	.07
❑ 45T	Marty Cordova	.15	.07
❑ 46T	Dave Mlicki	.15	.07
❑ 47T	Bronson Arroyo	1.50	.70
❑ 48T	John Burkett	.15	.07
❑ 49T	J.D. Smart	.50	.23
❑ 50T	Mickey Tettleton	.15	.07
❑ 51T	Todd Stottlemyre	.15	.07
❑ 52T	Mike Perez	.15	.07
❑ 53T	Terry Mulholland	.15	.07
❑ 54T	Edgardo Alfonzo	.30	.14
❑ 55T	Zane Smith	.15	.07
❑ 56T	Jacob Brumfield	.15	.07
❑ 57T	Andujar Cedeno	.15	.07
❑ 58T	Jose Parra	.15	.07
❑ 59T	Manny Alexander	.15	.07
❑ 60T	Tony Tarasco	.15	.07
❑ 61T	Orel Hershiser	.30	.14
❑ 62T	Tim Scott	.15	.07
❑ 63T	Felix Rodriguez	.15	.07
❑ 64T	Ken Hill	.15	.07
❑ 65T	Marquis Grissom	.30	.14
❑ 66T	Lee Smith	.30	.14
❑ 67T	Jason Bates	.15	.07
❑ 68T	Felipe Lira	.15	.07
❑ 69T	Alex Hernandez	1.50	.70
❑ 70T	Tony Fernandez	.15	.07
❑ 71T	Scott Radinsky	.15	.07
❑ 72T	Jose Canseco	.60	.25
❑ 73T	Mark Grudzielanek	.50	.23
❑ 74T	Ben Davis	8.00	3.60
❑ 75T	Jim Abbott	.30	.14
❑ 76T	Roger Bailey	.15	.07
❑ 77T	Gregg Jefferies	.15	.07
❑ 78T	Erik Hanson	.15	.07
❑ 79T	Brad Radke	1.00	.45
❑ 80T	Jaime Navarro	.15	.07
❑ 81T	John Wetteland	.30	.14
❑ 82T	Chad Fonville	.15	.07
❑ 83T	John Mabry	.15	.07
❑ 84T	Glenallen Hill	.15	.07
❑ 85T	Ken Caminiti	.40	.18
❑ 86T	Tom Goodwin	.15	.07
❑ 87T	Darren Bragg	.15	.07
❑ 88T	Pitching Prospects	3.00	1.35
	Pat Ahearne		
	Gary Rath		
	Larry Wimberly		
	Robbie Bell		
❑ 89T	Jeff Russell	.15	.07
❑ 90T	Dave Gallagher	.15	.07
❑ 91T	Steve Finley	.30	.14
❑ 92T	Vaughn Eshelman	.15	.07
❑ 93T	Kevin Jarvis	.15	.07
❑ 94T	Mark Gubicza	.15	.07
❑ 95T	Tim Wakefield	.30	.14
❑ 96T	Bob Tewksbury	.15	.07
❑ 97T	Sid Roberson	.15	.07
❑ 98T	Tom Henke	.15	.07
❑ 99T	Michael Tucker	.30	.14
❑ 100T	Jason Bates	.15	.07
❑ 101T	Otis Nixon	.15	.07
❑ 102T	Mark Whiten	.15	.07
❑ 103T	Dilson Torres	.15	.07
❑ 104T	Melvin Bunch	.15	.07
❑ 105T	Terry Pendleton	.15	.07
❑ 106T	Corey Jenkins	.60	.25
❑ 107T	Glenn Dishman	.30	.14
	Rob Grable		
❑ 108T	Reggie Taylor	2.50	1.10
❑ 109T	Curtis Goodwin	.15	.07
❑ 110T	David Cone	.40	.18
❑ 111T	Antonio Osuna	.15	.07
❑ 112T	Paul Shuey	.15	.07
❑ 113T	Doug Jones	.15	.07
❑ 114T	Mark McLemore	.15	.07
❑ 115T	Kevin Ritz	.15	.07
❑ 116T	John Kruk	.30	.14
❑ 117T	Trevor Wilson	.15	.07
❑ 118T	Jerald Clark	.15	.07
❑ 119T	Julian Tavarez	.15	.07
❑ 120T	Tim Pugh	.15	.07
❑ 121T	Todd Zeile	.15	.07
❑ 122T	Prospects	10.00	4.50
	Mark Sweeney UER		
	George Arias		
	Richie Sexson		
	Brian Schneider		
❑ 123T	Bobby Witt	.15	.07
❑ 124T	Hideo Nomo	1.25	.55
❑ 125T	Joey Cora	.30	.14
❑ 126T	Jim Scharrer	.15	.07
❑ 127T	Paul Quantrill	.15	.07
❑ 128T	Chipper Jones ROY	1.25	.55
❑ 129T	Kenny James	.15	.07
❑ 130T	Lyle Mouton	.60	.25
	Mariano Rivera		
❑ 131T	Tyler Green	.15	.07
❑ 132T	Brad Clontz	.15	.07
❑ 133T	Jon Nunnally	.15	.07
❑ 134T	Dave Magadan	.15	.07
❑ 135T	Al Leiter	.30	.14
❑ 136T	Bret Barberie	.15	.07
❑ 137T	Bill Swift	.15	.07

❑ 138T Scott Cooper .15 .07
❑ 139T Roberto Kelly .15 .07
❑ 140T Charlie Hayes .15 .07
❑ 141T Pete Harnisch .15 .07
❑ 142T Rich Amaral .15 .07
❑ 143T Rudy Seanez .15 .07
❑ 144T Pat Listach .15 .07
❑ 145T Quilvio Veras .15 .07
❑ 146T Jose Olmeda .15 .07
❑ 147T Roberto Petagine .15 .07
❑ 148T Kevin Brown .40 .18
❑ 149T Phil Plantier .15 .07
❑ 150T Carlos Perez .30 .14
❑ 151T Pat Borders .15 .07
❑ 152T Tyler Green .15 .07
❑ 153T Stan Belinda .15 .07
❑ 154T Dave Stewart .30 .14
❑ 155T Andre Dawson .40 .18
❑ 156T Frank Thomas AS .60 .25
Fred McGriff UER
(McGriff's team shown as Blue Jays)
❑ 157T Carlos Baerga AS .30 .14
Craig Biggio
❑ 158T Wade Boggs AS .30 .14
Matt Williams
❑ 159T Cal Ripken AS .60 .25
Ozzie Smith
❑ 160T Ken Griffey Jr. AS .75 .35
Tony Gwynn
❑ 161T Albert Belle AS .40 .18
Barry Bonds
❑ 162T Kirby Puckett .60 .25
Len Dykstra
❑ 163T Ivan Rodriguez AS .60 .25
Mike Piazza
❑ 164T Randy Johnson AS .75 .35
Hideo Nomo
❑ 165T Checklist .15 .07

1995 Topps Traded Power Boosters

	MINT	NRMT
COMPLETE SET (10)	120.00	55.00
COMMON CARD (1-10)	4.00	1.80

❑ 1 Frank Thomas 20.00 9.00
❑ 2 Ken Griffey Jr. 30.00 13.50
❑ 3 Barry Bonds 8.00 3.60
❑ 4 Albert Belle 8.00 3.60
❑ 5 Cal Ripken 25.00 11.00
❑ 6 Mike Piazza 20.00 9.00
❑ 7 Tony Gwynn 15.00 6.75
❑ 8 Jeff Bagwell 10.00 4.50
❑ 9 Mo Vaughn 8.00 3.60
❑ 10 Matt Williams 4.00 1.80

1996 Topps

	MINT	NRMT
COMPLETE SET (440)	30.00	13.50
COMP.HOBBY SET (449)	60.00	27.00
COMP.CEREAL SET (444)	50.00	22.00
COMPLETE SERIES 1 (220)	15.00	6.75
COMPLETE SERIES 2 (220)	15.00	6.75
COMMON CARD (1-440)	.10	.05

❑ 1 Tony Gwynn STP .50 .23

❑ 2 Mike Piazza STP .60 .25
❑ 3 Greg Maddux STP .60 .25
❑ 4 Jeff Bagwell STP .40 .18
❑ 5 Larry Walker STP .20 .09
❑ 6 Barry Larkin STP .10 .05
❑ 7 Mickey Mantle 4.00 1.80
❑ 8 Tom Glavine STP UER .20 .09
Won 21 games in June 95
❑ 9 Craig Biggio STP .20 .09
❑ 10 Barry Bonds STP .30 .14
❑ 11 Heathcliff Slocumb STP .10 .05
❑ 12 Matt Williams STP .10 .05
❑ 13 Todd Helton 2.00 .90
❑ 14 Mark Redman .10 .05
❑ 15 Michael Barrett .60 .25
❑ 16 Ben Davis .50 .23
❑ 17 Juan LeBron .20 .09
❑ 18 Tony McKnight .10 .05
❑ 19 Ryan Jaroncyk .10 .05
❑ 20 Corey Jenkins .10 .05
❑ 21 Jim Scharrer .10 .05
❑ 22 Mark Bellhorn .40 .18
❑ 23 Jarrod Washburn .40 .18
❑ 24 Geoff Jenkins .60 .25
❑ 25 Sean Casey 1.25 .55
❑ 26 Brett Tomko .40 .18
❑ 27 Tony Fernandez .10 .05
❑ 28 Rich Becker .10 .05
❑ 29 Andujar Cedeno .10 .05
❑ 30 Paul Molitor .40 .18
❑ 31 Brent Gates .10 .05
❑ 32 Glenallen Hill .10 .05
❑ 33 Mike Macfarlane .10 .05
❑ 34 Manny Alexander .10 .05
❑ 35 Todd Zeile .10 .05
❑ 36 Joe Girardi .10 .05
❑ 37 Tony Tarasco .10 .05
❑ 38 Tim Belcher .10 .05
❑ 39 Tom Goodwin .10 .05
❑ 40 Orel Hershiser .20 .09
❑ 41 Tripp Cromer .10 .05
❑ 42 Sean Bergman .10 .05
❑ 43 Troy Percival .20 .09
❑ 44 Kevin Stocker .10 .05
❑ 45 Albert Belle .50 .23
❑ 46 Tony Eusebio .10 .05
❑ 47 Sid Roberson .10 .05
❑ 48 Todd Hollandsworth .10 .05
❑ 49 Mark Wohlers .10 .05
❑ 50 Kirby Puckett .60 .25
❑ 51 Darren Holmes .10 .05
❑ 52 Ron Karkovice .10 .05
❑ 53 Al Martin .10 .05
❑ 54 Pat Rapp .10 .05
❑ 55 Mark Grace .30 .14
❑ 56 Greg Gagne .10 .05
❑ 57 Stan Javier .10 .05
❑ 58 Scott Sanders .10 .05
❑ 59 J.T. Snow .20 .09
❑ 60 David Justice .40 .18
❑ 61 Royce Clayton .10 .05
❑ 62 Kevin Foster .10 .05
❑ 63 Tim Naehring .10 .05
❑ 64 Orlando Miller .10 .05
❑ 65 Mike Mussina .40 .18
❑ 66 Jim Eisenreich .10 .05
❑ 67 Felix Fermin .10 .05
❑ 68 Bernie Williams .40 .18
❑ 69 Robb Nen .10 .05
❑ 70 Ron Gant .10 .05
❑ 71 Felipe Lira .10 .05
❑ 72 Jacob Brumfield .10 .05
❑ 73 John Mabry .10 .05
❑ 74 Mark Carreon .10 .05
❑ 75 Carlos Baerga .20 .09
❑ 76 Jim Dougherty .10 .05
❑ 77 Ryan Thompson .10 .05
❑ 78 Scott Leius .10 .05
❑ 79 Roger Pavlik .10 .05
❑ 80 Gary Sheffield .30 .14
❑ 81 Julian Tavarez .10 .05
❑ 82 Andy Ashby .10 .05
❑ 83 Mark Lemke .10 .05
❑ 84 Omar Vizquel .20 .09
❑ 85 Darren Daulton .20 .09
❑ 86 Mike Lansing .10 .05
❑ 87 Rusty Greer .30 .14
❑ 88 Dave Stevens .10 .05
❑ 89 Jose Offerman .10 .05
❑ 90 Tom Henke .10 .05
❑ 91 Troy O'Leary .20 .09
❑ 92 Michael Tucker .20 .09
❑ 93 Marvin Freeman .10 .05
❑ 94 Alex Diaz .10 .05
❑ 95 John Wetteland .20 .09
❑ 96 Cal Ripken 2131 2.00 .90
❑ 97 Mike Mimbs .10 .05
❑ 98 Bobby Higginson .40 .18
❑ 99 Edgardo Alfonzo .20 .09
❑ 100 Frank Thomas 1.25 .55
❑ 101 Steve Gibralter .40 .18
Bob Abreu
❑ 102 Brian Givens .10 .05
T.J. Mathews
❑ 103 Chris Pritchett .10 .05
Trenidad Hubbard
❑ 104 Eric Owens .20 .09
Butch Huskey
❑ 105 Doug Drabek .10 .05
❑ 106 Tomas Perez .10 .05
❑ 107 Mark Leiter .10 .05
❑ 108 Joe Oliver .10 .05
❑ 109 Tony Castillo .10 .05
❑ 110 Checklist (1-110) .10 .05
❑ 111 Kevin Seitzer .10 .05
❑ 112 Pete Schourek .10 .05
❑ 113 Sean Berry .10 .05
❑ 114 Todd Stottlemyre .10 .05
❑ 115 Joe Carter .20 .09
❑ 116 Jeff King .10 .05
❑ 117 Dan Wilson .10 .05
❑ 118 Kurt Abbott .10 .05
❑ 119 Lyle Mouton .10 .05
❑ 120 Jose Rijo .10 .05
❑ 121 Curtis Goodwin .10 .05
❑ 122 Jose Valentin .10 .05
❑ 123 Ellis Burks .20 .09
❑ 124 David Cone .30 .14
❑ 125 Eddie Murray .40 .18
❑ 126 Brian Jordan .20 .09
❑ 127 Darrin Fletcher .10 .05
❑ 128 Curt Schilling .20 .09
❑ 129 Ozzie Guillen .10 .05
❑ 130 Kenny Rogers .10 .05
❑ 131 Tom Pagnozzi .10 .05
❑ 132 Garret Anderson .20 .09
❑ 133 Bobby Jones .10 .05
❑ 134 Chris Gomez .10 .05
❑ 135 Mike Stanley .10 .05
❑ 136 Hideo Nomo .60 .25
❑ 137 Jon Nunnally .10 .05
❑ 138 Tim Wakefield .20 .09
❑ 139 Steve Finley .20 .09
❑ 140 Ivan Rodriguez .50 .23
❑ 141 Quilvio Veras .10 .05
❑ 142 Mike Fetters .10 .05
❑ 143 Mike Greenwell .10 .05
❑ 144 Bill Pulsipher .10 .05
❑ 145 Mark McGwire 2.00 .90
❑ 146 Frank Castillo .10 .05
❑ 147 Greg Vaughn .20 .09
❑ 148 Pat Hentgen .20 .09
❑ 149 Walt Weiss .10 .05

❑	150	Randy Johnson	.40	.18
❑	151	David Segui	.20	.09
❑	152	Benji Gil	.10	.05
❑	153	Tom Candiotti	.10	.05
❑	154	Geronimo Berroa	.10	.05
❑	155	John Franco	.20	.09
❑	156	Jay Bell	.20	.09
❑	157	Mark Gubicza	.10	.05
❑	158	Hal Morris	.10	.05
❑	159	Wilson Alvarez	.20	.09
❑	160	Derek Bell	.20	.09
❑	161	Ricky Bottalico	.20	.09
❑	162	Bret Boone	.20	.09
❑	163	Brad Radke	.20	.09
❑	164	John Valentin	.20	.09
❑	165	Steve Avery	.10	.05
❑	166	Mark McLemore	.10	.05
❑	167	Danny Jackson	.10	.05
❑	168	Tino Martinez	.40	.18
❑	169	Shane Reynolds	.20	.09
❑	170	Terry Pendleton	.10	.05
❑	171	Jim Edmonds	.30	.14
❑	172	Esteban Loaiza	.10	.05
❑	173	Ray Durham	.20	.09
❑	174	Carlos Perez	.20	.09
❑	175	Raul Mondesi	.30	.14
❑	176	Steve Ontiveros	.10	.05
❑	177	Chipper Jones	1.00	.45
❑	178	Otis Nixon	.10	.05
❑	179	John Burkett	.10	.05
❑	180	Gregg Jefferies	.10	.05
❑	181	Denny Martinez	.20	.09
❑	182	Ken Caminiti	.30	.14
❑	183	Doug Jones	.10	.05
❑	184	Brian McRae	.10	.05
❑	185	Don Mattingly	.60	.25
❑	186	Mel Rojas	.10	.05
❑	187	Marty Cordova	.10	.05
❑	188	Vinny Castilla	.30	.14
❑	189	John Smoltz	.20	.09
❑	190	Travis Fryman	.20	.09
❑	191	Chris Hoiles	.10	.05
❑	192	Chuck Finley	.20	.09
❑	193	Ryan Klesko	.20	.09
❑	194	Alex Fernandez	.10	.05
❑	195	Dante Bichette	.20	.09
❑	196	Eric Karros	.20	.09
❑	197	Roger Clemens	.75	.35
❑	198	Randy Myers	.10	.05
❑	199	Tony Phillips	.10	.05
❑	200	Cal Ripken	1.50	.70
❑	201	Rod Beck	.10	.05
❑	202	Chad Curtis	.10	.05
❑	203	Jack McDowell	.10	.05
❑	204	Gary Gaetti	.20	.09
❑	205	Ken Griffey Jr.	2.00	.90
❑	206	Ramon Martinez	.20	.09
❑	207	Jeff Kent	.20	.09
❑	208	Brad Ausmus	.10	.05
❑	209	Devon White	.20	.09
❑	210	Jason Giambi	.20	.09
❑	211	Nomar Garciaparra	1.50	.70
❑	212	Billy Wagner	.20	.09
❑	213	Todd Greene	.20	.09
❑	214	Paul Wilson	.10	.05
❑	215	Johnny Damon	.20	.09
❑	216	Alan Benes	.20	.09
❑	217	Karim Garcia	.20	.09
❑	218	Dustin Hermanson	.20	.09
❑	219	Derek Jeter	1.25	.55
❑	220	Checklist (111-220)	.10	.05
❑	221	Kirby Puckett STP	.40	.18
❑	222	Cal Ripken STP	.75	.35
❑	223	Albert Belle STP	.30	.14
❑	224	Randy Johnson STP	.20	.09
❑	225	Wade Boggs STP	.20	.09
❑	226	Carlos Baerga STP	.10	.05
❑	227	Ivan Rodriguez STP	.30	.14
❑	228	Mike Mussina STP	.20	.09
❑	229	Frank Thomas STP	.60	.25
❑	230	Ken Griffey Jr. STP	1.00	.45
❑	231	Jose Mesa STP	.10	.05
❑	232	Matt Morris	.60	.25
❑	233	Craig Wilson	.25	.11
❑	234	Alvie Shepherd	.10	.05
❑	235	Randy Winn	.30	.14
❑	236	David Yocum	.30	.14
❑	237	Jason Brester	.30	.14
❑	238	Shane Monahan	.40	.18
❑	239	Brian McNichol	.20	.09
❑	240	Reggie Taylor	.20	.09
❑	241	Garrett Long	.20	.09
❑	242	Jonathan Johnson	.20	.09
❑	243	Jeff Liefer	.25	.11
❑	244	Brian Powell	.20	.09
❑	245	Brian Buchanan	.10	.05
❑	246	Mike Piazza	1.25	.55
❑	247	Edgar Martinez	.20	.09
❑	248	Chuck Knoblauch	.40	.18
❑	249	Andres Galarraga	.40	.18
❑	250	Tony Gwynn	1.00	.45
❑	251	Lee Smith	.20	.09
❑	252	Sammy Sosa	1.00	.45
❑	253	Jim Thome	.40	.18
❑	254	Frank Rodriguez	.10	.05
❑	255	Charlie Hayes	.10	.05
❑	256	Bernard Gilkey	.10	.05
❑	257	John Smiley	.10	.05
❑	258	Brady Anderson	.20	.09
❑	259	Rico Brogna	.10	.05
❑	260	Kirt Manwaring	.10	.05
❑	261	Len Dykstra	.20	.09
❑	262	Tom Glavine	.40	.18
❑	263	Vince Coleman	.10	.05
❑	264	John Olerud	.20	.09
❑	265	Orlando Merced	.10	.05
❑	266	Kent Mercker	.10	.05
❑	267	Terry Steinbach	.20	.09
❑	268	Brian L. Hunter	.20	.09
❑	269	Jeff Fassero	.10	.05
❑	270	Jay Buhner	.20	.09
❑	271	Jeff Brantley	.10	.05
❑	272	Tim Raines	.20	.09
❑	273	Jimmy Key	.20	.09
❑	274	Mo Vaughn	.50	.23
❑	275	Andre Dawson	.30	.14
❑	276	Jose Mesa	.10	.05
❑	277	Brett Butler	.20	.09
❑	278	Luis Gonzalez	.10	.05
❑	279	Steve Sparks	.10	.05
❑	280	Chili Davis	.20	.09
❑	281	Carl Everett	.10	.05
❑	282	Jeff Cirillo	.20	.09
❑	283	Thomas Howard	.10	.05
❑	284	Paul O'Neill	.20	.09
❑	285	Pat Meares	.10	.05
❑	286	Mickey Tettleton	.10	.05
❑	287	Rey Sanchez	.10	.05
❑	288	Bip Roberts	.10	.05
❑	289	Roberto Alomar	.40	.18
❑	290	Ruben Sierra	.10	.05
❑	291	John Flaherty	.10	.05
❑	292	Bret Saberhagen	.20	.09
❑	293	Barry Larkin	.30	.14
❑	294	Sandy Alomar	.20	.09
❑	295	Ed Sprague	.10	.05
❑	296	Gary DiSarcina	.10	.05
❑	297	Marquis Grissom	.20	.09
❑	298	John Frascatore	.10	.05
❑	299	Will Clark	.40	.18
❑	300	Barry Bonds	.50	.23
❑	301	Ozzie Smith	.50	.23
❑	302	Dave Nilsson	.10	.05
❑	303	Pedro Martinez	.40	.18
❑	304	Joey Cora	.20	.09
❑	305	Rick Aguilera	.10	.05
❑	306	Craig Biggio	.40	.18
❑	307	Jose Vizcaino	.10	.05
❑	308	Jeff Montgomery	.10	.05
❑	309	Moises Alou	.30	.14
❑	310	Robin Ventura	.20	.09
❑	311	David Wells	.30	.14
❑	312	Delino DeShields	.10	.05
❑	313	Trevor Hoffman	.20	.09
❑	314	Andy Benes	.20	.09
❑	315	Deion Sanders	.20	.09
❑	316	Jim Bullinger	.10	.05
❑	317	John Jaha	.10	.05
❑	318	Greg Maddux	1.25	.55
❑	319	Tim Salmon	.40	.18
❑	320	Ben McDonald	.10	.05
❑	321	Sandy Martinez	.10	.05
❑	322	Dan Miceli	.10	.05
❑	323	Wade Boggs	.40	.18
❑	324	Ismael Valdes	.20	.09
❑	325	Juan Gonzalez	1.00	.45
❑	326	Charles Nagy	.20	.09
❑	327	Ray Lankford	.20	.09
❑	328	Mark Portugal	.10	.05
❑	329	Bobby Bonilla	.20	.09
❑	330	Reggie Sanders	.20	.09
❑	331	Jamie Brewington	.10	.05
❑	332	Aaron Sele	.20	.09
❑	333	Pete Harnisch	.10	.05
❑	334	Cliff Floyd	.20	.09
❑	335	Cal Eldred	.10	.05
❑	336	Jason Bates	.10	.05
❑	337	Tony Clark	.40	.18
❑	338	Jose Herrera	.10	.05
❑	339	Alex Ochoa	.10	.05
❑	340	Mark Loretta	.10	.05
❑	341	Donne Wall	.10	.05
❑	342	Jason Kendall	.40	.18
❑	343	Shannon Stewart	.20	.09
❑	344	Brooks Kieschnick	.10	.05
❑	345	Chris Snopek	.10	.05
❑	346	Ruben Rivera	.20	.09
❑	347	Jeff Suppan	.10	.05
❑	348	Phil Nevin	.10	.05
❑	349	John Wasdin	.10	.05
❑	350	Jay Payton	.10	.05
❑	351	Tim Crabtree	.10	.05
❑	352	Rick Krivda	.10	.05
❑	353	Bob Wolcott	.10	.05
❑	354	Jimmy Haynes	.10	.05
❑	355	Herb Perry	.10	.05
❑	356	Ryne Sandberg	.50	.23
❑	357	Harold Baines	.20	.09
❑	358	Chad Ogea	.10	.05
❑	359	Lee Tinsley	.10	.05
❑	360	Matt Williams	.20	.09
❑	361	Randy Velarde	.10	.05
❑	362	Jose Canseco	.40	.18
❑	363	Larry Walker	.40	.18
❑	364	Kevin Appier	.20	.09
❑	365	Darryl Hamilton	.10	.05
❑	366	Jose Lima	.10	.05
❑	367	Javy Lopez	.20	.09
❑	368	Dennis Eckersley	.20	.09
❑	369	Jason Isringhausen	.10	.05
❑	370	Mickey Morandini	.10	.05
❑	371	Scott Cooper	.10	.05
❑	372	Jim Abbott	.20	.09
❑	373	Paul Sorrento	.10	.05
❑	374	Chris Hammond	.10	.05
❑	375	Lance Johnson	.10	.05
❑	376	Kevin Brown	.40	.18
❑	377	Luis Alicea	.10	.05
❑	378	Andy Pettitte	.30	.14
❑	379	Dean Palmer	.20	.09
❑	380	Jeff Bagwell	.60	.25
❑	381	Jaime Navarro	.10	.05
❑	382	Rondell White	.20	.09
❑	383	Erik Hanson	.10	.05
❑	384	Pedro Munoz	.10	.05
❑	385	Heathcliff Slocumb	.10	.05
❑	386	Wally Joyner	.20	.09
❑	387	Bob Tewksbury	.10	.05
❑	388	David Bell	.10	.05
❑	389	Fred McGriff	.30	.14
❑	390	Mike Henneman	.10	.05
❑	391	Robby Thompson	.10	.05
❑	392	Norm Charlton	.10	.05
❑	393	Cecil Fielder	.20	.09
❑	394	Benito Santiago	.10	.05
❑	395	Rafael Palmeiro	.30	.14
❑	396	Ricky Bones	.10	.05
❑	397	Rickey Henderson	.40	.18
❑	398	C.J. Nitkowski	.10	.05
❑	399	Shawon Dunston	.10	.05
❑	400	Manny Ramirez	.40	.18
❑	401	Bill Swift	.10	.05
❑	402	Chad Fonville	.10	.05
❑	403	Joey Hamilton	.20	.09
❑	404	Alex Gonzalez	.10	.05

❑ 405 Roberto Hernandez .... .10 .05
❑ 406 Jeff Blauser .... .10 .05
❑ 407 LaTroy Hawkins .... .10 .05
❑ 408 Greg Colbrunn................ .10 .05
❑ 409 Todd Hundley .... .20 .09
❑ 410 Glenn Dishman .... .10 .05
❑ 411 Joe Vitiello...................... .10 .05
❑ 412 Todd Worrell .... .10 .05
❑ 413 Wil Cordero .... .10 .05
❑ 414 Ken Hill .... .10 .05
❑ 415 Carlos Garcia .... .10 .05
❑ 416 Bryan Rekar .... .10 .05
❑ 417 Shawn Green .... .20 .09
❑ 418 Tyler Green .... .10 .05
❑ 419 Mike Blowers................... .10 .05
❑ 420 Kenny Lofton.................... .40 .18
❑ 421 Denny Neagle .... .20 .09
❑ 422 Jeff Conine .... .20 .09
❑ 423 Mark Langston .... .10 .05
❑ 424 Steve Cox .... .60 .25
Jesse Ibarra
Derrek Lee
Ron Wright
❑ 425 Jim Bonnici .... .75 .35
Billy Owens
Richie Sexson
Daryle Ward
❑ 426 Kevin Jordan .... .20 .09
Bobby Morris
Desi Relaford
Adam Riggs
❑ 427 Tim Harkrider .... .20 .09
Rey Ordonez
Neifi Perez
Enrique Wilson
❑ 428 Bartolo Colon .... .50 .23
Doug Million
Rafael Orellano
Ray Ricken
❑ 429 Jeff D'Amico .... .20 .09
Marty Janzen
Gary Rath
Clint Sodowsky
❑ 430 Matt Drews .... .20 .09
Rich Hunter
Matt Ruebel
Bret Wagner
❑ 431 Jaime Bluma .... .30 .14
David Coggin
Steve Montgomery
Brandon Reed
❑ 432 Mike Figga........................ .60 .25
Raul Ibanez
Paul Konerko
Julio Mosquera
❑ 433 Brian Barber .... .20 .09
Marc Kroon
Marc Valdes
Don Wengert
❑ 434 George Arias .... 1.50 .70
Chris Haas
Scott Rolen
Scott Spiezio
❑ 435 Brian Banks.................. 2.00 .90
Vladimir Guerrero
Andruw Jones
Billy McMillon
❑ 436 Roger Cedeno 3.00 1.35
Derrick Gibson
Ben Grieve
Shane Spencer
❑ 437 Anton French.................. .25 .11
Demond Smith
DaRond Stovall
Keith Williams
❑ 438 Michael Coleman .... .50 .23
Jacob Cruz
Richard Hidalgo
Charles Peterson
❑ 439 Trey Beamon.................. .20 .09
Yamil Benitez
Jermaine Dye
Angel Echevarria
❑ 440 Checklist .... .10 .05
❑ F7 Mickey Mantle Last Day 15.00 6.75

1996 Topps Classic Confrontations

	MINT	NRMT
COMPLETE SET (15)	6.00	2.70
COMMON CARD (CC1-CC15)	.10	.05

❑ CC1 Ken Griffey Jr. .... 1.50 .70
❑ CC2 Cal Ripken .... 1.25 .55
❑ CC3 Edgar Martinez............. .25 .11
❑ CC4 Kirby Puckett .... .60 .25
❑ CC5 Frank Thomas .... 1.00 .45
❑ CC6 Barry Bonds .... .60 .25
❑ CC7 Reggie Sanders .... .10 .05
❑ CC8 Andres Galarraga.......... .60 .25
❑ CC9 Tony Gwynn.................. .75 .35
❑ CC10 Mike Piazza .... 1.00 .45
❑ CC11 Randy Johnson .... .60 .25
❑ CC12 Mike Mussina.............. .60 .25
❑ CC13 Roger Clemens .... .75 .35
❑ CC14 Tom Glavine................ .60 .25
❑ CC15 Greg Maddux .... 1.00 .45

1996 Topps Mantle

	MINT	NRMT
COMPLETE SET (19)	150.00	70.00
COMMON MANTLE (1-14)	8.00	3.60
COMMON MANTLE SP (15-19)	12.00	5.50

❑ 1 Mickey Mantle 15.00 6.75
1951 Bowman
❑ 2 Mickey Mantle 20.00 9.00
1952 Topps
❑ 3 Mickey Mantle 10.00 4.50
1953 Topps
❑ 4 Mickey Mantle 8.00 3.60
1954 Bowman
❑ 5 Mickey Mantle 8.00 3.60
1955 Bowman
❑ 6 Mickey Mantle 8.00 3.60
1956 Topps
❑ 7 Mickey Mantle 8.00 3.60
1957 Topps
❑ 8 Mickey Mantle 8.00 3.60
1958 Topps
❑ 9 Mickey Mantle 8.00 3.60
1959 Topps
❑ 10 Mickey Mantle 8.00 3.60
1960 Topps
❑ 11 Mickey Mantle 8.00 3.60
1961 Topps
❑ 12 Mickey Mantle 8.00 3.60
1962 Topps
❑ 13 Mickey Mantle 8.00 3.60
1963 Topps
❑ 14 Mickey Mantle 8.00 3.60
1964 Topps
❑ 15 Mickey Mantle 12.00 5.50
1965 Topps
❑ 16 Mickey Mantle 12.00 5.50
1966 Topps
❑ 17 Mickey Mantle 12.00 5.50
1967 Topps
❑ 18 Mickey Mantle 12.00 5.50
1968 Topps
❑ 19 Mickey Mantle 12.00 5.50
1969 Topps

1996 Topps Mantle Case

	MINT	NRMT
COMPLETE SET (19)	1000.00	450.00
COMMON MANTLE (1-14)	50.00	22.00
COMMON MANTLE SP (15-19)	60.00	27.00

❑ 1 Mickey Mantle 100.00 45.00
1951 Bowman
❑ 2 Mickey Mantle 120.00 55.00
1952 Topps
❑ 3 Mickey Mantle 60.00 27.00
1953 Topps
❑ 4 Mickey Mantle 50.00 22.00
1954 Bowman
❑ 5 Mickey Mantle 50.00 22.00
1955 Bowman
❑ 6 Mickey Mantle 50.00 22.00
1956 Topps
❑ 7 Mickey Mantle 50.00 22.00
1957 Topps
❑ 8 Mickey Mantle 50.00 22.00
1958 Topps
❑ 9 Mickey Mantle 50.00 22.00
1959 Topps
❑ 10 Mickey Mantle 50.00 22.00
1960 Topps
❑ 11 Mickey Mantle 50.00 22.00
1961 Topps
❑ 12 Mickey Mantle 50.00 22.00
1962 Topps
❑ 13 Mickey Mantle 50.00 22.00
1963 Topps
❑ 14 Mickey Mantle 50.00 22.00
1964 Topps
❑ 15 Mickey Mantle 60.00 27.00
1965 Topps
❑ 16 Mickey Mantle 60.00 27.00
1966 Topps
❑ 17 Mickey Mantle 60.00 27.00
1967 Topps
❑ 18 Mickey Mantle 60.00 27.00
1968 Topps
❑ 19 Mickey Mantle 60.00 27.00
1969 Topps

1996 Topps Mantle Finest

	MINT	NRMT
COMPLETE SET (19)	150.00	70.00
COMMON MANTLE (1-14)	8.00	3.60
COMMON MANTLE SP (15-19)	12.00	5.50

❑ 1 Mickey Mantle 15.00 6.75
1951 Bowman
❑ 2 Mickey Mantle 20.00 9.00
1952 Topps
❑ 3 Mickey Mantle 10.00 4.50
1953 Topps
❑ 4 Mickey Mantle 8.00 3.60
1954 Bowman
❑ 5 Mickey Mantle 8.00 3.60
1955 Bowman

	MINT	NRMT
❑ 6 Mickey Mantle 1956 Topps	8.00	3.60
❑ 7 Mickey Mantle 1957 Topps	8.00	3.60
❑ 8 Mickey Mantle 1958 Topps	8.00	3.60
❑ 9 Mickey Mantle 1959 Topps	8.00	3.60
❑ 10 Mickey Mantle 1960 Topps	8.00	3.60
❑ 11 Mickey Mantle 1961 Topps	8.00	3.60
❑ 12 Mickey Mantle 1962 Topps	8.00	3.60
❑ 13 Mickey Mantle 1963 Topps	8.00	3.60
❑ 14 Mickey Mantle 1964 Topps	8.00	3.60
❑ 15 Mickey Mantle 1965 Topps	12.00	5.50
❑ 16 Mickey Mantle 1966 Topps	12.00	5.50
❑ 17 Mickey Mantle 1967 Topps	12.00	5.50
❑ 18 Mickey Mantle 1968 Topps	12.00	5.50
❑ 19 Mickey Mantle 1969 Topps	12.00	5.50

1996 Topps Mantle Finest Refractors

	MINT	NRMT
COMPLETE SET (19)	500.00	220.00
COMMON MANTLE (1-14)	30.00	13.50
COMMON MANTLE SP (15-19)	40.00	18.00
❑ 1 Mickey Mantle 1951 Bowman	60.00	27.00
❑ 2 Mickey Mantle 1952 Topps	80.00	36.00
❑ 3 Mickey Mantle 1953 Topps	40.00	18.00
❑ 4 Mickey Mantle 1954 Bowman	30.00	13.50
❑ 5 Mickey Mantle 1955 Bowman	30.00	13.50
❑ 6 Mickey Mantle 1956 Topps	30.00	13.50
❑ 7 Mickey Mantle 1957 Topps	30.00	13.50
❑ 8 Mickey Mantle 1958 Topps	30.00	13.50
❑ 9 Mickey Mantle 1959 Topps	30.00	13.50
❑ 10 Mickey Mantle 1960 Topps	30.00	13.50
❑ 11 Mickey Mantle 1961 Topps	30.00	13.50
❑ 12 Mickey Mantle 1962 Topps	30.00	13.50
❑ 13 Mickey Mantle 1963 Topps	30.00	13.50
❑ 14 Mickey Mantle 1964 Topps	30.00	13.50
❑ 15 Mickey Mantle 1965 Topps	40.00	18.00
❑ 16 Mickey Mantle 1966 Topps	40.00	18.00
❑ 17 Mickey Mantle 1967 Topps	40.00	18.00
❑ 18 Mickey Mantle 1968 Topps	40.00	18.00
❑ 19 Mickey Mantle 1969 Topps	40.00	18.00

1996 Topps Mantle Redemption

	MINT	NRMT
COMPLETE SET (19)	300.00	135.00
COMMON MANTLE (1-19)	15.00	6.75
❑ 1 Mickey Mantle 1951 Bowman (2)	30.00	13.50
❑ 2 Mickey Mantle 1952 Topps (1)	40.00	18.00
❑ 3 Mickey Mantle 1953 Topps (4)	20.00	9.00
❑ 4 Mickey Mantle 1954 Bowman (2)	15.00	6.75
❑ 5 Mickey Mantle 1955 Bowman (3)	15.00	6.75
❑ 6 Mickey Mantle 1956 Topps (2)	15.00	6.75
❑ 7 Mickey Mantle 1957 Topps (2)	15.00	6.75
❑ 8 Mickey Mantle 1958 Topps (2)	15.00	6.75
❑ 9 Mickey Mantle 1959 Topps (3)	15.00	6.75
❑ 10 Mickey Mantle 1960 Topps (3)	15.00	6.75
❑ 11 Mickey Mantle 1961 Topps (3)	15.00	6.75
❑ 12 Mickey Mantle 1962 Topps (3)	15.00	6.75
❑ 13 Mickey Mantle 1963 Topps (3)	15.00	6.75
❑ 14 Mickey Mantle 1964 Topps (6)	15.00	6.75
❑ 15 Mickey Mantle 1965 Topps (3)	15.00	6.75
❑ 16 Mickey Mantle 1966 Topps (10)	15.00	6.75
❑ 17 Mickey Mantle 1967 Topps (10)	15.00	6.75
❑ 18 Mickey Mantle 1968 Topps (10)	15.00	6.75
❑ 19 Mickey Mantle 1969 Topps (4)	15.00	6.75

1996 Topps Masters of the Game

	MINT	NRMT
COMPLETE SET (20)	30.00	13.50
COMMON CARD (1-20)	.50	.23
❑ 1 Dennis Eckersley	.50	.23
❑ 2 Denny Martinez	.50	.23
❑ 3 Eddie Murray	1.50	.70
❑ 4 Paul Molitor	1.50	.70
❑ 5 Ozzie Smith	1.50	.70
❑ 6 Rickey Henderson	1.50	.70
❑ 7 Tim Raines	.50	.23
❑ 8 Lee Smith	.50	.23
❑ 9 Cal Ripken	8.00	3.60
❑ 10 Chili Davis	.50	.23
❑ 11 Wade Boggs	1.50	.70
❑ 12 Tony Gwynn	5.00	2.20
❑ 13 Don Mattingly	4.00	1.80
❑ 14 Bret Saberhagen	.50	.23
❑ 15 Kirby Puckett	4.00	1.80
❑ 16 Joe Carter	.50	.23
❑ 17 Roger Clemens	3.00	1.35
❑ 18 Barry Bonds	1.50	.70
❑ 19 Greg Maddux	6.00	2.70
❑ 20 Frank Thomas	6.00	2.70

1996 Topps Mystery Finest

	MINT	NRMT
COMPLETE SET (26)	150.00	70.00
COMMON CARD (M1-M26)	1.50	.70
COMP.REF.SET (22)	400.00	180.00

REFRACTORS: 1.25X TO 3X BASIC MYSTERY FINEST
REF.SER.1 ODDS 1:216 HOB/RET, 1:36 JUM

	MINT	NRMT
❑ M1 Hideo Nomo	6.00	2.70
❑ M2 Greg Maddux	12.00	5.50
❑ M3 Randy Johnson	4.00	1.80
❑ M4 Chipper Jones	10.00	4.50
❑ M5 Marty Cordova	1.50	.70
❑ M6 Garret Anderson	2.00	.90
❑ M7 Cal Ripken	15.00	6.75
❑ M8 Kirby Puckett	6.00	2.70
❑ M9 Tony Gwynn	10.00	4.50
❑ M10 Manny Ramirez	4.00	1.80
❑ M11 Jim Edmonds	2.50	1.10
❑ M12 Mike Piazza	12.00	5.50
❑ M13 Barry Bonds	5.00	2.20
❑ M14 Raul Mondesi	2.50	1.10
❑ M15 Sammy Sosa	10.00	4.50
❑ M16 Ken Griffey Jr.	20.00	9.00
❑ M17 Albert Belle	5.00	2.20
❑ M18 Dante Bichette	2.00	.90
❑ M19 Mo Vaughn	5.00	2.20
❑ M20 Jeff Bagwell	6.00	2.70
❑ M21 Frank Thomas	12.00	5.50
❑ M22 Hideo Nomo	6.00	2.70
❑ M23 Cal Ripken	15.00	6.75
❑ M24 Mike Piazza	12.00	5.50
❑ M25 Ken Griffey Jr.	20.00	9.00
❑ M26 Frank Thomas	12.00	5.50

1996 Topps Power Boosters

	MINT	NRMT
COMP. STAR POWER SET (11)	50.00	22.00
COMMON STAR POW. (1-6/8-12)	1.00	.45
COMP. DRAFT PICKS SET (14)	60.00	27.00
COMMON DRAFT PICK (12-26)	2.00	.90
❑ 1 Tony Gwynn	10.00	4.50
❑ 2 Mike Piazza	12.00	5.50

Card	MINT	NRMT
❑ 3 Greg Maddux	12.00	5.50
❑ 4 Jeff Bagwell	6.00	2.70
❑ 5 Larry Walker	4.00	1.80
❑ 6 Barry Larkin	2.50	1.10
❑ 8 Tom Glavine	4.00	1.80
❑ 9 Craig Biggio	4.00	1.80
❑ 10 Barry Bonds	5.00	2.20
❑ 11 Heathcliff Slocumb	1.00	.45
❑ 12 Matt Williams	1.50	.70
❑ 13 Todd Helton	20.00	9.00
❑ 14 Mark Redman	2.00	.90
❑ 15 Michael Barrett	15.00	6.75
❑ 16 Ben Davis	10.00	4.50
❑ 17 Juan LeBron	4.00	1.80
❑ 18 Tony McKnight	2.00	.90
❑ 19 Ryan Jaroncyk	2.00	.90
❑ 20 Corey Jenkins	2.00	.90
❑ 21 Jim Scharrer	2.00	.90
❑ 22 Mark Bellhorn	4.00	1.80
❑ 23 Jarrod Washburn	4.00	1.80
❑ 24 Geoff Jenkins	6.00	2.70
❑ 25 Sean Casey	12.00	5.50
❑ 26 Brett Tomko	4.00	1.80

1996 Topps Profiles

	MINT	NRMT
COMPLETE SET (40)	40.00	18.00
COMPLETE SERIES 1 (20)	30.00	13.50
COMPLETE SERIES 2 (20)	10.00	4.50
COMMON CARD (AL1-NL20)	.25	.11
❑ AL1 Roberto Alomar	1.00	.45
❑ AL2 Carlos Baerga	.50	.23
❑ AL3 Albert Belle	1.00	.45
❑ AL4 Cecil Fielder	.50	.23
❑ AL5 Ken Griffey Jr.	5.00	2.20
❑ AL6 Randy Johnson	1.00	.45
❑ AL7 Paul O'Neill	.50	.23
❑ AL8 Cal Ripken	4.00	1.80
❑ AL9 Frank Thomas	3.00	1.35
❑ AL10 Mo Vaughn	1.00	.45
❑ AL11 Jay Buhner	.50	.23
❑ AL12 Marty Cordova	.25	.11
❑ AL13 Jim Edmonds	.75	.35
❑ AL14 Juan Gonzalez	2.50	1.10
❑ AL15 Kenny Lofton	1.00	.45
❑ AL16 Edgar Martinez	.50	.23
❑ AL17 Don Mattingly	2.00	.90
❑ AL18 Mark McGwire	5.00	2.20
❑ AL19 Rafael Palmeiro	.75	.35
❑ AL20 Tim Salmon	1.00	.45
❑ NL1 Jeff Bagwell	1.50	.70
❑ NL2 Derek Bell	.50	.23
❑ NL3 Barry Bonds	1.00	.45
❑ NL4 Greg Maddux	3.00	1.35
❑ NL5 Fred McGriff	.75	.35
❑ NL6 Raul Mondesi	.75	.35
❑ NL7 Mike Piazza	3.00	1.35
❑ NL8 Reggie Sanders	.50	.23
❑ NL9 Sammy Sosa	2.50	1.10
❑ NL10 Larry Walker	1.00	.45
❑ NL11 Dante Bichette	.50	.23
❑ NL12 Andres Galarraga	1.00	.45
❑ NL13 Ron Gant	.25	.11
❑ NL14 Tom Glavine	1.00	.45
❑ NL15 Chipper Jones	2.50	1.10
❑ NL16 David Justice	1.00	.45
❑ NL17 Barry Larkin	.75	.35
❑ NL18 Hideo Nomo	1.25	.55
❑ NL19 Gary Sheffield	.75	.35
❑ NL20 Matt Williams	.50	.23

1996 Topps Road Warriors

	MINT	NRMT
COMPLETE SET (20)	12.00	5.50
COMMON CARD (RW1-RW20)	.25	.11
❑ RW1 Derek Bell	.30	.14
❑ RW2 Albert Belle	.75	.35
❑ RW3 Craig Biggio	.75	.35
❑ RW4 Barry Bonds	.75	.35
❑ RW5 Jay Buhner	.30	.14
❑ RW6 Jim Edmonds	.50	.23
❑ RW7 Gary Gaetti	.30	.14
❑ RW8 Ron Gant	.25	.11
❑ RW9 Edgar Martinez	.30	.14
❑ RW10 Tino Martinez	.75	.35
❑ RW11 Mark McGwire	4.00	1.80
❑ RW12 Mike Piazza	3.00	1.35
❑ RW13 Manny Ramirez	.75	.35
❑ RW14 Tim Salmon	.75	.35
❑ RW15 Reggie Sanders	.30	.14
❑ RW16 Frank Thomas	2.50	1.10
❑ RW17 John Valentin	.30	.14
❑ RW18 Mo Vaughn	.75	.35
❑ RW19 Robin Ventura	.30	.14
❑ RW20 Matt Williams	.30	.14

1996 Topps Wrecking Crew

	MINT	NRMT
COMPLETE SET (15)	70.00	32.00
COMMON CARD (1-15)	1.50	.70
❑ WC1 Jeff Bagwell	6.00	2.70
❑ WC2 Albert Belle	5.00	2.20
❑ WC3 Barry Bonds	5.00	2.20
❑ WC4 Jose Canseco	4.00	1.80
❑ WC5 Joe Carter	2.00	.90
❑ WC6 Cecil Fielder	2.00	.90
❑ WC7 Ron Gant	1.50	.70
❑ WC8 Juan Gonzalez	10.00	4.50
❑ WC9 Ken Griffey Jr	20.00	9.00
❑ WC10 Fred McGriff	2.50	1.10
❑ WC11 Mark McGwire	20.00	9.00
❑ WC12 Mike Piazza	12.00	5.50
❑ WC13 Frank Thomas	12.00	5.50
❑ WC14 Mo Vaughn	5.00	2.20
❑ WC15 Matt Williams	2.00	.90

1997 Topps

	MINT	NRMT
COMPLETE SET (495)	50.00	22.00
COMPLETE SERIES 1 (275)	25.00	11.00
COMPLETE SERIES 2 (220)	25.00	11.00
COMMON CARD (1-496)	.10	.05
❑ 1 Barry Bonds	.50	.23
❑ 2 Tom Pagnozzi	.10	.05
❑ 3 Terrell Wade	.10	.05
❑ 4 Jose Valentin	.10	.05
❑ 5 Mark Clark	.10	.05
❑ 6 Brady Anderson	.20	.09
❑ 8 Wade Boggs	.40	.18
❑ 9 Scott Stahoviak	.10	.05
❑ 10 Andres Galarraga	.40	.18
❑ 11 Steve Avery	.10	.05
❑ 12 Rusty Greer	.20	.09
❑ 13 Derek Jeter	1.25	.55
❑ 14 Ricky Bottalico	.20	.09
❑ 15 Andy Ashby	.10	.05
❑ 16 Paul Shuey	.10	.05
❑ 17 F.P. Santangelo	.10	.05
❑ 18 Royce Clayton	.10	.05
❑ 19 Mike Mohler	.10	.05
❑ 20 Mike Piazza	1.25	.55
❑ 21 Jaime Navarro	.10	.05
❑ 22 Billy Wagner	.20	.09
❑ 23 Mike Timlin	.10	.05
❑ 24 Garret Anderson	.20	.09
❑ 25 Ben McDonald	.10	.05
❑ 26 Mel Rojas	.10	.05
❑ 27 John Burkett	.10	.05
❑ 28 Jeff King	.10	.05
❑ 29 Reggie Jefferson	.10	.05
❑ 30 Kevin Appier	.20	.09
❑ 31 Felipe Lira	.10	.05
❑ 32 Kevin Tapani	.10	.05
❑ 33 Mark Portugal	.10	.05
❑ 34 Carlos Garcia	.10	.05
❑ 35 Joey Cora	.20	.09
❑ 36 David Segui	.20	.09
❑ 37 Mark Grace	.30	.14
❑ 38 Erik Hanson	.10	.05
❑ 39 Jeff D'Amico	.10	.05
❑ 40 Jay Buhner	.20	.09
❑ 41 B.J. Surhoff	.20	.09
❑ 42 Jackie Robinson TRIB	2.00	.90
❑ 43 Roger Pavlik	.10	.05
❑ 44 Hal Morris	.10	.05
❑ 45 Mariano Duncan	.10	.05
❑ 46 Harold Baines	.20	.09
❑ 47 Jorge Fabregas	.10	.05
❑ 48 Jose Herrera	.10	.05
❑ 49 Jeff Cirillo	.20	.09
❑ 50 Tom Glavine	.40	.18
❑ 51 Pedro Astacio	.10	.05
❑ 52 Mark Gardner	.10	.05
❑ 53 Arthur Rhodes	.10	.05
❑ 54 Troy O'Leary	.20	.09

❑	55	Bip Roberts	.10	.05
❑	56	Mike Lieberthal	.10	.05
❑	57	Shane Andrews	.10	.05
❑	58	Scott Karl	.10	.05
❑	59	Gary DiSarcina	.10	.05
❑	60	Andy Pettitte	.30	.14
❑	61	Kevin Elster	.10	.05
❑	62	Mark McGwire	2.00	.90
❑	63	Dan Wilson	.10	.05
❑	64	Mickey Morandini	.10	.05
❑	65	Chuck Knoblauch	.40	.18
❑	66	Tim Wakefield	.20	.09
❑	67	Raul Mondesi	.30	.14
❑	68	Todd Jones	.10	.05
❑	69	Albert Belle	.50	.23
❑	70	Trevor Hoffman	.20	.09
❑	71	Eric Young	.20	.09
❑	72	Robert Perez	.10	.05
❑	73	Butch Huskey	.10	.05
❑	74	Brian McRae	.10	.05
❑	75	Jim Edmonds	.30	.14
❑	76	Mike Henneman	.10	.05
❑	77	Frank Rodriguez	.10	.05
❑	78	Danny Tartabull	.10	.05
❑	79	Robb Nen	.10	.05
❑	80	Reggie Sanders	.20	.09
❑	81	Ron Karkovice	.10	.05
❑	82	Benito Santiago	.10	.05
❑	83	Mike Lansing	.10	.05
❑	84	Mike Fetters UER	.10	.05
		Card numbered 61		
❑	85	Craig Biggio	.40	.18
❑	86	Mike Bordick	.10	.05
❑	87	Ray Lankford	.20	.09
❑	88	Charles Nagy	.20	.09
❑	89	Paul Wilson	.10	.05
❑	90	John Wetteland	.20	.09
❑	91	Tom Candiotti	.10	.05
❑	92	Carlos Delgado	.20	.09
❑	93	Derek Bell	.20	.09
❑	94	Mark Lemke	.10	.05
❑	95	Edgar Martinez	.20	.09
❑	96	Rickey Henderson	.40	.18
❑	97	Greg Myers	.10	.05
❑	98	Jim Leyritz	.10	.05
❑	99	Mark Johnson	.10	.05
❑	100	Dwight Gooden HL	.10	.05
❑	101	Al Leiter HL	.20	.09
❑	102	John Mabry HL	.10	.05
❑	103	Alex Ochoa HL	.10	.05
❑	104	Mike Piazza HL	.60	.25
❑	105	Jim Thome	.40	.18
❑	106	Ricky Otero	.10	.05
❑	107	Jamey Wright	.10	.05
❑	108	Frank Thomas	1.25	.55
❑	109	Jody Reed	.10	.05
❑	110	Orel Hershiser	.20	.09
❑	111	Terry Steinbach	.20	.09
❑	112	Mark Loretta	.10	.05
❑	113	Turk Wendell	.10	.05
❑	114	Marvin Benard	.10	.05
❑	115	Kevin Brown	.30	.14
❑	116	Robert Person	.10	.05
❑	117	Joey Hamilton	.20	.09
❑	118	Francisco Cordova	.10	.05
❑	119	John Smiley	.10	.05
❑	120	Travis Fryman	.20	.09
❑	121	Jimmy Key	.20	.09
❑	122	Tom Goodwin	.10	.05
❑	123	Mike Greenwell	.10	.05
❑	124	Juan Gonzalez	1.00	.45
❑	125	Pete Harnisch	.10	.05
❑	126	Roger Cedeno	.10	.05
❑	127	Ron Gant	.10	.05
❑	128	Mark Langston	.20	.09
❑	129	Tim Crabtree	.10	.05
❑	130	Greg Maddux	1.25	.55
❑	131	William VanLandingham	.10	.05
❑	132	Wally Joyner	.20	.09
❑	133	Randy Myers	.10	.05
❑	134	John Valentin	.20	.09
❑	135	Bret Boone	.20	.09
❑	136	Bruce Ruffin	.10	.05
❑	137	Chris Snopek	.10	.05
❑	138	Paul Molitor	.40	.18
❑	139	Mark McLemore	.10	.05
❑	140	Rafael Palmeiro	.30	.14
❑	141	Herb Perry	.10	.05
❑	142	Luis Gonzalez	.10	.05
❑	143	Doug Drabek	.10	.05
❑	144	Ken Ryan	.10	.05
❑	145	Todd Hundley	.20	.09
❑	146	Ellis Burks	.20	.09
❑	147	Ozzie Guillen	.10	.05
❑	148	Rich Becker	.10	.05
❑	149	Sterling Hitchcock	.20	.09
❑	150	Bernie Williams	.40	.18
❑	151	Mike Stanley	.10	.05
❑	152	Roberto Alomar	.40	.18
❑	153	Jose Mesa	.10	.05
❑	154	Steve Trachsel	.10	.05
❑	155	Alex Gonzalez	.10	.05
❑	156	Troy Percival	.20	.09
❑	157	John Smoltz	.20	.09
❑	158	Pedro Martinez	.40	.18
❑	159	Jeff Conine	.20	.09
❑	160	Bernard Gilkey	.10	.05
❑	161	Jim Eisenreich	.10	.05
❑	162	Mickey Tettleton	.10	.05
❑	163	Justin Thompson	.20	.09
❑	164	Jose Offerman	.10	.05
❑	165	Tony Phillips	.10	.05
❑	166	Ismael Valdes	.20	.09
❑	167	Ryne Sandberg	.50	.23
❑	168	Matt Mieske	.10	.05
❑	169	Geronimo Berroa	.10	.05
❑	170	Otis Nixon	.10	.05
❑	171	John Mabry	.10	.05
❑	172	Shawon Dunston	.10	.05
❑	173	Omar Vizquel	.20	.09
❑	174	Chris Hoiles	.10	.05
❑	175	Dwight Gooden	.20	.09
❑	176	Wilson Alvarez	.20	.09
❑	177	Todd Hollandsworth	.10	.05
❑	178	Roger Salkeld	.10	.05
❑	179	Rey Sanchez	.10	.05
❑	180	Rey Ordonez	.20	.09
❑	181	Denny Martinez	.20	.09
❑	182	Ramon Martinez	.20	.09
❑	183	Dave Nilsson	.10	.05
❑	184	Marquis Grissom	.20	.09
❑	185	Randy Velarde	.10	.05
❑	186	Ron Coomer	.10	.05
❑	187	Tino Martinez	.40	.18
❑	188	Jeff Brantley	.10	.05
❑	189	Steve Finley	.20	.09
❑	190	Andy Benes	.20	.09
❑	191	Terry Adams	.10	.05
❑	192	Mike Blowers	.10	.05
❑	193	Russ Davis	.20	.09
❑	194	Darryl Hamilton	.10	.05
❑	195	Jason Kendall	.30	.14
❑	196	Johnny Damon	.20	.09
❑	197	Dave Martinez	.10	.05
❑	198	Mike Macfarlane	.10	.05
❑	199	Norm Charlton	.10	.05
❑	200	Doug Million	.25	.11
		Damian Moss		
		Bobby Rodgers		
❑	201	Geoff Jenkins	.20	.09
		Raul Ibanez		
		Mike Cameron		
❑	202	Sean Casey	.40	.18
		Jim Bonnici		
		Dmitri Young		
❑	203	Jed Hansen	.10	.05
		Homer Bush		
		Felipe Crespo		
❑	204	Kevin Orie	.20	.09
		Gabe Alvarez		
		Aaron Boone		
❑	205	Ben Davis	.20	.09
		Kevin Brown		
		Bobby Estalella		
❑	206	Billy McMillon	.25	.11
		Bubba Trammell		
		Dante Powell		
❑	207	Jarrod Washburn	.20	.09
		Marc Wilkins		
		Glendon Rusch		
❑	208	Brian Hunter	.20	.09
❑	209	Jason Giambi	.20	.09
❑	210	Henry Rodriguez	.20	.09
❑	211	Edgar Renteria	.20	.09
❑	212	Edgardo Alfonzo	.20	.09
❑	213	Fernando Vina	.10	.05
❑	214	Shawn Green	.20	.09
❑	215	Ray Durham	.20	.09
❑	216	Joe Randa	.10	.05
❑	217	Armando Reynoso	.10	.05
❑	218	Eric Davis	.20	.09
❑	219	Bob Tewksbury	.10	.05
❑	220	Jacob Cruz	.10	.05
❑	221	Glenallen Hill	.10	.05
❑	222	Gary Gaetti	.10	.05
❑	223	Donne Wall	.10	.05
❑	224	Brad Clontz	.10	.05
❑	225	Marty Janzen	.10	.05
❑	226	Todd Worrell	.10	.05
❑	227	John Franco	.20	.09
❑	228	David Wells	.30	.14
❑	229	Gregg Jefferies	.10	.05
❑	230	Tim Naehring	.10	.05
❑	231	Thomas Howard	.10	.05
❑	232	Roberto Hernandez	.10	.05
❑	233	Kevin Ritz	.10	.05
❑	234	Julian Tavarez	.10	.05
❑	235	Ken Hill	.10	.05
❑	236	Greg Gagne	.10	.05
❑	237	Bobby Chouinard	.10	.05
❑	238	Joe Carter	.20	.09
❑	239	Jermaine Dye	.10	.05
❑	240	Antonio Osuna	.10	.05
❑	241	Julio Franco	.20	.09
❑	242	Mike Grace	.10	.05
❑	243	Aaron Sele	.20	.09
❑	244	David Justice	.40	.18
❑	245	Sandy Alomar Jr.	.20	.09
❑	246	Jose Canseco	.40	.18
❑	247	Paul O'Neill	.20	.09
❑	248	Sean Berry	.10	.05
❑	249	Nick Bierbrodt	.30	.14
		Kevin Sweeney		
❑	250	Larry Rodriguez	.25	.11
		Vladimir Nunez		
❑	251	Ron Hartman	.25	.11
		David Hayman		
❑	252	Alex Sanchez	.25	.11
		Matthew Quatraro		
❑	253	Ronni Seberino	.25	.11
		Pablo Ortego		
❑	254	Rex Hudler	.10	.05
❑	255	Orlando Miller	.10	.05
❑	256	Mariano Rivera	.20	.09
❑	257	Brad Radke	.20	.09
❑	258	Bobby Higginson	.30	.14
❑	259	Jay Bell	.20	.09
❑	260	Mark Grudzielanek	.20	.09
❑	261	Lance Johnson	.10	.05
❑	262	Ken Caminiti	.30	.14
❑	263	J.T. Snow	.20	.09
❑	264	Gary Sheffield	.30	.14
❑	265	Darrin Fletcher	.10	.05
❑	266	Eric Owens	.10	.05
❑	267	Luis Castillo	.20	.09
❑	268	Scott Rolen	1.00	.45
❑	269	Todd Noel	.25	.11
		John Oliver		
❑	270	Robert Stratton	.25	.11
		Corey Lee		
❑	271	Gil Meche	.50	.23
		Matt Halloran		
❑	272	Eric Milton	1.00	.45
		Dermal Brown		
❑	273	Josh Garrett	.25	.11
		Chris Reitsma		
❑	274	A.J.Zapp	.60	.25
		Jason Marquis		
❑	275	Checklist	.10	.05
❑	276	Checklist	.10	.05
❑	277	Chipper Jones UER	1.00	.45
		incorrectly numbered 276		
❑	278	Orlando Merced	.10	.05
❑	279	Ariel Prieto	.10	.05
❑	280	Al Leiter	.20	.09

❑ 281 Pat Meares .10 .05
❑ 282 Darryl Strawberry .20 .09
❑ 283 Jamie Moyer .10 .05
❑ 284 Scott Servais .10 .05
❑ 285 Delino DeShields .10 .05
❑ 286 Danny Graves .10 .05
❑ 287 Gerald Williams .10 .05
❑ 288 Todd Greene .20 .09
❑ 289 Rico Brogna .10 .05
❑ 290 Derrick Gibson .30 .14
❑ 291 Joe Girardi .10 .05
❑ 292 Darren Lewis .10 .05
❑ 293 Nomar Garciaparra 1.25 .55
❑ 294 Greg Colbrunn .10 .05
❑ 295 Jeff Bagwell .60 .25
❑ 296 Brent Gates .10 .05
❑ 297 Jose Vizcaino .10 .05
❑ 298 Alex Ochoa .10 .05
❑ 299 Sid Fernandez .10 .05
❑ 300 Ken Griffey Jr. 2.00 .90
❑ 301 Chris Gomez .10 .05
❑ 302 Wendell Magee .10 .05
❑ 303 Darren Oliver .10 .05
❑ 304 Mel Nieves .10 .05
❑ 305 Sammy Sosa 1.00 .45
❑ 306 George Arias .10 .05
❑ 307 Jack McDowell .10 .05
❑ 308 Stan Javier .10 .05
❑ 309 Kimera Bartee .10 .05
❑ 310 James Baldwin .20 .09
❑ 311 Rocky Coppinger .10 .05
❑ 312 Keith Lockhart .10 .05
❑ 313 C.J. Nitkowski .10 .05
❑ 314 Allen Watson .10 .05
❑ 315 Darryl Kile .20 .09
❑ 316 Amaury Telemaco .10 .05
❑ 317 Jason Isringhausen .10 .05
❑ 318 Manny Ramirez .40 .18
❑ 319 Terry Pendleton .10 .05
❑ 320 Tim Salmon .40 .18
❑ 321 Eric Karros .20 .09
❑ 322 Mark Whiten .10 .05
❑ 323 Rick Krivda .10 .05
❑ 324 Brett Butler .20 .09
❑ 325 Randy Johnson .40 .18
❑ 326 Eddie Taubensee .10 .05
❑ 327 Mark Leiter .10 .05
❑ 328 Kevin Gross .10 .05
❑ 329 Ernie Young .10 .05
❑ 330 Pat Hentgen .20 .09
❑ 331 Rondell White .20 .09
❑ 332 Bobby Witt .10 .05
❑ 333 Eddie Murray .40 .18
❑ 334 Tim Raines .20 .09
❑ 335 Jeff Fassero .10 .05
❑ 336 Chuck Finley .20 .09
❑ 337 Willie Adams .10 .05
❑ 338 Chan Ho Park .40 .18
❑ 339 Jay Powell .10 .05
❑ 340 Ivan Rodriguez .50 .23
❑ 341 Jermaine Allensworth .10 .05
❑ 342 Jay Payton .10 .05
❑ 343 T.J. Mathews .10 .05
❑ 344 Tony Batista .10 .05
❑ 345 Ed Sprague .10 .05
❑ 346 Jeff Kent .20 .09
❑ 347 Scott Erickson .20 .09
❑ 348 Jeff Suppan .10 .05
❑ 349 Pete Schourek .10 .05
❑ 350 Kenny Lofton .40 .18
❑ 351 Alan Benes .20 .09
❑ 352 Fred McGriff .30 .14
❑ 353 Charlie O'Brien .10 .05
❑ 354 Darren Bragg .10 .05
❑ 355 Alex Fernandez .10 .05
❑ 356 Al Martin .10 .05
❑ 357 Bob Wells .10 .05
❑ 358 Chad Mottola .10 .05
❑ 359 Devon White .20 .09
❑ 360 David Cone .30 .14
❑ 361 Bobby Jones .10 .05
❑ 362 Scott Sanders .10 .05
❑ 363 Karim Garcia .20 .09
❑ 364 Kirt Manwaring .10 .05
❑ 365 Chili Davis .20 .09
❑ 366 Mike Hampton .10 .05
❑ 367 Chad Ogea .10 .05
❑ 368 Curt Schilling .20 .09
❑ 369 Phil Nevin .10 .05
❑ 370 Roger Clemens .75 .35
❑ 371 Willie Greene .20 .09
❑ 372 Kenny Rogers .10 .05
❑ 373 Jose Rijo .10 .05
❑ 374 Bobby Bonilla .20 .09
❑ 375 Mike Mussina .40 .18
❑ 376 Curtis Pride .10 .05
❑ 377 Todd Walker .40 .18
❑ 378 Jason Bere .10 .05
❑ 379 Heathcliff Slocumb .10 .05
❑ 380 Dante Bichette .20 .09
❑ 381 Carlos Baerga .20 .09
❑ 382 Livan Hernandez .20 .09
❑ 383 Jason Schmidt .10 .05
❑ 384 Kevin Stocker .10 .05
❑ 385 Matt Williams .20 .09
❑ 386 Bartolo Colon .20 .09
❑ 387 Will Clark .40 .18
❑ 388 Dennis Eckersley .20 .09
❑ 389 Brooks Kieschnick .10 .05
❑ 390 Ryan Klesko .20 .09
❑ 391 Mark Carreon .10 .05
❑ 392 Tim Worrell .10 .05
❑ 393 Dean Palmer .20 .09
❑ 394 Wil Cordero .10 .05
❑ 395 Javy Lopez .20 .09
❑ 396 Rich Aurilia .10 .05
❑ 397 Greg Vaughn .20 .09
❑ 398 Vinny Castilla .30 .14
❑ 399 Jeff Montgomery .10 .05
❑ 400 Cal Ripken 1.50 .70
❑ 401 Walt Weiss .10 .05
❑ 402 Brad Ausmus .10 .05
❑ 403 Ruben Rivera .20 .09
❑ 404 Mark Wohlers .10 .05
❑ 405 Rick Aguilera .10 .05
❑ 406 Tony Clark .30 .14
❑ 407 Lyle Mouton .10 .05
❑ 408 Bill Pulsipher .10 .05
❑ 409 Jose Rosado .10 .05
❑ 410 Tony Gwynn 1.00 .45
❑ 411 Cecil Fielder .20 .09
❑ 412 John Flaherty .10 .05
❑ 413 Lenny Dykstra .20 .09
❑ 414 Ugueth Urbina .20 .09
❑ 415 Brian Jordan .20 .09
❑ 416 Bob Abreu .20 .09
❑ 417 Craig Paquette .10 .05
❑ 418 Sandy Martinez .10 .05
❑ 419 Jeff Blauser .10 .05
❑ 420 Barry Larkin .30 .14
❑ 421 Kevin Seitzer .10 .05
❑ 422 Tim Belcher .10 .05
❑ 423 Paul Sorrento .10 .05
❑ 424 Cal Eldred .10 .05
❑ 425 Robin Ventura .20 .09
❑ 426 John Olerud .20 .09
❑ 427 Bob Wolcott .10 .05
❑ 428 Matt Lawton .20 .09
❑ 429 Rod Beck .10 .05
❑ 430 Shane Reynolds .20 .09
❑ 431 Mike James .10 .05
❑ 432 Steve Wojciechowski .10 .05
❑ 433 Vladimir Guerrero .75 .35
❑ 434 Dustin Hermanson .20 .09
❑ 435 Marty Cordova .10 .05
❑ 436 Marc Newfield .10 .05
❑ 437 Todd Stottlemyre .10 .05
❑ 438 Jeffrey Hammonds .20 .09
❑ 439 Dave Stevens .10 .05
❑ 440 Hideo Nomo .50 .23
❑ 441 Mark Thompson .10 .05
❑ 442 Mark Lewis .10 .05
❑ 443 Quinton McCracken .20 .09
❑ 444 Cliff Floyd .20 .09
❑ 445 Denny Neagle .20 .09
❑ 446 John Jaha .10 .05
❑ 447 Mike Sweeney .10 .05
❑ 448 John Wasdin .10 .05
❑ 449 Chad Curtis .10 .05
❑ 450 Mo Vaughn .50 .23
❑ 451 Donovan Osborne .10 .05
❑ 452 Ruben Sierra .10 .05
❑ 453 Michael Tucker .20 .09
❑ 454 Kurt Abbott .10 .05
❑ 455 Andruw Jones UER .60 .25
Birthdate is incorrectly listed as 1-22-67, should be 1-22-77
❑ 456 Shannon Stewart .20 .09
❑ 457 Scott Brosius .20 .09
❑ 458 Juan Guzman .10 .05
❑ 459 Ron Villone .10 .05
❑ 460 Moises Alou .30 .14
❑ 461 Larry Walker .40 .18
❑ 462 Eddie Murray SH .20 .09
❑ 463 Paul Molitor SH .20 .09
❑ 464 Hideo Nomo SH .50 .23
❑ 465 Barry Bonds SH .20 .09
❑ 466 Todd Hundley SH .10 .05
❑ 467 Rheal Cormier .10 .05
❑ 468 Jason Conti .75 .35
Jhensy Sandoval
❑ 469 Rod Barajas .30 .14
Jackie Rexrode
❑ 470 Cedric Bowers .75 .35
Jared Sandberg
❑ 471 Chei Gunner .25 .11
Paul Wilder
❑ 472 Mike Decelle .25 .11
Marcus McCain
❑ 473 Todd Zeile .10 .05
❑ 474 Neifi Perez .10 .05
❑ 475 Jeromy Burnitz .20 .09
❑ 476 Trey Beamon .10 .05
❑ 477 Braden Looper .50 .23
John Patterson
❑ 478 Danny Peoples .40 .18
Jake Westbrook
❑ 479 Eric Chavez 2.50 1.10
Adam Eaton
❑ 480 Joe Lawrence .40 .18
Pete Tucci
❑ 481 Kris Benson .50 .23
Billy Koch
❑ 482 John Nicholson .30 .14
Andy Prater
❑ 483 Mark Johnson .75 .35
Mark Kotsay
❑ 484 Armando Benitez .10 .05
❑ 485 Mike Matheny .10 .05
❑ 486 Jeff Reed .10 .05
❑ 487 Mark Bellhorn .20 .09
Russ Johnson
Enrique Wilson
❑ 488 Ben Grieve 1.00 .45
Richard Hidalgo
Scott Morgan
❑ 489 Paul Konerko .40 .18
Derrek Lee UER
spelled Derek on back
Ron Wright
❑ 490 Wes Helms .50 .23
Bill Mueller
Brad Seitzer
❑ 491 Jeff Abbott .20 .09
Shane Monahan
Edgard Velazquez
❑ 492 Jimmy Anderson .25 .11
Ron Blazier
Gerald Witasick
❑ 493 Darin Blood .30 .14
Heath Murray
Carl Pavano
❑ 494 Nelson Figueroa .25 .11
Mark Redman
Mike Villano
❑ 495 Checklist .10 .05
❑ 496 Checklist .10 .05
❑ NNO Derek Jeter AU 100.00 45.00

1997 Topps All-Stars

	MINT	NRMT
COMPLETE SET (22)	60.00	27.00
COMMON CARD (AS1-AS22)	1.50	.70

❑ AS1 Ivan Rodriguez 4.00 1.80

		MINT	NRMT
❑ AS2	Todd Hundley	1.50	.70
❑ AS3	Frank Thomas	10.00	4.50
❑ AS4	Andres Galarraga	3.00	1.35
❑ AS5	Chuck Knoblauch	3.00	1.35
❑ AS6	Eric Young	1.50	.70
❑ AS7	Jim Thome	3.00	1.35
❑ AS8	Chipper Jones	8.00	3.60
❑ AS9	Cal Ripken	12.00	5.50
❑ AS10	Barry Larkin	2.00	.90
❑ AS11	Albert Belle	4.00	1.80
❑ AS12	Barry Bonds	4.00	1.80
❑ AS13	Ken Griffey Jr.	15.00	6.75
❑ AS14	Ellis Burks	1.50	.70
❑ AS15	Juan Gonzalez	8.00	3.60
❑ AS16	Gary Sheffield	2.00	.90
❑ AS17	Andy Pettitte	2.00	.90
❑ AS18	Tom Glavine	3.00	1.35
❑ AS19	Pat Hentgen	1.50	.70
❑ AS20	John Smoltz	1.50	.70
❑ AS21	Roberto Hernandez	1.50	.70
❑ AS22	Mark Wohlers	1.50	.70

1997 Topps Awesome Impact

	MINT	NRMT
COMPLETE SET (20)	100.00	45.00
COMMON CARD (AI1-AI20)	1.50	.70

		MINT	NRMT
❑ AI1	Jaime Bluma	1.50	.70
❑ AI2	Tony Clark	3.00	1.35
❑ AI3	Jermaine Dye	1.50	.70
❑ AI4	Nomar Garciaparra	20.00	9.00
❑ AI5	Vladimir Guerrero	10.00	4.50
❑ AI6	Todd Hollandsworth	1.50	.70
❑ AI7	Derek Jeter	15.00	6.75
❑ AI8	Andruw Jones	8.00	3.60
❑ AI9	Chipper Jones	15.00	6.75
❑ AI10	Jason Kendall	3.00	1.35
❑ AI11	Brooks Kieschnick	1.50	.70
❑ AI12	Alex Ochoa	1.50	.70
❑ AI13	Rey Ordonez	2.50	1.10
❑ AI14	Neifi Perez	1.50	.70
❑ AI15	Edgar Renteria	2.50	1.10
❑ AI16	Mariano Rivera	2.50	1.10
❑ AI17	Ruben Rivera	2.50	1.10
❑ AI18	Scott Rolen	12.00	5.50
❑ AI19	Billy Wagner	2.50	1.10
❑ AI20	Todd Walker	5.00	2.20

1997 Topps Hobby Masters

	MINT	NRMT
COMPLETE SET (20)	110.00	50.00
COMPLETE SERIES 1 (10)	60.00	27.00
COMPLETE SERIES 2 (10)	50.00	22.00
COMMON CARD (HM1-HM20)	2.00	.90

		MINT	NRMT
❑ HM1	Ken Griffey Jr.	15.00	6.75
❑ HM2	Cal Ripken	12.00	5.50
❑ HM3	Greg Maddux	10.00	4.50
❑ HM4	Albert Belle	4.00	1.80
❑ HM5	Tony Gwynn	8.00	3.60
❑ HM6	Jeff Bagwell	5.00	2.20
❑ HM7	Randy Johnson	3.00	1.35
❑ HM8	Raul Mondesi	2.00	.90
❑ HM9	Juan Gonzalez	8.00	3.60
❑ HM10	Kenny Lofton	3.00	1.35
❑ HM11	Frank Thomas	10.00	4.50
❑ HM12	Mike Piazza	10.00	4.50
❑ HM13	Chipper Jones	8.00	3.60
❑ HM14	Brady Anderson	2.00	.90
❑ HM15	Ken Caminiti	2.00	.90
❑ HM16	Barry Bonds	4.00	1.80
❑ HM17	Mo Vaughn	4.00	1.80
❑ HM18	Derek Jeter	8.00	3.60
❑ HM19	Sammy Sosa	8.00	3.60
❑ HM20	Andres Galarraga	3.00	1.35

1997 Topps Inter-League Finest

	MINT	NRMT
COMPLETE SET (14)	60.00	27.00
COMMON CARD (ILM1-ILM14)	1.50	.70

		MINT	NRMT
❑ ILM1	Mark McGwire Barry Bonds	15.00	6.75
❑ ILM2	Tim Salmon Mike Piazza	10.00	4.50
❑ ILM3	Ken Griffey Jr. Dante Bichette	15.00	6.75
❑ ILM4	Juan Gonzalez Tony Gwynn	10.00	4.50
❑ ILM5	Frank Thomas Sammy Sosa	15.00	6.75
❑ ILM6	Albert Belle Barry Larkin	4.00	1.80
❑ ILM7	Johnny Damon Brian Jordan	1.50	.70
❑ ILM8	Paul Molitor Jeff King	3.00	1.35
❑ ILM9	John Jaha Jeff Bagwell	5.00	2.20
❑ ILM10	Bernie Williams Todd Hundley	3.00	1.35
❑ ILM11	Joe Carter Henry Rodriguez	1.50	.70
❑ ILM12	Cal Ripken Gregg Jefferies	12.00	5.50
❑ ILM13	Mo Vaughn Chipper Jones	10.00	4.50
❑ ILM14	Travis Fryman Gary Sheffield	3.00	1.35

1997 Topps Mantle

	MINT	NRMT
COMPLETE SET (16)	125.00	55.00
COMMON MANTLE (21-36)	8.00	3.60

		MINT	NRMT
❑ 21	Mickey Mantle Hank Bauer Yogi Berra 1953 Bowman	8.00	3.60
❑ 22	Mickey Mantle 1953 Bowman	8.00	3.60
❑ 23	Mickey Mantle Yogi Berra 1957 Topps	8.00	3.60
❑ 24	Mickey Mantle Hank Aaron 1958 Topps	8.00	3.60
❑ 25	Mickey Mantle 1958 Topps AS	8.00	3.60
❑ 26	Mickey Mantle 1959 Topps HL	8.00	3.60
❑ 27	Mickey Mantle 1959 Topps AS	8.00	3.60
❑ 28	Mickey Mantle Ken Boyer 1960 Topps	8.00	3.60
❑ 29	Mickey Mantle 1960 Topps AS	8.00	3.60
❑ 30	Mickey Mantle 1961 Topps HL	8.00	3.60
❑ 31	Mickey Mantle 1961 Topps MVP	8.00	3.60
❑ 32	Mickey Mantle 1961 Topps AS	8.00	3.60
❑ 33	Mickey Mantle Willie Mays 1962 Topps Hank Aaron and Ernie Banks in background	8.00	3.60
❑ 34	Mickey Mantle 1962 Topps IA	8.00	3.60
❑ 35	Mickey Mantle 1962 AS	8.00	3.60
❑ 36	Mickey Mantle Roger Maris Al Kaline Norm Cash 1964 Topps	8.00	3.60

1997 Topps Mays

	MINT	NRMT
COMPLETE SET (27)	100.00	45.00
COMMON MAYS (1-27)	4.00	1.80
❑ 1 Willie Mays 1951 Bowman	8.00	3.60
❑ 2 Willie Mays 1952 Topps	6.00	2.70
❑ 3 Willie Mays 1953 Topps	4.00	1.80
❑ 4 Willie Mays 1954 Bowman	4.00	1.80
❑ 5 Willie Mays 1954 Topps	4.00	1.80
❑ 6 Willie Mays 1955 Bowman	4.00	1.80
❑ 7 Willie Mays 1955 Topps	4.00	1.80
❑ 8 Willie Mays 1956 Topps	4.00	1.80
❑ 9 Willie Mays 1957 Topps	4.00	1.80
❑ 10 Willie Mays 1958 Topps	4.00	1.80
❑ 11 Willie Mays 1959 Topps	4.00	1.80
❑ 12 Willie Mays 1960 Topps	4.00	1.80
❑ 13 Willie Mays 1960 Topps AS	4.00	1.80
❑ 14 Willie Mays 1961 Topps	4.00	1.80
❑ 15 Willie Mays 1961 Topps AS	4.00	1.80
❑ 16 Willie Mays 1962 Topps	4.00	1.80
❑ 17 Willie Mays 1963 Topps	4.00	1.80
❑ 18 Willie Mays 1964 Topps	4.00	1.80
❑ 19 Willie Mays 1965 Topps	4.00	1.80
❑ 20 Willie Mays 1966 Topps	4.00	1.80
❑ 21 Willie Mays 1967 Topps	4.00	1.80
❑ 22 Willie Mays 1968 Topps	4.00	1.80
❑ 23 Willie Mays 1969 Topps	4.00	1.80
❑ 24 Willie Mays 1970 Topps	4.00	1.80
❑ 25 Willie Mays 1971 Topps	4.00	1.80
❑ 26 Willie Mays 1972 Topps	4.00	1.80
❑ 27 Willie Mays 1973 Topps	4.00	1.80
❑ J261 Willie Mays 1952 Jumbo	10.00	4.50
❑ NNO Willie Mays AU	100.00	45.00

1997 Topps Season's Best

	MINT	NRMT
COMPLETE SET (25)	25.00	11.00
COMMON CARD (1-25)	.50	.23
❑ SB1 Tony Gwynn	4.00	1.80
❑ SB2 Frank Thomas	5.00	2.20
❑ SB3 Ellis Burks	.75	.35
❑ SB4 Paul Molitor	1.50	.70
❑ SB5 Chuck Knoblauch	1.50	.70
❑ SB6 Mark McGwire	8.00	3.60
❑ SB7 Brady Anderson	.75	.35
❑ SB8 Ken Griffey Jr.	8.00	3.60
❑ SB9 Albert Belle	1.50	.70
❑ SB10 Andres Galarraga	1.50	.70
❑ SB11 Andres Galarraga	1.50	.70
❑ SB12 Albert Belle	1.50	.70
❑ SB13 Juan Gonzalez	4.00	1.80
❑ SB14 Mo Vaughn	2.00	.90
❑ SB15 Rafael Palmeiro	1.00	.45
❑ SB16 John Smoltz	.75	.35
❑ SB17 Andy Pettitte	1.00	.45
❑ SB18 Pat Hentgen	.75	.35
❑ SB19 Mike Mussina	1.50	.70
❑ SB20 Andy Benes	.75	.35
❑ SB21 Kenny Lofton	1.50	.70
❑ SB22 Tom Goodwin	.50	.23
❑ SB23 Otis Nixon	.50	.23
❑ SB24 Eric Young	.75	.35
❑ SB25 Lance Johnson	.50	.23

1997 Topps Sweet Strokes

	MINT	NRMT
COMPLETE SET (15)	40.00	18.00
COMMON CARD (SS1-SS15)	1.25	.55
❑ SS1 Roberto Alomar	2.00	.90
❑ SS2 Jeff Bagwell	3.00	1.35
❑ SS3 Albert Belle	2.50	1.10
❑ SS4 Barry Bonds	2.50	1.10
❑ SS5 Mark Grace	1.50	.70
❑ SS6 Ken Griffey Jr.	10.00	4.50
❑ SS7 Tony Gwynn	5.00	2.20
❑ SS8 Chipper Jones	5.00	2.20
❑ SS9 Edgar Martinez	1.25	.55
❑ SS10 Mark McGwire	10.00	4.50
❑ SS11 Rafael Palmeiro	1.50	.70
❑ SS12 Mike Piazza	6.00	2.70
❑ SS13 Gary Sheffield	1.50	.70
❑ SS14 Frank Thomas	6.00	2.70
❑ SS15 Mo Vaughn	2.50	1.10

1997 Topps Team Timber

	MINT	NRMT
COMPLETE SET (16)	50.00	22.00
COMMON CARD (TT1-TT16)	1.50	.70
❑ TT1 Ken Griffey Jr.	12.00	5.50
❑ TT2 Ken Caminiti	2.00	.90
❑ TT3 Bernie Williams	2.50	1.10
❑ TT4 Jeff Bagwell	4.00	1.80
❑ TT5 Frank Thomas	8.00	3.60
❑ TT6 Andres Galarraga	2.50	1.10
❑ TT7 Barry Bonds	3.00	1.35
❑ TT8 Rafael Palmeiro	2.00	.90
❑ TT9 Brady Anderson	1.50	.70
❑ TT10 Juan Gonzalez	6.00	2.70
❑ TT11 Mo Vaughn	3.00	1.35
❑ TT12 Mark McGwire	12.00	5.50
❑ TT13 Gary Sheffield	2.00	.90
❑ TT14 Albert Belle	4.00	1.80
❑ TT15 Chipper Jones	6.00	2.70
❑ TT16 Mike Piazza	8.00	3.60

1998 Topps

	MINT	NRMT
COMPLETE SET (503)	45.00	20.00
COMPLETE SERIES 1 (282)	25.00	11.00
COMPLETE SERIES 2 (221)	20.00	9.00
COMP.HOBBY SET (511)	80.00	36.00
COMP.RETAIL SET (511)	60.00	27.00
COMP.X-MAS SET (511)	40.00	18.00
COMMON CARD (1-504)	.10	.05
❑ 1 Tony Gwynn	1.00	.45
❑ 2 Larry Walker	.40	.18
❑ 3 Billy Wagner	.15	.07
❑ 4 Denny Neagle	.15	.07
❑ 5 Vladimir Guerrero	.60	.25
❑ 6 Kevin Brown	.25	.11
❑ 8 Mariano Rivera	.15	.07
❑ 9 Tony Clark	.25	.11
❑ 10 Deion Sanders	.15	.07
❑ 11 Francisco Cordova	.10	.05
❑ 12 Matt Williams	.15	.07
❑ 13 Carlos Baerga	.15	.07
❑ 14 Mo Vaughn	.50	.23
❑ 15 Bobby Witt	.10	.05
❑ 16 Matt Stairs	.15	.07

❑ 17 Chan Ho Park .40 .18
❑ 18 Mike Bordick .10 .05
❑ 19 Michael Tucker .15 .07
❑ 20 Frank Thomas 1.25 .55
❑ 21 Roberto Clemente 1.00 .45
❑ 22 Dmitri Young .15 .07
❑ 23 Steve Trachsel .10 .05
❑ 24 Jeff Kent .15 .07
❑ 25 Scott Rolen 1.00 .45
❑ 26 John Thomson .10 .05
❑ 27 Joe Vitiello .10 .05
❑ 28 Eddie Guardado .10 .05
❑ 29 Charlie Hayes .10 .05
❑ 30 Juan Gonzalez 1.00 .45
❑ 31 Garret Anderson .15 .07
❑ 32 John Jaha .10 .05
❑ 33 Omar Vizquel .15 .07
❑ 34 Brian Hunter .15 .07
❑ 35 Jeff Bagwell .60 .25
❑ 36 Mark Lemke .10 .05
❑ 37 Doug Glanville .15 .07
❑ 38 Dan Wilson .10 .05
❑ 39 Steve Cooke .10 .05
❑ 40 Chili Davis .15 .07
❑ 41 Mike Cameron .15 .07
❑ 42 F.P. Santangelo .10 .05
❑ 43 Brad Ausmus .10 .05
❑ 44 Gary DiSarcina .10 .05
❑ 45 Pat Hentgen .15 .07
❑ 46 Wilton Guerrero .10 .05
❑ 47 Devon White .15 .07
❑ 48 Danny Patterson .10 .05
❑ 49 Pat Meares .10 .05
❑ 50 Rafael Palmeiro .25 .11
❑ 51 Mark Gardner .10 .05
❑ 52 Jeff Blauser .10 .05
❑ 53 Dave Hollins .10 .05
❑ 54 Carlos Garcia .10 .05
❑ 55 Ben McDonald .10 .05
❑ 56 John Mabry .10 .05
❑ 57 Trevor Hoffman .15 .07
❑ 58 Tony Fernandez .10 .05
❑ 59 Rich Loiselle .15 .07
❑ 60 Mark Leiter .10 .05
❑ 61 Pat Kelly .10 .05
❑ 62 John Flaherty .10 .05
❑ 63 Roger Bailey .10 .05
❑ 64 Tom Gordon .15 .07
❑ 65 Ryan Klesko .15 .07
❑ 66 Darryl Hamilton .10 .05
❑ 67 Jim Eisenreich .10 .05
❑ 68 Butch Huskey .10 .05
❑ 69 Mark Grudzielanek .15 .07
❑ 70 Marquis Grissom .15 .07
❑ 71 Mark McLemore .10 .05
❑ 72 Gary Gaetti .10 .05
❑ 73 Greg Gagne .10 .05
❑ 74 Lyle Mouton .10 .05
❑ 75 Jim Edmonds .25 .11
❑ 76 Shawn Green .15 .07
❑ 77 Greg Vaughn .15 .07
❑ 78 Terry Adams .10 .05
❑ 79 Kevin Polcovich .10 .05
❑ 80 Troy O'Leary .15 .07
❑ 81 Jeff Shaw .15 .07
❑ 82 Rich Becker .10 .05
❑ 83 David Wells .25 .11
❑ 84 Steve Karsay .10 .05
❑ 85 Charles Nagy .15 .07
❑ 86 B.J. Surhoff .15 .07
❑ 87 Jamey Wright .10 .05
❑ 88 James Baldwin .15 .07
❑ 89 Edgardo Alfonzo .15 .07
❑ 90 Jay Buhner .15 .07
❑ 91 Brady Anderson .15 .07
❑ 92 Scott Servais .10 .05
❑ 93 Edgar Renteria .15 .07
❑ 94 Mike Lieberthal .10 .05
❑ 95 Rick Aguilera .10 .05
❑ 96 Walt Weiss .15 .07
❑ 97 Deivi Cruz .10 .05
❑ 98 Kurt Abbott .10 .05
❑ 99 Henry Rodriguez .15 .07
❑ 100 Mike Piazza 1.25 .55
❑ 101 Bill Taylor .10 .05
❑ 102 Todd Zeile .15 .07
❑ 103 Rey Ordonez .15 .07
❑ 104 Willie Greene .15 .07
❑ 105 Tony Womack .15 .07
❑ 106 Mike Sweeney .10 .05
❑ 107 Jeffrey Hammonds .15 .07
❑ 108 Kevin Orie .10 .05
❑ 109 Alex Gonzalez .10 .05
❑ 110 Jose Canseco .40 .18
❑ 111 Paul Sorrento .10 .05
❑ 112 Joey Hamilton .15 .07
❑ 113 Brad Radke .15 .07
❑ 114 Steve Avery .10 .05
❑ 115 Esteban Loaiza .10 .05
❑ 116 Stan Javier .10 .05
❑ 117 Chris Gomez .10 .05
❑ 118 Royce Clayton .10 .05
❑ 119 Orlando Merced .10 .05
❑ 120 Kevin Appier .15 .07
❑ 121 Mel Nieves .10 .05
❑ 122 Joe Girardi .10 .05
❑ 123 Rico Brogna .15 .07
❑ 124 Kent Mercker .10 .05
❑ 125 Manny Ramirez .40 .18
❑ 126 Jeromy Burnitz .15 .07
❑ 127 Kevin Foster .10 .05
❑ 128 Matt Morris .15 .07
❑ 129 Jason Dickson .15 .07
❑ 130 Tom Glavine .40 .18
❑ 131 Wally Joyner .15 .07
❑ 132 Rick Reed .10 .05
❑ 133 Todd Jones .10 .05
❑ 134 Dave Martinez .10 .05
❑ 135 Sandy Alomar .15 .07
❑ 136 Mike Lansing .10 .05
❑ 137 Sean Berry .10 .05
❑ 138 Doug Jones .10 .05
❑ 139 Todd Stottlemyre .15 .07
❑ 140 Jay Bell .15 .07
❑ 141 Jaime Navarro .10 .05
❑ 142 Chris Hoiles .10 .05
❑ 143 Joey Cora .15 .07
❑ 144 Scott Spiezio .10 .05
❑ 145 Joe Carter .15 .07
❑ 146 Jose Guillen .15 .07
❑ 147 Damion Easley .15 .07
❑ 148 Lee Stevens .10 .05
❑ 149 Alex Fernandez .10 .05
❑ 150 Randy Johnson .40 .18
❑ 151 J.T. Snow .15 .07
❑ 152 Chuck Finley .15 .07
❑ 153 Bernard Gilkey .10 .05
❑ 154 David Segui .15 .07
❑ 155 Dante Bichette .15 .07
❑ 156 Kevin Stocker .10 .05
❑ 157 Carl Everett .10 .05
❑ 158 Jose Valentin .10 .05
❑ 159 Pokey Reese .10 .05
❑ 160 Derek Jeter 1.00 .45
❑ 161 Roger Pavlik .10 .05
❑ 162 Mark Wohlers .10 .05
❑ 163 Ricky Bottalico .15 .07
❑ 164 Ozzie Guillen .10 .05
❑ 165 Mike Mussina .40 .18
❑ 166 Gary Sheffield .25 .11
❑ 167 Hideo Nomo .50 .23
❑ 168 Mark Grace .25 .11
❑ 169 Aaron Sele .15 .07
❑ 170 Darryl Kile .15 .07
❑ 171 Shawn Estes .15 .07
❑ 172 Vinny Castilla .25 .11
❑ 173 Ron Coomer .10 .05
❑ 174 Jose Rosado .10 .05
❑ 175 Kenny Lofton .40 .18
❑ 176 Jason Giambi .15 .07
❑ 177 Hal Morris .10 .05
❑ 178 Darren Bragg .10 .05
❑ 179 Orel Hershiser .15 .07
❑ 180 Ray Lankford .15 .07
❑ 181 Hideki Irabu .25 .11
❑ 182 Kevin Young .15 .07
❑ 183 Javy Lopez .15 .07
❑ 184 Jeff Montgomery .10 .05
❑ 185 Mike Holtz .10 .05
❑ 186 George Williams .10 .05
❑ 187 Cal Eldred .10 .05
❑ 188 Tom Candiotti .10 .05
❑ 189 Glenallen Hill .10 .05
❑ 190 Brian Giles .15 .07
❑ 191 Dave Mlicki .10 .05
❑ 192 Garrett Stephenson .10 .05
❑ 193 Jeff Frye .10 .05
❑ 194 Joe Oliver .10 .05
❑ 195 Bob Hamelin .10 .05
❑ 196 Luis Sojo .10 .05
❑ 197 LaTroy Hawkins .10 .05
❑ 198 Kevin Elster .10 .05
❑ 199 Jeff Reed .10 .05
❑ 200 Dennis Eckersley .15 .07
❑ 201 Bill Mueller .15 .07
❑ 202 Russ Davis .15 .07
❑ 203 Armando Benitez .10 .05
❑ 204 Quilvio Veras .10 .05
❑ 205 Tim Naehring .10 .05
❑ 206 Quinton McCracken .15 .07
❑ 207 Raul Casanova .10 .05
❑ 208 Matt Lawton .15 .07
❑ 209 Luis Alicea .10 .05
❑ 210 Luis Gonzalez .10 .05
❑ 211 Allen Watson .10 .05
❑ 212 Gerald Williams .10 .05
❑ 213 David Bell .10 .05
❑ 214 Todd Hollandsworth .10 .05
❑ 215 Wade Boggs .40 .18
❑ 216 Jose Mesa .10 .05
❑ 217 Jamie Moyer .10 .05
❑ 218 Darren Daulton .15 .07
❑ 219 Mickey Morandini .10 .05
❑ 220 Rusty Greer .15 .07
❑ 221 Jim Bullinger .10 .05
❑ 222 Jose Offerman .10 .05
❑ 223 Matt Karchner .10 .05
❑ 224 Woody Williams .10 .05
❑ 225 Mark Loretta .10 .05
❑ 226 Mike Hampton .10 .05
❑ 227 Willie Adams .10 .05
❑ 228 Scott Hatteberg .10 .05
❑ 229 Rich Amaral .10 .05
❑ 230 Terry Steinbach .15 .07
❑ 231 Glendon Rusch .10 .05
❑ 232 Bret Boone .15 .07
❑ 233 Robert Person .10 .05
❑ 234 Jose Hernandez .10 .05
❑ 235 Doug Drabek .10 .05
❑ 236 Jason McDonald .10 .05
❑ 237 Chris Widger .10 .05
❑ 238 Tom Martin .10 .05
❑ 239 Dave Burba .10 .05
❑ 240 Pete Rose Jr. .15 .07
❑ 241 Bobby Ayala .10 .05
❑ 242 Tim Wakefield .10 .05
❑ 243 Dennis Springer .10 .05
❑ 244 Tim Belcher .10 .05
❑ 245 Jon Garland .15 .07
Geoff Goetz
❑ 246 Glenn Davis .40 .18
Lance Berkman
❑ 247 Vernon Wells .25 .11
Aaron Akin
❑ 248 Adam Kennedy .15 .07
Jason Romano
❑ 249 Jason Dellaero .15 .07
Troy Cameron
❑ 250 Alex Sanchez .40 .18
Jared Sandberg
❑ 251 Pablo Ortega .15 .07
James Manias
❑ 252 Jason Conti .40 .18
Mike Stoner
❑ 253 John Patterson .15 .07
Larry Rodriguez
❑ 254 Adrian Beltre .60 .25
Ryan Minor
Aaron Boone
❑ 255 Ben Grieve .75 .35
Brian Buchanan
Dermal Brown
❑ 256 Kerry Wood 2.00 .90
Carl Pavano
Gil Meche

❑	257	David Ortiz	.15	.07
		Daryle Ward		
		Richie Sexson		
❑	258	Randy Winn	.15	.07
		Juan Encarnacion		
		Andrew Vessel		
❑	259	Kris Benson	.25	.11
		Travis Smith		
		Courtney Duncan		
❑	260	Chad Hermansen	.40	.18
		Brent Butler		
		Warren Morris		
❑	261	Ben Davis	.15	.07
		Eli Marrero		
		Ramon Hernandez		
❑	262	Eric Chavez	.60	.25
		Russell Branyan		
		Russ Johnson		
❑	263	Todd Dunwoody	.25	.11
		John Barnes		
		Ryan Jackson		
❑	264	Matt Clement	.25	.11
		Roy Halladay		
		Brian Fuentes		
❑	265	Randy Johnson SH	.15	.07
❑	266	Kevin Brown SH	.10	.05
❑	267	Ricardo Rincon SH	.10	.05
		Francisco Cordova		
❑	268	Nomar Garciaparra SH	.60	.25
❑	269	Tino Martinez SH	.15	.07
❑	270	Chuck Knoblauch IL	.15	.07
❑	271	Pedro Martinez IL	.15	.07
❑	272	Denny Neagle IL	.10	.05
❑	273	Juan Gonzalez IL	.50	.23
❑	274	Andres Galarraga IL	.15	.07
❑	275	Checklist	.10	.05
❑	276	Checklist	.10	.05
❑	277	Moises Alou WS	.15	.07
❑	278	Sandy Alomar WS	.15	.07
❑	279	Gary Sheffield WS	.15	.07
❑	280	Matt Williams WS	.15	.07
❑	281	Livan Hernandez WS	.15	.07
❑	282	Chad Ogea WS	.15	.07
❑	283	Marlins Champs	.15	.07
❑	284	Tino Martinez	.40	.18
❑	285	Roberto Alomar	.40	.18
❑	286	Jeff King	.15	.07
❑	287	Brian Jordan	.15	.07
❑	288	Darin Erstad	.50	.23
❑	289	Ken Caminiti	.25	.11
❑	290	Jim Thome	.40	.18
❑	291	Paul Molitor	.40	.18
❑	292	Ivan Rodriguez	.50	.23
❑	293	Bernie Williams	.40	.18
❑	294	Todd Hundley	.15	.07
❑	295	Andres Galarraga	.40	.18
❑	296	Greg Maddux	1.25	.55
❑	297	Edgar Martinez	.15	.07
❑	298	Ron Gant	.10	.05
❑	299	Derek Bell	.15	.07
❑	300	Roger Clemens	.75	.35
❑	301	Rondell White	.15	.07
❑	302	Barry Larkin	.25	.11
❑	303	Robin Ventura	.15	.07
❑	304	Jason Kendall	.15	.07
❑	305	Chipper Jones	1.00	.45
❑	306	John Franco	.15	.07
❑	307	Sammy Sosa	1.00	.45
❑	308	Troy Percival	.15	.07
❑	309	Chuck Knoblauch	.40	.18
❑	310	Ellis Burks	.15	.07
❑	311	Al Martin	.10	.05
❑	312	Tim Salmon	.40	.18
❑	313	Moises Alou	.25	.11
❑	314	Lance Johnson	.10	.05
❑	315	Justin Thompson	.15	.07
❑	316	Will Clark	.40	.18
❑	317	Barry Bonds	.50	.23
❑	318	Craig Biggio	.40	.18
❑	319	John Smoltz	.15	.07
❑	320	Cal Ripken	1.50	.70
❑	321	Ken Griffey Jr.	2.00	.90
❑	322	Paul O'Neill	.15	.07
❑	323	Todd Helton	.50	.23
❑	324	John Olerud	.15	.07
❑	325	Mark McGwire	2.50	1.10
❑	326	Jose Cruz Jr.	.50	.23
❑	327	Jeff Cirillo	.15	.07
❑	328	Dean Palmer	.15	.07
❑	329	John Wetteland	.15	.07
❑	330	Steve Finley	.15	.07
❑	331	Albert Belle	.50	.23
❑	332	Curt Schilling	.15	.07
❑	333	Raul Mondesi	.25	.11
❑	334	Andruw Jones	.50	.23
❑	335	Nomar Garciaparra	1.25	.55
❑	336	David Justice	.40	.18
❑	337	Andy Pettitte	.25	.11
❑	338	Pedro Martinez	.40	.18
❑	339	Travis Miller	.10	.05
❑	340	Chris Stynes	.10	.05
❑	341	Gregg Jefferies	.10	.05
❑	342	Jeff Fassero	.10	.05
❑	343	Craig Counsell	.10	.05
❑	344	Wilson Alvarez	.15	.07
❑	345	Bip Roberts	.10	.05
❑	346	Kelvim Escobar	.15	.07
❑	347	Mark Bellhorn	.15	.07
❑	348	Cory Lidle	.10	.05
❑	349	Fred McGriff	.25	.11
❑	350	Chuck Carr	.10	.05
❑	351	Bob Abreu	.15	.07
❑	352	Juan Guzman	.10	.05
❑	353	Fernando Vina	.10	.05
❑	354	Andy Benes	.15	.07
❑	355	Dave Nilsson	.10	.05
❑	356	Bobby Bonilla	.15	.07
❑	357	Ismael Valdes	.15	.07
❑	358	Carlos Perez	.15	.07
❑	359	Kirk Rueter	.10	.05
❑	360	Bartolo Colon	.15	.07
❑	361	Mel Rojas	.10	.05
❑	362	Johnny Damon	.15	.07
❑	363	Geronimo Berroa	.10	.05
❑	364	Reggie Sanders	.15	.07
❑	365	Jermaine Allensworth	.10	.05
❑	366	Orlando Cabrera	.15	.07
❑	367	Jorge Fabregas	.10	.05
❑	368	Scott Stahoviak	.10	.05
❑	369	Ken Cloude	.15	.07
❑	370	Donovan Osborne	.10	.05
❑	371	Roger Cedeno	.10	.05
❑	372	Neifi Perez	.15	.07
❑	373	Chris Holt	.10	.05
❑	374	Cecil Fielder	.15	.07
❑	375	Marty Cordova	.10	.05
❑	376	Tom Goodwin	.10	.05
❑	377	Jeff Suppan	.10	.05
❑	378	Jeff Brantley	.10	.05
❑	379	Mark Langston	.10	.05
❑	380	Shane Reynolds	.15	.07
❑	381	Mike Fetters	.10	.05
❑	382	Todd Greene	.15	.07
❑	383	Ray Durham	.15	.07
❑	384	Carlos Delgado	.15	.07
❑	385	Jeff D'Amico	.10	.05
❑	386	Brian McRae	.10	.05
❑	387	Alan Benes	.15	.07
❑	388	Heathcliff Slocumb	.10	.05
❑	389	Eric Young	.15	.07
❑	390	Travis Fryman	.15	.07
❑	391	David Cone	.25	.11
❑	392	Otis Nixon	.10	.05
❑	393	Jeremi Gonzalez	.15	.07
❑	394	Jeff Juden	.10	.05
❑	395	Jose Vizcaino	.10	.05
❑	396	Ugueth Urbina	.15	.07
❑	397	Ramon Martinez	.15	.07
❑	398	Robb Nen	.15	.07
❑	399	Harold Baines	.15	.07
❑	400	Delino DeShields	.10	.05
❑	401	John Burkett	.10	.05
❑	402	Sterling Hitchcock	.15	.07
❑	403	Mark Clark	.10	.05
❑	404	Terrell Wade	.10	.05
❑	405	Scott Brosius	.15	.07
❑	406	Chad Curtis	.10	.05
❑	407	Brian Johnson	.10	.05
❑	408	Roberto Kelly	.10	.05
❑	409	Dave Dellucci	.50	.23
❑	410	Michael Tucker	.15	.07
❑	411	Mark Kotsay	.25	.11
❑	412	Mark Lewis	.10	.05
❑	413	Ryan McGuire	.10	.05
❑	414	Shawon Dunston	.10	.05
❑	415	Brad Rigby	.10	.05
❑	416	Scott Erickson	.15	.07
❑	417	Bobby Jones	.10	.05
❑	418	Darren Oliver	.10	.05
❑	419	John Smiley	.10	.05
❑	420	T.J. Mathews	.10	.05
❑	421	Dustin Hermanson	.15	.07
❑	422	Mike Timlin	.10	.05
❑	423	Willie Blair	.10	.05
❑	424	Manny Alexander	.10	.05
❑	425	Bob Tewksbury	.10	.05
❑	426	Pete Schourek	.10	.05
❑	427	Reggie Jefferson	.10	.05
❑	428	Ed Sprague	.10	.05
❑	429	Jeff Conine	.15	.07
❑	430	Roberto Hernandez	.10	.05
❑	431	Tom Pagnozzi	.10	.05
❑	432	Jaret Wright	.50	.23
❑	433	Livan Hernandez	.15	.07
❑	434	Andy Ashby	.10	.05
❑	435	Todd Dunn	.10	.05
❑	436	Bobby Higginson	.25	.11
❑	437	Rod Beck	.15	.07
❑	438	Jim Leyritz	.10	.05
❑	439	Matt Williams	.15	.07
❑	440	Brett Tomko	.15	.07
❑	441	Joe Randa	.10	.05
❑	442	Chris Carpenter	.15	.07
❑	443	Dennis Reyes	.15	.07
❑	444	Al Leiter	.15	.07
❑	445	Jason Schmidt	.10	.05
❑	446	Ken Hill	.10	.05
❑	447	Shannon Stewart	.15	.07
❑	448	Enrique Wilson	.15	.07
❑	449	Fernando Tatis	.15	.07
❑	450	Jimmy Key	.15	.07
❑	451	Darrin Fletcher	.10	.05
❑	452	John Valentin	.15	.07
❑	453	Kevin Tapani	.10	.05
❑	454	Eric Karros	.15	.07
❑	455	Jay Bell	.15	.07
❑	456	Walt Weiss	.15	.07
❑	457	Devon White	.15	.07
❑	458	Carl Pavano	.15	.07
❑	459	Mike Lansing	.10	.05
❑	460	John Flaherty	.10	.05
❑	461	Richard Hidalgo	.15	.07
❑	462	Quinton McCracken	.15	.07
❑	463	Karim Garcia	.15	.07
❑	464	Miguel Cairo	.15	.07
❑	465	Edwin Diaz	.10	.05
❑	466	Bobby Smith	.15	.07
❑	467	Yamil Benitez	.10	.05
❑	468	Rich Butler	.25	.11
❑	469	Ben Ford	.25	.11
❑	470	Bubba Trammell	.15	.07
❑	471	Brent Brede	.10	.05
❑	472	Brooks Kieschnick	.10	.05
❑	473	Carlos Castillo	.10	.05
❑	474	Brad Radke SH	.10	.05
❑	475	Roger Clemens SH	.40	.18
❑	476	Curt Schilling SH	.10	.05
❑	477	John Olerud SH	.10	.05
❑	478	Mark McGwire SH	1.25	.55
❑	479	Mike Piazza	1.00	.45
		Ken Griffey Jr. IL		
❑	480	Jeff Bagwell	.60	.25
		Frank Thomas IL		
❑	481	Chipper Jones	.60	.25
		Nomar Garciaparra IL		
❑	482	Larry Walker	.50	.23
		Juan Gonzalez IL		
❑	483	Gary Sheffield	.15	.07
		Tino Martinez IL		
❑	484	Derrick Gibson	.25	.11
		Michael Coleman		
		Norm Hutchins		
❑	485	Braden Looper	.15	.07
		Cliff Politte		
		Brian Rose		

		MINT	NRMT
❑ 486	Eric Milton Jason Marquis Corey Lee	.15	.07
❑ 487	A.J.Hinch Mark Osborne Robert Fick	.50	.23
❑ 488	Aramis Ramirez Alex Gonzalez Sean Casey	.50	.23
❑ 489	Donnie Bridges Tim Drew	.25	.11
❑ 490	Ntema Ndungidi Darnell McDonald	1.00	.45
❑ 491	Ryan Anderson Mark Mangum	1.50	.70
❑ 492	J.J.Davis Troy Glaus	2.00	.90
❑ 493	Jayson Werth Dan Reichert	.25	.11
❑ 494	John Curtice Michael Cuddyer	.60	.25
❑ 495	Jack Cust Jason Standridge	.60	.25
❑ 496	Brian Anderson	.10	.05
❑ 497	Tony Saunders	.10	.05
❑ 498	Vladimir Nunez Jhensy Sandoval	.40	.18
❑ 499	Brad Penny Nick Bierbrodt	.25	.11
❑ 500	Dustin Carr Luis Cruz	.25	.11
❑ 501	Cedric Bowers Marcus McCain	.15	.07
❑ 502	Checklist	.10	.05
❑ 503	Checklist	.10	.05
❑ 504	Alex Rodriguez	2.50	1.10

1998 Topps Baby Boomers

	MINT	NRMT
COMPLETE SET (15)	80.00	36.00
COMMON CARD (BB1-BB15)	1.50	.70

		MINT	NRMT
❑ BB1	Derek Jeter	10.00	4.50
❑ BB2	Scott Rolen	10.00	4.50
❑ BB3	Nomar Garciaparra	12.00	5.50
❑ BB4	Jose Cruz Jr.	5.00	2.20
❑ BB5	Darin Erstad	5.00	2.20
❑ BB6	Todd Helton	5.00	2.20
❑ BB7	Tony Clark	2.50	1.10
❑ BB8	Jose Guillen	1.50	.70
❑ BB9	Andruw Jones	5.00	2.20
❑ BB10	Vladimir Guerrero	6.00	2.70
❑ BB11	Mark Kotsay	2.50	1.10
❑ BB12	Todd Greene	1.50	.70
❑ BB13	Andy Pettitte	2.50	1.10
❑ BB14	Justin Thompson	1.50	.70
❑ BB15	Alan Benes	1.50	.70

1998 Topps Clemente

	MINT	NRMT
COMPLETE SET (19)	110.00	50.00
COMPLETE SERIES 1 (10)	60.00	27.00
COMPLETE SERIES 2 (9)	50.00	22.00
COMMON CARD (1-19)	6.00	2.70

		MINT	NRMT
❑ 1	Roberto Clemente 1955	12.00	5.50
❑ 2	Roberto Clemente 1956	6.00	2.70
❑ 3	Roberto Clemente 1957	6.00	2.70
❑ 4	Roberto Clemente 1958	6.00	2.70
❑ 5	Roberto Clemente 1959	6.00	2.70
❑ 6	Roberto Clemente 1960	6.00	2.70
❑ 7	Roberto Clemente 1961	6.00	2.70
❑ 8	Roberto Clemente 1962	6.00	2.70
❑ 9	Roberto Clemente 1963	6.00	2.70
❑ 10	Roberto Clemente 1964	6.00	2.70
❑ 11	Roberto Clemente 1965	6.00	2.70
❑ 12	Roberto Clemente 1966	6.00	2.70
❑ 13	Roberto Clemente 1967	6.00	2.70
❑ 14	Roberto Clemente 1968	6.00	2.70
❑ 15	Roberto Clemente 1969	6.00	2.70
❑ 16	Roberto Clemente 1970	6.00	2.70
❑ 17	Roberto Clemente 1971	6.00	2.70
❑ 18	Roberto Clemente 1972	6.00	2.70
❑ 19	Roberto Clemente 1973	6.00	2.70

1998 Topps Clemente Finest

	MINT	NRMT
COMPLETE SET (19)	180.00	80.00
COMPLETE SERIES 1 (9)	80.00	36.00
COMPLETE SERIES 2 (10)	100.00	45.00
COMMON CARD (1-19)	12.00	5.50

		MINT	NRMT
❑ 1	Roberto Clemente 1955	25.00	11.00
❑ 2	Roberto Clemente 1956	12.00	5.50
❑ 3	Roberto Clemente 1957	12.00	5.50
❑ 4	Roberto Clemente 1958	12.00	5.50
❑ 5	Roberto Clemente 1959	12.00	5.50
❑ 6	Roberto Clemente 1960	12.00	5.50
❑ 7	Roberto Clemente 1961	12.00	5.50
❑ 8	Roberto Clemente 1962	12.00	5.50
❑ 9	Roberto Clemente 1963	12.00	5.50
❑ 10	Roberto Clemente 1964	12.00	5.50
❑ 11	Roberto Clemente 1965	12.00	5.50
❑ 12	Roberto Clemente 1966	12.00	5.50
❑ 13	Roberto Clemente 1967	12.00	5.50
❑ 14	Roberto Clemente 1968	12.00	5.50
❑ 15	Roberto Clemente 1969	12.00	5.50
❑ 16	Roberto Clemente 1970	12.00	5.50
❑ 17	Roberto Clemente 1971	12.00	5.50
❑ 18	Roberto Clemente 1972	12.00	5.50
❑ 19	Roberto Clemente 1973	12.00	5.50

1998 Topps Clemente Tribute

	MINT	NRMT
COMPLETE SET (5)	8.00	3.60
COMMON CARD (RC1-RC5)	2.00	.90

		MINT	NRMT
❑ RC1	Roberto Clemente Picking Bat from Rack	2.00	.90
❑ RC2	Roberto Clemente Posed batting shot	2.00	.90
❑ RC3	Roberto Clemente Follow through on swing	2.00	.90
❑ RC4	Roberto Clemente Portrait	2.00	.90
❑ RC5	Roberto Clemente	2.00	.90

1998 Topps Clout Nine

	MINT	NRMT
COMPLETE SET (9)	70.00	32.00
COMMON CARD (C1-C9)	1.00	.45

		MINT	NRMT
❑ C1	Edgar Martinez	2.00	.90
❑ C2	Mike Piazza	15.00	6.75
❑ C3	Frank Thomas	15.00	6.75
❑ C4	Craig Biggio	5.00	2.20
❑ C5	Vinny Castilla	3.00	1.35
❑ C6	Jeff Blauser	1.00	.45
❑ C7	Barry Bonds	6.00	2.70
❑ C8	Ken Griffey Jr.	25.00	11.00
❑ C9	Larry Walker	5.00	2.20

1998 Topps Etch-A-Sketch

	MINT	NRMT
COMPLETE SET (9)	50.00	22.00
COMMON CARD (ES1-ES9)	2.50	1.10

		MINT	NRMT
❑ ES1	Albert Belle	3.00	1.35
❑ ES2	Barry Bonds	3.00	1.35
❑ ES3	Ken Griffey Jr.	12.00	5.50
❑ ES4	Greg Maddux	8.00	3.60
❑ ES5	Hideo Nomo	3.00	1.35
❑ ES6	Mike Piazza	8.00	3.60
❑ ES7	Cal Ripken	10.00	4.50
❑ ES8	Frank Thomas	8.00	3.60
❑ ES9	Mo Vaughn	3.00	1.35

1998 Topps Flashback

	MINT	NRMT
COMPLETE SET (10)	80.00	36.00
COMMON CARD (FB1-FB10)	2.50	1.10
❑ FB1 Barry Bonds	8.00	3.60
❑ FB2 Ken Griffey Jr.	30.00	13.50
❑ FB3 Paul Molitor	6.00	2.70
❑ FB4 Randy Johnson	6.00	2.70
❑ FB5 Cal Ripken	25.00	11.00
❑ FB6 Tony Gwynn	15.00	6.75
❑ FB7 Kenny Lofton	6.00	2.70
❑ FB8 Gary Sheffield	4.00	1.80
❑ FB9 Deion Sanders	2.50	1.10
❑ FB10 Brady Anderson	2.50	1.10

1998 Topps Focal Points

	MINT	NRMT
COMPLETE SET (15)	120.00	55.00
COMMON CARD (FP1-FP15)	3.00	1.35
❑ FP1 Juan Gonzalez	10.00	4.50
❑ FP2 Nomar Garciaparra	12.00	5.50
❑ FP3 Jose Cruz Jr.	4.00	1.80
❑ FP4 Cal Ripken	15.00	6.75
❑ FP5 Ken Griffey Jr.	20.00	9.00
❑ FP6 Ivan Rodriguez	5.00	2.20
❑ FP7 Larry Walker	4.00	1.80
❑ FP8 Barry Bonds	5.00	2.20
❑ FP9 Roger Clemens	8.00	3.60
❑ FP10 Frank Thomas	12.00	5.50
❑ FP11 Chuck Knoblauch	3.00	1.35
❑ FP12 Mike Piazza	12.00	5.50
❑ FP13 Greg Maddux	12.00	5.50
❑ FP14 Vladimir Guerrero	5.00	2.20
❑ FP15 Andruw Jones	4.00	1.80

1998 Topps HallBound

	MINT	NRMT
COMPLETE SET (15)	100.00	45.00
COMMON CARD (HB1-HB15)	2.00	.90
❑ HB1 Paul Molitor	4.00	1.80
❑ HB2 Tony Gwynn	10.00	4.50
❑ HB3 Wade Boggs	4.00	1.80
❑ HB4 Roger Clemens	8.00	3.60

	MINT	NRMT
❑ HB5 Dennis Eckersley	2.00	.90
❑ HB6 Cal Ripken	15.00	6.75
❑ HB7 Greg Maddux	12.00	5.50
❑ HB8 Rickey Henderson	4.00	1.80
❑ HB9 Ken Griffey Jr.	20.00	9.00
❑ HB10 Frank Thomas	12.00	5.50
❑ HB11 Mark McGwire	25.00	11.00
❑ HB12 Barry Bonds	5.00	2.20
❑ HB13 Mike Piazza	12.00	5.50
❑ HB14 Juan Gonzalez	10.00	4.50
❑ HB15 Randy Johnson	4.00	1.80

1998 Topps Milestones

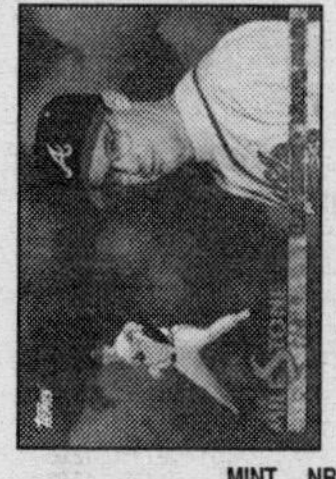

	MINT	NRMT
COMPLETE SET (10)	80.00	36.00
COMMON CARD (MS1-MS10)	1.50	.70
❑ MS1 Barry Bonds	4.00	1.80
❑ MS2 Roger Clemens	6.00	2.70
❑ MS3 Dennis Eckersley	1.50	.70
❑ MS4 Juan Gonzalez	8.00	3.60
❑ MS5 Ken Griffey Jr.	15.00	6.75
❑ MS6 Tony Gwynn	8.00	3.60
❑ MS7 Greg Maddux	10.00	4.50
❑ MS8 Mark McGwire	20.00	9.00
❑ MS9 Cal Ripken	12.00	5.50
❑ MS10 Frank Thomas	10.00	4.50

1998 Topps Mystery Finest

	MINT	NRMT
COMPLETE SET (20)	150.00	70.00
COMMON CARD (ILM1-ILM20)	2.00	.90
❑ ILM1 Chipper Jones	12.00	5.50
❑ ILM2 Cal Ripken	20.00	9.00
❑ ILM3 Greg Maddux	15.00	6.75
❑ ILM4 Rafael Palmeiro	3.00	1.35
❑ ILM5 Todd Hundley	2.00	.90
❑ ILM6 Derek Jeter	15.00	6.75
❑ ILM7 John Olerud	2.00	.90
❑ ILM8 Tino Martinez	5.00	2.20
❑ ILM9 Larry Walker	5.00	2.20
❑ ILM10 Ken Griffey Jr.	25.00	11.00
❑ ILM11 Andres Galarraga	5.00	2.20
❑ ILM12 Randy Johnson	5.00	2.20
❑ ILM13 Mike Piazza	15.00	6.75
❑ ILM14 Jim Edmonds	3.00	1.35
❑ ILM15 Eric Karros	2.00	.90
❑ ILM16 Tim Salmon	5.00	2.20
❑ ILM17 Sammy Sosa	12.00	5.50
❑ ILM18 Frank Thomas	15.00	6.75
❑ ILM19 Mark Grace	3.00	1.35
❑ ILM20 Albert Belle	6.00	2.70

1998 Topps Mystery Finest Bordered

	MINT	NRMT
COMPLETE SET (20)	200.00	90.00
COMMON CARD (M1-M20)	4.00	1.80
❑ M1 Nomar Garciaparra	15.00	6.75
❑ M2 Chipper Jones	12.00	5.50
❑ M3 Scott Rolen	10.00	4.50
❑ M4 Albert Belle	6.00	2.70
❑ M5 Mo Vaughn	6.00	2.70
❑ M6 Jose Cruz Jr.	5.00	2.20
❑ M7 Mark McGwire	30.00	13.50
❑ M8 Derek Jeter	12.00	5.50
❑ M9 Tony Gwynn	12.00	5.50
❑ M10 Frank Thomas	15.00	6.75
❑ M11 Tino Martinez	4.00	1.80
❑ M12 Greg Maddux	15.00	6.75
❑ M13 Juan Gonzalez	12.00	5.50
❑ M14 Larry Walker	5.00	2.20
❑ M15 Mike Piazza	15.00	6.75
❑ M16 Cal Ripken	20.00	9.00
❑ M17 Jeff Bagwell	8.00	3.60
❑ M18 Andruw Jones	5.00	2.20
❑ M19 Barry Bonds	6.00	2.70
❑ M20 Ken Griffey Jr.	25.00	11.00

1998 Topps Rookie Class

	MINT	NRMT
COMPLETE SET (10)	12.00	5.50
COMMON CARD (R1-R10)	1.00	.45
❑ R1 Travis Lee	4.00	1.80
❑ R2 Richard Hidalgo	1.00	.45
❑ R3 Todd Helton	2.50	1.10
❑ R4 Paul Konerko	2.00	.90
❑ R5 Mark Kotsay	1.50	.70
❑ R6 Derrek Lee	1.00	.45
❑ R7 Eli Marrero	1.00	.45

❑ R8 Fernando Tatis .... 1.00 .45
❑ R9 Juan Encarnacion.......... 1.00 .45
❑ R10 Ben Grieve 4.00 1.80

1999 Topps

	MINT	NRMT
COMPLETE SERIES 1 (241) ..	25.00	11.00
COMMON CARD (1-6/8-242)......	.10	.05
COMP.MCGWIRE 220 SET (70)	800.00	350.00
MCGWIRE 220 HR 1	25.00	11.00
MCGWIRE 220 HR 2-60	12.00	5.50
MCGWIRE 220 HR 61	30.00	13.50
MCGWIRE 220 HR 62	40.00	18.00
MCGWIRE 220 HR 63-69	20.00	9.00
MCWGIRE 220 HR 70	80.00	36.00

❑ 1 Roger Clemens .... .75 .35
❑ 2 Andres Galarraga
❑ 3 Scott Brosius...................... .15 .07
❑ 4 John Flaherty .... .10 .05
❑ 5 Jim Leyritz........................... .10 .05
❑ 6 Ray Durham .... .15 .07
❑ 8 Jose Vizcaino .... .10 .05
❑ 9 Will Clark
❑ 10 David Wells........................ .25 .11
❑ 11 Jose Guillen .... .15 .07
❑ 12 Scott Hatteberg................. .10 .05
❑ 13 Edgardo Alfonzo .... .15 .07
❑ 14 Mike Bordick .... .10 .05
❑ 15 Manny Ramirez
❑ 16 Greg Maddux .... 1.25 .55
❑ 17 David Segui........................ .15 .07
❑ 18 Darryl Strawberry .... .15 .07
❑ 19 Brad Radke .... .15 .07
❑ 20 Kerry Wood .... 1.00 .45
❑ 21 Matt Anderson.................. .15 .07
❑ 22 Derrek Lee .... .15 .07
❑ 23 Mickey Morandini .... .10 .05
❑ 24 Paul Konerko
❑ 25 Travis Lee .... .50 .23
❑ 26 Ken Hill .... .10 .05
❑ 27 Kenny Rogers .... .10 .05
❑ 28 Paul Sorrento .... .10 .05
❑ 29 Quilvio Veras.................... .10 .05
❑ 30 Todd Walker .... .25 .11
❑ 31 Ryan Jackson .... .10 .05
❑ 32 John Olerud....................... .15 .07
❑ 33 Doug Glanville................... .15 .07
❑ 34 Nolan Ryan .... 2.00 .90
❑ 35 Ray Lankford..................... .15 .07
❑ 36 Mark Loretta .... .10 .05
❑ 37 Jason Dickson................... .15 .07
❑ 38 Sean Bergman .... .10 .05
❑ 39 Quinton McCracken .... .15 .07
❑ 40 Bartolo Colon .... .15 .07
❑ 41 Brady Anderson .... .15 .07
❑ 42 Chris Stynes .... .10 .05
❑ 43 Jorge Posada .... .15 .07
❑ 44 Justin Thompson.............. .15 .07
❑ 45 Johnny Damon .... .15 .07
❑ 46 Armando Benitez............. .10 .05
❑ 47 Brant Brown .... .15 .07
❑ 48 Charlie Hayes .... .10 .05
❑ 49 Darren Dreifort .... .10 .05
❑ 50 Juan Gonzalez .... 1.00 .45
❑ 51 Chuck Knoblauch .... .25 .11
❑ 52 Todd Helton....................... .50 .23
❑ 53 Rick Reed .... .10 .05
❑ 54 Chris Gomez .... .10 .05
❑ 55 Gary Sheffield .... .25 .11
❑ 56 Rod Beck............................ .15 .07
❑ 57 Rey Sanchez..................... .10 .05
❑ 58 Garret Anderson .... .15 .07
❑ 59 Jimmy Haynes................... .10 .05
❑ 60 Steve Woodard .... .15 .07
❑ 61 Rondell White .... .15 .07
❑ 62 Vladimir Guerrero .... .60 .25
❑ 63 Eric Karros .... .15 .07
❑ 64 Russ Davis .... .10 .05
❑ 65 Mo Vaughn .... .50 .23
❑ 66 Sammy Sosa.................. 1.00 .45
❑ 67 Troy Percival .... .15 .07
❑ 68 Kenny Lofton
❑ 69 Bill Taylor .... .10 .05
❑ 70 Mark McGwire 2.50 1.10
❑ 71 Roger Cedeno................... .10 .05
❑ 72 Javy Lopez .... .15 .07
❑ 73 Damion Easley .... .15 .07
❑ 74 Andy Pettitte .... .25 .11
❑ 75 Tony Gwynn .... 1.00 .45
❑ 76 Ricardo Rincon .... .10 .05
❑ 77 F.P. Santangelo .... .10 .05
❑ 78 Jay Bell .... .15 .07
❑ 79 Scott Servais..................... .10 .05
❑ 80 Jose Canseco
❑ 81 Roberto Hernandez.......... .10 .05
❑ 82 Todd Dunwoody .... .15 .07
❑ 83 John Wetteland .... .15 .07
❑ 84 Mike Caruso .... .15 .07
❑ 85 Derek Jeter .... 1.00 .45
❑ 86 Aaron Sele .... .15 .07
❑ 87 Jose Lima .... .10 .05
❑ 88 Ryan Christenson .... .10 .05
❑ 89 Jeff Cirillo .... .15 .07
❑ 90 Jose Hernandez .... .10 .05
❑ 91 Mark Kotsay .... .15 .07
❑ 92 Darren Bragg..................... .10 .05
❑ 93 Albert Belle .... .40 .18
❑ 94 Matt Lawton....................... .15 .07
❑ 95 Pedro Martinez
❑ 96 Greg Vaughn..................... .15 .07
❑ 97 Neifi Perez .... .15 .07
❑ 98 Gerald Williams .... .10 .05
❑ 99 Derek Bell .... .15 .07
❑ 100 Ken Griffey Jr. .... 2.00 .90
❑ 101 David Cone .... .25 .11
❑ 102 Brian Johnson .... .10 .05
❑ 103 Dean Palmer .... .15 .07
❑ 104 Javier Valentin............... .15 .07
❑ 105 Trevor Hoffman .... .15 .07
❑ 106 Butch Huskey .... .10 .05
❑ 107 Dave Martinez .... .10 .05
❑ 108 Billy Wagner .... .15 .07
❑ 109 Shawn Green .... .15 .07
❑ 110 Ben Grieve .... .75 .35
❑ 111 Tom Goodwin .... .10 .05
❑ 112 Jaret Wright
❑ 113 Aramis Ramirez
❑ 114 Dmitri Young .... .15 .07
❑ 115 Hideki Irabu .... .25 .11
❑ 116 Roberto Kelly.................. .10 .05
❑ 117 Jeff Fassero .... .10 .05
❑ 118 Mark Clark....................... .10 .05
❑ 119 Jason McDonald .... .10 .05
❑ 120 Matt Williams.................. .15 .07
❑ 121 Dave Burba .... .10 .05
❑ 122 Bret Saberhagen .... .15 .07
❑ 123 Deivi Cruz .... .10 .05
❑ 124 Chad Curtis .... .10 .05
❑ 125 Scott Rolen .... 1.00 .45
❑ 126 Lee Stevens .... .10 .05
❑ 127 J.T. Snow .... .15 .07
❑ 128 Rusty Greer..................... .15 .07
❑ 129 Brian Meadows .... .10 .05
❑ 130 Jim Edmonds .... .25 .11
❑ 131 Ron Gant......................... .10 .05
❑ 132 A.J. Hinch .... .15 .07
❑ 133 Shannon Stewart............ .15 .07
❑ 134 Brad Fullmer .... .15 .07
❑ 135 Cal Eldred .... .10 .05
❑ 136 Matt Walbeck .... .10 .05
❑ 137 Carl Everett .... .10 .05
❑ 138 Walt Weiss .... .15 .07
❑ 139 Fred McGriff .... .25 .11
❑ 140 Darin Erstad .... .50 .23
❑ 141 Dave Nilsson................... .10 .05
❑ 142 Eric Young....................... .10 .05
❑ 143 Dan Wilson .... .10 .05
❑ 144 Jeff Reed......................... .10 .05
❑ 145 Brett Tomko..................... .15 .07
❑ 146 Terry Steinbach .... .15 .07
❑ 147 Seth Greisinger .... .15 .07
❑ 148 Pat Meares .... .10 .05
❑ 149 Livan Hernandez .... .15 .07
❑ 150 Jeff Bagwell..................... .60 .25
❑ 151 Bob Wickman .... .10 .05
❑ 152 Omar Vizquel .... .15 .07
❑ 153 Eric Davis .... .15 .07
❑ 154 Larry Sutton.................... .10 .05
❑ 155 Magglio Ordonez............ .15 .07
❑ 156 Eric Milton .... .15 .07
❑ 157 Darren Lewis .... .10 .05
❑ 158 Rick Aguilera .... .10 .05
❑ 159 Mike Lieberthal .... .10 .05
❑ 160 Robb Nen .... .15 .07
❑ 161 Brian Giles...................... .15 .07
❑ 162 Jeff Brantley .... .10 .05
❑ 163 Gary DiSarcina .... .10 .05
❑ 164 John Valentin .... .15 .07
❑ 165 David Dellucci .... .15 .07
❑ 166 Chan Ho Park
❑ 167 Masato Yoshii .... .15 .07
❑ 168 Jason Schmidt................ .15 .07
❑ 169 LaTroy Hawkins .... .10 .05
❑ 170 Bret Boone .... .15 .07
❑ 171 Jerry DiPoto .... .10 .05
❑ 172 Mariano Rivera .... .15 .07
❑ 173 Mike Cameron................. .15 .07
❑ 174 Scott Erickson .... .15 .07
❑ 175 Charles Johnson .... .15 .07
❑ 176 Bobby Jones .... .10 .05
❑ 177 Francisco Cordova .... .10 .05
❑ 178 Todd Jones .... .10 .05
❑ 179 Jeff Montgomery .... .15 .07
❑ 180 Mike Mussina
❑ 181 Bob Abreu .... .15 .07
❑ 182 Ismael Valdes .... .15 .07
❑ 183 Andy Fox .... .10 .05
❑ 184 Woody Williams.............. .10 .05
❑ 185 Denny Neagle .... .15 .07
❑ 186 Jose Valentin.................. .10 .05
❑ 187 Darrin Fletcher .... .10 .05
❑ 188 Gabe Alvarez .... .15 .07
❑ 189 Eddie Taubensee .... .10 .05
❑ 190 Edgar Martinez .... .15 .07
❑ 191 Jason Kendall .... .15 .07
❑ 192 Darryl Kile .... .15 .07
❑ 193 Jeff King .... .15 .07
❑ 194 Rey Ordonez .... .15 .07
❑ 195 Andruw Jones .... .50 .23
❑ 196 Tony Fernandez .... .10 .05
❑ 197 Jamey Wright .... .10 .05
❑ 198 B.J. Surhoff .... .15 .07
❑ 199 Vinny Castilla .... .25 .11
❑ 200 David Wells HL .... .25 .11
❑ 201 Mark McGwire HL 2.50 1.10
❑ 202 Sammy Sosa HL .... 1.00 .45
❑ 203 Roger Clemens HL .... .40 .18
❑ 204 Kerry Wood HL .... .50 .23
❑ 205 Lance Berkman .... .75 .35
Mike Frank

		MINT	NRMT
	Gabe Kapler		
❑ 206	Alex Escobar	1.00	.45
	Ricky Ledee		
	Mike Stoner		
❑ 207	Peter Bergeron	.50	.23
	Jeremy Giambi		
	George Lombard		
❑ 208	Michael Barrett	.25	.11
	Ben Davis		
	Robert Fick		
❑ 209	Pat Cline	.25	.11
	Ramon Hernandez		
	Jayson Werth		
❑ 210	Bruce Chen	.50	.23
	Chris Enochs		
	Ryan Anderson		
❑ 211	Mike Lincoln	.25	.11
	Octavio Dotel		
	Brad Penny		
❑ 212	Chuck Abbott	.25	.11
	Brent Butler		
	Danny Klassen		
❑ 213	Chris C.Jones	.50	.23
	Jeff Urban		
❑ 214	Arturo McDowell	.50	.23
	Tony Torcato		
❑ 215	Josh McKinley	.50	.23
	Jason Tyner		
❑ 216	Matt Burch	.50	.23
	Seth Etheron		
	UER back Etherton		
❑ 217	Mamon Tucker	.50	.23
	Rick Elder		
❑ 218	J.M.Gold	1.00	.45
	Ryan Mills		
❑ 219	Adam Brown	.50	.23
	Choo Freeman		
❑ 221	Larry Walker LL		
❑ 222	Bernie Williams LL		
❑ 223	Mark McGwire LL	2.50	1.10
❑ 224	Ken Griffey Jr. LL	2.00	.90
❑ 225	Sammy Sosa LL	1.00	.45
❑ 226	Juan Gonzalez LL	1.00	.45
❑ 227	Dante Bichette LL	.15	.07
❑ 228	Alex Rodriguez LL	1.25	.55
❑ 229	Sammy Sosa LL	1.00	.45
❑ 230	Derek Jeter LL	1.00	.45
❑ 231	Greg Maddux LL	1.25	.55
❑ 232	Roger Clemens LL	.75	.35
❑ 233	Ricky Ledee WS	.25	.11
❑ 234	Chuck Knoblauch WS	.25	.11
❑ 235	Bernie Williams WS		
❑ 236	Tino Martinez WS		
❑ 237	Orlando Hernandez WS	.60	.25
❑ 238	Scott Brosius WS	.15	.07
❑ 239	Andy Pettitte WS	.25	.11
❑ 240	Mariano Rivera WS	.15	.07
❑ 241	Checklist 1	.10	.05
❑ 242	Checklist 2	.10	.05

1999 Topps Oversize

	MINT	NRMT
COMPLETE SET (8)	40.00	18.00
COMMON CARD (1-8)	4.00	1.80

		MINT	NRMT
❑ 1	Roger Clemens	4.00	1.80
❑ 2	Greg Maddux	6.00	2.70
❑ 3	Kerry Wood	5.00	2.20
❑ 4	Juan Gonzalez	5.00	2.20
❑ 5	Sammy Sosa	5.00	2.20
❑ 6	Mark McGwire	12.00	5.50
❑ 7	Ken Griffey Jr.	10.00	4.50
❑ 8	Ben Grieve	4.00	1.80

1999 Topps Autographs

	MINT	NRMT
COMPLETE SET (8)	600.00	275.00
COMMON CARD (A1-A8)	30.00	13.50

		MINT	NRMT
❑ A1	Roger Clemens	120.00	55.00
❑ A2	Chipper Jones	120.00	55.00
❑ A3	Scott Rolen	80.00	36.00
❑ A4	Alex Rodriguez	150.00	70.00
❑ A5	Andres Galarraga	40.00	18.00
❑ A6	Rondell White	30.00	13.50
❑ A7	Ben Grieve	80.00	36.00
❑ A8	Troy Glaus	80.00	36.00

1999 Topps Hall of Fame Collection

	MINT	NRMT
COMPLETE SET (10)	20.00	9.00
COMMON CARD (HOF1-HOF10)	1.50	.70

		MINT	NRMT
❑ HOF1	Mike Schmidt	3.00	1.35
❑ HOF2	Brooks Robinson	2.00	.90
❑ HOF3	Stan Musial	3.00	1.35
❑ HOF4	Willie McCovey	2.00	.90
❑ HOF5	Eddie Matthews	2.00	.90
❑ HOF6	Reggie Jackson	3.00	1.35
❑ HOF7	Ernie Banks	3.00	1.35
❑ HOF8	Whitey Ford	2.00	.90
❑ HOF9	Bob Feller	2.00	.90
❑ HOF10	Yogi Berra	3.00	1.35

1999 Topps Lords of the Diamond

	MINT	NRMT
COMPLETE SET (15)	60.00	27.00
COMMON CARD (LD1-LD15)	1.50	.70

		MINT	NRMT
❑ LD1	Ken Griffey Jr.	10.00	4.50
❑ LD2	Chipper Jones	5.00	2.20
❑ LD3	Sammy Sosa	5.00	2.20
❑ LD4	Frank Thomas	6.00	2.70
❑ LD5	Mark McGwire	12.00	5.50
❑ LD6	Jeff Bagwell	3.00	1.35
❑ LD7	Alex Rodriguez	6.00	2.70
❑ LD8	Juan Gonzalez	5.00	2.20
❑ LD9	Barry Bonds	2.50	1.10
❑ LD10	Nomar Garciaparra	6.00	2.70
❑ LD11	Darin Erstad	2.50	1.10
❑ LD12	Tony Gwynn	5.00	2.20
❑ LD13	Andres Galarraga	2.50	1.10
❑ LD14	Mike Piazza	6.00	2.70
❑ LD15	Greg Maddux	6.00	2.70

1999 Topps New Breed

	MINT	NRMT
COMPLETE SET (15)	30.00	13.50
COMMON CARD (NB1-NB15)	.75	.35

		MINT	NRMT
❑ NB1	Darin Erstad	2.00	.90
❑ NB2	Brad Fullmer	.75	.35
❑ NB3	Kerry Wood	4.00	1.80
❑ NB4	Nomar Garciaparra	5.00	2.20
❑ NB5	Travis Lee	2.50	1.10
❑ NB6	Scott Rolen	4.00	1.80
❑ NB7	Todd Helton	2.00	.90
❑ NB8	Vladimir Guerrero	2.50	1.10
❑ NB9	Derek Jeter	4.00	1.80
❑ NB10	Alex Rodriguez	5.00	2.20
❑ NB11	Ben Grieve	3.00	1.35
❑ NB12	Andruw Jones	2.00	.90
❑ NB13	Paul Konerko	1.50	.70
❑ NB14	Aramis Ramirez	1.50	.70
❑ NB15	Adrian Beltre	1.50	.70

1999 Topps Picture Perfect

	MINT	NRMT
COMPLETE SET (10)	15.00	6.75
COMMON CARD (P1-P10)	.40	.18

		MINT	NRMT
❑ P1	Ken Griffey Jr.	4.00	1.80
❑ P2	Kerry Wood	2.00	.90
❑ P3	Pedro Martinez	.75	.35
❑ P4	Mark McGwire	5.00	2.20
❑ P5	Greg Maddux	2.50	1.10
❑ P6	Sammy Sosa	2.00	.90
❑ P7	Greg Vaughn	.40	.18
❑ P8	Juan Gonzalez	2.00	.90

	MINT	NRMT
❑ P9 Jeff Bagwell	1.25	.55
❑ P10 Derek Jeter	2.00	.90

1999 Topps Power Brokers

	MINT	NRMT
COMPLETE SET (20)	150.00	70.00
COMMON CARD (PB1-PB20)	2.00	.90
❑ PB1 Mark McGwire	25.00	11.00
❑ PB2 Andres Galarraga	4.00	1.80
❑ PB3 Ken Griffey Jr.	20.00	9.00
❑ PB4 Sammy Sosa	10.00	4.50
❑ PB5 Juan Gonzalez	10.00	4.50
❑ PB6 Alex Rodriguez	12.00	5.50
❑ PB7 Frank Thomas	12.00	5.50
❑ PB8 Jeff Bagwell	6.00	2.70
❑ PB9 Vinny Castilla	3.00	1.35
❑ PB10 Mike Piazza	12.00	5.50
❑ PB11 Greg Vaughn	2.00	.90
❑ PB12 Barry Bonds	5.00	2.20
❑ PB13 Mo Vaughn	5.00	2.20
❑ PB14 Jim Thome	4.00	1.80
❑ PB15 Larry Walker	4.00	1.80
❑ PB16 Chipper Jones	10.00	4.50
❑ PB17 Nomar Garciaparra	12.00	5.50
❑ PB18 Manny Ramirez	4.00	1.80
❑ PB19 Roger Clemens	8.00	3.60
❑ PB20 Kerry Wood	10.00	4.50

1999 Topps Ryan

	MINT	NRMT
COMPLETE SERIES 1 (14)	80.00	36.00
COMMON CARD (1-27)	6.00	2.70
❑ 1 Nolan Ryan 1968	12.00	5.50
❑ 3 Nolan Ryan 1970	6.00	2.70
❑ 5 Nolan Ryan 1972	6.00	2.70
❑ 7 Nolan Ryan 1974	6.00	2.70
❑ 9 Nolan Ryan 1976	6.00	2.70
❑ 11 Nolan Ryan 1978	6.00	2.70
❑ 13 Nolan Ryan 1980	6.00	2.70
❑ 15 Nolan Ryan 1982	6.00	2.70
❑ 17 Nolan Ryan 1984	6.00	2.70
❑ 19 Nolan Ryan 1986	6.00	2.70
❑ 21 Nolan Ryan 1988	6.00	2.70
❑ 23 Nolan Ryan 1990	6.00	2.70
❑ 25 Nolan Ryan 1992	6.00	2.70
❑ 27 Nolan Ryan 1994	6.00	2.70
❑ NNO Nolan Ryan AU	300.00	135.00

1999 Topps Ryan Finest

	MINT	NRMT
COMPLETE SERIES 1 (13)	120.00	55.00
COMMON CARD (2-26)	12.00	5.50
❑ 2 Nolan Ryan 1969	12.00	5.50
❑ 4 Nolan Ryan 1971	12.00	5.50
❑ 6 Nolan Ryan 1973	12.00	5.50
❑ 8 Nolan Ryan 1975	12.00	5.50
❑ 10 Nolan Ryan 1977	12.00	5.50
❑ 12 Nolan Ryan 1979	12.00	5.50
❑ 14 Nolan Ryan 1981	12.00	5.50
❑ 16 Nolan Ryan 1983	12.00	5.50
❑ 18 Nolan Ryan 1985	12.00	5.50
❑ 20 Nolan Ryan 1987	12.00	5.50
❑ 22 Nolan Ryan 1989	12.00	5.50
❑ 24 Nolan Ryan 1991	12.00	5.50
❑ 26 Nolan Ryan 1993	12.00	5.50

1996 Topps Chrome

	MINT	NRMT
COMPLETE SET (165)	80.00	36.00
COMMON CARD (1-165)	.40	.18
❑ 1 Tony Gwynn STP	2.00	.90
❑ 2 Mike Piazza STP	2.50	1.10
❑ 3 Greg Maddux STP	2.50	1.10
❑ 4 Jeff Bagwell STP	1.50	.70
❑ 5 Larry Walker STP	.75	.35
❑ 6 Barry Larkin STP	.40	.18
❑ 7 Mickey Mantle COMM	15.00	6.75
❑ 8 Tom Glavine STP	.75	.35
❑ 9 Craig Biggio STP	.75	.35
❑ 10 Barry Bonds STP	1.00	.45
❑ 11 Heathcliff Slocumb STP	.40	.18
❑ 12 Matt Williams STP	.40	.18
❑ 13 Todd Helton	15.00	6.75
❑ 14 Paul Molitor	1.50	.70
❑ 15 Glenallen Hill	.40	.18
❑ 16 Troy Percival	.75	.35
❑ 17 Albert Belle	2.00	.90
❑ 18 Mark Wohlers	.40	.18
❑ 19 Kirby Puckett	2.50	1.10
❑ 20 Mark Grace	1.00	.45
❑ 21 J.T. Snow	.75	.35
❑ 22 David Justice	1.50	.70
❑ 23 Mike Mussina	1.50	.70
❑ 24 Bernie Williams	1.50	.70
❑ 25 Ron Gant	.40	.18
❑ 26 Carlos Baerga	.75	.35
❑ 27 Gary Sheffield	1.00	.45
❑ 28 Cal Ripken 2131	6.00	2.70
❑ 29 Frank Thomas	5.00	2.20
❑ 30 Kevin Seitzer	.40	.18
❑ 31 Joe Carter	.75	.35
❑ 32 Jeff King	.40	.18
❑ 33 David Cone	1.00	.45
❑ 34 Eddie Murray	1.50	.70
❑ 35 Brian Jordan	.75	.35
❑ 36 Garret Anderson	.75	.35
❑ 37 Hideo Nomo	2.50	1.10
❑ 38 Steve Finley	.75	.35
❑ 39 Ivan Rodriguez	2.00	.90
❑ 40 Quilvio Veras	.40	.18
❑ 41 Mark McGwire	8.00	3.60
❑ 42 Greg Vaughn	.75	.35
❑ 43 Randy Johnson	1.50	.70
❑ 44 David Segui	.75	.35
❑ 45 Derek Bell	.75	.35
❑ 46 John Valentin	.75	.35
❑ 47 Steve Avery	.40	.18
❑ 48 Tino Martinez	1.50	.70
❑ 49 Shane Reynolds	.75	.35
❑ 50 Jim Edmonds	1.00	.45
❑ 51 Raul Mondesi	1.00	.45
❑ 52 Chipper Jones	4.00	1.80
❑ 53 Gregg Jefferies	.40	.18
❑ 54 Ken Caminiti	1.00	.45
❑ 55 Brian McRae	.40	.18
❑ 56 Don Mattingly	2.50	1.10
❑ 57 Marty Cordova	.40	.18
❑ 58 Vinny Castilla	1.00	.45
❑ 59 John Smoltz	.75	.35
❑ 60 Travis Fryman	.75	.35
❑ 61 Ryan Klesko	.75	.35
❑ 62 Alex Fernandez	.40	.18
❑ 63 Dante Bichette	.75	.35
❑ 64 Eric Karros	.75	.35
❑ 65 Roger Clemens	3.00	1.35
❑ 66 Randy Myers	.40	.18
❑ 67 Cal Ripken	6.00	2.70
❑ 68 Rod Beck	.40	.18
❑ 69 Jack McDowell	.40	.18
❑ 70 Ken Griffey Jr.	8.00	3.60
❑ 71 Ramon Martinez	.75	.35
❑ 72 Jason Giambi	.75	.35
❑ 73 Nomar Garciaparra FS	6.00	2.70
❑ 74 Billy Wagner	.75	.35
❑ 75 Todd Greene	.75	.35
❑ 76 Paul Wilson	.40	.18
❑ 77 Johnny Damon	.75	.35
❑ 78 Alan Benes	.75	.35
❑ 79 Karim Garcia FS	.75	.35
❑ 80 Derek Jeter FS	5.00	2.20
❑ 81 Kirby Puckett STP	1.50	.70
❑ 82 Cal Ripken STP	3.00	1.35
❑ 83 Albert Belle STP	1.00	.45
❑ 84 Randy Johnson STP	.75	.35
❑ 85 Wade Boggs STP	.75	.35
❑ 86 Carlos Baerga STP	.40	.18
❑ 87 Ivan Rodriguez STP	1.00	.45
❑ 88 Mike Mussina STP	.75	.35
❑ 89 Frank Thomas STP	2.50	1.10
❑ 90 Ken Griffey Jr. STP	4.00	1.80

Card	MINT	NRMT
❑ 91 Jose Mesa STP	.40	.18
❑ 92 Matt Morris	6.00	2.70
❑ 93 Mike Piazza	5.00	2.20
❑ 94 Edgar Martinez	.75	.35
❑ 95 Chuck Knoblauch	1.50	.70
❑ 96 Andres Galarraga	1.50	.70
❑ 97 Tony Gwynn	4.00	1.80
❑ 98 Lee Smith	.75	.35
❑ 99 Sammy Sosa	4.00	1.80
❑ 100 Jim Thome	1.50	.70
❑ 101 Bernard Gilkey	.40	.18
❑ 102 Brady Anderson	.75	.35
❑ 103 Rico Brogna	.40	.18
❑ 104 Len Dykstra	.75	.35
❑ 105 Tom Glavine	1.50	.70
❑ 106 John Olerud	.75	.35
❑ 107 Terry Steinbach	.75	.35
❑ 108 Brian Hunter	.75	.35
❑ 109 Jay Buhner	.75	.35
❑ 110 Mo Vaughn	2.00	.90
❑ 111 Jose Mesa	.40	.18
❑ 112 Brett Butler	.75	.35
❑ 113 Chili Davis	.75	.35
❑ 114 Paul O'Neill	.75	.35
❑ 115 Roberto Alomar	1.50	.70
❑ 116 Barry Larkin	1.00	.45
❑ 117 Marquis Grissom	.75	.35
❑ 118 Will Clark	1.50	.70
❑ 119 Barry Bonds	2.00	.90
❑ 120 Ozzie Smith	2.00	.90
❑ 121 Pedro Martinez	1.50	.70
❑ 122 Craig Biggio	1.50	.70
❑ 123 Moises Alou	1.00	.45
❑ 124 Robin Ventura	.75	.35
❑ 125 Greg Maddux	5.00	2.20
❑ 126 Tim Salmon	1.50	.70
❑ 127 Wade Boggs	1.50	.70
❑ 128 Ismael Valdes	.75	.35
❑ 129 Juan Gonzalez	4.00	1.80
❑ 130 Ray Lankford	.75	.35
❑ 131 Bobby Bonilla	.75	.35
❑ 132 Reggie Sanders	.75	.35
❑ 133 Alex Ochoa	.40	.18
❑ 134 Mark Loretta	.40	.18
❑ 135 Jason Kendall	1.50	.70
❑ 136 Brooks Kieschnick	.40	.18
❑ 137 Chris Snopek	.40	.18
❑ 138 Ruben Rivera NOW	.75	.35
❑ 139 Jeff Suppan	.40	.18
❑ 140 John Wasdin	.40	.18
❑ 141 Jay Payton	.40	.18
❑ 142 Rick Krivda	.40	.18
❑ 143 Jimmy Haynes	.40	.18
❑ 144 Ryne Sandberg	2.00	.90
❑ 145 Matt Williams	.75	.35
❑ 146 Jose Canseco	1.50	.70
❑ 147 Larry Walker	1.50	.70
❑ 148 Kevin Appier	.75	.35
❑ 149 Javy Lopez	.75	.35
❑ 150 Dennis Eckersley	.75	.35
❑ 151 Jason Isringhausen	.40	.18
❑ 152 Dean Palmer	.75	.35
❑ 153 Jeff Bagwell	2.50	1.10
❑ 154 Rondell White	.75	.35
❑ 155 Wally Joyner	.75	.35
❑ 156 Fred McGriff	1.00	.45
❑ 157 Cecil Fielder	.75	.35
❑ 158 Rafael Palmeiro	1.00	.45
❑ 159 Rickey Henderson	1.50	.70
❑ 160 Shawon Dunston	.40	.18
❑ 161 Manny Ramirez	1.50	.70
❑ 162 Alex Gonzalez	.40	.18
❑ 163 Shawn Green	.75	.35
❑ 164 Kenny Lofton	1.50	.70
❑ 165 Jeff Conine	.75	.35

1996 Topps Chrome Refractors

	MINT	NRMT
COMPLETE SET (165)	2500.00	1100.00
COMMON CARD (1-165)	6.00	2.70

*STARS: 6X TO 15X BASIC CARDS
*YOUNG STARS: 5X TO 12X BASIC CARDS
*ROOKIES/PROSPECTS: 2X TO 4X BASIC CARDS

1996 Topps Chrome Masters of the Game

	MINT	NRMT
COMPLETE SET (20)	60.00	27.00
COMMON CARD (1-20)	1.50	.70
COMP.REF.SET (20)	200.00	90.00

*REFRACTORS: 1.25X TO 3X BASIC CHROME MASTERS
REF.STATED ODDS 1:36 HOBBY

Card	MINT	NRMT
❑ 1 Dennis Eckersley	1.50	.70
❑ 2 Denny Martinez	1.50	.70
❑ 3 Eddie Murray	4.00	1.80
❑ 4 Paul Molitor	4.00	1.80
❑ 5 Ozzie Smith	5.00	2.20
❑ 6 Rickey Henderson	4.00	1.80
❑ 7 Tim Raines	1.50	.70
❑ 8 Lee Smith	1.50	.70
❑ 9 Cal Ripken	15.00	6.75
❑ 10 Chili Davis	1.50	.70
❑ 11 Wade Boggs	4.00	1.80
❑ 12 Tony Gwynn	10.00	4.50
❑ 13 Don Mattingly	6.00	2.70
❑ 14 Bret Saberhagen	1.50	.70
❑ 15 Kirby Puckett	6.00	2.70
❑ 16 Joe Carter	1.50	.70
❑ 17 Roger Clemens	8.00	3.60
❑ 18 Barry Bonds	5.00	2.20
❑ 19 Greg Maddux	12.00	5.50
❑ 20 Frank Thomas	12.00	5.50

1996 Topps Chrome Wrecking Crew

	MINT	NRMT
COMPLETE SET (15)	80.00	36.00
COMMON CARD (WC1-WC15)	2.00	.90
COMP.REF.SET (15)	250.00	110.00

*REFRACTORS: 1.25X TO 3X BASIC CHROME WRECKING
REF.STATED ODDS 1:72 HOBBY

Card	MINT	NRMT
❑ WC1 Jeff Bagwell	8.00	3.60
❑ WC2 Albert Belle	6.00	2.70
❑ WC3 Barry Bonds	6.00	2.70
❑ WC4 Jose Canseco	5.00	2.20
❑ WC5 Joe Carter	2.00	.90
❑ WC6 Cecil Fielder	2.00	.90
❑ WC7 Ron Gant	2.00	.90
❑ WC8 Juan Gonzalez	12.00	5.50
❑ WC9 Ken Griffey Jr.	25.00	11.00
❑ WC10 Fred McGriff	3.00	1.35
❑ WC11 Mark McGwire	25.00	11.00
❑ WC12 Mike Piazza	15.00	6.75
❑ WC13 Frank Thomas	15.00	6.75
❑ WC14 Mo Vaughn	6.00	2.70
❑ WC15 Matt Williams	2.00	.90

1997 Topps Chrome

	MINT	NRMT
COMPLETE SET (165)	80.00	36.00
COMMON CARD (1-165)	.40	.18

Card	MINT	NRMT
❑ 1 Barry Bonds	2.00	.90
❑ 2 Jose Valentin	.40	.18
❑ 3 Brady Anderson	.75	.35
❑ 4 Wade Boggs	1.50	.70
❑ 5 Andres Galarraga	1.50	.70
❑ 6 Rusty Greer	.75	.35
❑ 7 Derek Jeter	5.00	2.20
❑ 8 Ricky Bottalico	.75	.35
❑ 9 Mike Piazza	5.00	2.20
❑ 10 Garret Anderson	.75	.35
❑ 11 Jeff King	.40	.18
❑ 12 Kevin Appier	.75	.35
❑ 13 Mark Grace	1.00	.45
❑ 14 Jeff D'Amico	.40	.18
❑ 15 Jay Buhner	.75	.35
❑ 16 Hal Morris	.40	.18
❑ 17 Harold Baines	.75	.35
❑ 18 Jeff Cirillo	.75	.35
❑ 19 Tom Glavine	1.50	.70
❑ 20 Andy Pettitte	1.00	.45
❑ 21 Mark McGwire	8.00	3.60
❑ 22 Chuck Knoblauch	1.50	.70
❑ 23 Raul Mondesi	1.00	.45
❑ 24 Albert Belle	2.00	.90
❑ 25 Trevor Hoffman	.75	.35
❑ 26 Eric Young	.75	.35
❑ 27 Brian McRae	.40	.18
❑ 28 Jim Edmonds	1.00	.45
❑ 29 Robb Nen	.40	.18
❑ 30 Reggie Sanders	.75	.35
❑ 31 Mike Lansing	.40	.18
❑ 32 Craig Biggio	1.50	.70
❑ 33 Ray Lankford	.75	.35
❑ 34 Charles Nagy	.75	.35
❑ 35 Paul Wilson	.40	.18
❑ 36 John Wetteland	.75	.35
❑ 37 Derek Bell	.75	.35
❑ 38 Edgar Martinez	.75	.35
❑ 39 Rickey Henderson	1.50	.70
❑ 40 Jim Thome	1.50	.70
❑ 41 Frank Thomas	5.00	2.20
❑ 42 Jackie Robinson	5.00	2.20
❑ 43 Terry Steinbach	.75	.35
❑ 44 Kevin Brown	1.00	.45
❑ 45 Joey Hamilton	.75	.35
❑ 46 Travis Fryman	.75	.35
❑ 47 Juan Gonzalez	4.00	1.80
❑ 48 Ron Gant	.40	.18
❑ 49 Greg Maddux	5.00	2.20
❑ 50 Wally Joyner	.75	.35
❑ 51 John Valentin	.75	.35
❑ 52 Bret Boone	.75	.35

❑ 53	Paul Molitor	1.50	.70
❑ 54	Rafael Palmeiro	1.00	.45
❑ 55	Todd Hundley	.75	.35
❑ 56	Ellis Burks	.75	.35
❑ 57	Bernie Williams	1.50	.70
❑ 58	Roberto Alomar	1.50	.70
❑ 59	Jose Mesa	.40	.18
❑ 60	Troy Percival	.75	.35
❑ 61	John Smoltz	.75	.35
❑ 62	Jeff Conine	.75	.35
❑ 63	Bernard Gilkey	.40	.18
❑ 64	Mickey Tettleton	.40	.18
❑ 65	Justin Thompson	.75	.35
❑ 66	Tony Phillips	.40	.18
❑ 67	Ryne Sandberg	2.00	.90
❑ 68	Geronimo Berroa	.40	.18
❑ 69	Todd Hollandsworth	.40	.18
❑ 70	Rey Ordonez	.75	.35
❑ 71	Marquis Grissom	.75	.35
❑ 72	Tino Martinez	1.50	.70
❑ 73	Steve Finley	.75	.35
❑ 74	Andy Benes	.75	.35
❑ 75	Jason Kendall	1.00	.45
❑ 76	Johnny Damon	.75	.35
❑ 77	Jason Giambi	.75	.35
❑ 78	Henry Rodriguez	.75	.35
❑ 79	Edgar Renteria	.75	.35
❑ 80	Ray Durham	.75	.35
❑ 81	Gregg Jefferies	.40	.18
❑ 82	Roberto Hernandez	.40	.18
❑ 83	Joe Carter	.75	.35
❑ 84	Jermaine Dye	.40	.18
❑ 85	Julio Franco	.75	.35
❑ 86	David Justice	1.50	.70
❑ 87	Jose Canseco	1.50	.70
❑ 88	Paul O'Neill	.75	.35
❑ 89	Mariano Rivera	.75	.35
❑ 90	Bobby Higginson	1.00	.45
❑ 91	Mark Grudzielanek	.75	.35
❑ 92	Lance Johnson	.40	.18
❑ 93	Ken Caminiti	1.00	.45
❑ 94	Gary Sheffield	1.00	.45
❑ 95	Luis Castillo	.75	.35
❑ 96	Scott Rolen	4.00	1.80
❑ 97	Chipper Jones	4.00	1.80
❑ 98	Darryl Strawberry	.75	.35
❑ 99	Nomar Garciaparra	5.00	2.20
❑ 100	Jeff Bagwell	2.50	1.10
❑ 101	Ken Griffey Jr.	8.00	3.60
❑ 102	Sammy Sosa	4.00	1.80
❑ 103	Jack McDowell	.40	.18
❑ 104	James Baldwin	.75	.35
❑ 105	Rocky Coppinger	.40	.18
❑ 106	Manny Ramirez	1.50	.70
❑ 107	Tim Salmon	1.50	.70
❑ 108	Eric Karros	.75	.35
❑ 109	Brett Butler	.75	.35
❑ 110	Randy Johnson	1.50	.70
❑ 111	Pat Hentgen	.75	.35
❑ 112	Rondell White	.75	.35
❑ 113	Eddie Murray	1.50	.70
❑ 114	Ivan Rodriguez	2.00	.90
❑ 115	Jermaine Allensworth	.40	.18
❑ 116	Ed Sprague	.40	.18
❑ 117	Kenny Lofton	1.50	.70
❑ 118	Alan Benes	.75	.35
❑ 119	Fred McGriff	1.00	.45
❑ 120	Alex Fernandez	.40	.18
❑ 121	Al Martin	.40	.18
❑ 122	Devon White	.75	.35
❑ 123	David Cone	1.00	.45
❑ 124	Karim Garcia	.75	.35
❑ 125	Chili Davis	.75	.35
❑ 126	Roger Clemens	3.00	1.35
❑ 127	Bobby Bonilla	.75	.35
❑ 128	Mike Mussina	1.50	.70
❑ 129	Todd Walker	1.50	.70
❑ 130	Dante Bichette	.75	.35
❑ 131	Carlos Baerga	.75	.35
❑ 132	Matt Williams	.75	.35
❑ 133	Will Clark	1.50	.70
❑ 134	Dennis Eckersley	.75	.35
❑ 135	Ryan Klesko	.75	.35
❑ 136	Dean Palmer	.75	.35
❑ 137	Javy Lopez	.75	.35
❑ 138	Greg Vaughn	.75	.35
❑ 139	Vinny Castilla	1.00	.45
❑ 140	Cal Ripken	6.00	2.70
❑ 141	Ruben Rivera	.75	.35
❑ 142	Mark Wohlers	.40	.18
❑ 143	Tony Clark	1.00	.45
❑ 144	Jose Rosado	.40	.18
❑ 145	Tony Gwynn	4.00	1.80
❑ 146	Cecil Fielder	.75	.35
❑ 147	Brian Jordan	.75	.35
❑ 148	Bob Abreu	.75	.35
❑ 149	Barry Larkin	1.00	.45
❑ 150	Robin Ventura	.75	.35
❑ 151	John Olerud	.75	.35
❑ 152	Rod Beck	.40	.18
❑ 153	Vladimir Guerrero	3.00	1.35
❑ 154	Marty Cordova	.40	.18
❑ 155	Todd Stottlemyre	.40	.18
❑ 156	Hideo Nomo	2.00	.90
❑ 157	Denny Neagle	.75	.35
❑ 158	John Jaha	.40	.18
❑ 159	Mo Vaughn	2.00	.90
❑ 160	Andruw Jones	2.50	1.10
❑ 161	Moises Alou	1.00	.45
❑ 162	Larry Walker	1.50	.70
❑ 163	Eddie Murray SH	.75	.35
❑ 164	Paul Molitor SH	.75	.35
❑ 165	Checklist	.40	.18

1997 Topps Chrome Refractors

	MINT	NRMT
COMPLETE SET (165)	2000.00	900.00
COMMON CARD (1-165)	6.00	2.70

*STARS: 6X TO 15X BASE CARDS
*YOUNG STARS: 5X TO 12X BASE CARDS

1997 Topps Chrome All-Stars

	MINT	NRMT
COMPLETE SET (22)	120.00	55.00
COMMON CARD (AS1-AS22)	1.50	.70
COMP.REF.SET (22)	400.00	180.00

*REFRACTORS: 1.25X TO 3X BASIC CARDS
REFRACTOR STATED ODDS 1:72

❑ AS1	Ivan Rodriguez	6.00	2.70
❑ AS2	Todd Hundley	2.50	1.10
❑ AS3	Frank Thomas	15.00	6.75
❑ AS4	Andres Galarraga	5.00	2.20
❑ AS5	Chuck Knoblauch	5.00	2.20
❑ AS6	Eric Young	2.50	1.10
❑ AS7	Jim Thome	5.00	2.20
❑ AS8	Chipper Jones	12.00	5.50
❑ AS9	Cal Ripken	20.00	9.00
❑ AS10	Barry Larkin	3.00	1.35
❑ AS11	Albert Belle	6.00	2.70
❑ AS12	Barry Bonds	6.00	2.70
❑ AS13	Ken Griffey Jr.	25.00	11.00
❑ AS14	Ellis Burks	2.50	1.10
❑ AS15	Juan Gonzalez	12.00	5.50
❑ AS16	Gary Sheffield	3.00	1.35
❑ AS17	Andy Pettitte	3.00	1.35
❑ AS18	Tom Glavine	5.00	2.20
❑ AS19	Pat Hentgen	2.50	1.10
❑ AS20	John Smoltz	2.50	1.10
❑ AS21	Roberto Hernandez	1.50	.70
❑ AS22	Mark Wohlers	1.50	.70

1997 Topps Chrome Diamond Duos

	MINT	NRMT
COMPLETE SET (10)	100.00	45.00
COMMON CARD (DD1-DD10)	4.00	1.80
COMP.REF.SET (10)	300.00	135.00

*REFRACTORS: 1.25X TO 3X BASIC CARDS
REFRACTOR STATED ODDS 1:108

❑ DD1	Chipper Jones Andruw Jones	12.00	5.50
❑ DD2	Derek Jeter Bernie Williams	10.00	4.50
❑ DD3	Ken Griffey Jr. Jay Buhner	20.00	9.00
❑ DD4	Kenny Lofton Manny Ramirez	4.00	1.80
❑ DD5	Jeff Bagwell Craig Biggio	6.00	2.70
❑ DD6	Juan Gonzalez Ivan Rodriguez	10.00	4.50
❑ DD7	Cal Ripken Brady Anderson	15.00	6.75
❑ DD8	Mike Piazza Hideo Nomo	12.00	5.50
❑ DD9	Andres Galarraga Dante Bichette	4.00	1.80
❑ DD10	Frank Thomas Albert Belle	12.00	5.50

1997 Topps Chrome Season's Best

	MINT	NRMT
COMPLETE SET (25)	100.00	45.00
COMMON CARD (1-25)	1.00	.45
COMP.REF.SET (25)	300.00	135.00

*REFRACTORS: 1.25X TO 3X BASIC CARDS
REFRACTOR STATED ODDS 1:54

❑ 1	Tony Gwynn	10.00	4.50
❑ 2	Frank Thomas	12.00	5.50
❑ 3	Ellis Burks	2.00	.90
❑ 4	Paul Molitor	4.00	1.80

Card	Player	MINT	NRMT
❑ 5	Chuck Knoblauch	4.00	1.80
❑ 6	Mark McGwire	20.00	9.00
❑ 7	Brady Anderson	2.00	.90
❑ 8	Ken Griffey Jr.	20.00	9.00
❑ 9	Albert Belle	5.00	2.20
❑ 10	Andres Galarraga	4.00	1.80
❑ 11	Andres Galarraga	4.00	1.80
❑ 12	Albert Belle	5.00	2.20
❑ 13	Juan Gonzalez	10.00	4.50
❑ 14	Mo Vaughn	5.00	2.20
❑ 15	Rafael Palmeiro	2.50	1.10
❑ 16	John Smoltz	2.00	.90
❑ 17	Andy Pettitte	2.50	1.10
❑ 18	Pat Hentgen	2.00	.90
❑ 19	Mike Mussina	4.00	1.80
❑ 20	Andy Benes	2.00	.90
❑ 21	Kenny Lofton	4.00	1.80
❑ 22	Tom Goodwin	1.00	.45
❑ 23	Otis Nixon	1.00	.45
❑ 24	Eric Young	2.00	.90
❑ 25	Lance Johnson	1.00	.45

1998 Topps Chrome

	MINT	NRMT
COMPLETE SET (503)	400.00	180.00
COMPLETE SERIES 1 (282)	200.00	90.00
COMPLETE SERIES 2 (221)	200.00	90.00
COMMON CARD (1-504)	.50	.23

Card	Player	MINT	NRMT
❑ 1	Tony Gwynn	5.00	2.20
❑ 2	Larry Walker	2.00	.90
❑ 3	Billy Wagner	.75	.35
❑ 4	Denny Neagle	.75	.35
❑ 5	Vladimir Guerrero	3.00	1.35
❑ 6	Kevin Brown	1.25	.55
❑ 8	Mariano Rivera	.75	.35
❑ 9	Tony Clark	1.25	.55
❑ 10	Deion Sanders	.75	.35
❑ 11	Francisco Cordova	.50	.23
❑ 12	Matt Williams	.75	.35
❑ 13	Carlos Baerga	.75	.35
❑ 14	Mo Vaughn	2.50	1.10
❑ 15	Bobby Witt	.50	.23
❑ 16	Matt Stairs	.75	.35
❑ 17	Chan Ho Park	2.00	.90
❑ 18	Mike Bordick	.50	.23
❑ 19	Michael Tucker	.75	.35
❑ 20	Frank Thomas	6.00	2.70
❑ 21	Roberto Clemente	5.00	2.20
❑ 22	Dmitri Young	.75	.35
❑ 23	Steve Trachsel	.50	.23
❑ 24	Jeff Kent	.75	.35
❑ 25	Scott Rolen	5.00	2.20
❑ 26	John Thomson	.50	.23
❑ 27	Joe Vitiello	.50	.23
❑ 28	Eddie Guardado	.50	.23
❑ 29	Charlie Hayes	.50	.23
❑ 30	Juan Gonzalez	5.00	2.20
❑ 31	Garret Anderson	.75	.35
❑ 32	John Jaha	.50	.23
❑ 33	Omar Vizquel	.75	.35
❑ 34	Brian Hunter	.75	.35
❑ 35	Jeff Bagwell	3.00	1.35
❑ 36	Mark Lemke	.50	.23
❑ 37	Doug Glanville	.75	.35
❑ 38	Dan Wilson	.50	.23
❑ 39	Steve Cooke	.50	.23
❑ 40	Chili Davis	.75	.35
❑ 41	Mike Cameron	.75	.35
❑ 42	F.P. Santangelo	.50	.23
❑ 43	Brad Ausmus	.50	.23
❑ 44	Gary DiSarcina	.50	.23
❑ 45	Pat Hentgen	.75	.35
❑ 46	Wilton Guerrero	.50	.23
❑ 47	Devon White	.75	.35
❑ 48	Danny Patterson	.50	.23
❑ 49	Pat Meares	.50	.23
❑ 50	Rafael Palmeiro	1.25	.55
❑ 51	Mark Gardner	.50	.23
❑ 52	Jeff Blauser	.50	.23
❑ 53	Dave Hollins	.50	.23
❑ 54	Carlos Garcia	.50	.23
❑ 55	Ben McDonald	.50	.23
❑ 56	John Mabry	.50	.23
❑ 57	Trevor Hoffman	.75	.35
❑ 58	Tony Fernandez	.50	.23
❑ 59	Rich Loiselle	.75	.35
❑ 60	Mark Leiter	.50	.23
❑ 61	Pat Kelly	.50	.23
❑ 62	John Flaherty	.50	.23
❑ 63	Roger Bailey	.50	.23
❑ 64	Tom Gordon	.75	.35
❑ 65	Ryan Klesko	.75	.35
❑ 66	Darryl Hamilton	.50	.23
❑ 67	Jim Eisenreich	.50	.23
❑ 68	Butch Huskey	.50	.23
❑ 69	Mark Grudzielanek	.75	.35
❑ 70	Marquis Grissom	.75	.35
❑ 71	Mark McLemore	.50	.23
❑ 72	Gary Gaetti	.50	.23
❑ 73	Greg Gagne	.50	.23
❑ 74	Lyle Mouton	.50	.23
❑ 75	Jim Edmonds	1.25	.55
❑ 76	Shawn Green	.75	.35
❑ 77	Greg Vaughn	.75	.35
❑ 78	Terry Adams	.50	.23
❑ 79	Kevin Polcovich	.50	.23
❑ 80	Troy O'Leary	.75	.35
❑ 81	Jeff Shaw	.75	.35
❑ 82	Rich Becker	.50	.23
❑ 83	David Wells	1.25	.55
❑ 84	Steve Karsay	.50	.23
❑ 85	Charles Nagy	.75	.35
❑ 86	B.J. Surhoff	.75	.35
❑ 87	Jamey Wright	.50	.23
❑ 88	James Baldwin	.75	.35
❑ 89	Edgardo Alfonzo	.75	.35
❑ 90	Jay Buhner	.75	.35
❑ 91	Brady Anderson	.75	.35
❑ 92	Scott Servais	.50	.23
❑ 93	Edgar Renteria	.75	.35
❑ 94	Mike Lieberthal	.50	.23
❑ 95	Rick Aguilera	.50	.23
❑ 96	Walt Weiss	.75	.35
❑ 97	Deivi Cruz	.50	.23
❑ 98	Kurt Abbott	.50	.23
❑ 99	Henry Rodriguez	.75	.35
❑ 100	Mike Piazza	6.00	2.70
❑ 101	Billy Taylor	.50	.23
❑ 102	Todd Zeile	.75	.35
❑ 103	Rey Ordonez	.75	.35
❑ 104	Willie Greene	.75	.35
❑ 105	Tony Womack	.75	.35
❑ 106	Mike Sweeney	.50	.23
❑ 107	Jeffrey Hammonds	.75	.35
❑ 108	Kevin Orie	.50	.23
❑ 109	Alex Gonzalez	.50	.23
❑ 110	Jose Canseco	2.00	.90
❑ 111	Paul Sorrento	.50	.23
❑ 112	Joey Hamilton	.75	.35
❑ 113	Brad Radke	.75	.35
❑ 114	Steve Avery	.50	.23
❑ 115	Esteban Loaiza	.50	.23
❑ 116	Stan Javier	.50	.23
❑ 117	Chris Gomez	.50	.23
❑ 118	Royce Clayton	.50	.23
❑ 119	Orlando Merced	.50	.23
❑ 120	Kevin Appier	.75	.35
❑ 121	Mel Nieves	.50	.23
❑ 122	Joe Girardi	.50	.23
❑ 123	Rico Brogna	.75	.35
❑ 124	Kent Mercker	.50	.23
❑ 125	Manny Ramirez	2.00	.90
❑ 126	Jeromy Burnitz	.75	.35
❑ 127	Kevin Foster	.50	.23
❑ 128	Matt Morris	.75	.35
❑ 129	Jason Dickson	.75	.35
❑ 130	Tom Glavine	2.00	.90
❑ 131	Wally Joyner	.75	.35
❑ 132	Rick Reed	.50	.23
❑ 133	Todd Jones	.50	.23
❑ 134	Dave Martinez	.50	.23
❑ 135	Sandy Alomar	.75	.35
❑ 136	Mike Lansing	.50	.23
❑ 137	Sean Berry	.50	.23
❑ 138	Doug Jones	.50	.23
❑ 139	Todd Stottlemyre	.75	.35
❑ 140	Jay Bell	.75	.35
❑ 141	Jaime Navarro	.50	.23
❑ 142	Chris Hoiles	.50	.23
❑ 143	Joey Cora	.75	.35
❑ 144	Scott Spiezio	.50	.23
❑ 145	Joe Carter	.75	.35
❑ 146	Jose Guillen	.75	.35
❑ 147	Damion Easley	.75	.35
❑ 148	Lee Stevens	.50	.23
❑ 149	Alex Fernandez	.50	.23
❑ 150	Randy Johnson	2.00	.90
❑ 151	J.T. Snow	.75	.35
❑ 152	Chuck Finley	.75	.35
❑ 153	Bernard Gilkey	.50	.23
❑ 154	David Segui	.75	.35
❑ 155	Dante Bichette	.75	.35
❑ 156	Kevin Stocker	.50	.23
❑ 157	Carl Everett	.50	.23
❑ 158	Jose Valentin	.50	.23
❑ 159	Pokey Reese	.50	.23
❑ 160	Derek Jeter	5.00	2.20
❑ 161	Roger Pavlik	.50	.23
❑ 162	Mark Wohlers	.50	.23
❑ 163	Ricky Bottalico	.75	.35
❑ 164	Ozzie Guillen	.50	.23
❑ 165	Mike Mussina	2.00	.90
❑ 166	Gary Sheffield	1.25	.55
❑ 167	Hideo Nomo	2.50	1.10
❑ 168	Mark Grace	1.25	.55
❑ 169	Aaron Sele	.75	.35
❑ 170	Darryl Kile	.75	.35
❑ 171	Shawn Estes	.75	.35
❑ 172	Vinny Castilla	1.25	.55
❑ 173	Ron Coomer	.50	.23
❑ 174	Jose Rosado	.50	.23
❑ 175	Kenny Lofton	2.00	.90
❑ 176	Jason Giambi	.75	.35
❑ 177	Hal Morris	.50	.23
❑ 178	Darren Bragg	.50	.23
❑ 179	Orel Hershiser	.75	.35
❑ 180	Ray Lankford	.75	.35
❑ 181	Hideki Irabu	1.25	.55
❑ 182	Kevin Young	.75	.35
❑ 183	Javy Lopez	.75	.35
❑ 184	Jeff Montgomery	.50	.23
❑ 185	Mike Holtz	.50	.23
❑ 186	George Williams	.50	.23
❑ 187	Cal Eldred	.50	.23
❑ 188	Tom Candiotti	.50	.23
❑ 189	Glenallen Hill	.50	.23
❑ 190	Brian Giles	.75	.35
❑ 191	Dave Mlicki	.50	.23
❑ 192	Garrett Stephenson	.50	.23
❑ 193	Jeff Frye	.50	.23
❑ 194	Joe Oliver	.50	.23
❑ 195	Bob Hamelin	.50	.23
❑ 196	Luis Sojo	.50	.23
❑ 197	LaTroy Hawkins	.50	.23
❑ 198	Kevin Elster	.50	.23
❑ 199	Jeff Reed	.50	.23
❑ 200	Dennis Eckersley	.75	.35
❑ 201	Bill Mueller	.75	.35
❑ 202	Russ Davis	.75	.35
❑ 203	Armando Benitez	.50	.23
❑ 204	Quilvio Veras	.50	.23
❑ 205	Tim Naehring	.50	.23
❑ 206	Quinton McCracken	.75	.35
❑ 207	Raul Casanova	.50	.23
❑ 208	Matt Lawton	.75	.35
❑ 209	Luis Alicea	.50	.23

❑ 210	Luis Gonzalez	.50	.23
❑ 211	Allen Watson	.50	.23
❑ 212	Gerald Williams	.50	.23
❑ 213	David Bell	.50	.23
❑ 214	Todd Hollandsworth	.50	.23
❑ 215	Wade Boggs	2.00	.90
❑ 216	Jose Mesa	.50	.23
❑ 217	Jamie Moyer	.50	.23
❑ 218	Darren Daulton	.75	.35
❑ 219	Mickey Morandini	.50	.23
❑ 220	Rusty Greer	.75	.35
❑ 221	Jim Bullinger	.50	.23
❑ 222	Jose Offerman	.50	.23
❑ 223	Matt Karchner	.50	.23
❑ 224	Woody Williams	.50	.23
❑ 225	Mark Loretta	.50	.23
❑ 226	Mike Hampton	.50	.23
❑ 227	Willie Adams	.50	.23
❑ 228	Scott Hatteberg	.50	.23
❑ 229	Rich Amaral	.50	.23
❑ 230	Terry Steinbach	.75	.35
❑ 231	Glendon Rusch	.50	.23
❑ 232	Bret Boone	.75	.35
❑ 233	Robert Person	.50	.23
❑ 234	Jose Hernandez	.50	.23
❑ 235	Doug Drabek	.50	.23
❑ 236	Jason McDonald	.50	.23
❑ 237	Chris Widger	.50	.23
❑ 238	Tom Martin	.50	.23
❑ 239	Dave Burba	.50	.23
❑ 240	Pete Rose Jr.	.75	.35
❑ 241	Bobby Ayala	.50	.23
❑ 242	Tim Wakefield	.50	.23
❑ 243	Dennis Springer	.50	.23
❑ 244	Tim Belcher	.50	.23
❑ 245	Jon Garland	2.50	1.10
	Geoff Goetz		
❑ 246	Glenn Davis	4.00	1.80
	Lance Berkman		
❑ 247	Vernon Wells	2.50	1.10
	Aaron Akin		
❑ 248	Adam Kennedy	2.50	1.10
	Jason Romano		
❑ 249	Jason Dellaero	2.50	1.10
	Troy Cameron		
❑ 250	Alex Sanchez	6.00	2.70
	Jared Sandberg		
❑ 251	Pablo Ortega	2.50	1.10
	James Manias		
❑ 252	Jason Conti	6.00	2.70
	Mike Stoner		
❑ 253	John Patterson	2.50	1.10
	Larry Rodriguez		
❑ 254	Adrian Beltre	8.00	3.60
	Ryan Minor		
	Aaron Boone		
❑ 255	Ben Grieve	8.00	3.60
	Brian Buchanan		
	Dermal Brown		
❑ 256	Kerrry Wood	20.00	9.00
	Carl Pavano		
	Gil Meche		
❑ 257	David Ortiz	4.00	1.80
	Daryle Ward		
	Richie Sexson		
❑ 258	Randy Winn	2.50	1.10
	Juan Encarnacion		
	Andrew Vessel		
❑ 259	Kris Benson	2.50	1.10
	Travis Smith		
	Courtney Duncan		
❑ 260	Chad Hermansen	4.00	1.80
	Brent Butler		
	Warren Morris		
❑ 261	Ben Davis	4.00	1.80
	Eli Marrero		
	Ramon Hernandez		
❑ 262	Eric Chavez	6.00	2.70
	Russell Branyan		
	Russ Johnson		
❑ 263	Todd Dunwoody	2.50	1.10
	John Barnes		
	Ryan Jackson		
❑ 264	Matt Clement	2.50	1.10
	Roy Halladay		
	Brian Fuentes		
❑ 265	Randy Johnson SH	.75	.35
❑ 266	Kevin Brown SH	.50	.23
❑ 267	Ricardo Rincon SH	.50	.23
❑ 268	Nomar Garciaparra SH	3.00	1.35
❑ 269	Tino Martinez SH	.75	.35
❑ 270	Chuck Knoblauch IL	.75	.35
❑ 271	Pedro Martinez IL	.75	.35
❑ 272	Denny Neagle IL	.50	.23
❑ 273	Juan Gonzalez IL	2.50	1.10
❑ 274	Andres Galarraga IL	.75	.35
❑ 275	Checklist	.50	.23
❑ 276	Checklist	.50	.23
❑ 277	Moises Alou WS	.75	.35
❑ 278	Sandy Alomar WS	.75	.35
❑ 279	Gary Sheffield WS	.75	.35
❑ 280	Matt Williams WS	.75	.35
❑ 281	Livan Hernandez WS	.75	.35
❑ 282	Chad Ogea WS	.75	.35
❑ 283	Marlins Champs	.75	.35
❑ 284	Tino Martinez	2.00	.90
❑ 285	Roberto Alomar	2.00	.90
❑ 286	Jeff King	.75	.35
❑ 287	Brian Jordan	.75	.35
❑ 288	Darin Erstad	2.50	1.10
❑ 289	Ken Caminiti	1.25	.55
❑ 290	Jim Thome	2.00	.90
❑ 291	Paul Molitor	2.00	.90
❑ 292	Ivan Rodriguez	2.50	1.10
❑ 293	Bernie Williams	2.00	.90
❑ 294	Todd Hundley	.75	.35
❑ 295	Andres Galarraga	2.00	.90
❑ 296	Greg Maddux	6.00	2.70
❑ 297	Edgar Martinez	.75	.35
❑ 298	Ron Gant	.50	.23
❑ 299	Derek Bell	.75	.35
❑ 300	Roger Clemens	4.00	1.80
❑ 301	Rondell White	.75	.35
❑ 302	Barry Larkin	1.25	.55
❑ 303	Robin Ventura	.75	.35
❑ 304	Jason Kendall	.75	.35
❑ 305	Chipper Jones	5.00	2.20
❑ 306	John Franco	.75	.35
❑ 307	Sammy Sosa	5.00	2.20
❑ 308	Troy Percival	.75	.35
❑ 309	Chuck Knoblauch	2.00	.90
❑ 310	Ellis Burks	.75	.35
❑ 311	Al Martin	.50	.23
❑ 312	Tim Salmon	2.00	.90
❑ 313	Moises Alou	1.25	.55
❑ 314	Lance Johnson	.50	.23
❑ 315	Justin Thompson	.75	.35
❑ 316	Will Clark	2.00	.90
❑ 317	Barry Bonds	2.50	1.10
❑ 318	Craig Biggio	2.00	.90
❑ 319	John Smoltz	.75	.35
❑ 320	Cal Ripken	8.00	3.60
❑ 321	Ken Griffey Jr.	10.00	4.50
❑ 322	Paul O'Neill	.75	.35
❑ 323	Todd Helton	2.50	1.10
❑ 324	John Olerud	.75	.35
❑ 325	Mark McGwire	12.00	5.50
❑ 326	Jose Cruz Jr.	2.50	1.10
❑ 327	Jeff Cirillo	.75	.35
❑ 328	Dean Palmer	.75	.35
❑ 329	John Wetteland	.75	.35
❑ 330	Steve Finley	.75	.35
❑ 331	Albert Belle	2.50	1.10
❑ 332	Curt Schilling	.75	.35
❑ 333	Raul Mondesi	1.25	.55
❑ 334	Andruw Jones	2.50	1.10
❑ 335	Nomar Garciaparra	6.00	2.70
❑ 336	David Justice	2.00	.90
❑ 337	Andy Pettitte	1.25	.55
❑ 338	Pedro Martinez	2.00	.90
❑ 339	Travis Miller	.50	.23
❑ 340	Chris Stynes	.50	.23
❑ 341	Gregg Jefferies	.50	.23
❑ 342	Jeff Fassero	.50	.23
❑ 343	Craig Counsell	.50	.23
❑ 344	Wilson Alvarez	.75	.35
❑ 345	Bip Roberts	.50	.23
❑ 346	Kelvim Escobar	.75	.35
❑ 347	Mark Bellhorn	.75	.35
❑ 348	Cory Lidle	.50	.23
❑ 349	Fred McGriff	1.25	.55
❑ 350	Chuck Carr	.50	.23
❑ 351	Bob Abreu	.75	.35
❑ 352	Juan Guzman	.50	.23
❑ 353	Fernando Vina	.50	.23
❑ 354	Andy Benes	.75	.35
❑ 355	Dave Nilsson	.50	.23
❑ 356	Bobby Bonilla	.75	.35
❑ 357	Ismael Valdes	.75	.35
❑ 358	Carlos Perez	.75	.35
❑ 359	Kirk Rueter	.50	.23
❑ 360	Bartolo Colon	.75	.35
❑ 361	Mel Rojas	.50	.23
❑ 362	Johnny Damon	.75	.35
❑ 363	Geronimo Berroa	.50	.23
❑ 364	Reggie Sanders	.75	.35
❑ 365	Jermaine Allensworth	.50	.23
❑ 366	Orlando Cabrera	.75	.35
❑ 367	Jorge Fabregas	.50	.23
❑ 368	Scott Stahoviak	.50	.23
❑ 369	Ken Cloude	.75	.35
❑ 370	Donovan Osborne	.50	.23
❑ 371	Roger Cedeno	.50	.23
❑ 372	Neifi Perez	.75	.35
❑ 373	Chris Holt	.50	.23
❑ 374	Cecil Fielder	.75	.35
❑ 375	Marty Cordova	.50	.23
❑ 376	Tom Goodwin	.50	.23
❑ 377	Jeff Suppan	.50	.23
❑ 378	Jeff Brantley	.50	.23
❑ 379	Mark Langston	.50	.23
❑ 380	Shane Reynolds	.75	.35
❑ 381	Mike Fetters	.50	.23
❑ 382	Todd Greene	.75	.35
❑ 383	Ray Durham	.75	.35
❑ 384	Carlos Delgado	.75	.35
❑ 385	Jeff D'Amico	.50	.23
❑ 386	Brian McRae	.50	.23
❑ 387	Alan Benes	.75	.35
❑ 388	Heathcliff Slocumb	.50	.23
❑ 389	Eric Young	.75	.35
❑ 390	Travis Fryman	.75	.35
❑ 391	David Cone	1.25	.55
❑ 392	Otis Nixon	.50	.23
❑ 393	Jeremi Gonzalez	.75	.35
❑ 394	Jeff Juden	.50	.23
❑ 395	Jose Vizcaino	.50	.23
❑ 396	Ugueth Urbina	.75	.35
❑ 397	Ramon Martinez	.75	.35
❑ 398	Robb Nen	.75	.35
❑ 399	Harold Baines	.75	.35
❑ 400	Delino DeShields	.50	.23
❑ 401	John Burkett	.50	.23
❑ 402	Sterling Hitchcock	.75	.35
❑ 403	Mark Clark	.50	.23
❑ 404	Terrell Wade	.50	.23
❑ 405	Scott Brosius	.75	.35
❑ 406	Chad Curtis	.50	.23
❑ 407	Brian Johnson	.50	.23
❑ 408	Roberto Kelly	.50	.23
❑ 409	Dave Dellucci	6.00	2.70
❑ 410	Michael Tucker	.75	.35
❑ 411	Mark Kotsay	1.25	.55
❑ 412	Mark Lewis	.50	.23
❑ 413	Ryan McGuire	.50	.23
❑ 414	Shawon Dunston	.50	.23
❑ 415	Brad Rigby	.50	.23
❑ 416	Scott Erickson	.75	.35
❑ 417	Bobby Jones	.50	.23
❑ 418	Darren Oliver	.50	.23
❑ 419	John Smiley	.50	.23
❑ 420	T.J. Mathews	.50	.23
❑ 421	Dustin Hermanson	.75	.35
❑ 422	Mike Timlin	.50	.23
❑ 423	Willie Blair	.50	.23
❑ 424	Manny Alexander	.50	.23
❑ 425	Bob Tewksbury	.50	.23
❑ 426	Pete Schourek	.50	.23
❑ 427	Reggie Jefferson	.50	.23
❑ 428	Ed Sprague	.50	.23
❑ 429	Jeff Conine	.75	.35
❑ 430	Roberto Hernandez	.50	.23
❑ 431	Tom Pagnozzi	.50	.23
❑ 432	Jaret Wright	2.50	1.10
❑ 433	Livan Hernandez	.75	.35
❑ 434	Andy Ashby	.50	.23

❑ 435 Todd Dunn .50 .23
❑ 436 Bobby Higginson 1.25 .55
❑ 437 Rod Beck .75 .35
❑ 438 Jim Leyritz .50 .23
❑ 439 Matt Williams .75 .35
❑ 440 Brett Tomko .75 .35
❑ 441 Joe Randa .50 .23
❑ 442 Chris Carpenter .75 .35
❑ 443 Dennis Reyes .75 .35
❑ 444 Al Leiter .75 .35
❑ 445 Jason Schmidt .50 .23
❑ 446 Ken Hill .50 .23
❑ 447 Shannon Stewart .75 .35
❑ 448 Enrique Wilson .75 .35
❑ 449 Fernando Tatis .75 .35
❑ 450 Jimmy Key .75 .35
❑ 451 Darrin Fletcher .50 .23
❑ 452 John Valentin .75 .35
❑ 453 Kevin Tapani .50 .23
❑ 454 Eric Karros .75 .35
❑ 455 Jay Bell .75 .35
❑ 456 Walt Weiss .75 .35
❑ 457 Devon White .75 .35
❑ 458 Carl Pavano .75 .35
❑ 459 Mike Lansing .50 .23
❑ 460 John Flaherty .50 .23
❑ 461 Richard Hidalgo .75 .35
❑ 462 Quinton McCracken .75 .35
❑ 463 Karim Garcia .75 .35
❑ 464 Miguel Cairo .75 .35
❑ 465 Edwin Diaz .50 .23
❑ 466 Bobby Smith .75 .35
❑ 467 Yamil Benitez .50 .23
❑ 468 Rich Butler 3.00 1.35
❑ 469 Ben Ford 2.50 1.10
❑ 470 Bubba Trammell .75 .35
❑ 471 Brent Brede .50 .23
❑ 472 Brooks Kieschnick .50 .23
❑ 473 Carlos Castillo .50 .23
❑ 474 Brad Radke SH .50 .23
❑ 475 Roger Clemens SH 2.00 .90
❑ 476 Curt Schilling SH .50 .23
❑ 477 John Olerud SH .50 .23
❑ 478 Mark McGwire SH 6.00 2.70
❑ 479 Mike Piazza IL 5.00 2.20
Ken Griffey Jr.
❑ 480 Jeff Bagwell 3.00 1.35
Frank Thomas
❑ 481 Chipper Jones 3.00 1.35
Nomar Garciaparra IL
❑ 482 Larry Walker IL 2.50 1.10
Juan Gonzalez IL
❑ 483 Gary Sheffield IL .75 .35
Tino Martinez IL
❑ 484 Derrick Gibson 3.00 1.35
Michael Coleman
Norm Hutchins
❑ 485 Braden Looper 2.50 1.10
Cliff Politte
Brian Rose
❑ 486 Eric Milton 2.50 1.10
Jason Marquis
Corey Lee
❑ 487 A.J.Hinch 6.00 2.70
Mark Osborne
Robert Fick
❑ 488 Aramis Ramirez 5.00 2.20
Alex Gonzalez
Sean Casey
❑ 489 Donnie Bridges 3.00 1.35
Tim Drew
❑ 490 Ntema Ndungidi 12.00 5.50
Darnell McDonald
❑ 491 Ryan Anderson 20.00 9.00
Mark Mangum
❑ 492 J.J.Davis 25.00 11.00
Troy Glaus
❑ 493 Jayson Werth 3.00 1.35
Dan Reichert
❑ 494 John Curtice 8.00 3.60
Michael Cuddyer
❑ 495 Jack Cust 8.00 3.60
Jason Standridge
❑ 496 Brian Anderson .75 .35
❑ 497 Tony Saunders .50 .23
❑ 498 Vladimir Nunez 6.00 2.70
Jhensy Sandoval
❑ 499 Brad Penny 4.00 1.80
Nick Bierbrodt
❑ 500 Dustin Carr 3.00 1.35
Luis Cruz
❑ 501 Cedric Bowers 2.50 1.10
Marcus McCain
❑ 502 Checklist .50 .23
❑ 503 Checklist .50 .23
❑ 504 Alex Rodriguez 6.00 2.70

1998 Topps Chrome Refractors

	MINT	NRMT
COMPLETE SET (503)	5000.00	2200.00
COMPLETE SERIES 1 (282)	2500.00	1100.00
COMPLETE SERIES 2 (221)	2500.00	1100.00
COMMON CARD (1-504)	6.00	2.70

*STARS: 5X TO 12X BASIC CARDS
*YOUNG STARS: 4X TO 10X BASIC CARDS
*ROOKIES/PROSPECTS: 2.5X TO 5X BASIC CARDS

1998 Topps Chrome Baby Boomers

	MINT	NRMT
COMPLETE SET (15)	100.00	45.00
COMMON CARD (BB1-BB15)	2.50	1.10

❑ BB1 Derek Jeter 15.00 6.75
❑ BB2 Scott Rolen 15.00 6.75
❑ BB3 Nomar Garciaparra 20.00 9.00
❑ BB4 Jose Cruz Jr. 8.00 3.60
❑ BB5 Darin Erstad 8.00 3.60
❑ BB6 Todd Helton 8.00 3.60
❑ BB7 Tony Clark 4.00 1.80
❑ BB8 Jose Guillen 2.50 1.10
❑ BB9 Andruw Jones 8.00 3.60
❑ BB10 Vladimir Guerrero 10.00 4.50
❑ BB11 Mark Kotsay 4.00 1.80
❑ BB12 Todd Greene 2.50 1.10
❑ BB13 Andy Pettitte 4.00 1.80
❑ BB14 Justin Thompson 2.50 1.10
❑ BB15 Alan Benes 2.50 1.10

1998 Topps Chrome Clout Nine

	MINT	NRMT
COMPLETE SET (9)	80.00	36.00
COMMON CARD (C1-C9)	1.50	.70

❑ C1 Edgar Martinez 2.50 1.10
❑ C2 Mike Piazza 20.00 9.00
❑ C3 Frank Thomas 20.00 9.00
❑ C4 Craig Biggio 6.00 2.70
❑ C5 Vinny Castilla 4.00 1.80
❑ C6 Jeff Blauser 1.50 .70
❑ C7 Barry Bonds 8.00 3.60
❑ C8 Ken Griffey Jr. 30.00 13.50
❑ C9 Larry Walker 6.00 2.70

1998 Topps Chrome Flashback

	MINT	NRMT
COMPLETE SET (10)	80.00	36.00
COMMON CARD (FB1-FB10)	2.50	1.10

❑ FB1 Barry Bonds 8.00 3.60
❑ FB2 Ken Griffey Jr. 30.00 13.50
❑ FB3 Paul Molitor 6.00 2.70
❑ FB4 Randy Johnson 6.00 2.70
❑ FB5 Cal Ripken 25.00 11.00
❑ FB6 Tony Gwynn 15.00 6.75
❑ FB7 Kenny Lofton 6.00 2.70
❑ FB8 Gary Sheffield 4.00 1.80
❑ FB9 Deion Sanders 2.50 1.10
❑ FB10 Brady Anderson 2.50 1.10

1998 Topps Chrome HallBound

	MINT	NRMT
COMPLETE SET (15)	200.00	90.00
COMMON CARD (HB1-HB15)	4.00	1.80

❑ HB1 Paul Molitor 8.00 3.60
❑ HB2 Tony Gwynn 20.00 9.00
❑ HB3 Wade Boggs 8.00 3.60
❑ HB4 Roger Clemens 15.00 6.75
❑ HB5 Dennis Eckersley 4.00 1.80
❑ HB6 Cal Ripken 30.00 13.50

	MINT	NRMT
❑ HB7 Greg Maddux	25.00	11.00
❑ HB8 Rickey Henderson	8.00	3.60
❑ HB9 Ken Griffey Jr.	40.00	18.00
❑ HB10 Frank Thomas	25.00	11.00
❑ HB11 Mark McGwire	50.00	22.00
❑ HB12 Barry Bonds	10.00	4.50
❑ HB13 Mike Piazza	25.00	11.00
❑ HB14 Juan Gonzalez	20.00	9.00
❑ HB15 Randy Johnson	8.00	3.60

1998 Topps Chrome Milestones

	MINT	NRMT
COMPLETE SET (10)	120.00	55.00
COMMON CARD (MS1-MS10)	3.00	1.35
MINOR STARS	3.00	1.35
SEMISTARS	4.00	1.80
UNLISTED STARS	6.00	2.70
❑ MS1 Barry Bonds	8.00	3.60
❑ MS2 Roger Clemens	12.00	5.50
❑ MS3 Dennis Eckersley	3.00	1.35
❑ MS4 Juan Gonzalez	15.00	6.75
❑ MS5 Ken Griffey Jr.	30.00	13.50
❑ MS6 Tony Gwynn	15.00	6.75
❑ MS7 Greg Maddux	20.00	9.00
❑ MS8 Mark McGwire	40.00	18.00
❑ MS9 Cal Ripken	25.00	11.00
❑ MS10 Frank Thomas	20.00	9.00

1998 Topps Chrome Rookie Class

	MINT	NRMT
COMPLETE SET (10)	25.00	11.00
COMMON CARD (R1-R10)	1.50	.70
❑ R1 Travis Lee	6.00	2.70
❑ R2 Richard Hidalgo	1.50	.70
❑ R3 Todd Helton	4.00	1.80
❑ R4 Paul Konerko	3.00	1.35
❑ R5 Mark Kotsay	2.50	1.10
❑ R6 Derrek Lee	1.50	.70
❑ R7 Eli Marrero	1.50	.70
❑ R8 Fernando Tatis	1.50	.70
❑ R9 Juan Encarnacion	1.50	.70
❑ R10 Ben Grieve	6.00	2.70

1996 Topps Gallery

	MINT	NRMT
COMPLETE SET (180)	40.00	18.00
COMMON CARD (1-180)	.25	.11
❑ 1 Tom Glavine	1.00	.45
❑ 2 Carlos Baerga	.50	.23
❑ 3 Dante Bichette	.50	.23
❑ 4 Mark Langston	.25	.11
❑ 5 Ray Lankford	.50	.23
❑ 6 Moises Alou	.75	.35
❑ 7 Marquis Grissom	.50	.23
❑ 8 Ramon Martinez	.50	.23
❑ 9 Steve Finley	.50	.23
❑ 10 Todd Hundley	.50	.23
❑ 11 Brady Anderson	.50	.23
❑ 12 John Valentin	.50	.23
❑ 13 Heathcliff Slocumb	.25	.11
❑ 14 Ruben Sierra	.25	.11
❑ 15 Jeff Conine	.50	.23
❑ 16 Jay Buhner	.50	.23
❑ 17 Sammy Sosa	2.50	1.10
❑ 18 Doug Drabek	.25	.11
❑ 19 Jose Mesa	.25	.11
❑ 20 Jeff King	.25	.11
❑ 21 Mickey Tettleton	.25	.11
❑ 22 Jeff Montgomery	.25	.11
❑ 23 Alex Fernandez	.25	.11
❑ 24 Greg Vaughn	.50	.23
❑ 25 Chuck Finley	.50	.23
❑ 26 Terry Steinbach	.50	.23
❑ 27 Rod Beck	.25	.11
❑ 28 Jack McDowell	.25	.11
❑ 29 Mark Wohlers	.25	.11
❑ 30 Len Dykstra	.50	.23
❑ 31 Bernie Williams	1.00	.45
❑ 32 Travis Fryman	.50	.23
❑ 33 Jose Canseco	1.00	.45
❑ 34 Ken Caminiti	.75	.35
❑ 35 Devon White	.50	.23
❑ 36 Bobby Bonilla	.50	.23
❑ 37 Paul Sorrento	.25	.11
❑ 38 Ryne Sandberg	1.25	.55
❑ 39 Derek Bell	.50	.23
❑ 40 Bobby Jones	.25	.11
❑ 41 J.T. Snow	.50	.23
❑ 42 Denny Neagle	.50	.23
❑ 43 Tim Wakefield	.50	.23
❑ 44 Andres Galarraga	1.00	.45
❑ 45 David Segui	.50	.23
❑ 46 Lee Smith	.50	.23
❑ 47 Mel Rojas	.25	.11
❑ 48 John Franco	.50	.23
❑ 49 Pete Schourek	.25	.11
❑ 50 John Wetteland	.50	.23
❑ 51 Paul Molitor	1.00	.45
❑ 52 Ivan Rodriguez	1.25	.55
❑ 53 Chris Hoiles	.25	.11
❑ 54 Mike Greenwell	.25	.11
❑ 55 Orel Hershiser	.50	.23
❑ 56 Brian McRae	.25	.11
❑ 57 Geronimo Berroa	.25	.11
❑ 58 Craig Biggio	1.00	.45
❑ 59 David Justice	1.00	.45
❑ 60 Lance Johnson	.25	.11
❑ 61 Andy Ashby	.25	.11
❑ 62 Randy Myers	.25	.11
❑ 63 Gregg Jefferies	.25	.11
❑ 64 Kevin Appier	.50	.23
❑ 65 Rick Aguilera	.25	.11
❑ 66 Shane Reynolds	.50	.23
❑ 67 John Smoltz	.50	.23
❑ 68 Ron Gant	.25	.11
❑ 69 Eric Karros	.50	.23
❑ 70 Jim Thome	1.00	.45
❑ 71 Terry Pendleton	.25	.11
❑ 72 Kenny Rogers	.25	.11
❑ 73 Robin Ventura	.50	.23
❑ 74 Dave Nilsson	.25	.11
❑ 75 Brian Jordan	.50	.23
❑ 76 Glenallen Hill	.25	.11
❑ 77 Greg Colbrunn	.25	.11
❑ 78 Roberto Alomar	1.00	.45
❑ 79 Rickey Henderson	1.00	.45
❑ 80 Carlos Garcia	.25	.11
❑ 81 Dean Palmer	.50	.23
❑ 82 Mike Stanley	.25	.11
❑ 83 Hal Morris	.25	.11
❑ 84 Wade Boggs	1.00	.45
❑ 85 Chad Curtis	.25	.11
❑ 86 Roberto Hernandez	.25	.11
❑ 87 John Olerud	.50	.23
❑ 88 Frank Castillo	.25	.11
❑ 89 Rafael Palmeiro	.75	.35
❑ 90 Trevor Hoffman	.50	.23
❑ 91 Marty Cordova	.25	.11
❑ 92 Hideo Nomo	1.50	.70
❑ 93 Johnny Damon	.50	.23
❑ 94 Bill Pulsipher	.25	.11
❑ 95 Garret Anderson	.50	.23
❑ 96 Ray Durham	.50	.23
❑ 97 Ricky Bottalico	.50	.23
❑ 98 Carlos Perez	.50	.23
❑ 99 Troy Percival	.50	.23
❑ 100 Chipper Jones	2.50	1.10
❑ 101 Esteban Loaiza	.25	.11
❑ 102 John Mabry	.25	.11
❑ 103 Jon Nunnally	.25	.11
❑ 104 Andy Pettitte	.75	.35
❑ 105 Lyle Mouton	.25	.11
❑ 106 Jason Isringhausen	.25	.11
❑ 107 Brian L.Hunter	.50	.23
❑ 108 Quilvio Veras	.25	.11
❑ 109 Jim Edmonds	.75	.35
❑ 110 Ryan Klesko	.50	.23
❑ 111 Pedro Martinez	1.00	.45
❑ 112 Joey Hamilton	.50	.23
❑ 113 Vinny Castilla	.75	.35
❑ 114 Alex Gonzalez	.25	.11
❑ 115 Raul Mondesi	.75	.35
❑ 116 Rondell White	.50	.23
❑ 117 Dan Miceli	.25	.11
❑ 118 Tom Goodwin	.25	.11
❑ 119 Bret Boone	.50	.23
❑ 120 Shawn Green	.50	.23
❑ 121 Jeff Cirillo	.50	.23
❑ 122 Rico Brogna	.25	.11
❑ 123 Chris Gomez	.25	.11
❑ 124 Ismael Valdes	.50	.23
❑ 125 Javy Lopez	.50	.23
❑ 126 Manny Ramirez	1.00	.45
❑ 127 Paul Wilson	.25	.11
❑ 128 Billy Wagner	.50	.23
❑ 129 Eric Owens	.25	.11
❑ 130 Todd Greene	.50	.23
❑ 131 Karim Garcia	.50	.23
❑ 132 Jimmy Haynes	.25	.11
❑ 133 Michael Tucker	.50	.23
❑ 134 John Wasdin	.25	.11
❑ 135 Brooks Kieschnick	.25	.11
❑ 136 Alex Ochoa	.25	.11
❑ 137 Ariel Prieto	.25	.11
❑ 138 Tony Clark	1.00	.45
❑ 139 Mark Loretta	.25	.11
❑ 140 Rey Ordonez	.50	.23
❑ 141 Chris Snopek	.25	.11
❑ 142 Roger Cedeno	.25	.11
❑ 143 Derek Jeter	3.00	1.35
❑ 144 Jeff Suppan	.25	.11
❑ 145 Greg Maddux	3.00	1.35
❑ 146 Ken Griffey Jr.	5.00	2.20
❑ 147 Tony Gwynn	2.50	1.10

Card	MINT	NRMT
❑ 148 Darren Daulton	.50	.23
❑ 149 Will Clark	1.00	.45
❑ 150 Mo Vaughn	1.25	.55
❑ 151 Reggie Sanders	.50	.23
❑ 152 Kirby Puckett	1.50	.70
❑ 153 Paul O'Neill	.50	.23
❑ 154 Tim Salmon	1.00	.45
❑ 155 Mark McGwire	5.00	2.20
❑ 156 Barry Bonds	1.25	.55
❑ 157 Albert Belle	1.25	.55
❑ 158 Edgar Martinez	.50	.23
❑ 159 Mike Mussina	1.00	.45
❑ 160 Cecil Fielder	.50	.23
❑ 161 Kenny Lofton	1.00	.45
❑ 162 Randy Johnson	1.00	.45
❑ 163 Juan Gonzalez	2.50	1.10
❑ 164 Jeff Bagwell	1.50	.70
❑ 165 Joe Carter	.50	.23
❑ 166 Mike Piazza	3.00	1.35
❑ 167 Eddie Murray	1.00	.45
❑ 168 Cal Ripken	4.00	1.80
❑ 169 Barry Larkin	.75	.35
❑ 170 Chuck Knoblauch	1.00	.45
❑ 171 Chili Davis	.50	.23
❑ 172 Fred McGriff	.75	.35
❑ 173 Matt Williams	.50	.23
❑ 174 Roger Clemens	2.00	.90
❑ 175 Frank Thomas	3.00	1.35
❑ 176 Dennis Eckersley	.50	.23
❑ 177 Gary Sheffield	.75	.35
❑ 178 David Cone	.75	.35
❑ 179 Larry Walker	1.00	.45
❑ 180 Mark Grace	.75	.35
❑ NNO M. Mantle Masterpiece	20.00	9.00

1996 Topps Gallery Expressionists

	MINT	NRMT
COMPLETE SET (20)	80.00	36.00
COMMON CARD (1-20)	1.25	.55

Card	MINT	NRMT
❑ 1 Mike Piazza	12.00	5.50
❑ 2 J.T. Snow	2.00	.90
❑ 3 Ken Griffey Jr.	20.00	9.00
❑ 4 Kirby Puckett	6.00	2.70
❑ 5 Carlos Baerga	1.25	.55
❑ 6 Chipper Jones	10.00	4.50
❑ 7 Hideo Nomo	6.00	2.70
❑ 8 Mark McGwire	20.00	9.00
❑ 9 Gary Sheffield	2.50	1.10
❑ 10 Randy Johnson	4.00	1.80
❑ 11 Ray Lankford	2.00	.90
❑ 12 Sammy Sosa	10.00	4.50
❑ 13 Denny Martinez	2.00	.90
❑ 14 Jose Canseco	4.00	1.80
❑ 15 Tony Gwynn	10.00	4.50
❑ 16 Edgar Martinez	2.00	.90
❑ 17 Reggie Sanders	1.25	.55
❑ 18 Andres Galarraga	4.00	1.80
❑ 19 Albert Belle	8.00	3.60
❑ 20 Barry Larkin	2.50	1.10

1996 Topps Gallery Photo Gallery

	MINT	NRMT
COMPLETE SET (15)	100.00	45.00
COMMON CARD (PG1-PG15)	1.25	.55

Card	MINT	NRMT
❑ PG1 Eddie Murray	5.00	2.20
❑ PG2 Randy Johnson	5.00	2.20
❑ PG3 Cal Ripken	20.00	9.00
❑ PG4 Bret Boone	2.00	.90
❑ PG5 Frank Thomas	15.00	6.75
❑ PG6 Jeff Conine	1.25	.55
❑ PG7 Johnny Damon	2.00	.90
❑ PG8 Roger Clemens	10.00	4.50
❑ PG9 Albert Belle	6.00	2.70
❑ PG10 Ken Griffey Jr.	25.00	11.00
❑ PG11 Kirby Puckett	8.00	3.60
❑ PG12 David Justice	5.00	2.20
❑ PG13 Bobby Bonilla	2.00	.90
❑ PG14 Colorado Rockies	5.00	2.20
❑ PG15 Atlanta Braves	5.00	2.20

1997 Topps Gallery

	MINT	NRMT
COMPLETE SET (180)	60.00	27.00
COMMON CARD (1-180)	.25	.11

Card	MINT	NRMT
❑ 1 Paul Molitor	1.00	.45
❑ 2 Devon White	.50	.23
❑ 3 Andres Galarraga	1.00	.45
❑ 4 Cal Ripken	4.00	1.80
❑ 5 Tony Gwynn	2.50	1.10
❑ 6 Mike Stanley	.25	.11
❑ 7 Orel Hershiser	.50	.23
❑ 8 Jose Canseco	1.00	.45
❑ 9 Chili Davis	.50	.23
❑ 10 Harold Baines	.50	.23
❑ 11 Rickey Henderson	1.00	.45
❑ 12 Darryl Strawberry	.50	.23
❑ 13 Todd Worrell	.25	.11
❑ 14 Cecil Fielder	.50	.23
❑ 15 Gary Gaetti	.25	.11
❑ 16 Bobby Bonilla	.50	.23
❑ 17 Will Clark	1.00	.45
❑ 18 Kevin Brown	.75	.35
❑ 19 Tom Glavine	1.00	.45
❑ 20 Wade Boggs	1.00	.45
❑ 21 Edgar Martinez	.50	.23
❑ 22 Lance Johnson	.25	.11
❑ 23 Gregg Jefferies	.25	.11
❑ 24 Bip Roberts	.25	.11
❑ 25 Tony Phillips	.25	.11
❑ 26 Greg Maddux	3.00	1.35
❑ 27 Mickey Tettleton	.25	.11
❑ 28 Terry Steinbach	.50	.23
❑ 29 Ryne Sandberg	1.25	.55
❑ 30 Wally Joyner	.50	.23
❑ 31 Joe Carter	.50	.23
❑ 32 Ellis Burks	.50	.23
❑ 33 Fred McGriff	.75	.35
❑ 34 Barry Larkin	.75	.35
❑ 35 John Franco	.50	.23
❑ 36 Rafael Palmeiro	.75	.35
❑ 37 Mark McGwire	5.00	2.20
❑ 38 Ken Caminiti	.75	.35
❑ 39 David Cone	.75	.35
❑ 40 Julio Franco	.50	.23
❑ 41 Roger Clemens	2.00	.90
❑ 42 Barry Bonds	1.25	.55
❑ 43 Dennis Eckersley	.50	.23
❑ 44 Eddie Murray	1.00	.45
❑ 45 Paul O'Neill	.50	.23
❑ 46 Craig Biggio	1.00	.45
❑ 47 Roberto Alomar	1.00	.45
❑ 48 Mark Grace	.75	.35
❑ 49 Matt Williams	.50	.23
❑ 50 Jay Buhner	.50	.23
❑ 51 John Smoltz	.50	.23
❑ 52 Randy Johnson	1.00	.45
❑ 53 Ramon Martinez	.50	.23
❑ 54 Curt Schilling	.50	.23
❑ 55 Gary Sheffield	.75	.35
❑ 56 Jack McDowell	.25	.11
❑ 57 Brady Anderson	.50	.23
❑ 58 Dante Bichette	.50	.23
❑ 59 Ron Gant	.25	.11
❑ 60 Alex Fernandez	.25	.11
❑ 61 Moises Alou	.75	.35
❑ 62 Travis Fryman	.50	.23
❑ 63 Dean Palmer	.50	.23
❑ 64 Todd Hundley	.50	.23
❑ 65 Jeff Brantley	.25	.11
❑ 66 Bernard Gilkey	.25	.11
❑ 67 Geronimo Berroa	.25	.11
❑ 68 John Wetteland	.50	.23
❑ 69 Robin Ventura	.50	.23
❑ 70 Ray Lankford	.50	.23
❑ 71 Kevin Appier	.50	.23
❑ 72 Larry Walker	1.00	.45
❑ 73 Juan Gonzalez	2.50	1.10
❑ 74 Jeff King	.25	.11
❑ 75 Greg Vaughn	.50	.23
❑ 76 Steve Finley	.50	.23
❑ 77 Brian McRae	.25	.11
❑ 78 Paul Sorrento	.25	.11
❑ 79 Ken Griffey Jr.	5.00	2.20
❑ 80 Omar Vizquel	.50	.23
❑ 81 Jose Mesa	.25	.11
❑ 82 Albert Belle	1.25	.55
❑ 83 Glenallen Hill	.25	.11
❑ 84 Sammy Sosa	2.50	1.10
❑ 85 Andy Benes	.50	.23
❑ 86 David Justice	1.00	.45
❑ 87 Marquis Grissom	.50	.23
❑ 88 John Olerud	.50	.23
❑ 89 Tino Martinez	1.00	.45
❑ 90 Frank Thomas	3.00	1.35
❑ 91 Raul Mondesi	.75	.35
❑ 92 Steve Trachsel	.25	.11
❑ 93 Jim Edmonds	.75	.35
❑ 94 Rusty Greer	.50	.23
❑ 95 Joey Hamilton	.50	.23
❑ 96 Ismael Valdes	.50	.23
❑ 97 Dave Nilsson	.25	.11
❑ 98 John Jaha	.25	.11
❑ 99 Alex Gonzalez	.25	.11
❑ 100 Javy Lopez	.50	.23
❑ 101 Ryan Klesko	.50	.23
❑ 102 Tim Salmon	1.00	.45
❑ 103 Bernie Williams	1.00	.45
❑ 104 Roberto Hernandez	.25	.11
❑ 105 Chuck Knoblauch	1.00	.45
❑ 106 Mike Lansing	.25	.11

		MINT	NRMT
❑ 107	Vinny Castilla	.75	.35
❑ 108	Reggie Sanders	.50	.23
❑ 109	Mo Vaughn	1.00	.45
❑ 110	Rondell White	.50	.23
❑ 111	Ivan Rodriguez	1.25	.55
❑ 112	Mike Mussina	1.00	.45
❑ 113	Carlos Baerga	.50	.23
❑ 114	Jeff Conine	.50	.23
❑ 115	Jim Thome	1.00	.45
❑ 116	Manny Ramirez	1.00	.45
❑ 117	Kenny Lofton	1.00	.45
❑ 118	Wilson Alvarez	.50	.23
❑ 119	Eric Karros	.50	.23
❑ 120	Robb Nen	.25	.11
❑ 121	Mark Wohlers	.25	.11
❑ 122	Ed Sprague	.25	.11
❑ 123	Pat Hentgen	.50	.23
❑ 124	Juan Guzman	.25	.11
❑ 125	Derek Bell	.50	.23
❑ 126	Jeff Bagwell	1.50	.70
❑ 127	Eric Young	.50	.23
❑ 128	John Valentin	.50	.23
❑ 129	Al Martin UER Picture of Javy Lopez	.25	.11
❑ 130	Trevor Hoffman	.50	.23
❑ 131	Henry Rodriguez	.50	.23
❑ 132	Pedro Martinez	1.00	.45
❑ 133	Mike Piazza	3.00	1.35
❑ 134	Brian Jordan	.50	.23
❑ 135	Jose Valentin	.25	.11
❑ 136	Jeff Cirillo	.50	.23
❑ 137	Chipper Jones	2.50	1.10
❑ 138	Ricky Bottalico	.50	.23
❑ 139	Hideo Nomo	1.25	.55
❑ 140	Troy Percival	.50	.23
❑ 141	Rey Ordonez	.50	.23
❑ 142	Edgar Renteria	.50	.23
❑ 143	Luis Castillo	.50	.23
❑ 144	Vladimir Guerrero	2.00	.90
❑ 145	Jeff D'Amico	.25	.11
❑ 146	Andruw Jones	1.50	.70
❑ 147	Darin Erstad	1.50	.70
❑ 148	Bob Abreu	.50	.23
❑ 149	Carlos Delgado	.50	.23
❑ 150	Jamey Wright	.25	.11
❑ 151	Nomar Garciaparra	3.00	1.35
❑ 152	Jason Kendall	.75	.35
❑ 153	Jermaine Allensworth	.25	.11
❑ 154	Scott Rolen	2.50	1.10
❑ 155	Rocky Coppinger	.25	.11
❑ 156	Paul Wilson	.25	.11
❑ 157	Garret Anderson	.50	.23
❑ 158	Mariano Rivera	.50	.23
❑ 159	Ruben Rivera	.50	.23
❑ 160	Andy Pettitte	.75	.35
❑ 161	Derek Jeter	3.00	1.35
❑ 162	Neifi Perez	.25	.11
❑ 163	Ray Durham	.50	.23
❑ 164	James Baldwin	.50	.23
❑ 165	Marty Cordova	.25	.11
❑ 166	Tony Clark	.75	.35
❑ 167	Michael Tucker	.50	.23
❑ 168	Mike Sweeney	.25	.11
❑ 169	Johnny Damon	.50	.23
❑ 170	Jermaine Dye	.25	.11
❑ 171	Alex Ochoa	.25	.11
❑ 172	Jason Isringhausen	.25	.11
❑ 173	Mark Grudzielanek	.50	.23
❑ 174	Jose Rosado	.25	.11
❑ 175	Todd Hollandsworth	.25	.11
❑ 176	Alan Benes	.50	.23
❑ 177	Jason Giambi	.50	.23
❑ 178	Billy Wagner	.50	.23
❑ 179	Justin Thompson	.50	.23
❑ 180	Todd Walker	1.00	.45

1997 Topps Gallery Gallery of Heroes

	MINT	NRMT
COMPLETE SET (10)	180.00	80.00
COMMON CARD (GH1-GH10)	10.00	4.50

		MINT	NRMT
❑ GH1	Derek Jeter	20.00	9.00
❑ GH2	Chipper Jones	20.00	9.00
❑ GH3	Frank Thomas	25.00	11.00
❑ GH4	Ken Griffey Jr.	40.00	18.00
❑ GH5	Cal Ripken	30.00	13.50
❑ GH6	Mark McGwire	40.00	18.00
❑ GH7	Mike Piazza	25.00	11.00
❑ GH8	Jeff Bagwell	12.00	5.50
❑ GH9	Tony Gwynn	20.00	9.00
❑ GH10	Mo Vaughn	10.00	4.50

1997 Topps Gallery Peter Max Serigraphs

	MINT	NRMT
COMPLETE SET (10)	100.00	45.00
COMMON CARD (1-10)	3.00	1.35

*AUTOGRAPHS: 10X TO 20X BASIC SERIGRAPHS
AUTOGRAPHS: RANDOM INS.IN PACKS
AUTO. PRINT RUN 40 SERIAL #'d SETS

		MINT	NRMT
❑ 1	Derek Jeter	12.00	5.50
❑ 2	Albert Belle	6.00	2.70
❑ 3	Ken Caminiti	3.00	1.35
❑ 4	Chipper Jones	12.00	5.50
❑ 5	Ken Griffey Jr.	25.00	11.00
❑ 6	Frank Thomas	15.00	6.75
❑ 7	Cal Ripken	20.00	9.00
❑ 8	Mark McGwire	25.00	11.00
❑ 9	Barry Bonds	6.00	2.70
❑ 10	Mike Piazza	15.00	6.75

1997 Topps Gallery Photo Gallery

	MINT	NRMT
COMPLETE SET (16)	180.00	80.00
COMMON CARD (PG1-PG16)	2.00	.90

		MINT	NRMT
❑ PG1	John Wetteland	2.00	.90
❑ PG2	Paul Molitor	8.00	3.60
❑ PG3	Eddie Murray	8.00	3.60
❑ PG4	Ken Griffey Jr.	40.00	18.00
❑ PG5	Chipper Jones	20.00	9.00
❑ PG6	Derek Jeter	20.00	9.00
❑ PG7	Frank Thomas	25.00	11.00
❑ PG8	Mark McGwire	40.00	18.00
❑ PG9	Kenny Lofton	8.00	3.60
❑ PG10	Gary Sheffield	6.00	2.70
❑ PG11	Mike Piazza	25.00	11.00
❑ PG12	Vinny Castilla	6.00	2.70
❑ PG13	Andres Galarraga	8.00	3.60
❑ PG14	Andy Pettitte	6.00	2.70
❑ PG15	Robin Ventura	4.00	1.80
❑ PG16	Barry Larkin	6.00	2.70

1998 Topps Gallery

	MINT	NRMT
COMPLETE SET (150)	55.00	25.00
COMMON CARD (1-150)	.25	.11

		MINT	NRMT
❑ 1	Andruw Jones	1.25	.55
❑ 2	Fred McGriff	.60	.25
❑ 3	Wade Boggs	1.00	.45
❑ 4	Pedro Martinez	1.00	.45
❑ 5	Matt Williams	.40	.18
❑ 6	Wilson Alvarez	.40	.18
❑ 7	Henry Rodriguez	.40	.18
❑ 8	Jay Bell	.40	.18
❑ 9	Marquis Grissom	.40	.18
❑ 10	Darryl Kile	.40	.18
❑ 11	Chuck Knoblauch	1.00	.45
❑ 12	Kenny Lofton	1.00	.45
❑ 13	Quinton McCracken	.40	.18
❑ 14	Andres Galarraga	1.00	.45
❑ 15	Brian Jordan	.40	.18
❑ 16	Mike Lansing	.25	.11
❑ 17	Travis Fryman	.40	.18
❑ 18	Tony Saunders	.25	.11
❑ 19	Moises Alou	.60	.25
❑ 20	Travis Lee	2.00	.90
❑ 21	Garret Anderson	.40	.18
❑ 22	Ken Caminiti	.60	.25
❑ 23	Pedro Astacio	.25	.11
❑ 24	Ellis Burks	.40	.18
❑ 25	Albert Belle	1.00	.45
❑ 26	Alan Benes	.40	.18
❑ 27	Jay Buhner	.40	.18
❑ 28	Derek Bell	.40	.18
❑ 29	Jeromy Burnitz	.40	.18
❑ 30	Kevin Appier	.40	.18
❑ 31	Jeff Cirillo	.40	.18
❑ 32	Bernard Gilkey	.25	.11
❑ 33	David Cone	.60	.25
❑ 34	Jason Dickson	.40	.18
❑ 35	Jose Cruz Jr.	1.25	.55
❑ 36	Marty Cordova	.25	.11
❑ 37	Ray Durham	.40	.18
❑ 38	Jaret Wright	1.25	.55
❑ 39	Billy Wagner	.40	.18

	Player	MINT	NRMT
❑ 40	Roger Clemens	2.00	.90
❑ 41	Juan Gonzalez	2.50	1.10
❑ 42	Jeremi Gonzalez	.40	.18
❑ 43	Mark Grudzielanek	.40	.18
❑ 44	Tom Glavine	1.00	.45
❑ 45	Barry Larkin	.60	.25
❑ 46	Lance Johnson	.25	.11
❑ 47	Bobby Higginson	.60	.25
❑ 48	Mike Mussina	1.00	.45
❑ 49	Al Martin	.25	.11
❑ 50	Mark McGwire	6.00	2.70
❑ 51	Todd Hundley	.40	.18
❑ 52	Ray Lankford	.40	.18
❑ 53	Jason Kendall	.40	.18
❑ 54	Javy Lopez	.40	.18
❑ 55	Ben Grieve	2.00	.90
❑ 56	Randy Johnson	1.00	.45
❑ 57	Jeff King	.40	.18
❑ 58	Mark Grace	.60	.25
❑ 59	Rusty Greer	.40	.18
❑ 60	Greg Maddux	3.00	1.35
❑ 61	Jeff Kent	.40	.18
❑ 62	Rey Ordonez	.40	.18
❑ 63	Hideo Nomo	1.25	.55
❑ 64	Charles Nagy	.40	.18
❑ 65	Rondell White	.40	.18
❑ 66	Todd Helton	1.25	.55
❑ 67	Jim Thome	1.00	.45
❑ 68	Denny Neagle	.40	.18
❑ 69	Ivan Rodriguez	1.25	.55
❑ 70	Vladimir Guerrero	1.50	.70
❑ 71	Jorge Posada	.40	.18
❑ 72	J.T. Snow	.40	.18
❑ 73	Reggie Sanders	.40	.18
❑ 74	Scott Rolen	2.50	1.10
❑ 75	Robin Ventura	.40	.18
❑ 76	Mariano Rivera	.40	.18
❑ 77	Cal Ripken	4.00	1.80
❑ 78	Justin Thompson	.40	.18
❑ 79	Mike Piazza	3.00	1.35
❑ 80	Kevin Brown	.60	.25
❑ 81	Sandy Alomar	.40	.18
❑ 82	Craig Biggio	1.00	.45
❑ 83	Vinny Castilla	.60	.25
❑ 84	Eric Young	.40	.18
❑ 85	Bernie Williams	1.00	.45
❑ 86	Brady Anderson	.40	.18
❑ 87	Bobby Bonilla	.40	.18
❑ 88	Tony Clark	.60	.25
❑ 89	Dan Wilson	.25	.11
❑ 90	John Wetteland	.40	.18
❑ 91	Barry Bonds	1.25	.55
❑ 92	Chan Ho Park	1.00	.45
❑ 93	Carlos Delgado	.40	.18
❑ 94	David Justice	1.00	.45
❑ 95	Chipper Jones	2.50	1.10
❑ 96	Shawn Estes	.40	.18
❑ 97	Jason Giambi	.40	.18
❑ 98	Ron Gant	.25	.11
❑ 99	John Olerud	.40	.18
❑ 100	Frank Thomas	3.00	1.35
❑ 101	Jose Guillen	.40	.18
❑ 102	Brad Radke	.40	.18
❑ 103	Troy Percival	.40	.18
❑ 104	John Smoltz	.40	.18
❑ 105	Edgardo Alfonzo	.40	.18
❑ 106	Dante Bichette	.40	.18
❑ 107	Larry Walker	1.00	.45
❑ 108	John Valentin	.40	.18
❑ 109	Roberto Alomar	1.00	.45
❑ 110	Mike Cameron	.40	.18
❑ 111	Eric Davis	.40	.18
❑ 112	Johnny Damon	.40	.18
❑ 113	Darin Erstad	1.25	.55
❑ 114	Omar Vizquel	.40	.18
❑ 115	Derek Jeter	2.50	1.10
❑ 116	Tony Womack	.40	.18
❑ 117	Edgar Renteria	.40	.18
❑ 118	Raul Mondesi	.60	.25
❑ 119	Tony Gwynn	2.50	1.10
❑ 120	Ken Griffey Jr.	5.00	2.20
❑ 121	Jim Edmonds	.60	.25
❑ 122	Brian Hunter	.40	.18
❑ 123	Neifi Perez	.40	.18
❑ 124	Dean Palmer	.40	.18
❑ 125	Alex Rodriguez	3.00	1.35
❑ 126	Tim Salmon	1.00	.45
❑ 127	Curt Schilling	.40	.18
❑ 128	Kevin Orie	.25	.11
❑ 129	Andy Pettitte	.60	.25
❑ 130	Gary Sheffield	.60	.25
❑ 131	Jose Rosado	.25	.11
❑ 132	Manny Ramirez	1.00	.45
❑ 133	Rafael Palmeiro	.60	.25
❑ 134	Sammy Sosa	2.50	1.10
❑ 135	Jeff Bagwell	1.50	.70
❑ 136	Delino DeShields	.25	.11
❑ 137	Ryan Klesko	.40	.18
❑ 138	Mo Vaughn	1.25	.55
❑ 139	Steve Finley	.40	.18
❑ 140	Nomar Garciaparra	3.00	1.35
❑ 141	Paul Molitor	1.00	.45
❑ 142	Pat Hentgen	.40	.18
❑ 143	Eric Karros	.40	.18
❑ 144	Bobby Jones	.25	.11
❑ 145	Tino Martinez	1.00	.45
❑ 146	Matt Morris	.40	.18
❑ 147	Livan Hernandez	.40	.18
❑ 148	Edgar Martinez	.40	.18
❑ 149	Paul O'Neill	.40	.18
❑ 150	Checklist	.25	.11

1998 Topps Gallery Gallery Proofs

	MINT	NRMT
COMMON CARD (1-150)	12.00	5.50

*STARS: 20X TO 50X BASIC CARDS
*YOUNG STARS: 15X TO 40X BASIC CARDS
*ROOKIES/PROSPECTS: 10X TO 25X BASIC CARDS

1998 Topps Gallery Player's Private Issue

	MINT	NRMT
COMPLETE SET (150)	3000.00	1350.00
COMMON CARD (1-150)	8.00	3.60

*STARS: 12.5X TO 30X BASIC CARDS
*YOUNG STARS: 10X TO 25X BASIC CARDS
*RC'S/PROSPECTS: 6X TO 15X BASIC CARDS

1998 Topps Gallery Player's Private Issue Auction

	MINT	NRMT
COMPLETE SET (150)	100.00	45.00
COMMON CARD	.25	.11

*STARS: .75X TO 2X BASIC CARDS

1998 Topps Gallery Awards Gallery

	MINT	NRMT
COMPLETE SET (10)	100.00	45.00
COMMON CARD (AG1-AG10)	2.00	.90

	Player	MINT	NRMT
❑ AG1	Ken Griffey Jr.	25.00	11.00
❑ AG2	Larry Walker	5.00	2.20
❑ AG3	Roger Clemens	10.00	4.50
❑ AG4	Pedro Martinez	5.00	2.20
❑ AG5	Nomar Garciaparra	15.00	6.75
❑ AG6	Scott Rolen	10.00	4.50
❑ AG7	Frank Thomas	15.00	6.75
❑ AG8	Tony Gwynn	12.00	5.50
❑ AG9	Mark McGwire	30.00	13.50
❑ AG10	Livan Hernandez	2.00	.90

1998 Topps Gallery Gallery of Heroes

	MINT	NRMT
COMPLETE SET (15)	200.00	90.00
COMMON CARD (GH1-GH15)	6.00	2.70
❑ GH1 Ken Griffey Jr.	30.00	13.50
❑ GH2 Derek Jeter	15.00	6.75
❑ GH3 Barry Bonds	8.00	3.60
❑ GH4 Alex Rodriguez	20.00	9.00
❑ GH5 Frank Thomas	20.00	9.00
❑ GH6 Nomar Garciaparra	20.00	9.00
❑ GH7 Mark McGwire	40.00	18.00
❑ GH8 Mike Piazza	20.00	9.00
❑ GH9 Cal Ripken	25.00	11.00
❑ GH10 Jose Cruz Jr.	6.00	2.70
❑ GH11 Jeff Bagwell	10.00	4.50
❑ GH12 Chipper Jones	15.00	6.75
❑ GH13 Juan Gonzalez	15.00	6.75
❑ GH14 Hideo Nomo	8.00	3.60
❑ GH15 Greg Maddux	20.00	9.00

1998 Topps Gallery Photo Gallery

	MINT	NRMT
COMPLETE SET (10)	100.00	45.00
COMMON CARD (PG1-PG10)	4.00	1.80
❑ PG1 Alex Rodriguez	15.00	6.75
❑ PG2 Frank Thomas	15.00	6.75
❑ PG3 Derek Jeter	12.00	5.50
❑ PG4 Cal Ripken	20.00	9.00
❑ PG5 Ken Griffey Jr.	25.00	11.00
❑ PG6 Mike Piazza	15.00	6.75
❑ PG7 Nomar Garciaparra	15.00	6.75
❑ PG8 Tim Salmon	4.00	1.80
❑ PG9 Jeff Bagwell	8.00	3.60
❑ PG10 Barry Bonds	6.00	2.70

1998 Topps Gold Label Class 1

	MINT	NRMT
COMP.GOLD SET (100)	100.00	45.00
COMMON GOLD (1-100)	.40	.18
❑ 1 Kevin Brown	1.00	.45
❑ 2 Greg Maddux	5.00	2.20
❑ 3 Albert Belle	1.50	.70
❑ 4 Andres Galarraga	1.25	.55
❑ 5 Craig Biggio	1.25	.55
❑ 6 Matt Williams	.60	.25
❑ 7 Derek Jeter	4.00	1.80
❑ 8 Randy Johnson	1.50	.70
❑ 9 Jay Bell	.60	.25
❑ 10 Jim Thome	1.50	.70
❑ 11 Roberto Alomar	1.50	.70
❑ 12 Tom Glavine	1.50	.70
❑ 13 Reggie Sanders	.60	.25
❑ 14 Tony Gwynn	4.00	1.80
❑ 15 Mark McGwire	10.00	4.50
❑ 16 Jeromy Burnitz	.60	.25
❑ 17 Andruw Jones	2.00	.90
❑ 18 Jay Buhner	.60	.25
❑ 19 Robin Ventura	.60	.25
❑ 20 Jeff Bagwell	2.50	1.10
❑ 21 Roger Clemens	3.00	1.35
❑ 22 Masato Yoshii	1.25	.55
❑ 23 Travis Fryman	.60	.25
❑ 24 Rafael Palmeiro	1.00	.45
❑ 25 Alex Rodriguez	5.00	2.20
❑ 26 Sandy Alomar Jr.	.60	.25
❑ 27 Chipper Jones	4.00	1.80
❑ 28 Rusty Greer	.60	.25
❑ 29 Cal Ripken	6.00	2.70
❑ 30 Tony Clark	1.00	.45
❑ 31 Derek Bell	.60	.25
❑ 32 Fred McGriff	1.00	.45
❑ 33 Paul O'Neill	.60	.25
❑ 34 Moises Alou	1.00	.45
❑ 35 Henry Rodriguez	.60	.25
❑ 36 Steve Finley	.60	.25
❑ 37 Marquis Grissom	.60	.25
❑ 38 Jason Giambi	.60	.25
❑ 39 Javy Lopez	.60	.25
❑ 40 Damion Easley	.60	.25
❑ 41 Mariano Rivera	.60	.25
❑ 42 Mo Vaughn	2.00	.90
❑ 43 Mike Mussina	1.50	.70
❑ 44 Jason Kendall	.60	.25
❑ 45 Pedro Martinez	1.50	.70
❑ 46 Frank Thomas	5.00	2.20
❑ 47 Jim Edmonds	1.00	.45
❑ 48 Hideki Irabu	1.25	.55
❑ 49 Eric Karros	.60	.25
❑ 50 Juan Gonzalez	4.00	1.80
❑ 51 Ellis Burks	.60	.25
❑ 52 Dean Palmer	.60	.25
❑ 53 Scott Rolen	4.00	1.80
❑ 54 Raul Mondesi	1.00	.45
❑ 55 Quinton McCracken	.60	.25
❑ 56 John Olerud	.60	.25
❑ 57 Ken Caminiti	1.00	.45
❑ 58 Brian Jordan	.60	.25
❑ 59 Wade Boggs	1.50	.70
❑ 60 Mike Piazza	5.00	2.20
❑ 61 Darin Erstad	2.00	.90
❑ 62 Curt Schilling	.60	.25
❑ 63 David Justice	1.25	.55
❑ 64 Kenny Lofton	1.50	.70
❑ 65 Barry Bonds	2.00	.90
❑ 66 Ray Lankford	.60	.25
❑ 67 Brian Hunter	.60	.25
❑ 68 Chuck Knoblauch	1.25	.55
❑ 69 Vinny Castilla	1.00	.45
❑ 70 Vladimir Guerrero	2.50	1.10
❑ 71 Tim Salmon	1.25	.55
❑ 72 Larry Walker	1.50	.70
❑ 73 Paul Molitor	1.50	.70
❑ 74 Barry Larkin	1.00	.45
❑ 75 Edgar Martinez	.60	.25
❑ 76 Bernie Williams	1.50	.70
❑ 77 Dante Bichette	.60	.25
❑ 78 Nomar Garciaparra	5.00	2.20
❑ 79 Ben Grieve	3.00	1.35
❑ 80 Ivan Rodriguez	2.00	.90
❑ 81 Todd Helton	2.00	.90
❑ 82 Ryan Klesko	.60	.25
❑ 83 Sammy Sosa	4.00	1.80
❑ 84 Travis Lee	3.00	1.35
❑ 85 Jose Cruz Jr.	2.00	.90
❑ 86 Mark Kotsay	1.00	.45
❑ 87 Richard Hidalgo	.60	.25
❑ 88 Rondell White	.60	.25
❑ 89 Greg Vaughn	.60	.25
❑ 90 Gary Sheffield	1.00	.45
❑ 91 Paul Konerko	1.25	.55
❑ 92 Mark Grace	1.00	.45
❑ 93 Kevin Millwood	4.00	1.80
❑ 94 Manny Ramirez	1.50	.70
❑ 95 Tino Martinez	1.25	.55
❑ 96 Brad Fullmer	.60	.25
❑ 97 Todd Walker	1.00	.45
❑ 98 Carlos Delgado	.60	.25
❑ 99 Kerry Wood	8.00	3.60
❑ 100 Ken Griffey Jr.	8.00	3.60

1998 Topps Gold Label Class 2

	MINT	NRMT
COMP.GOLD SET (100)	200.00	90.00
COMMON GOLD (1-100)	.75	.35
CLASS 2 GOLD STATED ODDS 1:2		
COMP.BLACK SET (100)	1000.00	450.00
COMMON BLACK (1-100)	3.00	1.35
*CLASS 2 BLACK: 1.5X TO 4X CLASS 2 GOLD		
CLASS 2 BLACK STATED ODDS 1:16		
COMMON RED (1-100)	25.00	11.00
*CLASS 2 RED: 12.5X TO 30X BASIC CARDS		
CLASS 2 RED STATED ODDS 1:198		
CLASS 2 RED PRINT RUN 50 SERIAL #'d SETS		
CLASS 2: SPARKLING SILVER TEXT ON FRONT		

1998 Topps Gold Label Class 3

	MINT	NRMT
COMP.GOLD SET (100)	300.00	135.00
COMMON GOLD (1-100)	1.25	.55
*GOLD: X TO X CLASS 1 GOLD		
COMP.BLACK SET (100)	1500.00	700.00
COMMON BLACK (1-100)	5.00	2.20
*CLASS 3 BLACK: 1.5X TO 4X CLASS 3 GOLD		
CLASS 3 BLACK STATED ODDS 1:32		
COMMON RED (1-100)	40.00	18.00
*CLASS 3 RED: 15X TO 30X CLASS 3 GOLD		
CLASS 3 RED STATED ODDS 1:396		
CLASS 3 RED PRINT RUN 25 SERIAL #'d SETS		
CLASS 3: SPARKLING GOLD TEXT ON FRONT		

1998 Topps Gold Label Home Run Race

	MINT	NRMT
COMPLETE SET (4)	60.00	27.00
COMMON CARD (HR1-HR4)..	10.00	4.50
COMP.BLACK HR SET (4) ..	200.00	90.00
*BLACK HR: 1.25X TO 3X GOLD HR		
BLACK HR STATED ODDS 1:48		
COMP.RED HR SET (4)......	1200.00	550.00
*RED HR: 10X TO 20X GOLD HR		
RED HR STATED ODDS 1:4055 HTA		
RED HR STATED PRINT RUN 61 SETS		

	MINT	NRMT
❑ HR1 Roger Maris	12.00	5.50
❑ HR2 Mark McGwire	25.00	11.00
❑ HR3 Ken Griffey Jr.	20.00	9.00
❑ HR4 Sammy Sosa	10.00	4.50

1996 Topps Laser

	MINT	NRMT
COMPLETE SET (128)	100.00	45.00
COMPLETE SERIES 1 (64)	50.00	22.00
COMPLETE SERIES 2 (64)	50.00	22.00
COMMON CARD (1-128)	.50	.23

	MINT	NRMT
❑ 1 Moises Alou	1.50	.70
❑ 2 Derek Bell	1.00	.45
❑ 3 Joe Carter	1.00	.45
❑ 4 Jeff Conine	1.00	.45
❑ 5 Darren Daulton	1.00	.45
❑ 6 Jim Edmonds	1.50	.70
❑ 7 Ron Gant	.50	.23
❑ 8 Juan Gonzalez	5.00	2.20
❑ 9 Brian Jordan	1.00	.45
❑ 10 Ryan Klesko	1.00	.45
❑ 11 Paul Molitor	2.00	.90
❑ 12 Tony Phillips	.50	.23
❑ 13 Manny Ramirez	2.00	.90
❑ 14 Sammy Sosa	5.00	2.20
❑ 15 Devon White	1.00	.45
❑ 16 Bernie Williams	2.00	.90
❑ 17 Garrett Anderson	1.00	.45
❑ 18 Jay Bell	1.00	.45
❑ 19 Craig Biggio	2.00	.90
❑ 20 Bobby Bonilla	1.00	.45
❑ 21 Ken Caminiti	1.50	.70
❑ 22 Shawon Dunston	.50	.23
❑ 23 Mark Grace	1.50	.70
❑ 24 Gregg Jefferies	.50	.23
❑ 25 Jeff King	.50	.23
❑ 26 Javy Lopez	1.00	.45
❑ 27 Edgar Martinez	1.00	.45
❑ 28 Dean Palmer	1.00	.45
❑ 29 J.T. Snow	1.00	.45
❑ 30 Mike Stanley	.50	.23
❑ 31 Terry Steinbach	1.00	.45
❑ 32 Robin Ventura	1.00	.45
❑ 33 Roberto Alomar	2.00	.90
❑ 34 Jeff Bagwell	3.00	1.35
❑ 35 Dante Bichette	1.00	.45
❑ 36 Wade Boggs	2.00	.90
❑ 37 Barry Bonds	2.50	1.10
❑ 38 Jose Canseco	2.00	.90
❑ 39 Vinny Castilla	1.50	.70
❑ 40 Will Clark	2.00	.90
❑ 41 Marty Cordova	.50	.23
❑ 42 Ken Griffey Jr.	10.00	4.50
❑ 43 Tony Gwynn	5.00	2.20
❑ 44 Rickey Henderson	2.00	.90
❑ 45 Chipper Jones	5.00	2.20
❑ 46 Mark McGwire	10.00	4.50
❑ 47 Brian McRae	.50	.23
❑ 48 Ryne Sandberg	2.50	1.10
❑ 49 Andy Ashby	.50	.23
❑ 50 Alan Benes	1.00	.45
❑ 51 Andy Benes	1.00	.45
❑ 52 Roger Clemens	4.00	1.80
❑ 53 Doug Drabek	.50	.23
❑ 54 Dennis Eckersley	1.00	.45
❑ 55 Tom Glavine	2.00	.90
❑ 56 Randy Johnson	2.00	.90
❑ 57 Mark Langston	.50	.23
❑ 58 Denny Martinez	1.00	.45
❑ 59 Jack McDowell	.50	.23
❑ 60 Hideo Nomo	3.00	1.35
❑ 61 Shane Reynolds	1.00	.45
❑ 62 John Smoltz	1.00	.45
❑ 63 Paul Wilson	.50	.23
❑ 64 Mark Wohlers	.50	.23
❑ 65 Shawn Green	1.00	.45
❑ 66 Marquis Grissom	1.00	.45
❑ 67 Dave Hollins	.50	.23
❑ 68 Todd Hundley	1.00	.45
❑ 69 David Justice	2.00	.90
❑ 70 Eric Karros	1.00	.45
❑ 71 Ray Lankford	1.00	.45
❑ 72 Fred McGriff	1.50	.70
❑ 73 Hal Morris	.50	.23
❑ 74 Eddie Murray	2.00	.90
❑ 75 Paul O'Neill	1.00	.45
❑ 76 Rey Ordonez	1.00	.45
❑ 77 Reggie Sanders	1.00	.45
❑ 78 Gary Sheffield	1.50	.70
❑ 79 Jim Thome	2.00	.90
❑ 80 Rondell White	1.00	.45
❑ 81 Travis Fryman	1.00	.45
❑ 82 Derek Jeter	6.00	2.70
❑ 83 Chuck Knoblauch	2.00	.90
❑ 84 Barry Larkin	1.50	.70
❑ 85 Tino Martinez	2.00	.90
❑ 86 Raul Mondesi	1.50	.70
❑ 87 John Olerud	1.00	.45
❑ 88 Rafael Palmeiro	1.50	.70
❑ 89 Mike Piazza	6.00	2.70
❑ 90 Cal Ripken	8.00	3.60
❑ 91 Ivan Rodriguez	2.50	1.10
❑ 92 Frank Thomas	6.00	2.70
❑ 93 John Valentin	1.00	.45
❑ 94 Mo Vaughn	2.50	1.10
❑ 95 Quilvio Veras	.50	.23
❑ 96 Matt Williams	1.00	.45
❑ 97 Brady Anderson	1.00	.45
❑ 98 Carlos Baerga	1.00	.45
❑ 99 Albert Belle	2.50	1.10
❑ 100 Jay Buhner	1.00	.45
❑ 101 Johnny Damon	1.00	.45
❑ 102 Chili Davis	1.00	.45
❑ 103 Ray Durham	1.00	.45
❑ 104 Len Dykstra	1.00	.45
❑ 105 Cecil Fielder	1.00	.45
❑ 106 Andres Galarraga	2.00	.90
❑ 107 Brian L.Hunter	1.00	.45
❑ 108 Kenny Lofton	2.00	.90
❑ 109 Kirby Puckett	3.00	1.35
❑ 110 Tim Salmon	2.00	.90
❑ 111 Greg Vaughn	1.00	.45
❑ 112 Larry Walker	2.00	.90
❑ 113 Rick Aguilera	.50	.23
❑ 114 Kevin Appier	1.00	.45
❑ 115 Kevin Brown	2.00	.90
❑ 116 David Cone	1.50	.70
❑ 117 Alex Fernandez	.50	.23
❑ 118 Chuck Finley	1.00	.45
❑ 119 Joey Hamilton	1.00	.45
❑ 120 Jason Isringhausen	.50	.23
❑ 121 Greg Maddux	6.00	2.70
❑ 122 Pedro Martinez	2.00	.90
❑ 123 Jose Mesa	.50	.23
❑ 124 Jeff Montgomery	.50	.23
❑ 125 Mike Mussina	2.00	.90
❑ 126 Randy Myers	.50	.23
❑ 127 Kenny Rogers	.50	.23
❑ 128 Ismael Valdes	1.00	.45

1996 Topps Laser Bright Spots

	MINT	NRMT
COMPLETE SET (16)	100.00	45.00
COMPLETE SERIES 1 (8)	40.00	18.00
COMPLETE SERIES 2 (8)	60.00	27.00
COMMON CARD (1-16)	3.00	1.35

	MINT	NRMT
❑ 1 Brian L.Hunter	5.00	2.20
❑ 2 Derek Jeter	15.00	6.75
❑ 3 Jason Kendall	10.00	4.50
❑ 4 Brooks Kieschnick	3.00	1.35
❑ 5 Rey Ordonez	5.00	2.20
❑ 6 Jason Schmidt	3.00	1.35
❑ 7 Chris Snopek	3.00	1.35
❑ 8 Bob Wolcott	3.00	1.35
❑ 9 Alan Benes	5.00	2.20
❑ 10 Marty Cordova	3.00	1.35
❑ 11 Jimmy Haynes	3.00	1.35
❑ 12 Todd Hollandsworth	3.00	1.35
❑ 13 Derek Jeter	15.00	6.75
❑ 14 Chipper Jones	15.00	6.75
❑ 15 Hideo Nomo	10.00	4.50
❑ 16 Paul Wilson	3.00	1.35

1996 Topps Laser Power Cuts

	MINT	NRMT
COMPLETE SET (16)	160.00	70.00
COMPLETE SERIES 1 (8)	80.00	36.00
COMPLETE SERIES 2 (8)	80.00	36.00
COMMON CARD (1-16)	4.00	1.80
❑ 1 Albert Belle	10.00	4.50
❑ 2 Jay Buhner	4.00	1.80
❑ 3 Fred McGriff	6.00	2.70
❑ 4 Mike Piazza	25.00	11.00
❑ 5 Tim Salmon	8.00	3.60
❑ 6 Frank Thomas	25.00	11.00
❑ 7 Mo Vaughn	10.00	4.50
❑ 8 Matt Williams	4.00	1.80
❑ 9 Jeff Bagwell	12.00	5.50
❑ 10 Barry Bonds	10.00	4.50
❑ 11 Jose Canseco	8.00	3.60
❑ 12 Cecil Fielder	4.00	1.80
❑ 13 Juan Gonzalez	20.00	9.00
❑ 14 Ken Griffey Jr.	40.00	18.00
❑ 15 Sammy Sosa	20.00	9.00
❑ 16 Larry Walker	8.00	3.60

1996 Topps Laser Stadium Stars

	MINT	NRMT
COMPLETE SET (16)	240.00	110.00
COMPLETE SERIES 1 (8)	120.00	55.00
COMPLETE SERIES 2 (8)	120.00	55.00
COMMON CARD (1-16)	5.00	2.20
❑ 1 Carlos Baerga	5.00	2.20
❑ 2 Barry Bonds	12.00	5.50
❑ 3 Andres Galarraga	10.00	4.50
❑ 4 Ken Griffey Jr.	50.00	22.00
❑ 5 Barry Larkin	8.00	3.60
❑ 6 Raul Mondesi	8.00	3.60
❑ 7 Kirby Puckett	15.00	6.75
❑ 8 Cal Ripken	40.00	18.00
❑ 9 Will Clark	10.00	4.50
❑ 10 Roger Clemens	20.00	9.00
❑ 11 Tony Gwynn	25.00	11.00
❑ 12 Randy Johnson	10.00	4.50
❑ 13 Kenny Lofton	10.00	4.50
❑ 14 Edgar Martinez	6.00	2.70
❑ 15 Ryne Sandberg	12.00	5.50
❑ 16 Frank Thomas	30.00	13.50

1997 Topps Screenplays

	MINT	NRMT
COMPLETE SET (20)	150.00	70.00
COMMON CARD (1-20)	4.00	1.80
❑ 1 Jeff Bagwell	8.00	3.60
❑ 2 Albert Belle	6.00	2.70
❑ 3 Barry Bonds	6.00	2.70
❑ 4 Andres Galarraga	4.00	1.80
❑ 5 Nomar Garciaparra	15.00	6.75
❑ 6 Juan Gonzalez	12.00	5.50
❑ 7 Ken Griffey Jr.	25.00	11.00
❑ 8 Tony Gwynn	12.00	5.50
❑ 9 Derek Jeter	15.00	6.75
❑ 10 Randy Johnson	5.00	2.20
❑ 11 Andruw Jones	8.00	3.60
❑ 12 Chipper Jones	12.00	5.50
❑ 13 Kenny Lofton	5.00	2.20
❑ 14 Mark McGwire	25.00	11.00
❑ 15 Paul Molitor	5.00	2.20
❑ 16 Hideo Nomo	6.00	2.70
❑ 17 Cal Ripken	20.00	9.00
❑ 18 Sammy Sosa	12.00	5.50
❑ 19 Frank Thomas	15.00	6.75
❑ 20 Jim Thome	5.00	2.20

1997 Topps Screenplays Premium Series

	MINT	NRMT
COMPLETE SET (6)	300.00	135.00
COMMON CARD (1-6)	15.00	6.75
❑ 1 Ken Griffey Jr.	80.00	36.00
❑ 2 Chipper Jones	40.00	18.00
❑ 3 Mike Piazza	50.00	22.00
❑ 4 Cal Ripken	60.00	27.00
❑ 5 Frank Thomas	50.00	22.00
❑ 6 Larry Walker	15.00	6.75

1997 Topps Stars

	MINT	NRMT
COMPLETE SET (125)	80.00	36.00
COMMON CARD (1-125)	.15	.07
❑ 1 Larry Walker	.60	.25
❑ 2 Tino Martinez	.60	.25
❑ 3 Cal Ripken	2.50	1.10
❑ 4 Ken Griffey Jr.	3.00	1.35
❑ 5 Chipper Jones	1.50	.70
❑ 6 David Justice	.60	.25
❑ 7 Mike Piazza	2.00	.90
❑ 8 Jeff Bagwell	1.00	.45
❑ 9 Ron Gant	.15	.07
❑ 10 Sammy Sosa	1.50	.70
❑ 11 Tony Gwynn	1.50	.70
❑ 12 Carlos Baerga	.30	.14
❑ 13 Frank Thomas	2.00	.90
❑ 14 Moises Alou	.40	.18
❑ 15 Barry Larkin	.40	.18
❑ 16 Ivan Rodriguez	.75	.35
❑ 17 Greg Maddux	2.00	.90
❑ 18 Jim Edmonds	.40	.18
❑ 19 Jose Canseco	.60	.25
❑ 20 Rafael Palmeiro	.40	.18
❑ 21 Paul Molitor	.60	.25
❑ 22 Kevin Appier	.30	.14
❑ 23 Raul Mondesi	.40	.18
❑ 24 Lance Johnson	.15	.07
❑ 25 Edgar Martinez	.30	.14
❑ 26 Andres Galarraga	.60	.25
❑ 27 Mo Vaughn	.75	.35
❑ 28 Ken Caminiti	.40	.18
❑ 29 Cecil Fielder	.30	.14
❑ 30 Harold Baines	.30	.14
❑ 31 Roberto Alomar	.60	.25
❑ 32 Shawn Estes	.30	.14
❑ 33 Tom Glavine	.60	.25
❑ 34 Dennis Eckersley	.30	.14
❑ 35 Manny Ramirez	.60	.25
❑ 36 John Olerud	.30	.14
❑ 37 Juan Gonzalez	1.50	.70
❑ 38 Chuck Knoblauch	.60	.25
❑ 39 Albert Belle	.75	.35
❑ 40 Vinny Castilla	.40	.18
❑ 41 John Smoltz	.30	.14
❑ 42 Barry Bonds	.75	.35
❑ 43 Randy Johnson	.60	.25
❑ 44 Brady Anderson	.30	.14
❑ 45 Jeff Blauser	.15	.07
❑ 46 Craig Biggio	.60	.25
❑ 47 Jeff Conine	.30	.14
❑ 48 Marquis Grissom	.30	.14
❑ 49 Mark Grace	.40	.18
❑ 50 Roger Clemens	1.25	.55
❑ 51 Mark McGwire	3.00	1.35
❑ 52 Fred McGriff	.40	.18
❑ 53 Gary Sheffield	.40	.18
❑ 54 Bobby Jones	.15	.07
❑ 55 Eric Young	.30	.14
❑ 56 Robin Ventura	.30	.14
❑ 57 Wade Boggs	.60	.25
❑ 58 Joe Carter	.30	.14
❑ 59 Ryne Sandberg	.75	.35
❑ 60 Matt Williams	.30	.14
❑ 61 Todd Hundley	.30	.14
❑ 62 Dante Bichette	.30	.14
❑ 63 Chili Davis	.30	.14
❑ 64 Kenny Lofton	.60	.25
❑ 65 Jay Buhner	.30	.14
❑ 66 Will Clark	.60	.25
❑ 67 Travis Fryman	.30	.14
❑ 68 Pat Hentgen	.30	.14
❑ 69 Ellis Burks	.30	.14
❑ 70 Mike Mussina	.60	.25
❑ 71 Hideo Nomo	.75	.35
❑ 72 Sandy Alomar	.30	.14
❑ 73 Bobby Bonilla	.30	.14
❑ 74 Rickey Henderson	.60	.25
❑ 75 David Cone	.40	.18
❑ 76 Terry Steinbach	.30	.14
❑ 77 Pedro Martinez	.60	.25
❑ 78 Jim Thome	.60	.25
❑ 79 Rod Beck	.15	.07
❑ 80 Randy Myers	.15	.07
❑ 81 Charles Nagy	.30	.14
❑ 82 Mark Wohlers	.15	.07
❑ 83 Paul O'Neill	.30	.14
❑ 84 Curt Schilling	.30	.14
❑ 85 Joey Cora	.30	.14
❑ 86 John Franco	.30	.14
❑ 87 Kevin Brown	.40	.18
❑ 88 Benito Santiago	.15	.07
❑ 89 Ray Lankford	.30	.14
❑ 90 Bernie Williams	.60	.25

		MINT	NRMT
❑ 91	Jason Dickson	.30	.14
❑ 92	Jeff Cirillo	.30	.14
❑ 93	Nomar Garciaparra	2.00	.90
❑ 94	Mariano Rivera	.30	.14
❑ 95	Javy Lopez	.30	.14
❑ 96	Tony Womack	2.00	.90
❑ 97	Jose Rosado	.15	.07
❑ 98	Denny Neagle	.30	.14
❑ 99	Darryl Kile	.30	.14
❑ 100	Justin Thompson	.30	.14
❑ 101	Juan Encarnacion	.30	.14
❑ 102	Brad Fullmer	.40	.18
❑ 103	Kris Benson	3.00	1.35
❑ 104	Todd Helton	1.25	.55
❑ 105	Paul Konerko	.60	.25
❑ 106	Travis Lee	15.00	6.75
❑ 107	Todd Greene	.30	.14
❑ 108	Mark Kotsay	5.00	2.20
❑ 109	Carl Pavano	.60	.25
❑ 110	Kerry Wood	35.00	16.00
❑ 111	Jason Romano	1.50	.70
❑ 112	Geoff Goetz	1.25	.55
❑ 113	Scott Hodges	1.25	.55
❑ 114	Aaron Akin	1.00	.45
❑ 115	Vernon Wells	5.00	2.20
❑ 116	Chris Stowe	.75	.35
❑ 117	Brett Caradonna	3.00	1.35
❑ 118	Adam Kennedy	1.50	.70
❑ 119	Jayson Werth	6.00	2.70
❑ 120	Glenn Davis	1.50	.70
❑ 121	Troy Cameron	3.00	1.35
❑ 122	J.J. Davis	4.00	1.80
❑ 123	Jason Dellaero	1.50	.70
❑ 124	Jason Standridge	1.50	.70
❑ 125	Lance Berkman	10.00	4.50
❑ NNO	Checklist	.15	.07

1997 Topps Stars Always Mint

	MINT	NRMT
COMPLETE SET (125)	1000.00	450.00
COMMON CARD (1-125)	2.50	1.10

*STARS: 7.5X TO 15X BASIC CARDS
*YOUNG STARS: 6X TO 12X BASIC CARDS
*ROOKIES: 2X TO 4X BASIC CARDS

1997 Topps Stars '97 All-Stars

		MINT	NRMT
COMPLETE SET (20)		300.00	135.00
COMMON CARD (AS1-AS20)		5.00	2.20
❑ AS1	Greg Maddux	40.00	18.00
❑ AS2	Randy Johnson	12.00	5.50
❑ AS3	Tino Martinez	12.00	5.50
❑ AS4	Jeff Bagwell	20.00	9.00
❑ AS5	Ivan Rodriguez	15.00	6.75
❑ AS6	Mike Piazza	40.00	18.00
❑ AS7	Cal Ripken	50.00	22.00
❑ AS8	Ken Caminiti	8.00	3.60
❑ AS9	Tony Gwynn	30.00	13.50
❑ AS10	Edgar Martinez	5.00	2.20
❑ AS11	Craig Biggio	12.00	5.50
❑ AS12	Roberto Alomar	12.00	5.50
❑ AS13	Larry Walker	12.00	5.50
❑ AS14	Brady Anderson	5.00	2.20
❑ AS15	Barry Bonds	15.00	6.75
❑ AS16	Ken Griffey Jr.	60.00	27.00
❑ AS17	Ray Lankford	5.00	2.20
❑ AS18	Paul O'Neill	5.00	2.20
❑ AS19	Jeff Blauser	5.00	2.20
❑ AS20	Sandy Alomar	5.00	2.20

1997 Topps Stars All-Star Memories

		MINT	NRMT
COMPLETE SET (10)		80.00	36.00
COMMON CARD (ASM1-ASM10)		2.00	.90
❑ ASM1	Cal Ripken	20.00	9.00
❑ ASM2	Jeff Conine	2.00	.90
❑ ASM3	Mike Piazza	15.00	6.75
❑ ASM4	Randy Johnson	5.00	2.20
❑ ASM5	Ken Griffey Jr.	25.00	11.00
❑ ASM6	Fred McGriff	3.00	1.35
❑ ASM7	Moises Alou	3.00	1.35
❑ ASM8	Hideo Nomo	6.00	2.70
❑ ASM9	Larry Walker	5.00	2.20
❑ ASM10	Sandy Alomar	2.00	.90

1997 Topps Stars Future All-Stars

		MINT	NRMT
COMPLETE SET (15)		50.00	22.00
COMMON CARD (FAS1-FAS15)		1.00	.45
❑ FAS1	Derek Jeter	10.00	4.50
❑ FAS2	Andruw Jones	5.00	2.20
❑ FAS3	Vladimir Guerrero	6.00	2.70
❑ FAS4	Scott Rolen	8.00	3.60
❑ FAS5	Jose Guillen	3.00	1.35
❑ FAS6	Jose Cruz Jr.	8.00	3.60
❑ FAS7	Darin Erstad	5.00	2.20
❑ FAS8	Tony Clark	2.00	.90
❑ FAS9	Scott Spiezio	1.00	.45
❑ FAS10	Kevin Orie	1.00	.45
❑ FAS11	Calvin Reese	1.00	.45
❑ FAS12	Billy Wagner	1.50	.70
❑ FAS13	Matt Morris	1.50	.70
❑ FAS14	Jeremi Gonzalez	2.00	.90
❑ FAS15	Hideki Irabu	5.00	2.20

1997 Topps Stars Rookie Reprints

		MINT	NRMT
COMPLETE SET (15)		60.00	27.00
COMMON CARD (1-15)		4.00	1.80
❑ 1	Luis Aparicio	4.00	1.80
❑ 2	Richie Ashburn	4.00	1.80
❑ 3	Jim Bunning	4.00	1.80
❑ 4	Bob Feller	4.00	1.80
❑ 5	Rollie Fingers	4.00	1.80
❑ 6	Monte Irvin	4.00	1.80
❑ 7	Al Kaline	6.00	2.70
❑ 8	Ralph Kiner	4.00	1.80
❑ 9	Eddie Mathews	5.00	2.20
❑ 10	Hal Newhouser	4.00	1.80
❑ 11	Gaylord Perry	4.00	1.80
❑ 12	Robin Roberts	4.00	1.80
❑ 13	Brooks Robinson	5.00	2.20
❑ 14	Enos Slaughter	4.00	1.80
❑ 15	Earl Weaver	4.00	1.80

1997 Topps Stars Rookie Reprint Autographs

		MINT	NRMT
COMPLETE SET (14)		350.00	160.00
COMMON CARD (1/3-15)		20.00	9.00
❑ 1	Luis Aparicio	30.00	13.50
❑ 3	Jim Bunning	30.00	13.50
❑ 4	Bob Feller	25.00	11.00
❑ 5	Rollie Fingers	20.00	9.00
❑ 6	Monte Irvin	20.00	9.00
❑ 7	Al Kaline	50.00	22.00
❑ 8	Ralph Kiner	30.00	13.50
❑ 9	Eddie Mathews	40.00	18.00
❑ 10	Hal Newhouser	20.00	9.00
❑ 11	Gaylord Perry	20.00	9.00
❑ 12	Robin Roberts	25.00	11.00
❑ 13	Brooks Robinson	40.00	18.00
❑ 14	Enos Slaughter	25.00	11.00
❑ 15	Earl Weaver	25.00	11.00

1998 Topps Stars

	MINT	NRMT
COMP.RED SET (150)	80.00	36.00
COMMON RED (1-150)	.40	.18
RED MINOR STARS	.60	.25
RED SEMISTARS	1.00	.45
RED UNLISTED STARS	1.50	.70

Card	MINT	NRMT
❑ 1 Greg Maddux	5.00	2.20
❑ 2 Darryl Kile	.60	.25
❑ 3 Rod Beck	.60	.25
❑ 4 Ellis Burks	.60	.25
❑ 5 Gary Sheffield	1.00	.45
❑ 6 David Ortiz	.60	.25
❑ 7 Marquis Grissom	.60	.25
❑ 8 Tony Womack	.60	.25
❑ 9 Mike Mussina	1.50	.70
❑ 10 Bernie Williams	1.50	.70
❑ 11 Andy Benes	.60	.25
❑ 12 Rusty Greer	.60	.25
❑ 13 Carlos Delgado	.60	.25
❑ 14 Jim Edmonds	1.00	.45
❑ 15 Raul Mondesi	1.00	.45
❑ 16 Andres Galarraga	1.50	.70
❑ 17 Wade Boggs	1.50	.70
❑ 18 Paul O'Neill	.60	.25
❑ 19 Edgar Renteria	.60	.25
❑ 20 Tony Clark	1.00	.45
❑ 21 Vladimir Guerrero	2.50	1.10
❑ 22 Moises Alou	1.00	.45
❑ 23 Bernard Gilkey	.40	.18
❑ 24 Lance Johnson	.40	.18
❑ 25 Ben Grieve	3.00	1.35
❑ 26 Sandy Alomar	.60	.25
❑ 27 Ray Durham	.60	.25
❑ 28 Shawn Estes	.60	.25
❑ 29 David Segui	.60	.25
❑ 30 Javy Lopez	.60	.25
❑ 31 Steve Finley	.60	.25
❑ 32 Rey Ordonez	.60	.25
❑ 33 Derek Jeter	4.00	1.80
❑ 34 Henry Rodriguez	.60	.25
❑ 35 Mo Vaughn	2.00	.90
❑ 36 Richard Hidalgo	.60	.25
❑ 37 Omar Vizquel	.60	.25
❑ 38 Johnny Damon	.60	.25
❑ 39 Brian Hunter	.60	.25
❑ 40 Matt Williams	.60	.25
❑ 41 Chuck Finley	.60	.25
❑ 42 Jeromy Burnitz	.60	.25
❑ 43 Livan Hernandez	.60	.25
❑ 44 Delino DeShields	.40	.18
❑ 45 Charles Nagy	.60	.25
❑ 46 Scott Rolen	4.00	1.80
❑ 47 Neifi Perez	.60	.25
❑ 48 John Wetteland	.60	.25
❑ 49 Eric Milton	.60	.25
❑ 50 Mike Piazza	5.00	2.20
❑ 51 Cal Ripken	6.00	2.70
❑ 52 Mariano Rivera	.60	.25
❑ 53 Butch Huskey	.40	.18
❑ 54 Quinton McCracken	.60	.25
❑ 55 Jose Cruz Jr.	2.00	.90
❑ 56 Brian Jordan	.60	.25
❑ 57 Hideo Nomo	2.00	.90
❑ 58 Masato Yoshii	1.25	.55
❑ 59 Cliff Floyd	.60	.25
❑ 60 Jose Guillen	.60	.25
❑ 61 Jeff Shaw	.60	.25
❑ 62 Edgar Martinez	.60	.25
❑ 63 Rondell White	.60	.25
❑ 64 Hal Morris	.40	.18
❑ 65 Barry Larkin	1.00	.45
❑ 66 Eric Young	.60	.25
❑ 67 Ray Lankford	.60	.25
❑ 68 Derek Bell	.60	.25
❑ 69 Charles Johnson	.60	.25
❑ 70 Robin Ventura	.60	.25
❑ 71 Chuck Knoblauch	1.50	.70
❑ 72 Kevin Brown	1.00	.45
❑ 73 Jose Valentin	.40	.18
❑ 74 Jay Buhner	.60	.25
❑ 75 Tony Gwynn	4.00	1.80
❑ 76 Andy Pettitte	1.00	.45
❑ 77 Edgardo Alfonzo	.60	.25
❑ 78 Kerry Wood	8.00	3.60
❑ 79 Darin Erstad	2.00	.90
❑ 80 Paul Konerko	1.50	.70
❑ 81 Jason Kendall	.60	.25
❑ 82 Tino Martinez	1.50	.70
❑ 83 Brad Radke	.60	.25
❑ 84 Jeff King	.60	.25
❑ 85 Travis Lee	3.00	1.35
❑ 86 Jeff Kent	.60	.25
❑ 87 Trevor Hoffman	.60	.25
❑ 88 David Cone	1.00	.45
❑ 89 Jose Canseco	1.50	.70
❑ 90 Juan Gonzalez	4.00	1.80
❑ 91 Todd Hundley	.60	.25
❑ 92 John Valentin	.60	.25
❑ 93 Sammy Sosa	4.00	1.80
❑ 94 Jason Giambi	.60	.25
❑ 95 Chipper Jones	4.00	1.80
❑ 96 Jeff Blauser	.40	.18
❑ 97 Brad Fullmer	.60	.25
❑ 98 Derrek Lee	.60	.25
❑ 99 Denny Neagle	.60	.25
❑ 100 Ken Griffey Jr.	8.00	3.60
❑ 101 David Justice	1.50	.70
❑ 102 Tim Salmon	1.50	.70
❑ 103 J.T. Snow	.60	.25
❑ 104 Fred McGriff	1.00	.45
❑ 105 Brady Anderson	.60	.25
❑ 106 Larry Walker	1.50	.70
❑ 107 Jeff Cirillo	.60	.25
❑ 108 Andruw Jones	2.00	.90
❑ 109 Manny Ramirez	1.50	.70
❑ 110 Justin Thompson	.60	.25
❑ 111 Vinny Castilla	1.00	.45
❑ 112 Chan Ho Park	1.50	.70
❑ 113 Mark Grudzielanek	.60	.25
❑ 114 Mark Grace	1.00	.45
❑ 115 Ken Caminiti	1.00	.45
❑ 116 Ryan Klesko	.60	.25
❑ 117 Rafael Palmeiro	1.00	.45
❑ 118 Pat Hentgen	.60	.25
❑ 119 Eric Karros	.60	.25
❑ 120 Randy Johnson	1.50	.70
❑ 121 Roberto Alomar	1.50	.70
❑ 122 John Olerud	.60	.25
❑ 123 Paul Molitor	1.50	.70
❑ 124 Dean Palmer	.60	.25
❑ 125 Nomar Garciaparra	5.00	2.20
❑ 126 Curt Schilling	.60	.25
❑ 127 Jay Bell	.60	.25
❑ 128 Craig Biggio	1.50	.70
❑ 129 Marty Cordova	.40	.18
❑ 130 Ivan Rodriguez	2.00	.90
❑ 131 Todd Helton	2.00	.90
❑ 132 Jim Thome	1.50	.70
❑ 133 Albert Belle	1.50	.70
❑ 134 Mike Lansing	.40	.18
❑ 135 Mark McGwire	10.00	4.50
❑ 136 Roger Clemens	3.00	1.35
❑ 137 Tom Glavine	1.50	.70
❑ 138 Ron Gant	.40	.18
❑ 139 Alex Rodriguez	5.00	2.20
❑ 140 Jeff Bagwell	2.50	1.10
❑ 141 John Smoltz	.60	.25
❑ 142 Kenny Lofton	1.50	.70
❑ 143 Dante Bichette	.60	.25
❑ 144 Pedro Martinez	1.50	.70
❑ 145 Barry Bonds	2.00	.90
❑ 146 Travis Fryman	.60	.25
❑ 147 Bobby Jones	.40	.18
❑ 148 Bobby Higginson	1.00	.45
❑ 149 Reggie Sanders	.60	.25
❑ 150 Frank Thomas	5.00	2.20

1998 Topps Stars Galaxy Bronze

	MINT	NRMT
COMPLETE SET (10)	800.00	350.00
COMMON CARD (G1-G10)	30.00	13.50

*SILVER: .5X TO 1.2X BRONZE
SILVER STATED ODDS 1:910
SILVER PRINT RUN 75 SERIAL #'d SETS
*GOLD: .6X TO 1.5X BRONZE
GOLD STATED ODDS 1:1364
GOLD PRINT RUN 50 SERIAL #'d SETS
GOLD RAINBOW STATED ODDS 1:13643
GOLD RBW.PRINT RUN 5 SERIAL #'d SETS
BRONZE CARDS LISTED BELOW!

Card	MINT	NRMT
❑ G1 Barry Bonds	60.00	27.00
❑ G2 Jeff Bagwell	80.00	36.00
❑ G3 Nomar Garciaparra	150.00	70.00
❑ G4 Chipper Jones	120.00	55.00
❑ G5 Ken Griffey Jr.	250.00	110.00
❑ G6 Sammy Sosa	120.00	55.00
❑ G7 Larry Walker	50.00	22.00
❑ G8 Alex Rodriguez	150.00	70.00
❑ G9 Craig Biggio	50.00	22.00
❑ G10 Raul Mondesi	30.00	13.50

1998 Topps Stars Luminaries Bronze

	MINT	NRMT
COMPLETE SET (15)	1200.00	550.00
COMMON CARD (L1-L15)	20.00	9.00

*SILVER: .5X TO 1.2X BRONZE
SILVER STATED ODDS 1:606
SILVER PRINT RUN 75 SERIAL #'d SETS
*GOLD: .6X TO 1.5X BRONZE
GOLD STATED ODDS 1:910
GOLD PRINT RUN 50 SERIAL #'d SETS
GOLD RAINBOW STATED ODDS 1:9095
GOLD RBW.PRINT RUN 5 SERIAL #'d SETS

		MINT	NRMT
❑ L1	Ken Griffey Jr.	250.00	110.00
❑ L2	Mark McGwire	300.00	135.00
❑ L3	Juan Gonzalez	120.00	55.00
❑ L4	Tony Gwynn	120.00	55.00
❑ L5	Frank Thomas	150.00	70.00
❑ L6	Mike Piazza	150.00	70.00
❑ L7	Chuck Knoblauch	40.00	18.00
❑ L8	Kenny Lofton	40.00	18.00
❑ L9	Barry Bonds	60.00	27.00
❑ L10	Matt Williams	20.00	9.00
❑ L11	Raul Mondesi	30.00	13.50
❑ L12	Ivan Rodriguez	60.00	27.00
❑ L13	Alex Rodriguez	150.00	70.00
❑ L14	Nomar Garciaparra	150.00	70.00
❑ L15	Ken Caminiti	30.00	13.50

1998 Topps Stars Rookie Reprints

	MINT	NRMT
COMPLETE SET (5)	40.00	18.00
COMMON CARD (1-5)	6.00	2.70
❑ 1 Johnny Bench	10.00	4.50
❑ 2 Whitey Ford	6.00	2.70
❑ 3 Joe Morgan	6.00	2.70
❑ 4 Mike Schmidt	12.00	5.50
❑ 5 Carl Yastrzemski	10.00	4.50

1998 Topps Stars Rookie Reprints Autographs

	MINT	NRMT
COMPLETE SET (5)	400.00	180.00
COMMON CARD (1-5)	60.00	27.00
❑ 1 Johnny Bench	100.00	45.00
❑ 2 Whitey Ford	60.00	27.00
❑ 3 Joe Morgan	60.00	27.00
❑ 4 Mike Schmidt	120.00	55.00
❑ 5 Carl Yastrzemski	100.00	45.00

1998 Topps Stars Supernovas Bronze

	MINT	NRMT
COMPLETE SET (10)	500.00	220.00

	MINT	NRMT
COMMON CARD (S1-S10)	20.00	9.00

*SILVER: .5X TO 1.2X BRONZE
SILVER STATED ODDS 1:910
SILVER PRINT RUN 75 SERIAL #'d SETS
*GOLD: .6X TO 1.5X BRONZE
GOLD STATED ODDS 1:1364
GOLD PRINT RUN 50 SERIAL #'d SETS
GOLD RAINBOW STATED ODDS 1:13643
GOLD RBW.PRINT RUN 5 SERIAL #'d SETS

		MINT	NRMT
❑ S1	Ben Grieve	80.00	36.00
❑ S2	Travis Lee	80.00	36.00
❑ S3	Todd Helton	50.00	22.00
❑ S4	Adrian Beltre		
❑ S5	Derrek Lee		
❑ S6	David Ortiz		
❑ S7	Brad Fullmer		
❑ S8	Mark Kotsay	30.00	13.50
❑ S9	Paul Konerko		
❑ S10	Kerry Wood	200.00	90.00

1998 Topps Stars 'N Steel

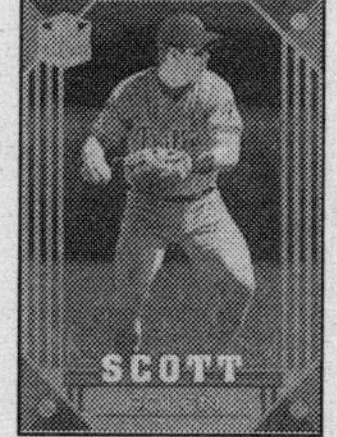

	MINT	NRMT
COMPLETE SET (44)	180.00	80.00
COMMON CARD (1-44)	2.00	.90
❑ 1 Roberto Alomar	5.00	2.20
❑ 2 Jeff Bagwell	8.00	3.60
❑ 3 Albert Belle	5.00	2.20
❑ 4 Dante Bichette	2.00	.90
❑ 5 Barry Bonds	6.00	2.70
❑ 6 Jay Buhner	2.00	.90
❑ 7 Ken Caminiti	3.00	1.35
❑ 8 Vinny Castilla	3.00	1.35
❑ 9 Roger Clemens	10.00	4.50
❑ 10 Jose Cruz Jr.	5.00	2.20
❑ 11 Andres Galarraga	5.00	2.20
❑ 12 Nomar Garciaparra	15.00	6.75
❑ 13 Juan Gonzalez	12.00	5.50
❑ 14 Mark Grace	3.00	1.35
❑ 15 Ken Griffey Jr.	25.00	11.00
❑ 16 Tony Gwynn	12.00	5.50
❑ 17 Todd Hundley	2.00	.90
❑ 18 Derek Jeter	12.00	5.50
❑ 19 Randy Johnson	5.00	2.20
❑ 20 Andruw Jones	5.00	2.20
❑ 21 Chipper Jones	12.00	5.50
❑ 22 David Justice	5.00	2.20
❑ 23 Ray Lankford	2.00	.90
❑ 24 Barry Larkin	3.00	1.35
❑ 25 Kenny Lofton	5.00	2.20
❑ 26 Greg Maddux	15.00	6.75
❑ 27 Edgar Martinez	2.00	.90
❑ 28 Tino Martinez	5.00	2.20
❑ 29 Mark McGwire	30.00	13.50
❑ 30 Paul Molitor	5.00	2.20
❑ 31 Rafael Palmeiro	3.00	1.35
❑ 32 Mike Piazza	15.00	6.75
❑ 33 Manny Ramirez	5.00	2.20
❑ 34 Cal Ripken	20.00	9.00
❑ 35 Ivan Rodriguez	6.00	2.70
❑ 36 Scott Rolen	10.00	4.50
❑ 37 Tim Salmon	5.00	2.20
❑ 38 Gary Sheffield	3.00	1.35
❑ 39 Sammy Sosa	12.00	5.50
❑ 40 Frank Thomas	15.00	6.75
❑ 41 Jim Thome	5.00	2.20
❑ 42 Mo Vaughn	6.00	2.70
❑ 43 Larry Walker	5.00	2.20
❑ 44 Bernie Williams	5.00	2.20

1999 Topps Stars 'N Steel

	MINT	NRMT
COMPLETE SET (44)	150.00	70.00
COMMON CARD (1-44)	2.00	.90
❑ 1 Kerry Wood	12.00	5.50
❑ 2 Ben Grieve	8.00	3.60
❑ 3 Chipper Jones	12.00	5.50
❑ 4 Alex Rodriguez	15.00	6.75
❑ 5 Mo Vaughn	6.00	2.70
❑ 6 Bernie Williams	5.00	2.20
❑ 7 Juan Gonzalez	12.00	5.50
❑ 8 Vinny Castilla	3.00	1.35
❑ 9 Tony Gwynn	12.00	5.50
❑ 10 Manny Ramirez	5.00	2.20
❑ 11 Raul Mondesi	3.00	1.35
❑ 12 Roger Clemens	10.00	4.50
❑ 13 Darin Erstad	5.00	2.20
❑ 14 Barry Bonds	6.00	2.70
❑ 15 Cal Ripken	20.00	9.00
❑ 16 Barry Larkin	3.00	1.35
❑ 17 Scott Rolen	10.00	4.50
❑ 18 Albert Belle	5.00	2.20
❑ 19 Craig Biggio	5.00	2.20
❑ 20 Tony Clark	3.00	1.35
❑ 21 Mark McGwire	30.00	13.50
❑ 22 Andres Galarraga	5.00	2.20
❑ 23 Kenny Lofton	5.00	2.20
❑ 24 Pedro Martinez	5.00	2.20
❑ 25 Paul O'Neill	2.50	1.10
❑ 26 Ken Griffey Jr.	25.00	11.00
❑ 27 Travis Lee	6.00	2.70
❑ 28 Tim Salmon	5.00	2.20
❑ 29 Frank Thomas	15.00	6.75
❑ 30 Larry Walker	5.00	2.20
❑ 31 Moises Alou	3.00	1.35
❑ 32 Vladimir Guerrero	6.00	2.70
❑ 33 Ivan Rodriguez	6.00	2.70
❑ 34 Derek Jeter	12.00	5.50
❑ 35 Greg Vaughn	2.50	1.10
❑ 36 Gary Sheffield	3.00	1.35
❑ 37 Carlos Delgado	2.50	1.10

	MINT	NRMT
❑ 38 Greg Maddux	15.00	6.75
❑ 39 Sammy Sosa	12.00	5.50
❑ 40 Mike Piazza	15.00	6.75
❑ 41 Nomar Garciaparra	15.00	6.75
❑ 42 Dante Bichette	2.50	1.10
❑ 43 Jeff Bagwell	8.00	3.60
❑ 44 Jim Thome	5.00	2.20

1999 Topps Stars 'N Steel Gold

	MINT	NRMT
COMPLETE SET (44)	1000.00	450.00
COMMON CARD (1-44)	8.00	3.60

*GOLD: 1.25X TO 3X BASIC CARDS

1999 Topps Stars 'N Steel Gold Domed Holographic

	MINT	NRMT
COMPLETE SET (44)	2000.00	900.00
COMMON CARD (1-44)	15.00	6.75

*STARS: 3X TO 6X BASIC CARDS

1998 Topps SuperChrome

	MINT	NRMT
COMPLETE SET (36)	50.00	22.00
COMMON CARD (1-36)	.40	.18
❑ 1 Tony Gwynn	2.50	1.10
❑ 2 Larry Walker	1.00	.45
❑ 3 Vladimir Guerrero	1.50	.70
❑ 4 Mo Vaughn	1.25	.55
❑ 5 Frank Thomas	3.00	1.35
❑ 6 Barry Larkin	.60	.25
❑ 7 Scott Rolen	2.50	1.10
❑ 8 Juan Gonzalez	2.50	1.10
❑ 9 Jeff Bagwell	1.50	.70
❑ 10 Ryan Klesko	.50	.23
❑ 11 Mike Piazza	3.00	1.35
❑ 12 Randy Johnson	1.00	.45
❑ 13 Derek Jeter	2.50	1.10
❑ 14 Gary Sheffield	.60	.25
❑ 15 Hideo Nomo	1.25	.55
❑ 16 Tino Martinez	1.00	.45
❑ 17 Ivan Rodriguez	1.25	.55
❑ 18 Bernie Williams	1.00	.45
❑ 19 Greg Maddux	3.00	1.35
❑ 20 Roger Clemens	2.00	.90
❑ 21 Roberto Clemente	2.50	1.10
❑ 22 Chipper Jones	2.50	1.10
❑ 23 Sammy Sosa	2.50	1.10
❑ 24 Tony Clark	.60	.25
❑ 25 Barry Bonds	1.25	.55
❑ 26 Craig Biggio	1.00	.45
❑ 27 Cal Ripken	4.00	1.80
❑ 28 Ken Griffey Jr.	5.00	2.20
❑ 29 Todd Helton	1.25	.55
❑ 30 Mark McGwire	6.00	2.70
❑ 31 Jose Cruz Jr.	1.25	.55
❑ 32 Albert Belle	1.00	.45
❑ 33 Andruw Jones	1.25	.55
❑ 34 Nomar Garciaparra	3.00	1.35
❑ 35 Andy Pettitte	.60	.25
❑ 36 Alex Rodriguez	3.00	1.35

1998 Topps SuperChrome Refractors

	MINT	NRMT
COMPLETE SET (36)	600.00	275.00
COMMON CARD (1-36)	3.00	1.35

*STARS: 5X TO 12X BASIC CARDS

1998 Topps Tek

	MINT	NRMT
COMPLETE SET (90)	150.00	70.00
COMMON CARD (1-90)	.50	.23
❑ 1 Ben Grieve	3.00	1.35
❑ 2 Kerry Wood	8.00	3.60
❑ 3 Barry Bonds	2.50	1.10
❑ 4 John Olerud	.75	.35
❑ 5 Ivan Rodriguez	2.50	1.10
❑ 6 Frank Thomas	6.00	2.70
❑ 7 Bernie Williams	2.00	.90
❑ 8 Dante Bichette	.75	.35
❑ 9 Alex Rodriguez	6.00	2.70
❑ 10 Tom Glavine	2.00	.90
❑ 11 Eric Karros	.75	.35
❑ 12 Craig Biggio	2.00	.90
❑ 13 Mark McGwire	12.00	5.50
❑ 14 Derek Jeter	5.00	2.20
❑ 15 Nomar Garciaparra	6.00	2.70
❑ 16 Brady Anderson	.75	.35
❑ 17 Vladimir Guerrero	2.50	1.10
❑ 18 David Justice	2.00	.90
❑ 19 Chipper Jones	5.00	2.20
❑ 20 Jim Edmonds	1.25	.55
❑ 21 Roger Clemens	4.00	1.80
❑ 22 Mark Kotsay	1.25	.55
❑ 23 Tony Gwynn	5.00	2.20
❑ 24 Todd Walker	1.25	.55
❑ 25 Tino Martinez	2.00	.90
❑ 26 Andruw Jones	2.00	.90
❑ 27 Sandy Alomar Jr.	.75	.35
❑ 28 Sammy Sosa	5.00	2.20
❑ 29 Gary Sheffield	1.25	.55
❑ 30 Ken Griffey Jr.	10.00	4.50
❑ 31 Aramis Ramirez	2.00	.90
❑ 32 Curt Schilling	.75	.35
❑ 33 Robin Ventura	.75	.35
❑ 34 Larry Walker	2.00	.90
❑ 35 Darin Erstad	2.00	.90
❑ 36 Todd Dunwoody	.75	.35
❑ 37 Paul O'Neill	.75	.35
❑ 38 Vinny Castilla	1.25	.55
❑ 39 Randy Johnson	2.00	.90
❑ 40 Rafael Palmeiro	1.25	.55
❑ 41 Pedro Martinez	2.00	.90
❑ 42 Derek Bell	.75	.35
❑ 43 Carlos Delgado	.75	.35
❑ 44 Matt Williams	.75	.35
❑ 45 Kenny Lofton	2.00	.90
❑ 46 Edgar Renteria	.75	.35
❑ 47 Albert Belle	2.00	.90
❑ 48 Jeromy Burnitz	.75	.35
❑ 49 Adrian Beltre	2.00	.90
❑ 50 Greg Maddux	6.00	2.70
❑ 51 Cal Ripken	8.00	3.60
❑ 52 Jason Kendall	.75	.35
❑ 53 Ellis Burks	.75	.35
❑ 54 Paul Molitor	2.00	.90
❑ 55 Moises Alou	1.25	.55
❑ 56 Raul Mondesi	1.25	.55
❑ 57 Barry Larkin	1.25	.55
❑ 58 Tony Clark	1.25	.55
❑ 59 Travis Lee	3.00	1.35
❑ 60 Juan Gonzalez	5.00	2.20
❑ 61 Troy Glaus	8.00	3.60
❑ 62 Jose Cruz Jr.	2.00	.90
❑ 63 Paul Konerko	2.00	.90
❑ 64 Edgar Martinez	.75	.35
❑ 65 Javy Lopez	.75	.35
❑ 66 Manny Ramirez	2.00	.90
❑ 67 Roberto Alomar	2.00	.90
❑ 68 Ken Caminiti	1.25	.55
❑ 69 Todd Helton	2.00	.90
❑ 70 Chuck Knoblauch	2.00	.90
❑ 71 Kevin Brown	1.25	.55
❑ 72 Tim Salmon	2.00	.90
❑ 73 Orlando Hernandez	8.00	3.60
❑ 74 Jeff Bagwell	3.00	1.35
❑ 75 Brian Jordan	.75	.35
❑ 76 Derrek Lee	.75	.35
❑ 77 Brad Fullmer	.75	.35
❑ 78 Mark Grace	1.25	.55
❑ 79 Jeff King	.75	.35
❑ 80 Mike Mussina	2.00	.90
❑ 81 Jay Buhner	.75	.35

Card	MINT	NRMT
❑ 82 Quinton McCracken	.75	.35
❑ 83 A.J. Hinch	.75	.35
❑ 84 Richard Hidalgo	.75	.35
❑ 85 Andres Galarraga	2.00	.90
❑ 86 Mike Piazza	6.00	2.70
❑ 87 Mo Vaughn	2.50	1.10
❑ 88 Scott Rolen	4.00	1.80
❑ 89 Jim Thome	2.00	.90
❑ 90 Ray Lankford	.75	.35

1998 Topps Tek Diffractors

	MINT	NRMT
COMPLETE SET (90)	1000.00	450.00
COMMON CARD (1-90)	3.00	1.35

*STARS: 3X TO 6X BASIC CARDS
*ROOKIES: 2.5X TO 5X BASIC CARDS

1995 UC3

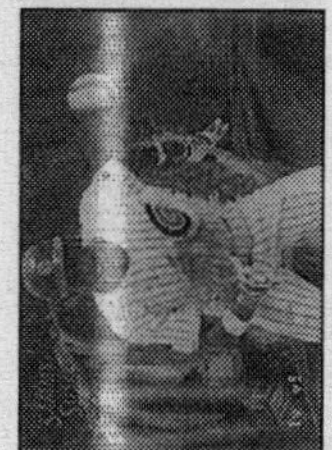

	MINT	NRMT
COMPLETE SET (147)	20.00	9.00
COMMON CARD (1-147)	.15	.07

Card	MINT	NRMT
❑ 1 Frank Thomas	2.00	.90
❑ 2 Wil Cordero	.15	.07
❑ 3 John Olerud	.30	.14
❑ 4 Deion Sanders	.30	.14
❑ 5 Mike Mussina	.60	.25
❑ 6 Mo Vaughn	.75	.35
❑ 7 Will Clark	.60	.25
❑ 8 Chili Davis	.30	.14
❑ 9 Jimmy Key	.30	.14
❑ 10 John Valentin	.30	.14
❑ 11 Tony Tarasco	.15	.07
❑ 12 Alan Trammell	.30	.14
❑ 13 David Cone	.40	.18
❑ 14 Tim Salmon	.60	.25
❑ 15 Danny Tartabull	.15	.07
❑ 16 Aaron Sele	.30	.14
❑ 17 Alex Fernandez	.15	.07
❑ 18 Barry Bonds	.75	.35
❑ 19 Andres Galarraga	.60	.25
❑ 20 Don Mattingly	1.00	.45
❑ 21 Kevin Appier	.30	.14
❑ 22 Paul Molitor	.60	.25
❑ 23 Omar Vizquel	.30	.14
❑ 24 Andy Benes	.30	.14
❑ 25 Rafael Palmeiro	.40	.18
❑ 26 Barry Larkin	.40	.18
❑ 27 Bernie Williams	.60	.25
❑ 28 Gary Sheffield	.40	.18
❑ 29 Wally Joyner	.30	.14
❑ 30 Wade Boggs	.60	.25
❑ 31 Rico Brogna	.15	.07
❑ 32 Ken Caminiti	.40	.18
❑ 33 Kirby Puckett	1.00	.45
❑ 34 Bobby Bonilla	.30	.14
❑ 35 Hal Morris	.15	.07
❑ 36 Moises Alou	.40	.18
❑ 37 Jim Thome	.60	.25
❑ 38 Chuck Knoblauch	.60	.25
❑ 39 Mike Piazza	2.00	.90
❑ 40 Travis Fryman	.30	.14
❑ 41 Rickey Henderson	.60	.25
❑ 42 Jack McDowell	.15	.07
❑ 43 Carlos Baerga	.30	.14
❑ 44 Gregg Jefferies	.15	.07
❑ 45 Kirk Gibson	.30	.14
❑ 46 Bret Saberhagen	.30	.14
❑ 47 Cecil Fielder	.30	.14
❑ 48 Manny Ramirez	.60	.25
❑ 49 Marquis Grissom	.30	.14
❑ 50 Dave Winfield	.60	.25
❑ 51 Mark McGwire	3.00	1.35
❑ 52 Dennis Eckersley	.30	.14
❑ 53 Robin Ventura	.30	.14
❑ 54 Ryan Klesko	.30	.14
❑ 55 Jeff Bagwell	1.00	.45
❑ 56 Ozzie Smith	.75	.35
❑ 57 Brian McRae	.15	.07
❑ 58 Albert Belle	.75	.35
❑ 59 Darren Daulton	.30	.14
❑ 60 Jose Canseco	.60	.25
❑ 61 Greg Maddux	2.00	.90
❑ 62 Ben McDonald	.15	.07
❑ 63 Lenny Dykstra	.30	.14
❑ 64 Randy Johnson	.60	.25
❑ 65 Fred McGriff	.40	.18
❑ 66 Ray Lankford	.30	.14
❑ 67 Dave Justice	.60	.25
❑ 68 Paul O'Neill	.30	.14
❑ 69 Tony Gwynn	1.50	.70
❑ 70 Matt Williams	.30	.14
❑ 71 Dante Bichette	.30	.14
❑ 72 Craig Biggio	.60	.25
❑ 73 Ken Griffey Jr.	3.00	1.35
❑ 74 Juan Gonzalez	1.50	.70
❑ 75 Cal Ripken	2.50	1.10
❑ 76 Jay Bell	.30	.14
❑ 77 Joe Carter	.30	.14
❑ 78 Roberto Alomar	.60	.25
❑ 79 Mark Langston	.15	.07
❑ 80 Dave Hollins	.15	.07
❑ 81 Tom Glavine	.60	.25
❑ 82 Ivan Rodriguez	.75	.35
❑ 83 Mark Whiten	.15	.07
❑ 84 Raul Mondesi	.40	.18
❑ 85 Kenny Lofton	.60	.25
❑ 86 Ruben Sierra	.15	.07
❑ 87 Mark Grace	.40	.18
❑ 88 Royce Clayton	.15	.07
❑ 89 Billy Ashley	.15	.07
❑ 90 Larry Walker	.60	.25
❑ 91 Sammy Sosa	1.50	.70
❑ 92 Jason Bere	.15	.07
❑ 93 Bob Hamelin	.15	.07
❑ 94 Greg Vaughn	.30	.14
❑ 95 Roger Clemens	1.25	.55
❑ 96 Scott Ruffcorn	.15	.07
❑ 97 Hideo Nomo	2.50	1.10
❑ 98 Michael Tucker	.30	.14
❑ 99 J.R. Phillips	.15	.07
❑ 100 Roberto Petagine	.15	.07
❑ 101 Chipper Jones	1.50	.70
❑ 102 Armando Benitez	.15	.07
❑ 103 Orlando Miller	.15	.07
❑ 104 Carlos Delgado	.30	.14
❑ 105 Jeff Cirillo	.30	.14
❑ 106 Shawn Green	.30	.14
❑ 107 Joe Randa	.15	.07
❑ 108 Vaughn Eshelman	.15	.07
❑ 109 Frank Rodriguez	.15	.07
❑ 110 Russ Davis	.30	.14
❑ 111 Todd Hollandsworth	.15	.07
❑ 112 Mark Grudzielanek	.50	.23
❑ 113 Jose Oliva	.15	.07
❑ 114 Ray Durham	.30	.14
❑ 115 Alex Rodriguez	2.50	1.10
❑ 116 Alex Gonzalez	.15	.07
❑ 117 Midre Cummings	.15	.07
❑ 118 Marty Cordova	.15	.07
❑ 119 John Mabry	.15	.07
❑ 120 Jason Jacome	.15	.07
❑ 121 Joe Vitiello	.15	.07
❑ 122 Charles Johnson	.30	.14
❑ 123 Cal Ripken ID	1.25	.55
❑ 124 Ken Griffey Jr. ID	1.50	.70
❑ 125 Frank Thomas ID	1.00	.45
❑ 126 Mike Piazza ID	1.00	.45
❑ 127 Matt Williams ID	.15	.07
❑ 128 Barry Bonds ID	.40	.18
❑ 129 Greg Maddux ID	1.00	.45
❑ 130 Randy Johnson ID	.30	.14
❑ 131 Albert Belle ID	.30	.14
❑ 132 Will Clark ID	.30	.14
❑ 133 Tony Gwynn ID	.75	.35
❑ 134 Manny Ramirez ID	.30	.14
❑ 135 Raul Mondesi ID	.15	.07
❑ 136 Mo Vaughn ID	.40	.18
❑ 137 Mark McGwire ID	1.50	.70
❑ 138 Kirby Puckett ID	.60	.25
❑ 139 Don Mattingly ID	.60	.25
❑ 140 Carlos Baerga ID	.15	.07
❑ 141 Roger Clemens ID	.60	.25
❑ 142 Fred McGriff ID	.15	.07
❑ 143 Kenny Lofton ID	.30	.14
❑ 144 Jeff Bagwell ID	.60	.25
❑ 145 Larry Walker ID	.30	.14
❑ 146 Joe Carter ID	.15	.07
❑ 147 Rafael Palmeiro ID	.15	.07

1995 UC3 Clear Shots

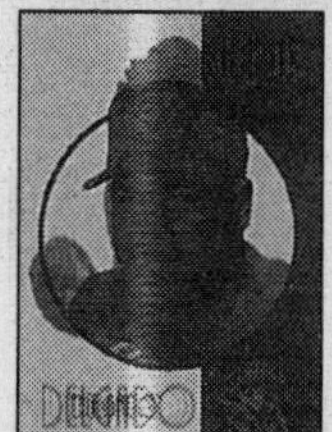

	MINT	NRMT
COMPLETE SET (12)	60.00	27.00
COMMON CARD (CS1-CS12)	1.00	.45

Card	MINT	NRMT
❑ CS1 Alex Rodriguez	20.00	9.00
❑ CS2 Shawn Green	1.50	.70
❑ CS3 Hideo Nomo	12.00	5.50
❑ CS4 Charles Johnson	1.50	.70
❑ CS5 Orlando Miller	1.00	.45
❑ CS6 Billy Ashley	1.00	.45
❑ CS7 Carlos Delgado	1.50	.70
❑ CS8 Cliff Floyd	1.50	.70
❑ CS9 Chipper Jones	15.00	6.75
❑ CS10 Alex Gonzalez	1.00	.45
❑ CS11 J.R. Phillips	1.00	.45
❑ CS12 Michael Tucker	1.50	.70
❑ PCS8 Cliff Floyd Promo	2.00	.90
❑ PCS10 Alex Gonzalez Promo	1.00	.45

1995 UC3 Cyclone Squad

	MINT	NRMT
COMPLETE SET (20)	20.00	9.00
COMMON CARD (CS1-CS20)	.40	.18

	MINT	NRMT
❑ CS1 Frank Thomas	2.50	1.10
❑ CS2 Ken Griffey Jr.	4.00	1.80
❑ CS3 Jeff Bagwell	1.25	.55
❑ CS4 Cal Ripken	3.00	1.35
❑ CS5 Barry Bonds	.75	.35
❑ CS6 Mike Piazza	2.50	1.10
❑ CS7 Matt Williams	.40	.18
❑ CS8 Kirby Puckett	.75	.35
❑ CS9 Jose Canseco	.75	.35
❑ CS10 Will Clark	.75	.35
❑ CS11 Don Mattingly	1.00	.45
❑ CS12 Albert Belle	.75	.35
❑ CS13 Tony Gwynn	2.00	.90
❑ CS14 Raul Mondesi	.50	.23
❑ CS15 Bobby Bonilla	.40	.18
❑ CS16 Rafael Palmeiro	.50	.23
❑ CS17 Fred McGriff	.50	.23
❑ CS18 Tim Salmon	.75	.35
❑ CS19 Kenny Lofton	.75	.35
❑ CS20 Joe Carter	.40	.18

1995 UC3 In Motion

	MINT	NRMT
COMPLETE SET (10)	40.00	18.00
COMMON CARD (IM1-IM10)	.75	.35
❑ IM1 Cal Ripken	6.00	2.70
❑ IM2 Ken Griffey Jr.	8.00	3.60
❑ IM3 Frank Thomas	5.00	2.20
❑ IM4 Mike Piazza	5.00	2.20
❑ IM5 Barry Bonds	1.50	.70
❑ IM6 Matt Williams	.75	.35
❑ IM7 Kirby Puckett	1.50	.70
❑ IM8 Greg Maddux	5.00	2.20
❑ IM9 Don Mattingly	2.50	1.10
❑ IM10 Will Clark	1.50	.70

1997 UD3

	MINT	NRMT
COMPLETE SET (60)	60.00	27.00
COMMON CARD (1-60)	.50	.23
❑ 1 Mark McGwire	6.00	2.70
❑ 2 Brady Anderson	.50	.23
❑ 3 Ken Griffey Jr.	6.00	2.70
❑ 4 Albert Belle	1.50	.70
❑ 5 Andres Galarraga	1.25	.55
❑ 6 Juan Gonzalez	3.00	1.35
❑ 7 Jay Buhner	.50	.23
❑ 8 Mo Vaughn	1.50	.70
❑ 9 Barry Bonds	1.50	.70
❑ 10 Gary Sheffield	.75	.35
❑ 11 Todd Hundley	.50	.23
❑ 12 Ellis Burks	.50	.23
❑ 13 Ken Caminiti	.75	.35
❑ 14 Vinny Castilla	.75	.35
❑ 15 Sammy Sosa	3.00	1.35
❑ 16 Frank Thomas	4.00	1.80
❑ 17 Rafael Palmeiro	.75	.35
❑ 18 Mike Piazza	4.00	1.80
❑ 19 Matt Williams	.50	.23
❑ 20 Eddie Murray	1.25	.55
❑ 21 Roger Clemens	2.50	1.10
❑ 22 Tim Salmon	1.25	.55
❑ 23 Robin Ventura	.50	.23
❑ 24 Ron Gant	.50	.23
❑ 25 Cal Ripken	5.00	2.20
❑ 26 Bernie Williams	1.25	.55
❑ 27 Hideo Nomo	1.50	.70
❑ 28 Ivan Rodriguez	1.50	.70
❑ 29 John Smoltz	.50	.23
❑ 30 Paul Molitor	1.25	.55
❑ 31 Greg Maddux	4.00	1.80
❑ 32 Raul Mondesi	.75	.35
❑ 33 Roberto Alomar	1.25	.55
❑ 34 Barry Larkin	.75	.35
❑ 35 Tony Gwynn	3.00	1.35
❑ 36 Jim Thome	1.25	.55
❑ 37 Kenny Lofton	1.25	.55
❑ 38 Jeff Bagwell	2.00	.90
❑ 39 Ozzie Smith	1.50	.70
❑ 40 Kirby Puckett	2.00	.90
❑ 41 Andruw Jones	2.00	.90
❑ 42 Vladimir Guerrero	2.50	1.10
❑ 43 Edgar Renteria	.50	.23
❑ 44 Luis Castillo	.50	.23
❑ 45 Darin Erstad	2.00	.90
❑ 46 Nomar Garciaparra	4.00	1.80
❑ 47 Todd Greene	.50	.23
❑ 48 Jason Kendall	.75	.35
❑ 49 Rey Ordonez	.50	.23
❑ 50 Alex Rodriguez	4.00	1.80
❑ 51 Manny Ramirez	1.25	.55
❑ 52 Todd Walker	1.25	.55
❑ 53 Ruben Rivera	.50	.23
❑ 54 Andy Pettitte	.75	.35
❑ 55 Derek Jeter	4.00	1.80
❑ 56 Todd Hollandsworth	.50	.23
❑ 57 Rocky Coppinger	.50	.23
❑ 58 Scott Rolen	3.00	1.35
❑ 59 Jermaine Dye	.50	.23
❑ 60 Chipper Jones	3.00	1.35

1997 UD3 Generation Next

	MINT	NRMT
COMPLETE SET (20)	120.00	55.00
COMMON CARD (1-20)	1.50	.70
❑ GN1 Alex Rodriguez	20.00	9.00
❑ GN2 Vladimir Guerrero	10.00	4.50
❑ GN3 Luis Castillo	2.50	1.10
❑ GN4 Rey Ordonez	2.50	1.10
❑ GN5 Andruw Jones	8.00	3.60
❑ GN6 Darin Erstad	8.00	3.60
❑ GN7 Edgar Renteria	2.50	1.10
❑ GN8 Jason Kendall	3.00	1.35
❑ GN9 Jermaine Dye	1.50	.70
❑ GN10 Chipper Jones	15.00	6.75
❑ GN11 Rocky Coppinger	1.50	.70
❑ GN12 Andy Pettitte	3.00	1.35
❑ GN13 Todd Greene	2.50	1.10
❑ GN14 Todd Hollandsworth	1.50	.70
❑ GN15 Derek Jeter	15.00	6.75
❑ GN16 Ruben Rivera	2.50	1.10
❑ GN17 Todd Walker	5.00	2.20
❑ GN18 Nomar Garciaparra	20.00	9.00
❑ GN19 Scott Rolen	12.00	5.50
❑ GN20 Manny Ramirez	5.00	2.20

1997 UD3 Marquee Attraction

	MINT	NRMT
COMPLETE SET (10)	500.00	220.00
COMMON CARD (MA1-MA10)	20.00	9.00
❑ MA1 Ken Griffey Jr.	100.00	45.00
❑ MA2 Mark McGwire	100.00	45.00
❑ MA3 Juan Gonzalez	50.00	22.00
❑ MA4 Barry Bonds	25.00	11.00
❑ MA5 Frank Thomas	60.00	27.00
❑ MA6 Albert Belle	25.00	11.00
❑ MA7 Mike Piazza	60.00	27.00
❑ MA8 Cal Ripken	80.00	36.00
❑ MA9 Mo Vaughn	25.00	11.00
❑ MA10 Alex Rodriguez	60.00	27.00

1997 UD3 Superb Signatures

	MINT	NRMT
COMPLETE SET (4)	1000.00	450.00
COMMON CARD	80.00	36.00
❑ 1 Ken Caminiti	80.00	36.00
❑ 2 Ken Griffey Jr.	600.00	275.00
❑ 3 Vladimir Guerrero	150.00	70.00
❑ 4 Derek Jeter	250.00	110.00

1998 UD3

	MINT	NRMT
COMPLETE SET (270)	750.00	350.00
COMP.FUTURE FX SET (30)	100.00	45.00
COMMON FUTURE FX (1-30)	1.00	.45
COMP.POWER FX SET (30)	40.00	18.00
COMMON POWER FX (31-60)	.25	.11
COMP.EST.FX SET (30)	60.00	27.00
COMMON EST.FX (61-90)	.60	.25
COMP.FUTURE EMB.SET (30)	60.00	27.00
COM.FUTURE EMB. (91-120)	.60	.25
COMP.POWER EMB.SET (30)	60.00	27.00
COM.POWER EMB. (121-150)	.40	.18
COMP.EST.EMB.SET (30)	20.00	9.00
COMMON EST.EMB. (151-180)	.20	.09
COMP.FUTURE RBW. SET (30)	25.00	11.00
COM.FUTURE RBW (181-210)	.25	.11
COMP.POWER RBW.SET (30)	200.00	90.00
COM.POWER RBW (211-240)	1.25	.55
COMP.EST.RBW.SET (30)	200.00	90.00
COMMON EST.RBW (241-270)	2.00	.90

Card	MINT	NRMT
1 Travis Lee FF	8.00	3.60
2 A.J. Hinch FF	1.50	.70
3 Mike Caruso FF	1.50	.70
4 Miguel Tejada FF	1.50	.70
5 Brad Fullmer FF	1.50	.70
6 Eric Milton FF	1.50	.70
7 Mark Kotsay FF	2.50	1.10
8 Darin Erstad FF	5.00	2.20
9 Magglio Ordonez FF	5.00	2.20
10 Ben Grieve FF	8.00	3.60
11 Brett Tomko FF	1.50	.70
12 Mike Kinkade FF	4.00	1.80
13 Rolando Arrojo FF	6.00	2.70
14 Todd Helton FF	5.00	2.20
15 Scott Rolen FF	10.00	4.50
16 Bruce Chen FF	1.50	.70
17 Daryle Ward FF	1.50	.70
18 Jaret Wright FF	5.00	2.20
19 Sean Casey FF	1.50	.70
20 Paul Konerko FF	4.00	1.80
21 Kerry Wood FF	20.00	9.00
22 Russell Branyan FF	1.50	.70
23 Gabe Alvarez FF	1.50	.70
24 Juan Encarnacion FF	1.50	.70
25 Andruw Jones FF	5.00	2.20
26 Vladimir Guerrero FF	6.00	2.70
27 Eli Marrero FF	1.50	.70
28 Matt Clement FF	1.50	.70
29 Gary Matthews Jr. FF	4.00	1.80
30 Derrek Lee FF	1.50	.70
31 Ken Caminiti PF	.60	.25
32 Gary Sheffield PF	.60	.25
33 Jay Buhner PF	.40	.18
34 Ryan Klesko PF	.40	.18
35 Nomar Garciaparra PF	3.00	1.35
36 Vinny Castilla PF	.60	.25
37 Tony Clark PF	.60	.25
38 Sammy Sosa PF	2.50	1.10
39 Tino Martinez PF	1.00	.45
40 Mike Piazza PF	3.00	1.35
41 Manny Ramirez PF	1.00	.45
42 Larry Walker PF	1.00	.45
43 Jose Cruz Jr. PF	1.00	.45
44 Matt Williams PF	.40	.18
45 Frank Thomas PF	3.00	1.35
46 Jim Edmonds PF	.60	.25
47 Raul Mondesi PF	.60	.25
48 Alex Rodriguez PF	3.00	1.35
49 Albert Belle PF	2.00	.90
50 Mark McGwire PF	6.00	2.70
51 Tim Salmon PF	1.00	.45
52 Andres Galarraga PF	1.00	.45
53 Jeff Bagwell PF	1.50	.70
54 Jim Thome PF	1.00	.45
55 Barry Bonds PF	1.25	.55
56 Carlos Delgado PF	.40	.18
57 Mo Vaughn PF	1.25	.55
58 Chipper Jones PF	2.50	1.10
59 Juan Gonzalez PF	2.50	1.10
60 Ken Griffey Jr. PF	5.00	2.20
61 David Cone EF	1.50	.70
62 Hideo Nomo EF	3.00	1.35
63 Edgar Martinez EF	1.00	.45
64 Fred McGriff EF	1.50	.70
65 Cal Ripken EF	10.00	4.50
66 Todd Hundley EF	1.00	.45
67 Barry Larkin EF	1.50	.70
68 Dennis Eckersley EF	1.00	.45
69 Randy Johnson EF	2.50	1.10
70 Paul Molitor EF	2.50	1.10
71 Eric Karros EF	1.00	.45
72 Rafael Palmeiro EF	1.50	.70
73 Chuck Knoblauch EF	2.50	1.10
74 Ivan Rodriguez EF	3.00	1.35
75 Greg Maddux EF	8.00	3.60
76 Dante Bichette EF	1.00	.45
77 Brady Anderson EF	1.00	.45
78 Craig Biggio EF	2.50	1.10
79 Derek Jeter EF	6.00	2.70
80 Roger Clemens EF	5.00	2.20
81 Roberto Alomar EF	2.50	1.10
82 Wade Boggs EF	2.50	1.10
83 Charles Johnson EF	1.00	.45
84 Mark Grace EF	1.50	.70
85 Kenny Lofton EF	2.50	1.10
86 Mike Mussina EF	2.50	1.10
87 Pedro Martinez EF	2.50	1.10
88 Curt Schilling EF	1.00	.45
89 Bernie Williams EF	2.50	1.10
90 Tony Gwynn EF	6.00	2.70
91 Travis Lee FE	5.00	2.20
92 A.J. Hinch FE	1.00	.45
93 Mike Caruso FE	1.00	.45
94 Miguel Tejada FE	1.00	.45
95 Brad Fullmer FE	1.00	.45
96 Eric Milton FE	1.00	.45
97 Mark Kotsay FE	1.50	.70
98 Darin Erstad FE	3.00	1.35
99 Magglio Ordonez FE	3.00	1.35
100 Ben Grieve FE	5.00	2.20
101 Brett Tomko FE	1.00	.45
102 Mike Kinkade FE	2.50	1.10
103 Rolando Arrojo FE	4.00	1.80
104 Todd Helton FE	3.00	1.35
105 Scott Rolen FE	6.00	2.70
106 Bruce Chen FE	1.00	.45
107 Daryle Ward FE	1.00	.45
108 Jaret Wright FE	3.00	1.35
109 Sean Casey FE	1.00	.45
110 Paul Konerko FE	2.50	1.10
111 Kerry Wood FE	12.00	5.50
112 Russell Branyan FE	1.00	.45
113 Gabe Alvarez FE	1.00	.45
114 Juan Encarnacion FE	1.00	.45
115 Andruw Jones FE	3.00	1.35
116 Vladimir Guerrero FE	4.00	1.80
117 Eli Marrero FE	1.00	.45
118 Matt Clement FE	1.00	.45
119 Gary Matthews Jr. FE	2.50	1.10
120 Derrek Lee FE	1.00	.45
121 Ken Caminiti PE	1.00	.45
122 Gary Sheffield PE	1.00	.45
123 Jay Buhner PE	.60	.25
124 Ryan Klesko PE	.60	.25
125 Nomar Garciaparra PE	5.00	2.20
126 Vinny Castilla PE	1.00	.45
127 Tony Clark PE	1.00	.45
128 Sammy Sosa PE	4.00	1.80
129 Tino Martinez PE	1.50	.70
130 Mike Piazza PE	5.00	2.20
131 Manny Ramirez PE	1.50	.70
132 Larry Walker PE	1.50	.70
133 Jose Cruz Jr. PE	2.00	.90
134 Matt Williams PE	.60	.25
135 Frank Thomas PE	5.00	2.20
136 Jim Edmonds PE	1.00	.45
137 Raul Mondesi PE	1.00	.45
138 Alex Rodriguez PE	5.00	2.20
139 Albert Belle PE	1.50	.70
140 Mark McGwire PE	10.00	4.50
141 Tim Salmon PE	1.50	.70
142 Andres Galarraga PE	1.50	.70
143 Jeff Bagwell PE	2.50	1.10
144 Jim Thome PE	1.50	.70
145 Barry Bonds PE	2.00	.90
146 Carlos Delgado PE	.60	.25
147 Mo Vaughn PE	2.00	.90
148 Chipper Jones PE	4.00	1.80
149 Juan Gonzalez PE	4.00	1.80
150 Ken Griffey Jr. PE	8.00	3.60
151 David Cone EE	.50	.23
152 Hideo Nomo EE	1.00	.45
153 Edgar Martinez EE	.30	.14
154 Fred McGriff EE	.50	.23
155 Cal Ripken EE	3.00	1.35
156 Todd Hundley EE	.30	.14
157 Barry Larkin EE	.50	.23
158 Dennis Eckersley EE	.30	.14
159 Randy Johnson EE	.75	.35
160 Paul Molitor EE	.75	.35
161 Eric Karros EE	.30	.14
162 Rafael Palmeiro EE	.50	.23
163 Chuck Knoblauch EE	.75	.35
164 Ivan Rodriguez EE	1.00	.45
165 Greg Maddux EE	2.50	1.10
166 Dante Bichette EE	.30	.14
167 Brady Anderson EE	.30	.14
168 Craig Biggio EE	.75	.35
169 Derek Jeter EE	2.00	.90
170 Roger Clemens EE	1.50	.70
171 Roberto Alomar EE	.75	.35
172 Wade Boggs EE	.75	.35
173 Charles Johnson EE	.30	.14
174 Mark Grace EE	.50	.23
175 Kenny Lofton EE	.75	.35
176 Mike Mussina EE	.75	.35
177 Pedro Martinez EE	.75	.35
178 Curt Schilling EE	.30	.14
179 Bernie Williams EE	.75	.35
180 Tony Gwynn EE	2.00	.90
181 Travis Lee FR	2.00	.90
182 A.J. Hinch FR	.40	.18
183 Mike Caruso FR	.40	.18
184 Miguel Tejada FR	.40	.18
185 Brad Fullmer FR	.40	.18
186 Eric Milton FR	.40	.18
187 Mark Kotsay FR	.60	.25
188 Darin Erstad FR	1.25	.55
189 Magglio Ordonez FR	1.25	.55
190 Ben Grieve FR	2.00	.90
191 Brett Tomko FR	.40	.18
192 Mike Kinkade FR	.75	.35
193 Rolando Arrojo FR	1.50	.70
194 Todd Helton FR	1.25	.55
195 Scott Rolen FR	2.50	1.10
196 Bruce Chen FR	.40	.18
197 Daryle Ward FR	.40	.18

❑ 198 Jaret Wright FR .... 1.25 .55
❑ 199 Sean Casey FR .... .40 .18
❑ 200 Paul Konerko FR .... 1.00 .45
❑ 201 Kerry Wood FR 5.00 2.20
❑ 202 Russell Branyan FR ...... .40 .18
❑ 203 Gabe Alvarez FR .... .40 .18
❑ 204 Juan Encarnacion FR .... .40 .18
❑ 205 Andruw Jones FR .... 1.25 .55
❑ 206 Vladimir Guerrero FR .. 1.50 .70
❑ 207 Eli Marrero FR .... .40 .18
❑ 208 Matt Clement FR .... .40 .18
❑ 209 Gary Matthews Jr. FR .... .75 .35
❑ 210 Derrek Lee FR .... .40 .18
❑ 211 Ken Caminiti PR 3.00 1.35
❑ 212 Gary Sheffield PR 3.00 1.35
❑ 213 Jay Buhner PR .... 2.00 .90
❑ 214 Ryan Klesko PR .... 2.00 .90
❑ 215 Nomar Garciaparra PR 15.00 6.75
❑ 216 Vinny Castilla PR 3.00 1.35
❑ 217 Tony Clark PR 3.00 1.35
❑ 218 Sammy Sosa PR 12.00 5.50
❑ 219 Tino Martinez PR 5.00 2.20
❑ 220 Mike Piazza PR 15.00 6.75
❑ 221 Manny Ramirez PR 5.00 2.20
❑ 222 Larry Walker PR 5.00 2.20
❑ 223 Jose Cruz Jr. PR 5.00 2.20
❑ 224 Matt Williams PR .... 2.00 .90
❑ 225 Frank Thomas PR 15.00 6.75
❑ 226 Jim Edmonds PR 3.00 1.35
❑ 227 Raul Mondesi PR 3.00 1.35
❑ 228 Alex Rodriguez PR 15.00 6.75
❑ 229 Albert Belle PR 8.00 3.60
❑ 230 Mark McGwire PR 30.00 13.50
❑ 231 Tim Salmon PR 5.00 2.20
❑ 232 Andres Galarraga PR .. 5.00 2.20
❑ 233 Jeff Bagwell PR 8.00 3.60
❑ 234 Jim Thome PR 5.00 2.20
❑ 235 Barry Bonds PR 6.00 2.70
❑ 236 Carlos Delgado PR ...... 2.00 .90
❑ 237 Mo Vaughn PR 6.00 2.70
❑ 238 Chipper Jones PR 12.00 5.50
❑ 239 Juan Gonzalez PR 12.00 5.50
❑ 240 Ken Griffey Jr. PR 25.00 11.00
❑ 241 David Cone ER 5.00 2.20
❑ 242 Hideo Nomo ER 10.00 4.50
❑ 243 Edgar Martinez ER 3.00 1.35
❑ 244 Fred McGriff ER 5.00 2.20
❑ 245 Cal Ripken ER 30.00 13.50
❑ 246 Todd Hundley ER 3.00 1.35
❑ 247 Barry Larkin ER 5.00 2.20
❑ 248 Dennis Eckersley ER .. 3.00 1.35
❑ 249 Randy Johnson ER 8.00 3.60
❑ 250 Paul Molitor ER 8.00 3.60
❑ 251 Eric Karros ER 3.00 1.35
❑ 252 Rafael Palmeiro ER 5.00 2.20
❑ 253 Chuck Knoblauch ER .. 8.00 3.60
❑ 254 Ivan Rodriguez ER 10.00 4.50
❑ 255 Greg Maddux ER 25.00 11.00
❑ 256 Dante Bichette ER 3.00 1.35
❑ 257 Brady Anderson ER 3.00 1.35
❑ 258 Craig Biggio ER 8.00 3.60
❑ 259 Derek Jeter ER 20.00 9.00
❑ 260 Roger Clemens ER 15.00 6.75
❑ 261 Roberto Alomar ER 8.00 3.60
❑ 262 Wade Boggs ER 8.00 3.60
❑ 263 Charles Johnson ER 3.00 1.35
❑ 264 Mark Grace ER 5.00 2.20
❑ 265 Kenny Lofton ER 8.00 3.60
❑ 266 Mike Mussina ER 8.00 3.60
❑ 267 Pedro Martinez ER 8.00 3.60
❑ 268 Curt Schilling ER 3.00 1.35
❑ 269 Bernie Williams ER 8.00 3.60
❑ 270 Tony Gwynn ER 20.00 9.00
❑ S1 Ken Griffey Jr. PE Sample 5.00 2.20

1998 UD3 Die Cuts

	MINT	NRMT
COMPLETE SET (270)	5500.00	2500.00
COMP.FX SET (90)	500.00	220.00
COMMON CARD (1-90)	2.00	.90

*DIE CUTS 1-30: .6X TO 1.5X BASIC 1-30
*DIE CUTS 31-60: 3X TO 8X BASIC 31-60
*DIE CUTS 61-90: 1.25X TO 3X BASIC 61-90

COMP.EMBOSSED SET (90)	1000.00	450.00
COMMON CARD 91-180	4.00	1.80

*DIE CUTS 91-120: 2X TO 5X BASIC 91-120
*DIE CUTS 121-150: 4X TO 10X BASIC 121-150
*DIE CUTS 151-180: 8X TO 20X BASIC 151-180

COMP.RAINBOW SET (90)	4000.00	1800.00
COMMON CARD (181-270)	15.00	6.75

*DC'S 181-210: 15X TO 40X BASIC 181-210
*DC RC'S 181-210: 12.5X TO 30X BASIC 181-210
*DIE CUTS 211-240: 5X TO 12X BASIC 211-240
*DIE CUTS 241-270: 3X TO 8X BASIC 241-270

1991 Ultra

	MINT	NRMT
COMPLETE SET (400)	20.00	9.00
COMMON CARD (1-400)	.10	.05

❑ 1 Steve Avery .... .10 .05
❑ 2 Jeff Blauser .... .10 .05
❑ 3 Francisco Cabrera .... .10 .05
❑ 4 Ron Gant .... .20 .09
❑ 5 Tom Glavine .... .40 .18
❑ 6 Tommy Gregg .... .10 .05
❑ 7 Dave Justice .... .50 .23
❑ 8 Oddibe McDowell .... .10 .05
❑ 9 Greg Olson .... .10 .05
❑ 10 Terry Pendleton .... .20 .09
❑ 11 Lonnie Smith .... .10 .05
❑ 12 John Smoltz .... .40 .18
❑ 13 Jeff Treadway .... .10 .05
❑ 14 Glenn Davis .... .10 .05
❑ 15 Mike Devereaux .... .10 .05
❑ 16 Leo Gomez .... .10 .05
❑ 17 Chris Hoiles .... .10 .05
❑ 18 Dave Johnson .... .10 .05
❑ 19 Ben McDonald .... .10 .05
❑ 20 Randy Milligan .... .10 .05
❑ 21 Gregg Olson .... .10 .05
❑ 22 Joe Orsulak .... .10 .05
❑ 23 Bill Ripken .... .10 .05
❑ 24 Cal Ripken .... 1.50 .70
❑ 25 David Segui .... .20 .09
❑ 26 Craig Worthington .... .10 .05
❑ 27 Wade Boggs .... .40 .18
❑ 28 Tom Bolton .... .10 .05
❑ 29 Tom Brunansky .... .10 .05
❑ 30 Ellis Burks .... .20 .09
❑ 31 Roger Clemens .... .75 .35
❑ 32 Mike Greenwell .... .10 .05
❑ 33 Greg A. Harris .... .10 .05
❑ 34 Daryl Irvine .... .10 .05
❑ 35 Mike Marshall UER .... .10 .05
(1990 in stats is shown as 990)
❑ 36 Tim Naehring .... .20 .09
❑ 37 Tony Pena .... .10 .05
❑ 38 Phil Plantier .... .10 .05
❑ 39 Carlos Quintana .... .10 .05
❑ 40 Jeff Reardon .... .20 .09
❑ 41 Jody Reed .... .10 .05
❑ 42 Luis Rivera .... .10 .05
❑ 43 Jim Abbott .... .20 .09
❑ 44 Chuck Finley .... .20 .09
❑ 45 Bryan Harvey .... .10 .05
❑ 46 Donnie Hill .... .10 .05
❑ 47 Jack Howell .... .10 .05
❑ 48 Wally Joyner .... .20 .09
❑ 49 Mark Langston .... .10 .05
❑ 50 Kirk McCaskill .... .10 .05
❑ 51 Lance Parrish .... .10 .05
❑ 52 Dick Schofield .... .10 .05
❑ 53 Lee Stevens .... .10 .05
❑ 54 Dave Winfield .... .40 .18
❑ 55 George Bell .... .10 .05
❑ 56 Damon Berryhill .... .10 .05
❑ 57 Mike Bielecki .... .10 .05
❑ 58 Andre Dawson .... .40 .18
❑ 59 Shawon Dunston .... .10 .05
❑ 60 Joe Girardi UER .... .20 .09
(Bats right, LH hitter shown is Doug Dascenzo)
❑ 61 Mark Grace .... .40 .18
❑ 62 Mike Harkey .... .10 .05
❑ 63 Les Lancaster .... .10 .05
❑ 64 Greg Maddux .... 1.25 .55
❑ 65 Derrick May .... .10 .05
❑ 66 Ryne Sandberg .... .50 .23
❑ 67 Luis Salazar .... .10 .05
❑ 68 Dwight Smith .... .10 .05
❑ 69 Hector Villanueva .... .10 .05
❑ 70 Jerome Walton .... .10 .05
❑ 71 Mitch Williams .... .10 .05
❑ 72 Carlton Fisk .... .40 .18
❑ 73 Scott Fletcher .... .10 .05
❑ 74 Ozzie Guillen .... .10 .05
❑ 75 Greg Hibbard .... .10 .05
❑ 76 Lance Johnson .... .10 .05
❑ 77 Steve Lyons .... .10 .05
❑ 78 Jack McDowell .... .10 .05
❑ 79 Dan Pasqua .... .10 .05
❑ 80 Melido Perez .... .10 .05
❑ 81 Tim Raines .... .20 .09
❑ 82 Sammy Sosa .... 2.00 .90
❑ 83 Cory Snyder .... .10 .05
❑ 84 Bobby Thigpen .... .10 .05
❑ 85 Frank Thomas .... 2.00 .90
(Card says he is an outfielder)
❑ 86 Robin Ventura .... .40 .18
❑ 87 Todd Benzinger .... .10 .05
❑ 88 Glenn Braggs .... .10 .05
❑ 89 Tom Browning UER .... .10 .05
(Front photo actually Norm Charlton)
❑ 90 Norm Charlton .... .10 .05
❑ 91 Eric Davis .... .20 .09
❑ 92 Rob Dibble .... .10 .05
❑ 93 Bill Doran .... .10 .05
❑ 94 Mariano Duncan UER .... .10 .05
(Right back photo is Billy Hatcher)
❑ 95 Billy Hatcher .... .10 .05
❑ 96 Barry Larkin .... .40 .18
❑ 97 Randy Myers .... .20 .09
❑ 98 Hal Morris .... .10 .05
❑ 99 Joe Oliver .... .10 .05
❑ 100 Paul O'Neill .... .20 .09
❑ 101 Jeff Reed .... .10 .05
(See also 104)
❑ 102 Jose Rijo .... .10 .05
❑ 103 Chris Sabo .... .10 .05
(See also 106)
❑ 104 Beau Allred UER .... .10 .05
(Card number is 101)
❑ 105 Sandy Alomar Jr. .... .20 .09
❑ 106 Carlos Baerga UER .... .20 .09
(Card number is 103)

❑ 107 Albert Belle .50 .23
❑ 108 Jerry Browne .10 .05
❑ 109 Tom Candiotti .10 .05
❑ 110 Alex Cole .10 .05
❑ 111 John Farrell .10 .05
(See also 114)
❑ 112 Felix Fermin .10 .05
❑ 113 Brook Jacoby .10 .05
❑ 114 Chris James UER .10 .05
(Card number is 111)
❑ 115 Doug Jones .10 .05
❑ 116 Steve Olin .10 .05
(See also 119)
❑ 117 Greg Swindell .10 .05
❑ 118 Turner Ward .10 .05
❑ 119 Mitch Webster UER .10 .05
(Card number is 116)
❑ 120 Dave Bergman .10 .05
❑ 121 Cecil Fielder .20 .09
❑ 122 Travis Fryman .40 .18
❑ 123 Mike Henneman .10 .05
❑ 124 Lloyd Moseby .10 .05
❑ 125 Dan Petry .10 .05
❑ 126 Tony Phillips .10 .05
❑ 127 Mark Salas .10 .05
❑ 128 Frank Tanana .10 .05
❑ 129 Alan Trammell .30 .14
❑ 130 Lou Whitaker .20 .09
❑ 131 Eric Anthony .10 .05
❑ 132 Craig Biggio .40 .18
❑ 133 Ken Caminiti .40 .18
❑ 134 Casey Candaele .10 .05
❑ 135 Andujar Cedeno .10 .05
❑ 136 Mark Davidson .10 .05
❑ 137 Jim Deshaies .10 .05
❑ 138 Mark Portugal .10 .05
❑ 139 Rafael Ramirez .10 .05
❑ 140 Mike Scott .10 .05
❑ 141 Eric Yelding .10 .05
❑ 142 Gerald Young .10 .05
❑ 143 Kevin Appier .20 .09
❑ 144 George Brett .75 .35
❑ 145 Jeff Conine .50 .23
❑ 146 Jim Eisenreich .10 .05
❑ 147 Tom Gordon .20 .09
❑ 148 Mark Gubicza .10 .05
❑ 149 Bo Jackson .20 .09
❑ 150 Brent Mayne .10 .05
❑ 151 Mike Macfarlane .10 .05
❑ 152 Brian McRae .40 .18
❑ 153 Jeff Montgomery .20 .09
❑ 154 Bret Saberhagen .20 .09
❑ 155 Kevin Seitzer .10 .05
❑ 156 Terry Shumpert .10 .05
❑ 157 Kurt Stillwell .10 .05
❑ 158 Danny Tartabull .10 .05
❑ 159 Tim Belcher .10 .05
❑ 160 Kal Daniels .10 .05
❑ 161 Alfredo Griffin .10 .05
❑ 162 Lenny Harris .10 .05
❑ 163 Jay Howell .10 .05
❑ 164 Ramon Martinez .20 .09
❑ 165 Mike Morgan .10 .05
❑ 166 Eddie Murray .40 .18
❑ 167 Jose Offerman .10 .05
❑ 168 Juan Samuel .10 .05
❑ 169 Mike Scioscia .10 .05
❑ 170 Mike Sharperson .10 .05
❑ 171 Darryl Strawberry .20 .09
❑ 172 Greg Brock .10 .05
❑ 173 Chuck Crim .10 .05
❑ 174 Jim Gantner .10 .05
❑ 175 Ted Higuera .10 .05
❑ 176 Mark Knudson .10 .05
❑ 177 Tim McIntosh .10 .05
❑ 178 Paul Molitor .40 .18
❑ 179 Dan Plesac .10 .05
❑ 180 Gary Sheffield .40 .18
❑ 181 Bill Spiers .10 .05
❑ 182 B.J. Surhoff .20 .09
❑ 183 Greg Vaughn .40 .18
❑ 184 Robin Yount .40 .18
❑ 185 Rick Aguilera .20 .09
❑ 186 Greg Gagne .10 .05
❑ 187 Dan Gladden .10 .05
❑ 188 Brian Harper .10 .05
❑ 189 Kent Hrbek .20 .09
❑ 190 Gene Larkin .10 .05
❑ 191 Shane Mack .10 .05
❑ 192 Pedro Munoz .10 .05
❑ 193 Al Newman .10 .05
❑ 194 Junior Ortiz .10 .05
❑ 195 Kirby Puckett .60 .25
❑ 196 Kevin Tapani .10 .05
❑ 197 Dennis Boyd .10 .05
❑ 198 Tim Burke .10 .05
❑ 199 Ivan Calderon .10 .05
❑ 200 Delino DeShields .20 .09
❑ 201 Mike Fitzgerald .10 .05
❑ 202 Steve Frey .10 .05
❑ 203 Andres Galarraga .40 .18
❑ 204 Marquis Grissom .40 .18
❑ 205 Dave Martinez .10 .05
❑ 206 Dennis Martinez .20 .09
❑ 207 Junior Noboa .10 .05
❑ 208 Spike Owen .10 .05
❑ 209 Scott Ruskin .10 .05
❑ 210 Tim Wallach .10 .05
❑ 211 Daryl Boston .10 .05
❑ 212 Vince Coleman .10 .05
❑ 213 David Cone .20 .09
❑ 214 Ron Darling .10 .05
❑ 215 Kevin Elster .10 .05
❑ 216 Sid Fernandez .10 .05
❑ 217 John Franco .20 .09
❑ 218 Dwight Gooden .20 .09
❑ 219 Tom Herr .10 .05
❑ 220 Todd Hundley .40 .18
❑ 221 Gregg Jefferies .10 .05
❑ 222 Howard Johnson .10 .05
❑ 223 Dave Magadan .10 .05
❑ 224 Kevin McReynolds .10 .05
❑ 225 Keith Miller .10 .05
❑ 226 Mackey Sasser .10 .05
❑ 227 Frank Viola .10 .05
❑ 228 Jesse Barfield .10 .05
❑ 229 Greg Cadaret .10 .05
❑ 230 Alvaro Espinoza .10 .05
❑ 231 Bob Geren .10 .05
❑ 232 Lee Guetterman .10 .05
❑ 233 Mel Hall .10 .05
❑ 234 Andy Hawkins UER .10 .05
(Back center photo
is not him)
❑ 235 Roberto Kelly .10 .05
❑ 236 Tim Leary .10 .05
❑ 237 Jim Leyritz .20 .09
❑ 238 Kevin Maas .10 .05
❑ 239 Don Mattingly .60 .25
❑ 240 Hensley Meulens .10 .05
❑ 241 Eric Plunk .10 .05
❑ 242 Steve Sax .10 .05
❑ 243 Todd Burns .10 .05
❑ 244 Jose Canseco .40 .18
❑ 245 Dennis Eckersley .20 .09
❑ 246 Mike Gallego .10 .05
❑ 247 Dave Henderson .10 .05
❑ 248 Rickey Henderson .40 .18
❑ 249 Rick Honeycutt .10 .05
❑ 250 Carney Lansford .20 .09
❑ 251 Mark McGwire 2.00 .90
❑ 252 Mike Moore .10 .05
❑ 253 Terry Steinbach .20 .09
❑ 254 Dave Stewart .20 .09
❑ 255 Walt Weiss .10 .05
❑ 256 Bob Welch .10 .05
❑ 257 Curt Young .10 .05
❑ 258 Wes Chamberlain .10 .05
❑ 259 Pat Combs .10 .05
❑ 260 Darren Daulton .20 .09
❑ 261 Jose DeJesus .10 .05
❑ 262 Len Dykstra .20 .09
❑ 263 Charlie Hayes .10 .05
❑ 264 Von Hayes .10 .05
❑ 265 Ken Howell .10 .05
❑ 266 John Kruk .20 .09
❑ 267 Roger McDowell .10 .05
❑ 268 Mickey Morandini .10 .05
❑ 269 Terry Mulholland .10 .05
❑ 270 Dale Murphy .40 .18
❑ 271 Randy Ready .10 .05
❑ 272 Dickie Thon .10 .05
❑ 273 Stan Belinda .10 .05
❑ 274 Jay Bell .20 .09
❑ 275 Barry Bonds .50 .23
❑ 276 Bobby Bonilla .20 .09
❑ 277 Doug Drabek .10 .05
❑ 278 Carlos Garcia .10 .05
❑ 279 Neal Heaton .10 .05
❑ 280 Jeff King .20 .09
❑ 281 Bill Landrum .10 .05
❑ 282 Mike LaValliere .10 .05
❑ 283 Jose Lind .10 .05
❑ 284 Orlando Merced .20 .09
❑ 285 Gary Redus .10 .05
❑ 286 Don Slaught .10 .05
❑ 287 Andy Van Slyke .20 .09
❑ 288 Jose DeLeon .10 .05
❑ 289 Pedro Guerrero .10 .05
❑ 290 Ray Lankford .40 .18
❑ 291 Joe Magrane .10 .05
❑ 292 Jose Oquendo .10 .05
❑ 293 Tom Pagnozzi .10 .05
❑ 294 Bryn Smith .10 .05
❑ 295 Lee Smith .20 .09
❑ 296 Ozzie Smith UER .50 .23
(Born 12-26, 54,
should have hyphen)
❑ 297 Milt Thompson .10 .05
❑ 298 Craig Wilson .10 .05
❑ 299 Todd Zeile .20 .09
❑ 300 Shawn Abner .10 .05
❑ 301 Andy Benes .20 .09
❑ 302 Paul Faries .10 .05
❑ 303 Tony Gwynn 1.00 .45
❑ 304 Greg W. Harris .10 .05
❑ 305 Thomas Howard .10 .05
❑ 306 Bruce Hurst .10 .05
❑ 307 Craig Lefferts .10 .05
❑ 308 Fred McGriff .40 .18
❑ 309 Dennis Rasmussen .10 .05
❑ 310 Bip Roberts .10 .05
❑ 311 Benito Santiago .10 .05
❑ 312 Garry Templeton .10 .05
❑ 313 Ed Whitson .10 .05
❑ 314 Dave Anderson .10 .05
❑ 315 Kevin Bass .10 .05
❑ 316 Jeff Brantley .10 .05
❑ 317 John Burkett .10 .05
❑ 318 Will Clark .40 .18
❑ 319 Steve Decker .10 .05
❑ 320 Scott Garrelts .10 .05
❑ 321 Terry Kennedy .10 .05
❑ 322 Mark Leonard .10 .05
❑ 323 Darren Lewis .20 .09
❑ 324 Greg Litton .10 .05
❑ 325 Willie McGee .20 .09
❑ 326 Kevin Mitchell .10 .05
❑ 327 Don Robinson .10 .05
❑ 328 Andres Santana .10 .05
❑ 329 Robby Thompson .10 .05
❑ 330 Jose Uribe .10 .05
❑ 331 Matt Williams .40 .18
❑ 332 Scott Bradley .10 .05
❑ 333 Henry Cotto .10 .05
❑ 334 Alvin Davis .10 .05
❑ 335 Ken Griffey Sr. .10 .05
❑ 336 Ken Griffey Jr. 3.00 1.35
❑ 337 Erik Hanson .10 .05
❑ 338 Brian Holman .10 .05
❑ 339 Randy Johnson .50 .23
❑ 340 Edgar Martinez UER .40 .18
(Listed as playing SS)
❑ 341 Tino Martinez .40 .18
❑ 342 Pete O'Brien .10 .05
❑ 343 Harold Reynolds .10 .05
❑ 344 Dave Valle .10 .05
❑ 345 Omar Vizquel .40 .18
❑ 346 Brad Amsberg .10 .05
❑ 347 Kevin Brown .30 .14
❑ 348 Julio Franco .10 .05
❑ 349 Jeff Huson .10 .05
❑ 350 Rafael Palmeiro .40 .18
❑ 351 Geno Petralli .10 .05
❑ 352 Gary Pettis .10 .05

No.	Player	MINT	NRMT
353	Kenny Rogers	.10	.05
354	Jeff Russell	.10	.05
355	Nolan Ryan	1.50	.70
356	Ruben Sierra	.10	.05
357	Bobby Witt	.10	.05
358	Roberto Alomar	.40	.18
359	Pat Borders	.10	.05
360	Joe Carter UER (Reverse negative on back photo)	.20	.09
361	Kelly Gruber	.10	.05
362	Tom Henke	.10	.05
363	Glenallen Hill	.10	.05
364	Jimmy Key	.20	.09
365	Manny Lee	.10	.05
366	Rance Mulliniks	.10	.05
367	John Olerud UER (Throwing left on card; back has throws right; he does throw lefty)	.20	.09
368	Dave Stieb	.20	.09
369	Duane Ward	.10	.05
370	David Wells	.20	.09
371	Mark Whiten	.10	.05
372	Mookie Wilson	.20	.09
373	Willie Banks MLP	.10	.05
374	Steve Carter MLP	.10	.05
375	Scott Chiamparino MLP	.10	.05
376	Steve Chitren MLP	.10	.05
377	Darrin Fletcher MLP	.10	.05
378	Rich Garces MLP	.10	.05
379	Reggie Jefferson MLP	.30	.14
380	Eric Karros MLP	.75	.35
381	Pat Kelly MLP	.10	.05
382	Chuck Knoblauch MLP	.50	.23
383	Denny Neagle MLP	1.00	.45
384	Dan Opperman MLP	.10	.05
385	John Ramos MLP	.10	.05
386	Henry Rodriguez MLP	.60	.25
387	Mo Vaughn MLP	.75	.35
388	Gerald Williams MLP	.10	.05
389	Mike York MLP	.10	.05
390	Eddie Zosky MLP	.10	.05
391	Barry Bonds EP	.40	.18
392	Cecil Fielder EP	.10	.05
393	Rickey Henderson EP	.20	.09
394	Dave Justice EP	.20	.09
395	Nolan Ryan EP	.75	.35
396	Bobby Thigpen EP	.10	.05
397	Gregg Jefferies CL	.10	.05
398	Von Hayes CL	.10	.05
399	Terry Kennedy CL	.10	.05
400	Nolan Ryan CL	.40	.18

1991 Ultra Gold

	MINT	NRMT
COMPLETE SET (10)	10.00	4.50
COMMON CARD (1-10)	.25	.11

No.	Player	MINT	NRMT
1	Barry Bonds	1.00	.45
2	Will Clark	.75	.35
3	Doug Drabek	.25	.11
4	Ken Griffey Jr.	6.00	2.70
5	Rickey Henderson	.75	.35
6	Bo Jackson	.40	.18
7	Ramon Martinez	.40	.18
8	Kirby Puckett UER (Boggs won 1988 batting title, so Puckett didn't win consecutive titles)	1.25	.55
9	Chris Sabo	.25	.11
10	Ryne Sandberg UER (Johnson and Hornsby didn't hit 40 homers in 1990, Fielder did hit 51 in '90)	1.00	.45

1991 Ultra Update

	MINT	NRMT
COMP.FACT.SET (120)	50.00	22.00
COMMON CARD (1-120)	.25	.11

No.	Player	MINT	NRMT
1	Dwight Evans	.50	.23
2	Chito Martinez	.25	.11
3	Bob Melvin	.25	.11
4	Mike Mussina	6.00	2.70
5	Jack Clark	.50	.23
6	Dana Kiecker	.25	.11
7	Steve Lyons	.25	.11
8	Gary Gaetti	.50	.23
9	Dave Gallagher	.25	.11
10	Dave Parker	.50	.23
11	Luis Polonia	.25	.11
12	Luis Sojo	.25	.11
13	Wilson Alvarez	1.00	.45
14	Alex Fernandez	.50	.23
15	Craig Grebeck	.25	.11
16	Ron Karkovice	.25	.11
17	Warren Newson	.25	.11
18	Scott Radinsky	.25	.11
19	Glenallen Hill	.25	.11
20	Charles Nagy	1.00	.45
21	Mark Whiten	.25	.11
22	Milt Cuyler	.25	.11
23	Paul Gibson	.25	.11
24	Mickey Tettleton	.50	.23
25	Todd Benzinger	.25	.11
26	Storm Davis	.25	.11
27	Kirk Gibson	.50	.23
28	Bill Pecota	.25	.11
29	Gary Thurman	.25	.11
30	Darryl Hamilton	.25	.11
31	Jaime Navarro	.25	.11
32	Willie Randolph	.50	.23
33	Bill Wegman	.25	.11
34	Randy Bush	.25	.11
35	Chili Davis	.50	.23
36	Scott Erickson	1.25	.55
37	Chuck Knoblauch	3.00	1.35
38	Scott Leius	.25	.11
39	Jack Morris	.50	.23
40	John Habyan	.25	.11
41	Pat Kelly	.25	.11
42	Matt Nokes	.25	.11
43	Scott Sanderson	.25	.11
44	Bernie Williams	8.00	3.60
45	Harold Baines	.50	.23
46	Brook Jacoby	.25	.11
47	Earnest Riles	.25	.11
48	Willie Wilson	.25	.11
49	Jay Buhner	1.00	.45
50	Rich DeLucia	.25	.11
51	Mike Jackson	.50	.23
52	Bill Krueger	.25	.11
53	Bill Swift	.25	.11
54	Brian Downing	.25	.11
55	Juan Gonzalez	30.00	13.50
56	Dean Palmer	1.50	.70
57	Kevin Reimer	.25	.11
58	Ivan Rodriguez	12.00	5.50
59	Tom Candiotti	.25	.11
60	Juan Guzman	.50	.23
61	Bob MacDonald	.25	.11
62	Greg Myers	.25	.11
63	Ed Sprague	.25	.11
64	Devon White	.25	.11
65	Rafael Belliard	.25	.11
66	Juan Berenguer	.25	.11
67	Brian R. Hunter	.25	.11
68	Kent Mercker	.25	.11
69	Otis Nixon	.50	.23
70	Danny Jackson	.25	.11
71	Chuck McElroy	.25	.11
72	Gary Scott	.25	.11
73	Heathcliff Slocumb	1.00	.45
74	Chico Walker	.25	.11
75	Rick Wilkins	.25	.11
76	Chris Hammond	.25	.11
77	Luis Quinones	.25	.11
78	Herm Winningham	.25	.11
79	Jeff Bagwell	15.00	6.75
80	Jim Corsi	.25	.11
81	Steve Finley	1.00	.45
82	Luis Gonzalez	1.00	.45
83	Pete Harnisch	.25	.11
84	Darryl Kile	1.00	.45
85	Brett Butler	.50	.23
86	Gary Carter	1.00	.45
87	Tim Crews	.25	.11
88	Orel Hershiser	.50	.23
89	Bob Ojeda	.25	.11
90	Bret Barberie	.25	.11
91	Barry Jones	.25	.11
92	Gilberto Reyes	.25	.11
93	Larry Walker	2.00	.90
94	Hubie Brooks	.25	.11
95	Tim Burke	.25	.11
96	Rick Cerone	.25	.11
97	Jeff Innis	.25	.11
98	Wally Backman	.25	.11
99	Tommy Greene	.25	.11
100	Ricky Jordan	.25	.11
101	Mitch Williams	.25	.11
102	John Smiley	.25	.11
103	Randy Tomlin	.25	.11
104	Gary Varsho	.25	.11
105	Cris Carpenter	.25	.11
106	Ken Hill	.50	.23
107	Felix Jose	.25	.11
108	Omar Olivares	.25	.11
109	Gerald Perry	.25	.11
110	Jerald Clark	.25	.11
111	Tony Fernandez	.25	.11
112	Darrin Jackson	.25	.11
113	Mike Maddux	.25	.11
114	Tim Teufel	.25	.11
115	Bud Black	.25	.11
116	Kelly Downs	.25	.11
117	Mike Felder	.25	.11
118	Willie McGee	.50	.23
119	Trevor Wilson	.25	.11
120	Checklist 1-120	.25	.11

1992 Ultra

	MINT	NRMT
COMPLETE SET (600)	30.00	13.50
COMPLETE SERIES 1 (300)	20.00	9.00
COMPLETE SERIES 2 (300)	10.00	4.50
COMMON CARD (1-600)	.10	.05

No.	Player	MINT	NRMT
1	Glenn Davis	.10	.05
2	Mike Devereaux	.10	.05
3	Dwight Evans	.20	.09
4	Leo Gomez	.10	.05
5	Chris Hoiles	.10	.05
6	Sam Horn	.10	.05
7	Chito Martinez	.10	.05
8	Randy Milligan	.10	.05

Card	Mint	Nrmt
❑ 9 Mike Mussina	.60	.25
❑ 10 Billy Ripken	.10	.05
❑ 11 Cal Ripken	1.50	.70
❑ 12 Tom Brunansky	.10	.05
❑ 13 Ellis Burks	.20	.09
❑ 14 Jack Clark	.20	.09
❑ 15 Roger Clemens	.75	.35
❑ 16 Mike Greenwell	.10	.05
❑ 17 Joe Hesketh	.10	.05
❑ 18 Tony Pena	.10	.05
❑ 19 Carlos Quintana	.10	.05
❑ 20 Jeff Reardon	.20	.09
❑ 21 Jody Reed	.10	.05
❑ 22 Luis Rivera	.10	.05
❑ 23 Mo Vaughn	.60	.25
❑ 24 Gary DiSarcina	.10	.05
❑ 25 Chuck Finley	.20	.09
❑ 26 Gary Gaetti	.10	.05
❑ 27 Bryan Harvey	.10	.05
❑ 28 Lance Parrish	.10	.05
❑ 29 Luis Polonia	.10	.05
❑ 30 Dick Schofield	.10	.05
❑ 31 Luis Sojo	.10	.05
❑ 32 Wilson Alvarez	.20	.09
❑ 33 Carlton Fisk	.40	.18
❑ 34 Craig Grebeck	.10	.05
❑ 35 Ozzie Guillen	.10	.05
❑ 36 Greg Hibbard	.10	.05
❑ 37 Charlie Hough	.20	.09
❑ 38 Lance Johnson	.10	.05
❑ 39 Ron Karkovice	.10	.05
❑ 40 Jack McDowell	.10	.05
❑ 41 Donn Pall	.10	.05
❑ 42 Melido Perez	.10	.05
❑ 43 Tim Raines	.20	.09
❑ 44 Frank Thomas	1.25	.55
❑ 45 Sandy Alomar Jr.	.20	.09
❑ 46 Carlos Baerga	.10	.05
❑ 47 Albert Belle	.50	.23
❑ 48 Jerry Browne UER (Reversed negative on card back)	.10	.05
❑ 49 Felix Fermin	.10	.05
❑ 50 Reggie Jefferson UER (Born 1968, not 1966)	.20	.09
❑ 51 Mark Lewis	.10	.05
❑ 52 Carlos Martinez	.10	.05
❑ 53 Steve Olin	.10	.05
❑ 54 Jim Thome	1.00	.45
❑ 55 Mark Whiten	.10	.05
❑ 56 Dave Bergman	.10	.05
❑ 57 Milt Cuyler	.10	.05
❑ 58 Rob Deer	.10	.05
❑ 59 Cecil Fielder	.20	.09
❑ 60 Travis Fryman	.20	.09
❑ 61 Scott Livingstone	.10	.05
❑ 62 Tony Phillips	.10	.05
❑ 63 Mickey Tettleton	.10	.05
❑ 64 Alan Trammell	.30	.14
❑ 65 Lou Whitaker	.20	.09
❑ 66 Kevin Appier	.20	.09
❑ 67 Mike Boddicker	.10	.05
❑ 68 George Brett	.75	.35
❑ 69 Jim Eisenreich	.10	.05
❑ 70 Mark Gubicza	.10	.05
❑ 71 David Howard	.10	.05
❑ 72 Joel Johnson	.10	.05
❑ 73 Mike Macfarlane	.10	.05
❑ 74 Brent Mayne	.10	.05
❑ 75 Brian McRae	.20	.09
❑ 76 Jeff Montgomery	.20	.09
❑ 77 Danny Tartabull	.10	.05
❑ 78 Don August	.10	.05
❑ 79 Dante Bichette	.30	.14
❑ 80 Ted Higuera	.10	.05
❑ 81 Paul Molitor	.40	.18
❑ 82 Jaime Navarro	.10	.05
❑ 83 Gary Sheffield	.40	.18
❑ 84 Bill Spiers	.10	.05
❑ 85 B.J. Surhoff	.20	.09
❑ 86 Greg Vaughn	.20	.09
❑ 87 Robin Yount	.40	.18
❑ 88 Rick Aguilera	.20	.09
❑ 89 Chili Davis	.20	.09
❑ 90 Scott Erickson	.20	.09
❑ 91 Brian Harper	.10	.05
❑ 92 Kent Hrbek	.20	.09
❑ 93 Chuck Knoblauch	.40	.18
❑ 94 Scott Leius	.10	.05
❑ 95 Shane Mack	.10	.05
❑ 96 Mike Pagliarulo	.10	.05
❑ 97 Kirby Puckett	.60	.25
❑ 98 Kevin Tapani	.10	.05
❑ 99 Jesse Barfield	.10	.05
❑ 100 Alvaro Espinoza	.10	.05
❑ 101 Mel Hall	.10	.05
❑ 102 Pat Kelly	.10	.05
❑ 103 Roberto Kelly	.10	.05
❑ 104 Kevin Maas	.10	.05
❑ 105 Don Mattingly	.60	.25
❑ 106 Hensley Meulens	.10	.05
❑ 107 Matt Nokes	.10	.05
❑ 108 Steve Sax	.10	.05
❑ 109 Harold Baines	.20	.09
❑ 110 Jose Canseco	.40	.18
❑ 111 Ron Darling	.10	.05
❑ 112 Mike Gallego	.10	.05
❑ 113 Dave Henderson	.10	.05
❑ 114 Rickey Henderson	.40	.18
❑ 115 Mark McGwire	2.00	.90
❑ 116 Terry Steinbach	.20	.09
❑ 117 Dave Stewart	.20	.09
❑ 118 Todd Van Poppel	.10	.05
❑ 119 Bob Welch	.10	.05
❑ 120 Greg Briley	.10	.05
❑ 121 Jay Buhner	.30	.14
❑ 122 Rick DeLucia	.10	.05
❑ 123 Ken Griffey Jr.	2.50	1.10
❑ 124 Erik Hanson	.10	.05
❑ 125 Randy Johnson	.40	.18
❑ 126 Edgar Martinez	.30	.14
❑ 127 Tino Martinez	.40	.18
❑ 128 Pete O'Brien	.10	.05
❑ 129 Harold Reynolds	.10	.05
❑ 130 Dave Valle	.10	.05
❑ 131 Julio Franco	.10	.05
❑ 132 Juan Gonzalez	1.25	.55
❑ 133 Jeff Huson (Shows Jose Canseco sliding into second)	.20	.09
❑ 134 Mike Jeffcoat	.10	.05
❑ 135 Terry Mathews	.10	.05
❑ 136 Rafael Palmeiro	.30	.14
❑ 137 Dean Palmer	.20	.09
❑ 138 Geno Petralli	.10	.05
❑ 139 Ivan Rodriguez	.75	.35
❑ 140 Jeff Russell	.10	.05
❑ 141 Nolan Ryan	1.50	.70
❑ 142 Ruben Sierra	.10	.05
❑ 143 Roberto Alomar	.40	.18
❑ 144 Pat Borders	.10	.05
❑ 145 Joe Carter	.20	.09
❑ 146 Kelly Gruber	.10	.05
❑ 147 Jimmy Key	.20	.09
❑ 148 Manny Lee	.10	.05
❑ 149 Rance Mulliniks	.10	.05
❑ 150 Greg Myers	.10	.05
❑ 151 John Olerud	.20	.09
❑ 152 Dave Stieb	.10	.05
❑ 153 Todd Stottlemyre	.20	.09
❑ 154 Duane Ward	.10	.05
❑ 155 Devon White	.10	.05
❑ 156 Eddie Zosky	.10	.05
❑ 157 Steve Avery	.10	.05
❑ 158 Rafael Belliard	.10	.05
❑ 159 Jeff Blauser	.10	.05
❑ 160 Sid Bream	.10	.05
❑ 161 Ron Gant	.20	.09
❑ 162 Tom Glavine	.30	.14
❑ 163 Brian Hunter	.10	.05
❑ 164 Dave Justice	.40	.18
❑ 165 Mark Lemke	.10	.05
❑ 166 Greg Olson	.10	.05
❑ 167 Terry Pendleton	.10	.05
❑ 168 Lonnie Smith	.10	.05
❑ 169 John Smoltz	.30	.14
❑ 170 Mike Stanton	.10	.05
❑ 171 Jeff Treadway	.10	.05
❑ 172 Paul Assenmacher	.10	.05
❑ 173 George Bell	.10	.05
❑ 174 Shawon Dunston	.10	.05
❑ 175 Mark Grace	.30	.14
❑ 176 Danny Jackson	.10	.05
❑ 177 Les Lancaster	.10	.05
❑ 178 Greg Maddux	1.25	.55
❑ 179 Luis Salazar	.10	.05
❑ 180 Rey Sanchez	.10	.05
❑ 181 Ryne Sandberg	.50	.23
❑ 182 Jose Vizcaino	.10	.05
❑ 183 Chico Walker	.10	.05
❑ 184 Jerome Walton	.10	.05
❑ 185 Glenn Braggs	.10	.05
❑ 186 Tom Browning	.10	.05
❑ 187 Rob Dibble	.10	.05
❑ 188 Bill Doran	.10	.05
❑ 189 Chris Hammond	.10	.05
❑ 190 Billy Hatcher	.10	.05
❑ 191 Barry Larkin	.30	.14
❑ 192 Hal Morris	.10	.05
❑ 193 Joe Oliver	.10	.05
❑ 194 Paul O'Neill	.20	.09
❑ 195 Jeff Reed	.10	.05
❑ 196 Jose Rijo	.10	.05
❑ 197 Chris Sabo	.10	.05
❑ 198 Jeff Bagwell	1.00	.45
❑ 199 Craig Biggio	.40	.18
❑ 200 Ken Caminiti	.30	.14
❑ 201 Andujar Cedeno	.10	.05
❑ 202 Steve Finley	.20	.09
❑ 203 Luis Gonzalez	.10	.05
❑ 204 Pete Harnisch	.10	.05
❑ 205 Xavier Hernandez	.10	.05
❑ 206 Darryl Kile	.20	.09
❑ 207 Al Osuna	.10	.05
❑ 208 Curt Schilling	.30	.14
❑ 209 Brett Butler	.20	.09
❑ 210 Kal Daniels	.10	.05
❑ 211 Lenny Harris	.10	.05
❑ 212 Stan Javier	.10	.05
❑ 213 Ramon Martinez	.20	.09
❑ 214 Roger McDowell	.10	.05
❑ 215 Jose Offerman	.10	.05
❑ 216 Juan Samuel	.10	.05
❑ 217 Mike Scioscia	.10	.05
❑ 218 Mike Sharperson	.10	.05
❑ 219 Darryl Strawberry	.20	.09
❑ 220 Delino DeShields	.20	.09
❑ 221 Tom Foley	.10	.05
❑ 222 Steve Frey	.10	.05
❑ 223 Dennis Martinez	.20	.09
❑ 224 Spike Owen	.10	.05
❑ 225 Gilberto Reyes	.10	.05
❑ 226 Tim Wallach	.10	.05
❑ 227 Daryl Boston	.10	.05
❑ 228 Tim Burke	.10	.05
❑ 229 Vince Coleman	.10	.05
❑ 230 David Cone	.20	.09
❑ 231 Kevin Elster	.10	.05
❑ 232 Dwight Gooden	.20	.09
❑ 233 Todd Hundley	.20	.09
❑ 234 Jeff Innis	.10	.05
❑ 235 Howard Johnson	.10	.05
❑ 236 Dave Magadan	.10	.05
❑ 237 Mackey Sasser	.10	.05
❑ 238 Anthony Young	.10	.05
❑ 239 Wes Chamberlain	.10	.05
❑ 240 Darren Daulton	.20	.09
❑ 241 Len Dykstra	.20	.09

❑ 242 Tommy Greene .10 .05
❑ 243 Charlie Hayes .10 .05
❑ 244 Dave Hollins .10 .05
❑ 245 Ricky Jordan .10 .05
❑ 246 John Kruk .20 .09
❑ 247 Mickey Morandini .10 .05
❑ 248 Terry Mulholland .10 .05
❑ 249 Dale Murphy .40 .18
❑ 250 Jay Bell .20 .09
❑ 251 Barry Bonds .50 .23
❑ 252 Steve Buechele .10 .05
❑ 253 Doug Drabek .10 .05
❑ 254 Mike LaValliere .10 .05
❑ 255 Jose Lind .10 .05
❑ 256 Lloyd McClendon .10 .05
❑ 257 Orlando Merced .10 .05
❑ 258 Don Slaught .10 .05
❑ 259 John Smiley .10 .05
❑ 260 Zane Smith .10 .05
❑ 261 Randy Tomlin .10 .05
❑ 262 Andy Van Slyke .20 .09
❑ 263 Pedro Guerrero .10 .05
❑ 264 Felix Jose .10 .05
❑ 265 Ray Lankford .40 .18
❑ 266 Omar Olivares .10 .05
❑ 267 Jose Oquendo .10 .05
❑ 268 Tom Pagnozzi .10 .05
❑ 269 Bryn Smith .10 .05
❑ 270 Lee Smith UER .20 .09
(1991 record listed as 61-61)
❑ 271 Ozzie Smith UER .50 .23
(Comma before year of birth on card back)
❑ 272 Milt Thompson .10 .05
❑ 273 Todd Zeile .10 .05
❑ 274 Andy Benes .20 .09
❑ 275 Jerald Clark .10 .05
❑ 276 Tony Fernandez .10 .05
❑ 277 Tony Gwynn 1.00 .45
❑ 278 Greg W. Harris .10 .05
❑ 279 Thomas Howard .10 .05
❑ 280 Bruce Hurst .10 .05
❑ 281 Mike Maddux .10 .05
❑ 282 Fred McGriff .30 .14
❑ 283 Benito Santiago .10 .05
❑ 284 Kevin Bass .10 .05
❑ 285 Jeff Brantley .10 .05
❑ 286 John Burkett .10 .05
❑ 287 Will Clark .40 .18
❑ 288 Royce Clayton .10 .05
❑ 289 Steve Decker .10 .05
❑ 290 Kelly Downs .10 .05
❑ 291 Mike Felder .10 .05
❑ 292 Darren Lewis .10 .05
❑ 293 Kirt Manwaring .10 .05
❑ 294 Willie McGee .20 .09
❑ 295 Robby Thompson .10 .05
❑ 296 Matt Williams .30 .14
❑ 297 Trevor Wilson .10 .05
❑ 298 Checklist 1-100 .10 .05
❑ 299 Checklist 101-200 .10 .05
❑ 300 Checklist 201-300 .10 .05
❑ 301 Brady Anderson .30 .14
❑ 302 Todd Frohwirth .10 .05
❑ 303 Ben McDonald .10 .05
❑ 304 Mark McLemore .10 .05
❑ 305 Jose Mesa .10 .05
❑ 306 Bob Milacki .10 .05
❑ 307 Gregg Olson .10 .05
❑ 308 David Segui .20 .09
❑ 309 Rick Sutcliffe .10 .05
❑ 310 Jeff Tackett .10 .05
❑ 311 Wade Boggs .40 .18
❑ 312 Scott Cooper .10 .05
❑ 313 John Flaherty .10 .05
❑ 314 Wayne Housie .10 .05
❑ 315 Peter Hoy .10 .05
❑ 316 John Marzano .10 .05
❑ 317 Tim Naehring .20 .09
❑ 318 Phil Plantier .10 .05
❑ 319 Frank Viola .10 .05
❑ 320 Matt Young .10 .05
❑ 321 Jim Abbott .20 .09
❑ 322 Hubie Brooks .10 .05
❑ 323 Chad Curtis .40 .18
❑ 324 Alvin Davis .10 .05
❑ 325 Junior Felix .10 .05
❑ 326 Von Hayes .10 .05
❑ 327 Mark Langston .10 .05
❑ 328 Scott Lewis .10 .05
❑ 329 Don Robinson .10 .05
❑ 330 Bobby Rose .10 .05
❑ 331 Lee Stevens .10 .05
❑ 332 George Bell .10 .05
❑ 333 Esteban Beltre .10 .05
❑ 334 Joey Cora .20 .09
❑ 335 Alex Fernandez .20 .09
❑ 336 Roberto Hernandez .20 .09
❑ 337 Mike Huff .10 .05
❑ 338 Kirk McCaskill .10 .05
❑ 339 Dan Pasqua .10 .05
❑ 340 Scott Radinsky .10 .05
❑ 341 Steve Sax .10 .05
❑ 342 Bobby Thigpen .10 .05
❑ 343 Robin Ventura .20 .09
❑ 344 Jack Armstrong .10 .05
❑ 345 Alex Cole .10 .05
❑ 346 Dennis Cook .10 .05
❑ 347 Glenallen Hill .10 .05
❑ 348 Thomas Howard .10 .05
❑ 349 Brook Jacoby .10 .05
❑ 350 Kenny Lofton .75 .35
❑ 351 Charles Nagy .20 .09
❑ 352 Rod Nichols .10 .05
❑ 353 Junior Ortiz .10 .05
❑ 354 Dave Otto .10 .05
❑ 355 Tony Perezchica .10 .05
❑ 356 Scott Scudder .10 .05
❑ 357 Paul Sorrento .10 .05
❑ 358 Skeeter Barnes .10 .05
❑ 359 Mark Carreon .10 .05
❑ 360 John Doherty .10 .05
❑ 361 Dan Gladden .10 .05
❑ 362 Bill Gullickson .10 .05
❑ 363 Shawn Hare .10 .05
❑ 364 Mike Henneman .10 .05
❑ 365 Chad Kreuter .10 .05
❑ 366 Mark Leiter .10 .05
❑ 367 Mike Munoz .10 .05
❑ 368 Kevin Ritz .10 .05
❑ 369 Mark Davis .10 .05
❑ 370 Tom Gordon .20 .09
❑ 371 Chris Gwynn .10 .05
❑ 372 Gregg Jefferies .10 .05
❑ 373 Wally Joyner .20 .09
❑ 374 Kevin McReynolds .10 .05
❑ 375 Keith Miller .10 .05
❑ 376 Rico Rossy .10 .05
❑ 377 Curtis Wilkerson .10 .05
❑ 378 Ricky Bones .10 .05
❑ 379 Chris Bosio .10 .05
❑ 380 Cal Eldred .10 .05
❑ 381 Scott Fletcher .10 .05
❑ 382 Jim Gantner .10 .05
❑ 383 Darryl Hamilton .10 .05
❑ 384 Doug Henry .10 .05
❑ 385 Pat Listach .10 .05
❑ 386 Tim McIntosh .10 .05
❑ 387 Edwin Nunez .10 .05
❑ 388 Dan Plesac .10 .05
❑ 389 Kevin Seitzer .10 .05
❑ 390 Franklin Stubbs .10 .05
❑ 391 William Suero .10 .05
❑ 392 Bill Wegman .10 .05
❑ 393 Willie Banks .10 .05
❑ 394 Jarvis Brown .10 .05
❑ 395 Greg Gagne .10 .05
❑ 396 Mark Guthrie .10 .05
❑ 397 Bill Krueger .10 .05
❑ 398 Pat Mahomes .10 .05
❑ 399 Pedro Munoz .10 .05
❑ 400 John Smiley .10 .05
❑ 401 Gary Wayne .10 .05
❑ 402 Lenny Webster .10 .05
❑ 403 Carl Willis .10 .05
❑ 404 Greg Cadaret .10 .05
❑ 405 Steve Farr .10 .05
❑ 406 Mike Gallego .10 .05
❑ 407 Charlie Hayes .10 .05
❑ 408 Steve Howe .10 .05
❑ 409 Dion James .10 .05
❑ 410 Jeff Johnson .10 .05
❑ 411 Tim Leary .10 .05
❑ 412 Jim Leyritz .10 .05
❑ 413 Melido Perez .10 .05
❑ 414 Scott Sanderson .10 .05
❑ 415 Andy Stankiewicz .10 .05
❑ 416 Mike Stanley .10 .05
❑ 417 Danny Tartabull .10 .05
❑ 418 Lance Blankenship .10 .05
❑ 419 Mike Bordick .10 .05
❑ 420 Scott Brosius .50 .23
❑ 421 Dennis Eckersley .20 .09
❑ 422 Scott Hemond .10 .05
❑ 423 Carney Lansford .20 .09
❑ 424 Henry Mercedes .10 .05
❑ 425 Mike Moore .10 .05
❑ 426 Gene Nelson .10 .05
❑ 427 Randy Ready .10 .05
❑ 428 Bruce Walton .10 .05
❑ 429 Willie Wilson .10 .05
❑ 430 Rich Amaral .10 .05
❑ 431 Dave Cochrane .10 .05
❑ 432 Henry Cotto .10 .05
❑ 433 Calvin Jones .10 .05
❑ 434 Kevin Mitchell .20 .09
❑ 435 Clay Parker .10 .05
❑ 436 Omar Vizquel .20 .09
❑ 437 Floyd Bannister .10 .05
❑ 438 Kevin Brown .30 .14
❑ 439 John Cangelosi .10 .05
❑ 440 Brian Downing .10 .05
❑ 441 Monty Fariss .10 .05
❑ 442 Jose Guzman .10 .05
❑ 443 Donald Harris .10 .05
❑ 444 Kevin Reimer .10 .05
❑ 445 Kenny Rogers .10 .05
❑ 446 Wayne Rosenthal .10 .05
❑ 447 Dickie Thon .10 .05
❑ 448 Derek Bell .20 .09
❑ 449 Juan Guzman .10 .05
❑ 450 Tom Henke .10 .05
❑ 451 Candy Maldonado .10 .05
❑ 452 Jack Morris .20 .09
❑ 453 David Wells .20 .09
❑ 454 Dave Winfield .40 .18
❑ 455 Juan Berenguer .10 .05
❑ 456 Damon Berryhill .10 .05
❑ 457 Mike Bielecki .10 .05
❑ 458 Marvin Freeman .10 .05
❑ 459 Charlie Leibrandt .10 .05
❑ 460 Kent Mercker .10 .05
❑ 461 Otis Nixon .20 .09
❑ 462 Alejandro Pena .10 .05
❑ 463 Ben Rivera .10 .05
❑ 464 Deion Sanders .40 .18
❑ 465 Mark Wohlers .20 .09
❑ 466 Shawn Boskie .10 .05
❑ 467 Frank Castillo .10 .05
❑ 468 Andre Dawson .30 .14
❑ 469 Joe Girardi .20 .09
❑ 470 Chuck McElroy .10 .05
❑ 471 Mike Morgan .10 .05
❑ 472 Ken Patterson .10 .05
❑ 473 Bob Scanlan .10 .05
❑ 474 Gary Scott .10 .05
❑ 475 Dave Smith .10 .05
❑ 476 Sammy Sosa 1.00 .45
❑ 477 Hector Villanueva .10 .05
❑ 478 Scott Bankhead .10 .05
❑ 479 Tim Belcher .10 .05
❑ 480 Freddie Benavides .10 .05
❑ 481 Jacob Brumfield .10 .05
❑ 482 Norm Charlton .10 .05
❑ 483 Dwayne Henry .10 .05
❑ 484 Dave Martinez .10 .05
❑ 485 Bip Roberts .10 .05
❑ 486 Reggie Sanders .10 .05
❑ 487 Greg Swindell .10 .05
❑ 488 Ryan Bowen .10 .05
❑ 489 Casey Candaelé .10 .05
❑ 490 Juan Guerrero UER .10 .05
(photo on front is Andujar Cedeno
❑ 491 Pete Incaviglia .10 .05

Card	MINT	NRMT
❑ 492 Jeff Juden	.10	.05
❑ 493 Rob Murphy	.10	.05
❑ 494 Mark Portugal	.10	.05
❑ 495 Rafael Ramirez	.10	.05
❑ 496 Scott Servais	.10	.05
❑ 497 Ed Taubensee	.20	.09
❑ 498 Brian Williams	.10	.05
❑ 499 Todd Benzinger	.10	.05
❑ 500 John Candelaria	.10	.05
❑ 501 Tom Candiotti	.10	.05
❑ 502 Tim Crews	.10	.05
❑ 503 Eric Davis	.20	.09
❑ 504 Jim Gott	.10	.05
❑ 505 Dave Hansen	.10	.05
❑ 506 Carlos Hernandez	.10	.05
❑ 507 Orel Hershiser	.20	.09
❑ 508 Eric Karros	.40	.18
❑ 509 Bob Ojeda	.10	.05
❑ 510 Steve Wilson	.10	.05
❑ 511 Moises Alou	.40	.18
❑ 512 Bret Barberie	.10	.05
❑ 513 Ivan Calderon	.10	.05
❑ 514 Gary Carter	.40	.18
❑ 515 Archi Cianfrocco	.10	.05
❑ 516 Jeff Fassero	.20	.09
❑ 517 Darrin Fletcher	.10	.05
❑ 518 Marquis Grissom	.20	.09
❑ 519 Chris Haney	.10	.05
❑ 520 Ken Hill	.10	.05
❑ 521 Chris Nabholz	.10	.05
❑ 522 Bill Sampen	.10	.05
❑ 523 John Vander Wal	.10	.05
❑ 524 Dave Wainhouse	.10	.05
❑ 525 Larry Walker	.40	.18
❑ 526 John Wetteland	.20	.09
❑ 527 Bobby Bonilla	.20	.09
❑ 528 Sid Fernandez	.10	.05
❑ 529 John Franco	.20	.09
❑ 530 Dave Gallagher	.10	.05
❑ 531 Paul Gibson	.10	.05
❑ 532 Eddie Murray	.40	.18
❑ 533 Junior Noboa	.10	.05
❑ 534 Charlie O'Brien	.10	.05
❑ 535 Bill Pecota	.10	.05
❑ 536 Willie Randolph	.20	.09
❑ 537 Bret Saberhagen	.20	.09
❑ 538 Dick Schofield	.10	.05
❑ 539 Pete Schourek	.10	.05
❑ 540 Ruben Amaro	.10	.05
❑ 541 Andy Ashby	.20	.09
❑ 542 Kim Batiste	.10	.05
❑ 543 Cliff Brantley	.10	.05
❑ 544 Mariano Duncan	.10	.05
❑ 545 Jeff Grotewold	.10	.05
❑ 546 Barry Jones	.10	.05
❑ 547 Julio Peguero	.10	.05
❑ 548 Curt Schilling	.30	.14
❑ 549 Mitch Williams	.10	.05
❑ 550 Stan Belinda	.10	.05
❑ 551 Scott Bullett	.10	.05
❑ 552 Cecil Espy	.10	.05
❑ 553 Jeff King	.20	.09
❑ 554 Roger Mason	.10	.05
❑ 555 Paul Miller	.10	.05
❑ 556 Denny Neagle	.30	.14
❑ 557 Vicente Palacios	.10	.05
❑ 558 Bob Patterson	.10	.05
❑ 559 Tom Prince	.10	.05
❑ 560 Gary Redus	.10	.05
❑ 561 Gary Varsho	.10	.05
❑ 562 Juan Agosto	.10	.05
❑ 563 Cris Carpenter	.10	.05
❑ 564 Mark Clark	.10	.05
❑ 565 Jose DeLeon	.10	.05
❑ 566 Rich Gedman	.10	.05
❑ 567 Bernard Gilkey	.20	.09
❑ 568 Rex Hudler	.10	.05
❑ 569 Tim Jones	.10	.05
❑ 570 Donovan Osborne	.10	.05
❑ 571 Mike Perez	.10	.05
❑ 572 Gerald Perry	.10	.05
❑ 573 Bob Tewksbury	.10	.05
❑ 574 Todd Worrell	.10	.05
❑ 575 Dave Eiland	.10	.05
❑ 576 Jeremy Hernandez	.10	.05
❑ 577 Craig Lefferts	.10	.05
❑ 578 Jose Melendez	.10	.05
❑ 579 Randy Myers	.20	.09
❑ 580 Gary Pettis	.10	.05
❑ 581 Rich Rodriguez	.10	.05
❑ 582 Gary Sheffield	.40	.18
❑ 583 Craig Shipley	.10	.05
❑ 584 Kurt Stillwell	.10	.05
❑ 585 Tim Teufel	.10	.05
❑ 586 Rod Beck	.40	.18
❑ 587 Dave Burba	.10	.05
❑ 588 Craig Colbert	.10	.05
❑ 589 Bryan Hickerson	.10	.05
❑ 590 Mike Jackson	.20	.09
❑ 591 Mark Leonard	.10	.05
❑ 592 Jim McNamara	.10	.05
❑ 593 John Patterson	.10	.05
❑ 594 Dave Righetti	.10	.05
❑ 595 Cory Snyder	.10	.05
❑ 596 Bill Swift	.10	.05
❑ 597 Ted Wood	.10	.05
❑ 598 Checklist 301-400	.10	.05
❑ 599 Checklist 401-500	.10	.05
❑ 600 Checklist 501-600	.10	.05

1992 Ultra All-Rookies

	MINT	NRMT
COMPLETE SET (10)	12.00	5.50
COMMON CARD (1-10)	.50	.23
❑ 1 Eric Karros	2.00	.90
❑ 2 Andy Stankiewicz	.50	.23
❑ 3 Gary DiSarcina	.50	.23
❑ 4 Archi Cianfrocco	.50	.23
❑ 5 Jim McNamara	.50	.23
❑ 6 Chad Curtis	2.00	.90
❑ 7 Kenny Lofton	5.00	2.20
❑ 8 Reggie Sanders	.50	.23
❑ 9 Pat Mahomes	.50	.23
❑ 10 Donovan Osborne	.50	.23

1992 Ultra All-Stars

	MINT	NRMT
COMPLETE SET (20)	25.00	11.00
COMMON CARD (1-20)	.25	.11
❑ 1 Mark McGwire	8.00	3.60
❑ 2 Roberto Alomar	1.25	.55
❑ 3 Cal Ripken Jr.	5.00	2.20
❑ 4 Wade Boggs	1.25	.55
❑ 5 Mickey Tettleton	.25	.11
❑ 6 Ken Griffey Jr.	8.00	3.60
❑ 7 Roberto Kelly	.25	.11
❑ 8 Kirby Puckett	2.00	.90
❑ 9 Frank Thomas	4.00	1.80
❑ 10 Jack McDowell	.25	.11
❑ 11 Will Clark	1.25	.55
❑ 12 Ryne Sandberg	1.50	.70
❑ 13 Barry Larkin	.75	.35
❑ 14 Gary Sheffield	1.25	.55
❑ 15 Tom Pagnozzi	.25	.11
❑ 16 Barry Bonds	2.00	.90
❑ 17 Deion Sanders	1.25	.55
❑ 18 Darryl Strawberry	.50	.23
❑ 19 David Cone	.50	.23
❑ 20 Tom Glavine	.75	.35

1992 Ultra Award Winners

	MINT	NRMT
COMPLETE SET (25)	50.00	22.00
COMMON CARD (1-25)	.50	.23
❑ 1 Jack Morris	1.00	.45
❑ 2 Chuck Knoblauch	1.50	.70
❑ 3 Jeff Bagwell	5.00	2.20
❑ 4 Terry Pendleton	.50	.23
❑ 5 Cal Ripken	8.00	3.60
❑ 6 Roger Clemens	4.00	1.80
❑ 7 Tom Glavine	1.25	.55
❑ 8 Tom Pagnozzi	.50	.23
❑ 9 Ozzie Smith	2.50	1.10
❑ 10 Andy Van Slyke	1.00	.45
❑ 11 Barry Bonds	2.50	1.10
❑ 12 Tony Gwynn	5.00	2.20
❑ 13 Matt Williams	1.25	.55
❑ 14 Will Clark	1.50	.70
❑ 15 Robin Ventura	1.00	.45
❑ 16 Mark Langston	.50	.23
❑ 17 Tony Pena	.50	.23
❑ 18 Devon White	.50	.23
❑ 19 Don Mattingly	3.00	1.35
❑ 20 Roberto Alomar	1.50	.70
❑ 21A Cal Ripken ERR (Reversed negative on card back)	15.00	6.75
❑ 21B Cal Ripken COR	8.00	3.60
❑ 22 Ken Griffey Jr.	12.00	5.50
❑ 23 Kirby Puckett	3.00	1.35
❑ 24 Greg Maddux	6.00	2.70
❑ 25 Ryne Sandberg	2.50	1.10

1992 Ultra Gwynn

	MINT	NRMT
COMPLETE SET (10)	10.00	4.50
COMMON GWYNN (1-10)	1.00	.45
COMMON MAIL-IN (S1-S2)	1.00	.45
❑ 1 Tony Gwynn (Leaping and catching ball at outfield wall)	1.00	.45
❑ 2 Tony Gwynn (Batting stance, brown Padres' uniform)	1.00	.45
❑ 3 Tony Gwynn	1.00	.45

	MINT	NRMT
(Awaiting flyball, glove above head)		
❑ 4 Tony Gwynn	1.00	.45
(Follow-through on swing)		
❑ 5 Tony Gwynn	1.00	.45
(Leading off base; crouching at the knees)		
❑ 6 Tony Gwynn	1.00	.45
(Posed with silver bat and Gold Glove trophy)		
❑ 7 Tony Gwynn	1.00	.45
(Bunting)		
❑ 8 Tony Gwynn	1.00	.45
(Full body shot; swinging)		
❑ 9 Tony Gwynn	1.00	.45
(Taking off for first)		
❑ 10 Tony Gwynn	1.00	.45
(Batting, following through, sunglasses on)		
❑ S1 Tony Gwynn	1.00	.45
(Batting)		
❑ S2 Tony Gwynn	1.00	.45
(Fielding)		
❑ AU0 Tony Gwynn AU	175.00	80.00
(Autographed with certified signature)		

1993 Ultra

	MINT	NRMT
COMPLETE SET (650)	30.00	13.50
COMPLETE SERIES 1 (300)	15.00	6.75
COMPLETE SERIES 2 (350)	15.00	6.75
COMMON CARD (1-650)	.15	.07

	MINT	NRMT
❑ 1 Steve Avery	.15	.07
❑ 2 Rafael Belliard	.15	.07
❑ 3 Damon Berryhill	.15	.07
❑ 4 Sid Bream	.15	.07
❑ 5 Ron Gant	.30	.14
❑ 6 Tom Glavine	.40	.18
❑ 7 Ryan Klesko	.60	.25
❑ 8 Mark Lemke	.15	.07
❑ 9 Javier Lopez	.60	.25
❑ 10 Greg Olson	.15	.07
❑ 11 Terry Pendleton	.15	.07
❑ 12 Deion Sanders	.40	.18
❑ 13 Mike Stanton	.15	.07
❑ 14 Paul Assenmacher	.15	.07
❑ 15 Steve Buechele	.15	.07
❑ 16 Frank Castillo	.15	.07
❑ 17 Shawon Dunston	.15	.07
❑ 18 Mark Grace	.40	.18
❑ 19 Derrick May	.15	.07
❑ 20 Chuck McElroy	.15	.07
❑ 21 Mike Morgan	.15	.07
❑ 22 Bob Scanlan	.15	.07
❑ 23 Dwight Smith	.15	.07
❑ 24 Sammy Sosa	1.50	.70
❑ 25 Rick Wilkins	.15	.07
❑ 26 Tim Belcher	.15	.07
❑ 27 Jeff Branson	.15	.07
❑ 28 Bill Doran	.15	.07
❑ 29 Chris Hammond	.15	.07
❑ 30 Barry Larkin	.40	.18
❑ 31 Hal Morris	.15	.07
❑ 32 Joe Oliver	.15	.07
❑ 33 Jose Rijo	.15	.07
❑ 34 Bip Roberts	.15	.07
❑ 35 Chris Sabo	.15	.07
❑ 36 Reggie Sanders	.15	.07
❑ 37 Craig Biggio	.60	.25
❑ 38 Ken Caminiti	.40	.18
❑ 39 Steve Finley	.30	.14
❑ 40 Luis Gonzalez	.15	.07
❑ 41 Juan Guerrero	.15	.07
❑ 42 Pete Harnisch	.15	.07
❑ 43 Xavier Hernandez	.15	.07
❑ 44 Doug Jones	.15	.07
❑ 45 Al Osuna	.15	.07
❑ 46 Eddie Taubensee	.15	.07
❑ 47 Scooter Tucker	.15	.07
❑ 48 Brian Williams	.15	.07
❑ 49 Pedro Astacio	.15	.07
❑ 50 Rafael Bournigal	.15	.07
❑ 51 Brett Butler	.30	.14
❑ 52 Tom Candiotti	.15	.07
❑ 53 Eric Davis	.30	.14
❑ 54 Lenny Harris	.15	.07
❑ 55 Orel Hershiser	.30	.14
❑ 56 Eric Karros	.40	.18
❑ 57 Pedro Martinez	.75	.35
❑ 58 Roger McDowell	.15	.07
❑ 59 Jose Offerman	.15	.07
❑ 60 Mike Piazza	3.00	1.35
❑ 61 Moises Alou	.30	.14
❑ 62 Kent Bottenfield	.15	.07
❑ 63 Archi Cianfrocco	.15	.07
❑ 64 Greg Colbrunn	.15	.07
❑ 65 Wil Cordero	.15	.07
❑ 66 Delino DeShields	.30	.14
❑ 67 Darrin Fletcher	.15	.07
❑ 68 Ken Hill	.15	.07
❑ 69 Chris Nabholz	.15	.07
❑ 70 Mel Rojas	.15	.07
❑ 71 Larry Walker	.60	.25
❑ 72 Sid Fernandez	.15	.07
❑ 73 John Franco	.30	.14
❑ 74 Dave Gallagher	.15	.07
❑ 75 Todd Hundley	.40	.18
❑ 76 Howard Johnson	.15	.07
❑ 77 Jeff Kent	.30	.14
❑ 78 Eddie Murray	.60	.25
❑ 79 Bret Saberhagen	.30	.14
❑ 80 Chico Walker	.15	.07
❑ 81 Anthony Young	.15	.07
❑ 82 Kyle Abbott	.15	.07
❑ 83 Ruben Amaro	.15	.07
❑ 84 Juan Bell	.15	.07
❑ 85 Wes Chamberlain	.15	.07
❑ 86 Darren Daulton	.30	.14
❑ 87 Mariano Duncan	.15	.07
❑ 88 Dave Hollins	.15	.07
❑ 89 Ricky Jordan	.15	.07
❑ 90 John Kruk	.30	.14
❑ 91 Mickey Morandini	.15	.07
❑ 92 Terry Mulholland	.15	.07
❑ 93 Ben Rivera	.15	.07
❑ 94 Mike Williams	.15	.07
❑ 95 Stan Belinda	.15	.07
❑ 96 Jay Bell	.30	.14
❑ 97 Jeff King	.30	.14
❑ 98 Mike LaValliere	.15	.07
❑ 99 Lloyd McClendon	.15	.07
❑ 100 Orlando Merced	.15	.07
❑ 101 Zane Smith	.15	.07
❑ 102 Randy Tomlin	.15	.07
❑ 103 Andy Van Slyke	.30	.14
❑ 104 Tim Wakefield	.30	.14
❑ 105 John Wehner	.15	.07
❑ 106 Bernard Gilkey	.15	.07
❑ 107 Brian Jordan	.30	.14
❑ 108 Ray Lankford	.40	.18
❑ 109 Donovan Osborne	.15	.07
❑ 110 Tom Pagnozzi	.15	.07
❑ 111 Mike Perez	.15	.07
❑ 112 Lee Smith	.30	.14
❑ 113 Ozzie Smith	.75	.35
❑ 114 Bob Tewksbury	.15	.07
❑ 115 Todd Zeile	.15	.07
❑ 116 Andy Benes	.30	.14
❑ 117 Greg W. Harris	.15	.07
❑ 118 Darrin Jackson	.15	.07
❑ 119 Fred McGriff	.40	.18
❑ 120 Rich Rodriguez	.15	.07
❑ 121 Frank Seminara	.15	.07
❑ 122 Gary Sheffield	.60	.25
❑ 123 Craig Shipley	.15	.07
❑ 124 Kurt Stillwell	.15	.07
❑ 125 Dan Walters	.15	.07
❑ 126 Rod Beck	.30	.14
❑ 127 Mike Benjamin	.15	.07
❑ 128 Jeff Brantley	.15	.07
❑ 129 John Burkett	.15	.07
❑ 130 Will Clark	.60	.25
❑ 131 Royce Clayton	.15	.07
❑ 132 Steve Hosey	.15	.07
❑ 133 Mike Jackson	.15	.07
❑ 134 Darren Lewis	.15	.07
❑ 135 Kirt Manwaring	.15	.07
❑ 136 Bill Swift	.15	.07
❑ 137 Robby Thompson	.15	.07
❑ 138 Brady Anderson	.40	.18
❑ 139 Glenn Davis	.15	.07
❑ 140 Leo Gomez	.15	.07
❑ 141 Chito Martinez	.15	.07
❑ 142 Ben McDonald	.15	.07
❑ 143 Alan Mills	.15	.07
❑ 144 Mike Mussina	.60	.25
❑ 145 Gregg Olson	.15	.07
❑ 146 David Segui	.15	.07
❑ 147 Jeff Tackett	.15	.07
❑ 148 Jack Clark	.15	.07
❑ 149 Scott Cooper	.15	.07
❑ 150 Danny Darwin	.15	.07
❑ 151 John Dopson	.15	.07
❑ 152 Mike Greenwell	.15	.07
❑ 153 Tim Naehring	.15	.07
❑ 154 Tony Pena	.15	.07
❑ 155 Paul Quantrill	.15	.07
❑ 156 Mo Vaughn	.75	.35
❑ 157 Frank Viola	.15	.07
❑ 158 Bob Zupcic	.15	.07
❑ 159 Chad Curtis	.30	.14
❑ 160 Gary DiSarcina	.15	.07
❑ 161 Damion Easley	.30	.14
❑ 162 Chuck Finley	.30	.14
❑ 163 Tim Fortugno	.15	.07
❑ 164 Rene Gonzales	.15	.07
❑ 165 Joe Grahe	.15	.07
❑ 166 Mark Langston	.15	.07
❑ 167 John Orton	.15	.07
❑ 168 Luis Polonia	.15	.07
❑ 169 Julio Valera	.15	.07
❑ 170 Wilson Alvarez	.30	.14
❑ 171 George Bell	.15	.07
❑ 172 Joey Cora	.30	.14
❑ 173 Alex Fernandez	.30	.14
❑ 174 Lance Johnson	.15	.07
❑ 175 Ron Karkovice	.15	.07
❑ 176 Jack McDowell	.15	.07
❑ 177 Scott Radinsky	.15	.07
❑ 178 Tim Raines	.30	.14
❑ 179 Steve Sax	.15	.07
❑ 180 Bobby Thigpen	.15	.07
❑ 181 Frank Thomas	2.00	.90
❑ 182 Sandy Alomar	.30	.14
❑ 183 Carlos Baerga	.15	.07
❑ 184 Felix Fermin	.15	.07
❑ 185 Thomas Howard	.15	.07

❑ 186	Mark Lewis	.15	.07
❑ 187	Derek Lilliquist	.15	.07
❑ 188	Carlos Martinez	.15	.07
❑ 189	Charles Nagy	.30	.14
❑ 190	Scott Scudder	.15	.07
❑ 191	Paul Sorrento	.15	.07
❑ 192	Jim Thome	1.25	.55
❑ 193	Mark Whiten	.15	.07
❑ 194	Milt Cuyler UER (Reversed negative on card front)	.15	.07
❑ 195	Rob Deer	.15	.07
❑ 196	John Doherty	.15	.07
❑ 197	Travis Fryman	.30	.14
❑ 198	Dan Gladden	.15	.07
❑ 199	Mike Henneman	.15	.07
❑ 200	John Kiely	.15	.07
❑ 201	Chad Kreuter	.15	.07
❑ 202	Scott Livingstone	.15	.07
❑ 203	Tony Phillips	.15	.07
❑ 204	Alan Trammell	.40	.18
❑ 205	Mike Boddicker	.15	.07
❑ 206	George Brett	1.25	.55
❑ 207	Tom Gordon	.30	.14
❑ 208	Mark Gubicza	.15	.07
❑ 209	Gregg Jefferies	.15	.07
❑ 210	Wally Joyner	.30	.14
❑ 211	Kevin Koslofski	.15	.07
❑ 212	Brent Mayne	.15	.07
❑ 213	Brian McRae	.15	.07
❑ 214	Kevin McReynolds	.15	.07
❑ 215	Rusty Meacham	.15	.07
❑ 216	Steve Shifflett	.15	.07
❑ 217	James Austin	.15	.07
❑ 218	Cal Eldred	.15	.07
❑ 219	Darryl Hamilton	.15	.07
❑ 220	Doug Henry	.15	.07
❑ 221	John Jaha	.15	.07
❑ 222	Dave Nilsson	.30	.14
❑ 223	Jesse Orosco	.15	.07
❑ 224	B.J. Surhoff	.30	.14
❑ 225	Greg Vaughn	.30	.14
❑ 226	Bill Wegman	.15	.07
❑ 227	Robin Yount UER (Born in Illinois, not in Virginia)	.40	.18
❑ 228	Rick Aguilera	.15	.07
❑ 229	J.T. Bruett	.15	.07
❑ 230	Scott Erickson	.15	.07
❑ 231	Kent Hrbek	.30	.14
❑ 232	Terry Jorgensen	.15	.07
❑ 233	Scott Leius	.15	.07
❑ 234	Pat Mahomes	.15	.07
❑ 235	Pedro Munoz	.15	.07
❑ 236	Kirby Puckett	1.00	.45
❑ 237	Kevin Tapani	.15	.07
❑ 238	Lenny Webster	.15	.07
❑ 239	Carl Willis	.15	.07
❑ 240	Mike Gallego	.15	.07
❑ 241	John Habyan	.15	.07
❑ 242	Pat Kelly	.15	.07
❑ 243	Kevin Maas	.15	.07
❑ 244	Don Mattingly	1.00	.45
❑ 245	Hensley Meulens	.15	.07
❑ 246	Sam Militello	.15	.07
❑ 247	Matt Nokes	.15	.07
❑ 248	Melido Perez	.15	.07
❑ 249	Andy Stankiewicz	.15	.07
❑ 250	Randy Velarde	.15	.07
❑ 251	Bob Wickman	.15	.07
❑ 252	Bernie Williams	.60	.25
❑ 253	Lance Blankenship	.15	.07
❑ 254	Mike Bordick	.15	.07
❑ 255	Jerry Browne	.15	.07
❑ 256	Ron Darling	.15	.07
❑ 257	Dennis Eckersley	.30	.14
❑ 258	Rickey Henderson	.60	.25
❑ 259	Vince Horsman	.15	.07
❑ 260	Troy Neel	.15	.07
❑ 261	Jeff Parrett	.15	.07
❑ 262	Terry Steinbach	.15	.07
❑ 263	Bob Welch	.15	.07
❑ 264	Bobby Witt	.15	.07
❑ 265	Rich Amaral	.15	.07
❑ 266	Bret Boone	.30	.14
❑ 267	Jay Buhner	.40	.18
❑ 268	Dave Fleming	.15	.07
❑ 269	Randy Johnson	.60	.25
❑ 270	Edgar Martinez	.40	.18
❑ 271	Mike Schooler	.15	.07
❑ 272	Russ Swan	.15	.07
❑ 273	Dave Valle	.15	.07
❑ 274	Omar Vizquel	.30	.14
❑ 275	Kerry Woodson	.15	.07
❑ 276	Kevin Brown	.40	.18
❑ 277	Julio Franco	.15	.07
❑ 278	Jeff Frye	.15	.07
❑ 279	Juan Gonzalez	1.50	.70
❑ 280	Jeff Huson	.15	.07
❑ 281	Rafael Palmeiro	.40	.18
❑ 282	Dean Palmer	.30	.14
❑ 283	Roger Pavlik	.15	.07
❑ 284	Ivan Rodriguez	.75	.35
❑ 285	Kenny Rogers	.15	.07
❑ 286	Derek Bell	.30	.14
❑ 287	Pat Borders	.15	.07
❑ 288	Joe Carter	.30	.14
❑ 289	Bob MacDonald	.15	.07
❑ 290	Jack Morris	.30	.14
❑ 291	John Olerud	.40	.18
❑ 292	Ed Sprague	.15	.07
❑ 293	Todd Stottlemyre	.15	.07
❑ 294	Mike Timlin	.15	.07
❑ 295	Duane Ward	.15	.07
❑ 296	David Wells	.30	.14
❑ 297	Devon White	.15	.07
❑ 298	Ray Lankford CL	.30	.14
❑ 299	Bobby Witt CL	.15	.07
❑ 300	Mike Piazza CL	.60	.25
❑ 301	Steve Bedrosian	.15	.07
❑ 302	Jeff Blauser	.15	.07
❑ 303	Francisco Cabrera	.15	.07
❑ 304	Marvin Freeman	.15	.07
❑ 305	Brian Hunter	.15	.07
❑ 306	David Justice	.60	.25
❑ 307	Greg Maddux	2.00	.90
❑ 308	Greg McMichael	.15	.07
❑ 309	Kent Mercker	.15	.07
❑ 310	Otis Nixon	.15	.07
❑ 311	Pete Smith	.15	.07
❑ 312	John Smoltz	.30	.14
❑ 313	Jose Guzman	.15	.07
❑ 314	Mike Harkey	.15	.07
❑ 315	Greg Hibbard	.15	.07
❑ 316	Candy Maldonado	.15	.07
❑ 317	Randy Myers	.30	.14
❑ 318	Dan Plesac	.15	.07
❑ 319	Rey Sanchez	.15	.07
❑ 320	Ryne Sandberg	.75	.35
❑ 321	Tommy Shields	.15	.07
❑ 322	Jose Vizcaino	.15	.07
❑ 323	Matt Walbeck	.15	.07
❑ 324	Willie Wilson	.15	.07
❑ 325	Tom Browning	.15	.07
❑ 326	Tim Costo	.15	.07
❑ 327	Rob Dibble	.15	.07
❑ 328	Steve Foster	.15	.07
❑ 329	Roberto Kelly	.15	.07
❑ 330	Randy Milligan	.15	.07
❑ 331	Kevin Mitchell	.30	.14
❑ 332	Tim Pugh	.15	.07
❑ 333	Jeff Reardon	.30	.14
❑ 334	John Roper	.15	.07
❑ 335	Juan Samuel	.15	.07
❑ 336	John Smiley	.15	.07
❑ 337	Dan Wilson	.30	.14
❑ 338	Scott Aldred	.15	.07
❑ 339	Andy Ashby	.30	.14
❑ 340	Freddie Benavides	.15	.07
❑ 341	Dante Bichette	.30	.14
❑ 342	Willie Blair	.15	.07
❑ 343	Daryl Boston	.15	.07
❑ 344	Vinny Castilla	.75	.35
❑ 345	Jerald Clark	.15	.07
❑ 346	Alex Cole	.15	.07
❑ 347	Andres Galarraga	.60	.25
❑ 348	Joe Girardi	.30	.14
❑ 349	Ryan Hawblitzel	.15	.07
❑ 350	Charlie Hayes	.15	.07
❑ 351	Butch Henry	.15	.07
❑ 352	Darren Holmes	.15	.07
❑ 353	Dale Murphy	.40	.18
❑ 354	David Nied	.15	.07
❑ 355	Jeff Parrett	.15	.07
❑ 356	Steve Reed	.15	.07
❑ 357	Bruce Ruffin	.15	.07
❑ 358	Danny Sheaffer	.15	.07
❑ 359	Bryn Smith	.15	.07
❑ 360	Jim Tatum	.15	.07
❑ 361	Eric Young	.60	.25
❑ 362	Gerald Young	.15	.07
❑ 363	Luis Aquino	.15	.07
❑ 364	Alex Arias	.15	.07
❑ 365	Jack Armstrong	.15	.07
❑ 366	Bret Barberie	.15	.07
❑ 367	Ryan Bowen	.15	.07
❑ 368	Greg Briley	.15	.07
❑ 369	Cris Carpenter	.15	.07
❑ 370	Chuck Carr	.15	.07
❑ 371	Jeff Conine	.15	.07
❑ 372	Steve Decker	.15	.07
❑ 373	Orestes Destrade	.15	.07
❑ 374	Monty Fariss	.15	.07
❑ 375	Junior Felix	.15	.07
❑ 376	Chris Hammond	.15	.07
❑ 377	Bryan Harvey	.15	.07
❑ 378	Trevor Hoffman	.60	.25
❑ 379	Charlie Hough	.30	.14
❑ 380	Joe Klink	.15	.07
❑ 381	Richie Lewis	.15	.07
❑ 382	Dave Magadan	.15	.07
❑ 383	Bob McClure	.15	.07
❑ 384	Scott Pose	.15	.07
❑ 385	Rich Renteria	.15	.07
❑ 386	Benito Santiago	.15	.07
❑ 387	Walt Weiss	.15	.07
❑ 388	Nigel Wilson	.15	.07
❑ 389	Eric Anthony	.15	.07
❑ 390	Jeff Bagwell	1.00	.45
❑ 391	Andujar Cedeno	.15	.07
❑ 392	Doug Drabek	.15	.07
❑ 393	Darryl Kile	.30	.14
❑ 394	Mark Portugal	.15	.07
❑ 395	Karl Rhodes	.15	.07
❑ 396	Scott Servais	.15	.07
❑ 397	Greg Swindell	.15	.07
❑ 398	Tom Goodwin	.15	.07
❑ 399	Kevin Gross	.15	.07
❑ 400	Carlos Hernandez	.15	.07
❑ 401	Ramon Martinez	.30	.14
❑ 402	Raul Mondesi	.75	.35
❑ 403	Jody Reed	.15	.07
❑ 404	Mike Sharperson	.15	.07
❑ 405	Cory Snyder	.15	.07
❑ 406	Darryl Strawberry	.30	.14
❑ 407	Rick Trlicek	.15	.07
❑ 408	Tim Wallach	.15	.07
❑ 409	Todd Worrell	.15	.07
❑ 410	Tavo Alvarez	.15	.07
❑ 411	Sean Berry	.15	.07
❑ 412	Frank Bolick	.15	.07
❑ 413	Cliff Floyd	.60	.25
❑ 414	Mike Gardiner	.15	.07
❑ 415	Marquis Grissom	.30	.14
❑ 416	Tim Laker	.15	.07
❑ 417	Mike Lansing	.30	.14
❑ 418	Dennis Martinez	.30	.14
❑ 419	John Vander Wal	.15	.07
❑ 420	John Wetteland	.30	.14
❑ 421	Rondell White	.40	.18
❑ 422	Bobby Bonilla	.30	.14
❑ 423	Jeromy Burnitz	.30	.14
❑ 424	Vince Coleman	.15	.07
❑ 425	Mike Draper	.15	.07
❑ 426	Tony Fernandez	.15	.07
❑ 427	Dwight Gooden	.30	.14
❑ 428	Jeff Innis	.15	.07
❑ 429	Bobby Jones	.40	.18
❑ 430	Mike Maddux	.15	.07
❑ 431	Charlie O'Brien	.15	.07
❑ 432	Joe Orsulak	.15	.07
❑ 433	Pete Schourek	.15	.07
❑ 434	Frank Tanana	.15	.07
❑ 435	Ryan Thompson	.15	.07
❑ 436	Kim Batiste	.15	.07

❑ 437 Mark Davis .15 .07
❑ 438 Jose DeLeon .15 .07
❑ 439 Len Dykstra .30 .14
❑ 440 Jim Eisenreich .15 .07
❑ 441 Tommy Greene .15 .07
❑ 442 Pete Incaviglia .15 .07
❑ 443 Danny Jackson .15 .07
❑ 444 Todd Pratt .15 .07
❑ 445 Curt Schilling .30 .14
❑ 446 Milt Thompson .15 .07
❑ 447 David West .15 .07
❑ 448 Mitch Williams .15 .07
❑ 449 Steve Cooke .15 .07
❑ 450 Carlos Garcia .15 .07
❑ 451 Al Martin .15 .07
❑ 452 Blas Minor .15 .07
❑ 453 Dennis Moeller .15 .07
❑ 454 Denny Neagle .30 .14
❑ 455 Don Slaught .15 .07
❑ 456 Lonnie Smith .15 .07
❑ 457 Paul Wagner .15 .07
❑ 458 Bob Walk .15 .07
❑ 459 Kevin Young .15 .07
❑ 460 Rene Arocha .15 .07
❑ 461 Brian Barber .15 .07
❑ 462 Rheal Cormier .15 .07
❑ 463 Gregg Jefferies .15 .07
❑ 464 Joe Magrane .15 .07
❑ 465 Omar Olivares .15 .07
❑ 466 Geronimo Pena .15 .07
❑ 467 Allen Watson .15 .07
❑ 468 Mark Whiten .15 .07
❑ 469 Derek Bell .30 .14
❑ 470 Phil Clark .15 .07
❑ 471 Pat Gomez .15 .07
❑ 472 Tony Gwynn 1.50 .70
❑ 473 Jeremy Hernandez .15 .07
❑ 474 Bruce Hurst .15 .07
❑ 475 Phil Plantier .15 .07
❑ 476 Scott Sanders .15 .07
❑ 477 Tim Scott .15 .07
❑ 478 Darrell Sherman .15 .07
❑ 479 Guillermo Velasquez .15 .07
❑ 480 Tim Worrell .15 .07
❑ 481 Todd Benzinger .15 .07
❑ 482 Bud Black .15 .07
❑ 483 Barry Bonds .75 .35
❑ 484 Dave Burba .15 .07
❑ 485 Bryan Hickerson .15 .07
❑ 486 Dave Martinez .15 .07
❑ 487 Willie McGee .30 .14
❑ 488 Jeff Reed .15 .07
❑ 489 Kevin Rogers .15 .07
❑ 490 Matt Williams .40 .18
❑ 491 Trevor Wilson .15 .07
❑ 492 Harold Baines .30 .14
❑ 493 Mike Devereaux .15 .07
❑ 494 Todd Frohwirth .15 .07
❑ 495 Chris Hoiles .15 .07
❑ 496 Luis Mercedes .15 .07
❑ 497 Sherman Obando .15 .07
❑ 498 Brad Pennington .15 .07
❑ 499 Harold Reynolds .15 .07
❑ 500 Arthur Rhodes .15 .07
❑ 501 Cal Ripken 2.50 1.10
❑ 502 Rick Sutcliffe .15 .07
❑ 503 Fernando Valenzuela .30 .14
❑ 504 Mark Williamson .15 .07
❑ 505 Scott Bankhead .15 .07
❑ 506 Greg Blosser .15 .07
❑ 507 Ivan Calderon .15 .07
❑ 508 Roger Clemens 1.25 .55
❑ 509 Andre Dawson .40 .18
❑ 510 Scott Fletcher .15 .07
❑ 511 Greg A. Harris .15 .07
❑ 512 Billy Hatcher .15 .07
❑ 513 Bob Melvin .15 .07
❑ 514 Carlos Quintana .15 .07
❑ 515 Luis Rivera .15 .07
❑ 516 Jeff Russell .15 .07
❑ 517 Ken Ryan .15 .07
❑ 518 Chili Davis .30 .14
❑ 519 Jim Edmonds 1.50 .70
❑ 520 Gary Gaetti .15 .07
❑ 521 Torey Lovullo .15 .07
❑ 522 Troy Percival .40 .18
❑ 523 Tim Salmon .60 .25
❑ 524 Scott Sanderson .15 .07
❑ 525 J.T. Snow .75 .35
❑ 526 Jerome Walton .15 .07
❑ 527 Jason Bere .15 .07
❑ 528 Rod Bolton .15 .07
❑ 529 Ellis Burks .30 .14
❑ 530 Carlton Fisk .60 .25
❑ 531 Craig Grebeck .15 .07
❑ 532 Ozzie Guillen .15 .07
❑ 533 Roberto Hernandez .30 .14
❑ 534 Bo Jackson .30 .14
❑ 535 Kirk McCaskill .15 .07
❑ 536 Dave Stieb .30 .14
❑ 537 Robin Ventura .30 .14
❑ 538 Albert Belle .75 .35
❑ 539 Mike Bielecki .15 .07
❑ 540 Glenallen Hill .15 .07
❑ 541 Reggie Jefferson .30 .14
❑ 542 Kenny Lofton .60 .25
❑ 543 Jeff Mutis .15 .07
❑ 544 Junior Ortiz .15 .07
❑ 545 Manny Ramirez 1.25 .55
❑ 546 Jeff Treadway .15 .07
❑ 547 Kevin Wickander .15 .07
❑ 548 Cecil Fielder .30 .14
❑ 549 Kirk Gibson .30 .14
❑ 550 Greg Gohr .15 .07
❑ 551 David Haas .15 .07
❑ 552 Bill Krueger .15 .07
❑ 553 Mike Moore .15 .07
❑ 554 Mickey Tettleton .15 .07
❑ 555 Lou Whitaker .30 .14
❑ 556 Kevin Appier .30 .14
❑ 557 Billy Brewer .15 .07
❑ 558 David Cone .30 .14
❑ 559 Greg Gagne .15 .07
❑ 560 Mark Gardner .15 .07
❑ 561 Phil Hiatt .15 .07
❑ 562 Felix Jose .15 .07
❑ 563 Jose Lind .15 .07
❑ 564 Mike Macfarlane .15 .07
❑ 565 Keith Miller .15 .07
❑ 566 Jeff Montgomery .30 .14
❑ 567 Hipolito Pichardo .15 .07
❑ 568 Ricky Bones .15 .07
❑ 569 Tom Brunansky .15 .07
❑ 570 Joe Kmak .15 .07
❑ 571 Pat Listach .15 .07
❑ 572 Graeme Lloyd .15 .07
❑ 573 Carlos Maldonado .15 .07
❑ 574 Josias Manzanillo .15 .07
❑ 575 Matt Mieske .15 .07
❑ 576 Kevin Reimer .15 .07
❑ 577 Bill Spiers .15 .07
❑ 578 Dickie Thon .15 .07
❑ 579 Willie Banks .15 .07
❑ 580 Jim Deshaies .15 .07
❑ 581 Mark Guthrie .15 .07
❑ 582 Brian Harper .15 .07
❑ 583 Chuck Knoblauch .60 .25
❑ 584 Gene Larkin .15 .07
❑ 585 Shane Mack .15 .07
❑ 586 David McCarty .15 .07
❑ 587 Mike Pagliarulo .15 .07
❑ 588 Mike Trombley .15 .07
❑ 589 Dave Winfield .40 .18
❑ 590 Jim Abbott .30 .14
❑ 591 Wade Boggs .60 .25
❑ 592 Russ Davis .60 .25
❑ 593 Steve Farr .15 .07
❑ 594 Steve Howe .15 .07
❑ 595 Mike Humphreys .15 .07
❑ 596 Jimmy Key .30 .14
❑ 597 Jim Leyritz .15 .07
❑ 598 Bobby Munoz .15 .07
❑ 599 Paul O'Neill .30 .14
❑ 600 Spike Owen .15 .07
❑ 601 Mike Stanley .15 .07
❑ 602 Danny Tartabull .15 .07
❑ 603 Scott Brosius .15 .07
❑ 604 Storm Davis .15 .07
❑ 605 Eric Fox .15 .07
❑ 606 Rich Gossage .30 .14
❑ 607 Scott Hemond .15 .07
❑ 608 Dave Henderson .15 .07
❑ 609 Mark McGwire 3.00 1.35
❑ 610 Mike Mohler .15 .07
❑ 611 Edwin Nunez .15 .07
❑ 612 Kevin Seitzer .15 .07
❑ 613 Ruben Sierra .15 .07
❑ 614 Chris Bosio .15 .07
❑ 615 Norm Charlton .15 .07
❑ 616 Jim Converse .15 .07
❑ 617 John Cummings .15 .07
❑ 618 Mike Felder .15 .07
❑ 619 Ken Griffey Jr. 3.00 1.35
❑ 620 Mike Hampton .40 .18
❑ 621 Erik Hanson .15 .07
❑ 622 Bill Haselman .15 .07
❑ 623 Tino Martinez .60 .25
❑ 624 Lee Tinsley .30 .14
❑ 625 Fernando Vina .40 .18
❑ 626 David Wainhouse .15 .07
❑ 627 Jose Canseco .60 .25
❑ 628 Benji Gil .15 .07
❑ 629 Tom Henke .15 .07
❑ 630 David Hulse .15 .07
❑ 631 Manuel Lee .15 .07
❑ 632 Craig Lefferts .15 .07
❑ 633 Robb Nen .40 .18
❑ 634 Gary Redus .15 .07
❑ 635 Bill Ripken .15 .07
❑ 636 Nolan Ryan 2.50 1.10
❑ 637 Dan Smith .15 .07
❑ 638 Matt Whiteside .15 .07
❑ 639 Roberto Alomar .60 .25
❑ 640 Juan Guzman .15 .07
❑ 641 Pat Hentgen .40 .18
❑ 642 Darrin Jackson .15 .07
❑ 643 Randy Knorr .15 .07
❑ 644 Domingo Martinez .15 .07
❑ 645 Paul Molitor .60 .25
❑ 646 Dick Schofield .15 .07
❑ 647 Dave Stewart .30 .14
❑ 648 Rey Sanchez CL .15 .07
❑ 649 Jeremy Hernandez CL .15 .07
❑ 650 Junior Ortiz CL .15 .07

1993 Ultra All-Rookies

	MINT	NRMT
COMPLETE SET (10)	15.00	6.75
COMMON CARD (1-10)	.50	.23

❑ 1 Rene Arocha .50 .23
❑ 2 Jeff Conine .50 .23
❑ 3 Phil Hiatt .50 .23
❑ 4 Mike Lansing .75 .35
❑ 5 Al Martin .50 .23
❑ 6 David Nied .50 .23
❑ 7 Mike Piazza 12.00 5.50
❑ 8 Tim Salmon 3.00 1.35
❑ 9 J.T. Snow 2.00 .90
❑ 10 Kevin Young .75 .35

1993 Ultra All-Stars

	MINT	NRMT
COMPLETE SET (20)	40.00	18.00
COMMON CARD (1-20)	.75	.35

		MINT	NRMT
❑ 1	Darren Daulton	1.00	.45
❑ 2	Will Clark	2.00	.90
❑ 3	Ryne Sandberg	3.00	1.35
❑ 4	Barry Larkin	1.50	.70
❑ 5	Gary Sheffield	2.00	.90
❑ 6	Barry Bonds	3.00	1.35
❑ 7	Ray Lankford	1.00	.45
❑ 8	Larry Walker	2.50	1.10
❑ 9	Greg Maddux	8.00	3.60
❑ 10	Lee Smith	1.00	.45
❑ 11	Ivan Rodriguez	3.00	1.35
❑ 12	Mark McGwire	12.50	5.50
❑ 13	Carlos Baerga	.75	.35
❑ 14	Cal Ripken	10.00	4.50
❑ 15	Edgar Martinez	1.50	.70
❑ 16	Juan Gonzalez	6.00	2.70
❑ 17	Ken Griffey Jr.	12.00	5.50
❑ 18	Kirby Puckett	4.00	1.80
❑ 19	Frank Thomas	8.00	3.60
❑ 20	Mike Mussina	2.50	1.10

1993 Ultra Award Winners

	MINT	NRMT
COMPLETE SET (25)	40.00	18.00
COMMON CARD (1-25)	.50	.23

		MINT	NRMT
❑ 1	Greg Maddux	8.00	3.60
❑ 2	Tom Pagnozzi	.50	.23
❑ 3	Mark Grace	1.50	.70
❑ 4	Jose Lind	.50	.23
❑ 5	Terry Pendleton	.50	.23
❑ 6	Ozzie Smith	3.00	1.35
❑ 7	Barry Bonds	3.00	1.35
❑ 8	Andy Van Slyke	.50	.23
❑ 9	Larry Walker	2.50	1.10
❑ 10	Mark Langston	.50	.23
❑ 11	Ivan Rodriguez	3.00	1.35
❑ 12	Don Mattingly	4.00	1.80
❑ 13	Roberto Alomar	2.50	1.10
❑ 14	Robin Ventura	1.00	.45
❑ 15	Cal Ripken	10.00	4.50
❑ 16	Ken Griffey	12.00	5.50
❑ 17	Kirby Puckett	4.00	1.80
❑ 18	Devon White	.50	.23
❑ 19	Pat Listach	.50	.23
❑ 20	Eric Karros	1.50	.70
❑ 21	Pat Borders	.50	.23
❑ 22	Greg Maddux	8.00	3.60
❑ 23	Dennis Eckersley	1.00	.45
❑ 24	Barry Bonds	3.00	1.35
❑ 25	Gary Sheffield	2.00	.90

1993 Ultra Eckersley

	MINT	NRMT
COMPLETE SET (10)	4.00	1.80
COMMON CARD (1-10)	.50	.23
COMMON MAIL-IN (11-12)	1.00	.45

		MINT	NRMT
❑ 1	Dennis Eckersley Perfection	.50	.23
❑ 2	Dennis Eckersley The Kid	.50	.23
❑ 3	Dennis Eckersley The Warrior	.50	.23
❑ 4	Dennis Eckersley Beantown Blazer	.50	.23
❑ 5	Dennis Eckersley Eckspeak	.50	.23
❑ 6	Dennis Eckersley Down to Earth	.50	.23
❑ 7	Dennis Eckersley Wrigley Bound	.50	.23
❑ 8	Dennis Eckersley No Relief	.50	.23
❑ 9	Dennis Eckersley In Control	.50	.23
❑ 10	Dennis Eckersley Simply the Best	.50	.23
❑ 11	Dennis Eckersley Reign of Perfection	1.00	.45
❑ 12	Dennis Eckersley Leaving His Mark	1.00	.45
❑ P1	Dennis Eckersley Promo with Paul Mullan	4.00	1.80
❑ AU0	Dennis Eckersley AU (Certified autograph)	40.00	18.00

1993 Ultra Home Run Kings

	MINT	NRMT
COMPLETE SET (10)	15.00	6.75
COMMON CARD (1-10)	1.00	.45

		MINT	NRMT
❑ 1	Juan Gonzalez	8.00	3.60
❑ 2	Mark McGwire	15.00	6.75
❑ 3	Cecil Fielder	1.50	.70
❑ 4	Fred McGriff	2.00	.90
❑ 5	Albert Belle	4.00	1.80
❑ 6	Barry Bonds	4.00	1.80
❑ 7	Joe Carter	1.50	.70
❑ 8	Gary Sheffield	2.50	1.10
❑ 9	Darren Daulton	1.50	.70
❑ 10	Dave Hollins	1.00	.45

1993 Ultra Performers

	MINT	NRMT
COMPLETE SET (10)	25.00	11.00
COMMON CARD (1-10)	.50	.23

		MINT	NRMT
❑ 1	Barry Bonds	2.00	.90
❑ 2	Juan Gonzalez	4.00	1.80
❑ 3	Ken Griffey Jr.	10.00	4.50
❑ 4	Eric Karros	1.25	.55
❑ 5	Pat Listach	.50	.23
❑ 6	Greg Maddux	6.00	2.70
❑ 7	David Nied	.50	.23
❑ 8	Gary Sheffield	2.00	.90
❑ 9	J.T. Snow	1.50	.70
❑ 10	Frank Thomas	6.00	2.70

1993 Ultra Strikeout Kings

	MINT	NRMT
COMPLETE SET (5)	20.00	9.00
COMMON CARD (1-5)	1.00	.45

		MINT	NRMT
❑ 1	Roger Clemens	8.00	3.60
❑ 2	Juan Guzman	1.00	.45
❑ 3	Randy Johnson	2.50	1.10
❑ 4	Nolan Ryan	15.00	6.75
❑ 5	John Smoltz	1.50	.70

1994 Ultra

	MINT	NRMT
COMPLETE SET (600)	40.00	18.00
COMPLETE SERIES 1 (300)	20.00	9.00
COMPLETE SERIES 2 (300)	20.00	9.00
COMMON CARD (1-600)	.15	.07

		MINT	NRMT
❑ 1	Jeffrey Hammonds	.30	.14
❑ 2	Chris Hoiles	.15	.07
❑ 3	Ben McDonald	.15	.07
❑ 4	Mark McLemore	.15	.07

❑ 5 Alan Mills .15 .07
❑ 6 Jamie Moyer .15 .07
❑ 7 Brad Pennington .15 .07
❑ 8 Jim Poole .15 .07
❑ 9 Cal Ripken Jr. 2.50 1.10
❑ 10 Jack Voigt .15 .07
❑ 11 Roger Clemens 1.25 .55
❑ 12 Danny Darwin .15 .07
❑ 13 Andre Dawson .40 .18
❑ 14 Scott Fletcher .15 .07
❑ 15 Greg A Harris .15 .07
❑ 16 Billy Hatcher .15 .07
❑ 17 Jeff Russell .15 .07
❑ 18 Aaron Sele .30 .14
❑ 19 Mo Vaughn .75 .35
❑ 20 Mike Butcher .15 .07
❑ 21 Rod Correia .15 .07
❑ 22 Steve Frey .15 .07
❑ 23 Phil Leftwich .15 .07
❑ 24 Torey Lovullo .15 .07
❑ 25 Ken Patterson .15 .07
❑ 26 Eduardo Perez UER .15 .07
(listed as a Twin instead of Angel)
❑ 27 Tim Salmon .60 .25
❑ 28 J.T. Snow .30 .14
❑ 29 Chris Turner .15 .07
❑ 30 Wilson Alvarez .30 .14
❑ 31 Jason Bere .15 .07
❑ 32 Joey Cora .30 .14
❑ 33 Alex Fernandez .15 .07
❑ 34 Roberto Hernandez .15 .07
❑ 35 Lance Johnson .15 .07
❑ 36 Ron Karkovice .15 .07
❑ 37 Kirk McCaskill .15 .07
❑ 38 Jeff Schwarz .15 .07
❑ 39 Frank Thomas 2.00 .90
❑ 40 Sandy Alomar Jr. .30 .14
❑ 41 Albert Belle .75 .35
❑ 42 Felix Fermin .15 .07
❑ 43 Wayne Kirby .15 .07
❑ 44 Tom Kramer .15 .07
❑ 45 Kenny Lofton .60 .25
❑ 46 Jose Mesa .15 .07
❑ 47 Eric Plunk .15 .07
❑ 48 Paul Sorrento .15 .07
❑ 49 Jim Thome .75 .35
❑ 50 Bill Wertz .15 .07
❑ 51 John Doherty .15 .07
❑ 52 Cecil Fielder .30 .14
❑ 53 Travis Fryman .30 .14
❑ 54 Chris Gomez .15 .07
❑ 55 Mike Henneman .15 .07
❑ 56 Chad Kreuter .15 .07
❑ 57 Bob MacDonald .15 .07
❑ 58 Mike Moore .15 .07
❑ 59 Tony Phillips .15 .07
❑ 60 Lou Whitaker .30 .14
❑ 61 Kevin Appier .30 .14
❑ 62 Greg Gagne .15 .07
❑ 63 Chris Gwynn .15 .07
❑ 64 Bob Hamelin .15 .07
❑ 65 Chris Haney .15 .07
❑ 66 Phil Hiatt .15 .07
❑ 67 Felix Jose .15 .07
❑ 68 Jose Lind .15 .07
❑ 69 Mike Macfarlane .15 .07
❑ 70 Jeff Montgomery .15 .07
❑ 71 Hipolito Pichardo .15 .07
❑ 72 Juan Bell .15 .07
❑ 73 Cal Eldred .15 .07
❑ 74 Darryl Hamilton .15 .07
❑ 75 Doug Henry .15 .07
❑ 76 Mike Ignasiak .15 .07
❑ 77 John Jaha .15 .07
❑ 78 Graeme Lloyd .15 .07
❑ 79 Angel Miranda .15 .07
❑ 80 Dave Nilsson .15 .07
❑ 81 Troy O'Leary .30 .14
❑ 82 Kevin Reimer .15 .07
❑ 83 Willie Banks .15 .07
❑ 84 Larry Casian .15 .07
❑ 85 Scott Erickson .30 .14
❑ 86 Eddie Guardado .15 .07
❑ 87 Kent Hrbek .30 .14
❑ 88 Terry Jorgensen .15 .07
❑ 89 Chuck Knoblauch .60 .25
❑ 90 Pat Meares .15 .07
❑ 91 Mike Trombley .15 .07
❑ 92 Dave Winfield .60 .25
❑ 93 Wade Boggs .60 .25
❑ 94 Scott Kamieniecki .15 .07
❑ 95 Pat Kelly .15 .07
❑ 96 Jimmy Key .30 .14
❑ 97 Jim Leyritz .30 .14
❑ 98 Bobby Munoz .15 .07
❑ 99 Paul O'Neill .30 .14
❑ 100 Melido Perez .15 .07
❑ 101 Mike Stanley .15 .07
❑ 102 Danny Tartabull .15 .07
❑ 103 Bernie Williams .60 .25
❑ 104 Kurt Abbott .15 .07
❑ 105 Mike Bordick .15 .07
❑ 106 Ron Darling .15 .07
❑ 107 Brent Gates .15 .07
❑ 108 Miguel Jimenez .15 .07
❑ 109 Steve Karsay .15 .07
❑ 110 Scott Lydy .15 .07
❑ 111 Mark McGwire 3.00 1.35
❑ 112 Troy Neel .15 .07
❑ 113 Craig Paquette .15 .07
❑ 114 Bob Welch .15 .07
❑ 115 Bobby Witt .15 .07
❑ 116 Rich Amaral .15 .07
❑ 117 Mike Blowers .15 .07
❑ 118 Jay Buhner .30 .14
❑ 119 Dave Fleming .15 .07
❑ 120 Ken Griffey Jr. 3.00 1.35
❑ 121 Tino Martinez .60 .25
❑ 122 Marc Newfield .15 .07
❑ 123 Ted Power .15 .07
❑ 124 Mackey Sasser .15 .07
❑ 125 Omar Vizquel .30 .14
❑ 126 Kevin Brown .30 .14
❑ 127 Juan Gonzalez 1.50 .70
❑ 128 Tom Henke .15 .07
❑ 129 David Hulse .15 .07
❑ 130 Dean Palmer .30 .14
❑ 131 Roger Pavlik .15 .07
❑ 132 Ivan Rodriguez .75 .35
❑ 133 Kenny Rogers .15 .07
❑ 134 Doug Strange .15 .07
❑ 135 Pat Borders .15 .07
❑ 136 Joe Carter .30 .14
❑ 137 Darnell Coles .15 .07
❑ 138 Pat Hentgen .30 .14
❑ 139 Al Leiter .30 .14
❑ 140 Paul Molitor .60 .25
❑ 141 John Olerud .30 .14
❑ 142 Ed Sprague .15 .07
❑ 143 Dave Stewart .30 .14
❑ 144 Mike Timlin .15 .07
❑ 145 Duane Ward .15 .07
❑ 146 Devon White .30 .14
❑ 147 Steve Avery .15 .07
❑ 148 Steve Bedrosian .15 .07
❑ 149 Damon Berryhill .15 .07
❑ 150 Jeff Blauser .15 .07
❑ 151 Tom Glavine .60 .25
❑ 152 Chipper Jones 2.00 .90
❑ 153 Mark Lemke .15 .07
❑ 154 Fred McGriff .40 .18
❑ 155 Greg McMichael .15 .07
❑ 156 Deion Sanders .30 .14
❑ 157 John Smoltz .30 .14
❑ 158 Mark Wohlers .15 .07
❑ 159 Jose Bautista .15 .07
❑ 160 Steve Buechele .15 .07
❑ 161 Mike Harkey .15 .07
❑ 162 Greg Hibbard .15 .07
❑ 163 Chuck McElroy .15 .07
❑ 164 Mike Morgan .15 .07
❑ 165 Kevin Roberson .15 .07
❑ 166 Ryne Sandberg .75 .35
❑ 167 Jose Vizcaino .15 .07
❑ 168 Rick Wilkins .15 .07
❑ 169 Willie Wilson .15 .07
❑ 170 Willie Greene .30 .14
❑ 171 Roberto Kelly .15 .07
❑ 172 Larry Luebbers .15 .07
❑ 173 Kevin Mitchell .15 .07
❑ 174 Joe Oliver .15 .07
❑ 175 John Roper .15 .07
❑ 176 Johnny Ruffin .15 .07
❑ 177 Reggie Sanders .30 .14
❑ 178 John Smiley .15 .07
❑ 179 Jerry Spradlin .15 .07
❑ 180 Freddie Benavides .15 .07
❑ 181 Dante Bichette .30 .14
❑ 182 Willie Blair .15 .07
❑ 183 Kent Bottenfield .15 .07
❑ 184 Jerald Clark .15 .07
❑ 185 Joe Girardi .15 .07
❑ 186 Roberto Mejia .15 .07
❑ 187 Steve Reed .15 .07
❑ 188 Armando Reynoso .15 .07
❑ 189 Bruce Ruffin .15 .07
❑ 190 Eric Young .15 .07
❑ 191 Luis Aquino .15 .07
❑ 192 Bret Barberie .15 .07
❑ 193 Ryan Bowen .15 .07
❑ 194 Chuck Carr .15 .07
❑ 195 Orestes Destrade .15 .07
❑ 196 Richie Lewis .15 .07
❑ 197 Dave Magadan .15 .07
❑ 198 Bob Natal .15 .07
❑ 199 Gary Sheffield .60 .25
❑ 200 Matt Turner .15 .07
❑ 201 Darrell Whitmore .15 .07
❑ 202 Eric Anthony .15 .07
❑ 203 Jeff Bagwell 1.00 .45
❑ 204 Andujar Cedeno .15 .07
❑ 205 Luis Gonzalez .15 .07
❑ 206 Xavier Hernandez .15 .07
❑ 207 Doug Jones .15 .07
❑ 208 Darryl Kile .30 .14
❑ 209 Scott Servais .15 .07
❑ 210 Greg Swindell .15 .07
❑ 211 Brian Williams .15 .07
❑ 212 Pedro Astacio .15 .07
❑ 213 Brett Butler .30 .14
❑ 214 Omar Daal .15 .07
❑ 215 Jim Gott .15 .07
❑ 216 Raul Mondesi .60 .25
❑ 217 Jose Offerman .15 .07
❑ 218 Mike Piazza 2.00 .90
❑ 219 Cory Snyder .15 .07
❑ 220 Tim Wallach .15 .07
❑ 221 Todd Worrell .15 .07
❑ 222 Moises Alou .40 .18
❑ 223 Sean Berry .15 .07
❑ 224 Wil Cordero .15 .07
❑ 225 Jeff Fassero .15 .07
❑ 226 Darrin Fletcher .15 .07
❑ 227 Cliff Floyd .30 .14
❑ 228 Marquis Grissom .30 .14
❑ 229 Ken Hill .15 .07
❑ 230 Mike Lansing .30 .14
❑ 231 Kirk Rueter .15 .07
❑ 232 John Wetteland .30 .14
❑ 233 Rondell White .30 .14
❑ 234 Tim Bogar .15 .07
❑ 235 Jeromy Burnitz .30 .14
❑ 236 Dwight Gooden .30 .14
❑ 237 Todd Hundley .30 .14
❑ 238 Jeff Kent .30 .14
❑ 239 Josias Manzanillo .15 .07
❑ 240 Joe Orsulak .15 .07

❑	241	Ryan Thompson	.15	.07
❑	242	Kim Batiste	.15	.07
❑	243	Darren Daulton	.30	.14
❑	244	Tommy Greene	.15	.07
❑	245	Dave Hollins	.15	.07
❑	246	Pete Incaviglia	.15	.07
❑	247	Danny Jackson	.15	.07
❑	248	Ricky Jordan	.15	.07
❑	249	John Kruk	.30	.14
❑	250	Mickey Morandini	.15	.07
❑	251	Terry Mulholland	.15	.07
❑	252	Ben Rivera	.15	.07
❑	253	Kevin Stocker	.15	.07
❑	254	Jay Bell	.30	.14
❑	255	Steve Cooke	.15	.07
❑	256	Jeff King	.15	.07
❑	257	Al Martin	.15	.07
❑	258	Danny Miceli	.15	.07
❑	259	Blas Minor	.15	.07
❑	260	Don Slaught	.15	.07
❑	261	Paul Wagner	.15	.07
❑	262	Tim Wakefield	.30	.14
❑	263	Kevin Young	.15	.07
❑	264	Rene Arocha	.15	.07
❑	265	Richard Batchelor	.15	.07
❑	266	Gregg Jefferies	.15	.07
❑	267	Brian Jordan	.30	.14
❑	268	Jose Oquendo	.15	.07
❑	269	Donovan Osborne	.15	.07
❑	270	Erik Pappas	.15	.07
❑	271	Mike Perez	.15	.07
❑	272	Bob Tewksbury	.15	.07
❑	273	Mark Whiten	.15	.07
❑	274	Todd Zeile	.15	.07
❑	275	Andy Ashby	.15	.07
❑	276	Brad Ausmus	.15	.07
❑	277	Phil Clark	.15	.07
❑	278	Jeff Gardner	.15	.07
❑	279	Ricky Gutierrez	.15	.07
❑	280	Tony Gwynn	1.50	.70
❑	281	Tim Mauser	.15	.07
❑	282	Scott Sanders	.15	.07
❑	283	Frank Seminara	.15	.07
❑	284	Wally Whitehurst	.15	.07
❑	285	Rod Beck	.15	.07
❑	286	Barry Bonds	.75	.35
❑	287	Dave Burba	.15	.07
❑	288	Mark Carreon	.15	.07
❑	289	Royce Clayton	.15	.07
❑	290	Mike Jackson	.15	.07
❑	291	Darren Lewis	.15	.07
❑	292	Kirt Manwaring	.15	.07
❑	293	Dave Martinez	.15	.07
❑	294	Billy Swift	.15	.07
❑	295	Salomon Torres	.15	.07
❑	296	Matt Williams	.40	.18
❑	297	Checklist 1-75	.15	.07
❑	298	Checklist 76-150	.15	.07
❑	299	Checklist 151-225	.15	.07
❑	300	Checklist 226-300	.15	.07
❑	301	Brady Anderson	.30	.14
❑	302	Harold Baines	.30	.14
❑	303	Damon Buford	.15	.07
❑	304	Mike Devereaux	.15	.07
❑	305	Sid Fernandez	.15	.07
❑	306	Rick Krivda	.15	.07
❑	307	Mike Mussina	.60	.25
❑	308	Rafael Palmeiro	.40	.18
❑	309	Arthur Rhodes	.15	.07
❑	310	Chris Sabo	.15	.07
❑	311	Lee Smith	.30	.14
❑	312	Gregg Zaun	.15	.07
❑	313	Scott Cooper	.15	.07
❑	314	Mike Greenwell	.15	.07
❑	315	Tim Naehring	.15	.07
❑	316	Otis Nixon	.15	.07
❑	317	Paul Quantrill	.15	.07
❑	318	John Valentin	.30	.14
❑	319	Dave Valle	.15	.07
❑	320	Frank Viola	.15	.07
❑	321	Brian Anderson	.40	.18
❑	322	Garret Anderson	.60	.25
❑	323	Chad Curtis	.15	.07
❑	324	Chili Davis	.30	.14
❑	325	Gary DiSarcina	.15	.07
❑	326	Damion Easley	.30	.14
❑	327	Jim Edmonds	.60	.25
❑	328	Chuck Finley	.30	.14
❑	329	Joe Grahe	.15	.07
❑	330	Bo Jackson	.30	.14
❑	331	Mark Langston	.15	.07
❑	332	Harold Reynolds	.15	.07
❑	333	James Baldwin	.30	.14
❑	334	Ray Durham	1.00	.45
❑	335	Julio Franco	.15	.07
❑	336	Craig Grebeck	.15	.07
❑	337	Ozzie Guillen	.15	.07
❑	338	Joe Hall	.15	.07
❑	339	Darrin Jackson	.15	.07
❑	340	Jack McDowell	.15	.07
❑	341	Tim Raines	.30	.14
❑	342	Robin Ventura	.30	.14
❑	343	Carlos Baerga	.30	.14
❑	344	Derek Lilliquist	.15	.07
❑	345	Dennis Martinez	.30	.14
❑	346	Jack Morris	.30	.14
❑	347	Eddie Murray	.60	.25
❑	348	Chris Nabholz	.15	.07
❑	349	Charles Nagy	.30	.14
❑	350	Chad Ogea	.30	.14
❑	351	Manny Ramirez	.75	.35
❑	352	Omar Vizquel	.30	.14
❑	353	Tim Belcher	.15	.07
❑	354	Eric Davis	.30	.14
❑	355	Kirk Gibson	.30	.14
❑	356	Rick Greene	.15	.07
❑	357	Mickey Tettleton	.15	.07
❑	358	Alan Trammell	.40	.18
❑	359	David Wells	.40	.18
❑	360	Stan Belinda	.15	.07
❑	361	Vince Coleman	.15	.07
❑	362	David Cone	.40	.18
❑	363	Gary Gaetti	.30	.14
❑	364	Tom Gordon	.15	.07
❑	365	Dave Henderson	.15	.07
❑	366	Wally Joyner	.30	.14
❑	367	Brent Mayne	.15	.07
❑	368	Brian McRae	.15	.07
❑	369	Michael Tucker	.40	.18
❑	370	Ricky Bones	.15	.07
❑	371	Brian Harper	.15	.07
❑	372	Tyrone Hill	.15	.07
❑	373	Mark Kiefer	.15	.07
❑	374	Pat Listach	.15	.07
❑	375	Mike Matheny	.15	.07
❑	376	Jose Mercedes	.15	.07
❑	377	Jody Reed	.15	.07
❑	378	Kevin Seitzer	.15	.07
❑	379	B.J. Surhoff	.30	.14
❑	380	Greg Vaughn	.30	.14
❑	381	Turner Ward	.15	.07
❑	382	Wes Weger	.15	.07
❑	383	Bill Wegman	.15	.07
❑	384	Rick Aguilera	.15	.07
❑	385	Rich Becker	.15	.07
❑	386	Alex Cole	.15	.07
❑	387	Steve Dunn	.15	.07
❑	388	Keith Garagozzo	.15	.07
❑	389	LaTroy Hawkins	.30	.14
❑	390	Shane Mack	.15	.07
❑	391	David McCarty	.15	.07
❑	392	Pedro Munoz	.15	.07
❑	393	Derek Parks	.15	.07
❑	394	Kirby Puckett	1.00	.45
❑	395	Kevin Tapani	.15	.07
❑	396	Matt Walbeck	.15	.07
❑	397	Jim Abbott	.30	.14
❑	398	Mike Gallego	.15	.07
❑	399	Xavier Hernandez	.15	.07
❑	400	Don Mattingly	1.00	.45
❑	401	Terry Mulholland	.15	.07
❑	402	Matt Nokes	.15	.07
❑	403	Luis Polonia	.15	.07
❑	404	Bob Wickman	.15	.07
❑	405	Mark Acre	.15	.07
❑	406	Fausto Cruz	.15	.07
❑	407	Dennis Eckersley	.30	.14
❑	408	Rickey Henderson	.60	.25
❑	409	Stan Javier	.15	.07
❑	410	Carlos Reyes	.15	.07
❑	411	Ruben Sierra	.15	.07
❑	412	Terry Steinbach	.30	.14
❑	413	Bill Taylor	.15	.07
❑	414	Todd Van Poppel	.15	.07
❑	415	Eric Anthony	.15	.07
❑	416	Bobby Ayala	.15	.07
❑	417	Chris Bosio	.15	.07
❑	418	Tim Davis	.15	.07
❑	419	Randy Johnson	.60	.25
❑	420	Kevin King	.15	.07
❑	421	Anthony Manahan	.15	.07
❑	422	Edgar Martinez	.30	.14
❑	423	Keith Mitchell	.15	.07
❑	424	Roger Salkeld	.15	.07
❑	425	Mac Suzuki	.30	.14
❑	426	Dan Wilson	.15	.07
❑	427	Duff Brumley	.15	.07
❑	428	Jose Canseco	.60	.25
❑	429	Will Clark	.60	.25
❑	430	Steve Dreyer	.15	.07
❑	431	Rick Helling	.30	.14
❑	432	Chris James	.15	.07
❑	433	Matt Whiteside	.15	.07
❑	434	Roberto Alomar	.60	.25
❑	435	Scott Brow	.15	.07
❑	436	Domingo Cedeno	.15	.07
❑	437	Carlos Delgado	.40	.18
❑	438	Juan Guzman	.15	.07
❑	439	Paul Spoljaric	.15	.07
❑	440	Todd Stottlemyre	.15	.07
❑	441	Woody Williams	.15	.07
❑	442	David Justice	.60	.25
❑	443	Mike Kelly	.15	.07
❑	444	Ryan Klesko	.30	.14
❑	445	Javier Lopez	.40	.18
❑	446	Greg Maddux	2.00	.90
❑	447	Kent Mercker	.15	.07
❑	448	Charlie O'Brien	.15	.07
❑	449	Terry Pendleton	.15	.07
❑	450	Mike Stanton	.15	.07
❑	451	Tony Tarasco	.15	.07
❑	452	Terrell Wade	.15	.07
❑	453	Willie Banks	.15	.07
❑	454	Shawon Dunston	.15	.07
❑	455	Mark Grace	.40	.18
❑	456	Jose Guzman	.15	.07
❑	457	Jose Hernandez	.15	.07
❑	458	Glenallen Hill	.15	.07
❑	459	Blaise Ilsley	.15	.07
❑	460	Brooks Kieschnick	.30	.14
❑	461	Derrick May	.15	.07
❑	462	Randy Myers	.15	.07
❑	463	Karl Rhodes	.15	.07
❑	464	Sammy Sosa	1.50	.70
❑	465	Steve Trachsel	.15	.07
❑	466	Anthony Young	.15	.07
❑	467	Eddie Zambrano	.15	.07
❑	468	Bret Boone	.30	.14
❑	469	Tom Browning	.15	.07
❑	470	Hector Carrasco	.15	.07
❑	471	Rob Dibble	.15	.07
❑	472	Erik Hanson	.15	.07
❑	473	Thomas Howard	.15	.07
❑	474	Barry Larkin	.40	.18
❑	475	Hal Morris	.15	.07
❑	476	Jose Rijo	.15	.07
❑	477	John Burke	.15	.07
❑	478	Ellis Burks	.30	.14
❑	479	Marvin Freeman	.15	.07
❑	480	Andres Galarraga	.60	.25
❑	481	Greg W. Harris	.15	.07
❑	482	Charlie Hayes	.15	.07
❑	483	Darren Holmes	.15	.07
❑	484	Howard Johnson	.15	.07
❑	485	Marcus Moore	.15	.07
❑	486	David Nied	.15	.07
❑	487	Mark Thompson	.15	.07
❑	488	Walt Weiss	.15	.07
❑	489	Kurt Abbott	.15	.07
❑	490	Matias Carrillo	.15	.07
❑	491	Jeff Conine	.30	.14
❑	492	Chris Hammond	.15	.07
❑	493	Bryan Harvey	.15	.07
❑	494	Charlie Hough	.15	.07
❑	495	Yorkis Perez	.15	.07

Card	MINT	NRMT
❑ 496 Pat Rapp	.15	.07
❑ 497 Benito Santiago	.15	.07
❑ 498 David Weathers	.15	.07
❑ 499 Craig Biggio	.60	.25
❑ 500 Ken Caminiti	.40	.18
❑ 501 Doug Drabek	.15	.07
❑ 502 Tony Eusebio	.15	.07
❑ 503 Steve Finley	.30	.14
❑ 504 Pete Harnisch	.15	.07
❑ 505 Brian L.Hunter	.30	.14
❑ 506 Domingo Jean	.15	.07
❑ 507 Todd Jones	.15	.07
❑ 508 Orlando Miller	.15	.07
❑ 509 James Mouton	.15	.07
❑ 510 Roberto Petagine	.15	.07
❑ 511 Shane Reynolds	.30	.14
❑ 512 Mitch Williams	.15	.07
❑ 513 Billy Ashley	.15	.07
❑ 514 Tom Candiotti	.15	.07
❑ 515 Delino DeShields	.15	.07
❑ 516 Kevin Gross	.15	.07
❑ 517 Orel Hershiser	.30	.14
❑ 518 Eric Karros	.30	.14
❑ 519 Ramon Martinez	.30	.14
❑ 520 Chan Ho Park	2.50	1.10
❑ 521 Henry Rodriguez	.30	.14
❑ 522 Joey Eischen	.15	.07
❑ 523 Rod Henderson	.15	.07
❑ 524 Pedro Martinez	.75	.35
❑ 525 Mel Rojas	.15	.07
❑ 526 Larry Walker	.60	.25
❑ 527 Gabe White	.15	.07
❑ 528 Bobby Bonilla	.30	.14
❑ 529 Jonathan Hurst	.15	.07
❑ 530 Bobby Jones	.15	.07
❑ 531 Kevin McReynolds	.15	.07
❑ 532 Bill Pulsipher	.30	.14
❑ 533 Bret Saberhagen	.30	.14
❑ 534 David Segui	.30	.14
❑ 535 Pete Smith	.15	.07
❑ 536 Kelly Stinnett	.15	.07
❑ 537 Dave Telgheder	.15	.07
❑ 538 Quilvio Veras	.15	.07
❑ 539 Jose Vizcaino	.15	.07
❑ 540 Pete Walker	.15	.07
❑ 541 Ricky Bottalico	.30	.14
❑ 542 Wes Chamberlain	.15	.07
❑ 543 Mariano Duncan	.15	.07
❑ 544 Lenny Dykstra	.30	.14
❑ 545 Jim Eisenreich	.15	.07
❑ 546 Phil Geisler	.15	.07
❑ 547 Wayne Gomes	.15	.07
❑ 548 Doug Jones	.15	.07
❑ 549 Jeff Juden	.15	.07
❑ 550 Mike Lieberthal	.15	.07
❑ 551 Tony Longmire	.15	.07
❑ 552 Tom Marsh	.15	.07
❑ 553 Bobby Munoz	.15	.07
❑ 554 Curt Schilling	.30	.14
❑ 555 Carlos Garcia	.15	.07
❑ 556 Ravelo Manzanillo	.15	.07
❑ 557 Orlando Merced	.15	.07
❑ 558 Will Pennyfeather	.15	.07
❑ 559 Zane Smith	.15	.07
❑ 560 Andy Van Slyke	.30	.14
❑ 561 Rick White	.15	.07
❑ 562 Luis Alicea	.15	.07
❑ 563 Brian Barber	.15	.07
❑ 564 Clint Davis	.15	.07
❑ 565 Bernard Gilkey	.15	.07
❑ 566 Ray Lankford	.30	.14
❑ 567 Tom Pagnozzi	.15	.07
❑ 568 Ozzie Smith	.75	.35
❑ 569 Rick Sutcliffe	.15	.07
❑ 570 Allen Watson	.15	.07
❑ 571 Dmitri Young	.30	.14
❑ 572 Derek Bell	.30	.14
❑ 573 Andy Benes	.30	.14
❑ 574 Archi Cianfrocco	.15	.07
❑ 575 Joey Hamilton	.60	.25
❑ 576 Gene Harris	.15	.07
❑ 577 Trevor Hoffman	.30	.14
❑ 578 Tim Hyers	.15	.07
❑ 579 Brian Johnson	.15	.07
❑ 580 Keith Lockhart	.15	.07
❑ 581 Pedro A. Martinez	.15	.07
❑ 582 Ray McDavid	.15	.07
❑ 583 Phil Plantier	.15	.07
❑ 584 Bip Roberts	.15	.07
❑ 585 Dave Staton	.15	.07
❑ 586 Todd Benzinger	.15	.07
❑ 587 John Burkett	.15	.07
❑ 588 Bryan Hickerson	.15	.07
❑ 589 Willie McGee	.30	.14
❑ 590 John Patterson	.15	.07
❑ 591 Mark Portugal	.15	.07
❑ 592 Kevin Rogers	.15	.07
❑ 593 Joe Rosselli	.15	.07
❑ 594 Steve Soderstrom	.15	.07
❑ 595 Robby Thompson	.15	.07
❑ 596 125th Anniversary Card	.15	.07
❑ 597 Checklist	.15	.07
❑ 598 Checklist	.15	.07
❑ 599 Checklist	.15	.07
❑ 600 Checklist	.15	.07
❑ P243 Darren Daulton Promo	2.00	.90
❑ P249 John Kruk Promo	2.00	.90

1994 Ultra All-Rookies

	MINT	NRMT
COMPLETE SET (10)	10.00	4.50
COMMON CARD (1-10)	.50	.23

*JUMBOS: 1X TO 2X BASIC CARDS
ONE JUMBO SET PER HOBBY CASE

Card	MINT	NRMT
❑ 1 Kurt Abbott	.50	.23
❑ 2 Carlos Delgado	1.50	.70
❑ 3 Cliff Floyd	1.00	.45
❑ 4 Jeffrey Hammonds	1.00	.45
❑ 5 Ryan Klesko	1.00	.45
❑ 6 Javier Lopez	1.50	.70
❑ 7 Raul Mondesi	2.00	.90
❑ 8 James Mouton	.50	.23
❑ 9 Chan Ho Park	2.00	.90
❑ 10 Dave Staton	.50	.23

1994 Ultra All-Stars

	MINT	NRMT
COMPLETE SET (20)	18.00	8.00
COMMON CARD (1-20)	.25	.11

Card	MINT	NRMT
❑ 1 Chris Hoiles	.25	.11
❑ 2 Frank Thomas	3.00	1.35
❑ 3 Roberto Alomar	1.00	.45
❑ 4 Cal Ripken Jr.	4.00	1.80
❑ 5 Robin Ventura	.50	.23
❑ 6 Albert Belle	1.25	.55
❑ 7 Juan Gonzalez	2.50	1.10
❑ 8 Ken Griffey Jr.	5.00	2.20
❑ 9 John Olerud	.50	.23
❑ 10 Jack McDowell	.25	.11
❑ 11 Mike Piazza	3.00	1.35
❑ 12 Fred McGriff	.75	.35
❑ 13 Ryne Sandberg	1.25	.55
❑ 14 Jay Bell	.50	.23
❑ 15 Matt Williams	.75	.35
❑ 16 Barry Bonds	1.00	.45
❑ 17 Lenny Dykstra	.50	.23
❑ 18 David Justice	1.00	.45
❑ 19 Tom Glavine	1.00	.45
❑ 20 Greg Maddux	3.00	1.35

1994 Ultra Award Winners

	MINT	NRMT
COMPLETE SET (25)	15.00	6.75
COMMON CARD (1-25)	.25	.11

Card	MINT	NRMT
❑ 1 Ivan Rodriguez	1.00	.45
❑ 2 Don Mattingly	1.25	.55
❑ 3 Roberto Alomar	1.00	.45
❑ 4 Robin Ventura	.50	.23
❑ 5 Omar Vizquel	.50	.23
❑ 6 Ken Griffey Jr.	5.00	2.20
❑ 7 Kenny Lofton	1.00	.45
❑ 8 Devon White	.50	.23
❑ 9 Mark Langston	.25	.11
❑ 10 Kirt Manwaring	.25	.11
❑ 11 Mark Grace	.75	.35
❑ 12 Robby Thompson	.25	.11
❑ 13 Matt Williams	.75	.35
❑ 14 Jay Bell	.50	.23
❑ 15 Barry Bonds	1.00	.45
❑ 16 Marquis Grissom	.50	.23
❑ 17 Larry Walker	1.00	.45
❑ 18 Greg Maddux	3.00	1.35
❑ 19 Frank Thomas	3.00	1.35
❑ 20 Barry Bonds	1.00	.45
❑ 21 Paul Molitor	1.00	.45
❑ 22 Jack McDowell	.25	.11
❑ 23 Greg Maddux	3.00	1.35
❑ 24 Tim Salmon	1.00	.45
❑ 25 Mike Piazza	3.00	1.35

1994 Ultra Career Achievement

	MINT	NRMT
COMPLETE SET (5)	12.00	5.50
COMMON CARD (1-5)	1.00	.45

Card	MINT	NRMT
❑ 1 Joe Carter	1.00	.45
❑ 2 Paul Molitor	2.00	.90
❑ 3 Cal Ripken Jr.	8.00	3.60
❑ 4 Ryne Sandberg	2.50	1.10
❑ 5 Dave Winfield	2.00	.90

1994 Ultra Firemen

	MINT	NRMT
COMPLETE SET (10)	5.00	2.20
COMMON CARD (1-10)	.50	.23

	MINT	NRMT
❑ 1 Jeff Montgomery	.50	.23
❑ 2 Duane Ward	.50	.23
❑ 3 Tom Henke	.50	.23
❑ 4 Roberto Hernandez	.50	.23
❑ 5 Dennis Eckersley	.75	.35
❑ 6 Randy Myers	.50	.23
❑ 7 Rod Beck	.50	.23
❑ 8 Bryan Harvey	.50	.23
❑ 9 John Wetteland	.75	.35
❑ 10 Mitch Williams	.50	.23

1994 Ultra Hitting Machines

	MINT	NRMT
COMPLETE SET (10)	12.00	5.50
COMMON CARD (1-10)	.25	.11

	MINT	NRMT
❑ 1 Roberto Alomar	1.00	.45
❑ 2 Carlos Baerga	.25	.11
❑ 3 Barry Bonds	1.00	.45
❑ 4 Andres Galarraga	1.00	.45
❑ 5 Juan Gonzalez	2.50	1.10
❑ 6 Tony Gwynn	2.50	1.10
❑ 7 Paul Molitor	1.00	.45
❑ 8 John Olerud	.50	.23
❑ 9 Mike Piazza	3.00	1.35
❑ 10 Frank Thomas	3.00	1.35

1994 Ultra Home Run Kings

	MINT	NRMT
COMPLETE SET (12)	80.00	36.00
COMMON CARD (1-12)	1.50	.70

	MINT	NRMT
❑ 1 Juan Gonzalez	12.00	5.50
❑ 2 Ken Griffey Jr.	25.00	11.00
❑ 3 Frank Thomas	15.00	6.75
❑ 4 Albert Belle	4.00	1.80
❑ 5 Rafael Palmeiro	2.00	.90
❑ 6 Joe Carter	1.50	.70
❑ 7 Barry Bonds	4.00	1.80
❑ 8 David Justice	4.00	1.80
❑ 9 Matt Williams	2.00	.90
❑ 10 Fred McGriff	2.00	.90
❑ 11 Ron Gant	1.50	.70
❑ 12 Mike Piazza	15.00	6.75

1994 Ultra League Leaders

	MINT	NRMT
COMPLETE SET (10)	5.00	2.20
COMMON CARD (1-10)	.25	.11

	MINT	NRMT
❑ 1 John Olerud	.50	.23
❑ 2 Rafael Palmeiro	1.00	.45
❑ 3 Kenny Lofton	1.50	.70
❑ 4 Jack McDowell	.25	.11
❑ 5 Randy Johnson	1.50	.70
❑ 6 Andres Galarraga	1.50	.70
❑ 7 Lenny Dykstra	.50	.23
❑ 8 Chuck Carr	.25	.11
❑ 9 Tom Glavine	1.50	.70
❑ 10 Jose Rijo	.25	.11

1994 Ultra On-Base Leaders

	MINT	NRMT
COMPLETE SET (12)	120.00	55.00
COMMON CARD (1-12)	3.00	1.35

	MINT	NRMT
❑ 1 Roberto Alomar	10.00	4.50
❑ 2 Barry Bonds	12.00	5.50
❑ 3 Lenny Dykstra	6.00	2.70
❑ 4 Andres Galarraga	10.00	4.50
❑ 5 Mark Grace	6.00	2.70
❑ 6 Ken Griffey Jr.	50.00	22.00
❑ 7 Gregg Jefferies	3.00	1.35
❑ 8 Orlando Merced	3.00	1.35
❑ 9 Paul Molitor	10.00	4.50
❑ 10 John Olerud	6.00	2.70
❑ 11 Tony Phillips	3.00	1.35
❑ 12 Frank Thomas	30.00	13.50

1994 Ultra Phillies Finest

	MINT	NRMT
COMPLETE SET (20)	10.00	4.50
COMPLETE SERIES 1 (10)	5.00	2.20
COMPLETE SERIES 2 (10)	5.00	2.20
COMMON DAULTON (1-5/11-15)	.50	.23
COMMON KRUK (6-10/16-20)	.50	.23
COMMON MAIL-IN (M1-M4)	1.00	.45

	MINT	NRMT
❑ 1 Darren Daulton (Standing behind home plate)	.50	.23
❑ 2 Darren Daulton (Swinging at a pitch)	.50	.23
❑ 3 Darren Daulton (Blocking home plate)	.50	.23
❑ 4 Darren Daulton (Just completed swing and is headed for first)	.50	.23
❑ 5 Darren Daulton (Looking skyward after connecting with a pitch)	.50	.23
❑ 6 John Kruk (Swinging at a pitch)	.50	.23
❑ 7 John Kruk (Fielding)	.50	.23
❑ 8 John Kruk (Just completed a swing)	.50	.23
❑ 9 John Kruk (On deck)	.50	.23
❑ 10 John Kruk (Breaking out of batters box)	.50	.23
❑ 11 Darren Daulton (Looking skyward after swing)	.50	.23

	MINT	NRMT
❑ 12 Darren Daulton	.50	.23
❑ 13 Darren Daulton (Anticipating throw home)	.50	.23
❑ 14 Darren Daulton (Standing at home with ball in hand)	.50	.23
❑ 15 Darren Daulton (Running up first base line with in catching gear)	.50	.23
❑ 16 John Kruk (Follow through of swing)	.50	.23
❑ 17 John Kruk (Waiting on deck)	.50	.23
❑ 18 John Kruk (Follow through from first base dugout angle)	.50	.23
❑ 19 John Kruk (Swinging at pitch) chest high)	.50	.23
❑ 20 John Kruk (Looking out toward left field afer swinging)	.50	.23
❑ M1 Darren Daulton (About to throw down to second base)	1.00	.45
❑ M2 John Kruk (Fielding position)	1.00	.45
❑ M3 Darren Daulton (Awaiting pitch)	1.00	.45
❑ M4 John Kruk (Running)	1.00	.45
❑ AU1 Darren Daulton Certified Autograph	40.00	18.00
❑ AU2 John Kruk Certified Autograph	40.00	18.00

1994 Ultra RBI Kings

	MINT	NRMT
COMPLETE SET (12)	150.00	70.00
COMMON CARD (1-12)	4.00	1.80
❑ 1 Albert Belle	15.00	6.75
❑ 2 Frank Thomas	40.00	18.00
❑ 3 Joe Carter	6.00	2.70
❑ 4 Juan Gonzalez	30.00	13.50
❑ 5 Cecil Fielder	6.00	2.70
❑ 6 Carlos Baerga	4.00	1.80
❑ 7 Barry Bonds	15.00	6.75
❑ 8 David Justice	12.00	5.50
❑ 9 Ron Gant	6.00	2.70
❑ 10 Mike Piazza	40.00	18.00
❑ 11 Matt Williams	8.00	3.60
❑ 12 Darren Daulton	6.00	2.70

1994 Ultra Rising Stars

	MINT	NRMT
COMPLETE SET (12)	120.00	55.00
COMMON CARD (1-12)	4.00	1.80
❑ 1 Carlos Baerga	6.00	2.70
❑ 2 Jeff Bagwell	20.00	9.00
❑ 3 Albert Belle	15.00	6.75
❑ 4 Cliff Floyd	6.00	2.70
❑ 5 Travis Fryman	6.00	2.70
❑ 6 Marquis Grissom	6.00	2.70
❑ 7 Kenny Lofton	12.00	5.50
❑ 8 John Olerud	6.00	2.70
❑ 9 Mike Piazza	40.00	18.00
❑ 10 Kirk Rueter	4.00	1.80
❑ 11 Tim Salmon	12.00	5.50
❑ 12 Aaron Sele	6.00	2.70

1994 Ultra Second Year Standouts

	MINT	NRMT
COMPLETE SET (10)	10.00	4.50
COMMON CARD (1-10)	.25	.11
❑ 1 Jason Bere	.25	.11
❑ 2 Brent Gates	.25	.11
❑ 3 Jeffrey Hammonds	.50	.23
❑ 4 Tim Salmon	1.00	.45
❑ 5 Aaron Sele	.50	.23
❑ 6 Chuck Carr	.25	.11
❑ 7 Jeff Conine	.50	.23
❑ 8 Greg McMichael	.25	.11
❑ 9 Mike Piazza	8.00	3.60
❑ 10 Kevin Stocker	.25	.11

1994 Ultra Strikeout Kings

	MINT	NRMT
COMPLETE SET (5)	5.00	2.20
COMMON CARD (1-5)	.25	.11
❑ 1 Randy Johnson	1.00	.45
❑ 2 Mark Langston	.25	.11
❑ 3 Greg Maddux	3.00	1.35
❑ 4 Jose Rijo	.25	.11
❑ 5 John Smoltz	.50	.23

1995 Ultra

	MINT	NRMT
COMPLETE SET (450)	30.00	13.50
COMPLETE SERIES 1 (250)	18.00	8.00
COMPLETE SERIES 2 (200)	12.00	5.50
COMMON CARD (1-450)	.15	.07
❑ 1 Brady Anderson	.30	.14
❑ 2 Sid Fernandez	.15	.07
❑ 3 Jeffrey Hammonds	.30	.14
❑ 4 Chris Hoiles	.15	.07
❑ 5 Ben McDonald	.15	.07
❑ 6 Mike Mussina	.60	.25
❑ 7 Rafael Palmeiro	.40	.18
❑ 8 Jack Voigt	.15	.07
❑ 9 Wes Chamberlain	.15	.07
❑ 10 Roger Clemens	1.25	.55
❑ 11 Chris Howard	.15	.07
❑ 12 Tim Naehring	.15	.07
❑ 13 Otis Nixon	.15	.07
❑ 14 Rich Rowland	.15	.07
❑ 15 Ken Ryan	.15	.07
❑ 16 John Valentin	.30	.14
❑ 17 Mo Vaughn	.75	.35
❑ 18 Brian Anderson	.30	.14
❑ 19 Chili Davis	.30	.14
❑ 20 Damion Easley	.30	.14
❑ 21 Jim Edmonds	.40	.18
❑ 22 Mark Langston	.15	.07
❑ 23 Tim Salmon	.60	.25
❑ 24 J.T. Snow	.30	.14
❑ 25 Chris Turner	.15	.07
❑ 26 Wilson Alvarez	.30	.14
❑ 27 Joey Cora	.30	.14
❑ 28 Alex Fernandez	.15	.07
❑ 29 Roberto Hernandez	.15	.07
❑ 30 Lance Johnson	.15	.07
❑ 31 Ron Karkovice	.15	.07
❑ 32 Kirk McCaskill	.15	.07
❑ 33 Tim Raines	.30	.14
❑ 34 Frank Thomas	2.00	.90
❑ 35 Sandy Alomar Jr.	.30	.14
❑ 36 Albert Belle	.75	.35
❑ 37 Mark Clark	.15	.07
❑ 38 Kenny Lofton	.60	.25
❑ 39 Eddie Murray	.60	.25
❑ 40 Eric Plunk	.15	.07
❑ 41 Manny Ramirez	.60	.25
❑ 42 Jim Thome	.60	.25
❑ 43 Omar Vizquel	.30	.14
❑ 44 Danny Bautista	.15	.07
❑ 45 Junior Felix	.15	.07
❑ 46 Cecil Fielder	.30	.14
❑ 47 Chris Gomez	.15	.07
❑ 48 Chad Kreuter	.15	.07
❑ 49 Mike Moore	.15	.07
❑ 50 Tony Phillips	.15	.07
❑ 51 Alan Trammell	.30	.14
❑ 52 David Wells	.40	.18
❑ 53 Kevin Appier	.30	.14
❑ 54 Billy Brewer	.15	.07
❑ 55 David Cone	.40	.18

56	Greg Gagne	.15	.07
57	Bob Hamelin	.15	.07
58	Jose Lind	.15	.07
59	Brent Mayne	.15	.07
60	Brian McRae	.15	.07
61	Terry Shumpert	.15	.07
62	Ricky Bones	.15	.07
63	Mike Fetters	.15	.07
64	Darryl Hamilton	.15	.07
65	John Jaha	.15	.07
66	Graeme Lloyd	.15	.07
67	Matt Mieske	.15	.07
68	Kevin Seitzer	.15	.07
69	Jose Valentin	.15	.07
70	Turner Ward	.15	.07
71	Rick Aguilera	.15	.07
72	Rich Becker	.15	.07
73	Alex Cole	.15	.07
74	Scott Leius	.15	.07
75	Pat Meares	.15	.07
76	Kirby Puckett	1.00	.45
77	Dave Stevens	.15	.07
78	Kevin Tapani	.15	.07
79	Matt Walbeck	.15	.07
80	Wade Boggs	.60	.25
81	Scott Kamieniecki	.15	.07
82	Pat Kelly	.15	.07
83	Jimmy Key	.30	.14
84	Paul O'Neill	.30	.14
85	Luis Polonia	.15	.07
86	Mike Stanley	.15	.07
87	Danny Tartabull	.15	.07
88	Bob Wickman	.15	.07
89	Mark Acre	.15	.07
90	Geronimo Berroa	.15	.07
91	Mike Bordick	.15	.07
92	Ron Darling	.15	.07
93	Stan Javier	.15	.07
94	Mark McGwire	3.00	1.35
95	Troy Neel	.15	.07
96	Ruben Sierra	.15	.07
97	Terry Steinbach	.30	.14
98	Eric Anthony	.15	.07
99	Chris Bosio	.15	.07
100	Dave Fleming	.15	.07
101	Ken Griffey Jr.	3.00	1.35
102	Reggie Jefferson	.15	.07
103	Randy Johnson	.60	.25
104	Edgar Martinez	.30	.14
105	Bill Risley	.15	.07
106	Dan Wilson	.15	.07
107	Cris Carpenter	.15	.07
108	Will Clark	.60	.25
109	Juan Gonzalez	1.50	.70
110	Rusty Greer	.60	.25
111	David Hulse	.15	.07
112	Roger Pavlik	.15	.07
113	Ivan Rodriguez	.75	.35
114	Doug Strange	.15	.07
115	Matt Whiteside	.15	.07
116	Roberto Alomar	.60	.25
117	Brad Cornett	.15	.07
118	Carlos Delgado	.30	.14
119	Alex Gonzalez	.30	.14
120	Darren Hall	.15	.07
121	Pat Hentgen	.30	.14
122	Paul Molitor	.60	.25
123	Ed Sprague	.15	.07
124	Devon White	.30	.14
125	Tom Glavine	.60	.25
126	David Justice	.60	.25
127	Roberto Kelly	.15	.07
128	Mark Lemke	.15	.07
129	Greg Maddux	2.00	.90
130	Greg McMichael	.15	.07
131	Kent Mercker	.15	.07
132	Charlie O'Brien	.15	.07
133	John Smoltz	.30	.14
134	Willie Banks	.15	.07
135	Steve Buechele	.15	.07
136	Kevin Foster	.15	.07
137	Glenallen Hill	.15	.07
138	Rey Sanchez	.15	.07
139	Sammy Sosa	1.50	.70
140	Steve Trachsel	.15	.07
141	Rick Wilkins	.15	.07
142	Jeff Brantley	.15	.07
143	Hector Carrasco	.15	.07
144	Kevin Jarvis	.15	.07
145	Barry Larkin	.40	.18
146	Chuck McElroy	.15	.07
147	Jose Rijo	.15	.07
148	Johnny Ruffin	.15	.07
149	Deion Sanders	.30	.14
150	Eddie Taubensee	.15	.07
151	Dante Bichette	.30	.14
152	Ellis Burks	.30	.14
153	Joe Girardi	.15	.07
154	Charlie Hayes	.15	.07
155	Mike Kingery	.15	.07
156	Steve Reed	.15	.07
157	Kevin Ritz	.15	.07
158	Bruce Ruffin	.15	.07
159	Eric Young	.15	.07
160	Kurt Abbott	.15	.07
161	Chuck Carr	.15	.07
162	Chris Hammond	.15	.07
163	Bryan Harvey	.15	.07
164	Terry Mathews	.15	.07
165	Yorkis Perez	.15	.07
166	Pat Rapp	.15	.07
167	Gary Sheffield	.40	.18
168	Dave Weathers	.15	.07
169	Jeff Bagwell	1.00	.45
170	Ken Caminiti	.40	.18
171	Doug Drabek	.15	.07
172	Steve Finley	.30	.14
173	John Hudek	.15	.07
174	Todd Jones	.15	.07
175	James Mouton	.15	.07
176	Shane Reynolds	.30	.14
177	Scott Servais	.15	.07
178	Tom Candiotti	.15	.07
179	Omar Daal	.15	.07
180	Darren Dreifort	.30	.14
181	Eric Karros	.30	.14
182	Ramon J.Martinez	.30	.14
183	Raul Mondesi	.40	.18
184	Henry Rodriguez	.30	.14
185	Todd Worrell	.15	.07
186	Moises Alou	.40	.18
187	Sean Berry	.15	.07
188	Wil Cordero	.15	.07
189	Jeff Fassero	.15	.07
190	Darrin Fletcher	.15	.07
191	Butch Henry	.15	.07
192	Ken Hill	.15	.07
193	Mel Rojas	.15	.07
194	John Wetteland	.30	.14
195	Bobby Bonilla	.30	.14
196	Rico Brogna	.15	.07
197	Bobby Jones	.15	.07
198	Jeff Kent	.30	.14
199	Josias Manzanillo	.15	.07
200	Kelly Stinnett	.15	.07
201	Ryan Thompson	.15	.07
202	Jose Vizcaino	.15	.07
203	Lenny Dykstra	.30	.14
204	Jim Eisenreich	.15	.07
205	Dave Hollins	.15	.07
206	Mike Lieberthal	.15	.07
207	Mickey Morandini	.15	.07
208	Bobby Munoz	.15	.07
209	Curt Schilling	.30	.14
210	Heathcliff Slocumb	.15	.07
211	David West	.40	.18
212	Dave Clark	.15	.07
213	Steve Cooke	.15	.07
214	Midre Cummings	.15	.07
215	Carlos Garcia	.15	.07
216	Jeff King	.15	.07
217	Jon Lieber	.15	.07
218	Orlando Merced	.15	.07
219	Don Slaught	.15	.07
220	Rick White	.15	.07
221	Rene Arocha	.15	.07
222	Bernard Gilkey	.15	.07
223	Brian Jordan	.30	.14
224	Tom Pagnozzi	.15	.07
225	Vicente Palacios	.15	.07
226	Geronimo Pena	.15	.07
227	Ozzie Smith	.75	.35
228	Allen Watson	.15	.07
229	Mark Whiten	.15	.07
230	Brad Ausmus	.15	.07
231	Derek Bell	.30	.14
232	Andy Benes	.30	.14
233	Tony Gwynn	1.50	.70
234	Joey Hamilton	.30	.14
235	Luis Lopez	.15	.07
236	Pedro A.Martinez	.15	.07
237	Scott Sanders	.15	.07
238	Eddie Williams	.15	.07
239	Rod Beck	.15	.07
240	Dave Burba	.15	.07
241	Darren Lewis	.15	.07
242	Kirt Manwaring	.15	.07
243	Mark Portugal	.15	.07
244	Darryl Strawberry	.30	.14
245	Robby Thompson	.15	.07
246	Wm.VanLandingham	.15	.07
247	Matt Williams	.30	.14
248	Checklist	.15	.07
249	Checklist	.15	.07
250	Checklist	.15	.07
251	Harold Baines	.30	.14
252	Bret Barberie	.15	.07
253	Armando Benitez	.15	.07
254	Mike Devereaux	.15	.07
255	Leo Gomez	.15	.07
256	Jamie Moyer	.15	.07
257	Arthur Rhodes	.15	.07
258	Cal Ripken	2.50	1.10
259	Luis Alicea	.15	.07
260	Jose Canseco	.60	.25
261	Scott Cooper	.15	.07
262	Andre Dawson	.40	.18
263	Mike Greenwell	.15	.07
264	Aaron Sele	.30	.14
265	Garret Anderson	.30	.14
266	Chad Curtis	.15	.07
267	Gary DiSarcina	.15	.07
268	Chuck Finley	.30	.14
269	Rex Hudler	.15	.07
270	Andrew Lorraine	.15	.07
271	Spike Owen	.15	.07
272	Lee Smith	.30	.14
273	Jason Bere	.15	.07
274	Ozzie Guillen	.15	.07
275	Norberto Martin	.15	.07
276	Scott Ruffcorn	.15	.07
277	Robin Ventura	.30	.14
278	Carlos Baerga	.30	.14
279	Jason Grimsley	.15	.07
280	Dennis Martinez	.30	.14
281	Charles Nagy	.30	.14
282	Paul Sorrento	.15	.07
283	Dave Winfield	.60	.25
284	John Doherty	.15	.07
285	Travis Fryman	.30	.14
286	Kirk Gibson	.30	.14
287	Lou Whitaker	.30	.14
288	Gary Gaetti	.30	.14
289	Tom Gordon	.15	.07
290	Mark Gubicza	.15	.07
291	Wally Joyner	.30	.14
292	Mike Macfarlane	.15	.07
293	Jeff Montgomery	.15	.07
294	Jeff Cirillo	.30	.14
295	Cal Eldred	.15	.07
296	Pat Listach	.15	.07
297	Jose Mercedes	.15	.07
298	Dave Nilsson	.15	.07
299	Duane Singleton	.15	.07
300	Greg Vaughn	.30	.14
301	Scott Erickson	.30	.14
302	Denny Hocking	.15	.07
303	Chuck Knoblauch	.60	.25
304	Pat Mahomes	.15	.07
305	Pedro Munoz	.15	.07
306	Erik Schullstrom	.15	.07
307	Jim Abbott	.30	.14
308	Tony Fernandez	.15	.07
309	Sterling Hitchcock	.30	.14
310	Jim Leyritz	.30	.14

❑ 311 Don Mattingly 1.00 .45
❑ 312 Jack McDowell .15 .07
❑ 313 Melido Perez .15 .07
❑ 314 Bernie Williams .60 .25
❑ 315 Scott Brosius .30 .14
❑ 316 Dennis Eckersley .30 .14
❑ 317 Brent Gates .15 .07
❑ 318 Rickey Henderson .60 .25
❑ 319 Steve Karsay .15 .07
❑ 320 Steve Ontiveros .15 .07
❑ 321 Bill Taylor .15 .07
❑ 322 Todd Van Poppel .15 .07
❑ 323 Bob Welch .15 .07
❑ 324 Bobby Ayala .15 .07
❑ 325 Mike Blowers .15 .07
❑ 326 Jay Buhner .30 .14
❑ 327 Felix Fermin .15 .07
❑ 328 Tino Martinez .60 .25
❑ 329 Marc Newfield .15 .07
❑ 330 Greg Pirkl .15 .07
❑ 331 Alex Rodriguez 2.50 1.10
❑ 332 Kevin Brown .40 .18
❑ 333 John Burkett .15 .07
❑ 334 Jeff Frye .15 .07
❑ 335 Kevin Gross .15 .07
❑ 336 Dean Palmer .30 .14
❑ 337 Joe Carter .30 .14
❑ 338 Shawn Green .30 .14
❑ 339 Juan Guzman .15 .07
❑ 340 Mike Huff .15 .07
❑ 341 Al Leiter .30 .14
❑ 342 John Olerud .30 .14
❑ 343 Dave Stewart .30 .14
❑ 344 Todd Stottlemyre .15 .07
❑ 345 Steve Avery .15 .07
❑ 346 Jeff Blauser .15 .07
❑ 347 Chipper Jones 1.50 .70
❑ 348 Mike Kelly .15 .07
❑ 349 Ryan Klesko .30 .14
❑ 350 Javier Lopez .30 .14
❑ 351 Fred McGriff .40 .18
❑ 352 Jose Oliva .15 .07
❑ 353 Terry Pendleton .15 .07
❑ 354 Mike Stanton .15 .07
❑ 355 Tony Tarasco .15 .07
❑ 356 Mark Wohlers .15 .07
❑ 357 Jim Bullinger .15 .07
❑ 358 Shawon Dunston .15 .07
❑ 359 Mark Grace .40 .18
❑ 360 Derrick May .15 .07
❑ 361 Randy Myers .15 .07
❑ 362 Karl Rhodes .15 .07
❑ 363 Bret Boone .30 .14
❑ 364 Brian Dorsett .15 .07
❑ 365 Ron Gant .15 .07
❑ 366 Brian R.Hunter .15 .07
❑ 367 Hal Morris .15 .07
❑ 368 Jack Morris .30 .14
❑ 369 John Roper .15 .07
❑ 370 Reggie Sanders .30 .14
❑ 371 Pete Schourek .15 .07
❑ 372 John Smiley .15 .07
❑ 373 Marvin Freeman .15 .07
❑ 374 Andres Galarraga .60 .25
❑ 375 Mike Munoz .15 .07
❑ 376 David Nied .15 .07
❑ 377 Walt Weiss .15 .07
❑ 378 Greg Colbrunn .15 .07
❑ 379 Jeff Conine .30 .14
❑ 380 Charles Johnson .30 .14
❑ 381 Kurt Miller .15 .07
❑ 382 Robb Nen .15 .07
❑ 383 Benito Santiago .15 .07
❑ 384 Craig Biggio .60 .25
❑ 385 Tony Eusebio .15 .07
❑ 386 Luis Gonzalez .15 .07
❑ 387 Brian L.Hunter .30 .14
❑ 388 Darryl Kile .30 .14
❑ 389 Orlando Miller .15 .07
❑ 390 Phil Plantier .15 .07
❑ 391 Greg Swindell .15 .07
❑ 392 Billy Ashley .15 .07
❑ 393 Pedro Astacio .15 .07
❑ 394 Brett Butler .30 .14
❑ 395 Delino DeShields .15 .07
❑ 396 Orel Hershiser .30 .14
❑ 397 Garey Ingram .15 .07
❑ 398 Chan Ho Park .75 .35
❑ 399 Mike Piazza 2.00 .90
❑ 400 Ismael Valdes .30 .14
❑ 401 Tim Wallach .15 .07
❑ 402 Cliff Floyd .30 .14
❑ 403 Marquis Grissom .30 .14
❑ 404 Mike Lansing .15 .07
❑ 405 Pedro J.Martinez .60 .25
❑ 406 Kirk Rueter .15 .07
❑ 407 Tim Scott .15 .07
❑ 408 Jeff Shaw .15 .07
❑ 409 Larry Walker .60 .25
❑ 410 Rondell White .30 .14
❑ 411 John Franco .30 .14
❑ 412 Todd Hundley .30 .14
❑ 413 Jason Jacome .15 .07
❑ 414 Joe Orsulak .15 .07
❑ 415 Bret Saberhagen .30 .14
❑ 416 David Segui .30 .14
❑ 417 Darren Daulton .30 .14
❑ 418 Mariano Duncan .15 .07
❑ 419 Tommy Greene .15 .07
❑ 420 Gregg Jefferies .15 .07
❑ 421 John Kruk .30 .14
❑ 422 Kevin Stocker .15 .07
❑ 423 Jay Bell .30 .14
❑ 424 Al Martin .15 .07
❑ 425 Denny Neagle .30 .14
❑ 426 Zane Smith .15 .07
❑ 427 Andy Van Slyke .30 .14
❑ 428 Paul Wagner .15 .07
❑ 429 Tom Henke .15 .07
❑ 430 Danny Jackson .15 .07
❑ 431 Ray Lankford .30 .14
❑ 432 John Mabry .15 .07
❑ 433 Bob Tewksbury .15 .07
❑ 434 Todd Zeile .15 .07
❑ 435 Andy Ashby .15 .07
❑ 436 Andujar Cedeno .15 .07
❑ 437 Donnie Elliott .15 .07
❑ 438 Bryce Florie .15 .07
❑ 439 Trevor Hoffman .30 .14
❑ 440 Melvin Nieves .15 .07
❑ 441 Bip Roberts .15 .07
❑ 442 Barry Bonds .75 .35
❑ 443 Royce Clayton .15 .07
❑ 444 Mike Jackson .15 .07
❑ 445 John Patterson .15 .07
❑ 446 J.R. Phillips .15 .07
❑ 447 Bill Swift .15 .07
❑ 448 Checklist .15 .07
❑ 449 Checklist .15 .07
❑ 450 Checklist .15 .07

1995 Ultra All-Rookies

	MINT	NRMT
COMPLETE SET (10)	5.00	2.20
COMMON CARD (1-10)	.25	.11

*GOLD MEDAL: 2X TO 5X BASIC CARDS
GM SER.2 STATED ODDS 1:50

❑ 1 Cliff Floyd .50 .23
❑ 2 Chris Gomez .25 .11
❑ 3 Rusty Greer 1.25 .55
❑ 4 Bob Hamelin .25 .11
❑ 5 Joey Hamilton .50 .23
❑ 6 John Hudek .25 .11
❑ 7 Ryan Klesko .50 .23
❑ 8 Raul Mondesi .75 .35
❑ 9 Manny Ramirez 1.25 .55
❑ 10 Steve Trachsel .25 .11

1995 Ultra All-Stars

	MINT	NRMT
COMPLETE SET (20)	20.00	9.00
COMMON CARD (1-20)	.50	.23

*GOLD MEDAL: 1.25X TO 3X BASIC CARDS
GM SER.2 STATED ODDS 1:40

❑ 1 Moises Alou .75 .35
❑ 2 Albert Belle 1.00 .45
❑ 3 Craig Biggio 1.00 .45
❑ 4 Wade Boggs 1.00 .45
❑ 5 Barry Bonds 1.00 .45
❑ 6 David Cone .75 .35
❑ 7 Ken Griffey Jr. 5.00 2.20
❑ 8 Tony Gwynn 2.00 .90
❑ 9 Chuck Knoblauch 1.00 .45
❑ 10 Barry Larkin .75 .35
❑ 11 Kenny Lofton 1.00 .45
❑ 12 Greg Maddux 3.00 1.35
❑ 13 Fred McGriff .75 .35
❑ 14 Paul O'Neill .50 .23
❑ 15 Mike Piazza 3.00 1.35
❑ 16 Kirby Puckett 1.00 .45
❑ 17 Cal Ripken 4.00 1.80
❑ 18 Ivan Rodriguez 1.00 .45
❑ 19 Frank Thomas 3.00 1.35
❑ 20 Matt Williams .50 .23

1995 Ultra Award Winners

	MINT	NRMT
COMPLETE SET (25)	20.00	9.00
COMMON CARD (1-25)	.25	.11

*GOLD MEDAL: 1.25X TO 3X BASIC CARDS
GM SER.1 STATED ODDS 1:40

❑ 1 Ivan Rodriguez 1.00 .45
❑ 2 Don Mattingly 1.50 .70
❑ 3 Roberto Alomar 1.00 .45
❑ 4 Wade Boggs 1.00 .45
❑ 5 Omar Vizquel .50 .23

		MINT	NRMT
❑ 6	Ken Griffey Jr.	5.00	2.20
❑ 7	Kenny Lofton	1.00	.45
❑ 8	Devon White	.50	.23
❑ 9	Mark Langston	.25	.11
❑ 10	Tom Pagnozzi	.25	.11
❑ 11	Jeff Bagwell	1.50	.70
❑ 12	Craig Biggio	1.00	.45
❑ 13	Matt Williams	.50	.23
❑ 14	Barry Larkin	.75	.35
❑ 15	Barry Bonds	1.00	.45
❑ 16	Marquis Grissom	.50	.23
❑ 17	Darren Lewis	.25	.11
❑ 18	Greg Maddux	3.00	1.35
❑ 19	Frank Thomas	3.00	1.35
❑ 20	Jeff Bagwell	1.50	.70
❑ 21	David Cone	.75	.35
❑ 22	Greg Maddux	3.00	1.35
❑ 23	Bob Hamelin	.25	.11
❑ 24	Raul Mondesi	.75	.35
❑ 25	Moises Alou	.75	.35

1995 Ultra Gold Medallion Rookies

	MINT	NRMT
COMPLETE SET (20)	12.00	5.50
COMMON CARD (M1-M20)	.25	.11

		MINT	NRMT
❑ M1	Manny Alexander	.25	.11
❑ M2	Edgardo Alfonzo	.30	.14
❑ M3	Jason Bates	.25	.11
❑ M4	Andres Berumen	.25	.11
❑ M5	Darren Bragg	.25	.11
❑ M6	Jamie Brewington	.25	.11
❑ M7	Jason Christiansen	.25	.11
❑ M8	Brad Clontz	.25	.11
❑ M9	Marty Cordova	.25	.11
❑ M10	Johnny Damon	.30	.14
❑ M11	Vaughn Eshelman	.25	.11
❑ M12	Chad Fonville	.25	.11
❑ M13	Curtis Goodwin	.25	.11
❑ M14	Tyler Green	.25	.11
❑ M15	Bob Higginson	3.00	1.35
❑ M16	Jason Isringhausen	.30	.14
❑ M17	Hideo Nomo	5.00	2.20
❑ M18	Jon Nunnally	.25	.11
❑ M19	Carlos Perez	.30	.14
❑ M20	Julian Tavarez	.25	.11

1995 Ultra Golden Prospects

	MINT	NRMT
COMPLETE SET (10)	12.00	5.50
COMMON CARD (1-10)	.50	.23

*GOLD MEDAL: 1X TO 2X BASIC CARDS
GM SER.1 STATED ODDS 1:80

		MINT	NRMT
❑ 1	James Baldwin	.75	.35
❑ 2	Alan Benes	.75	.35
❑ 3	Armando Benitez	.50	.23
❑ 4	Ray Durham	.75	.35
❑ 5	LaTroy Hawkins	.50	.23
❑ 6	Brian L.Hunter	.75	.35
❑ 7	Derek Jeter	5.00	2.20
❑ 8	Charles Johnson	.75	.35
❑ 9	Alex Rodriguez	6.00	2.70
❑ 10	Michael Tucker	.75	.35

1995 Ultra Hitting Machines

	MINT	NRMT
COMPLETE SET (10)	12.00	5.50
COMMON CARD (1-10)	.50	.23

*GOLD MEDAL: 1.25X TO 3X BASIC CARDS
GM SER.2 STATED ODDS 1:80 RETAIL

		MINT	NRMT
❑ 1	Jeff Bagwell	1.50	.70
❑ 2	Albert Belle	1.00	.45
❑ 3	Dante Bichette	.50	.23
❑ 4	Barry Bonds	1.00	.45
❑ 5	Jose Canseco	1.00	.45
❑ 6	Ken Griffey Jr.	5.00	2.20
❑ 7	Tony Gwynn	2.00	.90
❑ 8	Fred McGriff	.75	.35
❑ 9	Mike Piazza	3.00	1.35
❑ 10	Frank Thomas	3.00	1.35

1995 Ultra Home Run Kings

	MINT	NRMT
COMPLETE SET (10)	30.00	13.50
COMMON CARD (1-10)	1.00	.45

*GOLD MEDAL: 3X TO 8X BASIC CARDS
GM SER.1 STATED ODDS 1:80 RETAIL

		MINT	NRMT
❑ 1	Ken Griffey Jr.	12.00	5.50
❑ 2	Frank Thomas	8.00	3.60
❑ 3	Albert Belle	2.50	1.10
❑ 4	Jose Canseco	2.50	1.10
❑ 5	Cecil Fielder	1.00	.45
❑ 6	Matt Williams	1.00	.45
❑ 7	Jeff Bagwell	4.00	1.80
❑ 8	Barry Bonds	2.50	1.10
❑ 9	Fred McGriff	1.50	.70
❑ 10	Andres Galarraga	2.50	1.10

1995 Ultra League Leaders

	MINT	NRMT
COMPLETE SET (10)	6.00	2.70
COMMON CARD (1-10)	.25	.11

*GOLD MEDAL: 1.25X TO 3X BASIC CARDS
GM SER.1 STATED ODDS 1:30

		MINT	NRMT
❑ 1	Paul O'Neill	.25	.11
❑ 2	Kenny Lofton	.75	.35
❑ 3	Jimmy Key	.25	.11
❑ 4	Randy Johnson	.75	.35
❑ 5	Lee Smith	.25	.11
❑ 6	Tony Gwynn	2.00	.90
❑ 7	Craig Biggio	.75	.35
❑ 8	Greg Maddux	3.00	1.35
❑ 9	Andy Benes	.25	.11
❑ 10	John Franco	.25	.11

1995 Ultra On-Base Leaders

	MINT	NRMT
COMPLETE SET (10)	40.00	18.00
COMMON CARD (1-10)	2.00	.90

*GOLD MEDAL: 5X TO 12X BASIC CARDS
GM SER.2 STATED ODDS 1:80 JUMBO

		MINT	NRMT
❑ 1	Jeff Bagwell	6.00	2.70
❑ 2	Albert Belle	4.00	1.80
❑ 3	Craig Biggio	4.00	1.80
❑ 4	Wade Boggs	4.00	1.80
❑ 5	Barry Bonds	4.00	1.80
❑ 6	Will Clark	4.00	1.80
❑ 7	Tony Gwynn	10.00	4.50
❑ 8	David Justice	4.00	1.80
❑ 9	Paul O'Neill	2.00	.90
❑ 10	Frank Thomas	12.00	5.50

1995 Ultra Power Plus

	MINT	NRMT
COMPLETE SET (6)	50.00	22.00
COMMON CARD (1-6)	3.00	1.35

*GOLD MEDAL: 5X TO 12X BASIC CARDS
GM SER.1 STATED ODDS 1:370

	MINT	NRMT
❑ 1 Albert Belle	4.00	1.80
❑ 2 Ken Griffey Jr.	20.00	9.00
❑ 3 Frank Thomas	12.00	5.50
❑ 4 Jeff Bagwell	6.00	2.70
❑ 5 Barry Bonds	4.00	1.80
❑ 6 Matt Williams	3.00	1.35

1995 Ultra RBI Kings

	MINT	NRMT
COMPLETE SET (10)	50.00	22.00
COMMON CARD (1-10)	1.00	.45

*GOLD MEDAL: 5X TO 12X BASIC CARDS
GM SER.1 STATED ODDS 1:110 JUMBO

	MINT	NRMT
❑ 1 Kirby Puckett	4.00	1.80
❑ 2 Joe Carter	2.00	.90
❑ 3 Albert Belle	4.00	1.80
❑ 4 Frank Thomas	12.00	5.50
❑ 5 Julio Franco	1.00	.45
❑ 6 Jeff Bagwell	6.00	2.70
❑ 7 Matt Williams	2.00	.90
❑ 8 Dante Bichette	2.00	.90
❑ 9 Fred McGriff	2.50	1.10
❑ 10 Mike Piazza	12.00	5.50

1995 Ultra Rising Stars

	MINT	NRMT
COMPLETE SET (9)	60.00	27.00
COMMON CARD (1-9)	3.00	1.35

*GOLD MEDAL: .75X TO 2X BASIC RISING STARS
GM SER.2 STATED ODDS 1:370

	MINT	NRMT
❑ 1 Moises Alou	3.00	1.35
❑ 2 Jeff Bagwell	10.00	4.50
❑ 3 Albert Belle	8.00	3.60
❑ 4 Juan Gonzalez	15.00	6.75
❑ 5 Chuck Knoblauch	6.00	2.70
❑ 6 Kenny Lofton	6.00	2.70
❑ 7 Raul Mondesi	4.00	1.80
❑ 8 Mike Piazza	20.00	9.00
❑ 9 Frank Thomas	20.00	9.00

1995 Ultra Second Year Standouts

	MINT	NRMT
COMPLETE SET (15)	10.00	4.50
COMMON CARD (1-15)	.50	.23

*GOLD MEDAL: 3X TO 8X BASIC CARDS
GM SER.1 STATED ODDS 1:60

	MINT	NRMT
❑ 1 Cliff Floyd	1.00	.45
❑ 2 Chris Gomez	.50	.23
❑ 3 Rusty Greer	2.00	.90
❑ 4 Darren Hall	.50	.23
❑ 5 Bob Hamelin	.50	.23
❑ 6 Joey Hamilton	1.00	.45
❑ 7 Jeffrey Hammonds	1.00	.45
❑ 8 John Hudek	.50	.23
❑ 9 Ryan Klesko	1.00	.45
❑ 10 Raul Mondesi	1.50	.70
❑ 11 Manny Ramirez	2.00	.90
❑ 12 Bill Risley	.50	.23
❑ 13 Steve Trachsel	.50	.23
❑ 14 W.VanLandingham	.50	.23
❑ 15 Rondell White	1.00	.45

1995 Ultra Strikeout Kings

	MINT	NRMT
COMPLETE SET (6)	5.00	2.20
COMMON CARD (1-6)	.25	.11

*GOLD MEDAL: 1X TO 2X BASIC CARDS
GM SER.2 STATED ODDS 1:50

	MINT	NRMT
❑ 1 Andy Benes	.75	.35
❑ 2 Roger Clemens	2.00	.90
❑ 3 Randy Johnson	1.00	.45
❑ 4 Greg Maddux	3.00	1.35
❑ 5 Pedro Martinez	1.00	.45
❑ 6 Jose Rijo	.25	.11

1996 Ultra

	MINT	NRMT
COMPLETE SET (600)	60.00	27.00
COMPLETE SERIES 1 (300)	30.00	13.50
COMPLETE SERIES 2 (300)	30.00	13.50
COMMON CARD (1-600)	.15	.07

	MINT	NRMT
❑ 1 Manny Alexander	.15	.07
❑ 2 Brady Anderson	.30	.14
❑ 3 Bobby Bonilla	.30	.14
❑ 4 Scott Erickson	.30	.14
❑ 5 Curtis Goodwin	.15	.07
❑ 6 Chris Hoiles	.15	.07
❑ 7 Doug Jones	.15	.07
❑ 8 Jeff Manto	.15	.07
❑ 9 Mike Mussina	.60	.25
❑ 10 Rafael Palmeiro	.40	.18
❑ 11 Cal Ripken	2.50	1.10
❑ 12 Rick Aguilera	.15	.07
❑ 13 Luis Alicea	.15	.07
❑ 14 Stan Belinda	.15	.07
❑ 15 Jose Canseco	.60	.25
❑ 16 Roger Clemens	1.25	.55
❑ 17 Mike Greenwell	.15	.07
❑ 18 Mike Macfarlane	.15	.07
❑ 19 Tim Naehring	.15	.07
❑ 20 Troy O'Leary	.30	.14
❑ 21 John Valentin	.30	.14
❑ 22 Mo Vaughn	.75	.35
❑ 23 Tim Wakefield	.30	.14
❑ 24 Brian Anderson	.30	.14
❑ 25 Garret Anderson	.30	.14
❑ 26 Chili Davis	.30	.14
❑ 27 Gary DiSarcina	.15	.07
❑ 28 Jim Edmonds	.40	.18
❑ 29 Jorge Fabregas	.15	.07
❑ 30 Chuck Finley	.30	.14
❑ 31 Mark Langston	.15	.07
❑ 32 Troy Percival	.30	.14
❑ 33 Tim Salmon	.60	.25
❑ 34 Lee Smith	.30	.14
❑ 35 Wilson Alvarez	.30	.14
❑ 36 Ray Durham	.30	.14
❑ 37 Alex Fernandez	.15	.07
❑ 38 Ozzie Guillen	.15	.07
❑ 39 Roberto Hernandez	.15	.07
❑ 40 Lance Johnson	.15	.07
❑ 41 Ron Karkovice	.15	.07
❑ 42 Lyle Mouton	.15	.07
❑ 43 Tim Raines	.30	.14
❑ 44 Frank Thomas	2.00	.90
❑ 45 Carlos Baerga	.30	.14
❑ 46 Albert Belle	.75	.35
❑ 47 Orel Hershiser	.30	.14
❑ 48 Kenny Lofton	.60	.25
❑ 49 Dennis Martinez	.30	.14
❑ 50 Jose Mesa	.15	.07

❑ 51 Eddie Murray .60 .25
❑ 52 Chad Ogea .15 .07
❑ 53 Manny Ramirez .60 .25
❑ 54 Jim Thome .60 .25
❑ 55 Omar Vizquel .30 .14
❑ 56 Dave Winfield .60 .25
❑ 57 Chad Curtis .15 .07
❑ 58 Cecil Fielder .30 .14
❑ 59 John Flaherty .15 .07
❑ 60 Travis Fryman .30 .14
❑ 61 Chris Gomez .15 .07
❑ 62 Bob Higginson .60 .25
❑ 63 Felipe Lira .15 .07
❑ 64 Brian Maxcy .15 .07
❑ 65 Alan Trammell .40 .18
❑ 66 Lou Whitaker .30 .14
❑ 67 Kevin Appier .30 .14
❑ 68 Gary Gaetti .30 .14
❑ 69 Tom Goodwin .15 .07
❑ 70 Tom Gordon .15 .07
❑ 71 Jason Jacome .15 .07
❑ 72 Wally Joyner .30 .14
❑ 73 Brent Mayne .15 .07
❑ 74 Jeff Montgomery .15 .07
❑ 75 Jon Nunnally .15 .07
❑ 76 Joe Vitiello .15 .07
❑ 77 Ricky Bones .15 .07
❑ 78 Jeff Cirillo .30 .14
❑ 79 Mike Fetters .15 .07
❑ 80 Darryl Hamilton .15 .07
❑ 81 David Hulse .15 .07
❑ 82 Dave Nilsson .15 .07
❑ 83 Kevin Seitzer .15 .07
❑ 84 Steve Sparks .15 .07
❑ 85 B.J. Surhoff .30 .14
❑ 86 Jose Valentin .15 .07
❑ 87 Greg Vaughn .30 .14
❑ 88 Marty Cordova .15 .07
❑ 89 Chuck Knoblauch .60 .25
❑ 90 Pat Meares .15 .07
❑ 91 Pedro Munoz .15 .07
❑ 92 Kirby Puckett 1.00 .45
❑ 93 Brad Radke .30 .14
❑ 94 Scott Stahoviak .15 .07
❑ 95 Dave Stevens .15 .07
❑ 96 Mike Trombley .15 .07
❑ 97 Matt Walbeck .15 .07
❑ 98 Wade Boggs .60 .25
❑ 99 Russ Davis .30 .14
❑ 100 Jim Leyritz .15 .07
❑ 101 Don Mattingly 1.00 .45
❑ 102 Jack McDowell .15 .07
❑ 103 Paul O'Neill .30 .14
❑ 104 Andy Pettitte .40 .18
❑ 105 Mariano Rivera .30 .14
❑ 106 Ruben Sierra .15 .07
❑ 107 Darryl Strawberry .30 .14
❑ 108 John Wetteland .30 .14
❑ 109 Bernie Williams .60 .25
❑ 110 Geronimo Berroa .15 .07
❑ 111 Scott Brosius .30 .14
❑ 112 Dennis Eckersley .30 .14
❑ 113 Brent Gates .15 .07
❑ 114 Rickey Henderson .60 .25
❑ 115 Mark McGwire 3.00 1.35
❑ 116 Ariel Prieto .15 .07
❑ 117 Terry Steinbach .30 .14
❑ 118 Todd Stottlemyre .15 .07
❑ 119 Todd Van Poppel .15 .07
❑ 120 Steve Wojciechowski .15 .07
❑ 121 Rich Amaral .15 .07
❑ 122 Bobby Ayala .15 .07
❑ 123 Mike Blowers .15 .07
❑ 124 Chris Bosio .15 .07
❑ 125 Joey Cora .30 .14
❑ 126 Ken Griffey Jr. 3.00 1.35
❑ 127 Randy Johnson .60 .25
❑ 128 Edgar Martinez .30 .14
❑ 129 Tino Martinez .60 .25
❑ 130 Alex Rodriguez 2.00 .90
❑ 131 Dan Wilson .15 .07
❑ 132 Will Clark .60 .25
❑ 133 Jeff Frye .15 .07
❑ 134 Benji Gil .15 .07
❑ 135 Juan Gonzalez 1.50 .70
❑ 136 Rusty Greer .40 .18
❑ 137 Mark McLemore .15 .07
❑ 138 Roger Pavlik .15 .07
❑ 139 Ivan Rodriguez .75 .35
❑ 140 Kenny Rogers .15 .07
❑ 141 Mickey Tettleton .15 .07
❑ 142 Roberto Alomar .60 .25
❑ 143 Joe Carter .30 .14
❑ 144 Tony Castillo .15 .07
❑ 145 Alex Gonzalez .15 .07
❑ 146 Shawn Green .30 .14
❑ 147 Pat Hentgen .30 .14
❑ 148 Sandy Martinez .15 .07
❑ 149 Paul Molitor .60 .25
❑ 150 John Olerud .30 .14
❑ 151 Ed Sprague .15 .07
❑ 152 Jeff Blauser .15 .07
❑ 153 Brad Clontz .15 .07
❑ 154 Tom Glavine .60 .25
❑ 155 Marquis Grissom .30 .14
❑ 156 Chipper Jones 1.50 .70
❑ 157 David Justice .60 .25
❑ 158 Ryan Klesko .30 .14
❑ 159 Javier Lopez .30 .14
❑ 160 Greg Maddux 2.00 .90
❑ 161 John Smoltz .30 .14
❑ 162 Mark Wohlers .15 .07
❑ 163 Jim Bullinger .15 .07
❑ 164 Frank Castillo .15 .07
❑ 165 Shawon Dunston .15 .07
❑ 166 Kevin Foster .15 .07
❑ 167 Luis Gonzalez .15 .07
❑ 168 Mark Grace .40 .18
❑ 169 Rey Sanchez .15 .07
❑ 170 Scott Servais .15 .07
❑ 171 Sammy Sosa 1.50 .70
❑ 172 Ozzie Timmons .15 .07
❑ 173 Steve Trachsel .15 .07
❑ 174 Bret Boone .30 .14
❑ 175 Jeff Branson .15 .07
❑ 176 Jeff Brantley .15 .07
❑ 177 Dave Burba .15 .07
❑ 178 Ron Gant .15 .07
❑ 179 Barry Larkin .40 .18
❑ 180 Darren Lewis .15 .07
❑ 181 Mark Portugal .15 .07
❑ 182 Reggie Sanders .30 .14
❑ 183 Pete Schourek .15 .07
❑ 184 John Smiley .15 .07
❑ 185 Jason Bates .15 .07
❑ 186 Dante Bichette .30 .14
❑ 187 Ellis Burks .30 .14
❑ 188 Vinny Castilla .40 .18
❑ 189 Andres Galarraga .60 .25
❑ 190 Darren Holmes .15 .07
❑ 191 Armando Reynoso .15 .07
❑ 192 Kevin Ritz .15 .07
❑ 193 Bill Swift .15 .07
❑ 194 Larry Walker .60 .25
❑ 195 Kurt Abbott .15 .07
❑ 196 John Burkett .15 .07
❑ 197 Greg Colbrunn .15 .07
❑ 198 Jeff Conine .30 .14
❑ 199 Andre Dawson .40 .18
❑ 200 Chris Hammond .15 .07
❑ 201 Charles Johnson .30 .14
❑ 202 Robb Nen .15 .07
❑ 203 Terry Pendleton .15 .07
❑ 204 Quilvio Veras .15 .07
❑ 205 Jeff Bagwell 1.00 .45
❑ 206 Derek Bell .30 .14
❑ 207 Doug Drabek .15 .07
❑ 208 Tony Eusebio .15 .07
❑ 209 Mike Hampton .15 .07
❑ 210 Brian L. Hunter .30 .14
❑ 211 Todd Jones .15 .07
❑ 212 Orlando Miller .15 .07
❑ 213 James Mouton .15 .07
❑ 214 Shane Reynolds .30 .14
❑ 215 Dave Veres .15 .07
❑ 216 Billy Ashley .15 .07
❑ 217 Brett Butler .30 .14
❑ 218 Chad Fonville .15 .07
❑ 219 Todd Hollandsworth .15 .07
❑ 220 Eric Karros .30 .14
❑ 221 Ramon Martinez .30 .14
❑ 222 Raul Mondesi .40 .18
❑ 223 Hideo Nomo 1.00 .45
❑ 224 Mike Piazza 2.00 .90
❑ 225 Kevin Tapani .15 .07
❑ 226 Ismael Valdes .30 .14
❑ 227 Todd Worrell .15 .07
❑ 228 Moises Alou .40 .18
❑ 229 Wil Cordero .15 .07
❑ 230 Jeff Fassero .15 .07
❑ 231 Darrin Fletcher .15 .07
❑ 232 Mike Lansing .15 .07
❑ 233 Pedro J.Martinez .60 .25
❑ 234 Carlos Perez .30 .14
❑ 235 Mel Rojas .15 .07
❑ 236 David Segui .30 .14
❑ 237 Tony Tarasco .15 .07
❑ 238 Rondell White .30 .14
❑ 239 Edgardo Alfonzo .30 .14
❑ 240 Rico Brogna .15 .07
❑ 241 Carl Everett .15 .07
❑ 242 Todd Hundley .30 .14
❑ 243 Butch Huskey .15 .07
❑ 244 Jason Isringhausen .15 .07
❑ 245 Bobby Jones .15 .07
❑ 246 Jeff Kent .30 .14
❑ 247 Bill Pulsipher .15 .07
❑ 248 Jose Vizcaino .15 .07
❑ 249 Ricky Bottalico .30 .14
❑ 250 Darren Daulton .30 .14
❑ 251 Jim Eisenreich .15 .07
❑ 252 Tyler Green .15 .07
❑ 253 Charlie Hayes .15 .07
❑ 254 Gregg Jefferies .15 .07
❑ 255 Tony Longmire .15 .07
❑ 256 Michael Mimbs .15 .07
❑ 257 Mickey Morandini .15 .07
❑ 258 Paul Quantrill .15 .07
❑ 259 Heathcliff Slocumb .15 .07
❑ 260 Jay Bell .30 .14
❑ 261 Jacob Brumfield .15 .07
❑ 262 Angelo Encarnacion .15 .07
❑ 263 John Ericks .15 .07
❑ 264 Mark Johnson .15 .07
❑ 265 Esteban Loaiza .15 .07
❑ 266 Al Martin .15 .07
❑ 267 Orlando Merced .15 .07
❑ 268 Dan Miceli .15 .07
❑ 269 Denny Neagle .30 .14
❑ 270 Brian Barber .15 .07
❑ 271 Scott Cooper .15 .07
❑ 272 Tripp Cromer .15 .07
❑ 273 Bernard Gilkey .15 .07
❑ 274 Tom Henke .15 .07
❑ 275 Brian Jordan .30 .14
❑ 276 John Mabry .15 .07
❑ 277 Tom Pagnozzi .15 .07
❑ 278 Mark Petkovsek .15 .07
❑ 279 Ozzie Smith .75 .35
❑ 280 Andy Ashby .15 .07
❑ 281 Brad Ausmus .15 .07
❑ 282 Ken Caminiti .40 .18
❑ 283 Glenn Dishman .15 .07
❑ 284 Tony Gwynn 1.50 .70
❑ 285 Joey Hamilton .30 .14
❑ 286 Trevor Hoffman .30 .14
❑ 287 Phil Plantier .15 .07
❑ 288 Jody Reed .15 .07
❑ 289 Eddie Williams .15 .07
❑ 290 Barry Bonds .75 .35
❑ 291 Jamie Brewington .15 .07
❑ 292 Mark Carreon .15 .07
❑ 293 Royce Clayton .15 .07
❑ 294 Glenallen Hill .15 .07
❑ 295 Mark Leiter .15 .07
❑ 296 Kirt Manwaring .15 .07
❑ 297 J.R. Phillips .15 .07
❑ 298 Deion Sanders .30 .14
❑ 299 Wm. VanLandingham .15 .07
❑ 300 Matt Williams .30 .14
❑ 301 Roberto Alomar .60 .25
❑ 302 Armando Benitez .15 .07
❑ 303 Mike Devereaux .15 .07
❑ 304 Jeffrey Hammonds .30 .14
❑ 305 Jimmy Haynes .15 .07

❑ 306	Scott McClain	.15	.07
❑ 307	Kent Mercker	.15	.07
❑ 308	Randy Myers	.15	.07
❑ 309	B.J. Surhoff	.30	.14
❑ 310	Tony Tarasco	.15	.07
❑ 311	David Wells	.40	.18
❑ 312	Wil Cordero	.15	.07
❑ 313	Alex Delgado	.15	.07
❑ 314	Tom Gordon	.15	.07
❑ 315	Dwayne Hosey	.15	.07
❑ 316	Jose Malave	.15	.07
❑ 317	Kevin Mitchell	.15	.07
❑ 318	Jamie Moyer	.15	.07
❑ 319	Aaron Sele	.30	.14
❑ 320	Heathcliff Slocumb	.15	.07
❑ 321	Mike Stanley	.15	.07
❑ 322	Jeff Suppan	.15	.07
❑ 323	Jim Abbott	.30	.14
❑ 324	George Arias	.15	.07
❑ 325	Todd Greene	.30	.14
❑ 326	Bryan Harvey	.15	.07
❑ 327	J.T. Snow	.30	.14
❑ 328	Randy Velarde	.15	.07
❑ 329	Tim Wallach	.15	.07
❑ 330	Harold Baines	.30	.14
❑ 331	Jason Bere	.15	.07
❑ 332	Darren Lewis	.15	.07
❑ 333	Norberto Martin	.15	.07
❑ 334	Tony Phillips	.15	.07
❑ 335	Bill Simas	.15	.07
❑ 336	Chris Snopek	.15	.07
❑ 337	Kevin Tapani	.15	.07
❑ 338	Danny Tartabull	.15	.07
❑ 339	Robin Ventura	.30	.14
❑ 340	Sandy Alomar Jr.	.30	.14
❑ 341	Julio Franco	.15	.07
❑ 342	Jack McDowell	.15	.07
❑ 343	Charles Nagy	.30	.14
❑ 344	Julian Tavarez	.15	.07
❑ 345	Kimera Bartee	.15	.07
❑ 346	Greg Keagle	.15	.07
❑ 347	Mark Lewis	.15	.07
❑ 348	Jose Lima	.15	.07
❑ 349	Melvin Nieves	.15	.07
❑ 350	Mark Parent	.15	.07
❑ 351	Eddie Williams	.15	.07
❑ 352	Johnny Damon	.30	.14
❑ 353	Sal Fasano	.15	.07
❑ 354	Mark Gubicza	.15	.07
❑ 355	Bob Hamelin	.15	.07
❑ 356	Chris Haney	.15	.07
❑ 357	Keith Lockhart	.15	.07
❑ 358	Mike Macfarlane	.15	.07
❑ 359	Jose Offerman	.15	.07
❑ 360	Bip Roberts	.15	.07
❑ 361	Michael Tucker	.30	.14
❑ 362	Chuck Carr	.15	.07
❑ 363	Bobby Hughes	.15	.07
❑ 364	John Jaha	.15	.07
❑ 365	Mark Loretta	.15	.07
❑ 366	Mike Matheny	.15	.07
❑ 367	Ben McDonald	.15	.07
❑ 368	Matt Mieske	.15	.07
❑ 369	Angel Miranda	.15	.07
❑ 370	Fernando Vina	.15	.07
❑ 371	Rick Aguilera	.15	.07
❑ 372	Rich Becker	.15	.07
❑ 373	LaTroy Hawkins	.15	.07
❑ 374	Dave Hollins	.15	.07
❑ 375	Roberto Kelly	.15	.07
❑ 376	Matt Lawton	.60	.25
❑ 377	Paul Molitor	.60	.25
❑ 378	Dan Naulty	.15	.07
❑ 379	Rich Robertson	.15	.07
❑ 380	Frank Rodriguez	.15	.07
❑ 381	David Cone	.40	.18
❑ 382	Mariano Duncan	.15	.07
❑ 383	Andy Fox	.15	.07
❑ 384	Joe Girardi	.15	.07
❑ 385	Dwight Gooden	.30	.14
❑ 386	Derek Jeter	2.00	.90
❑ 387	Pat Kelly	.15	.07
❑ 388	Jimmy Key	.30	.14
❑ 389	Matt Luke	.15	.07
❑ 390	Tino Martinez	.60	.25
❑ 391	Jeff Nelson	.15	.07
❑ 392	Melido Perez	.15	.07
❑ 393	Tim Raines	.30	.14
❑ 394	Ruben Rivera	.30	.14
❑ 395	Kenny Rogers	.15	.07
❑ 396	Tony Batista	.15	.07
❑ 397	Allen Battle	.15	.07
❑ 398	Mike Bordick	.15	.07
❑ 399	Steve Cox	.15	.07
❑ 400	Jason Giambi	.30	.14
❑ 401	Doug Johns	.15	.07
❑ 402	Pedro Munoz	.15	.07
❑ 403	Phil Plantier	.15	.07
❑ 404	Scott Spiezio	.15	.07
❑ 405	George Williams	.15	.07
❑ 406	Ernie Young	.15	.07
❑ 407	Darren Bragg	.15	.07
❑ 408	Jay Buhner	.30	.14
❑ 409	Norm Charlton	.15	.07
❑ 410	Russ Davis	.30	.14
❑ 411	Sterling Hitchcock	.30	.14
❑ 412	Edwin Hurtado	.15	.07
❑ 413	Raul Ibanez	.15	.07
❑ 414	Mike Jackson	.15	.07
❑ 415	Luis Sojo	.15	.07
❑ 416	Paul Sorrento	.15	.07
❑ 417	Bob Wolcott	.15	.07
❑ 418	Damon Buford	.15	.07
❑ 419	Kevin Gross	.15	.07
❑ 420	Darryl Hamilton UER	.15	.07
❑ 421	Mike Henneman	.15	.07
❑ 422	Ken Hill	.15	.07
❑ 423	Dean Palmer	.30	.14
❑ 424	Bobby Witt	.15	.07
❑ 425	Tilson Brito	.15	.07
❑ 426	Giovanni Carrara	.15	.07
❑ 427	Domingo Cedeno	.15	.07
❑ 428	Felipe Crespo	.15	.07
❑ 429	Carlos Delgado	.30	.14
❑ 430	Juan Guzman	.15	.07
❑ 431	Erik Hanson	.15	.07
❑ 432	Marty Janzen	.15	.07
❑ 433	Otis Nixon	.15	.07
❑ 434	Robert Perez	.15	.07
❑ 435	Paul Quantrill	.15	.07
❑ 436	Bill Risley	.15	.07
❑ 437	Steve Avery	.15	.07
❑ 438	Jermaine Dye	.15	.07
❑ 439	Mark Lemke	.15	.07
❑ 440	Marty Malloy	.30	.14
❑ 441	Fred McGriff	.40	.18
❑ 442	Greg McMichael	.15	.07
❑ 443	Wonderful Monds	.15	.07
❑ 444	Eddie Perez	.15	.07
❑ 445	Jason Schmidt	.15	.07
❑ 446	Terrell Wade	.15	.07
❑ 447	Terry Adams	.15	.07
❑ 448	Scott Bullett	.15	.07
❑ 449	Robin Jennings	.15	.07
❑ 450	Doug Jones	.15	.07
❑ 451	Brooks Kieschnick	.15	.07
❑ 452	Dave Magadan	.15	.07
❑ 453	Jason Maxwell	.15	.07
❑ 454	Brian McRae	.15	.07
❑ 455	Rodney Myers	.15	.07
❑ 456	Jaime Navarro	.15	.07
❑ 457	Ryne Sandberg	.60	.25
❑ 458	Vince Coleman	.15	.07
❑ 459	Eric Davis	.30	.14
❑ 460	Steve Gibralter	.15	.07
❑ 461	Thomas Howard	.15	.07
❑ 462	Mike Kelly	.15	.07
❑ 463	Hal Morris	.15	.07
❑ 464	Eric Owens	.15	.07
❑ 465	Jose Rijo	.15	.07
❑ 466	Chris Sabo	.15	.07
❑ 467	Eddie Taubensee	.15	.07
❑ 468	Trenidad Hubbard	.15	.07
❑ 469	Curt Leskanic	.15	.07
❑ 470	Quinton McCracken	.30	.14
❑ 471	Jayhawk Owens	.15	.07
❑ 472	Steve Reed	.15	.07
❑ 473	Bryan Rekar	.15	.07
❑ 474	Bruce Ruffin	.15	.07
❑ 475	Bret Saberhagen	.30	.14
❑ 476	Walt Weiss	.15	.07
❑ 477	Eric Young	.15	.07
❑ 478	Kevin Brown	.60	.25
❑ 479	Al Leiter	.30	.14
❑ 480	Pat Rapp	.15	.07
❑ 481	Gary Sheffield	.40	.18
❑ 482	Devon White	.30	.14
❑ 483	Bob Abreu	.30	.14
❑ 484	Sean Berry	.15	.07
❑ 485	Craig Biggio	.60	.25
❑ 486	Jim Dougherty	.15	.07
❑ 487	Richard Hidalgo	.30	.14
❑ 488	Darryl Kile	.30	.14
❑ 489	Derrick May	.15	.07
❑ 490	Greg Swindell	.15	.07
❑ 491	Rick Wilkins	.15	.07
❑ 492	Mike Blowers	.15	.07
❑ 493	Tom Candiotti	.15	.07
❑ 494	Roger Cedeno	.15	.07
❑ 495	Delino DeShields	.15	.07
❑ 496	Greg Gagne	.15	.07
❑ 497	Karim Garcia	.30	.14
❑ 498	Wilton Guerrero	.50	.23
❑ 499	Chan Ho Park	.60	.25
❑ 500	Isreal Alcantara	.15	.07
❑ 501	Shane Andrews	.15	.07
❑ 502	Yamil Benitez	.15	.07
❑ 503	Cliff Floyd	.30	.14
❑ 504	Mark Grudzielanek	.30	.14
❑ 505	Ryan McGuire	.15	.07
❑ 506	Sherman Obando	.15	.07
❑ 507	Jose Paniagua	.15	.07
❑ 508	Henry Rodriguez	.30	.14
❑ 509	Kirk Rueter	.15	.07
❑ 510	Juan Acevedo	.15	.07
❑ 511	John Franco	.30	.14
❑ 512	Bernard Gilkey	.15	.07
❑ 513	Lance Johnson	.15	.07
❑ 514	Rey Ordonez	.30	.14
❑ 515	Robert Person	.15	.07
❑ 516	Paul Wilson	.15	.07
❑ 517	Toby Borland	.15	.07
❑ 518	David Doster	.15	.07
❑ 519	Lenny Dykstra	.30	.14
❑ 520	Sid Fernandez	.15	.07
❑ 521	Mike Grace	.15	.07
❑ 522	Rich Hunter	.15	.07
❑ 523	Benito Santiago	.15	.07
❑ 524	Gene Schall	.15	.07
❑ 525	Curt Schilling	.30	.14
❑ 526	Kevin Sefcik	.15	.07
❑ 527	Lee Tinsley	.15	.07
❑ 528	David West	.15	.07
❑ 529	Mark Whiten	.15	.07
❑ 530	Todd Zeile	.15	.07
❑ 531	Carlos Garcia	.15	.07
❑ 532	Charlie Hayes	.15	.07
❑ 533	Jason Kendall	.60	.25
❑ 534	Jeff King	.15	.07
❑ 535	Mike Kingery	.15	.07
❑ 536	Nelson Liriano	.15	.07
❑ 537	Dan Plesac	.15	.07
❑ 538	Paul Wagner	.15	.07
❑ 539	Luis Alicea	.15	.07
❑ 540	David Bell	.15	.07
❑ 541	Alan Benes	.30	.14
❑ 542	Andy Benes	.30	.14
❑ 543	Mike Busby	.15	.07
❑ 544	Royce Clayton	.15	.07
❑ 545	Dennis Eckersley	.30	.14
❑ 546	Gary Gaetti	.30	.14
❑ 547	Ron Gant	.15	.07
❑ 548	Aaron Holbert	.15	.07
❑ 549	Ray Lankford	.30	.14
❑ 550	T.J. Mathews	.15	.07
❑ 551	Willie McGee	.30	.14
❑ 552	Miguel Mejia	.15	.07
❑ 553	Todd Stottlemyre	.15	.07
❑ 554	Sean Bergman	.15	.07
❑ 555	Willie Blair	.15	.07
❑ 556	Andujar Cedeno	.15	.07
❑ 557	Steve Finley	.30	.14
❑ 558	Rickey Henderson	.60	.25
❑ 559	Wally Joyner	.30	.14
❑ 560	Scott Livingstone	.15	.07

		MINT	NRMT
❑ 561	Marc Newfield	.15	.07
❑ 562	Bob Tewksbury	.15	.07
❑ 563	Fernando Valenzuela	.30	.14
❑ 564	Rod Beck	.15	.07
❑ 565	Doug Creek	.15	.07
❑ 566	Shawon Dunston	.15	.07
❑ 567	Osvaldo Fernandez	.15	.07
❑ 568	Stan Javier	.15	.07
❑ 569	Marcus Jensen	.15	.07
❑ 570	Steve Scarsone	.15	.07
❑ 571	Robby Thompson	.15	.07
❑ 572	Allen Watson	.15	.07
❑ 573	Roberto Alomar STA	.30	.14
❑ 574	Jeff Bagwell STA	.60	.25
❑ 575	Albert Belle STA	.40	.18
❑ 576	Wade Boggs STA	.30	.14
❑ 577	Barry Bonds STA	.40	.18
❑ 578	Juan Gonzalez STA	.75	.35
❑ 579	Ken Griffey Jr. STA	1.50	.70
❑ 580	Tony Gwynn STA	.75	.35
❑ 581	Randy Johnson STA	.30	.14
❑ 582	Chipper Jones STA	.75	.35
❑ 583	Barry Larkin STA	.15	.07
❑ 584	Kenny Lofton STA	.30	.14
❑ 585	Greg Maddux STA	1.00	.45
❑ 586	Raul Mondesi STA	.15	.07
❑ 587	Mike Piazza STA	1.00	.45
❑ 588	Cal Ripken STA	1.25	.55
❑ 589	Tim Salmon STA	.30	.14
❑ 590	Frank Thomas STA	1.00	.45
❑ 591	Mo Vaughn STA	.40	.18
❑ 592	Matt Williams STA	.15	.07
❑ 593	Marty Cordova RAW	.15	.07
❑ 594	Jim Edmonds RAW	.15	.07
❑ 595	Cliff Floyd RAW	.15	.07
❑ 596	Chipper Jones RAW	.75	.35
❑ 597	Ryan Klesko RAW	.15	.07
❑ 598	Raul Mondesi RAW	.15	.07
❑ 599	Manny Ramirez RAW	.30	.14
❑ 600	Ruben Rivera RAW	.15	.07
❑ DD1	Cal Ripken Dia. Dust Issued through dealers Serial numbered to 2131	.15	.07
❑ DD2	Cal Ripken Dia. Dust Issued through a wrapper redemption	.15	.07

1996 Ultra Call to the Hall

	MINT	NRMT
COMPLETE SET (10)	80.00	36.00
COMMON CARD (1-10)	1.50	.70

*GOLD MEDAL: .75X TO 2X BASIC CALL TO HALL
GM SER.2 STATED ODDS 1:240

❑ 1	Barry Bonds	5.00	2.20
❑ 2	Ken Griffey Jr.	20.00	9.00
❑ 3	Tony Gwynn	10.00	4.50
❑ 4	Rickey Henderson	4.00	1.80
❑ 5	Greg Maddux	12.00	5.50
❑ 6	Eddie Murray	1.50	.70
❑ 7	Cal Ripken	15.00	6.75
❑ 8	Ryne Sandberg	5.00	2.20
❑ 9	Ozzie Smith	5.00	2.20
❑ 10	Frank Thomas	12.00	5.50

1996 Ultra Checklists

	MINT	NRMT
COMPLETE SERIES 1 (10)	10.00	4.50
COMPLETE SERIES 2 (10)	8.00	3.60
COMMON CARD (A1-B10)	.40	.18

*GOLD MEDAL: 1X TO 2.5X BASIC CARDS
GM STATED ODDS 1:40

❑ A1	Jeff Bagwell	1.25	.55
❑ A2	Barry Bonds	1.00	.45
❑ A3	Juan Gonzalez	2.00	.90
❑ A4	Ken Griffey Jr.	4.00	1.80
❑ A5	Chipper Jones	2.00	.90
❑ A6	Mike Piazza	2.50	1.10
❑ A7	Manny Ramirez	.75	.35
❑ A8	Cal Ripken	3.00	1.35
❑ A9	Frank Thomas	2.50	1.10
❑ A10	Matt Williams	.40	.18
❑ B1	Albert Belle	.75	.35
❑ B2	Cecil Fielder	.40	.18
❑ B3	Ken Griffey Jr.	4.00	1.80
❑ B4	Tony Gwynn	2.00	.90
❑ B5	Derek Jeter	2.50	1.10
❑ B6	Jason Kendall	.75	.35
❑ B7	Ryan Klesko	.40	.18
❑ B8	Greg Maddux	2.50	1.10
❑ B9	Cal Ripken	3.00	1.35
❑ B10	Frank Thomas	2.50	1.10

1996 Ultra Diamond Producers

	MINT	NRMT
COMPLETE SET (12)	60.00	27.00
COMMON CARD (1-12)	3.00	1.35

*GOLD MEDAL: 4X TO 10X BASIC CARDS
GM SER.1 STATED ODDS 1:200

❑ 1	Albert Belle	3.00	1.35
❑ 2	Barry Bonds	3.00	1.35
❑ 3	Ken Griffey Jr.	15.00	6.75
❑ 4	Tony Gwynn	8.00	3.60
❑ 5	Greg Maddux	10.00	4.50
❑ 6	Hideo Nomo	4.00	1.80
❑ 7	Mike Piazza	10.00	4.50
❑ 8	Kirby Puckett	6.00	2.70
❑ 9	Cal Ripken	12.00	5.50
❑ 10	Frank Thomas	10.00	4.50
❑ 11	Mo Vaughn	3.00	1.35
❑ 12	Matt Williams	3.00	1.35

1996 Ultra Fresh Foundations

	MINT	NRMT
COMPLETE SET (10)	3.00	1.35
COMMON CARD (1-10)	.15	.07

*GOLD MEDAL: .75X TO 2X BASIC CARDS
GM SER.1 STATED ODDS 1:30

❑ 1	Garret Anderson	.25	.11
❑ 2	Marty Cordova	.15	.07
❑ 3	Jim Edmonds	.40	.18
❑ 4	Brian L.Hunter	.25	.11
❑ 5	Chipper Jones	1.50	.70
❑ 6	Ryan Klesko	.25	.11
❑ 7	Raul Mondesi	.40	.18
❑ 8	Hideo Nomo	.60	.25
❑ 9	Manny Ramirez	.60	.25
❑ 10	Rondell White	.25	.11

1996 Ultra Golden Prospects

	MINT	NRMT
COMPLETE SET (10)	5.00	2.20
COMMON CARD (1-10)	.25	.11

*GOLD MEDAL: 1.5X TO 4X BASIC CARDS
GM SER.1 STATED ODDS 1:50 HOBBY

❑ 1	Yamil Benitez	.25	.11
❑ 2	Alberto Castillo	.25	.11
❑ 3	Roger Cedeno	.25	.11
❑ 4	Johnny Damon	.50	.23
❑ 5	Micah Franklin	.25	.11
❑ 6	Jason Giambi	.50	.23
❑ 7	Jose Herrera	.25	.11
❑ 8	Derek Jeter	5.00	2.20
❑ 9	Kevin Jordan	.25	.11
❑ 10	Ruben Rivera	.50	.23

1996 Ultra Golden Prospects Hobby

	MINT	NRMT
COMPLETE SET (15)	100.00	45.00
COMMON CARD (1-15)	6.00	2.70

*GOLD MEDAL: .75X TO 2X BASIC CARDS
GM SER.2 STATED ODDS 1:720 HOBBY

❑ 1 Bob Abreu	12.00	5.50
❑ 2 Israel Alcantara	6.00	2.70
❑ 3 Tony Batista	6.00	2.70
❑ 4 Mike Cameron	20.00	9.00
❑ 5 Steve Cox	6.00	2.70
❑ 6 Jermaine Dye	6.00	2.70
❑ 7 Wilton Guerrero	8.00	3.60
❑ 8 Richard Hidalgo	15.00	6.75
❑ 9 Raul Ibanez	6.00	2.70
❑ 10 Marty Janzen	6.00	2.70
❑ 11 Robin Jennings	6.00	2.70
❑ 12 Jason Maxwell	6.00	2.70
❑ 13 Scott McClain	6.00	2.70
❑ 14 Wonderful Monds	6.00	2.70
❑ 15 Chris Singleton	6.00	2.70

1996 Ultra Hitting Machines

	MINT	NRMT
COMPLETE SET (10)	400.00	180.00
COMMON CARD (1-10)	15.00	6.75

*GOLD MEDAL: .75X TO 2X BASIC CARDS
GM SER.2 STATED ODDS 1:2880

❑ 1 Albert Belle	30.00	13.50
❑ 2 Barry Bonds	30.00	13.50
❑ 3 Juan Gonzalez	60.00	27.00
❑ 4 Ken Griffey Jr.	120.00	55.00
❑ 5 Edgar Martinez	15.00	6.75
❑ 6 Rafael Palmeiro	15.00	6.75
❑ 7 Mike Piazza	80.00	36.00
❑ 8 Tim Salmon	25.00	11.00
❑ 9 Frank Thomas	80.00	36.00
❑ 10 Matt Williams	15.00	6.75

1996 Ultra Home Run Kings

	MINT	NRMT
COMPLETE SET (12)	60.00	27.00
COMMON CARD (1-12)	1.50	.70

*GOLD MEDAL: 5X TO 10X BASIC HR KINGS
GM SER.1 STATED ODDS 1:750
*REDEMPTION: .4X TO 1X BASIC HR KINGS
ONE RDMP.CARD VIA MAIL PER HR CARD

❑ 1 Albert Belle	5.00	2.20
❑ 2 Dante Bichette	1.50	.70
❑ 3 Barry Bonds	5.00	2.20
❑ 4 Jose Canseco	4.00	1.80
❑ 5 Juan Gonzalez	10.00	4.50
❑ 6 Ken Griffey Jr.	20.00	9.00
❑ 7 Mark McGwire	20.00	9.00
❑ 8 Manny Ramirez	4.00	1.80
❑ 9 Tim Salmon	4.00	1.80
❑ 10 Frank Thomas	12.00	5.50
❑ 11 Mo Vaughn	5.00	2.20
❑ 12 Matt Williams	1.50	.70

1996 Ultra On-Base Leaders

	MINT	NRMT
COMPLETE SET (10)	5.00	2.20
COMMON CARD (1-10)	.50	.23

*GOLD MEDAL: 1X TO 2.5X BASIC CARDS
GM SER.2 STATED ODDS 1:40

❑ 1 Wade Boggs	.75	.35
❑ 2 Barry Bonds	.75	.35
❑ 3 Tony Gwynn	2.00	.90
❑ 4 Rickey Henderson	.75	.35
❑ 5 Chuck Knoblauch	.75	.35
❑ 6 Edgar Martinez	.50	.23
❑ 7 Mike Piazza	2.50	1.10
❑ 8 Tim Salmon	.75	.35
❑ 9 Frank Thomas	2.50	1.10
❑ 10 Jim Thome	.75	.35

1996 Ultra Power Plus

	MINT	NRMT
COMPLETE SET (12)	25.00	11.00
COMMON CARD (1-12)	.50	.23

*GOLD MEDAL: 2.5X TO 6X BASIC CARDS
GM SER.1 STATED ODDS 1:100

❑ 1 Jeff Bagwell	3.00	1.35
❑ 2 Barry Bonds	2.00	.90
❑ 3 Ken Griffey Jr.	10.00	4.50
❑ 4 Raul Mondesi	1.50	.70
❑ 5 Rafael Palmeiro	1.50	.70
❑ 6 Mike Piazza	6.00	2.70
❑ 7 Manny Ramirez	2.00	.90
❑ 8 Tim Salmon	2.00	.90
❑ 9 Reggie Sanders	.50	.23
❑ 10 Frank Thomas	8.00	3.60
❑ 11 Larry Walker	2.00	.90
❑ 12 Matt Williams	1.00	.45

1996 Ultra Prime Leather

	MINT	NRMT
COMPLETE SET (18)	25.00	11.00
COMMON CARD (1-18)	.50	.23

*GOLD MEDAL: 2.5X TO 6X BASIC CARDS
GM SER.1 STATED ODDS 1:80

❑ 1 Ivan Rodriguez	2.00	.90
❑ 2 Will Clark	2.00	.90
❑ 3 Roberto Alomar	2.00	.90
❑ 4 Cal Ripken	8.00	3.60
❑ 5 Wade Boggs	2.00	.90
❑ 6 Ken Griffey Jr.	10.00	4.50
❑ 7 Kenny Lofton	2.00	.90
❑ 8 Kirby Puckett	4.00	1.80
❑ 9 Tim Salmon	2.00	.90
❑ 10 Mike Piazza	6.00	2.70
❑ 11 Mark Grace	1.50	.70
❑ 12 Craig Biggio	2.00	.90
❑ 13 Barry Larkin	1.50	.70
❑ 14 Matt Williams	1.00	.45
❑ 15 Barry Bonds	2.00	.90
❑ 16 Tony Gwynn	5.00	2.20
❑ 17 Brian McRae	.50	.23
❑ 18 Raul Mondesi	1.50	.70

1996 Ultra Rawhide

	MINT	NRMT
COMPLETE SET (10)	15.00	6.75
COMMON CARD (1-10)	1.00	.45

*GOLD MEDAL: 1.5X BASIC CARDS
GM SER.2 STATED ODDS 1:80

	MINT	NRMT
❑ 1 Roberto Alomar	1.25	.55
❑ 2 Barry Bonds	1.25	.55
❑ 3 Mark Grace	1.00	.45
❑ 4 Ken Griffey Jr.	6.00	2.70
❑ 5 Kenny Lofton	1.25	.55
❑ 6 Greg Maddux	4.00	1.80
❑ 7 Raul Mondesi	1.00	.45
❑ 8 Mike Piazza	4.00	1.80
❑ 9 Cal Ripken	5.00	2.20
❑ 10 Matt Williams	1.00	.45

1996 Ultra RBI Kings

	MINT	NRMT
COMPLETE SET (10)	30.00	13.50
COMMON CARD (1-10)	1.00	.45

*GOLD MEDAL: .75X TO 2X BASIC RBI KINGS
GM SER.1 STATED ODDS 1:50 RETAIL

	MINT	NRMT
❑ 1 Derek Bell	1.50	.70
❑ 2 Albert Belle	5.00	2.20
❑ 3 Dante Bichette	1.50	.70
❑ 4 Barry Bonds	5.00	2.20
❑ 5 Jim Edmonds	2.50	1.10
❑ 6 Manny Ramirez	4.00	1.80
❑ 7 Reggie Sanders	1.00	.45
❑ 8 Sammy Sosa	10.00	4.50
❑ 9 Frank Thomas	12.00	5.50
❑ 10 Mo Vaughn	5.00	2.20

1996 Ultra Respect

	MINT	NRMT
COMPLETE SET (10)	60.00	27.00
COMMON CARD (1-10)	1.50	.70

*GOLD MEDAL: 4X TO 10X BASIC CARDS
GM SER.2 STATED ODDS 1:180

	MINT	NRMT
❑ 1 Joe Carter	1.50	.70
❑ 2 Ken Griffey Jr.	15.00	6.75
❑ 3 Tony Gwynn	8.00	3.60
❑ 4 Greg Maddux	10.00	4.50
❑ 5 Eddie Murray	3.00	1.35
❑ 6 Kirby Puckett	6.00	2.70
❑ 7 Cal Ripken	12.00	5.50
❑ 8 Ryne Sandberg	3.00	1.35
❑ 9 Frank Thomas	10.00	4.50
❑ 10 Mo Vaughn	3.00	1.35

1996 Ultra Rising Stars

	MINT	NRMT
COMPLETE SET (10)	4.00	1.80
COMMON CARD (1-10)	.25	.11

*GOLD MEDAL: .75X BASIC CARDS
GM SER.2 STATED ODDS 1:40

	MINT	NRMT
❑ 1 Garret Anderson	.40	.18
❑ 2 Marty Cordova	.25	.11
❑ 3 Jim Edmonds	.60	.25
❑ 4 Cliff Floyd	.40	.18
❑ 5 Brian L.Hunter	.40	.18
❑ 6 Chipper Jones	2.00	.90
❑ 7 Ryan Klesko	.40	.18
❑ 8 Hideo Nomo	1.00	.45
❑ 9 Manny Ramirez	.75	.35
❑ 10 Rondell White	.40	.18

1996 Ultra Season Crowns

	MINT	NRMT
COMPLETE SET (10)	30.00	13.50
COMMON CARD (1-10)	.50	.23

*GOLD MEDAL: 2.5X TO 6X BASIC CARDS
GM SER.1 STATED ODDS 1:100

	MINT	NRMT
❑ 1 Barry Bonds	1.50	.70
❑ 2 Tony Gwynn	5.00	2.20
❑ 3 Randy Johnson	1.50	.70
❑ 4 Kenny Lofton	1.50	.70
❑ 5 Greg Maddux	6.00	2.70
❑ 6 Edgar Martinez	.50	.23
❑ 7 Hideo Nomo	2.50	1.10
❑ 8 Cal Ripken	8.00	3.60
❑ 9 Frank Thomas	6.00	2.70
❑ 10 Tim Wakefield	.50	.23

1996 Ultra Thunderclap

	MINT	NRMT
COMPLETE SET (20)	500.00	220.00
COMMON CARD (1-20)	8.00	3.60

*GOLD MEDAL: 1.25X TO 3X BASIC THUNDERCLAP

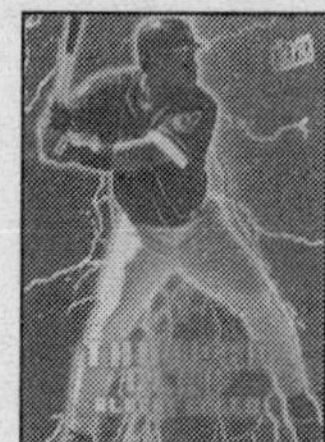

GM SER.2 STATED ODDS 1:720 RETAIL

	MINT	NRMT
❑ 1 Albert Belle	25.00	11.00
❑ 2 Barry Bonds	25.00	11.00
❑ 3 Bobby Bonilla	8.00	3.60
❑ 4 Jose Canseco	12.00	5.50
❑ 5 Joe Carter	8.00	3.60
❑ 6 Will Clark	12.00	5.50
❑ 7 Andre Dawson	12.00	5.50
❑ 8 Cecil Fielder	8.00	3.60
❑ 9 Andres Galarraga	20.00	9.00
❑ 10 Juan Gonzalez	50.00	22.00
❑ 11 Ken Griffey Jr.	100.00	45.00
❑ 12 Fred McGriff	12.00	5.50
❑ 13 Mark McGwire	100.00	45.00
❑ 14 Eddie Murray	20.00	9.00
❑ 15 Rafael Palmeiro	12.00	5.50
❑ 16 Kirby Puckett	40.00	18.00
❑ 17 Cal Ripken	80.00	36.00
❑ 18 Ryne Sandberg	30.00	13.50
❑ 19 Frank Thomas	60.00	27.00
❑ 20 Matt Williams	12.00	5.50

1997 Ultra

	MINT	NRMT
COMPLETE SET (553)	60.00	27.00
COMPLETE SERIES 1 (300)	30.00	13.50
COMPLETE SERIES 2 (253)	30.00	13.50
COMMON CARD (1-450)	.15	.07
COMMON CARD (451-553)	.20	.09

	MINT	NRMT
❑ 1 Roberto Alomar	.60	.25
❑ 2 Brady Anderson	.30	.14
❑ 3 Rocky Coppinger	.15	.07
❑ 4 Jeffrey Hammonds	.30	.14
❑ 5 Chris Hoiles	.15	.07
❑ 6 Eddie Murray	.60	.25
❑ 7 Mike Mussina	.60	.25
❑ 8 Jimmy Myers	.15	.07
❑ 9 Randy Myers	.15	.07
❑ 10 Arthur Rhodes	.15	.07
❑ 11 Cal Ripken	2.50	1.10
❑ 12 Jose Canseco	.60	.25
❑ 13 Roger Clemens	1.25	.55
❑ 14 Tom Gordon	.15	.07
❑ 15 Jose Malave	.15	.07
❑ 16 Tim Naehring	.15	.07
❑ 17 Troy O'Leary	.30	.14
❑ 18 Bill Selby	.15	.07
❑ 19 Heathcliff Slocumb	.15	.07

❑	20	Mike Stanley	.15	.07
❑	21	Mo Vaughn	.75	.35
❑	22	Garret Anderson	.30	.14
❑	23	George Arias	.15	.07
❑	24	Chili Davis	.30	.14
❑	25	Jim Edmonds	.40	.18
❑	26	Darin Erstad	1.00	.45
❑	27	Chuck Finley	.30	.14
❑	28	Todd Greene	.30	.14
❑	29	Troy Percival	.30	.14
❑	30	Tim Salmon	.60	.25
❑	31	Jeff Schmidt	.15	.07
❑	32	Randy Velarde	.15	.07
❑	33	Shad Williams	.15	.07
❑	34	Wilson Alvarez	.30	.14
❑	35	Harold Baines	.30	.14
❑	36	James Baldwin	.30	.14
❑	37	Mike Cameron	.30	.14
❑	38	Ray Durham	.30	.14
❑	39	Ozzie Guillen	.15	.07
❑	40	Roberto Hernandez	.15	.07
❑	41	Darren Lewis	.15	.07
❑	42	Jose Munoz	.15	.07
❑	43	Tony Phillips	.15	.07
❑	44	Frank Thomas	2.00	.90
❑	45	Sandy Alomar Jr.	.30	.14
❑	46	Albert Belle	.75	.35
❑	47	Mark Carreon	.15	.07
❑	48	Julio Franco	.30	.14
❑	49	Orel Hershiser	.30	.14
❑	50	Kenny Lofton	.60	.25
❑	51	Jack McDowell	.15	.07
❑	52	Jose Mesa	.15	.07
❑	53	Charles Nagy	.30	.14
❑	54	Manny Ramirez	.60	.25
❑	55	Julian Tavarez	.15	.07
❑	56	Omar Vizquel	.30	.14
❑	57	Raul Casanova	.15	.07
❑	58	Tony Clark	.40	.18
❑	59	Travis Fryman	.30	.14
❑	60	Bob Higginson	.40	.18
❑	61	Melvin Nieves	.15	.07
❑	62	Curtis Pride	.15	.07
❑	63	Justin Thompson	.30	.14
❑	64	Alan Trammell	.30	.14
❑	65	Kevin Appier	.30	.14
❑	66	Johnny Damon	.30	.14
❑	67	Keith Lockhart	.15	.07
❑	68	Jeff Montgomery	.15	.07
❑	69	Jose Offerman	.15	.07
❑	70	Bip Roberts	.15	.07
❑	71	Jose Rosado	.15	.07
❑	72	Chris Stynes	.15	.07
❑	73	Mike Sweeney	.15	.07
❑	74	Jeff Cirillo	.30	.14
❑	75	Jeff D'Amico	.15	.07
❑	76	John Jaha	.15	.07
❑	77	Scott Karl	.15	.07
❑	78	Mike Matheny	.15	.07
❑	79	Ben McDonald	.15	.07
❑	80	Matt Mieske	.15	.07
❑	81	Marc Newfield	.15	.07
❑	82	Dave Nilsson	.15	.07
❑	83	Jose Valentin	.15	.07
❑	84	Fernando Vina	.15	.07
❑	85	Rick Aguilera	.15	.07
❑	86	Marty Cordova	.15	.07
❑	87	Chuck Knoblauch	.60	.25
❑	88	Matt Lawton	.30	.14
❑	89	Pat Meares	.15	.07
❑	90	Paul Molitor	.60	.25
❑	91	Greg Myers	.15	.07
❑	92	Dan Naulty	.15	.07
❑	93	Kirby Puckett	1.00	.45
❑	94	Frank Rodriguez	.15	.07
❑	95	Wade Boggs	.60	.25
❑	96	Cecil Fielder	.30	.14
❑	97	Joe Girardi	.15	.07
❑	98	Dwight Gooden	.30	.14
❑	99	Derek Jeter	2.00	.90
❑	100	Tino Martinez	.60	.25
❑	101	Ramiro Mendoza	.50	.23
❑	102	Andy Pettitte	.40	.18
❑	103	Mariano Rivera	.30	.14
❑	104	Ruben Rivera	.30	.14
❑	105	Kenny Rogers	.15	.07
❑	106	Darryl Strawberry	.30	.14
❑	107	Bernie Williams	.60	.25
❑	108	Tony Batista	.15	.07
❑	109	Geronimo Berroa	.15	.07
❑	110	Bobby Chouinard	.15	.07
❑	111	Brent Gates	.15	.07
❑	112	Jason Giambi	.30	.14
❑	113	Damon Mashore	.15	.07
❑	114	Mark McGwire	3.00	1.35
❑	115	Scott Spiezio	.15	.07
❑	116	John Wasdin	.15	.07
❑	117	Steve Wojciechowski	.15	.07
❑	118	Ernie Young	.15	.07
❑	119	Norm Charlton	.15	.07
❑	120	Joey Cora	.30	.14
❑	121	Ken Griffey Jr.	3.00	1.35
❑	122	Sterling Hitchcock	.30	.14
❑	123	Raul Ibanez	.15	.07
❑	124	Randy Johnson	.60	.25
❑	125	Edgar Martinez	.30	.14
❑	126	Alex Rodriguez	2.00	.90
❑	127	Matt Wagner	.15	.07
❑	128	Bob Wells	.15	.07
❑	129	Dan Wilson	.15	.07
❑	130	Will Clark	.60	.25
❑	131	Kevin Elster	.15	.07
❑	132	Juan Gonzalez	1.50	.70
❑	133	Rusty Greer	.30	.14
❑	134	Darryl Hamilton	.15	.07
❑	135	Mike Henneman	.15	.07
❑	136	Ken Hill	.15	.07
❑	137	Mark McLemore	.15	.07
❑	138	Dean Palmer	.30	.14
❑	139	Roger Pavlik	.15	.07
❑	140	Ivan Rodriguez	.75	.35
❑	141	Joe Carter	.30	.14
❑	142	Carlos Delgado	.30	.14
❑	143	Alex Gonzalez	.15	.07
❑	144	Juan Guzman	.15	.07
❑	145	Pat Hentgen	.30	.14
❑	146	Marty Janzen	.15	.07
❑	147	Otis Nixon	.15	.07
❑	148	Charlie O'Brien	.15	.07
❑	149	John Olerud	.30	.14
❑	150	Robert Perez	.15	.07
❑	151	Jermaine Dye	.15	.07
❑	152	Tom Glavine	.60	.25
❑	153	Andruw Jones	1.00	.45
❑	154	Chipper Jones	1.50	.70
❑	155	Ryan Klesko	.30	.14
❑	156	Javier Lopez	.30	.14
❑	157	Greg Maddux	2.00	.90
❑	158	Fred McGriff	.40	.18
❑	159	Wonderful Monds	.15	.07
❑	160	John Smoltz	.30	.14
❑	161	Terrell Wade	.15	.07
❑	162	Mark Wohlers	.15	.07
❑	163	Brant Brown	.30	.14
❑	164	Mark Grace	.40	.18
❑	165	Tyler Houston	.15	.07
❑	166	Robin Jennings	.15	.07
❑	167	Jason Maxwell	.15	.07
❑	168	Ryne Sandberg	.75	.35
❑	169	Sammy Sosa	1.50	.70
❑	170	Amaury Telemaco	.15	.07
❑	171	Steve Trachsel	.15	.07
❑	172	Pedro Valdes	.15	.07
❑	173	Tim Belk	.15	.07
❑	174	Bret Boone	.30	.14
❑	175	Jeff Brantley	.15	.07
❑	176	Eric Davis	.30	.14
❑	177	Barry Larkin	.40	.18
❑	178	Chad Mottola	.15	.07
❑	179	Mark Portugal	.15	.07
❑	180	Reggie Sanders	.30	.14
❑	181	John Smiley	.15	.07
❑	182	Eddie Taubensee	.15	.07
❑	183	Dante Bichette	.30	.14
❑	184	Ellis Burks	.30	.14
❑	185	Andres Galarraga	.60	.25
❑	186	Curt Leskanic	.15	.07
❑	187	Quinton McCracken	.30	.14
❑	188	Jeff Reed	.15	.07
❑	189	Kevin Ritz	.15	.07
❑	190	Walt Weiss	.15	.07
❑	191	Jamey Wright	.15	.07
❑	192	Eric Young	.30	.14
❑	193	Kevin Brown	.40	.18
❑	194	Luis Castillo	.30	.14
❑	195	Jeff Conine	.30	.14
❑	196	Andre Dawson	.40	.18
❑	197	Charles Johnson	.30	.14
❑	198	Al Leiter	.30	.14
❑	199	Ralph Milliard	.15	.07
❑	200	Robb Nen	.15	.07
❑	201	Edgar Renteria	.30	.14
❑	202	Gary Sheffield	.40	.18
❑	203	Bob Abreu	.30	.14
❑	204	Jeff Bagwell	1.00	.45
❑	205	Derek Bell	.30	.14
❑	206	Sean Berry	.15	.07
❑	207	Richard Hidalgo	.30	.14
❑	208	Todd Jones	.15	.07
❑	209	Darryl Kile	.30	.14
❑	210	Orlando Miller	.15	.07
❑	211	Shane Reynolds	.30	.14
❑	212	Billy Wagner	.30	.14
❑	213	Donne Wall	.15	.07
❑	214	Roger Cedeno	.15	.07
❑	215	Greg Gagne	.15	.07
❑	216	Karim Garcia	.30	.14
❑	217	Wilton Guerrero	.15	.07
❑	218	Todd Hollandsworth	.15	.07
❑	219	Ramon Martinez	.30	.14
❑	220	Raul Mondesi	.40	.18
❑	221	Hideo Nomo	.75	.35
❑	222	Chan Ho Park	.60	.25
❑	223	Mike Piazza	2.00	.90
❑	224	Ismael Valdes	.30	.14
❑	225	Moises Alou	.40	.18
❑	226	Derek Aucoin	.15	.07
❑	227	Yamil Benitez	.15	.07
❑	228	Jeff Fassero	.15	.07
❑	229	Darrin Fletcher	.15	.07
❑	230	Mark Grudzielanek	.30	.14
❑	231	Barry Manuel	.15	.07
❑	232	Pedro Martinez	.60	.25
❑	233	Henry Rodriguez	.30	.14
❑	234	Ugueth Urbina	.30	.14
❑	235	Rondell White	.30	.14
❑	236	Carlos Baerga	.30	.14
❑	237	John Franco	.30	.14
❑	238	Bernard Gilkey	.15	.07
❑	239	Todd Hundley	.30	.14
❑	240	Butch Huskey	.15	.07
❑	241	Jason Isringhausen	.15	.07
❑	242	Lance Johnson	.15	.07
❑	243	Bobby Jones	.15	.07
❑	244	Alex Ochoa	.15	.07
❑	245	Rey Ordonez	.30	.14
❑	246	Paul Wilson	.15	.07
❑	247	Ron Blazier	.15	.07
❑	248	David Doster	.15	.07
❑	249	Jim Eisenreich	.15	.07
❑	250	Mike Grace	.15	.07
❑	251	Mike Lieberthal	.15	.07
❑	252	Wendell Magee	.15	.07
❑	253	Mickey Morandini	.15	.07
❑	254	Ricky Otero	.15	.07
❑	255	Scott Rolen	1.50	.70
❑	256	Curt Schilling	.30	.14
❑	257	Todd Zeile	.15	.07
❑	258	Jermaine Allensworth	.15	.07
❑	259	Trey Beamon	.15	.07
❑	260	Carlos Garcia	.15	.07
❑	261	Mark Johnson	.15	.07
❑	262	Jason Kendall	.40	.18
❑	263	Jeff King	.15	.07
❑	264	Al Martin	.15	.07
❑	265	Denny Neagle	.30	.14
❑	266	Matt Ruebel	.15	.07
❑	267	Marc Wilkins	.15	.07
❑	268	Alan Benes	.30	.14
❑	269	Dennis Eckersley	.30	.14
❑	270	Ron Gant	.15	.07
❑	271	Aaron Holbert	.15	.07
❑	272	Brian Jordan	.30	.14
❑	273	Ray Lankford	.30	.14
❑	274	John Mabry	.15	.07

❑ 275 T.J. Mathews .15 .07
❑ 276 Ozzie Smith .75 .35
❑ 277 Todd Stottlemyre .15 .07
❑ 278 Mark Sweeney .15 .07
❑ 279 Andy Ashby .15 .07
❑ 280 Steve Finley .30 .14
❑ 281 John Flaherty .15 .07
❑ 282 Chris Gomez .15 .07
❑ 283 Tony Gwynn 1.50 .70
❑ 284 Joey Hamilton .30 .14
❑ 285 Rickey Henderson .60 .25
❑ 286 Trevor Hoffman .30 .14
❑ 287 Jason Thompson .15 .07
❑ 288 Fernando Valenzuela .30 .14
❑ 289 Greg Vaughn .30 .14
❑ 290 Barry Bonds .75 .35
❑ 291 Jay Canizaro .15 .07
❑ 292 Jacob Cruz .15 .07
❑ 293 Shawon Dunston .15 .07
❑ 294 Shawn Estes .30 .14
❑ 295 Mark Gardner .15 .07
❑ 296 Marcus Jensen .15 .07
❑ 297 Bill Mueller .75 .35
❑ 298 Chris Singleton .15 .07
❑ 299 Allen Watson .15 .07
❑ 300 Matt Williams .30 .14
❑ 301 Rod Beck .15 .07
❑ 302 Jay Bell .30 .14
❑ 303 Shawon Dunston .15 .07
❑ 304 Reggie Jefferson .15 .07
❑ 305 Darren Oliver .15 .07
❑ 306 Benito Santiago .15 .07
❑ 307 Gerald Williams .15 .07
❑ 308 Damon Buford .15 .07
❑ 309 Jeromy Burnitz .30 .14
❑ 310 Sterling Hitchcock .30 .14
❑ 311 Dave Hollins .15 .07
❑ 312 Mel Rojas .15 .07
❑ 313 Robin Ventura .30 .14
❑ 314 David Wells .40 .18
❑ 315 Cal Eldred .15 .07
❑ 316 Gary Gaetti .15 .07
❑ 317 John Hudek .15 .07
❑ 318 Brian Johnson .15 .07
❑ 319 Denny Neagle .30 .14
❑ 320 Larry Walker .60 .25
❑ 321 Russ Davis .30 .14
❑ 322 Delino DeShields .15 .07
❑ 323 Charlie Hayes .15 .07
❑ 324 Jermaine Dye .15 .07
❑ 325 John Ericks .15 .07
❑ 326 Jeff Fassero .15 .07
❑ 327 Nomar Garciaparra 2.00 .90
❑ 328 Willie Greene .30 .14
❑ 329 Greg McMichael .15 .07
❑ 330 Damion Easley .30 .14
❑ 331 Ricky Bones .15 .07
❑ 332 John Burkett .15 .07
❑ 333 Royce Clayton .15 .07
❑ 334 Greg Colbrunn .15 .07
❑ 335 Tony Eusebio .15 .07
❑ 336 Gregg Jefferies .15 .07
❑ 337 Wally Joyner .30 .14
❑ 338 Jim Leyritz .15 .07
❑ 339 Paul O'Neill .30 .14
❑ 340 Bruce Ruffin .15 .07
❑ 341 Michael Tucker .30 .14
❑ 342 Andy Benes .30 .14
❑ 343 Craig Biggio .60 .25
❑ 344 Rex Hudler .15 .07
❑ 345 Brad Radke .30 .14
❑ 346 Deion Sanders .30 .14
❑ 347 Moises Alou .40 .18
❑ 348 Brad Ausmus .15 .07
❑ 349 Armando Benitez .15 .07
❑ 350 Mark Gubicza .15 .07
❑ 351 Terry Steinbach .30 .14
❑ 352 Mark Whiten .15 .07
❑ 353 Ricky Bottalico .30 .14
❑ 354 Brian Giles .75 .35
❑ 355 Eric Karros .30 .14
❑ 356 Jimmy Key .30 .14
❑ 357 Carlos Perez .30 .14
❑ 358 Alex Fernandez .15 .07
❑ 359 J.T. Snow .30 .14
❑ 360 Bobby Bonilla .30 .14
❑ 361 Scott Brosius .30 .14
❑ 362 Greg Swindell .15 .07
❑ 363 Jose Vizcaino .15 .07
❑ 364 Matt Williams .30 .14
❑ 365 Darren Daulton .30 .14
❑ 366 Shane Andrews .15 .07
❑ 367 Jim Eisenreich .15 .07
❑ 368 Ariel Prieto .15 .07
❑ 369 Bob Tewksbury .15 .07
❑ 370 Mike Bordick .15 .07
❑ 371 Rheal Cormier .15 .07
❑ 372 Cliff Floyd .30 .14
❑ 373 David Justice .60 .25
❑ 374 John Wetteland .30 .14
❑ 375 Mike Blowers .15 .07
❑ 376 Jose Canseco .60 .25
❑ 377 Roger Clemens 1.25 .55
❑ 378 Kevin Mitchell .15 .07
❑ 379 Todd Zeile .15 .07
❑ 380 Jim Thome .60 .25
❑ 381 Turk Wendell .15 .07
❑ 382 Rico Brogna .15 .07
❑ 383 Eric Davis .30 .14
❑ 384 Mike Lansing .15 .07
❑ 385 Devon White .30 .14
❑ 386 Marquis Grissom .30 .14
❑ 387 Todd Worrell .15 .07
❑ 388 Jeff Kent .30 .14
❑ 389 Mickey Tettleton .15 .07
❑ 390 Steve Avery .15 .07
❑ 391 David Cone .40 .18
❑ 392 Scott Cooper .15 .07
❑ 393 Lee Stevens .15 .07
❑ 394 Kevin Elster .15 .07
❑ 395 Tom Goodwin .15 .07
❑ 396 Shawn Green .30 .14
❑ 397 Pete Harnisch .15 .07
❑ 398 Eddie Murray .60 .25
❑ 399 Joe Randa .15 .07
❑ 400 Scott Sanders .15 .07
❑ 401 John Valentin .30 .14
❑ 402 Todd Jones .15 .07
❑ 403 Terry Adams .15 .07
❑ 404 Brian Hunter .30 .14
❑ 405 Pat Listach .15 .07
❑ 406 Kenny Lofton .60 .25
❑ 407 Hal Morris .15 .07
❑ 408 Ed Sprague .15 .07
❑ 409 Rich Becker .15 .07
❑ 410 Edgardo Alfonzo .30 .14
❑ 411 Albert Belle .75 .35
❑ 412 Jeff King .15 .07
❑ 413 Kirt Manwaring .15 .07
❑ 414 Jason Schmidt .15 .07
❑ 415 Allen Watson .15 .07
❑ 416 Lee Tinsley .15 .07
❑ 417 Brett Butler .30 .14
❑ 418 Carlos Garcia .15 .07
❑ 419 Mark Lemke .15 .07
❑ 420 Jaime Navarro .15 .07
❑ 421 David Segui .30 .14
❑ 422 Ruben Sierra .15 .07
❑ 423 B.J. Surhoff .30 .14
❑ 424 Julian Tavarez .15 .07
❑ 425 Billy Taylor .15 .07
❑ 426 Ken Caminiti .40 .18
❑ 427 Chuck Carr .15 .07
❑ 428 Benji Gil .15 .07
❑ 429 Terry Mulholland .15 .07
❑ 430 Mike Stanton .15 .07
❑ 431 Wil Cordero .15 .07
❑ 432 Chili Davis .30 .14
❑ 433 Mariano Duncan .15 .07
❑ 434 Orlando Merced .15 .07
❑ 435 Kent Mercker .15 .07
❑ 436 John Olerud .30 .14
❑ 437 Quilvio Veras .15 .07
❑ 438 Mike Fetters .15 .07
❑ 439 Glenallen Hill .15 .07
❑ 440 Bill Swift .15 .07
❑ 441 Tim Wakefield .30 .14
❑ 442 Pedro Astacio .15 .07
❑ 443 Vinny Castilla .40 .18
❑ 444 Doug Drabek .15 .07
❑ 445 Alan Embree .15 .07
❑ 446 Lee Smith .30 .14
❑ 447 Darryl Hamilton .15 .07
❑ 448 Brian McRae .15 .07
❑ 449 Mike Timlin .15 .07
❑ 450 Bob Wickman .15 .07
❑ 451 Jason Dickson .40 .18
❑ 452 Chad Curtis .20 .09
❑ 453 Mark Leiter .20 .09
❑ 454 Damon Berryhill .20 .09
❑ 455 Kevin Orie .20 .09
❑ 456 Dave Burba .20 .09
❑ 457 Chris Holt .20 .09
❑ 458 Ricky Ledee 3.00 1.35
❑ 459 Mike Devereaux .20 .09
❑ 460 Pokey Reese .20 .09
❑ 461 Tim Raines .40 .18
❑ 462 Ryan Jones .20 .09
❑ 463 Shane Mack .20 .09
❑ 464 Darren Dreifort .40 .18
❑ 465 Mark Parent .20 .09
❑ 466 Mark Portugal .20 .09
❑ 467 Dante Powell .40 .18
❑ 468 Craig Grebeck .20 .09
❑ 469 Ron Villone .20 .09
❑ 470 Dmitri Young .40 .18
❑ 471 Shannon Stewart .40 .18
❑ 472 Rick Helling .40 .18
❑ 473 Bill Haselman .20 .09
❑ 474 Albie Lopez .20 .09
❑ 475 Glendon Rusch .20 .09
❑ 476 Derrick May .20 .09
❑ 477 Chad Ogea .20 .09
❑ 478 Kirk Rueter .20 .09
❑ 479 Chris Hammond .20 .09
❑ 480 Russ Johnson .20 .09
❑ 481 James Mouton .20 .09
❑ 482 Mike Macfarlane .20 .09
❑ 483 Scott Ruffcorn .20 .09
❑ 484 Jeff Frye .20 .09
❑ 485 Richie Sexson .50 .23
❑ 486 Emil Brown .50 .23
❑ 487 Desi Wilson .20 .09
❑ 488 Brent Gates .20 .09
❑ 489 Tony Graffanino .20 .09
❑ 490 Dan Miceli .20 .09
❑ 491 Orlando Cabrera .50 .23
❑ 492 Tony Womack .75 .35
❑ 493 Jerome Walton .20 .09
❑ 494 Mark Thompson .20 .09
❑ 495 Jose Guillen .75 .35
❑ 496 Willie Blair .20 .09
❑ 497 T.J. Staton .50 .23
❑ 498 Scott Kamieniecki .20 .09
❑ 499 Vince Coleman .20 .09
❑ 500 Jeff Abbott .40 .18
❑ 501 Chris Widger .20 .09
❑ 502 Kevin Tapani .20 .09
❑ 503 Carlos Castillo .50 .23
❑ 504 Luis Gonzalez .20 .09
❑ 505 Tim Belcher .20 .09
❑ 506 Armando Reynoso .20 .09
❑ 507 Jamie Moyer .20 .09
❑ 508 Randall Simon 1.50 .70
❑ 509 Vladimir Guerrero 1.50 .70
❑ 510 Wady Almonte .50 .23
❑ 511 Dustin Hermanson .40 .18
❑ 512 Deivi Cruz .75 .35
❑ 513 Luis Alicea .20 .09
❑ 514 Felix Heredia .40 .18
❑ 515 Don Slaught .20 .09
❑ 516 Shigetoshi Hasegawa .50 .23
❑ 517 Matt Walbeck .20 .09
❑ 518 David Arias-Ortiz 2.00 .90
❑ 519 Brady Raggio .20 .09
❑ 520 Rudy Pemberton .20 .09
❑ 521 Wayne Kirby .20 .09
❑ 522 Calvin Maduro .20 .09
❑ 523 Mark Lewis .20 .09
❑ 524 Mike Jackson .20 .09
❑ 525 Sid Fernandez .20 .09
❑ 526 Mike Bielecki .20 .09
❑ 527 Bubba Trammell .60 .25
❑ 528 Brent Brede .20 .09
❑ 529 Matt Morris .40 .18

❑ 530 Joe Borowski	.20	.09
❑ 531 Orlando Miller	.20	.09
❑ 532 Jim Bullinger	.20	.09
❑ 533 Robert Person	.20	.09
❑ 534 Doug Glanville	.40	.18
❑ 535 Terry Pendleton	.20	.09
❑ 536 Jorge Posada	.40	.18
❑ 537 Marc Sagmoen	.20	.09
❑ 538 Fernando Tatis	1.50	.70
❑ 539 Aaron Sele	.40	.18
❑ 540 Brian Banks	.20	.09
❑ 541 Derrek Lee	.50	.23
❑ 542 John Wasdin	.20	.09
❑ 543 Justin Towle	.60	.25
❑ 544 Pat Cline	.40	.18
❑ 545 Dave Magadan	.20	.09
❑ 546 Jeff Blauser	.20	.09
❑ 547 Phil Nevin	.20	.09
❑ 548 Todd Walker	.75	.35
❑ 549 Eli Marrero	.40	.18
❑ 550 Bartolo Colon	.40	.18
❑ 551 Jose Cruz Jr.	4.00	1.80
❑ 552 Todd Dunwoody	.40	.18
❑ 553 Hideki Irabu	2.50	1.10
❑ P11 Cal Ripken Promo Three Card Strip	4.00	1.80

1997 Ultra Autographstix Emeralds

	MINT	NRMT
COMPLETE SET (6)	60.00	27.00
COMMON CARD (1-6)	5.00	2.20
❑ 1 Alex Ochoa	5.00	2.20
❑ 2 Todd Walker	6.00	2.70
❑ 3 Scott Rolen	15.00	6.75
❑ 4 Darin Erstad	10.00	4.50
❑ 5 Alex Rodriguez	25.00	11.00
❑ 6 Todd Hollandsworth	5.00	2.20

1997 Ultra Baseball Rules

	MINT	NRMT
COMPLETE SET (10)	120.00	55.00
COMMON CARD (1-10)	1.50	.70
❑ 1 Barry Bonds	6.00	2.70
❑ 2 Ken Griffey Jr.	25.00	11.00
❑ 3 Derek Jeter	12.00	5.50
❑ 4 Chipper Jones	12.00	5.50
❑ 5 Greg Maddux	15.00	6.75
❑ 6 Mark McGwire	25.00	11.00
❑ 7 Troy Percival	1.50	.70
❑ 8 Mike Piazza	15.00	6.75
❑ 9 Cal Ripken	20.00	9.00
❑ 10 Frank Thomas	15.00	6.75

1997 Ultra Checklists

	MINT	NRMT
COMPLETE SERIES 1 (10)	8.00	3.60
COMPLETE SERIES 2 (10)	12.00	5.50
COMMON CARD (A1-B10)	.25	.11
❑ A1 Dante Bichette	.25	.11
❑ A2 Barry Bonds	.75	.35
❑ A3 Ken Griffey Jr.	3.00	1.35
❑ A4 Greg Maddux	2.00	.90
❑ A5 Mark McGwire	3.00	1.35
❑ A6 Mike Piazza	2.00	.90
❑ A7 Cal Ripken	2.00	.90
❑ A8 John Smoltz	.25	.11
❑ A9 Sammy Sosa	.50	.23
❑ A10 Frank Thomas	1.50	.70
❑ B1 Andruw Jones	1.25	.55
❑ B2 Ken Griffey Jr.	3.00	1.35
❑ B3 Frank Thomas	1.50	.70
❑ B4 Alex Rodriguez	2.00	.90
❑ B5 Cal Ripken	2.00	.90
❑ B6 Mike Piazza	2.00	.90
❑ B7 Greg Maddux	2.00	.90
❑ B8 Chipper Jones	1.50	.70
❑ B9 Derek Jeter	2.00	.90
❑ B10 Juan Gonzalez	1.50	.70

1997 Ultra Diamond Producers

	MINT	NRMT
COMPLETE SET (12)	600.00	275.00
COMMON CARD (1-12)	12.00	5.50
❑ 1 Jeff Bagwell	30.00	13.50
❑ 2 Barry Bonds	25.00	11.00
❑ 3 Ken Griffey Jr.	100.00	45.00
❑ 4 Chipper Jones	50.00	22.00
❑ 5 Kenny Lofton	20.00	9.00
❑ 6 Greg Maddux	60.00	27.00
❑ 7 Mark McGwire	100.00	45.00
❑ 8 Mike Piazza	60.00	27.00
❑ 9 Cal Ripken	80.00	36.00
❑ 10 Alex Rodriguez	60.00	27.00
❑ 11 Frank Thomas	60.00	27.00
❑ 12 Matt Williams	12.00	5.50

1997 Ultra Double Trouble

	MINT	NRMT
COMPLETE SET (20)	12.00	5.50
COMMON CARD (1-20)	.25	.11
❑ 1 Roberto Alomar Cal Ripken	2.00	.90
❑ 2 Mo Vaughn Jose Canseco	.60	.25
❑ 3 Jim Edmonds Tim Salmon	.75	.35
❑ 4 Harold Baines Frank Thomas	1.50	.70
❑ 5 Albert Belle Kenny Lofton	.60	.25
❑ 6 Marty Cordova Chuck Knoblauch	.75	.35
❑ 7 Derek Jeter Andy Pettitte	1.25	.55
❑ 8 Jason Giambi Mark McGwire	2.50	1.10
❑ 9 Ken Griffey Jr. Alex Rodriguez	3.00	1.35
❑ 10 Juan Gonzalez Will Clark	1.25	.55
❑ 11 Greg Maddux Chipper Jones	2.00	.90
❑ 12 Mark Grace Sammy Sosa	1.25	.55
❑ 13 Dante Bichette Andres Galarraga	.75	.35
❑ 14 Jeff Bagwell Derek Bell	.75	.35
❑ 15 Hideo Nomo Mike Piazza	1.50	.70
❑ 16 Henry Rodriguez Moises Alou	.25	.11
❑ 17 Rey Ordonez Alex Ochoa	.25	.11
❑ 18 Ray Lankford Ron Gant	.25	.11
❑ 19 Tony Gwynn Rickey Henderson	1.25	.55
❑ 20 Barry Bonds Matt Williams	.60	.25

1997 Ultra Fame Game

	MINT	NRMT
COMPLETE SET (18)	70.00	32.00
COMMON CARD (1-18)	2.00	.90
❑ 1 Ken Griffey Jr.	12.00	5.50
❑ 2 Frank Thomas	8.00	3.60
❑ 3 Alex Rodriguez	8.00	3.60
❑ 4 Cal Ripken	10.00	4.50
❑ 5 Mike Piazza	8.00	3.60
❑ 6 Greg Maddux	8.00	3.60

❑ 7 Derek Jeter	6.00	2.70
❑ 8 Jeff Bagwell	4.00	1.80
❑ 9 Juan Gonzalez	6.00	2.70
❑ 10 Albert Belle	3.00	1.35
❑ 11 Tony Gwynn	6.00	2.70
❑ 12 Mark McGwire	12.00	5.50
❑ 13 Andy Pettitte	2.00	.90
❑ 14 Kenny Lofton	2.50	1.10
❑ 15 Roberto Alomar	2.50	1.10
❑ 16 Ryne Sandberg	3.00	1.35
❑ 17 Barry Bonds	3.00	1.35
❑ 18 Eddie Murray	2.50	1.10

1997 Ultra Fielder's Choice

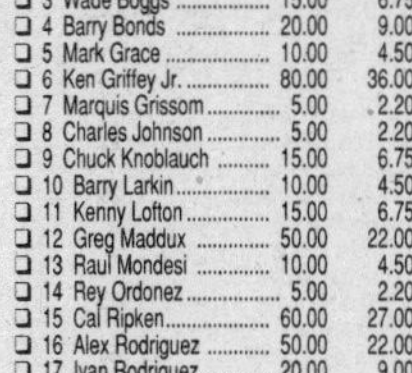

	MINT	NRMT
COMPLETE SET (18)	300.00	135.00
COMMON CARD (1-18)	5.00	2.20
❑ 1 Roberto Alomar	15.00	6.75
❑ 2 Jeff Bagwell	25.00	11.00
❑ 3 Wade Boggs	15.00	6.75
❑ 4 Barry Bonds	20.00	9.00
❑ 5 Mark Grace	10.00	4.50
❑ 6 Ken Griffey Jr.	80.00	36.00
❑ 7 Marquis Grissom	5.00	2.20
❑ 8 Charles Johnson	5.00	2.20
❑ 9 Chuck Knoblauch	15.00	6.75
❑ 10 Barry Larkin	10.00	4.50
❑ 11 Kenny Lofton	15.00	6.75
❑ 12 Greg Maddux	50.00	22.00
❑ 13 Raul Mondesi	10.00	4.50
❑ 14 Rey Ordonez	5.00	2.20
❑ 15 Cal Ripken	60.00	27.00
❑ 16 Alex Rodriguez	50.00	22.00
❑ 17 Ivan Rodriguez	20.00	9.00
❑ 18 Matt Williams	8.00	3.60

1997 Ultra Golden Prospects

	MINT	NRMT
COMPLETE SET (10)	6.00	2.70
COMMON CARD (1-10)	.40	.18
❑ 1 Andruw Jones	1.50	.70
❑ 2 Vladimir Guerrero	1.50	.70
❑ 3 Todd Walker	.75	.35
❑ 4 Karim Garcia	.40	.18
❑ 5 Kevin Orie	.40	.18
❑ 6 Brian Giles	.40	.18
❑ 7 Jason Dickson	.40	.18
❑ 8 Jose Guillen	1.00	.45
❑ 9 Ruben Rivera	.40	.18
❑ 10 Derrek Lee	.50	.23

1997 Ultra Hitting Machines

	MINT	NRMT
COMPLETE SET (18)	200.00	90.00
COMMON CARD (1-18)	4.00	1.80
❑ 1 Andruw Jones	8.00	3.60
❑ 2 Ken Griffey Jr.	30.00	13.50
❑ 3 Frank Thomas	20.00	9.00
❑ 4 Alex Rodriguez	20.00	9.00
❑ 5 Cal Ripken	25.00	11.00
❑ 6 Mike Piazza	20.00	9.00
❑ 7 Derek Jeter	15.00	6.75
❑ 8 Albert Belle	8.00	3.60
❑ 9 Tony Gwynn	15.00	6.75
❑ 10 Jeff Bagwell	10.00	4.50
❑ 11 Mark McGwire	30.00	13.50
❑ 12 Kenny Lofton	6.00	2.70
❑ 13 Manny Ramirez	6.00	2.70
❑ 14 Roberto Alomar	6.00	2.70
❑ 15 Ryne Sandberg	8.00	3.60
❑ 16 Eddie Murray	6.00	2.70
❑ 17 Sammy Sosa	15.00	6.75
❑ 18 Ken Caminiti	4.00	1.80

1997 Ultra Home Run Kings

	MINT	NRMT
COMPLETE SET (12)	100.00	45.00
COMMON CARD (1-12)	2.50	1.10
❑ 1 Albert Belle	6.00	2.70
❑ 2 Barry Bonds	6.00	2.70
❑ 3 Juan Gonzalez	12.00	5.50
❑ 4 Ken Griffey Jr.	25.00	11.00
❑ 5 Todd Hundley	2.50	1.10
❑ 6 Ryan Klesko	2.50	1.10
❑ 7 Mark McGwire	25.00	11.00
❑ 8 Mike Piazza	15.00	6.75
❑ 9 Sammy Sosa	12.00	5.50
❑ 10 Frank Thomas	15.00	6.75
❑ 11 Mo Vaughn	6.00	2.70
❑ 12 Matt Williams	2.50	1.10

1997 Ultra Leather Shop

	MINT	NRMT
COMPLETE SET (12)	20.00	9.00
COMMON CARD (1-12)	.50	.23
❑ 1 Ken Griffey Jr.	5.00	2.20
❑ 2 Alex Rodriguez	3.00	1.35
❑ 3 Cal Ripken	4.00	1.80
❑ 4 Derek Jeter	3.00	1.35
❑ 5 Juan Gonzalez	2.50	1.10
❑ 6 Tony Gwynn	2.50	1.10
❑ 7 Jeff Bagwell	1.50	.70
❑ 8 Roberto Alomar	1.00	.45
❑ 9 Ryne Sandberg	1.25	.55
❑ 10 Ken Caminiti	.75	.35
❑ 11 Kenny Lofton	1.00	.45
❑ 12 John Smoltz	.50	.23

1997 Ultra Power Plus

	MINT	NRMT
COMPLETE SERIES 1 (12)	100.00	45.00
COMMON CARD (A1-A12)	2.50	1.10
COMPLETE SERIES 2 (12)	30.00	13.50
COMMON CARD (B1-B12)	1.50	.70
❑ A1 Jeff Bagwell	6.00	2.70

❑ A2 Barry Bonds	5.00	2.20
❑ A3 Juan Gonzalez	10.00	4.50
❑ A4 Ken Griffey Jr.	20.00	9.00
❑ A5 Chipper Jones	10.00	4.50
❑ A6 Mark McGwire	20.00	9.00
❑ A7 Mike Piazza	12.00	5.50
❑ A8 Cal Ripken	15.00	6.75
❑ A9 Alex Rodriguez	12.00	5.50
❑ A10 Sammy Sosa	10.00	4.50
❑ A11 Frank Thomas	12.00	5.50
❑ A12 Matt Williams	2.50	1.10
❑ B1 Ken Griffey Jr.	6.00	2.70
❑ B2 Frank Thomas	5.00	2.20
❑ B3 Alex Rodriguez	4.00	1.80
❑ B4 Cal Ripken	5.00	2.20
❑ B5 Mike Piazza	4.00	1.80
❑ B6 Chipper Jones	4.00	1.80
❑ B7 Albert Belle	1.50	.70
❑ B8 Juan Gonzalez	3.00	1.35
❑ B9 Jeff Bagwell	2.50	1.10
❑ B10 Mark McGwire	2.50	1.10
❑ B11 Mo Vaughn	1.50	.70
❑ B12 Barry Bonds	1.50	.70

1997 Ultra RBI Kings

	MINT	NRMT
COMPLETE SET (10)	50.00	22.00
COMMON CARD (1-10)	1.50	.70
❑ 1 Jeff Bagwell	5.00	2.20
❑ 2 Albert Belle	4.00	1.80
❑ 3 Dante Bichette	1.50	.70
❑ 4 Barry Bonds	4.00	1.80
❑ 5 Jay Buhner	1.50	.70
❑ 6 Juan Gonzalez	8.00	3.60
❑ 7 Ken Griffey Jr.	15.00	6.75
❑ 8 Sammy Sosa	8.00	3.60
❑ 9 Frank Thomas	10.00	4.50
❑ 10 Mo Vaughn	4.00	1.80

1997 Ultra Rookie Reflections

	MINT	NRMT
COMPLETE SET (10)	4.00	1.80
COMMON CARD (1-10)	.25	.11
❑ 1 James Baldwin	.40	.18
❑ 2 Jermaine Dye	.25	.11
❑ 3 Darin Erstad	1.25	.55
❑ 4 Todd Hollandsworth	.25	.11
❑ 5 Derek Jeter	2.50	1.10
❑ 6 Jason Kendall	.50	.23
❑ 7 Alex Ochoa	.25	.11
❑ 8 Rey Ordonez	.40	.18
❑ 9 Edgar Renteria	.40	.18
❑ 10 Scott Rolen	2.00	.90

1997 Ultra Season Crowns

	MINT	NRMT
COMPLETE SET (12)	15.00	6.75
COMMON CARD (1-12)	.50	.23
❑ 1 Albert Belle	1.00	.45
❑ 2 Dante Bichette	.50	.23
❑ 3 Barry Bonds	1.25	.55
❑ 4 Kenny Lofton	1.00	.45
❑ 5 Edgar Martinez	.50	.23
❑ 6 Mark McGwire	6.00	2.70
❑ 7 Andy Pettitte	.75	.35
❑ 8 Mike Piazza	3.00	1.35
❑ 9 Alex Rodriguez	3.00	1.35
❑ 10 John Smoltz	.50	.23
❑ 11 Sammy Sosa	3.00	1.35
❑ 12 Frank Thomas	3.00	1.35

1997 Ultra Starring Role

	MINT	NRMT
COMPLETE SET (12)	600.00	275.00
COMMON CARD (1-12)	20.00	9.00
❑ 1 Andruw Jones	25.00	11.00
❑ 2 Ken Griffey Jr.	100.00	45.00
❑ 3 Frank Thomas	60.00	27.00
❑ 4 Alex Rodriguez	60.00	27.00
❑ 5 Cal Ripken	80.00	36.00
❑ 6 Mike Piazza	60.00	27.00
❑ 7 Greg Maddux	60.00	27.00
❑ 8 Chipper Jones	50.00	22.00
❑ 9 Derek Jeter	50.00	22.00
❑ 10 Juan Gonzalez	50.00	22.00
❑ 11 Albert Belle	25.00	11.00
❑ 12 Tony Gwynn	50.00	22.00

1997 Ultra Thunderclap

	MINT	NRMT
COMPLETE SET (10)	80.00	36.00
COMMON CARD (1-10)	4.00	1.80
❑ 1 Barry Bonds	4.00	1.80
❑ 2 Mo Vaughn	4.00	1.80
❑ 3 Mark McGwire	15.00	6.75
❑ 4 Jeff Bagwell	5.00	2.20
❑ 5 Juan Gonzalez	8.00	3.60
❑ 6 Alex Rodriguez	10.00	4.50
❑ 7 Chipper Jones	8.00	3.60
❑ 8 Ken Griffey Jr.	15.00	6.75
❑ 9 Mike Piazza	10.00	4.50
❑ 10 Frank Thomas	10.00	4.50

1997 Ultra Top 30

	MINT	NRMT
COMPLETE SET (30)	40.00	18.00
COMMON CARD (1-30)	.40	.18
COMP.G.MED.SET (30)	300.00	135.00

*GOLD MEDALLION: 5X TO 12X BASIC CARDS
G.MED SER.2 STATED ODDS 1:18 RETAIL

❑ 1 Andruw Jones	1.50	.70
❑ 2 Ken Griffey	4.00	1.80
❑ 3 Frank Thomas	2.50	1.10
❑ 4 Alex Rodriguez	2.50	1.10
❑ 5 Cal Ripken	3.00	1.35
❑ 6 Mike Piazza	2.50	1.10
❑ 7 Greg Maddux	2.50	1.10
❑ 8 Chipper Jones	2.00	.90
❑ 9 Derek Jeter	2.50	1.10
❑ 10 Juan Gonzalez	2.00	.90
❑ 11 Albert Belle	.75	.35
❑ 12 Tony Gwynn	2.00	.90
❑ 13 Jeff Bagwell	1.25	.55
❑ 14 Mark McGwire	4.00	1.80
❑ 15 Andy Pettitte	.50	.23
❑ 16 Mo Vaughn	1.00	.45
❑ 17 Kenny Lofton	.75	.35
❑ 18 Manny Ramirez	.75	.35
❑ 19 Roberto Alomar	.75	.35
❑ 20 Ryne Sandberg	1.00	.45
❑ 21 Hideo Nomo	2.00	.90
❑ 22 Barry Bonds	1.00	.45
❑ 23 Eddie Murray	.75	.35
❑ 24 Ken Caminiti	.50	.23

❑ 25 John Smoltz .40 .18
❑ 26 Pat Hentgen .40 .18
❑ 27 Todd Hollandsworth .40 .18
❑ 28 Matt Williams .40 .18
❑ 29 Bernie Williams .75 .35
❑ 30 Brady Anderson .40 .18

1998 Ultra

	MINT	NRMT
COMPLETE SET (501)	300.00	135.00
COMPLETE SERIES 1 (250)	180.00	80.00
COMPLETE SERIES 2 (251)	120.00	55.00
COMP.SER.1 w/o SP's (210)	15.00	6.75
COMP.SER.2 w/o SP's (226)	15.00	6.75
COMMON 1 (1-220/246-250)	.15	.07
COMMON 2 (251-475/501)	.15	.07
COMMON SP 1 (211-245)	.75	.35
COMMON SP 2 (476-500)	2.00	.90

❑ 1 Ken Griffey Jr. 3.00 1.35
❑ 2 Matt Morris .25 .11
❑ 3 Roger Clemens 1.25 .55
❑ 4 Matt Williams .25 .11
❑ 5 Roberto Hernandez .15 .07
❑ 6 Rondell White .25 .11
❑ 7 Tim Salmon .60 .25
❑ 8 Brad Radke .25 .11
❑ 9 Brett Butler .25 .11
❑ 10 Carl Everett .15 .07
❑ 11 Chili Davis .25 .11
❑ 12 Chuck Finley .25 .11
❑ 13 Darryl Kile .25 .11
❑ 14 Deivi Cruz .15 .07
❑ 15 Gary Gaetti .15 .07
❑ 16 Matt Stairs .25 .11
❑ 17 Pat Meares .15 .07
❑ 18 Will Cunnane .15 .07
❑ 19 Steve Woodard .25 .11
❑ 20 Andy Ashby .15 .07
❑ 21 Bobby Higginson .40 .18
❑ 22 Brian Jordan .25 .11
❑ 23 Craig Biggio .60 .25
❑ 24 Jim Edmonds .40 .18
❑ 25 Ryan McGuire .15 .07
❑ 26 Scott Hatteberg .15 .07
❑ 27 Willie Greene .25 .11
❑ 28 Albert Belle .75 .35
❑ 29 Ellis Burks .25 .11
❑ 30 Hideo Nomo .75 .35
❑ 31 Jeff Bagwell 1.00 .45
❑ 32 Kevin Brown .40 .18
❑ 33 Nomar Garciaparra 2.00 .90
❑ 34 Pedro Martinez .60 .25
❑ 35 Raul Mondesi .40 .18
❑ 36 Ricky Bottalico .25 .11
❑ 37 Shawn Estes .25 .11
❑ 38 Otis Nixon .15 .07
❑ 39 Terry Steinbach .25 .11
❑ 40 Tom Glavine .60 .25
❑ 41 Todd Dunwoody .25 .11
❑ 42 Deion Sanders .25 .11
❑ 43 Gary Sheffield .40 .18
❑ 44 Mike Lansing .15 .07
❑ 45 Mike Lieberthal .15 .07
❑ 46 Paul Sorrento .15 .07
❑ 47 Paul O'Neill .25 .11
❑ 48 Tom Goodwin .15 .07
❑ 49 Andruw Jones .75 .35
❑ 50 Barry Bonds .75 .35
❑ 51 Bernie Williams .60 .25
❑ 52 Jeremi Gonzalez .25 .11
❑ 53 Mike Piazza 2.00 .90
❑ 54 Russ Davis .25 .11
❑ 55 Vinny Castilla .40 .18
❑ 56 Rod Beck .25 .11
❑ 57 Andres Galarraga .60 .25
❑ 58 Ben McDonald .15 .07
❑ 59 Billy Wagner .25 .11
❑ 60 Charles Johnson .25 .11
❑ 61 Fred McGriff .40 .18
❑ 62 Dean Palmer .25 .11
❑ 63 Frank Thomas 2.00 .90
❑ 64 Ismael Valdes .25 .11
❑ 65 Mark Bellhorn .25 .11
❑ 66 Jeff King .25 .11
❑ 67 John Wetteland .25 .11
❑ 68 Mark Grace .40 .18
❑ 69 Mark Kotsay .40 .18
❑ 70 Scott Rolen 1.50 .70
❑ 71 Todd Hundley .25 .11
❑ 72 Todd Worrell .15 .07
❑ 73 Wilson Alvarez .25 .11
❑ 74 Bobby Jones .15 .07
❑ 75 Jose Canseco .60 .25
❑ 76 Kevin Appier .25 .11
❑ 77 Neifi Perez .25 .11
❑ 78 Paul Molitor .60 .25
❑ 79 Quilvio Veras .15 .07
❑ 80 Randy Johnson .60 .25
❑ 81 Glendon Rusch .15 .07
❑ 82 Curt Schilling .25 .11
❑ 83 Alex Rodriguez 2.00 .90
❑ 84 Rey Ordonez .25 .11
❑ 85 Jeff Juden .15 .07
❑ 86 Mike Cameron .25 .11
❑ 87 Ryan Klesko .25 .11
❑ 88 Trevor Hoffman .25 .11
❑ 89 Chuck Knoblauch .60 .25
❑ 90 Larry Walker .60 .25
❑ 91 Mark McLemore .15 .07
❑ 92 B.J. Surhoff .25 .11
❑ 93 Darren Daulton .25 .11
❑ 94 Ray Durham .25 .11
❑ 95 Sammy Sosa 1.50 .70
❑ 96 Eric Young .25 .11
❑ 97 Gerald Williams .15 .07
❑ 98 Javy Lopez .25 .11
❑ 99 John Smiley .15 .07
❑ 100 Juan Gonzalez 1.50 .70
❑ 101 Shawn Green .25 .11
❑ 102 Charles Nagy .25 .11
❑ 103 David Justice .60 .25
❑ 104 Joey Hamilton .25 .11
❑ 105 Pat Hentgen .25 .11
❑ 106 Raul Casanova .15 .07
❑ 107 Tony Phillips .15 .07
❑ 108 Tony Gwynn 1.50 .70
❑ 109 Will Clark .60 .25
❑ 110 Jason Giambi .25 .11
❑ 111 Jay Bell .25 .11
❑ 112 Johnny Damon .25 .11
❑ 113 Alan Benes .25 .11
❑ 114 Jeff Suppan .15 .07
❑ 115 Kevin Polcovich .15 .07
❑ 116 Shigetoshi Hasegawa .25 .11
❑ 117 Steve Finley .25 .11
❑ 118 Tony Clark .40 .18
❑ 119 David Cone .40 .18
❑ 120 Jose Guillen .25 .11
❑ 121 Kevin Millwood 1.50 .70
❑ 122 Greg Maddux 2.00 .90
❑ 123 Dave Nilsson .15 .07
❑ 124 Hideki Irabu .40 .18
❑ 125 Jason Kendall .25 .11
❑ 126 Jim Thome .60 .25
❑ 127 Delino DeShields .15 .07
❑ 128 Edgar Renteria .25 .11
❑ 129 Edgardo Alfonzo .25 .11
❑ 130 J.T. Snow .25 .11
❑ 131 Jeff Abbott .25 .11
❑ 132 Jeffrey Hammonds .25 .11
❑ 133 Todd Greene .25 .11
❑ 134 Vladimir Guerrero 1.00 .45
❑ 135 Jay Buhner .25 .11
❑ 136 Jeff Cirillo .25 .11
❑ 137 Jeromy Burnitz .25 .11
❑ 138 Mickey Morandini .15 .07
❑ 139 Tino Martinez .60 .25
❑ 140 Jeff Shaw .25 .11
❑ 141 Rafael Palmeiro .40 .18
❑ 142 Bobby Bonilla .25 .11
❑ 143 Cal Ripken 2.50 1.10
❑ 144 Chad Fox .15 .07
❑ 145 Dante Bichette .25 .11
❑ 146 Dennis Eckersley .25 .11
❑ 147 Mariano Rivera .25 .11
❑ 148 Mo Vaughn .75 .35
❑ 149 Reggie Sanders .25 .11
❑ 150 Derek Jeter 1.50 .70
❑ 151 Rusty Greer .25 .11
❑ 152 Brady Anderson .25 .11
❑ 153 Brett Tomko .25 .11
❑ 154 Jaime Navarro .15 .07
❑ 155 Kevin Orie .15 .07
❑ 156 Roberto Alomar .60 .25
❑ 157 Edgar Martinez .25 .11
❑ 158 John Olerud .25 .11
❑ 159 John Smoltz .25 .11
❑ 160 Ryne Sandberg .75 .35
❑ 161 Billy Taylor .15 .07
❑ 162 Chris Holt .15 .07
❑ 163 Damion Easley .25 .11
❑ 164 Darin Erstad .75 .35
❑ 165 Joe Carter .25 .11
❑ 166 Kelvim Escobar .25 .11
❑ 167 Ken Caminiti .40 .18
❑ 168 Pokey Reese .15 .07
❑ 169 Ray Lankford .25 .11
❑ 170 Livan Hernandez .25 .11
❑ 171 Steve Kline .15 .07
❑ 172 Tom Gordon .25 .11
❑ 173 Travis Fryman .25 .11
❑ 174 Al Martin .15 .07
❑ 175 Andy Pettitte .40 .18
❑ 176 Jeff Kent .25 .11
❑ 177 Jimmy Key .25 .11
❑ 178 Mark Grudzielanek .25 .11
❑ 179 Tony Saunders .15 .07
❑ 180 Barry Larkin .40 .18
❑ 181 Bubba Trammell .25 .11
❑ 182 Carlos Delgado .25 .11
❑ 183 Carlos Baerga .25 .11
❑ 184 Derek Bell .25 .11
❑ 185 Henry Rodriguez .25 .11
❑ 186 Jason Dickson .25 .11
❑ 187 Ron Gant .15 .07
❑ 188 Tony Womack .25 .11
❑ 189 Justin Thompson .25 .11
❑ 190 Fernando Tatis .25 .11
❑ 191 Mark Wohlers .15 .07
❑ 192 Takashi Kashiwada .40 .18
❑ 193 Garret Anderson .25 .11
❑ 194 Jose Cruz Jr. .75 .35
❑ 195 Ricardo Rincon .15 .07
❑ 196 Tim Naehring .15 .07
❑ 197 Moises Alou .40 .18
❑ 198 Eric Karros .25 .11
❑ 199 John Jaha .15 .07
❑ 200 Marty Cordova .15 .07
❑ 201 Ken Hill .15 .07
❑ 202 Chipper Jones 1.50 .70
❑ 203 Kenny Lofton .60 .25
❑ 204 Mike Mussina .60 .25
❑ 205 Manny Ramirez .60 .25
❑ 206 Todd Hollandsworth .15 .07
❑ 207 Cecil Fielder .25 .11
❑ 208 Mark McGwire 4.00 1.80
❑ 209 Jim Leyritz .15 .07
❑ 210 Ivan Rodriguez .75 .35
❑ 211 Jeff Bagwell SC 4.00 1.80
❑ 212 Barry Bonds SC 3.00 1.35
❑ 213 Roger Clemens SC 5.00 2.20
❑ 214 Nomar Garciaparra SC 8.00 3.60
❑ 215 Ken Griffey Jr. SC 12.00 5.50
❑ 216 Tony Gwynn SC 6.00 2.70
❑ 217 Randy Johnson SC 2.50 1.10
❑ 218 Mark McGwire SC 15.00 6.75

❑ 219	Scott Rolen SC	6.00	2.70
❑ 220	Frank Thomas SC	8.00	3.60
❑ 221	Matt Perisho PROS	.75	.35
❑ 222	Wes Helms PROS	1.50	.70
❑ 223	Dave Dellucci PROS	4.00	1.80
❑ 224	Todd Helton PROS	4.00	1.80
❑ 225	Brian Rose PROS	1.50	.70
❑ 226	Aaron Boone PROS	.75	.35
❑ 227	Keith Foulke PROS	.75	.35
❑ 228	Homer Bush PROS	.75	.35
❑ 229	Shannon Stewart PROS	1.50	.70
❑ 230	Richard Hidalgo PROS	1.50	.70
❑ 231	Russ Johnson PROS	.75	.35
❑ 232	Henry Blanco PROS	.75	.35
❑ 233	Paul Konerko PROS	2.50	1.10
❑ 234	Antone Williamson PROS	.75	.35
❑ 235	Shane Bowers PROS	.75	.35
❑ 236	Jose Vidro PROS	.75	.35
❑ 237	Derek Wallace PROS	.75	.35
❑ 238	Ricky Ledee PROS	1.50	.70
❑ 239	Ben Grieve PROS	6.00	2.70
❑ 240	Lou Collier PROS	.75	.35
❑ 241	Derrek Lee PROS	1.50	.70
❑ 242	Ruben Rivera PROS	1.50	.70
❑ 243	Jorge Velandia PROS	.75	.35
❑ 244	Andrew Vessel PROS	.75	.35
❑ 245	Chris Carpenter PROS	1.50	.70
❑ 246	Ken Griffey Jr. CL	1.50	.70
❑ 247	Alex Rodriguez CL	1.00	.45
❑ 248	Diamond Ink CL	.15	.07
❑ 249	Frank Thomas CL	1.00	.45
❑ 250	Cal Ripken CL	1.25	.55
❑ 251	Carlos Perez	.25	.11
❑ 252	Larry Sutton	.15	.07
❑ 253	Gary Sheffield	.40	.18
❑ 254	Wally Joyner	.25	.11
❑ 255	Todd Stottlemyre	.25	.11
❑ 256	Nerio Rodriguez	.25	.11
❑ 257	Charles Johnson	.25	.11
❑ 258	Pedro Astacio	.15	.07
❑ 259	Cal Eldred	.15	.07
❑ 260	Chili Davis	.25	.11
❑ 261	Freddy Garcia	.15	.07
❑ 262	Bobby Witt	.15	.07
❑ 263	Michael Coleman	.25	.11
❑ 264	Mike Caruso	.25	.11
❑ 265	Mike Lansing	.15	.07
❑ 266	Dennis Reyes	.25	.11
❑ 267	F.P. Santangelo	.15	.07
❑ 268	Darryl Hamilton	.15	.07
❑ 269	Mike Fetters	.15	.07
❑ 270	Charlie Hayes	.15	.07
❑ 271	Royce Clayton	.15	.07
❑ 272	Doug Drabek	.15	.07
❑ 273	James Baldwin	.25	.11
❑ 274	Brian Hunter	.25	.11
❑ 275	Chan Ho Park	.60	.25
❑ 276	John Franco	.25	.11
❑ 277	David Wells	.40	.18
❑ 278	Eli Marrero	.25	.11
❑ 279	Kerry Wood	3.00	1.35
❑ 280	Donnie Sadler	.25	.11
❑ 281	Scott Winchester	.25	.11
❑ 282	Hal Morris	.15	.07
❑ 283	Brad Fullmer	.25	.11
❑ 284	Bernard Gilkey	.15	.07
❑ 285	Ramiro Mendoza	.25	.11
❑ 286	Kevin Brown	.40	.18
❑ 287	David Segui	.25	.11
❑ 288	Willie McGee	.15	.07
❑ 289	Darren Oliver	.15	.07
❑ 290	Antonio Alfonseca	.15	.07
❑ 291	Eric Davis	.25	.11
❑ 292	Mickey Morandini	.15	.07
❑ 293	Frank Catalanotto	.25	.11
❑ 294	Derrek Lee	.25	.11
❑ 295	Todd Zeile	.25	.11
❑ 296	Chuck Knoblauch	.60	.25
❑ 297	Wilson Delgado	.25	.11
❑ 298	Bobby Bonilla	.25	.11
❑ 299	Orel Hershiser	.25	.11
❑ 300	Ozzie Guillen	.15	.07
❑ 301	Aaron Sele	.25	.11
❑ 302	Joe Carter	.25	.11
❑ 303	Darryl Kile	.25	.11
❑ 304	Shane Reynolds	.25	.11
❑ 305	Todd Dunn	.15	.07
❑ 306	Bob Abreu	.25	.11
❑ 307	Doug Strange	.15	.07
❑ 308	Jose Canseco	.60	.25
❑ 309	Lance Johnson	.15	.07
❑ 310	Harold Baines	.25	.11
❑ 311	Todd Pratt	.15	.07
❑ 312	Greg Colbrunn	.15	.07
❑ 313	Masato Yoshii	.50	.23
❑ 314	Felix Heredia	.15	.07
❑ 315	Dennis Martinez	.25	.11
❑ 316	Geronimo Berroa	.15	.07
❑ 317	Darren Lewis	.15	.07
❑ 318	Bill Ripken	.15	.07
❑ 319	Enrique Wilson	.25	.11
❑ 320	Alex Ochoa	.15	.07
❑ 321	Doug Glanville	.25	.11
❑ 322	Mike Stanley	.15	.07
❑ 323	Gerald Williams	.15	.07
❑ 324	Pedro Martinez	.60	.25
❑ 325	Jaret Wright	.75	.35
❑ 326	Terry Pendleton	.25	.11
❑ 327	LaTroy Hawkins	.15	.07
❑ 328	Emil Brown	.25	.11
❑ 329	Walt Weiss	.25	.11
❑ 330	Omar Vizquel	.25	.11
❑ 331	Carl Everett	.15	.07
❑ 332	Fernando Vina	.15	.07
❑ 333	Mike Blowers	.15	.07
❑ 334	Dwight Gooden	.25	.11
❑ 335	Mark Lewis	.15	.07
❑ 336	Jim Leyritz	.15	.07
❑ 337	Kenny Lofton	.60	.25
❑ 338	John Halama	.15	.07
❑ 339	Jose Valentin	.15	.07
❑ 340	Desi Relaford	.15	.07
❑ 341	Dante Powell	.25	.11
❑ 342	Ed Sprague	.15	.07
❑ 343	Reggie Jefferson	.15	.07
❑ 344	Mike Hampton	.15	.07
❑ 345	Marquis Grissom	.25	.11
❑ 346	Heathcliff Slocumb	.15	.07
❑ 347	Francisco Cordova	.15	.07
❑ 348	Ken Cloude	.25	.11
❑ 349	Benito Santiago	.15	.07
❑ 350	Denny Neagle	.25	.11
❑ 351	Sean Casey	.25	.11
❑ 352	Robb Nen	.25	.11
❑ 353	Orlando Merced	.15	.07
❑ 354	Adrian Brown	.25	.11
❑ 355	Gregg Jefferies	.15	.07
❑ 356	Otis Nixon	.15	.07
❑ 357	Michael Tucker	.25	.11
❑ 358	Eric Milton	.25	.11
❑ 359	Travis Fryman	.25	.11
❑ 360	Gary DiSarcina	.15	.07
❑ 361	Mario Valdez	.25	.11
❑ 362	Craig Counsell	.15	.07
❑ 363	Jose Offerman	.15	.07
❑ 364	Tony Fernandez	.15	.07
❑ 365	Jason McDonald	.15	.07
❑ 366	Sterling Hitchcock	.25	.11
❑ 367	Donovan Osborne	.15	.07
❑ 368	Troy Percival	.25	.11
❑ 369	Henry Rodriguez	.25	.11
❑ 370	Dmitri Young	.25	.11
❑ 371	Jay Powell	.15	.07
❑ 372	Jeff Conine	.25	.11
❑ 373	Orlando Cabrera	.25	.11
❑ 374	Butch Huskey	.15	.07
❑ 375	Mike Lowell	.60	.25
❑ 376	Kevin Young	.25	.11
❑ 377	Jamie Moyer	.15	.07
❑ 378	Jeff D'Amico	.15	.07
❑ 379	Scott Erickson	.25	.11
❑ 380	Magglio Ordonez	.75	.35
❑ 381	Melvin Nieves	.15	.07
❑ 382	Ramon Martinez	.25	.11
❑ 383	A.J. Hinch	.25	.11
❑ 384	Jeff Brantley	.15	.07
❑ 385	Kevin Elster	.15	.07
❑ 386	Allen Watson	.15	.07
❑ 387	Moises Alou	.40	.18
❑ 388	Jeff Blauser	.15	.07
❑ 389	Pete Harnisch	.15	.07
❑ 390	Shane Andrews	.15	.07
❑ 391	Rico Brogna	.25	.11
❑ 392	Stan Javier	.15	.07
❑ 393	David Howard	.15	.07
❑ 394	Darryl Strawberry	.25	.11
❑ 395	Kent Mercker	.15	.07
❑ 396	Juan Encarnacion	.25	.11
❑ 397	Sandy Alomar Jr.	.25	.11
❑ 398	Al Leiter	.25	.11
❑ 399	Tony Graffanino	.15	.07
❑ 400	Terry Adams	.15	.07
❑ 401	Bruce Aven	.15	.07
❑ 402	Derrick Gibson	.25	.11
❑ 403	Jose Cabrera	.15	.07
❑ 404	Rich Becker	.15	.07
❑ 405	David Ortiz	.25	.11
❑ 406	Brian McRae	.15	.07
❑ 407	Bobby Estalella	.25	.11
❑ 408	Bill Mueller	.25	.11
❑ 409	Dennis Eckersley	.25	.11
❑ 410	Sandy Martinez	.15	.07
❑ 411	Jose Vizcaino	.15	.07
❑ 412	Jermaine Allensworth	.15	.07
❑ 413	Miguel Tejada	.25	.11
❑ 414	Turner Ward	.15	.07
❑ 415	Glenallen Hill	.15	.07
❑ 416	Lee Stevens	.15	.07
❑ 417	Cecil Fielder	.25	.11
❑ 418	Ruben Sierra	.15	.07
❑ 419	Jon Nunnally	.15	.07
❑ 420	Rod Myers	.15	.07
❑ 421	Dustin Hermanson	.25	.11
❑ 422	James Mouton	.15	.07
❑ 423	Dan Wilson	.15	.07
❑ 424	Roberto Kelly	.15	.07
❑ 425	Antonio Osuna	.15	.07
❑ 426	Jacob Cruz	.15	.07
❑ 427	Brent Mayne	.15	.07
❑ 428	Matt Karchner	.15	.07
❑ 429	Damian Jackson	.15	.07
❑ 430	Roger Cedeno	.15	.07
❑ 431	Rickey Henderson	.60	.25
❑ 432	Joe Randa	.15	.07
❑ 433	Greg Vaughn	.25	.11
❑ 434	Andres Galarraga	.60	.25
❑ 435	Rod Beck	.25	.11
❑ 436	Curtis Goodwin	.15	.07
❑ 437	Brad Ausmus	.15	.07
❑ 438	Bob Hamelin	.15	.07
❑ 439	Todd Walker	.40	.18
❑ 440	Scott Brosius	.25	.11
❑ 441	Len Dykstra	.25	.11
❑ 442	Abraham Nunez	.25	.11
❑ 443	Brian Johnson	.15	.07
❑ 444	Randy Myers	.25	.11
❑ 445	Bret Boone	.25	.11
❑ 446	Oscar Henriquez	.25	.11
❑ 447	Mike Sweeney	.15	.07
❑ 448	Kenny Rogers	.15	.07
❑ 449	Mark Langston	.15	.07
❑ 450	Luis Gonzalez	.15	.07
❑ 451	John Burkett	.15	.07
❑ 452	Bip Roberts	.15	.07
❑ 453	Travis Lee	1.25	.55
❑ 454	Felix Rodriguez	.15	.07
❑ 455	Andy Benes	.25	.11
❑ 456	Willie Blair	.15	.07
❑ 457	Brian Anderson	.25	.11
❑ 458	Jay Bell	.25	.11
❑ 459	Matt Williams	.25	.11
❑ 460	Devon White	.25	.11
❑ 461	Karim Garcia	.25	.11
❑ 462	Jorge Fabregas	.15	.07
❑ 463	Wilson Alvarez	.25	.11
❑ 464	Roberto Hernandez	.15	.07
❑ 465	Tony Saunders	.15	.07
❑ 466	Rolando Arrojo	1.00	.45
❑ 467	Wade Boggs	.60	.25
❑ 468	Fred McGriff	.40	.18
❑ 469	Paul Sorrento	.15	.07
❑ 470	Kevin Stocker	.15	.07
❑ 471	Bubba Trammell	.25	.11
❑ 472	Quinton McCracken	.25	.11
❑ 473	Ken Griffey Jr. CL	1.50	.70

		MINT	NRMT
❑ 474	Cal Ripken CL	1.25	.55
❑ 475	Frank Thomas CL	1.00	.45
❑ 476	Ken Griffey Jr. PZ	10.00	4.50
❑ 477	Cal Ripken PZ	8.00	3.60
❑ 478	Frank Thomas PZ	6.00	2.70
❑ 479	Alex Rodriguez PZ	6.00	2.70
❑ 480	Nomar Garciaparra PZ	6.00	2.70
❑ 481	Derek Jeter PZ	5.00	2.20
❑ 482	Andruw Jones PZ	2.50	1.10
❑ 483	Chipper Jones PZ	5.00	2.20
❑ 484	Greg Maddux PZ	6.00	2.70
❑ 485	Mike Piazza PZ	6.00	2.70
❑ 486	Juan Gonzalez PZ	5.00	2.20
❑ 487	Jose Cruz Jr. PZ	2.50	1.10
❑ 488	Jaret Wright PZ	2.50	1.10
❑ 489	Hideo Nomo PZ	2.50	1.10
❑ 490	Scott Rolen PZ	5.00	2.20
❑ 491	Tony Gwynn PZ	5.00	2.20
❑ 492	Roger Clemens PZ	4.00	1.80
❑ 493	Darin Erstad PZ	2.50	1.10
❑ 494	Mark McGwire PZ	12.00	5.50
❑ 495	Jeff Bagwell PZ	3.00	1.35
❑ 496	Mo Vaughn PZ	2.50	1.10
❑ 497	Albert Belle PZ	2.00	.90
❑ 498	Kenny Lofton PZ	2.00	.90
❑ 499	Ben Grieve PZ	4.00	1.80
❑ 500	Barry Bonds PZ	2.50	1.10
❑ 501	Mike Piazza	2.00	.90
❑ S100	Alex Rodriguez AU/750	150.00	70.00

1998 Ultra Gold Medallion

	MINT	NRMT
COMPLETE SET (501)	400.00	180.00
COMPLETE SERIES 1 (250)	200.00	90.00
COMPLETE SERIES 2 (251)	200.00	90.00
COMMON CARD (1-501)	.50	.23

*STARS: 1.5X TO 4X BASIC CARDS
*YOUNG STARS: 1.25X TO 3X BASIC CARDS
*ROOKIES: 1X TO 2.5X BASIC CARDS
*SEASON CROWNS: .4X TO 1X BASIC SC
*PROSPECTS: .3X TO .8X BASIC PROSPECTS
*CHECKLISTS: 1.5X TO 4X BASIC CL'S
*PIZZAZZ: .5X TO 1.2X BASIC PIZZAZZ

1998 Ultra Platinum Medallion

	MINT	NRMT
COMMON CARD (1-501)	15.00	6.75
MINOR STARS	30.00	13.50
SEMISTARS	50.00	22.00
UNLISTED STARS	80.00	36.00

*STARS: 50X TO 100X BASIC CARDS
*YNG.STARS: 40X TO 80X BASIC CARDS
*ROOKIES: 25X TO 50X BASIC CARDS
*SEASON CROWNS: 6X TO 12X BASIC SC
*PROSPECTS: 7.5X TO 15X BASIC PROSP.
*CHECKLISTS: 50X TO 100X BASIC CL'S
*PIZZAZZ: 7.5X TO 15X BASIC PIZZAZZ

1998 Ultra Artistic Talents

		MINT	NRMT
COMPLETE SET (18)		80.00	36.00
COMMON CARD (1-18)		1.50	.70
❑ 1	Ken Griffey Jr.	10.00	4.50
❑ 2	Andruw Jones	2.50	1.10
❑ 3	Alex Rodriguez	6.00	2.70
❑ 4	Frank Thomas	6.00	2.70
❑ 5	Cal Ripken	8.00	3.60
❑ 6	Derek Jeter	5.00	2.20
❑ 7	Chipper Jones	5.00	2.20
❑ 8	Greg Maddux	6.00	2.70
❑ 9	Mike Piazza	6.00	2.70
❑ 10	Albert Belle	2.50	1.10
❑ 11	Darin Erstad	2.50	1.10
❑ 12	Juan Gonzalez	5.00	2.20
❑ 13	Jeff Bagwell	3.00	1.35
❑ 14	Tony Gwynn	5.00	2.20
❑ 15	Mark McGwire	12.00	5.50
❑ 16	Scott Rolen	5.00	2.20
❑ 17	Barry Bonds	2.50	1.10
❑ 18	Kenny Lofton	1.50	.70

1998 Ultra Back to the Future

		MINT	NRMT
COMPLETE SET (15)		20.00	9.00
COMMON CARD (1-15)		.50	.23
❑ 1	Andruw Jones	1.50	.70
❑ 2	Alex Rodriguez	4.00	1.80
❑ 3	Derek Jeter	3.00	1.35
❑ 4	Darin Erstad	1.50	.70
❑ 5	Mike Cameron	.50	.23
❑ 6	Scott Rolen	3.00	1.35
❑ 7	Nomar Garciaparra	4.00	1.80
❑ 8	Hideki Irabu	.75	.35
❑ 9	Jose Cruz Jr.	1.50	.70
❑ 10	Vladimir Guerrero	2.00	.90
❑ 11	Mark Kotsay	.75	.35
❑ 12	Tony Womack	.50	.23
❑ 13	Jason Dickson	.50	.23
❑ 14	Jose Guillen	.50	.23
❑ 15	Tony Clark	.75	.35

1998 Ultra Big Shots

		MINT	NRMT
COMPLETE SET (15)		12.00	5.50
COMMON CARD (1-15)		.30	.14
❑ 1	Ken Griffey Jr.	4.00	1.80
❑ 2	Frank Thomas	2.50	1.10
❑ 3	Chipper Jones	2.00	.90
❑ 4	Albert Belle	1.00	.45
❑ 5	Juan Gonzalez	2.00	.90
❑ 6	Jeff Bagwell	1.25	.55
❑ 7	Mark McGwire	5.00	2.20
❑ 8	Barry Bonds	1.00	.45
❑ 9	Manny Ramirez	.75	.35
❑ 10	Mo Vaughn	1.00	.45
❑ 11	Matt Williams	.30	.14
❑ 12	Jim Thome	.75	.35
❑ 13	Tino Martinez	.75	.35
❑ 14	Mike Piazza	2.50	1.10
❑ 15	Tony Clark	.50	.23

1998 Ultra Diamond Immortals

		MINT	NRMT
COMPLETE SET (15)		1000.00	450.00
COMMON CARD (1-15)		25.00	11.00
❑ 1	Ken Griffey Jr.	120.00	55.00
❑ 2	Frank Thomas	80.00	36.00
❑ 3	Alex Rodriguez	80.00	36.00
❑ 4	Cal Ripken	100.00	45.00
❑ 5	Mike Piazza	80.00	36.00
❑ 6	Mark McGwire	150.00	70.00
❑ 7	Greg Maddux	80.00	36.00
❑ 8	Andruw Jones	25.00	11.00
❑ 9	Chipper Jones	60.00	27.00
❑ 10	Derek Jeter	60.00	27.00
❑ 11	Tony Gwynn	60.00	27.00
❑ 12	Juan Gonzalez	60.00	27.00
❑ 13	Jose Cruz Jr.	25.00	11.00
❑ 14	Roger Clemens	50.00	22.00
❑ 15	Barry Bonds	30.00	13.50

1998 Ultra Diamond Producers

		MINT	NRMT
COMPLETE SET (15)		1000.00	450.00
COMMON CARD (1-15)		25.00	11.00
❑ 1	Ken Griffey Jr.	120.00	55.00

		MINT	NRMT
❑ 2	Andruw Jones	25.00	11.00
❑ 3	Alex Rodriguez	80.00	36.00
❑ 4	Frank Thomas	80.00	36.00
❑ 5	Cal Ripken	100.00	45.00
❑ 6	Derek Jeter	60.00	27.00
❑ 7	Chipper Jones	60.00	27.00
❑ 8	Greg Maddux	80.00	36.00
❑ 9	Mike Piazza	80.00	36.00
❑ 10	Juan Gonzalez	60.00	27.00
❑ 11	Jeff Bagwell	40.00	18.00
❑ 12	Tony Gwynn	60.00	27.00
❑ 13	Mark McGwire	150.00	70.00
❑ 14	Barry Bonds	30.00	13.50
❑ 15	Jose Cruz Jr.	25.00	11.00

1998 Ultra Double Trouble

		MINT	NRMT
COMPLETE SET (20)		12.00	5.50
COMMON CARD (1-20)		.25	.11
❑ 1	Ken Griffey Jr.	4.00	1.80
	Alex Rodriguez		
❑ 2	Vladimir Guerrero	1.00	.45
	Pedro Martinez		
❑ 3	Andruw Jones	.50	.23
	Kenny Lofton		
❑ 4	Chipper Jones	2.50	1.10
	Greg Maddux		
❑ 5	Derek Jeter	1.50	.70
	Tino Martinez		
❑ 6	Frank Thomas	2.00	.90
	Albert Belle		
❑ 7	Cal Ripken	2.50	1.10
	Roberto Alomar		
❑ 8	Mike Piazza	2.00	.90
	Hideo Nomo		
❑ 9	Darin Erstad	.75	.35
	Jason Dickson		
❑ 10	Juan Gonzalez	2.00	.90
	Ivan Rodriguez		
❑ 11	Jeff Bagwell	1.00	.45
	Darryl Kile		
	UER front Kyle		
❑ 12	Tony Gwynn	1.50	.70
	Steve Finley		
❑ 13	Mark McGwire	4.00	1.80
	Ray Lankford		
❑ 14	Barry Bonds	.75	.35
	Jeff Kent		
❑ 15	Andy Pettitte	.50	.23
	Bernie Williams		
❑ 16	Mo Vaughn	2.00	.90
	Nomar Garciaparra		
❑ 17	Matt Williams	.50	.23
	Jim Thome		
❑ 18	Hideki Irabu	.25	.11
	Mariano Rivera		
❑ 19	Roger Clemens	1.25	.55
	Jose Cruz Jr.		
❑ 20	Manny Ramirez	.50	.23
	David Justice		

1998 Ultra Fall Classics

		MINT	NRMT
COMPLETE SET (15)		120.00	55.00
COMMON CARD (1-15)		4.00	1.80
❑ 1	Ken Griffey Jr.	20.00	9.00
❑ 2	Andruw Jones	4.00	1.80
❑ 3	Alex Rodriguez	12.00	5.50
❑ 4	Frank Thomas	12.00	5.50
❑ 5	Cal Ripken	15.00	6.75
❑ 6	Derek Jeter	10.00	4.50
❑ 7	Chipper Jones	10.00	4.50
❑ 8	Greg Maddux	12.00	5.50
❑ 9	Mike Piazza	12.00	5.50
❑ 10	Albert Belle	5.00	2.20
❑ 11	Juan Gonzalez	10.00	4.50
❑ 12	Jeff Bagwell	6.00	2.70
❑ 13	Tony Gwynn	10.00	4.50
❑ 14	Mark McGwire	25.00	11.00
❑ 15	Barry Bonds	5.00	2.20

1998 Ultra Kid Gloves

		MINT	NRMT
COMPLETE SET (12)		20.00	9.00
COMMON CARD (1-12)		.50	.23
❑ 1	Andruw Jones	1.50	.70
❑ 2	Alex Rodriguez	4.00	1.80
❑ 3	Derek Jeter	3.00	1.35
❑ 4	Chipper Jones	3.00	1.35
❑ 5	Darin Erstad	1.50	.70
❑ 6	Todd Walker	.75	.35
❑ 7	Scott Rolen	3.00	1.35
❑ 8	Nomar Garciaparra	4.00	1.80
❑ 9	Jose Cruz Jr.	1.50	.70
❑ 10	Charles Johnson	.50	.23
❑ 11	Rey Ordonez	.50	.23
❑ 12	Vladimir Guerrero	2.00	.90

1998 Ultra Millennium Men

		MINT	NRMT
COMPLETE SET (15)		150.00	70.00
COMMON CARD (1-15)		5.00	2.20
❑ 1	Jose Cruz Jr.	5.00	2.20
❑ 2	Ken Griffey Jr.	25.00	11.00
❑ 3	Cal Ripken	20.00	9.00
❑ 4	Derek Jeter	12.00	5.50
❑ 5	Andruw Jones	5.00	2.20
❑ 6	Alex Rodriguez	15.00	6.75
❑ 7	Chipper Jones	12.00	5.50
❑ 8	Scott Rolen	10.00	4.50
❑ 9	Nomar Garciaparra	15.00	6.75
❑ 10	Frank Thomas	15.00	6.75
❑ 11	Mike Piazza	15.00	6.75
❑ 12	Greg Maddux	15.00	6.75
❑ 13	Juan Gonzalez	12.00	5.50
❑ 14	Ben Grieve	8.00	3.60
❑ 15	Jaret Wright	5.00	2.20

1998 Ultra Notables

		MINT	NRMT
COMPLETE SET (20)		40.00	18.00
COMMON CARD (1-20)		.50	.23
❑ 1	Frank Thomas	4.00	1.80
❑ 2	Ken Griffey Jr.	6.00	2.70
❑ 3	Edgar Renteria	.50	.23
❑ 4	Albert Belle	1.25	.55
❑ 5	Juan Gonzalez	3.00	1.35
❑ 6	Jeff Bagwell	2.00	.90
❑ 7	Mark McGwire	8.00	3.60
❑ 8	Barry Bonds	1.50	.70
❑ 9	Scott Rolen	2.50	1.10
❑ 10	Mo Vaughn	1.50	.70
❑ 11	Andruw Jones	1.25	.55
❑ 12	Chipper Jones	3.00	1.35
❑ 13	Tino Martinez	1.25	.55
❑ 14	Mike Piazza	4.00	1.80
❑ 15	Tony Clark	.75	.35
❑ 16	Jose Cruz Jr.	1.25	.55
❑ 17	Nomar Garciaparra	4.00	1.80
❑ 18	Cal Ripken	5.00	2.20
❑ 19	Alex Rodriguez	4.00	1.80
❑ 20	Derek Jeter	3.00	1.35

1998 Ultra Power Plus

		MINT	NRMT
COMPLETE SET (10)		120.00	55.00
COMMON CARD (1-10)		6.00	2.70
❑ 1	Ken Griffey Jr.	30.00	13.50
❑ 2	Andruw Jones	6.00	2.70
❑ 3	Alex Rodriguez	20.00	9.00
❑ 4	Frank Thomas	20.00	9.00
❑ 5	Mike Piazza	20.00	9.00
❑ 6	Albert Belle	8.00	3.60
❑ 7	Juan Gonzalez	15.00	6.75
❑ 8	Jeff Bagwell	10.00	4.50

	MINT	NRMT
❑ 9 Barry Bonds	8.00	3.60
❑ 10 Jose Cruz Jr.	6.00	2.70

1998 Ultra Prime Leather

	MINT	NRMT
COMPLETE SET (18)	600.00	275.00
COMMON CARD (1-18)	12.00	5.50
❑ 1 Ken Griffey Jr.	80.00	36.00
❑ 2 Andruw Jones	15.00	6.75
❑ 3 Alex Rodriguez	50.00	22.00
❑ 4 Frank Thomas	50.00	22.00
❑ 5 Cal Ripken	60.00	27.00
❑ 6 Derek Jeter	40.00	18.00
❑ 7 Chipper Jones	40.00	18.00
❑ 8 Greg Maddux	50.00	22.00
❑ 9 Mike Piazza	50.00	22.00
❑ 10 Albert Belle	15.00	6.75
❑ 11 Darin Erstad	15.00	6.75
❑ 12 Juan Gonzalez	40.00	18.00
❑ 13 Jeff Bagwell	25.00	11.00
❑ 14 Tony Gwynn	40.00	18.00
❑ 15 Roberto Alomar	15.00	6.75
❑ 16 Barry Bonds	20.00	9.00
❑ 17 Kenny Lofton	12.00	5.50
❑ 18 Jose Cruz Jr.	15.00	6.75

1998 Ultra Rocket to Stardom

	MINT	NRMT
COMPLETE SET (15)	40.00	18.00
COMMON CARD (1-15)	1.00	.45
❑ 1 Ben Grieve	8.00	3.60
❑ 2 Magglio Ordonez	5.00	2.20
❑ 3 Travis Lee	8.00	3.60
❑ 4 Mike Caruso	1.50	.70
❑ 5 Brian Rose	1.50	.70
❑ 6 Brad Fullmer	1.50	.70
❑ 7 Michael Coleman	1.50	.70
❑ 8 Juan Encarnacion	1.50	.70
❑ 9 Karim Garcia	1.50	.70
❑ 10 Todd Helton	5.00	2.20
❑ 11 Richard Hidalgo	1.50	.70
❑ 12 Paul Konerko	4.00	1.80
❑ 13 Rod Myers	1.00	.45
❑ 14 Jaret Wright	5.00	2.20
❑ 15 Miguel Tejada	1.50	.70

1998 Ultra Ticket Studs

	MINT	NRMT
COMPLETE SET (15)	600.00	275.00
COMMON CARD (1-15)	15.00	6.75
❑ 1 Travis Lee	25.00	11.00
❑ 2 Tony Gwynn	40.00	18.00
❑ 3 Scott Rolen	30.00	13.50
❑ 4 Nomar Garciaparra	50.00	22.00
❑ 5 Mike Piazza	50.00	22.00
❑ 6 Mark McGwire	100.00	45.00
❑ 7 Ken Griffey Jr.	80.00	36.00
❑ 8 Juan Gonzalez	40.00	18.00
❑ 9 Jose Cruz Jr.	15.00	6.75
❑ 10 Frank Thomas	50.00	22.00
❑ 11 Derek Jeter	40.00	18.00
❑ 12 Chipper Jones	40.00	18.00
❑ 13 Cal Ripken	60.00	27.00
❑ 14 Andruw Jones	15.00	6.75
❑ 15 Alex Rodriguez	50.00	22.00

1998 Ultra Top 30

	MINT	NRMT
COMPLETE SET (30)	40.00	18.00
COMMON CARD (1-30)	.40	.18
❑ 1 Barry Bonds	1.00	.45
❑ 2 Ivan Rodriguez	1.00	.45
❑ 3 Kenny Lofton	.75	.35
❑ 4 Albert Belle	.75	.35
❑ 5 Mo Vaughn	1.00	.45
❑ 6 Jeff Bagwell	1.25	.55
❑ 7 Mark McGwire	5.00	2.20
❑ 8 Darin Erstad	1.00	.45
❑ 9 Roger Clemens	1.50	.70
❑ 10 Tony Gwynn	2.00	.90
❑ 11 Scott Rolen	2.00	.90
❑ 12 Hideo Nomo	1.00	.45
❑ 13 Juan Gonzalez	2.00	.90
❑ 14 Mike Piazza	2.50	1.10
❑ 15 Greg Maddux	2.50	1.10
❑ 16 Chipper Jones	2.00	.90
❑ 17 Andruw Jones	1.00	.45
❑ 18 Derek Jeter	2.00	.90
❑ 19 Nomar Garciaparra	2.50	1.10
❑ 20 Alex Rodriguez	2.50	1.10
❑ 21 Frank Thomas	2.50	1.10
❑ 22 Cal Ripken	3.00	1.35
❑ 23 Ken Griffey Jr.	4.00	1.80
❑ 24 Jose Cruz Jr.	1.00	.45
❑ 25 Jaret Wright	1.00	.45
❑ 26 Travis Lee	1.50	.70
❑ 27 Wade Boggs	.75	.35
❑ 28 Chuck Knoblauch	.75	.35
❑ 29 Joe Carter	.40	.18
❑ 30 Ben Grieve	1.50	.70

1998 Ultra Win Now

	MINT	NRMT
COMPLETE SET (20)	400.00	180.00
COMMON CARD (1-20)	10.00	4.50
❑ 1 Alex Rodriguez	30.00	13.50
❑ 2 Andruw Jones	10.00	4.50
❑ 3 Cal Ripken	40.00	18.00
❑ 4 Chipper Jones	25.00	11.00
❑ 5 Darin Erstad	10.00	4.50
❑ 6 Derek Jeter	25.00	11.00
❑ 7 Frank Thomas	30.00	13.50
❑ 8 Greg Maddux	30.00	13.50
❑ 9 Hideo Nomo	12.00	5.50
❑ 10 Jeff Bagwell	15.00	6.75
❑ 11 Jose Cruz Jr.	10.00	4.50
❑ 12 Juan Gonzalez	25.00	11.00
❑ 13 Ken Griffey Jr.	50.00	22.00
❑ 14 Mark McGwire	60.00	27.00
❑ 15 Mike Piazza	30.00	13.50
❑ 16 Mo Vaughn	12.00	5.50
❑ 17 Nomar Garciaparra	30.00	13.50
❑ 18 Roger Clemens	20.00	9.00
❑ 19 Scott Rolen	20.00	9.00
❑ 20 Tony Gwynn	25.00	11.00

1999 Ultra

	MINT	NRMT
COMPLETE SERIES 1 (250)	180.00	80.00
COMP.SER.1 w/o SP's (215)	20.00	9.00
COMMON CARD (1-215)	.15	.07
COMMON SC (216-225)	1.50	.70
COMMON PROSPECT (226-250)	2.00	.90
❑ 1 Greg Maddux	2.00	.90
❑ 2 Greg Vaughn	.25	.11
❑ 3 John Wetteland	.25	.11
❑ 4 Tino Martinez	.60	.25

❑ 5 Todd Walker .40 .18
❑ 6 Troy O'Leary .25 .11
❑ 7 Barry Larkin .40 .18
❑ 8 Mike Lansing .15 .07
❑ 9 Delino DeShields .15 .07
❑ 10 Brett Tomko .25 .11
❑ 11 Carlos Perez .15 .07
❑ 12 Mark Langston .15 .07
❑ 13 Jamie Moyer .15 .07
❑ 14 Jose Guillen .25 .11
❑ 15 Bartolo Colon .25 .11
❑ 16 Brady Anderson .25 .11
❑ 17 Walt Weiss .25 .11
❑ 18 Shane Reynolds .25 .11
❑ 19 David Segui .25 .11
❑ 20 Vladimir Guerrero 1.00 .45
❑ 21 Freddy Garcia .15 .07
❑ 22 Carl Everett .15 .07
❑ 23 Jose Cruz Jr. .60 .25
❑ 24 David Ortiz .25 .11
❑ 25 Andruw Jones .75 .35
❑ 26 Darren Lewis .15 .07
❑ 27 Ray Lankford .25 .11
❑ 28 Wally Joyner .25 .11
❑ 29 Charles Johnson .25 .11
❑ 30 Derek Jeter 1.50 .70
❑ 31 Sean Casey .25 .11
❑ 32 Bobby Bonilla .25 .11
❑ 33 Todd Zeile .25 .11
❑ 34 Todd Helton .75 .35
❑ 35 David Wells .40 .18
❑ 36 Darin Erstad .75 .35
❑ 37 Ivan Rodriguez .75 .35
❑ 38 Antonio Osuna .15 .07
❑ 39 Mickey Morandini .15 .07
❑ 40 Rusty Greer .25 .11
❑ 41 Rod Beck .25 .11
❑ 42 Larry Sutton .15 .07
❑ 43 Edgar Renteria .25 .11
❑ 44 Otis Nixon .15 .07
❑ 45 Eli Marrero .25 .11
❑ 46 Reggie Jefferson .15 .07
❑ 47 Trevor Hoffman .25 .11
❑ 48 Andres Galarraga .60 .25
❑ 49 Scott Brosius .25 .11
❑ 50 Vinny Castilla .40 .18
❑ 51 Bret Boone .25 .11
❑ 52 Masato Yoshii .25 .11
❑ 53 Matt Williams .25 .11
❑ 54 Robin Ventura .25 .11
❑ 55 Jay Powell .15 .07
❑ 56 Dean Palmer .25 .11
❑ 57 Eric Milton .25 .11
❑ 58 Willie McGee .25 .11
❑ 59 Tony Gwynn 1.50 .70
❑ 60 Tom Gordon .25 .11
❑ 61 Dante Bichette .25 .11
❑ 62 Jaret Wright .60 .25
❑ 63 Devon White .25 .11
❑ 64 Frank Thomas 2.00 .90
❑ 65 Mike Piazza 2.00 .90
❑ 66 Jose Offerman .15 .07
❑ 67 Pat Meares .15 .07
❑ 68 Brian Meadows .15 .07
❑ 69 Nomar Garciaparra 2.00 .90
❑ 70 Mark McGwire 4.00 1.80
❑ 71 Tony Graffanino .15 .07
❑ 72 Ken Griffey Jr. 3.00 1.35
❑ 73 Ken Caminiti .40 .18
❑ 74 Todd Jones .15 .07
❑ 75 A.J. Hinch .25 .11
❑ 76 Marquis Grissom .25 .11
❑ 77 Jay Buhner .25 .11
❑ 78 Albert Belle .60 .25
❑ 79 Brian Anderson .25 .11
❑ 80 Quinton McCracken .25 .11
❑ 81 Omar Vizquel .25 .11
❑ 82 Todd Stottlemyre .25 .11
❑ 83 Cal Ripken 2.50 1.10
❑ 84 Magglio Ordonez .25 .11
❑ 85 John Olerud .25 .11
❑ 86 Hal Morris .15 .07
❑ 87 Derrek Lee .25 .11
❑ 88 Doug Glanville .25 .11
❑ 89 Marty Cordova .15 .07
❑ 90 Kevin Brown .40 .18
❑ 91 Kevin Young .25 .11
❑ 92 Rico Brogna .25 .11
❑ 93 Wilson Alvarez .15 .07
❑ 94 Bob Wickman .15 .07
❑ 95 Jim Thome .60 .25
❑ 96 Mike Mussina .60 .25
❑ 97 Al Leiter .15 .07
❑ 98 Travis Lee 1.00 .45
❑ 99 Jeff King .25 .11
❑ 100 Kerry Wood 1.50 .70
❑ 101 Cliff Floyd .25 .11
❑ 102 Jose Valentin .15 .07
❑ 103 Manny Ramirez .60 .25
❑ 104 Butch Huskey .15 .07
❑ 105 Scott Erickson .25 .11
❑ 106 Ray Durham .25 .11
❑ 107 Johnny Damon .25 .11
❑ 108 Craig Counsell .15 .07
❑ 109 Rolando Arrojo .60 .25
❑ 110 Bob Abreu .25 .11
❑ 111 Tony Womack .15 .07
❑ 112 Mike Stanley .15 .07
❑ 113 Kenny Lofton .60 .25
❑ 114 Eric Davis .25 .11
❑ 115 Jeff Conine .25 .11
❑ 116 Carlos Baerga .25 .11
❑ 117 Rondell White .25 .11
❑ 118 Billy Wagner .25 .11
❑ 119 Ed Sprague .15 .07
❑ 120 Jason Schmidt .25 .11
❑ 121 Edgar Martinez .25 .11
❑ 122 Travis Fryman .25 .11
❑ 123 Armando Benitez .15 .07
❑ 124 Matt Stairs .25 .11
❑ 125 Roberto Hernandez .15 .07
❑ 126 Jay Bell .25 .11
❑ 127 Justin Thompson .25 .11
❑ 128 John Jaha .15 .07
❑ 129 Mike Caruso .25 .11
❑ 130 Miguel Tejada .25 .11
❑ 131 Geoff Jenkins .25 .11
❑ 132 Wade Boggs .60 .25
❑ 133 Andy Benes .25 .11
❑ 134 Aaron Sele .25 .11
❑ 135 Bret Saberhagen .25 .11
❑ 136 Mariano Rivera .25 .11
❑ 137 Neifi Perez .25 .11
❑ 138 Paul Konerko .60 .25
❑ 139 Barry Bonds .75 .35
❑ 140 Garret Anderson .25 .11
❑ 141 Bernie Williams .60 .25
❑ 142 Gary Sheffield .40 .18
❑ 143 Rafael Palmeiro .40 .18
❑ 144 Orel Hershiser .25 .11
❑ 145 Craig Biggio .60 .25
❑ 146 Dmitri Young .25 .11
❑ 147 Damion Easley .25 .11
❑ 148 Henry Rodriguez .25 .11
❑ 149 Brad Radke .25 .11
❑ 150 Pedro Martinez .60 .25
❑ 151 Mike Lieberthal .15 .07
❑ 152 Jim Leyritz .15 .07
❑ 153 Chuck Knoblauch .40 .18
❑ 154 Darryl Kile .25 .11
❑ 155 Brian Jordan .25 .11
❑ 156 Chipper Jones 1.50 .70
❑ 157 Pete Harnisch .15 .07
❑ 158 Moises Alou .40 .18
❑ 159 Ismael Valdes .25 .11
❑ 160 Stan Javier .15 .07
❑ 161 Mark Grace .40 .18
❑ 162 Jason Giambi .25 .11
❑ 163 Chuck Finley .15 .07
❑ 164 Juan Encarnacion .25 .11
❑ 165 Chan Ho Park .60 .25
❑ 166 Randy Johnson .60 .25
❑ 167 J.T. Snow .25 .11
❑ 168 Tim Salmon .60 .25
❑ 169 Brian L.Hunter .25 .11
❑ 170 Rickey Henderson .60 .25
❑ 171 Cal Eldred .15 .07
❑ 172 Curt Schilling .25 .11
❑ 173 Alex Rodriguez 2.00 .90
❑ 174 Dustin Hermanson .25 .11
❑ 175 Mike Hampton .15 .07
❑ 176 Shawn Green .25 .11
❑ 177 Roberto Alomar .60 .25
❑ 178 Sandy Alomar Jr. .25 .11
❑ 179 Larry Walker .60 .25
❑ 180 Mo Vaughn .75 .35
❑ 181 Raul Mondesi .40 .18
❑ 182 Hideki Irabu .40 .18
❑ 183 Jim Edmonds .40 .18
❑ 184 Shawn Estes .25 .11
❑ 185 Tony Clark .40 .18
❑ 186 Dan Wilson .15 .07
❑ 187 Michael Tucker .15 .07
❑ 188 Jeff Shaw .25 .11
❑ 189 Mark Grudzielanek .25 .11
❑ 190 Roger Clemens 1.25 .55
❑ 191 Juan Gonzalez 1.50 .70
❑ 192 Sammy Sosa 1.50 .70
❑ 193 Troy Percival .25 .11
❑ 194 Robb Nen .25 .11
❑ 195 Bill Mueller .25 .11
❑ 196 Ben Grieve 1.25 .55
❑ 197 Luis Gonzalez .15 .07
❑ 198 Will Clark .60 .25
❑ 199 Jeff Cirillo .25 .11
❑ 200 Scott Rolen 1.50 .70
❑ 201 Reggie Sanders .15 .07
❑ 202 Fred McGriff .40 .18
❑ 203 Denny Neagle .25 .11
❑ 204 Brad Fullmer .25 .11
❑ 205 Royce Clayton .15 .07
❑ 206 Jose Canseco .60 .25
❑ 207 Jeff Bagwell 1.00 .45
❑ 208 Hideo Nomo .75 .35
❑ 209 Karim Garcia .25 .11
❑ 210 Kenny Rogers .15 .07
❑ 211 Kerry Wood CL .75 .35
❑ 212 Alex Rodriguez CL 1.00 .45
❑ 213 Cal Ripken CL 1.25 .55
❑ 214 Frank Thomas CL 1.00 .45
❑ 215 Ken Griffey Jr. CL 1.50 .70
❑ 216 Alex Rodriguez SC 5.00 2.20
❑ 217 Greg Maddux SC 5.00 2.20
❑ 218 Juan Gonzalez SC 4.00 1.80
❑ 219 Ken Griffey Jr. SC 8.00 3.60
❑ 220 Kerry Wood SC 5.00 2.20
❑ 221 Mark McGwire SC 10.00 4.50
❑ 222 Mike Piazza SC 5.00 2.20
❑ 223 Rickey Henderson SC 1.50 .70
❑ 224 Sammy Sosa SC 4.00 1.80
❑ 225 Travis Lee SC 2.50 1.10
❑ 226 Gabe Alvarez PROS 2.00 .90
❑ 227 Matt Anderson PROS 2.00 .90
❑ 228 Adrian Beltre PROS 4.00 1.80
❑ 229 Orlando Cabrera PROS 2.00 .90
❑ 230 Orlando Hernandez PROS 6.00 2.70
❑ 231 Aramis Ramirez PROS 3.00 1.35
❑ 232 Troy Glaus PROS 8.00 3.60
❑ 233 Gabe Kapler PROS 8.00 3.60
❑ 234 Jeremy Giambi PROS 3.00 1.35
❑ 235 Derrick Gibson PROS 2.00 .90
❑ 236 Carlton Loewer PROS 2.00 .90
❑ 237 Mike Frank PROS 2.00 .90
❑ 238 Carlos Guillen PROS 2.00 .90
❑ 239 Alex Gonzalez PROS 2.00 .90
❑ 240 Enrique Wilson PROS 2.00 .90
❑ 241 J.D. Drew PROS 30.00 13.50
❑ 242 Bruce Chen PROS 2.50 1.10

		MINT	NRMT
❑ 243	Ryan Minor PROS	2.50	1.10
❑ 244	Preston Wilson PROS	2.00	.90
❑ 245	Josh Booty PROS	2.00	.90
❑ 246	Luis Ordaz PROS	2.00	.90
❑ 247	George Lombard PROS	2.50	1.10
❑ 248	Matt Clement PROS	2.00	.90
❑ 249	Eric Chavez PROS	5.00	2.20
❑ 250	Corey Koskie PROS	2.00	.90

1999 Ultra Gold Medallion

	MINT	NRMT
COMPLETE SERIES 1 (250)	500.00	220.00
COMMON CARD (1-215)	.50	.23
*STARS: 1.5X TO 4X BASIC CARDS		
*YOUNG STARS: 1.25X TO 3X BASIC CARDS		
COMMON SC (216-225)	8.00	3.60
*SC STARS: 2X TO 5X BASIC SC		
COMMON PROSPECT (226-250)	5.00	2.20
*PROSPECTS: 1X TO 2.5X BASIC PROSPECTS		

1999 Ultra Platinum Medallion

	MINT	NRMT
COMMON CARD (1-215)	12.00	5.50
*STARS: 30X TO 80X BASIC CARDS		
*YOUNG STARS: 25X TO 60X BASIC CARDS		
COMMON SC (216-225)	80.00	36.00
*SC STARS: 20X TO 50X BASIC SC		
COMMON PROSPECT (226-250)	20.00	9.00
*PROSPECTS: 4X TO 10X BASIC PROSPECTS		

1999 Ultra The Book On

	MINT	NRMT
COMPLETE SET (20)	60.00	27.00
COMMON CARD (1-20)	1.50	.70

		MINT	NRMT
❑ 1	Kerry Wood	5.00	2.20
❑ 2	Ken Griffey Jr.	8.00	3.60
❑ 3	Frank Thomas	5.00	2.20
❑ 4	Albert Belle	1.50	.70
❑ 5	Juan Gonzalez	4.00	1.80
❑ 6	Jeff Bagwell	2.50	1.10
❑ 7	Mark McGwire	10.00	4.50
❑ 8	Barry Bonds	2.00	.90
❑ 9	Andruw Jones	2.00	.90
❑ 10	Mo Vaughn	2.00	.90
❑ 11	Scott Rolen	4.00	1.80
❑ 12	Travis Lee	2.50	1.10
❑ 13	Tony Gwynn	4.00	1.80
❑ 14	Greg Maddux	5.00	2.20
❑ 15	Mike Piazza	5.00	2.20
❑ 16	Chipper Jones	4.00	1.80
❑ 17	Nomar Garciaparra	5.00	2.20
❑ 18	Cal Ripken	6.00	2.70
❑ 19	Derek Jeter	4.00	1.80
❑ 20	Alex Rodriguez	5.00	2.20

1999 Ultra Damage Inc.

	MINT	NRMT
COMPLETE SET (15)	300.00	135.00
COMMON CARD (1-15)	10.00	4.50

		MINT	NRMT
❑ 1	Alex Rodriguez	25.00	11.00
❑ 2	Greg Maddux	25.00	11.00
❑ 3	Cal Ripken	30.00	13.50
❑ 4	Chipper Jones	20.00	9.00
❑ 5	Derek Jeter	20.00	9.00
❑ 6	Frank Thomas	25.00	11.00
❑ 7	Juan Gonzalez	20.00	9.00
❑ 8	Ken Griffey Jr.	40.00	18.00
❑ 9	Kerry Wood	20.00	9.00
❑ 10	Mark McGwire	50.00	22.00
❑ 11	Mike Piazza	25.00	11.00
❑ 12	Nomar Garciaparra	25.00	11.00
❑ 13	Scott Rolen	15.00	6.75
❑ 14	Tony Gwynn	20.00	9.00
❑ 15	Travis Lee	10.00	4.50

1999 Ultra Diamond Producers

	MINT	NRMT
COMPLETE SET (10)	600.00	275.00
COMMON CARD (1-10)	50.00	22.00

		MINT	NRMT
❑ 1	Ken Griffey Jr.	100.00	45.00
❑ 2	Frank Thomas	60.00	27.00
❑ 3	Alex Rodriguez	60.00	27.00
❑ 4	Cal Ripken	80.00	36.00
❑ 5	Mike Piazza	60.00	27.00
❑ 6	Mark McGwire	120.00	55.00
❑ 7	Greg Maddux	60.00	27.00
❑ 8	Kerry Wood	50.00	22.00
❑ 9	Chipper Jones	50.00	22.00
❑ 10	Derek Jeter	50.00	22.00

1999 Ultra RBI Kings

	MINT	NRMT
COMPLETE SET (30)	40.00	18.00
COMMON CARD (1-30)	.50	.23

		MINT	NRMT
❑ 1	Rafael Palmeiro	.75	.35
❑ 2	Mo Vaughn	1.00	.45
❑ 3	Ivan Rodriguez	1.00	.45
❑ 4	Barry Bonds	1.00	.45
❑ 5	Albert Belle	.75	.35
❑ 6	Jeff Bagwell	1.25	.55
❑ 7	Mark McGwire	5.00	2.20
❑ 8	Darin Erstad	1.00	.45
❑ 9	Manny Ramirez	.75	.35
❑ 10	Chipper Jones	2.00	.90
❑ 11	Jim Thome	.75	.35
❑ 12	Scott Rolen	2.00	.90
❑ 13	Tony Gwynn	2.00	.90
❑ 14	Juan Gonzalez	2.00	.90
❑ 15	Mike Piazza	2.50	1.10
❑ 16	Sammy Sosa	2.00	.90
❑ 17	Andruw Jones	1.00	.45
❑ 18	Derek Jeter	2.00	.90
❑ 19	Nomar Garciaparra	2.50	1.10
❑ 20	Alex Rodriguez	2.50	1.10
❑ 21	Frank Thomas	2.50	1.10
❑ 22	Cal Ripken	3.00	1.35
❑ 23	Ken Griffey Jr.	4.00	1.80
❑ 24	Travis Lee	1.25	.55
❑ 25	Paul O'Neill	.50	.23
❑ 26	Greg Vaughn	.50	.23
❑ 27	Andres Galarraga	.75	.35
❑ 28	Tino Martinez	.75	.35
❑ 29	Jose Canseco	.75	.35
❑ 30	Ben Grieve	1.50	.70

1999 Ultra Thunderclap

	MINT	NRMT
COMPLETE SET (15)	150.00	70.00
COMMON CARD (1-15)	4.00	1.80

		MINT	NRMT
❑ 1	Alex Rodriguez	12.00	5.50
❑ 2	Andruw Jones	5.00	2.20
❑ 3	Cal Ripken	15.00	6.75
❑ 4	Chipper Jones	10.00	4.50

❑ 5 Darin Erstad	5.00	2.20
❑ 6 Derek Jeter	10.00	4.50
❑ 7 Frank Thomas	12.00	5.50
❑ 8 Jeff Bagwell	6.00	2.70
❑ 9 Juan Gonzalez	10.00	4.50
❑ 10 Ken Griffey Jr.	20.00	9.00
❑ 11 Mark McGwire	25.00	11.00
❑ 12 Mike Piazza	12.00	5.50
❑ 13 Travis Lee	5.00	2.20
❑ 14 Nomar Garciaparra	12.00	5.50
❑ 15 Scott Rolen	8.00	3.60

1999 Ultra World Premiere

	MINT	NRMT
COMPLETE SET (15)	80.00	36.00
COMMON CARD (1-15)	2.00	.90
❑ 1 Gabe Alvarez	2.00	.90
❑ 2 Kerry Wood	15.00	6.75
❑ 3 Orlando Hernandez	8.00	3.60
❑ 4 Mike Caruso	2.00	.90
❑ 5 Matt Anderson	2.00	.90
❑ 6 Randall Simon	2.00	.90
❑ 7 Adrian Beltre	5.00	2.20
❑ 8 Scott Elarton	2.00	.90
❑ 9 Karim Garcia	2.00	.90
❑ 10 Mike Frank	2.00	.90
❑ 11 Richard Hidalgo	2.00	.90
❑ 12 Paul Konerko	3.00	1.35
❑ 13 Travis Lee	8.00	3.60
❑ 14 J.D. Drew	30.00	13.50
❑ 15 Miguel Tejada	2.00	.90

1989 Upper Deck

	MINT	NRMT
COMPLETE SET (800)	160.00	70.00
COMP.FACT.SET (800)	180.00	80.00
COMPLETE LO SET (700)	110.00	50.00
COMPLETE HI SET (100)	10.00	4.50
COMP.HI FACT.SET (100)	8.00	3.60
COMMON CARD (1-800)	.20	.09
❑ 1 Ken Griffey Jr.	135.00	60.00
❑ 2 Luis Medina	.20	.09
❑ 3 Tony Chance	.20	.09
❑ 4 Dave Otto	.20	.09
❑ 5 Sandy Alomar Jr. UER (Born 6/16/66, should be 6/18/66)	2.00	.90
❑ 6 Rolando Roomes	.20	.09
❑ 7 Dave West	.20	.09
❑ 8 Cris Carpenter	.20	.09
❑ 9 Gregg Jefferies	.30	.14
❑ 10 Doug Dascenzo	.20	.09
❑ 11 Ron Jones	.20	.09
❑ 12 Luis DeLosSantos	.20	.09
❑ 13 Gary Sheffield COR	3.00	1.35
❑ 13A Gary Sheffield ERR (SS upside down on card front)	3.00	1.35
❑ 14 Mike Harkey	.20	.09
❑ 15 Lance Blankenship	.20	.09
❑ 16 William Brennan	.20	.09
❑ 17 John Smoltz	2.50	1.10
❑ 18 Ramon Martinez	1.00	.45
❑ 19 Mark Lemke	.50	.23
❑ 20 Juan Bell	.20	.09
❑ 21 Rey Palacios	.20	.09
❑ 22 Felix Jose	.20	.09
❑ 23 Van Snider	.20	.09
❑ 24 Dante Bichette	2.00	.90
❑ 25 Randy Johnson	6.00	2.70
❑ 26 Carlos Quintana	.20	.09
❑ 27 Star Rookie CL	.20	.09
❑ 28 Mike Schooler	.20	.09
❑ 29 Randy St.Claire	.20	.09
❑ 30 Jerald Clark	.20	.09
❑ 31 Kevin Gross	.20	.09
❑ 32 Dan Firova	.20	.09
❑ 33 Jeff Calhoun	.20	.09
❑ 34 Tommy Hinzo	.20	.09
❑ 35 Ricky Jordan	.30	.14
❑ 36 Larry Parrish	.20	.09
❑ 37 Bret Saberhagen UER (Hit total 931, should be 1031)	.30	.14
❑ 38 Mike Smithson	.20	.09
❑ 39 Dave Dravecky	.30	.14
❑ 40 Ed Romero	.20	.09
❑ 41 Jeff Musselman	.20	.09
❑ 42 Ed Hearn	.20	.09
❑ 43 Rance Mulliniks	.20	.09
❑ 44 Jim Eisenreich	.20	.09
❑ 45 Sil Campusano	.20	.09
❑ 46 Mike Krukow	.20	.09
❑ 47 Paul Gibson	.20	.09
❑ 48 Mike LaCoss	.20	.09
❑ 49 Larry Herndon	.20	.09
❑ 50 Scott Garrelts	.20	.09
❑ 51 Dwayne Henry	.20	.09
❑ 52 Jim Acker	.20	.09
❑ 53 Steve Sax	.20	.09
❑ 54 Pete O'Brien	.20	.09
❑ 55 Paul Runge	.20	.09
❑ 56 Rick Rhoden	.20	.09
❑ 57 John Dopson	.20	.09
❑ 58 Casey Candaele UER (No stats for Astros for '88 season)	.20	.09
❑ 59 Dave Righetti	.20	.09
❑ 60 Joe Hesketh	.20	.09
❑ 61 Frank DiPino	.20	.09
❑ 62 Tim Laudner	.20	.09
❑ 63 Jamie Moyer	.20	.09
❑ 64 Fred Toliver	.20	.09
❑ 65 Mitch Webster	.20	.09
❑ 66 John Tudor	.20	.09
❑ 67 John Cangelosi	.20	.09
❑ 68 Mike Devereaux	.20	.09
❑ 69 Brian Fisher	.20	.09
❑ 70 Mike Marshall	.20	.09
❑ 71 Zane Smith	.20	.09
❑ 72A Brian Holton ERR (Photo actually Shawn Hillegas)	1.00	.45
❑ 72B Brian Holton COR	.30	.14
❑ 73 Jose Guzman	.20	.09
❑ 74 Rick Mahler	.20	.09
❑ 75 John Shelby	.20	.09
❑ 76 Jim Deshaies	.20	.09
❑ 77 Bobby Meacham	.20	.09
❑ 78 Bryn Smith	.20	.09
❑ 79 Joaquin Andujar	.20	.09
❑ 80 Richard Dotson	.20	.09
❑ 81 Charlie Lea	.20	.09
❑ 82 Calvin Schiraldi	.20	.09
❑ 83 Les Straker	.20	.09
❑ 84 Les Lancaster	.20	.09
❑ 85 Allan Anderson	.20	.09
❑ 86 Junior Ortiz	.20	.09
❑ 87 Jesse Orosco	.20	.09
❑ 88 Felix Fermin	.20	.09
❑ 89 Dave Anderson	.20	.09
❑ 90 Rafael Belliard UER (Born '61, not '51)	.20	.09
❑ 91 Franklin Stubbs	.20	.09
❑ 92 Cecil Espy	.20	.09
❑ 93 Albert Hall	.20	.09
❑ 94 Tim Leary	.20	.09
❑ 95 Mitch Williams	.20	.09
❑ 96 Tracy Jones	.20	.09
❑ 97 Danny Darwin	.20	.09
❑ 98 Gary Ward	.20	.09
❑ 99 Neal Heaton	.20	.09
❑ 100 Jim Pankovits	.20	.09
❑ 101 Bill Doran	.20	.09
❑ 102 Tim Wallach	.20	.09
❑ 103 Joe Magrane	.20	.09
❑ 104 Ozzie Virgil	.20	.09
❑ 105 Alvin Davis	.20	.09
❑ 106 Tom Brookens	.20	.09
❑ 107 Shawon Dunston	.20	.09
❑ 108 Tracy Woodson	.20	.09
❑ 109 Nelson Liriano	.20	.09
❑ 110 Devon White UER (Doubles total 46, should be 56)	.30	.14
❑ 111 Steve Balboni	.20	.09
❑ 112 Buddy Bell	.30	.14
❑ 113 German Jimenez	.20	.09
❑ 114 Ken Dayley	.20	.09
❑ 115 Andres Galarraga	.75	.35
❑ 116 Mike Scioscia	.20	.09
❑ 117 Gary Pettis	.20	.09
❑ 118 Ernie Whitt	.20	.09
❑ 119 Bob Boone	.30	.14
❑ 120 Ryne Sandberg	1.00	.45
❑ 121 Bruce Benedict	.20	.09
❑ 122 Hubie Brooks	.20	.09
❑ 123 Mike Moore	.20	.09
❑ 124 Wallace Johnson	.20	.09
❑ 125 Bob Horner	.20	.09
❑ 126 Chili Davis	.30	.14
❑ 127 Manny Trillo	.20	.09
❑ 128 Chet Lemon	.20	.09
❑ 129 John Cerutti	.20	.09
❑ 130 Orel Hershiser	.30	.14
❑ 131 Terry Pendleton	.20	.09
❑ 132 Jeff Blauser	.30	.14
❑ 133 Mike Fitzgerald	.20	.09
❑ 134 Henry Cotto	.20	.09
❑ 135 Gerald Young	.20	.09
❑ 136 Luis Salazar	.20	.09
❑ 137 Alejandro Pena	.20	.09
❑ 138 Jack Howell	.20	.09
❑ 139 Tony Fernandez	.20	.09
❑ 140 Mark Grace	.75	.35
❑ 141 Ken Caminiti	1.00	.45
❑ 142 Mike Jackson	.50	.23
❑ 143 Larry McWilliams	.20	.09

❑ 144 Andres Thomas .20 .09
❑ 145 Nolan Ryan 3X 3.00 1.35
❑ 146 Mike Davis .20 .09
❑ 147 DeWayne Buice .20 .09
❑ 148 Jody Davis .20 .09
❑ 149 Jesse Barfield .20 .09
❑ 150 Matt Nokes .20 .09
❑ 151 Jerry Reuss .20 .09
❑ 152 Rick Cerone .20 .09
❑ 153 Storm Davis .20 .09
❑ 154 Marvell Wynne .20 .09
❑ 155 Will Clark .75 .35
❑ 156 Luis Aguayo .20 .09
❑ 157 Willie Upshaw .20 .09
❑ 158 Randy Bush .20 .09
❑ 159 Ron Darling .20 .09
❑ 160 Kal Daniels .20 .09
❑ 161 Spike Owen .20 .09
❑ 162 Luis Polonia .20 .09
❑ 163 Kevin Mitchell UER .30 .14
('88/total HR's 18/52,
should be 19/53)
❑ 164 Dave Gallagher .20 .09
❑ 165 Benito Santiago .20 .09
❑ 166 Greg Gagne .20 .09
❑ 167 Ken Phelps .20 .09
❑ 168 Sid Fernandez .20 .09
❑ 169 Bo Diaz .20 .09
❑ 170 Cory Snyder .20 .09
❑ 171 Eric Show .20 .09
❑ 172 Robby Thompson .20 .09
❑ 173 Marty Barrett .20 .09
❑ 174 Dave Henderson .20 .09
❑ 175 Ozzie Guillen .20 .09
❑ 176 Barry Lyons .20 .09
❑ 177 Kelvin Torve .20 .09
❑ 178 Don Slaught .20 .09
❑ 179 Steve Lombardozzi .20 .09
❑ 180 Chris Sabo .20 .09
❑ 181 Jose Uribe .20 .09
❑ 182 Shane Mack .20 .09
❑ 183 Ron Karkovice .20 .09
❑ 184 Todd Benzinger .20 .09
❑ 185 Dave Stewart .30 .14
❑ 186 Julio Franco .20 .09
❑ 187 Ron Robinson .20 .09
❑ 188 Wally Backman .20 .09
❑ 189 Randy Velarde .20 .09
❑ 190 Joe Carter .75 .35
❑ 191 Bob Welch .20 .09
❑ 192 Kelly Paris .20 .09
❑ 193 Chris Brown .20 .09
❑ 194 Rick Reuschel .20 .09
❑ 195 Roger Clemens 1.50 .70
❑ 196 Dave Concepcion .30 .14
❑ 197 Al Newman .20 .09
❑ 198 Brook Jacoby .20 .09
❑ 199 Mookie Wilson .30 .14
❑ 200 Don Mattingly 1.25 .55
❑ 201 Dick Schofield .20 .09
❑ 202 Mark Gubicza .20 .09
❑ 203 Gary Gaetti .30 .14
❑ 204 Dan Pasqua .20 .09
❑ 205 Andre Dawson .75 .35
❑ 206 Chris Speier .20 .09
❑ 207 Kent Tekulve .20 .09
❑ 208 Rod Scurry .20 .09
❑ 209 Scott Bailes .20 .09
❑ 210 Rickey Henderson UER .75 .35
(Throws Right)
❑ 211 Harold Baines .30 .14
❑ 212 Tony Armas .20 .09
❑ 213 Kent Hrbek .30 .14
❑ 214 Darrin Jackson .20 .09
❑ 215 George Brett 1.50 .70
❑ 216 Rafael Santana .20 .09
❑ 217 Andy Allanson .20 .09
❑ 218 Brett Butler .30 .14
❑ 219 Steve Jeltz .20 .09
❑ 220 Jay Buhner .75 .35
❑ 221 Bo Jackson .50 .23
❑ 222 Angel Salazar .20 .09
❑ 223 Kirk McCaskill .20 .09
❑ 224 Steve Lyons .20 .09
❑ 225 Bert Blyleven .30 .14
❑ 226 Scott Bradley .20 .09
❑ 227 Bob Melvin .20 .09
❑ 228 Ron Kittle .20 .09
❑ 229 Phil Bradley .20 .09
❑ 230 Tommy John .30 .14
❑ 231 Greg Walker .20 .09
❑ 232 Juan Berenguer .20 .09
❑ 233 Pat Tabler .20 .09
❑ 234 Terry Clark .20 .09
❑ 235 Rafael Palmeiro .75 .35
❑ 236 Paul Zuvella .20 .09
❑ 237 Willie Randolph .30 .14
❑ 238 Bruce Fields .20 .09
❑ 239 Mike Aldrete .20 .09
❑ 240 Lance Parrish .20 .09
❑ 241 Greg Maddux 4.00 1.80
❑ 242 John Moses .20 .09
❑ 243 Melido Perez .20 .09
❑ 244 Willie Wilson .20 .09
❑ 245 Mark McLemore .20 .09
❑ 246 Von Hayes .20 .09
❑ 247 Matt Williams .75 .35
❑ 248 John Candelaria UER .20 .09
(Listed as Yankee for
part of '87,
should be Mets)
❑ 249 Harold Reynolds .20 .09
❑ 250 Greg Swindell .20 .09
❑ 251 Juan Agosto .20 .09
❑ 252 Mike Felder .20 .09
❑ 253 Vince Coleman .20 .09
❑ 254 Larry Sheets .20 .09
❑ 255 George Bell .20 .09
❑ 256 Terry Steinbach .30 .14
❑ 257 Jack Armstrong .20 .09
❑ 258 Dickie Thon .20 .09
❑ 259 Ray Knight .20 .09
❑ 260 Darryl Strawberry .30 .14
❑ 261 Doug Sisk .20 .09
❑ 262 Alex Trevino .20 .09
❑ 263 Jeffrey Leonard .20 .09
❑ 264 Tom Henke .20 .09
❑ 265 Ozzie Smith 1.00 .45
❑ 266 Dave Bergman .20 .09
❑ 267 Tony Phillips .20 .09
❑ 268 Mark Davis .20 .09
❑ 269 Kevin Elster .20 .09
❑ 270 Barry Larkin .75 .35
❑ 271 Manny Lee .20 .09
❑ 272 Tom Brunansky .20 .09
❑ 273 Craig Biggio 4.00 1.80
❑ 274 Jim Gantner .20 .09
❑ 275 Eddie Murray .75 .35
❑ 276 Jeff Reed .20 .09
❑ 277 Tim Teufel .20 .09
❑ 278 Rick Honeycutt .20 .09
❑ 279 Guillermo Hernandez .20 .09
❑ 280 John Kruk .30 .14
❑ 281 Luis Alicea .20 .09
❑ 282 Jim Clancy .20 .09
❑ 283 Billy Ripken .20 .09
❑ 284 Craig Reynolds .20 .09
❑ 285 Robin Yount .75 .35
❑ 286 Jimmy Jones .20 .09
❑ 287 Ron Oester .20 .09
❑ 288 Terry Leach .20 .09
❑ 289 Dennis Eckersley .50 .23
❑ 290 Alan Trammell .50 .23
❑ 291 Jimmy Key .30 .14
❑ 292 Chris Bosio .20 .09
❑ 293 Jose DeLeon .20 .09
❑ 294 Jim Traber .20 .09
❑ 295 Mike Scott .20 .09
❑ 296 Roger McDowell .20 .09
❑ 297 Garry Templeton .20 .09
❑ 298 Doyle Alexander .20 .09
❑ 299 Nick Esasky .20 .09
❑ 300 Mark McGwire UER 5.00 2.20
(Doubles total 52,
should be 51)
❑ 301 Darryl Hamilton .20 .09
❑ 302 Dave Smith .20 .09
❑ 303 Rick Sutcliffe .20 .09
❑ 304 Dave Stapleton .20 .09
❑ 305 Alan Ashby .20 .09
❑ 306 Pedro Guerrero .20 .09
❑ 307 Ron Guidry .30 .14
❑ 308 Steve Farr .20 .09
❑ 309 Curt Ford .20 .09
❑ 310 Claudell Washington .20 .09
❑ 311 Tom Prince .20 .09
❑ 312 Chad Kreuter .20 .09
❑ 313 Ken Oberkfell .20 .09
❑ 314 Jerry Browne .20 .09
❑ 315 R.J. Reynolds .20 .09
❑ 316 Scott Bankhead .20 .09
❑ 317 Milt Thompson .20 .09
❑ 318 Mario Diaz .20 .09
❑ 319 Bruce Ruffin .20 .09
❑ 320 Dave Valle .20 .09
❑ 321A Gary Varsho ERR 2.00 .90
(Back photo actually
Mike Bielecki bunting)
❑ 321B Gary Varsho COR .20 .09
(In road uniform)
❑ 322 Paul Mirabella .20 .09
❑ 323 Chuck Jackson .20 .09
❑ 324 Drew Hall .20 .09
❑ 325 Don August .20 .09
❑ 326 Israel Sanchez .20 .09
❑ 327 Denny Walling .20 .09
❑ 328 Joel Skinner .20 .09
❑ 329 Danny Tartabull .20 .09
❑ 330 Tony Pena .20 .09
❑ 331 Jim Sundberg .20 .09
❑ 332 Jeff D. Robinson .20 .09
❑ 333 Oddibe McDowell .20 .09
❑ 334 Jose Lind .20 .09
❑ 335 Paul Kilgus .20 .09
❑ 336 Juan Samuel .20 .09
❑ 337 Mike Campbell .20 .09
❑ 338 Mike Maddux .20 .09
❑ 339 Darnell Coles .20 .09
❑ 340 Bob Dernier .20 .09
❑ 341 Rafael Ramirez .20 .09
❑ 342 Scott Sanderson .20 .09
❑ 343 B.J. Surhoff .30 .14
❑ 344 Billy Hatcher .20 .09
❑ 345 Pat Perry .20 .09
❑ 346 Jack Clark .20 .09
❑ 347 Gary Thurman .20 .09
❑ 348 Tim Jones .20 .09
❑ 349 Dave Winfield .75 .35
❑ 350 Frank White .30 .14
❑ 351 Dave Collins .20 .09
❑ 352 Jack Morris .30 .14
❑ 353 Eric Plunk .20 .09
❑ 354 Leon Durham .20 .09
❑ 355 Ivan DeJesus .20 .09
❑ 356 Brian Holman .20 .09
❑ 357A Dale Murphy ERR 15.00 6.75
(Front has
reverse negative)
❑ 357B Dale Murphy COR .30 .14
❑ 358 Mark Portugal .20 .09
❑ 359 Andy McGaffigan .20 .09
❑ 360 Tom Glavine .75 .35
❑ 361 Keith Moreland .20 .09
❑ 362 Todd Stottlemyre .50 .23
❑ 363 Dave Leiper .20 .09
❑ 364 Cecil Fielder .30 .14
❑ 365 Carmelo Martinez .20 .09
❑ 366 Dwight Evans .30 .14
❑ 367 Kevin McReynolds .20 .09
❑ 368 Rich Gedman .20 .09
❑ 369 Len Dykstra .30 .14
❑ 370 Jody Reed .20 .09
❑ 371 Jose Canseco UER .75 .35
(Strikeout total 391,
should be 491)
❑ 372 Rob Murphy .20 .09
❑ 373 Mike Henneman .20 .09
❑ 374 Walt Weiss .20 .09
❑ 375 Rob Dibble .30 .14
❑ 376 Kirby Puckett 1.50 .70
(Mark McGwire
in background)
❑ 377 Dennis Martinez .30 .14
❑ 378 Ron Gant .30 .14
❑ 379 Brian Harper .20 .09

❑ 380 Nelson Santovenia .20 .09
❑ 381 Lloyd Moseby .20 .09
❑ 382 Lance McCullers .20 .09
❑ 383 Dave Stieb .20 .09
❑ 384 Tony Gwynn 2.00 .90
❑ 385 Mike Flanagan .20 .09
❑ 386 Bob Ojeda .20 .09
❑ 387 Bruce Hurst .20 .09
❑ 388 Dave Magadan .20 .09
❑ 389 Wade Boggs .75 .35
❑ 390 Gary Carter .50 .23
❑ 391 Frank Tanana .20 .09
❑ 392 Curt Young .20 .09
❑ 393 Jeff Treadway .20 .09
❑ 394 Darrell Evans .30 .14
❑ 395 Glenn Hubbard .20 .09
❑ 396 Chuck Cary .20 .09
❑ 397 Frank Viola .20 .09
❑ 398 Jeff Parrett .20 .09
❑ 399 Terry Blocker .20 .09
❑ 400 Dan Gladden .20 .09
❑ 401 Louie Meadows .20 .09
❑ 402 Tim Raines .30 .14
❑ 403 Joey Meyer .20 .09
❑ 404 Larry Andersen .20 .09
❑ 405 Rex Hudler .20 .09
❑ 406 Mike Schmidt 1.00 .45
❑ 407 John Franco .30 .14
❑ 408 Brady Anderson 2.00 .90
❑ 409 Don Carman .20 .09
❑ 410 Eric Davis .30 .14
❑ 411 Bob Stanley .20 .09
❑ 412 Pete Smith .20 .09
❑ 413 Jim Rice .30 .14
❑ 414 Bruce Sutter .20 .09
❑ 415 Oil Can Boyd .20 .09
❑ 416 Ruben Sierra .20 .09
❑ 417 Mike LaValliere .20 .09
❑ 418 Steve Buechele .20 .09
❑ 419 Gary Redus .20 .09
❑ 420 Scott Fletcher .20 .09
❑ 421 Dale Sveum .20 .09
❑ 422 Bob Knepper .20 .09
❑ 423 Luis Rivera .20 .09
❑ 424 Ted Higuera .20 .09
❑ 425 Kevin Bass .20 .09
❑ 426 Ken Gerhart .20 .09
❑ 427 Shane Rawley .20 .09
❑ 428 Paul O'Neill .30 .14
❑ 429 Joe Orsulak .20 .09
❑ 430 Jackie Gutierrez .20 .09
❑ 431 Gerald Perry .20 .09
❑ 432 Mike Greenwell .20 .09
❑ 433 Jerry Royster .20 .09
❑ 434 Ellis Burks .50 .23
❑ 435 Ed Olwine .20 .09
❑ 436 Dave Rucker .20 .09
❑ 437 Charlie Hough .30 .14
❑ 438 Bob Walk .20 .09
❑ 439 Bob Brower .20 .09
❑ 440 Barry Bonds 1.50 .70
❑ 441 Tom Foley .20 .09
❑ 442 Rob Deer .20 .09
❑ 443 Glenn Davis .20 .09
❑ 444 Dave Martinez .20 .09
❑ 445 Bill Wegman .20 .09
❑ 446 Lloyd McClendon .20 .09
❑ 447 Dave Schmidt .20 .09
❑ 448 Darren Daulton .30 .14
❑ 449 Frank Williams .20 .09
❑ 450 Don Aase .20 .09
❑ 451 Lou Whitaker .30 .14
❑ 452 Goose Gossage .30 .14
❑ 453 Ed Whitson .20 .09
❑ 454 Jim Walewander .20 .09
❑ 455 Damon Berryhill .20 .09
❑ 456 Tim Burke .20 .09
❑ 457 Barry Jones .20 .09
❑ 458 Joel Youngblood .20 .09
❑ 459 Floyd Youmans .20 .09
❑ 460 Mark Salas .20 .09
❑ 461 Jeff Russell .20 .09
❑ 462 Darrell Miller .20 .09
❑ 463 Jeff Kunkel .20 .09
❑ 464 Sherman Corbett .20 .09
❑ 465 Curtis Wilkerson .20 .09
❑ 466 Bud Black .20 .09
❑ 467 Cal Ripken 3.00 1.35
❑ 468 John Farrell .20 .09
❑ 469 Terry Kennedy .20 .09
❑ 470 Tom Candiotti .20 .09
❑ 471 Roberto Alomar 1.25 .55
❑ 472 Jeff M. Robinson .20 .09
❑ 473 Vance Law .20 .09
❑ 474 Randy Ready UER .20 .09
(Strikeout total 136, should be 115)
❑ 475 Walt Terrell .20 .09
❑ 476 Kelly Downs .20 .09
❑ 477 Johnny Paredes .20 .09
❑ 478 Shawn Hillegas .20 .09
❑ 479 Bob Brenly .20 .09
❑ 480 Otis Nixon .30 .14
❑ 481 Johnny Ray .20 .09
❑ 482 Geno Petralli .20 .09
❑ 483 Stu Cliburn .20 .09
❑ 484 Pete Incaviglia .20 .09
❑ 485 Brian Downing .20 .09
❑ 486 Jeff Stone .20 .09
❑ 487 Carmen Castillo .20 .09
❑ 488 Tom Niedenfuer .20 .09
❑ 489 Jay Bell .50 .23
❑ 490 Rick Schu .20 .09
❑ 491 Jeff Pico .20 .09
❑ 492 Mark Parent .20 .09
❑ 493 Eric King .20 .09
❑ 494 Al Nipper .20 .09
❑ 495 Andy Hawkins .20 .09
❑ 496 Daryl Boston .20 .09
❑ 497 Ernie Riles .20 .09
❑ 498 Pascual Perez .20 .09
❑ 499 Bill Long UER .20 .09
(Games started total 70, should be 44)
❑ 500 Kirt Manwaring .20 .09
❑ 501 Chuck Crim .20 .09
❑ 502 Candy Maldonado .20 .09
❑ 503 Dennis Lamp .20 .09
❑ 504 Glenn Braggs .20 .09
❑ 505 Joe Price .20 .09
❑ 506 Ken Williams .20 .09
❑ 507 Bill Pecota .20 .09
❑ 508 Rey Quinones .20 .09
❑ 509 Jeff Bittiger .20 .09
❑ 510 Kevin Seitzer .20 .09
❑ 511 Steve Bedrosian .20 .09
❑ 512 Todd Worrell .30 .14
❑ 513 Chris James .20 .09
❑ 514 Jose Oquendo .20 .09
❑ 515 David Palmer .20 .09
❑ 516 John Smiley .20 .09
❑ 517 Dave Clark .20 .09
❑ 518 Mike Dunne .20 .09
❑ 519 Ron Washington .20 .09
❑ 520 Bob Kipper .20 .09
❑ 521 Lee Smith .30 .14
❑ 522 Juan Castillo .20 .09
❑ 523 Don Robinson .20 .09
❑ 524 Kevin Romine .20 .09
❑ 525 Paul Molitor .75 .35
❑ 526 Mark Langston .20 .09
❑ 527 Donnie Hill .20 .09
❑ 528 Larry Owen .20 .09
❑ 529 Jerry Reed .20 .09
❑ 530 Jack McDowell .30 .14
❑ 531 Greg Mathews .20 .09
❑ 532 John Russell .20 .09
❑ 533 Dan Quisenberry .20 .09
❑ 534 Greg Gross .20 .09
❑ 535 Danny Cox .20 .09
❑ 536 Terry Francona .30 .14
❑ 537 Andy Van Slyke .30 .14
❑ 538 Mel Hall .20 .09
❑ 539 Jim Gott .20 .09
❑ 540 Doug Jones .20 .09
❑ 541 Craig Lefferts .20 .09
❑ 542 Mike Boddicker .20 .09
❑ 543 Greg Brock .20 .09
❑ 544 Atlee Hammaker .20 .09
❑ 545 Tom Bolton .20 .09
❑ 546 Mike Macfarlane .20 .09
❑ 547 Rich Renteria .20 .09
❑ 548 John Davis .20 .09
❑ 549 Floyd Bannister .20 .09
❑ 550 Mickey Brantley .20 .09
❑ 551 Duane Ward .20 .09
❑ 552 Dan Petry .20 .09
❑ 553 Mickey Tettleton UER .30 .14
(Walks total 175, should be 136)
❑ 554 Rick Leach .20 .09
❑ 555 Mike Witt .20 .09
❑ 556 Sid Bream .20 .09
❑ 557 Bobby Witt .20 .09
❑ 558 Tommy Herr .20 .09
❑ 559 Randy Milligan .20 .09
❑ 560 Jose Cecena .20 .09
❑ 561 Mackey Sasser .20 .09
❑ 562 Carney Lansford .30 .14
❑ 563 Rick Aguilera .30 .14
❑ 564 Ron Hassey .20 .09
❑ 565 Dwight Gooden .30 .14
❑ 566 Paul Assenmacher .20 .09
❑ 567 Neil Allen .20 .09
❑ 568 Jim Morrison .20 .09
❑ 569 Mike Pagliarulo .20 .09
❑ 570 Ted Simmons .30 .14
❑ 571 Mark Thurmond .20 .09
❑ 572 Fred McGriff .75 .35
❑ 573 Wally Joyner .30 .14
❑ 574 Jose Bautista .20 .09
❑ 575 Kelly Gruber .20 .09
❑ 576 Cecilio Guante .20 .09
❑ 577 Mark Davidson .20 .09
❑ 578 Bobby Bonilla UER .50 .23
(Total steals 2 in '87, should be 3)
❑ 579 Mike Stanley .20 .09
❑ 580 Gene Larkin .20 .09
❑ 581 Stan Javier .20 .09
❑ 582 Howard Johnson .20 .09
❑ 583A Mike Gallego ERR 1.00 .45
(Front reversed negative)
❑ 583B Mike Gallego COR .75 .35
❑ 584 David Cone .75 .35
❑ 585 Doug Jennings .20 .09
❑ 586 Charles Hudson .20 .09
❑ 587 Dion James .20 .09
❑ 588 Al Leiter .75 .35
❑ 589 Charlie Puleo .20 .09
❑ 590 Roberto Kelly .30 .14
❑ 591 Thad Bosley .20 .09
❑ 592 Pete Stanicek .20 .09
❑ 593 Pat Borders .30 .14
❑ 594 Bryan Harvey .20 .09
❑ 595 Jeff Ballard .20 .09
❑ 596 Jeff Reardon .30 .14
❑ 597 Doug Drabek .20 .09
❑ 598 Edwin Correa .20 .09
❑ 599 Keith Atherton .20 .09
❑ 600 Dave LaPoint .20 .09
❑ 601 Don Baylor .30 .14
❑ 602 Tom Pagnozzi .20 .09
❑ 603 Tim Flannery .20 .09
❑ 604 Gene Walter .20 .09
❑ 605 Dave Parker .30 .14
❑ 606 Mike Diaz .20 .09
❑ 607 Chris Gwynn .20 .09
❑ 608 Odell Jones .20 .09
❑ 609 Carlton Fisk .75 .35
❑ 610 Jay Howell .20 .09
❑ 611 Tim Crews .20 .09
❑ 612 Keith Hernandez .30 .14
❑ 613 Willie Fraser .20 .09
❑ 614 Jim Eppard .20 .09
❑ 615 Jeff Hamilton .20 .09
❑ 616 Kurt Stillwell .20 .09
❑ 617 Tom Browning .20 .09
❑ 618 Jeff Montgomery .30 .14
❑ 619 Jose Rijo .20 .09
❑ 620 Jamie Quirk .20 .09
❑ 621 Willie McGee .30 .14
❑ 622 Mark Grant UER .20 .09
(Glove on wrong hand)

❑ 623 Bill Swift .20 .09
❑ 624 Orlando Mercado .20 .09
❑ 625 John Costello .20 .09
❑ 626 Jose Gonzalez .20 .09
❑ 627A Bill Schroeder ERR 1.00 .45
(Back photo actually
Ronn Reynolds buckling
shin guards)
❑ 627B Bill Schroeder COR .75 .35
❑ 628A Fred Manrique ERR .75 .35
(Back photo actually
Ozzie Guillen throwing)
❑ 628B Fred Manrique COR .20 .09
(Swinging bat on back)
❑ 629 Ricky Horton .20 .09
❑ 630 Dan Plesac .20 .09
❑ 631 Alfredo Griffin .20 .09
❑ 632 Chuck Finley .30 .14
❑ 633 Kirk Gibson .30 .14
❑ 634 Randy Myers .30 .14
❑ 635 Greg Minton .20 .09
❑ 636A Herm Winningham .75 .35
ERR (W1nningham
on back)
❑ 636B Herm Winningham COR .20 .09
❑ 637 Charlie Leibrandt .20 .09
❑ 638 Tim Birtsas .20 .09
❑ 639 Bill Buckner .30 .14
❑ 640 Danny Jackson .20 .09
❑ 641 Greg Booker .20 .09
❑ 642 Jim Presley .20 .09
❑ 643 Gene Nelson .20 .09
❑ 644 Rod Booker .20 .09
❑ 645 Dennis Rasmussen .20 .09
❑ 646 Juan Nieves .20 .09
❑ 647 Bobby Thigpen .20 .09
❑ 648 Tim Belcher .20 .09
❑ 649 Mike Young .20 .09
❑ 650 Ivan Calderon .20 .09
❑ 651 Oswaldo Peraza .20 .09
❑ 652A Pat Sheridan ERR 2.00 .90
(No position on front)
❑ 652B Pat Sheridan COR .20 .09
❑ 653 Mike Morgan .20 .09
❑ 654 Mike Heath .20 .09
❑ 655 Jay Tibbs .20 .09
❑ 656 Fernando Valenzuela .30 .14
❑ 657 Lee Mazzilli .20 .09
❑ 658 Frank Viola AL CY .20 .09
❑ 659A Jose Canseco AL MVP .30 .14
(Eagle logo in black)
❑ 659B Jose Canseco AL MVP .30 .14
(Eagle logo in blue)
❑ 660 Walt Weiss AL ROY .20 .09
❑ 661 Orel Hershiser NL CY .30 .14
❑ 662 Kirk Gibson NL MVP .20 .09
❑ 663 Chris Sabo NL ROY .20 .09
❑ 664 Dennis Eckersley .20 .09
ALCS MVP
❑ 665 Orel Hershiser .30 .14
NLCS MVP
❑ 666 Kirk Gibson WS .75 .35
❑ 667 Orel Hershiser WS MVP .30 .14
❑ 668 Wally Joyner TC .20 .09
❑ 669 Nolan Ryan TC 1.00 .45
❑ 670 Jose Canseco TC .30 .14
❑ 671 Fred McGriff TC .30 .14
❑ 672 Dale Murphy TC .30 .14
❑ 673 Paul Molitor TC .30 .14
❑ 674 Ozzie Smith TC .50 .23
❑ 675 Ryne Sandberg TC .50 .23
❑ 676 Kirk Gibson TC .20 .09
❑ 677 Andres Galarraga TC .30 .14
❑ 678 Will Clark TC .30 .14
❑ 679 Cory Snyder TC .20 .09
❑ 680 Alvin Davis TC .20 .09
❑ 681 Darryl Strawberry TC .20 .09
❑ 682 Cal Ripken TC 1.00 .45
❑ 683 Tony Gwynn TC 1.00 .45
❑ 684 Mike Schmidt TC .50 .23
❑ 685 Andy Van Slyke TC UER .20 .09
(96 Junior Ortiz)
❑ 686 Ruben Sierra TC .20 .09
❑ 687 Wade Boggs TC .30 .14
❑ 688 Eric Davis TC .20 .09
❑ 689 George Brett TC .75 .35
❑ 690 Alan Trammell TC .30 .14
❑ 691 Frank Viola TC .20 .09
❑ 692 Harold Baines TC .20 .09
❑ 693 Don Mattingly TC .50 .23
❑ 694 Checklist 1-100 .20 .09
❑ 695 Checklist 101-200 .20 .09
❑ 696 Checklist 201-300 .20 .09
❑ 697 Checklist 301-400 .20 .09
❑ 698 Checklist 401-500 UER .20 .09
(467 Cal Ripkin Jr.)
❑ 699 Checklist 501-600 UER .20 .09
(543 Greg Booker)
❑ 700 Checklist 601-700 .20 .09
❑ 701 Checklist 701-800 .20 .09
❑ 702 Jesse Barfield .20 .09
❑ 703 Walt Terrell .20 .09
❑ 704 Dickie Thon .20 .09
❑ 705 Al Leiter .75 .35
❑ 706 Dave LaPoint .20 .09
❑ 707 Charlie Hayes .75 .35
❑ 708 Andy Hawkins .20 .09
❑ 709 Mickey Hatcher .20 .09
❑ 710 Lance McCullers .20 .09
❑ 711 Ron Kittle .20 .09
❑ 712 Bert Blyleven .30 .14
❑ 713 Rick Dempsey .20 .09
❑ 714 Ken Williams .20 .09
❑ 715 Steve Rosenberg .20 .09
❑ 716 Joe Skalski .20 .09
❑ 717 Spike Owen .20 .09
❑ 718 Todd Burns .20 .09
❑ 719 Kevin Gross .20 .09
❑ 720 Tommy Herr .20 .09
❑ 721 Rob Ducey .20 .09
❑ 722 Gary Green .20 .09
❑ 723 Gregg Olson .75 .35
❑ 724 Greg W. Harris .20 .09
❑ 725 Craig Worthington .20 .09
❑ 726 Tom Howard .20 .09
❑ 727 Dale Mohorcic .20 .09
❑ 728 Rich Yett .20 .09
❑ 729 Mel Hall .20 .09
❑ 730 Floyd Youmans .20 .09
❑ 731 Lonnie Smith .20 .09
❑ 732 Wally Backman .20 .09
❑ 733 Trevor Wilson .20 .09
❑ 734 Jose Alvarez .20 .09
❑ 735 Bob Milacki .20 .09
❑ 736 Tom Gordon .75 .35
❑ 737 Wally Whitehurst .20 .09
❑ 738 Mike Aldrete .20 .09
❑ 739 Keith Miller .20 .09
❑ 740 Randy Milligan .20 .09
❑ 741 Jeff Parrett .20 .09
❑ 742 Steve Finley 1.00 .45
❑ 743 Junior Felix .20 .09
❑ 744 Pete Harnisch .30 .14
❑ 745 Bill Spiers .20 .09
❑ 746 Hensley Meulens .20 .09
❑ 747 Juan Bell .20 .09
❑ 748 Steve Sax .20 .09
❑ 749 Phil Bradley .20 .09
❑ 750 Rey Quinones .20 .09
❑ 751 Tommy Gregg .20 .09
❑ 752 Kevin Brown 2.50 1.10
❑ 753 Derek Lilliquist .20 .09
❑ 754 Todd Zeile .75 .35
❑ 755 Jim Abbott .75 .35
(Triple exposure)
❑ 756 Ozzie Canseco .20 .09
❑ 757 Nick Esasky .20 .09
❑ 758 Mike Moore .20 .09
❑ 759 Rob Murphy .20 .09
❑ 760 Rick Mahler .20 .09
❑ 761 Fred Lynn .20 .09
❑ 762 Kevin Blankenship .20 .09
❑ 763 Eddie Murray .75 .35
❑ 764 Steve Searcy .20 .09
❑ 765 Jerome Walton .75 .35
❑ 766 Erik Hanson .30 .14
❑ 767 Bob Boone .30 .14
❑ 768 Edgar Martinez .75 .35
❑ 769 Jose DeJesus .20 .09
❑ 770 Greg Briley .20 .09
❑ 771 Steve Peters .20 .09
❑ 772 Rafael Palmeiro .75 .35
❑ 773 Jack Clark .20 .09
❑ 774 Nolan Ryan 3.00 1.35
(Throwing football)
❑ 775 Lance Parrish .20 .09
❑ 776 Joe Girardi .75 .35
❑ 777 Willie Randolph .30 .14
❑ 778 Mitch Williams .20 .09
❑ 779 Dennis Cook .20 .09
❑ 780 Dwight Smith .30 .14
❑ 781 Lenny Harris .20 .09
❑ 782 Torey Lovullo .20 .09
❑ 783 Norm Charlton .30 .14
❑ 784 Chris Brown .20 .09
❑ 785 Todd Benzinger .20 .09
❑ 786 Shane Rawley .20 .09
❑ 787 Omar Vizquel 2.00 .90
❑ 788 LaVel Freeman .20 .09
❑ 789 Jeffrey Leonard .20 .09
❑ 790 Eddie Williams .20 .09
❑ 791 Jamie Moyer .20 .09
❑ 792 Bruce Hurst UER .20 .09
(Workd Series)
❑ 793 Julio Franco .20 .09
❑ 794 Claudell Washington .20 .09
❑ 795 Jody Davis .20 .09
❑ 796 Oddibe McDowell .20 .09
❑ 797 Paul Kilgus .20 .09
❑ 798 Tracy Jones .20 .09
❑ 799 Steve Wilson .20 .09
❑ 800 Pete O'Brien .20 .09

1990 Upper Deck

	MINT	NRMT
COMPLETE SET (800)	30.00	13.50
COMP.FACT.SET (800)	30.00	13.50
COMPLETE LO SET (700)	16.00	7.25
COMPLETE HI SET (100)	4.00	1.80
COMP.HI FACT.SET (100)	4.00	1.80
COMMON CARD (1-800)	.10	.05

❑ 1 Star Rookie Checklist .10 .05
❑ 2 Randy Nosek .10 .05
❑ 3 Tom Drees UER .10 .05
(11th line, hulred,
should be hurled)
❑ 4 Curt Young .10 .05
❑ 5 Devon White TC .10 .05
❑ 6 Luis Salazar .10 .05
❑ 7 Von Hayes TC .10 .05
❑ 8 Jose Bautista .10 .05
❑ 9 Marquis Grissom .50 .23
❑ 10 Orel Hershiser TC .10 .05
❑ 11 Rick Aguilera .20 .09
❑ 12 Benito Santiago TC .10 .05
❑ 13 Deion Sanders .40 .18
❑ 14 Marvell Wynne .10 .05
❑ 15 Dave West .10 .05
❑ 16 Bobby Bonilla TC .10 .05
❑ 17 Sammy Sosa 8.00 3.60
❑ 18 Steve Sax TC .10 .05
❑ 19 Jack Howell .10 .05
❑ 20 Mike Schmidt Special .50 .23
UER (Suprising,
should be surprising)
❑ 21 Robin Ventura UER .40 .18

(Samta Maria)
❑ 22 Brian Meyer .10 .05
❑ 23 Blaine Beatty .10 .05
❑ 24 Ken Griffey Jr. TC 1.25 .55
❑ 25 Greg Vaughn UER .75 .35
(Association misspelled as assiocation)
❑ 26 Xavier Hernandez .10 .05
❑ 27 Jason Grimsley .10 .05
❑ 28 Eric Anthony UER .10 .05
(Ashville, should be Asheville)
❑ 29 Tim Raines TC UER .10 .05
(Wallach listed before Walker)
❑ 30 David Wells .30 .14
❑ 31 Hal Morris .10 .05
❑ 32 Bo Jackson TC .20 .09
❑ 33 Kelly Mann .10 .05
❑ 34 Nolan Ryan Special .75 .35
❑ 35 Scott Service UER .10 .05
(Born Cincinatti on 7/27/67, should be Cincinnati 2/27)
❑ 36 Mark McGwire TC .40 .18
❑ 37 Tino Martinez .75 .35
❑ 38 Chili Davis .20 .09
❑ 39 Scott Sanderson .10 .05
❑ 40 Kevin Mitchell TC .10 .05
❑ 41 Lou Whitaker TC .10 .05
❑ 42 Scott Coolbaugh UER .10 .05
(Definately)
❑ 43 Jose Cano UER .10 .05
(Born 9/7/62, should be 3/7/62)
❑ 44 Jose Vizcaino .40 .18
❑ 45 Bob Hamelin .40 .18
❑ 46 Jose Offerman UER .50 .23
(Posesses)
❑ 47 Kevin Blankenship .10 .05
❑ 48 Kirby Puckett TC .40 .18
❑ 49 Tommy Greene UER .10 .05
(Livest, should be liveliest)
❑ 50 Will Clark Special .40 .18
UER (Perenial, should be perennial)
❑ 51 Rob Nelson .10 .05
❑ 52 Chris Hammond UER .10 .05
(Chatanooga)
❑ 53 Joe Carter TC .10 .05
❑ 54A Ben McDonald ERR 2.00 .90
(No Rookie designation on card front)
❑ 54B Ben McDonald COR .30 .14
❑ 55 Andy Benes UER .40 .18
(Whichita)
❑ 56 John Olerud 1.00 .45
❑ 57 Roger Clemens TC .40 .18
❑ 58 Tony Armas .10 .05
❑ 59 George Canale .10 .05
❑ 60A Mickey Tettleton TC 2.00 .90
ERR (683 Jamie Weston)
❑ 60B Mickey Tettleton TC .10 .05
COR (683 Mickey Weston)
❑ 61 Mike Stanton .10 .05
❑ 62 Dwight Gooden TC .10 .05
❑ 63 Kent Mercker UER .10 .05
(Albuguerque)
❑ 64 Francisco Cabrera .10 .05
❑ 65 Steve Avery UER .10 .05
(Born NJ, should be MI, Merker should be Mercker)
❑ 66 Jose Canseco .40 .18
❑ 67 Matt Merullo .10 .05
❑ 68 Vince Coleman TC UER .10 .05
(Guererro)
❑ 69 Ron Karkovice .10 .05
❑ 70 Kevin Maas .20 .09
❑ 71 Dennis Cook UER .10 .05
(Shown with righty glove on card back)
❑ 72 Juan Gonzalez UER 5.00 2.20
(135 games for Tulsa in '89, should be 133)
❑ 73 Andre Dawson TC .20 .09
❑ 74 Dean Palmer UER .50 .23
(Permanent misspelled as perminant)
❑ 75 Bo Jackson Special .20 .09
UER (Monsterous, should be monstrous)
❑ 76 Rob Richie .10 .05
❑ 77 Bobby Rose UER .10 .05
(Pickin, should be pick in)
❑ 78 Brian DuBois UER .10 .05
(Commiting)
❑ 79 Ozzie Guillen TC .10 .05
❑ 80 Gene Nelson .10 .05
❑ 81 Bob McClure .10 .05
❑ 82 Julio Franco TC .10 .05
❑ 83 Greg Minton .10 .05
❑ 84 John Smoltz TC UER .20 .09
(Oddibe not Odibbe)
❑ 85 Willie Fraser .10 .05
❑ 86 Neal Heaton .10 .05
❑ 87 Kevin Tapani UER .20 .09
(24th line has excpet, should be except)
❑ 88 Mike Scott TC .10 .05
❑ 89A Jim Gott ERR 2.50 1.10
(Photo actually Rick Reed)
❑ 89B Jim Gott COR .10 .05
❑ 90 Lance Johnson .10 .05
❑ 91 Robin Yount TC UER .20 .09
(Checklist on back has 178 Rob Deer and 176 Mike Felder)
❑ 92 Jeff Parrett .10 .05
❑ 93 Julio Machado UER .10 .05
(Valenzuelan, should be Venezuelan)
❑ 94 Ron Jones .10 .05
❑ 95 George Bell TC .10 .05
❑ 96 Jerry Reuss .10 .05
❑ 97 Brian Fisher .10 .05
❑ 98 Kevin Ritz UER .10 .05
(Amercian)
❑ 99 Barry Larkin TC .20 .09
❑ 100 Checklist 1-100 .10 .05
❑ 101 Gerald Perry .10 .05
❑ 102 Kevin Appier .30 .14
❑ 103 Julio Franco .10 .05
❑ 104 Craig Biggio .40 .18
❑ 105 Bo Jackson UER .20 .09
('89 BA wrong, should be .256)
❑ 106 Junior Felix .10 .05
❑ 107 Mike Harkey .10 .05
❑ 108 Fred McGriff .40 .18
❑ 109 Rick Sutcliffe .10 .05
❑ 110 Pete O'Brien .10 .05
❑ 111 Kelly Gruber .10 .05
❑ 112 Dwight Evans .20 .09
❑ 113 Pat Borders .10 .05
❑ 114 Dwight Gooden .20 .09
❑ 115 Kevin Batiste .10 .05
❑ 116 Eric Davis .20 .09
❑ 117 Kevin Mitchell UER .10 .05
(Career HR total 99, should be 100)
❑ 118 Ron Oester .10 .05
❑ 119 Brett Butler .20 .09
❑ 120 Danny Jackson .10 .05
❑ 121 Tommy Gregg .10 .05
❑ 122 Ken Caminiti .40 .18
❑ 123 Kevin Brown .40 .18
❑ 124 George Brett UER .75 .35
(133 runs, should be 1300)
❑ 125 Mike Scott .10 .05
❑ 126 Cory Snyder .10 .05
❑ 127 George Bell .10 .05
❑ 128 Mark Grace .40 .18
❑ 129 Devon White .10 .05
❑ 130 Tony Fernandez .10 .05
❑ 131 Don Aase .10 .05
❑ 132 Rance Mulliniks .10 .05
❑ 133 Marty Barrett .10 .05
❑ 134 Nelson Liriano .10 .05
❑ 135 Mark Carreon .10 .05
❑ 136 Candy Maldonado .10 .05
❑ 137 Tim Birtsas .10 .05
❑ 138 Tom Brookens .10 .05
❑ 139 John Franco .20 .09
❑ 140 Mike LaCoss .10 .05
❑ 141 Jeff Treadway .10 .05
❑ 142 Pat Tabler .10 .05
❑ 143 Darrell Evans .20 .09
❑ 144 Rafael Ramirez .10 .05
❑ 145 Oddibe McDowell UER .10 .05
(Misspelled Odibbe)
❑ 146 Brian Downing .10 .05
❑ 147 Curt Wilkerson .10 .05
❑ 148 Ernie Whitt .10 .05
❑ 149 Bill Schroeder .10 .05
❑ 150 Domingo Ramos UER .10 .05
(Says throws right, but shows him throwing lefty)
❑ 151 Rick Honeycutt .10 .05
❑ 152 Don Slaught .10 .05
❑ 153 Mitch Webster .10 .05
❑ 154 Tony Phillips .10 .05
❑ 155 Paul Kilgus .10 .05
❑ 156 Ken Griffey Jr. UER 5.00 2.20
(Simultaniously)
❑ 157 Gary Sheffield .40 .18
❑ 158 Wally Backman .10 .05
❑ 159 B.J. Surhoff .20 .09
❑ 160 Louie Meadows .10 .05
❑ 161 Paul O'Neill .20 .09
❑ 162 Jeff McKnight .10 .05
❑ 163 Alvaro Espinoza .10 .05
❑ 164 Scott Scudder .10 .05
❑ 165 Jeff Reed .10 .05
❑ 166 Gregg Jefferies .20 .09
❑ 167 Barry Larkin .40 .18
❑ 168 Gary Carter .40 .18
❑ 169 Robby Thompson .10 .05
❑ 170 Rolando Roomes .10 .05
❑ 171 Mark McGwire UER 2.00 .90
(Total games 427 and hits 479, should be 467 and 427)
❑ 172 Steve Sax .10 .05
❑ 173 Mark Williamson .10 .05
❑ 174 Mitch Williams .10 .05
❑ 175 Brian Holton .10 .05
❑ 176 Rob Deer .10 .05
❑ 177 Tim Raines .20 .09
❑ 178 Mike Felder .10 .05
❑ 179 Harold Reynolds .10 .05
❑ 180 Terry Francona .20 .09
❑ 181 Chris Sabo .10 .05
❑ 182 Darryl Strawberry .20 .09
❑ 183 Willie Randolph .20 .09
❑ 184 Bill Ripken .10 .05
❑ 185 Mackey Sasser .10 .05
❑ 186 Todd Benzinger .10 .05
❑ 187 Kevin Elster UER .10 .05
(16 homers in 1989, should be 10)
❑ 188 Jose Uribe .10 .05
❑ 189 Tom Browning .10 .05
❑ 190 Keith Miller .10 .05
❑ 191 Don Mattingly .60 .25
❑ 192 Dave Parker .20 .09
❑ 193 Roberto Kelly UER .10 .05
(96 RBI, should be 62)
❑ 194 Phil Bradley .10 .05
❑ 195 Ron Hassey .10 .05
❑ 196 Gerald Young .10 .05
❑ 197 Hubie Brooks .10 .05
❑ 198 Bill Doran .10 .05
❑ 199 Al Newman .10 .05
❑ 200 Checklist 101-200 .10 .05
❑ 201 Terry Puhl .10 .05
❑ 202 Frank DiPino .10 .05
❑ 203 Jim Clancy .10 .05
❑ 204 Bob Ojeda .10 .05
❑ 205 Alex Trevino .10 .05
❑ 206 Dave Henderson .10 .05
❑ 207 Henry Cotto .10 .05

❑ 208 Rafael Belliard UER ...... .10 .05
(Born 1961, not 1951)
❑ 209 Stan Javier .... .10 .05
❑ 210 Jerry Reed .... .10 .05
❑ 211 Doug Dascenzo .... .10 .05
❑ 212 Andres Thomas .... .10 .05
❑ 213 Greg Maddux .... 1.25 .55
❑ 214 Mike Schooler .... .10 .05
❑ 215 Lonnie Smith .... .10 .05
❑ 216 Jose Rijo .... .10 .05
❑ 217 Greg Gagne .... .10 .05
❑ 218 Jim Gantner .... .10 .05
❑ 219 Allan Anderson .... .10 .05
❑ 220 Rick Mahler .... .10 .05
❑ 221 Jim Deshaies .... .10 .05
❑ 222 Keith Hernandez .... .20 .09
❑ 223 Vince Coleman .... .10 .05
❑ 224 David Cone .... .40 .18
❑ 225 Ozzie Smith .... .50 .23
❑ 226 Matt Nokes .... .10 .05
❑ 227 Barry Bonds .... .50 .23
❑ 228 Felix Jose .... .10 .05
❑ 229 Dennis Powell .... .10 .05
❑ 230 Mike Gallego .... .10 .05
❑ 231 Shawon Dunston UER .. .10 .05
('89 stats are
Andre Dawson's)
❑ 232 Ron Gant .... .20 .09
❑ 233 Omar Vizquel .... .40 .18
❑ 234 Derek Lilliquist .... .10 .05
❑ 235 Erik Hanson .... .10 .05
❑ 236 Kirby Puckett UER .... .60 .25
(824 games, should
be 924)
❑ 237 Bill Spiers .... .10 .05
❑ 238 Dan Gladden .... .10 .05
❑ 239 Bryan Clutterbuck .... .10 .05
❑ 240 John Moses .... .10 .05
❑ 241 Ron Darling .... .10 .05
❑ 242 Joe Magrane .... .10 .05
❑ 243 Dave Magadan .... .10 .05
❑ 244 Pedro Guerrero UER ...... .10 .05
(Misspelled Guererro)
❑ 245 Glenn Davis .... .10 .05
❑ 246 Terry Steinbach .... .20 .09
❑ 247 Fred Lynn .... .10 .05
❑ 248 Gary Redus .... .10 .05
❑ 249 Ken Williams .... .10 .05
❑ 250 Sid Bream .... .10 .05
❑ 251 Bob Welch UER .... .10 .05
(2587 career strike-
outs, should be 1587)
❑ 252 Bill Buckner .... .10 .05
❑ 253 Carney Lansford .... .20 .09
❑ 254 Paul Molitor .... .40 .18
❑ 255 Jose DeJesus .... .10 .05
❑ 256 Orel Hershiser .... .20 .09
❑ 257 Tom Brunansky .... .10 .05
❑ 258 Mike Davis .... .10 .05
❑ 259 Jeff Ballard .... .10 .05
❑ 260 Scott Terry .... .10 .05
❑ 261 Sid Fernandez .... .10 .05
❑ 262 Mike Marshall .... .10 .05
❑ 263 Howard Johnson UER .... .10 .05
(192 SO, should be 592)
❑ 264 Kirk Gibson UER .... .20 .09
(659 runs, should
be 669)
❑ 265 Kevin McReynolds .... .10 .05
❑ 266 Cal Ripken .... 1.50 .70
❑ 267 Ozzie Guillen UER .... .10 .05
(Career triples 27,
should be 29)
❑ 268 Jim Traber .... .10 .05
❑ 269 Bobby Thigpen UER ...... .10 .05
(31 saves in 1989,
should be 34)
❑ 270 Joe Orsulak .... .10 .05
❑ 271 Bob Boone .... .20 .09
❑ 272 Dave Stewart UER .... .20 .09
(Totals wrong due to
omission of '86 stats)
❑ 273 Tim Wallach .... .10 .05
❑ 274 Luis Aquino UER .... .10 .05
(Says throws lefty,
but shows him
throwing righty)
❑ 275 Mike Moore .... .10 .05
❑ 276 Tony Pena .... .10 .05
❑ 277 Eddie Murray UER .... .40 .18
(Several typos in
career total stats)
❑ 278 Milt Thompson .... .10 .05
❑ 279 Alejandro Pena .... .10 .05
❑ 280 Ken Dayley .... .10 .05
❑ 281 Carmen Castillo .... .10 .05
❑ 282 Tom Henke .... .10 .05
❑ 283 Mickey Hatcher .... .10 .05
❑ 284 Roy Smith .... .10 .05
❑ 285 Manny Lee .... .10 .05
❑ 286 Dan Pasqua .... .10 .05
❑ 287 Larry Sheets .... .10 .05
❑ 288 Garry Templeton .... .10 .05
❑ 289 Eddie Williams .... .10 .05
❑ 290 Brady Anderson UER .... .40 .18
(Home: Silver Springs,
not Siver Springs)
❑ 291 Spike Owen .... .10 .05
❑ 292 Storm Davis .... .10 .05
❑ 293 Chris Bosio .... .10 .05
❑ 294 Jim Eisenreich .... .10 .05
❑ 295 Don August .... .10 .05
❑ 296 Jeff Hamilton .... .10 .05
❑ 297 Mickey Tettleton .... .20 .09
❑ 298 Mike Scioscia .... .10 .05
❑ 299 Kevin Hickey .... .10 .05
❑ 300 Checklist 201-300 .... .10 .05
❑ 301 Shawn Abner .... .10 .05
❑ 302 Kevin Bass .... .10 .05
❑ 303 Bip Roberts .... .10 .05
❑ 304 Joe Girardi .... .30 .14
❑ 305 Danny Darwin .... .10 .05
❑ 306 Mike Heath .... .10 .05
❑ 307 Mike Macfarlane .... .10 .05
❑ 308 Ed Whitson .... .10 .05
❑ 309 Tracy Jones .... .10 .05
❑ 310 Scott Fletcher .... .10 .05
❑ 311 Darnell Coles .... .10 .05
❑ 312 Mike Brumley .... .10 .05
❑ 313 Bill Swift .... .10 .05
❑ 314 Charlie Hough .... .20 .09
❑ 315 Jim Presley .... .10 .05
❑ 316 Luis Polonia .... .10 .05
❑ 317 Mike Morgan .... .10 .05
❑ 318 Lee Guetterman .... .10 .05
❑ 319 Jose Oquendo .... .10 .05
❑ 320 Wayne Tolleson .... .10 .05
❑ 321 Jody Reed .... .10 .05
❑ 322 Damon Berryhill .... .10 .05
❑ 323 Roger Clemens .... .75 .35
❑ 324 Ryne Sandberg .... .50 .23
❑ 325 Benito Santiago UER .... .10 .05
(Misspelled Santago
on card back)
❑ 326 Bret Saberhagen UER .. .20 .09
(1140 hits, should be
1240; 56 CG, should
be 52)
❑ 327 Lou Whitaker .... .20 .09
❑ 328 Dave Gallagher .... .10 .05
❑ 329 Mike Pagliarulo .... .10 .05
❑ 330 Doyle Alexander .... .10 .05
❑ 331 Jeffrey Leonard .... .10 .05
❑ 332 Torey Lovullo .... .10 .05
❑ 333 Pete Incaviglia .... .10 .05
❑ 334 Rickey Henderson .... .40 .18
❑ 335 Rafael Palmeiro .... .40 .18
❑ 336 Ken Hill .... .30 .14
❑ 337 Dave Winfield UER .... .40 .18
(1418 RBI, should
be 1438)
❑ 338 Alfredo Griffin .... .10 .05
❑ 339 Andy Hawkins .... .10 .05
❑ 340 Ted Power .... .10 .05
❑ 341 Steve Wilson .... .10 .05
❑ 342 Jack Clark UER .... .20 .09
(916 BB, should be
1006; 1142 SO,
should be 1130)
❑ 343 Ellis Burks .... .30 .14
❑ 344 Tony Gwynn UER .... 1.00 .45
(Doubles stats on
card back are wrong)
❑ 345 Jerome Walton UER ...... .10 .05
(Total At Bats 476,
should be 475)
❑ 346 Roberto Alomar UER .... .40 .18
(61 doubles, should
be 51)
❑ 347 Carlos Martinez UER .... .10 .05
(Born 8/11/64, should
be 8/11/65)
❑ 348 Chet Lemon .... .10 .05
❑ 349 Willie Wilson .... .10 .05
❑ 350 Greg Walker .... .10 .05
❑ 351 Tom Bolton .... .10 .05
❑ 352 German Gonzalez .... .10 .05
❑ 353 Harold Baines .... .20 .09
❑ 354 Mike Greenwell .... .10 .05
❑ 355 Ruben Sierra .... .10 .05
❑ 356 Andres Galarraga .... .40 .18
❑ 357 Andre Dawson .... .40 .18
❑ 358 Jeff Brantley .... .10 .05
❑ 359 Mike Bielecki .... .10 .05
❑ 360 Ken Oberkfell .... .10 .05
❑ 361 Kurt Stillwell .... .10 .05
❑ 362 Brian Holman .... .10 .05
❑ 363 Kevin Seitzer UER .... .10 .05
(Career triples total
does not add up)
❑ 364 Alvin Davis .... .10 .05
❑ 365 Tom Gordon .... .30 .14
❑ 366 Bobby Bonilla UER .... .20 .09
(Two steals in 1987,
should be 3)
❑ 367 Carlton Fisk .... .40 .18
❑ 368 Steve Carter UER .... .10 .05
(Charlotesville)
❑ 369 Joel Skinner .... .10 .05
❑ 370 John Cangelosi .... .10 .05
❑ 371 Cecil Espy .... .10 .05
❑ 372 Gary Wayne .... .10 .05
❑ 373 Jim Rice .... .20 .09
❑ 374 Mike Dyer .... .10 .05
❑ 375 Joe Carter .... .20 .09
❑ 376 Dwight Smith .... .10 .05
❑ 377 John Wetteland .... .40 .18
❑ 378 Earnie Riles .... .10 .05
❑ 379 Otis Nixon .... .20 .09
❑ 380 Vance Law .... .10 .05
❑ 381 Dave Bergman .... .10 .05
❑ 382 Frank White .... .20 .09
❑ 383 Scott Bradley .... .10 .05
❑ 384 Israel Sanchez UER ...... .10 .05
(Totals don't in-
clude '89 stats)
❑ 385 Gary Pettis .... .10 .05
❑ 386 Donn Pall .... .10 .05
❑ 387 John Smiley .... .10 .05
❑ 388 Tom Candiotti .... .10 .05
❑ 389 Junior Ortiz .... .10 .05
❑ 390 Steve Lyons .... .10 .05
❑ 391 Brian Harper .... .10 .05
❑ 392 Fred Manrique .... .10 .05
❑ 393 Lee Smith .... .20 .09
❑ 394 Jeff Kunkel .... .10 .05
❑ 395 Claudell Washington ...... .10 .05
❑ 396 John Tudor .... .10 .05
❑ 397 Terry Kennedy UER ...... .10 .05
(Career totals all
wrong)
❑ 398 Lloyd McClendon .... .10 .05
❑ 399 Craig Lefferts .... .10 .05
❑ 400 Checklist 301-400 .... .10 .05
❑ 401 Keith Moreland .... .10 .05
❑ 402 Rich Gedman .... .10 .05
❑ 403 Jeff D. Robinson .... .10 .05
❑ 404 Randy Ready .... .10 .05
❑ 405 Rick Cerone .... .10 .05
❑ 406 Jeff Blauser .... .10 .05
❑ 407 Larry Andersen .... .10 .05
❑ 408 Joe Boever .... .10 .05
❑ 409 Felix Fermin .... .10 .05
❑ 410 Glenn Wilson .... .10 .05
❑ 411 Rex Hudler .... .10 .05
❑ 412 Mark Grant .... .10 .05
❑ 413 Dennis Martinez .... .20 .09

❑	414	Darrin Jackson	.10	.05
❑	415	Mike Aldrete	.10	.05
❑	416	Roger McDowell	.10	.05
❑	417	Jeff Reardon	.20	.09
❑	418	Darren Daulton	.20	.09
❑	419	Tim Laudner	.10	.05
❑	420	Don Carman	.10	.05
❑	421	Lloyd Moseby	.10	.05
❑	422	Doug Drabek	.10	.05
❑	423	Lenny Harris UER (Walks 2 in '89, should be 20)	.10	.05
❑	424	Jose Lind	.10	.05
❑	425	Dave Johnson (P)	.10	.05
❑	426	Jerry Browne	.10	.05
❑	427	Eric Yelding	.10	.05
❑	428	Brad Komminsk	.10	.05
❑	429	Jody Davis	.10	.05
❑	430	Mariano Duncan	.10	.05
❑	431	Mark Davis	.10	.05
❑	432	Nelson Santovenia	.10	.05
❑	433	Bruce Hurst	.10	.05
❑	434	Jeff Huson	.10	.05
❑	435	Chris James	.10	.05
❑	436	Mark Guthrie	.10	.05
❑	437	Charlie Hayes	.10	.05
❑	438	Shane Rawley	.10	.05
❑	439	Dickie Thon	.10	.05
❑	440	Juan Berenguer	.10	.05
❑	441	Kevin Romine	.10	.05
❑	442	Bill Landrum	.10	.05
❑	443	Todd Frohwirth	.10	.05
❑	444	Craig Worthington	.10	.05
❑	445	Fernando Valenzuela	.20	.09
❑	446	Joey Belle	2.00	.90
❑	447	Ed Whited UER (Ashville, should be Asheville)	.10	.05
❑	448	Dave Smith	.10	.05
❑	449	Dave Clark	.10	.05
❑	450	Juan Agosto	.10	.05
❑	451	Dave Valle	.10	.05
❑	452	Kent Hrbek	.20	.09
❑	453	Von Hayes	.10	.05
❑	454	Gary Gaetti	.20	.09
❑	455	Greg Briley	.10	.05
❑	456	Glenn Braggs	.10	.05
❑	457	Kirt Manwaring	.10	.05
❑	458	Mel Hall	.10	.05
❑	459	Brook Jacoby	.10	.05
❑	460	Pat Sheridan	.10	.05
❑	461	Rob Murphy	.10	.05
❑	462	Jimmy Key	.20	.09
❑	463	Nick Esasky	.10	.05
❑	464	Rob Ducey	.10	.05
❑	465	Carlos Quintana UER (Internatinoal)	.10	.05
❑	466	Larry Walker	2.00	.90
❑	467	Todd Worrell	.10	.05
❑	468	Kevin Gross	.10	.05
❑	469	Terry Pendleton	.20	.09
❑	470	Dave Martinez	.10	.05
❑	471	Gene Larkin	.10	.05
❑	472	Len Dykstra UER ('89 and total runs understated by 10)	.20	.09
❑	473	Barry Lyons	.10	.05
❑	474	Terry Mulholland	.10	.05
❑	475	Chip Hale	.10	.05
❑	476	Jesse Barfield	.10	.05
❑	477	Dan Plesac	.10	.05
❑	478A	Scott Garrelts ERR (Photo actually Bill Bathe)	2.00	.90
❑	478B	Scott Garrelts COR	.10	.05
❑	479	Dave Righetti	.10	.05
❑	480	Gus Polidor UER (Wearing 14 on front, but 10 on back)	.10	.05
❑	481	Mookie Wilson	.20	.09
❑	482	Luis Rivera	.10	.05
❑	483	Mike Flanagan	.10	.05
❑	484	Dennis Boyd	.10	.05
❑	485	John Cerutti	.10	.05
❑	486	John Costello	.10	.05
❑	487	Pascual Perez	.10	.05
❑	488	Tommy Herr	.10	.05
❑	489	Tom Foley	.10	.05
❑	490	Curt Ford	.10	.05
❑	491	Steve Lake	.10	.05
❑	492	Tim Teufel	.10	.05
❑	493	Randy Bush	.10	.05
❑	494	Mike Jackson	.20	.09
❑	495	Steve Jeltz	.10	.05
❑	496	Paul Gibson	.10	.05
❑	497	Steve Balboni	.10	.05
❑	498	Bud Black	.10	.05
❑	499	Dale Sveum	.10	.05
❑	500	Checklist 401-500	.10	.05
❑	501	Tim Jones	.10	.05
❑	502	Mark Portugal	.10	.05
❑	503	Ivan Calderon	.10	.05
❑	504	Rick Rhoden	.10	.05
❑	505	Willie McGee	.20	.09
❑	506	Kirk McCaskill	.10	.05
❑	507	Dave LaPoint	.10	.05
❑	508	Jay Howell	.10	.05
❑	509	Johnny Ray	.10	.05
❑	510	Dave Anderson	.10	.05
❑	511	Chuck Crim	.10	.05
❑	512	Joe Hesketh	.10	.05
❑	513	Dennis Eckersley	.30	.14
❑	514	Greg Brock	.10	.05
❑	515	Tim Burke	.10	.05
❑	516	Frank Tanana	.10	.05
❑	517	Jay Bell	.20	.09
❑	518	Guillermo Hernandez	.10	.05
❑	519	Randy Kramer UER (Codiroli misspelled as Codoroli)	.10	.05
❑	520	Charles Hudson	.10	.05
❑	521	Jim Corsi (Word "originally" is misspelled on back)	.10	.05
❑	522	Steve Rosenberg	.10	.05
❑	523	Cris Carpenter	.10	.05
❑	524	Matt Winters	.10	.05
❑	525	Melido Perez	.10	.05
❑	526	Chris Gwynn UER (Albeguergue)	.10	.05
❑	527	Bert Blyleven UER (Games career total is wrong, should be 644)	.20	.09
❑	528	Chuck Cary	.10	.05
❑	529	Daryl Boston	.10	.05
❑	530	Dale Mohorcic	.10	.05
❑	531	Geronimo Berroa	.10	.05
❑	532	Edgar Martinez	.40	.18
❑	533	Dale Murphy	.40	.18
❑	534	Jay Buhner	.40	.18
❑	535	John Smoltz UER (HEA Stadium)	.40	.18
❑	536	Andy Van Slyke	.20	.09
❑	537	Mike Henneman	.10	.05
❑	538	Miguel Garcia	.10	.05
❑	539	Frank Williams	.10	.05
❑	540	R.J. Reynolds	.10	.05
❑	541	Shawn Hillegas	.10	.05
❑	542	Walt Weiss	.10	.05
❑	543	Greg Hibbard	.10	.05
❑	544	Nolan Ryan	1.50	.70
❑	545	Todd Zeile	.20	.09
❑	546	Hensley Meulens	.10	.05
❑	547	Tim Belcher	.10	.05
❑	548	Mike Witt	.10	.05
❑	549	Greg Cadaret UER (Aquiring, should be Acquiring)	.10	.05
❑	550	Franklin Stubbs	.10	.05
❑	551	Tony Castillo	.10	.05
❑	552	Jeff M. Robinson	.10	.05
❑	553	Steve Olin	.20	.09
❑	554	Alan Trammell	.30	.14
❑	555	Wade Boggs 4X (Bo Jackson in background)	.40	.18
❑	556	Will Clark	.40	.18
❑	557	Jeff King	.20	.09
❑	558	Mike Fitzgerald	.10	.05
❑	559	Ken Howell	.10	.05
❑	560	Bob Kipper	.10	.05
❑	561	Scott Bankhead	.10	.05
❑	562A	Jeff Innis ERR (Photo actually David West)	2.00	.90
❑	562B	Jeff Innis COR	.10	.05
❑	563	Randy Johnson	.60	.25
❑	564	Wally Whitehurst	.10	.05
❑	565	Gene Harris	.10	.05
❑	566	Norm Charlton	.10	.05
❑	567	Robin Yount UER (7602 career hits, should be 2606)	.20	.09
❑	568	Joe Oliver UER (Fl.orida)	.10	.05
❑	569	Mark Parent	.10	.05
❑	570	John Farrell UER (Loss total added wrong)	.10	.05
❑	571	Tom Glavine	.40	.18
❑	572	Rod Nichols	.10	.05
❑	573	Jack Morris	.20	.09
❑	574	Greg Swindell	.10	.05
❑	575	Steve Searcy	.10	.05
❑	576	Ricky Jordan	.10	.05
❑	577	Matt Williams	.40	.18
❑	578	Mike LaValliere	.10	.05
❑	579	Bryn Smith	.10	.05
❑	580	Bruce Ruffin	.10	.05
❑	581	Randy Myers	.20	.09
❑	582	Rick Wrona	.10	.05
❑	583	Juan Samuel	.10	.05
❑	584	Les Lancaster	.10	.05
❑	585	Jeff Musselman	.10	.05
❑	586	Rob Dibble	.10	.05
❑	587	Eric Show	.10	.05
❑	588	Jesse Orosco	.10	.05
❑	589	Herm Winningham	.10	.05
❑	590	Andy Allanson	.10	.05
❑	591	Dion James	.10	.05
❑	592	Carmelo Martinez	.10	.05
❑	593	Luis Quinones	.10	.05
❑	594	Dennis Rasmussen	.10	.05
❑	595	Rich Yett	.10	.05
❑	596	Bob Walk	.10	.05
❑	597A	Andy McGaffigan ERR (Photo actually Rich Thompson)	.20	.09
❑	597B	Andy McGaffigan COR	.10	.05
❑	598	Billy Hatcher	.10	.05
❑	599	Bob Knepper	.10	.05
❑	600	Checklist 501-600 UER (599 Bob Kneppers)	.10	.05
❑	601	Joey Cora	.30	.14
❑	602	Steve Finley	.40	.18
❑	603	Kal Daniels UER (12 hits in '87, should be 123; 335 runs, should be 235)	.10	.05
❑	604	Gregg Olson	.10	.05
❑	605	Dave Stieb	.20	.09
❑	606	Kenny Rogers (Shown catching football)	.20	.09
❑	607	Zane Smith	.10	.05
❑	608	Bob Geren UER (Origionally)	.10	.05
❑	609	Chad Kreuter	.10	.05
❑	610	Mike Smithson	.10	.05
❑	611	Jeff Wetherby	.10	.05
❑	612	Gary Mielke	.10	.05
❑	613	Pete Smith	.10	.05
❑	614	Jack Daugherty UER (Born 7/30/60, should be 7/3/60)	.10	.05
❑	615	Lance McCullers	.10	.05
❑	616	Don Robinson	.10	.05
❑	617	Jose Guzman	.10	.05
❑	618	Steve Bedrosian	.10	.05
❑	619	Jamie Moyer	.10	.05
❑	620	Atlee Hammaker	.10	.05
❑	621	Rick Luecken UER (Innings pitched wrong)	.10	.05
❑	622	Greg W. Harris	.10	.05
❑	623	Pete Harnisch	.10	.05
❑	624	Jerald Clark	.10	.05

❑ 625 Jack McDowell UER ...... .10 .05
(Career totals for Games and GS don't include 1987 season)
❑ 626 Frank Viola .... .10 .05
❑ 627 Teddy Higuera................ .10 .05
❑ 628 Marty Pevey .... .10 .05
❑ 629 Bill Wegman .... .10 .05
❑ 630 Eric Plunk .... .10 .05
❑ 631 Drew Hall........................ .10 .05
❑ 632 Doug Jones .... .10 .05
❑ 633 Geno Petralli UER.......... .10 .05
(Sacremento)
❑ 634 Jose Alvarez .... .10 .05
❑ 635 Bob Milacki .... .10 .05
❑ 636 Bobby Witt...................... .10 .05
❑ 637 Trevor Wilson .... .10 .05
❑ 638 Jeff Russell UER............ .10 .05
(Shutout stats wrong)
❑ 639 Mike Krukow .... .10 .05
❑ 640 Rick Leach .... .10 .05
❑ 641 Dave Schmidt .... .10 .05
❑ 642 Terry Leach.................... .10 .05
❑ 643 Calvin Schiraldi .... .10 .05
❑ 644 Bob Melvin .... .10 .05
❑ 645 Jim Abbott .... .30 .14
❑ 646 Jaime Navarro................ .10 .05
❑ 647 Mark Langston UER ...... .10 .05
(Several errors in stats totals)
❑ 648 Juan Nieves .... .10 .05
❑ 649 Damaso Garcia .... .10 .05
❑ 650 Charlie O'Brien .... .10 .05
❑ 651 Eric King .... .10 .05
❑ 652 Mike Boddicker .... .10 .05
❑ 653 Duane Ward .... .10 .05
❑ 654 Bob Stanley.................... .10 .05
❑ 655 Sandy Alomar Jr............. .30 .14
❑ 656 Danny Tartabull UER .... .10 .05
(395 BB, should be 295)
❑ 657 Randy McCament .... .10 .05
❑ 658 Charlie Leibrandt........... .10 .05
❑ 659 Dan Quisenberry .... .10 .05
❑ 660 Paul Assenmacher .... .10 .05
❑ 661 Walt Terrell .... .10 .05
❑ 662 Tim Leary .... .10 .05
❑ 663 Randy Milligan................ .10 .05
❑ 664 Bo Diaz .... .10 .05
❑ 665 Mark Lemke UER .... .10 .05
(Richmond misspelled as Richomond)
❑ 666 Jose Gonzalez .... .10 .05
❑ 667 Chuck Finley UER.......... .20 .09
(Born 11/16/62, should be 11/26/62)
❑ 668 John Kruk .... .20 .09
❑ 669 Dick Schofield .... .10 .05
❑ 670 Tim Crews....................... .10 .05
❑ 671 John Dopson .... .10 .05
❑ 672 John Orton .... .10 .05
❑ 673 Eric Hetzel...................... .10 .05
❑ 674 Lance Parrish .... .10 .05
❑ 675 Ramon Martinez .... .30 .14
❑ 676 Mark Gubicza .... .10 .05
❑ 677 Greg Litton .... .10 .05
❑ 678 Greg Mathews................ .10 .05
❑ 679 Dave Dravecky .... .20 .09
❑ 680 Steve Farr .... .10 .05
❑ 681 Mike Devereaux .... .10 .05
❑ 682 Ken Griffey Sr................. .10 .05
❑ 683A Mickey Weston ERR.. 2.00 .90
(Listed as Jamie on card)
❑ 683B Mickey Weston COR .. .10 .05
(Technically still an error as birthdate is listed as 3/26/81)
❑ 684 Jack Armstrong .... .10 .05
❑ 685 Steve Buechele .... .10 .05
❑ 686 Bryan Harvey .... .10 .05
❑ 687 Lance Blankenship .... .10 .05
❑ 688 Dante Bichette................ .40 .18
❑ 689 Todd Burns .... .10 .05
❑ 690 Dan Petry .... .10 .05
❑ 691 Kent Anderson .... .10 .05
❑ 692 Todd Stottlemyre............ .20 .09
❑ 693 Wally Joyner UER........... .20 .09
(Several stats errors)
❑ 694 Mike Rochford .... .10 .05
❑ 695 Floyd Bannister .... .10 .05
❑ 696 Rick Reuschel .... .10 .05
❑ 697 Jose DeLeon .... .10 .05
❑ 698 Jeff Montgomery .... .20 .09
❑ 699 Kelly Downs .... .10 .05
❑ 700A Checklist 601-700 ...... 2.00 .90
(683 Jamie Weston)
❑ 700B Checklist 601-700 .... .10 .05
(683 Mickey Weston)
❑ 701 Jim Gott.......................... .10 .05
❑ 702 Rookie Threats .... .50 .23
Delino DeShields
Marquis Grissom
Larry Walker
❑ 703 Alejandro Pena .... .10 .05
❑ 704 Willie Randolph .... .20 .09
❑ 705 Tim Leary .... .10 .05
❑ 706 Chuck McElroy .... .10 .05
❑ 707 Gerald Perry .... .10 .05
❑ 708 Tom Brunansky.............. .10 .05
❑ 709 John Franco .... .20 .09
❑ 710 Mark Davis .... .10 .05
❑ 711 David Justice............... 1.50 .70
❑ 712 Storm Davis.................... .10 .05
❑ 713 Scott Ruskin .... .10 .05
❑ 714 Glenn Braggs .... .10 .05
❑ 715 Kevin Bearse.................. .10 .05
❑ 716 Jose Nunez .... .10 .05
❑ 717 Tim Layana .... .10 .05
❑ 718 Greg Myers .... .10 .05
❑ 719 Pete O'Brien .... .10 .05
❑ 720 John Candelaria .... .10 .05
❑ 721 Craig Grebeck................ .10 .05
❑ 722 Shawn Boskie .... .10 .05
❑ 723 Jim Leyritz...................... .40 .18
❑ 724 Bill Sampen..................... .10 .05
❑ 725 Scott Radinsky .... .10 .05
❑ 726 Todd Hundley .... .75 .35
❑ 727 Scott Hemond .... .10 .05
❑ 728 Lenny Webster .... .10 .05
❑ 729 Jeff Reardon .... .20 .09
❑ 730 Mitch Webster .... .10 .05
❑ 731 Brian Bohanon .... .10 .05
❑ 732 Rick Parker .... .10 .05
❑ 733 Terry Shumpert .... .10 .05
❑ 734A Ryan's 6th No-Hitter .. 2.50 1.10
(No stripe on front)
❑ 734B Ryan's 6th No-Hitter ..... .75 .35
(stripe added on card front for 300th win)
❑ 735 John Burkett .... .20 .09
❑ 736 Derrick May .... .20 .09
❑ 737 Carlos Baerga .... .50 .23
❑ 738 Greg Smith .... .10 .05
❑ 739 Scott Sanderson .... .10 .05
❑ 740 Joe Kraemer .... .10 .05
❑ 741 Hector Villanueva .... .10 .05
❑ 742 Mike Fetters .... .10 .05
❑ 743 Mark Gardner .... .10 .05
❑ 744 Matt Nokes .... .10 .05
❑ 745 Dave Winfield .... .40 .18
❑ 746 Delino DeShields............ .40 .18
❑ 747 Dann Howitt.................... .10 .05
❑ 748 Tony Pena...................... .10 .05
❑ 749 Oil Can Boyd.................. .10 .05
❑ 750 Mike Benjamin................ .10 .05
❑ 751 Alex Cole........................ .10 .05
❑ 752 Eric Gunderson .... .10 .05
❑ 753 Howard Farmer .... .10 .05
❑ 754 Joe Carter .... .20 .09
❑ 755 Ray Lankford................ 1.00 .45
❑ 756 Sandy Alomar Jr............. .30 .14
❑ 757 Alex Sanchez .... .10 .05
❑ 758 Nick Esasky.................... .10 .05
❑ 759 Stan Belinda .... .10 .05
❑ 760 Jim Presley .... .10 .05
❑ 761 Gary DiSarcina .... .40 .18
❑ 762 Wayne Edwards .... .10 .05
❑ 763 Pat Combs .... .10 .05
❑ 764 Mickey Pina.................... .10 .05
❑ 765 Wilson Alvarez .... .50 .23
❑ 766 Dave Parker .... .20 .09
❑ 767 Mike Blowers.................. .20 .09
❑ 768 Tony Phillips .... .10 .05
❑ 769 Pascual Perez................ .10 .05
❑ 770 Gary Pettis .... .10 .05
❑ 771 Fred Lynn .... .10 .05
❑ 772 Mel Rojas .... .40 .18
❑ 773 David Segui.................... .50 .23
❑ 774 Gary Carter .... .40 .18
❑ 775 Rafael Valdez .... .10 .05
❑ 776 Glenallen Hill.................. .10 .05
❑ 777 Keith Hernandez .... .20 .09
❑ 778 Billy Hatcher .... .10 .05
❑ 779 Marty Clary .... .10 .05
❑ 780 Candy Maldonado .... .10 .05
❑ 781 Mike Marshall .... .10 .05
❑ 782 Billy Joe Robidoux.......... .10 .05
❑ 783 Mark Langston .... .10 .05
❑ 784 Paul Sorrento .... .40 .18
❑ 785 Dave Hollins .... .40 .18
❑ 786 Cecil Fielder .... .20 .09
❑ 787 Matt Young .... .10 .05
❑ 788 Jeff Huson...................... .10 .05
❑ 789 Lloyd Moseby .... .10 .05
❑ 790 Ron Kittle........................ .10 .05
❑ 791 Hubie Brooks.................. .10 .05
❑ 792 Craig Lefferts.................. .10 .05
❑ 793 Kevin Bass .... .10 .05
❑ 794 Bryn Smith...................... .10 .05
❑ 795 Juan Samuel .... .10 .05
❑ 796 Sam Horn .... .10 .05
❑ 797 Randy Myers .... .20 .09
❑ 798 Chris James .... .10 .05
❑ 799 Bill Gullickson .... .10 .05
❑ 800 Checklist 701-800 .... .10 .05

1990 Upper Deck Jackson Heroes

	MINT	NRMT
COMPLETE SET (10)	15.00	6.75
COMMON REGGIE (1-9)	1.50	.70

❑ 1 Reggie Jackson................ 1.50 .70
1969 Emerging Superstar
❑ 2 Reggie Jackson................ 1.50 .70
1973 An MVP Year
❑ 3 Reggie Jackson................ 1.50 .70
1977 Mr. October
❑ 4 Reggie Jackson................ 1.50 .70
1978 vs. Bob Welch
❑ 5 Reggie Jackson................ 1.50 .70
1982 Under the Halo
❑ 6 Reggie Jackson................ 1.50 .70
1984 500 Homers
❑ 7 Reggie Jackson................ 1.50 .70
1986 Moving Up the List
❑ 8 Reggie Jackson................ 1.50 .70
1987 A Great Career Ends
❑ 9 Jackson Heroes art/CL .... 1.50 .70
❑ AU1 Reggie Jackson AU 200.00 90.00
(Signed and Numbered out of 2500)
❑ NNO0 Reggie Jackson........ 3.00 1.35
Header Card

1991 Upper Deck

	MINT	NRMT
COMPLETE SET (800)	20.00	9.00
COMP.FACT.SET (800)	20.00	9.00
COMPLETE LO SET (700)	16.00	7.25
COMPLETE HI SET (100)	4.00	1.80
COMMON CARD (1-800)	.05	.02

	No.	Card	MINT	NRMT
❑	1	Star Rookie Checklist	.05	.02
❑	2	Phil Plantier	.05	.02
❑	3	D.J. Dozier	.05	.02
❑	4	Dave Hansen	.05	.02
❑	5	Maurice Vaughn	.40	.18
❑	6	Leo Gomez	.05	.02
❑	7	Scott Aldred	.05	.02
❑	8	Scott Chiamparino	.05	.02
❑	9	Lance Dickson	.05	.02
❑	10	Sean Berry	.10	.05
❑	11	Bernie Williams	.30	.14
❑	12	Brian Barnes UER (Photo either not him or in wrong jersey)	.05	.02
❑	13	Narciso Elvira	.05	.02
❑	14	Mike Gardiner	.05	.02
❑	15	Greg Colbrunn	.05	.02
❑	16	Bernard Gilkey	.10	.05
❑	17	Mark Lewis	.05	.02
❑	18	Mickey Morandini	.05	.02
❑	19	Charles Nagy	.20	.09
❑	20	Geronimo Pena	.05	.02
❑	21	Henry Rodriguez	.40	.18
❑	22	Scott Cooper	.05	.02
❑	23	Andujar Cedeno UER (Shown batting left, back says right)	.05	.02
❑	24	Eric Karros	.50	.23
❑	25	Steve Decker UER (Lewis-Clark State College, not Lewis and Clark)	.05	.02
❑	26	Kevin Belcher	.05	.02
❑	27	Jeff Conine	.25	.11
❑	28	Dave Stewart TC	.05	.02
❑	29	Carlton Fisk TC	.10	.05
❑	30	Rafael Palmeiro TC	.10	.05
❑	31	Chuck Finley TC	.05	.02
❑	32	Harold Reynolds TC	.05	.02
❑	33	Bret Saberhagen TC	.05	.02
❑	34	Gary Gaetti TC	.05	.02
❑	35	Scott Leius	.05	.02
❑	36	Neal Heaton	.05	.02
❑	37	Terry Lee	.05	.02
❑	38	Gary Redus	.05	.02
❑	39	Barry Jones	.05	.02
❑	40	Chuck Knoblauch	.25	.11
❑	41	Larry Andersen	.05	.02
❑	42	Darryl Hamilton	.05	.02
❑	43	Mike Greenwell TC	.05	.02
❑	44	Kelly Gruber TC	.05	.02
❑	45	Jack Morris TC	.05	.02
❑	46	Sandy Alomar Jr. TC	.05	.02
❑	47	Gregg Olson TC	.05	.02
❑	48	Dave Parker TC	.05	.02
❑	49	Roberto Kelly TC	.05	.02
❑	50	Top Prospect Checklist	.05	.02
❑	51	Kyle Abbott	.05	.02
❑	52	Jeff Juden	.05	.02
❑	53	Todd Van Poppel UER (Born Arlington and attended John Martin HS, should say Hinsdale and James Martin HS)	.05	.02
❑	54	Steve Karsay	.10	.05
❑	55	Chipper Jones	5.00	2.20
❑	56	Chris Johnson UER (Called Tim on back)	.05	.02
❑	57	John Ericks	.05	.02
❑	58	Gary Scott	.05	.02
❑	59	Kiki Jones	.05	.02
❑	60	Wil Cordero	.05	.02
❑	61	Royce Clayton	.15	.07
❑	62	Tim Costo	.05	.02
❑	63	Roger Salkeld	.05	.02
❑	64	Brook Fordyce	.05	.02
❑	65	Mike Mussina	1.25	.55
❑	66	Dave Staton	.05	.02
❑	67	Mike Lieberthal	.20	.09
❑	68	Kurt Miller	.05	.02
❑	69	Dan Peltier	.05	.02
❑	70	Greg Blosser	.05	.02
❑	71	Reggie Sanders	.25	.11
❑	72	Brent Mayne	.05	.02
❑	73	Rico Brogna	.15	.07
❑	74	Willie Banks	.05	.02
❑	75	Len Brutcher	.05	.02
❑	76	Pat Kelly	.05	.02
❑	77	Chris Sabo TC	.05	.02
❑	78	Ramon Martinez TC	.05	.02
❑	79	Matt Williams TC	.10	.05
❑	80	Roberto Alomar TC	.10	.05
❑	81	Glenn Davis TC	.05	.02
❑	82	Ron Gant TC	.05	.02
❑	83	Cecil Fielder FEAT	.05	.02
❑	84	Orlando Merced	.10	.05
❑	85	Domingo Ramos	.05	.02
❑	86	Tom Bolton	.05	.02
❑	87	Andres Santana	.05	.02
❑	88	John Dopson	.05	.02
❑	89	Kenny Williams	.05	.02
❑	90	Marty Barrett	.05	.02
❑	91	Tom Pagnozzi	.05	.02
❑	92	Carmelo Martinez	.05	.02
❑	93	Bobby Thigpen SAVE	.05	.02
❑	94	Barry Bonds TC	.20	.09
❑	95	Gregg Jefferies TC	.05	.02
❑	96	Tim Wallach TC	.05	.02
❑	97	Len Dykstra TC	.05	.02
❑	98	Pedro Guerrero TC	.05	.02
❑	99	Mark Grace TC	.10	.05
❑	100	Checklist 1-100	.05	.02
❑	101	Kevin Elster	.05	.02
❑	102	Tom Brookens	.05	.02
❑	103	Mackey Sasser	.05	.02
❑	104	Felix Fermin	.05	.02
❑	105	Kevin McReynolds	.05	.02
❑	106	Dave Stieb	.10	.05
❑	107	Jeffrey Leonard	.05	.02
❑	108	Dave Henderson	.05	.02
❑	109	Sid Bream	.05	.02
❑	110	Henry Cotto	.05	.02
❑	111	Shawon Dunston	.05	.02
❑	112	Mariano Duncan	.05	.02
❑	113	Joe Girardi	.10	.05
❑	114	Billy Hatcher	.05	.02
❑	115	Greg Maddux	.60	.25
❑	116	Jerry Browne	.05	.02
❑	117	Juan Samuel	.05	.02
❑	118	Steve Olin	.05	.02
❑	119	Alfredo Griffin	.05	.02
❑	120	Mitch Webster	.05	.02
❑	121	Joel Skinner	.05	.02
❑	122	Frank Viola	.05	.02
❑	123	Cory Snyder	.05	.02
❑	124	Howard Johnson	.05	.02
❑	125	Carlos Baerga	.10	.05
❑	126	Tony Fernandez	.05	.02
❑	127	Dave Stewart	.10	.05
❑	128	Jay Buhner	.20	.09
❑	129	Mike LaValliere	.05	.02
❑	130	Scott Bradley	.05	.02
❑	131	Tony Phillips	.05	.02
❑	132	Ryne Sandberg	.25	.11
❑	133	Paul O'Neill	.10	.05
❑	134	Mark Grace	.20	.09
❑	135	Chris Sabo	.05	.02
❑	136	Ramon Martinez	.10	.05
❑	137	Brook Jacoby	.05	.02
❑	138	Candy Maldonado	.05	.02
❑	139	Mike Scioscia	.05	.02
❑	140	Chris James	.05	.02
❑	141	Craig Worthington	.05	.02
❑	142	Manny Lee	.05	.02
❑	143	Tim Raines	.10	.05
❑	144	Sandy Alomar Jr.	.10	.05
❑	145	John Olerud	.10	.05
❑	146	Ozzie Canseco (With Jose)	.10	.05
❑	147	Pat Borders	.05	.02
❑	148	Harold Reynolds	.05	.02
❑	149	Tom Henke	.05	.02
❑	150	R.J. Reynolds	.05	.02
❑	151	Mike Gallego	.05	.02
❑	152	Bobby Bonilla	.10	.05
❑	153	Terry Steinbach	.10	.05
❑	154	Barry Bonds	.25	.11
❑	155	Jose Canseco	.20	.09
❑	156	Gregg Jefferies	.05	.02
❑	157	Matt Williams	.20	.09
❑	158	Craig Biggio	.20	.09
❑	159	Daryl Boston	.05	.02
❑	160	Ricky Jordan	.05	.02
❑	161	Stan Belinda	.05	.02
❑	162	Ozzie Smith	.25	.11
❑	163	Tom Brunansky	.05	.02
❑	164	Todd Zeile	.10	.05
❑	165	Mike Greenwell	.05	.02
❑	166	Kal Daniels	.05	.02
❑	167	Kent Hrbek	.10	.05
❑	168	Franklin Stubbs	.05	.02
❑	169	Dick Schofield	.05	.02
❑	170	Junior Ortiz	.05	.02
❑	171	Hector Villanueva	.05	.02
❑	172	Dennis Eckersley	.10	.05
❑	173	Mitch Williams	.05	.02
❑	174	Mark McGwire	1.00	.45
❑	175	Fernando Valenzuela 3X	.10	.05
❑	176	Gary Carter	.20	.09
❑	177	Dave Magadan	.05	.02
❑	178	Robby Thompson	.05	.02
❑	179	Bob Ojeda	.05	.02
❑	180	Ken Caminiti	.20	.09
❑	181	Don Slaught	.05	.02
❑	182	Luis Rivera	.05	.02
❑	183	Jay Bell	.10	.05
❑	184	Jody Reed	.05	.02
❑	185	Wally Backman	.05	.02
❑	186	Dave Martinez	.05	.02
❑	187	Luis Polonia	.05	.02
❑	188	Shane Mack	.05	.02
❑	189	Spike Owen	.05	.02
❑	190	Scott Bailes	.05	.02
❑	191	John Russell	.05	.02
❑	192	Walt Weiss	.05	.02
❑	193	Jose Oquendo	.05	.02
❑	194	Carney Lansford	.10	.05
❑	195	Jeff Huson	.05	.02
❑	196	Keith Miller	.05	.02
❑	197	Eric Yelding	.05	.02
❑	198	Ron Darling	.05	.02
❑	199	John Kruk	.10	.05
❑	200	Checklist 101-200	.05	.02
❑	201	John Shelby	.05	.02
❑	202	Bob Geren	.05	.02
❑	203	Lance McCullers	.05	.02
❑	204	Alvaro Espinoza	.05	.02
❑	205	Mark Salas	.05	.02
❑	206	Mike Pagliarulo	.05	.02
❑	207	Jose Uribe	.05	.02
❑	208	Jim Deshaies	.05	.02
❑	209	Ron Karkovice	.05	.02
❑	210	Rafael Ramirez	.05	.02
❑	211	Donnie Hill	.05	.02
❑	212	Brian Harper	.05	.02
❑	213	Jack Howell	.05	.02
❑	214	Wes Gardner	.05	.02
❑	215	Tim Burke	.05	.02
❑	216	Doug Jones	.05	.02

❑ 217 Hubie Brooks .05 .02
❑ 218 Tom Candiotti .05 .02
❑ 219 Gerald Perry .05 .02
❑ 220 Jose DeLeon .05 .02
❑ 221 Wally Whitehurst .05 .02
❑ 222 Alan Mills .05 .02
❑ 223 Alan Trammell .15 .07
❑ 224 Dwight Gooden .10 .05
❑ 225 Travis Fryman .20 .09
❑ 226 Joe Carter .10 .05
❑ 227 Julio Franco .05 .02
❑ 228 Craig Lefferts .05 .02
❑ 229 Gary Pettis .05 .02
❑ 230 Dennis Rasmussen .05 .02
❑ 231A Brian Downing ERR .05 .02
(No position on front)
❑ 231B Brian Downing COR .15 .07
(DH on front)
❑ 232 Carlos Quintana .05 .02
❑ 233 Gary Gaetti .10 .05
❑ 234 Mark Langston .05 .02
❑ 235 Tim Wallach .05 .02
❑ 236 Greg Swindell .05 .02
❑ 237 Eddie Murray .20 .09
❑ 238 Jeff Manto .05 .02
❑ 239 Lenny Harris .05 .02
❑ 240 Jesse Orosco .05 .02
❑ 241 Scott Lusader .05 .02
❑ 242 Sid Fernandez .05 .02
❑ 243 Jim Leyritz .10 .05
❑ 244 Cecil Fielder .10 .05
❑ 245 Darryl Strawberry .10 .05
❑ 246 Frank Thomas UER 1.00 .45
(Comiskey Park
misspelled Comisky)
❑ 247 Kevin Mitchell .05 .02
❑ 248 Lance Johnson .05 .02
❑ 249 Rick Reuschel .05 .02
❑ 250 Mark Portugal .05 .02
❑ 251 Derek Lilliquist .05 .02
❑ 252 Brian Holman .05 .02
❑ 253 Rafael Valdez UER .05 .02
(Born 4/17/68,
should be 12/17/67)
❑ 254 B.J. Surhoff .10 .05
❑ 255 Tony Gwynn .50 .23
❑ 256 Andy Van Slyke .10 .05
❑ 257 Todd Stottlemyre .10 .05
❑ 258 Jose Lind .05 .02
❑ 259 Greg Myers .05 .02
❑ 260 Jeff Ballard .05 .02
❑ 261 Bobby Thigpen .05 .02
❑ 262 Jimmy Kremers .05 .02
❑ 263 Robin Ventura .20 .09
❑ 264 John Smoltz .20 .09
❑ 265 Sammy Sosa 1.00 .45
❑ 266 Gary Sheffield .20 .09
❑ 267 Len Dykstra .10 .05
❑ 268 Bill Spiers .05 .02
❑ 269 Charlie Hayes .05 .02
❑ 270 Brett Butler .10 .05
❑ 271 Bip Roberts .05 .02
❑ 272 Rob Deer .05 .02
❑ 273 Fred Lynn .05 .02
❑ 274 Dave Parker .10 .05
❑ 275 Andy Benes .10 .05
❑ 276 Glenallen Hill .05 .02
❑ 277 Steve Howard .05 .02
❑ 278 Doug Drabek .05 .02
❑ 279 Joe Oliver .05 .02
❑ 280 Todd Benzinger .05 .02
❑ 281 Eric King .05 .02
❑ 282 Jim Presley .05 .02
❑ 283 Ken Patterson .05 .02
❑ 284 Jack Daugherty .05 .02
❑ 285 Ivan Calderon .05 .02
❑ 286 Edgar Diaz .05 .02
❑ 287 Kevin Bass .05 .02
❑ 288 Don Carman .05 .02
❑ 289 Greg Brock .05 .02
❑ 290 John Franco .10 .05
❑ 291 Joey Cora .10 .05
❑ 292 Bill Wegman .05 .02
❑ 293 Eric Show .05 .02
❑ 294 Scott Bankhead .05 .02
❑ 295 Garry Templeton .05 .02
❑ 296 Mickey Tettleton .10 .05
❑ 297 Luis Sojo .05 .02
❑ 298 Jose Rijo .05 .02
❑ 299 Dave Johnson .05 .02
❑ 300 Checklist 201-300 .05 .02
❑ 301 Mark Grant .05 .02
❑ 302 Pete Harnisch .05 .02
❑ 303 Greg Olson .05 .02
❑ 304 Anthony Telford .05 .02
❑ 305 Lonnie Smith .05 .02
❑ 306 Chris Hoiles .05 .02
❑ 307 Bryn Smith .05 .02
❑ 308 Mike Devereaux .05 .02
❑ 309A Milt Thompson ERR .20 .09
(Under yr information
has print dot)
❑ 309B Milt Thompson COR .05 .02
(Under yr information
says 86)
❑ 310 Bob Melvin .05 .02
❑ 311 Luis Salazar .05 .02
❑ 312 Ed Whitson .05 .02
❑ 313 Charlie Hough .10 .05
❑ 314 Dave Clark .05 .02
❑ 315 Eric Gunderson .05 .02
❑ 316 Dan Petry .05 .02
❑ 317 Dante Bichette UER .20 .09
(Assists misspelled
as assissts)
❑ 318 Mike Heath .05 .02
❑ 319 Damon Berryhill .05 .02
❑ 320 Walt Terrell .05 .02
❑ 321 Scott Fletcher .05 .02
❑ 322 Dan Plesac .05 .02
❑ 323 Jack McDowell .05 .02
❑ 324 Paul Molitor .20 .09
❑ 325 Ozzie Guillen .05 .02
❑ 326 Gregg Olson .05 .02
❑ 327 Pedro Guerrero .05 .02
❑ 328 Bob Milacki .05 .02
❑ 329 John Tudor UER .05 .02
('90 Cardinals,
should be '90 Dodgers)
❑ 330 Steve Finley UER .20 .09
(Born 3/12/65,
should be 5/12)
❑ 331 Jack Clark .10 .05
❑ 332 Jerome Walton .05 .02
❑ 333 Andy Hawkins .05 .02
❑ 334 Derrick May .05 .02
❑ 335 Roberto Alomar .20 .09
❑ 336 Jack Morris .10 .05
❑ 337 Dave Winfield .20 .09
❑ 338 Steve Searcy .05 .02
❑ 339 Chili Davis .10 .05
❑ 340 Larry Sheets .05 .02
❑ 341 Ted Higuera .05 .02
❑ 342 David Segui .10 .05
❑ 343 Greg Cadaret .05 .02
❑ 344 Robin Yount .20 .09
❑ 345 Nolan Ryan .75 .35
❑ 346 Ray Lankford .20 .09
❑ 347 Cal Ripken .75 .35
❑ 348 Lee Smith .10 .05
❑ 349 Brady Anderson .20 .09
❑ 350 Frank DiPino .05 .02
❑ 351 Hal Morris .05 .02
❑ 352 Deion Sanders .10 .05
❑ 353 Barry Larkin .20 .09
❑ 354 Don Mattingly .30 .14
❑ 355 Eric Davis .10 .05
❑ 356 Jose Offerman .05 .02
❑ 357 Mel Rojas .10 .05
❑ 358 Rudy Seanez .05 .02
❑ 359 Oil Can Boyd .05 .02
❑ 360 Nelson Liriano .05 .02
❑ 361 Ron Gant .10 .05
❑ 362 Howard Farmer .05 .02
❑ 363 David Justice .25 .11
❑ 364 Delino DeShields .10 .05
❑ 365 Steve Avery .05 .02
❑ 366 David Cone .10 .05
❑ 367 Lou Whitaker .10 .05
❑ 368 Von Hayes .05 .02
❑ 369 Frank Tanana .05 .02
❑ 370 Tim Teufel .05 .02
❑ 371 Randy Myers .10 .05
❑ 372 Roberto Kelly .05 .02
❑ 373 Jack Armstrong .05 .02
❑ 374 Kelly Gruber .05 .02
❑ 375 Kevin Maas .05 .02
❑ 376 Randy Johnson .25 .11
❑ 377 David West .05 .02
❑ 378 Brent Knackert .05 .02
❑ 379 Rick Honeycutt .05 .02
❑ 380 Kevin Gross .05 .02
❑ 381 Tom Foley .05 .02
❑ 382 Jeff Blauser .05 .02
❑ 383 Scott Ruskin .05 .02
❑ 384 Andres Thomas .05 .02
❑ 385 Dennis Martinez .10 .05
❑ 386 Mike Henneman .05 .02
❑ 387 Felix Jose .05 .02
❑ 388 Alejandro Pena .05 .02
❑ 389 Chet Lemon .05 .02
❑ 390 Craig Wilson .05 .02
❑ 391 Chuck Crim .05 .02
❑ 392 Mel Hall .05 .02
❑ 393 Mark Knudson .05 .02
❑ 394 Norm Charlton .05 .02
❑ 395 Mike Felder .05 .02
❑ 396 Tim Layana .05 .02
❑ 397 Steve Frey .05 .02
❑ 398 Bill Doran .05 .02
❑ 399 Dion James .05 .02
❑ 400 Checklist 301-400 .05 .02
❑ 401 Ron Hassey .05 .02
❑ 402 Don Robinson .05 .02
❑ 403 Gene Nelson .05 .02
❑ 404 Terry Kennedy .05 .02
❑ 405 Todd Burns .05 .02
❑ 406 Roger McDowell .05 .02
❑ 407 Bob Kipper .05 .02
❑ 408 Darren Daulton .10 .05
❑ 409 Chuck Cary .05 .02
❑ 410 Bruce Ruffin .05 .02
❑ 411 Juan Berenguer .05 .02
❑ 412 Gary Ward .05 .02
❑ 413 Al Newman .05 .02
❑ 414 Danny Jackson .05 .02
❑ 415 Greg Gagne .05 .02
❑ 416 Tom Herr .05 .02
❑ 417 Jeff Parrett .05 .02
❑ 418 Jeff Reardon .10 .05
❑ 419 Mark Lemke .05 .02
❑ 420 Charlie O'Brien .05 .02
❑ 421 Willie Randolph .10 .05
❑ 422 Steve Bedrosian .05 .02
❑ 423 Mike Moore .05 .02
❑ 424 Jeff Brantley .05 .02
❑ 425 Bob Welch .05 .02
❑ 426 Terry Mulholland .05 .02
❑ 427 Willie Blair .05 .02
❑ 428 Darrin Fletcher .05 .02
❑ 429 Mike Witt .05 .02
❑ 430 Joe Boever .05 .02
❑ 431 Tom Gordon .10 .05
❑ 432 Pedro Munoz .05 .02
❑ 433 Kevin Seitzer .05 .02
❑ 434 Kevin Tapani .05 .02
❑ 435 Bret Saberhagen .10 .05
❑ 436 Ellis Burks .10 .05
❑ 437 Chuck Finley .10 .05
❑ 438 Mike Boddicker .05 .02
❑ 439 Francisco Cabrera .05 .02
❑ 440 Todd Hundley .20 .09
❑ 441 Kelly Downs .05 .02
❑ 442 Dann Howitt .05 .02
❑ 443 Scott Garrelts .05 .02
❑ 444 Rickey Henderson 3X .20 .09
❑ 445 Will Clark .20 .09
❑ 446 Ben McDonald .05 .02
❑ 447 Dale Murphy .20 .09
❑ 448 Dave Righetti .05 .02
❑ 449 Dickie Thon .05 .02
❑ 450 Ted Power .05 .02
❑ 451 Scott Coolbaugh .05 .02
❑ 452 Dwight Smith .05 .02
❑ 453 Pete Incaviglia .05 .02

❑ 454	Andre Dawson	.20	.09
❑ 455	Ruben Sierra	.05	.02
❑ 456	Andres Galarraga	.20	.09
❑ 457	Alvin Davis	.05	.02
❑ 458	Tony Castillo	.05	.02
❑ 459	Pete O'Brien	.05	.02
❑ 460	Charlie Leibrandt	.05	.02
❑ 461	Vince Coleman	.05	.02
❑ 462	Steve Sax	.05	.02
❑ 463	Omar Olivares	.05	.02
❑ 464	Oscar Azocar	.05	.02
❑ 465	Joe Magrane	.05	.02
❑ 466	Karl Rhodes	.05	.02
❑ 467	Benito Santiago	.05	.02
❑ 468	Joe Klink	.05	.02
❑ 469	Sil Campusano	.05	.02
❑ 470	Mark Parent	.05	.02
❑ 471	Shawn Boskie UER	.05	.02
	(Depleted misspelled as depleated)		
❑ 472	Kevin Brown	.15	.07
❑ 473	Rick Sutcliffe	.05	.02
❑ 474	Rafael Palmeiro	.20	.09
❑ 475	Mike Harkey	.05	.02
❑ 476	Jaime Navarro	.05	.02
❑ 477	Marquis Grissom UER	.20	.09
	(DeShields misspelled as DeSheilds)		
❑ 478	Marty Clary	.05	.02
❑ 479	Greg Briley	.05	.02
❑ 480	Tom Glavine	.20	.09
❑ 481	Lee Guetterman	.05	.02
❑ 482	Rex Hudler	.05	.02
❑ 483	Dave LaPoint	.05	.02
❑ 484	Terry Pendleton	.10	.05
❑ 485	Jesse Barfield	.05	.02
❑ 486	Jose DeJesus	.05	.02
❑ 487	Paul Abbott	.05	.02
❑ 488	Ken Howell	.05	.02
❑ 489	Greg W. Harris	.05	.02
❑ 490	Roy Smith	.05	.02
❑ 491	Paul Assenmacher	.05	.02
❑ 492	Geno Petralli	.05	.02
❑ 493	Steve Wilson	.05	.02
❑ 494	Kevin Reimer	.05	.02
❑ 495	Bill Long	.05	.02
❑ 496	Mike Jackson	.10	.05
❑ 497	Oddibe McDowell	.05	.02
❑ 498	Bill Swift	.05	.02
❑ 499	Jeff Treadway	.05	.02
❑ 500	Checklist 401-500	.05	.02
❑ 501	Gene Larkin	.05	.02
❑ 502	Bob Boone	.10	.05
❑ 503	Allan Anderson	.05	.02
❑ 504	Luis Aquino	.05	.02
❑ 505	Mark Guthrie	.05	.02
❑ 506	Joe Orsulak	.05	.02
❑ 507	Dana Kiecker	.05	.02
❑ 508	Dave Gallagher	.05	.02
❑ 509	Greg A. Harris	.05	.02
❑ 510	Mark Williamson	.05	.02
❑ 511	Casey Candaele	.05	.02
❑ 512	Mookie Wilson	.10	.05
❑ 513	Dave Smith	.05	.02
❑ 514	Chuck Carr	.05	.02
❑ 515	Glenn Wilson	.05	.02
❑ 516	Mike Fitzgerald	.05	.02
❑ 517	Devon White	.05	.02
❑ 518	Dave Hollins	.05	.02
❑ 519	Mark Eichhorn	.05	.02
❑ 520	Otis Nixon	.10	.05
❑ 521	Terry Shumpert	.05	.02
❑ 522	Scott Erickson	.10	.05
❑ 523	Danny Tartabull	.05	.02
❑ 524	Orel Hershiser	.10	.05
❑ 525	George Brett	.40	.18
❑ 526	Greg Vaughn	.20	.09
❑ 527	Tim Naehring	.10	.05
❑ 528	Curt Schilling	.20	.09
❑ 529	Chris Bosio	.05	.02
❑ 530	Sam Horn	.05	.02
❑ 531	Mike Scott	.05	.02
❑ 532	George Bell	.05	.02
❑ 533	Eric Anthony	.05	.02
❑ 534	Julio Valera	.05	.02
❑ 535	Glenn Davis	.05	.02
❑ 536	Larry Walker UER	.30	.14
	(Should have comma after Expos in text)		
❑ 537	Pat Combs	.05	.02
❑ 538	Chris Nabholz	.05	.02
❑ 539	Kirk McCaskill	.05	.02
❑ 540	Randy Ready	.05	.02
❑ 541	Mark Gubicza	.05	.02
❑ 542	Rick Aguilera	.10	.05
❑ 543	Brian McRae	.20	.09
❑ 544	Kirby Puckett	.30	.14
❑ 545	Bo Jackson	.10	.05
❑ 546	Wade Boggs	.20	.09
❑ 547	Tim McIntosh	.05	.02
❑ 548	Randy Milligan	.05	.02
❑ 549	Dwight Evans	.10	.05
❑ 550	Billy Ripken	.05	.02
❑ 551	Erik Hanson	.05	.02
❑ 552	Lance Parrish	.05	.02
❑ 553	Tino Martinez	.20	.09
❑ 554	Jim Abbott	.10	.05
❑ 555	Ken Griffey Jr. UER	1.50	.70
	(Second most votes for 1991 All-Star Game)		
❑ 556	Milt Cuyler	.05	.02
❑ 557	Mark Leonard	.05	.02
❑ 558	Jay Howell	.05	.02
❑ 559	Lloyd Moseby	.05	.02
❑ 560	Chris Gwynn	.05	.02
❑ 561	Mark Whiten	.05	.02
❑ 562	Harold Baines	.10	.05
❑ 563	Junior Felix	.05	.02
❑ 564	Darren Lewis	.10	.05
❑ 565	Fred McGriff	.20	.09
❑ 566	Kevin Appier	.10	.05
❑ 567	Luis Gonzalez	.20	.09
❑ 568	Frank White	.10	.05
❑ 569	Juan Agosto	.05	.02
❑ 570	Mike Macfarlane	.05	.02
❑ 571	Bert Blyleven	.10	.05
❑ 572	Ken Griffey Sr.	.50	.23
	Ken Griffey Jr.		
❑ 573	Lee Stevens	.05	.02
❑ 574	Edgar Martinez	.20	.09
❑ 575	Wally Joyner	.10	.05
❑ 576	Tim Belcher	.05	.02
❑ 577	John Burkett	.05	.02
❑ 578	Mike Morgan	.05	.02
❑ 579	Paul Gibson	.05	.02
❑ 580	Jose Vizcaino	.05	.02
❑ 581	Duane Ward	.05	.02
❑ 582	Scott Sanderson	.05	.02
❑ 583	David Wells	.10	.05
❑ 584	Willie McGee	.10	.05
❑ 585	John Cerutti	.05	.02
❑ 586	Danny Darwin	.05	.02
❑ 587	Kurt Stillwell	.05	.02
❑ 588	Rich Gedman	.05	.02
❑ 589	Mark Davis	.05	.02
❑ 590	Bill Gullickson	.05	.02
❑ 591	Matt Young	.05	.02
❑ 592	Bryan Harvey	.05	.02
❑ 593	Omar Vizquel	.20	.09
❑ 594	Scott Lewis	.05	.02
❑ 595	Dave Valle	.05	.02
❑ 596	Tim Crews	.05	.02
❑ 597	Mike Bielecki	.05	.02
❑ 598	Mike Sharperson	.05	.02
❑ 599	Dave Bergman	.05	.02
❑ 600	Checklist 501-600	.05	.02
❑ 601	Steve Lyons	.05	.02
❑ 602	Bruce Hurst	.05	.02
❑ 603	Donn Pall	.05	.02
❑ 604	Jim Vatcher	.05	.02
❑ 605	Dan Pasqua	.05	.02
❑ 606	Kenny Rogers	.05	.02
❑ 607	Jeff Schulz	.05	.02
❑ 608	Brad Arnsberg	.05	.02
❑ 609	Willie Wilson	.05	.02
❑ 610	Jamie Moyer	.05	.02
❑ 611	Ron Oester	.05	.02
❑ 612	Dennis Cook	.05	.02
❑ 613	Rick Mahler	.05	.02
❑ 614	Bill Landrum	.05	.02
❑ 615	Scott Scudder	.05	.02
❑ 616	Tom Edens	.05	.02
❑ 617	1917 Revisited	.10	.05
	(White Sox in vintage uniforms)		
❑ 618	Jim Gantner	.05	.02
❑ 619	Darrel Akerfelds	.05	.02
❑ 620	Ron Robinson	.05	.02
❑ 621	Scott Radinsky	.05	.02
❑ 622	Pete Smith	.05	.02
❑ 623	Melido Perez	.05	.02
❑ 624	Jerald Clark	.05	.02
❑ 625	Carlos Martinez	.05	.02
❑ 626	Wes Chamberlain	.05	.02
❑ 627	Bobby Witt	.05	.02
❑ 628	Ken Dayley	.05	.02
❑ 629	John Barfield	.05	.02
❑ 630	Bob Tewksbury	.05	.02
❑ 631	Glenn Braggs	.05	.02
❑ 632	Jim Neidlinger	.05	.02
❑ 633	Tom Browning	.05	.02
❑ 634	Kirk Gibson	.10	.05
❑ 635	Rob Dibble	.05	.02
❑ 636	Rickey Henderson SB	.30	.14
	Lou Brock		
	May 1, 1991 on front		
❑ 636A	Rickey Henderson SB	.20	.09
	Lou Brock		
	no date on card		
❑ 637	Jeff Montgomery	.10	.05
❑ 638	Mike Schooler	.05	.02
❑ 639	Storm Davis	.05	.02
❑ 640	Rich Rodriguez	.05	.02
❑ 641	Phil Bradley	.05	.02
❑ 642	Kent Mercker	.05	.02
❑ 643	Carlton Fisk	.20	.09
❑ 644	Mike Bell	.05	.02
❑ 645	Alex Fernandez	.10	.05
❑ 646	Juan Gonzalez	.75	.35
❑ 647	Ken Hill	.10	.05
❑ 648	Jeff Russell	.05	.02
❑ 649	Chuck Malone	.05	.02
❑ 650	Steve Buechele	.05	.02
❑ 651	Mike Benjamin	.05	.02
❑ 652	Tony Pena	.05	.02
❑ 653	Trevor Wilson	.05	.02
❑ 654	Alex Cole	.05	.02
❑ 655	Roger Clemens	.40	.18
❑ 656	Mark McGwire BASH	.50	.23
❑ 657	Joe Grahe	.05	.02
❑ 658	Jim Eisenreich	.05	.02
❑ 659	Dan Gladden	.05	.02
❑ 660	Steve Farr	.05	.02
❑ 661	Bill Sampen	.05	.02
❑ 662	Dave Rohde	.05	.02
❑ 663	Mark Gardner	.05	.02
❑ 664	Mike Simms	.05	.02
❑ 665	Moises Alou	.20	.09
❑ 666	Mickey Hatcher	.05	.02
❑ 667	Jimmy Key	.10	.05
❑ 668	John Wetteland	.20	.09
❑ 669	John Smiley	.05	.02
❑ 670	Jim Acker	.05	.02
❑ 671	Pascual Perez	.05	.02
❑ 672	Reggie Harris UER	.05	.02
	(Opportunity misspelled as oppurtinity)		
❑ 673	Matt Nokes	.05	.02
❑ 674	Rafael Novoa	.05	.02
❑ 675	Hensley Meulens	.05	.02
❑ 676	Jeff M. Robinson	.05	.02
❑ 677	Ground Breaking	.10	.05
	(New Comiskey Park; Carlton Fisk and Robin Ventura)		
❑ 678	Johnny Ray	.05	.02
❑ 679	Greg Hibbard	.05	.02
❑ 680	Paul Sorrento	.10	.05
❑ 681	Mike Marshall	.05	.02
❑ 682	Jim Clancy	.05	.02
❑ 683	Rob Murphy	.05	.02
❑ 684	Dave Schmidt	.05	.02
❑ 685	Jeff Gray	.05	.02
❑ 686	Mike Hartley	.05	.02
❑ 687	Jeff King	.10	.05

❑ 688 Stan Javier	.05	.02
❑ 689 Bob Walk	.05	.02
❑ 690 Jim Gott	.05	.02
❑ 691 Mike LaCoss	.05	.02
❑ 692 John Farrell	.05	.02
❑ 693 Tim Leary	.05	.02
❑ 694 Mike Walker	.05	.02
❑ 695 Eric Plunk	.05	.02
❑ 696 Mike Fetters	.05	.02
❑ 697 Wayne Edwards	.05	.02
❑ 698 Tim Drummond	.05	.02
❑ 699 Willie Fraser	.05	.02
❑ 700 Checklist 601-700	.05	.02
❑ 701 Mike Heath	.05	.02
❑ 702 Rookie Threats	.75	.35
Luis Gonzalez		
Karl Rhodes		
Jeff Bagwell		
❑ 703 Jose Mesa	.05	.02
❑ 704 Dave Smith	.05	.02
❑ 705 Danny Darwin	.05	.02
❑ 706 Rafael Belliard	.05	.02
❑ 707 Rob Murphy	.05	.02
❑ 708 Terry Pendleton	.10	.05
❑ 709 Mike Pagliarulo	.05	.02
❑ 710 Sid Bream	.05	.02
❑ 711 Junior Felix	.05	.02
❑ 712 Dante Bichette	.20	.09
❑ 713 Kevin Gross	.05	.02
❑ 714 Luis Sojo	.05	.02
❑ 715 Bob Ojeda	.05	.02
❑ 716 Julio Machado	.05	.02
❑ 717 Steve Farr	.05	.02
❑ 718 Franklin Stubbs	.05	.02
❑ 719 Mike Boddicker	.05	.02
❑ 720 Willie Randolph	.10	.05
❑ 721 Willie McGee	.10	.05
❑ 722 Chili Davis	.10	.05
❑ 723 Danny Jackson	.05	.02
❑ 724 Cory Snyder	.05	.02
❑ 725 MVP Lineup	.20	.09
Andre Dawson		
George Bell		
Ryne Sandberg		
❑ 726 Rob Deer	.05	.02
❑ 727 Rich DeLucia	.05	.02
❑ 728 Mike Perez	.05	.02
❑ 729 Mickey Tettleton	.10	.05
❑ 730 Mike Blowers	.05	.02
❑ 731 Gary Gaetti	.10	.05
❑ 732 Brett Butler	.10	.05
❑ 733 Dave Parker	.10	.05
❑ 734 Eddie Zosky	.05	.02
❑ 735 Jack Clark	.10	.05
❑ 736 Jack Morris	.10	.05
❑ 737 Kirk Gibson	.10	.05
❑ 738 Steve Bedrosian	.05	.02
❑ 739 Candy Maldonado	.05	.02
❑ 740 Matt Young	.05	.02
❑ 741 Rich Garces	.05	.02
❑ 742 George Bell	.05	.02
❑ 743 Deion Sanders	.10	.05
❑ 744 Bo Jackson	.10	.05
❑ 745 Luis Mercedes	.05	.02
❑ 746 Reggie Jefferson UER	.15	.07
(Throwing left on card;		
back has throws right)		
❑ 747 Pete Incaviglia	.05	.02
❑ 748 Chris Hammond	.05	.02
❑ 749 Mike Stanton	.05	.02
❑ 750 Scott Sanderson	.05	.02
❑ 751 Paul Faries	.05	.02
❑ 752 Al Osuna	.05	.02
❑ 753 Steve Chitren	.05	.02
❑ 754 Tony Fernandez	.05	.02
❑ 755 Jeff Bagwell UER	2.50	1.10
(Strikeout and walk		
totals reversed)		
❑ 756 Kirk Dressendorfer	.05	.02
❑ 757 Glenn Davis	.05	.02
❑ 758 Gary Carter	.20	.09
❑ 759 Zane Smith	.05	.02
❑ 760 Vance Law	.05	.02
❑ 761 Denis Boucher	.05	.02
❑ 762 Turner Ward	.05	.02
❑ 763 Roberto Alomar	.20	.09
❑ 764 Albert Belle	.25	.11
❑ 765 Joe Carter	.10	.05
❑ 766 Pete Schourek	.10	.05
❑ 767 Heathcliff Slocumb	.20	.09
❑ 768 Vince Coleman	.05	.02
❑ 769 Mitch Williams	.05	.02
❑ 770 Brian Downing	.05	.02
❑ 771 Dana Allison	.05	.02
❑ 772 Pete Harnisch	.05	.02
❑ 773 Tim Raines	.10	.05
❑ 774 Darryl Kile	.20	.09
❑ 775 Fred McGriff	.20	.09
❑ 776 Dwight Evans	.10	.05
❑ 777 Joe Slusarski	.05	.02
❑ 778 Dave Righetti	.05	.02
❑ 779 Jeff Hamilton	.05	.02
❑ 780 Ernest Riles	.05	.02
❑ 781 Ken Dayley	.05	.02
❑ 782 Eric King	.05	.02
❑ 783 Devon White	.05	.02
❑ 784 Beau Allred	.05	.02
❑ 785 Mike Timlin	.05	.02
❑ 786 Ivan Calderon	.05	.02
❑ 787 Hubie Brooks	.05	.02
❑ 788 Juan Agosto	.05	.02
❑ 789 Barry Jones	.05	.02
❑ 790 Wally Backman	.05	.02
❑ 791 Jim Presley	.05	.02
❑ 792 Charlie Hough	.10	.05
❑ 793 Larry Andersen	.05	.02
❑ 794 Steve Finley	.20	.09
❑ 795 Shawn Abner	.05	.02
❑ 796 Jeff M. Robinson	.05	.02
❑ 797 Joe Bitker	.05	.02
❑ 798 Eric Show	.05	.02
❑ 799 Bud Black	.05	.02
❑ 800 Checklist 701-800	.05	.02
❑ HH1 Hank Aaron Hologram	1.50	.70
❑ SP1 Michael Jordan SP	15.00	6.75
(Shown batting in		
White Sox uniform)		
❑ SP2 Rickey Henderson	1.50	.70
Nolan Ryan		
May 1, 1991 Records		

1991 Upper Deck Aaron Heroes

	MINT	NRMT
COMPLETE SET (10)	5.00	2.20
COMMON AARON (19-27)	.50	.23
❑ 19 Hank Aaron	.50	.23
1954 Rookie Year		
❑ 20 Hank Aaron	.50	.23
1957 MVP		
❑ 21 Hank Aaron	.50	.23
1966 Move to Atlanta		
❑ 22 Hank Aaron	.50	.23
1970 3,000 Hits		
❑ 23 Hank Aaron	.50	.23
1974 715 Homers		
❑ 24 Hank Aaron	.50	.23
1975 Return to Milwaukee		
❑ 25 Hank Aaron	.50	.23
1976 755 Homers		
❑ 26 Hank Aaron	.50	.23
1982 Hall of Fame		
❑ 27 Checklist 19-27	.50	.23
❑ AU3 Hank Aaron AU	250.00	110.00
(Signed and Numbered		
out of 2500)		
❑ NNO0 Title/Header card SP	1.00	.45

1991 Upper Deck Heroes of Baseball

	MINT	NRMT
COMPLETE SET (4)	20.00	9.00
COMMON CARD (H1-H4)	5.00	2.20
❑ H1 Harmon Killebrew	5.00	2.20
❑ H2 Gaylord Perry	5.00	2.20
❑ H3 Ferguson Jenkins	5.00	2.20
❑ H4 Harmon Killebrew ART	5.00	2.20
Ferguson Jenkins		
Gaylord Perry		
❑ AU1 H. Killebrew AU/3000	50.00	22.00
❑ AU2 G. Perry AU/3000	50.00	22.00
❑ AU3 F. Jenkins AU/3000	50.00	22.00

1991 Upper Deck Ryan Heroes

	MINT	NRMT
COMPLETE SET (10)	5.00	2.20
COMMON RYAN (10-18)	.50	.23
❑ 10 Nolan Ryan	.50	.23
Tom Seaver		
Jerry Koosman		
1968 Victory 1		
❑ 11 Nolan Ryan	.50	.23
1973 A Career Year		
❑ 12 Nolan Ryan	.50	.23
1975 Double Milestone		
❑ 13 Nolan Ryan	.50	.23
1979 Back Home		
❑ 14 Nolan Ryan	.50	.23
1981 All Time Leader		
❑ 15 Nolan Ryan	.50	.23
1989 5,000 K's		
❑ 16 Nolan Ryan	.50	.23
1990 6th No-Hitter		
❑ 17 Nolan Ryan	.50	.23
1990 And Still Counting		

❑ 18	NBlan Ryan	.50	.23
	Checklist Card Vernon Wells drawing with 5 poses of Ryan including each team he played for		
❑ AU2	Nolan Ryan AU	500.00	220.00
	(Signed and Numbered out of 2500)		
❑ NNO0	Baseball Heroes SP	1.00	.45
	(Header card)		

1991 Upper Deck Silver Sluggers

	MINT	NRMT
COMPLETE SET (18)	15.00	6.75
COMMON CARD (SS1-SS18)	.50	.23

		MINT	NRMT
❑ SS1	Julio Franco	.50	.23
❑ SS2	Alan Trammell	1.00	.45
❑ SS3	Rickey Henderson	1.25	.55
❑ SS4	Jose Canseco	1.25	.55
❑ SS5	Barry Bonds	2.00	.90
❑ SS6	Eddie Murray	1.25	.55
❑ SS7	Kelly Gruber	.50	.23
❑ SS8	Ryne Sandberg	2.00	.90
❑ SS9	Darryl Strawberry	.75	.35
❑ SS10	Ellis Burks	.75	.35
❑ SS11	Lance Parrish	.50	.23
❑ SS12	Cecil Fielder	.75	.35
❑ SS13	Matt Williams	1.25	.55
❑ SS14	Dave Parker	.75	.35
❑ SS15	Bobby Bonilla	.75	.35
❑ SS16	Don Robinson	.50	.23
❑ SS17	Benito Santiago	.50	.23
❑ SS18	Barry Larkin	1.25	.55

1991 Upper Deck Final Edition

	MINT	NRMT
COMP.FACT.SET (100)	5.00	2.20
COMMON CARD (1F-100F)	.05	.02

		MINT	NRMT
❑ 1F	Ryan Klesko CL	.20	.09
	Reggie Sanders		
❑ 2F	Pedro Martinez	1.25	.55
❑ 3F	Lance Dickson	.05	.02
❑ 4F	Royce Clayton	.15	.07
❑ 5F	Scott Bryant	.05	.02
❑ 6F	Dan Wilson	.25	.11
❑ 7F	Dmitri Young	.30	.14
❑ 8F	Ryan Klesko	.40	.18
❑ 9F	Tom Goodwin	.10	.05
❑ 10F	Rondell White	.40	.18
❑ 11F	Reggie Sanders	.15	.07
❑ 12F	Todd Van Poppel	.05	.02
❑ 13F	Arthur Rhodes	.10	.05
❑ 14F	Eddie Zosky	.05	.02
❑ 15F	Gerald Williams	.05	.02
❑ 16F	Robert Eenhoorn	.05	.02
❑ 17F	Jim Thome	1.00	.45
❑ 18F	Marc Newfield	.10	.05
❑ 19F	Kerwin Moore	.05	.02
❑ 20F	Jeff McNeely	.05	.02
❑ 21F	Frankie Rodriguez	.10	.05
❑ 22F	Andy Mota	.05	.02
❑ 23F	Chris Haney	.05	.02
❑ 24F	Kenny Lofton	.75	.35
❑ 25F	Dave Nilsson	.20	.09
❑ 26F	Derek Bell	.20	.09
❑ 27F	Frank Castillo	.05	.02
❑ 28F	Candy Maldonado	.05	.02
❑ 29F	Chuck McElroy	.05	.02
❑ 30F	Chito Martinez	.05	.02
❑ 31F	Steve Howe	.05	.02
❑ 32F	Freddie Benavides	.05	.02
❑ 33F	Scott Kamieniecki	.05	.02
❑ 34F	Denny Neagle	.40	.18
❑ 35F	Mike Humphreys	.05	.02
❑ 36F	Mike Remlinger	.05	.02
❑ 37F	Scott Coolbaugh	.05	.02
❑ 38F	Darren Lewis	.10	.05
❑ 39F	Thomas Howard	.05	.02
❑ 40F	John Candelaria	.05	.02
❑ 41F	Todd Benzinger	.05	.02
❑ 42F	Wilson Alvarez	.20	.09
❑ 43F	Patrick Lennon	.05	.02
❑ 44F	Rusty Meacham	.05	.02
❑ 45F	Ryan Bowen	.05	.02
❑ 46F	Rick Wilkins	.05	.02
❑ 47F	Ed Sprague	.05	.02
❑ 48F	Bob Scanlan	.05	.02
❑ 49F	Tom Candiotti	.05	.02
❑ 50F	Dennis Martinez	.05	.02
	(Perfecto)		
❑ 51F	Oil Can Boyd	.05	.02
❑ 52F	Glenallen Hill	.05	.02
❑ 53F	Scott Livingstone	.05	.02
❑ 54F	Brian R. Hunter	.05	.02
❑ 55F	Ivan Rodriguez	1.25	.55
❑ 56F	Keith Mitchell	.05	.02
❑ 57F	Roger McDowell	.05	.02
❑ 58F	Otis Nixon	.10	.05
❑ 59F	Juan Bell	.05	.02
❑ 60F	Bill Krueger	.05	.02
❑ 61F	Chris Donnels	.05	.02
❑ 62F	Tommy Greene	.05	.02
❑ 63F	Doug Simons	.05	.02
❑ 64F	Andy Ashby	.25	.11
❑ 65F	Anthony Young	.05	.02
❑ 66F	Kevin Morton	.05	.02
❑ 67F	Bret Barberie	.05	.02
❑ 68F	Scott Servais	.05	.02
❑ 69F	Ron Darling	.05	.02
❑ 70F	Tim Burke	.05	.02
❑ 71F	Vicente Palacios	.05	.02
❑ 72F	Gerald Alexander	.05	.02
❑ 73F	Reggie Jefferson	.15	.07
❑ 74F	Dean Palmer	.10	.05
❑ 75F	Mark Whiten	.05	.02
❑ 76F	Randy Tomlin	.05	.02
❑ 77F	Mark Wohlers	.10	.05
❑ 78F	Brook Jacoby	.05	.02
❑ 79F	Ken Griffey Jr. CL	.40	.18
	Ryne Sandberg		
❑ 80F	Jack Morris AS	.05	.02
❑ 81F	Sandy Alomar Jr. AS	.10	.05
❑ 82F	Cecil Fielder AS	.05	.02
❑ 83F	Roberto Alomar AS	.10	.05
❑ 84F	Wade Boggs AS	.10	.05
❑ 85F	Cal Ripken AS	.40	.18
❑ 86F	Rickey Henderson AS	.10	.05
❑ 87F	Ken Griffey Jr. AS	.75	.35
❑ 88F	Dave Henderson AS	.05	.02
❑ 89F	Danny Tartabull AS	.05	.02
❑ 90F	Tom Glavine AS	.10	.05
❑ 91F	Benito Santiago AS	.05	.02
❑ 92F	Will Clark AS	.10	.05
❑ 93F	Ryne Sandberg AS	.20	.09
❑ 94F	Chris Sabo AS	.05	.02
❑ 95F	Ozzie Smith AS	.20	.09
❑ 96F	Ivan Calderon AS	.05	.02
❑ 97F	Tony Gwynn AS	.25	.11
❑ 98F	Andre Dawson AS	.10	.05
❑ 99F	Bobby Bonilla AS	.05	.02
❑ 100F	Checklist 1-100	.05	.02

1992 Upper Deck

	MINT	NRMT
COMPLETE SET (800)	15.00	6.75
COMP.FACT.SET (800)	20.00	9.00
COMPLETE LO SET (700)	12.00	5.50
COMPLETE HI SET (100)	3.00	1.35
COMMON CARD (1-800)	.05	.02

		MINT	NRMT
❑ 1	Ryan Klesko CL	.40	.18
	Jim Thome		
❑ 2	Royce Clayton SR	.05	.02
❑ 3	Brian Jordan SR	.40	.18
❑ 4	Dave Fleming SR	.05	.02
❑ 5	Jim Thome SR	.50	.23
❑ 6	Jeff Juden SR	.05	.02
❑ 7	Roberto Hernandez SR	.10	.05
❑ 8	Kyle Abbott SR	.05	.02
❑ 9	Chris George SR	.05	.02
❑ 10	Rob Maurer SR	.05	.02
❑ 11	Donald Harris SR	.05	.02
❑ 12	Ted Wood SR	.05	.02
❑ 13	Patrick Lennon SR	.05	.02
❑ 14	Willie Banks SR	.05	.02
❑ 15	Roger Salkeld SR UER	.05	.02
	(Bill was his grand- father, not his father)		
❑ 16	Wil Cordero SR	.05	.02
❑ 17	Arthur Rhodes SR	.05	.02
❑ 18	Pedro Martinez SR	.60	.25
❑ 19	Andy Ashby SR	.10	.05
❑ 20	Tom Goodwin SR	.05	.02
❑ 21	Braulio Castillo SR	.05	.02
❑ 22	Todd Van Poppel SR	.05	.02
❑ 23	Brian Williams SR	.05	.02
❑ 24	Ryan Klesko SR	.25	.11
❑ 25	Kenny Lofton SR	.40	.18
❑ 26	Derek Bell SR	.10	.05
❑ 27	Reggie Sanders SR	.05	.02
❑ 28	Dave Winfield's 400th	.10	.05
❑ 29	David Justice TC	.10	.05
❑ 30	Rob Dibble TC	.05	.02
❑ 31	Craig Biggio TC	.10	.05
❑ 32	Eddie Murray TC	.10	.05
❑ 33	Fred McGriff TC	.10	.05
❑ 34	Willie McGee TC	.05	.02
❑ 35	Shawon Dunston TC	.05	.02
❑ 36	Delino DeShields TC	.05	.02
❑ 37	Howard Johnson TC	.05	.02
❑ 38	John Kruk TC	.05	.02
❑ 39	Doug Drabek TC	.05	.02
❑ 40	Todd Zeile TC	.05	.02
❑ 41	Steve Avery	.05	.02

Playoff Perfection
❑ 42 Jeremy Hernandez .05 .02
❑ 43 Doug Henry .05 .02
❑ 44 Chris Donnels .05 .02
❑ 45 Mo Sanford .05 .02
❑ 46 Scott Kamieniecki .05 .02
❑ 47 Mark Lemke .05 .02
❑ 48 Steve Farr .05 .02
❑ 49 Francisco Oliveras .05 .02
❑ 50 Ced Landrum .05 .02
❑ 51 Rondell White CL .20 .09
Mark Newfield
❑ 52 Eduardo Perez TP .05 .02
❑ 53 Tom Nevers TP .05 .02
❑ 54 David Zancanaro TP .05 .02
❑ 55 Shawn Green TP .50 .23
❑ 56 Mark Wohlers TP .05 .02
❑ 57 Dave Nilsson TP .10 .05
❑ 58 Dmitri Young TP .20 .09
❑ 59 Ryan Hawblitzel TP .05 .02
❑ 60 Raul Mondesi TP .30 .14
❑ 61 Rondell White TP .20 .09
❑ 62 Steve Hosey TP .05 .02
❑ 63 Manny Ramirez TP 1.50 .70
❑ 64 Marc Newfield TP .05 .02
❑ 65 Jeromy Burnitz TP .20 .09
❑ 66 Mark Smith TP .05 .02
❑ 67 Joey Hamilton TP .25 .11
❑ 68 Tyler Green TP .05 .02
❑ 69 Jon Farrell TP .05 .02
❑ 70 Kurt Miller TP .05 .02
❑ 71 Jeff Plympton TP .05 .02
❑ 72 Dan Wilson TP .10 .05
❑ 73 Joe Vitiello TP .05 .02
❑ 74 Rico Brogna TP .10 .05
❑ 75 David McCarty TP .05 .02
❑ 76 Bob Wickman TP .05 .02
❑ 77 Carlos Rodriguez TP .05 .02
❑ 78 Jim Abbott .05 .02
Stay In School
❑ 79 Ramon Martinez .25 .11
Pedro Martinez
❑ 80 Kevin Mitchell .05 .02
Keith Mitchell
❑ 81 Sandy Alomar Jr. .20 .09
Roberto Alomar
❑ 82 Cal Ripken .50 .23
Billy Ripken
❑ 83 Tony Gwynn .20 .09
Chris Gwynn
❑ 84 Dwight Gooden .15 .07
Gary Sheffield
❑ 85 Ken Griffey Sr. .60 .25
Ken Griffey Jr.
Craig Griffey
❑ 86 Jim Abbott TC .05 .02
❑ 87 Frank Thomas TC .40 .18
❑ 88 Danny Tartabull TC .05 .02
❑ 89 Scott Erickson TC .05 .02
❑ 90 Rickey Henderson TC .10 .05
❑ 91 Edgar Martinez TC .10 .05
❑ 92 Nolan Ryan TC .40 .18
❑ 93 Ben McDonald TC .05 .02
❑ 94 Ellis Burks TC .05 .02
❑ 95 Greg Swindell TC .05 .02
❑ 96 Cecil Fielder TC .05 .02
❑ 97 Greg Vaughn TC .05 .02
❑ 98 Kevin Maas TC .05 .02
❑ 99 Dave Stieb TC .05 .02
❑ 100 Checklist 1-100 .05 .02
❑ 101 Joe Oliver .05 .02
❑ 102 Hector Villanueva .05 .02
❑ 103 Ed Whitson .05 .02
❑ 104 Danny Jackson .05 .02
❑ 105 Chris Hammond .05 .02
❑ 106 Ricky Jordan .05 .02
❑ 107 Kevin Bass .05 .02
❑ 108 Darrin Fletcher .05 .02
❑ 109 Junior Ortiz .05 .02
❑ 110 Tom Bolton .05 .02
❑ 111 Jeff King .10 .05
❑ 112 Dave Magadan .05 .02
❑ 113 Mike LaValliere .05 .02
❑ 114 Hubie Brooks .05 .02
❑ 115 Jay Bell .10 .05
❑ 116 David Wells .10 .05
❑ 117 Jim Leyritz .05 .02
❑ 118 Manuel Lee .05 .02
❑ 119 Alvaro Espinoza .05 .02
❑ 120 B.J. Surhoff .10 .05
❑ 121 Hal Morris .05 .02
❑ 122 Shawon Dawson .05 .02
❑ 123 Chris Sabo .05 .02
❑ 124 Andre Dawson .15 .07
❑ 125 Eric Davis .10 .05
❑ 126 Chili Davis .10 .05
❑ 127 Dale Murphy .20 .09
❑ 128 Kirk McCaskill .05 .02
❑ 129 Terry Mulholland .05 .02
❑ 130 Rick Aguilera .10 .05
❑ 131 Vince Coleman .05 .02
❑ 132 Andy Van Slyke .10 .05
❑ 133 Gregg Jefferies .05 .02
❑ 134 Barry Bonds .25 .11
❑ 135 Dwight Gooden .10 .05
❑ 136 Dave Stieb .05 .02
❑ 137 Albert Belle .25 .11
❑ 138 Teddy Higuera .05 .02
❑ 139 Jesse Barfield .05 .02
❑ 140 Pat Borders .05 .02
❑ 141 Bip Roberts .05 .02
❑ 142 Rob Dibble .05 .02
❑ 143 Mark Grace .15 .07
❑ 144 Barry Larkin .15 .07
❑ 145 Ryne Sandberg .25 .11
❑ 146 Scott Erickson .10 .05
❑ 147 Luis Polonia .05 .02
❑ 148 John Burkett .05 .02
❑ 149 Luis Sojo .05 .02
❑ 150 Dickie Thon .05 .02
❑ 151 Walt Weiss .05 .02
❑ 152 Mike Scioscia .05 .02
❑ 153 Mark McGwire 1.00 .45
❑ 154 Matt Williams .15 .07
❑ 155 Rickey Henderson .20 .09
❑ 156 Sandy Alomar Jr. .10 .05
❑ 157 Brian McRae .10 .05
❑ 158 Harold Baines .10 .05
❑ 159 Kevin Appier .10 .05
❑ 160 Felix Fermin .05 .02
❑ 161 Leo Gomez .05 .02
❑ 162 Craig Biggio .20 .09
❑ 163 Ben McDonald .05 .02
❑ 164 Randy Johnson .20 .09
❑ 165 Cal Ripken .75 .35
❑ 166 Frank Thomas .60 .25
❑ 167 Delino DeShields .10 .05
❑ 168 Greg Gagne .05 .02
❑ 169 Ron Karkovice .05 .02
❑ 170 Charlie Leibrandt .05 .02
❑ 171 Dave Righetti .05 .02
❑ 172 Dave Henderson .05 .02
❑ 173 Steve Decker .05 .02
❑ 174 Darryl Strawberry .10 .05
❑ 175 Will Clark .20 .09
❑ 176 Ruben Sierra .05 .02
❑ 177 Ozzie Smith .25 .11
❑ 178 Charles Nagy .10 .05
❑ 179 Gary Pettis .05 .02
❑ 180 Kirk Gibson .10 .05
❑ 181 Randy Milligan .05 .02
❑ 182 Dave Valle .05 .02
❑ 183 Chris Hoiles .05 .02
❑ 184 Tony Phillips .05 .02
❑ 185 Brady Anderson .15 .07
❑ 186 Scott Fletcher .05 .02
❑ 187 Gene Larkin .05 .02
❑ 188 Lance Johnson .05 .02
❑ 189 Greg Olson .05 .02
❑ 190 Melido Perez .05 .02
❑ 191 Lenny Harris .05 .02
❑ 192 Terry Kennedy .05 .02
❑ 193 Mike Gallego .05 .02
❑ 194 Willie McGee .10 .05
❑ 195 Juan Samuel .05 .02
❑ 196 Jeff Huson .10 .05
(Shows Jose Canseco
sliding into second)
❑ 197 Alex Cole .05 .02
❑ 198 Ron Robinson .05 .02
❑ 199 Joel Skinner .05 .02
❑ 200 Checklist 101-200 .05 .02
❑ 201 Kevin Reimer .05 .02
❑ 202 Stan Belinda .05 .02
❑ 203 Pat Tabler .05 .02
❑ 204 Jose Guzman .05 .02
❑ 205 Jose Lind .05 .02
❑ 206 Spike Owen .05 .02
❑ 207 Joe Orsulak .05 .02
❑ 208 Charlie Hayes .05 .02
❑ 209 Mike Devereaux .05 .02
❑ 210 Mike Fitzgerald .05 .02
❑ 211 Willie Randolph .10 .05
❑ 212 Rod Nichols .05 .02
❑ 213 Mike Boddicker .05 .02
❑ 214 Bill Spiers .05 .02
❑ 215 Steve Olin .05 .02
❑ 216 David Howard .05 .02
❑ 217 Gary Varsho .05 .02
❑ 218 Mike Harkey .05 .02
❑ 219 Luis Aquino .05 .02
❑ 220 Chuck McElroy .05 .02
❑ 221 Doug Drabek .05 .02
❑ 222 Dave Winfield .20 .09
❑ 223 Rafael Palmeiro .15 .07
❑ 224 Joe Carter .10 .05
❑ 225 Bobby Bonilla .10 .05
❑ 226 Ivan Calderon .05 .02
❑ 227 Gregg Olson .05 .02
❑ 228 Tim Wallach .05 .02
❑ 229 Terry Pendleton .05 .02
❑ 230 Gilberto Reyes .05 .02
❑ 231 Carlos Baerga .05 .02
❑ 232 Greg Vaughn .10 .05
❑ 233 Bret Saberhagen .10 .05
❑ 234 Gary Sheffield .20 .09
❑ 235 Mark Lewis .05 .02
❑ 236 George Bell .05 .02
❑ 237 Danny Tartabull .05 .02
❑ 238 Willie Wilson .05 .02
❑ 239 Doug Dascenzo .05 .02
❑ 240 Bill Pecota .05 .02
❑ 241 Julio Franco .05 .02
❑ 242 Ed Sprague .05 .02
❑ 243 Juan Gonzalez .60 .25
❑ 244 Chuck Finley .10 .05
❑ 245 Ivan Rodriguez .40 .18
❑ 246 Len Dykstra .10 .05
❑ 247 Deion Sanders .20 .09
❑ 248 Dwight Evans .10 .05
❑ 249 Larry Walker .20 .09
❑ 250 Billy Ripken .05 .02
❑ 251 Mickey Tettleton .05 .02
❑ 252 Tony Pena .05 .02
❑ 253 Benito Santiago .05 .02
❑ 254 Kirby Puckett .30 .14
❑ 255 Cecil Fielder .10 .05
❑ 256 Howard Johnson .05 .02
❑ 257 Andujar Cedeno .05 .02
❑ 258 Jose Rijo .05 .02
❑ 259 Al Osuna .05 .02
❑ 260 Todd Hundley .10 .05
❑ 261 Orel Hershiser .10 .05
❑ 262 Ray Lankford .20 .09
❑ 263 Robin Ventura .10 .05
❑ 264 Felix Jose .05 .02
❑ 265 Eddie Murray .20 .09
❑ 266 Kevin Mitchell .10 .05
❑ 267 Gary Carter .20 .09
❑ 268 Mike Benjamin .05 .02
❑ 269 Dick Schofield .05 .02
❑ 270 Jose Uribe .05 .02
❑ 271 Pete Incaviglia .05 .02
❑ 272 Tony Fernandez .05 .02
❑ 273 Alan Trammell .15 .07
❑ 274 Tony Gwynn .50 .23
❑ 275 Mike Greenwell .05 .02
❑ 276 Jeff Bagwell .50 .23
❑ 277 Frank Viola .05 .02
❑ 278 Randy Myers .10 .05
❑ 279 Ken Caminiti .15 .07
❑ 280 Bill Doran .05 .02
❑ 281 Dan Pasqua .05 .02
❑ 282 Alfredo Griffin .05 .02
❑ 283 Jose Oquendo .05 .02

❑ 284	Kal Daniels	.05	.02
❑ 285	Bobby Thigpen	.05	.02
❑ 286	Robby Thompson	.05	.02
❑ 287	Mark Eichhorn	.05	.02
❑ 288	Mike Felder	.05	.02
❑ 289	Dave Gallagher	.05	.02
❑ 290	Dave Anderson	.05	.02
❑ 291	Mel Hall	.05	.02
❑ 292	Jerald Clark	.05	.02
❑ 293	Al Newman	.05	.02
❑ 294	Rob Deer	.05	.02
❑ 295	Matt Nokes	.05	.02
❑ 296	Jack Armstrong	.05	.02
❑ 297	Jim Deshaies	.05	.02
❑ 298	Jeff Innis	.05	.02
❑ 299	Jeff Reed	.05	.02
❑ 300	Checklist 201-300	.05	.02
❑ 301	Lonnie Smith	.05	.02
❑ 302	Jimmy Key	.10	.05
❑ 303	Junior Felix	.05	.02
❑ 304	Mike Heath	.05	.02
❑ 305	Mark Langston	.05	.02
❑ 306	Greg W. Harris	.05	.02
❑ 307	Brett Butler	.10	.05
❑ 308	Luis Rivera	.05	.02
❑ 309	Bruce Ruffin	.05	.02
❑ 310	Paul Faries	.05	.02
❑ 311	Terry Leach	.05	.02
❑ 312	Scott Brosius	.25	.11
❑ 313	Scott Leius	.05	.02
❑ 314	Harold Reynolds	.05	.02
❑ 315	Jack Morris	.10	.05
❑ 316	David Segui	.10	.05
❑ 317	Bill Gullickson	.05	.02
❑ 318	Todd Frohwirth	.05	.02
❑ 319	Mark Leiter	.05	.02
❑ 320	Jeff M. Robinson	.05	.02
❑ 321	Gary Gaetti	.05	.02
❑ 322	John Smoltz	.15	.07
❑ 323	Andy Benes	.10	.05
❑ 324	Kelly Gruber	.05	.02
❑ 325	Jim Abbott	.10	.05
❑ 326	John Kruk	.10	.05
❑ 327	Kevin Seitzer	.05	.02
❑ 328	Darrin Jackson	.05	.02
❑ 329	Kurt Stillwell	.05	.02
❑ 330	Mike Maddux	.05	.02
❑ 331	Dennis Eckersley	.10	.05
❑ 332	Dan Gladden	.05	.02
❑ 333	Jose Canseco	.20	.09
❑ 334	Kent Hrbek	.10	.05
❑ 335	Ken Griffey Sr.	.10	.05
❑ 336	Greg Swindell	.05	.02
❑ 337	Trevor Wilson	.05	.02
❑ 338	Sam Horn	.05	.02
❑ 339	Mike Henneman	.05	.02
❑ 340	Jerry Browne	.05	.02
❑ 341	Glenn Braggs	.05	.02
❑ 342	Tom Glavine	.15	.07
❑ 343	Wally Joyner	.10	.05
❑ 344	Fred McGriff	.15	.07
❑ 345	Ron Gant	.10	.05
❑ 346	Ramon Martinez	.10	.05
❑ 347	Wes Chamberlain	.05	.02
❑ 348	Terry Shumpert	.05	.02
❑ 349	Tim Teufel	.05	.02
❑ 350	Wally Backman	.05	.02
❑ 351	Joe Girardi	.10	.05
❑ 352	Devon White	.05	.02
❑ 353	Greg Maddux	.60	.25
❑ 354	Ryan Bowen	.05	.02
❑ 355	Roberto Alomar	.20	.09
❑ 356	Don Mattingly	.30	.14
❑ 357	Pedro Guerrero	.05	.02
❑ 358	Steve Sax	.05	.02
❑ 359	Joey Cora	.10	.05
❑ 360	Jim Gantner	.05	.02
❑ 361	Brian Barnes	.05	.02
❑ 362	Kevin McReynolds	.05	.02
❑ 363	Bret Barberie	.05	.02
❑ 364	David Cone	.10	.05
❑ 365	Dennis Martinez	.10	.05
❑ 366	Brian Hunter	.05	.02
❑ 367	Edgar Martinez	.15	.07
❑ 368	Steve Finley	.10	.05
❑ 369	Greg Briley	.05	.02
❑ 370	Jeff Blauser	.05	.02
❑ 371	Todd Stottlemyre	.10	.05
❑ 372	Luis Gonzalez	.05	.02
❑ 373	Rick Wilkins	.05	.02
❑ 374	Darryl Kile	.10	.05
❑ 375	John Olerud	.10	.05
❑ 376	Lee Smith	.10	.05
❑ 377	Kevin Maas	.05	.02
❑ 378	Dante Bichette	.15	.07
❑ 379	Tom Pagnozzi	.05	.02
❑ 380	Mike Flanagan	.05	.02
❑ 381	Charlie O'Brien	.05	.02
❑ 382	Dave Martinez	.05	.02
❑ 383	Keith Miller	.05	.02
❑ 384	Scott Ruskin	.05	.02
❑ 385	Kevin Elster	.05	.02
❑ 386	Alvin Davis	.05	.02
❑ 387	Casey Candaele	.05	.02
❑ 388	Pete O'Brien	.05	.02
❑ 389	Jeff Treadway	.05	.02
❑ 390	Scott Bradley	.05	.02
❑ 391	Mookie Wilson	.10	.05
❑ 392	Jimmy Jones	.05	.02
❑ 393	Candy Maldonado	.05	.02
❑ 394	Eric Yelding	.05	.02
❑ 395	Tom Henke	.05	.02
❑ 396	Franklin Stubbs	.05	.02
❑ 397	Milt Thompson	.05	.02
❑ 398	Mark Carreon	.05	.02
❑ 399	Randy Velarde	.05	.02
❑ 400	Checklist 301-400	.05	.02
❑ 401	Omar Vizquel	.10	.05
❑ 402	Joe Boever	.05	.02
❑ 403	Bill Krueger	.05	.02
❑ 404	Jody Reed	.05	.02
❑ 405	Mike Schooler	.05	.02
❑ 406	Jason Grimsley	.05	.02
❑ 407	Greg Myers	.05	.02
❑ 408	Randy Ready	.05	.02
❑ 409	Mike Timlin	.05	.02
❑ 410	Mitch Williams	.05	.02
❑ 411	Garry Templeton	.05	.02
❑ 412	Greg Cadaret	.05	.02
❑ 413	Donnie Hill	.05	.02
❑ 414	Wally Whitehurst	.05	.02
❑ 415	Scott Sanderson	.05	.02
❑ 416	Thomas Howard	.05	.02
❑ 417	Neal Heaton	.05	.02
❑ 418	Charlie Hough	.10	.05
❑ 419	Jack Howell	.05	.02
❑ 420	Greg Hibbard	.05	.02
❑ 421	Carlos Quintana	.05	.02
❑ 422	Kim Batiste	.05	.02
❑ 423	Paul Molitor	.20	.09
❑ 424	Ken Griffey Jr.	1.25	.55
❑ 425	Phil Plantier	.05	.02
❑ 426	Denny Neagle	.15	.07
❑ 427	Von Hayes	.05	.02
❑ 428	Shane Mack	.05	.02
❑ 429	Darren Daulton	.10	.05
❑ 430	Dwayne Henry	.05	.02
❑ 431	Lance Parrish	.05	.02
❑ 432	Mike Humphreys	.05	.02
❑ 433	Tim Burke	.05	.02
❑ 434	Bryan Harvey	.05	.02
❑ 435	Pat Kelly	.05	.02
❑ 436	Ozzie Guillen	.05	.02
❑ 437	Bruce Hurst	.05	.02
❑ 438	Sammy Sosa	.50	.23
❑ 439	Dennis Rasmussen	.05	.02
❑ 440	Ken Patterson	.05	.02
❑ 441	Jay Buhner	.15	.07
❑ 442	Pat Combs	.05	.02
❑ 443	Wade Boggs	.20	.09
❑ 444	George Brett	.40	.18
❑ 445	Mo Vaughn	.30	.14
❑ 446	Chuck Knoblauch	.20	.09
❑ 447	Tom Candiotti	.05	.02
❑ 448	Mark Portugal	.05	.02
❑ 449	Mickey Morandini	.05	.02
❑ 450	Duane Ward	.05	.02
❑ 451	Otis Nixon	.10	.05
❑ 452	Bob Welch	.05	.02
❑ 453	Rusty Meacham	.05	.02
❑ 454	Keith Mitchell	.05	.02
❑ 455	Marquis Grissom	.10	.05
❑ 456	Robin Yount	.20	.09
❑ 457	Harvey Pulliam	.05	.02
❑ 458	Jose DeLeon	.05	.02
❑ 459	Mark Gubicza	.05	.02
❑ 460	Darryl Hamilton	.05	.02
❑ 461	Tom Browning	.05	.02
❑ 462	Monty Fariss	.05	.02
❑ 463	Jerome Walton	.05	.02
❑ 464	Paul O'Neill	.10	.05
❑ 465	Dean Palmer	.10	.05
❑ 466	Travis Fryman	.10	.05
❑ 467	John Smiley	.05	.02
❑ 468	Lloyd Moseby	.05	.02
❑ 469	John Wehner	.05	.02
❑ 470	Skeeter Barnes	.05	.02
❑ 471	Steve Chitren	.05	.02
❑ 472	Kent Mercker	.05	.02
❑ 473	Terry Steinbach	.10	.05
❑ 474	Andres Galarraga	.20	.09
❑ 475	Steve Avery	.05	.02
❑ 476	Tom Gordon	.10	.05
❑ 477	Cal Eldred	.05	.02
❑ 478	Omar Olivares	.05	.02
❑ 479	Julio Machado	.05	.02
❑ 480	Bob Milacki	.05	.02
❑ 481	Les Lancaster	.05	.02
❑ 482	John Candelaria	.05	.02
❑ 483	Brian Downing	.05	.02
❑ 484	Roger McDowell	.05	.02
❑ 485	Scott Scudder	.05	.02
❑ 486	Zane Smith	.05	.02
❑ 487	John Cerutti	.05	.02
❑ 488	Steve Buechele	.05	.02
❑ 489	Paul Gibson	.05	.02
❑ 490	Curtis Wilkerson	.05	.02
❑ 491	Marvin Freeman	.05	.02
❑ 492	Tom Foley	.05	.02
❑ 493	Juan Berenguer	.05	.02
❑ 494	Ernest Riles	.05	.02
❑ 495	Sid Bream	.05	.02
❑ 496	Chuck Crim	.05	.02
❑ 497	Mike Macfarlane	.05	.02
❑ 498	Dale Sveum	.05	.02
❑ 499	Storm Davis	.05	.02
❑ 500	Checklist 401-500	.05	.02
❑ 501	Jeff Reardon	.10	.05
❑ 502	Shawn Abner	.05	.02
❑ 503	Tony Fossas	.05	.02
❑ 504	Cory Snyder	.05	.02
❑ 505	Matt Young	.05	.02
❑ 506	Allan Anderson	.05	.02
❑ 507	Mark Lee	.05	.02
❑ 508	Gene Nelson	.05	.02
❑ 509	Mike Pagliarulo	.05	.02
❑ 510	Rafael Belliard	.05	.02
❑ 511	Jay Howell	.05	.02
❑ 512	Bob Tewksbury	.05	.02
❑ 513	Mike Morgan	.05	.02
❑ 514	John Franco	.10	.05
❑ 515	Kevin Gross	.05	.02
❑ 516	Lou Whitaker	.10	.05
❑ 517	Orlando Merced	.05	.02
❑ 518	Todd Benzinger	.05	.02
❑ 519	Gary Redus	.05	.02
❑ 520	Walt Terrell	.05	.02
❑ 521	Jack Clark	.10	.05
❑ 522	Dave Parker	.10	.05
❑ 523	Tim Naehring	.10	.05
❑ 524	Mark Whiten	.05	.02
❑ 525	Ellis Burks	.10	.05
❑ 526	Frank Castillo	.05	.02
❑ 527	Brian Harper	.05	.02
❑ 528	Brook Jacoby	.05	.02
❑ 529	Rick Sutcliffe	.05	.02
❑ 530	Joe Klink	.05	.02
❑ 531	Terry Bross	.05	.02
❑ 532	Jose Offerman	.05	.02
❑ 533	Todd Zeile	.05	.02
❑ 534	Eric Karros	.20	.09
❑ 535	Anthony Young	.05	.02
❑ 536	Milt Cuyler	.05	.02
❑ 537	Randy Tomlin	.05	.02
❑ 538	Scott Livingstone	.05	.02

❑ 539 Jim Eisenreich .05 .02
❑ 540 Don Slaught .05 .02
❑ 541 Scott Cooper .05 .02
❑ 542 Joe Grahe .05 .02
❑ 543 Tom Brunansky .05 .02
❑ 544 Eddie Zosky .05 .02
❑ 545 Roger Clemens .40 .18
❑ 546 David Justice .20 .09
❑ 547 Dave Stewart .10 .05
❑ 548 David West .05 .02
❑ 549 Dave Smith .05 .02
❑ 550 Dan Plesac .05 .02
❑ 551 Alex Fernandez .10 .05
❑ 552 Bernard Gilkey .10 .05
❑ 553 Jack McDowell .05 .02
❑ 554 Tino Martinez .20 .09
❑ 555 Bo Jackson .10 .05
❑ 556 Bernie Williams .20 .09
❑ 557 Mark Gardner .05 .02
❑ 558 Glenallen Hill .05 .02
❑ 559 Oil Can Boyd .05 .02
❑ 560 Chris James .05 .02
❑ 561 Scott Servais .05 .02
❑ 562 Rey Sanchez .05 .02
❑ 563 Paul McClellan .05 .02
❑ 564 Andy Mota .05 .02
❑ 565 Darren Lewis .05 .02
❑ 566 Jose Melendez .05 .02
❑ 567 Tommy Greene .05 .02
❑ 568 Rich Rodriguez .05 .02
❑ 569 Heathcliff Slocumb .05 .02
❑ 570 Joe Hesketh .05 .02
❑ 571 Carlton Fisk .20 .09
❑ 572 Erik Hanson .05 .02
❑ 573 Wilson Alvarez .10 .05
❑ 574 Rheal Cormier .05 .02
❑ 575 Tim Raines .10 .05
❑ 576 Bobby Witt .05 .02
❑ 577 Roberto Kelly .05 .02
❑ 578 Kevin Brown .15 .07
❑ 579 Chris Nabholz .05 .02
❑ 580 Jesse Orosco .05 .02
❑ 581 Jeff Brantley .05 .02
❑ 582 Rafael Ramirez .05 .02
❑ 583 Kelly Downs .05 .02
❑ 584 Mike Simms .05 .02
❑ 585 Mike Remlinger .05 .02
❑ 586 Dave Hollins .05 .02
❑ 587 Larry Andersen .05 .02
❑ 588 Mike Gardiner .05 .02
❑ 589 Craig Lefferts .05 .02
❑ 590 Paul Assenmacher .05 .02
❑ 591 Bryn Smith .05 .02
❑ 592 Donn Pall .05 .02
❑ 593 Mike Jackson .10 .05
❑ 594 Scott Radinsky .05 .02
❑ 595 Brian Holman .05 .02
❑ 596 Geronimo Pena .05 .02
❑ 597 Mike Jeffcoat .05 .02
❑ 598 Carlos Martinez .05 .02
❑ 599 Geno Petralli .05 .02
❑ 600 Checklist 501-600 .05 .02
❑ 601 Jerry Don Gleaton .05 .02
❑ 602 Adam Peterson .05 .02
❑ 603 Craig Grebeck .05 .02
❑ 604 Mark Guthrie .05 .02
❑ 605 Frank Tanana .05 .02
❑ 606 Hensley Meulens .05 .02
❑ 607 Mark Davis .05 .02
❑ 608 Eric Plunk .05 .02
❑ 609 Mark Williamson .05 .02
❑ 610 Lee Guetterman .05 .02
❑ 611 Bobby Rose .05 .02
❑ 612 Bill Wegman .05 .02
❑ 613 Mike Hartley .05 .02
❑ 614 Chris Beasley .05 .02
❑ 615 Chris Bosio .05 .02
❑ 616 Henry Cotto .05 .02
❑ 617 Chico Walker .05 .02
❑ 618 Russ Swan .05 .02
❑ 619 Bob Walk .05 .02
❑ 620 Billy Swift .05 .02
❑ 621 Warren Newson .05 .02
❑ 622 Steve Bedrosian .05 .02
❑ 623 Ricky Bones .05 .02
❑ 624 Kevin Tapani .05 .02
❑ 625 Juan Guzman .05 .02
❑ 626 Jeff Johnson .05 .02
❑ 627 Jeff Montgomery .10 .05
❑ 628 Ken Hill .05 .02
❑ 629 Gary Thurman .05 .02
❑ 630 Steve Howe .05 .02
❑ 631 Jose DeJesus .05 .02
❑ 632 Kirk Dressendorfer .05 .02
❑ 633 Jaime Navarro .05 .02
❑ 634 Lee Stevens .05 .02
❑ 635 Pete Harnisch .05 .02
❑ 636 Bill Landrum .05 .02
❑ 637 Rich DeLucia .05 .02
❑ 638 Luis Salazar .05 .02
❑ 639 Rob Murphy .05 .02
❑ 640 Jose Canseco CL .20 .09
Rickey Henderson
❑ 641 Roger Clemens DS .20 .09
❑ 642 Jim Abbott DS .05 .02
❑ 643 Travis Fryman DS .05 .02
❑ 644 Jesse Barfield DS .05 .02
❑ 645 Cal Ripken DS .20 .09
❑ 646 Wade Boggs DS .10 .05
❑ 647 Cecil Fielder DS .05 .02
❑ 648 Rickey Henderson DS .10 .05
❑ 649 Jose Canseco DS .10 .05
❑ 650 Ken Griffey Jr. DS 1.00 .45
❑ 651 Kenny Rogers .05 .02
❑ 652 Luis Mercedes .05 .02
❑ 653 Mike Stanton .05 .02
❑ 654 Glenn Davis .05 .02
❑ 655 Nolan Ryan .75 .35
❑ 656 Reggie Jefferson .10 .05
❑ 657 Javier Ortiz .05 .02
❑ 658 Greg A. Harris .05 .02
❑ 659 Mariano Duncan .05 .02
❑ 660 Jeff Shaw .05 .02
❑ 661 Mike Moore .05 .02
❑ 662 Chris Haney .05 .02
❑ 663 Joe Slusarski .05 .02
❑ 664 Wayne Housie .05 .02
❑ 665 Carlos Garcia .05 .02
❑ 666 Bob Ojeda .05 .02
❑ 667 Bryan Hickerson .05 .02
❑ 668 Tim Belcher .05 .02
❑ 669 Ron Darling .05 .02
❑ 670 Rex Hudler .05 .02
❑ 671 Sid Fernandez .05 .02
❑ 672 Chito Martinez .05 .02
❑ 673 Pete Schourek .05 .02
❑ 674 Armando Reynoso .05 .02
❑ 675 Mike Mussina .30 .14
❑ 676 Kevin Morton .05 .02
❑ 677 Norm Charlton .05 .02
❑ 678 Danny Darwin .05 .02
❑ 679 Eric King .05 .02
❑ 680 Ted Power .05 .02
❑ 681 Barry Jones .05 .02
❑ 682 Carney Lansford .10 .05
❑ 683 Mel Rojas .05 .02
❑ 684 Rick Honeycutt .05 .02
❑ 685 Jeff Fassero .10 .05
❑ 686 Cris Carpenter .05 .02
❑ 687 Tim Crews .05 .02
❑ 688 Scott Terry .05 .02
❑ 689 Chris Gwynn .05 .02
❑ 690 Gerald Perry .05 .02
❑ 691 John Barfield .05 .02
❑ 692 Bob Melvin .05 .02
❑ 693 Juan Agosto .05 .02
❑ 694 Alejandro Pena .05 .02
❑ 695 Jeff Russell .05 .02
❑ 696 Carmelo Martinez .05 .02
❑ 697 Bud Black .05 .02
❑ 698 Dave Otto .05 .02
❑ 699 Billy Hatcher .05 .02
❑ 700 Checklist 601-700 .05 .02
❑ 701 Clemente Nunez .10 .05
❑ 702 Rookie Threats .05 .02
Mark Clark
Donovan Osborne
Brian Jordan
❑ 703 Mike Morgan .05 .02
❑ 704 Keith Miller .05 .02
❑ 705 Kurt Stillwell .05 .02
❑ 706 Damon Berryhill .05 .02
❑ 707 Von Hayes .05 .02
❑ 708 Rick Sutcliffe .05 .02
❑ 709 Hubie Brooks .05 .02
❑ 710 Ryan Turner .05 .02
❑ 711 Barry Bonds CL .10 .05
Andy Van Slyke
❑ 712 Jose Rijo DS .05 .02
❑ 713 Tom Glavine DS .10 .05
❑ 714 Shawon Dunston DS .05 .02
❑ 715 Andy Van Slyke DS .05 .02
❑ 716 Ozzie Smith DS .20 .09
❑ 717 Tony Gwynn DS .25 .11
❑ 718 Will Clark DS .10 .05
❑ 719 Marquis Grissom DS .05 .02
❑ 720 Howard Johnson DS .05 .02
❑ 721 Barry Bonds DS .20 .09
❑ 722 Kirk McCaskill .05 .02
❑ 723 Sammy Sosa 1.00 .45
❑ 724 George Bell .05 .02
❑ 725 Gregg Jefferies .05 .02
❑ 726 Gary DiSarcina .05 .02
❑ 727 Mike Bordick .05 .02
❑ 728 Eddie Murray .20 .09
400 Home Run Club
❑ 729 Rene Gonzales .05 .02
❑ 730 Mike Bielecki .05 .02
❑ 731 Calvin Jones .05 .02
❑ 732 Jack Morris .10 .05
❑ 733 Frank Viola .05 .02
❑ 734 Dave Winfield .20 .09
❑ 735 Kevin Mitchell .10 .05
❑ 736 Bill Swift .05 .02
❑ 737 Dan Gladden .05 .02
❑ 738 Mike Jackson .10 .05
❑ 739 Mark Carreon .05 .02
❑ 740 Kirt Manwaring .05 .02
❑ 741 Randy Myers .10 .05
❑ 742 Kevin McReynolds .05 .02
❑ 743 Steve Sax .05 .02
❑ 744 Wally Joyner .10 .05
❑ 745 Gary Sheffield .20 .09
❑ 746 Danny Tartabull .05 .02
❑ 747 Julio Valera .05 .02
❑ 748 Denny Neagle .15 .07
❑ 749 Lance Blankenship .05 .02
❑ 750 Mike Gallego .05 .02
❑ 751 Bret Saberhagen .10 .05
❑ 752 Ruben Amaro .05 .02
❑ 753 Eddie Murray .20 .09
❑ 754 Kyle Abbott .05 .02
❑ 755 Bobby Bonilla .10 .05
❑ 756 Eric Davis .10 .05
❑ 757 Eddie Taubensee .10 .05
❑ 758 Andres Galarraga .20 .09
❑ 759 Pete Incaviglia .05 .02
❑ 760 Tom Candiotti .05 .02
❑ 761 Tim Belcher .05 .02
❑ 762 Ricky Bones .05 .02
❑ 763 Bip Roberts .05 .02
❑ 764 Pedro Munoz .05 .02
❑ 765 Greg Swindell .05 .02
❑ 766 Kenny Lofton .40 .18
❑ 767 Gary Carter .20 .09
❑ 768 Charlie Hayes .05 .02
❑ 769 Dickie Thon .05 .02
❑ 770 Donovan Osborne DD CL .05 .02
❑ 771 Bret Boone DD .10 .05
❑ 772 Archi Cianfrocco DD .05 .02
❑ 773 Mark Clark DD .05 .02
❑ 774 Chad Curtis DD .20 .09
❑ 775 Pat Listach DD .05 .02
❑ 776 Pat Mahomes DD .05 .02
❑ 777 Donovan Osborne DD .05 .02
❑ 778 John Patterson DD .05 .02
❑ 779 Andy Stankiewicz DD .05 .02
❑ 780 Turk Wendell DD .10 .05
❑ 781 Bill Krueger .05 .02
❑ 782 Rickey Henderson .10 .05
Grand Theft
❑ 783 Kevin Seitzer .05 .02
❑ 784 Dave Martinez .05 .02
❑ 785 John Smiley .05 .02
❑ 786 Matt Stairs .20 .09

❑ 787	Scott Scudder	.05	.02
❑ 788	John Wetteland	.10	.05
❑ 789	Jack Armstrong	.05	.02
❑ 790	Ken Hill	.05	.02
❑ 791	Dick Schofield	.05	.02
❑ 792	Mariano Duncan	.05	.02
❑ 793	Bill Pecota	.05	.02
❑ 794	Mike Kelly	.05	.02
❑ 795	Willie Randolph	.10	.05
❑ 796	Butch Henry	.05	.02
❑ 797	Carlos Hernandez	.05	.02
❑ 798	Doug Jones	.05	.02
❑ 799	Melido Perez	.05	.02
❑ 800	Checklist 701-800	.05	.02
❑ HH2	Ted Williams Hologram (Top left corner says 91 Upper Deck 92)	2.00	.90
❑ SP3	Deion Sanders FB/BB	.50	.23
❑ SP4	Tom Selleck Frank Thomas SP (Mr. Baseball)	1.50	.70

1992 Upper Deck Bench/Morgan Heroes

		MINT	NRMT
COMPLETE SET (10)		10.00	4.50
COMMON CARD (37-45)		1.00	.45
❑ 37	Johnny Bench 1968 Rookie-of-the-Year	1.00	.45
❑ 38	Johnny Bench 1968-77 Ten Straight Gold Gloves	1.00	.45
❑ 39	Johnny Bench 1970 and 1972 MVP	1.00	.45
❑ 40	Joe Morgan 1965 Rookie Year	1.00	.45
❑ 41	Joe Morgan 1975-76 Back-to-Back MVP	1.00	.45
❑ 42	Johnny Bench 1980-83 The Golden Years	1.00	.45
❑ 43	Johnny Bench Joe Morgan 1972-79 Big Red Machine	1.00	.45
❑ 44	Johnny Bench Joe Morgan 1989 and 1990 Hall of Fame	1.00	.45
❑ 45	Checklist-Heroes 37-45	1.00	.45
❑ AU5	Johnny Bench and Joe Morgan AU (Signed and Numbered of 2500)	150.00	70.00
❑ NNO0	Baseball Heroes SP (Header card)	2.50	1.10

1992 Upper Deck Heroes of Baseball

		MINT	NRMT
COMPLETE SET (4)		6.00	2.70
COMMON CARD (H5-H8)		.50	.23
❑ H5	Vida Blue	.50	.23
❑ H6	Lou Brock	3.00	1.35
❑ H7	Rollie Fingers	1.00	.45
❑ H8	Vida Blue ART Lou Brock Rollie Fingers	2.00	.90
❑ AU5	Vida Blue AU/3000	10.00	4.50
❑ AU6	Lou Brock AU/3000	50.00	22.00
❑ AU7	R.Fingers AU/3000	20.00	9.00

1992 Upper Deck Home Run Heroes

		MINT	NRMT
COMPLETE SET (26)		12.00	5.50
COMMON CARD (HR1-HR26)		.25	.11
❑ HR1	Jose Canseco	.75	.35
❑ HR2	Cecil Fielder	.40	.18
❑ HR3	Howard Johnson	.25	.11
❑ HR4	Cal Ripken	2.00	.90
❑ HR5	Matt Williams	.60	.25
❑ HR6	Joe Carter	.40	.18
❑ HR7	Ron Gant	.40	.18
❑ HR8	Frank Thomas	2.00	.90
❑ HR9	Andre Dawson	.60	.25
❑ HR10	Fred McGriff	.60	.25
❑ HR11	Danny Tartabull	.25	.11
❑ HR12	Chili Davis	.40	.18
❑ HR13	Albert Belle	.75	.35
❑ HR14	Jack Clark	.25	.11
❑ HR15	Paul O'Neill	.40	.18
❑ HR16	Darryl Strawberry	.40	.18
❑ HR17	Dave Winfield	.75	.35
❑ HR18	Jay Buhner	.60	.25
❑ HR19	Juan Gonzalez	2.00	.90
❑ HR20	Greg Vaughn	.40	.18
❑ HR21	Barry Bonds	.75	.35
❑ HR22	Matt Nokes	.25	.11
❑ HR23	John Kruk	.40	.18
❑ HR24	Ivan Calderon	.25	.11
❑ HR25	Jeff Bagwell	1.50	.70
❑ HR26	Todd Zeile	.25	.11

1992 Upper Deck Scouting Report

		MINT	NRMT
COMPLETE SET (25)		15.00	6.75
COMMON CARD (SR1-SR25)		.50	.23

❑ SR1	Andy Ashby	1.00	.45
❑ SR2	Willie Banks	.50	.23
❑ SR3	Kim Batiste	.50	.23
❑ SR4	Derek Bell	1.00	.45
❑ SR5	Archi Cianfrocco	.50	.23
❑ SR6	Royce Clayton	.50	.23
❑ SR7	Gary DiSarcina	.50	.23
❑ SR8	Dave Fleming	.50	.23
❑ SR9	Butch Henry	.50	.23
❑ SR10	Todd Hundley	1.00	.45
❑ SR11	Brian Jordan	2.00	.90
❑ SR12	Eric Karros	1.50	.70
❑ SR13	Pat Listach	.50	.23
❑ SR14	Scott Livingstone	.50	.23
❑ SR15	Kenny Lofton	5.00	2.20
❑ SR16	Pat Mahomes	.50	.23
❑ SR17	Denny Neagle	1.25	.55
❑ SR18	Dave Nilsson	1.00	.45
❑ SR19	Donovan Osborne	.50	.23
❑ SR20	Reggie Sanders	.50	.23
❑ SR21	Andy Stankiewicz	.50	.23
❑ SR22	Jim Thome	6.00	2.70
❑ SR23	Julio Valera	.50	.23
❑ SR24	Mark Wohlers	1.00	.45
❑ SR25	Anthony Young	.50	.23

1992 Upper Deck Williams Best

		MINT	NRMT
COMPLETE SET (20)		25.00	11.00
COMMON CARD (T1-T20)		.50	.23
❑ T1	Wade Boggs	1.50	.70
❑ T2	Barry Bonds	1.50	.70
❑ T3	Jose Canseco	1.00	.45
❑ T4	Will Clark	1.00	.45
❑ T5	Cecil Fielder	.75	.35
❑ T6	Tony Gwynn	2.50	1.10
❑ T7	Rickey Henderson	1.00	.45
❑ T8	Fred McGriff	1.00	.45
❑ T9	Kirby Puckett	2.00	.90
❑ T10	Ruben Sierra	.50	.23
❑ T11	Roberto Alomar	1.50	.70
❑ T12	Jeff Bagwell	3.00	1.35
❑ T13	Albert Belle	1.25	.55
❑ T14	Juan Gonzalez	4.00	1.80
❑ T15	Ken Griffey Jr.	8.00	3.60
❑ T16	Chris Hoiles	.50	.23
❑ T17	David Justice	1.50	.70

Card	MINT	NRMT
❑ T18 Phil Plantier	.50	.23
❑ T19 Frank Thomas	5.00	2.20
❑ T20 Robin Ventura	.75	.35

1992 Upper Deck Williams Heroes

	MINT	NRMT
COMPLETE SET (10)	6.00	2.70
COMMON T.WILLIAMS (28-36)	.50	.23
❑ 28 Ted Williams	.50	.23
1939 Rookie Year		
❑ 29 Ted Williams	.50	.23
1941 .406 BA		
❑ 30 Ted Williams	.50	.23
1942 Triple Crown Year		
❑ 31 Ted Williams	.50	.23
1946 and 1949 MVP		
❑ 32 Ted Williams	.50	.23
1947 2nd Triple Crown		
❑ 33 Ted Williams	.50	.23
1950s Player of the Decade		
❑ 34 Ted Williams	.50	.23
1960 500 Home Run Club		
❑ 35 Ted Williams	.50	.23
1966 Hall of Fame		
❑ 36 Baseball Heroes CL	.50	.23
❑ AU4 Ted Williams	500.00	220.00
(Signed and Numbered of 2500)		
❑ NNO0 Baseball Heroes SP	2.00	.90
(Header card)		

1993 Upper Deck

	MINT	NRMT
COMPLETE SET (840)	30.00	13.50
COMP.FACT.SET (840)	40.00	18.00
COMPLETE SERIES 1 (420)	15.00	6.75
COMPLETE SERIES 2 (420)	15.00	6.75
COMMON CARD (1-840)	.10	.05
❑ 1 Tim Salmon CL	.30	.14
❑ 2 Mike Piazza SR	2.00	.90
❑ 3 Rene Arocha SR	.10	.05
❑ 4 Willie Greene SR	.10	.05
❑ 5 Manny Alexander	.10	.05
❑ 6 Dan Wilson	.20	.09
❑ 7 Dan Smith	.10	.05
❑ 8 Kevin Rogers	.10	.05
❑ 9 Kurt Miller SR	.10	.05
❑ 10 Joe Vitko	.10	.05
❑ 11 Tim Costo	.10	.05
❑ 12 Alan Embree SR	.10	.05
❑ 13 Jim Tatum SR	.10	.05
❑ 14 Cris Colon	.10	.05
❑ 15 Steve Hosey	.10	.05
❑ 16 Sterling Hitchcock SR	.40	.18
❑ 17 Dave Mlicki	.10	.05
❑ 18 Jessie Hollins	.10	.05
❑ 19 Bobby Jones SR	.30	.14
❑ 20 Kurt Miller	.10	.05
❑ 21 Melvin Nieves SR	.10	.05
❑ 22 Billy Ashley SR	.10	.05
❑ 23 J.T. Snow SR	.50	.23
❑ 24 Chipper Jones SR	2.00	.90
❑ 25 Tim Salmon SR	.40	.18
❑ 26 Tim Pugh SR	.10	.05
❑ 27 David Nied SR	.10	.05
❑ 28 Mike Trombley	.10	.05
❑ 29 Javier Lopez SR	.40	.18
❑ 30 Jim Abbott CH CL	.10	.05
❑ 31 Jim Abbott CH	.10	.05
❑ 32 Dale Murphy CH	.20	.09
❑ 33 Tony Pena CH	.10	.05
❑ 34 Kirby Puckett CH	.40	.18
❑ 35 Harold Reynolds CH	.10	.05
❑ 36 Cal Ripken CH	.75	.35
❑ 37 Nolan Ryan CH	.75	.35
❑ 38 Ryne Sandberg CH	.30	.14
❑ 39 Dave Stewart CH	.10	.05
❑ 40 Dave Winfield CH	.20	.09
❑ 41 Joe Carter CL	.40	.18
Mark McGwire		
❑ 42 Blockbuster Trade	.40	.18
Joe Carter		
Roberto Alomar		
❑ 43 Brew Crew	.40	.18
Paul Molitor		
Pat Listach		
Robin Yount		
❑ 44 Iron and Steel	.40	.18
Cal Ripken		
Brady Anderson		
❑ 45 Youthful Tribe	.20	.09
Albert Belle		
Sandy Alomar Jr.		
Jim Thome		
Carlos Baerga		
Kenny Lofton		
❑ 46 Motown Mashers	.20	.09
Cecil Fielder		
Mickey Tettleton		
❑ 47 Yankee Pride	.20	.09
Roberto Kelly		
Don Mattingly		
❑ 48 Boston Cy Sox	.20	.09
Frank Viola		
Roger Clemens		
❑ 49 Bash Brothers	.20	.09
Ruben Sierra		
Mark McGwire		
❑ 50 Twin Titles	.40	.18
Kent Hrbek		
Kirby Puckett		
❑ 51 Southside Sluggers	.40	.18
Robin Ventura		
Frank Thomas		
❑ 52 Latin Stars	.50	.23
Juan Gonzalez		
Jose Canseco		
Ivan Rodriguez		
Rafael Palmeiro		
❑ 53 Lethal Lefties	.10	.05
Mark Langston		
Jim Abbott		
Chuck Finley		
❑ 54 Royal Family	.10	.05
Wally Joyner		
Gregg Jefferies		
George Brett		
❑ 55 Pacific Sock Exchange	.50	.23
Kevin Mitchell		
Ken Griffey Jr.		
Jay Buhner		
❑ 56 George Brett	.75	.35
❑ 57 Scott Cooper	.10	.05
❑ 58 Mike Maddux	.10	.05
❑ 59 Rusty Meacham	.10	.05
❑ 60 Wil Cordero	.10	.05
❑ 61 Tim Teufel	.10	.05
❑ 62 Jeff Montgomery	.20	.09
❑ 63 Scott Livingstone	.10	.05
❑ 64 Doug Dascenzo	.10	.05
❑ 65 Bret Boone	.20	.09
❑ 66 Tim Wakefield	.20	.09
❑ 67 Curt Schilling	.20	.09
❑ 68 Frank Tanana	.10	.05
❑ 69 Len Dykstra	.20	.09
❑ 70 Derek Lilliquist	.10	.05
❑ 71 Anthony Young	.10	.05
❑ 72 Hipolito Pichardo	.10	.05
❑ 73 Rod Beck	.20	.09
❑ 74 Kent Hrbek	.20	.09
❑ 75 Tom Glavine	.30	.14
❑ 76 Kevin Brown	.30	.14
❑ 77 Chuck Finley	.20	.09
❑ 78 Bob Walk	.10	.05
❑ 79 Rheal Cormier UER	.10	.05
(Born in New Brunswick, not British Columbia)		
❑ 80 Rick Sutcliffe	.10	.05
❑ 81 Harold Baines	.20	.09
❑ 82 Lee Smith	.20	.09
❑ 83 Geno Petralli	.10	.05
❑ 84 Jose Oquendo	.10	.05
❑ 85 Mark Gubicza	.10	.05
❑ 86 Mickey Tettleton	.10	.05
❑ 87 Bobby Witt	.10	.05
❑ 88 Mark Lewis	.10	.05
❑ 89 Kevin Appier	.20	.09
❑ 90 Mike Stanton	.10	.05
❑ 91 Rafael Belliard	.10	.05
❑ 92 Kenny Rogers	.10	.05
❑ 93 Randy Velarde	.10	.05
❑ 94 Luis Sojo	.10	.05
❑ 95 Mark Leiter	.10	.05
❑ 96 Jody Reed	.10	.05
❑ 97 Pete Harnisch	.10	.05
❑ 98 Tom Candiotti	.10	.05
❑ 99 Mark Portugal	.10	.05
❑ 100 Dave Valle	.10	.05
❑ 101 Shawon Dunston	.10	.05
❑ 102 B.J. Surhoff	.20	.09
❑ 103 Jay Bell	.20	.09
❑ 104 Sid Bream	.10	.05
❑ 105 Frank Thomas CL	.40	.18
❑ 106 Mike Morgan	.10	.05
❑ 107 Bill Doran	.10	.05
❑ 108 Lance Blankenship	.10	.05
❑ 109 Mark Lemke	.10	.05
❑ 110 Brian Harper	.10	.05
❑ 111 Brady Anderson	.30	.14
❑ 112 Bip Roberts	.10	.05
❑ 113 Mitch Williams	.10	.05
❑ 114 Craig Biggio	.40	.18
❑ 115 Eddie Murray	.40	.18
❑ 116 Matt Nokes	.10	.05
❑ 117 Lance Parrish	.10	.05
❑ 118 Bill Swift	.10	.05
❑ 119 Jeff Innis	.10	.05
❑ 120 Mike LaValliere	.10	.05
❑ 121 Hal Morris	.10	.05
❑ 122 Walt Weiss	.10	.05
❑ 123 Ivan Rodriguez	.50	.23
❑ 124 Andy Van Slyke	.20	.09
❑ 125 Roberto Alomar	.40	.18
❑ 126 Robby Thompson	.10	.05
❑ 127 Sammy Sosa	1.00	.45
❑ 128 Mark Langston	.10	.05
❑ 129 Jerry Browne	.10	.05
❑ 130 Chuck McElroy	.10	.05
❑ 131 Frank Viola	.10	.05
❑ 132 Leo Gomez	.10	.05
❑ 133 Ramon Martinez	.20	.09
❑ 134 Don Mattingly	.60	.25
❑ 135 Roger Clemens	.75	.35
❑ 136 Rickey Henderson	.40	.18
❑ 137 Darren Daulton	.20	.09
❑ 138 Ken Hill	.10	.05

❑ 139 Ozzie Guillen .10 .05
❑ 140 Jerald Clark .10 .05
❑ 141 Dave Fleming .10 .05
❑ 142 Delino DeShields .20 .09
❑ 143 Matt Williams .30 .14
❑ 144 Larry Walker .40 .18
❑ 145 Ruben Sierra .10 .05
❑ 146 Ozzie Smith .50 .23
❑ 147 Chris Sabo .10 .05
❑ 148 Carlos Hernandez .10 .05
❑ 149 Pat Borders .10 .05
❑ 150 Orlando Merced .10 .05
❑ 151 Royce Clayton .10 .05
❑ 152 Kurt Stillwell .10 .05
❑ 153 Dave Hollins .10 .05
❑ 154 Mike Greenwell .10 .05
❑ 155 Nolan Ryan 1.50 .70
❑ 156 Felix Jose .10 .05
❑ 157 Junior Felix .10 .05
❑ 158 Derek Bell .20 .09
❑ 159 Steve Buechele .10 .05
❑ 160 John Burkett .10 .05
❑ 161 Pat Howell .10 .05
❑ 162 Milt Cuyler .10 .05
❑ 163 Terry Pendleton .10 .05
❑ 164 Jack Morris .20 .09
❑ 165 Tony Gwynn 1.00 .45
❑ 166 Deion Sanders .30 .14
❑ 167 Mike Devereaux .10 .05
❑ 168 Ron Darling .10 .05
❑ 169 Orel Hershiser .20 .09
❑ 170 Mike Jackson .10 .05
❑ 171 Doug Jones .10 .05
❑ 172 Dan Walters .10 .05
❑ 173 Darren Lewis .10 .05
❑ 174 Carlos Baerga .10 .05
❑ 175 Ryne Sandberg .50 .23
❑ 176 Gregg Jefferies .10 .05
❑ 177 John Jaha .10 .05
❑ 178 Luis Polonia .10 .05
❑ 179 Kirt Manwaring .10 .05
❑ 180 Mike Magnante .10 .05
❑ 181 Billy Ripken .10 .05
❑ 182 Mike Moore .10 .05
❑ 183 Eric Anthony .10 .05
❑ 184 Lenny Harris .10 .05
❑ 185 Tony Pena .10 .05
❑ 186 Mike Felder .10 .05
❑ 187 Greg Olson .10 .05
❑ 188 Rene Gonzales .10 .05
❑ 189 Mike Bordick .10 .05
❑ 190 Mel Rojas .10 .05
❑ 191 Todd Frohwirth .10 .05
❑ 192 Darryl Hamilton .10 .05
❑ 193 Mike Fetters .10 .05
❑ 194 Omar Olivares .10 .05
❑ 195 Tony Phillips .10 .05
❑ 196 Paul Sorrento .10 .05
❑ 197 Trevor Wilson .10 .05
❑ 198 Kevin Gross .10 .05
❑ 199 Ron Karkovice .10 .05
❑ 200 Brook Jacoby .10 .05
❑ 201 Mariano Duncan .10 .05
❑ 202 Dennis Cook .10 .05
❑ 203 Daryl Boston .10 .05
❑ 204 Mike Perez .10 .05
❑ 205 Manuel Lee .10 .05
❑ 206 Steve Olin .10 .05
❑ 207 Charlie Hough .20 .09
❑ 208 Scott Scudder .10 .05
❑ 209 Charlie O'Brien .10 .05
❑ 210 Barry Bonds CL .40 .18
❑ 211 Jose Vizcaino .10 .05
❑ 212 Scott Leius .10 .05
❑ 213 Kevin Mitchell .20 .09
❑ 214 Brian Barnes .10 .05
❑ 215 Pat Kelly .10 .05
❑ 216 Chris Hammond .10 .05
❑ 217 Rob Deer .10 .05
❑ 218 Cory Snyder .10 .05
❑ 219 Gary Carter .30 .14
❑ 220 Danny Darwin .10 .05
❑ 221 Tom Gordon .20 .09
❑ 222 Gary Sheffield .40 .18
❑ 223 Joe Carter .20 .09
❑ 224 Jay Buhner .30 .14
❑ 225 Jose Offerman .10 .05
❑ 226 Jose Rijo .10 .05
❑ 227 Mark Whiten .10 .05
❑ 228 Randy Milligan .10 .05
❑ 229 Bud Black .10 .05
❑ 230 Gary DiSarcina .10 .05
❑ 231 Steve Finley .20 .09
❑ 232 Dennis Martinez .20 .09
❑ 233 Mike Mussina .40 .18
❑ 234 Joe Oliver .10 .05
❑ 235 Chad Curtis .20 .09
❑ 236 Shane Mack .10 .05
❑ 237 Jaime Navarro .10 .05
❑ 238 Brian McRae .10 .05
❑ 239 Chili Davis .20 .09
❑ 240 Jeff King .20 .09
❑ 241 Dean Palmer .20 .09
❑ 242 Danny Tartabull .10 .05
❑ 243 Charles Nagy .20 .09
❑ 244 Ray Lankford .30 .14
❑ 245 Barry Larkin .30 .14
❑ 246 Steve Avery .10 .05
❑ 247 John Kruk .20 .09
❑ 248 Derrick May .10 .05
❑ 249 Stan Javier .10 .05
❑ 250 Roger McDowell .10 .05
❑ 251 Dan Gladden .10 .05
❑ 252 Wally Joyner .20 .09
❑ 253 Pat Listach .10 .05
❑ 254 Chuck Knoblauch .40 .18
❑ 255 Sandy Alomar Jr. .20 .09
❑ 256 Jeff Bagwell .60 .25
❑ 257 Andy Stankiewicz .10 .05
❑ 258 Darrin Jackson .10 .05
❑ 259 Brett Butler .20 .09
❑ 260 Joe Orsulak .10 .05
❑ 261 Andy Benes .20 .09
❑ 262 Kenny Lofton .35 .16
❑ 263 Robin Ventura .20 .09
❑ 264 Ron Gant .20 .09
❑ 265 Ellis Burks .20 .09
❑ 266 Juan Guzman .10 .05
❑ 267 Wes Chamberlain .10 .05
❑ 268 John Smiley .10 .05
❑ 269 Franklin Stubbs .10 .05
❑ 270 Tom Browning .10 .05
❑ 271 Dennis Eckersley .20 .09
❑ 272 Carlton Fisk .40 .18
❑ 273 Lou Whitaker .20 .09
❑ 274 Phil Plantier .10 .05
❑ 275 Bobby Bonilla .20 .09
❑ 276 Ben McDonald .10 .05
❑ 277 Bob Zupcic .10 .05
❑ 278 Terry Steinbach .10 .05
❑ 279 Terry Mulholland .10 .05
❑ 280 Lance Johnson .10 .05
❑ 281 Willie McGee .20 .09
❑ 282 Bret Saberhagen .20 .09
❑ 283 Randy Myers .20 .09
❑ 284 Randy Tomlin .10 .05
❑ 285 Mickey Morandini .10 .05
❑ 286 Brian Williams .10 .05
❑ 287 Tino Martinez .40 .18
❑ 288 Jose Melendez .10 .05
❑ 289 Jeff Huson .10 .05
❑ 290 Joe Grahe .10 .05
❑ 291 Mel Hall .10 .05
❑ 292 Otis Nixon .10 .05
❑ 293 Todd Hundley .30 .14
❑ 294 Casey Candaele .10 .05
❑ 295 Kevin Seitzer .10 .05
❑ 296 Eddie Taubensee .10 .05
❑ 297 Moises Alou .20 .09
❑ 298 Scott Radinsky .10 .05
❑ 299 Thomas Howard .10 .05
❑ 300 Kyle Abbott .10 .05
❑ 301 Omar Vizquel .20 .09
❑ 302 Keith Miller .10 .05
❑ 303 Rick Aguilera .10 .05
❑ 304 Bruce Hurst .10 .05
❑ 305 Ken Caminiti .30 .14
❑ 306 Mike Pagliarulo .10 .05
❑ 307 Frank Seminara .10 .05
❑ 308 Andre Dawson .30 .14
❑ 309 Jose Lind .10 .05
❑ 310 Joe Boever .10 .05
❑ 311 Jeff Parrett .10 .05
❑ 312 Alan Mills .10 .05
❑ 313 Kevin Tapani .10 .05
❑ 314 Darryl Kile .20 .09
❑ 315 Will Clark CL .20 .09
❑ 316 Mike Sharperson .10 .05
❑ 317 John Orton .10 .05
❑ 318 Bob Tewksbury .10 .05
❑ 319 Xavier Hernandez .10 .05
❑ 320 Paul Assenmacher .10 .05
❑ 321 John Franco .20 .09
❑ 322 Mike Timlin .10 .05
❑ 323 Jose Guzman .10 .05
❑ 324 Pedro Martinez .50 .23
❑ 325 Bill Spiers .10 .05
❑ 326 Melido Perez .10 .05
❑ 327 Mike Macfarlane .10 .05
❑ 328 Ricky Bones .10 .05
❑ 329 Scott Bankhead .10 .05
❑ 330 Rich Rodriguez .10 .05
❑ 331 Geronimo Pena .10 .05
❑ 332 Bernie Williams .40 .18
❑ 333 Paul Molitor .40 .18
❑ 334 Carlos Garcia .10 .05
❑ 335 David Cone .20 .09
❑ 336 Randy Johnson .40 .18
❑ 337 Pat Mahomes .10 .05
❑ 338 Erik Hanson .10 .05
❑ 339 Duane Ward .10 .05
❑ 340 Al Martin .10 .05
❑ 341 Pedro Munoz .10 .05
❑ 342 Greg Colbrunn .10 .05
❑ 343 Julio Valera .10 .05
❑ 344 John Olerud .30 .14
❑ 345 George Bell .10 .05
❑ 346 Devon White .10 .05
❑ 347 Donovan Osborne .10 .05
❑ 348 Mark Gardner .10 .05
❑ 349 Zane Smith .10 .05
❑ 350 Wilson Alvarez .20 .09
❑ 351 Kevin Koslofski .10 .05
❑ 352 Roberto Hernandez .20 .09
❑ 353 Glenn Davis .10 .05
❑ 354 Reggie Sanders .10 .05
❑ 355 Ken Griffey Jr. 2.00 .90
❑ 356 Marquis Grissom .20 .09
❑ 357 Jack McDowell .10 .05
❑ 358 Jimmy Key .20 .09
❑ 359 Stan Belinda .10 .05
❑ 360 Gerald Williams .10 .05
❑ 361 Sid Fernandez .10 .05
❑ 362 Alex Fernandez .20 .09
❑ 363 John Smoltz .20 .09
❑ 364 Travis Fryman .20 .09
❑ 365 Jose Canseco .40 .18
❑ 366 David Justice .40 .18
❑ 367 Pedro Astacio .10 .05
❑ 368 Tim Belcher .10 .05
❑ 369 Steve Sax .10 .05
❑ 370 Gary Gaetti .10 .05
❑ 371 Jeff Frye .10 .05
❑ 372 Bob Wickman .10 .05
❑ 373 Ryan Thompson .10 .05
❑ 374 David Hulse .10 .05
❑ 375 Cal Eldred .10 .05
❑ 376 Ryan Klesko .40 .18
❑ 377 Damion Easley .20 .09
❑ 378 John Kiely .10 .05
❑ 379 Jim Bullinger .10 .05
❑ 380 Brian Bohanon .10 .05
❑ 381 Rod Brewer .10 .05
❑ 382 Fernando Ramsey .10 .05
❑ 383 Sam Militello .10 .05
❑ 384 Arthur Rhodes .10 .05
❑ 385 Eric Karros .30 .14
❑ 386 Rico Brogna .20 .09
❑ 387 John Valentin .20 .09
❑ 388 Kerry Woodson .10 .05
❑ 389 Ben Rivera .10 .05
❑ 390 Matt Whiteside .10 .05
❑ 391 Henry Rodriguez .20 .09
❑ 392 John Wetteland .20 .09
❑ 393 Kent Mercker .10 .05

❑ 394 Bernard Gilkey .10 .05
❑ 395 Doug Henry .10 .05
❑ 396 Mo Vaughn .50 .23
❑ 397 Scott Erickson .10 .05
❑ 398 Bill Gullickson .10 .05
❑ 399 Mark Guthrie .10 .05
❑ 400 Dave Martinez .10 .05
❑ 401 Jeff Kent .20 .09
❑ 402 Chris Hoiles .10 .05
❑ 403 Mike Henneman .10 .05
❑ 404 Chris Nabholz .10 .05
❑ 405 Tom Pagnozzi .10 .05
❑ 406 Kelly Gruber .10 .05
❑ 407 Bob Welch .10 .05
❑ 408 Frank Castillo .10 .05
❑ 409 John Dopson .10 .05
❑ 410 Steve Farr .10 .05
❑ 411 Henry Cotto .10 .05
❑ 412 Bob Patterson .10 .05
❑ 413 Todd Stottlemyre .10 .05
❑ 414 Greg A. Harris .10 .05
❑ 415 Denny Neagle .20 .09
❑ 416 Bill Wegman .10 .05
❑ 417 Willie Wilson .10 .05
❑ 418 Terry Leach .10 .05
❑ 419 Willie Randolph .20 .09
❑ 420 Mark McGwire CL .40 .18
❑ 421 Calvin Murray CL .10 .05
❑ 422 Pete Janicki TP .10 .05
❑ 423 Todd Jones TP .20 .09
❑ 424 Mike Neill TP .10 .05
❑ 425 Carlos Delgado TP .40 .18
❑ 426 Jose Oliva TP .10 .05
❑ 427 Tyrone Hill TP .10 .05
❑ 428 Dmitri Young TP .40 .18
❑ 429 Derek Wallace TP .10 .05
❑ 430 Michael Moore TP .10 .05
❑ 431 Cliff Floyd TP .40 .18
❑ 432 Calvin Murray TP .10 .05
❑ 433 Manny Ramirez TP .75 .35
❑ 434 Marc Newfield TP .10 .05
❑ 435 Charles Johnson TP .40 .18
❑ 436 Butch Huskey TP .30 .14
❑ 437 Brad Pennington TP .10 .05
❑ 438 Ray McDavid TP .10 .05
❑ 439 Chad McConnell TP .10 .05
❑ 440 Midre Cummings TP .10 .05
❑ 441 Benji Gil TP .10 .05
❑ 442 Frankie Rodriguez TP .10 .05
❑ 443 Chad Mottola TP .10 .05
❑ 444 John Burke TP .10 .05
❑ 445 Michael Tucker TP .40 .18
❑ 446 Rick Greene TP .10 .05
❑ 447 Rich Becker TP .20 .09
❑ 448 Mike Robertson TP .10 .05
❑ 449 Derek Jeter TP 4.00 1.80
❑ 450 Ivan Rodriguez CL .20 .09
David McCarty
❑ 451 Jim Abbott IN .10 .05
❑ 452 Jeff Bagwell IN .40 .18
❑ 453 Jason Bere IN .10 .05
❑ 454 Delino DeShields IN .10 .05
❑ 455 Travis Fryman IN .10 .05
❑ 456 Alex Gonzalez IN .30 .14
❑ 457 Phil Hiatt IN .10 .05
❑ 458 Dave Hollins IN .10 .05
❑ 459 Chipper Jones IN 1.00 .45
❑ 460 David Justice IN .20 .09
❑ 461 Ray Lankford IN .20 .09
❑ 462 David McCarty IN .10 .05
❑ 463 Mike Mussina IN .20 .09
❑ 464 Jose Offerman IN .10 .05
❑ 465 Dean Palmer IN .10 .05
❑ 466 Geronimo Pena IN .10 .05
❑ 467 Eduardo Perez IN .10 .05
❑ 468 Ivan Rodriguez IN .40 .18
❑ 469 Reggie Sanders IN .10 .05
❑ 470 Bernie Williams IN .40 .18
❑ 471 Barry Bonds CL .40 .18
Matt Williams
Will Clark
❑ 472 Strike Force .40 .18
Greg Maddux
Steve Avery
John Smoltz
Tom Glavine
❑ 473 Red October .10 .05
Jose Rijo
Rob Dibble
Roberto Kelly
Reggie Sanders
Barry Larkin
❑ 474 Four Corners .30 .14
Gary Sheffield
Phil Plantier
Tony Gwynn
Fred McGriff
❑ 475 Shooting Stars .10 .05
Doug Drabek
Craig Biggio
Jeff Bagwell
❑ 476 Giant Sticks .30 .14
Will Clark
Barry Bonds
Matt Williams
❑ 477 Boyhood Friends .20 .09
Eric Davis
Darryl Strawberry
❑ 478 Rock Solid Foundation .30 .14
Dante Bichette
David Nied
Andres Galarraga
❑ 479 Inaugural Catch .10 .05
Dave Magadan
Orestes Destrade
Bret Barberie
Jeff Conine
❑ 480 Steel City Champions .10 .05
Tim Wakefield
Andy Van Slyke
Jay Bell
❑ 481 Les Grandes Etoiles .20 .09
Marquis Grissom
Delino DeShields
Dennis Martinez
Larry Walker
❑ 482 Runnin' Redbirds .20 .09
Geronimo Pena
Ray Lankford
Ozzie Smith
Bernard Gilkey
❑ 483 Ivy Leaguers .20 .09
Randy Myers
Ryne Sandberg
Mark Grace
❑ 484 Big Apple Power Switch .20 .09
Eddie Murray
Howard Johnson
Bobby Bonilla
❑ 485 Hammers and Nails .10 .05
John Kruk
Dave Hollins
Darren Daulton
Len Dykstra
❑ 486 Barry Bonds AW .40 .18
❑ 487 Dennis Eckersley AW .10 .05
❑ 488 Greg Maddux AW .60 .25
❑ 489 Dennis Eckersley AW .10 .05
❑ 490 Eric Karros AW .10 .05
❑ 491 Pat Listach AW .10 .05
❑ 492 Gary Sheffield AW .20 .09
❑ 493 Mark McGwire AW 1.00 .45
❑ 494 Gary Sheffield AW .20 .09
❑ 495 Edgar Martinez AW .20 .09
❑ 496 Fred McGriff AW .20 .09
❑ 497 Juan Gonzalez AW .50 .23
❑ 498 Darren Daulton AW .10 .05
❑ 499 Cecil Fielder AW .10 .05
❑ 500 Brent Gates CL .10 .05
❑ 501 Tavo Alvarez DD .10 .05
❑ 502 Rod Bolton .10 .05
❑ 503 John Cummings DD .10 .05
❑ 504 Brent Gates DD .10 .05
❑ 505 Tyler Green .10 .05
❑ 506 Jose Martinez DD .10 .05
❑ 507 Troy Percival .30 .14
❑ 508 Kevin Stocker DD .10 .05
❑ 509 Matt Walbeck DD .10 .05
❑ 510 Rondell White DD .30 .14
❑ 511 Billy Ripken .10 .05
❑ 512 Mike Moore .10 .05
❑ 513 Jose Lind .10 .05
❑ 514 Chito Martinez .10 .05
❑ 515 Jose Guzman .10 .05
❑ 516 Kim Batiste .10 .05
❑ 517 Jeff Tackett .10 .05
❑ 518 Charlie Hough .20 .09
❑ 519 Marvin Freeman .10 .05
❑ 520 Carlos Martinez .10 .05
❑ 521 Eric Young .40 .18
❑ 522 Pete Incaviglia .10 .05
❑ 523 Scott Fletcher .10 .05
❑ 524 Orestes Destrade .10 .05
❑ 525 Ken Griffey Jr. CL .40 .18
❑ 526 Ellis Burks .20 .09
❑ 527 Juan Samuel .10 .05
❑ 528 Dave Magadan .10 .05
❑ 529 Jeff Parrett .10 .05
❑ 530 Bill Krueger .10 .05
❑ 531 Frank Bolick .10 .05
❑ 532 Alan Trammell .30 .14
❑ 533 Walt Weiss .10 .05
❑ 534 David Cone .20 .09
❑ 535 Greg Maddux 1.25 .55
❑ 536 Kevin Young .10 .05
❑ 537 Dave Hansen .10 .05
❑ 538 Alex Cole .10 .05
❑ 539 Greg Hibbard .10 .05
❑ 540 Gene Larkin .10 .05
❑ 541 Jeff Reardon .20 .09
❑ 542 Felix Jose .10 .05
❑ 543 Jimmy Key .20 .09
❑ 544 Reggie Jefferson .20 .09
❑ 545 Gregg Jefferies .10 .05
❑ 546 Dave Stewart .20 .09
❑ 547 Tim Wallach .10 .05
❑ 548 Spike Owen .10 .05
❑ 549 Tommy Greene .10 .05
❑ 550 Fernando Valenzuela .20 .09
❑ 551 Rich Amaral .10 .05
❑ 552 Bret Barberie .10 .05
❑ 553 Edgar Martinez .30 .14
❑ 554 Jim Abbott .20 .09
❑ 555 Frank Thomas 1.25 .55
❑ 556 Wade Boggs .40 .18
❑ 557 Tom Henke .10 .05
❑ 558 Milt Thompson .10 .05
❑ 559 Lloyd McClendon .10 .05
❑ 560 Vinny Castilla .50 .23
❑ 561 Ricky Jordan .10 .05
❑ 562 Andujar Cedeno .10 .05
❑ 563 Greg Vaughn .20 .09
❑ 564 Cecil Fielder .20 .09
❑ 565 Kirby Puckett .60 .25
❑ 566 Mark McGwire 2.00 .90
❑ 567 Barry Bonds .50 .23
❑ 568 Jody Reed .10 .05
❑ 569 Todd Zeile .10 .05
❑ 570 Mark Carreon .10 .05
❑ 571 Joe Girardi .20 .09
❑ 572 Luis Gonzalez .10 .05
❑ 573 Mark Grace .30 .14
❑ 574 Rafael Palmeiro .30 .14
❑ 575 Darryl Strawberry .20 .09
❑ 576 Will Clark .40 .18
❑ 577 Fred McGriff .30 .14
❑ 578 Kevin Reimer .10 .05
❑ 579 Dave Righetti .10 .05
❑ 580 Juan Bell .10 .05
❑ 581 Jeff Brantley .10 .05
❑ 582 Brian Hunter .10 .05
❑ 583 Tim Naehring .10 .05
❑ 584 Glenallen Hill .10 .05
❑ 585 Cal Ripken 1.50 .70
❑ 586 Albert Belle .50 .23
❑ 587 Robin Yount .30 .14
❑ 588 Chris Bosio .10 .05
❑ 589 Pete Smith .10 .05
❑ 590 Chuck Carr .10 .05
❑ 591 Jeff Blauser .10 .05
❑ 592 Kevin McReynolds .10 .05
❑ 593 Andres Galarraga .40 .18
❑ 594 Kevin Maas .10 .05
❑ 595 Eric Davis .20 .09
❑ 596 Brian Jordan .20 .09
❑ 597 Tim Raines .20 .09

		MINT	NRMT
❑ 598	Rick Wilkins	.10	.05
❑ 599	Steve Cooke	.10	.05
❑ 600	Mike Gallego	.10	.05
❑ 601	Mike Munoz	.10	.05
❑ 602	Luis Rivera	.10	.05
❑ 603	Junior Ortiz	.10	.05
❑ 604	Brent Mayne	.10	.05
❑ 605	Luis Alicea	.10	.05
❑ 606	Damon Berryhill	.10	.05
❑ 607	Dave Henderson	.10	.05
❑ 608	Kirk McCaskill	.10	.05
❑ 609	Jeff Fassero	.10	.05
❑ 610	Mike Harkey	.10	.05
❑ 611	Francisco Cabrera	.10	.05
❑ 612	Rey Sanchez	.10	.05
❑ 613	Scott Servais	.10	.05
❑ 614	Darrin Fletcher	.10	.05
❑ 615	Felix Fermin	.10	.05
❑ 616	Kevin Seitzer	.10	.05
❑ 617	Bob Scanlan	.10	.05
❑ 618	Billy Hatcher	.10	.05
❑ 619	John Vander Wal	.10	.05
❑ 620	Joe Hesketh	.10	.05
❑ 621	Hector Villanueva	.10	.05
❑ 622	Randy Milligan	.10	.05
❑ 623	Tony Tarasco	.10	.05
❑ 624	Russ Swan	.10	.05
❑ 625	Willie Wilson	.10	.05
❑ 626	Frank Tanana	.10	.05
❑ 627	Pete O'Brien	.10	.05
❑ 628	Lenny Webster	.10	.05
❑ 629	Mark Clark	.10	.05
❑ 630	Roger Clemens CL	.40	.18
❑ 631	Alex Arias	.10	.05
❑ 632	Chris Gwynn	.10	.05
❑ 633	Tom Bolton	.10	.05
❑ 634	Greg Briley	.10	.05
❑ 635	Kent Bottenfield	.10	.05
❑ 636	Kelly Downs	.10	.05
❑ 637	Manuel Lee	.10	.05
❑ 638	Al Leiter	.20	.09
❑ 639	Jeff Gardner	.10	.05
❑ 640	Mike Gardiner	.10	.05
❑ 641	Mark Gardner	.10	.05
❑ 642	Jeff Branson	.10	.05
❑ 643	Paul Wagner	.10	.05
❑ 644	Sean Berry	.10	.05
❑ 645	Phil Hiatt	.10	.05
❑ 646	Kevin Mitchell	.20	.09
❑ 647	Charlie Hayes	.10	.05
❑ 648	Jim Deshaies	.10	.05
❑ 649	Dan Pasqua	.10	.05
❑ 650	Mike Maddux	.10	.05
❑ 651	Domingo Martinez	.10	.05
❑ 652	Greg McMichael	.10	.05
❑ 653	Eric Wedge	.10	.05
❑ 654	Mark Whiten	.10	.05
❑ 655	Roberto Kelly	.10	.05
❑ 656	Julio Franco	.10	.05
❑ 657	Gene Harris	.10	.05
❑ 658	Pete Schourek	.10	.05
❑ 659	Mike Bielecki	.10	.05
❑ 660	Ricky Gutierrez	.10	.05
❑ 661	Chris Hammond	.10	.05
❑ 662	Tim Scott	.10	.05
❑ 663	Norm Charlton	.10	.05
❑ 664	Doug Drabek	.10	.05
❑ 665	Dwight Gooden	.20	.09
❑ 666	Jim Gott	.10	.05
❑ 667	Randy Myers	.20	.09
❑ 668	Darren Holmes	.10	.05
❑ 669	Tim Spehr	.10	.05
❑ 670	Bruce Ruffin	.10	.05
❑ 671	Bobby Thigpen	.10	.05
❑ 672	Tony Fernandez	.10	.05
❑ 673	Darrin Jackson	.10	.05
❑ 674	Gregg Olson	.10	.05
❑ 675	Rob Dibble	.10	.05
❑ 676	Howard Johnson	.10	.05
❑ 677	Mike Lansing	.20	.09
❑ 678	Charlie Leibrandt	.10	.05
❑ 679	Kevin Bass	.10	.05
❑ 680	Hubie Brooks	.10	.05
❑ 681	Scott Brosius	.10	.05
❑ 682	Randy Knorr	.10	.05
❑ 683	Dante Bichette	.20	.09
❑ 684	Bryan Harvey	.10	.05
❑ 685	Greg Gohr	.10	.05
❑ 686	Willie Banks	.10	.05
❑ 687	Robb Nen	.30	.14
❑ 688	Mike Scioscia	.10	.05
❑ 689	John Farrell	.10	.05
❑ 690	John Candelaria	.10	.05
❑ 691	Damon Buford	.10	.05
❑ 692	Todd Worrell	.10	.05
❑ 693	Pat Hentgen	.30	.14
❑ 694	John Smiley	.10	.05
❑ 695	Greg Swindell	.10	.05
❑ 696	Derek Bell	.20	.09
❑ 697	Terry Jorgensen	.10	.05
❑ 698	Jimmy Jones	.10	.05
❑ 699	David Wells	.20	.09
❑ 700	Dave Martinez	.10	.05
❑ 701	Steve Bedrosian	.10	.05
❑ 702	Jeff Russell	.10	.05
❑ 703	Joe Magrane	.10	.05
❑ 704	Matt Mieske	.10	.05
❑ 705	Paul Molitor	.40	.18
❑ 706	Dale Murphy	.30	.14
❑ 707	Steve Howe	.10	.05
❑ 708	Greg Gagne	.10	.05
❑ 709	Dave Eiland	.10	.05
❑ 710	David West	.10	.05
❑ 711	Luis Aquino	.10	.05
❑ 712	Joe Orsulak	.10	.05
❑ 713	Eric Plunk	.10	.05
❑ 714	Mike Felder	.10	.05
❑ 715	Joe Klink	.10	.05
❑ 716	Lonnie Smith	.10	.05
❑ 717	Monty Fariss	.10	.05
❑ 718	Craig Lefferts	.10	.05
❑ 719	John Habyan	.10	.05
❑ 720	Willie Blair	.10	.05
❑ 721	Darnell Coles	.10	.05
❑ 722	Mark Williamson	.10	.05
❑ 723	Bryn Smith	.10	.05
❑ 724	Greg W. Harris	.10	.05
❑ 725	Graeme Lloyd	.10	.05
❑ 726	Cris Carpenter	.10	.05
❑ 727	Chico Walker	.10	.05
❑ 728	Tracy Woodson	.10	.05
❑ 729	Jose Uribe	.10	.05
❑ 730	Stan Javier	.10	.05
❑ 731	Jay Howell	.10	.05
❑ 732	Freddie Benavides	.10	.05
❑ 733	Jeff Reboulet	.10	.05
❑ 734	Scott Sanderson	.10	.05
❑ 735	Ryne Sandberg CL	.40	.18
❑ 736	Archi Cianfrocco	.10	.05
❑ 737	Daryl Boston	.10	.05
❑ 738	Craig Grebeck	.10	.05
❑ 739	Doug Dascenzo	.10	.05
❑ 740	Gerald Young	.10	.05
❑ 741	Candy Maldonado	.10	.05
❑ 742	Joey Cora	.20	.09
❑ 743	Don Slaught	.10	.05
❑ 744	Steve Decker	.10	.05
❑ 745	Blas Minor	.10	.05
❑ 746	Storm Davis	.10	.05
❑ 747	Carlos Quintana	.10	.05
❑ 748	Vince Coleman	.10	.05
❑ 749	Todd Burns	.10	.05
❑ 750	Steve Frey	.10	.05
❑ 751	Ivan Calderon	.10	.05
❑ 752	Steve Reed	.10	.05
❑ 753	Danny Jackson	.10	.05
❑ 754	Jeff Conine	.10	.05
❑ 755	Juan Gonzalez	1.00	.45
❑ 756	Mike Kelly	.10	.05
❑ 757	John Doherty	.10	.05
❑ 758	Jack Armstrong	.10	.05
❑ 759	John Wehner	.10	.05
❑ 760	Scott Bankhead	.10	.05
❑ 761	Jim Tatum	.10	.05
❑ 762	Scott Pose	.10	.05
❑ 763	Andy Ashby	.20	.09
❑ 764	Ed Sprague	.10	.05
❑ 765	Harold Baines	.20	.09
❑ 766	Kirk Gibson	.20	.09
❑ 767	Troy Neel	.10	.05
❑ 768	Dick Schofield	.10	.05
❑ 769	Dickie Thon	.10	.05
❑ 770	Butch Henry	.10	.05
❑ 771	Junior Felix	.10	.05
❑ 772	Ken Ryan	.10	.05
❑ 773	Trevor Hoffman	.40	.18
❑ 774	Phil Plantier	.10	.05
❑ 775	Bo Jackson	.20	.09
❑ 776	Benito Santiago	.10	.05
❑ 777	Andre Dawson	.30	.14
❑ 778	Bryan Hickerson	.10	.05
❑ 779	Dennis Moeller	.10	.05
❑ 780	Ryan Bowen	.10	.05
❑ 781	Eric Fox	.10	.05
❑ 782	Joe Kmak	.10	.05
❑ 783	Mike Hampton	.30	.14
❑ 784	Darrell Sherman	.10	.05
❑ 785	J.T. Snow	.40	.18
❑ 786	Dave Winfield	.30	.14
❑ 787	Jim Austin	.10	.05
❑ 788	Craig Shipley	.10	.05
❑ 789	Greg Myers	.10	.05
❑ 790	Todd Benzinger	.10	.05
❑ 791	Cory Snyder	.10	.05
❑ 792	David Segui	.10	.05
❑ 793	Armando Reynoso	.10	.05
❑ 794	Chili Davis	.20	.09
❑ 795	Dave Nilsson	.20	.09
❑ 796	Paul O'Neill	.20	.09
❑ 797	Jerald Clark	.10	.05
❑ 798	Jose Mesa	.10	.05
❑ 799	Brain Holman	.10	.05
❑ 800	Jim Eisenreich	.10	.05
❑ 801	Mark McLemore	.10	.05
❑ 802	Luis Sojo	.10	.05
❑ 803	Harold Reynolds	.10	.05
❑ 804	Dan Plesac	.10	.05
❑ 805	Dave Stieb	.20	.09
❑ 806	Tom Brunansky	.10	.05
❑ 807	Kelly Gruber	.10	.05
❑ 808	Bob Ojeda	.10	.05
❑ 809	Dave Burba	.10	.05
❑ 810	Joe Boever	.10	.05
❑ 811	Jeremy Hernandez	.10	.05
❑ 812	Tim Salmon TC	.30	.14
❑ 813	Jeff Bagwell TC	.40	.18
❑ 814	Dennis Eckersley TC	.10	.05
❑ 815	Roberto Alomar TC	.20	.09
❑ 816	Steve Avery TC	.10	.05
❑ 817	Pat Listach TC	.10	.05
❑ 818	Gregg Jefferies TC	.10	.05
❑ 819	Sammy Sosa TC	.50	.23
❑ 820	Darryl Strawberry TC	.10	.05
❑ 821	Dennis Martinez TC	.10	.05
❑ 822	Robby Thompson TC	.10	.05
❑ 823	Albert Belle TC	.40	.18
❑ 824	Randy Johnson TC	.20	.09
❑ 825	Nigel Wilson TC	.10	.05
❑ 826	Bobby Bonilla TC	.10	.05
❑ 827	Glenn Davis TC	.10	.05
❑ 828	Gary Sheffield TC	.20	.09
❑ 829	Darren Daulton TC	.10	.05
❑ 830	Jay Bell TC	.10	.05
❑ 831	Juan Gonzalez TC	.50	.23
❑ 832	Andre Dawson TC	.20	.09
❑ 833	Hal Morris TC	.10	.05
❑ 834	David Nied TC	.10	.05
❑ 835	Felix Jose TC	.10	.05
❑ 836	Travis Fryman TC	.10	.05
❑ 837	Shane Mack TC	.10	.05
❑ 838	Robin Ventura TC	.20	.09
❑ 839	Danny Tartabull TC	.10	.05
❑ 840	Roberto Alomar CL	.40	.18
❑ SP5	George Brett Robin Yount 3,000th Hit	1.00	.45
❑ SP6	Nolan Ryan	2.00	.90

1993 Upper Deck Clutch Performers

	MINT	NRMT
COMPLETE SET (20)	20.00	9.00
COMMON CARD (R1-R20)	.25	.11

❑ R1 Roberto Alomar	1.00	.45
❑ R2 Wade Boggs	1.00	.45
❑ R3 Barry Bonds	1.25	.55
❑ R4 Jose Canseco	1.00	.45
❑ R5 Joe Carter	.50	.23
❑ R6 Will Clark	1.00	.45
❑ R7 Roger Clemens	2.00	.90
❑ R8 Dennis Eckersley	.50	.23
❑ R9 Cecil Fielder	.50	.23
❑ R10 Juan Gonzalez	2.50	1.10
❑ R11 Ken Griffey Jr.	5.00	2.20
❑ R12 Rickey Henderson	1.00	.45
❑ R13 Barry Larkin	.75	.35
❑ R14 Don Mattingly	2.00	.90
❑ R15 Fred McGriff	.75	.35
❑ R16 Terry Pendleton	.25	.11
❑ R17 Kirby Puckett	1.50	.70
❑ R18 Ryne Sandberg	1.25	.55
❑ R19 John Smoltz	.50	.23
❑ R20 Frank Thomas	3.00	1.35

1993 Upper Deck Fifth Anniversary

	MINT	NRMT
COMPLETE SET (15)	20.00	9.00
COMMON CARD (A1-A15)	.25	.11
*JUMBO CARDS: 2X VALUE		
❑ A1 Ken Griffey Jr.	5.00	2.20
❑ A2 Gary Sheffield	1.00	.45
❑ A3 Roberto Alomar	1.00	.45
❑ A4 Jim Abbott	.50	.23
❑ A5 Nolan Ryan	4.00	1.80
❑ A6 Juan Gonzalez	2.50	1.10
❑ A7 David Justice	1.00	.45
❑ A8 Carlos Baerga	.25	.11
❑ A9 Reggie Jackson	1.00	.45
❑ A10 Eric Karros	.75	.35
❑ A11 Chipper Jones	5.00	2.20
❑ A12 Ivan Rodriguez	1.25	.55
❑ A13 Pat Listach	.25	.11
❑ A14 Frank Thomas	3.00	1.35
❑ A15 Tim Salmon	1.00	.45

1993 Upper Deck Future Heroes

	MINT	NRMT
COMPLETE SET (10)	12.00	5.50

COMMON CARD (55-63)	.25	.11
❑ 55 Roberto Alomar	1.00	.45
❑ 56 Barry Bonds	1.25	.55
❑ 57 Roger Clemens	2.00	.90
❑ 58 Juan Gonzalez	2.50	1.10
❑ 59 Ken Griffey Jr.	5.00	2.20
❑ 60 Mark McGwire	6.00	2.70
❑ 61 Kirby Puckett	1.50	.70
❑ 62 Frank Thomas	3.00	1.35
❑ 63 Checklist	.25	.11
❑ NNO Header Card SP	.75	.35

1993 Upper Deck Home Run Heroes

	MINT	NRMT
COMPLETE SET (28)	15.00	6.75
COMMON CARD (HR1-HR28)	.25	.11
❑ HR1 Juan Gonzalez	2.50	1.10
❑ HR2 Mark McGwire	6.00	2.70
❑ HR3 Cecil Fielder	.50	.23
❑ HR4 Fred McGriff	.75	.35
❑ HR5 Albert Belle	1.25	.55
❑ HR6 Barry Bonds	1.00	.45
❑ HR7 Joe Carter	.50	.23
❑ HR8 Darren Daulton	.50	.23
❑ HR9 Ken Griffey Jr.	5.00	2.20
❑ HR10 Dave Hollins	.25	.11
❑ HR11 Ryne Sandberg	1.25	.55
❑ HR12 George Bell	.25	.11
❑ HR13 Danny Tartabull	.25	.11
❑ HR14 Mike Devereaux	.25	.11
❑ HR15 Greg Vaughn	.50	.23
❑ HR16 Larry Walker	1.00	.45
❑ HR17 David Justice	.50	.23
❑ HR18 Terry Pendleton	.25	.11
❑ HR19 Eric Karros	.75	.35
❑ HR20 Ray Lankford	.75	.35
❑ HR21 Matt Williams	.75	.35
❑ HR22 Eric Anthony	.25	.11
❑ HR23 Bobby Bonilla	.50	.23
❑ HR24 Kirby Puckett	1.50	.70
❑ HR25 Mike Macfarlane	.25	.11
❑ HR26 Tom Brunansky	.25	.11
❑ HR27 Paul O'Neill	.50	.23
❑ HR28 Gary Gaetti	.25	.11

1993 Upper Deck Iooss Collection

	MINT	NRMT
COMPLETE SET (27)	25.00	11.00
COMMON CARD (WI1-WI26)	.25	.11
*JUMBO CARDS: 2X VALUE		
❑ WI1 Tim Salmon	1.25	.55
❑ WI2 Jeff Bagwell	2.00	.90
❑ WI3 Mark McGwire	7.50	3.40
❑ WI4 Roberto Alomar	1.00	.45
❑ WI5 Steve Avery	.25	.11
❑ WI6 Paul Molitor	1.00	.45
❑ WI7 Ozzie Smith	1.50	.70
❑ WI8 Mark Grace	.75	.35
❑ WI9 Eric Karros	.75	.35
❑ WI10 Delino DeShields	.25	.11
❑ WI11 Will Clark	1.00	.45
❑ WI12 Albert Belle	1.50	.70
❑ WI13 Ken Griffey Jr.	6.00	2.70
❑ WI14 Howard Johnson	.25	.11
❑ WI15 Cal Ripken Jr.	5.00	2.20
❑ WI16 Fred McGriff	.75	.35
❑ WI17 Darren Daulton	.50	.23
❑ WI18 Andy Van Slyke	.25	.11
❑ WI19 Nolan Ryan	5.00	2.20
❑ WI20 Wade Boggs	1.00	.45
❑ WI21 Barry Larkin	.75	.35
❑ WI22 George Brett	2.50	1.10
❑ WI23 Cecil Fielder	.50	.23
❑ WI24 Kirby Puckett	2.00	.90
❑ WI25 Frank Thomas	4.00	1.80
❑ WI26 Don Mattingly	2.50	1.10
❑ NNO Title Card Iooss Header	.50	.23

1993 Upper Deck Mays Heroes

	MINT	NRMT
COMPLETE SET (10)	3.00	1.35
COMMON CARD (46-54/HDR)	.50	.23
❑ 46 Willie Mays 1951 Rookie-of-the-Year	.50	.23
❑ 47 Willie Mays 1954 The Catch	.50	.23
❑ 48 Willie Mays 1956-57 30-30 Club	.50	.23

Card	Mint	NrMt
❑ 49 Willie Mays 1961 Four-Homer Game	.50	.23
❑ 50 Willie Mays 1965 Most Valuable Player	.50	.23
❑ 51 Willie Mays 1969 600-Home Run Club	.50	.23
❑ 52 Willie Mays 1972 New York Homecoming	.50	.23
❑ 53 Willie Mays 1979 Hall of Fame	.50	.23
❑ 54 Baseball Heroes CL Vernon Wells Portrait	.50	.23
❑ NNO0 Baseball Heroes SP (Header card)	.50	.23

1993 Upper Deck On Deck

	MINT	NRMT
COMPLETE SET (25)	20.00	9.00
COMMON CARD (D1-D25)	.25	.11
❑ D1 Jim Abbott	.50	.23
❑ D2 Roberto Alomar	1.00	.45
❑ D3 Carlos Baerga	.25	.11
❑ D4 Albert Belle	1.25	.55
❑ D5 Wade Boggs	1.00	.45
❑ D6 George Brett	2.00	.90
❑ D7 Jose Canseco	1.00	.45
❑ D8 Will Clark	1.00	.45
❑ D9 Roger Clemens	2.00	.90
❑ D10 Dennis Eckersley	.50	.23
❑ D11 Cecil Fielder	.50	.23
❑ D12 Juan Gonzalez	2.50	1.10
❑ D13 Ken Griffey Jr.	5.00	2.20
❑ D14 Tony Gwynn	2.50	1.10
❑ D15 Bo Jackson	.50	.23
❑ D16 Chipper Jones	5.00	2.20
❑ D17 Eric Karros	.75	.35
❑ D18 Mark McGwire	6.00	2.70
❑ D19 Kirby Puckett	1.50	.70
❑ D20 Nolan Ryan	4.00	1.80
❑ D21 Tim Salmon	1.00	.45
❑ D22 Ryne Sandberg	1.25	.55
❑ D23 Darryl Strawberry	.50	.23
❑ D24 Frank Thomas	3.00	1.35
❑ D25 Andy Van Slyke	.25	.11

1993 Upper Deck Season Highlights

	MINT	NRMT
COMPLETE SET (20)	150.00	70.00
COMMON CARD (HI1-HI20)	2.50	1.10
MINOR STARS	4.00	1.80
SEMISTARS	5.00	2.20
UNLISTED STARS	10.00	4.50
❑ HI1 Roberto Alomar	10.00	4.50
❑ HI2 Steve Avery	2.50	1.10
❑ HI3 Harold Baines	4.00	1.80
❑ HI4 Damon Berryhill	2.50	1.10
❑ HI5 Barry Bonds	12.00	5.50
❑ HI6 Bret Boone	4.00	1.80
❑ HI7 George Brett	20.00	9.00
❑ HI8 Francisco Cabrera	2.50	1.10
❑ HI9 Ken Griffey Jr.	50.00	22.00

Card	Mint	NrMt
❑ HI10 Rickey Henderson	10.00	4.50
❑ HI11 Kenny Lofton	10.00	4.50
❑ HI12 Mickey Morandini	2.50	1.10
❑ HI13 Eddie Murray	10.00	4.50
❑ HI14 David Nied	2.50	1.10
❑ HI15 Jeff Reardon	4.00	1.80
❑ HI16 Bip Roberts	2,50	1.10
❑ HI17 Nolan Ryan	50.00	22.00
❑ HI18 Ed Sprague	2.50	1.10
❑ HI19 Dave Winfield	5.00	2.20
❑ HI20 Robin Yount	5.00	2.20

1993 Upper Deck Then And Now

	MINT	NRMT
COMPLETE SET (18)	50.00	22.00
COMPLETE SERIES 1 (9)	20.00	9.00
COMPLETE SERIES 2 (9)	30.00	13.50
COMMON CARD (TN1-TN18)	.50	.23
❑ TN1 Wade Boggs	1.50	.70
❑ TN2 George Brett	4.00	1.80
❑ TN3 Rickey Henderson	1.50	.70
❑ TN4 Cal Ripken	8.00	3.60
❑ TN5 Nolan Ryan	8.00	3.60
❑ TN6 Ryne Sandberg	2.50	1.10
❑ TN7 Ozzie Smith	2.50	1.10
❑ TN8 Darryl Strawberry	.75	.35
❑ TN9 Dave Winfield	1.00	.45
❑ TN10 Dennis Eckersley	.75	.35
❑ TN11 Tony Gwynn	5.00	2.20
❑ TN12 Howard Johnson	.50	.23
❑ TN13 Don Mattingly	4.00	1.80
❑ TN14 Eddie Murray	1.50	.70
❑ TN15 Robin Yount	1.00	.45
❑ TN16 Reggie Jackson	2.50	1.10
❑ TN17 Mickey Mantle	15.00	6.75
❑ TN18 Willie Mays	8.00	3.60

1993 Upper Deck Triple Crown

	MINT	NRMT
COMPLETE SET (10)	25.00	11.00
COMMON CARD (TC1-TC10)	1.25	.55
❑ TC1 Barry Bonds	2.50	1.10
❑ TC2 Jose Canseco	2.00	.90

Card	Mint	NrMt
❑ TC3 Will Clark	2.00	.90
❑ TC4 Ken Griffey Jr.	10.00	4.50
❑ TC5 Fred McGriff	1.25	.55
❑ TC6 Kirby Puckett	3.00	1.35
❑ TC7 Cal Ripken Jr.	8.00	3.60
❑ TC8 Gary Sheffield	2.00	.90
❑ TC9 Frank Thomas	6.00	2.70
❑ TC10 Larry Walker	2.00	.90

1994 Upper Deck

	MINT	NRMT
COMPLETE SET (550)	50.00	22.00
COMPLETE SERIES 1 (280)	30.00	13.50
COMPLETE SERIES 2 (270)	20.00	9.00
COMMON CARD (1-550)	.15	.07
❑ 1 Brian Anderson	.40	.18
❑ 2 Shane Andrews	.15	.07
❑ 3 James Baldwin	.30	.14
❑ 4 Rich Becker	.15	.07
❑ 5 Greg Blosser	.15	.07
❑ 6 Ricky Bottalico	.30	.14
❑ 7 Midre Cummings	.15	.07
❑ 8 Carlos Delgado	.40	.18
❑ 9 Steve Dreyer	.15	.07
❑ 10 Joey Eischen	.15	.07
❑ 11 Carl Everett	.15	.07
❑ 12 Cliff Floyd UER (text indicates he throws left; should be right)	.30	.14
❑ 13 Alex Gonzalez	.15	.07
❑ 14 Jeff Granger	.15	.07
❑ 15 Shawn Green	.30	.14
❑ 16 Brian L. Hunter	.30	.14
❑ 17 Butch Huskey	.30	.14
❑ 18 Mark Hutton	.15	.07
❑ 19 Michael Jordan	10.00	4.50
❑ 20 Steve Karsay	.15	.07
❑ 21 Jeff McNeely	.15	.07
❑ 22 Marc Newfield	.15	.07
❑ 23 Manny Ramirez	.75	.35
❑ 24 Alex Rodriguez	12.00	5.50
❑ 25 Scott Ruffcorn UER (photo on back is Robert Ellis)	.15	.07
❑ 26 Paul Spoljaric UER (Expos logo on back)	.15	.07
❑ 27 Salomon Torres	.15	.07
❑ 28 Steve Trachsel	.15	.07
❑ 29 Chris Turner	.15	.07
❑ 30 Gabe White	.15	.07

	Card	Player	Mint	Nr Mt
❑	31	Randy Johnson FT	.30	.14
❑	32	John Wetteland FT	.15	.07
❑	33	Mike Piazza FT	1.00	.45
❑	34	Rafael Palmeiro FT	.15	.07
❑	35	Roberto Alomar FT	.30	.14
❑	36	Matt Williams FT	.15	.07
❑	37	Travis Fryman FT	.15	.07
❑	38	Barry Bonds FT	.60	.25
❑	39	Marquis Grissom FT	.15	.07
❑	40	Albert Belle FT	.40	.18
❑	41	Steve Avery FUT	.15	.07
❑	42	Jason Bere FUT	.15	.07
❑	43	Alex Fernandez FUT	.15	.07
❑	44	Mike Mussina FUT	.30	.14
❑	45	Aaron Sele FUT	.15	.07
❑	46	Rod Beck FUT	.15	.07
❑	47	Mike Piazza FUT	1.00	.45
❑	48	John Olerud FUT	.15	.07
❑	49	Carlos Baerga FUT	.15	.07
❑	50	Gary Sheffield FUT	.30	.14
❑	51	Travis Fryman FUT	.15	.07
❑	52	Juan Gonzalez FUT	.75	.35
❑	53	Ken Griffey Jr. FUT	1.50	.70
❑	54	Tim Salmon FUT	.30	.14
❑	55	Frank Thomas FUT	1.00	.45
❑	56	Tony Phillips	.15	.07
❑	57	Julio Franco	.15	.07
❑	58	Kevin Mitchell	.15	.07
❑	59	Raul Mondesi	.60	.25
❑	60	Rickey Henderson	.60	.25
❑	61	Jay Buhner	.30	.14
❑	62	Bill Swift	.15	.07
❑	63	Brady Anderson	.30	.14
❑	64	Ryan Klesko	.30	.14
❑	65	Darren Daulton	.30	.14
❑	66	Damion Easley	.30	.14
❑	67	Mark McGwire	3.00	1.35
❑	68	John Roper	.15	.07
❑	69	Dave Telgheder	.15	.07
❑	70	Dave Nied	.15	.07
❑	71	Mo Vaughn	.75	.35
❑	72	Tyler Green	.15	.07
❑	73	Dave Magadan	.15	.07
❑	74	Chili Davis	.30	.14
❑	75	Archi Cianfrocco	.15	.07
❑	76	Joe Girardi	.15	.07
❑	77	Chris Hoiles	.15	.07
❑	78	Ryan Bowen	.15	.07
❑	79	Greg Gagne	.15	.07
❑	80	Aaron Sele	.30	.14
❑	81	Dave Winfield	.60	.25
❑	82	Chad Curtis	.15	.07
❑	83	Andy Van Slyke	.30	.14
❑	84	Kevin Stocker	.15	.07
❑	85	Deion Sanders	.30	.14
❑	86	Bernie Williams	.60	.25
❑	87	John Smoltz	.30	.14
❑	88	Ruben Santana	.15	.07
❑	89	Dave Stewart	.30	.14
❑	90	Don Mattingly	1.00	.45
❑	91	Joe Carter	.30	.14
❑	92	Ryne Sandberg	.75	.35
❑	93	Chris Gomez	.15	.07
❑	94	Tino Martinez	.60	.25
❑	95	Terry Pendleton	.15	.07
❑	96	Andre Dawson	.40	.18
❑	97	Wil Cordero	.15	.07
❑	98	Kent Hrbek	.30	.14
❑	99	John Olerud	.30	.14
❑	100	Kirt Manwaring	.15	.07
❑	101	Tim Bogar	.15	.07
❑	102	Mike Mussina	.60	.25
❑	103	Nigel Wilson	.15	.07
❑	104	Ricky Gutierrez	.15	.07
❑	105	Roberto Mejia	.15	.07
❑	106	Tom Pagnozzi	.15	.07
❑	107	Mike Macfarlane	.15	.07
❑	108	Jose Bautista	.15	.07
❑	109	Luis Ortiz	.15	.07
❑	110	Brent Gates	.15	.07
❑	111	Tim Salmon	.60	.25
❑	112	Wade Boggs	.60	.25
❑	113	Tripp Cromer	.15	.07
❑	114	Denny Hocking	.15	.07
❑	115	Carlos Baerga	.30	.14
❑	116	J.R. Phillips	.15	.07
❑	117	Bo Jackson	.30	.14
❑	118	Lance Johnson	.15	.07
❑	119	Bobby Jones	.15	.07
❑	120	Bobby Witt	.15	.07
❑	121	Ron Karkovice	.15	.07
❑	122	Jose Vizcaino	.15	.07
❑	123	Danny Darwin	.15	.07
❑	124	Eduardo Perez	.15	.07
❑	125	Brian Looney	.15	.07
❑	126	Pat Hentgen	.30	.14
❑	127	Frank Viola	.15	.07
❑	128	Darren Holmes	.15	.07
❑	129	Wally Whitehurst	.15	.07
❑	130	Matt Walbeck	.15	.07
❑	131	Albert Belle	.75	.35
❑	132	Steve Cooke	.15	.07
❑	133	Kevin Appier	.30	.14
❑	134	Joe Oliver	.15	.07
❑	135	Benji Gil	.15	.07
❑	136	Steve Buechele	.15	.07
❑	137	Devon White	.30	.14
❑	138	Sterling Hitchcock UER (two losses for career; should be four)	.30	.14
❑	139	Phil Leftwich	.15	.07
❑	140	Jose Canseco	.60	.25
❑	141	Rick Aguilera	.15	.07
❑	142	Rod Beck	.15	.07
❑	143	Jose Rijo	.15	.07
❑	144	Tom Glavine	.60	.25
❑	145	Phil Plantier	.15	.07
❑	146	Jason Bere	.15	.07
❑	147	Jamie Moyer	.15	.07
❑	148	Wes Chamberlain	.15	.07
❑	149	Glenallen Hill	.15	.07
❑	150	Mark Whiten	.15	.07
❑	151	Bret Barberie	.15	.07
❑	152	Chuck Knoblauch	.60	.25
❑	153	Trevor Hoffman	.30	.14
❑	154	Rick Wilkins	.15	.07
❑	155	Juan Gonzalez	1.50	.70
❑	156	Ozzie Guillen	.15	.07
❑	157	Jim Eisenreich	.15	.07
❑	158	Pedro Astacio	.15	.07
❑	159	Joe Magrane	.15	.07
❑	160	Ryan Thompson	.15	.07
❑	161	Jose Lind	.15	.07
❑	162	Jeff Conine	.30	.14
❑	163	Todd Benzinger	.15	.07
❑	164	Roger Salkeld	.15	.07
❑	165	Gary DiSarcina	.15	.07
❑	166	Kevin Gross	.15	.07
❑	167	Charlie Hayes	.15	.07
❑	168	Tim Costo	.15	.07
❑	169	Wally Joyner	.30	.14
❑	170	Johnny Ruffin	.15	.07
❑	171	Kirk Rueter	.15	.07
❑	172	Lenny Dykstra	.30	.14
❑	173	Ken Hill	.15	.07
❑	174	Mike Bordick	.15	.07
❑	175	Billy Hall	.15	.07
❑	176	Rob Butler	.15	.07
❑	177	Jay Bell	.30	.14
❑	178	Jeff Kent	.30	.14
❑	179	David Wells	.40	.18
❑	180	Dean Palmer	.30	.14
❑	181	Mariano Duncan	.15	.07
❑	182	Orlando Merced	.15	.07
❑	183	Brett Butler	.30	.14
❑	184	Milt Thompson	.15	.07
❑	185	Chipper Jones	2.00	.90
❑	186	Paul O'Neill	.30	.14
❑	187	Mike Greenwell	.15	.07
❑	188	Harold Baines	.30	.14
❑	189	Todd Stottlemyre	.15	.07
❑	190	Jeromy Burnitz	.30	.14
❑	191	Rene Arocha	.15	.07
❑	192	Jeff Fassero	.15	.07
❑	193	Robby Thompson	.15	.07
❑	194	Greg W. Harris	.15	.07
❑	195	Todd Van Poppel	.15	.07
❑	196	Jose Guzman	.15	.07
❑	197	Shane Mack	.15	.07
❑	198	Carlos Garcia	.15	.07
❑	199	Kevin Roberson	.15	.07
❑	200	David McCarty	.15	.07
❑	201	Alan Trammell	.40	.18
❑	202	Chuck Carr	.15	.07
❑	203	Tommy Greene	.15	.07
❑	204	Wilson Alvarez	.30	.14
❑	205	Dwight Gooden	.30	.14
❑	206	Tony Tarasco	.15	.07
❑	207	Darren Lewis	.15	.07
❑	208	Eric Karros	.30	.14
❑	209	Chris Hammond	.15	.07
❑	210	Jeffrey Hammonds	.30	.14
❑	211	Rich Amaral	.15	.07
❑	212	Danny Tartabull	.15	.07
❑	213	Jeff Russell	.15	.07
❑	214	Dave Staton	.15	.07
❑	215	Kenny Lofton	.60	.25
❑	216	Manuel Lee	.15	.07
❑	217	Brian Koelling	.15	.07
❑	218	Scott Lydy	.15	.07
❑	219	Tony Gwynn	1.50	.70
❑	220	Cecil Fielder	.30	.14
❑	221	Royce Clayton	.15	.07
❑	222	Reggie Sanders	.30	.14
❑	223	Brian Jordan	.30	.14
❑	224	Ken Griffey Jr.	3.00	1.35
❑	225	Fred McGriff	.40	.18
❑	226	Felix Jose	.15	.07
❑	227	Brad Pennington	.15	.07
❑	228	Chris Bosio	.15	.07
❑	229	Mike Stanley	.15	.07
❑	230	Willie Greene	.30	.14
❑	231	Alex Fernandez	.15	.07
❑	232	Brad Ausmus	.15	.07
❑	233	Darrell Whitmore	.15	.07
❑	234	Marcus Moore	.15	.07
❑	235	Allen Watson	.15	.07
❑	236	Jose Offerman	.15	.07
❑	237	Rondell White	.30	.14
❑	238	Jeff King	.15	.07
❑	239	Luis Alicea	.15	.07
❑	240	Dan Wilson	.15	.07
❑	241	Ed Sprague	.15	.07
❑	242	Todd Hundley	.30	.14
❑	243	Al Martin	.15	.07
❑	244	Mike Lansing	.30	.14
❑	245	Ivan Rodriguez	.75	.35
❑	246	Dave Fleming	.15	.07
❑	247	John Doherty	.15	.07
❑	248	Mark McLemore	.15	.07
❑	249	Bob Hamelin	.15	.07
❑	250	Curtis Pride	.15	.07
❑	251	Zane Smith	.15	.07
❑	252	Eric Young	.15	.07
❑	253	Brian McRae	.15	.07
❑	254	Tim Raines	.30	.14
❑	255	Javier Lopez	.40	.18
❑	256	Melvin Nieves	.15	.07
❑	257	Randy Myers	.15	.07
❑	258	Willie McGee	.30	.14
❑	259	Jimmy Key UER (birthdate missing on back)	.30	.14
❑	260	Tom Candiotti	.15	.07
❑	261	Eric Davis	.30	.14
❑	262	Craig Paquette	.15	.07
❑	263	Robin Ventura	.30	.14
❑	264	Pat Kelly	.15	.07
❑	265	Gregg Jefferies	.15	.07
❑	266	Cory Snyder	.15	.07
❑	267	David Justice HFA	.30	.14
❑	268	Sammy Sosa HFA	.75	.35
❑	269	Barry Larkin HFA	.15	.07
❑	270	Andres Galarraga HFA	.30	.14
❑	271	Gary Sheffield HFA	.30	.14
❑	272	Jeff Bagwell HFA	.75	.35
❑	273	Mike Piazza HFA	1.00	.45
❑	274	Larry Walker HFA	.30	.14
❑	275	Bobby Bonilla HFA	.15	.07
❑	276	John Kruk HFA	.15	.07
❑	277	Jay Bell HFA	.15	.07
❑	278	Ozzie Smith HFA	.60	.25
❑	279	Tony Gwynn HFA	.75	.35
❑	280	Barry Bonds HFA	.60	.25
❑	281	Cal Ripken Jr. HFA	1.25	.55
❑	282	Mo Vaughn HFA	.40	.18

283	Tim Salmon HFA	.30	.14
284	Frank Thomas HFA	1.00	.45
285	Albert Belle HFA	.40	.18
286	Cecil Fielder HFA	.15	.07
287	Wally Joyner HFA	.15	.07
288	Greg Vaughn HFA	.15	.07
289	Kirby Puckett HFA	.60	.25
290	Don Mattingly HFA	.40	.18
291	Terry Steinbach HFA	.15	.07
292	Ken Griffey Jr. HFA	1.50	.70
293	Juan Gonzalez HFA	.75	.35
294	Paul Molitor HFA	.30	.14
295	Tavo Alvarez UDCA	.15	.07
296	Matt Brunson UDC	.15	.07
297	Shawn Green UDC	.15	.07
298	Alex Rodriguez UDC	2.50	1.10
299	Shannon Stewart UDCA	.30	.14
300	Frank Thomas	2.00	.90
301	Mickey Tettleton	.15	.07
302	Pedro Munoz	.15	.07
303	Jose Valentin	.15	.07
304	Orestes Destrade	.15	.07
305	Pat Listach	.15	.07
306	Scott Brosius	.30	.14
307	Kurt Miller	.15	.07
308	Rob Dibble	.15	.07
309	Mike Blowers	.15	.07
310	Jim Abbott	.30	.14
311	Mike Jackson	.15	.07
312	Craig Biggio	.60	.25
313	Kurt Abbott	.15	.07
314	Chuck Finley	.30	.14
315	Andres Galarraga	.60	.25
316	Mike Moore	.15	.07
317	Doug Strange	.15	.07
318	Pedro Martinez	.75	.35
319	Kevin McReynolds	.15	.07
320	Greg Maddux	2.00	.90
321	Mike Henneman	.15	.07
322	Scott Leius	.15	.07
323	John Franco	.30	.14
324	Jeff Blauser	.15	.07
325	Kirby Puckett	1.00	.45
326	Darryl Hamilton	.15	.07
327	John Smiley	.15	.07
328	Derrick May	.15	.07
329	Jose Vizcaino	.15	.07
330	Randy Johnson	.60	.25
331	Jack Morris	.30	.14
332	Graeme Lloyd	.15	.07
333	Dave Valle	.15	.07
334	Greg Myers	.15	.07
335	John Wetteland	.30	.14
336	Jim Gott	.15	.07
337	Tim Naehring	.15	.07
338	Mike Kelly	.15	.07
339	Jeff Montgomery	.15	.07
340	Rafael Palmeiro	.40	.18
341	Eddie Murray	.60	.25
342	Xavier Hernandez	.15	.07
343	Bobby Munoz	.15	.07
344	Bobby Bonilla	.30	.14
345	Travis Fryman	.30	.14
346	Steve Finley	.30	.14
347	Chris Sabo	.15	.07
348	Armando Reynoso	.15	.07
349	Ramon Martinez	.30	.14
350	Will Clark	.60	.25
351	Moises Alou	.40	.18
352	Jim Thome	.75	.35
353	Bob Tewksbury	.15	.07
354	Andujar Cedeno	.15	.07
355	Orel Hershiser	.30	.14
356	Mike Devereaux	.15	.07
357	Mike Perez	.15	.07
358	Dennis Martinez	.30	.14
359	Dave Nilsson	.15	.07
360	Ozzie Smith	.75	.35
361	Eric Anthony	.15	.07
362	Scott Sanders	.15	.07
363	Paul Sorrento	.15	.07
364	Tim Belcher	.15	.07
365	Dennis Eckersley	.30	.14
366	Mel Rojas	.15	.07
367	Tom Henke	.15	.07
368	Randy Tomlin	.15	.07
369	B.J. Surhoff	.30	.14
370	Larry Walker	.60	.25
371	Joey Cora	.30	.14
372	Mike Harkey	.15	.07
373	John Valentin	.30	.14
374	Doug Jones	.15	.07
375	David Justice	.60	.25
376	Vince Coleman	.15	.07
377	David Hulse	.15	.07
378	Kevin Seitzer	.15	.07
379	Pete Harnisch	.15	.07
380	Ruben Sierra	.15	.07
381	Mark Lewis	.15	.07
382	Bip Roberts	.15	.07
383	Paul Wagner	.15	.07
384	Stan Javier	.15	.07
385	Barry Larkin	.40	.18
386	Mark Portugal	.15	.07
387	Roberto Kelly	.15	.07
388	Andy Benes	.30	.14
389	Felix Fermin	.15	.07
390	Marquis Grissom	.30	.14
391	Troy Neel	.15	.07
392	Chad Kreuter	.15	.07
393	Gregg Olson	.15	.07
394	Charles Nagy	.30	.14
395	Jack McDowell	.15	.07
396	Luis Gonzalez	.15	.07
397	Benito Santiago	.15	.07
398	Chris James	.15	.07
399	Terry Mulholland	.15	.07
400	Barry Bonds	.75	.35
401	Joe Grahe	.15	.07
402	Duane Ward	.15	.07
403	John Burkett	.15	.07
404	Scott Servais	.15	.07
405	Bryan Harvey	.15	.07
406	Bernard Gilkey	.15	.07
407	Greg McMichael	.15	.07
408	Tim Wallach	.15	.07
409	Ken Caminiti	.40	.18
410	John Kruk	.30	.14
411	Darrin Jackson	.15	.07
412	Mike Gallego	.15	.07
413	David Cone	.40	.18
414	Lou Whitaker	.30	.14
415	Sandy Alomar Jr.	.30	.14
416	Bill Wegman	.15	.07
417	Pat Borders	.15	.07
418	Roger Pavlik	.15	.07
419	Pete Smith	.15	.07
420	Steve Avery	.15	.07
421	David Segui	.30	.14
422	Rheal Cormier	.15	.07
423	Harold Reynolds	.15	.07
424	Edgar Martinez	.30	.14
425	Cal Ripken Jr.	2.50	1.10
426	Jaime Navarro	.15	.07
427	Sean Berry	.15	.07
428	Bret Saberhagen	.30	.14
429	Bob Welch	.15	.07
430	Juan Guzman	.15	.07
431	Cal Eldred	.15	.07
432	Dave Hollins	.15	.07
433	Sid Fernandez	.15	.07
434	Willie Banks	.15	.07
435	Darryl Kile	.30	.14
436	Henry Rodriguez	.30	.14
437	Tony Fernandez	.15	.07
438	Walt Weiss	.15	.07
439	Kevin Tapani	.15	.07
440	Mark Grace	.40	.18
441	Brian Harper	.15	.07
442	Kent Mercker	.15	.07
443	Anthony Young	.15	.07
444	Todd Zeile	.15	.07
445	Greg Vaughn	.30	.14
446	Ray Lankford	.30	.14
447	Dave Weathers	.15	.07
448	Bret Boone	.30	.14
449	Charlie Hough	.15	.07
450	Roger Clemens	1.25	.55
451	Mike Morgan	.15	.07
452	Doug Drabek	.15	.07
453	Danny Jackson	.15	.07
454	Dante Bichette	.30	.14
455	Roberto Alomar	.60	.25
456	Ben McDonald	.15	.07
457	Kenny Rogers	.15	.07
458	Bill Gullickson	.15	.07
459	Darrin Fletcher	.15	.07
460	Curt Schilling	.30	.14
461	Billy Hatcher	.15	.07
462	Howard Johnson	.15	.07
463	Mickey Morandini	.15	.07
464	Frank Castillo	.15	.07
465	Delino DeShields	.15	.07
466	Gary Gaetti	.30	.14
467	Steve Farr	.15	.07
468	Roberto Hernandez	.15	.07
469	Jack Armstrong	.15	.07
470	Paul Molitor	.60	.25
471	Melido Perez	.15	.07
472	Greg Hibbard	.15	.07
473	Jody Reed	.15	.07
474	Tom Gordon	.15	.07
475	Gary Sheffield	.60	.25
476	John Jaha	.15	.07
477	Shawon Dunston	.15	.07
478	Reggie Jefferson	.15	.07
479	Don Slaught	.15	.07
480	Jeff Bagwell	1.00	.45
481	Tim Pugh	.15	.07
482	Kevin Young	.15	.07
483	Ellis Burks	.30	.14
484	Greg Swindell	.15	.07
485	Mark Langston	.15	.07
486	Omar Vizquel	.30	.14
487	Kevin Brown	.30	.14
488	Terry Steinbach	.30	.14
489	Mark Lemke	.15	.07
490	Matt Williams	.40	.18
491	Pete Incaviglia	.15	.07
492	Karl Rhodes	.15	.07
493	Shawn Green	.30	.14
494	Hal Morris	.15	.07
495	Derek Bell	.30	.14
496	Luis Polonia	.15	.07
497	Otis Nixon	.15	.07
498	Ron Darling	.15	.07
499	Mitch Williams	.15	.07
500	Mike Piazza	2.00	.90
501	Pat Meares	.15	.07
502	Scott Cooper	.15	.07
503	Scott Erickson	.30	.14
504	Jeff Juden	.15	.07
505	Lee Smith	.30	.14
506	Bobby Ayala	.15	.07
507	Dave Henderson	.15	.07
508	Erik Hanson	.15	.07
509	Bob Wickman	.15	.07
510	Sammy Sosa	1.50	.70
511	Hector Carrasco	.15	.07
512	Tim Davis	.15	.07
513	Joey Hamilton DD	.60	.25
514	Robert Eenhoorn	.15	.07
515	Jorge Fabregas	.15	.07
516	Tim Hyers	.15	.07
517	John Hudek DD	.15	.07
518	James Mouton DD	.15	.07
519	Herbert Perry DD	.15	.07
520	Chan Ho Park DD	2.50	1.10
521	W.Van Landingham DD	.15	.07
522	Paul Shuey DD	.15	.07
523	Ryan Hancock TP	.15	.07
524	Billy Wagner TP	.75	.35
525	Jason Giambi	.40	.18
526	Jose Silva TP	.30	.14
527	Terrell Wade TP	.15	.07
528	Todd Dunn TP	.30	.14
529	Alan Benes TP	.75	.35
530	Brooks Kieschnick TP	.30	.14
531	Todd Hollandsworth TP	.15	.07
532	Brad Fullmer TP	2.00	.90
533	Steve Soderstrom TP	.15	.07
534	Daron Kirkreit	.15	.07
535	Arquimedez Pozo TP	.30	.14
536	Charles Johnson TP	.30	.14
537	Preston Wilson	.30	.14

❑ 538 Alex Ochoa	.15	.07
❑ 539 Derrek Lee TP	2.00	.90
❑ 540 Wayne Gomes TP	.15	.07
❑ 541 Jermaine Allensworth TP	.30	.14
❑ 542 Mike Bell TP	.15	.07
❑ 543 Trot Nixon TP	.75	.35
❑ 544 Pokey Reese	.30	.14
❑ 545 Neifi Perez TP	.75	.35
❑ 546 Johnny Damon TP	.30	.14
❑ 547 Matt Brunson TP	.15	.07
❑ 548 LaTroy Hawkins TP	.30	.14
❑ 549 Eddie Pearson TP	.30	.14
❑ 550 Derek Jeter TP	2.50	1.10
❑ A298 Alex Rodriguez AU	150.00	70.00
❑ P224 Ken Griffey Jr. Promo	3.00	1.35
❑ GM1 Ken Griffey Jr. AU Mickey Mantle AU/1000	1200.00	550.00
❑ KG1 Ken Griffey Jr. AU1000	250.00	110.00
❑ MM1 Mickey Mantle AU1000	600.00	275.00

1994 Upper Deck Diamond Collection

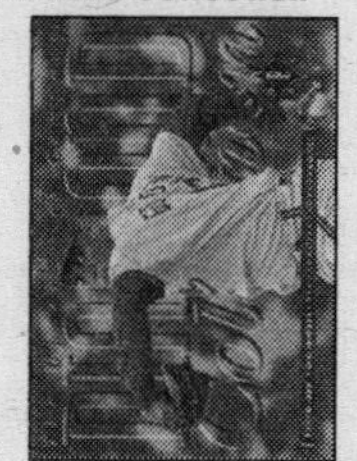

	MINT	NRMT
COMPLETE SET (30)	300.00	135.00
COMPLETE CENTRAL (10)	140.00	65.00
COMPLETE EAST (10)	60.00	27.00
COMPLETE WEST (10)	100.00	45.00
COMMON CARD	2.50	1.10

❑ C1 Jeff Bagwell	12.00	5.50
❑ C2 Michael Jordan	50.00	22.00
❑ C3 Barry Larkin	5.00	2.20
❑ C4 Kirby Puckett	12.00	5.50
❑ C5 Manny Ramirez	10.00	4.50
❑ C6 Ryne Sandberg	10.00	4.50
❑ C7 Ozzie Smith	10.00	4.50
❑ C8 Frank Thomas	25.00	11.00
❑ C9 Andy Van Slyke	2.50	1.10
❑ C10 Robin Yount	8.00	3.60
❑ E1 Roberto Alomar	8.00	3.60
❑ E2 Roger Clemens	15.00	6.75
❑ E3 Lenny Dykstra	2.50	1.10
❑ E4 Cecil Fielder	4.00	1.80
❑ E5 Cliff Floyd	2.50	1.10
❑ E6 Dwight Gooden	4.00	1.80
❑ E7 David Justice	8.00	3.60
❑ E8 Don Mattingly	12.00	5.50
❑ E9 Cal Ripken Jr.	30.00	13.50
❑ E10 Gary Sheffield	8.00	3.60
❑ W1 Barry Bonds	10.00	4.50
❑ W2 Andres Galarraga	8.00	3.60
❑ W3 Juan Gonzalez	20.00	9.00
❑ W4 Ken Griffey Jr.	40.00	18.00
❑ W5 Tony Gwynn	20.00	9.00
❑ W6 Rickey Henderson	8.00	3.60
❑ W7 Bo Jackson	4.00	1.80
❑ W8 Mark McGwire	40.00	18.00
❑ W9 Mike Piazza	25.00	11.00
❑ W10 Tim Salmon	8.00	3.60

1994 Upper Deck Griffey Jumbos

	MINT	NRMT
COMPLETE SET (4)	20.00	9.00
COMMON GRIFFEY (CL1-CL4)	4.00	1.80

❑ CL1 Numerical CL TP	4.00	1.80
❑ CL2 Alphabetical CL DP	5.00	2.20
❑ CL3 Team CL	6.00	2.70
❑ CL4 Insert CL SP	8.00	3.60

1994 Upper Deck Mantle Heroes

	MINT	NRMT
COMPLETE SET (10)	100.00	45.00
COMMON CARD (64-72/HDR)	12.00	5.50

❑ 64 Mickey Mantle 1951 The Early Years	12.00	5.50
❑ 65 Mickey Mantle 1953 Tape-Measure Home Runs	12.00	5.50
❑ 66 Mickey Mantle 1956 Triple Crown Season	12.00	5.50
❑ 67 Mickey Mantle 1957 Second Consecutive MVP	12.00	5.50
❑ 68 Mickey Mantle 1961 Chasing the Babe	12.00	5.50
❑ 69 Mickey Mantle 1964 Series Home Run Record	12.00	5.50
❑ 70 Mickey Mantle 1967 500th Home Run	12.00	5.50
❑ 71 Mickey Mantle 1974 Hall of Fame	12.00	5.50
❑ 72 Mickey Mantle Checklist	12.00	5.50
❑ NNO0 Mickey Mantle Header Card	12.00	5.50

1994 Upper Deck Mantle's Long Shots

	MINT	NRMT
COMPLETE SET (21)	50.00	22.00
COMMON CARD (MM1-MM21)	.50	.23
COMP.ELEC.DIAM.SET (21)	60.00	27.00

*ELEC.DIAMOND VERSIONS: 1.5X TO 4X BASIC CARDS
ONE ED SET VIA MAIL PER BLUE TRADE CARD
TRADES: RANDOM INS.IN SER.1 HOB.PACKS

❑ MM1 Jeff Bagwell	3.00	1.35
❑ MM2 Albert Belle	2.00	.90
❑ MM3 Barry Bonds	2.00	.90
❑ MM4 Jose Canseco	2.00	.90
❑ MM5 Joe Carter	1.00	.45
❑ MM6 Carlos Delgado	1.50	.70
❑ MM7 Cecil Fielder	1.00	.45
❑ MM8 Cliff Floyd	.50	.23
❑ MM9 Juan Gonzalez	5.00	2.20
❑ MM10 Ken Griffey Jr.	10.00	4.50
❑ MM11 David Justice	2.00	.90
❑ MM12 Fred McGriff	1.50	.70
❑ MM13 Mark McGwire	10.00	4.50
❑ MM14 Dean Palmer	1.00	.45
❑ MM15 Mike Piazza	6.00	2.70
❑ MM16 Manny Ramirez	2.00	.90
❑ MM17 Tim Salmon	2.00	.90
❑ MM18 Frank Thomas	6.00	2.70
❑ MM19 Mo Vaughn	2.00	.90
❑ MM20 Matt Williams	1.50	.70
❑ MM21 Mickey Mantle	15.00	6.75
❑ NNO M.Mantle Blue ED Trade	12.00	5.50
❑ NNO M.Mantle Silver Trade	6.00	2.70

1994 Upper Deck Next Generation

	MINT	NRMT
COMPLETE SET (18)	150.00	70.00
COMMON CARD (1-18)	1.50	.70
COMP.ELEC.DIAM.SET (18)	180.00	80.00

*ELEC.DIAMOND: .5X BASIC CARDS
ONE ED SET VIA MAIL PER ED TRADE CARD
TRADES: RANDOM INS.IN SER.2 HOB.PACKS

❑ 1 Roberto Alomar	6.00	2.70
❑ 2 Carlos Delgado	4.00	1.80
❑ 3 Cliff Floyd	2.50	1.10
❑ 4 Alex Gonzalez	1.50	.70
❑ 5 Juan Gonzalez	15.00	6.75
❑ 6 Ken Griffey Jr.	30.00	13.50
❑ 7 Jeffrey Hammonds	2.50	1.10
❑ 8 Michael Jordan	40.00	18.00
❑ 9 David Justice	6.00	2.70
❑ 10 Ryan Klesko	2.50	1.10
❑ 11 Javier Lopez	4.00	1.80
❑ 12 Raul Mondesi	6.00	2.70
❑ 13 Mike Piazza	20.00	9.00
❑ 14 Kirby Puckett	10.00	4.50
❑ 15 Manny Ramirez	8.00	3.60

#	Player	MINT	NRMT
16	Alex Rodriguez	40.00	18.00
17	Tim Salmon	6.00	2.70
18	Gary Sheffield	6.00	2.70
NNO	Expired NG Trade Card	4.00	1.80
NNO	Expired NG Trade Card	4.00	1.80

1995 Upper Deck

	MINT	NRMT
COMPLETE SET (450)	60.00	27.00
COMPLETE SERIES 1 (225)	30.00	13.50
COMPLETE SERIES 2 (225)	30.00	13.50
COMMON CARD (1-450)	.15	.07
COMP.TRADE SET (45)	20.00	9.00
COMMON TRADE (451T-495T)	.25	.11

#	Player	MINT	NRMT
1	Ruben Rivera	.30	.14
2	Bill Pulsipher	.15	.07
3	Ben Grieve	4.00	1.80
4	Curtis Goodwin	.15	.07
5	Damon Hollins	.15	.07
6	Todd Greene	.30	.14
7	Glenn Williams	.30	.14
8	Bret Wagner	.15	.07
9	Karim Garcia	1.00	.45
10	Nomar Garciaparra	4.00	1.80
11	Raul Casanova	.15	.07
12	Matt Smith	.15	.07
13	Paul Wilson	.15	.07
14	Jason Isringhausen	.30	.14
15	Reid Ryan	.30	.14
16	Lee Smith	.30	.14
17	Chili Davis	.30	.14
18	Brian Anderson	.30	.14
19	Gary DiSarcina	.15	.07
20	Bo Jackson	.30	.14
21	Chuck Finley	.30	.14
22	Darryl Kile	.30	.14
23	Shane Reynolds	.30	.14
24	Tony Eusebio	.15	.07
25	Craig Biggio	.60	.25
26	Doug Drabek	.15	.07
27	Brian L. Hunter	.30	.14
28	James Mouton	.15	.07
29	Geronimo Berroa	.15	.07
30	Rickey Henderson	.60	.25
31	Steve Karsay	.15	.07
32	Steve Ontiveros	.15	.07
33	Ernie Young	.15	.07
34	Dennis Eckersley	.30	.14
35	Mark McGwire	3.00	1.35
36	Dave Stewart	.30	.14
37	Pat Hentgen	.30	.14
38	Carlos Delgado	.30	.14
39	Joe Carter	.30	.14
40	Roberto Alomar	.60	.25
41	John Olerud	.30	.14
42	Devon White	.30	.14
43	Roberto Kelly	.15	.07
44	Jeff Blauser	.15	.07
45	Fred McGriff	.40	.18
46	Tom Glavine	.60	.25
47	Mike Kelly	.15	.07
48	Javier Lopez	.30	.14
49	Greg Maddux	2.00	.90
50	Matt Mieske	.15	.07
51	Troy O'Leary	.30	.14
52	Jeff Cirillo	.30	.14
53	Cal Eldred	.15	.07
54	Pat Listach	.15	.07
55	Jose Valentin	.15	.07
56	John Mabry	.15	.07
57	Bob Tewksbury	.15	.07
58	Brian Jordan	.30	.14
59	Gregg Jefferies	.15	.07
60	Ozzie Smith	.75	.35
61	Geronimo Pena	.15	.07
62	Mark Whiten	.15	.07
63	Rey Sanchez	.15	.07
64	Willie Banks	.15	.07
65	Mark Grace	.40	.18
66	Randy Myers	.15	.07
67	Steve Trachsel	.15	.07
68	Derrick May	.15	.07
69	Brett Butler	.30	.14
70	Eric Karros	.30	.14
71	Tim Wallach	.15	.07
72	Delino DeShields	.15	.07
73	Darren Dreifort	.30	.14
74	Orel Hershiser	.30	.14
75	Billy Ashley	.15	.07
76	Sean Berry	.15	.07
77	Ken Hill	.15	.07
78	John Wetteland	.30	.14
79	Moises Alou	.40	.18
80	Cliff Floyd	.30	.14
81	Marquis Grissom	.30	.14
82	Larry Walker	.60	.25
83	Rondell White	.30	.14
84	William VanLandingham	.15	.07
85	Matt Williams	.30	.14
86	Rod Beck	.15	.07
87	Darren Lewis	.15	.07
88	Robby Thompson	.15	.07
89	Darryl Strawberry	.30	.14
90	Kenny Lofton	.60	.25
91	Charles Nagy	.30	.14
92	Sandy Alomar Jr.	.30	.14
93	Mark Clark	.15	.07
94	Dennis Martinez	.30	.14
95	Dave Winfield	.60	.25
96	Jim Thome	.60	.25
97	Manny Ramirez	.60	.25
98	Goose Gossage	.30	.14
99	Tino Martinez	.60	.25
100	Ken Griffey Jr.	3.00	1.35
101	Greg Maddux ANA	1.00	.45
102	Randy Johnson ANA	.30	.14
103	Barry Bonds ANA	.40	.18
104	Juan Gonzalez ANA	.75	.35
105	Frank Thomas ANA	1.00	.45
106	Matt Williams ANA	.15	.07
107	Paul Molitor ANA	.30	.14
108	Fred McGriff ANA	.15	.07
109	Carlos Baerga ANA	.15	.07
110	Ken Griffey Jr. ANA	1.50	.70
111	Reggie Jefferson	.15	.07
112	Randy Johnson	.60	.25
113	Marc Newfield	.15	.07
114	Robb Nen	.15	.07
115	Jeff Conine	.30	.14
116	Kurt Abbott	.15	.07
117	Charlie Hough	.15	.07
118	Dave Weathers	.15	.07
119	Juan Castillo	.15	.07
120	Bret Saberhagen	.30	.14
121	Rico Brogna	.15	.07
122	John Franco	.30	.14
123	Todd Hundley	.30	.14
124	Jason Jacome	.15	.07
125	Bobby Jones	.15	.07
126	Bret Barberie	.15	.07
127	Ben McDonald	.15	.07
128	Harold Baines	.30	.14
129	Jeffrey Hammonds	.30	.14
130	Mike Mussina	.60	.25
131	Chris Hoiles	.15	.07
132	Brady Anderson	.30	.14
133	Eddie Williams	.15	.07
134	Andy Benes	.30	.14
135	Tony Gwynn	1.50	.70
136	Bip Roberts	.15	.07
137	Joey Hamilton	.30	.14
138	Luis Lopez	.15	.07
139	Ray McDavid	.15	.07
140	Lenny Dykstra	.30	.14
141	Mariano Duncan	.15	.07
142	Fernando Valenzuela	.30	.14
143	Bobby Munoz	.15	.07
144	Kevin Stocker	.15	.07
145	John Kruk	.30	.14
146	Jon Lieber	.15	.07
147	Zane Smith	.15	.07
148	Steve Cooke	.15	.07
149	Andy Van Slyke	.30	.14
150	Jay Bell	.30	.14
151	Carlos Garcia	.15	.07
152	John Dettmer	.15	.07
153	Darren Oliver	.15	.07
154	Dean Palmer	.30	.14
155	Otis Nixon	.15	.07
156	Rusty Greer	.60	.25
157	Rick Helling	.30	.14
158	Jose Canseco	.60	.25
159	Roger Clemens	1.25	.55
160	Andre Dawson	.40	.18
161	Mo Vaughn	.75	.35
162	Aaron Sele	.30	.14
163	John Valentin	.30	.14
164	Brian R. Hunter	.15	.07
165	Bret Boone	.30	.14
166	Hector Carrasco	.15	.07
167	Pete Schourek	.15	.07
168	Willie Greene	.30	.14
169	Kevin Mitchell	.15	.07
170	Deion Sanders	.30	.14
171	John Roper	.15	.07
172	Charlie Hayes	.15	.07
173	David Nied	.15	.07
174	Ellis Burks	.30	.14
175	Dante Bichette	.30	.14
176	Marvin Freeman	.15	.07
177	Eric Young	.15	.07
178	David Cone	.40	.18
179	Greg Gagne	.15	.07
180	Bob Hamelin	.15	.07
181	Wally Joyner	.30	.14
182	Jeff Montgomery	.15	.07
183	Jose Lind	.15	.07
184	Chris Gomez	.15	.07
185	Travis Fryman	.30	.14
186	Kirk Gibson	.30	.14
187	Mike Moore	.15	.07
188	Lou Whitaker	.30	.14
189	Sean Bergman	.15	.07
190	Shane Mack	.15	.07
191	Rick Aguilera	.15	.07
192	Denny Hocking	.15	.07
193	Chuck Knoblauch	.60	.25
194	Kevin Tapani	.15	.07
195	Kent Hrbek	.15	.07
196	Ozzie Guillen	.15	.07
197	Wilson Alvarez	.30	.14
198	Tim Raines	.30	.14
199	Scott Ruffcorn	.15	.07
200	Michael Jordan	3.00	1.35
201	Robin Ventura	.30	.14
202	Jason Bere	.15	.07
203	Darrin Jackson	.15	.07
204	Russ Davis	.30	.14
205	Jimmy Key	.30	.14
206	Jack McDowell	.15	.07
207	Jim Abbott	.30	.14
208	Paul O'Neill	.30	.14
209	Bernie Williams	.60	.25
210	Don Mattingly	1.00	.45
211	Orlando Miller	.15	.07
212	Alex Gonzalez	.15	.07
213	Terrell Wade	.15	.07
214	Jose Oliva	.15	.07
215	Alex Rodriguez	2.50	1.10
216	Garret Anderson	.30	.14
217	Alan Benes	.30	.14
218	Armando Benitez	.15	.07
219	Dustin Hermanson	.30	.14
220	Charles Johnson	.30	.14
221	Julian Tavarez	.15	.07
222	Jason Giambi	.30	.14

❑ 223	LaTroy Hawkins	.15	.07
❑ 224	Todd Hollandsworth	.15	.07
❑ 225	Derek Jeter	2.00	.90
❑ 226	Hideo Nomo	2.50	1.10
❑ 227	Tony Clark	.60	.25
❑ 228	Roger Cedeno	.15	.07
❑ 229	Scott Stahoviak	.15	.07
❑ 230	Michael Tucker	.30	.14
❑ 231	Joe Rosselli	.15	.07
❑ 232	Antonio Osuna	.15	.07
❑ 233	Bobby Higginson	1.50	.70
❑ 234	Mark Grudzielanek	.50	.23
❑ 235	Ray Durham	.30	.14
❑ 236	Frank Rodriguez	.15	.07
❑ 237	Quilvio Veras	.15	.07
❑ 238	Darren Bragg	.15	.07
❑ 239	Ugueth Urbina	.15	.07
❑ 240	Jason Bates	.15	.07
❑ 241	David Bell	.15	.07
❑ 242	Ron Villone	.15	.07
❑ 243	Joe Randa	.15	.07
❑ 244	Carlos Perez	.50	.23
❑ 245	Brad Clontz	.15	.07
❑ 246	Steve Rodriguez	.15	.07
❑ 247	Joe Vitiello	.15	.07
❑ 248	Ozzie Timmons	.15	.07
❑ 249	Rudy Pemberton	.15	.07
❑ 250	Marty Cordova	.15	.07
❑ 251	Tony Graffanino	.15	.07
❑ 252	Mark Johnson	.15	.07
❑ 253	Tomas Perez	.30	.14
❑ 254	Jimmy Hurst	.15	.07
❑ 255	Edgardo Alfonzo	.30	.14
❑ 256	Jose Malave	.15	.07
❑ 257	Brad Radke	.75	.35
❑ 258	Jon Nunnally	.15	.07
❑ 259	Dilson Torres	.15	.07
❑ 260	Esteban Loaiza	.15	.07
❑ 261	Freddy Garcia	.15	.07
❑ 262	Don Wengert	.15	.07
❑ 263	Robert Person	.15	.07
❑ 264	Tim Unroe	.15	.07
❑ 265	Juan Acevedo	.15	.07
❑ 266	Eduardo Perez	.15	.07
❑ 267	Tony Phillips	.15	.07
❑ 268	Jim Edmonds	.40	.18
❑ 269	Jorge Fabregas	.15	.07
❑ 270	Tim Salmon	.60	.25
❑ 271	Mark Langston	.15	.07
❑ 272	J.T. Snow	.30	.14
❑ 273	Phil Plantier	.15	.07
❑ 274	Derek Bell	.30	.14
❑ 275	Jeff Bagwell	1.00	.45
❑ 276	Luis Gonzalez	.15	.07
❑ 277	John Hudek	.15	.07
❑ 278	Todd Stottlemyre	.15	.07
❑ 279	Mark Acre	.15	.07
❑ 280	Ruben Sierra	.15	.07
❑ 281	Mike Bordick	.15	.07
❑ 282	Ron Darling	.15	.07
❑ 283	Brent Gates	.15	.07
❑ 284	Todd Van Poppel	.15	.07
❑ 285	Paul Molitor	.60	.25
❑ 286	Ed Sprague	.15	.07
❑ 287	Juan Guzman	.15	.07
❑ 288	David Cone	.40	.18
❑ 289	Shawn Green	.30	.14
❑ 290	Marquis Grissom	.30	.14
❑ 291	Kent Mercker	.15	.07
❑ 292	Steve Avery	.15	.07
❑ 293	Chipper Jones	1.50	.70
❑ 294	John Smoltz	.30	.14
❑ 295	David Justice	.60	.25
❑ 296	Ryan Klesko	.30	.14
❑ 297	Joe Oliver	.15	.07
❑ 298	Ricky Bones	.15	.07
❑ 299	John Jaha	.15	.07
❑ 300	Greg Vaughn	.30	.14
❑ 301	Dave Nilsson	.15	.07
❑ 302	Kevin Seitzer	.15	.07
❑ 303	Bernard Gilkey	.15	.07
❑ 304	Allen Battle	.15	.07
❑ 305	Ray Lankford	.30	.14
❑ 306	Tom Pagnozzi	.15	.07
❑ 307	Allen Watson	.15	.07
❑ 308	Danny Jackson	.15	.07
❑ 309	Ken Hill	.15	.07
❑ 310	Todd Zeile	.15	.07
❑ 311	Kevin Roberson	.15	.07
❑ 312	Steve Buechele	.15	.07
❑ 313	Rick Wilkins	.15	.07
❑ 314	Kevin Foster	.15	.07
❑ 315	Sammy Sosa	1.50	.70
❑ 316	Howard Johnson	.15	.07
❑ 317	Greg Hansell	.15	.07
❑ 318	Pedro Astacio	.15	.07
❑ 319	Rafael Bournigal	.15	.07
❑ 320	Mike Piazza	2.00	.90
❑ 321	Ramon Martinez	.30	.14
❑ 322	Raul Mondesi	.40	.18
❑ 323	Ismael Valdes	.30	.14
❑ 324	Wil Cordero	.15	.07
❑ 325	Tony Tarasco	.15	.07
❑ 326	Roberto Kelly	.15	.07
❑ 327	Jeff Fassero	.15	.07
❑ 328	Mike Lansing	.15	.07
❑ 329	Pedro J. Martinez	.60	.25
❑ 330	Kirk Rueter	.15	.07
❑ 331	Glenallen Hill	.15	.07
❑ 332	Kirt Manwaring	.15	.07
❑ 333	Royce Clayton	.15	.07
❑ 334	J.R. Phillips	.15	.07
❑ 335	Barry Bonds	.75	.35
❑ 336	Mark Portugal	.15	.07
❑ 337	Terry Mulholland	.15	.07
❑ 338	Omar Vizquel	.30	.14
❑ 339	Carlos Baerga	.30	.14
❑ 340	Albert Belle	.75	.35
❑ 341	Eddie Murray	.60	.25
❑ 342	Wayne Kirby	.15	.07
❑ 343	Chad Ogea	.15	.07
❑ 344	Tim Davis	.15	.07
❑ 345	Jay Buhner	.30	.14
❑ 346	Bobby Ayala	.15	.07
❑ 347	Mike Blowers	.15	.07
❑ 348	Dave Fleming	.15	.07
❑ 349	Edgar Martinez	.30	.14
❑ 350	Andre Dawson	.40	.18
❑ 351	Darrell Whitmore	.15	.07
❑ 352	Chuck Carr	.15	.07
❑ 353	John Burkett	.15	.07
❑ 354	Chris Hammond	.15	.07
❑ 355	Gary Sheffield	.40	.18
❑ 356	Pat Rapp	.15	.07
❑ 357	Greg Colbrunn	.15	.07
❑ 358	David Segui	.30	.14
❑ 359	Jeff Kent	.30	.14
❑ 360	Bobby Bonilla	.30	.14
❑ 361	Pete Harnisch	.15	.07
❑ 362	Ryan Thompson	.15	.07
❑ 363	Jose Vizcaino	.15	.07
❑ 364	Brett Butler	.30	.14
❑ 365	Cal Ripken Jr.	2.50	1.10
❑ 366	Rafael Palmeiro	.40	.18
❑ 367	Leo Gomez	.15	.07
❑ 368	Andy Van Slyke	.30	.14
❑ 369	Arthur Rhodes	.15	.07
❑ 370	Ken Caminiti	.40	.18
❑ 371	Steve Finley	.30	.14
❑ 372	Melvin Nieves	.15	.07
❑ 373	Andujar Cedeno	.15	.07
❑ 374	Trevor Hoffman	.30	.14
❑ 375	Fernando Valenzuela	.30	.14
❑ 376	Ricky Bottalico	.30	.14
❑ 377	Dave Hollins	.15	.07
❑ 378	Charlie Hayes	.15	.07
❑ 379	Tommy Greene	.15	.07
❑ 380	Darren Daulton	.30	.14
❑ 381	Curt Schilling	.30	.14
❑ 382	Midre Cummings	.15	.07
❑ 383	Al Martin	.15	.07
❑ 384	Jeff King	.15	.07
❑ 385	Orlando Merced	.15	.07
❑ 386	Denny Neagle	.30	.14
❑ 387	Don Slaught	.15	.07
❑ 388	Dave Clark	.15	.07
❑ 389	Kevin Gross	.15	.07
❑ 390	Will Clark	.60	.25
❑ 391	Ivan Rodriguez	.75	.35
❑ 392	Benji Gil	.15	.07
❑ 393	Jeff Frye	.15	.07
❑ 394	Kenny Rogers	.15	.07
❑ 395	Juan Gonzalez	1.50	.70
❑ 396	Mike Macfarlane	.15	.07
❑ 397	Lee Tinsley	.15	.07
❑ 398	Tim Naehring	.15	.07
❑ 399	Tim Vanegmond	.15	.07
❑ 400	Mike Greenwell	.15	.07
❑ 401	Ken Ryan	.15	.07
❑ 402	John Smiley	.15	.07
❑ 403	Tim Pugh	.15	.07
❑ 404	Reggie Sanders	.30	.14
❑ 405	Barry Larkin	.40	.18
❑ 406	Hal Morris	.15	.07
❑ 407	Jose Rijo	.15	.07
❑ 408	Lance Painter	.15	.07
❑ 409	Joe Girardi	.15	.07
❑ 410	Andres Galarraga	.60	.25
❑ 411	Mike Kingery	.15	.07
❑ 412	Roberto Mejia	.15	.07
❑ 413	Walt Weiss	.15	.07
❑ 414	Bill Swift	.15	.07
❑ 415	Larry Walker	.60	.25
❑ 416	Billy Brewer	.15	.07
❑ 417	Pat Borders	.15	.07
❑ 418	Tom Gordon	.15	.07
❑ 419	Kevin Appier	.30	.14
❑ 420	Gary Gaetti	.30	.14
❑ 421	Greg Gohr	.15	.07
❑ 422	Felipe Lira	.15	.07
❑ 423	John Doherty	.15	.07
❑ 424	Chad Curtis	.15	.07
❑ 425	Cecil Fielder	.30	.14
❑ 426	Alan Trammell	.30	.14
❑ 427	David McCarty	.15	.07
❑ 428	Scott Erickson	.30	.14
❑ 429	Pat Mahomes	.15	.07
❑ 430	Kirby Puckett	1.00	.45
❑ 431	Dave Stevens	.15	.07
❑ 432	Pedro Munoz	.15	.07
❑ 433	Chris Sabo	.15	.07
❑ 434	Alex Fernandez	.15	.07
❑ 435	Frank Thomas	2.00	.90
❑ 436	Roberto Hernandez	.15	.07
❑ 437	Lance Johnson	.15	.07
❑ 438	Jim Abbott	.30	.14
❑ 439	John Wetteland	.30	.14
❑ 440	Melido Perez	.15	.07
❑ 441	Tony Fernandez	.15	.07
❑ 442	Pat Kelly	.15	.07
❑ 443	Mike Stanley	.15	.07
❑ 444	Danny Tartabull	.15	.07
❑ 445	Wade Boggs	.60	.25
❑ 446	Robin Yount	.60	.25
❑ 447	Ryne Sandberg	.75	.35
❑ 448	Nolan Ryan	2.50	1.10
❑ 449	George Brett	1.25	.55
❑ 450	Mike Schmidt	.75	.35
❑ 451	Jim Abbott TRADE	.35	.16
❑ 452	Danny Tartabull TRADE	.25	.11
❑ 453	Ariel Prieto TRADE	.25	.11
❑ 454	Scott Cooper TRADE	.25	.11
❑ 455	Tom Henke TRADE	.25	.11
❑ 456	Todd Zeile TRADE	.25	.11
❑ 457	Brian McRae TRADE	.25	.11
❑ 458	Luis Gonzalez TRADE	.25	.11
❑ 459	Jaime Navarro TRADE	.25	.11
❑ 460	Todd Worrell TRADE	.25	.11
❑ 461	Roberto Kelly TRADE	.25	.11
❑ 462	Chad Fonville TRADE	.25	.11
❑ 463	Shane Andrews TRADE	.25	.11
❑ 464	David Segui TRADE	.35	.16
❑ 465	Deion Sanders TRADE	.35	.16
❑ 466	Orel Hershiser TRADE	.35	.16
❑ 467	Ken Hill TRADE	.25	.11
❑ 468	Andy Benes TRADE	.35	.16
❑ 469	Terry Pendleton TRADE	.25	.11
❑ 470	Bobby Bonilla TRADE	.35	.16
❑ 471	Scott Erickson TRADE	.35	.16
❑ 472	Kevin Brown TRADE	.50	.23
❑ 473	Glenn Dishman TRADE	.35	.16
❑ 474	Phil Plantier TRADE	.25	.11
❑ 475	Gregg Jefferies TRADE	.25	.11
❑ 476	Tyler Green TRADE	.25	.11
❑ 477	H. Slocumb TRADE	.25	.11

❑ 478 Mark Whiten TRADE...... .25 .11
❑ 479 Mickey Tettleton TRADE .25 .11
❑ 480 Tim Wakefield TRADE .. .35 .16
❑ 481 V. Eshelman TRADE...... .25 .11
❑ 482 Rick Aguilera TRADE .... .25 .11
❑ 483 Erik Hanson TRADE ...... .25 .11
❑ 484 Willie McGee TRADE ...... .35 .16
❑ 485 Troy O'Leary TRADE .... .35 .16
❑ 486 Benito Santiago TRADE .25 .11
❑ 487 Darren Lewis TRADE .... .25 .11
❑ 488 Dave Burba TRADE ...... .25 .11
❑ 489 Ron Gant TRADE .... .25 .11
❑ 490 Bret Saberhagen TRADE .35 .16
❑ 491 Vinny Castilla TRADE .... .50 .23
❑ 492 Frank Rodriguez TRADE .35 .16
❑ 493 Andy Pettitte TRADE.... 6.00 2.70
❑ 494 Ruben Sierra TRADE .... .25 .11
❑ 495 David Cone TRADE ...... .50 .23
❑ J159 R. Clemens Jumbo AU 50.00 22.00
❑ J215 A. Rodriguez Jumbo AU 80.00 36.00
❑ P100 Ken Griffey Jr. Promo 3.00 1.35
❑ TC1 Orel Hershiser .... 1.00 .45
❑ TC2 Terry Pendleton .... 1.00 .45
❑ TC3 Benito Santiago .... 1.00 .45
❑ TC4 Kevin Brown .... 1.00 .45
❑ TC5 Gregg Jefferies............ 1.00 .45

1995 Upper Deck Autographs

	MINT	NRMT
COMPLETE SET (5)	250.00	110.00
COMMON CARD	30.00	13.50

❑ 1 Roger Clemens.............. 60.00 27.00
❑ 2 Reggie Jackson............. 40.00 18.00
❑ 3 Willie Mays 100.00 45.00
❑ 4 Raul Mondesi 30.00 13.50
❑ 5 Frank Robinson.............. 40.00 18.00

1995 Upper Deck Checklists

	MINT	NRMT
COMPLETE SET (5)	15.00	6.75
COMPLETE SERIES 1 (5)........	6.00	2.70
COMPLETE SERIES 2 (5)......	10.00	4.50
COMMON CARD (1A-5B)	.75	.35

❑ 1A Montreal Expos................ .75 .35
❑ 2A Fred McGriff .... 1.25 .55
❑ 3A John Valentin .... 1.00 .45
❑ 4A Kenny Rogers.................. .75 .35
❑ 5A Greg Maddux 6.00 2.70
❑ 1B Cecil Fielder .... 1.00 .45
❑ 2B Tony Gwynn 3.00 1.35
❑ 3B Greg Maddux 6.00 2.70
❑ 4B Randy Johnson............... 1.25 .55
❑ 5B Mike Schmidt 2.50 1.10

1995 Upper Deck Predictor Award Winners

	MINT	NRMT
COMPLETE SET (40)	100.00	45.00
COMPLETE SERIES 1 (20)....	60.00	27.00
COMPLETE SERIES 2 (20)....	40.00	18.00
COMMON CARD (H1-H40)	.50	.23
COMP.SER.1 EXCH.SET (20)	15.00	6.75
COMP.SER.2 EXCH.SET (20)	10.00	4.50

*AW EXCH.CARDS: .4X BASIC CARDS
ONE EXCH.SET VIA MAIL PER PRED.WINNER

❑ H1 Albert Belle MVP .... 2.00 .90
❑ H2 Juan Gonzalez MVP...... 5.00 2.20
❑ H3 Ken Griffey Jr. MVP 10.00 4.50
❑ H4 Kirby Puckett MVP .... 2.00 .90
❑ H5 Frank Thomas MVP 6.00 2.70
❑ H6 Jeff Bagwell MVP 3.00 1.35
❑ H7 Barry Bonds MVP.......... 2.00 .90
❑ H8 Mike Piazza MVP 6.00 2.70
❑ H9 Matt Williams MVP .... 1.00 .45
❑ H10 MVP Wild Card.............. .50 .23
❑ H11 Armando Benitez ROY.. .50 .23
❑ H12 Alex Gonzalez ROY ...... .50 .23
❑ H13 Shawn Green ROY...... 1.00 .45
❑ H14 Derek Jeter ROY 8.00 3.60
❑ H15 Alex Rodriguez ROY .. 8.00 3.60
❑ H16 Alan Benes ROY .... 1.00 .45
❑ H17 Brian L.Hunter ROY .... 1.00 .45
❑ H18 Charles Johnson ROY 1.00 .45
❑ H19 Jose Oliva ROY .... .50 .23
❑ H20 ROY Wild Card.............. .50 .23
❑ H21 Cal Ripken MVP 8.00 3.60
❑ H22 Don Mattingly MVP...... 3.00 1.35
❑ H23 Roberto Alomar MVP .. 2.00 .90
❑ H24 Kenny Lofton MVP ...... 2.00 .90
❑ H25 Will Clark MVP .... 2.00 .90
❑ H26 Mark McGwire MVP .. 10.00 4.50
❑ H27 Greg Maddux MVP...... 6.00 2.70
❑ H28 Fred McGriff MVP....... 1.50 .70
❑ H29 Andres Galarraga MVP 2.00 .90
❑ H30 Jose Canseco MVP .... 2.00 .90
❑ H31 Ray Durham ROY........ 1.00 .45
❑ H32 Mark Grudzielanek ROY 2.00 .90
❑ H33 Scott Ruffcorn ROY ...... .50 .23
❑ H34 Michael Tucker ROY .. 1.00 .45
❑ H35 Garret Anderson ROY 1.00 .45
❑ H36 Darren Bragg ROY .... .50 .23
❑ H37 Quilvio Veras ROY .... .50 .23
❑ H38 Hideo Nomo ROY W .. 4.00 1.80
❑ H39 Chipper Jones ROY 5.00 2.20
❑ H40 Marty Cordova ROY W.. .50 .23

1995 Upper Deck Predictor League Leaders

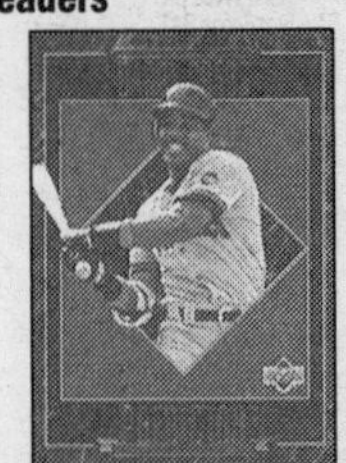

	MINT	NRMT
COMPLETE SET (60)	130.00	57.50
COMPLETE SERIES 1 (30)....	80.00	36.00
COMPLETE SERIES 2 (30)....	50.00	22.00
COMMON CARD (R1-R60)........	.50	.23
COMP.SER.1 EXCH.SET (30)	20.00	9.00
COMP.SER.2 EXCH.SET (30)	12.00	5.50

*LL EXCH.CARDS: .4X BASIC CARDS
ONE EXCH.SET VIA MAIL PER PRED.WINNER

❑ R1 Albert Belle HR W.......... 2.50 1.10
❑ R2 Jose Canseco HR.......... 2.00 .90
❑ R3 Juan Gonzalez HR 5.00 2.20
❑ R4 Ken Griffey Jr. HR 10.00 4.50
❑ R5 Frank Thomas HR 6.00 2.70
❑ R6 Jeff Bagwell HR 3.00 1.35
❑ R7 Barry Bonds HR .... 2.00 .90
❑ R8 Fred McGriff HR .... 1.50 .70
❑ R9 Matt Williams HR .... 1.00 .45
❑ R10 HR WC W (Bichette) .... .50 .23
❑ R11 Albert Belle RBI W .... 2.00 .90
❑ R12 Joe Carter RBI .... 1.00 .45
❑ R13 Cecil Fielder RBI.......... 1.00 .45
❑ R14 Kirby Puckett RBI .... 2.00 .90
❑ R15 Frank Thomas RBI 6.00 2.70
❑ R16 Jeff Bagwell RBI 3.00 1.35
❑ R17 Barry Bonds RBI.......... 2.00 .90
❑ R18 Mike Piazza RBI 6.00 2.70
❑ R19 Matt Williams RBI .... 1.00 .45
❑ R20 RBI WC W (M.Vaughn) .50 .23
❑ R21 Wade Boggs BAT........ 2.00 .90
❑ R22 Kenny Lofton BAT ...... 2.00 .90
❑ R23 Paul Molitor BAT.......... 2.00 .90
❑ R24 Paul O'Neill BAT.......... 1.00 .45
❑ R25 Frank Thomas BAT 6.00 2.70
❑ R26 Jeff Bagwell BAT 3.00 1.35
❑ R27 Tony Gwynn BAT W.... 5.00 2.20
❑ R28 Gregg Jefferies BAT...... .50 .23
❑ R29 Hal Morris BAT .... .50 .23
❑ R30 Batting WC W (E.Martinez) .50
.23
❑ R31 Joe Carter HR.............. 1.00 .45
❑ R32 Cecil Fielder HR .... 1.00 .45
❑ R33 Rafael Palmeiro HR .... 1.50 .70
❑ R34 Larry Walker HR.......... 2.00 .90
❑ R35 Manny Ramirez HR .... 2.00 .90
❑ R36 Tim Salmon HR .... 2.00 .90
❑ R37 Mike Piazza HR 6.00 2.70
❑ R38 Andres Galarraga HR.. 2.00 .90
❑ R39 David Justice HR .... 2.00 .90
❑ R40 Gary Sheffield HR........ 1.50 .70
❑ R41 Juan Gonzalez RBI...... 5.00 2.20
❑ R42 Jose Canseco RBI ...... 2.00 .90
❑ R43 Will Clark RBI .... 2.00 .90
❑ R44 Rafael Palmeiro RBI.... 1.50 .70
❑ R45 Ken Griffey Jr. RBI 10.00 4.50
❑ R46 Ruben Sierra RBI .... .50 .23
❑ R47 Larry Walker RBI .... 2.00 .90
❑ R48 Fred McGriff RBI.......... 1.50 .70
❑ R49 Dante Bichette RBI W.. 1.00 .45
❑ R50 Darren Daulton RBI .... 1.00 .45
❑ R51 Will Clark BAT .... 2.00 .90
❑ R52 Ken Griffey Jr. BAT.... 10.00 4.50

❑ R53 Don Mattingly BAT	4.00	1.80
❑ R54 John Olerud BAT	1.00	.45
❑ R55 Kirby Puckett BAT	2.00	.90
❑ R56 Raul Mondesi BAT	1.50	.70
❑ R57 Moises Alou BAT	.50	.23
❑ R58 Bret Boone BAT	1.00	.45
❑ R59 Albert Belle BAT	2.00	.90
❑ R60 Mike Piazza BAT	6.00	2.70

1995 Upper Deck Ruth Heroes

	MINT	NRMT
COMPLETE SET (10)	120.00	55.00
COMMON CARD (73-81/HDR)	15.00	6.75

Card	MINT	NRMT
❑ 73 Babe Ruth	15.00	6.75
1914-18 Pitching Career		
❑ 74 Babe Ruth	15.00	6.75
1919 Move to Outfield		
❑ 75 Babe Ruth	15.00	6.75
1920 Renaissance Man		
❑ 76 Babe Ruth	15.00	6.75
1923 House that Ruth Built		
❑ 77 Babe Ruth	15.00	6.75
1927 60-home run Season		
❑ 78 Babe Ruth	15.00	6.75
1928 Three Homers in Game 4		
❑ 79 Babe Ruth	15.00	6.75
1932 The Called Shot		
❑ 80 Babe Ruth	15.00	6.75
1930-35 Milestones		
❑ 81 Babe Ruth	15.00	6.75
1935 The Last Hurrah		
❑ NNO Babe Ruth Header Card	15.00	6.75
An American Hero		

1995 Upper Deck Special Edition

	MINT	NRMT
COMPLETE SET (270)	160.00	70.00
COMPLETE SERIES 1 (135)	80.00	36.00
COMPLETE SERIES 2 (135)	80.00	36.00
COMMON CARD (1-270)	.40	.18

Card	MINT	NRMT
❑ 1 Cliff Floyd	.60	.25
❑ 2 Wil Cordero	.40	.18
❑ 3 Pedro J. Martinez	1.50	.70
❑ 4 Larry Walker	1.50	.70
❑ 5 Derek Jeter	5.00	2.20
❑ 6 Mike Stanley	.40	.18
❑ 7 Melido Perez	.40	.18
❑ 8 Jim Leyritz	.60	.25
❑ 9 Danny Tartabull	.40	.18
❑ 10 Wade Boggs	1.50	.70
❑ 11 Ryan Klesko	.60	.25
❑ 12 Steve Avery	.40	.18
❑ 13 Damon Hollins	.40	.18
❑ 14 Chipper Jones	4.00	1.80
❑ 15 David Justice	1.50	.70
❑ 16 Glenn Williams	.60	.25
❑ 17 Jose Oliva	.40	.18
❑ 18 Terrell Wade	.40	.18
❑ 19 Alex Fernandez	.40	.18
❑ 20 Frank Thomas	5.00	2.20
❑ 21 Ozzie Guillen	.40	.18
❑ 22 Roberto Hernandez	.40	.18
❑ 23 Albie Lopez	.40	.18
❑ 24 Eddie Murray	1.50	.70
❑ 25 Albert Belle	2.50	1.10
❑ 26 Omar Vizquel	.60	.25
❑ 27 Carlos Baerga	.60	.25
❑ 28 Jose Rijo	.40	.18
❑ 29 Hal Morris	.40	.18
❑ 30 Reggie Sanders	.60	.25
❑ 31 Jack Morris	.60	.25
❑ 32 Raul Mondesi	1.00	.45
❑ 33 Karim Garcia	2.50	1.10
❑ 34 Todd Hollandsworth	.40	.18
❑ 35 Mike Piazza	5.00	2.20
❑ 36 Chan Ho Park	2.00	.90
❑ 37 Ramon Martinez	.60	.25
❑ 38 Kenny Rogers	.40	.18
❑ 39 Will Clark	1.50	.70
❑ 40 Juan Gonzalez	4.00	1.80
❑ 41 Ivan Rodriguez	2.00	.90
❑ 42 Orlando Miller	.40	.18
❑ 43 John Hudek	.40	.18
❑ 44 Luis Gonzalez	.40	.18
❑ 45 Jeff Bagwell	3.00	1.35
❑ 46 Cal Ripken	6.00	2.70
❑ 47 Mike Oquist	.40	.18
❑ 48 Armando Benitez	.40	.18
❑ 49 Ben McDonald	.40	.18
❑ 50 Rafael Palmeiro	1.00	.45
❑ 51 Curtis Goodwin	.40	.18
❑ 52 Vince Coleman	.40	.18
❑ 53 Tom Gordon	.40	.18
❑ 54 Mike Macfarlane	.40	.18
❑ 55 Brian McRae	.40	.18
❑ 56 Matt Smith	.40	.18
❑ 57 David Segui	.60	.25
❑ 58 Paul Wilson	.40	.18
❑ 59 Bill Pulsipher	.40	.18
❑ 60 Bobby Bonilla	.60	.25
❑ 61 Jeff Kent	.60	.25
❑ 62 Ryan Thompson	.40	.18
❑ 63 Jason Isringhausen	.60	.25
❑ 64 Ed Sprague	.40	.18
❑ 65 Paul Molitor	1.50	.70
❑ 66 Juan Guzman	.40	.18
❑ 67 Alex Gonzalez	.40	.18
❑ 68 Shawn Green	.60	.25
❑ 69 Mark Portugal	.40	.18
❑ 70 Barry Bonds	2.00	.90
❑ 71 Robby Thompson	.40	.18
❑ 72 Royce Clayton	.40	.18
❑ 73 Ricky Bottalico	.60	.25
❑ 74 Doug Jones	.40	.18
❑ 75 Darren Daulton	.60	.25
❑ 76 Gregg Jefferies	.40	.18
❑ 77 Scott Cooper	.40	.18
❑ 78 Nomar Garciaparra	10.00	4.50
❑ 79 Ken Ryan	.40	.18
❑ 80 Mike Greenwell	.60	.25
❑ 81 LaTroy Hawkins	.40	.18
❑ 82 Rich Becker	.60	.25
❑ 83 Scott Erickson	.60	.25
❑ 84 Pedro Munoz	.40	.18
❑ 85 Kirby Puckett	3.00	1.35
❑ 86 Orlando Merced	.40	.18
❑ 87 Jeff King	.40	.18
❑ 88 Midre Cummings	.40	.18
❑ 89 Bernard Gilkey	.40	.18
❑ 90 Ray Lankford	.60	.25
❑ 91 Todd Zeile	.40	.18
❑ 92 Alan Benes	.60	.25
❑ 93 Bret Wagner	.40	.18
❑ 94 Rene Arocha	.40	.18
❑ 95 Cecil Fielder	.60	.25
❑ 96 Alan Trammell	.60	.25
❑ 97 Tony Phillips	.40	.18
❑ 98 Junior Felix	.40	.18
❑ 99 Brian Harper	.40	.18
❑ 100 Greg Vaughn	.60	.25
❑ 101 Ricky Bones	.40	.18
❑ 102 Walt Weiss	.40	.18
❑ 103 Lance Painter	.40	.18
❑ 104 Roberto Mejia	.40	.18
❑ 105 Andres Galarraga	1.50	.70
❑ 106 Todd Van Poppel	.40	.18
❑ 107 Ben Grieve	10.00	4.50
❑ 108 Brent Gates	.40	.18
❑ 109 Jason Giambi	.60	.25
❑ 110 Ruben Sierra	.40	.18
❑ 111 Terry Steinbach	.60	.25
❑ 112 Chris Hammond	.40	.18
❑ 113 Charles Johnson	.60	.25
❑ 114 Jesus Tavarez	.40	.18
❑ 115 Gary Sheffield	1.00	.45
❑ 116 Chuck Carr	.40	.18
❑ 117 Bobby Ayala	.40	.18
❑ 118 Randy Johnson	1.50	.70
❑ 119 Edgar Martinez	.60	.25
❑ 120 Alex Rodriguez	6.00	2.70
❑ 121 Kevin Foster	.40	.18
❑ 122 Kevin Roberson	.40	.18
❑ 123 Sammy Sosa	4.00	1.80
❑ 124 Steve Trachsel	.40	.18
❑ 125 Eduardo Perez	.40	.18
❑ 126 Tim Salmon	1.50	.70
❑ 127 Todd Greene	.60	.25
❑ 128 Jorge Fabregas	.40	.18
❑ 129 Mark Langston	.40	.18
❑ 130 Mitch Williams	.40	.18
❑ 131 Raul Casanova	.40	.18
❑ 132 Mel Nieves	.40	.18
❑ 133 Andy Benes	.60	.25
❑ 134 Dustin Hermanson	.60	.25
❑ 135 Trevor Hoffman	.60	.25
❑ 136 Mark Grudzielanek	1.50	.70
❑ 137 Ugueth Urbina	.40	.18
❑ 138 Moises Alou	1.00	.45
❑ 139 Roberto Kelly	.40	.18
❑ 140 Rondell White	.60	.25
❑ 141 Paul O'Neill	.60	.25
❑ 142 Jimmy Key	.60	.25
❑ 143 Jack McDowell	.40	.18
❑ 144 Ruben Rivera	.60	.25
❑ 145 Don Mattingly	2.50	1.10
❑ 146 John Wetteland	.60	.25
❑ 147 Tom Glavine	1.50	.70
❑ 148 Marquis Grissom	.60	.25
❑ 149 Javier Lopez	.60	.25
❑ 150 Fred McGriff	1.00	.45
❑ 151 Greg Maddux	5.00	2.20
❑ 152 Chris Sabo	.40	.18
❑ 153 Ray Durham	.60	.25
❑ 154 Robin Ventura	.60	.25
❑ 155 Jim Abbott	.60	.25
❑ 156 Jimmy Hurst	.40	.18
❑ 157 Tim Raines	.60	.25
❑ 158 Dennis Martinez	.60	.25
❑ 159 Kenny Lofton	1.50	.70
❑ 160 Dave Winfield	1.50	.70
❑ 161 Manny Ramirez	1.50	.70
❑ 162 Jim Thome	1.50	.70
❑ 163 Barry Larkin	1.00	.45
❑ 164 Bret Boone	.60	.25
❑ 165 Deion Sanders	.60	.25
❑ 166 Ron Gant	.40	.18
❑ 167 Benito Santiago	.40	.18
❑ 168 Hideo Nomo	6.00	2.70
❑ 169 Billy Ashley	.40	.18
❑ 170 Roger Cedeno	.40	.18
❑ 171 Ismael Valdes	.60	.25
❑ 172 Eric Karros	.60	.25
❑ 173 Rusty Greer	1.50	.70

Card	MINT	NRMT
❑ 174 Rick Helling	.60	.25
❑ 175 Nolan Ryan	6.00	2.70
❑ 176 Dean Palmer	.60	.25
❑ 177 Phil Plantier	.40	.18
❑ 178 Darryl Kile	.60	.25
❑ 179 Derek Bell	.60	.25
❑ 180 Doug Drabek	.40	.18
❑ 181 Craig Biggio	1.50	.70
❑ 182 Kevin Brown	1.00	.45
❑ 183 Harold Baines	.60	.25
❑ 184 Jeffrey Hammonds	.60	.25
❑ 185 Chris Hoiles	.40	.18
❑ 186 Mike Mussina	1.50	.70
❑ 187 Bob Hamelin	.40	.18
❑ 188 Jeff Montgomery	.40	.18
❑ 189 Michael Tucker	.60	.25
❑ 190 George Brett	3.00	1.35
❑ 191 Edgardo Alfonzo	.60	.25
❑ 192 Brett Butler	.60	.25
❑ 193 Bobby Jones	.40	.18
❑ 194 Todd Hundley	.60	.25
❑ 195 Bret Saberhagen	.60	.25
❑ 196 Pat Hentgen	.60	.25
❑ 197 Roberto Alomar	1.50	.70
❑ 198 David Cone	1.00	.45
❑ 199 Carlos Delgado	.60	.25
❑ 200 Joe Carter	.60	.25
❑ 201 Wm. VanLandingham	.40	.18
❑ 202 Rod Beck	.40	.18
❑ 203 J.R. Phillips	.40	.18
❑ 204 Darren Lewis	.40	.18
❑ 205 Matt Williams	.60	.25
❑ 206 Lenny Dykstra	.60	.25
❑ 207 Dave Hollins	.40	.18
❑ 208 Mike Schmidt	2.00	.90
❑ 209 Charlie Hayes	.40	.18
❑ 210 Mo Vaughn	2.00	.90
❑ 211 Jose Malave	.40	.18
❑ 212 Roger Clemens	3.00	1.35
❑ 213 Jose Canseco	1.50	.70
❑ 214 Mark Whiten	.40	.18
❑ 215 Marty Cordova	.40	.18
❑ 216 Rick Aguilera	.40	.18
❑ 217 Kevin Tapani	.60	.25
❑ 218 Chuck Knoblauch	1.50	.70
❑ 219 Al Martin	.40	.18
❑ 220 Jay Bell	.60	.25
❑ 221 Carlos Garcia	.40	.18
❑ 222 Freddy Garcia	.40	.18
❑ 223 Jon Lieber	.40	.18
❑ 224 Danny Jackson	.40	.18
❑ 225 Ozzie Smith	2.00	.90
❑ 226 Brian Jordan	.60	.25
❑ 227 Ken Hill	.40	.18
❑ 228 Scott Cooper	.40	.18
❑ 229 Chad Curtis	.40	.18
❑ 230 Lou Whitaker	.60	.25
❑ 231 Kirk Gibson	.60	.25
❑ 232 Travis Fryman	.60	.25
❑ 233 Jose Valentin	.40	.18
❑ 234 Dave Nilsson	.40	.18
❑ 235 Cal Eldred	.40	.18
❑ 236 Matt Mieske	.40	.18
❑ 237 Bill Swift	.40	.18
❑ 238 Marvin Freeman	.40	.18
❑ 239 Jason Bates	.40	.18
❑ 240 Larry Walker	1.50	.70
❑ 241 Dave Nied	.40	.18
❑ 242 Dante Bichette	.60	.25
❑ 243 Dennis Eckersley	.60	.25
❑ 244 Todd Stottlemyre	.40	.18
❑ 245 Rickey Henderson	1.50	.70
❑ 246 Geronimo Berroa	.40	.18
❑ 247 Mark McGwire	8.00	3.60
❑ 248 Quilvio Veras	.40	.18
❑ 249 Terry Pendleton	.40	.18
❑ 250 Andre Dawson	1.00	.45
❑ 251 Jeff Conine	.60	.25
❑ 252 Kurt Abbott	.40	.18
❑ 253 Jay Buhner	.60	.25
❑ 254 Darren Bragg	.40	.18
❑ 255 Ken Griffey Jr.	8.00	3.60
❑ 256 Tino Martinez	1.50	.70
❑ 257 Mark Grace	1.00	.45
❑ 258 Ryne Sandberg	2.00	.90
❑ 259 Randy Myers	.40	.18
❑ 260 Howard Johnson	.40	.18
❑ 261 Lee Smith	.60	.25
❑ 262 J.T. Snow	.60	.25
❑ 263 Chili Davis	.60	.25
❑ 264 Chuck Finley	.60	.25
❑ 265 Eddie Williams	.40	.18
❑ 266 Joey Hamilton	.60	.25
❑ 267 Ken Caminiti	1.00	.45
❑ 268 Andujar Cedeno	.40	.18
❑ 269 Steve Finley	.60	.25
❑ 270 Tony Gwynn	4.00	1.80

1995 Upper Deck Steal of a Deal

	MINT	NRMT
COMPLETE SET (15)	80.00	36.00
COMMON CARD (SD1-SD15)	1.50	.70

Card	MINT	NRMT
❑ SD1 Mike Piazza	20.00	9.00
❑ SD2 Fred McGriff	4.00	1.80
❑ SD3 Kenny Lofton	6.00	2.70
❑ SD4 Jose Oliva	1.50	.70
❑ SD5 Jeff Bagwell	10.00	4.50
❑ SD6 Roberto Alomar Joe Carter	6.00	2.70
❑ SD7 Steve Karsay	1.50	.70
❑ SD8 Ozzie Smith	8.00	3.60
❑ SD9 Dennis Eckersley	2.50	1.10
❑ SD10 Jose Canseco	6.00	2.70
❑ SD11 Carlos Baerga	2.50	1.10
❑ SD12 Cecil Fielder	2.50	1.10
❑ SD13 Don Mattingly	10.00	4.50
❑ SD14 Bret Boone	2.50	1.10
❑ SD15 Michael Jordan	30.00	13.50

1996 Upper Deck

	MINT	NRMT
COMPLETE SET (480)	70.00	32.00
COMP.FACT.SET (510)	80.00	36.00
COMPLETE SERIES 1 (240)	40.00	18.00
COMPLETE SERIES 2 (240)	30.00	13.50
COMMON CARD (1-480)	.15	.07
COMP.UPDATE SET (30)	10.00	4.50
COMMON UPDATE (481U-510U)	.25	.11

Card	MINT	NRMT
❑ 1 Cal Ripken 2131	4.00	1.80
❑ 2 Eddie Murray 3000 Hits	.60	.25
❑ 3 Mark Wohlers	.15	.07
❑ 4 David Justice	.60	.25
❑ 5 Chipper Jones	1.50	.70
❑ 6 Javier Lopez	.30	.14
❑ 7 Mark Lemke	.15	.07
❑ 8 Marquis Grissom	.30	.14
❑ 9 Tom Glavine	.60	.25
❑ 10 Greg Maddux	2.00	.90
❑ 11 Manny Alexander	.15	.07
❑ 12 Curtis Goodwin	.15	.07
❑ 13 Scott Erickson	.30	.14
❑ 14 Chris Hoiles	.15	.07
❑ 15 Rafael Palmeiro	.40	.18
❑ 16 Rick Krivda	.15	.07
❑ 17 Jeff Manto	.15	.07
❑ 18 Mo Vaughn	.75	.35
❑ 19 Tim Wakefield	.30	.14
❑ 20 Roger Clemens	1.25	.55
❑ 21 Tim Naehring	.15	.07
❑ 22 Troy O'Leary	.30	.14
❑ 23 Mike Greenwell	.15	.07
❑ 24 Stan Belinda	.15	.07
❑ 25 John Valentin	.30	.14
❑ 26 J.T. Snow	.30	.14
❑ 27 Gary DiSarcina	.15	.07
❑ 28 Mark Langston	.15	.07
❑ 29 Brian Anderson	.30	.14
❑ 30 Jim Edmonds	.40	.18
❑ 31 Garret Anderson	.30	.14
❑ 32 Orlando Palmeiro	.15	.07
❑ 33 Brian McRae	.15	.07
❑ 34 Kevin Foster	.15	.07
❑ 35 Sammy Sosa	1.50	.70
❑ 36 Todd Zeile	.15	.07
❑ 37 Jim Bullinger	.15	.07
❑ 38 Luis Gonzalez	.15	.07
❑ 39 Lyle Mouton	.15	.07
❑ 40 Ray Durham	.30	.14
❑ 41 Ozzie Guillen	.15	.07
❑ 42 Alex Fernandez	.15	.07
❑ 43 Brian Keyser	.15	.07
❑ 44 Robin Ventura	.30	.14
❑ 45 Reggie Sanders	.30	.14
❑ 46 Pete Schourek	.15	.07
❑ 47 John Smiley	.15	.07
❑ 48 Jeff Brantley	.15	.07
❑ 49 Thomas Howard	.15	.07
❑ 50 Bret Boone	.30	.14
❑ 51 Kevin Jarvis	.15	.07
❑ 52 Jeff Branson	.15	.07
❑ 53 Carlos Baerga	.30	.14
❑ 54 Jim Thome	.60	.25
❑ 55 Manny Ramirez	.60	.25
❑ 56 Omar Vizquel	.30	.14
❑ 57 Jose Mesa	.15	.07
❑ 58 Julian Tavarez UER	.15	.07
❑ 59 Orel Hershiser	.30	.14
❑ 60 Larry Walker	.60	.25
❑ 61 Bret Saberhagen	.30	.14
❑ 62 Vinny Castilla	.40	.18
❑ 63 Eric Young	.15	.07
❑ 64 Bryan Rekar	.15	.07
❑ 65 Andres Galarraga	.60	.25
❑ 66 Steve Reed	.15	.07
❑ 67 Chad Curtis	.15	.07
❑ 68 Bobby Higginson	.60	.25
❑ 69 Phil Nevin	.15	.07
❑ 70 Cecil Fielder	.30	.14
❑ 71 Felipe Lira	.15	.07
❑ 72 Chris Gomez	.15	.07
❑ 73 Charles Johnson	.30	.14
❑ 74 Quilvio Veras	.15	.07
❑ 75 Jeff Conine	.30	.14
❑ 76 John Burkett	.15	.07
❑ 77 Greg Colbrunn	.15	.07
❑ 78 Terry Pendleton	.15	.07
❑ 79 Shane Reynolds	.30	.14
❑ 80 Jeff Bagwell	1.00	.45
❑ 81 Orlando Miller	.15	.07
❑ 82 Mike Hampton	.15	.07
❑ 83 James Mouton	.15	.07
❑ 84 Brian L. Hunter	.30	.14
❑ 85 Derek Bell	.30	.14
❑ 86 Kevin Appier	.30	.14
❑ 87 Joe Vitiello	.15	.07

88	Wally Joyner	.30	.14
89	Michael Tucker	.30	.14
90	Johnny Damon	.30	.14
91	Jon Nunnally	.15	.07
92	Jason Jacome	.15	.07
93	Chad Fonville	.15	.07
94	Chan Ho Park	.60	.25
95	Hideo Nomo	1.00	.45
96	Ismael Valdes	.30	.14
97	Greg Gagne	.15	.07
98	Diamondbacks-Devil Rays	.60	.25
99	Raul Mondesi	.40	.18
100	Dave Winfield YH	.30	.14
101	Dennis Eckersley YH	.15	.07
102	Andre Dawson YH	.15	.07
103	Dennis Martinez YH	.15	.07
104	Lance Parrish YH	.15	.07
105	Eddie Murray YH	.30	.14
106	Alan Trammell YH	.15	.07
107	Lou Whitaker YH	.15	.07
108	Ozzie Smith YH	.60	.25
109	Paul Molitor YH	.30	.14
110	Rickey Henderson YH	.30	.14
111	Tim Raines YH	.15	.07
112	Harold Baines YH	.15	.07
113	Lee Smith YH	.15	.07
114	Fernando Valenzuela YH	.15	.07
115	Cal Ripken YH	1.25	.55
116	Tony Gwynn YH	.75	.35
117	Wade Boggs	.60	.25
118	Todd Hollandsworth	.15	.07
119	Dave Nilsson	.15	.07
120	Jose Valentin	.15	.07
121	Steve Sparks	.15	.07
122	Chuck Carr	.15	.07
123	John Jaha	.15	.07
124	Scott Karl	.15	.07
125	Chuck Knoblauch	.60	.25
126	Brad Radke	.30	.14
127	Pat Meares	.15	.07
128	Ron Coomer	.15	.07
129	Pedro Munoz	.15	.07
130	Kirby Puckett	1.00	.45
131	David Segui	.30	.14
132	Mark Grudzielanek	.30	.14
133	Mike Lansing	.15	.07
134	Sean Berry	.15	.07
135	Rondell White	.30	.14
136	Pedro J. Martinez	.60	.25
137	Carl Everett	.15	.07
138	Dave Mlicki	.15	.07
139	Bill Pulsipher	.15	.07
140	Jason Isringhausen	.15	.07
141	Rico Brogna	.15	.07
142	Edgardo Alfonzo	.30	.14
143	Jeff Kent	.30	.14
144	Andy Pettitte	.40	.18
145	Mike Piazza BO	1.00	.45
146	Cliff Floyd BO	.15	.07
147	Jason Isringhausen BO	.15	.07
148	Tim Wakefield BO	.15	.07
149	Chipper Jones BO	.75	.35
150	Hideo Nomo BO	.75	.35
151	Mark McGwire BO	1.50	.70
152	Ron Gant BO	.15	.07
153	Gary Gaetti BO	.15	.07
154	Don Mattingly	1.00	.45
155	Paul O'Neill	.30	.14
156	Derek Jeter	2.00	.90
157	Joe Girardi	.15	.07
158	Ruben Sierra	.15	.07
159	Jorge Posada	.30	.14
160	Geronimo Berroa	.15	.07
161	Steve Ontiveros	.15	.07
162	George Williams	.15	.07
163	Doug Johns	.15	.07
164	Ariel Prieto	.15	.07
165	Scott Brosius	.30	.14
166	Mike Bordick	.15	.07
167	Tyler Green	.15	.07
168	Mickey Morandini	.15	.07
169	Darren Daulton	.30	.14
170	Gregg Jefferies	.15	.07
171	Jim Eisenreich	.15	.07
172	Heathcliff Slocumb	.15	.07
173	Kevin Stocker	.15	.07
174	Esteban Loaiza	.15	.07
175	Jeff King	.15	.07
176	Mark Johnson	.15	.07
177	Denny Neagle	.30	.14
178	Orlando Merced	.15	.07
179	Carlos Garcia	.15	.07
180	Brian Jordan	.30	.14
181	Mike Morgan	.15	.07
182	Mark Petkovsek	.15	.07
183	Bernard Gilkey	.15	.07
184	John Mabry	.15	.07
185	Tom Henke	.15	.07
186	Glenn Dishman	.15	.07
187	Andy Ashby	.15	.07
188	Bip Roberts	.15	.07
189	Melvin Nieves	.15	.07
190	Ken Caminiti	.40	.18
191	Brad Ausmus	.15	.07
192	Deion Sanders	.30	.14
193	Jamie Brewington	.15	.07
194	Glenallen Hill	.15	.07
195	Barry Bonds	.75	.35
196	Wm. Van Landingham	.15	.07
197	Mark Carreon	.15	.07
198	Royce Clayton	.15	.07
199	Joey Cora	.30	.14
200	Ken Griffey Jr.	3.00	1.35
201	Jay Buhner	.30	.14
202	Alex Rodriguez	2.00	.90
203	Norm Charlton	.15	.07
204	Andy Benes	.30	.14
205	Edgar Martinez	.30	.14
206	Juan Gonzalez	1.50	.70
207	Will Clark	.60	.25
208	Kevin Gross	.15	.07
209	Roger Pavlik	.15	.07
210	Ivan Rodriguez	.75	.35
211	Rusty Greer	.40	.18
212	Angel Martinez	.15	.07
213	Tomas Perez	.15	.07
214	Alex Gonzalez	.15	.07
215	Joe Carter	.30	.14
216	Shawn Green	.30	.14
217	Edwin Hurtado	.15	.07
218	Edgar Martinez Tony Pena CL	.30	.14
219	Chipper Jones Barry Larkin CL	.75	.35
220	Orel Hershiser CL	.15	.07
221	Mike Devereaux CL	.15	.07
222	Tom Glavine CL	.30	.14
223	Karim Garcia	.30	.14
224	Arquimedez Pozo	.15	.07
225	Billy Wagner	.30	.14
226	John Wasdin	.15	.07
227	Jeff Suppan	.15	.07
228	Steve Gibralter	.15	.07
229	Jimmy Haynes	.15	.07
230	Ruben Rivera	.30	.14
231	Chris Snopek	.15	.07
232	Alex Ochoa	.15	.07
233	Shannon Stewart	.30	.14
234	Quinton McCracken	.30	.14
235	Trey Beamon	.15	.07
236	Billy McMillon	.15	.07
237	Steve Cox	.15	.07
238	George Arias	.15	.07
239	Jose Herrera	.15	.07
240	Todd Greene	.30	.14
241	Jason Kendall	.60	.25
242	Brooks Kieschnick	.15	.07
243	Osvaldo Fernandez	.15	.07
244	Livan Hernandez	1.25	.55
245	Rey Ordonez	.30	.14
246	Mike Grace	.15	.07
247	Jay Canizaro	.15	.07
248	Bob Wolcott	.15	.07
249	Jermaine Dye	.15	.07
250	Jason Schmidt	.15	.07
251	Mike Sweeney	.40	.18
252	Marcus Jensen	.15	.07
253	Mendy Lopez	.15	.07
254	Wilton Guerrero	.50	.23
255	Paul Wilson	.15	.07
256	Edgar Renteria	.30	.14
257	Richard Hidalgo	.30	.14
258	Bob Abreu	.30	.14
259	Robert Smith	.60	.25
260	Sal Fasano	.15	.07
261	Enrique Wilson	.30	.14
262	Rich Hunter	.15	.07
263	Sergio Nunez	.15	.07
264	Dan Serafini	.15	.07
265	David Doster	.15	.07
266	Ryan McGuire	.15	.07
267	Scott Spiezio	.15	.07
268	Rafael Orellano	.15	.07
269	Steve Avery	.15	.07
270	Fred McGriff	.40	.18
271	John Smoltz	.30	.14
272	Ryan Klesko	.30	.14
273	Jeff Blauser	.15	.07
274	Brad Clontz	.15	.07
275	Roberto Alomar	.60	.25
276	B.J. Surhoff	.30	.14
277	Jeffrey Hammonds	.15	.07
278	Brady Anderson	.30	.14
279	Bobby Bonilla	.30	.14
280	Cal Ripken	2.50	1.10
281	Mike Mussina	.60	.25
282	Wil Cordero	.15	.07
283	Mike Stanley	.15	.07
284	Aaron Sele	.30	.14
285	Jose Canseco	.60	.25
286	Tom Gordon	.15	.07
287	Heathcliff Slocumb	.15	.07
288	Lee Smith	.30	.14
289	Troy Percival	.30	.14
290	Tim Salmon	.60	.25
291	Chuck Finley	.30	.14
292	Jim Abbott	.30	.14
293	Chili Davis	.30	.14
294	Steve Trachsel	.15	.07
295	Mark Grace	.40	.18
296	Rey Sanchez	.15	.07
297	Scott Servais	.15	.07
298	Jaime Navarro	.15	.07
299	Frank Castillo	.15	.07
300	Frank Thomas	2.00	.90
301	Jason Bere	.15	.07
302	Danny Tartabull	.15	.07
303	Darren Lewis	.15	.07
304	Roberto Hernandez	.15	.07
305	Tony Phillips	.15	.07
306	Wilson Alvarez	.30	.14
307	Jose Rijo	.15	.07
308	Hal Morris	.15	.07
309	Mark Portugal	.15	.07
310	Barry Larkin	.40	.18
311	Dave Burba	.15	.07
312	Ed Taubensee	.15	.07
313	Sandy Alomar Jr.	.30	.14
314	Dennis Martinez	.30	.14
315	Albert Belle	.75	.35
316	Eddie Murray	.60	.25
317	Charles Nagy	.30	.14
318	Chad Ogea	.15	.07
319	Kenny Lofton	.60	.25
320	Dante Bichette	.30	.14
321	Armando Reynoso	.15	.07
322	Walt Weiss	.15	.07
323	Ellis Burks	.30	.14
324	Kevin Ritz	.15	.07
325	Bill Swift	.15	.07
326	Jason Bates	.15	.07
327	Tony Clark	.60	.25
328	Travis Fryman	.30	.14
329	Mark Parent	.15	.07
330	Alan Trammell	.40	.18
331	C.J. Nitkowski	.15	.07
332	Jose Lima	.15	.07
333	Phil Plantier	.15	.07
334	Kurt Abbott	.15	.07
335	Andre Dawson	.40	.18
336	Chris Hammond	.15	.07
337	Robb Nen	.15	.07
338	Pat Rapp	.15	.07
339	Al Leiter	.30	.14
340	Gary Sheffield UER (HR total says 17	.40	.18

Card	Player	MINT	NRMT
❑ 341	Todd Jones	.15	.07
❑ 342	Doug Drabek	.15	.07
❑ 343	Greg Swindell	.15	.07
❑ 344	Tony Eusebio	.15	.07
❑ 345	Craig Biggio	.60	.25
❑ 346	Darryl Kile	.30	.14
❑ 347	Mike Macfarlane	.15	.07
❑ 348	Jeff Montgomery	.15	.07
❑ 349	Chris Haney	.15	.07
❑ 350	Bip Roberts	.15	.07
❑ 351	Tom Goodwin	.15	.07
❑ 352	Mark Gubicza	.15	.07
❑ 353	Joe Randa	.15	.07
❑ 354	Ramon Martinez	.30	.14
❑ 355	Eric Karros	.30	.14
❑ 356	Delino DeShields	.15	.07
❑ 357	Brett Butler	.30	.14
❑ 358	Todd Worrell	.15	.07
❑ 359	Mike Blowers	.15	.07
❑ 360	Mike Piazza	2.00	.90
❑ 361	Ben McDonald	.15	.07
❑ 362	Ricky Bones	.15	.07
❑ 363	Greg Vaughn	.30	.14
❑ 364	Matt Mieske	.15	.07
❑ 365	Kevin Seitzer	.15	.07
❑ 366	Jeff Cirillo	.30	.14
❑ 367	LaTroy Hawkins	.15	.07
❑ 368	Frank Rodriguez	.15	.07
❑ 369	Rick Aguilera	.15	.07
❑ 370	Roberto Alomar BG	.30	.14
❑ 371	Albert Belle BG	.40	.18
❑ 372	Wade Boggs BG	.30	.14
❑ 373	Barry Bonds BG	.40	.18
❑ 374	Roger Clemens BG	.60	.25
❑ 375	Dennis Eckersley BG	.15	.07
❑ 376	Ken Griffey Jr. BG	1.50	.70
❑ 377	Tony Gwynn BG	.75	.35
❑ 378	Rickey Henderson BG	.30	.14
❑ 379	Greg Maddux BG	1.00	.45
❑ 380	Fred McGriff BG	.15	.07
❑ 381	Paul Molitor BG	.30	.14
❑ 382	Eddie Murray BG	.30	.14
❑ 383	Mike Piazza BG	1.00	.45
❑ 384	Kirby Puckett BG	.60	.25
❑ 385	Cal Ripken BG	1.25	.55
❑ 386	Ozzie Smith BG	.60	.25
❑ 387	Frank Thomas BG	1.00	.45
❑ 388	Matt Walbeck	.15	.07
❑ 389	Dave Stevens	.15	.07
❑ 390	Marty Cordova	.15	.07
❑ 391	Darrin Fletcher	.15	.07
❑ 392	Cliff Floyd	.30	.14
❑ 393	Mel Rojas	.15	.07
❑ 394	Shane Andrews	.15	.07
❑ 395	Moises Alou	.40	.18
❑ 396	Carlos Perez	.30	.14
❑ 397	Jeff Fassero	.15	.07
❑ 398	Bobby Jones	.15	.07
❑ 399	Todd Hundley	.30	.14
❑ 400	John Franco	.30	.14
❑ 401	Jose Vizcaino	.15	.07
❑ 402	Bernard Gilkey	.15	.07
❑ 403	Pete Harnisch	.15	.07
❑ 404	Pat Kelly	.15	.07
❑ 405	David Cone	.40	.18
❑ 406	Bernie Williams	.60	.25
❑ 407	John Wetteland	.30	.14
❑ 408	Scott Kamieniecki	.15	.07
❑ 409	Tim Raines	.30	.14
❑ 410	Wade Boggs	.60	.25
❑ 411	Terry Steinbach	.30	.14
❑ 412	Jason Giambi	.30	.14
❑ 413	Todd Van Poppel	.15	.07
❑ 414	Pedro Munoz	.15	.07
❑ 415	Eddie Murray SBT	.30	.14
❑ 416	Dennis Eckersley SBT	.15	.07
❑ 417	Bip Roberts SBT	.15	.07
❑ 418	Glenallen Hill SBT	.15	.07
❑ 419	John Hudek SBT	.15	.07
❑ 420	Derek Bell SBT	.15	.07
❑ 421	Larry Walker SBT	.30	.14
❑ 422	Greg Maddux SBT	1.00	.45
❑ 423	Ken Caminiti SBT	.15	.07
❑ 424	Brent Gates	.15	.07
❑ 425	Mark McGwire	3.00	1.35
❑ 426	Mark Whiten	.15	.07
❑ 427	Sid Fernandez	.15	.07
❑ 428	Ricky Bottalico	.30	.14
❑ 429	Mike Mimbs	.15	.07
❑ 430	Lenny Dykstra	.30	.14
❑ 431	Todd Zeile	.15	.07
❑ 432	Benito Santiago	.15	.07
❑ 433	Danny Miceli	.15	.07
❑ 434	Al Martin	.15	.07
❑ 435	Jay Bell	.30	.14
❑ 436	Charlie Hayes	.15	.07
❑ 437	Mike Kingery	.15	.07
❑ 438	Paul Wagner	.15	.07
❑ 439	Tom Pagnozzi	.15	.07
❑ 440	Ozzie Smith	.75	.35
❑ 441	Ray Lankford	.30	.14
❑ 442	Dennis Eckersley	.30	.14
❑ 443	Ron Gant	.15	.07
❑ 444	Alan Benes	.30	.14
❑ 445	Rickey Henderson	.60	.25
❑ 446	Jody Reed	.15	.07
❑ 447	Trevor Hoffman	.30	.14
❑ 448	Andujar Cedeno	.15	.07
❑ 449	Steve Finley	.30	.14
❑ 450	Tony Gwynn	1.50	.70
❑ 451	Joey Hamilton	.30	.14
❑ 452	Mark Leiter	.15	.07
❑ 453	Rod Beck	.15	.07
❑ 454	Kirt Manwaring	.15	.07
❑ 455	Matt Williams	.30	.14
❑ 456	Robby Thompson	.15	.07
❑ 457	Shawon Dunston	.15	.07
❑ 458	Russ Davis	.30	.14
❑ 459	Paul Sorrento	.15	.07
❑ 460	Randy Johnson	.60	.25
❑ 461	Chris Bosio	.15	.07
❑ 462	Luis Sojo	.15	.07
❑ 463	Sterling Hitchcock	.30	.14
❑ 464	Benji Gil	.15	.07
❑ 465	Mickey Tettleton	.15	.07
❑ 466	Mark McLemore	.15	.07
❑ 467	Darryl Hamilton	.15	.07
❑ 468	Ken Hill	.15	.07
❑ 469	Dean Palmer	.30	.14
❑ 470	Carlos Delgado	.30	.14
❑ 471	Ed Sprague	.15	.07
❑ 472	Otis Nixon	.15	.07
❑ 473	Pat Hentgen	.30	.14
❑ 474	Juan Guzman	.15	.07
❑ 475	John Olerud	.30	.14
❑ 476	Buck Showalter CL	.15	.07
❑ 477	Bobby Cox CL	.15	.07
❑ 478	Tommy Lasorda CL	.30	.14
❑ 479	Buck Showalter CL	.15	.07
❑ 480	Sparky Anderson CL	.30	.14
❑ 481U	Randy Myers	.25	.11
❑ 482U	Kent Mercker	.25	.11
❑ 483U	David Wells	.75	.35
❑ 484U	Kevin Mitchell	.25	.11
❑ 485U	Randy Velarde	.25	.11
❑ 486U	Ryne Sandberg	1.50	.70
❑ 487U	Doug Jones	.25	.11
❑ 488U	Terry Adams	.25	.11
❑ 489U	Kevin Tapani	.25	.11
❑ 490U	Harold Baines	.50	.23
❑ 491U	Eric Davis	.50	.23
❑ 492U	Julio Franco	.25	.11
❑ 493U	Jack McDowell	.25	.11
❑ 494U	Devon White	.50	.23
❑ 495U	Kevin Brown	.50	.23
❑ 496U	Rick Wilkins	.25	.11
❑ 497U	Sean Berry	.25	.11
❑ 498U	Keith Lockhart	.25	.11
❑ 499U	Mark Loretta	.25	.11
❑ 500U	Paul Molitor	1.25	.55
❑ 501U	Roberto Kelly	.25	.11
❑ 502U	Lance Johnson	.25	.11
❑ 503U	Tino Martinez	1.00	.45
❑ 504U	Kenny Rogers	.25	.11
❑ 505U	Todd Stottlemyre	.25	.11
❑ 506U	Gary Gaetti	.50	.23
❑ 507U	Royce Clayton	.25	.11
❑ 508U	Andy Benes	.50	.23
❑ 509U	Wally Joyner	.50	.23
❑ 510U	Erik Hanson	.25	.11

1996 Upper Deck Blue Chip Prospects

	MINT	NRMT
COMPLETE SET (20)	200.00	90.00
COMMON CARD (BC1-BC20)	5.00	2.20
❑ BC1 Hideo Nomo	20.00	9.00
❑ BC2 Johnny Damon	6.00	2.70
❑ BC3 Jason Isringhausen	5.00	2.20
❑ BC4 Bill Pulsipher	5.00	2.20
❑ BC5 Marty Cordova	5.00	2.20
❑ BC6 Michael Tucker	6.00	2.70
❑ BC7 John Wasdin	5.00	2.20
❑ BC8 Karim Garcia	6.00	2.70
❑ BC9 Ruben Rivera	6.00	2.70
❑ BC10 Chipper Jones	30.00	13.50
❑ BC11 Billy Wagner	6.00	2.70
❑ BC12 Brooks Kieschnick	5.00	2.20
❑ BC13 Alan Benes	6.00	2.70
❑ BC14 Roger Cedeno	5.00	2.20
❑ BC15 Alex Rodriguez	40.00	18.00
❑ BC16 Jason Schmidt	5.00	2.20
❑ BC17 Derek Jeter	30.00	13.50
❑ BC18 Brian L.Hunter	6.00	2.70
❑ BC19 Garret Anderson	6.00	2.70
❑ BC20 Manny Ramirez	12.00	5.50

1996 Upper Deck Diamond Destiny

	MINT	NRMT
COMPLETE SET (40)	120.00	55.00
COMMON CARD (DD1-DD40)	1.00	.45
COMP.GOLD DD SET (40)	1500.00	700.00

*GOLD DD: 20X TO 50X BASIC CARDS
GOLD DD STATED ODDS 1:143 UD TECH

	MINT	NRMT
COMP.SILVER DD SET (40)	500.00	220.00

*SILVER DD: 6X TO 15X BASIC CARDS
SILVER DD STATED ODDS 1:35 UD TECH

Card	MINT	NRMT
❑ DD1 Chipper Jones	10.00	4.50
❑ DD2 Fred McGriff	1.50	.70
❑ DD3 John Smoltz	1.00	.45
❑ DD4 Ryan Klesko	1.00	.45
❑ DD5 Greg Maddux	10.00	4.50
❑ DD6 Cal Ripken	12.00	5.50
❑ DD7 Roberto Alomar	2.00	.90
❑ DD8 Eddie Murray	2.00	.90

☐ DD9 Brady Anderson	1.00	.45
☐ DD10 Mo Vaughn	2.00	.90
☐ DD11 Roger Clemens	4.00	1.80
☐ DD12 Darin Erstad	10.00	4.50
☐ DD13 Sammy Sosa	2.00	.90
☐ DD14 Frank Thomas	12.00	5.50
☐ DD15 Barry Larkin	1.50	.70
☐ DD16 Albert Belle	4.00	1.80
☐ DD17 Manny Ramirez	2.00	.90
☐ DD18 Kenny Lofton	2.00	.90
☐ DD19 Dante Bichette	1.00	.45
☐ DD20 Gary Sheffield	1.50	.70
☐ DD21 Jeff Bagwell	6.00	2.70
☐ DD22 Hideo Nomo	6.00	2.70
☐ DD23 Mike Piazza	10.00	4.50
☐ DD24 Kirby Puckett	6.00	2.70
☐ DD25 Paul Molitor	2.00	.90
☐ DD26 Chuck Knoblauch	2.00	.90
☐ DD27 Wade Boggs	2.00	.90
☐ DD28 Derek Jeter	10.00	4.50
☐ DD29 Rey Ordonez	1.00	.45
☐ DD30 Mark McGwire	6.00	2.70
☐ DD31 Ozzie Smith	2.00	.90
☐ DD32 Tony Gwynn	8.00	3.60
☐ DD33 Barry Bonds	2.00	.90
☐ DD34 Matt Williams	1.00	.45
☐ DD35 Ken Griffey Jr.	15.00	6.75
☐ DD36 Jay Buhner	1.00	.45
☐ DD37 Randy Johnson	2.00	.90
☐ DD38 Alex Rodriguez	10.00	4.50
☐ DD39 Juan Gonzalez	8.00	3.60
☐ DD40 Joe Carter	1.00	.45

1996 Upper Deck Future Stock Prospects

	MINT	NRMT
COMPLETE SET (20)	10.00	4.50
COMMON CARD (FS1-FS20)	1.00	.45
☐ FS1 George Arias	1.00	.45
☐ FS2 Brian Barber	1.00	.45
☐ FS3 Trey Beamon	1.00	.45
☐ FS4 Yamil Benitez	1.00	.45
☐ FS5 Jamie Brewington	1.00	.45
☐ FS6 Tony Clark	2.50	1.10
☐ FS7 Steve Cox	1.00	.45
☐ FS8 Carlos Delgado	1.50	.70
☐ FS9 Chad Fonville	1.00	.45
☐ FS10 Alex Ochoa	1.00	.45
☐ FS11 Curtis Goodwin	1.00	.45
☐ FS12 Todd Greene	1.50	.70
☐ FS13 Jimmy Haynes	1.00	.45
☐ FS14 Quinton McCracken	1.50	.70
☐ FS15 Billy McMillon	1.00	.45
☐ FS16 Chan Ho Park	2.50	1.10
☐ FS17 Arquimedez Pozo	1.00	.45
☐ FS18 Chris Snopek	1.00	.45
☐ FS19 Shannon Stewart	1.50	.70
☐ FS20 Jeff Suppan	1.00	.45

1996 Upper Deck Gameface

	MINT	NRMT
COMPLETE SET (10)	12.00	5.50
COMMON CARD (GF1-GF10)	.40	.18
☐ GF1 Ken Griffey Jr.	3.00	1.35
☐ GF2 Frank Thomas	2.00	.90
☐ GF3 Barry Bonds	.75	.35
☐ GF4 Albert Belle	.60	.25
☐ GF5 Cal Ripken	2.50	1.10
☐ GF6 Mike Piazza	2.00	.90
☐ GF7 Chipper Jones	1.50	.70
☐ GF8 Matt Williams	.40	.18
☐ GF9 Hideo Nomo	1.00	.45
☐ GF10 Greg Maddux	2.00	.90

1996 Upper Deck Hot Commodities

	MINT	NRMT
COMPLETE SET (20)	150.00	70.00
COMMON CARD (HC1-HC20)	4.00	1.80
☐ HC1 Ken Griffey Jr.	30.00	13.50
☐ HC2 Hideo Nomo	10.00	4.50
☐ HC3 Roberto Alomar	6.00	2.70
☐ HC4 Paul Wilson	4.00	1.80
☐ HC5 Albert Belle	8.00	3.60
☐ HC6 Manny Ramirez	6.00	2.70
☐ HC7 Kirby Puckett	10.00	4.50
☐ HC8 Johnny Damon	5.00	2.20
☐ HC9 Randy Johnson	6.00	2.70
☐ HC10 Greg Maddux	20.00	9.00
☐ HC11 Chipper Jones	15.00	6.75
☐ HC12 Barry Bonds	8.00	3.60
☐ HC13 Mo Vaughn	8.00	3.60
☐ HC14 Mike Piazza	20.00	9.00
☐ HC15 Cal Ripken	25.00	11.00
☐ HC16 Tim Salmon	6.00	2.70
☐ HC17 Sammy Sosa	15.00	6.75
☐ HC18 Kenny Lofton	6.00	2.70
☐ HC19 Tony Gwynn	15.00	6.75
☐ HC20 Frank Thomas	20.00	9.00

1996 Upper Deck V.J. Lovero Showcase

	MINT	NRMT
COMPLETE SET (19)	25.00	11.00
COMMON CARD (VJ1-VJ19)	.50	.23
☐ VJ1 Jim Abbott	.50	.23
☐ VJ2 Hideo Nomo	2.00	.90
☐ VJ3 Derek Jeter	5.00	2.20
☐ VJ4 Barry Bonds	1.50	.70
☐ VJ5 Greg Maddux	5.00	2.20
☐ VJ6 Mark McGwire	5.00	2.20
☐ VJ7 Jose Canseco	1.50	.70
☐ VJ8 Ken Caminiti	1.00	.45
☐ VJ9 Raul Mondesi	1.00	.45
☐ VJ10 Ken Griffey Jr.	8.00	3.60
☐ VJ11 Jay Buhner	.50	.23
☐ VJ12 Randy Johnson	1.50	.70
☐ VJ13 Roger Clemens	2.00	.90
☐ VJ14 Brady Anderson	.50	.23
☐ VJ15 Frank Thomas	4.00	1.80
☐ VJ16 Garret Anderson Jim Edmonds Tim Salmon	1.50	.70
☐ VJ17 Mike Piazza	5.00	2.20
☐ VJ18 Dante Bichette	.50	.23
☐ VJ19 Tony Gwynn	4.00	1.80

1996 Upper Deck Nomo Highlights

	MINT	NRMT
COMPLETE SET (5)	20.00	9.00
COMMON CARD (1-5)	5.00	2.20
☐ 1 Hideo Nomo Dodgers at Giants First Career Start	5.00	2.20
☐ 2 Hideo Nomo	5.00	2.20
☐ 3 Hideo Nomo 1995 All-Star Game	5.00	2.20
☐ 4 Hideo Nomo Dodgers at Giants One-Hitter	5.00	2.20
☐ 5 Hideo Nomo Dodgers at Padres Season-Ending Performance	5.00	2.20

1996 Upper Deck Power Driven

	MINT	NRMT
COMPLETE SET (20)	120.00	55.00
COMMON CARD (PD1-PD20)	2.50	1.10
☐ PD1 Albert Belle	8.00	3.60
☐ PD2 Barry Bonds	8.00	3.60
☐ PD3 Jay Buhner	3.00	1.35

❑ PD4 Jose Canseco	6.00	2.70
❑ PD5 Cecil Fielder	3.00	1.35
❑ PD6 Juan Gonzalez	15.00	6.75
❑ PD7 Ken Griffey Jr.	30.00	13.50
❑ PD8 Eric Karros	3.00	1.35
❑ PD9 Fred McGriff	4.00	1.80
❑ PD10 Mark McGwire	30.00	13.50
❑ PD11 Rafael Palmeiro	4.00	1.80
❑ PD12 Mike Piazza	20.00	9.00
❑ PD13 Manny Ramirez	6.00	2.70
❑ PD14 Tim Salmon	6.00	2.70
❑ PD15 Reggie Sanders	2.50	1.10
❑ PD16 Sammy Sosa	15.00	6.75
❑ PD17 Frank Thomas	20.00	9.00
❑ PD18 Mo Vaughn	8.00	3.60
❑ PD19 Larry Walker	6.00	2.70
❑ PD20 Matt Williams	3.00	1.35

1996 Upper Deck Predictor Hobby

	MINT	NRMT
COMPLETE SET (60)	110.00	50.00
COMPLETE SERIES 1 (30)	60.00	27.00
COMPLETE SERIES 2 (30)	50.00	22.00
COMMON CARD (H1-H60)	1.00	.45
COMP.AL PLAY.EXCH.SET (10)	20.00	9.00
COMP.AL PITCH.EXCH.SET (10)	6.00	2.70
COMP.AL ROOK.EXCH.SET (10)	8.00	3.60
COMP.NL PLAY.EXCH.SET (10)	12.00	5.50
COMP.NL PITCH.EXCH.SET (10)	8.00	3.60
COMP.NL ROOK.EXCH.SET (10)	6.00	2.70

*EXCH.CARDS: .6X TO 1.5X BASIC CARDS
ONE EXCH.SET VIA MAIL PER PRED.WINNER

❑ H1 Albert Belle	2.00	.90
❑ H2 Kenny Lofton	2.00	.90
❑ H3 Rafael Palmeiro	1.50	.70
❑ H4 Ken Griffey Jr.	10.00	4.50
❑ H5 Tim Salmon	2.00	.90
❑ H6 Cal Ripken	8.00	3.60
❑ H7 Mark McGwire W	10.00	4.50
❑ H8 Frank Thomas W	6.00	2.70
❑ H9 Mo Vaughn W	2.00	.90
❑ H10 Player of Month LS W	1.00	.45
❑ H11 Roger Clemens	3.00	1.35
❑ H12 David Cone	1.50	.70
❑ H13 Jose Mesa	1.00	.45
❑ H14 Randy Johnson	2.00	.90
❑ H15 Chuck Finley	1.25	.55
❑ H16 Mike Mussina	2.00	.90
❑ H17 Kevin Appier	1.25	.55
❑ H18 Kenny Rogers	1.00	.45
❑ H19 Lee Smith	1.25	.55
❑ H20 Pitcher of Month LS W	1.00	.45
❑ H21 George Arias	1.00	.45
❑ H22 Jose Herrera	1.00	.45
❑ H23 Tony Clark	2.00	.90
❑ H24 Todd Greene	1.25	.55
❑ H25 Derek Jeter W	6.00	2.70
❑ H26 Arquimedez Pozo	1.00	.45
❑ H27 Matt Lawton	2.00	.90
❑ H28 Shannon Stewart	1.25	.55
❑ H29 Chris Snopek	1.00	.45
❑ H30 Most Rookie Hits LS	1.00	.45
❑ H31 Jeff Bagwell W	3.00	1.35
❑ H32 Dante Bichette	1.25	.55
❑ H33 Barry Bonds W	2.00	.90
❑ H34 Tony Gwynn	5.00	2.20
❑ H35 Chipper Jones	5.00	2.20
❑ H36 Eric Karros	1.25	.55
❑ H37 Barry Larkin	1.50	.70
❑ H38 Mike Piazza	6.00	2.70
❑ H39 Matt Williams	1.25	.55
❑ H40 Long Shot Card	1.00	.45
❑ H41 Osvaldo Fernandez	1.00	.45
❑ H42 Tom Glavine	2.00	.90
❑ H43 Jason Isringhausen	1.00	.45
❑ H44 Greg Maddux	6.00	2.70
❑ H45 Pedro Martinez	2.00	.90
❑ H46 Hideo Nomo	2.50	1.10
❑ H47 Pete Schourek	1.00	.45
❑ H48 Paul Wilson	1.00	.45
❑ H49 Mark Wohlers	1.00	.45
❑ H50 Long Shot Card	1.00	.45
❑ H51 Bob Abreu	1.25	.55
❑ H52 Trey Beamon	1.00	.45
❑ H53 Yamil Benitez	1.00	.45
❑ H54 Roger Cedeno	1.00	.45
❑ H55 Todd Hollandsworth	1.00	.45
❑ H56 Marvin Benard	1.00	.45
❑ H57 Jason Kendall	2.00	.90
❑ H58 Brooks Kieschnick	1.00	.45
❑ H59 Rey Ordonez W	1.25	.55
❑ H60 Long Shot Card	1.00	.45

1996 Upper Deck Predictor Retail

	MINT	NRMT
COMPLETE SET (60)	150.00	70.00
COMPLETE SERIES 1 (30)	100.00	45.00
COMPLETE SERIES 2 (30)	50.00	22.00
COMMON CARD (R1-R60)	1.00	.45
COMP.AL HR EXCH.SET (10)	20.00	9.00
COMP.AL RBI EXCH.SET (10)	15.00	6.75
COMP.AL AVG.EXCH.SET (10)	15.00	6.75
COMP.NL HR EXCH.SET (10)	10.00	4.50
COMP.NL RBI EXCH.SET (10)	8.00	3.60
COMP.NL AVG.EXCH.SET (10)	10.00	4.50

*EXCHANGE CARDS: .6X TO 1.5X BASIC CARDS
ONE EXCH.SET VIA MAIL PER PRED.WINNER

❑ R1 Albert Belle W	2.00	.90
❑ R2 Jay Buhner W	1.25	.55
❑ R3 Juan Gonzalez	5.00	2.20
❑ R4 Ken Griffey Jr.	10.00	4.50
❑ R5 Mark McGwire W	10.00	4.50
❑ R6 Rafael Palmeiro	1.50	.70
❑ R7 Tim Salmon	2.00	.90
❑ R8 Frank Thomas	6.00	2.70
❑ R9 Mo Vaughn W	2.00	.90
❑ R10 Monthly HR Ldr LS W	1.00	.45
❑ R11 Albert Belle W	2.00	.90
❑ R12 Jay Buhner	1.25	.55
❑ R13 Jim Edmonds	1.50	.70
❑ R14 Cecil Fielder	1.25	.55
❑ R15 Ken Griffey Jr.	10.00	4.50
❑ R16 Edgar Martinez	1.25	.55
❑ R17 Manny Ramirez	2.00	.90
❑ R18 Frank Thomas	6.00	2.70
❑ R19 Mo Vaughn W	2.00	.90
❑ R20 Monthly RBI Ldr LS W	1.00	.45
❑ R21 Roberto Alomar W	2.00	.90
❑ R22 Carlos Baerga	1.25	.55
❑ R23 Wade Boggs	2.00	.90
❑ R24 Ken Griffey Jr.	10.00	4.50
❑ R25 Chuck Knoblauch	2.00	.90
❑ R26 Kenny Lofton	2.00	.90
❑ R27 Edgar Martinez	1.25	.55
❑ R28 Tim Salmon	2.00	.90
❑ R29 Frank Thomas	6.00	2.70
❑ R30 Monthly Hits Ldr Longshot W	1.00	.45
❑ R31 Dante Bichette	1.25	.55
❑ R32 Barry Bonds W	2.00	.90
❑ R33 Ron Gant	1.00	.45
❑ R34 Chipper Jones	5.00	2.20
❑ R35 Fred McGriff	1.50	.70
❑ R36 Mike Piazza	6.00	2.70
❑ R37 Sammy Sosa	5.00	2.20
❑ R38 Larry Walker	2.00	.90
❑ R39 Matt Williams	1.25	.55
❑ R40 Long Shot Card	1.00	.45
❑ R41 Jeff Bagwell W	3.00	1.35
❑ R42 Dante Bichette	1.25	.55
❑ R43 Barry Bonds W	2.00	.90
❑ R44 Jeff Conine	1.25	.55
❑ R45 Andres Galarraga	2.00	.90
❑ R46 Mike Piazza	6.00	2.70
❑ R47 Reggie Sanders	1.25	.55
❑ R48 Sammy Sosa	5.00	2.20
❑ R49 Matt Williams	1.25	.55
❑ R50 Long Shot Card	1.00	.45
❑ R51 Jeff Bagwell	3.00	1.35
❑ R52 Derek Bell	1.25	.55
❑ R53 Dante Bichette	1.25	.55
❑ R54 Craig Biggio	2.00	.90
❑ R55 Barry Bonds	2.00	.90
❑ R56 Bret Boone	1.25	.55
❑ R57 Tony Gwynn	5.00	2.20
❑ R58 Barry Larkin	1.50	.70
❑ R59 Mike Piazza W	6.00	2.70
❑ R60 Long Shot Card	1.00	.45

1996 Upper Deck Ripken Collection

	MINT	NRMT
COMPLETE SET (23)	120.00	55.00
COMP.COLC SER.1 (5)	12.00	5.50
COMP.UD SER.1 (4)	25.00	11.00
COMP.COLC SER.2 (4)	10.00	4.50
COMP.UD SER.2 (5)	25.00	11.00

COMPLETE SP SET (5).......... 50.00 22.00
COMMON COLC (1-4/9-12)...... 3.00 1.35
COMMON UD (5-8/13-17) 6.00 2.70
COMMON SP (18-22) 12.00 5.50

❑ 1 Cal Ripken COLC 3.00 1.35
After playing in 2,131 consecutive games
❑ 2 Cal Ripken COLC 3.00 1.35
Barry Bonds
1995 All-Star Game
❑ 3 Cal Ripken COLC 3.00 1.35
300th home run
❑ 4 Cal Ripken COLC 3.00 1.35
Chasing Pop-up
1994
❑ 5 Cal Ripken UD 6.00 2.70
Running to first
1995
❑ 6 Cal Ripken UD 6.00 2.70
Brian McRae sliding into second
1992
❑ 7 Cal Ripken UD 6.00 2.70
1992 Roberto Clemente Award
❑ 8 Cal Ripken UD 6.00 2.70
Batting pose
1991
❑ 9 Cal Ripken COLC 3.00 1.35
Batting follow-through
1991
❑ 10 Cal Ripken COLC 3.00 1.35
1991 1st Gold Glove
❑ 11 Cal Ripken COLC 3.00 1.35
Midway through swing
1991
❑ 12 Cal Ripken COLC 3.00 1.35
Fielding and throwing Ball
1990
❑ 13 Cal Ripken UD 6.00 2.70
Black uniform top in field
1990
❑ 14 Cal Ripken UD 6.00 2.70
Batting follow-through
1987
❑ 15 Cal Ripken UD 6.00 2.70
In Backswing
1986
❑ 16 Cal Ripken UD 6.00 2.70
Midway through swing
1984
❑ 17 Cal Ripken UD 6.00 2.70
Ball about to enter glove
1983
❑ 18 Cal Ripken SP.............. 12.00 5.50
Throwing
1983
❑ 19 Cal Ripken SP.............. 12.00 5.50
Batting, Orange Uniform
1983
❑ 20 Cal Ripken SP.............. 12.00 5.50
Batting follow-through
1982
❑ 21 Cal Ripken SP.............. 12.00 5.50
Fielding at third
Mark Belanger in background
1981
❑ 22 Cal Ripken SP.............. 12.00 5.50
Eddie Murray
1981
❑ NNO Cal Ripken Header COLC 4.00 1.80

1996 Upper Deck Run Producers

	MINT	NRMT
COMPLETE SET (20)	200.00	90.00
COMMON CARD (RP1-RP20)..	4.00	1.80

❑ RP1 Albert Belle................ 10.00 4.50
❑ RP2 Dante Bichette 4.00 1.80
❑ RP3 Barry Bonds 10.00 4.50
❑ RP4 Jay Buhner.................. 4.00 1.80
❑ RP5 Jose Canseco 8.00 3.60
❑ RP6 Juan Gonzalez 20.00 9.00

❑ RP7 Ken Griffey Jr. 40.00 18.00
❑ RP8 Tony Gwynn.............. 20.00 9.00
❑ RP9 Kenny Lofton 8.00 3.60
❑ RP10 Edgar Martinez.......... 4.00 1.80
❑ RP11 Fred McGriff 6.00 2.70
❑ RP12 Mark McGwire 40.00 18.00
❑ RP13 Rafael Palmeiro 6.00 2.70
❑ RP14 Mike Piazza 25.00 11.00
❑ RP15 Manny Ramirez 8.00 3.60
❑ RP16 Tim Salmon 8.00 3.60
❑ RP17 Sammy Sosa 20.00 9.00
❑ RP18 Frank Thomas 25.00 11.00
❑ RP19 Mo Vaughn.............. 10.00 4.50
❑ RP20 Matt Williams 4.00 1.80

1997 Upper Deck

	MINT	NRMT
COMP.MASTER SET (550) ..	200.00	90.00
COMPLETE SET (490)	135.00	60.00
COMPLETE SERIES 1 (240) ..	35.00	16.00
COMPLETE SERIES 2 (250)	100.00	45.00
COMP.SER.2 w/o GHL (240) ..	20.00	9.00
COMMON (1-240/271-520)	.15	.07
COMP.UPDATE SET (30)	50.00	22.00
COMMON UPDATE (241-270)....	.50	.23
COMP.TRADE SET (30)	20.00	9.00
COMMON TRADE (521-550)......	.30	.14

❑ 1 Jackie Robinson .... .50 .23
The Beginnings
❑ 2 Jackie Robinson .... .50 .23
Breaking the Barrier
❑ 3 Jackie Robinson .... .50 .23
The MVP Season, 1949
❑ 4 Jackie Robinson .... .50 .23
1951 season
❑ 5 Jackie Robinson .... .50 .23
1952 and 1953 seasons
❑ 6 Jackie Robinson .... .50 .23
1954 season
❑ 7 Jackie Robinson .... .50 .23
1955 season
❑ 8 Jackie Robinson .... .50 .23
1956 season
❑ 9 Jackie Robinson .... .50 .23
Hall of Fame
❑ 10 Chipper Jones................ 1.50 .70
❑ 11 Marquis Grissom............ .30 .14
❑ 12 Jermaine Dye .... .15 .07
❑ 13 Mark Lemke .... .15 .07
❑ 14 Terrell Wade.................... .15 .07
❑ 15 Fred McGriff .... .40 .18
❑ 16 Tom Glavine .... .60 .25
❑ 17 Mark Wohlers .... .15 .07
❑ 18 Randy Myers.................. .15 .07
❑ 19 Roberto Alomar.............. .60 .25
❑ 20 Cal Ripken...................... 2.50 1.10
❑ 21 Rafael Palmeiro.............. .40 .18
❑ 22 Mike Mussina .... .60 .25
❑ 23 Brady Anderson .... .30 .14
❑ 24 Jose Canseco .... .60 .25
❑ 25 Mo Vaughn .... .75 .35
❑ 26 Roger Clemens .... 1.25 .55
❑ 27 Tim Naehring.................. .15 .07
❑ 28 Jeff Suppan .... .15 .07
❑ 29 Troy Percival .... .30 .14
❑ 30 Sammy Sosa .... 1.50 .70
❑ 31 Amaury Telemaco .... .15 .07
❑ 32 Rey Sanchez .... .15 .07
❑ 33 Scott Servais .... .15 .07
❑ 34 Steve Trachsel .... .15 .07
❑ 35 Mark Grace .... .40 .18
❑ 36 Wilson Alvarez .... .30 .14
❑ 37 Harold Baines .... .30 .14
❑ 38 Tony Phillips .... .15 .07
❑ 39 James Baldwin .... .30 .14
❑ 40 Frank Thomas UER ...... 2.00 .90
Bio information is Ken Griffey Jr.'s
❑ 41 Lyle Mouton.................... .15 .07
❑ 42 Chris Snopek.................. .15 .07
❑ 43 Hal Morris .... .15 .07
❑ 44 Eric Davis .... .30 .14
❑ 45 Barry Larkin.................... .40 .18
❑ 46 Reggie Sanders .... .30 .14
❑ 47 Pete Schourek................ .15 .07
❑ 48 Lee Smith .... .30 .14
❑ 49 Charles Nagy .... .30 .14
❑ 50 Albert Belle .... .75 .35
❑ 51 Julio Franco.................... .30 .14
❑ 52 Kenny Lofton .... .60 .25
❑ 53 Orel Hershiser .... .30 .14
❑ 54 Omar Vizquel .... .30 .14
❑ 55 Eric Young...................... .30 .14
❑ 56 Curtis Leskanic .... .15 .07
❑ 57 Quinton McCracken .... .30 .14
❑ 58 Kevin Ritz .... .15 .07
❑ 59 Walt Weiss .... .15 .07
❑ 60 Dante Bichette................ .30 .14
❑ 61 Mark Lewis .... .15 .07
❑ 62 Tony Clark...................... .40 .18
❑ 63 Travis Fryman .... .30 .14
❑ 64 John Smoltz SF.............. .15 .07
❑ 65 Greg Maddux SF .... 1.00 .45
❑ 66 Tom Glavine SF .... .30 .14
❑ 67 Mike Mussina SF............ .30 .14
❑ 68 Andy Pettitte SF .... .15 .07
❑ 69 Mariano Rivera SF .... .15 .07
❑ 70 Hideo Nomo SF.............. .75 .35
❑ 71 Kevin Brown SF .... .15 .07
❑ 72 Randy Johnson SF .... .30 .14
❑ 73 Felipe Lira .... .15 .07
❑ 74 Kimera Bartee .... .15 .07
❑ 75 Alan Trammell................. .30 .14
❑ 76 Kevin Brown .... .40 .18
❑ 77 Edgar Renteria .... .30 .14
❑ 78 Al Leiter.......................... .30 .14
❑ 79 Charles Johnson .... .30 .14
❑ 80 Andre Dawson................ .40 .18
❑ 81 Billy Wagner .... .30 .14
❑ 82 Donne Wall .... .15 .07
❑ 83 Jeff Bagwell.................. 1.00 .45
❑ 84 Keith Lockhart .... .15 .07
❑ 85 Jeff Montgomery .... .15 .07
❑ 86 Tom Goodwin .... .15 .07
❑ 87 Tim Belcher.................... .15 .07
❑ 88 Mike Macfarlane .... .15 .07
❑ 89 Joe Randa...................... .15 .07
❑ 90 Brett Butler .... .30 .14
❑ 91 Todd Worrell .... .15 .07
❑ 92 Todd Hollandsworth .... .15 .07
❑ 93 Ismael Valdes .... .30 .14
❑ 94 Hideo Nomo .... .75 .35
❑ 95 Mike Piazza.................. 2.00 .90
❑ 96 Jeff Cirillo .... .30 .14
❑ 97 Ricky Bones .... .15 .07

❑ 98 Fernando Vina .15 .07
❑ 99 Ben McDonald .15 .07
❑ 100 John Jaha .15 .07
❑ 101 Mark Loretta .15 .07
❑ 102 Paul Molitor .60 .25
❑ 103 Rick Aguilera .15 .07
❑ 104 Marty Cordova .15 .07
❑ 105 Kirby Puckett 1.00 .45
❑ 106 Dan Naulty .15 .07
❑ 107 Frank Rodriguez .15 .07
❑ 108 Shane Andrews .15 .07
❑ 109 Henry Rodriguez .30 .14
❑ 110 Mark Grudzielanek .30 .14
❑ 111 Pedro Martinez .60 .25
❑ 112 Ugueth Urbina .30 .14
❑ 113 David Segui .30 .14
❑ 114 Rey Ordonez .30 .14
❑ 115 Bernard Gilkey .15 .07
❑ 116 Butch Huskey .15 .07
❑ 117 Paul Wilson .15 .07
❑ 118 Alex Ochoa .15 .07
❑ 119 John Franco .30 .14
❑ 120 Dwight Gooden .30 .14
❑ 121 Ruben Rivera .30 .14
❑ 122 Andy Pettitte .40 .18
❑ 123 Tino Martinez .60 .25
❑ 124 Bernie Williams .60 .25
❑ 125 Wade Boggs .60 .25
❑ 126 Paul O'Neill .30 .14
❑ 127 Scott Brosius .30 .14
❑ 128 Ernie Young .15 .07
❑ 129 Doug Johns .15 .07
❑ 130 Geronimo Berroa .15 .07
❑ 131 Jason Giambi .30 .14
❑ 132 John Wasdin .15 .07
❑ 133 Jim Eisenreich .15 .07
❑ 134 Ricky Otero .15 .07
❑ 135 Ricky Bottalico .30 .14
❑ 136 Mark Langston DG .15 .07
❑ 137 Greg Maddux DG 1.00 .45
❑ 138 Ivan Rodriguez DG .40 .18
❑ 139 Charles Johnson DG .15 .07
❑ 140 J.T. Snow DG .15 .07
❑ 141 Mark Grace DG .15 .07
❑ 142 Roberto Alomar DG .30 .14
❑ 143 Craig Biggio DG .30 .14
❑ 144 Ken Caminiti DG .15 .07
❑ 145 Matt Williams DG .15 .07
❑ 146 Omar Vizquel DG .15 .07
❑ 147 Cal Ripken DG 1.25 .55
❑ 148 Ozzie Smith DG .60 .25
❑ 149 Rey Ordonez DG .15 .07
❑ 150 Ken Griffey Jr. DG 1.50 .70
❑ 151 Devon White DG .15 .07
❑ 152 Barry Bonds DG .30 .14
❑ 153 Kenny Lofton DG .30 .14
❑ 154 Mickey Morandini .15 .07
❑ 155 Gregg Jefferies .15 .07
❑ 156 Curt Schilling .30 .14
❑ 157 Jason Kendall .40 .18
❑ 158 Francisco Cordova .15 .07
❑ 159 Dennis Eckersley .30 .14
❑ 160 Ron Gant .15 .07
❑ 161 Ozzie Smith .75 .35
❑ 162 Brian Jordan .30 .14
❑ 163 John Mabry .15 .07
❑ 164 Andy Ashby .15 .07
❑ 165 Steve Finley .30 .14
❑ 166 Fernando Valenzuela .30 .14
❑ 167 Archi Cianfrocco .15 .07
❑ 168 Wally Joyner .30 .14
❑ 169 Greg Vaughn .30 .14
❑ 170 Barry Bonds .75 .35
❑ 171 William VanLandingham .15 .07
❑ 172 Marvin Benard .15 .07
❑ 173 Rich Aurilia .15 .07
❑ 174 Jay Canizaro .15 .07
❑ 175 Ken Griffey Jr. 3.00 1.35
❑ 176 Bob Wells .15 .07
❑ 177 Jay Buhner .30 .14
❑ 178 Sterling Hitchcock .30 .14
❑ 179 Edgar Martinez .30 .14
❑ 180 Rusty Greer .30 .14
❑ 181 Dave Nilsson GI .15 .07
❑ 182 Larry Walker GI .30 .14
❑ 183 Edgar Renteria GI .15 .07
❑ 184 Rey Ordonez GI .15 .07
❑ 185 Rafael Palmeiro GI .15 .07
❑ 186 Osvaldo Fernandez GI .15 .07
❑ 187 Raul Mondesi GI .15 .07
❑ 188 Manny Ramirez GI .30 .14
❑ 189 Sammy Sosa GI .75 .35
❑ 190 Robert Eenhoorn GI .15 .07
❑ 191 Devon White GI .15 .07
❑ 192 Hideo Nomo GI .75 .35
❑ 193 Mac Suzuki GI .15 .07
❑ 194 Chan Ho Park GI .30 .14
❑ 195 Fernando Valenzuela GI .15 .07
❑ 196 Andruw Jones GI .75 .35
❑ 197 Vinny Castilla GI .15 .07
❑ 198 Dennis Martinez GI .15 .07
❑ 199 Ruben Rivera GI .15 .07
❑ 200 Juan Gonzalez GI .75 .35
❑ 201 Roberto Alomar GI .30 .14
❑ 202 Edgar Martinez GI .15 .07
❑ 203 Ivan Rodriguez GI .40 .18
❑ 204 Carlos Delgado GI .15 .07
❑ 205 Andres Galarraga GI .30 .14
❑ 206 Ozzie Guillen GI .15 .07
❑ 207 Midre Cummings GI .15 .07
❑ 208 Roger Pavlik .15 .07
❑ 209 Darren Oliver .15 .07
❑ 210 Dean Palmer .30 .14
❑ 211 Ivan Rodriguez .75 .35
❑ 212 Otis Nixon .15 .07
❑ 213 Pat Hentgen .30 .14
❑ 214 Ozzie Smith .30 .14
Andre Dawson
Kirby Puckett
HL/CL (1-27)
❑ 215 Barry Bonds .30 .14
Gary Sheffield
Brady Anderson
HL/CL (28-54)
❑ 216 Ken Caminiti SH CL .15 .07
❑ 217 John Smoltz SH CL .15 .07
❑ 218 Eric Young SH CL .15 .07
❑ 219 Juan Gonzalez SH CL .75 .35
❑ 220 Eddie Murray SH CL .30 .14
❑ 221 Tommy Lasorda SH CL .15 .07
❑ 222 Paul Molitor SH CL .30 .14
❑ 223 Luis Castillo .30 .14
❑ 224 Justin Thompson .30 .14
❑ 225 Rocky Coppinger .15 .07
❑ 226 Jermaine Allensworth .15 .07
❑ 227 Jeff D'Amico .15 .07
❑ 228 Jamey Wright .15 .07
❑ 229 Scott Rolen 1.50 .70
❑ 230 Darin Erstad 1.00 .45
❑ 231 Marty Janzen .15 .07
❑ 232 Jacob Cruz .15 .07
❑ 233 Raul Ibanez .15 .07
❑ 234 Nomar Garciaparra 2.00 .90
❑ 235 Todd Walker .60 .25
❑ 236 Brian Giles .75 .35
❑ 237 Matt Beech .15 .07
❑ 238 Mike Cameron .30 .14
❑ 239 Jose Paniagua .15 .07
❑ 240 Andruw Jones 1.00 .45
❑ 241 Brant Brown UPD 1.00 .45
❑ 242 Robin Jennings UPD .50 .23
❑ 243 Willie Adams UPD .50 .23
❑ 244 Ken Caminiti UPD .25 .11
❑ 245 Brian Jordan UPD 1.00 .45
❑ 246 Chipper Jones UPD 5.00 2.20
❑ 247 Juan Gonzalez UPD 5.00 2.20
❑ 248 Bernie Williams UPD 2.00 .90
❑ 249 Roberto Alomar UPD 2.00 .90
❑ 250 Bernie Williams UPD 2.00 .90
❑ 251 David Wells UPD .25 .11
❑ 252 Cecil Fielder UPD 1.00 .45
❑ 253 Darryl Strawberry UPD 1.00 .45
❑ 254 Andy Pettitte UPD .25 .11
❑ 255 Javier Lopez UPD 1.00 .45
❑ 256 Gary Gaetti UPD .50 .23
❑ 257 Ron Gant UPD .50 .23
❑ 258 Brian Jordan UPD 1.00 .45
❑ 259 John Smoltz UPD 1.00 .45
❑ 260 Greg Maddux UPD 6.00 2.70
❑ 261 Tom Glavine UPD 2.00 .90
❑ 262 Andruw Jones UPD 3.00 1.35
❑ 263 Greg Maddux UPD 6.00 2.70
❑ 264 David Cone UPD .25 .11
❑ 265 Jim Leyritz UPD .50 .23
❑ 266 Andy Pettitte UPD .25 .11
❑ 267 John Wetteland UPD 1.00 .45
❑ 268 Dario Veras UPD .50 .23
❑ 269 Neifi Perez UPD .50 .23
❑ 270 Bill Mueller UPD 2.50 1.10
❑ 271 Vladimir Guerrero 1.25 .55
❑ 272 Dmitri Young .30 .14
❑ 273 Nerio Rodriguez .30 .14
❑ 274 Kevin Orie .15 .07
❑ 275 Felipe Crespo .15 .07
❑ 276 Danny Graves .15 .07
❑ 277 Rod Myers .30 .14
❑ 278 Felix Heredia .30 .14
❑ 279 Ralph Milliard .15 .07
❑ 280 Greg Norton .15 .07
❑ 281 Derek Wallace .15 .07
❑ 282 Trot Nixon .30 .14
❑ 283 Bobby Chouinard .15 .07
❑ 284 Jay Witasick .15 .07
❑ 285 Travis Miller .15 .07
❑ 286 Brian Bevil .15 .07
❑ 287 Bobby Estalella .30 .14
❑ 288 Steve Soderstrom .15 .07
❑ 289 Mark Langston .30 .14
❑ 290 Tim Salmon .60 .25
❑ 291 Jim Edmonds .40 .18
❑ 292 Garret Anderson .30 .14
❑ 293 George Arias .15 .07
❑ 294 Gary DiSarcina .15 .07
❑ 295 Chuck Finley .30 .14
❑ 296 Todd Greene .30 .14
❑ 297 Randy Velarde .15 .07
❑ 298 David Justice .60 .25
❑ 299 Ryan Klesko .30 .14
❑ 300 John Smoltz .30 .14
❑ 301 Javier Lopez .30 .14
❑ 302 Greg Maddux 2.00 .90
❑ 303 Denny Neagle .30 .14
❑ 304 B.J. Surhoff .30 .14
❑ 305 Chris Hoiles .15 .07
❑ 306 Eric Davis .30 .14
❑ 307 Scott Erickson .30 .14
❑ 308 Mike Bordick .15 .07
❑ 309 John Valentin .30 .14
❑ 310 Heathcliff Slocumb .15 .07
❑ 311 Tom Gordon .15 .07
❑ 312 Mike Stanley .15 .07
❑ 313 Reggie Jefferson .15 .07
❑ 314 Darren Bragg .15 .07
❑ 315 Troy O'Leary .30 .14
❑ 316 John Mabry SH CL .15 .07
❑ 317 Mark Whiten SH CL .15 .07
❑ 318 Edgar Martinez SH CL .15 .07
❑ 319 Alex Rodriguez SH CL 1.00 .45
❑ 320 Mark McGwire SH CL 1.50 .70
❑ 321 Hideo Nomo SH CL .75 .35
❑ 322 Todd Hundley SH CL .15 .07
❑ 323 Barry Bonds SH CL .30 .14
❑ 324 Andruw Jones SH CL .75 .35
❑ 325 Ryne Sandberg .75 .35
❑ 326 Brian McRae .15 .07
❑ 327 Frank Castillo .15 .07
❑ 328 Shawon Dunston .15 .07
❑ 329 Ray Durham .30 .14
❑ 330 Robin Ventura .30 .14
❑ 331 Ozzie Guillen .15 .07
❑ 332 Roberto Hernandez .15 .07
❑ 333 Albert Belle .75 .35
❑ 334 Dave Martinez .15 .07
❑ 335 Willie Greene .30 .14
❑ 336 Jeff Brantley .15 .07
❑ 337 Kevin Jarvis .15 .07
❑ 338 John Smiley .15 .07
❑ 339 Eddie Taubensee .15 .07
❑ 340 Bret Boone .30 .14
❑ 341 Kevin Seitzer .15 .07
❑ 342 Jack McDowell .15 .07
❑ 343 Sandy Alomar Jr. .30 .14
❑ 344 Chad Curtis .15 .07
❑ 345 Manny Ramirez .60 .25
❑ 346 Chad Ogea .15 .07

❑ 347 Jim Thome .60 .25
❑ 348 Mark Thompson .15 .07
❑ 349 Ellis Burks .30 .14
❑ 350 Andres Galarraga .60 .25
❑ 351 Vinny Castilla .40 .18
❑ 352 Kirt Manwaring .15 .07
❑ 353 Larry Walker .60 .25
❑ 354 Omar Olivares .15 .07
❑ 355 Bobby Higginson .40 .18
❑ 356 Melvin Nieves .15 .07
❑ 357 Brian Johnson .15 .07
❑ 358 Devon White .30 .14
❑ 359 Jeff Conine .30 .14
❑ 360 Gary Sheffield .40 .18
❑ 361 Robb Nen .15 .07
❑ 362 Mike Hampton .15 .07
❑ 363 Bob Abreu .30 .14
❑ 364 Luis Gonzalez .15 .07
❑ 365 Derek Bell .30 .14
❑ 366 Sean Berry .15 .07
❑ 367 Craig Biggio .60 .25
❑ 368 Darryl Kile .30 .14
❑ 369 Shane Reynolds .30 .14
❑ 370 Jeff Bagwell CF .60 .25
❑ 371 Ron Gant CF .15 .07
❑ 372 Andy Benes CF .15 .07
❑ 373 Gary Gaetti CF .15 .07
❑ 374 Ramon Martinez CF .15 .07
❑ 375 Raul Mondesi CF .30 .14
❑ 376 Steve Finley CF .15 .07
❑ 377 Ken Caminiti CF .15 .07
❑ 378 Tony Gwynn CF .75 .35
❑ 379 Dario Veras .40 .18
❑ 380 Andy Pettitte CF .15 .07
❑ 381 Ruben Rivera CF .15 .07
❑ 382 David Cone CF .15 .07
❑ 383 Roberto Alomar CF .30 .14
❑ 384 Edgar Martinez CF .15 .07
❑ 385 Ken Griffey Jr. CF 1.50 .70
❑ 386 Mark McGwire CF 1.50 .70
❑ 387 Rusty Greer CF .15 .07
❑ 388 Jose Rosado .15 .07
❑ 389 Kevin Appier .30 .14
❑ 390 Johnny Damon .30 .14
❑ 391 Jose Offerman .15 .07
❑ 392 Michael Tucker .30 .14
❑ 393 Craig Paquette .15 .07
❑ 394 Bip Roberts .15 .07
❑ 395 Ramon Martinez .30 .14
❑ 396 Greg Gagne .15 .07
❑ 397 Chan Ho Park .60 .25
❑ 398 Karim Garcia .30 .14
❑ 399 Wilton Guerrero .15 .07
❑ 400 Eric Karros .30 .14
❑ 401 Raul Mondesi .40 .18
❑ 402 Matt Mieske .15 .07
❑ 403 Mike Fetters .15 .07
❑ 404 Dave Nilsson .15 .07
❑ 405 Jose Valentin .15 .07
❑ 406 Scott Karl .15 .07
❑ 407 Marc Newfield .15 .07
❑ 408 Cal Eldred .15 .07
❑ 409 Rich Becker .15 .07
❑ 410 Terry Steinbach .30 .14
❑ 411 Chuck Knoblauch .60 .25
❑ 412 Pat Meares .15 .07
❑ 413 Brad Radke .30 .14
❑ 414 Kirby Puckett UER 1.00 .45
Card numbered 415
❑ 415 Andruw Jones GHL SP 5.00 2.20
❑ 416 Chipper Jones GHL SP 8.00 3.60
❑ 417 Mo Vaughn GHL SP 4.00 1.80
❑ 418 Frank Thomas GHL SP 10.00 4.50
❑ 419 Albert Belle GHL SP 3.00 1.35
❑ 420 Mark McGwire GHL SP 15.00 6.75
❑ 421 Derek Jeter GHL SP 8.00 3.60
❑ 422 Alex Rodriguez GHL SP 10.00 4.50
❑ 423 Juan Gonzalez GHL SP 8.00 3.60
❑ 424 Ken Griffey Jr. GHL SP 15.00 6.75
❑ 425 Rondell White .30 .14
❑ 426 Darrin Fletcher .15 .07
❑ 427 Cliff Floyd .30 .14
❑ 428 Mike Lansing .15 .07
❑ 429 F.P. Santangelo .15 .07
❑ 430 Todd Hundley .30 .14
❑ 431 Mark Clark .15 .07
❑ 432 Pete Harnisch .15 .07
❑ 433 Jason Isringhausen .15 .07
❑ 434 Bobby Jones .15 .07
❑ 435 Lance Johnson .15 .07
❑ 436 Carlos Baerga .30 .14
❑ 437 Mariano Duncan .15 .07
❑ 438 David Cone .40 .18
❑ 439 Mariano Rivera .30 .14
❑ 440 Derek Jeter 2.00 .90
❑ 441 Joe Girardi .15 .07
❑ 442 Charlie Hayes .15 .07
❑ 443 Tim Raines .30 .14
❑ 444 Darryl Strawberry .30 .14
❑ 445 Cecil Fielder .30 .14
❑ 446 Ariel Prieto .15 .07
❑ 447 Tony Batista .15 .07
❑ 448 Brent Gates .15 .07
❑ 449 Scott Spiezio .15 .07
❑ 450 Mark McGwire 3.00 1.35
❑ 451 Don Wengert .15 .07
❑ 452 Mike Lieberthal .15 .07
❑ 453 Lenny Dykstra .30 .14
❑ 455 Darren Daulton .30 .14
❑ 456 Kevin Stocker .15 .07
❑ 457 Trey Beamon .15 .07
❑ 458 Midre Cummings .15 .07
❑ 459 Mark Johnson .15 .07
❑ 460 Al Martin .15 .07
❑ 461 Kevin Elster .15 .07
❑ 462 Jon Lieber .15 .07
❑ 463 Jason Schmidt .15 .07
❑ 464 Paul Wagner .15 .07
❑ 465 Andy Benes .30 .14
❑ 466 Alan Benes .30 .14
❑ 467 Royce Clayton .15 .07
❑ 468 Gary Gaetti .15 .07
❑ 469 Curt Lyons .15 .07
❑ 470 Eugene Kingsale DD .30 .14
❑ 471 Damian Jackson DD .15 .07
❑ 472 Wendell Magee DD .15 .07
❑ 473 Kevin L. Brown DD .15 .07
❑ 474 Raul Casanova DD .15 .07
❑ 475 Ramiro Mendoza DD .50 .23
❑ 476 Todd Dunn DD .15 .07
❑ 477 Chad Mottola DD .15 .07
❑ 478 Andy Larkin DD .15 .07
❑ 479 Jaime Bluma DD .15 .07
❑ 480 Mac Suzuki DD .15 .07
❑ 481 Brian Banks DD .15 .07
❑ 482 Desi Wilson DD .15 .07
❑ 483 Einar Diaz DD .15 .07
❑ 484 Tom Pagnozzi .15 .07
❑ 485 Ray Lankford .30 .14
❑ 486 Todd Stottlemyre .15 .07
❑ 487 Donovan Osborne .15 .07
❑ 488 Trevor Hoffman .30 .14
❑ 489 Chris Gomez .15 .07
❑ 490 Ken Caminiti .40 .18
❑ 491 John Flaherty .15 .07
❑ 492 Tony Gwynn 1.50 .70
❑ 493 Joey Hamilton .30 .14
❑ 494 Rickey Henderson .60 .25
❑ 495 Glenallen Hill .15 .07
❑ 496 Rod Beck .15 .07
❑ 497 Osvaldo Fernandez .15 .07
❑ 498 Rick Wilkins .15 .07
❑ 499 Joey Cora .30 .14
❑ 500 Alex Rodriguez 2.00 .90
❑ 501 Randy Johnson .60 .25
❑ 502 Paul Sorrento .15 .07
❑ 503 Dan Wilson .15 .07
❑ 504 Jamie Moyer .15 .07
❑ 505 Will Clark .60 .25
❑ 506 Mickey Tettleton .15 .07
❑ 507 John Burkett .15 .07
❑ 508 Ken Hill .15 .07
❑ 509 Mark McLemore .15 .07
❑ 510 Juan Gonzalez 1.50 .70
❑ 511 Bobby Witt .15 .07
❑ 512 Carlos Delgado .30 .14
❑ 513 Alex Gonzalez .15 .07
❑ 514 Shawn Green .30 .14
❑ 515 Joe Carter .30 .14
❑ 516 Juan Guzman .15 .07
❑ 517 Charlie O'Brien .15 .07
❑ 518 Ed Sprague .15 .07
❑ 519 Mike Timlin .15 .07
❑ 520 Roger Clemens 1.25 .55
❑ 521 Eddie Murray TRADE 1.25 .55
❑ 522 Jason Dickson TRADE .60 .25
❑ 523 Jim Leyritz TRADE .30 .14
❑ 524 Michael Tucker TRADE .60 .25
❑ 525 Kenny Lofton TRADE 1.25 .55
❑ 526 Jimmy Key TRADE .60 .25
❑ 527 Mel Rojas TRADE .30 .14
❑ 528 Deion Sanders TRADE .60 .25
❑ 529 Bartolo Colon TRADE .60 .25
❑ 530 Matt Williams TRADE .60 .25
❑ 531 Marquis Grissom TRADE .60 .25
❑ 532 David Justice TRADE 1.25 .55
❑ 533 Bubba Trammell TRADE 1.00 .45
❑ 534 Moises Alou TRADE .75 .35
❑ 535 Bobby Bonilla TRADE .60 .25
❑ 536 Alex Fernandez TRADE .30 .14
❑ 537 Jay Bell TRADE .60 .25
❑ 538 Chili Davis TRADE .60 .25
❑ 539 Jeff King TRADE .30 .14
❑ 540 Todd Zeile TRADE .30 .14
❑ 541 John Olerud TRADE .60 .25
❑ 542 Jose Guillen TRADE 1.25 .55
❑ 543 Derrek Lee TRADE .75 .35
❑ 544 Dante Powell TRADE .60 .25
❑ 545 J.T. Snow TRADE .60 .25
❑ 546 Jeff Kent TRADE .60 .25
❑ 547 Jose Cruz Jr. TRADE 8.00 3.60
❑ 548 John Wetteland TRADE .60 .25
❑ 549 Orlando Merced TRADE .30 .14
❑ 550 Hideki Irabu TRADE 5.00 2.20

1997 Upper Deck Amazing Greats

	MINT	NRMT
COMPLETE SET (20)	500.00	220.00
COMMON CARD (AG1-AG20)	8.00	3.60

❑ AG1 Ken Griffey Jr. 60.00 27.00
❑ AG2 Roberto Alomar 12.00 5.50
❑ AG3 Alex Rodriguez 40.00 18.00
❑ AG4 Paul Molitor 12.00 5.50
❑ AG5 Chipper Jones 30.00 13.50
❑ AG6 Tony Gwynn 30.00 13.50
❑ AG7 Kenny Lofton 12.00 5.50
❑ AG8 Albert Belle 20.00 9.00
❑ AG9 Matt Williams 8.00 3.60
❑ AG10 Frank Thomas 40.00 18.00
❑ AG11 Greg Maddux 40.00 18.00
❑ AG12 Sammy Sosa 30.00 13.50
❑ AG13 Kirby Puckett 20.00 9.00
❑ AG14 Jeff Bagwell 20.00 9.00
❑ AG15 Cal Ripken 50.00 22.00
❑ AG16 Manny Ramirez 12.00 5.50
❑ AG17 Barry Bonds 15.00 6.75
❑ AG18 Mo Vaughn 15.00 6.75
❑ AG19 Eddie Murray 12.00 5.50
❑ AG20 Mike Piazza 40.00 18.00

1997 Upper Deck Blue Chip Prospects

	MINT	NRMT
COMPLETE SET (20)	400.00	180.00
COMMON CARD (BC1-BC20)	5.00	2.20
❑ BC1 Andruw Jones	30.00	13.50
❑ BC2 Derek Jeter	50.00	22.00
❑ BC3 Scott Rolen	50.00	22.00
❑ BC4 Manny Ramirez	20.00	9.00
❑ BC5 Todd Walker	20.00	9.00
❑ BC6 Rocky Coppinger	5.00	2.20
❑ BC7 Nomar Garciaparra	60.00	27.00
❑ BC8 Darin Erstad	30.00	13.50
❑ BC9 Jermaine Dye	5.00	2.20
❑ BC10 Vladimir Guerrero	40.00	18.00
❑ BC11 Edgar Renteria	10.00	4.50
❑ BC12 Bob Abreu	10.00	4.50
❑ BC13 Karim Garcia	10.00	4.50
❑ BC14 Jeff D'Amico	5.00	2.20
❑ BC15 Chipper Jones	50.00	22.00
❑ BC16 Todd Hollandsworth	5.00	2.20
❑ BC17 Andy Pettitte	25.00	11.00
❑ BC18 Ruben Rivera	10.00	4.50
❑ BC19 Jason Kendall	12.00	5.50
❑ BC20 Alex Rodriguez	60.00	27.00

1997 Upper Deck Game Jersey

	MINT	NRMT
COMPLETE SET (3)	1000.00	450.00
COMMON CARD (GJ1-GJ3)	80.00	36.00
❑ GJ1 Ken Griffey Jr.	700.00	325.00
❑ GJ2 Tony Gwynn	300.00	135.00
❑ GJ3 Rey Ordonez	80.00	36.00

1997 Upper Deck Hot Commodities

	MINT	NRMT
COMPLETE SET (20)	100.00	45.00
COMMON CARD (HC1-HC20)	1.00	.45
❑ HC1 Alex Rodriguez	6.00	2.70
❑ HC2 Andruw Jones	3.00	1.35
❑ HC3 Derek Jeter	5.00	2.20
❑ HC4 Frank Thomas	6.00	2.70
❑ HC5 Ken Griffey Jr.	10.00	4.50
❑ HC6 Chipper Jones	5.00	2.20
❑ HC7 Juan Gonzalez	5.00	2.20
❑ HC8 Cal Ripken	8.00	3.60
❑ HC9 John Smoltz	1.00	.45
❑ HC10 Mark McGwire	10.00	4.50
❑ HC11 Barry Bonds	2.50	1.10
❑ HC12 Albert Belle	3.00	1.35
❑ HC13 Mike Piazza	6.00	2.70
❑ HC14 Manny Ramirez	2.00	.90
❑ HC15 Mo Vaughn	2.50	1.10
❑ HC16 Tony Gwynn	5.00	2.20
❑ HC17 Vladimir Guerrero	4.00	1.80
❑ HC18 Hideo Nomo	2.50	1.10
❑ HC19 Greg Maddux	8.00	3.60
❑ HC20 Kirby Puckett	3.00	1.35

1997 Upper Deck Long Distance Connection

	MINT	NRMT
COMPLETE SET (20)	150.00	70.00
COMMON CARD (LD1-LD20)	3.00	1.35
❑ LD1 Mark McGwire	30.00	13.50
❑ LD2 Brady Anderson	4.00	1.80
❑ LD3 Ken Griffey Jr.	30.00	13.50
❑ LD4 Albert Belle	10.00	4.50
❑ LD5 Juan Gonzalez	15.00	6.75
❑ LD6 Andres Galarraga	6.00	2.70
❑ LD7 Jay Buhner	4.00	1.80
❑ LD8 Mo Vaughn	8.00	3.60
❑ LD9 Barry Bonds	8.00	3.60
❑ LD10 Gary Sheffield	5.00	2.20
❑ LD11 Todd Hundley	3.00	1.35
❑ LD12 Frank Thomas	20.00	9.00
❑ LD13 Sammy Sosa	15.00	6.75
❑ LD14 Rafael Palmeiro	5.00	2.20
❑ LD15 Alex Rodriguez	20.00	9.00
❑ LD16 Mike Piazza	20.00	9.00
❑ LD17 Ken Caminiti	5.00	2.20
❑ LD18 Chipper Jones	15.00	6.75
❑ LD19 Manny Ramirez	6.00	2.70
❑ LD20 Andruw Jones	8.00	3.60

1997 Upper Deck Memorable Moments

	MINT	NRMT
COMPLETE SERIES 1 (10)	15.00	6.75
COMMON CARD (A1-B10)	.60	.25
COMPLETE SERIES 2 (10)	15.00	6.75
❑ A1 Andruw Jones	1.25	.55
❑ A2 Chipper Jones	1.50	.70
❑ A3 Cal Ripken	2.50	1.10
❑ A4 Frank Thomas	2.00	.90
❑ A5 Manny Ramirez	.60	.25
❑ A6 Mike Piazza	2.00	.90
❑ A7 Mark McGwire	3.00	1.35
❑ A8 Barry Bonds	.75	.35
❑ A9 Ken Griffey Jr.	3.00	1.35
❑ A10 Alex Rodriguez	2.00	.90
❑ B1 Ken Griffey Jr.	3.00	1.35
❑ B2 Albert Belle	1.25	.55
❑ B3 Derek Jeter	2.00	.90
❑ B4 Greg Maddux	2.00	.90
❑ B5 Tony Gwynn	1.50	.70
❑ B6 Ryne Sandberg	.75	.35
❑ B7 Juan Gonzalez	1.50	.70
❑ B8 Roger Clemens	1.25	.55
❑ B9 Jose Cruz Jr.	2.50	1.10
❑ B10 Mo Vaughn	.75	.35

1997 Upper Deck Power Package

	MINT	NRMT
COMPLETE SET (20)	100.00	45.00
COMMON CARD (PP1-PP20)	2.50	1.10
❑ PP1 Ken Griffey Jr.	25.00	11.00
❑ PP2 Joe Carter	3.00	1.35
❑ PP3 Rafael Palmeiro	4.00	1.80
❑ PP4 Jay Buhner	3.00	1.35
❑ PP5 Sammy Sosa	12.00	5.50
❑ PP6 Fred McGriff	4.00	1.80
❑ PP7 Jeff Bagwell	8.00	3.60
❑ PP8 Albert Belle	8.00	3.60
❑ PP9 Matt Williams	3.00	1.35
❑ PP10 Mark McGwire	25.00	11.00
❑ PP11 Gary Sheffield	4.00	1.80
❑ PP12 Tim Salmon	5.00	2.20
❑ PP13 Ryan Klesko	2.50	1.10

		MINT	NRMT
❑ PP14	Manny Ramirez	5.00	2.20
❑ PP15	Mike Piazza	15.00	6.75
❑ PP16	Barry Bonds	6.00	2.70
❑ PP17	Mo Vaughn	6.00	2.70
❑ PP18	Jose Canseco	5.00	2.20
❑ PP19	Juan Gonzalez	12.00	5.50
❑ PP20	Frank Thomas	15.00	6.75

1997 Upper Deck Predictor

	MINT	NRMT
COMPLETE SET (30)	30.00	13.50
COMMON CARD (1-30)	.40	.18

*SCRATCHED LOSER: .25X TO .6X UNSCRATCHED
*EXCHANGED WINNERS: 1.25X TO 3X BASIC CARDS
SER.2 STATED ODDS 1:5

		MINT	NRMT
❑ 1	Andruw Jones L	1.50	.70
❑ 2	Chipper Jones L	2.00	.90
❑ 3	Greg Maddux W Complete Game Shutout	2.50	1.10
❑ 4	Fred McGriff W 4 Hits/2HR/3B	.50	.23
❑ 5	John Smoltz W Complete Game Shutout	.40	.18
❑ 6	Brady Anderson W Leadoff HR	.40	.18
❑ 7	Cal Ripken W Grand Slam	3.00	1.35
❑ 8	Mo Vaughn W 3HR/6RBI	1.00	.45
❑ 9	Sammy Sosa L	2.50	1.10
❑ 10	Albert Belle W Grand Slam/9th HR	1.00	.45
❑ 11	Frank Thomas L	2.50	1.10
❑ 12	Kenny Lofton W 5 Hits	.75	.35
❑ 13	Jim Thome L	.75	.35
❑ 14	Dante Bichette W 6RBI's	.40	.18
❑ 15	Andres Galarraga L	.75	.35
❑ 16	Gary Sheffield L	.50	.23
❑ 17	Hideo Nomo W Base Hit	2.00	.90
❑ 18	Mike Piazza W Steal/9th HR	2.50	1.10
❑ 19	Derek Jeter W 2HR	2.50	1.10
❑ 20	Bernie Williams L	.75	.35
❑ 21	Mark McGwire W Grand Slam/4HR	4.00	1.80
❑ 22	Ken Caminiti W 5RBI's	.50	.23
❑ 23	Tony Gwynn W 2 2B/3RBI	2.00	.90
❑ 24	Barry Bonds W 5RBI's	1.00	.45
❑ 25	Jay Buhner W 5RBI's	.40	.18
❑ 26	Ken Griffey Jr. W 3HR's	4.00	1.80
❑ 27	Alex Rodriguez W Cycle	2.50	1.10
❑ 28	Juan Gonzalez W 5RBI's/4 Hits	2.00	.90
❑ 29	Dean Palmer W 2HR's/5RBI's	.40	.18
❑ 30	Roger Clemens W Complete Game Shutout	1.50	.70

1997 Upper Deck Rock Solid Foundation

	MINT	NRMT
COMPLETE SET (20)	50.00	22.00
COMMON CARD (RS1-RS20)	1.00	.45

		MINT	NRMT
❑ RS1	Alex Rodriguez	10.00	4.50
❑ RS2	Rey Ordonez	1.50	.70
❑ RS3	Derek Jeter	8.00	3.60
❑ RS4	Darin Erstad	5.00	2.20
❑ RS5	Chipper Jones	8.00	3.60
❑ RS6	Johnny Damon	1.50	.70
❑ RS7	Ryan Klesko	1.50	.70
❑ RS8	Charles Johnson	1.50	.70
❑ RS9	Andy Pettitte	2.00	.90
❑ RS10	Manny Ramirez	3.00	1.35
❑ RS11	Ivan Rodriguez	4.00	1.80
❑ RS12	Jason Kendall	2.00	.90
❑ RS13	Rondell White	1.50	.70
❑ RS14	Alex Ochoa	1.00	.45
❑ RS15	Javier Lopez	1.50	.70
❑ RS16	Pedro Martinez	3.00	1.35
❑ RS17	Carlos Delgado	1.50	.70
❑ RS18	Paul Wilson	1.00	.45
❑ RS19	Alan Benes	1.50	.70
❑ RS20	Raul Mondesi	2.00	.90

1997 Upper Deck Run Producers

	MINT	NRMT
COMPLETE SET (24)	350.00	160.00
COMMON CARD (RP1-RP24)	6.00	2.70

		MINT	NRMT
❑ RP1	Ken Griffey Jr.	60.00	27.00
❑ RP2	Barry Bonds	15.00	6.75
❑ RP3	Albert Belle	15.00	6.75
❑ RP4	Mark McGwire	60.00	27.00
❑ RP5	Frank Thomas	40.00	18.00
❑ RP6	Juan Gonzalez	30.00	13.50
❑ RP7	Brady Anderson	6.00	2.70
❑ RP8	Andres Galarraga	12.00	5.50
❑ RP9	Rafael Palmeiro	8.00	3.60
❑ RP10	Alex Rodriguez	40.00	18.00
❑ RP11	Jay Buhner	6.00	2.70
❑ RP12	Gary Sheffield	8.00	3.60
❑ RP13	Sammy Sosa	30.00	13.50
❑ RP14	Dante Bichette	6.00	2.70
❑ RP15	Mike Piazza	40.00	18.00
❑ RP16	Manny Ramirez	12.00	5.50
❑ RP17	Kenny Lofton	12.00	5.50
❑ RP18	Mo Vaughn	15.00	6.75
❑ RP19	Tim Salmon	12.00	5.50
❑ RP20	Chipper Jones	30.00	13.50
❑ RP21	Jim Thome	12.00	5.50
❑ RP22	Ken Caminiti	8.00	3.60
❑ RP23	Jeff Bagwell	20.00	9.00
❑ RP24	Paul Molitor	12.00	5.50

1997 Upper Deck Star Attractions

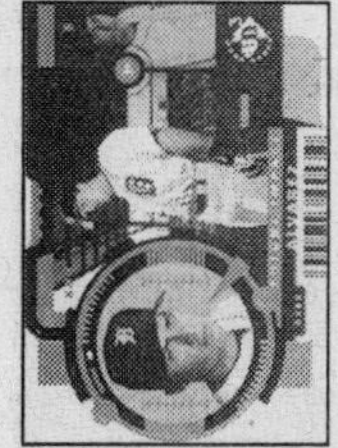

	MINT	NRMT
COMPLETE SET (20)	30.00	13.50
COMMON CARD (1-20)	.75	.35

		MINT	NRMT
❑ 1	Ken Griffey Jr.	4.00	1.80
❑ 2	Barry Bonds	1.00	.45
❑ 3	Jeff Bagwell	1.25	.55
❑ 4	Nomar Garciaparra	2.00	.90
❑ 5	Tony Gwynn	2.00	.90
❑ 6	Roger Clemens	1.50	.70
❑ 7	Chipper Jones	2.00	.90
❑ 8	Tino Martinez	.75	.35
❑ 9	Albert Belle	1.00	.45
❑ 10	Kenny Lofton	1.00	.45
❑ 11	Alex Rodriguez	2.50	1.10
❑ 12	Mark McGwire	4.00	1.80
❑ 13	Cal Ripken	3.00	1.35
❑ 14	Larry Walker	.75	.35
❑ 15	Mike Piazza	2.50	1.10
❑ 16	Frank Thomas	2.50	1.10
❑ 17	Juan Gonzalez	2.00	.90
❑ 18	Greg Maddux	2.50	1.10
❑ 19	Jose Cruz Jr.	3.00	1.35
❑ 20	Mo Vaughn	1.00	.45

1997 Upper Deck Ticket To Stardom

	MINT	NRMT
COMPLETE SET (20)	100.00	45.00
COMMON CARD (TS1-TS20)	1.50	.70

	Player		
❑ TS1	Chipper Jones	15.00	6.75
❑ TS2	Jermaine Dye	1.50	.70
❑ TS3	Rey Ordonez	3.00	1.35
❑ TS4	Alex Ochoa	1.50	.70
❑ TS5	Derek Jeter	15.00	6.75
❑ TS6	Ruben Rivera	3.00	1.35
❑ TS7	Billy Wagner	3.00	1.35
❑ TS8	Jason Kendall	5.00	2.20
❑ TS9	Darin Erstad	10.00	4.50
❑ TS10	Alex Rodriguez	20.00	9.00
❑ TS11	Bob Abreu	3.00	1.35
❑ TS12	Richard Hidalgo	3.00	1.35
❑ TS13	Karim Garcia	3.00	1.35
❑ TS14	Andruw Jones	10.00	4.50
❑ TS15	Carlos Delgado	3.00	1.35
❑ TS16	Rocky Coppinger	1.50	.70
❑ TS17	Jeff D'Amico	1.50	.70
❑ TS18	Johnny Damon	3.00	1.35
❑ TS19	John Wasdin	1.50	.70
❑ TS20	Manny Ramirez	6.00	2.70

1998 Upper Deck

	MINT	NRMT
COMPLETE SET (751)	200.00	90.00
COMPLETE SERIES 1 (270)	50.00	22.00
COMPLETE SERIES 2 (270)	50.00	22.00
COMPLETE SERIES 3 (211)	100.00	45.00
COMMON (1-600/631-750)	.15	.07
COMMON EP (601-630)	1.25	.55

	Player		
❑ 1	Tino Martinez HIST	.25	.11
❑ 2	Jimmy Key HIST	.15	.07
❑ 3	Jay Buhner HIST	.15	.07
❑ 4	Mark Gardner HIST	.15	.07
❑ 5	Greg Maddux HIST	1.00	.45
❑ 6	Pedro Martinez HIST	.25	.11
❑ 7	Hideo Nomo HIST	.60	.25
❑ 8	Sammy Sosa HIST	.75	.35
❑ 9	Mark McGwire GHL	4.00	1.80
❑ 10	Ken Griffey Jr. GHL	3.00	1.35
❑ 11	Larry Walker GHL	.25	.11
❑ 12	Tino Martinez GHL	.25	.11
❑ 13	Mike Piazza GHL	2.00	.90
❑ 14	Jose Cruz Jr. GHL	.75	.35
❑ 15	Tony Gwynn GHL	1.50	.70
❑ 16	Greg Maddux GHL	2.00	.90
❑ 17	Roger Clemens GHL	1.25	.55
❑ 18	Alex Rodriguez GHL	2.00	.90
❑ 19	Shigetoshi Hasegawa	.25	.11
❑ 20	Eddie Murray	.60	.25
❑ 21	Jason Dickson	.25	.11
❑ 22	Darin Erstad	.75	.35
❑ 23	Chuck Finley	.25	.11
❑ 24	Dave Hollins	.15	.07
❑ 25	Garret Anderson	.25	.11
❑ 26	Michael Tucker	.25	.11
❑ 27	Kenny Lofton	.60	.25
❑ 28	Javier Lopez	.25	.11
❑ 29	Fred McGriff	.40	.18
❑ 30	Greg Maddux	2.00	.90
❑ 31	Jeff Blauser	.15	.07
❑ 32	John Smoltz	.25	.11
❑ 33	Mark Wohlers	.15	.07
❑ 34	Scott Erickson	.25	.11
❑ 35	Jimmy Key	.25	.11
❑ 36	Harold Baines	.25	.11
❑ 37	Randy Myers	.25	.11
❑ 38	B.J. Surhoff	.25	.11
❑ 39	Eric Davis	.25	.11
❑ 40	Rafael Palmeiro	.40	.18
❑ 41	Jeffrey Hammonds	.25	.11
❑ 42	Mo Vaughn	.75	.35
❑ 43	Tom Gordon	.25	.11
❑ 44	Tim Naehring	.15	.07
❑ 45	Darren Bragg	.15	.07
❑ 46	Aaron Sele	.25	.11
❑ 47	Troy O'Leary	.25	.11
❑ 48	John Valentin	.25	.11
❑ 49	Doug Glanville	.25	.11
❑ 50	Ryne Sandberg	.75	.35
❑ 51	Steve Trachsel	.15	.07
❑ 52	Mark Grace	.40	.18
❑ 53	Kevin Foster	.15	.07
❑ 54	Kevin Tapani	.15	.07
❑ 55	Kevin Orie	.15	.07
❑ 56	Lyle Mouton	.15	.07
❑ 57	Ray Durham	.25	.11
❑ 58	Jaime Navarro	.15	.07
❑ 59	Mike Cameron	.25	.11
❑ 60	Albert Belle	.75	.35
❑ 61	Doug Drabek	.15	.07
❑ 62	Chris Snopek	.15	.07
❑ 63	Ed Taubensee	.15	.07
❑ 64	Terry Pendleton	.25	.11
❑ 65	Barry Larkin	.40	.18
❑ 66	Willie Greene	.25	.11
❑ 67	Deion Sanders	.25	.11
❑ 68	Pokey Reese	.15	.07
❑ 69	Jeff Shaw	.25	.11
❑ 70	Jim Thome	.60	.25
❑ 71	Orel Hershiser	.25	.11
❑ 72	Omar Vizquel	.25	.11
❑ 73	Brian Giles	.25	.11
❑ 74	David Justice	.60	.25
❑ 75	Bartolo Colon	.25	.11
❑ 76	Sandy Alomar Jr.	.25	.11
❑ 77	Neifi Perez	.25	.11
❑ 78	Dante Bichette	.25	.11
❑ 79	Vinny Castilla	.40	.18
❑ 80	Eric Young	.25	.11
❑ 81	Quinton McCracken	.25	.11
❑ 82	Jamey Wright	.15	.07
❑ 83	John Thomson	.15	.07
❑ 84	Damion Easley	.25	.11
❑ 85	Justin Thompson	.25	.11
❑ 86	Willie Blair	.15	.07
❑ 87	Raul Casanova	.15	.07
❑ 88	Bobby Higginson	.40	.18
❑ 89	Bubba Trammell	.25	.11
❑ 90	Tony Clark	.40	.18
❑ 91	Livan Hernandez	.25	.11
❑ 92	Charles Johnson	.25	.11
❑ 93	Edgar Renteria	.25	.11
❑ 94	Alex Fernandez	.15	.07
❑ 95	Gary Sheffield	.40	.18
❑ 96	Moises Alou	.40	.18
❑ 97	Tony Saunders	.15	.07
❑ 98	Robb Nen	.25	.11
❑ 99	Darryl Kile	.25	.11
❑ 100	Craig Biggio	.60	.25
❑ 101	Chris Holt	.15	.07
❑ 102	Bob Abreu	.25	.11
❑ 103	Luis Gonzalez	.15	.07
❑ 104	Billy Wagner	.25	.11
❑ 105	Brad Ausmus	.15	.07
❑ 106	Chili Davis	.25	.11
❑ 107	Tim Belcher	.15	.07
❑ 108	Dean Palmer	.25	.11
❑ 109	Jeff King	.25	.11
❑ 110	Jose Rosado	.15	.07
❑ 111	Mike Macfarlane	.15	.07
❑ 112	Jay Bell	.25	.11
❑ 113	Todd Worrell	.15	.07
❑ 114	Chan Ho Park	.60	.25
❑ 115	Raul Mondesi	.40	.18
❑ 116	Brett Butler	.25	.11
❑ 117	Greg Gagne	.15	.07
❑ 118	Hideo Nomo	.75	.35
❑ 119	Todd Zeile	.25	.11
❑ 120	Eric Karros	.25	.11
❑ 121	Cal Eldred	.15	.07
❑ 122	Jeff D'Amico	.15	.07
❑ 123	Antone Williamson	.15	.07
❑ 124	Doug Jones	.15	.07
❑ 125	Dave Nilsson	.15	.07
❑ 126	Gerald Williams	.15	.07
❑ 127	Fernando Vina	.15	.07
❑ 128	Ron Coomer	.15	.07
❑ 129	Matt Lawton	.25	.11
❑ 130	Paul Molitor	.60	.25
❑ 131	Todd Walker	.40	.18
❑ 132	Rick Aguilera	.15	.07
❑ 133	Brad Radke	.25	.11
❑ 134	Bob Tewksbury	.15	.07
❑ 135	Vladimir Guerrero	1.00	.45
❑ 136	Tony Gwynn DG	.75	.35
❑ 137	Roger Clemens DG	.60	.25
❑ 138	Dennis Eckersley DG	.15	.07
❑ 139	Brady Anderson DG	.15	.07
❑ 140	Ken Griffey Jr. DG	1.50	.70
❑ 141	Derek Jeter DG	.75	.35
❑ 142	Ken Caminiti DG	.15	.07
❑ 143	Frank Thomas DG	1.00	.45
❑ 144	Barry Bonds DG	.40	.18
❑ 145	Cal Ripken DG	1.25	.55
❑ 146	Alex Rodriguez DG	1.00	.45
❑ 147	Greg Maddux DG	1.00	.45
❑ 148	Kenny Lofton DG	.25	.11
❑ 149	Mike Piazza DG	1.00	.45
❑ 150	Mark McGwire DG	2.00	.90
❑ 151	Andruw Jones DG	.40	.18
❑ 152	Rusty Greer DG	.15	.07
❑ 153	F.P. Santangelo DG	.15	.07
❑ 154	Mike Lansing	.15	.07
❑ 155	Lee Smith	.25	.11
❑ 156	Carlos Perez	.25	.11
❑ 157	Pedro Martinez	.60	.25
❑ 158	Ryan McGuire	.15	.07
❑ 159	F.P. Santangelo	.15	.07
❑ 160	Rondell White	.25	.11
❑ 161	Takashi Kashiwada	.40	.18
❑ 162	Butch Huskey	.15	.07
❑ 163	Edgardo Alfonzo	.25	.11
❑ 164	John Franco	.25	.11
❑ 165	Todd Hundley	.25	.11
❑ 166	Rey Ordonez	.25	.11
❑ 167	Armando Reynoso	.15	.07
❑ 168	John Olerud	.25	.11
❑ 169	Bernie Williams	.60	.25
❑ 170	Andy Pettitte	.40	.18
❑ 171	Wade Boggs	.60	.25
❑ 172	Paul O'Neill	.25	.11
❑ 173	Cecil Fielder	.25	.11
❑ 174	Charlie Hayes	.15	.07
❑ 175	David Cone	.40	.18
❑ 176	Hideki Irabu	.40	.18
❑ 177	Mark Bellhorn	.25	.11
❑ 178	Steve Karsay	.15	.07
❑ 179	Damon Mashore	.15	.07
❑ 180	Jason McDonald	.15	.07
❑ 181	Scott Spiezio	.15	.07
❑ 182	Ariel Prieto	.15	.07
❑ 183	Jason Giambi	.25	.11
❑ 184	Wendell Magee	.15	.07
❑ 185	Rico Brogna	.25	.11
❑ 186	Garrett Stephenson	.15	.07
❑ 187	Wayne Gomes	.15	.07
❑ 188	Ricky Bottalico	.25	.11
❑ 189	Mickey Morandini	.15	.07
❑ 190	Mike Lieberthal	.15	.07
❑ 191	Kevin Polcovich	.15	.07
❑ 192	Francisco Cordova	.15	.07
❑ 193	Kevin Young	.25	.11
❑ 194	Jon Lieber	.15	.07
❑ 195	Kevin Elster	.15	.07
❑ 196	Tony Womack	.25	.11
❑ 197	Lou Collier	.15	.07
❑ 198	Mike Difelice	.15	.07
❑ 199	Gary Gaetti	.15	.07
❑ 200	Dennis Eckersley	.25	.11
❑ 201	Alan Benes	.25	.11
❑ 202	Willie McGee	.15	.07
❑ 203	Ron Gant	.15	.07
❑ 204	Fernando Valenzuela	.25	.11
❑ 205	Mark McGwire	4.00	1.80
❑ 206	Archi Cianfrocco	.15	.07

		Card	Price 1	Price 2
❑	207	Andy Ashby	.15	.07
❑	208	Steve Finley	.25	.11
❑	209	Quilvio Veras	.15	.07
❑	210	Ken Caminiti	.40	.18
❑	211	Rickey Henderson	.60	.25
❑	212	Joey Hamilton	.25	.11
❑	213	Derrek Lee	.25	.11
❑	214	Bill Mueller	.25	.11
❑	215	Shawn Estes	.25	.11
❑	216	J.T. Snow	.25	.11
❑	217	Mark Gardner	.15	.07
❑	218	Terry Mulholland	.15	.07
❑	219	Dante Powell	.25	.11
❑	220	Jeff Kent	.25	.11
❑	221	Jamie Moyer	.15	.07
❑	222	Joey Cora	.25	.11
❑	223	Jeff Fassero	.15	.07
❑	224	Dennis Martinez	.25	.11
❑	225	Ken Griffey Jr.	3.00	1.35
❑	226	Edgar Martinez	.25	.11
❑	227	Russ Davis	.25	.11
❑	228	Dan Wilson	.15	.07
❑	229	Will Clark	.60	.25
❑	230	Ivan Rodriguez	.75	.35
❑	231	Benji Gil	.15	.07
❑	232	Lee Stevens	.15	.07
❑	233	Mickey Tettleton	.15	.07
❑	234	Julio Santana	.15	.07
❑	235	Rusty Greer	.25	.11
❑	236	Bobby Witt	.15	.07
❑	237	Ed Sprague	.15	.07
❑	238	Pat Hentgen	.25	.11
❑	239	Kelvim Escobar	.25	.11
❑	240	Joe Carter	.25	.11
❑	241	Carlos Delgado	.25	.11
❑	242	Shannon Stewart	.25	.11
❑	243	Benito Santiago	.15	.07
❑	244	Tino Martinez SH	.25	.11
❑	245	Ken Griffey Jr. SH	1.50	.70
❑	246	Kevin Brown SH	.15	.07
❑	247	Ryne Sandberg SH	.40	.18
❑	248	Mo Vaughn SH	.40	.18
❑	249	Darryl Hamilton SH	.15	.07
❑	250	Randy Johnson SH	.25	.11
❑	251	Steve Finley SH	.15	.07
❑	252	Bobby Higginson SH	.15	.07
❑	253	Brett Tomko	.25	.11
❑	254	Mark Kotsay	.40	.18
❑	255	Jose Guillen	.25	.11
❑	256	Eli Marrero	.25	.11
❑	257	Dennis Reyes	.25	.11
❑	258	Richie Sexson	.40	.18
❑	259	Pat Cline	.25	.11
❑	260	Todd Helton	.75	.35
❑	261	Juan Melo	.25	.11
❑	262	Matt Morris	.25	.11
❑	263	Jeremi Gonzalez	.25	.11
❑	264	Jeff Abbott	.25	.11
❑	265	Aaron Boone	.15	.07
❑	266	Todd Dunwoody	.25	.11
❑	267	Jaret Wright	.75	.35
❑	268	Derrick Gibson	.25	.11
❑	269	Mario Valdez	.25	.11
❑	270	Fernando Tatis	.25	.11
❑	271	Craig Counsell	.15	.07
❑	272	Brad Rigby	.15	.07
❑	273	Danny Clyburn	.15	.07
❑	274	Brian Rose	.25	.11
❑	275	Miguel Tejada	.25	.11
❑	276	Jason Varitek	.15	.07
❑	277	Dave Dellucci	.75	.35
❑	278	Michael Coleman	.25	.11
❑	279	Adam Riggs	.15	.07
❑	280	Ben Grieve	1.25	.55
❑	281	Brad Fullmer	.25	.11
❑	282	Ken Cloude	.25	.11
❑	283	Tom Evans	.25	.11
❑	284	Kevin Millwood	1.50	.70
❑	285	Paul Konerko	.60	.25
❑	286	Juan Encarnacion	.25	.11
❑	287	Chris Carpenter	.25	.11
❑	288	Tom Fordham	.15	.07
❑	289	Gary DiSarcina	.15	.07
❑	290	Tim Salmon	.60	.25
❑	291	Troy Percival	.25	.11
❑	292	Todd Greene	.25	.11
❑	293	Ken Hill	.15	.07
❑	294	Dennis Springer	.15	.07
❑	295	Jim Edmonds	.40	.18
❑	296	Allen Watson	.15	.07
❑	297	Brian Anderson	.25	.11
❑	298	Keith Lockhart	.15	.07
❑	299	Tom Glavine	.60	.25
❑	300	Chipper Jones	1.50	.70
❑	301	Randall Simon	.25	.11
❑	302	Mark Lemke	.15	.07
❑	303	Ryan Klesko	.25	.11
❑	304	Denny Neagle	.25	.11
❑	305	Andruw Jones	.75	.35
❑	306	Mike Mussina	.60	.25
❑	307	Brady Anderson	.25	.11
❑	308	Chris Hoiles	.15	.07
❑	309	Mike Bordick	.15	.07
❑	310	Cal Ripken	2.50	1.10
❑	311	Geronimo Berroa	.15	.07
❑	312	Armando Benitez	.15	.07
❑	313	Roberto Alomar	.60	.25
❑	314	Tim Wakefield	.15	.07
❑	315	Reggie Jefferson	.15	.07
❑	316	Jeff Frye	.15	.07
❑	317	Scott Hatteberg	.15	.07
❑	318	Steve Avery	.15	.07
❑	319	Robinson Checo	.25	.11
❑	320	Nomar Garciaparra	2.00	.90
❑	321	Lance Johnson	.15	.07
❑	322	Tyler Houston	.15	.07
❑	323	Mark Clark	.15	.07
❑	324	Terry Adams	.15	.07
❑	325	Sammy Sosa	1.50	.70
❑	326	Scott Servais	.15	.07
❑	327	Manny Alexander	.15	.07
❑	328	Norberto Martin	.15	.07
❑	329	Scott Eyre	.15	.07
❑	330	Frank Thomas	2.00	.90
❑	331	Robin Ventura	.25	.11
❑	332	Matt Karchner	.15	.07
❑	333	Keith Foulke	.15	.07
❑	334	James Baldwin	.25	.11
❑	335	Chris Stynes	.15	.07
❑	336	Bret Boone	.25	.11
❑	337	Jon Nunnally	.15	.07
❑	338	Dave Burba	.15	.07
❑	339	Eduardo Perez	.15	.07
❑	340	Reggie Sanders	.25	.11
❑	341	Mike Remlinger	.15	.07
❑	342	Pat Watkins	.15	.07
❑	343	Chad Ogea	.15	.07
❑	344	John Smiley	.15	.07
❑	345	Kenny Lofton	.60	.25
❑	346	Jose Mesa	.15	.07
❑	347	Charles Nagy	.25	.11
❑	348	Enrique Wilson	.25	.11
❑	349	Bruce Aven	.15	.07
❑	350	Manny Ramirez	.60	.25
❑	351	Jerry DiPoto	.15	.07
❑	352	Ellis Burks	.25	.11
❑	353	Kirt Manwaring	.15	.07
❑	354	Vinny Castilla	.40	.18
❑	355	Larry Walker	.60	.25
❑	356	Kevin Ritz	.15	.07
❑	357	Pedro Astacio	.15	.07
❑	358	Scott Sanders	.15	.07
❑	359	Deivi Cruz	.15	.07
❑	360	Brian L. Hunter	.25	.11
❑	361	Pedro Martinez HM	.25	.11
❑	362	Tom Glavine HM	.25	.11
❑	363	Willie McGee HM	.15	.07
❑	364	J.T. Snow HM	.15	.07
❑	365	Rusty Greer HM	.15	.07
❑	366	Mike Grace HM	.15	.07
❑	367	Tony Clark HM	.15	.07
❑	368	Ben Grieve HM	.60	.25
❑	369	Gary Sheffield HM	.15	.07
❑	370	Joe Oliver	.15	.07
❑	371	Todd Jones	.15	.07
❑	372	Frank Catalanotto	.25	.11
❑	373	Brian Moehler	.15	.07
❑	374	Cliff Floyd	.25	.11
❑	375	Bobby Bonilla	.25	.11
❑	376	Al Leiter	.25	.11
❑	377	Josh Booty	.15	.07
❑	378	Darren Daulton	.25	.11
❑	379	Jay Powell	.15	.07
❑	380	Felix Heredia	.15	.07
❑	381	Jim Eisenreich	.15	.07
❑	382	Richard Hidalgo	.25	.11
❑	383	Mike Hampton	.15	.07
❑	384	Shane Reynolds	.25	.11
❑	385	Jeff Bagwell	1.00	.45
❑	386	Derek Bell	.25	.11
❑	387	Ricky Gutierrez	.15	.07
❑	388	Bill Spiers	.15	.07
❑	389	Jose Offerman	.15	.07
❑	390	Johnny Damon	.25	.11
❑	391	Jermaine Dye	.15	.07
❑	392	Jeff Montgomery	.15	.07
❑	393	Glendon Rusch	.15	.07
❑	394	Mike Sweeney	.15	.07
❑	395	Kevin Appier	.25	.11
❑	396	Joe Vitiello	.15	.07
❑	397	Ramon Martinez	.25	.11
❑	398	Darren Dreifort	.25	.11
❑	399	Wilton Guerrero	.15	.07
❑	400	Mike Piazza	2.00	.90
❑	401	Eddie Murray	.60	.25
❑	402	Ismael Valdes	.25	.11
❑	403	Todd Hollandsworth	.15	.07
❑	404	Mark Loretta	.15	.07
❑	405	Jeromy Burnitz	.25	.11
❑	406	Jeff Cirillo	.25	.11
❑	407	Scott Karl	.15	.07
❑	408	Mike Matheny	.15	.07
❑	409	Jose Valentin	.15	.07
❑	410	John Jaha	.15	.07
❑	411	Terry Steinbach	.25	.11
❑	412	Torii Hunter	.15	.07
❑	413	Pat Meares	.15	.07
❑	414	Marty Cordova	.15	.07
❑	415	Jaret Wright PH	.40	.18
❑	416	Mike Mussina PH	.25	.11
❑	417	John Smoltz PH	.15	.07
❑	418	Devon White PH	.15	.07
❑	419	Denny Neagle PH	.15	.07
❑	420	Livan Hernandez PH	.15	.07
❑	421	Kevin Brown PH	.15	.07
❑	422	Marquis Grissom PH	.15	.07
❑	423	Mike Mussina PH	.25	.11
❑	424	Eric Davis PH	.15	.07
❑	425	Tony Fernandez PH	.15	.07
❑	426	Moises Alou PH	.15	.07
❑	427	Sandy Alomar Jr. PH	.15	.07
❑	428	Gary Sheffield PH	.15	.07
❑	429	Jaret Wright PH	.40	.18
❑	430	Livan Hernandez PH	.15	.07
❑	431	Chad Ogea PH	.15	.07
❑	432	Edgar Renteria PH	.15	.07
❑	433	LaTroy Hawkins	.15	.07
❑	434	Rich Robertson	.15	.07
❑	435	Chuck Knoblauch	.60	.25
❑	436	Jose Vidro	.15	.07
❑	437	Dustin Hermanson	.25	.11
❑	438	Jim Bullinger	.15	.07
❑	439	Orlando Cabrera	.25	.11
❑	440	Vladimir Guerrero	1.00	.45
❑	441	Ugueth Urbina	.25	.11
❑	442	Brian McRae	.15	.07
❑	443	Matt Franco	.15	.07
❑	444	Bobby Jones	.15	.07
❑	445	Bernard Gilkey	.15	.07
❑	446	Dave Mlicki	.15	.07
❑	447	Brian Bohanon	.15	.07
❑	448	Mel Rojas	.15	.07
❑	449	Tim Raines	.25	.11
❑	450	Derek Jeter	1.50	.70
❑	451	Roger Clemens UE	.60	.25
❑	452	Nomar Garciaparra UE	1.00	.45
❑	453	Mike Piazza UE	1.00	.45
❑	454	Mark McGwire UE	2.00	.90
❑	455	Ken Griffey Jr. UE	1.50	.70
❑	456	Larry Walker UE	.25	.11
❑	457	Alex Rodriguez UE	1.00	.45
❑	458	Tony Gwynn UE	.75	.35
❑	459	Frank Thomas UE	1.00	.45
❑	460	Tino Martinez	.60	.25
❑	461	Chad Curtis	.15	.07

❑ 462	Ramiro Mendoza	.25	.11
❑ 463	Joe Girardi	.15	.07
❑ 464	David Wells	.40	.18
❑ 465	Mariano Rivera	.25	.11
❑ 466	Willie Adams	.15	.07
❑ 467	George Williams	.15	.07
❑ 468	Dave Telgheder	.15	.07
❑ 469	Dave Magadan	.15	.07
❑ 470	Matt Stairs	.25	.11
❑ 471	Bill Taylor	.15	.07
❑ 472	Jimmy Haynes	.15	.07
❑ 473	Gregg Jefferies	.15	.07
❑ 474	Midre Cummings	.15	.07
❑ 475	Curt Schilling	.25	.11
❑ 476	Mike Grace	.15	.07
❑ 477	Mark Leiter	.15	.07
❑ 478	Matt Beech	.15	.07
❑ 479	Scott Rolen	1.50	.70
❑ 480	Jason Kendall	.25	.11
❑ 481	Esteban Loaiza	.15	.07
❑ 482	Jermaine Allensworth	.15	.07
❑ 483	Mark Smith	.15	.07
❑ 484	Jason Schmidt	.15	.07
❑ 485	Jose Guillen	.25	.11
❑ 486	Al Martin	.15	.07
❑ 487	Delino DeShields	.15	.07
❑ 488	Todd Stottlemyre	.25	.11
❑ 489	Brian Jordan	.25	.11
❑ 490	Ray Lankford	.25	.11
❑ 491	Matt Morris	.25	.11
❑ 492	Royce Clayton	.15	.07
❑ 493	John Mabry	.15	.07
❑ 494	Wally Joyner	.25	.11
❑ 495	Trevor Hoffman	.25	.11
❑ 496	Chris Gomez	.15	.07
❑ 497	Sterling Hitchcock	.25	.11
❑ 498	Pete Smith	.15	.07
❑ 499	Greg Vaughn	.25	.11
❑ 500	Tony Gwynn	1.50	.70
❑ 501	Will Cunnane	.15	.07
❑ 502	Darryl Hamilton	.15	.07
❑ 503	Brian Johnson	.15	.07
❑ 504	Kirk Rueter	.15	.07
❑ 505	Barry Bonds	.75	.35
❑ 506	Osvaldo Fernandez	.15	.07
❑ 507	Stan Javier	.15	.07
❑ 508	Julian Tavarez	.15	.07
❑ 509	Rich Aurilia	.15	.07
❑ 510	Alex Rodriguez	2.00	.90
❑ 511	David Segui	.25	.11
❑ 512	Rich Amaral	.15	.07
❑ 513	Raul Ibanez	.15	.07
❑ 514	Jay Buhner	.25	.11
❑ 515	Randy Johnson	.60	.25
❑ 516	Heathcliff Slocumb	.15	.07
❑ 517	Tony Saunders	.15	.07
❑ 518	Kevin Elster	.15	.07
❑ 519	John Burkett	.15	.07
❑ 520	Juan Gonzalez	1.50	.70
❑ 521	John Wetteland	.25	.11
❑ 522	Domingo Cedeno	.15	.07
❑ 523	Darren Oliver	.15	.07
❑ 524	Roger Pavlik	.15	.07
❑ 525	Jose Cruz Jr.	.75	.35
❑ 526	Woody Williams	.15	.07
❑ 527	Alex Gonzalez	.15	.07
❑ 528	Robert Person	.15	.07
❑ 529	Juan Guzman	.15	.07
❑ 530	Roger Clemens	1.25	.55
❑ 531	Shawn Green	.25	.11
❑ 532	Francisco Cordova SH Ricardo Rincon Mark Smith	.15	.07
❑ 533	Nomar Garciaparra SH	1.00	.45
❑ 534	Roger Clemens SH	.60	.25
❑ 535	Mark McGwire SH	2.00	.90
❑ 536	Larry Walker SH	.25	.11
❑ 537	Mike Piazza SH	1.00	.45
❑ 538	Curt Schilling SH	.15	.07
❑ 539	Tony Gwynn SH	.75	.35
❑ 540	Ken Griffey Jr. SH	1.50	.70
❑ 541	Carl Pavano	.25	.11
❑ 542	Shane Monahan	.25	.11
❑ 543	Gabe Kapler	3.00	1.35
❑ 544	Eric Milton	.25	.11
❑ 545	Gary Matthews Jr.	.50	.23
❑ 546	Mike Kinkade	.50	.23
❑ 547	Ryan Christenson	.25	.11
❑ 548	Corey Koskie	.60	.25
❑ 549	Norm Hutchins	.25	.11
❑ 550	Russell Branyan	.25	.11
❑ 551	Masato Yoshii	.50	.23
❑ 552	Jesus Sanchez	.40	.18
❑ 553	Anthony Sanders	.25	.11
❑ 554	Edwin Diaz	.15	.07
❑ 555	Gabe Alvarez	.25	.11
❑ 556	Carlos Lee	1.00	.45
❑ 557	Mike Darr	.25	.11
❑ 558	Kerry Wood	3.00	1.35
❑ 559	Carlos Guillen	.25	.11
❑ 560	Sean Casey	.25	.11
❑ 561	Manny Aybar	.25	.11
❑ 562	Octavio Dotel	.25	.11
❑ 563	Jarrod Washburn	.25	.11
❑ 564	Mark L. Johnson	.15	.07
❑ 565	Ramon Hernandez	.25	.11
❑ 566	Rich Butler	.40	.18
❑ 567	Mike Caruso	.25	.11
❑ 568	Cliff Politte	.25	.11
❑ 569	Scott Elarton	.25	.11
❑ 570	Magglio Ordonez	.75	.35
❑ 571	Adam Butler	.25	.11
❑ 572	Marlon Anderson	.25	.11
❑ 573	Julio Ramirez	.75	.35
❑ 574	Darron Ingram	.50	.23
❑ 575	Bruce Chen	.25	.11
❑ 576	Steve Woodard	.25	.11
❑ 577	Hiram Bocachica	.25	.11
❑ 578	Kevin Witt	.25	.11
❑ 579	Javier Vazquez	.25	.11
❑ 580	Alex Gonzalez	.25	.11
❑ 581	Brian Powell	.15	.07
❑ 582	Wes Helms	.25	.11
❑ 583	Ron Wright	.25	.11
❑ 584	Rafael Medina	.25	.11
❑ 585	Daryle Ward	.25	.11
❑ 586	Geoff Jenkins	.25	.11
❑ 587	Preston Wilson	.25	.11
❑ 588	Jim Chamblee	.25	.11
❑ 589	Mike Lowell	.60	.25
❑ 590	A.J. Hinch	.25	.11
❑ 591	Francisco Cordero	.25	.11
❑ 592	Rolando Arrojo	1.00	.45
❑ 593	Braden Looper	.25	.11
❑ 594	Sidney Ponson	.25	.11
❑ 595	Matt Clement	.25	.11
❑ 596	Carlton Loewer	.25	.11
❑ 597	Brian Meadows	.15	.07
❑ 598	Danny Klassen	.25	.11
❑ 599	Larry Sutton	.15	.07
❑ 600	Travis Lee	1.25	.55
❑ 601	Randy Johnson EP	1.50	.70
❑ 602	Greg Maddux EP	5.00	2.20
❑ 603	Roger Clemens EP	3.00	1.35
❑ 604	Jaret Wright EP	2.00	.90
❑ 605	Mike Piazza EP	5.00	2.20
❑ 606	Tino Martinez EP	1.25	.55
❑ 607	Frank Thomas EP	5.00	2.20
❑ 608	Mo Vaughn EP	2.00	.90
❑ 609	Todd Helton EP	2.00	.90
❑ 610	Mark McGwire EP	10.00	4.50
❑ 611	Jeff Bagwell EP	2.50	1.10
❑ 612	Travis Lee EP	3.00	1.35
❑ 613	Scott Rolen EP	4.00	1.80
❑ 614	Cal Ripken EP	6.00	2.70
❑ 615	Chipper Jones EP	4.00	1.80
❑ 616	Nomar Garciaparra EP	5.00	2.20
❑ 617	Alex Rodriguez EP	5.00	2.20
❑ 618	Derek Jeter EP	4.00	1.80
❑ 619	Tony Gwynn EP	4.00	1.80
❑ 620	Ken Griffey Jr. EP	8.00	3.60
❑ 621	Kenny Lofton EP	1.25	.55
❑ 622	Juan Gonzalez EP	4.00	1.80
❑ 623	Jose Cruz Jr. EP	2.00	.90
❑ 624	Larry Walker EP	1.50	.70
❑ 625	Barry Bonds EP	2.00	.90
❑ 626	Ben Grieve EP	3.00	1.35
❑ 627	Andruw Jones EP	2.00	.90
❑ 628	Vladimir Guerrero EP	2.50	1.10
❑ 629	Paul Konerko EP	1.25	.55
❑ 630	Paul Molitor EP	1.50	.70
❑ 631	Cecil Fielder	.25	.11
❑ 632	Jack McDowell	.15	.07
❑ 633	Mike James	.15	.07
❑ 634	Brian Anderson	.25	.11
❑ 635	Jay Bell	.25	.11
❑ 636	Devon White	.25	.11
❑ 637	Andy Stankiewicz	.15	.07
❑ 638	Tony Batista	.15	.07
❑ 639	Omar Daal	.15	.07
❑ 640	Matt Williams	.25	.11
❑ 641	Brent Brede	.15	.07
❑ 642	Jorge Fabregas	.15	.07
❑ 643	Karim Garcia	.25	.11
❑ 644	Felix Rodriguez	.15	.07
❑ 645	Andy Benes	.25	.11
❑ 646	Willie Blair	.15	.07
❑ 647	Jeff Suppan	.15	.07
❑ 648	Yamil Benitez	.15	.07
❑ 649	Walt Weiss	.25	.11
❑ 650	Andres Galarraga	.60	.25
❑ 651	Doug Drabek	.15	.07
❑ 652	Ozzie Guillen	.15	.07
❑ 653	Joe Carter	.25	.11
❑ 654	Dennis Eckersley	.25	.11
❑ 655	Pedro Martinez	.60	.25
❑ 656	Jim Leyritz	.15	.07
❑ 657	Henry Rodriguez	.25	.11
❑ 658	Rod Beck	.25	.11
❑ 659	Mickey Morandini	.15	.07
❑ 660	Jeff Blauser	.15	.07
❑ 661	Ruben Sierra	.15	.07
❑ 662	Mike Sirotka	.15	.07
❑ 663	Pete Harnisch	.15	.07
❑ 664	Damian Jackson	.15	.07
❑ 665	Dmitri Young	.25	.11
❑ 666	Steve Cooke	.15	.07
❑ 667	Geronimo Berroa	.15	.07
❑ 668	Shawon Dunston	.15	.07
❑ 669	Mike Jackson	.15	.07
❑ 670	Travis Fryman	.25	.11
❑ 671	Dwight Gooden	.25	.11
❑ 672	Paul Assenmacher	.15	.07
❑ 673	Eric Plunk	.15	.07
❑ 674	Mike Lansing	.15	.07
❑ 675	Darryl Kile	.25	.11
❑ 676	Luis Gonzalez	.15	.07
❑ 677	Frank Castillo	.15	.07
❑ 678	Joe Randa	.15	.07
❑ 679	Bip Roberts	.15	.07
❑ 680	Derrek Lee	.25	.11
❑ 681	Mike Piazza SP New York Mets	5.00	2.20
❑ 681A	Mike Piazza SP Florida Marlins	5.00	2.20
❑ 682	Sean Berry	.15	.07
❑ 683	Ramon Garcia	.15	.07
❑ 684	Carl Everett	.15	.07
❑ 685	Moises Alou	.40	.18
❑ 686	Hal Morris	.15	.07
❑ 687	Jeff Conine	.25	.11
❑ 688	Gary Sheffield	.40	.18
❑ 689	Jose Vizcaino	.15	.07
❑ 690	Charles Johnson	.25	.11
❑ 691	Bobby Bonilla	.25	.11
❑ 692	Marquis Grissom	.25	.11
❑ 693	Alex Ochoa	.15	.07
❑ 694	Mike Morgan	.15	.07
❑ 695	Orlando Merced	.15	.07
❑ 696	David Ortiz	.25	.11
❑ 697	Brent Gates	.15	.07
❑ 698	Otis Nixon	.15	.07
❑ 699	Trey Moore	.15	.07
❑ 700	Derrick May	.15	.07
❑ 701	Rich Becker	.15	.07
❑ 702	Al Leiter	.25	.11
❑ 703	Chili Davis	.25	.11
❑ 704	Scott Brosius	.25	.11
❑ 705	Chuck Knoblauch	.60	.25
❑ 706	Kenny Rogers	.15	.07
❑ 707	Mike Blowers	.15	.07
❑ 708	Mike Fetters	.15	.07
❑ 709	Tom Candiotti	.15	.07
❑ 710	Rickey Henderson	.60	.25
❑ 711	Bob Abreu	.25	.11

Card	Mint	NrMt
❑ 712 Mark Lewis	.15	.07
❑ 713 Doug Glanville	.25	.11
❑ 714 Desi Relaford	.15	.07
❑ 715 Kent Mercker	.15	.07
❑ 716 Kevin Brown	.40	.18
❑ 717 James Mouton	.15	.07
❑ 718 Mark Langston	.15	.07
❑ 719 Greg Myers	.15	.07
❑ 720 Orel Hershiser	.25	.11
❑ 721 Charlie Hayes	.15	.07
❑ 722 Robb Nen	.25	.11
❑ 723 Glenallen Hill	.15	.07
❑ 724 Tony Saunders	.15	.07
❑ 725 Wade Boggs	.60	.25
❑ 726 Kevin Stocker	.15	.07
❑ 727 Wilson Alvarez	.25	.11
❑ 728 Albie Lopez	.15	.07
❑ 729 Dave Martinez	.15	.07
❑ 730 Fred McGriff	.40	.18
❑ 731 Quinton McCracken	.25	.11
❑ 732 Bryan Rekar	.15	.07
❑ 733 Paul Sorrento	.15	.07
❑ 734 Roberto Hernandez	.15	.07
❑ 735 Bubba Trammell	.25	.11
❑ 736 Miguel Cairo	.25	.11
❑ 737 John Flaherty	.15	.07
❑ 738 Terrell Wade	.15	.07
❑ 739 Roberto Kelly	.15	.07
❑ 740 Mark McLemore	.15	.07
❑ 741 Danny Patterson	.15	.07
❑ 742 Aaron Sele	.25	.11
❑ 743 Tony Fernandez	.15	.07
❑ 744 Randy Myers	.25	.11
❑ 745 Jose Canseco	.60	.25
❑ 746 Darrin Fletcher	.15	.07
❑ 747 Mike Stanley	.15	.07
❑ 748 Marquis Grissom SH CL	.15	.07
❑ 749 Fred McGriff SH CL	.15	.07
❑ 750 Travis Lee SH CL	.60	.25

1998 Upper Deck 10th Anniversary Preview

	MINT	NRMT
COMPLETE SET (60)	120.00	55.00
COMMON CARD (1-60)	.50	.23

*RETAIL VERSION: .1X BASIC CARDS

Card	Mint	NrMt
❑ 1 Greg Maddux	8.00	3.60
❑ 2 Mike Mussina	2.50	1.10
❑ 3 Roger Clemens	5.00	2.20
❑ 4 Hideo Nomo	3.00	1.35
❑ 5 David Cone	1.50	.70
❑ 6 Tom Glavine	2.50	1.10
❑ 7 Andy Pettitte	1.50	.70
❑ 8 Jimmy Key	1.00	.45
❑ 9 Randy Johnson	2.50	1.10
❑ 10 Dennis Eckersley	1.00	.45
❑ 11 Lee Smith	1.00	.45
❑ 12 John Franco	1.00	.45
❑ 13 Randy Myers	1.00	.45
❑ 14 Mike Piazza	8.00	3.60
❑ 15 Ivan Rodriguez	3.00	1.35
❑ 16 Todd Hundley	1.00	.45
❑ 17 Sandy Alomar Jr.	1.00	.45
❑ 18 Frank Thomas	8.00	3.60
❑ 19 Rafael Palmeiro	1.50	.70
❑ 20 Mark McGwire	15.00	6.75
❑ 21 Mo Vaughn	3.00	1.35
❑ 22 Fred McGriff	1.50	.70
❑ 23 Andres Galarraga	2.50	1.10
❑ 24 Mark Grace	1.50	.70
❑ 25 Jeff Bagwell	4.00	1.80
❑ 26 Roberto Alomar	2.50	1.10
❑ 27 Chuck Knoblauch	2.50	1.10
❑ 28 Ryne Sandberg	3.00	1.35
❑ 29 Eric Young	.50	.23
❑ 30 Craig Biggio	2.50	1.10
❑ 31 Carlos Baerga	.50	.23
❑ 32 Robin Ventura	1.00	.45
❑ 33 Matt Williams	1.00	.45
❑ 34 Wade Boggs	2.50	1.10
❑ 35 Dean Palmer	1.00	.45
❑ 36 Chipper Jones	6.00	2.70
❑ 37 Vinny Castilla	1.50	.70
❑ 38 Ken Caminiti	1.50	.70
❑ 39 Omar Vizquel	1.00	.45
❑ 40 Cal Ripken	10.00	4.50
❑ 41 Derek Jeter	6.00	2.70
❑ 42 Alex Rodriguez	8.00	3.60
❑ 43 Barry Larkin	1.50	.70
❑ 44 Mark Grudzielanek	.50	.23
❑ 45 Albert Belle	3.00	1.35
❑ 46 Manny Ramirez	2.50	1.10
❑ 47 Jose Canseco	2.50	1.10
❑ 48 Ken Griffey Jr.	12.00	5.50
❑ 49 Juan Gonzalez	6.00	2.70
❑ 50 Kenny Lofton	2.50	1.10
❑ 51 Sammy Sosa	6.00	2.70
❑ 52 Larry Walker	2.50	1.10
❑ 53 Gary Sheffield	1.50	.70
❑ 54 Rickey Henderson	2.50	1.10
❑ 55 Tony Gwynn	6.00	2.70
❑ 56 Barry Bonds	3.00	1.35
❑ 57 Paul Molitor	2.50	1.10
❑ 58 Edgar Martinez	1.00	.45
❑ 59 Chili Davis	1.00	.45
❑ 60 Eddie Murray	2.50	1.10

1998 Upper Deck A Piece of the Action 1

	MINT	NRMT
COMPLETE SET (10)	2000.00	900.00
COMMON CARD	50.00	22.00

Card	Mint	NrMt
❑ 1 Jay Buhner Bat	60.00	27.00
❑ 2 Tony Gwynn Bat	250.00	110.00
❑ 3 Tony Gwynn Jersey	300.00	135.00
❑ 4 Todd Hollandsworth Bat	50.00	22.00
❑ 5 Todd Hollandsworth Jersey	60.00	27.00
❑ 6 Greg Maddux Jersey	400.00	180.00
❑ 7 Alex Rodriguez Bat	300.00	135.00
❑ 8 Alex Rodriguez Jersey	400.00	180.00
❑ 9 Gary Sheffield Bat	80.00	36.00
❑ 10 Gary Sheffield Jersey	100.00	45.00

1998 Upper Deck A Piece of the Action 2

	MINT	NRMT
COMPLETE SET (4)	600.00	275.00
COMMON CARD	100.00	45.00

Card	Mint	NrMt
❑ AJ Andruw Jones	200.00	90.00
❑ GS Gary Sheffield	120.00	55.00
❑ JB Jay Buhner	100.00	45.00
❑ RA Roberto Alomar	200.00	90.00

1998 Upper Deck A Piece of the Action 3

	MINT	NRMT
COMMON CARD	200.00	90.00

Card	Mint	NrMt
❑ BG Ben Grieve/200	300.00	135.00
❑ JC Jose Cruz Jr./200	200.00	90.00
❑ KG Ken Griffey Jr./300	750.00	350.00
❑ KGS Ken Griffey Jr. AU/24	5000.00	2200.00
❑ TL Travis Lee/200	300.00	135.00

1998 Upper Deck All-Star Credentials

	MINT	NRMT
COMPLETE SET (30)	120.00	55.00
COMMON CARD (AS1-AS30)	2.00	.90

Card	Mint	NrMt
❑ AS1 Ken Griffey Jr.	12.00	5.50
❑ AS2 Travis Lee	4.00	1.80
❑ AS3 Ben Grieve	4.00	1.80
❑ AS4 Jose Cruz Jr.	2.50	1.10
❑ AS5 Andruw Jones	2.50	1.10
❑ AS6 Craig Biggio	2.00	.90
❑ AS7 Hideo Nomo	3.00	1.35
❑ AS8 Cal Ripken	10.00	4.50

		MINT	NRMT
❑ AS9	Jaret Wright	2.50	1.10
❑ AS10	Mark McGwire	15.00	6.75
❑ AS11	Derek Jeter	6.00	2.70
❑ AS12	Scott Rolen	5.00	2.20
❑ AS13	Jeff Bagwell	4.00	1.80
❑ AS14	Manny Ramirez	2.50	1.10
❑ AS15	Alex Rodriguez	8.00	3.60
❑ AS16	Chipper Jones	6.00	2.70
❑ AS17	Larry Walker	2.50	1.10
❑ AS18	Barry Bonds	3.00	1.35
❑ AS19	Tony Gwynn	6.00	2.70
❑ AS20	Mike Piazza	8.00	3.60
❑ AS21	Roger Clemens	5.00	2.20
❑ AS22	Greg Maddux	8.00	3.60
❑ AS23	Jim Thome	2.50	1.10
❑ AS24	Tino Martinez	2.00	.90
❑ AS25	Nomar Garciaparra	8.00	3.60
❑ AS26	Juan Gonzalez	6.00	2.70
❑ AS27	Kenny Lofton	2.00	.90
❑ AS28	Randy Johnson	2.50	1.10
❑ AS29	Todd Helton	2.50	1.10
❑ AS30	Frank Thomas	8.00	3.60

1998 Upper Deck Amazing Greats

	MINT	NRMT
COMPLETE SET (30)	600.00	275.00
COMMON CARD (AG1-AG30)	8.00	3.60
COMP.DIE CUT SET (30)	1500.00	700.00

*DIE CUT STARS: 1X TO 2.5X BASIC CARDS
DIE CUT PRINT RUN 250 SERIAL #'d SETS

		MINT	NRMT
❑ AG1	Ken Griffey Jr.	60.00	27.00
❑ AG2	Derek Jeter	30.00	13.50
❑ AG3	Alex Rodriguez	40.00	18.00
❑ AG4	Paul Molitor	12.00	5.50
❑ AG5	Jeff Bagwell	20.00	9.00
❑ AG6	Larry Walker	12.00	5.50
❑ AG7	Kenny Lofton	12.00	5.50
❑ AG8	Cal Ripken Jr.	50.00	22.00
❑ AG9	Juan Gonzalez	30.00	13.50
❑ AG10	Chipper Jones	30.00	13.50
❑ AG11	Greg Maddux	40.00	18.00
❑ AG12	Roberto Alomar	12.00	5.50
❑ AG13	Mike Piazza	40.00	18.00
❑ AG14	Andres Galarraga	12.00	5.50
❑ AG15	Barry Bonds	15.00	6.75
❑ AG16	Andy Pettitte	8.00	3.60
❑ AG17	Nomar Garciaparra	40.00	18.00
❑ AG18	Tino Martinez	12.00	5.50
❑ AG19	Tony Gwynn	30.00	13.50
❑ AG20	Frank Thomas	40.00	18.00
❑ AG21	Roger Clemens	25.00	11.00
❑ AG22	Sammy Sosa	30.00	13.50
❑ AG23	Jose Cruz Jr.	12.00	5.50
❑ AG24	Manny Ramirez	12.00	5.50
❑ AG25	Mark McGwire	80.00	36.00
❑ AG26	Randy Johnson	12.00	5.50
❑ AG27	Mo Vaughn	15.00	6.75
❑ AG28	Gary Sheffield	8.00	3.60
❑ AG29	Andruw Jones	12.00	5.50
❑ AG30	Albert Belle	20.00	9.00

1998 Upper Deck Blue Chip Prospects

	MINT	NRMT
COMPLETE SET (30)	400.00	180.00
COMMON CARD (BC1-BC30)	4.00	1.80

		MINT	NRMT
❑ BC1	Nomar Garciaparra	50.00	22.00
❑ BC2	Scott Rolen	30.00	13.50
❑ BC3	Jason Dickson	6.00	2.70
❑ BC4	Darin Erstad	15.00	6.75
❑ BC5	Brad Fullmer	6.00	2.70
❑ BC6	Jaret Wright	15.00	6.75
❑ BC7	Justin Thompson	6.00	2.70
❑ BC8	Matt Morris	6.00	2.70
❑ BC9	Fernando Tatis	6.00	2.70
❑ BC10	Alex Rodriguez	50.00	22.00
❑ BC11	Todd Helton	15.00	6.75
❑ BC12	Andy Pettitte	10.00	4.50
❑ BC13	Jose Cruz Jr.	15.00	6.75
❑ BC14	Mark Kotsay	10.00	4.50
❑ BC15	Derek Jeter	40.00	18.00
❑ BC16	Paul Konerko	12.00	5.50
❑ BC17	Todd Dunwoody	6.00	2.70
❑ BC18	Vladimir Guerrero	20.00	9.00
❑ BC19	Miguel Tejada	6.00	2.70
❑ BC20	Chipper Jones	40.00	18.00
❑ BC21	Kevin Orie	4.00	1.80
❑ BC22	Juan Encarnacion	6.00	2.70
❑ BC23	Brian Rose	6.00	2.70
❑ BC24	Livan Hernandez	6.00	2.70
❑ BC25	Andruw Jones	15.00	6.75
❑ BC26	Brian Giles	6.00	2.70
❑ BC27	Brett Tomko	6.00	2.70
❑ BC28	Jose Guillen	6.00	2.70
❑ BC29	Aaron Boone	4.00	1.80
❑ BC30	Ben Grieve	25.00	11.00

1998 Upper Deck Clearly Dominant

	MINT	NRMT
COMPLETE SET (30)	2000.00	900.00
COMMON CARD (CD1-CD30)	15.00	6.75

		MINT	NRMT
❑ CD1	Mark McGwire	250.00	110.00
❑ CD2	Derek Jeter	100.00	45.00
❑ CD3	Alex Rodriguez	120.00	55.00
❑ CD4	Paul Molitor	40.00	18.00
❑ CD5	Jeff Bagwell	60.00	27.00
❑ CD6	Ivan Rodriguez	50.00	22.00
❑ CD7	Kenny Lofton	40.00	18.00
❑ CD8	Cal Ripken	150.00	70.00
❑ CD9	Albert Belle	50.00	22.00
❑ CD10	Chipper Jones	100.00	45.00
❑ CD11	Gary Sheffield	25.00	11.00
❑ CD12	Roberto Alomar	40.00	18.00
❑ CD13	Mo Vaughn	50.00	22.00
❑ CD14	Andres Galarraga	40.00	18.00
❑ CD15	Nomar Garciaparra	120.00	55.00
❑ CD16	Randy Johnson	40.00	18.00
❑ CD17	Mike Mussina	40.00	18.00
❑ CD18	Greg Maddux	120.00	55.00
❑ CD19	Tony Gwynn	100.00	45.00
❑ CD20	Frank Thomas	120.00	55.00
❑ CD21	Roger Clemens	80.00	36.00
❑ CD22	Dennis Eckersley	15.00	6.75
❑ CD23	Juan Gonzalez	100.00	45.00
❑ CD24	Tino Martinez	40.00	18.00
❑ CD25	Andruw Jones	40.00	18.00
❑ CD26	Larry Walker	40.00	18.00
❑ CD27	Ken Caminiti	25.00	11.00
❑ CD28	Mike Piazza	120.00	55.00
❑ CD29	Barry Bonds	50.00	22.00
❑ CD30	Ken Griffey Jr.	200.00	90.00

1998 Upper Deck Destination Stardom

	MINT	NRMT
COMPLETE SET (60)	150.00	70.00
COMMON CARD (DS1-DS60)	.75	.35

		MINT	NRMT
❑ DS1	Travis Lee	6.00	2.70
❑ DS2	Nomar Garciaparra	10.00	4.50
❑ DS3	Alex Gonzalez	1.50	.70
❑ DS4	Richard Hidalgo	1.50	.70
❑ DS5	Jaret Wright	4.00	1.80
❑ DS6	Mike Kinkade	2.50	1.10
❑ DS7	Matt Morris	1.50	.70
❑ DS8	Gary Matthews Jr.	2.50	1.10
❑ DS9	Brett Tomko	1.50	.70
❑ DS10	Todd Helton	4.00	1.80
❑ DS11	Scott Elarton	1.50	.70
❑ DS12	Scott Rolen	8.00	3.60
❑ DS13	Jose Cruz Jr.	4.00	1.80
❑ DS14	Jarrod Washburn	1.50	.70
❑ DS15	Sean Casey	1.50	.70
❑ DS16	Magglio Ordonez	4.00	1.80
❑ DS17	Gabe Alvarez	1.50	.70
❑ DS18	Todd Dunwoody	1.50	.70
❑ DS19	Kevin Witt	1.50	.70
❑ DS20	Ben Grieve	6.00	2.70
❑ DS21	Daryle Ward	1.50	.70
❑ DS22	Matt Clement	1.50	.70
❑ DS23	Carlton Loewer	1.50	.70
❑ DS24	Javier Vazquez	1.50	.70
❑ DS25	Paul Konerko	2.50	1.10
❑ DS26	Preston Wilson	1.50	.70
❑ DS27	Wes Helms	1.50	.70
❑ DS28	Derek Jeter	8.00	3.60
❑ DS29	Corey Koskie	3.00	1.35
❑ DS30	Russell Branyan	1.50	.70
❑ DS31	Vladimir Guerrero	5.00	2.20
❑ DS32	Ryan Christenson	1.50	.70
❑ DS33	Carlos Lee	5.00	2.20

- ❑ DS34 Dave Dellucci 4.00 1.80
- ❑ DS35 Bruce Chen 1.50 .70
- ❑ DS36 Ricky Ledee 1.50 .70
- ❑ DS37 Ron Wright 1.50 .70
- ❑ DS38 Derrek Lee 1.50 .70
- ❑ DS39 Miguel Tejada 1.50 .70
- ❑ DS40 Brad Fullmer 1.50 .70
- ❑ DS41 Rich Butler 2.00 .90
- ❑ DS42 Chris Carpenter 1.50 .70
- ❑ DS43 Alex Rodriguez 10.00 4.50
- ❑ DS44 Darron Ingram 2.50 1.10
- ❑ DS45 Kerry Wood 15.00 6.75
- ❑ DS46 Jason Varitek .75 .35
- ❑ DS47 Ramon Hernandez 1.50 .70
- ❑ DS48 Aaron Boone .75 .35
- ❑ DS49 Juan Encarnacion 1.50 .70
- ❑ DS50 A.J. Hinch 1.50 .70
- ❑ DS51 Mike Lowell 2.50 1.10
- ❑ DS52 Fernando Tatis 1.50 .70
- ❑ DS53 Jose Guillen 1.50 .70
- ❑ DS54 Mike Caruso 1.50 .70
- ❑ DS55 Carl Pavano 1.50 .70
- ❑ DS56 Chris Clemons .75 .35
- ❑ DS57 Mark L. Johnson .75 .35
- ❑ DS58 Ken Cloude 1.50 .70
- ❑ DS59 Rolando Arrojo 5.00 2.20
- ❑ DS60 Mark Kotsay 2.00 .90

1998 Upper Deck Griffey Home Run Chronicles

	MINT	NRMT
COMPLETE SET (56)	220.00	100.00
COMPLETE SERIES 1 (30)	120.00	55.00
COMPLETE SERIES 2 (26)	100.00	45.00
COMMON GRIFFEY (1-56)	5.00	2.20

1998 Upper Deck National Pride

	MINT	NRMT
COMPLETE SET (42)	300.00	135.00
COMMON CARD (NP1-NP42)	2.50	1.10

- ❑ NP1 Dave Nilsson 2.50 1.10
- ❑ NP2 Larry Walker 10.00 4.50
- ❑ NP3 Edgar Renteria 4.00 1.80
- ❑ NP4 Jose Canseco 10.00 4.50
- ❑ NP5 Rey Ordonez 4.00 1.80
- ❑ NP6 Rafael Palmeiro 6.00 2.70
- ❑ NP7 Livan Hernandez 4.00 1.80
- ❑ NP8 Andruw Jones 10.00 4.50
- ❑ NP9 Manny Ramirez 10.00 4.50
- ❑ NP10 Sammy Sosa 25.00 11.00
- ❑ NP11 Raul Mondesi 6.00 2.70
- ❑ NP12 Moises Alou 6.00 2.70
- ❑ NP13 Pedro Martinez 10.00 4.50
- ❑ NP14 Vladimir Guerrero 12.00 5.50
- ❑ NP15 Chili Davis 4.00 1.80
- ❑ NP16 Hideo Nomo 12.00 5.50
- ❑ NP17 Hideki Irabu 6.00 2.70
- ❑ NP18 Shigetoshi Hasegawa 4.00 1.80
- ❑ NP19 Takashi Kashiwada 6.00 2.70
- ❑ NP20 Chan Ho Park 10.00 4.50
- ❑ NP21 Fernando Valenzuela 4.00 1.80
- ❑ NP22 Vinny Castilla 6.00 2.70
- ❑ NP23 Armando Reynoso 2.50 1.10
- ❑ NP24 Karim Garcia 4.00 1.80
- ❑ NP25 Marvin Benard 2.50 1.10
- ❑ NP26 Mariano Rivera 4.00 1.80
- ❑ NP27 Juan Gonzalez 25.00 11.00
- ❑ NP28 Roberto Alomar 10.00 4.50
- ❑ NP29 Ivan Rodriguez 12.00 5.50
- ❑ NP30 Carlos Delgado 4.00 1.80
- ❑ NP31 Bernie Williams 10.00 4.50
- ❑ NP32 Edgar Martinez 4.00 1.80
- ❑ NP33 Frank Thomas 30.00 13.50
- ❑ NP34 Barry Bonds 12.00 5.50
- ❑ NP35 Mike Piazza 30.00 13.50
- ❑ NP36 Chipper Jones 25.00 11.00
- ❑ NP37 Cal Ripken Jr. 40.00 18.00
- ❑ NP38 Alex Rodriguez 30.00 13.50
- ❑ NP39 Ken Griffey Jr. 50.00 22.00
- ❑ NP40 Andres Galarraga 10.00 4.50
- ❑ NP41 Omar Vizquel 4.00 1.80
- ❑ NP42 Ozzie Guillen 2.50 1.10

1998 Upper Deck Prime Nine

	MINT	NRMT
COMPLETE SET (60)	300.00	135.00
COMMON GRIFFEY (1-7)	10.00	4.50
COMMON PIAZZA (8-14)	6.00	2.70
COMMON F.THOMAS (15-21)	6.00	2.70
COMMON MCGWIRE (22-28)	12.00	5.50
COMMON RIPKEN (29-35)	8.00	3.60
COMMON J.GONZALEZ (36-42)	5.00	2.20
COMMON GWYNN (43-49)	5.00	2.20
COMMON BONDS (50-55)	2.50	1.10
COMMON MADDUX (56-60)	6.00	2.70

1998 Upper Deck Retrospectives

	MINT	NRMT
COMPLETE SET (30)	250.00	110.00
COMMON CARD (1-30)	3.00	1.35

- ❑ 1 Dennis Eckersley 3.00 1.35
- ❑ 2 Rickey Henderson 6.00 2.70
- ❑ 3 Harold Baines 3.00 1.35
- ❑ 4 Cal Ripken 25.00 11.00
- ❑ 5 Tony Gwynn 15.00 6.75
- ❑ 6 Wade Boggs 6.00 2.70
- ❑ 7 Orel Hershiser 3.00 1.35
- ❑ 8 Joe Carter 3.00 1.35
- ❑ 9 Roger Clemens 12.00 5.50
- ❑ 10 Barry Bonds 8.00 3.60
- ❑ 11 Mark McGwire 40.00 18.00
- ❑ 12 Greg Maddux 20.00 9.00
- ❑ 13 Fred McGriff 4.00 1.80
- ❑ 14 Rafael Palmeiro 4.00 1.80
- ❑ 15 Craig Biggio 6.00 2.70
- ❑ 16 Brady Anderson 3.00 1.35
- ❑ 17 Randy Johnson 6.00 2.70
- ❑ 18 Gary Sheffield 4.00 1.80
- ❑ 19 Albert Belle 6.00 2.70
- ❑ 20 Ken Griffey Jr. 30.00 13.50
- ❑ 21 Juan Gonzalez 15.00 6.75
- ❑ 22 Larry Walker 6.00 2.70
- ❑ 23 Tino Martinez 6.00 2.70
- ❑ 24 Frank Thomas 20.00 9.00
- ❑ 25 Jeff Bagwell 10.00 4.50
- ❑ 26 Kenny Lofton 6.00 2.70
- ❑ 27 Mo Vaughn 8.00 3.60
- ❑ 28 Mike Piazza 20.00 9.00
- ❑ 29 Alex Rodriguez 20.00 9.00
- ❑ 30 Chipper Jones 15.00 6.75

1998 Upper Deck Rookie Edition Preview

	MINT	NRMT
COMPLETE SET (10)	10.00	4.50
COMMON CARD (1-10)	.40	.18

- ❑ 1 Nomar Garciaparra 3.00 1.35
- ❑ 2 Scott Rolen 2.50 1.10
- ❑ 3 Mark Kotsay .60 .25
- ❑ 4 Todd Helton 1.25 .55
- ❑ 5 Paul Konerko 1.00 .45
- ❑ 6 Juan Encarnacion .40 .18
- ❑ 7 Brad Fullmer .40 .18
- ❑ 8 Miguel Tejada .40 .18
- ❑ 9 Richard Hidalgo .40 .18
- ❑ 10 Ben Grieve 2.00 .90

1998 Upper Deck Tape Measure Titans

	MINT	NRMT
COMPLETE SET (30)	250.00	110.00
COMMON CARD (1-30)	2.50	1.10

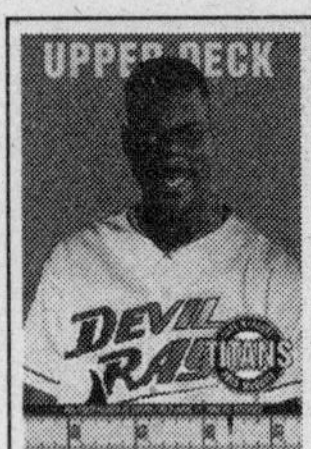

❑ 1 Mark McGwire	40.00	18.00
❑ 2 Andres Galarraga	6.00	2.70
❑ 3 Jeff Bagwell	10.00	4.50
❑ 4 Larry Walker	6.00	2.70
❑ 5 Frank Thomas	20.00	9.00
❑ 6 Rafael Palmeiro	4.00	1.80
❑ 7 Nomar Garciaparra	20.00	9.00
❑ 8 Mo Vaughn	8.00	3.60
❑ 9 Albert Belle	8.00	3.60
❑ 10 Ken Griffey Jr.	30.00	13.50
❑ 11 Manny Ramirez	6.00	2.70
❑ 12 Jim Thome	6.00	2.70
❑ 13 Tony Clark	4.00	1.80
❑ 14 Juan Gonzalez	15.00	6.75
❑ 15 Mike Piazza	20.00	9.00
❑ 16 Jose Canseco	6.00	2.70
❑ 17 Jay Buhner	2.50	1.10
❑ 18 Alex Rodriguez	20.00	9.00
❑ 19 Jose Cruz Jr.	6.00	2.70
❑ 20 Tino Martinez	6.00	2.70
❑ 21 Carlos Delgado	2.50	1.10
❑ 22 Andruw Jones	6.00	2.70
❑ 23 Chipper Jones	15.00	6.75
❑ 24 Fred McGriff	4.00	1.80
❑ 25 Matt Williams	2.50	1.10
❑ 26 Sammy Sosa	15.00	6.75
❑ 27 Vinny Castilla	4.00	1.80
❑ 28 Tim Salmon	6.00	2.70
❑ 29 Ken Caminiti	4.00	1.80
❑ 30 Barry Bonds	8.00	3.60

1998 Upper Deck Unparalleled

	MINT	NRMT
COMPLETE SET (20)	500.00	220.00
COMMON CARD (1-20)	10.00	4.50
❑ 1 Ken Griffey Jr.	60.00	27.00
❑ 2 Travis Lee	20.00	9.00
❑ 3 Ben Grieve	20.00	9.00
❑ 4 Jose Cruz Jr.	12.00	5.50
❑ 5 Nomar Garciaparra	40.00	18.00
❑ 6 Hideo Nomo	15.00	6.75
❑ 7 Kenny Lofton	10.00	4.50
❑ 8 Cal Ripken	50.00	22.00
❑ 9 Roger Clemens	25.00	11.00
❑ 10 Mike Piazza	40.00	18.00
❑ 11 Jeff Bagwell	20.00	9.00
❑ 12 Chipper Jones	30.00	13.50
❑ 13 Greg Maddux	40.00	18.00
❑ 14 Randy Johnson	12.00	5.50
❑ 15 Alex Rodriguez	40.00	18.00
❑ 16 Barry Bonds	15.00	6.75
❑ 17 Frank Thomas	40.00	18.00
❑ 18 Juan Gonzalez	30.00	13.50
❑ 19 Tony Gwynn	30.00	13.50
❑ 20 Mark McGwire	80.00	36.00

1999 Upper Deck

	MINT	NRMT
COMPLETE SERIES 1 (255)	60.00	27.00
COMMON CARD (1-255)	.15	.07
❑ 1 Troy Glaus SR	5.00	2.20
❑ 2 Adrian Beltre SR	2.50	1.10
❑ 3 Matt Anderson SR	1.00	.45
❑ 4 Eric Chavez SR	3.00	1.35
❑ 5 Jin Ho Cho SR	2.00	.90
❑ 6 Robert Smith SR	1.00	.45
❑ 7 George Lombard SR	1.00	.45
❑ 8 Mike Kinkade SR	1.00	.45
❑ 9 Seth Greisinger SR	1.00	.45
❑ 10 J.D. Drew SR	20.00	9.00
❑ 11 Aramis Ramirez SR	2.00	.90
❑ 12 Carlos Guillen SR	1.00	.45
❑ 13 Justin Baughman SR	1.00	.45
❑ 14 Jim Parque SR	1.00	.45
❑ 15 Ryan Jackson SR	1.00	.45
❑ 16 Ramon E.Martinez SR	1.50	.70
❑ 17 Orlando Hernandez SR	4.00	1.80
❑ 18 Jeremy Giambi SR	2.00	.90
❑ 19 Gary DiSarcina	.15	.07
❑ 20 Darin Erstad	.75	.35
❑ 21 Troy Glaus	1.25	.55
❑ 22 Chuck Finley	.15	.07
❑ 23 Dave Hollins	.15	.07
❑ 24 Troy Percival	.25	.11
❑ 25 Tim Salmon	.60	.25
❑ 26 Brian Anderson	.25	.11
❑ 27 Jay Bell	.25	.11
❑ 28 Andy Benes	.25	.11
❑ 29 Brent Brede	.15	.07
❑ 30 David Dellucci	.25	.11
❑ 31 Karim Garcia	.25	.11
❑ 32 Travis Lee	1.00	.45
❑ 33 Andres Galarraga	.60	.25
❑ 34 Ryan Klesko	.25	.11
❑ 35 Keith Lockhart	.15	.07
❑ 36 Kevin Millwood	.25	.11
❑ 37 Denny Neagle	.25	.11
❑ 38 John Smoltz	.25	.11
❑ 39 Michael Tucker	.15	.07
❑ 40 Walt Weiss	.25	.11
❑ 41 Dennis Martinez	.25	.11
❑ 42 Javy Lopez	.25	.11
❑ 43 Brady Anderson	.25	.11
❑ 44 Harold Baines	.25	.11
❑ 45 Mike Bordick	.15	.07
❑ 46 Roberto Alomar	.60	.25
❑ 47 Scott Erickson	.25	.11
❑ 48 Mike Mussina	.60	.25
❑ 49 Cal Ripken	2.50	1.10
❑ 50 Darren Bragg	.15	.07
❑ 51 Dennis Eckersley	.25	.11
❑ 52 Nomar Garciaparra	2.00	.90
❑ 53 Scott Hatteberg	.15	.07
❑ 54 Troy O'Leary	.25	.11
❑ 55 Bret Saberhagen	.25	.11
❑ 56 John Valentin	.25	.11
❑ 57 Rod Beck	.25	.11
❑ 58 Jeff Blauser	.15	.07
❑ 59 Brant Brown	.25	.11
❑ 60 Mark Clark	.15	.07
❑ 61 Mark Grace	.40	.18
❑ 62 Kevin Tapani	.15	.07
❑ 63 Henry Rodriguez	.25	.11
❑ 64 Mike Cameron	.25	.11
❑ 65 Mike Caruso	.25	.11
❑ 66 Ray Durham	.25	.11
❑ 67 Jaime Navarro	.15	.07
❑ 68 Magglio Ordonez	.25	.11
❑ 69 Mike Sirotka	.15	.07
❑ 70 Sean Casey	.25	.11
❑ 71 Barry Larkin	.40	.18
❑ 72 Jon Nunnally	.15	.07
❑ 73 Paul Konerko	.60	.25
❑ 74 Chris Stynes	.15	.07
❑ 75 Brett Tomko	.25	.11
❑ 76 Dmitri Young	.25	.11
❑ 77 Sandy Alomar Jr.	.25	.11
❑ 78 Bartolo Colon	.25	.11
❑ 79 Travis Fryman	.25	.11
❑ 80 Brian Giles	.25	.11
❑ 81 David Justice	.60	.25
❑ 82 Omar Vizquel	.25	.11
❑ 83 Jaret Wright	.60	.25
❑ 84 Jim Thome	.60	.25
❑ 85 Charles Nagy	.25	.11
❑ 86 Pedro Astacio	.15	.07
❑ 87 Todd Helton	.75	.35
❑ 88 Darryl Kile	.25	.11
❑ 89 Mike Lansing	.15	.07
❑ 90 Neifi Perez	.25	.11
❑ 91 John Thomson	.15	.07
❑ 92 Larry Walker	.60	.25
❑ 93 Tony Clark	.40	.18
❑ 94 Deivi Cruz	.15	.07
❑ 95 Damion Easley	.25	.11
❑ 96 Brian L.Hunter	.25	.11
❑ 97 Todd Jones	.15	.07
❑ 98 Brian Moehler	.15	.07
❑ 99 Gabe Alvarez	.25	.11
❑ 100 Craig Counsell	.15	.07
❑ 101 Cliff Floyd	.25	.11
❑ 102 Livan Hernandez	.25	.11
❑ 103 Andy Larkin	.15	.07
❑ 104 Derrek Lee	.25	.11
❑ 105 Brian Meadows	.15	.07
❑ 106 Moises Alou	.40	.18
❑ 107 Sean Berry	.15	.07
❑ 108 Craig Biggio	.60	.25
❑ 109 Ricky Gutierrez	.15	.07
❑ 110 Mike Hampton	.15	.07
❑ 111 Jose Lima	.15	.07
❑ 112 Billy Wagner	.25	.11
❑ 113 Hal Morris	.15	.07
❑ 114 Johnny Damon	.25	.11
❑ 115 Jeff King	.25	.11
❑ 116 Jeff Montgomery	.25	.11
❑ 117 Glendon Rusch	.15	.07
❑ 118 Larry Sutton	.15	.07
❑ 119 Bobby Bonilla	.25	.11
❑ 120 Jim Eisenreich	.15	.07
❑ 121 Eric Karros	.25	.11
❑ 122 Matt Luke	.15	.07
❑ 123 Ramon Martinez	.25	.11
❑ 124 Gary Sheffield	.40	.18
❑ 125 Eric Young	.15	.07
❑ 126 Charles Johnson	.25	.11
❑ 127 Jeff Cirillo	.25	.11
❑ 128 Marquis Grissom	.25	.11
❑ 129 Jeromy Burnitz	.25	.11
❑ 130 Bob Wickman	.15	.07
❑ 131 Scott Karl	.15	.07
❑ 132 Mark Loretta	.15	.07
❑ 133 Fernando Vina	.15	.07
❑ 134 Matt Lawton	.25	.11
❑ 135 Pat Meares	.15	.07
❑ 136 Eric Milton	.25	.11
❑ 137 Paul Molitor	.60	.25
❑ 138 David Ortiz	.25	.11

❑ 139 Todd Walker .40 .18
❑ 140 Shane Andrews .15 .07
❑ 141 Brad Fullmer .25 .11
❑ 142 Vladimir Guerrero 1.00 .45
❑ 143 Dustin Hermanson .25 .11
❑ 144 Ryan McGuire .15 .07
❑ 145 Ugueth Urbina .25 .11
❑ 146 John Franco .25 .11
❑ 147 Butch Huskey .15 .07
❑ 148 Bobby Jones .15 .07
❑ 149 John Olerud .25 .11
❑ 150 Rey Ordonez .25 .11
❑ 151 Mike Piazza 2.00 .90
❑ 152 Hideo Nomo .75 .35
❑ 153 Masato Yoshii .25 .11
❑ 154 Derek Jeter 1.50 .70
❑ 155 Chuck Knoblauch .40 .18
❑ 156 Paul O'Neill .25 .11
❑ 157 Andy Pettitte .40 .18
❑ 158 Mariano Rivera .25 .11
❑ 159 Darryl Strawberry .25 .11
❑ 160 David Wells .40 .18
❑ 161 Jorge Posada .25 .11
❑ 162 Ramiro Mendoza .25 .11
❑ 163 Miguel Tejada .25 .11
❑ 164 Ryan Christenson .15 .07
❑ 165 Rickey Henderson .60 .25
❑ 166 A.J. Hinch .25 .11
❑ 167 Ben Grieve 1.25 .55
❑ 168 Kenny Rogers .15 .07
❑ 169 Matt Stairs .25 .11
❑ 170 Bob Abreu .25 .11
❑ 171 Rico Brogna .25 .11
❑ 172 Doug Glanville .25 .11
❑ 173 Mike Grace .15 .07
❑ 174 Desi Relaford .15 .07
❑ 175 Scott Rolen 1.50 .70
❑ 176 Jose Guillen .25 .11
❑ 177 Francisco Cordova .15 .07
❑ 178 Al Martin .15 .07
❑ 179 Jason Schmidt .25 .11
❑ 180 Turner Ward .15 .07
❑ 181 Kevin Young .25 .11
❑ 182 Mark McGwire 4.00 1.80
❑ 183 Delino DeShields .15 .07
❑ 184 Eli Marrero .25 .11
❑ 185 Tom Lampkin .15 .07
❑ 186 Ray Lankford .25 .11
❑ 187 Willie McGee .15 .07
❑ 188 Matt Morris .25 .11
❑ 189 Andy Ashby .15 .07
❑ 190 Kevin Brown .40 .18
❑ 191 Ken Caminiti .40 .18
❑ 192 Trevor Hoffman .25 .11
❑ 193 Wally Joyner .25 .11
❑ 194 Greg Vaughn .25 .11
❑ 195 Danny Darwin .15 .07
❑ 196 Shawn Estes .25 .11
❑ 197 Orel Hershiser .25 .11
❑ 198 Jeff Kent .25 .11
❑ 199 Bill Mueller .25 .11
❑ 200 Robb Nen .25 .11
❑ 201 J.T. Snow .25 .11
❑ 202 Ken Cloude .25 .11
❑ 203 Russ Davis .15 .07
❑ 204 Jeff Fassero .15 .07
❑ 205 Ken Griffey Jr. 3.00 1.35
❑ 206 Shane Monahan .25 .11
❑ 207 David Segui .25 .11
❑ 208 Dan Wilson .15 .07
❑ 209 Wilson Alvarez .15 .07
❑ 210 Wade Boggs .60 .25
❑ 211 Miguel Cairo .25 .11
❑ 212 Bubba Trammell .25 .11
❑ 213 Quinton McCracken .25 .11
❑ 214 Paul Sorrento .15 .07
❑ 215 Kevin Stocker .15 .07
❑ 216 Will Clark .60 .25
❑ 217 Rusty Greer .25 .11
❑ 218 Rick Helling .25 .11
❑ 219 Mark McLemore .15 .07
❑ 220 Ivan Rodriguez .75 .35
❑ 221 John Wetteland .25 .11
❑ 222 Jose Canseco .60 .25
❑ 223 Roger Clemens 1.25 .55
❑ 224 Carlos Delgado .25 .11
❑ 225 Darrin Fletcher .15 .07
❑ 226 Alex Gonzalez .15 .07
❑ 227 Jose Cruz Jr. .60 .25
❑ 228 Shannon Stewart .25 .11
❑ 229 Rolando Arrojo FF .60 .25
❑ 230 Livan Hernandez FF .40 .18
❑ 231 Orlando Hernandez FF 1.00 .45
❑ 232 Raul Mondesi FF .50 .23
❑ 233 Moises Alou FF .50 .23
❑ 234 Pedro Martinez FF .60 .25
❑ 235 Sammy Sosa FF 1.50 .70
❑ 236 Vladimir Guerrero FF 1.00 .45
❑ 237 Bartolo Colon FF .40 .18
❑ 238 Miguel Tejada FF .40 .18
❑ 239 Ismael Valdes FF .40 .18
❑ 240 Mariano Rivera FF .40 .18
❑ 241 Jose Cruz Jr. FF .60 .25
❑ 242 Juan Gonzalez FF 1.50 .70
❑ 243 Ivan Rodriguez FF .75 .35
❑ 244 Sandy Alomar Jr. FF .40 .18
❑ 245 Roberto Alomar FF .60 .25
❑ 246 Magglio Ordonez FF .40 .18
❑ 247 Kerry Wood SH CL 1.00 .45
❑ 248 Mark McGwire SH CL 2.00 .90
❑ 249 David Wells SH CL .15 .07
❑ 250 Rolando Arrojo SH CL .25 .11
❑ 251 Ken Griffey Jr. SH CL 1.50 .70
❑ 252 Trevor Hoffman SH CL
❑ 253 Travis Lee SH CL .60 .25
❑ 254 Roberto Alomar SH CL .25 .11
❑ 255 Sammy Sosa SH CL .75 .35
❑ NNO Ken Griffey Jr. '89 AU

1999 Upper Deck Exclusives Level 1

	MINT	NRMT
COMMON CARD (1-255)	10.00	4.50

*STARS: 25X TO 60X BASIC CARDS
*YOUNG STARS: 20X TO 50X BASIC CARDS
*FOREIGN FOCUS: 12.5X TO 30X BASIC FF
*STAR ROOKIES: 4X TO 10X BASIC SR

1999 Upper Deck 10th Anniversary Team

	MINT	NRMT
COMPLETE SET (30)	60.00	27.00
COMMON CARD (X1-X30)	.50	.23

❑ X1 Mike Piazza 5.00 2.20
❑ X2 Mark McGwire 10.00 4.50
❑ X3 Roberto Alomar 1.50 .70
❑ X4 Chipper Jones 4.00 1.80
❑ X5 Cal Ripken 6.00 2.70
❑ X6 Ken Griffey Jr. 8.00 3.60
❑ X7 Barry Bonds 2.00 .90
❑ X8 Tony Gwynn 4.00 1.80
❑ X9 Nolan Ryan 8.00 3.60
❑ X10 Randy Johnson 1.50 .70
❑ X11 Dennis Eckersley .75 .35
❑ X12 Ivan Rodriguez 2.00 .90
❑ X13 Frank Thomas 5.00 2.20
❑ X14 Craig Biggio 1.50 .70
❑ X15 Wade Boggs 1.50 .70
❑ X16 Alex Rodriguez 5.00 2.20
❑ X17 Albert Belle 1.50 .70
❑ X18 Juan Gonzalez 4.00 1.80
❑ X19 Rickey Henderson 1.50 .70
❑ X20 Greg Maddux 5.00 2.20
❑ X21 Tom Glavine 1.50 .70
❑ X22 Randy Myers .50 .23
❑ X23 Sandy Alomar Jr. .75 .35
❑ X24 Jeff Bagwell 2.50 1.10
❑ X25 Derek Jeter 4.00 1.80
❑ X26 Matt Williams .75 .35
❑ X27 Kenny Lofton 1.50 .70
❑ X28 Sammy Sosa 4.00 1.80
❑ X29 Larry Walker 1.50 .70
❑ X30 Roger Clemens 3.00 1.35

1999 Upper Deck A Piece of History

	MINT	NRMT
COMMON CARD	2500.00	1100.00

❑ PH Babe Ruth 2500.00 1100.00
❑ LCPH Babe Ruth AU/3

1999 Upper Deck Crowning Glory

	MINT	NRMT
COMPLETE SET (3)	100.00	45.00
COMMON CARD (CG1-CG3)	25.00	11.00

❑ CG1 Roger Clemens 25.00 11.00
Kerry Wood

		MINT	NRMT
❑ CG2	Mark McGwire Barry Bonds	40.00	18.00
❑ CG3	Ken Griffey Jr. Mark McGwire	50.00	22.00

1999 Upper Deck Game Jerseys

	MINT	NRMT
COMPLETE SET (11)	2000.00	900.00
COMMON CARD	100.00	45.00

		MINT	NRMT
❑ AB	Adrian Beltre H	100.00	45.00
❑ AR	Alex Rodriguez H/R	300.00	135.00
❑ BG	Ben Grieve H	150.00	70.00
❑ CJ	Charles Johnson H/R	100.00	45.00
❑ DE	Darin Erstad H	100.00	45.00
❑ IR	Ivan Rodriguez H	120.00	55.00
❑ JG	Juan Gonzalez H/R	250.00	110.00
❑ KG	Ken Griffey Jr. H	400.00	180.00
❑ KW	Kerry Wood H/R	300.00	135.00
❑ MP	Mike Piazza H/R	300.00	135.00
❑ TL	Travis Lee H	120.00	55.00
❑ KGAU	Ken Griffey Jr. AU/24		
❑ KWAU	Kerry Wood AU/34		

1999 Upper Deck Immaculate Perception

	MINT	NRMT
COMPLETE SET (27)	300.00	135.00
COMMON CARD (I1-I27)	3.00	1.35

		MINT	NRMT
❑ I1	Jeff Bagwell	10.00	4.50
❑ I2	Craig Biggio	6.00	2.70
❑ I3	Barry Bonds	8.00	3.60
❑ I4	Roger Clemens	12.00	5.50
❑ I5	Jose Cruz Jr.	6.00	2.70
❑ I6	Nomar Garciaparra	20.00	9.00
❑ I7	Tony Clark	4.00	1.80
❑ I8	Ben Grieve	10.00	4.50
❑ I9	Ken Griffey Jr.	30.00	13.50
❑ I10	Tony Gwynn	15.00	6.75
❑ I11	Randy Johnson	6.00	2.70
❑ I12	Chipper Jones	15.00	6.75
❑ I13	Travis Lee	8.00	3.60
❑ I14	Kenny Lofton	6.00	2.70
❑ I15	Greg Maddux	20.00	9.00
❑ I16	Mark McGwire	40.00	18.00
❑ I17	Hideo Nomo	8.00	3.60
❑ I18	Mike Piazza	20.00	9.00
❑ I19	Manny Ramirez	6.00	2.70
❑ I20	Cal Ripken	25.00	11.00
❑ I21	Alex Rodriguez	20.00	9.00
❑ I22	Scott Rolen	12.00	5.50
❑ I23	Frank Thomas	20.00	9.00
❑ I24	Kerry Wood	15.00	6.75
❑ I25	Larry Walker	6.00	2.70
❑ I26	Vinny Castilla	4.00	1.80
❑ I27	Derek Jeter	15.00	6.75

1999 Upper Deck Wonder Years

	MINT	NRMT
COMPLETE SET (30)	120.00	55.00
COMMON CARD (W1-W30)	2.00	.90

		MINT	NRMT
❑ W1	Kerry Wood	6.00	2.70
❑ W2	Travis Lee	3.00	1.35
❑ W3	Jeff Bagwell	4.00	1.80
❑ W4	Barry Bonds	3.00	1.35
❑ W5	Roger Clemens	5.00	2.20
❑ W6	Jose Cruz Jr.	2.50	1.10
❑ W7	Andres Galarraga	2.50	1.10
❑ W8	Nomar Garciaparra	8.00	3.60
❑ W9	Juan Gonzalez	6.00	2.70
❑ W10	Ken Griffey Jr.	12.00	5.50
❑ W11	Tony Gwynn	6.00	2.70
❑ W12	Derek Jeter	6.00	2.70
❑ W13	Randy Johnson	2.50	1.10
❑ W14	Andruw Jones	2.50	1.10
❑ W15	Chipper Jones	6.00	2.70
❑ W16	Kenny Lofton	2.50	1.10
❑ W17	Greg Maddux	8.00	3.60
❑ W18	Tino Martinez	2.50	1.10
❑ W19	Mark McGwire	15.00	6.75
❑ W20	Paul Molitor	2.50	1.10
❑ W21	Mike Piazza	8.00	3.60
❑ W22	Manny Ramirez	2.50	1.10
❑ W23	Cal Ripken	10.00	4.50
❑ W24	Alex Rodriguez	8.00	3.60
❑ W25	Sammy Sosa	6.00	2.70
❑ W26	Frank Thomas	8.00	3.60
❑ W27	Mo Vaughn	3.00	1.35
❑ W28	Larry Walker	2.50	1.10
❑ W29	Scott Rolen	5.00	2.20
❑ W30	Ben Grieve	4.00	1.80

1999 Upper Deck Black Diamond

	MINT	NRMT
COMPLETE SET (120)	180.00	80.00
COMP.SET w/o DD's (90)	40.00	18.00
COMMON CARD (1-90)	.20	.09
COMMON DIAM.DEB (91-120)	2.50	1.10

		MINT	NRMT
❑ 1	Darin Erstad	1.00	.45
❑ 2	Tim Salmon	.75	.35
❑ 3	Jim Edmonds	.50	.23
❑ 4	Matt Williams	.30	.14
❑ 5	David Dellucci	.30	.14
❑ 6	Jay Bell	.30	.14
❑ 7	Andres Galarraga	.75	.35
❑ 8	Chipper Jones	2.00	.90
❑ 9	Greg Maddux	2.50	1.10
❑ 10	Andruw Jones	1.00	.45
❑ 11	Cal Ripken	3.00	1.35
❑ 12	Rafael Palmeiro	.50	.23
❑ 13	Brady Anderson	.30	.14
❑ 14	Mike Mussina	.75	.35
❑ 15	Nomar Garciaparra	2.50	1.10
❑ 16	Mo Vaughn	1.00	.45
❑ 17	Pedro Martinez	.75	.35
❑ 18	Sammy Sosa	2.00	.90
❑ 19	Henry Rodriguez	.30	.14
❑ 20	Frank Thomas	2.50	1.10
❑ 21	Magglio Ordonez	.30	.14
❑ 22	Albert Belle	.75	.35
❑ 23	Paul Konerko	.75	.35
❑ 24	Sean Casey	.30	.14
❑ 25	Jim Thome	.75	.35
❑ 26	Kenny Lofton	.75	.35
❑ 27	Sandy Alomar Jr.	.30	.14
❑ 28	Jaret Wright	.75	.35
❑ 29	Larry Walker	.75	.35
❑ 30	Todd Helton	1.00	.45
❑ 31	Vinny Castilla	.50	.23
❑ 32	Tony Clark	.50	.23
❑ 33	Damion Easley	.30	.14
❑ 34	Mark Kotsay	.30	.14
❑ 35	Derrek Lee	.30	.14
❑ 36	Moises Alou	.50	.23
❑ 37	Jeff Bagwell	1.25	.55
❑ 38	Craig Biggio	.75	.35
❑ 39	Randy Johnson	.75	.35
❑ 40	Dean Palmer	.30	.14
❑ 41	Johnny Damon	.30	.14
❑ 42	Chan Ho Park	.75	.35
❑ 43	Raul Mondesi	.50	.23
❑ 44	Gary Sheffield	.50	.23
❑ 45	Jeromy Burnitz	.30	.14
❑ 46	Marquis Grissom	.30	.14
❑ 47	Jeff Cirillo	.30	.14
❑ 48	Paul Molitor	.75	.35
❑ 49	Todd Walker	.50	.23
❑ 50	Vladimir Guerrero	1.25	.55
❑ 51	Brad Fullmer	.30	.14
❑ 52	Mike Piazza	2.50	1.10
❑ 53	Hideo Nomo	1.00	.45
❑ 54	Carlos Baerga	.30	.14
❑ 55	John Olerud	.30	.14
❑ 56	Derek Jeter	2.00	.90
❑ 57	Hideki Irabu	.50	.23
❑ 58	Tino Martinez	.75	.35
❑ 59	Bernie Williams	.75	.35
❑ 60	Miguel Tejada	.30	.14
❑ 61	Ben Grieve	1.50	.70
❑ 62	Jason Giambi	.30	.14
❑ 63	Scott Rolen	2.00	.90
❑ 64	Doug Glanville	.30	.14
❑ 65	Desi Relaford	.20	.09
❑ 66	Tony Womack	.20	.09
❑ 67	Jason Kendall	.30	.14
❑ 68	Jose Guillen	.30	.14
❑ 69	Tony Gwynn	2.00	.90
❑ 70	Ken Caminiti	.50	.23
❑ 71	Greg Vaughn	.30	.14
❑ 72	Kevin Brown	.50	.23
❑ 73	Barry Bonds	1.00	.45
❑ 74	J.T. Snow	.30	.14
❑ 75	Jeff Kent	.30	.14
❑ 76	Ken Griffey Jr.	4.00	1.80

❑ 77 Alex Rodriguez	2.50	1.10
❑ 78 Edgar Martinez	.30	.14
❑ 79 Jay Buhner	.30	.14
❑ 80 Mark McGwire	5.00	2.20
❑ 81 Delino DeShields	.20	.09
❑ 82 Brian Jordan	.30	.14
❑ 83 Quinton McCracken	.30	.14
❑ 84 Fred McGriff	.50	.23
❑ 85 Juan Gonzalez	2.00	.90
❑ 86 Ivan Rodriguez	1.00	.45
❑ 87 Will Clark	.75	.35
❑ 88 Roger Clemens	1.50	.70
❑ 89 Jose Cruz Jr.	.75	.35
❑ 90 Babe Ruth	5.00	2.20
❑ 91 Troy Glaus DD	10.00	4.50
❑ 92 Jarrod Washburn DD	3.00	1.35
❑ 93 Travis Lee DD	8.00	3.60
❑ 94 Bruce Chen DD	3.00	1.35
❑ 95 Mike Caruso DD	3.00	1.35
❑ 96 Jim Parque DD	3.00	1.35
❑ 97 Kerry Wood DD	15.00	6.75
❑ 98 Jeremy Giambi DD	4.00	1.80
❑ 99 Matt Anderson DD	3.00	1.35
❑ 100 Seth Greisinger DD	3.00	1.35
❑ 101 Gabe Alvarez DD	3.00	1.35
❑ 102 Rafael Medina DD	3.00	1.35
❑ 103 Daryle Ward DD	3.00	1.35
❑ 104 Alex Cora DD	3.00	1.35
❑ 105 Adrian Beltre DD	5.00	2.20
❑ 106 Geoff Jenkins DD	3.00	1.35
❑ 107 Eric Milton DD	3.00	1.35
❑ 108 Carl Pavano DD	3.00	1.35
❑ 109 Eric Chavez DD	6.00	2.70
❑ 110 Orlando Hernandez DD	8.00	3.60
❑ 111 A.J. Hinch DD	3.00	1.35
❑ 112 Carlton Loewer DD	3.00	1.35
❑ 113 Aramis Ramirez DD	4.00	1.80
❑ 114 Cliff Politte DD	2.50	1.10
❑ 115 Matt Clement DD	3.00	1.35
❑ 116 Alex Gonzalez DD	3.00	1.35
❑ 117 J.D. Drew DD	40.00	18.00
❑ 118 Shane Monahan DD	3.00	1.35
❑ 119 Rolando Arrojo DD	4.00	1.80
❑ 120 George Lombard DD	3.00	1.35

1999 Upper Deck Black Diamond Double

	MINT	NRMT
COMPLETE SET (120)	600.00	275.00
COMMON CARD (1-120)	1.25	.55

*STARS: 2.5X TO 6X BASIC CARDS
*DIAM.DEB: .6X TO 1.2X BASIC DIAM.DEB.

❑ 18 Sammy Sosa/1998	20.00	9.00
❑ 76 Ken Griffey Jr./1998	40.00	18.00
❑ 80 Mark McGwire/1998	50.00	22.00
❑ 117 J.D. Drew DD	50.00	22.00

1999 Upper Deck Black Diamond Triple

	MINT	NRMT
COMPLETE SET (120)	1200.00	550.00
COMMON CARD (1-120)	2.50	1.10

*STARS: 5X TO 12X BASIC CARDS

*DIAM.DEB: 1X TO 2.5X BASIC DIAM.DEB.

❑ 18 Sammy Sosa/273	60.00	27.00
❑ 76 Ken Griffey Jr./350	100.00	45.00
❑ 80 Mark McGwire/457	120.00	55.00
❑ 117 J.D. Drew DD	100.00	45.00

1999 Upper Deck Black Diamond Quadruple

	MINT	NRMT
COMPLETE SET (120)		
COMMON CARD (1-120)	10.00	4.50

*STARS: 20X TO 50X BASIC CARDS
*DIAM.DEB: 2.5X TO 6X BASIC DIAM.DEB.

❑ 18 Sammy Sosa/66	120.00	55.00
❑ 76 Ken Griffey Jr./56	250.00	110.00
❑ 80 Mark McGwire/70	300.00	135.00
❑ 117 J.D. Drew DD	250.00	110.00

1999 Upper Deck Black Diamond A Piece of History

	MINT	NRMT
COMPLETE SET (6)	1500.00	700.00
COMMON CARD	100.00	45.00

❑ BW Bernie Williams	100.00	45.00
❑ JG Juan Gonzalez	250.00	110.00
❑ MM Mark McGwire	600.00	275.00
❑ MV Mo Vaughn	120.00	55.00
❑ SS Sammy Sosa	250.00	110.00
❑ TG Tony Gwynn	250.00	110.00

1999 Upper Deck Black Diamond Dominance

	MINT	NRMT
COMPLETE SET (30)	400.00	180.00
COMMON CARD (D1-D30)	5.00	2.20

❑ D1 Kerry Wood	20.00	9.00
❑ D2 Derek Jeter	20.00	9.00
❑ D3 Alex Rodriguez	25.00	11.00
❑ D4 Frank Thomas	25.00	11.00
❑ D5 Jeff Bagwell	12.00	5.50
❑ D6 Mo Vaughn	10.00	4.50
❑ D7 Ivan Rodriguez	10.00	4.50
❑ D8 Cal Ripken	30.00	13.50
❑ D9 Rolando Arrojo	8.00	3.60
❑ D10 Chipper Jones	20.00	9.00
❑ D11 Kenny Lofton	8.00	3.60
❑ D12 Paul Konerko	8.00	3.60
❑ D13 Mike Piazza	25.00	11.00
❑ D14 Ben Grieve	12.00	5.50
❑ D15 Nomar Garciaparra	25.00	11.00
❑ D16 Travis Lee	10.00	4.50
❑ D17 Scott Rolen	15.00	6.75
❑ D18 Juan Gonzalez	20.00	9.00
❑ D19 Tony Gwynn	20.00	9.00
❑ D20 Tony Clark		
❑ D21 Roger Clemens	15.00	6.75
❑ D22 Sammy Sosa	20.00	9.00
❑ D23 Larry Walker	8.00	3.60
❑ D24 Ken Griffey Jr.	40.00	18.00
❑ D25 Mark McGwire	50.00	22.00
❑ D26 Barry Bonds	10.00	4.50
❑ D27 Vladimir Guerrero	10.00	4.50
❑ D28 Tino Martinez	8.00	3.60
❑ D29 Greg Maddux	25.00	11.00
❑ D30 Babe Ruth	50.00	22.00

1999 Upper Deck Black Diamond Mystery Numbers

	MINT	NRMT
COMPLETE SET (30)	1000.00	450.00
COMMON CARD (M1-M30)	5.00	2.20
MINOR STARS		
SEMISTARS		
UNLISTED STARS		

❑ M1 Babe Ruth/100	200.00	90.00
❑ M2 Ken Griffey Jr./200	150.00	70.00
❑ M3 Kerry Wood/300	80.00	36.00
❑ M4 Mark McGwire/400	120.00	55.00
❑ M5 Alex Rodriguez/500	60.00	27.00
❑ M6 Chipper Jones/600	40.00	18.00
❑ M7 Nomar Garciaparra/700	50.00	22.00
❑ M8 Derek Jeter/800	40.00	18.00
❑ M9 Mike Piazza/900	50.00	22.00
❑ M10 Roger Clemens/1000	25.00	11.00
❑ M11 Greg Maddux/1100	40.00	18.00
❑ M12 Scott Rolen/1200	25.00	11.00
❑ M13 Cal Ripken/1300	50.00	22.00
❑ M14 Ben Grieve/1400	20.00	9.00
❑ M15 Troy Glaus/1500	20.00	9.00
❑ M16 Sammy Sosa/1600	25.00	11.00
❑ M17 Darin Erstad/1700	10.00	4.50
❑ M18 Juan Gonzalez/1800	25.00	11.00
❑ M19 Pedro Martinez/1900	10.00	4.50
❑ M20 Larry Walker/2000	8.00	3.60
❑ M21 Vladimir Guerrero/2100	10.00	4.50
❑ M22 Jeff Bagwell/2200	12.00	5.50
❑ M23 Jaret Wright/2300	6.00	2.70
❑ M24 Travis Lee/2400	10.00	4.50
❑ M25 Barry Bonds/2500	8.00	3.60
❑ M26 Orlando Hernandez/2600	10.00	4.50
❑ M27 Frank Thomas/2700	20.00	9.00

Card	MINT	NRMT
❑ M28 Tony Gwynn/2800	15.00	6.75
❑ M29 Andres Galarraga/2900	5.00	2.20
❑ M30 Craig Biggio/3000	5.00	2.20

1998 Upper Deck Retro

	MINT	NRMT
COMPLETE SET (129)	60.00	27.00
COMMON CARD (1-81/83-130)	.20	.09

Card	MINT	NRMT
❑ 1 Jim Edmonds	.50	.23
❑ 2 Darin Erstad	1.00	.45
❑ 3 Tim Salmon	.75	.35
❑ 4 Jay Bell	.30	.14
❑ 5 Matt Williams	.30	.14
❑ 6 Andres Galarraga	.75	.35
❑ 7 Andruw Jones	1.00	.45
❑ 8 Chipper Jones	2.00	.90
❑ 9 Greg Maddux	2.50	1.10
❑ 10 Rafael Palmeiro	.50	.23
❑ 11 Cal Ripken	3.00	1.35
❑ 12 Brooks Robinson	.75	.35
❑ 13 Nomar Garciaparra	2.50	1.10
❑ 14 Pedro Martinez	.75	.35
❑ 15 Mo Vaughn	1.00	.45
❑ 16 Ernie Banks	1.00	.45
❑ 17 Mark Grace	.50	.23
❑ 18 Gary Matthews Sr.	.30	.14
❑ 19 Sammy Sosa	2.00	.90
❑ 20 Albert Belle	.75	.35
❑ 21 Carlton Fisk	.75	.35
❑ 22 Frank Thomas	2.50	1.10
❑ 23 Ken Griffey Sr.	.30	.14
❑ 24 Paul Konerko	.75	.35
❑ 25 Barry Larkin	.50	.23
❑ 26 Sean Casey	.30	.14
❑ 27 Tony Perez	.30	.14
❑ 28 Bob Feller	.75	.35
❑ 29 Kenny Lofton	.75	.35
❑ 30 Manny Ramirez	.75	.35
❑ 31 Jim Thome	.75	.35
❑ 32 Omar Vizquel	.30	.14
❑ 33 Dante Bichette	.30	.14
❑ 34 Larry Walker	.75	.35
❑ 35 Tony Clark	.50	.23
❑ 36 Damion Easley	.30	.14
❑ 37 Cliff Floyd	.30	.14
❑ 38 Livan Hernandez	.30	.14
❑ 39 Jeff Bagwell	1.25	.55
❑ 40 Craig Biggio	.75	.35
❑ 41 Al Kaline	.75	.35
❑ 42 Johnny Damon	.30	.14
❑ 43 Dean Palmer	.30	.14
❑ 44 Charles Johnson	.30	.14
❑ 45 Eric Karros	.30	.14
❑ 46 Gaylord Perry	.30	.14
❑ 47 Raul Mondesi	.50	.23
❑ 48 Gary Sheffield	.50	.23
❑ 49 Eddie Mathews	.75	.35
❑ 50 Warren Spahn	.75	.35
❑ 51 Jeromy Burnitz	.30	.14
❑ 52 Jeff Cirillo	.30	.14
❑ 53 Marquis Grissom	.30	.14
❑ 54 Paul Molitor	.75	.35
❑ 55 Kirby Puckett	1.25	.55
❑ 56 Brad Radke	.30	.14
❑ 57 Todd Walker	.50	.23
❑ 58 Vladimir Guerrero	1.25	.55
❑ 59 Brad Fullmer	.30	.14
❑ 60 Rondell White	.30	.14
❑ 61 Bobby Jones	.20	.09
❑ 62 Hideo Nomo	1.00	.45
❑ 63 Mike Piazza	2.50	1.10
❑ 64 Tom Seaver	1.00	.45
❑ 65 Frank Thomas	.20	.09
❑ 66 Yogi Berra	1.00	.45
❑ 67 Derek Jeter	2.00	.90
❑ 68 Tino Martinez	.75	.35
❑ 69 Paul O'Neill	.30	.14
❑ 70 Andy Pettitte	.50	.23
❑ 71 Rollie Fingers	.30	.14
❑ 72 Rickey Henderson	.75	.35
❑ 73 Matt Stairs	.30	.14
❑ 74 Scott Rolen	2.00	.90
❑ 75 Curt Schilling	.30	.14
❑ 76 Jose Guillen	.30	.14
❑ 77 Jason Kendall	.30	.14
❑ 78 Lou Brock	.75	.35
❑ 79 Bob Gibson	.75	.35
❑ 80 Ray Lankford	.30	.14
❑ 81 Mark McGwire	5.00	2.20
❑ 83 Kevin Brown	.50	.23
❑ 84 Ken Caminiti	.50	.23
❑ 85 Tony Gwynn	2.00	.90
❑ 86 Greg Vaughn	.30	.14
❑ 87 Barry Bonds	1.00	.45
❑ 88 Willie Stargell	.50	.23
❑ 89 Willie McCovey	.75	.35
❑ 90 Ken Griffey Jr.	4.00	1.80
❑ 91 Randy Johnson	.75	.35
❑ 92 Alex Rodriguez	2.50	1.10
❑ 93 Quinton McCracken	.30	.14
❑ 94 Fred McGriff	.50	.23
❑ 95 Juan Gonzalez	2.00	.90
❑ 96 Ivan Rodriguez	1.00	.45
❑ 97 Nolan Ryan	3.00	1.35
❑ 98 Jose Canseco	.75	.35
❑ 99 Roger Clemens	1.50	.70
❑ 100 Jose Cruz Jr.	1.00	.45
❑ 101 Justin Baughman FUT	.40	.18
❑ 102 David Dellucci FUT	1.00	.45
❑ 103 Travis Lee FUT	1.50	.70
❑ 104 Troy Glaus FUT	4.00	1.80
❑ 105 Kerry Wood FUT	4.00	1.80
❑ 106 Mike Caruso FUT	.30	.14
❑ 107 Jim Parque FUT	.75	.35
❑ 108 Brett Tomko FUT	.30	.14
❑ 109 Russell Branyan FUT	.30	.14
❑ 110 Jaret Wright FUT	1.00	.45
❑ 111 Todd Helton FUT	1.00	.45
❑ 112 Gabe Alvarez FUT	.30	.14
❑ 113 Matt Anderson FUT	.75	.35
❑ 114 Alex Gonzalez FUT	.30	.14
❑ 115 Mark Kotsay FUT	.50	.23
❑ 116 Derrek Lee FUT	.30	.14
❑ 117 Richard Hidalgo FUT	.30	.14
❑ 118 Adrian Beltre FUT	1.00	.45
❑ 119 Geoff Jenkins FUT	.30	.14
❑ 120 Eric Milton FUT	.30	.14
❑ 121 Brad Fullmer FUT	.30	.14
❑ 122 Vladimir Guerrero FUT	1.25	.55
❑ 123 Carl Pavano FUT	.30	.14
❑ 124 Orlando Hernandez FUT	4.00	1.80
❑ 125 Ben Grieve FUT	1.50	.70
❑ 126 A.J. Hinch FUT	.30	.14
❑ 127 Matt Clement FUT	.30	.14
❑ 128 Gary Matthews Jr. FUT	.60	.25
❑ 129 Aramis Ramirez FUT	.75	.35
❑ 130 Rolando Arrojo FUT	1.25	.55

1998 Upper Deck Retro Big Boppers

	MINT	NRMT
COMPLETE SET (30)	600.00	275.00
COMMON CARD (BB1-BB30)	6.00	2.70

Card	MINT	NRMT
❑ BB1 Darin Erstad	12.00	5.50
❑ BB2 Rafael Palmeiro	8.00	3.60
❑ BB3 Cal Ripken	50.00	22.00
❑ BB4 Nomar Garciaparra	40.00	18.00
❑ BB5 Mo Vaughn	15.00	6.75
❑ BB6 Frank Thomas	40.00	18.00
❑ BB7 Albert Belle	12.00	5.50
❑ BB8 Jim Thome	12.00	5.50
❑ BB9 Manny Ramirez	12.00	5.50
❑ BB10 Tony Clark	8.00	3.60
❑ BB11 Tino Martinez	12.00	5.50
❑ BB12 Ben Grieve	20.00	9.00
❑ BB13 Ken Griffey Jr.	60.00	27.00
❑ BB14 Alex Rodriguez	40.00	18.00
❑ BB15 Jay Buhner	6.00	2.70
❑ BB16 Juan Gonzalez	30.00	13.50
❑ BB17 Jose Cruz Jr.	12.00	5.50
❑ BB18 Jose Canseco	12.00	5.50
❑ BB19 Travis Lee	20.00	9.00
❑ BB20 Chipper Jones	30.00	13.50
❑ BB21 Andres Galarraga	12.00	5.50
❑ BB22 Andruw Jones	12.00	5.50
❑ BB23 Sammy Sosa	30.00	13.50
❑ BB24 Vinny Castilla	8.00	3.60
❑ BB25 Larry Walker	12.00	5.50
❑ BB26 Jeff Bagwell	20.00	9.00
❑ BB27 Gary Sheffield	8.00	3.60
❑ BB28 Mike Piazza	40.00	18.00
❑ BB29 Mark McGwire	80.00	36.00
❑ BB30 Barry Bonds	15.00	6.75

1998 Upper Deck Retro Groovy Kind of Glove

	MINT	NRMT
COMPLETE SET (30)	200.00	90.00
COMMON CARD (G1-G30)	1.50	.70

Card	MINT	NRMT
❑ G1 Roberto Alomar	4.00	1.80
❑ G2 Cal Ripken	15.00	6.75
❑ G3 Nomar Garciaparra	12.00	5.50
❑ G4 Frank Thomas	12.00	5.50
❑ G5 Robin Ventura	1.50	.70
❑ G6 Omar Vizquel	1.50	.70
❑ G7 Kenny Lofton	4.00	1.80
❑ G8 Ben Grieve	6.00	2.70
❑ G9 Alex Rodriguez	12.00	5.50
❑ G10 Ken Griffey Jr.	20.00	9.00
❑ G11 Ivan Rodriguez	5.00	2.20
❑ G12 Travis Lee	6.00	2.70
❑ G13 Matt Williams	1.50	.70
❑ G14 Greg Maddux	12.00	5.50
❑ G15 Andres Galarraga	4.00	1.80
❑ G16 Andruw Jones	4.00	1.80
❑ G17 Kerry Wood	15.00	6.75
❑ G18 Mark Grace	2.50	1.10

❑ G19 Craig Biggio 4.00 1.80
❑ G20 Charles Johnson .... 1.50 .70
❑ G21 Raul Mondesi 2.50 1.10
❑ G22 Mike Piazza 12.00 5.50
❑ G23 Rey Ordonez .... 1.50 .70
❑ G24 Derek Jeter 20.00 9.00
❑ G25 Scott Rolen 8.00 3.60
❑ G26 Mark McGwire 25.00 11.00
❑ G27 Ken Caminiti 2.50 1.10
❑ G28 Tony Gwynn 10.00 4.50
❑ G29 J.T. Snow .... 1.50 .70
❑ G30 Barry Bonds 5.00 2.20

1998 Upper Deck Retro Lunchboxes

	MINT	NRMT
COMPLETE SET (6)	100.00	45.00
COMMON BOX	10.00	4.50

❑ 1 Nomar Garciaparra 15.00 6.75
❑ 2 Ken Griffey Jr. 25.00 11.00
❑ 3 Chipper Jones 12.00 5.50
❑ 4 Travis Lee 10.00 4.50
❑ 5 Mark McGwire 30.00 13.50
❑ 6 Cal Ripken 20.00 9.00

1998 Upper Deck Retro New Frontier

	MINT	NRMT
COMPLETE SET (30)	150.00	70.00
COMMON CARD (NF1-NF30)	2.50	1.10
MINOR STARS	2.50	1.10
SEMISTARS	3.00	1.35
UNLISTED STARS	4.00	1.80

❑ NF1 Justin Baughman 4.00 1.80
❑ NF2 David Dellucci 5.00 2.20
❑ NF3 Travis Lee 12.00 5.50
❑ NF4 Troy Glaus 25.00 11.00
❑ NF5 Mike Caruso 2.50 1.10
❑ NF6 Jim Parque 4.00 1.80
❑ NF7 Kerry Wood 30.00 13.50
❑ NF8 Brett Tomko 2.50 1.10
❑ NF9 Russell Branyan 2.50 1.10
❑ NF10 Jaret Wright 8.00 3.60
❑ NF11 Todd Helton 8.00 3.60
❑ NF12 Gabe Alvarez 2.50 1.10
❑ NF13 Matt Anderson 4.00 1.80
❑ NF14 Alex Gonzalez 2.50 1.10
❑ NF15 Mark Kotsay 3.00 1.35
❑ NF16 Derrek Lee 2.50 1.10
❑ NF17 Richard Hidalgo 2.50 1.10
❑ NF18 Adrian Beltre 8.00 3.60
❑ NF19 Geoff Jenkins 2.50 1.10
❑ NF20 Eric Milton 2.50 1.10
❑ NF21 Brad Fullmer 2.50 1.10
❑ NF22 Vladimir Guerrero 10.00 4.50
❑ NF23 Carl Pavano 2.50 1.10
❑ NF24 Orlando Hernandez 20.00 9.00
❑ NF25 Ben Grieve 12.00 5.50
❑ NF26 A.J. Hinch 2.50 1.10
❑ NF27 Matt Clement 2.50 1.10
❑ NF28 Gary Matthews Jr. 3.00 1.35
❑ NF29 Aramis Ramirez 6.00 2.70
❑ NF30 Rolando Arrojo 6.00 2.70

1998 Upper Deck Retro Quantum Leap

	MINT	NRMT
COMPLETE SET (30)	5000.00	2200.00
COMMON CARD (Q1-Q30)	60.00	27.00

❑ Q1 Darin Erstad 80.00 36.00
❑ Q2 Cal Ripken 300.00 135.00
❑ Q3 Nomar Garciaparra 250.00 110.00
❑ Q4 Frank Thomas 250.00 110.00
❑ Q5 Kenny Lofton 80.00 36.00
❑ Q6 Ben Grieve 120.00 55.00
❑ Q7 Ken Griffey Jr. 400.00 180.00
❑ Q8 Alex Rodriguez 250.00 110.00
❑ Q9 Juan Gonzalez 200.00 90.00
❑ Q10 Jose Cruz Jr. 80.00 36.00
❑ Q11 Roger Clemens 150.00 70.00
❑ Q12 Travis Lee 120.00 55.00
❑ Q13 Chipper Jones 200.00 90.00
❑ Q14 Greg Maddux 250.00 110.00
❑ Q15 Kerry Wood 300.00 135.00
❑ Q16 Jeff Bagwell 120.00 55.00
❑ Q17 Mike Piazza 250.00 110.00
❑ Q18 Scott Rolen 150.00 70.00
❑ Q19 Mark McGwire 500.00 220.00
❑ Q20 Tony Gwynn 200.00 90.00
❑ Q21 Larry Walker 80.00 36.00
❑ Q22 Derek Jeter 200.00 90.00
❑ Q23 Sammy Sosa 200.00 90.00
❑ Q24 Barry Bonds 100.00 45.00
❑ Q25 Mo Vaughn 100.00 45.00
❑ Q26 Roberto Alomar 80.00 36.00
❑ Q27 Todd Helton 80.00 36.00
❑ Q28 Ivan Rodriguez 100.00 45.00
❑ Q29 Vladimir Guerrero 100.00 45.00
❑ Q30 Albert Belle 80.00 36.00

1998 Upper Deck Retro Sign of the Times

	MINT	NRMT
COMMON CARD (AK-)	20.00	9.00

❑ AK Al Kaline/600 .... 60.00 27.00
❑ BF Bob Feller/600 .... 40.00 18.00
❑ BR Brooks Robinson/300 .... 60.00 27.00
❑ CF Carlton Fisk/600 .... 50.00 22.00
❑ EB Ernie Banks/300 .... 60.00 27.00
❑ EM Eddie Matthews/600 .... 60.00 27.00
❑ FT Frank Thomas/600 .... 20.00 9.00
❑ GP Gaylord Perry/1000 .... 40.00 18.00
❑ JC Jose Cruz Jr./300 .... 50.00 22.00

❑ KP Kirby Puckett/450 .... 120.00 55.00
❑ KW Kerry Wood/200 .... 180.00 80.00
❑ LB Lou Brock/300 .... 60.00 27.00
❑ NR Nolan Ryan/500 .... 300.00 135.00
❑ PK Paul Konerko/750 .... 30.00 13.50
❑ RB Russell Branyan/750 .... 25.00 11.00
❑ RF Rollie Fingers/600 .... 40.00 18.00
❑ SR Scott Rolen/300 .... 80.00 36.00
❑ TG Tony Gwynn/200 .... 150.00 70.00
❑ TP Tony Perez/600 .... 40.00 18.00
❑ TS Tom Seaver/300 .... 80.00 36.00
❑ WM Willie McCovey/600 .... 50.00 22.00
❑ WS Warren Spahn/600 .... 60.00 27.00
❑ YB Yogi Berra/150
❑ BGI Bob Gibson/300 .... 60.00 27.00
❑ BGR Ben Grieve/300 .... 80.00 36.00
❑ GMJ Gary Matthews Jr./750 30.00 13.50
❑ GMS Gary Matthews Sr./600 30.00 13.50
❑ KGJ Ken Griffey Jr./100
❑ KGS Ken Griffey Sr./600 .... 40.00 18.00
❑ TLE Travis Lee/300 .... 80.00 36.00
❑ WIS Willie Stargell/600 .... 50.00 22.00

1998 Upper Deck Retro Time Capsule

	MINT	NRMT
COMPLETE SET (50)	150.00	70.00
COMMON CARD (TC1-TC50)	1.00	.45

❑ TC1 Mike Mussina 2.50 1.10
❑ TC2 Rafael Palmeiro .... 1.50 .70
❑ TC3 Cal Ripken 10.00 4.50
❑ TC4 Nomar Garciaparra 8.00 3.60
❑ TC5 Pedro Martinez 2.50 1.10
❑ TC6 Mo Vaughn 3.00 1.35
❑ TC7 Albert Belle 2.50 1.10
❑ TC8 Frank Thomas 8.00 3.60
❑ TC9 David Justice 2.50 1.10
❑ TC10 Kenny Lofton 2.50 1.10
❑ TC11 Manny Ramirez 2.50 1.10
❑ TC12 Jim Thome 2.50 1.10
❑ TC13 Derek Jeter 6.00 2.70
❑ TC14 Tino Martinez 2.50 1.10
❑ TC15 Ben Grieve 5.00 2.20
❑ TC16 Rickey Henderson 2.50 1.10
❑ TC17 Ken Griffey Jr. 12.00 5.50
❑ TC18 Randy Johnson 2.50 1.10
❑ TC19 Alex Rodriguez 8.00 3.60
❑ TC20 Wade Boggs 2.50 1.10

❑ TC21 Fred McGriff 1.50 .70
❑ TC22 Juan Gonzalez 6.00 2.70
❑ TC23 Ivan Rodriguez 3.00 1.35
❑ TC24 Nolan Ryan 10.00 4.50
❑ TC25 Jose Canseco 2.50 1.10
❑ TC26 Roger Clemens 5.00 2.20
❑ TC27 Jose Cruz Jr. 3.00 1.35
❑ TC28 Travis Lee 5.00 2.20
❑ TC29 Matt Williams 1.00 .45
❑ TC30 Andres Galarraga 2.50 1.10
❑ TC31 Andruw Jones 3.00 1.35
❑ TC32 Chipper Jones 6.00 2.70
❑ TC33 Greg Maddux 8.00 3.60
❑ TC34 Kerry Wood 12.00 5.50
❑ TC35 Barry Larkin 1.50 .70
❑ TC36 Dante Bichette 1.00 .45
❑ TC37 Larry Walker 2.50 1.10
❑ TC38 Livan Hernandez 1.00 .45
❑ TC39 Jeff Bagwell 4.00 1.80
❑ TC40 Craig Biggio 2.50 1.10
❑ TC41 Charles Johnson 1.00 .45
❑ TC42 Gary Sheffield 1.50 .70
❑ TC43 Marquis Grissom 1.00 .45
❑ TC44 Mike Piazza 8.00 3.60
❑ TC45 Scott Rolen 6.00 2.70
❑ TC46 Curt Schilling 1.00 .45
❑ TC47 Mark McGwire 15.00 6.75
❑ TC48 Ken Caminiti 1.50 .70
❑ TC49 Tony Gwynn 6.00 2.70
❑ TC50 Barry Bonds 3.00 1.35

1998 Upper Deck Special F/X

	MINT	NRMT
COMPLETE SET (150)	60.00	27.00
COMMON CARD (1-150)	.25	.11

❑ 1 Ken Griffey Jr. GHL 5.00 2.20
❑ 2 Mark McGwire GHL 6.00 2.70
❑ 3 Alex Rodriguez GHL 3.00 1.35
❑ 4 Larry Walker GHL 1.00 .45
❑ 5 Tino Martinez GHL 1.00 .45
❑ 6 Mike Piazza GHL 3.00 1.35
❑ 7 Jose Cruz Jr. GHL 1.25 .55
❑ 8 Greg Maddux GHL 3.00 1.35
❑ 9 Tony Gwynn GHL 2.50 1.10
❑ 10 Roger Clemens GHL 2.00 .90
❑ 11 Jason Dickson .40 .18
❑ 12 Darin Erstad 1.25 .55
❑ 13 Chuck Finley .40 .18
❑ 14 Dave Hollins .25 .11
❑ 15 Garret Anderson .40 .18
❑ 16 Michael Tucker .40 .18
❑ 17 Javier Lopez .40 .18
❑ 18 John Smoltz .40 .18
❑ 19 Mark Wohlers .25 .11
❑ 20 Greg Maddux 3.00 1.35
❑ 21 Scott Erickson .40 .18
❑ 22 Jimmy Key .40 .18
❑ 23 B.J. Surhoff .40 .18
❑ 24 Eric Davis .40 .18
❑ 25 Rafael Palmeiro .60 .25
❑ 26 Tim Naehring .25 .11
❑ 27 Darren Bragg .25 .11
❑ 28 Troy O'Leary .40 .18
❑ 29 John Valentin .40 .18
❑ 30 Mo Vaughn 1.25 .55
❑ 31 Mark Grace .60 .25
❑ 32 Kevin Foster .25 .11
❑ 33 Kevin Tapani .25 .11
❑ 34 Kevin Orie .25 .11
❑ 35 Albert Belle 1.25 .55
❑ 36 Ray Durham .40 .18
❑ 37 Jaime Navarro .25 .11
❑ 38 Mike Cameron .40 .18
❑ 39 Eddie Taubensee .25 .11
❑ 40 Barry Larkin .60 .25
❑ 41 Willie Greene .40 .18
❑ 42 Jeff Shaw .40 .18
❑ 43 Omar Vizquel .40 .18
❑ 44 Brian Giles .40 .18
❑ 45 Jim Thome 1.00 .45
❑ 46 David Justice 1.00 .45
❑ 47 Sandy Alomar Jr. .40 .18
❑ 48 Neifi Perez .40 .18
❑ 49 Dante Bichette .40 .18
❑ 50 Vinny Castilla .60 .25
❑ 51 John Thomson .25 .11
❑ 52 Damion Easley .40 .18
❑ 53 Justin Thompson .40 .18
❑ 54 Bobby Higginson .60 .25
❑ 55 Tony Clark .60 .25
❑ 56 Charles Johnson .40 .18
❑ 57 Edgar Renteria .40 .18
❑ 58 Alex Fernandez .25 .11
❑ 59 Gary Sheffield .60 .25
❑ 60 Livan Hernandez .40 .18
❑ 61 Craig Biggio 1.00 .45
❑ 62 Chris Holt .25 .11
❑ 63 Billy Wagner .40 .18
❑ 64 Brad Ausmus .25 .11
❑ 65 Dean Palmer .40 .18
❑ 66 Tim Belcher .25 .11
❑ 67 Jeff King .40 .18
❑ 68 Jose Rosado .25 .11
❑ 69 Chan Ho Park 1.00 .45
❑ 70 Raul Mondesi .60 .25
❑ 71 Hideo Nomo 1.25 .55
❑ 72 Todd Zeile .40 .18
❑ 73 Eric Karros .40 .18
❑ 74 Cal Eldred .25 .11
❑ 75 Jeff D'Amico .25 .11
❑ 76 Doug Jones .25 .11
❑ 77 Dave Nilsson .25 .11
❑ 78 Todd Walker .60 .25
❑ 79 Rick Aguilera .25 .11
❑ 80 Paul Molitor 1.00 .45
❑ 81 Brad Radke .40 .18
❑ 82 Vladimir Guerrero 1.50 .70
❑ 83 Carlos Perez .40 .18
❑ 84 F.P. Santangelo .25 .11
❑ 85 Rondell White .40 .18
❑ 86 Butch Huskey .25 .11
❑ 87 Edgardo Alfonzo .40 .18
❑ 88 John Franco .40 .18
❑ 89 John Olerud .40 .18
❑ 90 Todd Hundley .40 .18
❑ 91 Bernie Williams 1.00 .45
❑ 92 Andy Pettitte .60 .25
❑ 93 Paul O'Neill .40 .18
❑ 94 David Cone .60 .25
❑ 95 Jason Giambi .40 .18
❑ 96 Damon Mashore .25 .11
❑ 97 Scott Spiezio .25 .11
❑ 98 Ariel Prieto .25 .11
❑ 99 Rico Brogna .40 .18
❑ 100 Mike Lieberthal .25 .11
❑ 101 Garrett Stephenson .25 .11
❑ 102 Ricky Bottalico .40 .18
❑ 103 Kevin Polcovich .25 .11
❑ 104 Jon Lieber .25 .11
❑ 105 Kevin Young .40 .18
❑ 106 Tony Womack .40 .18
❑ 107 Gary Gaetti .25 .11
❑ 108 Alan Benes .40 .18
❑ 109 Willie McGee .25 .11
❑ 110 Mark McGwire 6.00 2.70
❑ 111 Ron Gant .25 .11
❑ 112 Andy Ashby .25 .11
❑ 113 Steve Finley .40 .18
❑ 114 Quilvio Veras .25 .11
❑ 115 Ken Caminiti .60 .25
❑ 116 Joey Hamilton .40 .18
❑ 117 Bill Mueller .40 .18
❑ 118 Mark Gardner .25 .11
❑ 119 Shawn Estes .40 .18
❑ 120 J.T. Snow .40 .18
❑ 121 Dante Powell .40 .18
❑ 122 Jeff Kent .40 .18
❑ 123 Jamie Moyer .25 .11
❑ 124 Joey Cora .40 .18
❑ 125 Ken Griffey Jr. 5.00 2.20
❑ 126 Jeff Fassero .25 .11
❑ 127 Edgar Martinez .40 .18
❑ 128 Will Clark 1.00 .45
❑ 129 Lee Stevens .25 .11
❑ 130 Ivan Rodriguez 1.25 .55
❑ 131 Rusty Greer .40 .18
❑ 132 Ed Sprague .25 .11
❑ 133 Pat Hentgen .40 .18
❑ 134 Shannon Stewart .40 .18
❑ 135 Carlos Delgado .40 .18
❑ 136 Brett Tomko .40 .18
❑ 137 Jose Guillen .40 .18
❑ 138 Eli Marrero .40 .18
❑ 139 Dennis Reyes .40 .18
❑ 140 Mark Kotsay .60 .25
❑ 141 Richie Sexson .60 .25
❑ 142 Todd Helton 1.25 .55
❑ 143 Jeremi Gonzalez .40 .18
❑ 144 Jeff Abbott .40 .18
❑ 145 Matt Morris .40 .18
❑ 146 Aaron Boone .25 .11
❑ 147 Todd Dunwoody .40 .18
❑ 148 Mario Valdez .40 .18
❑ 149 Fernando Tatis .40 .18
❑ 150 Jaret Wright 1.25 .55

1998 Upper Deck Special F/X Power Zone

	MINT	NRMT
COMPLETE SET (20)	80.00	36.00
COMMON CARD (PZ1-PZ20)	1.00	.45

❑ PZ1 Jose Cruz Jr. 2.50 1.10
❑ PZ2 Frank Thomas 8.00 3.60
❑ PZ3 Juan Gonzalez 6.00 2.70
❑ PZ4 Mike Piazza 8.00 3.60
❑ PZ5 Mark McGwire 15.00 6.75
❑ PZ6 Barry Bonds 3.00 1.35
❑ PZ7 Greg Maddux 8.00 3.60
❑ PZ8 Alex Rodriguez 8.00 3.60
❑ PZ9 Nomar Garciaparra 8.00 3.60
❑ PZ10 Ken Griffey Jr. 12.00 5.50
❑ PZ11 John Smoltz 1.00 .45
❑ PZ12 Andruw Jones 2.50 1.10
❑ PZ13 Sandy Alomar Jr. 1.00 .45
❑ PZ14 Roberto Alomar 2.50 1.10
❑ PZ15 Chipper Jones 6.00 2.70
❑ PZ16 Kenny Lofton 2.50 1.10
❑ PZ17 Larry Walker 2.50 1.10
❑ PZ18 Jeff Bagwell 4.00 1.80
❑ PZ19 Mo Vaughn 3.00 1.35
❑ PZ20 Tom Glavine 2.50 1.10

1998 Upper Deck Special F/X Power Zone OctoberBest

	MINT	NRMT
COMPLETE SET (15)	200.00	90.00
COMMON CARD (PZ1-PZ15)	4.00	1.80

Card	Player	MINT	NRMT
❑ PZ1	Frank Thomas	25.00	11.00
❑ PZ2	Juan Gonzalez	20.00	9.00
❑ PZ3	Mike Piazza	25.00	11.00
❑ PZ4	Mark McGwire	50.00	22.00
❑ PZ5	Jeff Bagwell	12.00	5.50
❑ PZ6	Barry Bonds	10.00	4.50
❑ PZ7	Ken Griffey Jr.	40.00	18.00
❑ PZ8	John Smoltz	4.00	1.80
❑ PZ9	Andruw Jones	8.00	3.60
❑ PZ10	Greg Maddux	25.00	11.00
❑ PZ11	Sandy Alomar Jr.	4.00	1.80
❑ PZ12	Roberto Alomar	8.00	3.60
❑ PZ13	Chipper Jones	20.00	9.00
❑ PZ14	Kenny Lofton	8.00	3.60
❑ PZ15	Tom Glavine	8.00	3.60

1998 Upper Deck Special F/X Power Zone Power Driven

	MINT	NRMT
COMPLETE SET (10)	200.00	90.00
COMMON CARD (PZ1-PZ10)	8.00	3.60

Card	Player	MINT	NRMT
❑ PZ1	Frank Thomas	30.00	13.50
❑ PZ2	Juan Gonzalez	25.00	11.00
❑ PZ3	Mike Piazza	30.00	13.50
❑ PZ4	Larry Walker	10.00	4.50
❑ PZ5	Mark McGwire	60.00	27.00
❑ PZ6	Jeff Bagwell	15.00	6.75
❑ PZ7	Mo Vaughn	12.00	5.50
❑ PZ8	Barry Bonds	12.00	5.50
❑ PZ9	Tino Martinez	8.00	3.60
❑ PZ10	Ken Griffey Jr.	50.00	22.00

1998 Upper Deck Special F/X Power Zone Superstar Xcitement

	MINT	NRMT
COMPLETE SET (10)	1000.00	450.00
COMMON CARD (PZ1-PZ10)	40.00	18.00

Card	Player	MINT	NRMT
❑ PZ1	Jose Cruz Jr.	40.00	18.00
❑ PZ2	Frank Thomas	120.00	55.00
❑ PZ3	Juan Gonzalez	100.00	45.00
❑ PZ4	Mike Piazza	120.00	55.00
❑ PZ5	Mark McGwire	250.00	110.00
❑ PZ6	Barry Bonds	50.00	22.00
❑ PZ7	Greg Maddux	120.00	55.00
❑ PZ8	Alex Rodriguez	120.00	55.00
❑ PZ9	Nomar Garciaparra	120.00	55.00
❑ PZ10	Ken Griffey Jr.	200.00	90.00

1995 Zenith

	MINT	NRMT
COMPLETE SET (150)	40.00	18.00
COMMON CARD (1-150)	.20	.09

Card	Player	MINT	NRMT
❑ 1	Albert Belle	1.25	.55
❑ 2	Alex Fernandez	.20	.09
❑ 3	Andy Benes	.40	.18
❑ 4	Barry Larkin	.75	.35
❑ 5	Barry Bonds	1.00	.45
❑ 6	Ben McDonald	.20	.09
❑ 7	Bernard Gilkey	.20	.09
❑ 8	Billy Ashley	.20	.09
❑ 9	Bobby Bonilla	.40	.18
❑ 10	Bret Saberhagen	.40	.18
❑ 11	Brian Jordan	.40	.18
❑ 12	Cal Ripken	3.00	1.35
❑ 13	Carlos Baerga	.40	.18
❑ 14	Carlos Delgado	.40	.18
❑ 15	Cecil Fielder	.40	.18
❑ 16	Chili Davis	.40	.18
❑ 17	Chuck Knoblauch	.75	.35
❑ 18	Craig Biggio	.75	.35
❑ 19	Danny Tartabull	.20	.09
❑ 20	Dante Bichette	.40	.18
❑ 21	Darren Daulton	.40	.18
❑ 22	David Justice	.75	.35
❑ 23	Dave Winfield	.75	.35
❑ 24	David Cone	.75	.35
❑ 25	Dean Palmer	.40	.18
❑ 26	Deion Sanders	.40	.18
❑ 27	Dennis Eckersley	.40	.18
❑ 28	Derek Bell	.40	.18
❑ 29	Don Mattingly	1.25	.55
❑ 30	Edgar Martinez	.40	.18
❑ 31	Eric Karros	.40	.18
❑ 32	James Mouton	.20	.09
❑ 33	Frank Thomas	2.50	1.10
❑ 34	Fred McGriff	.75	.35
❑ 35	Gary Sheffield	.75	.35
❑ 36	Gary Gaetti	.40	.18
❑ 37	Greg Maddux	2.50	1.10
❑ 38	Gregg Jefferies	.20	.09
❑ 39	Ivan Rodriguez	1.00	.45
❑ 40	Kenny Rogers	.20	.09
❑ 41	J.T. Snow	.40	.18
❑ 42	Hal Morris	.20	.09
❑ 43	Eddie Murray 3000th Hit	.40	.18
❑ 44	Javier Lopez	.40	.18
❑ 45	Jay Bell	.40	.18
❑ 46	Jeff Conine	.40	.18
❑ 47	Jeff Bagwell	1.25	.55
❑ 48	Hideo Nomo Japanese	3.00	1.35
❑ 49	Jeff Kent	.40	.18
❑ 50	Jeff King	.20	.09
❑ 51	Jim Thome	.75	.35
❑ 52	Jimmy Key	.40	.18
❑ 53	Joe Carter	.40	.18
❑ 54	John Valentin	.40	.18
❑ 55	John Olerud	.40	.18
❑ 56	Jose Canseco	.75	.35
❑ 57	Jose Rijo	.20	.09
❑ 58	Jose Offerman	.20	.09
❑ 59	Juan Gonzalez	2.00	.90
❑ 60	Ken Caminiti	.75	.35
❑ 61	Ken Griffey Jr.	4.00	1.80
❑ 62	Kenny Lofton	.75	.35
❑ 63	Kevin Appier	.40	.18
❑ 64	Kevin Seitzer	.20	.09
❑ 65	Kirby Puckett	1.25	.55
❑ 66	Kirk Gibson	.40	.18
❑ 67	Larry Walker	.75	.35
❑ 68	Lenny Dykstra	.40	.18
❑ 69	Manny Ramirez	.75	.35
❑ 70	Mark Grace	.75	.35
❑ 71	Mark McGwire	4.00	1.80
❑ 72	Marquis Grissom	.40	.18
❑ 73	Jim Edmonds	.75	.35
❑ 74	Matt Williams	.40	.18
❑ 75	Mike Mussina	.75	.35
❑ 76	Mike Piazza	2.50	1.10
❑ 77	Mo Vaughn	1.00	.45
❑ 78	Moises Alou	.75	.35
❑ 79	Ozzie Smith	1.00	.45
❑ 80	Paul O'Neill	.40	.18
❑ 81	Paul Molitor	.75	.35
❑ 82	Rafael Palmeiro	.75	.35
❑ 83	Randy Johnson	.75	.35
❑ 84	Raul Mondesi	.75	.35
❑ 85	Ray Lankford	.40	.18
❑ 86	Reggie Sanders	.40	.18
❑ 87	Rickey Henderson	.75	.35
❑ 88	Rico Brogna	.20	.09
❑ 89	Roberto Alomar	.75	.35
❑ 90	Robin Ventura	.40	.18
❑ 91	Roger Clemens	1.50	.70
❑ 92	Ron Gant	.20	.09
❑ 93	Rondell White	.40	.18
❑ 94	Royce Clayton	.20	.09
❑ 95	Ruben Sierra	.20	.09
❑ 96	Rusty Greer	.75	.35
❑ 97	Ryan Klesko	.40	.18
❑ 98	Sammy Sosa	2.00	.90
❑ 99	Shawon Dunston	.20	.09
❑ 100	Steve Ontiveros	.20	.09
❑ 101	Tim Naehring	.20	.09
❑ 102	Tim Salmon	.75	.35
❑ 103	Tino Martinez	.75	.35
❑ 104	Tony Gwynn	2.00	.90
❑ 105	Travis Fryman	.40	.18
❑ 106	Vinny Castilla	.75	.35
❑ 107	Wade Boggs	.75	.35
❑ 108	Wally Joyner	.40	.18
❑ 109	Wil Cordero	.20	.09
❑ 110	Will Clark	.75	.35
❑ 111	Chipper Jones	2.00	.90
❑ 112	Armando Benitez	.20	.09
❑ 113	Curtis Goodwin	.20	.09
❑ 114	Gabe White	.20	.09
❑ 115	Vaughn Eshelman	.20	.09
❑ 116	Marty Cordova	.20	.09
❑ 117	Dustin Hermanson	.40	.18
❑ 118	Rich Becker	.20	.09
❑ 119	Ray Durham	.40	.18
❑ 120	Shane Andrews	.20	.09
❑ 121	Scott Ruffcorn	.20	.09
❑ 122	Mark Grudzielanek	.60	.25
❑ 123	James Baldwin	.40	.18
❑ 124	Carlos Perez	.60	.25
❑ 125	Julian Tavarez	.20	.09
❑ 126	Joe Vitiello	.20	.09
❑ 127	Jason Bates	.20	.09

- ❑ 128 Edgardo Alfonzo .40 .18
- ❑ 129 Juan Acevedo .20 .09
- ❑ 130 Bill Pulsipher .20 .09
- ❑ 131 Bob Higginson 2.00 .90
- ❑ 132 Russ Davis .40 .18
- ❑ 133 Charles Johnson .40 .18
- ❑ 134 Derek Jeter 2.50 1.10
- ❑ 135 Orlando Miller .20 .09
- ❑ 136 LaTroy Hawkins .20 .09
- ❑ 137 Brian L.Hunter .40 .18
- ❑ 138 Roberto Petagine .20 .09
- ❑ 139 Midre Cummings .20 .09
- ❑ 140 Garret Anderson .40 .18
- ❑ 141 Ugueth Urbina .20 .09
- ❑ 142 Antonio Osuna .20 .09
- ❑ 143 Michael Tucker .40 .18
- ❑ 144 Benji Gil .20 .09
- ❑ 145 Jon Nunnally .20 .09
- ❑ 146 Alex Rodriguez 3.00 1.35
- ❑ 147 Todd Hollandsworth .20 .09
- ❑ 148 Alex Gonzalez .20 .09
- ❑ 149 Hideo Nomo 3.00 1.35
- ❑ 150 Shawn Green .40 .18

1995 Zenith All-Star Salute

	MINT	NRMT
COMPLETE SET (18)	50.00	22.00
COMMON CARD (1-18)	.50	.23

- ❑ 1 Cal Ripken 8.00 3.60
- ❑ 2 Frank Thomas 6.00 2.70
- ❑ 3 Mike Piazza 6.00 2.70
- ❑ 4 Kirby Puckett 2.00 .90
- ❑ 5 Manny Ramirez 2.00 .90
- ❑ 6 Tony Gwynn 5.00 2.20
- ❑ 7 Hideo Nomo 5.00 2.20
- ❑ 8 Matt Williams 1.00 .45
- ❑ 9 Randy Johnson 2.00 .90
- ❑ 10 Raul Mondesi 1.50 .70
- ❑ 11 Albert Belle 2.00 .90
- ❑ 12 Ivan Rodriguez 2.00 .90
- ❑ 13 Barry Bonds 2.00 .90
- ❑ 14 Carlos Baerga 1.00 .45
- ❑ 15 Ken Griffey Jr. 10.00 4.50
- ❑ 16 Jeff Conine 1.00 .45
- ❑ 17 Frank Thomas 6.00 2.70
- ❑ 18 Cal Ripken 6.00 2.70
  Barry Bonds

1995 Zenith Rookie Roll Call

	MINT	NRMT
COMPLETE SET (18)	150.00	70.00
COMMON CARD (1-18)	6.00	2.70

- ❑ 1 Alex Rodriguez 50.00 22.00
- ❑ 2 Derek Jeter 40.00 18.00
- ❑ 3 Chipper Jones 40.00 18.00
- ❑ 4 Shawn Green 10.00 4.50
- ❑ 5 Todd Hollandsworth 6.00 2.70
- ❑ 6 Bill Pulsipher 6.00 2.70
- ❑ 7 Hideo Nomo 30.00 13.50
- ❑ 8 Ray Durham 10.00 4.50
- ❑ 9 Curtis Goodwin 6.00 2.70

- ❑ 10 Brian L.Hunter 10.00 4.50
- ❑ 11 Julian Tavarez 6.00 2.70
- ❑ 12 Marty Cordova UER 6.00 2.70
  Kevin Maas pictured
- ❑ 13 Michael Tucker 10.00 4.50
- ❑ 14 Edgardo Alfonzo 10.00 4.50
- ❑ 15 LaTroy Hawkins 6.00 2.70
- ❑ 16 Carlos Perez 10.00 4.50
- ❑ 17 Charles Johnson 10.00 4.50
- ❑ 18 Benji Gil 6.00 2.70

1995 Zenith Z-Team

	MINT	NRMT
COMPLETE SET (18)	300.00	135.00
COMMON CARD (1-18)	8.00	3.60

- ❑ 1 Cal Ripken 50.00 22.00
- ❑ 2 Ken Griffey Jr. 60.00 27.00
- ❑ 3 Frank Thomas 40.00 18.00
- ❑ 4 Matt Williams 10.00 4.50
- ❑ 5 Mike Piazza UER 40.00 18.00
  (Card says started at first base Piazza is a catcher)
- ❑ 6 Barry Bonds 15.00 6.75
- ❑ 7 Raul Mondesi 10.00 4.50
- ❑ 8 Greg Maddux 40.00 18.00
- ❑ 9 Jeff Bagwell 20.00 9.00
- ❑ 10 Manny Ramirez 12.00 5.50
- ❑ 11 Larry Walker 12.00 5.50
- ❑ 12 Tony Gwynn 30.00 13.50
- ❑ 13 Will Clark 12.00 5.50
- ❑ 14 Albert Belle 15.00 6.75
- ❑ 15 Kenny Lofton 12.00 5.50
- ❑ 16 Rafael Palmeiro 10.00 4.50
- ❑ 17 Don Mattingly 20.00 9.00
- ❑ 18 Carlos Baerga 10.00 4.50

1996 Zenith

	MINT	NRMT
COMPLETE SET (150)	30.00	13.50
COMMON CARD (1-150)	.15	.07

- ❑ 1 Ken Griffey Jr. 3.00 1.35
- ❑ 2 Ozzie Smith .75 .35
- ❑ 3 Greg Maddux 2.00 .90
- ❑ 4 Rondell White .30 .14
- ❑ 5 Mark McGwire 3.00 1.35
- ❑ 6 Jim Thome .60 .25
- ❑ 7 Ivan Rodriguez .75 .35

- ❑ 8 Marc Newfield .15 .07
- ❑ 9 Travis Fryman .30 .14
- ❑ 10 Fred McGriff .60 .25
- ❑ 11 Shawn Green .30 .14
- ❑ 12 Mike Piazza 2.00 .90
- ❑ 13 Dante Bichette .30 .14
- ❑ 14 Tino Martinez .60 .25
- ❑ 15 Sterling Hitchcock .30 .14
- ❑ 16 Ryne Sandberg .75 .35
- ❑ 17 Rico Brogna .15 .07
- ❑ 18 Roberto Alomar .60 .25
- ❑ 19 Barry Larkin .60 .25
- ❑ 20 Bernie Williams .60 .25
- ❑ 21 Gary Sheffield .60 .25
- ❑ 22 Frank Thomas 2.00 .90
- ❑ 23 Gregg Jefferies .15 .07
- ❑ 24 Jeff Bagwell 1.00 .45
- ❑ 25 Marty Cordova .15 .07
- ❑ 26 Jim Edmonds .60 .25
- ❑ 27 Jay Bell .30 .14
- ❑ 28 Ben McDonald .15 .07
- ❑ 29 Barry Bonds .75 .35
- ❑ 30 Mo Vaughn .75 .35
- ❑ 31 Johnny Damon .30 .14
- ❑ 32 Dean Palmer .30 .14
- ❑ 33 Ismael Valdes .30 .14
- ❑ 34 Manny Ramirez .60 .25
- ❑ 35 Edgar Martinez .30 .14
- ❑ 36 Cecil Fielder .30 .14
- ❑ 37 Ryan Klesko .30 .14
- ❑ 38 Ray Lankford .30 .14
- ❑ 39 Tim Salmon .60 .25
- ❑ 40 Joe Carter .30 .14
- ❑ 41 Jason Isringhausen .15 .07
- ❑ 42 Rickey Henderson .60 .25
- ❑ 43 Lenny Dykstra .30 .14
- ❑ 44 Andre Dawson .60 .25
- ❑ 45 Paul O'Neill .30 .14
- ❑ 46 Ray Durham .30 .14
- ❑ 47 Raul Mondesi .60 .25
- ❑ 48 Jay Buhner .30 .14
- ❑ 49 Eddie Murray .60 .25
- ❑ 50 Henry Rodriguez .30 .14
- ❑ 51 Hal Morris .15 .07
- ❑ 52 Mike Mussina .60 .25
- ❑ 53 Wally Joyner .30 .14
- ❑ 54 Will Clark .60 .25
- ❑ 55 Chipper Jones 1.50 .70
- ❑ 56 Brian Jordan .30 .14
- ❑ 57 Larry Walker .60 .25
- ❑ 58 Wade Boggs .60 .25
- ❑ 59 Melvin Nieves .15 .07
- ❑ 60 Charles Johnson .30 .14
- ❑ 61 Juan Gonzalez 1.50 .70
- ❑ 62 Carlos Delgado .30 .14
- ❑ 63 Reggie Sanders .30 .14
- ❑ 64 Brian L.Hunter .30 .14
- ❑ 65 Edgardo Alfonzo .30 .14
- ❑ 66 Kenny Lofton .60 .25
- ❑ 67 Paul Molitor .60 .25
- ❑ 68 Mike Bordick .15 .07
- ❑ 69 Garret Anderson .30 .14
- ❑ 70 Orlando Merced .15 .07
- ❑ 71 Craig Biggio .60 .25
- ❑ 72 Chuck Knoblauch .60 .25
- ❑ 73 Mark Grace .60 .25
- ❑ 74 Jack McDowell .15 .07
- ❑ 75 Randy Johnson .60 .25

❑ 76 Cal Ripken	2.50	1.10
❑ 77 Matt Williams	.30	.14
❑ 78 Benji Gil	.15	.07
❑ 79 Moises Alou	.60	.25
❑ 80 Robin Ventura	.30	.14
❑ 81 Greg Vaughn	.30	.14
❑ 82 Carlos Baerga	.30	.14
❑ 83 Roger Clemens	1.25	.55
❑ 84 Hideo Nomo	1.00	.45
❑ 85 Pedro Martinez	.60	.25
❑ 86 John Valentin	.30	.14
❑ 87 Andres Galarraga	.60	.25
❑ 88 Andy Pettitte	.60	.25
❑ 89 Derek Bell	.30	.14
❑ 90 Kirby Puckett	1.00	.45
❑ 91 Tony Gwynn	1.50	.70
❑ 92 Brady Anderson	.30	.14
❑ 93 Derek Jeter	2.00	.90
❑ 94 Michael Tucker	.30	.14
❑ 95 Albert Belle	1.00	.45
❑ 96 David Cone	.60	.25
❑ 97 J.T. Snow	.30	.14
❑ 98 Tom Glavine	.60	.25
❑ 99 Alex Rodriguez	2.00	.90
❑ 100 Sammy Sosa	1.50	.70
❑ 101 Karim Garcia	.30	.14
❑ 102 Alan Benes	.30	.14
❑ 103 Chad Mottola	.15	.07
❑ 104 Robin Jennings	.15	.07
❑ 105 Bob Abreu	.30	.14
❑ 106 Tony Clark	.60	.25
❑ 107 George Arias	.15	.07
❑ 108 Jermaine Dye	.15	.07
❑ 109 Jeff Suppan	.15	.07
❑ 110 Ralph Milliard	.15	.07
❑ 111 Ruben Rivera	.30	.14
❑ 112 Billy Wagner	.30	.14
❑ 113 Jason Kendall	.60	.25
❑ 114 Mike Grace	.15	.07
❑ 115 Edgar Renteria	.30	.14
❑ 116 Jason Schmidt	.15	.07
❑ 117 Paul Wilson	.15	.07
❑ 118 Rey Ordonez	.30	.14
❑ 119 Rocky Coppinger	.60	.25
❑ 120 Wilton Guerrero	.50	.23
❑ 121 Brooks Kieschnick	.15	.07
❑ 122 Raul Casanova	.15	.07
❑ 123 Alex Ochoa	.15	.07
❑ 124 Chan Ho Park	.60	.25
❑ 125 John Wasdin	.15	.07
❑ 126 Eric Owens	.15	.07
❑ 127 Justin Thompson	.30	.14
❑ 128 Chris Snopek	.15	.07
❑ 129 Terrell Wade	.15	.07
❑ 130 Darin Erstad	5.00	2.20
❑ 131 Albert Belle HON	.60	.25
❑ 132 Cal Ripken HON	1.25	.55
❑ 133 Frank Thomas HON	1.00	.45
❑ 134 Greg Maddux HON	1.00	.45
❑ 135 Ken Griffey Jr. HON	1.50	.70
❑ 136 Mo Vaughn HON	.60	.25
❑ 137 Chipper Jones HON	.75	.35
❑ 138 Mike Piazza HON	1.00	.45
❑ 139 Ryan Klesko HON	.15	.07
❑ 140 Hideo Nomo HON	1.00	.45
❑ 141 Roberto Alomar HON	.30	.14
❑ 142 Manny Ramirez HON	.30	.14
❑ 143 Gary Sheffield HON	.15	.07
❑ 144 Barry Bonds HON	.60	.25
❑ 145 Matt Williams HON	.30	.14
❑ 146 Jim Edmonds HON	.15	.07
❑ 147 Derek Jeter HON	1.00	.45
❑ 148 Sammy Sosa HON	.75	.35
❑ 149 Kirby Puckett HON	.30	.14
❑ 150 Tony Gwynn HON	.75	.35

1996 Zenith Diamond Club

	MINT	NRMT
COMPLETE SET (20)	200.00	90.00
COMMON CARD (1-20)	1.50	.70

*REAL DIAMONDS: 2X TO 5X BASIC DIAM.CLUB
REAL DIAMONDS STATED ODDS 1:350

❑ 1 Albert Belle	8.00	3.60
❑ 2 Mo Vaughn	6.00	2.70
❑ 3 Ken Griffey Jr.	25.00	11.00
❑ 4 Mike Piazza	15.00	6.75
❑ 5 Cal Ripken	20.00	9.00
❑ 6 Jermaine Dye	1.50	.70
❑ 7 Jeff Bagwell	8.00	3.60
❑ 8 Frank Thomas	15.00	6.75
❑ 9 Alex Rodriguez	15.00	6.75
❑ 10 Ryan Klesko	3.00	1.35
❑ 11 Roberto Alomar	5.00	2.20
❑ 12 Sammy Sosa	12.00	5.50
❑ 13 Matt Williams	3.00	1.35
❑ 14 Gary Sheffield	3.00	1.35
❑ 15 Ruben Rivera	3.00	1.35
❑ 16 Darin Erstad	20.00	9.00
❑ 17 Randy Johnson	5.00	2.20
❑ 18 Greg Maddux	15.00	6.75
❑ 19 Karim Garcia	3.00	1.35
❑ 20 Chipper Jones	12.00	5.50

1996 Zenith Mozaics

	MINT	NRMT
COMPLETE SET (25)	150.00	70.00
COMMON CARD (1-25)	2.50	1.10
❑ 1 Greg Maddux Chipper Jones Ryan Klesko	15.00	6.75
❑ 2 Juan Gonzalez Will Clark Ivan Rodriguez	10.00	4.50
❑ 3 Frank Thomas Robin Ventura Ray Durham	12.00	5.50
❑ 4 Matt Williams Barry Bonds Osvaldo Fernandez	5.00	2.20
❑ 5 Ken Griffey Jr. Randy Johnson Alex Rodriguez	25.00	11.00
❑ 6 Sammy Sosa Ryne Sandberg Mark Grace	10.00	4.50
❑ 7 Jim Edmonds Tim Salmon Garret Anderson	6.00	2.70
❑ 8 Cal Ripken Roberto Alomar Mike Mussina	15.00	6.75
❑ 9 Mo Vaughn Roger Clemens John Valentin	8.00	3.60
❑ 10 Barry Larkin Reggie Sanders Hal Morris	4.00	1.80
❑ 11 Ray Lankford Brian Jordan Ozzie Smith	6.00	2.70
❑ 12 Dante Bichette Larry Walker Andres Galarraga	6.00	2.70
❑ 13 Mike Piazza Hideo Nomo Raul Mondesi	12.00	5.50
❑ 14 Ben McDonald Greg Vaughn Kevin Seitzer	2.50	1.10
❑ 15 Joe Carter Carlos Delgado Alex Gonzalez	3.00	1.35
❑ 16 Gary Sheffield Charles Johnson Jeff Conine	6.00	2.70
❑ 17 Rondell White Moises Alou Henry Rodriguez	3.00	1.35
❑ 18 Albert Belle Manny Ramirez Carlos Baerga	6.00	2.70
❑ 19 Kirby Puckett Paul Molitor Chuck Knoblauch	8.00	3.60
❑ 20 Tony Gwynn Rickey Henderson Wally Joyner	10.00	4.50
❑ 21 Mark McGwire Mike Bordick Scott Brosius	20.00	9.00
❑ 22 Paul O'Neill Bernie Williams Wade Boggs	6.00	2.70
❑ 23 Jay Bell Orlando Merced Jason Kendall	3.00	1.35
❑ 24 Rico Brogna Paul Wilson Jason Isringhausen	2.50	1.10
❑ 25 Jeff Bagwell Craig Biggio Derek Bell	8.00	3.60

1996 Zenith Z-Team

	MINT	NRMT
COMPLETE SET (18)	400.00	180.00
COMMON CARD (1-18)	8.00	3.60
❑ 1 Ken Griffey Jr.	60.00	27.00
❑ 2 Albert Belle	20.00	9.00
❑ 3 Cal Ripken	50.00	22.00
❑ 4 Frank Thomas	40.00	18.00
❑ 5 Greg Maddux	40.00	18.00
❑ 6 Mo Vaughn	15.00	6.75
❑ 7 Chipper Jones	30.00	13.50
❑ 8 Mike Piazza	40.00	18.00
❑ 9 Ryan Klesko	8.00	3.60
❑ 10 Hideo Nomo	20.00	9.00

❑ 11 Roberto Alomar	12.00	5.50
❑ 12 Manny Ramirez	12.00	5.50
❑ 13 Gary Sheffield	10.00	4.50
❑ 14 Barry Bonds	15.00	6.75
❑ 15 Matt Williams	8.00	3.60
❑ 16 Jim Edmonds	10.00	4.50
❑ 17 Kirby Puckett	20.00	9.00
❑ 18 Sammy Sosa	30.00	13.50

1997 Zenith

	MINT	NRMT
COMPLETE SET (50)	40.00	18.00
COMMON CARD (1-50)	.40	.18
❑ 1 Frank Thomas	2.50	1.10
❑ 2 Tony Gwynn	2.00	.90
❑ 3 Jeff Bagwell	1.25	.55
❑ 4 Paul Molitor	.75	.35
❑ 5 Roberto Alomar	.75	.35
❑ 6 Mike Piazza	2.50	1.10
❑ 7 Albert Belle	1.00	.45
❑ 8 Greg Maddux	2.50	1.10
❑ 9 Barry Larkin	.60	.25
❑ 10 Tony Clark	.60	.25
❑ 11 Larry Walker	.75	.35
❑ 12 Chipper Jones	2.00	.90
❑ 13 Juan Gonzalez	2.00	.90
❑ 14 Barry Bonds	1.00	.45
❑ 15 Ivan Rodriguez	1.00	.45
❑ 16 Sammy Sosa	2.00	.90
❑ 17 Derek Jeter	2.50	1.10
❑ 18 Hideo Nomo	1.00	.45
❑ 19 Roger Clemens	1.50	.70
❑ 20 Ken Griffey Jr.	4.00	1.80
❑ 21 Andy Pettitte	.60	.25
❑ 22 Alex Rodriguez	2.50	1.10
❑ 23 Tino Martinez	.75	.35
❑ 24 Bernie Williams	.75	.35
❑ 25 Ken Caminiti	.60	.25
❑ 26 John Smoltz	.60	.25
❑ 27 Javier Lopez	.60	.25
❑ 28 Mark McGwire	4.00	1.80
❑ 29 Gary Sheffield	.60	.25
❑ 30 David Justice	.75	.35
❑ 31 Randy Johnson	.75	.35
❑ 32 Chuck Knoblauch	.75	.35
❑ 33 Mike Mussina	.75	.35
❑ 34 Deion Sanders	.60	.25
❑ 35 Cal Ripken	3.00	1.35
❑ 36 Darin Erstad	1.25	.55
❑ 37 Kenny Lofton	.75	.35
❑ 38 Jay Buhner	.60	.25
❑ 39 Brady Anderson	.60	.25
❑ 40 Edgar Martinez	.60	.25
❑ 41 Mo Vaughn	1.00	.45
❑ 42 Ryne Sandberg	1.00	.45
❑ 43 Andruw Jones	1.25	.55
❑ 44 Nomar Garciaparra	2.50	1.10
❑ 45 Hideki Irabu	2.00	.90
❑ 46 Wilton Guerrero	.40	.18
❑ 47 Jose Cruz Jr.	3.00	1.35
❑ 48 Vladimir Guerrero	1.50	.70
❑ 49 Scott Rolen	2.00	.90
❑ 50 Jose Guillen	.75	.35

1997 Zenith 8 x 10

	MINT	NRMT
COMPLETE SET (24)	40.00	18.00
COMMON CARD (1-24)	.50	.23
COMP.DUFEX SET (24)	80.00	36.00

*DUFEX: 1X TO 2.5X BASIC CARDS
ONE DUFEX PER PACK

❑ 1 Frank Thomas	3.00	1.35
❑ 2 Tony Gwynn	2.50	1.10
❑ 3 Jeff Bagwell	1.50	.70
❑ 4 Ken Griffey Jr.	5.00	2.20
❑ 5 Mike Piazza	3.00	1.35
❑ 6 Greg Maddux	3.00	1.35
❑ 7 Ken Caminiti	.50	.23
❑ 8 Albert Belle	.75	.35
❑ 9 Ivan Rodriguez	1.50	.70
❑ 10 Sammy Sosa	3.00	1.35
❑ 11 Mark McGwire	5.00	2.20
❑ 12 Roger Clemens	2.00	.90
❑ 13 Alex Rodriguez	3.00	1.35
❑ 14 Chipper Jones	2.50	1.10
❑ 15 Juan Gonzalez	2.50	1.10
❑ 16 Barry Bonds	1.50	.70
❑ 17 Derek Jeter	3.00	1.35
❑ 18 Hideo Nomo	2.50	1.10
❑ 19 Cal Ripken	4.00	1.80
❑ 20 Hideki Irabu	1.50	.70
❑ 21 Andruw Jones	2.00	.90
❑ 22 Nomar Garciaparra	3.00	1.35
❑ 23 Vladimir Guerrero	2.00	.90
❑ 24 Scott Rolen	2.50	1.10

1997 Zenith V-2

	MINT	NRMT
COMPLETE SET (8)	250.00	110.00
COMMON CARD (1-8)	15.00	6.75
❑ 1 Ken Griffey Jr.	60.00	27.00
❑ 2 Andruw Jones	15.00	6.75
❑ 3 Frank Thomas	40.00	18.00
❑ 4 Mike Piazza	40.00	18.00
❑ 5 Alex Rodriguez	40.00	18.00
❑ 6 Cal Ripken	50.00	22.00
❑ 7 Derek Jeter	30.00	13.50
❑ 8 Vladimir Guerrero	20.00	9.00

1997 Zenith Z-Team

	MINT	NRMT
COMPLETE SET (9)	600.00	275.00
COMMON CARD (1-9)	25.00	11.00
❑ 1 Ken Griffey Jr.	120.00	55.00
❑ 2 Larry Walker	25.00	11.00
❑ 3 Frank Thomas	80.00	36.00
❑ 4 Alex Rodriguez	80.00	36.00
❑ 5 Mike Piazza	80.00	36.00
❑ 6 Cal Ripken	100.00	45.00
❑ 7 Derek Jeter	60.00	27.00
❑ 8 Andruw Jones	30.00	13.50
❑ 9 Roger Clemens	50.00	22.00

1998 Zenith

	MINT	NRMT
COMPLETE SET (100)	100.00	45.00
COMMON CARD (1-100)	.30	.14
❑ 1 Larry Walker	1.25	.55
❑ 2 Ken Griffey Jr.	6.00	2.70
❑ 3 Cal Ripken	5.00	2.20
❑ 4 Sammy Sosa	3.00	1.35
❑ 5 Andruw Jones	1.50	.70
❑ 6 Frank Thomas	4.00	1.80
❑ 7 Tony Gwynn	3.00	1.35
❑ 8 Rafael Palmeiro	.75	.35
❑ 9 Tim Salmon	1.25	.55
❑ 10 Randy Johnson	1.25	.55
❑ 11 Juan Gonzalez	3.00	1.35
❑ 12 Greg Maddux	4.00	1.80
❑ 13 Vladimir Guerrero	2.00	.90
❑ 14 Mike Piazza	4.00	1.80
❑ 15 Andres Galarraga	1.25	.55
❑ 16 Alex Rodriguez	4.00	1.80
❑ 17 Derek Jeter	3.00	1.35
❑ 18 Nomar Garciaparra	4.00	1.80
❑ 19 Ivan Rodriguez	1.50	.70
❑ 20 Chipper Jones	3.00	1.35
❑ 21 Barry Larkin	.75	.35
❑ 22 Mo Vaughn	1.50	.70
❑ 23 Albert Belle	1.25	.55
❑ 24 Scott Rolen	3.00	1.35
❑ 25 Sandy Alomar Jr.	.50	.23
❑ 26 Roberto Alomar	1.25	.55
❑ 27 Andy Pettitte	.75	.35
❑ 28 Chuck Knoblauch	1.25	.55
❑ 29 Jeff Bagwell	2.00	.90
❑ 30 Mike Mussina	1.25	.55
❑ 31 Fred McGriff	.75	.35
❑ 32 Roger Clemens	2.50	1.10
❑ 33 Rusty Greer	.50	.23
❑ 34 Edgar Martinez	.50	.23
❑ 35 Paul Molitor	1.25	.55
❑ 36 Mark Grace	.75	.35
❑ 37 Darin Erstad	1.50	.70
❑ 38 Kenny Lofton	1.25	.55
❑ 39 Tom Glavine	1.25	.55
❑ 40 Javier Lopez	.50	.23
❑ 41 Will Clark	1.25	.55
❑ 42 Tino Martinez	1.25	.55
❑ 43 Raul Mondesi	.75	.35
❑ 44 Brady Anderson	.50	.23

		MINT	NRMT
❑ 45	Chan Ho Park	1.25	.55
❑ 46	Jason Giambi	.50	.23
❑ 47	Manny Ramirez	1.25	.55
❑ 48	Jay Buhner	.50	.23
❑ 49	Dante Bichette	.50	.23
❑ 50	Jose Cruz Jr.	1.50	.70
❑ 51	Charles Johnson	.50	.23
❑ 52	Bernard Gilkey	.30	.14
❑ 53	Johnny Damon	.50	.23
❑ 54	David Justice	1.25	.55
❑ 55	Justin Thompson	.50	.23
❑ 56	Bobby Higginson	.75	.35
❑ 57	Todd Hundley	.50	.23
❑ 58	Gary Sheffield	.75	.35
❑ 59	Barry Bonds	1.50	.70
❑ 60	Mark McGwire	8.00	3.60
❑ 61	John Smoltz	.50	.23
❑ 62	Tony Clark	.75	.35
❑ 63	Brian Jordan	.50	.23
❑ 64	Jason Kendall	.50	.23
❑ 65	Mariano Rivera	.50	.23
❑ 66	Pedro Martinez	1.25	.55
❑ 67	Jim Thome	1.25	.55
❑ 68	Neifi Perez	.50	.23
❑ 69	Kevin Brown	.75	.35
❑ 70	Hideo Nomo	1.50	.70
❑ 71	Craig Biggio	1.25	.55
❑ 72	Bernie Williams	1.25	.55
❑ 73	Jose Guillen	.50	.23
❑ 74	Ken Caminiti	.75	.35
❑ 75	Livan Hernandez	.50	.23
❑ 76	Ray Lankford	.50	.23
❑ 77	Jim Edmonds	.75	.35
❑ 78	Matt Williams	.50	.23
❑ 79	Mark Kotsay	.75	.35
❑ 80	Moises Alou	.75	.35
❑ 81	Antone Williamson	.30	.14
❑ 82	Jaret Wright	1.50	.70
❑ 83	Jacob Cruz	.30	.14
❑ 84	Abraham Nunez	.50	.23
❑ 85	Raul Ibanez	.30	.14
❑ 86	Miguel Tejada	.50	.23
❑ 87	Derrek Lee	.50	.23
❑ 88	Juan Encarnacion	.50	.23
❑ 89	Todd Helton	1.50	.70
❑ 90	Travis Lee	2.50	1.10
❑ 91	Ben Grieve	2.50	1.10
❑ 92	Ryan McGuire	.30	.14
❑ 93	Richard Hidalgo	.50	.23
❑ 94	Paul Konerko	1.25	.55
❑ 95	Shannon Stewart	.50	.23
❑ 96	Homer Bush	.30	.14
❑ 97	Lou Collier	.30	.14
❑ 98	Jeff Abbott	.50	.23
❑ 99	Brett Tomko	.50	.23
❑ 100	Fernando Tatis	.50	.23

1998 Zenith 5 x 7

	MINT	NRMT
COMPLETE SET (80)	120.00	55.00
COMMON CARD (1-80)	.40	.18

❑ 1	Nomar Garciaparra	5.00	2.20
❑ 2	Andres Galarraga	1.50	.70
❑ 3	Greg Maddux	5.00	2.20
❑ 4	Frank Thomas	5.00	2.20
❑ 5	Mark McGwire	10.00	4.50
❑ 6	Rafael Palmeiro	1.00	.45
❑ 7	John Smoltz	.60	.25
❑ 8	Jeff Bagwell	2.50	1.10
❑ 9	Andruw Jones	2.00	.90
❑ 10	Rusty Greer	.60	.25
❑ 11	Paul Molitor	1.50	.70
❑ 12	Bernie Williams	1.50	.70
❑ 13	Kenny Lofton	1.50	.70
❑ 14	Alex Rodriguez	5.00	2.20
❑ 15	Derek Jeter	4.00	1.80
❑ 16	Scott Rolen	4.00	1.80
❑ 17	Albert Belle	1.50	.70
❑ 18	Mo Vaughn	2.00	.90
❑ 19	Chipper Jones	4.00	1.80
❑ 20	Chuck Knoblauch	1.50	.70
❑ 21	Mike Piazza	5.00	2.20
❑ 22	Tony Gwynn	4.00	1.80
❑ 23	Juan Gonzalez	4.00	1.80

❑ 24	Andy Pettitte	1.00	.45
❑ 25	Tim Salmon	1.50	.70
❑ 26	Brady Anderson	.60	.25
❑ 27	Mike Mussina	1.50	.70
❑ 28	Edgar Martinez	.60	.25
❑ 29	Jose Guillen	.60	.25
❑ 30	Hideo Nomo	2.00	.90
❑ 31	Jim Thome	1.50	.70
❑ 32	Mark Grace	1.00	.45
❑ 33	Darin Erstad	2.00	.90
❑ 34	Bobby Higginson	1.00	.45
❑ 35	Ivan Rodriguez	2.00	.90
❑ 36	Todd Hundley	.60	.25
❑ 37	Sandy Alomar Jr.	.60	.25
❑ 38	Gary Sheffield	1.00	.45
❑ 39	David Justice	1.50	.70
❑ 40	Ken Griffey Jr.	8.00	3.60
❑ 41	Vladimir Guerrero	2.50	1.10
❑ 42	Larry Walker	1.50	.70
❑ 43	Barry Bonds	2.00	.90
❑ 44	Randy Johnson	1.50	.70
❑ 45	Roger Clemens	3.00	1.35
❑ 46	Raul Mondesi	1.00	.45
❑ 47	Tino Martinez	1.50	.70
❑ 48	Jason Giambi	.60	.25
❑ 49	Matt Williams	.60	.25
❑ 50	Cal Ripken	6.00	2.70
❑ 51	Barry Larkin	1.00	.45
❑ 52	Jim Edmonds	1.00	.45
❑ 53	Ken Caminiti	1.00	.45
❑ 54	Sammy Sosa	4.00	1.80
❑ 55	Tony Clark	1.00	.45
❑ 56	Manny Ramirez	1.50	.70
❑ 57	Bernard Gilkey	.40	.18
❑ 58	Jose Cruz Jr.	2.00	.90
❑ 59	Brian Jordan	.60	.25
❑ 60	Kevin Brown	1.00	.45
❑ 61	Craig Biggio	1.50	.70
❑ 62	Javier Lopez	.60	.25
❑ 63	Jay Buhner	.60	.25
❑ 64	Roberto Alomar	1.50	.70
❑ 65	Justin Thompson	.60	.25
❑ 66	Todd Helton	2.00	.90
❑ 67	Travis Lee	3.00	1.35
❑ 68	Paul Konerko	1.50	.70
❑ 69	Jaret Wright	2.00	.90
❑ 70	Ben Grieve	3.00	1.35
❑ 71	Juan Encarnacion	.60	.25
❑ 72	Ryan McGuire	.40	.18
❑ 73	Derrek Lee	.60	.25
❑ 74	Abraham Nunez	.60	.25
❑ 75	Richard Hidalgo	.60	.25
❑ 76	Miguel Tejada	.60	.25
❑ 77	Jacob Cruz	.40	.18
❑ 78	Homer Bush	.40	.18
❑ 79	Jeff Abbott	.60	.25
❑ 80	Lou Collier	.40	.18

1998 Zenith Z-Gold

	MINT	NRMT
COMMON CARD (1-100)	15.00	6.75

*STARS: 20X TO 50X BASIC CARDS
*YOUNG STARS: 15X TO 40X BASIC CARDS

1998 Zenith Z-Silver

	MINT	NRMT
COMPLETE SET (100)	600.00	275.00
COMMON CARD (1-100)	2.00	.90

*STARS: 2.5X TO 6X BASIC CARDS
*YOUNG STARS: 2X TO 5X BASIC CARDS

1998 Zenith 5 x 7 Gold Impulse

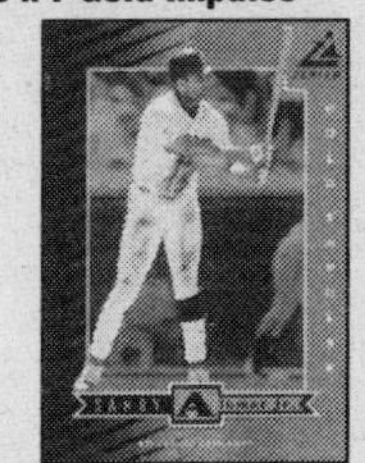

	MINT	NRMT
COMMON CARD (1-80)	15.00	6.75

*STARS: 15X TO 40X BASIC 5 X 7'S
*YOUNG STARS: 12.5X TO 30X BASIC 5 X 7'S

1998 Zenith 5 x 7 Impulse

	MINT	NRMT
COMPLETE SET (80)	600.00	275.00
COMMON CARD (1-80)	2.00	.90

*STARS: 2X TO 5X BASIC 5 X 7'S
*YOUNG STARS: 1.5X TO 4X BASIC 5 X 7'S

1998 Zenith Raising the Bar

	MINT	NRMT
COMPLETE SET (15)	300.00	135.00
COMMON CARD (1-15)	10.00	4.50
❑ 1 Ken Griffey Jr.	50.00	22.00
❑ 2 Frank Thomas	30.00	13.50
❑ 3 Alex Rodriguez	30.00	13.50
❑ 4 Tony Gwynn	25.00	11.00
❑ 5 Mike Piazza	30.00	13.50
❑ 6 Ivan Rodriguez	12.00	5.50
❑ 7 Cal Ripken	40.00	18.00
❑ 8 Greg Maddux	30.00	13.50
❑ 9 Hideo Nomo	12.00	5.50
❑ 10 Mark McGwire	60.00	27.00
❑ 11 Juan Gonzalez	25.00	11.00
❑ 12 Andruw Jones	10.00	4.50
❑ 13 Jeff Bagwell	15.00	6.75
❑ 14 Chipper Jones	25.00	11.00
❑ 15 Nomar Garciaparra	30.00	13.50

1998 Zenith Rookie Thrills

	MINT	NRMT
COMPLETE SET (15)	60.00	27.00
COMMON CARD (1-15)	1.50	.70
❑ 1 Travis Lee	12.00	5.50
❑ 2 Juan Encarnacion	2.50	1.10
❑ 3 Derrek Lee	2.50	1.10
❑ 4 Raul Ibanez	1.50	.70
❑ 5 Ryan McGuire	1.50	.70
❑ 6 Todd Helton	8.00	3.60
❑ 7 Jacob Cruz	1.50	.70
❑ 8 Abraham Nunez	2.50	1.10
❑ 9 Paul Konerko	6.00	2.70
❑ 10 Ben Grieve	12.00	5.50
❑ 11 Jeff Abbott	2.50	1.10
❑ 12 Richard Hidalgo	2.50	1.10
❑ 13 Jaret Wright	8.00	3.60
❑ 14 Lou Collier	1.50	.70
❑ 15 Miguel Tejada	2.50	1.10

1998 Zenith Z-Team

	MINT	NRMT
COMPLETE SET (18)	400.00	180.00
COMMON CARD (1-18)	8.00	3.60
❑ 1 Frank Thomas	30.00	13.50
❑ 2 Ken Griffey Jr.	50.00	22.00
❑ 3 Mike Piazza	30.00	13.50
❑ 4 Cal Ripken	40.00	18.00
❑ 5 Alex Rodriguez	30.00	13.50
❑ 6 Greg Maddux	30.00	13.50
❑ 7 Derek Jeter	25.00	11.00
❑ 8 Chipper Jones	25.00	11.00
❑ 9 Roger Clemens	20.00	9.00
❑ 10 Ben Grieve	20.00	9.00
❑ 11 Derrek Lee	8.00	3.60
❑ 12 Jose Cruz Jr.	12.00	5.50
❑ 13 Nomar Garciaparra	30.00	13.50
❑ 14 Travis Lee	20.00	9.00
❑ 15 Todd Helton	12.00	5.50
❑ 16 Paul Konerko	8.00	3.60
❑ 17 Miguel Tejada	8.00	3.60
❑ 18 Scott Rolen	25.00	11.00

1998 Zenith Z-Team 5 x 7

	MINT	NRMT
COMPLETE SET (9)	300.00	135.00
COMMON CARD (1-9)	25.00	11.00
❑ 1 Frank Thomas	40.00	18.00
❑ 2 Ken Griffey Jr.	60.00	27.00
❑ 3 Mike Piazza	40.00	18.00
❑ 4 Cal Ripken	50.00	22.00
❑ 5 Alex Rodriguez	40.00	18.00
❑ 6 Greg Maddux	40.00	18.00
❑ 7 Derek Jeter	30.00	13.50
❑ 8 Chipper Jones	30.00	13.50
❑ 9 Roger Clemens	25.00	11.00

Acknowledgments

Each year we refine the process of developing the most accurate and up-to-date information for this book. I believe this year's Price Guide is our best yet. Thanks again to all the contributors nationwide (listed below) as well as our staff here in Dallas.

Those who have worked closely with us on this and many other books have again proven themselves invaluable: Ed Allan, Frank and Vivian Baining, David Berman, Brian Bigelow, Levi Bleam and Jim Fleck (707 Sportscards), Peter Brennan, Ray Bright, Card Collectors Co., Cartophilium (Andrew Pywowarczuk), Dwight Chapin, Barry Colla, Bill and Diane Dodge, David Festberg, Fleer/SkyBox (Rich Bradley, Doug Drotman and Ted Taylor), Steve Freedman, Gervise Ford, Larry and Jeff Fritsch, Tony Galovich, Georgia Music and Sports (Dick DeCourcey), Dick Gilkeson, Steve Gold (AU Sports), Bill Goodwin (St. Louis Baseball Cards), Mike and Howard Gordon, George Grauer, Steve Green (STB Sports), John Greenwald, Greg's Cards, Bill Henderson, Jerry and Etta Hersh, Mike Hersh, Neil Hoppenworth, Hunt Action, Jay and Mary Kasper (Jay's Emporium), Jerry Katz, Pete Kennedy, David Kohler (SportsCards Plus), Paul Lewicki, Robert Lifsen (Robert Edward Auction), Lew Lipset (Four Base Hits), Mike Livingston (University Trading Cards), Mark Macrae, Bill Madden, Bill Mastro, Dr.William McAvoy, Michael McDonald, Mid-Atlantic Sports Cards (Bill Bossert), Gary Mills, Ernie Montella, Brian Morris, Mike Mosier (Columbia City Collectibles Co.), B.A. Murry, Ralph Nozaki, Mike O'Brien, Oldies and Goodies (Nigel Spill), Oregon Trail Auctions, Pacific Trading Cards (Mike Cramer and Mike Monson), Jack Pollard, Jeff Prillaman, Pat Quinn, Jerald Reichstein (Fabulous Cardboard), Tom Reid, Gavin Riley, Clifton Rouse, John Rumierz, Kevin Savage (Sports Gallery), Gary Sawatski, Mike Schechter, Barry Sloate, John E. Spalding, Phil Spector, Frank Steele, Murvin Sterling, Lee Temanson, Topps (Marty Appel, Brian Parkinson), Treat (Harold Anderson), Ed Twombly (New England Bullpen), Upper Deck (Steve Ryan, Marilyn Van Dyke), Wayne Varner, Bill Vizas, Bill Wesslund (Portland Sports Card Co.), Kit Young and Bob Ivanjack (Kit Young Cards), Rick Young, Ted Zanidakis, Robert Zanze (Z-Cards and Sports), Bill Zimpleman and Dean Zindler. Finally we give a special acknowledgment to the late Dennis W. Eckes, "Mr. Sport Americana." The success of the Beckett Price Guides has always been the result of a team effort.

It is very difficult to be "accurate" — one can only do one's best. But this job is especially difficult since we're shooting at a moving target: Prices are fluctuating all the time. Having several full-time pricing experts has definitely proven to be better than just one, and I thank all of them for working together to provide you, our readers, with the most accurate prices possible.

Many people have provided price input, illustrative material, checklist verifications, errata, and/or background information. We should like to individually thank AbD Cards (Dale Wesolewski), Action Card Sales, Jerry Adamic, Johnny and Sandy Adams, Alex's MVP Cards & Comics, Doug Allen (Round Tripper Sportscards), Will Allison, Dennis Anderson, Ed Anderson, Shane Anderson, Bruce W. Andrews, Ellis Anmuth, Tom Antonowicz, Alan Applegate, Ric Apter, Jason Arasate, Clyde Archer, Randy Archer, Matt Argento, Burl Armstrong, Neil Armstrong (World Series Cards), Todd Armstrong, B and J Sportscards, Shawn Bailey, Ball Four Cards (Frank and Steve Pemper), Bob Bartosz, Nathan Basford, Carl Berg, Beulah Sports (Jeff Blatt), George Birsic, B.J. Sportscollectables, David Boedicker (The Wild Pitch Inc.), Bob Boffa, Louis Bollman, Tim Bond (Tim's Cards & Comics), Andrew Bosarge, Brian W. Bottles, Bill Brandt, Jeff Breitenfield, John Brigandi, John

Broggi, Chuck Brooks, Dan Bruner, Lesha Bundrick, Michael Bunker, John E. Burick, Ed Burkey Jr., Bubba Bennett, Virgil Burns, California Card Co., Capital Cards, Danny Cariseo, Carl Carlson (C.T.S.), Jim Carr, Patrick Carroll, Ira Cetron, Don Chaffee, Michael Chan, Sandy Chan, Ric Chandgie, Ray Cherry, Bigg Wayne Christian, Josh Chidester, Dick Cianciotto, Michael and Abe Citron, Dr. Jeffrey Clair, Derrick F. Clark, Bill Cochran, Don Coe, Michael Cohen, Tom Cohoon (Cardboard Dreams), Collection de Sport AZ (Ronald Villaneuve), Gary Collett, Andrew T. Collier, Charles A. Collins, Curt Cooter, Steven Cooter, Pedro Cortes, Rick Cosmen (RC Card Co.), Lou Costanzo (Champion Sports), Mike Coyne, Paul and Ryan Crabb, Tony Craig (T.C. Card Co.), Kevin Crane, Taylor Crane, Chad Cripe, Brian Cunningham, Allen Custer, Donald L. Cutler, Eugene C. Dalager, Dave Dame, Brett Daniel, Tony Daniele III, Scott Dantio, Roy Datema, John Davidson, Travis Deaton, Dee's Baseball Cards (Dee Robinson), Joe Delgrippo, Tim DelVecchio, Steve Dempski, John Derossett, Mark Diamond, Gilberto Diaz Jr., Ken Dinerman (California Cruizers), Cliff Dolgins, Discount Dorothy, Walter J. Dodds Sr., Bill Dodson, Richard Dolloff (Dolloff Coin Center), Ron Dorsey, Double Play Baseball Cards, Richard Duglin (Baseball Cards-N-More), The Dugout, Kyle Dunbar, B.M. Dungan, Ken Edick (Home Plate of Utah), Randall Edwards, Rick Einhorn, Mark Ely, Todd Entenman, Doak Ewing, Bryan Failing, R.J. Faletti, Terry Falkner, Mike and Chris Fanning, John Fedak, Stephen A. Ferradino, Tom Ferrara, Dick Fields, Louis Fineberg, Jay Finglass, L.V. Fischer, Bob Flitter, Fremont Fong, Perry Fong, Craig Frank, Mark Franke, Walter Franklin, Tom Freeman, Bob Frye, Chris Gala, Richard Galasso, Ray Garner, David Garza, David Gaumer, Georgetown Card Exchange, Richard Gibson Jr., Glenn A. Giesey, David Giove, Dick Goddard, Alvin Goldblum, Brian Goldner, Jeff Goldstein, Ron Gomez, Rich Gove, Joseph Griffin, Mike Grimm, Neil Gubitz (What-A-Card), Hall's Nostalgia, Hershell Hanks, Gregg Hara, Zac Hargis, Floyd Haynes (H and H Baseball Cards), Ben Heckert, Kevin Heffner, Kevin Heimbigner, Dennis Heitland, Joel Hellman, Arthur W. Henkel, Hit and Run Cards (Jon, David, and Kirk Peterson), Gary Holcomb, Lyle Holcomb, Rich Hovorka, John Howard, Mark Hromalik, H.P. Hubert, Dennis Hughes, Harold Hull, Johnny Hustle Card Co., Tom Imboden, Chris Imbriaco, Vern Isenberg, Dale Jackson, Marshall Jackson, Mike Jardina, Hal Jarvis, Paul Jastrzembski, Jeff's Sports Cards, David Jenkins, Donn Jennings Cards, George Johnson, Robe Johnson, Stephen Jones, Al Julian, Chuck Juliana, Dave Jurgensmeier, John Just, Robert Just, Nick Kardoulias, Scott Kashner, Frank J. Katen, Mark Kauffman, Allan Kaye, Rick Keplinger, Sam Kessler, Kevin's Kards, Larry B. Killian, Kingdom Collectibles, Inc., John Klassnik, Steve Kloloack, Philip C. Klutts, Don Knutsen, Steven Koenigsberg, Bob & Bryan Kornfield, Blake Krier, Neil Krohn, Scott Ku, Thomas Kunnecke, Gary Lambert, Matthew Lancaster (MC's Card and Hobby), Jason Lassic, Allan Latawiec, Howard Lau, Gerald A. Lavelle, Dan Lavin, Richard S. Lawrence, William Lawrence, Brent Lee, W.H. Lee, Morley Leeking, Ronald Lenhardt, Brian Lentz, Irv Lerner, Larry and Sally Levine, Lisa Licitra, James Litopoulos, Larry Loeschen (A and J Sportscards), Neil Lopez, Allan Lowenberg, Kendall Loyd (Orlando Sportscards South), Robert Luce, David Macaray, Jim Macie, Joe Maddigan, David Madison, Rob Maerten, Frank Magaha, Pierre Marceau, Paul Marchant, Jim Marsh, Rich Markus, Bob Marquette, Brad L. Marten, Ronald L. Martin, Scott Martinez, Frank J. Masi, Duane Matthes, James S. Maxwell Jr., Michael McCormick, Paul McCormick, McDag Productions Inc., Tony McLaughlin, Mendal Mearkle, Carlos Medina, Ken Melanson, William Mendel, Eric Meredith, Blake Meyer (Lone Star Sportscards), Tim Meyer, Joe Michalowicz, Lee Milazzo, Jimmy Milburn, Cary

S. Miller, David (Otis) Miller, Eldon Miller, George Miller, Wayne Miller, Dick Millerd, Mitchell's Baseball Cards, Perry Miyashita, Douglas Mo, John Morales, William Munn, Mark Murphy, John Musacchio, Robert Nappe, National Sportscard Exchange, Roger Neufeldt, Bud Obermeyer, Francisco Ochoa, John O'Hara, Glenn Olson, Mike Orth, Ron Oser, Luther Owen, Earle Parrish, Clay Pasternack, Mickey Payne, Michael Perrotta, Doug and Zachary Perry, Tom Pfirrmann, Bob Pirro, George Pollitt, Don Prestia, Coy Priest, Loran Pulver, Bob Ragonese, Richard H. Ranck, Bryan Rappaport, Robert M. Ray, R.W. Ray, Phil Regli, Glenn Renick, Rob Resnick, John Revell, Carson Ritchey, Bill Rodman, Craig Roehrig, David H. Rogers, Michael H. Rosen, Martin Rotunno, Michael Runyan, Mark Rush, George Rusnak, Mark Russell, Terry Sack, Joe Sak, Jennifer Salems, Barry Sanders, Everett Sands, Jon Sands, Tony Scarpa, John Schad, Dave Schau (Baseball Cards), Bruce M. Schwartz, Keith A. Schwartz, Charlie Seaver, Tom Shanyfelt, Steven C. Sharek, Eddie Silard (Eddie's Sports Den), Art Smith, Ben Smith, Michael Smith, Jerry Sorice, Don Spagnolo, Carl Specht, Sports Card Fan-Attic, The Sport Hobbyist, Dauer Stackpole, Norm Stapleton, Bill Steinberg, Bob Stern, Lisa Stellato (Never Enough Cards), Jason Stern, Andy Stoltz, Bill Stone, Tim Strandberg (East Texas Sports Cards), Edward Strauss, Strike Three, Richard Strobino, Superior Sport Card, Dr. Richard Swales, Paul Taglione, George Tahinos, Ian Taylor, Lyle Telfer, The Thirdhand Shoppe, Scott A. Thomas, Paul Thornton, Carl N. Thrower, Jim Thurtell, John Tomko, Bud Tompkins (Minnesota Connection), Philip J. Tremont, Ralph Triplette, Mike Trotta, Umpire's Choice Inc., Eric Unglaub, Hoyt Vanderpool, Rob Veres, Nathan Voss, Steven Wagman, Jonathan Waldman, Terry Walker, T. Wall, Gary A. Walter, Mark Weber, Joe and John Weisenburger (The Wise Guys), Brian Wentz, Richard West, Mike Wheat, Richard Wiercinski, Don Williams (Robin's Nest of Dolls), Jeff Williams, John Williams, Kent Williams, Craig Williamson, Opry Winston, Brandon Witz, Rich Wojtasick, John Wolf Jr., Jay Wolt (Cavalcade of Sports), Carl Womack, Pete Wooten, Peter Yee, Wes Young, Mark Zubrensky and Tim Zwick.

Every year we make active solicitations for expert input. We are particularly appreciative of help (however extensive or cursory) provided for this volume. We receive many inquiries, comments and questions regarding material within this book. In fact, each and every one is read and digested. Time constraints, however, prevent us from personally replying. But keep sharing your knowledge. Your letters and input are part of the "big picture" of hobby information we can pass along to readers in our books and magazines. Even though we cannot respond to each letter, you are making significant contributions to the hobby through your interest and comments.

The effort to continually refine and improve this book also involves a growing number of people and types of expertise on our home team. Our company boasts a substantial Sports Data Publishing team, which strengthens our ability to provide comprehensive analysis of the marketplace. SDP capably handled numerous technical details and provided able assistance in the preparation of this edition.

Our baseball analysts played a major part in compiling this year's book, traveling thousands of miles during the past year to attend sports card shows and visit card shops around the United States and Canada. The Beckett baseball specialists are, Mark Anderson, Steve Judd, Rich Klein and Grant Sandground (Senior Price Guide Editor). Their pricing analysis and careful proofreading were key contributions to the accuracy of this annual.

Grant Sandground's coordination and reconciling of prices as Beckett Baseball Card Monthly Price Guide Editor helped immeasurably. Rich Klein, as research analyst, contributed detailed pricing analysis and hours of proofing. They were ably assisted by Jeany Finch and Beverly Mills, who helped enter new sets and pricing information, and ably handled administration of our contributor Price Guide surveys. Card librarian Gabriel Rangel handled the ever-growing quantity of cards we need organized for efforts such as this.

The effort was led by the Manager of Sport Data Publishing Dan Hitt. They were ably assisted by the rest of the Price Guide analysts: Pat Blandford, Wayne Grove, Denny Parsons, Rob Springs and Bill Sutherland.

The price gathering and analytical talents of this fine group of hobbyists have helped make our Beckett team stronger, while making this guide and its companion monthly Price Guide more widely recognized as the hobby's most reliable and relied upon sources of pricing information.

The Beckett Interactive Department, ably headed by Mark Harwell, played a critical role in technology. Working with software designed by assistant manager Eric Best, they spent countless hours programming, testing, and implementing it to simplify the handling of thousands of prices that must be checked and updated for each edition.

In the Production Department, Airey Baringer and Paul Kerutis were responsible for the typesetting and for the card photos you see throughout the book.

In the years since this guide debuted, Beckett Publications has grown beyond any rational expectation. A great many talented and hard working individuals have been instrumental in this growth and success. Our whole team is to be congratulated for what we together have accomplished.

Our Beckett Publications team is led by President Jeff Amano, Executive Vice President Claire Backus, Vice Presidents Joe Galindo, Mark Harwell, Margaret Steele, C.R. Conant, and Chuck Robison and Directors Jeff Anthony, Beth Harwell and Rudy Klancnik. They are ably assisted by Pete Adauto, Dana Alecknavage, John Ayres, Kaye Ball, Airey Baringer, Jeff Bauzon, Therese Bellar, Louise Bird, Bill Bridgeforth, Amy Brougher, Bob Brown, Joel Brown, Angie Calandro, Randall Calvert, Victor Camara, Cara Carmichael, Albert Chavez, Allen Christopherson, Marty Click, Susan Denniston, Aaron Derr, Ryan Duckworth, Amy Durett, Mitchell Dyson, Mila Egusquiza, Ron Espy, Craig Ferris, Gean Paul Figari, Kathy Flood, Carol Fowler, Laura Garbeff, Mary Gonzalez-Davis, Rosanna Gonzalez-Oleachea, Jeff Greer, Robert Gregory, Jenifer Grellhesl, Julie Grove, Barry Hacker, Tracy Hackler, Patti Harris, Mark Hartley, Pepper Hastings, Joanna Hayden, Jana Haynes, Steve Hunt, Mike Jaspersen, Bob Johnson, Jamie Joyce, Justin Kanoya, Eddie Kelly, Kevin King, Gayle Klancnik, Tom Layberger, Jane Ann Layton, Benedito Leme, Lori Lindsey, Stanley Lira, John Marshall, Mike McAllister, Matt McGuire, Brandon Medcalf, Omar Mediano, Sherry Monday, Daniel Moscoso Jr., Allan Muir, Hugh Murphy, Mike Obert, Stacy Olivieri, Mike Pagel, Wendy Pallugna, Clark Palomino, Missy Patrello, Andrea Paul, Mike Payne, Tim Polzer, Bob Richardson, Ed Rue, Wade Rugenstein, Lisa Runyon, Christine Seibert, Brett Setter, Len Shelton, Dave Sliepka, Judi Smalling, Quentin Smith, Sheri Smith, Jeff Stanton, Donald Stephens, Marcia Stoesz, Mark Stokes, Phaedra Strecher, Dawn Sturgeon, Margie Swoyer, Doree Tate, Jim Tereschuk, Chuck Thomas, Jim Thompson, Susan Thompson, Bud Walden, Michelle Wilson, Steve Wilson, Ed Wornson, David Yandry, Bryan Winstead, Mark Zeske and Jay Zwerner. The whole Beckett Publications team has my thanks for jobs well done. Thank you, everyone.

NOTES

NOTES

NOTES

NOTES

NOTES

NOTES

NOTES

NOTES